DK ILLUSTRATED
OXFORD
DICTIONARY

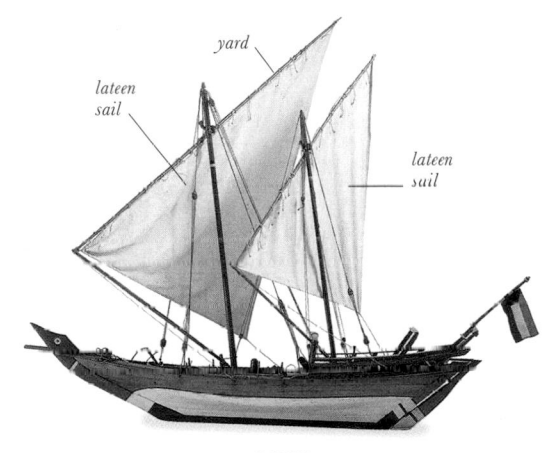

yard

lateen
sail

lateen
sail

DHOW

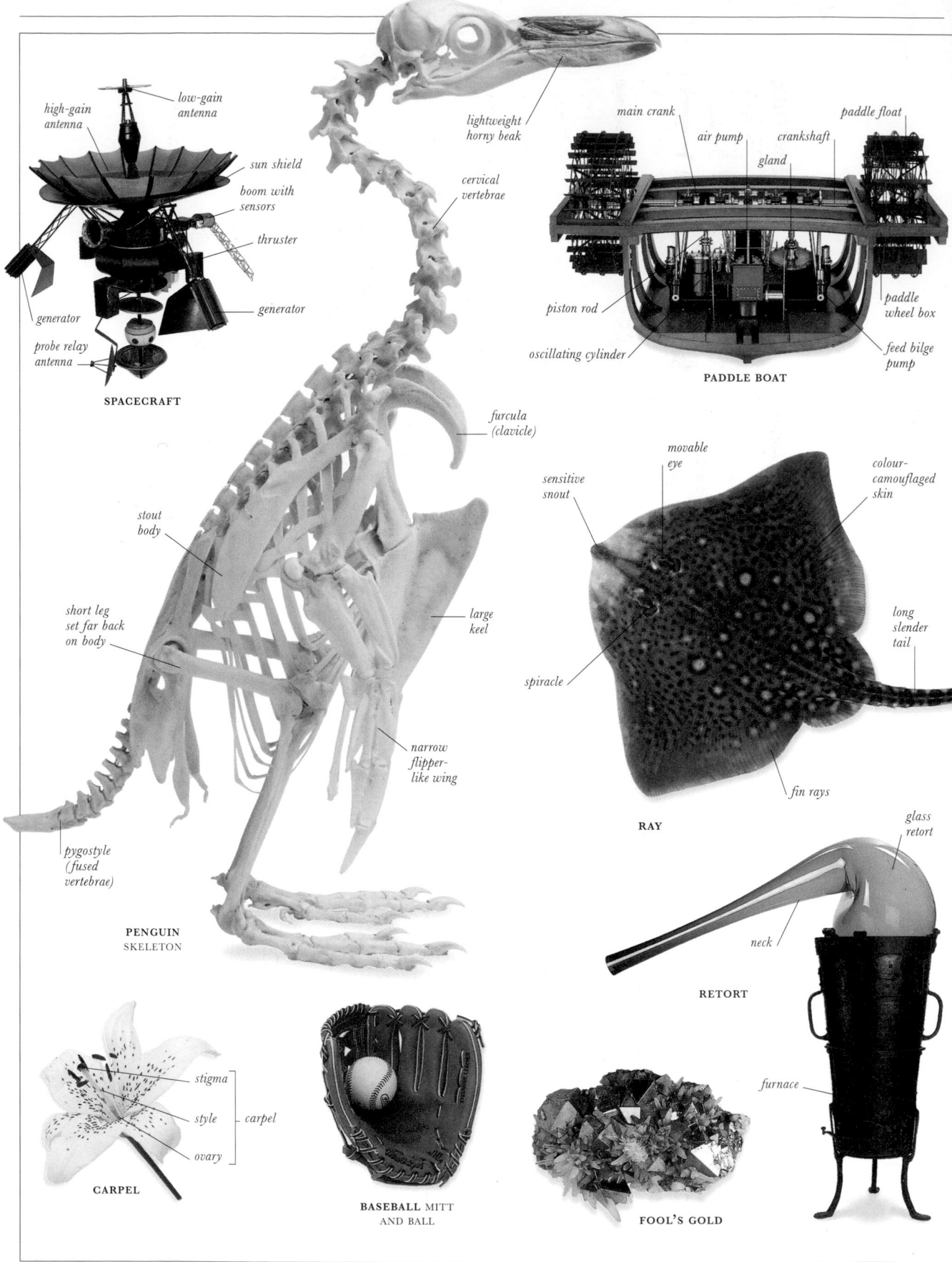

SPACECRAFT

high-gain antenna

low-gain antenna

sun shield

boom with sensors

thruster

generator

generator

probe relay antenna

PADDLE BOAT

main crank

air pump

gland

crankshaft

paddle float

piston rod

oscillating cylinder

paddle wheel box

feed bilge pump

lightweight horny beak

cervical vertebrae

furcula (clavicle)

stout body

short leg set far back on body

large keel

narrow flipper-like wing

pygostyle (fused vertebrae)

PENGUIN
SKELETON

RAY

movable eye

sensitive snout

colour-camouflaged skin

spiracle

long slender tail

fin rays

RETORT

glass retort

neck

furnace

CARPEL

stigma

style

ovary

carpel

BASEBALL MITT
AND BALL

FOOL'S GOLD

DK ILLUSTRATED
OXFORD
DICTIONARY

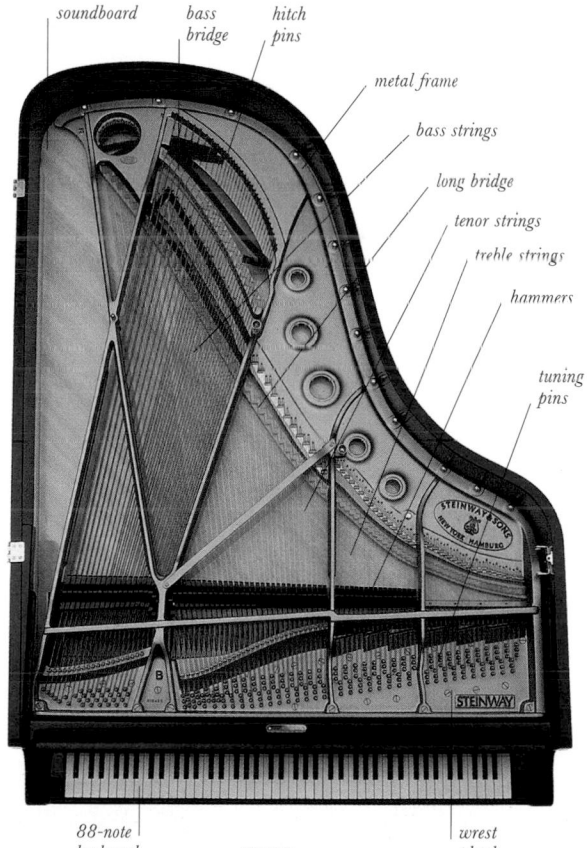

soundboard   bass bridge   hitch pins   metal frame   bass strings   long bridge   tenor strings   treble strings   hammers   tuning pins

88-note keyboard   **PIANO**   wrest plank

DORLING KINDERSLEY
London • New York • Sydney • Moscow

OXFORD UNIVERSITY PRESS
Oxford • New York

Published, created, and produced in Great Britain in 1998 by
DORLING KINDERSLEY LIMITED and OXFORD UNIVERSITY PRESS

Lexicographic text copyright © 1998 Oxford University Press being the text
of *The Oxford Compact English Dictionary* (1998) with updating and additions.

Images copyright © 1998 Dorling Kindersley Limited, London
Non-lexicographic text copyright © 1998 Dorling Kindersley Limited, London
Layout and design copyright © 1998 Dorling Kindersley Limited, London

A CIP catalogue record for this book is available from the British Library.

ISBN 0-7513-1110-3

2   4   6   8   10   9   7   5   3   1

Colour reproduction by Colourpath, London, England
Printed and bound in Germany by Mohndruck GmbH, Gütersloh

———— OXFORD UNIVERSITY PRESS ————
Great Clarendon Street, Oxford OX2 6DP

OXFORD   NEW YORK   ATHENS   AUCKLAND   BANGKOK   BOGOTA   BOMBAY   BUENOS AIRES   CALCUTTA
CAPE TOWN   DAR ES SALAAM   DELHI   FLORENCE   HONG KONG   ISTANBUL   KARACHI   KUALA LUMPUR
MADRAS   MADRID   MELBOURNE   MEXICO CITY   NAIROBI   PARIS   SINGAPORE   TAIPEI
TOKYO   TORONTO   and associated companies in   BERLIN   IBADAN

Oxford is a trade mark of Oxford University Press

———— DORLING KINDERSLEY LIMITED ————
9 Henrietta Street, London WC2E 8PS
LONDON   NEW YORK   SYDNEY   MOSCOW

Visit us on the World Wide Web at http://www.dk.com

CONTENTS

FOREWORD 7

HOW TO USE THE DICTIONARY *8–14*

HOW TO USE THE DICTIONARY *8–9* • STRUCTURE OF ENTRIES *10–11*
PRONUNCIATION *12* • LABELS *12* • FORMS *13* • ABBREVIATIONS *14*

THE ILLUSTRATED DICTIONARY
15–972

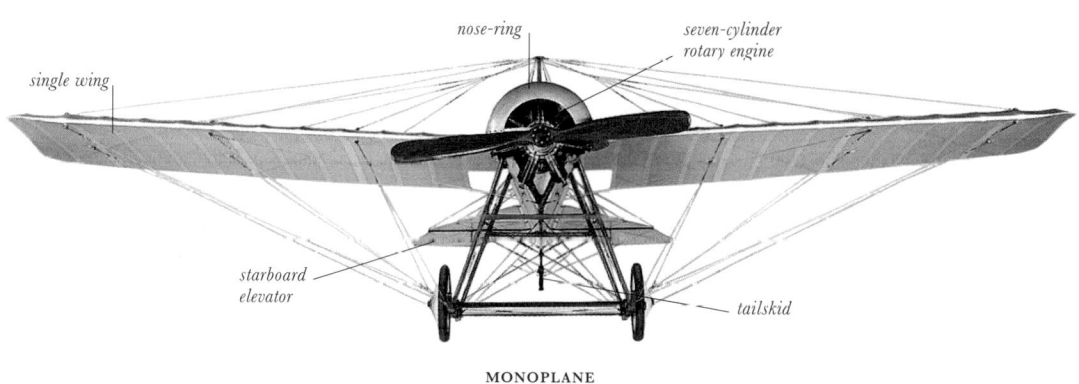

nose-ring

*seven-cylinder
rotary engine*

single wing

*starboard
elevator*

tailskid

MONOPLANE

REFERENCE SECTION *973–1007*

POLITICAL MAP OF THE WORLD *974–975* • PHYSICAL MAP OF THE WORLD *976–977*
COUNTRIES OF THE WORLD *978–985* • THE NIGHT SKY *986–987*
MEASUREMENTS *988–989* • NUMBERS AND SYMBOLS *990–991*
TIME *992–993* • MISCELLANEOUS INFORMATION *994–995*
THE LIVING WORLD *996–997* • THE ANIMAL KINGDOM *998–999*
GEOLOGICAL TIME PERIODS *1000–1001* • GRAMMAR AND STYLE *1002–1007*

ACKNOWLEDGEMENTS *1008*

STAFF AND CONTRIBUTORS

DORLING KINDERSLEY

MANAGING EDITOR
Jonathan Metcalf

MANAGING ART EDITORS
Peter Cross, Steve Knowlden

SENIOR ART EDITOR
Ina Stradins

PROJECT ART EDITOR
Elaine Hewson

PROJECT EDITORS
Monica Byles, Angeles Gavira

EDITORS
Michael Ellis, Michael Fullalove,
Phil Hunt, Irene Lyford, Gerard McLaughlin,
Sean O'Connor, Victoria Sorzano,
Geoffrey Stalker, Nichola Thomasson

DESIGNERS
Alistair Carlisle, Pauline Clarke, Martin Cropper,
Jane Felstead, Alison Greenhalgh, Des Hemsley,
Spencer Holbrook, Mark Johnson Davies, Elly King

ADMINISTRATIVE SUPPORT
Sarah Coverdale, Simon Maughan, James Nugent

DESIGN ASSISTANT
Corinne Manches

PICTURE RESEARCHERS
Martin Copeland, Denise O'Brien, Andrew Sansom

PRODUCTION CONTROLLER
Michelle Thomas

DTP PROJECT MANAGER
Robert Campbell

———

EDITORIAL DIRECTOR
Jackie Douglas

ART DIRECTOR
Peter Luff

OXFORD UNIVERSITY PRESS

MANAGING EDITOR
Della Thompson

ASSOCIATE EDITORS
Jeremy Marshall, Maurice Waite

CHIEF SCIENCE EDITOR
William Trumble

NATURAL HISTORY EDITOR
David Shirt

SENIOR EDITOR
Glynnis Chantrell

ASSISTANT EDITOR
Andrew Hodgson

EDITORIAL ASSISTANT
Louise Jones

CHIEF EDITOR, CURRENT ENGLISH DICTIONARIES
Patrick Hanks

MARKET HOUSE BOOKS LTD, AYLESBURY

MANAGING EDITOR
John Daintith

EDITOR
Robert Hine

ILLUSTRATION CONSULTANTS

David Alderton MA
Richard C.F. Baker PhD, DIC, FHG
Emma Rose Barber MA
Roger Bridgman MSc
David Burnie BSc
Jack Challoner ARCS, PGCE
Philip Eden MSc

Elwyn Hartley Edwards
Mike Flynn
Captain P.M. Gurnell MRIN
Dr Alan Guy MA, DPhil, FRHISTS
Laurie Milner
Sean C. Mulshaw PhD, FGS, MIMM
Dr Gabrielle Murphy

Iain Nicolson BSc, FRAS
Julia Parker
Des Pawson
Dominic Sagar
Simon Stephens
Michael Tambini MA
Richard Walker PhD, PGCE

FOREWORD

WHEN THE OPPORTUNITY AROSE for Dorling Kindersley to collaborate with Oxford University Press on an illustrated dictionary, it seemed like a perfect marriage of talents. The harnessing of the complementary strengths of the two houses generated the possibility of creating a new landmark in this area of publishing. I believe that this has been realised. The double branding of Oxford, the most renowned name in the world for the English language, and DK, recognized as a quality imprint on illustrated home reference, offers the reader not only care, expertise, and high production values but also a volume that reaches beyond the traditional confines of a language-only dictionary.

This is no mere dictionary with pictures. The rationale behind the choice of illustrations has been as rigorous as for word selection. To have added pictures whose value was simply decorative would not have afforded any benefits beyond the coffee table. The selection of images has been governed by their usefulness, their accuracy, their capacity to bring the unfamiliar to life, their potential for expanding a definition, for shedding light on the obscure, or illuminating those dark corners where the reach of verbal description is challenged. Illustration panels have been created to provide a wide range of themes with additional information: the wordfields of annotation placed around images expand the reader's vocabulary; cutaway diagrams and cross-sections deepen understanding and add detail to a variety of subjects; galleries of images demonstrate the diversity between objects or types defined by a single word.

These benefits are genuinely substantial, and the fact that the dictionary itself is a handsome object to have and to hold is an additional bonus. We are proud to be associated with it.

STAINED-GLASS WINDOW

THE TEXT OF THE *Dorling Kindersley Illustrated Oxford Dictionary* has – like that of all Oxford dictionaries – benefited from Oxford's unrivalled language research programmes. Oxford dictionary editors rely on a wide range of editorial tools to extend our knowledge of English as it is used throughout the world. Central to these is the Oxford World Reading Programme – a 60-strong international network of readers who send new words, idioms, examples, and meanings to Oxford's editorial offices for analysis. Once sufficient evidence has built up to extend or alter an existing meaning or to add a new entry, specialist lexicographers undertake further research on the item, from pronunciation to etymology. Disputed facts are often checked with the Oxford Special Subject Advisors – a 150-strong international consultative body working in renowned institutions such as the Royal Botanic Gardens at Kew, London, and the IBM Laboratories. Finally, new entries are deposited with The Oxford Bank of New Words, the database that feeds new editions of all Oxford's dictionaries – including this one – and which, at any one time, holds over 3,000 authenticated new words.

Using computer search-and-analysis techniques, Oxford's lexicographers also consult databases of real language to research complex aspects of grammar, usage, and meaning. The Oxford Historical Corpus is used to investigate archaic words and holds the texts of some 700 titles dating from medieval times to the early twentieth century. A corpus of American English clarifies differences between American and British English, while the British National Corpus, representing every kind of writing and speech in English, answers questions on current English. Together, these databases ensure definitions and guidance to usage are as authoritative as possible.

CHRISTOPHER DAVIS
PUBLISHER, DORLING KINDERSLEY

THOMAS WEBSTER
PUBLISHING DIRECTOR FOR REFERENCE,
OXFORD UNIVERSITY PRESS

HOW TO USE THE DICTIONARY

THE FOLLOWING PAGES (8–14) illustrate and explain all the features and conventions that are used throughout this dictionary – from the structure and content of individual word entries to a complete list of abbreviations. The ILLUSTRATED DICTIONARY itself appears on pages 15–972,

and is followed by a comprehensive selection of ready-reference material (pages 973–1007). With the exception of feature panels (see opposite), all illustrations appear in alphabetical order, and can be found below or adjacent to the precise definition to which they are relevant.

NEW SECTION
Each alphabetical section of the dictionary begins on a new page, and is introduced by a large capital letter to make it easier to find.

ALPHABETICAL ORDER
Words are listed in 'letter by letter' alphabetical order, with spaces and hyphens disregarded.

QUICK-REFERENCE GUIDE TO WORD ENTRIES

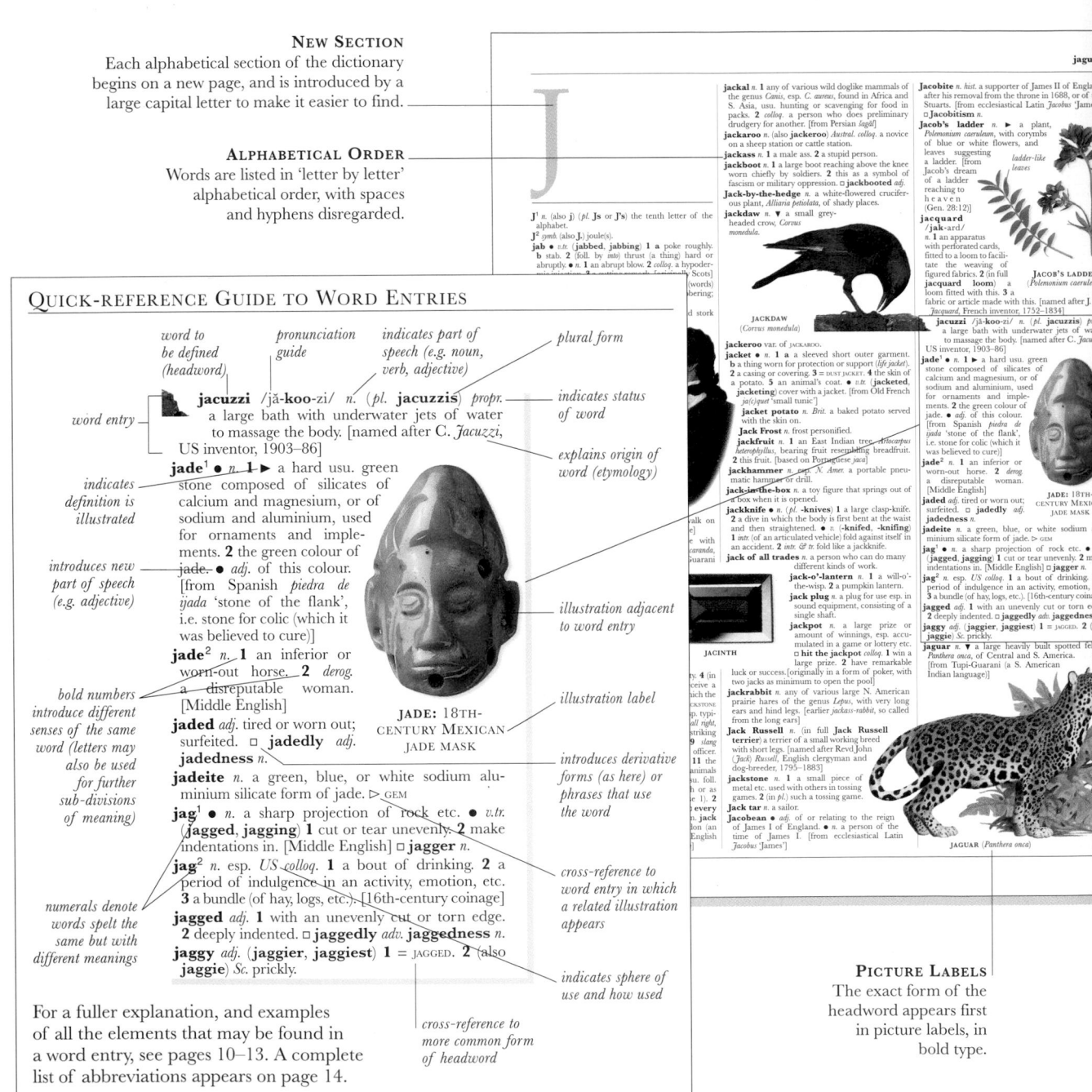

word to be defined (headword)

pronunciation guide

indicates part of speech (e.g. noun, verb, adjective)

plural form

word entry

jacuzzi /jǎ-koo-zi/ n. (pl. **jacuzzis**) propr. a large bath with underwater jets of water to massage the body. [named after C. Jacuzzi, US inventor, 1903–86]

indicates status of word

indicates definition is illustrated

jade¹ ● n. **1** ▶ a hard usu. green stone composed of silicates of calcium and magnesium, or of sodium and aluminium, used for ornaments and implements. **2** the green colour of jade. ● adj. of this colour. [from Spanish *piedra de ijada* 'stone of the flank', i.e. stone for colic (which it was believed to cure)]

explains origin of word (etymology)

introduces new part of speech (e.g. adjective)

jade² n. **1** an inferior or worn-out horse. **2** derog. a disreputable woman. [Middle English]

illustration adjacent to word entry

jaded adj. tired or worn out; surfeited. □ **jadedly** adj. **jadedness** n.

bold numbers introduce different senses of the same word (letters may also be used for further sub-divisions of meaning)

JADE: 18TH-CENTURY MEXICAN JADE MASK

illustration label

jadeite n. a green, blue, or white sodium aluminium silicate form of jade. ▷ GEM

introduces derivative forms (as here) or phrases that use the word

jag¹ ● n. a sharp projection of rock etc. ● v.tr. (**jagged**, **jagging**) **1** cut or tear unevenly. **2** make indentations in. [Middle English] □ **jagger** n.

jag² n. esp. US colloq. **1** a bout of drinking. **2** a period of indulgence in an activity, emotion, etc. **3** a bundle (of hay, logs, etc.). [16th-century coinage]

cross-reference to word entry in which a related illustration appears

numerals denote words spelt the same but with different meanings

jagged adj. **1** with an unevenly cut or torn edge. **2** deeply indented. □ **jaggedly** adv. **jaggedness** n.

jaggy adj. (**jaggier**, **jaggiest**) **1** = JAGGED. **2** (also **jaggie**) Sc. prickly.

indicates sphere of use and how used

cross-reference to more common form of headword

For a fuller explanation, and examples of all the elements that may be found in a word entry, see pages 10–13. A complete list of abbreviations appears on page 14.

Right column dictionary text

J¹ n. (also **j**) (pl. **Js** or **J's**) the tenth letter of the alphabet.

J² symb. Physics joule(s).

jab ● v.tr. (**jabbed**, **jabbing**) **1 a** poke roughly. **b** stab. **2** (foll. by *into*) thrust (a thing) hard or abruptly. ● n. **1** an abrupt blow. **2** colloq. a hypodermic injection. **3** a cutting remark. [originally Scots] (words bering;

stork

jackal n. **1** any of various wild doglike mammals of the genus *Canis*, esp. *C. aureus*, found in Africa and S. Asia, usu. hunting or scavenging for food in packs. **2** colloq. a person who does preliminary drudgery for another. [from Persian *šagāl*]

jackaroo n. (also **jackeroo**) Austral. colloq. a novice on a sheep station or cattle station.

jackass n. **1** a male ass. **2** a stupid person.

jackboot n. **1** a large boot reaching above the knee worn chiefly by soldiers. **2** this as a symbol of fascism or military oppression. □ **jackbooted** adj.

Jack-by-the-hedge n. a white-flowered cruciferous plant, *Alliaria petiolata*, of shady places.

jackdaw n. ▼ a small grey-headed crow, *Corvus monedula*.

JACKDAW (*Corvus monedula*)

jackeroo var. of JACKAROO.

jacket n. **1 a** a sleeved short outer garment. **b** a thing worn for protection or support (*life jacket*). **2** a casing or covering. **3** = DUST JACKET. **4** the skin of a potato. **5** an animal's coat. ● v.tr. (**jacketed**, **jacketing**) cover with a jacket. [from Old French *ja(c)quet* 'small tunic']

jacket potato n. Brit. a baked potato served with the skin on.

Jack Frost n. frost personified.

jackfruit n. **1** an East Indian tree, *Artocarpus heterophyllus*, bearing fruit resembling breadfruit. **2** this fruit. [based on Portuguese *jaca*]

jackhammer n. esp. N. Amer. a portable pneumatic hammer or drill.

jack-in-the-box n. a toy figure that springs out of a box when it is opened.

jackknife n. (pl. **-knives**) **1** a large clasp-knife. **2** a dive in which the body is first bent at the waist and then straightened. ● v. (**-knifed**, **-knifing**) **1** intr. (of an articulated vehicle) fold against itself in an accident. **2** intr. & tr. fold like a jackknife.

jack of all trades n. a person who can do many different kinds of work.

jack-o'-lantern n. **1** a will-o'-the-wisp. **2** a pumpkin lantern.

jack plug n. a plug for use esp. in sound equipment, consisting of a single shaft.

jackpot n. a large prize or amount of winnings, esp. accumulated in a game or lottery etc. □ **hit the jackpot** colloq. **1** win a large prize. **2** have remarkable luck or success. [originally in a form of poker, with two jacks as minimum to open the pool]

jackrabbit n. any of various large N. American prairie hares of the genus *Lepus*, with very long ears and hind legs. [earlier *jackass-rabbit*, so called from the long ears]

Jack Russell n. (in full **Jack Russell terrier**) a terrier of a small working breed with short legs. [named after Revd John (Jack) Russell, English clergyman and dog-breeder, 1795–1883]

jackstone n. **1** a small piece of metal etc. used with others in tossing games. **2** (in pl.) such a tossing game.

Jack tar n. a sailor.

Jacobean ● adj. of or relating to the reign of James I of England. ● n. a person of the time of James I. [from ecclesiastical Latin *Jacobus* 'James']

Jacobite n. hist. a supporter of James II of England after his removal from the throne in 1688, or of the Stuarts. [from ecclesiastical Latin *Jacobus* 'James'] □ **Jacobitism** n.

Jacob's ladder n. ▶ a plant, *Polemonium caeruleum*, with corymbs of blue or white flowers, and leaves suggesting a ladder. [from Jacob's dream of a ladder reaching to heaven (Gen. 28:12)]

ladder-like leaves

JACOB'S LADDER (*Polemonium caeruleu*)

jacquard /jak-ard/ n. **1** an apparatus with perforated cards, fitted to a loom to facilitate the weaving of figured fabrics. **2** (in full **jacquard loom**) a loom fitted with this. **3** a fabric or article made with this. [named after J. M. Jacquard, French inventor, 1752–1834]

jacuzzi /jǎ-koo-zi/ n. (pl. **jacuzzis**) pro a large bath with underwater jets of wat to massage the body. [named after C. Jacuz US inventor, 1903–86]

jade¹ ● n. **1** ▶ a hard usu. green stone composed of silicates of calcium and magnesium, or of sodium and aluminium, used for ornaments and implements. **2** the green colour of jade. ● adj. of this colour. [from Spanish *piedra de ijada* 'stone of the flank', i.e. stone for colic (which it was believed to cure)]

jade² n. **1** an inferior or worn-out horse. **2** derog. a disreputable woman. [Middle English]

JADE: 18TH-CENTURY MEXIC JADE MASK

jaded adj. tired or worn out; surfeited. □ **jadedly** adj. **jadedness** n.

jadeite n. a green, blue, or white sodium a minium silicate form of jade. ▷ GEM

jag¹ ● n. a sharp projection of rock etc. ● (**jagged**, **jagging**) **1** cut or tear unevenly. **2** ma indentations in. [Middle English] □ **jagger** n.

jag² n. esp. US colloq. **1** a bout of drinking. **2** period of indulgence in an activity, emotion, **3** a bundle (of hay, logs, etc.). [16th-century coinag

jagged adj. **1** with an unevenly cut or torn ed **2** deeply indented. □ **jaggedly** adj. **jaggedness**

jaggy adj. (**jaggier**, **jaggiest**) **1** = JAGGED. **2** (al **jaggie**) Sc. prickly.

jaguar n. ▼ a large heavily built spotted fel *Panthera onca*, of Central and S. America. [from Tupi-Guarani (a S. American Indian language)]

JACINTH

JAGUAR (*Panthera onca*)

PICTURE LABELS
The exact form of the headword appears first in picture labels, in bold type.

FEATURE PANELS

Feature panels give more detailed explanations of words, and often employ larger illustrations or series of illustrations to aid understanding. Associated vocabulary may be introduced in the picture annotation. Feature panels appear on the same double-page spread as the word defined; picture symbols (e.g. ▲) indicate the direction in which to look.

PAGE HEADINGS

The left-hand page heading identifies the first word entry to appear in full on that page; the right-hand heading identifies the last entry to appear.

JUPITER

Jupiter is the largest, most massive planet in the solar system. Its rapid rate of rotation in 9 hours 55 minutes causes the clouds in its atmosphere to form dark, low-altitude 'belts' and bright, high-altitude 'zones' – both with huge storm systems – which encircle the planet parallel with the equator. Jupiter has two faint rings, and is orbited by 16 known moons, of which Ganymede, Callisto, Io, and Europa (the Galileans) are the largest.

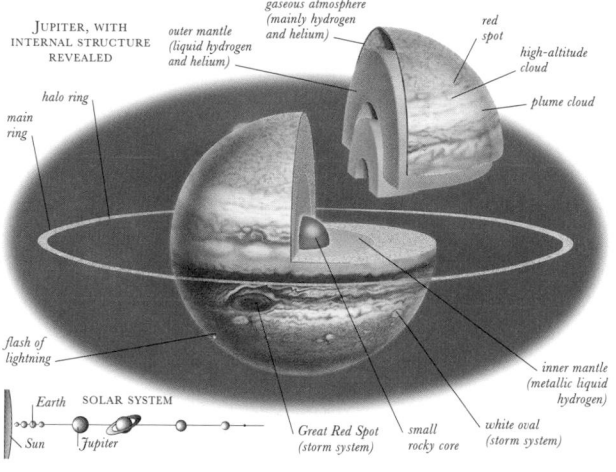

JUPITER, WITH INTERNAL STRUCTURE REVEALED

gaseous atmosphere (mainly hydrogen and helium)

outer mantle (liquid hydrogen and helium)

red spot

high-altitude cloud

halo ring

main ring

plume cloud

flash of lightning

inner mantle (metallic liquid hydrogen)

Earth

SOLAR SYSTEM

Sun

Jupiter

Great Red Spot (storm system)

small rocky core

white oval (storm system)

---

jaguarundi

jaguarundi n. (pl. jaguarundis) a long-tailed slender feline, Felis yaguarondi, of Central and S. American (a. S. American Indian language)]

jam¹ n. also Brit. gaol) n. 1 a place to which persons are committed by a court for detention. 2 confinement in a jail. ● v.tr. put in jail. [from Old Northern French gaol]

jailbait n. (collect.) slang a girl, or girls, under the age of consent.

jailbird n. (also Brit. gaolbird) a prisoner or habitual criminal.

jailbreak n. (also Brit. gaolbreak) an escape from jail.

jailer n. (also Brit. gaoler) a person in charge of a jail or of the prisoners in it.

jailhouse n. esp. N. Amer. a prison.

Jain /jyn/ n. an adherent of a non-theistic Indian religion. ● adj. of or relating to this religion. [from Sanskrit janas 'saint, victor'] □ Jainism n.

jake adj. N. Amer., Austral., & NZ slang all right; satisfactory. [20th-century coinage]

JALAPEÑO PEPPER

jalapeño /hal-ă-payn-yoh/ n. (pl. -os) jalapeño pepper ◄ a very hot green chilli pepper, used esp. in Mexican-style cooking. [Mexican Spanish]

jalopy /jă-lop-i/ n. (pl. -ies) colloq. a dilapidated old motor vehicle. [20th-century coinage]

jalousie /zhal-oo-zee/ n. a blind or shutter made of a row of angled slats to keep out rain etc. and control the influx of light. [French]

jam¹ ● n. (jammed, jamming) 1 a tr. squeeze or wedge into a space. b intr. become wedged. 2 a tr. cause (machinery or a component) to become wedged so immovable so that it cannot work. b intr. become jammed in this way. 3 tr. cram together in a compact mass. 4 intr. (foll. by in, on to) push or crowd (they jammed on to the bus). 5 tr. a block (a passage, road, etc.) by crowding or obstructing. b (foll. by in) obstruct the exit of (we were jammed in). 6 tr. (usu. foll. by on) apply (brakes etc.) forcefully or abruptly. 7 tr. make (a radio transmission) unintelligible by causing interference. 8 intr. colloq. (in jazz etc.) extemporize with other musicians ● n. 1 a squeeze or crush. 2 a crowded mass (traffic jam). 3 colloq. a predicament. 4 a stoppage (on a machine etc.) due to jamming. 5 (in full jam session) colloq. improvised playing by a group of usu. jazz musicians. □ jammer n.

jam² ● n. 1 a conserve of fruit and sugar boiled to a thick consistency. 2 Brit. colloq. something easy or pleasant (money for jam). □ jam tomorrow Brit. a pleasant thing often promised but never forthcoming.

jamb n. Archit. a side post or surface of a doorway, window, or fireplace. [from Late Latin gamba 'hoof']

jambalaya /jam-bă-lyr/ n. a Cajun dish of rice with shrimps, chicken, etc. [Louisiana French from modern Provençal jambalaia]

jamboree n. 1 a celebration. 2 a large rally of Scouts. [19th-century coinage]

jam jar n. 1 a glass jar for containing jam. 2 Brit. rhyming slang a car.

jammy adj. (jammier, jammiest) 1 covered with jam. 2 Brit. colloq. a lucky. b profitable.

jam-packed adj. colloq. full to capacity.

jam session see jam¹ n. 5.

Jan. abbr. January.

jane n. plain jane an unattractive girl or woman.

jangle ● n. 1 intr. & tr. make, or cause (a bell etc.) to make, a harsh metallic sound. 2 tr. irritate (the nerves etc.) by discordant sound or speech etc. ● n. a harsh metallic sound. [from Old French jangler]

janitor n. 1 a doorkeeper. 2 a caretaker of a building. [Latin, based on janua 'door'] □ janitorial adj.

janizary n. (also janissary) (pl. -ies) 1 hist. a member of the Turkish infantry forming the Sultan's guard in the 14th–19th c. 2 a devoted follower. [based on Turkish yeni 'new' + çeri 'troops']

January n. (pl. -ies) the first month of the year. [from Latin Januarius (mensis) '(month)' of Janus, guardian god of doors and beginnings]

Jap n. & adj. colloq. offens. = JAPANESE.

japan ● n. ▼ a hard usu. black varnish, esp. of a kind brought originally from Japan. ● v.tr. (japanned, japanning) 1 varnish with japan. 2 make black and glossy.

JAPAN: JAPANNED AND LACQUERED ANTIQUE SCREEN

japanned finish

Japanese ● n. (pl. same) 1 a a native or national of Japan. b a person of Japanese descent. 2 the language of Japan. ● adj. of or relating to Japan, its people, or its language.

Japanese quince n. = JAPONICA.

jape ● n. a practical joke. ● v.intr. play a joke. [Middle English] □ japery n.

Japlish n. a blend of Japanese and English, used in Japan.

japonica n. any flowering shrub of the genus Chaenomeles, esp. C. speciosa, with round white, green, or yellow edible fruits and bright red flowers. [modern Latin fem. of japonicus 'Japanese']

jar¹ n. 1 a a container of glass, earthenware, plastic, etc., usu. cylindrical. b the contents of this. 2 Brit. colloq. a glass of beer. [from Arabic jarra] □ jarful n.

jar² ● n. (jarred, jarring) 1 intr. (of sound, words, manner, etc.) sound discordant or grating (on the nerves etc.). 2 a tr. (foll. by against, on) strike or cause to strike with vibration or a grating sound. b intr. (of a body affected) vibrate gratingly. 3 tr. send a shock through (a part of the body) (the fall jarred his neck). 4 intr. (of an opinion, fact, etc.) be at variance; be in conflict or in dispute. ● n. 1 a jarring sound or sensation. 2 a physical shock or jolt. 3 lack of harmony; disagreement. [Middle English]

jardinière /zhar-din-yair/ n. 1 an ornamental pot or stand for the display of growing plants. 2 a dish of mixed vegetables. [French, literally 'female gardener']

jargon n. 1 words or expressions used by a particular group or profession (medical jargon). 2 barbarous or debased language. [from Old French]

jasmine n. (also jasmin, jessamin, jessamine) ▼ any of various ornamental shrubs of the genus Jasminum usu. with white or yellow flowers. [from Persian yāsmīn]

JASMINE: YELLOW JASMINE (Jasminum humile)

jasper n. ▶ an opaque variety of quartz, usu. red, yellow, or brown. [from Latin iaspis]

JASPER: RED JASPER

jaundice ● n. 1 Med. a condition with yellowing of the skin or whites of the eyes, often caused by obstruction of the bile duct or by liver disease. 2 disordered (esp. mental) vision. 3 envy. ● v.tr. 1 affect with jaundice. 2 (esp. as jaundiced adj.) affect (a person) with envy. [from Old French jaunisse 'yellowness']

jaunt ● n. a short excursion for enjoyment. ● v.intr. take a jaunt. [16th-century coinage]

jaunty adj. (jauntier, jauntiest) 1 cheerful and self-confident. 2 dashing, pert (jaunty hat). [earlier jentee, from French gentil 'noble'] □ jauntily adv. jauntiness n.

Javanese ● n. (pl. same) 1 a a native or inhabitant of Java in Indonesia. b a person of Javanese descent. 2 the Austronesian language of central Java. ● adj. of or relating to Java, its people, or its language.

javelin n. 1 a light spear thrown in a competitive sport or as a weapon. 2 the athletic event or sport of throwing the javelin. [from Gallo-Roman gabalottus]

jaw n. 1 a each of the upper and lower bony structures in vertebrates forming the framework of the mouth and containing the teeth. b the parts of certain invertebrates for the ingestion of food. 2 a (in pl.) the mouth with its bones and teeth. b the narrow mouth of a valley, channel, etc. c the gripping parts of a tool or machine. d gripping-power (jaws of death). 3 colloq. a talkativeness (hold your jaw). b sermonizing talk. ● v. colloq. 1 intr. speak esp. at tedious length. 2 tr. persuade by talking. b admonish or lecture. [from Old French joe 'cheek, jaw'] □ jawless adj.

jawbone n. a bone of the jaw, esp. that of the lower jaw, or either half of this. ▷ VERTEBRATE

jawline n. the outline of the jaw.

jay n. 1 ▶ a noisy European bird, Garrulus glandarius, with vivid pinkish-brown, blue, black, and white plumage. ▷ PASSERINE. 2 any other bird of the subfamily Garrulinae. [from Late Latin gaius]

JAY (Garrulus glandarius)

jaywalk v.intr. cross or walk in the street or road without regard for traffic. □ jaywalker n.

jazz ● n. 1 music of African-American origin characterized by improvisation, syncopation, and usu. a forceful rhythm. 2 colloq. pretentious talk or behaviour (all that jazz). ● v.intr. play or dance to jazz. □ jazz up brighten or enliven. [20th-century coinage] □ jazzer n.

jazzman n. (pl. -men) a male jazz musician.

jazzy adj. (jazzier, jazziest) 1 of or like jazz. 2 vivid, showy. □ jazzily adv.

JCB n. Brit. propr. a type of mechanical excavator with a shovel at the front and a digging arm at the rear. [from J. C. Bamford, the makers]

J-cloth n. (also J cloth propr.) a type of cloth used esp. for household cleaning. [from Johnson and Johnson, original makers]

431

MARGINAL MARKERS

Alphabetical sections are easily located by using the coloured tabs, which are positioned further down the page with each new letter.

J

SEPARATE ENTRIES

Compounds are given their own entry, rather than being grouped under one general heading (e.g. **jawbone** appears separately, rather than under **jaw**).

USAGE NOTES

usage notes are placed between horizontal lines after main part of entry

jobber n. **1** (in the UK) a principal or wholesaler dealing on the Stock Exchange. **2** US **a** a wholesaler. **b** derog. = BROKER 2. **3** a person who jobs.

■ **Usage** The term *jobber* in sense 1 was officially replaced by *broker-dealer* in 1986, broker-dealers being entitled to act as both agents and principals in share dealings.

Usage notes directly after word entries alert the reader to a difficulty or controversy attached to particular uses; they are not intended to prescribe usage. Further notes on grammar and style appear on pages 1002–1007 of the REFERENCE SECTION.

KEY TO SYMBOLS

- ● Introduces a new part of speech (e.g. noun, verb, adjective)
- □ Introduces a section containing phrases or derivatives
- ■ Introduces a usage note (see right)
- ▷ Introduces a headword where a relevant illustration can be found
- ▶ Indicates that a definition is illustrated, and in which direction to look

STRUCTURE OF ENTRIES

These two pages contain examples from the dictionary, illustrating all elements found in word entries. Annotation identifies the typographic style and location of each part, and explains the editorial approach where appropriate. Proper names are not listed in the dictionary, but only those vocabulary items to which they have given rise (e.g. *Jonah*). More detailed information on forms and labels appears on pages 12–13, and a list of abbreviations on page 14. Grammar and style are further clarified on pages 1002–1007 of the REFERENCE SECTION.

HEADWORDS

DIFFERENT FORMS

headword printed in bold type

variant spelling (where applicable)

different forms of the headword are given for different parts of speech

cosy (*US* **cozy**) ● *adj.* (**cosier**, **cosiest**) **1** comfortable and warm. **2** *derog.* complacent; expedient, self-serving. **3** warm and friendly. ● *n.* (*pl.* **-ies**) a cover to keep something hot, esp. a teapot or a boiled egg. ● *v.tr.* (**-ies**, **-ied**) (often foll. by *along*) *colloq.* reassure, esp. deceptively. [originally Scots] □ **cosily** *adv.* **cosiness** *n.*

symbol introduces derivative forms of the headword (as here) or phrases (see below)

fizzle ● *v.intr.* make a feeble hiss. ● *n.* such a sound. □ **fizzle out** end feebly.

symbol introduces phrasal verb (or idioms and derivatives elsewhere)

foreign headword printed in bold italic type

pronunciation guide (with stress indicated in bold type)

idée fixe /ee-day **feeks**/ *n.* (*pl.* **idées fixes** *pronunc.* same) an idea that dominates the mind; an obsession. [French, literally 'fixed idea']

indicates that pronunciation is the same, despite change in form of headword

compounds are entered as headwords in their own right, rather than under general headings

zoom lens *n.* a lens allowing a camera to zoom by varying the focal length. ▷ CAMCORDER

DIVISION OF ENTRIES INTO DIFFERENT SENSES

different senses are numbered, and ordered by currency or comparative significance

letters are used to indicate closely related subdivisions within a sense

bull[1] ● *n.* **1 a** an uncastrated male bovine animal. **b** a male of the whale, elephant, and other large animals. **2** (**the Bull**) the zodiacal sign or constellation Taurus. **3** *Brit.* the bull's-eye of a target. **4** *Stock Exch.* a person who buys shares hoping to sell them at a higher price later. ● *attrib.adj.* like that of a bull (*bull neck*). [from Old Norse *boli*]

bull[2] *n.* a papal edict. [from Latin *bulla* 'rounded object']

superior numerals are used to denote separate entries for words spelt the same but with different meanings or origins

spelling change applicable to a specific sense

LABELLING

PARTS OF SPEECH (E.G. VERB, NOUN, ADJECTIVE)

a bullet introduces each successive part of speech within a word entry

labels indicate intransitive and transitive subdivisions of a verb

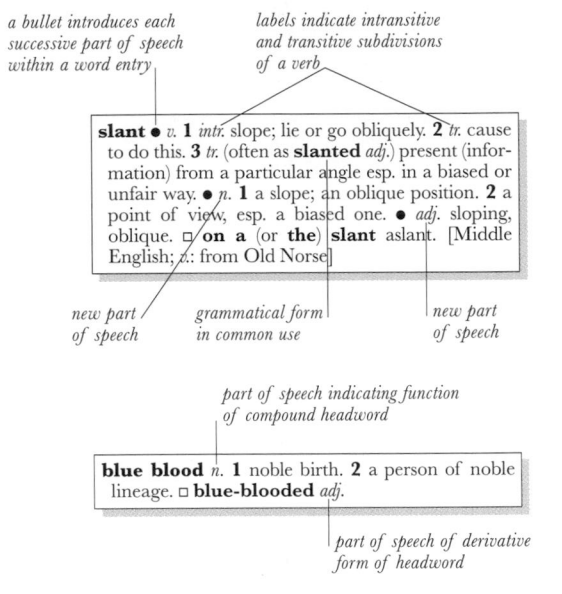

slant ● *v.* **1** *intr.* slope; lie or go obliquely. **2** *tr.* cause to do this. **3** *tr.* (often as **slanted** *adj.*) present (information) from a particular angle esp. in a biased or unfair way. ● *n.* **1** a slope; an oblique position. **2** a point of view, esp. a biased one. ● *adj.* sloping, oblique. □ **on a** (or **the**) **slant** aslant. [Middle English; *z.*: from Old Norse]

new part of speech

grammatical form in common use

new part of speech

part of speech indicating function of compound headword

blue blood *n.* **1** noble birth. **2** a person of noble lineage. □ **blue-blooded** *adj.*

part of speech of derivative form of headword

USAGE ADVICE WITHIN WORD ENTRIES

grammatical information

bracketed information indicates subject area(s)

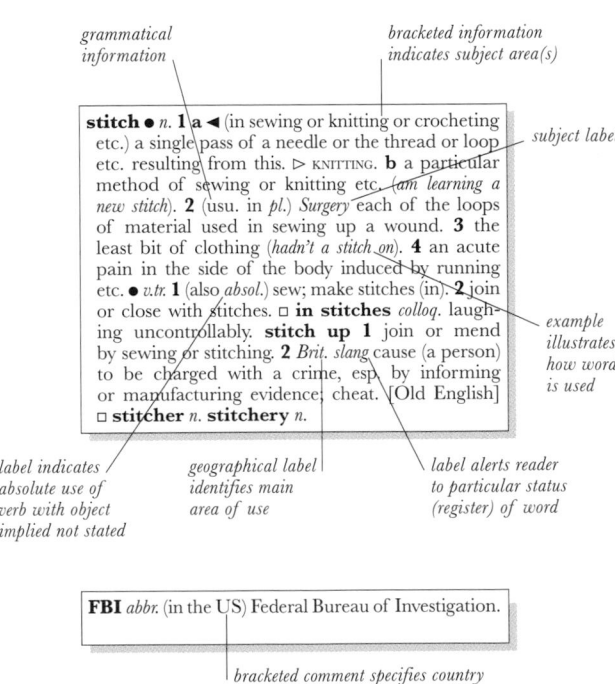

stitch ● *n.* **1 a** ◄ (in sewing or knitting or crocheting etc.) a single pass of a needle or the thread or loop etc. resulting from this. ▷ KNITTING. **b** a particular method of sewing or knitting etc. (*am learning a new stitch*). **2** (usu. in *pl.*) *Surgery* each of the loops of material used in sewing up a wound. **3** the least bit of clothing (*hadn't a stitch on*). **4** an acute pain in the side of the body induced by running etc. ● *v.tr.* **1** (also *absol.*) sew; make stitches (in). **2** join or close with stitches. □ **in stitches** *colloq.* laughing uncontrollably. **stitch up 1** join or mend by sewing or stitching. **2** *Brit. slang* cause (a person) to be charged with a crime, esp. by informing or manufacturing evidence; cheat. [Old English] □ **stitcher** *n.* **stitchery** *n.*

subject label

example illustrates how word is used

label indicates absolute use of verb with object implied not stated

geographical label identifies main area of use

label alerts reader to particular status (register) of word

FBI *abbr.* (in the US) Federal Bureau of Investigation.

bracketed comment specifies country associated with the defined institution

conscious *adj.* **1** awake and aware of one's surroundings and identity. **2** (usu. foll. by *of*, or *that* + clause) aware (*conscious of his inferiority*). **3** (of actions, emotions, etc.) realized or recognized by the doer (*made a conscious effort not to laugh*). [from Latin *conscius* 'knowing with others or in oneself'] □ **consciously** *adv.*

— *specifies formula for grammatical construction*

indicates limited use of word in this sense

use restricted to predicative position in this sense

fond *adj.* **1** (*predic.*; foll. by *of*) having affection or a liking for. **2** (*attrib.*) affectionate, loving, doting. **3** (*attrib.*) (of beliefs etc.) foolishly optimistic or credulous; naive. [Middle English, from obsolete *fon* 'to be foolish'] □ **fondly** *adv.* **fondness** *n.*

adjective used attributively in these senses

ETYMOLOGY

The etymologies aim to highlight noteworthy features in the history or composition of the headword, of particular interest in terms of origin, sense, form, etc. Information common to a set (e.g. **exclaim**, **exclamation**, **exclamatory**) is not repeated where neighbouring entries provide ease of reference. Cross-references are kept to a minimum and speculative derivations are not pursued. Notes on etymology are given in square brackets at the end of the main entry, before any derivative forms; examples of various types are shown below.

aardvark *n.* a nocturnal mammal of southern Africa, *Orycteropus afer*, with a tubular snout and long extensible tongue, that feeds on termites. Also called *ant-bear*, *earth-pig*. ▷ MAMMAL. [Afrikaans, from *aarde* 'earth' + *varken* 'pig']

etymology given in square brackets

banal /bă-nahl/ *adj.* trite, feeble, commonplace. [originally in sense 'compulsory', hence 'common to all'] □ **banality** *n.* (*pl.* -**ies**).

etymology appears before derivative forms

blotto *adj.* *slang* very drunk, esp. unconscious from drinking. [20th-century coinage]

etymology

hornpipe *n.* **1** a lively dance (esp. associated with sailors). **2** the music for this. [Middle English: originally the name of a wind instrument partly of horn]

etymology

CROSS-REFERENCES

variant spelling appears as bold headword

aging var. of AGEING.

headword where definition appears

decanal *adj.* **1** of a dean or deanery. **2** of the south side of a choir, the side on which the dean sits. [based on Late Latin *decanus* (see DEAN)]

indicates further information is to be found at headword named

antonym given for consultation

statics *n.pl.* (usu. treated as *sing.*) **1** the science of bodies at rest or of forces in equilibrium (opp. DYNAMICS 1a). **2** = STATIC *n.*

small capitals used to indicate headword entry appearing elsewhere

cross-reference to the noun sense of the headword **static**

calves *pl.* of CALF[1], CALF[2].

irregular forms appear as cross-referenced bold headwords, when they are three or more entries away from main headword

trodden *past part.* of TREAD.

PICTURES

symbol indicates that definition is illustrated, and points in direction of illustration

calyx *n.* (also **calix**) (*pl.* **calyces** or **calyxes**) **1** *Bot.* ▼ the sepals collectively, forming the protective layer of a flower in bud. **2** *Biol.* any cuplike cavity or structure. [from Greek *kalux* 'bud case, husk']

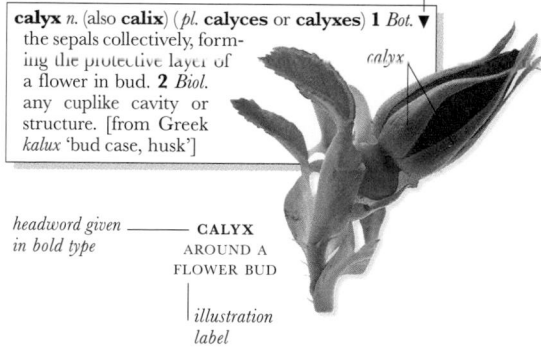

calyx

headword given in bold type — **CALYX** AROUND A FLOWER BUD

illustration label

fisher *n.* **1** an animal that catches fish, esp. the pekan, a tree-living N. American marten, *Martes pennanti*, valued for its fur. ▷ MUSTELID. **2** *archaic* a fisherman.

symbol introduces headword where relevant illustration appears

PRONUNCIATION

A guide to pronunciation is given for difficult words. The pronunciation given represents the standard speech of southern England. It is shown between diagonal slashes, usually just after the word itself. Words are broken up into small units, usually of one syllable. The syllable that is spoken with most stress in a word of two or more syllables is shown in bold type, like **this**. An apostrophe (') is occasionally used to show either a slight break between sounds, as in /**sy**-ki-k'l/ for *psychical*, or that two letters are pronounced with their own separate sounds (and not as they might appear when together), as in /s'**yoo**-doh/ for *pseudo* or /th'**ee**-tă/ for *theta*. A consonant is sometimes doubled to avoid misinterpretation, as in /**day**-iss/ for *dais*. The pronunciation of a word is sometimes indicated by giving a well-known word that rhymes with it, as in /*rhymes with* roof/ for *woof* [2].

The sounds represented are as follows:

a *as in* cat	ee *as in* meet	kh *as in* loch	or *as in* corn	uu *as in* book
ă *as in* ago	eer *as in* beer	l *as in* leg	ow *as in* cow	v *as in* van
ah *as in* calm	er *as in* her	m *as in* man	oy *as in* boy	w *as in* will
air *as in* hair	ew *as in* few	n *as in* not	p *as in* pen	y *as in* yes
ar *as in* bar	ewr *as in* pure	ng *as in* sing, finger	r *as in* red	or when preceded by a
aw *as in* law	f *as in* fat	nk *as in* thank	s *as in* sit	consonant = I *as in* cry,
ay *as in* say	g *as in* get	o *as in* top	sh *as in* shop	realize
b *as in* bat	h *as in* hat	ŏ *as in* lemon	t *as in* top	yoo *as in* unit
ch *as in* chin	i *as in* pin	oh *as in* most	th *as in* thin	yoor *as in* Europe
d *as in* day	I *as in* eye	oi *as in* join	*th as in* this	yr *as in* fire
e *as in* bed	j *as in* jam	oo *as in* soon	u *as in* cup	z *as in* zebra
ě *as in* taken	k *as in* king	oor *as in* poor	ŭ *as in* circus	*zh as in* vision

LABELS

These are used to clarify the particular context in which a word or phrase is normally used. They appear in italic type, often in abbreviated form (an alphabetical list of all abbreviations is given on page 14).

SUBJECT

Some subject labels are used to indicate the particular relevance of a term or subject with which it is associated, e.g. *Mus.* (music), *Law*, *Physics*. They are not used when this is sufficiently clear from the definition itself.

GEOGRAPHICAL

The geographical label *Brit.* (British) indicates that the use of a word or phrase is found chiefly in British English (and often in other parts of the Commonwealth) but not in American English. *US* indicates that the use is found chiefly in American English but not in British English except as a conscious Americanism. Other geographical labels, such as *Austral.* (Australian) and *Canad.* (Canadian) show that use is generally restricted to the area named.

REGISTER (E.G. FORMAL, SLANG, DISPUTED)

● *formal, colloq., slang*

Words and phrases more common in formal (esp. written English) are labelled *formal*. Those more common in informal spoken English are labelled *colloq.* (colloquial) or, especially if very informal or restricted to a particular social group, *slang*.

● *coarse slang, offens.*

Two categories of deprecated usage are indicated by special markings: *coarse slang* indicates a word that, although widely found, is still unacceptable to many people; *offens.* (offensive) indicates a use that is regarded as offensive by members of a particular religious, ethnic, or other group. Words regarded as offensive have not been excluded from the dictionary; instead they have been included and marked for the information of the reader as basic guidance.

● *disp.*

Where usage is disputed or controversial, *disp.* (disputed) alerts the user to a danger or difficulty; any further information is given in a usage note at the end of the entry (see page 9).

STYLE

● *literary, poet.*

Words or phrases found mainly in literature are indicated by *literary* whereas *poet.* (poetical) indicates that use is confined generally to poetry or other contexts with romantic connotations.

● *joc., derog.*

Where use is intended to be humorous, the label *joc.* (jocular) is given; *derog.* (derogatory) denotes the intentionally disparaging use of the word or phrase.

CURRENCY

● *archaic, hist.*

For words that have lost currency except perhaps in special contexts such as legal or religious use, *archaic* is given; *hist.* (historical) denotes a word or use that is confined to historical reference, normally because the thing referred to no longer exists.

STATUS

● *propr.*

The label *propr.* (proprietary) indicates a term that has the status of a trade mark (see the Note on Proprietary Status on page 4).

FORMS

In general, different forms of nouns, verbs, adjectives, and adverbs are given when the form is irregular (as described further below) or when, though regular, it causes difficulty (as with forms such as **budgeted**, **coos**, and **taxis**).

PLURALS OF NOUNS

For nouns that form their plural regularly by adding -s (or -es when they end in -s, -x, -z, -sh, or soft -ch), the plural form is not shown. Other plural forms are given, notably for:

- nouns ending in -i or -o (e.g. **alibi**, **gazebo**).
- nouns ending in Latinate forms such as -a and -um (e.g. **amphora**, **ileum**).
- nouns ending in the suffix -y (e.g. **colloquy**).
- nouns with more than one plural form (e.g. **fish**, **aquarium**).
- nouns with plurals showing a change in the stem (e.g. **foot**).
- nouns with a plural form unchanged from the singular form (e.g. **sheep**).
- nouns in -ful (e.g. **handful**).

FORMS OF VERBS

The following forms are regarded as regular:

- third person singular present forms adding -s to the stem (or -es to stems ending in -s, -x, -z, -sh, or soft -ch).
- past tenses and past participles dropping a final silent e and adding -ed to the stem (e.g. **changed**, **danced**).
- present participles dropping a final silent e and adding -ing to the stem (e.g. **changing**, **dancing**).

Other forms are given, notably for:

- verbs which change form by doubling a consonant (e.g. **bat**, **batted**, **batting**). Where practice differs in American usage this is noted (e.g. at **cavil**).
- verbs with strong and irregular forms showing a change in the stem (e.g. **go**, **went**, **gone**).
- verbs ending in -y which change form by substituting -i for -y (e.g. **try**, **tries**, **tried**).

COMPARATIVE AND SUPERLATIVE OF ADJECTIVES

For the following regular forms, changes in form are not given:

- Words of one syllable adding -er and -est (e.g. **greater**, **greatest**).
- Words of one syllable dropping a final silent e and adding -er and -est (e.g. **braver**, **bravest**).

Other forms are given, notably for:

- Those adjectives that double a final consonant (e.g. **hot**, **hotter**, **hottest**).
- Two-syllable words that have comparative and superlative forms in -er and -est (of which very many are words ending in -y, e.g. **happy**, **happier**, **happiest**), and their negative forms (e.g. **unhappy**, **unhappier**, **unhappiest**).

Specification of the above forms indicates only that they are available; it is usually also possible to form comparatives with *more* and superlatives with *most* (e.g. *more happy*, *most unhappy*).

ADJECTIVES IN -ABLE

These are given as derivative forms when there is sufficient evidence of their currency, and as headwords when further definition is called for. In general they are formed as follows:

- Verbs drop silent final -e except after c and g (e.g. **movable**, **abridgeable**).
- Verbs of more than one syllable ending in -y (preceded by a consonant or qu) change y to i (e.g. **enviable**).

A final consonant is often doubled as in a normal form change (e.g. **conferrable**, **regrettable**).

PREFIXES, SUFFIXES, AND COMBINING FORMS

A selection of these is given in the main body of the text; prefixes are given in the form **ex-**, **re-**, etc., and suffixes in the form **-able**, **-ably**, etc.

For a usage note on combining forms see the entry COMBINING FORM in the dictionary itself.

ABBREVIATIONS

Most abbreviations appear in italics. Abbreviations in general use (such as *etc.*) are explained in the dictionary itself.

abbr.	abbreviation
absol.	absolute
adj.	adjective
adv.	adverb
Aeron.	Aeronautics
Amer.	American
Anat.	Anatomy
Anglo-Ind.	Anglo-Indian
Anthropol.	Anthropology
Antiq.	Antiquities; Antiquity
Archaeol.	Archaeology
Archit.	Architecture
assim.	assimilated
Astrol.	Astrology
Astron.	Astronomy
attrib.	attributive(ly)
attrib.adj.	attributive adjective
Austral.	Australian
aux.	auxiliary
Bibl.	Biblical
Biochem.	Biochemistry
Biol.	Biology
Bot.	Botany
Brit.	British
Canad.	Canadian
Chem.	Chemistry; chemical
Cinematog.	Cinematography
collect.	collective
colloq.	colloquial
comb.	combination; combining
compar.	comparative
compl.	complement
conj.	conjunction
contr.	contraction
Crystallog.	Crystallography
derog.	derogatory
det.	determiner
dial.	dialect
disp.	disputed
Eccl.	Ecclesiastical
Ecol.	Ecology
Econ.	Economics
Electr.	Electricity
ellipt.	elliptical(ly)
emphat.	emphatic
Engin.	Engineering
esp.	especially
euphem.	euphemistic

fem.	feminine
foll.	followed
Geog.	Geography
Geol.	Geology
Geom.	Geometry
Gk	Greek
Gram.	Grammar
Hist.	History
hist.	with historical reference
imper.	imperative
infin.	infinitive
int.	interjection
interrog.	interrogative
interrog.adv.	interrogative adverb
interrog.pron.	interrogative pronoun
intr.	intransitive
Ir.	Irish
iron.	ironical
joc.	jocular
masc.	masculine
Math.	Mathematics
Mech.	Mechanics
Med.	Medicine
Meteorol.	Meteorology
Mil.	Military
Mineral.	Mineralogy
Mus.	Music
Mythol.	Mythology
n.	noun
N. Amer.	North American
Naut.	Nautical
neg.	negative
N.Engl.	Northern English
neut.	neuter
n.pl.	noun plural
NZ	New Zealand
offens.	offensive
opp.	opposite; (as) opposed (to)
orig.	originally
Parl.	Parliament
part.	participle
past part.	past participle
Pharm.	Pharmacy; Pharmacology
Philol.	Philology
Philos.	Philosophy
Phonet.	Phonetics
Photog.	Photography
phr.	phrase

phrs.	phrases
Physiol.	Physiology
pl.	plural
poet.	poetical
Polit.	Politics
poss.	possessive
prec.	preceded
predet.	predeterminer
predic.	predicate; predicative(ly)
predic.adj.	predicative adjective
prep.	preposition
pres. part.	present participle
pron.	pronoun
pronunc.	pronunciation
propr.	proprietary term
Psychol.	Psychology
RC Ch.	Roman Catholic Church
refl.	reflexive
rel.adv.	relative adverb
rel.det.	relative determiner
Relig.	Religion
rel.pron.	relative pronoun
Rhet.	Rhetoric
Rom.	Roman
S.Afr.	South African
Sc.	Scottish
Sci.	Science
sing.	singular
Stock Exch.	Stock Exchange
superl.	superlative
symb.	symbol
Telev.	Television
Theatr.	Theatre
Theol.	Theology
tr.	transitive
US	American; United States
usu.	usually
v.	verb
var.	variant(s)
v.aux	auxiliary verb
v.intr.	intransitive verb
v.refl.	reflexive verb
v.tr.	transitive verb
W.Ind.	West Indian
Zool.	Zoology

THE ILLUSTRATED DICTIONARY

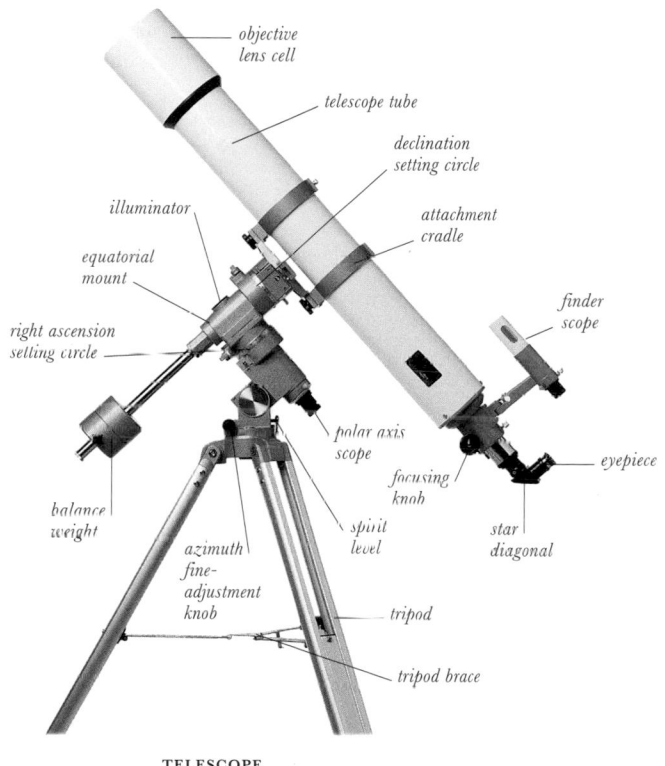

objective
lens cell

telescope tube

declination
setting circle

illuminator

attachment
cradle

equatorial
mount

finder
scope

right ascension
setting circle

polar axis
scope

eyepiece

focusing
knob

balance
weight

spirit
level

star
diagonal

azimuth
fine-
adjustment
knob

tripod

tripod brace

TELESCOPE

A

A¹ *n.* (also **a**) (*pl.* **As** or **A's**) **1** the first letter of the alphabet. **2** *Mus.* the sixth note of the diatonic scale of C major. ▷ NOTATION. **3** the first hypothetical person or example. **4** the highest class or category (of roads, academic marks, etc.). **5** (usu. *a*) *Algebra* the first known quantity. **6** a human blood type of the ABO system. □ **from A to B** from one place to another. **from A to Z** over the entire range; completely.

A² *abbr.* (also **A.**) **1** ace. **2** = A LEVEL. **3** answer. **4** atomic (*A-bomb*).

A³ *symb.* ampere(s).

Å *abbr.* ångström(s).

a¹ *det.* (also **an** before a vowel) (called *the indefinite article*) **1** one, some, any (used when referring to something for the first time in a text or conversation) (cf. THE). **2** one like (*a Judas*). **3** one single (*not a thing in sight*). **4** the same (*all of a size*). **5** in, to, or for each (*twice a year; seven a side*). [Old English *ān* 'one']

■ **Usage** See Usage Note at AN.

a² *prep.* (usu. as *prefix*) **1** to, towards (*ashore; aside*). **2** (with verb in pres. part. or infin.) in the process of; in a specified state (*a-wandering; aflutter*). **3** on (*afire; afoot*). [Old English]

a³ *abbr.* (also **a.**) **1** arrives. **2** before.

a- *prefix* not, without (*amoral; agnostic*).

A1 ● *n.* *Naut.* a first class vessel in Lloyd's Register of Shipping. ● *adj.* *colloq.* **1** excellent; first-class. **2** fit; in excellent health.

A3 *n.* a standard European size of paper, 420 × 297 mm.

A4 *n.* a standard European size of paper, 210 × 297 mm.

A5 *n.* a standard European size of paper, 210 × 148 mm.

AA *abbr.* **1** (in the UK) Automobile Association. **2** Alcoholics Anonymous. **3** *Mil.* anti-aircraft.

aardvark *n.* a nocturnal mammal of southern Africa, *Orycteropus afer*, with a tubular snout and long extensible tongue, that feeds on termites. Also called *ant-bear, earth-pig.* ▷ MAMMAL. [Afrikaans, from *aarde* 'earth' + *varken* 'pig']

Aaron's rod *n.* any of several tall plants, esp. the great mullein (*Verbascum thapsus*). [with reference to Num. 17:8]

AB *n.* a human blood type of the ABO system.

aback *adv. archaic* backwards, behind. □ **take aback** surprise, disconcert (*was taken aback by the news*). [Old English]

abacus *n.* (*pl.* **abacuses**) ▼ an oblong frame with rows of wires or grooves along which beads are slid, used for calculating. [from Greek *abax abakos* 'slab, drawing board']

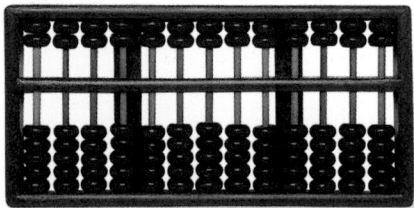

ABACUS

ABBEY

The layout of buildings within an abbey complex often follows a common pattern. Essential to the pattern is the abbey church, with a cloistered quadrant adjacent to it. Surrounding the quadrant on the remaining three sides are buildings housing a refectory and kitchens, a dormitory, and a chapter house. Other buildings within the complex might include an abbot's house and a hostel for visiting pilgrims.

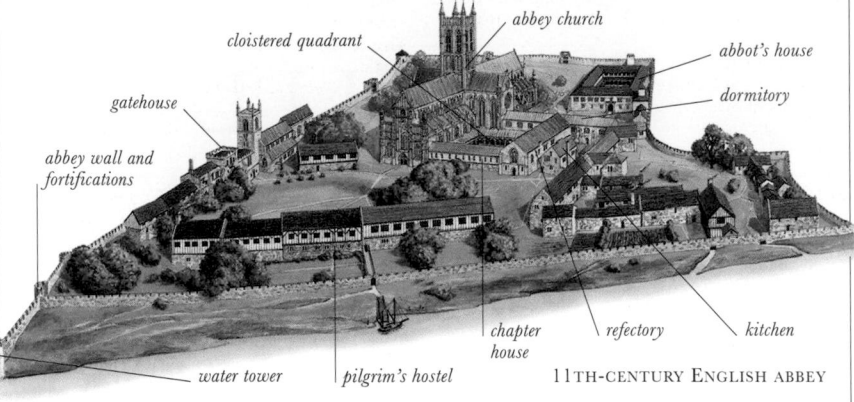

cloistered quadrant
abbey church
abbot's house
gatehouse
dormitory
abbey wall and fortifications
chapter house
refectory
kitchen
water tower
pilgrim's hostel

11TH-CENTURY ENGLISH ABBEY

abaft *Naut.* ● *adv.* in the stern half of a ship. ● *prep.* nearer the stern than; aft of. [Middle English, from earlier *beæftan* 'at the back']

abalone /ab-ă-loh-ni/ *n.* ▼ a mollusc of the genus *Haliotis*, with a shallow ear-shaped shell lined with mother-of-pearl, e.g. the ormer. [from Latin American Spanish *abulón*]

abandon ● *v.tr.* **1** give up completely or before completion (*abandoned hope; abandoned the game*). **2** forsake or desert (a person or a post of responsibility). **3 a** give up to another's control or mercy. **b** *refl.* yield oneself completely to a passion or impulse. ● *n.* lack of inhibition or restraint. [Middle English, based on Old French *à bandon* 'under control'] □ **abandonment** *n.*

ABALONE SHELL (INTERIOR)

abandoned *adj.* (of a person or behaviour) unrestrained, profligate.

abase *v.tr. & refl.* humiliate or degrade. [based on Late Latin *bassus* 'short of stature'] □ **abasement** *n.*

abash *v.tr.* (usu. as **abashed** *adj.*) embarrass, disconcert. [from Old French *esbaïr* 'to astound'] □ **abashment** *n.*

abate *v.* **1** *tr. & intr.* make or become less strong, severe, etc. **2** *tr. Law* **a** quash (a writ or action). **b** put an end to (a nuisance). [based on Latin *batt(u)ere* 'to beat'] □ **abatement** *n.*

abattoir /ab-ă-twah/ *n.* a slaughterhouse. [French]

abbacy *n.* (*pl.* **-ies**) the office, jurisdiction, or period of office of an abbot or abbess. [from ecclesiastical Latin *abbacia*, related to ABBOT]

abbatial *adj.* of an abbey, abbot, or abbess. [from medieval Latin *abbatialis*, related to ABBOT]

abbé *n.* (in France) an abbot; a man entitled to wear ecclesiastical dress. [French]

abbess *n.* a woman who is the head of certain communities of nuns.

abbey *n.* (*pl.* **-eys**) **1** ▲ the building(s) occupied by a community of monks or nuns. **2** the community itself. **3** a church or house that was once an abbey. [from medieval Latin *abbatia*, related to ABBOT]

abbot *n.* a man who is the head of an abbey of monks. [from Aramaic *'abbā* 'father'] □ **abbotship** *n.*

abbreviate *v.tr.* shorten (esp. a word etc.). [based on Latin *brevis* 'short']

abbreviation *n.* **1** an abbreviated form, esp. a shortened form of a word or phrase. **2** the process or result of abbreviating.

ABC¹ *n.* **1** the alphabet. **2** the rudiments of any subject. **3** an alphabetical guide.

ABC² *abbr.* **1** Australian Broadcasting Corporation. **2** American Broadcasting Company.

abdicate *v.tr.* give up or renounce (the throne, a duty, etc.). [based on Latin *dicare* 'to declare'] □ **abdication** *n.*

abdomen *n.* **1** the part of the body containing the stomach, bowels, reproductive organs, etc. **2** *Zool.* the hinder part of an insect, crustacean, spider, etc. ▷ INSECT, SPIDER. [Latin] □ **abdominal** *adj.*

abduct *v.tr.* carry off or kidnap (a person) illegally by force or deception. [based on Latin *abductus* 'led away'] □ **abduction** *n.* **abductor** *n.*

abeam *adv.* (often foll. by *of*) on a line at right angles to the middle of a ship's or an aircraft's length.

abed *adv. archaic* in bed. [Middle English]

abele *n.* the white poplar, *Populus alba*. [based on Latin *albus* 'white']

Aberdeen Angus *n.* ▼ an animal of a Scottish breed of hornless black beef cattle. [from *Aberdeenshire* and *Angus*, former Scottish counties]

ABERDEEN ANGUS

Aberdonian ● *adj.* of Aberdeen. ● *n.* a native or citizen of Aberdeen. [from medieval Latin]

aberrant *adj.* departing from an accepted standard or normal type. [from Latin *aberrant-* 'straying from'] □ **aberrance** *n.* **aberrancy** *n.*

aberration *n.* **1** a departure from what is normal or accepted or regarded as right. **2** a moral or mental lapse. **3** *Optics* the failure of rays to converge at one focus because of a defect in a lens or mirror. **4** *Astron.* the apparent displacement of a celestial object from its true position caused by the observer's relative motion. [from Latin *aberratio*]

abet *v.tr.* (**abetted**, **abetting**) (usu. in **aid and abet**) encourage or assist (an offender or offence). [based on Old French *beter* 'to bait'] □ **abetment** *n.* **abetter** *n.* (also **abettor**).

abeyance *n.* (usu. prec. by *in*, *into*) temporary disuse or suspension. [based on Old French *abeer* 'to aspire after']

ABH *abbr.* actual bodily harm.

abhor *v.tr.* (**abhorred**, **abhorring**) regard with disgust and hatred. [based on Latin *horrēre* 'to shudder'] □ **abhorrer** *n.*

abhorrence *n.* **1** disgust; detestation. **2** a detested thing.

abhorrent *adj.* (often foll. by *to*) (of conduct etc.) inspiring disgust; repugnant, hateful, detestable.

abide *v.* (*past* and *past part.* **abided** or rarely **abode**) **1** *tr.* (usu. in *neg.* or *interrog.*) tolerate, endure. **2** *intr.* (foll. by *by*) act in accordance with (rules etc. or a promise). **3** *intr. archaic* dwell. [Old English] □ **abidance** *n.*

abiding *adj.* enduring, permanent (*an abiding sense of loss*). □ **abidingly** *adv.*

ability *n.* (*pl.* **-ies**) **1** (often foll. by *to* + infin.) capacity or power. **2** cleverness, talent; mental power (*a person of great ability; has many abilities*). [related to ABLE]

-ability *suffix* forming nouns of quality from, or corresponding to, adjectives in *-able* (*capability; vulnerability*).

ab initio /ab in-**ish**-i-oh/ *adv.* from the beginning. [Latin]

abiogenesis *n.* **1** the formation of organic matter without the action of living organisms. **2** the supposed spontaneous generation of living organisms.

abject *adj.* **1** miserable, wretched. **2** degraded, self-abasing, humble. **3** despicable. [from Latin *abjectus* 'rejected'] □ **abjectly** *adv.* **abjectness** *n.*

abjection *n.* a state of misery or degradation. [based on Latin *abjectus* 'rejected']

abjure *v.tr.* renounce on oath (an opinion, cause, claim, etc.). [based on Latin *jurare* 'to swear'] □ **abjuration** *n.*

ablation *n.* **1** the surgical removal of body tissue. **2** *Geol.* the wasting or erosion of a glacier, iceberg, or rock by melting or the action of water. □ **ablate** *v.tr.* [based on Latin *ablatus* 'carried away']

ablative *Gram.* ● *n.* the case (esp. in Latin) of nouns and pronouns (and words in grammatical agreement with them) indicating an agent, instrument, or location. ● *adj.* of or in the ablative.

ablaut *n.* a change of vowel in related words or forms, arising from differences of accent and stress in the parent language, e.g. in *sing, sang, sung.* [German, based on *Laut* 'sound']

ablaze *predic.adj.* & *adv.* **1** on fire (*set it ablaze; the house was ablaze*). **2** (often foll. by *with*) glittering, glowing, radiant.

able *adj.* (**abler**, **ablest**) **1** (often foll. by *to* + infin.) having the capacity or power (*was not able to come*). **2** clever, skilful. [based on Latin *habēre* 'to hold']

-able *suffix* forming adjectives meaning: **1** that may or must be (*forgivable; payable*). **2** that can be made the subject of (*objectionable*). **3** that is relevant to or in accordance with (*fashionable*). **4** (with active sense, in earlier word-formations) that may (*comfortable; suitable*).

able-bodied *adj.* fit, healthy.

able-bodied rating *n.* (also **able-bodied seaman**) *Naut.* a rating able to perform all duties.

abled *adj.* having a full range of physical or mental abilities; able-bodied.

ableism *n.* (also **ablism**) discrimination in favour of able-bodied people.

ablution *n.* (usu. in *pl.*) **1** the ceremonial washing of parts of the body or of sacred vessels etc. **2** *colloq.* the ordinary washing of the body. [based on Latin *luere* 'to wash'] □ **ablutionary** *adj.*

ably *adv.* capably, cleverly, competently.

-ably *suffix* forming adverbs corresponding to adjectives in *-able.*

ABM *abbr.* anti-ballistic missile.

abnegate *v.tr.* **1** give up or deny oneself (a pleasure etc.). **2** renounce or reject (a right or belief). [based on Latin *negare* 'to deny'] □ **abnegation** *n.* **abnegator** *n.*

abnormal *adj.* deviating from what is normal or usual; exceptional. [from Greek *anōmalos* 'anomalous'] □ **abnormally** *adv.*

abnormality *n.* (*pl.* **-ies**) **1** an abnormal quality, occurrence, etc. **2** the state of being abnormal.

Abo (also **abo**) *Austral. slang offens.* ● *n.* (*pl.* **Abos**) an Aborigine. ● *adj.* Aboriginal.

aboard *adv.* & *prep.* **1** on or into (a ship, aircraft, train, etc.). **2** alongside. [Middle English]

abode[1] *n.* habitual residence; a house or home. [verbal noun of ABIDE]

abode[2] *past* of ABIDE.

abolish *v.tr.* put an end to (esp. a custom or institution). [from Latin *abolēre* 'to destroy'] □ **abolishment** *n.*

abolition *n.* the act or process of abolishing or being abolished.

abolitionist *n.* a person who favours the abolition of esp. capital punishment or (formerly) slavery. □ **abolitionism** *n.*

abomasum *n.* (*pl.* **abomasa**) the fourth stomach of a ruminant. ▷ RUMINANT. [modern Latin]

A-bomb *n.* = ATOM BOMB.

abominable *adj.* **1** detestable; loathsome; morally reprehensible. **2** *colloq.* very bad or unpleasant (*abominable weather*). [based on Latin *abominari* 'to deprecate'] □ **abominably** *adv.*

Abominable Snowman *n.* an unidentified manlike or bearlike animal said to exist in the Himalayas; a yeti.

abominate *v.tr.* detest, loathe. [based on Latin *abominatus* 'deprecated as an ill omen']

abomination *n.* **1** an object of disgust. **2** an odious or degrading habit or act. **3** loathing.

aboriginal ● *adj.* **1** inhabiting or existing in a land from the earliest times or from before the arrival of colonists. **2** (**Aboriginal**) of the Australian Aboriginals or their languages. ● *n.* **1** an aboriginal inhabitant. **2** (**Aboriginal**) = ABORIGINE 2. **3** (**Aboriginal**) any of the Australian Aboriginal languages.

aborigine /ab-er-ij-in-ee/ *n.* (usu. in *pl.*) **1** an aboriginal inhabitant, plant, or animal. **2** (**Aborigine**) an aboriginal inhabitant of Australia. [from Latin, probably from *ab origine* 'from the beginning']

abort *v.* **1** *intr.* **a** (of a woman) undergo abortion; miscarry. **b** (of a foetus) suffer abortion. **2** *tr.* **a** effect the abortion of (a foetus). **b** effect abortion in (a mother). **3 a** *tr.* cause to end fruitlessly or prematurely. **b** *intr.* end unsuccessfully or prematurely. **4** *tr.* (also *absol.*) abandon or terminate (esp. a space flight) before its completion. [based on Latin *abortus* 'disappeared, miscarried']

abortifacient ● *adj.* effecting abortion. ● *n.* a drug or other agent that effects abortion.

abortion *n.* **1** the expulsion of a foetus (naturally or esp. by medical induction) from the womb before it is able to survive independently, esp. in the first 28 weeks of a human pregnancy. **2** a stunted or deformed creature or thing.

abortionist *n.* a person who carries out abortions, esp. illegally.

abortive *adj.* **1** fruitless, unsuccessful, unfinished. **2** resulting in or from abortion. □ **abortively** *adv.*

ABO system *n.* a system of four types (A, AB, B, and O) by which human blood may be classified, based on the presence or absence of certain inherited antigens.

abound *v.intr.* **1** be plentiful. **2** (foll. by *in*, *with*) teem, be infested. [from Latin *abundare* 'to overflow']

about ● *prep.* **1 a** on the subject of; in connection with (*a book about birds*). **b** relating to (*something funny about this*). **c** in relation to (*symmetry about a plane*). **d** so as to affect (*what are you going to do about it?*). **2** at a time near to (*come about four*). **3 a** in, round, surrounding (*wandered about the town; a scarf about her neck*). **b** all round from a centre (*look about you*). **4** here and there in (*toys lying about the house*). **5** at a point or points near to (*fighting going on about us*). **6** carried with (*have no money about me*). **7** occupied with (*what are you about?*). ● *adv.* **1 a** approximately. **b** *colloq.* used to indicate understatement (*just about had enough*). **2** here and there (*a lot of flu about; I've seen him about recently*). **3** all round; in every direction (*look about*). **4** on the move; in action (*out and about*). **5** in partial rotation or alteration from a given position (*the wrong way about*). **6** in rotation or succession (*turn and turn about*). **7** *Naut.* on or to the opposite tack (*go about; put about*). □ **be about** *colloq.* have as its most important aim (*it's about caring*). **be about to** be on the point of (doing something) (*was about to laugh*). [Old English]

about-face ● *n.* & *v.intr.* esp. *US* = ABOUT-TURN *n.* & *v.* ● *int.* = ABOUT-TURN.

about-turn ● *n.* **1** a turn made so as to face the opposite direction. **2** a change of opinion or policy etc. ● *v.intr.* make an about-turn. ● *int.* (**about turn**) *Mil.* a command to make an about-turn.

above ● *prep.* **1** over; on the top of; higher than; over the surface of. **2** more than (*above average*). **3** higher in rank, position, importance, etc. than. **4 a** too great or good for (*above one's station; is not above cheating*). **b** beyond the reach of; not affected by (*above my understanding; above suspicion*). ● *adv.* **1** at or to a higher point; overhead (*the floor above; the clouds above*). **2** (of a text reference) further back on a page or in a book (*as noted above*). **3** on the upper side (*looks similar above and below*). **4** *literary* in heaven (*Lord above!*). ● *adj.* mentioned earlier; preceding (*the above argument*). ● *n.* (prec. by *the*) what is mentioned above (*the above holds true*). □ **above all** more than anything else; most of all. **above one's head** see HEAD. **above oneself** conceited, arrogant. [Old English]

above board *adj.* & *adv.* without concealment; fair or fairly; open or openly.

abracadabra *int.* a supposedly magic word used by conjurors in performing a trick. [Latin, from Greek]

abrade *v.tr.* scrape or wear away by rubbing. [based on Latin *radere* 'to scrape'] □ **abrader** *n.*

abrasion *n.* **1** scraping or wearing away. **2** a damaged area resulting from this. [related to ABRADE]

abrasive ● *adj.* **1 a** tending to rub or graze. **b** capable of polishing by rubbing or grinding. **2** harsh or hurtful in manner. ● *n.* an abrasive substance. [related to ABRADE]

abreaction *n.* *Psychol.* the free expression and consequent release of a previously repressed emotion. [influenced by German *Abreagierung*] □ **abreact** *v.tr.* **abreactive** *adj.*

abreast *adv.* **1** side by side and facing the same way. **2 a** (often foll. by *with*) up to date. **b** (foll. by *of*) well informed (*abreast of all the changes*). [Middle English]

abridge *v.tr.* shorten (a book, film, etc.). [based on Latin *brevis* 'short'] □ **abridgeable** *adj.* **abridger** *n.*

abridgement *n.* (also **abridgment**) **1** a shortened version, esp. of a book; an abstract. **2** the process of producing this.

abroad *adv.* **1** in or to a foreign country or countries. **2** over a wide area; in different directions. **3** at large; in circulation. □ **from abroad** from another country. [Middle English]

abrogate *v.tr.* repeal, annul, or abolish (a law or custom). [based on Latin *rogare* 'to propose a law'] □ **abrogation** *n.*

abrupt *adj.* **1** sudden and unexpected; hasty (*his abrupt departure*). **2** (of speech, manner, etc.) lacking continuity; curt. **3** steep. [from Latin *abruptus* 'broken off'] □ **abruptly** *adv.* **abruptness** *n.*

ABS *abbr.* anti-lock braking system (for motor vehicles).

A

ABSCESS

An abscess is a sac of pus formed from destroyed tissue cells. The destroyed cells are the result of a localized infection, and are made up of leucocytes and micro-organisms, such as bacteria. A pyogenic membrane, or lining, contains the pus.

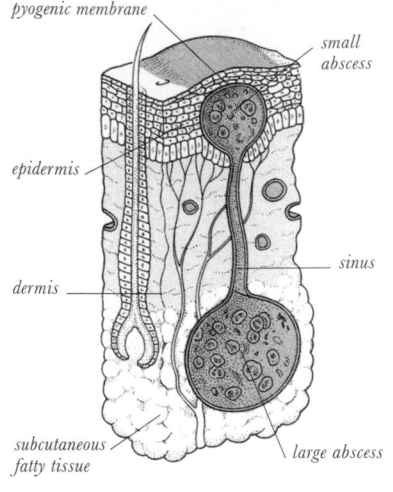

SECTION OF HUMAN SKIN SHOWING A
COLLAR-AND-STUD (DOUBLE) ABSCESS

abscess *n.* ▲ a swollen area accumulating pus within a body tissue. [from Latin *abscessus* 'a going away', from the elimination of bad matter via the pus] □ **abscessed** *adj.*

abscissa *n.* (*pl.* **abscissae** /-see/ or **abscissas**) *Math.* (in a system of coordinates) the shortest distance from a point to the vertical or *y*-axis; the *x*-coordinate (cf. ORDINATE). [from modern Latin *abscissa (linea)* 'cut-off (line)']

abscission *n.* the act or an instance of cutting off. [based on Latin *scindere sciss-* 'to cut']

abscond *v.intr.* depart hurriedly and furtively, esp. unlawfully or to avoid arrest. [from Latin *abscondere* 'to hide, put away'] □ **absconder** *n.*

abseil /**ab**-sayl/ esp. *Brit.* ● *v.intr.* ▼ descend a steep rock face etc. by using a doubled rope coiled round the body and fixed at a higher point, or by using

ABSEIL: CLIMBER ABSEILING

modern variable friction devices. ● *n.* a descent made by abseiling. [from German *abseilen*, based on *Seil* 'rope']

absence *n.* **1** the state of being away from a place or person. **2** the duration of being away. **3** (foll. by *of*) the non-existence or lack of. □ **absence of mind** inattentiveness. [from Latin *absentia*]

absent ● *adj.* /**ab**-sĕnt/ **1** (often foll. by *from*) not present (at or in). **2** not existing. **3** inattentive. ● *v.refl.* /ab-**sent**/ **1** stay away. **2** withdraw. [based on Latin *abesse* 'to be absent'] □ **absently** *adv.* (in sense 3 of *adj.*).

absentee *n.* a person not present, esp. one who is absent from work or school.

absenteeism *n.* the practice of absenting oneself from work or school etc., esp. frequently or illicitly.

absentee landlord *n.* a landlord who lets a property while living elsewhere.

absent-minded *adj.* habitually forgetful or in-attentive; with one's mind on other things. □ **absent-mindedly** *adv.* **absent-mindedness** *n.*

absinthe *n.* (also **absinth**) a green aniseed-flavoured liqueur originally made with wormwood. [from Greek *apsinthion* 'wormwood']

absolute ● *adj.* **1** utter, perfect (*an absolute fool*). **2** unconditional, unlimited (*absolute authority*). **3** despotic; ruling arbitrarily or with unrestricted power. **4** (of a standard or other concept) univer-sally valid; not relative or comparative. **5** *Gram.* **a** (of a construction) syntactically independent of the rest of the sentence, as in *dinner being over, we left the table*; *let us toss for it, loser to pay*. **b** (of an adjective or transitive verb) used or usable without an expressed noun or object (e.g. *the deaf, guns kill*). **6** (of a legal decree etc.) final. ● *n. Philos.* a value, standard, etc. which is objective and universally valid, not subjective or relative. [from Latin *abso-lutus* 'freed, completed'] □ **absoluteness** *n.*

absolutely *adv.* **1** utterly, perfectly (*absolutely marvel-lous*; *he absolutely denies it*). **2** (foll. by *neg.*) (no or none) at all (*absolutely no chance*; *absolutely nowhere*). **3** *Gram.* in an absolute way, esp. (of a verb) without a stated object. **4** *colloq.* (used in reply) quite so; yes.

absolute majority *n.* **1** a majority over all others combined. **2** more than half.

absolute pitch *n. Mus.* **1** the ability to recognize the pitch of a note or produce any given note. **2** a fixed standard of pitch defined by the rate of vibration.

absolute temperature *n.* a temperature measur-ed from absolute zero.

absolute zero *n.* a theoretical lowest possible temperature, calculated as −273.15°C (zero on the Kelvin scale).

absolution *n.* **1** a formal release from guilt, obliga-tion, or punishment. **2** a declaration of forgiveness of sins. [from Latin *absolutio*]

absolutism *n.* the acceptance of or belief in absolute principles in political, philosophical, or theological matters. □ **absolutist** *n. & adj.*

absolve *v.tr.* **1** (often foll. by *from, of*) **a** set or pro-nounce free from blame or obligation etc. **b** acquit; pronounce not guilty. **2** pardon or give absolution for (a sin etc.). [from Latin *absolvere*]

absorb *v.tr.* **1** include or incorporate as part of itself or oneself. **2** take in; suck up (liquid, heat, knowledge, etc.). **3** reduce the effect or intensity of; deal easily with (an impact, sound, difficulty, etc.). **4** consume (income, time, etc.). **5** engross the attention of (*television absorbs them completely*). [based on Latin *sorbere* 'to suck in'] □ **absorbable** *adj.* **absorber** *n.*

absorbed *predic.adj.* intensely engaged or inter-ested. □ **absorbedly** *adv.*

absorbent ● *adj.* having a tendency to absorb (esp. liquids). ● *n.* an absorbent substance or thing. [from Latin *absorbent-* 'sucking away from'] □ **ab-sorbency** *n.*

absorbing *adj.* engrossing; intensely interesting. □ **absorbingly** *adv.*

absorption *n.* **1** the process or action of absorbing or being absorbed. **2** mental engrossment. [from Latin *absorptio*] □ **absorptive** *adj.*

abstain *v.intr.* **1 a** (usu. foll. by *from*) restrain oneself; refrain from indulging in (*abstained from sweets*). **b** refrain from drinking alcohol. **2** formally decline to use one's vote. [based on Latin *tenēre* 'to hold'] □ **abstainer** *n.*

abstemious *adj.* moderate, esp. in eating and drinking. [based on Latin *temetum* 'a strong drink'] □ **abstemiously** *adv.* **abstemiousness** *n.*

abstention *n.* the act or an instance of abstaining, esp. from voting. [based on Latin *abstentus* 'held away from'] □ **abstentionism** *n.*

abstinence *n.* the act of abstaining, esp. from food, alcohol, or sexual activity.

abstinent *adj.* practising abstinence. [from Latin *abstinent-* 'withholding']

abstract ● *adj.* /**ab**-strakt/ **1 a** to do with or exist-ing in thought rather than matter, or in theory rather than practice. **b** (of a word, esp. a noun) denoting a quality, condition, or intangible thing rather than a concrete object. **2** ▶ (of art) achiev-ing its effect by grouping shapes and colours in satisfying patterns rather than by the recognizable representation of physical reality. ● *v.tr.* /ăb-**strakt**/ **1** (often foll. by *from*) take out of; extract; remove. **2** summarize (an article, book, etc.). **3** also *refl.* (often foll. by *from*) distract. **4** (foll. by *from*) consider abstractly or separately from something else. ● *n.* /**ab**-strakt/ **1** a summary or statement of the contents of a book etc. **2** an abstract work of art. **3** an abstraction or abstract term. □ **in the abstract** in theory rather than in practice. [from Latin *abstractus* 'drawn away'] □ **abstractly** *adv.* **abstractor** *n.* (in sense 2 of *v.*).

abstracted *adj.* inattentive; preoccupied. □ **abstractedly** *adv.*

abstraction *n.* **1** abstracting or taking away. **2** an abstract or visionary idea. **3** abstract qualities (esp. in art). **4** absent-mindedness.

abstruse *adj.* hard to understand; obscure; profound. [from Latin *abstrusus* 'pushed away'] □ **abstrusely** *adv.* **abstruseness** *n.*

absurd ● *adj.* wildly unreasonable, illogical, or ludi-crous. ● *n.* (**the absurd**) that which is absurd, esp. human existence in a purposeless chaotic universe. [from Latin *absurdus* 'inharmonious, foolish', based on *surdus* 'deaf, insufferable to the ear'] □ **absurdly** *adv.* **absurdness** *n.*

absurdity *n.* (*pl.* **-ies**) **1** absurdness. **2** an absurd statement or act.

ABTA /**ab**-tă/ *abbr.* Association of British Travel Agents.

abundance *n.* **1** a very great quantity, esp. more than enough. **2** wealth, affluence. [from Latin *abundantia*]

abundant *adj.* **1** existing or available in large quan-tities; plentiful. **2** (foll. by *in*) having an abundance of. [from Latin *abundant-* 'overflowing'] □ **abun-dantly** *adv.*

abuse ● *v.tr.* /ă-**bewz**/ **1** use to bad effect or for a bad purpose (*abused his power*). **2** insult verbally. **3** maltreat; assault (esp. sexually). ● *n.* /ă-**bewss**/ **1** incorrect or improper use (*the abuse of power*). **2** insulting language (*a torrent of abuse*). **3** unjust or corrupt practice. **4** maltreatment or (esp. sexual) assault of a person (*child abuse*). [based on Latin *abusus* 'misused'] □ **abuser** *n.*

abusive *adj.* **1** using insulting language. **2** (of language) insulting. □ **abusively** *adv.* **abusiveness** *n.*

abut *v.* (**abutted, abutting**) **1** *intr.* (foll. by *on*) (of estates, countries, etc.) adjoin (another). **2** *intr.* (foll. by *on, against*) (of part of a building) touch or lean upon (another) with a projecting end or point (*the shed abutted on the side of the house*). **3** *tr.* abut on. [based on Old French *but* 'end']

abutment *n.* the lateral supporting structure of a bridge, arch, etc. ▷ ARCH

abuzz *adv. & adj.* in a state of excitement or activity.

ABSTRACT

Although the term abstract can be attributed to art throughout its history, it is specifically applied to an artistic style that began among avant-garde movements in Europe and the USA in the early 20th century. Such movements rejected recognizable styles of representation, and instead chose either to reduce subjects to simplified forms, as exemplified by the sculpture of Brancusi or Henry Moore, or to create work without a physical subject in the real world, as evident in works by Kandinsky, and Mondrian after 1917.

Composition in Red, Blue, Yellow and Black (1929), PIET MONDRIAN

TIMELINE

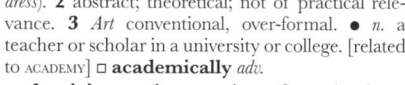

| 1500 | 1550 | 1600 | 1650 | 1700 | 1750 | 1800 | 1850 | 1900 | 1950 | 2000 |

A

volute

acanthus leaf

ACANTHUS: CORINTHIAN CAPITAL WITH ACANTHUS-LEAF DECORATION

---

abysmal *adj* **1** *colloq* extremely bad (*the standard is abysmal*). **2** profound, utter (*abysmal ignorance*). [related to ABYSS] □ **abysmally** *adv.*

abyss *n.* **1** a deep or seemingly bottomless chasm. **2 a** an immeasurable depth (*abyss of despair*). **b** a catastrophic situation as contemplated (*his loss brought him a step nearer the abyss*). [from Greek *abussos* 'bottomless']

abyssal *adj.* at or of the ocean depths or floor.

AC *abbr.* **1** (also **ac**) alternating current. **2** aircraftman. **3** *appellation contrôlée.*

Ac *symb. Chem.* the element actinium.

a/c *abbr.* account.

acacia /ă-**kay**-shă/ *n.* **1** (also **acacia tree**) ▶ a leguminous tree of the genus *Acacia*, with yellow or white flowers. **2** (also **false acacia**) the locust tree, *Robinia pseudoacacia.* [from Greek]

academe *n.* **1** the world of learning. **2** universities collectively. [related to ACADEMY]

academia *n.* the academic world; scholastic life. [modern Latin]

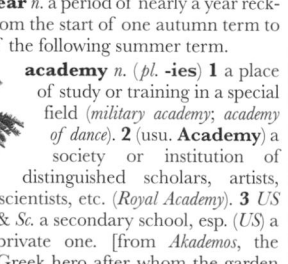

ACACIA: SILVER WATTLE (*Acacia dealbata*)

academic ● *adj.* **1 a** scholarly; to do with learning. **b** of or relating to a scholarly institution (*academic dress*). **2** abstract; theoretical; not of practical relevance. **3** *Art* conventional, over-formal. ● *n.* a teacher or scholar in a university or college. [related to ACADEMY] □ **academically** *adv.*

academician *n.* **1** a member of an Academy. **2** *US* an academic; an intellectual.

academicism *n.* (also **academism**) academic principles or their application in art.

academic year *n.* a period of nearly a year reckoned usu. from the start of one autumn term to the end of the following summer term.

academy *n.* (*pl.* **-ies**) **1** a place of study or training in a special field (*military academy; academy of dance*). **2** (usu. **Academy**) a society or institution of distinguished scholars, artists, scientists, etc. (*Royal Academy*). **3** *US & Sc.* a secondary school, esp. (*US*) a private one. [from *Akademos*, the Greek hero after whom the garden where Plato taught was named]

---

acanthus *n.* **1** any herbaceous plant or shrub of the genus *Acanthus*, with spiny leaves. **2** *Archit.* ▲ a conventionalized representation of an acanthus leaf, esp. on Corinthian column capitals. [from Greek *akantha* 'thorn']

a cappella *adj. & adv. Mus.* (of choral music) unaccompanied. [Italian, literally 'in church style']

acarid *n.* any small arachnid of the order Acarina, including mites and ticks. [from Greek *akari* 'mite']

ACAS /**ay**-kass/ *abbr.* (in the UK) Advisory, Conciliation, and Arbitration Service.

accede *v.intr.* (often foll. by *to*) **1** take office, esp. become monarch. **2** assent or agree (*acceded to the proposal*). **3** (foll. by *to*) formally subscribe to a treaty or other agreement. [from Latin *accedere* 'to come to']

accelerando *adj., adv., & n. Mus.* ● *adj. & adv.* with a gradual increase of speed. ● *n.* (*pl.* **accelerandos** or **accelerandi**) a passage performed accelerando. [Italian]

accelerate *v.* **1** *intr.* **a** (of a moving body, esp. a vehicle) move or begin to move more quickly; increase speed. **b** (of a process) happen or reach completion more quickly. **2** *tr.* cause to accelerate. [based on Latin *celer* 'swift'] □ **accelerative** *adj.*

acceleration *n.* **1** the process or act of accelerating or being accelerated. **2** (of a vehicle etc.) the capacity to gain speed (*the car has good acceleration*).

accelerator *n.* **1** a device for increasing speed, esp. the pedal that controls the speed of a vehicle's engine. **2** *Physics* an apparatus for imparting high speeds to charged particles. **3** *Chem.* a substance that speeds up a chemical reaction.

accelerator board *n.* (also **accelerator card**) *Computing* an accessory circuit board which can be plugged into a small computer to increase its speed of operation.

accent ● *n.* /**ak**-sĕnt/ **1** a mode of pronunciation, esp. one associated with a region or group. **2** prominence given to a syllable by stress or pitch. **3** a mark on a letter or word to indicate pitch, stress, or the quality of a vowel. **4** emphasis (*with the accent on comfort*). **5** *Mus.* emphasis on a particular note or chord. ● *v.tr.* /ak-**sent**/ **1** pronounce with an accent; emphasize (a word or syllable). **2** write or print accents on (words etc.). **3** *Mus.* play (a note etc.) with an accent. [from Latin *accentus*, a rendering of Greek *prosōidia*, literally 'song added to'] □ **accentual** *adj.*

accentuate *v.tr.* emphasize; make prominent. □ **accentuation** *n.*

accept *v.tr.* **1** (also *absol.*) consent to receive (a thing offered). **2** (also *absol.*) give an affirmative answer to (an offer or proposal). **3** regard favourably; treat as welcome (*her mother-in-law never accepted her*). **4 a** believe or receive (an opinion, explanation, etc.) as adequate, valid, or correct. **b** be prepared to subscribe to (a belief, philosophy, etc.). **5** receive as suitable (*the hotel accepts cheques*). **6 a** tolerate; submit to (*accepted the umpire's decision*). **b** (often foll. by *that* + clause) esp. *Brit.* be willing to believe (*we accept that you meant well*). [from Latin *acceptare*, based on *capere* 'to take'] □ **accepter** *n.*

A

acceptable *adj.* **1 a** worthy of being accepted. **b** pleasing, welcome. **2** adequate, satisfactory. **3** tolerable (*an acceptable risk*). □ **acceptability** *n.* **acceptably** *adv.*

acceptance *n.* **1** willingness to receive or accept. **2** an affirmative answer to an invitation or proposal. **3 a** approval, belief (*found wide acceptance*). **b** willingness or ability to tolerate.

access ● *n.* **1** a way of approaching or reaching or entering (*a building with rear access*). **2 a** (often foll. by *to*) the right or opportunity to reach, use, or visit; admittance (*has access to secret files*). **b** accessibility. **3** (often foll. by *of*) an attack or outburst (*an access of anger*). **●** *v.tr.* esp. *Computing* gain access to (data, a file, etc.). [based on Latin *accedere access-* 'to come to']

■ **Usage** The use of the verb in contexts other than computing (as in *The kitchen can be accessed from the dining room*) is considered incorrect by some people.

accessary var. of ACCESSORY.

accessible *adj.* (often foll. by *to*) **1** that can readily be reached, entered, or used. **2** (of a person) readily available (esp. to subordinates). **3** (in a form) easy to understand. □ **accessibility** *n.* **accessibly** *adv.*

accession ● *n.* **1** entering upon an office (esp. the throne) or a condition (as manhood). **2** (often foll. by *to*) a thing added (e.g. a book to a library). **3** *Law* the incorporation of one item of property in another. **●** *v.tr.* record the addition of (a new item) to a library or museum. [from Latin *accessio*, related to ACCEDE]

accessorize *v.tr.* (also **-ise**) provide (an outfit etc.) with accessories.

accessory (also **accessary**) **●** *n.* (*pl.* **-ies**) **1** an additional or extra thing. **2** (usu. in *pl.*) **a** a small attachment or fitting. **b** a small item of (esp. a woman's) dress (e.g. shoes, gloves, handbag). **3** (often foll. by *to*) a person who helps in or knows the details of an (esp. illegal) act, without taking part in it. **●** *adj.* additional; contributing or aiding in a minor way; dispensable. □ **accessory before** (or **after**) **the fact** a person who incites (or assists) another to commit a crime. [related to ACCEDE] □ **accessorial** *adj.*

acciaccatura /ă-chak-ă-**toor**-ă/ *n. Mus.* a grace note performed as quickly as possible before an essential note of a melody. [Italian]

accident *n.* **1** an event that is without apparent cause, or is unexpected. **2** an unfortunate event, esp. one causing physical harm or damage, brought about unintentionally. **3** chance; the working of fortune (*accident accounts for much in life*). □ **by accident** unintentionally. [based on Latin *accidere* 'to fall, happen']

accidental ● *adj.* **1** happening by chance, unintentionally, or unexpectedly. **2** not essential to a conception; subsidiary. **●** *n.* **1** *Mus.* a sign indicating a momentary departure from the key signature by raising or lowering a note. ▷ NOTATION. **2** something not essential to a conception. □ **accidentally** *adv.*

accident-prone *adj.* (of a person) subject to frequent accidents.

accidie /**ak**-si-di/ *n.* laziness, sloth, apathy. [from medieval Latin *accidia*]

acclaim ● *v.tr.* **1** welcome or applaud enthusiastically; praise publicly. **2** (foll. by compl.) hail as (*was acclaimed the winner*). **●** *n.* **1** applause; welcome; public praise. **2** a shout of acclaim. [based on Latin *clamare* 'to shout']

acclamation *n.* **1** loud and eager assent to a proposal. **2** (usu. in *pl.*) shouting in a person's honour. **3** the act or process of acclaiming. [related to ACCLAIM]

acclimate *v.tr.* **1** esp. *N. Amer.* acclimatize. **2** *Biol.* adapt physiologically to environmental stress. [based on French *à* 'to' + *climat* 'climate'] □ **acclimation** *n.*

acclimatize *v.* (also **-ise**) **1** *tr.* accustom to a new climate or to new conditions. **2** *intr.* become acclimatized. □ **acclimatization** *n.*

acclivity *n.* (*pl.* **-ies**) an upward slope. [based on Latin *clivus* 'slope'] □ **acclivitous** *adj.*

accolade *n.* the awarding of praise; an acknowledgement of merit. [French, based on Latin *collum* 'neck']

accommodate *v.tr.* **1** provide lodging or room for. **2** adapt, harmonize, reconcile (*must accommodate ourselves to new surroundings*). **3** do a service or favour to; oblige (a person). [based on Latin *commodus* 'fitting']

accommodating *adj.* obliging, compliant. □ **accommodatingly** *adv.*

accommodation *n.* **1** (in *sing.* or *US* in *pl.*) room for receiving people, esp. a place to live or lodgings. **2** an adjustment or adaptation to suit a special or different purpose. **3** a convenient arrangement; a settlement or compromise.

accommodation address *n. Brit.* an address used on letters to a person who is unable or unwilling to give a permanent address.

accompaniment *n.* **1** *Mus.* an instrumental or orchestral part supporting or partnering a solo instrument, voice, or group. **2** an accompanying thing.

accompanist *n.* person who provides a musical accompaniment.

accompany *v.tr.* (**-ies**, **-ied**) **1** go with; escort, attend. **2** (usu. in *passive*; foll. by *with*, *by*) be done or found with; supplement (*speech accompanied with gestures*). **3** *Mus.* support or partner with accompaniment. [from French *accompagner*, related to COMPANY]

accomplice *n.* a partner or helper, esp. in a crime or wrongdoing. [based on Latin *complex complicis* 'closely connected']

accomplish *v.tr.* perform; complete; succeed in doing. [based on Latin *complēre* 'to complete']

accomplished *adj.* clever, skilled; well trained or educated.

accomplishment *n.* **1** the fulfilment or completion (of a task etc.). **2** an acquired skill, esp. a social one. **3** a thing done or achieved.

accord ● v. 1 *intr.* (often foll. by *with*) (esp. of a thing) be in harmony; be consistent. **2** *tr.* **a** grant (permission, a request, etc.). **b** give (a welcome etc.). **●** *n.* **1** agreement, consent. **2** harmonious correspondence in pitch, tone, colour, etc. □ **of one's own accord** on one's own initiative; voluntarily. **with one accord** unanimously; in a united way. [based on Latin *cor cordis* 'heart']

accordance *n.* harmony, agreement. □ **in accordance with** in a manner corresponding to (*in accordance with your wishes*).

accordant *adj.* (often foll. by *with*) in tune; agreeing. [from Old French *acordant*]

according *adv.* (foll. by *to*) **1** as stated by or in (*according to my sister*). **2** in a manner corresponding to; in proportion to (*he lives according to his principles*).

accordingly *adv.* **1** as suggested or required by the (stated) circumstances. **2** consequently, therefore.

accordion *n.* ▶ a portable musical instrument with metal reeds blown by bellows, played by means of keys and buttons. [based on Italian *accordare* 'to tune'] □ **accordionist** *n.*

accost *v.tr.* approach and address (a person), esp. boldly. [based on Latin *costa* 'rib, side']

account ● *n.* **1** a narration or description. **2 a** an arrangement or facility at a bank or building society etc. for commercial or financial transactions, esp. for depositing and withdrawing money. **b** esp. *Brit.* an arrangement at a shop for buying goods on credit. **3 a** (often in *pl.*) a record or statement of money, goods, or services received or expended, with the balance. **b** (in *pl.*) the practice of accounting or reckoning (*is good at accounts*). **●** *v.tr.* (foll. by *to be* or compl.) regard as (*account him to be*

guilty; *account him wise*). □ **account for 1** serve as or provide an explanation or reason for (*that accounts for my absence*). **2 a** give a reckoning of or answer for (money etc. entrusted). **b** answer for (one's conduct). **3** succeed in killing, destroying, disposing of, or defeating. **4** supply or make up a specified amount or proportion of (*rent accounts for 50% of expenditure*). **by all accounts** in everyone's opinion. **call to account** require an explanation from (a person). **give a good** (or **bad**) **account of oneself** make a favourable (or unfavourable) impression; be successful (or unsuccessful). **keep account of** keep a record of; follow closely. **leave out of account** fail or decline to consider. **of no account** unimportant. **of some account** important. **on account 1** (of goods) to be paid for later. **2** (of money) in part payment. **on one's account** for one's benefit (*don't do it on my account*). **on account of** because of. **on no account** under no circumstances; certainly not. **on one's own account** for one's own purposes; at one's own risk. **take account of** (or **take into account**) consider along with other factors (*took their age into account*). **turn to account** (or **good account**) turn to one's advantage. [from Old French, related to COUNT[1] and COMPUTE]

accountable *adj.* responsible; required to account for one's conduct. □ **accountability** *n.* **accountably** *adv.*

accountancy *n.* the profession or duties of an accountant.

accountant *n.* a professional keeper or inspector of accounts.

accounting *n.* the process of or skill in keeping and verifying accounts.

account rendered *n.* a bill which has been sent but is not yet paid.

accounts payable *n.pl.* money owed by a company.

accounts receivable *n.pl.* money owed to a company.

accoutre *v.tr.* (*US* **accouter**) (usu. as **accoutred**, *US* **-tered** *adj.*) attire, equip, esp. with a special outfit. [based on Old French *couture* 'sewing']

accoutrement *n.* (*US* also **accouterment**) (usu. in *pl.*) **1** equipment, trappings. **2** *Mil.* a soldier's outfit other than weapons and garments.

accredit *v.tr.* (**accredited**, **accrediting**) **1** (foll. by *to*) attribute (a saying etc.) to (a person). **2** (foll. by *with*) credit (a person) with (a saying etc.). **3** (usu. foll. by *to*, *at*) send (an ambassador etc.) with credentials; recommend by documents as an envoy

keyboard
carrying straps
bellows
sound grill
bass and chord buttons

ACCORDION: 20TH-CENTURY ITALIAN ACCORDION

A

(*was accredited to the sovereign*). **4** recognize officially. [from French *accréditer*] □ **accreditation** *n.*

accredited *adj.* (of a person or organization) officially recognized.

accrete *v.* **1** *intr.* grow together or into one. **2** *intr.* (often foll. by *to*) form round or on, as round a nucleus. **3** *tr.* attract (such additions). [based on Latin *crescere* 'to grow']

accretion *n.* **1 a** the addition of external matter or things. **b** a thing formed by such growth. **2** an extraneous addition to something. **3** the growing together of separate things to form one. □ **accretive** *adj.*

accrue *v.* (**accrues, accrued, accruing**) **1** *intr.* (often foll. by *to*) come as a natural increase or advantage, esp. financial. **2** *tr.* accumulate; collect. [based on Anglo-French *acru(e)* 'increased'] □ **accrual** *n.* **accrued** *adj.*

acculturate *v.* **1** *intr.* adapt to or adopt a different culture. **2** *tr.* cause to do this. □ **acculturation** *n.* **acculturative** *adj.*

accumulate *v.* **1** *tr.* **a** acquire an increasing number or quantity of; heap up. **b** produce or acquire (a resulting whole) in this way. **2** *intr.* form an increasing mass or quantity. [based on Latin *cumulus* 'heap']

accumulation *n.* **1** the act or process of accumulating or being accumulated. **2** an accumulated mass or quantity.

accumulative *adj.* **1** arising from accumulation; cumulative (*accumulative evidence*). **2** arranged so as to accumulate.

accumulator *n.* **1** *Brit.* a rechargeable electric cell. **2** *Brit.* a bet placed on a sequence of events, the winnings and stake from each being placed on the next. **3** a person who accumulates things.

accuracy *n.* (*pl.* **-ies**) **1** exactness or precision, esp. arising from careful effort. **2** the degree of refinement in measurement or specification.

accurate *adj.* **1** careful, precise; lacking errors. **2** conforming exactly with the truth or with a given standard. [from Latin *accuratus* 'done carefully'] □ **accurately** *adv.*

accursed *adj.* (archaic **accurst**) **1** lying under a curse; ill-fated. **2** *colloq.* annoying.

accusation *n.* **1** the act or process of accusing or being accused. **2** a statement charging a person with an offence.

accusative *Gram.* ● *n.* the case of nouns, pronouns, and adjectives, expressing the object of an action or the goal of motion. ● *adj.* of or in this case. [from Latin *(casus) accusativus* 'the case showing cause']

accusatorial *adj.* *Law* (of proceedings) involving accusation by a prosecutor and a verdict reached by an impartial judge or jury (opp. INQUISITORIAL 3).

accusatory *adj.* of or implying accusation.

accuse *v.tr.* **1** (foll. by *of*) charge (a person etc.) with a fault or crime; indict (*accused them of murder*). **2** lay the blame on. [from Latin *accusare* 'to call to account'] □ **accuser** *n.* **accusingly** *adv.*

accustom *v.tr. & refl.* (foll. by *to*) make (a person or thing or oneself) used to (*the army accustomed him to discipline*). [related to CUSTOM]

accustomed *adj.* **1** (foll. by *to*) used to (*accustomed to hard work*). **2** customary, usual.

ace ● *n.* **1** ▼ a playing card, domino, etc. with a single spot and generally having the value 'one' or, in card games, the highest value in each suit. **2 a** a person who excels in some activity. **b** a pilot who has shot down many enemy aircraft. **3** *Tennis* an unreturnable service. **4** *Golf* a hole in one. ● *adj.* *slang* excellent. □ **within an ace of** on the verge of. [from Latin *as* 'unity']

acellular *adj.* *Biol.* **1** having no cells; not consisting of cells. **2** consisting of one cell only.

acephalous *adj.* **1** headless. **2** having no chief. **3** *Zool.* ▼ having no part of the body specially organized as a head. [from Greek *akephalos* 'headless'] **4** *Prosody* lacking a syllable or syllables in the first foot. [medieval Latin *acephalus*, from Greek *akephalos* 'headless']

ACEPHALOUS ORGANISM (STARFISH)

acer *n.* a tree or shrub of the genus *Acer*, which includes maples and the European sycamore. [Latin, literally 'maple']

acerbic *adj.* **1** astringently sour; harsh tasting. **2** bitter in speech, manner etc. [from Latin *acerbus* 'sour-tasting'] □ **acerbically** *adv.*

acerbity *n.* (*pl.* **-ies**)

acetaldehyde /ass-i-**tal**-di-hyd/ *n.* a colourless volatile liquid aldehyde.

acetaminophen /ă-set-ă-**min**-ŏ-fen/ *n. N. Amer.* = PARACETAMOL.

acetate /**ass**-i-tayt/ *n.* **1** a salt or ester of acetic acid. **2** a fabric made from cellulose acetate.

acetic /ă-**see**-tik/ *adj.* of or like vinegar or acetic acid. [based on Latin *acetum* 'vinegar'] □ **acetous** *adj.*

acetic acid *n.* the clear liquid acid that gives vinegar its characteristic taste.

acetone /**ass**-i-tohn/ *n.* a colourless volatile liquid ketone valuable as a solvent of organic compounds esp. paints etc.

acetyl /**ass**-i-tyl/ *n. Chem.* the monovalent radical of acetic acid, $CH_3CO–$.

acetylcholine /ass-i-til-**koh**-leen/ *n.* a compound serving to transmit impulses from nerve fibres.

acetylene /ă-**set**-i-leen/ *n.* a colourless hydrocarbon gas used esp. in welding.

acetylsalicylic acid /ass-i-tyl-sal-i-**sil**-ik/ *n.* = ASPIRIN.

Achaean /ă-**kee**-ăn/ ● *adj.* **1** of or relating to Achaea in ancient Greece. **2** *literary* Greek. ● *n.* **1** an inhabitant of Achaea. **2** (usu. in *pl.*) *literary* a Greek. [from Greek *Akhaios*]

ache ● *n.* **1** a continuous or prolonged dull pain. **2** mental distress. ● *v.intr.* **1** suffer from or be the source of an ache (*my left leg ached*). **2** (foll. by *to* + infin.) desire greatly (*we ached to be at home again*). [Old English] □ **achingly** *adv.* **achy** *adj.*

achieve *v.tr.* **1 a** attain by effort (*achieved victory*). **b** acquire, gain (*achieved notoriety*). **2** accomplish or

carry out (a feat or task). **3** *absol.* attain a desired level of performance. [from Old French phrase *à chief (venir)* '(to come or bring) to a head'] □ **achievable** *adj.* **achievement** *n.* **achiever** *n.*

Achilles heel /ă-**kil**-eez/ *n.* a person's vulnerable point. [from *Achilles*, Latin name of Greek hero *Akhilleus*, invulnerable except in the heel]

Achilles tendon *n.* ◄ the tendon connecting the heel with the calf muscles. ▷ MUSCULATURE

calf

Achilles tendon

heel

ACHILLES TENDON

achondroplasia /ă-kon-drŏ-**play**-ziă/ *n. Med.* a hereditary condition in which the growth of long bones by ossification of cartilage is retarded. [based on Greek *khondros* 'cartilage' + *plasis* 'moulding'] □ **achondroplasic** *adj.*

achondroplastic *adj.*

achromatic *adj.* *Optics* **1** that transmits light without separating it into constituent colours (*achromatic lens*). **2** without colour (*achromatic fringe*). [based on Greek *khrōma* 'colour'] □ **achromaticity** *n.* **achromatism** *n.*

acid ● *n.* **1** *Chem.* ▼ any of a class of substances that liberate hydrogen ions in water, are usu. sour and corrosive, turn litmus red, and have a pH of less than 7. ▷ ACID RAIN, pH. **2** (in general use) any sour substance. **3** *slang* the drug LSD. ● *adj.* **1** sharp-tasting. **2** biting (*an acid wit*). **3** *Chem.* having the essential properties of an acid. **4** (of a colour) intense, bright. [based on Latin *acēre* 'to be sour'] □ **acidic** *adj.* **acidimetry** *n.* **acidly** *adv.*

acid drop *n. Brit.* a kind of sweet with a sharp taste.

acid house *n.* a kind of synthesized music with a simple repetitive beat, often associated with the taking of hallucinogenic drugs.

acidify *v.tr. & intr.* (**-ies, -ied**) make or become acid. □ **acidification** *n.*

acidity *n.* an acid quality or state, esp. an excessively acid condition of the stomach.

acidophilic /ass-id-**off**-i-lik/ *adj.* esp. *Bot.* growing best in acidic conditions.

acidophilus /ass-id-**off**-i-lŭs/ *n.* a bacterium, *Lactobacillus acidophilus*, used to make yogurt and to supplement the intestinal flora. [modern Latin, literally 'acid-loving']

acidosis *n.* an over-acid condition of the body fluids or tissues. □ **acidotic** *adj.*

ACID

In chemistry, an acid is a water-soluble substance, capable of donating protons (hydrogen ions, H^+) when dissolved in water. The protons attach to water molecules (H_2O) to produce hydroxonium ions (H_3O^+). In neutral water, there are equal numbers of hydroxonium ions and hydroxide ions (OH^-), but in an acid solution there are more hydroxonium ions. The greater their concentration, the stronger the acid.

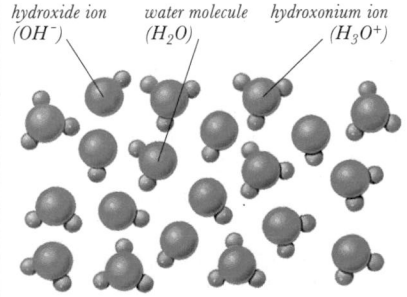

hydroxide ion (OH^-)   *water molecule* (H_2O)   *hydroxonium ion* (H_3O^+)

MOLECULES AND IONS IN NEUTRAL WATER

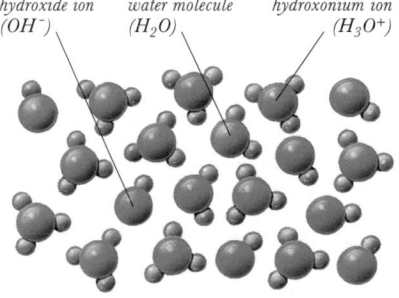

hydroxide ion (OH^-)   *water molecule* (H_2O)   *hydroxonium ion* (H_3O^+)

MOLECULES AND IONS IN AN ACID SOLUTION

A

ACID RAIN

The clouds that produce acid rain are formed when polluting gases, such as sulphur dioxide and nitrogen oxide, combine with oxygen and moisture in the air. The resultant precipitation – acid rain – is a dilute mixture of sulphuric acid and nitric acid. Acid rain causes forestry damage, as well as hastening the erosion of many ancient buildings and sculptures.

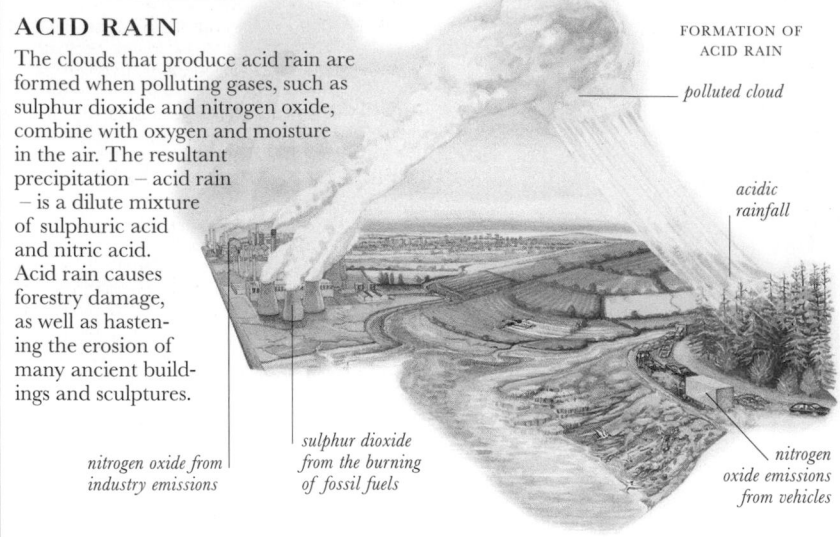

FORMATION OF ACID RAIN

polluted cloud

acidic rainfall

nitrogen oxide from industry emissions

sulphur dioxide from the burning of fossil fuels

nitrogen oxide emissions from vehicles

---

acid rain *n.* ▲ rain containing acid formed in the atmosphere esp. from industrial waste gases.

acid test *n.* **1** a severe or conclusive test. **2** a test in which acid is used to test for gold etc.

acidulate *v.tr.* make somewhat acid. [based on Latin *acidulus* 'somewhat sour'] □ **acidulation** *n.*

acidulous *adj.* somewhat acid.

ack-ack *colloq.* ● *adj.* anti-aircraft. ● *n.* an anti-aircraft gun etc. [formerly signallers' name for the letters *AA*]

ackee *n.* (also **akee**) **1** a tropical tree, *Blighia sapida*. **2** its fruit. [from Kru (a language of Liberia)]

ack emma *adv. & n.* Brit. *colloq.* = A.M. [formerly signallers' name for the letters *AM*]

acknowledge *v.tr.* **1 a** recognize; accept (*acknowledged the failure of the plan*). **b** (often foll. by *to be* + compl. or *that* + clause) admit that something is so (*acknowledged it to be a great success*). **2** confirm the receipt of (*acknowledged her letter*). **3 a** show that one has noticed (*acknowledged my arrival with a grunt*). **b** express appreciation of (a service etc.). [probably based on obsolete verb *to knowledge*] □ **acknowledgeable** *adj.*

acknowledgement *n.* (also **acknowledgment**) **1** the act or an instance of acknowledging. **2 a** a thing given or done in return for a service etc. **b** a letter confirming receipt of something. **3** (usu. in *pl.*) an author's statement of indebtedness to others.

acme *n.* the highest point or period; the peak of perfection. [Greek, literally 'highest point']

acne *n.* a skin condition characterized by red pimples. [from an erroneous Greek form, based on *akmē* 'facial eruption, acme'] □ **acned** *adj.*

acolyte *n.* **1** a person assisting a priest. **2** an assistant; a beginner. [from Greek *akolouthos* 'follower']

aconite *n.* **1 a** any poisonous plant of the genus *Aconitum* (buttercup family). **b** = ACONITINE. **2** (in full **winter aconite**) any related plant of the genus *Eranthis*, with yellow flowers. [from Greek *akoniton*]

aconitine *n.* *Chem.* a poisonous alkaloid obtained from the aconite.

acorn *n.* the fruit of the oak, a smooth nut in a rough cuplike base. ▷ OAK. [Old English, related to OAK and CORN[1]]

acoustic ● *adj.* **1** relating to sound or the sense of hearing. **2** ▶ (of a musical instrument etc.) not having electrical amplification (*acoustic guitar*). **3** (of building materials) used for soundproofing or modifying sound. ● *n.* **1** (usu. in *pl.*) the properties or qualities (esp. of a room or hall etc.) in

transmitting sound (*good acoustics*). **2** (in *pl.*; usu. treated as *sing.*) the science of sound. [based on Greek *akouein* 'to hear'] □ **acoustical** *adj.* **acoustically** *adv.*

acoustic coupler *n.* *Computing* a modem which converts digital signals into audible signals and vice versa.

acoustician *n.* an expert in acoustics.

acquaint *v.tr. & refl.* (usu. foll. by *with*) make (a person or oneself) aware of or familiar with (*acquaint me with the facts*). □ **be acquainted with** have personal knowledge of. [from Late Latin *accognitare* 'to come to know']

acquaintance *n.* **1** (usu. foll. by *with*) slight knowledge (of a person or thing). **2** the fact or process of being acquainted (*our acquaintance lasted a year*). **3** a person one knows slightly. □ **make the acquaintance of** (or **make a person's acquaintance**) meet (a person) for the first time; come to know. □ **acquaintanceship** *n.*

acquaintance rape *n.* the rape of a person by a person known to them.

acquiesce *v.intr.* (often foll. by *in*, *to*) agree, esp. tacitly; accept (an arrangement). [based on Latin *quiescere* 'to rest'] □ **acquiescence** *n.* **acquiescent** *adj.*

acquire *v.tr.* **1** gain by and for oneself; obtain. **2** come into possession of. [based on Latin *quaerere* 'to seek'] □ **acquirable** *adj.* **acquirement** *n.* **acquirer** *n.*

acquired characteristic *n.* *Biol.* a characteristic caused by the environment, not inherited.

acquired immune deficiency syndrome see AIDS.

acquired taste *n.* **1** a liking gained by experience. **2** the object of such a liking.

acquisition *n.* **1** something acquired, esp. if regarded as useful. **2** the act or an instance of acquiring. [related to ACQUIRE]

acquisitive *adj.* keen to acquire things; avaricious; materialistic. □ **acquisitively** *adv.* **acquisitiveness** *n.*

hollow wooden body

sound hole

string

fret

neck   tuning key

bridge   scratch-plate   **ACOUSTIC GUITAR**

acquit *v.tr.* (**acquitted**, **acquitting**) **1** (often foll. by *of*) declare (a person) not guilty (*were acquitted of the offence*). **2** *refl.* **a** conduct oneself (*acquitted ourselves well*). **b** (foll. by *of*) discharge (a duty or responsibility). [from medieval Latin *acquitare* 'to pay a debt']

acquittal *n.* **1** the process of freeing or being freed from a charge, esp. by a judgement of not guilty. **2** performance of a duty.

acquittance *n.* **1** payment of or release from a debt. **2** a written receipt attesting settlement of a debt.

acre *n.* **1** a measure of land, 4,840 sq. yards, 0.405 hectare. **2** (in *pl.*; usu. foll. by *of*) a large area or amount. [Old English] □ **acreage** *n.* **acred** *adj.* (esp. in *comb.*).

acrid *adj.* **1** bitterly pungent; corrosive. **2** bitter in manner etc. [from Latin *acer acris* 'keen'] □ **acridity** *n.* **acridly** *adv.*

acrimonious *adj.* bitter in manner or temper. □ **acrimoniously** *adv.*

acrimony *n.* (*pl.* **-ies**) bitterness; ill feeling. [related to ACRID]

acrobat *n.* a performer of spectacular gymnastic feats. [based on Greek *akron* 'summit' + *bainein* 'to walk'] □ **acrobatic** *adj.* **acrobatically** *adv.*

acrobatics *n.pl.* **1** acrobatic feats. **2** (treated as *sing.*) the art of performing these.

acromegaly *n.* *Med.* abnormal growth of the hands, feet, and face, caused by overproduction of growth hormone by the pituitary gland. [based on Greek *akron* 'extremity' + *megas megal-* 'great'] □ **acromegalic** *adj.*

acronym *n.* a word, usu. pronounced as such, formed from the initial letters of other words (e.g. *Ernie*, *laser*, *Nato*). [from Greek *akron* 'end' + *onoma* 'name']

acrophobia *n.* *Psychol.* an abnormal dread of heights. [based on Greek *akron* 'peak'] □ **acrophobic** *adj.*

acropolis *n.* **1** ▲ a citadel or upper fortified part of an ancient Greek city. **2** (**Acropolis**) ▲ the ancient citadel at Athens. [from Greek *akron* 'summit' + *polis* 'city']

across ● *prep.* **1** to or on the other side of (*lives across the river*). **2** from one side to another side of (*stretched across the opening*). **3** at or forming an angle (esp. a right angle) with (*deep cuts across his legs*). ● *adv.* **1** to or on the other side (*ran across*). **2** from one side to another (*a blanket stretched across*). **3** forming a cross (*with cuts across*). **4** (of a crossword clue or answer) read horizontally. □ **across the board** applying to all. [from Old French *a croix* 'in a cross']

acrostic *n.* a poem, puzzle, etc. in which certain letters in each line form a word or words. [from Greek *akron* 'end' + *stikhos* 'row, line of verse']

acrylic ● *adj.* **1** made with a synthetic polymer derived from acrylic acid. **2** *Chem.* of or derived from acrylic acid. ● *n.* **1** an acrylic textile fibre. **2** (also in *pl.*) acrylic paint. [based on Latin *acer acris* 'pungent' + *olēre* 'to smell']

acrylic acid *n.* a pungent liquid organic acid.

act ● *n.* **1** something done; an action. **2** the process of doing something (*caught in the act*). **3 a** a piece of entertainment. **b** the performer(s) of this. **4** a pretence (*it was all an act*). **5** a main division of a play or opera. **6 a** (also **Act**) a written ordinance of a legislative body. **b** a document attesting a legal transaction. **7** (often in *pl.*) the recorded decisions or proceedings of a committee, etc. **8** (**Acts**) in full **Acts of the Apostles**) the New Testament book relating the growth of the early Church. ● *v.* **1** *intr.* behave. **2** *intr.* perform actions or functions; operate effectively (*act as referee*; *the brakes failed to act*). **3** *intr.* (also foll. by *on*) exert energy or influence (*alcohol acts on the brain*). **4** *intr.* **a** perform a part in a play, film, etc. **b** pretend. **5** *tr.* **a** perform the part of (*acts the fool*). **b** perform (a play etc.). **c** portray (an incident) by actions. **d** feign (*we acted indifference*). □ **act for** be the (esp. legal) representative of. **act of God** an instance of uncontrollable

ACROPOLIS

An acropolis is an ancient Greek citadel, situated on an area of high ground in order to protect it from attack. The best known is the Acropolis in Athens, constructed in the 5th century BC, which contains the remnants of several temple buildings, including the Parthenon.

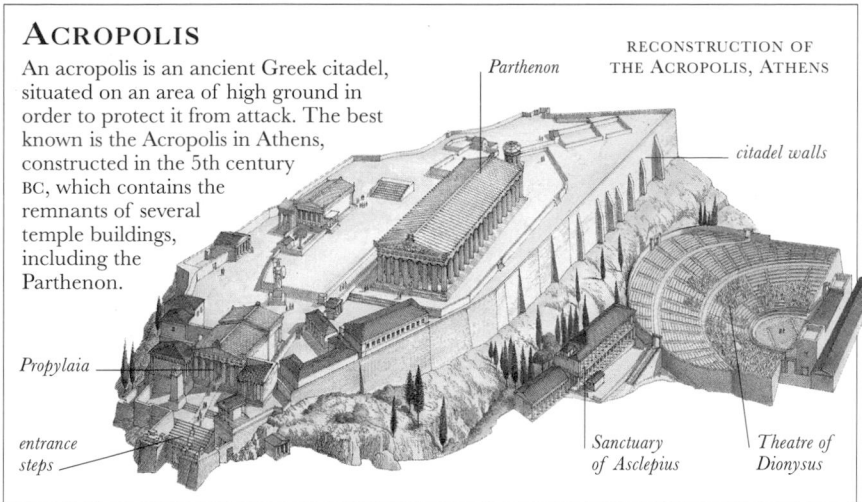

RECONSTRUCTION OF THE ACROPOLIS, ATHENS

Parthenon

citadel walls

Propylaia

entrance steps

Sanctuary of Asclepius

Theatre of Dionysus

A

natural forces in operation. **act out 1** translate (ideas etc.) into action. **2** *Psychol.* represent (one's subconscious desires etc.) in action. **act up** *colloq.* give trouble (*my car is acting up again*). **get one's act together** *slang* become properly organized. **get in on the act** *slang* become a participant (esp. for profit). **put on an act** *colloq.* carry out a pretence. [based on Latin *agere* 'to do']

actin *n.* a protein which with myosin forms the contractile filaments of muscle fibres. [based on Greek *aktis -inos* 'ray']

acting ● *n.* **1** the art or occupation of performing parts in plays, films, etc. **2** in senses of ACT *v.* **●** *attrib.adj.* serving on behalf of another or others (*acting manager; Acting Captain*).

acting pilot officer *n.* a rank in the RAF above warrant officer and below pilot officer.

actinide series *n. Chem.* the series of 15 radioactive elements from actinium to lawrencium.

actinism *n.* the property of short-wave radiation that produces chemical changes, as in photography. [based on Greek *aktis -inos* 'ray'] **□ actinic** *adj.*

actinium *n. Chem.* a radioactive metallic element of the actinide series, occurring naturally in pitchblende. [based on Greek *aktis -inos* 'ray']

action ● *n.* **1** the fact or process of doing or acting (*put ideas into action*). **2** energy as a characteristic (*a woman of action*). **3** the exertion of energy or influence (*the action of acid on metal*). **4** something done; an act (*not aware of his own actions*). **5 a** a series of events represented in a story, play, etc. **b** *slang* exciting activity (*want some action*). **6** armed conflict; fighting (*killed in action*). **7 a** the way in which a machine etc. works (*the action of an air rifle*). **b** the mode of movement of an animal or human (*a runner with good action*). **8** a lawsuit (*bring an action*). **9** (in *imper.*) a word of command to begin, used by a film director etc. **●** *v.tr.* bring a legal action against. **□ go into action** start work. **out of action** not working. **take action** begin to act (esp. in protest). [Middle English, related to ACT]

actionable *adj.* giving cause for legal action.

action-packed *adj.* full of action or excitement.

action painting *n.* ▶ an aspect of abstract art with paint applied by random or spontaneous gestures.

action replay *n. Brit.* a playback of part of a television broadcast, esp. a sporting event, often in slow motion.

action stations *n.pl.* esp. *Brit.* positions taken up in readiness for action, esp. by troops preparing for battle.

activate *v.tr.* **1** make active; bring into action. **2** *Chem.* cause reaction in (a substance, molecules, etc.). **3** *Physics* make radioactive. **□ activation** *n.* **activator** *n.*

activated carbon *n.* carbon, esp. charcoal, treated to increase its adsorptive power.

activated sludge *n.* aerated sewage containing aerobic micro-organisms to break it down.

active ● *adj.* **1 a** consisting in or marked by action; energetic; diligent (*leads an active life*). **b** able to move about or accomplish practical tasks (*infirmity made him less active*). **2** working (*an active volcano*). **3** originating action; not merely inert (*active ingredients*). **4** radioactive. **5** *Gram.* designating the voice that attributes the action of a verb to the person or thing from which it logically proceeds (e.g. of the verbs in *guns kill; we saw him*). **●** *n. Gram.* the active form or voice of a verb. [from Latin *activus*, based on *agere* 'to do'] **□ actively** *adv.* **activeness** *n.*

active birth *n.* childbirth during which the mother is encouraged to be active and move around freely.

active carbon *n.* = ACTIVATED CARBON.

active citizen *n.* a person who plays an active role in the community, esp. in crime prevention etc.

active duty *n.* participation in policing or military operational activities.

active matrix *n. Electronics* a display system in which each pixel is individually controlled (also *attrib.*: *active matrix LCD*).

active service *n.* participation in warfare as a member of the armed forces.

activism *n.* a policy of vigorous action in a cause, esp. in politics. **□ activist** *n.*

activity *n.* (*pl.* **-ies**) **1 a** the condition of being active or moving about. **b** the exertion of energy. **2** (often in *pl.*) a particular pursuit (*outdoor activities*). **3** = RADIOACTIVITY. [from Late Latin *activitas*]

actor *n.* (*fem.* **actress**) **1** a person who acts a part in a play etc. **2** a person whose profession is performing such parts. [Latin, literally 'doer']

actual *adj.* (usu. *attrib.*) **1** existing in fact; real (often as distinct from ideal). **2** existing now. [based on Latin noun *actus* 'an act'] **□ actualize** *v.tr.* (also **-ise**). **actualization** *n.*

■ **Usage** Redundant use, as in *Tell me the actual facts*, is common but to be avoided in formal contexts.

actual bodily harm *n.* injury inflicted intentionally on a person but less serious than grievous bodily harm.

actuality *n.* (*pl.* **-ies**) **1** reality; what is the case. **2** (in *pl.*) existing conditions.

actually *adv.* **1** as a fact, really (*I asked for ten, but actually got nine*). **2** strange as it may seem (*he actually refused!*).

actuary *n.* (*pl.* **-ies**) an expert in statistics and probability theory, esp. one who calculates insurance risks. **□ actuarial** *adj.* **actuarially** *adv.*

actuate *v.tr.* **1** communicate motion to (a machine etc.). **2** cause the operation of (an electrical device etc.). **3** cause (a person) to act. [based on medieval Latin *actuatus* 'brought to action'] **□ actuation** *n.* **actuator** *n.*

ACTION PAINTING

A method of painting that originated in the USA during the 1940s, action painting is associated with a wider artistic movement called abstract expressionism. Artists producing action paintings intended their works to be a record of the act of painting itself, to the exclusion of all other subject matter.

The paintings are often extremely vibrant, conveying the spontaneity and impulsiveness of their creation. This is best exemplified in the work of Jackson Pollock, whose paintings clearly show the energetic gestures of the artist, who splashed, dripped, flicked, and threw paint on to the canvas.

TIMELINE

Convergence (1952), JACKSON POLLOCK

| 1500 | 1550 | 1600 | 1650 | 1700 | 1750 | 1800 | 1850 | 1900 | 1950 | 2000 |

A

acuity *n.* sharpness, acuteness. [based on Latin *acuere* 'to sharpen']

acumen *n.* keen insight. [Latin, literally 'point']

acupressure *n.* = SHIATSU. [blend of ACUPUNCTURE and PRESSURE]

acupuncture *n.* a method (originally Chinese) of treating medical conditions by pricking the skin or tissues with needles. [from Latin *acu punctura* 'a pricking with a needle'] □ **acupuncturist** *n.*

acute ● *adj.* (**acuter**, **acutest**) **1** (of sensation or senses) keen, penetrating. **2** shrewd (*an acute critic*). **3** (of a disease) coming sharply to a crisis; severe. **4** (of a difficulty) critical, serious. **5 a** (of an angle) less than 90°. ▷ TRIANGLE. **b** pointed. **6** (of a sound) shrill. ● *n.* = ACUTE ACCENT. [from Latin *acutus* 'sharpened'] □ **acutely** *adv.* **acuteness** *n.*

acute accent *n.* a mark (´) placed over letters in some languages to show pronunciation (e.g. *rosé*) etc.

acyl /**ay**-syl/ *n. Chem.* the monovalent radical of a carboxylic acid. [German]

AD *abbr.* (of a date) of the Christian era. [Latin *Anno Domini* 'in the year of the Lord']

■ **Usage** Strictly, AD should precede a date (e.g. AD 410), but uses such as *the tenth century* AD are well established.

ad *n. colloq.* an advertisement.

adage /**ad**-ij/ *n.* a traditional maxim; a proverb. [from Latin *adagium*]

adagio /ă-**dah**-ji-oh/ *Mus.* ● *adv. & adj.* in slow time. ● *n.* (*pl.* **-os**) an adagio movement or passage. [Italian, from *ad agio* 'at ease']

Adam *n.* the first man, in the biblical and Koranic traditions. □ **not know a person from Adam** be unable to recognize the person in question. [from Hebrew *ādām* 'man']

adamant ● *adj.* stubbornly resolute. ● *n. archaic* diamond or other hard substance. [from Latin *adamas adamant-* 'untameable'] □ **adamance** *n.* **adamantine** *adj.* **adamantly** *adv.*

Adam's ale *n.* water.

Adam's apple *n.* ▼ the projection at the front of the neck formed by the thyroid cartilage of the larynx.

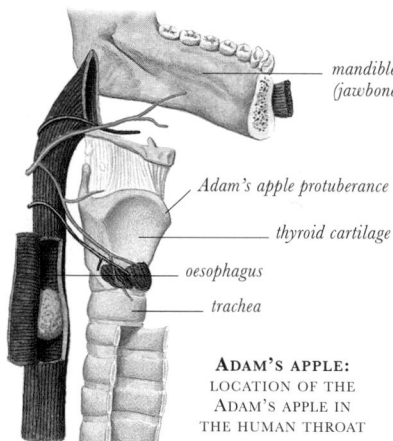

mandible (jawbone)

Adam's apple protuberance

thyroid cartilage

oesophagus

trachea

ADAM'S APPLE:
LOCATION OF THE
ADAM'S APPLE IN
THE HUMAN THROAT

adapt *v.* **1** *tr.* **a** (foll. by *to*) fit, adjust (one thing to another). **b** (foll. by *to*, *for*) make suitable for a purpose. **c** alter or modify (esp. a text). **2** *intr. & refl.* (usu. foll. by *to*) become adjusted to new conditions. [from Latin *adaptare*] □ **adaptive** *adj.*

adaptable *adj.* **1** able to adapt oneself to new conditions. **2** that can be adapted. □ **adaptability** *n.* **adaptably** *adv.*

adaptation *n.* **1** the act or process of adapting or being adapted. **2** a thing that has been adapted.

adaptor *n.* (also **adapter**) **1** a device for making equipment compatible. **2** *Brit.* a device for connecting several electrical plugs to one socket. **3** a person who adapts.

ADC *abbr.* **1** aide-de-camp. **2** analogue-digital converter.

add *v.tr.* **1** join (one thing to another) as a supplement (*add insult to injury*). **2** put together (numbers) to find their combined value. **3** say in addition. □ **add in** include. **add to** increase (*this adds to our difficulties*). **add up 1** find the total of. **2** (foll. by *to*) constitute (*adds up to a disaster*). **3** *colloq.* make sense. [from Latin *addere*] □ **added** *adj.*

addendum *n.* (*pl.* **addenda**) a thing (usu. something omitted) to be added, esp. (in *pl.*) as additional matter at the end of a book. [Latin, literally 'thing to be added']

adder *n.* a small often venomous snake, esp. the common viper, *Vipera berus*. [Old English *nædre*: *n* lost later by wrong division of *a naddre*]

addict ● *v.tr. & refl.* (usu. foll. by *to*) devote or apply habitually or compulsively; make addicted. ● *n.* **1** a person addicted to a habit (*drug addict*). **2** *colloq.* an enthusiastic devotee of a pastime. [based on Latin *addictus* 'assigned, devoted'] □ **addicted** *adj.*

addiction *n.* the fact or process of being addicted.

addictive *adj.* (of a drug, habit, etc.) causing addiction.

addition *n.* **1** the act or process of adding or being added. **2** a person or thing added (*a useful addition to the team*). □ **in addition** (often foll. by *to*) as something added.

additional *adj.* added, extra, supplementary. □ **additionally** *adv.*

additive ● *n.* a thing added (*food additive*). ● *adj.* **1** characterized by addition (*additive process*). **2** to be added. [from Late Latin *additivus*]

addle ● *v.* **1** *tr.* muddle, confuse. **2** *intr.* (of an egg) become addled. ● *adj.* (in *comb.*) muddled, unsound (*addle-brained*; *addle-head*). [Old English *adela* 'liquid filth']

addled *adj.* **1** (of an egg) rotten, producing no chick. **2** muddled.

add-on *n.* something added to an existing object or quantity (also *attrib.*: *add-on features are available*).

address ● *n.* **1 a** the place where a person lives or an organization is situated. **b** particulars of this, esp. for postal purposes. **c** *Computing* the location of an item of stored information. **2** a discourse delivered to an audience. **3** skill, dexterity, readiness. **4** (in *pl.*) a courteous approach; courtship (*pay one's addresses to*). ● *v.tr.* **1** write the name and address of the intended recipient on (an envelope, packet, etc.). **2** direct in speech or writing (remarks, a protest, etc.). **3** speak or write to (*addressed the audience*). **4** direct one's attention to. **5** *Golf* take aim at or prepare to hit (the ball). □ **address oneself to 1** speak or write to. **2** attend to. [based on Latin *directus* 'direct'] □ **addressable** *adj.*

addressee *n.* the person to whom something is addressed.

adduce *v.tr.* cite as an instance or as proof or evidence. [from Latin *adducere*]

adenine *n.* a purine derivative found in all living tissue as a component base of DNA or RNA. ▷ DNA. [from German]

adenoids *n.pl. Med.* ▶ a mass of enlarged lymphatic tissue between the back of the nose and the throat, often hindering speaking and breathing in the young. [based on Greek *adēn* 'gland'] □ **adenoidal** *adj.*

adenoma *n.* (*pl.* **adenomas** or **adenomata**) a glandlike benign tumour. [modern Latin]

adept ● *adj.* (foll. by *at*, *in*) thoroughly proficient. ● *n.* a skilled performer; an expert. [from Latin *adeptus* 'attained'] □ **adeptly** *adv.* **adeptness** *n.*

adequate *adj.* **1** sufficient, satisfactory. **2** proportionate. **3** barely sufficient. [from Latin *adaequatus* 'made equal'] □ **adequacy** *n.* **adequately** *adv.*

adhere *v.intr.* **1** (usu. foll. by *to*) (of a substance) stick fast to a surface, another substance, etc. **2** (foll. by *to*) behave according to (*adhered to our plan*). **3** (foll. by *to*) give support or allegiance to. [based on Latin *haerēre* 'to stick']

adherent ● *n.* **1** a supporter of a party, person, etc. **2** a devotee of an activity. ● *adj.* (often foll. by *to*) (of a substance) sticking fast. □ **adherence** *n.*

■ **Usage** See Usage Note at ADHESION.

adhesion *n.* **1** the act or process of adhering. **2** the capacity of a substance to stick fast. **3** *Med.* an abnormal union of surfaces due to inflammation or injury. **4** the maintenance of contact between a vehicle's wheels and the road. **5** the giving of support or allegiance. [related to ADHERE]

■ **Usage** Adhesion is more common in physical senses (e.g. *The glue has good adhesion*), with *adherence* used in abstract senses (e.g. *adherence to principles*).

adhesive ● *adj.* enabling surfaces or substances to adhere to one another. ● *n.* an adhesive substance. [from French *adhésif -ive*] □ **adhesiveness** *n.*

ad hoc *adv. & adj.* for a particular purpose (*an ad hoc decision*). [Latin, literally 'to this']

ad hominem *adv. & adj.* relating to or associated with a particular person. [Latin, literally 'to the person']

adiabatic *Physics* ● *adj.* **1** impassable to heat. **2** occurring without heat entering or leaving the system. ● *n.* a curve or formula for adiabatic phenomena. [from Greek *adiabatos* 'impassable'] □ **adiabatically** *adv.*

adieu /ă-**dew**/ ● *int.* goodbye. ● *n.* (*pl.* **adieus** or **adieux** /ă-**dewz**/) a goodbye. [from (Old) French, from *à Dieu* 'to God']

ad infinitum *adv.* without limit; for ever. [Latin, literally 'to infinity']

adipose *adj.* of or characterized by fat, esp. as stored in the body tissues; fatty. ▷ BREAST, FAT. [based on Latin *adeps adipis* 'fat'] □ **adiposity** *n.*

adit *n.* a horizontal entrance or passage in a mine.

adjacent *adj.* (often foll. by *to*) lying near or adjoining. [from Latin *adjacent-* 'lying near to'] □ **adjacency** *n.*

adjective *n.* a word or phrase naming an attribute, added to or grammatically related to a noun. [based on Latin *adjicere adject-* 'to throw to, attribute'] □ **adjectival** *adj.* **adjectivally** *adv.*

adjoin *v.tr.* be next to and joined with. [from Latin *adjungere*]

adjourn *v.* **1** *tr.* **a** put off; postpone. **b** break off (a meeting, discussion, etc.) with the intention of resuming later. **2** *intr.* (of persons at a meeting) **a** break off proceedings and disperse. **b** (foll. by *to*) transfer the meeting to another place. [based on Old French *jorn* 'day'] □ **adjournment** *n.*

adjudge *v.tr.* **1** adjudicate (a matter). **2** pronounce judicially. **3** (foll. by *to*) award judicially. **4** *archaic* condemn. [from Latin *adjudicare*]

adjudicate *v.* **1** *intr.* act as judge in a court, competition, tribunal, etc. **2** *tr.* decide judicially regarding (a claim etc.). [based on Latin *judex -icis* 'judge'] □ **adjudication** *n.* **adjudicative** *adj.* **adjudicator** *n.*

adjunct *n.* **1** (foll. by *to*, *of*) a subordinate or incidental thing. **2** an assistant. [from Latin *adjunctus* 'joined to'] □ **adjunctive** *adj.*

adjure *v.tr.* (usu. foll. by *to* + infin.) charge or request (a

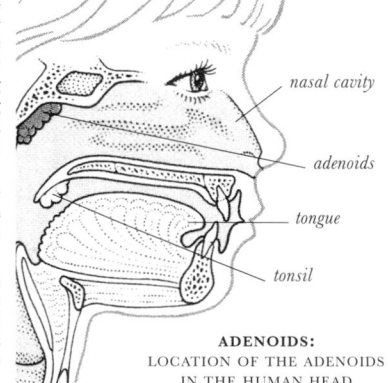

nasal cavity

adenoids

tongue

tonsil

ADENOIDS:
LOCATION OF THE ADENOIDS
IN THE HUMAN HEAD

person) solemnly or earnestly, esp. under oath. [from Late Latin *adjurare* 'to put a person to an oath'] □ **adjuration** *n.*

adjust *v.* **1 a** *tr.* arrange; put in the correct order or position. **b** regulate, esp. by a small amount. **2** *tr.* (usu. foll. by *to*) make suitable. **3** *tr.* harmonize (discrepancies). **4** *tr.* assess (loss or damages). **5** *intr.* (usu. foll. by *to*) make oneself suited to; become familiar with (*adjust to one's surroundings*). [based on Latin *juxta* 'near'] □ **adjustable** *adj.* **adjustability** *n.* **adjuster** *n.* **adjustment** *n.*

adjutant *n.* **1 a** *Mil.* an officer who assists superior officers by communicating orders, conducting correspondence, etc. **b** an assistant. **2** (in full **adjutant bird**) a large black and white S. Asian stork of the genus *Leptoptilos*. [based on Latin *adjutare* 'to assist']

Adjutant General *n.* (*pl.* **Adjutant Generals**) a high-ranking army administrative officer.

adjuvant ● *adj.* **1** helpful, auxiliary. **2** *Med.* (of therapy) applied after initial treatment for cancer, esp. to suppress secondary tumour formation. ● *n.* **1** an adjuvant person or thing. **2** *Med.* a substance which enhances the body's immune response to an antigen. [from Latin *adjuvant-* 'helping']

ad lib ● *v.intr.* (**ad libbed**, **ad libbing**) speak or perform without preparation; improvise. ● *adj.* improvised. ● *adv.* as one pleases; to any desired extent. ● *n.* something spoken or played extempore. [abbreviation of Latin *ad libitum* 'at (one's) pleasure']

adman *n.* (*pl.* **admen**) *colloq.* a person who produces advertisements commercially.

admin *n. Brit. colloq.* administration.

administer *v.* **1** *tr.* attend to the running of (business affairs etc.); manage. **2** *tr.* **a** be responsible for the implementation of (the law, a punishment, etc.). **b** *Eccl.* perform the rites of (a sacrament). **c** (usu. foll. by *to*) direct the taking of (an oath). **3** *tr.* **a** provide, apply (a remedy). **b** deliver (a rebuke). **4** *intr.* act as administrator. [from Latin *administrare*] □ **administrable** *adj.*

administrate *v. tr. & intr.* administer (esp. business affairs); act as an administrator.

administration *n.* **1 a** management of a business, institution, etc. **b** (prec. by *the*) *N. Amer.* the people responsible for this. **2** the management of public affairs; government. **3** the government in power. **4** *N. Amer.* the term of office of a political leader or government. **5** (**Administration**) (in the US) a government agency (*the Food and Drug Administration*). **6** *Law* the management of another person's estate. **7** (foll. by *of*) **a** the administering of justice, an oath, etc. **b** application of remedies.

administrative *adj.* of or relating to the management of affairs. □ **administratively** *adv.*

administrator *n.* **1** a person who administers a business or public affairs. **2** a person capable of organizing. **3** (*fem.* **administratrix**) *Law* a person appointed to manage the estate of a person who has died intestate.

admirable *adj.* **1** deserving admiration. **2** excellent. [from Latin *admirabilis*] □ **admirably** *adv.*

admiral *n.* **1 a** the commander-in-chief of a country's navy. **b** a naval officer of high rank; the commander of a fleet or naval squadron. **c** (**Admiral**) an admiral of the second grade. **2** ▶ a boldly patterned nymphalid butterfly (*red admiral; white admiral*). [based on Arabic *'amīr* 'commander']

Admiral of the Fleet *n.* an admiral of the first grade.

Admiralty *n.* (*pl.* **-ies**) **1** (*hist.* except in titles) (in the UK) the department administering the Royal Navy. **2** (**admiralty**) *Law* the maritime branch of the administration of justice.

admiration *n.* **1** pleased contemplation. **2** respect; warm approval. **3** an object of this (*was the admiration of the whole town*).

admire *v.tr.* **1** regard with approval, respect, or satisfaction. **2** express one's admiration of. [from Latin *admirari* 'to wonder at'] □ **admiring** *adj.* **admiringly** *adv.*

admirer *n.* **1** a woman's suitor. **2** a person who admires.

admissible *adj.* **1** (of an idea) worth considering. **2** *Law* allowable as evidence. **3** (foll. by *to*) capable of being admitted. [related to ADMIT] □ **admissibility** *n.*

admission *n.* **1** an acknowledgement (*admission of error*). **2 a** the process or right of entering or being admitted. **b** a charge for this (*admission is £5*). **3** a person admitted to a hospital. [Middle English, related to ADMIT]

admit *v.* (**admitted**, **admitting**) **1** *tr.* **a** acknowledge; recognize as true. **b** accept as valid. **2** *intr.* (foll. by *to*) acknowledge responsibility for (a deed, fault, etc.). **3** *tr.* **a** allow (a person) entrance or access. **b** allow (a person) to be a member of (a group etc.) or to share in (a privilege etc.). **c** (of a hospital etc.) bring in (a person) for residential treatment. **4** *tr.* (of an enclosed space) have room for. **5** *intr.* (foll. by *of*) allow as possible. [Middle English, from Latin *admittere* 'to let into']

admittance *n.* the right or process of admitting or being admitted (*no admittance except on business*).

admittedly *adv.* as an acknowledged fact (*admittedly there are problems*).

admix *v.* **1** *tr. & intr.* (foll. by *with*) mingle. **2** *tr.* add as an ingredient.

admixture *n.* **1** a thing added, esp. a minor ingredient. **2** the act of adding this. [based on Latin *admiscēre admixt-* 'to mix in']

admonish *v.tr.* **1** reprove. **2** (foll. by *to* + infin., or *that* + clause) urge. **3** give earnest advice to. **4** (foll. by *of*) warn. [from Latin *admonēre* 'to warn'] □ **admonishment** *n.* **admonition** *n.* **admonitory** *adj.*

ad nauseam *adv.* to a disgusting degree. [Latin, literally 'to sickness']

ado *n.* busy activity, fuss, trouble. □ **without more** (or **further**) **ado** immediately. [from Old Norse]

adobe /ă-**doh**bi/ *n.* **1** an unburnt sun-dried brick. **2** the clay used for these. [from Arabic]

adolescent ● *adj.* between childhood and adulthood. ● *n.* an adolescent person. [from Latin *adolescent-* 'growing up'] □ **adolescence** *n.*

Adonis *n.* a handsome young man. [from Greek *Adōnis*, name of a youth loved by Aphrodite]

adopt *v.tr.* **1** take (a person) into a relationship, esp. another's child as one's own. **2** choose to follow (a course of action etc.). **3** take over (an idea etc.) from another person. **4** *Brit.* choose as a candidate for office. **5** *Brit.* (of a local authority) accept responsibility for the maintenance of (a road etc.). **6** accept; formally approve (a report, accounts, etc.). [from Latin *adoptare* 'to choose for oneself'] □ **adoption** *n.*

adoptive *attrib.adj.* as a result of adoption (*adoptive parents*). □ **adoptively** *adv.*

adorable *adj.* **1** deserving adoration. **2** *colloq.* delightful, charming. □ **adorably** *adv.*

ADMIRAL BUTTERFLIES

INDIAN RED ADMIRAL (*Vanessa indica*)

BLUE ADMIRAL (*Vanessa canace*)

adore *v.tr.* **1** regard with honour and deep affection. **2** worship as divine. **3** *colloq.* like very much. [from Latin *adorare* 'to worship'] □ **adoration** *n.* **adorer** *n.* **adoring** *adj.* **adoringly** *adv.*

adorn *v.tr.* **1** add beauty to; be an ornament to. **2** decorate. [from Latin *adornare* 'to deck out'] □ **adornment** *n.*

adrenal /ă-**dree**-năl/ ● *adj.* **1** at or near the kidneys. **2** of the adrenal glands. ● *n.* (in full **adrenal gland**) ▼ either of two ductless glands above the kidneys, secreting adrenalin etc. ▷ ENDOCRINE. [based on Latin *renes* 'kidneys']

adrenal gland   inferior vena cava

adrenal gland

aorta

kidney

renal artery

renal vein

ADRENAL GLANDS

adrenal cortex *n. Anat.* the outer part of the adrenal glands, secreting corticosteroids etc. ▷ KIDNEY

adrenalin /ă-**dren**-ă-lin/ *n.* (also **adrenaline**) **1** a hormone secreted by the adrenal glands, causing excitement and stimulation.

adrift *adv. & predic.adj.* **1** drifting. **2** at the mercy of circumstances. **3** *Brit. colloq.* **a** unfastened. **b** out of touch. **c** absent without leave. **d** (often foll. by *of*) failing to reach a target. **e** out of order.

adroit *adj.* dexterous, skilful. [from French *à droit* 'correctly'] □ **adroitly** *adv.* **adroitness** *n.*

adsorb *v.tr.* (usu. of a solid) hold (molecules) to its surface, causing a thin film to form. [related to ABSORB] □ **adsorbable** *adj.* **adsorbent** *adj. & n.* **adsorption** *n.* (also **adsorbtion**).

aduki *var.* of ADZUKI.

adulate *v.tr.* flatter obsequiously. [based on Latin *adulatus* 'fawned upon'] □ **adulation** *n.* **adulatory** *adj.*

adult ● *adj.* **1** mature, grown-up. **2 a** of or for adults (*adult education*). **b** *euphem.* sexually explicit (*adult films*). ● *n.* **1** an adult person. **2** *Law* a person who has reached the age of majority. [from Latin *adultus* 'grown up'] □ **adulthood** *n.*

adulterate *v.tr.* debase (esp. foods) by adding other substances. [based on Latin *adulteratus* 'corrupted'] □ **adulteration** *n.* **adulterator** *n.*

adulterer *n.* (*fem.* **adulteress**) a person who commits adultery. [from obsolete verb *adulter*]

adultery *n.* (*pl.* **-ies**) voluntary sexual intercourse between a married person and a person other than his or her spouse. [based on Old French *avoutre* 'adulterer', assimilated to Latin *adulterium*] □ **adulterous** *adj.*

adumbrate *v.tr.* **1** indicate faintly. **2** represent in outline. **3** foreshadow, typify. **4** overshadow. [based on Latin *adumbratus* 'overshadowed'] □ **adumbration** *n.*

advance ● *v.* **1** *tr. & intr.* move or put forward. **2** *intr.* make progress. **3** *tr.* **a** pay (money) before it is due. **b** lend (money). **4** *tr.* promote (a person, cause, or plan). **5** *tr.* put forward (a claim or suggestion). **6** *tr.* cause (an event) to occur at an earlier date. **7** *tr.* raise (a price). **8** *intr.* rise (in price). **9** *tr.* (as **advanced** *adj.*) **a** far on in progress (*the work is well advanced*). **b** ahead of the times (*advanced ideas*).

A

● *n.* **1** an act of going forward. **2** progress. **3** a payment made before the due time. **4** a loan. **5** (esp. in *pl.*; often foll. by *to*) an amorous or friendly approach. **6** a rise in price. ● *attrib.adj.* done or supplied beforehand (*advance warning*). □ **advance on** approach threateningly. **in advance** ahead in place or time. [based on Late Latin *abante* 'in front']

advanced level *n.* a GCE examination of a standard higher than ordinary level and GCSE.

advanced supplementary level *n.* a GCE examination with a smaller syllabus than advanced levels.

advance guard *n.* a body of soldiers preceding the main body of an army.

advancement *n.* the promotion of a person, cause, or plan.

advantage ● *n.* **1** a beneficial feature. **2** benefit, profit (*is not to your advantage*). **3** (often foll. by *over*) a better position; superiority in a particular respect. **4** *Tennis* the next point won after deuce. ● *v.tr.* **1** be beneficial or favourable to. **2** further, promote. □ **take advantage of 1** make good use of (a favourable circumstance). **2** exploit (a person), esp. unfairly. **3** *euphem.* seduce. **to advantage** in a way which exhibits the merits (*was seen to advantage*). [from Old French *avantage* (n.), *avantager* (v.), related to ADVANCE] □ **advantageous** *adj.* **advantageously** *adv.*

Advent *n.* **1** the season before Christmas. **2** the coming or second coming of Christ. **3** (**advent**) the arrival of a person or thing. [from Latin *adventus* 'arrival']

Adventist *n.* a member of a Christian sect that believes in the imminent second coming of Christ. □ **Adventism** *n.*

adventitious *adj.* **1** accidental, casual. **2** added from outside. **3** *Biol.* formed accidentally or in an unusual anatomical position. ▷ BULB. □ **adventitiously** *adv.*

Advent Sunday *n.* the first Sunday in Advent.

adventure ● *n.* **1** an unusual and exciting experience. **2** a daring enterprise; a hazardous activity. **3** enterprise (*the spirit of adventure*). **4** a commercial speculation. ● *v.intr.* **1** (often foll. by *into*, *upon*) dare to go or come. **2** (foll. by *on*, *upon*) dare to undertake. **3** engage in adventure. [from Latin *adventurus* 'about to happen'] □ **adventuresome** *adj.*

adventure playground *n. Brit.* a children's playground with materials for climbing on, building with, etc.

adventurer *n.* (*fem.* **adventuress**) **1** a person who seeks adventure. **2** a financial speculator.

adventurism *n.* a tendency to take risks. □ **adventurist** *n.*

adventurous *adj.* **1** rash, venturesome; enterprising. **2** characterized by adventures. □ **adventurously** *adv.* **adventurousness** *n.*

adverb *n.* a word or phrase that modifies or qualifies another word or a word-group, expressing a relation of place, time, manner, cause, degree, etc. (e.g. *gently, quite, then, there*). [from Latin *adverbium*] □ **adverbial** *adj.*

adversarial *adj.* **1** involving conflict or opposition. **2** opposed, hostile.

adversary *n.* (*pl.* **-ies**) **1** an enemy. **2** an opponent in a sport or game. [from Latin *adversarius*, related to ADVERSE]

adverse *adj.* (often foll. by *to*) **1** contrary, hostile. **2** injurious. [from Latin *adversus*, based on *vertere* 'to turn'] □ **adversely** *adv.*

adversity *n.* (*pl.* **-ies**) **1** adverse fortune. **2** a misfortune. [from Latin *adversitas*, related to ADVERSE]

advert[1] /ad-vert/ *n. Brit. colloq.* an advertisement. [abbreviation]

advert[2] /ăd-vert/ *v.intr.* (foll. by *to*) *literary* refer in speaking or writing. [from Latin *advertere*]

advertise *v.* **1** *tr.* (also *absol.*) draw attention to or describe favourably (goods, services, or vacant positions) in a public medium in order to sell, or to seek employees. **2** *tr.* make generally or publicly known. **3** *intr.* (foll. by *for*) seek by public notice. [from Old French *a(d)vertir*] □ **advertiser** *n.*

advertisement *n.* **1 a** a public notice or announcement, esp. one advertising goods or services in newspapers or in broadcasts. **b** *colloq.* a person or thing regarded as a means of conveying the merits of something (*he's a good advertisement for a healthy lifestyle*). **2** the act or process of advertising.

advice *n.* **1** words offered as a recommendation about future action or behaviour. **2** information given; news. **3** formal notice of a transaction. [from (Old) French *avis*]

advisable *adj.* to be recommended; expedient. □ **advisability** *n.*

advise *v.* **1** *tr.* (also *absol.*) give advice to. **2** *tr.* recommend; offer as advice (*they advise caution; advised me to rest*). **3** *tr.* inform, notify. **4** *intr.* (foll. by *with*) *US* consult. [based on Latin *visare* 'to see to']

advised *adj.* deliberate, considered. □ **advisedly** *adv.*

adviser *n.* (also *disp.* **advisor**) a person who advises, esp. one appointed to do so.

■ **Usage** The variant form *advisor* is fairly common, but is considered incorrect by some people.

advisory *adj.* **1** giving advice (*an advisory body*). **2** consisting in giving advice.

advocaat *n.* a liqueur of eggs, sugar, and brandy. [Dutch, literally 'advocate', being originally an advocate's drink]

advocacy *n.* (usu. foll. by *of*) verbal support for a cause, policy, etc. **2** the function of an advocate. [related to ADVOCATE]

advocate ● *n.* **1** (foll. by *of*) a person who speaks in favour. **2** a person who pleads for another. **3 a** a professional pleader in a court of justice. **b** *Sc.* a barrister. ● *v.tr.* **1** recommend or support by argument (a cause, policy, etc.). **2** plead for, defend. [from Latin *advocatus* 'called to']

adze (*US* also **adz**) ● *n.* a tool like an axe with an arched blade at right angles to the handle, used for cutting away the surface of wood. ● *v.tr.* dress or cut with an adze. [Old English]

adzuki *n.* (in full **adzuki bean**) (also **aduki**) **1** an annual leguminous plant, *Vigna angularis*, native to China and Japan. **2** ▶ the small dark red edible bean of this plant. [from Japanese *azuki*]

aegis /ee-jis/ *n.* □ **under the aegis of** under the auspices of. [Latin, from Greek *aigis*, the mythical shield of Zeus or Athene]

aegrotat /I-grŏ-tat/ *n. Brit.* **1** a certificate that a university student is too ill to attend an examination. **2** an examination pass awarded in such circumstances. [Latin, literally 'is sick']

aeolian /ee-oh-li-ăn/ *adj.* (*US* **eolian**) wind-borne. [based on Latin *Aeolus*, god of the winds]

aeolian harp *n.* a stringed instrument or toy that produces musical sounds when the wind passes through it.

Aeolian mode *n. Mus.* the mode represented by the natural diatonic scale A–A. [Latin *Aeolius* 'from *Aeolis*' (in Asia Minor), from Greek *Aiolis*]

aeon /ee-ŏn/ *n.* (also **eon**) **1** a very long or indefinite period. **2** an age of the universe. **3** *Astron.* a thousand million years. [from Greek *aiōn* 'age']

aerate *v.tr.* **1** charge (a liquid) with a gas. **2** expose to the mechanical or chemical action of the air. [based on Latin *aer* 'air'] □ **aeration** *n.* **aerator** *n.*

aerial ● *n.* a structure by which signals are transmitted or received as part of a radio or television transmission or receiving system. ● *adj.* **1** by or from or involving aircraft (*aerial photography*). **2 a** existing, moving, or happening in the air. **b** of or in the atmosphere; atmospheric. [based on Greek *aēr* 'air'] □ **aerially** *adv.*

aerialist *n.* a high-wire or trapeze artist.

aerial torpedo see TORPEDO *n.* 1b.

aerie var. of EYRIE.

aero- *comb. form* **1** air. **2** aircraft. [Greek]

aerobatics *n.pl.* feats of expert flying and manoeuvring of aircraft.

aerobe *n.* a micro-organism usu. growing in the presence of air, or needing oxygen for growth. [from Greek *aēr* 'air' + *bios* 'life']

aerobic *adj.* **1** of or relating to aerobics. **2** *Biol.* relating to or requiring free oxygen.

aerobics *n.pl.* (often treated as *sing.*) vigorous exercises designed to increase the body's oxygen intake.

aerodrome *n. Brit.* a small airport or airfield.

aerodynamics *n.pl.* (usu. treated as *sing.*) the study of the interaction between the air and solid bodies moving through it. □ **aerodynamic** *adj.* **aerodynamically** *adv.* **aerodynamicist** *n.*

aerofoil *n. Brit.* ▼ a structure with curved surfaces (e.g. a wing, fin, or tailplane) designed to give lift in flight. ▷ AIRCRAFT, INDYCAR

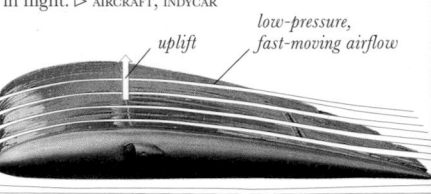

uplift
low-pressure, fast-moving airflow
high-pressure, slower-moving airflow

AEROFOIL: AEROPLANE WING

aeronautics *n.pl.* (usu. treated as *sing.*) the science of motion or travel in the air. □ **aeronautic** *adj.* **aeronautical** *adj.*

aeroplane *n.* esp. *Brit.* a powered heavier-than-air flying vehicle with fixed wings. ▷ AIRCRAFT, FIGHTER. [French *aéroplane*]

aerosol *n.* **1 a** a substance packed under pressure and able to be released as a fine spray. **b** a container holding this. **2** a system of colloidal particles dispersed in a gas (e.g. fog or smoke).

aerospace *n.* **1** the Earth's atmosphere and outer space. **2** the technology of aviation in this region.

aesthete /eess-th'eet/ *n.* (*US* **esthete**) a person who has or professes to have a special appreciation of beauty. [from Greek *aisthētēs* 'a person who perceives']

aesthetic /eess-thet-ik/ (*US* also **esthetic**) ● *adj.* **1** concerned with beauty or the appreciation of beauty. **2** having such appreciation; sensitive to beauty. **3** in accordance with good taste. ● *n.* **1** (in *pl.*) the philosophy of the beautiful. **2** a set of principles of good taste and the appreciation of beauty. [based on Greek *aisthēta* 'things perceived'] □ **aesthetically** *adv.* **aestheticism** *n.*

aesthetician *n.* (*US* also **esthetician**) **1** a person versed in or devoted to aesthetics. **2** *N. Amer.* a beautician.

aestival /eest-i-văl/ *adj.* (*US* **estival**) *formal* belonging to or appearing in summer. [Middle English via Old French from Latin *aestivalis*]

aestivate /eest-i-vayt/ *v.intr.* (*US* **estivate**) **1** *Zool.* spend the summer or dry season in a state of torpor. **2** *formal* pass the summer. □ **aestivation** *n.*

aether var. of ETHER 2, 3.

aetiology /ee-ti-ol-ŏji/ *n.* (*US* **etiology**) **1** the assignment of a cause or reason. **2** the study of causation. **3** *Med.* the causation of diseases and disorders as a subject of investigation. [from Greek *aitiologia*] □ **aetiologic** *adj.* **aetiological** *adj.* **aetiologically** *adv.*

AF *abbr.* audio frequency.

ADZUKI BEANS

afar *adv.* at or to a distance. □ **from afar** from a distance. [Middle English]

affable *adj.* friendly, good-natured. [from Latin *affabilis*] □ **affability** *n.* **affably** *adv.*

affair *n.* **1** a concern; a business; a matter to be attended to (*that is my affair*). **2** a celebrated or noteworthy happening or sequence of events. **3** = LOVE AFFAIR. **4** (in *pl.*) **a** ordinary pursuits of life. **b** business dealings. **c** public matters (*current affairs*). [from Old French *afaire*, from *à faire* 'to do']

affect[1] *v.tr.* **1** produce an effect on (*the recession did not affect business*). **2** touch the feelings of (*affected me deeply*). [based on Latin *affectus* 'influenced'] □ **affecting** *adj.* **affectingly** *adv.*

■ **Usage** *Affect* should not be confused with *effect* which means 'to bring about', e.g. *The government effected great changes.*

affect[2] *v.tr.* **1** pretend to have or feel (*affected indifference*). **2** (foll. by *to* + infin.) pretend. **3** assume the character or manner of (*affect the freethinker*). **4** make a show of liking or using (*she affects fancy hats*). [from Latin *affectare* 'to aim at', related to AFFECT[1]]

affectation *n.* **1** a contrived manner of behaviour. **2** (foll. by *of*) a studied display. **3** pretence. [related to AFFECT[2]]

affected *adj.* **1** in senses of AFFECT[1], AFFECT[2]. **2** artificially assumed (*an affected air of innocence*). **3** (of a person) full of affectation; artificial. □ **affectedly** *adv.*

affection *n.* fond feeling. [related to AFFECT[1]]

affectionate *adj.* fond; showing love or tenderness. [from medieval Latin *affectionatus*] □ **affectionately** *adv.*

affective *adj.* concerning the affections; emotional. □ **affectivity** *n.*

afferent *adj. Physiol.* conducting inwards or towards (*afferent nerves*) (opp. EFFERENT). [from Latin *afferent-* 'bringing to']

affiance *v.tr.* (usu. in *passive*) *literary* promise to give in marriage. [from medieval Latin *affidare* 'to swear on oath']

affiant *n. N. Amer.* a person who makes an affidavit.

affidavit *n.* a written statement confirmed by oath, for use as evidence in court. [medieval Latin, literally 'has stated on oath']

affiliate ● *v.* **1** *tr.* (usu. in *passive*; foll. by *to, with*) connect (a person or society) with a larger organization. **2** *tr.* (of an institution) adopt (a person) as a member of a society) as a branch. **3** *intr.* (foll. by *to, with*) associate oneself with a society or political party. ● *n.* an affiliated person or organization. [from medieval Latin *affiliatus* 'adopted'] □ **affiliation** *n.* **affiliative** *adj.*

affiliation order *n. Brit.* a legal order that the man judged to be the father of an illegitimate child must help to support it.

affinity *n.* (*pl.* **-ies**) **1** a natural attraction to a person or thing. **2** relationship, esp. by marriage. **3** resemblance in structure between animals, plants, or languages. **4** a similarity of characteristics; family likeness. **5** *Chem.* the tendency of certain substances to combine with others. [based on Latin *affinis* 'related']

affinity card *n.* **1** a discount card issued to people with a common interest. **2** (in the UK) a bank card for which the bank donates to a specific charity etc. a portion of the money spent using the card.

affirm *v.* **1** *tr.* assert strongly; state as a fact. **2** *intr.* **a** *Law* make an affirmation. **b** make a formal declaration. [from Latin *affirmare*]

affirmation *n.* **1** the act or process of affirming or being affirmed. **2** *Law* a solemn declaration by a person who conscientiously declines to take an oath.

affirmative ● *adj.* **1** asserting that a thing is so. **2** (of a vote) expressing approval. ● *n.* **1** an affirmative statement, reply, or word. **2** (prec. by *the*) a positive or affirming position. ● *int.* esp. *N. Amer.* yes.

□ **in the affirmative** so as to accept or agree to a proposal; yes (*the answer was in the affirmative*). [from Late Latin *affirmativus*] □ **affirmatively** *adv.*

affirmative action *n.* esp. *N. Amer.* action favouring those who suffer from discrimination.

affix ● *v.tr.* /ă-**fiks**/ **1** (usu. foll. by *to, on*) attach, fasten. **2** add in writing. **3** impress (a seal or stamp). ● *n.* /**af**-iks/ **1** an appendage; an addition. **2** *Gram.* an addition or element placed at the beginning (*prefix*) or end (*suffix*) of a root, stem, or word, or in the body of a word (*infix*), to modify its meaning. [from medieval Latin *affixare*] □ **affixation** *n.*

afflict *v.tr.* inflict suffering on. □ **afflicted with** suffering from. [from Latin *afflictare*]

■ **Usage** See Usage Note at INFLICT.

affliction *n.* **1** physical or mental distress. **2** a cause of this.

affluence *n.* an abundant supply of money etc.; wealth. [from Latin *affluentia*, related to AFFLUENT]

affluent *adj.* **1** wealthy, rich. **2** abundant. [from Latin *affluent-* 'flowing towards'] □ **affluently** *adv.*

afford *v.tr.* **1** (prec. by *can* or *be able to*) **a** have enough money, time, etc. for; be able to spare (*cannot afford to buy a car*; *can afford £50*). **b** be in a position to do something (*can't afford to lose*). **2** provide (*affords a view of the sea*). [Old English *geforthian* 'to promote'] □ **affordable** *adj.* **affordability** *n.*

afforest *v.tr.* convert into forest; plant with trees. [from medieval Latin *afforestare*] □ **afforestation** *n.*

affray *n.* a breach of the peace by fighting or rioting. [based on Old French *esfreer* 'to frighten']

affront ● *n.* an open insult (*feel it an affront*). ● *v.tr.* **1** insult openly. **2** offend. [from Old French *afronter* 'to slap in the face']

Afghan ● *n.* **1 a** a native or national of Afghanistan. **b** a person of Afghan descent. **2** the official language of Afghanistan; also called PASHTO. ● *adj.* of or relating to Afghanistan, its people, or its language. [from Pashto (official language of Afghanistan)]

Afghan hound *n.* ▼ a tall hunting dog of a breed with long silky hair. ▷ DOG

AFGHAN HOUND

aficionado /ă-fis-yŏ-**nah**-doh/ *n.* (*pl.* **-os**) a devotee of a sport or pastime. [Spanish]

afield *adv.* away from home; to or at a distance (esp. in phr. **far afield**). [Middle English]

afire *adv. & predic.adj.* **1** on fire. **2** intensely roused or excited.

aflame *adv. & predic.adj.* **1** in flames. **2** = AFIRE 2.

afloat *adv. & predic.adj.* **1** floating in water or air. **2** at sea; on board ship. **3** out of debt or difficulty. **4** in general circulation. **5** full of or covered with a liquid. [Old English]

AFM *abbr.* (in the UK) Air Force Medal.

afoot *adv. & predic.adj.* in operation; progressing.

afore *prep., conj., & adv. archaic* or *dial.* before; previously; in front (of). [Old English]

afore- *prefix* before, previously (*aforementioned*).

aforethought *adj.* premeditated (following a noun: *malice aforethought*).

a fortiori *adv. & adj.* with a yet stronger reason (than a conclusion already accepted). [Latin]

afoul *adv.* (in phrs. **fall afoul of**, **run afoul of**) *N. Amer.* foul (see FALL, RUN).

afraid *predic.adj.* **1** (often foll. by *of*, or *that* or *lest* + clause) frightened. **2** (foll. by *to* + infin.) reluctant for fear of the consequences (*afraid to go in*). □ **be afraid** (foll. by *that* + clause) *colloq.* admit or declare with regret (*I'm afraid there's none left*). [based on Old French *esfreer* 'to frighten']

afresh *adv.* anew; with a fresh beginning.

African ● *n.* **1** a native of Africa (esp. a dark-skinned person). **2** a person of African descent. ● *adj.* of or relating to Africa. [from Latin *Africanus*]

African-American ● *n.* a black American. ● *adj.* of or relating to black Americans.

Africanize *v.tr.* (also **-ise**) **1** make African in character. **2** place under the control of African blacks. □ **Africanization** *n.*

African violet *n.* ◀ a small E. African plant of the genus *Saintpaulia*, with velvety leaves and blue, purple, or pink flowers, esp. *S. ionantha*.

Afrikaans *n.* the language of the Afrikaner people, developed from Dutch. [Dutch, literally 'African']

Afrikaner *n.* an Afrikaans-speaking white person in S. Africa, esp. of Dutch descent. [Afrikaans, on the pattern of *Hollander* 'Dutchman' etc.]

Afro ● *adj.* (of a hairstyle) long and bushy, as grown by some blacks. ● *n.* (*pl.* **-os**) an Afro hairstyle.

Afro- *comb. form* African.

Afro-American *adj. & n.* = AFRICAN-AMERICAN.

Afrocentric *adj.* centring on African or Afro-American culture.

afrormosia *n.* **1** an African tree, *Pericopsis elata*, yielding a hardwood resembling teak. **2** this wood.

aft *adv. Naut. & Aeron.* at or towards the stern or tail.

after ● *prep.* **1 a** following in time; later than (*after six months*; *after midnight*). **b** *N. Amer.* in specifying time (*a quarter after eight*). **2** in view of (*after your behaviour tonight what do you expect?*). **3** in spite of (*after all my efforts I've still not succeeded*). **4** behind (*shut the door after you*). **5** in pursuit or quest of (*run after them*; *is after a job*). **6** about, concerning (*asked after her*). **7** in allusion to (*named him William after the prince*). **8** in imitation of (*a painting after Rubens*). **9** next in importance to (*the best book on the subject after mine*). **10** according to (*after a fashion*). ● *conj.* in or at a time later than that when (*left after they arrived*). ● *adv.* **1** later in time (*soon after*). **2** behind in place (*followed on after*). ● *adj.* **1** later, following (*in after years*). **2** *Naut.* nearer the stern (*after cabins*). □ **after all 1** in spite of all that has happened or has been said etc. (*after all, what does it matter?*). **2** in spite of one's exertions, expectations, etc. (*tried for an hour and failed after all*; *he came after all!*). [Old English]

afterbirth *n.* the placenta and foetal membranes discharged from the womb after the birth of offspring.

afterburner *n.* an auxiliary burner in a jet engine to increase thrust.

aftercare *n.* **1** care of a person after a stay in hospital or on release from prison. **2 a** subsequent maintenance. **b** support offered to a customer following the purchase of a product.

after-effect *n.* an effect that follows after an interval or after the primary action of something.

afterglow *n.* **1** a light or radiance remaining after its source has disappeared. **2** a pleasant feeling remaining after a pleasurable experience.

AFRICAN VIOLET
(*Saintpaulia* 'Bright Eyes')

A

after-hours *attrib.adj.* taking place after normal hours.

after-image *n.* an image retained by a sense organ and producing a sensation after the cessation of the stimulus.

afterlife *n.* **1** *Relig.* life after death. **2** life at a later time.

aftermarket *n.* **1** a market in spare parts and components. **2** *Stock Exch.* a market in shares after their original issue.

aftermath *n.* **1** consequences or after-effects (*the aftermath of war*). **2** *dial.* new grass growing after mowing. [earlier in sense 'later mowing': based on obsolete *math* 'mowing']

aftermost *adj. Naut.* furthest aft.

afternoon *n.* the time from noon or lunchtime to evening (*this afternoon; during the afternoon*).

afters *n.pl. Brit. colloq.* the course following the main course of a meal; dessert.

aftershave *n.* an astringent lotion for use after shaving.

aftershock *n.* a lesser shock following the main shock of an earthquake.

aftertaste *n.* a taste remaining after eating or drinking.

afterthought *n.* an item or thing that is thought of or added later.

afterwards *adv.* (*US* also **afterward**) later, subsequently. [Middle English]

afterword *n.* concluding remarks in a book.

Ag[1] *symb. Chem.* the element silver. [Latin *argentum*]

Ag[2] *abbr.* antigen.

Aga *n. Brit. propr.* a type of heavy heat-retaining cooking stove or range intended for continuous heating. [from Svenska Aktienbolaget *Gas-ackumulator* (Swedish Gas Accumulator Company), the original manufacturer]

aga *n.* (in Muslim countries, esp. under the Ottoman Empire) a commander; a chief. [from Turkish *ağa* 'master']

again *adv.* **1** another time; once more. **2** as in a previous position or condition (*back again; quite well again*). **3** in addition (*half as many again*). **4** further, besides (*again, what about the children?*). **5** on the other hand (*I might, and again I might not*). [Old English]

against *prep.* **1** in opposition to (*fight against crime; am against hanging; against the law*). **2** into collision or in contact with (*ran against a rock; lean against the wall*). **3** to the disadvantage of (*his age is against him*). **4** in contrast to (*against a dark background*). **5** in anticipation of or preparation for (*against a rainy day*). **6** as a compensating factor to (*income against expenditure*). **7** in return for (*issued against payment of the fee*). [Middle English]

Aga Khan *n.* the spiritual leader of the Nizari sect of Shi'ite Muslims.

agamospermy *n. Bot.* asexual reproduction by division of an unfertilized ovule. [Greek *agamos* 'unmarried' + *sperma* 'seed']

AGARIC:
SHAGGY PARASOL
(*Macrolepiota rhacodes*)

agapanthus *n.* any lilylike plant of the African genus *Agapanthus*. [from Greek *agapē* 'love' + *anthos* 'flower']

agape[1] *adv. & predic.adj.* gaping, esp. with wonder.

agape[2] /**ag**-ă-pi/ *n.* **1** a Christian feast in token of fellowship. **2** *Theol.* Christian love, esp. as distinct from erotic love. [Greek, literally 'brotherly love']

agar /**ay**-gar/ *n.* a gelatinous substance obtained from seaweed and used in making soups, biological culture media, etc. [Malay]

agaric *n.* ◄ any fungus of the family Agaricaceae, including the common edible mushroom. ▷ MUSHROOM, TOADSTOOL. [from Greek *agarikon*]

agate /**ag**-īt/ *n.* ► a hard usu. banded variety of chalcedony. [from Greek *akhatēs*]

agave /ă-**gay**-vi/ *n.* any plant of the genus *Agave*, e.g. the American aloe. [based on Greek *agauos* 'illustrious']

age ● *n.* **1 a** the length of time that a person or thing has existed. **b** a particular point in or part of one's life (*old age; voting age*). **2 a** (often in *pl.*) *colloq.* a long time (*for ages*). **b** a distinct period of the past (*golden age; Middle Ages*). **c** *Geol.* a period of time. **d** a generation. **3** old age (*the peevishness of age*). ● *v.* (*pres. part.* **ageing**, **aging**) **1** *intr.* show signs of advancing age (*has aged recently*). **2** *intr.* grow old. **3** *intr.* mature. **4** *tr.* cause or allow to age. □ **come of age** reach adult status. [based on Latin *aevum* 'an age of time']

aged *adj.* **1** /ayjd/ **a** of the age of (*aged ten*). **b** that has been subjected to ageing. **2** /**ay**-jid/ having lived long; old.

age group *n.* a number of persons or things classed together as of similar age.

ageing *n.* (also **aging**) **1** growing old. **2** giving the appearance of advancing age.

ageism *n.* discrimination on the grounds of age. □ **ageist** *adj. & n.*

ageless *adj.* **1** never growing or appearing old or outmoded. **2** eternal, timeless.

age-long *adj.* lasting for a very long time.

agency *n.* (*pl.* **-ies**) **1** the business, establishment, or function of an agent (*travel agency*). **2 a** active operation; action (*free agency*). **b** intervening action (*fertilized by the agency of insects*). **c** action personified (*an invisible agency*). **3** (also **Agency**) a department or body providing a specific service for a government, etc. (*United Nations relief agency*). [based on Latin *agere* 'to do']

agenda *n.* (*pl.* **agendas**) **1** a list of items of business to be considered at a meeting. **2** a series of things to be done; a plan of action. [Latin, literally 'things to be done']

agent *n.* **1 a** a person who acts for another in business etc. (*literary agent*). **b** a person or company that acts as broker and provides a specified service (*estate agent*). **c** a travelling salesman or saleswoman. **d** a spy. **2** a person or thing that exerts power or produces an effect (*oxidizing agent*). [based on Latin *agere* 'to do']

agent noun *n.* a noun denoting an agent or agency (e.g. *lawyer, accelerator*).

agent provocateur /*a*zh-ahn prŏ-vok-ă-**ter**/ *n.* (*pl.* **agents provocateurs** *pronunc.* same) a person employed to tempt suspected offenders to self-incriminating action. [French, literally 'provocative agent']

age of consent *n.* the age at which consent to sexual intercourse is valid in law.

age-old *adj.* having existed for a very long time.

agglomerate ● *v.tr. & intr.* **1** collect into a mass; accumulate in a disorderly way. ● *n.* a mass or collection of things. ● *adj.* collected into a mass. [from Latin *agglomeratus* 'added to'] □ **agglomeration** *n.* **agglomerative** *adj.*

agglutinate *v.* **1** *tr.* unite as with glue. **2** *tr. & intr. Biol.* cause or undergo rapid clumping (of bacteria etc.). [based on Latin *gluten -inis* 'glue'] □ **agglutination** *n.* **agglutinative** *adj.*

agglutinin *n. Biol.* an antibody or other substance causing agglutination.

aggrandize *v.tr.* (also **-ise**) **1** increase the power, rank, or wealth of. **2** cause to appear greater than is the case. [from French *agrandir*] □ **aggrandizement** *n.*

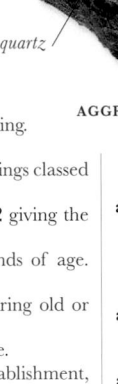

AGATE:
POLISHED SLICE

feldspar

quartz

mica

AGGREGATE ROCK

aggravate *v.tr.* **1** increase the gravity of (*the war was aggravating the situation*). **2** *disp.* annoy, exasperate (a person). [based on Latin *aggravatus* 'made heavy'] □ **aggravating** *adj. disp.* in sense 2. **aggravation** *n. disp.* in sense 2.

■ **Usage** The use of *aggravate* to mean 'annoy, exasperate', is regarded by some people as incorrect but is common in informal use and dates back to the 17th century.

aggregate ● *n.* **1** a collection of, or the total of, disparate elements. **2** pieces of crushed stone, gravel, etc. used in making concrete. **3 a** *Geol.* ◄ a mass of minerals formed into solid rock. **b** a mass of particles. ● *adj.* **1** (of disparate elements) collected into one mass. **2** constituted by the collection of many units into one body. **3** *Bot.* (of a group of species) comprising several very similar species formerly regarded as a single species. ● *v.tr. & intr.* collect together; combine into a whole. □ **in the aggregate** as a whole. [from Latin *aggregatus* 'herd together, associated'] □ **aggregation** *n.* **aggregative** *adj.*

aggression *n.* **1** the act or practice of attacking without provocation. **2** an unprovoked attack. **3** forcefulness. **4** *Psychol.* a hostile or destructive tendency; such behaviour. [from Latin *aggressio* 'attack']

aggressive *adj.* **1** (of a person) **a** given to aggression. **b** forceful. **2** (of an act) hostile. **3** of aggression. □ **aggressively** *adv.* **aggressiveness** *n.*

aggressor *n.* a person who attacks without provocation. [Late Latin]

aggrieved *adj.* having a grievance. [based on Old French *agrever* 'to make heavier'] □ **aggrievedly** *adv.*

aggro *n. Brit. slang* **1** aggressive trouble-making. **2** trouble.

aghast *predic.adj.* filled with consternation or dismay. [Middle English]

agile *adj.* quick-moving, nimble, active. [from Latin *agilis*] □ **agilely** *adv.* **agility** *n.*

aging var. of AGEING.

agitate *v.* **1** *tr.* disturb or excite (a person or feelings). **2** *intr.* stir up interest or concern, esp. publicly. **3** *tr.* shake or move. [based on Latin *agitatus* 'moved to and fro'] □ **agitatedly** *adv.* **agitator** *n.*

agitation *n.* **1** agitating or being agitated. **2** mental anxiety.

AGM *abbr. Brit.* annual general meeting.

agnail *n.* **1** a piece of torn skin at the root of a fingernail. **2** soreness from this. [Old English]

agnate ● *adj.* **1** descended esp. by male line from the same male ancestor. **2** of the same clan or nation. **3** akin. ● *n.* a person who is descended esp. by male line from the same male ancestor. [based on Latin *natus* 'born'] □ **agnatic** *adj.* **agnation** *n.*

agnosia *n. Med.* the loss of the ability to interpret sensations. [from Greek *agnōsia* 'ignorance']

agnostic ● *n.* a person who believes that nothing is known of the existence or nature of God or of anything beyond material phenomena. ● *adj.* of or relating to agnostics or agnosticism. [based on Greek *gnōsis* 'knowledge'] □ **agnosticism** *n.*

ago *adv.* earlier; before the present (*ten years ago*). [Middle English, from obsolete verb *ago* 'to pass']

agog ● *adv.* eagerly, expectantly. ● *predic.adj.* eager, expectant. [from Old French *en gogues* 'in merry mood']

à gogo *adv.* in abundance (*whisky à gogo*). [French]

agonistic *adj.* polemical, combative. [from Greek *agōnistikos*, related to AGONY]

agonize *v.* (also **-ise**) **1** *intr.* undergo (esp. mental) anguish. **2** *tr.* (as **agonized** *adj.*) expressing agony (*an agonized look*). [from Greek *agōnizesthai* 'to contend'] □ **agonizingly** *adv.*

agony *n.* (*pl.* **-ies**) **1** extreme suffering. **2** a severe struggle. [based on Greek *agōn* 'contest']

agony aunt *n.* (*masc.* **agony uncle**) *Brit. colloq.* a person who answers letters in an agony column.

agony column *n. Brit. colloq.* **1** a column in a periodical offering personal advice to readers who write in. **2** = PERSONAL COLUMN.

agoraphobia *n. Psychol.* an abnormal fear of open spaces or public places. [based on Greek *agora* 'place of assembly'] □ **agoraphobe** *n.* **agoraphobic** *adj. & n.*

AGR *abbr.* advanced gas-cooled (nuclear) reactor.

agrarian *adj.* **1** of or relating to the land or its cultivation. **2** relating to landed property. [based on Latin *ager agri* 'field']

agree *v.* (**agrees**, **agreed**, **agreeing**) **1** *intr.* hold a similar opinion (*I agree with you*). **2** *intr.* (often foll. by *to*, or *to* + infin.) consent (*agreed to go*). **3** *intr.* (often foll. by *with*) **a** become or be in harmony. **b** suit; be good for (*caviar didn't agree with him*). **c** *Gram.* have the same number, gender, case, or person as. **4** *tr. Brit.* reach agreement about (*agreed a price*). **5** *tr. Brit.* consent to or approve of (terms, a proposal, etc.). **6** *tr. Brit.* bring into harmony. **7** *intr.* (foll. by *on*) decide by mutual consent (*agreed on a compromise*). □ **agree to differ** leave a difference of opinion unresolved. **be agreed** have reached the same opinion. [based on Latin *gratus* 'pleasing']

agreeable *adj.* **1** pleasing. **2** (often foll. by *to*) (of a person) willing to agree (*was agreeable to going*). **3** conformable. [based on Old French *agreer* 'to agree'] □ **agreeableness** *n.* **agreeably** *adv.*

agreement *n.* **1** the act of agreeing; the holding of the same opinion (*reached agreement*). **2** mutual understanding. **3** an arrangement between parties as to a course of action etc. **4** *Gram.* having the same number, gender, case, or person. **5** mutual conformity; harmony.

agribusiness *n.* **1** agriculture conducted on strictly commercial principles, esp. using advanced technology. **2** an organization engaged in this. □ **agribusinessman** *n.* (*pl.* **-men**)

agriculture *n.* the science or practice of cultivating the soil and rearing animals. [based on Latin *ager agri* 'field'] □ **agricultural** *adj.* **agriculturalist** *n.* **agriculturally** *adv.* **agriculturist** *n.*

agrimony *n.* (*pl.* **-ies**) ◄ any perennial plant of the genus *Agrimonia*, esp. *A. eupatoria* with small yellow flowers. [from Greek *argemōnē* 'poppy']

agro- *comb. form* agricultural. [from Greek *agros* 'field']

agrochemical *n.* a chemical used in agriculture.

agroforestry *n.* agriculture incorporating the cultivation and conservation of trees.

agronomy *n.* the science of soil management and crop production. [based on Greek *agros* 'field' + *nemōein* 'to arrange'] □ **agronomic** *adj.* **agronomist** *n.*

aground *predic.adj. & adv.* (of a ship) on or on to the bottom of shallow water (*run aground*). [Middle English]

ague /ay-gew/ *n.* **1** *hist.* a malarial fever. **2** a shivering fit. [from medieval Latin *acuta (febris)* 'acute (fever)'] □ **agued** *adj.*

AH *abbr.* in the year of the Hegira (AD 622); of the Muslim era.

ah *int.* expressing surprise, pleasure, realization, resignation, etc.

aha *int.* expressing surprise, triumph, irony, etc.

ahead *adv.* **1** further forward in space or time. **2** in the lead (*ahead on points*). **3** in the line of one's forward motion (*roadworks ahead*). **4** straight forwards. [originally nautical]

AGRIMONY
(*Agrimonia eupatoria*)

---

ahem *int.* used to attract attention, gain time, or express disapproval.

ahoy *int. Naut.* a call used in hailing.

AI *abbr.* **1** artificial insemination. **2** artificial intelligence.

AID *abbr.* artificial insemination by donor.

aid ● *n.* **1** help. **2** financial or material help given by one country to another. **3** a person or thing that helps. ● *v.tr.* **1** help. **2** encourage (*sleep will aid recovery*). □ **in aid of** *Brit.* in support of. [based on Latin *adjuvare* 'to help']

aide *n.* **1** an aide-de-camp. **2** an assistant.

aide-de-camp /ayd-dĕ-kahng/ *n.* (*pl.* **aides-de-camp** *pronunc.* same) an officer acting as a confidential assistant to a senior officer. [French, literally 'camp adjutant']

aide-mémoire /ayd-mem-**wah**/ *n.* (*pl.* **aides-mémoires** or **aides-mémoire** *pronunc.* same) an aid to the memory. [French, literally 'help-memory']

Aids *n.* (also **AIDS**) acquired immune deficiency syndrome, a viral condition marked by severe loss of resistance to infection and so ultimately fatal. [acronym]

aigrette *n.* **1** a white plume from an egret. **2** a tuft of feathers or hair. **3** a spray of gems or similar ornament. [French]

aikido *n.* a Japanese form of self-defence and martial art. [Japanese, literally 'way of integrating the spirit']

ail *v.* **1** *tr. archaic* trouble or afflict (*what ails him?*). **2** *intr.* be ill. [Old English]

aileron *n.* ▼ a hinged surface in the trailing edge of an aeroplane wing, used to control lateral balance. ▷ WING. [French, literally 'little wing']

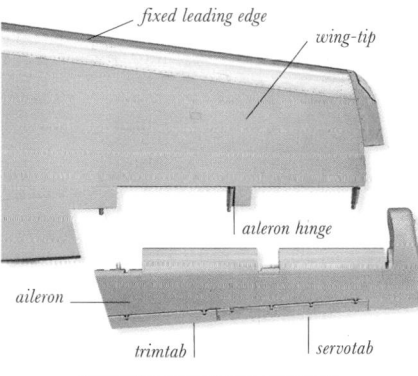

fixed leading edge
wing-tip
aileron hinge
aileron
trimtab
servotab

AILERON: AEROPLANE WING-TIP
WITH AILERON DETACHED

ailing *adj.* **1** ill, esp. chronically. **2** in poor condition.

ailment *n.* an illness, esp. a minor one.

aim ● *v.* **1** *intr.* intend or try (*aim at winning*; *aim to win*). **2** *tr.* direct or point (a weapon, remark, etc.). **3** *intr.* take aim. **4** *intr.* (foll. by *at, for*) seek to attain or achieve. ● *n.* **1** a purpose or design; an object aimed at. **2** the directing of a weapon, missile, etc., at an object. □ **take aim** direct a weapon etc. at an object. [from Latin *aestimare* 'to reckon']

aimless *adj.* without aim or purpose. □ **aimlessly** *adv.* **aimlessness** *n.*

ain't *contr. colloq.* **1** am not; are not; is not (*she ain't nice*). **2** has not; have not (*we ain't seen him*).

▪ **Usage** *Ain't* is generally unacceptable in spoken and written English, except in representations of dialect speech.

air ● *n.* **1** an invisible gaseous substance surrounding the Earth, a mixture mainly of oxygen and nitrogen. **2 a** the Earth's atmosphere. **b** the free space in the atmosphere (*birds of the air; in the open air*). **c** the atmosphere as a place where aircraft operate or as a medium for transmitting radio

---

waves. **3 a** a distinctive characteristic (*an air of absurdity*). **b** one's manner, esp. a confident one (*with a triumphant air*). **c** (esp. in *pl.*) an affected manner (*gave himself airs*). **4** *Mus.* a melody. **5** a breeze or light wind. ● *v.tr.* **1** *Brit.* warm (washed laundry) to remove damp. **2** expose (a room etc.) to the open air; ventilate. **3** express publicly (an opinion, grievance, etc.). □ **airs and graces** affected elegance designed to impress. **in the air** (of opinions or feelings) prevalent; gaining currency. **on** (or **off**) **the air** in (or not in) the process of broadcasting. **tread** (or **walk**) **on air** feel elated. **up in the air** (of projects etc.) uncertain; not decided. [from Greek *aēr*]

air bag *n.* ▼ a safety device that fills with air or nitrogen on impact to protect the occupants of a vehicle in a collision.

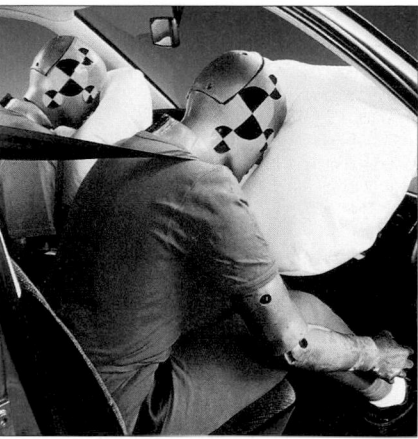

AIR BAG: CAR IMPACT TEST WITH
INFLATABLE AIR BAGS

airbase *n.* a base for the operation of military aircraft.

air-bed *n. Brit.* an inflatable mattress.

air bladder *n.* a bladder or sac filled with air in fish or some plants (cf. SWIM-BLADDER).

airborne *adj.* **1** transported by air. **2** (of aircraft) in the air after taking off.

air brake *n.* **1** a brake worked by air pressure. **2** a movable flap or other device on an aircraft to reduce its speed.

airbrick *n. Brit.* a brick perforated with small holes for ventilation.

air bridge *n. Brit.* a portable bridge or walkway put against an aircraft door.

airbrush ● *n.* ▼ an artist's device for spraying paint by means of compressed air. ● *v.tr.* paint or paint over with an airbrush, esp. for the purpose of enhancement.

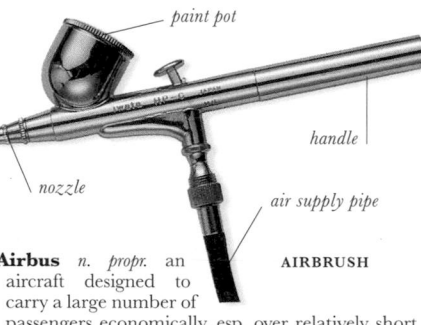

paint pot
handle
nozzle
air supply pipe

AIRBRUSH

Airbus *n. propr.* an aircraft designed to carry a large number of passengers economically, esp. over relatively short routes.

Air Chief Marshal *n.* an RAF officer of high rank, below Marshal of the RAF and above Air Marshal.

Air Commodore *n.* an RAF officer next above Group Captain.

AIRCRAFT

Aeroplanes, helicopters, and microlights use aerodynamics to overcome gravity. An upward force, known as lift, is achieved by creating more air pressure beneath the wings (or rotary blades) than above them. The degree of lift depends on the surface area of the wings or blades, and the speed of airflow across them. These factors can be varied by increasing or decreasing engine power and by adjusting wing dynamics. Hot-air balloons and airships become airborne using light gas or heated air within a balloon envelope. Gliders must be towed or winched into the air, but, once airborne, their light, aerodynamic construction prolongs descent.

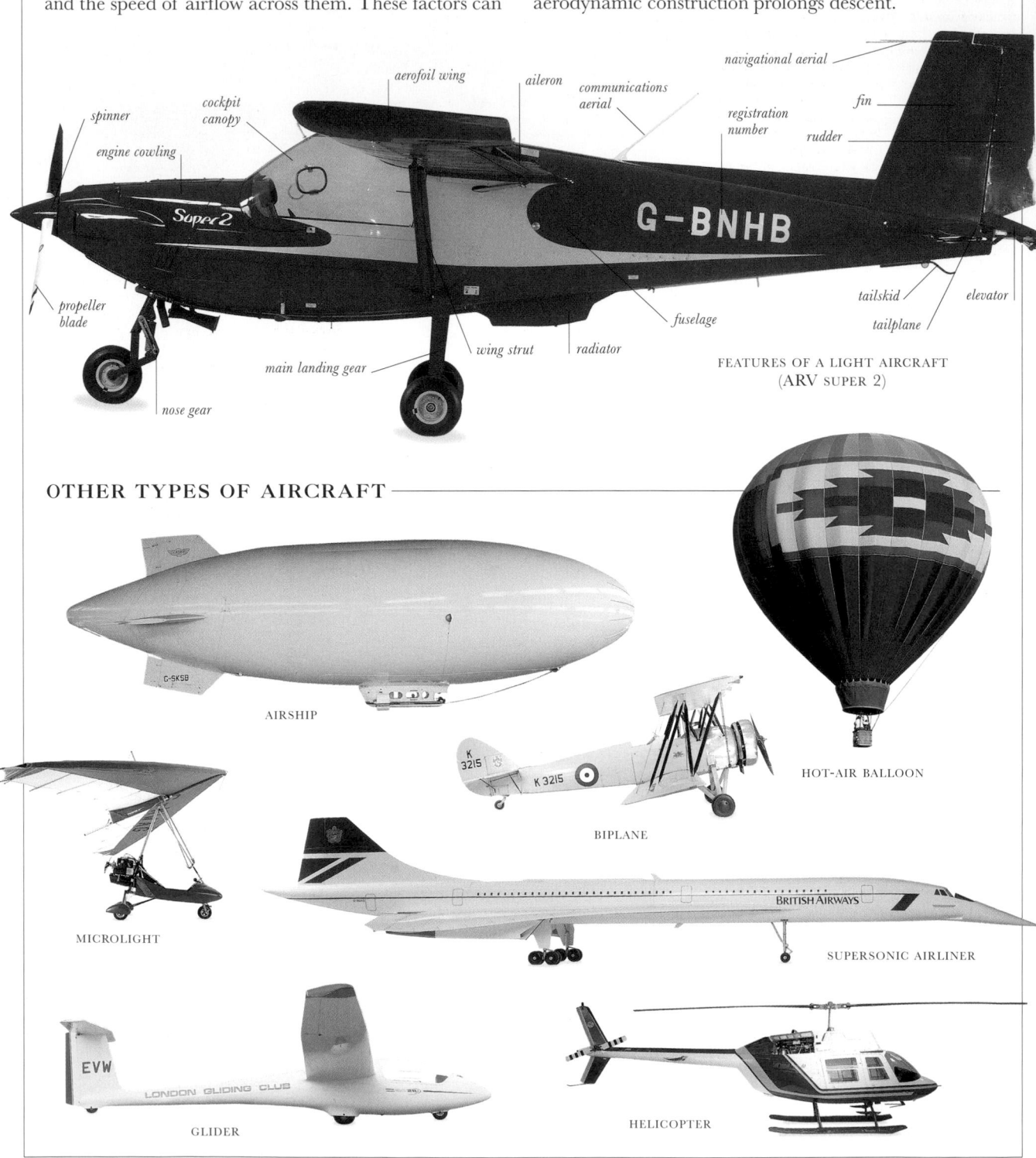

spinner

engine cowling

cockpit canopy

aerofoil wing

aileron

communications aerial

registration number

navigational aerial

fin

rudder

Super 2

G-BNHB

propeller blade

main landing gear

nose gear

wing strut

radiator

fuselage

tailskid

tailplane

elevator

FEATURES OF A LIGHT AIRCRAFT
(ARV SUPER 2)

OTHER TYPES OF AIRCRAFT

AIRSHIP

HOT-AIR BALLOON

BIPLANE

MICROLIGHT

SUPERSONIC AIRLINER

GLIDER

HELICOPTER

A

air-conditioning n. ▶ a system for regulating the humidity, ventilation, and temperature in a building or vehicle. □ **air-conditioned** adj. **air-conditioner** n.

air corridor n. = CORRIDOR 4.

aircraft n. (pl. same) ◀ a machine capable of flight, esp. an aeroplane or helicopter.

aircraft carrier n. a warship that carries aeroplanes.

aircraftman n. (pl. **-men**; fem. **aircraftwoman**, pl. **-women**) the lowest rank in the RAF.

air cushion n. **1** an inflatable cushion. **2** the layer of air supporting a hovercraft or similar vehicle.

airdrop ● n. the act or an instance of dropping supplies, troops, etc. by parachute. ● v.tr. (**dropped**, **-dropping**) drop (supplies etc.) by parachute.

Airedale n. ◀ a large terrier of a rough-coated breed. ▷ DOG. [from the name of a Yorkshire district]

airer n. Brit. a frame or stand for airing or drying clothes etc.

airfield n. an area of land where aircraft take off and land, are maintained, etc.

airflow n. the flow of air, esp. that encountered by a moving aircraft or vehicle.

AIREDALE

air force n. the branch of the armed forces concerned with defence in the air.

airgun n. ▶ a gun using compressed air to propel pellets.

airhead n. **1** Mil. a forward base for aircraft in enemy territory. **2** slang a silly or foolish person.

air hostess n. Brit. a stewardess in a passenger aircraft.

airing n. **1** exposure to fresh air, esp. for exercise or an excursion. **2** Brit. exposure (of laundry etc.) to warm air. **3** public expression of an opinion etc.

cocking lever and barrel

piston

trigger

hand grip   pellets

AIRGUN: REFLEXED AIR PISTOL

air lane n. a path or course regularly used by aircraft.

airless adj. **1** stuffy. **2** without wind or breeze. □ **airlessness** n.

air letter n. a sheet of light paper forming an airmail letter.

airlift ● n. the transport of troops and supplies by air, esp. in an emergency. ● v.tr. transport in this way.

airline n. an organization providing a regular public service of air transport on one or more routes.

airliner n. a large passenger aircraft. ▷ AIRCRAFT

airlock n. **1** a stoppage of the flow in a pump or pipe, caused by an air bubble. **2** a compartment with controlled pressure and parallel sets of doors, to permit movement between areas at different pressures.

airmail n. **1** a system of transporting mail by air. **2** mail carried by air.

airman n. (pl. **-men**) **1** a pilot or member of the crew of an aircraft. **2** a member of the RAF below commissioned rank.

Air Marshal n. an RAF officer of high rank, below Air Chief Marshal and above Air Vice-Marshal.

air mile n. **1** a nautical mile used as a measure of distance flown by aircraft. **2** (**Air Miles**) pl. propr. points (equivalent to miles of free air travel) accumulated by buyers of airline tickets and other products.

airmiss n. Brit. a circumstance in which two aircraft in flight on different routes are less than a prescribed distance apart.

AIR-CONDITIONING

An all-season air-conditioning system controls air temperature and humidity. In summer, air is passed through a cooling unit, where heat is absorbed by a liquid refrigerant evaporating in a cooling pipe. In winter, air is blown over a heating element and carried through ducts to warm the building's rooms. A moisture unit regulates the air's humidity.

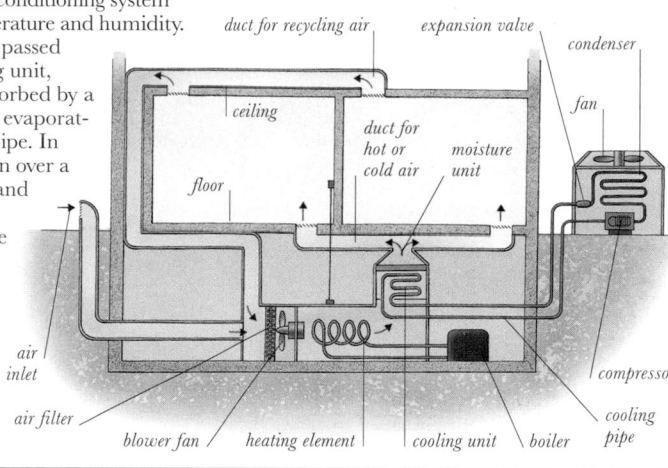

CROSS-SECTION OF A BUILDING SHOWING AN ALL-SEASON AIR-CONDITIONING SYSTEM

duct for recycling air · expansion valve · condenser · ceiling · duct for hot or cold air · moisture unit · fan · floor · air inlet · air filter · blower fan · heating element · cooling unit · boiler · compressor · cooling pipe

airmobile adj.(of troops) that can be moved about by air.

Air Officer n. any RAF officer above the rank of Group Captain.

airplane n. N. Amer. = AEROPLANE.

air plant n. ▶ a plant growing naturally without soil.

airplay n. broadcasting (of recorded music).

air pocket n. **1** a cavity containing air. **2** a region of low pressure etc. causing an aircraft to lose height suddenly.

airport n. a complex of runways and buildings for the take-off, landing, and maintenance of civil aircraft, with facilities for passengers.

air raid n. an attack by aircraft.

air rifle n. a rifle using compressed air to propel pellets.

air sac n. an extension of the lungs in birds or of the tracheae in insects. ▷ SONGBIRD

airship n. a power-driven aircraft that is lighter than air. ▷ AIRCRAFT

air show n. a show at which aircraft are on view and perform aerial displays.

airsick adj. affected with nausea due to travel in an aircraft. □ **airsickness** n

airspace n. the air available to aircraft to fly in, esp. the part subject to the jurisdiction of a particular country.

airstrip n. a strip of ground suitable for the take-off and landing of aircraft.

air terminal n. **1** Brit. an airline office in a town to which passengers report and which serves as a base for transport to and from an airport. **2** = TERMINAL n. 3.

airtight adj. not allowing air to pass through.

airtime n. time allotted for a broadcast.

air traffic control n. the control of air traffic by giving radio instructions to pilots concerning route, altitude, take-off, and landing. □ **air traffic controller** n.

Air Vice-Marshal n. an RAF officer of high rank, just below Air Marshal.

airwaves n.pl. radio waves used in broadcasting.

airway n. **1** a passage by which air reaches the lungs. **2 a** a recognized route followed by aircraft. **b** (often in pl.) = AIRLINE.

airwoman n. (pl. **-women**) **1** a woman pilot or member of the crew of an aircraft. **2** a female member of the RAF below commissioned rank.

AIR PLANT
(Tillandsia caput-medusae)

airy adj. (**airier**, **airiest**) **1** well-ventilated, breezy. **2** flippant, superficial. **3 a** light as air. **b** graceful, delicate. **4** insubstantial, ethereal, immaterial. □ **airily** adv. **airiness** n.

airy-fairy adj. colloq. unrealistic, impractical, foolishly idealistic.

aisle /rhymes with mile/ n. **1** part of a church parallel to the nave, choir, or transept. **2** a passage between rows of pews, seats, shelves of goods, etc. [from Latin ala 'wing']

aitch n. the name of the letter H. □ **drop one's aitches** fail to pronounce the initial h in words. [from Old French ache]

aitchbone n. **1** the buttock or rump bone of cattle. **2** a cut of beef lying over this. [Middle English nache-bone 'buttock': for loss of n cf. ADDER]

ajar adv. & predic.adj. (of a door) slightly open. [from earlier on char: Old English cerr 'a turn']

aka abbr. also known as.

akee var. of ACKEE.

Akela n. colloq. the adult leader of a group of Cub Scouts, officially termed Cub Scout Leader. [from the name of the wolves' leader in Kipling's Jungle Book (1894–5)]

akimbo adv. (of the arms) with hands on the hips and elbows turned outwards. [Middle English]

akin predic.adj. **1** related by blood. **2** of similar or kindred character.

akvavit var. of AQUAVIT.

Al symb. Chem. the element aluminium.

à la /ah lah/ prep. after the manner of (à la russe). [French]

alabaster ● n. a translucent usu. white form of gypsum. ● adj. **1** of alabaster. **2** like alabaster in whiteness or smoothness. [from Greek alabast(r)os]

à la carte adv. & adj. ordered as separately priced item(s) from a menu, not as part of a set meal. [French, literally 'according to the card (menu)']

alack int. (also **alack-a-day**) archaic an expression of regret or surprise.

alacrity n. briskness or cheerful readiness. [based on Latin alacer 'brisk']

à la mode adv. & adj. **1** fashionable. **2 a** (of beef) braised in wine. **b** N. Amer. served with ice cream. [French, literally 'in the fashion']

Alar n. propr. a growth retardant sprayed on fruit and vegetables to enhance the quality of the crop. [20th-century coinage]

A

alarm ● *n.* **1** a warning of danger etc. **2 a** a warning sound or device. **b** = ALARM CLOCK. **3** frightened expectation of danger or difficulty. ● *v.tr.* **1** frighten or disturb. **2** arouse to a sense of danger. [from Italian *all' arme!* 'to arms!'] □ **alarming** *adj.* **alarmingly** *adv.*

alarm clock *n.* a clock with a device that can be made to sound at the time set in advance. ▷ CLOCK

alarmist ● *n.* a person given to spreading needless alarm. ● *adj.* creating needless alarm. □ **alarmism** *n.*

alas *int.* an expression of grief, pity, or concern.

alb *n.* a white vestment reaching to the feet, worn by clergy and servers in some Christian Churches. [from ecclesiastical Latin *alba* (fem.) 'white']

albacore *n.* **1** a long-finned tunny, *Thunnus alalunga*. **2** any of various other related fish. [from Arabic *al bakr* 'the young camel' or *al bakūr* 'the precocious one']

Albanian ● *n.* **1 a** a native or national of Albania in SE Europe. **b** a person of Albanian descent. **2** the language of Albania. ● *adj.* of or relating to Albania, its people, or its language.

albatross *n.* **1 a** ▼ any long-winged bird of the family Diomedeidae, inhabiting the Pacific and Southern Oceans. ▷ SEABIRD. **b** an encumbrance (in allusion to Coleridge's *The Rime of the Ancient Mariner*). **2** *Brit. Golf* a score of three strokes under par at any hole. [alteration (influenced by Latin *albus* 'white') of 17th century coinage *alcatras*, applied to various seabirds]

albeit *conj.* though (*he tried, albeit without success*). [literally 'although it be (that)']

albino *n.* (*pl.* **-os**) ▼ a person or animal having a congenital absence of pigment in the skin, hair, and eyes. [Spanish & Portuguese, based on Latin *albus* 'white'] □ **albinism** *n.*

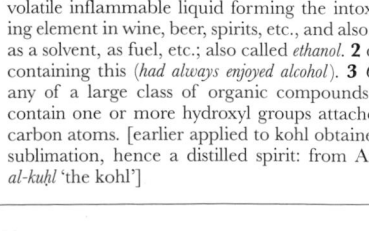

ALBINO: AFRICAN
CLAWED TOAD
(*Xenopus laevis*)

Albion *n.* Britain or England. [Old English via Latin from Celtic, probably related to Latin *albus* 'white' with reference to the white cliffs of Dover]

album *n.* **1** a blank book for inserting photographs etc. **2 a** a long-playing gramophone record. **b** a set of recordings issued together. [Latin, literally 'a blank tablet']

albumen *n.* **1** egg white. ▷ EGG. **2** *Bot.* the substance found between the skin and germ of many seeds; = ENDOSPERM.

albumin *n.* any of a class of water-soluble proteins found in egg white, milk, blood, etc. [from French *albumine*] □ **albuminous** *adj.*

alchemy *n.* (*pl.* **-ies**) **1** the medieval forerunner of chemistry, esp. seeking to turn base metals into gold or silver. **2** a miraculous transformation or the means of achieving this. [based on Greek *khēmia* 'art of transmuting metals'] □ **alchemical** *adj.* **alchemist** *n.*

alcohol *n.* **1** (in full **ethyl alcohol**) a colourless volatile inflammable liquid forming the intoxicating element in wine, beer, spirits, etc., and also used as a solvent, as fuel, etc.; also called *ethanol*. **2** drink containing this (*had always enjoyed alcohol*). **3** *Chem.* any of a large class of organic compounds that contain one or more hydroxyl groups attached to carbon atoms. [earlier applied to kohl obtained by sublimation, hence a distilled spirit: from Arabic *al-kuḥl* 'the kohl']

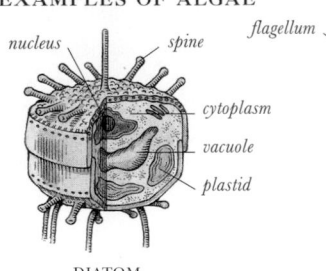

colony of cells
daughter colony
gelatinous sheath

GREEN ALGA
(*Volvox* species)

EXAMPLES OF ALGAE

nucleus   spine   flagellum
cytoplasm
cytoplasm
vacuole
nucleus
plastid
chloroplast
protein body
reproductive chamber
stalk
rhizoid

DIATOM
(*Thalassiosira* species)

GREEN ALGA
(*Chlamydomonas* species)

GREEN ALGA
(*Acetabularia* species)

alcoholic ● *adj.* of, relating to, containing, or caused by alcohol. ● *n.* a person suffering from alcoholism.

alcoholic soft drink *n.* a traditionally soft drink such as lemonade, which has an alcoholic content.

alcoholism *n.* **1** an addiction to the consumption of alcohol. **2** the diseased condition resulting from this.

alcove *n.* a recess, esp. in the wall of a room or a garden. [from Arabic *al-kubba* 'the vault']

aldehyde *n. Chem.* any of a class of compounds formed by the oxidation of alcohols. [abbreviation of modern Latin *alcohol dehydrogenatum* 'alcohol deprived of hydrogen'] □ **aldehydic** *adj.*

al dente /al den-tay/ *adj. & adv.* (of pasta etc.) (cooked) so as to be still firm when bitten. [Italian, literally 'to the tooth']

alder *n.* **1** (also **alder tree**) a tree of the genus *Alnus*, related to the birch, bearing catkins and toothed leaves, esp. *A. glutinosa*, common in damp ground. **2** the wood of this tree. [Old English]

alderman *n.* (*pl.* **-men**) **1** esp. *hist.* a co-opted member of an English county or borough council, next in dignity to the Mayor. **2** (*fem.* **alderwoman**, *pl.* **-women**) *N. Amer.* & *Austral.* an elected member of a city council. [Old English, from *aldor* 'patriarch'] □ **aldermanic** *adj.*

aldosterone /al-dos-tĕ-rohn/ *n. Physiol.* a corticosteroid hormone which stimulates absorption of sodium by the kidneys and so regulates water and salt balance.

ale *n.* **1** esp. *Brit.* beer (now usu. as a trade word). **2** *N. Amer.* a type of beer fermented rapidly at high temperatures. [Old English]

aleatoric *adj.* depending on the throw of a die or on chance. [based on Latin *alea* 'die']

aleatory *adj.* = ALEATORIC.

alehouse *n. hist.* a tavern.

alembic *n. hist.* ▶ an apparatus formerly used in distilling. [from Arabic *al-'anbīk* 'the still']

alert ● *adj.* **1** vigilant; ready to take action. **2** nimble (esp. of mental faculties); attentive. ● *n.* a warning call or alarm. ● *v.tr.* make alert; warn (*were alerted to the danger*). □ **on the alert** on the lookout against danger or attack. [based on Italian *all' erta* 'to the watchtower'] □ **alertly** *adv.* **alertness** *n.*

A level *n. Brit.* = ADVANCED LEVEL.

alexandrine ● *adj.* (of a line of verse) having six iambic feet. ● *n.* an alexandrine line. [based on French *Alexandre* 'Alexander the Great', the subject of an Old French poem in this metre]

alexandrite *n. Mineral.* ▼ a green to red variety of chrysoberyl, originally found in the Urals. [named after Tsar *Alexander* II of Russia]

alexia *n.* the inability to see words or to read, caused by a defect of the brain. [based on Greek *lexis* 'speech' from *legein* 'to speak', confused with Latin *legere* 'to read']

alfalfa *n.* a clover-like plant, *Medicago sativa*, grown for fodder. [from Arabic *al-faṣfaṣa*, a green fodder]

ALEXANDRITE

alfresco *adv. & adj.* in the open air (*we lunched alfresco*). [from Italian *al fresco* 'in the fresh (air)']

alga *n.* (*pl.* **algae** /al-ji/) (usu. in *pl.*) ▲ a non-flowering stemless usu. aquatic plant. □ **algal** *adj.*

algebra *n.* the branch of mathematics that uses letters to represent numbers and quantities in formulae and equations. [from Arabic *al-jabr* 'the reunion of broken parts'] □ **algebraic** *adj.* **algebraically** *adv.*

-algia *comb. form Med.* denoting pain in a part specified by the first element (*neuralgia*). [from Greek *algos* 'pain'] □ **-algic** *comb. form* forming adjectives.

algicide *n.* a preparation for destroying algae.

alginate *n. Chem.* a salt or ester of alginic acid.

alginic acid *n. Chem.* an insoluble carbohydrate found (chiefly as salts) in many brown seaweeds.

Algol *n.* a high-level computer programming language. [blend of *algorithmic* and LANGUAGE]

Algonquian (also **Algonkian**) ● *n.* **1** a member of any of a large group of scattered N. American Indian peoples. **2** any of the family of languages used by them, including Cree and Ojibwa. ● *adj.* of or relating to these peoples or their languages. [from *Algonquin*, N. American tribal name]

algorithm *n. Math.* a process or set of rules used for calculation or problem-solving. [from Arabic *al-Kuwārizmī*, cognomen of a 9th-century mathematician] □ **algorithmic** *adj.* **algorithmically** *adv.*

alias /ay-li-ăs/ ● *adv.* also named or known as. ● *n.* a false name. [Latin, = otherwise, at another time]

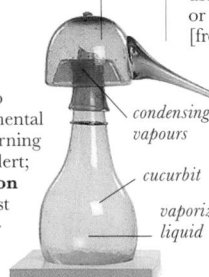

alembic head
condensing vapours
cucurbit
vaporizing liquid
distilled liquid
ALEMBIC

ALBATROSS:
WANDERING
ALBATROSS
(*Diomedea exulans*)

alibi /**al**-i-by/ n. (pl. **alibis**) **1** a claim, or the evidence supporting it, that when an alleged act took place one was elsewhere. **2** disp. an excuse. [Latin, literally 'elsewhere']

■ **Usage** The use of *alibi* in sense 2 is informal and to some people unacceptable.

alien ● adj. **1 a** (often foll. by *to*) unfamiliar; not in accordance; unfriendly, hostile; repugnant (*army discipline was alien to him; struck an alien note*). **b** different or separated. **2** from a foreign country (*help from alien powers*). **3** of or relating to beings from other worlds. **4** *Bot.* (of a plant species) introduced from elsewhere and naturalized. ● n. **1** a foreigner. **2** a being from another world. **3** an alien species. [from Latin *alienus* 'belonging to another'] □ **alienness** n.

alienable adj. *Law* able to be transferred to new ownership. □ **alienability** n.

alienate v.tr. **1 a** cause (a person) to become hostile. **b** cause (a person) to feel estranged from (friends, society, etc.). **2** transfer ownership of (property) to another person etc. □ **alienation** n.

alienist n. *US* a psychiatrist.

alight¹ v.intr. (**alighted**) **1** esp. *Brit.* **a** descend from a vehicle. **b** dismount from a horse. **2** descend and settle; come to Earth from the air. **3** (foll. by *on*) find by chance; notice. [Old English]

alight² adv. & predic.adj. **1** on fire; burning (*set the shed alight; is the fire still alight?*). **2** lit up; excited (*eyes alight with expectation*). [Middle English]

align v.tr. **1** put in a straight line or bring into line (*books neatly aligned on the shelf*). **2** (usu. foll. by *with*) bring (oneself etc.) into alliance with (a cause, policy, political party, etc.). [based on French *à ligne* 'into line'] □ **alignment** n.

alike ● adj. (usu. *predic.*) like one another; indistinguishable. ● adv. in a similar way. [Old English]

alimentary adj. of, relating to, or providing nourishment. [based on Latin *alere* 'to nourish']

alimentary canal n. *Anat.* the passage along which food passes through the body from mouth to anus during digestion. ▷ DIGESTION

alimentation n. **1** nourishment; feeding. **2** maintenance, support. [based on Late Latin *alimentare* 'to supply with food']

alimony n. esp. *US* money payable by a man to his wife or former wife or by a woman to her husband or former husband after they are separated or divorced. [from Latin *alimonia* 'nutriment']

A-line adj. (of a garment) having a narrow waist or shoulders and a slightly flared skirt.

aliphatic adj. *Chem.* of, denoting, or relating to organic compounds in which carbon atoms form open chains, not aromatic rings. [based on Greek *aleiphar -atos* 'fat']

aliquot ● adj. *Math.* (of a part or portion) contained by the whole an integral or whole number of times (*4 is an aliquot part of 12*). ● n. **1** *Math.* an aliquot part; an integral factor. **2** a known fraction of a whole; a sample. [Latin, literally 'some, so many']

alive adj. (usu. *predic.*) **1** (of a person, animal, plant, etc.) living. **2 a** (of a thing) continuing; in operation or action (*kept his interest alive*). **b** provoking interest (*the topic is still very much alive today*). **3** lively, active. **4** charged with an electric current; connected to a source of electricity. **5** (foll. by *to*) alert or responsive to. **6** (foll. by *with*) **a** swarming or teeming with. **b** full of. □ **alive and kicking** *colloq.* very active; lively. **alive and well** still alive or active. [Old English] □ **aliveness** n.

alkali n. (pl. **alkalis**) **1** *Chem.* ▲ any of a class of substances which neutralize acids and turn litmus blue, containing free hydroxide ions; a soluble base. ▷ PH. **2** any soluble salt present in excess in the soil. [from Arabic *al-ḳalī* 'calcined ashes']

alkaline adj. of, relating to, or having the nature of an alkali. □ **alkalinity** n.

alkaloid n. *Chem.* any of a series of nitrogenous organic compounds of plant origin, many of which are used as drugs. [German, related to ALKALI]

ALKALI

An alkali is a water-soluble substance capable of accepting protons (hydrogen ions). When an alkali is added to water, it accepts protons (H^+), from some of the hydroxonium ions (H_3O^+) and water molecules (H_2O) present, forming more water molecules and hydroxide ions (OH^-). The greater the number of hydroxide ions in the solution, the stronger is its alkalinity and the higher its pH value.

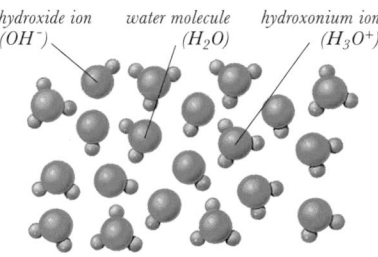
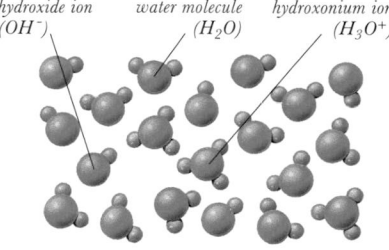

hydroxide ion (OH^-)   water molecule (H_2O)   hydroxonium ion (H_3O^+)

MOLECULES AND IONS IN NEUTRAL WATER

hydroxide ion (OH^-)   water molecule (H_2O)   hydroxonium ion (H_3O^+)

MOLECULES AND IONS IN ALKALINE SOLUTION

---

alkalosis n. *Med.* an excessive alkaline condition of the body fluids or tissues.

alkane n. *Chem.* ▼ any of a series of saturated aliphatic hydrocarbons having the general formula C_nH_{2n+2}.

alkene n. *Chem.* ▼ any of a series of unsaturated aliphatic hydrocarbons containing a double bond and having the general formula C_nH_{2n}.

alkyd n. (usu. *attrib.*) *Chem.* any of a group of synthetic resins derived from various alcohols and acids.

alkyl n. (usu. *attrib.*) *Chem.* a radical derived from an alkane by the removal of a hydrogen atom. [based on German *Alkohol*]

alkylate v.tr. *Chem.* introduce an alkyl radical into (a compound).

alkyne n. *Chem.* ▼ any of a series of unsaturated aliphatic hydrocarbons containing a triple bond and having the general formula C_nH_{2n-2}. [based on ALKYL]

all ● predet. **1 a** the whole amount, quantity, or extent of (*all the upheaval; all this clutter; waited all day; all his life*). **b** (with *pl.*) the entire number of (*all the others left, all ten men*). **2** any whatever (*beyond all doubt*). **3** greatest possible (*with all speed*). ● pron. **1 a** all the persons or things concerned (*all were present*). **b** everything (*that is all*). **2** (foll. by *of*) **a** the whole of (*take all of it*). **b** every one of (*all of us*). **c** *colloq.* as much as (*all of six feet tall*). **d** *colloq.* in a state of (*all of a dither*). ● n. (prec. by *my, your*, etc.) one's whole strength or resources (*gave his all*). ● adv. **1 a** entirely (*dressed all in black; all round the room*). **b** as an intensifier (*a book all about ships; stop all this grumbling; it was all too clear*). **2** *Brit. colloq.* very (*went all shy*). **3** (foll. by *the + compar.*) **a** to that extent (*if they go, all the better*). **b** in the full degree to be expected (*that makes it all the worse*). **4** (in games) on both sides (*two goals all*). □ **all along** all the time (*he was joking all along*). **all and sundry** everyone. **all but** very nearly (*he was all but drowned*). **all for** *colloq.* strongly in favour of. **all in** *colloq.* exhausted. **all in all** everything considered. **all manner of** see MANNER. **all one** (or **the same**) a matter of indifference (*it's all one to me*). **all out** involving all one's strength or resources; at full speed (also, with hyphen, *attrib.: an all-out effort*). **all over 1** completely finished. **2** in or on all parts of (esp. the body) (*went hot and cold all over; mud all over the carpet*). **3** *colloq.* typically (*that is you all over*). **4** *slang* effusively attentive to (a person). **all right** predic.adj. satisfactory; safe and sound; in good condition. ● adv. **1** satisfactorily (*it worked out all right*). **2** as an intensifier (*that's the one all right*). ● int. an interjection expressing consent or assent to a proposal or order. **all round** (*US* also **all around**) **1** in all respects (*a good performance all round*). **2** for each person (*he bought drinks all round*). **all the same** nevertheless, in spite of this (*he was innocent but was punished all the same*). **all set** *colloq.* ready to start. **all there** (usu. in *neg.*) *colloq.* mentally

---

ALKANE, ALKENE, ALKYNE

Alkanes, alkenes, and alkynes are all hydrocarbons (compounds made up of hydrogen and carbon only). The three differ in the type of bonds that exist between their atoms. Alkanes have only single covalent bonds, meaning that the bonds are formed by two carbon atoms sharing a pair of electrons. Alkenes have one or more double bonds between carbon atoms, where two pairs of electrons are shared. Alkynes have one or more triple bonds, the carbon atoms sharing three pairs of electrons.

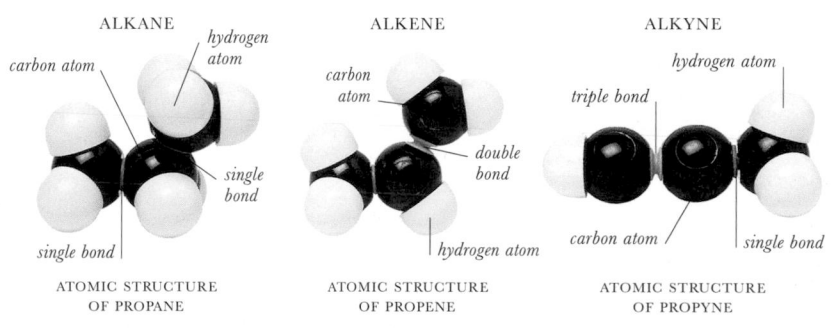

ALKANE

carbon atom   hydrogen atom   single bond

ATOMIC STRUCTURE OF PROPANE

ALKENE

carbon atom   double bond   hydrogen atom

ATOMIC STRUCTURE OF PROPENE

ALKYNE

hydrogen atom   triple bond   carbon atom   single bond

ATOMIC STRUCTURE OF PROPYNE

A

ALLEGORY

This complex allegorical painting is based upon Classical mythology, and warns of dangers and deceit disguised in false love. Venus, the Goddess of Love, is seducing Cupid with a kiss while reaching to steal the arrow from his quiver. Behind the central figures are Fraud, depicted as an empty mask, and Pleasure, portrayed as a young girl offering honey, but possessing the hindquarters of a serpent. Time is pictured reaching to expose Fraud, and in the shadows the distraught figure of Jealousy pulls at her hair.

Fraud — *Time* — *Folly* — *Jealousy* — *Pleasure* — *Cupid* — *Venus*

An Allegory (Venus, Cupid, Folly, and Time)
(1540–45), AGNOLO BRONZINO

alert; not mentally deficient. **all the way** the whole distance; completely. **all together** all at once; all in one place or in a group (*they came all together*) (cf. ALTOGETHER). **all told** in all. **all very well** *colloq.* an expression used to imply scepticism about a favourable or consoling remark. **at all** (with *neg.* or *interrog.*) to any extent (*did not swim at all; did you like it at all?*). **in all** in total number (*there were 10 people in all*). [Old English]

Allah *n.* the name of God among Arabs and Muslims. [Arabic *'allāh*, from *al'ilāh* 'the god']

all-American *adj.* **1** representing the whole of (or only) America or the US. **2** truly American (*all-American boy*).

allay *v.tr.* **1** diminish (fear, suspicion, etc.). **2** relieve or alleviate (pain, hunger, etc.). [Old English]

all-clear *n.* a signal that danger or difficulty is over (*had further tests and was given the all-clear*).

all comers *n.pl.* any applicants, participants, or challengers.

all day *attrib.adj.* lasting throughout the day.

allegation *n.* **1** an assertion; an accusation. **2** the act or an instance of alleging or accusing. [based on Latin *allegare* 'to allege']

allege *v.tr.* **1** declare to be the case, esp. without proof. **2** advance as an argument or excuse. [from Old French *esligier* 'to clear at law', confused with Latin *allegare* 'to allege'] □ **alleged** *adj.*

allegedly *adv.* as is alleged.

allegiance *n.* **1** loyalty. **2** the duty of a subject to his or her sovereign or government. [based on Old French *ligeance*]

allegorical *adj.* consisting of or relating to allegory; by means of allegory. □ **allegorically** *adv.*

allegorize *v.tr.* (also **-ise**) treat as or by means of an allegory. □ **allegorization** *n.*

allegory *n.* (*pl.* **-ies**) **1** ▲ a story, play, poem, picture, etc., in which the meaning or message is represented symbolically. **2** the use of such symbols. **3** a symbol. [from Greek *allēgoria*]

allegro *Mus.* ● *adv. & adj.* in a brisk tempo. ● *n.* (*pl.* **-os**) an allegro passage or movement. [Italian, literally 'lively, gay']

allele /al-eel/ *n.* (also **allel**) one of the alternative forms of a gene, found at the same place on a chromosome. [from German *Allel*, abbreviation of *allelomorph*] □ **allelic** *adj.*

alleluia (also **alleluya**, **hallelujah**) ● *int.* God be praised. ● *n.* **1** praise to God. **2** a song of praise to God. [from Hebrew *hallĕlūyāh* 'praise ye the Lord']

Allen key *n. propr.* ▼ a spanner designed to fit into and turn an Allen screw. [from *Allen*, name of the US manufacturer]

Allen screw *n. propr.* a screw with a hexagonal socket in the head.

ALLEN KEYS

allergen *n.* any substance that causes an allergic reaction. □ **allergenic** *adj.*

allergic *adj.* **1** (foll. by *to*) having an allergy to. **2** caused by or relating to an allergy.

allergy *n.* (*pl.* **-ies**) *Med.* a damaging immune response by the body to a substance to which it has become hypersensitive. [based on Greek *allos* 'other'] □ **allergist** *n.*

alleviate *v.tr.* make less severe (pain, suffering, etc.). [based on Late Latin *alleviatus* 'lightened'] □ **alleviation** *n.*

alley *n.* (*pl.* **-eys**) **1** (also **alleyway**) **a** a narrow street. **b** a narrow passageway between or behind buildings. **2** a path in a park or garden. **3** an enclosure for skittles, bowling, etc. [based on Latin *ambulare* 'to walk']

All Fools' Day var. of APRIL FOOL'S DAY.

All Hallows *n.* All Saints' Day, 1 Nov.

alliaceous *adj.* **1** of or relating to the genus *Allium*, which includes onion, garlic, leek, etc. **2** tasting or smelling like onion or garlic. [based on Latin *allium* 'garlic']

alliance *n.* **1 a** a union or agreement to cooperate, esp. of states by treaty or families by marriage. **b** the parties involved. **2** a relationship resulting from an affinity in nature or qualities etc. (*the old alliance between logic and metaphysics*). [from Old French *aliance*, related to ALLY]

allied *adj.* **1** united or associated in an alliance. **2** connected or related (*studied medicine and allied subjects*).

alligator *n.* **1** ▶ a large reptile of the order Crocodilia native to the Americas and China, with a head broader and shorter than that of the crocodile. ▷ CROCODILE. **2** (in general use) any of several large members of this order. **3** the skin of such an animal or material resembling it. [from Spanish *el lagarto* 'the lizard']

alligator clip *n.* a clip with teeth for gripping.

all-important *adj.* crucial; vitally important.

all-in *attrib.adj. Brit.* inclusive of all.

all-in-one *adj.* combined in a single unit.

all-in wrestling *n.* esp. *Brit.* wrestling with few or no restrictions.

alliteration *n.* the occurrence of the same letter or sound at the beginning of adjacent or closely connected words (e.g. *cool, calm, and collected*). [based on Latin *littera* 'letter'] □ **alliterate** *v.tr. & intr.* **alliterative** *adj.*

allium *n.* ▶ any plant of the genus *Allium*, usu. bulbous and strong-smelling. [Latin, literally 'garlic']

allo- *comb. form* other. [from Greek *allos* 'other']

allocate *v.tr.* assign or devote to (a purpose, person, or place). [from medieval Latin *allocare allocat-*] □ **allocable** *adj.* **allocation** *n.*

allograft *n.* a tissue graft from a donor of the same species as the recipient but not genetically identical (cf. HOMOGRAFT).

allopathy *n.* the treatment of disease by conventional means, i.e. with drugs having opposite effects to the symptoms (cf. HOMOEOPATHY). [from German *Allopathie*] □ **allopathic** *adj.*

allopatric *adj. Biol.* occurring in separate geographical areas (cf. SYMPATRIC).

ALLIUM:
WILD GARLIC
(*Allium ursinum*)

allot *v.tr.* (**allotted, allotting**) **1** give or apportion to (a person) as a share or task; distribute officially to (*they allotted us each a pair of boots; the men were allotted duties*). **2** (foll. by *to*) give or distribute officially to (*a sum was allotted to each charity*). [from Old French *aloter*]

allotment *n.* **1** *Brit.* a small piece of land rented for cultivation. **2** a share allotted. **3** the action of allotting.

allotrope *n.* ▲ each of two or more different physical forms in which an element can exist (*graphite, charcoal, and diamond are all allotropes of carbon*). [from Greek *allotropos* 'of another form']

allottee *n.* a person to whom something is allotted.

all-out see *all out* (ALL).

allow *v.* **1** *tr.* permit (*smoking is not allowed; we allowed them to speak*). **2** *tr.* give or provide; permit (a person) to have (a limited quantity or sum) (*we were allowed £500 a year*). **3** *tr.* set aside for a purpose; add or deduct in consideration of something (*allow 10% for inflation*). **4** *tr.* admit, concede (*he allowed that it was so*). **b** *dial.* be of the opinion. **5** *refl.* permit oneself, indulge oneself in (conduct) (*allowed herself to be persuaded*). **6** *intr.* (foll. by *of*) admit of. **7** *intr.* (foll. by *for*) take into consideration; make addition or deduction corresponding to (*allowing for wastage*). [partly from Latin *allaudare* 'to praise', partly from medieval Latin *allocare* 'to place'] □ **allowable** *adj.*

allowance ● *n.* **1 a** an amount allowed to a person, esp. regularly. **b** *N. Amer.* = POCKET MONEY **2**. **2** an amount allowed in reckoning. **3** a deduction or

rounded snout — *protruding eye* — ALLIGATOR: AMERICAN ALLIGATOR (*Alligator mississippiensis*)
cone-shaped teeth — *short leg*

ALLOTROPE

An element such as carbon has several allotropic forms. In each case the carbon atoms link up differently to produce distinct forms, with very different properties. Shown here are two allotropes of carbon: diamond and graphite. The pyramidal configuration of atoms in a diamond produces a very strong structure, whereas graphite is composed of layers of carbon atoms, with only weak bonds between the layers.

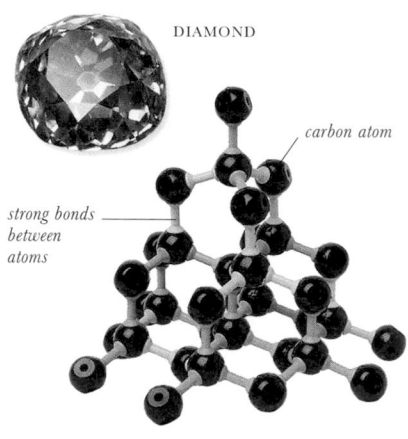

DIAMOND

carbon atom

strong bonds between atoms

STRUCTURE OF CARBON ATOMS
IN A DIAMOND

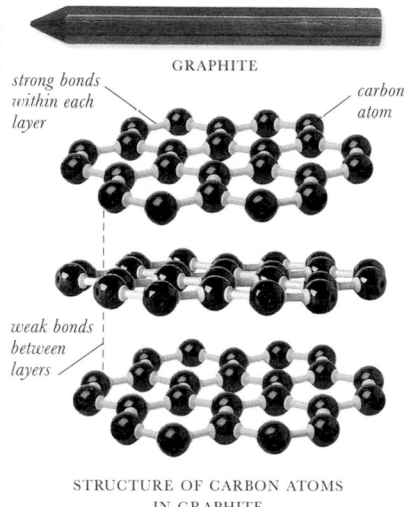

GRAPHITE

strong bonds within each layer

carbon atom

weak bonds between layers

STRUCTURE OF CARBON ATOMS
IN GRAPHITE

A

---

discount (*an allowance on your old cooker*). **4** (foll. by *of*) tolerance of. ● *v.tr.* **1** make an allowance to (a person). **2** supply in limited quantities. □ **make allowances** (often foll. by *for*) **1** take into consideration (mitigating circumstances) (*made allowances for his demented state*). **2** look with tolerance upon; make excuses for (a person, bad behaviour, etc.).

alloy ● *n.* /ˈal-oy/ **1** a mixture of two or more chemical elements at least one of which is a metal. **2** an inferior metal mixed esp. with gold or silver. ● *v.tr.* /ă-ˈloy/ **1** mix (metals). **2 a** debase (a pure substance) by admixture. **b** spoil the character of a thing by adding something else. [from Old French *aloier, aleier* 'to combine']

all-party *attrib.adj.* involving all (esp. political) parties.

all-points bulletin *n.* US a general alert issued among police officers, esp. one giving information for the capture of a suspected criminal.

all-powerful *adj.* having complete power; almighty.

all-purpose *adj.* suitable for many uses.

all-right *attrib.adj. colloq.* fine, acceptable (*an all-right guy*).

all right see ALL.

all-round *attrib.adj.* (of a person) versatile.

all-rounder *n. Brit.* a versatile person or thing.

All Saints' Day *n.* a Christian festival in honour of the saints, 1 Nov.

all-seater *adj.* (usu. *attrib.*) (of a sports stadium etc.) providing only seats and no standing places.

All Souls' Day *n.* a Roman Catholic festival with prayers for the souls of the dead, 2 Nov.

allspice *n.* **1 a** ◀ the aromatic spice obtained from the ground berry of the W. Indian tree *Pimenta dioica*. **b** this plant. Also called PIMENTO. ▷ SPICE. **2** any of various other aromatic shrubs.

ground spice

allspice berries

ALLSPICE

all-ticket *adj.* (usu. *attrib.*) (of an event) that may be attended only by those with tickets purchased in advance.

all-time *attrib.adj.* (of a record etc.) hitherto unsurpassed.

---

allude *v.intr.* (foll. by *to*) **1** refer to indirectly. **2** *disp.* mention. [from Latin *alludere* 'to touch lightly upon']

■ **Usage** *Allude to* should not be used simply as a synonym for *mention*. The sentence *Mr Smith was alluded to several times, though not actually mentioned by name, in the president's speech* illustrates the difference.

allure ● *v.tr.* attract, charm, or fascinate. ● *n.* attractiveness, personal charm; fascination. [from Old French *alurer*] □ **allurement** *n.*

allusion *n.* an indirect or passing reference. [related to ALLUDE]

■ **Usage** Care should be taken not to confuse *allusion* with *illusion*. See also Usage Note at ALLUDE.

allusive *adj.* **1** containing an allusion. **2** containing many allusions. □ **allusively** *adv.*

alluvial *adj.* of or relating to alluvium.

alluvium *n.* (*pl.* **alluvia** or **alluviums**) a deposit of soil left during a time of flood. ▷ ERODE, SEDIMENT.

ally ● *n.* /ˈal-I/ (*pl.* **-ies**) **1** a state formally cooperating or united with another for a special purpose, esp. by a treaty. **2** a person or organization that cooperates with or helps another. ● *v.tr.* /ă-ˈly/ (**-ies, -ied**) (often foll. by *with*) combine or unite in alliance. [from Latin *alligare* 'to bind']

Alma Mater *n.* (also **alma mater**) the university, school, or college one attends or attended. [Latin, literally 'bounteous mother']

almanac *n.* (also **almanack**) **1** an annual table, or book of tables, containing a calendar and usu. astronomical data and other information. **2** a usu. annual directory or handbook containing statistical and other information. [from Greek *almenikhiaka*]

almighty ● *adj.* **1** having complete power; omnipotent. **2** *slang* very great (*an almighty crash*). ● *n.* (**the Almighty**) God. ● *adv. slang* extremely; very much.

almond *n.* **1** the oval nutlike seed (kernel) of the stone fruit from the tree *Prunus dulcis*. ▷ NUT. **2** (in full **almond tree**) the tree itself, of the rose family and allied to the peach and plum. [from Greek *amugdalē*]

almond paste *n.* = MARZIPAN.

almoner *n. Brit. hist.* a social worker attached to a hospital and seeing to the aftercare of patients. [based on medieval Latin *eleēmosynarius*, related to ALMS]

---

almost *adv.* all but; very nearly. [Old English]

alms *n.pl. hist.* charitable donations of money or food to the poor. [based on Greek *eleos* 'compassion']

almshouse *n. hist.* a house founded by charity for the poor.

aloe *n.* **1** any plant of the genus *Aloe*, usu. having toothed fleshy leaves. ▷ XEROPHYTE. **2** (in *pl.*) (in full **bitter aloes**) a strong laxative obtained from the bitter juice of various species of aloe. **3** (also **American aloe**) an agave native to Central America, which flowers only once in many years, and from whose sap tequila is made. [from Greek]

aloe vera *n.* **1** a Caribbean aloe, *Aloe vera*, yielding a gelatinous substance used esp. in cosmetics as an emollient. **2** this substance. [modern Latin, literally 'true aloe']

aloft *predic.adj. & adv.* **1** high up; overhead. **2** upwards. [from Old Norse *á lopt* 'in air']

alone *predic.adj. & adv.* **1 a** without others present. **b** without others' help. **c** lonely and wretched (*felt alone*). **2** (often foll. by *in*) standing by oneself in an opinion etc. (*was alone in thinking this*). **3** only, exclusively (*you alone can help me*). □ **go it alone** act by oneself without assistance. [Middle English, from *all one*] □ **aloneness** *n.*

along ● *prep.* **1** from one end to the other end of (*a cliff with trees along the edge*). **2** on or through any part of the length of (*was walking along the road*). **3** beside or through the length of (*shelves stood along the wall*). ● *adv.* **1** onward; into a more advanced state (*come along*). **2** at or to a particular place; arriving (*I'll be along soon*). **3** in company with a person, esp. oneself (*bring a book along*). **4** beside or through part or the whole length of a thing. □ **along with** together with. [Old English]

alongshore *adv.* along or by the shore.

alongside ● *adv.* at or to the side (of a ship etc.). ● *prep.* close to the side of; next to. □ **alongside of** side by side with; together or simultaneously with.

aloof ● *adj.* distant, unsympathetic. ● *adv.* away, apart (*he kept aloof from us all*). [originally nautical, related to LUFF] □ **aloofly** *adv.* **aloofness** *n.*

alopecia /al-ō-ˈpee-shă/ *n. Med.* the abnormal absence (complete or partial) of hair. [from Greek *alōpekia* 'fox-mange']

aloud *adv.* audibly; not silently or in a whisper.

alp *n.* **1** a high mountain. **2** (**the Alps**) the range of mountains in Switzerland and adjoining countries. [from Greek *Alpeis*]

alpaca *n.* **1** ▼ a S. American mammal, *Lama pacos*, related to the llama, with long shaggy hair. **2** wool from this animal. **3** fabric made from this wool. [Spanish]

ALPACA
(*Lama pacos*)

alpenstock *n.* a long iron-tipped staff used in hill-walking. [German]

alpha *n.* **1** the first letter of the Greek alphabet (A, α). **2** *Brit.* a first-class mark given for a piece of work or in an examination. □ **alpha and omega** the beginning and the end; the most important features. [Middle English, from Greek]

A

alphabet *n.* the set of letters used in writing a language (*the Russian alphabet*). [from Greek *alpha*, *bēta*, first two letters of the alphabet]

alphabetical *adj.* (also **alphabetic**) **1** of or relating to an alphabet. **2** in the order of the letters of the alphabet.

alphabetize *v.tr.* (also **-ise**) arrange (words, names, etc.) in alphabetical order. □ **alphabetization** *n.*

alpha decay *n.* radioactive decay in which an alpha particle is emitted. ▷ RADIOACTIVITY

alphanumeric *adj.* containing both alphabetical and numerical symbols.

alpha particle *n.* (also **alpha ray**) a helium nucleus emitted by a radioactive substance, originally regarded as a ray. ▷ RADIOACTIVITY

alpine ● *adj.* **1 a** of or relating to high mountains. **b** growing or found on high mountains. **2** (**Alpine**) of or relating to the Alps. **3** (**Alpine**) (of skiing) involving fast downhill racing. ● *n.* **1** a plant native to mountain districts. **2** a plant suited to rock gardens.

Alpinist *n.* (also **alpinist**) a climber of high mountains, esp. in the Alps.

already *adv.* **1** before the time in question (*I knew that already*). **2** as early or as soon as this (*already at the age of six*).

alright *adj., adv., & int. disp.* = all right (see ALL).

■ **Usage** Although widely used, *alright* is still nonstandard and considered incorrect by many people.

Alsatian ● *n.* **1** *Brit.* a large dog of a breed used as guard dogs etc. and for police work. **2** a native of Alsace, a region of eastern France. ● *adj.* of or relating to Alsace or its inhabitants. [from *Alsatia*, ancient name of Alsace]

also *adv.* in addition; likewise; besides. [Old English]

also-ran *n.* **1** a horse or dog etc. not among the winners in a race. **2** an undistinguished person.

altar *n.* **1** ▶ a table or flat-topped block, often of stone, for making sacrifices or offerings to a deity. ▷ CATHEDRAL, CHURCH. **2** a Communion table. [from Latin *altaria* 'burnt offerings']

altarpiece *n.* a piece of art, esp. a painting, set above or behind an altar.

alter *tr. & intr.* make or become different; change. [based on Latin *alter* 'other'] □ **alterable** *adj.* **alteration** *n.*

alterative *adj.* tending to produce alteration.

altercate *v.intr.* (often foll. by *with*) dispute hotly; wrangle. [from Latin *altercari altercat-*] □ **altercation** *n.*

alter ego *n.* (*pl.* **alter egos**) **1** a person's secondary or alternative personality. **2** an intimate and trusted friend. [Latin, literally 'other self']

alternate ● *v.* /**awl**-ter-nayt/ **1** *intr.* (often foll. by *with*) (of two things) succeed each other by turns (*elation alternated with depression*). **2** *intr.* (foll. by *between*) change repeatedly (between two conditions) (*the patient alternated between hot and cold fevers*). **3** *tr.* (often foll. by *with*) cause (two things) to succeed each other by turns (*the band alternated fast and slow tunes*). ● *adj.* /awl-**ter**-năt/ **1** (with noun in *pl.*) every other (*comes on alternate days*). **2** (of things of two kinds) each following and succeeded by one of the other kind (*alternate joy and misery*). **3** (of a sequence etc.) consisting of alternate things. **4** esp. *N. Amer.* = ALTERNATIVE 1 (*an alternate route*). ● *n.* /awl-**ter**-năt/ esp. *N. Amer.* a deputy or substitute. [from Latin *alternatus* 'done by turns'] □ **alternately** *adv.*

■ **Usage** See Usage Note at ALTERNATIVE.

ALTAR IN 19TH-CENTURY CATHOLIC CHURCH, IRELAND

ALTERNATING CURRENT

An alternating current is produced by a type of generator known as an alternator. Within the alternator, a wire is coiled round an armature situated between opposing poles of a magnet. When the armature is rotated by an external power source, the magnet induces current in the wire, which can be conducted for use in an electrical appliance such as a light. With each half-turn of the armature, the current changes direction.

SECOND HALF-TURN OF THE ARMATURE

south pole of magnet

armature

brush contact

light bulb

FIRST HALF-TURN OF THE ARMATURE

south pole of magnet

slip ring conducting current

north pole of magnet

direction of current

slip ring conducting current

armature

direction of spin

direction of current

brush contact

north pole of magnet

GENERATION OF AN ALTERNATING CURRENT

---

alternate angles *n.pl.* two angles, not adjoining one another, that are formed on opposite sides of a line that intersects two other lines.

alternating current *n.* ▲ an electric current that reverses its direction at regular intervals.

alternation *n.* the action or result of alternating.

alternative ● *adj.* **1** (of one or more things) available or usable instead of another (*an alternative route*). **2** (of two things) mutually exclusive. **3** of or relating to practices that offer a substitute for the conventional ones (*alternative theatre*). ● *n.* any of two or more possibilities. □ **alternatively** *adv.*

■ **Usage** Use of the adjective in sense 1 with reference to more than two options (e.g. *many alternative methods*) is common and acceptable. *Alternative* should not be used in place of *alternate* in the sense 'every other', e.g. *There was a dance on alternate Saturdays.*

alternative energy *n.* energy fuelled in ways that do not harm the environment. ▷ SOLAR PANEL

alternative medicine *n.* any of a range of medical therapies not regarded as orthodox by the medical profession, e.g. homoeopathy and reflexology.

alternator *n.* a dynamo that generates an alternating current.

although *conj.* = THOUGH *conj.* 1, 3, 4. [Middle English]

altimeter /al-**tim**-i-ter/ *n.* an instrument for showing height above sea or ground level, esp. one fitted to an aircraft. ▷ INSTRUMENT PANEL [based on Latin *altus* 'high']

altitude *n.* the height of an object in relation to a given point, esp. sea level or the horizon. [based on Latin 'altus' high] □ **altitudinal** *adj.*

alto *n.* (*pl.* **-os**) **1** = CONTRALTO. **2 a** the highest adult male singing voice, above tenor. **b** a singer with this voice. **c** a part written for it. **3** (*attrib.*) denoting the member of a family of instruments pitched second or third highest. [from Italian *alto (canto)* 'high (singing)']

altocumulus *n. Meteorol.* rounded masses of cloud with a level base, at medium altitude. ▷ CLOUD. [from Latin *altus* 'high' + *cumulus* 'pile']

altogether *adv.* **1** totally, completely (*you are altogether wrong*). **2** on the whole (*altogether it had been a good day*). **3** in total. □ **in the altogether** *colloq.* naked. [Old English]

■ **Usage** Note that *altogether* means 'in total', as in *there are six bedrooms altogether*, whereas *all together* is used to mean 'all in one place' or 'all at once', as in *there are six bedrooms all together*; *they came in all together.*

altostratus *n. Meteorol.* continuous uniform cloud at medium altitude. ▷ CLOUD. [based on Latin *altus* 'high' + *sternere strat-* 'to spread']

altruism *n.* **1** regard for others as a principle of action. **2** unselfishness; concern for other people. [based on Italian *altrui* 'somebody else'] □ **altruist** *n.* **altruistic** *adj.* **altruistically** *adv.*

alum *n. Chem.* a double sulphate of aluminium and potassium. [from Latin *alumen aluminis*]

alumina *n.* the compound aluminium oxide occurring naturally as corundum and emery. [from Latin *alumen aluminis*]

aluminium *n.* (*N. Amer.* **aluminum**) a silvery light and malleable metallic element resistant to tarnishing by air. ▷ ORE. [alteration on the pattern of *sodium* etc., related to ALUM]

aluminize *v.tr.* (also **-ise**) coat with aluminium. □ **aluminization** *n.*

aluminosilicate *n. Mineral.* a silicate containing aluminium, esp. a rock-forming mineral of this kind, e.g. a feldspar, a clay mineral.

alumnus *n.* (*pl.* **alumni** /-nee/; *fem.* **alumna**, *pl.* **alumnae** /-nee/) a former pupil or student of a particular school, college, or university. [Latin, literally 'nursling']

alveolus *n.* (*pl.* **alveoli**) **1** a small cavity, pit, or hollow. **2** any of the many tiny air sacs of the lungs which allow for rapid gaseous exchange. ▷ LUNG. **3** the bony socket for the root of a tooth. **4** the cell of a honeycomb. [Latin, literally 'little cavity'] □ **alveolar** *adj.* **alveolate** *adj.*

always *adv.* **1** at all times; on all occasions (*always late*). **2** whatever the circumstances (*can always sleep on the floor*). **3** repeatedly; often (*they are always complaining*). **4** for ever; for all time (*he will always be a fool*). [Middle English]

A

alyssum *n.* a cruciferous plant of the genus *Alyssum*, widely cultivated and usu. having yellow or white flowers. [from Greek *alusson*]

Alzheimer's disease /alts-hy-merz/ *n.* a serious disorder of the brain manifesting itself in premature senility. [named after A. *Alzheimer*, German neurologist, 1864–1915, who first identified it]

AM *abbr.* amplitude modulation.

Am *symb. Chem.* the element americium.

am *1st person sing. present of* BE.

a.m. *abbr.* before noon. [Latin *ante meridiem*]

amah *n.* (in the Far East and India) a nursemaid or maid. [from Portuguese]

amalgam *n.* **1** a mixture or blend. **2** an alloy of mercury with one or more other metals, used esp. in dentistry. [based on Greek *malagma* 'an emollient']

amalgamate *v.* **1** *tr. & intr.* combine or unite to form one structure, organization, etc. **2** *intr.* (of metals) alloy with mercury. □ **amalgamation** *n.*

amanuensis *n.* (*pl.* **amanuenses**) **1** a person who writes from dictation or copies manuscripts. **2** a literary assistant. [based on Latin *(servus) a manu* 'slave' at hand(writing)]

amaryllis *n.* a bulbous lily-like plant, *Amaryllis belladonna*, native to S. Africa, with white or rose-pink flowers. [from Greek *Amarullis*, a name for a country girl in pastoral poetry]

amass *v.tr.* **1** gather or heap together. **2** accumulate (esp. riches). [related to MASS] □ **amasser** *n.*

amateur *n.* **1** a person who engages in a pursuit as a pastime rather than a profession. **2** (*attrib.*) for or done by amateurs (*amateur athletics*). **3** (foll. by *of*) a person who is fond of (a thing). [from Latin *amator* 'lover'] □ **amateurism** *n.*

amateurish *adj.* characteristic of an amateur, esp. *derog.* unskilful or inept. □ **amateurishly** *adv.* **amateurishness** *n.*

amatory *adj.* of or relating to sexual love or desire. [based on Latin *amare* 'to love']

amaze *v.tr.* (often foll. by *at*, or *that* + clause, or *to* + infin.) surprise greatly; overwhelm with wonder. [Old English] □ **amazement** *n.* **amazing** *adj.* **amazingly** *adv.* **amazingness** *n.*

Amazon *n.* **1** ▼ a member of a legendary race of female warriors. **2** (**amazon**) a very tall or athletic woman. [from Greek: explained by the Greeks as 'breastless', but probably of foreign origin] □ **Amazonian** *adj.*

AMAZON WARRIOR BEING SLAIN BY THE ANCIENT GREEK HERO ACHILLES

ambassador *n.* **1** an accredited diplomat sent by a state on a mission to, or as its permanent representative in, a foreign country. **2** a representative or promoter of a specified thing (*an ambassador of peace*). [based on Latin *ambactus* 'servant'] □ **ambassadorial** *adj.* **ambassadorship** *n.*

ambassadress *n.* **1** a female ambassador. **2** an ambassador's wife.

---

amber ● *n.* **1 a** ▶ a yellowish translucent fossilized resin deriving from extinct (esp. coniferous) trees and used in jewellery. ▷ GEM. **b** the honey-yellow colour of this. **2** a cautionary yellow light, esp. a traffic light showing between green for 'go' and red for 'stop'. ● *adj.* made of or coloured like amber. [from Arabic *'anbar*]

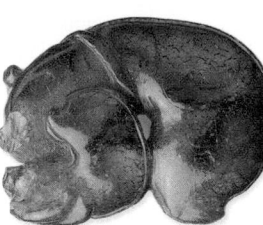

ambergris *n.* a strong-smelling waxlike secretion of the intestine of the sperm whale, used in perfume manufacture. [Old French *ambre gris* 'grey amber']

ambidextrous *adj.* able to use the right and left hands equally well. [based on Latin *ambi* 'on both sides' + *dexter* 'right-handed'] □ **ambidexterity** *n.* **ambidextrously** *adv.* **ambidextrousness** *n.*

ambience *n.* (also **ambiance**) the surroundings or atmosphere of a place.

ambient *adj.* surrounding; of the surroundings (*ambient temperature*). [from Latin *ambient-* 'going round']

ambiguity *n.* (*pl.* **-ies**) **1** double meaning (*tried to avoid ambiguity in setting out the rules*). **2** an expression able to be interpreted in more than one way (e.g. *dogs must be carried*).

ambiguous *adj.* having an obscure or double meaning. [from Latin *ambiguus* 'doubtful'] □ **ambiguously** *adv.* **ambiguousness** *n.*

ambit *n.* the scope, extent, or bounds of something. [from Latin *ambitus* 'circuit']

ambition *n.* **1** drive to succeed or progress (*full of ambition to succeed*). **2** a strong desire or aspiration. [from Latin *ambitio*]

ambitious *adj.* **1** full of ambition. **2** showing ambition (*an ambitious attempt*). □ **ambitiously** *adv.* **ambitiousness** *n.*

ambivalence *n.* the coexistence in one person's mind of opposing feelings, esp. love and hate, in a single context. [based on Latin *ambo* 'both' + *valēre* 'to be worth'] □ **ambivalent** *adj.* **ambivalently** *adv.*

amble ● *v.intr.* **1** move at an easy pace. **2** (of a horse etc.) move by lifting the two feet on one side together. **3** ride an ambling horse; ride at an easy pace. ● *n.* **1** an easy pace. **2** the gait of an ambling horse. [from Latin *ambulare* 'to walk']

ambrosia *n.* **1** (in Greek and Roman mythology) the food of the gods; the elixir of life. **2** anything very pleasing to taste or smell. [from Greek, literally 'elixir of life'] □ **ambrosial** *adj.* **ambrosian** *adj.*

ambulance *n.* **1** a vehicle for conveying the sick or injured to and from hospital. **2** a mobile hospital following an army. [French, replacing *hôpital ambulant*, a mobile (horse-drawn) field ambulance]

ambulant *adj. Med.* **1** able to walk about; not confined to bed. **2** (of treatment) not confining a patient to bed. [from Latin *ambulant-* 'walking']

ambulatory ● *adj.* **1** = AMBULANT. **2** of or adapted for walking. ● *n.* (*pl.* **-ies**) a place for walking, esp. an aisle or cloister in a church or monastery.

ambush ● *n.* **1** a surprise attack by persons (e.g. troops) in a concealed position. **2 a** the concealment of troops etc. to make such an attack. **b** the place where they are concealed. ● *v.tr.* attack by means of an ambush. [from Old French *embuschier* 'to put in a wood']

ameba *US* var. of AMOEBA. □ **amebic** *adj.* **ameboid** *adj.*

ameer var. of AMIR.

ameliorate *v.tr. & intr. formal* make or become better; improve. [alteration of earlier *meliorate*] □ **amelioration** *n.* **ameliorative** *adj.* **ameliorator** *n.*

amen ● *int.* uttered at the end of a prayer or hymn etc., meaning 'so be it'. ● *n.* an utterance of 'amen'. [from Hebrew *'āmēn* 'certainly']

---

amenable *adj.* **1** responsive, tractable. **2** (often foll. by *to*) (of a person) responsible to law. **3** (foll. by *to*) (of a thing) subject or liable. [based on Late Latin *minare* 'to drive (animals)'] □ **amenability** *n.* **amenably** *adv.*

amend *v.tr.* **1** make minor improvements in (a text or a written proposal). **2** correct an error or errors in (a document). [from Latin *emendare* 'to correct'] □ **amendable** *adj.* **amender** *n.*

▪ **Usage** *Amend* should not be confused with *emend*, a more technical word used in the context of textual correction.

amendment *n.* **1** a minor improvement in a document (esp. a legal or statutory one). **2** an article added to the US Constitution.

amends *n.* **make amends** (often foll. by *for*) compensate or make up (for).

amenity *n.* (*pl.* **-ies**) **1** (usu. in *pl.*) a pleasant or useful feature. **2** pleasantness (of a place, person, etc.). [from Latin *amoenitas* 'pleasantness']

amenorrhoea /ă-men-ŏ-ree-ă/ *n.* (*US* **amenorrhea**) *Med.* an abnormal absence of menstruation.

American ● *adj.* **1** of, relating to, or characteristic of the United States or its inhabitants. **2** (usu. in *comb.*) of or relating to the continents of America (*Latin American*). ● *n.* **1** a native or citizen of the United States. **2** (usu. in *comb.*) a native or inhabitant of the continents of America (*North Americans*). **3** the English language as it is used in the United States. [from the Latinized name of *Amerigo* Vespucci, Italian navigator]

Americana *n.pl.* things connected with America, esp. with the United States.

American aloe var. of ALOE 3.

American football *n.* a kind of football played with an oval ball, evolved from rugby. ▷ FOOTBALL

American Indian *n.* a member of a group of indigenous peoples of N. and S. America and the Caribbean.

▪ **Usage** The term *Native American* is now often, though not universally, preferred.

Americanism *n.* **1 a** a word, sense, or phrase peculiar to or originating from the United States. **b** a thing or feature characteristic of or peculiar to the United States. **2** attachment to or sympathy for the United States.

Americanize *v.* (also **-ise**) **1** *tr.* **a** make American in character. **b** naturalize as an American. **2** *intr.* become American in character. □ **Americanization** *n.*

American plaice see PLAICE 2.

americium *n. Chem.* an artificially made transuranic radioactive metallic element. [based on *America*, where first made]

Amerind *adj. & n.* (also **Amerindian**) = AMERICAN INDIAN.

amethyst *n.* a precious stone of a violet or purple variety of quartz. ▷ GEM, QUARTZ. [from Greek *amethustos* 'not drunken', the stone being supposed to prevent intoxication] □ **amethystine** *adj.*

Amex *abbr.* **1** *propr.* American Express. **2** American Stock Exchange.

amiable *adj.* friendly and pleasant in temperament. [from Late Latin *amicabilis* 'amicable': the spelling from confusion with French *aimable* 'lovable'] □ **amiability** *n.* **amiably** *adv.*

amicable *adj.* showing or done in a friendly spirit (*an amicable meeting*). [from Late Latin *amicabilis*] □ **amicably** *adv.*

amice /am-iss/ *n.* a white linen cloth worn on the neck and shoulders by a priest celebrating the Eucharist. [from Latin *amictus* 'outer garment']

amid *prep.* (also **amidst**) **1** in the middle of. **2** in the course of. [Middle English]

A

amide *n. Chem.* a compound formed from ammonia by replacement of one or more hydrogen atoms by a metal or an acyl radical.

amidships *adv.* (*US* also **amidship**) in or into the middle of a ship.

amine *n. Chem.* a compound formed from ammonia by replacement of one or more hydrogen atoms by an organic radical or radicals.

amino *n.* (used *attrib.*) *Chem.* the monovalent group –NH₂.

amino acid *n. Biochem.* any of a group of simple organic compounds, many occurring naturally in plant and animal tissues and forming the basic constituents of proteins.

amir *n.* (also **ameer**) the title of some Arab rulers. [from Arabic 'amīr 'commander']

Amish ● *adj.* belonging to a strict US Mennonite sect. ● *n.pl.* (prec. by *the*) the members of this sect. [from J. *Amen*, 17th-century Swiss Mennonite preacher]

amiss ● *predic.adj.* wrong; out of order; faulty (*something was amiss*). ● *adv.* wrong; wrongly; inappropriately (*everything went amiss*). □ **take amiss** be offended by (*took my words amiss*). [Middle English]

amitosis *n. Biol.* a form of nuclear division that does not involve mitosis.

amity *n.* friendship; friendly relations. [based on Latin *amicus* 'friend']

ammeter *n.* an instrument for measuring electric current in amperes. ▷ INDUCTION

ammo *n. colloq.* ammunition.

ammonia *n. Chem.* **1** a colourless gas with a characteristic pungent smell. **2** (in general use) a strongly alkaline solution of ammonia gas in water. [modern Latin] □ **ammoniacal** *adj.* **ammoniated** *adj.*

ammonite *n.* ◀ an extinct cephalopod mollusc of the order Ammonoidea, with a flat coiled spiral shell found as a fossil. ▷ FOSSIL. [based on medieval Latin *cornu Ammonis* 'horn of Ammon', from the shape of the shell]

AMMONITE FOSSIL

ammonium *n.* the monovalent ion NH₄⁺, formed from ammonia. [modern Latin]

ammunition *n.* **1** a supply of projectiles (esp. bullets, shells, and grenades). **2** points used or usable to advantage in an argument. [from French, corruption of (*la*) *munition* '(the) munition']

amnesia *n.* a partial or total loss of memory. [from Greek, literally 'forgetfulness'] □ **amnesiac** *n.* **amnesic** *adj. & n.*

amnesty ● *n.* (*pl.* **-ies**) a general pardon, esp. for political offences. ● *v.tr.* (**-ies**, **-ied**) grant an amnesty to. [from Greek *amnēstia* 'oblivion']

amniocentesis /am-ni-oh-sen-*tee*-sis/ *n.* (*pl.* **amniocenteses**) *Med.* the sampling of amniotic fluid to determine the condition of a foetus. [from AMNION + Greek *kentēsis* 'pricking']

amnion *n.* (*pl.* **amnia**) *Zool. & Physiol.* the innermost membrane that encloses the embryo of a reptile, bird, or mammal. ▷ EGG. [Greek, literally 'caul'] □ **amniotic** *adj.*

amniotic fluid *n.* the fluid surrounding a foetus within the amnion. ▷ FOETUS

amoeba /ă-*mee*-bă/ *n.* (*US* also **ameba**) (*pl.* **amoebas** or **amoebae** /-bee/) ▶ any usu. aquatic protozoan of the genus *Amoeba*, esp. *A. proteus*, capable of changing shape. ▷ PSEUDOPODIUM. [from Greek *amoibē* 'change'] □ **amoebic** *adj.* **amoeboid** *adj.*

amok *adv.* (also **amuck**) □ **run amok** run about wildly in an uncontrollable violent rage. [Malay]

AMOEBA
(*Amoeba* species)

among *prep.* (also esp. *Brit.* **amongst**) **1** surrounded by; in the company of. **2** in the number of (*among us were those who disagreed*). **3** an example of; in the class or category of (*is among the richest men alive*). **4** between; shared by (*had £5 among us; divide it among you*). **5** with one another; by the reciprocal action of (*was decided among the participants; talked among themselves*). [Old English]

amoral *adj.* **1** not concerned with or outside the scope of morality (cf. IMMORAL). **2** having no moral principles. □ **amoralism** *n.* **amoralist** *n.* **amorality** *n.*

amorous *adj.* **1** showing, feeling, or inclined to sexual love. **2** of or relating to sexual love. [based on Latin *amor* 'love'] □ **amorously** *adv.* **amorousness** *n.*

amorphous *adj.* **1** shapeless. **2** vague, ill-organized. **3** *Mineral. & Chem.* non-crystalline; having neither definite form nor structure. [from Greek *amorphos* 'shapeless'] □ **amorphously** *adv.* **amorphousness** *n.*

amortize *v.tr.* (also **-ise**) *Commerce* **1** gradually extinguish (a debt) by money put aside. **2** gradually write off the initial cost of (assets). [based on Latin *ad mortem* 'to death'] □ **amortization** *n.*

amount ● *n.* a quantity, esp. the total of a thing or things in number, size, value, extent, etc. (*a large amount of money*). ● *v.intr.* (foll. by *to*) be equivalent to in number, size, significance, etc. (*amounted to £100; amounted to a disaster*). □ **any amount of** a great deal of. **no amount of** not even the greatest possible amount of. [based on Old French *amont* 'upward']

amour /a-*moor*/ *n.* a love affair, esp. a secret one. [French, literally 'love']

amour propre /am-oor *propr*/ *n.* self-respect. [French]

amp¹ *n. Electr.* an ampere.

amp² *n. colloq.* an amplifier. [abbreviation]

amperage *n. Electr.* the strength of an electric current in amperes.

ampere *n. Electr.* the SI base unit of electric current. [named after A. M. *Ampère*, French physicist, 1775–1836]

ampersand *n.* the sign & (= *and*, Latin *et*). [corruption of *and per se and*]

amphetamine *n.* a synthetic drug used esp. as a stimulant. [from alpha-methyl *phen*ethyl*amine*]

amphi- *comb. form* **1** both. **2** of both kinds. **3** on both sides. **4** around. [Greek]

AMPHIBIAN

Beginning life as larvae or tadpoles, amphibians go through a metamorphosis as they grow into their adult state. All but the caecilians grow legs, and most develop lungs, which supersede gills for oxygen intake. Many amphibians are also able to absorb oxygen through their skin. The three main divisions of the Amphibia class are shown here.

URODELA
(newts, salamanders)
▷ NEWT, SALAMANDER

ANURA
(frogs, toads)
▷ FROG, TOAD

APODA
(caecilians)

amphibian ● *adj.* **1** living both on land and in water. **2** *Zool.* of or relating to the class Amphibia. **3** (of a vehicle) able to operate on land and water. ● *n.* **1** *Zool.* ▲ any vertebrate of the class Amphibia, including frogs, toads, newts, and salamanders. **2** (in general use) a creature living both on land and in water. **3** an amphibian vehicle. [from Greek *amphibion*]

amphibious *adj.* **1** living both on land and in water. **2** of or relating to or suited for both land and water. **3** *Mil.* **a** (of a military operation) involving forces landed from the sea. **b** (of forces) trained for such operations. □ **amphibiously** *adv.*

amphibole *n. Mineral.* any of a class of rock-forming silicate and aluminosilicate minerals with fibrous or columnar crystals. [from Latin *amphibolus* 'ambiguous', so called because of their varied structure]

amphitheatre *n.* (*US* **amphitheater**) **1** ▶ a round, usu. unroofed building with tiers of seats surrounding a central space. **2** a semicircular gallery in a theatre. [from Greek *amphitheatron*]

amphora *n.* (*pl.* **amphorae** /-ree/ or **amphoras**) ▼ a Greek or Roman vessel with two handles and a narrow neck. [Latin, from Greek *amphoreus*]

ampicillin *n. Pharm.* a type of penicillin used esp. in treating infections of the urinary and respiratory tracts.

ample *adj.* (**ampler**, **amplest**) **1 a** plentiful, abundant, extensive. **b** *euphem.* (esp. of a person) large, stout. **2** enough or more than enough. [from Latin *amplus*] □ **ampleness** *n.* **amply** *adv.*

amplifier *n.* an electronic device for increasing the strength of electrical signals, used esp. in sound reproduction.

amplify *v.* (**-ies**, **-ied**) **1** *tr.* increase the volume or strength of (sound, electrical signals, etc.). **2** *tr.* enlarge upon or add detail to (a story etc.). **3** *intr.* expand what is said or written. [based on Latin *amplus* 'abundant'] □ **amplification** *n.*

AMPHORA:
8TH-CENTURY BC
GREEK AMPHORA

amplitude *n.* **1 a** *Physics* the maximum extent of a vibration or oscillation from the position of equilibrium. **b** *Electr.* the maximum departure of the value of an alternating current or wave from the average value. **2 a** spaciousness, breadth; wide range. **b** abundance. [related to AMPLE]

amplitude modulation *n. Electr.* the modulation of a wave by variation of its amplitude, esp. as a means of carrying an audio signal by radio. ▷ WAVELENGTH

ampoule *n.* (also esp. *US* **ampul** or **ampule**) a small capsule in which a measured quantity of liquid or solid, esp. for injecting, is sealed ready for use. [from Latin *ampulla* 'receptacle']

ampulla *n.* (*pl.* **ampullae** /-lee/) **1** a Roman globular flask with two handles. **2** a vessel for sacred uses. [Latin]

amputate *v.tr.* cut off by surgical operation (a part of the body, esp. a limb). [based on Latin *putare* 'to prune'] □ **amputation** *n.* **amputator** *n.*

amputee *n.* a person who has lost a limb etc. by amputation.

amtrac *n.* (also **amtrak**) *US* an amphibious tracked vehicle used for landing assault troops on a shore. [from *amphibious* + *tractor*]

amu *abbr.* atomic mass unit.

amuck var. of AMOK.

amulet *n.* an ornament or small piece of jewellery worn as a charm against evil. [from Latin *amuletum*]

amuse *v.tr.* **1** cause (a person) to laugh or smile. **2** (also *refl.*; often foll. by *with, by*) interest or occupy; keep (a person) entertained. [from Old French *amuser* 'to cause to muse'] □ **amusing** *adj.* **amusingly** *adv.*

amusement *n.* **1** something that amuses, esp. a pleasant diversion, game, or pastime. **2** the state of being amused. **3** *Brit.* a mechanical device (e.g. a roundabout) for entertainment at a fairground etc.

amusement arcade *n. Brit.* an indoor area for entertainment with automatic game machines.

amusement park *n.* a large outdoor area with fairground amusements etc.

amyl *n.* (used *attrib.*) *Chem.* the monovalent group C_5H_{11}-, derived from pentane. [from Latin *amylum* 'starch']

amylase *n. Biochem.* an enzyme that converts starch and glycogen into simple sugars.

an *det.* the form of the indefinite article (see A[1]) used before words beginning with a vowel sound (*an egg; an hour; an MP*).

■ **Usage** Some people retain the use of *an* before words beginning with a sounded *h* e.g. *an hotel, an historian.* Historically this was justifiable because the *h-* was dropped in these words, but today this is not the case and *a hotel, a historian* are now the preferred forms.

an- *prefix* not, without (*anarchy*) (cf. A-). [Greek]

-ana *suffix* forming plural nouns meaning 'things associated with' (*Victoriana; Americana*).

Anabaptism *n.* the doctrine that baptism should only be administered to believing adults. [from Greek *anabaptismos*] □ **Anabaptist** *n.*

anabolic *adj. Biochem.* of or relating to anabolism.

anabolic steroid *n.* a synthetic steroid hormone used to increase muscle size.

anabolism *n. Biochem.* the synthesis of complex molecules in living organisms from simpler ones together with the storage of energy; constructive metabolism (opp. CATABOLISM). [based on Greek *anaballein* 'to ascend, throw upwards']

anachronism *n.* **1 a** the attribution of a custom, event, etc. to a period to which it does not belong. **b** a thing attributed in this way. **2** an old-fashioned or out-of-date person or thing. [based on Greek *khronos* 'time'] □ **anachronistic** *adj.* **anachronistically** *adv.*

anacoluthon *n.* (*pl.* **anacolutha**) a sentence or construction which lacks grammatical sequence (e.g. *while in the garden the door banged shut*). [based on Greek *akolouthos* 'following'] □ **anacoluthic** *adj.*

anaconda *n.* ▶ a S. American boa of the genus *Eunectes*, esp. the very large semi-aquatic *E. murinus*. ▷ SNAKE. [from Sinhalese *henakandayā* 'whip snake']

anaemia /ă-nee-miă/ *n.* (*US* **anemia**) a deficiency in the blood, usu. of red cells or their haemoglobin, resulting in pallor and weariness. [from Greek *anaimia*]

anaemic /ă-nee-mik/ *adj.* (*US* **anemic**) **1** relating to or suffering from anaemia. **2** pale; lacking in vitality.

anaerobic *adj. Biol.* living or taking place in the absence of free oxygen. □ **anaerobe** *n.*

anaesthesia /an-iss-th'ee-ziă/ *n.* (*US* **anesthesia**) the absence of sensation, esp. artificially induced insensitivity to pain. [from Greek *anaisthēsia*] □ **anaesthesiology** *n.*

anaesthetic /an-iss-thet-ik/ (*US* **anesthetic**) ● *n.* a substance that produces insensibility to pain etc. ● *adj.* producing insensibility to pain etc.

anaesthetist /ă neess-thĕ-tist/ *n.* a specialist in the administration of anaesthetics.

anaesthetize /ă neess-thĕ-tyz/ *v.tr.* (also -ise, *US* **anesthetize**) **1** administer an anaesthetic to. **2** deprive of physical or mental sensation. □ **anaesthetization** *n.*

Anaglypta *n. propr.* a type of thick embossed wallpaper, usu. for painting over. [Latin, literally 'work in low relief']

anagram *n.* a word or phrase formed by transposing the letters of another word or phrase. [based on Greek *gramma* 'letter'] □ **anagrammatic** *adj.* **anagrammatical** *adj.* **anagrammatize** *v.tr.* (also **-ise**)

anal *adj.* relating to or situated near the anus. [from modern Latin *analis*] □ **anally** *adv.*

analeptic ● *adj.* (of a drug etc.) restorative. ● *n.* a restorative medicine or drug. [based on Greek *analambanein* 'to take back']

analgesia *n.* the absence or relief of pain. [from Greek, literally 'painlessness']

analgesic ● *adj.* relieving pain. ● *n.* an analgesic drug.

analog *US* var. of ANALOGUE.

analogize *v.* (also **-ise**) **1** *tr.* represent or explain by analogy. **2** *intr.* use analogy.

analogous *adj.* (often foll. by *to*) **1** partially similar or parallel; showing analogy. **2** *Biol.* performing a similar function but having a different evolutionary origin (opp. HOMOLOGOUS 2). [from Greek *analogos* 'proportionate'] □ **analogously** *adv.*

■ **Usage** *Analogous* means 'similar in certain respects'. It should not be used as a mere synonym for *similar*.

analogue (*US* also **analog**) ● *n.* an analogous or parallel thing. ● *adj.* (usu. **analog**) **1** relating to or using signals or information represented by a continuously variable quantity such as spatial position, voltage, etc. ▷ DIGITIZE, RECORD. **2** (of a watch etc.) showing the time by means of hands or a pointer rather than displayed digits (cf. DIGITAL *adj.* 2). [from Greek *analogon*]

analogy *n.* (*pl.* **-ies**) **1** (usu. foll. by *to, with, between*) correspondence or partial similarity. **2** *Biol.* the resemblance of function between organs essentially different. **3** an analogue. [from Greek *analogia* 'proportion'] □ **analogical** *adj.* **analogically** *adv.*

anal-retentive *adj.* (of a person) excessively orderly and fussy (supposedly owing to conflict over toilet-training in infancy). □ **anal retention** *n.* **anal retentiveness** *n.*

analyse *v.tr.* (*US* **analyze**) **1** examine in detail the elements or structure of. **2** *Chem.* ascertain the constituents of (a sample of a mixture or compound). **3** find or show the essence or structure of (a book, piece of music, etc.). **4** psychoanalyse. [based on medieval Latin *analysis*] □ **analysable** *adj.* **analyser** *n.*

analysis *n.* (*pl.* **analyses**) **1 a** a detailed examination of the elements or structure of a substance etc. **b** a statement of the result of this. **2** *Chem.* the determination of the constituent parts of a mixture or compound. **3** psychoanalysis. □ **in the final** (or **last**) **analysis** after all due consideration; in the end. [based on Greek *analuein* 'to unloose']

analyst *n.* **1** a person skilled in (esp. chemical) analysis. **2** a psychoanalyst.

analytic *adj.* of or relating to analysis.

analytical *adj.* using analytic methods. □ **analytically** *adv.*

analytical geometry *n.* geometry using coordinates.

analyze *US* var. of ANALYSE.

anamnesis *n.* (*pl.* **anamneses**) recollection (esp. of a supposed previous existence). [Greek, literally 'remembrance']

anapaest *n.* (*US* **anapest**) *Prosody* a foot consisting of two short or unstressed syllables followed by one long or stressed syllable. [from Greek *anapaistos* 'reversed' (because the reverse of a dactyl)] □ **anapaestic** *adj.*

ANACONDA
(*Eunectes murinus*)

AMPHITHEATRE

An amphitheatre is a circular or elliptical building, with tiers of seating surrounding a central arena. This architectural form was originated by the ancient Romans, who erected such buildings in all their major cities. Amphitheatres such as the Colosseum were able to hold up to 50,000 spectators, who gathered to watch athletic contests, gladiatorial fights, and other spectacles enacted within the arena.

tiers of seating

poles to support a canopy

arena

colonnades decorated with statues

one of 80 entrances

internal corridors

cages for animals and slaves

RECONSTRUCTION OF THE
COLOSSEUM, ROME (AD 72)

A

anaphora /ă-**naf**-ŏ-ră/ n. **1** Rhet. the repetition of a word or phrase at the beginning of successive clauses. **2** Gram. the use of a word referring to or replacing a word used earlier in a sentence, to avoid repetition (e.g. do in I like it and so do they). [from Greek, literally 'repetition'] □ **anaphoric** adj.

anaphrodisiac ● adj. tending to reduce sexual desire. ● n. an anaphrodisiac drug.

anaphylaxis n. Med. an extreme, often life-threatening, reaction to an antigen, e.g. to a bee sting, due to hypersensitivity following an earlier dose. [based on Greek phulaxis 'guarding'] □ **anaphylactic** adj.

anaptyxis n. Phonet. the insertion of a vowel between two consonants to aid pronunciation (as in went thataway). □ **anaptyctic** adj. [modern Latin from Greek anaptuxis]

anarchism n. the doctrine that all government should be abolished.

anarchist ● n. an advocate of anarchism or of political disorder. ● adj. relating to anarchism or its advocates. □ **anarchistic** adj.

anarchy n. **1** disorder, esp. political or social. **2** lack of government in a society. [based on Greek arkhē 'rule'] □ **anarchic** adj. **anarchical** adj. **anarchically** adv.

anastigmat n. a lens or lens system made free from astigmatism by correction. [from German anastigmatisch]

anastigmatic adj. (of a lens) free from astigmatism. [related to ASTIGMATISM]

anastomosis n. (pl. **anastomoses**) a cross-connection of arteries, rivers, etc. [based on Greek anastomoun 'to provide with an outlet'] □ **anastomose** v.intr.

anathema /ă-**nath**-ĕmă/ n. (pl. **anathemas**) **1** a detested thing or person (is anathema to me). **2 a** a curse of the Church, excommunicating a person or denouncing a doctrine. **b** a cursed thing or person. [ecclesiastical Latin, literally 'excommunicated person, excommunication']

anathematize v.tr. & intr. (also **-ise**) curse.

anatomical adj. **1** of or relating to anatomy. **2** of or relating to bodily structure. □ **anatomically** adv.

anatomist n. a person skilled in anatomy.

anatomize v.tr. (also **-ise**) **1** examine in detail. **2** dissect.

anatomy n. (pl. **-ies**) **1** the science of the bodily structure of animals and plants. **2** this structure. **3** colloq. a human body. **4** analysis. [from Greek anatomē 'a cutting up']

anatta (also **anatto**) var. of ANNATTO.

ANC abbr. African National Congress.

ancestor n. (fem. **ancestress**) **1** any (esp. remote) person from whom one is descended. **2** an early type of animal or plant from which others have evolved. **3** an early prototype or forerunner (ancestor of the computer). [based on Latin antecedere 'to go before']

ancestral adj. belonging to or inherited from one's ancestors.

ancestry n. (pl. **-ies**) **1** one's (esp. remote) family descent. **2** one's ancestors collectively. [Middle English alteration of Old French ancesserie]

anchor ● n. **1** a device used to moor a ship to the sea bottom or a balloon to the ground. ▷ MAN-OF-WAR, SHIP. **2** = ANCHORPERSON. ● v. **1** tr. (also absol.) secure (a ship or balloon) by means of an anchor. **2** tr. fix firmly. **3** intr. be moored by means of an anchor. □ **cast** (or **come to**) **anchor** let down the anchor. **weigh anchor** take up the anchor. [from Greek agkura]

anchorage n. a place where a ship may be anchored.

anchorite n. (fem. **anchoress**) **1** a hermit; a religious recluse. **2** a person of secluded habits. [based on Greek anakhōrein 'to retire'] □ **anchoretic** adj. **anchoritic** adj.

anchorman n. (pl. **-men**; fem. **anchorwoman**, pl. **-women**) **1** a person who coordinates activities, esp. as compère in a broadcast. **2** a person who plays a crucial part, esp. at the back of a tug-of-war team or as the last runner in a relay race.

anchorperson n. (pl. **anchorpersons** or **anchorpeople**) an anchorman or anchorwoman (used as a neutral alternative).

anchovy n. (pl. **-ies**) any of various small silvery fish of the herring family, usu. preserved in salt and oil and having a strong taste. [from Spanish & Portuguese ancho(v)a]

anchusa /ăng-**kew**-ză/ n. any plant of the genus Anchusa, akin to borage. [from Greek agkhousa]

anchylose var. of ANKYLOSE (see ANKYLOSIS).

anchylosis var. of ANKYLOSIS.

ancien régime /on-see-ăn ray-**zheem**/ n. (pl. **anciens régimes** pronunc. same) **1** the political and social system in France before the Revolution of 1789. **2** any superseded regime. [French, literally 'old rule']

ancient adj. **1** of long ago. **2** having existed long. □ **the ancients** the people of ancient times, esp. the Greeks and Romans. [based on Latin ante 'before'] □ **ancientness** n.

ancient history n. **1** the history of the ancient civilizations of the Mediterranean area and the Near East before the fall of the Western Roman Empire in AD 476. **2** something already long familiar.

ancient lights n.pl. Brit. a window that a neighbour may not deprive of light by erecting a building.

anciently adv. long ago.

ancient world n. the region around the Mediterranean and the Near East before the fall of the Roman Empire in AD 476.

ancillary ● adj. **1** providing essential support to a central service or industry, esp. the medical service. **2** (often foll. by to) subordinate. ● n. (pl. **-ies**) **1** an ancillary worker. **2** something which is ancillary. [based on Latin ancilla 'maidservant']

and conj. **1 a** connecting words, clauses, or sentences, that are to be taken jointly (cakes and buns; buy and sell; two hundred and forty). **b** implying progression (better and better). **c** implying causation (do that and I'll hit you). **d** implying great duration (he cried and cried). **e** implying a great number (miles and miles). **f** implying addition (two and two are four). **g** implying variety (there are books and books). **h** implying succession (walking two and two). **2** colloq. to (try and open it). **3** in relation to (Britain and the EU). [Old English]

Andalusian adj. of or relating to Andalusia in southern Spain, its inhabitants, or its language.

andante Mus. ● adv. & adj. in a moderately slow tempo. ● n. an andante passage or movement. [Italian, literally 'going']

andiron n. a metal stand for supporting burning wood in a fireplace; a firedog. [from Old French andier; assimilated to IRON]

androgen n. any of a group of male sex hormones, esp. testosterone, involved in developing and maintaining certain male sexual characteristics. [based on Greek anēr andros 'male'] □ **androgenic** adj.

androgynous adj. **1** having a partly male, partly female appearance; of ambiguous gender. **2** Bot. with stamens and pistils in the same flower or inflorescence. **3** = HERMAPHRODITE.

androgyny n. **1** androgynous character. **2** Biol. hermaphroditism.

android n. a robot with a human appearance. [based on Greek anēr andros 'male']

anecdote n. a short account or (painting etc.) of an entertaining or interesting incident. [from Greek anekdota 'things unpublished'] □ **anecdotal** adj. **anecdotalist** n. **anecdotally** adv.

anechoic adj. free from echo.

anemia US var. of ANAEMIA.

anemic US var. of ANAEMIC.

anemometer n. ▶ an instrument for measuring or indicating the force of the wind. [based on Greek anemos 'wind']

ANEMOMETER

anemone n. **1** any plant of the genus Anemone, akin to the buttercup, with flowers of various vivid colours. **2** = SEA ANEMONE. [from Greek anemōnē 'windflower']

aneroid ● adj. (of a barometer) that measures air pressure by its action on the elastic lid of an evacuated box. ● n. an aneroid barometer. [from French anéroïde]

anesthesia etc. US var. of ANAESTHESIA etc.

aneurysm n. (also **aneurism**) an excessive localized enlargement of an artery. [from Greek aneurusma, based on eurus 'wide'] □ **aneurysmal** adj. (also **aneurismal**).

anew adv. **1** again. **2** in a different way. [Middle English]

angel n. **1 a** an attendant or messenger of God. **b** a representation of this in human form with wings. **c** an attendant spirit (evil angel; guardian angel). **2** a very virtuous or obliging person. **3** a messenger or bringer of something (angel of mercy). **4** slang a financial backer of an enterprise, esp. in the theatre. **5** an unexplained radar echo. [from Greek aggelos 'messenger']

angel dust n. slang the hallucinogenic drug phencyclidine hydrochloride.

Angeleno n. (in full **Los Angeleno**) (pl. **-os**) esp. US a native or inhabitant of Los Angeles in California. [American Spanish]

angelfish n. (pl. same). ◀ any of various fish, esp. Pterophyllum scalare, with large dorsal and ventral fins.

angelic adj. **1** like or relating to angels. **2** having characteristics attributed to angels, esp. sublime beauty or innocence. □ **angelical** adj. **angelically** adv.

angelica n. **1** an aromatic umbelliferous plant, Angelica archangelica. **2** its candied stalks. [from medieval Latin (herba) angelica 'angelic (herb)']

angelus n. **1** a Roman Catholic devotion said at morning, noon, and sunset. **2** a bell announcing this. [from the opening words Angelus domini (Latin, literally 'angel of the Lord')]

anger ● n. extreme or passionate displeasure. ● v.tr. make angry; enrage. [from Old Norse angr 'grief']

angina /an-**jy**-nă/ n. **1** (in full **angina pectoris**) pain in the chest brought on by exertion, owing to an inadequate blood supply to the heart. **2** an attack of intense constricting pain, esp. in the throat. [Latin, literally 'quinsy']

angiogram n. a radiograph of blood and lymph vessels, made by introducing a substance opaque to X-rays. [based on Greek aggeion 'vessel'] □ **angiography** n.

angiosperm n. ▶ a plant of the subdivision Angiospermae producing flowers and reproducing by seeds enclosed within a carpel. [from Greek aggeion 'vessel' + sperma 'seed'] □ **angiospermous** adj.

Angle n. (usu. in pl.) a member of a tribe from Schleswig that settled in eastern Britain in the 5th c. [from Angul, a district of Schleswig, now in N. Germany] □ **Anglian** adj.

dorsal fin

ANGELFISH: DEEP ANGELFISH (Pterophyllum altum)

pelvic fins

anal fin

ANGIOSPERM

The angiosperms, or flowering plants, number at least 250,000 species, and form the largest division in the plant world. Unlike other seed plants, such as conifers, they produce seeds inside protective ovaries, which later ripen to form fruits. There are over 250 families of angiosperm, divided into two unequal groups. The dicotyledons, which make up the largest group, all have two seed-leaves or cotyledons. They include a huge variety of herbaceous plants, shrubs, and all broad-leaved trees. The monocotyledons have a single seed-leaf (cotyledon). They are mainly herbaceous, and include only a few treelike forms, such as palms.

EXAMPLES OF DICOTYLEDON FAMILIES

CRUCIFERAE
(cabbage family)

MYRTACEAE
(myrtle family)

ERICACEAE
(heather family)

UMBELLIFERAE
(carrot family)

SOLANACEAE
(nightshade family)

EUPHORBIACEAE
(spurge family)

LEGUMINOSAE
(pea family)

LABIATAE
(mint family)

ROSACEAE
(rose family)
▷ ROSE

COMPOSITAE
(daisy family)
▷ COMPOSITE

EXAMPLES OF MONOCOTYLEDON FAMILIES

GRAMINEAE
(grasses)
▷ GRASS

CYPERACEAE
(rush family)

LILIACEAE
(lily family)

PALMAE
(palm family)

ORCHIDACEAE
(orchid family)
▷ ORCHID

A

angle[1] ● *n.* **1** the space between or inclination of two meeting lines or surfaces. **2 a** a corner. **b** a sharp projection. **3 a** the direction from which a photograph etc. is taken. **b** the aspect from which a matter is considered. ● *v.* **1** *tr. & intr.* move or place obliquely. **2** *tr.* present (information) from a particular point of view (*was angled in favour of the victim*). [from Latin *angulus* 'corner'] □ **angled** *adj.*

angle[2] *v.intr.* **1** (often foll. by *for*) fish with hook and line. ▷ FISHING. **2** (foll. by *for*) seek an objective by devious or calculated means. [Old English] □ **angler** *n.*

anglepoise *n.* (often *attrib.*) *propr.* a type of desk lamp with a sprung and jointed adjustable arm.

angler fish *n.* any of various fishes that prey upon small fish, attracting them by filaments arising from the dorsal fin.

Anglican ● *adj.* of or relating to the Church of England or any Church in communion with it. ● *n.* a member of an Anglican Church. [based on *Anglus* 'Angle', member of a N. German tribe] □ **Anglicanism** *n.*

anglice /anglisee/ *adv.* in English. [medieval Latin]

Anglicism *n.* **1** a peculiarly English word or custom. **2** Englishness. **3** preference for what is English.

Anglicize *v.tr.* (also **-ise**) make English in form or character.

Anglo ● *n.* (*pl.* **Anglos**) **1** esp. *N. Amer.* **a** a person of British or northern European origin, esp. (*US*) as distinct from a Hispanic American. **b** an English-speaking person, esp. a white N. American who is not (*US*) of Hispanic descent or (*Canad.*) of French descent. **2** *Brit.* a Scottish, Irish, or Welsh sports player who plays for an English club. ● *adj.* of or relating to Anglos.

Anglo- *comb. form* **1** English (*Anglo-Catholic*). **2** of English origin (*an Anglo-American*). **3** English or *disp.* British and (*an Anglo-American agreement*).

Anglo-Catholic ● *adj.* of a High Church Anglican group which emphasizes its Catholic tradition. ● *n.* a member of this group.

Anglo-French ● *adj.* **1** English (or British) and French. **2** of Anglo-French. ● *n.* the French language as retained and separately developed in England after the Norman Conquest.

Anglo-Indian ● *adj.* **1** of or relating to England and India. **2 a** of British descent or birth but living or having lived long in India. **b** of mixed British and Indian parentage. **3** (of a word) adopted into English from an Indian language. ● *n.* an Anglo-Indian person.

Anglo-Irish ● *adj.* **1** of English descent but born or resident in Ireland. **2** of mixed English and Irish parentage. **3** of or belonging to both Britain and the Republic of Ireland. ● *n.* **1** (prec. by *the*; treated as *pl.*) Anglo-Irish people. **2** the English language as used in Ireland.

Anglo-Latin ● *adj.* of Latin as used in medieval England. ● *n.* this form of Latin.

Anglo-Norman ● *adj.* **1** English and Norman. **2** of the Normans in England after the Norman Conquest. **3** = ANGLO-FRENCH *adj.* 2. ● *n.* = ANGLO-FRENCH *n.*

Anglophobia *n.* intense hatred or fear of England or the English.

anglophone ● *adj.* English-speaking. ● *n.* an English-speaking person.

Anglo-Saxon ● *adj.* **1** of the English Saxons (as distinct from the Old Saxons of the Continent, and from the Angles) before the Norman Conquest. **2** of the Old English people as a whole before the Norman Conquest. **3** of English descent. ● *n.* **1** an Anglo-Saxon person. **2** the Old English language. **3** *colloq.* plain (esp. crude) English. **4** *US* the modern English language.

angora *n.* (often *attrib.*) **1** a fabric made from the hair of the angora goat or rabbit. **2** ◄ a long-haired variety of cat, goat, or rabbit. ▷ CAT. [from *Angora*, former name of Ankara in Turkey]

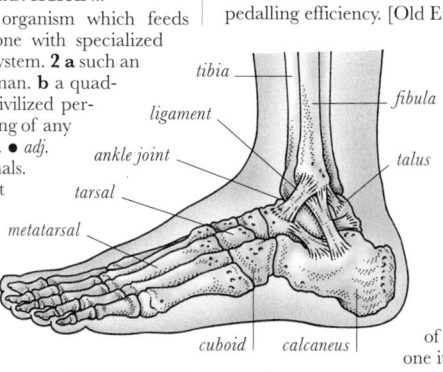
ANGORA GOAT

angora wool *n.* a mixture of sheep's wool and angora rabbit hair.

angostura *n.* (in full **angostura bark**) an aromatic bitter bark used as a flavouring, and formerly used as a tonic and to reduce fever. [from *Angostura*, a town in Venezuela, now named Ciudad Bolívar]

Angostura Bitters *n.pl. propr.* a kind of tonic first made in Angostura.

angry *adj.* (**angrier**, **angriest**) **1** feeling or showing anger; extremely displeased or resentful. **2** (of a sore etc.) inflamed, painful. **3** suggesting anger (*an angry sky*). [Middle English] □ **angrily** *adv.*

angst *n.* **1** anxiety. **2** a feeling of guilt or remorse. [German]

angstrom *n.* (also **ångström**) a unit of length equal to 10^{-10} metre. [named after A.J. *Ångström*, Swedish physicist, 1814–1874]

anguine *adj.* of or resembling a snake. [Latin *anguinus* from *anguis* 'snake']

anguish *n.* severe mental or physical pain or suffering. [from Latin *angustia* 'tightness'] □ **anguished** *adj.*

angular *adj.* **1 a** having angles or sharp corners. **b** (of a person) having sharp features. **c** awkward in manner. **2** forming an angle. **3** measured by angle (*angular distance*). [related to ANGLE[1]] □ **angularity** *n.* **angularly** *adv.*

anhydrous *adj. Chem.* without water, esp. as an essential part of the structure of some crystals. [based on Greek *hudōr* 'water']

aniline *n.* a colourless oily liquid, used in the manufacture of dyes, drugs, and plastics. [based on Arabic *an-nīl* 'indigo', from which it was obtained]

aniline dye *n.* a synthetic dye, esp. one made from aniline.

anima *n. Psychol.* **1** the inner personality (opp. PERSONA 1). **2** Jung's term for the feminine part of a man's personality (opp. ANIMUS 4). [Latin, literally 'mind, soul']

animadvert *v.intr.* (foll. by *on*) criticize, censure (conduct, a fault, etc.). [from Latin *animadvertere* 'to turn the mind to'] □ **animadversion** *n.*

animal ● *n.* **1** a living organism which feeds on organic matter, usu. one with specialized sense organs and nervous system. **2 a** such an organism other than a human. **b** a quadruped. **3** a brutish or uncivilized person. **4** *colloq.* a person or thing of any kind (*there is no such animal*). ● *adj.* **1** characteristic of animals. **2** of animals as distinct from plants (*animal charcoal*). **3** characteristic of the physical needs of animals; carnal, sensual. [from Latin *animale* '(thing) having breath'] □ **animalize** *v.tr.* (also **-ise**)

animalism *n.* **1** the nature and activity of animals. **2** the belief that humans are not superior to other animals. **3** concern with physical matters; sensuality.

animality *n.* **1** the animal world. **2** the nature or behaviour of animals.

animal liberation *n.* the liberation of animals from exploitation by humans.

animal rights *n.pl.* the natural right of animals to live free from human exploitation (often *attrib.*: *animal rights activists*).

animate ● *adj.* **1** having life. **2** lively. ● *v.tr.* **1** enliven, make lively. **2** give life to. **3** inspire, actuate; encourage. **4** (esp. as **animated** *adj.*) *Cinematog.* give (a film, cartoon figure, etc.) the appearance of movement using animation techniques. [from Latin *animatus* 'given life']

animated *adj.* **1** lively, vigorous. **2** having life. □ **animatedly** *adv.*

animateur *n.* a person who enlivens or encourages something, esp. a promoter of artistic projects. [French]

animation *n.* **1** vivacity, ardour. **2** the state of being alive. **3** *Cinematog.* the technique of filming successive drawings or positions of puppets or models to create an illusion of movement when the film is shown as a sequence. □ **animator** *n.*

animatronics *n.pl.* (treated as *sing.*) the technique of making and operating lifelike robots. [blend of ANIMATED and ELECTRONICS] □ **animatronic** *adj.*

animism *n.* the attribution of a living soul to plants, inanimate objects, and natural phenomena. [based on Latin *anima* 'life, soul'] □ **animist** *n.* **animistic** *adj.*

animosity *n.* (*pl.* **-ies**) a spirit or feeling of strong hostility. [from Late Latin *animositas*]

animus *n.* **1** a display of animosity. **2** ill feeling. **3** a motivating spirit or feeling. **4** *Psychol.* Jung's term for the masculine part of a woman's personality (opp. ANIMA 2). [Latin, literally 'spirit, mind']

anion /an-I-ŏn/ *n. Chem.* a negatively charged ion; an ion that is attracted to the anode in electrolysis. [from Greek, literally '(thing) going up'] □ **anionic** *adj.*

anise *n.* an umbelliferous plant, *Pimpinella anisum*, having aromatic seeds. [from Greek *anison* 'anise, dill']

aniseed *n.* ► the seed of the anise, used to flavour liqueurs and sweets.

anisette *n.* a liqueur flavoured with aniseed.

ground aniseed

whole aniseed

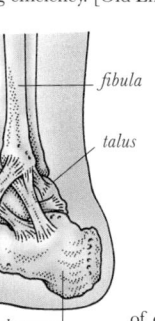
ANISEED

ankh *n.* a device consisting of a looped bar with a shorter crossbar, used in ancient Egypt as a symbol of life. [Egyptian, literally 'life, soul']

ankle ● *n.* **1** ▼ the joint connecting the foot with the leg. ▷ JOINT. **2** the part of the leg between this and the calf. ● *v.intr.* flex the ankles while cycling to increase pedalling efficiency. [Old English & Old Norse]

anklet *n.* an ornament or fetter worn round the ankle.

ankylosis *n.* (also **anchylosis**) **1** the abnormal stiffening and immobility of a joint by fusion of the bones. **2** such fusion. □ **ankylose** *v.tr. & intr.* (also **anchylose**). **ankylotic** *adj.*

annal *n.* **1** the annals of one year. **2** a record of one item in a chronicle.

annalist *n.* a writer of annals. □ **annalistic** *adj.*

tibia
fibula
ligament
ankle joint
talus
tarsal
metatarsal
cuboid   calcaneus

ANKLE JOINT IN THE HUMAN FOOT

annals *n.pl.* **1** a narrative of events year by year. **2** historical records. [from Latin *annales (libri)* 'yearly (books)']

annatto *n.* (also **anatta**, **anatto**) an orange-red dye from the pulp of a tropical fruit, used for colouring foods. [Carib name of the fruit tree]

anneal ● *v.tr.* **1** heat (metal or glass) and allow it to cool slowly, esp. to toughen it. **2** toughen. ● *n.* treatment by annealing. [Old English] □ **annealer** *n.*

annelid *n.* ▼ a segmented worm of the phylum Annelida, which includes earthworms, lugworms, etc. [based on Latin *anellus* 'little ring']

ANNELID:
EARTHWORM
(*Lumbricus terrestris*)

prostomium (head)

pygidium (tail)

segment

dorsal surface

clitellum (saddle)

annex ● *v.tr.* **1** add as a subordinate part; append. **2** incorporate (territory of another) into one's own. **3** add as a condition or consequence. **4** *colloq.* take without right. ● *n.* = ANNEXE. [based on Latin *annectere annex-* 'to bind to'] □ **annexation** *n.*

annexe *n.* esp. *Brit.* **1** a separate or added building. **2** an addition to a document. [from Latin *annexum* 'that which is joined']

annihilate *v.tr.* **1** completely destroy. **2** defeat utterly; make insignificant. [based on Latin *nihil* 'nothing'] □ **annihilation** *n.* **annihilator** *n.*

anniversary *n.* (*pl.* **-ies**) **1** the date of an event in a previous year. **2** the celebration of this. [from Latin *anniversarius*]

Anno Domini ● *adv.* in the year of our Lord, in the year of the Christian era. ● *n. colloq.* advancing age (*suffering from Anno Domini*). [Latin, literally 'in the year of the Lord']

annotate *v.tr.* add explanatory notes to (a book, document, etc.). [based on Latin *nota* 'mark'] □ **annotatable** *adj.* **annotation** *n.* **annotator** *n.*

announce *v.tr.* **1** (often foll. by *that*) make publicly known. **2** make known the arrival or imminence of (a guest, dinner, etc.). **3** be a sign of. [based on Latin *nuntius* 'messenger'] □ **announcement** *n.*

announcer *n.* a person who announces, esp. introducing programmes in broadcasting.

annoy *v.tr.* **1** cause slight anger or mental distress to. **2** (in *passive*) be somewhat angry (*am annoyed with you*). **3** harass repeatedly. [based on Latin *in odio* 'hateful'] □ **annoyance** *n.* **annoyer** *n.*

annual ● *adj.* **1** reckoned by the year. **2** occurring every year. **3** living or lasting for one year. ● *n.* **1** a book etc. published once a year. **2** a plant that lives only for a year or less. [based on Latin *annus* 'year'] □ **annually** *adv.*

annual general meeting *n. Brit.* a yearly meeting of members or shareholders.

annualized *adj.* (also **-ised**) (of rates of interest, inflation, etc.) calculated on an annual basis, as a projection from figures obtained for a shorter period.

annual ring *n.* a ring in the cross-section of a plant, esp. a tree, produced by one year's growth.

annuity *n.* (*pl.* **-ies**) **1** a yearly grant or allowance. **2** an investment of money entitling the investor to a series of equal annual sums over a stated period. [based on Latin *annuus* 'yearly'] □ **annuitant** *n.*

annul *v.tr.* (**annulled**, **annulling**) **1** declare (a marriage etc.) invalid. **2** cancel, abolish. [from Late Latin *annullare*] □ **annulment** *n.*

annular *adj.* ring-shaped. □ **annularly** *adv.*

annulate *adj.* marked with or formed of rings. □ **annulation** *n.*

annulus /*an*-yuu-lŭs/ *n.* (*pl.* **annuli**) esp. *Math.* & *Biol.* a ring. [Latin]

annunciation *n.* **1** (**Annunciation**) **a** the announcing of the Incarnation related in Luke 1:26–38. **b** the festival commemorating this on 25 March. **2 a** the act or process of announcing. **b** an announcement. □ **annunciate** *v.tr.*

annunciator *n.* **1** a device that indicates which of several electrical circuits has been activated, the position of a train, etc. **2** an announcer.

annus horribilis /ho-*ree*-bi-lis/ *n.* a horrible year. [modern Latin]

annus mirabilis /mi-*rah*-bi-lis/ *n.* a remarkable or auspicious year. [modern Latin, literally 'wonderful year']

anode *n. Electr.* **1** the positively charged electrode by which electrons leave an electrical device. **2** the negatively charged electrode of a device supplying current, for example a primary cell. [from Greek *anodos* 'way up'] □ **anodal** *adj.* **anodic** *adj.*

anodize *v.tr.* (also **-ise**) coat (a metal, esp. aluminium) with a protective oxide layer by electrolysis. □ **anodizer** *n.*

anodyne *adj.* **1** able to relieve pain. **2** mentally soothing. [from Greek *anōdunos* 'painless']

anoint *v.tr.* **1** apply oil or ointment to, esp. as a religious ceremony. **2** (usu. foll. by *with*) smear, rub. [from Latin *inungere inunct-* 'to smear oil upon'] □ **anointer** *n.*

anomalous *adj.* having an irregular or deviant feature. [from Greek *anōmalos* 'not even'] □ **anomalously** *adv.* **anomalousness** *n.*

anomaly *n.* (*pl.* **-ies**) **1** an anomalous circumstance or thing; an irregularity. **2** irregularity of motion, behaviour, etc. [from Greek *anōmalia*]

anomie *n.* (also **anomy**) lack of the usual social or ethical standards in an individual or group. [based on Greek *anomos* 'lawless'] □ **anomic** *adj.*

anon *adv. archaic* or *literary* soon, shortly (*more of this anon*). [Old English]

anon. *abbr.* anonymous; an anonymous author.

anonymous *adj.* **1** of unknown name. **2** of unknown or undeclared source or authorship. **3** without character; featureless, impersonal. [from Greek *anōnumos* 'nameless'] □ **anonymity** *n.* **anonymously** *adv.*

anopheles /ă-*nof*-i-leez/ *n.* a mosquito of the genus Anopheles, which includes many that are carriers of the malarial parasite. [from Greek *anōphelēs* 'unprofitable']

anorak *n.* **1** a waterproof jacket of cloth or plastic, usu. with a hood, of a kind originally used in polar regions. **2** *colloq. derog.* a boring, studious, or socially inept person with unfashionable interests. [from Greenland Eskimo *anoraq*]

anorexia *n.* **1** a lack or loss of appetite for food. **2** (in full **anorexia nervosa**) a psychological illness characterized by an obsessive desire to lose weight by refusing to eat. [from Greek, literally 'lack of appetite'] □ **anorexic** *adj.* & *n.* (also **anorectic**).

anosmia *n.* the loss of the sense of smell. [based on Greek *osmē* 'smell'] □ **anosmic** *adj.*

another ● *det.* **1** an additional; one more (*have another cake*). **2** a person comparable to (*another Callas*). **3** a different (*quite another matter*). **4** some or any other (*will not do another man's work*). ● *pron.* **1** an additional one (*have another*). **2** a different one (*take this book away and bring me another*). **3** some or any other one (*I love another*). **4** *Brit.* an unnamed additional party to a legal action (*X versus Y and another*). **5** (usu. **A. N. Other**) *Brit.* a player unnamed or not yet selected. □ **such another** another of the same sort. [Middle English]

anovulant *Pharm.* ● *n.* a drug preventing ovulation. ● *adj.* preventing ovulation. [related to OVULATE]

anschluss *n.* a unification, esp. (**Anschluss**) the annexation of Austria by Germany in 1938. [German, from *anschliessen* 'join']

ANSI *abbr.* American National Standards Institute.

answer ● *n.* **1** something said or done in reaction to a question, statement, or circumstance. **2** the solution to a problem. ● *v.* **1** *tr.* (also *absol.*) make an answer to (*answer me*). **2** *tr.* respond to the summons or signal of (*answer the telephone*). **3** *tr.* be satisfactory for (a purpose or need). **4** *intr.* (foll. by *for, to*) be responsible (*you will answer to me for your conduct*). **5** *intr.* (foll. by *to*) correspond, esp. to a description. **6** *intr.* be satisfactory or successful. □ **answer back** answer a rebuke etc. impudently. **answer to the name of** be called. [Old English *andswarian* 'to swear against (charge)'] □ **answerable** *adj.*

answering machine *n.* a tape recorder which supplies a recorded answer to a telephone call.

answering service *n.* a business that receives and answers telephone calls for its clients.

answerphone *n. Brit.* a telephone answering machine.

ant ● *n.* ▼ any small insect of the widely distributed hymenopterous family Formicidae, living in complex social colonies, wingless (except for adults at the time of mating), and proverbial for industry. ● *v.intr.* & *refl.* (usu. as **anting** *n.*) (of a bird) place or rub ants on the feathers to repel parasites. □ **have ants in one's pants** *colloq.* be fidgety or restless. [Old English]

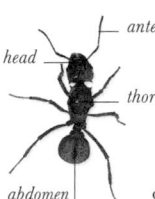

antenna

head

thorax

abdomen

ANT

ant- assim. form of ANTI- before a vowel or *h* (*Antarctic*).

antacid ● *n.* a substance that prevents or corrects acidity esp. in the stomach. ● *adj.* having these properties.

antagonist *n.* **1** an opponent or adversary. **2** *Biol.* a substance or organ that partially or completely opposes the action of another. [based on Greek *agōn* 'contest'] □ **antagonism** *n.* **antagonistic** *adj.* **antagonistically** *adv.*

antagonize *v.tr.* (also **-ise**) **1** evoke hostility or opposition in. **2** (of one force etc.) counteract or tend to neutralize (another). [from Greek *antagōnizesthai* 'to struggle against'] □ **antagonization** *n.*

Antarctic ● *adj.* of the south polar regions. ● *n.* these regions. [from Greek *antarktikos*]

Antarctic Circle *n.* ◄ the parallel of latitude 66° 33' S., forming an imaginary line round the Antarctic regions.

Antarctic Ocean *n.* = SOUTHERN OCEAN.

ant-bear *n.* = AARDVARK.

ante ● *n.* **1** a stake put up by a player in poker etc. before receiving cards. **2** (esp. in phr. **up the ante**) an amount to be paid in advance; a stake. ● *v.tr.* (**antes**, **anted**) **1** put up as an ante. **2 a** bet, stake. **b** (foll. by *up*) pay. [Latin, literally 'before']

ante- *prefix* forming nouns and adjectives meaning 'before, preceding' (*ante-room*; *antenatal*; *ante-post*). [Latin, literally 'before']

anteater *n.* ▼ a mammal that feeds on ants and termites, esp. one of the edentate family Myrmecophagidae, with a long snout and sticky tongue.

ANTEATER:
GIANT ANTEATER
(*Myrmecophaga tridactyla*)

Antarctic Circle

Antarctic regions

ANTARCTIC CIRCLE

A

antecedent • *n.* **1** a preceding thing or circumstance. **2** *Gram.* a word or phrase etc. to which a later word (esp. a relative pronoun) refers. **3** (in *pl.*) past history, esp. of a person. • *adj.* **1** (often foll. by *to*) previous. **2** presumptive, a priori. [from Latin *antecedent-* 'going before'] □ **antecedence** *n.* **antecedently** *adv.*

antechamber *n.* a small room leading to a main one. [from Italian *anticamera*]

antedate • *v.tr.* **1** exist or occur at a date earlier than. **2** assign an earlier date to (a document, event, etc.). • *n.* a date earlier than the actual one.

antediluvian *adj.* **1** of or belonging to the time before the biblical Flood. **2** *colloq.* very old or out of date. [based on Latin *diluvium* 'deluge']

antelope *n.* (*pl.* same or **antelopes**) **1** a deerlike ruminant of the family Bovidae, mainly found in Africa, e.g. gazelles, gnus, kudus, and impala. **2** leather made from the skin of any of these. **3** *N. Amer.* = PRONGHORN. [from late Greek *antholops*]

antenatal *adj.* esp. *Brit.* **1** existing or occurring before birth. **2** relating to the period of pregnancy.

antenna *n.* **1** (*pl.* **antennae** /-nee/) *Zool.* ◀ each of a pair of mobile appendages on the heads of insects, crustaceans, etc., sensitive to touch and taste; a feeler. ▷ CRUSTACEAN, HOUSEFLY. **2** (*pl.* **antennas**) = AERIAL *n.* [Latin, literally 'yard (of a ship)', used in pl. to translate Greek *keraioi* 'horns (of insects)'] □ **antennal** *adj.* (in sense 1). **antennary** *adj.* (in sense 1).

ANTENNAE
OF A BEETLE
(*Simianellus cyaneicollis*) **antenuptial** *adj.* esp. *Brit.* existing or occurring before marriage. [from Late Latin *antenuptialis*]

antepenultimate *adj.* last but two.

anterior *adj.* **1** nearer the front. **2** (often foll. by *to*) earlier, prior. [based on Latin *ante* 'before'] □ **anteriority** *n.* **anteriorly** *adv.*

ante-room *n.* **1** a small room leading to a main one. **2** *Mil.* a sitting room in an officers' mess.

antheap *n.* = ANTHILL.

anthelmintic • *n.* (also **anthelminthic**) any drug or agent used to destroy parasitic, esp. intestinal worms, e.g. tapeworms, roundworms, and flukes. • *adj.* having the power to eliminate or destroy parasitic worms. [based on Greek *helmins helminthos* 'worm']

anthem *n.* **1** an elaborate choral composition usu. based on a passage of scripture for church use. **2 a** a solemn hymn of praise etc., esp. = NATIONAL ANTHEM. **b** a popular song that is identified with a person, group, etc. (*rock anthem*). **3** a composition sung antiphonally. [from Late Latin *antiphona* 'antiphon']

anther *n.* *Bot.* ▶ the apical portion of a stamen containing pollen. ▷ FLOWER. [based on Greek *anthos* 'flower'] □ **antheral** *adj.*

anthill *n.* **1** a moundlike nest built by ants or termites. **2** a community teeming with people.

anthology *n.* (*pl.* **-ies**) a published collection (of poems), songs, reproductions of paintings, etc. [from Greek *anthologia*] □ **anthologist** *n.* **anthologize** *v.tr. & intr.* (also **-ise**)

anthozoan • *n.* a sessile marine cnidarian of the class Anthozoa which includes anemones, corals, and sea pens. ▷ CNIDARIAN. • *adj.* of or relating to this class. [modern Latin *Anthozoa*, from Greek *anthos* 'flower' + *zōia* 'animals']

anthracite *n.* coal of a hard variety containing relatively pure carbon and burning with little smoke. ▷ COAL. [from Greek *anthrakitis*, a kind of coal] □ **anthracitic** *adj.*

anthrax *n.* a fatal bacterial disease of sheep and cattle, transmissible to humans. [originally in sense 'carbuncle': from Greek]

anthropic principle *n.* the cosmological principle that theories of the origin of the universe are constrained by the necessity to allow individual human existence.

anthropo- *comb. form* human, humankind. [from Greek *anthrōpos* 'human being']

anthropocentric *adj.* regarding humankind as the centre of existence. □ **anthropocentrism** *n.*

anthropogenesis *n.* the study of the origin of man.

anthropoid • *adj.* **1** resembling a human being in form, esp. (of an ape) tailless and often bipedal. **2** of or relating to the primate suborder Anthropoidea, which includes monkeys, apes, and humans. ▷ PRIMATE. **3** *colloq.* (of a person) apelike. • *n.* a being that is human in form only.

anthropology *n.* **1** the study of humankind. **2** the study of the structure and evolution of humans as animals. □ **anthropological** *adj.* **anthropologist** *n.*

anthropomorphism *n.* the attribution of a human form or personality to a god, animal, or thing. [based on Greek *morphē* 'form'] □ **anthropomorphic** *adj.* **anthropomorphically** *adv.* **anthropomorphize** *v.tr.* (also **-ise**)

anthropomorphous *adj.* human in form.

anthropophagy *n.* the eating of human flesh; cannibalism. [based on Greek *phagein* 'to eat'] □ **anthropophagous** *adj.*

anti • *prep.* (also *absol.*) opposed to (*is anti everything*). • *n.* (*pl.* **antis**) a person opposed to a particular policy etc. [from Greek, literally 'against']

anti- *prefix* (also **ant-** before a vowel or *h*) forming nouns and adjectives meaning: **1** opposed to; against (*antivivisectionism*). **2** preventing (*antiscorbutic*). **3** the opposite of (*anticlimax*). **4** rival (*antipope*). **5** unlike the conventional form (*anti-hero*). **6** *Physics* the antiparticle of a specified particle (*antiproton*).

anti-abortion *attrib.adj.* opposing abortion. □ **anti-abortionist** *n.*

anti-aircraft *attrib.adj.* (of a gun, missile, etc.) used to attack enemy aircraft.

antibacterial *adj.* active against bacteria.

antibiotic *n.* *Pharm.* any of various substances (e.g. penicillin) produced by micro-organisms or made synthetically, that can inhibit or destroy susceptible micro-organisms. [from French *antibiotique*, based on Greek *biōtikos* 'fit for life']

antibody *n.* (*pl.* **-ies**) any of a class of blood proteins (immunoglobulins) produced in response to and counteracting antigens.

antic *n.* **1** (usu. in *pl.*) absurd or foolish behaviour. **2** an absurd or silly action. [from Italian *antico* 'antique']

Antichrist *n.* **1** an arch-enemy of Christ. **2** a postulated personal opponent of Christ expected by the early Church to appear before the end of the world.

anticipate *v.tr.* **1** be aware of in advance and act accordingly (*anticipated his opponent's moves*). **2** *disp.* expect (*did not anticipate any difficulty*). **3** forestall (*was about to announce the discovery but was anticipated by his pupil*). **4** look forward to (*I anticipated the interview with pleasure*). **5** cause (a future event) to happen earlier. [based on Latin *anticipatus* 'taken beforehand'] □ **anticipation** *n.* **anticipative** *adj.* **anticipatory** *adj.*

■ **Usage** The use of *anticipate* in sense 2 above is well established in informal use, but is regarded as incorrect by some people.

anticlerical • *adj.* opposed to the influence of the clergy, esp. in politics. • *n.* an anticlerical person. □ **anticlericalism** *n.*

ANTHER: LILY
FLOWER SHOWING
ANTHERS
filament
style   *anther*
stamen

anticlimax *n.* a trivial conclusion to something significant, esp. where a climax was expected. □ **anticlimactic** *adj.*

anticline *n.* *Geol.* ▼ a ridge or fold of stratified rock in which the strata slope down from the crest. [based on Greek *klinein* 'to lean'] □ **anticlinal** *adj.*

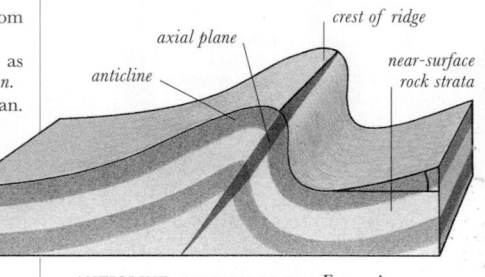

crest of ridge
axial plane
anticline
near-surface rock strata

ANTICLINE: SECTION OF THE EARTH'S CRUST
SHOWING THE STRUCTURE OF AN ANTICLINE

anticlockwise *Brit.* • *adv.* in a curve opposite in direction to the movement of the hands of a clock. • *adj.* moving anticlockwise.

anticoagulant • *n.* any drug or agent that retards or inhibits coagulation, esp. of the blood. • *adj.* retarding or inhibiting coagulation.

anticonvulsant • *n.* any drug or agent that prevents or reduces the severity of convulsions. • *adj.* preventing or reducing convulsions.

anticyclone *n.* a system of winds rotating outwards from an area of high barometric pressure, producing fine weather. □ **anticyclonic** *adj.*

antidepressant *n.* any drug or agent that alleviates depression.

antidote *n.* (often foll. by *to*, *for*, *against*) **1** a medicine etc. taken or given to counteract poison. **2** anything that counteracts something unpleasant or evil (*antidote to jet lag*). [from Greek *antidoton* '(thing) given against'] □ **antidotal** *adj.*

anti-establishment *adj.* (also **anti-Establishment**) against the Establishment or established authority.

antifreeze *n.* a substance (usu. ethylene glycol) added to water to lower its freezing point, esp. in the radiator of a motor vehicle.

antigen *n.* a foreign substance (e.g. a toxin) which induces an immune response in the body, esp. the production of antibodies. [German] □ **antigenic** *adj.*

anti-gravity • *n.* *Physics* a hypothetical force opposing gravity. • *adj.* (of clothing for an astronaut etc.) designed to counteract the effects of high acceleration.

anti-hero *n.* (*pl.* **-oes**) a central character in a story or drama who notably lacks conventional heroic attributes.

antihistamine *n.* a substance that counteracts the effects of histamine, used esp. in the treatment of allergies.

anti-inflammatory • *adj.* (of a drug etc.) reducing inflammation. • *n.* (*pl.* **-ies**) an anti-inflammatory drug.

anti-lock *attrib.adj.* (of brakes) set up so as to prevent locking and skidding if applied suddenly.

antilog *n.* = ANTILOGARITHM. [abbreviation]

antilogarithm *n.* the number to which a logarithm belongs (*100 is the common antilogarithm of 2*).

antimacassar *n.* a decorative protective covering put over the back of a chair. [based on *Macassar*, a kind of hair oil]

antimatter *n.* *Physics* matter composed solely of antiparticles.

antimony *n.* *Chem.* a brittle silvery-white metallic element used esp. in alloys with lead. [from medieval Latin *antimonium*] □ **antimonial** *adj.* **antimonic** *adj.* **antimonious** *adj.*

antinode *n.* *Physics* the position of maximum displacement in a standing wave system.

antinomian ● *adj.* of or relating to the view that Christians are released from the obligation of observing the moral law. [from medieval Latin *Antinomi*, name of a sect in Germany (1535)] □ **antinomianism** *n.*

antinomy /an-tin-ŏ-mi/ *n.* (*pl.* **-ies**) 1 a contradiction between two beliefs or conclusions that are in themselves reasonable; a paradox. 2 a conflict between two laws or authorities. [from Latin *antinomia*, based on Greek *nomos* 'law']

anti-nuclear *adj.* opposed to the development of nuclear weapons or nuclear power.

antioxidant *n.* 1 *Chem.* an agent that inhibits oxidation, esp. used to counteract deterioration of stored food products. 2 *Biol.* a substance (e.g. vitamin C or E) that removes potentially damaging oxidizing agents in a living organism.

antiparticle *n. Physics* a subatomic particle having the same mass as a given particle but opposite electric or magnetic properties.

antipasto *n.* (*pl.* **antipasti**) an hors d'oeuvre, esp. in an Italian meal. [Italian]

antipathy *n.* (*pl.* **-ies**) (often foll. by *to*, *for*, *between*) a strong or deep-seated aversion or dislike. [based on Greek *antipathēs* 'opposed in feeling'] □ **antipathetic** *adj.* **antipathetically** *adv.*

anti-personnel *attrib.adj.* (of a bomb, mine, etc.) designed to kill or injure people rather than to damage buildings or equipment.

antiperspirant ● *n.* a substance applied to the skin to prevent or reduce perspiration. ● *adj.* that acts as an antiperspirant.

antiphon *n.* 1 a hymn or psalm, the parts of which are sung or recited alternately by two groups. 2 a versicle or phrase from this. [ecclesiastical Latin *antiphona*, from Greek *phōnē* 'sound'] □ **antiphonal** *adj.* & *n.* **antiphonally** *adv.*

antiphonary *n.* (*pl.* **-ies**) a book of antiphons. [ecclesiastical Latin *antiphonarium* (as ANTIPHON)]

antiphony *n.* (*pl.* **-ies**) 1 antiphonal singing or chanting. 2 a response or echo.

antipodes /an-tip-ŏ-deez/ *n.pl.* 1 a (also **Antipodes**) a place diametrically opposite to another, esp. Australasia relative to Europe. b places diametrically opposite to each other. 2 (usu. foll. by *of*, *to*) the exact opposite. [from Greek *antipodes* 'having the feet opposite'] □ **antipodal** *adj.* **antipodean** *adj.* & *n.*

antipope *n.* a person set up as pope in opposition to one (held by others to be) canonically chosen.

antiproton *n. Physics* the negatively charged antiparticle of a proton.

antipruritic ● *adj.* relieving itching. ● *n.* an antipruritic drug or agent.

antipyretic ● *adj.* preventing or reducing fever. ● *n.* an antipyretic drug or agent.

antiquarian ● *adj.* 1 of or dealing in antiques or rare books. 2 of the study of antiquities. ● *n.* an antiquary. □ **antiquarianism** *n.*

antiquary *n.* (*pl.* **-ies**) a student or collector of antiques or antiquities. [from Latin *antiquarius*]

antiquated *adj.* old-fashioned; out of date.

antique ● *n.* an object of considerable age, esp. an item of furniture or the decorative arts having a high value. ● *adj.* 1 of or existing from an early date. 2 old-fashioned, archaic. 3 of ancient times. [from Latin *antiquus* 'former, ancient']

antiquity *n.* (*pl.* **-ies**) 1 ancient times, esp. the period before the Middle Ages. 2 great age (*a city of great antiquity*). 3 (usu. in *pl.*) physical remains or relics from ancient times, esp. buildings and works of art. 4 (in *pl.*) customs, events, etc., of ancient times. [related to ANTIQUE]

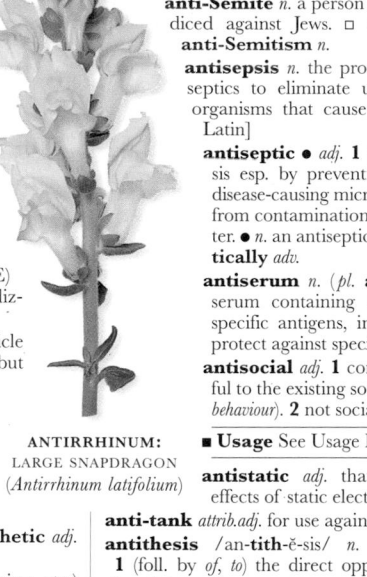

ANTIRRHINUM:
LARGE SNAPDRAGON
(*Antirrhinum latifolium*)

antirrhinum *n.* ◄ a plant of the genus *Antirrhinum* (figwort family), with tubular two-lipped flowers. [based on Greek *rhis rhinos* 'nose', from the resemblance of the flower to an animal's snout]

antiscorbutic *adj.* preventing or curing scurvy.

anti-Semite *n.* a person hostile to or prejudiced against Jews. □ **anti-Semitic** *adj.* **anti-Semitism** *n.*

antisepsis *n.* the process of using antiseptics to eliminate undesirable microorganisms that cause disease. [modern Latin]

antiseptic ● *adj.* 1 counteracting sepsis esp. by preventing the growth of disease-causing micro-organisms. 2 free from contamination. 3 lacking character. ● *n.* an antiseptic agent. □ **antiseptically** *adv.*

antiserum *n.* (*pl.* **antisera**) a blood serum containing antibodies against specific antigens, injected to treat or protect against specific diseases.

antisocial *adj.* 1 contrary to or harmful to the existing social order (*antisocial behaviour*). 2 not sociable.

■ **Usage** See Usage Note at UNSOCIABLE.

antistatic *adj.* that counteracts the effects of static electricity.

anti-tank *attrib.adj.* for use against tanks.

antithesis /an-tith-ĕ-sis/ *n.* (*pl.* **antitheses**) 1 (foll. by *of*, *to*) the direct opposite. 2 (usu. foll. by *of*, *between*) contrast or opposition between two things, ideas, etc. [based on Greek *antitithenai* 'to set against'] □ **antithetical** *adj.* (also **antithetic**). **antithetically** *adv.*

antitoxin *n.* an antibody that counteracts a toxin. □ **antitoxic** *adj.*

antitrades *n.pl.* winds that blow in the opposite direction to (and usu. above) a trade wind.

antiviral *adj.* effective against viruses.

antivivisectionism *n.* opposition to vivisection. □ **antivivisectionist** *n.* & *adj.*

antler *n.* 1 each of the branched horns of a usu. male deer. ▷ DEER. 2 a branch of this. [variant of Old French *antoillier*] □ **antlered** *adj.*

ant-lion *n.* ▼ a dragonfly-like neuropterous insect with predatory larvae which trap other insects in conical pits.

antenna

double pair of wings   *long, delicate thorax*

ANT-LION
(*Palpares libelluloides*)

antonym *n.* a word opposite in meaning to another in the same language (e.g. *bad* and *good*). [from French *antonyme*] □ **antonymous** *adj.*

antrum *n.* (*pl.* **antra**) *Anat.* 1 a natural chamber or cavity in the body, esp. in a bone. 2 the part of the stomach just inside its opening into the duodenum. [Latin] □ **antral** *adj.*

ant's eggs *n.pl. colloq.* the pupae of ants.

anuran ● *n.* any tailless amphibian of the order Anura, including frogs and toads. ▷ FROG, TOAD. ● *adj.* of or relating to this order. [based on Greek *oura* 'tail']

anus *n. Anat.* the excretory opening at the end of the alimentary canal. ▷ INTESTINE. [Latin]

anvil *n.* a block (usu. of iron) with a flat top, concave sides, and often a pointed end, on which metals are worked in forging. [Old English]

anxiety *n.* (*pl.* **-ies**) 1 the state of being anxious. 2 concern about an imminent or future difficulty, etc. 3 (foll. by *for*, or *to* + infin.) anxious desire. 4 *Psychol.* a nervous disorder characterized by a state of excessive uneasiness. [related to ANXIOUS]

anxious *adj.* 1 uneasy in the mind. 2 causing or marked by anxiety (*an anxious moment*). 3 (foll. by *for*, or *to* + infin.) earnestly or uneasily wanting (*anxious to please*). [from Latin *anxius*, based on *angere* 'to choke'] □ **anxiously** *adv.* **anxiousness** *n.*

any ● *det.* 1 (with *interrog.*, *neg.*, or conditional expressed or implied) a one, no matter which, of several (*cannot find any answer*; *are there any good films on?*). b some, no matter how much or many or of what sort (*if any books arrive*; *have you any sugar?*). 2 a minimal amount of (*hardly any difference*). 3 whichever might be chosen (*any fool knows that*). 4 a an appreciable (*did not stay for any length of time*). b a very large (*has any amount of money*). ● *pron.* 1 any one (*did not know any of them*). 2 any number (*are any of them yours?*). 3 any amount (*is there any left?*). ● *adv.* (usu. with *neg.* or *interrog.*) at all; in some degree (*is that any good?*; *without being any the wiser*). □ **any more** to any further extent (*don't like you any more*). [Old English]

■ **Usage** The pronoun *any* can be used with either a singular or a plural verb depending on the context (see examples above).

anybody *n.* & *pron.* 1 a a person, no matter who. b a person of any kind. c whatever person is chosen. 2 a person of importance (*are you anybody?*).

anyhow *adv.* 1 anyway. 2 in a disorderly manner or state (*does his work anyhow*; *things are all anyhow*).

anymore *adv.* esp. *N. Amer.* = any more (see ANY).

anyone *pron.* anybody.

■ **Usage** *Anyone* is written as two words to imply a numerical sense, as in *Any one of us can do it.*

anyplace *adv. N. Amer. colloq.* anywhere.

any road *adv. esp. N.Engl.* = ANYWAY 2, 3.

anything *pron.* 1 a thing, no matter which. 2 a thing of any kind. 3 whatever thing is chosen. □ **anything but** not at all (*was anything but honest*).

anyway *adv.* 1 (also **any way**) in any way or manner. 2 in any case. 3 to resume (*anyway, as I was saying*).

anyways *adv. N. Amer. colloq.* or *dial.* = ANYWAY.

anywhere ● *adv.* in or to any place. ● *pron.* any place (*anywhere will do*).

Anzac *n.* 1 a soldier in the Australian and New Zealand Army Corps (1914–18). 2 a person from Australia or New Zealand. [acronym]

Anzac Day *n.* (in Australia and New Zealand) the day (25 April) commemorating the Anzac landing at Gallipoli in 1915.

AOB *abbr. Brit.* any other business.

A-OK *abbr. N. Amer. colloq.* excellent; in good order. [from *all systems OK*]

aorist *Gram.* ● *n.* an unqualified past tense of a verb, without reference to duration or completion. ● *adj.* of or designating this tense. [from Greek *aoristos* 'indefinite']

aorta *n.* (*pl.* **aortas**) the main artery of the body, supplying oxygenated blood to the circulatory system, in humans passing over the heart from the left ventricle and running down in front of the backbone. ▷ CARDIOVASCULAR, HEART. [from Greek *aortē*] □ **aortic** *adj.*

apace *adv. literary* swiftly, quickly. [from Old French *à pas* 'at (a considerable) pace']

Apache ● *n.* 1 /ă-pach-i/ a (*pl.* same or **Apaches**) a member of a N. American Indian people of New Mexico and Arizona. b the language of this people. 2 (**apache** /ă-pash/) (*pl.* **apaches** *pronunc.* same) a violent street ruffian, originally in Paris. ● *adj.* /ă-pach-i/ of or relating to the Apache or their language. [Mexican Spanish]

A

apart *adv.* **1** separately; not together (*keep your feet apart*). **2** into pieces (*came apart in my hands*). **3 a** to or on one side. **b** out of consideration (placed after noun: *joking apart*). **4** to or at a distance. □ **apart from** excepting; not considering. [from French *à part* 'to one side'] □ **apartness** *n.*

apartheid /ă-**par**-tayt/ *n. hist.* (esp. in S. Africa) a policy or system of segregation or discrimination on grounds of race. [Afrikaans]

apartment *n.* **1** (in *pl.*) a suite of rooms. **2** a single room in a house. **3** *N. Amer.* **a** a flat. **b** = APARTMENT BUILDING. [from Italian *appartamento*, based on *a parte* 'apart']

apartment building *n. N. Amer.* a block of flats.

apartment house *n.* esp. *US* = APARTMENT BUILDING.

apathetic *adj.* having no emotion or interest. □ **apathetically** *adv.*

apathy *n.* lack of interest or feeling. [from Greek *apatheia* 'absence of feeling']

apatosaurus *n.* ▼ a huge plant-eating dinosaur of the genus *Apatosaurus* (formerly *Brontosaurus*), of the Jurassic and Cretaceous periods, with a long tail and trunklike legs. [from Greek *apatē* 'deceit' + *sauros* 'lizard']

APATOSAURUS

ape ● *n.* **1** any of the various primates of the family Pongidae characterized by the absence of a tail. **2** (in general use) any monkey. **3 a** an imitator. **b** an apelike person. ● *v.tr.* imitate, mimic. □ **go ape** *slang* become crazy. [Old English]

apeman *n.* (*pl.* **-men**) any of various extinct apelike primates held to be related to present-day humans.

aperçu *n.* **1** a summary or survey. **2** an insight. [French]

aperient ● *adj.* laxative. ● *n.* a laxative medicine. [from Latin *aperient-* 'opening']

aperiodic *adj.* **1** not periodic; irregular. **2** (of an oscillation or vibration) without a regular period.

aperitif *n.* an alcoholic drink taken before a meal to stimulate the appetite. [based on Latin *aperire* 'to open']

aperture *n.* **1** a gap. **2** ▼ a space through which light passes in an optical or photographic instrument. ▷ CAMERA. [based on Latin *aperire* ' to open']

APERTURE

The iris in a camera lens alters the size of the aperture through which light falls on to photographic film. A wide aperture, indicated by a low f-number, lets in the most light, but reduces the depth of field (the range of the subject that is in focus). Conversely, a small aperture, indicated by a higher f-number, lets little light in, but allows the greatest depth of field.

EXTRA-WIDE APERTURE (F/2.8)

WIDE APERTURE (F/4)

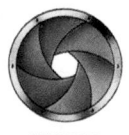

MEDIUM APERTURE (F/8)

Apex *n.* (also **APEX**) (often *attrib.*) a system of reduced fares for scheduled airline flights when paid for before a certain period in advance of departure. [acronym from *Advance Purchase Excursion*]

apex *n.* (*pl.* **apexes** or **apices** /**ay**-pi-seez/) **1** the highest point. **2** a climax. **3** the vertex of a triangle or cone. **4** a tip or pointed end. [Latin, literally 'peak, tip']

aphasia *n. Med.* the loss of ability to understand or express speech, owing to brain damage. [Greek, based on *aphatos* 'speechless'] □ **aphasic** *adj. & n.*

aphelion *n.* (*pl.* **aphelia**) the point in the orbit of a planet, comet, etc., at which it is furthest from the Sun. [based on Greek *aph' hēliou* 'from the Sun']

aphid *n.* a small insect of the family Aphididae, feeding by sucking sap from leaves, stems, or roots of plants. ▷ HEMIPTERA

aphis *n.* (*pl.* **aphides**) an aphid, esp. of the genus *Aphis* which includes the greenfly. [modern Latin]

aphorism *n.* a short pithy maxim. [from Greek *aphorismos* 'definition'] □ **aphoristic** *adj.*

aphrodisiac ● *adj.* that arouses sexual desire. ● *n.* an aphrodisiac drug. [based on Greek *Aphroditē*, goddess of love]

apiary *n.* (*pl.* **-ies**) a place where bees are kept. ▷ BEEHIVE. [based on Latin *apis* 'bee']

apical *adj.* of, at, or forming an apex. [related to APEX]

apices *pl.* of APEX.

apiculture *n.* bee-keeping. [based on Latin *apis* 'bee'] □ **apicultural** *adj.* **apiculturist** *n.*

apiece *adv.* for each one; severally (*had five pounds apiece*).

apish *adj.* **1** of or like an ape. **2** silly. □ **apishly** *adv.* **apishness** *n.*

aplenty *adv.* in plenty.

aplomb *n.* assurance; self-confidence. [French, literally 'perpendicularity']

apnoea /ap-**nee**-ă/ *n.* (*US* **apnea**) *Med.* a temporary cessation of breathing. [based on Greek *apnous* 'breathless']

apo- *prefix* **1** away from (*apogee*). **2** separate.

apocalypse *n.* **1** (**the Apocalypse**) = REVELATION 3. **2** a revelation. **3** a grand or violent event resembling those described in the Apocalypse. [based on Greek *apokaluptein* 'to uncover, disclose']

apocalyptic *adj.* **1** of or resembling the Apocalypse. **2** revelatory, prophetic.

Apocrypha *n.pl.* (also treated as *sing.*) **1** biblical writings not forming part of the accepted canon. **2** (**apocrypha**) writings or reports not considered genuine. [from ecclesiastical Latin *apocrypha (scripta)* 'hidden (writings)']

■ **Usage** The Old Testament Apocrypha include those writings appearing in the Septuagint and Vulgate versions but not in the Hebrew Bible; they are accepted by the Roman Catholic Church as the 'deuterocanonical' books.

apocryphal *adj.* **1** of doubtful authenticity. **2** invented, mythical (*an apocryphal story*). **3** of or belonging to the Apocrypha.

apogee *n.* **1** the point in a body's orbit at which it is furthest from the Earth (opp. PERIGEE). **2** the most distant or highest point. [from Greek *apogeion* 'away from Earth']

apolitical *adj.* not interested in or concerned with politics.

apologetic ● *adj.* **1** regretfully acknowledging an offence. **2** diffident. **3** of reasoned defence. ● *n.* (usu. in *pl.*) a reasoned defence. [based on

Greek *apologeisthai* 'to speak in defence'] □ **apologetically** *adv.*

apologia *n.* a formal defence of one's opinions or conduct. [Latin]

apologist *n.* a person who defends something by argument.

apologize *v.intr.* (also **-ise**) make an apology.

apologue *n.* a moral fable. [from Greek *apologos* 'story']

apology *n.* (*pl.* **-ies**) **1** a regretful acknowledgement of an offence. **2** an assurance that no offence was intended. **3** an explanation or defence. **4** (foll. by *for*) a poor specimen of (*this apology for a letter*). [from Greek *apologia* 'speech in defence']

apolune *n.* the point at which a body orbiting the Moon is furthest from it (opp. PERILUNE). [based on Latin *luna* 'Moon', on the pattern of *apogee*]

apophthegm /**ap**-ŏ-th'em/ *n.* (*US* also **apothegm**) a terse saying or maxim, an aphorism. [from Greek *apophthegma* 'something clearly spoken'] □ **apophthegmatic** *adj.*

apoplectic *adj.* **1** of, causing, suffering, or liable to apoplexy. **2** *colloq.* enraged. [based on Greek *apoplēssein* 'to strike completely']

apoplexy *n.* **1** *Med.* = STROKE *n.* 2. **2** *colloq.* a rush of extreme emotion, esp. anger. [from Greek *apoplēxia*]

aporia *n.* **1** *Rhet.* an expression of doubt. **2** a perplexing difficulty. [based on Greek *aporos* 'impassable']

apostasy *n.* (*pl.* **-ies**) **1** renunciation of a belief or faith. **2** abandonment of principles or of a party. **3** an instance of apostasy. [from Greek *apostasis* 'defection']

apostate ● *n.* a person who renounces a belief etc. ● *adj.* engaged in apostasy. [from Greek *apostatēs* 'deserter']

apostatize *v.intr.* (also **-ise**) renounce a former belief etc.

a posteriori ● *adj.* (of reasoning) inductive, empirical; proceeding from effects to causes. ● *adv.* inductively, empirically; from effects to causes. [Latin, literally 'from what comes after']

apostle *n.* **1 a** (**Apostle**) each of the twelve chief disciples of Jesus Christ. **b** any of a number of early Christian teachers ranked with these. **c** the first successful Christian missionary in a country or to a people. **2** a leader or outstanding figure, esp. of a reform movement (*apostle of temperance*). **3** a messenger or representative. [from Greek *apostolos* 'messenger']

apostolate *n.* **1** the position or authority of an Apostle. **2** leadership in reform.

apostolic *adj.* **1** of or relating to the Apostles. **2** of the Pope regarded as the successor of St Peter. **3** of the character of an Apostle.

apostolic succession *n.* the uninterrupted transmission of spiritual authority from the Apostles through successive popes and bishops.

apostrophe[1] /ă-**pos**-trŏ-fi/ *n.* a punctuation mark used to indicate: **1** the omission of letters or numbers (e.g. *can't*; *1 Jan. '92*). **2** the possessive case (e.g. *Harry's book*). [from Greek *apostrophos* 'accent of elision']

apostrophe[2] /ă-**pos**-trŏ-fi/ *n.* an exclamatory passage in a speech or poem, addressed to a person or thing. [from Greek, literally 'a turning away'] □ **apostrophize** *v.tr. & intr.* (also **-ise**)

apothecaries' measure *n.* (also **apothecaries' weight**) *hist.* units of weight and liquid volume formerly used in pharmacy (12 ounces = one pound; 20 fluid ounces = one pint).

apothecary *n.* (*pl.* **-ies**) *archaic* a chemist licensed to dispense medicines. [based on Greek *apothēkē* 'storehouse']

apothegm *US* var. of APOPHTHEGM.

apotheosis *n.* (*pl.* **apotheoses**) **1** elevation to divine status; deification. **2** a glorification of a thing; a sublime example (*apotheosis of the dance*). [based on Greek *apotheoun* 'to deify']

apotheosize *v.tr.* (also **-ise**) **1** make divine; deify. **2** idealize, glorify.

apotropaic *adj.* supposedly having the power to avert an evil influence. [from Greek *apotropaios*, based on *trepein* 'to turn']

appal *v.tr.* (*US* **appall**) (**appalled**, **appalling**) **1** greatly dismay. **2** (as **appalling** *adj.*) *colloq.* shocking; unpleasant; bad. [from Old French *apalir* 'to grow pale'] □ **appallingly** *adv.*

apparatus *n.* **1** the equipment needed for a particular purpose or function. **2** a complex organization. [based on Latin *adparare adparat-* 'to make ready for']

apparel *n. US* or *formal* clothing, dress. [from Old French *apareillier*]

apparent *adj.* **1** readily visible or perceivable. **2** seeming. [from Latin *apparent-* 'appearing'] □ **apparently** *adv.*

apparent magnitude *n.* the magnitude, i.e. brightness, of a celestial object as seen from the Earth.

apparition *n.* a sudden or dramatic appearance; a visible ghost. [related to APPEAR]

appeal ● *v.* **1** *intr.* make an earnest request; plead (*appealed for calm; appealed to us not to leave*). **2** *intr.* be attractive or of interest; be pleasing. **3** *intr.* (foll. by *to*) resort to or cite for support. **4** *Law* **a** *intr.* apply (to a higher court) for a reconsideration of the decision of a lower court. **b** *tr.* refer to a higher court to review (a case). **c** *intr.* (foll. by *against*) apply to a higher court to reconsider (a verdict or sentence). **5** *intr. Cricket* call on the umpire for a decision on whether a batsman is out. ● *n.* **1** the act or an instance of appealing. **2** a formal or urgent request for public support for a cause. **3** *Law* the referral of a case to a higher court. **4** attractiveness; appealing quality (*sex appeal*). [from Latin *appellare* 'to address']

appealable *adj. Law* (of a case) that can be referred to a higher court for review.

appealing *adj.* attractive, likeable. □ **appealingly** *adv.*

appear *v.intr.* **1** become or be visible. **2** be evident (*a new problem then appeared*). **3** seem; have the appearance of being (*you appear to be right*). **4** present oneself publicly or formally, esp. on stage or as the accused or counsel in a law court. **5** be published (*it appeared in the papers; a new edition will appear*). [from Latin *apparēre* 'to come in sight']

appearance *n.* **1** the act or an instance of appearing. **2** an outward form as perceived, esp. visually (*smartened up his appearance; gives an appearance of scalded skin*). **3** a semblance (*lend an appearance of legitimacy*). □ **keep up appearances** maintain an impression or pretence of virtue, affluence, etc. **make** (or **put in**) **an appearance** be present, esp. briefly. **to all appearances** as far as can be seen; apparently.

appease *v.tr.* **1** make calm or quiet, esp. by making concessions. **2** satisfy (an appetite, scruples). [from Old French *apaisier*] □ **appeasement** *n.* **appeaser** *n.*

appellant *n. Law* a person who appeals. [from Old French *apelant*]

appellate *adj. Law* concerned with appeals. [from Latin *appellatus* 'appealed to']

appellation *n. formal* a name or title; nomenclature. [related to APPEAL]

appellation contrôlée /ap-ĕ-las-yon kon-**troh**-lay/ *n.* (also **appellation d'origine contrôlée** /do-ri-**zh**een/) a guarantee of the description of a bottle of French wine or of a foodstuff as to its origin, in conformity with statutory regulations. [French, literally 'controlled appellation']

append *v.tr.* attach, affix, add, esp. to a written document etc. [from Latin *appendere* 'to hang']

appendage *n.* **1** something attached; an addition. **2** *Zool.* a leg or other projecting part of an arthropod.

appendant ● *adj.* (usu. foll. by *to*) attached in a subordinate capacity. ● *n.* an appendant person or thing. [Old French *apendant* from *apendre*]

appendectomy *n.* (*pl.* **-ies**) the surgical removal of the appendix.

appendicitis *n.* inflammation of the appendix.

appendix *n.* (*pl.* **appendices** or **appendixes**) **1** (in full **vermiform appendix**) *Anat.* ▼ a small outgrowth of tissue forming a tube-shaped sac attached to the lower end of the large intestine. ▷ INTESTINE. **2** subsidiary matter at the end of a book or document. [Latin]

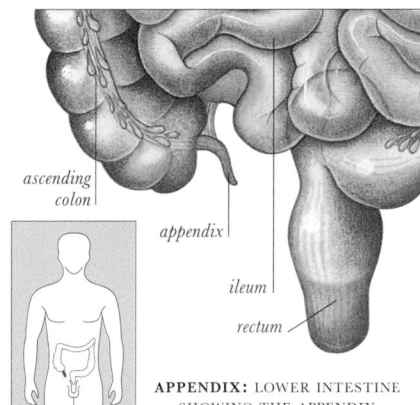

ascending colon

appendix

ileum

rectum

APPENDIX: LOWER INTESTINE
SHOWING THE APPENDIX

appertain *v.intr.* (foll. by *to*) **1** relate. **2** belong as a possession or right. **3** be appropriate. [based on Latin *pertinēre* 'to pertain']

appetite *n.* **1** a natural desire to satisfy bodily needs, esp. for food or sexual activity. **2** (usu. foll. by *for*) an inclination or desire. [based on Latin *appetere* 'to seek after'] □ **appetitive** *adj.*

appetizer *n.* (also **-iser**) a small amount to stimulate an appetite.

appetizing *adj.* (also **-ising**) stimulating an appetite. □ **appetizingly** *adv.*

applaud *v.* **1** *intr.* express strong approval, esp. by clapping. **2** *tr.* express approval of (a person or action) verbally or by clapping. [from Latin *applaudere*]

applause *n.* **1** approval shown by clapping the hands. **2** warm approval.

apple *n.* **1** the fruit of a tree of the genus *Malus*, rounded in form and with a crisp flesh. ▷ FRUIT, SEED. **2** (in full **apple tree**) the tree bearing this. □ **apple of one's eye** (prec. by *the*) a cherished person or thing. **upset the apple-cart** spoil careful plans. [Old English]

applejack *n. N. Amer.* a spirit distilled from fermented apple juice.

apple-pie bed *n.* a bed made (as a joke) with the sheets folded short, so that the legs cannot be accommodated.

appliance *n.* a device or piece of equipment used for a specific task, esp. a machine for domestic use.

applicable *adj.* **1** that may be applied. **2** having reference; appropriate. □ **applicability** *n.*

applicant *n.* a person who applies for something.

application *n.* **1** the act of applying, esp. medicinal ointment to the skin. **2** a formal request for employment, membership, etc. **3 a** relevance. **b** the use to which something can or should be put. **4** sustained effort; diligence.

applicator *n.* a device for applying a substance to a surface or for inserting something into a cavity.

applied *adj.* (of a subject of study) put to practical use as opposed to being theoretical.

applied mathematics see MATHEMATICS.

appliqué /ap-lee-kay/ ● *n.* ► ornamental work in which fabric is cut out and attached, usu. sewn, to the surface of another fabric to form pictures or patterns. ● *adj.* executed in appliqué.

● *v.tr.* (**appliqués**, **appliquéd**, **appliquéing**) decorate with appliqué; make using appliqué technique. [French, literally 'applied']

apply *v.* (**-ies**, **-ied**) **1** *intr.* make a formal request for something to be done, given, etc. (*apply for a job; apply for help to the governors; applied to be sent overseas*). **2** *intr.* have relevance (*does not apply in this case*). **3** *tr.* **a** make use of as relevant or suitable (*apply the rules*). **b** operate (*apply the handbrake*). **4** *tr.* **a** put or spread on (*applied the ointment to the cut*). **b** administer (*applied common sense to the problem*). **5** *refl.* devote oneself (*applied myself to the task*). [from Latin *applicare* 'to fold, fasten to']

appoggiatura /ă poj-ă-**tyoo**ră/ *n. Mus.* a grace note performed before an essential note of a melody and normally taking half its time value. [Italian, literally 'lean upon, rest']

appoint *v.tr.* **1** assign a post or office to (*appoint him governor; appoint him to govern; appointed to the post*). **2** fix, decide on (a time, place, etc.) (*8.30 was the appointed time*). **3** prescribe; ordain (*Holy Writ appointed by the Church*). **4** *Law* **a** (also *absol.*) declare the destination of (property etc.). **b** declare (a person) as having an interest in property etc. (*Jones was appointed in the will*). **5** (as **appointed** *adj.*) equipped, furnished (*a badly appointed hotel*). [from Old French *apointer*] □ **appointee** *n.* **appointive** *adj.* esp. *N. Amer.* (in sense 1 of *v.*).

appointment *n.* **1** an arrangement to meet at a specific time and place. **2 a** a post available for applicants, or recently filled (*took up the appointment on Monday*). **b** a person appointed. **3** (usu. in *pl.*) **a** furniture, fittings. **b** equipment.

apportion *v.tr.* share out; assign as a share. [from medieval Latin *apportionare*] □ **apportionment** *n.*

apposite *adj.* **1** apt; well chosen. **2** well expressed. [from Latin *appositus* 'put to'] □ **appositely** *adv.* **appositeness** *n.*

apposition *n.* **1** placing side by side; juxtaposition. **2** *Gram.* the placing of a word next to another, esp. the addition of one noun to another, in order to qualify or explain the first (e.g. *William the Conqueror; my friend Sue*). □ **appositional** *adj.*

appraisal *n.* **1** the act or an instance of appraising. **2** a formal evaluation of the performance of an employee over a particular period.

appraise *v.tr.* **1** estimate the quality of (*appraised her skills*). **2** set a price on; value. **3** evaluate the performance of (an employee) formally. [from archaic *apprize*, by assimilation to PRAISE] □ **appraisee** *n.* **appraiser** *n.* **appraisingly** *adv.* **appraisive** *adj.*

appreciable *adj.* large enough to be noticed; significant; considerable (*appreciable progress has been made*). [from (Old) French *appréciable*] □ **appreciably** *adv.*

appreciate *v.* **1** *tr.* **a** esteem highly; value. **b** be grateful for (*we appreciate your sympathy*). **c** be sensitive to (*appreciate the nuances*). **2** *tr.* (often foll. by *that* + clause) understand; recognize. **3 a** *intr.* (of property etc.) rise in value. **b** *tr.* raise in value. [from Late Latin *appretiare* 'to appraise'] □ **appreciative** *adj.* **appreciatively** *adv.* **appreciator** *n.*

appreciation *n.* **1** favourable or grateful recognition. **2** an estimation or judgement; sensitive understanding (*a quick appreciation of the problem*). **3** an increase in value. **4** a (usu. favourable) review of a book, film, etc.

APPLIQUÉ DETAIL ON
19TH-CENTURY AMERICAN QUILT

apprehend *v.tr.* **1** understand, perceive (*apprehend your meaning*). **2** seize, arrest (*apprehended the criminal*). [from Latin *apprehendere* 'to lay hold of']

apprehensible *adj.* capable of being apprehended by the senses or the intellect (*an apprehensible change in her expression*).

apprehension *n.* **1** uneasiness. **2** understanding. **3** arrest, capture. **4** an idea; a conception. [related to APPREHEND]

A

apprehensive *adj.* uneasily fearful; anxious. □ **apprehensively** *adv.* **apprehensiveness** *n.*

apprentice ● *n.* **1** a person who is learning a trade by being employed in it for an agreed period at low wages. **2** a beginner; a novice. ● *v.* **1** *tr.* engage as an apprentice (*was apprenticed to a builder*). **2** *intr. N. Amer.* serve as an apprentice (*she apprenticed at a hairdresser's*). [from Old French *aprentis*] □ **apprenticeship** *n.*

apprise *v.tr.* (foll. by *of*) inform. □ **be apprised of** be aware of. [based on French *apprise* (fem.) 'learnt, taught']

appro *n. Brit. colloq.* □ **on appro** = on approval (see APPROVAL).

approach ● *v.* **1** *tr.* come near or nearer to (a place or time). **2** *intr.* come near or nearer in space or time (*the hour approaches*). **3** *tr.* make a tentative proposal to (*approached me about a loan*). **4** *tr.* **a** be similar in character, quality, etc., to (*doesn't approach her for artistic skill*). **b** approximate to (*a population approaching 5 million*). **5** *tr.* attempt to influence or bribe. **6** *tr.* set about (a task etc.). **7** *intr. Golf* play an approach shot. ● *n.* **1** an act or means of approaching (*made an approach; an approach lined with trees*). **2** an approximation (*an approach to an apology*). **3** a way of dealing with a person or thing (*needs a new approach*). **4** (usu. in *pl.*) a sexual advance. **5** *Golf* a stroke from the fairway to the green. **6** *Aeron.* the final part of a flight before landing. [from ecclesiastical Latin *appropiare*]

approachable *adj.* **1** friendly; easy to talk to. **2** able to be approached. □ **approachability** *n.*

approach road *n. Brit.* a road by which traffic enters a motorway.

approbation *n.* approval, consent. [from Latin *approbatio*] □ **approbatory** *adj.*

appropriate ● *adj.* **1** suitable or proper. **2** *formal* belonging or particular. ● *v.tr.* **1** take possession of. **2** devote (money etc.) to special purposes. [from Late Latin *appropriatus* 'made (one's) own'] □ **appropriately** *adv.* **appropriateness** *n.* **appropriation** *n.* **appropriator** *n.*

approval *n.* **1** the act of approving. **2** consent; a favourable opinion (*with your approval; looked at him with approval*). □ **on approval** (of goods supplied) to be returned if not satisfactory.

approve *v.* **1** *tr.* confirm; sanction (*approved his application*). **2** *intr.* give or have a favourable opinion. **3** *tr.* commend (*approved the new hat*). □ **approve of** pronounce or consider good or satisfactory; commend. [from Latin *approbare*] □ **approvingly** *adv.*

approx. *abbr.* **1** approximate. **2** approximately.

approximate ● *adj.* fairly correct or accurate; near to the actual (*the approximate time of arrival; an approximate guess*). ● *v.tr. & intr.* bring or come near (esp. in quality, number, etc.), but not exactly (*approximates to the truth; approximates the amount required*). [from Late Latin *approximatus* 'drawn near to'] □ **approximately** *adv.* **approximation** *n.*

appurtenance *n.* (usu. in *pl.*) a belonging; an appendage; an accessory. [based on Latin *pertinēre* 'to pertain']

APR *abbr.* annual or annualized percentage rate (esp. of interest on loans or credit).

Apr. *abbr.* April.

après-ski ● *n.* the evening, esp. its social activities, following a day's skiing. ● *attrib.adj.* (of clothes, drinks, etc.) appropriate to social activities following skiing. [French]

apricot ● *n.* **1 a** a juicy soft fruit of an orange-yellow colour. **b** (in full **apricot tree**) the tree, *Prunus armeniaca*, bearing it. **2** the ripe fruit's orange-yellow colour. ● *adj.* of an orange-yellow colour. [based on Latin *praecoquum*, variant of *praecox* 'early-ripe']

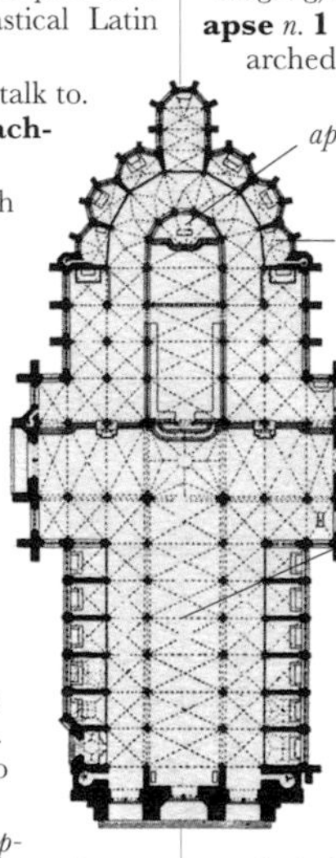

April *n.* the fourth month of the year. [from Latin *Aprilis*]

April Fool *n.* a person successfully tricked on 1 April.

April Fool's Day *n.* (also **April Fools' Day**, **All Fools' Day**) 1 April.

a priori ● *adj.* **1** (of reasoning) deductive; proceeding from causes to effects. **2** (of concepts, knowledge, etc.) logically independent of experience; not derived from experience. **3** not submitted to critical investigation (*an a priori conjecture*). ● *adv.* **1** in an a priori manner. **2** as far as one knows. [Latin, literally 'from what is before'] □ **apriorism** *n.*

apron *n.* **1** a garment covering and protecting the front of a person's clothes, either from chest or waist level, and tied at the back. **2** *Theatr.* the part of a stage in front of the curtain. **3** the hard-surfaced area on an airfield used for manoeuvring or loading aircraft. **4** an endless conveyor belt. [based on Old French *nape* 'tablecloth': for loss of *n* cf. ADDER] □ **aproned** *adj.* **apronful** *n.* (*pl.* **-fuls**).

apropos /ap-rŏ-poh/ ● *adj.* to the point; appropriate (*his comment was apropos*). ● *prep.* (often foll. by *of*) *colloq.* in respect of; concerning (*apropos the meeting; apropos of the talk*). ● *adv.* **1** appropriately (*spoke apropos*). **2** (*absol.*) by the way; incidentally (*apropos, she's not going*). [from French *à propos*]

apse *n.* **1** ▼ a large semicircular or polygonal recess, arched or with a domed roof, esp. at the eastern end of a church. ▷ BASILICA. **2** = APSIS. [from Latin *apsis*] □ **apsidal** *adj.*

[diagram labels:]
apse

row of apsidal chapels

nave

APSE: PLAN OF AMIENS CATHEDRAL, FRANCE, SHOWING THE APSE

apsis *n.* (*pl.* **apsides**) either of two points on the orbit of a planet or satellite that are nearest to or furthest from the body round which it moves. [from Greek *(h)apsis* 'arch, vault'] □ **apsidal** *adj.*

apt *adj.* **1** appropriate, suitable (*an apt moment*). **2** (foll. by *to* + infin.) having a tendency, prone, likely (*apt to lose his temper*). **3** clever; quick to learn. [from Latin *aptus* 'fitted'] □ **aptly** *adv.* **aptness** *n.*

apteryx *n.* = KIWI 1. [modern Latin]

aptitude *n.* **1** a natural propensity or talent (*an aptitude for drawing*). **2** ability or suitability. [from Late Latin *aptitudo* 'fitness']

aqua ● *n.* the colour aquamarine. ● *adj.* of this colour. [abbreviation]

aqualung *n.* ▼ a portable breathing apparatus for divers, consisting of cylinders of compressed air strapped on the back, feeding air through a mask or mouthpiece. ▷ SCUBA-DIVING. [based on Latin *aqua* 'water']

[diagram labels:]
mouthpiece to inflate buoyancy jacket

mouthpiece and demand valve

cylinder stop valve

buoyancy jacket

main air cylinde..

compass

air, time, and depth display

emergenc.. air cylin..

AQUALUNG

aquamarine ● *n.* **1** ► a light bluish-green beryl. **2** its colour. ▷ GEM. ● *adj.* of a bluish-green colour. [from Latin *aqua marina* 'sea water']

AQUAMARINE

aquaplane ● *n.* a board for riding on water, pulled by a speedboat. ● *v.intr.* **1** ride on an aquaplane. **2** (of a vehicle) glide uncontrollably on the wet surface of a road.

aqua regia *n. Chem.* a mixture of concentrated nitric and hydrochloric acids, a highly corrosive liquid attacking many substances unaffected by other reagents. [Latin, literally, 'royal water']

aquarelle *n.* a painting in thin watercolours. [French, based on Latin *aqua* 'water']

aquarium *n.* (*pl.* **aquaria** or **aquariums**) ▼ an artificial environment designed for keeping live aquatic plants and animals for study or exhibition, esp. a tank of water with transparent sides. [Latin, literally '(thing) of water']

AQUARIUM

Fishkeeping dates back to Roman times, and first became a popular hobby in Europe in the 1600s. Four types of fish are kept in home aquaria: tropical freshwater species, tropical marine species, coldwater freshwater species, and coldwater marine species. An aquarium's features are usually chosen to imitate the natural habitat of the fish.

[diagram labels:]
power filter

reef rock

vagabond butterfly fish

malu anemone

coral sand

power head for oxygenation

glass-sided tank

squirrelfish

crushed coral

'CORAL-REEF' MARINE AQUARIUM

A

Aquarius *n.* **1** *Astron.* ▶ a large constellation (the Water-carrier or Water-bearer), said to represent a man pouring water from a jar. **2** *Astrol.* **a** the eleventh sign of the zodiac, which the Sun enters about 21 Jan. ▷ ZODIAC. **b** a person born when the Sun is in this sign. [Latin, literally 'water-carrier'] □ **Aquarian** *adj. & n.*

aquatic ● *adj.* **1** living in or near water. **2** (of a sport) played in or on water. ● *n.* **1** an aquatic plant or animal. **2** (in *pl.*) aquatic sports. [based on Latin *aqua* 'water']

aquatint *n.* **1** a print resembling a watercolour, produced from a copper plate etched with nitric acid. **2** the process of producing this. [from Italian *acqua tinta* 'coloured water']

aquavit *n.* (also **akvavit**) an alcoholic spirit made from potatoes etc. [Scandinavian]

aqua vitae *n.* a strong alcoholic spirit. [Latin, literally 'water of life']

aqueduct *n.* ▼ an artificial channel for conveying water, esp. in the form of a bridge supported by tall columns across a valley. [from Latin *aquae ductus* 'conduit']

water channel   *river valley*

AQUEDUCT
BUILT BY THE
ANCIENT ROMANS

aqueous /ay-kwi-ŭs/ *adj.* **1** of, containing, or like water. **2** *Geol.* produced by water (*aqueous rocks*). [from medieval Latin *aqueus*]

aqueous humour *n.* *Anat.* the clear fluid in the eye between the lens and the cornea. ▷ EYE

aquifer *n.* *Geol.* a layer of rock or soil able to hold or transmit much water. ▷ ARTESIAN WELL. [from Latin *aqua* 'water' and *-fer* 'bearing']

aquilegia *n.* a plant of the genus *Aquilegia* (buttercup family) with flowers having backward-pointing spurs. [medieval Latin]

aquiline *adj.* **1** of or like an eagle. **2** (of a nose) curved like an eagle's beak. [based on Latin *aquila* 'eagle']

Ar *symb. Chem.* the element argon.

Arab ● *n.* **1** a member of a Semitic people inhabiting originally Saudi Arabia and adjoining countries, now the Middle East generally. **2** a horse of a breed originally native to Arabia. ▷ HORSE. ● *adj.* of or relating to the Arabs. [from Arabic *'arab*]

arabesque *n.* **1** *Ballet* a posture with one leg extended horizontally backwards, torso extended forwards, and arms outstretched. ▷ GYMNASTICS. **2** a design of intertwined leaves, scrolls, etc. **3** *Mus.* a florid melodic section or composition. [from Italian *arabesco* 'in the Arabic style']

Arabian ● *adj.* of or relating to Arabia (*the Arabian desert*). ● *n.* **1** a native of Arabia. **2** *US* = ARAB *n.* 2. [Middle English, from Old French *arabi*]

■ **Usage** In the sense 'a native of Arabia', the usual term is now *Arab*.

Arabian camel *n.* a domesticated one-humped camel, *Camelus dromedarius*, native to the deserts of N. Africa and the Near East. ▷ CAMEL

Arabic ● *n.* the Semitic language of the Arabs. ● *adj.* of or relating to Arabia (esp. with reference to language or literature). [from Greek *arabikos*]

arabica *n.* **1** coffee from the most widely grown species of the coffee plant, *Coffea arabica*. **2** this plant. [modern Latin]

AQUARIUS:
FIGURE OF A WATER-CARRIER FORMED FROM
THE STARS OF AQUARIUS

Arabic numeral *n.* any of the numerals 0, 1, 2, 3, 4, 5, 6, 7, 8, and 9 (cf. ROMAN NUMERAL).

arable ● *adj.* **1** (of land) suitable for crop production. **2** (of crops) that can be grown on arable land. ● *n.* arable land or crops. [based on Latin *arare* 'to plough']

arachnid *n.* ▼ any arthropod of the class Arachnida, having four pairs of legs and usu. pincers or fangs e.g. scorpions, spiders, mites, and ticks. [from Greek *arakhne* 'spider'] □ **arachnidan** *adj. & n.*

arachnoid *n.* (in full **arachnoid membrane**) *Anat.* one of the three membranes (see MENINX) that surround the brain and spinal cord of vertebrates. [from Greek *arakhnoeidēs* 'like a cobweb']

arachnophobia *n.* an abnormal fear of spiders. □ **arachnophobe** *n.* **arachnophobic** *adj.*

Aramaic ● *n.* a branch of the Semitic family of languages, esp. the language of Syria used as a lingua franca in the Near East from the sixth century BC. ● *adj.* of or in Aramaic. [from Greek *Aramaios* 'of Aram', biblical name of Syria]

Aran *attrib.adj.* designating a type of knitwear with traditional patterns, esp. raised cable stitch and large diamond designs. [from the *Aran* islands, off the W. coast of Ireland]

araucaria *n.* an evergreen conifer of the genus *Araucaria*, native to the southern hemisphere, e.g. the monkey-puzzle tree. [modern Latin, from *Arauco*, the name of a province in Chile]

arbiter *n.* (*fem.* **arbitress**) **1 a** an arbitrator in a dispute. **b** a judge; an authority (*arbiter of taste*). **2** a person who has entire control of something.

arbitrage /ar-bi-**trahzh**/ *n.* the buying and selling of stocks or bills of exchange to take advantage of varying prices in different markets. [French]

arbitrageur /ar-bi-trah-**zher**/ *n.* (also **arbitrager** /**ar**-bi-trij-er/) a person who engages in arbitrage.

arbitral *adj.* concerning arbitration. [from (Old) French]

arbitrary *adj.* **1** based on or derived from uninformed opinion or random choice; capricious. **2** despotic. □ **arbitrarily** *adv.* **arbitrariness** *n.*

arbitrate *v.tr. & intr.* decide by arbitration. [based on Latin *arbiter* 'judge']

arbitration *n.* the settlement of a dispute by an arbitrator.

arbitrator *n.* a person appointed to settle a dispute; an arbiter.

arbitress see ARBITER.

arbor[1] *n.* **1** an axle or spindle on which something revolves. **2** a device holding a tool in a lathe etc. [from Latin *arbor* 'tree']

arbor[2] *US* var. of ARBOUR.

Arbor Day *n.* a day dedicated annually to public tree-planting in the US, Australia, and other countries.

arboreal *adj.* of, living in, or connected with trees. [based on Latin *arbor* 'tree']

arborescent *adj.* treelike in growth or general appearance. [from Latin *arborescent-* 'growing into a tree'] □ **arborescence** *n.*

arboretum *n.* (*pl.* **arboretums** or **arboreta**) a botanical garden devoted to trees. [Latin]

arboriculture *n.* the cultivation of trees and shrubs. □ **arboricultural** *adj.* **arboriculturist** *n.*

arbor vitae *n.* = THUJA. [Latin, literally 'tree of life']

arbour /**ar**-ber/ *n.* (*US* **arbor**) a shady garden alcove with the sides and roof formed by trees or climbing plants. [based on Latin *herba* 'grass, undergrowth'] □ **arboured** *adj.*

arc ● *n.* **1** part of the circumference of a circle or any other curve. **2** *Electr.* a luminous discharge between two electrodes. ● *v.intr.* (**arced**, **arcing**) form an arc. [Middle English via Old French, from Latin *arcus* 'bow, curve']

arcade *n.* **1** a passage with an arched roof. **2** esp. *Brit.* any covered walk, esp. with shops along one or both sides. **3** *Archit.* a series of arches supporting or set along a wall. ▷ NORMAN, ROMANESQUE. [from Italian *arcata*] □ **arcaded** *adj.* **arcading** *n.*

Arcadian ● *n.* an idealized peasant or country dweller, esp. in poetry. ● *adj. poet.* of or relating to

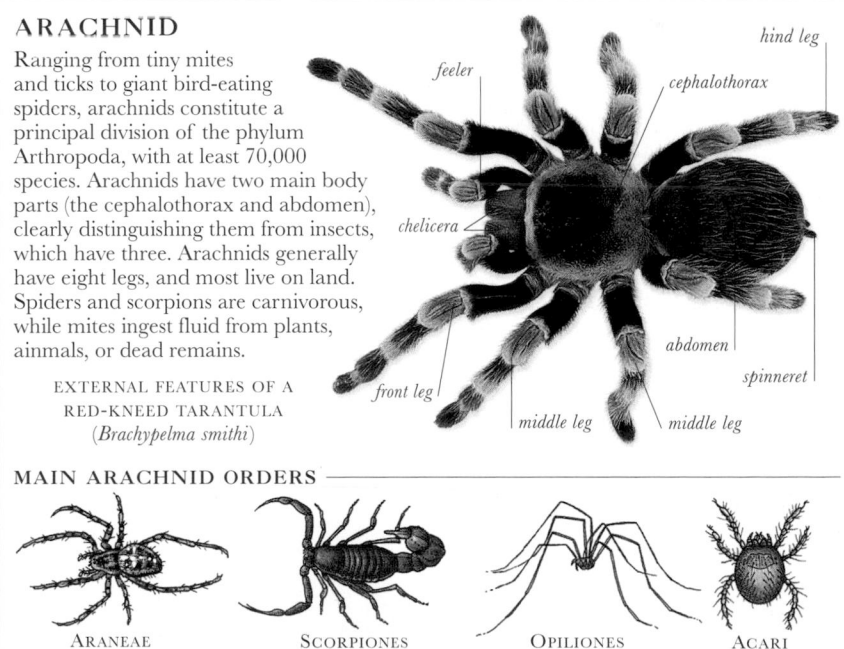

ARACHNID

Ranging from tiny mites and ticks to giant bird-eating spiders, arachnids constitute a principal division of the phylum Arthropoda, with at least 70,000 species. Arachnids have two main body parts (the cephalothorax and abdomen), clearly distinguishing them from insects, which have three. Arachnids generally have eight legs, and most live on land. Spiders and scorpions are carnivorous, while mites ingest fluid from plants, aimnals, or dead remains.

feeler   *hind leg*   *cephalothorax*   *chelicera*   *abdomen*   *spinneret*   *front leg*   *middle leg*   *middle leg*

EXTERNAL FEATURES OF A
RED-KNEED TARANTULA
(*Brachypelma smithi*)

MAIN ARACHNID ORDERS

ARANEAE (spiders) ▷ SPIDER   SCORPIONES (scorpions) ▷ SCORPION   OPILIONES (harvestmen)   ACARI (mites, ticks)

A

Arcady; ideally rustic. [from Greek *Arkadia*, a mountain district in the Peloponnese] □ **Arcadianism** *n.*

Arcady *n. poet.* an ideal rustic paradise.

arcane *adj.* mysterious, secret; understood by few. [from Latin *arcanus*, based on *arca* 'chest'] □ **arcanely** *adv.*

arch¹ ● *n.* **1 a** ▶ a curved structure as an opening or a support for a bridge, roof, floor, etc. **b** ▶ an arch used in building as an ornament. **2** any arch-shaped curve, e.g. as on the inner side of the foot, the eyebrows, etc. ● *v.* **1** *tr.* provide with or form into an arch. **2** *intr.* form an arch. [related to ARC]

arch² *adj.* self-consciously or affectedly playful or teasing. [earlier in sense 'crafty', as in *arch rogue* etc.] □ **archly** *adv.* **archness** *n.*

arch- *comb. form* **1** chief, superior (*archbishop*; *archdiocese*; *archduke*). **2** pre-eminent of its kind (esp. in unfavourable senses) (*arch-enemy*). [from Greek *arkhos* 'chief']

Archaean /ar-**kee**-ăn/ (*US* **Archean**) ● *adj.* of or relating to the earlier part of the Precambrian era, characterized by the absence of life (cf. PROTEROZOIC). ● *n.* this period. [based on Greek *arkhē* 'beginning']

archaeology *n.* (*US* also **archeology**) the study of human history and prehistory through the excavation of sites and the analysis of physical remains. [from Greek *arkhaiologia* 'ancient history'] □ **archaeological** *adj.* **archaeologically** *adv.* **archaeologist** *n.*

archaeopteryx *n.* ▼ the oldest known fossil bird, *Archaeopteryx lithographica*, of the late Jurassic period, which has wings and feathers, but teeth and a bony tail. [from Greek *arkhaios* 'ancient' + *pterux* 'wing']

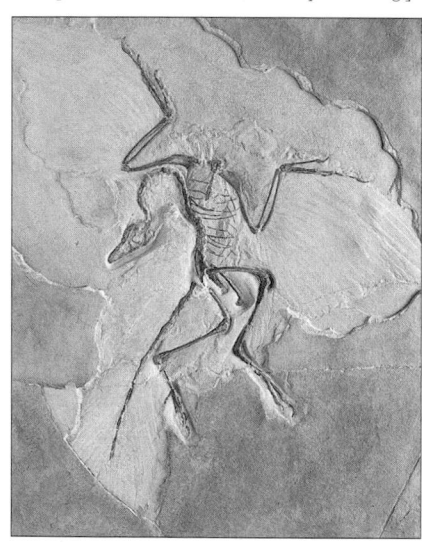

ARCHAEOPTERYX: FOSSILIZED SKELETON OF *Archaeopteryx lithographica*

archaic *adj.* **1 a** antiquated. **b** (of a word etc.) no longer in ordinary use, though retained for special purposes. **2** primitive. **3** of an early period of art or culture. [from Greek *arkhaïkos* 'old-fashioned'] □ **archaically** *adv.* **archaize** *v.tr. & intr.* (also **-ise**).

archaism *n.* **1** the retention or imitation of the old or obsolete, esp. in language or art. **2** an archaic word or expression. [based on Greek *arkhaizein* 'to copy the ancients'] □ **archaistic** *adj.*

archangel *n.* **1** an angel of the highest rank. **2** a member of the eighth order of the nine ranks of heavenly beings (see ORDER *n.* 15). □ **archangelic** *adj.*

archbishop *n.* the chief bishop of a province.

archbishopric *n.* the office or diocese of an archbishop.

archdeacon *n.* **1** an Anglican cleric ranking below

ARCH

The curve of an arch displaces weight from above, directing it to the spring line, where it is then supported vertically by abutments or pillars. In a classical arch, such as the basket type, the curve is formed from a series of interlocking blocks (voussoirs), with the central stone referred to as the keystone. A reinforcing piece of stonework, known as the impost, is situated at the spring line. The first curved arches were built by the Etruscans, but as architectural styles have varied in different locations and eras, so too has the form of the arch.

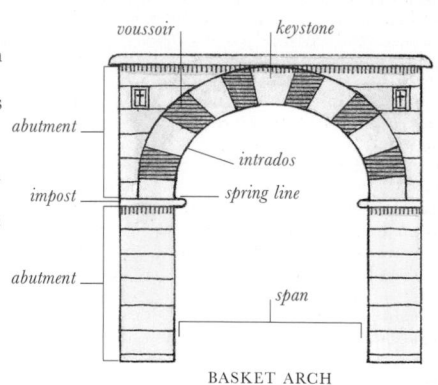

BASKET ARCH

OTHER TYPES OF ARCH

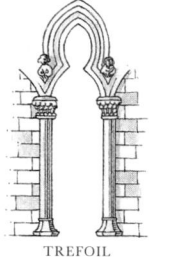
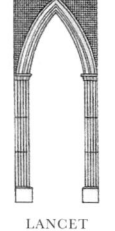

CALIPHAL NASRID TREFOIL LANCET TUDOR

a bishop. **2** a member of the clergy of similar rank in other Churches. □ **archdeaconry** *n.* (*pl.* **-ies**).

archdiocese *n.* the diocese of an archbishop. □ **archdiocesan** *adj.*

archduke *n.* (*fem.* **archduchess**) *hist.* the chief duke (esp. as the title of a son of the Emperor of Austria). □ **archducal** *adj.* **archduchy** *n.* (*pl.* **-ies**).

Archean *US* var. of ARCHAEAN.

archeology *US* var. of ARCHAEOLOGY.

archer *n.* **1** a person who shoots with a bow and arrows. **2** (**the Archer**) the zodiacal sign or constellation Sagittarius. ▷ SAGITTARIUS, ZODIAC. [based on Latin *arcus* 'bow']

archery *n.* ▼ shooting with a bow and arrows, esp. as a sport.

archetype /**ar**-ki-typ/ *n.* **1** a prototype; an original model. **2** a typical specimen. [from Greek *arkhetupon*] □ **archetypal** *adj.* **archetypical** *adj.*

archidiaconal *adj.* of or relating to an archdeacon. [from medieval Latin *archidiaconalis*] □ **archidiaconate** *n.*

archiepiscopal *adj.* of or relating to an archbishop. [based on Greek *arkhiepiskopos* 'archbishop'] □ **archiepiscopate** *n.*

archipelago *n.* (*pl.* **-os** or **-oes**) a group of islands. [from Greek *arkhi-* 'chief' + *pelagos* 'sea', originally the Aegean Sea]

architect *n.* **1** a designer who prepares plans for buildings, ships, etc., and supervises their construction. **2** (foll. by *of*) a person who brings about a specified thing (*the architect of his own fortune*). [from Greek *arkhitektōn*]

architectonic ● *adj.* **1** of or relating to architecture or architects. **2** of or relating to the systematization of knowledge. ● *n.* (in *pl.*; usu. treated as *sing.*) **1** the scientific study of architecture. **2** the study of the systematization of knowledge.

ARCHERY

Archery's origins lie in hunting and warfare, but today it is practised mainly as a sport. In competition, arrows are fired at targets at distances ranging from 30 m (98 ft) to 90 m (295 ft), with the highest score accorded to the centre circle, or bull's-eye. Modern bows are made of strong but flexible materials, and incorporate stabilizers and sophisticated sights.

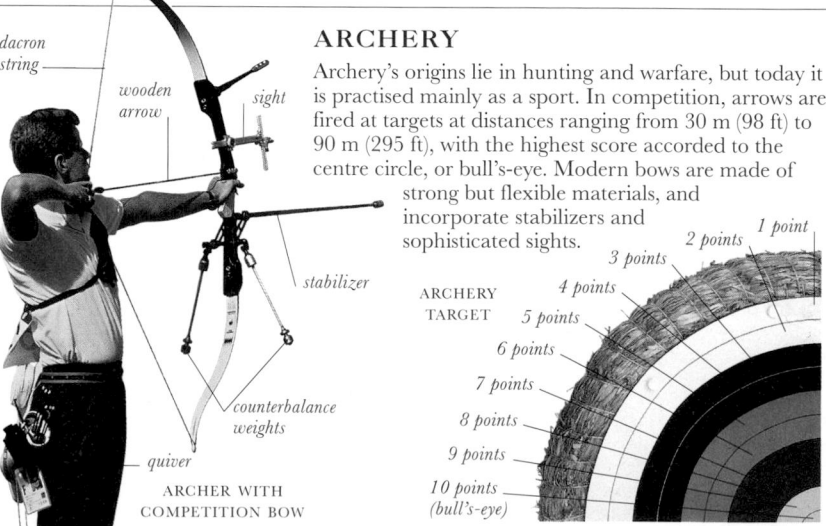

ARCHER WITH COMPETITION BOW

ARCHERY TARGET

architecture n. **1** the art or science of designing and constructing buildings. **2** the style of a building as regards design and construction. **3** buildings or other structures collectively. **4** the conceptual structure and logical organization of a computer system. [based on Greek *tektōn* 'builder'] □ **architectural** adj. **architecturally** adv.

architrave n. **1** (in classical architecture) a main beam resting across the tops of columns. ▷ COLUMN, ENTABLATURE. **2** the moulded frame around a doorway or window. [based on Latin *trabs trabis* 'beam']

archive /ar-kyv/ ● n. (usu. in *pl.*) **1** a collection of esp. public or corporate documents or records. **2** the place where these are kept. ● v.tr. place or store in an archive. [from Greek *arkheia* 'public records'] □ **archival** adj.

archivist /ar-kiv-ist/ n. a person who maintains archives.

archway n. **1** a vaulted passage. **2** an arched entrance.

arc lamp n. (also **arc light**) a light source using an electric arc.

Arctic ● adj. **1** of or relating to the north polar regions. **2** (**arctic**) colloq. (esp. of weather) very cold. ● n. the regions north of the Arctic Circle. [based on Greek *arktos* 'bear, Ursa Major, pole star']

Arctic Circle n. ▶ the parallel of latitude 66° 33' N., forming an imaginary line round the Arctic regions.

Arctic Ocean n. the partly ice-covered expanse of ocean surrounding the North Pole. ▷ OCEAN

arcuate adj. shaped like a bow; curved. ▷ DELTA. [from Latin *arcuatus* 'curved']

arc welding n. a method of welding using an electric arc to melt metals to be welded.

ardent adj. eager, zealous; (of persons or feelings) fervent, passionate. [from Latin *ardent-* 'burning'] □ **ardency** n. **ardently** adv.

ardour /ar-der/ n. (US **ardor**) zeal; burning enthusiasm; passion. [based on Latin *ardēre* 'to burn']

arduous adj. hard to achieve or overcome; laborious, strenuous. [from Latin *arduus* 'steep, difficult'] □ **arduously** adv. **arduousness** n.

are[1] 2nd sing. present & 1st, 2nd, 3rd pl. present of BE.

are[2] n. a metric unit of measure, equal to 100 square metres. [from Latin *area*]

area n. **1** the extent or measure of a surface (*over a large area; 3 acres in area; the area of a triangle*). **2** a region or tract (*the southern area*). **3** a space allocated for a specific purpose (*dining area*). **4** the scope or range of an activity or study. **5** (prec. by *the*) *Football* = PENALTY AREA. [Latin, literally 'vacant piece of level ground'] □ **areal** adj.

areca /a-ri-kǎ, ǎ-ree-kǎ/ n. a tropical Asian palm of the genus *Areca*. [Portuguese]

areca nut n. the astringent seed of a species of areca, *A. catechu*.

arena n. **1** the central part of an amphitheatre etc., where contests take place. ▷ AMPHITHEATRE. **2** a scene of conflict; a sphere of action or discussion. [from Latin *(h)arena* 'sand, sand-strewn place of combat']

aren't contr. **1** are not. **2** (in *interrog.*) am not (*aren't I coming too?*).

areola /ǎ-ree-ŏ-lǎ/ n. (pl. **areolae** /-lee/) *Anat.* a circular pigmented area, esp. that surrounding a nipple. ▷ BREAST. [Latin, literally 'little area'] □ **areolar** adj.

arête n. a sharp mountain ridge. ▷ GLACIER

argentiferous adj. containing natural deposits of silver.

Argentine (also **Argentinian**) ● adj. of or relating to Argentina. ● n. **1** a native or national of Argentina. **2** a person of Argentine descent.

□ **the Argentine** Argentina. [based on Latin *argentum* 'silver', a major historical export]

argil n. clay, esp. that used in pottery. [based on Greek *argos* 'white'] □ **argillaceous** adj.

argon n. *Chem.* an inert gaseous element of the noble gas group. [Greek, literally 'idle thing']

argosy n. (pl. **-ies**) *poet.* a large merchant ship, originally esp. from Ragusa (now Dubrovnik) or Venice.

argot /ar-goh/ n. the jargon of a group or class, formerly esp. of criminals. [French]

arguable adj. open to argument; debatable. □ **arguably** adv.

argue v. (**argues**, **argued**, **arguing**) **1** intr. (often foll. by *with*, *about*, etc.) exchange views or opinions, especially heatedly or contentiously. **2** tr. & intr. (often foll. by *that* + clause) maintain by reasoning. **3** intr. (foll. by *for*, *against*) reason (*argued against joining*). **4** tr. treat by reasoning (*argue the point*). □ **argue the toss** esp. *Brit. colloq.* dispute a decision or choice already made. [from Latin *argutari* 'to prattle'] □ **arguer** n.

argument n. **1** an exchange of views, esp. a heated or contentious one. **2** (often foll. by *for*, *against*) a reason advanced (*an argument for abolition*). **3** a summary of the line of reasoning of a book etc. [based on Latin *arguere* 'to make clear']

argumentation n. **1** methodical reasoning. **2** debate or argument.

argumentative adj. **1** fond of arguing; quarrelsome. **2** using methodical reasoning. □ **argumentatively** adv. **argumentativeness** n.

Argus n. a watchful guardian. [from Greek *Argos*, a mythical watchman with a hundred eyes]

Argus-eyed adj. vigilant.

argy-bargy *joc.* esp. *Brit.* ● n. (pl. **-ies**) a dispute or wrangle. ● v.intr. (**-ies**, **-ied**) quarrel, esp. loudly. [originally Scots]

aria /ar-iǎ/ n. *Mus.* a long accompanied song for solo voice in an opera, oratorio, etc. [Italian, literally 'tune']

arid adj. **1 a** (of ground, climate, etc.) dry, parched. **b** too dry to support vegetation, barren. **2** uninteresting. [from Latin *aridus*] □ **aridity** n. **aridly** adv. **aridness** n.

Aries n. (pl. same) **1** *Astron.* ▼ a small constellation (the Ram), said to represent the ram whose Golden Fleece was sought by Jason and the Argonauts. **2** *Astrol.* **a** the first sign of the zodiac, which the Sun enters at the vernal equinox (about 20 Mar.). ▷ ZODIAC. **b** a person born when the Sun is in this sign. [from Latin, literally 'ram'] □ **Arian** adj. & n.

ARIES: FIGURE OF A RAM FORMED FROM THE STARS OF ARIES

aright adv. rightly.

aril n. *Bot.* ▼ an extra seed-covering, often coloured and fleshy, e.g. around a nutmeg seed. [from modern Latin *arillus*] □ **arillate** adj.

arioso *Mus.* ● adj. & adv. in a melodious songlike style. ● n. (pl. **-os**) a piece of music to be performed in this way. [Italian]

arise v.intr. (past **arose**; past part. **arisen**) **1** begin to exist; originate. **2** (usu. foll. by *from*, *out of*) result (*accidents can arise from carelessness*). **3** come to one's notice (*the question of payment arose*). **4** archaic or poet. rise or get up. [Old English]

aril (mace)

seed / uncovered seed

ARIL: NUTMEG SEED WITH AND WITHOUT ARIL

aristocracy n. (pl. **-ies**) **1** the highest class in society; the nobility. **2 a** government by the nobility or a privileged group. **b** a state governed in this way. [from Greek *aristokratia*]

aristocrat n. a member of the nobility.

aristocratic adj. **1** of or relating to the aristocracy. **2** distinguished in manners or bearing. □ **aristocratically** adv.

Aristotelian ● n. a disciple or student of the Greek philosopher Aristotle (d. 322 BC). ● adj. of or concerning Aristotle or his ideas.

arithmetic ● n. /ǎ-rith-mě-tik/ **1** the science of numbers. **2** the use of numbers; computation (*a problem involving arithmetic*). ● adj. /a-rith-**met**-ik/ (also **arithmetical**) of or concerning arithmetic. [from Greek *arithmētikē* 'art of counting'] □ **arithmetician** n.

arithmetic mean n. the central number in an arithmetic progression.

arithmetic progression n. **1** an increase or decrease by a constant quantity (e.g. 1, 2, 3, 4, etc., 9, 7, 5, 3, etc.). **2** a sequence of numbers showing this.

-arium suffix forming nouns usu. denoting a place (*aquarium*; *planetarium*). [Latin neuter inflection]

ark n. **1** the ship in which (according to the Bible) Noah, his family, and the animals were saved. **2** *archaic* a chest or box. [from Latin *arca* 'chest']

Ark of the Covenant n. (also **Ark of the Testimony**) ▶ a chest or cupboard containing the scrolls or tables of Jewish Law.

shields protecting the Torah scrolls

ARK OF THE COVENANT IN AN 18TH-CENTURY DUTCH SYNAGOGUE

arm[1] n. **1** each of the two upper limbs of the human body from the shoulder to the hand. **2 a** the forelimb of an animal. **b** the flexible limb of an invertebrate animal (e.g. an octopus). ▷ OCTOPUS. **3 a** the sleeve of a garment. **b** the side part of a chair etc., used to support a sitter's arm. **c** a thing resembling an arm in branching from a main stem (*an arm of the sea*). **4** a subsidiary company or specialist branch of a business, institution, etc. □ **an arm and a leg** colloq. a large sum of money. **arm in arm** (of two or more persons) with arms linked. **at arm's length 1** as far as an arm can reach. **2** far enough to avoid undue familiarity. **in arms** (of a baby) too young to walk. **under one's arm** between the arm and the body. **with open arms** cordially. [Old English] □ **armful** n. (pl. **-fuls**). **armless** adj.

arm[2] ● n. **1** (usu. in *pl.*) **a** a weapon. **b** = FIREARM. **2** (in *pl.*) the military profession. **3** a branch of the military (e.g. infantry, cavalry, artillery). **4** (in *pl.*) heraldic devices (*coat of arms*). ● v.tr. & refl. **1** supply with weapons. **2** supply with tools or other requisites or advantages (*armed with the truth*). **3** make (a bomb etc.) able to explode. □ **in arms** armed. **lay down one's arms** cease fighting. **take up arms** begin fighting. **under arms** ready for war or battle. **up in arms** (usu. foll. by *against*, *about*) actively rebelling. [from Latin *arma* 'arms, fittings'] □ **armless** adj.

A

armada *n.* a fleet of warships, esp. that sent by Spain against England in 1588. [Spanish]

armadillo *n.* (*pl.* **-os**) ▼ a nocturnal insect-eating mammal of the family Dasypodidae, native to Central and S. America, with large claws for digging and a body covered in bony plates, often rolling itself into a ball when threatened. ▷ EDENTATE. [Spanish, literally 'little armed man']

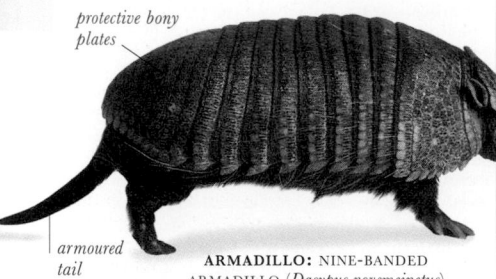

protective bony plates

armoured tail

ARMADILLO: NINE-BANDED ARMADILLO (*Dasypus novemcinctus*)

Armageddon *n.* **1** (in the New Testament) the last battle between good and evil before the Day of Judgement. **2** a bloody battle or struggle on a huge scale. [from Hebrew *har megiddōn* 'hill of Megiddo' (see Rev. 16:16)]

armament *n.* **1** (often in *pl.*) military weapons and equipment, esp. guns on a warship. **2** the process of equipping for war. [from Latin *armamentum*]

armature *n.* **1** the rotating coil or coils of a dynamo or electric motor. ▷ ALTERNATING CURRENT. **2** = KEEPER 5. **3** *Biol.* the protective covering of an animal or plant. **4** a metal framework on which a sculpture is moulded. [from Latin *armatura* 'armour']

armband *n.* a band worn around the upper arm to hold up a shirtsleeve or as a form of identification etc.

armchair *n.* **1** a comfortable, usu. upholstered, chair with side supports for the arms. **2** (*attrib.*) theoretical rather than active or practical (*an armchair critic*).

armed forces *n.pl.* the army, navy, and air force.

Armenian ● *n.* **1 a** a native of Armenia in the Caucasus. **b** a person of Armenian descent. **2** the language of Armenia. ● *adj.* of or relating to Armenia, its language, or the Christian Church established there *c.*300.

armhole *n.* each of two holes in a garment through which the arms are put, usu. into a sleeve.

armistice *n.* a stopping of hostilities by agreement of the opposing sides; a truce. [from Latin *arma* 'arms' + *-stitium* 'stoppage']

Armistice Day *n.* the anniversary of the armistice of 11 Nov. 1918 (cf. REMEMBRANCE SUNDAY).

armlet *n.* a band worn round the arm.

armoire *n.* a cupboard or wardrobe, esp. one that is ornate or antique. [French]

armor *US* var. of ARMOUR.

armorer *US* var. of ARMOURER.

armory[1] *n.* (*pl.* **-ies**) heraldry. □ **armorial** *adj.*

armory[2] *US* var. of ARMOURY.

armour (*US* **armor**) ● *n.* **1** ▶ a defensive covering, usu. of metal, formerly worn to protect the body in fighting. ▷ SAMURAI. **2 a** (in full **armour-plate**) a protective metal covering for an armed vehicle, ship, etc. **b** armoured fighting vehicles collectively. **3** a protective covering or shell on certain animals and plants. ● *v.tr.* (usu. as **armoured** *adj.*) provide with a protective covering, and often with guns (*armoured car*). [related to ARMATURE]

armourer *n.* (*US* **armorer**) **1** a maker or repairer of arms or armour. **2** an official in charge of a ship's or a regiment's arms.

armoury *n.* (*US* also **armory**) (*pl.* **-ies**) **1** a place where arms are kept; an arsenal. **2** an array of weapons, defensive resources, usable material, etc. **3** *US* a place where arms are manufactured. [from Old French *armoirie*]

armpit *n.* the hollow under the arm at the shoulder.

armrest *n.* = ARM[1] 3b.

army *n.* (*pl.* **-ies**) **1** an organized force armed for fighting on land. **2** (prec. by *the*) the military profession. **3** (often foll. by *of*) a very large number (*an army of locusts; army of helpers*). **4** an organized body regarded as fighting for a particular cause (*Salvation Army*). [based on Latin *armare* 'to arm']

arnica *n.* **1** a plant of the genus *Arnica* (daisy family), having yellow daisy-like flower heads, e.g. mountain tobacco. **2** a medicine prepared from this, used for bruises etc. [modern Latin]

aroma *n.* **1** a fragrance; a distinctive and pleasing smell, often of food. **2** a subtle pervasive quality. [Latin, from Greek *arōma* 'spice']

aromatherapy *n.* the use of aromatic plant extracts and essential oils in massage or other treatment. □ **aromatherapeutic** *adj.* **aromatherapist** *n.*

aromatic ● *adj.* **1** fragrant, spicy; (of a smell) pleasantly pungent. **2** *Chem.* (of an organic compound) having an unsaturated ring, esp. a benzene ring. ● *n.* an aromatic substance. [from Greek *arōmatikos*] □ **aromatically** *adv.* **aromaticity** *n.*

arose past of ARISE.

around ● *adv.* **1** on every side; all round. **2** in various places; here and there; at random (*fool around; shop around*). **3** *colloq.* **a** in existence; available. **b** near at hand. **4** approximately. ● *prep.* **1** on or along the circuit of. **2** on every side of; enveloping. **3** here and there in; here and there near (*chairs around the room*). **4** *N. Amer.* (and increasingly *Brit.*)

a round (*the church around the corner*). **b** approximately at; at a time near to (*come around four o'clock*). □ **have been around** *colloq.* be widely experienced.

arouse *v.tr.* **1** induce; call into existence (esp. a feeling, emotion, etc.). **2** awake from sleep. **3** stir into activity. **4** stimulate sexually. □ **arousable** *adj.* **arousal** *n.*

arpeggio /ar-pej-i-oh/ *n.* (*pl.* **-os**) *Mus.* the notes of a chord played in succession. [Italian, based on *arpeggiare* 'to play the harp']

arr. *abbr.* **1** *Mus.* arranged by. **2** arrives.

arraign *v.tr.* **1** indict before a tribunal; accuse. **2** find fault with; call into question (an action or statement). [from Old French *araisnier*] □ **arraignment** *n.*

arrange *v.* **1** *tr.* put into the required order; classify. **2** *tr.* plan or provide for; cause to occur (*arranged a meeting*). **3** *intr.* take measures; form plans; give instructions (*arrange to be there at eight; arranged for a taxi to come*). **4** *intr.* come to an agreement (*arranged with her to meet later*). **5** *tr.* *Mus.* adapt (a composition) for performance with instruments or voices other than those originally specified. [from Old French *arangier*] □ **arrangeable** *adj.* **arranger** *n.* (esp. in sense 5).

arrangement *n.* **1** the act or process of arranging or being arranged. **2** the manner in which a thing is arranged. **3** something arranged. **4** (in *pl.*) plans, measures (*make your own arrangements*). **5** *Mus.* a composition arranged for performance by different instruments or voices.

arrant *attrib.adj.* downright, utter, notorious (*arrant liar; arrant nonsense*). [Middle English variant of ERRANT] □ **arrantly** *adv.*

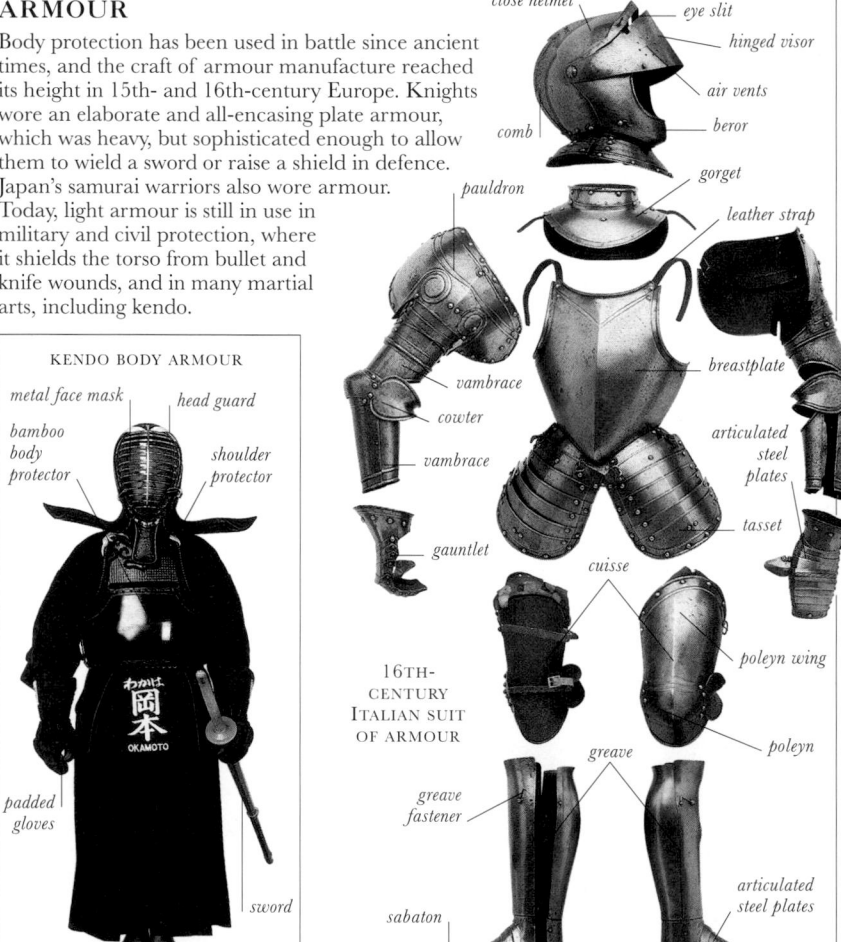

ARMOUR

Body protection has been used in battle since ancient times, and the craft of armour manufacture reached its height in 15th- and 16th-century Europe. Knights wore an elaborate and all-encasing plate armour, which was heavy, but sophisticated enough to allow them to wield a sword or raise a shield in defence. Japan's samurai warriors also wore armour. Today, light armour is still in use in military and civil protection, where it shields the torso from bullet and knife wounds, and in many martial arts, including kendo.

close helmet · *eye slit* · *hinged visor* · *air vents* · *beror* · *comb* · *pauldron* · *gorget* · *leather strap* · *vambrace* · *cowter* · *vambrace* · *gauntlet* · *breastplate* · *articulated steel plates* · *tasset* · *cuisse* · *poleyn wing* · *poleyn* · *greave* · *greave fastener* · *sabaton* · *articulated steel plates*

16TH-CENTURY ITALIAN SUIT OF ARMOUR

KENDO BODY ARMOUR

metal face mask · *head guard* · *bamboo body protector* · *shoulder protector* · *padded gloves* · *sword*

OKAMOTO

ART DECO

The term art deco originates from an exhibition of decorative and industrial design held in Paris in 1925. Owing something to art nouveau, but with a greater emphasis on geometry rather than organic forms, it became the most fashionable style of the 1920s and 1930s. With high regard to fine workmanship and materials, the style affected jewellery and furniture, as well as interior design and architecture. William van Alen's Chrysler Building epitomizes art deco style, from the overall structure to interior detailing, such as the elevator doors shown here.

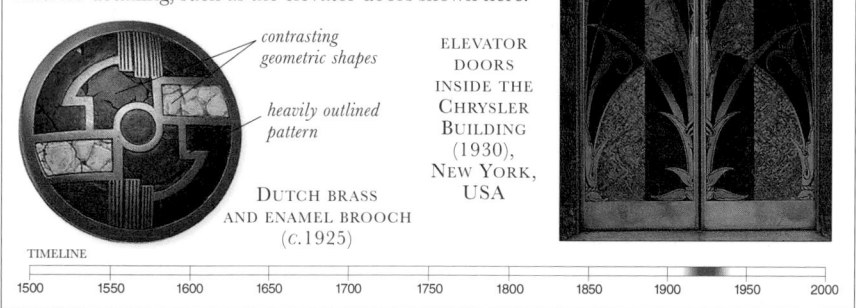

contrasting geometric shapes

heavily outlined pattern

DUTCH BRASS AND ENAMEL BROOCH (*c.*1925)

ELEVATOR DOORS INSIDE THE CHRYSLER BUILDING (1930), NEW YORK, USA

TIMELINE
1500   1550   1600   1650   1700   1750   1800   1850   1900   1950   2000

arras *n. hist.* a rich tapestry, often hung on the wall. [from *Arras*, a town in NE France famous for the fabric]

array • *n.* **1** an imposing or well-ordered series or display. **2** an ordered arrangement, esp. of troops (*battle array*). • *v.tr.* **1** deck, adorn. **2** set in order; marshal (forces). [from Old French *areer*]

arrears *n.pl.* an amount still outstanding or uncompleted. □ **in arrears** (or **arrear**) behindhand, esp. in payment. [based on medieval Latin *adretro* 'in a backwards direction'] □ **arrearage** *n.*

arrest • *v.tr.* **1 a** seize (a person) and take into custody, esp. by legal authority. **b** seize (a ship) by legal authority. **2** stop or check (esp. a process or moving thing). **3** attract (a person's attention). • *n.* **1** the act of arresting or being arrested, esp. the legal seizure of a person. **2** a stoppage or check (*cardiac arrest*). [based on Latin *restare* 'to remain, stop'] □ **arrestingly** *adv.*

arrestable *adj. Law* (esp. of an offence) such that the offender may be arrested without a warrant.

arrester *n.* (also **arrestor**) a device for slowing an aircraft after landing.

arrival *n.* **1** the act or an instance of arriving. **2** a person or thing that has arrived. [from Anglo-French *arrivaille*]

arrive *v.intr.* (often foll. by *at, in*) **1** reach a destination; come to the end of a journey or a specified part of a journey (*arrived in Tibet*; *arrived late*). **2** (foll. by *at*) reach (a conclusion, decision, etc.). **3** *colloq.* establish one's reputation or position. **4** *colloq.* (of a child) be born. **5** (of a time) come (*her birthday arrived at last*). [based on Latin *ripa* 'shore']

arriviste *n.* an ambitious or ruthlessly self-seeking person. [French]

arrogant *adj.* aggressively assertive or presumptuous; overbearing. □ **arrogance** *n.* **arrogantly** *adv.*

arrogate *v.tr.* **1** (often foll. by *to oneself*) claim (power, responsibility, etc.) without justification. **2** (often foll. by *to*) attribute unjustly (to a person). [based on Latin *arrogatus* 'claimed for oneself'] □ **arrogation** *n.*

arrow • *n.* **1** a sharp pointed wooden or metal stick shot from a bow as a weapon. ▷ ARCHERY. **2** a drawn or printed etc. representation of an arrow indicating a direction. • *v.tr.* (as **arrowed** *adj.*) provided or marked with an arrow or arrows. [Old English] □ **arrowy** *adj.*

arrow-grass *n.* a marsh plant of the genus *Triglochin*.

arrowhead *n.* **1** the pointed end of an arrow. **2** a decorative device resembling an arrowhead.

arrowroot *n.* a plant of the family Marantaceae from which a starch is prepared and used in food and medicines. [from the use of its tubers to absorb poison from arrow wounds]

arse (*N. Amer.* **ass**) *coarse slang* • *n.* the buttocks. • *v.intr.* (usu. foll. by *about, around*) play the fool. [Old English]

arsehole *n.* (*N. Amer.* **asshole**) *coarse slang* **1** the anus. **2** *offens.* a term of contempt for a person.

arse-licking *n.* (*N. Amer.* **ass-licking**) *coarse slang* obsequiousness for the purpose of gaining favour; toadying. □ **arse-licker** *n.*

arsenal *n.* **1** a store of weapons. **2** a government establishment for the storage and manufacture of weapons and ammunition. **3** resources of anything compared with weapons (e.g. terms of abuse). [based on Arabic *dār* 'house' + *sinā'a* 'industry']

arsenic *n.* **1** a non-scientific name for arsenic trioxide, a highly poisonous substance used in weedkillers, rat poison, etc. **2** *Chem.* a brittle semi-metallic element, used in semiconductors and alloys.

arsenical • *adj.* of or containing arsenic. • *n.* a drug containing arsenic.

arson *n.* the act of maliciously setting fire to property. [based on Latin *ardēre ars-* 'to burn'] □ **arsonist** *n.*

art *n.* **1 a** human creative skill or its application. **b** work exhibiting this. **2 a** (in *pl.*; prec. by *the*) the various branches of creative activity, e.g. painting, music, writing, considered collectively. **b** any one of these branches. **3** creative activity, esp. painting and drawing, resulting in visual representation (*interested in music but not art*). **4** human skill or workmanship as opposed to the work of nature. **5** (often foll. by *of*) a skill, aptitude, or knack (*the art of writing clearly*). **6** (in *pl.*; usu. prec. by *the*) those branches of learning (esp. languages, literature, and history) associated with creative skill as opposed to scientific, technical, or vocational skills. [from Latin *ars artis*]

art. *abbr.* article.

art deco *n.* ◀ the predominant decorative art style of the period 1910–30, characterized by precise and boldly delineated geometric motifs, shapes, and strong colours. [shortened from French *art décoratif*]

artefact *n.* (*US* **artifact**) a product of human art and workmanship. [from Latin *arte factum* 'thing made by art'] □ **artefactual** *adj.*

arterial *adj.* **1** of or relating to an artery (*arterial blood*). **2** (esp. of a road) main, important, esp. linking large cities or towns. [based on French *artère* 'artery']

arteriosclerosis *n.* loss of elasticity and thickening of the walls of the arteries, esp. in old age. □ **arteriosclerotic** *adj.*

artery *n.* (*pl.* **-ies**) **1** ▼ any of the muscular-walled tubes forming part of the blood circulation system of the body. ▷ CARDIOVASCULAR. **2** a main road or railway line. [from Greek *artēria*] □ **arteritis** *n.*

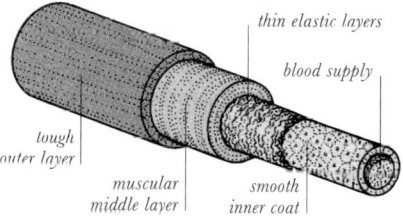

thin elastic layers

blood supply

tough outer layer

muscular middle layer

smooth inner coat

ARTERY: CUTAWAY SECTION OF A HUMAN ARTERY

artesian well *n.* ▼ a well bored perpendicularly, esp. through rock, into water bearing strata lying at an angle, so that natural pressure produces a constant supply of water. [based on *Artois*, old French province where such wells were first made]

ARTESIAN WELL

An artesian well makes use of hydrostatic pressure to raise water to the Earth's surface. Such a well may be bored into an aquifer (a saturated stratum of rock or earth) that is sandwiched between layers of impermeable rock. Provided the water table is higher than ground level at the well head, water will naturally rise to the surface.

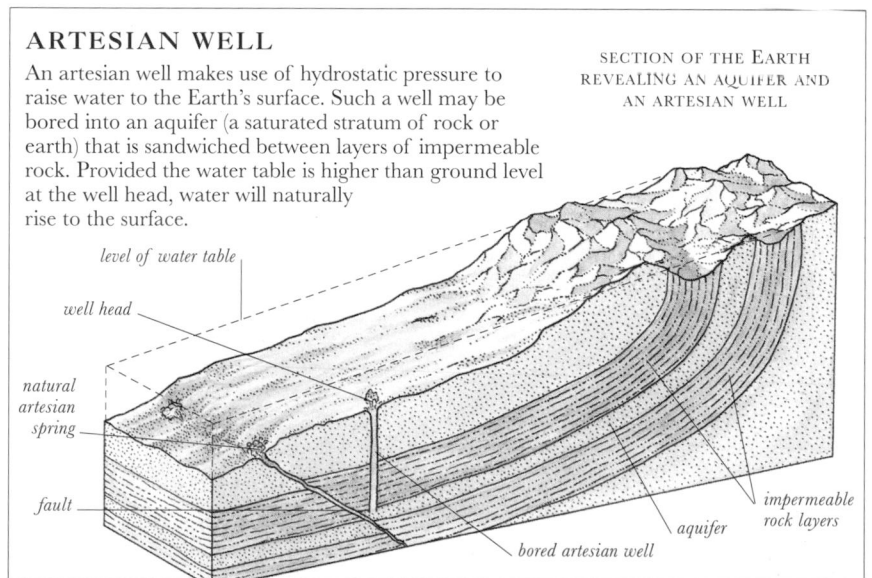

SECTION OF THE EARTH REVEALING AN AQUIFER AND AN ARTESIAN WELL

level of water table

well head

natural artesian spring

fault

bored artesian well

aquifer

impermeable rock layers

A

ARTHROPOD

Arthropods are the largest invertebrate group, with more than one million known species existing on land and in water. All have jointed bodies protected by a tough, waterproof exoskeleton, which is shed several times as they grow into their adult state. The main groups of arthropods are shown here.

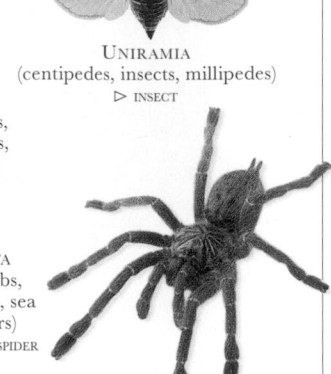

UNIRAMIA
(centipedes, insects, millipedes)
▷ INSECT

CRUSTACEA (barnacles, crabs, lobsters, shrimps, water fleas, woodlice)
▷ CRAB, CRUSTACEAN

CHELICERATA (horseshoe crabs, mites, scorpions, sea spiders, spiders)
▷ ARACHNID, CRAB, SPIDER

artful *adj.* **1** (of a person or action) crafty, deceitful. **2** skilful, clever. □ **artfully** *adv.* **artfulness** *n.*

arthritis *n.* a disease, esp. rheumatoid arthritis or osteoarthritis, involving pain and stiffness of the joints. [based on Greek *arthron* 'joint'] □ **arthritic** *adj. & n.*

arthropod *n. Zool.* ▲ any invertebrate animal of the phylum Arthropoda, with a segmented body, jointed limbs, and an external skeleton, e.g. an insect, spider, or crustacean. [from Greek *arthron* 'joint' + *pous podos* 'foot']

Arthurian *adj.* relating to or associated with King Arthur, the legendary British ruler, or his court.

artichoke *n.* **1** a European plant, *Cynara scolymus*, allied to the thistle. **2** (in full **globe artichoke**) the flower head of the artichoke, the bracts of which have edible bases (see also JERUSALEM ARTICHOKE). ▷ GLOBE ARTICHOKE. [from Arabic *al-ḵaršūfa*]

article ● *n.* **1** (often in *pl.*) an item or commodity, usu. not further distinguished (*a collection of odd articles*). **2** a non-fictional essay, esp. one included with others in a newspaper, magazine, journal etc. **3 a** a particular part (*an article of faith*). **b** a separate clause or portion of any document (*articles of apprenticeship*). **4** *Gram.* the definite or indefinite article. ● *v.tr.* bind by articles of apprenticeship. [from Latin *articulus* 'little joint']

articled clerk *n.* a trainee solicitor.

articular *adj.* of or relating to the joints. [based on Latin *articulus* 'little joint']

articulate ● *adj.* **1** able to speak fluently and coherently. **2** (of sound or speech) having clearly distinguishable parts. **3** having joints. ● *v.* **1** *tr.* **a** pronounce (words, syllables, etc.) clearly and distinctly. **b** express (an idea etc.) coherently. **2** *intr.* speak distinctly (*was quite unable to articulate*). **3** *tr.* (usu. in *passive*) connect by joints. **4** *tr.* mark with apparent joints. **5** *intr.* (often foll. by *with*) form a joint. [from Latin *articulatus*, related to ARTICLE] □ **articulacy** *n.* **articulately** *adv.* **articulateness** *n.* **articulator** *n.*

articulated lorry *n. Brit.* a lorry consisting of two or more sections connected by a flexible joint.

articulation *n.* **1 a** the act of speaking. **b** articulate utterance; speech. **2** the act or a mode of jointing. [based on Latin *articulare* 'to divide into parts']

artifact *US* var. of ARTEFACT.

artifice *n.* **1** a clever device; a contrivance. **2 a** cunning. **b** an instance of this. **3** skill, dexterity. [from Latin *artificium*, based on *facere* 'to make']

artificer *n.* **1** an inventor. **2** a craftsman. **3** a skilled mechanic in the armed forces.

artificial *adj.* **1** produced by human art or effort rather than originating naturally (*an artificial lake*).

2 imitation, fake (*artificial flowers*). **3** affected, insincere (*an artificial smile*). [related to ARTIFICE] □ **artificiality** *n.* **artificially** *adv.*

artificial insemination *n.* the injection of semen into the vagina or uterus other than by sexual intercourse.

artificial intelligence *n.* the theory and development of computer systems able to perform tasks normally requiring human intelligence, such as decision-making and speech recognition.

artificial kidney *n.* (also **kidney machine**) an apparatus that performs the functions of the human kidney (outside the body), when one or both organs are damaged. ▷ DIALYSIS

artificial respiration *n.* the restoration or initiation of breathing by manual, mechanical, or mouth-to-mouth methods.

artificial silk *n.* rayon.

artillery *n.* (*pl.* **-ies**) **1** large-calibre guns used in warfare on land. **2** a branch of the armed forces that uses these. [from Old French *artillerie*] □ **artillerist** *n.*

artilleryman *n.* (*pl.* **-men**) a member of the artillery.

artiodactyl *Zool.* ● *adj.* ▶ of or relating to the order Artiodactyla of ungulate mammals with two main toes on each foot, including camels, pigs, and ruminants. ● *n.* an animal of this order. ▷ UNGULATE. [modern Latin *Artiodactyla*, from Greek *artios* 'even' + *daktulos* 'finger, toe']

artisan *n.* a skilled (esp. manual) worker; a craftsman. [based on Latin *artitus* 'instructed in the arts']

artist *n.* **1** a painter. **2** a person who practises any of the arts. **3** an artiste. **4** *colloq.* a practiser of a specified (usu. reprehensible) activity (*con artist*). [based on Latin *ars artis* 'art'] □ **artistry** *n.*

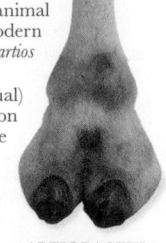

ARTIODACTYL:
TWO-TOED
CAMEL HOOF

artiste /ar-*teest*/ *n.* a professional performer, esp. a singer or dancer. [French]

artistic *adj.* **1** having natural skill in art. **2** made or done with art. **3** of art or artists. □ **artistically** *adv.*

artless *adj.* **1** guileless, ingenuous. **2** not resulting from or displaying art. □ **artlessly** *adv.*

art nouveau *n.* ▼ a European art style of the late 19th c. characterized by flowing lines and natural organic forms. [French, literally 'new art']

arts and crafts *n.pl.* decorative design and handicraft.

artwork *n.* the illustrations in a printed work.

arty *adj.* (also esp. *N. Amer.* **artsy**) (**-ier**, **-iest**) *colloq.* pretentiously artistic. □ **artiness** *n.*

arum *n.* a plant of the genus *Arum*, e.g. cuckoo-pint. [from Greek *aron*]

arum lily *n.* esp. *Brit.* a tall lily-like plant of the genus *Zantedeschia*.

arvo *n.* (*pl.* **-os**) *Austral. slang* afternoon. [abbreviation]

Aryan ● *n.* **1** a member of the peoples speaking Indo-European (esp. Indo-Iranian) languages. **2** = INDO-EUROPEAN *n.* 2. **3** (in Nazi ideology) a Caucasian not of Jewish descent. ● *adj.* of or relating to Aryan or the Aryans. [from Sanskrit *āryas* 'noble']

As *symb. Chem.* the element arsenic.

as[1] ● *adv. & conj.* (*adv.* as antecedent in main sentence; *conj.* in relative clause expressed or implied) … to the extent to which … is or does etc. (*I am as tall as he; am as tall as he is; am not so tall as he;*

ART NOUVEAU

Popular throughout Europe and influential in the USA, the style of art nouveau was characterized by the use of extended, flowing lines based on organic forms such as plants, waves, and the human body. Taking its name from a Parisian shop of the time, art nouveau was most prevalent in the fields of decorative art and architecture. One of its leading exponents was the French architect Hector Guimard. He is best known for his elaborate entrances to the metro stations in Paris, which are characterized by shell-shaped canopies made of glass and wrought iron.

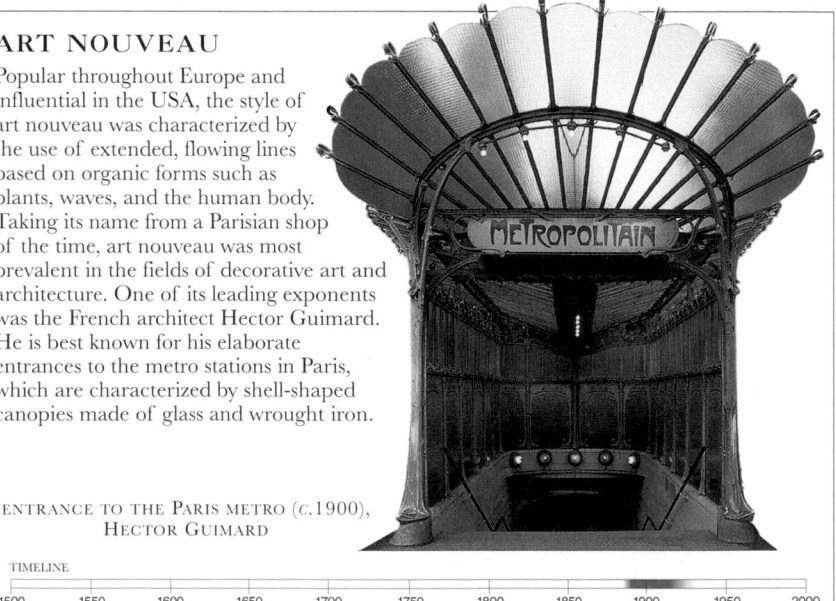

ENTRANCE TO THE PARIS METRO (*c.*1900),
HECTOR GUIMARD

TIMELINE

| 1500 | 1550 | 1600 | 1650 | 1700 | 1750 | 1800 | 1850 | 1900 | 1950 | 2000 |

(*colloq.*) *am as tall as him; as many as six; as recently as last week*. ● *conj.* (with relative clause expressed or implied) **1** (with antecedent *so*) expressing result or purpose (*came early so as to meet us*). **2** (with antecedent adverb omitted) having concessive force (*good as it is* = although it is good). **3** (without antecedent adverb) **a** in the manner in which (*do as you like*). **b** in the capacity or form of (*I speak as your friend; as a matter of fact*). **c** during or at the time that (*came up as I was speaking; fell just as I reached the door*). **d** for the reason that; seeing that (*as you are here, we can talk*). ● *rel.pron.* (with verb of relative clause expressed or implied) **1** that, who, which (*I had the same trouble as you; he is a writer, as is his wife; such countries as France*). **2** (with sentence as antecedent) a fact that (*he lost, as you know*). **as for** with regard to (*as for you, I think you are wrong*). **as from** esp. *Brit.* on and after (a specified date). **as if** (or **though**) as would be the case if (*acts as if he were in charge; looks as though we've won*). **as it is** (or **as is**) in the existing circumstances or state. **as it were** in a way; to a certain extent (*he is, as it were, infatuated*). **as long as** see LONG[1]. **as much** see MUCH. **as of 1** = *as from*. **2** at a (specified time). **as per** see PER 3. **as regards** see REGARD. **as soon as** see SOON. **as such** see SUCH. **as though** see *as if*. **as to** with respect to; concerning (*said nothing as to money*). **as was** *Brit.* in the previously existing circumstances or state. **as well** see WELL[1]. **as yet** until now or a particular time in the past (usu. with neg.: *have received no news as yet*). [reduced form of Old English *alswā* 'also']

■ **Usage** In comparisons expressed by *as … as*, the pronoun standing for the subject of the second half of the phrase should, strictly, be in the nominative case, i.e. *I am not as wealthy as he/she/they*. However, in all but very formal contexts, the accusative or object case is now acceptable, i.e. *I am not as wealthy as her/him/them*. These comments also apply to *as … as* and the *same … as*, e.g. *We're not so eager as them/*(formal*) they; I live in the same street as her/*(formal*) she*.

as[2] /ass/ *n.* (*pl.* **asses**) a Roman copper coin. [Latin]

a.s.a.p. *abbr.* as soon as possible.

asbestos *n.* **1** a fibrous silicate mineral that is incombustible. **2** this used as a heat-resistant or insulating material. [from Greek *asbestos* 'unquenchable'] □ **asbestine** *adj.*

asbestosis *n.* a lung disease resulting from the inhalation of asbestos particles.

ascend *v.* **1** *intr.* move upwards; rise. **2** *intr.* slope upwards. **3** *tr.* climb; go up. **4** *intr.* rise in rank or status. **5** *intr.* (of sound) rise in pitch. □ **ascend the throne** become king or queen. [from Latin *ascendere*]

ascendancy *n.* (also **ascendency**) (often foll. by *over*) a superior or dominant condition or position.

ascendant ● *adj.* **1** rising. **2** *Astron.* rising towards the zenith. **3** *Astrol.* just above the eastern horizon. **4** predominant. ● *n. Astrol.* the point of the Sun's apparent path that is ascendant at a given time (*Aries in the ascendant*). □ **in the ascendant 1** supreme or dominating. **2** rising; gaining power or authority.

ascension *n.* **1** the act or an instance of ascending. **2** (**Ascension**) the ascent of Christ into heaven on the fortieth day after the Resurrection. [from Latin *ascensio*] □ **ascensional** *adj.*

Ascension Day *n.* the Thursday forty days after Easter on which Christ's ascension is celebrated.

ascent *n.* **1** the act or an instance of ascending. **2 a** an upward movement or rise. **b** advancement or progress (*the ascent of man*). **3** a way by which one may ascend; an upward slope.

ascertain *v.tr.* **1** find out as a definite fact. **2** get to know. [from Old French *acertener*] □ **ascertainable** *adj.* **ascertainment** *n.*

ascesis *n.* the practice of self-discipline. [from Greek *askēsis* 'training']

ascetic ● *n.* a person who practises severe self-discipline and abstains from pleasure, esp. for religious or spiritual reasons. ● *adj.* relating to or characteristic of ascetics or asceticism. [from Greek *askētikos*] □ **ascetically** *adv.* **asceticism** *n.*

ASCII /ass-ki/ *abbr. Computing* American Standard Code for Information Interchange.

ascites /ă-sy-teez/ *n.* (*pl.* same) *Med.* the accumulation of fluid in the abdominal cavity, causing swelling. [based on Greek *askos* 'wineskin']

ascorbic acid *n.* a vitamin found in citrus fruits and green vegetables, a deficiency of which results in scurvy. [based on medieval Latin *scorbutus* 'scurvy']

ascribe *v.tr.* (usu. foll. by *to*) **1** attribute or impute (*ascribes his well-being to a sound constitution*). **2** regard as belonging. [based on Latin (*ad*) *scribere* 'to write (in addition to)'] □ **ascribable** *adj.* **ascription** *n.*

asdic *n.* esp. *Brit.* an early form of echo-sounder. [from *A*llied *S*ubmarine *D*etection *I*nvestigation *C*ommittee]

asepsis *n.* the absence of harmful bacteria, viruses, or other micro-organisms.

aseptic *adj.* free from contamination caused by harmful bacteria, viruses, or other micro-organisms.

asexual *adj.* **1** *Biol.* without sex or sexual organs. **2** *Biol.* (of reproduction) not involving the fusion of gametes. □ **asexuality** *n.* **asexually** *adv.*

ash[1] *n.* **1** (often in *pl.*) the powdery residue left after the burning of any substance. **2** (in *pl.*) the remains of the human body after cremation or disintegration. **3** (**the Ashes**) *Cricket* a trophy competed for regularly by Australia and England. [Old English]

ash[2] *n.* **1** (also **ash tree**) ◀ any forest tree of the genus *Fraxinus*, with silver-grey bark, compound leaves, and hard, tough, pale wood. **2** its wood. ▷ WOOD. [Old English]

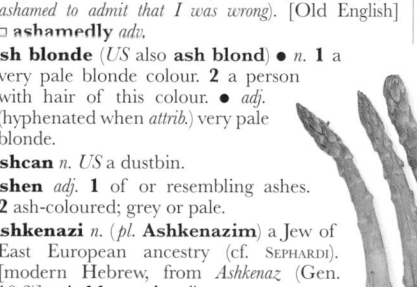

pinnate leaf

seed pods

ASH: EUROPEAN ASH (*Fraxinus excelsior*)

ashamed *adj.* (usu. *predic.*) **1** (often foll. by *of* (= with regard to), *for* (= on account of), or *to* + *infin.*) embarrassed by shame (*ashamed of his aunt; ashamed of having lied; ashamed to be seen with him*). **2** (foll. by *to* + *infin.*) hesitant, reluctant (*am ashamed to admit that I was wrong*). [Old English] □ **ashamedly** *adv.*

ash blonde (*US* also **ash blond**) ● *n.* **1** a very pale blonde colour. **2** a person with hair of this colour. ● *adj.* (hyphenated when *attrib.*) very pale blonde.

ashcan *n. US* a dustbin.

ashen *adj.* **1** of or resembling ashes. **2** ash-coloured; grey or pale.

Ashkenazi *n.* (*pl.* **Ashkenazim**) a Jew of East European ancestry (cf. SEPHARDI). [modern Hebrew, from *Ashkenaz* (Gen. 10:3)] □ **Ashkenazic** *adj.*

ashlar *n.* masonry made of large square-cut stones. [based on Latin *axilla* 'little board']

ashore *adv.* towards or on the shore or land (*sailed ashore; stayed ashore*).

ashram *n.* (in the Indian subcontinent) a place of religious retreat; a hermitage. [from Sanskrit *āshrama* 'hermitage']

ashtray *n.* a small receptacle for cigarette ash, stubs, etc.

Ash Wednesday *n.* the first day of Lent. [from the custom of marking the foreheads of penitents with ashes on that day]

ashy *adj.* **1** = ASHEN. **2** covered with ashes.

Asian ● *n.* **1** a native of Asia. **2** a person of Asian descent. ● *adj.* of or relating to Asia or its people, customs, or languages.

■ **Usage** In Britain *Asian* is the usual term for people who come from (or whose parents came from) the Indian subcontinent, while in North America it commonly also includes people from the Far East.

Asiatic ● *n. offens.* an Asian. ● *adj.* (*offens.* if used of people) Asian.

■ **Usage** *Asiatic* is now acceptable only as an adjective, and is found chiefly in geographical, zoological, and medical contexts, e.g. *Asiatic coastal regions; Asiatic golden plover; Asiatic cholera*.

A-side *n.* the side of a gramophone record regarded as the main one.

aside ● *adv.* **1** to or on one side; away. **2** out of consideration (placed after noun: *joking aside*). ● *n.* **1** words spoken in a play for the audience to hear, but supposed not to be heard by the other characters. **2** an incidental remark. □ **aside from** apart from. **set aside 1** put to one side. **2** keep for a special purpose or future use. **3** reject or disregard. **4** annul. **5** remove (land) from agricultural production for fallow, forestry, or other use. **take aside** engage (a person) esp. for a private conversation. [originally *on side*]

asinine *adj.* stupid. [based on Latin *asinus* 'ass'] □ **asininity** *n.*

ask *v.* **1** *tr.* call for an answer from, about, or to (*ask her about it; ask a question of him*). **2** *tr.* seek to obtain from another person (*ask a favour of; ask to be allowed*). **3** *tr.* (usu. foll. by *out* or *over*, or to (a function etc.)) invite. **4** *intr.* (foll. by *for*) seek to obtain, meet, or be directed to (*ask for a donation*). □ **ask after** enquire about (esp. a person). **ask for it** *colloq.* invite trouble. **for the asking** for nothing. **if you ask me** *colloq.* in my opinion. [Old English] □ **asker** *n.*

askance *adv.* (also **askant**) sideways or squinting. □ **look askance at** regard with suspicion or disapproval. [15th-century coinage]

askew ● *adv.* obliquely; awry. ● *predic.adj.* oblique; awry.

asking price *n.* the price of an object set by the seller.

aslant ● *adv.* obliquely or at a slant. ● *prep.* obliquely across (*lay aslant the path*).

asleep *predic.adj. & adv.* **1** in or into a state of sleep (*he fell asleep*). **2** (of a limb etc.) numb. **3** *euphem.* dead.

asocial *adj.* **1** not social; antisocial. **2** inconsiderate of or hostile to others.

asp *n.* **1** a small viper, *Vipera aspis*, native to southern Europe. **2** the Egyptian cobra, *Naja haje*, found throughout Africa. [from Greek]

asparagus *n.* **1** any plant of the genus *Asparagus*. **2** ◀ one species of this, *A. officinalis*, with edible young shoots and leaves. [from Greek *asparagos*]

asparagus fern *n.* a decorative plant, *Asparagus setaceus*.

aspartame *n.* a very sweet low-calorie substance used as a sweetener.

aspartic acid *n. Biochem.* an acidic amino acid present in many proteins, important in animal metabolism, and also acting as a neurotransmitter. [from French *aspartique*]

aspect *n.* **1 a** a particular component or feature of a matter (*only one aspect of the problem*). **b** a particular way in which a matter may be considered. **2 a** a facial expression; a look (*a cheerful aspect*). **b** the appearance of a person or thing (*has a frightening aspect*). **3** the side of a building or location facing a particular direction (*southern aspect*). [from Latin *aspectus*, based on *specere* 'to look']

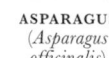

ASPARAGUS (*Asparagus officinalis*)

A

aspect ratio *n.* **1** *Aeron.* the ratio of the span to the mean chord of an aerofoil. **2** *Telev.* the ratio of picture width to height.

aspen *n.* a poplar tree, *Populus tremula*, with especially tremulous leaves. [Middle English]

asperity *n.* (*pl.* **-ies**) **1** harshness or sharpness of temper or tone. **2** roughness. [from Latin *asperitas*]

aspersion *n.* □ **cast aspersions on** attack the reputation or integrity of.

asphalt ● *n.* **1** a dark bituminous pitch occurring naturally or made from petroleum. **2** a mixture of this with sand, gravel, etc., for surfacing roads etc. ● *v.tr.* surface with asphalt. [from Greek *asphalton*] □ **asphaltic** *adj.*

asphodel *n.* **1** ▼ any of various plants of the genus *Asphodelus* and related genera of the lily family. **2** *poet.* an immortal flower growing in Elysium. [from Greek *asphodelos*]

asphyxia *n.* a lack of oxygen in the blood, causing unconsciousness or death; suffocation. [from Greek *asphuxia*] □ **asphyxiant** *adj. & n.*

asphyxiate *v.tr.* cause (a person) to have asphyxia; suffocate. □ **asphyxiation** *n.*

aspic *n.* a savoury meat jelly used as a garnish or to contain game, eggs, etc. [French, literally 'asp', from comparison with the colours of the jelly]

aspidistra *n.* a plant of the genus *Aspidistra*, with broad tapering leaves, native to the Far East. [based on *aspis -idos* 'shield', from the shape of the leaves]

aspirant ● *adj.* aspiring. ● *n.* a person who aspires. [from Latin *aspirant-* 'seeking to reach']

aspirate ● *adj.* *Phonet.* **1** pronounced with an exhalation of breath. **2** blended with the sound of *h*. ● *n.* *Phonet.* **1** a consonant pronounced in this way. **2** the sound of *h*. ● *v.* *Phonet.* **1** *tr.* pronounce with a breath. **b** *intr.* make the sound of *h*. **2** *tr.* draw (fluid) by suction from a vessel or cavity. [from Latin *aspiratus* 'breathed at']

ASPHODEL *(Asphodelus aestivus)*

aspiration *n.* **1** an ambition. **2** the act or process of drawing breath. **3** the action of aspirating. □ **aspirational** *adj.*

aspirator *n.* an apparatus for aspirating fluid.

aspire *v.intr.* **1** have ambition. **2** *poet.* rise high. [from Latin *aspirare* 'to breathe upon, seek to reach']

aspirin *n.* (*pl.* same or **aspirins**) **1** a white compound, acetylsalicylic acid, used to relieve pain and fever and in the prevention of thrombosis. **2** a tablet of this.

ass[1] *n.* **1 a** either of two kinds of four-legged long-eared mammal of the horse genus *Equus*, *E. africanus* of Africa and *E. hemionus* of Asia. **b** (in general use) a donkey. **2** a stupid person. [from Latin *asinus*]

ass[2] *N. Amer.* var. of ARSE.

assagai var. of ASSEGAI.

assail *v.tr.* **1** make a concerted attack on. **2** make a resolute start on (a task). **3** make a constant verbal attack on (*was assailed with angry questions*). [from Latin *assilire*, based on *salire* 'to leap'] □ **assailable** *adj.*

assailant *n.* a person who attacks another.

assassin *n.* a killer. [from Arabic *ḥašīšī* 'hashish-eater']

assassinate *v.tr.* **1** kill from political or religious motives. **2** destroy or injure (esp. a person's reputation). □ **assassination** *n.* **assassinator** *n.*

assault ● *n.* **1** a violent attack. **2 a** *Law* an act that threatens physical harm to a person. **b** *euphem.* an act of rape. **3** a vigorous start made to a lengthy or difficult task. **4** a final rush on a fortified place. **5** (*attrib.*) relating to or used in an assault (*assault troops*). ● *v.tr.* **1** make an assault on. **2** *euphem.* rape. [based on Latin *salire* salt- 'to leap'] □ **assaulter** *n.* **assaultive** *adj.*

assault course *n.* *Brit.* an obstacle course used in training soldiers etc.

assay ● *n.* **1** the testing of a metal or ore to determine its ingredients and quality. **2** *Chem.* etc. the determination of the content or concentration of a substance. ● *v.* **1** *tr.* make an assay of (a metal or ore). **2** *tr.* *Chem.* etc. determine the concentration of (a substance). **3** *tr.* show (content) on being assayed. **4** *intr.* make an assay. [from Old French *assaier*] □ **assayer** *n.*

assay office *n.* **1** *Brit.* an establishment which awards hallmarks. **2** esp. *N. Amer.* an office for the assaying of ores.

assegai *n.* (also **assagai**) ► a slender iron-tipped spear of hardwood, used by southern African peoples. [based on Arabic *al zaḡāyah* 'the spear']

assemblage *n.* **1** the act or an instance of bringing or coming together. **2** a collection of things or gathering of people.

assemble *v.* **1** *tr. & intr.* gather together; collect. **2** *tr.* arrange in order. **3** *tr.* esp. *Mech.* fit together the parts of. [based on Latin *simul* 'together']

assembler *n.* **1** a person who assembles a machine or its parts. **2** *Computing* **a** a program for converting instructions written in low-level symbolic code into machine code. **b** the low-level symbolic code itself; an assembly language.

assembly *n.* (*pl.* **-ies**) **1** the act or an instance of assembling or gathering together. **2 a** a group of persons gathered together. **b** a gathering of the entire membership or a section of a school. **3** the assembling of a machine or structure or its parts.

assembly language *n.* *Computing* the low-level symbolic code converted by an assembler.

assembly line *n.* machinery arranged in stages by which the components of a product are progressively assembled.

assembly rooms *n.pl.* esp. *Brit.* public rooms in which meetings or social functions are held.

assent ● *v.intr.* **1** express agreement (*assented to my view*). **2** consent (*assented to my request*). ● *n.* **1** mental or inward acceptance or agreement (*a nod of assent*). **2** consent or sanction. [from Latin *assentari*]

assert *v.tr.* **1** declare; state clearly (*assert one's beliefs; assert that it is so*). **2** *refl.* insist on one's rights or opinions; demand recognition. **3** vindicate a claim to (*assert one's rights*). [based on Latin *assertus* 'claimed, declared']

assertion *n.* **1** a declaration; a forthright statement. **2** the act or an instance of asserting. **3** (also **self-assertion**) insistence on the recognition of one's rights or claims.

assertive *adj.* **1** tending to assert oneself; forthright, positive. **2** dogmatic. □ **assertively** *adv.* **assertiveness** *n.*

assess *v.tr.* **1 a** estimate the size or quality of. **b** estimate the value of (a property) for taxation etc. **2 a** fix the amount of (a tax etc.) and impose it on a person or community. **b** fine or tax (a person, community, etc.) in or at a specific amount (*assessed them at £100*). [from Latin *assidēre* 'to sit by' (in judgement)] □ **assessable** *adj.* **assessment** *n.*

assessor *n.* **1** a person who assesses taxes or estimates the value of property for taxation or *Brit.* insurance purposes. **2** a person called upon to advise a judge, committee of inquiry, etc., on technical questions.

asset *n.* **1 a** a useful or valuable quality. **b** a person or thing possessing such a quality or qualities (*is an asset to the firm*). **2** (usu. in *pl.*) property and possessions, esp. regarded as having value in meeting debts, commitments, etc. [based on Old French *asez* 'enough']

asset-stripping *n.* the practice of taking over a company and selling off its assets to make a profit. □ **asset-stripper** *n.*

asseverate *v.tr.* declare solemnly or emphatically. [from Latin *asseverare*, based on *severus* 'severe'] □ **asseveration** *n.*

asshole *N. Amer.* var. of ARSEHOLE.

assiduity *n.* constant or close attention to what one is doing. [from Latin *assiduitas*]

assiduous *adj.* persevering, hard-working. [based on Latin *assidēre* 'to sit by', hence 'to apply oneself closely to'] □ **assiduously** *adv.* **assiduousness** *n.*

assign ● *v.tr.* **1 a** allot a share or responsibility. **b** appoint to a position, task, etc. **2** fix (a time, place, etc.) for a specific purpose. **3** (foll. by *to*) ascribe or refer to (a reason, date, etc.) (*assigned the manuscript to 1832*). **4** (foll. by *to*) transfer formally to. ● *n.* a person to whom property or rights are legally transferred. [from Latin *assignare* 'to mark out to'] □ **assignable** *adj.*

assignation *n.* **1 a** an appointment to meet. **b** a secret appointment, esp. between illicit lovers. **2** the act or an instance of assigning or being assigned.

assignee *n.* **1** a person appointed to act for another. **2** an assign.

assignment *n.* **1** something assigned, esp. a task allotted to a person. **2** the act or an instance of assigning or being assigned. **3 a** a legal transfer. **b** the document effecting this.

assimilate *v.tr.* **1 a** absorb (food etc.) into the body. **b** absorb (information etc.) into the mind. **c** absorb (people) into a larger group. **2** make like; cause to resemble. [based on Latin *assimilatus* 'likened'] □ **assimilable** *adj.* **assimilation** *n.* **assimilative** *adj.* **assimilator** *n.* **assimilatory** *adj.*

assist *v.* **1** *tr.* help (a person, process, etc.) (*assisted them in running the playgroup*). **2** *intr.* attend or be present (*assisted in the ceremony*). [from Latin *assistere* 'to take one's stand by'] □ **assistance** *n.*

assistant *n.* **1** a helper. **2** (often *attrib.*) a person who assists. **3** *Brit.* = SHOP ASSISTANT.

assize *n.* (usu. in *pl.*) *hist.* a court sitting at intervals in each county of England and Wales to administer the civil and criminal law. [from Old French *as(s)ise* 'sitting, assessment']

ass-licking *N. Amer.* var. of ARSE-LICKING.

associate ● *v.* **1** *tr.* connect in the mind (*associate holly with Christmas*). **2** *tr.* join or combine. **3** *refl.* make oneself a partner; declare oneself in agreement (*associate myself in your endeavour*). **4** *intr.* combine for a common purpose. **5** *intr.* meet frequently or have dealings. ● *n.* **1** a business partner or colleague. **2** a friend or companion. **3** a subordinate member of a body, institute, etc. ● *adj.* **1** joined in companionship, function, or dignity. **2** allied. **3** of less than full status (*associate member*). [from Latin *associatus*] □ **associateship** *n.*

association *n.* **1** a group of people organized for a joint purpose. **2** the act or an instance of associating. **3** fellowship; human contact or cooperation. **4** a mental connection between ideas. □ **associational** *adj.*

Association Football *n.* *Brit.* football played by teams of 11 players with a round ball which may not be handled during play except by the goalkeepers. ▷ FOOTBALL

associative *adj.* of or involving association.

assonance *n.* the resemblance of sound between two syllables in nearby words, arising from the rhyming of two or more accented vowels, but not consonants, or the use of identical consonants with different vowels. [based on Latin *assonare* 'to respond to']

assort *v.* **1** *tr.* classify or arrange in groups. **2** *intr.* suit; harmonize with (usu. in *phrs.* **assort ill** or **well with**). [from Old French *assortir*]

assorted *adj.* **1** of various sorts put together; miscellaneous. **2** sorted into groups. **3** matched (*ill-assorted; poorly assorted*).

assortment *n.* a set of various sorts of things or people put together.

ASSEGAI

ASTEROID

Asteroids are small bodies, composed of rock and iron, that were unable to form distinct planets when the solar system was born. They orbit the Sun, most of them travelling in a belt between Mars and Jupiter. Jupiter's gravitational pull can send asteroids into erratic orbits, causing them to collide with planets and other asteroids.

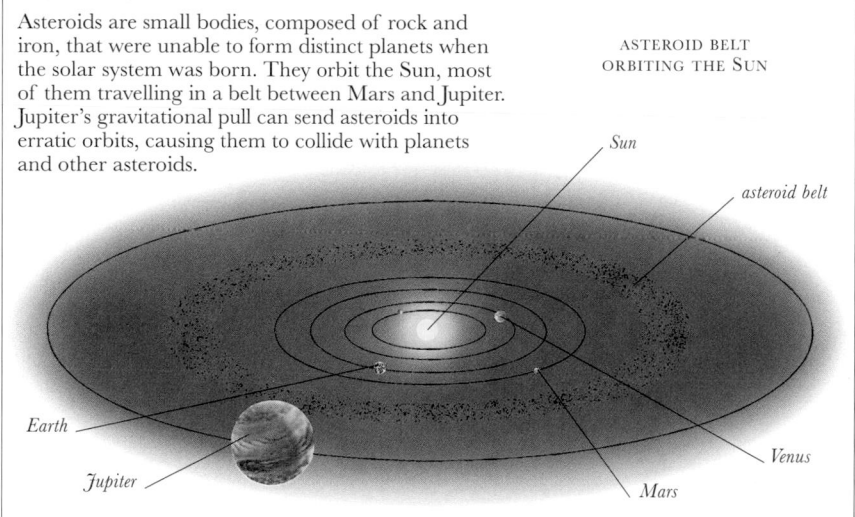

ASTEROID BELT ORBITING THE SUN

Sun

asteroid belt

Earth

Jupiter

Venus

Mars

A

---

assuage /ă-**swayj**/ v.tr. **1** soothe (a person, pain, etc.). **2** appease or relieve (an appetite or desire). [based on Latin *suavis* 'sweet'] □ **assuagement** n.

assume v.tr. **1** accept as being true, without proof, for the purpose of argument or action. **2** pretend (ignorance etc.). **3** undertake (an office or duty). **4** take or put on oneself or itself (an aspect, attribute, etc.) (*the problem assumed immense proportions*). **5** arrogate, usurp, or seize (credit, power, etc.) (*assumed to himself the right of veto*). [from Latin *(ad) sumere* 'to take (to oneself)']

assumption n. **1** the act or an instance of assuming. **2 a** the act or an instance of accepting without proof. **b** a thing assumed in this way. **3** arrogance. **4** (**Assumption**) the reception of the Virgin Mary bodily into heaven, according to Roman Catholic doctrine. [related to ASSUME]

assurance n. **1** a positive declaration that a thing is true. **2** a solemn promise or guarantee. **3** esp. *Brit.* insurance. **4** certainty. **5 a** self-confidence. **b** impudence.

assure v.tr. **1 a** make (a person) sure; convince (*assured him of my sincerity*). **b** tell (a person) confidently (*assured him the bus went to Westminster*). **2 a** make certain of; ensure the happening etc. of (*will assure her success*). **b** make safe (against overthrow etc.). **3** esp. *Brit.* insure. **4** (as **assured** adj.) **a** guaranteed. **b** self-confident. [based on Latin *securus* 'safe, secure'] □ **assurer** n.

assuredly adv. certainly.

astatine /**ass**-tă-teen/ n. *Chem.* a radioactive element, the heaviest of the halogens, which occurs naturally.

aster n. a plant of the genus *Aster* (daisy family), with bright rayed flowers. [from Greek *astēr* 'star']

asterisk ● n. a symbol (*) used in printing and writing to mark words etc. for reference, to stand for omitted matter, etc. ● v.tr. mark with an asterisk. [from Greek *asteriskos* 'little star']

astern adv. *Naut.* & *Aeron.* **1** aft; away to the rear. **2** backwards.

asteroid n. **1** ▲ a small rocky body orbiting the Sun. **2** *Zool.* a starfish. ▷ ECHINODERM, STARFISH. [based on Greek *astēr* 'star'] □ **asteroidal** adj.

asthma n. a respiratory disease, often with paroxysms of difficult breathing. [based on Greek *azein* 'to breathe hard']

asthmatic ● adj. relating to or suffering from asthma. ● n. a person suffering from asthma. □ **asthmatically** adv.

astigmatism n. a defect in the eye or in a lens resulting in distorted images, as light rays are

prevented from meeting at a common focus. [based on Greek *a-* 'without' + *stigma* 'point'] □ **astigmatic** adj.

astilbe n. a plant of the genus *Astilbe* (saxifrage family), with plumelike heads of tiny white or red flowers. [from Greek *a-* 'not' + *stilbē* (fem.) 'glittering', from the inconspicuous (individual) flowers]

astir predic.adj. & adv. **1** in motion. **2** awake and out of bed (*already astir*). **3** excited.

astonish v.tr. amaze; surprise greatly. [based on Latin *tonare* 'to thunder'] □ **astonishing** adj. **astonishingly** adv. **astonishment** n.

astound v.tr. shock with alarm or surprise; amaze. [related to ASTONISH] □ **astounding** adj. **astoundingly** adv.

astral adj. **1** of or connected with the stars. **2** consisting of stars; starry. [based on Late Latin *astrum* 'star']

astray adv. & predic.adj. **1** in or into error or sin (esp. in phr. **lead astray**). **2** out of the right way. □ **go astray** be lost or mislaid. [probably from Old French *estraié* 'strayed']

astride ● adv. **1** with a leg on each side. **2** with legs apart. ● prep. with a leg on each side of.

astringent ● adj. **1** causing the contraction of body tissues. **2** checking bleeding. **3** severe, austere. ● n. an astringent substance or drug. [from Latin *astringent-* 'binding together'] □ **astringency** n. **astringently** adv.

astro- comb. form **1** relating to the stars or celestial objects. **2** relating to outer space. [from Greek *astron* 'star']

astrolabe n. ▶ an instrument formerly used to make astronomical measurements, esp. of the altitudes of celestial bodies, and as an aid in navigation. [from Greek *astrolabon* 'star-taking (instrument)']

astrology n. the study of the movements and relative positions of celestial bodies interpreted as having an influence on human affairs. [from Latin *astrologia*] ▷ ZODIAC. □ **astrologer** n. **astrological** adj. **astrologist** n.

astronaut n. a person who is trained to travel in a spacecraft. □ **astronautical** adj.

astronautics n. the science of space travel.

astronomical adj. (also **astronomic**) **1** of or relating to astronomy. **2** extremely large; too large to contemplate. □ **astronomically** adv.

astronomy n. the scientific study of celestial objects, of space, and of the physical universe as a whole. [from Greek *astronomia* 'star-arranging (matters)'] □ **astronomer** n.

astrophysics n. a branch of astronomy concerned with the physics of celestial bodies. □ **astrophysical** adj. **astrophysicist** n.

astute adj. **1** shrewd; sagacious. **2** crafty. [from Latin *astutus*, based on *astus* 'craft'] □ **astutely** adv. **astuteness** n.

asunder adv. *literary* apart. [Old English]

asylum n. **1** sanctuary; protection (*seek asylum*). **2** esp. *hist.* any of various kinds of institution offering shelter to distressed individuals, esp. the mentally ill. [from Greek *asulon* 'refuge']

asymmetry n. (pl. **-ies**) lack of symmetry. [from Greek *asummetria*] □ **asymmetric** adj. **asymmetrical** adj. **asymmetrically** adv.

asymptomatic adj. producing or showing no symptoms.

asynchronous adj. not synchronous. □ **asynchronously** adv.

At symb. *Chem.* the element astatine.

at prep. **1** expressing position, exact or approximate (*wait at the corner; met at Bath; is at school; at a distance*). **2** expressing a point in time (*see you at three; went at dawn*). **3** expressing a point in a scale or range (*at boiling point; at his best*). **4** expressing engagement or involvement in a state or activity (*at work; at odds*). **5** expressing a value or rate (*sell at £10 each*). **6 a** with or with reference to; in terms of (*at a disadvantage; annoyed at losing; good at cricket; sick at heart; at short notice*). **b** in response to (*starts at a touch*). **c** by means of (*drank it at a gulp*). **7** expressing: **a** motion towards (*went at them*). **b** aim towards or pursuit of (*aim at the target; guess at the truth; laughed at us; has been at the milk again*). □ **at that** moreover (*found one, and a good one at that*). [Old English]

atavism n. **1** a resemblance to remote ancestors rather than to parents in plants or animals. **2** reversion to an earlier type. [based on Latin *atavus* 'great grandfather's grandfather'] □ **atavistic** adj. **atavistically** adv.

ataxia n. *Med.* the loss of full control of bodily movements. [based on Greek *taxis* 'order'] □ **ataxic** adj.

ate past of EAT.

atelier n. a workshop or studio. [French]

atheism n. the belief that God does not exist. [based on Greek *atheos* 'without God'] □ **atheist** n. **atheistic** adj. **atheistical** adj.

atherosclerosis n. a form of arteriosclerosis characterized by the degeneration of the arteries because of the build-up of fatty deposits. [from German *Atherosklerose*] □ **atherosclerotic** adj.

athirst predic.adj. *poet.* **1** eager (*athirst for knowledge*). **2** thirsty.

athlete n. **1** a skilled performer in physical exercises, esp. *Brit.* in track and field events. **2** a healthy person with natural athletic ability. [based on Greek *athlon* 'prize']

athlete's foot n. a fungal foot condition.

athletic adj. **1** of or relating to athletes or athletics (*an athletic competition*). **2** muscular or physically powerful. □ **athletically** adv. **athleticism** n.

athletics n.pl. (usu. treated as *sing.*) **1** esp. *Brit.* **a** track and field events (often *attrib.*: *athletics meeting*). **b** the practice of these. ▷ TRACK. **2** *N. Amer.* physical sports and games of any kind.

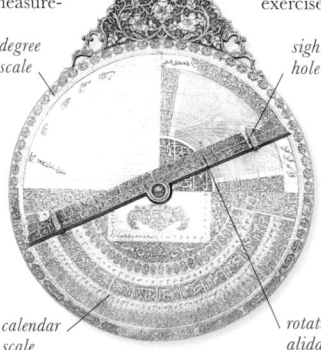

degree scale

sight hole

calendar scale

rotating alidade

ASTROLABE: 18TH-CENTURY PERSIAN ASTROLABE

A

ATMOSPHERE

The Earth's atmosphere is about 700 km (430 miles) deep and is divided into five main layers according to the way the temperature changes with height. The lowest layer, the troposphere, contains over 75 per cent of all the gas in the atmosphere, as well as vast quantities of water. Air movement within this layer produces the Earth's weather. Above the troposphere are the stratosphere, mesosphere, thermosphere, and exosphere. The ozone layer lies within the stratosphere, providing protection from the Sun's harmful ultraviolet rays. Radio signals transmit by bouncing off the ionosphere, a layer within the thermosphere that is made up of electrically charged (ionized) gas particles.

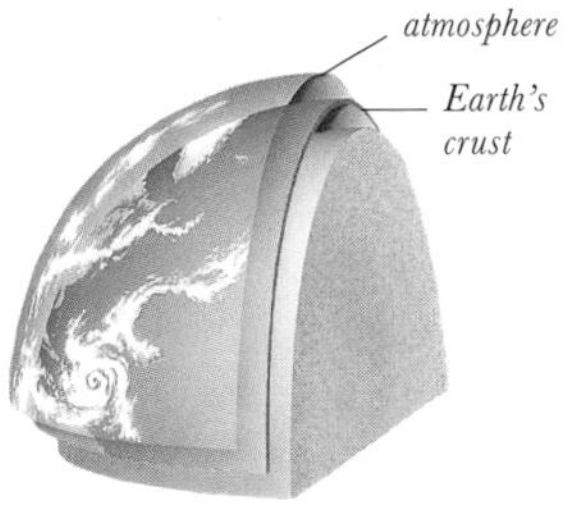

exosphere

satellite

high-level aurora

meteor

thermosphere

atmosphere

Earth's crust

SECTION OF THE
EARTH SHOWING THE
RELATIVE THICKNESS
OF ITS ATMOSPHERE

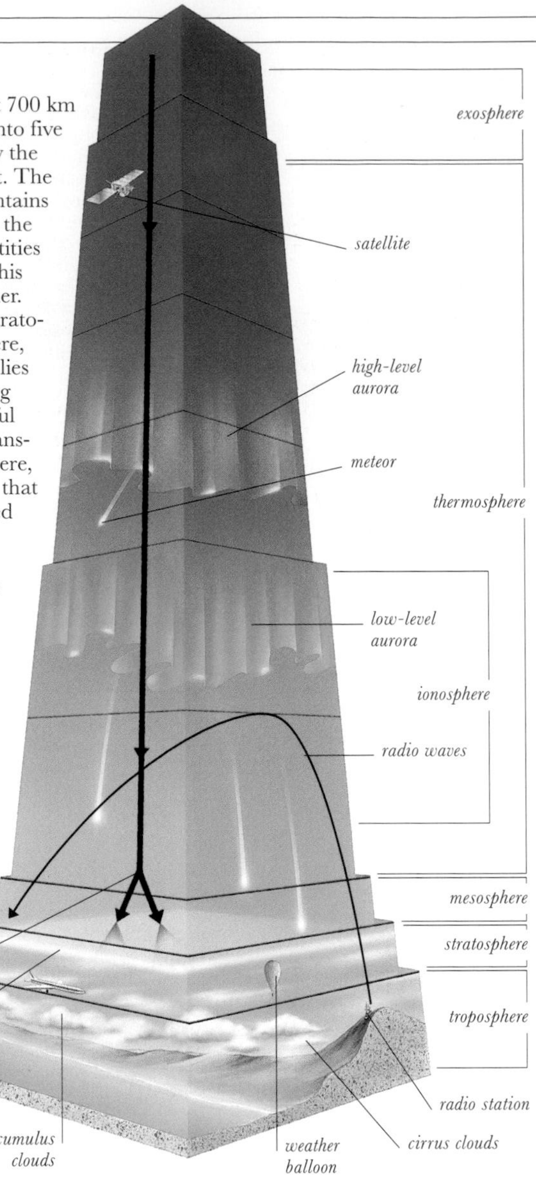

low-level aurora

ionosphere

radio waves

mesosphere

stratosphere

troposphere

ultraviolet rays

ozone layer

radio station

DIVISIONS OF THE
EARTH'S ATMOSPHERE

cumulus clouds

weather balloon

cirrus clouds

at-home *n.* a social reception in a person's home.

athwart ● *adv.* **1** across from side to side. **2** perversely or in opposition. ● *prep.* **1** from side to side of. **2** in opposition to.

Atlantic Ocean *n.* the ocean between Europe and Africa to the east, and America to the west. ▷ OCEAN

atlas *n.* a book of maps or charts. [from Greek *Atlas*, a Titan who held up the pillars of the universe, illustrated in early atlases]

ATM *abbr.* automated teller machine.

atmosphere *n.* **1 a** ▲ the envelope of gases surrounding the Earth, any other planet, or any substance. **b** the air in any particular place. **2 a** the pervading tone or mood of a place or situation, esp. with reference to the feelings or emotions evoked. **b** the feelings or emotions evoked by a work or art, a piece of music, etc. **3** *Physics* a unit of pressure equal to mean atmospheric

pressure at sea level. [from Greek *atmos* 'vapour' + *sphaira* 'ball'] □ **atmospheric** *adj.* **atmospherically** *adv.*

atmospherics *n.pl.* **1** electrical disturbance in the atmosphere. **2** interference with telecommunications caused by this.

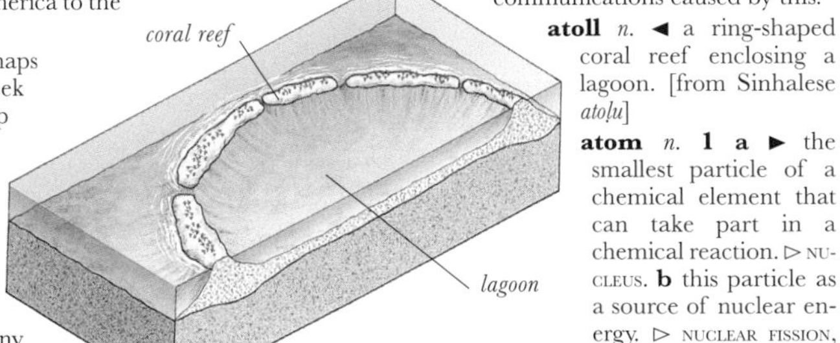

coral reef

atoll *n.* ◀ a ring-shaped coral reef enclosing a lagoon. [from Sinhalese *atolu*]

atom *n.* **1 a** ▶ the smallest particle of a chemical element that can take part in a chemical reaction. ▷ NUCLEUS. **b** this particle as a source of nuclear energy. ▷ NUCLEAR FISSION, NUCLEAR FUSION. **2** (usu. with *neg*) the least portion of a thing or quality (*not an atom of pity*). [from Greek *atomos* 'indivisible (one)']

lagoon

ATOLL: SECTION
THROUGH AN ATOLL

atom bomb *n.* a bomb which derives its power from the release of energy by nuclear fission.

atomic *adj.* **1** concerned with or using atomic energy or atom bombs. **2** of or relating to an atom or atoms. □ **atomically** *adv.*

atomic bomb *n.* = ATOM BOMB.

atomic clock *n.* ▼ a clock in which the timescale is regulated by the vibrations of an atomic or molecular system such as caesium.

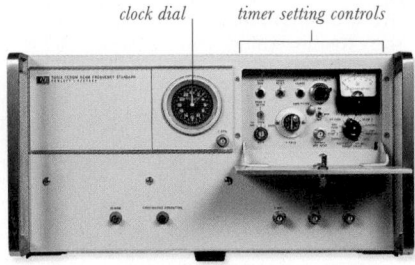

clock dial   *timer setting controls*

ATOMIC CLOCK

atomic energy *n.* nuclear energy. ▷ NUCLEAR POWER

atomicity *n.* **1** the number of atoms in the molecules of an element. **2** the state or fact of being composed of atoms.

atomic mass *n.* the mass of an atom measured in atomic mass units.

atomic mass unit *n.* a unit of mass used to express atomic and molecular weights that is equal to one-twelfth of the mass of an atom of carbon-12.

atomic number *n.* the number of protons in the nucleus of an atom, which is characteristic of a chemical element and determines its place in the periodic table.

atomic physics *n.* the branch of physics concerned with the structure of the atom and the characteristics of the subatomic particles.

atomic pile *n.* a nuclear reactor.

atomic power *n.* nuclear power. ▷ NUCLEAR POWER

atomic theory *n.* **1** *Physics* the theory that atoms are composed of subatomic particles. **2** the theory that all matter is made up of tiny indivisible particles called atoms.

atomic weight *n.* = RELATIVE ATOMIC MASS.

atomize *v.tr.* (also **-ise**) reduce to atoms or fine particles. □ **atomization** *n.*

atomizer *n.* (also **-iser**) an instrument for emitting liquids as a fine spray.

atonal /ay-toh-năl/ *adj. Mus.* not written in any key or mode. □ **atonality** *n.*

ATOM

Inside an atom is a nucleus made up of protons and neutrons. The nucleus is orbited by electrons, travelling so fast that they seem to form a solid shell. The atom of carbon-12 shown is so named because its nucleus comprises six protons and six neutrons. Electrons surround its nucleus in two separate layers.

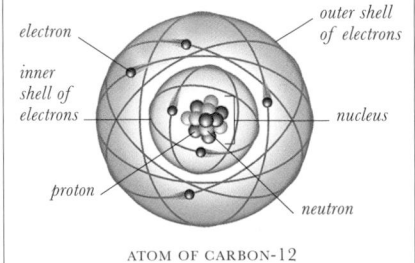

electron

inner shell of electrons

outer shell of electrons

nucleus

proton

neutron

ATOM OF CARBON-12

A

atone *v.intr.* (usu. foll. by *for*) make amends; expiate (a wrong).

atonement *n.* **1** expiation; reparation for a wrong or injury. **2** the reconciliation of God and man. □ the **Atonement** the expiation by Christ of mankind's sin. [based on *at one*, from obsolete verb *one* 'to unite']

atop ● *adv.* on the top. ● *prep.* on the top of.

atrium *n.* (*pl.* **atriums** or **atria**) **1 a** the central court of an ancient Roman house. **b** ► a central court rising through several storeys with galleries and rooms opening off at each level. **c** (in a modern house) a central hall or glazed court with rooms opening off it. **2** *Anat.* a cavity in the body, esp. one of the two upper cavities of the heart, receiving blood from the veins. ▷ HEART. [Latin] □ **atrial** *adj.*

ATRIUM IN A 19TH-CENTURY AUSTRALIAN SHOPPING ARCADE

atrocious *adj.* **1** very bad or unpleasant (*atrocious weather; their manners were atrocious*). **2** extremely savage or wicked (*atrocious cruelty*). [from Latin *atrox -ocis* 'cruel'] □ **atrociously** *adv.*

atrocity *n.* (*pl.* **-ies**) **1** an extremely wicked or cruel act. **2** extreme wickedness. [based on Latin *atrox -ocis* 'cruel']

atrophy ● *v.* (**-ies, -ied**) **1** *intr.* waste away through undernourishment, ageing, or lack of use. **2** *tr.* cause to atrophy. ● *n.* the process of atrophying. [from Late Latin *atrophia*]

atropine *n.* a poisonous alkaloid found in deadly nightshade, used in medicine. [based on modern Latin *Atropa belladonna* 'deadly nightshade']

attach *v.* **1** *tr.* fasten, affix, join. **2** *tr.* (in *passive*; foll. by *to*) be very fond of or devoted to (*am deeply attached to her*). **3** *tr.* attribute, assign (some function, quality, or characteristic) (*attaches great importance to it*). **4 a** *tr.* include; cause to form part of a thing (*no conditions are attached*). **b** *intr.* (foll. by *to*) be an attribute or characteristic (*great prestige attaches to the job*). **5** *refl.* take part in; join (*attached themselves to the expedition*). **6** *tr.* appoint for special or temporary duties. **7** *tr. Law* seize (a person or property) by legal authority. [from Old French *estachier*] □ **attachable** *adj.*

attaché /ă-**tash**-ay/ *n.* a person appointed to an ambassador's staff, usu. with a special sphere of activity (*military attaché; press attaché*). [French]

attaché case *n.* a small flat rectangular case for carrying documents etc.

attachment *n.* **1** a thing attached or to be attached. **2** affection, devotion. **3** a means of attaching. **4** the act of attaching or the state of being attached. **5** legal seizure. **6** *Brit.* a temporary position in, or secondment to, an organization.

attack ● *v.* **1** *tr.* act against with force. **2** *tr.* seek to hurt or defeat. **3** *tr.* criticize adversely. **4** *tr.* act harmfully upon (*a virus attacking the nervous system; rust had attacked the metal*). **5** *tr.* vigorously apply oneself to (*attacked his meal with gusto*). **6** *tr.* (in various games) try to score goals, points, etc. against (one's opponents). **7** *intr.* make an attack. **8** *intr.* be in a mode of attack. ● *n.* **1** an act, or the process, of acting against a person or thing with force; an offensive operation or mode of behaviour. **2** a sudden occurrence of an illness. **3** gusto, vigour. **4** *Mus.* the action or manner of beginning a piece, passage, etc. **5** a player or players seeking to score goals etc. [from Italian *attacco*] □ **attacker** *n.*

attain *v.* **1** *tr.* arrive at; reach (a goal etc.). **2** *tr.* gain, accomplish (an aim, distinction, etc.). **3** *intr.* (foll. by *to*) arrive at by conscious development or effort. [from Latin *attingere*, based on *tangere* 'to touch'] □ **attainability** *n.* **attainable** *adj.*

attainment *n.* **1** something attained or achieved. **2** the act or an instance of attaining.

attar *n.* (also **otto**) a fragrant essential oil. [from Arabic *'iṭr* 'perfume']

attempt ● *v.tr.* **1** seek to achieve or complete (a task or action) (*attempted the exercise; attempted to explain*). **2** seek to climb or master (a mountain etc.). ● *n.* **1** an act of attempting; an endeavour (*made an attempt at winning; an attempt to succeed*). **2** (foll. by *on*) an attack; an effort to overcome (*an attempt on his life; attempt on the world record*). [from Latin *attemptare*]

attend *v.* **1** *tr.* **a** be present at (*attended the meeting*). **b** go regularly to (*attends the local school*). **2** *intr.* **a** be present (*many members failed to attend*). **b** be present in a serving capacity; wait. **3 a** *tr.* escort, accompany (*the king was attended by soldiers*). **b** *intr.* (foll. by *on*) wait on; serve. **4** *intr.* **a** turn or apply one's mind; focus one's attention (*attend to what I am saying*). **b** (foll. by *to*) deal with (*shall attend to the matter myself*). **5** *tr.* follow as a result from (*the error was attended by serious consequences*). [from Latin *adtendere* 'to stretch to'] □ **attendee** *n.* **attender** *n.*

attendance *n.* **1** the act of attending or being present. **2** the number of people present.

attendance allowance *n.* (in the UK) a state benefit paid to disabled people in need of constant care at home.

attendance centre *n.* (in the UK) a place where young offenders report by order of a court as a minor penalty.

attendant ● *n.* a person employed to wait on others or provide a service. ● *adj.* **1** accompanying (*attendant circumstances*). **2** waiting on (*ladies attendant on the queen*). [Middle English]

attention *n.* **1** the act or faculty of applying one's mind (*attract his attention*). **2** consideration; care (*special attention*). **3** (in *pl.*) **a** ceremonious politeness (*he paid his attentions to her*). **b** wooing; courting (*she was the subject of his attentions*). **4** *Mil.* an erect attitude of readiness (*stand at attention*). ● *int.* **1** (in full **stand at** or **to attention!**) *Mil.* an order to assume an attitude of attention. **2** an imperative warning, to gain attention (*attention please!*). [Middle English, related to ATTEND] □ **attentional** *adj.*

attentive *adj.* **1** paying attention. **2** assiduously polite. **3** heedful. [related to ATTEND] □ **attentively** *adv.* **attentiveness** *n.*

attenuate ● *v.tr.* **1** make thin. **2** reduce in force, value, or virulence. ● *adj.* **1** slender. **2** tapering gradually. **3** rarefied. [based on Latin *tenuis* 'thin'] □ **attenuated** *adj.* **attenuation** *n.* **attenuator** *n.*

attest *v.* **1** *tr.* **a** certify the validity of. **b** be evidence of. **2** *intr.* (foll. by *to*) bear witness to. [based on Latin *testis* 'witness'] □ **attestable** *adj.* **attestation** *n.* **attestor** *n.*

Attic ● *adj.* of or relating to ancient Athens or Attica, or the form of Greek spoken there. ● *n.* the form of Greek used by the ancient Athenians. [from Greek *Attikos*]

attic *n.* **1** the uppermost storey in a house, usu. under the roof. **2** a room in the attic area. [related to ATTIC: originally (*Archit.*) a small order (column and entablature) above a taller one]

attire *formal* ● *v.tr.* dress, esp. in fine clothes or formal wear. ● *n.* clothes, esp. fine or formal. [from Old French *atir(i)er* 'to equip']

attitude *n.* **1 a** a settled opinion or way of thinking. **b** behaviour reflecting this (*I don't like his attitude*). **2 a** a bodily posture. **b** a pose adopted for dramatic effect (*strike an attitude*). **3** esp. *N. Amer. slang* truculence; arrogance. **b** style, swagger. [from Late Latin *aptitudo*] □ **attitudinal** *adj.* **attitudinize** *v.intr.*

attorney *n.* (*pl.* **-eys**) **1** a person appointed to act for another in business or legal matters. **2** *US* a qualified lawyer, esp. one representing a client in a law court. [from Old French *atorné* 'assigned'] □ **attorneyship** *n.*

Attorney-General *n.* the chief legal officer in England, the US, and other countries.

attract *v.tr.* **1** (also *absol.*) draw or bring to oneself or itself (*attracts many admirers*). **2** be attractive to; fascinate. **3** (of a magnet, etc.) exert a pull on (an object). [based on Latin *attractus* 'drawn to'] □ **attractable** *adj.* **attractant** *n. & adj.* **attractor** *n.*

attraction *n.* **1 a** the act or power of attracting (*the attraction of foreign travel*). **b** a person or thing that attracts by arousing interest (*the fair is a big attraction*). **2** *Physics* the force by which bodies attract or approach each other.

attractive *adj.* **1** attracting or capable of attracting (*an attractive proposition*). **2** aesthetically pleasing. □ **attractively** *adv.* **attractiveness** *n.*

attribute ● *v.tr.* /ă-**tri**-bewt/ (foll. by *to*) **1** ascribe to or regard as the effect of (a stated cause) (*delays were attributed to the heavy traffic*). **2** regard as having been created or originated by (*attributed to Shakespeare*). **3** regard as characteristic of; regard as possessing or having (*attributed magical powers to their gods*). ● *n.* /**at**-ri-bewt/ **1 a** a quality ascribed to a person or thing. **b** a characteristic quality. **2** a material object recognized as appropriate to a person, office, or status (*a large car is an attribute of seniority*). [from Latin *attribuere attribut-* 'to assign to'] □ **attributable** *adj.* **attribution** *n.*

attributive *adj. Gram.* (of an adjective or noun) preceding the word it qualifies or modifies and expressing an attribute, as *old* in *the old dog* (but not in *the dog is old*) and *expiry* in *expiry date* (opp. PREDICATIVE 1). □ **attributively** *adv.*

attrition *n.* **1** the act or process of gradually wearing out, esp. by friction. **2** abrasion. [from Late Latin *attritio*, based on *atterere* 'to rub'] □ **attritional** *adj.*

attune *v.tr.* **1** adjust (a person or thing) to a situation. **2** bring (an orchestra, instrument, etc.) into musical accord.

atypical *adj.* not typical; not conforming to a type. □ **atypically** *adv.*

Au *symb. Chem.* the element gold. [Latin *aurum*]

aubergine /**oh**-ber-*zheen*/ esp. *Brit.* ● *n.* **1** a tropical plant, *Solanum melongena*, having erect or spreading branches bearing egg-shaped fruit. **2** ◄ this fruit eaten as a vegetable. **3** the dark purple colour of this fruit. ● *adj.* dark purple. [French, literally 'little peach']

AUBERGINE
(*Solanum melongena*)

aubrietia /aw-**bree**-shă/ *n.* (also **aubretia**) a dwarf perennial rock plant of the genus *Aubrieta*, having purple or pink flowers in spring. [named after Claude *Aubriet*, French botanist, 1668–1743]

auburn ● *adj.* (usu. of a person's hair) reddish-brown. ● *n.* this colour. [originally in sense 'yellowish white': from Latin *alburnus* 'whitish']

auction ● *n.* a sale of goods in which articles are sold to the highest bidder. ● *v.tr.* sell by auction. [from Latin *auctio* 'increase, auction']

auctioneer *n.* a person who conducts auctions professionally, by calling for bids and declaring goods sold. □ **auctioneering** *n.*

auction house *n.* a company that runs auctions.

auction room *n.* (often in *pl.*) the premises where auctions take place.

AUDITORIUM

A myriad of seating variations have been devised to allow an audience to appreciate a performance within a theatre or concert hall fully. Most make use of tiered seating, angled to give spectators an unobstructed view of the stage. In the auditorium shown here, balconies and seating behind the stage have been added to maximize audience capacity.

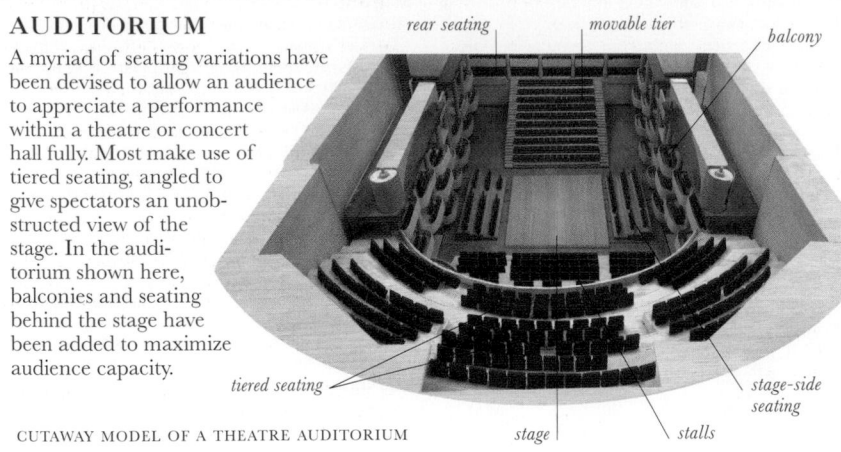

rear seating   *movable tier*   *balcony*

tiered seating   *stage-side seating*

stage   *stalls*

CUTAWAY MODEL OF A THEATRE AUDITORIUM

---

auction sale *n.* = AUCTION *n.*

audacious *adj.* **1** daring, bold. **2** impudent. [from Latin *audax -acis*] □ **audaciously** *adv.* **audaciousness** *n.* **audacity** *n.*

audible *adj.* capable of being heard. [based on Latin *audire* 'to hear'] □ **audibility** *n.* **audibly** *adv.*

audience *n.* **1 a** the assembled listeners or spectators at an event. **b** the people addressed by a film, play, etc. **2** a formal interview with a person in authority. **3** *archaic* a hearing (*give audience to my plea*). [from Latin *audientia*]

audio *n.* (usu. *attrib.*) sound or the reproduction of sound.

audio- *comb. form* hearing or sound.

audio cassette *n.* a cassette of audiotape.

audiology *n.* the science of hearing. □ **audiologist** *n.*

audiotape *n.* (also **audio tape**) **1 a** magnetic tape on which sound can be recorded. **b** a length of this, esp. an audio cassette. **2** a sound recording on tape.

audio-visual *adj.* (esp. of teaching methods) using both sight and sound.

audit ● *n.* an official examination of accounts. ● *v.tr.* (**audited**, **auditing**) conduct an audit of. [from Latin *auditus* 'hearing']

audition ● *n.* an interview for a role as a singer, actor, etc., consisting of a practical demonstration of suitability. ● *v.* **1** *tr.* interview (a candidate) at an audition. **2** *intr.* be interviewed at an audition. [based on Latin *audire audit-* 'to hear']

auditor *n.* **1** a person who conducts an audit. **2** a listener. [Middle English, from Latin *auditor*] □ **auditorial** *adj.*

auditorium *n.* (*pl.* **auditoriums** or **auditoria**) ▲ the part of a theatre etc. in which the audience sits. ▷ AMPHITHEATRE, THEATRE. [Latin]

auditory *adj.* **1** concerned with hearing. **2** received by the ear.

au fait /oh **fay**/ *predic.adj.* (usu. foll. by *with*) having current knowledge (*au fait with the arrangements*). [French, literally 'to the fact, to the point']

Aug. *abbr.* August.

Augean *adj. literary* filthy. [from Greek *Augeias*, mythological owner of stables which Hercules cleaned by diversion of a river]

auger *n.* **1** a tool resembling a large corkscrew, for boring holes. ▷ COMBINE HARVESTER. [Old English]

aught *n.* (usu. implying *neg.*) *archaic* anything at all. [Old English]

augment *v.tr. & intr.* make or become greater; increase. [based on Latin *augēre* 'to increase'] □ **augmentation** *n.* **augmentative** *n.* **augmenter** *n.*

au gratin /oh **gra**-tan/ *adj.* sprinkled with breadcrumbs or grated cheese and browned. [French, literally 'with crumbs']

augur ● *v.* **1** *intr.* (of an event, circumstance, etc.) suggest a specified outcome (usu. **augur well** or **ill**). **2** *tr.* **a** foresee, predict. **b** portend. ● *n. hist.* an ancient Roman religious official who observed natural signs, esp. the behaviour of birds, interpreting these as an indication of divine approval or disapproval of a proposed action. [Latin] □ **augural** *adj.*

augury *n.* (*pl.* **-ies**) **1** an omen. **2** the interpretation of omens.

August *n.* the eighth month of the year. [from Latin *Augustus* Caesar, the first Roman emperor]

august /aw-**gust**/ *adj.* inspiring reverence and admiration. [from Latin *augustus* 'consecrated, venerable'] □ **augustly** *adv.* **augustness** *n.*

Augustan ● *adj.* **1** relating to the reign of the Roman emperor Augustus, esp. as an outstanding period of Latin literature. **2** (of a nation's literature) refined and classical in style (in England of the literature of the 17th–18th c.). ● *n.* a writer of the Augustan age of any literature.

Augustinian ● *adj.* **1** of or relating to St Augustine or his doctrines. **2** belonging to a religious order observing a rule derived from St Augustine's writings. ● *n.* a member of an Augustinian order.

auk *n.* ▶ any marine diving bird of the family Alcidae, native to the northern oceans, with heavy body, short wings, and black and white plumage, e.g. the puffin. ▷ SEABIRD. [from Old Norse]

auld /awld, ahld/ *adj. Sc.* old. [Old English *ald*]

auld lang syne *n.* times long past. [Scots, literally 'old long since']

au naturel *predic.adj. & adv.* **1** uncooked; (cooked) in the simplest way. **2** in its natural state. [French, literally 'in the natural state']

aunt *n.* **1** the sister of one's father or mother. **2** an uncle's wife. **3** *colloq.* an unrelated woman friend of a child or children. □ **my** (or **my sainted** etc.) **aunt** esp. *Brit. slang* an exclamation of surprise, disbelief, etc. [from Latin *amita*]

auntie *n.* (also **aunty**) (*pl.* **-ies**) *colloq.* = AUNT.

Aunt Sally *n. Brit.* **1** a game in which players throw sticks or balls at a wooden dummy. **2** the object of unreasonable attack.

au pair *n.* a young foreign person, esp. a woman, helping with housework etc. in exchange for room, board, and pocket money. [French, literally 'on equal terms']

aura *n.* (*pl.* **aurae** /-ree/ or **auras**) **1** the distinctive atmosphere diffused by or attending a person, place, etc. **2** (in mystic or spiritualistic use) a supposed subtle emanation, surrounding the body of a living creature. **3** a subtle emanation or aroma from flowers etc. **4** *Med.* premonitory symptom(s) in epilepsy etc. [from Greek, literally 'breeze, breath'] □ **aural** *adj.* **auric** *adj.*

aural *adj.* of or relating to or received by the ear. [based on Latin *auris* 'ear'] □ **aurally** *adv.*

■ **Usage** *Aural* is sometimes pronounced with the first syllable rhyming with *cow*, in order to distinguish it from *oral*. Some people regard this as incorrect.

aureate *adj.* **1** golden, gold-coloured. **2** resplendent. [from Latin *aureus* 'golden']

aureole *n.* (also **aureola**) **1** a halo or circle of light. **2** a corona round the Sun or Moon. [from Latin *aureola (corona)* 'golden (crown)']

au revoir /oh rĕ-**vwah**/ *int. & n.* goodbye (until we meet again). [French, literally 'to the seeing again']

auricle *n. Anat.* **1 a** a small muscular pouch on the surface of each atrium of the heart. **b** the atrium itself. **2** the external part of the ear. ▷ EAR. [related to AURICULA] □ **auricular** *adj.*

auricula *n.* a primula, *Primula auricula*, with leaves shaped like bears' ears. [Latin, literally 'little ear']

auriferous *adj.* naturally bearing gold. [based on Latin *aurum* 'gold']

aurochs *n.* (*pl.* same) an extinct wild ox, *Bos primigenius*, ancestor of domestic cattle and formerly native to many parts of the world. [from Old High German *ūrohso*]

aurora *n.* (*pl.* **auroras** or **aurorae** /-ree/) **1** ▼ a luminous electrical atmospheric phenomenon, usu. of streamers of light in the sky, esp. **aurora australis** /or-**stray**-lis/ above southern regions and **aurora borealis** /bor-i-**ay**-lis/ above northern regions. ▷ ATMOSPHERE. **2** *poet.* the dawn. [Latin, literally 'dawn'] □ **auroral** *adj.*

AUK:
LITTLE AUK
(*Alle alle*)

AURORA

The aurora borealis (northern lights), and their equivalent in the southern hemisphere, the aurora australis, are colourful lights, seen in the sky near the polar regions. The lights are caused by charged particles carried from the Sun by the solar wind. As they enter the Earth's atmosphere, they create an incandescent light display.

AURORA BOREALIS

auscultation *n.* the act of listening to sounds from the heart, lungs, etc., as part of medical diagnosis. [based on Latin *auscultare* 'to listen to'] □ **auscultatory** *adj.*

auspice *n.* **1** (in *pl.*) patronage (esp. in phr. **under the auspices of**). **2** a forecast. [originally in sense 'observation of bird-flight in divination', from Latin *auspicium*]

auspicious *adj.* **1** of good omen; favourable. **2** prosperous. □ **auspiciously** *adv.* **auspiciousness** *n.*

Aussie (also **Ossie**, **Ozzie**) *colloq.* ● *n.* an Australian. ● *adj.* Australian. [abbreviation]

austere *adj.* (**austerer**, **austerest**) **1** severely simple. **2** morally strict; stern. [from Greek *austēros* 'severe'] □ **austerely** *adv.* **austerity** *n.* (*pl.* **-ies**).

austral *adj.* **1** southern. **2** (**Austral**) of Australia or Australasia (*Austral English*). [from Latin *australis*]

Australasian *adj.* of or relating to Australasia, a region consisting of Australia and islands of the SW Pacific.

Australian ● *n.* **1** a native or national of Australia. **2** a person of Australian descent. ● *adj.* of or relating to Australia. [based on Latin *Terra Australis* 'southern land'] □ **Australianism** *n.*

Australian salmon see SALMON 2a.

Austrian ● *n.* **1** a native or national of Austria. **2** a person of Austrian descent. ● *adj.* of or relating to Austria.

Austro- *comb. form* Austrian; Austrian and (*Austro-Hungarian*).

autarchy *n.* (*pl.* **-ies**) **1** absolute sovereignty. **2** despotism. **3** an autarchic country or society. [from Greek *autarkhia*, based on *arkhein* 'to rule'] □ **autarchic** *adj.* **autarchical** *adj.*

autarky *n.* (*pl.* **-ies**) **1** self-sufficiency, esp. as an economic system. **2** a state etc. run according to such a system. [from Greek *autarkeia*, based on *arkein* 'to suffice'] □ **autarkic** *adj.* **autarkist** *n.*

authentic *adj.* **1** of undisputed origin; genuine. **2** reliable or trustworthy. [from Greek *authentikos* 'principal, genuine'] □ **authentically** *adv.* **authenticity** *n.*

authenticate *v.tr.* **1** establish the truth or genuineness of. **2** validate. □ **authentication** *n.* **authenticator** *n.*

author ● *n.* (*fem.* **authoress**) **1** a writer, esp. of books. **2** the originator of an event etc (*the author of all my woes*). ● *v.tr.* **1** *disp.* be the author or originator of. [from Latin *auctor*, based on *augēre* 'to increase, originate'] □ **authorial** *adj.*

■ **Usage** *Author* can be used of both male and female writers and many women writers prefer it to *authoress*. The use of the verb *author* as a mere synonym for *write* (as in *he authored several books on the subject*) is deplored by many people, although *author* is different from *write* in that it implies publication of the text produced. In addition, *author* is often used in contexts where the person or people responsible for the text (often a committee) did not actually write it themselves, and where the thing written is a report, article, or document, rather than a book. Unlike *author*, *co-author* is generally acceptable as a verb. It may be convenient to use *author* when contrasting it with *co-author*, e.g. *he authored or co-authored several publications on the wildlife of Australia.*

authoring *n.* *Computing* the creation of programs, databases, etc. for computer applications.

authoritarian *adj.* **1** favouring, encouraging, or enforcing strict obedience to authority. **2** tyrannical or domineering. □ **authoritarianism** *n.*

authoritative *adj.* **1** being recognized as true or dependable. **2** (of a person, behaviour, etc.) commanding or self-confident. **3** official; supported by authority (*an authoritative document*). □ **authoritatively** *adv.* **authoritativeness** *n.*

authority *n.* (*pl.* **-ies**) **1 a** the power or right to enforce obedience. **b** (often foll. by *for*, or *to* + infin.) delegated power. **2** (esp. in *pl.*) a person or body having authority. **3 a** an influence exerted on opinion because of recognized expertise. **b** such an influence expressed in a book etc. **c** an expert in a subject. [from Latin *auctoritas*, related to AUTHOR]

authorize *v.tr.* (also **-ise**) **1** sanction. **2** (foll. by *to* + infin.) **a** give authority. **b** commission (a person or body). □ **authorization** *n.*

Authorized Version *n.* esp. *Brit.* an English translation of the Bible made in 1611.

authorship *n.* **1** the origin of a book or other written work (*of unknown authorship*). **2** the occupation of writing.

autism *n.* a mental condition characterized by complete self-absorption and a reduced ability to respond to the outside world. [from modern Latin *autismus*] □ **autistic** *adj.*

auto *n.* (*pl.* **-os**) (usu. *attrib.*) *N. Amer. colloq.* a motor car. [abbreviation of AUTOMOBILE]

auto- *comb. form* (usu. **aut-** before a vowel) **1** self (*autism*). **2** one's own (*autobiography*). **3** by oneself or spontaneous (*auto-suggestion*). **4** automatic (*automobile*). [from Greek *autos* 'self']

autobahn *n.* a German, Austrian, or Swiss motorway. [German]

autobiography *n.* (*pl.* **-ies**) **1** a personal account of one's own life. **2** this as a process or literary form. □ **autobiographer** *n.* **autobiographic** *adj.* **autobiographical** *adj.*

autochthon /aw-tok-thŏn/ *n.* (*pl.* **autochthons** or **autochthones**) (usu. in *pl.*) an aboriginal. [Greek, literally 'sprung from the earth']

autochthonous *adj.* **1** indigenous, native. **2** of independent or local formation.

autoclave *n.* **1** a strong vessel used for chemical reactions at high pressures and temperatures. **2** a sterilizer using high-pressure steam. [based on Latin *clavis* 'key', so called because self-fastening]

autocracy *n.* (*pl.* **-ies**) **1** absolute government by one person. **2** the power exercised by such a person. **3** an autocratic country or society. [from Greek *autokrateia*]

autocrat *n.* **1** an absolute ruler. **2** a dictatorial person. [based on Greek *kratos* 'power'] □ **autocratic** *adj.* **autocratically** *adv.*

autocross *n.* motor racing across country or on unmade roads.

autocue *n.* esp. *Brit. propr.* a device, unseen by the audience, displaying a television script as an aid to memory (cf. TELEPROMPTER).

auto-da-fé *n.* (*pl.* **autos-da-fé**) **1** a sentence of punishment by the Spanish Inquisition. **2** the execution of such a sentence, esp. the burning of a heretic. [Portuguese, literally 'act of the faith']

autodidact *n.* a self-taught person. [from Greek *autodidactos*] □ **autodidactic** *adj.*

auto-erotism *n.* (also **auto-eroticism**) *Psychol.* sexual excitement generated by stimulating one's own body; masturbation. □ **auto-erotic** *adj.*

autograph ● *n.* **1 a** a signature, esp. that of a celebrity. **b** handwriting. **2** a manuscript in an author's handwriting. **3** a document signed by its author. ● *v.tr.* **1** sign (a photograph etc.). **2** write (a letter etc.) by hand. [from Greek *autographon*]

autoharp *n.* a kind of zither with a mechanical device to allow the playing of chords.

autoimmune *adj.* *Med.* (of a disease) caused by antibodies or lymphocytes produced against substances naturally present in the body. □ **autoimmunity** *n.*

automat *n.* *US* a slot machine that dispenses goods. [German]

automate *v.tr.* convert to operation by automatic equipment. □ **automation** *n.*

automatic ● *adj.* **1** working by itself, without direct human intervention. **2 a** done spontaneously, without conscious intention (*an automatic reaction*). **b** necessary and inevitable (*an automatic penalty*). **3** *Psychol.* performed unconsciously or subconsciously. **4** (of a firearm) that continues firing until the ammunition is exhausted or the pressure on the trigger is released. **5** (of a motor vehicle or its transmission) using gears that change automatically. ● *n.* **1** an automatic device. **2** *colloq.* a vehicle with automatic transmission. □ **automatically** *adv.* **automaticity** *n.* **automatism** *n.* **automatize** *v.tr.* (also **-ise**). **automatization** *n.*

automatic pilot *n.* a device for keeping an aircraft on a set course.

automaton *n.* (*pl.* **automata** or **automatons**) **1** a mechanism with concealed motive power. **2** a person who behaves mechanically. [Greek, literally '(thing) acting of itself']

automobile *n.* esp. *N. Amer.* a motor car. ▷ CAR. [French]

automotive *adj.* concerned with motor vehicles.

autonomic *adj.* esp. *Physiol.* functioning involuntarily.

autonomic nervous system *n.* ▼ the part of the nervous system responsible for control of the bodily functions not consciously directed, e.g. heartbeat. ▷ PERIPHERAL NERVOUS SYSTEM

autonomous *adj.* **1** having self-government. **2** acting independently or having the freedom to do so. [from Greek *autonomos*] □ **autonomously** *adv.*

autonomy *n.* (*pl.* **-ies**) **1** the right of self-government. **2** personal freedom. **3** freedom of the will. **4** a self-governing community. [based on Greek *autos* 'self' + *nomos* 'law'] □ **autonomist** *n.*

AUTONOMIC NERVOUS SYSTEM

The autonomic nervous system comprises those nerves of the peripheral nervous system that transmit nerve impulses to the glands and visceral organs. It controls involuntary functions, such as heart rate, sweating, and digestion, and is itself divided into the sympathetic and parasympathetic systems. The sympathetic system works in response to stress, increasing heart rate and blood pressure; the parasympathetic system counteracts these effects, decreasing heart rate and blood pressure, as well as stimulating the digestive system.

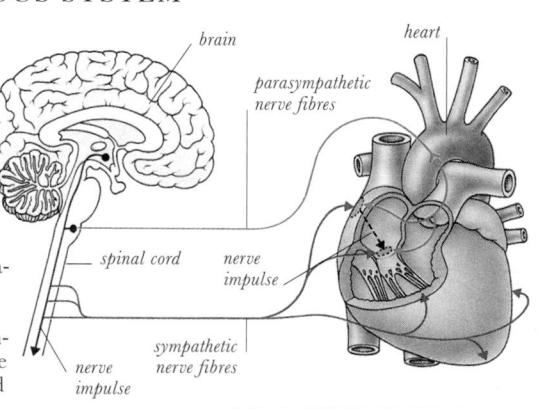

HUMAN AUTONOMIC NERVE CONNECTIONS TO THE HEART

A

autopilot *n.* an automatic pilot.

autopsy *n.* (*pl.* **-ies**) **1** a post-mortem examination. **2** any critical analysis. **3** a personal inspection. [based on Greek *autoptēs* 'eye-witness']

autoroute *n.* a French motorway. [French]

autostrada *n.* an Italian motorway. [Italian]

auto-suggestion *n.* a self-induced or subconscious suggestion affecting reaction, behaviour, etc.

autumn *n.* **1** the third season of the year, when crops and fruits are gathered, and leaves fall. ▷ SEASON. **2** *Astron.* the period from the autumnal equinox to the winter solstice. [from Latin *autumnus*] □ **autumnal** *adj.*

autumn equinox *n.* (also **autumnal equinox**) **1** the equinox in autumn, on about 22 Sept. in the northern hemisphere and 20 Mar. in the southern hemisphere. **2** *Astron.* the equinox in September.

auxiliary ● *adj.* **1** (of a person or thing) that gives help. **2** (of services or equipment) subsidiary, additional. ● *n.* (*pl.* **-ies**) **1** an auxiliary person or thing. **2** (in *pl.*) *Mil.* auxiliary troops. [based on Latin *auxilium* 'help']

auxiliary verb *n. Gram.* a verb used in forming the tenses, moods, and voices of other verbs.

auxin *n.* any of a group of plant hormones that regulate growth. [based on Greek *auxein* 'to increase']

avail ● *v.* **1** *tr.* help, benefit. **2** *refl.* (foll. by *of*) profit by; take advantage of. **3** *intr.* **a** provide help. **b** be of use or value. ● *n.* (usu. in *neg.* or *interrog.* phrases) use, profit (*of what avail?*). [based on Latin *valēre* 'to be worth']

available *adj.* (often foll. by *to*, *for*) **1** capable of being used; at one's disposal. **2** obtainable; within one's reach. **3 a** (of a person) free, not otherwise occupied. **b** able to be contacted. **4** *sexually* unattached. □ **availability** *n.* **availableness** *n.* **availably** *adv.*

avalanche *n.* **1** a mass of snow and ice, tumbling rapidly down a mountain. **2** a sudden arrival of anything in large quantities (*faced with an avalanche of work*). [French, alteration of dialect *lavanche*, influenced by *avaler* 'to descend']

avant-garde /av-ahn-gard/ ● *n.* pioneers or innovators. ● *adj.* (of art, ideas, etc.) new, progressive. [French, literally 'vanguard'] □ **avant-gardism** *n.* **avant-gardist** *n.*

AVENUE: VIA APPIA, ITALY

avarice *n.* extreme greed for money or gain; cupidity. [based on Latin *avarus* 'greedy'] □ **avaricious** *adj.* **avariciously** *adv.* **avariciousness** *n.*

avast *int. Naut.* stop, cease. [from Dutch *houd vast* 'hold fast!']

avatar *n.* **1** *Hinduism* the descent of a deity or released soul to Earth in bodily form. **2** incarnation; manifestation. **3** a manifestation or phase. [from Sanskrit *avatāra* 'descent']

Ave. *abbr.* Avenue.

ave *int.* **1** welcome. **2** farewell. [Latin, literally 'fare well']

avenge *v.tr.* **1** inflict retribution on behalf of. **2** take vengeance for (*the loss of the aircraft would be avenged*). □ **be avenged** avenge oneself. [based on Latin *vindicare* 'to vindicate'] □ **avenger** *n.*

■ **Usage** Where necessary, though uncommon, the preposition *on* (or *upon*) is used with *avenge*, to introduce the person on whom vengeance is being taken, e.g. *swore he would be avenged on their leader. Avenge* usually implies that the retribution inflicted is justifiable, whereas *revenge* often implies that the main aim of retribution is to satisfy the injured party's resentment.

avenue *n.* **1** ◀ a broad road, street, or approach, often with trees at regular intervals along its sides. **2** a way of dealing with something (*explored every avenue*). **3** (in many American cities) a road running perpendicular to another, esp. east-west. [from French, literally 'approached']

aver /ă-ver/ *v.tr.* (**averred, averring**) *formal* assert, affirm. [based on Latin *verus* 'true'] □ **averment** *n.*

average ● *n.* **1 a** the usual amount, extent, or rate. **b** the ordinary standard. **2** an amount obtained by dividing the total of given amounts by the number of amounts in the set. ● *adj.* **1 a** usual, ordinary. **b** mediocre. **2** estimated or calculated by average. ● *v.tr.* **1** amount on average to (*sales averaged one hundred a day*). **2** do on average (*averages six hours' work a day*). **3** estimate the average of. □ **average out (at)** result in an average (of). **on** (or **on an**) **average** as an average rate or estimate. [originally in sense '(maritime) charge': from French *avarie* 'damage to ship or cargo'] □ **averagely** *adv.*

averse *predic.adj.* (usu. foll. by *to*; also foll. by *from*) opposed, disinclined (*not averse to helping*). [from Latin *aversus*, related to AVERT]

■ **Usage** Although condemned in the past as etymologically improper (the literal meaning being 'turned *from*'), *averse* is now more often followed by *to* than *from*. This can be justified by analogy with semantically related words such as *disinclined, hostile, opposed*, etc., which are also used with *to*.

aversion *n.* **1** (usu. foll. by *to, from, for*) a dislike or unwillingness. **2** an object of dislike (*my pet aversion*). □ **aversive** *adj.*

avert *v.tr.* **1** (often foll. by *from*) turn away (one's eyes or thoughts). **2** prevent or ward off (an undesirable occurrence). [from Latin *avertere* 'to turn from'] □ **avertible** *adj.* (also **avertable**).

■ **Usage** Care should be taken not to confuse sense 2 of *avert* with *avoid*, e.g. *Disaster was narrowly averted* and *He narrowly avoided being arrested. Avert* incorporates the idea of taking action to ward off an undesirable event in advance, while *avoid* means 'to escape' or 'evade'.

Avesta *n.* (usu. prec. by *the*) the sacred writings of Zoroastrianism. [Persian] □ **Avestan** *adj.*

aviary *n.* (*pl.* **-ies**) ▼ a large enclosure or building for keeping birds. [based on Latin *avis* 'bird']

aviation *n.* **1** the skill or practice of operating aircraft. **2** aircraft manufacture. [based on Latin *avis* 'bird'] □ **aviate** *v.tr. & intr.* **aviator** *n.*

avid *adj.* eager, greedy. [from Latin *avidus*] □ **avidity** *n.* **avidly** *adv.*

avocado *n.* (*pl.* **-os**) **1** (in full **avocado pear**) ▼ a pear-shaped fruit with smooth oily edible flesh and a large stone. **2** the tropical evergreen tree, *Persea americana*, bearing this fruit. **3** the light green colour of the flesh of this fruit. [Spanish, literally 'advocate' (substituted for Aztec *ahuacatl*)]

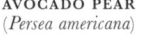

AVOCADO PEAR (*Persea americana*)

avocation *n.* **1** a minor occupation. **2** *colloq.* a vocation or calling. [from Latin *avocatio* 'a calling away']

avocet *n.* ▼ a wading bird of the genus *Recurvirostra* with long legs and a long slender upward-curved bill. ▷ WADING BIRD. [from Italian *avosetta*]

Avogadro's law *n. Phys.* a law stating that equal volumes of gases at the same temperature and pressure contain equal numbers of molecules.

avoid *v.tr.* **1** keep away from. **2** escape; evade. **3** *Law* nullify; quash. [from Old French] □ **avoidable** *adj.* **avoidably** *adv.* **avoidance** *n.* **avoider** *n.*

■ **Usage** See Usage Note at AVERT.

avoirdupois *n.* (in full **avoirdupois weight**) a system of weights based on a pound of 16 ounces or 7,000 grains. [from Old French]

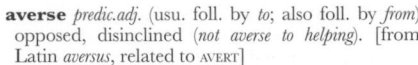

AVOCET: PIED AVOCET (*Recurvirostra avosetta*)

avouch *v.tr. & intr. archaic* or *literary* guarantee, affirm, confess. [from Latin *advocare*] □ **avouchment** *n.*

avow *v.tr.* **1** admit. **2** *refl.* admit that one is (*avowed himself the author*). [from Latin *advocare*] □ **avowal** *n.* **avowedly** *adv.*

avuncular *adj.* like or of an uncle. [based on Latin *avunculus* 'maternal uncle']

AVIARY

Many birds can be housed in an outdoor aviary for at least part of the year in temperate climes. The birds are essentially confined to two sections: the flight and the shelter. The flight is an area, partially open to the elements, where the birds have a certain amount of freedom to fly. The shelter is protected from the elements; here birds are fed and encouraged to roost. A third section, the safety porch, allows the keeper to enter the aviary without birds escaping.

TYPICAL DESIGN FOR AN AVIARY

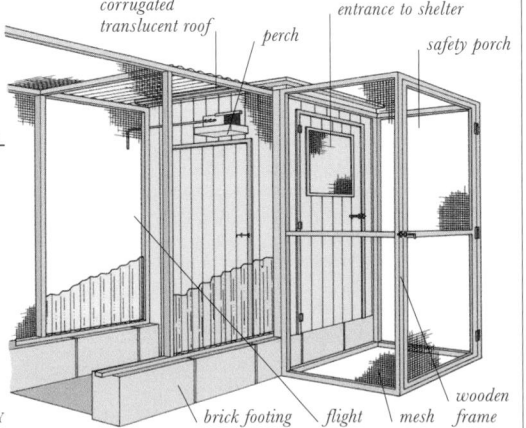

corrugated translucent roof · perch · entrance to shelter · safety porch · brick footing · flight · mesh · wooden frame

AWACS /**ay**-waks/ *n.* a long-range airborne radar system for detecting enemy aircraft. [acronym from *airborne warning and control system*]

await *v.tr.* **1** wait for. **2** be in store for. [from Anglo-French *awaitier*]

awake ● *v.* (*past* **awoke**; *past part.* **awoken**) **1** *intr.* **a** cease to sleep. **b** become active. **2** *intr.* (foll. by *to*) become aware of. **3** *tr.* rouse. ● *predic.adj.* **1 a** not asleep. **b** vigilant. **2** (foll. by *to*) aware of. [Old English]

■ **Usage** See Usage Note at AWAKEN.

awaken *v.* **1** *v.tr. & intr.* = AWAKE *v.* **2** *tr.* (often foll. by *to*) make aware.

■ **Usage** *Awake* and *awaken* are largely interchangeable, but *awaken* is much rarer than *awake* as an intransitive verb, and has an extra transitive usage (sense 2 above), as in *The strike had awakened them to the possibilities of resistance.*

award ● *v.tr.* **1** give or order to be given as a payment or prize. **2** grant, assign. ● *n.* **1** a payment or prize awarded. **2** a judicial decision. [from Anglo-French *awarder*] □ **awarder** *n.*

aware *predic.adj.* **1** (often foll. by *of*, or *that* + clause) conscious; having knowledge. **2** well informed (often in *comb.*: *politically aware*). [Old English] □ **awareness** *n.*

■ **Usage** In popular use, *aware* is sometimes used in sense 2 to mean 'well informed', without any qualifying word, as in *she's a very aware person*. This should be avoided in formal contexts.

awash *predic.adj.* level with the surface of water which just washes over; flooded.

away ● *adv.* **1** to or at a distance from the place, person, or thing in question (*go away*; *they are away*). **2** towards or into non-existence (*sounds die away*; *explain it away*). **3** constantly, persistently, continuously (*laugh away*). **4** without hesitation (*ask away*). ● *adj. Sport* played on an opponent's ground etc. (*away match*). ● *n. Sport* an away match or win. □ **away with** (as *imper.*) take away; let us be rid of. [Old English *onweg*, *aweg* 'on one's way']

awe ● *n.* reverential fear or wonder. ● *v.tr.* inspire with awe. [from Old Norse *agi*]

aweigh *predic.adj. Naut.* (of an anchor) clear of the sea or river bed; hanging.

awe-inspiring *adj.* causing awe or wonder; amazing, magnificent.

awesome *adj.* **1** inspiring awe; dreaded. **2** *slang* excellent. □ **awesomely** *adv.* **awesomeness** *n.*

awful *adj.* **1** *colloq.* **a** unpleasant (*awful weather*). **b** poor in quality (*has awful writing*). **c** (*attrib.*) remarkably large (*an awful lot of money*). **2** *poet.* inspiring awe. □ **awfully** *adv.* **awfulness** *n.*

awhile *adv.* for a short time. [Old English]

awkward *adj.* **1** ill-adapted for use. **2** clumsy or bungling. **3 a** esp. *Brit.* ill at ease (*felt awkward about it*). **b** embarrassing (*an awkward situation*). **4** esp. *Brit.* difficult to deal with (*an awkward customer*). □ **the awkward age** adolescence. [based on obsolete *awk* 'backhanded, untoward'] □ **awkwardly** *adv.* **awkwardness** *n.*

awl *n.* a small pointed tool used for piercing holes, esp. in leather. [Old English]

awn *n.* ◀ a stiff bristle, esp. one growing from the sheath around the seed of cereals and other grasses. [from Old Norse *ögn*] □ **awned** *adj.*

awn

seed sheath

AWN: EAR OF WHEAT WITH AWNED SHEATHS

awning *n.* a sheet of canvas or similar material stretched on a frame and used to shade a shop window, doorway, ship's deck, or other area from the sun or rain. [17th-century nautical coinage]

awoke *past* of AWAKE.

awoken *past part.* of AWAKE.

AWOL /**ay**-wol/ *abbr. colloq.* absent without leave.

awry /ă-**ry**/ ● *adv.* **1** askew. **2** amiss. ● *predic.adj.* crooked; unsound (*his theory is awry*). □ **go awry** go or do wrong. [Middle English]

axe (*US* usu. **ax**) ● *n.* **1** a chopping tool, usu. with a steel edge and wooden handle. **2** (**the axe**) the drastic cutting of staff etc. ● *v.tr.* (**axing**) **1** cut (services etc.) drastically. **2** abandon (a project). □ **an axe to grind** private ends to serve. [Old English]

axes *pl.* of AXIS.

axial *adj.* **1** forming or belonging to an axis. **2** round an axis. □ **axially** *adv.*

axil *n. Bot.* ◀ the upper angle between a leaf and the stem it springs from, or between a branch and the trunk. [from Latin *axilla*]

axilla *n.* (*pl.* **axillae** /-lee/) **1** *Anat.* the armpit. **2** *Bot.* an axil. [Latin, literally 'armpit']

axillary *adj.* **1** *Anat.* of or relating to the armpit. **2** *Bot.* in or growing from the axil.

axiom *n.* **1** an established or widely accepted principle. **2** esp. *Geom.* a self-evident truth. [based on Greek *axios* 'worthy']

axiomatic *adj.* **1** self-evident. **2** relating to or containing axioms. □ **axiomatically** *adv.*

axis[1] *n.* (*pl.* **axes** /**ak**-seez/) **1 a** an imaginary line about which a body rotates or about which a plane figure is conceived as generating a solid. **b** a line which divides a regular figure symmetrically. **2** *Math.* ▲ a fixed reference line for the measurement of coordinates etc. **3** *Bot.* the central column of an inflorescence or other growth. **4** *Anat.* the second cervical vertebra. **5** an agreement or alliance between two or more countries forming a centre for an eventual larger grouping of nations sharing an ideal or objective. **5** (**the Axis**) **a** the alliance of Germany and Italy formed before and during the Second World War, later extended to include Japan and other countries. **b** these countries as a group. [Latin, literally 'axle, pivot']

axillary bud

stem — *axil*

AXIL BETWEEN AN OAK LEAF AND STEM

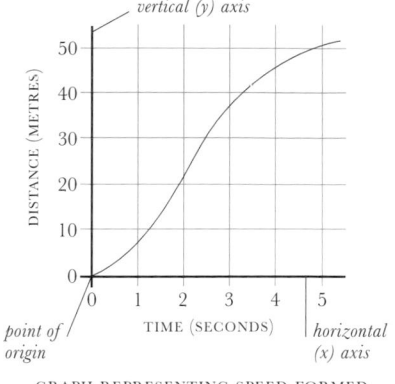

AXOLOTL (*Ambystoma mexicanum*)

AXIS

Axes provide the framework to visualize an equation. Speed, for example, is an equation of distance divided by time. If distance is shown on the *y* axis and time on the *x* axis, a line representing speed can be plotted on the grid they form.

vertical (y) axis

DISTANCE (METRES): 50, 40, 30, 20, 10, 0

TIME (SECONDS): 0, 1, 2, 3, 4, 5

point of origin

horizontal (x) axis

GRAPH REPRESENTING SPEED FORMED WITHIN THE AXES OF DISTANCE AND TIME

axis[2] *n.* (*pl.* same) a white-spotted deer, *Cervus axis*, of S. Asia. Also called *chital*. [Latin]

axle *n.* a spindle on which a wheel is fixed or turns. [originally *axle-tree*: from Old Norse *öxull-tré*]

Axminster *n.* (in full **Axminster carpet**) a kind of machine-woven patterned carpet with a cut pile. [the town of *Axminster* in S. England, where such carpets are made]

axolotl *n.* ▼ an aquatic newtlike salamander, *Ambystoma mexicanum*, from Mexico. [Aztec, from *atl xolotl* 'water servant']

axon *n. Anat. & Zool.* ▼ a long threadlike part of a nerve cell, conducting impulses from the cell body. ▷ NERVOUS SYSTEM. [from Greek *axōn* 'axis']

ayah *n.* a nurse or maidservant, esp. of Europeans in former British territories abroad. [Anglo-Indian]

ayatollah *n.* a Shi'ite religious leader in Iran. [from Arabic, literally 'token of God']

aye[1] (also **ay**) ● *adv.* **1** *archaic* or *dial.* yes. **2** (as **aye aye**) *Naut.* a response accepting an order. ● *n.* an affirmative answer, esp. in voting. [16th-century coinage]

AXON

An axon is a sinuous extension of a nerve cell body that conveys impulses to targets such as muscles, glands, and other nerve cells. Axons range from a few millimetres to two metres or more in length, and are protected by cells that form a myelin sheath around them. Intermittent gaps in the sheath are referred to as the nodes of Ranvier.

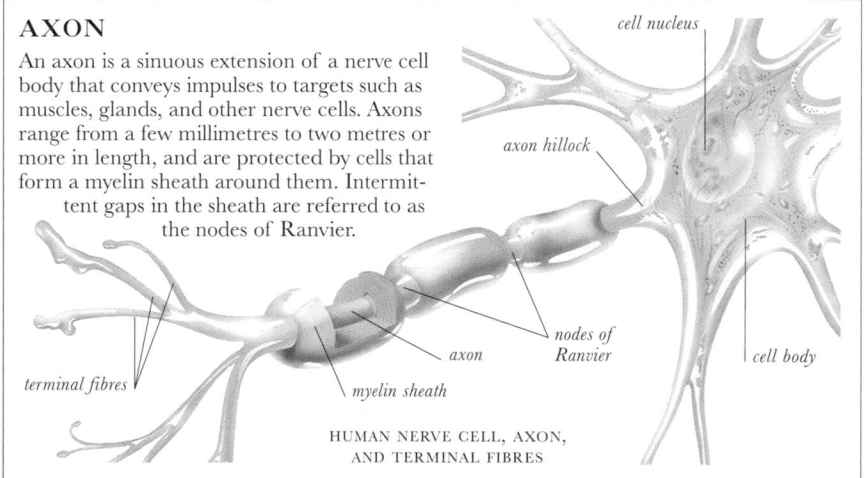

cell nucleus

axon hillock

nodes of Ranvier

axon

myelin sheath

terminal fibres

cell body

HUMAN NERVE CELL, AXON, AND TERMINAL FIBRES

A

aye[2] *adv. archaic* always. □ **for aye** for ever. [from Old Norse]

aye-aye *n.* ▼ an arboreal nocturnal lemur, *Daubentonia madagascariensis*, native to Madagascar. [French, from Malagasy *aiay*]

AYE-AYE
(*Daubentonia madagascariensis*)

azalea *n.* any of various flowering deciduous shrubs of the genus *Rhododendron*, with large pink, purple, white, or yellow flowers. [based on Greek *azaleos* 'dry' (from the dry soil in which it was believed to flourish)]

Azerbaijani *n.* (*pl.* **Azerbaijanis**) **1** a native or inhabitant of Azerbaijan in the Caucasus. **2** the Turkic language of Azerbaijan.

Azeri *n.* (*pl.* **Azeris**) **1** a member of a Turkic people living mainly in Azerbaijan, Armenia, and northern Iran. **2** their language. [from Persian, literally 'fire']

azimuth *n.* **1** the angular distance from a north or south point of the horizon to the intersection with the horizon of a vertical circle passing through a given celestial object. **2** the horizontal angle or direction of a compass bearing. [based on Arabic *al* 'the' + *sumūt* 'directions'] □ **azimuthal** *adj.*

azimuthal projection *n.* ▼ a map projection in which a region of the Earth is projected on to a plane tangential to the surface, usually at the pole or equator.

azoic *adj.* **1** having no trace of life. **2** *Geol.* (of an age etc.) having left no organic remains [Greek *azōos* 'without life']

AZT *abbr. propr.* the drug zidovudine.

Aztec *n.* **1** a member of the native people dominant in Mexico before the Spanish conquest of the 16th c. **2** the language of the Aztecs. [from Aztec *aztecatl* 'men of the north']

azuki var. of ADZUKI.

azure ● *n.* **1 a** a deep sky-blue colour. **b** *Heraldry* blue. **2** *poet.* the clear sky. ● *adj* **1 a** of the colour azure. **b** *Heraldry* blue. **2** *poet.* serene, untroubled. [based on Persian *lāžward* 'lapis lazuli']

azygous *Anat.* ● *adj.* (of any organic structure) single; not existing in pairs. ● *n.* an organic structure occurring singly. [Greek *azugos* 'unyoked']

AZIMUTHAL PROJECTION

An azimuthal projection shows half of the Earth at once. It is produced as though a light were shone through the globe from its centre. The grid of longitudinal and latitudinal lines on the globe's surface is projected on to the flat plane of the map. The best use of an azimuthal projection is to show the true direction between two points on the Earth.

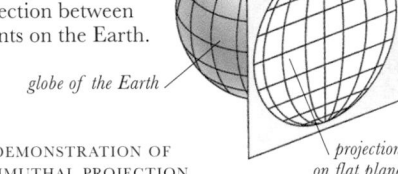

globe of the Earth

DEMONSTRATION OF
AZIMUTHAL PROJECTION

*projection
on flat plane*

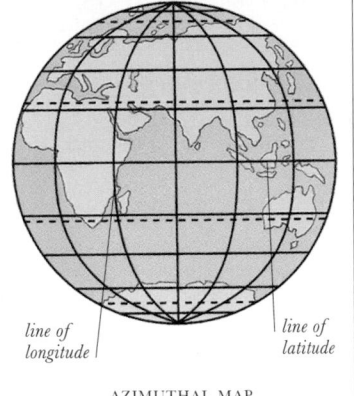

*line of
longitude*   *line of
latitude*

AZIMUTHAL MAP

B

B[1] *n.* (also **b**) (*pl.* **Bs** or **B's**) **1** the second letter of the alphabet. **2** *Mus.* the seventh note of the diatonic scale of C major. ▷ NOTATION. **3** the second hypothetical person or example. **4** the second highest class or category. **5** (usu. **b**) *Algebra* the second known quantity. **6** a human blood type of the ABO system.

B[2] *abbr.* (also **B.**) **1** black (pencil lead). **2** *Chess* bishop.

B[3] *symb. Chem.* the element boron.

b *abbr.* (also **b.**) **1** born. **2** *Cricket* **a** bowled by. **b** bye.

BA *abbr.* Bachelor of Arts.

Ba *symb. Chem.* the element barium.

baa *v.intr.* (**baas**, **baaed** or **baa'd**) (of a sheep etc.) bleat.

babble ● *v.* **1** *intr.* **a** talk in an incoherent manner. **b** chatter excessively. **c** (of a stream etc.) murmur. **2** *tr.* divulge through chatter. ● *n.* **1 a** incoherent speech. **b** idle or childish talk. **2** the murmur of voices, water, etc. [from Middle Low German *babbelen*] □ **babbler** *n.*

babe *n.* **1** *literary* a baby. **2** an innocent or helpless person (*babes in the wood*). **3** *slang, esp. N. Amer.* often *offens.* a young woman (often as a form of address). [Middle English]

babel /bay-bĕl/ *n.* **1** a confused noise, esp. of voices. **2** a noisy assembly. **3** a scene of confusion. [from Semitic *bāb ili* 'gate of god', with reference to the biblical account (Gen. 11) of the Tower of Babel]

cheek pouch

callosity

BABOON: HAMADRYAS BABOON
(*Papio hamadryas*)

baboon *n.* ◄ any of various large Old World monkeys of the genera *Papio* and *Mandrillus*, having a long snout, large teeth, and callosities on the buttocks. [from medieval Latin *babewynus*]

babu *n.* **1** (in the Indian subcontinent) a title of respect, esp. to Hindus. **2** *Anglo-Ind. offens.* an Indian clerk or official who has a superficial knowledge of English. [from Hindi *bābū* 'father']

babushka *n.* **1** (in Russia) an old woman; a grandmother. **2** a headscarf tied under the chin. [Russian, literally 'grandmother']

baby ● *n.* (*pl.* **-ies**) **1** a very young child or infant. **2** an unduly childish person (*is a baby about injections*). **3** the youngest member of a family, team, etc. **4** (often *attrib.*) **a** a young or newly born animal. **b** a thing that is small of its kind (*baby rose*). **5** *slang* a young woman; a sweetheart (often as a form of address). **6** one's own responsibility, invention, etc., regarded in a personal way. ● *v.tr.* (**-ies, -ied**) **1** treat like a baby. **2** pamper. [Middle English] □ **babyish** *adj.* **babyishly** *adv.* **babyhood** *n.*

baby boom *n. colloq.* a temporary marked increase in the birth rate.

baby bouncer *n. Brit.* a frame supported by elastic or springs, into which a baby is harnessed to exercise its limbs.

baby buggy *n.* **1** *Brit. propr.* a kind of child's collapsible pushchair. **2** *N. Amer.* a pram.

baby face *n.* **1** a smooth round face like a baby's. **2** a person with such a face. □ **baby-faced** *adj.*

baby grand *n.* the smallest size of grand piano.

Babygro *n.* (*pl.* **-os**) *Brit. propr.* a kind of all-in-one stretch garment for babies.

babysit *v.intr.* (**-sitting**; *past* and *past part.* **-sat**) look after a child while the parents are out. □ **babysitter** *n.*

baby talk *n.* childish talk used by or to young children.

baby walker *n.* ► a wheeled frame in which a baby can learn to walk.

baccalaureate /bak-ă-lor-iăt/ *n.* **1** an examination intended to qualify successful candidates for higher education. **2** the university degree of bachelor. [from medieval Latin *baccalaureatus*]

BABY WALKER

baccarat /bak-er-ah/ *n.* a gambling card game played by punters in turn against the banker. [from French *baccara*]

bacchanal ● *n.* **1** a wild and drunken revelry. **2** a drunken reveller. **3.** **a** priest, worshipper, or follower of Bacchus, the Greek or Roman god of wine. ● *adj.* **1** of or like Bacchus or his rites. **2** riotous, roistering. [based on Greek *Bakkhos*, god of wine]

Bacchanalia *n.pl.* **1** the Roman festival of Bacchus. **2** (**bacchanalia**) a drunken revelry. [Latin] □ **Bacchanalian** *adj. & n.*

baccy *n. colloq.* tobacco.

bachelor *n.* **1** an unmarried man. **2** a man or woman who has taken the degree of Bachelor of Arts or Science etc. [from Old French *bacheler* 'aspirant to knighthood'] □ **bachelorhood** *n.*

bacillary /bă-sil-ări/ *adj.* relating to or caused by bacilli.

bacillus /bă-sil-us/ *n.* (*pl.* **bacilli**) **1** any rod-shaped bacterium. **2** any pathogenic bacterium. [Late Latin, literally 'little stick']

back ● *n.* **1 a** the rear surface of the human body from the shoulders to the hips. **b** the corresponding upper surface of an animal's body. **c** the spine (*fell and broke his back*). **2 a** any surface regarded as corresponding to the human back, e.g. of the head or hand, or of a chair. **b** the part of a garment that covers the back. **3 a** the less important part of something functional, e.g. of a knife or a piece of paper (*write it on the back*). **b** the part normally away from the spectator or the direction of motion or attention, e.g. of a car, house, or room (*stood at the back*). **4 a** a defensive player in field games. **b** this position. ● *adv.* **1** to the rear; away from what is considered to be the front (*go back a bit*; *ran off without looking back*). **2 a** in or into an earlier position or condition (*came back late*; *ran back to the car*; *put it back on the shelf*). **b** in return (*pay back*). **3** in or into the past (*back in June*; *three years back*). **4** at a distance (*stand back from the road*). **5** in check (*hold him back*). **6** (foll. by *of*) *N. Amer.* behind (*was back of the house*). ● *v.* **1** *tr.* **a** help with moral or financial support. **b** bet on the success of (a horse etc.). **2** *tr. & intr.* move, or cause (a vehicle etc.) to move, backwards. **3** *tr.* **a** put or serve as a back, background, or support to. **b** *Mus.* accompany. **4** *tr.* lie at the back of (*a beach backed by steep cliffs*). **5** *intr.* (of the wind) move round in an anticlockwise direction. ● *attrib.adj.* **1** situated behind (*back entrance*; *back teeth*). **2** of or relating to the past (*back pay*; *back issue*). **3** reversed (*back flow*). □ **at the back of one's mind** remembered but not consciously thought of. **back and forth** to and fro. **back down** withdraw one's claim; concede defeat in an argument etc. **the back of beyond** a very remote or inaccessible place. **back off 1** draw back, retreat. **2** abandon one's intention, stand, etc. **back on to** have its back adjacent to (*the house backs on to a field*). **back out** withdraw from a commitment. **back up 1** give support to. **2** *Computing* make a spare copy of (data, a disk, etc.). **3** (of running water) accumulate behind an obstruction. **4** reverse (a vehicle) into a desired position. **5** form a queue of vehicles etc. **get** (or **put**) **a person's back up** annoy or anger a person. **get off a person's back** stop troubling a person. **go back on** fail to honour (a promise or commitment). **on the back burner** see BURNER. **put one's back into** approach (a task etc.) with vigour. **see the back of** see SEE[1]. **turn one's back on 1** abandon. **2** ignore. **with one's back to** (or **up against**) **the wall** in a desperate situation; hard-pressed. [Old English] □ **backer** *n.* (in sense 1 of *v.*). **backless** *adj.*

backache *n.* a (usu. prolonged) pain in one's back.

backbeat *n. Mus.* a strong accent on one of the normally unaccented beats of the bar.

backbench *n. Brit.* a backbencher's seat in the House of Commons.

backbencher *n. Brit.* a Member of Parliament not holding a senior office.

backbiting ● *n.* malicious talk. ● *attrib.adj.* speaking ill of another or others. □ **backbiter** *n.*

back boiler *n. Brit.* a boiler behind and integral with a domestic fire.

backbone *n.* **1** the spine. **2** the main support of a structure. **3** firmness of character.

back-breaking *adj.* (esp. of manual work) extremely hard.

backchat *n. Brit. colloq.* the practice of replying rudely or impudently.

backcloth *n. Brit.* **1** *Theatr.* a painted cloth at the back of the stage as a main part of the scenery. ▷ THEATRE. **2** the background to a scene or situation.

backcomb *v.tr. Brit.* comb (the hair) towards the top of the head to make it look thicker.

backcountry *n. esp. N. Amer.* an area away from settled districts.

backdate *v.tr.* **1** put an earlier date to (an agreement etc.) than the actual one. **2** *Brit.* make retrospectively valid.

back door ● *n.* **1** the door at the back of a building. **2** a secret means of gaining an objective. ● *attrib.adj.* (**back-door**) clandestine, underhand (*back-door deal*).

backdrop *n.* = BACKCLOTH.

backfill *v.tr.* refill (an excavated hole) with the material dug out of it.

backfire ● *v.intr.* **1** undergo a mistimed explosion in the cylinder or exhaust of an internal-combustion engine. **2** (of a plan etc.) have the opposite effect to what was intended. ● *n.* an instance of backfiring.

back-formation *n.* **1** the formation of a word from its seeming derivative (e.g. *laze* from *lazy*). **2** a word formed in this way.

backgammon *n.* a game for two played on a board with pieces moved according to throws of the dice.

background *n.* **1** part of a scene, picture, or description, that serves as a setting to the chief figures or objects and foreground. **2** an inconspicuous position (*kept in the background*). **3** a person's education, knowledge, or social circumstances. **4** explanatory information.

backhand *n. Tennis* etc. **1** ► a stroke played with the back of the hand turned towards the opponent. **2** (*attrib.*) of or made with a backhand (*backhand volley*).

BACKHAND
TENNIS STROKE

B

backhanded adj. **1** (of a blow etc.) delivered with the back of the hand, or in a direction opposite to the usual one. **2** indirect; ambiguous (*a backhanded compliment*). **3** = BACKHAND 2.

backhander n. **1 a** a backhand stroke. **b** a backhanded blow. **2** colloq. an indirect attack. **3** Brit. slang a bribe.

backhoe n. N. Amer. a mechanical excavator which draws towards itself a bucket attached to a hinged boom.

backing n. **1 a** support. **b** a body of supporters. **c** material used to form a back or support. **2** musical accompaniment.

backlash n. **1** a marked adverse reaction. **2 a** a sudden recoil or reaction between parts of a mechanism. **b** excessive play between such parts.

backlight n. illumination from behind. □ **backlit** adj.

backlog n. arrears of uncompleted work etc.

backmarker n. Brit. a competitor who has the least favourable handicap in a race etc.

backmost adj. furthest back.

back number n. **1** an issue of a periodical earlier than the current one. **2** slang an out-of-date person or thing.

backpack ● n. a rucksack. ● v.intr. travel with a backpack. □ **backpacker** n.

back passage n. Brit. colloq. the rectum.

back-pedal v.intr. (**-pedalled**, **-pedalling**; US **-pedaled**, **-pedaling**) **1** pedal backwards. **2** reverse one's previous action or opinion.

back-projection n. the projection of a picture from behind a translucent screen for viewing or filming.

backrest n. a support for the back.

back room n. (often, with hyphen, attrib.) a place where secret work is done.

back seat n. an inferior position or status.

back-seat driver n. a person who is eager to advise without responsibility (originally of a passenger in a car etc.).

backsheesh var. of BAKSHEESH.

backside n. colloq. the buttocks.

back slang n. slang using words spelt backwards (e.g. *yob*).

backslash n. a reverse solidus (\).

backslide v.intr. (past **-slid**; past part. **-slid** or **-slidden**) relapse into bad ways or error. □ **backslider** n.

backspace v.intr. move a typewriter carriage or computer cursor back one or more spaces.

backspin n. a backward spin imparted to a ball causing it to fly off at an angle on hitting a surface.

backstage ● adv. **1** Theatr. out of view of the audience. **2** not known to the public. ● adj. that is backstage; concealed.

backstairs n.pl. **1** stairs at the back of a building. **2** (also **backstair**) (attrib.) denoting underhand or clandestine activity.

backstitch ● n. sewing with overlapping stitches. ▷ STITCH. ● v.tr. & intr. sew using backstitch.

backstop n. **1 a** Cricket etc. a fielder directly behind the wicketkeeper. **b** Baseball = CATCHER 2. **c** these fielding positions. **2** an emergency precaution; a last resort.

backstreet n. **1** a street away from the main streets. **2** (attrib.) denoting illicit activity (*a backstreet abortion*).

backstroke n. a swimming stroke performed on the back with the arms lifted alternately out of the water in a backward circular motion and the legs extended in a kicking action.

back talk n. N. Amer. colloq. = BACKCHAT.

back-to-back ● attrib.adj. **1** esp. Brit. (of houses) with a party wall at the rear. **2** esp. N. Amer. consecutive. ● n. a back-to-back house. ● adv. (**back to back**) **1** with backs adjacent and opposite each other (*we stood back to back*). **2** esp. N. Amer. consecutively.

back to front adj. **1** with the back at the front and the front at the back. **2** in disorder.

backtrack v.intr. **1** retrace one's steps. **2** reverse one's previous action or opinion.

back-up n. **1** moral or technical support (*called for extra back-up*). **2** a reserve. **3** (often attrib.) Computing **a** the procedure for making security copies of data (*back-up facilities*). **b** the copy itself (*made a back-up*). **4** N. Amer. a queue of vehicles etc.

backup light n. US a reversing light.

backveld n. S.Afr. remote country districts.

backward ● adv. = BACKWARDS. ● adj. **1** directed to the rear or starting point (*a backward look*). **2** reversed. **3** mentally retarded. **4** reluctant, shy, unassertive. **5** Cricket (of a fielding position) behind a line through the stumps at right angles to the wicket. [earlier *abackward*] □ **backwardness** n.

■ **Usage** *Backward* is both an adjective and an adverb, while *backwards* is only an adverb and more common than *backward* as such.

backwards adv. **1** away from one's front (*lean backwards*). **2 a** with the back foremost (*walk backwards*). **b** in reverse of the usual way (*count backwards*). **3 a** into a worse state (*new policies are taking us backwards*). **b** into the past (*looked backwards over the years*). **c** back towards the starting point (*rolled backwards*). □ **backwards and forwards** to and fro. **bend over backwards** or **fall** or **lean** **over backwards** colloq. make every effort. **know backwards** be entirely familiar with.

■ **Usage** See Usage Note at BACKWARD.

backwash n. **1 a** a receding waves created by the motion of a ship etc. **b** a backward current of air created by a moving aircraft. **2** repercussions.

backwater n. **1** a place or condition remote from the centre of activity or thought. **2** stagnant water fed from a stream.

backwoods n.pl. **1** uncleared forest land. **2** any sparsely inhabited region.

backwoodsman n. (pl. **-men**) **1** an inhabitant of backwoods. **2** an uncouth person. **3** a peer who very rarely attends the House of Lords.

backyard n. **1** Brit. a yard at the back of a house etc. **2** N. Amer. a back garden. □ **in one's own backyard** colloq. near one's home; in one's own area.

baclava var. of BAKLAVA.

bacon n. cured meat from the back or sides of a pig. □ **bring home the bacon** colloq. **1** succeed in one's undertaking. **2** supply material provision or support. [from Frankish *bako* 'ham, flitch']

bactericide n. a substance capable of destroying bacteria. □ **bactericidal** adj.

bacteriology n. the study of bacteria. □ **bacteriological** adj. **bacteriologist** n.

bacterium n. (pl. **bacteria**) ▼ a member of a large group of unicellular micro-organisms lacking organelles and an organized nucleus. [from Greek *baktērion* 'little stick'] □ **bacterial** adj.

ribosome

plasma membrane

flagellum

BACTERIUM:
SECTION THROUGH
A BACTERIUM

■ **Usage** A very common mistake is the use of *bacteria* as the singular form, e.g. *The salmonella bacteria accounts for the majority of food poisoning cases today.* This is wrong and the form *bacterium* should be used here instead.

Bactrian camel n. a camel with two humps, *Camelus ferus*, native to central Asia. ▷ CAMEL

bad ● adj. (**worse**, **worst**) **1** inferior, inadequate, defective (*bad work; a bad driver; bad light*). **2 a** unpleasant (*bad weather; bad news*). **b** unfortunate (*a bad business*). **3** harmful (*is bad for you*). **4 a** (of food) decayed. **b** (of the atmosphere) polluted, unhealthy (*bad air*). **5** colloq. ill, injured (*am feeling bad today; a bad leg*). **6** colloq. regretful, ashamed (*feels bad about it*). **7** (of an unwelcome thing) serious, severe (*a bad mistake*). **8 a** morally wicked or offensive (*a bad man; bad language*). **b** naughty; badly behaved (*a bad child*). **9** not valid (*a bad cheque*). **10** (**badder**, **baddest**) esp. US slang good, excellent. ● n. **1 a** ill fortune (*take the bad with the good*). **b** ruin; a degenerate condition (*go to the bad*). **2** the debit side of an account (*£500 to the bad*). **3** (treated as pl.; prec. by *the*) bad people. ● adv. N. Amer. colloq. badly (*took it bad*). □ **in a bad way** ill; in trouble (*looked in a bad way*). **too bad** colloq. (of circumstances etc.) regrettable but now beyond retrieval. [Middle English] □ **badness** n.

bad blood n. ill feeling.

bad break n. colloq. **1** a piece of bad luck. **2** a mistake or blunder.

bad breath n. unpleasant-smelling breath; halitosis.

bad debt n. a debt that is not recoverable.

baddy n. (also **baddie**) (pl. **-ies**) colloq. a villain.

bade see BID.

bad form n. an offence against current social conventions.

badge n. **1** a distinctive emblem worn as a mark of office, membership, achievement, licensed employment, etc. **2** any feature which reveals a characteristic condition or quality. [Middle English]

badger ● n. **1** ▼ an omnivorous greyish-black nocturnal Eurasian mammal, *Meles meles*, of the weasel family, having a white head with two black stripes, and living in burrows called setts. ▷ VERTEBRATE. **2** a related N. American animal, *Taxidea taxus*. ● v.tr. pester, harass, tease. [16th-century coinage]

BADGER
(*Meles meles*)

badinage /bad-in-ah*zh*/ n. humorous or playful ridicule. [French]

badlands n.pl. extensive uncultivable eroded tracts in arid areas. [translation of French *mauvaises terres*]

bad lot n. a person of bad character.

badly adv. (**worse**, **worst**) **1** in a bad manner (*works badly*). **2** colloq. very much (*wants it badly*). **3** severely (*was badly defeated*).

badminton n. ▲ a game with rackets in which a shuttlecock is played back and forth across a net. [from *Badminton* in S. England, a country house where the game was first played]

bad mouth N. Amer. slang ● n. malicious gossip or criticism. ● v.tr. (**bad-mouth**) criticize maliciously; abuse.

bad news n. colloq. an unpleasant or troublesome person or thing.

bad-tempered adj. irritable; easily annoyed.

baffle ● v.tr. **1** confuse or perplex. **2 a** frustrate or hinder (*plans etc.*). **b** restrain or regulate the progress of (fluids, sounds, etc.). ● n. (also **baffle plate**) a device used to restrain the flow of fluid, gas, etc., or to limit the emission of sound, light, etc. □ **bafflement** n. **baffling** adj. **bafflingly** adv.

BAFTA /baf-tă/ abbr. British Academy of Film and Television Arts.

bag ● n. **1** a receptacle of flexible material with an opening at the top. **2 a** a piece of luggage (*put the bags in the boot*). **b** a woman's handbag. **3** (in pl.) esp.

BADMINTON

Usually an indoor sport, played on a court with a high net, badminton singles is played by two opponents, and doubles by teams of two people. The object of the game is to hit the shuttlecock to the floor on the opposite side of the net, so that the shot cannot be returned. Only the serving player can score a point from a rally.

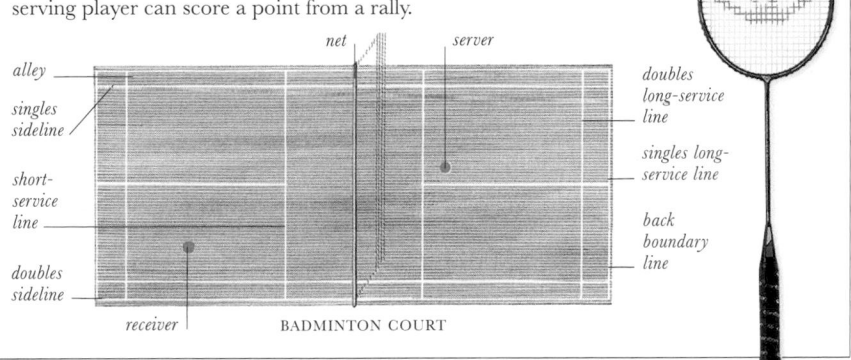

BADMINTON RACKET

SHUTTLECOCK

alley

singles sideline

short-service line

doubles sideline

net

server

receiver

doubles long-service line

singles long-service line

back boundary line

BADMINTON COURT

Brit. colloq. a large amount (*bags of time*). **4** (in *pl.*) *Brit. colloq.* trousers. **5** *slang derog.* a woman, esp. regarded as unattractive or unpleasant. **6** (usu. in *pl.*) baggy folds of skin under the eyes. ● *v.* (**bagged**, **bagging**) **1** *tr.* put in a bag. **2** *tr.* **a** *colloq.* secure; get hold of (*bagged the best seat*). **b** *colloq.* steal. **c** shoot (game). **d** (often in phr. **bags I**) *Brit. colloq.* claim on grounds of being the first to do so (*bags I go first*). **3 a** *intr.* hang loosely; bulge. **b** *tr.* cause to do this. **4** *tr. Austral. slang* criticize, disparage. □ **bag and baggage** with all one's belongings. **bag of bones** an emaciated person or animal. **bag of nerves** a very tense or timid person. **in the bag** *colloq.* achieved; as good as secured. [Middle English] □ **bagful** *n.* (*pl.* **-fuls**).

bagatelle *n.* **1** a game in which small balls are struck into numbered holes on a board, with pins as obstructions. **2** a mere trifle. **3** *Mus.* a short piece of music. [from Italian *bagatella*]

bagel /bay-gĕl/ *n.* a hard-crusted bread roll in the shape of a ring. [from Yiddish]

baggage *n.* **1** everyday belongings packed up in suitcases etc. for travelling. **2** the portable equipment of an army. **3** *joc.* or *derog.* a girl or woman. **4** mental encumbrances. [based on Old French *baguer* 'to tie up']

baggy *adj.* (**baggier**, **baggiest**) **1** hanging in loose folds. **2** puffed out. □ **bagginess** *n.*

bag lady *n.* esp. *N. Amer.* a homeless woman who carries her possessions around in shopping bags.

bagpipe *n.* (usu. in *pl.*) ◄ a musical instrument consisting of a windbag squeezed by the player's arm to force air into reeded pipes.

baguette /ba-get/ *n.* a long narrow French loaf. [French, from Italian *bacchetto* 'little rod']

bah *int.* an expression of contempt or disbelief.

Baha'i /bah-**hah**-i/ *n.* (*pl.* **Baha'is**) an adherent of a monotheistic religion founded in 1863 as a branch of Babism (an offshoot of Islam), emphasizing religious unity and world peace. □ **Baha'ism** *n.*

Bahutu *pl.* of HUTU.

bail[1] ● *n.* **1** money etc. required as security against the

drone

bag

mouthpiece

chanter

BAGPIPES: MID-19TH-CENTURY FRENCH SHEEPSKIN BINIOU

temporary release of a prisoner pending trial. **2** a person or persons giving such security. ● *v.tr.* (usu. foll. by *out*) **1** release or secure the release of (a prisoner) on payment of bail. **2** (also **bale** by association with *bale out* 1: see BALE[1]) release from a difficulty; come to the rescue of. □ **forfeit** (or *colloq.* **jump**) **bail** fail to appear for trial after being released on bail. **go** (or **stand**) **bail** act as surety (for an accused person). [based on Latin *bajulare* 'to bear a burden']

bail[2] *n.* **1** *Cricket* either of the two crosspieces bridging the stumps. ▷ CRICKET. **2** the bar on a typewriter holding the paper against the platen. **3** a bar separating horses in an open stable. [from Old French *bail(e)* 'enclosure']

bail[3] *v.tr.* (also *Brit.* **bale**) **1** (usu. foll. by *out*) scoop water out of (a boat etc.). **2** scoop (water etc.) out. □ **bail out** var. of *bale out* 1 (see BALE[1]). [based on Latin *bajulus* 'carrier']

bailey *n.* (*pl.* **-eys**) **1** the outer wall of a castle. **2** ▶ a court enclosed by it. ▷ CASTLE. [related to BAIL[2]]

Bailey bridge *n.* a temporary bridge of lattice steel designed for rapid assembly from prefabricated standard parts. [named after Sir D. Bailey, 1901–85, its designer]

bailie *n.* esp. *hist.* a municipal officer and magistrate in Scotland. [from Old French *bailli(s)* 'bailiff']

bailiff *n.* **1** esp. *Brit.* a sheriff's officer who executes writs and processes and carries out distraints and arrests. **2** *Brit.* the agent or steward of a landlord. **3** *N. Amer.* an official in a court of law who keeps order, looks after prisoners, etc. [related to BAIL[3]]

bailiwick *n.* **1** *joc.* a person's sphere of operations or particular area of interest. **2** *Law* the district or jurisdiction of a bailie or bailiff.

bailout *n.* financial assistance given to a failing business, economy, etc., to save it from collapse.

bain-marie /ban mă-**ree**/ *n.* (*pl.* **bains-marie** *pronunc.* same) a cooking utensil consisting of a vessel of hot water in which a receptacle can be slowly and gently heated. [French, translation of medieval Latin *balneum Mariae* 'bath of *Maria*', alleged Jewish alchemist]

bairn *n. Sc.* & *N.Engl.* a child. [Old English]

bait ● *n.* **1** food used to entice a prey. **2** an allurement; something intended to tempt or entice. ● *v.tr.* **1 a** harass or annoy (a person). **b** torment

(a chained animal). **2** put bait on (a hook, trap, etc.) to entice a prey. [from Old Norse *beita* 'to hunt, chase']

baize *n.* a coarse woollen material used as a covering or lining. ▷ POOL. [from French *baies*, fem. pl. of *bai* 'chestnut-coloured']

bake ● *v.* **1 a** *tr.* cook (food) by dry heat in an oven or on a hot surface, without direct exposure to a flame. **b** *intr.* undergo the process of being baked. **2** *intr. colloq.* **a** (usu. as **be baking**) (of weather etc.) be very hot. **b** (of a person) be hot. **3 a** *tr.* harden (clay etc.) by heat. **b** *intr.* (of clay etc.) be hardened by heat. ● *n.* **1** the act or an instance of baking. **2** a batch of baking. **3** *US* a social gathering at which baked food is eaten. □ **bake blind** see BLIND. [Old English]

baked Alaska *n.* sponge cake and ice cream in a meringue covering. [from *Alaska*, name of a US state]

baked beans *n.pl.* baked haricot beans, usu. *Brit.* tinned in tomato sauce or *US* cooked with salt pork.

bakehouse *n.* = BAKERY.

Bakelite *n. propr.* ▶ any of various thermosetting resins or plastics made from formaldehyde and phenol and used for cables, buttons, plates, etc. ▷ COSTUME JEWELLERY. [from L.H. *Baekeland*, its Belgian-born inventor, 1863–1944]

BAKELITE BABY ALARM (1937)

baker *n.* a person who bakes and sells bread, cakes, etc., esp. professionally. [Old English]

baker's dozen *n.* thirteen (so called from the former bakers' custom of adding an extra loaf to a dozen sold; the exact reason for this is unclear).

bakery *n.* (*pl.* **-ies**) a place where bread and cakes are made or sold.

baking powder *n.* a mixture of sodium bicarbonate, cream of tartar, etc., used instead of yeast in baking.

motte

bailey

baking soda *n.* sodium bicarbonate.

baklava *n.* (also **baclava**) a rich dessert of flaky pastry, honey, and nuts. [Turkish]

baksheesh *n.* (also **backsheesh**) (in some oriental countries) a small sum of money given as a gratuity or as alms. [from Persian *bakšīš*]

BAILEY: NORMAN MOTTE AND BAILEY CASTLE

balaclava *n.* (in full **balaclava helmet**) a tight woollen garment covering the whole head and neck except for parts of the face, worn originally by soldiers on active service in the Crimean War. [from *Balaclava* in the Crimea, site of a battle (1854)]

balalaika /bal-ă-**ly**-kă/ *n.* ▼ a guitar-like musical instrument having a triangular body and from two to four strings. ▷ STRINGED. [Russian]

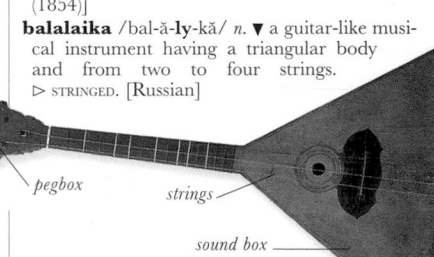

pegbox

strings

sound box

BALALAIKA

B

balance ● *n.* **1** an apparatus for weighing, esp. one with a central pivot, beam, and two scales. **2 a** a counteracting weight or force. **b** (in full **balance wheel**) the regulating device in a clock etc. **3 a** an even distribution of weight or amount. **b** stability of body or mind (*regained his balance*). **4** a preponderating weight or amount (*the balance of opinion*). **5 a** an agreement between or the difference between credits and debits in an account. **b** the difference between an amount due and an amount paid (*will pay the balance next week*). **c** an amount left over; the rest. **6 a** *Art* harmony of design and proportion. **b** *Mus.* the relative volume of various sources of sound (*bad balance between violins and trumpets*). **7** (**the Balance**) the zodiacal sign or constellation Libra. ▷ LIBRA. ● *v.* **1** *tr.* (foll. by *with, against*) offset or compare (one thing) with another (*must balance the advantages with the disadvantages*). **2** *tr.* counteract, equal, or neutralize the weight or importance of. **3 a** *tr.* bring into or keep in equilibrium (*balanced a book on her head*). **b** *intr.* be in equilibrium (*balanced on one leg*). **4** *tr.* (usu. as **balanced** *adj.*) establish equal or appropriate proportions of elements in (*a balanced diet*). **5** *tr.* weigh (arguments etc.) against each other. **6 a** *tr.* compare and esp. equalize debits and credits of (an account). **b** *intr.* (of an account) have credits and debits equal. □ **in the balance** uncertain; at a critical stage. **on balance** all things considered. **strike a balance** choose a moderate course or compromise. [from Late Latin *bilancia*, based on *libra bilanx* 'balance having two scale-pans'] □ **balancer** *n.*

balance of payments *n.* the difference in value between payments into and out of a country.

balance of power *n.* **1** a situation in which states of the world have roughly equal power. **2** the power held by a small group when larger groups are of equal strength.

balance of trade *n.* the difference in value between imports and exports.

balance sheet *n.* a written statement of the balance of assets and liabilities of an organization.

balance wheel see BALANCE *n.* 2b.

balancing act *n.* an action or activity that requires achieving a delicate balance between different requirements.

balcony *n.* (*pl.* **-ies**) **1** a usu. balustraded platform on the outside of a building, with access from an upper-floor window or door. **2 a** the tier of seats in a theatre above the dress circle. **b** the upstairs seats in a cinema etc. **c** *N. Amer.* the dress circle in a theatre. [from Italian *balcone*] □ **balconied** *adj.*

bald *adj.* **1** with the scalp wholly or partly lacking hair. **2** not covered by the usual hair, feathers, leaves, etc. **3** *colloq.* with the surface worn away (*a bald tyre*). **4 a** blunt, unelaborated (*a bald statement*). **b** undisguised (*the bald effrontery*). **5** meagre or dull (*a bald style*). **6** marked with white, esp. on the face (*a bald horse*). [originally in sense 'having a white blaze': Middle English] □ **balding** *adj.* (in senses 1–3). **baldly** *adv.* (in sense 4). **baldness** *n.*

baldachin /bal-dă-kin/ *n.* (also **baldaquin**) a ceremonial canopy over an altar, throne, etc. [based on Italian *Baldacco* 'Baghdad', source of rich brocade]

bald eagle *n.* a white-headed eagle, *Haliaeetus leucocephalus*, used as the emblem of the United States. ▷ EAGLE

balderdash *n.* senseless talk or writing; nonsense [earlier (17th c.) in the sense 'a mixture of drinks', then 'a senseless jumble of words': origin unknown]

baldhead *n.* a person with a bald head.

bale[1] ● *n.* **1** a bundle of merchandise or hay etc. tightly wrapped and bound with cords or hoops. **2** the quantity in a bale as a measure. ● *v.tr.* make up into bales. □ **bale** (or **bail**) **out 1** (of a pilot etc.) make an emergency parachute descent from an aircraft (cf. BAIL[3]). **2** = BAIL[1] *v.* 2. [Middle English, related to BALL[1]]

bale[2] *Brit.* var. of BAIL[3] [Old English]

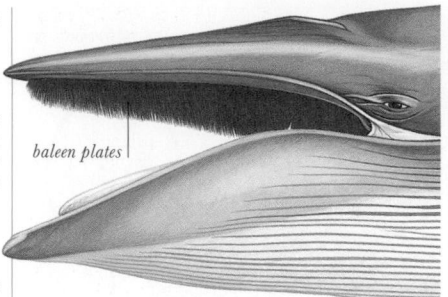

BALEEN WHALE: BLUE WHALE
(*Balaenoptera musculus*)

baleen whale *n.* ▲ any of various whales of the suborder Mysticeti, having plates of whalebone in the mouth for straining plankton from the water. ▷ FILTER-FEEDING, WHALE

baleful *adj.* **1** gloomy, menacing. **2** harmful, malignant, destructive. □ **balefully** *adv.*

baler *n.* a machine for making bales of hay, straw, metal, etc.

balk var. of BAULK.

Balkan ● *adj.* **1** of or relating to the region of SE Europe bounded by the Adriatic, the Aegean, and the Black Sea. **2** of or relating to its peoples or countries. ● *n.* (**the Balkans**) the Balkan countries. [Turkish]

Balkanize *v.tr.* (also **-ise**) divide (an area) into smaller mutually hostile states. □ **Balkanization** *n.*

ball[1] ● *n.* **1** a solid or hollow sphere, esp. for use in a game. **2 a** a ball-shaped object (*ball of wool*). **b** a rounded part of the body (*ball of the foot*). **3** a solid non-explosive missile for a cannon etc. **4** a single delivery of a ball in cricket, baseball, etc., or passing of a ball in football. **5** (in *pl.*) *coarse slang* **a** the testicles. **b** *Brit.* nonsense, rubbish. **c** courage. ● *v.* **1** *tr.* squeeze or wind into a ball. **2** *intr.* form into a ball or balls. □ **the ball is in your** etc. **court** you etc. must be next to act. **balls** (or *Brit.* **ball**) **up** *coarse slang* bungle; make a mess of. **on the ball** *colloq.* alert. **play ball** *colloq.* cooperate. **start** etc. **the ball rolling** set an activity in motion. [from Old Norse *böllr*]

ball[2] *n.* **1** a formal social gathering for dancing. **2** *slang* an enjoyable time (esp. *have a ball*). [based on Late Latin *ballare* 'to dance']

ballad *n.* **1** a poem or song narrating a popular story. **2** a slow sentimental or romantic song. [from Provençal *balada* 'dancing-song']

ballade /ba-lahd/ *n.* **1** a poem of one or more triplets of stanzas with a repeated refrain and a short stanza in conclusion. **2** *Mus.* a short lyrical piece. [earlier spelling of BALLAD]

balladry *n.* ballad poetry.

ball-and-socket joint *n.* a joint in which a rounded end lies in a concave socket. ▷ JOINT

ballast ● *n.* **1** any heavy material placed in a ship or the car of a balloon etc. to secure stability. **2** coarse stone etc. used to form the bed of a railway track or road. **3** a mixture of coarse and fine aggregate for making concrete. ● *v.tr.* **1** provide with ballast. **2** afford stability or weight to. [16th-century coinage]

ball-bearing *n.* ▶ a bearing in which the two halves are separated by a ring of small metal balls which reduce friction. **2** one of these balls.

ballboy *n.* (*fem.* **ballgirl**) *Tennis* etc. a boy or girl who retrieves balls that go out of play.

ballcock *n.* a floating ball on a hinged arm, whose movement up and down controls the water level in a cistern etc.

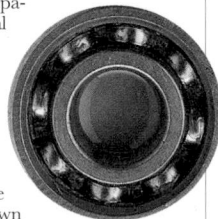

BALL-BEARING

ballerina *n.* a female ballet dancer. [Italian, 'dancing mistress']

ballet *n.* **1 a** a dramatic or representational style of dancing and mime, using set steps and techniques and usu. accompanied by music. **b** a particular piece or performance of ballet. **c** the music for this. **2** a company performing ballet. [from Italian *balletto* 'little dance'] □ **balletic** *adj.*

balletomane *n.* a devotee of ballet.

ball game *n.* **1 a** any game played with a ball. **b** *N. Amer.* a game of baseball. **2** esp. *N. Amer. colloq.* a particular affair or concern (*a whole new ball game*).

ballgirl see BALLBOY.

ballistic *adj.* **1** of or relating to projectiles. **2** moving under the force of gravity only. □ **go ballistic** esp. *N. Amer. slang* become furious.

ballistic missile *n.* ▶ a missile which is initially powered and guided but falls under gravity on its target.

ballistics *n.* the science of projectiles and firearms.

ball lightning *n.* a rare globular form of lightning.

ballocks var. of BOLLOCKS.

balloon ● *n.* **1** a small inflatable rubber pouch with a neck, used as a child's toy or as decoration. **2** a large bag inflatable with hot air or gas to make it rise in the air, often carrying a basket for passengers. ▷ HOT-AIR BALLOON. **3** *colloq.* a balloon shape enclosing the words or thoughts of characters in a comic strip. **4** a large globular drinking glass. ● *v.* **1** *intr. & tr.* swell out or cause to swell out like a balloon. **2** *intr.* travel by balloon. □ **when the balloon goes up** *colloq.* when the action or trouble starts. [from French *ballon* 'large ball'] □ **balloonist** *n.*

ballot ● *n.* **1** a process of voting, in writing and usu. secret. **2** the total of votes recorded in a ballot. **3** the drawing of lots. **4** a paper or ticket etc. used in voting. ● *v.* (**balloted, balloting**) **1** *intr.* (usu. foll. by *for*) **a** hold a ballot; give a vote. **b** draw lots for precedence etc. **2** *tr.* take a ballot of (*the union balloted its members*). [Italian *ballotta*, 'little ball' diminutive of *balla* BALL[1] (from the practice of registering votes by placing coloured balls in a container)]

ballot box *n.* a sealed box into which voters put completed ballot papers.

ballot paper *n. Brit.* a slip of paper used to register a vote.

ballpark *n. N. Amer.* **1** a baseball ground. **2** (*attrib.*) *colloq.* approximate, rough (*a ballpark figure*). □ **in the right ballpark** *colloq.* close to one's objective; approximately correct.

ballpoint *n.* (in full **ballpoint pen**) a pen with a tiny ball as its writing point.

ball-race *n.* **1** a ring-shaped groove in which the balls of a ball-bearing move. **2** a ball-bearing.

ballroom *n.* a large room for dancing.

ballroom dancing *n.* formal social dancing as a recreation or performed competitively.

balls-up *n. Brit. coarse slang* a confused or bungled situation.

ballsy *adj. slang* **1** manly, powerful. **2** courageous. [based on BALL[1] *n.* 5c]

ball valve *n.* a valve opened or closed by a ball which fits into a cup-shaped opening.

bally *adj. & adv. Brit. slang* a mild form of *bloody* (see BLOODY *adj.* 3) (*took the bally lot*). [alteration of BLOODY]

ballyhoo *n.* **1** a loud noise or fuss; a confused state or commotion. **2** extravagant or sensational publicity. [19th-century coinage, originally US: origin unknown]

nose-cone

whistle

BALLISTIC MISSILE: FIRST WORLD WAR MESSAGE ROCKET

rocket body

stabilizing fin

balm *n.* **1** an aromatic ointment for anointing, soothing, or healing. **2** a fragrant and medicinal exudation from certain trees and plants. **3** a soothing influence. **4** ▶ any aromatic herb, esp. one of the genus *Melissa*. **5** a pleasant perfume or fragrance. [Middle English, related to BALSAM]

balmy *adj.* (**balmier**, **balmiest**) **1** mild and fragrant; soothing. **2** yielding balm. **3** esp. *Brit. slang* = BARMY.

baloney *n.* (also **boloney**) (*pl.* **-eys**) *slang* **1** humbug, nonsense. **2** *N. Amer.* a large smoked sausage made of bacon, veal, pork, suet, and other meats, and sold ready for eating. [alteration of *Bologna*, a city in Italy]

BALM:
LEMON BALM
(*Melissa officinalis*)

balsa *n.* **1** (in full **balsa wood**) a type of tough lightweight wood used for making models, rafts, etc. **2** the tropical American tree, *Ochroma lagopus*, from which it comes. [Spanish, literally 'raft']

balsam *n.* **1** an aromatic resinous exudation obtained from various trees and shrubs and used as a base for certain fragrances and medical preparations. **2** an ointment, esp. one composed of a substance dissolved in oil or turpentine. **3** any of various trees or shrubs which yield balsam. **4** any of several flowering plants of the genus *Impatiens*. [from Latin *balsamum*] □ **balsamic** *adj.*

balsam fir *n.* a N. American tree, *Abies balsamea*, which yields balsam.

balsamic vinegar *n.* a dark, sweet, Italian vinegar, matured in wooden barrels.

Balti *n.* a type of Pakistani curry, usu. cooked and served in a dish like a shallow wok. [20th-century coinage]

baluster *n.* each of a series of usu. ornamental short posts or pillars supporting a rail or coping etc. [from Greek *balaustion* 'wild-pomegranate flower', which the baluster resembles in shape]

■ **Usage** *Baluster* is sometimes confused with *banister* because their meanings overlap. A *baluster* is usually a curved ornamental post forming part of a *balustrade* which is mainly found around a gallery, bridge, or terrace.

A *banister* is a post supporting the handrail of a staircase. It can also mean the posts together with the rail. In this case it is often used in the plural.

Occasionally, a large staircase in a grand house may have ornamental carved banisters, in which case they may be called *balusters*.

balustrade *n.* a railing supported by balusters. [French, related to BALUSTER] □ **balustraded** *adj.*

bambino /bam-bee-noh/ *n.* (*pl.* **bambini** /-nee/) *colloq.* a young child. [Italian, literally 'little silly']

bamboo *n.* **1** ◀ a giant woody grass of the mainly tropical subfamily Bambusidae. **2** its hollow jointed stem, used as a stick or to make furniture etc. [from Malay]

bamboo shoot *n.* a young shoot of bamboo, eaten as a vegetable.

bamboozle *v.tr. colloq.* cheat, hoax, mystify. [18th-century coinage]

BAMBOO:
BLACK BAMBOO
(*Phyllostachys nigra*)

ban ● *v.tr.* (**banned**, **banning**) forbid, prohibit. esp. formally. ● *n.* a formal or authoritative prohibition (*a ban on smoking*). [from Old French *ban* 'public proclamation']

banal /bă-nahl/ *adj.* trite, feeble, commonplace. [originally in sense 'compulsory', hence 'common to all'] □ **banality** *n.* (*pl.* **-ies**).

banana *n.* **1** a long curved fruit with soft pulpy flesh and yellow skin when ripe. ▷ BERRY. **2** (in full **banana tree**) the tropical and subtropical treelike plant, *Musa sapientum*, bearing this. □ **go bananas** *slang* become crazy or angry. [from a native name in Guinea]

banana plug *n.* a single-pole connector having a curved spring along its tip, used for electronic devices.

banana republic *n. derog.* a small state economically dependent on one trade and therefore dependent on foreign capital.

banana skin *n.* **1** the skin of a banana. **2** a cause of upset or humiliation; a blunder.

banana split *n.* a sweet dish made with split bananas, ice cream, sauce, etc.

band[1] ● *n.* **1** a flat, thin strip or loop of material put round something (*headband*). **2 a** a strip of material forming part of a garment (*hatband*; *waistband*). **b** a stripe of a different colour or material on an object. **3** a range or category within which items fall (*tax band*; *top band of the fifth form*). **4 a** a range of frequencies or wavelengths in a spectrum. **b** a range of values within a series. **5** a plain gold ring. **6** *Mech.* a belt connecting wheels or pulleys. **7** (in *pl.*) a collar having two hanging strips, worn by some lawyers, ministers, and academics in formal dress. ● *v.tr.* **1** put a band on. **2 a** mark with stripes. **b** (as **banded** *adj.*) *Bot.* & *Zool.* marked with coloured bands or stripes. **3 a** divide into, or arrange in, bands or ranges with a view to treating the bands differently. **b** group (pupils) on the basis of ability. [from Old French; sense 6: from Old Norse]

band[2] ● *n.* **1 a** a group of musicians who play together (*brass band*; *rock band*). **b** *colloq.* an orchestra. **2** an organized group of people having a common object, esp. of a criminal nature (*band of cut-throats*). ● *v.tr.* & *intr.* form into a group for a purpose (*band together for mutual protection*). [from medieval Latin *banda*]

bandage ● *n.* **1** a strip of material for binding up a wound etc. **2** a piece of material used as a blindfold. ● *v.tr.* bind (a wound etc.) with a bandage. [French]

Band-Aid *n.* (also **band-aid**) *propr.* **a** a type of sticking plaster with a gauze pad. **b** a piece of this. **2** a makeshift or temporary solution.

bandanna *n.* a large coloured handkerchief or neckerchief.

B. & B. *abbr.* (also **b. & b.**) bed and breakfast.

bandbox *n.* a cardboard box for carrying hats, used originally for neckbands. □ **out of a bandbox** extremely neat.

bandeau /ban-doh/ *n.* (*pl.* **bandeaux** /-dohz/) a narrow band worn round the head. [French]

banderilla *n.* a decorated dart thrust into a bull's neck or shoulders during a bullfight. [Spanish, literally 'little banner']

bandicoot *n.* **1** ▶ any mainly insect eating marsupial of the family Peramelidae, of Australia and New Guinea. **2** (in full **bandicoot rat**) a destructive Asian rat of the genus *Bandicota*. [from Telugu (a language of SE India) *pandikokku* 'pig-rat']

BANDICOOT:
RABBIT-EARED
BANDICOOT
(*Macrotis lagrotis*)

banding *n.* **1** the presence or formation of visible bands or stripes. **2** division into a series of categories.

bandit *n.* (*pl.* **bandits** or **banditti**) **1** a robber or murderer, esp. a member of a gang. **2** an outlaw. [from Italian *bandito* 'banned'] □ **banditry** *n.*

bandleader *n.* the leader of a musical band.

bandmaster *n.* the conductor of a (esp. military or brass) band.

BANDOLIER:
FIRST WORLD WAR
BRITISH BANDOLIER

buckle

ammunition pouch

waist-belt loop

bandolier /ban-dŏ-leer/ *n.* (also **bandoleer**) ▼ a shoulder-belt with loops or pockets for cartridges. [from French *bandoulière*]

bandsaw *n.* an endless saw, consisting of a steel belt with a serrated edge running over wheels.

bandsman *n.* (*pl.* **-men**) a player in a band.

bandstand *n.* a covered outdoor platform for a band to play on.

bandwagon *n.* orig. *US* a wagon used for carrying a band in a parade etc. □ **climb** (or **jump**) **on the bandwagon** join a group that seems likely to succeed.

bandwidth *n.* the range of frequencies within a given band (see BAND[1] *n.* 4a).

bandy[1] *adj.* (**bandier**, **bandiest**) **1** (of the legs) curved so as to be wide apart at the knees. **2** (also **bandy-legged**) (of a person) having bandy legs.

bandy[2] *v.tr.* (**-ies**, **-ied**) **1 a** pass (a story, rumour, etc.) to and fro. **b** throw or pass (a ball etc.) to and fro. **2** discuss disparagingly (*bandied her name about*). **3** exchange (blows, insults, etc.) (*don't bandy words with me*).

bane *n.* **1** the cause of ruin or trouble (esp. *the bane of one's life*). **2** *poet.* ruin; woe. **3** *archaic* (except in *comb.*) poison (*ratsbane*). [Old English] □ **baneful** *adj.*

bang ● *n.* **1 a** a loud short sound. **b** an explosion. **c** the report of a gun. **2 a** a sharp blow. **b** the sound of this. **3** (in *pl.*) esp. *N. Amer.* a fringe of hair cut straight across the forehead. ● *v.* **1** *tr.* & *intr.* strike or shut noisily (*banged on the table*). **2** *tr.* & *intr.* make or cause to make the sound of a blow or an explosion. **3** *tr.* esp. *N. Amer.* cut (hair) in bangs. ● *adv.* **1** with a bang or sudden impact. **2** *esp. Brit. colloq.* exactly (*bang in the middle*). □ **bang on** *Brit. colloq.* exactly right. **bang on about** talk tediously and at length about. **bang up 1** *Brit. colloq.* imprison (a person). **2** *N. Amer.* damage or injure (a person or thing). **go bang 1** (of a door etc.) shut noisily. **2** explode. **3** *colloq.* be suddenly destroyed (*bang went their chances*). **go with a bang** go successfully. [16th-century coinage]

banger *n.* esp. *Brit.* **1** *slang* a sausage. **2** *slang* an old car. **3** a loud firework.

Bangladeshi ● *n.* (*pl.* same or **Bangladeshis**) a native or inhabitant of Bangladesh, in the northeast of the Indian subcontinent. ● *adj.* of or relating to Bangladesh or its people.

bangle *n.* a rigid ornamental band worn round the arm. [from Hindi *bangli* 'glass bracelet']

banian var. of BANYAN.

banish *v.tr.* **1** formally expel. **2** dismiss from one's presence or mind. [Middle English] □ **banishment** *n.*

banister *n.* (also **bannister**) **1** (often in *pl.*) the uprights and handrail at the side of a staircase. **2** each of these uprights. ▷ NEWEL. [earlier *barrister*, corruption of BALUSTER]

■ **Usage** See Usage Note at BALUSTER.

banjo *n.* (*pl.* **-os** or **-oes**) a stringed musical instrument with a neck and head like a guitar and an open-backed body consisting of parchment stretched over a metal hoop. [based on Greek *pandoura* 'three-stringed lute']

B

bank[1] ● *n.* **1 a** the sloping edge of land by a river. **b** the area of ground alongside a river. **2 a** a raised shelf of ground; a slope. **3** an elevation in the sea or a river bed. **4 a** the artificial slope of a road etc., enabling vehicles to maintain speed round a curve. **b** the sideways tilt of an aircraft when turning in flight. **5** a mass of cloud, fog, snow, etc. ● *v.* **1** *tr.* & *intr.* heap or rise into banks. **2** *tr.* heap up (a fire) tightly so that it burns slowly. **3 a** *intr.* (of a vehicle or aircraft or its occupant) travel with one side higher than the other in rounding a curve. **b** *tr.* cause (a vehicle or aircraft) to do this. [from Old Norse *bakki*]

bank[2] ● *n.* **1 a** a financial establishment which uses money deposited by customers for investment, pays it out when required, makes loans at interest, etc. **b** a building in which this business takes place. **2** the money or tokens held by the banker in some gambling games. **b** the banker in such games. **3** a place for storing anything for future use (*data bank*). ● *v.* **1** *tr.* deposit in a bank. **2** *intr.* engage in business as a banker. **3** *intr.* keep money (at a bank). □ **bank on** rely on (*I'm banking on your help*). [originally in sense 'a money-dealers' bench': from medieval Latin *banca, bancus*]

bank[3] *n.* **1** a row of similar objects, esp. of keys, lights, or switches. **2** a tier of oars. [from Old French *banc*]

bankable *adj.* **1** certain to bring profit. **2** acceptable at a bank. **3** reliable (*a bankable reputation*). □ **bankability** *n.*

bank balance *n.* the amount of money held in a bank account.

bank card *n.* = CHEQUE CARD.

banker *n.* **1** a person who manages or owns a bank. **2** a keeper of the bank or dealer in some gambling games. **3** *Brit.* a result forecast identically in several football-pool entries on one coupon.

banker's order *n. Brit.* an instruction to a bank to pay money or deliver property.

bank holiday *n.* a day on which banks are officially closed, (in the UK) usu. kept as a public holiday.

banking *n.* the business transactions of a bank.

banknote *n.* ▼ a banker's promissory note, payable to the bearer on demand, and serving as money.

BANKNOTE: ITALIAN 10,000-LIRE NOTE

denomination   *central bank*   *serial number*

bankroll orig. *N. Amer.* ● *n.* **1** a roll of banknotes. **2** funds. ● *v.tr. colloq.* support financially.

bankrupt ● *adj.* **1** insolvent; declared in law unable to pay debts. **2** undergoing the legal process resulting from this. ● *n.* **1** an insolvent person whose estate is administered and disposed of for the benefit of the creditors. **2** an insolvent debtor. ● *v.tr.* make bankrupt. [from Italian *banca rotta* 'broken bench', related to BANK[2]] □ **bankruptcy** *n.* (*pl.* **-ies**).

banksia *n.* an evergreen flowering shrub of the genus *Banksia*, native to Australia. [named after Sir J. *Banks*, English naturalist, 1743–1820]

bank statement *n.* a printed statement of transactions and balance issued periodically to the holder of a bank account.

banner *n.* **1 a** a large rectangular sign bearing a slogan or design and usu. carried on two side-poles or a crossbar in a demonstration or procession. **b** a long strip of cloth etc. bearing a slogan. **2 a** a slogan or phrase used to represent a belief or principle.

3 a flag on a pole used as the standard of a king, knight, etc. [from Old French *baniere*]

banner headline *n.* a large newspaper headline.

bannister var. of BANISTER.

bannock *n. Sc. & N.Engl.* a round flat loaf, usu. unleavened. [Old English]

banns *n.pl.* a notice read out on three successive Sundays in a parish church, announcing an intended marriage and giving the opportunity for objections. [pl. variant of BAN]

banoffi pie *n.* a pie with a banana and toffee filling. [from blend of BANANA and TOFFEE]

banquet ● *n.* **1** an elaborate feast. **2** a dinner for many people followed by speeches. ● *v.* (**banqueted, banqueting**) **1** *intr.* hold a banquet. **2** *tr.* entertain with a banquet. [from French, literally 'little bench']

banquette /bang-ket/ *n.* an upholstered bench along a wall. [from Italian *banchetta* 'little bench']

banshee *n. Ir. & Sc.* a female spirit whose wailing warns of a death in a house. [from Old Irish *ben síde* 'woman of the fairies']

BANTAM: PEKIN BANTAM COCK

bantam *n.* **1** ◄ a breed of small domestic fowl, of which the cock is aggressive. **2** a small but aggressive person. [apparently from *Banten* in Java, although the fowl is not native there]

bantamweight *n.* **1** a weight in certain sports intermediate between flyweight and featherweight. **2** a boxer etc. of this weight.

banter ● *n.* good-humoured teasing. ● *v.* **1** *tr.* ridicule in a good-humoured way. **2** *intr.* talk teasingly. [17th-century coinage]

Bantu ● *n.* (*pl.* same or **Bantus**) **1** *offens.* **a** a large group of Negroid peoples of central and southern Africa. **b** a member of any of these peoples. **2** the group of languages spoken by them. ● *adj.* of or relating to these peoples (*offens.*), or languages. [Bantu, literally 'people']

■ **Usage** *Bantu*, originally a neutral 'scientific' term, became strongly associated with apartheid policies in South Africa and is therefore regarded as offensive with reference to the peoples.

Bantustan *n. S.Afr. hist. colloq. derog.* = HOMELAND 2.

banyan *n.* (also **banian**) (also **banyan tree**) an Indian fig tree, *Ficus benghalensis*, the branches of which hang down and root themselves. [from Gujarati *vāṇiyo* 'man of trading caste', applied originally to a tree sheltering the pagoda of Hindu traders]

banzai ● *int.* a Japanese battle-cry. ● *attrib.adj.* reckless. [Japanese, literally 'ten thousand years (of life to you)']

baobab *n.* **1** ► an African tree, *Adansonia digitata*, with an enormously thick trunk and large edible pulpy fruit hanging down on stalks. **2** a related Australian tree, *Adansonia gregorii*.

bap *n. Brit.* a soft flattish bread roll. [16th-century coinage]

baptism *n.* **1 a** the religious rite, symbolizing admission to the Christian Church, of sprinkling or pouring water on to the forehead, or (usu. only with adults) of immersion, generally accompanied by name-giving. **b** the act of baptizing or being baptized. **2** an initiation, e.g. into battle. [from ecclesiastical Greek *baptismos* 'ceremonial washing'] □ **baptismal** *adj.*

baptism of fire *n.* **1** initiation into battle. **2** a painful new undertaking or experience.

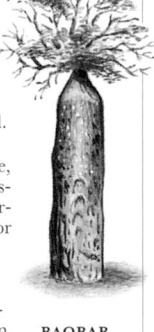

BAOBAB (*Adansonia digitata*)

baptist *n.* **1** a person who baptizes, esp. John the Baptist. **2** (**Baptist**) a member of a Protestant Christian denomination advocating baptism only of adult believers by total immersion. [based on Greek *baptizein* 'to baptize']

baptistery *n.* (also **baptistry**) (*pl.* **-ies**) **1** the part of a church used for baptism. **2** (in a Baptist chapel) a sunken receptacle used for total immersion.

baptize *v.tr.* (also **-ise**) **1** (also *absol.*) administer baptism to. **2** give a name or nickname to. [from Greek *baptizein* 'to baptize']

bar[1] ● *n.* **1** a long rod or piece of rigid wood, metal, etc. **2** a something resembling a bar (*bar of soap; bar of chocolate*). **b** the heating element of an electric fire. **c** *Brit.* a metal strip below the clasp of a medal, awarded as an extra distinction. **d** a sandbank or shoal at the mouth of a harbour or an estuary. **3 a** a barrier of any shape. **b** a restriction (*a bar to promotion*). **4 a** a counter across which alcohol or refreshments are served. **b** a room in a public house in which customers may sit and drink. **c** a public house. **d** a small shop or stall serving refreshments (*snack bar*). **e** a specialized department in a large store (*heel bar*). **5 a** an enclosure in which a prisoner stands in a law court. **b** a particular court of law. **6** *Mus.* **a** any of the sections of usu. equal time value into which a musical composition is divided by vertical lines across the staff. ▷ NOTATION. **b** = BAR LINE. **7** (**the Bar**) *Law* **a** barristers collectively. **b** the profession of barrister. ● *v.tr.* (**barred, barring**) **1 a** fasten with a bar or bars. **b** (usu. foll. by *in, out*) shut or keep in or out. **2** obstruct (*bar his progress*). **3** (usu. foll. by *from*) exclude (*bar them from attending*). **4** mark with stripes. ● *prep.* **1** esp. *Brit.* except (*all bar a few*). **2** *Brit. Racing* except (the horses indicated, used in stating the odds) (*33–1 bar three*). □ **bar none** with no exceptions. **be called to the bar** *Brit.* be admitted as a barrister. **behind bars** in prison. [from Old French *barre* (n.), *barrer* (v.)]

bar[2] *n.* esp. *Meteorol.* a unit of pressure, 10^5 newton per square metre, approx. one atmosphere. [from Greek *baros* 'weight']

barathea /ba-ră-th'ee-ă/ *n.* a fine woollen cloth, sometimes mixed with silk or cotton, used esp. for coats, suits, etc. [19th-century coinage]

barb ● *n.* **1** ► an angled projection from an arrow, fish-hook, etc. ▷ FLUKE. **2** a deliberately hurtful remark. **3** a beardlike filament at the mouth of some fish. ● *v.tr.* **1** provide (an arrow etc.) with a barb or barbs. **2** (as **barbed** *adj.*) (of a *barb* remark etc.) deliberately hurtful. [from Latin *barba* 'beard'] □ **barbless** *adj.*

barb

barbarian ● *n.* **1** an uncultured or brutish person. **2** a member of a primitive community or tribe. ● *adj.* **1** rough and uncultured. **2** uncivilized. [originally of any foreigner: based on Greek *barbaros* 'foreign'] □ **barbaric** *adj.* **barbarically** *adv.*

BARBS ON AN ARROWHEAD

barbarism *n.* **1 a** the absence of culture and civilized standards; ignorance and rudeness. **b** an example of this. **2** a word or expression not considered correct; a solecism. **3** anything considered to be in bad taste. [based on Greek *barbarizein* 'to speak like a foreigner']

barbarity *n.* (*pl.* **-ies**) **1** savage cruelty. **2** an example of this.

barbarize *v.tr. & intr.* (also **-ise**) make or become barbarous. □ **barbarization** *n.*

barbarous *adj.* **1** uncivilized. **2** cruel. **3** coarse and unrefined. □ **barbarously** *adv.* **barbarousness** *n.*

barbecue ● *n.* **1 a** a meal cooked on an open fire out of doors, esp. meat grilled on a metal appliance. **b** a party at which such a meal is cooked. **2 a** the metal appliance used for the preparation of a barbecue. **b** a usu. brick structure containing such an appliance. ● *v.tr.* (**barbecues**, **barbecued**, **barbecuing**) cook (esp. meat) on a barbecue. [from Spanish *barbacoa* 'wooden frame on posts']

barbecue sauce *n.* a highly seasoned sauce in which meat may be cooked.

barbed wire *n.* wire bearing sharp pointed spikes close together and used in fencing, or in warfare as an obstruction.

barbel *n.* **1** ► any large European freshwater fish of the genus *Barbus*, with fleshy filaments hanging from its mouth. **2** such a filament growing from the mouth of any fish. [from Late Latin *barbellus* 'little barbel or beard']

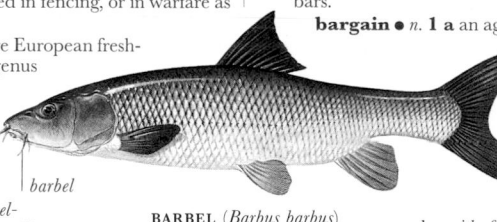

BARBEL (*Barbus barbus*)

barbell *n.* ▼ an iron bar with a series of graded discs at each end, used for weightlifting exercises.

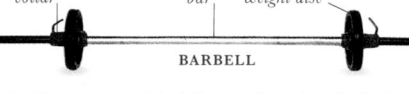

collar | bar | weight disc

BARBELL

barber *n.* a men's hairdresser. [based on Latin *barba* 'beard']

barberry *n.* (*pl.* **-ies**) **1** any shrub of the genus *Berberis*, with spiny shoots, yellow flowers, and ovoid red berries. **2** its berry. [from Old French *berberis*]

barber-shop *n.* a popular style of close harmony singing, esp. for four male voices.

barber's pole *n.* a spirally painted striped red and white pole hung outside barbers' shops as a business sign.

barbican *n.* the outer defence of a city, castle, etc., esp. a double tower above a gate or drawbridge. [from Old French *barbacane*]

barbitone *n.* (*US* **barbital**) a sedative drug.

barbiturate *n.* any derivative of barbituric acid used in the preparation of sedative and sleep-inducing drugs.

barbituric acid *n. Chem.* an organic acid from which various sedatives are derived.

Barbour /bah-ber/ *n.* (in full **Barbour jacket**) *propr.* a type of green waxed jacket. [named after J. *Barbour*, died 1918, English draper who sold waterproof clothing]

barbwire *n. N. Amer.* — BARBED WIRE.

barcarole *n.* (also **barcarolle**) **1** a song sung by Venetian gondoliers. **2** music in imitation of this. [from Venetian Italian *barcarola* 'boatman's song']

bar chart *n.* (also **bar graph**) a chart or graph using bars to represent quantity.

bar code *n.* ► a machine-readable code in the form of a pattern of stripes printed on and identifying a commodity.

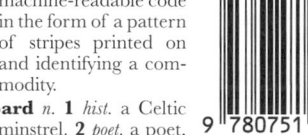

BAR CODE

bard *n.* **1** *hist.* a Celtic minstrel. **2** *poet.* a poet, esp. one treating heroic themes. [from Celtic] □ **bardic** *adj.*

bare ● *adj.* **1** (esp. of part of the body) unclothed or uncovered (*with bare head*). **2** without appropriate covering or contents: **a** (of a tree) leafless. **b** empty (*bare rooms; the cupboard was bare*). **c** (of a floor) uncarpeted. **3 a** undisguised (*the bare truth*). **b** unadorned (*bare facts*). **4** (*attrib.*) **a** scanty (*a bare majority*). **b** mere (*bare necessities*). ● *v.tr.* uncover; reveal. □ **bare of** without. **with one's bare hands** without using tools or weapons. [Old English] □ **bareness** *n.*

bareback *adj. & adv.* on an unsaddled horse etc.

barefaced *adj.* undisguised; impudent (*barefaced cheek*). □ **barefacedly** *adv.*

barefoot *adj. & adv.* (also **barefooted**) with nothing on the feet.

bareheaded *adj. & adv.* without a covering for the head.

barely *adv.* **1** only just; scarcely (*barely escaped*). **2** scantily (*barely furnished*). **3** *archaic* openly, explicitly.

barfly *n.* (*pl.* **-flies**) *colloq.* a person who frequents bars.

bargain ● *n.* **1 a** an agreement on the terms of a transaction or sale. **b** this seen from the buyer's viewpoint (*a bad bargain*). **2** something acquired or offered cheaply. ● *v.intr.* (often foll. by *with*, *for*) discuss the terms of a transaction. □ **bargain for** (or *colloq.* **on**) (usu. with *neg.* actual or implied) expect (*didn't bargain for bad weather*). **bargain on** rely on. **into** (*US* **in**) **the bargain** in addition to what was expected. [from Old French *bargaine* (n.), *bargaignier* (v.)] □ **bargainer** *n.*

barge ● *n.* **1** a long flat-bottomed boat for carrying freight on canals etc. **2** a long ornamental boat used for pleasure or ceremony. **3** a boat used by the chief officers of a warship. ● *v.* **1** *intr.* (often foll. by *around*) lurch or rush clumsily about. **2** *intr.* (foll. by *in*, *into*) **a** interrupt rudely (*barged in while we were kissing*). **b** collide with (*barged into her*). **3** *tr.* convey by barge. [from Greek *baris* 'Egyptian boat']

bargeboard *n.* a board (often ornamental) fixed to the gable-end of a roof to hide the ends of the roof timbers.

bargee *n. Brit.* a person in charge of or working on a barge.

bargepole *n.* a long pole used for punting barges etc. □ **would not touch with a bargepole** *Brit.* refuse to be associated or concerned with.

bar graph var. of BAR CHART.

barite /ba-ryt/ *n.* (also **baryte**) ▼ a mineral form of barium sulphate.

baritone *n.* **1 a** the second lowest adult male singing voice. **b** a singer with this voice. **c** a part written for it. **2** an instrument that is second lowest in pitch in its family. [from Greek *barutonos*]

barium /bair-i-ŭm/ *n.* **1** *Chem.* a white reactive soft metallic element. **2** a mixture of barium sulphate and water, opaque to X-rays, which is given to patients requiring radiological examination of the stomach or intestines (*barium meal*).

BARITE

bark[1] ● *n.* **1** the sharp explosive cry of a dog, fox, etc. **2** a sound resembling this. ● *v.* **1** *intr.* give a bark. **2** *tr. & intr.* speak or utter sharply or brusquely. □ **bark up the wrong tree** be on the wrong track. [Old English]

bark[2] ● *n.* the tough protective outer sheath of branches etc. or woody shrubs. ▷ WOOD. [from Old Norse *börkr* bark-]

barker *n.* a tout at a sideshow etc., who calls out for custom to passers-by. [related to BARK[1]]

barley *n.* **1** any of various hardy awned cereals of the genus *Hordeum* widely used as food and in malt liquors. **2** the grain produced from this. ▷ GRAIN. [Old English]

barleycorn *n.* **1** the grain of barley. **2** a former unit of measure (about a third of an inch) based on the length of a grain of barley.

barley sugar *n.* an amber-coloured sweet made of boiled sugar, traditionally shaped as a twisted stick.

barley water *n.* a drink made from water and a boiled barley mixture.

bar line *n. Mus.* a vertical line used to mark divisions between bars. ▷ NOTATION

barm *n.* **1** the froth on fermenting malt liquor. **2** *archaic* or *dial.* yeast or leaven. [Old English]

barmaid *n.* **1** *Brit.* a woman serving behind the bar of a public house, hotel, etc. **2** *US* a waitress who serves drinks.

barman *n.* (*pl.* **-men**) esp. *Brit.* a man serving behind the bar of a public house, hotel, etc.

bar mitzvah *n.* **1** the religious initiation ceremony of a Jewish boy who has reached the age of 13. **2** a boy undergoing this ceremony. [Hebrew, literally 'son of the commandment']

barmy *adj.* (**barmier**, **barmiest**) esp. *Brit. slang* crazy, stupid. [originally in sense 'frothy', related to BARM] □ **barmily** *adv.* **barminess** *n.*

barn *n.* **1** a large farm building for storing grain etc. or *N. Amer.* housing livestock. **2** *derog.* a large plain or unattractive building. **3** *N. Amer.* a large shed for storing vehicles. [Old English, from *bere ern* 'barley house']

barnacle *n.* ◄ any of various small marine crustaceans of the class Cirripedia which in adult form cling to rocks, ships' bottoms, etc., forming a rough encrustation. ▷ CRUSTACEAN. [Middle English] □ **barnacled** *adj.*

cirrus

carina
plate

BARNACLE (*Balanus* species)

barn dance *n.* **1** an informal social gathering for country dancing, originally in a barn. **2** a dance for a number of couples forming a line or circle and moving along it in turn.

barney *n.* (*pl.* **-eys**) *Brit. colloq.* a noisy quarrel. [perhaps dialect]

barn owl *n.* a kind of owl, *Tyto alba*, frequenting barns. ▷ OWL

barnstorm *v.intr.* **1** tour rural districts giving theatrical performances (formerly often in barns). **2** *N. Amer.* make a rapid tour, esp. for political meetings. □ **barnstormer** *n.*

barnyard *n.* the area around a barn.

barograph *n.* a barometer that records its readings on a moving chart. [based on Greek *baros* 'weight']

barometer /bă-rom-i-ter/ *n.* **1** ► an instrument measuring atmospheric pressure esp. in forecasting the weather and determining altitude. **2** anything which reflects changes in circumstances, opinions etc. [based on Greek *baros* 'weight'] □ **barometric** *adj.* **barometrical** *adj.*

pressure scale

pointer

BAROMETER: ANEROID BAROMETER

baron *n.* **1 a** a member of the lowest order of the British nobility. **b** a similar member of a foreign nobility. **2** an important businessman or other powerful or influential person (*sugar baron; newspaper baron*). **3** *hist.* a person who held lands or property from the sovereign or a powerful overlord. [from medieval Latin *baro* 'man, warrior'] □ **baronial** *adj.*

baronage *n.* **1** barons or nobles collectively. **2** an annotated list of barons or peers.

baroness *n.* **1** a woman holding the rank of baron either as a life peerage or as a hereditary rank. **2** the wife or widow of a baron.

baronet *n.* a member of the lowest hereditary titled British order. □ **baronetcy** *n.* (*pl.* **-ies**).

B

B

BAROQUE

The baroque style emerged in Rome during the 17th century, rising from the growing confidence of the Roman Catholic Church. Originally it was developed to appeal to the increasing number of new members within the congregation, and to lure others away from the more austere Protestantism. Characterized by religious subjects, this ornate and theatrical style travelled across Italy, into other parts of Europe, and to the American colonies, as the influence of Catholicism spread internationally. The style was adopted by many of the architects, sculptors, and painters of the period.

Ecstasy of Teresa (1646), GIANLORENZO BERNINI

TIMELINE

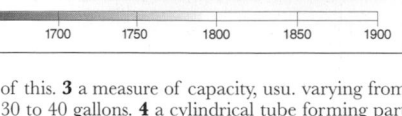

1400 1450 1500 1550 1600 1650 1700 1750 1800 1850 1900

---

baronetcy *n.* (*pl.* **-ies**) the domain, rank or tenure of a baronet.

baron of beef *n. Brit.* an undivided double sirloin.

barony *n.* (*pl.* **-ies**) **1** the domain, rank, or tenure of a baron. **2** (in Ireland) a division of a county. **3** (in Scotland) a large manor or estate.

baroque /bă-rok/ ● *adj.* **1** ▲ highly ornate and extravagant in style, esp. of European art etc. of the 17th and 18th c. **2** of or relating to this period. ● *n.* **1** the baroque style. **2** baroque art collectively. [from Portuguese *barroco* 'irregular pearl']

barque /bahk/ *n.* **1** a sailing ship with the rear mast fore-and-aft-rigged and the remaining masts square-rigged. **2** *poet.* any boat. [from Latin *barca* 'ship's boat']

barrack[1] *n.* (usu. in *pl.*; often treated as *sing.*) **1** a building or complex used to house soldiers. **2** a large building of a bleak or plain appearance. [from Spanish *barraca* 'soldier's tent']

barrack[2] *v. Brit., Austral., & NZ* **1** *tr.* (also *absol.*) shout or jeer at. **2** *intr.* (foll. by *for*) cheer for, encourage (a team etc.).

barrack-room lawyer *n. Brit.* a pompously argumentative person.

barrack square *n. Brit.* a drill ground near a barracks.

barracouta *n.* (*pl.* same or **barracoutas**) a long slender fish, *Thyrsites atun*, usu. found in southern oceans. [variant of BARRACUDA]

barracuda *n.* (*pl.* same or **barracudas**) ▼ a large and voracious tropical marine fish of the family Sphyraenidae. [Latin American Spanish]

BARRACUDA: GREAT BARRACUDA
(*Sphyraena barracuda*)

barrage *n.* **1** a concentrated artillery bombardment over a wide area. **2** a rapid succession of questions or criticisms. **3** *Brit.* an artificial barrier, esp. in a river. [French]

barrage balloon *n. hist.* a large anchored balloon, often with netting suspended from it, used as a defence against low-flying aircraft.

barratry *n.* fraud or gross negligence of a ship's master or crew at the expense of its owners or users. [from Old French *baraterie*] □ **barratrous** *adj.*

barre *n.* a horizontal bar at waist level used in dance exercises. [French]

barrel ● *n.* **1** a cylindrical container usu. bulging out in the middle, traditionally made of wooden staves with metal hoops round them. **2** the contents of this. **3** a measure of capacity, usu. varying from 30 to 40 gallons. **4** a cylindrical tube forming part of an object such as a gun. ▷ BLUNDERBUSS, CANNON. ● *v.tr.* (**barrelled**, **barrelling**; *US* **barreled**, **barreling**) put into a barrel or barrels. □ **over a barrel** *colloq.* in a helpless position; at a person's mercy. [from medieval Latin *barrillus* 'small cask']

barrel-chested *adj.* having a large rounded chest.

barrel organ *n.* a mechanical musical instrument in which a rotating pin-studded cylinder acts on a series of pipe-valves, strings, or metal tongues.

barrel vault *n. Archit.* a vault forming a half cylinder. ▷ VAULT. □ **barrel-vaulted** *adj.*

barren *adj.* (**barrener**, **barrenest**) **1** unable to bear young, fruit, etc. **2** meagre, unprofitable. **3** dull, unstimulating. **4** (foll. by *of*) lacking in (*barren of wit*). [from Old French *barhaine*] □ **barrenly** *adv.* **barrenness** *n.*

barricade ● *n.* a barrier, esp. one improvised across a street etc. ● *v.tr.* block or defend with a barricade. [based on Spanish *barrica* 'cask']

barrier *n.* **1** a fence or other obstacle that bars advance or access. **2** an obstacle or circumstance that keeps people or things apart (*class barriers; a language barrier*). [from Old French *barriere*]

barrier cream *n. Brit.* a cream used to protect the skin from damage or infection.

barrier reef *n.* a coral reef separated from the shore by a broad deep channel.

barring *prep.* except, not including.

barrio *n.* (*pl.* **-os**) (in the US) the Spanish-speaking quarter of a town or city. [Spanish, literally 'district of a town']

barrister *n.* (in full **barrister-at-law**) esp. *Brit.* a person called to the bar and entitled to practise as an advocate in the higher courts. [Middle English, based on BAR[1]]

barrow[1] *n.* **1** *Brit.* a two-wheeled handcart used esp. by street vendors. **2** = WHEELBARROW. [Old English] □ **barrowload** *n.*

barrow[2] *n. Archaeol.* ▼ an ancient grave mound or tumulus. [Old English]

main passage
grave chamber
blocking stone

BARROW: SECTION THROUGH NEOLITHIC LONG BARROW (*c*.2,500 BC)

Bart. *abbr.* Baronet.

bartender *n.* a person serving behind the bar of a public house.

barter ● *v.tr.* (also *absol.*) exchange (goods or services) without using money. ● *n.* trade by exchange of goods. □ **barterer** *n.*

baryon *n. Physics* a subatomic particle that has a mass equal to or greater than that of a proton. [based on Greek *barus* 'heavy'] □ **baryonic** *adj.*

barysphere *n.* the dense interior of the Earth, including the mantle and core, enclosed by the lithosphere. [from Greek *barus* 'heavy' + *sphaira* 'sphere']

baryte var. of BARITE.

basal /bay-săl/ *adj.* of, at, or forming a base.

basal cell carcinoma *n. Med.* a slow-growing malignant tumour of the face.

basalt /ba-sawlt/ *n.* **1** ▶ a dark basic volcanic rock whose deposits sometimes form columns. ▷ ROCK CYCLE. **2** a kind of black stoneware resembling basalt. [based on Greek *basanos* 'touchstone'] □ **basaltic** *adj.*

BASALT

base[1] ● *n.* **1 a** a part that supports from beneath or serves as a foundation. **b** a notional structure on which something depends (*economic base*). **2** a principle or starting point. **3** esp. *Mil.* a place from which activity is directed. **4 a** a main or important ingredient. **b** a substance, e.g. water, in combination with which pigment forms paint etc. **5** a substance used as a foundation for make-up. **6** *Chem.* a substance capable of reacting with an acid to form a salt and water, or (more broadly) of accepting or neutralizing hydrogen ions. **7** *Math.* a number in terms of which other numbers or logarithms are expressed (see RADIX 1). **8** *Baseball* etc. one of the four stations that must be reached in turn to score a run. ▷ BASEBALL. ● *v.tr.* **1** (usu. foll. by *on, upon*) establish (*a theory based on speculation*). **2** (foll. by *at, in*, etc.) station (*troops were based in Malta*). [from Latin *basis* 'step, pedestal']

base[2] *adj.* **1** cowardly, despicable. **2** menial. **3** alloyed (*base coin*). **4** (of a metal) not regarded as precious. [from medieval Latin *bassus* 'short'] □ **basely** *adv.* **baseness** *n.*

baseball *n.* ▶ a game played with teams of nine, a bat and ball, and a circuit of four bases which the batter must complete to score. ▷ HOMEPLATE

baseboard *n. N. Amer.* a skirting board.

base camp *n.* a camp from which expeditions set out or operations are conducted.

basehead *n. US slang* a person who habitually takes either of the drugs freebase or crack. [blend of FREEBASE and HEAD]

baseless *adj.* unfounded, groundless. □ **baselessly** *adv.* **baselessness** *n.*

baseline *n.* **1** a line used as a base or starting point. **2** (in tennis etc.) the line marking each end of a court. ▷ TENNIS

basement *n.* the lowest floor of a building, usu. at least partly below ground level.

base rate *n. Brit.* the interest rate set by the Bank of England, used as the basis for other banks' rates.

bases *pl.* of BASE[1], BASIS.

base unit *n.* a unit that is defined arbitrarily and not by combinations of other units.

bash ● *v.* **1** *tr.* **a** strike bluntly or heavily. **b** (often foll. by *up*) *colloq.* attack violently. **c** esp. *N. Amer.* criticize severely. **2** *intr.* (foll. by *into*) collide with. ● *n.* **1** a heavy blow. **2** *Brit. colloq.* an attempt (*a bash at painting*). **3** *slang* a social event.

bashful *adj.* **1** shy, self-conscious. **2** sheepish. [based on obsolete verb *bash* 'to abash'] □ **bashfully** *adv.* **bashfulness** *n.*

basho *n.* (*pl.* same or **-os**) a sumo wrestling tournament. [Japanese, from *ba* 'place' + *shō* 'victory']

BASIC *n.* a computer programming language using familiar English words, widely used on microcomputers. [acronym from *B*eginner's *A*ll-purpose *S*ymbolic *I*nstruction *C*ode]

basic ● *adj.* **1** forming or serving as a base. **2** fundamental. **3 a** simplest or lowest in level (*basic requirements*). **b** vulgar (*basic humour*). **4** *Chem.* having the properties of or containing a base. ● *n.* (usu. in *pl.*) the fundamental facts or principles. [based on Latin *basis* 'pedestal']

basically *adv.* **1** fundamentally. **2** (qualifying a sentence or clause) in fact, actually.

basic wage *n.* a minimum wage earned before possible additional payments such as overtime etc.

basil *n.* an aromatic herb of the genus *Ocimum*, esp. *O. basilicum* (in full **sweet basil**), whose leaves are used in savoury dishes. ▷ HERB. [based on Greek *basilikos* 'royal']

basilar *adj.* of or at the base (esp. of the skull). [from modern Latin *basilaris*, related to BASIS]

basilica *n.* **1** ▼ an ancient Roman public hall with an apse and colonnades. **2** a similar building used as a Christian church. **3** a church having special privileges from the Pope. [from Greek *basilikē (oikiastoa)* 'royal (house, portico)'] □ **basilican** *adj.*

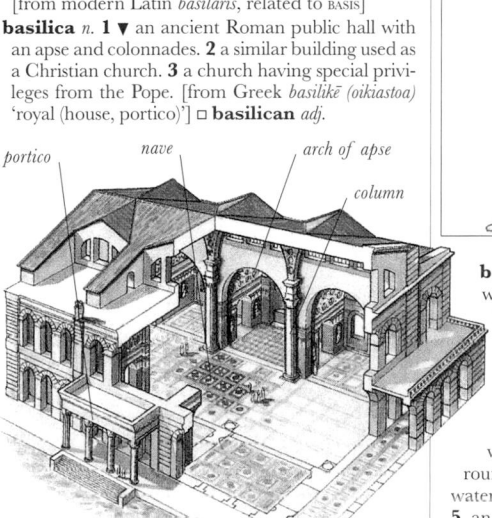

BASILICA:
SECTION THROUGH A
4TH-CENTURY ROMAN BASILICA

portico *nave* *arch of apse* *column*

BASKETBALL

Basketball is a fast-moving non-contact sport in which players move the ball across the court by dribbling and passing. The aim of the game is to take possession of the ball, then to score points by throwing it into the opposing team's basket.

net
basketball
backboard
JUMP SHOT

backboard *basket* *endline*
restraining circle
player's bench
semicircle
referee
right guard
left guard
centre
centreline
referee
left forward
right forward
centre circle
sideline
three-point line
free-throw line
BASKETBALL COURT
15 m (49 ft)

basilisk *n.* **1** a mythical reptile with a lethal breath and look. **2** ▶ any small American lizard of the genus *Basiliscus*, with a crest from its back to its tail. [from Greek *basiliskos* 'little king, serpent']

basin *n.* **1 a** = WASHBASIN. **b** a wide round open container. **2** a hollow rounded depression. **3** any sheltered area of water for mooring boats. **4** a round valley. **5** an area drained by rivers and tributaries. [from medieval Latin *ba(s)cinus*] □ **basinful** *n.* (*pl.* -**fuls**).

BASILISK LIZARD
(*Basiliscus plumifrons*)

basis *n.* (*pl.* **bases** /**bay**-seez/) **1** the foundation or support of esp. an idea or argument. **2** the main or determining principle (*on a purely friendly basis*). [Latin, literally 'pedestal', from Greek]

bask *v.intr.* **1** sit or lie back lazily in warmth and light. **2** (foll. by *in*) derive great pleasure (from) (*basking in glory*). [Middle English]

basket *n.* **1** a container made of interwoven cane etc. **2** a container resembling this. **3** the amount held by a basket. **4** the goal in basketball, or a goal scored. ▷ BASKETBALL. [from Anglo-Latin *baskettum*] □ **basketful** *n.* (*pl.* -**fuls**).

basketball *n.* ▲ a game between two teams of five, in which goals are scored by making the ball drop through hooped nets fixed high up at each end of a court.

basketry *n.* **1** the art of making baskets. **2** baskets collectively.

basket weave *n.* a weave resembling that of a basket.

basketwork *n.* **1** material woven in the style of a basket. **2** the art of making this.

basmati *n.* (in full **basmati rice**) a kind of long-grain Indian rice, with a delicate nutty flavour. [Hindi, literally 'fragrant']

Basque *n.* **1** a member of a people of the western Pyrenees. **2** the language of this people. [French, from Latin *Vasco*]

basque *n.* a close-fitting bodice extending from the shoulders to the waist and often with a short continuation below waist level.

bas-relief *n.* *Sculpture* **1** = *low relief* (see RELIEF 6a). **2** a sculpture, carving, etc. in low relief. [alteration of Italian *basso-rilievo* to French form]

bass[1] /bayss/ ● *n.* **1 a** the lowest adult male singing voice. **b** a singer with this voice. **c** a part written for it. **2** the lowest part in harmonized music. **3 a** an instrument that is the lowest in pitch in its family. **b** a player of such an instrument. **4** *colloq.* a bass guitar or double bass. **5** the low-frequency output of a radio etc., corresponding to the bass in music. ● *adj.* **1** lowest in musical pitch. **2** deep-sounding. [alteration of BASE[2], influenced by BASSO] □ **bassist** *n.* (in sense 4 of *n.*).

BASEBALL

Baseball is played by two teams of nine players who take it in turns to bat and field. The pitcher aims the ball at the 'strike zone' of the batter, who has up to three attempts to hit the ball. The batter then runs around the four bases to score a run; he is out if he fails to strike, his strike is caught, or he is tagged as he runs.

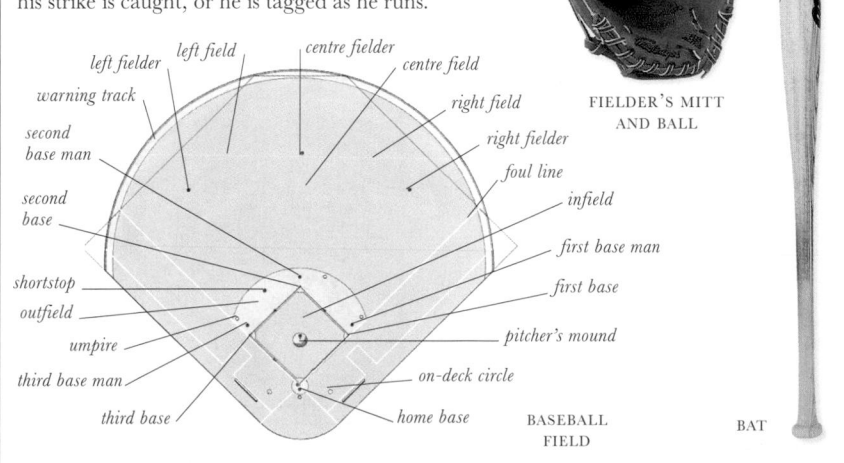

left fielder *left field* *centre fielder* *centre field*
warning track *right field*
second base man *right fielder*
second base *foul line*
shortstop *infield*
outfield *first base man*
umpire *first base*
third base man *pitcher's mound*
third base *on-deck circle*
home base
BASEBALL FIELD

FIELDER'S MITT AND BALL

BAT

B

bass² /*rhymes with* lass/ *n.* (*pl.* same or **basses**) **1** the common European freshwater perch. **2** ▼ a similar marine fish of the family Percichthyidae (alias Moronidae), esp. *Dicentrarchus*. **3** (in full **sea bass**) a similar marine fish of the family Serranidae, esp. of the genus *Centropristis*. [Middle English]

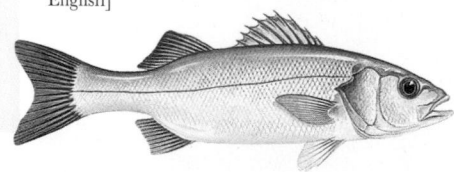

BASS: EUROPEAN SEA BASS (*Dicentrarchus labrax*)

bass³ *n.* = BAST. [alteration of BAST]

bass clef *n.* a clef placing F below middle C on the second highest line of the staff. ▷ NOTATION

basset *n.* (in full **basset-hound**) a sturdy hunting dog of a breed with a long body, short legs, and big ears. [French, literally 'rather low']

basset-horn *n.* an alto clarinet in F. [translation of Italian *corno di bassetto*]

bassinet *n.* a child's wicker cradle. [French, literally 'little basin']

basso *n.* (*pl.* **-os** or **bassi**) a singer with a bass voice. [Italian]

bassoon *n.* ▼ a bass instrument of the oboe family. ▷ ORCHESTRA, WOODWIND. [from French *basson*] □ **bassoonist** *n.*

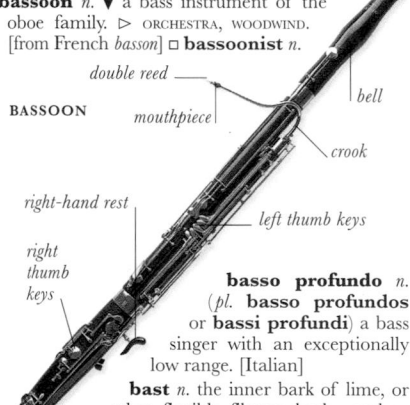

BASSOON

double reed
mouthpiece
bell
crook
right-hand rest
left thumb keys
right thumb keys

basso profundo *n.* (*pl.* **basso profundos** or **bassi profundi**) a bass singer with an exceptionally low range. [Italian]

bast *n.* the inner bark of lime, or other flexible fibrous bark, used as fibre in matting etc. [Old English]

bastard ● *n.* **1** *archaic* or *offens.* a person born of an unmarried mother. **2** *coarse slang* **a** an unpleasant or despicable person. **b** a person of a specified kind (*poor bastard*). **3** *coarse slang* a difficult or awkward thing. ● *adj.* (usu. *attrib.*) **1** *archaic* or *offens.* illegitimate. **2** (of things): **a** unauthorized, counterfeit. **b** hybrid. [from medieval Latin *bastardus*] □ **bastardy** *n.* (in sense 1 of *n. archaic*).

bastardize *v.tr.* (also **-ise**) **1** declare (a person) illegitimate. **2** corrupt, debase. □ **bastardization** *n.*

baste¹ *v.tr.* moisten (meat) with gravy or melted fat during cooking. [15th-century coinage]

baste² *v.tr. Needlework* tack. [from Old French *bastir* 'to sew lightly']

baste³ *v.tr.* beat soundly.

bastinado *n.* punishment by beating with a stick on the soles of the feet. [from Spanish *bastonada*]

bastion *n.* **1** a projecting part of a fortification built at an angle of, or against the line of, a wall. **2** a thing regarded as protecting (*bastion of freedom*). [based on Italian *bastire* 'to build']

bat¹ ● *n.* **1** an implement with a handle and a flat or curved surface, used for hitting balls in games. ▷ CRICKET. **2** *Cricket* a turn at using this. **3** a batsman described in some way (*an excellent bat*). **4** (usu. in *pl.*) an object like a table tennis bat used to guide aircraft when taxiing. ● *v.* (**batted**, **batting**) **1** *tr.* hit with or as with a bat. **2** *intr.* take a turn at using a bat; have an innings at cricket etc. □ **off one's own bat** *Brit.* unprompted, unaided. [Old English]

BAT

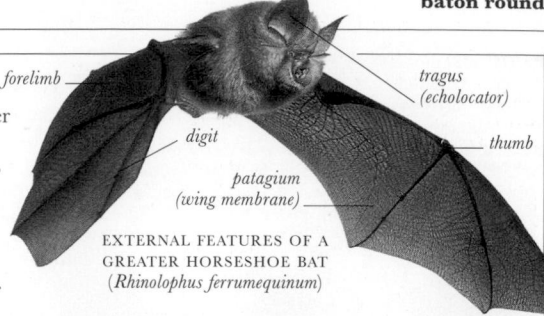

Bats form the second largest order of mammals, with almost 1,000 species. Divided into two groups, fruit-eating megabats find food by sight and smell, while mainly insect-eating microbats locate their prey using sound waves, by a process known as echolocation.

forelimb
digit
patagium (wing membrane)
tragus (echolocator)
thumb

EXTERNAL FEATURES OF A GREATER HORSESHOE BAT (*Rhinolophus ferrumequinum*)

EXAMPLES OF OTHER BATS

COMMON VAMPIRE BAT (*Desmodus rotundus*)

PROBOSCIS BAT (*Rhynchonycteris naso*)

FRANQUET'S FRUITBAT (*Epomops franqueti*)

NOCTULE BAT (*Nyctalus noctula*)

FUNNEL-EARED BAT (*Natalus tumidirostris*)

---

bat² *n.* **1** ▲ any mouselike nocturnal mammal of the order Chiroptera, capable of flight by means of membranous wings extending from its forelimbs. **2** (esp. in phr. **old bat**) *derog.* a woman, esp. regarded as unattractive or unpleasant. □ **have bats in the belfry** be eccentric or crazy. **like a bat out of hell** very fast. [16th-century alteration of Middle English *bakke*]

bat³ *v.tr.* (**batted**, **batting**) □ **not** (or **never**) **bat an eyelid** (or **eye**) *colloq.* show no reaction. [variant of obsolete *bate* 'to flutter']

batch ● *n.* **1** a number of things or persons forming a group. **2** an instalment (*sent off the last batch*). **3** the loaves produced at one baking. **4** (*attrib.*) using or dealt with in batches, not as a continuous flow (*batch production*). **5** *Computing* a group of records processed as a single unit. ● *v.tr.* arrange or deal with in batches. [Middle English, from earlier *bacan* 'to bake']

batch processing *n.* **1** the performance of an industrial process on material in batches. **2** *Computing* the processing of previously collected data or jobs in batches, esp. automatically.

bated *adj.* □ **with bated breath** very anxiously. [originally in sense 'restrained': from obsolete *bate*]

bath ● *n.* (*pl.* **baths**) **1 a** a container for liquid, usu. water, used for immersing and washing the body. **b** this with its contents (*your bath is ready*). **2** the act or process of immersing the body for washing or therapy (*have a bath*). **3 a** a vessel containing liquid in which something is immersed in film developing etc. **b** this with its contents. **4** (usu. in *pl.*) a building with baths or a swimming pool, usu. open to the public. ● *v.* **1** *tr.* wash (esp. a person) in a bath. **2** *intr.* take a bath. [Old English]

bath chair *n.* esp. *hist.* a kind of wheelchair for invalids. [from *Bath* in S. England, named for its hot springs thought to have curative powers]

bath cube *n. Brit.* a cube of compacted bath salts.

bathe ● *v.* **1** *intr.* immerse oneself in water, esp. (*Brit.*) to swim or (esp. *N. Amer.*) to wash oneself. **2** *tr.* **a** treat with liquid for cleansing or medicinal purposes. **b** *N. Amer.* wash (esp. a person) in a bath. **3** *tr.* (of sunlight etc.) envelop. ● *n.* an act of immersing oneself or part of the body in liquid. [Old English] □ **bather** *n.*

bathhouse *n.* a building with baths for public use.

batholith *n.* a dome of igneous rock extending inwards to an unknown depth. [German from Greek *bathos* 'depth' + -LITH]

bathos /*bay*-thos/ *n.* **1** an unintentional lapse in mood from the sublime to the absurd or trivial. **2** a commonplace or ridiculous feature offsetting an otherwise sublime situation. [Greek, literally 'depth'] □ **bathetic** *adj.* **bathotic** *adj.*

bathrobe *n.* a loose coat usu. of towelling worn esp. before and after taking a bath; a dressing gown.

bathroom *n.* **1 a** a room containing a bath and usu. other washing facilities. **b** bathroom fitments or units esp. as sold together. **2** esp. *N. Amer.* a room containing a lavatory.

bath salts *n.pl.* soluble salts used for softening or scenting bathwater.

bathtub *n.* = BATH *n.* 1.

bathwater *n.* the water in a bath.

bathyscaphe *n.* ▼ a manned vessel for deep-sea diving. [from Greek *bathus* 'deep' + *skaphos* 'ship']

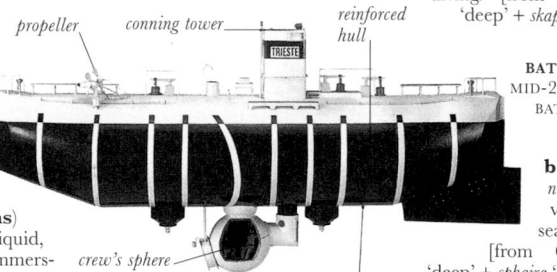

BATHYSCAPHE: MID-20TH-CENTURY BATHYSCAPHE

propeller
conning tower
reinforced hull
crew's sphere
mushroom anchor

bathysphere *n.* a spherical vessel for deep-sea observation. [from Greek *bathus* 'deep' + *sphaira* 'ball']

batik *n.* **1** a method (originally used in Java) of producing coloured designs on textiles by applying wax to the parts to be left uncoloured. **2** a piece of cloth treated in this way. [Javanese, literally 'painted']

batiste ● *n.* a fine linen or cotton cloth. ● *adj.* made of batiste. [French]

batman *n.* (*pl.* **-men**) *Mil.* (in the British forces) an attendant serving an officer. [based on medieval Latin *bastum* 'packsaddle']

baton *n.* **1** a thin stick used by a conductor to direct an orchestra etc. **2** *Athletics* a short stick or tube carried and passed on in a relay race. **3** a long stick carried and twirled by a drum major. **4** a staff of office or authority, esp. a field marshal's. **5** esp. *Brit.* a police officer's truncheon. [from Late Latin *bastum* 'stick']

baton round *n. Brit.* a rubber or plastic bullet used esp. in riot control.

batrachian /bă-**tray**-ki-ăn/ ● *n.* a frog or toad. ▷ FROG, TOAD. ● *adj.* of or relating to frogs or toads. [from Greek *batrakhos* 'frog']

bats *predic.adj. slang* crazy. [from the phrase *have bats in the belfry*]

batsman *n.* (*pl.* **-men**) **1** a person who bats or is batting, esp. in cricket. ▷ CRICKET. **2** a signaller using bats to guide aircraft on the ground. □ **batsmanship** *n.* (in sense 1).

battalion *n.* **1** a large body of troops ready for battle, esp. an infantry unit forming part of a brigade. **2** a large group of people pursuing a common aim or sharing a common undertaking. [based on Italian *battaglia* 'battle']

batten[1] ● *n.* a long flat strip of squared timber or metal, esp. used to hold something in place or as a fastening against a wall etc. ● *v.tr.* strengthen or fasten with battens. □ **batten down the hatches 1** *Naut.* secure a ship's tarpaulins. **2** prepare for a difficulty or crisis. [based on Latin *battuere* 'to beat']

batten[2] *v.intr.* (foll. by *on*) thrive or prosper at another's expense. [from Old Norse *batna* 'to get better']

batter[1] *v.* **1 a** *tr.* strike repeatedly with hard blows. **b** *intr.* (often foll. by *against, at,* etc.) pound heavily and insistently. **2** *tr.* (often in *passive*) handle roughly, esp. over a long period. [from Latin *battuere* 'to beat'] □ **batterer** *n.*

batter[2] *n.* a fluid mixture of flour, egg, and milk or water, used in cooking, for pancakes and for coating food before frying. [related to BATTER[1]]

batter[3] *n. Sport* a player batting, esp. in baseball. ▷ HOMEPLATE

battered *adj.* (esp. of fish) coated in batter and deep-fried.

battered wife *n.* a wife subjected to repeated violence by her husband.

battering ram *n.* **1** *hist.* a heavy beam, originally with an end in the form of a ram's head, used in breaching fortifications. **2** a means of forceful persuasion.

battery *n.* (*pl.* **-ies**) **1** ▼ a usu. portable container of a cell or cells carrying an electric charge, as a source of current. **2** (often *attrib.*) esp. *Brit.* a series of cages for the intensive breeding and rearing of poultry or cattle. **3** (usu. foll. by *of*) an extensive series, sequence, or range. **4 a** a fortified emplacement for heavy guns. **b** an artillery unit of guns, men, and vehicles. **5** *Law* an act, including touching, inflicting unlawful personal violence on another person, even if no physical harm is done. [based on Latin *battuere* 'to beat']

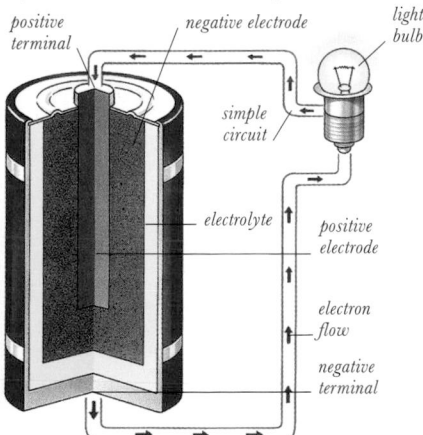

positive terminal · negative electrode · light bulb · simple circuit · electrolyte · positive electrode · electron flow · negative terminal

BATTERY: DEMONSTRATION OF A DRY-CELL BATTERY AS A SOURCE OF CURRENT

battle ● *n.* **1** a prolonged fight between esp. large organized armed forces. **2** a contest (*a battle of wits*). ● *v.* **1** *intr.* fight persistently (*battled against the elements*). **2** *tr.* fight (one's way etc.). [from Late Latin *battualia* 'gladiatorial exercises'] □ **battler** *n.*

---

battleaxe *n.* **1** ◀ a large axe used in ancient warfare. **2** *colloq.* a formidable or domineering older woman.

BATTLEAXE

battlebus *n.* a bus used as a mobile operational centre during an election campaign.

battlecruiser *n. hist.* a heavy-gunned ship faster and more lightly armoured than a battleship.

battle-cry *n.* a cry or slogan of participants in a battle or contest.

battledore *n. hist.* **1** (in full **battledore and shuttlecock**) a game played with a shuttlecock and rackets. **2** the racket used in this. [Middle English]

battledress *n. archaic* = COMBAT DRESS.

battlefield *n.* (also **battleground**) the scene of a battle.

battlement *n.* (usu. in *pl.*) **1** a parapet with recesses along the top of a wall, as part of a fortification. **2** a section of roof enclosed by this. [based on Old French *bataillier* 'to furnish with ramparts'] □ **battlemented** *adj.*

battle royal *n.* (*pl.* **battles royal**) **1** a battle in which several combatants or all available forces engage; a free fight. **2** a heated argument.

battleship *n.* ▶ a warship with the heaviest armour and the largest guns. ▷ WARSHIP

batty *adj.* (**battier, battiest**) *slang* crazy. □ **battily** *adv.* **battiness** *n.*

batwing *attrib.adj.* (esp. of a sleeve) shaped like the wing of a bat.

bauble *n.* **1** a showy trinket or toy of little value. **2** a baton formerly used as an emblem by jesters. [from Old French *ba(u)bel* 'child's toy']

baud *n.* (*pl.* same or **bauds**) *Computing* etc. a unit of speed of electronic code signals, corresponding to one information unit per second. [named after J. M. E. Baudot, French engineer, 1845–1903]

baulk (also esp. *US* **balk**) ● *v.* **1** *intr.* **a** refuse to go on. **b** (often foll. by *at*) hesitate. **2** *tr.* **a** thwart. **b** disappoint. **3** *tr.* let slip (a chance etc.). **b** ignore, shirk. ● *n.* **1** a stumbling block. **2** a roughly squared timber beam. [Old English]

bauxite *n.* ▶ a claylike mineral containing varying proportions of alumina. ▷ ORE. [French, from *Les Baux* near Arles in SE France, where first found] □ **bauxitic** *adj.*

bawdy *adj.* (**bawdier, bawdiest**) humorously indecent or coarse. □ **bawdily** *adv.* **bawdiness** *n.*

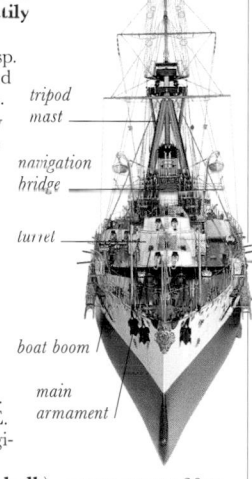

BAUXITE

bawdy house *n.* a brothel.

bawl *v.* **1** *tr.* speak or call out noisily. **2** *intr.* weep loudly. □ **bawl out** *colloq.* reprimand angrily.

bay[1] *n.* a broad inlet of the sea where the land curves inwards. [from Old Spanish *bahia*]

---

bay[2] *n.* **1** (in full **bay laurel** or **bay tree**) ▶ a laurel, *Laurus nobilis*, having deep green leaves and purple berries; also called *sweet bay*. ▷ HERB. **2** (in *pl.*) a wreath made of bay leaves, for a victor or poet. [from Latin *baca* 'berry']

BAY: SWEET BAY (*Laurus nobilis*)

bay[3] *n.* **1** a space created by a window-line projecting outwards from a wall. **2** a recess. **3** a compartment (*bomb bay*). **4** an area specially allocated (*loading bay*). [based on medieval Latin *batare* 'to gape']

bay[4] ● *adj.* (esp. of a horse) dark reddish brown. ● *n.* ▼ a bay horse with a black mane and tail. [from Latin *badius* 'chestnut-coloured']

BAY: CLEVELAND BAY

bay[5] ● *v.* **1** *intr.* (esp. of a large dog) bark or howl loudly and plaintively. **2** *tr.* bay at. ● *n.* the sound of baying, esp. in chorus from hounds in close pursuit. □ **at bay 1** cornered, apparently unable to escape. **2** in a desperate situation. **hold** (or **keep**) **at bay** hold off (a pursuer). [from Italian *baiare* 'to bark']

bay laurel see BAY[2] 1.

bay leaf *n.* the aromatic (usu. dried) leaf of the bay tree, used in cooking.

bayonet ● *n.* **1** ▶ a stabbing blade attachable to the muzzle of a rifle. **2** a fitting engaged by being pushed into a socket and twisted. ● *v.tr.* (**bayoneted, bayonecting**) stab with a bayonet. [from French *baïonnette*]

bayou /by-oo/ *n.* a marshy offshoot of a river etc. in the southern US. [Louisiana French]

bay tree see BAY[2] 1.

bay window *n.* a window built into a bay.

bazaar *n.* **1** a market in an oriental country. **2** a fund-raising sale of goods, esp. for charity. **3** a large shop selling fancy goods etc. [from Persian *bāzār*]

bazooka *n.* a tubular short-range rocket launcher used against tanks.

BBC *abbr.* British Broadcasting Corporation.

BBFC *abbr.* British Board of Film Classification (formerly *British Board of Film Censors*).

BBQ *abbr.* barbecue.

BBSRC *abbr.* (in the UK) Biotechnology and Biological Sciences Research Council.

BC *abbr.* (of a date) before Christ.

BCE *abbr.* before the Common Era.

BCG *abbr.* Bacillus Calmette-Guérin, an anti-tuberculosis vaccine.

BD *abbr.* Bachelor of Divinity.

bdellium /**del**-iŭm/ *n.* **1** any of various trees, esp. of the genus *Commiphora*, yielding resin. **2** this fragrant resin used in perfumes. [from Hebrew *b'dhōlah*]

BDS *abbr.* Bachelor of Dental Surgery.

BE *abbr.* **1** Bachelor of Education. **2** Bachelor of Engineering.

Be *symb. Chem.* the element beryllium.

be (*sing. present* **am, are, is**; *pl. present* **are**; *1st and 3rd sing. past* **was**; *2nd sing. past and pl. past* **were**; *present subjunctive* **be**; *past subjunctive* **were**; *pres. part.* **being**; *past part.* **been**) ● *v.intr.* **1** (often prec. by *there*) exist; live (*there once was a man*). **2 a** take place (*dinner is at eight*). **b** occupy a position in space (*he is in the garden*). **3** remain, continue (*let it be*). **4** linking subject and

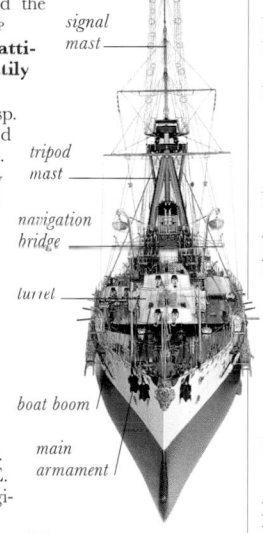

signal mast · tripod mast · navigation bridge · turret · boat boom · main armament

BATTLESHIP: 20TH-CENTURY BRAZILIAN BATTLESHIP

BAYONET: SOCKET BAYONET

B

B

predicate, expressing: **a** identity (*today is Thursday*). **b** condition (*he is ill today*). **c** state or quality (*he is very kind*). **d** opinion (*I am against hanging*). **e** total (*two and two are four*). **f** cost or significance (*it is £5 to enter*). ● *v.aux.* **1** with a past participle to form the passive mood (*it was done*). **2** with a present participle to form continuous tenses (*we are coming*). **3** with an infinitive to express duty or commitment, intention, possibility, destiny, or hypothesis (*he is to come at four; if I were to die*). **4** *archaic* with the past participle of intransitive verbs to form perfect tenses (*Babylon is fallen*). □ **be about** occupy oneself with (*is about his business*). **be at** occupy oneself with (*what is he at?*). **be off** *colloq.* go away; leave. **be that as it may** see MAY. **-to-be** of the future (in *comb.*: *bride-to-be*). [Old English]

beach ● *n.* a pebbly or sandy shore. ▷ LONGSHORE DRIFT. ● *v.tr.* run or haul up (a boat etc.) on to a beach. [16th-century coinage]

beach ball *n.* a large inflated ball for games on the beach.

beachcomber *n.* **1** a vagrant who lives by searching beaches for articles of value. **2** a long wave rolling in from the sea.

beachhead *n. Mil.* a fortified position established on a beach by landing forces.

beachwear *n.* clothing suitable for wearing on the beach.

beacon *n.* **1 a** a fire or light set up in a high or prominent position as a warning etc. **b** *Brit.* a hill suitable for this. **2** a visible guiding point or device (e.g. a lighthouse). **3** a radio transmitter whose signal helps fix the position of a ship or aircraft. [Old English]

bead ● *n.* **1 a** a small usu. rounded and perforated piece of glass, stone, etc., for threading with others. **b** (in *pl.*) a string of beads; a rosary. **2** a drop of liquid. **3** a small knob in the foresight of a gun. ● *v.* **1** *tr.* furnish or decorate with beads. **2** *tr.* string together. **3** *intr.* form or grow into beads. □ **draw a bead on** take aim at. [Old English, originally in sense 'prayer' (for which beads were first used)] □ **beaded** *adj.*

beading *n.* **1** decoration in the form of or resembling a row of beads, esp. looped edging. **2** the inner edge of a tyre. ▷ TYRE

beadle *n.* **1** *Brit.* a ceremonial officer of a college etc. **2** *Sc.* a church officer attending on the minister. **3** *Brit. hist.* a minor parish officer dealing with petty offenders etc. [from Old French *bedel*]

beady *adj.* (**beadier**, **beadiest**) **1** (of the eyes) small, round, and bright. **2** covered with beads or drops. □ **beadily** *adv.* **beadiness** *n.*

beady-eyed *adj.* **1** having beady eyes. **2** observant.

beagle ● *n.* ▶ a small hound of a breed with a short coat, used for hunting hares. ▷ DOG. ● *v.intr.* (often as **beagling** *n.*) hunt with beagles. [from Old French *beegueule* 'noisy person'] □ **beagler** *n.*

beak[1] *n.* **1 a** ▼ a bird's horny projecting jaws; a bill. **b** the similar projecting jaw of other animals, e.g. a turtle. **2** *slang* a hooked nose. **3** a spout. [from Latin *beccus*] □ **beaked** *adj.* **beaky** *adj.*

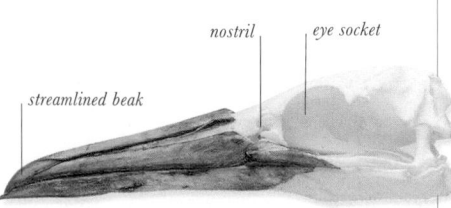

BEAGLE

BEAK AND SKULL OF A GANNET
(*Sula bassana*)

streamlined beak

nostril

eye socket

BEAR

There are seven species of bear, all of which belong to the mammalian order Carnivora. Despite this, only the polar bear is wholly carnivorous, feeding on seals and fish. Other bears eat plant material when meat is not available. Bears have poor eyesight, and rely on hearing and an acute sense of smell to locate their food. With the exception of the polar bear, bears are forest animals. Those living in warmer areas are active throughout the year, while those in cooler regions hibernate in dens during the winter.

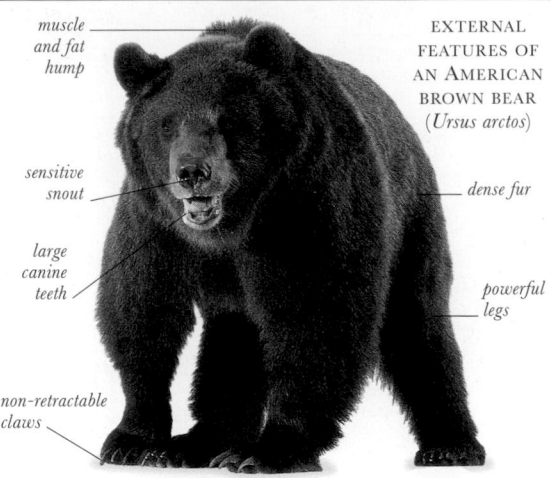

EXTERNAL FEATURES OF AN AMERICAN BROWN BEAR (*Ursus arctos*)

muscle and fat hump

sensitive snout

large canine teeth

non-retractable claws

dense fur

powerful legs

EXAMPLES OF OTHER BEARS

ASIAN BLACK BEAR (*Selenarctos thibetanus*)

POLAR BEAR (*Thalarctos maritimus*)

SPECTACLED BEAR (*Tremarctos ornatus*)

SLOTH BEAR (*Melursus ursinus*)

---

beak[2] *n. Brit. slang* **1** a magistrate. **2** a schoolmaster. [19th-century coinage]

beaker *n.* **1** *Brit.* a tall tumbler-shaped drinking vessel. **2** a lipped cylindrical glass vessel for scientific experiments. [from Old Norse *bikarr*]

be-all and end-all *n.* (often foll. by *of*) *colloq.* the whole being or essence.

beam ● *n.* **1** a long sturdy piece of squared timber or metal spanning an opening or room, usu. to support the structure above. ▷ QUEEN POST, ROOF. **2 a** a ray or shaft of light. **b** a directional flow of particles or radiation. **3** a bright look or smile. **4 a** a series of radio or radar signals as a guide to a ship or aircraft. **b** the course indicated by this (*off beam*). **5** the crossbar of a balance. **6 a** a ship's breadth at its widest point. **b** the width of a person's hips (esp. *broad in the beam*). **7** the side of a ship (*land on the port beam*). **8** the chief timber of a plough. ● *v.* **1** *tr.* emit or direct (light, radio waves, etc.). **2** *intr.* **a** shine. **b** look or smile radiantly. **3** (often foll. by *up*, *down*) (in science fiction) **a** *intr.* travel from one point to another along an invisible beam of energy. **b** *tr.* transport in this way. □ **off** (or **off the**) **beam** *colloq.* mistaken. **on one's beam-ends** near the end of one's resources. [Old English *bēam* 'tree']

bean ● *n.* **1 a** any kind of leguminous plant with edible usu. kidney-shaped seeds in long pods. ▷ VEGETABLE. **b** one of these seeds. **2** a similar seed of coffee and other plants. **3** *slang* the head. ● *v.tr.* esp. *N. Amer. slang* hit on the head. □ **full of beans** *colloq.* lively; in high spirits. **not a bean** *Brit. slang* no money. [Old English]

beanbag *n.* **1** a small bag filled with dried beans and used esp. in children's games. **2** a large cushion filled usu. with polystyrene beads and used as a seat.

bean-counter *n.* orig. *US colloq. derog.* an accountant.

bean curd *n.* jelly or paste made from beans, used esp. in Asian cookery.

beanfeast *n. Brit. colloq.* a celebration, originally an annual dinner with colleagues.

beanie *n.* a small close-fitting hat worn on the back of the head.

beano *n.* (*pl.* **-os**) *Brit. slang* a celebration; a party. [abbreviation of BEANFEAST]

beanpole *n.* **1** a stick for supporting bean plants. **2** *colloq.* a tall thin person.

bear[1] *v.* (*past* **bore**; *past part.* **borne**, **born**) **1** *tr.* carry, bring, or take (*bear gifts*). **2** *tr.* show; be marked by; have as an attribute or characteristic (*bear marks of violence; bears no relation to the case*). **3** *tr.* **a** produce, yield (fruit etc.). **b** give birth to (*has borne a son; was born last week*). **4** *tr.* **a** sustain (a weight, responsibility, cost, etc.). **b** stand, endure (an ordeal, difficulty, etc.). **5** *tr.* **a** tolerate; put up with (*can't bear him; how can you bear it?*). **b** admit of; be fit for (*does not bear thinking about*). **6** *tr.* carry in thought or memory (*bear a grudge*). **7** *intr.* veer in a given direction (*bear left*). □ **bear down** exert downward pressure. **bear down on** approach rapidly or purposefully. **bear fruit** have results. **bear hard on** oppress. **bear in mind** take into account having remembered. **bear on** (or **upon**) be relevant to. **bear out** support or confirm (an account or the person giving it). **bear up** raise one's spirits; not despair. **bear with** treat forbearingly; tolerate patiently. **bear witness** testify. [Old English]

■ **Usage** Note the difference between *borne* and *born*. *Borne* is the standard past participle of *bear* and is used in all senses above except one. *Born* is used only in the passive with reference to birth, e.g. *was born in July*, and then not if followed by *by* and the name of the mother (e.g. *was borne by Sarah*). Compare *a son was born to Sarah* which is also correct.

bear² *n.* **1** ◄ any large heavy mammal of the family Ursidae. **2** a rough, unmannerly, or uncouth person. **3** *Stock Exch.* a person who sells shares hoping to buy them back later at a lower price. **4** = TEDDY 1. [Old English]

bearable *adj.* that may be endured or tolerated.

beard ● *n.* **1** hair growing on the chin and lower cheeks. **2** a tuft of hair or similar growth or marking on the face or chin of an animal. ● *v.tr.* oppose openly; defy. [Old English] □ **bearded** *adj.* **beardless** *adj.*

bearer *n.* **1** a person or thing that bears, carries, or brings. **2** a carrier of equipment on an expedition etc. **3** a person who presents a cheque or other order to pay money.

bear-hug *n.* a tight embrace.

bearing *n.* **1** a person's bodily attitude or outward behaviour. **2** (foll. by *on, upon*) relation or relevance to (*his comments have no bearing on the subject*). **3** endurability (*beyond bearing*). **4** a part of a machine that supports a rotating or other moving part. **5** direction or position relative to a fixed point. **6** (in *pl.*) **a** one's position relative to one's surroundings. **b** awareness of this (*get one's bearings; lose one's bearings*).

bear market *n.* *Stock Exch.* a market with falling prices.

bearskin *n.* **1** the skin of a bear. **2** ▶ a tall furry hat worn ceremonially by some regiments.

beast *n.* **1** an animal other than a human being, esp. a wild quadruped. **2 a** a brutal person. **b** *colloq.* an objectionable or unpleasant person or thing **3** (prec. by *the*) the animal nature in man (*saw the beast in him*). [from Latin *bestia*]

beastly ● *adj.* (**beastlier**, **beastliest**) **1** *colloq.* objectionable, unpleasant. **2** like a beast; brutal. ● *adv. Brit. colloq.* very, extremely. □ **beastliness** *n.*

beast of burden *n.* an animal used for carrying loads.

BEARSKIN
OF A BRITISH
GRENADIER GUARD

beast of prey *n.* an animal which hunts animals for food.

beat ● *v.* (*past* **beat**; *past part.* **beaten**) **1** *tr.* **a** strike (a person or animal) persistently. **b** strike (a thing) repeatedly, e.g. to remove dust from (a carpet etc.), to sound (a drum etc.). **2** *intr.* pound or knock repeatedly (*beat at the door*). **3** *tr.* **a** overcome; surpass. **b** complete an activity before (another person etc.). **c** be too hard for. **4** *tr.* stir (eggs etc.) vigorously into a frothy mixture. **5** *tr.* shape (metal etc.) by blows. **6** *intr.* (of the heart, a drum, etc.) pulsate rhythmically. **7** *tr.* **a** indicate (a tempo or rhythm) by gestures, tapping, etc. **b** sound (a signal etc.) by striking a drum or other means (*beat a tattoo*). **8 a** *intr.* (of a bird's wings) move up and down. **b** *tr.* cause (wings) to move in this way. **9** *tr.* make (a path etc.) by trampling. **10** *tr.* strike (bushes etc.) to rouse game. ● *n.* **1 a** a main accent or rhythmic unit in music or verse (*three beats to the bar*). **b** the indication of rhythm by a conductor's movements (*watch the beat*). **c** (in popular music) a strong rhythm. **d** (*attrib.*) characterized by a strong rhythm (*beat music*). **2 a** a stroke or blow. **b** a measured sequence of strokes (*the beat of the waves on the rocks*). **c** a throbbing movement or sound (*the beat of his heart*). **3 a** a route or area allocated to a police officer etc. **b** a person's habitual round. ● *predic.adj. slang* exhausted, tired out. □ **beat about** search (for an excuse etc.). **beat about** (or *US* **around**) **the bush** discuss a matter without coming to the point. **beat the clock** complete a task within a stated time. **beat down 1 a** bargain with (a seller) to lower the price. **b** cause a seller to lower (the price). **2** strike (a resisting object) until it falls (*beat the door down*). **3** (of the sun, rain, etc.) radiate heat or fall continuously and vigorously. **beat in** crush. **beat it** *slang* go away. **beat off** drive back (an attack etc.). **beat a retreat** withdraw; abandon an undertaking. **beat time** indicate or follow a musical tempo with the feet, a baton, etc. **beat a person to it** arrive or achieve something before another person. **beat up** beat (a person) severely. [Old English] □ **beatable** *adj.* **beating** *n.*

beaten *adj.* **1** outwitted; defeated. **2** exhausted; dejected. **3** (of gold or any other metal) shaped by a hammer. **4** (of a path etc.) well-trodden, much used. □ **off the beaten track 1** in or into an isolated place. **2** unusual.

beater *n.* **1** an implement used for beating (esp. a carpet or eggs). ▷ DRUM, PERCUS-

SION. **2** a person employed to rouse game for shooting. **3** a person who beats metal.

beatific *adj.* **1** *colloq.* blissful (*a beatific smile*). **2 a** of or relating to blessedness. **b** making blessed. [based on Latin *beatus* 'blessed']

beatification *n.* *RC Ch.* the act of formally declaring a dead person 'blessed'.

beatify *v.tr.* (**-ies**, **-ied**) **1** *RC Ch.* announce the beatification of. **2** make happy. [based on Latin *beatus* 'blessed']

beatitude *n.* **1** blessedness. **2** (also **Beatitude**) a declaration of blessedness, a blessing, esp. (in *pl.*) those made by Jesus (Matt. 5:3-11).

beatnik *n.* a member of a movement of socially unconventional young people in the 1950s.

beat-up *adj. colloq.* in a state of disrepair.

beau /boh/ *n.* (*pl.* **beaux** /bohz/ or **beaus**) **1** *US* an admirer; a boyfriend. **2** a dandy. [French, literally 'handsome']

Beaufort scale /boh-fŏt/ *n.* ▼ a scale of wind speed ranging from 0 (calm) to 12 (hurricane). [named after the English admiral Sir F. *Beaufort*, 1774–1857, who devised it]

Beaujolais /boh-zhŏ-lay/ *n.* a red or white burgundy wine from the Beaujolais district of France.

Beaujolais Nouveau /noo-voh/ *n.* Beaujolais wine sold in the first year of a vintage. [French, literally 'new Beaujolais']

beau monde *n.* fashionable society. [French, literally 'fine world']

beaut *Austral. & NZ slang* ● *n.* (also *US*) an excellent or beautiful person or thing. ● *adj.* excellent; beautiful.

beauteous *adj. poet.* beautiful.

beautician *n.* **1** a person who gives beauty treatment. **2** a person who runs or owns a beauty salon.

beautiful *adj.* **1** delighting the aesthetic senses (*a beautiful voice*). **2** pleasant, enjoyable (*had a beautiful time*). **3** excellent (*a beautiful specimen*). □ **beautifully** *adv.*

beautify *v.tr.* (**-ies**, **-ied**) make beautiful; adorn. □ **beautification** *n.*

beauty *n.* (*pl.* **-ies**) **1 a** a combination of qualities that pleases the aesthetic senses. **b** a combination of qualities that pleases the intellect or moral sense (*the beauty of the argument*). **2** *colloq.* **a** an excellent specimen (*what a beauty!*). **b** an attractive feature; an advantage (*that's the beauty of it!*). **3** a beautiful woman. [from Old French *bealte*, based on Latin *bellus* 'beautiful']

B

BEAUFORT SCALE

Based on observation of wind effects on sailing vessels and waves, the Beaufort scale was devised in 1806 as a method of gauging wind force at sea. Later adapted for use on land, this scale continues to be utilized by some weather stations.

FORCE 0
CALM
(less than
1 knot,
1 k.p.h.)

FORCE 1
LIGHT AIR
(1–3 knots,
1–6 k.p.h.)

FORCE 2
LIGHT
BREEZE
(4–6 knots,
7–12 k.p.h.)

FORCE 3
GENTLE
BREEZE
(7–10 knots,
13–19 k.p.h.)

FORCE 4
MODERATE
BREEZE
(11–16 knots,
20–30 k.p.h.)

FORCE 5
FRESH
BREEZE
(17–21 knots,
31–39 k.p.h.)

FORCE 6
STRONG
BREEZE
(22–27 knots,
40–50 k.p.h.)

FORCE 7
NEAR GALE
(28–33 knots,
51–62 k.p.h.)

FORCE 8
GALE
(34–40 knots,
63–74 k.p.h.)

FORCE 9
STRONG
GALE
(41–47 knots,
75–87 k.p.h.)

FORCE 10
STORM
(48–55 knots,
88–102
k.p.h.)

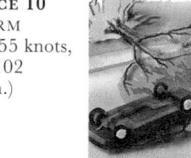

FORCE 11
VIOLENT
STORM
(56–63 knots,
103–117
k.p.h.)

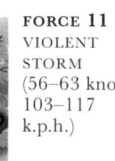

FORCE 12
HURRICANE
(equal to or
more than
64 knots,
118 k.p.h.)

B

BEE

All bees bear a sting, and have hairy bodies and a narrow waist between the thorax and abdomen. They are usually solitary creatures, but some species, such as the honey bee, live in complex social colonies. Important pollinators, they disperse pollen as they collect nectar, and are essential to the reproductive process of many flowers.

EXTERNAL FEATURES OF A HONEY BEE
(*Apis mellifera*)

compound eye · wing · waist · antenna · sting · tube-like mouthpart · thorax · claw · jointed leg · abdomen

EXAMPLES OF OTHER BEES

MOUNTAIN BUMBLE BEE
(*Bombus monticola*)

ORCHID BEE
(*Euglossa assarophora*)

ASIAN CARPENTER BEE
(*Xylocopa laticeps*)

PARASITIC BEE
(*Aglae caerulea*)

---

beauty parlour *n.* (also **beauty salon**) an establishment in which manicure, make-up, etc., are offered to women.

beauty queen *n.* the woman judged most beautiful in a competition.

beauty sleep *n.* sleep before midnight, supposed to be health-giving.

beauty spot *n.* **1** a place known for its beauty. **2** a small natural or artificial mark such as a mole on the face, considered to enhance another feature.

beauty treatment *n.* cosmetic treatment received in a beauty parlour.

beaux *pl.* of BEAU.

beaver ● *n.* (*pl.* same or **beavers**) **1** ▼ any large amphibious broad-tailed rodent of the genus *Castor*, native to N. America, Europe, and Asia, and able to gnaw through tree trunks and make dams. ▷ RODENT. **2** its soft light brown fur. **3** a hat of this. **4** (in full **beaver cloth**) a heavy woollen cloth like beaver fur. ● *v.intr.* (usu. foll. by *away*) *colloq.* work hard. [Old English]

BEAVER: AMERICAN BEAVER
(*Castor canadensis*)

bebop *n.* a type of jazz originating in the 1940s and characterized by complex harmony and rhythms.

becalm *v.tr.* (usu. in *passive*) deprive (a sailing ship) of wind.

became *past* of BECOME.

because *conj.* for the reason that; since. □ **because of** on account of; by reason of. [Middle English, from *by cause*]

■ **Usage** See Usage Note at REASON.

béchamel /bay-shă-mel/ *n.* a kind of thick white sauce. [invented by the Marquis de *Béchamel*, French courtier, 1630–1703]

beck[1] *n.* *N.Engl.* a brook; a mountain stream. [from Old Norse *bekkr*]

beck[2] *n.* □ **at a person's beck and call** having constantly to obey a person's orders. [from archaic *beck* 'to beckon']

beckon *v.* **1** *tr.* **a** attract the attention of; summon by gesture. **b** entice. **2** *intr.* make a signal to attract a person's attention; summon a person by doing this. [Old English, related to BEACON]

become *v.* (*past* **became**; *past part.* **become**) **1** *intr.* begin to be (*became president; will become famous*). **2** *tr.* **a** look well on; suit (*blue becomes him*). **b** befit (*it ill becomes you to complain*). **3** *intr.* (as **becoming** *adj.*) **a** flattering the appearance. **b** suitable; decorous. □ **become of** happen to (*what will become of me?*). [Old English] □ **becomingly** *adv.*

becquerel /bek-er-el/ *n.* *Physics* the SI unit of radioactivity. [named after A. H. *Becquerel*, French physicist, 1852–1908]

B.Ed. *abbr.* Bachelor of Education.

bed ● *n.* **1 a** a piece of furniture used for sleeping on. **b** a mattress, with or without coverings. **2** any place used by a person or animal for sleep or rest. **3 a** a garden plot. **b** a place where other things may be grown (*osier bed*). **4** the use of a bed: **a** *Brit. colloq.* for sexual intercourse. **b** *Brit.* for rest (*needs his bed*). **5** something flat, forming a support or base as in: **a** the bottom of the sea or a river. **b** the foundations of a road or railway. **6 a** a stratum. **b** a layer of oysters etc. ● *v.* (**bedded**, **bedding**) **1** *tr. & intr.* (usu. foll. by *down*) put or go to bed. **2** *tr. colloq.* have sexual intercourse with. **3** *tr.* (usu. foll. by *out*) plant in a garden bed. **4** *tr.* cover up or fix firmly in something. **5** *tr.* arrange as a layer. □ **bed of roses** a life of ease. **go to bed 1** retire for the night. **2** have sexual intercourse. **3** (of a newspaper) go to press. **make the bed** tidy and arrange the bed for use. **put to bed 1** cause to go to bed. **2** make (a newspaper) ready for press. **take to one's bed** retire to one's bed because of illness. [Old English]

bed and breakfast *n.* **1** one night's lodging and breakfast. **2** an establishment that provides this.

bedazzle *v.tr.* **1** dazzle. **2** confuse (a person).

bedbug *n.* either of two flat, wingless, evil-smelling insects of the genus *Cimex* infesting beds etc.

bedchamber *n.* archaic a bedroom.

bedclothes *n.pl.* coverings for a bed, such as sheets, blankets, etc.

bedcover *n.* **1** a bedspread. **2** (in *pl.*) = BEDCLOTHES.

beddable *adj. colloq.* considered seductive or sexually attractive.

bedding *n.* **1** a mattress and bedclothes. **2** litter for cattle, horses, etc. **3** a bottom layer. **4** *Geol.* the stratification of rocks.

bedding plant *n.* a plant set into a garden bed or container when it is about to bloom.

bedeck *v.tr.* adorn.

bedevil *v.tr.* (**bedevilled**, **bedevilling**; *US* **bedeviled**, **bedeviling**) **1** plague; afflict. **2** confound; confuse. **3** possess as if with a devil.

bedfellow *n.* **1** a person who shares a bed. **2** an associate.

bedhead *n.* the upper end of a bed.

bedizen /bi-dy-zĕn/ *v.tr.* poet. deck out gaudily. [from obsolete *dizen* 'to deck out']

bedjacket *n.* a jacket worn when sitting up in bed.

bedlam *n.* a scene of uproar and confusion. [from hospital of St Mary of *Bethlehem* in London]

bedlinen *n.* sheets, pillowcases, duvet covers, etc.

Bedouin (also **Beduin**) ● *n.* (*pl.* same) a nomadic Arab of the desert. ● *adj.* of or relating to the Bedouin. [from Arabic *badawīn* 'dwellers in the desert']

bedpan *n.* a receptacle used by a bedridden patient for urine and faeces.

bedpost *n.* any of the four upright supports of a bed.

bedraggle /bi-drag-ĕl/ *v.tr.* **1** wet (a garment etc.) by trailing it, or so that it hangs limp. **2** (as **bedraggled** *adj.*) untidy; dishevelled.

bedrest *n.* confinement of an invalid to bed.

bedridden *adj.* confined to bed by infirmity. [Middle English]

bedrock *n.* solid rock underlying alluvial deposits etc. ▷ GAS FIELD, SOIL

bedroll *n.* esp. *N. Amer.* portable bedding rolled into a bundle.

bedroom *n.* **1** a room for sleeping in. **2** (*attrib.*) of or referring to sexual relations (*bedroom farce*).

bedside *n.* **1** the space beside a bed. **2** (*attrib.*) of or relating to the side of a bed (*bedside lamp*).

bedside manner *n.* a doctor's approach or attitude to patients.

bedsitter *n.* (also **bedsit**) *Brit. colloq.* = BED-SITTING ROOM.

bed-sitting room *n.* *Brit.* a one-roomed unit of accommodation consisting of combined bedroom and sitting room.

bedsore *n.* a sore developed by an invalid because of pressure caused by lying in bed.

bedspread *n.* a cloth used to cover a bed when not in use.

bedstead *n.* the framework of a bed.

bedstraw *n.* **1** any herbaceous plant of the genus *Galium*, once used as straw for bedding. **2** (in full **lady's bedstraw**) a bedstraw, *G. verum*, with yellow flowers.

bedtime *n.* **1** the usual time for going to bed. **2** (*attrib.*) of or relating to bedtime (*bedtime drink*).

Beduin var. of BEDOUIN.

bed-wetting *n.* involuntary urination during the night. □ **bed-wetter** *n.*

bee *n.* **1 a** (in full **honey bee**) ▲ a stinging hymenopterous insect of the genus *Apis* which collects nectar and pollen, produces wax and honey, and lives in large communities. **b** ▲ a related insect of the superfamily Apoidea, either social or solitary. ▷ HYMENOPTERAN. **2** (usu. **busy bee**) a busy person. **3** esp. *US* a meeting for communal work or amusement (*spelling bee*). □ **a bee in one's bonnet** an obsession. **the bees' knees** *slang* something outstandingly good. [Old English]

Beeb *n.* (prec. by *the*) *Brit. colloq.* the BBC.

beech *n.* **1** (also **beech tree**) ◄ any large forest tree of the genus *Fagus*, having smooth grey bark and glossy leaves. **2** (also **beechwood**) its wood. **3** *Austral.* any of various similar trees in Australia. [Old English]

beechmast · leaf

BEECH: COMMON BEECH
(*Fagus sylvatica*)

beechmast *n.* (*pl.* same) the small rough-skinned fruit of the beech tree. ▷ BEECH

BEE-EATER:
CARMINE BEE-EATER
(*Merops nubicus*)

bee dance *n.* a dance performed by worker bees to inform the colony of the location of food.

bee-eater *n.* ▼ any bright-plumaged insect-eating bird of the family Meropidae with a long slender curved bill.

beef ● *n.* **1** the flesh of the ox, bull, or cow, for eating. ▷ CUT. **2** *colloq.* well-developed muscle. **3** (*pl.* **beeves**) a cow, bull, or ox fattened for beef; its carcass. **4** (*pl.* **beefs**) *slang* a complaint; a protest. ● *v.intr. slang* complain. □ **beef up** *slang* strengthen, reinforce. [from Latin *bos bovis* 'ox']

beefburger *n.* a cake of minced beef, usu. fried or grilled.

beefcake *n. slang* the display of muscular masculine physique.

beefeater *n.* a warder in the Tower of London.

beefsteak *n.* a thick slice of lean beef.

beefsteak tomato *n. N. Amer.* = BEEF TOMATO.

beef tea *n.* stewed extract of beef.

beef tomato *n. Brit.* an exceptionally large variety of tomato. ▷ TOMATO

beefy *adj.* (**beefier**, **beefiest**) **1** like beef. **2** solid; muscular.

beehive *n.* **1** ▶ an artificial habitation for bees. ▷ BEE. **2** a busy place. **3** anything resembling a wicker beehive in being domed.

bee-keeping *n.* the occupation of keeping bees. □ **bee-keeper** *n.*

beeline *n.* a straight line between two places. □ **make a beeline for** hurry directly to.

been *past part.* of BE.

beep ● *n.* **1** the sound of a motor car horn. **2** any similar short high-pitched sound. ● *v. intr.* emit a beep.

beeper *n.* **1** a device that emits beeps. **2** *N. Amer.* = BLEEPER.

beer *n.* **1 a** an alcoholic drink made from yeast-fermented malt etc., flavoured with hops. **b** a glass or can of this. **2** any of several other fermented drinks, e.g. ginger beer. [based on Latin *bibere* 'to drink']

beer belly *n.* a stomach which protrudes as a result of excessive consumption of beer.

beer garden *n.* a garden where beer is served.

beer gut *n.* = BEER BELLY.

beer mat *n. Brit* a small table mat for a beer glass.

beery *adj.* (**beerier**, **beeriest**) **1** showing the influence of drink. **2** smelling or tasting of beer.

beeswax ● *n.* **1** the wax secreted by bees to make

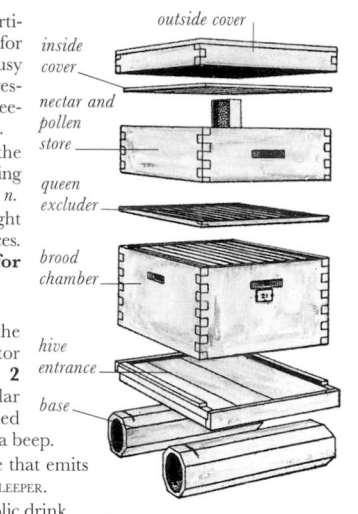

outside cover

inside cover

nectar and pollen store

queen excluder

brood chamber

hive entrance

base

BEEHIVE: EXPLODED VIEW OF A LANGSTROTH BEEHIVE

honeycombs. **2** this wax refined and used to polish wood. ● *v.tr.* polish (furniture etc.) with beeswax.

beet *n.* any plant of the genus *Beta* with an edible root (see BEETROOT, SUGAR BEET). [from Latin *beta*]

beetle[1] ● *n.* **1** ▼ any insect of the order Coleoptera, with modified front wings forming hard protective cases closing over the back wings. **2** *colloq.* any similar, usu. black insect. ● *v.intr.* (foll. by *about*, *away*, etc.) *colloq.* hurry, scurry. [Old English *bitula* 'biter']

beetle[2] ● *adj.* (esp. of the eyebrows) projecting, shaggy, scowling. ● *v.intr.* (usu. as **beetling** *adj.*) (of brows, cliffs, etc.) project; overhang threateningly. [Middle English]

beetle-browed *adj.* with shaggy, projecting, or scowling eyebrows.

beetroot *n. Brit.* **1** a beet, *Beta vulgaris*, with an edible spherical dark red root. **2** this root used as a vegetable.

beeves *pl.* of BEEF 3.

befall *v.* (*past* **befell**; *past part.* **befallen**) *poet.* **1** *intr.* happen (*so it befell*). **2** *tr.* happen to (a person etc.) (*what has befallen her?*). [Old English]

befit *v.tr.* (**befitted**, **befitting**) **1** be fitted or appropriate for; suit. **2** be incumbent on. □ **befitting** *adj.*

befog *v.tr.* (**befogged**, **befogging**) **1** confuse; obscure. **2** envelop in fog.

before ● *conj.* **1** earlier than the time when (*crawled before he walked*). **2** rather than that (*would starve before he stole*). ● *prep.* **1 a** in front of (*before her in the queue*). **b** ahead of (*crossed the line before him*). **c** under the

B

BEETLE

Beetles make up by far the largest order of insects, with over 375,000 species currently identified. They are found in almost all land habitats, and feed on a wide range of food from carrion, pollen, and plant sap to rotting wood. As adults, beetles have heavily armoured bodies, and hardened elytra, or forewings, which form a protective cover over the more delicate hindwings. Beetle larvae have softer bodies, and are usually protected by remaining hidden inside their food. Some beetles are important pests of crops or of stored food, but in nature beetles play a useful role in recycling the nutrients in dead remains. Some beetle larvae – particularly in wood-eating species – live for over 10 years before metamorphosis into adult form. The adults themselves typically live for a few weeks or months.

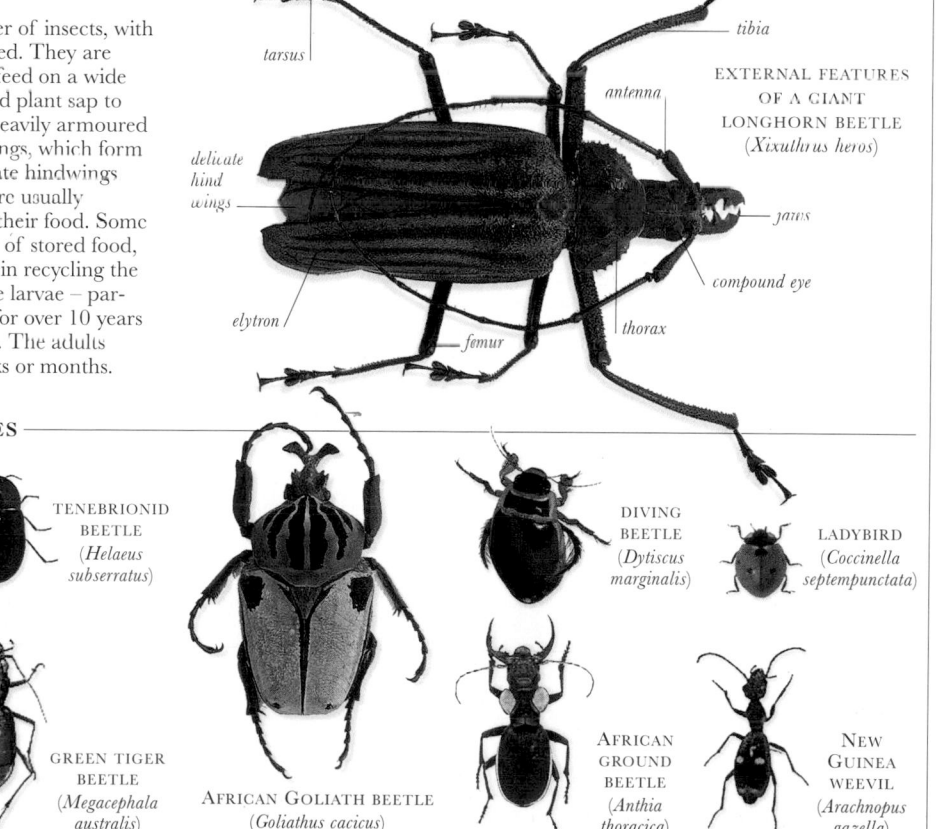

tarsus

tibia

antenna

delicate hind wings

jaws

elytron

compound eye

femur

thorax

EXTERNAL FEATURES OF A GIANT LONGHORN BEETLE (*Xixuthus heros*)

EXAMPLES OF OTHER BEETLES

MALAYAN FROG BEETLE (*Doryphorella langsdorfi*)

TENEBRIONID BEETLE (*Helaeus subserratus*)

DIVING BEETLE (*Dytiscus marginalis*)

LADYBIRD (*Coccinella septempunctata*)

STAG BEETLE (*Mesotopus tarandus*)

GREEN TIGER BEETLE (*Megacephala australis*)

AFRICAN GOLIATH BEETLE (*Goliathus cacicus*)

AFRICAN GROUND BEETLE (*Anthia thoracica*)

NEW GUINEA WEEVIL (*Arachnopus gazella*)

impulse of (*recoil before the attack*). **d** awaiting (*the future before them*). **2** earlier than; preceding (*Lent comes before Easter*). **3** rather than (*death before dishonour*). **4 a** in the presence of (*appear before the judge*). **b** for the attention of (*a plan put before the committee*). ● *adv.* **1 a** earlier than the time in question; already (*heard it before*). **b** in the past (*happened long before*). **2** ahead (*go before*). **3** on the front (*hit before and behind*). □ **before time** see TIME. [Old English]

before Christ *adv.* (of a date) reckoned backwards from the birth of Christ.

beforehand *adv.* in anticipation; in advance (*had prepared the meal beforehand*). [Middle English]

befoul *v.tr. poet.* **1** make foul or dirty. **2** degrade; defile (*befouled her name*).

befriend *v.tr.* act as a friend to; help.

befuddle *v.tr.* **1** make drunk. **2** confuse. □ **befuddlement** *n.*

beg *v.* (**begged**, **begging**) **1 a** *intr.* (foll. by *for*) ask for (*begged for alms*). **b** *tr.* ask for (food, money, etc.) as a gift. **c** *intr.* live by begging. **2** *tr.* & *intr.* ask earnestly or humbly. **3** *tr.* ask formally for (*beg leave*). **4** *intr.* (of a dog etc.) sit up with the front paws raised expectantly. **5** *tr.* take or ask leave (to do something) (*I beg to differ*). □ **beg off** decline to take part or attend. **beg the question 1** assume the truth of an argument or proposition to be proved. **2** *disp.* pose the question. **3** *colloq.* evade a difficulty. **go begging** (or *Brit.* **a-begging**) (of a chance or a thing) not be taken; be unwanted. [Middle English]

■ **Usage** Many people use the phrase *beg the question* in the disputed sense (sense 2 above). It originally meant, and still means, 'to assume the truth of the thing that is to be proved', e.g. *By asking why the policy has failed, he begs the question of whether it has failed.* Over the years *beg the question* has been misunderstood and another meaning has arisen, 'to raise the question', or 'invite the obvious question', and this is now the more common use of the phrase, e.g. *Most people continue to live in cities, which begs the question as to whether city life or country life is more desirable.* This use has been extended even further in phrases such as *The question that still needs to be begged is* ....

began *past* of BEGIN.

beget *v.tr.* (**begetting**; *past* **begot**; *archaic* **begat**; *past part.* **begotten**) *literary* **1** (usu. of a father, sometimes of a father and mother) procreate. **2** give rise to; cause (*beget strife*). [Old English] □ **begetter** *n.*

beggar ● *n.* **1** a person who begs, esp. one who lives by begging. **2** a poor person. **3** *colloq.* a person; a fellow (*poor beggar*). ● *v.tr.* **1** reduce to poverty. **2** outshine. **3** exhaust the resources of (*it beggars description*). [Middle English]

beggarly *adj.* **1** poverty-stricken; needy. **2** intellectually poor. **3** mean; sordid. **4** ungenerous.

beggary *n.* extreme poverty.

begin *v.* (**beginning**; *past* **began**; *past part.* **begun**) **1** *tr.* perform the first part of; start (*begin work*; *begin crying*; *begin to understand*). **2** *intr.* come into being; arise: **a** in time (*war began in 1939*). **b** in space (*Wales begins beyond the river*). **3** (with **to** + infin.) *tr.* start at a certain time (*then began to feel ill*). **4** *intr.* be begun (*the meeting will begin at 7*). **5 a** *tr.* & *intr.* start speaking (*'No,' he began*). **b** *intr.* be the first to do something (*who wants to begin?*). **6** *intr. colloq.* show any attempt or likelihood (*can't begin to compete*). [Old English]

beginner *n.* a person just beginning to learn a skill etc.

beginning *n.* **1** the time or place at which anything begins. **2** a source or origin. **3** the first part.

begone *int. poet.* go away at once!

begonia *n.* a plant of the genus *Begonia*, having flowers with brightly coloured sepals and no petals. [named after M. *Bégon*, French patron of science, 1638–1710]

begot *past* of BEGET.

begotten *past part.* of BEGET.

begrudge *v.tr.* **1** resent; be dissatisfied at. **2** envy (a person) the possession of. □ **begrudgingly** *adv.*

beguile *v.tr.* **1** charm; amuse. **2** divert attention pleasantly from (toil etc.). **3** delude; cheat (*beguiled him into paying*). [from obsolete *guile* 'to deceive'] □ **beguiling** *adj.* **beguilingly** *adv.*

begum *n.* (in the Indian subcontinent) **1** a Muslim woman of high rank. **2** (**Begum**) the title of a married Muslim woman, equivalent to Mrs. [from Eastern Turkish *bīgam* 'princess']

begun *past part.* of BEGIN.

behalf *n.* □ **on** (or esp. *US* **in**) **behalf of** (or **on a person's behalf**) **1** in the interests of (a person, principle, etc.). **2** as representative of (*acting on behalf of my client*). [mixture of earlier phrases *on his halve* and *bihalve him*, both literally 'on his side']

■ **Usage** *On behalf of* should not be confused with *on the part of*, which means 'proceeding from, done or initiated by'. *Behalf* cannot replace *part* in *His death was largely due to panic on his part.* Note the different senses expressed by *a long struggle on behalf of the strikers* (the struggle being carried out by people other than the strikers), and *a long struggle on the part of the strikers* (the struggle being carried out by the strikers).

behave *v.* **1** *intr.* **a** act or react (in a specified way) (*behaved well*). **b** conduct oneself properly. **2** *refl.* show good manners (*behaved herself*). [based on *to have* in reflexive 'to have or bear oneself']

behaviour *n.* (*US* **behavior**) **1 a** the way one conducts oneself. **b** the treatment of others; moral conduct. **2** the way in which a machine, chemical substance, etc., acts or works. □ **behavioural** *adj.*

behavioural science *n.* the scientific study of human and animal behaviour.

behaviourism *n.* (*US* **behaviorism**) *Psychol.* the theory that human behaviour is determined by conditioning rather than by thoughts or feelings, and that psychological disorders are best treated by altering behaviour patterns. □ **behaviourist** *n.* **behaviouristic** *adj.*

behead *v.tr.* cut off the head of (a person). [Old English]

beheld *past* and *past part.* of BEHOLD.

behemoth *n.* an enormous creature or thing. [from Hebrew *b'hēmôṯ* 'monstrous beast']

behest *n. literary* a command; an entreaty (*went at his behest*). [Old English]

behind ● *prep.* **1 a** in, towards, or to the rear of. **b** on the further side of (*behind the bush*). **c** hidden by (*something behind that remark*). **2 a** in the past in relation to (*trouble is behind me now*). **b** late in relation to (*behind schedule*). **3** inferior to; weaker than (*rather behind the others in his maths*). **4 a** in support of (*she's right behind us*). **b** responsible for; giving rise to (*the man behind the project*; *the reasons behind his resignation*). **5** in the tracks of; following. ● *adv.* **1 a** in or to or towards the rear; further back (*the street behind*). **b** on the further side (*a high wall with a field behind*). **2** remaining after the departure of most others (*stay behind*). **3 a** in arrears (*behind with the rent*). **b** late in accomplishing a task etc. (*working too slowly and getting behind*). **4** in a weak position; not advanced to the expected or normal level of learning (*behind in Latin*). **5** following (*his dog running behind*). ● *n. colloq.* the buttocks. □ **behind the scenes** see SCENE. **behind the times** antiquated. **come from behind** win after lagging. [Old English]

behindhand *adv.* & *predic.adj.* **1** late (in discharging a duty, paying a debt, etc.). **2** out of date; behind time.

behold *v.tr.* (*past* and *past part.* **beheld**) *literary* see, observe. [Old English] □ **beholder** *n.*

beholden *predic.adj.* under obligation.

behove *v.tr.* (*US* **behoove**) (prec. by *it* as subject; foll. by *to* + infin.) *formal* **1** be incumbent on. **2** befit (*ill behoves him to protest*). [Old English]

beige /bay*zh*/ ● *n.* a pale sandy fawn colour. ● *adj.* of this colour. [French]

being *n.* **1** existence. **2** the nature or essence (of a person etc.) (*his whole being revolted*). **3** a human being. **4** anything that exists or is imagined.

bejewelled *adj.* (*US* **bejeweled**) adorned with jewels.

bel *n.* a unit used in the comparison of power levels in electrical communication or intensities of sound, corresponding to an intensity ratio of 10 to 1 (cf. DECIBEL). [named after A. G. *Bell*, American inventor of telephone, 1847–1922]

belabour *v.tr.* (*US* **belabor**) **1 a** thrash; beat. **b** attack verbally. **2** argue or elaborate (a subject) in excessive detail.

belated *adj.* **1** coming late. **2** overtaken by darkness. [from obsolete verb *belate* 'to delay'] □ **belatedly** *adv.* **belatedness** *n.*

belay ● *v.* **1** *tr.* fix (a running rope) round a cleat, pin, rock, etc., to secure it. ▷ ROCK-CLIMBING. **2** *tr.* & *intr.* (usu. in *imper.*) *Naut. slang* stop; enough! (esp. *belay there!*). ● *n.* **1** an act of belaying. **2** a spike of rock etc. used for belaying. [from Dutch *beleggen*]

■ **Usage** In mountaineering contexts, this word is often stressed on the first syllable: /**bee**-lay/.

bel canto *n.* **1** a lyrical style of operatic singing using a full rich broad tone. **2** (*attrib.*) characterized by this type of singing. [Italian, literally 'fine song']

belch ● *v.* **1** *intr.* emit wind noisily from the stomach through the mouth. **2** *tr.* (of a chimney, volcano, gun, etc.) send (smoke etc.) out or up. ● *n.* an act of belching. [Old English]

beleaguer /bi-lee-ger/ *v.tr.* **1** besiege. **2** vex; harass. [from Dutch *belegeren* 'to camp round']

belfry *n.* (*pl.* **-ies**) **1** a bell tower or steeple housing bells. **2** a space for hanging bells in a church tower. ▷ CHURCH. □ **have bats in the belfry** see BAT[2]. [from Old French *berfrei*]

Belgian ● *n.* **1** a native or national of Belgium in W. Europe. **2** a person of Belgian descent. ● *adj.* of or relating to Belgium.

belie *v.tr.* (**belying**) **1** give a false notion of (*its appearance belies its age*). **2 a** fail to fulfil (a promise etc.). **b** fail to justify (a hope etc.). [Old English]

belief *n.* **1 a** a person's religion; religious conviction (*has no belief*). **b** a firm opinion (*my belief is that he did it*). **c** an acceptance (of a fact, statement, etc.) (*belief in the afterlife*). **2** (usu. foll. by *in*) trust or confidence. □ **beyond belief** incredible. [Middle English]

believe *v.* **1** *tr.* accept as true or as conveying the truth (*I believe it*; *don't believe him*). **2** *tr.* think, suppose (*I believe it's raining*). **3** *intr.* (foll. by *in*) **a** have faith in the existence of (*believes in God*). **b** have confidence in (*believes in alternative medicine*). **c** have trust in the advisability of (*believes in telling the truth*). **4** *intr.* have faith. [Old English] □ **believable** *adj.* **believability** *n.*

believer *n.* **1** an adherent of a specified religion. **2** a person who believes (*a great believer in exercise*).

Belisha beacon *n. Brit.* a flashing orange ball mounted on top of a striped post, marking some pedestrian crossings. [from L. Hore-*Belisha*, Minister of Transport in 1934]

belittle *v.tr.* **1** make seem unimportant; depreciate; disparage. **2** make small; diminish in size.

bell ● *n.* **1** a hollow object in the shape of a deep inverted cup, made to sound a clear musical note when struck (either externally or by means of a clapper inside). **2 a** a sound or stroke of a bell. **b** (prec. by a numeral) *Naut.* the time as indicated every half-hour of a watch by the striking of the ship's bell one to eight times. **3** anything that sounds like or functions as a bell. **4 a** a bell-shaped part of a musical instrument. ▷ BRASS. **b** the corolla of a flower when bell-shaped. **5** (in *pl.*) *Mus.* a set of cylindrical metal tubes of different lengths which are struck with a hammer. ● *v.tr.* provide with a bell or bells. □ **give a person a bell** *Brit. colloq.* telephone a person. **ring a bell** *colloq.* revive a distant recollection; sound familiar. [Old English]

belladonna *n.* **1** deadly nightshade. **2** *Med.* a drug prepared from this. [from Italian *bella donna* 'fair lady', perhaps from the use of its juice to dilate the pupils]

bell-bottom *n.* **1** a marked flare below the knee (of a trouser leg). **2** (in *pl.*) trousers with bell-bottoms. □ **bell-bottomed** *adj.*

bellboy *n.* esp. *N. Amer.* a page in a hotel or club.

belle n. **1** a beautiful woman. **2** a woman recognized as the most beautiful (*belle of the ball*). [from Latin *bella* (fem.) 'beautiful']

belles-lettres /bel-*letr*/ n.pl. (also treated as *sing.*) writings or studies of a literary nature, esp. essays and criticisms. [French, literally 'fine letters'] □ **belletrist** n. & adj.

bell-glass n. a bell-shaped glass cover for plants.

bellicose adj. eager to fight; warlike. [based on Latin *bellum* 'war'] □ **bellicosity** n.

belligerent ● adj. **1** engaged in war or conflict. **2** given to constant fighting; pugnacious. ● n. a nation or person engaged in war or conflict. [from Latin *belligerant-* 'waging war'] □ **belligerence** n. (also **belligerency**). **belligerently** adv.

bell jar n. a bell-shaped glass cover or container for use in a laboratory.

bell metal n. an alloy of copper and tin for making bells (the tin content being greater than in bronze).

bellow ● v. **1** *intr.* **a** emit a deep loud roar. **b** cry or shout with pain. **2** *tr.* utter loudly and usu. angrily. ● n. a bellowing sound. [Middle English]

bellows n.pl. (also treated as *sing.*) **1** a device with an air bag that emits a stream of air when squeezed, esp. (in full **pair of bellows**) a kind with two handles used for blowing air on to a fire. ▷ ACCORDION. **2** ▼ an expandable component, e.g. joining the lens to the body of a camera. [Middle English]

single-lens reflex camera   bellows

lens

mount

BELLOWS: CAMERA AND STANDARD
BELLOWS ON A MOUNT

bells and whistles n.pl. esp. *Computing* attractive additional features; gimmicks. [an allusion to old fairground organs]

bell tent n. a cone-shaped tent supported by a central pole.

bell-wether n. **1** the leading sheep of a flock, with a bell on its neck. **2** a ringleader.

belly n. (*pl.* **-ies**) **1** the part of the human body below the chest, containing the stomach and bowels. ▷ DIGESTION. **2** the stomach, representing the body's need for food. **3** the front of the body from the waist to the groin. **4** the underside of a four-legged animal. **5 a** a cavity or bulging part of anything. **b** the surface of an instrument of the violin family, across which the strings are placed. [Old English, originally in sense 'bag'] □ **bellyful** n. (*pl.* **-fuls**).

bellyache ● n. *colloq.* a stomach pain. ● v.intr. *slang* complain noisily or persistently. □ **bellyacher** n.

belly button n. *colloq.* the navel.

belly dance n. an oriental dance performed by a woman, involving voluptuous movements of the belly. □ **belly dancer** n. **belly dancing** n.

bellyflop n. *colloq.* a dive in which the body enters the water with the belly flat on the surface.

belly laugh n. a loud unrestrained laugh.

belong v.intr. **1** (foll. by *to*) **a** be the property of. **b** be rightly assigned to as a duty, right, part, member, characteristic, etc. **c** be a member of (a club etc.). **2** have the right qualities to be a member of a particular group (*he's nice but just doesn't belong*). **3** (foll. by *in*, *under*): **a** be rightly placed or classified. **b** fit a particular environment. [Middle English]

belongings n.pl. one's movable possessions or luggage.

Belorussian (also **Byelorussian**) ● n. **1** a native of Belarus in eastern Europe. **2** the East Slavonic language of Belarus, its people, or its language. ● adj. of or relating to Belarus, its people, or its language. [based on Russian *belyi* 'white' + *Russiya* 'Russia']

beloved ● adj. much loved. ● n. a much loved person.

below ● prep. **1** lower in position (down a slope etc.) than. **2** at or to a greater depth than (*below 500 feet*). **3** lower or less than in amount or degree (*below freezing point*). **4** lower in position or importance than. **5** unworthy of. ● adv. **1** at or to a lower point or level. **2 a** downstairs (*lives below*). **b** downstream. **3** (of a text reference) further forward in a book (*as noted above*). **4** on the lower side (*looks similar above and below*). □ **below stairs** *Brit.* in the basement of a house esp. as the part occupied by servants.

belt n. **1** a strip of leather or other material worn round the waist or across the chest. **2** a belt worn as a sign of rank or achievement. **3 a** a circular band used as a driving medium in machinery. **b** a conveyor belt. **c** a flexible strip carrying gun cartridges. **4** a strip of colour or texture etc. differing from that on each side. **5** a distinct region or extent (*commuter belt*). **6** *slang* a heavy blow. ● v. **1** *tr.* put a belt round. **2** *tr.* (often foll. by *on*) fasten with a belt. **3** *tr.* **a** beat with a belt. **b** *slang* hit hard. **4** *intr.* (usu. foll. by *along*, *down*, etc.) *slang* rush. □ **below the belt** unfair or unfairly. **belt out** *slang* sing or utter loudly and forcibly. **belt up 1** *slang* be quiet. **2** *colloq.* put on a seat belt. **tighten one's belt** live more frugally. **under one's belt 1** (of food) eaten. **2** securely acquired (*has a degree under her belt*). [from Latin *balteus*] □ **belter** n.

beltway n. *US* **1** a ring road. **2** (usu. **Beltway**) (often *attrib.*) Washington, DC.

beluga n. **1 a** a large kind of sturgeon, *Huso huso*. **b** caviar obtained from it. **2** ▼ a white whale. ▷ WHALE. [Russian]

BELUGA
(*Delphinapterus leucas*)

belvedere n. a summer house or open-sided gallery usu. at rooftop level. [Italian, from *bel* 'beautiful' + *vedere* 'to see']

belying *pres. part.* of BELIE.

BEM *abbr.* British Empire Medal.

bemoan v.tr. express regret or sorrow over; lament.

bemuse v.tr. bewilder (a person). □ **bemusedly** adv. **bemusement** n.

bench n. **1** a long seat of wood or stone. **2** a working-table for a carpenter etc. **3** (prec. by *the*) **a** the office of judge or magistrate. **b** a judge's seat in a law court. **c** a law court. **d** judges and magistrates collectively. **4** (often in *pl.*) an area to the side of a pitch, with seating where coaches and players not taking part can watch the game. □ **on the bench 1** appointed a judge or magistrate. **2** *Sport* acting as substitute or reserve. [Old English] □ **bencher** n. *Law*

benchmark n. **1** a surveyor's mark cut in a wall etc., used for reference in measuring altitudes. **2** a standard or point of reference.

bend[1] ● v. (*past* **bent**; *past part.* **bent** except in *bended knee*) **1 a** *tr.* force or adapt into a curve or angle. **b** *intr.* (of an object) be altered in this way. **2** *intr.* move in a curved course (*the road bends to the left*). **3** *intr.* & *tr.* (often foll. by *down*, *over*, etc.) incline or cause to incline from the vertical. **4** *tr.* interpret or modify (a rule). **5** *tr.* & *refl.* (foll. by *to*, *on*) direct or devote (oneself or one's attention, energies, etc.). **6** *tr.* turn (one's steps or eyes) in a new direction. **7** *tr.* (in *passive*; foll. by *on*) be determined (*was bent on selling*). **8 a** *intr.* stoop or submit (*bent before his master*).

b *tr.* force to submit. ● n. **1** a curve in a road or other course. **2** a departure from a straight course. **3** a bent part of anything. **4** (**the bends**) *colloq.* decompression sickness. □ **bend over backwards** see BACKWARDS. **round** (or *US* **around**) **the bend** *colloq.* insane. [Old English] □ **bendable** adj. **bendy** adj. (**bendier**, **bendiest**).

bend[2] n. **1** *Naut.* any of various knots for tying ropes. ▷ KNOT. **2** *Heraldry* **a** ◀ a diagonal stripe from top left to bottom right of a shield. **b** (**bend sinister**) a diagonal stripe from top right to bottom left, as a sign of bastardy. [Old English]

bender n. *slang* a wild drinking spree.

beneath ● prep. **1** too demeaning for (*beneath him to reply*). **2** below, under. ● adv. underneath. [Old English]

Benedictine n. /be-ni-*dik*-tin/ a monk or nun of an order following the rule of St Benedict. [from Latin name *Benedictus*]

benediction n. **1** the utterance of a blessing. **2** the state of being blessed. [based on Latin *benedictus* 'blessed']

benefaction n. **1** a donation or gift. **2** an act of giving or doing good. [from Late Latin *benefactio*, related to BENEFIT]

benefactor n. (*fem.* **benefactress**) a person who gives support (esp. financial) to a person or cause.

benefice n. **1** a living from a Church office. **2** the property attached to a Church office. [from Latin *beneficium* 'favour'] □ **beneficed** adj.

beneficent adj. doing good; actively kind. □ **beneficence** n. **beneficently** adv.

beneficial adj. advantageous; having benefits. [based on Latin *beneficium* 'favour'] □ **beneficially** adv.

beneficiary n. (*pl.* **-ies**) **1** a person who receives benefits under a will etc. **2** a holder of a Church living. [from Latin *beneficiarius*]

benefit ● n. **1** a favourable or helpful factor or circumstance; advantage, profit. **2** (often in *pl.*) payment made under insurance etc. (*sickness benefit*). **3** a public performance or game of which the proceeds go to a particular player, company, or charitable cause. ● v. (**benefited**, **benefiting**; *US* **benefitted**, **benefitting**) **1** *tr.* bring advantage to. **2** *intr.* (often foll. by *from*, *by*) receive an advantage or gain. □ **the benefit of the doubt** a concession that a person is innocent, correct, etc., although doubt exists. [based on Latin *bene facere* 'to do well']

benevolent adj. **1** wishing to do good; actively helpful. **2** charitable (*benevolent fund*). [from Latin *bene* 'well' + *volent-* 'wishing'] □ **benevolence** n. **benevolently** adv.

Bengali ● n. (*pl.* **Bengalis**) **1** a native of Bengal, a former Indian province. **2** the language of the Bengalis. ● adj. of or relating to Bengal or its people or language.

benighted adj. **1** intellectually or morally ignorant. **2** overtaken by darkness.

benign adj. /bi-*nyn*/ **1** gentle, kindly. **2** salutary. **3** (of the climate etc.) mild. **4** *Med.* not malignant. [from Latin *benignus*, from *bene* 'well' + *-genus* 'born'] □ **benignity** n. **benignly** adv.

benignant adj. **1** kindly, esp. to inferiors. **2** salutary, beneficial. **3** *Med.* = BENIGN 4. □ **benignancy** n. **benignantly** adv.

bent[1] *past* and *past part.* of BEND[1] v. ● adj. **1** curved or having an angle. **2** esp. *Brit. slang* dishonest, illicit. **3** *Brit. slang* offens. sexually deviant; homosexual. **4** (foll. by *on*) determined to do or have. ● n. **1** an inclination or bias. **2** (foll. by *for*) a talent (*a bent for mimicry*).

bent[2] n. **1 a** any stiff grass of the genus *Agrostis*. **b** any of various grasslike reeds, rushes, or sedges. **2** a stiff stalk of a grass. [Middle English]

BEND ON A
HERALDIC SHIELD

B

BERRY

Berries are produced by a wide range of flowering plants. Although many are cultivated for human consumption, their soft, succulent flesh originally evolved to attract animals and thereby aid seed dispersal. When an animal eats a berry, the fruit's flesh is digested, but the seeds pass through its body unharmed.

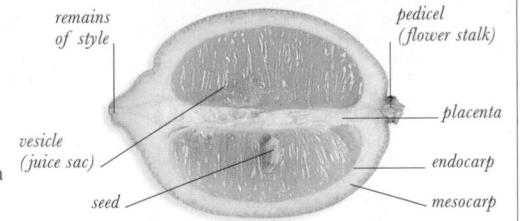

remains of style
pedicel (flower stalk)
placenta
endocarp
mesocarp
vesicle (juice sac)
seed

STRUCTURE OF A LEMON (*Citrus limon*)

EXAMPLES OF OTHER BERRIES

CAPE GOOSE-BERRY (*Physalis peruviana*)

BANANA (*Musa nana*)

TOMATO (*Lycopersicum esculentum*)

CACAO (*Theobroma cacao*)

CHARENTAIS MELON (*Cucumis melo*)

benthos *n.* the flora and fauna found at the bottom of a sea or lake. [Greek, literally 'depth of the sea'] □ **benthic** *adj.*

bentonite *n.* a kind of absorbent clay used esp. as a filler. [from Fort *Benton*, in Montana (US) where it is found]

bentwood *n.* wood that is artificially shaped for use in making furniture.

benumb *v.tr.* make numb.

Benzedrine *n. propr.* amphetamine.

benzene *n.* a colourless carcinogenic volatile liquid found in coal tar etc. □ **benzenoid** *adj.*

hydrogen atom

benzene ring *n.* ◄ the hexagonal unsaturated ring of six carbon atoms in the benzene molecule.

benzine *n.* (also **benzin**) a mixture of liquid hydrocarbons obtained from petroleum.

carbon atom
benzene ring

BENZENE RING IN A BENZENE MOLECULE

benzodiazepine *n. Pharm.* any class of heterocyclic organic compounds used as tranquillizers, including Librium and Valium.

benzoin *n.* a fragrant gum resin obtained from various E. Asian trees of the genus *Styrax*, and used in the manufacture of perfumes and incense. [based on Arabic *lubān jāwī* 'incense of Java']

benzol *n.* (also **benzole**) benzene, esp. unrefined and used as a fuel.

bequeath /bi-kweeth/ *v.tr.* **1** leave to a person by a will. **2** hand down to posterity. [Old English, related to QUOTH] □ **bequeathal** *n.* **bequeather** *n.*

bequest *n.* **1** the act or an instance of bequeathing. **2** a thing bequeathed. [Middle English, based on earlier *-cwiss* 'saying, testament']

berate *v.tr.* scold, rebuke.

bereave *v.tr.* (foll. by *of*) deprive of a relation etc. by death. [Old English] □ **bereaved** *adj.* **bereavement** *n.*

bereft *adj.* (foll. by *of*) deprived (*bereft of hope*). [past participle of BEREAVE]

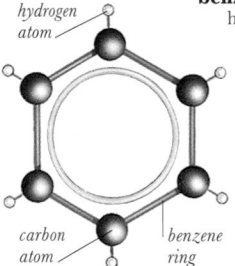

beret /be-ray/ *n.* ◄ a round flattish cap of felt or cloth. [from Provençal *berret*]

BERET

BERGAMOT (*Mentha citrata*)

berg *n.* = ICEBERG.

bergamot *n.* **1** ◄ an aromatic herb, esp. *Mentha citrata*. **2** an oily perfume extracted from the rind of the fruit of the citrus tree *Citrus bergamia*. **3** the tree itself. [from *Bergamo* in N. Italy]

beriberi *n.* a disease causing inflammation of the nerves, due to a deficiency of vitamin B_1. [Sinhalese, from *beri* 'weakness']

berk *n.* (also **burk**) *Brit. slang* a fool. [abbreviation of *Berkeley* or *Berkshire Hunt*, rhyming slang for *cunt*]

■ **Usage** Despite its etymology, this word is not usually considered to be obscene.

berkelium *n. Chem.* a transuranic radioactive metallic element. [modern Latin, based on *Berkeley* in California, where first made]

berm *n.* a narrow path or grass strip beside a road, canal, etc. [from Dutch]

Bermuda shorts *n.pl.* (also **Bermudas**) close-fitting shorts reaching the knees. [from *Bermuda* in the W. Atlantic]

berry *n.* (*pl.* **-ies**) **1** any small roundish juicy fruit without a stone. ▷ FRUIT. **2** *Bot.* ▲ a fruit with its seeds enclosed in a pulp (e.g. a banana). **3** any of various kernels or seeds (e.g. the coffee bean). [Old English] □ **berried** *adj.* (also in *comb.*).

berserk *adj.* (esp. in **go berserk**) wild; in a violent rage. [from Icelandic *berserkr*]

berth ● *n.* **1** a fixed bunk on a ship, train, etc., for sleeping in. **2** a ship's place at a wharf. **3** adequate sea room. **4** *colloq.* a situation or appointment. **5** the proper place for anything. ● *v.* **1** *tr.* moor (a ship) in its berth. **2** *tr.* provide a sleeping place for. **3** *intr.* (of a ship) come to its mooring place. □ **give a wide berth to** stay away from.

beryl *n.* **1** ► a kind of transparent precious stone, esp. pale green, blue, or yellow in a hexagonal form. **2** a mineral species which includes this, emerald, and aquamarine. [from Greek *bērullos*]

prismatic beryl crystal
rock groundmass
BERYL

beryllium *n. Chem.* a hard white metallic element used in the manufacture of light corrosion-resistant alloys.

beseech *v.tr.* (*past* and *past part.* **besought** or **beseeched**) **1** (foll. by *for*, or *to* + infin.) entreat. **2** ask earnestly for. [Middle English, based on *secan* 'to seek'] □ **beseeching** *adj.*

beset *v.tr.* (**besetting**; *past* and *past part.* **beset**) **1** harass persistently (*beset by worries*). **2** hem in (a person etc.). [Old English]

beside *prep.* **1** at the side of. **2** compared with. **3** irrelevant to (*beside the point*). □ **beside oneself** overcome with worry etc. [Old English]

besides ● *prep.* in addition to. ● *adv.* also; as well; moreover.

■ **Usage** Note the difference in meaning between the prepositions *beside* and *besides*. *Beside* was in the past used to mean 'in addition to, apart from', but this is now rare.

besiege *v.tr.* **1** lay siege to. **2** harass. [Middle English] □ **besieger** *n.*

besmirch *v.tr.* **1** soil, discolour. **2** dishonour; sully the reputation or name of.

besom /bee-zŏm/ *n.* ► a broom made of twigs tied round a stick. [Old English]

besotted *adj.* **1** infatuated. **2** confused. **3** intoxicated.

besought *past* and *past part.* of BESEECH.

bespatter *v.tr.* **1** spatter (an object) all over. **2** spatter (liquid etc.) about. **3** overwhelm with abuse etc.

bespeak *v.tr.* (*past* **bespoke**; *past part.* **bespoken** or as *adj.* **bespoke**) **1** engage in advance. **2** order (goods). **3** be evidence of (*bespeaks a kind heart*). [Old English]

bespectacled *adj.* wearing spectacles.

bespoke *past* and *past part.* of BESPEAK. ● *adj. Brit.* **1** (of goods, esp. clothing) made to order. **2** (of a tradesman) making goods to order.

bespoken *past part.* of BESPEAK.

BESOM

best ● *adj.* (*superl.* of GOOD) of the most excellent or outstanding or desirable kind (*my best work*). ● *adv.* (*superl.* of WELL[1]) **1** in the best manner (*does it best*). **2** to the greatest degree (*like it best*). **3** most usefully (*is best ignored*). ● *n.* **1** that which is best (*the best is yet to come*). **2** the chief merit or advantage (*brings out the best in him*). **3** (foll. by *of*) a winning majority of (a certain number of games etc. played) (*the best of five*). ● *v.tr. colloq.* defeat, outwit, outbid, etc. □ **as best one can** as well as possible under the circumstances. **at best** on the most optimistic view. **be for** (or **all for**) **the best** be desirable in the end. **the best part of** most of. **do one's best** do all one can. **get the best of** defeat, outwit. **had best** would find it wisest to. **to the best of one's ability, knowledge**, etc. as far as one can do, know, etc. [Old English]

best-before date *n.* = USE-BY DATE.

best boy *n.* esp. *US* the assistant to the chief electrician of a film crew.

bestial *adj.* **1** brutish, cruel, savage. **2** sexually depraved; lustful. **3** of or like a beast. [based on Latin *bestia* 'beast'] □ **bestialize** *v.tr.* (also **-ise**). **bestially** *adv.*

bestiality *n.* (*pl.* **-ies**) **1** bestial behaviour or an instance of this. **2** sexual intercourse between a person and an animal.

bestiary *n.* (*pl.* **-ies**) a moralizing medieval treatise on real and imaginary beasts.

bestir *v.refl.* (**bestirred, bestirring**) exert or rouse (oneself).

best-known *attrib.adj.* most famous.

best man *n.* the bridegroom's chief attendant.

bestow *v.tr.* **1** (foll. by *on*, *upon*) confer (a gift, right, etc.). **2** deposit. [Middle English, based on earlier *stow* 'a place'] □ **bestowal** *n.*

bestrew v.tr. (past part. **bestrewed** or **bestrewn**) **1** (foll. by with) cover (a surface). **2** scatter (things) about. **3** lie scattered over. [Old English]

bestride v.tr. (past part. **bestrode**; past part. **bestridden**) **1** sit astride on. **2** stand astride over. [Old English]

best-seller n. **1** a book or other item that has sold in large numbers. **2** Brit. the author of such a book. □ **best-selling** adj.

bet ● v. (**betting**; past and past part. **bet** or **betted**) **1** intr. (foll. by on or against with reference to the outcome) risk a sum of money etc. against another's on the basis of the outcome of an unpredictable event. **2** tr. risk (an amount) on such an outcome (bet £10 on a horse). **3** tr. risk a sum of money against (a person). **4** tr. colloq. feel sure (bet they've forgotten it). ● n. **1** the act of betting (make a bet). **2** the money etc. staked (put a bet on). **3** colloq. an opinion (my bet is that he won't come). **4** colloq. a choice or course of action (she's our best bet). □ **you bet** colloq. you may be sure. [16th-century coinage]

beta n. **1** the second letter of the Greek alphabet (Β, β). **2** Brit. a second-class mark given for a piece of work or in an examination. **3** the second member of a series. [from Greek]

beta blocker n. Pharm. a drug that prevents the stimulation of increased cardiac action, used to reduce high blood pressure.

beta decay n. radioactive decay in which an electron is emitted. ▷ RADIOACTIVITY

betake v.refl. (past **betook**; past part. **betaken**) (foll. by to) go to (a place or person).

beta particle n. (also **beta ray**) a fast-moving electron emitted by radioactive decay of substances (originally regarded as rays). ▷ RADIOACTIVITY

betatron n. Physics an apparatus for accelerating electrons in a circular path by magnetic induction.

betel /bee-těl/ n. the leaf of the Asian evergreen climbing plant Piper betle. [Portuguese]

betel-nut n. ▼ the areca nut.

nut kernel

BETEL-NUT
(Areca catechu)

half-ripe fruit

bête noire /bayt **nwah**/ n. (pl. **bêtes noires** pronunc. same) a person or thing one particularly dislikes or fears. [French, literally 'black beast']

bethink v.refl. (past and past part. **bethought**) (foll. by of, how, or that + clause) formal **1** reflect; stop to think. **2** be reminded by reflection. [Old English]

betide v. (only in infin. and 3rd sing. subjunctive) esp. poet. **1** happen to (woe betide him). **2** intr. happen (whate'er may betide). [from obsolete tide 'to befall']

betimes adv. literary early; in good time. [from obsolete betime (from by time)]

betoken v.tr. **1** be a sign of; indicate. **2** augur. [Middle English, from earlier tācnian 'to signify']

betony /bet-ŏni/ n. (pl. **-ies**) **1** ▶ a purple-flowered plant, Stachys officinalis. **2** any of various similar plants. [from Latin betonica]

betook past of BETAKE.

betray v.tr. **1** place (a person, one's country, etc.) in the power of an enemy. **2** be disloyal to (another person etc.). **3** reveal involuntarily (his shaking hand betrayed his fear). **4** lead into error. [based on Latin tradere 'to hand over'] □ **betrayal** n. **betrayer** n.

betroth v.tr. (usu. as **betrothed** adj.) bind with a promise to marry. [Middle English] □ **betrothal** n.

better[1] ● adj. **1** (compar. of GOOD) of a more excellent or outstanding or desirable kind (a better product; it would be better

to go home). **2** (compar. of WELL[1]) partly or fully recovered from illness (feeling better). ● adv. (compar. of WELL[1]) **1** in a better manner (she sings better). **2** to a greater degree (like it better). **3** more usefully or advantageously (is better forgotten). ● n. **1** that which is better (the better of the two). **2** (usu. in pl.; prec. by my etc.) one's superior in ability or rank (take notice of your betters). ● v. **1** tr. improve on; surpass. **2** tr. make better; improve. **3** refl. improve one's position etc. **4** intr. become better; improve. □ **the better part of** most of. **get the better of** defeat, outwit; win an advantage over. **go one better 1** outbid etc. by one. **2** outdo another person. **had better** would find it wiser to. [Old English] □ **betterment** n.

better[2] n. (also **bettor**) a person who bets.

better half n. colloq. one's wife or husband.

betting n. **1** gambling by risking money on an unpredictable outcome. **2** the odds offered in this.

betting shop n. Brit. a bookmaker's shop or office.

bettor var. of BETTER[2].

between ● prep. **1 a** at or to a point in the interval bounded by two or more other points in space, time, etc. (broke down between London and Dover; we must meet between now and Friday). **b** along the extent of such an interval (there are five shops between here and the main road; works best between five and six; the numbers between 10 and 20). **2** separating, physically or conceptually (the distance between here and Leeds; the difference between right and wrong). **3 a** by combining the resources of (between us we could afford it). **b** as the joint resources of (£5 between them). **c** by joint or reciprocal action (an agreement between us). **4** to and from (runs between London and Sheffield). **5** taking one and rejecting the other (decide between eating here and going out). ● adv. (also **in between**) at a point or in the area bounded by two or more other points in space, time, sequence, etc. (not fat or thin but in between). □ **between times** (or **whiles**) in the intervals between other actions; occasionally. [Old English betwēonum 'by two']

betwixt prep. & adv. archaic between. □ **betwixt and between** colloq. neither one thing nor the other. [Old English]

bevel ● n. **1** a slope from the horizontal or vertical in carpentry and stonework. **2** (in full **bevel square**) a tool for marking angles in carpentry and stonework. ● v. (**bevelled, bevelling**; US **beveled, beveling**) **1** tr. reduce (a square edge) to a sloping edge. **2** intr. slope at an angle; slant. [based on Old French baer 'to gape']

beverage n. esp. formal a drink. [based on Latin bibere 'to drink']

bevy n. (pl. **-ies**) **1** a flock of quails or larks. **2** a company or group (originally of women). [Middle English]

bewail v.tr. **1** greatly regret or lament. **2** wail over; mourn for.

beware v. (only in imper. or infin.) **1** intr. be cautious, take heed (beware of the dog; told us to beware; beware that you don't fall). **2** tr. be cautious of (beware the Ides of March).

bewilder v.tr. utterly perplex or confuse. [from obsolete wilder 'to lose one's way'] □ **bewilderedly** adv. **bewildering** adj. **bewilderment** n.

bewitch v.tr. **1** enchant; greatly delight. **2** cast a spell on. [Middle English, from earlier wiccian 'to enchant'] □ **bewitching** adj. **bewitchingly** adv.

beyond ● prep. **1** at or to the further side of (beyond the river). **2** outside the scope, range, or understanding of (beyond repair; beyond a joke; it is beyond me). **3** more than. ● adv. **1** at or to the further side. **2** further on. ● n. (prec. by the) the unknown after death. □ **the back of beyond** see BACK. [Old English]

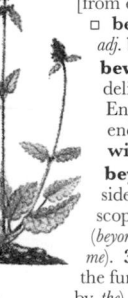

BETONY
(Stachys officinalis)

bezel /bez-ĕl/ n. **1** ◀ the sloped edge of a chisel. **2** the oblique faces of a cut gem. **3** a groove holding a watch-glass or gem. [from Old French]

bhaji n. (pl. **bhajis**) **1** an Indian dish of fried vegetables. **2** a small flat cake or ball of vegetables, fried in batter (onion bhaji). [from Hindi bhājī 'fried vegetables']

bhangra n. a kind of pop music that combines Punjabi folk traditions with Western pop music. [from Punjabi bhāngrā, a traditional folk dance]

Bi symb. Chem. the element bismuth.

bi- comb. form (often **bin-** before a vowel) forming nouns and adjectives meaning: **1** having two; a thing having two (bilateral; binaural). **2 a** occurring twice in every one or once in every two (bimonthly). **b** lasting for two (biennial). **3** doubly; in two ways (biconcave). **4** Chem. a substance having a double proportion of the acid etc. indicated by the simple word (bicarbonate). [Latin]

bezel

BEZEL OF A CHISEL

biannual adj. occurring, appearing, etc., twice a year. □ **biannually** adv.

bias ● n. **1** a predisposition or prejudice. **2** Statistics a systematic distortion of a statistical result due to a factor not allowed for in its derivation. **3** an edge cut obliquely across the weave of a fabric. ▷ WEFT. **4** Bowls **a** the irregular shape given to a bowl. **b** the oblique course this causes it to run. **5** Electr. a steady voltage, magnetic field, etc., applied to an electronic system or device. ● v.tr. (**biased, biasing**; **biassed, biassing**) **1** (esp. as **biased** adj.) influence (usu. unfairly); prejudice. **2** give a bias to. □ **on the bias** obliquely, diagonally. [from French biais]

bias binding n. a strip of fabric cut obliquely and used to bind edges.

biathlon n. Sport an athletic contest in skiing and shooting or in cycling and running. □ **biathlete** n.

bib n. **1** a piece of cloth or plastic fastened round a child's neck to keep the clothes clean while eating. **2** the top front part of an apron, pair of dungarees, etc. [Middle English]

bibelot /bib-ĕ-loh/ n. a small curio or artistic trinket. [French]

Bible n. **1 a** the Christian scriptures consisting of the Old and New Testaments. **b** the Jewish scriptures. **c** (**bible**) any copy of these (three bibles on the table). **d** a particular edition of the Bible (New English Bible). **2** colloq. any authoritative book (the Britannica is his Bible). **3** the scriptures of any religion. [from Greek biblia 'books']

Bible belt n. the areas of the southern and central US and western Canada where fundamentalist Protestant beliefs prevail.

biblical adj. (also **Biblical**) **1** of, concerning, or contained in the Bible. **2** resembling the language of the Authorized Version of the Bible. □ **biblically** adv.

biblio- comb. form denoting a book or books. [Greek]

bibliography n. (pl. **-ies**) **1 a** a list of the books referred to in a scholarly work. **b** a list of the books of a specific author or publisher, or on a specific subject, etc. **2 a** the history or description of books, including authors, editions, etc. **b** any book containing such information. [from modern Latin bibliographia] □ **bibliographer** n. **bibliographic** adj. **bibliographical** adj.

bibliophile n. a person who collects or is fond of books.

bibulous adj. given to drinking alcoholic liquor. [from Latin bibulus 'freely drinking']

bicameral adj. (of a parliament or legislative body) having two chambers. [based on Latin camera 'chamber'] □ **bicameralism** n.

bicarbonate n. **1** Chem. any acid salt of carbonic acid. **2** (in full **bicarbonate of soda**) sodium bicarbonate used as an antacid or in baking powder.

bicentenary ● n. (pl. **-ies**) **1** a two-hundredth anniversary. **2** a celebration of this. ● adj. of or concerning a bicentenary.

B

BICYCLE

The bicycle converts the energy of the cyclist into propulsion: pressure exerted on levers – the pedals – is transferred through the gear system to turn the wheels. The modern bicycle dates from the introduction of pneumatic tyres and gears at the end of the 19th century. A wide variety of types is now available, from general purpose bicycles to more specialized machines for off-road cycling and racing.

FEATURES OF A MOUNTAIN BICYCLE

saddle, seat bolt, handlebars, headset, brake cable, brake block, cantilever brake arm, top tube, front derailleur, cog, reflector, spoke, wheel rim, tyre, rear derailleur cage, presta valve, chain, pedal, toe clip, front fork blade, water bottle boss, quick-release hub clamp

EXAMPLES OF OTHER BICYCLES

RACING BICYCLE   RECUMBENT BICYCLE   SPEED-TRIAL BICYCLE

bicentennial ● *n.* a bicentenary. ● *adj.* **1** lasting two hundred years or occurring every two hundred years. **2** of or concerning a bicentenary.

biceps *n.* (*pl.* same) ▼ a muscle having two heads or attachments at one end, esp. the muscle which bends the elbow. ▷ MUSCULATURE. [Latin, literally 'two-headed']

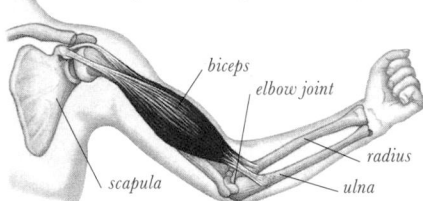

biceps, elbow joint, radius, scapula, ulna

BICEPS: HUMAN ARM SHOWING THE BICEPS

bicker *v.intr.* argue pettily. [Middle English]

biconcave *adj.* concave on both sides.

biconvex *adj.* convex on both sides.

bicultural *adj.* having or combining two cultures.

bicycle ● *n.* ▲ a vehicle of two wheels held in a frame one behind the other, propelled by pedals and steered with handlebars attached to the front wheel. ● *v.intr.* ride a bicycle. [based on Greek *kuklos* 'wheel'] □ **bicyclist** *n.* ▷ DERAILLEUR

bicycle clip *n.* a clip used to confine a cyclist's trouser leg at the ankle.

bid ● *v.* (**bidding**; *past* **bid**, *archaic* **bade**; *past part.* **bid**, *archaic* **bidden**) **1** *tr. & intr.* (*past* and *past part.* **bid**) **a** offer (a certain price) (*bid for the vase; bid against the dealer; bid £20*). **b** offer to do work etc. for a stated price. **2** *tr. archaic* or *literary* **a** command (*bid the soldiers shoot*). **b** invite (*bade her start*). **3** *tr. archaic* or *literary* utter (greeting or farewell) to (*I bade him welcome*). **4** (*past* and *past part.* **bid**) *Cards*

a *intr.* state before play how many tricks one intends to make. **b** *tr.* state (one's intended number of tricks). ● *n.* **1** an offer (of a price) (*a bid of £5*). **b** an offer (to do work, supply goods, etc.) at a stated price; a tender. **2** *Cards* a statement of the number of tricks a player proposes to make. **3** *colloq.* an attempt (*a bid for power*). □ **bid fair to** seem likely to. **make a bid for** try to gain (*made a bid for freedom*). [Old English] □ **bidder** *n.*

biddable *adj.* obedient.

bidding *n.* **1** the offers at an auction. **2** *Cards* the act of making a bid or bids. **3** a command, request, or invitation.

bidding prayer *n.* a prayer inviting the congregation to join in.

biddy *n.* (*pl.* **-ies**) *slang derog.* a woman (esp. *old biddy*). [pet form of the name *Bridget*]

bide *v.intr. archaic* or *dial.* remain; stay. □ **bide one's time** await one's best opportunity. [Old English]

bidet /bee-day/ *n.* a low oval basin used esp. for washing the genital area. [French, literally 'pony']

bidirectional *adj.* functioning in two directions.

Biedermeier /bee-der-myr/ *attrib.adj.* **1** (of styles, furnishings, etc.) characteristic of the period 1815–48 in Germany. **2** *derog.* conventional; bourgeois. [from *Biedermaier*, name of a fictitious German poet created (1854) by L. Eichrodt]

biennial ● *adj.* **1** lasting two years. **2** recurring every two years. ● *n.* **1** *Bot.* a plant that takes two years to grow from seed to fruition and die. **2** an event celebrated or taking place every two years. [based on Latin *annus* 'year']

bier *n.* a movable frame on which a coffin or a corpse is placed. [Old English]

biff *slang* ● *n.* a sharp blow. ● *v.tr.* strike (a person).

bifocal ● *adj.* having two focuses, esp. of a lens with a part for distant vision and a part for near vision. ● *n.* (in *pl.*) bifocal spectacles.

BIFU *abbr.* Banking, Insurance, and Finance Union.

bifurcate ● *v.tr. & intr.* divide into two branches; fork. ● *adj.* forked; branched. [based on Latin *bifurcus* 'two-forked'] □ **bifurcation** *n.*

big ● *adj.* (**bigger**, **biggest**) **1 a** of considerable size, amount, intensity, etc. (*a big mistake; a big helping*). **b** of a large or the largest size (*big toe; big drum*). **2** important; significant; outstanding (*my big chance*). **3 a** grown-up (*a big boy now*). **b** elder (*big sister*). **4** *colloq.* **a** boastful (*big words*). **b** often *iron.* generous (*big of him*). **c** ambitious (*big ideas*). **5** advanced in pregnancy; fecund (*big with child; big with consequences*). ● *adv. colloq.* in a big manner, esp.: **1** effectively (*went over big*). **2** boastfully (*talk big*). **3** ambitiously (*think big*). □ **the big time** *slang.* success in a profession. **in a big way 1** on a large scale. **2** *colloq.* with great enthusiasm, display, etc. **look** (or **talk**) **big** boast. [Middle English] □ **biggish** *adj.* **bigness** *n.*

bigamy *n.* (*pl.* **-ies**) the crime of marrying when already married to another person. [based on Greek *gamos* 'marriage'] □ **bigamist** *n.* **bigamous** *adj.*

Big Apple *n. N. Amer. slang* New York City.

big band *n.* a large jazz or pop orchestra.

big bang *n.* (also **Big Bang**) **1** ▼ the explosion of dense matter, postulated as the origin of the universe. **2** *Stock Exch.* (in the UK) the introduction in 1986 of important changes in the regulations and procedures for trading.

BIG BANG

Many astronomers subscribe to the big bang theory, which proposes that space, time, and matter were created by a huge explosion between 10 and 20 billion years ago.

At first a hot, dense fireball of particles and radiation, the universe continues to expand, with galaxies rushing away from each other.

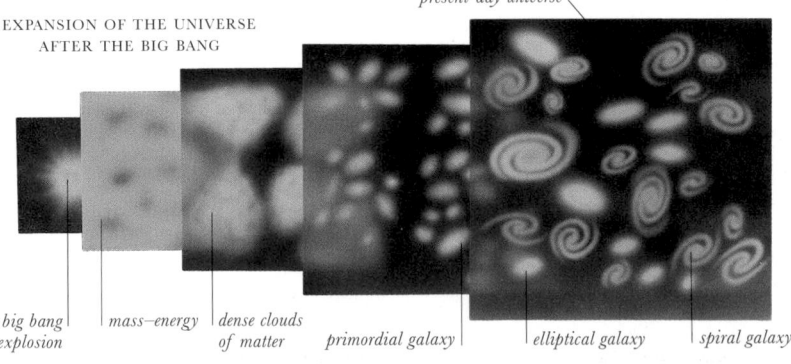

EXPANSION OF THE UNIVERSE AFTER THE BIG BANG

present-day universe

big bang explosion, mass–energy, dense clouds of matter, primordial galaxy, elliptical galaxy, spiral galaxy

Big Brother *n.* an all-powerful supposedly benevolent dictator (as in Orwell's *Nineteen Eighty-four*).

big business *n.* large-scale financial dealings, esp. when sinister or exploitative.

big deal *int. slang, iron.* I am not impressed.

big dipper *n.* **1** *Brit.* a fairground switchback. **2** *N. Amer.* (**Big Dipper**) = PLOUGH *n.* 3.

big end *n.* ▼ (in a motor vehicle) the end of the connecting rod that encircles the crankpin. ▷ INTERNAL COMBUSTION ENGINE

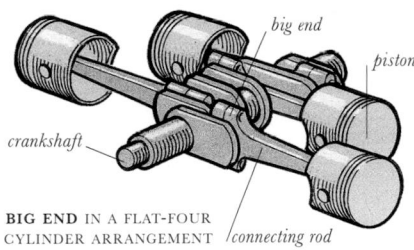

BIG END IN A FLAT-FOUR CYLINDER ARRANGEMENT

big game *n.* large animals hunted for sport.

biggie *n. colloq.* a big person or thing; an important event.

big-head *n. colloq.* a conceited person. □ **big-headed** *adj.*

big-hearted *adj.* generous.

bight *n.* **1** a curve or recess in a coastline, river, etc. **2** a loop of rope. [Old English].

big league *N. Amer.* ● *n.* a top league in a professional sport (often hyphenated when *attrib.*: *big-league teams*). ● *attrib.adj.* (**big-league**) *colloq.* major; top; outstanding.

big name *n.* a famous person.

big noise *n. Brit.* (also **big pot** *Brit.*, or **big shot**) *colloq.* = BIGWIG.

bigot *n.* an obstinate and intolerant believer in a religion, political theory, etc. [from French] □ **bigotry** *n.*

bigoted *adj.* unreasonably prejudiced and intolerant.

big top *n.* the main tent in a circus.

big tree *n. US* the giant sequoia, *Sequoiadendron giganteum*.

big wheel *n.* **1** a Ferris wheel. **2** *N. Amer. slang* = BIGWIG.

bigwig *n. colloq.* an important person.

bijou /*bee-zhoo*/ *attrib.adj.* small and elegant. [French, literally 'jewel']

bike ● *n.* a bicycle or motorcycle. ● *v.intr.* ride a bicycle or motorcycle.

biker *n.* a motorcyclist.

bikini *n.* a two-piece swimsuit for women. [from *Bikini*, atoll where an atom bomb was exploded (1946), from the supposed 'explosive' effect]

bilateral *adj.* **1** of, on, or with two sides. **2** affecting or between two parties, countries, etc. (*bilateral negotiations*). □ **bilaterally** *adv.*

bilateral symmetry *n.* ▶ the property of being divisible into symmetrical halves on either side of a unique plane.

bilberry *n.* (*pl.* **-ies**) **1** ◀ a hardy dwarf shrub, *Vaccinium myrtillus*, of N. Europe, growing on heaths and mountains, and having dark blue berries. **2** the berry of this species.

bile *n.* **1** a bitter greenish-brown alkaline fluid which aids digestion and is secreted by the liver and stored in the gall bladder. **2** peevish anger. [from Latin *bilis*]

BILBERRY (*Vaccinium myrtillus*)

bile duct *n.* the duct which conveys bile from the liver and the gall bladder to the duodenum. ▷ GALL BLADDER

bilge *n.* **1** the area on the outer surface of a ship's hull where the flat bottom meets the vertical sides. **2 a** (in *pl.*) the lowest internal portion of the hull. **b** (in full **bilge water**) filthy water that collects inside the bilge. **3** *slang* nonsense.

bilharzia *n.* a chronic disease, endemic in parts of Africa and S. America, caused by infestation with blood flukes (schistosomes). **2** = SCHISTOSOME. [named after T. *Bilharz*, German physician, 1825–62]

biliary *adj.* of the bile.

bilingual ● *adj.* **1** able to speak two languages. **2** spoken or written in two languages. ● *n.* a bilingual person. [based on Latin *lingua* 'tongue'] □ **bilingualism** *n.*

bilious *adj.* **1** affected by a disorder of the bile. **2** bad-tempered. □ **biliousness** *n.*

bilirubin *n.* an orange-yellow pigment formed by breakdown of haemoglobin and occurring in bile. [German, from Latin *bilis ruber* 'red bile']

bilk *v.tr. slang* **1** cheat. **2** give the slip to. **3** avoid paying (a creditor or debt).

bill¹ ● *n.* **1 a** a statement of charges for goods supplied or services rendered. **b** the amount owed (*ran up a bill of £300*). **2** a draft of a proposed law. **3 a** a poster; a placard. **b** = HANDBILL. **4 a** a printed list, esp. a theatre programme. **b** the entertainment itself (*top of the bill*). **5** *N. Amer.* a banknote (*ten-dollar bill*). ● *v.tr.* **1** put in the programme; announce. **2** (foll. by *as*) advertise. **3** send a note of charges to (*billed him for the books*). [from Anglo-Latin *billa* 'seal, bill'] □ **billable** *adj.*

bill² ● *n.* **1** the beak of a bird. ▷ DUCK. **2** the muzzle of a platypus. **3** a narrow promontory. ● *v.intr.* (of doves etc.) stroke a bill with a bill. □ **bill and coo** exchange caresses. [Old English] □ **billed** *adj.* (usu. in *comb.*).

bill³ *n.* **1** *hist.* a weapon like a halberd with a hook instead of a blade. **2** = BILLHOOK. [Old English]

billabong *n. Austral.* a branch of a river forming a backwater or a stagnant pool. [from Aboriginal *bilabang*]

billboard *n.* a large outdoor board for advertisements etc.

billet¹ ● *n.* **1 a** a place where troops etc. are lodged. **b** a written order requiring a householder to lodge the bearer. **2** *colloq.* a situation; a job. ● *v.tr.* (**billeted, billeting**) **1** quarter (soldiers etc.) **2** (of a householder) provide (a soldier etc.) with board and lodging. [from Anglo-Latin *billetta* 'little bill']

billet² *n.* **1** a thick piece of firewood. **2** a small metal bar. [from French *billette* 'small log']

billet-doux /*bi-li-doo*/ *n.* (*pl.* **billets-doux** /*-dooz*/) often *joc.* a love letter. [French, literally 'sweet note']

billfold *n. N. Amer.* a wallet for keeping banknotes.

billhook *n.* a sickle-shaped tool with a sharp inner edge, used for pruning, lopping, etc.

billiards *n.* **1** a game played on an oblong cloth-covered table, with three balls struck with cues into pockets round the edge of the table. **2** (**billiard**) (in *comb.*) used in billiards (*billiard ball*). [from French *billard* 'a cue']

billion ● *n.* (*pl.* same or (in sense 3 of *n.*) **billions**) (in *sing.* prec. by *a* or *one*) **1 a** thousand million (1,000,000,000 or 10⁹). **2** esp. *Brit.* a million million (1,000,000,000,000 or 10¹²). **3** (in *pl.*) *colloq.* a very large number (*billions of years*). ● *adj.* that amount to a billion. [French] □ **billionth** *adj. & n.*

billionaire *n.* a person possessing over a billion pounds, dollars, etc.

bill of exchange *n. Econ.* a written order to pay a sum of money on a given date to the drawer or to a named payee.

bill of fare *n.* a menu.

bill of health *n.* **1** *Naut.* a certificate regarding infectious disease on a ship or in a port at the time of sailing. **2** (in phr. **clean bill of health**) **a** such a certificate stating that there is no disease. **b** a declaration that a person or thing examined has been found to be free of illness or in good condition.

bill of lading *n. Naut.* **1** a detailed list of a ship's cargo. **2** *US* = WAYBILL.

Bill of Rights *n.* **1** *Law* the English constitutional settlement of 1689. **2** *Law* (in the US) the original constitutional amendments of 1791. **3** a statement of the rights of a class of people.

billow ● *n.* **1** a wave. **2** a soft upward-curving flow. **3** any large soft mass. ● *v.intr.* move in billows. [from Old Norse *bylgja*] □ **billowy** *adj.*

billposter *n.* (also **billsticker**) a person who pastes up advertisements on hoardings.

billy¹ *n.* (*pl.* **-ies**) (in full **billycan**) orig. *Austral.* a cooking pot with a lid and wire handle, for use out of doors.

billy² *n.* (*pl.* **-ies**) = BILLY GOAT.

billycan see BILLY¹.

billy goat *n.* a male goat.

biltong *n. S.Afr.* boneless meat salted and dried in strips. [from Dutch *bil* 'buttock' + *tong* 'tongue']

bimbo *n.* (*pl.* **-os**) *slang* usu. *derog.* **1** a woman, esp. a young empty-headed one. **2** a person. [Italian, literally 'little child']

bimetallic *adj.* made of two metals.

bimonthly ● *adj.* occurring twice a month or every two months. ● *adv.* twice a month or every two months. ● *n.* (*pl.* **-ies**) a periodical produced bimonthly.

■ **Usage** *Bimonthly* is often avoided, because of the ambiguity of meaning, in favour of *two-monthly* and *twice-monthly* or *every two months* and *twice a month*

bin ● *n.* a large receptacle for storage or for depositing rubbish. ● *v.tr.* (**binned, binning**) *colloq.* **1** store or put in a bin. **2** *Brit.* throw away. [Old English]

bin- *prefix* var. of BI- before a vowel.

binary ● *adj.* **1 a** dual. **b** of or involving pairs. **2** of the arithmetical system using 2 as a base. ● *n.* (*pl.* **-ies**) **1** something having two parts. **2** a binary number. **3** a binary star. [based on Late Latin *bini* 'two together']

binary code *n. Computing* a coding system using the binary digits 0 and 1.

binary compound *n. Chem.* a compound having two elements or radicals.

binary number *n.* (also **binary digit**) one of two digits (usu. 0 or 1) in a binary system of notation.

binary star *n.* ▶ a system of two stars orbiting each other.

binary system *n.* a system in which information can be expressed by combinations of the digits 0 and 1.

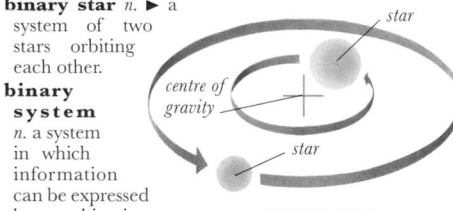

BINARY STAR

binaural *adj.* **1** of or used with both ears. **2** (of sound) recorded using two microphones.

bind ● *v.tr.* (*past* and *past part.* **bound**) (see also BOUNDEN). **1** tie or fasten tightly. **2 a** restrain; put in bonds. **b** (as **-bound** *adj.*) constricted, obstructed (*snowbound*). **3** *Cookery* cause (ingredients) to cohere. **4** fasten or hold together as a single mass. **5** compel; impose a duty on. **6 a** edge with braid etc. **b** fasten (the pages of a book) in a cover. **7** constipate. **8** (in *passive*) be required by an obligation or duty (*am bound to answer*). **9 a** put a bandage or other covering round. **b** fix together with something put round (*bound her hair*). ● *n. colloq.* a nuisance; a restriction. □ **be bound up with** be closely associated with. **bind over** *Law* order (a person) to do something, esp. keep the peace.

I'll be bound a statement of assurance, or guaranteeing the truth of something. [Old English]

binder n. **1** a cover for sheets of paper, for a book, etc. **2** a substance that acts cohesively. **3** a reaping machine that binds grain into sheaves. **4** a bookbinder.

bindery n. (pl. **-ies**) a workshop or factory for binding books.

binding ● n. something that binds, esp. the covers, glue, etc., of a book. ● adj. obligatory.

bindweed n. **1** convolvulus. **2** any of various climbing plants such as honeysuckle.

binge slang ● n. a period of uncontrolled eating, drinking, etc. ● v.intr. (**bingeing** or **binging**) indulge in uncontrolled eating, drinking, etc.

bingo ● n. a game for any number of players, each having a card of squares with numbers, which are marked off as numbers are randomly drawn by a caller. ● int. expressing sudden surprise, satisfaction, etc.

bin liner n. Brit. a bag for lining a rubbish bin.

binman n. (pl. **-men**) Brit. colloq. a dustman.

binnacle n. a built-in housing for a ship's compass. [earlier bittacle, based on Latin habitaculum 'habitation']

binocular adj. adapted for or using both eyes. [based on Latin oculus 'eye']

binoculars n.pl. ▼ an optical instrument with a lens for each eye, for viewing distant objects.

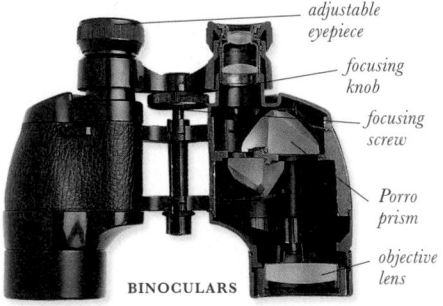

adjustable eyepiece

focusing knob

focusing screw

Porro prism

objective lens

BINOCULARS

binomial ● n. **1** an algebraic expression of the sum or the difference of two terms. **2** a two-part name, esp. in taxonomy. ● adj. consisting of two terms. [based on Greek nomos 'part, portion']

binomial nomenclature n. a system of classification using two terms, the first one indicating the genus and the second the species.

bint n. Brit. slang usu. offens. a girl or woman. [Arabic, literally 'daughter, girl']

bio- comb. form **1** life (biography). **2** biological (biotechnology). **3** of living beings (biophysics). [from Greek bios '(course of) human life']

bioactive adj. (of foods, cosmetic compounds, etc.) having an effect on or interacting with living tissue. □ **bioactivity** n.

biochemistry n. the study of the chemical and physico-chemical processes of living organisms. □ **biochemical** adj. **biochemist** n.

biocide n. **1** a poisonous substance, esp. a pesticide. **2** the destruction of life. [based on Greek bios 'life' (see -CIDE)]

biodegradable adj. capable of being decomposed by bacteria or other living organisms. □ **biodegradability** n. **biodegradation** n.

biodiversity n. diversity of plant and animal life.

bioengineering n. **1** the industrial use of biosynthetic processes. **2** the use of artificial tissues, organs, or organ components to replace damaged or absent parts of the body. □ **bioengineer** n. & v.

biofeedback n. the technique of using the feedback of a normally automatic bodily response to a stimulus, in order to acquire voluntary control of that response.

biogas n. gaseous fuel, esp. methane, produced by fermentation of organic matter.

biography n. (pl. **-ies**) **1 a** a written account of a person's life. **b** such writing as a branch of literature. **2** the course of a living being's life. [from medieval Greek] □ **biographer** n. **biographical** adj.

biohazard n. a risk to human health or the environment arising from biological work, esp. with micro-organisms.

biological adj. **1** of or relating to biology or living organisms. **2** (of a detergent etc.) containing enzymes to assist the process of cleaning. □ **biologically** adv.

biological clock n. an innate mechanism controlling the rhythmic physiological activities of an organism.

biological control n. the control of a pest by the introduction of a natural enemy.

biological warfare n. warfare involving the use of toxins or micro-organisms.

biology n. **1** the study of living organisms. **2** the plants and animals of a particular area. [from German Biologie] □ **biologist** n.

bioluminescence n. the emission of light by living organisms such as the firefly and glow-worm. □ **bioluminescent** adj.

biomass n. the total quantity or weight of organisms in a given area or volume.

biome n. **1** a large naturally occurring community of flora and fauna adapted to the particular conditions in which they occur, e.g. tundra. **2** the geographical region containing such a community.

biomechanics n. the study of the mechanical laws relating to the movement or structure of living organisms.

biometry /by-om-i-tri/ n. (also **biometrics**) the application of statistical analysis to biological data. □ **biometric** adj.

bionic adj. **1** having artificial body parts or superhuman powers resulting from these. **2** relating to bionics.

bionics n. the study of mechanical systems that function like living organisms or parts of living organisms.

biophysics n. the science of the application of the laws of physics to biological phenomena. □ **biophysical** adj. **biophysicist** n.

biopic /by-oh-pik/ n. colloq. a biographical film. [blend of biographical and PICTURE]

biopsy n. (pl. **-ies**) the examination of tissue removed from a living body to discover the presence, cause, or extent of a disease. [based on Greek bios 'life' + opsis 'sight']

biorhythm n. **1** any of the recurring cycles of biological processes thought to affect a person's emotional, intellectual, and physical activity. **2** any periodic change in the behaviour or physiology of an organism.

bioscope n. S.Afr. slang a cinema. [earlier in sense 'a view of life']

biosphere n. the regions of the Earth's crust and atmosphere occupied by living organisms. [from German Biosphäre]

biosynthesis n. the production of organic molecules by living organisms. □ **biosynthetic** adj.

biota /by-oh-tă/ n. the animal and plant life of a region. [from Greek biotē 'life']

biotechnology n. the exploitation of biological processes for industrial and other purposes, esp. genetic manipulation of micro-organisms (for the production of antibiotics, hormones, etc.).

biotic adj. **1** relating to life or to living things. **2** of biological origin.

biotin n. a vitamin of the B complex, found in egg yolk, liver, and yeast, and involved in the metabolism of carbohydrates, fats, and proteins. Also (esp. US) called vitamin H.

bipartisan adj. of or involving two parties. □ **bipartisanship** n.

bipartite adj. **1** consisting of two parts. **2** shared by or involving two parties. **3** Law (of a contract etc.) drawn up in two corresponding parts or between two parties.

biped /by-ped/ ● n. a two-footed animal. ● adj. two-footed. [based on Latin pes pedis 'foot'] □ **bipedal** adj.

biphenyl n. Chem. see PCB.

biplane n. ▼ an early type of aeroplane having two sets of wings, one above the other (cf. MONOPLANE). ▷ AIRCRAFT

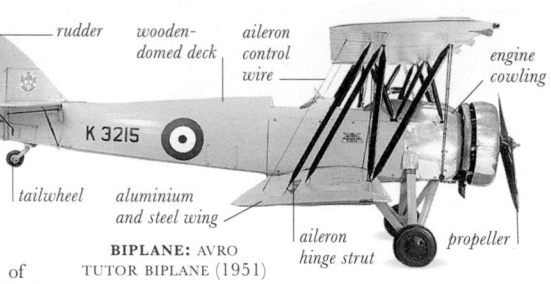

rudder — wooden-domed deck — aileron control wire — engine cowling

K 3215

K 3215

tailwheel — aluminium and steel wing — aileron hinge strut — propeller

BIPLANE: AVRO TUTOR BIPLANE (1951)

bipolar adj. having two poles or extremities. □ **bipolarity** n.

birch ● n. **1** (also **birch tree**) ◄ any tree of the genus Betula, bearing catkins, and found predominantly in northern temperate regions. **2** (in full **birchwood**) the hard fine-grained pale wood of these trees. **3** NZ any of various similar trees. **4** (in full **birch-rod**) a bundle of birch twigs used for flogging. ● v.tr. beat with a birch (in sense 4 of n.). [Old English]

catkin

BIRCH: PAPER BIRCH (Betula papyrifera)

bird n. **1** ► a feathered vertebrate of the class Aves with a beak, two wings, and two feet, egg-laying and usu. able to fly. **2** a game bird. **3** Brit. slang a young woman. **4** colloq. a person (an early bird). **5** Brit. slang **a** a prison. **b** rhyming slang a prison sentence (short for birdlime = time). □ **a bird in the hand** something secured or certain. **birds of a feather** people of like character. **for** (or **strictly for**) **the birds** colloq. trivial, uninteresting. [Old English]

birdbrain n. colloq. a stupid or flighty person.

birdcage n. **1** a cage for birds usu. made of wire or cane. **2** an object of a similar design.

bird cherry n. a wild cherry, Prunus padus.

birder n. esp. N. Amer. a birdwatcher. □ **birding** n.

birdie ● n. **1** colloq. a little bird. **2** Golf a score of one stroke less than par at any hole. ● v.tr. (**birdies**, **birdied**, **birdying**) Golf play (a hole) in a birdie.

birdlime n. sticky material painted on to twigs to trap small birds.

bird of paradise n. any bird of the family Paradiseidae, the males having very beautiful brilliantly coloured plumage.

bird of prey n. a bird which hunts animals for food. ▷ RAPTOR

birdseed n. a blend of seed for feeding birds.

bird's-eye view n. a general view from above.

bird's-foot trefoil n. a small leguminous plant, Lotus corniculatus, having yellow flowers streaked with red.

birdsong n. the musical cry of a bird or birds.

bird-strike n. a collision between a bird and an aircraft.

bird table n. Brit. a raised platform on which food for birds is placed.

birdwatcher n. a person who observes birds in their natural surroundings. □ **birdwatching** n.

BIRD

There are over 9,000 species of bird, living in a wide range of environments, from deserts to the open ocean. Birds are the only animals that have feathers, which they use for flight, insulation, camouflage, and for attracting mates. Flying birds have light-weight skeletons with air-filled bones, but in many diving and flightless species the bones are solid. Birds lack teeth but instead rely upon a muscular gizzard to grind up what they eat, using their beak or feet to collect or catch food. Birds lay hard-shelled eggs. In almost all species, these are incubated by the parents.

EXTERNAL FEATURES OF A
BLACK-HEADED STARLING
(*Sturnus pagodarum*)

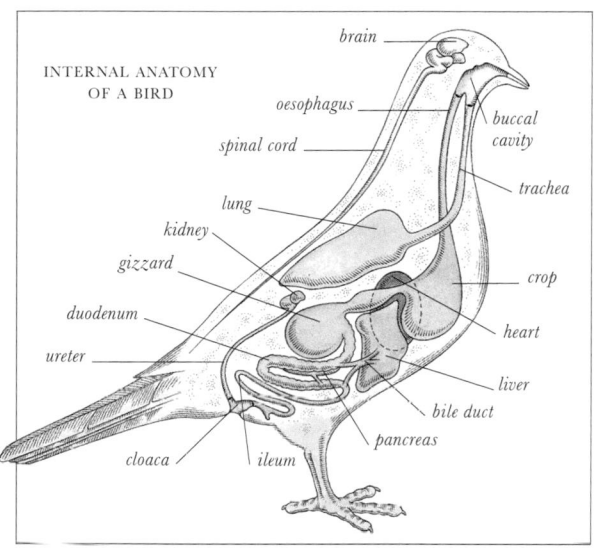

INTERNAL ANATOMY
OF A BIRD

MAIN BIRD ORDERS

STRUTHIONIFORMES
(ostriches)

SPHENISCIFORMES
(penguins)
▷ PENGUIN

CICONIIFORMES
(herons, ibises, storks)

ANSERIFORMES
(waterfowl)
▷ WATERFOWL

FALCONIFORMES
(birds of prey)
▷ RAPTOR

GALLIFORMES
(game birds)

CHARADRIIFORMES
(auks, gulls, terns, waders)
▷ SEABIRD, WADING BIRD

COLUMBIFORMES
(pigeons)

PSITTACIFORMES
(parrots)
▷ PARROT

CUCULIFORMES
(cuckoos, turacos)

STRIGIFORMES
(owls)
▷ OWLS

APODIFORMES
(hummingbirds, swifts)

CORACIIFORMES
(bee-eaters, hoopoes, kingfishers)

PICIFORMES
(barbets, toucans, woodpeckers)

PASSERIFORMES
(passerines)
▷ PASSERINE

biretta *n.* a square cap with three flat projections on top, worn by clergymen. [based on Late Latin *birrus* 'hooded cape']

biriani *n.* (also **biryani**) an Indian dish made with highly seasoned rice, and meat or fish etc. [Urdu]

biro *n.* (*pl.* **-os**) *Brit. propr.* a kind of ballpoint pen. [named after L. *Biró*, 1899–1985, Hungarian inventor of the ballpoint]

birth ● *n.* **1** the emergence of an infant or other young from the body of its mother. **2** *literary* the beginning of something (*the birth of socialism*). **3 a** origin, descent, ancestry (*of noble birth*). **b** noble birth; inherited position. ● *v.tr. N. Amer. colloq.* **1** (also *absol.*) give birth to. **2** assist (a woman) to give birth. □ **give birth** bear a child etc. **give birth to 1** produce (young) from the womb. **2** cause to begin. [from Old Norse *byrth*]

birth certificate *n.* an official document identifying a person by name, place, and date of birth.

birth control *n.* the control of the number of children one conceives.

birthday *n.* **1** the day on which a person etc. was born. **2** the anniversary of this. □ **in one's birthday suit** *joc.* naked.

birthing *n.* the act or process of giving birth (*birthing position*).

birthmark *n.* an unusual brown or red mark on one's body at or from birth.

birthplace *n.* the place where a person was born.

birth rate *n.* the number of live births per thousand of population per year.

birthright *n.* a right of possession or privilege one has from birth, esp. as the eldest son.

birthweight *n.* the weight of a baby at birth.

biryani var. of BIRIANI.

biscuit ● *n.* **1** *Brit.* a small unleavened cake, usu. flat and crisp and often sweet. **2** fired unglazed pottery. **3** a light brown colour. ● *adj.* light brown. [based on Latin *bis coctus* 'twice cooked'] □ **biscuity** *adj.*

bisect *v.tr.* divide into two (strictly, equal) parts. [based on Latin *secare sect-* 'to cut'] □ **bisection** *n.*

bisexual ● *adj.* **1** sexually attracted by persons of both sexes. **2** *Biol.* having characteristics of both sexes. ● *n.* a bisexual person. □ **bisexuality** *n.*

bishop *n.* **1** a senior member of the Christian clergy empowered to confer holy orders. **2** a chess piece with the top sometimes shaped like a mitre. ▷ CHESS. [from Greek *episkopos* 'overseer']

bishopric *n.* **1** the office of a bishop. **2** a diocese.

bismuth *n. Chem.* **1** ► a brittle grey metallic element with a reddish tinge or iridescent tarnish, occurring naturally and used in alloys. **2** any compound of this element used medicinally. [based on German *Wismut*]

BISMUTH

bison *n.* (*pl.* same) either of two wild humpbacked shaggy-haired oxen of the genus *Bison*, native to N. America (*B. bison*) or Europe (*B. bonasus*). [Latin]

bisque[1] *n.* a rich shellfish soup. [French]

bisque[2] *n. Tennis, Croquet, & Golf* an advantage of scoring one free point, or taking an extra turn or stroke. [French]

bisque[3] *n.* = BISCUIT 2.

bistable /by-stay-bŭl/ *adj.* (of an electrical circuit etc.) having two stable states.

bistre /**bis**-ter/ (*US* **bister**) ● *n.* **1** a brownish pigment made from the soot of burnt wood. **2** the brownish colour of this. ● *adj.* of this colour. [French]

bistro *n.* (*pl.* **-os**) a small restaurant. [French]

bisulphate *n.* (*US* **bisulfate**) *Chem.* a salt or ester of sulphuric acid.

bit[1] *n.* **1** a small piece or quantity (*a bit of cheese*). **2** (prec. by *a*) **a** a fair amount (*sold quite a bit*). **b** *colloq.* somewhat (*am a bit tired*). **c** (foll. by *of*) *colloq.* rather (*a bit of an idiot*). **3** a short time or distance (*wait a bit; move up a bit*). **4** *US slang* a unit of $12\frac{1}{2}$ cents (used only in even multiples). □ **bit by bit** gradually. **bit on the side** *slang* **1** a sexual relationship involving infidelity to one's partner. **2** the person with whom one is unfaithful. **bits and pieces** (or **bobs**) an assortment of small items. **do one's bit** *colloq.* make a useful contribution to an effort or cause. **not a bit** (or *Brit.* **not a bit of it**) not at all. **to bits 1** into pieces. **2** *colloq.* very much; to a great degree (*thrilled to bits*). [Old English, related to BITE]

bit[2] *past* of BITE.

bit[3] *n.* **1** a metal mouthpiece on a bridle, used to control a horse. ▷ BRIDLE. **2** a tool or piece for boring or drilling. ▷ DRILL. **3** the cutting or gripping part of a plane, pincers, etc. □ **take the bit between one's teeth 1** take decisive personal action. **2** escape from control. [Old English, related to BITE]

bit[4] *n. Computing* a unit of information expressed as a choice between two possibilities; a 0 or 1 in binary notation. [blend of BINARY and DIGIT]

bitch ● *n.* **1** a female dog or other canine animal. **2** *slang offens.* a spiteful woman. **3** *slang* a very unpleasant or difficult thing. ● *v. colloq.* **1** *intr.* **a** speak scathingly. **b** complain. **2** *tr.* be spiteful or unfair to. [Old English]

bitchy *adj.* (**bitchier**, **bitchiest**) *slang* spiteful; bad-tempered. □ **bitchiness** *n.*

bite ● *v.* (*past* **bit**; *past part.* **bitten**) **1** *tr.* cut or puncture using the teeth. **2** *tr.* (foll. by *off, away*, etc.) detach with the teeth. **3** *tr.* (of an insect, snake, etc.) wound with a sting, fangs, etc. **4** *intr.* (of a wheel, screw, etc.) grip, penetrate. **5** *intr.* accept bait. **6** *intr.* have a (desired) adverse effect. **7** *tr.* (in *passive*) **a** take in; swindle. **b** (foll. by *by, with*, etc.) be infected by (enthusiasm etc.). **8** *tr.* (as **bitten** *adj.*) cause a smarting pain to (*frostbitten*). **9** *intr.* (foll. by *at*) snap at. **10** *tr. colloq.* worry (*what's biting you?*). ● *n.* **1** an act of biting. **2** a wound or sore made by biting. **3 a** a mouthful of food. **b** a snack or light meal. **4** the taking of bait by a fish. **5** pungency. **6** incisiveness, sharpness. □ **bite back** restrain (one's speech etc.) by or as if by biting the lips. **bite** (or *Brit.* **bite on**) **the bullet** *slang* behave bravely or stoically. **bite the dust** *slang* **1** die. **2** fail; break down. **bite the hand that feeds one** hurt a benefactor. **bite a person's head off** *colloq.* respond fiercely or angrily. **bite off more than one can chew** take on a commitment one cannot fulfil. **put the bite on** *US slang* borrow or extort money from. [Old English] □ **biter** *n.*

biting *adj.* **1** stinging; intensely cold (*a biting wind*). **2** sharp; effective (*biting sarcasm*). □ **bitingly** *adv.*

bit part *n.* a minor part in a play or a film.

bitten *past part.* of BITE.

bitter ● *adj.* **1** having a harsh pungent taste as of quinine or of coffee that is too strong. **2 a** caused by or showing mental pain or resentment (*bitter memories; bitter rejoinder*). **b** painful or difficult to accept (*bitter disappointment*). **3 a** harsh; virulent (*bitter animosity*). **b** piercingly cold. ● *n.* **1** *Brit.* beer strongly flavoured with hops and having a bitter taste. **2** (in *pl.*) liquor with a bitter flavour used as an additive in cocktails. □ **to the bitter end** to the very end in spite of difficulties. [Old English] □ **bitterly** *adv.* **bitterness** *n.*

bitter aloes see ALOE 2.

bittern *n.* any of a group of wading birds of the heron family. [from Old French *butor*]

bitter pill *n.* something unpleasant that has to be accepted.

bitter-sweet ● *adj.* **1** sweet with a bitter aftertaste. **2** arousing pleasure tinged with pain or sorrow. ● *n.* **1 a** sweetness with a bitter aftertaste. **b** pleasure tinged with pain or sorrow. **2** = *woody nightshade* (see NIGHTSHADE).

bitty *adj.* (**bittier**, **bittiest**) **1** esp. *Brit.* made up of unrelated bits. **2** (esp. in phrs. **little bitty**, **itty-bitty**) *N. Amer. colloq.* tiny.

bitumen *n.* any of various tarlike mixtures of hydrocarbons derived from petroleum and used for road surfacing and roofing. ▷ FRACTIONAL DISTILLATION. [Latin]

bituminous *adj.* of, relating to, or containing bitumen.

bituminous coal *n.* a form of coal burning with a smoky flame. ▷ COAL

bivalve ● *n.* ► any of a group of aquatic molluscs of the class Bivalvia, with laterally compressed bodies enclosed within two hinged shells, e.g. oysters. ● *adj.* **1** with a hinged double shell. **2** *Biol.* having two valves, e.g. of a pea pod.

bivouac ● *n.* a temporary open encampment without tents. ● *v.intr.* (**bivouacked**, **bivouacking**) camp in a bivouac, esp. overnight. [French, originally in sense 'a night watch by a whole army']

biz *n. colloq.* business.

bizarre *adj.* strange; eccentric; grotesque. [French, literally 'handsome, brave'] □ **bizarrely** *adv.*

Bk *symb. Chem.* the element berkelium.

bk. *abbr.* book.

blab ● *v.* (**blabbed**, **blabbing**) **1** *intr.* **a** talk foolishly or indiscreetly. **b** reveal secrets. **2** *tr.* reveal (a secret etc.) by indiscreet talk. ● *n.* a person who blabs. [Middle English]

blabber ● *n.* (also **blabbermouth**) a person who blabs. ● *v.intr.* talk foolishly or inconsequentially, esp. at length.

black ● *adj.* **1** very dark, having no colour from the absorption of all or nearly all incident light (like coal or soot). **2** completely dark from the absence of a source of light (*black night*). **3** (also **Black**) **a** of the human group having dark-coloured skin. **b** of or relating to black people (*black rights*). **4** (of the sky, a cloud, etc.) dusky; heavily overcast. **5** angry, threatening (*a black look*). **6** implying disgrace or condemnation (*in his black books*). **7** sinister, deadly (*black-hearted*). **8** depressed, sullen (*a black mood*). **9** portending trouble or difficulty (*things looked black*). **10** (of hands, clothes, etc.) dirty, soiled. **11** (of humour or its representation) macabre (*black comedy*). **12** (of tea or coffee) without milk. **13** *Brit.* **a** (of industrial labour or its products) boycotted in an industrial dispute. **b** (of a person) doing work or handling goods that have been boycotted. **14** dark in colour as distinguished from a lighter variety (*black bear*). ● *n.* **1** a black colour or pigment. **2** black clothes or material (*dressed in black*). **3 a** (in a game or sport) a black piece, ball, etc. **b** the player using such pieces. **4** the credit side of an account (*in the black*). **5** (also **Black**) a member of a dark-skinned race. ● *v.tr.* **1** make black (*blacked his face*). **2** polish with blacking. **3** *Brit.* declare (goods etc.) 'black'. □ **black out 1 a** effect a blackout on. **b** undergo a blackout. **2** obscure windows etc. or extinguish all lights for protection esp. against an air attack. [Old English] □ **blackish** *adj.* **blackly** *adv.* **blackness** *n.*

■ **Usage** When referring to dark-skinned people, *black* (rather than *Negro* or *Coloured*) is now the preferred term. In Britain and the US it is generally used to designate people of African descent while in Australia it is used of Aboriginals. The term *African-American* is also common in the US for people of African descent.

black and blue *adj.* discoloured by bruises.

black and white ● *n.* writing or printing (*in black and white*). ● *adj.* **1** (of film etc.) not in colour. **2** consisting of extremes only, oversimplified.

black art *n.* (prec. by *the*) = BLACK MAGIC.

blackball *v.tr.* reject (a candidate) in a ballot (originally by voting with a black ball).

black belt *n.* **1** a black belt worn by an expert in judo, karate, etc. **2** a person qualified to wear this.

blackberry ● *n.* (*pl.* **-ies**) **1** a thorny climbing shrub, *Rubus fruticosus* (rose family), bearing white or pink flowers and purplish-black berries. **2** the edible berry of this plant. ▷ FRUIT. ● *v.intr.* (**-ies**, **-ied**) gather blackberries.

BIVALVE

Bivalves are molluscs whose shells consist of two hinged valves that protect the soft body; when faced with danger the two halves are pulled together by a powerful abductor muscle. Found in marine and freshwater habitats, molluscs are typically unable to extend far out of their shells, and live either embedded in sand or mud, or fastened to rocks. A few, such as scallops, can open and close their shell to propel themselves away from danger. Most bivalves have large gills that are used both for breathing and filter-feeding.

B

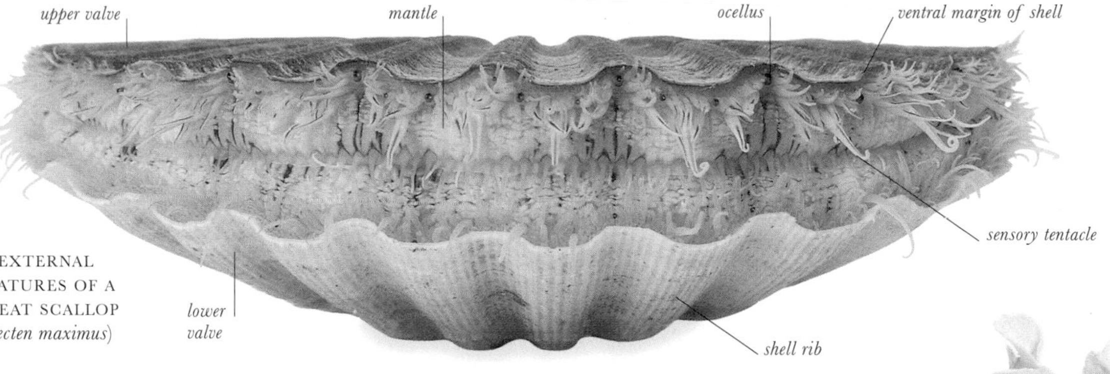

upper valve　　　*mantle*　　　*ocellus*　　　*ventral margin of shell*

sensory tentacle

EXTERNAL
FEATURES OF A
GREAT SCALLOP
(*Pecten maximus*)

*lower
valve*

shell rib

EXAMPLES OF OTHER BIVALVES

NEW ZEALAND MUSSEL
(*Mytilacea* species)

SWAN MUSSEL
(*Anodonta cygnea*)

ZEBRA MUSSEL
(*Dreissena polymorpha*)

GAPING
FILE SHELL
(*Lima hians*)

SPINY SAND COCKLE
(*Acanthoiardia echinata*)

COCKSCOMB OYSTER
(*Lopha cristagalli*)

THORNY OYSTER
(*Spondylus* species)

NOBLE PEN SHELL
(*Pinna nobilis*)

FLUTED GIANT CLAM
(*Tridacna squamosa*)

---

black bile *n. hist* one of the four bodily humours, characterized as cold and dry, and associated with a melancholy temperament (cf. HUMOUR *n.* 4). [translation of Greek *melagkholia*]

blackbird *n.* **1** a common thrush, *Turdus merula*, the male of which is black with an orange beak. **2** *US* any of various birds with black plumage.

blackboard *n.* a board with a smooth usu. dark surface for writing on with chalk.

black box *n.* **1** a flight recorder in an aircraft. **2** any complex piece of equipment with contents which are mysterious to the user.

black bread *n.* a coarse dark-coloured type of rye bread.

blackbuck *n.* a small Indian gazelle, *Antilope cervicapra*.

blackcap *n.* a small warbler, *Sylvia atricapilla*, the male of which has a black-topped head.

blackcurrant *n.* **1** a widely cultivated shrub, *Ribes nigrum*, bearing flowers in racemes. **2** the small round dark edible berry of this plant.

Black Death *n.* (prec. by *the*) the widespread epidemic of bubonic plague in Europe in the 14th c.

black economy *n.* unofficial economic activity.

blacken *v.* **1** *tr. & intr.* make or become black or dark. **2** *tr.* speak ill of, defame (*blacken someone's character*).

black English *n.* the form of English spoken by many black people, esp. as an urban dialect of the US.

black eye *n.* bruised skin around the eye resulting from a blow.

blackfly *n.* (*pl.* **-flies**) **1** any of various thrips or aphids infesting plants. **2** a biting fly of the genus *Simulium* or family Simuliidae.

Black Forest gateau *n.* (*N. Amer.* **Black Forest cake**) a chocolate sponge with layers of morello cherries or cherry jam and whipped cream, originally from S. Germany.

Black Friar *n.* a Dominican friar.

blackguard /**blag**-ard/ *n.* a villain; a scoundrel. [originally applied collectively to menials]

blackhead *n.* a dark plug of sebum in a hair follicle.

black hole *n.* **1** ▶ a region of space having a gravitational field so intense that no matter or radiation can escape. **2** a place of confinement for punishment.

black ice *n.* thin hard transparent ice.

blacking *n.* any black paste or polish.

blackjack *n.* **1** the card game pontoon. **2** *N. Amer.* a flexible leaded bludgeon.

blackleg *Brit.* ● *n.* (often *attrib.*) *derog.* a person who fails or declines to take part in industrial action. ● *v.intr.* (**-legged**, **-legging**) act as a blackleg.

black letter *n.* an early style of type with very thick verticals.

blacklist ● *n.* a list of people in disfavour, etc. ● *v.tr.* put the name of (a person) on a blacklist.

black magic *n.* magic involving invocation of evil spirits.

blackmail ● *n.* **1 a** an extortion of payment in return for not disclosing a secret etc. **b** any payment extorted in this way. **2** the use of threats or moral pressure. ● *v.tr.* **1** extort or try to extort money etc. from (a person) by blackmail. **2** threaten, coerce. [based on obsolete *mail* 'rent'] □ **blackmailer** *n.*

Black Maria *n. colloq.* a police vehicle for transporting prisoners. [apparently named after a *black woman, Maria* Lee, Boston landlady who helped the police in escorting disorderly customers to jail]

black mark *n.* a mark of discredit.

black market *n.* an illicit traffic in officially controlled or scarce commodities. □ **black marketeer** *n.*

black mass *n.* a travesty of the Roman Catholic Mass in worship of Satan.

BLACK HOLE

If the mass of the collapsed core of a supernova exceeds the mass of our Sun by three times, it continues to collapse, forming a black hole. Invisible because its gravity is so dense that light cannot escape, a black hole can be detected if gas from a companion star is drawn towards it.

quasar　　　*black hole*　　　*event horizon*

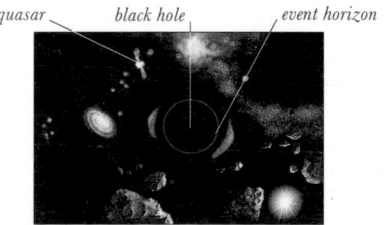

ARTIST'S IMPRESSION OF A BLACK HOLE

B

black Muslim n. US a member of an exclusively black Islamic sect proposing a separate black community.

black nationalism n. advocacy of the national civil rights of esp. US black people.

blackout n. 1 a temporary or complete loss of vision, consciousness, or memory. 2 a loss of power, radio reception, etc. 3 a compulsory period of darkness as a precaution against air raids. 4 a temporary suppression of the release of information. 5 a sudden darkening of a theatre stage.

black pepper n. ▶ the unripe ground or whole berries of *Piper nigrum* as a condiment.

black power n. a movement in support of rights and political power for black people.

black pudding n. Brit. a black sausage containing pork, dried pig's blood, suet, etc.

Black Rod n. Brit. the principal usher of the Lord Chamberlain's department, House of Lords, etc. [from the symbol of office]

black sheep n. colloq. a disreputable member of a family etc.; a misfit.

blackshirt n. a member of a Fascist organization. [from the colour of the Italian Fascist uniform]

blacksmith n. 1 a smith who works in iron. 2 N. Amer. = FARRIER 2.

black spot n. 1 Brit. a place of danger or difficulty (*an accident black spot*). 2 any of various diseases of plants, esp. of roses, producing black spots on leaves.

black swan n. an Australian swan, *Cygnus atratus*, with black plumage.

blackthorn n. 1 a thorny shrub, *Prunus spinosa* (rose family), bearing white-petalled flowers before the leaves appear, and blue-black fruits. 2 a cudgel or walking stick made from its wood.

black tea n. tea that is fully fermented before drying.

black tie n. 1 a black bow tie worn with a dinner jacket. 2 colloq. formal evening dress.

Black Watch n. (usu. prec. by *the*) the Royal Highland Regiment (so called from its dark tartan uniform).

black water n. domestic waste water and sewage from lavatories, or waste water that is heavily contaminated with human excrement. (cf. GREY WATER)

black widow n. ◀ a venomous N. American spider, *Latrodectus mactans*, the female of which devours its mate. ▷ SPIDER

BLACK WIDOW
(*Latrodectus mactans*)

bladder n. 1 a any of various membranous sacs in some animals, containing urine (**urinary bladder**), bile (**gall bladder**), or air (**swim-bladder**). ▷ FISH, GALL BLADDER, URINARY SYSTEM. b this or part of it or a similar object prepared for various uses. 2 an inflated pericarp or vesicle in various plants. 3 anything inflated and hollow. [Old English]

bladderwrack n. ▶ a common brown seaweed, *Fucus vesiculosus*, with fronds containing air bladders which give buoyancy.

BLADDERWRACK
(*Fucus vesiculosus*)

unripe fruit

black peppercorns
ground black pepper

BLACK PEPPER
(*Piper nigrum*)

blade n. 1 a the flat part of a knife, chisel, etc., that forms the cutting edge. b = RAZOR BLADE. 2 ▶ the flattened part of an oar, spade, propeller, etc. 3 a the flat narrow leaf of grass and cereals. b Bot. the broad thin part of a leaf. 4 (in full **blade-bone**) a flat bone. [Old English] □ **bladed** adj. (also in comb.).

blade

blag Brit. slang ● n. robbery; theft. ● v.tr. & intr. (**blagged, blagging**) rob; steal. [19th-century coinage] □ **blagger** n.

blame ● v.tr. 1 assign fault or responsibility to. 2 (foll. by on) assign the responsibility for (an error or wrong) to a person etc. (*blamed his death on a poor diet*). ● n. 1 responsibility for a bad result (*shared the blame equally*). 2 the act of blaming or attributing responsibility (*she got all the blame*). □ **be to blame** be responsible; deserve censure (*she is not to blame for the accident*). [from Greek *blasphēmein* to blaspheme]

blameless adj. innocent; free from blame. □ **blamelessly** adv. **blameworthy** adj. deserving blame. □ **blameworthiness** n.

blanch v. 1 tr. make white or pale by extracting colour. 2 intr. & tr. grow or make pale from shock, fear, etc. 3 tr. a peel (almonds etc.) by scalding. b immerse (vegetables or meat) briefly in boiling water. 4 tr. whiten (a plant) by depriving it of light. [based on (Old) French *blanc* 'white']

blancmange /blǎ-monj/ n. a sweet opaque gelatinous dessert made with flavoured cornflour and milk. [from Old French *blancmanger*, literally 'white to eat']

bland adj. 1 a mild, not irritating. b tasteless, unstimulating, insipid. 2 gentle in manner; suave. [from Latin *blandus* 'soft, smooth'] □ **blandly** adv. **blandness** n.

blandish v.tr. flatter; coax, cajole. [based on Latin *blandus* 'smooth']

blandishment n. (usu. in pl.) flattery; cajolery.

blank ● adj. 1 a (of paper) not written on or printed on. b (of a document) with spaces left for a signature or details. 2 a empty (*a blank space*). b unrelieved; sheer; plain (*a blank wall*). 3 a having or showing no interest or expression (*a blank face*). b void of incident or result. c puzzled, nonplussed. d having (temporarily) no knowledge (*my mind went blank*). 4 (with neg. import) complete, downright (*blank despair*). 5 euphem. used in place of an adjective regarded as coarse or abusive. ● n. 1 a a space left to be filled in a document. b a document having blank spaces to be filled. 2 (in full **blank cartridge**) a cartridge containing gunpowder but no bullet. 3 an empty space or period of time. 4 a a dash written instead of a word or letter. b euphem. used in place of a noun regarded as coarse. ● v.tr. (usu. foll. by *off, out*) screen, obscure (*clouds blanked out the Sun*). □ **draw a blank** elicit no response; fail. [from (Old) French *blanc* 'white'] □ **blankly** adv. **blankness** n.

blank cheque n. 1 a cheque with the amount left for the payee to fill in. 2 colloq. unlimited freedom of action (cf. CARTE BLANCHE).

blanket ● n. 1 a large piece of woollen or other material used esp. as a bed-covering or to wrap up a person or an animal for warmth. 2 a thick mass or layer that covers something (*blanket of fog; blanket of silence*). ● attrib.adj. covering all cases or classes; inclusive (*blanket condemnation; blanket agreement*). ● v.tr. (**blanketed, blanketing**) 1 cover with or as if with a blanket (*snow blanketed the land*). 2 stifle (*blanketed all discussion*). [from Old French *blancquet*]

BLADE
ON A
PADDLE

blanket bath n. Brit. a body wash given to a bedridden patient.

blanket stitch n. a stitch used to neaten the edges of a blanket or other material. ▷ STITCH

blank verse n. unrhymed verse, esp. iambic pentameters.

blare ● v. 1 tr. & intr. sound or utter loudly. 2 intr. make the sound of a trumpet. ● n. a loud sound resembling that of a trumpet. [from Middle Dutch *blaren*]

blarney n. 1 cajoling talk; flattery. 2 nonsense. [from *Blarney*, an Irish castle with a stone said to confer a cajoling tongue on whoever kisses it]

blasé /blah-zay/ adj. unimpressed or indifferent because of overfamiliarity.[French]

blaspheme v. 1 intr. use religious names irreverently; treat a religious or sacred subject irreverently. 2 tr. talk irreverently about; use blasphemy against. [from Greek *blasphēmein*] □ **blasphemer** n.

blasphemy n. (pl. **-ies**) 1 irreverent talk or treatment of a religious or sacred thing. 2 an instance of this. □ **blasphemous** adj.

blast ● n. 1 a strong gust of air. 2 a a destructive wave of highly compressed air spreading outwards from an explosion. b such an explosion. 3 the single loud note of a wind instrument, car horn, etc. 4 colloq. a severe reprimand. 5 a strong current of air used in smelting etc. ● v. 1 tr. blow up (rocks etc.) with explosives. 2 intr. (of wind) blow fiercely. 3 tr. a wither, shrivel, or blight (a plant, animal, limb, etc.) (*blasted oak*). b ruin (*blasted her hopes*). c strike with divine anger. 4 intr. & tr. make or cause to make a loud noise (*blasted away on his trumpet*). 5 tr. colloq. reprimand severely. 6 colloq. a tr. shoot; shoot at. b int. shoot. ● int. Brit. expressing annoyance. □ **at full blast** colloq. working at maximum speed etc. **blast from the past** a forcefully nostalgic event or thing. **blast off** (of a rocket etc.) take off from a launching site. [Old English]

-blast comb. form Biol. an embryonic cell (cf. -CYTE). [from Greek *blastos* 'sprout']

blasted ● attrib.adj. damned; annoying (*that blasted dog!*). ● adv. Brit. colloq. damned; extremely (*it's blasted cold*).

blast furnace n. ▼ a smelting furnace into which compressed hot air is driven.

BLAST FURNACE

During the iron smelting process, coke burned within a blast furnace reacts with oxygen in the air to release carbon monoxide. This combines with iron oxide in iron ore to produce both carbon dioxide and molten iron. Limestone acts as a flux, helping to separate impurities from the iron by turning them into molten slag.

CUTAWAY VIEW OF A
BLAST FURNACE

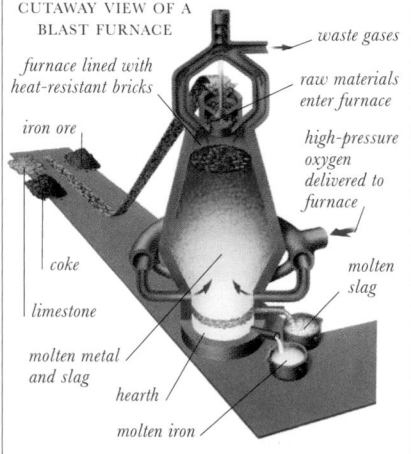

waste gases

furnace lined with
heat-resistant bricks

raw materials
enter furnace

iron ore

high-pressure
oxygen
delivered to
furnace

coke

molten
slag

limestone

molten metal
and slag

hearth

molten iron

blast-hole *n.* a hole containing an explosive charge for blasting.

blast-off *n.* **1** the launching of a rocket etc. **2** the initial thrust for this.

blatant *adj.* **1** flagrant, unashamed (*blatant attempt to steal*). **2** offensively noisy or obtrusive. [coined by Spenser (1596)] □ **blatancy** *n.* **blatantly** *adv.*

blather /bla*th*-er/ (also **blether**) ● *n.* foolish chatter. ● *v.intr.* chatter foolishly. [from Old Norse *blathra* 'to talk nonsense']

blaze[1] ● *n.* **1** a bright flame or fire. **2 a** a bright glaring light. **b** a full light (*a blaze of publicity*). **3** a violent outburst (of passion etc.). **4 a** a glow of colour (*roses were a blaze of scarlet*). **b** a bright display (*a blaze of glory*). ● *v.intr.* **1** burn with a bright flame. **2** be brilliantly lit. **3** be consumed with anger, excitement, etc. **4 a** show bright colours (*blazing with jewels*). **b** emit light (*stars blazing*). □ **blaze away 1** fire continuously with rifles etc. **2** work enthusiastically. **blaze up 1** burst into flame. **2** burst out in anger. **like blazes** *slang* **1** with great energy. **2** very fast. [Old English *blæse* 'torch'] □ **blazingly** *adv.*

blaze[2] ● *n.* **1** a white mark on an animal's face. **2** a mark made on a tree by slashing the bark. ● *v.tr.* mark (a tree or a path) by chipping bark. □ **blaze a trail 1** mark out a path or route. **2** be the first to do, invent, or study something; pioneer. [17th-century coinage]

blaze[3] *v.tr.* proclaim as with a trumpet. □ **blaze abroad** spread (news) about. [from Dutch *blāzen* 'to blow']

blazer *n.* **1** a coloured summer jacket worn by schoolchildren, sportsmen, etc., esp. as part of a uniform. **2** a man's plain jacket, not forming part of a suit. [based on BLAZE[1]]

blazon ● *v.tr.* **1** proclaim (esp. *blazon abroad*). **2** *Heraldry* **a** describe or paint (arms). **b** inscribe or paint (an object) with arms, names, etc. ● *n. Heraldry* a correct description of armorial bearings etc. ▷ HERALDRY. [from Old French *blason* 'shield'].

bleach ● *v.tr.* & *intr.* whiten by exposure to sunlight or by a chemical process. ● *n.* **1** a bleaching substance. **2** the process of bleaching. [Old English]

bleacher *n.* **1 a** a person who bleaches. **b** a vessel or chemical used in bleaching. **2** (usu. in *pl.*) esp. *N. Amer.* a cheap bench seat at a sports ground.

bleak *adj.* **1** bare, exposed; windswept. **2** unpromising; dreary (*bleak prospects*). [16th-century coinage] □ **bleakly** *adv.* **bleakness** *n.*

bleary *adj.* (**blearier**, **bleariest**) **1** (of the eyes) dim with sleep. **2** indistinct; blurred. □ **blearily** *adv.*

bleary-eyed *adj.* **1** having dim sight or wits. **2** half awake.

bleat ● *v.* **1** *intr.* (of a sheep, goat, or calf) make a weak, wavering cry. **2** *intr.* & *tr.* speak or say feebly, foolishly, or plaintively. ● *n.* **1** the sound made by a sheep, goat, etc. **2** a weak, plaintive, or foolish cry. [Old English]

bleb *n. Med.* a small blister on the skin.

bleed ● *v.* (*past* and *past part.* **bled**) **1** *intr.* emit blood. **2** *tr.* draw blood from surgically. **3** *tr. colloq.* extort money from. **4** *intr.* suffer wounds or violent death (*bled for the Revolution*). **5** *intr.* **a** (of a plant) emit sap. **b** (of dye) come out in water. **6** *tr.* **a** allow (fluid or gas) to escape from a closed system through a valve etc. **b** treat (such a system) in this way. **7** *intr. Printing* (of a printed area) extend to the cut edge of a sheet. ● *n.* an act of bleeding (cf. NOSEBLEED). □ **one's heart bleeds** usu. *iron.* one is very sorrowful. [Old English]

bleeder *n.* **1** *Brit. coarse slang* a person (esp. as a term of contempt or disrespect) (*lucky bleeder*). **2** *colloq.* a haemophiliac.

bleeding *adj.* & *adv. Brit. coarse slang* expressing annoyance or antipathy (*a bleeding nuisance*).

bleep ● *n.* an intermittent high-pitched sound made electronically. ● *v.* **1 a** *intr.* make such a sound. **b** *tr.* cause to make such a sound. **2** *tr. Brit.* summon with a bleeper.

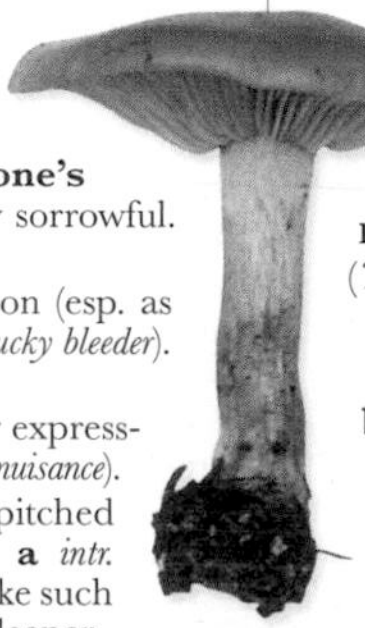

BLEWITS (*Tricholoma* species)

bleeper *n. Brit.* a small portable electronic device which emits bleeps when the wearer is contacted.

blemish ● *n.* a physical or moral defect; a stain; a flaw (*not a blemish on his character*). ● *v.tr.* spoil the beauty or perfection of (*spots blemished her complexion*). [from Old French *ble(s)mir* 'to make pale']

blench *v.intr.* flinch; quail. [Old English *blencan* 'to impose upon']

blend ● *v.* (*poet. past* and *past part.* **blent**) **1** *tr.* **a** mix together to produce a desired flavour etc. **b** produce by this method (*blended whisky*). **2** *intr.* form a harmonious compound; become one. **3 a** *tr.* & *intr.* mingle or be mingled (*blends well with the locals*). **b** *tr.* mix thoroughly. **4** *intr.* (esp. of colours): **a** pass imperceptibly into each other. **b** go well together; harmonize. ● *n.* **1 a** a mixture, esp. of various sorts of tea, spirits, tobacco, fibres, etc. **b** a combination (of different abstract or personal qualities). **2** a portmanteau word. [Middle English]

blende *n.* any naturally occurring metal sulphide. [German, from *blenden* 'to deceive', so called because though resembling galena, it yielded no lead]

blender *n.* **1** a mixing machine used in food preparation for liquidizing, chopping, or puréeing. **2 a** a thing that blends. **b** a person who blends.

blenny *n.* (*pl.* **-ies**) ► any of a family of small spiny-finned marine fish having scaleless skins. [from Greek *blennos* 'mucus', with reference to its mucous coating]

BLENNY: BUTTERFLY BLENNY (*Blennius ocellaris*)

bless *v.tr.* (*past* and *past part.* **blessed**, *poet.* **blest**) **1** confer or invoke divine favour upon. **2 a** consecrate. **b** sanctify by the sign of the cross. **3** call (God) holy; adore. **4** attribute one's good fortune to; thank (*bless the day I met her*). **5** (usu. in *passive*; often foll. by *with*) make happy or successful (*they were truly blessed*). **6** *euphem.* curse; damn (*bless the boy!*). □ **bless me** (or **my soul**) an exclamation of surprise, pleasure, indignation, etc. **bless you! 1** an exclamation of endearment, gratitude, etc. **2** an exclamation made to a person who has just sneezed. [Old English, based on *blōd* 'blood', hence 'to mark with blood, consecrate']

blessed /bless-id/ *adj.* (also *poet.* **blest**) **1 a** consecrated (*Blessed Sacrament*). **b** revered. **2** (usu. foll. by *with*) often *iron.* fortunate (in the possession of) (*blessed with children*). **3** *euphem.* cursed; damned (*blessed nuisance!*). **4 a** in paradise. **b** *RC Ch.* a title given to a dead person as an acknowledgement of his or her holy life. **5** bringing happiness; blissful (*blessed ignorance*). □ **blessedly** *adv.*

blessedness *n.* **1** happiness. **2** the enjoyment of divine favour.

blessing *n.* **1** the act of declaring, invoking, or bestowing favour (*sought God's blessing; mother gave them her blessing*). **2** grace said before or after a meal. **3** a gift of God, nature, etc.; a thing one is glad of (*what a blessing he brought it!*).

blest *poet.* var. of BLESSED.

blether *Brit.* var. of BLATHER.

blew *past* of BLOW[1].

blewits *n.* ◄ any fungus of the genus *Tricholoma*, with edible lilac-stemmed mushrooms. ▷ MUSHROOM

blight ● *n.* **1** a plant disease caused by mildews, fungi, or insects. **2** an insect or parasite causing such a disease. **3** any obscure force which is harmful. **4** an ugly urban area. ● *v.tr.* **1** affect with blight. **2** harm, destroy. [17th-century coinage]

blighter *n. Brit. colloq.* a person (esp. as a term of contempt or disparagement).

Blighty *n. Brit. slang* (used originally by soldiers during the First World War) Britain or England; home. [corruption of Urdu *bilāyatī* 'foreign, European']

blimey *int.* (also **cor blimey**) *Brit. coarse slang* an expression of surprise, excitement, alarm, etc. [corruption of (*God*) *blind me!*]

blimp *n.* **1** (also **(Colonel) Blimp**) *Brit.* a proponent of reactionary Establishment opinions. **2 a** a small non-rigid airship. **b** a barrage balloon. [20th-century coinage; sense 1: a character invented by cartoonist David Low, 1891–1963] □ **blimpish** *adj.*

blind ● *adj.* **1** lacking the power of sight. **2 a** without foresight, discernment, intellectual perception, or adequate information. **b** (foll. by *to*) unwilling or unable to appreciate (a factor, circumstance, etc.) (*blind to argument*). **3** not governed by purpose or reason (*blind forces*). **4** reckless (*blind hitting*). **5 a** concealed (*blind ditch*). **b** (of a door, window, etc.) walled up. **c** closed at one end. **6** *Aeron.* (of flying) without direct observation, using instruments only. ● *v.* **1** *tr.* deprive of sight (*blinded by tears*). **2** *tr.* rob of judgement; deceive (*blinded them to the danger*). **3** *intr. Brit. slang* go very fast and dangerously. ● *n.* **1 a** a screen for a window (*roller blind; Venetian blind*). **b** *Brit.* an awning over a shop window. **2 a** something designed or used to hide the truth. **b** *Brit.* a legitimate business concealing a criminal enterprise. **3** any obstruction to sight or light. **4** *Brit. slang* a heavy drinking bout. ● *adv.* blindly (*fly blind*). □ **bake blind** bake (a flan case etc.) without a filling. **blind with science** *Brit.* overawe with a display of (often spurious) knowledge. **turn a** (or **one's**) **blind eye to** pretend not to notice. [Old English] □ **blindly** *adv.* **blindness** *n.*

blind alley *n.* **1** a cul-de-sac. **2** a course of action leading nowhere.

blind corner *n.* a corner round which a motorist etc. cannot see.

blind date *n.* **1** a social engagement between a man and a woman who have not previously met. **2** either of the couple on a blind date.

blind drunk *adj. colloq.* extremely drunk.

blinder *n. colloq.* **1** *Brit.* an excellent performance in a game etc. **2** (in *pl.*) *N. Amer.* blinkers.

blindfold ● *v.tr.* deprive (a person) of sight by covering the eyes, esp. with a tied cloth. ● *n.* a bandage or cloth used to blindfold. ● *adj.* & *adv.* **1** (also **blindfolded**) with eyes bandaged. **2** (also **blindfolded**) without care or circumspection (*went into it blindfold*). [earlier *blindfelled* 'struck blind']

blind spot *n.* **1** *Anat.* the point of entry of the optic nerve on the retina, insensitive to light. **2** an area in which a person lacks understanding or impartiality.

blind stitch ● *n.* sewing visible on one side only. ● *v.tr.* & *intr.* (**blind-stitch**) sew with this stitch.

blindworm *n.* = SLOW-WORM.

blink ● *v.* **1** *intr.* shut and open the eyes quickly. **2** *tr.* **a** (often foll. by *back*) prevent (tears) by blinking. **b** (often foll. by *away, from*) clear (dust etc.) from the eyes by blinking. **3** *tr.* & (foll. by *at*) *intr.* ignore. **4** *intr.* **a** shine with an intermittent light. **b** cast a momentary gleam. **5** *tr.* blink with (eyes). ● *n.* **1** an act of blinking. **2** a momentary gleam or glimpse. □ **on the blink** *slang* out of order, esp. intermittently. [variant of Middle English *blenk* 'to blench']

blinker ● *n.* **1** (usu. in *pl.*) ► either of a pair of screens attached to a horse's bridle to prevent it from seeing sideways. **2** a device that blinks. ● *v.tr.* **1** obscure with blinkers. **2** (as **blinkered** *adj.*) having narrow views.

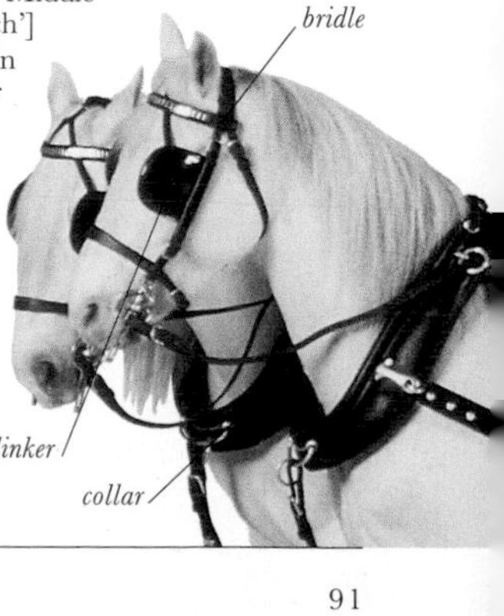

BLINKER

B

blinking adj. & adv. Brit. slang an intensive, esp. expressing disapproval (a blinking idiot). [euphemism for BLOODY]

blip • n. 1 a minor deviation or error. 2 a quick popping sound, as of dripping water or an electronic device. 3 a small intermittent image on a radar screen. • v.intr. (**blipped**, **blipping**) make a blip.

bliss n. 1 a perfect joy or happiness. b enjoyment; gladness. 2 a being in heaven. b a state of blessedness. [Old English] □ **blissful** adj. **blissfully** adv. **blissfulness** n.

blister • n. 1 a small bubble on the skin filled with serum and caused by burning etc. 2 a similar swelling on any other surface. • v. 1 tr. raise a blister on. 2 intr. come up in a blister or blisters. 3 tr. attack sharply (blistered by his criticisms). [Middle English]

blister gas n. a poison gas causing blisters on the skin.

blister pack n. a bubble pack.

blithe adj. 1 poet. gay, joyous. 2 careless, casual (with blithe indifference). [Old English] □ **blithely** adv. **blitheness** n. **blithesome** adj.

blithering adj. colloq. 1 senselessly talkative. 2 (attrib.) contemptible (esp. blithering idiot). [variant of blathering]

B.Litt. abbr. Bachelor of Letters. [Latin Baccalaureus Litterarum]

blitz colloq. • n. 1 a an intensive or sudden (esp. aerial) attack. b an energetic intensive attack (must have a blitz on this room). 2 (**the Blitz**) the German air raids on London in 1940. • v.tr. attack, damage, or destroy by a blitz. [abbreviation of BLITZKRIEG]

blitzkrieg /blits-kreeg/ n. an intense military campaign intended to bring about a swift victory. [German, literally 'lightning war']

blizzard n. a severe snowstorm with high winds.

bloat v. 1 tr. & intr. inflate, swell (bloated with gas). 2 tr. (as **bloated** adj.) a swollen. b puffed up with pride or wealth (bloated plutocrat). 3 tr. cure (a herring) by salting and smoking lightly. [from obsolete bloat 'swollen, soft and wet']

bloater n. a herring cured by bloating.

blob n. 1 a small roundish mass; a drop of matter. 2 a drop of liquid. 3 a spot of colour.

bloc n. a combination of governments, groups, etc. sharing a common purpose. [French, literally 'block']

block • n. 1 a solid hewn or unhewn piece of hard material (block of ice). 2 a flat-topped base for chopping, hammering on, etc. 3 a esp. Brit. a large building, esp. when subdivided (block of flats). b a compact mass of buildings bounded by (usu. four) streets. 4 an obstruction. 5 a pulley or system of pulleys mounted in a case. 6 (in pl.) any of a set of cubes used as a child's toy. 7 a piece of wood or metal engraved for printing. 8 slang the head (knock his block off). 9 N. Amer. a the area between streets in a town or suburb. b the length of such an area (lives three blocks away). 10 a large quantity of things treated as a unit, esp. shares, theatre seats, etc. 11 esp. Brit. a set of sheets of esp. drawing paper, glued along one edge. 12 Athletics = STARTING BLOCK. 13 Amer. Football a blocking action. 14 Austral. a a tract of land offered to an individual settler by a government. b a large area of land. c an urban or suburban building plot. • v.tr. 1 a (often foll. by up) obstruct (a passage etc.) (you are blocking my view). b put obstacles in the way of (progress etc.). 2 restrict the use or conversion of (currency or any other asset). 3 Sport stop or impede. • attrib.adj. treating (many similar things) as one unit (block booking). □ **block in 1** plan in outline. 2 confine. **block out 1 a** shut out (light, noise, etc.). b exclude from memory, as being too painful. 2 plan in outline. **block up 1** shut (a person etc.) in. 2 infill with

bricks etc. **put the blocks on** prevent from proceeding. [from Middle Dutch blok] □ **blocker** n.

blockade • n. 1 the surrounding or blocking of a place, esp. a port, by an enemy. 2 anything that prevents access or progress. 3 N. Amer. an obstruction by snow etc. • v.tr. subject to a blockade. □ **run a blockade** enter or leave a blockaded port by evading the blockading force. □ **blockader** n.

blockage n. an obstruction.

block and tackle n. ◄ a system of pulleys and ropes, esp. for lifting.

blockboard n. Brit. a plywood board with a core of wooden strips.

blockbuster n. slang 1 something of great power or size, esp. an epic film or a best-selling book. 2 a huge aerial bomb. □ **blockbusting** adj.

block capitals n.pl. letters printed without serifs, or written with each letter separate and in capitals.

block diagram n. a diagram showing the general arrangement of parts of an apparatus.

blockhead n. a stupid person. □ **blockheaded** adj.

blockhouse n. 1 a reinforced concrete shelter used as an observation point etc. 2 hist. a one-storeyed timber building with loopholes, used as a fort. 3 a house made of squared logs.

block letters n.pl. = BLOCK CAPITALS.

block vote n. (also **bloc vote**) a vote proportional in power to the number of people a delegate represents.

bloke n. Brit. colloq. a man, a fellow. [Shelta]

blond • adj. 1 (of hair) light-coloured; fair. 2 (of the complexion, esp. as an indication of race) light-coloured. • n. a person with fair hair and skin. [from medieval Latin blondus 'yellow'] □ **blondish** adj. **blondness** n.

blonde • adj. (of a woman or a woman's hair) blond. • n. a blond-haired woman. [fem. of French blond]

blood • n. 1 ▼ a liquid, usually red and circulating in the arteries and veins of vertebrates, that carries oxygen to and carbon dioxide from the tissues of the body. 2 a corresponding fluid in inverte-

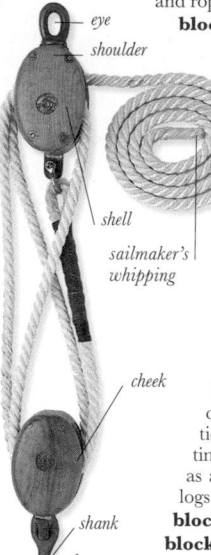

BLOCK AND TACKLE

eye
shoulder
shell
sailmaker's whipping
cheek
shank

brates. 3 bloodshed, esp. killing. 4 passion, temperament. 5 race, parentage (of the same blood). • v.tr. initiate by experience. □ **blood-and-thunder** (attrib.) colloq. sensational, melodramatic. **one's blood is up** one is in a fighting mood. **first blood 1** the first shedding of blood, esp. in boxing. 2 the first point gained in a contest etc. **in one's blood** inherent in one's character. **make one's blood boil** infuriate one. **make one's blood run cold** horrify one. **new** (or **fresh**) **blood** new members admitted to a group, esp. as an invigorating force. **of the blood** royal. **young blood 1** a younger member or members of a group. 2 a rake or fashionable young man. [Old English]

blood bank n. a place where supplies of blood or plasma for transfusion are stored.

bloodbath n. a massacre.

blood brother n. a brother by birth or by the ceremonial mingling of blood.

blood cell n. any of the kinds of cell normally circulating in the blood.

blood count n. 1 the counting of the number of corpuscles in a specific volume of blood. 2 the number itself.

blood-curdling adj. horrifying.

blood donor n. a person who gives blood for transfusion.

blood feud n. a feud between families involving killing or injury.

blood fluke n. a flatworm parasitic in the blood, esp. a schistosome.

blood group n. any of the various types of human blood whose antigen characteristics determine compatibility in transfusion.

bloodhound n. ► a large hound of a breed used in tracking and having a very keen sense of smell.

bloodless adj. 1 without blood or bloodshed (a bloodless coup). 2 unemotional. 3 pale. 4 feeble. □ **bloodlessly** adv. **bloodlessness** n.

bloodletting n. the surgical removal of some of a patient's blood.

blood money n. 1 money paid to the next of kin of a person who has been killed. 2 money paid to a hired murderer. 3 money paid for information about a murder or murderer.

BLOODHOUND

blood orange n. a red-fleshed orange.

blood poisoning n. a disease due to microorganisms or their toxins in the blood.

blood pressure n. the pressure of the blood in the circulatory system, often measured for diagnosis. ▷ SPHYGMOMANOMETER

blood red • n. the bright red colour of blood. • adj. (hyphenated when attrib.) of this colour.

blood relation n. (also **blood relative**) a relative by blood, not by marriage.

bloodshed n. 1 the spilling of blood. 2 slaughter.

bloodshot adj. (of an eyeball) inflamed.

blood sport n. a sport involving the wounding or killing of animals, esp. hunting.

bloodstain n. a discoloration caused by blood.

bloodstained adj. 1 stained with blood. 2 guilty of bloodshed.

bloodstream n. the blood in circulation.

bloodsucker n. 1 an animal or insect that sucks blood, esp. a leech. 2 an extortioner. □ **bloodsucking** adj.

blood sugar n. the amount of glucose in the blood.

blood test n. a scientific examination of blood, esp. for diagnosis.

bloodthirsty adj. (**bloodthirstier**, **bloodthirstiest**) eager for bloodshed. □ **bloodthirstily** adv. **bloodthirstiness** n.

BLOOD

Nutrients and hormones are transported around the body in blood. Its constituent fluid is plasma, in which blood cells are suspended. White blood cells (neutrophils and lymphocytes) guard against infection, red blood cells (erythrocytes) transport oxygen, and platelets help the blood to clot.

CROSS-SECTION OF A CAPILLARY

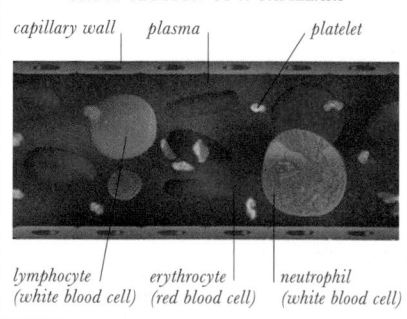

capillary wall   plasma   platelet

lymphocyte   erythrocyte   neutrophil
(white blood cell)   (red blood cell)   (white blood cell)

B

blood transfusion *n.* the injection of a volume of donated blood into a patient.

blood vessel *n.* a vein, artery, or capillary carrying blood. ▷ BLOOD, CARDIOVASCULAR

bloody ● *adj.* (**bloodier**, **bloodiest**) **1 a** of or like blood. **b** running or smeared with blood. **2 a** involving bloodshed (*bloody battle*). **b** sanguinary; cruel (*bloody butcher*). **3** esp. *Brit. coarse slang* expressing annoyance or antipathy, or as an intensive (*a bloody shame*). **4** red. ● *adv.* esp. *Brit. coarse slang* as an intensive (*I'll bloody thump him*). ● *v.tr.* (**-ies**, **-ied**) make bloody; stain with blood. [Old English] □ **bloodily** *adv.* **bloodiness** *n.*

bloody-minded *adj. Brit. colloq.* deliberately unco-operative. □ **bloody-mindedly** *adv.* **bloody-mindedness** *n.*

bloom ● *n.* **1 a** a flower, esp. one cultivated for its beauty. **b** the state of flowering (*in bloom*). **2** a state of perfection or loveliness (*in full bloom*). **3 a** (of the complexion) a flush; a glow. **b** a delicate powdery surface deposit on plums, leaves, etc., indicating freshness. **c** a cloudiness on a shiny surface. **4** a rapid growth of microscopic algae in water. ● *v.* **1** *intr.* be in flower. **2** *intr.* **a** come into, or remain in, full beauty. **b** be in a healthy, vigorous state. **3** *tr. Photog.* coat (a lens) so as to reduce reflection from its surface. □ **take the bloom off** make stale. [from Old Norse *blóm* 'blossom']

bloomer[1] *n. Brit. slang* a blunder. [blend of BLOOMING and ERROR]

bloomer[2] *n. Brit.* an oblong loaf with a rounded diagonally slashed top. [20th-century coinage]

bloomer[3] *n.* **1** a plant that blooms (in a specified way) (*early autumn bloomer*). **2** *N. Amer.* a person who develops (in a specified way) (*she's a late bloomer*).

bloomers *n.pl.* **1** women's loose-fitting almost knee-length knickers. **2** *colloq.* any women's knickers. **3** *hist.* women's and girls' loose-fitting trousers, gathered at the knee or (originally) the ankle. [named after Mrs A. *Bloomer*, American social reformer, 1818–94, who advocated a similar garment]

blooming ● *adj.* **1** flourishing; healthy. **2** *Brit. slang* an intensive (*a blooming miracle*). ● *adv. Brit. slang* an intensive (*was blooming difficult*). [euphemism for BLOODY]

blossom ● *n.* **1** ▶ a flower or a mass of flowers, esp. of a fruit tree. **2** the state or time of flowering (*the cherry tree in blossom*). **3** a promising stage (*the blossom of youth*). ● *v.intr.* **1** open into flower. **2** mature, thrive. [Old English] □ **blossomy** *adj.*

BLOSSOM OF A CRAB APPLE (*Malus × lemoinei*)

blot ● *n.* **1** a spot or stain of ink etc. **2** a disgraceful act or quality. **3** any disfigurement or blemish. ● *v.* (**blotted**, **blotting**) **1 a** *tr.* spot or stain with ink. **b** *intr.* (of a pen etc.) make blots. **2** *tr.* **a** use blotting paper etc. to absorb excess ink from. **b** (of blotting paper etc.) soak up (esp. ink). **3** *tr.* disgrace (*blotted his reputation*). □ **blot one's copybook** *Brit.* damage one's reputation. **blot out 1** obliterate, obscure. **2** destroy. [Middle English]

blotch ● *n.* **1** a discoloured or inflamed patch on the skin. **2** an irregular patch of ink or colour. ● *v.tr.* cover with blotches. [17th-century coinage] □ **blotchy** *adj.* (**blotchier**, **blotchiest**).

blotter *n.* a sheet or sheets of blotting paper, usu. inserted into a frame.

blotting paper *n.* unglazed absorbent paper used for soaking up excess ink.

blotto *adj. slang* very drunk, esp. unconscious from drinking. [20th-century coinage]

blouse ● *n.* **1** a woman's upper garment, usu. buttoned and collared. **2** the upper part of a soldier's or airman's battledress. ● *v.tr.* make (a bodice etc.) loose like a blouse. [French]

blouson /bloo-zon/ *n.* a short blouse-shaped jacket. [French]

blow[1] ● *v.* (*past* **blew**; *past part.* **blown**) **1 a** *intr.* (of the wind or impersonally) move along; act as an air current (*it was blowing hard*). **b** *intr.* be driven by an air current (*waste paper blew along*). **c** *tr.* drive with an air current (*blew the door open*). **2 a** *tr.* send out (esp. air) by breathing (*blew cigarette smoke*). **b** *intr.* be driven by a directed air current from the mouth. **3** *tr. & intr.* sound or be sounded by blowing (*the whistle blew*). **4** *tr.* **a** direct an air current at (*blew the embers*). **b** (foll. by *off, away,* etc.) clear by means of an air current. **5** *tr.* (*past part.* **blowed**) (esp. in *imper.*) *Brit. slang* curse (*blow it!*). **6** *tr.* clear (the nose) of mucus by blowing. **7** *intr.* puff, pant. **8** *intr. slang* depart suddenly. **9** *tr.* shatter or send flying by an explosion. **10** *tr.* make or shape (glass or a bubble) by blowing air in. **11** *tr. & intr.* melt from overloading (*the fuse has blown*). **12** *intr.* (of a whale) eject air and water through a blowhole. **13** *tr.* break into (a safe etc.) with explosives. **14** *tr. slang* **a** spend recklessly (*blew £20 on a meal*). **b** bungle (an opportunity etc.) (*he's blown his chances*). **c** reveal (a secret etc.). **15** *tr.* (of flies) deposit eggs in. ● *n.* **1 a** an act of blowing (e.g. one's nose). **b** *colloq.* a turn or spell of playing jazz (on any instrument). **2 a** a gust of air. **b** exposure to fresh air. □ **be blowed if one will** *slang* be unwilling to. **blow away** *slang* **1** kill, defeat. **2** astound. **blow the gaff** *Brit.* reveal a secret inadvertently. **blow hot and cold** *colloq.* vacillate. **blow in 1** break inwards by an explosion. **2** *colloq.* arrive unexpectedly. **blow a person's mind** *slang* cause a person to have drug-induced hallucinations or a similar experience. **blow off 1** escape or allow (steam etc.) to escape forcibly. **2** *slang* break wind noisily. **blow out 1 a** extinguish by blowing. **b** send outwards by an explosion. **2** (of a tyre) burst. **3** (of a fuse etc.) melt. **blow over** fade away without serious consequences. **blow one's own trumpet** praise oneself. **blow one's top** (*N. Amer.* also **stack**) *colloq.* explode in rage. **blow up 1 a** shatter or destroy by an explosion. **b** erupt. **2** *Brit. colloq.* rebuke strongly. **3** inflate (a tyre etc.). **4** *colloq.* **a** enlarge (a photograph). **b** exaggerate. **5** *colloq.* arise. **6** *colloq.* lose one's temper. [Old English] □ **blowy** *adj.* (**blowier**, **blowiest**).

blow[2] *n.* **1** a hard stroke with a hand or weapon. **2** a sudden shock or misfortune. □ **come to blows** end up fighting. [15th-century coinage]

blow-by-blow *attrib.adj.* (of a description etc.) giving all the details in sequence.

blow-dry *v.tr.* arrange (the hair) while drying it with a hand-held dryer. □ **blow-dryer** *n.* (also **-drier**)

blower *n.* **1** in senses of BLOW[1] *v.* **2** a device for creating a current of air. **3** esp. *Brit. colloq.* a telephone.

blowfly *n.* (*pl.* **-flies**) a fly of the family Calliphoridae, laying its eggs on meat and carcasses, e.g. a bluebottle. ▷ BLUEBOTTLE

blowhole *n.* **1** ▼ the nostril of a whale, on the top of its head. ▷ CETACEAN. **2** a hole (esp. in ice) for breathing or fishing through. **3** a vent for smoke etc., in a tunnel etc.

blow job *n. coarse slang* an act of fellatio.

blowhole

BLOWHOLE OF A BOWHEAD WHALE (OVERHEAD VIEW)

blowlamp *n. Brit.* a portable device with a very hot flame used for burning off paint, soldering, etc.

blown *past part.* of BLOW[1].

blow-out *n.* **1** *colloq.* a burst tyre. **2** *colloq.* a melted fuse. **3** *colloq.* **a** a huge meal. **b** *N. Amer.* a large social gathering or party. **4** an uncontrolled uprush of oil or gas from a well. **5** *N. Amer. slang* a resounding defeat; failure.

blowpipe *n.* **1** a tube used esp. by primitive peoples for propelling darts by blowing. **2** a tube used to intensify the heat of a flame by blowing air or other gas through it at high pressure. **3** a tube used in glass-blowing.

blowtorch *n.* = BLOWLAMP.

blow-up *n.* **1** *colloq.* an enlargement (of a photograph etc.). **2** an explosion.

blowzy *adj.* (**blowzier**, **blowziest**) **1** coarse-looking; red-faced. **2** dishevelled. [from obsolete *blowze* 'beggar's wench']

blub *v.intr.* (**blubbed**, **blubbing**) *Brit. slang* sob.

blubber[1] ● *n.* ▼ whale fat. ● *v.* **1** *intr.* sob loudly. **2** *tr.* sob out (words). [Middle English] □ **blubberer** *n.* **blubbery** *adj.*

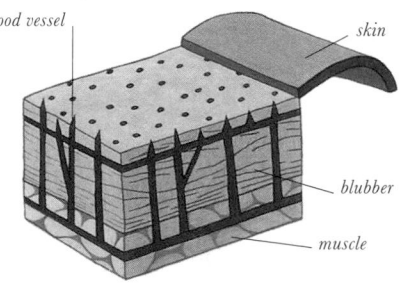

blood vessel   *skin*

blubber

muscle

BLUBBER: SECTION THROUGH WHALE BLUBBER

blubber[2] *adj.* (of the lips) swollen, protruding. [earlier *blabber, blobber*]

bludgeon ● *n.* a club with a heavy end. ● *v.tr.* **1** beat with a bludgeon. **2** coerce. [18th-century coinage]

bludger *n. Austral. & NZ slang* **1** a scrounger. **2** a loafer. [originally British slang, literally 'pimp']

blue[1] ● *adj.* (**bluer**, **bluest**) **1** having a colour like that of a clear sky. **2** sad, gloomy (*feel blue*). **3** pornographic (*a blue film*). **4** with bluish skin through cold, anger, etc. **5** *Brit.* politically conservative. ● *n.* **1** a blue colour or pigment. **2** blue clothes or material (*dressed in blue*). **3** *Brit.* **a** a person who has represented a university (esp. Oxford or Cambridge) in a sport. **b** this distinction. **4** *Brit.* a supporter of the Conservative Party. **5** *Austral. slang* **a** an argument or row. **b** (as a nickname) a red-headed person. **6** (*prec. by the*) the clear sky. ● *v.tr.* (**blues**, **blued**, **bluing** or **blueing**) make blue. □ **once in a blue moon** very rarely. **out of the blue** unexpectedly. [from (Old) French *bleu*]

blue[2] *v.tr.* (**blues**, **blued**, **bluing** or **blueing**) *Brit. slang* squander (money).

blue baby *n.* a baby with a blue complexion from lack of oxygen in the blood due to a congenital defect.

bluebell *n.* **1** ◀ a woodland plant of the lily family, *Hyacinthoides nonscripta*, with clusters of bell-shaped blue flowers on a stem arising from a rhizome. **2** *Sc.* = HAREBELL.

blueberry *n.* (*pl.* **-ies**) **1** any of several plants of the genus *Vaccinium* with small blue-black edible fruit, sometimes cultivated. **2** the fruit of these plants.

bluebird *n.* any of various N. American songbirds of the thrush family, esp. of the genus *Sialia*, with distinctive blue plumage usu. on the back or head.

BLUEBELL (*Hyacinthoides nonscripta*)

B

blue-black n. & adj. ● n. a black colour with a tinge of blue. ● adj. of this colour.

blue blood n. **1** noble birth. **2** a person of noble lineage. □ **blue-blooded** adj.

bluebottle n. ▼ a large buzzing fly, *Calliphora vomitoria*, with a metallic-blue body; a blowfly.

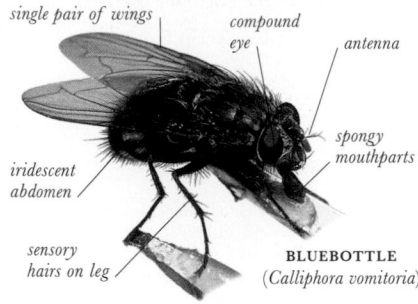

single pair of wings
compound eye
antenna
spongy mouthparts
iridescent abdomen
sensory hairs on leg

BLUEBOTTLE
(*Calliphora vomitoria*)

blue cheese n. cheese produced with veins of a bluish fungus, e.g. Stilton and Danish Blue. ▷ CHEESE

blue-chip attrib.adj. (of shares) of reliable investment, though less secure than gilt-edged stock. [from *blue chip*, a gambling counter of high value]

blue-collar attrib.adj. (of a worker or work) manual; industrial.

blue-eyed boy n. esp. *Brit. colloq.* usu. *derog.* a favourite.

blue funk n. *slang* **1** esp. *Brit.* a state of great terror or panic. **2** esp. *N. Amer.* a state of mild depression.

bluegrass n. **1** any of several bluish-green grasses, esp. of Kentucky. **2** a kind of instrumental country and western music characterized by virtuosic playing of banjos, guitars, etc.

blue-green alga n. = CYANOBACTERIUM.

bluegum n. ▶ any tree of the genus *Eucalyptus*, esp. *E. regnans* with blue-green aromatic leaves.

blue-pencil v.tr. (**-pencilled**, **-pencilling**; *US* **-penciled**, **-penciling**) censor (a film etc.).

Blue Peter n. a blue flag with a white square raised on board a ship leaving port.

blueprint n. **1** a photographic print of the final stage of esp. engineering plans in white on a blue background. **2** a detailed plan, esp. in the early stages of a project or idea.

BLUEGUM
(*Eucalyptus globulus*)

blue ribbon n. **1** a high honour. **2** *Brit.* the ribbon of the Order of the Garter.

blue rinse n. a preparation for tinting grey hair.

blues n.pl. **1** (prec. by *the*) a bout of depression. **2** (prec. by *the*; often treated as *sing.*) melancholic music of black American folk origin, often in a twelve-bar sequence. □ **bluesy** adj. (in sense 2).

bluestocking n. usu. *derog.* an intellectual or literary woman. [originally a (male) frequenter of the 'blue-stocking' literary assemblies held in London *c.*1750]

blue tit n. ◀ a common tit, *Parus caeruleus*, with a distinct blue crest on a black and white head.

blue whale n. a rorqual, *Balaenoptera musculus*, the largest known living mammal. ▷ WHALE

bluff¹ ● v. **1** intr. make a pretence of strength or confidence to gain an advantage. **2** tr. mislead by bluffing. ● n. an act of bluffing. □ **call a person's bluff** challenge a person

BLUE TIT
(*Parus caeruleus*)

thought to be bluffing. [19th-century coinage, originally used in poker: from Dutch *bluffen* 'to brag']

bluff² ● adj. **1** (of a cliff, or a ship's bows) having a vertical or steep broad front. **2** (of a person or manner) blunt, frank, hearty. ● n. a steep cliff or headland. [17th-century nautical coinage] □ **blufffly** adv. (in sense 2 of adj.). **bluffness** n. (in sense 2 of adj.).

bluish adj. somewhat blue.

blunder ● n. a clumsy or foolish mistake. ● v. **1** intr. make a blunder. **2** tr. deal incompetently with. **3** intr. move about clumsily. [Middle English] □ **blunderer** n. **blunderingly** adv.

blunderbuss n. *hist.* ▼ a short large-bored gun firing balls or slugs. [alteration of Dutch *donderbus* 'thunder gun']

flintlock mechanism
flared muzzle
barrel
ramrod

BLUNDERBUSS: 18TH-CENTURY
FLINTLOCK BLUNDERBUSS

blunt ● adj. **1** (of a knife, pencil, etc.) lacking a sharp edge or point; having a worn-down point or edge. **2** (of a person or manner) direct, outspoken. ● v.tr. make blunt or less sharp. [Middle English in sense 'dull, insensitive' (of perceptions or intellect)] □ **bluntly** adv. (in sense 2 of adj.). **bluntness** n.

blur ● v. (**blurred**, **blurring**) **1** tr. & intr. make or become unclear or less distinct. **2** tr. smear; partially efface. ● n. something that appears or sounds indistinct or unclear. [16th-century coinage] □ **blurry** adj. (**blurrier**, **blurriest**).

blurb n. a description of a book as promotion by its publishers. [coined by G. Burgess, American humorist, 1866–1951]

blurt v.tr. (usu. foll. by *out*) utter abruptly, thoughtlessly, or tactlessly.

blush ● v.intr. **1 a** develop a pink tinge in the face from embarrassment or shame. **b** (of the face) redden in this way. **2** feel embarrassed or ashamed. ● n. **1** the act of blushing. **2** a pink tinge. [Middle English]

blusher n. a cosmetic used to give a warmth of colour to the face. ▷ MAKE-UP

bluster ● v.intr. **1** behave pompously and boisterously. **2** (of the wind etc.) blow fiercely. ● n. **1** noisily self-assertive talk. **2** empty threats. [16th-century coinage] □ **blusterer** n. **blustery** adj.

BM abbr. **1** British Museum. **2** Bachelor of Medicine.

BMA abbr. British Medical Association.

B-movie n. a supporting film in a cinema programme; a low-budget film.

B.Mus. abbr. Bachelor of Music.

BMX n. a kind of bicycle used for racing on a dirt track. [abbreviation of *bicycle moto-cross*]

Bn. abbr. Battalion.

bn. abbr. billion.

BO abbr. *colloq.* body odour.

boa n. **1** a constrictor snake of the family Boidae. **2** any snake which is a constrictor, e.g. an Old World python. **3** a long thin stole made of feathers or fur. [Latin]

boa constrictor n. ▼ a large snake, *Boa constrictor*, native to tropical America and the W. Indies, which crushes its prey. ▷ SNAKE

boar n. **1** (in full **wild boar**) the tusked wild pig, *Sus scrofa*, from which domestic pigs are descended. **2** an uncastrated male pig. **3** its flesh. **4** a male guinea pig etc. [Old English]

board ● n. **1 a** a flat thin piece of sawn timber, usu. long and narrow. **b** a piece of material resembling this, made from compressed fibres. **c** a thin slab of wood or a similar substance, often with a covering, used for any of various purposes (*ironing board*; *noticeboard*). **d** thick stiff card used in bookbinding. **2** the provision of regular meals, usu. with accommodation, for payment. **3** the directors of a company; any other specially constituted administrative body. **4** (in *pl.*) the stage of a theatre (cf. *tread the boards*). ● v. **1** tr. **a** go on board (a ship etc.). **b** force one's way on board (a ship etc.) in attack. **2 a** intr. receive meals and lodging for payment. **b** tr. (often foll. by *out*) arrange accommodation away from home for (esp. a child). **c** tr. provide (a lodger etc.) with regular meals. **3** tr. (usu. foll. by *up*) cover with boards; seal. □ **go by the board** be neglected, omitted, or discarded. **on board** on or on to a ship, aircraft, oil rig, etc. **take on board** consider (a new idea etc.). [Old English]

boarder n. **1** a person who boards (see BOARD v. 2a), esp. a pupil at a boarding school. **2** a person who boards a ship, esp. an enemy.

board game n. a game played on a board.

boarding house n. an establishment providing board and lodging, esp. *Brit.* to holidaymakers.

boarding school n. a school where pupils are resident in term-time.

boardroom n. a room in which a board of directors etc. meets regularly.

boardsailing n. = WINDSURFING. □ **boardsailor** n. (also **boardsailer**).

boardwalk n. *N. Amer.* **1** a wooden walkway across sand, marsh, etc. **2** a promenade along a beach.

boast ● v. **1** intr. declare one's achievements, possessions, or abilities with indulgent pride and satisfaction. **2** tr. own or have as something praiseworthy etc. (*boasts magnificent views*). ● n. **1** an act of boasting. **2** something one is proud of. [from Anglo-French *bost*] □ **boaster** n. **boastingly** adv.

boastful adj. given to or characterized by boasting. □ **boastfully** adv. **boastfulness** n.

boat ● n. **1** ▶ a small vessel propelled on water by an engine, oars, or sails. **2** (in general use) a ship of any size. **3** a boat-shaped jug used for holding sauce etc. ● v.intr. travel in a boat, esp. for pleasure. □ **in the same boat** sharing the same adverse circumstances. **push the boat out** *Brit. colloq.* celebrate lavishly. [Old English]

boater n. a flat-topped hardened straw hat with a brim (originally worn while boating).

boat-hook n. a long pole with a hook and a spike at one end, for moving boats.

boathouse n. a shed at the edge of a river, lake, etc., for housing boats.

boating n. rowing or sailing in boats as a sport or form of recreation.

boatman n. (*pl.* **-men**) a person who hires out boats or provides transport by boat.

boat people n. refugees who have left a country by sea.

boat race n. a race between rowing crews, esp. (**the Boat Race**) the annual one between Oxford and Cambridge universities.

boatswain /boh-sŭn/ n. (also **bo'sun, bosun, bo's'n**) a ship's officer in charge of equipment and the crew. [Old English]

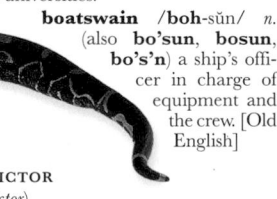

prey

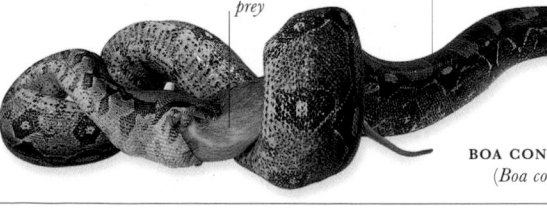

BOA CONSTRICTOR
(*Boa constrictor*)

BOAT

The term boat is generally applied to small, light, single-decked craft that travel on inland and coastal waters. The power source and design is determined by the role they fulfil. Rudimentary vessels, such as the logboat canoe, have been used since ancient times to transport people and goods, and craft like these still play an important role in both transportation and fishing across the world. However, many boats today are used exclusively for leisure and sport. Powerboats are designed mainly for racing, whereas dinghies and yachts are used for both competitive sailing and cruising. Other craft are built for more specific, practical functions. Lifeboats, for example, are used to rescue other vessels in distress, and so are designed to be rugged, buoyant, and manoeuvrable.

EXAMPLES OF BOATS

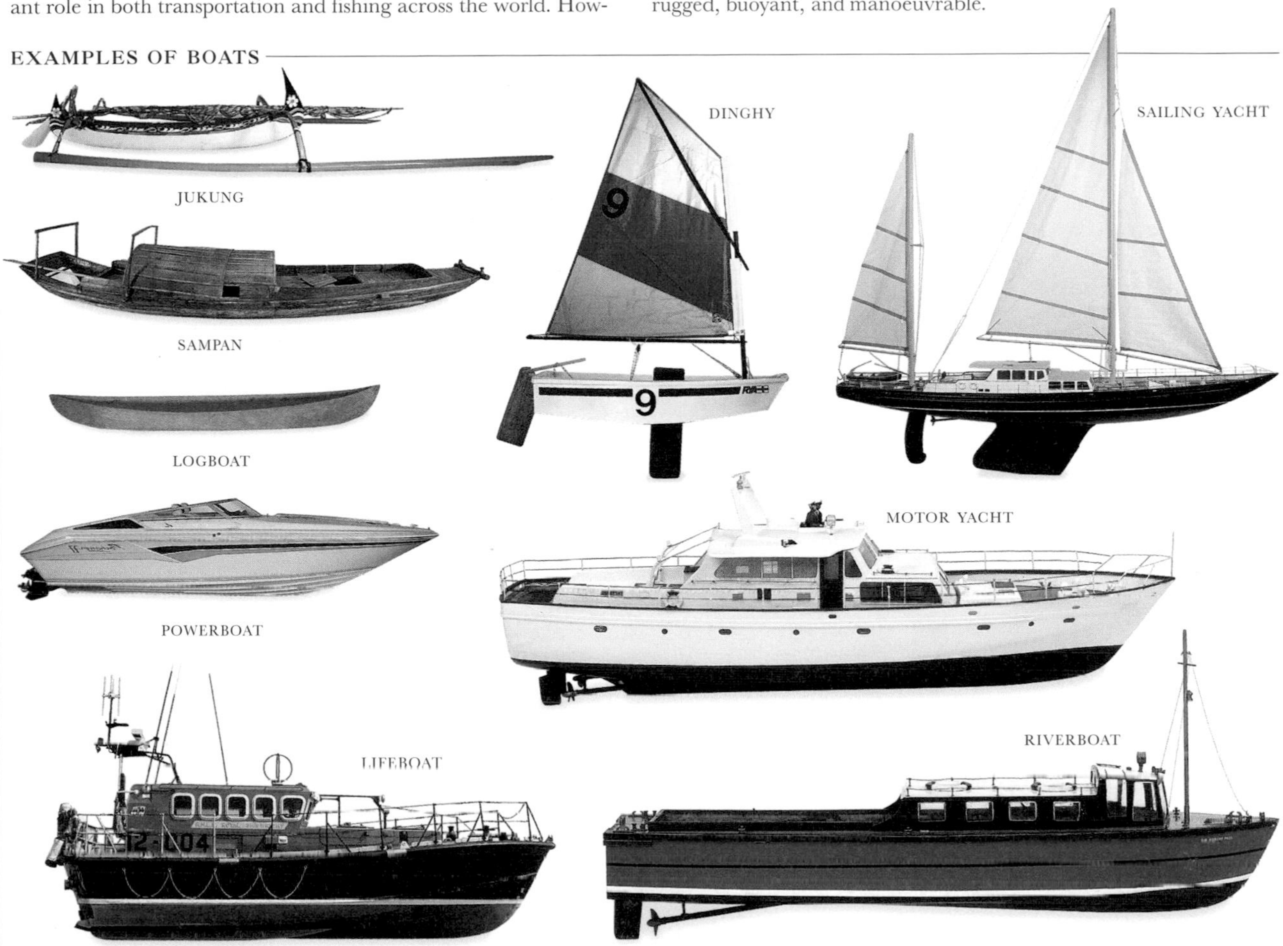

JUKUNG

SAMPAN

LOGBOAT

POWERBOAT

DINGHY

SAILING YACHT

MOTOR YACHT

LIFEBOAT

RIVERBOAT

---

boat-train *n.* a train scheduled to meet or go on a boat.

bob¹ ● *v.intr.* (**bobbed**, **bobbing**) **1** move quickly up and down. **2** (usu. foll. by *back*, *up*) **a** bounce buoyantly. **b** emerge suddenly; become active again. **3** curtsy. **4** (foll. by *for*) try to catch with the mouth alone (fruit etc. floating or hanging). ● *n.* **1** a jerking or bouncing movement, esp. upward. **2** a curtsy. [14th-century coinage]

bob² ● *n.* **1** a short hairstyle for women and children. **2** a weight on a pendulum, plumb line, or kite tail. **3** a horse's docked tail. ● *v.tr.* (**bobbed**, **bobbing**) cut (a woman's or child's hair) so that it hangs clear of the shoulders. [Middle English]

bob³ *n.* (*pl.* same) *Brit. slang hist.* a shilling (now = 5 decimal pence). [19th-century coinage]

bobbin *n.* **1** ◄ a cylinder or cone holding thread, yarn, wire, etc., used esp. in weaving and machine sewing. **2** a spool or reel. [from French *bobine*]

bobbin lace *n.* lace made by hand with thread wound on bobbins.

bobble *n.* a small woolly or tufted ball as a decoration or trimming. [based on BOB²] □ **bobbly** *adj.*

BOBBIN: COTTON REEL

bobby¹ *n.* (*pl.* **-ies**) *Brit. colloq.* a police officer. [from Sir *Robert Peel*, 1788–1850, founder of the Metropolitan Police Force]

bobby² *n.* (*pl.* **-ies**) (in full **bobby calf**) an unweaned calf slaughtered for veal. [dialect]

bobby-dazzler *n. Brit. colloq.* a remarkable or excellent person or thing. [dialect]

bobby pin *n. N. Amer., Austral., & NZ* a flat hairpin.

bobby socks *n.pl.* esp. *N. Amer.* short socks reaching just above the ankle. [based on BOB²] □ **bobby-soxer** *n.*

bobcat *n.* ▼ a small N. American lynx, *Felis rufus*, with a spotted reddish-brown coat and a short tail.

thick sidewhiskers

BOBCAT (*Felis rufus*)

bobsled *n. N. Amer.* = BOBSLEIGH. □ **bobsledding** *n.*

bobsleigh *n.* ▼ a mechanically steered and braked sledge used for racing down a steep ice-covered run. □ **bobsleighing** *n.*

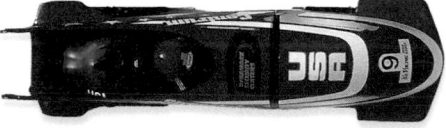

BOBSLEIGH: TWO-MAN BOBSLEIGH

Boche *n. slang derog.* (prec. by *the*) Germans, esp. German soldiers, collectively. [French slang, originally in sense 'rascal', applied to Germans in the First World War]

BOD *abbr.* biochemical oxygen demand.

bod *n. colloq.* **1** *Brit.* a person. **2** *N. Amer.* a body.

bodacious *adj. N. Amer. slang* **1** remarkable, excellent. **2** esp. *US* bold, audacious. [blend of BOLD and AUDACIOUS]

bode *v.tr.* **1** portend, promise. **2** foresee, foretell (evil). □ **bode well** (or **ill**) show good (or bad) signs for the future. [Old English]

bodge *Brit.* var. of BOTCH.

BODY

The human body consists of a number of interacting 'systems'. The skeleton forms a rigid framework, which, attached to the muscles, facilitates movement initiated by the nervous system – responsible for the body's reaction to stimuli. Hormones, produced by the endocrine system, control many functions, including growth and developmental changes such as puberty. The cardiovascular system circulates blood around the body, delivering oxygen and nutrients and collecting carbon dioxide and waste, while the respiratory system exchanges carbon dioxide for inhaled oxygen. The lymphatic system fights infection. The digestive system derives energy and nutrients for growth and repair from food, and with the urinary system eliminates waste; the urinary system also helps to regulate chemicals in the body. The reproductive system is concerned with producing offspring.

SYSTEMS OF THE HUMAN BODY

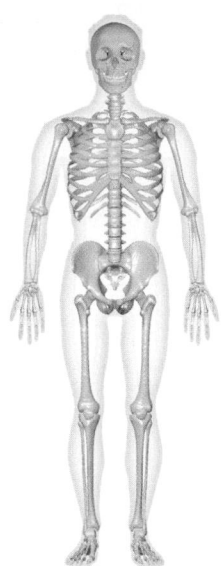

SKELETON
▷ SKELETON

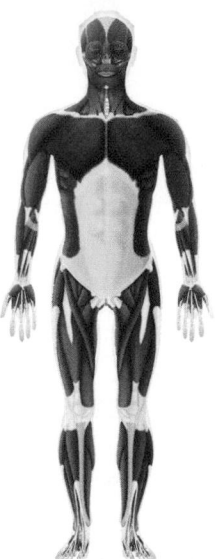

MUSCULAR SYSTEM
▷ MUSCULATURE

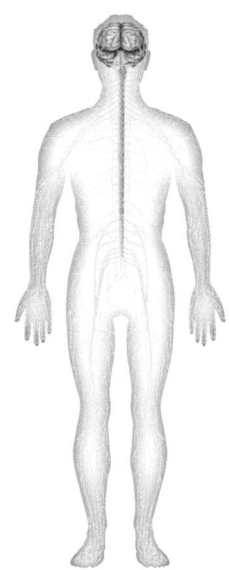

NERVOUS SYSTEM
▷ AUTONOMIC NERVOUS SYSTEM, NERVOUS SYSTEM, PERIPHERAL NERVOUS SYSTEM

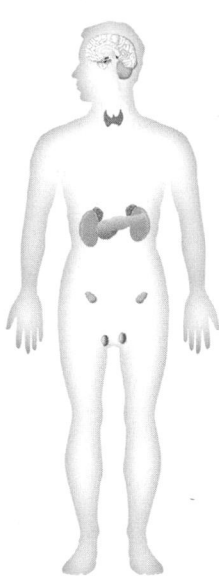

ENDOCRINE SYSTEM
▷ ENDOCRINE

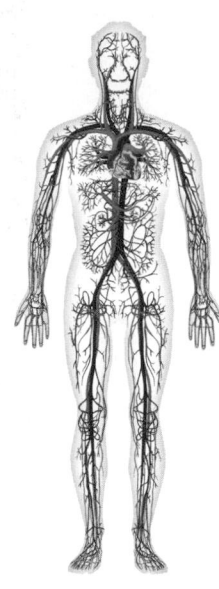

CARDIOVASCULAR SYSTEM
▷ CARDIOVASCULAR

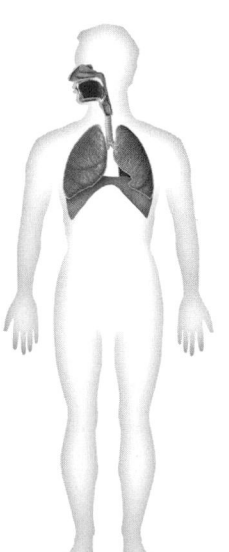

RESPIRATORY SYSTEM
▷ RESPIRATION

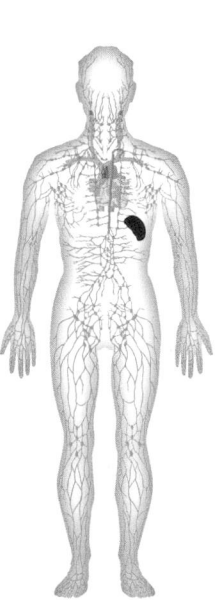

LYMPHATIC SYSTEM
▷ LYMPHATIC SYSTEM

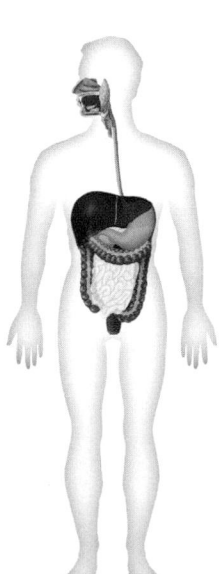

DIGESTIVE SYSTEM
▷ DIGESTION

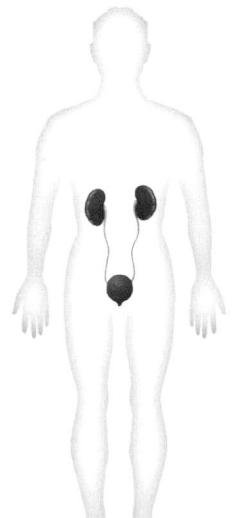

URINARY SYSTEM
▷ URINARY SYSTEM

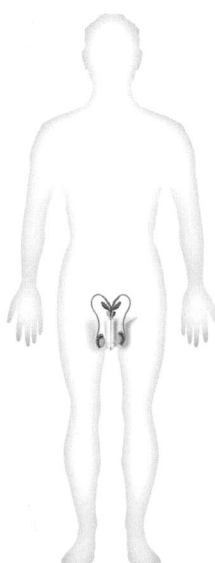

REPRODUCTIVE ORGANS
▷ REPRODUCTIVE ORGANS

bodice *n.* **1** the part of a woman's dress (excluding sleeves) which is above the waist. **2** a woman's undergarment for the same part of the body. [originally *(pair of) bodies* 'stays, corsets']

bodiless *adj.* **1** lacking a body. **2** insubstantial.

bodily ● *adj.* of or concerning the body. ● *adv.* **1** as a whole (*threw them bodily*). **2** as a person.

bodkin *n.* **1** a blunt thick needle with a large eye. **2** a long pin for fastening hair. **3** a small pointed instrument. [Middle English]

body ● *n.* (*pl.* **-ies**) **1** ◄ the physical structure, including the bones, flesh, and organs, of a person or an animal. **2** the trunk apart from the head and the limbs. **3** a woman's stretch undergarment which covers the torso, fastening at the crotch. **4 a** the main or central part of a thing (*body of the car*). **b** the majority (*body of opinion*). **5 a** a group of persons regarded collectively (*governing body*). **b** (usu. foll. by *of*) a collection (*body of facts*). **6** a quantity (*body of water*). **7** a material object (*celestial body*). **8** *colloq.* a person. **9** a substantial quality of flavour, tone, etc. ● *v.tr.* (**-ies**, **-ied**) (usu. foll. by *forth*) give body or substance to. [Old English] □ **-bodied** *adj.* (in *comb.*: *able-bodied*).

body bag *n.* a bag for carrying a corpse.

body blow *n.* a severe setback.

body-building *n.* the practice of strengthening the body, esp. enlarging the muscles, by exercise. □ **bodybuilder** *n.*

body-check ● *n.* a deliberate obstruction of one player by another. ● *v.tr.* obstruct in this way.

bodyguard *n.* a person or group of persons escorting and protecting another person.

body language *n.* the process of communicating through conscious or unconscious gestures and poses.

body odour *n.* the smell of the human body, esp. when unpleasant.

body piercing *n.* the piercing of holes in parts of the body other than the ear lobes.

body politic *n.* the nation or state as a corporate body.

body shop *n.* a workshop where repairs to the bodywork of vehicles are carried out.

body stocking *n.* a woman's undergarment which covers the torso.

bodysuit *n.* a close-fitting one-piece stretch garment for women.

body wave *n.* a soft light permanent wave designed to give the hair fullness.

bodywork *n.* the outer shell of a vehicle.

Boer /boor/ *n.* a South African of Dutch descent. [Dutch, literally 'farmer']

boffin *n.* esp. *Brit. colloq.* a person engaged in scientific (esp. military) research. [20th-century coinage]

bog ● *n.* **1 a** ▲ wet, usu. peaty, spongy ground. **b** a stretch of such ground. **2** *Brit. slang* a lavatory. ● *v.tr.* (**bogged**, **bogging**) (foll. by *down*; usu. in *passive*) impede (*bogged down by difficulties*). □ **bog standard** *Brit. slang* basic, standard, unexceptional. [Irish or Gaelic, from *bog* 'soft'] □ **boggy** *adj.* (**boggier**, **boggiest**). **bogginess** *n.*

bogey[1] *n. Golf* (*pl.* **-eys**) a score of one stroke more than par at any hole.

bogey[2] *n.* (also **bogy**) (*pl.* **-eys** or **-ies**) **1** an evil or mischievous spirit. **2** an awkward thing or circumstance. **3** *Brit. slang* a piece of nasal mucus. [19th-century coinage, originally a proper name applied to the Devil]

bogeyman *n.* (also **bogyman**) (*pl.* **-men**) a person (real or imaginary) causing fear or difficulty.

boggle *v.intr. colloq.* **1** be baffled (esp. *the mind boggles*). **2** (usu. foll. by *about*, *at*) hesitate.

bogie *n.* esp. *Brit.* a wheeled undercarriage pivoted below the end of a rail vehicle. ▷ LOCOMOTIVE. [19th-century northern dialect word]

bogus *adj.* sham, spurious. [19th-century US word] □ **bogusly** *adv.* **bogusness** *n.*

bogy var. of BOGEY[2].

BOG

Bogs form where plants invade lakes and pools, and where waterlogged conditions prevent those plants decomposing once they have died. As a result, their remains build up to form peat. Once the peat has begun to accumulate, the plants that grow on its surface – such as *Sphagnum* mosses – steadily add to it as they die. In blanket bogs, the peat forms connected pockets. In raised bogs, it forms a large dome that can be over 1 km (0.5 mile) across.

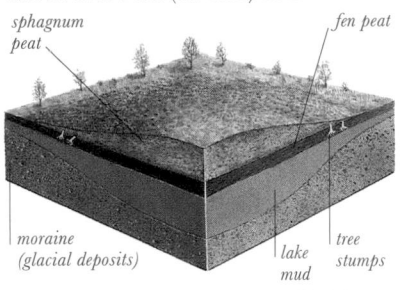

SECTION THROUGH A RAISED BOG

bogyman var. of BOGEYMAN.

Bohemian ● *n.* **1** a native of Bohemia, a former kingdom in central Europe; a Czech. **2** (also **bohemian**) a socially unconventional person. ● *adj.* **1** of or characteristic of Bohemia or its people. **2** socially unconventional. [sense 2: from French *bohémien* 'gypsy']

boil[1] ● *v.* **1** *intr.* **a** (of a liquid) start to bubble up and turn into vapour. **b** (of a vessel) contain boiling liquid (*the kettle is boiling*). **2 a** *tr.* bring (a liquid or vessel) to a temperature at which it boils. **b** *tr.* cook (food) by boiling. **c** *intr.* (of food) be cooked by boiling. **d** *tr.* subject to the heat of boiling water, e.g. to clean. **3** *intr.* **a** (of the sea etc.) seethe like boiling water. **b** (of a person or feelings) be agitated by anger. ● *n.* the act or process of boiling; boiling point (*on the boil*). □ **boil down 1** reduce volume by boiling. **2** reduce to essentials. **3** (foll. by *to*) signify basically. **boil over 1** spill over in boiling **2** lose one's temper. [from French *bullire* 'to bubble']

boil[2] *n.* an inflamed pus-filled swelling caused by infection of a hair follicle etc. [Old English]

boiled sweet *n. Brit.* a hard sweet made of boiled sugar.

boiler *n.* **1** a fuel-burning apparatus for heating water, esp. to supply a central heating system. **2** a tank for heating water to steam under pressure. ▷ STEAM ENGINE. **3** a metal tub for boiling laundry etc. **4** *Brit.* a fowl etc. suitable for cooking only by boiling.

boiler suit *n. Brit.* a one-piece suit worn as overalls for heavy manual work.

boiling *adj.* (also **boiling hot**) *colloq.* very hot.

boiling point *n.* the temperature at which a liquid starts to boil.

boisterous *adj.* **1** (of a person) rough; noisily exuberant. **2** (of the weather etc.) stormy. [variant of Middle English *boist(u)ous*] □ **boisterously** *adv.* **boisterousness** *n.*

bold *adj.* **1** confidently assertive; adventurous. **2** impudent. **3** vivid, distinct (*bold colour*). **4** (in full **boldface** or **boldfaced**) printed in a thick black typeface. [Old English *bald* 'dangerous'] □ **boldly** *adv.* **boldness** *n.*

bole *n.* the stem or trunk of a tree. [from Old Norse *bolr*]

bolero /bŏ-**lair**-oh/ *n.* (*pl.* **-os**) **1** a Spanish dance or music in simple triple time. **2** also /**bol**-ĕ-roh/ a woman's short open jacket. [Spanish]

boll *n.* a rounded capsule containing seeds, esp. flax or cotton. [from Middle Dutch *bolle* 'rounded object']

bollard *n.* **1** *Brit.* a short post in the road, esp. as part of a traffic island. **2** a short post on a quay or ship for securing a rope. [Middle English]

bollocking *n.* esp. *Brit. coarse slang* a severe reprimand.

bollocks *n.* (also **ballocks**) esp. *Brit. coarse slang* **1** the testicles. **2** nonsense, rubbish. [Old English]

boloney var. of BALONEY.

Bolshevik *n.* **1** *hist.* a member of the radical faction of the Russian Social Democratic party, which became the Communist party in 1918. **2** a Russian communist. **3** (in general use) any revolutionary socialist. [Russian, literally 'a member of the majority'] □ **Bolshevism** *n.* **Bolshevist** *n.*

Bolshie (also **Bolshy**) *slang* ● *adj.* (usu. **bolshie**) **1** *Brit.* uncooperative, rebellious. **2** socialist. ● *n.* (*pl.* **-ies**) a Bolshevik. □ **bolshiness** *n.* (in sense 1 of *adj.*).

bolster ● *n.* **1** a long thick pillow. **2** a pad or support, esp. in a machine. ● *v.tr.* (usu. foll. by *up*) **1** reinforce (*bolstered our morale*). **2** prop up. [Old English] □ **bolsterer** *n.*

bolt[1] ● *n.* **1** a sliding bar and socket used to fasten a door etc. **2** a large usu. metal pin with a head, used to hold things together. **3** a discharge of lightning. **4** a sudden dash for freedom. **5** an arrow for shooting from a crossbow. **6** a roll of fabric (originally as a measure). ● *v.* **1** *tr.* fasten or lock with a bolt. **2** *tr.* (foll. by *in*, *out*) keep from leaving or entering by bolting a door. **3** *tr.* fasten together with bolts. **4** *intr.* dash suddenly away. **5** *tr.* gulp down (food) unchewed. **6** *intr.* (of a plant) run to seed. ● *adv.* (usu. in **bolt upright**) rigidly, stiffly. □ **a bolt from the blue** a complete surprise. [Old English in sense 'arrow'] □ **bolter** *n.* (in sense 4 of *v.*).

bolt[2] *v.tr.* (also **boult**) sift (flour etc.). [from Old French *bulter*]

bomb ● *n.* **1 a** ◄ a container with explosive, gas, etc., designed to explode on impact or by means of a mechanism, lit fuse, etc. **b** an ordinary object fitted with an explosive device (*letter bomb*). **2** (prec. by *the*) the atomic or hydrogen bomb. **3** *Brit. slang* a large sum of money (*cost a bomb*). **4** *N. Amer. colloq.* a bad failure (esp. a theatrical one). ● *v.* **1** *tr.* drop bombs on. **2** *tr.* (foll. by *out*) drive out by using bombs. **3** *intr.* throw bombs. **4** *intr.* esp. *US slang* fail badly. **5** *intr.* (usu. foll. by *along*, *off*) *colloq.* go very quickly. □ **go down a bomb** *Brit. colloq.*, often *iron.* be very well received. [from Greek *bombos* 'boom']

BOMB: GERMAN SECOND WORLD WAR INCENDIARY DEVICES

bombard *v.tr.* **1** attack with bombs, shells, etc. **2** (often foll. by *with*) subject to persistent questioning etc. **3** *Physics* direct a stream of high-speed particles at (a substance). [based on medieval Latin *bombarda* 'a stone-throwing engine'] □ **bombardment** *n.*

bombardier *n.* **1** *Brit.* a non-commissioned officer in the artillery. **2** *N. Amer.* a member of a bomber crew responsible for sighting and releasing bombs.

bombasine var. of BOMBAZINE.

bombast *n.* pompous or extravagant language. [from medieval Latin *bombax*, alteration of *bombyx* 'silk'] □ **bombastic** *adj.* **bombastically** *adv.*

Bombay duck *n.* a dried fish, esp. bummalo, usu. eaten with curried dishes. [corruption of BUMMALO]

bombazine *n.* (also **bombasine**) a twilled dress material of worsted with or without an admixture of silk or cotton. [based on Greek *bombux* 'silkworm']

bomb disposal *n.* the defusing or removal and detonation of an unexploded bomb.

bombe /bomb/ *n.* a dome-shaped dish or confection, often frozen. [French, literally 'bomb']

B

starboard split rudder — weapon bay rear bulkhead — radar-resistant coating

fuel tank —

weapon bay front bulkhead —

two-seater cockpit

BOMBER: OVERHEAD VIEW OF AN AMERICAN STEALTH BOMBER

bomber *n.* **1** ▲ an aircraft equipped to carry and drop bombs. ▷ FIGHTER. **2** a person using bombs, esp. illegally.

bomber jacket *n.* a short leather or cloth jacket tightly gathered at the waist and cuffs.

bombshell *n.* **1** an overwhelming surprise or disappointment. **2** an artillery bomb. **3** *slang* a very attractive woman (*blonde bombshell*).

bomb-site *n.* an area where buildings have been destroyed by bombs.

bomb squad *n.* a division of a police force investigating crimes involving bombs.

bona fide /boh-nă fy-di/ ● *adj.* genuine; sincere. ● *adv.* genuinely; sincerely. [Latin, literally 'in good faith']

bona fides *n.* **1** *esp. Law* an honest intention; sincerity. **2** (treated as *pl.*) *colloq.* documentary evidence of acceptability. [Latin, literally 'good faith']

bonanza *n.* **1** a source of wealth or prosperity. **2** a large output (esp. of a mine). **3 a** prosperity; good luck. **b** a run of good luck. [Spanish, literally 'fair weather']

bonce *n. Brit.* **1** *slang* the head. **2** a large marble. [19th-century coinage]

bond ● *n.* **1 a** a thing that ties another down or together. **b** (usu. in *pl.*) a thing restraining bodily freedom (*broke his bonds*). **2** (often in *pl.*) **a** a uniting force (*sisterly bond*). **b** a restraint; a responsibility (*bonds of duty*). **3** a binding engagement (*his word is his bond*). **4** *Commerce* **a** a debenture. **b** a financial guarantee against the collapse of a company, esp. a tour operator. **5** adhesiveness. **6** *Law* a deed by which a person is bound to make payment to another. ● *v.* **1** *tr.* **a** (bricks) overlapping. **b** bind together (resin with fibres, etc.). **2** *intr.* adhere; hold together. **3** *tr.* connect with a bond. **4** *tr.* place (goods) in bond. **5 a** *intr.* become emotionally attached. **b** *tr.* link by an emotional or psychological bond. □ **in bond** (of goods) stored in a bonded warehouse until the importer pays the duty owing. [Middle English variant of BAND[1]]

bondage *n.* **1** slavery. **2** subjection to constraint, obligation, etc. **3** sadomasochistic practices, including the use of physical restraints or mental enslavement. [from Anglo-Latin *bondagium*]

bonded *adj.* **1** (of goods) placed in bond. **2** (of a travel company etc.) protected by a bond (see BOND *n.* 4b).

bonded warehouse *n.* a customs-controlled warehouse for the retention of imported goods until the duty owed is paid.

bond paper *n.* high-quality writing paper.

bondsman *n.* (*pl.* **-men**) **1** a slave. **2** a person in thrall to another. [based on archaic *bond* 'serf']

bone ● *n.* **1** ▶ any of the pieces of hard tissue making up the skeleton in vertebrates. ▷ SKELETON. **2** (in *pl.*) **a** the skeleton, esp. as remains after death. **b** the body, esp. as a seat of intuitive feeling (*felt it in my bones*). **3 a** the calcified material of which bones consist. **b** a similar substance such as ivory. **4** a thing made of bone. **5** (in *pl.*) the essential part of a thing (esp. *bare bones*). **6** a strip of stiffening in a corset etc. ● *v.tr.* **1** take out the bones from (meat or fish). **2** stiffen (a garment) with bone etc. **3** *Brit. slang* steal. □ **bone up** (often foll. by *on*) *colloq.* study (a

subject) intensively. **close to** (or **near**) **the bone 1 a** tactless to the point of offensiveness. **b** near the limit of decency. **2** destitute; hard up. **have a bone to pick** (usu. foll. by *with*) have a cause for dispute (with another person). **make no bones about 1** admit or allow without fuss. **2** not hesitate or scruple. [Old English] □ **boneless** *adj.*

bone china *n.* fine china made of clay mixed with the ash from bones.

bone dry *adj.* completely dry.

bonehead *n. slang* a stupid person. □ **boneheaded** *adj.*

bone idle *adj.* utterly idle.

bone marrow see MARROW 2.

bonemeal *n.* crushed or ground bones used esp. as a fertilizer.

bone of contention *n.* a source or ground of dispute.

boneshaker *n.* **1** a decrepit or uncomfortable old vehicle. **2** an old type of bicycle with solid tyres.

bonfire *n.* a large open-air fire. [earlier *bonefire*, bones being the chief material used]

Bonfire Night *n. Brit.* 5 Nov., on which fireworks are displayed and an effigy of Guy Fawkes burnt (see GUY[1]).

bongo *n.* (*pl.* **-os** or **-oes**) either of a pair of small long-bodied drums usu. held between the knees and played with the fingers. [from Latin American Spanish *bongó*]

bonhomie /bon-ŏ-mee/ *n.* good-natured friendliness. [French] □ **bonhomous** *adj.*

bonito *n.* (*pl.* **-os**) any of various striped tuna of warm seas. [Spanish]

bonk ● *v.* **1** *tr.* hit resoundingly. **2** *intr.* bang; bump. **3** *Brit. coarse slang* **a** *intr.* have sexual intercourse. **b** *tr.* have sexual intercourse with. ● *n.* an instance of bonking (*a bonk on the head*).

bonkers *predic.adj. slang* crazy. [20th-century coinage]

bon mot /bon moh/ *n.* (*pl.* **bons mots** *pronunc.* same or /bon **mohz**/) a witty saying. [French, literally 'good word']

bonnet *n.* **1 a** a hat tied under the chin and usu. with a brim framing the face. **b** a beret-like hat worn by men and boys in Scotland. **c** *colloq.* any hat. **2** *Brit.* a hinged cover over the engine of a motor vehicle. ▷ CAR. [from medieval Latin *abonnis* 'headgear']

bonny *adj.* (also **bonnie**) (**bonnier, bonniest**) esp. *Sc. & N.Engl.* **1 a** physically attractive. **b** healthy-looking. **2** good, fine, pleasant. [15th-century coinage] □ **bonnily** *adv.* **bonniness** *n.*

bonsai *n.* (*pl.* same) **1** the art of cultivating ornamental artificially dwarfed varieties of trees and shrubs. **2** (also **bonsai tree**) ◀ a tree or shrub grown by this method. [Japanese, literally 'tray planting']

BONSAI TREE: ENGLISH OAK (*Quercus robur*)

bonus *n.* **1** an unsought or unexpected extra benefit. **2 a** a gratuity to employees beyond their normal pay. **b** *Brit.* an extra dividend or issue paid to shareholders. **c** *Brit.* a distribution of profits to holders of an insurance policy. [Latin, literally 'good']

bon vivant /bon vee-von/ *n.* (*pl.* **bon vivants** or **bons vivants** *pronunc.* same) a person indulging in good living. [French, literally 'good living (person)']

bon viveur /bon vee-ver/ *n.* (*pl.* **bon viveurs** or **bons viveurs** *pronunc.* same) = BON VIVANT. [pseudo-French]

bon voyage /bon voy-ahzh/ *int.* an expression of good wishes to a departing traveller. [French, literally 'good journey']

bony *adj.* (**bonier, boniest**) **1** (of a person) thin with prominent bones. **2** having many bones. **3** of or like bone. **4** (of a fish) having bones rather than cartilage. ▷ FISH. □ **boniness** *n.*

bonze *n.* a Japanese or Chinese Buddhist priest. [French]

bonzer *adj. Austral. slang* excellent, first-rate.

boo ● *int.* **1** an expression of disapproval. **2** a sound intended to surprise. ● *n.* an utterance of *boo*, esp. expressing disapproval to a performer etc. ● *v.* (**boos, booed**) **1** *intr.* utter a boo or boos. **2** *tr.* jeer at (a performer etc.) by booing.

boob[1] *slang* ● *n.* (also **booboo**) **1** *Brit.* an embarrassing mistake. **2** a simpleton. ● *v.intr. Brit.* make an embarrassing mistake.

boob[2] *n. slang* a woman's breast. [earlier *bubby, booby*]

boob tube *n. slang* **1** *Brit.* a woman's low-cut close-fitting usu. strapless top. **2** (usu. prec. by *the*) *N. Amer.* television; one's television set.

booby *n.* (*pl.* **-ies**) **1** a stupid person. **2** a small gannet of the genus *Sula*.

booby prize *n.* a prize given to the least successful competitor in a contest.

booby trap ● *n.* **1** a trap intended as a practical joke. **2** *Mil.* an apparently harmless explosive device intended to kill or injure anyone touching it. ● *v.tr.* (**booby-trap**) place a booby trap or traps in or on.

boodle *n. slang* money, esp. when gained or used dishonestly. [from Dutch *boedel* 'possessions']

boogie ● *v.intr.* (**boogies, boogied, boogieing**) *slang* dance to pop music. ● *n.* **1** = BOOGIE-WOOGIE. **2** *slang* a dance to pop music. [20th-century coinage]

boogie-woogie *n.* a style of playing blues or jazz on the piano, marked by a persistent bass rhythm.

book ● *n.* **1 a** ▲ a written or printed work consisting of pages fixed together along one side and bound in covers. **b** a literary composition intended for publication (*is working on her book*). **2** a bound set of blank sheets for writing on. **3** a bound set of stamps, matches, cheques, etc. **4** (in *pl.*) a set of records or accounts. **5** a main division of a literary work, or of the Bible. **6** a libretto, script of a play, etc. **7** *colloq.* a magazine. **8** a telephone directory. **9** a record of bets made and money paid out at a

BONE

Each layer of a bone is composed of specialized cells, protein fibres, and minerals. The medullary cavity contains bone marrow, and is enclosed in a spongy cancellous layer. This is surrounded by hard cortical bone (made up of osteons), with an outer covering of periostium. This combination of layers makes bones strong and light.

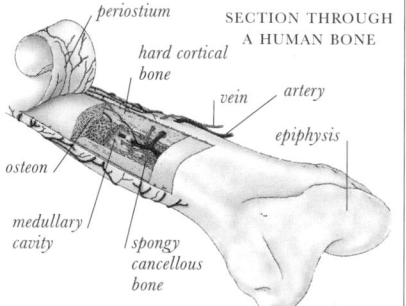

SECTION THROUGH A HUMAN BONE

periostium

hard cortical bone

vein   artery

epiphysis

osteon

medullary cavity

spongy cancellous bone

BOOK

The first books were written on papyrus by the ancient Egyptians. Religious scribes copied manuscripts by hand until book production was revolutionized by Johannes Gutenburg in 1455. He created a press with re-usable metal type, enabling the production of multiple copies. Books are now created with the aid of computers, and printing and binding are mechanized.

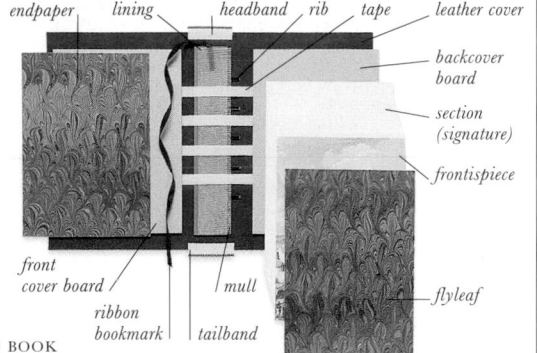

PARTS OF A LEATHER-BOUND BOOK

endpaper · lining · headband · rib · tape · leather cover · backcover board · section (signature) · frontispiece · front cover board · ribbon bookmark · mull · tailband · flyleaf

B

---

race meeting by a bookmaker. ● *v.* **1** *tr.* **a** engage (a seat etc.) in advance; make a reservation of. **b** engage (a guest etc.) for some occasion. **2** *tr.* **a** take the personal details of (an offender or rule-breaker). **b** enter in a book or list. **3** *tr.* make a reservation for (a person). **4** *intr.* make a reservation (*no need to book*). □ **book in** esp. *Brit.* register one's arrival at a hotel etc. **book up 1** *Brit.* buy tickets in advance for a theatre, concert, holiday, etc. **2** (as **booked up** *adj.*) with all places reserved. **bring to book** call to account. **go by the book** proceed according to the rules. **in a person's bad** (or **good**) **books** in disfavour (or favour) with a person. **in my book** in my opinion. **make a book** (or *US* **make book**) take bets and pay out winnings at a race meeting. **on the books** contained in a list of members etc. **suits my book** *Brit.* is convenient to me. **take a leaf out of a person's book** imitate a person. **throw the book at** *colloq.* charge or punish to the utmost. [Old English] □ **booker** *n.* **booking** *n.*

bookable *adj.* **1** that may be reserved or engaged in advance. **2** *Football* (of an offence) serious enough to be entered in the referee's book.

bookbinder *n.* a person who binds books professionally. □ **bookbinding** *n.*

bookcase *n.* a set of shelves for books in a frame.

book club *n.* a society selling members books on special terms.

bookend *n.* a usu. ornamental prop used to keep a row of books upright.

bookie *n.* *colloq.* = BOOKMAKER.

booking office *n.* a place where tickets are sold, esp. at a railway station or theatre.

bookish *adj.* **1** studious; fond of reading. **2** acquiring knowledge from books. **3** (of language etc.) literary. □ **bookishly** *adv.* **bookishness** *n.*

bookkeeper *n.* a person who keeps accounts for a trader etc. □ **bookkeeping** *n.*

book learning *n.* mere theory.

booklet *n.* a small book usu. with paper covers.

book-louse *n.* a minute insect of the order Psocoptera, often damaging to books.

bookmaker *n.* a person who takes bets, calculates odds, and pays out winnings. □ **bookmaking** *n.*

bookmark *n.* a strip of card etc. used to mark one's place in a book.

bookplate *n.* a decorative label stuck in the front of a book, bearing the owner's name.

book-rest *n.* an adjustable support for an open book on a table.

bookseller *n.* esp. *Brit.* a dealer in books.

bookshelf *n.* (*pl.* **-shelves**) a shelf on which books can be stored.

bookshop *n.* a shop where books are sold.

bookstall *n.* a stand for selling books, newspapers, etc.

bookstore *n.* *N. Amer.* = BOOKSHOP.

book token *n.* *Brit.* a voucher which can be exchanged for books.

---

bookwork *n.* the study of books (as opposed to practical work).

bookworm *n.* **1** *colloq.* a person devoted to reading. **2** the larva of a moth or beetle which feeds on the paper and glue used in books.

Boolean *adj.* denoting a system of algebraic notation to represent logical propositions. [from G. *Boole*, English mathematician, 1815–64]

Boolean logic *n.* the use of 'and', 'or', and 'not' in retrieving information from a computer database.

boom¹ ● *n.* a deep resonant sound. ● *v.intr.* make or speak with a boom.

boom² ● *n.* a period of prosperity or sudden activity in commerce. ● *v.intr.* be suddenly prosperous or successful. [19th-century US coinage]

boom³ *n.* **1** *Naut.* a pivoted spar to which the foot of a sail is attached, allowing the angle of the sail to be changed. ▷ DINGHY, SAILING BOAT. **2** a long pole over a television or film set, carrying equipment. **3** a floating barrier across the mouth of a harbour or river. [Dutch, literally 'beam']

boomerang ● *n.* a curved flat missile used by Australian Aboriginals to kill prey, and often able to return to the thrower. ● *v.intr.* **1** act as a boomerang. **2** (of a plan or action) backfire. [from Aboriginal *bumarin*]

boon¹ *n.* **1** an advantage; a blessing. **2** *archaic* **a** a request. **b** a gift; a favour. [Middle English, originally in sense 'prayer']

boon² *adj.* intimate, favourite (usu. *boon companion*). [from Latin *bonus* 'good']

boor *n.* a rude or clumsy person. [from Dutch *boer* 'farmer'] □ **boorish** *adj.* **boorishly** *adv.* **boorishness** *n.*

boost ● *v.tr.* **1 a** promote (a person, scheme, commodity, etc.) by praise or advertising; increase or assist (*boosted his spirits*; *boost sales*). **b** push from below (*boosted me up the tree*). **2 a** raise the voltage in (an electric circuit etc.). **b** amplify (a radio signal). ● *n.* an act, process, or result of boosting; a push. [19th-century US coinage]

booster *n.* **1** a device for increasing electrical power or voltage. **2** an auxiliary engine or rocket used to give initial acceleration. ▷ SPACECRAFT. **3** *Med.* a dose of an immunizing agent increasing or renewing the effect of an earlier one.

boot¹ ● *n.* **1** an outer foot-covering reaching above the ankle. **2** *Brit.* the luggage compartment of a motor car. ▷ CAR. **3** *colloq.* dismissal, esp. *Brit.* from employment (*gave them the boot*). ● *v.tr.* **1** kick, esp. hard. **2** (often foll. by *out*) dismiss (a person) forcefully. **3** (usu. foll. by *up*) put (a computer) in a state of readiness. □ **put the boot in** *Brit.* **1** kick brutally. **2** act decisively against a person. [from Old French *bote*] □ **booted** *adj.*

---

boot² *n.* □ **to boot** as well; to the good. [Old English, originally in sense 'advantage']

bootblack *n.* *N. Amer.* esp. *hist.* a person who polishes boots and shoes.

boot camp *n.* (esp. in the US) an institution for young offenders, having a tough quasi-military regime.

bootee *n.* **1** a soft shoe worn by a baby. **2** a woman's short boot.

booth *n.* **1** a small temporary roofed structure used esp. as a market stall, for puppet shows, etc. **2** a compartment for various purposes, e.g. telephoning or voting. **3** a set of a table and benches in a restaurant or bar. [from Scandinavian]

bootlace *n.* a cord or leather thong for lacing boots.

bootleg ● *adj.* (esp. of liquor) smuggled; illicitly sold; pirated. ● *v.tr.* (**-legged**, **-legging**) make, distribute, or smuggle (illicit goods, esp. alcohol); pirate (a musical recording). ● *n.* a pirated musical recording. [from the smugglers' practice of concealing bottles in their boots] □ **bootlegger** *n.*

bootlicker *n.* *colloq.* a person who behaves obsequiously.

boots *n.* *Brit.* a hotel servant who cleans boots and shoes, carries luggage, etc.

bootstrap *n.* **1** a loop at the back of a boot used to pull it on. **2** *Computing* a technique of loading a program into a computer by means of a few initial instructions which enable the introduction of the rest of the program from an input device.

booty *n.* **1** plunder gained esp. in war or by piracy. **2** *colloq.* something gained or won. [from Middle Dutch *būte*]

booze *colloq.* ● *n.* **1** alcoholic drink. **2** the drinking of this (*on the booze*). ● *v.intr.* drink alcoholic liquor, esp. excessively or habitually. [from Middle Dutch *būsen* 'to drink to excess']

boozer *n.* *colloq.* **1** a person who drinks alcohol, esp. to excess. **2** *Brit.* a public house.

booze-up *n.* *slang* a drinking bout.

boozy *adj.* (**boozier**, **booziest**) *colloq.* given to, or characterized by, boozing. □ **boozily** *adv.* **booziness** *n.*

bop¹ *colloq.* ● *n.* **1** = BEBOP. **2** *Brit.* **a** a spell of dancing, esp. to pop music. **b** an organized social occasion for this. ● *v.intr.* (**bopped**, **bopping**) move or dance, esp. to pop music. □ **bopper** *n.*

bop² *colloq.* ● *v.tr.* (**bopped**, **bopping**) hit, punch lightly. ● *n.* a light blow or hit.

boracic *adj.* of borax; containing boron. [based on medieval Latin *borax acis*]

boracic acid *n.* = BORIC ACID.

borage *n.* ◀ a plant of the genus *Borago*, esp. *Borago officinalis* with bright blue flowers and hairy leaves both used as flavouring. [from medieval Latin *borrago*]. ▷ HERB

borane *n.* *Chem.* any of the hydrides of boron.

borate *n.* a salt or ester of boric acid.

borax *n.* **1** ▶ the mineral salt sodium borate. **2** the purified form of this salt, used in making glass and china, and as an antiseptic. [from Persian *būrah*]

BORAGE
(*Borago officinalis*)

BORAX

bordello *n.* (*pl.* **-os**) esp. *N. Amer.* a brothel. [from Old French *bordel* 'cabin']

border ● *n.* **1** the edge or boundary of anything, or the part near it. **2 a** the line separating two political or geographical areas, esp. countries. **b** the district on each side of this. **3** a distinct edging round anything, esp. for strength or decoration. **4** a long narrow bed of flowers or shrubs. ● *v.* **1** *tr.* be a border to. **2** *tr.* provide with a

B

border. **3** *intr.* (usu. foll. by *on*, *upon*) **a** adjoin; come close to being. **b** approximate, resemble. [from Old French *bordure*]

Border collie *n.* a common working sheepdog.

borderer *n.* a person who lives near a border, esp. that between Scotland and England.

borderland *n.* **1** the district near a border. **2** an intermediate condition between two extremes. **3** an area for debate.

borderline ● *n.* **1** the line dividing two (often extreme) conditions. **2** a line marking a boundary. ● *adj.* **1** on the borderline. **2** verging on an extreme condition; only just acceptable.

Border terrier *n.* a small rough haired terrier.

bore[1] ● *v.* **1** *tr.* make a hole in, esp. with a revolving tool. **2** *tr.* hollow out (a tube etc.). **3** *tr.* make (a hole) by boring or excavation. **4** *intr.* drill a well (for oil etc.). ● *n.* **1** the hollow of a firearm barrel or of a cylinder in an internal-combustion engine. **2** the calibre of this. **3** = BORE-HOLE. [Old English]

bore[2] ● *n.* a tiresome or dull person or thing. ● *v.tr.* weary by tedious talk or dullness. [18th-century coinage] □ **boredom** *n.*

bore[3] *n.* a high tidal wave caused by the meeting of two tides, or by the constriction of a spring tide, rushing up a narrow estuary. [Middle English]

bore[4] *past* of BEAR[1].

boreal *adj.* of the North or northern regions. [based on Greek *Boreas* 'god of the north wind']

borehole *n.* a deep narrow hole, esp. one made in the earth to find water, oil, etc.

boric *adj.* of or containing boron.

boric acid *n.* an acid derived from borax, used as a mild antiseptic.

boring *adj.* that makes one bored; dull. □ **boringly** *adv.* **boringness** *n.*

born *adj.* **1** existing as a result of birth. **2 a** being such or likely to become such by natural ability or quality (*a born leader*). **b** (usu. foll. by *to* + infin.) having a specified destiny (*born lucky*). **3** (in *comb.*) of a certain status by birth (*French-born*). □ **in all one's born days** *colloq.* in one's life so far. **not born yesterday** *colloq.* not stupid; shrewd.

■ **Usage** See Usage Note at BEAR[1].

born-again *attrib.adj.* converted (esp. to fundamentalist Christianity).

borne ● *past part.* of BEAR[1]. ● *adj.* (in *comb.*) carried or transported by (*airborne*).

boron *n.* *Chem.* a non-metallic brown amorphous or black crystalline element extracted from borax and boracic acid and mainly used for hardening steel. [blend of BORAX and CARBON]

boronia *n.* *Austral.* any sweet-scented shrub of the genus *Boronia*. [named after F. *Borone*, Italian botanist, 1769–94]

borough *n.* **1** *Brit.* **a** a town (as distinct from a city) with a corporation and privileges granted by a royal charter. **b** *hist.* a town sending representatives to Parliament. **2** an administrative division of London. **3** a municipal corporation in certain US states. [Old English]

borrow *v.* **1 a** *tr.* acquire temporarily with the promise or intention of returning. **b** *intr.* obtain money in this way. **2** *tr.* use (an idea etc.) originated by another. □ **borrowed time** an unexpected extension, esp. of life. [Old English *borgian* 'to give a pledge'] □ **borrower** *n.* **borrowing** *n.*

Borstal *n.* *Brit. hist.* an institution for reforming and training young offenders. [from *Borstal* in S. England, where the first was established]

■ **Usage** The term *Borstal* has now been replaced by *detention centre* and *youth custody centre*.

---

bortsch *n.* (also **borsch**) a highly seasoned Russian or Polish soup of esp. beetroot and cabbage and served with sour cream. [from Russian *borshch*]

borzoi ▼ *n.* a large Russian wolfhound of a breed with a narrow head and silky, usu. white, coat. [Russian, from *borzyi* 'swift']

bosh *n. & int. slang* nonsense; foolish talk. [based on Turkish *boş* 'empty']

bosky *adj.* *literary* wooded, bushy. [16th-century coinage, from earlier *bosk* 'bush']

bo's'n var. of BOATSWAIN.

bosom /buu-zŏm/ *n.* **1 a** a person's breast or chest, esp. a woman's. **b** *colloq.* each of a woman's breasts. **c** the enclosure formed by a person's breast and arms. **2** an emotional centre (*bosom of one's family*). [Old English]

BORZOI

bosom friend *n.* a very close or intimate friend.

bosomy *adj.* (of a woman) having large breasts.

boss[1] *colloq.* ● *n.* **1** a person in charge. **2** *US* a person who controls or dominates a political organization. ● *v.tr.* **1** (usu. foll. by *about*, *around*) give constant peremptory orders to. **2** be the master or manager of. [from Dutch *baas* 'master'] □ **bossy** *adj.* (**bossier**, **bossiest**) *colloq.* **bossily** *adv.* **bossiness** *n.*

boss[2] *n.* **1** a round knob or other protuberance, esp. in ornamental work. ▷ SHIELD. **2** *Archit.* ◄ a piece of ornamental carving etc. covering the point where the ribs in a vault or ceiling cross. [from Old French *boce*]

bossa nova *n.* **1** a dance like the samba, originating in Brazil. **2** a piece of music for this or in its rhythm. [Portuguese, literally 'new style']

BOSS COVERING RIBS IN A CEILING

boss-eyed *adj.* *Brit. colloq.* **1** cross-eyed. **2** out of true. [based on dialect *boss* 'to miss, bungle']

boss-shot *n.* *Brit. dial. & slang* **1** a bad shot or aim. **2** an unsuccessful attempt.

bossy-boots *n.* *Brit. colloq.* a domineering person.

bosun (also **bo'sun**) var. of BOATSWAIN.

bot *n.* (also **bott**) any of various parasitic larvae of flies of the family Oestridae, infesting horses etc.

bot *abbr.* **1** bottle. **2** botanic; botanical; botany. **3** bought.

botanize *v.intr.* (also **-ise**) study plants, esp. in their habitat.

botany *n.* **1** the study of plants. **2** the plant life of a particular area or time. [based on Greek *botanē* 'plant'] □ **botanic** *adj.* **botanical** *adj.* **botanically** *adv.* **botanist** *n.*

botch (also **bodge**) ● *v.tr.* **1** bungle. **2** repair clumsily. ● *n.* bungled or spoilt work (*made a botch of it*). [Middle English] □ **botcher** *n.*

botfly *n.* (*pl.* **-flies**) a dipterous fly of the genus *Oestrus*, with a stout hairy body and parasitic larvae (see BOT).

both ● *predet. & pron.* the two, not only one (*both boys*; *the boys are both here*). ● *adv.* with equal truth in two cases (*both the boy and his sister are here*). [from Old Norse *báthir*]

■ **Usage** *Both* is widely used with *of*, esp. when followed by a pronoun (e.g. *both of us*) or a noun implying separate rather than collective consideration, e.g. *both of the boys* suggests *each boy* rather than the two together.

bother ● *v.* **1** *tr.* **a** worry, disturb. **b** *refl.* (often foll. by *about*) be concerned. **2** *intr.* **a** (often foll. by *about*, *with*, or *to* + infin.) worry or trouble oneself (*don't bother about that*). **b** (foll. by *with*) be concerned.

● *n.* **1 a** a person or thing that causes worry. **b** a minor nuisance. **2** trouble, fuss. ● *int.* esp. *Brit.* expressing annoyance or impatience. □ **cannot be bothered** will not make the effort needed. [earlier in sense 'noise, chatter']

botheration *n. & int. colloq.* = BOTHER *n.*, *int.*

bothersome *adj.* troublesome.

both ways *adj. & adv.* = EACH WAY.

bo tree *n.* ► the Indian fig tree, *Ficus religiosa*, regarded as sacred by Buddhists. [representing Sinhalese *bogaha* 'tree of knowledge', Buddha's enlightenment having occurred beneath such a tree]

BO TREE
(*Ficus religiosa*)

botrytis *n.* a fungus of the genus *Botrytis*, esp. the grey mould *B. cinerea*, deliberately cultivated on the grapes used for certain wines. [based on Greek *botrus* 'cluster of grapes']

bott var. of BOT.

bottle ● *n.* **1** a container, usu. of glass or plastic and with a narrow neck, for storing liquid. **2** the amount that will fill a bottle. **3** *Brit.* a baby's feeding bottle. **4** a metal cylinder for liquefied gas. **5** *Brit. slang* courage, confidence. ● *v.tr.* **1** put into bottles or jars. **2** *Brit.* preserve (fruit etc.) in jars. **3** (usu. foll. by *up*) **a** conceal or restrain for a time (esp. a feeling). **b** keep (an enemy force etc.) contained or entrapped. □ **bottle out** (often foll. by *of*) *Brit. slang* fail to carry out some activity through lack of nerve. **hit the bottle** *slang* drink heavily. **on the bottle** *slang* drinking (alcohol) heavily. [from medieval Latin *butticula* 'little butt']

bottle bank *n.* *Brit.* a place where used bottles may be deposited for recycling.

bottle-feed *v.tr.* (*past* and *past part.* **-fed**) feed (a baby) with milk by means of a bottle.

bottle green ● *n.* dark green. ● *adj.* (hyphenated when *attrib.*) of this colour.

bottleneck *n.* **1** a narrow place where the flow of traffic, production, etc., is constricted. **2** an obstruction to the flow of something (*information bottleneck*). **3** a device worn on a guitarist's finger, used to produce sliding effects on the strings.

bottlenose dolphin *n.* (also **bottlenosed dolphin**) a dolphin, *Tursiops truncatus*, with a bottle-shaped snout. ▷ DOLPHIN

bottle party *n.* *Brit.* a party to which guests bring bottles of drink.

bottom ● *n.* **1 a** the lowest point or part (*bottom of the stairs*). **b** the part on which a thing rests (*bottom of a saucepan*). **c** the underneath part (*scraped the bottom of the car*). **d** the furthest or inmost part (*bottom of the garden*). **2** *colloq.* **a** the buttocks. **b** the seat of a chair etc. **3 a** the less important or successful end of a class etc. (*at the bottom of the list of requirements*). **b** a person occupying this place (*he's always bottom of the class*). **4** the ground under the water of a lake etc. (*swam until he touched the bottom*). **5** (often in *pl.*) a garment for the lower part of the body, esp. matching one for the upper part (*a bikini bottom*; *he wore jogging bottoms*). **6** the basis (*he's at the bottom of it*). **7** the essential character. **8** *Naut.* a ship, esp. as a cargo carrier. ● *adj.* **1** lowest; last (*bottom button*; *bottom score*). **2** lower (*bottom half*). ● *v.* **1** *tr.* put a bottom to (a chair, saucepan, etc.). **2** *intr.* (of a ship) reach or touch the bottom. **3** *tr.* work out. **4** *tr.* touch the bottom or lowest point of. □ **at bottom** basically, essentially. **bet one's bottom dollar** *slang* **1** stake all. **2** be very sure. **bottom falls** (or **drops**) **out** collapse occurs. **bottom out** reach the lowest level. **bottoms up!** a call to drain one's glass. **get to the bottom of** fully investigate and explain.

knock the bottom out of *Brit.* make invalid or useless; prove (a thing) worthless. [Old English] □ **bottommost** *adj.*

bottom gear *n. Brit.* = FIRST GEAR.

bottomless *adj.* **1** without a bottom. **2** (of a supply etc.) inexhaustible.

bottom line *n. colloq.* the underlying or ultimate truth; the ultimate, esp. financial, criterion.

bottom-up *attrib.adj.* **1** proceeding from detail to general theory, or from the bottom upwards. **2** non-hierarchical.

botulism *n.* poisoning caused by a toxin produced by the bacillus *Clostridium botulinum* growing in poorly preserved food. [from German *Botulismus* 'sausage poisoning']

bouclé /**boo**-klay/ *n.* **1** a looped or curled yarn (esp. wool). **2** a fabric made of this. [French, literally 'buckled, curled']

boudoir /**bood**-wah/ *n.* a woman's small private room or bedroom. [French, literally 'sulking-place']

bouffant /**boo**-fon/ *adj.* (of a dress, hair, etc.) puffed out. [French, literally 'swelling']

bougainvillea *n.* (also **bougainvillaea**) any widely cultivated tropical plant of the genus *Bougainvillea*, with large coloured bracts. [named after L. A. de *Bougainville*, French navigator, 1729–1811]

bough *n.* a branch of a tree. [Old English]

bought *past* and *past part.* of BUY.

bouillon /**boo**-yawn/ *n.* thin soup; broth. [French]

boulder *n.* a large stone worn smooth by erosion. [shortening of Middle English *boulderstone*]

boulder clay *n.* a mixture of boulders etc. deposited by massive bodies of melting ice, giving distinctive glacial formations.

boule /**bool**/ *n.* (also **boules** *pronunc.* same) ▶ a French form of bowls, played on rough ground with usu. metal balls. [French]

boulevard *n.* **1** a broad tree-lined avenue. **2** esp. *US* a broad main road. [from German *Bollwerk* 'bulwark', originally of a promenade on a demolished fortification]

boult var. of BOLT[2].

bounce ● *v.* **1 a** *intr.* (of a ball etc.) rebound. **b** *tr.* cause to rebound. **c** *tr.* & *intr.* bounce repeatedly. **2** *intr. colloq.* (of a cheque) be returned by a bank, as insufficiently funded. **3** *intr.* **a** (foll. by *about, up*) (of a person, dog, etc.) jump or spring energetically. **b** (foll. by *in, out*, etc.) rush angrily, enthusiastically, etc. (*bounced out in a temper*). **4** *tr. Brit. colloq.* hustle (*bounced him into signing*). ● *n.* **1 a** a rebound. **b** the power of rebounding. **2** *Brit. colloq.* **a** self-confidence (*has a lot of bounce*). **b** liveliness. □ **bounce back** regain one's good health, spirits, etc. [from Dutch *bons* 'a thump'] □ **bouncy** *adj.* (**bouncier**, **bounciest**). **bouncily** *adv.* **bounciness** *n.*

bouncer *n.* **1** *colloq.* a person employed to eject troublemakers from a club etc. **2** *Cricket* a ball bowled fast and short which pitches high.

bouncing *adj.* **1** (esp. of a baby) big and healthy. **2** boisterous.

bound[1] ● *v.intr.* **1 a** spring (*bounded out of bed*). **b** move with leaping strides. **2** (of a ball etc.) recoil; bounce. ● *n.* **1** a leap. **2** a bounce. □ **by leaps and bounds** see LEAP. [from French *bondir*, originally 'to resound', later 'to rebound']

bound[2] ● *n.* (usu. in *pl.*) **1** a restriction (*beyond the bounds of possibility*). **2** a boundary. ● *v.tr.* **1** (esp. in *passive*; foll. by *by*) limit (*views bounded by prejudice*). **2** be the boundary of. □ **out of bounds 1** outside the area in which one is allowed to be. **2** beyond what is acceptable. [from medieval Latin *bodina*]

bound[3] *adj.* **1** (usu. foll. by *for*) ready to start or having started (*bound for stardom*). **2** (in *comb.*) moving in a specified direction (*northbound*). [from Old Norse *búinn* 'prepared']

bound[4] *past* and *past part.* of BIND. □ **bound to** certain to (*he's bound to come*).

boundary *n.* (*pl.* **-ies**) **1** a line marking the limits of an area, territory, etc. **2** *Cricket* a hit crossing the limits of the field. [related to BOUND[2]]

bounden *adj. archaic* obligatory.

bounder *n. Brit. colloq.* or *joc.* an ill-bred or dishonourable person.

boundless *adj.* unlimited; immense (*boundless enthusiasm*). □ **boundlessly** *adv.* **boundlessness** *n.*

bounteous *adj. poet.* generous, liberal. [based on (Old) French *bonté* 'bounty'] □ **bounteously** *adv.* **bounteousness** *n.*

bountiful *adj.* **1** = BOUNTEOUS. **2** ample. □ **bountifully** *adv.*

bounty *n.* (*pl.* **-ies**) **1** liberality. **2** a gift or reward, made usu. by the State. [from Latin *bonitas*, based on *bonus* 'good']

bounty hunter *n.* a person who pursues a criminal or seeks an achievement for the sake of the reward.

bouquet /**boo**-kay/ *n.* **1** a bunch of flowers. **2** the scent of wine etc. **3** a favourable comment; a compliment. [French, from dialect variant of Old French *bos* 'wood']

bouquet garni /**boo**-kay **gar**-ni/ *n.* (*pl.* **bouquets garnis**) a bunch of herbs used for flavouring stews etc. [French, literally 'garnished bouquet']

bourbon /**ber**-bŏn/ *n.* an American whiskey distilled from maize and rye. [from *Bourbon* County, Kentucky, where first made]

bourgeois /**boor**-zhwah/ *often derog.* ● *adj.* **1 a** conventionally middle-class. **b** unimaginative. **c** selfishly materialistic. **2** upholding the interests of the capitalist class. ● *n.* (*pl.* same) a bourgeois person. [French, from Late Latin *burgensis* 'town-dweller'] □ **bourgeoisie** /**boor**-zhwah-**zee**/ *n.*

bourn[1] *n.* a small stream. [Middle English: S. English variant of BURN[2]]

bourn[2] *n.* (also **bourne**) *archaic* **1** a goal; a destination. **2** a limit. [from Old French *bodne* 'limitation']

bourrée *n.* **1** a lively French dance like a gavotte. **2** the music for this dance. [French]

bourse /**boorss**/ *n.* **1** (**Bourse**) the Paris equivalent of the Stock Exchange. **2** a money market. [French, from medieval Latin *bursa* 'purse']

bout *n.* (often foll. by *of*) **1** a limited period or session. **2 a** a wrestling or boxing match. **b** a trial of strength. [16th-century coinage]

boutique *n.* a small shop or department of a store, selling (esp. fashionable) clothes or accessories. [French]

bouzouki *n.* a Greek form of mandolin. [modern Greek]

bovine *adj.* **1** of or relating to cattle. **2** stupid. [based on Latin *bos bovis* 'ox'] □ **bovinely** *adv.*

bovver *n. Brit. slang* deliberate trouble-making. [cockney pronunciation of BOTHER]

bovver boot *n. Brit. slang* a heavy laced boot worn typically by skinheads.

bow[1] /**boh**/ ● *n.* **1 a** a slip-knot with a double loop. **b** a ribbon etc., tied with this. **c** a decoration in the form of a bow. **2** a device for shooting arrows with a taut string joining the ends of a curved piece of wood etc. ▷ ARCHERY. **3** a rod with horsehair stretched along its length, used for playing the violin, cello, etc. ▷ STRINGED. **4** a shallow curve or bend. ● *v.tr.* (also *absol.*) use a bow on (a violin etc.). □ **have two** (or **many**) **strings to one's bow** *Brit.* have (many) more than one resource. [Old English]

bow[2] /*rhymes with* cow/ ● *v.* **1** *intr.* incline the head or trunk, in acknowledgement of applause etc.

B

2 *intr.* submit (*bowed to the inevitable*). **3** *tr.* cause to incline or submit (*bowed his head; bowed his will to hers*). **4** *tr.* (foll. by *in, out*) usher or escort obsequiously. ● *n.* an inclining of the head or body. □ **bow down 1** bend or kneel in submission or reverence. **2** (usu. in *passive*) crush with or as with a load (*was bowed down by care*). **bow out 1** make one's exit (esp. formally). **2** retire gracefully. **take a bow** acknowledge applause. [Old English]

bow[3] /*rhymes with* cow/ *n. Naut.* (often in *pl.*) the fore-end of a boat or a ship. ▷ MAN-OF-WAR. □ **on the bow** within 45° of the point directly ahead. **shot across the bows** a warning. [from Dutch *boeg*]

bowdlerize *v.tr.* (also **-ise**) expurgate (a book etc.). [from T. *Bowdler*, 1754–1825, expurgator of Shakespeare] □ **bowdlerism** *n.* **bowdlerization** *n.*

bowel *n.* **1** (often in *pl.*) the intestine. **2** (in *pl.*) the depths (*bowels of the Earth*). [from Latin *botellus* 'little sausage']

bowel movement *n.* discharge from the bowels.

bower ● *n.* **1** a secluded place enclosed by foliage; an arbour. **2** *poet.* a boudoir. ● *v.tr. poet.* embower. [Old English]

bowerbird *n.* **1** any of various birds of the family Ptilonorhynchidae, native to Australia and New Guinea, the males of which construct elaborate bowers during courtship.

bowhead *n.* an Arctic whale, *Balaena mysticetus*.

bowie *n.* (in full **bowie knife**) ▼ a long knife with a blade double-edged at the point. [named after J. *Bowie*, American soldier, 1796–1836, who popularized it]

BOWIE KNIFE

bowl[1] *n.* **1 a** a usu. round deep basin used for food or liquid. **b** the contents of a bowl. **2 a** any deep-sided container shaped like a bowl (*lavatory bowl*). **b** the bowl-shaped part of a tobacco pipe, spoon, balance, etc. **3** *Geog.* a natural basin. **4** esp. *US* an amphitheatre or stadium, esp. in names (*Hollywood Bowl*). [Old English] □ **bowlful** *n.*

bowl[2] ● *n.* **1 a** a slightly asymmetrical wooden or hard rubber ball used in the game of bowls. **b** a wooden ball or disc used in playing skittles. **c** a large ball with indents for gripping, used in tenpin bowling. **2** (in *pl.*; usu. treated as *sing.*) a game played with bowls. **3** a turn of bowling in cricket. ● *v.* **1 a** *tr.* roll (a hoop etc.) along the ground. **b** *intr.* play bowls or skittles. **2** *tr.* (also *absol.*) *Cricket* etc. **a** deliver (an over etc.). **b** (often foll. by *out, for*) dismiss (a batsman or a side) by knocking down the wicket with a ball. **3** *intr.* (often foll. by *along*) go along rapidly, esp. on wheels (*the cart bowled along the road*). □ **bowl out** *Cricket* etc. dismiss (a side) (see also sense 2b of *v.*). **bowl over 1** knock down. **2** *colloq.* **a** impress greatly. **b** overwhelm. [from Latin *bulla* 'bubble']

bow-legs *n.pl.* bandy legs. □ **bow-legged** *adj.*

bowler[1] *n.* **1** *Cricket* etc. a member of the fielding side who bowls. ▷ CRICKET. **2** a player at bowls.

bowler[2] *n.* (in full **bowler hat**) a man's hard felt hat with a round dome-shaped crown. ▷ HAT. [named after W. *Bowler*, a hatter, who designed it (1850)]

bowline /**boh**-lin/ *n. Naut.* ▼ a knot for forming a non-slipping loop at the end of a rope. ▷ KNOT

BOWLINE

BOULE: SET OF BALLS FOR PLAYING BOULE

B

bowling n. **1** *Bowls* the game of bowls as a sport or recreation. **2** *Cricket* the delivery of the ball (also *attrib.*: *bowling technique*).

bowling alley n. **1** a long enclosure for skittles or tenpin bowling. **2** a building containing these.

bowling green n. a smooth green for playing bowls.

bowman[1] /boh-măn/ n. (*pl.* **-men**) an archer.

bowman[2] /bow-măn; *first part rhymes with* cow/ n. (*pl.* **-men**) the rower nearest the bow of esp. a racing boat.

bowsaw n. a narrow saw stretched like a bowstring on a light frame.

bowser n. **1** *Brit.* a tanker used for fuelling aircraft etc., or for supplying water. **2** *propr.* a petrol pump. [trade name]

bowsprit n. *Naut.* ▼ a spar running out from a ship's bow to which the forestays are fastened. ▷ SAILING BOAT, SHIP

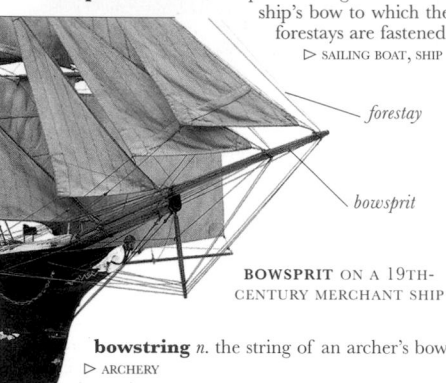

forestay

bowsprit

BOWSPRIT ON A 19TH-CENTURY MERCHANT SHIP

bowstring n. the string of an archer's bow. ▷ ARCHERY

bow tie n. a necktie in the form of a bow (see BOW[1] n. 1a).

bow wave n. a wave set up at the bows of a moving ship or in front of a body moving through a fluid.

bow window n. a curved bay window.

bowyer n. a maker or seller of archers' bows.

box[1] ● n. **1** a container, usu. with flat sides and of firm material, esp. for holding solids. **2** the amount that will fill a box. **3** a separate compartment, e.g. in a theatre. **4** an enclosure or receptacle for a special purpose (*money box*; *telephone box*). **5** a facility for receiving replies to an advertisement etc. **6** (prec. by *the*) *colloq.* television (*what's on the box?*). **7** a space or area of print on a page, enclosed by a border. **8** a protective casing for a piece of mechanism. **9** *Brit.* a light shield for protecting the genitals in sport, esp. in cricket. **10** (prec. by *the*) *Football colloq.* the penalty area. ● *v.tr.* **1** put in or provide with a box. **2** (foll. by *in*, *up*) confine. [based on Greek *puxos*] □ **boxful** n. **boxing** n. **boxlike** adj.

box[2] v. **1 a** *tr.* fight (an opponent) at boxing. **b** *intr.* practise boxing. **2** *tr.* slap (esp. a person's ears). □ **box clever** *Brit. colloq.* act in a clever or effective way. [Middle English]

box[3] n. **1** (also **box tree**) **a** an evergreen shrub or small tree of the genus *Buxus*, esp. *B. sempervirens*, often used in hedging. ▷ TOPIARY. **b** any of various similar trees in Australasia, esp. those of several species of *Eucalyptus*. **2** = BOXWOOD 1. [based on Greek *puxos*]

Box and Cox n. (often *attrib.*) *Brit.* two persons sharing accommodation etc., and using it at different times. [names of characters in a play (1847) by J. M. Morton]

box camera n. ▼ a simple box-shaped hand camera.

film winder   *eyepiece*   *lens*

BOX CAMERA: EARLY 20TH-CENTURY MODEL

boxcar n. *N. Amer.* an enclosed railway goods wagon, usu. with sliding doors on the sides.

boxer n. **1** a person who practises boxing, esp. for sport. **2** ▶ a medium-sized dog of a breed with a smooth brown coat and puglike face.

boxer shorts n.pl. men's underpants similar to shorts.

box girder n. a hollow girder square in cross-section.

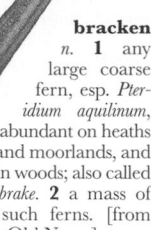

BOXER

Boxing Day n. the first day (strictly, the first weekday) after Christmas. [from the custom of giving tradesmen a Christmas box on this day]

boxing weight n. each of a series of fixed weight ranges at which boxers are matched.

box junction n. *Brit.* a road area at a junction marked with a yellow grid, which a vehicle should enter only if its exit from it is clear.

box number n. a number by which replies are made to a private advertisement in a newspaper.

box office n. **1** a ticket-office at a theatre etc. **2** the commercial aspect of the arts and entertainment (often *attrib.*: *a box-office failure*).

box pleat n. a pleat consisting of two parallel creases forming a raised band.

boxroom n. *Brit.* a small room esp. for storing boxes, cases, etc.

boxwood n. **1** the wood of the box tree, used esp. by engravers for the fineness of its grain and for its hardness. **2** = BOX[3] 1.

boxy adj. (**boxier**, **boxiest**) **1** (of a room or space) very cramped. **2** (of recorded sound) restricted in tone.

boy ● n. **1** a male child or youth. **2** a young man. **3** a male servant, attendant, etc. **4** (**the boys**) *colloq.* a group of men mixing socially. ● *int.* (also **oh boy**) expressing pleasure, surprise, etc. [Middle English] □ **boyhood** n. **boyish** adj. **boyishly** adv. **boyishness** n.

boycott ● *v.tr.* **1** combine in refusing relations with (a person, group, country, etc.). **2** refuse to handle (goods). ● n. such a refusal. [from Capt. C. C. Boycott, Irish land agent, 1832–97, so treated from 1880]

boyfriend n. a person's regular male companion or lover.

bozo n. (*pl.* **-os**) esp. *N. Amer. slang* a stupid or insignificant person. [20th-century coinage]

BP abbr. **1** boiling point. **2** blood pressure. **3** British Pharmacopoeia.

B.Phil. abbr. Bachelor of Philosophy.

bpi abbr. *Computing* bits per inch.

bps abbr. *Computing* bits per second.

Bq abbr. becquerel.

Br symb. Chem. the element bromine.

bra n. (*pl.* **bras**) an undergarment worn by women to support the breasts. □ **braless** adj.

brace ● n. **1 a** a device that clamps or fastens tightly. **b** a strengthening piece of iron or timber in building. ▷ QUEEN POST. **2** (in *pl.*) *Brit.* straps supporting trousers from the shoulders. **3** a wire device for straightening the teeth. **4** (*pl.* same) a pair. **5** a rope attached to the yard of a ship for trimming the sail. ▷ SHIP. **6** a connecting mark { or } used in printing. ● *v.tr.* **1** fasten tightly, give firmness to. **2** make steady by supporting. **3** (esp. as **bracing** adj.) invigorate, refresh. **4** (often *refl.*) prepare for a difficulty, shock, etc. [from Latin *bra(c)chia* 'arms'] □ **bracingly** adv.

brace and bit n. a revolving tool with a D-shaped central handle for boring. ▷ DRILL.

bracelet n. **1** an ornamental band, hoop, or chain worn on the wrist or arm. **2** *slang* a handcuff. [based on Latin *brac(c)hium* 'arm']

brachiopod n. ▶ a marine invertebrate of the phylum Brachiopoda, having a ciliated feeding arm and a two-valved shell, often found fossilized. Also called *lamp shell* [from Greek *brakhiōn* 'arm' + *pous podos* 'foot']

BRACHIOPOD SHELL

brachiosaurus n. ▼ any huge plant-eating dinosaur of the genus *Brachiosaurus*, with forelegs longer than its hind legs. [from Greek *brakhiōn* 'arm' + *sauros* 'lizard']

BRACHIOSAURUS (*Brachiosaurus* species)

bracken n. **1** any large coarse fern, esp. *Pteridium aquilinum*, abundant on heaths and moorlands, and in woods; also called *brake*. **2** a mass of such ferns. [from Old Norse]

bracket ● n. **1** a support attached to and projecting from a vertical surface. **2** a shelf fixed with such a support to a wall. **3** each of a pair of marks ( ) [ ] { } < > used to enclose words or figures. **4** a group classified as containing similar elements or falling between given limits (*income bracket*). ● *v.tr.* (**bracketed**, **bracketing**) **1 a** couple (names etc.) with a bracket. **b** imply a connection or equality between. **2 a** enclose in brackets as parenthetic or spurious. **b** *Math.* enclose in brackets as having specific relations to what precedes or follows. [from Spanish *bragueta* 'codpiece, bracket']

brackish adj. (of water etc.) slightly salty. [based on Middle Dutch *brac* 'worthless']

bract n. *Bot.* a modified leaf, with a flower or an inflorescence in its axil. ▷ POINSETTIA. [from Latin *bractea* 'gold leaf']

bradawl n. ▶ a small tool with a pointed end for boring holes by hand.

brae /bray/ n. *Sc.* a steep bank or hillside. [from Old Norse *brá* 'eyelash']

brag ● v. (**bragged**, **bragging**) **1** *intr.* talk boastfully. **2** *tr.* boast about. ● n. **1** a card game like poker. **2** a boastful statement; boastful talk. [Middle English]

braggadocio /brag-ă-**doh**-chee-oh/ n. empty boasting; a boastful manner of speech and behaviour. [from *Braggadochio*, a braggart in Spenser's *Faerie Queene*]

braggart ● n. a person given to bragging. ● adj. boastful. [based on French *braguer* 'to brag']

Brahman n. (also **brahman**) (*pl.* **-mans**) a member of the highest Hindu caste, the priesthood caste.

Brahmin n. **1** = BRAHMAN. **2** a socially or culturally superior person, esp. from New England.

BRADAWL

braid ● n. **1** a woven band used for edging or trimming. **2** a length of entwined hair. ● *v.tr.* **1** plait or intertwine (hair or thread). **2** trim or decorate with braid. [Old English]

Braille n. a system of writing and printing for the blind, in which characters are represented by patterns of raised dots. [named after L. *Braille*, French teacher, 1809–52, inventor of the system]

brain ● n. **1** ▲ an organ of soft nervous tissue contained in the skull of vertebrates, functioning as the coordinating centre of sensation, and of intellectual and nervous activity. ▷ HEAD, NERVOUS SYSTEM. **2** (in *pl.*) the substance of the brain, esp. as food. **3 a** a person's intellectual capacity (*has a poor brain*).

BRAIN

The brain, together with the spinal cord, constitutes the central nervous system. It is responsible for monitoring and regulating unconscious and voluntary actions and reactions in the body. It is also the intellectual centre that allows thought, learning, memory, and creativity.

OVERHEAD VIEW OF
THE HUMAN BRAIN

cerebrum   *cingulate gyrus*   *corpus callosum*   *fornix*

frontal lobe   *hippocampus*

sensory area

ventricle

motor area

frontal lobe

hypothalamus

sagittal section

parietal lobe

pituitary gland

coronal section

thalamus   *pons*   *medulla*

cerebellum

SAGITTAL SECTION
OF THE HUMAN BRAIN

b (often in *pl.*) intelligence; high intellectual capacity (*has a brain; has brains*). **4** (usu. in *pl.*; prec. by *the*) *colloq.* **a** the cleverest person in a group. **b** a person who originates a complex plan or idea (*the brains behind the robbery*). **5** an electronic device with functions comparable to those of a brain. ● *v.tr.* **1** dash out the brains of. **2** strike hard on the head. □ **on the brain** *colloq.* obsessively in one's thoughts. [Old English]

brainbox *n. Brit. colloq.* a clever person.

brainchild *n.* (*pl.* **-children**) *colloq.* an idea, plan, or invention regarded as the result of a person's mental effort.

brain-dead *adj.* **1** having suffered brain death. **2** *colloq. derog.* feeble-minded; lacking any vitality.

brain death *n.* irreversible brain damage causing the end of independent respiration, regarded as indicative of death.

brain drain *n. colloq.* the loss of academics and skilled personnel by emigration.

brainless *adj.* stupid, foolish.

brainpower *n.* mental ability or intelligence.

brainstem *n.* ▶ the central trunk of the brain, upon which the cerebrum and cerebellum are set, and which continues downwards to form the spinal cord. ▷ BRAIN, HEAD

BRAINSTEM

thalamus

midbrain

pons

medulla

spinal cord

brain-stem

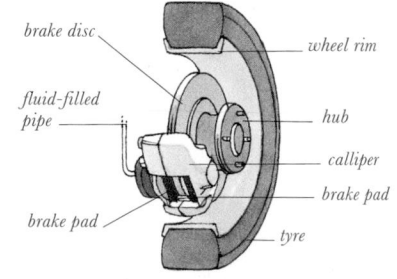

brainstorm ● *n.* **1** a violent or excited outburst often as a result of a sudden mental disturbance. **2** *colloq.* mental confusion. **3** *N. Amer.* = BRAINWAVE 2. **4** (also **brainstorming session**) a concerted intellectual treatment of a problem by discussing spontaneous ideas about it. ● *v.intr.* engage in a brainstorming session. □ **brainstorming** *n.* (in sense 4).

brains trust *n. Brit.* a group of experts who give impromptu answers to questions.

brain-teaser *n.* (also **brain-twister**) *colloq.* a puzzle or problem.

brain trust *n. US* a group of expert advisers.

brainwash *v.tr.* subject (a person) to a prolonged process by which ideas at variance with those already held are implanted in the mind. □ **brainwashing** *n.*

brainwave *n.* **1** (usu. in *pl.*) an electrical impulse in the brain. **2** *colloq.* a sudden bright idea.

brainy *adj.* (**brainier**, **brainiest**) intellectually clever or active.

braise *v.tr.* stew slowly with a little liquid in a closed container. [based on French *braise* 'live coals']

brake[1] ● *n.* **1** (often in *pl.*) ▼ a device for checking the motion of a mechanism, esp. a wheel or vehicle, or for keeping it at rest. **2** anything that hinders something (*put a brake on their enthusiasm*). ● *v.* **1** *intr.* apply a brake. **2** *tr.* retard or stop with a brake.

brake[2] *n. Brit.* a large estate car.

brake[3] *n.* **1** a thicket. **2** brushwood. [Old English]

brake[4] *archaic past* of BREAK.

brake block *n.* **1** a block which is applied to a bicycle wheel as a brake. **2** a block used to hold a brake shoe.

brake disc *n.* a disc attached to a wheel on which the brake pad presses in order to brake. ▷ BRAKE

brake drum *n.* a cylinder attached to a wheel on which the brake shoe presses in order to brake. ▷ BRAKE

brake fluid *n.* a fluid used in a hydraulic brake system.

brake horsepower *n.* the power of an engine reckoned in terms of the force needed to brake it.

brake lining *n.* a strip of fabric attached to a brake shoe to increase its friction. ▷ BRAKE

brake pad *n.* a block which presses on the brake disc when brakes are applied. ▷ BRAKE

brake shoe *n.* a long curved block which presses on the brake drum when brakes are applied. ▷ BRAKE

brakevan *n. Brit.* a railway coach or vehicle from which the train's brakes can be controlled.

bramble *n.* **1** any of various thorny shrubs of the rose family, esp. the blackberry bush, *Rubus fruticosus.* **2** *Brit.* the edible berry of these shrubs. **3** any of various other shrubs of the rose family with similar foliage, esp. the dog rose, *Rosa canina.* [Old English] □ **brambly** *adj.*

brambling *n.* a finch, *Fringilla montifringilla*, with brightly coloured plumage and a white rump.

bran *n.* grain husks separated from the flour. [from Old French]

branch ● *n.* **1** a limb extending from a tree or bough. **2** a lateral extension or subdivision, esp. of a river, road, or railway. **3** a subdivision of a family, knowledge, a subject, etc. **4** a local division or office etc. of a large business, library, etc. ● *v.intr.* **1** diverge from the main part. **2** divide into branches. **3** (of a tree) bear or send out branches. □ **branch out** extend one's field of interest. [from Late Latin *branca* 'paw'] □ **branched** *adj.* **branchlet** *n.*

brand ● *n.* **1 a** a particular make of goods. **b** (in full **brand name**) an identifying trade mark, label, etc. **2** a special or characteristic kind (*brand of humour*). **3** an identifying mark burned on livestock etc. with a hot iron. **4** an iron used for this. **5** a piece of burning, smouldering, or charred wood. **6** a stigma; a mark of disgrace. **7** *poet.* **a** a torch. **b** a sword. ● *v.tr.* **1** mark with a hot iron. **2** stigmatize; mark with disgrace (*they branded him a liar; was branded for life*). **3** impress unforgettably on one's mind. **4** assign a trade mark or label to. [Old English]

brandish *v.tr.* wave as a threat or in display. [related to BRAND]

brand leader *n.* the best-selling product of its type.

brandling *n.* a red earthworm, *Eisenia foetida*, with rings of a brighter colour, which is often found in manure and used as bait. [17th-century coinage]

brand name *n.* **1** see BRAND 1b. **2** a product with an identifying trade mark, label, etc.

brand new *adj.* completely new.

brandy *n.* (*pl.* **-ies**) a strong alcoholic spirit distilled from wine or fermented fruit juice [from Dutch *brandewijn* 'burnt (distilled) wine']

brandy butter *n. Brit.* an accompaniment to hot desserts, made from brandy, butter, and sugar.

brandy snap *n.* a crisp rolled gingerbread wafer

brant *US var.* of BRENT.

bran tub *n. Brit.* a lucky dip with prizes concealed in bran.

brash *adj.* **1** vulgarly or ostentatiously self-assertive. **2** hasty, rash. **3** impudent. [originally dialect] □ **brashly** *adv.* **brashness** *n.*

B

BRAKE

Brakes are essential to vehicle safety. Illustrated below are the main types of car brake. The disc brake is used on the front wheels of a car: when the footbrake is applied, hydraulic pressure forces pads inside the wheel to press against the disc, slowing the wheel. Drum brakes are often used for a car's rear or parking brakes: curved shoes inside the metal drum push outwards against the drum when the brake is applied.

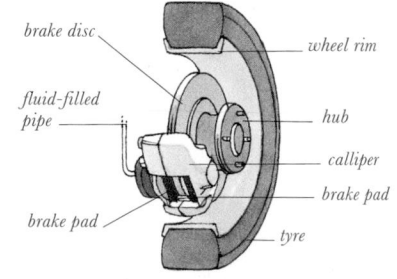

brake disc   *wheel rim*

fluid-filled pipe   *hub*

calliper

brake pad

brake pad   *tyre*

SECTION THROUGH A BRAKE DISC

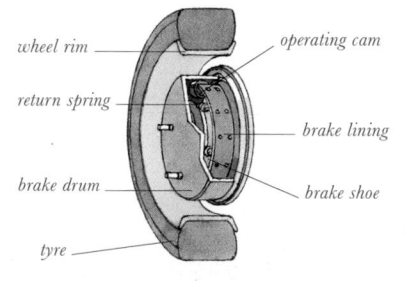

wheel rim   *operating cam*

return spring   *brake lining*

brake drum   *brake shoe*

tyre

SECTION THROUGH A BRAKE DRUM

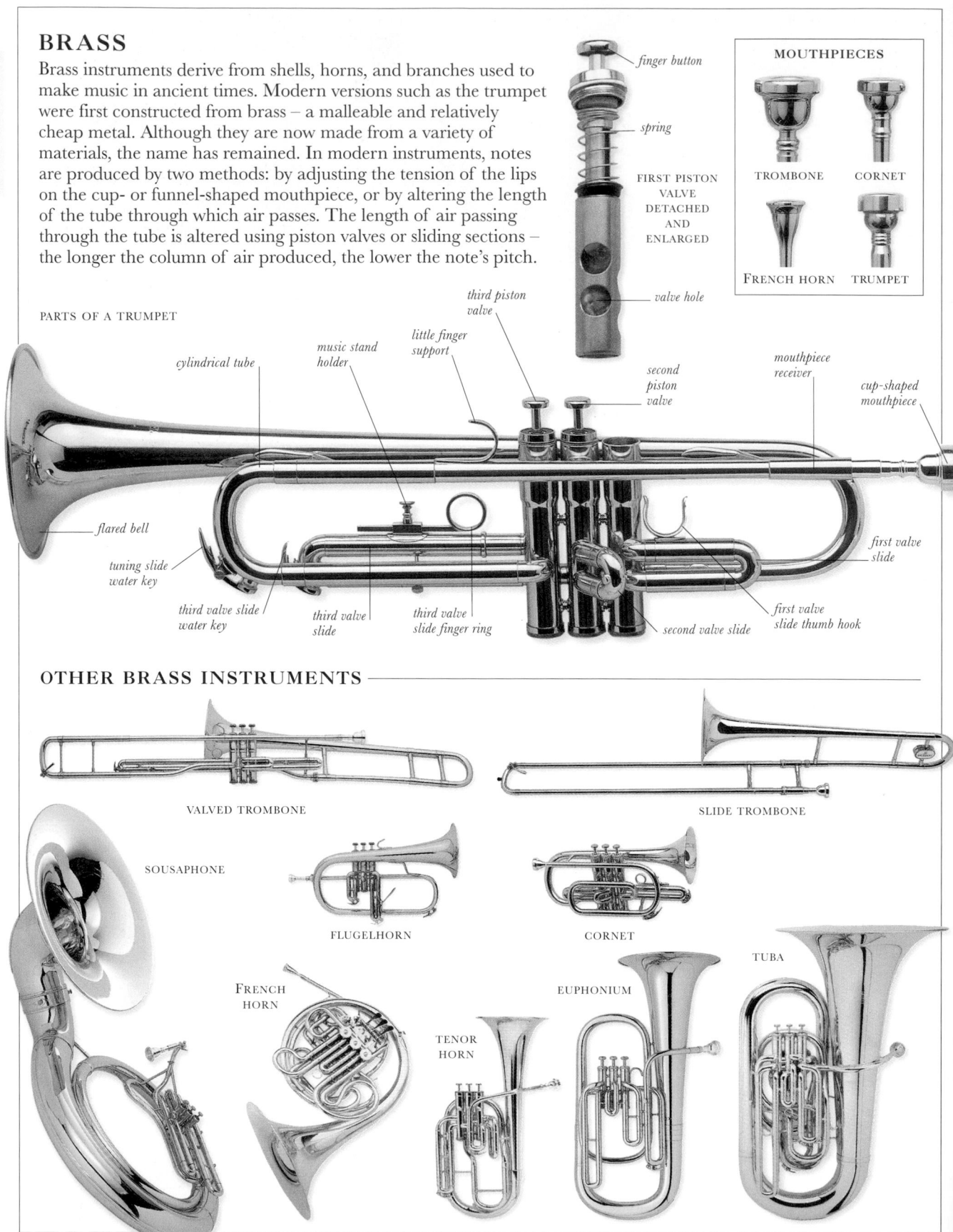

BRASS

Brass instruments derive from shells, horns, and branches used to make music in ancient times. Modern versions such as the trumpet were first constructed from brass – a malleable and relatively cheap metal. Although they are now made from a variety of materials, the name has remained. In modern instruments, notes are produced by two methods: by adjusting the tension of the lips on the cup- or funnel-shaped mouthpiece, or by altering the length of the tube through which air passes. The length of air passing through the tube is altered using piston valves or sliding sections – the longer the column of air produced, the lower the note's pitch.

B

finger button

spring

FIRST PISTON
VALVE
DETACHED
AND
ENLARGED

valve hole

third piston valve

MOUTHPIECES

TROMBONE   CORNET

FRENCH HORN   TRUMPET

PARTS OF A TRUMPET

cylindrical tube

music stand holder

little finger support

second piston valve

mouthpiece receiver

cup-shaped mouthpiece

flared bell

first valve slide

tuning slide water key

third valve slide water key

third valve slide

third valve slide finger ring

second valve slide

first valve slide thumb hook

OTHER BRASS INSTRUMENTS

VALVED TROMBONE

SLIDE TROMBONE

SOUSAPHONE

FLUGELHORN

CORNET

TUBA

FRENCH HORN

EUPHONIUM

TENOR HORN

brass • *n.* **1** a yellow alloy of copper and zinc. **2 a** a decorated piece of brass. **b** brass objects collectively. **3** *Mus.* ◄ brass wind instruments. ▷ ORCHESTRA. **4** *Brit. slang* money. **5** (in full **horse brass**) a round flat brass ornament for the harness of a draught horse. **6** (in full **top brass**) *colloq.* persons in authority or of high rank. **7** *Brit.* a memorial tablet of brass. **8** *colloq.* effrontery (*then had the brass to demand money*). • *adj.* made of brass. □ **brassed off** *Brit. slang* fed up. [Old English]

brassard *n.* a band worn on the sleeve. [based on French *bras* 'arm']

brass band *n.* a group of musicians playing brass instruments, sometimes also with percussion.

brasserie /**bras**-ĕ-ri/ *n.* a restaurant, originally one serving beer with food. [French, literally 'brewery']

brass hat *n. Brit. colloq.* an officer of high rank, usu. one with gold braid on the cap.

brassica *n.* any cruciferous plant of the genus *Brassica*, having tap roots and erect branched stems, including cabbage, swede, mustard, cauliflower, and turnip. [Latin, literally 'cabbage']

brassiere /**braz**-i-er/ *n.* = BRA. ▷ CORSELETTE. [French, literally 'child's vest']

brass rubbing *n.* **1** the rubbing of heelball etc. over paper laid on an engraved brass to take an impression of its design. **2** an impression obtained by this.

brass tacks *n.pl. slang* actual details; real business (*get down to brass tacks*).

brassy *adj.* (**brassier**, **brassiest**) **1** like brass, esp. in colour. **2** impudent. **3** pretentious, showy. **4** loud and blaring.

brat *n.* usu. *derog.* a child, esp. a badly behaved one. □ **bratty** *adj.*

brat pack *n. slang* a rowdy and ostentatious group of young celebrities. □ **brat packer** *n.*

bratwurst *n.* a type of small German pork sausage. [German, from *braten* 'to fry, roast' + *Wurst* 'sausage']

bravado *n.* a bold manner or a show of boldness. [related to BRAVE]

brave • *adj.* **1** able or ready to face and endure danger or pain. **2** *formal* splendid (*make a brave show*). • *n.* an American Indian warrior. • *v.tr.* defy; encounter bravely. [from Spanish *bravo* 'courageous, untamed'] □ **bravely** *adv.*

bravery *n.* **1** brave conduct. **2** a brave nature.

bravo[1] • *int.* expressing approval of a performer etc. • *n.* (*pl.* **-os**) a cry of bravo. [French, from Italian]

bravo[2] *n.* (*pl.* **-oes** or **-os**) a hired ruffian or killer. [Italian]

bravura /bră-**vewr**-ă/ *n.* (often *attrib.*) **1** a brilliant or ambitious action or display. **2 a** a style of music requiring exceptional ability. **b** a passage of this kind. **3** bravado. [Italian]

brawl • *n.* a noisy quarrel or fight. • *v.intr.* quarrel noisily or roughly. [Middle English] □ **brawler** *n.*

brawn *n.* **1** muscular strength. **2** muscle; lean flesh. **3** *Brit.* a jellied preparation of the chopped meat from a boiled pig's head. [from Old French *braon*]

brawny *adj.* (**brawnier**, **brawniest**) muscular, strong.

bray • *n.* **1** the cry of a donkey. **2** a sound like this cry. • *v.* **1** *intr.* make a braying sound. **2** *tr.* utter harshly. [from Old French *braire* 'to cry']

braze *v.tr.* solder with an alloy of copper and zinc at a high temperature. [from French *braser*]

brazen • *adj.* **1** (also **brazen-faced**) flagrant and shameless; insolent. **2** of or like brass. **3** harsh in sound. • *v.tr.* (foll. by *out*) face or undergo defiantly. □ **brazen it out** be defiantly unrepentant. [Old English] □ **brazenly** *adv.* **brazenness** *n.*

brazier[1] *n.* **1** a portable heater consisting of a pan or stand for holding lighted coals. **2** *N. Amer.* a charcoal grill for cooking. [based on French *braise* 'hot coals']

brazier[2] *n.* a worker in brass. [Middle English]

brazil *n.* **1** (in full **Brazil nut**) a large three-sided nut with an edible kernel, obtained from the S. American forest tree *Bertholletia excelsa*. ▷ NUT. **2** (in full **Brazil wood**) a hard red wood from any tropical tree of the genus *Caesalpinia*, yielding dyes. [from medieval Latin *brasilium*; the country *Brazil* is named from the wood]

breach • *n.* **1** the breaking of a law, contract, etc. **2 a** a breaking of relations. **b** a quarrel. **3 a** a broken state. **b** a gap. • *v.tr.* **1** break through; make a gap in. **2** break (a law, contract, etc.). □ **step into the breach** give help in a crisis, esp. by replacing someone. [from Old French]

breach of promise *n.* the breaking of a promise, esp. a promise to marry.

breach of the peace *n.* a violation of the public peace by any disturbance or riot etc.

bread • *n.* **1** baked dough made from flour usu. leavened with yeast and moistened. **2 a** necessary food. **b** (also **daily bread**) one's livelihood. **3** *slang* money. • *v.tr.* coat with breadcrumbs for cooking. □ **bread and wine** the Eucharist. **know which side one's bread is buttered** (or *US* **buttered on**) know where one's advantage lies. [Old English]

bread and butter *n.* **1** bread spread with butter. **2 a** one's livelihood. **b** routine work to ensure an income.

breadbasket *n.* **1** a basket for bread. **2** *slang* the stomach. **3** a region etc. that supplies cereals to another.

breadboard *n.* **1** a board for cutting bread on. **2** a board for making an experimental model of an electric circuit.

breadcrumb *n.* **1** a small fragment of bread. **2** (in *pl.*) bread crumbled for use in cooking.

breadfruit *n.* **1** (also **breadfruit tree**) a tropical evergreen tree, *Artocarpus altilis*, bearing edible fruit. **2** ► the fruit of this tree, which when roasted becomes soft like new bread.

BREADFRUIT
(*Artocarpus altilis*)

breadline *n.* **1** *Brit.* subsistence level (esp. *on the breadline*). **2** *N. Amer.* a queue of people waiting to receive free food.

bread sauce *n.* a white sauce thickened with breadcrumbs.

breadth *n.* **1** the distance or measurement from side to side of a thing. **2** a piece (of cloth etc.) of standard or full breadth. **3** extent, distance, room. **4** freedom from prejudice or intolerance (esp. *breadth of mind* or *view*). [related to BROAD]

breadwinner *n.* a person who earns the money to support a family.

break • *v.* (*past* **broke** or *archaic* **brake**; *past part.* **broken** or *archaic* **broke**) **1** *tr.* & *intr.* **a** separate into pieces under a blow or strain. **b** make or become inoperative (*the toaster has broken*). **c** break a bone in or dislocate (part of the body). **d** break the skin of (the head). **2 a** *tr.* cause an interruption in (*broke our journey*; *broke the silence*). **b** *intr.* have an interval between spells of work (*we broke for tea*). **3** *tr.* fail to keep (a law, promise, etc.). **4 a** *tr.* & *intr.* make or become subdued or weakened; yield or cause to yield (*broke his spirit*; *he broke under the strain*). **b** *tr.* weaken the effect of (a fall, blow, etc.). **c** *tr.* = *break in* 3c. **d** *tr.* defeat, destroy (*broke the enemy's power*). **e** *tr.* defeat the object of (a strike). **5** *tr.* surpass (a record). **6** *intr.* (foll. by *with*) cease association with (another person etc.). **7** *tr.* **a** be no longer subject to (a habit). **b** (foll. by *of*) cause (a person) to be free of a habit (*broke them of their addiction*). **8** *tr.* & *intr.* reveal or be revealed (*broke the news*; *the story broke on Friday*). **9** *intr.* **a** (of the weather) change suddenly. **b** (of waves) curl over and dissolve into foam. **c** (of the day) dawn. **d** (of clouds) move apart. **e** (of a storm) begin violently. **10** *tr. Electr.* disconnect (a circuit). **11** *intr.* **a** (of the voice) change with emotion. **b** (of a boy's voice) change in register etc. at puberty. **12** *tr.* ruin financially (see also BROKE *predic.adj.*). **13** *tr.* penetrate (e.g. a safe) by force. **14** *tr.* decipher (a code). **15** *tr.* make (a path etc.) by separating obstacles. **16** *intr.* burst forth (*the sun broke through the clouds*). **17** *Mil.* **a** *intr.* (of troops) disperse in confusion. **b** *tr.* make a rupture in (ranks). **18 a** *intr.* (usu. foll. by *free*, *loose*, *out*, etc.) escape from constraint by a sudden effort. **b** *tr.* escape or emerge from (prison, bounds, cover, etc.). **19** *tr. Tennis etc.* win a game against (an opponent serving). **20** *intr. Boxing* etc. (of two fighters) come out of a clinch. **21** *tr. Mil.* demote (an officer). **22** *intr.* esp. *Stock Exch.* (of prices) fall sharply. **23** *intr. Cricket* (of a bowled ball) change direction on bouncing. **24** *intr. Billiards* etc. make the first stroke at the beginning of a game. • *n.* **1 a** an act or instance of breaking. **b** a point where something is broken; a gap. **2** an interval, an interruption; a pause in work. **3** a sudden dash. **4** *colloq.* **a** a piece of good luck; a fair chance. **b** (also **bad break**) an unfortunate remark or action, a blunder. **5** *Cricket* a change in direction of a bowled ball on bouncing. **6** *Billiards* etc. **a** a series of points scored during one turn. **b** the opening shot that disperses the balls. **7** *Mus.* (in jazz etc.) a short unaccompanied passage for a soloist. **8** *Electr.* a discontinuity in a circuit. □ **break away** make or become free or separate (see also BREAKAWAY). **break the back of 1** do the hardest or greatest part of. **2** overburden (a person). **break down 1 a** fail in mechanical action; cease to function. **b** (of human relationships etc.) collapse. **c** fail in (esp. mental) health. **d** be overcome by emotion. **2 a** demolish. **b** overcome (resistance). **c** force (a person) to yield under pressure. **3** analyse into components (see also BREAKDOWN). **break even** emerge from a transaction etc. with neither profit nor loss. **break the ice 1** begin to overcome formality or shyness. **2** make a start. **break in 1** enter premises by force. **2** interrupt. **3 a** accustom to a habit etc. **b** wear etc. until comfortable. **c** esp. *Brit.* tame or discipline (an animal); accustom (a horse) to saddle and bridle etc. **4** *Austral.* & *NZ* bring (virgin land) into cultivation. **break into 1** enter forcibly or violently. **2 a** suddenly begin, burst forth with (a song, laughter, etc.). **b** suddenly change one's pace for (a faster one) (*broke into a gallop*). **3** interrupt. **break a leg** (as *int.*) *Theatr. slang* good luck. **break new** (or **fresh**) **ground** see GROUND[1]. **break of day** dawn. **break off 1** detach by breaking. **2** bring to an end. **3** cease talking etc. **break open** open forcibly. **break out 1** escape by force. **2** begin suddenly (*then violence broke out*). **3** (foll. by *in*) become covered in (a rash etc.). **4** exclaim. **5** *US* **a** open up (a receptacle) and remove its contents. **b** remove (articles) from a place of storage. **break step** get out of step. **break up 1** break into small pieces. **2** disperse. **3** *Brit.* end the school term. **4 a** terminate a relationship; disband. **b** cause to do this. **5** *Brit.* (of the weather) change suddenly. **6** esp. *US* **a** upset or be upset. **b** excite or be excited. **c** convulse or be convulsed (see also BREAK-UP). **break wind** release gas from the anus. [Old English]

breakable *adj.* & *n.* • *adj.* that may or is apt to be broken easily. • *n.* (esp. in *pl.*) a breakable thing

breakage *n.* **1** an act or instance of breaking. **2 a** a broken thing. **b** damage caused by breaking.

breakaway *n.* **1** the act or an instance of breaking away or seceding. **2** (*attrib.*) that breaks away or has broken away.

break-dancing *n.* an energetic and acrobatic style of street dancing, developed by US blacks.

breakdown *n.* **1 a** a mechanical failure. **b** a loss of (esp. mental) health. **2** a collapse (*breakdown of communication*). **3** a detailed analysis (of statistics etc.).

breaker *n.* **1** a person or thing that breaks something, esp. *Brit.* disused machinery. **2** a person who breaks in a horse. **3** a heavy wave that breaks.

breakfast • *n.* the first meal of the day. • *v.intr.* have breakfast. □ **have for breakfast** *slang* defeat easily. [from *break fast* (after the night's sleep)]

B

B

breakfast television n. early-morning television.

break-in n. an illegal forced entry into premises.

breaking and entering n. Brit. hist. & US Law the illegal entering of a building with intent to commit a felony.

breaking point n. the point of greatest strain, at which a thing breaks or a person gives way.

breakneck attrib.adj. (of speed) dangerously fast.

breakout n. a forcible escape.

break point n. **1** a place or time at which an interruption or change is made. **2** Tennis a point which would win the game for the player(s) receiving service (three break points). **3** = BREAKING POINT.

breakthrough n. **1** a major advance or discovery. **2** an act of breaking through an obstacle etc.

break-up n. **1** the disintegration or collapse of a thing. **2** a dispersal.

breakwater n. a barrier built out into the sea to break the force of waves.

bream n. (pl. same) **1** ▶ a yellowish deep-bodied freshwater fish, Abramis brama, of the carp family. **2** (in full **sea bream**) a similarly shaped marine fish of the family Sparidae, of the NE Atlantic. [from Old French bre(s)me]

BREAM:
BRONZE BREAM
(Abramis brama)

breast ● n. **1 a** ▲ either of two milk-secreting organs on the upper front of a woman's body. **b** the corresponding part of a man's body. **2 a** the chest. **b** the corresponding part of an animal. **3** the part of a garment that covers the breast. ● v.tr. **1** face, meet in full opposition (breast the wind). **2** contend with (breast it out against difficulties). **3** reach the top of (a hill). □ **breast the tape** see TAPE. **make a clean breast of** (esp. in phr. **make a clean breast of it**) confess fully. [Old English] □ **breasted** adj. (also in comb.).

breastbone n. a thin flat vertical bone and cartilage in the chest connecting the ribs. ▷ STERNUM

breastfeed v.tr. (past and past part. **-fed**) feed (a baby) from the breast.

breastplate n. ▶ a piece of armour covering the breast. ▷ ARMOUR, ROUNDHEAD

breaststroke n. a stroke made while swimming on the breast by extending arms forward and sweeping them back in unison.

breastwork n. a low temporary defence or parapet.

breath n. **1 a** the air taken into or expelled from the lungs. **b** one respiration of air. **c** an exhalation of air that can be seen, smelt, or heard (bad breath). **2 a** a slight movement of air. **b** a whiff of perfume etc. **3** a whisper, a murmur. **4** the power of breathing; life (is there breath in him?). □ **below** (or **under**) **one's breath** in a whisper. **breath of fresh air 1** a small amount of or a brief time in the fresh air. **2** a refreshing change. **catch one's breath 1** cease breathing momentarily in surprise etc. **2** rest after exercise to restore normal breathing. **draw breath** breathe; live. **hold one's breath** cease breathing temporarily. **out of breath** gasping for air. **take breath** pause for rest. **take one's breath away** astound; surprise; delight. [Old English]

breathable adj. **1** (of the air etc.) fit or pleasant to breathe. **2** (of material) admitting air to the skin and allowing sweat to evaporate.

breathalyser n. (US & propr. **breathalyzer**) an

strap to attach
backplate

lance-
rest

strap to attach
metal-plate skirt

BREASTPLATE:
16TH-CENTURY ITALIAN
BREASTPLATE

instrument for measuring the amount of alcohol in the breath of a driver. □ **breathalyse** v.tr. (US **-lyze**).

breathe v. **1** intr. **a** take air into and expel it from the lungs. **b** take in oxygen. **2** intr. be or seem alive (is she breathing?). **3** tr. **a** utter; say (breathed her forgiveness). **b** express (breathed defiance). **4** intr. take breath, pause. **5** tr. send out or take in (as if) with breathed air (breathed new life into them). **6** intr. **a** (of wine, the skin, etc.) be exposed to fresh air. **b** (of material) admit air or moisture. □ **breathe down a person's neck** follow or check up on a person, esp. menacingly. **breathe one's last** die. **not breathe a word** keep quite secret. [Middle English]

breather n. colloq. a brief pause for rest.

breathing-space n. time to breathe; a pause.

breathless adj. **1** out of breath. **2** holding, or as if holding, the breath because of excitement etc. **3** still. □ **breathlessly** adv. **breathlessness** n.

breathtaking adj. awe-inspiring. □ **breathtakingly** adv.

breath test n. a test of a person's alcohol consumption, using a breathalyser.

breathy adj. (**breathier**, **breathiest**) (of a singing voice etc.) containing the sound of breathing. □ **breathily** adv. **breathiness** n.

breccia /bre-chă/ ● n. ▶ a rock of angular stones etc. cemented by finer material. ● v.tr. form into breccia. [Italian, literally 'gravel'] □ **brecciate** v.tr. **brecciation** n.

bred past and past part. of BREED.

breech n. **1 a** the part of a cannon behind the bore. **b** the back part of a rifle or gun barrel. **2** archaic the buttocks. [Old English]

breech birth n. (also **breech delivery**) the delivery of a baby which is so positioned in the womb that the buttocks or feet are delivered first.

breeches /brich-iz/ n.pl. (also **pair of breeches** sing.) short trousers, esp. fastened below the knee.

breech-loader n. a gun loaded at the breech, not through the muzzle. □ **breech-loading** adj.

breed ● v. (past and past part. **bred**) **1** tr. & intr. bear, generate (offspring). **2** tr. & intr. propagate or cause to propagate; raise (livestock). **3** tr. **a** yield; result in (war breeds famine). **b** spread (discontent bred by rumour). **4** intr. arise; spread (disease breeds in the Tropics). **5** tr. bring up; train (Hollywood breeds stars). **6** tr. Physics create (fissile material) by nuclear reaction. ● n. **1** a stock of animals or plants within a species, having a similar appearance, and usu.

developed by deliberate selection. **2** a race; a lineage. **3** a sort, a kind. [Old English] □ **breeder** n.

breeder reactor n. a nuclear reactor that can create more fissile material than it consumes.

breeding n. **1** the process of developing or propagating (animals, plants, etc.). **2** the result of training or education; behaviour. **3** good manners (as produced by an aristocratic heredity).

breeze[1] ● n. **1** a gentle wind. **2** a wind blowing from land or sea during the day. **3** esp. Brit. colloq. a quarrel or display of temper. **4** esp. N. Amer. colloq. an easy task. ● v.intr. (foll. by in, out, along, etc.) colloq. come or go in a casual manner.

breeze[2] n. small cinders. [from French braise 'live coals']

breeze-block n. Brit. a lightweight building block, esp. one made from breeze mixed with sand and cement.

breezy adj. (**breezier**, **breeziest**) **1** slightly windy. **2** colloq. lively; jovial. **3** colloq. careless (breezy indifference). □ **breezily** adv. **breeziness** n.

Bren n. (in full **Bren gun**) a lightweight quick-firing machine-gun. [from Brno in the Czech Republic (where originally made) + Enfield in England (where later made)]

brent n. (US **brant**) (in full **brent-goose**) a small migratory goose, Branta bernicla. [16th-century coinage]

brethren see BROTHER.

Breton ● n. **1** a native of Brittany. **2** the Celtic language of Brittany. ● adj. of or relating to Brittany or its people or language. [from Old French, literally 'Briton']

breve n. **1** Mus. a note having the time value of two semibreves. ▷ NOTATION. **2** a written or printed mark (˘) indicating a short or unstressed vowel. [Middle English variant of brief]

BRECCIA

breviary n. (pl. **-ies**) RC Ch. a book containing the service for each day. [from Latin breviarium 'summary']

brevity n. **1** conciseness. **2** shortness (of time etc.) (the brevity of happiness). [from Old French brieveté, based on bref 'brief']

brew ● v. **1** tr. **a** make (beer etc.) by infusion, boiling, and fermentation. **b** make (tea etc.) by infusion or (punch etc.) by mixture. **2** intr. undergo either of these processes (the tea is brewing). **3** intr. (of trouble, a storm, etc.) threaten. **4** tr. bring about; concoct. ● n. **1** an amount (of beer etc.) brewed at one time (this year's brew). **2** what is brewed (a strong brew). **3** the process of brewing. □ **brew up** Brit. make tea. [Old English] □ **brewer** n.

brewery n. (pl. **-ies**) a place where beer etc. is brewed commercially.

brew-up n. Brit. colloq. an instance of making tea.

briar[1] var. of BRIER[1].

briar[2] var. of BRIER[2].

BREAST

Breasts are organs of fleshy tissue that overlie the pectoralis major muscles. The female breast contains 15–20 lobes of milk-producing glands, supported by ligaments. During pregnancy, under hormonal influence, these glands enlarge and prepare to secrete milk (lactate) to feed the suckling infant. Milk gathers in the lactiferous sinuses, and is released through the ducts when the nipple is sucked.

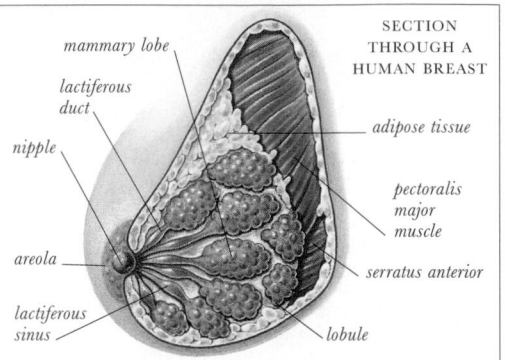

SECTION THROUGH A HUMAN BREAST

mammary lobe

lactiferous duct

nipple

areola

lactiferous sinus

adipose tissue

pectoralis major muscle

serratus anterior

lobule

BRICK

Strong, durable, and inexpensive, bricks have been made since ancient times, and are usually cast in standard sizes and shapes to simplify their laying. Styles of brickwork are typical of a particular region and era. The English bond was used in early brickwork of late medieval times, while the Flemish bond was popular during the early 17th century. The stretcher bond is often favoured for modern buildings.

TYPES OF BRICKWORK

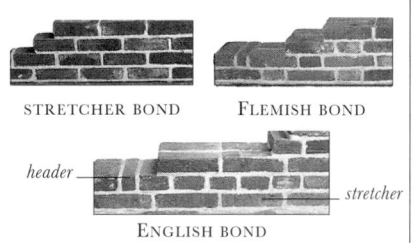

STRETCHER BOND   FLEMISH BOND

header — ENGLISH BOND — *stretcher*

bribe ● *v.tr.* persuade to act improperly in one's favour by a gift of money, services, etc. ● *n.* money or services offered in the process of bribing. [from Old French *briber* 'to beg'] □ **bribery** *n.*

bric-a-brac *n.* (also **bric-à-brac**, **bricabrac**) cheap ornaments, trinkets, etc. [French]

brick ● *n.* **1 a** ▲ a small block of fired or sun-dried clay, used in building. ▷ HOUSE. **b** the material used to make these. **c** a similar block of concrete etc. **2** *Brit.* a child's toy building block. **3** a brick-shaped solid object. **4** *slang* a generous or loyal person. ● *v.tr.* (foll. by *in*, *up*) close or block with brickwork. ● *adj.* **1** built of brick (*brick wall*). **2** of a dull red colour. [from Middle Dutch *bri(c)ke*]

brickbat *n.* **1** a piece of brick. **2** an uncomplimentary remark.

brickie *n. Brit. slang* a bricklayer.

bricklayer *n.* a worker who builds with bricks. □ **bricklaying** *n.*

brickwork *n.* **1** work executed in brick. ▷ BRICK. **2** bricklaying.

bridal *adj.* of or concerning a bride or a wedding.

bride *n.* a woman on her wedding day and for some time before and after it. [Old English]

bridegroom *n.* a man on his wedding day and for some time before and after it.

bridesmaid *n.* a girl or unmarried woman attending a bride on her wedding day.

bridge[1] ● *n.* (also *Sc.* & *N.Engl.* **brig**) **1 a** ▼ a structure carrying a road, path, railway, etc., across a stream, ravine, road, railway, etc. **b** anything providing a connection between different things. **2** the superstructure on a ship from which the officers direct operations. **3** the upper bony part of the nose. **4** *Mus.* an upright piece of wood on a violin etc. over which the strings are stretched. ▷ ACOUSTIC, STRINGED. **5** = BRIDGEWORK. ● *v.tr.* **1 a** be a bridge over (*a fallen tree bridges the stream*). **b** make a bridge over. **2** span as if with a bridge (*bridged their differences with understanding*). [Old English]

bridge[2] *n.* a card game derived from whist. [19th-century coinage]

bridge-building *n.* **1** the activity of building bridges. **2** the promotion of friendly relations, esp. between countries. □ **bridge-builder** *n.*

bridgehead *n. Mil.* a fortified position held on the enemy's side of a river or other obstacle.

bridge roll *n. Brit.* a small soft bread roll.

bridgework *n.* a dental structure used to cover a gap, joined to the teeth on either side.

bridging loan *n. esp. Brit.* a loan from a bank etc. to cover the short interval between buying a house etc. and selling another.

bridle ● *n.* ► the headgear used to control a horse, consisting of leather straps and a metal bit. ▷ HARNESS. ● *v.* **1** *tr.* put a bridle on (a horse etc.). **2** *tr.* bring under control. **3** *intr.* (often foll. by *at*, *up at*) express offence etc., esp. by throwing up the head and drawing in the chin. [Old English]

bridle path *n.* (also **bridleway**) a rough path fit only for riders or walkers, not vehicles.

Brie /bree/ *n.* a kind of soft cheese. ▷ CHEESE. [from *Brie* in N. France, where first made]

brief ● *adj.* **1** of short duration. **2** concise in expression. **3** brusque. **4** (of clothes) scanty. ● *n.* **1** (in *pl.*) close-fitting legless pants. **2** *Law* **a** *Brit.* a document instructing a barrister to appear as an advocate in court. **b** *US* a written summary of the legal points supporting one side of a case, for presentation to a court. **3** *esp. Brit.* instructions given for a task etc. **4** *RC Ch.* a letter from the Pope on a matter of discipline. ● *v.tr.* **1** *Brit. Law* instruct by brief. **2** instruct in preparation for a task. □ **hold a brief for 1** argue in favour of. **2** *Brit.* be retained as counsel for. **in brief** in short. [from Latin *brevis* 'short'] □ **briefing** *n.* **briefly** *adv.* **briefness** *n.*

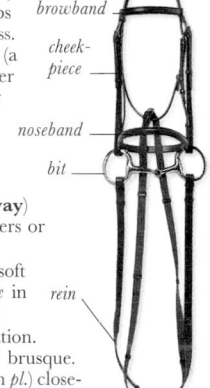

head piece
browband
cheek-piece
noseband
bit
rein

BRIDLE:
SNAFFLE
BRIDLE

briefcase *n.* a flat rectangular case for carrying documents etc.

brier[1] *n.* (also **briar**) any prickly bush esp. of a wild rose. [Old English]

brier[2] *n.* (also **briar**) **1** a white heath, *Erica arborea*, native to S. Europe. **2** a tobacco pipe made from its root. [from French *bruyère* 'heath']

Brig. *abbr.* Brigadier.

brig *n.* **1** a two-masted square-rigged ship, with an additional lower fore-and-aft sail on the gaff and a boom to the mainmast. **2** *slang* a prison, esp. on a warship. [abbreviation of BRIGANTINE]

brigade *n.* **1** *Mil.* **a** a subdivision of an army. **b** a British armoured or infantry unit consisting usu. of three battalions and forming part of a division. **2** an organized or uniformed band of workers (*fire brigade*). **3** *colloq.* a group of people with a characteristic in common (*the couldn't-care-less brigade*). [from Italian *brigata* 'company']

brigadier *n. Brit. Mil.* **1** an officer commanding a brigade. **2 a** a staff officer of similar standing, above a colonel and below a major general. **b** the titular rank granted to such an officer.

brigadier general *n.* an officer ranking next above colonel in the US army, air force, and marine corps.

brigand *n.* a member of a robber band living by pillage and ransom. [based on Italian *briga* 'strife'] □ **brigandage** *n.* **brigandry** *n.*

brigantine *n.* a two-masted sailing ship with a square-rigged foremast and a fore-and-aft-rigged mainmast. [earlier, a small vessel used by pirates: based on Italian *brigante* 'brigand']

bright ● *adj.* **1** emitting or reflecting much light. **2** (of colour) intense. **3** clever (*a bright idea*, *a bright child*). **4** cheerful. ● *adv. esp. poet.* brightly (*the moon shone bright*). [Old English] □ **brightish** *adj.* **brightly** *adv.* **brightness** *n.*

brighten *v.tr. & intr.* (often foll. by *up*) make or become brighter.

bright spark *n. colloq.* a witty, lively, or intelligent person.

brill[1] *n.* a European flatfish, *Scophthalmus rhombus*, resembling a turbot. [15th-century coinage]

brill[2] *Brit. colloq.* = BRILLIANT *adj.* 3.

brilliance *n.* (also **brilliancy**) **1** great brightness; radiant quality. **2** outstanding talent or intelligence.

brilliant ● *adj.* **1** very bright; sparkling. **2** outstandingly talented or intelligent. **3** *Brit. colloq.* excellent, superb. ● *n.* a diamond of the finest cut with many facets. ▷ DIAMOND, GEM. [based on Italian *brillare* 'to shine'] □ **brilliantly** *adv.*

brilliantine *n.* an oily liquid dressing for making the hair glossy.

brim ● *n.* **1** the edge or lip of a cup etc. or of a hollow. **2** the projecting edge of a hat. ▷ HAT. ● *v.tr. & intr.* (**brimmed**, **brimming**) fill or be full to the brim. □ **brim over** overflow. [Middle English] □ **brimmed** *adj.* (usu. in *comb.*).

brim-full *adj.* (also **brimful**) (often foll. by *of*) filled to the brim.

brimstone *n.* **1** *archaic* the element sulphur. **2** a butterfly, *Gonepteryx rhamni*, or moth, *Opisthograptis luteolata*, having yellow wings. [Middle English]

brindled *adj.* (also **brindle**) brownish or tawny with streaks of other colour (esp. of domestic animals). [variant of earlier *brinded*]

brine *n.* **1** water saturated or strongly impregnated with salt. **2** sea water. [Old English]

bring *v.tr.* (*past* and *past part.* **brought**) **1 a** come conveying esp. by carrying or leading. **b** come with. **2** cause to come (*what brings you here?*). **3** result in (*war brings misery*). **4** produce as income. **5 a** prefer (a charge). **b** initiate (legal action). **6** cause to become or to reach a particular condition (*brought them to their senses*). **7** adduce (evidence, an argument, etc.). □ **bring about 1** cause to happen. **2** turn (a ship) around. **bring back** call to mind. **bring down 1** cause to fall. **2** lower (a price). **3** *colloq.* damage the reputation of; demean. **bring forth** produce.

BRIDGE

Bridges vary in construction according to the gap they must span and their projected load. A cantilever bridge is ideal for supporting heavy loads, although an arch bridge is preferable where terrain prevents erection of pier supports. A suspension bridge may span widths of up to 1 km (0.6 miles).

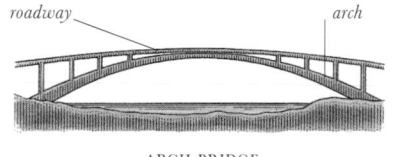

roadway   *arch*

ARCH BRIDGE

EXAMPLES OF BRIDGES

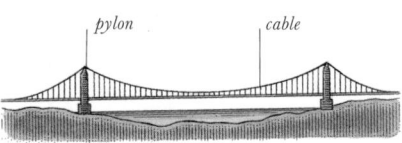

pylon   *cable*

SUSPENSION BRIDGE

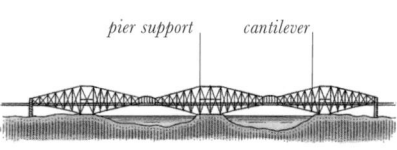

pier support   *cantilever*

CANTILEVER BRIDGE

B

bring forward 1 move to an earlier time. **2** transfer from the previous page or account. **3** draw attention to. **bring home to** cause to realize fully (*brought home to me that I was wrong*). **bring the house down** receive rapturous applause. **bring in 1** introduce (legislation, a custom, etc.). **2** yield as income or profit. **bring into play** activate. **bring low 1** overcome; deject. **2** humiliate. **bring off** achieve successfully. **bring on 1** cause to happen or appear. **2** accelerate the progress of. **bring out 1** make evident. **2** publish. **bring round** (or *US* **around**) **1** restore to consciousness. **2** persuade. **bring through** aid (a person) through adversity. **bring to 1** restore to consciousness (*brought him to*). **2** check the motion of. **bring to bear** (usu. foll. by *on*) direct and concentrate (forces). **bring to light** see LIGHT[1]. **bring to mind** recall. **bring to pass** cause to happen. **bring up 1** rear (a child). **2** vomit. **3** call attention to. **bring upon oneself** be responsible for (something one suffers). [Old English] □ **bringer** *n.*

bring-and-buy sale *n. Brit.* a charity sale at which people bring items for sale and buy what is brought by others.

brink *n.* **1** the extreme edge of land before a precipice etc. **2** the furthest point before something dangerous or exciting is discovered. □ **on the brink of** about to experience or suffer. [from Old Norse]

brinkmanship *n.* the art or policy of pursuing a dangerous course to the brink of catastrophe before desisting, esp in politics.

briny ● *adj.* of brine or the sea; salty. ● *n.* (prec. by *the*) *Brit. slang* the sea. □ **brininess** *n.*

brio *n.* dash, vigour, vivacity. [Italian]

brioche /bree-osh/ *n.* a small rounded sweet roll made with a light yeast dough. [French]

briquette /bri-ket/ *n.* (also **briquet**) a block of compressed coal dust used as fuel. [French, literally 'little brick']

brisk ● *adj.* **1** quick, lively (*a brisk pace*). **2** enlivening; fresh (*a brisk wind*). ● *v.tr. & intr.* (often foll. by *up*) make or grow brisk. □ **brisken** *v.tr. & intr.* **briskly** *adv.* **briskness** *n.*

brisket *n.* an animal's breast as a joint of meat. [from Old French *bruschet*]

brisling *n.* (*pl.* same or **brislings**) a small herring or sprat. [Norwegian & Danish, literally 'sprat']

bristle ● *n.* **1** a short stiff hair, esp. one of those on an animal's back. **2** such hairs, or a man-made substitute, used in clumps to make a brush. ● *v.* **1 a** *intr.* (of the hair) stand upright. **b** *tr.* make (the hair) do this. **2** *intr.* show irritation or defensiveness. **3** *intr.* (usu. foll. by *with*) be abundant (in) (*bristling with images*). [Middle English, from earlier *byrst*] □ **bristly** *adj.*

Brit *n. colloq.* a British person.

Britannia *n.* the personification of Britain, esp. as a helmeted woman with shield and trident. [Latin, from Greek *Brettania*, from *Brettanoi*, 'Britons']

Britannic *adj.* (esp. in **His** (or **Her**) **Britannic Majesty**) of Britain.

Briticism *n.* (also **Britishism**) an idiom used in Britain but not in other English-speaking countries.

British *adj.* **1** of or relating to Great Britain or the United Kingdom, its people or language. **2** of the British Commonwealth or (formerly) the British Empire (*British subject*). [Old English, from *Bret* Briton']

British English *n.* English as used in Great Britain, as distinct from that used elsewhere.

Britisher *n.* a British subject.

Britishism var. of BRITICISM.

British Summer Time *n.* time as advanced one hour ahead of Greenwich Mean Time for daylight saving between March and October.

British thermal unit *n.* the amount of heat needed to raise 1lb of water at maximum density through one degree Fahrenheit, equivalent to 1.055×10^3 joules.

Briton *n.* **1** one of the people of southern Britain before the Roman conquest. **2** a native or inhabitant of Great Britain or (formerly) of the British Empire.

brittle ● *adj.* hard and fragile; apt to break. ● *n.* a brittle sweet made from nuts and set melted sugar. [Middle English] □ **brittleness** *n.*

brittle-bone disease *n.* **1** = OSTEOPOROSIS. **2** a hereditary condition causing extreme fragility of the bones.

brittle-star ● *n.* ◄ an echinoderm of the class Ophiuroidea, with long flexible arms radiating from a small central body. ▷ ECHINODERM

BRITTLE-STAR: BLACK BRITTLE-STAR (*Ophiocomina nigra*)

broach ● *v.tr.* **1** raise (a subject) for discussion. **2** pierce (a cask) to draw liquor. **3** open and start using the contents of (a box etc.). ● *n.* **1** a bit for boring. **2** a roasting-spit. [based on Latin *brocc(h)us* 'projecting']

broad ● *adj.* **1** large in extent from one side to the other; wide. **2** in breadth (*2 metres broad*). **3** extensive (*broad acres*). **4** full and clear (*broad daylight*). **5** clear, explicit (*broad hint*). **6** general (*a broad inquiry*). **7** markedly regional (*broad Scots*). **8** principal (*the broad facts*). **9** widely inclusive (*take a broad view*). **10** somewhat coarse (*broad humour*). ● *n.* **1** the broad part of something (*broad of the back*). **2** *N. Amer. slang offens.* a woman. [Old English] □ **broadness** *n.*

broadband *attrib.adj.* relating to or using signals over a broad range of frequencies, esp. in high-capacity telecommunications.

broad bean *n.* **1** a kind of bean, *Vicia faba*, with pods containing large edible flat seeds. **2** one of these seeds. ▷ SEED

broad-brush *attrib.adj.* as if painted with a broad brush; general; lacking in detail (*adopted a broad-brush approach*).

broadcast ● *v.* (*past* **broadcast** and *past part.* **broadcast** or **broadcasted**) **1** *tr.* **a** transmit by radio or television. **b** disseminate (information) widely. **2** *intr.* undertake or take part in a radio or television transmission. **3** *tr.* scatter (seed etc.) over a large area. ● *n.* a radio or television transmission. ● *adj.* **1** transmitted by radio or television. **2** widely disseminated. ● *adv.* over a large area. □ **broadcaster** *n.* **broadcasting** *n.*

broad church *n.* a group allowing its members a wide range of opinion.

broadcloth *n.* a fine cloth of wool, cotton, or silk. [originally with reference to width and quality]

broaden *v.tr. & intr.* make or become broader.

broadleaved *adj.* (of a tree) having relatively broad flat leaves rather than needles; non-coniferous. □ **broadleaf** *n. & attrib.adj.*

broadloom *adj.* (esp. of carpet) woven in broad widths.

broadly *adv.* widely (*grinned broadly*). □ **broadly speaking** disregarding minor exceptions.

broad-minded *adj.* tolerant in one's views. □ **broad-mindedly** *adv.* **broad-mindedness** *n.*

broadsheet *n.* **1** a large sheet of paper printed on one side only, esp. with information. **2** a newspaper with a large format.

broadside *n.* **1** the firing of all guns from one side of a ship. **2** a vigorous verbal onslaught. □ **broadside on** sideways on.

broad spectrum *adj.* (of a drug) effective against a large variety of micro-organisms.

broadsword *n.* a sword with a broad blade, for cutting rather than thrusting. ▷ SWORD

broadway *n.* a large open or main road.

brocade *n.* ▶ a rich fabric with a silky finish woven with a raised pattern. [based on Italian *brocco* 'twisted thread']

broccoli *n.* a variety of cabbage, similar to the cauliflower, with a loose cluster of greenish flower buds. [Italian, literally 'little sprout']

brochure /broh-sher/ *n.* a pamphlet or leaflet, esp. one giving descriptive information. [French, literally 'a stitched work']

broderie anglaise *n.* open embroidery on white linen or cambric, esp. in floral patterns. [French, literally 'English embroidery']

BROCADE: 18TH-CENTURY BROCADE DRESS

brogue[1] *n.* **1** a strong outdoor shoe with perforated bands. **2** a rough shoe of untanned leather. [from Old Norse *brók*]

brogue[2] *n.* a marked accent, esp. Irish. [18th-century coinage]

broil *v.* esp. *N. Amer.* **1** *tr.* cook (meat) on a rack or a gridiron. **2** *tr. & intr.* make or become very hot. [from Old French *bruler* 'to burn']

broiler *n.* **1** a young chicken raised for broiling or roasting. **2** *N. Amer.* a gridiron etc. for broiling.

broke *past* of BREAK. ● *predic.adj. colloq.* having no money. □ **go for broke** *slang* risk everything in an all-out effort.

broken *past part.* of BREAK. ● *adj.* **1** that has been broken. **2** (of a person) reduced to despair. **3** spoken falteringly and with many mistakes (*broken English*). **4** interrupted. **5** uneven. □ **brokenly** *adv.* **brokenness** *n.*

broken-down *adj.* **1** worn out. **2** not functioning.

broken-hearted *adj.* overwhelmed with sorrow.

broken home *n.* a family in which the parents are divorced or separated.

broker ● *n.* **1** an agent who buys and sells for others. **2** a member of the Stock Exchange dealing in stocks and shares. **3** *Brit.* an official appointed to sell or appraise distrained goods. **4** a middleman, agent, or messenger. ● *v.tr* act as a broker for (negotiations etc.). [from Anglo-French *brocour*] □ **broking** *n. Brit.*

■ **Usage** The term *broker* in sense 2 was officially replaced in the UK by *broker-dealer* in 1986.

brokerage *n.* **1** the action or service of a broker. **2** a company providing such a service. **3** a broker's fee or commission.

broker-dealer *n.* a person combining the former functions of a broker and jobber on the Stock Exchange.

brolly *n.* (*pl.* **-ies**) *Brit.* **1** *colloq.* an umbrella. **2** *slang* a parachute.

bromate *n. Chem.* a salt or ester of bromic acid.

brome *n.* (in full **brome grass**) any oatlike grass of the genus *Bromus*, having slender stems with flowering spikes. [from Greek *bromos* 'oat']

bromelia *n.* (also **bromeliad**) ▶ any plant of the family Bromeliaceae (esp. of the genus *Bromelia*), native to the New World, having short stems with rosettes of stiff leaves, e.g. pineapple. ▷ EPIPHYTE. [named after O. *Bromel*, Swedish botanist,1639–1705].

BROMELIA (*Bromelia balansae*)

bromide *n.* **1** *Chem.* any compound of bromine with another element or group. **2** *Pharm.* a preparation of usu. potassium bromide, used as a sedative. **3** a trite remark.

bromide paper *n.* a photographic printing paper coated with silver bromide emulsion.

bromine *n. Chem.* a liquid element with a choking irritating smell used in the manufacture of chemicals for photography and medicine. [based on Greek *brōmos* 'a stink']

bronchi *pl.* of BRONCHUS.

bronchiole /brong-ki-ohl/ *n.* ▶ any of the minute divisions of a bronchus. ▷ LUNG. □ **bronchiolar** *adj.*

bronchitis /brong-**ky**-tis/ *n.* inflammation of the mucous membrane in the bronchial tubes. □ **bronchitic** *adj. & n.*

broncho- /brong-koh/ *comb. form* bronchi. [from Greek *brogkho-*]

bronchodilator *n.* a substance which causes widening of the bronchi, used esp. to alleviate asthma.

bronchopneumonia *n.* inflammation of the lungs, arising in the bronchi or bronchioles.

bronchus /**brong**-kŭs/ *n.* (*pl.* **bronchi** /-ky/) any of the major air passages of the lungs. ▷ LUNG. [from Greek *brogkhos* 'windpipe'] □ **bronchial** *adj.*

bronco *n.* (*pl.* **-os**) a wild or half-tamed horse of the western US. [Spanish, literally 'rough']

brontosaurus *n.* (also **brontosaur**) = APATOSAURUS. [from Greek *brontē* 'thunder' + *sauros* 'lizard']

bronze ● *n.* **1** an alloy of copper with up to one-third tin. **2** its brownish colour. **3** ▶ a thing made of bronze, esp. as a work of art. ● *adj.* made of or coloured like bronze. ● *v.* **1** *tr.* give a surface of bronze or resembling bronze to. **2** *tr. & intr.* tan. [from Italian *bronzo*] □ **bronzy** *adj.*

Bronze Age *n.* the period when weapons and tools were usu. made of bronze.

brooch /brohch/ *n.* an ornament fastened to clothing with a hinged pin. [variant of BROACH]

brood ● *n.* **1** the young of an animal (esp. a bird) produced at one hatching or birth. **2** *colloq.* the children in a family. **3** a group of related things. **4** bee or wasp larvae. **5** (*attrib.*) kept for breeding (*brood mare*). ● *v.* **1** *intr.* worry or ponder (esp. resentfully). **2 a** *intr.* sit as a hen on eggs to hatch them. **b** *tr.* sit on (eggs) to hatch them. **3** *intr.* (usu. foll. by *over*) (of silence, a storm, etc.) hang or hover closely. [Old English, related to BREED] □ **broodingly** *adv.*

broody *adj.* (**broodier**, **broodiest**) **1** (of a hen) wanting to brood. **2** sullenly thoughtful. **3** *Brit. colloq.* (of a woman) wanting to have a baby. □ **broodily** *adv.* **broodiness** *n.*

brook[1] *n.* a small stream. [Old English] □ **brooklet** *n.*

brook[2] *v.tr.* (usu. with *neg.*) *formal* tolerate. [Old English]

broom *n.* **1** a long-handled brush of bristles, twigs, etc. for sweeping. **2** any of various shrubs, esp. *Cytisus scoparius*, bearing bright yellow flowers. [Old English]

broomstick *n.* the handle of a broom, esp. as allegedly ridden through the air by witches.

Bros. *abbr.* Brothers (esp. in the name of a firm).

broth *n.* **1** a thin soup of meat or fish stock. **2** unclarified meat or fish stock. [Old English]

brothel *n.* a house etc. where prostitution takes place. [earlier in sense 'wretch': from Old English *brēothan* 'to go to ruin']

brother *n.* **1** a man or boy in relation to other sons

and daughters of his parents. **2 a** a close male friend or associate. **b** a male fellow member of a trade union etc. **3** (*pl.* also **brethren**) **a** a member of a male religious order. **b** a fellow member of a religion etc. **4** a fellow human being. [Old English] □ **brotherless** *adj.* **brotherly** *adj. & adv.* **brotherliness** *n.*

brother german see GERMAN 1.

brotherhood *n.* **1 a** the relationship between brothers. **b** brotherly friendliness. **2 a** an association or community of people linked by a common interest etc. **b** its members collectively. **3** *N. Amer.* a trade union. **4** community of feeling between all human beings.

brother-in-law *n.* (*pl.* **brothers-in-law**) **1** the brother of one's wife or husband. **2** the husband of one's sister. **3** the husband of one's sister-in-law.

brother uterine see UTERINE 2.

brought *past* and *past part.* of BRING.

brouhaha /broo-hah-hah/ *n.* commotion, sensation; uproar. [French]

brow *n.* **1** the forehead. **2** (usu. in *pl.*) an eyebrow. **3** the summit of a hill or pass. **4** the edge of a cliff etc. [Old English] □ **-browed** *adj.* (in *comb.*).

browbeat *v.tr.* (*past* **-beat**; *past part.* **-beaten**) intimidate with stern looks and words. □ **browbeater** *n.*

brown ● *adj.* **1** having the colour as of dark wood or rich soil. **2** dark-skinned or suntanned. **3** (of bread) made from a dark flour. ● *n.* **1** a brown colour or pigment. **2** brown clothes or material (*dressed in brown*). ● *v.tr. & intr.* make or become brown. [Old English] □ **brownish** *adj.* **brownness** *n.* **browny** *adj.*

brown bear *n.* a large brown bear, *Ursus arctos*, found in parts of Eurasia and N. America. ▷ BEAR

browned off *adj. Brit. slang* fed up.

brown goods *n.pl. Brit.* household goods such as television sets and audio equipment.

Brownian motion *n.* (also **Brownian movement**) *Physics* the erratic random movement of microscopic particles in a liquid, gas, etc., as a result of continuous bombardment from molecules of the surrounding medium. [named after R. *Brown*, Scots botanist, 1773–1858]

Brownie *n.* **1** (*Brit.* in full **Brownie Guide**) a member of the junior branch of the Guides Association. **2** (**brownie**) a benevolent elf said to do housework secretly.

brownie point *n. colloq.* a notional credit for something done to win favour.

browning *n. Brit.* browned flour or any other additive to colour gravy.

brown owl *n.* **1** any of various owls, esp. the tawny owl. **2** (**Brown Owl**) *Brit. colloq.* the adult leader of a pack of Brownie Guides, officially termed *Brownie Guider* since 1968.

brown rice *n.* unpolished rice with only the husk of the grain removed.

Brownshirt *n.* a Nazi; a member of a fascist organization.

brown sugar *n.* unrefined or partially refined sugar.

brown trout *n.* a common European trout, *Salmo trutta*, or a small dark non-migratory race found in small rivers and pools.

browse ● *v.* **1** *intr. & tr.* read or survey desultorily. **2** *intr.* (often foll. by *on*) feed (on leaves etc.). **3** *tr.* crop and eat. **4** *intr. & tr.* *Computing* read or survey (data

files etc.), esp. via a network. ● *n.* **1** young shoots etc. as fodder for cattle. **2** an act of browsing. [from Old French *brost* 'young shoot'] □ **browser** *n.*

brucellosis *n.* a disease caused by bacteria of the genus *Brucella*, affecting esp. cattle. [modern Latin, from Sir D. *Bruce*, Scots physician, 1855–1931]

bruise ● *n.* **1** an injury appearing as an area of discoloured skin on a human or animal body, caused by impact. **2** an area of damage on a fruit etc. ● *v.* **1** *tr.* inflict a bruise on. **2** *intr.* be susceptible to bruising. **3** *tr.* crush or pound (*bruised oats*). [Old English *brȳsan* 'to crush']

bruiser *n. colloq.* **1** a large tough-looking person. **2** a professional boxer.

bruit ● *v.tr.* (often foll. by *abroad*, *about*) spread (a report or rumour). ● *n. archaic* a report or rumour. [French, literally 'noise']

Brummagem *adj.* **1** cheap and showy (*Brummagem goods*). **2** counterfeit. [dialect form of *Birmingham*, England, with reference to counterfeiting done there]

Brummie (also **Brummy**) *Brit. colloq.* ● *n.* (*pl.* **-ies**) a native of Birmingham. ● *adj.* of or characteristic of a Brummie (*a Brummie accent*).

brunch *n.* a late-morning meal eaten as the first meal of the day. [blend of BREAKFAST and LUNCH]

brunette (*US* also **brunet**) ● *n.* a woman with dark brown hair. ● *adj.* (of a woman) having dark brown hair. [French]

brunt *n.* the chief impact of an attack, task, etc. (esp. *bear the brunt of*). [Middle English]

brush ● *n.* **1** an implement with bristles, hair, wire, etc. set into a block or projecting from the end of a handle, for any of various purposes, esp. cleaning or scrubbing, painting, arranging the hair, etc. ▷ CALLIGRAPHY. **2** the application of a brush; brushing. **3 a** a short encounter (*a brush with the law*). **b** a skirmish. **4 a** the bushy tail of a fox. **b** a brushlike tuft. **5** *Electr.* a piece of carbon or metal serving as an electrical contact. **6** esp. *N. Amer. & Austral.* **a** undergrowth; small trees and shrubs. **b** *US* such wood cut in faggots. **c** land covered with brush. **d** *Austral.* dense forest. ● *v.* **1** *tr.* **a** sweep or scrub or put in order with a brush. **b** treat (a surface) with a brush so as to change its nature or appearance. **2** *tr.* **a** remove (dust etc.) with a brush. **b** apply (a liquid preparation) to a surface with a brush. **3** *tr. & intr.* graze or touch in passing. **4** *intr.* perform a brushing action or motion. □ **brush aside** dismiss curtly or lightly. **brush off** rebuff; dismiss abruptly. **brush over** paint lightly. **brush up** **1** *Brit.* clean up or smarten. **2** (often foll. by *on*) revive one's former knowledge of (a subject). [from (Old) French *brosse*] □ **brushy** *adj.*

brushless *adj.* not requiring the use of a brush.

brush-off *n.* a rebuff.

brush-up *n. Brit.* the act of brushing up.

brushwood *n.* **1** cut or broken twigs etc. **2** undergrowth.

brushwork *n.* **1** manipulation of the brush in painting. **2** a painter's style in this.

brusque /broosk/ *adj.* abrupt or offhand in manner or speech. [from Italian *brusco* 'sour'] □ **brusquely** *adv.* **brusqueness** *n.*

Brussels sprout *n.* **1** a variety of cabbage producing many small compact buds borne close together along a tall single stem. **2** one of these buds used as a vegetable.

brut /broot/ *adj.* (of wine) unsweetened. [French, literally 'rough']

brutal *adj.* **1** savagely cruel. **2** harsh, merciless. □ **brutality** *n.* (*pl.* **-ies**). **brutally** *adv.*

brutalism *n.* **1** brutality. **2** a heavy plain style of architecture etc. □ **brutalist** *n. & adj.*

brutalize *v.tr.* (also **-ise**) **1** make brutal. **2** treat brutally. □ **brutalization** *n.*

brute ● *n.* **1 a** a brutal person or animal. **b** *colloq.* an unpleasant person. **2** an animal as opposed to a human being. ● *adj.* (usu. *attrib.*) **1** not possessing the capacity to reason. **2 a** cruel. **b** stupid, sensual.

trachea

tertiary bronchus

secondary bronchus

primary bronchus

bronchiole

BRONCHIOLE:
HUMAN
BRONCHIOLE

BRONZE DECORATION
FROM CELTIC CHARIOT
(c.100 BC–AD 100)

B

B

3 unthinking, merely material (*brute force*; *brute matter*). [from Latin *brutus* 'stupid'] □ **brutish** *adj*. **brutishness** *n*.

bryony *n*. (*pl*. **-ies**) any climbing plant of the genus *Bryonia*, esp. *B. dioica*, bearing greenish-white flowers and red berries. [from Greek *bruōnia*]

bryophyte *n*. ▶ a non-vascular plant of the division Bryophyta, comprising mosses and liverworts. [from Greek *bruon* 'moss' + *phuton* 'plant']

bryozoan ● *n*. any aquatic invertebrate animal of the phylum Bryozoa, forming colonies attached to rocks, seaweeds, etc. ● *adj*. of or relating to the phylum Bryozoa. [from Greek *bruon* 'moss' + *zōia* 'animals']

BS *abbr*. **1** *US* Bachelor of Science. **2** Bachelor of Surgery. **3** British Standard(s).

B.Sc. *abbr*. Bachelor of Science.

BSE *abbr*. bovine spongiform encephalopathy, a usu. fatal disease of cattle involving the central nervous system.

BSI *abbr*. British Standards Institution.

B-side *n*. the side of a gramophone record regarded as less important.

BST *abbr*. British Summer Time.

Bt. *abbr*. Baronet.

BTEC *abbr*. (also **Btec**) Business and Technician Education Council.

Btu *abbr*. (also **BTU**, **B.th.U.**) British thermal unit(s).

bubble ● *n*. **1 a** a thin sphere of liquid enclosing air etc. **b** an air-filled cavity in a liquid or a solidified liquid such as glass or amber. **2** the sound or appearance of bubbling; an agitated or bubbling motion. **3** a transparent domed cavity. ● *v.intr*. **1** rise in or send up bubbles. **2** make the sound of rising or bursting bubbles. □ **bubble over** be exuberant with laughter, excitement, anger, etc. [Middle English]

bubble and squeak *n*. *Brit*. cooked cabbage fried with cooked potatoes or meat. [from the cooking sounds]

bubble bath *n*. **1** a preparation for adding to bathwater to make it foam. **2** a bath with this added.

bubble chamber *n*. *Physics* an apparatus designed to make the tracks of ionizing particles visible as a row of bubbles in a liquid.

bubblegum *n*. chewing gum that can be blown into bubbles.

bubble wrap *n*. plastic wrapping material in sheets containing numerous small air-filled bladders.

bubbly ● *adj*. (**bubblier**, **bubbliest**) **1** having or resembling bubbles. **2** exuberant, vivacious. ● *n*. *colloq*. champagne.

bubo *n*. (*pl*. **-oes**) a swollen inflamed lymph node in the armpit or groin. [based on Greek *boubōn* 'groin'] □ **bubonic** *adj*.

bubonic plague *n*. see PLAGUE *n*. 1a.

buccaneer *n*. **1** a pirate. **2** an unscrupulous adventurer. [earlier in sense 'hunter of oxen': from French *boucaner* 'to cure on a barbecue'] □ **buccaneering** *n*. & *adj*.

buck[1] ● *n*. **1** the male of various animals, esp. the deer, hare, or rabbit. **2** (*attrib*.) a *slang* male (*buck antelope*). **b** *US Mil. slang* of the lowest rank (*buck private*). ● *v*. **1** *intr*. (of a horse) jump upwards with back arched and feet drawn together. **2** *tr*. **a** throw (a rider or burden) in this way. **b** esp. *N. Amer*. oppose, resist (*tried to buck the trend*). **3** *tr*. & *intr*. (usu. foll. by *up*) *colloq*. **a** make or become more cheerful. **b** *Brit*. make or become more vigorous or lively (*needs to buck up his ideas*). **4** *tr*. (as **bucked** *adj*.) *Brit. colloq*. encouraged, elated. [from Old Norse]

buck[2] *n*. *N. Amer*. & *Austral. slang* a dollar. □ **a fast buck** easy money. [19th-century coinage]

buck[3] *n*. *slang* an article placed as a reminder before a player whose turn it is to deal at poker. □ **pass the buck** *colloq*. shift responsibility (to another). [19th-century coinage]

bucket ● *n*. **1 a** a roughly cylindrical open container with a handle, used for carrying, drawing, or hold-

ing water etc. **b** the amount contained in this. **2** (in *pl*.) large quantities of liquid (*wept buckets*). **3** a compartment on the outer edge of a waterwheel. **4** the scoop of a dredger or a grain-elevator. ● *v*. (**bucketed**, **bucketing**) **1** *intr*. (of liquid, esp. rain) pour heavily. **2** *intr*. & *tr*. *Brit*. move or drive bumpily. [from Anglo-French *buket*] □ **bucketful** *n*. (*pl*. **-fuls**).

bucket seat *n*. a seat with a rounded back to fit one person, esp. in a car.

bucket shop *n*. **1** an unauthorized office for gambling in stocks etc. **2** *Brit. colloq*. a travel agency specializing in cheap air tickets.

buckle ● *n*. **1** a flat frame with a hinged pin, used for joining the ends of a belt, strap, etc. **2** a similarly shaped ornament. ● *v*. **1** *tr*. fasten with a buckle. **2** *intr*. & *tr*. give way or cause to give way under longitudinal pressure. □ **buckle down** make a determined effort. **buckle to** (or **down to**) prepare for, set about (work etc.). **buckle to** get to work, make a vigorous start. [from Latin *buccula* 'cheek-strap of a helmet'; *v*. sense 2: from French *boucler* 'to bulge']

buckler *n*. *hist*. a small round shield held by a handle. [from Old French *bocler* 'having a boss']

buckram *n*. a coarse linen or other cloth stiffened with gum or paste, and used as interfacing or in bookbinding. [from Old French *boquerant*]

buck rarebit *n*. *Brit*. Welsh rarebit with a poached egg on top.

Buck's Fizz *n*. *Brit*. a cocktail of champagne or sparkling white wine and orange juice. [from *Buck's* Club in London]

buckshee *adj*. & *adv*. *Brit. slang* free of charge. [corruption of BAKSHEESH]

buckshot *n*. coarse lead shot.

buckskin *n*. **1 a** the skin of a male deer. **b** leather made from such skin. **2** a thick smooth cloth.

buckthorn *n*. any thorny shrub of the genus *Rhamnus*, esp. *R. cathartica* with berries formerly used as a cathartic.

buck-tooth *n*. an upper tooth that projects. □ **buck-toothed** *adj*.

buckwheat *n*. a cereal plant of the genus *Fagopyrum*, esp. *F. esculentum* with seeds used for fodder and for flour. [from Middle Dutch *boecweite* 'beech wheat', its grains being shaped like beechmast]

bucolic *adj*. of or concerning shepherds or the pastoral life; rural. [based on Greek *boukolos* 'herdsman']

bud[1] ● *n*. **1 a** an immature knoblike shoot from which a stem, leaf, or flower develops. ▷ CALYX. **b** a flower or leaf that is not fully open. **2** *Biol*. an asexual outgrowth from a parent organism that separates to form a new individual. ● *v*. (**budded**, **budding**) **1** *intr*. *Bot*. & *Zool*. form a bud or buds. **2** *intr*. begin to develop (*a budding cricketer*). **3** *tr*. graft a bud (of a plant) on to another plant. □ **in bud** having newly formed buds. [Middle English]

bud[2] *n*. *N. Amer. colloq*. (as a form of address) = BUDDY.

Buddha *n*. **1** a title given to successive teachers of Buddhism, esp. to its founder, Gautama. **2** a statue or picture of the Buddha. [Sanskrit, literally 'enlightened']

Buddhism *n*. a widespread Asian religion or philosophy, founded by Gautama Buddha in India in the 5th c. BC, which teaches that elimination of the self and earthly desires is the highest goal. □ **Buddhist** *n*. & *adj*.

buddleia *n*. any shrub of the genus *Buddleia*, with fragrant flowers attractive to butterflies. [named after A. *Buddle*, 18th-century English botanist]

buddy esp. *N. Amer. colloq*. ● *n*. (*pl*. **-ies**) a close friend or mate. ● *v.intr*. (**-ies**, **-ied**) become friendly.

budge *v*. **1** *intr*. *Brit*. **a** make the slightest movement. **b** change one's opinion. **2** *tr*. cause or compel to budge (*nothing will budge him*). □ **budge up** (or **over**) *Brit*. make room for another person by moving. [based on Latin *bullire* 'to boil']

budgerigar *n*. a small parrot, *Melopsittacus undulatus*, native to Australia, and often kept as a cage bird. [Aboriginal, literally 'nice cockatoo']

budget ● *n*. **1** the amount of money needed or available. **2 a** (**the Budget**) a usu. annual estimate of national revenue and expenditure. **b** a similar estimate made by a company, etc. **3** (*attrib*.) inexpensive. ● *v.tr*. & *intr*. (**budgeted**, **budgeting**) allow or arrange for in a budget (*have budgeted for a new car*). □ **on a budget** with a restricted amount of money. [Middle English in sense 'pouch': based on Latin *bulga* 'knapsack'] □ **budgetary** *adj*.

budgie *n*. *colloq*. = BUDGERIGAR.

buff ● *adj*. yellowish beige. ● *n*. **1** a yellowish-beige colour. **2** *colloq*. an enthusiast (*railway buff*). **3 a** a velvety dull yellow ox-leather. **b** (*attrib*.) made of this. ● *v.tr*. **1** polish (metal, fingernails, etc.). **2** make (leather) velvety like buff. □ **in the buff** *colloq*. naked. [originally in sense 'buffalo'; *n*. sense 2: from buff uniforms worn by New York volunteer firemen, applied to enthusiastic fire-watchers]

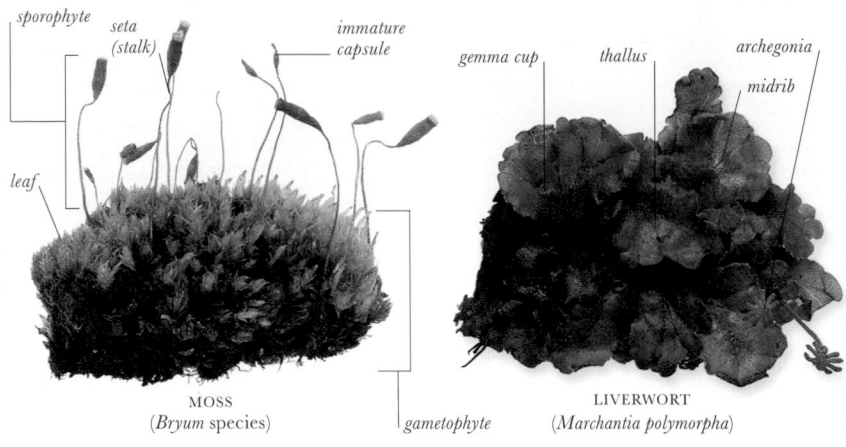

BRYOPHYTE

Bryophytes – liverworts and mosses – are simple low-growing plants, anchored to the ground or to tree bark by tiny filamentous rhizoids. They lack vascular tissue and an outer waterproof cuticle, and thrive best in moist habitats. Most mosses form cushion-like clumps, while liverworts are either leafy or flat and encrusting.

sporophyte
seta (stalk)
immature capsule
leaf

MOSS
(*Bryum* species)
gametophyte

gemma cup
thallus
archegonia
midrib

LIVERWORT
(*Marchantia polymorpha*)

B

buffalo n. (pl. same or **-oes**) **1 a** an Asiatic ox of the genus *Bubalus*, with heavy backswept horns, esp. (in full **water buffalo**) *B. arnee*, which is domesticated as a draught animal. **b** (in full **Cape buffalo**) a powerful wild ox, *Syncerus caffer*, of eastern and southern Africa. **2** a N. American bison, *Bison bison*. [from Greek *boubalos* 'antelope, wild ox']

buffalo grass n. **1** a grass, *Buchloe dactyloides*, of the N. American plains. **2** a grass, *Stenotaphrum secundatum*, of Australia and New Zealand.

buffalo wings n.pl. deep-fried chicken wings coated in spicy sauce.

buffer[1] ● n. **1 a** a device that protects against or reduces the effect of an impact. **b** *Brit.* such a device projecting from a cross-beam on the front and rear of a railway vehicle or at the end of a track. ▷ TENDER. **2** *Chem.* a substance that acts to minimize the change in hydrogen ion concentration of a solution when an acid or alkali is added. **3** *Computing* a temporary memory area or queue for data to aid its transfer between devices or programs operating at different speeds etc. ● v.tr. act as a buffer to.

buffer[2] n. *Brit. slang* a silly or incompetent old man (esp. *old buffer*). [18th-century coinage]

buffer state n. a small state situated between two larger ones potentially hostile to one another, whose existence is regarded as reducing the likelihood of open hostilities.

buffet[1] /buuf-ay/ n. **1** a room or counter where snacks may be bought. **2** a meal consisting of several dishes set out from which guests serve themselves (*buffet lunch*). [from Old French *buf(f)et* 'stool']

buffet[2] /buff-it/ ● v. (**buffeted**, **buffeting**) **1** tr. **a** strike or knock repeatedly (*wind buffeted the trees*). **b** strike with the hand or fist. **2** tr. (of fate etc.) treat badly; plague (*buffeted by misfortune*). **3 a** intr. struggle; fight one's way (through difficulties etc.). **b** tr. contend with (waves etc.). ● n. **1 a** blow, esp. of the hand. **2** a shock. [from Old French, literally 'little blow']

buffet car n. a railway coach serving light meals or snacks.

buffoon n. **1** a ludicrous person. **2** a jester; a mocker. [from medieval Latin *buffo* 'a clown'] □ **buffoonery** n. **buffoonish** adj.

bug ● n. **1 a** an insect of the order Hemiptera, with mouthparts modified for piercing and sucking. **b** any small insect. **2** *slang* a microorganism or a disease caused by it. **3** a concealed microphone. **4** an error in a computer program or system. **5** *colloq.* an obsession, enthusiasm, etc. ● v. (**bugged**, **bugging**) **1** tr. conceal a microphone in. **2** tr. *slang* annoy, bother. **3** intr. esp. *N. Amer. slang* **a** (often foll. by *out*) leave quickly. **b** (foll. by *off*) go away. [17th-century coinage]

bugbear n. **1** a cause of annoyance or anger. **2** an object of baseless fear. [based on obsolete *bug* 'bogey']

bug-eyed adj. with bulging eyes.

bugger *coarse slang* (except in sense 2 of n. and 3 of v.) ● n. **1** esp. *Brit.* **a** an unpleasant or awkward person or thing (*the bugger won't fit*). **b** a person of a specified kind (*he's a miserable bugger; clever bugger!*). **2** a person who commits buggery. ● v.tr. **1** as an exclamation of annoyance (*bugger the thing!*). **2** a ruin; spoil (*really buggered it up; it's no good, it's buggered*). **b** (esp. as **buggered** adj.) *Brit.* exhaust, tire out. **3** commit buggery with. ● int. expressing annoyance. □ **bugger about** (or **around**) *Brit.* **1** mess about. **2** hoax; persecute. **bugger all** *Brit.* nothing. **bugger off** (often in *imper.*) *Brit.* go away. [originally in sense 'heretic': from Old French *bougre*]

buggery n. **1** anal intercourse. **2** = BESTIALITY 2.

buggy n. (pl. **-ies**) **1** a light horse-drawn vehicle for one or two people. **2** a small, sturdy motor vehicle. **3** = BABY BUGGY 1, 2. [18th-century coinage]

bugle[1] n. (also **bugle-horn**) a brass instrument like a small trumpet, used esp. for military signals and in fox-hunting. [from Latin *buculus* 'little ox', from the use of an ox's horn as a bugle] □ **bugler** n.

bugle[2] n. a creeping labiate plant, *Ajuga reptans*, with blue flowers. [from Late Latin *bugula*]

bugloss /bew-gloss/ n. **1** any of various bristly plants related to borage, esp. of the genus *Anchusa* with bright blue tubular flowers. **2** = VIPER'S BUGLOSS. [from Greek *bouglōssos* 'ox-tongued', with reference to the leaves]

build ● v.tr. (*past* and *past. part.* **built**) **1 a** construct (a house, vehicle, fire, road, model, etc.) by putting parts or material together. **b** commission, finance, and oversee the building of (*the council built two new schools*). **2 a** establish, develop, make, or accumulate gradually (*built the business up from nothing*). **b** base (hopes, theories, etc.) (*ideas built on a false foundation*). **3** (as **built** adj.) having a specified build (*sturdily built; brick-built*). ● n. **1** the proportions of the body (*a slim build*). **2** a style of construction. □ **build in** incorporate as part of a structure. **build on** add (an extension etc.). **build up 1** increase in size or strength. **2** praise; boost. **3** gradually become established. **built on sand** unstable. [Old English]

builder n. **1** a contractor for building houses etc. **2** a person engaged as a bricklayer etc. on a building site.

builders' merchant n. a supplier of materials to builders.

building n. **1** a permanent fixed structure forming an enclosure and providing protection from the elements etc. **2** the constructing of such structures.

building site n. an area before or during the construction of a house etc.

building society n. *Brit.* a financial organization which accepts investments at interest and lends capital for mortgages on houses etc.

build-up n. **1** a favourable description in advance. **2** a gradual approach to a climax or maximum. **3** an accumulation or increase.

built *past* and *past part.* of BUILD.

built-in adj. **1** forming an integral part of a structure. **2** inherent, integral, innate.

built-up adj. **1** (of a locality) densely covered by houses etc. **2** increased in height etc. by the addition of parts. **3** composed of separately prepared parts.

bulb n. **1 a** ◀ a fleshy-leaved storage organ of some plants, sending roots downwards and leaves upwards. **b** a plant grown from this. **2** = LIGHT BULB. **3** any object or part shaped like a bulb. [from Greek *bolbos* 'onion']

bulbous adj. **1** shaped like a bulb; fat or bulging. **2** having a bulb or bulbs. **3** (of a plant) growing from a bulb.

bulgar n. (also **bulgur**) a cereal food of whole wheat partially boiled then dried, eaten esp. in Turkey. [Turkish]

Bulgarian ● n. **1 a** a native or national of Bulgaria. **b** a person of Bulgarian descent. **2** the language of Bulgaria. ● adj. of or relating to Bulgaria or its people or language. [from Late Latin *Bulgarus*]

bulge ● n. **1 a** a convex part of an otherwise flat or flatter surface. **b** an irregular swelling; a lump. **2** *colloq.* a temporary increase in quantity or number (*baby bulge*). ● v. **1** intr. swell outwards. **2** intr. be full or replete. **3** tr. swell (a bag, cheeks, etc.) by stuffing. [based on Latin *bulga* 'knapsack'] □ **bulgy** adj.

bulgur var. of BULGAR.

new foliage leaf

shoot

apical bud

protective leaf scale

scale leaf

stem

adventitious root

BULB: CROSS-SECTION OF AN AMARYLLIS BULB (*Hippeastrum* species)

bulimia n. *Med.* **1** insatiable overeating. **2** (in full **bulimia nervosa**) an emotional disorder in which bouts of extreme overeating are followed by self-induced vomiting etc. [based on Greek *bous* 'ox' + *limos* 'hunger'] □ **bulimic** adj. & n.

bulk ● n. **1** (usu. prec. by *the* and foll. by *of*; the verb agrees with the complement) the greater part or number (*the bulk of the applicants are women; the bulk of the book is boring*). **2 a** size, magnitude, or volume (*its bulk is enormous*). **b** a large mass. **c** great quantity or volume (often *attrib.: a bulk supplier*). **3** a large bodily frame (*jacket barely covered his bulk*). **4** roughage. ● v. **1** intr. seem large or important (*bulks large in his reckoning*). **2** tr. make (a book, a textile yarn, etc.) seem thicker by suitable treatment (*bulked it with irrelevant stories*). □ **in bulk** in large quantities.

bulk buying n. **1** buying in large amounts at a discount. **2** the purchase by one buyer of all or most of a producer's output.

bulkhead n. an upright partition separating the compartments in a ship, aircraft, vehicle, etc. ▷ SUBMARINE. [based on archaic *bulk* 'a stall']

bulky adj. (**bulkier**, **bulkiest**) **1** taking up much space, large. **2** awkwardly large. □ **bulkily** adv. **bulkiness** n.

bull[1] ● n. **1 a** an uncastrated male bovine animal. **b** a male of the whale, elephant, and other large animals. **2** (**the Bull**) the zodiacal sign or constellation Taurus. **3** *Brit.* the bull's-eye of a target. **4** *Stock Exch.* a person who buys shares hoping to sell them at a higher price later. ● attrib.adj. like that of a bull (*bull neck*). [from Old Norse *boli*]

bull[2] n. a papal edict. [from Latin *bulla* 'rounded object']

bull[3] n. **1** (also **Irish bull**) an expression containing a contradiction in terms. **2** *slang* **a** nonsense. **b** trivial or insincere talk or writing. **c** unnecessary routine tasks or discipline. [17th-century coinage]

bullace n. a thorny shrub, *Prunus insititia*, of which the damson is the cultivated form. [from Old French *buloce, beloce*]

bull bar n. a metal bar or framework fitted to the front of a vehicle for protection in the event of collision with a large animal.

bulldog n. ▶ a dog of a sturdy breed with a large head and smooth hair.

bulldog clip n. *propr.* a strong sprung clip for papers.

bulldoze v.tr. **1** clear with a bulldozer. **2** *colloq.* **a** intimidate. **b** make (one's way) forcibly. [from *US* sense 'to intimidate']

BULLDOG

bulldozer n. ▼ a powerful tractor with a broad curved upright blade at the front for clearing ground.

driver's cab

hydraulic system

steel bucket

cog

tread

crawler tracks

blade

BULLDOZER

B

bullet *n.* **1** ▶ a projectile of lead etc. for firing from a rifle, revolver, etc. **2** *Printing* a small usu. solid circle used to introduce and emphasize a line, etc. [from Latin *bulla* 'bubble']

bulletin *n.* **1** a short official statement of news. **2** a regular list of information etc. issued by a society. [from Italian *bullettino* 'little passport']

bulletin board *n.* **1** *N. Amer.* a noticeboard. **2** an information storage system for any authorized computer user to access and add to from a remote terminal.

bulletproof *adj.* (of a material) designed to resist the penetration of bullets.

bullet train *n.* a high-speed passenger train, esp. in Japan.

bullfight *n.* a public spectacle at which a bull is baited and usu. killed. □ **bullfighter** *n.* **bullfighting** *n.*

bullfinch *n.* a finch of the genus *Pyrrhula* with a short stout bill, esp. *P. pyrrhula*, which is mainly grey with a pink breast.

bullfrog *n.* ▶ a large frog, *Rana catesbiana*, native to N. America, with a deep croak.

bullion *n.* gold or silver in bulk before coining, or valued by weight. [from Anglo-French, literally 'mint', based on Latin *bullire* 'to boil']

bullish *adj.* **1** impetuous, aggressive. **2 a** *Stock Exch.* causing or associated with a rise in prices. **b** aggressively optimistic. □ **bullishly** *adv.* **bullishness** *n.*

bull market *n.* *Stock Exch.* a market with rising prices.

bull-nose *attrib.adj.* (also **bull-nosed**) with rounded end.

bullock *n.* a castrated male of domestic cattle, raised for beef. [Old English]

bullring *n.* an arena for bullfights.

bull's-eye *n.* **1 a** the centre of a target. **b** a shot that hits this. **2** a hemisphere or thick disc of glass in a ship's deck or side to admit light. **3** a small circular window. **4 a** a hemispherical lens. **b** a lantern fitted with this. **5** a boss of glass at the centre of a blown glass sheet.

bullshit *coarse slang* ● *n.* **1** (often as *int.*) nonsense. **2** trivial or insincere talk or writing. ● *v.intr. & tr.* (**-shitted, -shitting**) talk nonsense or as if one has specialist knowledge (to). □ **bullshitter** *n.*

bull terrier *n.* a short-haired dog of a breed that is a cross between a bulldog and a terrier.

bully[1] ● *n.* (*pl.* **-ies**) a person who uses strength or power to coerce others by fear. ● *v.tr.* (**-ies, -ied**) **1** persecute by force or threats. **2** (foll. by *into* + verbal noun) pressure (a person) to do something (*bullied into agreeing*). [originally as a term of endearment]

bully[2] *colloq.* ● *adj.* esp. *N. Amer.* very good. ● *int.* (foll. by *for*) expressing admiration or approval (often *iron.*: *bully for them!*).

bully[3] (in full **bully off**) ● *n.* (*pl.* **-ies**) the start of play in hockey in which two opponents strike each other's sticks three times and then go for the ball. ● *v.intr.* (**-ies, -ied**) start play in this way. [19th-century coinage]

bully[4] *n.* (in full **bully beef**) corned beef. [from French *bouilli* 'boiled beef']

bully boy *n.* a hired ruffian.

bulrush *n.* **1** = REED MACE. **2** a rushlike water plant, *Scirpus lacustris*, used for weaving. **3** *Bibl.* a papyrus plant.

bulwark *n.* **1** a defensive wall, esp. of earth; a breakwater. **2** a person, principle, etc., that acts as a defence. **3** (usu. in *pl.*) a ship's side above deck. [from Middle Dutch *bolwerk*]

bum[1] *n.* *Brit. slang* the buttocks. [Middle English]

bum[2] *slang* ● *n.* **1** *N. Amer.* a vagrant. **2** a habitual loafer. ● *v.* (**bummed, bumming**) **1** *intr.* (often foll. by *about*, *around*) loaf or wander around. **2** *tr.* cadge. ● *attrib.adj.* of poor quality.

bumbag *n.* *Brit. colloq.* a small pouch for valuables, on a belt worn round the waist.

bumble *v.intr.* **1** (foll. by *on*) speak in a rambling way. **2** (often as **bumbling** *adj.*) move or act ineptly. **3** make a buzz or hum. [based on BOOM[1] and its obsolete variant *bum*] □ **bumbler** *n.*

bumble-bee *n.* a large social bee of the genus *Bombus*, with a loud hum. ▷ BEE

bumf *n.* (also **bumph**) *Brit. colloq.* **1** usu. *derog.* documents. **2** lavatory paper. [abbreviation of *bum-fodder*]

bummalo *n.* (*pl.* same) a small fish, *Harpodon nehereus*, of S. Asian coasts, dried and used as food.

bummer *n.* esp. *N. Amer. slang* **1** an idler. **2** an unpleasant occurrence. [19th-century coinage]

bump ● *n.* **1** a dull-sounding blow or collision. **2** a swelling or dent caused by this. **3** an uneven patch on a surface. **4** *hist.* any prominence on the skull formerly thought to indicate a particular mental faculty. ● *v.* **1 a** *tr.* hit or come against with a bump. **b** *intr.* (of two objects) collide. **2** *intr.* (foll. by *against*, *into*) hit with a bump; collide with. **3** *tr.* hurt or damage by striking (*bumped my head on the ceiling*). **4** *intr.* move with much jolting (*bumped along the road*). **5** *tr.* *N. Amer.* displace, esp. by seniority. ● *adv.* with a bump; suddenly; violently. □ **bump into** *colloq.* meet by chance. **bump off** *slang* murder. **bump up** *colloq.* increase (prices etc.). [16th-century coinage]

bumper ● *n.* **1** a horizontal bar fixed across the front or back of a motor vehicle to reduce damage in a collision or as a trim. ▷ CAR. **2** (usu. *attrib.*) an unusually large or fine example (*a bumper crop*). **3** *Cricket* = BOUNCER 2. **4** a brim-full glass of wine etc.

bumph *var. of* BUMF.

bumpkin *n.* a rustic or socially inept person.

bump-start *n. & v.tr.* *Brit.* = PUSH-START.

bumptious *adj.* offensively self-assertive or conceited. □ **bumptiousness** *n.*

bumpy *adj.* (**bumpier, bumpiest**) **1** having many bumps (*a bumpy road*). **2** affected by bumps (*a bumpy ride*). □ **bumpily** *adv.* **bumpiness** *n.*

bun *n.* **1** a small usu. sweetened bread roll or cake. **2** *Sc.* a rich fruit cake or currant bread. **3** hair worn drawn back into a tight coil. **4** (in *pl.*) *N. Amer. slang* the buttocks. □ **have a bun in the oven** *slang* be pregnant. [Middle English]

bunch ● *n.* **1** a cluster of things growing or fastened together. **2** a collection; a lot (*best of the bunch*). **3** *colloq.* a group; a gang. ● *v.* **1** *tr.* make into a bunch; gather into close folds. **2** *intr.* form into a group or crowd. [Middle English] □ **bunchy** *adj.*

buncombe *var. of* BUNKUM.

bundle ● *n.* **1** a collection of things tied or fastened together. **2** a set of nerve fibres etc. banded together. **3** *slang* a large amount of money. ● *v.tr.* **1** tie in or make into a bundle (*bundled up my squash kit*). **2** throw or push, esp. quickly or confusedly (*bundled the papers into the drawer*). **3** send away hurriedly or unceremoniously (*bundled them off the premises*). **4** (foll. by *with*) (usu. as **bundled** *adj.*) *Computing* sell as a package with. □ **bundle up** dress warmly or cumbersomely. **go a bundle on** *Brit. slang* be very fond of. [Middle English]

bun fight *n.* *Brit. slang* a tea party.

bung ● *n.* a stopper for closing a hole in a container. ● *v.tr.* **1** stop with a bung. **2** *Brit. slang* throw, toss. □ **bunged up** closed, blocked. [from Middle Dutch *bonghe*]

bungalow *n.* a one-storeyed house. [based on Hindi *baṅglā* 'belonging to Bengal']

bungee /bun-jee/ *n.* (in full **bungee cord**, **rope**) an elasticated cord or rope.

bungee jumping *n.* the sport of jumping from a height while secured by a bungee from the ankles, or by a harness. □ **bungee jumper** *n.*

bungle ● *v.* **1** *tr.* mismanage or fail at (a task). **2** *intr.* work badly or clumsily. ● *n.* a bungled attempt; bungled work. □ **bungler** *n.*

bunion *n.* a swelling on the foot, esp. on the big toe. [based on Old French *buigne* 'bump on the head']

bunk[1] *n.* a shelf-like bed against a wall. [18th-century coinage]

bunk[2] *Brit. slang* ● *v.tr.* (also *absol.*) play truant from (school etc.). ● *n.* (in **do a bunk**) leave or abscond hurriedly. [19th-century coinage]

bunk[3] *n.* *slang* = BUNKUM.

bunk bed *n.* each of two or more beds one above the other, forming a unit.

bunker ● *n.* **1** a large container or compartment for storing fuel. **2** a reinforced underground shelter. **3** a hollow filled with sand, used as an obstacle in a golf course. ▷ FAIRWAY, GOLF. ● *v.tr.* **1** fill the fuel bunkers of (a ship etc.). **2** (usu. in *passive*) trap in a bunker (in sense 3). [19th-century coinage]

bunkhouse *n.* a house where workmen etc. are lodged.

bunkum *n.* (also **buncombe**) nonsense; humbug. [originally *buncombe* from *Buncombe* County in N. Carolina, mentioned in an inconsequential political speech *c*1820]

bunny *n.* (*pl.* **-ies**) a child's name for a rabbit. [from dialect *bun* 'rabbit']

Bunsen *n.* (in full **Bunsen burner**) ◀ a small adjustable gas burner used in scientific work as a source of great heat. [named after R. W. *Bunsen*, German chemist, 1811–99]

bunting[1] *n.* a seed-eating bird of the family Emberizidae, related to the finches. [Middle English]

bunting[2] *n.* **1** flags and other decorations. **2** a loosely woven fabric used for these. [18th-century coinage]

buoy /boy/ ● *n.* **1** ▶ an anchored float serving as a navigation mark or to show reefs etc. **2** a lifebuoy. ● *v.tr.* **1** (usu. foll. by *up*) **a** keep afloat. **b** sustain the spirits of (a person etc.); encourage. **2** mark with a buoy or buoys. [Middle English]

buoyancy /boy-ăn-si/ *n.* **1** the capacity to be or remain buoyant. **2** resilience. **3** cheerfulness.

buoyancy aid *n.* a sleeveless jacket lined with buoyant material, worn for watersports.

buoyant /boy-ănt/ *adj.* **1 a** able or apt to keep afloat. **b** (of a liquid or gas) able to keep something afloat. **2** lighthearted. [from Spanish *boyante* 'floating'] □ **buoyantly** *adv.*

bur *n.* (also **burr**) **1 a** a prickly clinging seed case or flower head. **b** any plant producing these. **2** = BURR *n.* 2. [Middle English]

burble ● *v.intr.* **1** speak ramblingly. **2** make a murmuring noise. ● *n.* **1** a murmuring noise. **2** rambling speech. [Middle English]

burbot *n.* ▼ an eel-like bearded freshwater fish, *Lota lota*. [from Old French *borbete*]

BULLFROG
(*Rana catesbiana*)

BULLET

BUNSEN BURNER
chimney / air valve / gas supply

BUOY: PILLAR MARK
top-mark / lantern support / lantern / solar panel / name-board / water-line / float

BURBOT
(*Lota lota*)
barbel

burden (also *archaic* **burthen**) ● *n.* **1** a load. **2** an oppressive duty, obligation, expense, emotion, etc. **3** the bearing of loads (*beast of burden*). **4** a ship's carrying capacity. **5 a** the refrain of a song. **b** the chief theme of a speech, book, poem, etc. ● *v.tr.* load with a burden; oppress. [Old English] □ **burdensome** *adj.*

burden of proof *n.* the obligation to prove one's case.

burdock *n.* ▶ any plant of the genus *Arctium*, with prickly flowers and dock-like leaves.

BURDOCK
(*Arctium lappa*)

bureau /bewr-oh/ *n.* (*pl.* **bureaux** or **bureaus** /-ohz/) **1 a** *Brit.* a writing desk with drawers and usu. an angled top opening downwards to form a writing surface. **b** *N. Amer.* a chest of drawers. **2** an office or department for transacting specific business. [French, literally 'desk']

bureaucracy /bewr-**rok**-ră-si/ *n.* (*pl.* **-ies**) **1 a** government by central administration. **b** a state or organization so governed. **2** the officials of such a government. **3** conduct typical of such officials.

bureaucrat *n.* **1** an official in a bureaucracy. **2** an inflexible or insensitive administrator. □ **bureaucratic** *adj.* **bureaucratically** *adv.*

bureaucratize *v.tr.* (also **-ise**) make bureaucratic. □ **bureaucratization** *n.*

burette *n.* (*US* **buret**) a graduated glass tube with a tap at one end, for measuring out small volumes of liquid in chemical analysis. [French]

burgeon *v.intr. literary* **1** begin to grow rapidly; flourish. **2** put forth young shoots; bud. [from Old French]

burger *n.* **1** *colloq.* a hamburger. **2** (in *comb.*) a certain kind of hamburger or variation of it (*beefburger*; *nutburger*).

burgess *n.* **1** *Brit.* an inhabitant of a town or borough. **2** *US* a borough magistrate or governor. [based on Late Latin *burgus* 'borough']

burgh /bu-ră/ *n. hist.* a Scottish borough or chartered town. [Scots form]

burgher /ber-ger/ *n.* a citizen of a Continental town. [from German *Burger* or Dutch *burger*]

burglar *n.* a person who commits burglary. [related to Old French *burgier* 'to pillage']

burglarize *v.tr. & intr.* (also **-ise**) *US* = BURGLE.

burglary *n.* (*pl.* **-ies**) **1** entry into a building illegally with intent to commit theft, do bodily harm, or do damage. **2** an instance of this.

burgle *v.* **1** *tr.* commit burglary on (a building or person). **2** *intr.* commit burglary.

burgundy ● *n.* (*pl.* **-ies**) **1 a** wine (usu. red) from Burgundy in eastern France. **b** a similar wine from another place. **2** the red colour of burgundy wine. ● *adj.* of this colour.

burial *n.* **1 a** the burying of a dead body. **b** a funeral. **2** *Archaeol.* a grave or its remains. [Middle English]

burial ground *n.* a cemetery.

burin /bewr-in/ *n.* **1** a steel tool for engraving on copper or wood. **2** *Archaeol.* a flint tool with a chisel point. [French]

burk var. of BERK.

burlap *n.* **1** coarse canvas, esp. of jute, used for sacking etc. **2** a similar lighter material for use in dressmaking or furnishing. [17th-century coinage]

burlesque ● *n.* **1 a** comic imitation, parody. **b** a performance or work of this kind. **c** bombast, mock-seriousness. **2** *US* a variety show, often including striptease. ● *adj.* of or in the nature of burlesque. ● *v.tr.* (**burlesques**, **burlesqued**, **burlesquing**) make or give a burlesque of. [from Italian *burlesco*]

burly *adj.* (**burlier**, **burliest**) of stout sturdy build; big and strong. [Middle English]

Burman *adj. & n.* (*pl.* **Burmans**) = BURMESE (except in sense 4 of *n.*).

Burmese ● *n.* (*pl.* same) **1 a** a native or national of Burma (now Myanmar) in SE Asia. **b** a person of Burmese descent. **2** a member of the largest ethnic group of Burma. **3** the language of this group. **4** (in full **Burmese cat**) ▶ a breed of short-coated domestic cat. ● *adj.* of or relating to Burma or its people or language.

BURMESE CAT

burn[1] ● *v.* (*past* and *past part.* **burnt** or **burned**) **1** *intr. & tr.* be or cause to be consumed or destroyed by fire. **2** *intr.* **a** blaze or glow with fire. **b** be in the state characteristic of fire. **3** *tr. & intr.* be or cause to be injured or damaged by fire or great heat or by radiation. **4** *tr. & intr.* use or be used as a source of heat, light, or other energy. **5** *tr. & intr.* char in cooking (*burned the meat*; *the meat is burning*). **6** *tr.* produce (a hole, a mark, etc.) by fire or heat. **7** *tr.* **a** subject (clay, chalk, etc.) to heat for a purpose. **b** harden (bricks) by fire. **c** make (lime or charcoal) by heat. **8** *tr.* colour, tan, or parch with heat or light. **9** *tr. & intr.* put or be put to death by fire. **10** *tr.* **a** cauterize, brand. **b** (foll. by *in*) imprint by burning. **11** *tr. & intr.* make, be, or feel hot, esp. painfully. **12** *tr. & intr.* make or be passionate; feel or cause to feel great emotion (*burn with shame*). **13** *intr.* (foll. by *into*) (of acid etc.) gradually penetrate (into) causing disintegration. ● *n.* **1** a mark or injury caused by burning. **2** the ignition of a rocket engine in flight, giving extra thrust. **3** *N. Amer.*, *Austral.*, & *NZ* **a** the clearing of vegetation by burning. **b** an area so cleared. □ **burn one's boats** (or esp. *N. Amer.* **bridges**) commit oneself irrevocably. **burn the candle at both ends** exhaust one's resources by undertaking too much. **burn down 1 a** destroy (a building) by burning. **b** (of a building) be destroyed by fire. **2** burn less vigorously as fuel less. **burn one's fingers** suffer on account of meddling or rashness. **burn a hole in one's pocket** (of money) be quickly spent. **burn low** (of fire) be nearly out. **burn the midnight oil** read or work late into the night. **burn out 1** be reduced to nothing by burning. **2** fail or cause to fail by burning. **3** (usu. *refl.*) suffer physical or emotional exhaustion. **4** consume the contents of by burning. **5** make (a person) homeless by burning his or her house. **burn up 1** get rid of by fire. **2** begin to blaze. **3** *colloq.* traverse at high speed. [Old English]

burn[2] *n. Sc. & N.Engl.* a small stream. [Old English]

burner *n.* the part of a gas cooker, lamp, etc. that emits and shapes the flame. ▷ HOT-AIR BALLOON. □ **on the back** (or **front**) **burner** *colloq.* receiving little (or much) attention.

burnet *n.* **1** a plant of the genus *Sanguisorba*, with globular pinkish flower heads. **2** any of several moths of the family Zygaenidae, with crimson spots. ▷ MOTH. [based on Old French *burnete* 'dark brown']

burning *adj.* **1** ardent, intense (*burning desire*). **2** hotly discussed, exciting; vital, urgent (*burning question*). **3** flagrant (*burning shame*). □ **burningly** *adv.*

burning bush *n.* **1** any of various shrubs with red fruits or red autumn leaves. **2** = FRAXINELLA. [with reference to Exod. 3:2]

burning-glass *n.* a lens for concentrating the sun's rays on an object to burn it.

burnish *v.tr.* polish by rubbing. [from Old French *burnir* 'to make brown'] □ **burnisher** *n.*

burnous /ber-**nooss**/ *n.* (*US* also **burnoose**) an Arab or Moorish hooded cloak. [from Greek *birros* 'cloak']

burn-out *n.* **1** physical or emotional exhaustion. **2** depression, disillusionment.

burnt *past* and *past part.* of BURN[1].

burnt-out *adj.* physically or emotionally exhausted.

burnt sienna (also **burnt umber**) ● *n.* a pigment darkened by burning. ● *adj.* of the colour of either of these pigments.

burp *colloq.* ● *v.* **1** *intr.* belch. **2** *tr.* make (a baby) belch. ● *n.* a belch.

burr ● *n.* **1 a** a whirring sound. **b** a rough sounding of the letter *r*. **2** (also **bur**) **a** a rough edge left on cut or punched metal or paper. **b** a surgeon's or dentist's small drill. **3** = BUR 1, 2. ● *v.* **1** *tr.* pronounce with a burr. **2** *intr.* make a whirring sound.

burrito /bu-**ree**-toh/ *n.* (*pl.* **-os**) a tortilla rolled round a savoury filling. [Latin American Spanish]

burrow ● *n.* ▼ a hole or tunnel dug by a small animal as a dwelling. ● *v.* **1** *intr.* make or live in a burrow. **2** *tr.* make (a hole etc.) by digging. **3** *intr.* hide oneself. **4** *intr.* (foll. by *into*) investigate, search. [Middle English] □ **burrower** *n.*

nest   *fortress*   *mole*

food supply   *hunting tunnels*

BURROW: CROSS-SECTION OF A MOLE BURROW

bursar *n.* **1** a treasurer, esp. the person in charge of the funds and other property of a college. **2** *Brit.* the holder of a bursary. [based on medieval Latin *bursa* 'bag']

bursary *n.* (*pl.* **-ies**) **1** *Brit.* a grant, esp. a scholarship. **2** the post or room of a bursar.

burst ● *v.* (*past* and *past part.* **burst**) **1 a** *intr.* break suddenly and violently apart by expansion of contents or internal pressure. **b** *tr.* cause to do this. **c** *tr.* cause (a container etc.) to split apart or puncture. **2 a** *tr.* open forcibly. **b** *intr.* come open or be opened forcibly. **3 a** *intr.* make one's way suddenly or by force. **b** *tr.* break away from or through (*the river burst its banks*). **4** *tr. & intr.* be full to overflowing. **5** *intr.* appear or come suddenly (*burst into flame*; *sun burst out*). **6** *intr.* (foll. by *into*) suddenly begin to shed or utter (esp. *burst into tears* or *laughter* or *song*). **7** *intr.* be as if about to burst because of effort, excitement, etc. **8** *tr.* suffer bursting of (*burst a blood vessel*). **9** *tr.* separate (continuous stationery) into single sheets. ● *n.* **1** the act of or an instance of bursting; a split. **2** a sudden issuing forth (*burst of flame*). **3** a sudden outbreak (*burst of applause*). **4 a** a sudden effort; a spurt. **b** a gallop. **5** an explosion. □ **burst out 1** suddenly begin (*burst out laughing*). **2** exclaim. [Old English] □ **burster** *n.*

burton *n.* □ **go for a burton** *Brit. slang* be lost or destroyed or killed. [20th-century coinage]

bur walnut *n.* walnut wood containing knots.

bury *v.tr.* (**-ies**, **-ied**) **1** place (a dead body) in the earth, in a tomb, or in the sea. **2** lose by death (*has buried three husbands*). **3** put under ground (*bury alive*). **b** hide in the earth. **c** cover up; submerge. **4 a** put out of sight (*buried his face in his hands*). **b** consign to obscurity (*the idea was buried*). **c** put away; forget. **5** involve deeply (*buried himself in his work*). □ **bury the hatchet** cease to quarrel. [Old English]

bus ● *n.* (*pl.* **buses** or *US* **busses**) **1** a large passenger vehicle, esp. one serving the public on a fixed route. **2** *colloq.* a motor car, aeroplane, etc. **3** *Computing* a defined set of conductors carrying data and

B

control signals within a computer. ▷ COMPUTER. ● v. (**buses** or **busses**, **bussed**, **bussing**) **1** intr. go by bus. **2** tr. esp. *N. Amer.* transport by bus, esp. to promote racial integration. [abbreviation of OMNIBUS]

busby n. (pl. **-ies**) (not in official use) a tall fur hat worn by hussars etc. [18th-century coinage]

bush¹ ● n. **1** a shrub or clump of shrubs. **2** a thing resembling this. **3** (esp. in Australia and Africa) an uncultivated district; woodland or forest. ● v.intr. spread like a bush. □ **go bush** *Austral.* leave one's usual surroundings; run wild. [from Old Norse]

bush² ● n. *Brit.* **1** a metal lining for a round hole enclosing a revolving shaft etc. **2** a sleeve providing electrical insulation. ▷ GEARBOX. ● v.tr. provide with a bush. [from Middle Dutch *busse* 'box']

bushbaby n. (pl. **-ies**) ▼ a small nocturnal tree-dwelling African primate of the family Lorisidae, with very large eyes. ▷ PROSIMIAN

BUSHBABY: LESSER BUSHBABY
(*Galago senegalensis*)

bushed adj. *colloq.* **1** *Austral.* & *NZ* **a** lost in the bush. **b** bewildered. **2** tired out.

bushel n. **1** *Brit.* a measure of capacity equal to 8 gallons and equivalent to 36.4 litres. **2** *US* a measure of capacity equal to 64 US pints. [from Old French *buissiel*]

bushfire n. a fire in a forest or in scrub, often spreading widely.

bushman n. (pl. **-men**) **1** a person who lives or travels in the Australian bush. **2** (**Bushman**) **a** a member of an aboriginal people in S. Africa. **b** the language of this people.

bush telegraph n. a rapid informal spreading of information, a rumour, etc.; the network by which this takes place.

bushwhack v. **1** intr. *US*, *Austral.*, & *NZ* **a** clear woods and bush country. **b** live or travel in bush country. **2** tr. *US* ambush.

bushy¹ adj. (**bushier**, **bushiest**) **1** growing thickly like a bush. **2** having many bushes. **3** covered with bush. □ **bushiness** n.

bushy² n. (pl. **-ies**) *Austral.* & *NZ colloq.* a person who lives in the bush (as distinct from in a town).

busily see BUSY.

business n. **1** one's regular occupation, profession. **2** a thing that is one's concern. **3 a** a task or duty. **b** a reason for coming (*what is your business?*). **4** serious activity (*get down to business*). **5** *derog.* a matter (*sick of the whole business*). **6** a thing to be dealt with (*the business of the day*). **7** buying and selling; trade. **8** a commercial firm. **9** *Theatr.* action on stage. **10** a difficult matter. **11** (**the business**) *Brit. colloq.* exactly what is required; an exemplary person or thing. □ **has no business to** has no right to. **in business 1** trading. **2** able to begin operations. **in the business of 1** engaged in. **2** intending to (*not in the business of surrendering*). **like nobody's business** *colloq.* extraordinarily. **mind one's own business** not meddle. **on business** with a definite purpose, esp. one relating to one's regular occupation. [Old English]

business card n. a card printed with one's name and professional details.

business end n. (prec. by *the*) *colloq.* the functional part of a tool or device.

businesslike adj. efficient, practical.

businessman n. (pl. **-men**; *fem.* **businesswoman**, pl. **-women**) a person engaged in trade or commerce, esp. at a senior level.

business park n. an area designed to accommodate businesses and light industry.

business person n. a businessman or businesswoman.

businesswoman see BUSINESSMAN.

busk v.intr. perform for voluntary donations. □ **busker** n.

bus lane n. a lane on a road marked off for use by buses.

busman n. (pl. **-men**) the driver of a bus.

busman's holiday n. leisure time spent in an activity similar to one's regular work.

bus shelter n. a shelter beside a bus stop.

bus station n. a centre where buses depart and arrive.

bus stop n. **1** a regular stopping place of a bus. **2** a sign marking this.

bust¹ n. **1 a** the human chest, esp. that of a woman; the bosom. **b** the circumference of the body at bust level (*a 36-inch bust*). **2** a sculpture of a person's head, shoulders, and chest. [from Italian *busto*]

bust² *colloq.* ● v. (*past* and *past part.* **busted** or **bust**) **1** tr. & intr. break, burst. **2** tr. esp. *US* reduce (a soldier etc.) to a lower rank; dismiss. **3** tr. esp. *N. Amer.* **a** raid, search. **b** arrest. ● n. **1** a sudden failure; a bankruptcy. **2** a police raid. ● adj. (also **busted**) **1** broken, burst, collapsed. **2** bankrupt. □ **bust up 1** bring or come to collapse; explode. **2** (of a couple) separate. **go bust** become bankrupt; fail. [originally a (dialect) pronunciation of BURST]

bustard n. any large terrestrial bird of the family Otididae, with long neck, long legs, and stout tapering body. [from Latin *avis tarda* 'slow bird']

buster n. **1** *slang* (esp. as a disrespectful form of address) mate; fellow. **2** a violent gale.

bustier n. a woman's strapless close-fitting bodice. [French]

bustle¹ ● v. **1** intr. **a** work etc. showily, energetically, and officiously. **b** scurry. **2** tr. make (a person) hurry or work hard (*bustled him into his overcoat*). **3** intr. (as **bustling** adj.) *colloq.* full of activity. ● n. excited activity; a fuss.

bustle² n. *hist.* ▶ a pad or frame worn under a skirt and puffing it out behind. [18th-century coinage]

bust-up n. **1** a quarrel. **2** a collapse; an explosion.

busy ● adj. (**busier**, **busiest**) **1** occupied or engaged in work etc. with the attention concentrated. **2** full of activity or detail; fussy (*a busy evening; a picture busy with detail*). **3** employed continuously; unresting. **4** meddlesome; prying. **5** esp. *N. Amer.* (of a telephone line) engaged. ● v.tr. (**-ies**, **-ied**) (often *refl.*) keep busy; occupy. ● n. (pl. **-ies**) *slang* a detective; a police officer. [Old English] □ **busily** adv. **busyness** n. (cf. BUSINESS).

busybody n. (pl. **-ies**) a meddlesome person.

busy Lizzie n. *Brit.* an E. African plant, *Impatiens walleriana*, with red, pink, or white flowers, often grown as a bedding plant or house plant.

but ● conj. **1 a** nevertheless, however (*tried hard but did not succeed*). **b** on the other hand; on the contrary (*I am old but you are young*). **2** (prec. by *can* etc.; in *neg.* or *interrog.*) except, other than, otherwise than (*cannot choose but do it; what could we do but run?*). **3** without the result that (*it never rains but it pours*). **4** prefixing an interruption to the speaker's train of thought (*the weather is ideal — but is that a cloud on the horizon?*). ● prep. except; apart from; other than (*everyone but me*). ● adv. **1** only; no more than; only just (*we can but try; is but a child; had but arrived*). **2** introducing emphatic repetition; definitely (*wanted to see nobody, but nobody*). **3** *Austral.*, *NZ*, & *Sc.* though, however (*didn't like it, but*). ● rel.pron. who not; that not (*there is not a man but feels pity*). ● n. an objection (*ifs and buts*). □ **but for** without the help or hindrance etc. of (*but for you I'd be rich by now*). **but one** (or **two** etc.) excluding one (or two etc.) from the number (*next door but one; last but one*). **but then** (or **yet**) however, (*I won, but then the others were beginners*). [Old English]

butane n. *Chem.* a gaseous hydrocarbon of the alkane series used in liquefied form as fuel.

butch adj. *slang* masculine; tough-looking.

butcher ● n. **1 a** a person who deals in meat. **b** a person who slaughters animals for food. **2** a person who kills indiscriminately or brutally. ● v.tr. **1** slaughter or cut up (an animal) for food. **2** kill wantonly or cruelly. **3** ruin through incompetence. [from Old French *bo(u)chier*]

butcher-bird n. a shrike (family Laniidae).

butcher's meat n. *Brit.* (also **butcher meat**) slaughtered fresh meat excluding game, poultry, and bacon.

butchery n. (pl. **-ies**) **1** wanton or cruel slaughter. **2** the butcher's trade. **3** *Brit.* a slaughterhouse.

butler n. the principal servant of a household. [from Old French *bouteillier* 'cup-bearer']

butt¹ ● v. **1** tr. & intr. push with the head or horns. **2 a** intr. (usu. foll. by *against*, *upon*) touch with one end flat, meet end to end, abut. **b** tr. (usu. foll. by *against*) place (timber etc.) with the end flat against a wall etc. ● n. **1** a push with the head. **2** a join of two edges. □ **butt in** interrupt, meddle. **butt out** *slang* **1** esp. *N. Amer.* stop interfering. **2** *N. Amer.* stop doing something. [from Old French *boter*]

butt² n. **1** an object (of ridicule etc.). **2 a** a mound behind a target. **b** (in *pl.*) a shooting range. **c** a target. [from Old French *but* 'goal']

butt³ n. **1** (also **butt-end**) the thicker end, esp. of a tool or a weapon (*gun butt*). ▷ MACHINE-GUN. **2** (also **butt-end**) **a** the stub of a cigar or a cigarette. **b** the remaining part. **3** esp. *N. Amer. slang* the buttocks. [from Dutch *bot* 'stumpy']

butt⁴ n. a cask. [from Late Latin *buttis*]

butte n. *N. Amer.* a high isolated steep-sided hill. ▷ ERODE. [French, literally 'mound'].

butter ● n. **1** a fatty substance made by churning cream and used as a spread or in cooking. **2** a substance of a similar consistency or appearance (*peanut butter*). ● v.tr. spread, cook, or serve with butter (*butter the bread; buttered carrots*). □ **butter up** *colloq.* flatter excessively. [from Greek *bouturon*]

butter-bean n. **1** a flat, dried, white, tropical American bean. ▷ PULSE. **2** a yellow-podded bean.

butter-cream n. a mixture of butter, icing sugar, etc. used as a filling etc. for a cake.

buttercup n. a plant of the genus *Ranunculus* (family Ranunculaceae), having bright yellow cup-shaped flowers.

butterfat n. the essential fats of pure butter.

butter-fingers n. *colloq.* a person prone to drop things.

butterfly n. (pl. **-flies**) **1** ▶ any insect of the order Lepidoptera which typically has two pairs of brightly coloured wings held erect when at rest. ▷ METAMORPHOSIS. **2** a showy or frivolous person. **3** (in *pl.*) *colloq.* a nervous sensation felt in the stomach. **4** (in full **butterfly stroke**) a stroke in swimming, with both arms raised out of the water and lifted forwards together. [Old English]

bustle

BUSTLE ON A 19TH-CENTURY DRESS

BUTTERFLY

Butterflies and moths form a single order of around 200,000 species, but it is sometimes difficult to distinguish between the two. Butterflies can usually be identified by their bright colours and clubbed antennae. They fly during the daytime and the base of the hindwing is expanded and strengthened to support the forewing in flight. When resting, butterflies fold their wings upright over their backs. Butterflies feed by sucking liquids through a long proboscis. All species undergo complete metamorphosis, developing as a larva (caterpillar) before emerging from a chrysalis as an adult butterfly.

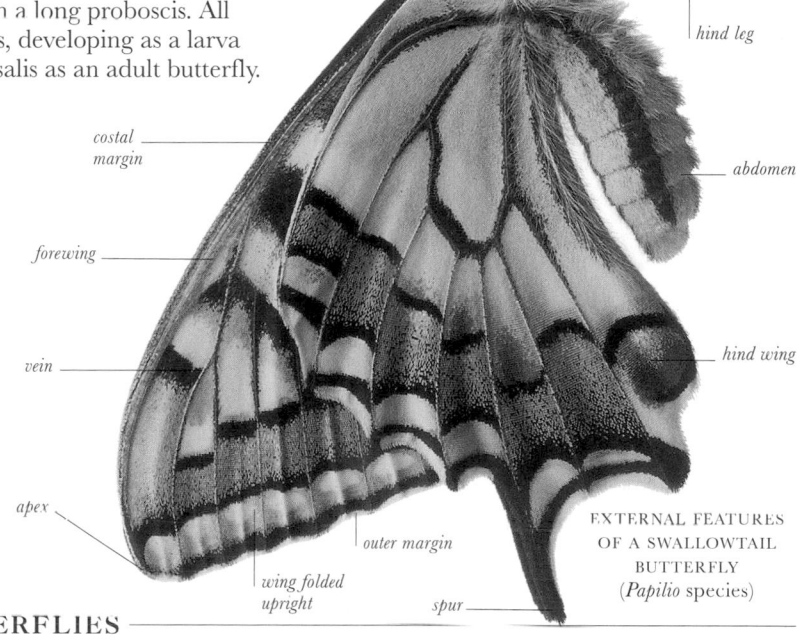

front leg
clubbed antenna
middle leg
proboscis
thorax
compound eye
pupal case
head
femur
tibia
hind leg

costal margin
abdomen
forewing
vein
hind wing
apex
outer margin
wing folded upright
spur

EXTERNAL FEATURES OF A SWALLOWTAIL BUTTERFLY
(*Papilio* species)

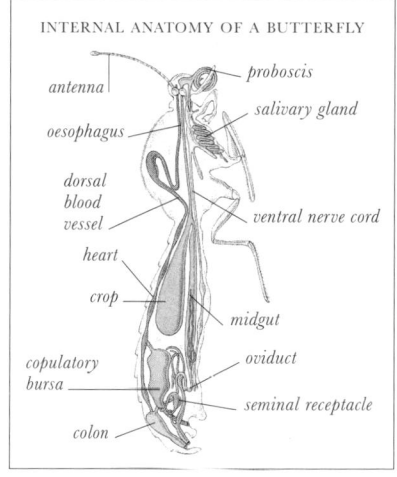

INTERNAL ANATOMY OF A BUTTERFLY

antenna
proboscis
oesophagus
salivary gland
dorsal blood vessel
ventral nerve cord
heart
crop
midgut
copulatory bursa
oviduct
seminal receptacle
colon

EXAMPLES OF OTHER BUTTERFLIES

| SWALLOWTAILS AND BIRDWINGS | SKIPPERS | WHITES AND RELATIVES | BLUES AND COPPERS | NYMPHALIDS |

CAIRNS BIRDWING
(*Ornithoptera priamus*)

SILVER-SPOTTED SKIPPER
(*Epargyreus clarus*)

LARGE WHITE
(*Pieris brassicae*)

ADONIS BLUE
(*Lysandra bellargus*)

CAMBERWELL BEAUTY
(*Nymphalis antiopa*)

TIGER SWALLOWTAIL
(*Papilio glaucus*)

REGENT SKIPPER
(*Euschemon rafflesia*)

BLACK-VEINED WHITE
(*Aporia crataegi*)

GREEN-UNDERSIDE BLUE
(*Glaucopsyche alexis*)

BLUE MORPHO
(*Morpho menelaus*)

APOLLO
(*Parnassius apollo*)

GUAVA SKIPPER
(*Phocides polybius*)

CLEOPATRA
(*Gonepteryx cleopatra*)

LARGE COPPER
(*Lycaena dispar*)

MONARCH BUTTERFLY
(*Danaus plexippus*)

butterfly stroke see BUTTERFLY 4.

butter-icing *n.* = BUTTER-CREAM.

buttermilk *n.* a slightly acid liquid left after churning butter.

butter muslin *n. Brit.* a thin, loosely woven cloth with a fine mesh, originally for wrapping butter.

butterscotch *n.* a brittle sweet made from butter, brown sugar, etc.

buttery[1] *n.* (*pl.* **-ies**) *Brit.* a room where provisions are kept and sold. [from Anglo-French *boterie* 'butt-store']

buttery[2] *adj.* like, containing, or spread with butter. □ **butteriness** *n.*

buttie var. of BUTTY.

buttock *n.* **1** either of the two fleshy protuberances on the lower rear part of the human body. **2** the corresponding part of an animal. [based on BUTT[3]]

button ● *n.* **1** a small disc or knob sewn on to a garment, either to fasten it by being pushed through a buttonhole, or as an ornament or badge. **2** a knob on a piece of equipment which is pressed to operate it. **3 a** a small disc-shaped object (*chocolate buttons*). **b** (*attrib.*) anything resembling a button (*button nose*). **4 a** a bud. **b** a button mushroom. **5** *Fencing* a terminal knob on a foil making it harmless. ● *v.* **1** *tr. & intr.* = button up 1. **2** *tr.* supply with buttons. □ **buttoned up** *colloq.* **1** formal and inhibited in manner. **2** silent. **button one's lip** *slang* remain silent. **button up 1** fasten with buttons. **2** *colloq.* complete satisfactorily. **3** *colloq.* become silent. **on the button** esp. *N. Amer. slang* precisely. [from (Old) French *bouton*] □ **buttoned** *adj.* **buttonless** *adj.*

buttonhole ● *n.* **1** a slit made in a garment to receive a button for fastening. **2** *Brit.* a flower or spray worn in a lapel buttonhole. ● *v.tr. colloq.* accost and detain (a reluctant listener).

button mushroom *n.* a young unopened mushroom.

button-through *adj. Brit.* (of a dress) fastened with buttons from neck to hem like a coat.

buttress ● *n.* **1 a** a projecting support built against a wall. ▷ CATHEDRAL. **b** a source of help or encouragement. **2** a projecting portion of a hill or mountain. ● *v.tr.* **1** support with a buttress. **2** support by argument etc. [from Old French (*ars*) *bouterez* 'thrusting (arch)']

butt weld *n.* a weld in which the pieces are joined end to end.

butty *n.* (also **buttie**) (*pl.* **-ies**) *N. Engl.* **1** a sandwich (*bacon butty*). **2** a slice of bread and butter. [18th-century coinage]

butyl *n. Chem.* the monovalent alkyl radical C_4H_9-.

butyl rubber *n.* a synthetic rubber used in the manufacture of tyre inner tubes and pond liners.

buxom *adj.* (esp. of a woman) plump and healthy-looking; busty. [earlier in sense 'pliant': from Old English *būgan* 'to bow']

buy ● *v.tr.* (**buys, buying**; *past* and *past part.* **bought**) **1 a** obtain in exchange for money etc. **b** serve to obtain (*money can't buy happiness*). **2 a** procure (the loyalty etc.) of a person by bribery, promises, etc. **b** win over (a person) in this way. **3** get by sacrifice, great effort, etc. (*dearly bought*). **4** *slang* accept, believe in, approve of. **5** *absol.* be a buyer for a store etc. (*buys for Selfridges*). ● *n. colloq.* a purchase (*a good buy*). □ **buy in 1** buy a stock of. **2** withdraw (an item) at auction because of failure to reach the reserve price. **buy into 1** buy a share in (an enterprise) by payment. **2** esp. *N. Amer. colloq.* support, embrace (an idea etc.). **buy it** (usu. in *past*) *slang* be killed. **buy off** get rid of (a claim, a claimant, a blackmailer) by payment. **buy oneself out** obtain one's release (esp. from the armed services) by payment. **buy out** pay (a person) to give up an ownership etc. **buy over** bribe. **buy time** delay an event, conclusion, etc., temporarily. **buy up 1** buy as much as possible of. **2** absorb (another firm etc.) by purchase. [Old English]

buy-back *n.* the buying-back or repurchase of goods, shares, etc., often by contractual agreement (often *attrib.*: *buy-back scheme*).

buyer *n.* **1** a person employed to select and purchase stock for a large store etc. **2** a purchaser, a customer.

buyer's market *n.* (also **buyers' market**) an economic position in which goods are plentiful and cheap and buyers have the advantage.

buyout *n.* the purchase of a controlling share in a company etc.

buzz ● *n.* **1** the hum of a bee etc. **2** the sound of a buzzer. **3 a** a confused low sound as of people talking; a murmur. **b** a stir (*a buzz of excitement*). **c** *colloq.* a rumour. **4** *slang* a telephone call. **5** *slang* a thrill; a euphoric sensation. ● *v.* **1** *intr.* make a humming sound. **2 a** *tr. & intr.* signal or signal to with a buzzer. **b** *tr. slang* telephone. **3** *intr.* a move or hover busily. **b** (of a place) have an air of excitement or purposeful activity. **4** *tr. Aeron. colloq.* fly fast and very close to (another aircraft, the ground, etc.). □ **buzz off** *slang* go or hurry away.

buzzard *n.* **1** any of a group of predatory birds of the hawk family with broad wings for soaring flight. **2** *N. Amer.* a vulture. [from Old French *busard*, based on Latin *buteo* 'falcon'].

buzzer *n.* **1** an electrical device that makes a buzzing noise. **2** a whistle or hooter.

buzz-saw *n. N. Amer.* a circular saw.

buzzword *n. slang* **1** a fashionable piece of jargon. **2** a catchword; a slogan.

bwana *n.* (in Africa) master, sir. [Swahili]

by ● *prep.* **1** near, beside (*a chair by the door*; *sit by me*). **2** through the agency, means, instrumentality, or causation of (*bought by a millionaire*; *a poem by Donne*; *went by bus*; *succeeded by persisting*; *divide four by two*). **3** not later than (*by next week*). **4 a** past, beyond (*drove by the church*). **b** passing through; via (*went by Paris*). **5** in the circumstances of (*by day*). **6** to the extent of (*missed by a foot*). **7** according to; using as a standard or unit (*judge by appearances*; *paid by the hour*). **8** with the succession of (*worse by the minute*). **9** concerning; in respect of (*did our duty by them*). **10** used in mild oaths (originally = as surely as one believes in) (*by God*). **11** placed between specified lengths in two directions (*three feet by two*). **12** avoiding, ignoring (*passed us by*). **13** (in names of compass points) inclining to (*north by east* between north and north-north-east; *north-east by north* between north-east and north-north-east). ● *adv.* **1** near (*sat by, watching*). **2** aside; in reserve (*put £5 by*). **3** past (*marched by*). ● *n.* (*pl.* **byes**) = BYE[1]. □ **by and by** before long; eventually. **by and large** on the whole, everything considered. **by the by** (or **bye**) incidentally, parenthetically. **by oneself 1 a** unaided. **b** without prompting. **2** alone. [Old English]

by- *prefix* (also **bye-**) subordinate, incidental, secondary (*by-product*; *byroad*).

bye[1] *n.* **1** *Cricket* a run scored from a ball that passes the batsman without being hit. **2** the status of an unpaired competitor in a sport, who proceeds to the next round by default. □ **by the bye** = *by the by*.

bye[2] *int. colloq.* = GOODBYE.

bye- *prefix* var. of BY-.

bye-bye *int. colloq.* = GOODBYE. [childish corruption]

bye-bye[2] *n.* (also **bye-byes**) (a child's word for) sleep. [Middle English, from the sound used in lullabies]

by-election *n. Brit.* the election of an MP in a single constituency to fill a vacancy arising during a government's term of office.

Byelorussian var. of BELORUSSIAN.

bygone ● *adj.* past, antiquated (*bygone years*). ● *n.* (in *pl.*) past offences (*let bygones be bygones*).

by-law *n.* (also **bye-law**) *Brit.* a regulation made by a local authority or corporation. [Middle English]

byline *n.* **1** a line in a newspaper etc. naming the writer of an article. **2** a secondary line of work. **3** a goal line or touchline.

bypass ● *n.* **1** a road passing round a town or its centre. **2 a** a secondary channel or pipe etc. to allow a flow when the main one is closed or blocked. **b** an alternative passage for the circulation of blood during a surgical operation on the heart. ▷ OPEN-HEART SURGERY. ● *v.tr.* **1** avoid; go round. **2** provide with a bypass.

byplay *n.* a secondary action, esp. in a play.

by-product *n.* **1** an incidental or secondary product made in the manufacture of something else. **2** a secondary result.

byre *n. Brit.* a cowshed. [Old English]

byroad *n.* a minor road.

bystander *n.* a person who stands by but does not take part.

byte *n. Computing* a group of binary digits (usu. eight), operated on as a unit. [20th-century coinage, based on BIT[4] and BITE]

byway *n.* **1** a minor road. **2** a minor activity.

byword *n.* **1** a person or thing cited as a notable example (*is a byword for luxury*). **2** a familiar saying.

Byzantine ● *adj.* **1** of Byzantium or the Eastern Roman Empire. **2** (of a political situation etc.): **a** extremely complicated. **b** inflexible. **c** carried on by underhand methods. **3** *Archit. & Art* ▼ of a highly decorated style developed in the Eastern Empire. ● *n.* a citizen of Byzantium or the Eastern Roman Empire.

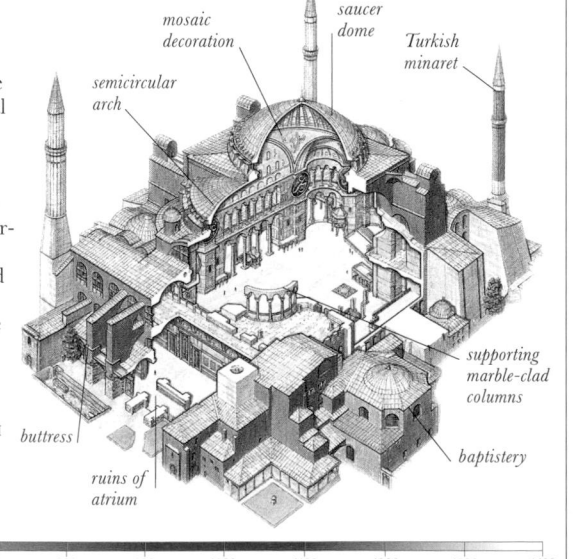

BYZANTINE

Following the division of the Roman Empire in AD 395, the Eastern section sited its capital in Byzantium (now Istanbul). Architects fused Roman and oriental styles, constructing buildings from brick and concrete, faced with marble. External walls were ornamented with decorative brickwork and internal walls with intricate mosaics. A large central dome was often surrounded by smaller domes.

CUTAWAY VIEW OF A 6TH-CENTURY BYZANTINE CHURCH (HAGIA SOPHIA, ISTANBUL, TURKEY), NOW A MOSQUE

mosaic decoration

saucer dome

semicircular arch

Turkish minaret

supporting marble-clad columns

buttress

baptistery

ruins of atrium

TIMELINE

400	500	600	700	800	900	1000	1100	1200	1300	1400

C[1] *n.* (also **c**) (*pl.* **Cs** or **C's**) **1** the third letter of the alphabet. **2** *Mus.* the first note of the diatonic scale of C major. ▷ NOTATION. **3** the third hypothetical person or example. **4** the third-highest class or category. **5** (usu. *c*) *Algebra* the third known quantity. **6** (as a Roman numeral) 100.

C[2] *abbr.* Celsius, Centigrade.

C[3] *symb.* **1** *Chem.* the element carbon. **2** (also ©) copyright.

c[1] *abbr.* (also **c.**) **1** century; centuries. **2** chapter. **3** cent(s). **4** cold. **5** (usu. *c.*) circa, about. **6** *Cricket* caught by.

c[2] *symb.* centi-.

c/- *abbr. Austral. & NZ* care of.

Ca *symb. Chem.* the element calcium.

ca. *abbr.* circa, about.

CAA *abbr.* (in the UK) Civil Aviation Authority.

CAB *abbr.* Citizens' Advice Bureau.

cab *n.* **1** a taxi. **2** the driver's compartment in a lorry, train, or crane. **3** *hist.* a hackney carriage. [abbreviation of CABRIOLET]

cabal *n.* **1** a secret intrigue. **2** a political clique or faction. [from medieval Latin *cabala*]

cabala 1 var. of CABBALA. **2** (**Cabala**) var. of KABBALAH.

cabaret /**kab**-ă-ray/ *n.* **1** an entertainment in a nightclub or restaurant while guests eat or drink at tables. **2** such a nightclub etc. [French, literally 'wooden structure, tavern']

cabbage *n.* **1 a** any of several cultivated varieties of *Brassica oleracea*, with thick green or purple leaves forming a round head. ▷ VEGETABLE. **b** these leaves eaten as a vegetable. **2** *Brit. colloq. derog.* a person who is inactive or lacks interest. [from Old French (Picard) *caboche* 'head'] □ **cabbagy** *adj.*

cabbage white *n.* ▼ a butterfly, *Pieris brassicae*, whose caterpillars feed on cabbage leaves.

CABBAGE WHITE
(*Pieris brassicae*)

cabbala *n.* **1** (also **cabala**, **kabbala**) any esoteric doctrine or occult lore. **2** (**Cabbala**) var. of KABBALAH. [from Rabbinical Hebrew *ḳabbālā* 'tradition'] □ **cabbalism** *n.* **cabbalist** *n.* **cabbalistic** *adj.*

cabby *n.* (also **cabbie**) (*pl.* **-ies**) *colloq.* a taxi driver.

caber *n.* a roughly trimmed tree trunk used in the Scottish Highland sport of tossing the caber. [from Gaelic *cabar* 'pole']

cabin *n.* **1** a small shelter or house. ▷ LOG CABIN. **2** a room or compartment in an aircraft or ship for passengers or crew. ▷ WING. **3** a driver's cab. [from Late Latin *capanna*]

cabin boy *n.* a boy who waits on a ship's officers or passengers.

cabin crew *n.* the crew members on an aeroplane attending to passengers and cargo.

cabin cruiser *n.* a large motor boat with living accommodation.

cabinet *n.* **1 a** ▼ a cupboard or case for storing or displaying articles. **b** a piece of furniture housing a radio or television set etc. **2** (**Cabinet**) **a** the committee of senior ministers responsible for controlling government policy. **b** (in the US) a body of advisers to the President, composed of the heads of the executive departments of the government. [based on CABIN]

open shelf   *projecting shelf*   *glazed display cupboard*

closed cupboard

CABINET: 19TH-CENTURY
ENGLISH MAHOGANY CABINET

cabinetmaker *n.* a skilled joiner. □ **cabinetmaking** *n.*

Cabinet minister *n. Brit.* a member of the Cabinet.

cabinetry *n.* cabinets regarded collectively.

cable ● *n.* **1** a thick rope of wire or hemp. **2 a** an encased group of insulated wires for transmitting electricity or electrical signals. **b** a cablegram. **c** = CABLE TELEVISION. **3** *Naut.* the chain of an anchor. **4** (in full **cable stitch**) a knitted stitch resembling twisted rope. ▷ KNITTING. ● *v.* **1 a** *tr.* transmit (a message) by cablegram. **b** *tr.* inform (a person) by cablegram. **c** *intr.* send a cablegram. **2** *tr.* furnish or fasten with a cable or cables. [from Arabic *ḥabl* 'halter']

cable car *n.* a small cabin suspended on an endless cable by which it is drawn up and down a mountainside etc.

cablegram *n.* a telegraph message sent by undersea cable etc.

cable release *n. Photog.* a cable attached to a camera to allow the photographer to open the shutter without having to hold the camera.

cable stitch see CABLE *n.* 4.

cable television *n.* a television broadcasting system with signals transmitted by cable to subscribers' sets.

cabochon /**kab**-ŏ-shon/ *n.* (also *attrib.*) ▶ a gem polished but not faceted. ▷ GEM. [French, literally 'little head'] □ **en cabochon** (of a gem) treated in this way.

CABOCHON:
SODALITE CABOCHON

caboodle *n.* □ **the whole caboodle** *slang* the whole lot (of persons or things). [19th-century US coinage]

caboose *n.* **1** *Brit.* a kitchen on a ship's deck. **2** *N. Amer.* a guard's van; a car on a freight train for workmen etc. [from Dutch *cabūse*]

cabriole *n.* a kind of curved leg characteristic of some 18th-century furniture, esp. that made or designed by the English cabinetmaker Thomas Chippendale (died 1779). [based on Italian *capriolare* 'to leap in the air', from the resemblance to a leaping animal's foreleg]

cabriolet /**kab**-ri-ŏ-lay/ *n.* **1** a light two-wheeled carriage with a hood, drawn by one horse. **2** a car with a folding top. [French, from *cabriole* 'goat's leap', applied to the carriage's motion]

cacao /kă-**kah**-oh/ *n.* (*pl.* **-os**) **1** a seed pod from which cocoa and chocolate are made. ▷ BERRY. **2** a small evergreen tree, *Theobroma cacao*, bearing these. [from Aztec *cacauatl*]

cachalot /**kash**-ă-lot/ *n.* a sperm whale. [French]

cache /kash/ ● *n.* **1** a hiding place for treasure, provisions, ammunition, etc. **2** what is hidden in a cache. ● *v.tr.* put in a cache. [French]

cachet /**kash**-ay/ *n.* **1** a distinguishing mark or seal. **2** prestige. **3** *Med.* a flat capsule enclosing a dose of unpleasant-tasting medicine. [French]

cack-handed *adj. Brit. colloq.* **1** awkward, clumsy. **2** left-handed. [based on dialect *cack* 'excrement'] □ **cack-handedly** *adv.* **cack-handedness** *n.*

cackle ● *n.* **1** a clucking sound as of a hen or a goose. **2** a loud silly laugh. **3** noisy inconsequential talk. ● *v.* **1** *intr.* emit a cackle. **2** *intr.* talk noisily and inconsequentially. **3** *tr.* utter or express with a cackle. [Middle English] □ **cut the cackle** *colloq.* stop talking aimlessly and come to the point.

cacophony *n.* (*pl.* **-ies**) **1** a harsh discordant mixture of sound. **2** dissonance; discord. [from Greek *kakos* 'bad' + *phōnē* 'sound'] □ **cacophonous** *adj.*

cactus *n.* (*pl.* **cacti** /-ty/ or **cactuses**) ▶ any succulent plant of the family Cactaceae, with a thick fleshy stem and usu. spines but no leaves. ▷ SUCCULENT, XEROPHYTE. [from Greek *kaktos* 'cardoon']

CAD *abbr.* computer-aided design.

cad *n.* a man who behaves dishonourably. [abbreviation of CADDIE in earlier sense 'odd job man'] □ **caddish** *adj.*

cadaver *n.* esp. *Med.* a corpse. [based on Latin *cadere* 'to fall'] □ **cadaveric** *adj.*

cadaverous *adj.* **1** corpselike. **2** deathly pale.

areole   *central spines*   *radial spines*

CACTUS:
SPINY CACTUS
(*Oreocereus intertexta*)

caddie (also **caddy**) ● *n.* (*pl.* **-ies**) a person who assists a golfer during a match, by carrying clubs etc. ● *v.intr.* (**caddies**, **caddied**, **caddying**) act as caddie. [originally Scots in sense 'errand boy', from French *cadet*]

caddie car *n.* (also **caddie cart**) *Brit.* a light two-wheeled trolley for transporting golf clubs during a game.

caddis-fly *n.* (*pl.* **-flies**) a small mothlike insect of the order Trichoptera, with aquatic larvae. ▷ LARVA. [17th-century coinage]

caddish see CAD.

caddis-worm *n.* (also **caddis**) the aquatic larva of a caddis-fly.

caddy[1] *n.* (*pl.* **-ies**) a box for tea. [earlier *catty*, a unit of weight of 1⅓ lb (0.61kg), from Malay]

C

caddy[2] var. of CADDIE.

cadence *n.* **1** a fall in pitch of the voice, esp. at the end of a phrase or sentence. **2** intonation, tonal inflection. **3** *Mus.* the close of a musical phrase. **4** rhythm; the measure or beat of sound or movement. [from Italian *cadenza*] □ **cadenced** *adj.*

cadential *adj.* of a cadence or cadenza.

cadenza *n. Mus.* a virtuosic passage for a solo instrument or voice, usu. near the close of a movement of a concerto. [Italian]

cadet *n.* **1** a young trainee in the armed services or police force. **2** a boy or girl of 13–18 who undergoes voluntary army, navy, or air force training, together with adventure training, occasionally also undertaking public duties. **3** *NZ* an apprentice in sheep farming. **4** a younger son. [French] □ **cadetship** *n.*

cadge *v.* **1** *tr.* get or seek by begging. **2** *intr.* beg. [19th-century coinage] □ **cadger** *n.*

cadi *n.* (also **kadi**) (*pl.* **-s**) a judge in a Muslim country. [Arabic *ḳāḍī*]

cadmium *n.* a soft bluish-white toxic metallic element occurring naturally with zinc ores, and used in the manufacture of solders and pigments and in electroplating. [based on Greek *kadm(e)ia* (*gē*) 'Cadmean (earth)', from *Kadmos*, legendary founder of Thebes]

cadmium yellow *n.* an intense yellow pigment containing cadmium sulphide and used in paints etc.

cadre /**kar**-der/ *n.* **1** a basic unit, esp. of servicemen, forming a nucleus for expansion when necessary. **2 a** a group of activists in a communist or other revolutionary party. **b** a member of such a group. [from Latin *quadrus* 'square']

caecilian /see-**sil**-yăn/ *n.* a burrowing wormlike amphibian of the order Apoda, having poorly developed eyes and no limbs. ▷ AMPHIBIAN. [Latin *caecilia* 'slow-worm']

caecum /**see**-kŭm/ *n.* (*US* **cecum**) (*pl.* **-ca**) *Anat.* a blind-ended pouch at the junction of the small and large intestines. ▷ COLON. [Latin, from *(intestinum) caecum* 'blind (gut)'] □ **caecal** *adj.*

Caerphilly *n.* a kind of mild white cheese originally made in Caerphilly in Wales.

Caesar *n.* **1** the title of the Roman emperors. **2** an autocrat. [Latin, family name of Gaius Julius *Caesar*, Roman statesman, 100–44 BC]

Caesarean /siz-**air**-iăn/ (also **Caesarian**) ● *adj.* **1** of Caesar or the Caesars. **2** (*US* also **Ces-**) (of a birth) effected by Caesarean section. ● *n.* a Caesarean section. [from Latin *Caesarianus*]

Caesarean section *n.* an operation for delivering a child by cutting through the wall of the mother's abdomen (Julius Caesar supposedly having been born this way).

caesium /**see**-zi-ŭm/ *n.* (*US* **cesium**) a rare soft silver-white element, occurring in certain minerals, and used in photoelectric cells and atomic clocks. [Latin neut. of *caesius* 'bluish or greyish green', from its spectrum lines]

caesura /siz-**yoor**-ă/ *n.* (*pl.* **caesuras**) *Prosody* a pause near the middle of a line. [Latin, literally 'cutting']

cafard /**kaf**-ar/ *n.* melancholia. [French, literally 'cockroach']

café *n.* (also **cafe**) **1** a small coffee house or restaurant. **2** *N. Amer.* a bar or nightclub. [French, literally 'coffee, coffee house']

cafeteria *n.* a restaurant in which customers collect their meals on trays at a counter and usu. pay before sitting down to eat. [from Latin American Spanish *cafetería* 'coffee shop']

cafetière /kaf-ĕt-**yair**/ *n. Brit.* a coffee pot with a plunger that pushes the grounds to the bottom. [French]

caff *n. Brit. slang* = CAFÉ.

caffeine *n.* an alkaloid drug with stimulant action, found in tea leaves and coffee beans. [from French]

caftan var. of KAFTAN.

cage ● *n.* **1** a structure of bars or wires for confining animals or birds. **2** any similar open framework, esp. an enclosed platform or lift in a mine or the compartment for passengers in a lift. ● *v.tr.* place or keep in a cage. [from Latin *cavea*]

cagey *adj.* (also **cagy**) (**cagier**, **cagiest**) *colloq.* cautious and uncommunicative. [20th-century US coinage] □ **cagily** *adv.* **caginess** *n.* (also **cageyness**).

cagoule *n.* a thin hooded outer jacket. [French, literally 'cowl']

cahoots *n.pl.* □ **in cahoots** *slang* in collusion. [19th-century coinage]

caiman var. of CAYMAN.

Cain *n.* □ **raise Cain** *colloq.* make a disturbance; create trouble. [from *Cain*, eldest son of Adam, who murdered his brother (Gen. 4)]

Cainozoic var. of CENOZOIC.

cairn *n.* **1** a mound of rough stones built as a monument or landmark. **2** (in full **cairn terrier**) ▼ a small terrier of a breed with short legs, a longish body, and a shaggy coat. [from Gaelic]

CAIRN TERRIER

cairngorm *n.* a semi-precious form of quartz. [found on *Cairngorm*, a mountain in Scotland]

caisson *n.* **1** a watertight chamber in which underwater construction work can be done. **2** a floating vessel used as a floodgate in docks. **3** an ammunition chest or wagon. [from Italian *cassone*]

cajole *v.tr.* (often foll. by *into*, *out of*) persuade by flattery, deceit, etc. [from French *cajoler*] □ **cajolery** *n.*

Cajun /**kay**-jŭn/ ● *n.* a French-speaking descendant of early settlers in Acadia, living esp. in the bayou areas of southern Louisiana. ● *adj.* of or relating to the Cajuns. [alteration of *Acadian*]

cake ● *n.* **1 a** a mixture of flour, butter, eggs, sugar, etc., baked in the oven. **b** a quantity of this baked in a flat round or ornamental shape. **2 a** other food in a flat round shape (*fish cake*). **b** = CATTLE CAKE. **3** a flattish compact mass (*a cake of soap*). ● *v.* **1** *tr.* & *intr.* form into a compact mass. **2** *tr.* cover (with a hard or sticky mass) (*boots caked with mud*). □ **have one's cake and eat it** *colloq.* enjoy both of two mutually exclusive alternatives. **a piece of cake** *colloq.* something easily achieved. **sell** (or **go**) **like hot cakes** be sold (or go) quickly; be popular. **a slice of the cake** *colloq.* participation in benefits. [Middle English]

cakewalk *n.* **1** a dance developed from an American black contest in graceful walking with a cake as a prize. **2** *colloq.* an easy task.

Cal. *abbr.* California.

cal *abbr.* calorie(s).

calabash *n.* **1 a** an evergreen tree, *Crescentia cujete*, bearing fruit in the form of large gourds. **b** a gourd from this tree. **2** the shell of this or a similar gourd used as a vessel etc. [from Spanish *calabaza*]

calabrese /kal-ă-**breess**, kal-ă-**bray**-si/ *n. Brit.* a large succulent variety of sprouting broccoli. [Italian, literally 'of *Calabria*', an Italian region]

calamari /kal-ă-**mar**-i/ *n.pl.* squid served as food. [Italian]

calamine *n.* a pink powder consisting of zinc carbonate and ferric oxide, used in lotions and ointments. [based on Latin *cadmia*, related to CADMIUM]

calamity *n.* (*pl.* **-ies**) **1** a disaster. **2 a** adversity. **b** deep distress. [from Latin *calamitas*] □ **calamitous** *adj.* **calamitously** *adv.*

calc- *comb. form* lime or calcium.

calcareous /kal-**kair**-iŭs/ *adj.* (also **calcarious**) of or containing calcium carbonate. [from Latin *calcarius*]

calceolaria /kal-si-ŏ-**lair**-iă/ *n.* a plant of the S. American genus *Calceolaria* (figwort family), with slipper-shaped flowers. [based on Latin *calceolus* 'little shoe']

calceolate *adj. Bot.* slipper-shaped.

calciferol /kal-**sif**-ĕ-rol/ *n.* one of the D vitamins, essential for the deposition of calcium in bones.

calciferous *adj.* yielding calcium salts, esp. calcium carbonate. [based on Latin *calx calc-* 'lime']

calcify *v.tr.* & *intr.* (**-ies**, **-ied**) **1** harden or become hardened by deposition of calcium salts. **2** convert or be converted to calcium carbonate. □ **calcification** *n.*

calcine *v.* **1** *tr.* **a** reduce, oxidize, or desiccate by strong heat. **b** burn to ashes; consume by fire. **c** reduce to calcium oxide by roasting or burning. **2** *tr.* consume or purify as if by fire. **3** *intr.* undergo any of these. [from Late Latin *calcina* 'lime'] □ **calcination** *n.*

calcite *n.* ▼ natural crystalline calcium carbonate. ▷ MATRIX. [from German *Calcit*]

CALCITE CRYSTALS

calcium *n.* a soft grey metallic element occurring naturally in limestone, chalk, gypsum, etc. [based on Latin *calx calc-* 'lime']

calcium carbonate *n.* a white insoluble solid occurring naturally as chalk, limestone, marble, and calcite, and used in the manufacture of lime and cement.

calcium hydroxide *n.* a white crystalline powder used in the manufacture of plaster and cement.

calcium oxide *n.* a white solid alkaline compound, commonly produced in the form of quicklime (see LIME[1] 1).

calcium phosphate *n.* the main constituent of animal bones, used as bone ash fertilizer.

calculable *adj.* able to be calculated or estimated. □ **calculability** *n.*

calculate *v.* **1** *tr.* ascertain or determine beforehand, esp. by mathematics or by reckoning. **2** *tr.* plan deliberately. **3** *intr.* (foll. by *on*, *upon*) make an essential part of one's reckoning (*calculated on a quick response*). [based on Late Latin *calculatus* 'counted, reckoned'] □ **calculative** *adj.*

calculated *adj.* **1** (of an action) done with awareness of the likely consequences. **2** (foll. by *to* + infin.) designed or suitable. □ **calculatedly** *adv.*

calculating *adj.* (of a person) shrewd, scheming. □ **calculatingly** *adv.*

calculation *n.* **1** the act or process of calculating. **2** a result got by calculating. **3** a reckoning or forecast.

calculator *n.* **1** a device used for making mathematical calculations. **2** a person or thing that calculates.

calculus *n.* (*pl.* **calculuses** or **calculi**) **1 a** a particular method of calculation or reasoning (*calculus of probabilities*). **b** *Math.* the infinitesimal calculuses of integration or differentiation (see INTEGRAL CALCULUS, DIFFERENTIAL CALCULUS). **2** *Med.* a stone

CALLIGRAPHY

Over the past 2,000 years the alphabet has been written in a wide range of scripts. Some are formal and have been used as an expression of authority. Cursive (joined-up) forms, meanwhile, are quickly written for everyday transactions. Today's calligraphers can also select the tool most appropriate to their choice of script – either traditional, such as a quill, or modern, like a dip pen. Each letter is then formed by a recommended sequence of strokes, as shown here.

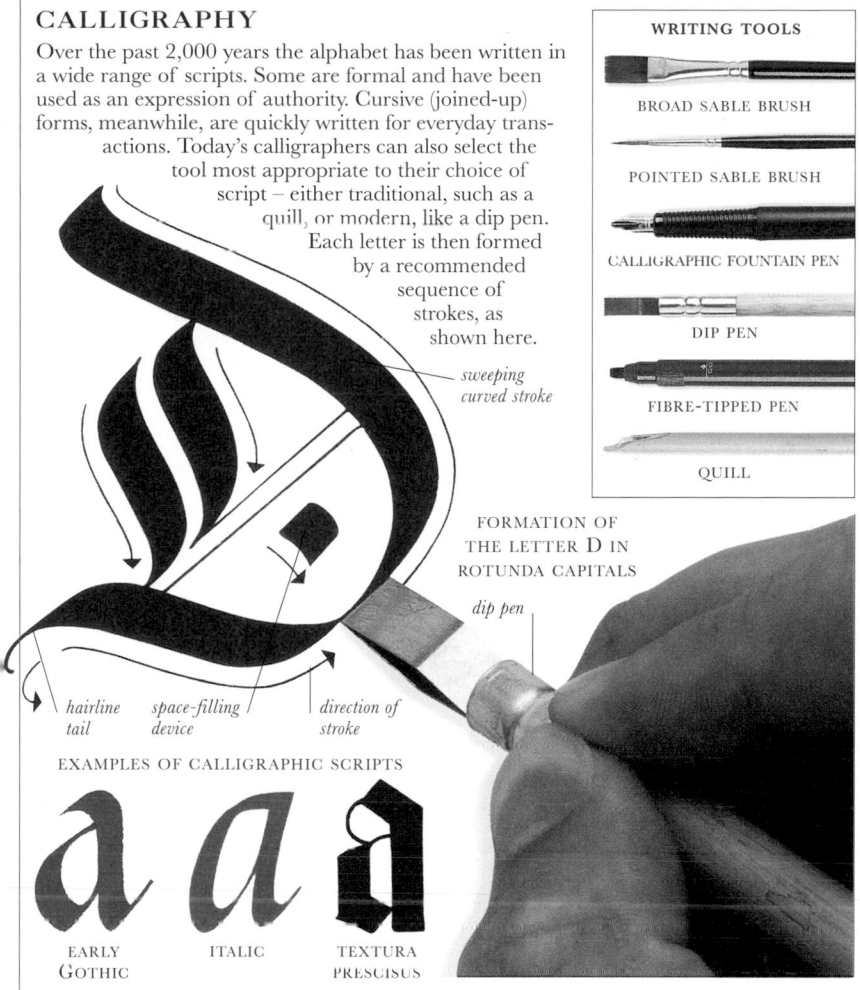

sweeping curved stroke

hairline tail

space-filling device

direction of stroke

WRITING TOOLS

BROAD SABLE BRUSH

POINTED SABLE BRUSH

CALLIGRAPHIC FOUNTAIN PEN

DIP PEN

FIBRE-TIPPED PEN

QUILL

FORMATION OF THE LETTER D IN ROTUNDA CAPITALS

dip pen

EXAMPLES OF CALLIGRAPHIC SCRIPTS

EARLY GOTHIC   ITALIC   TEXTURA PRESCISUS

C

or concretion of minerals formed within the body, esp. in the kidney or gall bladder. [Latin, literally 'small stone used in reckoning on an abacus']

caldron var. of CAULDRON.

Caledonian ● *adj.* **1** of or relating to Scotland. **2** *Geol.* of a mountain-forming period in Europe in the Palaeozoic era. ● *n.* a Scotsman. [from *Caledonia*, Latin name for northern Britain]

calendar *n.* **1** a system by which the beginning, length, and subdivisions of the year are fixed. **2** a chart or series of pages showing the days, weeks, and months of a particular year, or giving special seasonal information. **3** a timetable or programme of appointments, events, etc. [from Latin *calendarium* 'account book'] □ **calendric** *adj.* **calendrical** *adj.*

calendar month see MONTH 1.

calendar year see YEAR 2.

calender ● *n.* a machine in which cloth, paper, etc., is pressed by rollers to glaze or smooth it. ● *v.tr.* press in a calender. [from French *calendre(r)*]

calends *n.pl.* (also **kalends**) the first of the month in the ancient Roman calendar. [from Latin *kalendae*, first day of the month, when the order of days was proclaimed]

calendula *n.* any plant of the genus *Calendula* (daisy family), with large yellow or orange flowers. [modern Latin]

calf[1] *n.* (*pl.* **calves**) **1** a young bovine animal. **2** the young of other animals, e.g. elephant, deer, and whale. □ **in** (or **with**) **calf** (of a cow) pregnant. [Old English] □ **calflike** *adj.*

calf[2] *n.* (*pl.* **calves**) the fleshy hind part of the

human leg below the knee. [from Old Norse *kálfi*] □ **-calved** *adj.* (in *comb.*).

calf love *n.* romantic attachment or affection between adolescents.

calfskin *n.* calf leather.

calibrate *v.tr.* **1** mark (a gauge) with a standard scale of readings. **2** correlate the readings of (an instrument) with a standard. **3** determine the calibre of. **4** determine the correct capacity or value of. [based on CALIBRE] □ **calibrator** *n.*

calibration *n.* **1** the act or process of calibrating something. **2** each of a set of graduations on an instrument etc.

calibre *n.* (*US* **caliber**) **1 a** the internal diameter of a gun or tube. **b** the diameter of a bullet or shell. **2** strength or quality of character; ability, importance. [from Arabic *ḳālib* 'mould'] □ **calibred** *adj.* (also in *comb.*).

calico ● *n.* (*pl.* **-oes** or *N. Amer.* **-os**) **1** *Brit.* a cotton cloth, esp. plain white or unbleached. **2** *N. Amer.* a printed cotton fabric. ● *adj.* **1** made of calico. **2** *N. Amer.* multicoloured, piebald. [from *Calicut* (now Kozhikode), a port in India]

Californian ● *adj.* of or relating to California, a state on the Pacific coast of N. America. ● *n.* a native or inhabitant of California.

californium *n.* *Chem.* a transuranic radioactive metallic element produced artificially from curium. [based on *California*, where first made]

caliper var. of CALLIPER.

caliph *n.* esp. *hist.* the chief Muslim civil and reli-

gious ruler, regarded as the successor of Muhammad. [from Arabic *ḳalīfa* 'successor'] □ **caliphate** *n.*

calisthenics var. of CALLISTHENICS.

calix var. of CALYX.

calk *US* var. of CAULK.

call ● *v.* **1** *intr.* **a** cry, shout; speak loudly. **b** (of a bird or animal) emit its characteristic note or cry. **2** *tr.* communicate with by telephone or radio. **3** *tr.* **a** summon (*will you call the children?*). **b** arrange for (a person or thing) to come or be present (*called a taxi*). **4** *intr.* esp. *Brit.* pay a brief visit (*called at the house*; *called in to see you*). **5** *tr.* **a** order to take place; fix a time for (*called a meeting*). **b** direct to happen; announce (*call a halt*). **6 a** *intr.* require one's attention (*duty calls*). **b** *tr.* urge, invite, nominate (*call to the bar*). **7** *tr.* name; describe as (*call her Della*). **8** *tr.* regard or estimate as (*I call that silly*). **9** *tr.* rouse from sleep. **10** *intr.* guess the outcome of tossing a coin etc. **11** *intr.* (foll. by *for*) order, require (*called for silence*). **12** *tr.* (foll. by *over*) read out (a list of names to determine those present). **13** *intr.* (foll. by *on*, *upon*) appeal to; request or require (*called on us to be quiet*). **14** *tr.* *Cards* specify (a suit or contract) in bidding. ● *n.* **1** a shout or cry; an act of calling. **2 a** the characteristic cry of a bird or animal. **b** an imitation of this. **c** an instrument for imitating it. **3** a brief visit (*paid them a call*). **4** an act of telephoning. **b** a telephone conversation. **5 a** an invitation or summons. **b** an appeal or invitation to follow a certain profession, set of principles, etc. **6** (foll. by *for*, or *to* + infin.) a duty, need, or occasion (*no call for violence*). **7** (foll. by *for*, *on*) a demand (*not much call for it these days*; *a call on one's time*). **8** a signal on a bugle etc.; a signalling whistle. **9** *Cards* **a** a player's right or turn to make a bid. **b** a bid made. □ **at call** = *on call*. **call away** divert, distract. **call a person's bluff** see BLUFF[1]. **call forth** elicit. **call in 1** withdraw from circulation. **2** seek the advice or services of. **call in** (or **into**) **question** dispute; doubt the validity of. **call into play** give scope for; make use of. **call off 1** cancel (an arrangement etc.). **2** order (an attacker or pursuer) to desist. **call of nature** a need to urinate or defecate. **call out 1** summon (troops etc.) to action. **2** order (workers) to strike. **call the shots** (or **tune**) be in control; take the initiative. **call a spade a spade** see SPADE[1]. **call to account** see ACCOUNT. **call to mind** recollect; cause one to remember. **call to order 1** request to be orderly. **2** declare (a meeting) open. **call up 1** reach by telephone. **2** imagine, recollect. **3** summon, esp. to serve in the army. **on call 1** (of a doctor etc.) available if required but not actually on duty. **2** (of money lent) repayable on demand. **within call** near enough to be summoned by calling. [from Old Norse *kalla*]

call box *n.* esp. *Brit.* a public telephone box or kiosk.

caller *n.* **1** a person who pays a visit or makes a telephone call. **2** a person who calls out numbers in a game, directions in a dance, etc.

call-girl *n.* a prostitute who accepts appointments by telephone.

calligraphy *n.* **1** handwriting, esp. when fine. **2** ▲ the art of handwriting. [from Greek *kallos* 'beauty' + *graphia* 'writing'] □ **calligrapher** *n.* **calligraphic** *adj.*

calling *n.* **1** a profession or occupation. **2** an inwardly felt summons; a vocation.

calling card *n.* *N. Amer.* = VISITING CARD.

calliper (also **caliper**) ● *n.* **1** (in *pl.*) compasses with bowed legs for measuring the diameter of convex bodies, or with out-turned points for measuring internal dimensions. **2** (in full **calliper splint**) *Brit.* a metal splint to support the leg. ● *v.tr.* measure with callipers. [apparently variant of CALIBRE]

callisthenics *n.pl.* (*US* **calisthenics**) gymnastic exercises to achieve bodily fitness and grace of movement. [based on Greek *kallos* 'beauty' + *sthenos* 'strength']

callosity *n.* (*pl.* **-ies**) a hard thick area of skin.

callous ● *adj.* **1** unfeeling. **2** (of skin) hardened or hard. ● *n.* = CALLUS 1. [from Latin *callosus* 'calloused'] □ **calloused** *adj.* **callously** *adv.* (in sense 1 of *adj.*). **callousness** *n.*

C

call-out *n.* an instance of being called out, esp. in order to do repairs.

callow *adj.* inexperienced, immature. [Old English *calu*, in early sense 'bald', hence 'unfledged, immature'] □ **callowness** *n.*

call sign *n.* (also **call signal**) a broadcast signal identifying the radio transmitter used.

call-up *n.* the act or process of calling up (see *call up* 3).

callus *n.* **1** a hard thick area of skin or tissue. **2** a hard tissue formed round bone ends after a fracture. **3** *Bot.* a new protective tissue formed over a wound. [Latin, literally 'hardened skin']

calm ● *adj.* **1** tranquil, quiet, windless (*a calm sea*). **2** (of a person or disposition) settled; not agitated (*remained calm throughout the ordeal*). **3** confident (*his calm assumption that we would wait*). ● *n.* **1** a state of being calm; stillness, serenity. **2** a period without wind or storm. ● *v.tr. & intr.* make or become calm. [from Greek *kauma* 'heat (of the day)'] □ **calmly** *adv.* **calmness** *n.*

calmative *adj. Med.* tending to calm or sedate.

calomel *n.* mercury chloride, Hg_2Cl_2, a white powder formerly used as a purgative. [modern Latin]

Calor gas *n. Brit. propr.* liquefied butane gas stored under pressure in containers for domestic use. [from Latin *calor* 'heat']

caloric *adj.* of heat or calories.

calorie *n.* (also **calory**) (*pl.* **-ies**) a unit of heat energy: **1** (in full **small calorie**) the energy needed to raise the temperature of 1 gram of water through 1°C (now usu. defined as 4.1868 joules). **2** (in full **large calorie**) the energy needed to raise the temperature of 1 kilogram of water through 1°C, often used to measure the energy value of foods. [based on Latin *calor* 'heat']

calorific *adj.* producing heat. □ **calorifically** *adv.*

calorific value *n.* the amount of heat produced by a specified quantity of fuel, food, etc.

calorimeter *n.* any of various instruments for measuring quantity of heat. □ **calorimetric** *adj.* **calorimetry** *n.*

calory var. of CALORIE.

calumet *n.* ◀ a N. American Indian peace pipe. [French]

calumniate *v.tr.* slander. [based on Latin *calumniatus* 'slandered'] □ **calumniation** *n.* **calumniator** *n.* **calumniatory** *adj.*

calumny ● *n.* (*pl.* **-ies**) **1** slander; malicious representation. **2** an instance of this. ● *v.tr.* (**-ies, -ied**) slander. [from Latin *calumnia*] □ **calumnious** *adj.*

calvados *n.* an apple brandy. [name of a department of Normandy, France, where it is made.]

calve *v.* **1** *intr.* give birth to a calf. **2** *tr.* (esp. in *passive*) give birth to (a calf). **3** *tr.* (also *absol.*) (of an iceberg) break off or shed (a mass of ice).

calves *pl.* of CALF[1], CALF[2].

Calvinism *n.* the theology of the French theologian J. Calvin (d. 1564) or his followers, in which predestination and justification by faith are important elements. [from French *calvinisme*] □ **Calvinist** *n.* **Calvinistic** *adj.*

calypso *n.* (*pl.* **-os**) **1** a kind of W. Indian music in syncopated African rhythm, usu improvised on a topical theme. **2** a song in this style. [20th-century coinage]

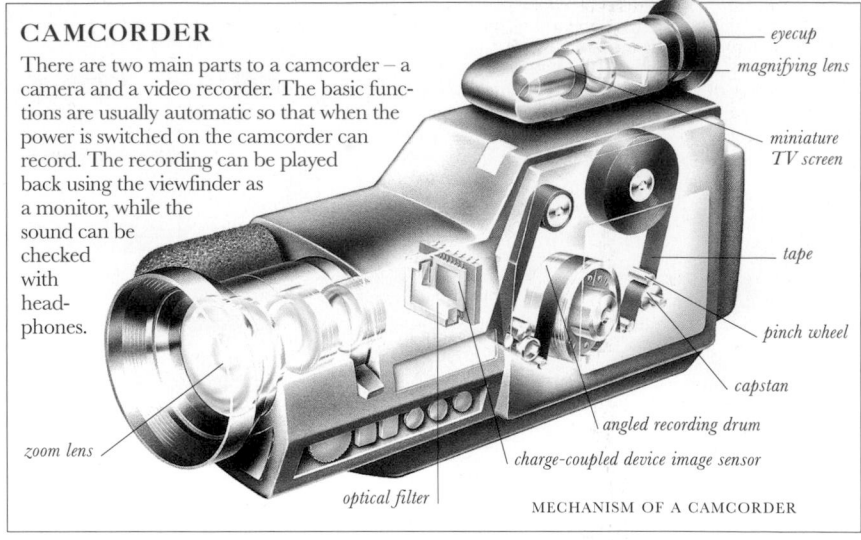

CAMCORDER

There are two main parts to a camcorder – a camera and a video recorder. The basic functions are usually automatic so that when the power is switched on the camcorder can record. The recording can be played back using the viewfinder as a monitor, while the sound can be checked with headphones.

eyecup
magnifying lens
miniature TV screen
tape
pinch wheel
capstan
angled recording drum
charge-coupled device image sensor
optical filter
zoom lens

MECHANISM OF A CAMCORDER

calyx *n.* (also **calix**) (*pl.* **calyces** or **calyxes**) **1** *Bot.* ▼ the sepals collectively, forming the protective layer of a flower in bud. **2** *Biol.* any cuplike cavity or structure. [from Greek *kalux* 'bud case, husk']

calyx

CALYX AROUND A FLOWER BUD

cam *n.* a projection on a rotating part in machinery, shaped to impart motion to the part in contact with it. [from Dutch *kam* 'comb', as in *kamrad* 'cogwheel']

camaraderie /kam-ă-**rah**-dĕ-ree/ *n.* mutual trust and sociability among friends. [French]

camber ● *n.* **1** the slightly convex or arched shape of the surface of a road, ship's deck, aircraft wing, etc. **2** *Brit.* = BANK[1] *n.* 4a. **3** the slight sideways inclination of the front wheel of a motor vehicle. ● *v.* **1** *intr.* (of a surface) have a camber. **2** *tr.* give a camber to. [based on Latin *camurus* 'curved inwards']

cambium *n.* (*pl.* **cambia** or **cambiums**) *Bot.* cellular plant tissue responsible for the increase in girth of stems and roots. ▷ STEM, WOOD. [medieval Latin, literally 'change, exchange']

Cambodian ● *n.* **1 a** a native or national of Cambodia (Kampuchea) in SE Asia. **b** a person of Cambodian descent. **2** the language of Cambodia. ● *adj.* of or relating to Cambodia or its people or language.

Cambrian ● *adj.* **1** Welsh. **2** *Geol.* of or relating to the first period in the Palaeozoic era. ● *n.* this period or system. [based on Welsh *Cymru* 'Wales']

cambric *n.* a fine white linen or cotton fabric. [from *Kamerijk*, Flemish form of *Cambrai* in N. France, where originally made]

Cambridge blue *Brit.* ● *n.* a pale blue. ● *adj.* (hyphenated when *attrib.*) of this colour. [adopted by *Cambridge* University in S. England]

camcorder *n.* ▲ a combined video camera and video recorder.

came *past* of COME.

camel ● *n.* **1** ▼ a large cud-chewing mammal, domesticated in parts of Africa and Asia, with slender legs, broad cushioned feet, and either one or two fatty humps on the back. **2** a yellowish-fawn colour. **3** an apparatus for providing additional buoyancy to ships etc. ● *adj.* yellowish fawn. [from Greek *kamēlos*]

cameleer *n.* a camel driver.

camel-hair *n.* (also **camel's-hair**) **1 a** the hair of a camel. **b** a fabric made of this (often *attrib.*: *camel-hair coat*). **2** a fine soft hair used in artists' brushes.

hollow wooden reed
eagle feathers
mouthpiece
CALUMET

CAMEL

There are two species of camel: the Arabian and the Bactrian. Both gain nourishment from desert plants, and store it in their humps. When food is scarce, fat in the humps is used up and they shrink. Arabian camels can lose up to one third of their body fluid; they can, however, drink 100 litres (about 20 gallons) at one time.

BACTRIAN CAMEL
(*Camelus bactrianus*)

ARABIAN CAMEL
(*Camelus dromedarius*)

CAMELLIA
(*Camellia* 'Dream Boat')

camellia /kă-mee-liă/ *n.* ◄ any evergreen shrub of the genus *Camellia*, native to E. Asia, with shiny leaves and showy flowers. [named after *J. Kamel*, 17th-century Jesuit botanist]

Camembert /kam-ĕm-bair/ *n.* a kind of rich soft creamy cheese. ▷ CHEESE. [from *Camembert* in N. France]

cameo *n.* (*pl.* **-os**) **1 a** ▶ a small piece of hard stone carved in relief with a background of a different colour. **b** a similar relief design using other materials. **2 a** a short descriptive literary sketch or acted scene. **b** a small character part in a play or film. [from medieval Latin *cammaeus*]

camera *n.* **1** ▶ an apparatus for taking photographs or moving film. **2** *Telev.* a piece of equipment which forms an optical image and converts it into electrical impulses for transmission or storage. □ **in camera 1** *Law* in a judge's private room. **2** privately; not in public. [Latin, literally 'vault, arched chamber']

CAMEO
CARVED IN
SARDONYX

cameraman *n.* (*pl.* **-men**) a person who operates a camera professionally, esp. in film-making or television.

camera obscura *n.* (*pl.* **camera obscuras**) ▼ a darkened box or room with a lens or aperture for projecting the image of an external object on to a screen inside. [Latin, literally 'dark chamber']

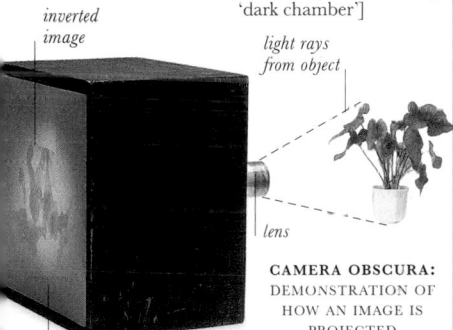

inverted image

light rays from object

lens

screen

CAMERA OBSCURA:
DEMONSTRATION OF
HOW AN IMAGE IS
PROJECTED

camera-ready *adj. Printing* (of copy) in a form suitable for immediate photographic reproduction.

camerawork *n.* the technique of using cameras in films or television.

camiknickers *n.pl. Brit.* a one-piece undergarment worn by women.

camisole *n.* a woman's under-bodice. [from Spanish *camisola*]

camomile *n.* (also **chamomile**) any of several aromatic plants of the daisy family with white and yellow daisy-like flowers, esp. *Chamaemelum nobile.* ▷ HERB. [from Greek *khamaimēlon* 'earth-apple', from the scent of its flowers]

camouflage /kam-ŏ-flah*zh*/ ● *n.* **1 a** the disguising of military equipment, vehicles, etc. to make them blend with their surroundings. **b** such a disguise. ▷ COMBAT DRESS. **2** ▶ the natural colouring of an animal which enables it to blend in with its surroundings. **3** any means of disguise or evasion.

butterfly's head

wing

CAMOUFLAGE: LEAF
BUTTERFLY AT REST

CAMERA

All cameras have the same basic design – a lightproof container with a lens opposite a light-sensitive surface. The 35 mm SLR (single-lens reflex) is the most popular format for stills photography. This is because of its unique viewing system, which allows both photographer and lens to see the subject framed in exactly the same way. Light from the subject enters the lens, reflects off a mirror, and travels through the pentaprism to the rear eyepiece. Pressing the shutter release flips the mirror out of the way, then operates the shutter to expose the film.

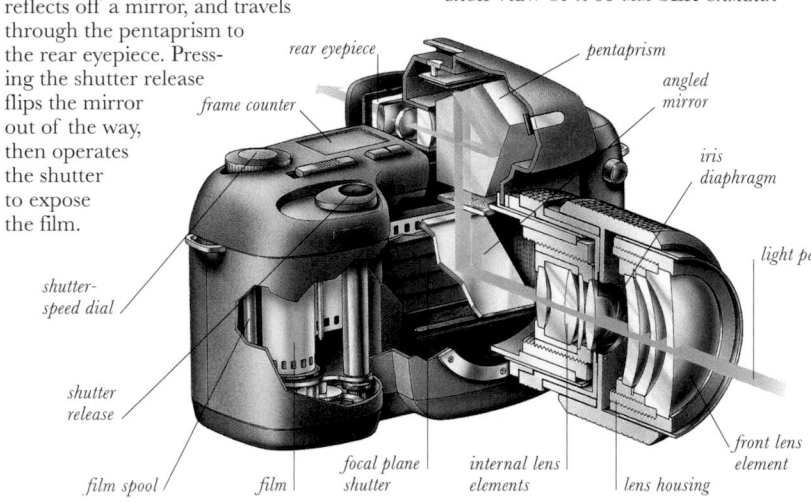

film cassette chamber   *eyepiece*   *shutter-speed dial*

BACK VIEW OF A 35 MM SLR CAMERA

rear eyepiece   *pentaprism*

frame counter   *angled mirror*

iris diaphragm

light path

shutter-speed dial

shutter release

film spool   *film*   *focal plane shutter*   *internal lens elements*   *lens housing*   *front lens element*

CUTAWAY VIEW OF A 35 MM SLR CAMERA

● *v.tr.* hide or disguise by means of camouflage. [based on Italian *camuffare* 'to disguise, deceive']

camp[1] ● *n.* **1** a place where troops are lodged or trained. **2** temporary overnight lodging in tents etc. in the open. **3 a** temporary accommodation of various kinds, usu. consisting of huts or tents, for detainees, homeless persons, etc. **b** a complex of buildings for holiday accommodation. **4** an ancient fortified site or its remains. **5** the adherents of a particular doctrine regarded collectively (*the monetarist camp*). ● *v.intr.* **1** set up or spend time in a camp (in sense 1 or 2 of *n.*). **2** lodge in temporary quarters or in the open. [from Latin *campus* 'level ground'] □ **camping** *n.*

camp[2] *colloq.* ● *adj.* **1** affected, effeminate. **2** homosexual. **3** done in an exaggerated way for effect. ● *n.* a camp manner or style. ● *v.intr. & tr.* behave or do in a camp way. □ **camp it up** overact; behave affectedly. [20th-century coinage] □ **campy** *adj.* (**campier, campiest**).

campaign ● *n.* **1** an organized course of action for a particular purpose, esp. to arouse public interest. **2 a** a series of military operations in a definite area or to achieve a particular objective. **b** military service in the field (*on campaign*). ● *v.intr.* conduct a campaign. [from Late Latin *campania* 'open country'] □ **campaigner** *n.*

campanile /kam-pă-**nee**-li/ *n.* a bell tower (usu. free-standing), esp. in Italy. [Italian, based on *campana* 'bell']

campanology *n.* **1** the study of bells. **2** the art or practice of bell-ringing. [based on Late Latin *campana* 'bell'] □ **campanologist** *n.*

campanula /kam-**pan**-yuu-lă/ *n.* any plant of the genus *Campanula*, with bell-shaped usu. blue, purple, or white flowers. [modern Latin, literally 'little bell']

camp bed *n. Brit.* a folding portable bed of a kind used in camping.

camper *n.* **1** a person who lives temporarily in a tent, hut, etc. **2** a large motor vehicle with accommodation for camping out.

campfire *n.* an open-air fire in a camp etc.

camp follower *n.* **1** a civilian worker in a military camp. **2** a disciple or adherent.

campground *n.* = CAMPSITE

camphor *n.* a white translucent crystalline volatile substance with aromatic smell and bitter taste, used to make celluloid and in medicine. [from Sanskrit *karpūram*]

camphorate *v.tr.* impregnate or treat with camphor.

campion *n.* **1** any plant of the genus *Silene* (pink family), with notched flowers. **2** a similar cultivated plant of the genus *Lychnis*.

campsite *n.* a place for camping.

campus *n.* (*pl.* **campuses**) the grounds and buildings of a university or college. [Latin, literally 'field']

campylobacter *n.* a curved or spiral bacterium of the genus *Campylobacter*, esp. as a cause of food poisoning. [from Greek *kampulos* 'bent' + *bakterion* 'little stick']

camshaft *n.* a shaft with one or more cams attached to it.

Can. *abbr.* Canada; Canadian.

can[1] *v.aux.* (3rd sing. present **can**; past **could**) (foll. by infin. without *to*, or *absol.*; present and past only in use) **1 a** be able to; know how to (*I can run fast; can he?*; *can you speak German?*). **b** be potentially capable of (*you can do it if you try*). **c** (in past) *colloq.* feel inclined to (*I could murder him*). **2** be permitted to (*can we go to the party?*). [Old English *cunnan* 'to know']

can[2] ● *n.* **1** a vessel for holding liquids. **2** a tin container in which food or drink is hermetically sealed to enable storage over long periods. **3** (in *pl.*) *Brit. slang* headphones. **4** (prec. by *the*) *slang* **a** a prison

C

C

(*sent to the can*). **b** *N. Amer.* lavatory. ● *v.tr.* (**canned, canning**) **1** put or preserve in a can. **2** record on film or tape for future use. **3** *N. Amer. colloq.* remove; dismiss (*he was canned from his job*). □ **in the can** *colloq.* completed. [Old English] □ **canner** *n.*

Canada goose *n.* a wild goose, *Branta canadensis*, with brownish-grey plumage and white cheeks and breast, native to N. America.

Canadian ● *n.* **1** a native or national of Canada. **2** a person of Canadian descent. ● *adj.* of or relating to Canada.

canal *n.* **1** an artificial waterway for inland navigation or irrigation. **2** any of various tubular ducts in a plant or animal, for carrying food, liquid, or air. [from Italian *canale* 'channel']

canal boat *n.* a long narrow boat for use on canals.

canalize *v.tr.* (also **-ise**) **1** make a canal through. **2** convert (a river) into a canal. **3** provide with canals. **4** give the desired direction or purpose to. □ **canalization** *n.*

canapé /kan-ă-pay/ *n.* a small piece of bread or pastry with a savoury on top. [French]

canard *n.* an unfounded rumour or story. [French, literally 'duck, hoax']

canary *n.* (*pl.* **-ies**) any of various small finches of the genus *Serinus*, esp. *S. canaria*, a songbird native to the Canary Islands, with mainly yellow plumage. [from Old Spanish *canario* 'of the *Canary* Islands', west of Africa]

canasta *n.* a card game using two packs and resembling rummy.

cancan *n.* a lively stage-dance with high kicking, performed by women in long skirts and petticoats. [French]

cancel *v.* (**cancelled, cancelling**; *US* also **canceled, canceling**) **1** *tr.* **a** revoke (a previous arrangement). **b** discontinue (an arrangement in progress). **2** *tr.* delete (writing etc.). **3** *tr.* mark or pierce (a stamp etc.) to invalidate it. **4** *tr.* annul; make void. **5** (often foll. by *out*) **a** *tr.* (of one factor or circumstance) neutralize (another). **b** *intr.* (of two factors or circumstances) neutralize each other. **6** *tr. Math.* strike out (an equal factor) on each side of an equation or from the numerator and denominator of a fraction. [from Latin *cancellare*] □ **canceller** *n.*

cancellation *n.* (*US* also **cancelation**) **1** the act or an instance of cancelling or being cancelled. **2** something that has been cancelled, esp. a booking or reservation.

cancellous *adj.* (of a bone) having pores. ▷ BONE. [based on Latin *cancelli* 'lattice']

cancer *n.* **1 a** any malignant tumour from an abnormal and uncontrolled division of body cells. **b** a disease caused by this. **2** an evil influence or corruption spreading uncontrollably. **3** (**Cancer**) **a** *Astron.* ◀ a constellation (the Crab), said to represent a crab crushed under the foot of Hercules. **b** *Astrol.* the fourth sign of the zodiac, which the Sun enters at the summer solstice (about 21 June). ▷ ZODIAC. **c** *Astrol.* a person born when the Sun is in this sign. □ **tropic of Cancer** see TROPIC *n.* 1. [Latin, literally 'crab, cancer'] □ **Cancerian** *n. & adj.* (in sense 3b, c). **cancerous** *adj.*

CANCER: FIGURE OF A CRAB FORMED FROM THE STARS OF CANCER

candela *n.* the SI unit of luminous intensity. [Latin, literally 'candle']

candelabrum *n.* (also **candelabra**) (*pl.* **candelabra, candelabras**; *US* also **candelabrums**) a large branched candlestick or lamp holder. [Latin]

■ **Usage** Strictly speaking, *candelabra* is the plural of *candelabrum* and is best kept so in written English. *Candelabra* (singular) and *candelabras* (plural) are

often found in informal use, while in American English *candelabrums* (plural) is also used.

candid *adj.* **1** frank; not hiding one's thoughts. **2** (of a photograph) taken informally, usu. without the subject's knowledge. [earlier in sense 'white', hence 'pure, ingenuous': from Latin *candidus* 'white'] □ **candidly** *adv.* **candidness** *n.*

candida *n.* any yeastlike parasitic fungus of the genus *Candida*, esp. *C. albicans*, which causes thrush. [modern Latin]

candidate *n.* **1** a person who seeks or is nominated for an office, award, etc. **2** a person or thing likely to gain some distinction or position. **3** a person entered for an examination. [from Latin *candidatus* 'white-robed', describing Roman candidates] □ **candidacy** *n.* **candidature** *n. Brit.*

candle *n.* **1** a cylinder or block of wax or tallow with a central wick, for giving light when burning. **2** = CANDLEPOWER. □ **cannot hold a candle to** is much inferior to. **not worth the candle** not justifying the cost or trouble. [based on Latin *candēre* 'to shine']

candleholder *n.* = CANDLESTICK.

candlelight *n.* light provided by candles. □ **candlelit** *adj.*

Candlemas *n.* a Christian feast with blessing of candles (2 Feb.), commemorating the purification of the Virgin Mary and the presentation of Christ in the Temple. [Old English]

candlepower *n.* a unit of luminous intensity.

candlestick *n.* a holder for one or more candles.

candlewick *n.* **1** a thick soft cotton yarn. **2** material made from this, usu. with a tufted pattern.

can-do *attrib.adj.* designating a determination or willingness to achieve something (*the American can-do philosophy*).

candour /kan-der/ *n.* (*US* **candor**) frankness. [from Latin *candor* 'whiteness', related to CANDID]

C. & W. *abbr.* country and western.

candy ● *n.* (*pl.* **-ies**) **1** (in full **sugar-candy**) *Brit.* sugar crystallized by repeated boiling and slow evaporation. **2** *N. Amer.* sweets; a sweet. ● *v.tr.* (**-ies, -ied**) (usu. as **candied** *adj.*) preserve by coating and impregnating with a sugar syrup (*candied fruit*). [based on Arabic *ḳand* 'sugar']

candyfloss *n. Brit.* a fluffy mass of spun sugar wrapped round a stick.

candytuft *n.* any of various cruciferous plants of the genus *Iberis*, with white, pink, or purple flowers in tufts. [based on *Candy*, obsolete form of *Candia* 'Crete']

cane ● *n.* **1 a** the hollow jointed stem of giant reeds or grasses (*bamboo cane*). **b** the solid stem of slender palms (*malacca cane*). **2** = SUGAR CANE. **3** a raspberry cane. **4** material of cane used for wickerwork etc.

5 a a cane used as a walking stick or a support for a plant or an instrument of punishment. **b** any slender walking stick. ● *v.tr.* **1** beat with a cane. **2** weave cane into (a chair etc.). [from Greek *kanna*] □ **caning** *n.*

cane sugar *n.* sugar obtained from sugar cane.

canine ● *adj.* **1** of a dog or dogs. **2** of or belonging to the family Canidae, including dogs, foxes, wolves, etc. ● *n.* **1** a dog. **2** (in full **canine tooth**) ▶ a pointed tooth between the incisors and premolars. ▷ DENTITION, TOOTH. [based on Latin *canis* 'dog']

upper canine
upper canine
INDIVIDUAL CANINE *lower canine* *lower canine*
CANINE PLAN OF HUMAN DENTITION

canister *n.* **1** a small, usu. metallic and cylindrical, container for storing tea etc. **2 a** a cylinder of shot, tear gas, etc. that explodes on impact. **b** such cylinders collectively. [from Greek *kanastron* 'wicker basket']

canker ● *n.* **1 a** a destructive fungal disease of trees and plants. **b** an open wound in the stem of a tree or plant. **2** *Zool.* an ulcerous ear disease of animals. **3** a corrupting influence. ● *v.tr.* **1** consume with canker. **2** corrupt. **3** (as **cankered** *adj.*) soured, malignant, crabbed. [from Latin *cancer* 'crab'] □ **cankerous** *adj.*

canna *n.* any tropical plant of the genus *Canna* with bright flowers and ornamental leaves. [Latin]

cannabis *n.* **1** a hemp plant of the genus *Cannabis*. **2** a preparation of parts of this used as an intoxicant or hallucinogen. [from Greek]

cannabis resin *n.* a sticky product containing the active principles of cannabis.

canned *adj.* **1** pre-recorded (*canned laughter*; *canned music*). **2** supplied in a can (*canned beer*). **3** *slang* drunk.

cannelloni *n.pl.* tubes of pasta stuffed with a meat or vegetable mixture. [Italian, from *cannello* 'stalk']

cannery *n.* (*pl.* **-ies**) a factory where food is canned.

cannibal ● *n.* **1** a person who eats human flesh. **2** an animal that feeds on flesh of its own species. ● *adj.* of or like a cannibal. [based on Spanish *Caribes*, name of a W. Indian nation] □ **cannibalism** *n.* **cannibalistic** *adj.*

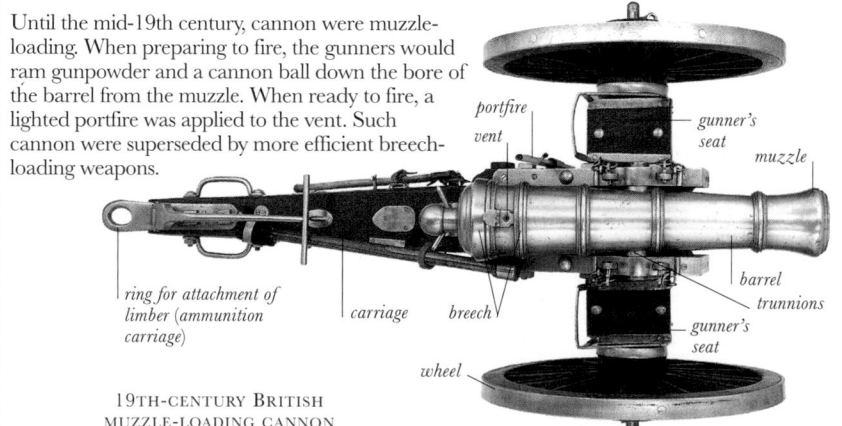

CANNON

Until the mid-19th century, cannon were muzzle-loading. When preparing to fire, the gunners would ram gunpowder and a cannon ball down the bore of the barrel from the muzzle. When ready to fire, a lighted portfire was applied to the vent. Such cannon were superseded by more efficient breech-loading weapons.

portfire
vent
gunner's seat
muzzle
ring for attachment of limber (ammunition carriage)
carriage
breech
barrel
trunnions
gunner's seat
wheel

19TH-CENTURY BRITISH MUZZLE-LOADING CANNON

cannibalize *v.tr.* (also **-ise**) use (a machine etc.) as a source of spare parts for others. □ **cannibalization** *n.*

cannon ● *n.* **1** (*pl.* usu. same) *hist.* ▼ a large heavy gun installed on a carriage or mounting. **2** an automatic aircraft gun firing shells. **3** *Brit. Billiards* the hitting of two balls successively by the cue ball. ● *v.intr. Brit.* **1** (usu. foll. by *against*, *into*) collide heavily or obliquely. **2** *Billiards* make a cannon shot. [from Italian *cannone* 'large tube'; Billiards sense from older *carom*]

cannonade ● *n.* a period of continuous heavy gunfire. ● *v.tr.* bombard with a cannonade. [French]

cannon ball *n. hist.* a large ball fired by a cannon.

cannon-bone *n.* the tubular bone between the hock and fetlock of a horse. ▷ HORSE

cannon fodder *n.* soldiers regarded merely as material to be expended in war.

cannot *v.aux.* can not.

cannula *n.* (*pl.* **cannulae** /-lee/ or **cannulas**) *Surgery* a small tube for inserting into the body to allow fluid to enter or escape. [Latin, literally 'little cane']

canny *adj.* (**cannier**, **canniest**) **1 a** shrewd, worldly-wise. **b** thrifty. **c** circumspect. **2** sly, drily humorous. [literally 'knowing', based on CAN[1]] □ **cannily** *adv.* **canniness** *n.*

canoe ● *n.* ▼ a small narrow boat with pointed ends usu. propelled by paddling. ▷ OUTRIGGER. ● *v.intr.* (**canoes**, **canoed**, **canoeing**) travel in a canoe. [from Carib *canaoua*] □ **canoeist** *n.*

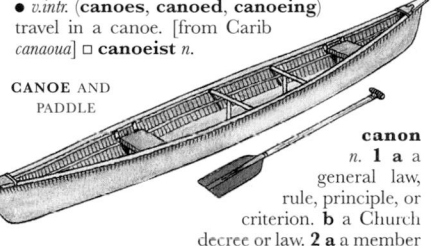

CANOE AND PADDLE

canon *n.* **1 a** a general law, rule, principle, or criterion. **b** a Church decree or law. **2 a** a member of a cathedral chapter. **b** (*fem.* **canoness**) a member of certain RC orders. **3 a** a collection of literary works, esp. of sacred books etc. accepted as genuine. **b** the recognized genuine works of a particular author. **4** the part of the Roman Catholic Mass containing the words of consecration. **5** *Mus.* a piece with different parts taking up the same theme successively. [from Greek *kanōn*]

cañon var. of CANYON.

canonical ● *adj.* **1 a** according to canon law. **b** included in the canon of Scripture. **2** authoritative, standard, accepted. **3** of a cathedral chapter or a member of it. **4** *Mus.* in canon form. ● *n.* (in *pl.*) the canonical dress of the clergy. □ **canonically** *adv.*

canonicity *n.* the status of being canonical.

canonize *v.tr.* (also **-ise**) **1 a** declare officially to be a saint. **b** regard as a saint. **2** admit to the canon of Scripture. **3** sanction by Church authority. □ **canonization** *n.*

canon law *n.* ecclesiastical law.

canon regular (also **regular canon**) see REGULAR *adj.* 8b.

canonry *n.* (*pl.* **-ies**) the office or benefice of a canon.

canoodle *v.intr. colloq.* kiss and cuddle amorously. [19th-century US coinage]

canopy *n.* (*pl.* **-ies**) **1 a** a covering hung or held up over a throne, bed, person, etc. **b** the sky. **c** an overhanging shelter. **2** *Archit.* a rooflike projection over a niche etc. **3** the uppermost layers of foliage etc. in a forest. ▷ RAINFOREST. **4 a** the expanding part of a parachute. **b** the cover of an aircraft's cockpit. ▷ AIRCRAFT. [from Greek *kōnōpeion* 'couch with mosquito-curtains']

cant[1] ● *n.* **1** insincere pious or moral talk. **2** ephemeral or fashionable catchwords. **3** language peculiar to a class, profession, sect, etc.; jargon. ● *v.intr.* use cant.

cant[2] ● *n.* **1 a** a slanting surface. **b** a bevel of a crystal etc. **2** an oblique push or movement that upsets

or partly upsets something. **3** a tilted position. ● *v.* **1** *tr.* push or pitch out of level; tilt. **2** *intr.* take or lie in a slanting position. **3** *tr.* impart a bevel to. [from Latin *cant(h)us* 'iron tire']

can't *contr.* can not.

Cantab *abbr.* of Cambridge University. [Latin *Cantabrigiensis*]

cantabile /kan-**tah**-bi-li/ *Mus.* ● *adv. & adj.* in a smooth singing style. ● *n.* a cantabile passage or movement. [Italian, literally 'singable']

Cantabrigian ● *adj.* of Cambridge or Cambridge University. ● *n.* **1** a member of Cambridge University. **2** a native of Cambridge. [from Latin *Cantabrigia* 'Cambridge']

cantaloupe *n.* (also **cantaloup**) ▶ a small round ribbed variety of melon with orange flesh. [from *Cantaluppi* near Rome]

cantankerous *adj.* bad-tempered, quarrelsome. □ **cantankerously** *adv.* **cantankerousness** *n.*

cantata *n. Mus.* a short narrative or descriptive composition with vocal solos and usu. chorus and orchestral accompaniment. [from Italian *cantata (aria)* 'sung (air)']

canteen *n.* **1 a** a restaurant for employees. **b** a shop selling provisions or liquor in a barracks or camp. **2** *Brit.* a case of cutlery. **3** a soldier's or camper's waterflask. [from Italian *cantina* 'cellar']

canter ● *n.* a gentle gallop. ● *v.* **1** *intr.* (of a horse or its rider) go at a canter. **2** *tr.* make (a horse) canter. [short for *Canterbury pace*, from the supposed easy pace of medieval pilgrims to Canterbury]

Canterbury bell *n.* a cultivated campanula with large flowers. [named after the bells on Canterbury pilgrims' horses (see CANTER)]

canticle *n.* song or chant with a biblical text, esp. one used in church services. [from Latin *canticulum*]

cantilever ● *n.* **1** a long bracket or beam etc. projecting from a wall to support a balcony etc. **2** a beam or girder fixed at only one end. ● *v.* **1** *intr. & tr.* project as a cantilever. **2** *tr.* support by a cantilever or cantilevers. [17th-century coinage]

cantilever bridge *n.* a bridge made of cantilevers projecting from the piers and connected by girders. ▷ BRIDGE

cantina *n.* a bar or wine shop. [Spanish & Italian]

canto *n.* (*pl.* **-os**) a division of a long poem. [Italian, literally 'song']

canton ● *n.* /kan-ton/ **1** a subdivision of a country. **2** a state of the Swiss Confederation. ● *v.tr.* /kan-**toon**/ *Brit.* put (troops) into quarters. [from Old French, literally 'corner'] □ **cantonal** *adj.*

Cantonese ● *adj.* of Canton or the Cantonese dialect of Chinese. ● *n.* (*pl.* same) **1** a native of Canton. **2** the dialect of Chinese spoken in SE China and Hong Kong. [from *Canton*, English name of the city of Guangzhou in China]

cantonment *n.* **1** a lodging assigned to troops. **2** *hist.* a permanent military station in India.

cantor *n.* **1** the leader of the singing in church; a precentor. **2** the precentor in a synagogue. [Latin, literally 'singer'] □ **cantorial** *adj.*

canvas *n.* **1 a** a strong coarse kind of cloth used for sails and tents etc. and as a surface for oil painting. **b** a piece of this. **2** a painting on canvas. **3** an open kind of canvas used as a basis for tapestry and embroidery. **4** (prec. by *the*) the canvas-covered floor of a boxing or wrestling ring. □ **by a canvas** (in boat racing) by a small margin (*win by a canvas*). **under canvas 1** in a tent or tents. **2** with sails spread. [from Latin *cannabis* 'hemp']

canvass ● *v.* **1 a** *intr.* solicit votes. **b** *tr.* solicit votes from. **2** *tr.* **a** ascertain the opinions of. **b** seek

custom from. **c** discuss thoroughly. **3** *tr. Brit.* propose (an idea or plan etc.). ● *n.* the process of or an instance of canvassing. [originally in sense 'to toss in a sheet, agitate'] □ **canvasser** *n.*

canyon *n.* (also **cañon**) a deep gorge. ▷ ERODE. [from Spanish *cañón* 'tube']

CAP *abbr.* Common Agricultural Policy (of the EU).

cap ● *n.* **1 a** a soft head covering, usu. with a peak but otherwise brimless. **b** a head covering worn in a particular profession (*nurse's cap*). **c** esp. *Brit.* a cap awarded as a sign of membership of a sports team. **d** an academic mortarboard or soft hat. **2 a** a cover like a cap in shape or position (*kneecap*; *toecap*). **b** a device to seal a bottle or protect the point of a pen, lens of a camera, etc. **3 a** = DUTCH CAP 1. **b** = PERCUSSION CAP. **4** = CROWN *n.* 8b. ● *v.tr.* (**capped**, **capping**) **1 a** put a cap on. **b** cover the top or end of. **c** set a limit to (expenditure etc.). **2 a** esp. *Brit.* award a sports cap to. **b** *Sc. & NZ* confer a university degree on. **3 a** lie on top of; form the cap of. **b** surpass, excel. **c** improve on (a story, quotation, etc.); esp. by producing a better or more apposite one. □ **cap in hand** humbly. **set one's cap at** (or *US* **for**) try to attract as a suitor. [from Late Latin *cappa*] □ **capping** *n.*

capability *n.* (*pl.* **-ies**) **1** ability, power; the condition of being capable. **2** an undeveloped or unused faculty.

capable *adj.* **1** competent, able, gifted. **2** (foll. by *of*) **a** having the ability, fitness, or necessary quality for. **b** susceptible of; admitting of (explanation or improvement etc.). [earlier in sense 'able to take in or understand': based on Latin *capere* 'to hold'] □ **capably** *adv.*

capacious *adj.* roomy; able to hold much. [from Latin *capax -acis*]

capacitance *n. Electr.* **1** the ability of a system to store an electric charge. **2** the ratio of the change in an electric charge in a system to the corresponding change in its electric potential.

capacitate *v.tr.* **1** (usu. foll. by *for*, or *to* + infin.) render capable. **2** make legally competent.

capacitor *n. Electr.* ▶ a device of one or more pairs of conductors separated by insulators used to store an electric charge. ▷ RADIO

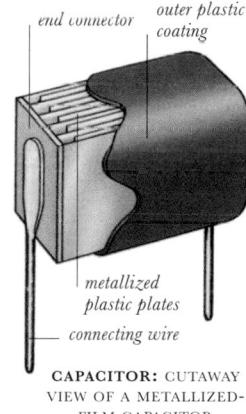

CAPACITOR: CUTAWAY VIEW OF A METALLIZED-FILM CAPACITOR

outer plastic coating
end connector
metallized plastic plates
connecting wire

capacity *n.* (*pl.* **-ies**) **1 a** the power of containing, receiving, experiencing, or producing (*capacity for heat, pain*, etc.). **b** the maximum amount that can be contained or produced etc. **c** the volume of the cylinders in an internal-combustion engine. **d** (*attrib.*) fully occupying the available space, resources, etc. (*a capacity audience*). **2** a mental power. **b** a faculty or talent. **3** a position or function (*in a civil capacity; in my capacity as a critic*). **4** legal competence. **5** *Electr.* capacitance. □ **to capacity** fully; using all resources (*working to capacity*). [from Latin *capacitas*]

caparison ● *n.* **1** (usu. in *pl.*) a horse's trappings. ▷ JOUST. **2** equipment, finery. ● *v.tr.* put caparisons on; adorn richly. [from Spanish *caparazón* 'saddle-cloth']

cape[1] *n.* **1** a sleeveless cloak. **2** a short sleeveless cloak as a fixed or detachable part of a longer cloak or coat. [from Late Latin *cappa* 'cap'] □ **caped** *adj.*

cape[2] *n.* **1** a headland or promontory. **2** (**the Cape**) **a** the Cape of Good Hope. **b** the S. African province containing it. [from Latin *caput* 'head']

Cape buffalo see BUFFALO *n.* 1b.

C

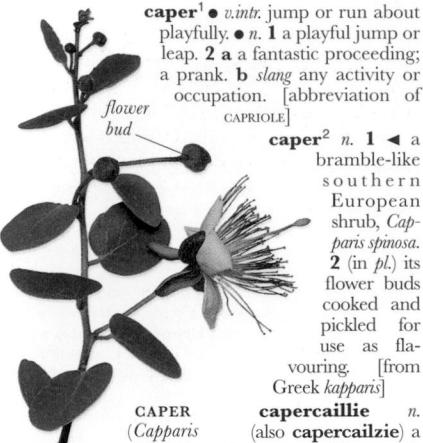

caper[1] ● *v.intr.* jump or run about playfully. ● *n.* **1** a playful jump or leap. **2 a** a fantastic proceeding; a prank. **b** *slang* any activity or occupation. [abbreviation of CAPRIOLE]

caper[2] *n.* **1** ◀ a bramble-like southern European shrub, *Capparis spinosa.* **2** (in *pl.*) its flower buds cooked and pickled for use as flavouring. [from Greek *kapparis*]

flower bud

CAPER (*Capparis spinosa*)

capercaillie *n.* (also **capercailzie**) a large grouse, *Tetrao urogallus,* of coniferous forests in northern Europe. ▷ DISPLAY. [from Gaelic *capull coille* 'horse of the wood']

capillarity *n.* = CAPILLARY ACTION.

capillary ● *adj.* **1** of or like a hair. **2** (of a tube) of hairlike internal diameter. **3** of one of the delicate ramified blood vessels intervening between arteries and veins. ▷ CARDIOVASCULAR. ● *n.* (*pl.* **-ies**) **1** a capillary tube. **2** a capillary blood vessel. ▷ CAPILLARY ACTION. [based on Latin *capillaris* 'hair']

capillary action *n.* ▼ the tendency of a liquid in a capillary tube or absorbent material to rise or fall as a result of surface tension. ▷ TRANSPIRE.

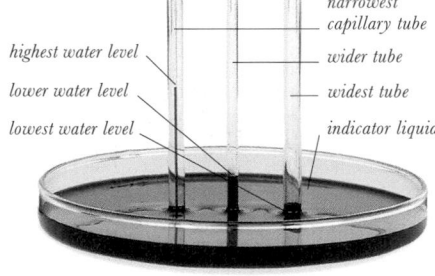

narrowest capillary tube
highest water level
wider tube
lower water level
widest tube
lowest water level
indicator liquid

CAPILLARY ACTION: DEMONSTRATION OF LIQUID RISING IN CAPILLARY TUBES

capital[1] ● *n.* **1** the most important town or city of a country or region, usu. its seat of government and administrative centre. **2 a** the money or other assets with which a company starts in business. **b** accumulated wealth. **c** money invested or lent at interest. **3** capitalists generally. **4** a capital letter. ● *adj.* **1 a** principal; most important; leading. **b** *colloq.* excellent, first-rate. **2 a** involving or punishable by death (*capital punishment; a capital offence*). **b** (of an error etc.) vitally harmful; fatal. **3** (of letters of the alphabet) large and of the form used to begin sentences and names etc. ● *int.* expressing approval or satisfaction. □ **make capital out** of use to one's advantage. **with a capital** — emphatically such (*art with a capital A*). [based on Latin *caput -itis* 'head'] □ **capitally** *adv.*

capital[2] *n. Archit.* ▼ the head or cornice of a pillar or column. ▷ ENTABLATURE. [from Late Latin *capitellum* 'little head']

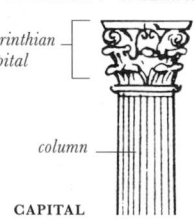

Corinthian capital
column
CAPITAL

capital gain *n.* a profit from the sale of investments or property.

capital gains tax *n.* a tax levied on the profit from the sale of investments or property.

capital goods *n.pl.* goods, esp. machinery, plant, etc., used or to be used in producing commodities (opp. CONSUMER GOODS).

capitalism *n.* **1 a** an economic system in which the production and distribution of goods depend on invested private capital and profit-making. **b** the possession of capital or wealth. **2** *Polit.* the dominance of private owners of capital and production for profit.

capitalist ● *n.* **1** a person using or possessing capital; a rich person. **2** an advocate of capitalism. ● *adj.* of or favouring capitalism. □ **capitalistic** *adj.* **capitalistically** *adv.*

capitalize *v.* (also **-ise**) **1** *tr.* **a** convert into or provide with capital. **b** calculate or realize the present value of an income. **c** reckon (the value of an asset) by setting future benefits against the cost of maintenance. **2** *tr.* **a** write (a letter of the alphabet) as a capital. **b** begin (a word) with a capital letter. **3** *intr.* (foll. by *on*) use to one's advantage; profit from. □ **capitalization** *n.*

capital sum *n.* a lump sum of money, esp. payable to an insured person.

capitation *n.* **1** a tax or fee at a set rate per person. **2** the levying of such a tax or fee. [from Late Latin *capitatio* 'poll tax']

capitation grant *n.* a grant of a sum calculated from the number of people to be catered for.

Capitol *n.* (usu. prec. by *the*) (in the US) a building housing a legislature, esp. the seat of the US Congress in Washington, DC.

capitulate *v.intr.* surrender, esp. on stated conditions. [based on medieval Latin *capitulatus* 'drawn up under headings']

capitulation *n.* **1** the act of capitulating; surrender. **2** a statement of the main divisions of a subject. **3** an agreement or set of conditions.

cap'n *n. colloq.* captain.

capo *n.* (*pl.* **capos**) *Mus.* ▼ a device secured across the neck of a fretted instrument to raise equally the tuning of all strings by the required amount. [from Italian *capo tasto* 'head stop']

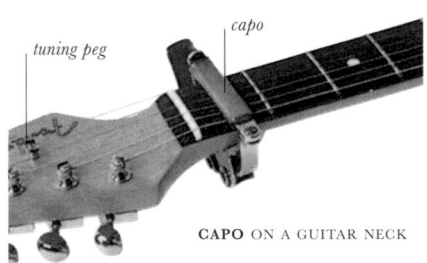

tuning peg
capo

CAPO ON A GUITAR NECK

capon *n.* a domestic cock castrated and fattened for eating. [from Latin *capo -onis*]

cappuccino /ka-puu-**chee**-noh/ *n.* (*pl.* **-os**) coffee with milk made frothy with pressurized steam. [Italian, literally 'Capuchin']

capriccio *n.* (*pl.* **-os**) **1** a lively musical composition. **2** a painting etc. representing a fantasy or a mixture of real and imaginary features. [Italian, literally 'sudden start']

caprice /kă-**preess**/ *n.* **1 a** a whimsical change of mind or conduct. **b** a tendency to this. **2** a work of lively fancy in painting, drawing, or music; a capriccio. [French]

capricious *adj.* **1** guided by or given to caprice. **2** irregular, unpredictable. □ **capriciously** *adv.* **capriciousness** *n.*

Capricorn *n.* **1** (usu. **Capricornus**) *Astron.* ▶ a constellation (the Goat), said to represent a goat with a fish's tail. **2** *Astrol.* **a** the tenth sign of the zodiac, which the Sun enters at the winter solstice (about 21 Dec.). ▷ ZODIAC. **b** a person born when the Sun is

CAPRICORN: FIGURE OF A GOAT FORMED FROM THE STARS OF CAPRICORNUS

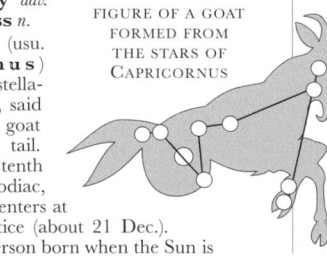

in this sign. □ **tropic of Capricorn** see TROPIC *n.* 1. [from Latin *caper* 'goat' + *cornu* 'horn'] □ **Capricornian** *n. & adj.*

caprine *adj.* of or like a goat. [based on Latin *caper* 'goat']

capriole ● *n.* **1** a leap or caper. **2** a trained horse's high leap and kick without advancing. ● *v.* **1** *intr.* (of a horse or its rider) perform a capriole. **2** *tr.* make (a horse) capriole. [from Italian *capriola* 'leap']

capsicum *n.* **1** any plant of the genus *Capsicum* (nightshade family), having edible capsular fruits containing many seeds, esp. *C. annuum* yielding chilli and sweet peppers. **2** the fruit of any of these plants. [modern Latin]

capsize *v.* **1** *tr.* upset or overturn (a boat). **2** *intr.* be capsized.

capstan *n.* **1** ▶ a thick revolving cylinder with a vertical axis, for winding an anchor cable or a halyard etc. ▷ SHIP. **2 a** motor-driven revolving spindle on a tape recorder that guides the tape past the head at constant speed. [from Latin *capistrum* 'halter']

drumhead
bar hole
barrel
whelp
tapered spindle (axis)
spigot
pin
CAPSTAN

capstan lathe *n.* a lathe with a revolving tool holder.

capstone *n.* a coping stone.

capsule *n.* **1** a small soluble case of gelatin enclosing a dose of medicine and swallowed with it. ▷ DRUG. **2 a** detachable compartment of a spacecraft or nose-cone of a rocket. ▷ SPACECRAFT. **3** an enclosing membrane in the body. **4** a top or cover for a bottle, esp. the foil or plastic covering the cork of a wine bottle. **5 a** a dry fruit that releases its seeds when ripe. ▷ FRUIT. **b** the spore-producing part of mosses and liverworts. **6** *Biol.* an enveloping layer surrounding certain bacteria. [from Latin *capsula*] □ **capsular** *adj.*

capsulize *v.tr.* (also **-ise**) put (information etc.) in compact form.

Capt. *abbr.* Captain.

captain ● *n.* **1 a** a chief or leader. **b** the leader of a team, esp. in sports. **c** a powerful or influential person (*captain of industry*). **2 a** the person in command of a merchant or passenger ship. **b** the pilot of a civil aircraft. **3** (as a title **Captain**) **a** an army or (in the US and Canada) air force officer next above lieutenant. **b** a navy officer in command of a warship; one ranking below commodore or rear admiral and above commander. **c** (in the US) a police officer in charge of a precinct, ranking below a chief. **4 a** *Brit.* a foreman. **b** a head boy or girl in a school. **c** *colloq.* the adult leader of a company of Guides, officially termed *Guide Guider* since 1968. **d** *N. Amer.* a supervisor of waiters or bellboys. ● *v.tr.* be captain of; lead. [from Late Latin *capitaneus* 'chief'] □ **captaincy** *n.* (*pl.* **-ies**).

caption ● *n.* **1** a title or brief explanation appended to an illustration, cartoon, etc. **2** wording appearing on a cinema or television screen as part of a film or broadcast. **3** the heading of a chapter or article etc. ● *v.tr.* provide with a caption. [earlier in sense 'capture, seizure', from Latin *captio*]

captious *adj.* given to finding fault or raising petty objections. [from Latin *captiosus*] □ **captiously** *adv.* **captiousness** *n.*

CAR

The first car was built by Lenoir in 1862. His innovation was a compact version of the internal-combustion engine powered by gas. Petrol-powered versions soon followed, and the design was widely adopted. The first mass-production car, the Model T Ford, was introduced in 1908, and by 1930 15 million had been sold. Today's engines work on similar principles, although cars now are designed for greater efficiency, safety, and comfort. Modern engines consume less fuel as a result of computerized ignition systems, fuel injectors, and multi-valve cylinder heads. Exhaust pollution is reduced by catalytic converters, while bodyshells with controlled stiffness, toughened windscreens, and airbags improve safety. Coil-spring suspension, pneumatic tyres, and padded seats enhance passenger comfort.

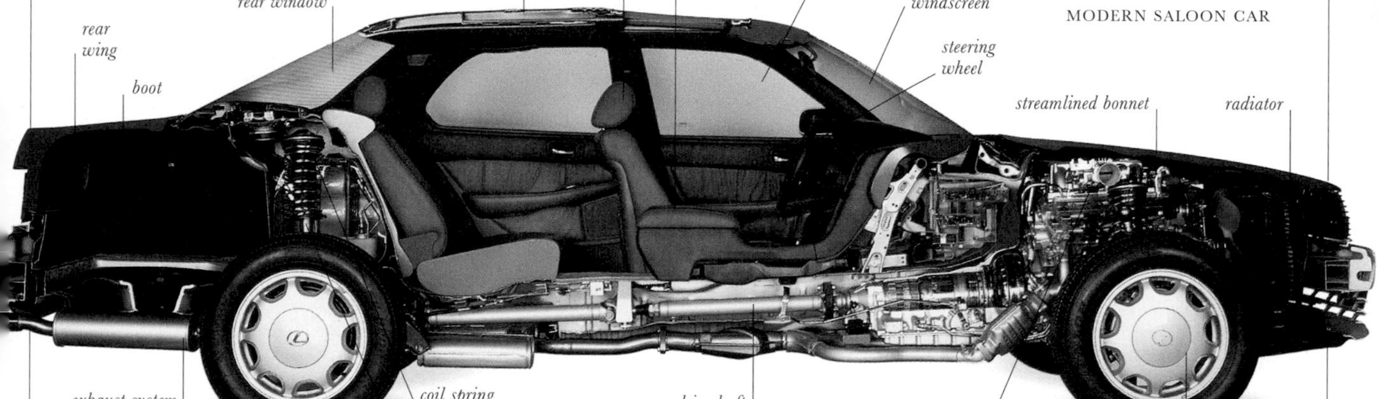

C

CUTAWAY VIEW OF A MODERN SALOON CAR

rear wing · boot · rear window · sound insulation · headrest · padded seat · side window · toughened glass windscreen · steering wheel · streamlined bonnet · radiator · exhaust system and catalytic converter · coil spring suspension · gas-filled shock absorbers · driveshaft · computerized fuel injection and ignition · pneumatic tyre · hubcap

MAIN TYPES OF CAR

ESTATE CAR  · HATCHBACK  · FAMILY SALOON  · PEOPLE CARRIER (MPV)

OFF-ROAD VEHICLE  · SPORTS CAR  · CONVERTIBLE CAR 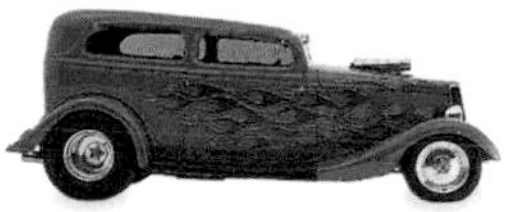 · CUSTOM CAR

captivate *v.tr.* **1** overwhelm with charm or affection. **2** fascinate. [based on Late Latin *captivatus* 'taken captive'] □ **captivation** *n.*

captive ● *n.* a person or animal that has been taken prisoner or confined. ● *adj.* **1 a** taken prisoner. **b** kept in confinement or under restraint. **2 a** unable to escape. **b** in a position of having to comply (*captive audience*; *captive market*). **3** of or like a prisoner (*captive state*). [from Latin *captivus*]

captivity *n.* (*pl.* **-ies**) **1** the condition or circumstances of being a captive. **2** a period of captivity.

captor *n.* a person who captures or holds captive (a person, group, etc.).

capture ● *v.tr.* **1 a** take prisoner; seize as a prize. **b** obtain by force or trickery. **2** portray in permanent form (*could not capture the likeness*). **3** *Physics* absorb (a subatomic particle). **4** (in board games) make a move that secures the removal of (an opposing piece) from the board. **5** cause (data) to be stored in a computer. **6** (of a stream) divert the upper course of (another stream) by encroaching on its basin. **7** *Astron.* (of a star, planet, etc.) bring (a less massive body) permanently within its gravitational influence. ● *n.* **1** the act of capturing. **2** a thing or person captured.

Capuchin *n.* **1** a Franciscan friar of the new rule of 1529. **2** a cloak and hood formerly worn by women. **3** (**capuchin**) **a** a monkey of the S. American genus *Cebus*, with cowl-like hair on the head. **b** a variety of pigeon with head and neck feathers resembling a cowl. [from Italian *cappuccino*]

capybara /kap-i-**bar**-ă/ *n.* ▼ a very large semi-aquatic rodent, *Hydrochoerus hydrochaeris*, native to S. America. [native name]

CAPYBARA (*Hydrochoerus hydrochaeris*)

car *n.* **1** (in full **motor car**) ▲ a road vehicle able to carry a small number of people and powered by an internal-combustion engine. **2** (in *comb.*) **a** a wheeled vehicle, esp. of a specified kind (*tramcar*). **b** a railway carriage of a specified type (*dining car*). **3** *N. Amer.* a railway carriage or van. **4** the passenger compartment of a lift, cableway, balloon, etc. [from Latin *carrum*] □ **carful** *n.* (*pl.* **-fuls**).

caracul var. of KARAKUL.

carafe /kă-**raf**/ *n.* a glass container for water or wine. [from Arabic *ġarrāfa* 'drinking vessel']

carambola *n.* **1** a small tree, *Averrhoa carambola*, native to SE Asia, bearing golden-yellow ribbed fruit. **2** this fruit. [Portuguese]

caramel ● *n.* **1 a** sugar or syrup heated until it turns brown, then used as a flavouring or to colour spirits etc. **b** a kind of soft toffee. **2** a light-brown colour. ● *adj.* of this colour. [from Spanish *caramelo*]

caramelize *v.* (also **-ise**) **1 a** *tr.* convert (sugar or syrup) into caramel. **b** *intr.* (of sugar or syrup) be converted into caramel. **2** *tr.* coat or cook (food) with caramelized sugar or syrup.

C

CARAPACE: STARRED
TORTOISE WITH A RIDGED
CARAPACE

carapace *n.* ◀ the hard upper shell of a tortoise or a crustacean. ▷ CRUSTACEAN. [from Spanish *carapacho*]

carat *n.* **1** a unit of weight for precious stones, now equivalent to 200 milligrams. **2** (*US* **karat**) a measure of purity of gold, pure gold being 24 carats. [earlier in sense 'carob fruit': from Greek *keration*]

caravan ● *n.* **1 a** *Brit.* a vehicle equipped for living in and usu. towed by a motor vehicle or a horse. **b** *N. Amer.* a covered wagon or lorry. **2** a company of merchants or pilgrims etc. travelling together, esp. across a desert in Asia or N. Africa. ● *v.intr.* (**caravanned, caravanning**) travel or live in a caravan. [from Persian *kārwān*] □ **caravanner** *n.*

caravanserai *n.* (*US* also **caravansary**) an Eastern inn with a central court where caravans (see CARAVAN 2) may rest. [from Persian *kārwānsarāy*]

caraway *n.* an umbelliferous plant, *Carum carvi*, bearing clusters of tiny white flowers. [from Arabic *alkarāwiyā*]

caraway seed *n.* the fruit of the caraway plant used as a flavouring and as a source of oil. ▷ SPICE

carb *n. colloq.* a carburettor.

carbide *n. Chem.* a binary compound of carbon.

carbine *n.* ▼ a short firearm, usu. a rifle, originally for cavalry use. [from French *carabine*, weapon of the *carabin* 'mounted musketeer']

carrying handle *foresight* *slip ring* *barrel* *plastic hand-guard* *bayonet lug* *trigger guard* *magazine*

CARBINE: US COLT
COMMANDO 5.56 MM
CARBINE

carbo- *comb. form* carbon (*carbohydrate*; *carbolic*; *carboxyl*).

carbohydrate *n. Biochem.* any of a large group of energy-producing organic compounds containing carbon, hydrogen, and oxygen, e.g. starch, glucose, and other sugars.

carbolic *n.* (in full **carbolic acid**) phenol, esp. when used as a disinfectant.

carbolic soap *n.* soap containing carbolic.

car bomb *n.* a terrorist bomb concealed in or under a parked car.

carbon *n.* **1** a non-metallic element occurring naturally as diamond, graphite, and charcoal, and in all organic compounds. ▷ ALLOTROPE, CARBON CYCLE. **2 a** = CARBON COPY 1. **b** = CARBON PAPER. **3** a rod of carbon in an arc lamp. [from Latin *carbo -onis* 'charcoal']

carbon-12 *n.* the commonest natural carbon isotope, of mass 12, used in calculations of atomic mass units.

carbon-14 *n.* a long-lived naturally occurring radioactive carbon isotope of mass 14, used in radiocarbon dating, and as a tracer in biochemistry.

carbonaceous *adj.* **1** consisting of or containing carbon. **2** of or like coal or charcoal.

carbonate ● *n. Chem.* a salt of carbonic acid. ● *v.tr.* **1** impregnate with carbon dioxide; aerate. **2** convert into a carbonate. [from modern Latin *carbonatum*] □ **carbonation** *n.*

CARBON CYCLE

Carbon is an essential element in the bodies of all living things. Present in gases in the atmosphere, it nourishes green plants and bacteria. Some of this carbon is absorbed when animals eat plants. It returns to the atmosphere as carbon dioxide when living things respire, defecate, or die and decay.

carbon dioxide in the atmosphere

carbon dioxide released by plants

carbon dioxide absorbed by plants

carbon dioxide exhaled by animals

carbon in animal dung

carbon in plants eaten by animals

decay of plants and animals releases carbon

carbon dioxide released by worms, fungi, and bacteria

carbon copy *n.* **1** a copy made with carbon paper. **2** a person or thing identical or similar to another (*is a carbon copy of his father*).

carbon cycle *n. Biol.* ▲ the cycle in which carbon compounds are interconverted, usu. by living organisms.

carbon dating *n.* the determination of the age of an organic object from the ratio of isotopes which changes as carbon-14 decays.

carbon dioxide *n.* a colourless odourless gas occurring naturally in the atmosphere and formed by respiration. ▷ CARBON CYCLE

carbonic *adj. Chem.* containing carbon.

carbonic acid *n.* a very weak acid formed from carbon dioxide dissolved in water.

carboniferous ● *adj.* **1** producing coal. **2** (**Carboniferous**) *Geol.* of or relating to the fifth period in the Palaeozoic era. ● *n.* (**Carboniferous**) *Geol.* this period or system.

carbonize *v.tr.* (also **-ise**) **1** convert into carbon by heating. **2** reduce to charcoal or coke. □ **carbonization** *n.*

carbon monoxide *n.* a colourless odourless toxic gas formed by the incomplete burning of carbon.

carbonnade /kar-bŏn-**ahd**/ *n.* a rich beef stew made with onions and beer. [French]

carbon paper *n.* a thin carbon-coated paper used for making (esp. typed) copies.

carbon steel *n.* a steel with properties dependent on the percentage of carbon present.

carbon tax *n.* a proposed tax on the carbon emissions that result from burning fossil fuels (e.g. in motor vehicles).

carbonyl *n.* (used *attrib.*) *Chem.* the divalent radical :C = O.

car boot sale *n. Brit.* a usu. outdoor sale at which participants sell unwanted possessions from the boots of their cars or from tables.

carborundum *n.* a compound of carbon and silicon used esp. as an abrasive.

carboxyl *n. Chem.* the monovalent acid radical –COOH, present in most organic acids.

carboxylic acid *n. Chem.* an organic acid containing the carboxyl group.

carboy *n.* a large globular glass bottle usu. protected by a frame. [from Persian *karāba* 'large glass flagon']

carbuncle *n.* **1** a severe abscess in the skin. **2** a bright red gem. [from Latin *carbunculus* 'small coal'] □ **carbuncular** *adj.*

carburation *n.* the process of charging air with a spray of liquid fuel, esp. in an internal-combustion engine. [based on Latin *carbo* 'charcoal']

carburettor *n.* (also **carburetter**, *US* **carburetor**) ▼ an apparatus for carburation of petrol and air in an internal-combustion engine.

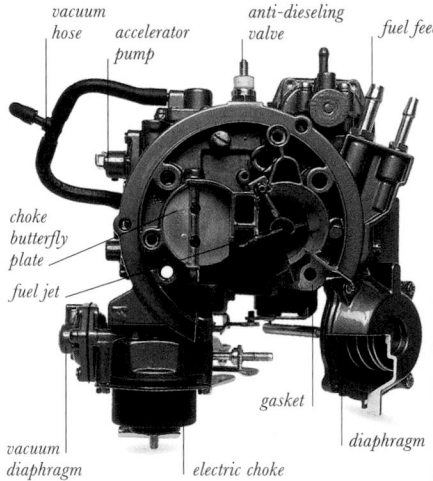

vacuum hose *accelerator pump* *anti-dieseling valve* *fuel feed*

choke butterfly plate

fuel jet

gasket

diaphragm

vacuum diaphragm *electric choke*

CARBURETTOR OF A PETROL-DRIVEN ENGINE

carcass *n.* (also *Brit.* **carcase**) **1** the dead body of an animal, esp. a trunk for cutting up as meat. **2** the bones of a cooked bird. **3** *derog.* the human body, living or dead. **4** the skeleton or framework of a building, ship, etc. **5** worthless remains. [from French *carcasse*]

carcinogen /kar-**sin**-ŏ-jĕn/ *n.* any substance that causes cancer. [based on CARCINOMA]

carcinogenic /kar-sin-ŏ-**jen**-ik/ *adj.* tending to cause cancer. □ **carcinogenicity** *n.*

carcinoma *n.* (*pl.* **carcinomata** or **carcinomas**) a cancer, esp. one arising in epithelial tissue. [based on Greek *karkinos* 'crab'] □ **carcinomatous** *adj.*

card[1] ● *n.* **1** thick stiff paper or thin pasteboard. **2 a** a flat piece of this, esp. for writing or printing on. **b** = POSTCARD. **c** a card used to send greetings, issue an invitation, etc. (*birthday card*). **d** = VISITING CARD. **e** = BUSINESS CARD. **f** a ticket of admission or membership etc. **3 a** = PLAYING CARD. **b** a similar card in a set designed for particular games, e.g. happy families. **c** (in *pl.*) card-playing; a card game. **4** (in *pl.*) *Brit. colloq.* an employee's documents, esp. for tax and national insurance, held by the employer. **5** a programme of events at a race meeting etc. **6 a** a small rectangular piece of plastic issued by a bank, building society, etc., with personal (often machine-readable) data on it, used chiefly to obtain cash or credit (*cheque card*; *credit card*; *do you have a card?*). **b** a similar piece of plastic, e.g. a phonecard, sold or issued for various purposes. ● *v.tr.* **1** fix to a card. **2** write on a card, esp. for indexing. □ **ask for** (or **get**) **one's cards** *Brit.* ask (or be told) to leave one's employment. **card up one's sleeve** *Brit.* a plan in reserve; a hidden advantage. **on** (*N. Amer.* **in**) **the cards** possible or likely. **put** (or **lay**) **one's cards on the table** reveal one's resources, intentions, etc. [from Greek *khartēs* 'papyrus leaf']

card[2] ● *n.* a toothed instrument, wire brush, etc., for raising a nap on cloth or for disentangling fibres before spinning. ● *v.tr.* brush, comb, cleanse, or scratch with a card. [from Latin *carere* 'to card'] □ **carder** *n.*

CARDAMOM SEED
CAPSULES
(*Elettaria cardamomum*)

cardamom *n.* (also **carda-mum**) **1** an aromatic SE Asian plant, *Elettaria cardamomum*. **2** ◄ the seed capsules of this used as a spice. ▷ SPICE. [from Greek *kardamōmon*]

cardboard ● *n.* pasteboard or stiff paper, esp. for making cards or boxes. ● *adj.* **1** made of cardboard. **2** flimsy, insubstantial.

cardboard city *n.* an urban area where homeless people make shelters at night from cardboard boxes etc.

card-carrying *attrib.adj.* registered as a member (esp. of a political party or trade union).

card game *n.* a game in which playing cards are used.

cardholder *n.* the holder of a credit card, discount card, etc.

cardiac *adj.* of or relating to the heart. ▷ HEART. [based on Greek *kardia* 'heart']

cardigan *n.* a knitted jacket fastening down the front, usu. with long sleeves. [named after the 7th Earl of *Cardigan*, 1797–1868, whose troops first wore such garments during the Crimean War]

cardinal ● *n.* (as a title **Cardinal**) a leading dignitary of the Roman Catholic Church, one of the college electing the Pope. ● *adj.* **1** chief, fundamental; on which something hinges. **2** of deep scarlet (like a cardinal's cassock). [earlier in sense 'that on which something hinges': based on Latin *cardo -inis* 'hinge'] □ **cardinalate** *n.* **cardinally** *adv.* **cardinalship** *n.*

cardinal humour see HUMOUR *n.* 4.

cardinal number *n.* a number denoting quantity (one, two, three, etc.), as opposed to an ordinal number (first, second, third, etc.).

cardinal point *n.* each of the four main points of the compass (N., S., E., W.). ▷ COMPASS

card index *n.* an index in which each item is entered on a separate card.

cardio- *comb. form* heart (*cardiogram*; *cardiology*). [from Greek *kardia* 'heart']

cardiogram *n.* a record of muscle activity within the heart, made esp. by an electrocardiograph.

cardiograph *n.* an instrument for recording heart muscle activity. □ **cardiographer** *n.* **cardiography** *n.*

CARDIOVASCULAR

The human cardiovascular (circulatory) system consists of the heart, the blood vessels, and, within them, the blood. Blood is pumped out of the heart through the arteries, carrying oxygen absorbed from the lungs, and nutrients absorbed from the gut, to all cells in the body. It also removes waste products from these cells and tissues, which are then excreted via the kidneys as urine, and by the lungs as carbon dioxide. Once deoxygenated, blood is returned to the heart through the veins. The entire circuit is completed in about one minute.

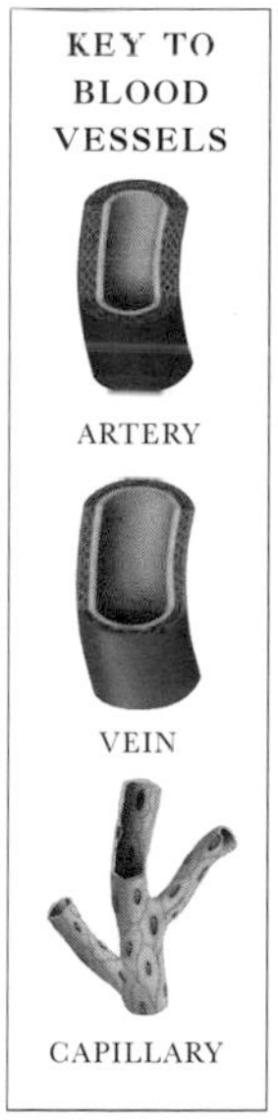

superficial temporal artery
superficial temporal vein
common carotid artery
internal jugular vein
aortic arch
subclavian vein
superior vena cava
pulmonary artery
pulmonary vein
heart
brachial vein
brachial artery
inferior vena cava
descending aorta
renal artery
renal vein
common iliac vein
common iliac artery
ulnar vein
great saphenous vein
femoral vein
popliteal vein
knee veins
anterior tibial artery
anterior tibial vein
posterior tibial vein
dorsal metatarsal arteries and veins

portal vein
branch of superior mesenteric artery
radial artery
ulnar artery
femoral artery
knee arteries
popliteal artery
posterior tibial artery
peroneal artery
dorsal digital veins and arteries

KEY TO BLOOD VESSELS
ARTERY
VEIN
CAPILLARY

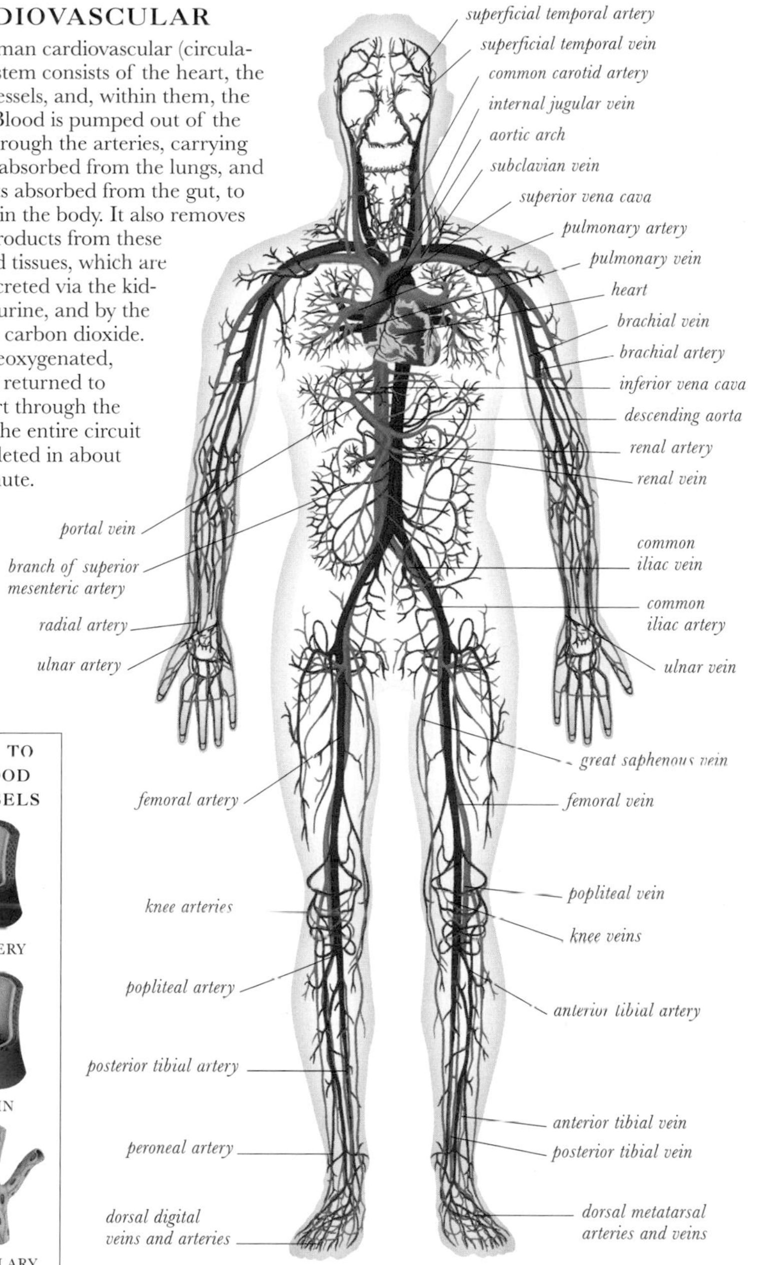

HUMAN CARDIOVASCULAR SYSTEM

cardiology *n.* the branch of medicine concerned with diseases and abnormalities of the heart. □ **cardiologist** *n.*

cardiopulmonary *adj. Med.* of or relating to the heart and the lungs.

cardiovascular *adj.* ▲ of or relating to the heart and blood vessels. ▷ BLOOD, HEART

cardoon *n.* a thistle-like plant, *Cynara cardunculus*, allied to the globe artichoke, with leaves used as a vegetable.

cardphone *n. Brit.* a public telephone operated by the insertion of a prepaid plastic machine-readable card instead of money.

card-playing *n.* the playing of card games.

card-sharp *n.* (also **card-sharper**) a swindler at card games.

card table *n.* a table (esp. folding) for card-playing.

card vote *n. Brit.* a block vote, esp. in trade-union meetings.

care ● *n.* **1** worry, anxiety. **2** an occasion for this. **3** serious attention; heed, caution, pains (*assembled with care*; *handle with care*). **4 a** protection, charge. **b** *Brit.* = CHILDCARE. **5** a thing to be done or seen to. ● *v.intr.* **1** (usu. foll. by *about, for, whether, if,* etc.) feel concern, interest, or emotion. **2** (foll. by *for, about,* and with neg. expressed or implied) feel liking, regard, or deference (*don't care for jazz*; *don't care about what he thinks*). **3** (foll. by *for,* or *to* + infin.) wish or be willing (*more times than I care to count*; *would you care for a drink?*). □ **care for** provide for; look after. **care of** at the address of (*sent it care of his sister*). **I** etc. **couldn't** (*US* also **could**) **care less** *colloq.* an expression of complete indifference. **in care** *Brit.* (of a child) taken into the care of a local authority.

C

take care 1 be careful. **2** (foll. by *to* + infin.) not fail or neglect. **take care of 1** look after; keep safe. **2** deal with. **3** dispose of. [Old English]

careen *v.* **1** *tr.* turn (a ship) on one side for cleaning, caulking, or repair. **2** *intr. N. Amer.* swerve about; career. **3a** *intr.* tilt; lean over. **b** *tr.* cause to do this. [based on Latin *carina* 'keel'] □ **careenage** *n.*

■ **Usage** Sense 2 of *careen* is influenced by *career* (v.).

career ● *n.* **1 a** one's advancement through life, esp. in a profession. **b** the progress through history of a group or institution. **2** a profession or occupation, esp. as offering advancement. **3** (*attrib.*) **a** pursuing or wishing to pursue a career (*career woman*). **b** working permanently in a specified profession (*career diplomat*). ● *v.intr.* **1** move or swerve about wildly. **2** go swiftly. [earlier in sense 'a racecourse or road': from Latin *carrus* 'wheeled conveyance']

careerist ● *n.* a person predominantly concerned with personal advancement in a career, esp. by unscrupulous means. ● *adj.* intent on such advancement. □ **careerism** *n.*

carefree *adj.* free from anxiety or responsibility; light-hearted. □ **carefreeness** *n.*

careful *adj.* **1** painstaking, thorough. **2** cautious. **3** done with care and attention. **4** (usu. foll. by *that* + clause, or *to* + infin.) taking care; not neglecting. **5** (foll. by *for, of*) concerned for; taking care of. □ **carefully** *adv.* **carefulness** *n.*

careless *adj.* **1** not taking care or paying attention. **2** unthinking, insensitive. **3** done without care; inaccurate. **4** (foll. by *of*) not concerned about; taking no heed of. **5** effortless; casual. □ **carelessly** *adv.* **carelessness** *n.*

carer *n. Brit.* a person who cares for a sick or elderly person, esp. a relative at home.

caress ● *v.tr.* **1** touch or stroke gently or lovingly; kiss. **2** treat fondly or kindly. ● *n.* a loving or gentle touch or kiss. [based on Latin *carus* 'dear'] □ **caressingly** *adv.*

caret *n.* a mark (∧, ⋏) indicating a proposed insertion in printing or writing. [Latin, literally 'is lacking']

caretaker *n.* **1** a person employed to look after something, esp. a house in the owner's absence, or *Brit.* a public building. **2** (*attrib.*) exercising temporary authority (*caretaker government*).

careworn *adj.* showing the effects of prolonged worry.

cargo *n.* (*pl.* **-oes** or **-os**) **1 a** goods carried on a ship or aircraft. **b** a load of such goods. **2** *US* **a** goods carried in a motor vehicle. **b** a load of such goods. [based on Late Latin *car(ri)care* 'to load']

Carib ● *n.* **1** an aboriginal inhabitant of the southern W. Indies or the adjacent coasts. **2** the language of the Caribs. ● *adj.* of or relating to the Caribs or their language. [from Haitian Creole]

Caribbean ● *n.* the part of the Atlantic between the southern W. Indies and Central America. ● *adj.* **1** of or relating to this region. **2** of the Caribs or their language or culture.

caribou *n.* (*pl.* same) a N. American reindeer. [Canadian French]

caricature ● *n.* **1** a grotesque usu. comic representation of a person by exaggeration of characteristic traits, in a picture, writing, or mime. **2** a ridiculously poor or absurd imitation or version. ● *v.tr.* make or give a caricature of. [from Italian *caricatura*] □ **caricatural** *adj.* **caricaturist** *n.*

caries /kair-eez/ *n.* (*pl.* same) decay and crumbling of a tooth or bone. [Latin]

carillon /kă-ril-yŏn/ *n.* **1** a set of bells sounded either from a keyboard or mechanically. **2** a tune played on bells. [from Old French *quarregnon* 'peal of four bells']

caring *adj.* **1** kind, humane. **2** (*attrib.*) concerned with looking after the sick, elderly, or disabled (*caring professions*).

cariogenic *adj.* causing caries.

carious *adj.* (of bones and teeth) decayed.

carjacking *n.* the hijacking of a car. □ **carjack** *v.tr.* **carjacker** *n.*

carload *n.* a quantity that can be carried in a car.

Carmelite ● *n.* a friar or nun of a contemplative order dedicated to Our Lady of Mount Carmel.

CARNIVORE

Mammals of the order Carnivora are predominantly flesh-eaters, and share features that reflect a hunting lifestyle. Powerful, agile limbs make them swift, while forward-facing eyes assist in judging distance accurately. All have strong canine teeth for cutting. Many also have specialized premolars and molars (carnassials) that operate like shears to slice through meat. One exception is the giant panda, which is almost entirely herbivorous, although most other members of the order Carnivora will supplement their diet with vegetation when necessary. In some systems of classification, pinnipeds are considered as members of the Carnivora.

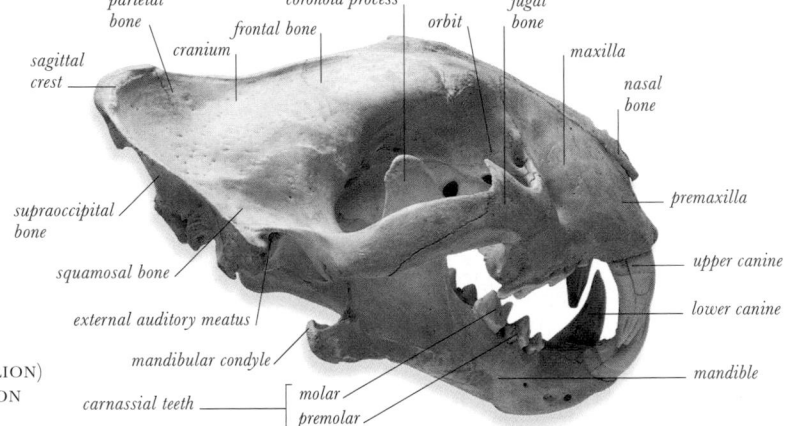

SKULL OF A CARNIVOROUS MAMMAL (LION)
SHOWING CHARACTERISTIC DENTITION

FAMILIES OF THE ORDER CARNIVORA

FELIDAE
(cats, cheetahs, lions) ▷ CAT

PROCYONIDAE
(raccoons, red pandas)

URSIDAE
(bears) ▷ BEAR

HYAENIDAE
(aardwolves, hyenas)

VIVERRIDAE
(civets, genets, mongooses)

MUSTELIDAE
(badgers, skunks, weasels) ▷ MUSTELID

CANIDAE
(dogs, foxes, wolves) ▷ DOG

● *adj.* of or relating to the Carmelites. [from Mount *Carmel* in Palestine, where the order was founded]

carmine ● *adj.* of a vivid crimson colour. ● *n.* this colour. [based on Arabic *ḳirmiz* 'kermes']

carnage *n.* great slaughter, esp. of human beings in battle. [based on Latin *caro carnis* 'flesh']

carnal *adj.* **1** of the body or flesh; worldly. **2** sensual, sexual. □ **carnality** *n.* **carnally** *adv.*

carnal knowledge *n.* esp. *Law* sexual intercourse.

carnation[1] *n.* a cultivated variety of clove pink, with variously coloured showy flowers.

carnation[2] ● *n.* a rosy pink colour. ● *adj.* of this colour. [based on Latin *caro carnis* 'flesh']

carnelian var. of CORNELIAN.

carnet /**kar**-nay/ *n.* **1** a customs permit to take a motor vehicle across a frontier for a limited period. **2** *Brit.* a permit allowing use of a campsite. [French, literally 'notebook']

carnival *n.* **1 a** the festivities usual during the period before Lent in Roman Catholic countries. **b** a festival usu. occurring at a regular date and involving a procession. **2** *N. Amer.* a travelling funfair or circus. [from medieval Latin *carnelevarium* 'period before Lent'] □ **carnivalesque** *adj.*

carnivore *n.* **1** ◄ any mammal of the order Carnivora, with jaws and teeth adapted for eating flesh, including cats, dogs, and bears. **2** any flesh-eating animal.

carnivorous *adj.* **1** (of an animal) feeding on flesh. **2** (of a plant) digesting trapped insects or other animal substances. **3** of or relating to the order Carnivora. [from Latin *carnivorus*]

carob *n.* **1** (in full **carob tree**) an evergreen tree, *Ceratonia siliqua*, native to the Mediterranean, bearing edible pods. **2** its bean-shaped edible seed pod. [from Arabic *ḵarrūba*]

carol ● *n.* a joyous song, esp. a Christmas hymn. ● *v.* (**carolled**, **carolling**; *US* **caroled**, **caroling**) **1** *intr.* sing carols, esp. outdoors at Christmas. **2** *tr.* & *intr.* sing joyfully. [from Old French *carole*] □ **caroller** *n.* (*US* **caroler**).

Carolingian ● *adj.* of or relating to the second Frankish dynasty, founded by Charlemagne (d. 814). ● *n.* a member of the Carolingian dynasty. [from French *carlovingien*]

carotene *n.* an orange or red plant pigment found in carrots etc. and acting as a source of vitamin A. [based on Latin *carota* 'carrot']

carotid /kă-**rot**-id/ ● *n.* each of the two main arteries carrying blood to the head and neck. ▷ CARDIOVASCULAR. ● *adj.* of or relating to either of these arteries. [from Greek *karōtides* (pl.)]

carouse ● *v.intr.* **1** have a noisy or lively drinking party. **2** drink heavily. ● *n.* a noisy or lively drinking party. [originally as adv. in phrase *drink carouse* (= drink right out), from German *gar aus trinken*] □ **carousal** *n.* **carouser** *n.*

carousel /ka-rŏ-**sel**/ *n.* **1** *N. Amer.* a merry-go-round or roundabout. **2** a rotating delivery or conveyor system, esp. for passengers' luggage at an airport. [from Italian *carosello*]

carp[1] *n.* (*pl.* same) ▼ any freshwater fish of the family Cyprinidae, esp. *Cyprinus carpio*, often bred for use as food. [from Late Latin *carpa*]

CARP: COMMON CARP
(*Cyprinus carpio*)

carp[2] *v.intr.* (usu. foll. by *at*) find fault; complain pettily. [from Latin *carpere* 'to pluck at, slander'] □ **carper** *n.*

carpal ● *adj.* of or relating to the bones in the wrist. ● *n.* any of the bones forming the wrist. ▷ HAND, SKELETON

car park *n.* an area for parking cars.

carpel *n. Bot.* ◄ the female reproductive organ of a flower, consisting of a stigma, style, and ovary. [based on Greek *karpos* 'fruit'] □ **carpellary** *adj.*

stigma

style ── carpel

ovary

CARPEL: LILY FLOWER SHOWING THE CARPEL

carpenter ● *n.* a person skilled in woodwork, esp. of a structural kind (cf. JOINER). ● *v.* **1** *intr.* do carpentry. **2** *tr.* make by means of carpentry. [from Late Latin *carpentarius* (*artifex*) 'carriage(-maker)']

carpentry *n.* **1** the work or occupation of a carpenter. **2** woodwork made by a carpenter.

carpet ● *n.* **1 a** thick fabric for covering a floor or stairs. **b** a usu. large rug. **2** an expanse or layer (*carpet of snow*). ● *v.tr.* (**carpeted**, **carpeting**) **1** cover with or as with a carpet. **2** *colloq.* reprimand, reprove. □ **on the carpet 1** *colloq.* being reprimanded. **2** under consideration. **sweep under the carpet** conceal (a problem or difficulty). [from obsolete Italian *carpita* 'woollen counterpane']

carpet-bag *n.* a travelling bag of a kind originally made of carpet-like material.

carpet-bagger *n.* **1** esp. *N. Amer.* a political candidate in an area where the candidate has no local connections. **2** an unscrupulous opportunist.

carpet beetle *n.* a small beetle of the genus *Anthrenus*, whose larvae are destructive to carpets and other materials.

carpet bombing *n.* intensive bombing.

carpeting *n.* **1** material for carpets. **2** carpets collectively.

carpet slipper *n.* a soft slipper.

carpet sweeper *n.* a household implement with a revolving brush or brushes for sweeping carpets.

car phone *n.* a radio-telephone for use in a car etc.

carport *n.* a roofed open-sided shelter for a car.

carrel *n.* **1** a small cubicle for a reader. **2** *hist.* a small study in a cloister. [from Old French *carole*]

carriage *n.* **1** *Brit.* a railway passenger vehicle. **2** a wheeled passenger vehicle, esp. one with four wheels and pulled by horses. **3** *Brit.* **a** the conveying of goods. **b** the cost of this (*carriage paid*). **4** the part of a machine (e.g. a typewriter) that carries other parts into the required position. **5** a manner of carrying oneself; one's bearing or deportment. [based on Old Northern French *carier* 'to carry']

carriageway *n. Brit.* the part of a road intended for vehicles.

carrier *n.* **1** a person or thing that carries. **2** a person or company undertaking to convey goods or passengers for payment. **3** *Brit.* = CARRIER BAG. **4** a part of a bicycle etc. for carrying luggage or a passenger. **5** a person or animal that may transmit a disease or a hereditary characteristic without suffering from or displaying it. **6** = AIRCRAFT CARRIER.

carrier bag *n. Brit.* a disposable plastic or paper bag with handles.

carrier pigeon *n.* a pigeon trained to carry messages tied to its neck or leg.

carrier wave *n.* a high-frequency electromagnetic wave modulated in amplitude or frequency to convey a signal.

carrion ● *n.* **1** dead putrefying flesh. **2** something vile or filthy. ● *adj.* rotten, loathsome. [from Latin *caro* 'flesh']

carrion crow *n.* a black crow, *Corvus corone*, native to Europe, feeding mainly on carrion.

carrot *n.* **1 a** an umbelliferous plant, *Daucus carota*, with a tapering orange-coloured root. **b** this root as a vegetable. ▷ VEGETABLE. **2** a means of enticement or persuasion (frequently opposed to *stick*). [from Greek *karōton*] □ **carroty** *adj.*

carry ● *v.* (**-ies**, **-ied**) **1** *tr.* support or hold up, esp. while moving. **2** *tr.* convey with one from one place to another. **3** *tr.* have on one's person (*carry a watch*). **4** *tr.* conduct or transmit (*pipe carries water*; *wire carries electric current*). **5** *tr.* take (a process etc.) to a specified point (*carry into effect*; *carry a joke too far*). **6** *tr.* (foll. by *to*) continue or prolong (*carry modesty to excess*). **7** *tr.* involve, imply; have as a feature or consequence (*carries a two-year guarantee*). **8** *tr.* (in reckoning) transfer (a figure) to a column of higher value. **9** *tr.* hold in a specified way (*carry oneself erect*). **10** *tr.* **a** (of a newspaper or magazine) publish; include in its contents, esp. regularly. **b** (of a radio or television station) broadcast, esp. regularly. **11** *tr.* (of a retailing outlet) keep a regular stock of (particular goods for sale). **12** *intr.* **a** (of sound, esp. a voice) be audible at a distance. **b** (of a missile) travel, penetrate. **13** *tr.* (of a gun etc.) propel to a specified distance. **14** *tr.* **a** win victory or acceptance for (a proposal etc.). **b** win acceptance from (*carried the audience with them*). **c** win, capture (a prize, a fortress, etc.). **d** *US* gain (a state or district) in an election. **15** *tr.* **a** endure the weight of; support (*columns carry the dome*). **b** be the chief cause of the effectiveness of; be the driving force in (*you carry the sales department*). **16** *tr.* be pregnant with (*is carrying twins*). ● *n.* (*pl.* **-ies**) **1** an act of carrying. **2** *Golf* the distance a ball travels before reaching the ground. **3** a portage between rivers etc. **4** the range of a gun etc. □ **carry away 1** remove. **2** inspire; affect emotionally or spiritually. **3** deprive of self-control (*got carried away*). **carry the can** *Brit. colloq.* bear the responsibility or blame. **carry the day** be victorious or successful. **carry forward** transfer to a new page or account. **carry it off** (or **carry it off well**) do well under difficulties. **carry off 1** take away, esp. by force. **2** win (a prize). **3** (esp. of a disease) kill. **4** render acceptable or passable. **carry on 1** continue (*carry on eating*; *carry on, don't mind me*). **2** engage in (a conversation or a business). **3** *colloq.* behave strangely or excitedly. **4** (often foll. by *with*) *Brit. colloq.* flirt or have a love affair. **carry out** put (ideas, instructions, etc.) into practice. **carry over 1** = *carry forward*. **2** postpone (work etc.). **carry through 1** complete successfully. **2** bring safely out of difficulties. **carry weight** be influential or important. **carry with one** bear in mind. [from Old Northern French *carier*]

carrycot *n. Brit.* a portable cot for a baby.

carryings-on *n.pl.* (also **carrying-on**) = CARRY-ON.

carry-on *n. Brit. slang* **1** a state of excitement or fuss. **2** a questionable piece of behaviour. **3** a flirtation or love affair.

carry-out *attrib.adj. & n.* esp. *Sc. & US* = TAKEAWAY.

carry-over *n.* something carried over.

carsick *adj.* affected with nausea caused by the motion of a car. □ **carsickness** *n.*

cart ● *n.* **1** a strong vehicle with two or four wheels for carrying loads, usu. drawn by a horse. **2** a light vehicle for pulling by hand. ● *v.tr. colloq.* carry (esp. a cumbersome thing) with difficulty or over a long distance. □ **cart off** remove, esp. by force. **in the cart** *Brit. slang* in trouble or difficulty. **put the cart before the horse 1** reverse the proper order or procedure. **2** take an effect for a cause. [from Old Norse *kartr*] □ **carter** *n.* **cartful** *n.* (*pl.* **-fuls**).

C

carte blanche /kart **blahnsh**/ *n.* full discretionary power. [French, literally 'blank paper']

cartel *n.* **1** an informal association of manufacturers or suppliers to maintain prices at a high level, and control production, marketing arrangements, etc. **2** a political combination between parties. [earlier in sense 'a written challenge or agreement': from Italian *cartello* 'little card'] □ **cartelize** *v.tr. & intr.* (also **-ise**).

Cartesian coordinates *n.pl.* a system for locating a point by reference to its distance from two or three axes intersecting at right angles. [Cartesian: from *Cartesius*, Latinized form of *Descartes*, French philosopher and mathematician]

carthorse *n.* a thickset horse.

Carthusian ● *n.* a monk or nun of an austere contemplative order founded by St Bruno in 1084. ● *adj.* of or relating to this order. [from Latin *Cart(h)usia* 'Chartreuse', France, where the order was founded]

cartilage *n.* a firm flexible connective tissue forming the infant skeleton, which is mainly replaced by bone in adulthood; gristle. ▷ EAR. [from Latin *cartilago*] □ **cartilaginous** *adj.*

cartilaginous fish *n.* ▼ a fish of the class Selachii, with a skeleton of cartilage rather than bone, e.g. a shark, a ray. ▷ ELASMOBRANCH, FISH, SHARK

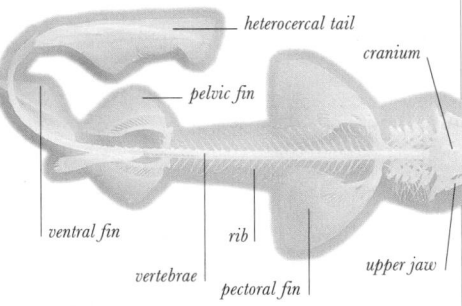

heterocercal tail
cranium
pelvic fin
ventral fin
rib
vertebrae
pectoral fin
upper jaw

CARTILAGINOUS FISH: DOGFISH SKELETON COMPOSED ENTIRELY OF CARTILAGE

cartload *n.* **1** an amount filling a cart. **2** a large quantity of anything.

cartography *n.* the science or practice of map-drawing. [based on French *carte* 'map, card'] □ **cartographer** *n.* **cartographic** *adj.* **cartographical** *adj.*

carton *n.* a light box or container, esp. one made of cardboard. [French]

cartoon ● *n.* **1** a humorous drawing in a newspaper, magazine, etc., esp. as a topical comment. **2** a sequence of drawings, often with speech indicated, telling a story. **3** a filmed sequence of drawings using the technique of animation. **4** a full-size drawing on stout paper as an artist's preliminary design for a painting, tapestry, mosaic, etc. ● *v.* **1** *tr.* draw a cartoon of. **2** *intr.* draw cartoons. [based on Italian *carta* 'card, map'] □ **cartoonish** *adj.* **cartoonist** *n.* **cartoony** *adj.*

cartoon strip *n.* = COMIC STRIP.

cartouche /kar-**toosh**/ *n.* **1** *Archit.* a scroll-like ornament, e.g. the volute of an Ionic capital. **2** *Archaeol.* an oval ring enclosing Egyptian hieroglyphs. [from Italian *cartoccio* 'cartridge']

cartridge *n.* **1** a casing containing a charge of propelling explosive for firearms or blasting, with the addition of a bullet or shot if for small arms. ▷ SHOTGUN. **2** a spool of film, magnetic tape, etc. in a sealed container ready for insertion. **3** a component carrying the stylus on the pick-up head of a record player. **4** an ink-container for insertion in a pen etc. [corruption of CARTOUCHE]

cartridge belt *n.* a belt with pockets or loops for cartridges (see CARTRIDGE 1).

cartridge paper *n.* thick rough paper used for cartridges, for drawing, and for strong envelopes.

cart track *n.* a track or road too rough for ordinary vehicles.

cartwheel *n.* **1** the wheel of a cart. **2** a circular sideways handspring with the arms and legs extended.

carve *v.tr.* **1** produce or shape (a statue, representation in relief, etc.) by cutting into a hard material (*carved a figure out of rock; carved it in wood*). **2** a cut patterns, designs, letters, etc. in (hard material). **b** (foll. by *into*) form a pattern, design, etc., from (*carved it into a bust*). **c** (foll. by *with*) cover or decorate (material) with figures or designs cut in it. **3** (also *absol.*) cut (meat etc.) into slices for eating. □ **carve out 1** take from a larger whole. **2** establish (a career etc.) purposefully. **carve up 1** divide into several pieces; subdivide (territory etc.). **2** *colloq.* drive aggressively into the path of (another vehicle). [Old English *ceorfan* 'to cut']

carver *n.* **1** a person who carves. **2 a** a knife for carving meat. **b** (in *pl.*) a knife and fork for carving. **3** *Brit.* the principal chair, with arms, in a set of dining chairs, intended for the person who carves.

carvery *n.* (*pl.* **-ies**) esp. *Brit.* a buffet or restaurant with cooked joints displayed, and carved as required, in front of customers.

carve-up *n. Brit. slang* a sharing-out, esp. of spoils.

carving *n.* a carved object, esp. as a work of art.

car wash *n.* **1** an establishment containing equipment for washing vehicles automatically. **2** the equipment itself.

Casanova *n.* a man notorious for seducing women. [from G. J. *Casanova* de Seingalt, Italian adventurer, 1725–98]

casbah var. of KASBAH.

cascade ● *n.* **1** a small waterfall, esp. forming part of a large broken waterfall. **2** a mass or quantity (of material, hair, etc.) in descending waves. **3 a** a process consisting of a series of similar stages with a cumulative effect. **b** a succession of devices, events, etc., each of which initiates the next. ● *v.intr.* fall in or like a cascade. [from Italian *cascata*]

case[1] *n.* **1** an instance of something occurring. **2** a state of affairs, hypothetical or actual. **3 a** an instance of a person receiving professional guidance or treatment, e.g. from a doctor or social worker. **b** this person or the circumstances involved. **4** a matter under official investigation, esp. by the police. **5** *Law* a cause or suit for trial. **6 a** the sum of the arguments on one side, esp. in a lawsuit (*that is our case*). **b** a set of arguments, esp. in relation to persuasiveness (*have a weak case*). **c** a valid set of arguments (*have no case*). **7** *Gram.* **a** the relation of a word to other words in a sentence. **b** a form of a noun, adjective, or pronoun expressing this. **8** one's position or circumstances (*in our case*). □ **in any case** whatever the truth is; whatever may happen; what's more. **in case** lest; in provision against a stated or implied possibility (*take an umbrella in case it rains; took it in case*). **in case of** in the event of. **in the case of** as regards. **is** (or **is not**) **the case** is (or is not) so. [from Latin *casus* 'a fall']

case[2] ● *n.* **1** a container or covering serving to enclose or contain. **2** the outer protective covering of a watch, book, seed vessel, sausage, etc. **3** *Brit.* an item of luggage, esp. a suitcase. **4** a glass box for showing specimens, curiosities, etc. ● *v.tr.* **1** enclose in a case. **2** (foll. by *with*) surround. **3** (esp. in phr. **case the joint**) *slang* reconnoitre (a house etc.), esp. with a view to robbery. [from Latin *capsa*]

casebook *n.* a book containing a record of legal or medical cases.

case-bound *adj.* (of a book) in a hard cover.

case-harden *v.tr.* harden the surface of, esp. give a steel surface to (iron) by carbonizing.

case history *n.* information about a person for use in professional treatment, e.g. by a doctor.

casein /**kay**-seen/ *n.* the main protein in milk, which occurs in coagulated form in cheese, and is used in plastics, adhesives, paint, etc. [based on Latin *caseus* 'cheese']

case knife *n.* a knife carried in a sheath.

case law *n.* the law as established by the outcome of former cases (cf. COMMON LAW, STATUTE LAW).

caseload *n.* the cases with which a doctor etc. is concerned at one time.

casement *n.* ▶ a window or part of a window hinged vertically to open like a door. ▷ WINDOW. [from Anglo-Latin *cassimentum*]

CASEMENT WINDOW

case-sensitive *adj. Computing* distinguishing between upper-case and lower-case letters for the purpose of making text searches.

case study *n.* the use of a particular instance as an exemplar of general principles.

casework *n.* social work concerned with individuals. □ **caseworker** *n.*

cash ● *n.* **1** money in coins or notes, as distinct from cheques or orders. **2** (also **cash down**) money paid as full payment at the time of purchase, as distinct from credit. **3** *colloq.* wealth. ● *v.tr.* give or obtain cash for (a note, cheque, etc.). □ **cash in 1** obtain cash for. **2** (usu. foll. by *on*) *colloq.* profit (from); take advantage (of). **cash up** *Brit.* count and check the day's takings. [earlier in sense 'a box for money': based on Latin *capsa* 'case'] □ **cashable** *adj.* **cashless** *adj.*

cash and carry *n.* **1** a system of wholesaling in which goods are paid for in cash and taken away by the purchaser. **2** a store where this system operates.

cash card *n. Brit.* a plastic card (see CARD[1] *n.* 6a) for withdrawing money from a cash dispenser.

cash cow *n. colloq.* a business, or part of one, that provides a steady cash flow.

cash crop *n.* a crop produced for sale.

cash desk *n.* a counter or compartment in a shop where goods are paid for.

cash dispenser *n. Brit.* ▼ an automatic machine from which customers of a bank etc. may withdraw cash, esp. by using a cash card.

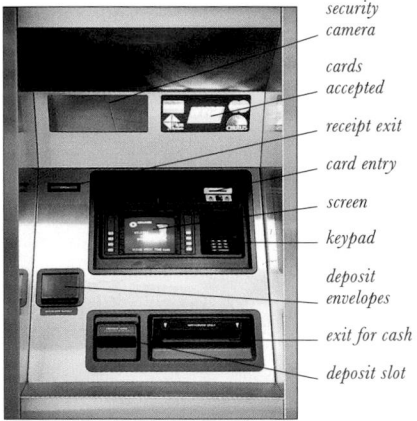

security camera
cards accepted
receipt exit
card entry
screen
keypad
deposit envelopes
exit for cash
deposit slot

CASH DISPENSER

cashew *n.* **1** (also **cashew tree**) a bushy evergreen tree, *Anacardium occidentale*, native to Central and S. America. **2** (in full **cashew nut**) the edible kidney-shaped nut of this tree. [Portuguese]

cash flow *n.* the movement of money into and out of a business.

cashier[1] *n.* a person dealing with cash transactions in a shop, bank, etc.

cashier[2] *v.tr.* dismiss from service, esp. with disgrace. [based on Latin *quassare* 'to quash']

cashmere *n.* a fine soft wool, esp. that of a breed of Himalayan goat. [from *Kashmir* in Asia]

cash on delivery *n.* a system of paying the carrier for goods when they are delivered.

cashpoint *n. Brit.* = CASH DISPENSER.

cash register *n.* a machine in a shop etc. with a drawer for money, recording the amount of each sale, totalling receipts, etc.

casing *n.* a protective or enclosing cover or shell.

casino *n.* (*pl.* **-os**) a public room or building for gambling. [Italian, literally 'little house']

cask *n.* a large barrel-like container made of wood, metal, or plastic, esp. one for alcoholic liquor. [from Spanish *casco* 'helmet']

casket *n.* **1** a small often ornamental box or chest for jewels, letters, etc. **2 a** *Brit.* a small wooden box for cremated ashes. **b** *N. Amer.* a coffin, esp. a rectangular one.

cassava *n.* **1 a** any plant of the genus *Manihot* (spurge family) having starchy tuberous roots. **b** the roots themselves. **2** a starch or flour obtained from these roots. See also TAPIOCA. [from Taino (Haitian) *casavi*]

casserole ● *n.* **1** a covered dish, usu. of earthenware or glass, in which food is cooked, esp. slowly in the oven. **2** food cooked in a casserole. ● *v.tr.* cook in a casserole. [based on Greek *kuathion* 'little cup']

cassette *n.* a sealed case containing a length of tape, ribbon, etc. ready for insertion in a machine, esp.: **1** a length of audiotape or videotape ready for insertion in a tape recorder or video recorder. **2** a length of photographic film, ready for insertion in a camera. [French, literally 'little case']

cassette player *n.* a tape recorder for playing back audio cassettes.

cassette recorder *n.* a tape recorder for recording and playing back audio cassettes.

cassette tape *n.* a cassette of esp. audiotape.

cassia *n.* **1** (also **cassia tree**) ▼ any tree of the genus *Cassia*, bearing leaves from which senna is extracted. **2** the cinnamon-like bark of this tree used as a spice. ▷ SENNA. [from Hebrew *kĕṣīʿāh* 'bark like cinnamon']

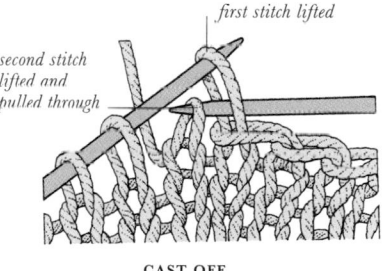

CASSIA LEAF
(*Cassia senna*)

stalk

leaflet

stipule

cassis *n.* a syrupy usu. alcoholic blackcurrant flavouring for drinks etc. [French, literally 'blackcurrant']

cassock *n.* a full-length usu. black or red garment worn by clergy, choirs, etc. [from Italian *casacca* 'horseman's coat'] □ **cassocked** *adj.*

cassoulet *n.* a ragout of meat and beans. [French]

cassowary *n.* (*pl.* **-ies**) a large flightless Australasian bird of the genus *Casuarius*, with heavy body, stout legs, a wattled neck, and a bony crest on its forehead. [from Malay *kasuārī*]

cast ● *v.tr.* (*past* and *past part.* **cast**) **1** throw, esp. deliberately or forcefully. **2** (often foll. by *on, over*) **a** direct or cause to fall (one's eyes, a glance, light, a shadow, a spell, etc.). **b** express (doubts, aspersions, etc.). **3** throw out (a net, fishing line, etc.) into the water. **4** let down (an anchor or plumb line). **5 a** throw off, get rid of. **b** shed (skin etc.), esp. in the process of growth. **6** record, register, or give (a vote). **7 a** shape (molten metal or plastic material) in a mould. **b** make (a product) in this way. **8 a** (usu. foll. by *as*) assign (an actor) to play a particular character. **b** allocate roles in (a play, film, etc.). **9** (foll. by *in, into*) arrange or formulate (facts etc.) in a specified form. ● *n.* **1** the throwing of a missile etc. **2** a throw of a net, plumb line, or fishing line. **3 a** an object of metal, clay, etc., made in a mould. **b** a moulded mass of solidified material, esp. plaster protecting a broken limb. **4** the actors taking part in a play, film, etc. **5** form, type, or quality (*cast of features*; *cast of mind*). **6** a tinge or shade of colour. **7** (in full **cast in the eye**) a slight squint. **8** a mass of earth excreted by a worm. □ **cast about** (or **around** or **round**) make an extensive search (actually or mentally) (*cast about for a solution*). **cast adrift** leave to drift. **cast ashore** (of waves etc.) throw to the shore. **cast aside** give up using; abandon. **cast away 1** reject. **2** (in *passive*) be shipwrecked and marooned. **cast down** deject. **cast loose** detach; detach oneself. **cast lots** see LOT. **cast off 1** abandon. **2** *Knitting* ▼ take the stitches off the needle by looping each over the next to finish the edge.

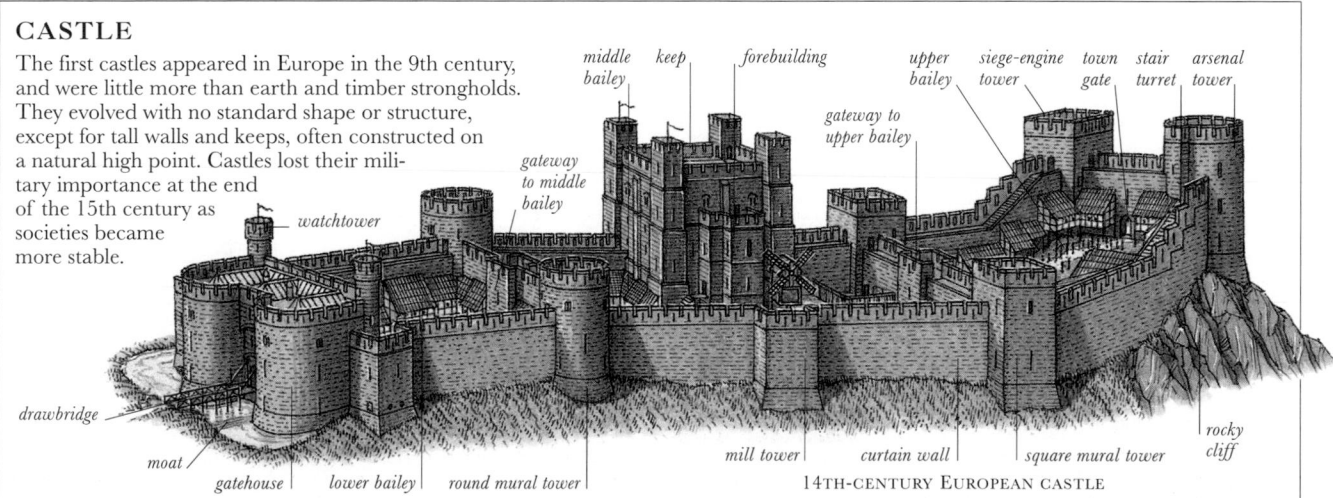

first stitch lifted

second stitch lifted and pulled through

CAST OFF

3 *Naut.* **a** set a ship free from a quay etc. **b** loosen and throw off (rope etc.). **cast on** *Knitting* make the first row of loops on the needle. **cast out** expel. **cast up** (of the sea) deposit on the shore. [from Old Norse *kasta*]

castanet *n.* (usu. in *pl.*) ▶ a small concave piece of hardwood, ivory, etc., in pairs held in the hands and clicked together by the fingers as a rhythmic accompaniment, esp. by Spanish dancers. ▷ ORCHESTRA, PERCUSSION. [from Spanish *castañeta* 'little chestnut']

CASTANETS

C

castaway ● *n.* a shipwrecked person. ● *adj.* shipwrecked.

caste *n.* **1** any of the Hindu hereditary classes, distinguished by relative degrees of purity or pollution, whose members have no social contact with other classes but are socially equal with one another and often follow the same occupations. **2** a more or less exclusive social class. □ **lose caste** descend in the social order. [from Spanish & Portuguese *casta* 'lineage, race'] □ **casteism** *n.* often *derog.*

castellated *adj.* **1** having battlements. **2** castle-like. □ **castellation** *n.*

caste mark *n.* a symbol on a person's forehead denoting his or her caste.

caster *n.* **1** var. of CASTOR. **2** a person who casts.

caster sugar *n.* (also **castor sugar**) *Brit.* finely granulated white sugar.

castigate *v.tr.* rebuke or punish severely. [based on Latin *castigatus* 'corrected, reproved'] □ **castigation** *n.* **castigator** *n.* **castigatory** *adj.*

Castilian ● *n.* **1** a native of Castile in Spain. **2** the language of Castile, standard spoken and literary Spanish. ● *adj.* of or relating to Castile or Castilian.

casting *n.* an object made by casting, esp. of metal.

casting couch *n.* *slang* a couch in a director's office on which actresses are said to be seduced in return for being awarded parts.

casting vote *n.* a deciding vote usu. given by the chairperson when the votes on two sides are equal. [from an obsolete sense of *cast* 'to turn the scale']

cast iron ● *n.* a hard alloy of iron, carbon, and silicon cast in a mould. ● *adj.* (**cast-iron**) **1** made of cast iron. **2** hard, unchallengeable, unchangeable.

castle ● *n.* **1 a** ▼ a large fortified building or group of buildings; a stronghold. ▷ KEEP. **b** a formerly fortified mansion. **2** *Chess* = ROOK[2]. ● *v.* *Chess* **1** *intr.* make a special move (once only in a game on

CASTLE

The first castles appeared in Europe in the 9th century, and were little more than earth and timber strongholds. They evolved with no standard shape or structure, except for tall walls and keeps, often constructed on a natural high point. Castles lost their military importance at the end of the 15th century as societies became more stable.

middle bailey   *keep*   *forebuilding*   *upper bailey*   *siege-engine tower*   *town gate*   *stair turret*   *arsenal tower*

gateway to upper bailey

gateway to middle bailey

watchtower

drawbridge

moat

gatehouse   *lower bailey*   *round mural tower*

mill tower   *curtain wall*   *square mural tower*

rocky cliff

14TH-CENTURY EUROPEAN CASTLE

CAT

Cats were domesticated by the ancient Egyptians over 8,000 years ago, yet it was only in the late 19th century that the first pedigree breeds were developed. Now more than 300 breeds and varieties are recognized, although they vary relatively little in appearance. Differing head shapes are one of the main distinguishing characteristics, as is length of hair. The latter feature is, perhaps, the most straightforward method of categorizing pedigree and non-pedigree cats. Shorthair breeds outnumber longhair ones.

EXTERNAL FEATURES OF A CHOCOLATE TORTOISESHELL BURMESE SHORTHAIR

pupil

whiskers

body

hips

nose leather

tail

chest

ribcage

thigh

heel

hind foot

front paw

rear paw

C

EXAMPLES OF CAT BREEDS

PEDIGREE LONGHAIR CATS

CHOCOLATE POINT LONGHAIR

RED PERSIAN LONGHAIR

BROWN CLASSIC TABBY MAINE COON

LILAC ANGORA

PEDIGREE SHORTHAIR CATS

USUAL ABYSSINIAN

CINNAMON SILVER CORNISH REX

BLUE EXOTIC

FOREIGN LILAC ORIENTAL SHORTHAIR

CREAM POINT COLOUR POINTED BRITISH SHORTHAIR

NON-PEDIGREE CATS

RED CLASSIC TABBY MANX

RED AND WHITE JAPANESE BOBTAIL

TORTOISESHELL AND WHITE SHORTHAIR

BLUE LONGHAIR

BROWN AND WHITE SPHYNX

SEAL POINT SIAMESE

BROWN SPOTTED SHORTHAIR

BLUE-CREAM SHORTHAIR

each side) in which the king is moved two squares along the back rank and the nearer rook is moved to the square passed over by the king. **2** *tr.* move (the king) by castling. [from Latin *castellum* 'little fort'] □ **castled** *adj.*

cast net *n.* a net thrown out and immediately drawn in.

cast-off ● *adj.* abandoned, discarded. ● *n.* a cast-off thing, esp. a garment.

castor *n.* (also **caster**) **1** a small swivelled wheel fixed to a leg (or the underside) of a piece of furniture. **2** a small container with holes in the top for sprinkling the contents.

castor oil *n.* an oil from the seeds of a plant, *Ricinus communis*, used as a purgative and lubricant. [18th-century coinage]

castor sugar var. of CASTER SUGAR.

castrate *v.tr.* **1** remove the testicles of; geld. **2** deprive of vigour. [based on Latin *castratus* 'pruned, deprived of vigour'] □ **castration** *n.* **castrator** *n.*

castrato /kass-**trah**-toh/ *n.* (*pl.* **castrati**) *hist.* a male singer castrated in boyhood so as to retain a soprano or alto voice. [Italian]

casual ● *adj.* **1** accidental; due to chance. **2** not regular or permanent; temporary, occasional (*casual work; a casual affair*). **3 a** unconcerned, uninterested (*was very casual about it*). **b** made or done without great care or thought (*a casual remark*). **c** acting carelessly or unmethodically. **4** (of clothes) informal. ● *n.* **1** a casual worker. **2** (usu. in *pl.*) casual clothes or shoes. [from Latin *casualis*] □ **casually** *adv.* **casualness** *n.*

casualty *n.* (*pl.* **-ies**) **1** a person killed or injured in a war or accident. **2** a thing lost or destroyed. **3** *Brit.* = CASUALTY DEPARTMENT.

casualty department *n.* (also **casualty ward**) the part of a hospital where casualties are treated.

casuist *n.* **1** a person, esp. a theologian, who resolves problems of conscience, duty, etc., often with clever but false reasoning. **2** a sophist or quibbler. [from Spanish *casuista*] □ **casuistic** *adj.* **casuistical** *adj.* **casuistically** *adv.* **casuistry** *n.*

CAT /kat/ *abbr.* **1** computer-assisted (or -aided) testing. **2** *Med.* computerized axial tomography (*CAT scanner*).

cat *n.* **1** ◄ a small soft-furred four-legged domesticated animal, *Felis catus*. **2** any wild animal of the family Felidae, e.g. a lion, tiger, or leopard. **3** a catlike animal of any other family (*civet cat*). **4** *colloq.* a malicious or spiteful woman. **5** = CAT-O'-NINE-TAILS. □ **let the cat out of the bag** reveal a secret, esp. involuntarily. **like a cat** *Brit.* on hot bricks (or **on a hot tin roof**) very agitated or agitatedly. **put** (or **set**) **the cat among the pigeons** *Brit.* cause trouble. **rain cats and dogs** rain very hard. **the cat's whiskers** (or **pyjamas**) *slang* an excellent person or thing. [Old English] □ **catlike** *adj.*

catabolism /kă-**tab**-ŏ-lizm/ *n. Biochem.* the breakdown of complex molecules in living organisms to form simpler ones with the release of energy; destructive metabolism (opp. ANABOLISM). [based on Greek *katabolē* 'descent'] □ **catabolic** *adj.*

cataclysm *n.* **1 a** a violent, esp. social or political, upheaval or disaster. **b** a great change. **2** a great flood or deluge. [based on Greek *klusmos* 'flood'] □ **cataclysmal** *adj.* **cataclysmic** *adj.* **cataclysmically** *adv.*

catacomb *n.* (often in *pl.*) **1** an underground cemetery, esp. a Roman subterranean gallery with recesses for tombs. **2** a cellar. [from Late Latin *catacumbas*, name given (5th c.) to the cemetery of St Sebastian near Rome]

catafalque *n.* a decorated wooden framework for supporting the coffin of a distinguished person. [from Italian *catafalco*]

Catalan ● *n.* **1** a native of Catalonia in Spain. **2** the language of Catalonia. ● *adj.* of or relating to Catalonia, its people, or its language. [from Spanish]

catalepsy *n.* a state of trance or seizure with loss of

sensation and consciousness accompanied by rigidity of the body. [based on Greek *lēpsis* 'seizure'] □ **cataleptic** *adj. & n.*

catalogue (*US* also **catalog**) ● *n.* **1** a complete list of items (e.g. articles for sale, books held by a library), usu. in alphabetical or other systematic order. **2** an extensive list (*a catalogue of crimes*). ● *v.tr.* (**catalogues, catalogued, cataloguing**; *US* **catalogs, cataloged, cataloging**) **1** make a catalogue of. **2** enter in a catalogue. [based on Greek *katalegein* 'to pick out'] □ **cataloguer** *n.* (*US* **cataloger**)

catalyse *v.tr.* (*US* **catalyze**) *Chem.* produce (a reaction) by catalysis.

catalyser *n. Brit.* = CATALYTIC CONVERTER.

catalysis *n.* (*pl.* **catalyses**) *Chem.* & *Biochem.* the acceleration of a chemical or biochemical reaction by a catalyst. [from Greek *katalusis* 'dissolution']

catalyst *n.* **1** *Chem.* a substance that, without itself undergoing any permanent chemical change, increases the rate of a reaction. **2** a person or thing that precipitates a change.

catalytic *adj. Chem.* relating to or involving catalysis.

catalytic converter *n.* ▼ a device in the exhaust system of a motor vehicle, with a catalyst for converting pollutant gases into less harmful ones. ▷ CAR

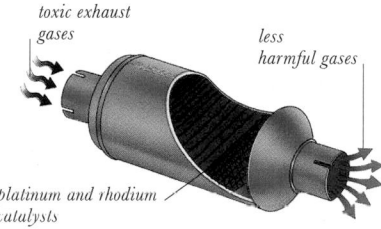

toxic exhaust gases

less harmful gases

platinum and rhodium catalysts

CATALYTIC CONVERTER: CUTAWAY VIEW

catalytic cracker *n.* a device for cracking (see CRACK *v.* 9) petroleum oils by catalysis.

catalyze *US* var. of CATALYSE.

catamaran *n.* **1** a boat with two hulls side by side. ▷ POWERBOAT. **2** a raft of yoked logs or boats. [from Tamil *kaṭṭumaram* 'tied wood']

catamite *n.* the passive partner in sodomy. [based on Greek *Ganumēdēs* 'Ganymede', name of Zeus' cupbearer]

cat-and-dog *adj.* (of a relationship etc.) full of quarrels.

cataplexy *n.* sudden temporary paralysis due to fright etc. [from Greek *kataplēxis* 'stupefaction'] □ **cataplectic** *adj.*

catapult ● *n.* **1** esp. *Brit.* a forked stick etc. with elastic for shooting stones. **2** *hist.* ▼ a military machine for hurling large stones etc. **3** a mechanical device for launching a glider, an aircraft from the deck of a ship, etc. ● *v.* **1** *tr.* **a** hurl from or launch with a catapult. **b** fling forcibly. **2** *intr.* leap or be hurled forcibly. [from Greek *katapeltēs*]

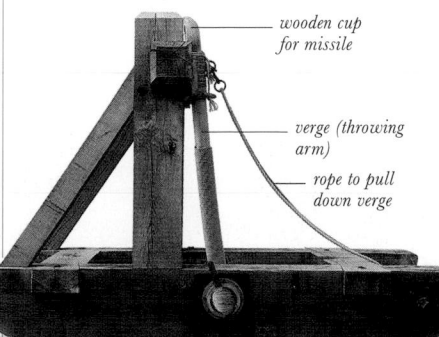

wooden cup for missile

verge (throwing arm)

rope to pull down verge

CATAPULT: REPLICA OF A 15TH-CENTURY MILITARY CATAPULT

cataract *n.* **1 a** a large waterfall or cascade. **b** a downpour; a rush of water. **2** *Med.* a condition in which the eye lens becomes progressively opaque. [from Greek *katarrhaktēs* 'down-rushing']

catarrh /kă-**tar**/ *n.* **1** inflammation of the mucous membrane of the nose, air passages, etc. **2** a watery discharge in the nose or throat due to this. [based on Greek *katarrhein* 'to flow down'] □ **catarrhal** *adj.*

catastrophe /kă-**tas**-trŏ-fi/ *n.* a great and usu. sudden disaster. [from Greek *katastrophē*] □ **catastrophic** *adj.* **catastrophically** *adv.*

catatonia *n.* **1** schizophrenia with intervals of catalepsy and sometimes violence. **2** catalepsy. [from German *Katatonie*] □ **catatonic** *adj. & n.*

cat burglar *n.* a burglar who enters by climbing to an upper storey.

catcall ● *n.* a shrill whistle of disapproval made at meetings etc. ● *v.intr.* make a catcall.

catch ● *v.* (*past* and *past part.* **caught**) **1** *tr.* **a** lay hold of so as to restrain or prevent from escaping; capture. **b** (also **catch hold of**) get into one's hands so as to retain, operate, etc. (*caught hold of the handle*). **2** *tr.* detect or surprise (esp. in a wrongful or embarrassing act) (*caught him smoking*). **3** *tr.* **a** intercept and hold (a moving thing) in the hands etc. (*catch the ball; catch the drips*). **b** *Cricket* dismiss (a batsman) by catching the ball before it reaches the ground. **4** *tr.* **a** contract (a disease) by infection or contagion. **b** acquire (a quality or feeling) from another's example (*caught their enthusiasm*). **5** *tr.* **a** reach in time and board (a train, bus, etc.). **b** be in time to see etc. (a person or thing about to leave or finish). **6** *tr.* **a** apprehend with the senses or the mind (esp. a thing occurring briefly) (*didn't catch what he said*). **b** (of an artist etc.) reproduce faithfully. **7 a** *intr.* become fixed or entangled (*the bolt began to catch*). **b** *tr.* cause to do this (*caught her tights on a nail*). **c** *tr.* (often foll. by *on*) hit, deal a blow to (*caught him on the nose; caught his elbow on the table*). **8** *tr.* draw the attention of; captivate (*caught his eye*). **9** *intr.* begin to burn. **10** *tr.* (often foll. by *up*) reach or overtake (a person etc. ahead). **11** *tr.* check suddenly (*caught his breath*). **12** *tr.* (foll. by *at*) grasp or try to grasp. ● *n.* **1 a** an act of catching. **b** *Cricket* a chance or act of catching the ball. **2 a** an amount of a thing caught, esp. of fish. **b** a thing or person caught or worth catching, esp. in marriage. **3 a** a question, trick, etc. intended to deceive, incriminate, etc. **b** an unexpected or hidden difficulty or disadvantage. **4** a device for fastening a door or window etc. **5** *Mus.* a round, esp. with words arranged to produce a humorous effect. □ **catch at a straw** see STRAW. **catch one's death of cold** see DEATH. **catch fire** see FIRE. **catch it** *colloq.* be punished or in trouble. **catch on** *colloq.* **1** (of a practice, fashion, etc.) become popular. **2** (of a person) understand what is meant. **catch out** *Brit.* **1** detect in a mistake etc. **2** take unawares. **3** = sense 3b of *v.* **catch the sun** be in a sunny position. **2** *Brit.* become sunburnt. **catch up 1 a** (often foll. by *with*) reach a person etc. ahead (*he caught up with us*). **b** (often foll. by *with, on*) make up arrears (of work etc.) (*must catch up with my chores*). **2** snatch or pick up hurriedly. **3** (often in *passive*) involve; entangle (*caught up in crime*). [from Latin *captare* 'to try to catch'] □ **catchable** *adj.*

catch-22 *n.* (often *attrib.*) *colloq.* a circumstance from which there is no escape because of mutually conflicting or dependent conditions. [title of a novel by J. Heller (1961) featuring such a dilemma]

catch-all *n.* (often *attrib.*) a thing designed to include everything.

catch-as-catch-can ● *n.* a style of wrestling with few holds barred. ● *adj.* using whatever is available (*a catch-as-catch-can repair*).

catch crop *n.* a crop grown between two staple crops (in position or time).

catcher *n.* **1** a person or thing that catches. **2** *Baseball* a fielder positioned behind the home plate. ▷ HOME PLATE

catching *adj.* **1 a** (of a disease) infectious. **b** (of a practice etc.) likely to be imitated. **2** attractive.

C

catchment *n.* the collection of rainfall.

catchment area *n.* **1** the area from which rainfall flows into a river etc. **2** the area served by a school etc.

catchpenny *adj.* intended merely to sell quickly.

catchphrase *n.* a phrase in frequent use.

catchweight ● *adj.* unrestricted as regards weight. ● *n.* unrestricted weight, as a weight category in sports.

catchword *n.* **1** a topical slogan. **2** a word so placed as to draw attention.

catchy *adj.* (**catchier**, **catchiest**) (of a tune) easy to remember; attractive. □ **catchily** *adv.* **catchiness** *n.*

catechism /kat-i-kizm/ *n.* **1 a** a summary of the principles of a religion in the form of questions and answers. **b** a book containing this. **2** a series of questions put to anyone. □ **catechismal** *adj.*

catechist /kat-i-kist/ *n.* a religious teacher, esp. one using a catechism.

catechize /kat-i-kyz/ *v.tr.* (also **-ise**) **1** instruct by means of question and answer, esp. from a catechism. **2** put questions to; examine. [from Greek *katēkhein* 'to instruct orally'] □ **catechizer** *n.*

catechumen /kat-i-**kew**-men/ *n.* a Christian convert under instruction before baptism. [based on Greek *katēkhein* 'to instruct orally']

categorical *adj.* (also **categoric**) unconditional; explicit, direct (*a categorical refusal*). □ **categorically** *adv.*

categorize *v.tr.* (also **-ise**) place in a category or categories. □ **categorization** *n.*

category *n.* (*pl.* **-ies**) a class or division. [from Greek *katēgoria* 'statement'] □ **categorial** *adj.*

catenary /kă-**tee**-nă-ri/ ● *n.* (*pl.* **-ies**) a curve formed by a uniform chain hanging freely from two points not in the same vertical line. ● *adj.* of or resembling such a curve. [based on Latin *catena* 'chain']

catenary bridge *n.* a suspension bridge hung from catenaries.

catenate *v.tr.* connect like links of a chain. □ **catenation** *n.*

cater *v.* **1 a** *intr.* (often foll. by *for*) provide food. **b** *tr.* (as **catered** *adj.*) esp. *N. Amer.* with food provided, esp. by a caterer (*catered party*). **2** *intr.* (foll. by *for, to*) provide what is desired or needed by. **3** *intr.* (foll. by *to*) pander to (esp. low tastes). [from archaic noun *cater* 'buyer': based on Latin *captare* 'to seize']

cater-cornered var. of KITTY-CORNER.

caterer *n.* a person who supplies food for social events, esp. professionally. □ **catering** *n.*

caterpillar *n.* **1 a** ◀ the larva of a butterfly or moth. **b** (in general use) any similar larva of various insects. ▷ META-MORPHOSIS. **2 a** (in full **caterpillar track** or **tread**) *propr.* ▼ an endless articulated steel band passing round the wheels of a tractor etc. for travel on rough ground. ▷ SNOWMOBILE. **b** a vehicle with these tracks, e.g. a tractor or tank.

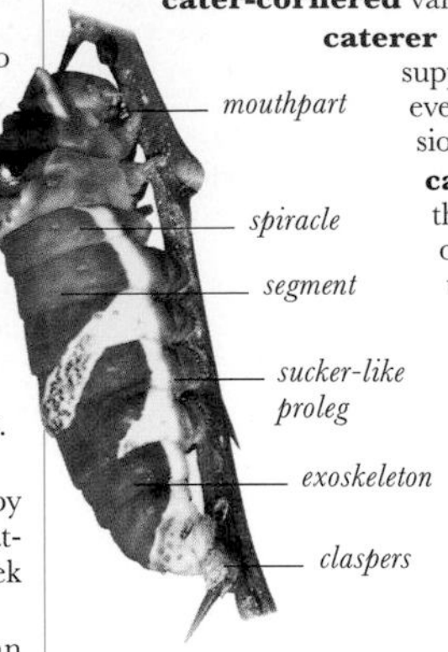

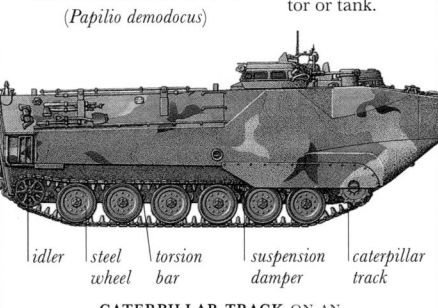

mouthpart
spiracle
segment
sucker-like proleg
exoskeleton
claspers

CATERPILLAR OF A CITRUS SWALLOWTAIL BUTTERFLY
(*Papilio demodocus*)

idler | steel wheel | torsion bar | suspension damper | caterpillar track

CATERPILLAR TRACK ON AN AMPHIBIOUS TRACTOR

caterwaul ● *v.intr.* make the shrill howl of a cat. ● *n.* a caterwauling noise. [Middle English]

catfish *n.* (*pl.* usu. same) ▼ any of various esp. freshwater fish, usu. having whisker-like barbels round the mouth.

barbel

CATFISH: BLUE CATFISH
(*Ictalurus furcatus*)

cat flap *n.* a small swinging flap in an outer door, for a cat to pass in and out.

catgut *n.* a material used for the strings of musical instruments and surgical sutures, made of the intestines of the sheep, horse, or ass (but not the cat).

Cath. *abbr.* **1** Cathedral. **2** Catholic.

catharsis *n.* (*pl.* **catharses**) **1** the release of repressed emotions through drama or art etc., or in psychotherapy. **2** *Med.* purgation. [from Greek *katharsis*]

cathartic ● *adj.* **1** effecting catharsis. **2** purgative. ● *n.* a cathartic drug. □ **cathartically** *adv.*

cathedral *n.* ▼ the principal church of a diocese, containing the bishop's throne. [based on Greek *kathedra* 'seat']

Catherine wheel *n.* a firework in the form of a flat coil which spins when fixed and lit. [based on Greek *Aikaterina*, name of a saint martyred on a spiked wheel]

catheter *n.* *Med.* a tube for insertion into a body cavity for introducing or removing fluid. [from Greek *kathetēr*] □ **catheterize** *v.tr.* (also **-ise**)

cathode *n.* *Electr.* **1** the positively charged electrode of a device supplying current, for example a primary cell. **2** the negatively charged electrode by which electrons enter an electrical device. [from Greek *kathodos* 'descent'] □ **cathodal** *adj.* **cathodic** *adj.*

CATHEDRAL

As Christianity spread some 1,000 years ago, larger churches were required. New building techniques of the time allowed for the construction of the first cathedrals. These had thinner walls, with taller windows that led the eye heavenwards and flooded the building with light. As Christian places of worship, many cathedrals, whatever their style, were built in the shape of a cross, with chapels in the arms (transepts), and the altar lying to the east to face the rising sun.

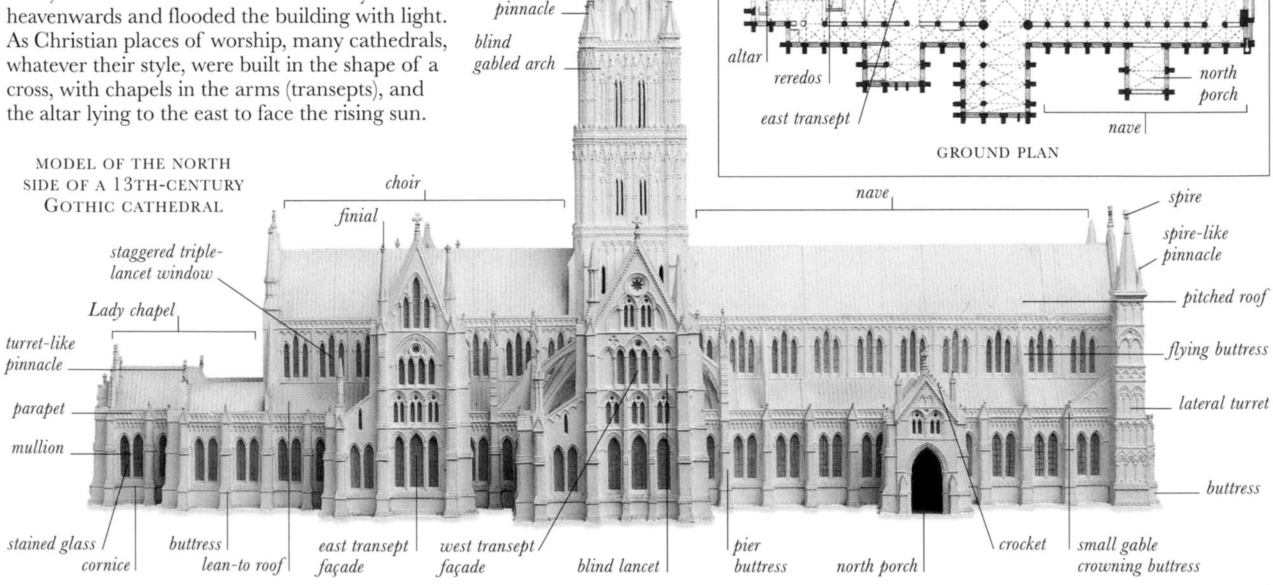

spire
spire-like pinnacle
blind gabled arch

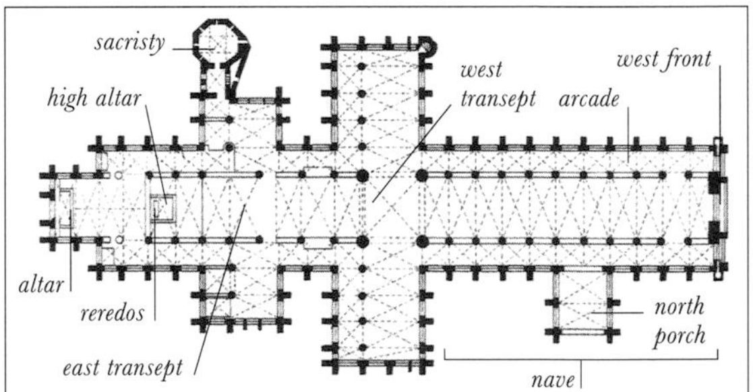

sacristy
high altar
west transept
arcade
west front
altar
reredos
east transept
north porch
nave

GROUND PLAN

MODEL OF THE NORTH SIDE OF A 13TH-CENTURY GOTHIC CATHEDRAL

choir
finial
staggered triple-lancet window
Lady chapel
turret-like pinnacle
parapet
mullion
stained glass
cornice
buttress
lean-to roof
east transept façade
west transept façade
blind lancet
nave
spire
spire-like pinnacle
pitched roof
flying buttress
lateral turret
buttress
pier buttress
north porch
crocket
small gable crowning buttress

cathode ray *n.* a beam of electrons emitted from the cathode of a high-vacuum tube.

cathode ray tube *n.* a high-vacuum tube in which cathode rays produce a luminous image on a fluorescent screen. ▷ TELEVISION

catholic ● *adj.* **1** universal. **2** of wide sympathies or interests (*catholic tastes*). **3** (**Catholic**) **a** of the Roman Catholic religion. **b** including all Christians. **c** including all of the Western Church. ● *n.* (**Catholic**) a Roman Catholic. [from Greek *katholikos* 'universal'] □ **catholically** *adv.* **Catholicism** *n.* **catholicity** *n.* **catholicly** *adv.*

cation /kat-I-ŏn/ *n.* a positively charged ion; an ion that is attracted to the cathode in electrolysis.

cationic /kat-I-on-ik/ *adj.* **1** of a cation or cations. **2** having an active cation.

catkin *n.* a spike of usu. downy or silky flowers hanging from a willow, hazel, etc. [from obsolete Dutch *katteken* 'kitten']

catmint *n.* esp. *Brit.* a plant, *Nepeta cataria* (mint family), with purple-spotted white flowers and a mintlike smell attractive to cats.

catnap ● *n.* a short sleep. ● *v.intr.* (**-napped, -napping**) have a catnap.

catnip *n.* = CATMINT. [based on dialect *nip* 'catmint', from Latin *nepeta*]

cat-o'-nine-tails *n. hist.* ▼ a rope whip with nine knotted lashes for flogging.

CAT-O'-NINE-TAILS

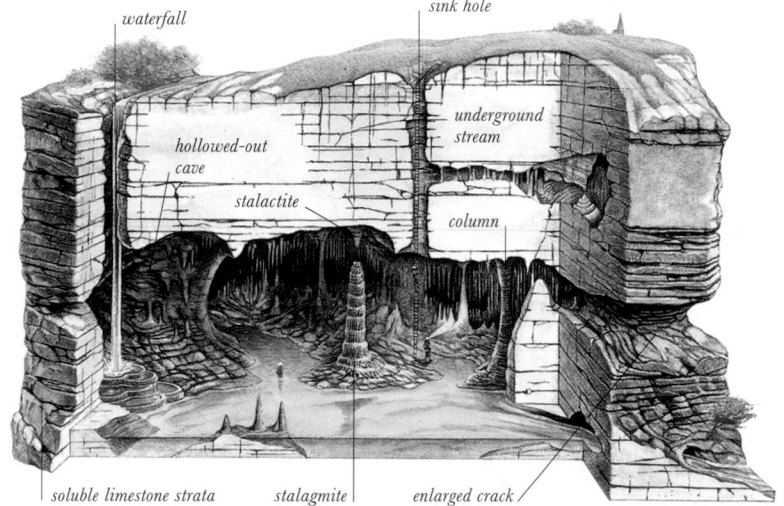

Catseye *n. Brit. propr.* one of a series of reflector studs set into a road.

cat's-eye *n.* a precious stone of Sri Lanka and the Malabar Coast

cat's-paw *n.* **1** a person used as a tool by another. **2** a slight breeze rippling the surface of water.

cat's-tail *n.* = REED MACE.

catsuit *n. Brit.* a close-fitting garment with trouser legs, covering the body from neck to feet.

catsup *US* var. of KETCHUP.

cattery *n.* (*pl.* **-ies**) a place where cats are boarded or bred.

cattle *n.pl.* large ruminant animals with horns and cloven hoofs, e.g. cows, bison, and buffalo, esp. of the genus *Bos*. ▷ RUMINANT. [from Old French *chatel* 'chattel']

cattle cake *n. Brit.* a concentrated food for cattle, in cake form.

cattle grid *n. Brit.* a grid covering a ditch, allowing vehicles to pass over but not cattle, sheep, etc.

cattle guard *n. N. Amer.* = CATTLE GRID.

catty *adj.* (**cattier, cattiest**) **1** spiteful. **2** catlike. □ **cattily** *adv.* **cattiness** *n.*

catty-corner (also **catty-cornered**) var. of KITTY-CORNER.

catwalk *n.* **1** a narrow footway along a bridge, above a theatre stage etc. **2** a narrow platform or gangway used in fashion shows etc.

Caucasian ● *adj.* **1** (also **Caucasoid**) of or relating to the light-skinned division of humankind. **2** of or relating to the Caucasus. ● *n.* a Caucasian person. [from *Caucasus*, mountains between the Black Sea and Caspian Sea, supposed place of origin of this people]

caucus ● *n.* (*pl.* **caucuses**) **1** (in N. America and New Zealand) **a** a meeting of the members of a legislative body belonging to a particular political party, to decide policy. **b** a bloc of such members. **2** often *derog.* (esp. in the UK) **a** a usu. secret meeting of a group within a larger organization. **b** such a group. ● *v.intr.* (**caucused, caucusing**) hold or form a caucus. [18th-century US coinage]

caudal *adj.* **1** of or like a tail. ▷ FISH. **2** of the posterior part of the body. [based on Latin *cauda* 'tail'] □ **caudally** *adv.*

caudate *adj.* having a tail.

caudillo *n.* (*pl.* **-os**) (in Spanish-speaking countries) a military or political leader. [Spanish]

caught *past* and *past part.* of CATCH.

caul *n.* the inner membrane enclosing a foetus. [Middle English]

cauldron *n.* (also **caldron**) a large deep bowl-shaped vessel for boiling over an open fire. [from Latin *caldarium* 'hot bath']

cauliflower *n.* **1** a variety of cabbage with a large immature flower head of small usu. creamy-white flower buds. **2** the head eaten as a vegetable. ▷ VEGETABLE. [earlier *cole-florie*, from obsolete French *chou fleuri* 'flowered cabbage']

cauliflower ear *n.* an ear thickened or deformed by repeated blows, esp. in boxing.

caulk (*US* also **calk**) ● *n.* a waterproof filler and sealant, used in building. ● *v.tr.* **1** seal (a seam etc.) with caulk. **2 a** stop up (the seams of a boat etc.) with oakum etc. and waterproofing material, or by driving plate-junctions together. **b** make watertight by this method. [from Latin *calcare* 'to tread'] □ **caulker** *n.*

causal *adj.* **1** of, forming, or expressing a cause or causes. **2** relating to cause and effect. □ **causally** *adv.*

causality *n.* **1** the relation of cause and effect. **2** the principle that everything has a cause.

causation *n.* **1** the act of causing or producing an effect. **2** = CAUSALITY 1.

causative *adj.* **1** acting as cause. **2** (foll. by *of*) producing. **3** *Gram.* expressing cause. □ **causatively** *adv.*

cause ● *n.* **1 a** that which produces an effect, or gives rise to an action, phenomenon, or condition. **b** a person or thing that occasions something. **c** a reason or motive; a ground (*cause for complaint*). **2** a reason adjudged adequate (*show cause*). **3** a principle, belief, or purpose (*faithful to the cause*). **4 a** a matter to be settled at law. **b** an individual's case offered at law (*plead a cause*). **5** a side taken in a dispute. ● *v.tr.* **1** be the cause of, produce, make happen (*caused a commotion*). **2** (foll. by *to* + infin.) induce (*caused me to smile*). □ **in the cause of** to defend or support (*in the cause of justice*). **make common cause with** join the side of. [from Latin *causa*] □ **causable** *adj.* **causeless** *adj.* **causer** *n.*

cause célèbre /kohz se-lebr/ *n.* (*pl.* **causes célèbres** *pronunc.* same) **1** a lawsuit that attracts much attention. **2** an issue that gives rise to widespread public discussion.

causeway *n.* **1** a raised road or track across low or wet ground or a stretch of water. **2** a raised path by a road. [based on Latin *calx* 'lime, limestone']

caustic ● *adj.* **1** that burns or corrodes organic tissue. **2** sarcastic, biting. **3** *Chem.* strongly alkaline. ● *n.* a caustic substance. [based on Greek *kaustos* 'burnt'] □ **caustically** *adv.* **causticity** *n.*

caustic potash *n.* potassium hydroxide.

caustic soda *n.* sodium hydroxide.

cauterize *v.tr.* (also **-ise**) *Med.* burn or coagulate (tissue) with a heated instrument or caustic substance, esp. to stop bleeding. [from Greek *kautēriazein*] □ **cauterization** *n.*

caution ● *n.* **1** attention to safety; prudence, carefulness. **2 a** esp. *Brit.* a warning, esp. a formal one in law. **b** a formal warning and reprimand. **3** *colloq.* an amusing or surprising person or thing. ● *v.tr.* **1** warn or admonish. **2** esp. *Brit.* issue a caution to. [from Latin *cautio* 'taking heed']

cautionary *adj.* that gives or serves as a warning.

cautious *adj.* careful, prudent; attentive to safety. □ **cautiously** *adv.* **cautiousness** *n.*

cavalcade *n.* a procession of riders, motor vehicles, etc. [based on Latin *caballus* 'packhorse']

cavalier ● *n.* **1** *hist.* (**Cavalier**) a supporter of Charles I in the Civil War. **2** a courtly gentleman. ● *adj.* offhand, supercilious, blasé. [based on Latin *caballus* 'horse'] □ **cavalierly** *adv.*

cavalry *n.* (*pl.* **-ies**) (usu. treated as *pl.*) soldiers on horseback or in armoured vehicles.

cavalryman *n.* (*pl.* **-men**) a soldier of a cavalry regiment.

cave ● *n.* ▼ a large hollow in the side of a cliff, hill, etc., or underground. ● *v.intr.* explore caves. □ **cave in 1 a** (of a wall, earth over a hollow, etc.) subside, collapse. **b** cause (a wall, earth, etc.) to do this. **2** yield; give up. [based on Latin *cavus* 'hollow'] □ **cavelike** *adj.* **caver** *n.*

caveat /kav-i-at/ *n.* **1** a warning or proviso. **2** *Law* a process in court to suspend proceedings. [Latin, literally 'let a person beware']

C

CAVE

Most caves occur in limestone since this type of rock is soluble in rainwater. Acidic rain seeps in, dissolving calcite out of the sedimentary rock and gradually producing hollows. As rain continues to drip in, it leaves behind tiny calcite sediments. These deposits accumulate to form stalactites and stalagmites, and columns where the two meet.

waterfall   sink hole

hollowed-out cave   underground stream

stalactite   column

soluble limestone strata   stalagmite   enlarged crack

CROSS-SECTION THROUGH A LIMESTONE CAVE

caveat emptor *n.* the principle that the buyer alone is responsible if dissatisfied. [Latin, literally 'let the buyer beware']

caveman *n.* (*pl.* **-men**; *fem.* **cavewoman**, *pl.* **-women**) **1** a prehistoric man living in a cave. **2** a primitive or crude man.

cavern *n.* a cave, esp. a large or dark one. [from Latin *caverna*] □ **cavernous** *adj.* **cavernously** *adv.*

caviar *n.* (also **caviare**) the pickled roe of sturgeon or other large fish, eaten as a delicacy. [from French]

cavil ● *v.intr.* (**cavilled**, **cavilling**; *US* **caviled**, **caviling**) (usu. foll. by *at, about*) make petty objections. ● *n.* a trivial objection. [from Latin *cavilla* 'mockery'] □ **caviller** *n.*

caving *n.* exploring caves as a sport or pastime.

cavity *n.* (*pl.* **-ies**) **1** a hollow within a solid body. **2** a decayed part of a tooth. [from Late Latin *cavitas*]

cavity wall *n.* a wall formed from two skins of brick or blockwork with a space between. ▷ HOUSE

cavort *v.intr. colloq.* caper excitedly. [originally US]

caw ● *n.* the harsh cry of a rook, crow, etc. ● *v.intr.* utter this cry.

cayenne pepper *n.* (in full **cayenne pepper**) a pungent red pepper prepared from ground dried chillies. ▷ CHILLI, SPICE. [from Tupi (Brazilian) *kynha*, assimilated to *Cayenne*, capital of French Guiana]

cayman *n.* (also **caiman**) ▼ any of several reptiles related to alligators. [from Carib *acayuman*]

CAYMAN: JUVENILE SPECTACLED CAYMAN
(*Caiman crocodilus*)

CB *abbr.* **1** citizens' band. **2** (in the UK) Companion of the Order of the Bath.

CBE *abbr.* Commander of the Order of the British Empire.

CBI *abbr.* (in the UK) Confederation of British Industry.

cc *abbr.* (also **c.c.**) **1** cubic centimetre(s). **2** carbon copy.

CD *abbr.* compact disc.

Cd *symb. Chem.* the element cadmium.

cd *abbr.* candela.

Cdr. *abbr. Mil.* Commander.

Cdre. *abbr.* Commodore.

CD-ROM *abbr.* compact disc read-only memory.

CDT *abbr.* **1** Central Daylight Time. **2** craft, design, and technology.

Ce *symb. Chem.* the element cerium.

cease ● *v.tr. & intr.* stop; bring or come to an end (*ceased breathing*). ● *n.* (in **without cease**) unendingly. □ **cease fire** *Mil.* stop firing. [from Latin *cessare*]

ceasefire *n. Mil.* **1** an order to stop firing. **2** a period of truce.

ceaseless *adj.* without end. □ **ceaselessly** *adv.*

cecum *US var. of* CAECUM.

cedar *n.* **1** ▼ any spreading evergreen conifer of the genus *Cedrus*, bearing tufts of small needles and cones of papery scales. **2** any of various similar conifers yielding timber. **3** = CEDARWOOD. [from Greek *kedros*]

CEDAR: CEDAR OF LEBANON
(*Cedrus libani*)

needle-like leaf

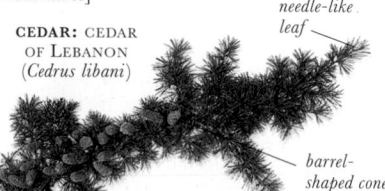

barrel-shaped cone

cedarwood *n.* the fragrant durable wood of any cedar tree.

cede *v.tr.* give up one's rights to or possession of. [from Latin *cedere* 'to yield']

cedilla *n.* **1** a mark written under the letter *c* to show that it is sibilant (as in *façade*). **2** a similar mark under *s*. [based on Greek *zēta*, the letter Z]

Ceefax *n. Brit. propr.* a teletext service provided by the BBC. [representing the pronunciation of *seeing* + *facsimile*]

ceilidh /**kay**-li/ *n.* orig. *Ir. & Sc.* an informal gathering for conversation, music, dancing, songs, and stories. [from Old Irish *céilide* 'visit, visiting']

ceiling *n.* **1 a** the upper interior surface of a room or other similar compartment. **b** the material forming this. **2** an upper limit on prices, wages, performance, etc. **3** *Aeron.* the maximum altitude a given aircraft can reach. [Middle English]

celandine *n.* either of two yellow-flowered plants, the greater celandine, *Chelidonium majus*, and the lesser celandine, *Ranunculus ficaria*. [based on Greek *khelidōn* 'swallow', the flowering being associated with the arrival of swallows]

celebrant *n.* a person who performs a rite.

celebrate *v.* **1** *tr.* mark (a festival or special event) with festivities etc. **2** *tr.* perform publicly and duly (a religious ceremony etc.). **3 a** *tr.* officiate at (the Eucharist). **b** *intr.* officiate. **4** *intr.* engage in festivities. **5** *tr.* (esp. as **celebrated** *adj.*) honour publicly, make widely known. [based on Latin *celeber* 'frequented, honoured'] □ **celebration** *n.* **celebrator** *n.* **celebratory** *adj.*

celebrity *n.* (*pl.* **-ies**) **1** a well-known person. **2** fame.

celeriac *n.* ▶ a variety of celery with a swollen turnip-like stem base used as a vegetable.

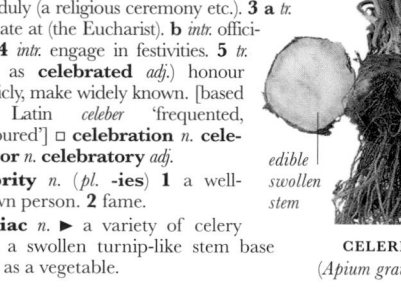

edible swollen stem

CELERIAC
(*Apium graveolens*)

celerity *n. archaic or literary* swiftness (esp. of a living creature). [from Latin *celeritas*]

celery *n.* an umbelliferous plant, *Apium graveolens*, with leaf-stalks used as a vegetable. [from Greek *selinon* 'parsley']

celesta *n. Mus.* a small keyboard instrument resembling a glockenspiel, with hammers striking steel plates suspended over wooden resonators. [from French]

celestial *adj.* **1** heavenly; divinely good or beautiful; sublime. **2** of the sky, or of outer space as observed in astronomy etc. [based on Latin *caelum* 'heaven'] □ **celestially** *adv.*

celestial equator *n.* the great circle of the sky in the plane perpendicular to the Earth's axis. ▷ CELESTIAL SPHERE

celestial navigation *n.* navigation by the stars etc.

celestial sphere *n.* ▼ an imaginary sphere of which the observer is the centre and in which celestial objects are represented as lying. ▷ ZODIAC

celiac *US var. of* COELIAC.

celibate ● *adj.* **1** committed to abstention from sexual relations and from marriage. **2** abstaining from sexual relations. ● *n.* a celibate person. [from Latin *caelibatus* 'unmarried state'] □ **celibacy** *n.*

cell *n.* **1** a small room, esp. in a prison or monastery. **2** a small compartment, e.g. in a honeycomb. **3** a small group as a nucleus of political activity, esp. of a subversive kind. **4** *Biol.* **a** ▶ the structural and functional unit of an organism, consisting of cytoplasm and a nucleus enclosed in a membrane. ▷ ALGA. **b** an enclosed cavity in an organism etc. **5** *Electr.* a vessel for containing electrodes within an electrolyte for current-generation or electrolysis. ▷ BATTERY. [from Latin *cella* 'storeroom, chamber'] □ **celled** *adj.* (also in *comb.*). **cell-like** *adj.*

CELESTIAL SPHERE

For the Earth-based observer, the positions of celestial bodies, such as the Sun, Moon, stars, and planets, can be described by locating them on an imaginary sphere – the celestial sphere – that is centred on the Earth, and which rotates around the Earth once a day. The north and south poles of the celestial sphere lie directly above those of the Earth, at the points where the Earth's axis of rotation intersects the sphere. The celestial equator marks a projection of the Earth's equator on to the sphere, while the ecliptic marks the path of the Sun across the sky as the Earth orbits the Sun.

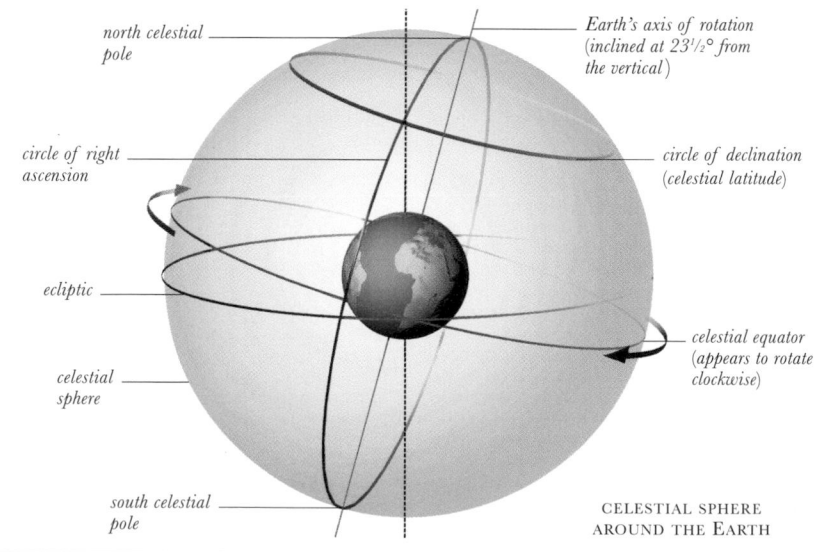

north celestial pole

Earth's axis of rotation (inclined at 23½° from the vertical)

circle of right ascension

circle of declination (celestial latitude)

ecliptic

celestial sphere

celestial equator (appears to rotate clockwise)

south celestial pole

CELESTIAL SPHERE AROUND THE EARTH

CELL

The cell is the basic structural unit of every living thing, and most plants and animals are composed of millions of them. Cells work in unison to perform the tasks necessary to keep an organism alive. They vary in shape according to function: a human red blood cell is disc-shaped, while a nerve cell is thread-like and may be a metre long. Unlike animal cells, plant cells can produce their own food through photosynthesis.

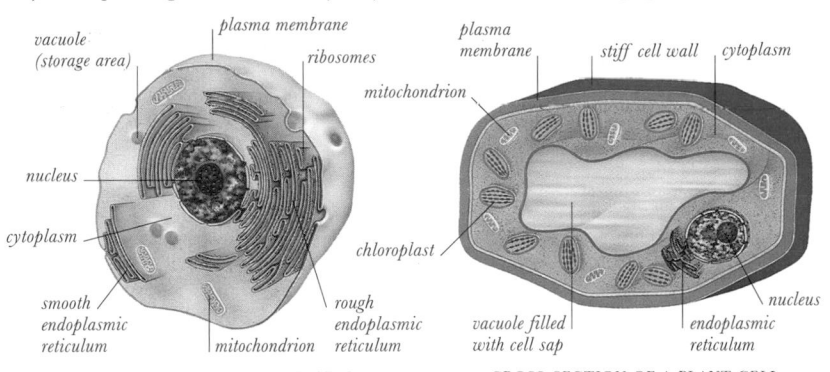

CROSS-SECTION OF AN ANIMAL CELL   CROSS-SECTION OF A PLANT CELL

cellar ● *n.* **1** a room below ground level in a house, used for storage. **2** a stock of wine in a cellar (*has a good cellar*). ● *v.tr.* store or put in a cellar. [from Late Latin *cellarium* 'storehouse']

Cellnet *n. propr.* a cellular telephone service.

cello /**chel**-oh/ *n.* (*pl.* **-os**) ▼ a bass instrument of the violin family. ▷ ORCHESTRA, STRINGED. [abbreviation of VIOLONCELLO] □ **cellist** *n.*

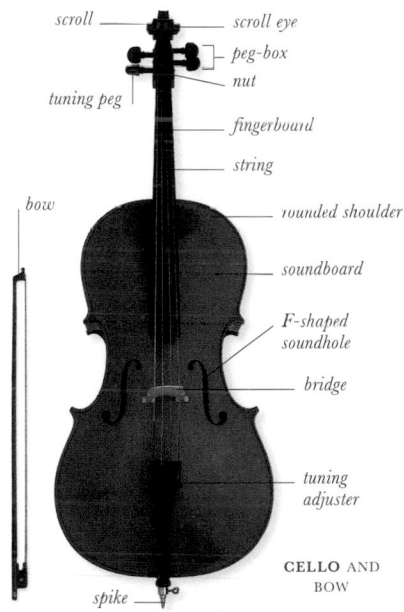

CELLO AND BOW

cellophane *n. propr.* a thin transparent wrapping material made from viscose. [based on CELLULOSE]

cellphone *n.* a small portable radio-telephone.

cellular *adj.* **1** of or having small compartments or cavities. **2** of open texture; porous. **3** *Physiol.* of or consisting of cells. **4** designating or relating to a mobile telephone system that uses a number of short-range radio stations to cover the area it serves. [from French *cellulaire*] □ **cellularity** *n.*

cellular blanket *n.* a blanket of open texture.

cellular phone *n.* (also **cellular radio**) a system of mobile radio-telephone transmission with an area divided into 'cells' each served by its own small transmitter.

cellule *n. Biol.* a small cell or cavity.

cellulite *n.* a lumpy form of fat, esp. on the hips and thighs of women, causing puckering of the skin.

celluloid *n.* **1** a transparent flammable plastic made from camphor and nitrocellulose. **2** cinema film. [based on CELLULOSE]

cellulose *n.* **1** *Biochem.* a carbohydrate forming the main constituent of plant cell walls, used in the production of textile fibres. ▷ CELL. **2** (in general use) a paint or lacquer consisting of esp. cellulose acetate or nitrate in solution. [French] □ **cellulosic** *adj.*

cell wall *n. Biol.* the rigid layer that encloses a plant or bacterial cell. ▷ CELL

Celsius *adj.* of or denoting a temperature on the Celsius scale. [named after A. *Celsius*, Swedish astronomer, 1701–44]

■ **Usage** See Usage Note at CENTIGRADE.

Celsius scale *n.* a scale of temperature on which water freezes at 0° and boils at 100° under standard conditions.

Celt *n.* a member of a group of western European peoples, including the pre-Roman inhabitants of Britain and Gaul and their descendants, esp. in Ireland, Wales, Scotland, Cornwall, Brittany, and the Isle of Man. [from Greek *Keltoi* 'Celts']

Celtic ● *adj.* of or relating to the Celts. ● *n.* a group of languages spoken by Celtic peoples, including Gaelic, Welsh, Cornish, and Breton. □ **Celticism** *n.*

Celtic cross *n.* ▶ a Latin cross with a circle round the centre.

cement ● *n.* **1** a powdery substance made by calcining lime and clay, mixed with water to form mortar or used in concrete (see also PORTLAND CEMENT). **2** any similar substance that hardens and fastens on setting. **3** a uniting factor or principle. **4** a substance for filling cavities in teeth. ● *v.tr.* **1 a** unite with or as with cement. **b** establish or strengthen (a friendship etc.). **2** apply cement to. **3** line or cover with cement. [from Latin *caementum* 'quarry stone'] □ **cementation** *n.*

cemetery *n.* (*pl.* **-ies**) a burial ground. [from Greek *koimētērion* 'dormitory']

cenobite *US* var. of COENOBITE.

cenotaph *n.* a tomblike monument to a dead person whose body is elsewhere. [from Greek *kenos* 'empty' + *taphos* 'tomb']

Cenozoic (also **Cainozoic**) *Geol.* ● *adj.* of or relating to the most recent era of geological time. ● *n.* this era (cf. MESOZOIC, PALAEOZOIC). [based on Greek *kainos* 'new' + *zōion* 'animal']

censer *n.* ▶ a vessel in which incense is burnt. [from Old French *censier*]

censor ● *n.* an official authorized to examine printed matter, films, news, etc., before public release, and to suppress any parts on the grounds of obscenity, a threat to security, etc. ● *v.tr.* **1** act as a censor of. **2** make deletions or changes in. [Latin, from *censēre* 'to assess'] □ **censorship** *n.*

■ **Usage** As a verb, *censor* is often confused with *censure* 'to criticize harshly'.

censorious *adj.* severely critical; faultfinding. □ **censoriously** *adv.* **censoriousness** *n.*

censure ● *v.tr.* criticize harshly; reprove. ● *n.* harsh criticism; expression of disapproval. [from Latin *censura*] □ **censurable** *adj.*

■ **Usage** See Usage Note at CENSOR.

census *n.* (*pl.* **censuses**) the official count of a population or of a class of things. [Latin]

cent *n.* **1 a** a monetary unit in various countries, equal to one-hundredth of a dollar or other decimal currency unit. **b** a coin of this value. **2** *colloq.* a very small sum of money. **3** see PER CENT. [from Latin *centum* 'hundred']

CENTAUR

centaur *n.* ◀ a creature in Greek mythology with the head, arms, and torso of a man and the body and legs of a horse. [from Greek *kentauros*, Greek name for a Thessalonian tribe of expert horsemen]

centenarian ● *n.* a person a hundred or more years old. ● *adj.* a hundred or more years old.

centenary ● *n.* (*pl.* **-ies**) **1** a hundredth anniversary. **2** a celebration of this. ● *adj.* of or relating to a centenary. [based on Latin *centum* 'a hundred']

centennial ● *adj.* **1** lasting for a hundred years. **2** occurring every hundred years. ● *n.* = CENTENARY *n.*

center *US* var. of CENTRE.

centerboard *US* var. of CENTREBOARD.

centerfold *US* var. of CENTREFOLD.

centering *US* var. of CENTRING.

centesimal *adj.* reckoning or reckoned by hundredths. [from Latin *centesimus* 'hundredth'] □ **centesimally** *adv.*

centi- *comb. form* **1** one-hundredth (*centigram*; *centilitre*). **2** hundred. [from Latin *centum* 'a hundred']

centigrade *adj.* **1** = CELSIUS. **2** having a scale of a hundred degrees. [based on Latin *gradus* 'step']

■ **Usage** In sense 1, *Celsius* is usually preferred in technical contexts.

centigram *n.* (also **centigramme**) a metric unit of mass, equal to one-hundredth of a gram.

centilitre *n.* (*US* **centiliter**) a metric unit of capacity, equal to one-hundredth of a litre.

centimetre *n.* (*US* **centimeter**) a metric unit of length, equal to one-hundredth of a metre.

CENSER

gilded chains

vessel for incense

CELTIC CROSS

C

centipede *n.* ▶ a predatory arthropod of the class Chilopoda, with a flattened elongated body of many segments, most bearing a pair of legs. [from Latin *centipeda*]

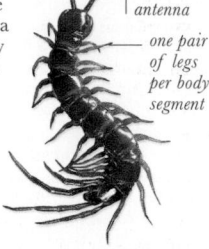

antenna

one pair of legs per body segment

CENTIPEDE
(*Lithobius* species)

central *adj.* **1** of, at, or forming the centre. **2** from the centre. **3** chief, essential, most important. □ **centrality** *n.* **centrally** *adv.*

central bank *n.* a national bank issuing currency etc.

central heating *n.* a method of warming a building by pipes, radiators, etc., fed from a central source of heat.

centralism *n.* a system that centralizes. □ **centralist** *n.*

centralize *v.* (also **-ise**) **1** *tr. & intr.* bring or come to a centre. **2** *tr.* **a** concentrate (administration) at a single centre. **b** subject (a state) to this system. □ **centralization** *n.*

central locking *n.* a locking system in motor vehicles whereby the locks of several doors can be operated from a single lock.

central nervous system *n. Anat.* the complex of nerve tissues that controls the activities of the body. ▷ NERVOUS SYSTEM

central processing unit *n.* (also **central processor**) the part of a computer in which the control and execution of operations occur. ▷ PCB

central reservation see RESERVATION 5.

centre (*US* **center**) ● *n.* **1** the middle point, esp. of a line, circle, or sphere. **2** a pivot or axis of rotation. **3 a** a place or group of buildings forming a central point in a district, city, etc., or a main area for an activity (*shopping centre*; *town centre*). **b** (with preceding word) equipment for a number of connected functions (*music centre*). **4** a point of concentration or dispersion; a nucleus or source. **5** a political group holding moderate opinions. **6** the filling in a chocolate etc. **7** *Sport* **a** the middle player in a line in some field games. ▷ RUGBY. **b** a kick or hit from the side to the centre of the pitch. ● *v.* **1** *intr.* (foll. by *in*, *on*; *disp.* foll. by *round*) have as its main centre; focus on. **2** *tr.* place in the centre. **3** *tr.* (foll. by *in*, *on*, etc.) concentrate or focus (a thing) in, around, etc. **4** *tr. Sport* kick or hit (the ball) from the side to the centre of the pitch. [from Greek *kentron* 'sharp point'] □ **centred** *adj.* (often in *comb.*). **centric** *adj.* **centricity** *n.*

■ **Usage** The use of the verb *centre* in sense 1 'to focus on' with *round* is common and found among good writers, but it is still considered incorrect by some people because *centre* designates a specific point. In such cases it is better to use *centre on*, e.g. *The discussion centred on ways of raising money.*

centre-back *n. Sport* a middle player or position in a back line.

centreboard *n.* (*US* **centerboard**) a board for lowering through a boat's keel to prevent leeway. ▷ DINGHY

centrefold *n.* (*US* **centerfold**) a printed and usu. illustrated sheet folded to form the centre spread of a magazine etc.

centre forward *n. Sport* the middle player or position in a forward line. ▷ FOOTBALL

centre half *n. Sport* the middle player or position in a defensive line. ▷ FOOTBALL

centre of gravity *n.* a point from which the weight of a body may be considered to act.

centre of mass *n.* a point representing the mean position of the matter in a body or system.

centrepiece *n.* **1** an ornament for the middle of a table. **2** a principal item.

centre spread *n.* the two facing middle pages of a newspaper etc.

centre stage ● *n.* **1** the centre of a stage. **2** the centre of attention. ● *adv.* in or into this position.

-centric *comb. form* forming adjectives with the sense 'having a (specified) centre' (*anthropocentric*; *eccentric*).

centrifugal *adj.* moving or tending to move from a centre. [based on Latin *centrum* 'centre' + *fugere* 'to flee']

centrifugal force *n.* an apparent force that acts outwards on a body moving about a centre, caused by the body's inertia.

centrifuge ● *n.* ▼ a machine with a rapidly rotating container designed to apply centrifugal force to its contents, usu. to separate liquids from solids, or fluids of different densities (e.g. cream from milk). ● *v.tr.* **1** subject to the action of a centrifuge. **2** separate by centrifuge. □ **centrifugation** *n.*

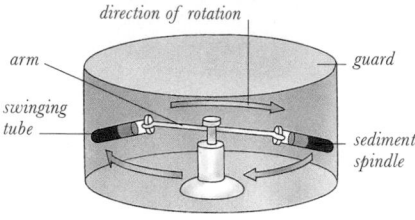

direction of rotation

arm   *guard*

swinging tube

sediment spindle

CENTRIFUGE

centripetal *adj.* moving or tending to move towards a centre. [based on Latin *centrum* 'centre' + *petere* 'to seek'] □ **centripetally** *adv.*

centripetal force *n.* a force acting on a moving body in the direction of the centre about which it is moving.

centrist *n. Polit.* often *derog.* a person who holds moderate views. □ **centrism** *n.*

centurion *n.* the commander of a century in the ancient Roman army. [from Latin *centurio*]

century *n.* (*pl.* **-ies**) **1 a** a period of one hundred years. **b** any of the centuries reckoned from the birth of Christ (*twentieth century* = 1901–2000; *fifth century* BC = 500–401 BC). **2 a** a score of a hundred, esp. a hundred runs by one batsman in cricket. **b** a group of a hundred things. **3** a company in the ancient Roman army, originally of 100 men. [from Latin *centuria*]

■ **Usage** Strictly speaking, since the first century ran from the year 1–100, the first year of a given

century should be that ending in 01. However, in popular use this has been moved back a year, and so the twenty-first century will commonly be regarded as running from 2000–2099.

century plant *n.* the American aloe, *Agave americana.*

cep *n.* ▶ an edible mushroom, *Boletus edulis*, with a stout stalk, a smooth brown cap, and pores rather than gills. [from Latin *cippus* 'stake']

CEP
(*Boletus edulis*)

cephalic /si-fal-ik/ *adj.* of or in the head. [based on Greek *kephalē* 'head']

cephalopod *n.* ▼ a marine mollusc of the class Cephalopoda, having a distinct head with large eyes and a ring of tentacles around a beaked mouth. [from Greek *kephalē* 'head' + *pous podos* 'foot']

ceramic ● *adj.* **1** made of clay and permanently hardened by heat (*a ceramic bowl*). **2** of or relating to ceramics (*the ceramic arts*). ● *n.* **1** ▶ a ceramic article or product. **2** a substance used to make ceramic articles. [based on Greek *keramos* 'pottery']

ceramicist *n.* a person who makes ceramics.

ceramics *n.pl.* **1** ceramic products collectively (*exhibition of ceramics*). **2** (usu. treated as *sing.*) the art of making ceramic articles.

cereal ● *n.* **1** (usu. in *pl.*) **a** any kind of grain used for food. ▷ GRAIN. **b** any grass producing this, e.g. wheat, maize, etc. **2** a breakfast food made from a cereal. ● *adj.* of or relating to edible grain or products of it. [based on *Ceres*, Roman goddess of agriculture]

cerebellum *n.* (*pl.* **cerebellums** or **cerebella**) the part of the brain at the back of the skull in vertebrates, which coordinates and regulates muscular activity. ▷ BRAIN, SPINAL CORD. [Latin, literally 'little brain'] □ **cerebellar** *adj.*

cerebral *adj.* **1** of the brain. **2** intellectual rather than emotional. □ **cerebrally** *adv.*

cerebral hemisphere *n.* each of the two halves of the vertebrate cerebrum. ▷ BRAIN

cerebral palsy *n.* a condition marked by weakness and impaired coordination of the limbs.

cerebration *n.* working of the brain. □ **cerebrate** *v.intr.*

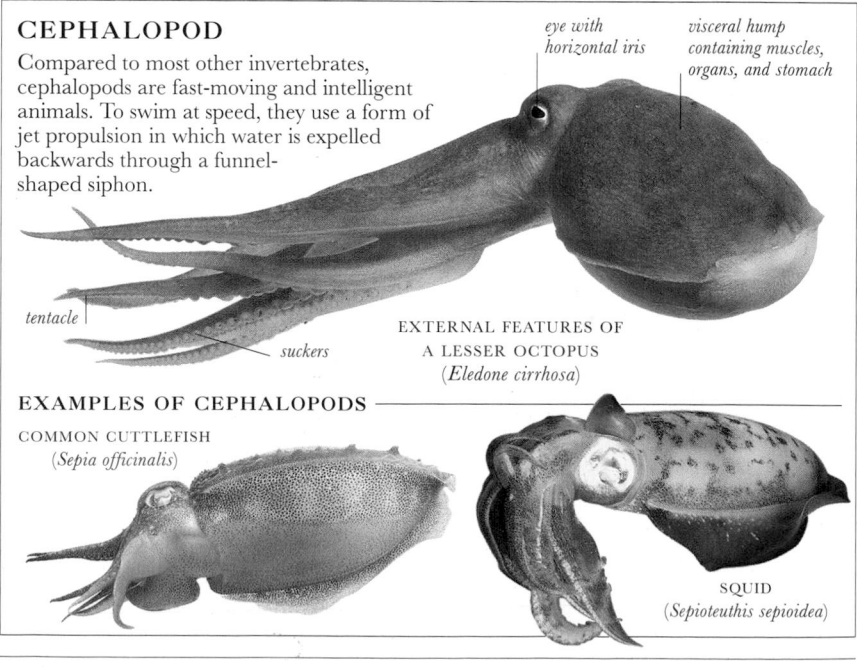

CEPHALOPOD

Compared to most other invertebrates, cephalopods are fast-moving and intelligent animals. To swim at speed, they use a form of jet propulsion in which water is expelled backwards through a funnel-shaped siphon.

eye with horizontal iris

visceral hump containing muscles, organs, and stomach

tentacle

suckers

EXTERNAL FEATURES OF
A LESSER OCTOPUS
(*Eledone cirrhosa*)

EXAMPLES OF CEPHALOPODS

COMMON CUTTLEFISH
(*Sepia officinalis*)

SQUID
(*Sepioteuthis sepioidea*)

CERAMIC

Fashioned from clay or other non-metallic minerals, ceramics were originally baked until hard in an open oven, but are now fired in a kiln or furnace. Widely used as decorative articles, they also have a more functional purpose: for building house walls, insulating cables, and mending broken teeth. New ceramics are being developed for car and aircraft engines. More durable than traditional kinds, they can be as strong as steel and are capable of withstanding extremely high temperatures.

EXAMPLES OF CERAMICS

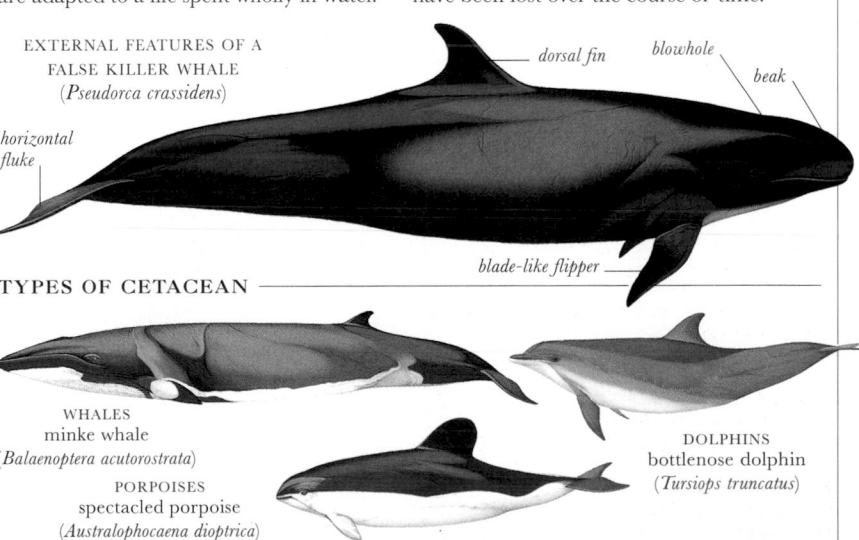

PORCELAIN

BRICK

GLAZED
CLAY BEADS

CEMENT

GLASS

---

cerebro- *comb. form* brain (*cerebrospinal*). [from Latin *cerebrum* 'brain']

cerebrospinal *adj.* of the brain and spine.

cerebrovascular *adj.* of the brain and its blood vessels. ▷ BRAIN

cerebrum *n.* (*pl.* **cerebra**) the principal part of the brain in vertebrates, located in the front area of the skull, which integrates complex sensory and neural functions. ▷ SPINAL CORD. [Latin, literally 'brain']

ceremonial ● *adj.* **1** with or concerning ritual or ceremony. **2** formal (*a ceremonial bow*). ● *n.* **1** a system of rites etc. **2** the formalities or behaviour proper to any occasion (*with all due ceremonial*). □ **ceremonialism** *n.* **ceremonialist** *n.* **ceremonially** *adv.*

ceremonious *adj.* **1** = CEREMONIAL *adj.* **2** full of ceremony; accompanied by rites. **3** having or showing a fondness for ritualistic observance or formality. □ **ceremoniously** *adv.* **ceremoniousness** *n.*

ceremony *n.* (*pl.* **-ies**) **1** a formal religious or public occasion. **2** formalities (*ceremony of exchanging compliments*). **3** excessively polite behaviour (*bowed low with great ceremony*). □ **stand on ceremony** insist on the observance of formalities. [from Latin *caerimonia* 'religious worship']

cerise /se-**reez**/ ● *adj.* of a light clear red colour. ● *n.* this colour. [French, literally 'cherry']

cerium *n. Chem.* a silvery metallic element of the lanthanide series used in the manufacture of lighter flints. [named after the asteroid *Ceres*, discovered at about the same time (1801)]

cert *n. Brit. slang* (esp. **dead cert**) **1** an event or result regarded as certain to happen. **2** a horse strongly tipped to win.

certain ● *adj.* **1 a** confident, convinced (*certain that I put it here*). **b** indisputable (*it is certain that he is guilty*). **2 a** that may be relied on to happen (*it is certain to rain*). **b** destined (*certain to become a star*). **3** definite, unfailing, reliable (*a certain indication of the coming storm; his touch is certain*). **4** (of a person, place, etc.) that might be specified, but is not (*a certain lady; of a certain age*). **5** some though not much (*a certain reluctance*). **6** (of a person, place, etc.) existing, though probably unknown to the reader or hearer (*a certain John Smith*). ● *pron.* (treated as *pl.*) some but not all (*certain of them were wounded*). □ **for certain** without doubt. **make certain** = *make sure* (see SURE). [from Latin *certus* 'settled']

certainly *adv.* **1** undoubtedly, definitely. **2** confidently. **3** yes; by all means.

certainty *n.* (*pl.* **-ies**) **1 a** an undoubted fact. **b** a certain prospect (*his return is a certainty*). **2** an absolute conviction (*has a certainty of his own worth*). **3** a thing or person that may be relied on (*a certainty to win the Derby*).

Cert. Ed. *abbr.* (in the UK) Certificate in Education.

certifiable *adj.* **1** able or needing to be certified. **2** *colloq.* insane.

certificate ● *n.* a formal document attesting a fact, esp. birth, marriage, or death, a medical condition, a level of achievement, a fulfilment of requirements, ownership of shares, etc. ● *v.tr.* (esp. as **certificated** *adj.*) provide with or license or attest by a certificate. [related to CERTIFY] □ **certification** *n.*

Certificate of Secondary Education *n. hist.* **1** an examination set for secondary-school pupils in England and Wales, replaced in 1988 by the General Certificate of Secondary Education (GCSE). **2** the certificate gained by passing it.

certified cheque *n.* a cheque the validity of which is guaranteed by a bank.

certified mail *n. N. Amer.* = RECORDED DELIVERY.

certify *v.tr.* (**-ies**, **-ied**) **1** make a formal statement of; attest; attest to (*certified that he had witnessed the crime*). **2** declare by certificate (that a person is qualified or competent) (*certified as a trained bookkeeper*).

3 officially declare insane. [based on Latin *certus* 'certain']

certitude *n.* a feeling of absolute certainty or conviction.

cerulean /si-**roo**-li-ăn/ *literary* ● *adj.* deep blue like a clear sky. ● *n.* this colour. [from Latin *caeruleus* 'sky blue']

cervelat /**ser**-vĕ-lah/ *n.* a kind of smoked pork sausage. [from Italian *cervellata*]

cervical *adj. Anat.* **1** of or relating to the neck (*cervical vertebrae*). ▷ VERTEBRA. **2** of or relating to the cervix. [based on Latin *cervix -icis* 'neck']

cervical screening *n.* examination of a large number of apparently healthy women for cervical cancer.

cervical smear *n.* esp. *Brit.* a specimen of cellular material from the neck of the womb spread on a microscope slide for examination for cancerous cells.

cervix *n.* (*pl.* **cervices** /**ser**-vi-seez/) *Anat.* **1** the neck. **2** the neck of the womb. ▷ REPRODUCTIVE ORGANS. [Latin]

Cesarean (also **Cesarian**) *US Med.* var. of CAESAREAN.

cesium *US* var. of CAESIUM.

cessation *n.* **1** a ceasing (*cessation of the truce*). **2** a pause (*resumed fighting after the cessation*). [based on Latin *cessare* 'to cease']

cession *n.* **1** the ceding or giving up (of rights, property, and esp. of territory by a state). **2** the territory etc. so ceded. [from Latin *cessio*]

cesspit *n.* **1** a pit for the disposal of refuse. **2** = CESSPOOL. [based on obsolete *cess* 'peatbog']

cesspool *n.* **1** an underground container for the temporary storage of liquid waste or sewage. **2** a centre of corruption, depravity, etc.

cetacean ● *n.* ▼ any marine mammal of the order Cetacea, with streamlined hairless body and dorsal blowhole for breathing. ▷ DOLPHIN, PORPOISE, WHALE. ● *adj.* of cetaceans. [based on Greek *kētos* 'whale']

cetane *n. Chem.* a colourless liquid hydrocarbon of the alkane series used in standardizing ratings of diesel fuel. [from spermaceti, from which it was derived]

Ceylon satinwood see SATINWOOD 1a.

Cf *symb. Chem.* the element californium.

CETACEAN

The order Cetacea comprises whales, porpoises, and dolphins. Like all other mammals, cetaceans breathe air, but they are adapted to a life spent wholly in water. They breathe through a blowhole, which can be closed on diving, and have flippers instead of front limbs. Their hind limbs have been lost over the course of time.

EXTERNAL FEATURES OF A
FALSE KILLER WHALE
(*Pseudorca crassidens*)

dorsal fin   blowhole

beak

horizontal
fluke

blade-like flipper

TYPES OF CETACEAN

WHALES
minke whale
(*Balaenoptera acutorostrata*)

PORPOISES
spectacled porpoise
(*Australophocaena dioptrica*)

DOLPHINS
bottlenose dolphin
(*Tursiops truncatus*)

cf. *abbr.* compare. [Latin *confer* 'compare']

c.f. *abbr.* carried forward.

CFC *abbr. Chem.* chlorofluorocarbon, any of a class of usu. gaseous compounds of carbon, hydrogen, chlorine, and fluorine, used in refrigerants, aerosol propellants, etc., and harmful to the ozone layer in the Earth's atmosphere.

CFE *abbr. Brit.* College of Further Education.

cg *abbr.* centigram(s).

cgs *abbr.* centimetre-gram-second.

cha var. of CHAR[3].

Chablis /**shab**-lee/ *n.* (*pl.* same) a dry white burgundy wine. [from *Chablis* in E. France, where it is produced]

cha-cha *n.* (also **cha-cha-cha**) **1** a ballroom dance with a Latin American rhythm. **2** music for or in the rhythm of a cha-cha. [Latin American Spanish]

chador *n.* (also **chadar**) a large piece of cloth worn in some countries by Muslim women, wrapped around the body to leave only the face exposed. [from Persian *čādar* 'sheet, veil']

chafe ● *v.* **1** *tr. & intr.* make or become sore or damaged by rubbing. **2** *tr.* rub. **3** *tr. & intr.* make or become annoyed; fret (*was chafed by the delay*). ● *n.* **1 a** an act of chafing. **b** a sore resulting from this. **2** a state of annoyance. [from Latin *calefacere* 'to heat']

chafer *n.* any of various large slow-moving strong-flying beetles of the family Scarabaeidae. [Old English]

chaff ● *n.* **1** the husks of corn or other seed separated by winnowing or threshing. **2** chopped hay and straw used as fodder. **3** light-hearted joking; banter. **4** worthless things; rubbish. ● *v.tr.* **1** tease; banter. **2** chop (straw etc.). [Old English]

chaffer *v.intr.* haggle; bargain. [Middle English] □ **chafferer** *n.* **chaffy** *adj.*

chaffinch *n.* a common European finch, *Fringilla coelebs*, the male of which has a blue-grey head with pinkish cheeks and breast. [Old English, literally 'chaff finch', from its foraging around barns etc.]

chafing dish *n.* **1** a cooking pot with an outer pan of hot water, used for keeping food warm. **2** a dish with a spirit lamp etc. for cooking at table. [from obsolete *chafe* 'to warm']

chagrin /**shag**-rin/ ● *n.* acute vexation or mortification. ● *v.tr.* affect with chagrin. [French]

chain ● *n.* **1 a** a connected flexible series of esp. metal links as decoration or for a practical purpose. **b** something resembling this (*formed a human chain*). **2** (in *pl.*) fetters used to confine prisoners. **3** a sequence, series, or set (*chain of events*; *mountain chain*). **4** a group of associated hotels, shops, etc. **5** a measure of length (66 ft). **6** *Chem.* a group of (esp. carbon) atoms bonded in sequence in a molecule. ● *v.tr.* **1** (often foll. by *up*) secure or confine with a chain. **2** confine or restrict (a person) (*is chained to the office*). [from Latin *catena*]

chain bridge *n.* a suspension bridge on chains.

chain gang *n.* a team of convicts chained together and forced to work in the open air.

chain letter *n.* one of a sequence of letters, each recipient in the sequence being requested to send copies to a specific number of other people.

chain link *adj.* made of wire in a diamond-shaped mesh (*chain link fencing*).

chain mail *n.* ▼ armour made of interlaced rings.

▷ JOUST, VIKING

chain reaction *n.* **1** *Physics* a self-sustaining nuclear reaction. **2** *Chem.* a self-sustaining molecular reaction. **3** a series of events, each caused by the previous one.

CHAIN MAIL:
ORIENTAL CHAIN-
MAIL SHIRT

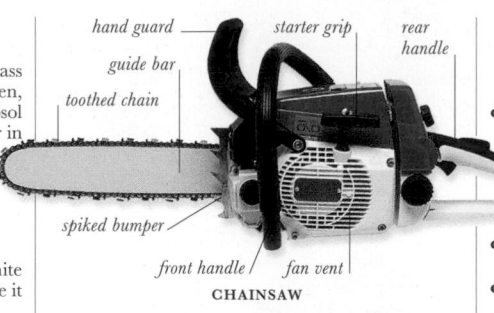

CHAINSAW

chainsaw *n.* ▲ a motor-driven saw with teeth on an endless chain. ▷ SAW

chain-smoker *n.* a person who smokes continually, esp. one who lights a cigarette etc. from the stub of the last one smoked. □ **chain-smoke** *v.tr. & intr.*

chain store *n.* one of a series of shops owned by one firm and selling the same sort of goods.

chair ● *n.* **1** a separate seat for one person, of various forms, usu. having a back and four legs. **2** a professorship. **3 a** a chairperson. **b** the seat or office of a chairperson (*will you take the chair?*; *I'm in the chair*). **4** *US* = ELECTRIC CHAIR. ● *v.tr.* **1** act as chairperson of or preside over (a meeting). **2** *Brit.* carry (a person) aloft in a chair or in a sitting position, in triumph. □ **take a chair** sit down. [from Greek *kathedra* 'seat']

chair-bed *n.* a chair that unfolds into a bed.

chair-car *n.* a railway carriage with chairs instead of long seats.

chairlift *n.* a series of chairs on an endless cable for carrying passengers up and down a mountain etc.

chairman *n.* (*pl.* **-men**; *fem.* also **chairwoman**, *pl.* **-women**) **1** a person chosen to preside over a meeting. **2** the permanent president of a committee, a board of directors, *Brit.* a firm, etc. **3** the master of ceremonies at an entertainment etc. □ **chairmanship** *n.*

chairperson *n.* a chairman or chairwoman (used as a neutral alternative).

chaise *n.* esp. *hist.* a horse-drawn carriage for one or two persons, esp. one with an open top and two wheels. [French]

chaise longue /shayz **long**'g/ *n.* (*pl.* **chaise longues** or **chaises longues** *pronunc.* same) **1** a sofa with a backrest at only one end. **2** a chair with a lengthened seat for reclining on; a sunbed. [French, literally 'long chair']

chalcedony /kal-**sed**-ŏ-ni/ *n.* (*pl.* **-ies**) a type of quartz occurring in several different forms, e.g. onyx, agate, etc. ▷ MINERAL. [from Greek *khalkēdōn*] □ **chalcedonic** *adj.*

chalet /**shal**-ay/ *n.* **1** a small suburban house or bungalow, esp. with an overhanging roof. **2** a small, usu. wooden, hut or house on a beach or in a holiday camp. **3** ▶ a Swiss hut or wooden cottage with overhanging eaves. [based on Latin *casa* 'hut, cottage']

CHALET:
TRADITIONAL
WOODEN
SWISS
CHALET

chalice *n.* **1** *literary* a goblet. **2** a wine cup used in the Communion service. [from Latin *calix -icis* 'cup']

chalk ● *n.* **1** a white soft earthy limestone (calcium carbonate) formed from the skeletal remains of sea creatures. **2 a** a similar substance (calcium sulphate), sometimes coloured, used for writing or drawing. **b** a piece of this (*a box of chalks*). **3** = FRENCH CHALK. ● *v.tr.* **1** rub, mark, draw, or write with chalk. **2** (foll. by *up*) **a** write or record with chalk. **b** regis-

ter (a success etc.). **c** *Brit.* charge (to an account). □ **by a long chalk** *Brit.* by far (from the use of chalk to mark the score in games). **chalk out** sketch or plan a thing to be accomplished. [from Latin *calx*]

chalkboard *n. N. Amer.* = BLACKBOARD.

chalk pit *n. Brit.* a quarry in which chalk is dug.

chalk-stripe *n.* a pattern of thin white stripes on a dark background. □ **chalk-striped** *adj.*

chalky *adj.* (**chalkier**, **chalkiest**) **1** abounding in chalk. **2** white as chalk. □ **chalkiness** *n.*

challenge ● *n.* **1 a** a summons to take part in a contest or a trial of strength etc., esp. a duel. **b** a summons to prove or justify something. **2** a demanding or difficult task. **3** *Law* an objection made to a jury member. **4** a call to respond, esp. a sentry's call for a password etc. ● *v.tr.* **1** (often foll. by *to* + infin.) **a** invite to take part in a contest, game, debate, duel, etc. **b** invite to prove or justify something. **2** dispute or deny (a statement etc.). **3 a** stretch, stimulate (*challenges him to produce his best*). **b** (as **challenging** *adj.*) demanding; stimulatingly difficult. **4** (of a sentry) call to respond. **5** *Law* object to (a jury member, evidence, etc.). [based on Latin *calumnia* 'trickery'] □ **challengeable** *adj.* **challenger** *n.* **challengingly** *adv.*

challenged *adj.* (in *comb.*) *euphem.* or *joc.* lacking a physical or mental attribute (*intellectually challenged*).

challis *n.* a lightweight soft clothing fabric.

chalybeate /kă-**lib**-i-ăt/ *adj.* (of mineral water etc.) impregnated with iron salts. [based on Greek *khalups -ubos* 'steel']

chamber *n.* **1 a** a hall used by a legislative or judicial body. **b** the body that meets in it. **2** (in *pl.*) *Law* **a** *Brit.* rooms used by a barrister or group of barristers, esp. in the Inns of Court. **b** a judge's room used for official proceedings not held in open court. **3** *poet.* or *archaic* a room, esp. a bedroom. **4** a large underground cavity; a cave. **5** (*attrib.*) *Mus.* of or for a small group of instruments (*chamber orchestra*; *chamber music*). **6** an enclosed space in machinery etc. (esp. the part of a gun bore that contains the charge). [from Latin *camera*] □ **chambered** *adj.*

chamberlain *n.* an officer managing the household of a sovereign or a great noble. [Middle English in sense 'servant in a bedchamber'] □ **chamberlainship** *n.*

chambermaid *n.* **1** a housemaid at a hotel etc. **2** *N. Amer.* a housemaid.

Chamber of Commerce *n.* an association to promote local commercial interests.

chamber pot *n.* a receptacle for urine etc., used in a bedroom.

chambray /**sham**-bray/ *n.* a linen-finished gingham cloth with a white weft and a coloured warp. [from *Cambrai* (see CAMBRIC)]

chambré *adj.* (of red wine) brought to room temperature. [French]

chameleon /kă-**mee**-li-ŏn/ *n.* **1** ▶ any of a family of small lizards having long tongues, protruding eyes, and the power of changing colour. ▷ LIZARD. **2** a variable or inconstant person. [from Greek *khamaileōn*, literally 'dwarf lion'] □ **chameleonic** *adj.*

chamfer ● *v.tr.* bevel symmetrically (a right-angled edge or corner). ● *n.* a bevelled surface at an edge or corner. [based on French *chant* 'edge']

CHAMELEON:
MADAGASCAN CHAMELEON
(*Chamaeleo ousteleti*)

chamois n. **1** /**sham**-wah/ (pl. same) ► an agile goat-antelope, *Rupicapra rupicapra*, native to the mountains of Europe and Asia. **2** /**sham**-i / (pl. same) (in full **chamois leather**) **a** a soft pliable leather from sheep, goats, deer, etc. **b** a piece of this for polishing etc. [French]

chamomile var. of CAMOMILE.

CHAMOIS
(*Rupicapra rupicapra*)

champ[1] ● v. **1** tr. & intr. munch or chew noisily. **2** tr. (of a horse etc.) work (the bit) noisily between the teeth. **3** intr. fret with impatience (*is champing to be away*). ● n. a chewing noise or motion. □ **champ at the bit** be restlessly impatient.

champ[2] n. colloq. a champion.

champagne /sham-**payn**/ n. **1 a** a white sparkling wine from Champagne. **b** (loosely) a similar wine from elsewhere. **2** a pale cream or straw colour. [from *Champagne*, former province in E. France where it is produced]

■ **Usage** The use of *champagne* in sense 1b is, strictly speaking, incorrect.

champion ● n. **1** (often *attrib.*) a person (esp. in a sport or game), an animal, plant, etc., that has defeated or surpassed all rivals in a competition etc. **2** a person who fights or argues for a cause or on behalf of another person. ● v.tr. support the cause of, defend, argue in favour of. ● adj. *Brit. colloq.* or *dial.* first-class, splendid. ● adv. *Brit. colloq.* or *dial.* splendidly, well. [based on Latin *campus* 'field, military exercise ground']

championship n. **1** (often in *pl.*) a contest for the position of champion in a sport etc. **2** the position of champion over all rivals. **3** the advocacy or defence of a cause etc.

chance ● n. **1 a** a possibility (*just a chance we will catch the train*). **b** (often in *pl.*) probability (*the chances are against it*). **2** a risk (*have to take a chance*). **3 a** an accidental occurrence (*just a chance that they met*). **b** the absence of design or discoverable cause (*here merely because of chance*). **4** an opportunity (*didn't have a chance to speak to him*). **5** (often **Chance**) the course of events regarded as a power; fate. ● adj. fortuitous, accidental (*a chance meeting*). ● v. **1** tr. colloq. risk (*we'll chance it and go*). **2** intr. (often foll. by *that* + clause, or *to* + infin.) happen without intention (*it chanced that I found it; I chanced to find it*). □ **by any chance** by chance; perhaps. **by chance** without design; unintentionally. **chance one's arm** *Brit.* make an attempt though unlikely to succeed. **chance on** (or **upon**) happen to find, meet, etc. **stand a chance** (usu. with *neg.* or *interrog.*) have a prospect of success etc. **take a chance** (or **chances**) behave riskily; risk failure. **take a** (or **one's**) **chance on** (or **with**) consent to take the consequences of; trust to luck. [from Old French *chéance*]

chancel n. the part of a church near the altar. [from Latin *cancelli* 'lattice']

chancellery n. (pl. **-ies**) **1 a** the position, office, department, etc., of a chancellor. **b** the official residence of a chancellor. **2** *US* an office attached to an embassy or consulate.

chancellor n. **1** a state or legal official of various kinds. **2** (**Chancellor**) **a** the head of the government in some European countries. **b** = CHANCELLOR OF THE EXCHEQUER. **3** esp. *Brit.* the non-resident honorary head of a university. [from Late Latin *cancellarius* 'porter, secretary'] □ **chancellorship** n.

Chancellor of the Exchequer n. the finance minister of the United Kingdom.

chancery n. (pl. **-ies**) **1** (**Chancery**) *Law* the Lord Chancellor's court, a division of the High Court of Justice. **2** an office attached to an embassy or consulate. [Middle English]

chancre /**shank**-er/ n. a painless ulcer developing in venereal disease etc. [from Latin *cancer* 'crab']

chancy adj. (**chancier**, **chanciest**) subject to chance; uncertain; risky. □ **chancily** adv. **chanciness** n.

chandelier /shan-dĕ-**leer**/ n. an ornamental branched hanging support for several candles or electric light bulbs. [French]

chandler n. a dealer in candles, oil, soap, paint, groceries, etc. [from Old French *chandelier* 'candle maker or seller']

chandlery n. goods sold by a chandler.

change ● n. **1** the act or an instance of making or becoming different. **2 a** money given in exchange for money in larger units or a different currency. **b** money returned as the balance of that given in payment. **c** = SMALL CHANGE 1. **3 a** the substitution of one thing for another; an exchange (*change of scene*). **b** a set of clothes etc. put on in place of another. **4** (in full **change of life**) colloq. the menopause. **5** (usu. in *pl.*) any of the different orders in which a peal of bells can be rung. ● v. **1** tr. & intr. undergo, show, or subject to change; make or become different (*the wig changed his appearance; changed from an introvert into an extrovert*). **2** tr. **a** take or use another instead of; go from one to another (*change one's socks; changed trains*). **b** (usu. foll. by *for*) give up or get rid of in exchange (*changed the car for a van*). **3** tr. **a** give or get change in smaller denominations for (*can you change a ten-pound note?*). **b** (foll. by *for*) exchange (a sum of money) for (*changed his dollars for pounds*). **4** tr. & intr. put fresh clothes or coverings on (*changed into something loose*). **5** tr. (often foll. by *with*) give and receive, exchange (*changed places with him; we changed places*). **6** intr. change trains etc. (*changed at Crewe*). □ **change down** *Brit.* engage a lower gear in a vehicle. **change gear** engage a different gear in a vehicle. **change hands** pass to a different owner. **change one's mind** adopt a different opinion or plan. **change of air** a different climate; variety. **change over** change from one system or situation to another. **change one's tune 1** voice a different opinion from that expressed previously. **2** change one's style of language or manner, esp. from an insolent to a respectful tone. **change up** *Brit.* engage a higher gear in a vehicle. **get no change out of** *Brit. colloq.* **1** fail to get information from. **2** fail to get the better of (in business etc.). **ring the changes (on)** vary the ways of expressing, arranging, or doing something. [from Latin *cambire* 'to barter'] □ **changeful** adj. **changer** n.

changeable adj. **1** irregular, inconstant. **2** that can change or be changed. □ **changeability** n. **changeably** adv.

changeless adj. unchanging. □ **changelessly** adv. **changelessness** n.

changeling n. a child believed to have been substituted for another by stealth, esp. by fairies.

change of heart n. a conversion to a different view.

change of life see CHANGE n. 4.

changeover n. a change from one system or situation to another.

change-ringing n. the ringing of a set of bells in a constantly varying order. □ **change-ringer** n.

channel ● n. **1 a** a length of water wider than a strait, joining two larger areas, esp. seas. **b** (**the Channel**) the English Channel between Britain and France. **2** a medium of communication; an agency for conveying information (*through the usual channels*). **3** *Broadcasting* **a** a band of frequencies used in radio and television transmission. **b** a station using this. **4** the course in which anything moves; a direction. **5** the navigable part of a waterway. **6** a tubular passage for liquid. **7** a groove or a flute, esp. in a column. ● v.tr. (**channelled**, **channelling**; *US* **channeled**, **channeling**) **1** guide, direct

(*channelled them through customs*). **2** form channels in; groove. [from Latin *canalis* 'canal'] □ **channelize** v.tr. (also **-ise**).

channel-surf v.intr. change frequently from one television channel to another, by means of a remote control.

chant ● n. **1** a spoken sing-song phrase. **2** *Mus.* **a** a short musical passage in two or more phrases used for singing unmetrical words, e.g. psalms, canticles. **b** the psalm or canticle so sung. ● v.tr. & intr. **1** talk or repeat monotonously. **2** sing or intone (a psalm etc.). [from Latin *cantare* 'to sing']

chanter n. *Mus.* the melody-pipe, with finger-holes, of a bagpipe. ▷ BAGPIPE

chanterelle /chahn-tĕ-**rel**/ n. ◄ an edible fungus, *Cantharellus cibarius*, with a yellow funnel-shaped cap and a smell of apricots. [based on Greek *kantharos*, a kind of drinking vessel]

chanteuse /shahn-**terz**/ n. a female singer of popular songs. [French]

chantry n. (pl. **-ies**) **1** an endowment for a priest or priests to celebrate masses for the founder's soul. **2** the priests, chapel, altar, etc., so endowed. [from Old French *chanterie*]

CHANTERELLE:
COMMON
CHANTERELLE
(*Cantharellus cibarius*)

chanty var. of SHANTY[2].

Chanukkah var. of HANUKKAH.

chaos n. **1** utter confusion. **2** the formless matter supposed to have existed before the creation of the universe. [from Greek *khaos*] □ **chaotic** adj. **chaotically** adv.

chap[1] ● v. (**chapped**, **chapping**) **1** intr. (esp. of the skin) crack in fissures, esp. because of exposure and dryness. **2** tr. (of the wind, cold, etc.) cause to chap. ● n. (usu. in *pl.*) a crack in the skin. [Middle English]

chap[2] n. esp. *Brit. colloq.* a man; a boy; a fellow. [abbreviation of CHAPMAN]

chaparajos /shap-ă-**ray**-hohss/ n.pl. *N. Amer.* ▼ a cowboy's leather protection for the front of the legs. [from Mexican Spanish *chaparreras*]

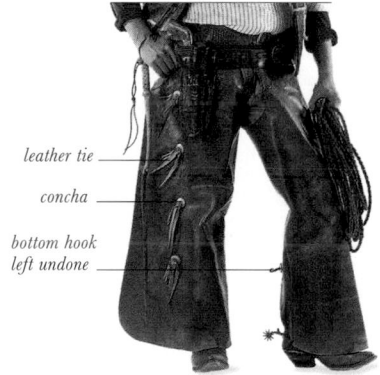

leather tie
concha
bottom hook left undone

CHAPARAJOS: TEXAN BATWING CHAPARAJOS

chaparral /shap-ă-**ral**/ n. *N. Amer.* dense tangled brushwood; undergrowth. [Spanish, from *chaparra* 'dwarf evergreen oak']

chapatti n. (also **chapati**, **chupatty**) (pl. **-is** or **chupatties**) (in Indian cookery) a flat thin cake of unleavened wholemeal bread. [from Hindi *capāti*]

chapel ● n. **1 a** a place for private Christian worship in a large church or esp. a cathedral (*Lady chapel*). ▷ CATHEDRAL. **b** a place of Christian worship attached to a private house or institution. **2** *Brit.* **a** a place of worship for Nonconformist bodies. **b** a chapel service. **c** attendance at a chapel. **3** a room or building for funeral services. **4** *Brit. Printing* the members or branch of a printers' trade union at a specific place of work. ● predic.adj. *Brit. colloq.* belonging to or

C

C

regularly attending a Nonconformist chapel. [from medieval Latin *cappella* 'little cloak': the first chapel held St Martin's sacred cloak]

chapel of rest *n. Brit.* an undertaker's mortuary.

chaperone /**shap**-ĕ-rohn/ (also **chaperon**) ● *n.* **1** a person, esp. an older woman, who ensures propriety by accompanying a young unmarried woman on social occasions. **2** a person who takes charge of esp. young people in public. ● *v.tr.* act as a chaperone to. [from French *chaperon* 'hood', regarded as giving protection] □ **chaperonage** *n.*

chap-fallen *adj.* dispirited, dejected. [based on *chap* 'lower jaw']

chaplain *n.* a member of the clergy attached to an institution, ship, regiment, etc. [from medieval Latin *cappellanus*, originally custodian of the cloak of St Martin (see CHAPEL)] □ **chaplaincy** *n.* (*pl.* -ies)

chaplet *n.* a garland or circlet for the head. [based on Late Latin *cappa* 'cap'] □ **chapleted** *adj.*

chapman *n.* (*pl.* -men) *Brit. hist.* a pedlar. [Old English]

chappal *n.* an Indian sandal, usu. of leather. [Hindi]

chappie *n. Brit. colloq.* = CHAP[2].

chaps *n.* = CHAPARAJOS.

chapter *n.* **1** a main division of a book. **2** a period of time (in a person's life, a nation's history, etc.). **3** a series or sequence (*a chapter of misfortunes*). **4 a** the canons of a cathedral or other religious community or knightly order. **b** a meeting of these. **5** *N. Amer.* a local branch of a society. □ **chapter and verse** an exact reference or authority. [from Latin *capitulum* 'little head']

chapter house *n.* **1** a building used for the meetings of a chapter. ▷ MONASTERY. **2** *US* the place where a college fraternity or sorority meets.

char[1] *v.tr. & intr.* (**charred**, **charring**) **1** make or become black by burning; scorch. **2** burn or be burnt to charcoal.

char[2] *Brit. colloq.* ● *n.* = CHARWOMAN. ● *v.intr.* (**charred**, **charring**) work as a charwoman. [Old English *cerr* 'a turn']

char[3] *n.* (also **cha**) *Brit. colloq.* tea. [from Chinese *cha*]

char[4] *n.* (also **charr**) (*pl.* same) ▼ any small troutlike fish of the genus *Salvelinus*. [17th-century coinage]

CHAR: LAKE CHAR
(*Salvelinus namaycush*)

charabanc /**sha**-ră-bang/ *n. Brit. hist.* ▼ an early form of motor coach. [from French *char à bancs* 'carriage with seats']

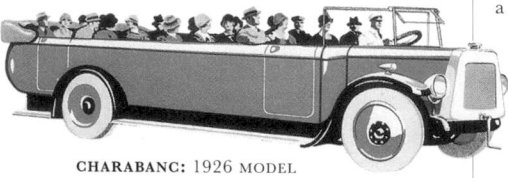

CHARABANC: 1926 MODEL

character *n.* **1** the collective qualities or characteristics, esp. mental and moral, that distinguish a person or thing. **2 a** moral strength (*has a weak character*). **b** reputation, esp. good reputation. **3** a person in a novel, play, etc. **4** *colloq.* a person, esp. an eccentric or outstanding individual (*he's a real character*). **5 a** a printed or written letter, symbol, or distinctive mark (*Chinese characters*). **b** *Computing* any of a group of symbols representing a letter etc.

□ **in** (or **out of**) **character** consistent (or inconsistent) with a person's character. [from Greek *kharaktēr* 'instrument for marking'] □ **characterful** *adj.* **characterfully** *adv.* **characterless** *adj.*

characteristic ● *adj.* typical, distinctive (*with characteristic expertise*). ● *n.* a characteristic feature or quality. □ **characteristically** *adv.*

characterize *v.tr.* (also **-ise**) **1** describe the character of. **2** be characteristic of. **3** impart character to. □ **characterization** *n.*

charade /shă-**rahd**/ *n.* **1** (usu. in *pl.*; treated as *sing.*) a game of guessing a word from a written or acted clue given for each syllable and for the whole. **2** an absurd pretence. [from modern Provençal *charrado* 'conversation']

charbroil *v.tr.* grill (meat etc.) on a rack over charcoal. [blend of CHARCOAL and BROIL]

charcoal ● *n.* **1 a** an amorphous form of carbon consisting of a porous black residue from wood, bones, etc., heated in the absence of air. **b** a piece of this used for drawing. **2** a drawing in charcoal. **3** (in full **charcoal grey**) a dark grey colour. ● *adj.* (in full **charcoal grey**; hyphenated when *attrib.*) dark grey. [Middle English, based on earlier *coal* 'charcoal']

CHARCOAL
STICK AND MARK

charcuterie /shar-**koo**-tĕ-ri/ *n.* cold cooked meats. [French]

chard *n.* (in full **Swiss chard**) a kind of beet, *Beta vulgaris*, with edible broad white leaf-stalks and green blades. ▷ VEGETABLE. [from French *carde*]

charge ● *v.* **1** *tr.* **a** ask (an amount) as a price (*charges £5 a ticket*). **b** ask (a person) for an amount as a price (*you forgot to charge me*). **2** *tr.* **a** (foll. by *to*, *up to*) debit the cost of to (a person or account). **b** debit (a person or an account) (*bought a new car and charged the company*). **3** *tr.* **a** (often foll. by *with*) accuse (of an offence) (*charged him with theft*). **b** (foll. by *that* + clause) make an accusation that. **4** *tr.* (foll. by *to* + infin.) instruct or urge. **5** *tr.* (foll. by *with*) entrust with. **6 a** *intr.* make a rushing attack; rush headlong. **b** *tr.* make a rushing attack on; throw oneself against. **7** (often foll. by *up*) **a** *tr.* give an electric charge to (a body); store energy in (a battery etc.). **b** *intr.* (of a battery etc.) receive and store energy. **8** *tr.* (often foll. by *with*) load or fill (a vessel, gun, etc.) to the full or proper extent. **9** *tr.* (usu. as **charged** *adj.*) (usu. foll. by *with*) pervaded (with strong feelings etc.) (*atmosphere charged with emotion; a charged atmosphere*). ● *n.* **1** a price asked for goods or services. **2** an accusation, esp. against a prisoner brought to trial. **3 a** a task, duty, or commission. **b** care, custody, responsible possession. **c** a person or thing entrusted. **4** an impetuous rush or attack, esp. in a battle. **5** the appropriate amount of material to be put into a receptacle, mechanism, etc. at one time, esp. of explosive for a gun. **6 a** a property of matter causing electrical phenomena. **b** the quantity of this carried by a body. **c** energy stored chemically for conversion into electricity. ▷ BATTERY. **d** the process of charging a battery. **7** *Heraldry* a device; a bearing. □ **free of charge** free, without charge. **in charge** having command. **put a person on a charge** *Brit.* charge a person with a specified offence. **return to the charge** begin again, esp. in argument. **take charge** (often foll. by *of*) assume control or direction. [from Late Latin *car(ri)care* 'to load'] □ **chargeable** *adj.*

charge account *n. N. Amer.* a credit account at a shop etc.

charge card *n.* a credit card for which the account must be paid in full when a statement is issued.

chargé d'affaires /shar-zhay da-**fair**/ *n.* (also **chargé**) (*pl.* **chargés** *pronunc.* same) **1** an ambassador's deputy. **2** an envoy to a minor country.

chargehand *n. Brit.* a worker, ranking below a foreman, in charge of others on a particular job.

charge nurse *n. Brit.* a nurse in charge of a ward.

charger[1] *n.* **1 a** a cavalry horse. **b** *poet.* any horse. **2** a device for charging a battery. **3** a person or thing that charges.

charger[2] *n. archaic* a large flat dish. [from Anglo-French *chargeour*]

chariot *n. hist.* ▼ a two-wheeled vehicle drawn by horses, used in ancient warfare and racing. [from Old French *char* 'car']

CHARIOT: REPLICA OF AN ANCIENT ROMAN CHARIOT
platform
shaft
spoked wheel

charioteer *n.* a chariot driver.

charisma /kă-**riz**-mă/ *n.* (*pl.* **charismata**) the ability to inspire followers with devotion and enthusiasm. [from Greek *kharisma* 'gift of grace']

charismatic /ka-riz-**mat**-ik/ ● *adj.* **1** having charisma; inspiring enthusiasm. **2** (of Christian worship) characterized by spontaneity, ecstatic utterances, etc. ● *n.* a person who claims divine inspiration; an adherent of charismatic worship. □ **charismatically** *adv.*

charitable *adj.* **1** generous in giving to those in need. **2** of, relating to, or connected with a charity or charities. **3** apt to judge persons, acts, and motives favourably. □ **charitableness** *n.* **charitably** *adv.*

charity *n.* (*pl.* -ies) **1 a** giving voluntarily to those in need; alms-giving. **b** the help, esp. money, so given. **2** an institution or organization for helping those in need. **3 a** kindness, benevolence. **b** tolerance in judging others. **c** love of one's fellows. [from Latin *caritas*]

charlady *n.* (*pl.* -ies) *Brit.* = CHARWOMAN.

charlatan /**shar**-lă-tăn/ *n.* a person falsely claiming a special knowledge or skill. [from Italian *ciarlatano* 'babbler'] □ **charlatanism** *n.* **charlatanry** *n.*

charleston (also **Charleston**) ● *n.* a lively dance of the 1920s with side-kicks from the knee. ● *v.intr.* dance the charleston. [named after *Charleston*, a city in S. Carolina, US]

charlotte /**shar**-lŏt/ *n.* a pudding made of stewed fruit with a casing or covering of bread, sponge cake, biscuits, or breadcrumbs (*apple charlotte*). [French]

charm ● *n.* **1 a** the power or quality of giving delight, arousing admiration, or influencing. **b** (usu. in *pl.*) an attractive or enticing quality. **2** a trinket on a bracelet etc. **3** an object, act, or word(s) supposedly having occult or magic power; a spell. **4** *Physics* a property of matter manifested by certain quarks. ● *v.tr.* **1** delight, captivate. **2** influence or protect as if by magic (*leads a charmed life*). **3** cast a spell on, bewitch. □ **like a charm** perfectly, wonderfully. [based on Latin *carmen* 'song'] □ **charmer** *n.*

charming *adj.* **1** delightful, attractive, pleasing. **2** (often as *int.*) *iron.* expressing displeasure or disapproval. □ **charmingly** *adv.*

charmless *adj.* lacking charm; unattractive; ungracious. □ **charmlessly** *adv.* **charmlessness** *n.*

charm offensive *n.* the deliberate use of charm or cooperation in order to achieve a (usu. political) goal.

charnel house *n.* a house or vault in which dead bodies or bones are piled. [from Old French *charnel* 'burying place']

charpoy *n. Anglo-Ind.* a light bedstead. [from Hindi *chārpāi*]

charr var. of CHAR[4].

chart ● *n.* **1** a geographical map or plan, esp. for navigation by sea or air. **2** a sheet of information in the form of a table, graph, or diagram. **3** (usu. in *pl.*) a listing of the currently most popular records, esp. pop singles. ● *v.tr.* make a chart of, map. [from Latin *charta* 'card']

chartbuster *n. colloq.* a best-selling popular song etc.

charter ● *n.* **1 a** a written grant of rights, by the sovereign or legislature, esp. the creation of a borough, company, university, etc. **b** a written constitution or description of an organization's functions etc. **2** a contract to hire an aircraft, ship, etc., for a special purpose. ● *v.tr.* **1** grant a charter to. **2** hire (an aircraft, ship, etc.). [from Latin *chartula* 'little card'] □ **charterer** *n.*

chartered *adj. Brit.* (of an accountant, engineer, librarian, etc.) qualified as a member of a professional body that has a royal charter.

charter flight *n.* a flight by a chartered aircraft.

Chartism *n. hist.* the principles of the UK parliamentary reform movement of 1837–48. [name taken from the manifesto 'People's Charter': based on Latin *charta* 'charter'] □ **Chartist** *n.*

chartreuse /shah-**trerz**/ ● *n.* **1** a pale green or pale yellow liqueur of brandy and aromatic herbs etc. **2** either colour of this. ● *adj.* pale green or pale yellow. [from La Grande *Chartreuse*, Carthusian monastery near Grenoble]

chart-topping *attrib.adj.* occupying the first place in a chart of popular records etc. □ **chart-topper** *n.*

charwoman *n.* (*pl.* **-women**) *Brit.* a woman employed as a cleaner in houses or offices.

chary *adj.* (**charier**, **chariest**) **1** cautious, wary. **2** sparing; ungenerous (*chary of giving praise*). **3** shy. [Old English, related to CARE] □ **charily** *adv.*

Charybdis see SCYLLA AND CHARYBDIS.

chase[1] ● *v.* **1** *tr.* pursue in order to catch. **2** *tr.* (foll. by *from, out of, to,* etc.) drive. **3** *intr.* **a** (foll. by *after*) hurry in pursuit of (a person). **b** (foll. by *round*) *colloq.* act or move about hurriedly. **4** *tr.* (usu. foll. by *up*) *Brit. colloq.* pursue (overdue work, payment, etc. or the person responsible for it). **5** *tr. colloq.* **a** try to attain. **b** court persistently and openly. ● *n.* **1** pursuit. **2** *Brit.* unenclosed hunting land. **3** (prec. by *the*) hunting, esp. as a sport. [based on Latin *capere* 'to take']

chase[2] *v.tr.* emboss or engrave (metal).

chaser *n.* **1** a person or thing that chases. **2** a horse for steeplechasing. **3** *colloq.* a drink taken after another of a different kind, e.g. spirits after beer.

chasm *n.* **1** a deep fissure or opening in the Earth, rock, etc. **2** a wide difference of feeling, interests, etc. [from Greek *khasma*] □ **chasmic** *adj.*

chassé /**shass**-ay/ ● *n.* a gliding step in dancing. ● *v.intr.* (**chasséd; chasséing**) make this step. [French, literally 'chased']

chassis /**shas**-i/ *n.* (*pl.* same) the base frame of a motor vehicle, carriage, etc. [based on Latin *capsa* 'case']

chaste *adj.* **1** abstaining from extramarital, or from all, sexual intercourse. **2** (of behaviour, speech, etc.) pure, virtuous, decent. [from Latin *castus*] □ **chastely** *adv.* **chasteness** *n.*

chasten *v.tr.* **1** (esp. as **chastening, chastened** *adjs.*) subdue, restrain. **2** discipline, punish. **3** moderate. [based on Latin *castigare* 'to castigate'] □ **chastener** *n.*

chastise *v.tr.* **1** rebuke or reprimand severely. **2** punish, esp. by beating. [related to CHASTEN] □ **chastisement** *n.* **chastiser** *n.*

chastity *n.* **1** being chaste. **2** sexual abstinence; virginity. [from Latin *castitas*]

chastity belt *n. hist.* a woman's garment designed to prevent her from having sexual intercourse.

chasuble *n.* a loose sleeveless usu. ornate outer vestment worn by a priest. ▷ VESTMENT. [from Latin *casula* 'hooded cloak, little cottage']

chat ● *v.intr.* (**chatted, chatting**) talk in a light familiar way. ● *n.* **1** informal conversation or talk. **2** an instance of this. □ **chat up** *colloq.* chat to, esp. flirtatiously or with an ulterior motive. [Middle English: shortening of CHATTER]

CHATEAU

During the 15th century, French society became less turbulent, allowing noblemen to design homes more for comfort and display than fortification. They converted, or had built, chateaux with large windows and luxurious state rooms. Defensive features, such as moats, were often maintained, but these served only as decoration.

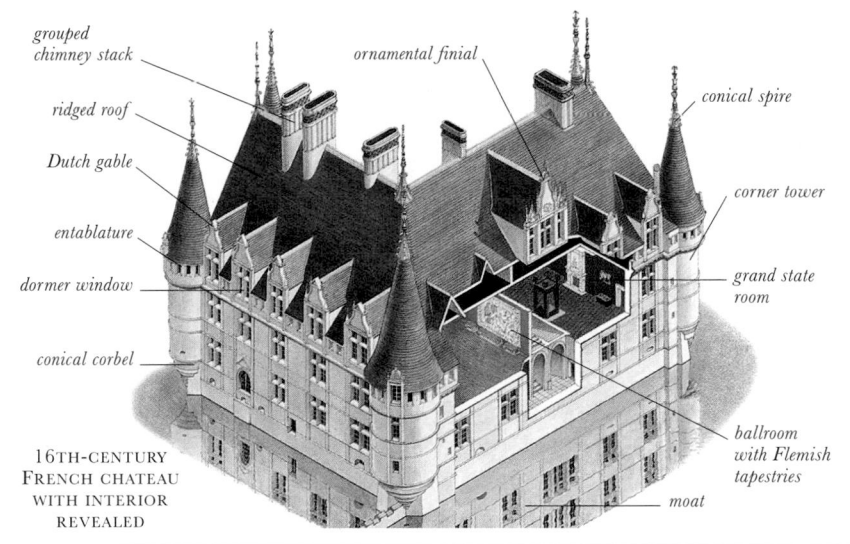

grouped chimney stack · ridged roof · Dutch gable · entablature · dormer window · conical corbel · ornamental finial · conical spire · corner tower · grand state room · ballroom with Flemish tapestries · moat

16TH-CENTURY FRENCH CHATEAU WITH INTERIOR REVEALED

chateau /**shat**-oh/ *n.* (also **château**) (*pl.* **-teaux** *pronunc.* same or /-ohz/) ▲ a large French country house or castle. [from Old French *chastel* 'castle']

chatelaine /**shat**-ĕ-layn/ *n.* **1** the mistress of a large house. **2** *hist.* a set of short chains attached to a woman's belt, for carrying keys etc. [based on medieval Latin *castellanus* 'lord of a castle']

chatline *n.* a telephone service which sets up conference calls esp. among young people.

chat show *n. Brit.* a television or radio programme in which celebrities are interviewed informally.

chattel *n.* (usu. in *pl.*) **1** *Law* any property other than freehold land, including tangible goods (**chattels personal**) and leasehold interests (**chattels real**). **2** (in general use) a personal possession. [from Old French *chatel*, related to CATTLE]

chatter ● *v.intr.* **1** talk quickly, incessantly, trivially, or indiscreetly. **2** (of a bird, monkey, etc.) emit short quick sounds. **3** (of the teeth) click repeatedly together (usu. from cold). **4** (of a tool) clatter from vibration. ● *n.* chattering talk or sounds. [Middle English] □ **chatterer** *n.* **chattery** *adj.*

chatterbox *n.* a talkative person.

chatty *adj.* (**chattier, chattiest**) **1** fond of chatting; talkative. **2** resembling chat; informal and lively (*a chatty letter*). □ **chattily** *adv.* **chattiness** *n.*

chauffeur /**shoh**-fer/ ● *n.* (*fem.* **chauffeuse**) a person employed to drive a motor car. ● *v.tr.* drive (a car or a passenger) as a chauffeur. [French, literally 'stoker']

chauvinism /**shoh**-vin-izm/ *n.* **1** exaggerated or aggressive patriotism. **2** excessive or prejudiced loyalty to one's cause or group or sex (*male chauvinism*). [named after N. *Chauvin*, Napoleonic veteran popularized in the Cogniards' *Cocarde Tricolore* (1831)]

chauvinist /**shoh**-vin-ist/ *n.* **1** a person exhibiting chauvinism. **2** (in full **male chauvinist**) a man who is prejudiced against or inconsiderate of women. □ **chauvinistic** *adj.* **chauvinistically** *adv.*

Ch.B. *abbr.* Bachelor of Surgery. [Latin *Chirurgiae Baccalaureus*]

cheap ● *adj.* **1** low in price; worth more than its cost. **2** charging low prices. **3** of poor quality; inferior (*cheap housing*). **4 a** costing little or acquired by discreditable means (*cheap popularity*). **b** contemptible; despicable (*a cheap criminal*). **5** *N. Amer. colloq.* stingy. ● *adv.* cheaply (*got it cheap*). □ **on the cheap** cheaply. [Old English *cēap* 'barter'] □ **cheapish** *adj.* **cheaply** *adv.* **cheapness** *n.*

cheapen *v.tr. & intr.* make or become cheap or cheaper; depreciate, degrade.

cheapjack ● *n.* a seller of inferior goods at low prices. ● *adj.* inferior, shoddy.

cheapo *adj.* (usu. *attrib.*) *slang* cheap.

cheapskate *n. colloq.* a stingy or parsimonious person; a miser [from *cheap* + *skate* 'a worn-out horse; a mean or dishonest person']

cheat ● *v.* **1** *tr.* **a** (often foll. by *into, out of*) deceive or trick (*cheated into parting with his savings*). **b** (foll. by *of*) deprive of (*cheated of a chance to reply*). **2** *intr.* gain unfair advantage by deception or breaking rules. ● *n.* **1** a person who cheats. **2** a trick, fraud, or deception. □ **cheat on** *colloq.* be sexually unfaithful to. [Middle English, from *achete* variant of ESCHEAT] □ **cheater** *n.*

Chechen ● *n.* (*pl.* **-s** or same) a member of a Muslim Caucasian people inhabiting Chechnya, an autonomous republic in SE Russia. ● *adj.* of or relating to this people. [from obsolete Russian *chechen*]

check[1] ● *v.* **1** *tr.* (also *absol.*) **a** examine the accuracy, quality, or condition of. **b** (often foll. by *that* + clause) make sure; verify; establish to one's satisfaction. **2** *tr.* **a** stop or slow the motion of; curb, restrain. **b** *colloq.* find fault with; rebuke. **3** *tr. Chess* move a piece into a position that directly threatens (the opposing king). **4** *intr. US* agree or correspond when compared. **5** *tr. US* mark with a tick etc. **6** *tr. N. Amer.* deposit (luggage etc.) for storage or dispatch. **7** *intr.* pause, esp. (of hounds) to ensure or regain scent. ● *n.* **1** a means or act of examining for accuracy, quality, satisfactory condition, etc. **2 a** a stopping or slowing of motion; a restraint on action. **b** a rebuff or rebuke. **c** a person or thing that restrains. **3** *Chess* **a** the exposure of a king to direct attack. **b** (as *int.*) an announcement of this. **4** *US* a bill in a restaurant. **5** (in full **baggage** or **luggage check**) esp. *N. Amer.* a token of identification for left luggage etc. ● *int. N. Amer. colloq.* expressing assent or agreement. □ **check in 1** arrive or

C

CHEESE

Cheese is made by curdling milk or cream with rennet or lactic acid. The solid curds are then removed, drained, and put into moulds; sometimes a bacterial culture is added. The nature of the finished product is greatly influenced by the duration of the ripening period, during which the characteristic flavour and texture develop, and also by the type of milk or cream used – whether wholefat or skimmed, cow's milk or goat's milk, etc. Blue-veined cheeses derive their colour from a particular mould.

EXAMPLES OF HARD CHEESES

JARLSBERG PARMESAN GRUYÈRE EMMENTAL TRADITIONAL CHEDDAR DOUBLE GLOUCESTER

EXAMPLES OF SOFT CHEESES

MONTEREY JACK BRIE LIVAROT WISCONSIN BRICK CAMEMBERT

EXAMPLES OF BLUE CHEESES

ROQUEFORT STILTON DANISH BLUE GORGONZOLA BRESSE BLEU

EXAMPLES OF GOAT'S OR SHEEP'S CHEESES

FETA BUCHERON BUCHETTE D'ANJOU CROTTIN DE CHAVIGNOL PYRENEES

register at a hotel, airport, etc. **2** record the arrival of. **check into** register one's arrival at (a hotel etc.). **check off** mark on a list etc. as having been examined or dealt with. **check on** examine carefully or in detail; ascertain the truth about; keep a watch on (a person, work done, etc.). **check out 1** (often foll. by *of*) leave a hotel etc. with due formalities. **2** *colloq.* investigate; examine for authenticity or suitability. **check over** examine for errors. **check through** inspect; verify successive items of. **check up** ascertain, verify, make sure. **check up on** = *check on.* **in check** under control, restrained. [from Old French *eschequier* 'to play chess, give check to'] □ **checkable** *adj.*

check² *n.* **1** a pattern of small squares. **2** fabric having this pattern. **3** (*attrib.*) so patterned. [Middle English]

check³ *US* var. of CHEQUE.

checked *adj.* having a check pattern.

checker¹ *n.* **1** a person or thing that verifies or examines, esp. in a factory etc. **2** *US* a cashier in a supermarket etc.

checker² *n.* **1** var. of CHEQUER. **2** *N. Amer.* (in *pl.*; usu. treated as *sing.*) the game of draughts.

checkerboard *US* var. of CHEQUERBOARD.

check-in *n.* **1** an act of checking in. **2** a place for checking in, esp. at an airport.

checking account *n.* *US* a current account at a bank.

checklist *n.* a list for reference and verification.

checkmate ● *n.* **1** *Chess* **a** a check from which a king cannot escape. **b** (as *int.*) an announcement of this. **2** a final defeat or deadlock. ● *v.tr.* **1** *Chess* put into checkmate. **2** defeat; frustrate. [from Persian *šāh māt* 'the king is dead']

checkout *n.* **1** an act of checking out. **2** a point at which goods are paid for in a supermarket etc.

checkpoint *n.* a place, esp. a barrier or manned entrance, where documents, vehicles, etc., are inspected.

check-up *n.* a thorough (esp. medical) examination.

Cheddar *n.* a kind of firm smooth yellow, white, or orange cheese originally made in Cheddar. ▷ CHEESE. [from *Cheddar*, a village in SW England]

cheek ● *n.* **1 a** the side of the face below the eye. **b** the side wall of the mouth. **2** impertinence; cool confidence (*had the cheek to ask for more*). **3** *slang* either

buttock. ● *v.tr.* speak impertinently to. □ **cheek by jowl** close together; intimate. **turn the other cheek** accept attack etc. meekly; refuse to retaliate. [Old English]

cheekbone *n.* the bone below the eye; the zygomatic bone.

cheeky *adj.* (**cheekier**, **cheekiest**) impertinent, impudent. □ **cheekily** *adv.* **cheekiness** *n.*

cheep ● *n.* the shrill cry of a young bird. ● *v.intr.* make such a cry.

cheer ● *n.* **1** a shout of encouragement or applause. **2** mood, disposition (*full of good cheer*). **3** (in *pl.*; *int.*) *colloq.* **a** expressing good wishes before drinking or *Brit.* before parting. **b** esp. *Brit.* expressing gratitude. ● *v.* **1** *tr.* **a** applaud with shouts. **b** (usu. foll. by *on*) urge or encourage with shouts. **2** *intr.* shout for joy. **3** *tr.* gladden; comfort. □ **cheer up** make or become less depressed. [Middle English in sense 'face, mood': from Greek *kara* 'head']

cheerful *adj.* **1** in good spirits, noticeably happy. **2** bright, pleasant (*a cheerful room*). **3** willing, not reluctant. □ **cheerfully** *adv.* **cheerfulness** *n.*

cheerio *int. Brit. colloq.* expressing good wishes on parting or *archaic* before drinking.

cheerleader *n.* a person who leads cheers of applause etc.

cheerless *adj.* gloomy, dreary, miserable. □ **cheerlessly** *adv.* **cheerlessness** *n.*

cheery *adj.* (**cheerier**, **cheeriest**) lively; in good spirits, genial, cheering. □ **cheerily** *adv.* **cheeriness** *n.*

cheese¹ *n.* **1** ◀ a food made from the pressed curds of milk. **2** a complete cake of this with rind. □ **hard cheese** *Brit. slang* bad luck. [from Latin *caseus*]

cheese² *v.tr. slang* (usu. as **cheesed** *adj.*) (often foll. by *off*) exasperate. [19th-century coinage]

cheese³ *n.* (also **big cheese**) *slang* an important person.

cheeseboard *n.* **1** a board from which cheese is served. **2** a selection of cheeses.

cheeseburger *n.* a beefburger with a slice of cheese on it, usu. served in a roll.

cheesecake *n.* a tart filled with sweetened curds etc.

cheesecloth *n.* thin loosely woven cloth, used originally for wrapping cheese.

cheesemonger *n. Brit.* a dealer in cheese, butter, etc.

cheese-paring ● *adj.* stingy. ● *n.* stinginess. □ **cheese-pare** *v.tr. & intr.*

cheese plant *n.* = SWISS CHEESE PLANT.

cheese straw *n.* a thin cheese-flavoured strip of pastry.

cheesy *adj.* (**cheesier**, **cheesiest**) like cheese in taste, smell, appearance, etc. □ **cheesiness** *n.*

cheetah *n.* a swift-running feline, *Acinonyx jubatus*, with a leopard-like spotted coat. [from Hindi *cītā*]

chef /shef/ *n.* a cook, esp. the chief cook in a restaurant etc. [French, literally 'head']

chef-d'œuvre /shay-dervr/ *n.* (*pl.* **chefs-d'œuvre** *pronunc.* same) a masterpiece. [French, literally 'chief (piece of) work']

chelonian /ki-loh-ni-ăn/ ● *n.* ▲ any reptile of the order Chelonia, including turtles, terrapins, and tortoises, having a shell of bony plates covered with horny scales. ● *adj.* of or relating to this order. [from Greek *khelōnē* 'tortoise']

Chelsea bun *n. Brit.* a kind of currant bun in the form of a flat spiral. [from *Chelsea* in London]

Chelsea pensioner *n.* (in the UK) an inmate of the Chelsea Royal Hospital for old or disabled soldiers.

chemical ● *adj.* of, made by, or employing chemistry or chemicals. ● *n.* a substance obtained or used in chemistry. [from medieval Latin *alchymicus* 'alchemical'] □ **chemically** *adv.*

chemical bond *n.* an interaction by which atoms are held together in a molecule or crystal.

CHELONIAN

Whether land- or water-dwelling, chelonians are protected by their shell. The underpart (plastron) guards the belly, while the carapace, composed of horny scales and a bony layer, covers the back. Inside is the true skeleton, which is partly fused to the shell.

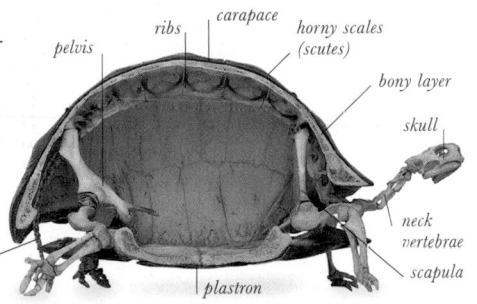

CROSS-SECTION THROUGH THE SHELL AND SKELETON OF A TORTOISE

pelvis · *ribs* · *carapace* · *horny scales (scutes)* · *bony layer* · *skull* · *neck vertebrae* · *scapula* · *caudal vertebrae* · *plastron*

TYPES OF CHELONIAN

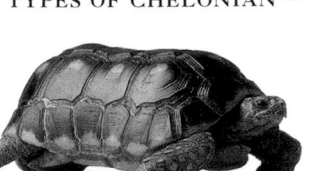

TORTOISES	TURTLES	TERRAPINS
red-footed tortoise (*Geochelone carbonaria*)	green turtle (*Chelonia mydas*)	red-eared slider terrapin (*Pseudemys cripta*)

chemical engineer *n.* an engineer specializing in the design and operation of industrial chemical plants. □ **chemical engineering** *n.*

chemical reaction *n.* a process that involves change in the structure of atoms, molecules, or ions.

chemical warfare *n.* warfare using poison gas and other chemicals.

chemical weapon *n.* a weapon depending for its effect on the release of a toxic or noxious substance.

chemico- *comb. form* chemical; chemical and (*chemico-physical*).

chemin de fer /shĕ-man dĕ **fair**/ *n.* a form of baccarat. [French, literally 'road of iron, railway']

chemise /shĕ-**meez**/ *n.* a woman's loose-fitting undergarment or dress hanging straight from the shoulders. [from Late Latin *camisia* 'shirt']

chemist *n.* **1** *Brit.* **a** a dealer in medicinal drugs, usu. also selling other medical goods and toiletries. **b** an authorized dispenser of medicines. **2** a person practising or trained in chemistry.

chemistry *n.* (*pl.* **-ies**) **1** the study of the elements and the compounds they form and the reactions they undergo. **2** the chemical composition and properties of a substance. **3** *colloq.* the attraction or interaction between people.

chemo- *comb. form* (also **chemi-**) chemical.

chemoreceptor *n. Biol.* a sensory organ responsive to chemical stimuli.

chemotherapy /kee-moh-**th'e**-ră-pi/ *n.* the treatment of disease, esp. cancer, by use of chemical substances. □ **chemotherapist** *n.*

chenille /shĕ-**neel**/ *n.* **1** a tufty velvety cord or yarn, used in trimming furniture etc. **2** fabric made from this. [French, literally 'hairy caterpillar']

cheque *n.* (*US* **check**) a written order to a bank to pay the stated sum from the drawer's account. [special use of CHECK[1] to mean 'device for checking an amount']

chequebook *n.* a book of forms for writing cheques.

cheque card *n. Brit.* a card issued by a bank to guarantee the honouring of cheques.

chequer (also **checker**) ● *n.* **1** (often in *pl.*) a pattern of squares often alternately coloured. **2** (in *pl.*) (usu. as **checkers**) *US* the game of draughts. ● *v.tr.* **1** mark with chequers. **2** (as **chequered** *adj.*) with varied fortunes (*a chequered career*). [Middle English, from EXCHEQUER]

chequerboard *n.* (*US* **checkerboard**) **1** a chessboard. **2** a pattern resembling it.

cherish *v.tr.* **1** protect or tend (a child, plant, etc.) lovingly. **2** hold dear, cling to (hopes, feelings, etc.). [based on Latin *carus* 'dear']

Cherokee ● *n.* **1 a** an American Indian tribe formerly inhabiting much of the southern US. **b** a member of this tribe. **2** the language of this tribe. ● *adj.* of or relating to the Cherokees or their language.

cheroot /shĕ-**root**/ *n.* a cigar with both ends open. [from Tamil *shuruṭṭu* 'roll']

cherry ● *n.* (*pl.* **-ies**) **1 a** a small soft round stone fruit. **b** (also **cherry tree**) ▼ any of several trees of the genus *Prunus* bearing this or grown for their ornamental flowers. **2** the wood of any of these trees. ▷ WOOD. **3** a bright deep red colour. ● *adj.* of a bright deep red colour. [from medieval Latin *ceresia*]

lanceolate leaf · *cherry fruit*

CHERRY: TIBETAN CHERRY (*Prunus serrula*)

cherry brandy *n.* a dark red liqueur of brandy in which cherries have been steeped.

cherry-pick *v.tr.* (also *absol.*) pick (the best) from a group.

cherry red ● *n.* = CHERRY *n.* 3. ● *adj.* (hyphenated when *attrib.*) = CHERRY *adj.*

cherry tomato *n.* a miniature tomato with a strong flavour. ▷ TOMATO

cherub *n.* **1** (*pl.* **cherubim**) an angelic being of the second order of the celestial hierarchy. **2 a** a representation of a winged child or the head of a winged child. **b** a beautiful or innocent child. [from Hebrew *kᵉrūb*, pl. *kᵉrubim*] □ **cherubic** *adj.* **cherubically** *adv.*

chervil *n.* ▶ an umbelliferous plant, *Anthriscus cerefolium*, with small white flowers, used as a herb for flavouring. [from Greek *khairephullon*]

Cheshire *n.* a kind of firm crumbly cheese. □ **like a Cheshire cat** with a broad fixed grin. [from *Cheshire*, a county in England]

chess *n.* ◀ a game for two with 16 men each, played on a chessboard. [from Old French *esches* (pl.)]

chessboard *n.* a chequered board of 64 squares on which chess and draughts are played. ▷ CHESS

chessman *n.* (*pl.* **-men**) a piece used in playing chess. ▷ CHESS

CHERVIL (*Anthriscus cerefolium*)

chess set *n.* a set of chessmen with a chessboard.

chest *n.* **1** a large strong box. **2 a** the part of a human or animal body enclosed by the ribs. **b** the circumference of the body at chest level. **c** the front surface of the body from neck to waist. **3** a small cabinet for medicines etc. □ **get a thing off one's chest** *colloq.* disclose a secret etc., to relieve one's anxiety about it. **play** (**one's cards, a thing,** etc.) **close to one's chest** *colloq.* be secretive about. [from Greek *kistē*] □ **-chested** *adj.* (in comb.).

chesterfield *n.* **1** a sofa with arms and back of the same height and curved outwards at the top. **2** a man's plain overcoat usu. with a velvet collar. [named after 19th-century Earl of *Chesterfield*]

CHESS

Devised some 1,400 years ago in India or China, chess is an imitation of warfare, with the sole object being to capture the opponent's king. The game is played on a board of 64 squares, with each of the two players having 16 chessmen. These represent different ranks and offices, and each is moved according to a predetermined pattern.

knight · *bishop* · *queen* · *king* · *bishop* · *knight* · *rook (castle)* · *rook (castle)* · *row of 8 pawns* · *16 black chessmen* · *square* · *chessboard* · *16 white chessmen*

CHESSBOARD AND CHESSMEN

C

chestnut ● *n.* **1** (also **chestnut tree**) **a** ► the tree *Castanea*, bearing flowers in catkins and nuts enclosed in a spiny fruit. **b** any other tree of the genus *Castanea*. **2** the glossy hard brown edible nut of *Castanea sativa*. ▷ NUT. **3** = HORSE CHESTNUT. **4** (in full **chestnut wood**) the heavy wood of any chestnut tree. **5** a horse of a reddish-brown colour. **6** *colloq.* a stale joke or anecdote. **7** (in full **chestnut brown**) a reddish-brown colour. ● *adj.* (in full **chestnut brown**; hyphenated when *attrib.*) of the colour chestnut. [from Greek *kastanea*]

coarse-toothed leaf margins

green fruit husk

ripe nuts

CHESTNUT: SWEET CHESTNUT (*Castanea sativa*)

chest of drawers *n.* a set of drawers in a frame.

chesty *adj.* (**chestier**, **chestiest**) **1** *Brit. colloq.* inclined to or symptomatic of chest disease. **2** *colloq.* having a large chest or prominent breasts. **3** *N. Amer. slang* arrogant. □ **chestily** *adv.* **chestiness** *n.*

cheval glass /shĕ-**val**/ *n.* a tall mirror swung on an upright frame. [from French *cheval* 'horse, frame']

chevalier /shev-ă-**leer**/ *n.* a member of certain orders of knighthood, and of certain modern French orders. [based on Latin *caballus* 'horse']

chevet *n.* the apsidal end of a church, sometimes with an attached group of apses. [French, literally 'pillow']

chèvre /shairvr/ *n.* a variety of goat's-milk cheese. [French, literally 'goat']

chevron /**shev**-rŏn/ *n.* **1** ► a badge in a V shape on the sleeve of a uniform indicating rank or length of service. **2** *Heraldry & Archit.* a bent bar of an inverted V shape. **3** any V-shaped line or stripe. [based on Latin *caper* 'goat': cf. Latin *capreoli* 'little goat' used to mean 'pair of rafters']

CHEVRON ON A NAPOLEONIC CORPORAL'S UNIFORM

chevrotain *n.* (also **chevrotin**) any small deerlike animal of the family Tragulidae, native to Africa and SE Asia, and having small tusks.

chevy var. of CHIVVY.

chew ● *v.tr.* (also *absol.*) work (food etc.) between the teeth; crush or indent with the teeth. ● *n.* **1** an act of chewing. **2** a chewy sweet. □ **chew the cud** reflect, ruminate. **chew the fat** (or **rag**) *slang* **1** chat. **2** grumble. **chew on** **1** work continuously between the teeth. **2** think about; meditate on. **chew out** *N. Amer. colloq.* reprimand. **chew over 1** discuss, talk over. **2** think about. [Old English] □ **chewable** *adj.* **chewer** *n.*

chewing gum *n.* flavoured gum, esp. chicle, for chewing.

chewy *adj.* (**chewier**, **chewiest**) **1** needing much chewing. **2** suitable for chewing. □ **chewiness** *n.*

chez /shay/ *prep.* at the home of. [from Latin *casa* 'cottage']

chi /ky/ *n.* the twenty-second letter of the Greek alphabet (Χ, χ). [from Greek *khi*]

Chianti /ki-**an**-ti/ *n.* (*pl.* **Chiantis**) a dry red Italian wine. [from *Chianti*, an area in Tuscany, Italy]

chiaroscuro /ki-ar-ŏ-**skoor**-oh/ *n.* **1** the treatment of light and shade in drawing and painting.

2 the use of contrast in literature etc. **3** (*attrib.*) half-revealed. [Italian, from *chiaro* 'bright' + *oscuro* 'dark']

chibouk *n.* (also **chibouque**) a long Turkish tobacco pipe.

chic /sheek/ ● *adj.* (**chic-er**, **chic-est**) stylish, elegant (in dress or appearance). ● *n.* stylishness, elegance. [French] □ **chicly** *adv.*

chicane /shi-**kayn**/ ● *n.* **1** an artificial barrier or obstacle, esp. a sharp double bend, on a motor-racing track. **2** chicanery. **3** *Bridge* a hand without trumps, or without cards of one suit. ● *v. archaic* **1** *intr.* use chicanery. **2** *tr.* (usu. foll. by *into, out of*, etc.) cheat (a person). [French, literally 'quibble']

chicanery /shi-**kayn**-ĕ-ri/ *n.* (*pl.* **-ies**) **1** clever but misleading talk; a false argument. **2** trickery, deception.

Chicano *n.* (*pl.* **-os**; *fem.* **Chicana**) esp. *US* an American of Mexican origin. [from Spanish *mejicano* 'Mexican']

chichi ● *adj.* **1** (of a thing) frilly, showy. **2** fussy, affected. ● *n.* over-refinement, pretentiousness, fussiness. [French]

chick *n.* **1** a young bird, esp. one newly hatched. **2** *slang* **a** a young woman. **b** a child.

chickadee *n.* *N. Amer.* ◄ any of various small birds of the tit family.

chicken ● *n.* **1** a domestic fowl, esp. a young bird. **2 a** a domestic fowl prepared as food. **b** its flesh. **3** a youthful person; a young and inexperienced person (usu. with *neg: is no chicken*). **4** *colloq.* a children's pastime testing courage, usu. recklessly. ● *adj. colloq.* cowardly. ● *v.intr.* (foll. by *out*) *colloq.* withdraw from or fail in some activity through fear. [Old English]

CHICKADEE: BLACK-CAPPED CHICKADEE (*Parus atricapillus*)

chicken feed *n.* **1** food for poultry. **2** *colloq.* an unimportant amount, esp. of money.

chicken-hearted *adj.* (also **chicken-livered**) easily frightened; lacking courage.

chickenpox *n.* an infectious disease, esp. of children, with a rash of small blisters.

chicken wire *n.* a light wire netting with a hexagonal mesh.

chickpea *n.* **1** a leguminous plant, *Cicer arietinum*, with pods containing yellow beaked seeds. **2** ► this seed used as a vegetable. [based on Latin *cicer* 'chickpea']

CHICKPEA SEEDS (*Cicer arietinum*)

chickweed *n.* any of numerous small plants of the pink family, esp. *Stellaria media*, a garden weed with slender stems and tiny white flowers.

chicle *n.* the milky juice of the sapodilla tree, used in the manufacture of chewing gum. [from Aztec *tzietli*]

chicory *n.* (*pl.* **-ies**) **1** a blue-flowered plant, *Cichorium intybus* (daisy family), cultivated for its salad leaves and its root. **2** its root, for use with or instead of coffee. **3** *N. Amer.* = ENDIVE 1. [from Greek *kikhorion*]

chide *v.tr. & intr.* (*past* **chided** or **chid**; *past part.* **chided** or **chidden**) esp. *archaic* or *literary* scold, rebuke. [Old English] □ **chider** *n.* **chidingly** *adv.*

chief ● *n.* **1 a** a leader or ruler. **b** the head of a tribe etc. **2** the head of a department; the highest official. ● *adj.* (usu. *attrib.*) **1** first in position, importance, etc. (*chief engineer*). **2** prominent, leading. [from Latin *caput* 'head'] □ **chiefdom** *n.*

Chief Constable *n. Brit.* the head of the police force of a county or other region.

chiefly *adv.* above all; mainly but not exclusively.

Chief of Staff *n.* the senior staff officer of a service or command.

chieftain *n.* (*fem.* **chieftainess**) the leader of a tribe etc. □ **chieftaincy** *n.* (*pl.* **-ies**). **chieftainship** *n.*

chief technician *n.* a non-commissioned officer in the RAF ranking above sergeant.

chiffchaff *n.* a small European warbler, *Phylloscopus collybita*, with a distinctive repetitive song.

chiffon /**shif**-on/ ● *n.* a light diaphanous fabric of silk, nylon, etc. ● *adj.* **1** made of chiffon. **2** (of a dessert etc.) light-textured. [French, from *chiffe* 'rag']

chiffonier *n.* **1** a movable low cupboard with a sideboard top. **2** *US* a tall chest of drawers. [from French *chiffonnier* 'rag-picker, chest of drawers for odds and ends']

chigger *n.* (also **jigger**) a tropical flea, *Tunga penetrans*, the females of which burrow beneath the skin causing painful sores. [variant of CHIGOE]

chignon /**sheen**-yon/ *n.* a coil or mass of hair at the back of a woman's head. [French, originally in sense 'nape of the neck']

chigoe *n.* = CHIGGER. [from a W. African language]

chihuahua /chi-**wah**-wă/ *n.* ▼ a very small dog of a smooth-haired large-eyed breed. [from *Chihuahua*, state and city in Mexico]

CHIHUAHUA: LONGHAIRED CHIHUAHUA

chilblain *n.* a painful itching swelling of the skin, caused by exposure to cold and by poor circulation. □ **chilblained** *adj.*

child *n.* (*pl.* **children**) **1 a** a young human being below the age of puberty. **b** an unborn or newborn human being. **2** one's son or daughter (at any age). **3** (foll. by *of*) a descendant, follower, adherent, or product of (*child of God; child of nature*). **4** a childish person. [Old English] □ **childless** *adj.* **childlessness** *n.*

child abuse *n.* maltreatment of a child, esp. by violence or sexual molestation.

childbearing *n.* (often *attrib.*) giving birth to a child or children.

childbed *n. archaic* = CHILDBIRTH.

child benefit *n.* (in the UK) regular payment by the state to the parents of a child up to a certain age.

childbirth *n.* the act of giving birth to a child.

childcare *n.* the care of a child or children while parents are working, or *Brit.* by a local authority when a normal home life is lacking.

child-centred *adj.* focusing on the needs etc. of the child.

childhood *n.* the state or period of being a child.

CHILLI

Often purchased in their dried form, chillies are also available as immature or ripe fruits, in colours ranging from orange to purplish-black. Many different varieties are grown commercially in the Tropics and subtropics. For the cook, they add a wide range of flavours to savoury dishes; in general, the smaller the fruit, the hotter it is.

EXAMPLES OF CHILLIES

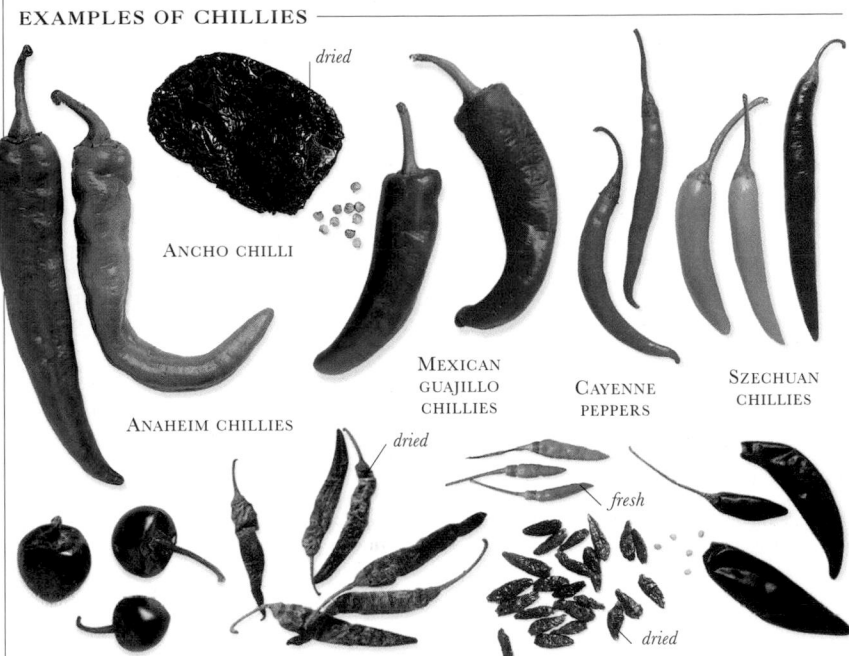

dried

ANCHO CHILLI

ANAHEIM CHILLIES

MEXICAN GUAJILLO CHILLIES

CAYENNE PEPPERS

SZECHUAN CHILLIES

dried

fresh

dried

CASCABEL CHILLIES   BUTTER CHILLIES   BIRD'S-EYE CHILLIES   SERRANO CHILLIES

---

childish *adj.* **1** of, like, or proper to a child. **2** immature, silly. □ **childishly** *adv.* **childishness** *n.*

childlike *adj.* having the good qualities of a child such as innocence, frankness, etc.

childminder *n. Brit.* a person who looks after children for payment, strictly a person registered with the local authority to give daytime care in his or her own home for children under eight.

childproof *adj.* that cannot be damaged or operated by a child.

children *pl.* of CHILD.

child's play *n.* an easy task.

chile var. of CHILLI.

Chilean ● *n.* **1** a native or national of Chile in S. America. **2** a person of Chilean descent. ● *adj.* of or relating to Chile.

chili var. of CHILLI.

chill ● *n.* **1 a** an unpleasant cold sensation. **b** a feverish cold (*catch a chill*). **2** unpleasant coldness. **3 a** a depressing influence (*cast a chill over*). **b** dread accompanied by coldness. **4** coldness of manner. ● *v.* **1** *tr. & intr.* make or become cold. **2** *tr.* **a** depress. **b** horrify. **3** *tr.* cool (food or drink); preserve by cooling. **4** *intr. esp. N. Amer. colloq.* (usu. foll. by *with*) pass time idly, hang around. ● *adj. literary* chilly. □ **chill out** *esp. N. Amer. colloq.* **1** relax. **2** = sense 4 of *v.* [Old English] □ **chillingly** *adv.* **chillness** *n.* **chillsome** *adj. literary.*

chiller *n.* **1** = SPINE-CHILLER. **2** a cold cabinet or refrigerator, esp. in a shop etc.

chill factor *n.* the perceived lowering of the air temperature caused by the wind etc.

chilli *n.* (also *chile* *pronunc.* same, *US* *chili*) (*pl.* **chillies, chiles,** or *US* **chilies**) **1** (in full **chilli pepper**) ▲ a small hot-tasting (dried) pod of a capsicum, *Capsicum anuum*, used in sauces etc. ▷ SPICE. **2** = CHILLI POWDER. **3** *esp. N. Amer.* = CHILLI CON CARNE. [Aztec]

chilli con carne *n.* a stew of chilli-flavoured minced beef and beans. [Spanish, literally 'chilli with meat']

chilli powder *n.* hot cayenne.

chilli sauce *n.* a hot sauce made with tomatoes, chillies, and spices.

chilly *adj.* (**chillier, chilliest**) **1** somewhat cold. **2** unfriendly; unemotional. □ **chilliness** *n.*

Chiltern Hundreds *n.pl.* (in the UK) a Crown manor, whose administration is a nominal office for which an MP applies as a way of resigning from the House of Commons. [from *Chiltern Hills* in S. England]

chime ● *n.* **1 a** a set of attuned bells. **b** the series of sounds given by this. **c** (usu. in *pl.*) a set of attuned bells as a doorbell. **2** agreement, correspondence, harmony. ● *v.* **1 a** *intr.* (of bells) ring. **b** *tr.* sound (a bell or chime) by striking. **2** *tr.* show (the hour) by chiming. **3** *intr.* be in agreement, harmonize. □ **chime in 1** interject a remark. **2** join in harmoniously. **3** (foll. by *with*) agree with. [Middle English] □ **chimer** *n.*

chimera /ky-meer-ă/ *n.* (also **chimaera**) **1** ▶ (in Greek mythology) a fire-breathing female monster with a lion's head, a goat's body, and a serpent's tail. **2** a fantastic or grotesque product of the imagination; a bogey. **3** any fabulous beast with parts taken from various animals. [from Greek *khimaira* 'she-goat, chimera'] □ **chimeric** *adj.* **chimerical** *adj.* **chimerically** *adv.*

chimney *n.* (*pl.* **-eys**) **1** a vertical channel conducting smoke or gases up and away from a fire, furnace, etc. **2** the part of this which projects above a roof. **3** a glass tube protecting the flame of a lamp. **4** a narrow vertical crack in a rock face. [from Greek *kaminos* 'oven']

chimney breast *n.* a projecting interior wall surrounding a chimney.

chimney piece *n. Brit.* an ornamental structure around a fireplace; a mantelpiece.

chimney pot *n.* a pipe at the top of a chimney, narrowing the aperture and increasing the updraught.

chimney stack *n.* **1** a number of chimneys grouped in one structure. **2** = CHIMNEY 2.

chimney sweep *n.* a person whose job is removing soot from inside chimneys.

chimp *n. colloq.* = CHIMPANZEE.

chimpanzee *n.* either of two anthropoid apes of central and W. Africa, *Pan troglodytes* and (in full **pygmy chimpanzee**) *Pan paniscus.* ▷ PRIMATE. [from French *chimpanzé*]

chin *n.* the front of the lower jaw. □ **chin up** *colloq.* cheer up. **keep one's chin up** *colloq.* remain cheerful. **take on the chin 1** suffer a severe blow from (a misfortune etc.). **2** endure courageously. [Old English] □ **-chinned** *adj.* (in comb.).

china ● *n.* **1** a kind of fine white or translucent ceramic ware, porcelain, etc. **2** things made from ceramic, esp. tableware. ● *adj.* made of china. [originally *China ware*: from Persian *chīnī*]

china clay *n.* kaolin.

chinagraph *n. Brit.* a waxy coloured pencil used to write on china, glass, etc.

Chinaman *n.* (*pl.* **-men**) **1** *archaic* or *derog.* (now usu. *offens.*) a native of China. **2** *Cricket* a ball bowled by a left-handed bowler that spins from off to leg.

China tea *n.* smoke-cured tea from a small-leaved tea plant grown in China.

Chinatown *n.* a district of a non-Chinese town in which the population is predominantly Chinese.

chinchilla *n.* **1 a** ▶ any small rodent of the genus *Chinchilla*, having silver-grey fur and a bushy tail. **b** its highly valued fur. **2 a** breed of cat or rabbit. [Spanish]

chin-chin *int. Brit. colloq.* a toast. [from Chinese]

chine[1] ● *n.* **1 a** a backbone. **b** a joint of meat containing this. **2** a ridge or arête. ● *v.tr.* cut (meat) across or along the backbone. [from Latin *spina* 'spine']

chine[2] *n.* a deep narrow ravine in the Isle of Wight or Dorset. [Old English *cinu* 'cleft, chink']

Chinese ● *adj.* **1** of or relating to China. **2** of Chinese descent. ● *n.* (*pl.* same) **1** the Chinese language. **2 a** a native or national of China. **b** a person of Chinese descent.

Chinese cabbage *n.* = CHINESE LEAF.

Chinese gooseberry *n.* = KIWI FRUIT.

Chinese lantern *n.* **1** a collapsible paper lantern. **2** a plant of the nightshade family, *Physalis alkekengi*, bearing white flowers and globular orange fruits enclosed in a papery calyx.

Chinese leaf *n.* a lettuce-like cabbage, *Brassica chinensis.*

Chinese puzzle *n.* a very intricate puzzle or problem.

Chinese water chestnut see WATER CHESTNUT 2.

Chinese white *n.* zinc oxide as a white pigment.

Chink *n. slang offens.* a Chinese.

chink[1] *n.* **1** an unintended crack that admits light or allows an attack. **2** a slit. [16th-century coinage, related to CHINE[2]]

CHINCHILLA
(Chinchilla laniger)

CHIMERA

C

chink[2] ● *v.* **1** *intr.* make a slight ringing sound, as of glasses striking together. **2** *tr.* cause to make this sound. ● *n.* this sound.

chinless *adj. colloq.* weak in character.

chinless wonder *n. Brit. colloq.* an ineffectual esp. upper-class person.

Chino- /chy-noh/ *comb. form* = SINO-.

chino /chee-noh/ *n.* (*pl.* **-os**) **1** a cotton twill fabric, usu. khaki-coloured. **2** (in *pl.*) trousers made from this. [Latin American Spanish, literally 'toasted']

chinoiserie /shin-wah-ze̬-ri/ *n.* **1** the imitation of Chinese motifs and techniques in Western art and architecture. **2** an object or objects in this style. [French]

chinook *n.* **1 a** a warm dry wind blowing east of the Rocky Mountains. **b** a warm wet southerly wind blowing west of the Rocky Mountains. **2** (**Chinook**) **a** (*pl.* same or **Chinooks**) a member of a N. American Indian people. **b** their language. [from American Indian *tsinúk*, name of the people]

chinook salmon *n.* a large salmon, *Oncorhynchus tshawytscha*, of the N. Pacific.

chintz ● *n.* a printed multicoloured cotton fabric with a glazed finish. ● *adj.* made from or upholstered with this fabric. [earlier *chints* (pl.), based on Sanskrit *citra* 'variegated']

chintzy *adj.* (**chintzier, chintziest**) **1** decorated or covered with chintz. **2** genteel, petit bourgeois. □ **chintzily** *adv.* **chintziness** *n.*

chin-up *n.* esp. *N. Amer.* = PULL-UP.

chinwag *Brit. slang* ● *n.* a talk or chat. ● *v.intr.* (**-wagged, -wagging**) have a gossip.

chionodoxa /ky-ŏn-ŏ-**dok**-să/ *n.* ▶ a plant of the genus *Chionodoxa* (lily family), with early-blooming blue flowers. Also called *glory of-the-snow*. [from Greek *khiōn* 'snow' + *doxa* 'glory']

CHIONODOXA
(*Chionodoxa luciliae*)

chip ● *n.* **1** a small piece removed by or in the course of chopping, cutting, or breaking, esp. from hard material such as wood or stone. **2** the place where such a chip has been made. **3 a** (usu. in *pl.*) esp. *Brit.* a strip of potato, deep-fried. **b** (in full **potato chip**) (usu. in *pl.*) *N. Amer.* a potato crisp. **4** a counter used in some gambling games to represent money. **5** *Electronics* = MICROCHIP. **6** *Football* etc. & *Golf* a short shot, kick, or pass with the ball describing an arc. ● *v.* (**chipped, chipping**) **1** *tr.* (often foll. by *off, away*) cut or break (a piece) from a hard material. **2** *intr.* (foll. by *at, away at*) cut pieces off (a hard material) to alter its shape, break it up, etc. **3** *intr.* (of china etc.) be susceptible to being chipped (*will chip easily*). **4** *tr.* (also *absol.*) *Football* etc. & *Golf* strike or kick (the ball) with a chip (cf. sense 6 of *n.*). **5** *tr.* (usu. as **chipped** *adj.*) *Brit.* cut (potatoes) into chips. □ **chip in** *colloq.* **1** *Brit.* interrupt or contribute abruptly to a conversation. **2** contribute (money or resources). **a chip off the old block** a child who resembles a parent. **a chip on one's shoulder** *colloq.* an inclination to feel resentful or aggrieved. **have had one's chips** *Brit. colloq.* be unable to avoid defeat, punishment, etc. **when the chips are down** *colloq.* when it comes to the point. [Middle English]

chipboard *n.* board made from compressed wood chips and resin.

chip heater *n. Austral.* & *NZ* a domestic water heater that burns wood chips.

chipmunk *n.* ◀ a N. American ground squirrel of the genus *Tamias*, having alternate light and dark stripes running down the body. ▷ RODENT. [Algonquian]

CHIPMUNK: EASTERN
CHIPMUNK
(*Tamias striatus*)

chipolata *n. Brit.* a small thin sausage. [from Italian *cipollata* 'dish of onions']

chipper *adj.* esp. *N. Amer. colloq.* **1** cheerful. **2** smartly dressed.

chipping *n. Brit.* **1** a small fragment of stone, wood, etc. **2** (in *pl.*) these used as a surface for roads etc.

chippy ● *n.* (also **chippie**) (*pl.* **-ies**) *Brit. colloq.* **1** a fish-and-chip shop. **2** a carpenter. ● *adj. colloq.* or *dial.* irritable.

Chips *n. Naut. slang* a ship's carpenter.

chip shot *n.* = CHIP n. 6.

chiral /**kyr**-ăl/ *adj. Chem.* (of an optically active compound) asymmetric and not superposable on its mirror image. [based on Greek *kheir* 'hand'] □ **chirality** *n.*

chiro- *comb. form* of the hand.

chirography *n.* handwriting, calligraphy.

chiromancy *n.* palmistry.

chiropody /ki-**rop**-ŏdi/ *n.* the treatment of the feet (originally also the hands) and their ailments. [based on Greek *kheir* 'hand' + *pous podos* 'foot'] □ **chiropodist** *n.*

chiropractic /ky-rŏ-**prak**-tik/ *n.* the manipulative treatment of disorders of the joints, esp. of the spinal column. [from Greek *kheir* 'hand' + *praktikos* 'practical'] □ **chiropractor** *n.*

chiropteran /ky-**rŏp**-ter-ăn/ *n.* any mammal of the order Chiroptera, which comprises the bats. ▷ BAT. [chiro- + Greek *pteron* 'wing']. □ **chiropterous** *adj.*

chirp ● *v.* **1** *intr.* (usu. of small birds, grasshoppers, etc.) utter a short sharp high-pitched note. **2** *tr.* & *intr.* (esp. of a child) speak or utter in a lively or jolly way. ● *n.* a chirping sound. [Middle English] □ **chirper** *n.*

chirpy *adj.* (**chirpier, chirpiest**) *colloq.* cheerful, lively. □ **chirpily** *adv.* **chirpiness** *n.*

chirrup ● *v.intr.* (**chirruped, chirruping**) (esp. of small birds) chirp, esp. repeatedly; twitter. ● *n.* a chirruping sound. □ **chirrupy** *adj.*

chisel ● *n.* ▼ a hand tool with a squared bevelled blade for shaping wood, stone, or metal. ▷ BEZEL. ● *v.* (**chiselled, chiselling**; *US* **chiseled, chiseling**) **1** *tr.* cut or shape with a chisel. **2** *tr.* (as **chiselled** *adj.*) (of facial features) clear-cut, fine. **3** *tr.* & *intr. slang* cheat, swindle. [based on Latin *caedere caes-* 'to cut'] □ **chiseller** *n.*

chi-square test *n.* a method of comparing observed and theoretical values in statistics.

chit[1] *n.* **1** *derog.* or *joc.* a young, small, or frail girl or woman (esp. *a chit of a girl*). **2** a young child. [Middle English in sense 'whelp']

chit[2] *n.* **1** a note of requisition; a note of a sum owed, esp. for food or drink. **2** esp. *Brit.* a note or memorandum. [from Sanskrit *citra* 'mark']

chit-chat *colloq.* ● *n.* light conversation; gossip. ● *v.intr.* (**-chatted, -chatting**) talk informally; gossip.

chitin *n. Chem.* ▼ a polysaccharide occurring in the exoskeleton of arthropods and in the cell walls of fungi. ▷ EXOSKELETON. [from French] □ **chitinous** *adj.*

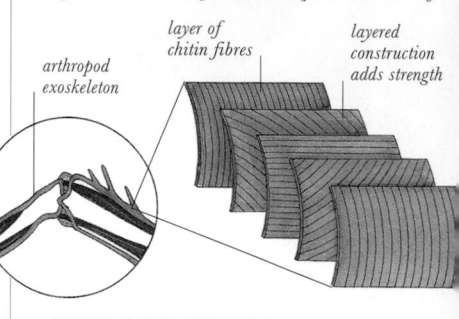

layer of
chitin fibres

layered
construction
adds strength

arthropod
exoskeleton

CHITIN: CROSS-SECTION OF AN ARTHROPOD
EXOSKELETON, WITH DETAIL OF CHITIN LAYERS

chitterling *n.* (usu. in *pl.*) the smaller intestines of pigs etc., esp. as cooked for food. [Middle English]

chitty *n.* (*pl.* **-ies**) *Brit.* = CHIT[2].

chivalrous /**shiv**-ăl-rŭs/ *adj.* (usu. of a male or his behaviour) gallant, honourable, courteous. □ **chivalrously** *adv.*

chivalry /**shiv**-ăl-ri/ *n.* **1** the medieval knightly system with its religious, moral, and social code. **2** the combination of qualities expected of an ideal knight. **3** a man's courteous behaviour, esp. towards women. [based on Late Latin *caballarius* 'horseman'] □ **chivalric** *adj.*

chive *n.* ▶ a small allium, *Allium schoenoprasum*, having long tubular leaves which are used as a herb. [from Latin *cepa* 'onion']

chivvy *v.tr.* (also **chivy, chevy**) (**-ies, -ied**) hurry (a person) up; nag; pursue. [probably from a skirmish described in the ballad of *Chevy Chase*, on the Scottish border]

chlamydia /klă-**mid**-iă/ *n.* (*pl.* **chlamydiae** /-di-I/) any small parasitic bacterium of the genus *Chlamydia*. [modern Latin]

chlor- var. of CHLORO-.

chloride *n. Chem.* any compound of chlorine with another element or group.

chlorinate *v.tr.* **1** impregnate or treat with chlorine. **2** *Chem.* cause to react or combine with chlorine. □ **chlorination** *n.* **chlorinator** *n.*

CHIVE
(*Allium
schoenoprasum*)

chlorine *n. Chem.* a poisonous greenish-yellow gaseous element occurring naturally esp. as sodium chloride, and used in disinfectants and bleaches. [based on Greek *khlōros* 'green']

chlorite *n. Mineral.* a dark green mineral found in many rocks, consisting of a basic aluminosilicate of magnesium, iron, etc.

chloro- *comb. form* (also **chlor-** esp. before a vowel) **1** *Biol.* & *Mineral.* green. **2** *Chem.* chlorine. [sense 1: from Greek *khlōros* 'green']

chlorofluorocarbon see CFC.

chloroform ● *n.* a colourless volatile sweet-smelling liquid used as a solvent and formerly as a general anaesthetic. ● *v.tr.* render unconscious with this. [from French *chloroforme*]

CHISEL

Chisels have specific functions. A bolster chisel is suitable for cutting masonry, lifting floorboards, or easing off tiles. The bevel-edge chisel is used for chipping out strips of wood, while the wood-cutting chisel is best for fashioning wooden joints.

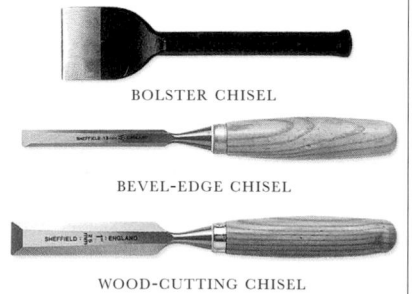

BOLSTER CHISEL

BEVEL-EDGE CHISEL

WOOD-CUTTING CHISEL

chlorophyll *n.* the green pigment found in most plants, responsible for light absorption to provide energy by photosynthesis. [from Greek *khlōros* 'green' + *phullon* 'leaf'] □ **chlorophyllous** *adj.*

chloroplast *n.* a plastid containing chlorophyll, found in plant cells undergoing photosynthesis. ▷ CELL. [German]

chlorosis *n.* **1** *Med.* a severe form of anaemia from iron deficiency esp. in young women, causing a greenish complexion (cf. GREENSICK). **2** *Bot.* a reduction or loss of the normal green coloration of leaves. □ **chlorotic** *adj.*

Ch.M. *abbr.* Master of Surgery. [Latin *Chirurgiae Magister*]

choc *n. & adj. Brit. colloq.* chocolate.

chocaholic var. of CHOCOHOLIC.

choc ice *n. Brit.* a bar of ice cream covered with a thin coating of chocolate.

chock ● *n.* a block or wedge used to check motion, esp. of a wheel. ● *v.tr.* fit or make fast with chocks. ● *adv.* as closely or tightly as possible.

chock-a-block *adj. & adv.* crammed close together; crammed full. [originally nautical, said of a tackle with the two blocks run close together]

chock-full *adj. & adv.* crammed full. [based on *chock* 'block']

chocoholic (also **chocaholic**) ● *n.* a person who is addicted to or very fond of chocolate. ● *adj.* of or relating to chocoholics.

chocolate ● *n.* **1 a** a food preparation made from roasted and ground cacao seeds, usually sweetened. **b** a sweet made of or coated with this. **c** a drink made with chocolate. **2** a deep brown colour. ● *adj.* **1** made from or of chocolate. **2** deep brown. [from Aztec *chocolatl*] □ **chocolatey** *adj.* (also **chocolaty**).

choice ● *n.* **1 a** the act or an instance of choosing. **b** a thing or person chosen. **2** a range from which to choose. **3** (usu. foll. by *of*) the elite, the best. **4** the opportunity to choose (*what choice have I?*). ● *adj.* of superior quality; carefully chosen. [from Old French *chois*]

choir *n.* **1** a regular group of singers, esp. taking part in church services. **2** the part of a cathedral or large church between the altar and the nave. ▷ CATHEDRAL, CHURCH. [from Latin *chorus*]

choirboy *n.* (*fem.* **choirgirl**) a boy or girl who sings in a church or cathedral choir.

choir stall *n.* = STALL[1] *n.* 3.

choke[1] ● *n* **1** *tr* hinder or impede the breathing of (a person or animal), esp. by constricting the wind pipe or (of gas, smoke, etc.) by being unbreathable. **2** *intr.* suffer a hindrance or stoppage of breath. **3** *tr. & intr.* make or become speechless from emotion. **4** *tr.* retard the growth of or kill (esp. plants) by the deprivation of light, air, nourishment, etc. **5** *tr.* (often foll. by *back*) suppress (feelings) with difficulty. **6** *tr.* block or clog (a passage, tube, etc.). **7** *tr.* (as **choked** *adj.*) *Brit. colloq.* disgusted, disappointed. ● *n.* **1** the valve in the carburettor of an internal-combustion engine that controls the intake of air, esp. to enrich the fuel mixture. ▷ CARBURETTOR. **2** *Electr.* an inductance coil used to smooth the variations of an alternating current or to alter its phase. □ **choke down** swallow with difficulty. **choke up** block (a channel etc.). [Middle English] □ **choky** *adj.* (**chokier, chokiest**).

choke[2] *n.* the centre part of an artichoke.

choke-damp *n.* carbon dioxide in mines, wells, etc.

choker *n.* **1** ▼ a close-fitting necklace or ornamental neckband. **2** a clerical or other high collar.

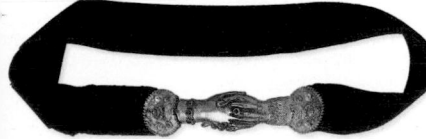

CHOKER: 18TH-CENTURY FABRIC CHOKER WITH ORNAMENTAL CLASP

choky *n.* (also **chokey**) (*pl.* **-ies** or **-eys**) *Brit. slang* prison. [from Hindi *caukī* 'shed']

chole- /kol-i-/ *comb. form* (also **chol-** esp. before a vowel) *Med. & Chem.* bile. [from Greek]

cholecalciferol *n.* one of the D vitamins, produced by the action of sunlight on a cholesterol derivative in the skin.

choler /kol-er/ *n.* **1** *hist.* = YELLOW BILE. **2** *poet.* or *archaic* anger, irascibility. [from Late Latin *cholera* in sense of Greek *kholē* 'bile, anger']

cholera *n. Med.* an infectious and often fatal disease of the small intestine caused by a mainly waterborne bacterium *Vibrio cholerae*, resulting in severe vomiting and diarrhoea. [from Greek *kholera*] □ **choleraic** *adj.*

choleric *adj.* irascible, angry.

cholesterol /kol-est-ě-rol/ *n. Biochem.* a sterol found in most body tissues, including the blood, where high concentrations can promote arteriosclerosis. [from Greek *kholē* 'bile' + *stereos* 'stiff']

chomp *v.tr.* = CHAMP[1] *v.* 1, 2.

choo-choo *n.* (also **choo-choo train**) *colloq.* (esp. as a child's word) a railway train or locomotive, esp. a steam engine.

chook *n.* (also **chookie**) *Austral. & NZ colloq.* a chicken or fowl. [English dialect]

choose *v.* (*past* **chose**; *past part.* **chosen**) **1** *tr.* select out of a greater number. **2** *intr.* (usu. foll. by *between, from*) take or select one or another. **3** *tr.* decide, be determined (*chose to stay behind*). **4** *tr.* (foll. by complement) select as (*was chosen king*). [Old English] □ **chooser** *n.*

choosy *adj.* (**choosier, choosiest**) *colloq.* fastidious. □ **choosily** *adv.* **choosiness** *n.*

chop[1] ● *v.tr.* (**chopped, chopping**) **1** (usu. foll. by *off, down,* etc.) cut or fell by a blow, usu. with an axe. **2** (often foll. by *up*) cut into small pieces. **3** strike (esp. a ball) with a short heavy edgewise blow. **4** cut as if by chopping; dispense with; reduce, shorten (*chopped the scene from the play*). ● *n.* **1** a cutting blow, esp. with an axe. **2** a thick slice of meat (esp. pork or lamb) usu. including a rib. ▷ CUT. **3** a short heavy edgewise stroke or blow in tennis, cricket, boxing, etc. **4** (prec. by *the*) *Brit. slang* a dismissal from employment. **b** the action of killing or being killed. **c** cancellation (of a project etc.). [Middle English variant of CHAP[1]]

chop[2] *n.* (usu. in *pl.*) the jaw of an animal etc. [Middle English]

chop[3] *v.intr.* (**chopped, chopping**) □ **chop and change** *Brit.* vacillate; change direction frequently. [Middle English in sense 'to barter, exchange']

chop-chop *adv. & int.* (pidgin English) quickly, quick. [from Chinese dialect *k'wâi-k'wâi*]

chop logic *v.intr.* argue pedantically. [based on CHOP[3]]

chopper *n.* **1 a** *Brit.* a short axe with a large blade. **b** a butcher's cleaver. **2** *colloq.* a helicopter. **3** a type of bicycle (**Chopper** *propr.*), or motorcycle, with high handlebars. **4** (in *pl.*) *slang* teeth.

choppy *adj.* (**choppier, choppiest**) (of the sea, the weather, etc.) fairly rough. [based on CHOP[1]] □ **choppily** *adv.* **choppiness** *n.*

chopstick *n.* each of a pair of small thin sticks of wood or ivory etc., held both in one hand as eating utensils by the Chinese, Japanese, etc. ▷ WOK. [pidgin English from *chop* 'quick' + STICK[1]]

chop suey *n.* (*pl.* **-eys**) a Chinese-style dish of meat stewed and fried with bean sprouts, bamboo shoots, onions, and served with rice. [from Cantonese *shap sui* 'mixed bits']

choral *adj.* of, for, or sung by a choir or chorus. □ **chorally** *adv.*

chorale *n.* (also **choral**) **1** a stately and simple hymn tune; a harmonized version of this. **2** esp. *US* a

choir or choral society. [from medieval Latin *cantus choralis* 'choral song']

choral society *n.* a group which meets regularly to sing choral music.

chord[1] *n. Mus.* a group of notes sounded together, as a basis of harmony. [originally *cord* from ACCORD: later confused with CHORD[2]] □ **chordal** *adj.*

chord[2] *n.* **1** *Math. & Aeron.* etc. ▶ a straight line joining the ends of an arc, the wings of an aeroplane, etc. **2** *Anat.* = CORD 2. **3** *Engin.* one of the two principal members, usu. horizontal, of a truss. □ **strike a chord 1** recall something to a person's memory. **2** elicit sympathy. **touch the right chord** appeal skilfully to the emotions. [16th century variant of CORD, reflecting Latin *chorda*] □ **chordal** *adj.*

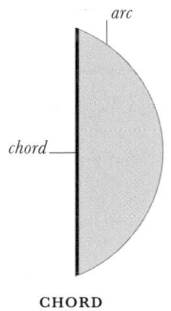

CHORD

chordate ● *n.* any animal of the phylum Chordata, possessing a notochord at some stage during its development. ● *adj.* of or relating to the chordates. [based on Latin *chorda* 'cord, string']

chording *n. Mus.* the playing, singing, or arrangement of chords. □ **chord** *v.intr.*

chore *n.* a tedious or routine task, esp. a domestic one. [originally dialect and US form of CHAR[2]]

chorea /ko-reer/ *n. Med.* a disorder characterized by jerky involuntary movements affecting esp. the shoulders, hips, and face. [from Greek *khoreia* 'dance']

choreograph /ko-ri-ŏ-grahf/ *v.tr.* compose the choreography for (a ballet etc.). □ **choreographer** *n.*

choreography /ko-ri-og-ră-fi/ *n.* **1** the design or arrangement of a ballet or other staged dance. **2** the sequence of steps and movements in dance. **3** the written notation for this. [based on Greek *khoreia* 'dance'] □ **choreographic** *adj.* **choreographically** *adv.*

choreology *n.* the study and description of the movements of dancing. □ **choreologist** *n.*

chorine *n.* a chorus girl. [based on CHORUS]

chorister *n.* **1** a member of a choir, esp. a choirboy or choirgirl. **2** *US* the leader of a church choir. [based on Old French *quer* 'choir']

choroid *n.* (in full **choroid coat** or **membrane**) a layer of the eyeball between the retina and the sclera. ▷ EYE. [based on Greek *khorion* 'chorion', an embryonic membrane]

chortle ● *v.intr.* chuckle gleefully. ● *n.* a gleeful chuckle. [portmanteau word coined by Lewis Carroll, probably from *chuckle* + *snort*]

chorus ● *n.* (*pl.* **choruses**) **1** a group (esp. a large one) of singers; a choir. **2** a piece of music composed for a choir. **3** the refrain of a popular song, in which a chorus participates. **4** any simultaneous utterance by many persons etc. (*a chorus of disapproval*). **5** a group of singers and dancers performing in concert in a musical, opera, etc. **6** *Gk Antiq.* **a** in Greek tragedy, a group of performers who comment together in voice and movement on the main action. **b** an utterance of the chorus. ● *v.tr. & intr.* (**chorused, chorusing**) (of a group) speak or utter simultaneously. □ **in chorus** (uttered) together; in unison. [from Greek *khoros*]

chorus girl *n.* a young woman who sings or dances in the chorus of a musical etc.

chose *past* of CHOOSE.

chosen *past part.* of CHOOSE.

chough /chuf/ *n.* ◀ a bird of the genus *Pyrrhocorax* (crow family), with glossy blue-black plumage and red legs. [Middle English]

CHOUGH: ALPINE CHOUGH (*Pyrrhocorax graculus*)

C

choux pastry /shoo/ *n.* very light pastry enriched with eggs. [from French *chou* 'cabbage, rosette': in English originally a round cream-filled pastry]

chow *n.* **1** *slang* food. **2** a dog of a Chinese breed with long hair and bluish-black tongue. [shortened from pidgin English *chow-chow*]

chowder *n. N. Amer.* a rich soup usu. containing fresh fish, clams, or corn with potatoes, onions, etc.

chow mein /mayn/ *n.* a Chinese-style dish of fried noodles with shredded meat or shrimps etc. and vegetables. [from Chinese *chao mian* 'fried flour']

chrism *n.* a consecrated oil or unguent used esp. for anointing in Catholic and Greek Orthodox rites. [from Greek *khrisma* 'anointing']

Christ ● *n.* **1** the title, also now treated as a name, given to Jesus of Nazareth. **2** the Messiah as prophesied in the Old Testament. [from Greek *khristos* 'anointed one'] □ **Christhood** *n.* **Christlike** *adj.* **Christly** *adj.*

christen *v.tr.* **1** give a Christian name to at baptism as a sign of admission to a Christian Church. **2** give a name to (a thing), esp. formally or with a ceremony. **3** *colloq.* use for the first time. [Old English *cristnian* 'to make Christian'] □ **christening** *n.*

Christendom *n.* Christians worldwide, regarded as a collective body.

Christian ● *adj.* **1** following, or believing in Christ's teaching or religion. **2** of the religion of Jesus Christ. **3** *colloq.* (of a person) kind, fair, decent. ● *n.* **1 a** a person who has received Christian baptism. **b** an adherent of Christ's teaching. **2** a person exhibiting Christian qualities. □ **Christianize** *v.tr. & intr.* (also **-ise**). **Christianization** *n.* **Christianly** *adv.*

Christian era *n.* the era reckoned from the traditional date of Christ's birth.

Christianity *n.* **1** the Christian religion; its beliefs and practices. **2** = CHRISTENDOM.

Christian name *n.* a forename, esp. as given at baptism.

Christian Science *n.* the beliefs and practices of The Church of Christ Scientist, a Christian body holding that only God and the mind have ultimate reality, sin and illness being illusions overcome by prayer and faith. □ **Christian Scientist** *n.*

Christingle *n.* a lighted candle symbolizing Christ as the light of the world, held by children esp. at Advent services.

Christmas *n.* (*pl.* **Christmases**) **1** (also **Christmas Day**) the annual festival of Christ's birth, celebrated on 25 Dec. **2** the season in which this occurs. □ **Christmassy** *adj.*

Christmas box *n. Brit.* a present or gratuity given at Christmas, esp. to tradesmen and employees.

Christmas cake *n. Brit.* a rich fruit cake usu. covered with marzipan and icing and eaten at Christmas.

Christmas card *n.* a card sent with greetings at Christmas.

Christmas Eve *n.* the day or the evening before Christmas Day.

Christmas pudding *n. Brit.* a rich boiled pudding eaten at Christmas, made with flour, suet, dried fruit, etc.

Christmas rose *n.* a small white-flowered winter-blooming plant, *Helleborus niger.*

Christmas stocking *n.* a real or ornamental stocking hung up by children on Christmas Eve for Father Christmas to fill with presents.

Christmas tree *n.* an evergreen (usu. spruce) or artificial tree set up with decorations at Christmas.

Christo- *comb. form* Christ.

chroma *n.* purity or intensity of colour. [from Greek]

chromatic *adj.* **1** of or produced by colour; in (esp. bright) colours. **2** *Mus.* **a** of or having notes not belonging to a diatonic scale. **b** (of a scale) ascending or descending by semitones. □ **chromatically** *adv.* **chromaticism** *n.*

chromaticity *n.* the quality of colour regarded independently of brightness.

chromatid *n. Biol.* either of two threadlike strands into which a chromosome divides longitudinally during cell division. ▷ CHROMOSOME, MEIOSIS, MITOSIS

chromatin *n. Biochem.* the material in a cell nucleus that stains with basic dyes and consists of protein, RNA, and DNA.

chromato- *comb. form* (also **chromo-**) colour. [from Greek *khrōma -atos* 'colour']

chromatography *n. Chem.* ▼ a technique for the separation of a mixture by passing it in solution or suspension through a medium in which the components move at different rates. [from German *Chromatographie*] □ **chromatograph** *n.* **chromatographic** *adj.*

blotting paper

constituent dyes separate out

black ink and water

CHROMATOGRAPHY: DEMONSTRATION OF SEPARATION OF BLACK INK ON BLOTTING PAPER

chrome *n.* **1** chromium, esp. as plating. **2** (in full **chrome yellow**) a yellow pigment obtained from a compound of chromium. [French, literally 'chromium']

chrome steel *n.* a hard fine-grained steel containing much chromium and used for tools etc.

chromite crystals

serpentinite groundmass

CHROMITE

chromite *n. Mineral.* ◀ a black mineral of chromium and iron oxides, which is the principal ore of chromium.

chromium *n. Chem.* a hard white metallic element, occurring naturally as chromite and used as a shiny decorative electroplated coating. [modern Latin]

chromium-plate ● *n.* an electrolytically deposited protective coating of chromium. ● *v.tr.* coat with this.

chromium steel *n.* = CHROME STEEL.

chromo- var. of CHROMATO-.

chromatid

centromere

supercoiled DNA

CHROMOSOME: HUMAN CHROMOSOME SEEN THROUGH A MICROSCOPE

chromolithograph ● *n.* a coloured picture printed by lithography. ● *v.tr.* print or produce by this process. □ **chromolithography** *n.*

chromosome *n. Biol.* ◀ each of the rodlike or threadlike structures of DNA and protein found in the nuclei of cells that carry the genetic information in the form of genes. ▷ GENE, MEIOSIS, MITOSIS. [from German *Chromosom*] □ **chromosomal** *adj.*

chromosome map *n.* a plan showing the relative positions of genes along the length of a chromosome.

chronic *adj.* **1** persisting for a long time (usu. of an illness or a personal or social problem). **2** having a chronic complaint. **3** *Brit. colloq.* very bad; intense, severe. [from Greek *khronikos*] □ **chronically** *adv.* **chronicity** *n.*

■ **Usage** The use of *chronic* in sense 3 is considered incorrect by some people.

chronic fatigue syndrome *n.* = ME.

chronicle ● *n.* **1** a register of events in order of their occurrence. **2** a narrative, a full account. ● *v.tr.* record (events) in the order of their occurrence. [from Greek *khronika* 'annals'] □ **chronicler** *n.*

chrono- *comb. form* time. [from Greek *khronos* 'time']

chronograph *n.* **1** an instrument for recording time with extreme accuracy. **2** a stopwatch. □ **chronographic** *adj.*

chronological *adj.* **1** (of a number of events) arranged or regarded in the order of their occurrence. **2** of or relating to chronology. □ **chronologically** *adv.*

chronology *n.* (*pl.* **-ies**) **1** the study of historical records to establish the dates of past events. **2 a** the arrangement of events, dates, etc. in the order of their occurrence. **b** a table or document displaying this. □ **chronologist** *n.*

chronometer *n.* a time-measuring instrument, esp. one used in navigation.

chronometry *n.* the science of accurate time-measurement. □ **chronometric** *adj.*

chrysalid *n.* = CHRYSALIS.

chrysalis *n.* (*pl.* **chrysalises** or **chrysalides** /kri-sal-i-deez/) **1** ▶ a quiescent pupa of a butterfly or moth. ▷ METAMORPHOSIS. **2** the hard outer case enclosing it. [from Greek *khrusallis*]

chrysalis

girdle

silken pad

CHRYSALIS OF A BUTTERFLY

chrysanthemum *n.* a plant of the genus *Chrysanthemum* or (if cultivated usu.) the genus *Dendranthema* (daisy family), having brightly coloured flowers. [from Greek *khrusanthemon*]

chrysoberyl *n.* ◀ a yellowish-green gem consisting of a beryllium salt. [from Greek *khrusos* 'gold' + *bērullos* 'beryl']

CHRYSOBERYL

chthonic /kthon-ik/ *adj.* (also **chthonian**) of, relating to, or inhabiting the underworld. [based on Greek *khthōn* 'Earth']

chub *n.* ▼ a thick-bodied coarse-fleshed river fish, *Leuciscus cephalus.* [15th-century coinage]

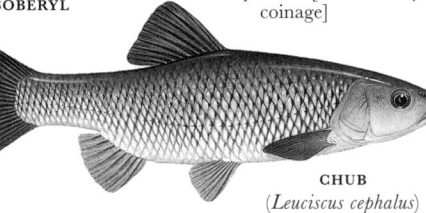

CHUB (*Leuciscus cephalus*)

Chubb *n.* (in full **Chubb lock**) *propr.* a lock with a device for fixing the bolt immovably should someone try to pick it. [from C. *Chubb*, 19th-century London locksmith]

chubby *adj.* (**chubbier**, **chubbiest**) plump and rounded (esp. of a person or a part of the body). □ **chubbily** *adv.* **chubbiness** *n.*

chuck[1] ● *v.tr.* **1** *colloq.* fling or throw carelessly or with indifference. **2** (often *Brit.*) foll. by *in, up*) *colloq.*

CHUNNEL

In 1994, the Chunnel (Channel tunnel) opened between Folkestone, in southern England, and Calais, in northern France. It is in reality a whole tunnel system, consisting of three separate tunnels linked by cross-passages. Lined with exceptionally strong concrete, the tunnels are 50.5 km (31 miles) long, of which 38 km (23 miles) are undersea. 'Le Shuttle' travels through one tunnel, carrying passengers with cars, and freight. On the other side is the 'Eurostar', a passenger train. In between lies the vital service tunnel.

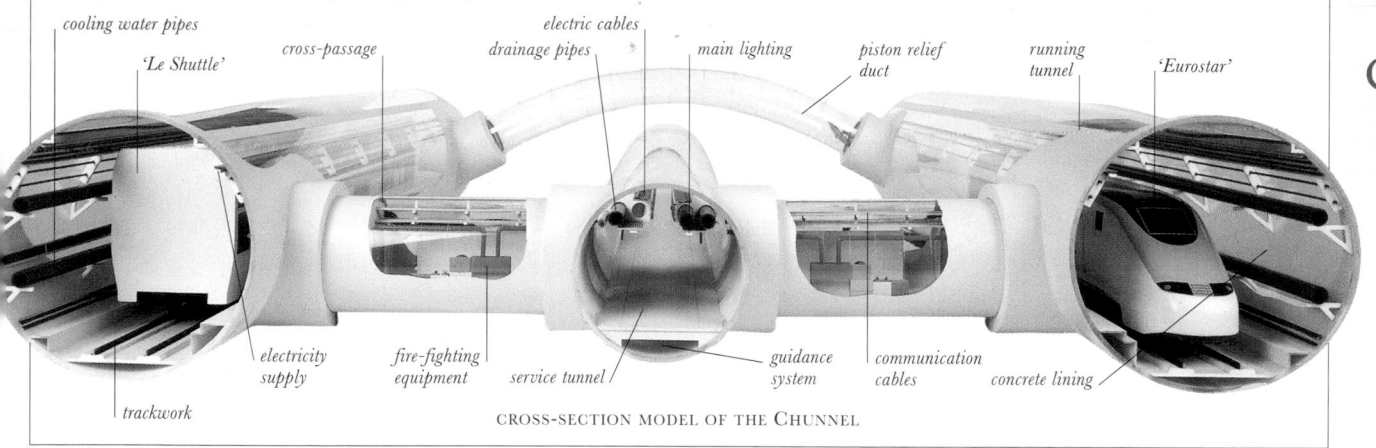

CROSS-SECTION MODEL OF THE CHUNNEL

C

give up; reject (*chucked in my job*). ● *n.* **1** a toss. **2** (prec. by *the*) *Brit. slang* dismissal (*he got the chuck*). **3** a playful touch under the chin. □ **chuck it** *slang* stop, desist. **chuck out** *colloq.* **1** expel (a person) from a gathering etc. **2** get rid of, discard. [16th-century coinage]

chuck² *n.* **1** a cut of beef between the neck and the ribs. **2** ◄ a device for holding a workpiece in a lathe or a tool in a drill. ▷ DRILL. [variant of CHOCK]

CHUCK ON A POWER DRILL

chuck³ *n. N. Amer. dial.* food, provisions. [19th-century coinage]

chuck⁴ *n. dial.* (as a form of address) dear, darling. [alteration of CHICK]

chucker-out *n. Brit. colloq.* a person employed to expel troublesome people from a gathering etc.

chuckle ● *v.intr.* laugh quietly or inwardly. ● *n.* a quiet or suppressed laugh. [based on *chuck* 'to cluck'] □ **chuckler** *n.*

chucklehead *n. colloq.* a stupid person. [*chuckle* 'clumsy', probably related to CHUCK²] □ **chuckle-headed** *adj.*

chuckwagon *n. N. Amer.* **1** ▼ a provision cart on a ranch etc. **2** a roadside eating place. [based on CHUCK³]

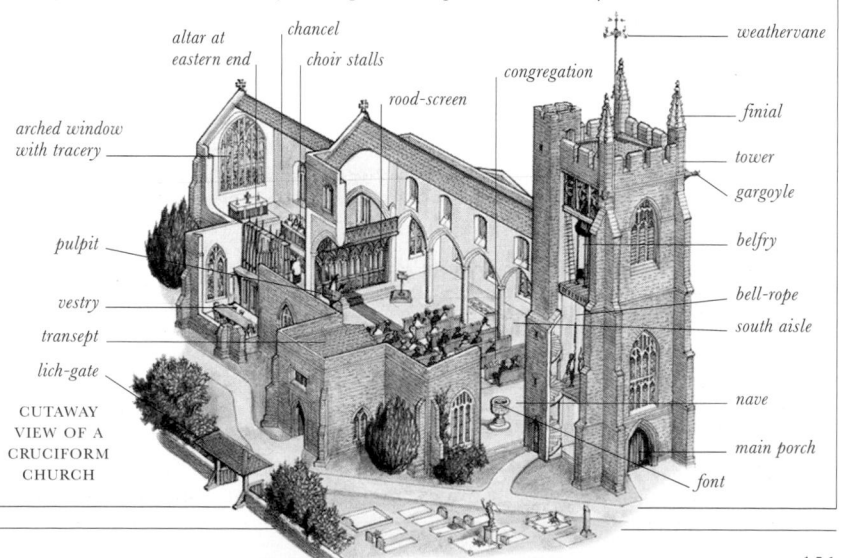

CHUCKWAGON: 19TH-CENTURY CHUCKWAGON

chuff *v.intr.* (of a steam engine etc.) work with a regular sharp puffing sound.

chuffed *adj. Brit. slang* delighted.

chug ● *v.intr.* (**chugged**, **chugging**) **1** emit a regular muffled explosive sound, as of an engine running slowly. **2** move with this sound. ● *n.* a chugging sound.

chukka *n.* (*US* **chukker**) each of the periods of play (7–7½ minutes) into which a game of polo is divided. [from Sanskrit *cakra* 'wheel']

chum ● *n. colloq.* (esp. among schoolchildren) a close friend. ● *v.intr.* (often foll. by *with*) share rooms. □ **chum up** (often foll. by *with*) become a close friend (of). [17th-century coinage] □ **chummy** *adj.* (**chummier**, **chummiest**). **chummily** *adv.* **chumminess** *n.*

chump *n.* **1** *colloq.* a foolish person. **2** *Brit.* the thick end, esp. of a loin of lamb or mutton (*chump chop*). **3** *Brit. slang* the head. □ **off one's chump** *Brit. slang* crazy. [18th-century coinage]

chunk *n.* **1** a thick solid slice or piece of something firm or hard. **2** a substantial amount or piece.

chunky *adj.* (**chunkier**, **chunkiest**) **1** containing or consisting of chunks. **2** short and thick; small and sturdy. **3** (of clothes) made of a thick material. □ **chunkiness** *n.*

Chunnel *n. colloq.* ▲ a tunnel under the English Channel linking England and France. [portmanteau word from *Channel tunnel*]

chunter *v.intr. Brit. colloq.* mutter, grumble.

chupatty var. of CHAPATTI.

church *n.* **1** ▼ a building for public (usu. Christian) worship. **2** a meeting for public worship in such a building (*go to church*; *met after church*). **3** (usu. **Church**) (prec. by *the*) the body of all Christians. **4** (usu. **Church**) the clergy or clerical profession. **5** (usu. **Church**) an organized Christian group or society of any time, country, or distinct principles of worship. [from Greek *kuriakon* (*dōma*) 'Lord's (house)']

CHURCH

The earliest churches were constructed in the Mediterranean region during the Roman Empire. They were small, with sufficient space for an altar and only a meagre congregation. As Christianity spread, larger churches with separate areas for the clergy and the followers were built, often in the shape of a cross to symbolize the crucifix.

CUTAWAY VIEW OF A CRUCIFORM CHURCH

C

churchgoer *n.* a person who goes to church, esp. regularly. □ **churchgoing** *n. & adj.*

churchman *n.* (*pl.* **-men**) **1** a member of the clergy or of a Church. **2** a supporter of the Church.

Church of England *n.* the English branch of the Western Christian Church.

church school *n.* **1** (in the UK) a school founded by or associated with the Church of England. **2** (in the US) a private school supported by a particular Church or church.

churchwarden *n.* **1 a** either of the two main elected lay representatives in an Anglican parish, formally responsible for movable church property and for keeping order in church. **b** *US* a church administrator. **2** *Brit.* a long-stemmed clay pipe.

churchwoman *n.* (*pl.* **-women**) **1** a woman member of the clergy or of a Church. **2** a woman supporter of the Church.

churchy *adj.* **1** obtrusively or intolerantly devoted to the Church or opposed to religious dissent. **2** like a church. □ **churchiness** *n.*

churchyard *n.* the enclosed ground around a church, esp. as used for burials.

churl *n.* an ill-bred person. [Old English in sense 'man']

churlish *adj.* surly; mean. □ **churlishly** *adv.* **churlishness** *n.*

churn ● *n.* **1** *Brit.* a large milk can. **2** ▶ a machine for making butter by agitating milk or cream. ● *v.* **1** *tr.* agitate (milk or cream) in a churn. **2** *tr.* produce (butter) in this way. **3** *tr.* (usu. foll. by *up*) cause distress to; upset, agitate. **4** *intr.* (of a liquid) seethe, foam violently (*the churning sea*). **5** *tr.* agitate or move (liquid) vigorously, causing it to foam. □ **churn out** produce routinely or mechanically, esp. in large quantities. [Old English]

chute *n.* a sloping channel or slide, with or without water, for conveying things to a lower level. [French, literally 'fall']

chutney *n.* (*pl.* **-eys**) a pungent condiment of fruits, vegetables, vinegar, spices, etc. [from Hindi *caṭnī*]

chutzpah /**khuutz**-pǎ/ *n.* *slang* shameless audacity; cheek. [Yiddish]

CIA *abbr.* (in the US) Central Intelligence Agency.

ciabatta /chǎ-**bah**-tǎ/ *n.* (*pl.* **ciabattas**) a type of moist aerated Italian bread made with olive oil. [Italian dialect, literally 'slipper', from its shape]

ciao /chow/ *int.* *colloq.* **1** goodbye. **2** hello. [Italian]

cicada /si-**kah**-dǎ/ *n.* (also **cicala**) any transparent-winged large insect of the family Cicadidae, the males of which make a loud rhythmic chirping sound. ▷ HEMIPTERA. [Latin]

cicatrice *n.* (also **cicatrix**) (*pl.* **cicatrices**) any mark left by a healed wound; a scar. [from Latin *cicatrix -icis*] □ **cicatricial** *adj.*

cicatrize *v.* (also **-ise**) **1** *tr.* heal (a wound) by scar formation. **2** *intr.* (of a wound) heal by scar formation. □ **cicatrization** *n.*

cicely *n.* (*pl.* **-ies**) any of various umbelliferous plants, esp. sweet cicely.

cichlid /**sik**-lid/ *n.* ▶ a tropical freshwater fish of the

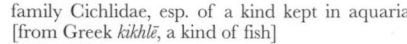

family Cichlidae, esp. of a kind kept in aquaria. [from Greek *kikhlē*, a kind of fish]

CID *abbr.* (in the UK) Criminal Investigation Department.

-cide *suffix* forming nouns meaning: **1** a person or substance that kills (*regicide; insecticide*). **2** the killing of (*infanticide; suicide*). [French from Latin, based on *caedere* 'to kill']

cider *n.* (also *Brit.* **cyder**) *Brit.* an alcoholic drink made from fermented apple juice. [from Hebrew *šēkār* 'strong drink']

cider press *n.* a press for crushing apples to make cider.

cigar *n.* a cylinder of tobacco rolled in tobacco leaves for smoking. [from Spanish *cigarro*]

cigarette *n.* (*US* **cigaret**) **1** a thin cylinder of finely cut tobacco rolled in paper for smoking. **2** a similar cylinder containing a narcotic, herbs, or a medicated substance. [French, literally 'little cigar']

cigarette card *n.* *Brit.* a small picture card of a kind formerly included in a packet of cigarettes.

cigarette end *n.* *Brit.* the unsmoked remainder of a cigarette.

cigarillo *n.* (*pl.* **-os**) a small cigar. [Spanish]

ciliary *adj.* **1** *Biol.* of or relating to cilia. **2** *Anat.* **a** of or relating to the eyelids or eyelashes. **b** of or denoting the part of the eye (**ciliary body**) connecting the iris to the choroid, and the muscle in it which controls the shape of the lens. ▷ EYE

cilium *n.* (*pl.* **cilia**) **1** *Anat. & Biol.* a short minute hairlike vibrating structure occurring, usu. in large numbers, on the surface of some cells or small organisms. **2** an eyelash. [Latin, literally 'eyelash'] □ **ciliated** *adj.* **ciliation** *n.*

cill var. of SILL.

cimbalom *n.* a dulcimer. [Hungarian]

C.-in-C. *abbr.* Commander-in-Chief.

cinch ● *n.* *colloq.* **a** a sure thing; a certainty. **b** an easy task. **2** a firm hold. ● *v.tr.* **1 a** tighten as with a cinch (*cinched at the waist with a belt*). **b** secure a grip on. **2** *slang* make certain of. [from Spanish *cincha*]

cincture *n.* *literary* a girdle, belt, or border. [from Latin *cinctura*]

cinder *n.* **1** the residue of coal or wood etc. that has stopped giving off flames but can still burn. **2** slag. **3** (in *pl.*) ashes. □ **burnt to a cinder** made useless by burning. [Old English] □ **cindery** *adj.*

Cinderella *n.* **1** a person or thing of unrecognized or disregarded merit or beauty. **2** a neglected or despised member of a group. [name of a girl in a fairy tale]

cine- /**sin**-i/ *comb. form* cinematographic. [abbreviation]

cineaste *n.* (also **cineast**) a cinema enthusiast. [from French]

cinema *n.* **1** *Brit.* a theatre where motion-picture films (see FILM *n.* 3a, b) are shown. **2 a** films collectively. **b** the production of films as an art or industry; cinematography. [from Greek *kinēma* 'movement']

cinematic *adj.* **1** having the qualities characteristic of the cinema. **2** of or relating to the cinema. □ **cinematically** *adv.*

cinematograph *n.* esp. *Brit. hist.* an apparatus for making or showing motion-picture films. [based on Greek *kinēma -atos* 'movement']

cinematography *n.* the art of making motion-picture films. □ **cinematographer** *n.* **cinematographic** *adj.* **cinematographically** *adv.*

cinephile *n.* a person who is fond of the cinema.

cineplex *n.* *N. Amer. & Austral.* a multiplex cinema.

cineraria *n.* a plant, *Pericallis cruenta* (daisy family), cultivated for its bright flowers.

[based on Latin *cinis -eris* 'ashes', from the ash-coloured down on the leaves]

cinerary *adj.* of ashes. [from Latin *cinerarius*]

cinerary urn *n.* an urn for holding the ashes after cremation.

cinnabar ● *n.* **1** ▶ a bright red mineral form of mercuric sulphide from which mercury is obtained. ▷ ORE. **2** vermilion. ● *adj.* bright red. [from Greek *kinnabari*]

cinnamon ● *n.* **1** an aromatic spice from the peeled, dried, and rolled bark of a SE Asian tree. ▷ SPICE. **2** any tree of the genus *Cinnamomum*, esp. *C. zeylanicum*, yielding the spice. **3** yellowish brown. ● *adj.* of this colour. [from Greek *kinnamon*]

CINNABAR

cinquefoil /**sink**-foil/ *n.* **1 a** herbaceous plant of the genus *Potentilla* (rose family), with compound leaves of five leaflets. **2** *Archit.* a five-cusped ornament in a circle or arch. [from Latin *quinque* 'five' + *folium* 'leaf']

Cinque Ports /sink/ *n.pl.* (in the UK) a group of ports (originally five only, Hastings, Sandwich, Dover, Romney, and Hythe, later also Rye and Winchelsea) on the SE coast of England with ancient privileges. [from Latin *quinque portus* 'five ports']

cion *US* var. of SCION 1.

cipher (also **cypher**) ● *n.* **1 a** a secret or disguised way of writing. **b** a thing written in this way. **c** the key to it. **2** the arithmetical symbol (0) denoting no amount but used to occupy a vacant place in decimal etc. numeration (as in 12.05). **3** a person or thing of no importance. **4** the interlaced initials of a person or company etc.; a monogram. ● *v.tr.* put into secret writing, encipher. [from Arabic *ṣifr* 'zero']

circa *prep.* (often preceding a date) about; approximately. [Latin]

circadian /ser-**kay**-di-ǎn/ *adj.* *Physiol.* occurring or recurring about once per day. [based on Latin *circa* 'about' + *dies* 'day']

circle ● *n.* **1 a** ▼ a plane figure whose circumference is everywhere equidistant from its centre. **b** the line enclosing a circle. **2** a roundish enclosure or structure. **3** a ring. **4** a curved upper tier of seats in a theatre etc. (*dress circle*). **5** a circular route. **6** *US* = CIRCUS *n.* 3. **7** *Archaeol.* a group of (usu. large embedded) stones arranged in a circle. **8** *Hockey* = STRIKING-CIRCLE. **9** persons grouped round a centre of interest. **10** a set or class or restricted group (*literary circles; not done in the best circles*). **11** (in full **vicious circle**) **a** an unbroken sequence of reciprocal cause and effect. **b** an action and reaction that intensify each other (cf. VIRTUOUS CIRCLE). **c** the fallacy of proving a proposition from another which depends on the first for its own proof. ● *v.* **1** *intr.* move in a circle. **2** *tr.* **a** revolve round. **b** form a circle round. □ **circle back** move in a wide loop towards the starting point. **come full circle** return to the starting point. **go round in circles** make no progress despite effort. **run round in circles** *colloq.* be fussily busy with little result. [from Latin *circulus* 'little ring']

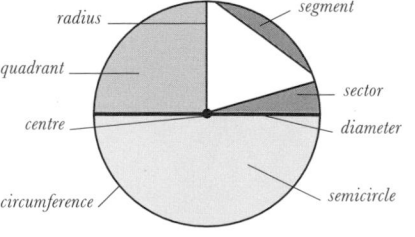

CHURN: 18TH-CENTURY END-OVER-END CHURN

lid clasp
glass peephole
crank handle
barrel
drainage hole

CICHLID: AFRICAN BUTTERFLY CICHLID (*Anomalochromis thomasi*)

radius   *segment*
quadrant
centre   *sector*
circumference   *diameter*
semicircle

CIRCLE AND ASSOCIATED PARTS

circlet *n.* **1** a small circle. **2** a circular band, esp. of gold or jewelled etc., as an ornament.

circlip *n.* a metal ring sprung into a slot or groove in a bar etc. to hold a thing in place.

circs *n.pl. colloq.* circumstances.

circuit *n.* **1 a** a line or course enclosing an area; the distance round. **b** the area enclosed. **2** *Electr.* **a** ▼ the path of a current. **b** the apparatus through which a current passes. **3 a** the journey of a judge in a particular district to hold courts. **b** this district. **4** *Brit.* a motor racing track. **5 a** a sequence of sporting events (*the US tennis circuit*). **b** a sequence of athletic exercises. **6** a roundabout journey. **7** a group of local Methodist Churches forming a minor administrative unit. **8** an itinerary or route followed by an entertainer, politician, etc.; a sphere of operation (*election circuit; cabaret circuit*). [from Latin *circuitus*]

circuit board *n.* a thin rigid board containing an electric circuit, esp. = PRINTED CIRCUIT. ▷ TELEPHONE, VIDEO RECORDER

circuit-breaker *n.* an automatic device for stopping the flow of current in an electric circuit.

circuitous /ser-kew-itŭs/ *adj.* **1** indirect (and usu. long). **2** going a long way round. □ **circuitously** *adv.* **circuitousness** *n.*

circuitry *n.* (*pl.* **-ies**) **1** a system of electric circuits. **2** the equipment forming this.

circular ● *adj.* **1 a** having the form of a circle. **b** moving or taking place along a circle (*circular tour*). **2** *Logic* (of reasoning) depending on a vicious circle. **3** (of a letter or advertisement etc.) for distribution to a large number of people. ● *n.* a circular letter, leaflet, etc. [based on Latin *circulus* 'circle'] □ **circularity** *n.* **circularly** *adv.*

circularize *v.tr.* (also **-ise**) **1** distribute circulars to. **2** *US* seek opinions of (people) by means of a questionnaire. □ **circularization** *n.*

circular saw *n.* a power saw with a rapidly rotating toothed disc. ▷ SAW

circulate *v.* **1** *intr.* go round from one place or person etc. to the next and so on; be in circulation. **2** *tr.* **a** cause to go round; put into circulation. **b** give currency to (a report etc.). **c** circularize. **3** *intr.* be actively sociable at a party, gathering, etc. □ **circulative** *adj.* **circulator** *n.*

circulating library *n. hist.* a small library with books lent for a small fee to subscribers.

circulating medium *n.* notes or gold etc. used in exchange.

circulation *n.* **1 a** movement to and fro, or from and back to a starting point, esp. of a fluid in a confined area or circuit. **b** the movement of blood to and from the tissues of the body. **2** the number of copies sold, esp. of journals and newspapers. **3** the movement or exchange of currency or coin in a country etc. □ **in** (or **out of**) **circulation** participating (or not participating) in activities etc.

circulatory *adj.* of or relating to the circulation of blood or sap.

circumcise *v.tr.* **1** cut off the foreskin of, as a Jewish or Muslim rite or a surgical operation. **2** cut off the clitoris (and sometimes the labia) of, as a traditional practice among some peoples. [based on Latin *circumcisus* 'cut round']

circumcision *n.* the act or rite of circumcising or being circumcised.

circumference *n.* **1** the enclosing boundary, esp. of a circle or other figure enclosed by a curve. ▷ CIRCLE. **2** the distance round. [from Latin *circumferentia*] □ **circumferential** *adj.* **circumferentially** *adv.*

circumflex *n.* (in full **circumflex accent**) a mark (˄ or ˆ) placed over a vowel in some languages to indicate a contraction, length, or a special quality. [from Latin *circumflexus* 'bent round']

circumlocution *n.* **1 a** a roundabout expression. **b** evasive talk. **2** the use of many words where fewer would do; verbosity. [from Latin *circumlocutio*, translation of Greek *periphrasis*] □ **circumlocutory** *adj.*

circumnavigate *v.tr.* sail round (esp. the world). [from Latin *circumnavigare*] □ **circumnavigation** *n.* **circumnavigator** *n.*

circumpolar *adj.* **1** *Geog.* around or near one of the Earth's poles. **2** *Astron.* (of a star or motion etc.) above the horizon at all times in a given latitude.

circumscribe *v.tr.* **1** (of a line etc.) enclose or outline. **2** lay down the limits of; confine, restrict. [from Latin *circumscribere*] □ **circumscription** *n.*

circumspect *adj.* wary, cautious; taking everything into account. [from Latin *circumspectus* 'having looked around'] □ **circumspection** *n.* **circumspectly** *adv.*

circumstance *n.* **1 a** a fact, occurrence, or condition, esp. (in *pl.*) the time, place, manner, cause, occasion, etc., or surroundings of an act or event. **b** (in *pl.*, or *sing.* as uncount noun) the external conditions that affect or might affect an action (*a victim of circumstance(s)*). **2** (often foll. by *that* + clause) an incident, occurrence, or fact (*the circumstance that he left early*). **3** (in *pl.*) one's state of financial or material welfare (*in reduced circumstances*). **4** ceremony, fuss (*pomp and circumstance*). □ **in** (or **under**) **the** (or **these**) **circumstances** the state of affairs being what it is. **in** (or **under**) **no circumstances** not at all; never. [from Latin *circumstantia*] □ **circumstanced** *adj.*

circumstantial *adj.* **1** given in full detail (*a circumstantial account*). **2** (of evidence, a legal case, etc.) tending to establish a conclusion by inference from known facts hard to explain otherwise. **3 a** depending on circumstances. **b** adventitious, incidental. □ **circumstantiality** *n.* **circumstantially** *adv.*

circumvent *v.tr.* **1 a** evade (a difficulty); find a way round. **b** baffle, outwit. **2** entrap (an enemy) by surrounding. [based on Latin *circumventus* 'surrounded'] □ **circumvention** *n.*

circus *n.* (*pl.* **circuses**) **1** a travelling show of performing animals, acrobats, clowns, etc. **2** *colloq.* a scene of lively action; a disturbance. **3** *Brit.* a rounded open space in a town, where several streets converge (*Piccadilly Circus*). **4** *Rom. Antiq.* a rounded or oval arena with tiers of seats, for equestrian and other sports and games. [Latin, literally 'ring']

cire perdue /seer pair-**dew**/ *n.* = LOST WAX. [French]

cirque /serk/ *n.* **1** *Geol.* ▲ a deep bowl-shaped hollow at the head of a valley or on a mountainside. **2** *poet.* **a** a ring. **b** an amphitheatre or arena. [French]

cirrhosis /si-**roh**-sis/ *n. Med.* a chronic disease of the liver as a result of alcoholism, hepatitis, etc. [modern Latin] □ **cirrhotic** *adj.*

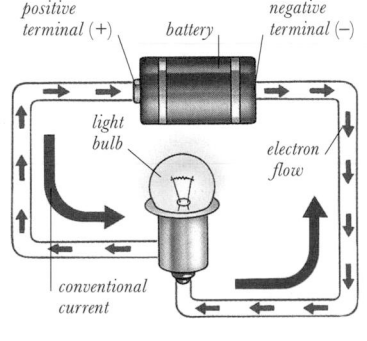

CIRQUE

As snow accumulates in shallow mountain hollows, it compresses into ice. The soil is loosened by frost wedging and abrasion, and the hollow deepens to form a cirque.

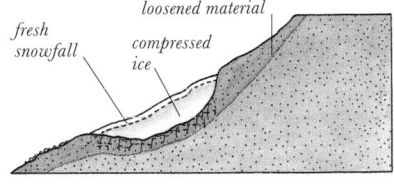

CROSS-SECTION THROUGH A CIRQUE

---

cirriped *n.* (also **cirripede**) any marine crustacean of the class Cirripedia, which comprises the barnacles. [from Latin *cirrus* 'curl' (from the form of the legs) + *pes pedis* 'foot']

cirro- *comb. form.* denoting cloud types formed at high altitudes (above 6 km or 20,000 feet). ▷ CLOUD

cirrus *n.* (*pl.* **cirri** /-ry/) **1** *Meteorol.* **a** a cloud formed at high altitude as delicate white wisps. ▷ CLOUD. **b** a cloud of this type. **2** *Bot.* a tendril. **3** *Zool.* a long slender appendage or filament. ▷ BARNACLE. [Latin, literally 'curl'] □ **cirrose** *adj.* **cirrous** *adj.*

CIS *abbr.* Commonwealth of Independent States (consisting of countries of the former Soviet Union).

cis- *prefix* on this side of; on the side nearer to the speaker or writer (*cisalpine*) (opp. TRANS- 2 or ULTRA- 1).

cisalpine /sis **al** pyn/ *adj.* on the southern side of the Alps.

cissy *var. of* SISSY.

Cistercian ● *n.* a monk or nun of an order founded as a stricter branch of the Benedictines. ● *adj.* of the Cistercians. [from Cistercium, Latin name of Cîteaux near Dijon in France]

cistern *n.* **1** a tank for storing water, esp. supplying taps or as part of a flushing lavatory. **2** an underground reservoir for rainwater. [from Latin *cisterna*]

cistus *n.* any shrub of the genus *Cistus*, with large white or red flowers. [from Greek *kistos*]

citadel *n.* **1** a fortress, usu. on high ground protecting or dominating a city. ▷ ACROPOLIS. **2** a meeting hall of the Salvation Army. [based on Latin *civitas* 'city']

citation *n.* **1** the citing of a book or other source; a passage cited. **2** a mention in an official dispatch. **3** a note accompanying an award, describing the reasons for it.

cite *v.tr.* **1** adduce as an instance. **2** quote (a passage, book, or author) in support of an argument etc. **3** mention in an official dispatch. [from Latin *citare*] □ **citable** *adj.*

CITES /**sy**-teez/ *abbr.* Convention on International Trade in Endangered Species.

citified *adj.* (also **cityfied**) usu. *derog.* city-like or urban in appearance or behaviour.

citizen *n.* **1** a member of a state or commonwealth (*British citizen*). **2 a** an inhabitant of a city. **b** a freeman of a city. **3** *US* a civilian. [based on Latin *civitas* 'city'] □ **citizenry** *n.* **citizenship** *n.*

Citizens' Advice Bureau *n.* (in the UK) an office at which the public can receive free advice on civil matters.

citizen's arrest *n.* an arrest by an ordinary person without a warrant.

citizens' band *n.* a system of local intercommunication by individuals on special radio frequencies.

Citizen's Charter *n. Polit.* a document guaranteeing citizens the right of redress where a public service fails to meet certain standards.

citrate *n. Chem.* a salt or ester of citric acid.

citric *adj.* derived from citrus fruit.

CITRUS FRUIT

Cultivated for at least 2,000 years in subtropical climates, citrus fruits are valued chiefly for their edible fruit, peel, and juice. They provide vital flavourings in food and drink, and are a rich source of vitamin C.

Cosmetics, scents, and aromatherapy also rely on essential oils yielded by their peel, leaves, and shoots, while soaps are made from the seed oils. Colds, coughs, and sore throats can all be soothed by citrus juices.

EXAMPLES OF CITRUS FRUITS

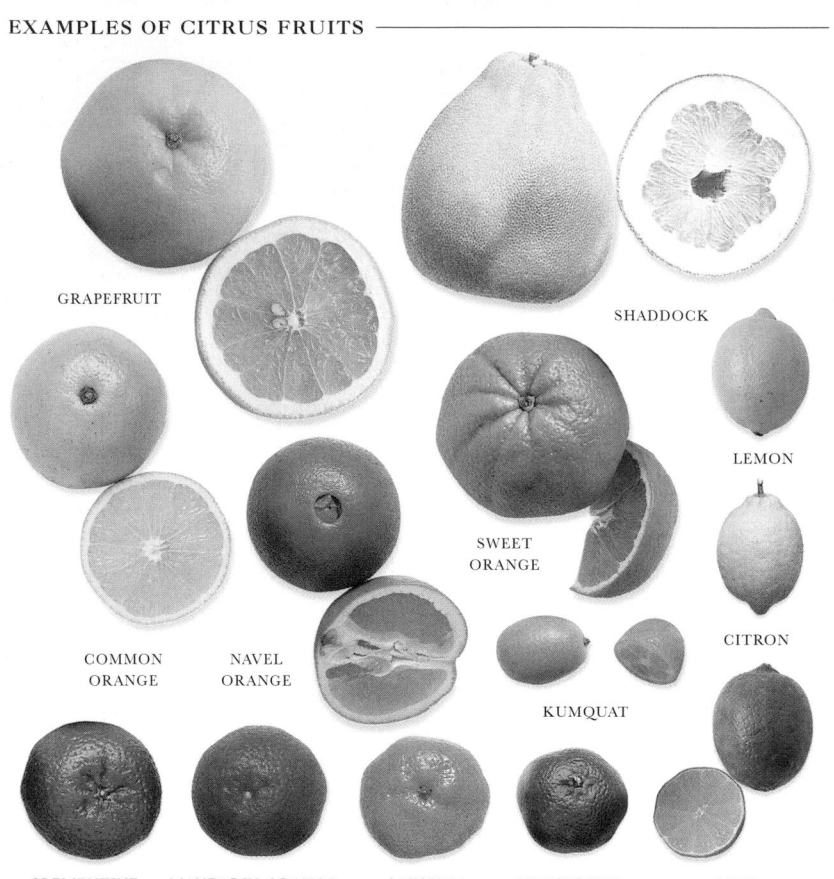

GRAPEFRUIT

SHADDOCK

LEMON

SWEET ORANGE

CITRON

COMMON ORANGE

NAVEL ORANGE

KUMQUAT

CLEMENTINE MANDARIN ORANGE SATSUMA TANGERINE LIME

citric acid *n.* a sharp-tasting water-soluble organic acid found in the juice of lemons and other sour fruits and used as a flavouring and setting agent.

citron *n.* **1** a shrubby tree, *Citrus medica*, bearing large lemon-like fruits with thick fragrant peel. **2** this fruit. ▷ CITRUS FRUIT. [French]

citronella *n.* **1** any fragrant grass of the genus *Cymbopogon*, native to S. Asia. **2** the scented oil from these, used in insect repellent, and in perfume and soap manufacture. [modern Latin]

citrus *n.* (*pl.* **citruses**) **1** any tree of the genus *Citrus*, including lemon, lime, orange, and grapefruit. **2** (in full **citrus fruit**) ▲ a fruit from such a tree. [Latin, literally 'citron tree'] □ **citrous** *adj.*

city *n.* (*pl.* **-ies**) **1 a** a large town. **b** *Brit.* (strictly) a town created a city by charter and containing a cathedral. **c** *US* a municipal state-chartered corporation occupying a definite area. **2** (**the City**) *Brit.* **a** the part of London governed by the Lord Mayor and the Corporation. **b** the business part of this. **c** commercial circles. **3** (*attrib.*) of a city or the City. [from Latin *civitas*] □ **cityward** *adj. & adv.* **citywards** *adv.*

City Company *n.* (in the UK) a corporation descended from an ancient trade guild.

city father *n.* (usu. in *pl.*) a person concerned with or experienced in the administration of a city.

cityfied *var.* of CITIFIED.

city hall *n. N. Amer.* municipal offices or officers.

cityscape *n.* **1** a view of a city (actual or depicted). **2** city scenery.

city slicker *n.* usu. *derog.* **1** a smart and sophisticated city dweller. **2** a plausible rogue as usu. found in cities.

city state *n.* esp. *hist.* a city that with its surrounding territory forms an independent state.

City Technology College *n.* a type of secondary school, set up mainly in towns and cities through partnerships between the Government and business and concentrating on technology and science.

civet *n.* **1** (in full **civet cat**) a slender catlike animal of the family Viverridae, esp. *Viverra civetta* of central Africa, having well-developed anal scent glands. **2** a strong musky perfume obtained from the secretions of these glands. [from medieval Latin *zibethum*, from Arabic]

civic *adj.* **1** of a city. **2** of or proper to citizens (*civic virtues*). **3** of citizenship. [from Latin *civicus*] □ **civically** *adv.*

civic centre *n.* the area in a town where municipal offices and other public buildings are situated; the buildings themselves.

civics *n.pl.* (usu. treated as *sing.*) the study of the rights and duties of citizenship.

civil *adj.* **1** of or belonging to citizens. **2** of ordinary citizens and their concerns, as distinct from military or naval or ecclesiastical matters. **3** polite, obliging. **4** *Law* relating to civil law, not criminal or political matters (*civil court*). **5** (of the length of a day, year, etc.) fixed by custom or law, not natural or astronomical. [based on Latin *civis* 'citizen'] □ **civilly** *adv.*

civil aviation *n.* non-military, esp. commercial, aviation.

civil commotion *n. Brit. Law* a riot or similar disturbance.

civil defence *n.* the organization of civilians for the protection of lives and property during and after attacks in wartime.

civil disobedience *n.* the refusal to comply with certain laws or to pay taxes etc. as a peaceful form of political protest.

civil engineer *n.* an engineer who designs or maintains roads, bridges, dams, etc. □ **civil engineering** *n.*

civilian ● *n.* a person not in the armed services or the police force. ● *adj.* of or for civilians.

civilianize *v.tr.* (also **-ise**) make civilian in character or function. □ **civilianization** *n.*

civility *n.* (*pl.* **-ies**) **1** politeness. **2** an act of politeness.

civilization *n.* (also **-isation**) **1** an advanced stage or system of social development. **2** those peoples of the world regarded as having this. **3** a people or nation (esp. of the past) regarded as an element of social evolution (*the Inca civilization*). **4** making or becoming civilized.

civilize *v.tr.* (also **-ise**) **1** bring out of a barbarous or primitive stage of society. **2** enlighten; refine and educate. □ **civilizer** *n.*

civil law *n.* **1** law concerning private rights (opp. CRIMINAL LAW). **2** Roman or non-ecclesiastical law, as of Quebec, France, or Germany (cf. COMMON LAW).

civil liberty *n.* (often in *pl.*) freedom of action and speech subject to the law.

Civil List *n.* (in the UK) an annual allowance voted by Parliament for the royal family's household expenses.

civil marriage *n.* a marriage solemnized as a civil contract without religious ceremony.

civil parish see PARISH 2.

civil rights *n.pl.* the rights of citizens to political and social freedom and equality.

civil servant *n.* a member of the civil service.

civil service *n.* the permanent professional branches of State administration, excluding military and judicial branches and elected politicians.

civil war *n.* a war between citizens of the same country.

civil year see YEAR 2.

civvy (*pl.* **-ies**) *slang* ● *n.* **1** (in *pl.*) civilian clothes. **2** a civilian. ● *adj.* civilian.

Civvy Street *n. Brit. slang* civilian life.

CJD *abbr.* Creutzfeldt–Jakob disease.

Cl *symb. Chem.* the element chlorine.

cl *abbr.* centilitre(s).

clack ● *v.intr.* **1** make a sharp sound as of boards struck together. **2** chatter. ● *n.* **1** a clacking sound. **2** clacking talk. [Middle English in sense 'to chatter'] □ **clacker** *n.*

clad¹ *adj.* **1** clothed (often in *comb.*: *leather-clad*; *scantily clad*). **2** provided with cladding. [past participle of CLOTHE]

clad² *v.tr.* (**cladding**; *past* and *past part.* **cladded** or **clad**) provide with cladding.

cladding *n.* a covering or coating on a structure or material etc.

clade *n. Biol.* a group of organisms evolved from a common ancestor. [from Greek *klados* 'branch']

cladistics *n. Biol.* a method of classification of animals and plants on the basis of those shared characteristics which are assumed to indicate common ancestry.

claim ● *v.tr.* **1 a** demand as one's due or property. **b** (usu. *absol.*) submit a request for payment under an insurance policy. **2 a** represent oneself as having or achieving (*claim victory*; *claim accuracy*). **b** (foll. by *to* + infin.) profess (*claimed to be the owner*). **c** assert, contend (*claim that one knows*). **3** have as an achievement or a consequence (*could claim five wins*; *fire claimed many victims*). **4** (of a thing) deserve (one's attention etc.). ● *n.* **1 a** a demand or request for something considered one's due (*lay claim to*; *put in a claim*). **b** an application for compensation under the terms of an insurance policy. **2** (foll. by *to*, *on*) a right or title to a thing (*his only claim to fame*; *have many claims on my time*). **3** a contention or assertion. **4** a thing claimed. **5** *Mining* a piece of land allotted or taken. [from Latin *clamare*] □ **claimable** *adj.* **claimer** *n.*

claimant *n.* a person making a claim, esp. in a lawsuit or for a state benefit.

clairvoyance *n.* **1** the supposed faculty of perceiving things or events in the future or beyond normal sensory contact. **2** exceptional insight.

clairvoyant ● *n.* a person having clairvoyance. ● *adj.* having clairvoyance. [French, literally 'seeing clearly'] □ **clairvoyantly** *adv.*

clam ● *n.* **1** ▼ any bivalve mollusc, esp. the edible N. American hard or round clam (*Venus mercenaria*) or the soft or long clam (*Mya arenaria*). ▷ BIVALVE. **2** *colloq.* a shy or withdrawn person. ● *v.intr.* (**clammed**, **clamming**) **1** dig for clams. **2** (foll. by *up*) *colloq.* refuse to talk. [16th-century coinage]

CLAM: SOFT-SHELL CLAM (*Mya arenaria*)

clamber ● *v.intr.* climb with hands and feet. ● *n.* a difficult climb. [Middle English]

clammy *adj.* (**clammier**, **clammiest**) **1** unpleasantly damp and sticky or slimy. **2** (of weather) cold and damp. [based on *clam* 'to daub'] □ **clammily** *adv.* **clamminess** *n.*

clamour (*US* **clamor**) ● *n.* **1** loud or vehement shouting or noise. **2** a protest or complaint; an appeal or demand. ● *v.* **1** *intr.* make a clamour. **2** *tr.* utter with a clamour. [from Latin *clamor*] □ **clamorous** *adj.* **clamorously** *adv.*

clamp[1] ● *n.* **1** a device for strengthening other materials or holding things together. **2** *Brit.* a device for immobilizing an illegally parked car. ● *v.tr.* **1** strengthen or fasten with a clamp. **2** place or hold firmly. **3** immobilize (an illegally parked car) by fixing a clamp to one of its wheels. □ **clamp down 1** be rigid in enforcing a rule etc. **2** (foll. by *on*) try to suppress. [Middle English]

clamp[2] *n.* **1** *Brit.* a heap of potatoes or other root vegetables stored under straw or earth. **2** a pile of bricks for firing. [16th-century coinage]

clampdown *n.* a rigid policy of suppression.

clamshell *n.* **1** the shell of a clam, formed of two roughly equal valves with a hinge. **2** a thing with a lid or opening section resembling this.

clan *n.* **1** a group of people with a common ancestor, esp. in the Scottish Highlands. **2** a large family as a social group. **3** a group with a strong common interest. [from Latin *planta* 'sprout']

clandestine *adj.* surreptitious, secret. [based on Latin *clam* 'secretly'] □ **clandestinely** *adv.* **clandestinity** *n.*

clang ● *n.* a loud resonant metallic sound. ● *v.* **1** *intr.* make a clang. **2** *tr.* cause to clang.

clanger *n.* esp. *Brit. slang* a mistake or blunder. □ **drop a clanger** commit a conspicuous indiscretion.

clangour *n.* (*US* **clangor**) **1** a prolonged or repeated clanging noise. **2** an uproar or commotion. [from Latin *clangor* 'noise (of trumpets etc.)'] □ **clangorous** *adj.*

clank ● *n.* a sound as of heavy pieces of metal meeting or a chain rattling. ● *v.* **1** *intr.* make a clanking sound. **2** *tr.* cause to clank. □ **clankingly** *adv.*

clannish *adj.* usu. *derog.* **1** (of a family or group) tending to hold together. **2** of or like a clan. □ **clannishness** *n.*

clansman *n.* (*pl.* **-men**; *fem.* **clanswoman**, *pl.* **-women**) a member or fellow member of a clan.

clap[1] ● *v.* (**clapped**, **clapping**) **1 a** *intr.* strike the palms of one's hands together as a signal or repeatedly as applause. **b** *tr.* strike (the hands) together in this way. **2** *tr.* applaud or show one's approval of in this way. **3** *tr.* (of a bird) flap (its wings) audibly. **4** *tr.* put or place quickly or with determination (*clapped him in prison*; *clap a tax on whisky*). ● *n.* **1** the act of clapping. **2** an explosive sound, esp. of thunder. **3** a slap, a pat. □ **clap eyes on** *colloq.* see. [Old English *clappian* 'to throb, beat']

clap[2] *n. coarse slang* venereal disease, esp. gonorrhoea. [from Old French *clapoir* 'venereal bubo']

clapboard *n.* *US* = WEATHERBOARD. [from Low German *klappholt* 'cask-stave']

clapped out *adj.* (hyphenated when *attrib.*). *Brit. slang* worn out; exhausted.

clapper *n.* the tongue or striker of a bell. □ **like the clappers** *Brit. slang* very fast or hard.

claptrap *n.* insincere or pretentious talk, nonsense.

claque /klak/ *n.* a group of people hired to applaud in a theatre etc. [French]

claret ● *n.* **1** red wine, esp. from Bordeaux. **2** a deep purplish red. ● *adj.* claret-coloured. [based on Latin *clarus* 'clear']

clarify *v.* (**-ies**, **-ied**) **1** *tr.* & *intr.* make or become clearer. **2** *tr.* **a** free (liquid, butter, etc.) from impurities. **b** make transparent. **c** purify. [based on Latin *clarus* 'clear'] □ **clarification** *n.* **clarificatory** *adj.* **clarifier** *n.*

clarinet *n.* ▶ a woodwind instrument with a single-reed mouthpiece, a cylindrical tube with a flared end, holes, and keys. ▷ ORCHESTRA, WOODWIND. [from French *clarinette* 'small clarion'] □ **clarinettist** *n.* (*US* **clarinetist**).

clarion ● *n.* **1** a clear rousing sound. **2** *hist.* a shrill narrow-tubed war trumpet. ● *adj.* clear and loud. [based on Latin *clarus* 'clear']

clarity *n.* the state or quality of being clear. [from Latin *claritas*]

clash ● *n.* **1 a** a loud jarring sound as of metal objects being struck together. **b** a collision, esp. with force. **2 a** a conflict or disagreement. **b** a discord of colours etc. ● *v.* **1 a** *intr.* make a clashing sound. **b** *tr.* cause to clash. **2** *intr.* coincide awkwardly. **3** *intr.* **a** come into conflict or be at variance. **b** (of colours) be discordant. □ **clasher** *n.*

clasp ● *n.* **1 a** a device for interlocking parts for fastening. **b** a buckle or brooch. **c** a metal fastening on a book cover. **2 a** an embrace. **b** a grasp or handshake. **3** a bar of silver on a medal-ribbon with the name of the battle etc. at which the wearer was present. ● *v.* **1** *tr.* fasten with or as with a clasp. **2 a** grasp, hold closely.

mouthpiece

barrel joint

head joint

keys for left hand

middle joint

keys for right hand

cork sealing ring

tube

flared end

CLARINET: SOPRANO CLARINET

b embrace, encircle. **3** *intr.* fasten a clasp. □ **clasp hands** shake hands with fervour or affection. **clasp one's hands** interlace one's fingers. [Middle English] □ **clasper** *n.*

clasp-knife *n.* a folding knife, usu. with a catch holding the blade when open.

class ● *n.* **1** any set of persons or things grouped together, or graded or differentiated from others esp. by quality (*first class*). **2 a** a division or order of society (*upper class*). **b** a caste system, a system of social classes. **3** *colloq.* distinction, high quality. **4 a** a group of students taught together. **b** the occasion when they meet. **c** their course of instruction. **5** *US* all the college or school students of the same standing or graduating in a given year (*the class of 1990*). **6** *Brit.* a division of candidates according to merit in an examination. **7** *Biol.* a grouping of organisms, the next major rank below a division or phylum. ● *v.tr.* assign to a class or category. ● *attrib.adj. colloq.* classy, stylish. □ **in a class of** (or **on**) **its** (or **one's**) **own** unequalled. [from Latin *classis* 'assembly']

class-conscious *adj.* aware of and reacting to social divisions or one's place in a system of social class. □ **class-consciousness** *n.*

classic ● *adj.* **1 a** of the first class; of acknowledged excellence. **b** remarkably typical (*a classic case*). **2 a** of ancient Greek and Latin literature, art, or culture. **b** (of style in art, music, etc.) simple, harmonious, well-proportioned (cf. ROMANTIC *adj.* 4). **3** having literary or historic associations (*classic ground*). **4** (of clothes) made in a simple elegant style not much affected by changes in fashion. ● *n.* **1 a** a classic writer, artist, work, or example. **2 a** an ancient Greek or Latin writer. **b** (in *pl.*) ancient Greek and Latin literature and history. **3** a garment in classic style. [based on Latin *classis* 'class']

classical *adj.* **1 a** of ancient Greek or Latin literature, art, or culture. **b** (of language) having the form used by the ancient standard authors (*classical Latin*; *classical Hebrew*). **c** based on the study of ancient Greek and Latin (*a classical education*). **2 a** (of music) serious or conventional; intended to be of permanent rather than ephemeral value (cf. POPULAR MUSIC, LIGHT[2] *adj.* 5a). **b** of the period from *c*.1750–1800. **3 a** ▶ in or following the restrained style of classical antiquity (cf. ROMANTIC *adj.* 4). **b** (of a form or period of art etc.) representing an exemplary standard. **4** *Physics* relating to the concepts which preceded relativity and quantum theory. □ **classically** *adv.*

CLASSICAL SCULPTURE: *The Three Graces* (1813), ANTONIO CANOVA

classicism *n.* **1** the following of a classic style. **2** classical scholarship. □ **classicist** *n.*

classicize *v.* (also **-ise**) **1** *tr.* make classic. **2** *intr.* imitate a classical style.

classified ● *adj.* **1** arranged in classes or categories. **2** (of information etc.) designated as officially secret. **3** *Brit.* (of a road) assigned to a category according to its importance. **4** (of advertisements) arranged in columns according to various categories. ● *n.* (in *pl.*) classified advertisements.

classify *v.tr.* (**-ies**, **-ied**) **1 a** arrange in classes or categories. **b** assign to a class or category. **2** designate as officially secret or not for general disclosure. □ **classifiable** *adj.* **classification** *n.* **classificatory** *adj.* **classifier** *n.*

classism *n.* discrimination on the grounds of social class. □ **classist** *adj.* & *n.*

C

classless *adj.* making or showing no distinction of classes (*classless society*). □ **classlessness** *n.*

class-list *n. Brit.* a list of candidates in an examination with the class achieved by each.

classmate *n.* a fellow member of a class, esp. at school.

classroom *n.* a room in which a class of students is taught.

class war *n.* conflict between social classes.

classy *adj.* (**classier, classiest**) *colloq.* superior, stylish. □ **classily** *adv.* **classiness** *n.*

clatter ● *n.* **1** a rattling sound as of many hard objects struck together. **2** noisy talk. ● *v.* **1** *intr.* **a** make a clatter. **b** fall or move etc. with a clatter. **2** *tr.* cause (plates etc.) to clatter. [Old English]

clause *n.* **1** *Gram.* a distinct part of a sentence, including a subject and predicate. **2** a single statement in a treaty, law, bill, or contract. [from Latin *clausula* 'conclusion'] □ **clausal** *adj.*

claustrophobia *n.* an abnormal fear of confined places. [based on Latin *claustrum* 'cloister']

claustrophobic *adj.* **1** suffering from claustrophobia. **2** inducing claustrophobia. □ **claustrophobically** *adv.*

clavichord *n.* a small keyboard instrument with a very soft tone. [from medieval Latin *clavichordium*]

clavicle *n.* ▶ the collarbone. ▷ SKELETON. [from Latin *clavicula* 'little key', from its shape] □ **clavicular** *adj.*

clavier *n. Mus.* **1** any keyboard instrument. **2** its keyboard. [from medieval Latin *claviarius*, originally in sense 'key-bearer']

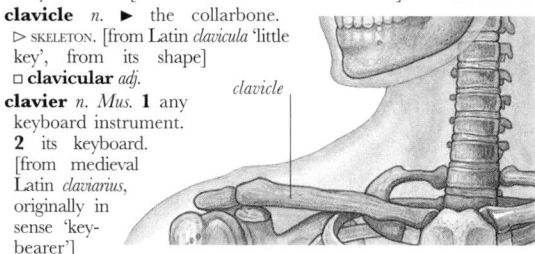

clavicle

CLAVICLE IN THE HUMAN SKELETON

claw ● *n.* **1 a** ◀ a pointed horny nail on an animal's or bird's foot. ▷ BIRD. **b** ◀ a foot bearing these. **2** the pincer of a crab or other crustacean. **3** a device for grappling, holding, etc. ● *v.* **1** *tr. & intr.* scratch, maul, or pull (a person or thing) with claws. **2** *tr.* make (one's way) with difficulty by pulling oneself (as if) using claws. **3** *tr. & intr. Sc.* scratch gently. **4** *intr. Naut.* beat to windward. □ **claw back** *Brit.* **1** regain laboriously or gradually. **2** recover (money paid out) from another source. [Old English] □ **clawed** *adj.* (also in *comb.*). **clawless** *adj.*

phalanx

claw   *claw*

CLAW: SKELETON OF A SNOWY OWL'S CLAW

claw hammer *n.* a hammer with one side of the head forked for extracting nails.

clay *n.* **1** a stiff sticky earth, used for making bricks, pottery, ceramics, etc. **2** *poet.* the substance of the human body. **3** (in full **clay pipe**) a tobacco pipe made of clay. [Old English] □ **clayey** *adj.* **clayish** *adj.* **claylike** *adj.*

claymore *n.* **1** *hist.* **a** ▼ a Scottish two-edged broadsword. **b** a broadsword, often with a single edge, having a hilt with a basketwork design. **2** a type of anti-personnel mine. [from Gaelic *claidheamh mór* 'great sword']

wooden grip

cross-guard

wheel-shaped pommel

two-edged blade

CLAYMORE:
17TH-CENTURY
SCOTTISH CLAYMORE

clay pigeon *n.* a breakable disc thrown up from a trap as a target for shooting.

clean ● *adj.* **1** free from dirt or contaminating matter, unsoiled. **2** clear; unused or unpolluted (*clean air, clean page*). **3** free from indecency. **4 a** attentive to cleanliness. **b** toilet-trained or house-trained. **5** complete, clear-cut, unobstructed, even. **6 a** (of a ship, aircraft, or car) streamlined, smooth. **b** well-formed, slender and shapely (*clean-limbed; the car has clean lines*). **7** skilful (*clean fielding*). **8** (of a nuclear weapon) producing relatively little fallout. **9 a** free from ceremonial defilement or from disease. **b** (of food) not prohibited. **10 a** free from any record of a crime, offence, etc. (*a clean driving licence*). **b** *slang* free from suspicion. **c** observing the rules of a sport or game; fair (*a clean fight*). **11** (of a taste, smell, etc.) sharp, fresh, distinctive. ● *adv.* **1** completely, outright, simply (*clean bowled; clean forgot*). **2** in a clean manner. ● *v.tr. &* (also foll. by *of*) *intr.* make or become clean. ● *n.* esp. *Brit.* the act or process of cleaning or being cleaned (*give it a clean*). □ **clean out 1** clean thoroughly. **2** *slang* empty or deprive. **clean up 1 a** clear (a mess) away. **b** (also *absol.*) put (things) tidy. **c** make (oneself) clean. **2** restore order or morality to. **3** *slang* **a** acquire as gain or profit. **b** make a gain or profit. **come clean** *colloq.* own up; confess everything. **make a clean breast of** see BREAST. **make a clean job of** *colloq.* do thoroughly. **make a clean sweep of** see SWEEP. [Old English] □ **cleanable** *adj.* **cleanish** *adj.* **cleanness** *n.*

clean bill of health see BILL OF HEALTH 2.

clean break *n.* a quick and final separation.

clean-cut *adj.* **1** sharply outlined. **2** (of a person) clean and neat.

cleaner *n.* **1** a person employed to clean the interior of a building. **2** (usu. in *pl.*) a commercial establishment for cleaning clothes. **3** a device or substance for cleaning. □ **take to the cleaners** *slang* **1** defraud or rob (a person) of all his or her money. **2** criticize severely.

clean hands *n.pl.* freedom from guilt.

clean-living *adj.* of upright character.

cleanly[1] **/kleen-li/** *adv.* **1** in a clean way. **2** efficiently; without difficulty.

cleanly[2] **/klen-li/** *adj.* (**cleanlier, cleanliest**) habitually clean; with clean habits. □ **cleanliness** *n.*

cleanse /klenz/ *v.tr.* **1** usu. *formal* make clean. **2** purify from sin or guilt. [Old English] □ **cleanser** *n.*

clean-shaven *adj.* without, whiskers, beard or moustache.

clean sheet *n.* freedom from commitments or imputations; the removal of these from one's record.

cleansing cream *n.* cream for removing unwanted matter from the face, hands, etc.

cleansing department *n. Brit.* a local service of refuse collection etc.

clean slate *n.* = CLEAN SHEET.

clean-up *n.* an act of cleaning up.

clear ● *adj.* **1** free from dirt or contamination. **2** (of weather, the sky, etc.) not dull. **3 a** transparent. **b** lustrous, shining. **4** (of soup) transparent. **5 a** distinct, easily perceived by the senses. **b** unambiguous, easily understood (*make oneself clear*). **c** manifest; not confused or doubtful (*clear evidence*). **6** that discerns readily and accurately (*clear thinking*). **7** confident, convinced. **8** (of a conscience) free from guilt. **9** (of a road etc.) unobstructed. **10 a** net, without deduction (*a clear £1,000*). **b** complete (*three clear days*). **11** free, unhampered; unencumbered by debt, commitments, etc. **12** (foll. by *of*) not obstructed by. ● *adv.* **1** clearly (*speak loud and clear*). **2** completely (*he got clear away*). **3** apart, out of contact (*stand clear of the doors*). **4** (foll. by *to*) *US* all the way. ● *v.* **1** *tr. & intr.* make or become clear. **2 a** *tr.* free from prohibition or obstruction. **b** *tr. & intr.* make or become empty or unobstructed. **c** *tr.* free (land) for cultivation or building by cutting down trees etc. **d** *tr.* cause people to leave (a room etc.). **3** *tr.* show (a person) to be innocent (*cleared them of complicity*). **4** *tr.* approve (a person) for special duty, access to information, etc. **5** *tr.* pass over or by, safely or without touching. **6** *tr.* make (an amount of money) as net gain or to balance expenses. **7** *tr.* pass (a cheque) through a clearing house. **8** *tr.* pass through (a customs office etc.). **9** *tr.* remove (an obstruction, an unwanted object, etc.) (*clear them out of the way*). **10** *intr.* disappear, gradually diminish (*mist cleared by lunchtime, my cold has cleared up*). □ **clear the air 1** make the air less sultry. **2** disperse an atmosphere of suspicion, tension, etc. **clear away 1** remove completely. **2** remove the remains of a meal from the table. **clear the decks** prepare for action. **clear off 1** get rid of. **2** *colloq.* go away. **clear out 1** empty. **2** remove. **3** *colloq.* go away. **clear one's throat** cough slightly to make one's voice clear. **clear up 1** tidy up. **2** solve (a mystery etc.). **3** (of weather) become fine. **clear the way 1** remove obstacles. **2** stand aside. **in the clear** free from suspicion or difficulty. [from Latin *clarus*] □ **clearly** *adv.* **clearness** *n.*

clearance *n.* **1 a** the removal of obstructions etc. **b** the removal of contents. **2** clear space allowed for the passing of two objects or two parts in machinery etc. **3** special authorization. **4 a** the clearing of a person, ship, etc., by customs. **b** a certificate showing this. **5** the clearing of cheques.

clearance sale *n.* a sale to get rid of superfluous stock.

clear-cut ● *adj.* sharply defined; obvious. ● *v.tr.* (**-cutting**; *past* and *past part.* **-cut**) cut down and remove every tree from (an area).

clearer *n.* **1** a clearing bank. **2** a person or thing that clears or clears away.

clear-headed *adj.* thinking clearly; sensible.

clearing *n.* **1** in senses of CLEAR *v.* **2** an area in a forest cleared for cultivation.

clearing bank *n. Brit.* a bank which is a member of a clearing house.

clearing house *n.* **1** a bankers' establishment where cheques and bills from member banks are exchanged, so that only the balances need be paid in cash. **2** an agency for collecting and distributing information etc.

clear-out *n.* an act or period of clearing out; a removal of unwanted items.

clear-sighted *adj.* seeing, thinking, or understanding clearly.

clearstory *US* var. of CLERESTORY.

clear-up *n.* **1** an act or period of clearing up. **2** (usu. *attrib.*) the solving of crimes (*clear-up rates*).

clearway *n. Brit.* a main road (other than a motorway) on which vehicles are not normally permitted to stop.

clearwing *n.* a day-flying moth with largely transparent wings, of the family Sesiidae.

cleat *n.* **1** a piece of metal, wood, etc., bolted on for fastening ropes to, or to strengthen woodwork etc. **2** a projecting piece on a spar, gangway, boot, etc., to give footing or prevent a rope from slipping. **3** a wedge. [Old English]

cleavage *n.* **1** the hollow between a woman's breasts. **2** a division or splitting. **3** ▲ the splitting of rocks, crystals, etc., in a preferred direction.

cleave[1] *v.* (*past* **clove** or **cleft** or **cleaved**; *past part.* **cloven** or **cleft** or **cleaved**) *literary* **1 a** *tr.* chop or break apart, split, esp. along the grain or the line of cleavage. **b** *intr.* come apart in this way. **2** *tr.* make one's way through (air or water). [Old English] □ **cleavable** *adj.*

cleave[2] *v.intr.* (*past* **cleaved**) (foll. by *to*) *literary* stick fast; adhere. [Old English]

cleaver *n.* a tool for cleaving, esp. a heavy chopping tool used by butchers.

clef *n. Mus.* any of several symbols placed at the beginning of a staff, indicating the pitch of the notes written on it. ▷ NOTATION. [from Latin *clavis* 'key']

cleft[1] *adj.* split, partly divided. □ **in a cleft stick** *Brit.* in a difficult position.

CLEAVAGE

When crystals break, some have a tendency to split along well-defined cleavage lines – planes of weakness between layers of atoms. In flaky cleavage, the crystals flake apart on one plane only, whereas a two-way break lies in two directions. Rhombic breaks and block breaks cleave on three planes, but the latter does so at right angles.

TYPES OF CLEAVAGE

FLAKY CLEAVAGE

TWO-WAY BREAK   BLOCK BREAK   RHOMBIC BREAK

cleft² *n.* a split or fissure; a space or division made by cleaving. [Old English]

cleft lip *n.* a congenital split in the upper lip.

cleft palate *n.* a congenital split in the roof of the mouth.

clematis *n.* ▶ a usu. climbing plant of the genus *Clematis* (buttercup family), bearing white, pink, or purple flowers. ▷ TRAVELLER'S JOY. [from Greek *klēmatis*]

clement *adj.* **1** mild (*clement weather*). **2** merciful. [from Latin *clemens -entis*] □ **clemency** *n.*

clementine *n.* a small tangerine-like citrus fruit. ▷ CITRUS FRUIT. [from French *clémentine*]

clench ● *v.tr.* **1** close (the teeth or fingers) tightly. **2** grasp firmly. **3** = CLINCH *v.* 4. ● *n.* **1** a clenching action. **2** a clenched state. [Old English, related to CLING]

CLEMATIS
(*Clematis* 'Carnaby')

clerestory /kleer-stor-i/ *n.* (*US* also **clearstory**) (*pl.* **-ies**) ◀ an upper row of windows in a cathedral or large church, above the level of the aisle roofs. ▷ FAÇADE. [Middle English]

clergy *n.* (*pl.* **-ies**) (usu. treated as *pl.*) **1** the body of all persons ordained for religious duties in the Christian Churches. **2** a number of such persons (*ten clergy were present*). [based on ecclesiastical Latin *clericus* 'cleric']

clergyman *n.* (*pl.* **-men**) a member of the clergy, esp. *Brit.* of the Church of England.

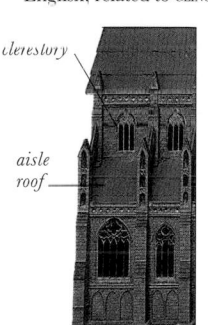

CLERESTORY
OF A GOTHIC
CATHEDRAL

cleric *n.* a member of the clergy. [based on Greek *klēros* 'lot, heritage' (Acts 1:26)]

clerical *adj.* **1** of the clergy or clergymen. **2** of or done by a clerk or clerks. □ **clericalism** *n.* **clericalist** *n.* **clerically** *adv.*

clerical collar *n.* a stiff upright white collar fastening at the back, as worn by the clergy in some Churches.

clerical error *n.* an error made in copying or writing out.

clerihew *n.* a short comic or nonsensical verse, usu. in two rhyming couplets with lines of unequal length and referring to a famous person. [named after E. *Clerihew* Bentley, English writer, 1875–1956, its inventor]

clerk /klark/ ● *n.* **1** a person employed in an office, bank, shop, etc., to keep records etc. **2** a secretary, agent, or record-keeper of a local council, court, etc. **3** a lay officer of a church, college chapel, etc. ● *v.intr.* work as a clerk. [from ecclesiastical Latin *clericus* 'cleric'] □ **clerkess** *n. Sc.* **clerkish** *adj.* **clerkly** *adj.* **clerkship** *n.*

clerk in holy orders *n. formal* a clergyman.

clerk of the course *n.* the judges' secretary etc. in horse or motor racing.

clerk of the works *n.* (also **clerk of works**) *Brit.* an overseer of building works etc.

clever *adj.* (**cleverer**, **cleverest**) **1 a** skilful, talented; quick to understand and learn. **b** *colloq.* sensible, wise. **2** adroit, dexterous. **3** (of the doer or the thing done) ingenious, cunning. [Middle English in sense 'adroit'] □ **cleverly** *adv.* **cleverness** *n.*

clever Dick *n. esp. Brit. colloq.* a person who is or purports to be smart or knowing.

clew *n.* **1** *Naut.* **a** ▶ a lower or after corner of a sail. **b** a set of small cords suspending a hammock. **2** *archaic* a ball of thread or yarn. [Old English]

cliché /klee-shay/ *n.* (also **cliche**) **1** a hackneyed phrase or opinion. **2** *Brit.* a metal casting of a stereotype or electrotype. [French, literally 'stereotyped']

clichéd *adj.* (also **cliché'd**, **cliched**) hackneyed; full of clichés.

click ● *n.* **1** a slight sharp sound. **2** a speech sound in some languages, produced as a type of plosive by sudden withdrawal of the tongue from the soft palate. **3** a catch in machinery acting with a slight sharp sound. ● *v.* **1 a** *intr.* make a click. **b** *tr.* cause (one's tongue, heels, etc.) to click. **2** *intr. colloq.* **a** become clear or understandable. **b** be successful, secure one's object. **c** (foll. by *with*) become friendly. **3** *intr.* & *tr.* (often foll. by *on*) *Computing* press (one of the buttons on a mouse); select (an item represented on the screen, a function, etc.) by so doing. □ **clicker** *n.*

click beetle *n.* a beetle of the family Elateridae, springing up with a click if turned on its back.

client *n.* **1** a person using the services of a lawyer, architect, social worker, or other professional person. **2** a customer. [from Latin *cliens -entis*] □ **clientship** *n.*

clientele /klee-on-tel/ *n.* **1** clients collectively. **2** customers. **3** the patrons of a theatre etc. [from Latin *clientela* 'clientship']

client-server *attrib. adj.* relating to a computer system in which a central server provides data to a number of networked outstations.

cliff *n.* a steep rock face, esp. *Brit.* at the edge of the sea. [Old English] □ **clifflike** *adj.* **cliffy** *adj.*

cliffhanger *n.* a story etc. with a strong element of

suspense; a suspenseful ending to an episode of a serial. □ **cliffhanging** *adj.*

climacteric *n.* **1** *Med.* the period of life when fertility and sexual activity are in decline. **2** a supposed critical period in life. [based on Greek *klimax -akos* 'ladder']

climactic *adj.* of or forming a climax. □ **climactically** *adv.*

climate *n.* **1** the prevailing weather conditions of an area. **2** a region with particular weather conditions. **3** the prevailing trend of opinion. [from Greek *klima klimat-* 'zone'] □ **climatic** *adj.* **climatical** *adj.* **climatically** *adv.*

climatology *n.* the scientific study of climate. □ **climatological** *adj.* **climatologist** *n.*

climax ● *n.* **1** the event or point of greatest intensity or interest; a culmination. **2** a sexual orgasm. **3** *Ecol.* a state of equilibrium reached by a plant community. ● *v.tr.* & *intr. colloq.* bring or come to a climax. [from Greek *klimax* 'ladder, climax']

climb ● *v.* **1** *tr.* & *intr.* ascend, go or come up. **2** *intr.* (of a plant) grow up a wall, trellis, etc. by clinging or twining. **3** *intr.* move along by grasping or clinging; clamber (*climbed across the ditch*; *climbed into bed*). **4** *intr.* make progress in social rank, intellectual or moral strength, etc. **5** *intr.* (of an aircraft, the Sun, etc.) go upwards. **6** *intr.* slope upwards. ● *n.* **1** an ascent by climbing. **2 a** a place climbed or to be climbed. **b** a recognized route up a mountain etc. □ **climb down 1** descend with the help of one's hands. **2** withdraw from a position taken up in argument, negotiation, etc. [Old English] □ **climbable** *adj.*

climbdown *n.* a withdrawal from a position taken up in argument, negotiation, etc.

climber *n.* **1** a mountaineer. **2** a climbing plant. **3** a person with strong social etc. aspirations.

climbing frame *n. Brit.* a structure of joined bars etc. for children to climb on.

clime *n. literary* **1** a region. **2** a climate. [related to CLIMATE]

clinch ● *v.* **1** *tr.* confirm or settle (an argument, bargain, etc.) conclusively. **2** *intr. Boxing* & *Wrestling* (of participants) become too closely engaged. **3** *intr. colloq.* embrace. **4** *tr.* secure (a nail or rivet) by driving the point sideways when through. ● *n.* **1 a** a clinching action. **b** a clinched state. **2** *colloq.* an embrace. **3** *Boxing* & *Wrestling* an action or state in which participants become too closely engaged. [16th-century variant of CLENCH]

clincher *n. colloq.* a remark or argument that settles a matter conclusively.

clincher-built var. of CLINKER-BUILT.

cline *n.* **1** *Biol.* a graded sequence of differences within a species etc. **2** a continuum with an infinite number of gradations. [based on Greek *klinein* 'to slope'] □ **clinal** *adj.*

cling *v.intr.* (*past* and *past part.* **clung**) **1** (foll. by *to*) adhere, stick, or hold on. **2** (foll. by *to*) remain persistently or stubbornly faithful. **3** maintain one's grasp; keep hold; resist separation. [Old English] □ **clinger** *n.*

cling film *n. Brit.* a very thin clinging transparent plastic film, used as a covering esp. for food.

clingy *adj.* (**clingier**, **clingiest**) liable to cling. □ **clinginess** *n.*

clinic *n.* **1** a private or specialized hospital. **2** a place or occasion for giving specialist medical treatment or advice (*eye clinic*; *fertility clinic*). **3** a gathering at a hospital bedside for the teaching of medicine or surgery. [from Greek *klinikē* (*tekhnē*), literally 'bedside (art)'] □ **clinician** *n.*

clinical *adj.* **1** *Med.* of or for the treatment of patients. **2** dispassionate, coldly detached. **3** (of a room, building, etc.) bare, functional. □ **clinically** *adv.*

clinical death *n.* death judged by observation of a person's condition.

clinical medicine *n.* medicine dealing with the observation and treatment of patients.

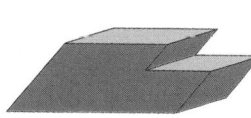

CLEW OF A
DINGHY SAIL

boom
clew / top block

C

C

clinical thermometer *n.* a thermometer with a small range, for taking a person's temperature.

clink[1] ● *n.* a sharp ringing sound. ● *v.* **1** *intr.* make a clink. **2** *tr.* cause (glasses etc.) to clink. [Middle English]

clink[2] *n. slang* prison. [16th-century coinage]

clinker *n.* **1** a mass of slag or lava. **2** a stony residue from burnt coal. [based on Dutch *klinken* 'to clink']

clinker-built *adj.* (also **clincher-built**) ▼ (of a boat) having external planks overlapping downwards and secured with clinched copper nails. [based on northern English *clink* 'to rivet']

overlapping planks   rope fender

CLINKER-BUILT DINGHY

clip[1] ● *n.* **1** a device for holding things together or for attachment to an object as a marker. **2** a piece of jewellery fastened by a clip. **3** a set of attached cartridges for a firearm. ● *v.tr.* (**clipped**, **clipping**) fix with a clip. [Old English *clyppan* 'to embrace']

clip[2] ● *v.tr.* (**clipped**, **clipping**) **1** cut with shears or scissors, esp. cut short or trim (hair, wool, etc.). **2** trim or remove the hair or wool of (a person or animal). **3** *colloq.* hit smartly. **4 a** curtail, diminish, cut short. **b** omit (a letter etc.) from a word; omit letters or syllables of (words pronounced). **5** *Brit.* remove a small piece of (a ticket) to show that it has been used. ● *n.* **1** an act of clipping, esp. shearing or hair-cutting. **2** *colloq.* a smart blow, esp. with the hand. **3** a short sequence from a motion picture. **4** the quantity of wool clipped from a sheep, flock, etc. [from Old Norse *klippa*] □ **clippable** *adj.*

clipboard *n.* a small board with a spring clip for holding papers etc. and providing support for writing.

clip joint *n. slang* a nightclub etc. charging exorbitant prices.

clip-on *adj.* attached by a clip.

clipper *n.* **1** (usu. in *pl.*) any of various instruments for clipping hair, fingernails, hedges, etc. **2** a fast sailing ship, esp. one with raking bows and masts.

clipping *n.* a piece clipped or cut from something, esp. from a newspaper.

clique /kleek/ *n.* a small exclusive group of people. [French] □ **cliquey** *adj.* (**cliquier**, **cliquiest**). **cliquish** *adj.* **cliquishness** *n.*

clitoris *n.* a small erectile part of the female genitals at the anterior end of the vulva. ▷ REPRODUCTIVE ORGANS. [from Greek *kleitoris*] □ **clitoral** *adj.*

cloaca /kloh-ay-kǎ/ *n.* (*pl.* **cloacae** /-see/) **1** the genital and excretory cavity at the end of the intestinal canal in birds, reptiles, etc. ▷ BIRD. **2** a sewer. [Latin, literally 'sewer'] □ **cloacal** *adj.*

cloak ● *n.* an outdoor overgarment, usu. sleeveless, hanging loosely from the shoulders. ● *v.tr.* **1** cover with a cloak. **2** conceal, disguise. [based on medieval Latin *clocca* 'bell', from its shape]

cloak-and-dagger *adj.* involving intrigue and espionage.

cloakroom *n.* **1** a room where outdoor clothes or luggage may be left. **2** *Brit. euphem.* a lavatory.

clobber[1] *n. Brit. slang* clothing or personal belongings. [19th-century coinage]

clobber[2] *v.tr. slang* **1** hit repeatedly; beat up. **2** defeat. **3** criticize severely. [20th-century coinage]

cloche /klosh/ *n.* **1** ◄ a small translucent cover for outdoor plants. **2** (in full

CLOCHE: INDIVIDUAL CLOCHE COVERING A LETTUCE PLANT

CLOCK

Mechanical clocks were invented in the 13th century. Worked by a falling weight and a swinging spindle, they had frequently to be corrected with a sundial. Greater accuracy was first achieved with the introduction of the mainspring, followed by the pendulum, and then the spiral balance wheel. Electricity and atomic power have since revolutionized the accuracy of timekeeping.

EXAMPLES OF CLOCKS

CARRIAGE CLOCK

CUCKOO CLOCK

WATER CLOCK   DIGITAL ALARM CLOCK   MECHANICAL ALARM CLOCK   GRANDFATHER CLOCK

---

cloche hat) a woman's close-fitting bell-shaped hat. [from medieval Latin *clocca* 'bell']

clock ● *n.* **1** ▲ an instrument for measuring time, indicating hours, minutes, etc., by hands on a dial or by displayed figures. **2** *colloq.* a speedometer, taximeter, or stopwatch. ● *v.tr.* **1** *colloq.* **a** (often foll. by *up*) attain or register (a stated time, distance, or speed, esp. in a race). **b** time (a race) with a stopwatch. **2** *Brit. slang* hit, esp. on the head. □ **clock in** (or **on**) register one's arrival at work, esp. by means of an automatic recording clock. **clock off** (or **out**) register one's departure similarly. **round the clock** all day and (usu.) night. [from medieval Latin *clocca* 'bell']

clockmaker *n.* a person who makes and repairs clocks and watches. □ **clockmaking** *n.*

clock radio *n.* a combined radio and alarm clock.

clock tower *n.* a tower displaying a large clock.

clockwise *adj. & adv.* in a curve corresponding in direction to the movement of the hands of a clock.

clockwork *n.* **1** ► the mechanism or works of a clock. **2** a mechanism like that of a mechanical clock, with a spring and gears. **3** (*attrib.*) **a** driven by clockwork. **b** regular, mechanical. □ **like clockwork** smoothly, regularly, automatically.

gear wheel   escape wheel

drive wheel for hands

hour hand

minute hand

weight

swinging pendulum

CLOCKWORK: MECHANISM OF A PENDULUM CLOCK

clod *n.* **1** a lump of earth, clay, etc. **2** *colloq.* a silly or foolish person. [Middle English, variant of CLOT]

cloddish *adj.* loutish, foolish, clumsy.

clodhopper *n. colloq.* **1** (usu. in *pl.*) a large heavy shoe. **2** = CLOD 2.

clodhopping *adj. colloq.* foolish, clumsy.

clog ● *n.* a shoe with a thick wooden sole. ● *v.* (**clogged**, **clogging**) **1** (often foll. by *up*) **a** *tr.* fill or obstruct, esp. by accumulation of glutinous or choking matter. **b** *intr.* fill or become obstructed. **2** *tr.* impede, hamper. [Middle English]

cloister ● *n.* a covered walk, esp. around a quadrangle in a monastery etc. ▷ MONASTERY. ● *v.tr.* seclude or shut up, usu. in a convent or monastery. [from Latin *claustrum*, *clostrum* 'lock, enclosed place'] □ **cloistral** *adj.*

cloistered *adj.* **1** secluded, sheltered. **2** monastic.

clomp var. of CLUMP *v.* 2.

clone ● *n.* **1 a** a group of cells or organisms produced asexually from one stock or ancestor. **b** one such cell or organism. **2** a person or thing regarded as identical with another. ● *v.tr.* propagate as a clone. [from Greek *klōn* 'twig, slip'] □ **clonal** *adj.*

clonk ● *n.* an abrupt heavy sound of impact. ● *v.* **1** *intr.* make such a sound. **2** *tr. colloq.* hit.

clop ● *n.* the sound made by a horse's hoofs. ● *v.intr.* (**clopped**, **clopping**) make this sound.

close[1] /klohss/ ● *adj.* **1** (often foll. by *to*) situated at only a short distance or interval. **2** having a strong, immediate, or intimate relation or connection (*close friend*; *close relative*). **3** in or almost in contact (*close combat*; *close proximity*). **4** dense, compact, with no or only slight intervals (*close texture*; *close formation*). **5** in which competitors are almost equal (*close contest*; *close election*). **6** concentrated, searching (*close examination*; *close attention*). **7** (of air etc.) stuffy or humid. **8** limited or restricted to certain persons etc. (*close corporation*). **9 a** hidden, secret, covered. **b** secretive. **10** (of a danger etc.) directly threatening, narrowly avoided (*that was close*). ● *adv.* (often foll. by *by*, *to*) at only a short distance or interval (*they live close by*; *close to the* church). ● *n.* **1** *Brit.* a street closed at one end. **2** *Brit.* the precinct of a cathedral. □ **close on** *Brit.* nearly, very near to (*it took close on three hours*). **close to the wind** see WIND[1]. [from Latin *clausus* 'shut'] □ **closely** *adv.* **closeness** *n.* **closish** *adj.*

close[2] /klohz/ ● *v.* **1 a** *tr.* shut (a lid, box, door, room, house, etc.). **b** *intr.* be shut (*the door closed slowly*). **c** *tr.* block up. **2 a** *tr.* bring or come to an end. **b** *intr.* finish speaking (*closed with an expression of thanks*). **c** *tr.* settle (a bargain etc.). **3 a** *intr.* end the day's business. **b** *tr.* end the day's business at (a shop, office, etc.). **4** *tr. & intr.* bring or come closer or into contact (*close ranks*). **5** *tr.* make (an electric circuit etc.) continuous. **6** *intr.* (often foll. by *with*) come within striking distance; grapple. ● *n.* a conclusion, an end. □ **close down 1** discontinue (or cause to discontinue) business, esp. permanently. **2** *Brit.* (of a broadcasting station) end transmission, esp. until the next day. **close in 1** enclose. **2** come nearer. **3** (of days) get successively shorter. **close up 1** (often foll. by *to*) move closer. **2** shut, esp. temporarily. **3** block up. **4** (of an aperture) grow smaller. [from Latin *claudere* 'to shut'] □ **closable** *adj.* **closer** *n.*

close-cropped *adj.* cut very short.

closed *adj.* **1** in senses of CLOSE[2]. **2** (of a society, system, etc.) self-contained; not communicating with others.

closed book *n.* a subject about which one is ignorant.

closed-circuit *attrib.adj.* (of television) transmitted by wires to a restricted set of receivers.

closed season *N. Amer.* var. of CLOSE SEASON.

closed shop *n.* a place of work etc. where all employees must belong to an agreed trade union.

close-fisted *adj.* niggardly.

close-fitting *adj.* (of a garment) fitting close to the body.

close-grained *adj.* without gaps between fibres etc.

close harmony *n.* harmony in which the notes of the chord are close together, esp. in vocal music.

close-in *attrib.adj.* **1** close-range. **2** close to the centre.

close-knit *adj.* tightly bound or interlocked; closely united in friendship.

close quarters *n.pl.* (usu. in phr. **at** or **from close quarters**) a very short distance.

close-range *attrib.adj.* **1** at or from a short distance. **2** (of a weapon) designed to be fired over a short distance.

close-run *attrib.adj.* (of a race, election, etc.) closely contested; almost even in outcome.

close season *n.* (*N. Amer.* **closed season**) the season when something, esp. the killing of game etc., is illegal.

close-set *adj.* set close together.

close shave *n. colloq.* a narrow escape.

closet ● *n.* **1** a small or private room. **2** a cupboard or recess. **3** *Brit.* = WATER CLOSET. **4** (*attrib.*) secret, covert (*closet homosexual*). ● *v.tr.* (**closeted, closeting**) shut away, esp. in private conference or study. [from Old French]

close-up ● *n.* a photograph etc. taken at close range. ● *attrib.adj.* at close range.

closure *n.* **1** the act or process of closing. **2** a closed condition. **3** something that closes or seals, e.g. a cap or tie. **4** esp. *Brit.* a procedure for ending a debate and taking a vote.

clot ● *n.* **1** ▲ a thick mass of coagulated liquid, esp. of blood. **2** *Brit. colloq.* a silly or foolish person. ● *v.tr. & intr.* (**clotted, clotting**) form into clots. [Old English]

cloth *n.* (*pl.* **cloths**) **1** woven or felted material. **2** a piece of this, esp. for a particular purpose; a tablecloth, dishcloth, etc. **3** woven fabric used

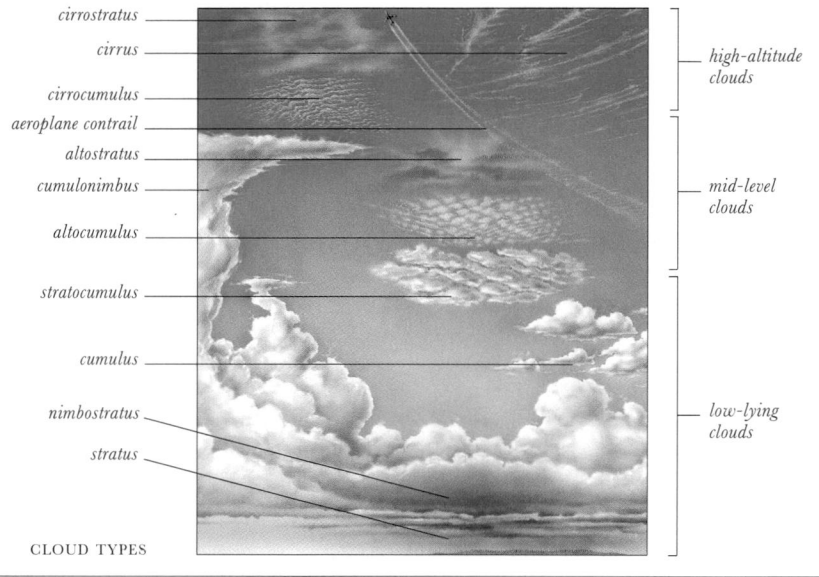

CLOUD

With the advent of aviation in the early 20th century, clouds were classified into ten main types, according to height and appearance. High-altitude clouds are wispy and thin, and composed of tiny ice crystals, with their bases 5–12 km (16,000–39,000 ft)

above ground. Sheet- or lump-like, mid-level clouds, at 2–5 km (7,000–16,000 ft), presage rain or snow. Low-lying clouds, below 2 km (7,000 ft), are heap-like, or form sheets. Cloud bases can, however, be affected by location, season, or time of day.

cirrostratus
cirrus
cirrocumulus
aeroplane contrail
altostratus
cumulonimbus
altocumulus
stratocumulus
cumulus
nimbostratus
stratus

high-altitude clouds
mid-level clouds
low-lying clouds

CLOUD TYPES

for clothes. **4** (prec. by *the*) the clergy. [Old English]

cloth-cap *adj. Brit.* relating to or associated with the working class.

clothe *v.tr.* (*past* and *past part.* **clothed** or *archaic* or *literary* **clad**) **1** put clothes on; provide with clothes (see also CLAD[1]). **2** cover as with clothes or a cloth. [Old English]

cloth-eared *adj. Brit. colloq.* somewhat deaf.

clothes *n.pl.* **1** garments worn to cover the body and limbs. **2** bedclothes. [Old English, plural of CLOTH]

clothes horse *n.* a frame for airing washed clothes.

clothes line *n.* a rope or wire etc. on which washed clothes are hung to dry.

clothes-moth see MOTH 2.

clothes-peg *n. Brit.* a clip or forked device for securing clothes to a clothes line.

clothier /kloh-*thi*-er/ *n.* a seller of men's clothes.

clothing *n.* clothes collectively.

cloth of gold *n.* (also **cloth of silver**) tissue of gold (or silver) threads interwoven with silk or wool.

clotted cream *n.* esp. *Brit.* thick cream obtained by slow scalding.

cloud ● *n.* **1** ▲ a visible mass of condensed watery vapour floating high above the ground. **2** a mass of smoke or dust. **3** (foll. by *of*) a great number of flying insects etc., moving together. **4** a state of gloom, trouble, or suspicion. ● *v.* **1** *tr.* cover or darken with clouds or gloom or trouble. **2** *intr.* (often foll. by *over*, *up*) become overcast or gloomy. **3** *tr.* make unclear. □ **in the clouds 1** unreal, imaginary, mystical. **2** abstracted, inattentive. **with one's head in the clouds** daydreaming, unrealistic. **under a cloud** out of favour, discredited, under suspicion. [Old English *clūd* 'mass of rock or earth'] □ **cloudless** *adj.* **cloudlessly** *adv.* **cloudlet** *n.*

cloud base *n.* the mass of cloud that is lowest in altitude.

blood clot
restricted blood flow
blood clot
blood clot
blood clot
normal blood flow

CLOT: BLOOD CLOTS IN A HUMAN VEIN

cloudburst *n.* a sudden violent rainstorm.

cloud-castle *n. Brit.* a daydream.

cloud chamber *n.* a device containing vapour for tracking the paths of charged particles, X-rays, and gamma rays.

cloud cover *n.* **1** a canopy of clouds. **2** the extent of this canopy.

cloud-cuckoo-land *n.* a fanciful or ideal place. [translation of Greek *Nephelokokkugia* (in Aristophanes' *Birds*)]

cloudy *adj.* (**cloudier, cloudiest**) **1 a** (of the sky) covered with clouds, overcast. **b** (of weather) characterized by clouds. **2** not transparent; unclear. □ **cloudily** *adv.* **cloudiness** *n.*

clout ● *n.* **1** a heavy blow. **2** *colloq.* influence, power of effective action, esp. in politics or business. **3** *dial.* a piece of cloth or clothing (*cast not a clout*). **4** a nail with a large flat head. ● *v.tr.* hit hard. [Old English]

clove[1] *n.* **1 a** a dried flower bud of a tropical plant, *Eugenia aromatica*, used as a spice. ▷ SPICE. **b** this plant. **2** (in full **clove gillyflower** or **clove pink**) a clove-scented pink, *Dianthus caryophyllus*, the ancestor of the carnation and other double pinks. [from Old French *clou* (*de girofle*) 'nail (of gillyflower)', from the nail-like shape of the dried bud]

clove[2] *n.* any of the small bulbs making up a compound bulb of garlic, shallot, etc. [Old English]

clove[3] *past* of CLEAVE[1].

clove hitch *n.* ► a knot by which a rope is secured to a spar or another rope that it crosses at right angles. ▷ KNOT. [from obsolete form of CLOVEN]

clove *adj.* split, partly divided.

cloven hoof *n.* (also **cloven foot**) the divided hoof of ruminant quadrupeds (e.g. oxen, sheep, goats); also ascribed to the Devil. □ **cloven-footed** *adj.* **cloven-hoofed** *adj.*

CLOVE HITCH

clover *n.* any leguminous fodder plant of the genus *Trifolium*, having leaves each consisting of usu. three leaflets. □ **in clover** in ease and luxury. [Old English]

clown ● *n.* **1** a comic entertainer, esp. in a pantomime or circus, usu. with traditional costume and make-up. **2** a silly, foolish, or playful person. ● *v.intr.* (often foll. by *about, around*) act foolishly or playfully. [16th-century coinage] □ **clownish** *adj.* **clownishly** *adv.* **clownishness** *n.*

cloy *v.tr.* (usu. foll. by *with*) satiate or sicken with an excess of sweetness, richness, etc. [from Old French *encloyer*] □ **cloyingly** *adv.*

club ● *n.* **1** a heavy stick with a thick end, used as a weapon etc. **2** a stick used in a game, esp. a stick with a head used in golf. **3 a** a playing card of a suit denoted by a black trefoil. **b** (in *pl.*) this suit. **4** an association of persons meeting periodically for a shared activity (*tennis club*). **5** an organization or premises offering members social amenities, meals and temporary residence, etc. **6** a commercial organization offering subscribers special deals (*book club*). ● *v.* (**clubbed, clubbing**) **1** *tr.* beat with or as with a club. **2** *intr.* (foll. by *together*) combine with others, esp. to make up a sum of money for a purpose. □ **in the club** *Brit. slang* pregnant. [from Old Norse *klumba*] □ **clubber** *n.*

clubbable *adj.* sociable; fit for membership of a club. □ **clubbability** *n.*

clubby *adj.* (**clubbier, clubbiest**) esp. *US* sociable; friendly.

club class *n. Brit.* a class of fare on aircraft etc. designed for the business traveller.

club foot *n.* a congenitally deformed foot. □ **club-footed** *adj.*

clubhouse *n.* the premises used by a club.

clubmate *n.* a fellow member of a sports club.

clubmoss *n.* ◄ a usu. small creeping plant of the family Lycopodiaceae, bearing upright spikes of spore cases.

clubroot *n.* a disease of cabbages etc. with swelling at the base of the stem.

club sandwich *n.* a sandwich with two layers of meat and salad between three slices of toast or bread.

cluck ● *n.* a guttural cry like that of a hen. ● *v.intr.* emit a cluck or clucks.

clue ● *n.* **1** a fact or idea that serves as a guide, or suggests a line of enquiry, in a problem or investigation. **2** a piece of evidence etc. in the detection of a crime. **3** a verbal formula serving as a hint as to what is to be inserted in a crossword. ● *v.tr.* (**clues, clued, cluing** or **clueing**) provide a clue to. □ **clue in** (or *Brit.* **up**) *slang* inform. **not have a clue** *colloq.* be ignorant or incompetent. [variant of CLEW]

clued-up *adj. Brit.* well informed, intelligent.

clueless *adj. colloq.* ignorant, stupid. □ **cluelessly** *adv.* **cluelessness** *n.*

clump ● *n.* (foll. by *of*) a cluster of plants, esp. trees or shrubs. ● *v.* **1 a** *intr.* form a clump. **b** *tr.* heap or plant together. **2** *intr.* (also **clomp**) walk with heavy tread. **3** *tr. colloq.* hit. [from Middle Dutch *klompe*] □ **clumpy** *adj.* (**clumpier, clumpiest**).

clumsy *adj.* (**clumsier, clumsiest**) **1** awkward in movement or shape; ungainly. **2** difficult to handle or use. **3** tactless. [from obsolete *clumse* 'numb with cold'] □ **clumsily** *adv.* **clumsiness** *n.*

clung *past* and *past part.* of CLING.

clunk ● *n.* a dull sound as of thick pieces of metal meeting. ● *v.intr.* make such a sound.

clunky *adj.* (**clunkier, clunkiest**) *colloq.* **1** making a clunking sound. **2** *N. Amer.* awkward, clumsy.

CLUBMOSS
(*Lycopodium* species)

---

cluster ● *n.* a close group or bunch of similar things growing or occurring together. ● *v.* **1** *tr.* bring into a cluster or clusters. **2** *intr.* be or come into a cluster or clusters. **3** *intr.* (foll. by *round, around*) gather. [Old English]

cluster bomb *n.* an anti-personnel bomb spraying pellets on impact.

clutch¹ ● *v.* **1** *tr.* seize eagerly; grasp tightly. **2** *intr.* (foll. by *at*) try, esp. desperately, to seize or grasp. ● *n.* **1 a** a tight grasp. **b** (foll. by *at*) an act of grasping. **2** (in *pl.*) grasping hands, esp. as representing a cruel or relentless grasp or control. **3 a** ► (in a motor vehicle) a device for connecting and disconnecting the engine and the transmission. **b** the pedal operating this. ▷ GEARBOX. [Old English *clyccan* 'to crook, clench']

clutch² *n.* **1** a set of eggs for hatching. **2** a brood of chickens. [18th-century coinage]

clutch bag *n.* a slim flat handbag without handles.

clutter ● *n.* **1** a crowded and untidy collection of things. **2** an untidy state. ● *v.tr.* (often foll. by *up, with*) crowd untidily, fill with clutter. [associated with CLUSTER, CLATTER, and *clotter* 'to coagulate']

Cm *symb. Chem.* the element curium.

cm *abbr.* centimetre(s).

Cmdr. *abbr.* Commander.

Cmdre. *abbr.* Commodore.

CMG *abbr.* (in the UK) Companion (of the Order) of St Michael and St George.

CND *abbr.* (in the UK) Campaign for Nuclear Disarmament.

cnidarian *n.* ▼ an aquatic invertebrate animal of the phylum Cnidaria (formerly called Coelenterata), typically having a simple tube-shaped or cup-shaped body, and including jellyfish, corals, and sea anemones. [based on Greek *knidē* 'nettle']

CNN *abbr.* Cable News Network.

CO *abbr.* **1** Commanding Officer. **2** conscientious objector.

Co *symb. Chem.* the element cobalt.

Co. *abbr.* **1** company. **2** county. □ **and Co.** *colloq.* and the rest of them; and similar things.

co- *prefix* **1** added to: **a** nouns, with the sense 'joint, mutual, common' (*co-author; co-equality*). **b** adjectives and adverbs, with the sense 'jointly, mutually' (*co-equal; co-equally*). **c** verbs, with the sense 'together with another or others' (*cooperate; co-author*). **2** *Math.* of the complement of an angle (*cosine*).

c/o *abbr.* care of.

coach ● *n.* **1** esp. *Brit.* a single-decker bus, usu. comfortably equipped for longer journeys. **2** a railway carriage. ▷ LOCOMOTIVE. **3** a horse-drawn carriage, usu. closed. **4 a** an instructor or trainer in sport. **b** a private tutor. **5** *N. Amer.* economy class seating in an aircraft. ● *v.tr.* train or teach (a pupil, sports team, etc.) as a coach. [from Hungarian *kocsi*]

coach-built *adj. Brit.* (of motor car bodies) individually built by craftsmen. □ **coachbuilder** *n.*

coach house *n.* an outhouse for carriages.

coachman *n.* (*pl.* **-men**) the driver of a horse-drawn carriage.

coach station *n.* a stopping place for a number of coaches, usu. with buildings and amenities.

coachwork *n.* the bodywork of a road or rail vehicle.

coadjutor *n.* an assistant, esp. an assistant bishop. [Late Latin]

coagulant /koh-**ag**-yuu-lănt/ *n.* a substance that produces coagulation.

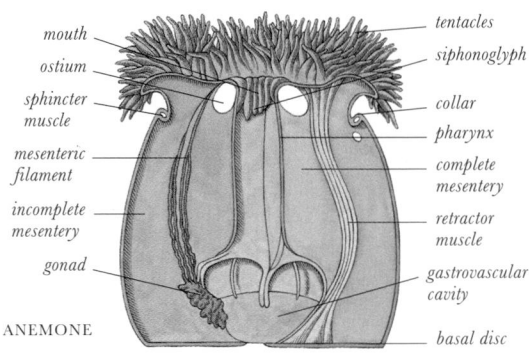

fibre plate
outer clutch drum
straight-cut primary-drive gear
pressure plate
springs
metal plate
key locks fibre plate to outer drum

CLUTCH: MULTIPLATE CLUTCH OF A MOTORCYCLE ENGINE

CNIDARIAN

Cnidarians have two different body forms. A polyp, such as a sea anemone, has a tube-shaped body, attached at one end to a solid object. Medusas, such as the jellyfish, move by contracting their cup-shaped bodies. Both feed by using stinging tentacles to draw food into a gastrovascular cavity.

mouth
ostium
sphincter muscle
mesenteric filament
incomplete mesentery
gonad
tentacles
siphonoglyph
collar
pharynx
complete mesentery
retractor muscle
gastrovascular cavity
basal disc

INTERNAL ANATOMY OF A SEA ANEMONE

EXAMPLES OF CNIDARIANS

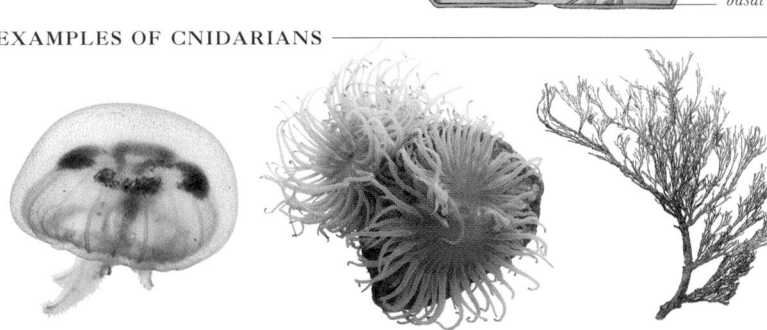

COMMON JELLYFISH
(*Aurelia aurita*)

SEA ANEMONE
(*Condylactis* species)

ORANGE SEA FAN CORAL
(*Gorgonia* species)

coagulate /koh-**ag**-yuu-layt/ *v.tr. & intr.* **1** change from a fluid to a solid or semi-solid state. **2** clot, curdle. [based on Latin *coagulum* 'rennet'] □ **coagulable** *adj.* **coagulative** *adj.* **coagulator** *n.*

coagulation /koh-ag-yuu-**lay**-shŏn/ *n.* the process by which a liquid changes to a semi-solid mass.

coal ● *n.* **1 a** ▼ a hard black rock, mainly carbonized plant matter, used as a fuel and in the manufacture of gas, tar, etc. ▷ SEDIMENT. **b** *Brit.* a piece of this for burning. **2** a red-hot piece of coal, wood, etc. in a fire. ● *v.* **1** *intr.* take in a supply of coal. **2** *tr.* put coal into (an engine, fire, etc.). □ **coals to Newcastle** something brought or sent to a place where it is already plentiful. **haul over the coals** reprimand. [Old English] □ **coaly** *adj.*

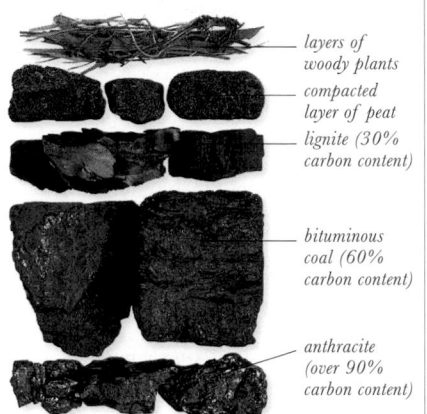

COAL: DIFFERENT STAGES IN
THE FORMATION OF COAL

layers of woody plants
compacted layer of peat
lignite (30% carbon content)
bituminous coal (60% carbon content)
anthracite (over 90% carbon content)

coal dust *n.* powdered coal.

coalesce *v.intr.* come together and form one whole. [from Latin *coalescere*] □ **coalescence** *n.* **coalescent** *adj.*

coalface *n.* an exposed surface of coal in a mine.

coalfield *n.* an extensive area with strata containing coal.

coalfish *n.* (*pl.* usu. same) = SAITHE.

coal gas *n.* mixed gases extracted from coal and used for lighting and heating.

coalition *n. Polit.* a temporary alliance for combined action, esp. of distinct parties forming a government. [from medieval Latin *coalitio*] □ **coalitionist** *n.*

coal mine *n.* a mine in which coal is dug. ▷ MINE. □ **coal miner** *n.* **coal mining** *n.* (often *attrib.*).

coal scuttle *n.* a container for coal to supply a domestic fire.

coal-seam *n.* a stratum of coal suitable for mining. ▷ MINE

coal tar *n.* a thick black oily liquid distilled from coal and used as a source of hydrocarbons.

coal tit *n.* (also **cole tit**) a small greyish bird, *Parus ater*, with a black head.

coaming *n.* a raised border round the hatches etc. of a ship to keep out water. [17th-century coinage]

coarse *adj.* **1 a** rough or loose in texture or grain; made of large particles. **b** (of a person's features) rough or large. **2** lacking refinement or delicacy; crude, obscene. [Middle English] □ **coarsely** *adv.* **coarseness** *n.* **coarsish** *adj.*

coarse fish *n. Brit.* any freshwater fish other than salmon and trout. □ **coarse fishing** *n.*

coarsen *v.tr. & intr.* make or become coarse.

coast ● *n.* the border of the land near the sea; the seashore. ● *v.intr.* **1** ride or move, usu. downhill, without use of power. **2** make progress without much effort. □ **the coast is clear** there is no danger of being observed or caught. [from Latin *costa* 'rib, flank, side'] □ **coastal** *adj.*

coaster *n.* **1** a ship that travels along the coast from port to port. **2** a small tray or mat for a bottle or glass.

coastguard *n.* **1** an organization keeping watch on the coasts and on local shipping to save life, prevent smuggling, etc. **2** a member of this.

coastline *n.* ▼ the line of the seashore, esp. with regard to its shape.

coast to coast *adj. & adv.* (usu. hyphenated when *attrib.*) across an island or continent.

coat ● *n.* **1** an outer garment with sleeves and often extending below the hips; an overcoat or jacket. **2** an animal's fur, hair, etc. **3** a covering of paint etc. laid on a surface at one time. ● *v.tr.* **1** (usu. foll. by *with*, *in*) apply a coat of paint etc. to. **2** (of paint etc.) form a covering to. [from Old French *cote*] □ **coated** *adj.* (also in *comb.*).

coat dress *n.* a woman's tailored dress resembling a coat.

coat-hanger see HANGER 2.

coating *n.* **1** a thin layer or covering of paint etc. **2** material for making coats.

coat of arms *n.* the heraldic bearings or shield of a person, family, or corporation. ▷ HERALDRY

coat of mail *n. hist.* a jacket covered with mail or composed of mail. ▷ CHAIN MAIL

coat-tail *n.* each of the flaps formed by the back of a tailcoat.

co-author ● *n.* a joint author. ● *v.tr.* be a joint author of.

■ **Usage** See Usage Note at AUTHOR.

coax *v.tr.* **1** (usu. foll. by *into*, or *to* + infin.) persuade (a person) gradually or by flattery. **2** (foll. by *out of*) obtain (a thing from a person) by coaxing. **3** manipulate (a thing) carefully or slowly. [16th-century coinage: from phrase *make a cokes* (= simpleton) *of*] □ **coaxer** *n.* **coaxingly** *adv.*

coaxial /koh-**aks**-iăl/ *adj.* **1** having a common axis. **2** *Electr.* (of a cable or line) transmitting by means of two concentric conductors separated by an insulator. □ **coaxially** *adv.*

C

COASTLINE

Coastlines evolve mainly by erosion and deposition. Depositional coasts are built up by rivers dropping sediment in deltas, or by waves transporting sand and small rocks (a process that includes longshore drift). Coasts are referred to as 'drowned' when land sinks or sea levels rise.

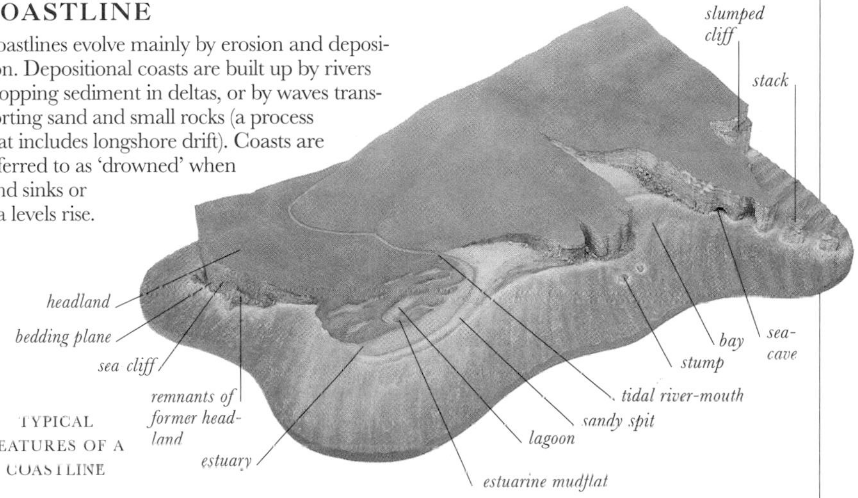

TYPICAL FEATURES OF A COASTLINE

headland
bedding plane
sea cliff
remnants of former headland
estuary
estuarine mudflat
lagoon
sandy spit
tidal river-mouth
stump
bay
sea-cave
sea-stack
slumped cliff
stack

MAIN TYPES OF COASTLINE

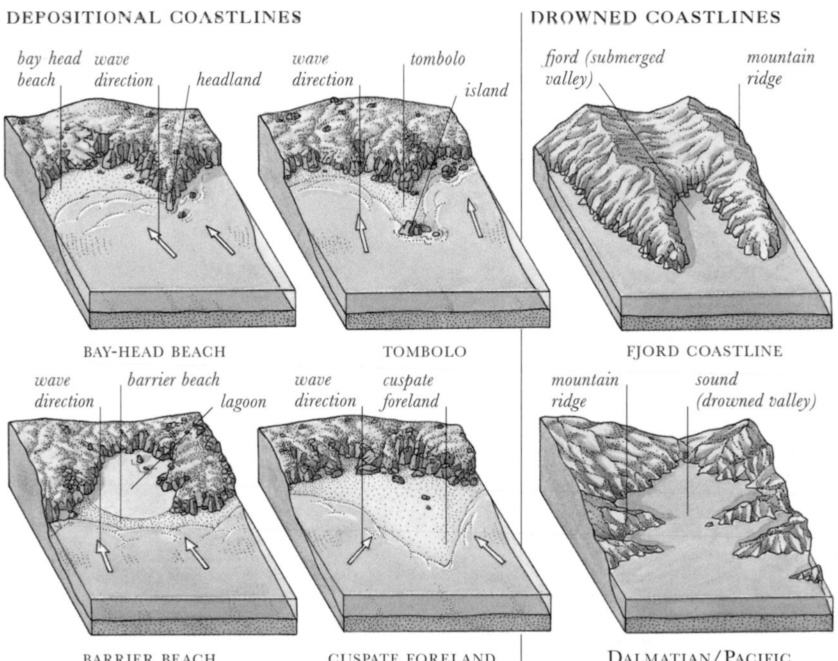

DEPOSITIONAL COASTLINES

bay head beach *wave direction* *headland*

BAY-HEAD BEACH

wave direction *tombolo* *island*

TOMBOLO

wave direction *barrier beach* *lagoon*

BARRIER BEACH

wave direction *cuspate foreland*

CUSPATE FORELAND

DROWNED COASTLINES

fjord (submerged valley) *mountain ridge*

FJORD COASTLINE

mountain ridge *sound (drowned valley)*

DALMATIAN/PACIFIC COASTLINE

cob *n.* **1** a roundish lump of coal etc. **2** *Brit.* a domed loaf of bread. **3** = CORN COB. **4** (in full **cobnut**) a large hazelnut. **5** ▼ a sturdy short-legged horse for riding. **6** a male swan. [Middle English]

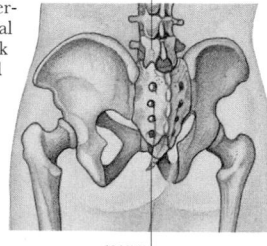

COB

cobalt ● *n.* *Chem.* a silvery-white magnetic metallic element. ● *n. & adj.* = COBALT BLUE. [from German *Kobalt* 'kobold' (an underground spirit): from the belief that cobalt was harmful to ores present with it] □ **cobaltic** *adj.* **cobaltous** *adj.*

cobalt blue ● *n.* **1** a pigment containing a cobalt salt. **2** the deep blue colour of this. ● *adj.* (hyphenated when *attrib.*) of this colour.

cobber *n.* *Austral. & NZ colloq.* a companion or friend. [19th-century coinage]

cobble[1] ● *n.* (in full **cobblestone**) a small rounded stone of a size used for paving. ● *v.tr.* pave with cobbles. [Middle English]

cobble[2] *v.tr.* **1** mend or patch up (esp. shoes). **2** (often foll. by *together*) join or assemble roughly.

cobbler *n.* **1** a person who mends shoes. **2 a** a pie topped with scones. **b** esp. *US* a fruit pie with a rich thick crust. **3** (in *pl.*) *Brit. slang* nonsense. [Middle English; sense 3: from rhyming slang *cobbler's awls* 'balls']

cobnut see COB 4.

COBOL /**koh**-bol/ *n.* a computer language for use in commerce. [acronym from *common business oriented language*]

cobra *n.* ► any venomous hooded snake of the genus *Naja*, native to Africa and Asia. ▷ SNAKE. [from Latin *colubra* 'snake']

cobweb *n.* a fine network of threads spun by a spider from a liquid extruded from its spinnerets. [Middle English] □ **cobwebbed** *adj.* **cobwebby** *adj.*

coca *n.* **1** a S. American shrub, *Erythroxylum coca*. **2** its dried leaves, chewed as a stimulant. [Spanish]

cocaine *n.* a drug from coca, used as a local anaesthetic and as a stimulant. [based on COCA]

coccus /**kok**-ŭs/ *n.* (*pl.* **cocci** /**kok**-i/) any spherical or roughly spherical bacterium. [from Greek *kokkos* 'berry'] □ **coccal** *adj.* **coccoid** *adj.*

coccyx /**kok**-siks/ *n.* (*pl.* **coccyges** /-jeez/ or **coccyxes**) ► the small triangular bone at the base of the spinal column. ▷ SPINE. [from Greek *kokkux* 'cuckoo', from its shape resembling a cuckoo's bill] □ **coccygeal** *adj.*

spinal column

coccyx

COCCYX: HUMAN LOWER TORSO (BACK VIEW) SHOWING THE COCCYX

cochineal *n.* **1** a scarlet dye used esp. for colouring food. **2** the dried bodies of the female of the Mexican insect, *Dactylopius coccus*, yielding this. ▷ DYE. [based on Latin *coccinus* 'scarlet']

cochlea /**kok**-liă/ *n.* (*pl.* **cochleae** /-li-ee/) the spiral cavity of the internal ear, in which sound vibrations are converted into nervous impulses. ▷ INNER EAR. [Latin, literally 'snail shell'] □ **cochlear** *adj.*

cock[1] ● *n.* **1** a male bird, esp. of a domestic fowl. **2** *Brit. slang* (usu. **old cock** as a form of address) a friend; a fellow. **3** *coarse slang* the penis. **4** *Brit. slang* nonsense. **5 a** a firing lever in a gun which can be raised to be released by the trigger. ▷ GUN. **b** the cocked position of this (*at full cock*). **6** a tap or valve controlling flow. ● *v.tr.* **1** raise or make upright or erect. **2** turn or move (the eye or ear) attentively or knowingly. **3** set aslant, or turn up the brim of (a hat). **4** raise the cock of (a gun). □ **at half cock** only partly ready. **cock a snook** see SNOOK. **cock up** *Brit. slang* bungle; make a mess of. [from Old French *coq*]

cock[2] *n.* a small pile of hay, straw, etc. with vertical sides and a rounded top. [Middle English]

cockade

cockade *n.* ◄ a rosette etc. worn in a hat as a badge of office or party, or as part of a livery. ▷ REDCOAT. [based on obsolete French *coquard* 'saucy'] □ **cockaded** *adj.*

cock-a-doodle-doo *n.* a cock's crow.

cock-a-hoop ● *adj.* exultant. ● *adv.* exultantly. [originally in phrase *set cock a hoop* denoting some action preliminary to hard drinking]

COCKADE ON A 19TH-CENTURY FRENCH OFFICER'S CZAPSKA

cock-a-leekie *n.* (also **cocky-leeky**) a soup traditionally made in Scotland with boiling fowl and leeks.

cock and bull story *n.* an absurd or incredible account.

cockatiel *n.* (also **cockateel**) *Austral.* a small delicately coloured crested parrot, *Nymphicus hollandicus*. [from Dutch *kaketielje*]

cockatoo *n.* an Australasian crested parrot of the family Cacatuidae. ▷ PARROT. [from Malay *kakatua*]

cockchafer *n.* a large nocturnal beetle, *Melolontha melolontha*.

cockcrow *n.* dawn.

cocked hat *n.* **1** a brimless triangular hat pointed at the front, back, and top. **2** *hist.* a hat with a wide brim permanently turned up towards the crown (e.g. a tricorne). □ **knock into a cocked hat** defeat utterly.

cocker *n.* (in full **cocker spaniel**) a small spaniel of a breed with a silky coat. [based on COCK[1], from the breed's use in hunting woodcocks etc.]

cockerel *n.* a young cock. [Middle English]

cock-eyed *adj.* *colloq.* **1** crooked, askew, not level. **2** (of a scheme etc.) absurd, not practical. [19th-century coinage]

cockfight *n.* a fight between cocks as sport. □ **cockfighting** *n.*

cockle[1] *n.* **1 a** any edible bivalve mollusc of the genus *Cardium*. ▷ BIVALVE. **b** its shell. **2** (in full **cockleshell**) a small shallow boat. □ **warm the cockles of one's heart** make one contented; be satisfying. [from Greek *kogkhulion* 'shell']

cockle[2] ● *v.* **1** *intr.* pucker, wrinkle. **2** *tr.* cause to cockle. ● *n.* a pucker or wrinkle in paper, glass, etc. [Old English]

cockney ● *n.* (*pl.* **-eys**) **1** a native of East London. **2** the dialect or accent typical of this area. ● *adj.* of or characteristic of cockneys or their dialect or accent. [Middle English *cokeney* 'cock's egg', later a derogatory term for a town-dweller] □ **cockneyism** *n.*

cockpit *n.* **1 a** a compartment for the pilot (and crew) of an aircraft or spacecraft. ▷ FIGHTER. **b** a similar compartment for the driver in a racing car. ▷ DRAGSTER. **c** a space for the helmsman in a sailing yacht. **2** an arena of war or other conflict. **3** a place where cockfights are held.

cockroach *n.* ► a stout-bodied beetle-like scavenging insect of the order Dictyoptera, esp. *Blatta orientalis* and *Periplaneta americana*, which infests kitchens, warehouses, etc. [from Spanish *cucaracha*]

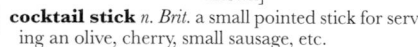

antenna

cercus

spiny leg

COCKROACH (*Periplaneta americana*)

cockscomb

cockscomb *n.* ◄ the crest or comb of a cock.

cock sparrow *n.* **1** a male sparrow. **2** *Brit.* a lively quarrelsome person.

cocksure *adj.* presumptuously or arrogantly confident. [based on archaic *cock*, alteration of *God*] □ **cocksureness** *n.*

COCKSCOMB

cocktail *n.* **1** a drink made by mixing various spirits, fruit juices, etc. **2** a dish of mixed ingredients (*fruit cocktail*; *prawn cocktail*). **3** any (esp. unpleasant or dangerous) mixture or concoction. [origin unknown]

cocktail stick *n.* *Brit.* a small pointed stick for serving an olive, cherry, small sausage, etc.

cock-up *n.* *Brit. slang* a muddle or mistake.

cocky *adj.* (**cockier**, **cockiest**) **1** conceited, arrogant. **2** saucy, impudent. □ **cockily** *adv.* **cockiness** *n.*

cocky-leeky var. of COCK-A-LEEKIE.

coco *n.* (also **cocoa**) (*pl.* **cocos** or **cocoas**) the coconut palm. [abbreviation of COCONUT]

cocoa *n.* **1** a powder made from crushed cacao seeds, often with other ingredients. **2** a drink made from this. [alteration of CACAO]

cocoa bean *n.* a cacao seed.

cocoa butter *n.* a fatty substance obtained from cocoa beans and used for confectionery, cosmetics, etc.

coconut *n.* (also **cocoanut**) **1** the large brown seed of a tall tropical palm, *Cocos nucifera*, with a fibrous husk around a hard shell lined with edible white flesh enclosing a white liquid. **2** (in full **coconut palm** or **tree**) the palm itself. **3** the flesh of a coconut. [based on Spanish *coco* 'grimace', from the facelike base of the shell]

coconut butter *n.* a solid fat obtained from the flesh of the coconut, and used in soap, candles, ointment, etc.

coconut ice *n.* *Brit.* a sweet of sugar and desiccated coconut.

coconut matting *n.* *Brit.* a matting made of fibre from coconut husks.

coconut palm see COCONUT 2.

coconut shy *n.* *Brit.* a fairground sideshow where balls are thrown to dislodge coconuts.

cocoon ● *n.* **1 a** a silky case spun by many insect larvae for protection as pupae. ▷ METAMORPHOSIS, SILKWORM. **b** a similar structure made by other animals. **2** a protective covering. ● *v.* **1** *tr.* (usu. as **cocooned** *adj.*) wrap (as) in a cocoon; protect, enclose. **2** *tr.* spray with a protective coating. **3** *intr.* form a cocoon. [from modern Provençal *coucoun*]

COBRA: INDIAN COBRA (*Naja naja*)

cocotte *n.* a heatproof dish for cooking and serving an individual portion of food. [French]

co-counselling *n.* a type of psychotherapy in which two individuals, after training in counselling techniques, form a partnership whereby each person acts as counsellor to the other in turn.

COD *abbr.* **1 a** cash on delivery. **b** *N. Amer.* collect on delivery. **2** Concise Oxford Dictionary.

cod[1] *n.* (*pl.* same) any large marine fish of the family Gadidae, esp. *Gadus morrhua*, an important food fish. [Middle English]

cod[2] *n. Brit. slang* nonsense. [abbreviation of CODSWALLOP]

cod[3] *n. Brit. slang* **1** a parody. **2** a hoax. **3** (*attrib.*) = MOCK *adj.* [19th-century coinage]

coda *n.* **1** *Mus.* the concluding passage of a piece or movement, usu. forming an addition to the basic structure. **2** *Ballet* the concluding section of a dance. [from Latin *cauda* 'tail']

coddle *v.tr.* **1** treat as an invalid; protect attentively. **2** cook (an egg) in water below boiling point. □ **coddler** *n.*

code ● *n.* **1** a system of words, letters, figures, or symbols, used to represent others for secrecy or brevity. **2** a system of pre-arranged signals, esp. used to ensure secrecy in transmitting messages. **3** *Computing* a piece of program text. **4** a systematic collection of laws etc. **5 a** the prevailing morality of a society or class (*code of honour*). **b** a person's standard of moral behaviour. ● *v.tr.* put (a message, program, etc.) into code. [from Latin *codex*] □ **coder** *n.*

codeine *n.* an alkaloid derived from morphine and used to relieve pain. [based on Greek *kōdeia* 'poppy-head']

code name *n.* (also **code number**) a word or symbol (or number) used for secrecy or convenience instead of the usual name. □ **code-named** *adj.*

codependency *n.* mutual emotional dependency on fulfilling a supportive role in a relationship. □ **co-dependent** *adj.* & *n.*

codex *n.* (*pl.* **codices** /koh-di-seez/ or **codexes**) **1** ▶ an ancient manuscript text in book form. **2** a collection of pharmaceutical descriptions of drugs etc. [Latin, literally 'block of wood, tablet, book']

codfish *n.* (*pl.* usu. same) = COD[1].

codger *n.* (usu. in **old codger**) *colloq.* a person, esp. an old or strange one.

codices *pl.* of CODEX.

codicil *n.* an addition to a will. [from Latin *codicillus* 'little book'] □ **codicillary** *adj.*

codify *v.tr.* (**-ies, -ied**) arrange (laws etc.) systematically into a code. □ **codification** *n.* **codifier** *n.*

codling[1] *n.* (also **codlin**) **1** *Brit.* any of several varieties of cooking apple. **2** (in full **codling moth**) a small moth, *Carpocapsa pomonella*, the larva of which feeds on apples. [from Anglo-French *quer de lion* 'lion-heart']

codling[2] *n.* a small codfish.

cod liver oil *n.* an oil pressed from the fresh liver of cod, which is rich in vitamins D and A.

codpiece *n. hist.* an appendage like a small bag or flap at the front of a man's breeches. [Middle English, based on *cod* 'scrotum']

co-driver *n.* a person who shares the driving of a vehicle with another, esp. in a race, rally, etc.

codswallop *n.* esp. *Brit. slang* nonsense. [20th-century coinage]

coed *colloq.* ● *n.* **1** *Brit.* a co-educational school. **2** *N. Amer.* a female student at a co-educational institution. ● *adj.* co-educational.

co-education *n.* the education of pupils of both sexes together. □ **co-educational** *adj.*

coefficient *n.* **1** *Math.* a quantity placed before and multiplying an algebraic expression (e.g. 4 in $4x^y$). **2** *Physics* a multiplier or factor that measures some property (*coefficient of expansion*).

coelacanth /see-lǎ-kanth/ *n.* ▼ a large bony marine fish, *Latimeria chalumnae*, known only from fossils until 1938. [based on Greek *koilos* 'hollow' + *akantha* 'spine']

COELACANTH
(*Latimeria chalumnae*)

coelenterate see CNIDARIAN.

coeliac /see-li-ak/ *adj.* (*US* **celiac**) *Med.* of or affecting the abdomen. [based on Greek *koilia* 'belly']

coeliac disease *n.* a disease in which chronic failure to digest food is triggered by hypersensitivity of the small intestine to gluten.

coenobite /see-nŏ-byt/ *n.* (*US* **cenobite**) a member of a monastic community. [based on Greek *koinobion* 'convent'] □ **coenobitic** *adj.*

coenzyme *n. Biochem.* a non-protein compound that is necessary for the functioning of an enzyme.

co-equal *archaic* or *literary* ● *adj.* equal with one another. ● *n.* an equal. □ **co-equality** *n.* **co-equally** *adv.*

coerce *v.tr.* (often foll. by *into*) persuade or restrain (an unwilling person) by force (*coerced you into signing*). [from Latin *coercēre* 'to restrain'] □ **coercion** *n.* **coercive** *adj.* **coercively** *adv.*

coeval /koh-eev-ǎl/ ● *adj.* **1** having the same age or date of origin. **2** living or existing at the same epoch. ● *n.* a coeval person, a contemporary. [from Late Latin *coaevus*] □ **coevality** *n.* **coevally** *adv.*

coexist *v.intr.* (often foll. by *with*) **1** exist together (in time or place). **2** (esp. of nations) exist in mutual tolerance. □ **coexistence** *n.* **coexistent** *adj.*

coextensive *adj.* extending over the same space or time.

C. of E. *abbr. Brit.* Church of England.

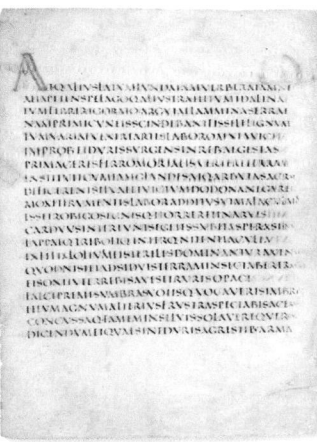

CODEX: DETAIL FROM
CODEX VATICANUS 3256

coffee ● *n.* **1 a** a drink made from the roasted and ground beanlike seeds of a tropical shrub of the genus *Coffea*. **b** a cup of this. **2 a** the shrub yielding these seeds. **b** these seeds raw, or roasted and ground. **3** a pale brown colour. ● *adj.* pale brown. [from Arabic *ḳahwa*]

coffee bar *n.* a bar or café serving coffee and light refreshments from a counter.

coffee bean *n.* the beanlike seed of the coffee shrub.

coffee grinder *n.* a machine for grinding roasted coffee beans.

coffee house *n.* a place serving coffee and other refreshments.

coffee-maker *n.* = PERCOLATOR.

coffee mill *n.* = COFFEE GRINDER.

coffee morning *n. Brit.* a morning gathering at which coffee is served, often in aid of charity.

coffee shop *n.* a small informal restaurant, esp. in a hotel or department store.

coffee table *n.* a small low table.

coffee-table book *n.* a large lavishly illustrated book.

coffer *n.* **1** a box, esp. a large strongbox for valuables. **2** (in *pl.*) a treasury or store of funds. **3** ▼ a sunken panel in a ceiling etc. [from Greek *kophinos* 'basket'] □ **coffered** *adj.*

carved mason's tools

coffer

COFFER: SQUARE COFFER
SET IN A VAULTED CEILING

coffer-dam *n.* a watertight enclosure pumped dry to permit work below the waterline on building bridges etc., or for repairing a ship.

coffin ● *n.* a box in which a corpse is buried or cremated. ● *v.tr.* (**coffined, coffining**) put in a coffin. [from Old French *cof(f)in* 'little basket']

coffin corner *n. Amer. Football* the corner formed by the goal line and sideline.

cog *n.* **1** ▶ each of a series of projections on the edge of a wheel or bar transferring motion by engaging with another series. ▷ BULLDOZER **2** an unimportant member of an organization etc. [Middle English] □ **cogged** *adj.*

cogent *adj.* (of arguments, reasons, etc.) convincing, compelling. [from Latin *cogent-* 'compelling'] □ **cogency** *n.* **cogently** *adv.*

cogitate *v.tr.* & *intr.* ponder, meditate. [based on Latin *cogitatus* 'thought over'] □ **cogitation** *n.* **cogitative** *adj.* **cogitator** *n.*

sloping-tooth cog

pinion wheel

crown wheel

cog

COGS ON A WOODEN BEVEL-TYPE GEAR

cognac *n.* a high-quality brandy, properly that distilled in Cognac in western France.

cognate ● *adj.* **1** related to or descended from a common ancestor (cf. AGNATE *adj.* 1). **2** *Philol.* (of a word) having the same linguistic family or derivation (as another). ● *n.* **1** a relative. **2** *Philol.* a cognate word. [from Latin *cognatus*] □ **cognately** *adv.* **cognateness** *n.*

cognate object *n. Gram.* an object that is related in origin and sense to the verb governing it (as in *live a good life*).

cognition *n.* **1** *Philos.* knowing, perceiving, or conceiving as an act or faculty distinct from emotion and volition. **2** a result of this. [from Latin *cognitio*] □ **cognitional** *adj.* **cognitive** *adj.* **cognitively** *adv.*

C

cognizance *n.* (also **cognisance**) **1** knowledge or awareness; perception, notice. **2** the sphere of one's observation or concern. **3** *Law* the right of a court to deal with a matter. □ **take cognizance of** attend to; take account of. [based on Latin *cognoscent-* 'knowing']

cognizant *adj.* (also **cognisant**) (foll. by *of*) having knowledge or being aware of.

cognomen *n.* **1** a nickname. **2** an ancient Roman's personal name or epithet, as in Marcus Tullius *Cicero*, Publius Cornelius Scipio *Africanus*. [Latin]

cognoscente /kon-yŏ-**shen**-ti/ *n.* (*pl.* **cognoscenti** *pronunc.* same) (usu. in *pl.*) a connoisseur. [Italian, literally 'a person who knows']

cogwheel *n.* a wheel with cogs.

cohabit *v.intr.* (**cohabited**, **cohabiting**) live together, esp. as husband and wife without being married to one another. [from Latin *cohabitare*] □ **cohabitant** *n.* **cohabitation** *n.* **cohabitee** *n.* **cohabiter** *n.*

cohere *v.intr.* **1** (of parts or a whole) stick together, remain united. **2** (of reasoning etc.) be logical or consistent. [from Latin *cohaerēre*]

coherent *adj.* **1** (of a person) able to speak intelligibly and articulately. **2** (of speech, an argument, etc.) logical and consistent; easily followed. **3** cohering; sticking together. **4** *Physics* (of waves) having a constant phase relationship. □ **coherence** *n.* **coherency** *n.* **coherently** *adv.*

cohesion *n.* **1 a** the act or condition of sticking together. **b** a tendency to cohere. **2** *Physics* the sticking together of molecules of the same substance. [based on Latin *cohaesus* 'stuck together'] □ **cohesive** *adj.* **cohesively** *adv.* **cohesiveness** *n.*

cohort *n.* **1** an ancient Roman military unit, equal to one-tenth of a legion. **2** a band of warriors. **3 a** persons banded or grouped together, esp. in a common cause. **b** a group of persons with a common statistical characteristic. [from Latin *cohors cohort-* 'enclosure, company']

coif ● *n.* **1** a close-fitting cap, now esp. as worn by nuns under a veil. **2** esp. *N. Amer.* a coiffure, esp. an elaborate one. ● *v.tr.* (**coiffed**, **coiffing**; *US* also **coifed**, **coifing**) **1** dress or arrange (the hair). **2** arrange the hair of (a person). [from Late Latin *cofia* 'helmet']

coiffeur /kwah-**fer**/ *n.* (*fem.* **coiffeuse**) a hairdresser. [French]

coiffure /kwahf-**yoor**/ *n.* a hairstyle. [French] □ **coiffured** *adj.*

coign /koin/ *n.* □ **coign of vantage** a favourable position for observation or action. [earlier spelling of COIN in sense 'cornerstone']

coil¹ ● *n.* **1** anything arranged in a joined sequence of concentric circles. **2** a single turn of something coiled, e.g. a snake. **3** an intrauterine contraceptive device. **4** *Electr.* an electrical device consisting of a length of wire arranged in a coil for converting the level of a voltage, producing a magnetic field, or adding inductance to a circuit. ▷ MAGLEV. **5** *Electr.* such a device for transmitting high voltage to the spark plugs of an internal-combustion engine. ● *v.* **1** *tr.* arrange in a series of concentric loops or rings. **2** *tr. & intr.* twist or be twisted into a circular or spiral shape. **3** *intr.* move sinuously. [from Latin *colligere* 'to collect']

coil² *n.* □ **this mortal coil** the bustle or turmoil of earthly life (with reference to Shakespeare's *Hamlet* III. i. 67). [16th-century coinage]

coin ● *n.* **1** a stamped metal disc issued as official money. **2** (*collect.*) metal money. ● *v.tr.* **1** make (coins) by stamping. **2** make (metal) into coins. **3** invent or devise (esp. a new word or phrase). □ **coin money** (or **coin it, coin it in**) make much money quickly. **to coin a phrase** *iron.* introducing a banal remark or cliché. [from Old French, literally 'stamping-die'] □ **coiner** *n.*

coinage *n.* **1** the act or process of coining. **2 a** coins

collectively. **b** a system or type of coins in use. **3** an invention, esp. of a new word or phrase.

coin box *n.* **1** *Brit.* a telephone operated by inserting coins. **2** the receptacle for these.

coincide *v.intr.* **1** occur at or during the same time. **2** occupy the same portion of space. **3** (often foll. by *with*) be in agreement. [from medieval Latin *coincidere*]

coincidence *n.* **1 a** occurring or being together. **b** an instance of this. **2** a remarkable concurrence of events or circumstances without apparent causal connection.

coincident *adj.* **1** occurring together in space or time. **2** (foll. by *with*) in agreement; harmonious. □ **coincidently** *adv.*

coincidental *adj.* in the nature of or resulting from a coincidence. □ **coincidentally** *adv.*

coir ◀ *n.* fibre from the outer husk of the coconut, used for ropes, matting, in potting compost, etc. ▷ ROPE. [from Malayalam (of southern India) *kāyar* 'cord']

COIR FIBRE ON A COCONUT HUSK

coition /koh-**ish**-ŏn/ *n. Med.* = COITUS.

coitus /**koh**-it-ŭs/ *n. Med.* sexual intercourse. [Latin] □ **coital** *adj.*

coitus interruptus *n.* sexual intercourse in which the penis is withdrawn before ejaculation.

coke¹ ● *n.* **1** a solid substance left after the gases have been extracted from coal. ▷ BLAST FURNACE. **2** a residue left after the incomplete combustion of petrol etc. ● *v.tr.* convert (coal) into coke.

coke² *n. slang* cocaine.

Col. *abbr.* Colonel.

col *n.* a depression in the summit-line of a chain of mountains, generally affording a pass from one slope to another. [from Latin *collum* 'neck']

col. *abbr.* column.

cola *n.* (also **kola**) **1** any small tree of the genus *Cola*, native to W. Africa, bearing seeds containing caffeine. **2** a carbonated drink usu. flavoured with these seeds. [Temne (a language of Sierra Leone)]

colander *n.* a perforated vessel used to strain off liquid in cookery. ▷ UTENSIL. [based on Latin *colare* 'to strain']

colchicine /**kol**-chi-seen/ *n.* a yellow alkaloid obtained from colchicum, used in the treatment of gout.

colchicum /**kol**-chi-kŭm/ *n.* **1** ▼ a plant of the genus *Colchicum* (lily family), esp. meadow saffron. **2** its dried corm or seed. [from Greek *kolkhikon* 'of *Kolkhis*', a region east of the Black Sea]

cold ● *adj.* **1** of or at a low or relatively low temperature. **2** not heated; cooled after being heated. **3** (of a person) feeling cold. **4** lacking ardour, friendliness, or affection. **5** depressing, uninteresting (*cold facts*). **6 a** dead. **b** *colloq.* unconscious. **7** *colloq.* at one's mercy (*had me cold*). **8** sexually frigid. **9** (of a scent in hunting) having become weak. **10** (in children's games) far from finding or guessing what is sought. **11** without preparation or rehearsal. ● *n.* **1 a** the prevalence of a low temperature. **b** cold weather or environment (*went out into the cold*). **2** an infection of the nose and throat with sneezing, sore throat, etc. ● *adv.* **1** unrehearsed. **2** esp. *US slang* completely (*was stopped cold mid-sentence*). □ **cold call** sell goods or services by making unsolicited calls on prospective customers by telephone or in person. **in cold blood** without feeling or passion.

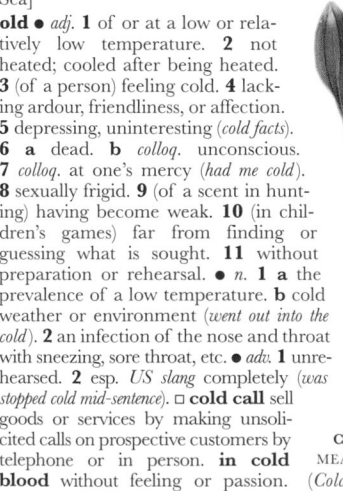

COLCHICUM: MEADOW SAFFRON (*Colchicum autumnale*)

throw (or **pour**) **cold water on** be discouraging or depreciatory about. [Old English] □ **coldish** *adj.* **coldly** *adv.* **coldness** *n.*

cold-blooded *adj.* **1** having a body temperature varying with that of the environment (e.g. of fish). **2** callous. □ **cold-bloodedly** *adv.* **cold-bloodedness** *n.*

cold chisel *n.* a chisel suitable for cutting metal.

cold comfort *n.* poor or inadequate consolation.

cold cream *n.* ointment for cleansing and softening the skin.

cold cuts *n.pl.* slices of cold cooked meats.

cold feet *n.pl. colloq.* loss of nerve or confidence.

cold frame *n.* ▶ an unheated frame with a glass top for growing small plants.

glass top   heat-retaining wooden frame

cold fusion *n.* nuclear fusion occurring at or close to room temperature.

cold-hearted *adj.* lacking affection or warmth; unfriendly. □ **cold-heartedly** *adv.* **cold-heartedness** *n.*

COLD FRAME

cold shoulder ● *n.* a show of intentional unfriendliness. ● *v.tr.* (**cold-shoulder**) be deliberately unfriendly to.

cold snap see SNAP *n.* 4.

cold sore *n.* inflammation and blisters in and around the mouth, caused by a virus infection.

cold start *n.* **1** the starting of an engine or machine at the ambient temperature. **2** the starting of a process, enterprise, etc. without prior preparation.

cold store *n.* a large refrigerated room for preserving usu. commercial food at very low temperatures.

cold sweat *n.* a state of sweating induced by fear or illness.

cold table *n. Brit.* a selection of dishes of cold food.

cold turkey *n. slang* abrupt withdrawal from addictive drugs; the symptoms of this.

cold war *n.* a state of hostility between nations without actual fighting.

cole *n.* (usu. in *comb.*) **1** cabbage. **2** = RAPE². [from Latin *caulis* 'stem, cabbage']

coleopteran /kol-i-**op**-tĕ-răn/ *n.* any insect of the order Coleoptera, comprising the beetles and weevils, which have the front wings modified into sheaths, and biting mouthparts. ▷ BEETLE. [from Greek *koleon* 'sheath' + *pteron* 'wing'] □ **coleopterist** *n.* **coleopterous** *adj.*

coleoptile /kol-i-**op**-tyl/ *n. Bot.* a sheath protecting a young shoot tip in grasses. [from Greek *koleon* 'sheath' + *ptilon* 'feather']

coleslaw *n.* a dressed salad of sliced raw cabbage, carrot, onion, etc. [from Dutch *koolsla*]

cole tit var. of COAL TIT.

coleus *n.* a plant of the genus *Solenostemon* (formerly *Coleus*), having variegated coloured leaves. [from Greek *koleon* 'sheath', from the way the stamens are joined together]

coley *n.* (*pl.* **-eys**) *Brit.* = SAITHE.

colic *n.* a severe spasmodic abdominal pain. [from Late Latin *colicus*] □ **colicky** *adj.*

colitis *n. Med.* inflammation of the lining of the colon.

Coll. *abbr.* College.

collaborate *v.intr.* (often foll. by *with*) **1** work jointly. **2** cooperate traitorously with an enemy. [based on Latin *laborare* 'to work'] □ **collaboration** *n.* **collaborationist** *n. & adj.* **collaborative** *adj.* **collaboratively** *adv.* **collaborator** *n.*

collage /kol-**ah**zh/ n. **1** a form of art in which various materials are arranged and glued to a backing. **2** ▶ a work of art done in this way. [French, literally 'gluing'] □ **collagist** n.

collagen n. Biochem. the main structural protein found in animal connective tissue. [based on Greek kolla 'glue']

collapse ● n. **1** the tumbling down or falling in of a structure. **2** a sudden failure of a plan etc. **3** a physical or mental breakdown. ● v. **1 a** intr. undergo or experience a collapse. **b** tr. cause to collapse. **2** intr. colloq. lie or sit down and relax, esp. after prolonged effort. **3 a** intr. (of furniture etc.) be foldable. **b** tr. fold up (furniture). [based on Latin collapsus 'fallen together'] □ **collapsible** adj. **collapsibility** n.

collar ● n. **1** the part of a shirt, dress, etc., that goes round the neck, either upright or turned over. **2** a band of linen, lace, etc., completing the upper part of a garment. **3** a band of leather or other material put round an animal's neck. **4** a restraining or connecting band, ring, or pipe in machinery. **5** ▶ a coloured marking resembling a collar round the neck of a bird or animal. **6** Brit. a piece of meat rolled up and tied. ● v.tr. **1** seize (a person) by the collar or neck. **2** apprehend. **3** colloq. accost. **4** slang take, esp. illicitly. [based on Latin collum 'neck'] □ **collared** adj. (also in comb.). **collarless** adj.

collarbone n. either of two bones joining the breastbone and the shoulder blades. ▷ CLAVICLE

collate v.tr. **1** analyse and compare (texts, statements, etc.) to identify points of agreement and difference. **2** assemble (information) from different sources. [based on Latin collatus 'brought together'] □ **collator** n

collateral ● n. **1** security pledged as a guarantee for repayment of a loan. **2** a person having the same descent as another but by a different line. ● adj. **1** descended from the same stock but by a different line. **2** side by side; parallel. **3 a** additional but subordinate. **b** contributory. **c** connected but aside from the main subject etc. [from medieval Latin collateralis] □ **collaterality** n. **collaterally** adv.

collateralize v.tr. (also **-ise**) (usu. in passive) secure (a loan etc.) with collateral.

collation n. **1** the act or an instance of collating. **2** a light meal. [sense 2: from Cassian's Collationes Patrum ('Lives of the Fathers') read by Benedictines and followed by a light meal]

colleague n. a fellow official or worker. [from Latin collega]

collect[1] ● v. **1** tr. & intr. bring or come together. **2** tr. systematically seek and acquire (books, stamps, etc.), esp. as a hobby. **3 a** tr. obtain (taxes etc.) from a number of people. **b** intr. colloq. receive money. **4** tr. fetch (went to collect the laundry). **5 a** refl. regain control of oneself esp. after a shock. **b** tr. concentrate (one's thoughts etc.). **c** tr. (as **collected** adj.) calm and cool. **6** tr. infer, gather, conclude. ● adj. & adv. N. Amer. to be paid for by the receiver (of a telephone call etc.). [based on Latin collectus 'gathered'] □ **collectedly** adv.

collect[2] n. a short prayer of the Anglican and Roman Catholic Church, esp. one assigned to a particular day or season. [from Latin collecta 'a gathering']

collectable (also **collectible**) ● adj. **1** worth collect-

ing. **2** able to be collected. ● n. an item sought by collectors. □ **collectability** n.

collection n. **1** the act or process of collecting or being collected. **2** a group of things collected together (e.g. works of art etc.), esp. systematically. **3** (foll. by of) an accumulation (a collection of dust). **4 a** the collecting of money, esp. for a charitable cause. **b** the amount collected. **5** the regular removal of mail for dispatch, refuse for disposal, etc.

collective ● adj. **1** formed by or constituting a collection. **2** taken as a whole (our collective opinion). **3** common. ● n. **1** a = COLLECTIVE FARM. **b** any cooperative enterprise. **c** its members. **2** = COLLECTIVE NOUN. □ **collectively** adv. **collectiveness** n. **collectivity** n.

collective bargaining n. negotiation of wages etc. by an organized body of employees.

collective farm n. a jointly-operated amalgamation of several smallholdings.

collective noun n. Gram. a singular noun denoting a collection or number of individuals (e.g. assembly, family, troop).

collective ownership n. ownership of land etc. by all for the benefit of all.

collectivism n. the theory and practice of collective ownership of land and the means of production. □ **collectivist** n. **collectivistic** adj.

collectivize v.tr. (also **-ise**) organize on the basis of collective ownership. □ **collectivization** n.

collector n. **1** a person who collects as a hobby. **2** a person who collects money etc. due (tax collector).

collector's item n. (also **collector's piece**) a valuable object, esp. one of interest to collectors.

colleen n. Ir. a girl. [from Irish cailín 'little country-woman']

college n. **1** an establishment for further, higher, or specialized education. **2** Brit. the buildings or premises of a college. **3** the students and teachers in a college. **4** Brit. a private secondary school. **5** an organized body of persons with shared functions (College of Physicians). [from Latin collegium]

college of education n. a training college for schoolteachers.

collegial adj. **1** = COLLEGIATE 1. **2** involving shared responsibility, as among a group of colleagues. □ **collegiality** n.

collegian n. a member of a college.

collegiate adj. **1** of the nature of, constituted as, or belonging to, a college. **2** (of a university) composed of different colleges. **3** designed for use by college students. □ **collegiately** adv.

collegiate church n. a church endowed for a chapter of canons but without a bishop's see.

collide v.intr. (often foll. by with) **1** come into abrupt or violent impact. **2** be in conflict. [from Latin collidere 'to strike together']

collie n. a sheepdog originally of a Scottish breed, with a long pointed nose and usu. dense long hair. ▷ DOG

collier n. **1** a coal miner. **2 a** a coal-

ship. **b** Brit. a member of its crew. [Middle English, based on COAL]

colliery n. (pl. **-ies**) a coal mine and its associated buildings. ▷ MINE

colligate v.tr. bring into connection (esp. isolated facts). [based on Latin colligatus 'bound together'] □ **colligation** n.

collinear adj. Geom. (of points) lying in the same straight line. □ **collinearity** n.

Collins n. (in full **Tom Collins**) an iced drink made of gin or whisky etc. with soda, lemon or lime juice, and sugar. [20th c.: origin unknown]

collision n. **1** a violent impact of a moving body with another or with a fixed object. **2** the clashing of opposed interests or considerations. **3** Physics the action of particles striking or coming together. [related to COLLIDE] □ **collisional** adj.

collision course n. a course or action that is bound to cause a collision or conflict.

collocate v.tr. **1** place together or side by side. **2** arrange; set in a particular place. [based on Latin collocatus 'placed together'] □ **collocation** n.

collocutor n. a person who takes part in a conversation.

collodion n. a syrupy solution of nitrocellulose in a mixture of alcohol and ether, used in photography and surgery. [Greek kollōdēs 'glue-like', from kolla 'glue']

colloid n. **1** Chem. ▶ a non-crystalline substance consisting of ultra-microscopic particles, esp. large single molecules, usu. dispersed through a second substance, as in gels, sols, and emulsions. **2** Med. a substance of a homogeneous gelatinous consistency. [based on Greek kolla 'glue'] □ **colloidal** adj.

collop n. a slice, esp. of meat or bacon, an escalope. [Middle English in sense 'fried bacon and eggs']

colloquial adj. belonging to or proper to ordinary or familiar conversation, not formal or literary. □ **colloquialism** n. **colloquially** adv.

colloquium n. (pl. **colloquiums** or **colloquia**) an academic conference or seminar.

colloquy n. (pl. **-quies**) **1** formal the act of conversing. **2** a conversation. [based on Latin loqui 'to speak']

collude v.intr. come to an understanding or conspire together. [from Latin colludere] □ **colluder** n.

collusion n. a secret understanding, esp. for a fraudulent purpose. □ **collusive** adj. **collusively** adv.

collyrium n. (pl. **collyria**) a medicated eye-lotion. [Latin from Greek kollurion 'poultice', from kollura 'coarse bread roll']

collywobbles n.pl. colloq. **1** a rumbling or pain in the stomach. **2** a feeling of strong apprehension. [fanciful, from COLIC + WOBBLE]

Colo. abbr. Colorado.

colobus n. ◀ any leaf-eating monkey of the genus Colobus, native to Africa, having shortened thumbs. [from Greek kolobos 'docked']

cologne /kŏ-**lohn**/ n. (in full **cologne water**) eau de Cologne or a similar scented toilet water. [from Cologne in Germany]

colon[1] n. a punctuation mark (:), used esp. to introduce a quotation, list of items, or to separate clauses when the second expands the first; also

COLLAGE: COILED, WOVEN, AND CUT PAPER LOW-RELIEF COLLAGE

coiled paper
woven paper
cut paper
corrugated paper

COLLAR ON A BLUE RING-NECKED PARAKEET

collar

COLLOID: HAIR GEL COMPOSED OF SOLID FAT PARTICLES SUSPENDED IN WATER

COLOBUS: BLACK-AND-WHITE COLOBUS (Colobus guereza)

C

between numbers in a statement of proportion (as in 10:1) and in biblical references (as in Exodus 3:2). [from Greek *kōlon* 'limb, clause']

colon[2] *n. Anat.* ▼ the part of the large intestine from the caecum to the rectum. ▷ DIGESTION. [from Greek *kolon* 'food, meat'] □ **colonic** *adj.*

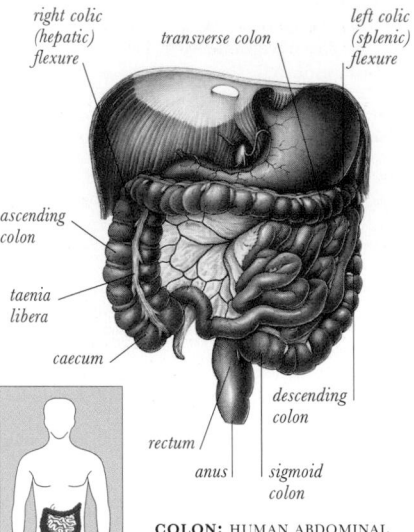

right colic (hepatic) flexure · transverse colon · left colic (splenic) flexure · ascending colon · taenia libera · caecum · descending colon · rectum · anus · sigmoid colon

COLON: HUMAN ABDOMINAL CAVITY, WITH LIVER REMOVED TO SHOW THE COLON

colonel /ker-něl/ *n.* **1** an army officer in command of a regiment, immediately below a brigadier in rank. **2** *US* an officer of corresponding rank in the Air Force. **3** = LIEUTENANT COLONEL. [from Italian *colonnello* 'column of soldiers'] □ **colonelcy** *n.* (*pl.* **-ies**).

Colonel Blimp see BLIMP *n.* 1.

colonial ● *adj.* **1** of a colony or colonies. **2** of colonialism. ● *n.* a native or inhabitant of a colony. □ **colonially** *adv.*

colonialism *n.* a policy of acquiring or maintaining colonies. □ **colonialist** *n.*

colonize *v.* (also **-ise**) **1** *tr.* **a** establish a colony in. **b** settle as colonists. **2** *intr.* establish or join a colony. □ **colonization** *n.* **colonizer** *n.*

colonnade *n.* ▼ a row of columns, esp. supporting an entablature or roof. ▷ AMPHITHEATRE, ROMANESQUE. [French, based on Latin *columna* 'column'] □ **colonnaded** *adj.*

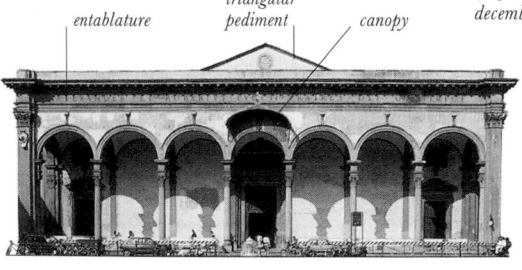

triangular pediment · canopy · entablature

COLONNADE OF A 15TH-CENTURY RENAISSANCE CHURCH

colonoscopy *n.* (*pl.* **-ies**) an examination of the colon by means of a flexible tube inserted through the anus. □ **colonoscope** *n.*

colony *n.* (*pl.* **-ies**) **1 a** a group of settlers in a new country fully or partly subject to the mother country. **b** the settlement or its territory. **2 a** people of one nationality or race or occupation in a city, esp. if living in isolation or in a special quarter. **b** a separate or segregated group (*nudist colony*). **3** *Biol.* a community of animals or plants of one kind forming a structure or living close together. ▷ ALGA. [from Latin *colonia*] □ **colonist** *n.*

colophon *n.* **1** a publisher's device or imprint, esp. on the title-page. **2** ► a tailpiece in a manuscript or book, often ornamental, giving the writer's or printer's name, the date, etc. [from Greek *kolophōn* 'summit, finishing touch']

colophony *n.* = ROSIN.

color etc. *US* var. of COLOUR etc.

Colorado beetle *n.* ◄ a yellow and black striped beetle, *Leptinotarsa decemlineata*, the larva of which is highly destructive to the potato plant.

COLORADO BEETLES (*Leptinotarsa decemlineata*)

coloration *n.* (also **colouration**) **1** colouring; a scheme or method of applying colour. **2** the natural (esp. variegated) colour of living things or animals.

coloratura /kol-ŏ-ră-**tewr**-ă/ *n.* **1** elaborate ornamentation of a vocal melody. **2** a soprano skilled in this. [based on Latin *colorare* 'to colour']

colorimeter *n.* an instrument for measuring the intensity of colour. [based on Latin *color* 'colour'] □ **colorimetric** *adj.* **colorimetry** *n.*

colossal *adj.* **1** of immense size. **2** *colloq.* remarkable, splendid. □ **colossally** *adv.*

colossus *n.* (*pl.* **colossi** /-sy/ or **colossuses**) **1** a statue much bigger than life size. **2** a gigantic person, animal, building, etc. **3** an imperial power personified. [from Greek *kolossos*]

colostomy *n.* (*pl.* **-ies**) *Surgery* an operation in which the colon is shortened and the cut end diverted to an opening in the abdominal wall. [based on COLON[2] + Greek *stoma* 'mouth']

colostrum *n.* the first secretion from the mammary glands occurring after giving birth. [Latin]

colour ● *n.* (*US* **color**) **1 a** the sensation produced on the eye by rays of light when resolved as by a prism etc. into different wavelengths. **b** ▲ perception of colour; a system of colours. **2** one, or any mixture, of the constituents into which light can be separated as in a spectrum or rainbow, sometimes including (loosely) black and white. **3** a colouring substance, esp. paint. **4** the use of all colours, not only black and white, as in photography and television. **5 a** pigmentation of the skin, esp. when dark.

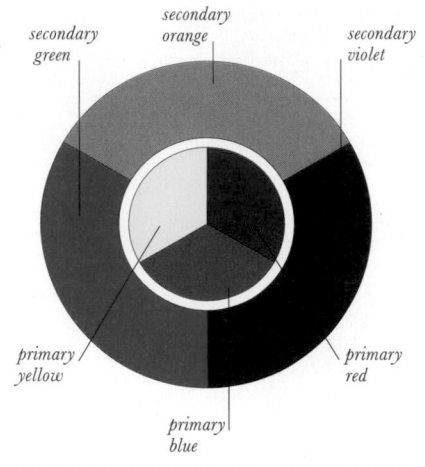

COLOPHON FROM AN EARLY FRENCH BOOK

b this as a ground for prejudice or discrimination. **6** ruddiness of complexion. **7** (in *pl.*) appearance or aspect (*see things in their true colours*). **8** (in *pl.*) **a** *Brit.* a coloured ribbon or uniform etc. worn to signify membership of a school, club, team, etc. **b** the flag of a regiment or ship. **c** a national flag. **9** quality, mood, or variety in music, literature, speech, etc. **10** a pretext (*under colour of*). ● *v.* **1** *tr.* apply colour to. **2** *tr.* influence (*coloured by experience*). **3** *tr.* misrepresent, exaggerate (*a highly coloured account*). **4** *intr.* blush. □ **show one's true colours** reveal one's true character or intentions. **with flying colours** see FLYING. [from Latin *color*]

colourable *adj.* (*US* **colorable**) **1** specious, plausible. **2** counterfeit. □ **colourably** *adv.*

colourant *n.* (*US* **colorant**) a colouring substance.

colouration var. of COLORATION.

colour bar *n.* the denial of services and facilities to non-white people.

colour-blind *adj.* unable to distinguish certain colours. □ **colour-blindness** *n.*

colour code ● *n.* the use of colours as a standard means of identification. ● *v.tr.* (**colour-code**) identify by means of a colour code.

coloured (*US* **colored**) ● *adj.* **1** having colour. **2** (often **Coloured**) often *offens.* **a** wholly or partly of non-white descent. **b** *S.Afr.* of mixed white and non-white descent. **c** of or relating to coloured people (*a coloured audience*). ● *n.* (often **Coloured**) often *offens.* **1** a coloured person. **2** *S.Afr.* a person of mixed descent speaking Afrikaans or English as the mother tongue.

■ **Usage** The use of *coloured* to refer to people of racial groups not considered white is regarded as offensive by many people and should be avoided by using black, Asian, etc., as appropriate.

colour fast *adj.* dyed in colours that will not fade or be washed out. □ **colour fastness** *n.*

colourful *adj.* (*US* **colorful**) **1** having much or varied colour; bright. **2** full of interest; vivid, lively. □ **colourfully** *adv.* **colourfulness** *n.*

colouring *n.* (*US* **coloring**) **1** the process of or skill in using colour. **2** the style in which a thing is coloured. **3** facial complexion.

colourist *n.* (*US* **colorist**) a person who uses colour, esp. in art.

colourless *adj.* (*US* **colorless**) **1** without colour. **2** lacking character or interest. □ **colourlessly** *adv.*

colour scheme *n.* an arrangement or planned combination of colours esp. in interior design.

colour-sergeant *n.* the senior sergeant of an infantry company.

colour supplement *n.* a magazine with coloured printing, as a supplement to a newspaper.

COLOUR

For the artist, there are three primary colours – yellow, blue, and red. Derived from these three are the secondary colours – green, orange, and violet. Their composition is shown in this double colour wheel. For example, blue mixed with its adjacent yellow produces secondary green. Similarly, blue and its neighbouring red combine to make violet. The wheel also illustrates complementary colours. These lie opposite each other, like violet and yellow. Laid side by side, they heighten and intensify one another.

DOUBLE COLOUR WHEEL SHOWING PRIMARY, SECONDARY, AND COMPLEMENTARY COLOURS

secondary green · secondary orange · secondary violet · primary yellow · primary red · primary blue

colour wash *n.* coloured distemper.

colourway *n.* (*US* **colorway**) a coordinated combination of colours.

colposcopy *n.* (*pl.* **-ies**) examination of the vagina and the neck of the womb. [based on Greek *kolpos* 'womb'] □ **colposcope** *n.*

colt *n.* **1** a young uncastrated male horse, usu. less than four years old. **2** *Brit. Sport* a young or inexperienced team player. [Old English] □ **colthood** *n.* **coltish** *adj.* **coltishly** *adv.* **coltishness** *n.*

colter *US* var. of COULTER.

coltsfoot *n.* (*pl.* **coltsfoots**) a plant of the daisy family, *Tussilago farfara*, with large leaves and yellow flowers.

colubrid *Zool.* ● *adj.* of or relating to the large family Colubridae to which most non-venomous snakes belong. ● *n.* a snake of this family. [based on Latin *coluber* 'snake']

columbine *n.* ◀ an aquilegia, esp. *Aquilegia vulgaris*, which has purple-blue flowers. [based on Latin *columba* 'dove', from the supposed resemblance of the flower to a cluster of 5 doves]

columbium *n.* esp. *N. Amer. Metallurgy* = NIOBIUM.

COLUMBINE
(*Aquilegia vulgaris*)

column *n.* **1** *Archit.* ▼ an upright cylindrical pillar often slightly tapering and usu. supporting an entablature or arch. ▷ FAÇADE. **2** a structure or part shaped like a column. **3** a vertical cylindrical mass of liquid or vapour. **4 a** a vertical division of a page, chart, etc., containing a sequence of figures or words. **b** the figures or words themselves. **5** a part of a newspaper regularly devoted to a particular subject. **6** an arrangement of troops or ships in successive lines, deep from front to rear but of narrow width. [from Latin *columna* 'pillar'] □ **columnar** *adj.* **columned** *adj.*

columnist /kol-ŭm-ist/ *n.* a journalist contributing regularly to a newspaper.

colza *n.* = RAPE[2]. [from French *kolza(t)*]

coma *n.* (*pl.* **comas**) a prolonged deep unconsciousness. [from Greek *kōma* 'deep sleep']

comatose *adj.* **1** in a coma. **2** drowsy.

comb ● *n.* **1** a toothed strip of rigid material for tidying or arranging the hair. **2** a part of a machine having a similar design or purpose. **3** the red fleshy crest of usu. a fowl. ▷ COCKSCOMB. **4** a honeycomb. ● *v.tr.* **1** arrange or tidy (the hair) by drawing a comb through. **2** curry (a horse). **3** dress (wool or flax)

with a comb. **4** search (a place) thoroughly. □ **comb out 1** tidy and arrange (the hair) loosely by combing. **2** remove with a comb. [Old English] □ **combed** *adj.*

combat ● *n.* a fight, struggle, or contest. ● *v.* (**combated**, **combating**) **1** *intr.* engage in combat. **2** *tr.* oppose; fight against. [French]

combatant ● *n.* a person engaged in fighting. ● *adj.* **1** fighting. **2** for fighting.

combat dress *n.* ▼ a soldier's uniform worn for combat and field training, usu. of olive-green, camouflage, or khaki fabric.

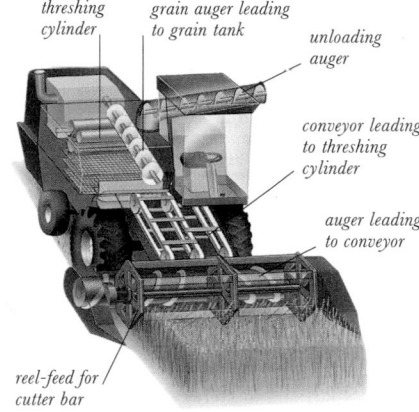

hood — *camouflage fabric*
shoulder strap — *drawstring*
patch pocket — *Velcro fastening*
foul-weather cuff

COMBAT DRESS: US ARMY URBAN-PATTERN CAMOUFLAGE JACKET

combative *adj.* ready to fight; pugnacious. □ **combatively** *adv.* **combativeness** *n.*

combe var. of COOMB.

comber *n.* **1** a person or thing that combs, esp. a machine for combing cotton or wool very fine. **2** a long curling wave; a breaker.

combi *n.* a machine etc. with a combined function or mode of action (often *attrib.*: *combi oven*).

combination *n.* **1** the act or an instance of combining; the process of being combined. **2** a combined state (*in combination with*). **3** a combined set of things or people. **4** a sequence of numbers or letters used to open a combination lock. **5** *Brit.* a motorcycle with sidecar attached. **6** (in *pl.*) a single undergarment for the body and legs. **7** *Chem.* a union of substances in a compound with new properties. □ **combinational** *adj.* **combinative** *adj.* **combinatory** *adj.* **combinatorial** *adj. Math.*

combination lock *n.* a lock that can be opened only by a specific sequence of movements.

combine ● *v.* /kŏm-byn/ **1** *tr. & intr.* join together; unite for a common purpose. **2** *tr.* possess (esp. disparate qualities) in combination (*combines charm and*

authority). **3 a** *intr.* coalesce in one substance. **b** *tr.* cause to do this. **c** *intr.* form a chemical compound. **4** *intr.* cooperate. **5** *tr.* harvest by means of a combine harvester. ● *n.* /kom-byn/ **1** a combination of esp. commercial interests to control prices etc. **2** = COMBINE HARVESTER. [based on Latin *bini* 'two'] □ **combinable** *adj.*

combine harvester *n.* ▼ a mobile machine that reaps and threshes in one operation.

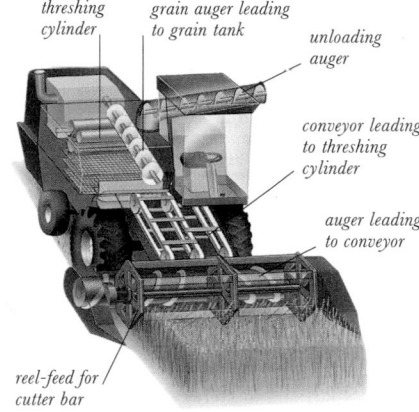

threshing cylinder — *grain auger leading to grain tank* — *unloading auger*
conveyor leading to threshing cylinder
auger leading to conveyor
reel-feed for cutter bar

COMBINE HARVESTER

combing *n.* **1** in senses of COMB *v.* **2** (in *pl.*) hairs combed off.

combing wool *n.* long-stapled wool, suitable for combing.

combining form *n. Gram.* a form of a word used (only) in compounds in combination with another element to form a word (e.g. *Anglo-* = English in *Anglo-Irish*, *bio-* = life in *biology*, *-cide* = killing in *biocide*).

■ **Usage** In this dictionary, *combining form* is used of an element that contributes to the particular sense of words (as with both elements of *biography*, as distinct from a prefix or suffix that adjusts the sense of or determines the function of words (as with *un-*, *-able*, and *-ation*).

combo *n.* (*pl.* **-os**) *slang* **1** a small jazz or dance band. **2** a combination; a combined unit.

combs /komz/ *n.pl. colloq.* combinations (see COMBINATION 6).

combust *v.tr.* subject to combustion. [based on Latin *combustus* 'burnt up']

combustible ● *adj.* capable of or used for burning. ● *n.* a combustible substance. □ **combustibility** *n.*

combustion *n.* **1** burning; consumption by fire. **2** *Chem.* the development of light and heat from the chemical combination of a substance with oxygen. □ **combustive** *adj.*

combustion chamber *n.* ▼ a space in which combustion takes place, e.g. of gases in a boiler-furnace or fuel in an internal-combustion engine. ▷ INTERNAL-COMBUSTION ENGINE

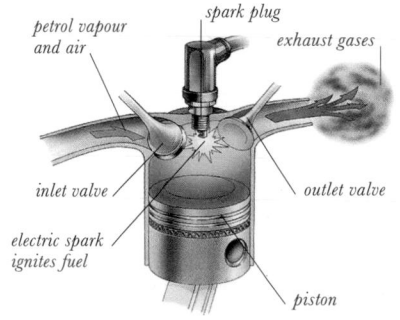

petrol vapour and air — *spark plug* — *exhaust gases*
inlet valve — *outlet valve*
electric spark ignites fuel — *piston*

COMBUSTION CHAMBER OF AN INTERNAL-COMBUSTION ENGINE

COLUMN

The ancient Egyptians and Greeks first incorporated columns into architectural designs. There were three orders, Doric, Ionic, and Corinthian, each with clearly defined conventions governing proportion and appearance. Roman and Renaissance architects imitated these, and devised two others: Composite and Tuscan.

TYPES OF COLUMN

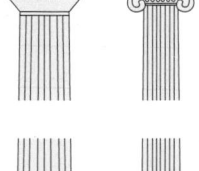
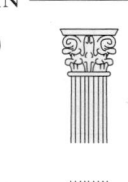

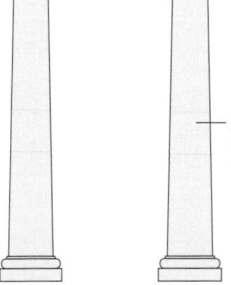

cornice — *frieze*
architrave — *capital*
plain round column

DORIC   IONIC   CORINTHIAN   COMPOSITE   TUSCAN (AND ENTABLATURE)

come *v.intr.* (*past* **came**, *past part.* **come**) **1** move, be brought towards, or reach a place thought of as near or familiar to the speaker or hearer (*come and see me*; *the books have come*). **2** reach or be brought to a specified situation or result (*you'll come to no harm*; *came to believe it*; *came into prominence*). **3** extend to a specified point (*the road comes within a mile of us*). **4** traverse or progress (with compl.: *have come a long way*). **5 a** get to be in a certain condition (*how did you come to break your leg?*). **b** (of time) arrive in due course (*the day soon came*). **6** take or occupy a specified position (*it comes on the third page*). **7** become perceptible or known (*the church came into sight*; *it will come to me*). **8** be available (*comes in three sizes*). **9** become (with compl.: *come loose*). **10** (foll. by *of*, *from*) **a** be descended from (*comes of a rich family*). **b** be the result of (*that comes from complaining*). **11** (foll. by *from*) **a** originate in; have as its source. **b** have as one's home. **12** *colloq.* play the part of; behave like (with compl.: *don't come the bully with me*). **13** *slang* have a sexual orgasm. **14** (in *subjunctive*) *colloq.* when a specified time is reached (*come next month*). **15** (also **come, come!**) (as *int.*) expressing caution or reserve (*come, it cannot be that bad*). □ **as ... as they come** typically or supremely so (*is as tough as they come*). **come about** happen; take place. **come across 1** meet or find by chance (*came across an old jacket*). **2** *colloq.* be effective or understood; give a specified impression. **3** (foll. by *with*) *slang* hand over what is wanted. **come again** *colloq.* **1** make a further effort. **2** (as *imper.*) what did you say? **come along 1** make progress; move forward. **2** (as *imper.*) hurry up. **come and go 1** pass to and fro; be transitory. **2** pay brief visits. **come apart** fall or break into pieces; disintegrate. **come at 1** reach, discover; get access to. **2** attack (*came at me with a knife*). **come away 1** become detached or broken off (*came away in my hands*). **2** (foll. by *with*) be left with (a feeling, impression, etc.). **come back 1** return. **2** recur to one's memory. **3** become fashionable or popular again. **4** *N. Amer.* reply, retort. **come before** be dealt with by (a judge etc.). **come between 1** interfere with the relationship of. **2** separate; prevent contact between. **come by 1** pass; go past. **2** call on a visit (*come by tomorrow*). **3** acquire (*came by a new bicycle*). **come clean** see CLEAN. **come down 1** come to a place or position regarded as lower. **2** lose position or wealth (*has come down in the world*). **3** be handed down by tradition or inheritance. **4** be reduced; show a downward trend (*prices are coming down*). **5** (foll. by *against*, *in favour of*, etc.) reach a decision or recommendation (*the report came down against change*). **6** (foll. by *to*) signify basically; be dependent on (a factor) (*it comes down to who is willing to go*). **7** (foll. by *on*) criticize harshly; punish. **8** (foll. by *with*) begin to suffer from (a disease). **come for 1** come to collect or receive. **2** attack (*came for me with a hammer*). **come forward 1** advance. **2** offer oneself for a task, post, etc. **come in 1** enter a house or room. **2** take a specified position in a race etc. (*came in third*). **3** become fashionable or seasonable. **4 a** have a useful role or function. **b** (with compl.) prove to be (*came in handy*). **c** have a part to play (*where do I come in?*). **5** be received (*news has just come in*). **6** begin speaking, esp. in radio transmission. **7** be elected; come to power. **8** *Cricket* begin an innings. **9** (foll. by *for*) receive; be the object of (*came in for much criticism*). **10** (foll. by *on*) join (an enterprise etc.). **11** (of a tide) turn to high tide. **12** (of a train, ship, or aircraft) approach its destination. **13** return to base (*come in, number 9*). **come into 1** see senses 2, 7. **2** receive, esp. as heir. **come near** see NEAR. **come of age** see AGE. **come off 1** *colloq.* (of an action) succeed; be accomplished. **2** (with compl.) fare; turn out (*came off badly*; *came off the winner*). **3** be detached or detachable (from). **4** *Brit.* fall (from). **5** be reduced or subtracted from (*£5 came off the price*). **come off it** (as *imper.*) *colloq.* an expression of disbelief or refusal to accept another's opinion, behaviour, etc. **come on 1** continue to come. **2** advance, esp. to attack. **3** make progress; thrive (*is really coming on*). **4** (foll. by *to* + infin.) *Brit.* begin (*it came on to rain*). **5** appear on the stage, field of play, etc. **6** be heard or seen on television, on the telephone, etc. **7** arise to be discussed. **8** (as *imper.*) expressing encouragement. **9** = *come upon*. **come out 1** emerge; become known (*it came out that he had left*). **2** appear or be published (*comes out every day*). **3 a** declare oneself as being for or against something; make a decision (*came out in favour of joining*). **b** openly declare something controversial (esp. that one is a homosexual). **4** *Brit.* go on strike. **5 a** be satisfactorily visible in a photograph etc., or present in a specified way (*the dog didn't come out*; *he came out badly*). **b** (of a photograph) be produced satisfactorily or in a specified way (*only three have come out*). **6** attain a specified result in an examination etc. **7** (of a stain etc.) be removed. **8** make one's debut in society. **9** (foll. by *in*) be covered with (*came out in spots*). **10** (of a problem) be solved. **11** (foll. by *with*) declare openly; disclose. **come over 1** come from some distance or nearer to the speaker (*came over from Paris*; *come over here*). **2** change sides or one's opinion. **3 a** (of a feeling etc.) overtake or affect (a person). **b** *Brit. colloq.* feel suddenly (*came over faint*). **4** appear or sound in a specified way (*you came over very well*; *the ideas came over clearly*). **come round** (or *US* also **around**) **1** pay an informal visit. **2** recover consciousness. **3** be converted to another person's opinion. **4** (of a date or regular occurrence) recur; be imminent again. **come through 1** be successful; survive. **2** be received by telephone. **3** survive or overcome (a difficulty) (*came through the ordeal*). **come to 1** (also *refl.*) recover consciousness. **2** *Naut.* bring a vessel to a stop. **3** reach in total; amount to. **4** *Brit. colloq.* stop being foolish. **5** have as a destiny; reach (*what is the world coming to?*). **come to hand** become available; be recovered. **come to light** see LIGHT[1]. **come to nothing** have no useful result in the end; fail. **come to pass** occur. **come to rest** cease moving. **come to one's senses** see SENSE. **come to that** *colloq.* in fact; if that is the case. **come under 1** be classified as or among. **2** be subject to (influence or authority). **come up 1** come to a place or position regarded as higher. **2** attain wealth or position (*come up in the world*). **3 a** (of an issue, problem, etc.) arise; be mentioned or discussed. **b** (of an event etc.) occur, happen (*coming up next on BBC1*). **4** (often foll. by *to*) **a** approach a person, esp. to talk. **b** (*US* also often foll. by *on*) approach a specified time etc. (*is coming up to noon*). **5** (foll. by *to*) match (a standard etc.). **6** (foll. by *with*) produce (an idea etc.), esp. in response to a challenge. **7** (of a plant etc.) spring up out of the ground. **8** become brighter (e.g. with polishing). **come up against** be faced with. **come upon 1** meet or find by chance. **2** attack by surprise. **come what may** no matter what happens. **have it coming to one** *colloq.* be about to get one's deserts. **how come?** *colloq.* how did that happen? **if it comes to that** in that case. **to come** future; in the future (*the year to come*; *many problems were still to come*). [Old English]

comeback *n.* **1** a return to a previous (esp. successful) state. **2** *slang* a retaliation.

comedian *n.* **1** a humorous entertainer. **2** an actor in comedy. **3** *slang* a buffoon.

comedienne *n.* a female comedian.

comedist *n.* a writer of comedies.

comedown *n.* **1** a loss of status; decline. **2** a disappointment.

comedy *n.* (*pl.* **-ies**) **1 a** a play, film, etc., of an amusing character, usu. with a happy ending. **b** the genre consisting of works of this kind (cf. TRAGEDY 3). **2** an amusing incident or series of incidents in everyday life. **3** humour, esp. in a work of art. [from Greek *kōmōidia*] □ **comedic** *adj.*

comedy of manners *n.* satirical portrayal of social behaviour, esp. of the upper classes.

come-hither *attrib.adj. colloq.* enticing, flirtatious.

comely *adj.* (**comelier**, **comeliest**) pleasant to look at. [Middle English] □ **comeliness** *n.*

come-on *n. slang* a lure or enticement.

comer *n.* **1** a person who comes, esp. as an applicant, participant, etc. (*offered the job to the first comer*). **2** *colloq.* a person likely to be a success.

comestible *n.* (usu. in *pl.*) *formal* or *joc.* food. [based on Latin *comedere comest-* 'to eat up']

comet *n.* ▼ a small body of ice and dust moving around the solar system, visible in the night sky with a tail of gas and dust when near the Sun. [from Greek *komētēs* 'long-haired (star)'] □ **cometary** *adj.*

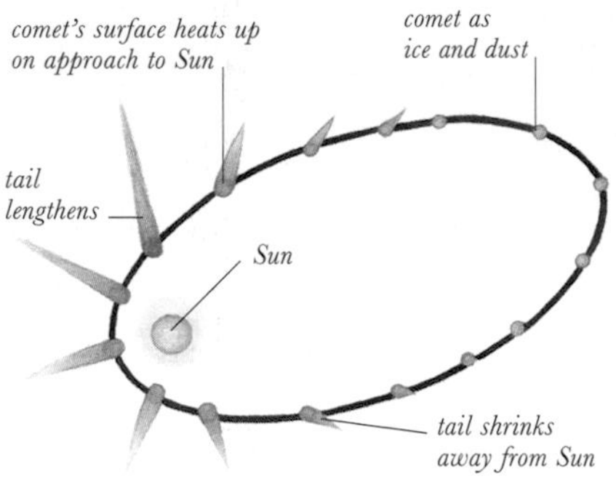
comet's surface heats up on approach to Sun
comet as ice and dust
tail lengthens
Sun
tail shrinks away from Sun

COMET: ORBIT OF A PERIODIC COMET IN THE INNER SOLAR SYSTEM

come-uppance *n. colloq.* one's deserved fate (*got his come-uppance*).

comfit *n. archaic* a sweet consisting of a nut etc. coated in sugar. [based on Latin *conficere confect-* 'to prepare']

comfort ● *n.* **1** consolation; relief in affliction. **2 a** a state of physical well-being (*live in comfort*). **b** (usu. in *pl.*) things that make life easy or pleasant. **3** a cause of satisfaction (*a comfort to me that you are here*). **4** a person who consoles or helps one (*he's a comfort to her in her old age*). ● *v.tr.* **1** soothe in grief; console. **2** make comfortable (*comforted by the warmth of the fire*). [from Late Latin *confortare* 'to strengthen'] □ **comforting** *adj.* **comfortingly** *adv.* **comfortless** *adj.*

comfortable *adj.* **1** giving ease (*a comfortable bed*). **2** free from discomfort; at ease. **3** *colloq.* having an adequate standard of living. **4** having an easy conscience (*did not feel comfortable about going*). **5** with a wide margin (*a comfortable win*). □ **comfortableness** *n.* **comfortably** *adv.*

comforter *n.* **1** a person who comforts. **2** *Brit.* a baby's dummy. **3** *archaic* a woollen scarf. **4** *N. Amer.* a warm quilt.

comfort station *n. N. Amer. euphem.* a public lavatory.

comfrey *n.* (*pl.* **-eys**) ► a plant of the genus *Symphytum* (borage family), esp. *S. officinale*, which has large hairy leaves and bell-shaped flowers. [from Latin *conferva* 'a boiling together, healing', referring to the plant's medicinal use]

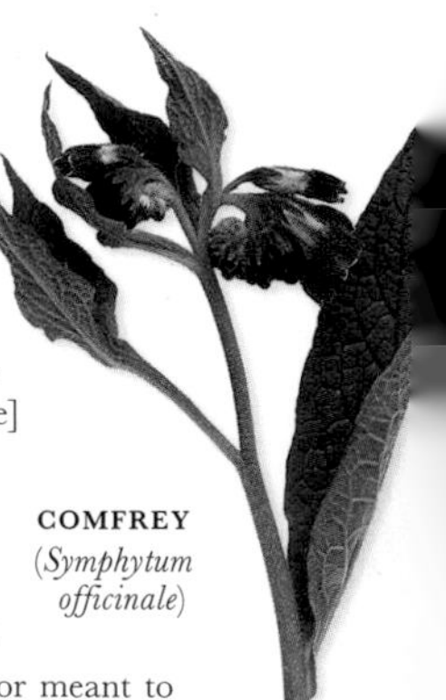

COMFREY (*Symphytum officinale*)

comfy *adj.* (**comfier**, **comfiest**) *colloq.* comfortable. □ **comfily** *adv.* **comfiness** *n.*

comic ● *adj.* **1** of, or in the style of, comedy (*comic opera*). **2** causing or meant to cause laughter. ● *n.* **1** a professional comedian. **2 a** a periodical mainly in the form of comic strips. **b** (in *pl.*) *US* comic strips. [based on Greek *kōmos* 'merry-making']

comical *adj.* funny. □ **comicality** *n.* **comically** *adv.*

comic opera *n.* **1** an opera with much spoken dialogue, usu. with humorous treatment. **2** this genre.

comic strip *n.* a series of drawings in a comic etc., telling a story.

coming ● *attrib.adj.* **1** approaching, next (*the coming week*). **2** of potential importance (*a coming man*). ● *n.* arrival; approach. □ **coming and going** (or **comings and goings**) activity, esp. intense.

comity *n.* (*pl.* **-ies**) **1** civility; consideration of others. **2 a** an association of nations etc. for mutual benefit. **b** (in full **comity of nations**) the mutual recognition by nations of the laws and customs of others. [based on Latin *comis* 'courteous']

comma *n.* a punctuation mark (,) indicating a pause between parts of a sentence, or dividing items in a list, string of figures, etc. [from Greek *komma* 'clause']

command ● *v.tr.* **1** give formal order or instructions to (*commands us to obey*; *commands that it be done*). **2** (also *absol.*) have authority over. **3** (often *refl.*) restrain, master. **4** gain the use of; have at one's disposal (skill, resources, etc.). **5** deserve and get (respect etc.). **6** *Mil.* dominate (a strategic position) from a superior height; look down over. ● *n.* **1** an order; an instruction. **2** mastery, control (*a good command of languages*). **3** the exercise or tenure of authority, esp. naval or military (*has command of this ship*). **4** *Mil.* **a** a body of troops etc. (*Bomber Command*). **b** a district under a commander (*Western Command*). **5** *Computing* **a** an instruction causing a computer to perform a basic function. **b** a signal initiating such an operation. □ **in command of** commanding. **under command of** commanded by. [from Late Latin *commandare* 'to commend']

commandant *n.* a commanding officer. □ **commandantship** *n.*

command economy *n.* = PLANNED ECONOMY.

commandeer *v.tr.* **1** seize (men or goods) for military purposes. **2** take possession of without authority. [from Afrikaans *kommanderen*]

commander *n.* **1** a person who commands, esp.: **a** a naval officer next in rank below captain. **b** = WING COMMANDER. **c** an officer in charge of a London police district. **2** (in full **knight commander**) a member of a higher class in some orders of knighthood. □ **commandership** *n.*

commander-in-chief *n.* (*pl.* **commanders-in-chief**) the supreme commander, esp. of a nation's forces.

commanding *adj.* **1** dignified, exalted, impressive. **2** (of a hill etc.) giving a wide view. **3** (of an advantage, a position, etc.) controlling; superior (*has a commanding lead*). □ **commandingly** *adv.*

commandment *n.* a divine command.

command module *n.* the control compartment in a spacecraft.

commando *n.* (*pl.* **-os**) *Mil.* **1** (often **Commando**) **a** a unit of British amphibious shock troops. **b** a member of such a unit. **c** a similar unit or member of such a unit elsewhere. **2 a** a party of men called out for military service. **b** a body of troops.

Command Paper *n.* (in the UK) a paper laid before Parliament by command of the Crown (in practice, by the Government).

command performance *n.* (in the UK) a theatrical or film performance given by royal command.

command post *n.* the headquarters of a military unit.

commemorate *v.tr.* **1** celebrate in speech or writing. **2 a** preserve in memory by some celebration. **b** (of a stone, plaque etc.) be a memorial of. [based on Latin *commemoratus* 'made mention of'] □ **commemoration** *n.* **commemorative** *adj.* **commemorator** *n.*

commence *v.tr. & intr. formal* begin. [from Old French *com(m)encier*]

commencement *n. formal* **1** a beginning. **2** esp. *N. Amer.* a ceremony of degree conferment.

commend *v.tr.* **1** entrust, commit (*commends his soul to God*). **2** praise. **3** (often *refl.*) recommend (*idea commends itself*; *has much to commend it*). [based on Latin *mandare* 'to entrust']

COMMENSALISM

Meaning 'eating at the same table', commensalism is a partnership between two species in which food is often involved. Usually, only one partner benefits, while the other is unaffected. Remoras live commensally with sharks. The remora fastens itself to the shark as a means of free transport, and detaches itself temporarily to feed.

remora

nurse shark

COMMENSALISM BETWEEN A NURSE SHARK AND A REMORA

---

commendable *adj.* praiseworthy. □ **commendably** *adv.*

commendation *n.* **1** an act of commending or recommending. **2** praise.

commendatory *adj.* commending, recommending.

commensal *Biol.* ● *adj.* of, relating to, or exhibiting commensalism. ● *n.* a commensal organism. [based on Latin *mensa* 'table'] □ **commensality** *n.*

commensalism *n. Biol.* ▲ an association between two organisms in which one benefits and the other derives neither benefit nor harm.

commensurable *adj.* **1** (often foll. by *with*, *to*) measurable by the same standard. **2** (foll. by *to*) proportionate to. **3** *Math.* (of numbers) in a ratio equal to the ratio of integers. [from Late Latin *commensurabilis*] □ **commensurability** *n.* **commensurably** *adv.*

commensurate *adj.* **1** (usu. foll. by *with*) having the same size, duration, etc. **2** proportionate. □ **commensurately** *adv.*

comment ● *n.* **1 a** a remark, esp. critical (*passed a comment on her hat*). **b** commenting; criticism (*his behaviour aroused much comment*). **2** an explanatory note (e.g. on a written text). ● *v.intr.* **1** make (esp. critical) remarks (*commented on her dress*). **2** (often foll. by *on*, *upon*) write explanatory notes. □ **no comment** *colloq.* I decline to answer your question. [from Latin *commentum* 'contrivance'] □ **commenter** *n.*

commentary *n.* (*pl.* **-ies**) **1** a set of explanatory or critical notes on a text etc. **2** a descriptive spoken account (esp. on radio or television) of an event as it happens.

commentate *v.intr.* (often foll. by *on*) act as a commentator.

commentator *n.* **1** a person who provides a commentary on an event etc. **2** the writer of a commentary. **3** a person who writes or speaks on current events.

commerce *n.* financial transactions, esp. the buying and selling of goods, on a large scale. [based on Latin *merx mercis* 'merchandise']

commercial ● *adj.* **1** of, engaged in, or concerned with, commerce. **2** having profit as a primary aim rather than artistic etc. value; philistine. **3** (of broadcasting) funded by advertising. ● *n.* a television or radio advertisement. □ **commerciality** *n.* **commercially** *adv.*

commercial art *n.* art used in advertising, selling, etc.

commercialism *n.* **1** the principles and practice of commerce. **2** (esp. excessive) emphasis on financial profit as a measure of worth.

commercialize *v.tr.* (also **-ise**) **1** exploit or spoil for profit. **2** make commercial. □ **commercialization** *n.*

commercial traveller *n. Brit.* a travelling salesman or saleswoman who visits shops to get orders.

commère *n. Brit.* a female compère. [French]

Commie *n. slang derog.* a Communist.

commination *n.* the threatening of divine vengeance. [based on Latin *comminari* 'to threaten']

comminatory *adj.* threatening.

commingle *v.tr. & intr. literary* mingle together.

comminute /kom-i-newt/ *v.tr.* **1** reduce to small fragments. **2** divide (property) into small portions. [based on Latin *minuere minut-* 'to lessen'] □ **comminution** *n.*

commis *n.* (*pl.* same) a junior chef or *Brit.* waiter. [French, literally 'entrusted']

commiserate *v.intr.* (usu. foll. by *with*) express or feel pity. [based on Latin *commiseratus* 'pitied'] □ **commiseration** *n.* **commiserative** *adj.*

commissar *n. hist.* an official of the Soviet Communist Party responsible for political education and organization. [related to COMMISSARY]

commissariat *n.* esp. *Mil.* **1** a department for the supply of food etc. **2** the food supplied. [related to COMMISSARY]

commissary *n.* (*pl.* **-ies**) **1** a deputy or delegate. **2** *N. Amer.* **a** a restaurant in a film studio etc. **b** the food supplied. **3** *N. Amer. Mil.* a store for the supply of food etc. to soldiers. [from medieval Latin *commissarius* 'person in charge'] □ **commissarial** *adj.* **commissaryship** *n.*

commission ● *n.* **1 a** the authority to perform a task or certain duties. **b** a person or group entrusted esp. by a government with such authority. **c** an instruction or duty given to such a group or person (*their commission was to simplify the procedure*). **2** an order for something, esp. a work of art, to be produced specially. **3** *Mil.* a warrant conferring the rank of officer in an army, navy, or air force. **b** the rank so conferred. **4 a** the authority to act as agent for a company etc. in trade. **b** a percentage paid to the agent from the business obtained (*his salary is low, but he gets 20% commission*). **5** the act of committing (a crime, sin, etc.). **6** the office or department of a commissioner. ● *v.tr.* **1** authorize or empower by a commission. **2 a** give (an artist etc.) a commission for a piece of work. **b** order (a work) to be written. **3** *Naut.* **a** give (an officer) the command of a ship. **b** prepare (a ship) for active service. **4** bring (a machine, equipment, etc.) into operation. □ **in commission** (of a warship etc.) manned, armed, and ready for service. **out of commission** (esp. of a ship) not in service; not in working order. [related to COMMIT]

commission agent *n. Brit.* a bookmaker.

C

C

commissionaire *n.* esp. *Brit.* a uniformed door attendant at a theatre, cinema, etc.

commissioner *n.* **1** a person appointed by a commission to perform a specific task. **2** (esp. in titles) a person appointed as a member of a government commission (*Civil Service Commissioner*). **3** a representative of the supreme authority in a district, department, etc.

Commissioner for Oaths *n. Brit.* a solicitor authorized to administer an oath to a person making an affidavit.

commissure *n.* **1** a junction, joint, or seam. **2** *Anat.* ▶ the line where the upper and lower lips, or eyelids, meet. [from Latin *commissura* 'junction'] □ **commissural** *adj.*

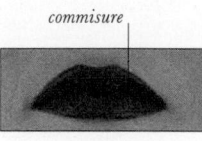

commisure

COMMISSURE

commit *v.tr.* (**committed, committing**) **1** entrust or consign for: **a** safe keeping (*I commit him to your care*). **b** treatment, usu. destruction (*committed the book to the flames*). **2** perpetrate, do (esp. a crime, sin, or blunder). **3** pledge, involve, or bind (esp. oneself) to a certain course or policy. **4** (as **committed** *adj.*) **a** morally dedicated or politically aligned (*a committed Christian; committed to the cause*). **b** obliged (to take certain action). □ **commit to memory** learn (a thing) so as to be able to recall it. **commit to prison** consign officially to custody, esp. on remand. [from Latin *committere* 'to join, entrust'] □ **committable** *adj.* **committer** *n.*

commitment *n.* **1** an engagement or obligation that restricts freedom of action. **2** the process or an instance of committing oneself.

committal *n.* **1** the act of committing a person to an institution, esp. prison or a psychiatric hospital. **2** the burial of a corpse.

committee *n.* **1** a body of persons appointed for a specific function by, and usu. out of, a larger body. **2** such a body appointed by Parliament etc. to consider the details of proposed legislation. **3** (**Committee**) (in the UK) the whole House of Commons when sitting as a committee.

committee man *n.* (*fem.* **committee woman**) a member of a committee, esp. a habitual member of committees.

committee stage *n. Brit.* the third of five stages of a bill's progress through Parliament when it may be considered in detail and amendments made.

commode *n.* **1** a chest of drawers. **2 a** a bedside table with a cupboard containing a chamber pot. **b** a chamber pot concealed in a chair with a hinged cover. [from Latin *commodus* 'convenient']

commodification *n.* the action of turning something into, or treating something as, a (mere) commodity. □ **commodify** *v.tr.* (**-ies, -ied**)

commodious *adj.* roomy and comfortable. □ **commodiously** *adv.* **commodiousness** *n.*

commodity *n.* (*pl.* **-ies**) **1** an article or raw material that can be bought and sold. **2** a useful thing.

commodore *n.* **1** a naval officer above a captain and below a rear admiral. **2** the commander of a squadron or other division of a fleet. **3** the president of a yacht club.

Commodore-in-Chief *n. Brit.* the supreme officer in the Royal Air Force.

common ● *adj.* (**commoner, commonest**) **1 a** occurring often (*a common mistake*). **b** ordinary; of ordinary qualities; without special rank or position (*no common mind; common soldier; the common people*). **2 a** shared by, coming from, or done by, more than one (*common knowledge; by common consent*). **b** belonging to, open to, or affecting, the whole community (*common land*). **3** *derog.* low-class; inferior (*a common little man*). **4** of the most familiar type (*common cold*). **5** *Math.* belonging to two or more quantities (*common factor*). **6** *Gram.* (of gender) referring to individuals of either sex (e.g. *teacher*). **7** *Mus.* having two

or four beats, esp. four crotchets, in a bar. ● *n.* a piece of open public land, esp. in a village or town. □ **common ground** a point or argument accepted by both sides in a dispute. **common or garden** *Brit. colloq.* ordinary. **in common 1** in joint use; shared. **2** of joint interest (*have little in common*). **in common with** in the same way as. **out of the common** *Brit.* unusual. [from Latin *communis*] □ **commonly** *adv.* **commonness** *n.*

commonality *n.* (*pl.* **-ies**) **1** the sharing of an attribute. **2** a common occurrence. **3** = COMMONALTY.

commonalty *n.* (*pl.* **-ies**) **1** the common people. **2** the general body (esp. of humankind). **3** a corporate body.

common crier *n.* = TOWN CRIER.

common denominator *n.* **1** a common multiple of the denominators of several fractions. **2** a common feature of members of a group.

commoner *n.* one of the common people, as opposed to the aristocracy.

Common Era *n.* the Christian era.

common law *n.* law derived from custom and judicial precedent (cf. CASE LAW, CIVIL LAW, STATUTE LAW).

common-law husband *n.* (*fem.* **common-law wife**) a partner in a marriage recognized in some jurisdictions as valid by common law, though not brought about by a civil or ecclesiastical ceremony.

Common Market *n.* the European Community.

common noun *n.* (also **common name**) *Gram.* a name denoting a class of objects or a concept as opposed to a particular individual (e.g. *boy, chocolate, beauty*).

commonplace ● *adj.* lacking originality; trite. ● *n.* **1 a** an everyday saying; a platitude. **b** an ordinary topic of conversation. **2** anything usual or trite. [translation of Latin *locus communis*] □ **commonplaceness** *n.*

commonplace book *n.* a book into which notable extracts from other works are copied for personal use.

Common Prayer *n.* the Church of England liturgy originally set forth in the *Book of Common Prayer* of Edward VI (1549), esp. as revised in 1662.

common property *n.* a thing known by most people.

common room *n.* esp. *Brit* **1** a room in some colleges, schools, etc., which members may use for relaxation or work. **2** the members who use this.

commons *n.pl.* **1** (**the Commons**) = HOUSE OF COMMONS. **2** the common people. **3** provisions shared in common.

common salt see SALT *n.* 1.

common sense *n.* sound practical sense, esp. in everyday matters.

commonsensical *adj.* possessing or marked by common sense.

Common Serjeant *n.* a circuit judge of the Central Criminal Court with duties in the City of London.

common soldier see SOLDIER *n.* 2.

common stock *n.pl. N. Amer.* = ORDINARY SHARE.

common valerian see VALERIAN 1.

common weal *n.* public welfare.

commonwealth *n.* **1** an independent state or community, esp. a democratic republic. **2** (**the Commonwealth**) **a** (in full **the Commonwealth of Nations**) an association of the UK together with states that were previously part of the British Empire, and dependencies. **b** the republican period of government in Britain 1649–60.

common year see YEAR 2.

commotion *n.* **1** a confused and noisy disturbance or outburst. **2** loud and confusing noise. [from Latin *commotio*]

communal *adj.* **1** relating to or benefiting a community; for common use (*communal baths*). **2** between different esp. ethnic or religious communities (*communal violence*). **3** of a commune, esp. the Paris Commune. □ **communality** *n.* **communally** *adv.*

communalism *n.* **1** a principle of political organization based on federated communes. **2** the principle of communal ownership etc.

communalize *v.tr.* (also **-ise**) make communal. □ **communalization** *n.*

communard *n.* **1** a member of a commune. **2** (also **Communard**) *hist.* a supporter of the Paris Commune (see COMMUNE[1] 3). [French]

commune[1] /kom-yoon/ *n.* **1 a** a group of people sharing living accommodation, goods, etc. **b** a communal settlement esp. for the pursuit of shared interests. **2** the smallest French territorial division for administrative purposes. **3** (**the Commune**) the communalistic government in Paris in 1871. [from medieval Latin *communia* 'things in common']

commune[2] /kŏ-mewn/ *v.intr.* (usu. foll. by *with*) **1** speak intimately. **2** feel in close touch (with nature etc.). [from Old French *comuner* 'to share']

communicable *adj.* (esp. of a disease) able to be passed on. □ **communicability** *n.* **communicably** *adv.*

communicant *n.* **1** a person who receives Holy Communion. **2** a person who imparts information.

communicate *v.* **1** *tr.* **a** transmit or pass on by speaking or writing. **b** transmit (heat, motion, etc.). **c** pass on (an infectious illness). **d** impart (feelings etc.) non-verbally. **2** *intr.* succeed in conveying information, evoking understanding, etc. (*he communicates well*). **3** *intr.* (often foll. by *with*) relate socially. **4** *intr.* (of a room etc.) have a common door (*my room communicates with yours*). [based on Latin *communicatus* 'made common'] □ **communicator** *n.* **communicatory** *adj.*

communication *n.* **1 a** the act of imparting, esp. news. **b** an instance of this. **c** the information etc. communicated. **2** a means of connecting different places. **3** social intercourse. **4** (in *pl.*) the science and practice of transmitting information.

communication cord *n. Brit.* a cord or chain that may be pulled to stop a train in an emergency.

communication satellite *n.* (also **communications satellite**) an artificial satellite used to relay telephone circuits or broadcast programmes.

communicative *adj.* ready to talk and impart information. □ **communicatively** *adv.*

communion *n.* **1** a sharing, esp. of thoughts etc.; fellowship. **2** participation; a sharing in common (*communion of interests*). **3** (**Communion, Holy Communion**) **a** the Eucharist. **b** participation in the Communion service. **4** a body or group within the Christian faith (*the Anglican communion*). [based on Latin *communis* 'common']

communiqué /kŏ-mew-ni-kay/ *n.* an official communication, esp. a news report. [French, literally 'communicated']

communism *n.* **1** a political theory advocating a society in which all property is publicly owned and each person is paid and works according to his or her needs and abilities. **2** (usu. **Communism**) **a** the communistic form of society established in the former USSR and elsewhere. **b** any movement or political doctrine advocating communism, esp. Marxism. **3** = COMMUNALISM. [based on French *commun* 'common']

communist ● *n.* **1** a person advocating or practising communism. **2** (**Communist**) a member of a Communist Party. ● *adj.* of or relating to communism (*a communist play*). □ **communistic** *adj.*

communitarian ● *n.* a member of a communistic community. ● *adj.* of or relating to such a community.

community *n.* (*pl.* **-ies**) **1** all the people living in a specific locality. **2** a body of people having a religion, a profession, etc., in common (*the immigrant community*). **3** fellowship; similarity (*community of intellect*). **4** a monastic, socialistic, etc. commune. **5** joint ownership or liability (*community of goods*). **6** (prec. by *the*) the public. **7** *Ecol.* a group of animals or plants living or growing together in the same area. [from Latin *communitas*, related to COMMON]

COMPACT DISC

Launched in 1982, compact discs (CDs) store sound as a sequence of millions of tiny pits, which capture the sound wave as a series of digital codes. As the disc spins, the CD player uses a laser beam to read the sequence of pits, and recreates the original waveform from the digital codes. Once amplified, this waveform drives a loudspeaker, reproducing the sound.

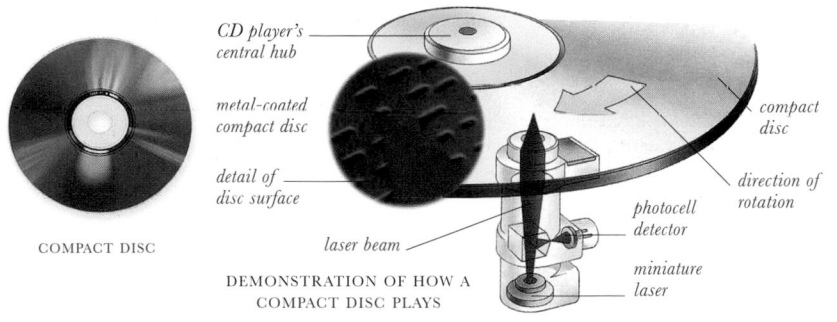

COMPACT DISC

CD player's central hub

metal-coated compact disc

detail of disc surface

laser beam

compact disc

direction of rotation

photocell detector

miniature laser

DEMONSTRATION OF HOW A
COMPACT DISC PLAYS

C

community centre *n.* a place providing social etc. facilities for a neighbourhood.

community charge *n. hist.* (in the UK) a short-lived tax levied locally on every adult in a community, replaced in 1993 by the council tax.

community chest *n.* a fund for charity and welfare work in a community.

community college *n. esp. N. Amer.* a college providing further and higher education for members of the local community.

community policing *n.* policing by officers intended to have personal knowledge of the community which they police. □ **community policeman** *n.*

community service *n.* work, esp. voluntary and unpaid, or stipulated by a community service order, in the community.

community service order *n. Brit.* an order for a convicted offender to perform a period of unpaid work in the community.

community singing *n.* singing by a large crowd or group, esp. of old popular songs or hymns.

community worker *n.* a person who works in a community to promote its welfare.

commutable *adj.* **1** convertible into money; exchangeable. **2** *Law* (of a punishment) able to be commuted. **3** within commuting distance. □ **commutability** *n.*

commutate *v.tr. Electr.* **1** regulate the direction of (an alternating current), esp. to make it a direct current. **2** reverse the direction (of an electric current). [related to COMMUTE]

commutation *n.* **1** the act or process of commuting or being commuted (in legal and exchange senses). **2** *Electr.* the act or process of commutating or being commutated. **3** *Math.* the reversal of the order of two quantities.

commutative *adj.* **1** relating to or involving substitution. **2** *Math.* unchanged in result by the interchange of the order of quantities.

commutator *n. Electr.* a device for reversing electric current.

commute *v.* **1** *intr.* travel some distance to and from one's daily work. **2** *tr.* (usu. foll. by *to*) *Law* change (a judicial sentence etc.) to another less severe. **3** *tr.* (often foll. by *into, for*) change (one kind of payment) for another. **4** *tr.* **a** exchange; interchange. **b** change (to another thing). [based on Latin *mutare* 'to change']

commuter *n.* a person who commutes to work.

compact[1] ● *adj.* /kŏm-**pakt**/ **1** closely or neatly packed together. **2** small and economically designed. **3** concise. **4** (esp. of the human body) small but well-proportioned. ● *v.tr.* /kŏm-**pakt**/ **1** join or press firmly together. **2** condense. ● *n.* /**kom**-pakt/ **1** a small flat case for face powder.

2 *N. Amer.* a medium-sized motor car. [from Latin *compactus* 'put together closely'] □ **compaction** *n.* **compactly** *adv.* **compactness** *n.* **compactor** *n.*

compact[2] /**kom**-pakt/ *n.* an agreement or contract. [from Latin *compactum*]

compact disc *n.* ▲ a disc on which information or sound is recorded digitally and reproduced by reflection of laser light. ▷ COMPUTER

compadre /kom-**pah**-dri/ *n.* (*pl.* **compadres**) esp. *US colloq.* a friend, companion. [Spanish, literally 'godfather']

companion[1] *n.* **1 a** a person who accompanies, associates with, or shares with, another. **b** a person employed to live with and assist another. **2** a handbook or reference book. **3** a thing that matches another. **4** (**Companion**) a member of the lowest grade of some orders of knighthood (*Companion of the Bath*). [from Latin, literally 'one who breaks bread with another']

companion[2] *n. Naut.* **1** a raised frame with windows let into the quarterdeck of a ship to allow light into the cabins etc. below. **2** = COMPANIONWAY. [from obsolete Dutch *kompanje* 'quarterdeck']

companionable *adj.* sociable, friendly. □ **companionableness** *n.* **companionably** *adv.*

companionate *adj.* **1** well-suited; (of clothes) matching. **2** of or like a companion.

companion-in-arms *n.* a fellow soldier.

companion ladder *n.* a ladder from a deck to a cabin.

companionship *n.* good fellowship; friendship.

companionway *n.* a staircase to a cabin.

company *n.* (*pl.* **-ies**) **1 a** a number of people assembled. **b** guests or a guest (*am expecting company*). **2** companionship, esp. of a specific kind (*enjoys low company; do not care for his company*). **3** a commercial business. **4** a troupe of actors or entertainers. **5** *Mil.* a subdivision of an infantry battalion. **6** *Brit.* a group of Guides. □ **in company** not alone. **in company with** together with. **keep company** (often foll. by *with*) associate habitually. **keep** (or *archaic* **bear**) **a person company** remain with a person to be sociable. **part company** (often foll. by *with*) cease to associate. [from Old French *compai(g)nie*]

company car *n.* a car provided by a company for the business and usu. private use of an employee.

comparable *adj.* **1** (often foll. by *with*) able to be compared. **2** (often foll. by *to*) fit to be compared; worth comparing. □ **comparability** *n.* **comparableness** *n.* **comparably** *adv.*

■ **Usage** The use of *comparable* with *to* and *with* corresponds to the senses at *compare*; *to* is more common.

comparative ● *adj.* **1** perceptible by comparison; relative (*in comparative comfort*). **2** estimated by comparison (*the comparative merits of the two ideas*). **3** of or involving comparison (*a comparative study*). **4** *Gram.* (of an adjective or adverb) expressing a higher degree of a quality (e.g. *braver*; *more fiercely*) (cf. POSITIVE *adj.* 3b, SUPERLATIVE *adj.* 2). ● *n. Gram.* **1** the comparative expression or form of a word. **2** a word in the comparative. □ **comparatively** *adv.*

compare ● *v.* **1** *tr.* (usu. foll. by *to*) express similarities in; liken (*compared the landscape to a painting*). **2** *tr.* (often foll. by *to, with*) estimate the similarity or dissimilarity of (*compared radio with television; that lacks quality compared to this*). **3** *intr.* (often foll. by *with*) bear comparison (*compares favourably with the rest*). ● *n. literary* comparison (*beyond compare*). □ **compare notes** exchange ideas or opinions. [based on Latin *par* 'equal']

■ **Usage** In sense 2 *to* and *with* are generally interchangeable, but *with* often implies a greater element of formal analysis.

comparison *n.* **1** the act or an instance of comparing. **2** a simile or semantic illustration. **3** capacity for being likened; similarity (*there's no comparison*). **4** (in full **degrees of comparison**) *Gram.* the positive, comparative, and superlative forms of adjectives and adverbs. □ **bear** (or **stand**) **comparison** (often foll. by *with*) be able to be compared favourably. **beyond comparison 1** totally different in quality. **2** greatly superior; excellent. **in** (or **by**) **comparison with** compared to.

compartment *n.* **1** a space within a larger space, separated from the rest by partitions. **2** *Naut.* a watertight division of a ship. [based on Late Latin *compartiri* 'to divide'] □ **compartmentation** *n.*

compartmental *adj.* consisting of or relating to compartments or a compartment. □ **compartmentally** *adv.*

compartmentalize *v.tr.* (also **-ise**) divide into compartments or categories. □ **compartmentalization** *n.*

compass ● *n.* **1** (in full **magnetic compass**) ◄ an instrument showing the direction of magnetic north and bearings from it (see also GYROCOMPASS). **2** (usu. in *pl.*) (also **pair of compasses** *sing.*) an instrument for taking measurements and describing circles, with two arms connected at one end by a movable joint. **3** a circumference or boundary. **4** area, extent; scope, range. ● *v.tr. literary* **1** hem in. **2** grasp mentally. [from Old French *compas* 'measure, pair of compasses'] □ **compassable** *adj.*

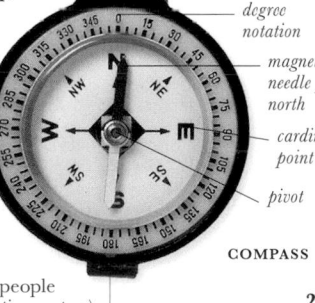

degree notation

magnetic needle points north

cardinal point (east)

pivot

COMPASS

compassion *n.* pity inclining one to help or be merciful. [from ecclesiastical Latin *compassio*]

compassionate *adj.* sympathetic, pitying. □ **compassionately** *adv.*

compassionate leave *n.* leave granted on grounds of bereavement etc.

compatible ● *adj.* **1** (often foll. by *with*) **a** able to coexist; well-suited; mutually tolerant. **b** consistent (*their views are not compatible with their actions*). **2** (of equipment etc.) capable of being used in combination. ● *n.* (usu. in *comb.*) *Computing* a piece of equipment that can use software etc. designed for another brand of the same equipment (*IBM compatibles*). [from medieval Latin *compatibilis*] □ **compatibility** *n.* **compatibly** *adv.*

C

compatriot *n.* a fellow countryman. [from Late Latin *compatriota*] □ **compatriotic** *adj.*

compeer *n.* **1** an equal; a peer. **2** a comrade. [from Old French *comper*]

compel *v.tr.* (**compelled**, **compelling**) **1** (usu. foll. by *to* + infin.) force, constrain. **2** bring about (an action) by force (*compel submission*). **3** (as **compelling** *adj.*) rousing strong interest, attention, conviction, or admiration. [based on Latin *pellere* 'to drive'] □ **compellingly** *adv.*

compellable *adj. Law* (of a witness etc.) that may be made to attend court or give evidence.

compendious *adj.* (esp. of a book etc.) comprehensive but fairly brief. [from Latin *compendiosus* 'brief'] □ **compendiously** *adv.* **compendiousness** *n.*

compendium *n.* (*pl.* **compendiums** or **compendia**) **1** esp. *Brit.* a usu. one-volume handbook or encyclopedia. **2 a** a summary or abstract of a larger work. **b** an abridgement. **3** (in full **compendium of games**) a collection of games in a box. [Latin, literally 'what is weighed together']

compensate *v.* **1** *tr.* (often foll. by *for*) recompense (a person) (*compensated him for his loss*). **2** *intr.* (usu. foll. by *for*) make amends (*compensated for the insult*). **3** *tr.* counterbalance; make up for; make amends for. **4** *intr. Psychol.* offset a disability or frustration by development in another direction. [based on Latin *compensatus* 'counterbalanced'] □ **compensative** *adj.* **compensator** *n.* **compensatory** *adj.*

compensation *n.* **1 a** the act of compensating. **b** the process of being compensated. **2** something, esp. money, given as a recompense. **3** *N. Amer.* a salary or wages. □ **compensational** *adj.*

compère *Brit.* ● *n.* a person who introduces and links the artistes in a variety show etc. ● *v.* **1** *tr.* act as a compère to. **2** *intr.* act as compère. [French, literally 'godfather']

compete *v.intr.* **1** (often foll. by *with*, *against* a person, *for* a thing) strive for superiority or supremacy (*compete for the job*). **2** (often foll. by *in*) take part (in a contest etc.). [from Latin *competere*, in late sense 'to strive after (something)']

competence *n.* (also **competency**) **1** (often foll. by *for*, or *to* + infin.) ability; the state of being competent. **2** *Law* the legal capacity (of a court, a magistrate, etc.) to deal with a matter.

competent *adj.* **1 a** (usu. foll. by *to* + infin. or *for*) adequately qualified or capable (*not competent to drive*). **b** effective (*a competent batsman*). **2** *Law* (of a judge, court, or witness) legally qualified or qualifying. [from Latin *competent-* 'being fit or proper'] □ **competently** *adv.*

competition *n.* **1** (often foll. by *for*) competing, esp. in an examination, in trade, etc. **2** an event or contest in which people compete. **3 a** the people competing against a person. **b** the opposition they represent.

competitive *adj.* **1** involving, offered for, or by competition (*competitive game*). **2** (of prices etc.) low enough to compare well with those of rival traders. **3** (of a person) having a strong urge to win. □ **competitively** *adv.* **competitiveness** *n.*

competitor *n.* **1** a person who competes. **2** a rival, esp. in business or commerce.

compilation *n.* **1 a** the act of compiling. **b** the process of being compiled. **2** something compiled, esp. a book etc. of separate articles, stories, etc.

compile *v.tr.* **1 a** collect (material) into a list, volume, etc. **b** make up (a volume etc.) from such material. **2** *Computing* produce (a machine-coded form of a high-level program). [from Old French *compiler*]

compiler *n.* **1** *Computing* a program for translating a high-level programming language into machine code. **2** a person who compiles.

complacent *adj.* **1** smugly self-satisfied. **2** calmly content. [from Latin *complacent-* 'pleasing'] □ **complacence** *n.* **complacency** *n.* **complacently** *adv.*

■ **Usage** *Complacent* should not be confused with *complaisant*.

complain *v.intr.* **1** (often foll. by *about*, *at*, or *that* + clause) express dissatisfaction. **2** (foll. by *of*) **a** announce that one is suffering from (an ailment) (*complained of a headache*). **b** state a grievance concerning (*complained of the delay*). [from medieval Latin *complangere* 'to bewail'] □ **complainer** *n.* **complainingly** *adv.*

complainant *n. Law* a plaintiff in certain lawsuits.

complaint *n.* **1 a** a grievance or cause for dissatisfaction (*I have no complaints*). **b** a statement of dissatisfaction (*make a complaint*). **2** an ailment or illness.

complaisant *adj.* **1** deferential. **2** willing to please; acquiescent. [French] □ **complaisance** *n.*

■ **Usage** *Complaisant* should not be confused with *complacent*.

compleat *archaic* var. of COMPLETE.

complement ● *n.* **1 a** something that completes. **b** one of two things that go together. **2** (often **full complement**) the full number needed to man a ship etc. **3** *Gram.* a word or phrase added to a verb to complete the predicate of a sentence. **4** *Geom.* ► the amount by which an angle is less than 90°. ● *v.tr.* **1** complete. **2** form a complement to (*the scarf complements her dress*). [from Latin *complementum*] □ **complemental** *adj.*

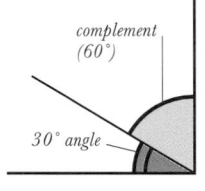

complement (60°)

30° angle

COMPLEMENT OF A 30° ANGLE

complementarity *n.* (*pl.* **-ies**) a complementary relationship or situation.

complementary *adj.* **1** completing; forming a complement. **2** (of two or more things) complementing each other. □ **complementarily** *adv.* **complementariness** *n.*

complementary angle *n.* either of two angles making up 90°.

complementary colour *n.* a colour that, combined with a given colour, makes white or black.

complementary medicine *n.* = ALTERNATIVE MEDICINE.

complete ● *adj.* **1** having all its parts; entire. **2** finished. **3** of the maximum extent or degree (*a complete surprise*; *a complete stranger*). ● *v.tr.* **1** finish. **2 a** make whole or perfect. **b** make up the amount of (*completes the quota*). **3** fill in the answers to (a questionnaire etc.). **4** (usu. *absol.*) *Law* conclude a sale of property. □ **complete with** having (as an important accessory) (*comes complete with instructions*). [from Latin *completus* 'filled up'] □ **completely** *adv.* **completeness** *n.* **completion** *n.*

completist *n.* an obsessive or indiscriminate collector.

complex ● *n.* **1** a building, a series of rooms, a network, etc. made up of related parts. **2** *Psychol.* a related group of usu. repressed feelings or thoughts which cause abnormal behaviour or mental states (*inferiority complex*; *Oedipus complex*). **3** (in general use) a preoccupation or obsession (*has a complex about punctuality*). ● *adj.* **1** consisting of related parts; composite. **2** complicated (*a complex problem*). [from Latin *complexus* 'embracing, interwoven'] □ **complexity** *n.* (*pl.* **-ies**). **complexly** *adv.*

complexion *n.* **1** the natural colour, texture, and appearance of the skin, esp. of the face. **2** an aspect; a character (*puts a different complexion on the matter*). [from Latin *complexio* 'combination, physical conformation'] □ **complexioned** *adj.* (also in *comb.*).

compliance *n.* **1** the act or an instance of complying. **2** unworthy acquiescence. □ **in compliance with** according to (a wish, command, etc.).

compliant *adj.* disposed to comply; yielding, obedient. □ **compliantly** *adv.*

complicate *v.tr. & intr.* **1** (often foll. by *with*) make or become difficult, confused, or complex. **2** (as **complicated** *adj.*) complex; intricate. [based on Latin *complicatus* 'folded together'] □ **complicatedly** *adv.* **complicatedness** *n.*

complication *n.* **1 a** an involved or confused condition or state. **b** a complicating circumstance; a difficulty. **2** *Med.* a secondary disease or condition aggravating a previous one.

complicity *n.* [based on Late Latin *complex conplicis* 'closely connected'] partnership in a crime or wrongdoing. □ **complicit** *adj.*

compliment ● *n.* **1 a** a spoken or written expression of praise. **b** an act or circumstance implying praise (*their success was a compliment to their efforts*). **2** (in *pl.*) **a** formal greetings, esp. as a written accompaniment to a gift etc. (*with the compliments of the management*). **b** praise (*my compliments to the cook*). ● *v.tr.* (often foll. by *on*) congratulate; praise. □ **pay a compliment** to praise. **return the compliment 1** give a compliment in return for another. **2** retaliate or recompense in kind. [based on Latin *complère* 'to fulfil' (the requirements of courtesy)]

complimentary *adj.* **1** expressing a compliment; praising. **2** (of a ticket for a play etc.) given free of charge.

compliments slip *n.* esp. *Brit.* a printed slip of paper sent with a gift etc., esp. from a business firm.

compline *n. Eccl.* the office of the seventh canonical hour of prayer, originally said at the end of the day. [based on Old French *complie* (fem.) 'completed']

comply *v.intr.* (**-ies**, **-ied**) (often foll. by *with*) act in accordance (with a wish, command, etc.). [from Latin *complère* 'to fill up, fulfil']

component ● *n.* **1** a part of a larger whole, esp. part of a motor vehicle. **2** *Math.* one of two or more vectors equivalent to a given vector. ● *adj.* being part of a larger whole (*assembled the component parts*). [from Latin *component-* 'composing'] □ **componential** *adj.*

comport *v.refl.* usu. *literary* conduct oneself; behave. [from Latin *comportare* 'to carry together'] □ **comportment** *n.*

compos *adj.* = COMPOS MENTIS.

compose *v.* **1 a** *tr.* construct or create (a work of art, esp. literature or music). **b** *intr.* compose music. **2** *tr.* constitute; make up (*six tribes which composed the German nation*). **3** *tr.* order, arrange (*composed the group for the photographer*). **4** *tr.* **a** (often *refl.*) calm; settle. **b** (as **composed** *adj.*) calm, settled. **5** *tr.* settle (a dispute etc.). **6** *tr. Printing* **a** ▼ set up (type) to form words and blocks of words. **b** set up (a manuscript etc.) in type. □ **composed of** made up of; consisting of. [from French *composer*] □ **composedly** *adv.*

■ **Usage** In sense 2, *compose* is preferable to *comprise* (see Usage Note at *comprise*).

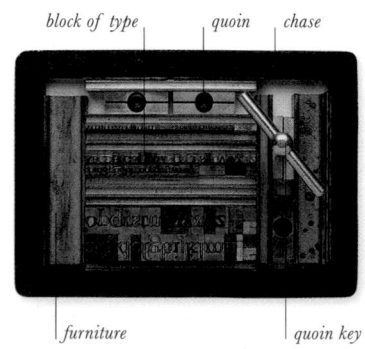

block of type   *quoin*   *chase*

furniture   *quoin key*

COMPOSE: TYPE COMPOSED IN A PRINTER'S FORME

composer *n.* a person who composes (esp. music).

composite /kom-pŏ-zit/ ● *adj.* **1** made up of various parts; blended. **2** (**Composite**) *Archit.* of the fifth classical order of architecture, consisting of elements of the Ionic and Corinthian orders. ▷ COLUMN.

COMPOSITE
FLOWER: WALL DAISY
(*Erigeron karvinskianus*)

disc-florets (small flowers in a head)

ray-floret

3 *Bot.* of the plant family Compositae. ● *n.* **1** a thing made up of several parts or elements. **2** *Bot.* ◀ a plant of the family Compositae, having many small flowers forming one bloom, e.g. the daisy. **3** /**kom**-pŏ-zyt/ *Polit.* a resolution composed of two or more related resolutions. ● *v.tr.* /**kom**-pŏ-zyt/ *Polit.* amalgamate (two or more related resolutions). [from Latin *compositus* 'put together'] □ **compositely** *adv.* **compositeness** *n.*

composition *n.* **1 a** the act of putting together; formation or construction. **b** something so composed; a mixture. **c** the constitution of such a mixture. **2 a** a literary or musical work. **b** the act or art of producing such a work. **c** an essay, esp. written by a schoolchild. **d** an artistic arrangement (of parts of a picture, subjects for a photograph, etc.). **3** (often *attrib.*) a compound artificial substance. **4** *Printing* the setting-up of type. **6** *Gram.* the formation of words into a compound word. □ **compositional** *adj.* **compositionally** *adv.*

compositor *n.* *Printing* a person who sets up type for printing.

compos mentis *adj.* having control of one's mind; sane. [Latin]

compost ● *n.* **1a** mixed manure, esp. of organic origin. **b** a loam soil or other medium with added compost, used for growing plants. **2** a mixture of ingredients (*a rich compost of lies and innuendo*). ● *v.tr.* **1** treat (soil) with compost. **2** make (manure, vegetable matter, etc.) into compost. [related to COMPOSITE]

compost heap *n.* a layered pile of garden refuse, soil, etc., which decays to become compost.

composure *n.* a tranquil manner; calmness.

compote *n.* fruit preserved or cooked in syrup. [French]

compound[1] ● *n.* /**kom**-pownd/ **1** a mixture of two or more things, qualities, etc. **2** (also **compound word**) a word made up of two or more existing words. **3** *Chem.* a substance formed from two or more

COMPOUND LEAF OF A ROWAN TREE

leaflet

elements chemically united in fixed proportions. ● *adj.* /**kom**-pownd/ **1 a** made up of several ingredients. **b** consisting of several parts. **2** combined; collective. **3** *Zool.* consisting of individual organisms. ● *v.tr.* /**kom**-**pownd**/ **1** mix or combine (ingredients, ideas, motives, etc.) (*grief compounded with fear*). **2** increase or complicate (difficulties etc.) (*anxiety compounded by discomfort*). **3** make up (a composite whole). **4** *Law* **a** condone (a liability or offence) in exchange for money etc. **b** forbear from prosecuting (a felony) from private motives. **5** combine (words or elements) into a word. [from Latin *componere* 'to put together'] □ **compoundable** *adj.*

compound[2] /**kom**-pownd/ *n.* **1** a large open enclosure for housing workers etc., esp. miners in S. Africa. **2** an enclosure, esp. in India, China, etc., in which a factory or a house stands. **3** a large enclosed space in a prison or prison camp. [from Malay]

compound eye *n.* ▶ an eye consisting of numerous visual units, as found in insects and crustaceans (cf. SIMPLE EYE).
▷ INSECT

compound fracture *n.* a fracture in which a bone pierces the skin, causing a risk of infection.

compound interest *n.* interest payable on both capital and the accumulated interest (cf. SIMPLE INTEREST).

compound leaf *n.* ◀ a leaf consisting of several leaflets.

compound sentence *n.* a sentence with more than one subject or predicate.

comprehend *v.tr.* **1** grasp mentally; understand. **2** include; take in. [from Latin *comprehendere*]

comprehensible *adj.* that can be understood; intelligible. □ **comprehensibility** *n.* **comprehensibly** *adv.*

comprehension *n.* **1 a** the act or capability of understanding. **b** *Brit.* a text with questions designed to test understanding of it. **2** inclusion.

comprehensive ● *adj.* **1** complete; including all or nearly all elements, aspects, etc. (a

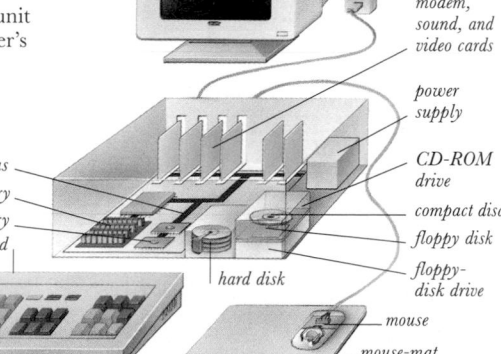

COMPOUND EYE:
CROSS-SECTION OF AN INSECT EYE

facet

conical lens

cuticular lens

rhabdome

cuticle

comprehensive grasp of the subject). **2** (of motor vehicle insurance) providing complete cover. ● *n.* (in full **comprehensive school**) *Brit.* a secondary school for children of all abilities. □ **comprehensively** *adv.* **comprehensiveness** *n.*

compress ● *v.tr.* /**kom**-press/ **1** squeeze together. **2** bring into a smaller space or shorter time. ● *n.* /**kom**-press/ a pad pressed on to part of the body to relieve inflammation, stop bleeding, etc. [from Late Latin *compressare* 'to keep pressing together'] □ **compressible** *adj.* **compressibility** *n.* **compressive** *adj.*

compressed air *n.* air at more than atmospheric pressure.

compression *n.* **1** the act of compressing or being compressed. **2** the reduction in volume (causing an increase in pressure) of the fuel mixture in an internal-combustion engine before ignition.

compressor *n.* an instrument or device for compressing, esp. a machine used for increasing the pressure of air or other gases. ▷ AIR CONDITIONING

comprise *v.* **1** *tr.* consist of, be made up of; contain (*the book comprises 350 pages*). **2** *tr. disp.* make up, compose. **3** *tr.* (in *passive*, foll. by *of*) *disp.* consist of. **4** *intr.* (foll. by *of*) *disp.* consist of. [from French *comprise* (fem.) 'comprehended'] □ **comprisable** *adj.*

■ **Usage** The use of *comprise* in senses 2 and 3 is still regarded as non-standard by some people and its use in sense 4, formed on analogy with *consist of*, is especially frowned upon. More acceptable alternatives are *consist of*, *be composed of*, or simply *comprise* without of (as in sense 1).

compromise /**kom**-prŏ-myz/ ● *n.* **1** the settlement of a dispute by mutual concession. **2** (often foll. by *between*) an intermediate state between conflicting opinions, actions, etc., reached by mutual concession. ● *v.* **1** *intr.* settle a dispute by mutual concession. **2** *tr.* bring into disrepute or danger esp. by indiscretion or folly. [from Late Latin *compromissum* 'bound together in a promise'] □ **compromiser** *n.* **compromisingly** *adv.*

comptroller /kŏn-**troh**-ler/ *n.* a controller (used in the title of some financial officers) (*Comptroller and Auditor General*). [variant of CONTROLLER]

compulsion *n.* **1** a constraint; an obligation. **2** *Psychol.* an irresistible urge to behave in a certain way, esp. against one's conscious wishes. □ **under compulsion** because one is compelled. [from Late Latin *compulsio*, related to COMPEL]

compulsive *adj.* **1** compelling. **2** resulting or acting from, or as if from, compulsion (*a compulsive gambler*). **3** irresistible (*compulsive viewing*). □ **compulsively** *adv.* **compulsiveness** *n.*

compulsory *adj.* required by law or a rule. □ **compulsorily** *adv.* **compulsoriness** *n.*

compulsory purchase *n. Brit.* the enforced purchase of land or property by a local authority etc., for public use.

compunction *n.* (usu. with *neg.*) **1** the pricking of the conscience; remorse. **2** slight regret; a scruple. [from ecclesiastical Latin *compunctio* 'sting of conscience']

computation *n.* **1** the act or an instance of reckoning; calculation. **2** the use of a computer. **3** a result obtained by calculation. □ **computational** *adj.* **computationally** *adv.*

compute *v.* **1** *tr.* (often foll. by *that* + clause) reckon or calculate (a number, an amount, etc.). **2** *intr.* make a reckoning, esp. using a computer. [from Latin *computare*] □ **computable** *adj.* **computability** *n.*

computer *n.* **1** ◀ a usu. electronic device for storing and processing data (usu. in binary form), according to instructions given to it in a variable program. **2** a person who computes or makes calculations.

COMPUTER

Developed in the Second World War (1939–45), computers are currently composed of four basic parts: an input unit, such as a keyboard, which feeds data into the computer; a central processing unit (CPU), which performs the computer's tasks; an output unit, such as a monitor, which displays the results; and a memory unit for storing information and instructions.

CUTAWAY VIEW OF A COMPUTER

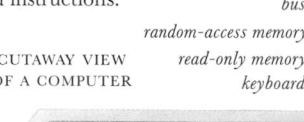

monitor

modem, sound, and video cards

power supply

CD-ROM drive

compact disc

floppy disk

floppy-disk drive

mouse

mouse-mat

bus

random-access memory

read-only memory

keyboard

hard disk

C

C

computerate *adj.* = COMPUTER-LITERATE.

computerize *v.tr.* (also **-ise**) **1** equip with a computer; install a computer in. **2** store, perform, or produce by computer. □ **computerization** *n.*

computer-literate *adj.* able to use computers; familiar with the operation of computers.

computer science *n.* the study of the principles and use of computers.

computer virus *n.* a hidden code within a computer program intended to corrupt a system or destroy data stored in it.

comrade *n.* **1** (also **comrade-in-arms**) **a** a workmate, friend, or companion. **b** a fellow soldier etc. **2** *Polit.* a fellow socialist or communist. [from Spanish *camarada* 'room-mate'] □ **comradely** *adj.* **comradeship** *n.*

Comsat *n. propr.* a communication satellite.

con[1] *slang* ● *n.* a confidence trick. ● *v.tr.* (**conned**, **conning**) swindle; deceive (*conned him into thinking he had won*). [abbreviation]

con[2] ● *n.* (usu. in *pl.*) a reason against. ● *prep. & adv.* against (cf. PRO[2]). [from Latin *contra* 'against']

con[3] *n. slang* a convict. [abbreviation]

con[4] *v.tr.* (*US* **conn**) (**conned**, **conning**) *Naut.* direct the steering of (a ship). [from Latin *conducere* 'to conduct']

con[5] *v.tr.* (**conned**, **conning**) *archaic* study, learn by heart (*conned his part well*). [Middle English, form of CAN[1]]

con amore *adv.* **1** with devotion or zeal. **2** *Mus.* tenderly. [Italian 'with love']

con brio *adv. Mus.* with vigour. [Italian]

concatenate ● *v.tr.* link together (a chain of events, things, etc.). ● *adj.* joined; linked. [from Late Latin *concatenatus* 'linked together'] □ **concatenation** *n.*

concave *adj.* having an outline or surface curved like the interior of a circle or sphere (cf. CONVEX). [based on Latin *cavus* 'hollow'] □ **concavely** *adv.* **concavity** *n.*

conceal *v.tr.* **1** (often foll. by *from*) keep secret (*concealed her motive from him*). **2** not allow to be seen; hide. [from Latin *concelare*] □ **concealer** *n.* **concealment** *n.*

concede *v.tr.* **1 a** (often foll. by *that* + clause) admit (a defeat etc.) to be true (*conceded that his work was inadequate*). **b** admit defeat in. **2** (often foll. by *to*) grant or surrender (a right, points in a game, etc.). **3** *Sport* fail to prevent an opponent from scoring (a goal etc.) or winning (a match etc.). [based on Latin *cedere* 'to yield'] □ **conceder** *n.*

conceit *n.* **1** personal vanity; pride. **2** *literary* **a** a far-fetched comparison. **b** a fanciful notion. [based on CONCEIVE, influenced by *deceit, deceive*, etc.]

conceited *adj.* vain, proud. □ **conceitedly** *adv.* **conceitedness** *n.*

conceivable *adj.* capable of being grasped or imagined; understandable. □ **conceivability** *n.* **conceivably** *adv.*

conceive *v.* **1** *intr.* become pregnant. **2** *tr.* become pregnant with (a child). **3** *tr.* (often foll. by *that* + clause) **a** imagine, fancy, think. **b** (usu. in *passive*) formulate, express (a belief, a plan, etc.). □ **conceive of** form in the mind; imagine. [from Latin *concipere* 'to take together']

concentrate ● *v.* **1** *intr.* (often foll. by *on, upon*) focus one's attention or mental ability. **2** *tr.* bring together (troops, power, attention, etc.) to one point. **3** *tr.* increase the strength of (a solution etc.) by removing water or other diluting agent. **4** *tr.* (as **concentrated** *adj.*) (of hate etc.) intense, strong. ● *n.* a concentrated substance. [from French *concentrer*] □ **concentratedly** *adv.* **concentrative** *adj.* **concentrator** *n.*

concentration *n.* **1** the act or power of focusing one's attention or mental ability. **2** the act of gathering or bringing together. **3** something so gathered. **4** *Chem.* **a** the act of strengthening a solution by the removal of solvent. **b** the strength of a

solution, esp. the amount of solute per unit volume of solution.

concentration camp *n.* a camp for the detention of political prisoners etc., esp. in Nazi Germany.

concentric *adj.* (often foll. by *with*) (esp. of circles) ▶ having a common centre (cf. ECCENTRIC *adj.* 2a). [from medieval Latin *concentricus*] □ **concentrically** *adv.* **concentricity** *n.*

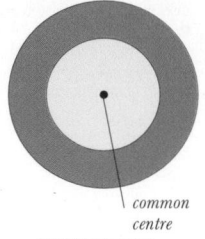

common centre

CONCENTRIC CIRCLES

concept *n.* **1** a general notion; an abstract idea (*the concept of evolution*). **2** *colloq.* an idea or invention to help sell or publicize a commodity (*a new concept in swimwear*). [from Late Latin *conceptus*]

conception *n.* **1** the act or an instance of conceiving; the process of being conceived. **2** an idea or plan, esp. as being new or daring. **3** (usu. foll. by *of*) understanding; ability to imagine (*has no conception of what it entails*). □ **conceptional** *adj.* **conceptive** *adj.*

conceptual *adj.* of mental conceptions or concepts. □ **conceptually** *adv.*

conceptualize *v.tr.* (also **-ise**) form a concept or idea of. □ **conceptualization** *n.*

concern ● *v.tr.* **1 a** be relevant or important to (*this concerns you*). **b** relate to; be about. **2** (usu. *refl.*; often foll. by *with, in, about*, or *to* + infin.) interest or involve oneself. **3** worry, affect. ● *n.* **1** anxiety, worry (*felt a deep concern*). **2 a** a matter of interest or importance to one (*no concern of mine*). **b** (usu. in *pl.*) affairs; private business. **3** a business; a firm. [based on Latin *cernere* 'to sift, discern']

concerned *adj.* **1** involved, interested (*the people concerned; concerned with proving his innocence*). **2** troubled, anxious (*concerned about him; concerned to hear that*). □ **be concerned** (often foll. by *in*) take part. **I am not concerned** it is not my business. □ **concernedly** *adv.* **concernedness** *n.*

concerning *prep.* about, regarding.

concernment *n. formal* **1** an affair or business. **2** importance. **3** a state of being concerned; anxiety.

concert ● *n.* /**kon**-sĕt/ **1** a musical performance of usu. several separate compositions. **2** agreement, harmony. **3** a combination of voices or sounds. ● *v.tr.* /kŏn-**sert**/ arrange (by mutual agreement or coordination). □ **in concert 1** (often foll. by *with*) acting jointly and accordantly. **2** (*predic.*) (of a musician) in a performance. [from Italian *concertare* 'to harmonize']

concerted *adj.* **1** jointly arranged or planned (*a concerted effort*). **2** *Mus.* arranged in parts for voices or instruments.

concert grand *n.* the largest size of grand piano, used for concerts. ▷ PIANO

concertina ● *n.* ◀ a musical instrument held in the hands and stretched and squeezed like bellows, having reeds and a set of buttons at each end to control the valves. ● *v.tr. & intr.* (**concertinas, concertinaed** or **concertina'd, concertinaing**) compress or collapse in folds like those of a concertina (*the car concertinaed into the bridge*). [based on CONCERT]

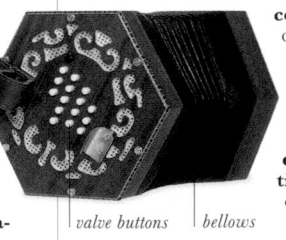

valve buttons   *bellows*

CONCERTINA

concert master *n.* esp. *N. Amer.* the leading first-violin player in some orchestras.

concerto /kŏn-**chair**-toh/ *n.* (*pl.* **-os** or **concerti**) *Mus.* a composition for a solo instrument or instruments accompanied by an orchestra. [Italian]

concert overture *n. Mus.* a piece like an overture but intended for independent performance.

concert performance *n. Brit.* a performance (of an opera etc.) without scenery, costumes, or action.

concert pitch *n. Mus.* the internationally agreed pitch, whereby the A above middle C = 440 Hz.

concession *n.* **1 a** the act or an instance of conceding something asked or required. **b** a thing conceded. **2** a reduction in price for a certain category of person. **3 a** the right to use land or other property. **b** the right to sell goods, esp. in a particular territory. **c** the land or property used or given. [from Latin *concessio*] □ **concessional** *adj.* **concessionary** *adj.*

concessionaire *n.* (also **concessionnaire**) the holder of a concession or grant.

concessive *adj.* **1** of or tending to concession. **2** *Gram.* **a** (of a preposition or conjunction) introducing a phrase or clause which might be expected to preclude the action of the main clause, but does not (e.g. *in spite of, although*). **b** (of a phrase or clause) introduced by a concessive preposition or conjunction.

conch /kongk, konch/ *n.* (*pl.* **conchs** or **conches**) **1** ◀ a thick heavy spiral shell of various marine gastropod molluscs of the family Strombidae. ▷ SHELL. **2** any of these gastropods. [from Greek *kogkhē* 'shell']

conchology *n. Zool.* the study of molluscs and their shells. □ **conchological** *adj.* **conchologist** *n.*

concierge /kon-si-**airzh**/ *n.* **1** (esp. in France) a doorkeeper or porter of a block of flats etc. **2** a person in a hotel employed to assist guests by booking tours, making reservations, etc. [French]

conciliar *adj.* of or concerning a council.

conciliate *v.tr.* **1** make calm and amenable; pacify. **2** gain (esteem or goodwill). [based on Latin *conciliatus* 'combined, gained'] □ **conciliation** *n.* **conciliator** *n.* **conciliatory** *adj.* **conciliatoriness** *n.*

CONCH: ROOSTER TAIL CONCH (*Strombus gallus*)

concise *adj.* (of speech, writing, style, or a person) brief but comprehensive in expression. [from Latin *concisus* 'cut up'] □ **concisely** *adv.* **conciseness** *n.* **concision** *n.*

conclave *n.* **1** a private meeting. **2** *RC Ch.* the assembly of cardinals for the election of a pope. [from Latin *conclave* 'lockable room']

conclude *v.* **1** *tr. & intr.* bring or come to an end. **2** *tr.* (often foll. by *from*, or *that* + clause) infer (from given premisses). **3** *tr.* settle, arrange (a treaty etc.). [based on Latin *claudere* 'to shut']

conclusion *n.* **1** a final result; a termination. **2** a judgement reached by reasoning. **3** a summing-up. **4** a settling; an arrangement (*the conclusion of peace*). **5** *Logic* a proposition that is reached from given premisses. □ **in conclusion** lastly, to conclude. [from Latin *conclusio*]

conclusive *adj.* decisive, convincing. □ **conclusively** *adv.* **conclusiveness** *n.*

concoct *v.tr.* **1** make by mixing ingredients. **2** invent (a story, a lie, etc.). [based on Latin *concoctus* 'boiled together'] □ **concocter** *n.* **concoction** *n.* **concoctor** *n.*

concomitant ● *adj.* coexisting; associated (*concomitant circumstances*). ● *n.* an accompanying thing. [based on Latin *comes -mitis* 'companion'] □ **concomitance** *n.* **concomitantly** *adv.*

concord *n.* **1** agreement or harmony between people or things. **2** a treaty. [from Latin *concordia* 'being of one mind']

concordance *n.* **1** agreement. **2** an alphabetical list of the important words used in a book or by an author.

concordant *adj.* (often foll. by *with*) agreeing, harmonious. □ **concordantly** *adv.*

concordat *n.* an agreement, esp. between the Roman Catholic Church and a state. [French]

concourse *n.* **1** a crowd. **2** a coming together; a gathering (*a concourse of ideas*). **3** an open central area in a large public building. [from Latin *concursus*]

concrete ● *adj.* **1 a** existing in a material form; real. **b** specific, definite (*concrete evidence; a concrete proposal*). **2** *Gram.* (of a noun) denoting a material object (opp. ABSTRACT). **●** *n.* (often *attrib.*) ▼ a composition of gravel, sand, cement, and water, used for building. ▷ HOUSE. **●** *v.tr.* **1** cover with concrete. **2** embed in concrete. [from Latin *concretus* 'grown together'] □ **concretely** *adv.* **concreteness** *n.*

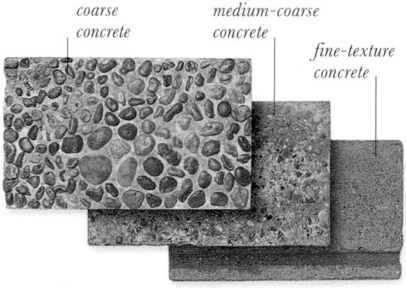

coarse concrete *medium-coarse concrete* *fine-texture concrete*

CONCRETE: THREE GRADES OF CONCRETE

concretion *n.* **1** a hard solid concreted mass. **2** the forming of this by coalescence. □ **concretionary** *adj.*

concretize *v.tr.* (also **-ise**) make concrete instead of abstract. □ **concretization** *n.*

concubine *n.* **1** a woman who cohabits with a man without being his wife. **2** (in polygamous societies) a secondary wife. [from Latin *concubina*]

concupiscence /kŏn-**kew**-pi-sĕnss/ *n. formal* sexual desire. [based on Latin *concupiscere* 'to begin to desire'] □ **concupiscent** *adj.*

concur *v.intr.* (**concurred, concurring**) **1** happen together; coincide. **2** (often foll. by *with*) **a** agree in opinion. **b** express agreement. [from Latin *concurrere* 'to run together']

concurrent *adj.* **1** (often foll. by *with*) **a** existing or in operation at the same time (*served two concurrent sentences*). **b** existing or acting together. **2** *Geom.* (of three or more lines) meeting at or tending towards one point. □ **concurrence** *n.* **concurrently** *adv.*

concuss *v.tr.* **1** subject to concussion. **2** shake violently. [based on Latin *concussus* 'shaken together'] □ **concussive** *adj.*

concussion *n.* **1** *Med.* temporary unconsciousness or incapacity due to a blow on the head. **2** violent shaking; shock.

condemn *v.tr.* **1** express utter disapproval of; censure. **2 a** find guilty; convict. **b** (usu. foll. by *to*) sentence to (a punishment, esp. death). **3** pronounce (a building etc.) unfit for use or habitation. **4** (usu. foll. by *to*) doom or assign (to something unwelcome or painful) (*condemned to a life of misery*). [from Latin *condemnare*] □ **condemnable** *adj.* **condemnation** *n.* **condemnatory** *adj.*

condensate *n.* a substance produced by condensation.

condensation *n.* **1** the act of condensing. ▷ MATTER. **2** any condensed material (esp. water on a cold surface). **3** an abridgement.

condense *v.* **1** *tr.* make denser or more concentrated. **2** *tr.* express in fewer words; make concise. **3** *tr. & intr.* reduce or be reduced from a gas or vapour to a liquid. [based on Latin *densus* 'thick'] □ **condensable** *adj.*

condensed milk *n.* milk thickened by evaporation and sweetened.

condenser *n.* **1** an apparatus or vessel for condensing vapour. ▷ DISTIL, REFRIGERATOR. **2** *Electr.* = CAPACITOR. **3** a lens or system of lenses for concentrating light.

condescend *v.intr.* **1** (usu. foll. by *to* + infin.) often *iron.* be gracious enough (to do a thing that one regards as below one's level of importance) (*condescended to speak to me*). **2** (foll. by *to*) *derog.* behave as if one is on equal terms with (a person), while maintaining an overt attitude of superiority (*condescends to the junior staff*). **3** (as **condescending** *adj.*) patronizing; superciliously kind. [from ecclesiastical Latin *condescendere*] □ **condescendingly** *adv.* **condescension** *n.*

condign /kŏn-**dyn**/ *adj.* (of a punishment etc.) severe and well-deserved. [from Latin *condignus* 'wholly worthy'] □ **condignly** *adv.*

condiment *n.* a seasoning or relish for food. [based on Latin *condire* 'to pickle']

condition ● *n.* **1** a stipulation; something upon the fulfilment of which something else depends. **2 a** the state of being or fitness of a person or thing (*arrived in bad condition*). **b** an ailment or abnormality (*a heart condition*). **3** (in *pl.*) circumstances, esp. those affecting the functioning or existence of something (*working conditions are good*). **●** *v.tr.* **1 a** bring into a good or desired state or condition. **b** make fit (esp. dogs or horses). **2** teach or accustom to adopt certain habits etc. (*conditioned by society*). **3** govern, determine. **4 a** impose conditions on. **b** be essential to. □ **in** (or **out of**) **condition** in good (or bad) condition. **in no condition to** certainly not fit to. **on condition that** with the stipulation that. [from Latin *condicio* 'agreement upon terms']

conditional ● *adj.* **1** (often foll. by *on*) dependent; not absolute; containing a condition or stipulation (*a conditional offer*). **2** *Gram.* (of a clause, mood, etc.) expressing a condition. **●** *n. Gram.* **1** a conditional clause etc. **2** the conditional mood. □ **conditionality** *n.* **conditionally** *adv.*

conditioner *n.* an agent that brings something into better condition, esp. a substance applied to the hair.

condo *n.* (*pl.* **-os**) *N. Amer. colloq.* a condominium.

condole *v.intr.* (foll. by *with*) express sympathy with (a person) over a loss, grief, etc. [from Late Latin *condolēre* 'to suffer with'] □ **condolatry** *adj.*

■ **Usage** *Condole* is often confused with *console* (see CONSOLE[1]). *Condole* 'to express sympathy' is always followed by *with*, e.g. *They condoled with him over the death of his brother.*

condolence *n.* (often in *pl.*) an expression of sympathy (*sent my condolences*).

condom *n.* a rubber sheath worn on the penis or (usu. **female condom**) in the vagina during sexual intercourse as a contraceptive or to prevent infection. [18th-century coinage]

condominium *n.* **1** the joint control of a state's affairs by other states. **2** *N. Amer.* **a** a building containing flats, or an area of land containing a complex of houses, which are individually owned. **b** such a flat or house. [modern Latin]

condone *v.tr.* **1** forgive or overlook (an offence or wrongdoing). **2** approve or sanction, usu. reluctantly. [from Latin *condonare* 'to permit a debt'] □ **condonation** *n.* **condoner** *n.*

condor *n.* ◄ a large vulture, *Vultur gryphus*, of S. America, having black plumage with a white neck ruff. [Spanish]

CONDOR:
ANDEAN CONDOR
(*Vultur gryphus*)

conduce *v.intr.* (foll. by *to*) contribute to (a result). [from Latin *conducere* 'to lead together']

conducive *adj.* (usu. foll. by *to*) contributing or helping (towards something).

conduct ● *n.* /**kon**-dukt/ **1** behaviour (esp. in its moral aspect). **2** the action or manner of directing or managing (business, war, etc.). **●** *v.* /kŏn-**dukt**/ **1** *tr.* lead or guide (a person). **2** *tr.* direct or manage (business etc.). **3** *tr.* (also *absol.*) be the conductor of (an orchestra etc.). **4** *tr. Physics* transmit (heat, electricity, etc.) by conduction. **5** *refl.* behave. [from Latin *conductus* 'led together'] □ **conductible** *adj.* **conductibility** *n.*

conductance *n. Physics* the power of a specified material to conduct electricity.

conducted tour *n.* a tour led by a guide on a fixed itinerary.

conduction *n.* the transmission of heat or electricity through a substance.

conductive *adj.* having the property of conducting (esp. heat, electricity, etc.). □ **conductively** *adv.*

conductivity *n.* the conducting power of a specified material.

conductor *n.* **1** a person who directs the performance of an orchestra or choir etc. **2** (*fem.* **conductress**) **a** a person who collects fares in a bus etc. **b** *US* an official in charge of a train. **3** *Physics* a thing that conducts or transmits heat or electricity. □ **conductorship** *n.*

conduit *n.* **1** a channel or pipe for conveying liquids. **2** a tube or trough for protecting insulated electric wires. [related to CONDUCT]

condyle *n. Anat.* ▼ a rounded process at the end of some bones, forming an articulation with another bone. ▷ SKELETON. □ **condylar** *adj.* **condyloid** *adj.*

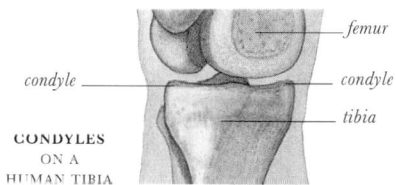

femur *condyle* *condyle* *tibia*

CONDYLES
ON A
HUMAN TIBIA

cone ● *n.* **1** ► a solid figure with a circular (or other curved) plane base, tapering to a point. **2** a thing of a similar shape, e.g. as used to mark off areas of roads. **3** the dry fruit of a conifer. ▷ CONIFER. **4** an ice-cream cornet. **5** any of the minute cone-shaped structures in the retina. **●** *v.tr.* **1** shape like a cone. **2** (foll. by *off*) *Brit.* mark off (a road etc.) with cones. [from Greek *kōnos*]

circular plane base

CONE

coney var. of CONY.

confab *colloq.* **●** *n.* a conversation; a chat. **●** *v.intr.* (**confabbed, confabbing**) = CONFABULATE.

confabulate *v.intr.* converse, chat. [based on Latin *fabula* 'tale'] □ **confabulation** *n.* **confabulatory** *adj.*

confection *n.* a dish or delicacy made with sweet ingredients. [from Latin *confectio*]

confectioner *n.* a maker or retailer of confectionery.

confectioner's sugar *n. US* icing sugar.

confectionery *n.* sweets and other confections.

confederacy *n.* (*pl.* **-ies**) **1** a league or alliance, esp. of confederate states. **2** (**the Confederacy**) the Confederate States.

confederate ● *adj.* esp. *Polit.* allied; joined by an agreement or treaty. **●** *n.* **1** an ally, esp. (pejoratively) an accomplice. **2** (**Confederate**) a supporter of the Confederate States. **●** *v.* (often foll. by *with*) **1** *tr.* bring (a person, state, or oneself) into alliance.

CONFEDERATE STATES

In 1860, Abraham Lincoln was elected President of the United States of America. Eleven southern states, fearing that his election would lead to restrictions on their right to own and trade in slaves, decided to secede, precipitating the American Civil War. Known as the Confederate States, they were effectively independent until April 1865, when southern armies under General Robert E. Lee finally surrendered to Union forces.

MAP OF THE 11
CONFEDERATE
STATES OF 1861

VIRGINIA

NORTH CAROLINA

TENNESSEE

ARKANSAS

SOUTH CAROLINA

MISSISSIPPI

GEORGIA

ALABAMA

TEXAS

LOUISIANA

ATLANTIC OCEAN

FLORIDA

GULF OF MEXICO

C

2 *intr.* come into alliance. [based on Latin *foedus -eris* 'league']

Confederate States *n.pl.* ▲ the southern states which seceded from the US in 1860–1.

confederation *n.* **1** a union or alliance of states etc. **2** the act or an instance of confederating; the state of being confederated.

confer *v.* (**conferred, conferring**) **1** *tr.* grant or bestow (a title, degree, favour, etc.). **2** *intr.* (often foll. by *with*) consult. [from Latin *conferre* 'to bring together'] □ **conferrable** *adj.*

conference *n.* **1** consultation, discussion. **2** a meeting for discussion, esp. a regular one held by an association or organization. □ **in conference** engaged in discussion.

conferment *n.* **1** the conferring of a degree, honour, etc. **2** an instance of this.

conferral *n.* esp. *US* = CONFERMENT.

confess *v.* **1 a** *tr.* (also *absol.*) acknowledge or admit (a fault, wrongdoing, etc.). **b** *intr.* (foll. by *to*) admit to (*confessed to having lied*). **2** *tr.* admit reluctantly (*confessed it would be difficult*). **3** *tr.* **a** (also *absol.*) declare (one's sins) to a priest. **b** (of a priest) hear the confession of. [based on Latin *confessus* 'avowed']

confessedly *adv.* by one's own or general admission.

confession *n.* **1 a** a confessing or acknowledgement of a fault, wrongdoing, a sin to a priest, etc. **b** an instance of this. **2** (in full **confession of faith**) **a** a declaration of one's religious beliefs. **b** a statement of one's principles. □ **confessionary** *adj.*

confessional ● *n.* an enclosed stall in a church in which a priest hears confessions. ● *adj.* of or relating to confession.

confessor *n.* **1** a person who makes a confession. **2** a priest who hears confessions and gives spiritual counsel.

confetti *n.* small pieces of coloured paper thrown by wedding guests at the bride and groom. [Italian, literally 'sweetmeats': from the sweets thrown during Italian carnivals]

confidant /kon-fi-dant/ *n.* (*fem.* **confidante** *pronunc.* same) a person trusted with knowledge of one's private affairs.

confide *v.* **1** *tr.* (usu. foll. by *to*) tell (a secret etc.) in confidence. **2** *tr.* (foll. by *to*) entrust (an object of care, a task, etc.) to. **3** *intr.* (foll. by *in*) talk confidentially to. [from Latin *confidere* 'to have full trust'] □ **confidingly** *adv.*

confidence *n.* **1** firm trust. **2 a** a feeling of reliance or certainty. **b** a sense of self-reliance; boldness. **3** some-thing told confidentially. □ **in confidence** as a secret. **in a person's confidence** trusted with a person's secrets. **take into one's confidence** confide in.

confidence man *n.* a man who robs or swindles by means of a confidence trick.

confidence trick *n.* (*US* **confidence game**) a swindle in which the victim is persuaded to trust the swindler. □ **confidence trickster** *n.*

confident *adj.* **1** feeling or showing confidence; self-assured, bold. **2** (often foll. by *of*, or *that* + clause) assured, trusting. □ **confidently** *adv.*

confidential *adj.* **1** spoken or written in confidence. **2** entrusted with secrets (*a confidential secretary*). **3** confiding. □ **confidentiality** *n.* **confidentially** *adv.*

configuration *n.* **1** an arrangement of parts or elements in a particular form or figure. **2** the form, shape, or figure resulting from such an arrangement. [from Late Latin *configuratio*] □ **configurational** *adj.* **configure** *v.tr.*

confine ● *v.tr.* **1** keep or restrict (within certain limits etc.). **2** hold captive; imprison. ● *n.* (usu. in *pl.*) a limit or boundary (*within the confines of the town*). □ **be confined** be in childbirth. [based on Latin *confinis* 'bordering']

confinement *n.* **1** the act or an instance of confining; the state of being confined. **2** the time of a woman's giving birth.

confirm *v.tr.* **1** provide support for the truth or correctness of; make definitely valid (*confirmed my suspicions; confirmed his arrival time*). **2** (foll. by *in*) encourage (a person) in (an opinion etc.). **3** ratify (a treaty, title, etc.); make formally valid. **4** establish more firmly (power, possession, etc.). **5** administer the religious rite of confirmation to. [from Latin *confirmare*] □ **confirmative** *adj.* **confirmatory** *adj.*

confirmand *n. Eccl.* a person who is to be or has just been confirmed.

confirmation *n.* **1** the act or an instance of confirming; the state or an instance of being confirmed. **2 a** a religious rite confirming a baptized person as a member of the Christian Church. **b** *Judaism* the ceremony of bar mitzvah.

confirmed *adj.* firmly settled in some habit or condition (*confirmed in his ways; a confirmed bachelor*).

confiscate *v.tr.* **1** seize by authority. **2** appropriate to the public treasury (by way of a penalty). [based on Latin *fiscus* 'treasury'] □ **confiscable** *adj.* **confiscation** *n.* **confiscator** *n.* **confiscatory** *adj.*

conflagration *n.* a great and destructive fire. [based on Latin *flagrare* 'to blaze']

conflate *v.tr.* blend or fuse together. [based on Latin *conflatus* 'blown together, fused'] □ **conflation** *n.*

conflict ● *n.* /kon-flikt/ **1 a** a state of opposition or hostilities. **b** a fight or struggle. **2** (often foll. by *of*) **a** the clashing of opposed principles etc. **b** an instance of this. ● *v.intr.* /kŏn-flikt/ **1** (often foll. by *with*) clash; be incompatible. **2** (as **conflicting** *adj.*) contradictory. □ **in conflict** conflicting. [from Latin *conflictus* 'striking together'] □ **confliction** *n.* **conflictual** *adj.*

confluence *n.* **1** a place where two rivers meet. **2** a coming together. [based on Latin *confluere* 'to flow together']

confluent ● *adj.* flowing together, uniting. ● *n.* a stream joining another.

conform *v.* **1** *intr.* comply with rules or custom. **2** *intr. & tr.* (often foll. by *to*) be or make in harmony or agreement. **3** *tr.* (often foll. by *to*) make similar. **4** *intr.* (foll. by *to*, *with*) comply with. [from Latin *conformare*] □ **conformer** *n.*

conformable *adj.* **1** (often foll. by *to*) similar. **2** (often foll. by *with*) consistent. **3** (often foll. by *to*) adapted. **4** tractable. □ **conformability** *n.* **conformably** *adv.*

conformation *n.* the way in which a thing is formed.

conformist ● *n.* a person who conforms to an established practice. ● *adj.* (of a person) conventional. □ **conformism** *n.*

conformity *n.* **1** (often foll. by *to*, *with*) action or behaviour in accordance with established practice. **2** (often foll. by *to*, *with*) likeness, agreement.

confound ● *v.tr.* **1** throw into perplexity. **2** confuse (in one's mind). **3** *archaic* overthrow. ● *int.* expressing annoyance (*confound you!*). [from Latin *confundere* 'to mix up']

confounded *adj. colloq.* damned (*a confounded nuisance!*). □ **confoundedly** *adv.*

confrère /kon-frair/ *n.* a fellow member of a profession, scientific body, etc. [based on Latin *frater* 'brother']

confront *v.tr.* **1 a** face in hostility or defiance. **b** face up to and deal with (a problem etc.). **2** (of a difficulty etc.) present itself to. **3** (foll. by *with*) **a** bring (a person) face to face with (a circumstance). **b** set (a thing) face to face with (another) for comparison. [from medieval Latin *confrontare*] □ **confrontation** *n.* **confrontational** *adj.*

Confucian *adj.* of or relating to Confucius, Chinese philosopher d. 479 BC, or his philosophy. [from *Confucius*, Latinization of *Kongfuze* 'Kong the master'] □ **Confucianism** *n.* **Confucianist** *n. & adj.*

confusable *adj.* that is able or liable to be confused. □ **confusability** *n.*

confuse *v.tr.* **1 a** disconcert, perplex. **b** embarrass. **2** mistake (one for another). **3** make indistinct (*that point confuses the issue*). **4** (as **confused** *adj.*) mentally decrepit or senile. **5** (often as **confused** *adj.*) throw into disorder (*a confused jumble of clothes*). [based on Latin *confusus* 'mixed up'] □ **confusedly** *adv.* **confusing** *adj.* **confusingly** *adv.*

confusion *n.* **1 a** the act of confusing (*the confusion of fact and fiction*). **b** a misunderstanding (*confusions arise from a lack of communication*). **2 a** a confused state (*thrown into confusion*). **b** (foll. by *of*) a disorderly jumble (*a confusion of ideas*).

confute *v.tr.* prove to be false or in error. **3** make indistinct [from Latin *confutare* 'to restrain'] □ **confutation** *n.*

conga *n.* **1** a Latin American dance of African origin, usu. with several persons in a single line, one behind the other. **2** (also **conga drum**) ▷ a tall, narrow, low-toned drum beaten with the hands. ▷ PERCUSSION. [Latin American Spanish, from *congo* 'of the Congo']

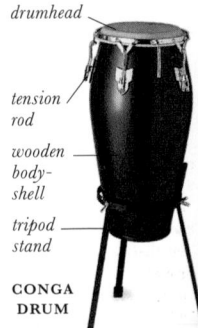

drumhead

tension rod

wooden body-shell

tripod stand

CONGA DRUM

CONIFER

All 550 species in the order Coniferales bear cones for reproduction. In most, pollen-forming male cones and seed-forming female cones develop on the same tree, and cross-fertilization between them is necessary. In cool parts of the world, conifers form dense forests, and are also common on mountains. Most bear narrow evergreen leaves, capable of withstanding drying winds.

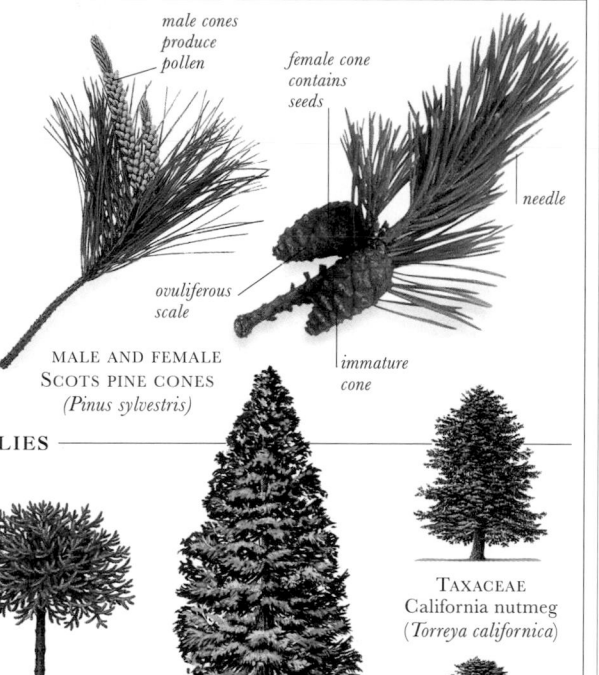

male cones produce pollen

female cone contains seeds

needle

ovuliferous scale

immature cone

MALE AND FEMALE
SCOTS PINE CONES
(*Pinus sylvestris*)

MAIN CONIFER FAMILIES

PINACEAE
Caucasian fir
(*Abies nordmanniana*)

ARAUCARIACEAE
monkey puzzle
(*Araucaria araucana*)

TAXODIACEAE
Wellingtonia
(*Sequoiadendron giganteum*)

CUPRESSACEAE
Monterey cypress
(*Cupressus macrocarpa*)

TAXACEAE
California nutmeg
(*Torreya californica*)

---

congeal *v.tr. & intr.* **1** make or become semi-solid by cooling. **2** (of blood etc.) coagulate. [from Latin *congelare* 'to freeze together'] □ **congealable** *adj.* **congealment** *n.*

congelation *n.* **1** the process of congealing. **2** a congealed state. **3** a congealed substance.

congener *n.* a thing or person of the same kind or category as another (*the raspberry and blackberry are congeners*). [Latin, literally 'of the same kind']

congeneric *adj.* **1** of the same genus, kind, or race. **2** akin. □ **congenerous** *adj.*

congenial *adj.* **1** agreeable (*congenial environment*). **2** (often foll. by *with, to*) (of a person, character, etc.) pleasant because akin to oneself in temperament or interests. **3** (often foll. by *to*) suited to the nature of anything (*congenial to my mood*). [based on GENIAL.] □ **congeniality** *n.* **congenially** *adv.*

congenital *adj.* **1** (esp. of a defect etc.) existing from birth. **2** as such from birth (*a congenital liar*). [based on Latin *congenitus* 'born together'] □ **congenitally** *adv.*

conger *n.* (in full **conger eel**) any large marine eel of the family Congridae. ▷ EEL. [from Greek *goggros*]

congeries /kon-**jeer**-eez/ *n.* (*pl.* same) a disorderly collection. [Latin]

■ **Usage** Although *congeries* looks like a plural form, it is a singular noun, e.g. *A congeries of problems was identified.*

congest *v.tr.* (esp. as **congested** *adj.*) affect with congestion. [based on Latin *congestus* 'carried together'] □ **congestive** *adj.*

congestion *n.* abnormal accumulation, crowding, or obstruction.

conglomerate ● *adj.* gathered into a rounded mass. ● *n.* **1** a number of things or parts forming a heterogeneous mass. **2** a group or corporation formed by the merging of separate and diverse firms. ● *v.tr. & intr.*

collect into a coherent mass. [from Latin *conglomeratus* 'rolled together'] □ **conglomeration** *n.*

Congolese ● *adj.* of or relating to Zaire or Congo, countries in central Africa, or the region surrounding the Zaire (formerly Congo) river. ● *n.* (*pl.* same) a native of any of these regions.

congrats *n.pl. & int. colloq.* congratulations.

congratulate *v.tr. & refl.* (often foll. by *on, upon*) **1** *tr.* express pleasure at the happiness or excellence of (a person). **2** *refl.* think oneself fortunate or clever. [based on Latin *congratulatus* 'having shown joy with'] □ **congratulatory** *adj.*

congratulation *n.* **1** congratulating. **2** (also as *int.*; usu. in *pl.*) an expression of this.

congregate *v.intr. & tr.* collect or gather into a crowd or mass. [based on Latin *grex gregis* 'flock']

congregation *n.* **1** the process or action of congregating. **2** a crowd or mass gathered together. **3** a body assembled for or regularly attending religious worship.

congregational *adj.* **1** of a congregation. **2** (**Congregational**) of or adhering to Congregationalism.

Congregationalism *n.* a system of ecclesiastical organization whereby individual churches are largely self-governing. □ **Congregationalist** *n.* **Congregationalize** *v.tr.* (also **-ise**)

congress *n.* **1** a formal meeting of delegates for discussion. **2** (**Congress**) a national legislative body, esp. that of the US. **3** a society or organization. **4** meeting. [from Latin *congressus*] □ **congressional** *adj.*

congressman *n.* (*pl.* **-men**; *fem.* **congresswoman**, *pl.* **-women**) a member of the US Congress.

congruence *n.* (also **congruency**) **1** agreement, consistency. **2** *Geom.* the state of being congruent.

congruent *adj.* **1** (often foll. by *with*) suitable, agreeing. **2** *Geom.* (of figures) coinciding exactly when

superimposed. [from Latin *congruent-* 'agreeing'] □ **congruently** *adv.*

congruous *adj.* (often foll. by *with*) suitable, fitting. □ **congruity** *n.* **congruously** *adv.*

conic *adj.* of a cone.

conical *adj.* cone-shaped. □ **conically** *adv.*

conic section *n.* ▶ a figure formed by the intersection of a cone and a plane.

conifer *n.* ◀ a tree of the order Coniferales, typically bearing cones and needle-like leaves. ▷ GYMNOSPERM, SEED. [Latin] □ **coniferous** *adj.*

conjecture ● *n.* **1** the formation of an opinion on incomplete information. **2** a conclusion reached in this way. ● *v.tr. & intr.* guess. [from Latin *conjectura* 'a throwing together'] □ **conjecturable** *adj.* **conjectural** *adj.* **conjecturally** *adv.*

conjoin *v.tr. & intr.* join, combine. [from Latin *conjungere*]

conjoint *adj.* associated, conjoined. □ **conjointly** *adv.*

conjugal *adj.* of marriage or the relation between husband and wife. [based on Latin *conjux conjug-* 'consort'] □ **conjugality** *n.* **conjugally** *adv.*

conjugate ● *v.* **1** *tr. Gram.* give the different forms of (a verb). **2** *intr. Biol.* **a** unite sexually. **b** (of gametes) become fused. ● *adj.* **1** joined together, esp. as a pair. **2** *Biol.* fused. ● *n.* a conjugate word or thing. [from Latin *conjugatus* 'yoked together'] □ **conjugation** *n.* **conjugational** *adj.*

conjunct *adj.* joined together; combined; associated. [from Latin *conjunctus*]

conjunction *n.* **1 a** the action of joining; the condition of being joined. **b** an instance of this. **2** *Gram.* a word used to connect clauses or sentences or words in the same clause (e.g. *and, but, if*). **3 a** a combination (of events or circumstances). **b** a number of associated persons or things. **4** *Astron. & Astrol.* ▼ the alignment of two bodies in the solar system so that they have the same longitude as seen from the Earth. □ **in conjunction with** together with. □ **conjunctional** *adj.*

CONIC SECTIONS

circle
ellipse
parabola
hyperbola

C

CONJUNCTION

A planet comes into conjunction with the Sun when it passes behind the Sun (superior conjunction), or between the Earth and the Sun (inferior conjunction). It then lies in the same direction (longitude) as the Sun when viewed from the Earth. An inferior planet (one orbiting closer to the Sun than the Earth) alternately passes through both inferior and superior conjunction; a superior planet (one further from the Sun than the Earth) can come only to superior conjunction.

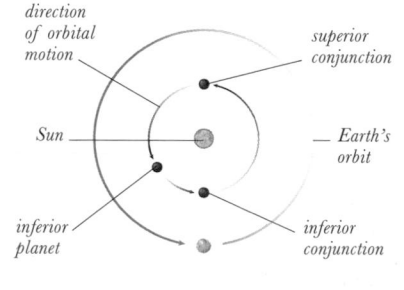

direction of orbital motion

superior conjunction

Sun

Earth's orbit

inferior planet

inferior conjunction

CONJUNCTION OF AN INFERIOR PLANET

C

conjunctiva *n.* (*pl.* **conjunctivas**) *Anat.* the mucous membrane that covers the front of the eye and lines the inside of the eyelids. ▷ EYE. [medieval Latin (*membrana*) *conjunctiva* 'conjunctive membrane'] □ **conjunctival** *adj.*

conjunctive *adj.* **1** serving to join. **2** *Gram.* of the nature of a conjunction. □ **conjunctively** *adv.*

conjunctivitis *n.* inflammation of the conjunctiva.

conjuncture *n.* a combination of events; a state of affairs.

conjure *v.* **1** *intr.* perform tricks which are seemingly magical, esp. by rapid movements of the hands. **2** *tr.* (usu. foll. by *out of, away, to,* etc.) cause to appear or disappear as if by magic. **3** *tr.* call upon (a spirit) to appear. □ **conjure up 1** bring into existence or cause to appear as if by magic. **2** evoke. [earlier in sense 'to oblige by oath, invoke (a spirit etc.)': from Latin *conjurare* 'to swear jointly']

conjuror *n.* (also **conjurer**) a performer of conjuring tricks.

conk[1] *v.intr.* (usu. foll. by *out*) *colloq.* **1** (of a machine etc.) break down. **2** (of a person) become exhausted and give up; faint; die. [20th-century coinage]

conk[2] *slang* ● *n.* **1 a** *Brit.* the nose. **b** the head. **2 a** a punch on the head or *Brit.* nose. **b** a blow. ● *v.tr.* punch on the head, *Brit.* nose etc. [19th-century coinage]

conker *n.* **1** ▶ the hard fruit of a horse chestnut. **2** (in *pl.*) *Brit.* a children's game played with conkers on strings. [from dialect *conker* 'snail shell', originally used in the game]

conman *n.* (*pl.* **-men**) *slang* = CONFIDENCE MAN.

con moto *adv. Mus.* with movement. [Italian]

conn *US* var. of CON[4].

connatural *adj.* **1** (often foll. by *to*) innate. **2** of like nature. □ **connaturally** *adv.*

connect *v.* **1 a** *tr.* (often foll. by *to, with*) join (one thing with another). **b** *tr.* join (two things) (*a track connected the two villages*). **c** *intr.* be joined or joinable (*the two parts do not connect*). **2** *tr.* (often foll. by *with*) associate mentally or practically (*did not connect the two ideas*). **3** *intr.* (foll. by *with*) (of a train etc.) be synchronized at its destination with another train etc., so that passengers can transfer. **4** *tr.* put into communication by telephone. **5 a** *tr.* (usu. in *passive*; foll. by *with*) unite or associate with others in relationships etc. (*am connected with the royal family*). **b** *intr.* form a logical sequence; be meaningful. [from Latin *connectere*] □ **connectable** *adj.* **connector** *n.*

connected *adj.* **1** joined in sequence. **2** (of ideas etc.) coherent. **3** related or associated. □ **connectedly** *adv.* **connectedness** *n.*

connecting rod *n.* ▶ the rod between the piston and the crankpin etc. in an internal-combustion engine or between the wheels of a locomotive. ▷ INTERNAL-COMBUSTION ENGINE

connection *n.* (also *Brit.* **connexion**) **1 a** the act of connecting; the state of being connected. **b** an instance of this. **2** the point at which two things are connected. **3** a link (*the only connection with the outside world*). **4** an arrangement or opportunity for catching a connecting train etc. (*missed the connection*). **5** *Electr.* **a** the linking up of an electric current by contact. **b** a

conker

spiny case

CONKER: HORSE CHESTNUT FRUIT (*Aesculus hippocastanum*)

piston

connecting rod

crankpin

crankshaft

counterweight

CONNECTING ROD OF A FOUR-STROKE INTERNAL-COMBUSTION ENGINE

device for effecting this. **6** (often in *pl.*) a relative or associate, esp. one with influence (*has connections in the Home Office*). **7** a relation of ideas; a context. □ **in connection with** with reference to. □ **connectional** *adj.*

connective ● *adj.* serving or tending to connect. ● *n.* something that connects.

connective tissue *n. Anat.* a tissue with relatively few cells in a non-living matrix that connects, supports, or separates other tissues or organs, esp. fibrous tissue rich in collagen. ▷ SKIN

connectivity *n.* **1** *Computing* capacity for interconnection of systems, applications, etc. **2** the property or degree of being connected or interconnected.

conning tower *n.* **1** the superstructure of a submarine which contains the periscope. ▷ SUBMARINE. **2** the armoured pilot house of a warship. ▷ WARSHIP

connivance *n.* **1** (often foll. by *at, in*) conniving (*connivance in the crime*). **2** tacit permission (*done with his connivance*).

connive *v.intr.* **1** (foll. by *at*) disregard or tacitly consent to (a wrongdoing). **2** (usu. foll. by *with*) conspire. [from Latin *connivēre* 'to shut the eyes (to)'] □ **conniver** *n.*

connoisseur /kon-ŏ-**ser**/ *n.* (often foll. by *of, in*) an expert judge in matters of taste. [from Old French, now *connaisseur*] □ **connoisseurship** *n.*

connotation *n.* that which is implied by a word etc. in addition to its literal or primary meaning.

connote *v.tr.* **1** (of a word etc.) imply in addition to the literal or primary meaning. **2** (of a fact) imply as a consequence or condition. **3** mean, signify. [from medieval Latin *connotare* 'to mark in addition'] □ **connotative** *adj.*

■ **Usage** *Connote* and *denote* are sometimes confused. *Connote* means 'to imply in addition to the primary meaning', e.g. *The words were harmless but the ideas they connoted were dangerous.* In popular usage it is frequently used to mean 'convey to the mind' or 'mean' and hence verges on the sense of *denote*.

connubial *adj.* of marriage or the relationship of husband and wife. [based on Latin *connubium* 'marriage'] □ **connubially** *adv.*

conquer *v.tr.* **1** (also *absol.*) overcome and control by military force. **2** overcome (a habit, disability, etc.) by effort. [from Latin *conquirere* 'to procure (by effort)'] □ **conquerable** *adj.* **conqueror** *n.*

conquest *n.* **1** the act or an instance of conquering; the state of being conquered. **2 a** a conquered territory. **b** something won. **3** a person whose affection has been won. **4** (**the Conquest, the Norman Conquest**) the conquest of England by William of Normandy in 1066. [related to CONQUER]

conquistador /kon-**kwist**-ă-dor/ *n.* (*pl.* **conquistadores** /-**dor**-ayz/ or **conquistadors**) a conqueror, esp. one of the Spanish conquerors of Mexico and Peru in the 16th c. [Spanish]

con-rod *n. Brit. colloq.* connecting rod.

Cons. *abbr.* Conservative.

consanguineous *adj.* descended from the same ancestor. [based on Latin *sanguis -inis* 'blood'] □ **consanguinity** *n.*

conscience *n.* **1** a moral sense of right and wrong. **2** an inner feeling as to the goodness or otherwise of one's behaviour (*has a guilty conscience*). □ **in all conscience** *colloq.* by any reasonable standard. **on one's conscience** causing one feelings of guilt. [earlier in sense 'knowledge': based on Latin *conscire* 'to be privy to'] □ **conscienceless** *adj.*

conscience clause *n.* a clause in a law, ensuring respect for the consciences of those affected.

conscience money *n.* a sum paid to relieve one's conscience.

conscience-stricken *adj.* (also **conscience-struck**) made uneasy by a bad conscience.

conscientious *adj.* (of a person or conduct) diligent

and scrupulous. □ **conscientiously** *adv.* **conscientiousness** *n.*

conscientious objector *n.* a person who for reasons of conscience objects to conforming to a requirement, esp. that of military service.

conscious *adj.* **1** awake and aware of one's surroundings and identity. **2** (usu. foll. by *of,* or *that* + clause) aware (*conscious of his inferiority*). **3** (of actions, emotions, etc.) realized or recognized by the doer (*made a conscious effort not to laugh*). [from Latin *conscius* 'knowing with others or in oneself'] □ **consciously** *adv.*

consciousness *n.* **1** the state of being conscious (*lost consciousness*). **2** awareness, perception (*no consciousness of being ridiculed*).

conscript ● *v.tr.* /kŏn-**skript**/ enlist by conscription. ● *n.* /**kon**-skript/ a person enlisted by conscription.

conscription *n.* compulsory enlistment for state service, esp. military service. [from Latin *conscriptio* 'enrolling']

consecrate *v.tr.* **1** make or declare sacred. **2** (foll. by *to*) devote (one's life etc.) to (a purpose). **3** ordain (esp. a bishop) to a sacred office. [based on Latin *consecratus* 'devoted as sacred'] □ **consecration** *n.* **consecrator** *n.* **consecratory** *adj.*

consecutive *adj.* **1 a** following continuously. **b** in unbroken or logical order. **2** *Gram.* expressing consequence. [from medieval Latin *consecutivus*] □ **consecutively** *adv.* **consecutiveness** *n.*

consensus *n.* (often foll. by *of*) **1 a** a general agreement (of opinion, testimony, etc.). **b** an instance of this. **2** (*attrib.*) majority view; collective opinion (*consensus politics*). [Latin, literally 'agreement'] □ **consensual** *adj.* **consensually** *adv.*

consent ● *v.intr.* (often foll. by *to*) give permission; agree. ● *n.* voluntary agreement; permission; compliance. [from Latin *consentire*]

consenting adult *n.* an adult who consents to something, esp. *Brit.* a homosexual act.

consequence *n.* **1** the result or effect of an action or condition. **2 a** importance (*of no consequence*). **b** social distinction (*persons of consequence*). □ **in consequence** as a result.

consequent ● *adj.* **1** (often foll. by *on, upon*) following as a result or consequence. **2** logically consistent. ● *n.* a thing that follows another. [from Latin *consequent-* 'following closely']

consequential *adj.* **1** following as a result or consequence. **2** resulting indirectly (*consequential damage*). **3** important. □ **consequentiality** *n.* **consequentially** *adv.*

consequently *adv. & conj.* as a result; therefore.

conservancy *n.* (*pl.* **-ies**) **1** *Brit.* a commission etc. controlling a port, river, etc. **2** a body concerned with the preservation of natural resources.

conservation *n.* preservation, esp. of the natural environment. □ **conservation of energy** (or **mass** or **momentum** etc.) *Physics* the principle that the total quantity of energy (or mass, momentum, etc.) remains constant in a system not subject to external influence. □ **conservational** *adj.* **conservationist** *n.*

conservation area *n.* an area specially protected by law against undesirable changes.

conservative ● *adj.* **1 a** averse to rapid change. **b** (of views, taste, etc.) avoiding extremes (*conservative in his dress*). **2** (of an estimate etc.) purposely low; moderate. **3** (**Conservative**) of or characteristic of Conservatives or the Conservative Party. **4** tending to conserve. ● *n.* **1** a conservative person. **2** (**Conservative**) a supporter or member of the Conservative Party. □ **conservatism** *n.* **conservatively** *adv.* **conservativeness** *n.*

Conservative Party *n.* **1** a British political party promoting free enterprise and private ownership. **2** a similar party elsewhere.

conservatoire /kŏn-**ser**-vă-twah/ *n.* a (usu. European) school of music or other arts. [French]

conservator *n.* a person who preserves something; an official custodian.

conservatory *n.* (*pl.* **-ies**) **1** ▼ a greenhouse for tender plants; a room, usu. communicating with a house, for the growing or displaying of plants. **2** = SUN LOUNGE. **3** esp. *N. Amer.* = CONSERVATOIRE. [from Late Latin *conservatorium*]

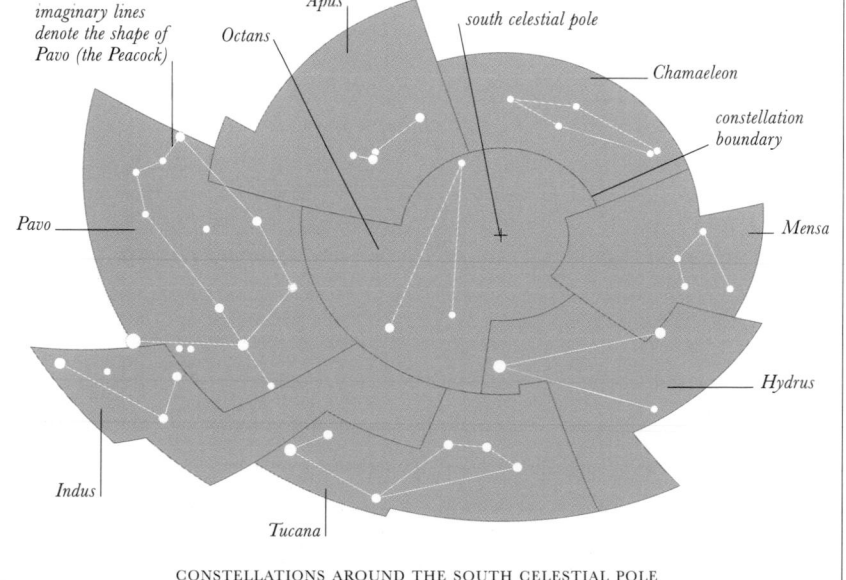

CONSERVATORY

conserve ● *v.tr.* /kŏn-**serv**/ **1** store up or preserve for later use. **2** *Physics* maintain a quantity of (heat etc.). ● *n.* /**kon**-serv/ **1** fruit etc. preserved in sugar. **2** fresh fruit jam. [based on Latin *servare* 'to keep']

consider *v.tr.* (often *absol.*) **1 a** contemplate mentally, esp. in order to reach a conclusion. **b** examine the merits of (a candidate, claim, etc.). **2** look attentively at. **3** take into account. **4** (foll. by *that* + clause) have the opinion. **5** (foll. by compl.) believe (*consider it settled*). **6** (as **considered** *adj.*) formed after careful thought (*a considered opinion*). □ **all things considered** taking everything into account. [from Latin *considerare* 'to examine']

considerable *adj.* **1** much; a lot of (*considerable pain*). **2** notable (*considerable achievement*). □ **considerably** *adv.*

considerate *adj.* thoughtful towards other people; careful not to cause hurt or inconvenience. □ **considerately** *adv.*

consideration *n.* **1** the act of considering; careful thought. **2** being considerate. **3** a fact or a thing taken into account. **4** compensation; a payment or reward. □ **in consideration of** in return for; on account of. **take into consideration** include as a factor, reason, etc. **under consideration** being considered.

considering ● *prep. & conj.* in view of; taking into consideration. ● *adv. colloq.* taking everything into account (*not so bad, considering*).

consign *v.tr.* (often foll. by *to*) **1** deliver to a person's possession or trust. **2** commit decisively or permanently (*consigned it to the dustbin*). **3** transmit or send (goods). [from Latin *consignare* 'to mark with a seal'] □ **consignee** *n.* **consignment** *n.* **consignor** *n.*

consist *v.intr.* **1** (foll. by *of*) have ingredients or elements as specified (*the house consists of five rooms*). **2** (foll. by *in*) have its essential features as specified (*its beauty consists in the use of colour*). [from Latin *consistere* 'to stand firm, exist']

consistency *n.* (also **consistence**) (*pl.* **-ies** or **-es**) **1 a** the degree of firmness with which a substance holds together. **b** the degree of density, esp. of thick liquids. **2** conformity with other or earlier attitudes, practice, etc.

consistent *adj.* (usu. foll. by *with*) **1** compatible or in harmony. **2** (of a person) constant to the same principles. □ **consistently** *adv.*

consistory *n.* (*pl.* **-ies**) *RC Ch.* the council of cardinals (with or without the Pope). □ **consistorial** *adj.*

consolation *n.* **1** the act or an instance of consoling; the state of being consoled. **2** a consoling thing, person, or circumstance. □ **consolatory** *adj.*

consolation prize *n.* a prize given to a competitor who just fails to win a main prize.

console[1] /kŏn-**sohl**/ *v.tr.* comfort, esp. in grief or disappointment. [from Latin *consolari*] □ **consolable** *adj.* **consoler** *n.* **consolingly** *adv.*

■ **Usage** See Usage Note at CONDOLE.

console[2] /**kon**-sohl/ *n.* **1** a panel or unit accommodating switches, controls, etc. **2** a cabinet for a television etc. **3** *Mus.* a cabinet with the keyboards, stops, pedals, etc., of an organ. **4** a bracket supporting a shelf etc. [French]

console table *n.* a table supported by a bracket against a wall.

consolidate *v.* **1** *tr. & intr.* make or become strong or solid. **2** *tr.* strengthen (one's position etc.). **3** *tr.* combine (territories, companies, debts, etc.) into one whole. [based on Latin *solidus* 'solid'] □ **consolidation** *n.* **consolidator** *n.* **consolidatory** *adj.*

consols *n.pl.* British government securities without redemption date and with fixed annual interest. [abbreviation of *consolidated annuities*]

consommé /kŏn-**som**-ay/ *n.* a clear soup made with meat stock. [French, literally 'completed', with reference to the end of the slow boiling process]

consonance *n.* agreement, harmony.

consonant ● *n.* **1** a speech sound in which the breath is at least partly obstructed, and which forms a syllable by combining with a vowel. **2** a letter or letters representing this. ● *adj.* (foll. by *with*, *to*) consistent; in agreement or harmony. [from Latin *consonant-* 'sounding together'] □ **consonantal** *adj.* **consonantly** *adv.*

consort[1] ● *n.* /**kon**-sort/ **1** a wife or husband, esp. of royalty (*prince consort*). **2** a companion; an associate. ● *v.intr.* /kŏn-**sort**/ (usu. foll. by *with*, *together*) **1** keep company; associate. **2** harmonize. [from Latin *consors* 'sharer, comrade']

consort[2] /**kon**-sort/ *n. Mus.* a group of musicians who regularly perform together, esp. playing early music (*recorder consort*). [earlier form of CONCERT]

consortium *n.* (*pl.* **consortia** or **consortiums**) an association, esp. of several business companies. [Latin, literally 'partnership']

conspecific *adj. Biol.* of the same species.

conspectus *n.* **1** a general or comprehensive survey. **2** a summary or synopsis. [Latin]

conspicuous *adj.* **1** clearly visible; striking to the eye. **2** noteworthy (*a conspicuous success*). **3** (of expenditure etc.) lavish, with a view to enhancing one's prestige. [from Latin *conspicuus*] □ **conspicuously** *adv.* **conspicuousness** *n.*

conspiracy *n.* (*pl.* **-ies**) **1** a secret plan to commit a crime or do harm; a plot. **2** the act of conspiring. [from Latin *conspiratio* 'plotting']

conspiracy of silence *n.* an agreement to say nothing.

conspiracy theory *n.* a belief that some covert but influential agency or organization is responsible for an unexplained event.

conspirator *n.* a person who takes part in a conspiracy. □ **conspiratorial** *adj.* **conspiratorially** *adv.*

conspire *v.intr.* **1** combine secretly to plan and prepare an unlawful or harmful act. **2** (of events or circumstances) seem to be working together, esp. disadvantageously. [from Latin *conspirare* 'to agree, plot']

constable *n.* **1** esp. *Brit.* **a** a policeman or policewoman. **b** (also **police constable**) a police officer of the lowest rank. **2** the governor of a royal castle. [from Late Latin *comes stabuli* 'officer of the stable']

constabulary *n.* (*pl.* **-ies**) a police force.

constancy *n.* the quality of being unchanging and dependable; faithfulness. [from Latin *constantia*]

constant ● *adj.* **1** continuous (*constant attention*). **2** occurring frequently (*constant complaints*). **3** unchanging, faithful, dependable. ● *n.* **1** anything that does not vary. **2** *Math. & Physics* a quantity or number that remains the same. [from Latin *constant-* 'standing firm'] □ **constantly** *adv.*

constellation *n.* **1** *Astron.* ◀ a group of stars that forms an imaginary pattern representing an object, animal, or person, as seen from the Earth. **2** ◀ one of the 88 areas into which the sky is divided by astronomers. **3** a group of associated persons etc. [based on Latin *stella* 'star'] □ **constellate** *v.tr.*

consternate *v.tr.* (usu. in *passive*) dismay; fill with anxiety. [based on Latin *sternere* 'to throw down']

consternation *n.* anxiety or dismay.

constipate *v.tr.* (esp. as **constipated** *adj.*) affect with constipation. [based on Latin *constipatus* 'pressed together']

C

CONSTELLATION

Astronomers divide the entire sky into 88 interlocking constellations, each with its own set boundaries. Within those boundaries, a pattern of stars, joined by imaginary lines, is visualized as representing an object, or human or animal figure. Although constellations may appear to be grouped in the sky as viewed from the Earth, generally speaking they are not in fact physically connected, and may be at different distances.

imaginary lines denote the shape of Pavo (the Peacock)

Apus

Octans

south celestial pole

Chamaeleon

constellation boundary

Pavo

Mensa

Hydrus

Indus

Tucana

CONSTELLATIONS AROUND THE SOUTH CELESTIAL POLE

C

constipation *n.* difficulty in emptying the bowels.

constituency *n.* (*pl.* **-ies**) **1** a body of voters in a specified area who elect a representative member to a legislative body. **2** *Brit.* the area represented in this way.

constituent ● *adj.* **1** composing or helping to make up a whole. **2** able to make or change a (political etc.) constitution (*constituent assembly*). **3** electing. ● *n.* **1** a member of a constituency. **2** a component part. [from Latin *constituent-* 'setting up']

constitute *v.tr.* **1** be the components or essence of; make up, form. **2 a** be equivalent or tantamount to (*this constitutes a warning*). **b** formally establish (*constitute a precedent*). **3** give legal or constitutional form to. [from Latin *constituere*]

constitution *n.* **1** the act or method of constituting; composition. **2** the body of fundamental principles according to which a state or other organization is governed. **3** a person's physical state as regards health, strength, etc. **4** a person's psychological make-up.

constitutional ● *adj.* **1** of or in line with a political constitution (*a constitutional monarchy*). **2** inherent (*constitutional weakness*). ● *n.* a walk taken regularly as healthy exercise. □ **constitutionality** *n.* **constitutionalize** *v.tr.* (also **-ise**). **constitutionally** *adv.*

constitutive *adj.* **1** able to form or appoint. **2** component. **3** essential. □ **constitutively** *adv.*

constrain *v.tr.* **1** compel. **2 a** confine forcibly; imprison. **b** restrict severely. **3** (as **constrained** *adj.*) forced, embarrassed (*a constrained manner*). [from Latin *constringere* 'to tie together'] □ **constrainedly** *adv.*

constraint *n.* **1** the act or result of constraining or being constrained. **2** a restriction. **3** self-control.

constrict *v.tr.* make narrow or tight; compress. [based on Latin *constrictus* 'tied together'] □ **constriction** *n.* **constrictive** *adj.*

constrictor *n.* **1** any snake that kills by compressing. ▷ SNAKE. **2** *Anat.* any muscle that contracts an organ or part of the body.

construct ● *v.tr.* /kŏn-**strukt**/ **1** make by fitting parts together; build, form. **2** *Geom.* draw or delineate (*construct a triangle*). ● *n.* /**kon**-strukt/ a thing constructed, esp. by the mind. [based on Latin *constructus* 'piled together'] □ **constructor** *n.*

construction *n.* **1** the act or a mode of constructing. **2** a thing constructed. **3** an interpretation or explanation. **4** *Gram.* an arrangement of words according to syntactical rules. □ **constructional** *adj.* **constructionally** *adv.*

construction site *n.* = BUILDING SITE.

constructive *adj.* **1** of construction; tending to construct. **2** tending to form a basis for ideas; helpful, positive (*constructive criticism*; *a constructive approach*). **3** derived by inference (*constructive permission*). □ **constructively** *adv.* **constructiveness** *n.*

constructive dismissal *n.* the changing of an employee's job or working conditions with the aim of forcing resignation.

construe *v.tr.* (**construes**, **construed**, **construing**) **1** interpret. **2** (often foll. by *with*) combine (words) grammatically ('*rely*' is construed with '*on*'). **3** analyse the syntax of (a sentence). **4** translate word for word. [from Latin *construere* 'to pile together'] □ **construable** *adj.* **construal** *n.*

consubstantial *adj.* *Theol.* of the same substance (esp. of the three persons of the Trinity). [from ecclesiastical Latin *consubstantialis*] □ **consubstantiality** *n.*

consubstantiation *n.* *Theol.* (the doctrine of) the real substantial presence of the body and blood of Christ together with the bread and wine in the Eucharist.

consuetude *n.* a custom, esp. one having legal force in Scotland. [based on Latin *consuetus* 'accustomed'] □ **consuetudinary** *adj.*

consul *n.* **1** an official appointed by a state to live in a foreign city and protect the state's citizens and interests there. **2** *hist.* either of two annually elected chief magistrates in ancient Rome. [Latin] □ **consular** *adj.* **consulship** *n.*

consulate *n.* **1** the building officially used by a consul. **2** the position or period of office of consul.

consult *v.* **1** *tr.* seek information or advice from. **2** *intr.* (often foll. by *with*) refer to a person for advice etc. **3** *tr.* seek permission or approval from (a person) for a proposed action. **4** *tr.* take into account (feelings, interests, etc.). [from Latin *consultare*] □ **consultative** *adj.*

consultancy *n.* (*pl.* **-ies**) the practice or position of a consultant.

consultant *n.* **1** a person providing professional advice etc. **2** *Brit.* a senior medical specialist in a hospital.

consultation *n.* **1** a meeting arranged to consult. **2** the act or an instance of consulting.

consulting *attrib.adj.* giving professional advice to others working in the same field or subject (*consulting physician*).

consumable ● *adj.* that can be consumed; intended for consumption. ● *n.* a commodity that is eventually used up, worn out, or eaten.

consume *v.tr.* **1** eat or drink. **2** completely destroy. **3** engross; dominate (often in *passive*, foll. by *with* or *by*: *consumed with rage*). **4** use up. [from Latin *consumere* 'to take up completely'] □ **consumingly** *adv.*

consumer *n.* **1** a person who consumes, esp. one who uses a product. **2** a purchaser of goods or services.

consumer durable *n.* a household product with a relatively long useful life (e.g. a radio or washing machine).

consumer goods *n.pl.* goods put to use by consumers, not used in producing other goods.

consumerism *n.* **1** the protection or promotion of consumers' interests. **2** often *derog.* a preoccupation with consumer goods and their acquisition. □ **consumerist** *adj. & n.*

consummate ● *v.tr.* /**kon**-sŭ-mayt/ **1** complete; make perfect. **2** complete (a marriage) by sexual intercourse. ● *adj.* /**kon**-sum-ăt/ complete, perfect; fully skilled. [based on Latin *summus* 'utmost'] □ **consummately** *adv.* **consummator** *n.*

consummation *n.* **1** completion, esp. of a marriage by sexual intercourse. **2** a desired end or goal; perfection.

consumption *n.* **1** the act or an instance of consuming; the process of being consumed. **2** an amount consumed. **3** the purchase and use of goods etc. **4** use by a particular group or group (*a film unfit for children's consumption*). **5** *archaic* any disease causing wasting of tissues, esp. pulmonary tuberculosis. [from Latin *consumptio*]

consumptive *archaic* ● *adj.* tending to or affected with pulmonary tuberculosis. ● *n.* a consumptive patient. [from medieval Latin *consumptivus*] □ **consumptively** *adv.*

cont. *abbr.* **1** contents. **2** continued.

contact ● *n.* **1** the state or condition of touching, meeting, or communicating. **2** a person who is or may be communicated with for information, assistance, etc. **3** *Electr.* **a** a connection for the passage of a current. **b** a device for providing this. ▷ ALTERNATING CURRENT, RHEOSTAT. **4** a person likely to carry a contagious disease through being near an infected person. **5** (usu. in *pl.*) *colloq.* a contact lens. ● *v.tr.* **1** get in touch with (a person). **2** begin correspondence or personal dealings with. [from Latin *contactus*] □ **contactable** *adj.*

contact lens *n.* a small lens placed on the eyeball to correct the vision.

contact sport *n.* a sport in which participants necessarily come into bodily contact with one another.

contagion *n.* **1 a** the communication of disease from one person to another by bodily contact. **b** a contagious disease. **2** a contagious or harmful influence. [from Latin *contagio* 'touching']

contagious *adj.* **1 a** (of a person) likely to transmit disease by contact. **b** (of a disease) transmitted in this way. **2** (of emotions etc.) likely to affect others (*contagious enthusiasm*). □ **contagiously** *adv.* **contagiousness** *n.*

contain *v.tr.* **1** hold or be capable of holding within itself; include, comprise. **2** (of measures) be equal to (*a gallon contains eight pints*). **3** prevent (an enemy, difficulty, etc.) from moving or extending. **4** control or restrain (feelings etc.). **5** (of a number) be divisible by (a factor) without a remainder. [from Latin *continēre*] □ **containable** *adj.*

container *n.* **1** a vessel, box, etc., for holding particular things. **2** a large boxlike receptacle of standard design for the transport of goods, esp. one readily transferable from one form of transport to another.

container-grown *adj.* (of a plant) grown in a container rather than in the ground.

containerize *v.tr.* (also **-ise**) pack in or transport by container. □ **containerization** *n.*

container port *n.* a port specializing in handling goods stored in containers.

container ship *n.* ▼ a ship designed to carry goods stored in containers.

bridge   *containers*   *stem*

propeller

CONTAINER SHIP

containment *n.* the action or policy of preventing the expansion of a hostile country or influence.

contaminate *v.tr.* **1** pollute, esp. with radioactivity. **2** infect; corrupt. [based on Latin *contaminatus* 'brought into contact'] □ **contaminant** *n.* **contamination** *n.* **contaminator** *n.*

Conté *attrib. adj.* designating a kind of pencil, crayon, or chalk. [N.J. *Conté*, French scientist, 1755–1805.]

contemn *v.tr.* *literary* despise; treat with disregard. [based on Latin *temnere* 'to despise'] □ **contemner** *n.* (also **contemnor**).

contemplate *v.tr.* **1** survey visually or mentally. **2** regard (an event) as possible. **3** intend (*we contemplate leaving tomorrow*). [based on Latin *templum* 'place for observations'] □ **contemplation** *n.* **contemplator** *n.*

contemplative ● *adj.* of or given to (esp. religious) contemplation; meditative. ● *n.* a person devoted to religious contemplation. □ **contemplatively** *adv.*

contemporaneous *adj.* (usu. foll. by *with*) existing or occurring at the same time. [based on Latin *tempus -oris* 'time'] □ **contemporaneity** *n.* **contemporaneously** *adv.* **contemporaneousness** *n.*

contemporary ● *adj.* **1** living or occurring at the same time. **2** approximately equal in age. **3** following modern ideas or fashion in style or design. ● *n.* (*pl.* **-ies**) a contemporary person or thing. [from medieval Latin *contemporarius*] □ **contemporarily** *adv.* **contemporariness** *n.*

contempt *n.* **1** a feeling that a person or a thing is beneath consideration or deserving scorn. **2** the condition of being held in contempt. **3** (in full **contempt of court**) disobedience to or disrespect for a court of law and its officers. □ **beneath contempt** utterly despicable. **hold in contempt** despise. [related to CONTEMN]

contemptible *adj.* deserving contempt; despicable. □ **contemptibility** *n.* **contemptibly** *adv.*

contemptuous *adj.* (often foll. by *of*) showing contempt, scornful. □ **contemptuously** *adv.* **contemptuousness** *n.*

CONTINENT

The land masses of the Earth are divisible into six main areas of land, known as continents. The continents are constantly moving over the Earth's surface as the lithospheric plates in which they are embedded move over the more liquid asthenosphere. This movement is thought to be driven by thermal convection in the Earth's mantle.

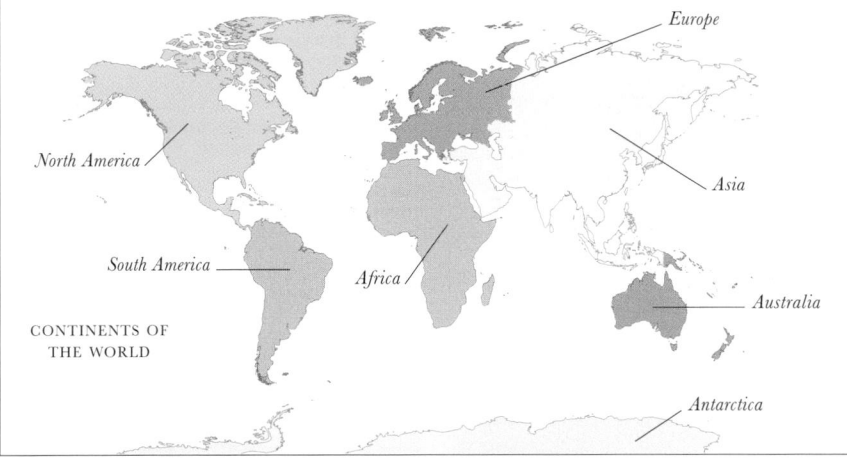

CONTINENTS OF
THE WORLD

contend *v.* **1** *intr.* (usu. foll. by *with*) strive, fight. **2** *intr.* (usu. foll. by *for, with*) compete (*contending for the title; contending emotions*). **3** *tr.* (usu. foll. by *that* + clause) maintain. [from Latin *contendere* 'to strive together'] □ **contender** *n.* (esp. in sense 2).

content[1] /kŏn-tent/ ● *predic.adj.* **1** satisfied; adequately happy. **2** (foll. by *to* + infin.) willing. ● *v.tr.* make content; satisfy. ● *n.* a contented state; satisfaction. □ **to one's heart's content** to the full extent of one's desires. [from Latin *contentus*] □ **contentment** *n.*

content[2] /kon-tent/ *n.* **1** (usu. in *pl.*) what is contained in something. **2** the amount of a constituent contained (*low sodium content*). **3** the substance dealt with (in a speech etc.) as distinct from its form. **4** the capacity or volume of a thing. **5** (in *pl.*; in full **table of contents**) a list of the titles of chapters etc. given at the front of a book etc. [from medieval Latin *contentum* 'thing contained']

contented *adj.* (often foll. by *with*, or *to* + infin.) **1** happy, satisfied. **2** (foll. by *with*) willing to be content. □ **contentedly** *adv.* **contentedness** *n.*

contention *n.* **1** a dispute or argument; rivalry. **2** a point contended for in an argument (*it is my contention that you are wrong*). □ **in contention** competing, esp. with a good chance of success. [related to CONTEND]

contentious *adj.* **1** argumentative, quarrelsome. **2** likely to cause an argument; disputed, controversial. □ **contentiously** *adv.* **contentiousness** *n.*

conterminous *adj.* (often foll. by *with*) **1** having a common boundary. **2** coextensive in space, time, or meaning. [based on Latin *terminus* 'boundary'] □ **conterminously** *adv.*

contest ● *n.* /kon-test/ **1** a process of contending; a competition. **2** a dispute; a controversy. ● *v.tr.* /kŏn-test/ **1** challenge or dispute (a decision etc.). **2** debate (a point, statement, etc.). **3** compete for (a prize, parliamentary seat, etc.); compete in (an election). [from Latin *contestari*] □ **contestable** *adj.* **contester** *n.*

contestant *n.* a person who takes part in a contest or competition.

context *n.* **1** parts that immediately precede and follow a word or passage and clarify its meaning. **2** relevant circumstances. □ **in** (or **out of**) **context** with (or without) the surrounding words or circumstances (*must be seen in context*). [from Latin *contextus* 'woven together'] □ **contextual** *adj.* **contextually** *adv.*

contextualize *v.tr.* (also **-ise**) place in a context; study in context. □ **contextualization** *n.*

contiguous *adj.* (usu. foll. by *with, to*) touching, esp. along a line; in contact. [from Latin *contiguus*] □ **contiguity** *n.* **contiguously** *adv.*

continent[1] *n.* **1** ▲ any of the main continuous expanses of land (Europe, Asia, Africa, N. and S. America, Australia, Antarctica). **2** (**the Continent**) the mainland of Europe as distinct from the British Isles. [from Latin *terra continens* 'continuous land']

continent[2] *adj.* **1** able to control movements of the bowels and bladder. **2** exercising self-restraint, esp. sexually. [from Latin *continent-* 'holding together'] □ **continence** *n.* **continently** *adv.*

continental *adj.* **1** of or characteristic of a continent. **2** (**Continental**) of, relating to, or characteristic of mainland Europe. □ **continentally** *adv.*

continental breakfast *n.* a light breakfast of coffee, rolls, etc.

continental drift *n.* the hypothesis that the continents are moving slowly over the surface of the Earth on a deep-lying plastic substratum. ▷ PLATE TECTONICS

continental quilt *n. Brit.* a duvet.

continental shelf *n.* ◀ an area of relatively shallow seabed between the shore of a continent and the deeper ocean. ▷ SEABED

ocean

continental land mass

continental shelf

CONTINENTAL SHELF OFF SOUTH AMERICA

contingency *n.* (*pl.* **-ies**) **1** an event regarded as likely to occur, or as influencing present action. **2** something dependent on another uncertain event. [from Late Latin *contingentia*]

contingency fund *n.* a fund to cover incidental or unforeseen expenses.

contingent ● *adj.* **1** (usu. foll. by *on, upon*) dependent (on an uncertain event or circumstance). **2** associated. **3** (usu. foll. by *to*) incidental. **4 a** that may or may not occur. **b** fortuitous. ● *n.* a body forming part of a larger group. [from Latin *contingent-* 'touching together'] □ **contingently** *adv.*

continual *adj.* constantly or frequently recurring; always happening. □ **continually** *adv.*

■ **Usage** Note the difference in meaning between *continual* and *continuous*. *Continual* means 'happening frequently (but with breaks in between each occurrence)', while *continuous* means 'uninterrupted, incessant'.

continuance *n.* **1** a state of continuing in existence or operation. **2** the duration of an event or action.

■ **Usage** Note the difference between *continuance* and *continuation*. *Continuance* relates mainly to the intransitive senses of *continue* 'to be still in existence', while *continuation* relates to its transitive senses 'to keep up, resume', e.g. *the Prime Minister's continuance in office; our continuation of the project*.

continuation *n.* **1** the act or an instance of continuing; the process of being continued. **2** a part that continues something else.

■ **Usage** See Usage Note at CONTINUANCE.

continue *v.* (**continues, continued, continuing**) **1** *tr.* (often foll. by verbal noun, or *to* + infin.) maintain, not stop (an action etc.). **2 a** *tr.* (also *absol.*) resume or prolong (a narrative, journey, etc.). **b** *intr.* recommence after a pause. **3** *tr.* be a sequel to. **4** *intr.* remain in existence or in a specified state (*the weather continued fine*). [from Latin *continuare* 'to make or be continuous'] □ **continuable** *adj.* **continuer** *n.*

continuing education *n.* education for adults consisting esp. of short or part-time courses.

continuity *n.* (*pl.* **-ies**) **1 a** the state of being continuous. **b** a logical sequence. **2** the detailed scenario of a film or broadcast. **3** the linking of broadcast items.

continuo *n.* (*pl.* **-os**) *Mus.* an accompaniment providing a bass line, often played on a keyboard instrument. [from Italian *basso continuo* 'continuous bass']

continuous *adj.* unbroken, uninterrupted, connected throughout in space or time. □ **continuously** *adv.* **continuousness** *n.*

■ **Usage** See Usage Note at CONTINUAL.

continuous stationery *n. Brit.* a continuous ream of paper, usu. perforated to form single sheets.

continuum *n.* (*pl.* **continua**) anything seen as having a continuous structure (*space time continuum*).

contort *v.tr.* twist or force out of normal shape. [based on Latin *contortus* 'twisted'] □ **contortion** *n.*

contortionist *n.* an entertainer who adopts contorted postures.

contour ● *n.* **1** an outline, esp. representing or bounding the shape or form of something. **2** the outline of a natural feature, e.g. a coast or mountain mass. **3** = CONTOUR LINE. ● *v.tr.* **1** mark with contour lines. **2** carry (a road or railway) round the side of a hill. [French, based on Italian *contornare* 'to draw in outline']

contour line *n.* a line on a map joining points of equal altitude. ▷ MAP

contour map *n.* ▼ a map marked with contour lines.

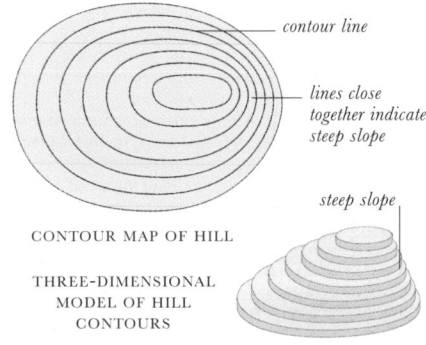

contour line

lines close together indicate steep slope

steep slope

CONTOUR MAP OF HILL

THREE-DIMENSIONAL MODEL OF HILL CONTOURS

CONTOUR MAP

C

contra- *prefix* **1** against, opposite (*contradict*). **2** *Mus.* (of instruments, organ stops, etc.) pitched an octave below (*contrabassoon*). [Latin *contra* 'against']

contraband ● *n.* **1** smuggled goods. **2** prohibited trade; smuggling. ● *adj.* forbidden to be imported or exported (at all or without payment of duty). [from Spanish *contrabanda*] □ **contrabandist** *n.*

contrabass *n.* *Mus.* = DOUBLE BASS.

contraception *n.* the intentional prevention of pregnancy. [based on CONCEPTION]

contraceptive ● *adj.* preventing pregnancy. ● *n.* a contraceptive device or drug.

contract ● *n.* /kon-trakt/ **1** a written or spoken agreement intended to be enforceable by law. **2** a document recording this. ● *v.* /kŏn-trakt/ **1** *tr.* & *intr.* **a** make or become smaller or shorter. **b** draw together or be drawn together. **2 a** *intr.* (usu. foll. by *with*) make a contract. **b** *tr.* (often foll. by *out*) arrange (work) to be done by contract. **c** *tr.* place under a contract. **3** *tr.* catch or develop (a disease). **4** *tr.* form or develop (a friendship, habit, etc.). **5** *tr.* enter into (marriage). **6** *tr.* incur (a debt etc.). □ **contract in** (or **out**) (also *refl.*) *Brit.* choose to be involved in (or withdraw or remain out of) a scheme or commitment. [from Latin *contractus* 'drawn together'] □ **contractive** *adj.*

contractable *adj.* (of a disease) that can be contracted.

contract bridge *n.* a form of bridge in which only tricks bid and won count towards the game.

contractible *adj.* that can be shrunk or drawn together.

contractile *adj.* capable of or producing contraction. □ **contractility** *n.*

contraction *n.* **1** the act of contracting. **2** (often in *pl.*) *Med.* a shortening of the uterine muscles during childbirth. **3** shrinking, diminution. **4 a** a shortening of a word by combination or elision. **b** a contracted word or group of words.

contractor *n.* a person who undertakes a contract, esp. to conduct building operations.

contractual *adj.* of or in the nature of a contract. □ **contractually** *adv.*

contradict *v.tr.* **1** deny (a statement). **2** express the opposite of a statement made by (a person). **3** be in opposition to or in conflict with. [based on Latin *contradictus* 'spoken against'] □ **contradiction** *n.* **contradictor** *n.*

contradictory *adj.* **1** expressing a denial or opposite statement. **2** (of statements etc.) mutually opposed or inconsistent. **3** (of a person) inclined to contradict. □ **contradictorily** *adv.*

contradistinction *n.* a distinction made by contrasting.

contraflow *n.* *Brit.* a flow (esp. of road traffic) alongside, and in a direction opposite to, an established or usual flow, esp. as a temporary arrangement.

contraindicate *v.tr.* *Med.* act as an indication against (the use of a particular substance or treatment). □ **contraindication** *n.*

contralto *n.* (*pl.* -**os**) **1 a** the lowest female singing voice. **b** a singer with this voice. **2** a part written for contralto. [Italian]

contraption *n.* often *derog.* or *joc.* a machine or device, esp. a strange or cumbersome one. [19th-century coinage]

contrapuntal *adj.* *Mus.* of or in counterpoint. [based on Italian *contrappunto* 'counterpoint'] □ **contrapuntally** *adv.* **contrapuntist** *n.*

contrariwise *adv.* **1** on the other hand. **2** in the opposite way. **3** perversely.

contrary /kon-tră-ri/ ● *adj.* **1** (usu. foll. by *to*) opposed in nature or tendency. **2** /kŏn-trair-i/ *colloq.* perverse, self-willed. **3** (of a wind) unfavourable. **4** mutually opposed. **5** opposite in position or direction. ● *n.* (*pl.* -**ies**) (prec. by *the*) the opposite. ● *adv.* (foll. by *to*) in opposition or contrast (*contrary to expectations it rained*). □ **on the contrary** intensifying a denial of what has just been implied

or stated. **to the contrary** to the opposite effect. [based on Latin *contra* 'against'] □ **contrarily** *adv.* **contrariness** *n.*

contrast ● *n.* /kon-trahst/ **1 a** a juxtaposition or comparison showing striking differences. **b** a difference so revealed. **2** (often foll. by *to*) a thing or person having qualities noticeably different from another. **3** ▼ the degree of difference between tones in a television picture or a photograph. ● *v.* /kŏn-trahst/ (often foll. by *with*) **1** *tr.* distinguish or set together so as to reveal a contrast. **2** *intr.* have or show a contrast. [from medieval Latin *contrastare* 'to withstand'] □ **contrastingly** *adv.* **contrastive** *adj.*

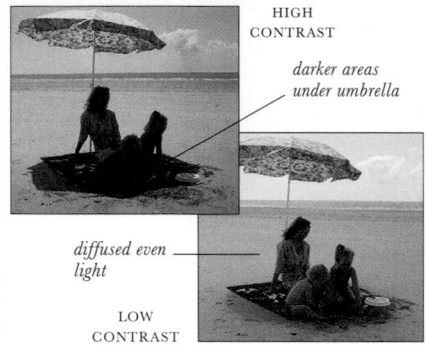

HIGH CONTRAST

darker areas under umbrella

diffused even light

LOW CONTRAST

CONTRAST IN TONES EXHIBITED BY TWO PHOTOGRAPHS

contrasty *adj.* (of a photograph etc.) showing a high degree of contrast.

contravene *v.tr.* **1** infringe (a law or code of conduct). **2** (of things) conflict with. [from Late Latin *contravenire* 'to oppose'] □ **contravener** *n.*

contravention *n.* **1** infringement. **2** an instance of this. □ **in contravention of** violating (a law etc.).

contretemps /kon-trĕ-tahng/ *n.* (*pl.* same /-tahngz/) **1** an awkward or unfortunate occurrence; an unexpected mishap. **2** *colloq.* a dispute or disagreement. [French, originally in sense 'motion out of time']

contribute *v.* (often foll. by *to*) **1** *tr.* give (money, an idea, help, etc.) towards a common purpose. **2** *intr.* help to bring about a result etc. (*contributed to their downfall*). **3** *tr.* (also *absol.*) supply (an article etc.) for publication with others in a journal etc. [based on Latin *contributus* 'brought together'] □ **contributive** *adj.* **contributor** *n.*

contribution *n.* **1** the act of contributing. **2** something contributed.

contributory *adj.* **1** that contributes. **2** using contributions (*contributory pension scheme*).

con-trick *n.* *slang* = CONFIDENCE TRICK.

contrite *adj.* **1** completely penitent. **2** feeling guilt. [from Latin *contritus* 'bruised'] □ **contritely** *adv.*

contriteness *n.* **contrition** *n.*

contrivance *n.* **1** something contrived, esp. a mechanical device or a plan. **2** an act of contriving, esp. deceitfully. **3** inventive capacity.

contrive *v.tr.* **1** devise. **2** (often foll. by *to* + infin.) manage. [from Old French *controver* 'to find, imagine'] □ **contrivable** *adj.* **contriver** *n.*

contrived *adj.* planned so carefully as to seem unnatural; forced.

control ● *n.* **1** command (*under the control of*). **2** the power of restraining, esp. self-restraint. **3** a means of restraint. **4** (usu. in *pl.*) a means of regulating prices etc. **5** (usu. in *pl.*) switches and other devices by which a machine is controlled (also *attrib.*: *control panel*). **6 a** a place where something is controlled or verified. **b** a person or group that controls something. **7** a standard of comparison for checking the results of a survey or experiment (also *attrib.*: *control sample*). ● *v.tr.*

(**controlled**, **controlling**) **1** have control or command of. **2** regulate. **3** restrain (*told him to control himself*). **4** serve as control to. **5** check, verify. □ **in control** (often foll. by *of*) directing an activity. **out of control** no longer subject to proper direction or restraint. **under control** being controlled. [from medieval Latin *contrarotulare* 'to keep a copy of a roll of accounts'] □ **controllability** *n.* **controllable** *adj.* **controllably** *adv.*

control group *n.* a group forming the standard of comparison in an experiment.

controller *n.* **1** a person or thing that controls. **2** a person in charge of expenditure. □ **controllership** *n.*

controlling interest *n.* a means of determining the policy of a business etc., esp. by ownership of a majority of the stock.

control tower *n.* ▼ a tall building at an airport etc. from which air traffic is controlled.

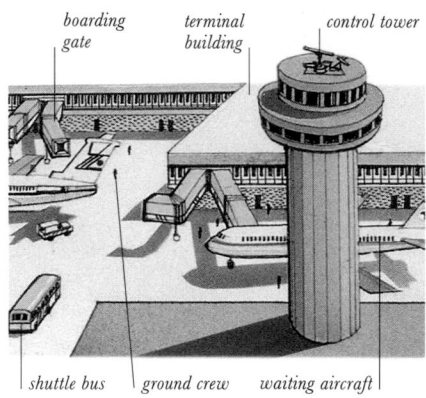

boarding gate *terminal building* *control tower*

shuttle bus *ground crew* *waiting aircraft*

CONTROL TOWER

controversial *adj.* **1** causing or subject to controversy. **2** of or relating to controversy. **3** prone to argue. □ **controversialism** *n.* **controversialist** *n.* **controversially** *adv.*

controversy *n.* (*pl.* -**ies**) **1** disagreement on a matter of opinion. **2** a prolonged argument or dispute, esp. when conducted publicly. [from Latin *controversia*]

controvert *v.tr.* dispute, deny. [based on Latin *controversus* 'disputed'] □ **controvertible** *adj.*

contumacious *adj.* stubbornly or wilfully disobedient. [from Latin *contumax contumac-*] □ **contumaciously** *adv.* □ **contumacy** *n.*

contumelious *adj.* reproachful, insulting, or insolent. □ **contumeliously** *adv.*

contumely *n.* **1** insolent or reproachful language or treatment. **2** disgrace. [from Latin *contumelia* 'reproach']

contuse *v.tr.* injure without breaking the skin; bruise. [based on Latin *contusus* 'beaten together'] □ **contusion** *n.*

conundrum *n.* **1** a riddle, esp. one with a pun in its answer. **2** a puzzling question. [16th-century coinage]

conurbation *n.* an extended urban area, esp. one consisting of several towns and merging suburbs. [based on Latin *urbs* 'city']

conure *n.* ◄ any medium-sized parrot of *Aratinga, Pyrrhura,* and related genera with mainly green plumage and a long gradated tail. [from Greek *kōnos* 'cone' + *oura* 'tail']

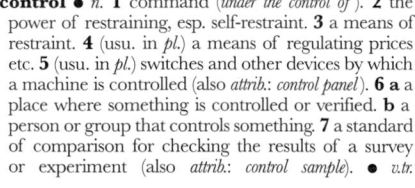

CONURE: SUN CONURE (*Aratinga solstitialis*)

C

convalesce *v.intr.* recover one's health after illness. [from Latin *convalescere*]

convalescent ● *adj.* recovering from an illness. ● *n.* a convalescent person. □ **convalescence** *n.*

convection *n.* **1** transference of heat by upward movement of a heated and less dense medium. **2** *Meteorol.* the transfer of heat by the upward flow of hot air or downward flow of cold air. ▷ FRONT. [from Late Latin *convectio*] □ **convectional** *adj.* **convective** *adj.*

convection current *n.* circulation that results from convection.

convector *n.* a heating appliance that circulates warm air by convection.

convene *v.* **1** *tr.* summon or arrange (a meeting etc.). **2** *intr.* assemble. **3** *tr.* summon (a person) before a tribunal. [from Latin *convenire* 'to assemble, agree, fit'] □ **convenable** *adj.*

convener *n.* (also **convenor**) **1** a person who convenes a meeting. **2** *Brit.* a senior trade union official at a workplace.

convenience *n.* **1** the quality of being convenient; suitability. **2** freedom from difficulty or trouble; material advantage (*for convenience*). **3** an advantage (*a great convenience*). **4** a useful thing, esp. an installation or piece of equipment. **5** *Brit.* a lavatory, esp. a public one. **at one's convenience** at a time or place that suits one. **at one's earliest convenience** as soon as one can. **make a convenience of** take advantage of (a person) insensitively. [from Latin *convenientia* 'conformity']

convenience food *n.* food sold in convenient form and requiring very little preparation.

convenience store *n.* a shop with extended opening hours, stocking a wide range of goods.

convenient *adj.* **1** (often foll. by *for, to*) **a** serving one's comfort or interests. **b** suitable. **c** free of trouble or difficulty. **2** available or occurring at a suitable time or place (*a convenient moment*). **3** easily accessible; well situated. □ **conveniently** *adv.*

convenor var. of CONVENER.

convent *n.* **1** a religious (usu. Christian) community, esp. of nuns, under vows. **2** the premises occupied by this. **3** (in full **convent school**) a school attached to and run by a convent. [from Latin *conventus* 'assembly']

conventicle *n.* esp. *hist.* **1** a secret or unlawful religious meeting, esp. of dissenters. **2** a building used for this. [from Latin *conventiculum* '(place of) assembly']

convention *n.* **1 a** general agreement, esp. agreement on social behaviour etc. by implicit consent of the majority. **b** a custom or customary practice. **2 a** formal assembly for a common purpose. **3 a** a formal agreement. **b** an agreement between states, esp. one less formal than a treaty. [related to CONVENE]

conventional *adj.* **1** depending on or according with convention. **2** (of a person) attentive to social conventions. **3** usual. **4** not spontaneous or sincere or original. **5** (of weapons or power) non-nuclear. □ **conventionalism** *n.* **conventionalist** *n.* **conventionality** *n.* (*pl.* **-ies**). **conventionalize** *v.tr.* (also **-ise**). **conventionally** *adv.*

conventioneer *n.* *US* a person attending a convention.

converge *v.intr.* **1** come together as if to meet or join. **2** (of lines) tend to meet at a point. **3** (foll. by *on, upon*) approach from different directions. [from Late Latin *convergere*] □ **convergence** *n.* **convergency** *n.* **convergent** *adj.*

conversant *adj.* (foll. by *with*) well acquainted with. □ **conversance** *n.* **conversancy** *n.*

conversation *n.* **1** the informal exchange of ideas, information, etc. by spoken words. **2** an instance of this.

conversational *adj.* **1** of or in conversation. **2** colloquial. □ **conversationally** *adv.*

conversationalist *n.* a person who is good at or fond of conversing.

converse[1] /kŏn-**verss**/ *v.intr.* (often foll. by *with*) engage in conversation. [from Latin *conversari* 'to keep company (with)'] □ **converser** *n.*

converse[2] /**kon**-verss/ ● *adj.* opposite, contrary, reversed. ● *n.* something, esp. a statement or proposition, that is opposite or contrary. [from Latin *conversus*] □ **conversely** *adv.*

conversion *n.* **1** the act or an instance of converting or the process of being converted, esp. in belief or religion. **2 a** an adaptation of a building for new purposes. **b** *Brit.* a converted building.

convert ● *v.* /kŏn-**vert**/ **1** *tr.* change in form, character, or function. **2** *tr.* cause (a person) to change beliefs etc. **3** *tr.* change (moneys etc.) into others of a different kind. **4** *tr.* make structural alterations in (a building) to serve a new purpose. **5** *tr.* (also *absol.*) *Rugby* score extra points from (a try) by a successful kick at goal. **6** *intr.* be converted or convertible (*the sofa converts into a bed*). ● *n.* /**kon**-vert/ (often foll. by *to*) a person who has been converted to a different belief, opinion, etc. [from Latin *convertere* 'to turn about']

converter *n.* (also **convertor**) **1** a person or thing that converts. **2** *Electr.* **a** an electrical apparatus for the interconversion of alternating current and direct current. **b** *Electronics* an apparatus for converting a signal from one frequency to another. **3** a reaction vessel used in making steel.

convertible ● *adj.* **1** that may be converted. **2** (of a car) having a folding or detachable roof. ● *n.* ▼ a car with a folding or detachable roof. □ **convertibility** *n.* **convertibly** *adv.*

convertible hood frame

fixed windscreen

steel hood cover

boot lid

CONVERTIBLE:
CADILLAC ELDORADO, 1954

convex *adj.* having an outline or surface curved like the exterior of a circle or sphere (cf. CONCAVE). [from Latin *convexus* 'vaulted, arched'] □ **convexity** *n.* **convexly** *adv.*

convey *v.tr.* **1** transport or carry (goods, passengers, etc.). **2** communicate (an idea, meaning, etc.). **3** *Law* transfer the title to (property). **4** transmit (sound, smell, etc.). [based on Latin *via* 'way'] □ **conveyable** *adj.*

conveyance *n.* **1** the act or process of carrying. **2** a means of transport; a vehicle. **3** *Law* **a** the transfer of property from one owner to another. **b** a document effecting this. □ **conveyancer** *n.* (in sense 3). **conveyancing** *n.* (in sense 3).

conveyor *n.* (also **conveyer**) a person or thing that conveys.

conveyor belt *n.* an endless moving belt for conveying articles or materials, esp. in a factory.

convict ● *v.tr.* /kŏn-**vikt**/ **1** (often foll. by *of*) prove to be guilty (of a crime etc.). **2** declare guilty by the verdict of a jury or the decision of a judge. ● *n.* /**kon**-vikt/ chiefly *hist.* a person serving a prison sentence. [from Latin *convictus* 'proved']

conviction *n.* **1 a** the act or process of proving or finding guilty. **b** an instance of this (*has two previous convictions*). **2 a** the action or resulting state of being convinced. **b** a firm belief or opinion.

convince *v.tr.* **1** persuade (a person) to believe or realize. **2** (as **convinced** *adj.*) firmly persuaded (*a convinced pacifist*). [from Latin *convincere* 'to prove'] □ **convincer** *n.* **convincible** *adj.*

convincing *adj.* **1** able to or such as to convince. **2** substantial (*a convincing victory*). □ **convincingly** *adv.*

convivial *adj.* **1** sociable and lively. **2** festive (*a convivial atmosphere*). [based on Latin *convivium* 'feast'] □ **conviviality** *n.* **convivially** *adv.*

convocation *n.* **1** the act of calling together. **2** a large formal gathering of people, esp.: **a** *Brit.* a provincial synod of the Anglican clergy. **b** *Brit.* a legislative or deliberative assembly of a university. [from Latin *convocatio*] □ **convocational** *adj.*

convoke *v.tr.* *formal* call (people) together; summon to assemble. [from Latin *convocare*]

convoluted *adj.* **1** coiled, twisted. **2** complex, intricate. [from Latin *convolutus*] □ **convolutedly** *adv.*

convolution *n.* **1** coiling, twisting. **2** a coil or twist. **3** complexity. **4** a sinuous fold in the surface of the brain. ▷ BRAIN. □ **convolutional** *adj.*

convolvulus *n.* (*pl.* **convolvuluses**) ▶ any twining plant of the genus *Convolvulus*, with trumpet-shaped flowers, e.g. bindweed. [Latin, literally 'bindweed']

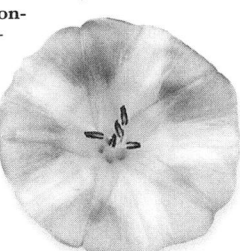

CONVOLVULUS
(*Convolvulus arvensis*)

convoy ● *n.* a group of ships or vehicles travelling together or under escort. ● *v.tr.* escort, esp. with armed protection. □ **in convoy** under escort with others; as a group. [from Old French *convoyer*, variant of *conveier* 'to convey']

convulsant *n.* *Pharm.* a drug that may produce convulsions. [French]

convulse *v.tr.* **1** (usu. in *passive*) affect with convulsions. **2** *colloq.* cause to laugh uncontrollably. **3** shake violently; agitate, disturb. [based on Latin *convulsus* 'wrenched'] □ **convulsive** *adj.* **convulsively** *adv.*

convulsion *n.* **1** (usu. in *pl.*) violent irregular motion of a limb or limbs or the body caused by involuntary contraction of muscles. **2** a violent disturbance or agitation. **3** (in *pl.*) *colloq.* uncontrollable laughter. □ **convulsionary** *adj.*

cony *n.* (also **coney**) (*pl.* **-ies** or **-eys**) **1 a** *Heraldry* or *dial.* a rabbit. **b** its fur. **2** *Bibl.* a hyrax. [from Latin *cuniculus*]

coo ● *n.* a soft murmuring sound like that of a dove or pigeon. ● *v.* (**coos**, **cooed**) **1** *intr.* make the sound of a coo. **2** *intr.* & *tr.* talk or say in a soft or amorous voice. ● *int.* *Brit.* *slang* expressing surprise or incredulity.

co-occur *v.intr.* (often foll. by *with*) occur together or simultaneously. □ **co-occurrence** *n.*

cooee *Brit.* *colloq.* ● *n.* & *int.* a sound used to attract attention, esp. at a distance. ● *v.intr.* (**cooees, cooeed, cooeeing**) make this sound. □ **within cooee** (or **a cooee**) **of** *Austral.* & *NZ* *colloq.* very near to. [imitative of a signal used by Australian Aboriginals and copied by settlers]

cook ● *v.* **1** *tr.* prepare (food) by heating it. **2** *intr.* (of food) undergo cooking. **3** *tr.* *colloq.* falsify (accounts etc.); alter to produce a desired result (esp. in **cook the books**). **4** *tr.* & *intr.* *US colloq.* do or proceed successfully. **5** *intr.* (as **be cooking**) *colloq.* be happening or about to happen (*went to find out what was cooking*). ● *n.* a person who cooks, esp. professionally or in a specified way (*a good cook*). □ **cook a person's goose** ruin a person's chances. **cook up** *colloq.* invent or concoct (a story, excuse, etc.). [based on Latin *coquus* 'a cook'] □ **cookable** *adj.* & *n.*

cookbook *n.* a cookery book.

cook-chill *attrib.adj.* *Brit.* designating food which has been cooked and refrigerated by the manufacturer ready for reheating by the consumer.

COOKWARE

Pans and dishes are designed for particular methods of cooking, although many fulfil several functions. Saucepans and frying pans are used on top of the stove, and are made from various metals, often with a non-stick coating. Casserole dishes and baking tins are used inside the oven, while cookware for microwaves must be non-metallic.

EXAMPLES OF COOKWARE

FRYING PAN

OVENPROOF DISH

MICROWAVE-PROOF DISH

SAUCEPAN

LOOSE-BASED FLAN TIN

CASSEROLE DISH

PATTY TINS

COOLING RACK

cooker n. **1 a** Brit. a stove used for cooking food. **b** (usu. in comb.) a container in which food is cooked (pressure cooker). **2** Brit. colloq. a fruit etc. (esp. an apple) that is more suitable for cooking than for eating raw.

cookery n. (pl. **-ies**) the art or practice of cooking.

cookery book n. Brit. a book containing recipes and other information about cooking.

cookie n. **1** N. Amer. a small sweet biscuit. **2** slang a person of a specified kind (tough cookie). [from Dutch koekje 'little cake']

cooking n. **1** the art or process by which food is cooked. **2** (attrib.) suitable for or used in cooking (cooking apple; cooking utensils).

cookware n. ▲ utensils for cooking, esp. dishes, pans, etc.

cool ● adj. **1** of or at a fairly low temperature; fairly cold (a cool day; a cool bath). **2** suggesting or achieving coolness (cool colours; cool clothes). **3** calm, unexcited. **4** lacking enthusiasm. **5** unfriendly; lacking cordiality (got a cool reception). **6** calmly audacious (a cool customer). **7** (prec. by a) colloq. (usu. as an intensive; esp. of large sums of money) not less than; a full (cost me a cool three thousand). **8** slang **a** excellent, marvellous. **b** fashionable; having street credibility. ● n. **1** coolness. **2** cool air; a cool place. **3** slang calmness, composure (keep/lose one's cool). ● v.tr. & intr. (often foll. by down, off) make or become cool. □ **cool one's heels** see HEEL[1]. **cool it** slang relax, calm down. [Old English] □ **coolish** adj. **coolly** adv. **coolness** n.

coolabah n. (also **coolibah**) Austral. any of various gum trees, esp. Eucalyptus microtheca. [from Aboriginal gulabaa]

coolant n. a cooling agent, esp. fluid, to remove heat from an engine, nuclear reactor, etc.

cool bag n. (also **cool box**) Brit. an insulated container for keeping food cool.

cooler n. **1** a vessel in which a thing is cooled. **2** N. Amer. **a** a refrigerator. **b** = COOL BAG. **3** slang prison or a prison cell.

cool-headed adj. not easily excited.

coolibah var. of COOLABAH.

coolie n. (also **cooly**) (pl. **-ies**) an unskilled native labourer in India, China, and some other Eastern countries. [from Hindi Kūlī 'day-labourer']

coolie hat n. a broad conical hat as worn by coolies.

cooling-off period n. an interval to allow for a change of mind before commitment to action.

cooling tower n. a tall structure for cooling hot water before reuse, esp. in industry. ▷ POWER STATION

coomb n. (also **combe**) Brit. **1** a valley or hollow on the side of a hill. **2** a short valley running up from the coast. [Old English]

coon n. **1** N. Amer. a raccoon. **2** slang offens. a black person.

coop ● n. **1** ▼ a cage or pen for poultry. **2** a small place of confinement, esp. a prison. ● v.tr. (often foll. by up, in) confine (a person) in a small space. [from Latin capa cask]

pop hole   hinged door

laying compartment

COOP FOR CHICKENS

co-op n. colloq. **1** Brit. a cooperative society or shop. **2** a cooperative business or enterprise.

cooper ● n. a maker or repairer of casks, barrels, etc. ● v.tr. make or repair (a cask). [based on Middle Low German kūpe 'coop']

cooperate v.intr. (also **co-operate**) **1** (often foll. by with) work or act together; help, assist. **2** be helpful and do as one is asked. [based on ecclesiastical Latin co-operatus 'acted together'] □ **cooperant** adj. **co-operation** n. **cooperator** n.

cooperative (also **co-operative**) ● adj. **1** of or affording cooperation. **2** willing to cooperate. **3** Econ. (of a farm, business, enterprise, etc.) owned and run jointly by its members, with profits or benefits shared among them. ● n. a cooperative farm or society or business. □ **cooperatively** adv. **cooperativeness** n.

co-opt v.tr. appoint to membership of a body by invitation of the existing members. [from Latin cooptare] □ **co-optation** n. **co-option** n. **co-optive** adj.

coordinate (also **co-ordinate**) ● v. /koh-**ord**-i-nayt/ **1** tr. bring (various parts, movements, etc.) into a proper or required relation. **2** intr. work or act together effectively. ● adj. /koh-**ord**-i-năt/ **1** equal in rank or importance. **2** Gram. (of parts of a compound sentence) equal in status. ● n. /koh-**ord**-i-năt/ **1** Math. each of a system of various magnitudes used to fix the position of a point, line, or plane. **2** (in pl.) matching items of clothing. [based on Latin ordinatus 'put in order'] □ **coordination** n. **coordinative** adj. **coordinator** n.

coot n. **1** ▼ any black aquatic bird of the genus Fulica, esp. F. atra with the upper mandible extended backwards to form a white plate on the forehead. **2** colloq. a stupid person. [Middle English]

COOT (Fulica atra)

co-own v.tr. own jointly with another person or persons. □ **co-owner** n. **co-ownership** n.

cop slang ● n. **1** a police officer. **2** Brit. a capture or arrest (it's a fair cop). ● v.tr. (**copped**, **copping**) **1** catch or arrest (an offender). **2** receive, suffer. **3** take, seize. □ **cop it** Brit. **1** get into trouble; be punished. **2** be killed. **cop out 1** withdraw; give up an attempt. **2** go back on a promise. **not much** (or **no**) **cop** Brit. of little or no value or use.

copal n. a resin from any of various tropical trees, used for varnish. [from Aztec copalli 'incense']

co-partner n. a partner or associate, esp. when sharing equally. □ **co-partnership** n.

cope[1] v.intr. (foll. by with) deal effectively or contend; manage. [earlier in sense 'to meet in battle': based on Greek kolaphos 'blow with the fist']

cope[2] ● n. Eccl. a long cloaklike vestment worn by a priest or bishop in ceremonies and processions. ● v.tr. cover with a cope or coping. [from Late Latin cappa 'cape']

copeck n. (also **kopeck**, **kopek**) a monetary unit of Russia etc., equal to one-hundredth of a rouble. [from Russian kopeĭka 'little lance', from the 1535 coin depicting Ivan IV bearing a lance]

Copernican system n. (also **Copernican theory**) Astron. the theory that the planets (including the Earth) move round the Sun (cf. PTOLEMAIC SYSTEM).

copiable adj. that can or may be copied.

copier n. a machine or person that copies (esp. documents).

co-pilot n. a second pilot in an aircraft.

coping stone

coping n. the top (usu. sloping) course of masonry in a wall or parapet.

coping stone n. ► a stone used in a coping.

course of bricks

COPING STONE

copious *adj.* **1** abundant, plentiful. **2** producing much. **3** providing much information. **4** profuse in speech. [based on Latin *copia* 'plenty'] □ **copiously** *adv.* **copiousness** *n.*

copita *n.* **1** a tulip-shaped sherry glass. **2** a glass of sherry. [Spanish]

cop-out *n.* **1** a cowardly or feeble evasion. **2** an escape; a way of escape.

copper[1] ● *n.* **1** *Chem.* a malleable red-brown metallic element used esp. for electrical wiring and in alloys. ▷ METAL. **2** (usu. in *pl.*) a bronze coin, esp. one of little value. **3** *Brit.* a large metal vessel for boiling esp. laundry. ● *adj.* ▶ made of or coloured like copper. ● *v.tr.* cover with copper. [from Latin *cyprium aes* 'Cyprus metal']

copper[2] *n. slang* a police officer.

copper beech *n.* a variety of beech with copper-coloured leaves.

copper belt *n.* a copper-mining area of central Africa.

copper-bottomed *adj.* **1** having a bottom sheathed with copper. **2** *Brit.* genuine or reliable, esp. financially.

copperhead *n.* **1** ▼ a venomous viper, *Agkistrodon contortrix*, native to N. America. **2** a venomous cobra, *Denisonia superba*, native to Australia.

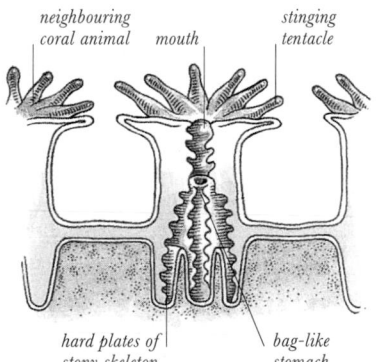

COPPER DISTILLER'S JUG

COPPERHEAD (*Agkistrodon contortrix*)

copperplate ● *n.* **1 a** a polished copper plate for engraving or etching. **b** a print made from this. **2** ▼ an ornate style of handwriting. ● *adj.* of or in copperplate writing.

Failings of others

COPPERPLATE: EXAMPLE OF ENGRAVED COPPERPLATE HANDWRITING

coppery *adj.* of or like copper, esp. in colour.

coppice ● *n.* an area of undergrowth and small trees, grown for periodic cutting. ● *v.tr.* cut back (young trees) periodically to stimulate growth of shoots. [based on medieval Latin *colpus* 'blow'] □ **coppiced** *adj.*

copra *n.* the dried kernels of the coconut. [Portuguese]

co-produce *v.tr.* produce (a play, broadcast, etc.) jointly. □ **co-producer** *n.* **co-production** *n.*

copse *n.* **1** = COPPICE. **2** (in general use) a small wood. [shortened from COPPICE]

copsewood *n.* undergrowth.

Copt *n.* **1** a native Egyptian in the Hellenistic and Roman periods. **2** a native Christian of the independent Egyptian Church. [based on Greek *Aiguptios* 'Egyptian']

Coptic ● *n.* the language of the Copts. ● *adj.* of or relating to the Copts or their language.

copula *n.* (*pl.* **copulas**) *Logic & Gram.* a connecting word, esp. a part of the verb *be* connecting a subject and predicate. [Latin] □ **copular** *adj.*

copulate *v.intr.* have sexual intercourse. [based on Latin *copulatus* 'linked'] □ **copulation** *n.* **copulatory** *adj.*

copy ● *n.* (*pl.* **-ies**) **1** a thing made to imitate or be identical to another. **2** a single specimen of a publication or issue. **3 a** a matter to be printed. **b** material for a newspaper or magazine article (*scandals make good copy*). ● *v.tr.* (**-ies, -ied**) **1 a** (often *absol.*) make a copy of. **b** (often foll. by *out*) transcribe. **2** (foll. by *to*) send a copy of (a letter) to a third party. **3** do the same as; imitate. [from medieval Latin *copia* 'transcript', cf. phrase *copiam describendi facere* 'to give permission to transcribe']

copybook *n.* **1** a book containing models of handwriting. **2** (*attrib.*) **a** a tritely conventional. **b** accurate, exemplary.

copycat *n.* **1** *colloq.* (esp. as a child's word) a person who copies another, esp. slavishly. **2** (*attrib.*) in imitation of a person, act, event, etc. (*copycat crimes*).

copy-edit *v.tr.* (**-edited, -editing**) edit (copy) for printing. □ **copy editor** *n.*

copyhold *n. Brit. hist.* **1** tenure of land based on manorial records. **2** land held in this way. □ **copyholder** *n.*

copyist *n.* a person who makes (esp. written) copies.

copyright ● *n.* the exclusive legal right to print, publish, perform, film, or record literary, artistic, or musical material. ● *adj.* (of such material) protected by copyright. ● *v.tr.* secure copyright for (material).

copy-typist *n.* a person who makes typewritten transcripts of documents.

copywriter *n.* a person who writes or prepares copy (esp. of advertising material) for publication. □ **copywriting** *n.*

coquette *n.* a woman who flirts. [French, literally 'wanton female'] □ **coquetry** *n.* (*pl.* **-ies**). **coquettish** *adj.* **coquettishly** *adv.* **coquettishness** *n.*

cor *int. Brit. slang* expressing surprise, excitement, alarm, etc. □ **cor blimey** see BLIMEY. [corruption of *God*]

coracle *n. Brit.* a small Welsh or Irish boat of wickerwork covered with watertight material. [from Welsh *corwgl*]

coral ● *n.* **1** a hard calcareous substance secreted by certain marine cnidarians and often forming large reefs. ▷ CNIDARIAN. **2** ▼ a sedentary and typically colonial cnidarian of warm and tropical seas with a calcareous, horny, or soft skeleton, which forms such reefs. **3** (in full **red coral**) a pinkish-red horny coral used in jewellery. **4** a pinkish-red colour. ● *adj.* **1** of a pinkish-red colour. **2** made of coral. [from Greek *korallion*] □ **coralloid** *adj. & n.*

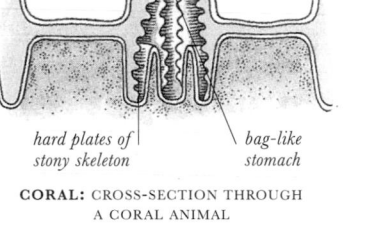

neighbouring coral animal   mouth   stinging tentacle

hard plates of stony skeleton   bag-like stomach

CORAL: CROSS-SECTION THROUGH A CORAL ANIMAL

coral island *n.* an island formed by the growth of coral.

coralline ● *n.* any seaweed of the genus *Corallin* having a calcareous jointed stem. ● *adj.* **1** = CORAL *adj.* 1. **2** of or like coral.

coral reef *n.* a reef formed by the growth of coral. ▷ ATOLL

cor anglais /kor ong-glay/ *n.* (*pl.* **cors anglais** *pronunc.* same) *Mus.* ▶ an alto woodwind instrument of the oboe family. ▷ ORCHESTRA, WOODWIND. [French, literally 'English horn']

corbel *n. Archit.* a projection of stone, timber, etc., jutting out from a wall to support a weight. ▷ CHATEAU. [from Old French, literally 'little crow']

cord ● *n.* **1 a** long thin flexible string or rope made from several twisted strands. **b** a piece of this. **2** *Anat.* a structure in the body resembling a cord (*spinal cord*). **3 a** ribbed fabric, esp. corduroy. **b** (in *pl.*) corduroy trousers. **4** an electric flex. ● *v.tr.* **1** fasten or bind with cord. **2** (as **corded** *adj.*) **a** (of cloth) ribbed. **b** provided with cords. [from Greek *khordē* 'gut, string of musical instrument'] □ **cordlike** *adj.*

cordate *adj.* ◀ heartshaped. [based on Latin *cor cordis* 'heart']

cordial ● *adj.* **1** heartfelt, sincere. **2** warm, friendly. ● *n.* **1** *Brit.* a fruit-flavoured drink. **2** a comforting or pleasant-tasting medicine. [based on Latin *cor cordis* 'heart'] □ **cordiality** *n.* **cordially** *adv.*

cordite *n.* a smokeless explosive. [based on CORD, from its appearance]

cordless *adj.* (of an electrical appliance, telephone, etc.) working without connection to a mains supply or central unit.

cordon ● *n.* **1** a line or circle of police, soldiers, etc., esp. preventing access to or from an area. **2** an ornamental cord or braid. **3** ▶ a fruit tree trained to grow as a single stem. ● *v.tr.* (often foll. by *off*) enclose or separate with a cordon of police etc. [related to CORD]

cordon bleu /kor-don bler/ *Cookery* ● *adj.* of the highest class. ● *n.* a cook of this class. [French, literally 'blue ribbon']

cordon sanitaire /kor-don san-i-tair/ *n.* **1** a guarded line between infected and uninfected districts. **2** any measure designed to prevent communication or the spread of undesirable influences. [French]

cordovan *n.* a kind of soft leather. [Spanish *cordovan* 'of Córdova', Spanish city where originally made]

corduroy *n.* **1** a thick cotton fabric with velvety ribs. **2** (in *pl.*) corduroy trousers. [18th-century coinage]

corduroy road *n.* a road made of tree trunks laid across a swamp.

cordwainer *n. Brit. archaic.* a shoemaker (usu. in names of guilds etc.). [from obsolete *cordwain* 'cordovan']

CORE *abbr.* (in the US) Congress of Racial Equality.

double reed

crook

upper joint conical wooden tube

C

key

middle joint

bell joint

bulb-shaped bell

COR ANGLAIS

CORDATE LEAF

CORDON

C

core ● *n.* **1** ▶ the horny central part of various fruits, containing the seeds. **2** the central or most important part of anything (also *attrib.*: *core curriculum*). **3** the central region of the Earth. ▷ EARTH. **4** the central part of a nuclear reactor, containing the fissile material. ▷ NUCLEAR POWER. **5** a magnetic structural unit in a computer, storing one bit of data (see BIT⁴). **6** the inner strand of an electric cable, rope, etc. **7** a piece of soft iron forming the centre of an electromagnet or an induction coil. ● *v.tr.* remove the core from. [Middle English] □ **corer** *n.* (usu. in *comb.*).

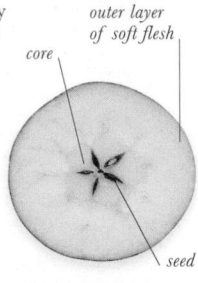

CORE: CROSS-SECTION OF AN APPLE SHOWING THE CORE

outer layer of soft flesh

core

seed

core memory *n.* the memory of a computer consisting of many cores.

coreopsis *n.* ▶ any plant of the genus *Coreopsis* (daisy family), having rayed usu. yellow flowers. [from Greek *koris* 'bug' + *opsis* 'appearance', with reference to the seed]

co-respondent *n.* (*US* **corespondent**) a person cited in a divorce case as having committed adultery with the respondent.

core time *n. Brit.* (in a flexitime system) the central part of the working day, when all employees must be present.

corgi *n.* (in full **Welsh corgi**) (*pl.* **corgis**) **1** ▼ a dog of a short-legged breed with fox-like head. **2** this breed. ▷ DOG. [from Welsh *cor* 'dwarf' + *ci* 'dog']

COREOPSIS
(*Coreopsis grandiflora*
'Early Sunrise')

CORGI:
WELSH CORGI

coriander *n.* **1** an umbelliferous plant, *Coriandrum sativum*, with leaves and fruits used for flavouring. ▷ HERB. **2** (also **coriander seed**) this fruit, dried. ▷ SPICE. [from Greek *koriannon*]

Corinthian ● *adj.* **1** of or relating to ancient Corinth in southern Greece. **2** *Archit.* ▲ of an order characterized by ornate decoration and flared capitals with acanthus leaves. ▷ COLUMN. ● *n.* a native of Corinth.

corium *n. Anat.* the dermis. [Latin, literally 'skin']

cork ● *n.* **1** ▶ the buoyant light brown material obtained from beneath the bark of the cork oak. **2** ▶ a bottle stopper of cork or other material. **3** a float of cork used in fishing

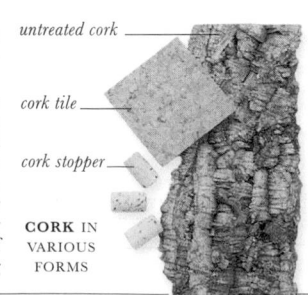

untreated cork

cork tile

cork stopper

CORK IN VARIOUS FORMS

CORINTHIAN

Corinthian is a term applied to one of the three principal orders of classical architecture. Invented in Athens in the 5th century BC, Corinthian architecture was also widely used by the ancient Romans, and borrowed some features from both the Doric and Ionian orders.

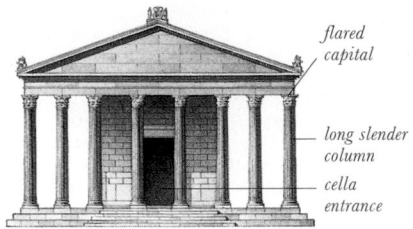

flared capital

long slender column

cella entrance

FRONT ELEVATION OF A CORINTHIAN TEMPLE

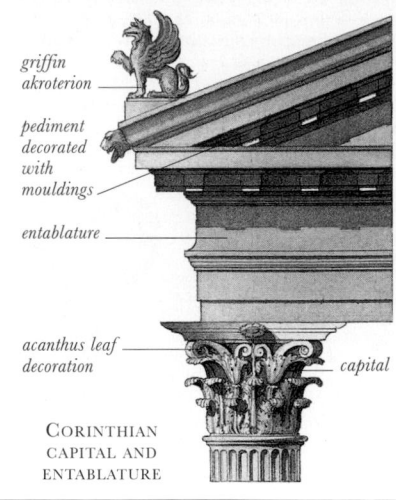

griffin akroterion

pediment decorated with mouldings

entablature

acanthus leaf decoration

capital

CORINTHIAN CAPITAL AND ENTABLATURE

---

etc. **4** (*attrib.*) made of cork. ● *v.tr.* (often foll. by *up*) **1** stop or confine. **2** restrain (feelings etc.). [from Spanish *alcorque* 'cork sole'] □ **corklike** *adj.*

corkage *n.* a charge made by a restaurant or hotel for serving wine etc. brought in by customers.

corked *adj.* **1** stopped with a cork. **2** (of wine) spoilt by a decayed cork.

corker *n. slang* an excellent or astonishing person or thing.

corking *adj.* esp. *Brit. slang* strikingly large or splendid.

cork oak *n.* ▶ an evergreen Mediterranean oak, *Quercus suber*, yielding cork.

corkscrew ● *n.* **1** a spiral device for extracting corks from bottles. **2** (often *attrib.*) a thing with a spiral shape. ● *v.tr. & intr.* move spirally; twist.

cork-tipped *adj. Brit.* (of a cigarette) having a filter of cork-like material.

corkwood *n.* **1** a shrub or tree yielding a light porous wood, esp. *Leitneria floridana* of the US and *Eritelea arborescens* of New Zealand. **2** this wood.

corky *adj.* (**corkier**, **corkiest**) **1** corklike. **2** (of wine) corked.

corm *n. Bot.* ▶ an underground swollen stem base of some plants, e.g. the crocus. [from Greek *kormos* 'trunk with boughs lopped off']

CORK OAK
(*Quercus suber*)

food storage tissue

cormel (young corm)

CORM: CROSS-SECTION OF A GLADIOLUS CORM

cormorant *n.* any diving seabird of the family Phalacrocoracidae, esp. *Phalacrocorax carbo*, which has lustrous black plumage. ▷ SEABIRD. [from medieval Latin *corvus marinus* 'sea-raven']

corn¹ ● *n.* **1 a** esp. *Brit.* any cereal before or after harvesting, esp. the chief crop of a region, e.g. wheat, oats, etc. **b** *US & Austral.*

= MAIZE. **c** a grain or seed of a cereal plant. **2** *colloq.* something corny or trite. ● *v.tr.* (as **corned** *adj.*) sprinkled or preserved with salt or brine (*corned beef*). [Old English]

corn² *n.* a small area of horny usu. tender skin esp. on the toes, extending into subcutaneous tissue. [from Latin *cornu* 'horn']

cornbread *n.* bread made of the meal of maize.

corn chandler *n.* a dealer in corn.

corn cob *n.* the cylindrical centre of the maize ear to which rows of grains are attached.

corn-cob pipe *n.* a tobacco pipe made from a corn cob.

corncrake *n.* a rail, *Crex crex*, with a rasping call, inhabiting grassland and nesting on the ground.

corn dog *n.* a hot dog sausage coated in cornmeal batter and deep-fried.

corn dolly *n. Brit.* a symbolic or decorative figure made of plaited straw.

cornea *n.* the transparent layer covering the front of the eye. ▷ EYE. [from medieval Latin *cornea tela* 'horny tissue'] □ **corneal** *adj.*

cornelian *n.* (also **carnelian**) **1** ▼ a dull red or reddish-white variety of chalcedony. ▷ GEM. **2** this colour. [from Old French *corneline*]

different coloured bands

CORNELIAN

corner ● *n.* **1** a place where converging sides or edges meet. **2** a projecting angle, esp. where two streets meet. **3** the internal space or recess formed by the meeting of two sides. **4** a difficult position, esp. one from which there is no escape (*driven into a corner*). **5** a secluded or remote place. **6** a region or quarter, esp. a remote one (*from the four corners of the Earth*). **7** the action or result of buying or controlling the whole available stock of a commodity, thereby dominating the market. **8** *Boxing & Wrestling* an angle of the ring, esp. one where a contestant rests between rounds. **9** *Football & Hockey* a free-kick or hit from a corner of the pitch. ● *v.* **1** *tr.* force (a person or animal) into a difficult or inescapable position. **2** *tr.* **a** establish a corner in (a commodity). **b** dominate (the market) in this way. **3** *intr.* (esp. of or in a vehicle) go round a corner. □ **just round** (or **around**) **the corner** *colloq.* very near; imminent. [based on Latin *cornu* 'horn']

cornerback n. (in American football etc.) a defensive player or position on the wing.

cornerstone n. **1** a stone in a projecting angle of a wall. **2** an indispensable part or basis of something.

cornerwise adv. diagonally.

cornet n. **1** Mus. ▼ a brass instrument resembling a trumpet but shorter and wider. ▷ BRASS. **2** Brit. a conical wafer for holding ice cream. [from Latin *cornu* 'horn'] □ **cornetist** n. (also **cornettist**).

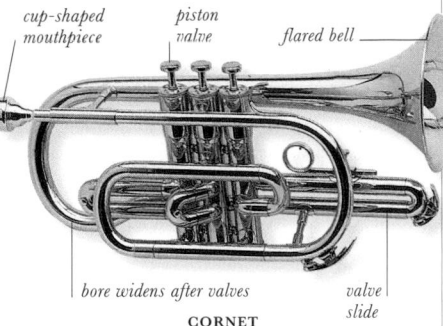

cup-shaped mouthpiece

piston valve

flared bell

bore widens after valves

valve slide

CORNET

corn exchange n. Brit. a place for trade in corn.

cornfield n. a field in which corn is being grown.

cornflake n. **1** (in pl.) a breakfast cereal of toasted flakes made from maize flour. **2** a flake of this cereal.

cornflour n. Brit. **1** a fine-ground maize flour. **2** a flour of rice or other grain.

cornflower n. any plant of the genus *Centaurea* (composite family), esp. *C. cyanus*, with deep blue flowers.

cornice n. Archit. **1** ▶ an ornamental moulding near the top of the wall of a room. **2** a horizontal moulded projection crowning a building or structure. ▷ ENTABLATURE. [from Italian] □ **corniced** adj.

cornice

moulded support

dentil

CORNICE FROM AN 18TH-CENTURY INTERIOR WALL

Cornish ● adj. of or relating to Cornwall in SW England, or its southern Celtic language. ● n. the ancient Celtic language of Cornwall. □ **Cornishman** n. (pl. **-men**).

Cornish cream n. clotted cream.

Cornish pasty n. a pasty containing seasoned meat and vegetables.

corn on the cob n. maize cooked and eaten from the corn cob.

corn salad n. = LAMB'S LETTUCE.

cornstarch n. = CORNFLOUR 1.

cornucopia n. **1 a** a symbol of plenty consisting of a goat's horn overflowing with flowers, fruit, and corn. **b** an ornamental vessel shaped like this. **2** an abundant supply. [from Latin *cornu copiae* 'horn of plenty'] □ **cornucopian** adj.

corn whiskey n. US whisky distilled from maize.

corny adj. (**cornier**, **corniest**) **1** colloq. trite. **2** feebly humorous. **3** sentimental. **4** old-fashioned; out of date. **5** of or abounding in corn. □ **cornily** adv. **corniness** n.

corolla n. Bot. a whorl or whorls of petals forming the inner envelope of a flower. [Latin, literally 'little crown']

corollary ● n. (pl. **-ies**) **1 a** a proposition that follows from (and is often appended to) one already proved. **b** an immediate deduction. **2** (often foll. by *of*) a natural consequence or result. ● adj. **1** supplementary, associated. **2** (often foll. by *to*) forming a corollary. [from Latin *corollarium* 'money paid for a garland, gratuity']

corona[1] /kŏ-roh-nă/ n. (pl. **coronae** /-nee/) **1 a** a small circle of light round the Sun or Moon. ▷ SUN. **b** the gaseous envelope of the Sun, seen as an area of light around the Moon's disc during a total solar eclipse. **2** Anat. a crown or crownlike structure. **3** Bot. ▶ a crownlike outgrowth from the inner side of a corolla. **4** Electr. the glow around a conductor at high potential. [Latin, literally 'crown'] □ **coronal** adj.

corona[2] n. a long cigar with straight sides. [originally a proprietary name]

coronary ● adj. Anat. resembling or encircling like a crown, esp. denoting or involving the arteries which supply blood to the heart. ● n. (pl. **-ies**) = CORONARY THROMBOSIS.

coronary thrombosis n. a blockage of the blood flow caused by a blood clot in a coronary artery.

coronation n. the ceremony of crowning a sovereign or a sovereign's consort.

coroner n. an official holding inquests on deaths thought to be violent or accidental, and Brit. inquiries in cases of treasure trove. [based on Anglo-French *cor(o)une* 'crown'] □ **coronership** n.

coronet n. **1** a small crown. **2** a circlet of precious materials, esp. as a headdress. [from Old French *coronet(e)*] □ **coroneted** adj.

Corp. abbr. **1** Corporal. **2** US Corporation.

corpora pl. of CORPUS.

corporal[1] n. a non-commissioned army or air force officer ranking next below sergeant. [from Italian *caporale*]

corporal[2] adj. of or relating to the human body. [from Latin *corporalis*] □ **corporally** adv.

corporality n. (pl. **-ies**) **1** material existence. **2** a body.

corporal punishment n. punishment inflicted on the body, esp. by beating.

corporate ● adj. **1** forming a corporation (*corporate body*). **2** forming one body of many individuals. **3** of or belonging to a corporation or group (*corporate responsibility*). ● n. a large industrial corporation. [from Latin *corporatus* 'formed into a body'] □ **corporately** adv. **corporatism** n. **corporatist** adj

corporate raider n. esp. US a person who mounts an unwelcome takeover bid by buying up a company's shares on the stock market.

corporation n. **1** a group of people authorized to act as an individual and recognized in law as a single entity, esp. in business. **2** Brit. the municipal authorities of a borough, town, or city. **3** joc. a protruding stomach.

corporative adj. **1** of a corporation. **2** governed by or organized in corporations, esp. of employers and employed. □ **corporativism** n.

corporeal /kor-por-iăl/ adj. bodily, physical, material, esp. as distinct from spiritual. [based on Latin *corpus -oris* 'body'] □ **corporeality** n. **corporeally** adv.

corps /kor/ n. (pl. **corps** /korz/) **1** Mil. **a** a body of troops with special duties (*intelligence corps*; *Royal Army Medical Corps*). **b** a main subdivision of an army in the field. **2** a body of people engaged in a special activity (*diplomatic corps*). [French, literally 'body']

corps de ballet /kor dĕ bal-ay/ n. the company of ensemble dancers in a ballet. [French]

corps diplomatique /dip-lŏ-ma-teek/ n. a diplomatic corps. [French]

corpse n. a dead (usu. human) body. [from Latin *corpus* 'body']

corpulent adj. bulky in body; fat. [from Latin *corpulentus*] □ **corpulence** n.

corpus n. (pl. **corpora** or **corpuses**) a body or

corona

corolla

CORONA OF A DAFFODIL

collection of writings, texts, spoken material, etc. [Latin, literally 'body']

corpuscle n. a minute body or cell in an organism, esp. (in pl.) the red or white cells in the blood of vertebrates. ▷ BLOOD. [from Latin *corpusculum*] □ **corpuscular** adj.

corpus delicti n. Law the facts and circumstances constituting a breach of a law. [Latin, literally 'body of offence']

corpus luteum n. Anat. a hormone-secreting structure developed in the ovary after discharge of the ovum, degenerating after a few days unless pregnancy has begun. ▷ OVARY. [Latin, literally 'yellow body']

corral /kŏ-rahl/ ● n. **1** N. Amer. a pen for cattle, horses, etc. **2** an enclosure for capturing wild animals. ● v.tr. (**corralled**, **corralling**) put or keep in a corral. [Spanish & Old Portuguese]

correct ● adj. **1** true, right, accurate. **2** (of conduct, manners, etc.) proper, right. ● v.tr. **1** set right; amend (an error, omission, etc., or person). **2** mark the errors in (work). **3** substitute the right thing for (the wrong one). **4 a** admonish or rebuke (a person). **b** punish (a person or fault). **5** counteract (a harmful quality). **6** adjust (an instrument etc.). [from Latin *correctus* 'made straight'] □ **correctable** adj. **correctly** adv. **correctness** n. **corrector** n.

correction n. **1 a** the act or process of correcting. **b** an instance of this. **2** a thing substituted for what is wrong. □ **correctional** adj.

correction fluid n. a usu. white liquid that is painted over a typed or written error leaving a blank space for typing or writing afresh.

correctitude n. correctness, esp. conscious correctness of conduct.

corrective ● adj. serving or tending to correct or counteract something undesired. ● n. a corrective measure or thing. □ **correctively** adv.

correlate ● v. **1** intr. (foll. by *with*, *to*) have a mutual relation. **2** tr. (usu. foll. by *with*) bring into a mutual relation. ● n. each of two related or complementary things.

correlation n. **1** a mutual relation between two or more things. **2** interdependence of variable quantities. **3** the act of correlating. [from medieval Latin *correlatio*] □ **correlational** adj.

correlative ● adj. **1** (often foll. by *with*, *to*) having a mutual relation. **2** Gram. (of words) corresponding to each other and regularly used together (as *neither* and *nor*). ● n. a correlative word or thing. [from medieval Latin *correlativus*] □ **correlatively** adv. **correlativity** n.

correspond v.intr. **1 a** (usu. foll. by *to*) be analogous or similar. **b** (usu. foll. by *to*) agree in amount, position, etc. **c** (usu. foll. by *with*, *to*) be in harmony or agreement. **2** (usu. foll. by *with*) communicate by interchange of letters. [from medieval Latin *correspondere*] □ **correspondingly** adv.

correspondence n. **1** (usu. foll. by *with*, *to*, *between*) agreement, similarity, or harmony. **2 a** communication by letters. **b** letters sent or received.

correspondence course n. a course of study conducted by post.

correspondent ● n. **1** a person who writes letters, esp. regularly. **2** a person employed to contribute material for a periodical or for broadcasting. ● adj. (often foll. by *to*, *with*) archaic corresponding.

corrida n. **1** a bullfight. **2** bullfighting. [from Spanish *corrida de toros* 'running of bulls']

corridor n. **1** a passage from which doors lead to rooms. **2** Brit. a passage in a railway carriage from which doors lead to compartments. **3** a strip of the territory of one state passing through that of another, esp. to the sea. **4** a route to which aircraft are restricted, esp. over a foreign country. [based on Italian *corridojo* 'running-place', by confusion with *corridore* 'runner']

corrie n. esp. Sc. a circular hollow on a mountainside; a cirque. [from Gaelic *coire* 'cauldron']

C

corrigendum *n.* (*pl.* **corrigenda**) an error to be corrected in a book. [Latin, literally 'thing to be corrected']

corrigible *adj.* **1** capable of being corrected. **2** (of a person) submissive; open to correction. [from medieval Latin *corrigibilis*] □ **corrigibly** *adv.*

corroborate *v.tr.* confirm or give support to (a statement or belief, or the person holding it). [based on Latin *corroboratus* 'strengthened'] □ **corroboration** *n.* **corroborative** *adj.* **corroborator** *n.* **corroboratory** *adj.*

corrode *v.* **1 a** *tr.* wear away, esp. by chemical action. **b** *intr.* be worn away; decay. **2** *tr.* destroy gradually. [from Latin *corrodere*] □ **corrodible** *adj.*

corrosion *n.* **1** the process of corroding, esp. of a rusting metal. **2** damage caused by corroding.

corrosive ● *adj.* tending to corrode or consume. ● *n.* a corrosive substance. [from Old French *corrosif -ive*] □ **corrosively** *adv.* **corrosiveness** *n.*

corrugate *v.tr.* (esp. as **corrugated** *adj.*) form into alternate ridges and grooves, esp. to strengthen (*corrugated iron*; *corrugated paper*). [based on Latin *ruga* 'wrinkle'] □ **corrugation** *n.*

corrupt ● *adj.* **1** morally depraved; wicked. **2** influenced by or using bribery or fraudulent activity. **3** (of a text, language, etc.) harmed (esp. made suspect or unreliable) by errors or alterations. ● *v.* **1** *tr. & intr.* make or become corrupt or depraved. **2** *tr.* affect or harm by errors or alterations. [from Latin *corruptus* 'ruined'] □ **corrupter** *n.* **corruptible** *adj.* **corruptibility** *n.* **corruptive** *adj.* **corruptly** *adv.*

corruption *n.* **1** moral deterioration, esp. widespread. **2** use of corrupt practices, esp. bribery or fraud. **3 a** irregular alteration (of a text, language, etc.) from its original state. **b** an irregularly altered form of a word.

corsage *n.* a small bouquet worn by a woman. [based on Old French *cors* 'body']

corsair *n.* **1** a pirate ship. **2** a pirate. [based on Latin *currere* 'to run']

corselet var. of CORSLET, CORSELETTE.

corselette *n.* (also **corselet**) ▶ a woman's garment combining corset and brassiere.

corset ● *n.* **1** a close-fitting undergarment worn by women to shape and support the abdomen. **2** a similar garment worn by men and women because of injury, weakness, or deformity. ● *v.tr.* (**corseted**, **corseting**) **1** provide with a corset. **2** control closely. □ **corseted** *adj.* **corsetry** *n.*

Corsican ● *adj.* of or relating to Corsica. ● *n.* a native of Corsica.

corslet *n.* (also **corselet**) **1** a garment (usu. tight-fitting) covering the trunk but not the limbs. **2** *hist.* a piece of armour covering the trunk. [from Old French *corselet* 'little body']

cortège /kor-**tayzh**/ *n.* a procession, esp. a funeral. [from Italian *corteggio*]

cortex *n.* (*pl.* **cortices** /kor-ti-seez/) *Anat.* the outer part of an organ, esp. of the brain (**cerebral cortex**) or kidneys (**renal cortex**). ▷ KIDNEY. [Latin, literally 'bark'] □ **cortical** *adj.*

corticate *adj.* (also **corticated**) **1** having bark or rind. **2** barklike.

corticosteroid *n.* **1** any of a group of steroid hormones produced in the adrenal cortex and concerned with regulation of salts and carbohy-

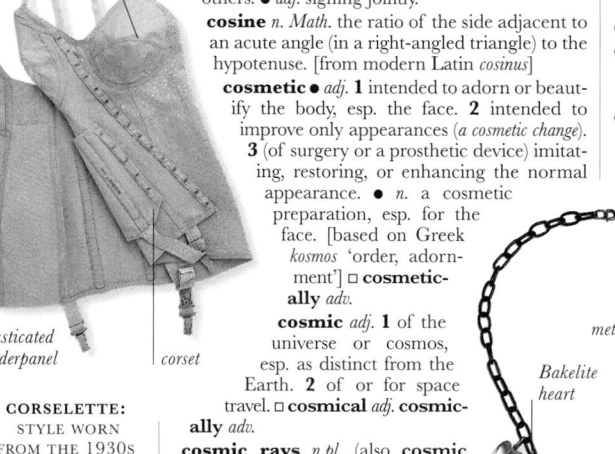

brassiere

elasticated underpanel

corset

CORSELETTE:
STYLE WORN
FROM THE 1930S
TO THE 1950S

drates, inflammation, and sexual physiology. **2** an analogous synthetic steroid.

cortisol *n.* = HYDROCORTISONE.

cortisone *n.* *Biochem.* a steroid hormone used medicinally esp. against inflammation and allergy. [from chemical name 17-hydroxy-11-dehydro*corti*coster*one*]

corundum *n.* *Mineral.* ▶ extremely hard crystallized alumina, used esp. as an abrasive, and varieties of which, e.g. ruby and sapphire, are used for gemstones. [from Sanskrit *kuruvinda* 'ruby']

coruscate *v.intr.* give off flashing light; sparkle. [based on Latin *coruscatus* 'vibrated, made to sparkle'] □ **coruscation** *n.*

CORUNDUM

corvette *n.* *Naut.* **1** a small naval escort vessel. **2** *hist.* a flush-decked warship with one tier of guns. [based on Middle Dutch *korf* 'basket, ship']

corvine *adj.* of or like a raven or crow. [based on Latin *corvus* 'raven']

corymb /ko-rimb/ *n.* *Bot.* a flat-topped cluster of flowers with the flower stalks proportionally longer lower down the stem. ▷ INFLORESCENCE. [from Greek *korumbos* 'cluster'] □ **corymbose** *adj.*

cos[1] *n.* a variety of lettuce with narrow leaves forming a long upright head. [from *Kōs* (formerly *Cos*), name of a Greek island]

cos[2] *abbr.* cosine.

cos[3] *conj. & adv.* (also **'cos**) *colloq.* because. [abbreviation]

cosec *abbr.* cosecant.

cosecant *n.* *Math.* the ratio of the hypotenuse (in a right-angled triangle) to the side opposite an acute angle; the reciprocal of sine.

cosh[1] *Brit. colloq.* ● *n.* a heavy blunt weapon. ● *v.tr.* hit with a cosh. [19th-century coinage]

cosh[2] *abbr.* *Math.* hyperbolic cosine.

co-signatory (*US* **cosignatory**) ● *n.* (*pl.* **-ies**) a person or state signing a treaty etc. jointly with others. ● *adj.* signing jointly.

cosine *n.* *Math.* the ratio of the side adjacent to an acute angle (in a right-angled triangle) to the hypotenuse. [from modern Latin *cosinus*]

cosmetic ● *adj.* **1** intended to adorn or beautify the body, esp. the face. **2** intended to improve only appearances (*a cosmetic change*). **3** (of surgery or a prosthetic device) imitating, restoring, or enhancing the normal appearance. ● *n.* a cosmetic preparation, esp. for the face. [based on Greek *kosmos* 'order, adornment'] □ **cosmetically** *adv.*

cosmic *adj.* **1** of the universe or cosmos, esp. as distinct from the Earth. **2** of or for space travel. □ **cosmical** *adj.* **cosmically** *adv.*

cosmic rays *n.pl.* (also **cosmic radiation**) radiation from space etc. that reaches the Earth from all directions.

cosmogony *n.* (*pl.* **-ies**) **1** the origin of the universe. **2** a theory about this. [from Greek *kosmogonia*] □ **cosmogonic** *adj.* **cosmogonical** *adj.* **cosmogonist** *n.*

cosmography *n.* (*pl.* **-ies**) a description or mapping of general features of the universe. □ **cosmographer** *n.* **cosmographical** *adj.*

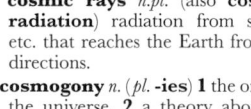

metal chain

Bakelite heart

emblem of King George VI

COSTUME JEWELLERY:
1930S BAKELITE
NECKLACE

cosmology *n.* **1** the science of the origin and development of the universe. **2** an account or theory of the origin of the universe. □ **cosmological** *adj.* **cosmologist** *n.*

cosmonaut *n.* a Russian astronaut. [Russian]

cosmopolitan ● *adj.* **1 a** of or from or knowing many parts of the world. **b** consisting of people from many or all parts. **2** free from national limitations or prejudices. ● *n.* a cosmopolitan person. [based on Greek *kosmopolitēs* 'citizen of the world'] □ **cosmopolitanism** *n.* **cosmopolitanize** *v.tr. & intr.* (also **-ise**).

cosmos *n.* the universe, esp. as a well-ordered whole. [from Greek *kosmos* 'order, world']

Cossack ● *n.* a member of a people of southern Russia, Ukraine, and Siberia. ● *adj.* of, relating to, or characteristic of the Cossacks. [from Turkic, literally 'vagabond']

cosset *v.tr.* (**cosseted**, **cosseting**) pamper. [dialect word, literally 'pet lamb']

cost ● *v.tr.* (*past* and *past part.* **cost**) **1** be obtainable for (a sum of money); have as a price (*what does it cost?*). **2** involve as a loss or sacrifice (*it cost him his life*). **3** (*past* and *past part.* **costed**) fix or estimate the cost or price of. ● *n.* **1** what a thing costs; its price. **2** a loss or sacrifice; an expenditure of time, effort, etc. **3** (in *pl.*) legal expenses. □ **at all costs** (or **at any cost**) no matter what the cost or risk may be. **to a person's cost** with loss or disadvantage to a person. [from Latin *constare* 'to stand firm, stand at a price']

costal *adj.* of the ribs. [based on Latin *costa* 'rib']

co-star ● *n.* a cinema or stage star appearing with another or others of equal importance. ● *v.* (**-starred**, **-starring**) **1** *intr.* take part as a co-star. **2** *tr.* (of a production) include as a co-star.

costard *n.* *Brit.* a large ribbed variety of apple.

costate *adj.* ribbed; having ribs or ridges.

cost-conscious *adj.* aware of cost or costs.

cost-cutting *n.* the cutting of costs (often *attrib.*: *cost-cutting measures*).

cost-effective *adj.* effective or productive in relation to its cost. □ **cost-effectively** *adv.* **cost-effectiveness** *n.*

cost-efficient *adj.* = COST-EFFECTIVE. □ **cost-efficiency** *n.*

coster *n.* *Brit.* = COSTERMONGER.

costermonger *n.* *Brit.* a person who sells fruit, vegetables, etc., in the street from a barrow. [based on COSTARD]

costing *n.* (often in *pl.*) **1** the determination of the cost of producing or undertaking something. **2** the cost so arrived at.

costive *adj.* **1** constipated. **2** niggardly. [from Latin *constipatus* 'pressed together'] □ **costively** *adv.* **costiveness** *n.*

costly *adj.* (**costlier**, **costliest**) **1** costing much; expensive. **2** of great value. □ **costliness** *n.*

cost of living *n.* the level of prices esp. of the basic necessities of life.

cost price *n.* *Brit.* the price paid for a thing by a person etc. who later sells it.

costume ● *n.* **1** a style or fashion of dress, esp. that of a particular place, time, or class. **2** a set of clothes. **3** clothing for a particular activity (*swimming costume*). **4** an actor's clothes for a part. **5** *Brit.* a woman's matching jacket and suit. ● *v.tr.* provide with a costume. [from Latin *consuetudo* 'custom']

costume jewellery *n.* ◀ artificial jewellery.

costume play *n.* (also **costume piece**) a play in which the actors wear historical costume.

costumier *n.* (also **costumer**) a person who makes or deals in costumes, esp. for theatrical use.

cosy (*US* **cozy**) ● *adj.* (**cosier, cosiest**) **1** comfortable and warm. **2** *derog.* complacent; expedient, self-serving. **3** warm and friendly. ● *n.* (*pl.* **-ies**) a cover to keep something hot, esp. a teapot or a boiled egg. ● *v.tr.* (**-ies, -ied**) (often foll. by *along*) *colloq.* reassure, esp. deceptively. [originally Scots] □ **cosily** *adv.* **cosiness** *n.*

cot[1] *n.* **1** *Brit.* a small bed with high sides, esp. for a baby. **2** a hospital bed. **3** *US* a small folding bed. [from Hindi *khāṭ* 'bedstead, hammock']

cot[2] *n.* **1** a small shelter; a cote (*sheep-cot*). **2** *poet.* a cottage. [Old English]

cot[3] *abbr. Math.* cotangent.

cotangent *n. Math.* the ratio of the side adjacent to an acute angle (in a right-angled triangle) to the opposite side.

cot death *n. Brit.* the unexplained death of a baby while sleeping.

cote *n.* a shelter, esp. for animals or birds; a shed or stall (*sheep-cote*). [Old English, related to COT[2]]

coterie *n.* an exclusive group of people sharing interests. [French, originally in sense 'association of tenants']

coterminous *adj.* (often foll. by *with*) having the same boundaries or extent (in space, time, or meaning).

coth /koth, kot-**aych**/ *abbr. Math.* hyperbolic cotangent.

cotoneaster /kŏ-toh-ni-**ass**-ter/ *n.* ◄ a shrub of the genus *Cotoneaster* (rose family), bearing usu. bright red berries. [based on Latin *cotoneum* 'quince']

cottage *n.* a small simple house, esp. in the country. [from Anglo-Latin *cotāgium*] □ **cottagey** *adj.*

cottage cheese *n.* soft white lumpy cheese made from curds of skimmed milk.

COTONEASTER
(*Cotoneaster frigidus*)

cottage garden *n.* an informal garden well-stocked with colourful traditional hardy plants.

cottage hospital *n. Brit.* a small hospital not having resident medical staff.

cottage industry *n.* a business activity partly or wholly carried on at home.

cottage pie *n. Brit.* a dish of minced meat topped with browned mashed potato.

cottager *n.* a person who lives in a cottage.

cotter *n.* **1** a bolt or wedge for securing parts of machinery etc. **2** (in full **cotter pin**) a split pin that opens after passing through a hole. [17th-century coinage, related to earlier *cotterel*]

cotton ● *n.* **1** a soft white fibrous substance covering the seeds of certain plants. **2** (in full **cotton plant**) ▼ a plant of the genus *Gossypium* (mallow family), grown for this fibre. **3** thread or cloth made from the fibre. ▷ ROPE. ● *v.intr.* (foll. by *to*) be attracted by (a person). □ **cotton on** (often foll. by *to*) *colloq.* begin to understand. [from Arabic *ḳuṭn*] □ **cottony** *adj.*

remains of fruit capsule

cotton cake *n.* compressed cotton seed used as food for cattle.

cotton candy *n. N. Amer.* candyfloss.

cotton grass *n.* any grasslike plant of the genus *Eriophorum*, with long white silky hairs.

seed-hairs (cotton)

COTTON BOLL

cotton-picking *adj. N. Amer. slang* unpleasant, wretched.

cotton waste *n.* refuse yarn used to clean machinery etc.

cottonwood *n.* **1** any of several poplars, native to N. America, having seeds covered in white cottony hairs. **2** any of several trees native to Australia, esp. a downy-leaved tree, *Bedfordia salicina.*

cotton wool *n.* **1** *esp. Brit.* fluffy wadding originally made from raw cotton. **2** *US* raw cotton.

cotyledon /kot-i-lee-dŏn/ *n.*
Bot. ► an embryonic leaf in seed bearing plants, one or more of which are the first leaves to appear from a germinating seed. [from Greek *kotulēdōn* 'cup-shaped cavity'] □ **cotyledonary** *adj.*

true leaf

cotyledons

couch[1] ● *n.* **1** an upholstered piece of furniture for several people; a sofa. **2** a long padded seat with a headrest at one end. ● *v.tr.* (foll. by *in*) express in words of a specified kind (*couched in simple language*). [based on Latin *collocare* 'to lodge, lay']

couch[2] *n.* (in full **couch grass**) any of several grasses of the genus *Agropyron*, esp. *A. repens*, having long creeping roots. ▷ GRASS. [variant of QUITCH]

COTYLEDONS ON A DICOTYLEDONOUS SEEDLING

couchette /koo-**shet**/ *n.* **1** a railway carriage with seats convertible into sleeping berths. **2** a berth in this. [French, literally 'little bed']

couch potato *n. esp. N. Amer. slang* a person who likes lazing at home, esp. watching television.

cougar /**koo**-ger/ *n. N. Amer.* a puma. [French]

cough ● *v.intr.* **1** expel air from the lungs with a sudden sharp sound to remove an obstruction or congestion. **2** (of an engine, gun, etc.) make a similar sound. **3** *Brit. slang* confess. ● *n.* **1** an act of coughing. **2** a condition of the respiratory organs causing coughing. □ **cough up 1** eject by coughing. **2** *colloq.* bring out or give (money or information) reluctantly. [Middle English]

cough drop *n.* (also **cough sweet**) a medicated lozenge for relieving a cough.

cough mixture *n.* a liquid medicine for relieving a cough.

could *past* of CAN[1].

couldn't *contr.* could not.

coulis /**koo**-li/ *n.* (*pl.* same) a fruit purée thin enough to pour. [French, from *couler* 'to flow']

coulomb /**koo**-lom/ *n. Electr.* the SI unit of electric charge. [named after C. A. de *Coulomb*, French physicist, 1736–1806]

coulter /**kohl**-ter/ *n.* (*US* **colter**) a vertical cutting blade fixed in front of a ploughshare. [from Latin *culter*]

council *n.* **1 a** an advisory, deliberative, or administrative body of people. **b** a meeting of such a body. **2** *Brit.* **a** the elected local administrative body of a parish, town, etc. **b** (*attrib.*) (esp. of housing) provided by a local council. [from Latin *concilium* 'convocation, assembly']

council chamber *n. Brit.* a room in which a council meets.

council house *n. Brit.* **1** a house owned and let by a local council. **2** a building in which a council meets.

councillor *n.* (*US* **councilor**) an elected member of a council, esp. *Brit.* a local council or *US* a deliberative council. □ **councillorship** *n.*

councilman *n.* (*pl.* **-men**; *fem.* **councilwoman**, *pl.* **-women**) esp. *US* a member of a council; a councillor.

council tax *n.* a tax levied by local authorities,

based on the estimated value of a property and the number of people living in it.

counsel ● *n.* **1** advice, esp. formally given. **2** consultation, esp. to seek or give advice. **3** (*pl.* same) a barrister or other legal adviser; a body of these in a case. ● *v.tr.* (**counselled, counselling**; *US* **counseled, counseling**) **1** (often foll. by *to* + infin.) advise (a person). **2** give advice to (a person) on personal problems, esp. professionally. **3** (often foll. by *that*) recommend (a course of action). □ **keep one's own counsel** not confide in others. **take counsel** (usu. foll. by *with*) consult. [from Latin *consilium* 'consultation, advice'] □ **counselling** *n.* (*US* **counseling**).

counsellor *n.* (*US* **counselor**) **1** an adviser. **2** a person trained to give guidance on personal problems. **3** a senior officer in the diplomatic service. **4** (also **counselor-at-law**) *US* a barrister.

counsel of despair *n.* action to be taken when all else fails.

counsel of perfection *n.* advice that is ideal but not feasible.

count[1] ● *v.* **1** *tr.* determine the total number or amount of, esp. by assigning successive numbers. **2** *intr.* repeat numbers in ascending order. **3 a** *tr.* (often foll. by *in*; often as **counting** *prep.*) include in one's reckoning or plan (*you can count me in*; *fifteen people, counting the guide*). **b** *intr.* be included in a reckoning or plan. **4** *tr.* consider (a thing or a person) to be (lucky etc.). **5** *intr.* (often foll. by *for*) have value; matter (*his opinion counts for a great deal*). ● *n.* **1 a** the act of counting (*after a count of fifty*). **b** the sum total of a reckoning (*pollen count*). **2** *Law* each charge in an indictment (*guilty on ten counts*). □ **count against** be reckoned to the disadvantage of. **count one's chickens** (**before they are hatched**) be over-optimistic or hasty in anticipating good fortune. **count the cost** consider the risks before taking action; calculate the damage resulting from an action. **count down** recite numbers backwards to zero, esp. as part of a rocket-launching procedure. **count on** (or **upon**) depend on, rely on; expect confidently. **count out 1** count while taking from a stock. **2** complete a count of ten seconds over (a fallen boxer etc.), indicating defeat. **3** *colloq.* exclude from a plan or reckoning (*I'm too tired, count me out*). **count up** find the sum of. **keep count** take note of how many there have been etc. **lose count** fail to take note of how many there have been etc.; forget the number noted in counting. **not counting** excluding from the reckoning (see sense 3a of the *v.*). **out for the count 1** *Boxing* defeated by being unable to rise within ten seconds. **2** soundly asleep; unconscious. [from Late Latin *computare* 'to compute']

count[2] *n.* a foreign noble corresponding to an earl. [from Latin *comes comitis* 'member of the imperial retinue'] □ **countship** *n.*

countable *adj.* that can be counted.

countable noun *n. Gram.* a noun that can form a plural or be used with the indefinite article (e.g. *book*, *kindness*, meaning 'a kind act'). Cf. UNCOUNTABLE NOUN, MASS NOUN.

countdown *n.* **1** the act of counting down, esp. at the launching of a rocket etc. **2** the final moments before any significant event.

countenance ● *n.* **1 a** the face. **b** the facial expression. **2** composure. **3** moral support. ● *v.tr.* **1** give approval to (an act etc.). **2** (often foll. by *in*) encourage (a person or a practice). □ **keep one's countenance** maintain composure, esp. by refraining from laughter. **out of countenance** disconcerted. [from Old French *contenance* 'bearing']

counter[1] *n.* **1 a** a long flat-topped fitment in a shop, bank, etc., across which business is conducted. **b** a similar structure used for serving food etc. in a cafeteria or bar. **c** *N. Amer.* = WORKTOP. **2 a** a small disc used for keeping the score etc. esp. in table games. **b** a token representing a coin. **c** something used in bargaining (*a counter in the struggle for power*). **3** an apparatus used for counting. □ **over the counter**

C

by ordinary retail purchase (see also OVER-THE-COUNTER). **under the counter** (esp. of the sale of scarce goods) surreptitiously, esp. illegally (see also UNDER-THE-COUNTER). [based on Latin *computare* 'to count']

counter² ● *v.* **1** *tr.* **a** oppose, contradict (*countered our proposal with their own*). **b** meet by a countermove. **2** *intr.* **a** make a countermove. **b** make an opposing statement. ● *adv.* **1** in the opposite direction (*ran counter to the fox*). **2** contrary (*his action was counter to my wishes*). ● *adj.* opposed; opposite. ● *n.* **1** a parry; a countermove. **2** something opposite or opposed. □ **run counter to** act contrary to. [from Latin *contra* 'against']

counter- *prefix* denoting: **1** retaliation, opposition, or rivalry (*counter-demonstration; counter-inflationary*). **2** opposite direction (*counter-current*). **3** correspondence, duplication, or substitution (*counterpart; countersign*).

counteract *v.tr.* **1** hinder or oppose by contrary action. **2** neutralize. □ **counteraction** *n.* **counteractive** *adj.*

counter-attack ● *n.* an attack in reply to an attack by an enemy or opponent. ● *v.tr. & intr.* attack in reply.

counter-attraction *n.* a rival attraction.

counterbalance ● *n.* **1** a weight balancing another. **2** an argument, force, etc., balancing another. ● *v.tr.* act as a counterbalance to.

counterblast *n.* (often foll. by *to*) an energetic or violent verbal or written reply to an argument etc.

countercharge ● *n.* a charge or accusation in return for one received. ● *v.tr.* make a countercharge against.

counter-claim ● *n.* **1** a claim made against another claim. **2** *Law* a claim made by a defendant in a suit against the plaintiff. ● *v.tr. & intr.* make a counter-claim (for).

counter-clockwise *adv. & adj.* N. Amer. = ANTICLOCKWISE.

counter-culture *n.* a way of life etc. opposed to that usually considered normal.

counter-espionage *n.* action taken to frustrate enemy spying.

counterfeit /kown-ter-fit/ ● *adj.* not genuine. ● *n.* a forgery; an imitation. ● *v.tr.* **1** imitate fraudulently (a coin, handwriting, etc.); forge. **2** simulate (feelings etc.) (*counterfeited interest*). [from Old French *countrefait* 'made in opposition'] □ **counterfeiter** *n.*

counterfoil *n.* esp. *Brit.* the part of a cheque, receipt, etc., retained by the issuer and containing details of the transaction.

counter-insurgency *n.* (usu. *attrib.*) action against insurrection (*counter-insurgency operations*).

counter-intelligence *n.* = COUNTER-ESPIONAGE.

counter-intuitive *adj.* contrary to intuition.

countermand *v.tr. Mil.* **1** revoke (an order or command). **2** recall (forces etc.) by a contrary order. [from medieval Latin *contramandare*]

countermarch ● *v.intr. & tr.* esp. *Mil.* march or cause to march in the opposite direction. ● *n.* an act of countermarching.

countermeasure *n.* an action taken to counteract a danger, threat, etc.

countermove ● *n.* a move or action in opposition to another. ● *v.intr.* make a countermove. □ **counter-movement** *n.*

counter-offensive *n.* esp. *Mil.* an attack made from a defensive position.

counterpane *n.* a bedspread. [from medieval Latin *culcita puncta* 'quilted mattress']

counterpart *n.* **1** a person or thing extremely like another. **2** a natural complement or equivalent.

counterplot ● *n.* a plot intended to defeat another plot. ● *v.intr.* (**-plotted**, **-plotting**) *intr.* make a counterplot.

counterpoint ● *n.* **1** *Mus.* **a** the art of writing melodies in conjunction with another, according to fixed rules. **b** a melody played in conjunction with another. **2** a contrasting argument, plot, idea, etc., used to set off the main element. ● *v.tr.* **1** *Mus.* add counterpoint to. **2** set (an argument, plot, etc.) in contrast to (a main element). [from medieval Latin *contrapunctum* 'pricked opposite']

counterpoise ● *n.* **1** a force etc. equivalent to another on the opposite side. **2** a state of equilibrium. ● *v.tr.* counterbalance. [from Old French *contrepois*]

counter-productive *adj.* having the opposite of the desired effect.

Counter-Reformation *n. hist.* the reform of the Church of Rome in the 16th and 17th c. which took place in response to the Protestant Reformation.

counter-revolution *n.* a revolution opposing a former one or reversing its results. □ **counter-revolutionary** *adj. & n.* (*pl.* **-ies**).

countersign ● *v.tr.* add a signature to (a document already signed by another). ● *n.* **1** a watchword or password spoken to a person on guard. **2** a mark used for identification etc. □ **counter-signature** *n.*

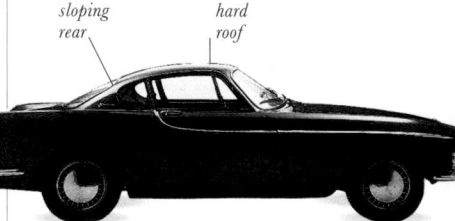

countersink drill bit

countersunk hole

COUNTERSINK

countersink *v.tr.* (*past* and *past part.* **-sunk**) **1** ◄ enlarge and bevel the rim of (a hole) so that a screw or bolt can be inserted flush with the surface. **2** sink (a screw etc.) in such a hole.

counterstroke *n.* a blow given in return for another.

counter-tenor *n. Mus.* **1 a** a male alto singing voice. **b** a singer with this voice. **2** a part written for counter-tenor.

countertop *n.* N. Amer. = WORKTOP.

countervail *v.* **1** *tr.* counterbalance. **2** *tr. & intr.* (often foll. by *against*) oppose forcefully and usu. successfully. [from Latin *contra valēre* 'to be of worth against']

counterweight *n.* a counterbalancing weight.

countess *n.* **1** the wife or widow of a count or an earl. **2** a woman holding the rank of count or earl.

counting house *n.* a place where accounts are kept.

countless *adj.* too many to be counted.

count noun *n. Gram.* = COUNTABLE NOUN.

Count Palatine *n. hist.* a high official of the Holy Roman Empire with royal authority within his domain.

countrified *adj.* (also **countryfied**) often *derog.* rural or rustic, esp. of manners, appearance, etc.

country *n.* (*pl.* **-ies**) **1 a** the territory of a nation with its own government; a state. **b** a territory possessing its own language, people, culture, etc. **2** (often *attrib.*) rural districts as opposed to towns or the capital. **3** the land of a person's birth or citizenship. **4** a territory, esp. an area of interest or knowledge. **5** a national population, esp. as voters (*the country won't stand for it*). □ **across country** not keeping to roads. **go** (or **appeal**) **to the country** *Brit.* test public opinion by dissolving Parliament and holding a general election. **line of country** *Brit.* a subject about which a person is knowledgeable. [from medieval Latin *contrata* (*terra*) '(land) lying opposite']

country and western *n.* rural or cowboy songs originating in the US, and usu. accompanied by a guitar etc.

country club *n.* a sporting and social club in a rural setting.

countryfied var. of COUNTRIFIED.

country gentleman *n.* a gentleman with landed property.

countryman *n.* (*pl.* **-men**; *fem.* **countrywoman**, *pl.* **-women**) **1** a person living in a rural area. **2 a** (also **fellow countryman**) a person of one's own

country or district. **b** (often in *comb.*) a person from a specified country or district (*north-countryman*).

country music *n.* = COUNTRY AND WESTERN.

countryside *n.* **1** a rural area. **2** rural areas in general.

countrywoman see COUNTRYMAN.

county ● *n.* (*pl.* **-ies**) **1** a territorial division of some countries, forming the chief unit of local administration. **2** *US* a political and administrative division of a state. ● *adj. Brit.* having the social status or characteristics of the gentry. [from Latin *comitatus* 'domain of a count']

county council *n.* the elected governing body of an administrative county. □ **county councillor** *n.*

county court *n.* a judicial court for civil cases (in the US for civil and criminal cases).

county town *n.* (*US* **county seat**) the administrative capital of a county.

coup /koo/ *n.* (*pl.* **coups**) **1** a notable or successful stroke or move. **2** = COUP D'ÉTAT. [French, literally 'blow']

coup de grâce /koo dĕ **grahss**/ *n.* (*pl.* **coups de grâce** *pronunc.* same) a finishing stroke, esp. to kill a wounded animal or person. [French, literally 'stroke of grace']

coup d'état /koo day-**tah**/ *n.* (*pl.* **coups d'état** *pronunc.* same) a violent and illegal seizure of power. [French, literally 'blow of State']

coupé /**koo**-pay/ *n.* (*US* **coupe** /koop/) ▼ a car with a hard roof, esp. one with two seats and a sloping rear. [French, literally 'cut']

sloping rear

hard roof

COUPÉ: 1961 VOLVO P1800
TWO-PLUS-TWO COUPÉ

couple ● *n.* **1** (usu. foll. by *of*; often treated as *sing.*) **a** two (*a couple of girls*). **b** about two (*a couple of hours*). **2** (often treated as *sing.*) a married, engaged, or similar pair. **b** a pair of partners in a dance, a game, etc. **3** (*pl.* **couple**) a pair of hunting dogs (*six couple of hounds*). ● *v.* **1** *tr.* fasten or link together; connect (esp. railway carriages). **2** *tr.* (often foll. by *together, with*) associate in thought or speech (*papers coupled their names*). **3** *tr. & intr.* (often foll. by *with, up* (*with*)) bring or come together as companions or partners. **4** *intr.* copulate. [from Latin *copula* 'connection']

coupler *n.* anything that connects two things, esp. a transformer used for connecting electric circuits.

couplet *n. Prosody* two successive lines of verse, usu. rhyming and of the same length.

coupling *n.* **1 a** a link connecting railway carriages etc. ▷ TENDER. **b** a device for connecting parts of machinery. **2** *Mus.* **a** the arrangement of items on a gramophone record. **b** each such item.

coupon *n.* **1** a form in a newspaper, to be filled in as an application for a purchase, information, etc. **2** *Brit.* a form for participation in a football pool or other competition. **3** a voucher for a discount on a purchase. **4 a** a detachable ticket entitling the holder to a ration of food, clothes, etc., esp. in wartime. **b** a similar ticket entitling the holder to payment, goods, services, etc. [French, literally 'piece cut off']

courage *n.* the ability to disregard one's fear; bravery. □ **have the courage of one's convictions** have the courage to act on one's beliefs. **lose courage** become less brave. **pluck up** (or **take**) **courage** muster one's courage. [based on Latin *cor* 'heart']

C

courageous *adj.* brave, fearless. □ **courageously** *adv.* **courageousness** *n.*

courgette /koor-**zhet**/ *n. Brit.* a small green variety of vegetable marrow. Also called ZUCCHINI. [French, literally 'little gourd']

courier *n.* **1** a person employed to guide and assist a group of tourists. **2** a special messenger. [based on Latin *currere* 'to run']

course ● *n.* **1** a continuous onward movement or progression. **2 a** a line along which a person or thing moves; a direction taken (*has changed course; the course of the winding river*). **3 a** a stretch of land or water used for races. **b** a golf course. **4** a series of lectures, lessons, etc., in a particular subject. **5** any of the successive parts of a meal. **6** *Med.* a sequence of medical treatment etc. (*prescribed a course of antibiotics*). **7** a line of conduct. **8** *Archit.* a continuous horizontal layer of brick, stone, etc., in a building. **9** a channel in which water flows. ● *v.* **1** *intr.* (esp. of liquid) run, esp. fast (*blood coursed through his veins*). **2** *tr.* (also *absol.*) **a** use hounds to hunt. **b** pursue (hares etc.) in hunting. □ **the course of nature** ordinary events or procedure. **in course of** in the process of. **in the course of** during. **of course** naturally; as is or was to be expected; admittedly. **on** (or **off**) **course** following (or deviating from) the desired direction or goal. [from Latin *cursus* 'a running'] □ **courser** *n.* (in sense 2 of *v.*).

courser *n. poet.* a swift horse. [from Old French *corsier*]

coursework *n.* the work done during a course of study, esp. when counting towards a student's final assessment.

court ● *n.* **1** (in full **court of law**) **a** a body of persons presided over by a judge, judges, or a magistrate, and acting as a tribunal in civil and criminal cases. **b** = COURTROOM. **2** an enclosed quadrangular area for games, which may be open or covered (*tennis court; squash court*). **3 a** a small enclosed street in a town, having a yard surrounded by houses, and adjoining a larger street. **b** *Brit.* = COURTYARD. **c** (**Court**) the name of a large house, block of flats, street, etc. (*Grosvenor Court*). **d** (at Cambridge University) a college quadrangle. **4 a** the establishment, retinue, and courtiers of a sovereign. **b** a sovereign and his or her councillors, constituting a ruling power. **c** a sovereign's residence. **d** an assembly held by a sovereign; a state reception. **5** attention paid to a person whose favour, love, or interest is sought (*paid court to her*). ● *v.tr.* **1 a** try to win the affection or favour of (a person). **b** pay amorous attention to (also *absol.*: *courting couples*). **2** seek to win (applause, fame, etc.). **3** invite (misfortune) by one's actions (*you are courting disaster*). □ **go to court** take legal action. **in court** appearing as a party or an advocate in a court of law. **out of court 1** before a hearing or judgement can take place. **2** not worthy of consideration (*that suggestion is out of court*). [from Latin *cohors cohort-* 'yard, retinue']

court card *n. Brit.* ◀ a playing card that is a king, queen, or jack.

courteous /**ker**-ti-ŭs/ *adj.* polite, kind, or considerate. [from Old French *corteis*] □ **courteously** *adv.* **courteousness** *n.*

courtesan /kor-ti-**zan**/ *n. literary* a prostitute, esp. one with wealthy or upper-class clients. [from Italian *cortigiana* 'female courtier']

courtesy /**ker**-ti-si/ *n.* (*pl.* **-ies**) **1** courteous behaviour. **2** a courteous act. □ **by**

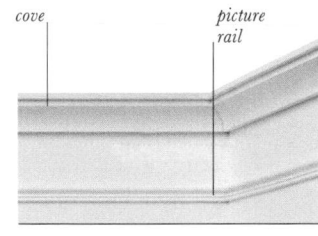

COURT CARDS

king

queen

jack

courtesy by favour, not by right. **by courtesy of** with the formal permission of (a person etc.). [from Old French *co(u)rtesie*]

courtesy light *n.* a light in a car that is switched on by opening a door.

courthouse *n.* **1** a building in which a judicial court is held. **2** *US* a building containing the administrative offices of a county.

courtier *n.* a person who attends or frequents a sovereign's court.

courtly *adj.* (**courtlier, courtliest**) polished or refined in manners. □ **courtliness** *n.*

courtly love *n.* the conventional medieval tradition of knightly love for a lady, and the etiquette used in its (esp. literary) expression.

court martial ● *n.* (*pl.* **courts martial**) a judicial court for trying members of the armed services. ● *v.tr.* (**court-martial**) (**-martialled, -martialling;** *US* **-martialed, -martialing**) try by a court martial.

Court of Appeal *n.* (*US* **Court of appeals**) a court of law hearing appeals against judgements in the Crown Court, High Court, County Court, etc.

court of law see COURT *n.* 1.

Court of Session *n.* the supreme civil court in Scotland.

Court of St James's *n.* the British sovereign's court.

court order *n.* a direction issued by a court or a judge, usu. requiring a person to do or not do something.

courtroom *n.* the place or room in which a court of law meets.

courtship *n.* **1 a** a courting with a view to marriage. **b** the courting behaviour of male animals, birds, etc. **c** a period of courting. **2** an attempt to gain advantage by flattery, attention, etc.

court shoe *n. Brit.* a woman's light, usu. high-heeled, shoe with a low-cut upper.

courtyard *n.* an area enclosed by walls or buildings, often opening off a street.

couscous /**kooss**-kooss/ *n.* **1** ▶ a type of N. African semolina in granules made from crushed durum wheat. **2** a spicy dish of this, usu. with meat or fruit added. [from Arabic *kuskus*]

cousin *n.* **1** (also **first cousin, cousin german** (*pl.* **cousins german**)) a child of one's uncle or aunt. **2** (usu. in *pl.*) applied to the people of kindred races or nations (*our American cousins*). □ **first cousin once removed 1** a child of one's first cousin. **2** one's parent's first cousin. **first cousin twice removed 1** a grandchild of one's first cousin. **2** one's grandparent's first cousin. **second cousin** a child of one's parent's first cousin. **second cousin once removed 1** a child of one's second cousin. **2** one's parent's second cousin. [from Latin *consobrinus* 'mother's sister's child'] □ **cousinhood** *n.* **cousinly** *adj.* **cousinship** *n.*

couth *adj. joc.* cultured; well-mannered. [back-formation as antonym of UNCOUTH]

couture /koo-**tewr**/ *n.* the design and manufacture of fashionable clothes; = HAUTE COUTURE. [French, literally 'sewing']

couturier /koo-**tewr**-i-ay/ *n.* (*fem.* **couturière** /koo-tewr-i-**air**/) a fashion designer or dressmaker.

couverture *n. Brit.* chocolate for covering sweets, cakes, etc. [French, = covering]

covalency *n. Chem.* **1** the linking of atoms by a covalent bond. **2** the number of pairs of electrons an atom can share with another.

covalent *adj. Chem.* ▶ of or designating chemical bonds formed by the sharing of electrons by two atoms in a molecule. ▷ ALKANE. [based on Late Latin *valentia* 'power'] □ **covalently** *adv.*

COUSCOUS

cove[1] ● *n.* **1** a small, esp. sheltered, bay or creek. **2** a sheltered recess. **3** *Archit.* ▼ a concave arch or arched moulding, esp. between a wall and a ceiling. ● *v.tr. Archit.* **1** provide (a room, ceiling, etc.) with a cove. **2** slope (the sides of a fireplace) inwards. [Old English *cofa* 'chamber']

cove　　　　　*picture rail*

COVE

cove[2] *n. Brit. slang* a fellow; a chap. [16th-century coinage]

coven /**kuv**-ĕn/ *n.* a group of witches. [variant of *covent*, from Latin *conventus* 'assembly']

covenant ● *n.* **1** an agreement; a contract. **2** *Law* a contract drawn up under a seal, esp. undertaking to make regular payments to a charity. **3** (**Covenant**) *Bibl.* the agreement between God and the Israelites (see ARK OF THE COVENANT). ● *v.tr. & intr.* agree, esp. by legal covenant. [from Old French, literally 'agreeing'] □ **covenantal** *adj.* **covenantor** *n.* (also **covenanter**).

Coventry *n.* □ **send a person to Coventry** esp. *Brit.* refuse to associate with or speak to a person. [from *Coventry*, a city in the W. Midlands]

cover ● *v.tr.* **1** (often foll. by *with*) protect or conceal by means of a cloth, lid, etc. **2 a** extend over; occupy the whole surface of (*covered in dirt; covered with writing*). **b** (often foll. by *with*) strew thickly or thoroughly (*covered the floor with straw*). **c** lie over; be a covering to (*the blanket scarcely covered him*). **3 a** protect; clothe. **b** (as **covered** *adj.*) wearing a hat; having a roof. **4** include; comprise; deal with (*the talk covered recent discoveries*). **5** travel (a specified distance) (*covered sixty miles*). **6** *Journalism* report (events, a meeting, etc.). **7** be enough to defray (expenses, a bill, etc.). **8 a** *refl.* take precautionary

COVALENT

Covalent compounds consist of molecules whose atoms are held together by covalent bonds. For example, an ammonia molecule is made up of three hydrogen atoms and one nitrogen atom. Each covalent bond consists of two shared electrons – one from the nitrogen atom and one from a hydrogen atom.

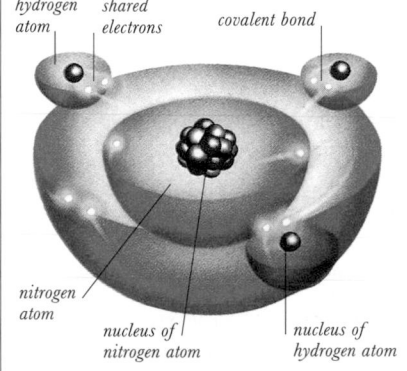

hydrogen atom　　*shared electrons*　　*covalent bond*

nitrogen atom

nucleus of nitrogen atom　　*nucleus of hydrogen atom*

COVALENT BONDS IN AN AMMONIA MOLECULE (NH_3)

C

measures so as to protect oneself (*had covered myself by saying I might be late*). **b** (*absol.*; foll. by *for*) deputize or stand in for (a colleague etc.) (*will you cover for me?*). **9** *Mil.* **a** aim a gun etc. at. **b** (of a fortress, guns, etc.) command (a territory). **c** protect (an exposed person etc.) by being able to return fire. **10** (in team games) mark (a corresponding player of the other side). **11** make a cover version of (a song etc.) **12** (of a stallion, a bull, etc.) copulate with. ● *n.* **1** something that covers or protects, esp.: **a** a lid. **b** the binding of a book. **c** either board of this. **d** an envelope or the wrapper of a parcel (*under separate cover*). **e** (in *pl.*) bedclothes. **2** a hiding place; a shelter. **3** woods or undergrowth sheltering game or covering the ground (cf. COVERT *n.* 1). **4 a** a pretence; a screen (*under cover of humility*). **b** a spy's pretended identity or activity. **c** *Mil.* a supporting force protecting an advance party from attack. **5** *Brit.* **a** funds, esp. obtained by insurance, to meet a liability or secure against a contingent loss. **b** the state of being so protected (*third-party cover*). **6** a place setting at table, esp. in a restaurant. **7** *Cricket* = COVER POINT. **8** (in full **cover version**) a recording of a previously recorded song etc. □ **break cover** (of game or a hunted person) leave a place of shelter, esp. vegetation. **cover one's tracks** conceal evidence of what one has done. **cover up 1** completely cover or conceal. **2** conceal (circumstances etc., esp. illicitly) (also *absol.*: *refused to cover up for them*). **from cover to cover** from beginning to end of a book etc. **take cover** use a natural or prepared shelter against an attack. [from Latin *cooperire*]

coverage *n.* **1** an area or an amount covered. **2** *Journalism* the amount of media publicity received by a particular story, person, etc.

coverall ● *n.* **1** something that covers entirely. **2** (usu. in *pl.*) a full-length protective outer garment often zipped up the front. ● *attrib.adj.* covering entirely (*a coverall term*).

cover charge *n.* an extra charge levied per head in a restaurant, nightclub, etc.

cover girl *n.* a female model whose picture appears on magazine covers etc.

covering *n.* something that covers, esp. a bedspread, blanket, etc., or clothing.

covering letter *n.* (also **covering note**) an explanatory letter (or note) sent with an enclosure.

coverlet *n.* a bedspread.

cover letter *n. N. Amer.* = COVERING LETTER.

cover note *n. Brit.* a temporary certificate of insurance.

cover point *n. Cricket* **1** a fielding position on the off side and halfway to the boundary. **2** a fielder at this position.

cover story *n.* a news story in a magazine, that is illustrated or advertised on the front cover.

covert ● *adj.* /kuv-ĕt, koh-vert/ secret or disguised (*a covert glance; covert operations*). ● *n.* /kuv-ĕt, kuv-er/ **1** a shelter, esp. a thicket hiding game. **2** a feather covering the base of a bird's flight feather. ▷ BIRD, FEATHER. [from Old French, literally 'covered'] □ **covertly** *adv.* **covertness** *n.*

cover-up *n.* an act of concealing circumstances, esp. illicitly.

cover version see COVER *n.* 8.

covet /kuv-it/ *v.tr.* (**coveted**, **coveting**) desire greatly (esp. something belonging to another person) (*coveted her friend's earrings*). [from Old French *coveiter*] □ **covetable** *adj.*

covetous *adj.* (usu. foll. by *of*) **1** greatly desirous (esp. of another person's property). **2** grasping, avaricious. □ **covetously** *adv.* **covetousness** *n.*

covey /kuv-i/ *n.* (*pl.* **-eys**) **1** a brood or flock of partridges. **2** a small party or group of people or things. [based on Latin *cubare* 'to lie']

coving *n.* = COVE[1] *n.* 3.

cow[1] *n.* **1** a fully grown female of any bovine animal, esp. of the genus *Bos*, used as a source of milk and beef. ▷ RUMINANT. **2** the female of other large animals, esp. the elephant, whale, and seal. **3** *colloq. derog.* **a** a woman. **b** *Austral. & NZ* an unpleasant person, thing, situation, etc. □ **till the cows come home** *colloq.* for an indefinitely long time. [Old English]

cow[2] *v.tr.* (usu. in *passive*) intimidate or dispirit (*cowed by ill-treatment*).

coward *n.* a person who is easily frightened or intimidated by danger or pain. [based on Latin *cauda* 'tail']

cowardice *n.* a lack of bravery.

cowardly *adj.* **1** of or like a coward; lacking courage. **2** (of an action) done against a person who cannot retaliate. □ **cowardliness** *n.*

cowbell *n.* ◀ a bell worn round a cow's neck for easy location of the animal.

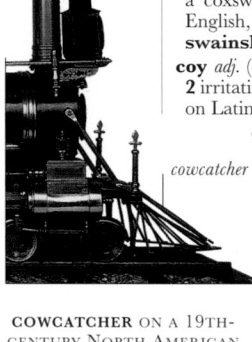
COWBELL

cowboy *n.* **1** (*fem.* **cowgirl**) a (usu. mounted) person who herds and tends cattle, esp. in the western US. **2** *colloq.* an unscrupulous or reckless person in business.

cowcatcher *n. N. Amer.* ▶ a peaked metal frame at the front of a locomotive for pushing aside obstacles on the line.

cowcatcher

COWCATCHER ON A 19TH-CENTURY NORTH AMERICAN LOCOMOTIVE

cower *v.intr.* crouch or shrink back, esp. in fear; cringe. [from Middle Low German *kūren* 'to lie in wait']

cowgirl see COWBOY 1.

cowherd *n.* a person who tends cattle.

cowhide *n.* **1** a cow's hide. **2** leather made from this.

cowl *n.* **1** the hood of a monk's habit. **2** the hood-shaped covering of a chimney or ventilating shaft. ▷ SHIP. **3** the removable cover of a vehicle or aircraft engine. ▷ AIRCRAFT, OUTBOARD. [from Latin *cucullus* 'hood of a cloak'] □ **cowled** *adj.* (in sense 1).

cow-lick *n.* a projecting lock of hair.

cowling *n.* = COWL 3.

cowl neck *n.* a neck on a woman's garment that hangs in draped folds (hyphenated when *attrib.*: *cowl-neck sweater*).

cowman *n.* (*pl.* **-men**) **1** = COWHERD. **2** *US* = COWBOY 1.

co-worker *n.* a person who works in collaboration with another.

cow-parsley *n.* a hedgerow plant, *Anthriscus sylvestris*, having lacelike umbels of flowers.

cow-pat *n.* a flat round piece of cow-dung.

cowpoke *n. N. Amer. colloq.* = COWBOY 1.

cowpox *n.* a disease of cows, of which the virus was formerly used in vaccination against smallpox.

cowpuncher *n. N. Amer. colloq.* = COWBOY 1.

cowrie *n.* (also **cowry**) (*pl.* **-ies**) **1** any gastropod mollusc of the family Cypraeidae, having a smooth, glossy, and often brightly coloured shell. ▷ SHELL. **2** ◀ its shell, formerly used as money in parts of Africa and S. Asia. [from Urdu & Hindi *kaurī*]

co-write *v.tr.* (*past* **co-wrote**; *past part.* **co-written**) write (a book, song, etc.) together with another person. □ **co-writer** *n.*

cowshed *n.* **1** a shed for cattle that are not at pasture. **2** a milking shed.

columellar lip   *outer lip*

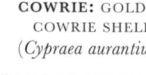

canal   *teeth*

COWRIE: GOLDEN COWRIE SHELL (*Cypraea aurantium*)

cowslip *n.* **1** ▶ a primula, *Primula veris*, with fragrant yellow flowers and growing in pastures. **2** *US* a marsh marigold. [Old English, from *cū* 'cow' + *slyppe* 'slimy substance', i.e. cowdung]

Cox *n.* (in full **Cox's orange pippin**) a variety of apple with a red-tinged green skin. [bred by R. Cox, English amateur fruit-grower, *c.*1776–1845]

COWSLIP (*Primula veris*)

cox ● *n.* a coxswain, esp. of a racing boat. ● *v.* **1** *intr.* act as a cox (*coxed for Cambridge*). **2** *tr.* act as cox for (*coxed the winning boat*).

coxcomb *n.* an ostentatiously conceited man; a dandy. [variant of COCKSCOMB, originally (a cap worn by) a jester] □ **coxcombry** *n.* (*pl.* **-ies**)

coxswain /kok-sŭn/ *n.* **1** the steersman of a ship's boat, lifeboat, racing boat, etc. **2** *Brit.* the senior petty officer in a small ship. ● *v.* **1** *intr.* act as a coxswain. **2** *tr.* act as a coxswain of. [Middle English, based on *cock* 'a small ship's boat'] □ **coxswainship** *n.*

coy *adj.* (**coyer**, **coyest**) **1** archly or affectedly shy. **2** irritatingly reticent (*always coy about her age*). [based on Latin *quietus* 'quiet'] □ **coyly** *adv.* **coyness** *n.*

coyote /koy-oh-ti/ *n.* (*pl.* same or **coyotes**) a wolflike wild dog, *Canis latrans*, native to N. America. [from Aztec *coyotl*]

coypu *n.* (*pl.* **coypus**) an aquatic beaver-like rodent, *Myocastor coypus*, native to S. America and kept in captivity for its fur. [Araucanian (a Chilean language)]

cozen *v. literary* **1** *tr.* (often foll. by *of, out of*) cheat, defraud. **2** *tr.* (often foll. by *into*) beguile; persuade. **3** *intr.* act deceitfully. [16th-century coinage] □ **cozenage** *n.*

cozy *US var. of* COSY.

Cpl *abbr.* Corporal.

CPO *abbr.* Chief Petty Officer.

CPS *abbr.* (in the UK) Crown Prosecution Service.

cps *abbr.* (also **c.p.s.**) **1** *Computing* characters per second. **2** cycles per second.

CPU *abbr. Computing* central processing unit.

Cr *symb. Chem.* the element chromium.

crab[1] *n.* **1 a** ▶ a ten-footed crustacean having the first pair of legs modified as pincers. **b** the flesh of a crab, esp. *Cancer pagurus*, as food. **2** (**the Crab**) the zodiacal sign or constellation Cancer. ▷ CANCER. **3** (in full **crab louse**) (often in *pl.*) a parasitic louse, *Phthirus pubis*, infesting hairy parts of the body. □ **catch a crab** *Rowing* jam the oar under water or miss the water altogether. [Old English] □ **crab-like** *adj.*

crab[2] *n.* **1** (in full **crab apple**) ▶ a small sour apple-like fruit. **2** (in full **crab tree** or **crab-apple tree**) a tree that bears such fruit, esp. the European wild apple, *Malus sylvestris*. [Middle English]

CRAB APPLE (*Malus* 'Crittenden')

crab[3] *v.* (**crabbed**, **crabbing**) *colloq.* **1** *tr. & intr.* criticize adversely or captiously; grumble. **2** *tr.* spoil (*the mistake crabbed his chances*). [from Middle Low German *krabben*]

crabbed *adj.* **1** = CRABBY. **2** (of handwriting) ill-formed and hard to decipher. [Middle English, based on CRAB[1]] □ **crabbedly** *adv.* **crabbedness** *n.*

CRAB

Crabs live in many different aquatic habitats, and – particularly in the Tropics – on dry land. All have a carapace, but there are two types of body shape. Brachyuran crabs, such as the edible crab (below), have broad bodies, with a small abdomen tucked beneath. Anomuran crabs are usually long-bodied, often with a soft curled abdomen. Hermit crabs protect their abdomens by taking over the empty shells of molluscs.

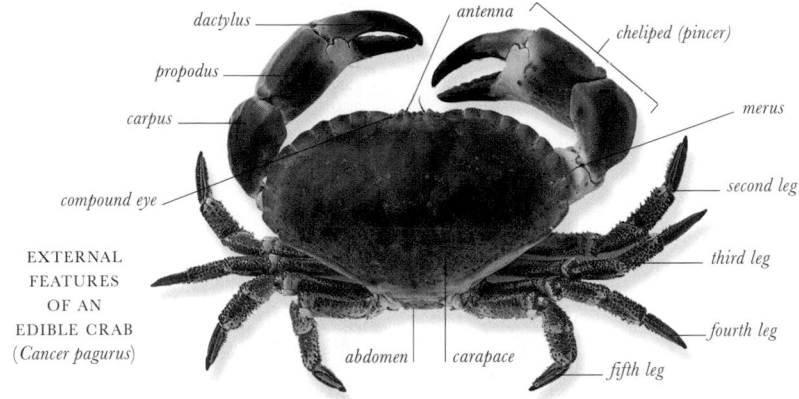

dactylus
propodus
carpus
compound eye
antenna
cheliped (pincer)
merus
second leg
third leg
fourth leg
abdomen
carapace
fifth leg

EXTERNAL
FEATURES
OF AN
EDIBLE CRAB
(*Cancer pagurus*)

EXAMPLES OF CRABS

BRACHYURANS

ANOMURANS

enlarged pincer (male only)
eye on long stalk
whelk shell
hermit crab

FIDDLER CRAB
(*Uca vocans*)

SHINY SPIDER CRAB
(*Maja squinado*)

HERMIT CRAB
(*Pagurus* species)

crabby *adj.* (**crabbier**, **crabbiest**) irritable; morose. □ **crabbily** *adv.* **crabbiness** *n.*

crabgrass *n.* a creeping grass.

crab louse see CRAB[1] 3.

crabmeat *n.* = CRAB[1] 1b.

crack ● *n.* **1 a** a sudden sharp or explosive noise, as of a whip or a rifle. **b** (in a voice) a sudden harshness or change in pitch. **2** a sharp blow (*a crack on the head*). **3 a** a narrow opening formed by a break. **b** a partial fracture, with the parts still joined. **c** a chink (*looked through the crack formed by the door*). **4** *colloq.* a mischievous or malicious remark or aside (*a nasty crack about my age*). **5** *colloq.* an attempt (*I'll have a crack at it*). **6** the exact moment (*the crack of dawn*). **7** *slang* a potent hard crystalline form of cocaine that is inhaled or smoked. ● *v.* **1** *tr. & intr.* break without a complete separation of the parts (*cracked the window*). **2** *intr. & tr.* make or cause to make a sudden sharp or explosive sound. **3** *intr. & tr.* break or cause to break with a sudden sharp sound. **4** *intr. & tr.* give way or cause to give way (under torture etc.); yield. **5** *intr.* (of the voice, esp. of an adolescent boy or a person under strain) become dissonant; break. **6** *tr. colloq.* find a solution to (a problem, code, etc.). **7** *tr.* say (a joke etc.). **8** *tr. colloq.* hit sharply or hard (*cracked her head on the ceiling*). **9** *tr. Chem.* decompose (heavy oils) to produce lighter hydrocarbons (such as petrol). **10** *tr.* break (wheat) into coarse pieces. ● *attrib.adj.* excellent; first-rate (*a crack shot*). □ **crack a bottle** open a bottle, esp. of wine, and drink it. **crack down on** *colloq.* take severe measures against. **cracked up to be** *colloq.* glowingly asserted to be. **crack up** *colloq.* **1** collapse under strain. **2** burst into laughter. **fair crack of the whip** *Brit. colloq.* a fair chance to participate etc.

get cracking *colloq.* begin promptly and vigorously. [Old English *cracian* 'to resound']

crack-brained *adj. colloq.* crazy.

crackdown *n. colloq.* severe measures (esp. against law-breakers etc.).

cracked *adj.* **1** having cracks. **2** (*predic.*) *slang* crazy.

cracked wheat *n.* wheat that has been crushed into small pieces.

cracker *n.* **1** a paper cylinder both ends of which are pulled at Christmas etc. making a sharp noise and releasing a small toy etc. **2** a firework exploding with a sharp noise. **3** (usu. in *pl.*) an instrument for cracking (*nutcrackers*). **4 a** a thin dry biscuit often eaten with cheese. **b** a light crisp made of rice or tapioca flour. **5** *Brit. slang* **a** an attractive person, esp. a woman. **b** a fine example of something. **6** *US offens.* = POOR WHITE.

cracker-barrel *attrib.adj. N. Amer.* unsophisticated.

crackers *predic.adj. slang* crazy.

cracking *Brit. slang* ● *adj.* **1** outstanding; very good (*a cracking performance*). **2** (*attrib.*) fast and exciting (*a cracking speed*). ● *adv.* outstandingly (*a cracking good time*).

crackle ● *v.intr.* (of a radio, fire, etc.) make a repeated slight cracking sound. ● *n.* such a sound. □ **crackly** *adj.*

crackling *n.* the crisp skin of roast pork.

cracknel *n.* a light crisp biscuit. [from Middle Dutch *krakelinc*]

crackpot *slang* ● *n.* an eccentric or impractical person. ● *adj.* mad, unworkable (*a crackpot scheme*).

crack-up *n. colloq.* a mental breakdown.

cradle ● *n.* **1 a** a child's bed or cot, esp. one mounted on rockers. **b** a place in which a thing begins, esp. a civilization etc. **2** a framework resembling a cradle, esp.: **a** that on which a ship, a boat, etc., rests during construction or repairs. **b** that on which a worker is suspended to work on a ceiling, a ship, the vertical side of a building, etc. **c** the part of a telephone on which the receiver rests when not in use. ● *v.tr.* **1** contain or shelter as if in a cradle (*cradled his head in her arms*). **2** place in a cradle. □ **from the cradle** from infancy. **from the cradle to the grave** from infancy till death. [Old English]

craft ● *n.* **1** skill, esp. in practical arts. **2 a** (esp. in *comb.*) a trade or an art (*statecraft*; *handicraft*; *priestcraft*; *the craft of pottery*). **b** the members of a craft. **3** (*pl.* **craft**) **a** a boat or other vessel. **b** an aircraft or spacecraft. **4** cunning or deceit. ● *v.tr.* make in a skilful way. [Old English]

craftsman *n.* (*pl.* **-men**; *fem.* **craftswoman**, *pl.* **-women**) **1** a skilled and usu. time-served worker. **2** a person who practises a handicraft. **3** *Brit.* a qualified private soldier in the Royal Electrical and Mechanical Engineers. □ **craftsmanship** *n.*

craftsperson *n.* (*pl.* **craftspeople**) a craftsman or craftswoman.

crafty *adj.* (**craftier**, **craftiest**) cunning, artful, wily. □ **craftily** *adv.* **craftiness** *n.*

crag *n.* a steep or rugged rock. [from Celtic]

craggy *adj.* (**craggier**, **craggiest**) **1** (esp. of a person's face) rugged; rough-textured. **2** (of a landscape) having crags. □ **craggily** *adv.* **cragginess** *n.*

crake *n.* a bird of the rail family, esp. a corncrake. [from Old Norse *kráka*]

cram *v.* (**crammed**, **cramming**) **1** *tr.* **a** fill to bursting; stuff (*the room was crammed*). **b** (foll. by *in*, *into*) force (a thing) into (*cram the sandwiches into the bag*). **2** *tr. & intr.* prepare for an examination by intensive study. **3** *tr.* (often foll. by *with*) feed (poultry etc.) to excess. **4** *tr. & intr. colloq.* eat greedily. [Old English]

cram-full *adj.* as full as possible.

crammer *n. Brit.* a person or institution that crams pupils for examinations.

cramp ● *n.* **1 a** a painful involuntary contraction of a muscle or muscles due to cold, exertion, etc. **b** = WRITER'S CRAMP. **2** (also **cramp-iron**) a metal bar with bent ends for holding masonry etc. together. **3** a portable tool for holding two planks etc. together; a clamp. **4** a restraint. ● *v.tr.* **1** affect with cramp. **2** confine narrowly. **3** restrict (energies etc.). **4** (as **cramped** *adj.*) (of handwriting) small and difficult to read. **5** fasten with a cramp. □ **cramp a person's style** prevent a person from acting freely or naturally. **cramp up** confine narrowly. [from Old High German *krampfo*, from an adjective meaning 'bent']

crampon *n.* (usu. in *pl.*) **1 ►** an iron plate with spikes fixed to a boot for walking on ice, climbing, etc. **2** a metal hook for lifting timber, rock, etc.; a grappling iron. [from French]

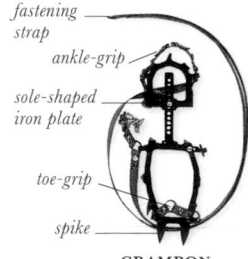

fastening strap
ankle-grip
sole-shaped iron plate
toe-grip
spike

CRAMPON

cranberry *n.* (*pl.* **-ies**) **1** any evergreen shrub of the genus *Vaccinium*, esp. *V. macrocarpon* of America and *V. oxycoccos* of Europe, yielding small red acid berries. **2** a berry from this used for a sauce and in cooking. Also called *fen-berry*. [named (17th c.) by American colonists from German *Kranbeere* 'crane-berry']

crane ● *n.* **1** a machine for moving heavy objects, usu. by suspending them from a projecting beam. **2** a tall bird of the family Gruidae, with long legs, long neck, and straight bill. **3** a moving platform supporting a television camera or cine-camera. ● *v.tr.* **1** (also *absol.*) stretch out (one's neck) in order to see something. **2** *tr.* move (an object) by a crane. [Old English]

C

crane-fly *n.* (*pl.* **-flies**) ▶ a large two-winged fly of the family Tipulidae, with very long legs. ▷ LEATHERJACKET

cranesbill *n.* any of various plants of the genus *Geranium*, with usu. purple, violet, or pink five-petalled flowers. [named from the long bill-like spur on the fruit]

CRANE-FLY: EUROPEAN
CRANE-FLY
(*Ctenophora ornata*)

cranial nerve *n. Anat.* each of twelve pairs of nerves arising directly from the brain, not from the spinal cord.

cranio- *comb. form* cranium.

craniology *n.* the scientific study of the shape and size of the human skull. □ **craniological** *adj.* **craniologist** *n.*

craniometry *n.* the scientific measurement of skulls. □ **craniometric** *adj.*

craniotomy *n.* (*pl.* **-ies**) **1** surgical removal of a portion of the skull. **2** surgical perforation of the skull of a dead foetus to ease delivery.

cranium *n.* (*pl.* **craniums** or **crania**) the skull, esp. the part that encloses the brain. ▷ SKELETON. [from Greek *kranion* 'skull'] □ **cranial** *adj.*

crank[1] ● *n.* part of an axle or shaft bent at right angles for interconverting reciprocal and circular motion. ● *v.tr.* cause to move by means of a crank. □ **crank up** start (a car engine) by turning a crank. [Old English]

crank[2] *n.* **1** an eccentric person. **2** *N. Amer.* a bad-tempered person. □ **cranky** *adj.* **crankily** *adv.* **crankiness** *n.*

crank[3] *adj. Naut.* liable to capsize.

crankcase *n.* a case enclosing a crankshaft.

crankpin *n.* a pin by which a connecting rod is attached to a crank. ▷ CRANKSHAFT

crankshaft *n.* ▼ a shaft driven by a crank (see CRANK[1] *n.*). ▷ INTERNAL-COMBUSTION ENGINE

crankshaft journal   *crankpin*   *balance weight*   *shaft*

CRANKSHAFT OF A CAR ENGINE

cranny *n.* (*pl.* **-ies**) a chink, a crevice. [based on popular Latin *crena* 'notch'] □ **crannied** *adj.*

crap *coarse slang* ● *n.* **1** (often as *int.*) nonsense, rubbish. **2** faeces. ● *v.intr.* (**crapped**, **crapping**) defecate. ● *adj.* of bad quality; useless. [earlier in senses 'chaff, refuse from fat-boiling': from Dutch *krappe*] □ **crappy** *adj.* (**crappier**, **crappiest**) *coarse slang*.

crape *n.* **1** crêpe, usu. of black silk or imitation silk, formerly used for mourning clothes. **2** a band of this formerly worn as a sign of mourning. [from French *crespe* 'curled'] □ **crapy** *adj.*

crape hair *n. Brit.* artificial hair used in stage make-up.

crap game *n.* a game of craps.

craps *n.pl. N. Amer.* a gambling game played with dice. □ **shoot craps** play craps. [19th-century coinage]

crapulent *adj. literary* **1** given to indulging in alcohol. **2** resulting from drunkenness. **3** drunk. [based on Greek *kraipalē* 'drunken headache'] □ **crapulence** *n.* **crapulous** *adj.*

crash[1] ● *v.* **1** *intr.* & *tr.* make or cause to make a loud smashing noise (*the cymbals crashed*). **2** *tr.* & *intr.* throw, drive, move, or fall with a loud smashing noise. **3** *intr.* & *tr.* **a** collide or cause (a vehicle) to collide violently with another vehicle, obstacle, etc. **b** fall or cause (an aircraft) to fall violently on to the land or the sea. **4** (usu. foll. by *into*) collide violently (*crashed into the window*). **5** *intr.* undergo financial ruin. **6** *tr. colloq.* enter without permission (*crashed the cocktail party*). **7** *intr. colloq.* be heavily defeated (*crashed to a 4–0 defeat*). **8** *intr. Computing* (of a machine or system) fail suddenly. **9** *tr. colloq.* pass (a red traffic light etc.). **10** *intr.* (often foll. by *out*) *slang* go to sleep. ● *n.* **1 a** a loud and sudden smashing noise. **b** a breakage (of crockery etc.). **2 a** a violent collision, esp. of one vehicle with another or with an object. **b** the violent fall of an aircraft on to the land or sea. **3** ruin, esp. financial. **4** *Computing* a sudden failure of a system. **5** (*attrib.*) done rapidly or urgently (*a crash diet*). ● *adv.* with a crash (*the window went crash*). [Middle English]

crash[2] *n.* a coarse plain linen, cotton, etc., fabric. [from Russian *krashenina* 'coloured linen']

crash barrier *n. Brit.* a barrier intended to prevent a vehicle from leaving the road etc.

crash-dive ● *v.* **1** *intr.* **a** (of a submarine or its pilot) dive hastily and steeply in an emergency. **b** (of an aircraft or its pilot) dive and crash. **2** *tr.* cause to crash-dive. ● *n.* such a dive.

crash helmet *n.* a helmet worn to protect the head in case of a crash.

crashing *adj. colloq.* overwhelming (*a crashing bore*).

crash-land *v.* **1** *intr.* (of an aircraft or its pilot) land hurriedly with a crash, usu. without lowering the undercarriage. **2** *tr.* cause (an aircraft) to crash-land. □ **crash landing** *n.*

crash pad *n. slang* a place to sleep.

crass *adj.* **1** grossly stupid. **2** gross (*crass stupidity*). **3** *literary* thick or gross. [from Latin *crassus* 'solid, thick'] □ **crassitude** *n.* **crassly** *adv.* **crassness** *n.*

-crat *comb. form* a member or supporter of a particular form of government or rule (*autocrat*; *democrat*). [from or suggested by French *-crate*]

crate ● *n.* **1** slatted wooden case etc. for conveying esp. fragile goods. **2** *slang* an old aeroplane or other vehicle. ● *v.tr.* pack in a crate. [Middle English] □ **crateful** *n.* (*pl.* **-fuls**).

crater ● *n.* **1** the mouth of a volcano. ▷ VOLCANO. **2** a bowl-shaped cavity, esp. that made by an explosion. **3** *Astron.* ▶ a hollow with a raised rim on the surface of a planet or moon, caused by impact. ▷ MOON. ● *v.tr.* form a crater in. [from Greek *kratēr* 'mixing-bowl'] □ **craterous** *adj.*

cravat *n.* a scarf worn by men inside an open-necked shirt. [from Serbo-Croat *Hrvat* 'Croat', from the scarf worn by Croatian mercenaries in France] □ **cravatted** *adj.*

crave *v.* **1** *tr.* **a** long for (*craved affection*). **b** beg for (*craves a blessing*). **2** (foll. by *for*) long for (*craved for comfort*). [Old English] □ **craver** *n.*

craven *adj.* (of a person, behaviour, etc.) cowardly; abject. [Middle English] □ **cravenly** *adv.* **cravenness** *n.*

craving *n.* (usu. foll. by *for*) a strong desire or longing.

craw *n. Zool.* the crop of a bird or insect. □ **stick in one's craw** be unacceptable. [Middle English]

crawfish ● *n.* (*pl.* same) esp. *N. Amer.* = CRAYFISH. ● *v.intr.* (often foll. by *out*) *US colloq.* retreat; back out. [variant of CRAYFISH]

crawl ● *v.intr.* **1** move slowly, esp. on hands and knees. **2** (of a snake etc.) move slowly with the body close to the ground etc. **3** proceed slowly (*the train crawled into the station*). **4** (often foll. by *to*) *colloq.* behave obsequiously or ingratiatingly in the hope of advantage. **5** (often foll. by *with*) be or appear to be covered or filled with crawling or moving things or people. **6** (esp. of the skin) feel a creepy sensation. ● *n.* **1** an act of crawling. **2** a slow rate of movement. **3** a high-speed swimming stroke with alternate overarm movements and rapid straight-legged kicks. **4** = PUB CRAWL. [Middle English] □ **crawly** *adj.* (in senses 5, 6 of *v.*).

crawler *n.* **1** *Brit. colloq.* a person who behaves obsequiously in the hope of advantage. **2** anything that crawls, such as an insect, a slow-moving vehicle, etc.

crawl space *n.* an underfloor space giving access to ducts.

crayfish *n.* (*pl.* same) **1** a small lobster-like freshwater crustacean, esp. of the genus *Astacus*. ▷ CRUSTACEAN. **2** = SPINY LOBSTER. [based on Old High German *krebiz* 'crab']

crayon ● *n.* **1** a stick or pencil of coloured chalk, wax, etc., used for drawing. **2** a drawing made with this. ● *v.tr.* draw with crayons. [French, based on Latin *creta* 'chalk']

craze ● *v.* **1** *tr.* (usu. as **crazed** *adj.*) make insane (*crazed with grief*). **2 a** *tr.* produce fine surface cracks on (pottery glaze etc.). **b** *intr.* develop such cracks. ● *n.* **1** a usu. temporary enthusiasm (*a craze for hula hoops*). **2** the object of this. [Middle English, originally in sense 'to break, shatter']

crazy ● *adj.* (**crazier**, **craziest**) **1** *colloq.* insane or mad; foolish. **2** (usu. foll. by *about*) *colloq.* extremely enthusiastic. **3** *slang* **a** exciting, unrestrained. **b** excellent. **4** (*attrib.*) (of paving etc.) made of irregular pieces fitted together. ● *n.* (*pl.* **-ies**) *colloq.* a crazy person or thing. □ **like crazy** *colloq.* = *like mad* (see MAD). □ **crazily** *adv.* **craziness** *n.*

CRC *abbr. Printing* camera-ready copy.

creak ● *n.* a harsh scraping or squeaking sound. ● *v.intr.* **1** make a creak. **2 a** move with a creaking noise. **b** move stiffly and awkwardly. **c** show weakness under strain. [Middle English] □ **creakingly** *adv.*

creaky *adj.* (**creakier**, **creakiest**) **1** liable to creak. **2 a** stiff or frail. **b** (of a practice etc.) decrepit, outmoded. □ **creakily** *adv.* **creakiness** *n.*

cream ● *n.* **1** the fatty content of milk. **2** the part of a liquid that gathers at the top. **3** (usu. prec. by *the*) the best or choicest part of something. **4** a cream-like preparation, esp. a cosmetic (*hand cream*). **5** a very pale yellow or off-white colour. **6 a** a dish or

CRATER

Meteoric craters are formed by lumps of interplanetary rock striking a planet's surface. Debris is blasted in all directions, creating a circular crater, while rock compressed by the impact rebounds. Gradually, the meteoric crater partly fills in as debris slips from the wall and peak.

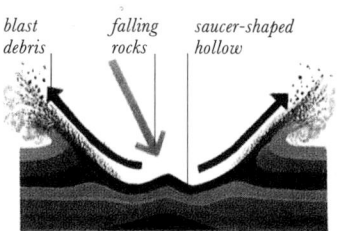

blast debris   *falling rocks*   *saucer-shaped hollow*

FORMATION OF A METEORIC CRATER

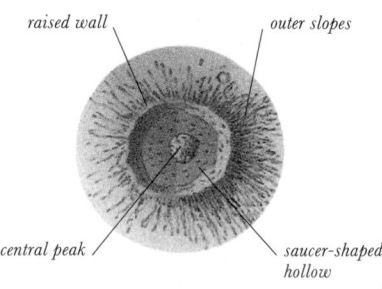

raised wall   *outer slopes*

central peak   *saucer-shaped hollow*

OVERHEAD VIEW OF A METEORIC CRATER

sweet like or made with cream. **b** a soup or sauce containing milk or cream. **c** a biscuit with a creamy sandwich filling. **d** a chocolate-covered fondant. ● *v.* **1** *tr.* **a** take the cream from (milk). **b** take the best or a specified part from. **2** *tr.* work (butter etc.) to a creamy consistency. **3** *tr.* add cream to (coffee etc.). **4** *intr.* (of milk or any other liquid) form a cream or scum. ● *adj.* pale yellow; off-white. □ **cream off** take (esp. the best part) from a whole. [from ecclesiastical Latin *chrisma* 'oil for anointing']

cream bun *n.* (also **cream cake**) *Brit.* a bun or cake filled or topped with cream.

cream cheese *n.* a soft rich cheese made from unskimmed milk and cream.

cream cracker *n. Brit.* a crisp dry unsweetened biscuit.

creamer *n.* **1** ▶ a flat dish used for skimming the cream off milk. **2** a machine used for separating cream from milk. **3** a cream or milk substitute for adding to coffee or tea. **4** *N. Amer.* a jug for cream.

creamery *n.* (*pl.* **-ies**) **1** a factory producing butter and cheese. **2** a dairy.

CREAMER

cream of tartar *n.* crystallized potassium hydrogen tartrate, used in medicine, baking powder, etc.

cream soda *n.* a carbonated vanilla-flavoured soft drink.

cream tea *n. Brit.* afternoon tea with scones, jam, and cream.

creamy *adj.* (**creamier**, **creamiest**) **1** like cream in consistency or colour. **2** rich in cream. □ **creamily** *adv.* **creaminess** *n.*

crease ● *n.* **1 a** a line in paper etc. caused by folding. **b** a fold or wrinkle. **2** *Cricket* a line marking the position of the bowler or batsman. ▷ CRICKET. ● *v.* **1** *tr.* make creases in (material). **2** *intr.* become creased (*linen creases badly*). **3** *tr. & intr.* (often foll. by *up*) *Brit. colloq.* make or become incapable through laughter. **4** *tr. esp. US slang* graze with a bullet. [earlier *creast* 'crest, ridge']

create *v.* **1** *tr.* **a** bring into existence (*poverty creates resentment*). **b** (of a person or persons) make or cause (*create a diversion*). **2** *tr.* originate (*an actor creates a part*). **3** *tr.* invest (a person) with a rank (*created him a lord*). **4** *intr. Brit. colloq.* make a fuss; grumble. [based on Latin *creatus* 'made, produced'] □ **creatable** *adj.*

creation *n.* **1 a** the act of creating. **b** an instance of this. **2 a** (usu. **the Creation**) the creating of the universe regarded as an act of God. **b** (usu. **Creation**) everything so created; the universe. **3** a product of human intelligence, esp. of imaginative thought or artistic ability. **4 a** the act of investing with a title or rank. **b** an instance of this.

creationism *n.* the belief that the universe and living organisms originate from specific acts of divine creation rather than by natural processes. □ **creationist** *n.*

creative *adj.* **1** inventive and imaginative. **2** creating or able to create. □ **creatively** *adv.* **creativeness** *n.* **creativity** *n.*

creative accountancy *n.* (also **creative accounting**) *colloq.* the exploitation of loopholes in financial legislation in order to gain advantage or present figures in a misleadingly favourable light.

creator *n.* **1** a person who creates. **2** (as **the Creator**) God.

creature *n.* **1 a** an animal, as distinct from a human being. **b** any living being (*we are all God's creatures*). **2** a person of a specified kind (*poor creature*). **3** a subservient person. **4** anything created. [from Latin *creatura* 'thing created'] □ **creaturely** *adj.*

creature comforts *n.pl.* material comforts such as good food, warmth, etc.

CREEL

crèche /kresh/ *n. Brit.* a day nursery for babies and young children. [French]

cred *n. colloq.* credibility.

credence *n.* belief. □ **give credence to** believe. [from medieval Latin *credentia*]

credential *n.* (usu. in *pl.*) **1** evidence of a person's achievements or trustworthiness, usu. in the form of certificates, references, etc. **2** a letter or letters of introduction.

credibility *n.* **1** the condition of being credible or believable. **2** reputation, status.

credible *adj.* **1** (of a person or statement) believable or worthy of belief. **2** (of a threat etc.) convincing. [based on Latin *credere* 'to believe'] □ **credibly** *adv.*

■ **Usage** Do not confuse *credible* 'able to be believed' with *credulous* 'too ready to believe'. The difference is illustrated by *he was such a credible trickster that he completely took in his credulous colleagues.*

credit ● *n.* **1** (usu. of a person) a source of honour, pride, etc. (*a credit to the school*). **2** the acknowledgement of merit (*must give him credit*). **3** a good reputation (*his credit stands high*). **4 a** belief or trust (*I place credit in that*). **b** something believable or trustworthy (*that statement has credit*). **5 a** a person's financial standing; the sum of money at a person's disposal in a bank etc. **b** the power to obtain goods etc. before payment. **6** (usu. in *pl.*) an acknowledgement of a contributor's services to a film etc. **7** *Brit.* a grade above a pass in an examination. **8** a reputation for solvency and honesty in business. **9** (in bookkeeping) **a** an entry in an account recording a payment received. **b** the sum entered. **c** the total of such sums. **d** the credit side of an account. **10** a unit of study counting towards a degree etc. ● *v.tr.* (**credited**, **crediting**) **1** believe (*cannot credit it*). **2** (usu. foll. by *to, with*; often in *passive*) **a** enter on the credit side of an account. **b** ascribe an achievement or good quality to (*he was credited with the goal*). **c** deem to be the originator or source of a thing (*now credited as its founder*). □ **do credit to** (or **do a person credit**) enhance the reputation of. **on credit** with an arrangement to pay later. **to one's credit** in one's praise or commendation. [from Latin *creditum* 'loan, thing entrusted']

creditable *adj.* (often foll. by *to*) bringing credit or honour. □ **creditability** *n.* **creditably** *adv.*

credit card *n.* a card from a bank etc. authorizing the obtaining of goods on credit.

credit note *n. Brit.* a note given by a shop etc. in return for goods returned, stating the value of goods owed to the customer.

creditor *n.* **1** a person to whom a debt is owing (cf. DEBTOR). **2** a person or company that gives credit for money or goods.

creditworthy *adj.* considered suitable to receive commercial credit. □ **creditworthiness** *n.*

credo *n.* (*pl.* **-os**) a statement of belief; a creed. [Latin, literally 'I believe']

credulous *adj.* too ready to believe; gullible. [from Latin *credulus*] □ **credulity** *n.* **credulously** *adv.* **credulousness** *n.*

■ **Usage** See Usage Note at CREDIBLE.

creed *n.* **1** a set of principles or opinions, esp. as a philosophy of life. **2** (also **Creed**) a brief formal summary of Christian belief. [Old English] □ **credal** *adj.* (also **creedal**)

creek *n.* **1** *Brit.* a small bay, harbour, or inlet. **2 a** esp. *US* a tributary of a river. **b** *Austral. & NZ* a stream or brook. □ **up the creek** *slang* **1** in difficulties. **2** crazy. [from Old Norse *kriki* 'nook']

creel *n.* ◀ a fisherman's large wicker basket. [Middle English, originally Scots]

creep ● *v.intr.* (*past* and *past part.* **crept**)

1 move with the body prone and close to the ground. **2** (often foll. by *in, out, up,* etc.) proceed slowly and stealthily or timidly. **3** enter slowly (into a person's awareness, etc.) (*a feeling crept over her*). **4** *colloq.* act obsequiously in the hope of advancement. **5** (of a plant) grow along the ground or up a wall. **6** (as **creeping** *adj.*) developing slowly and steadily (*creeping inflation*). **7** (of the flesh) feel as if insects etc. were creeping over it, as a result of fear etc. ● *n.* **1 a** the act of creeping. **b** an instance of this. **2** (in *pl.*; prec. by *the*) *colloq.* a feeling of revulsion or fear (*gives me the creeps*). **3** *colloq.* an unpleasant person. [Old English]

creeper *n.* **1** *Bot.* ▼ any climbing or creeping plant. **2** *slang* a soft-soled shoe. **3** any bird that climbs, esp. a treecreeper.

C

CREEPER: CREEPING JENNY
(*Lysimachia nummularia*)

creepy *adj.* (**creepier**, **creepiest**) **1** *colloq.* having or producing a creeping of the flesh (*a creepy film*). **2** given to creeping. □ **creepily** *adv.* **creepiness** *n.*

creepy-crawly *colloq.* ● *n.* (*pl.* **-ies**) an insect or other small crawling creature. ● *adj.* creeping and crawling.

cremate *v.tr.* burn (a corpse etc.) to ashes. [based on Latin *crematus* 'burnt'] □ **cremation** *n.* **cremator** *n.*

crematorium *n.* (*pl.* **crematoria** or **crematoriums**) a place for cremating corpses in a furnace.

crematory ● *adj.* of or relating to cremation. ● *n.* (*pl.* **-ies**) *N. Amer.* = CREMATORIUM.

crème de la crème /krem dĕ la **krem**/ *n.* the best part; the elite. [French, literally 'cream of the cream']

crème de menthe /krem dĕ **month**; *the vowel in* menthe *rhymes with* romp/ *n.* a peppermint-flavoured liqueur. [French, literally 'cream of mint']

crème fraîche *n.* a type of thick cream made from double cream with the addition of buttermilk, sour cream, or yogurt. [French *crème fraîche*, literally 'fresh cream']

crenellate *v.tr.* (also **crenelate**) ▶ provide (a tower etc.) with battlements or loopholes. [based on Latin *crena* 'notch'] □ **crenellation** *n.*

crenellated parapet

Creole ● *n.* **1 a** a descendant of European (esp. Spanish) settlers in the W. Indies or Central or S. America. **b** a white descendant of French settlers in the southern US. **c** a person of mixed European and black descent. **2** a mother tongue formed from the contact of a European language with another (esp. African) language. ● *adj.* **1** of or relating to a Creole or Creoles. **2** (usu. **creole**) of Creole origin or production (*creole cooking*). [from Spanish *criollo*]

CRENELLATE: SPANISH CASTLE TURRET WITH CRENELLATIONS

creosote ● *n.* **1** (in full **creosote oil**) a dark brown oil distilled from coal tar, used as a wood preservative. **2** a colourless oily fluid distilled from wood, used as an antiseptic. ● *v.tr.* treat with creosote. [from Greek *kreas* 'flesh' + *sōtēr* 'preserver', with reference to its antiseptic properties]

C

crêpe /krayp/ *n.* **1** a fine often gauzelike fabric with a wrinkled surface. **2** a thin pancake, usu. with a savoury or sweet filling. **3** (also **crêpe rubber**) a very hard-wearing wrinkled sheet rubber used for the soles of shoes etc. [from Latin *crispus* 'curly'] □ **crêpy** *adj.* (also **crêpey**).

crêpe de Chine /sheen/ *n.* a fine silk crêpe. [French, literally 'China crêpe']

crêpe paper *n.* thin crinkled paper.

crepitate *v.intr.* make a crackling sound. [based on Latin *crepitatus* 'crackled'] □ **crepitant** *adj.* **crepitation** *n.*

crept *past* and *past part.* of CREEP.

crepuscular *adj.* **1 a** of twilight. **b** dim. **2** *Zool.* appearing or active in twilight. [based on Latin *crepusculum* 'twilight']

crescendo /kri-**shen**-doh/ ● *n.* (*pl.* **-os** or **crescendi**) **1** *Mus.* **a** a gradual increase in loudness. **b** a passage to be performed with such an increase. **2** progress towards a climax (*a crescendo of emotions*). ● *adv. & adj. Mus.* with a gradual increase in loudness. [Italian, literally 'growing']

■ **Usage** When used figuratively, *crescendo* should mean 'progress towards a climax', not the climax itself.

crescent ● *n.* **1** the curved sickle shape of the waxing or waning Moon. ▷ LUNAR MONTH. **2** anything of this shape, esp. *Brit.* a street forming an arc. ● *adj.* **1** *poet.* increasing. **2** crescent-shaped. [from Latin *crescent-* 'growing, waxing'] □ **crescentic** *adj.*

cress *n.* any of various cruciferous plants usu. with pungent edible leaves. [Old English]

crest ● *n.* **1 a** a comb or tuft on a bird's or animal's head. ▷ LIZARD. **b** something resembling this. **2** the top of a mountain, wave, etc. **3** *Heraldry* **a** a device above the shield and helmet of a coat of arms. ▷ HERALDRY. **b** such a device reproduced on writing paper etc. ● *v.* **1** *tr.* reach the crest of (a hill, wave, etc.). **2** *tr.* **a** provide with a crest. **b** serve as a crest to. **3** *intr.* (of a wave) form into a crest. □ **on the crest of a wave** at the most favourable moment in one's progress. [from Latin *crista* 'tuft'] □ **crested** *adj.* (also in *comb.*). **crestless** *adj.*

crestfallen *adj.* dejected.

cretaceous ● *adj.* **1** of the nature of chalk. **2** (**Cretaceous**) *Geol.* of or relating to the last period of the Mesozoic era. ● *n.* (**Cretaceous**) *Geol.* this era or system. [based on Latin *creta* 'chalk']

cretin *n.* **1** a person who is deformed and mentally retarded as the result of a thyroid deficiency. **2** *colloq.* a stupid person. [from Latin *Christianus* 'Christian', in sense 'human creature'] □ **cretinism** *n.* **cretinize** *v.tr.* (also **-ise**). **cretinous** *adj.*

cretonne *n.* (often *attrib.*) a heavy cotton upholstery fabric, usu. with a floral pattern. [French]

Creutzfeldt–Jakob disease *n.* a type of spongiform encephalopathy affecting human beings, characterized by progressive dementia. [named after H. G. *Creutzfeldt*, 1885–1964, and A. *Jakob*, 1884–1931, German physicians]

crevasse /kri-**vass**/ *n.* **1** ▼ a deep open crack, esp. in a glacier. ▷ GLACIER. **2** *US* a breach in a river levee. [from Old French *crevace*]

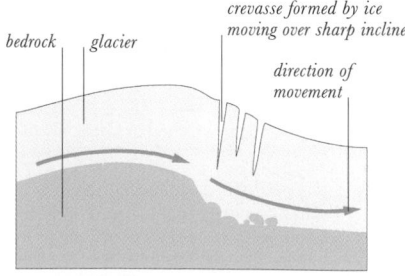

CREVASSE IN A DOWNWARD-MOVING GLACIER

crevice /**krev**-iss/ *n.* a narrow opening or fissure in a rock etc. [based on Latin *crepare* 'to burst']

crew[1] ● *n.* (often treated as *pl.*) **1 a** a body of people manning a ship, aircraft, train, etc. **b** such a body as distinguished from the captain or officers. **c** a body of people working together. **2** *colloq.* a company of people (*a motley crew*). ● *v.* **1** *tr.* supply or act as a crew or member of a crew for. **2** *intr.* act as a crew or member of a crew. [based on Latin *crescere* 'to grow (in size)']

crew[2] *past* of CROW[2].

crew-cut *n.* a very short haircut.

crewel *n.* a thin worsted yarn used for tapestry and embroidery. [Middle English]

crewman *n.* (*pl.* **-men**) a member of a crew.

crew neck *n.* a close-fitting round neckline.

crib ● *n.* **1 a** a child's bed; a cot. **b** *Brit.* a model of the Nativity of Christ, with a manger as a bed. **2** a barred rack for animal fodder. **3** *colloq.* **a** a translation of a text for the use of students. **b** plagiarized work etc. **4** *colloq.* cribbage. **5** *Austral. & NZ* a light meal; food. ● *v.tr.* (also *absol.*) (**cribbed**, **cribbing**) **1** *colloq.* copy (another person's work) unfairly or without acknowledgement. **2** confine in a small space. **3** *colloq.* pilfer, steal. [Old English] □ **cribber** *n.*

cribbage *n.* a card game for two, three, or four players. [17th-century coinage]

cribbage board *n.* a board with pegs and holes used for scoring at cribbage.

crick ● *n.* a sudden painful stiffness in the neck etc. ● *v.tr.* produce a crick in. [Middle English]

cricket[1] ● *n.* ▼ a game played on a grass pitch with two teams of 11 players taking turns to bowl at a wicket defended by a batting player of the other team. ● *v.intr.* (**cricketed**, **cricketing**) play cricket. □ **not cricket** *Brit. colloq.* dishonourable behaviour. [16th-century coinage] □ **cricketer** *n.*

cricket[2] *n.* any of various grasshopper-like insects of the order Orthoptera. ▷ ORTHOPTERAN. [based on Old French *criquer* 'to creak']

cried *past* and *past part.* of CRY.

crier *n.* (also **cryer**) a person who cries.

crikey *int. Brit. colloq.* an expression of astonishment. [euphemism for CHRIST]

crim *Austral. slang* = CRIMINAL.

crime *n.* **1 a** a serious offence punishable by law. **b** illegal acts as a whole (*resorted to crime*). **2** an evil act (*a crime against humanity*). [from Latin *crimen* 'judgement, offence']

crime sheet *n. Brit. Mil.* a record of a defendant's offences.

crime wave *n.* a sudden increase in crime.

crime writer *n.* a writer of detective fiction or thrillers.

criminal ● *n.* a person who has committed a crime. ● *adj.* **1** of, involving, or concerning crime (*criminal records; criminal offence*). **2** having committed a crime. **3** *Law* relating to or expert in criminal law (*criminal code; criminal lawyer*). **4** *colloq.* scandalous, deplorable. [from Late Latin *criminalis*] □ **criminality** *n.* **criminally** *adv.*

criminalize *v.tr.* (also **-ise**) **1** turn (an activity) into a criminal offence by making it illegal. **2** turn (a person) into a criminal, esp. by making his or her activities illegal. □ **criminalization** *n.*

criminal law *n.* law concerned with punishment of offenders (opp. CIVIL LAW 1).

criminal record see RECORD *n.* 6.

criminology *n.* the scientific study of crime. □ **criminological** *adj.* **criminologist** *n.*

crimp ● *v.tr.* **1** compress into small folds or ridges. **2** corrugate. **3** make waves in (the hair) with a hot iron. ● *n.* a crimped thing or form. [Middle English] □ **crimper** *n.* **crimpy** *adj.*

crimson ● *adj.* of a rich deep red inclining to purple. ● *n.* this colour. ● *v.tr. & intr.* make or become crimson. [from Arabic *kirmizī*]

cringe ● *v.intr.* (**cringing**) **1** shrink back in fear; cower. **2** behave obsequiously. ● *n.* the act or an instance of cringing. [Old English]

CRICKET

Originating in England in the 13th century, cricket is now an international sport, played over a fixed period (up to five days) or for a number of overs (one over being six bowls). Batsmen score runs by hitting the ball then running between the wickets, or by hitting the ball to or over the boundary. A batsman may be dismissed in several ways – by the bowler striking the wicket with the ball, for instance, or by the ball being caught.

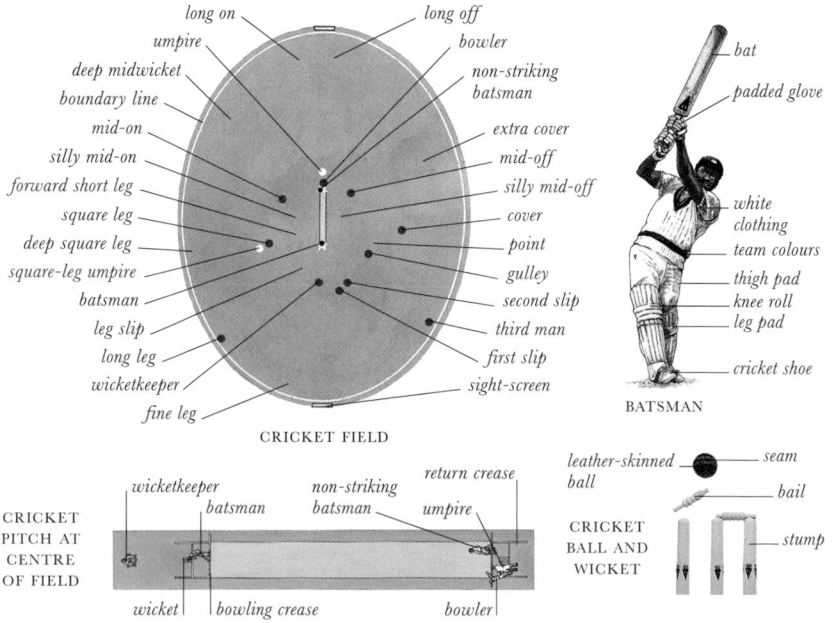

CRICKET FIELD

BATSMAN

CRICKET PITCH AT CENTRE OF FIELD

CRICKET BALL AND WICKET

crinkle ● *n.* a wrinkle or crease in paper, cloth, etc. ● *v.* **1** *intr.* form crinkles. **2** *tr.* form crinkles in. [Old English, based on *crincan* 'to curl up'] □ **crinkly** *adj.*

crinkle-cut *adj.* cut with wavy edges.

crinoline *n. hist.* ▶ a stiffened or hooped petticoat. [from Latin *crinis* 'hair' + *linum* 'thread']

cripple ● *n. archaic* or *offens.* a person who is permanently lame. ● *v.tr.* **1** make a cripple of. **2** disable, impair. **3** weaken or damage seriously (*crippled by the loss of funding*). [Old English] □ **crippler** *n.*

■ **Usage** The term *cripple* is no longer acceptable as a noun referring to a person. *Disabled person* is usually used instead.

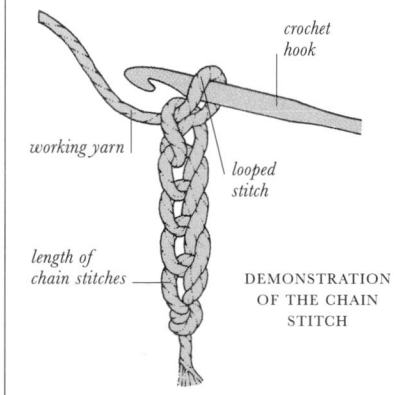

CRINOLINE: MID-19TH-CENTURY CRINOLINE

waist-tie

steel wires slotted through tapes

crisis *n.* (*pl.* **crises**) **1 a** a decisive moment. **b** a time of danger or great difficulty. **2** the turning point. [from Greek *krisis* 'decision']

crisis management *n.* the practice of taking managerial action only when a crisis has developed.

crisp ● *adj.* **1** hard but brittle. **2 a** (of air) bracing. **b** (of a style or manner) lively, brisk, and decisive. **c** (of features etc.) neat and clear-cut. **d** (of paper) stiff and crackling. **e** (of hair) closely curling. ● *n.* (in full **potato crisp**) *Brit.* a wafer-thin slice of potato fried until crisp. ● *v.tr. & intr.* make or become crisp. □ **burn to a crisp** make inedible or useless by burning. [from Latin *crispus* 'curled'] □ **crisply** *adv.* **crispness** *n.*

crispbread *n.* **1** a thin crisp biscuit of crushed rye etc. **2** these collectively (*a packet of crispbread*).

crisper *n.* a compartment in a refrigerator for storing fruit and vegetables.

crispy *adj.* (**crispier**, **crispiest**) **1** crisp, brittle. **2** curly. **3** brisk.

criss-cross ● *n.* **1** a pattern of crossing lines. **2** the crossing of lines or currents etc. ● *adj.* crossing; in cross lines (*criss-cross marking*). ● *adv.* crosswise; at cross purposes. ● *n.* **1** *intr.* **a** intersect repeatedly. **b** move crosswise. **2** *tr.* mark or make with a criss-cross pattern. [17th-century coinage, from *Christ's cross*]

criterion /kry-**teer**-iŏn/ *n.* (*pl.* **criteria**) a principle or standard that a thing is judged by. [from Greek *kritērion*] □ **criterial** *adj.*

■ **Usage** The plural form of *criterion*, *criteria*, is often used incorrectly as the singular. In the singular, *criterion* should always be used.

critic *n.* **1** a person who censures. **2** a person who reviews literary, artistic, or musical works etc. [based on Greek *krinein* 'to judge, decide']

critical *adj.* **1 a** making or involving adverse judgements. **b** expressing or involving criticism. **2** skilful at or engaged in criticism. **3** providing textual criticism (*a critical edition of Milton*). **4 a** of or at a crisis; involving risk or suspense (*in a critical condition*). **b** decisive, crucial (*at the critical moment*). **5 a** *Math. & Physics* marking a transition from one state etc. to another (*critical angle*). **b** *Physics* (of a nuclear reactor) maintaining a self-sustaining chain reaction. □ **criticality** *n.* (in sense 5). **critically** *adv.* **criticalness** *n.*

critical mass *n.* **1** the amount of fissile material needed to maintain a nuclear chain reaction. **2** the minimum size required to start a thing off or to keep a thing going.

critical path *n.* the sequence of stages determining the minimum time needed for an operation.

criticism *n.* **1 a** finding fault. **b** a statement expressing this. **2 a** the work of a critic. **b** an article, essay, etc., expressing or containing an analytical evaluation of something.

criticize *v.tr.* (also **-ise**) (also *absol.*) **1** find fault with. **2** discuss critically. □ **criticizable** *adj.*

critique ● *n.* a critical essay or analysis; an instance or the process of formal criticism. ● *v.tr.* (**critiques**, **critiqued**, **critiquing**) discuss critically. [from Greek *kritikē tekhnē* 'critical art']

croak ● *n.* **1** a deep hoarse sound as of a frog. **2** a sound resembling this. ● *v.* **1 a** *intr.* utter a croak. **b** *tr.* utter with a croak or in a dismal manner. **2** *slang* **a** *intr.* die. **b** *tr.* kill. [Middle English]

croaky *adj.* (**croakier**, **croakiest**) (of a voice) croaking; hoarse. □ **croakily** *adv.*

Croat ● *n.* **1 a** a native of Croatia in the former Yugoslavia. **b** a person of Croatian descent. **2** the Slavonic dialect of the Croats (cf. SERBO-CROAT). ● *adj.* of or relating to the Croats or their dialect. [from Serbo-Croatian *Hrvat*]

Croatian *n. & adj.* = CROAT.

crochet /**kroh**-shay/ ● *n.* **1** ▼ a handicraft in which yarn is made up into a patterned fabric by means of a hooked needle. **2** work made in this way. ● *v.* (**crocheted**, **crocheting**) **1** *tr.* make by crocheting. **2** *intr.* do crochet. [French, literally 'little hook'] □ **crocheter** *n.*

croci *pl.* of CROCUS.

crocidolite /kroh-**sid**-ŏ-lyt/ *n.* a fibrous blue or green silicate of iron and sodium; blue asbestos. [from Greek *krokis -idos* 'nap of cloth']

crock[1] *Brit. colloq.* ● *n.* **1** a broken-down or worn-out person. **2** a worn-out vehicle, ship, etc. ● *v.* **1** *intr.* (foll. by *up*) break down, collapse. **2** *tr.* disable, cause to collapse. [originally Scots]

crock[2] *n.* **1** an earthenware pot or jar. **2** a broken piece of earthenware. [Old English]

crockery *n.* earthenware or china dishes, plates, etc. [from obsolete *crocker* 'potter']

crocket *n. Archit.* a small carved ornament on the inclined side of a pinnacle etc. ▷ CATHEDRAL. [from a variant of Old French *crochet* 'little hook']

crocodile *n.* **1 a** ▼ a large tropical or subtropical amphibious reptile of the family Crocodylidae, with long jaws. **b** leather from its skin. **2** *Brit. colloq.* a line of schoolchildren etc. walking in pairs. [from Greek *krokodilos* 'worm of the stones']

CROCODILE: NILE CROCODILE (*Crocodilus niloticus*)

crocodile tears *n.pl.* insincere grief.

crocodilian ● *n.* any large predatory amphibious reptile of the order Crocodilia, with long jaws, short legs, and a powerful tail, including crocodiles, alligators, caymans, and gharials. ▷ ALLIGATOR, CROCODILE. ● *adj.* of or relating to the crocodilians.

crocus *n.* (*pl.* **crocuses** or **croci**) ▶ a small spring-flowering plant of the genus *Crocus* (iris family). [from Greek *krokos*]

Croesus *n.* a person of great wealth. [name of a king of Lydia (6th c. BC)]

croft *Brit.* ● *n.* **1** an enclosed piece of land. **2** a small rented farm in Scotland or northern England. ● *v.intr.* farm a croft; live as a crofter. [Old English]

crofter *n. Brit.* a person who rents a smallholding.

croissant /**krwus**-on/ *n.* a crescent-shaped roll made of rich yeast pastry. [French]

CROCUS (*Crocus versicolor*)

Cro-Magnon *adj. Anthropol.* of a tall broad-faced European race of late palaeolithic times. [name of a hill in the Dordogne, France, where remains were found (1868)]

C

CROCHET

The origins of crochet are difficult to trace, though the technique seems to have travelled extensively throughout the world. A length of yarn is formed into a looped fabric, using a hook, on which one stitch is worked at a time. Very fine yarns and the finest hooks form delicate open fabric. Thicker yarn on larger hooks is used for denser fabric. Flat pieces can be worked into tubular shapes or medallions.

crochet hook

working yarn

looped stitch

length of chain stitches

DEMONSTRATION OF THE CHAIN STITCH

EXAMPLES OF STITCHES

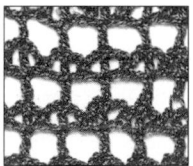

BAR AND LATTICE

LOOP STITCH

PEACOCK STITCH

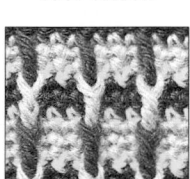

SPECKLE STITCH

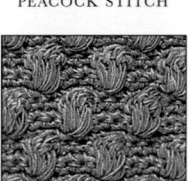

PINEAPPLE STITCH

SPIRAL HEXAGON

cromlech /krom-lek/ n. **1** (in Wales) a megalithic tomb. **2** (in Brittany) a stone circle. [Welsh, from *crom* (fem.) 'arched' + *llech* 'flat stone']

crone n. a withered old woman. [from Old Northern French *carogne* 'carrion']

cronk adj. Austral. colloq. **1** unsound; liable to collapse. **2 a** fraudulent. **b** (of a racehorse) dishonestly run, unfit.

crony n. (pl. **-ies**) often derog. a close friend or companion. [earlier *chrony*, Cambridge university slang, from Greek *khronios* 'long-standing']

crook ● n. **1** ▶ the hooked staff of a shepherd or bishop. **2 a** a bend, curve, or hook. **b** anything hooked or curved. **3** colloq. **a** a rogue; a swindler. **b** a professional criminal. ● v.tr. & intr. bend, curve. ● adj. **1** Brit. crooked. **2** Austral. & NZ colloq. **a** unsatisfactory, out of order; (of a person) unwell, injured. **b** unpleasant. **c** dishonest, unscrupulous. **d** bad-tempered, irritable, angry. □ **go crook** Austral. & NZ colloq. (usu. foll. by at, on) lose one's temper; become angry. [from Old Norse *krókr* 'hook'] □ **crookery** n.

crooked adj. (**crookeder, crookedest**) **1 a** not straight or level; bent. **b** deformed, bent with age. **2** colloq. not straightforward; dishonest. **3** Austral. & NZ slang = CROOK adj. 2. **4** (foll. by on) Austral. slang hostile to. □ **crookedly** adv. **crookedness** n.

croon ● v.tr. & intr. hum or sing in a low subdued voice. ● n. such singing. [from Middle Dutch *krōnen* 'to groan, lament'] □ **crooner** n.

crop ● n. **1 a** the produce of cultivated plants. **b** the season's yield of this (*a good crop*). **2** a group or an amount appearing at one time (*this year's crop of students*). **3** (in full **hunting crop**) the handle of a whip. **4 a** a style of hair cut very short. **b** the cropping of hair. **5** Zool. **a** the pouch in a bird's gullet where food is prepared for digestion. ▷ BIRD. **b** a similar organ in other animals. ● v. (**cropped, cropping**) **1** tr. **a** cut off. **b** bite off and eat (the tops of plants). **2** tr. cut (hair, cloth, edges of a book, etc.) short. **3** tr. gather or reap (produce). **4** tr. (foll. by with) sow or plant (land) with a crop. **5** intr. (of land) bear a crop. □ **crop up** (of a subject, circumstance, etc.) appear or come to one's notice unexpectedly. [Old English]

crop circle n. a usu. circular depression in a standing crop.

crop dusting n. the spraying of powdered insecticide or fertilizer on crops, esp. from the air.

crop-eared adj. having the ears (esp. of animals) or hair cut short.

crop-full adj. having a full crop or stomach.

cropper n. a crop-producing plant of specified quality (*a good cropper; a heavy cropper*). □ **come a cropper** colloq. **1** fall heavily. **2** fail badly.

croquet /kroh-kay/ ● n. **1** ◀ a game played on a lawn, with wooden balls which are driven through a series of hoops with mallets. **2** the act of croqueting a ball. ● v.tr. (**croqueted, croqueting**) drive away (one's opponent's ball in croquet) by placing one's own against it and striking one's own.

croquette /kroh-ket/ n. a fried breaded roll or ball of mashed potato or minced meat etc. [French]

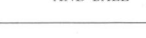

CROOK: ORNAMENTAL HEAD OF A BISHOP'S CROOK

— handle made of ash

— ball made of boxwood

CROQUET MALLET AND BALL

crore n. Anglo-Ind. **1** ten million. **2** one hundred lakhs. [from Sanskrit *koṭi* 'apex']

crosier n. (also **crozier**) a hooked staff carried by a bishop. [originally in sense 'bearer of a crook': based on Old French *crois*]

cross ● n. **1** an upright post with a transverse bar, as used in antiquity for crucifixion. **2 a** (**the Cross**) the cross on which Christ was crucified. **b** a representation of this as an emblem of Christianity. **3** a staff surmounted by a cross and borne in a religious procession. **4 a** a thing or mark shaped like a cross, esp. two short intersecting lines (+ or ×). **b** a monument in the form of a cross. **5** a cross-shaped decoration indicating rank in some orders of knighthood or awarded for personal valour. **6 a** an intermixture of animal breeds or plant varieties. **b** an animal or plant resulting from this. **7** (foll. by *between*) a mixture of two things. **8 a** a crosswise movement. **b** Football etc. a pass of the ball across the pitch. **c** Boxing a blow with a crosswise movement of the fist. **9** a trial or affliction (*bear one's crosses*). ● v. **1** tr. (often foll. by *over*; also *absol.*) go across or to the other side of (a road, river, sea, etc.). **2 a** intr. intersect or be across one another (*the roads cross near the bridge*). **b** tr. cause to do this; place crosswise (*cross one's legs*). **3** tr. **a** draw a line or lines across. **b** Brit. mark (a cheque) with two parallel lines to indicate that it must be paid into a named bank account. **4** tr. (foll. by *off, out, through*) cancel or obliterate or remove from a list with lines drawn across. **5** tr. (often *refl.*) make the sign of the cross on or over. **6** intr. **a** pass in opposite or different directions. **b** (of letters between two correspondents) each be dispatched before receipt of the other. **c** (of telephone lines) become wrongly interconnected so that intrusive calls can be heard. **7** tr. Football etc. pass (the ball) across the pitch. **8** tr. **a** cause to interbreed. **b** cross-fertilize (plants). **9** tr. thwart or frustrate (*crossed in love*). ● adj. **1** peevish, angry. **2** (usu. *attrib.*) transverse; reaching from side to side. **3** (usu. *attrib.*) intersecting. **4** (usu. *attrib.*) contrary, opposed, reciprocal. □ **at cross purposes** misunderstanding one another. **cross one's mind** (of a thought etc.) occur to one. **cross swords** have an argument or dispute. [from Old Irish *cros*, based on Latin *crux*] □ **crossly** adv. **crossness** n.

cross- comb. form **1** denoting movement or position across something (*cross-channel*). **2** denoting interaction (*cross-curricular; cross-fertilize*). **3 a** passing from side to side; transverse (*crossbar; cross-current*). **b** having a transverse part (*crossbow*). **4** describing the form or figure of a cross (*cross-keys; crossroads*).

crossbar n. a horizontal bar, esp. of a bicycle or of a football goal.

cross-bench n. Brit. a seat in Parliament (now only the House of Lords) occupied by a member not taking the whip from a political party. □ **cross-bencher** n.

crossbill n. ◀ a finch of the genus *Loxia*, having a bill with crossed mandibles with which it opens pine cones.

crossbow n. esp. hist. ▼ a bow fixed across a wooden stock, with a mechanism for drawing and releasing the string. □ **crossbowman** n. (pl. **-men**).

CROSSBILL: COMMON CROSSBILL (*Loxia curvirostra*)

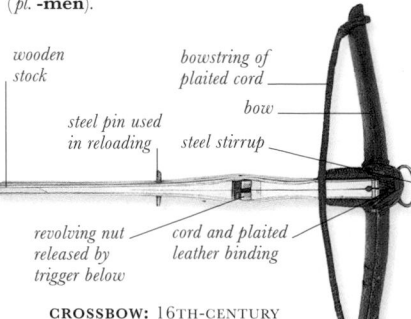

wooden stock

steel pin used in reloading

revolving nut released by trigger below

bowstring of plaited cord

bow

steel stirrup

cord and plaited leather binding

CROSSBOW: 16TH-CENTURY GERMAN CROSSBOW

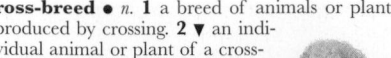

CROSS-BREED: LABRADOR RETRIEVER AND STANDARD POODLE (LABRADOODLE)

cross-breed ● n. **1** a breed of animals or plants produced by crossing. **2** ▼ an individual animal or plant of a cross-breed. ● v.tr. (*past* and *past part.* **-bred**) produce by crossing.

cross-check ● v.tr. check by an alternative method, or by several methods. ● n. an instance of cross-checking.

cross-country ● adj. & adv. **1** across open country. **2** not keeping to main roads. ● n. (pl. **-ies**) a cross-country race.

cross-cut ● adj. cut across the main grain. ● n. a diagonal cut, path, etc.

cross-cut saw n. a saw for cutting across the grain of wood.

cross-dressing n. the practice of wearing the clothes of the opposite sex. □ **cross-dress** v.intr. **cross-dresser** n.

crosse n. a stick with a triangular net at the end for conveying the ball in lacrosse. ▷ LACROSSE. [from Old French *croce* 'hook']

cross-examine v.tr. examine (esp. a witness in a law court) to check or extend testimony already given. □ **cross-examination** n. **cross-examiner** n.

cross-eyed adj. having one or both eyes turned permanently inwards towards the nose.

cross-fertilize v.tr. (also **-ise**) **1** fertilize (an animal or plant) from another. **2** help by the interchange of ideas etc. □ **cross-fertilization** n.

crossfire n. **1** firing in two crossing directions simultaneously. **2 a** attack or criticism from several sources at once. **b** a combative exchange of views etc.

cross-grain n. a grain in timber that runs across the regular grain (often *attrib.*: *cross-grain shrinkage*).

cross-grained adj. **1** (of timber) having a cross-grain. **2** perverse, intractable.

cross-hatch v.tr. ▶ shade with intersecting sets of parallel lines.

crossing n. **1** a place where things (esp. roads) cross. **2** a place at which one may cross a street etc. (*pedestrian crossing*). **3** a journey across water (*had a smooth crossing*). **4** the intersection of a church nave and transepts. **5** Biol. mating.

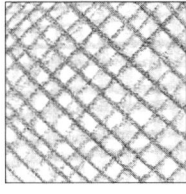

CROSS-HATCH: DETAIL FROM A PENCIL DRAWING

cross-legged adj. with one leg crossed over the other.

crossover ● n. **1** a point or place of crossing from one side to the other. **2** the process of crossing over, esp. from one style or genre to another. ● adj. **1** having a part that crosses over. **2** that crosses over, esp. from one style or genre to another.

cross-ownership n. ownership by a corporation of different companies having related commercial aims, esp. ownership of several media (e.g. a newspaper together with radio and television stations).

crosspatch n. colloq. a bad-tempered person. [based on obsolete *patch* 'fool, clown']

crosspiece n. a transverse beam etc.

cross-ply *adj. Brit.* (of a tyre) having fabric layers with cords lying crosswise.

cross-pollinate *v.tr.* pollinate (a plant) with pollen from another plant. □ **cross-pollination** *n.*

cross-question *v.tr.* = CROSS-EXAMINE.

cross-refer *v.intr.* (**-referred**, **-referring**) refer from one part of a book etc. to another.

cross-reference ● *n.* a reference from one part of a book etc. to another. ● *v.tr.* provide with cross-references.

crossroad *n.* **1** (usu. in *pl.*) an intersection of roads. **2** *US* a road that crosses a main road or joins two main roads. □ **at the crossroads** at a critical point in one's life.

cross-section *n.* **1 a** a cutting of a solid at right angles to an axis. **b** a plane surface produced in this way. **c** a representation of this. **2** a representative sample. □ **cross-sectional** *adj.*

cross stitch ● *n.* **1** a stitch formed of two stitches crossing each other. **2** ▶ needlework done using this stitch. ● *v.tr.* (**cross-stitch**) sew or embroider with cross stitches.

cross-subsidize *v.tr.* (also **-ise**) subsidize out of the profits of another business or activity. □ **cross-subsidy** *n.*

crosstalk *n.* **1** unwanted transfer of signals between communication channels. **2** *Brit.* witty repartee.

crosswalk *n. N. Amer.* & *Austral.* a pedestrian crossing.

crossways *adv.* = CROSSWISE.

crosswind *n.* a wind blowing across one's direction of travel.

crosswise *adj. & adv.* **1** in the form of a cross; intersecting. **2** transverse or transversely.

crossword *n.* (also **crossword puzzle**) a puzzle of a grid of squares and blanks into which words crossing vertically and horizontally have to be filled from clues.

crotch *n.* a place where something forks, esp. the legs of the human body or a garment (cf. CRUTCH 3).

crotchet *n.* **1** *Brit. Mus.* a note having the time value of a quarter of a semibreve and usu. representing one beat, drawn as a large dot with a stem. ▷ NOTATION. **2** a whimsical fancy. **3** a hook. [from Old French *crochet* 'little hook']

crotchety *adj.* peevish, irritable. □ **crotchetiness** *n.*

croton *n.* **1** any small tree or shrub of the genus *Croton*, producing a capsule-like fruit. **2** ▶ any small tree or shrub of the genus *Codiaeum*, esp. *C. variegatum*, with coloured ornamental leaves. [from Greek *krotōn* 'sheep-tick, croton', from the shape of its seeds]

crouch ● *v.intr.* lower the body with the limbs close to the chest; be in this position. ● *n.* an act of crouching; a crouching position. [Middle English]

croup[1] *n.* an inflammation of the larynx and trachea in children, with a hard cough and difficulty in breathing. [from dialect *croup* 'to croak'] □ **croupy** *adj.*

croup[2] *n.* the rump or hindquarters esp. of a horse. ▷ HORSE. [from Old French *croupe*]

croupier *n.* the person in charge of a gaming table, raking in and paying out money etc. [earlier in sense 'advisor standing behind a gambler': from original French sense 'rider on the croup']

CROSS STITCH:
EMBROIDERED CROSS
STITCH ON KNITTED
FABRIC

CROTON
(*Codiaeum*
'Gold Star')

crouton *n.* a small piece of fried or toasted bread served with soup or used as a garnish. [from French *croûte* 'crust']

crow[1] *n.* **1** ▶ any large bird of the genus *Corvus*, having a powerful black beak and black plumage. **2** any bird of the family Corvidae. □ **as the crow flies** in a straight line. **eat crow** *N. Amer.* submit to humiliation. [Old English]

crow[2] *v.intr.* **1** (*past* **crowed** or **crew**) (of a cock) utter its characteristic loud cry. **2** (of a baby) utter happy cries. **3** express unrestrained gleeful satisfaction. ● *n.* **1** the cry of a cock. **2** a happy cry of a baby. [Old English]

crowbar *n.* ▶ an iron bar with a flattened end, used as a lever.

crowd ● *n.* **1** a large number of people gathered together. **2** a mass of spectators; an audience. **3** *colloq.* a particular set of people. **4** (prec. by *the*) the mass or multitude of people. **5** a large number (of things). ● *v.* **1 a** *intr.* come together in a crowd. **b** *tr.* cause to do this. **c** *intr.* force one's way. **2** *tr.* **a** (foll. by *into*) force or compress into a confined space. **b** (often foll. by *with*; usu. in *passive*) fill or make abundant with (*was crowded with tourists*). **3** *tr.* **a** come aggressively close to. **b** *colloq.* harass or pressure (a person). □ **crowd out** exclude by crowding. [Old English *crūdan* 'to press, drive'] □ **crowdedness** *n.*

crowfoot *n.* any of various aquatic plants of the genus *Ranunculus*, with white buttercup-like flowers held above the water.

crown ● *n.* **1** a monarch's ornamental headdress. **2** (**the Crown**) **a** the monarch as head of state. **b** the power or authority residing in the monarchy. **3 a** a wreath worn on the head, esp. as an emblem of victory. **b** an award or distinction gained by a victory or achievement, esp. in sport. **4** a crown-shaped device or ornament. **5** the top part of a thing, esp. of the head or a hat. ▷ HAT. **6 a** the highest or central part of an arched or curved thing (*crown of the road*). **b** a thing that completes or forms the summit. **7** the part of a plant just above and below the ground. **8 a** the part of a tooth projecting from the gum. ▷ TOOTH. **b** an artificial replacement or covering for this. **9** a former British coin equal to five shillings (25p). ● *v.tr.* **1** put a crown on (a person or a person's head). **2** invest (a person) with a royal crown or authority. **3** be a crown to; rest on the top of. **4 a** (often as **crowning** *adj.*) be or cause to be the consummation, reward, or finishing touch to (*the crowning glory*). **b** bring (efforts) to a happy issue. **5** fit a crown to (a tooth). **6** *slang* hit on the head. [from Latin *corona*]

Crown Colony *n.* a British colony controlled by the Crown.

Crown Court *n.* a court of criminal jurisdiction in England and Wales.

crown green *n. Brit.* a kind of bowling green rising towards the middle.

crown jewels *n.pl.* the regalia and other jewellery worn by the sovereign on certain state occasions.

Crown prince *n.* a male heir to a sovereign throne.

Crown princess *n.* **1** the wife of a Crown prince. **2** a female heir to a sovereign throne.

crown roast *n.* a roast of rib-pieces of pork or lamb arranged like a crown.

CROW:
HOUSE CROW
(*Corvus splendens*)

flattened lever end

iron bar

clawed lever end

CROWBAR

crown wheel *n.* a wheel with teeth set at right angles to its plane.

crow's-foot *n.* (*pl.* **-feet**) (usu. in *pl.*) a wrinkle at the outer corner of a person's eye.

crow's-nest *n.* a shelter for a lookout fixed at the masthead of a sailing vessel.

crozier var. of CROSIER.

CRT *abbr.* cathode ray tube.

cruces *pl.* of CRUX.

crucial *adj.* **1** decisive, critical. **2** *disp.* very important. **3** *slang* excellent. [based on Latin *crux crucis* 'cross'] □ **cruciality** *n.* **crucially** *adv.*

■ **Usage** The use of *crucial* in sense 2 should be restricted to informal contexts.

cruciate ligament *n.* either of a pair of ligaments in the knee which cross each other and connect the femur and the tibia. [cruciate: from medieval Latin *cruciatus* 'cross-shaped']

crucible *n.* **1** a melting pot for metals etc. **2** a severe test or trial. [from medieval Latin *crucibulum* 'nightlamp, crucible']

cruciferous *adj. Bot.* of the plant family Cruciferae, having flowers with four petals arranged in a cross. [from Late Latin *crucifer*]

crucifix *n.* a model or image of a cross with a figure of Christ on it. ▷ ROSARY. [from Latin *cruci fixus* 'fixed to a cross']

crucifixion *n.* **1 a** a crucifying or being crucified. **b** an instance of this. **2** (**Crucifixion**) **a** the crucifixion of Christ. **b** a representation of this.

cruciform *adj.* cross-shaped. [based on Latin *crux crucis* 'cross']

crucify *v.tr.* (**-ies**, **-ied**) **1** put to death by fastening to a cross. **2 a** cause extreme pain to. **b** persecute, torment. **c** *slang* defeat thoroughly in an argument, match, etc.

crud *n. slang* unwanted impurities; dirt. [variant of CURD] □ **cruddy** *adj.* (**cruddier**, **cruddiest**).

crude ● *adj.* **1 a** in the natural or raw state; not refined. **b** unpolished; lacking finish. **2 a** (of an action or statement or manners) rude, blunt. **b** offensive, indecent. **3 a** *Statistics* (of figures) not adjusted or corrected. **b** rough (*a crude estimate*). ● *n.* natural mineral oil. [from Latin *crudus* 'raw, rough'] □ **crudely** *adv.* **crudeness** *n.* **crudity** *n.*

cruel *adj.* (**crueller**, **cruellest** or **crueler**, **cruelest**) **1** indifferent to or gratified by another's suffering. **2** causing pain or suffering. [from Latin *crudelis*] □ **cruelly** *adv.*

cruelty *n.* (*pl.* **-ies**) **1** a cruel act or attitude; indifference to another's suffering. **2** a succession of cruel acts; a continued cruel attitude (*suffered much cruelty*).

cruelty-free *adj.* (of cosmetics etc.) produced without involving cruelty to animals in the development or manufacturing process.

cruet *n. Brit.* **1** a small container for salt, pepper, oil, or vinegar for use at table. **2** (in full **cruet-stand**) a stand holding cruets. [from Old French *crue* 'pot']

cruise ● *v.intr.* **1** make a journey by sea calling at a series of ports usu. according to a predetermined plan, esp. for pleasure. **2** sail about without a precise destination. **3 a** (of a motor vehicle or aircraft) travel at a moderate or economical speed. **b** (of a vehicle or its driver) travel at random, esp. slowly. **4** achieve an objective, win a race etc., with ease. ● *n.* a cruising voyage.

cruise control *n.* a device which maintains a motor vehicle at a selected constant speed without the use of the accelerator pedal.

cruise missile *n.* a missile able to fly at a low altitude and guide itself by reference to the features of the region it traverses.

cruiser *n.* **1** a warship of high speed and medium armament. **2** = CABIN CRUISER. **3** *N. Amer.* a police patrol car.

cruiserweight *n.* esp. *Brit.* = LIGHT HEAVYWEIGHT.

C

cruising speed *n.* a comfortable and economical speed for a motor vehicle.

crumb ● *n.* **1 a** a small fragment, esp. of bread. **b** a small particle (*a crumb of comfort*). **2** the soft inner part of a loaf of bread. **3** *slang* an objectionable person. ● *v.tr.* **1** cover with breadcrumbs. **2** break into crumbs. [Old English]

crumble ● *v.* **1** *tr. & intr.* break or fall into fragments. **2** *intr.* (of power, a reputation, etc.) gradually disintegrate. ● *n.* **1** a mixture of flour and fat, rubbed to the texture of breadcrumbs and cooked as a topping for fruit etc. **2** a usu. specified dish having such a topping (*apple crumble; vegetable crumble*). [related to CRUMB]

crumbly *adj.* (**crumblier, crumbliest**) consisting of, or apt to fall into, crumbs or fragments.

crumbs *int. Brit. slang* expressing dismay or surprise. [euphemism for *Christ*]

crumby *adj.* (**crumbier, crumbiest**) **1** like or covered in crumbs. **2** *colloq.* = CRUMMY.

crumhorn var. of KRUMMHORN.

crummy *adj.* (**crummier, crummiest**) *colloq.* dirty, squalid; inferior, worthless. [variant of CRUMBY] □ **crumminess** *n.*

crumpet *n.* **1** a soft flat unsweetened cake of a yeast mixture eaten toasted and buttered. **2** *Brit. slang offens.* **a** a sexually attractive person, esp. a woman. **b** women regarded collectively, esp. as objects of sexual desire. [17th-century coinage]

crumple ● *v.* **1** *tr. & intr.* **a** crush or become crushed into creases. **b** ruffle, wrinkle. **2** *intr.* collapse, give way. ● *n.* a crease or wrinkle. [from obsolete *crump* 'to make or become curved'] □ **crumply** *adj.*

crumple zone *n.* a part of a motor vehicle designed to crumple easily in a crash and absorb impact.

crunch ● *v.* **1** *tr.* **a** crush noisily with the teeth. **b** grind (gravel, dry snow, etc.) under foot, wheels, etc. **2** *intr.* make a crunching sound in walking, moving, etc. ● *n.* **1** crunching; a crunching sound. **2** *colloq.* a decisive event or moment. [earlier *cra(u)nch*]

crunchy *adj.* (**crunchier, crunchiest**) hard and crispy. □ **crunchily** *adv.* **crunchiness** *n.*

crupper *n.* **1** a strap buckled to the back of a saddle and looped under the horse's tail to hold the harness back. ▷ TROTTING. **2** the hindquarters of a horse. [from Old French *cropiere*]

crusade ● *n.* **1 a** ◀ any of several medieval military expeditions made by Europeans to recover the Holy Land from the Muslims. **b** a war instigated by the Church for alleged religious ends. **2** a vigorous campaign in favour of a cause. ● *v.intr.* engage in a crusade. [from medieval Latin *cruciata* 'a marking with a cross'] □ **crusader** *n.*

cruse *n. archaic* an earthenware pot. [Old English]

crush ● *v.tr.* **1** compress with force or violence, so as to break, bruise, etc. **2** reduce to powder by pressure. **3** crease or crumple. **4** defeat or subdue completely (*crushed by my reply*). ● *n.* **1** an act of crushing. **2** a crowded mass of people. **3** a drink made from the juice of crushed fruit. **4** *colloq.* (usu. foll. by *on*) an infatuation. [from Old French *cruissir* 'to gnash (teeth),

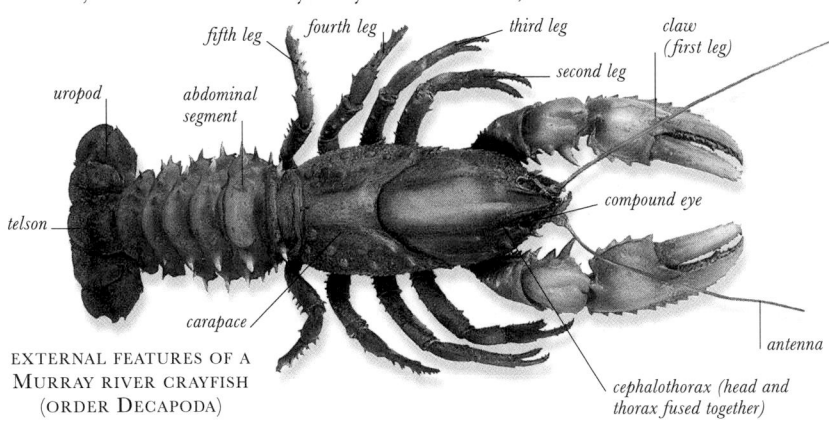

CRUSADE:
ENGLISH LATE
13TH-CENTURY
CRUSADER KNIGHT

pennon
lance
mail mitten
helm
mail coif
shield
surcoat
scabbard

crack'] □ **crushable** *adj.* **crusher** *n.* **crushing** *adj.* (esp. in sense 4 of *v.*). □ **crushingly** *adv.*

crust ● *n.* **1 a** the hard outer part of a loaf of bread. **b** a piece of this with some soft bread attached. **c** a hard dry scrap of bread. **d** esp. *Austral. slang* a livelihood (*what do you do for a crust?*). **2** the pastry covering of a pie. **3** a hard casing of a softer thing. **4** *Geol.* the outer rocky portion of the Earth. ▷ EARTH. **5 a** a coating or deposit on the surface of anything. **b** a hard dry formation on the skin, a scab. **6** a deposit of tartar formed in bottles of old wine. **7** *slang* impudence (*you have a crust!*). ● *v.tr. & intr.* **1** cover or become covered with a crust. **2** form into a crust. [from Latin *crusta* 'rind, shell'] □ **crustal** *adj.* (in sense 4 of *n.*).

crustacean ● *n.* ▼ any arthropod of the subphylum Crustacea, having a hard shell and numerous legs, and usu. aquatic, e.g. the crab, lobster, and shrimp. ▷ CRAB. ● *adj.* of or relating to crustaceans. [from modern Latin *crustaceus*] □ **crustaceous** *adj.*

crusted *adj.* **1 a** having a crust. **b** (of wine) having deposited a crust. **2** antiquated, venerable.

crustose *adj.* (esp. of a lichen) forming or resembling a crust.

crusty *adj.* (**crustier, crustiest**) **1** having a crisp crust (*a crusty loaf*). **2** irritable, curt. **3** hard, crust-like. □ **crustiness** *n.*

crutch *n.* **1** a support for a lame person, usu. with a crosspiece at the top fitting under the armpit (*pair of crutches*). **2** any support or prop. **3** the crotch of the human body or a garment. [Old English]

crux *n.* (*pl.* **cruxes** or **cruces** /kroo-seez/) **1** the decisive point at issue. **2** a difficult matter; a puzzle. [Latin, literally 'cross']

cry ● *v.* (**cries, cried**) **1** *intr.* make a loud or shrill sound, esp. to express pain, grief, etc., or to appeal for help. **2 a** *intr.* shed tears; weep. **b** *tr.* shed (tears). **3** *tr.* say or exclaim loudly or excitedly. **4** *intr.* (of an animal, esp. a bird) make a loud call. **5** *tr.* (of a hawker etc.) proclaim (wares etc.) in the street. ● *n.* (*pl.* **cries**) **1** a loud inarticulate utterance of grief, pain, fear, joy, etc. **2** a loud excited utterance of words. **3** an urgent appeal. **4** a spell of weeping. **5 a** public demand; a strong movement of opinion. **b** a rallying call. **6** the natural utterance of an animal. **7** the street-call of a hawker etc. □ **cry down** disparage. **cry off** *Brit. colloq.* withdraw from an undertaking. **cry out for** demand as a self-evident requirement or solution. **cry up** praise, extol. **cry wolf** see WOLF. **a far cry from 1** a long way from. **2** a very different thing from. **in full cry** (of hounds) in keen pursuit. [based on Latin *quiritare* 'to wail']

cry-baby *n.* a person who sheds tears frequently.

cryer var. of CRIER.

crying *attrib.adj.* (of an evil) flagrant, demanding redress (*a crying need; a crying shame*).

cryo- *comb. form* (extreme) cold. [from Greek *kruos* 'frost']

cryobiology *n.* the biology of organisms below their normal temperatures. □ **cryobiological** *adj.* **cryobiologist** *n.*

cryogen *n.* a freezing-mixture; a substance used to produce very low temperatures.

cryogenics *n.* the branch of physics dealing with the production and effects of very low temperatures. □ **cryogenic** *adj.*

cryonics *n.* the practice or technique of deep-freezing the bodies of those who have died of an incurable disease, in the hope of a future cure. □ **cryonic** *adj.*

cryosurgery *n.* surgery using the local application of intense cold for anaesthesia or therapy.

CRUSTACEAN

The subphylum Crustacea contains about 38,000 species, and is one of the largest groups in the phylum Arthropoda. Crustaceans are named after the hard carapace, or 'crust', that encloses their body. They vary greatly in size, but a typical species has compound eyes, antennae in pairs, and several pairs of jointed legs. They usually live in sea water, although a few, such as the woodlouse, live on land.

fifth leg   *fourth leg*   *third leg*   *claw (first leg)*
uropod   *abdominal segment*   *second leg*
telson   *compound eye*
carapace   *antenna*

EXTERNAL FEATURES OF A
MURRAY RIVER CRAYFISH
(ORDER DECAPODA)

cephalothorax (head and thorax fused together)

EXAMPLES OF OTHER CRUSTACEAN ORDERS —

EUPHAUSIACEA
krill
(*Euphausia superba*)

THORACICA
barnacle

HARPACTICOIDA
freshwater copepod

ISOPODA
woodlouse
(*Armadillidium vulgare*)

CRYSTAL

Crystals grow in a variety of forms, known as habits. Well-formed crystals have external faces with parallel edges, each face having a parallel on the opposite side of the crystal. Crystals of this type conform to certain systems, related to their axes of symmetry – imaginary lines around which they may rotate and still show identical aspects.

reflections of light   striation lines

plane of intersection

crystals in random growth directions

FEATURES OF A TWIN ROCK CRYSTAL

EXAMPLES OF CRYSTAL HABITS

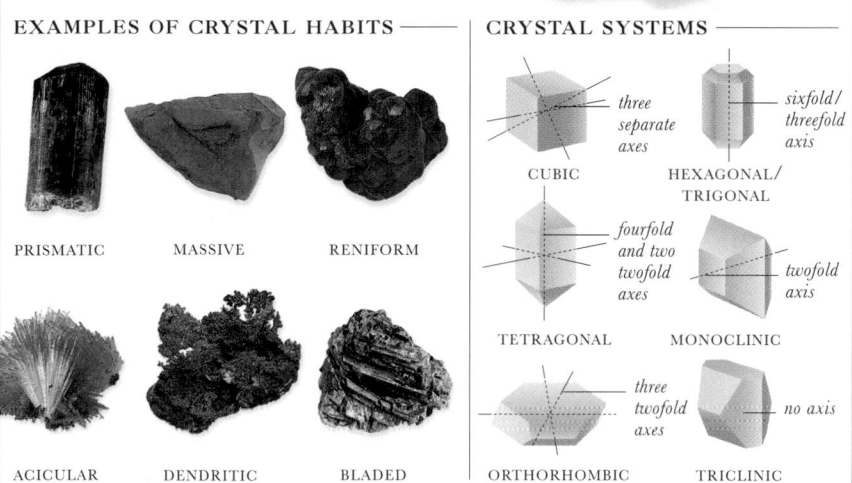

PRISMATIC   MASSIVE   RENIFORM

ACICULAR   DENDRITIC   BLADED

CRYSTAL SYSTEMS

three separate axes

CUBIC

sixfold/threefold axis

HEXAGONAL/TRIGONAL

fourfold and two twofold axes

TETRAGONAL

twofold axis

MONOCLINIC

three twofold axes

no axis

ORTHORHOMBIC   TRICLINIC

---

crypt *n.* an underground room or vault. [from Greek *kruptē*]

cryptic *adj.* **1 a** obscure in meaning. **b** (of a crossword clue etc.) indicating the solution in a way that is not obvious. **c** secret, mysterious. **2** *Zool.* (of coloration etc.) serving for concealment. □ **cryptically** *adv.*

crypto- *comb. form* concealed, secret (*crypto-communist*). [from Greek *kruptos* 'hidden']

cryptogam *n.* *Bot.* a plant that has no true flowers or seeds. [from Greek *kruptos* 'hidden' + *gamos* 'marriage'] □ **cryptogamic** *adj.* **cryptogamous** *adj.*

cryptogram *n.* a text written in cipher.

cryptography *n.* the art of writing or solving codes. □ **cryptographer** *n.* **cryptographic** *adj.*

cryptology *n.* = CRYPTOGRAPHY. □ **cryptologist** *n.* **cryptological** *adj.*

crystal ● *n.* **1 a** a clear transparent mineral, esp. rock crystal. **b** a piece of this. **2** (in full **crystal glass**) a highly transparent glass. **b** articles made of this. **3** *Electronics* a crystalline piece of semiconductor. **4** *Chem.* ▲ an aggregation of atoms or molecules with a regular internal structure and the external form of a solid enclosed by symmetrically arranged plane faces. ● *adj.* (usu. *attrib.*) made of, like, or clear as crystal. □ **crystal clear** (hyphenated when *attrib.*) **1** unclouded, transparent. **2** readily understood. [from Greek *krustallos*]

crystal ball *n.* a solid globe of glass or rock crystal, used in crystal-gazing.

crystal-gazing *n.* the process of concentrating one's gaze on a crystal ball supposedly in order to obtain a picture of future events etc.

crystalline *adj.* **1** of, like, or clear as crystal. **2** *Chem.* & *Mineral.* having the structure and form of a crystal. □ **crystallinity** *n.*

crystallize *v.* (also **-ise**) **1** *tr.* & *intr.* form or cause to form crystals. **2** (often foll. by *out*) **a** *intr.* (of ideas or plans) become definite. **b** *tr.* make definite. **3** *tr.* &

intr. coat or impregnate or become coated or impregnated with sugar (*crystallized fruit*). □ **crystallizable** *adj.* **crystallization** *n.* ▷ MATTER

crystallography *n.* the science of crystal form and structure. □ **crystallographer** *n.* **crystallographic** *adj.*

crystal system *n.* ▲ each of seven distinct symmetrical forms (cubic, tetragonal, orthorhombic, tri-

---

gonal, hexagonal, monoclinic, and triclinic) into which crystals can be classified according to the relations of their axes.

Cs *symb. Chem.* the element caesium.

c/s *abbr.* cycles per second.

CSE *abbr. hist.* (in the UK) Certificate of Secondary Education (replaced in 1988 by GCSE).

CS gas *n.* a tear gas used to control riots etc.

CSM *abbr.* (in the UK) Company Sergeant Major.

Cu *symb. Chem.* the element copper.

cu. *abbr.* cubic.

cub ● *n.* **1** the young of a fox, lion, etc. **2** an ill-mannered young man. **3** (**Cub**) (in full **Cub Scout**) a member of the junior branch of the Scout Association. ● *v.* (**cubbed, cubbing**) **1** *tr.* (also *absol.*) give birth to (cubs). **2** *intr.* hunt fox cubs. [16th-century coinage] □ **cubhood** *n.*

Cuban ● *adj.* of or relating to Cuba, an island republic in the Caribbean, or its people. ● *n.* a native or national of Cuba.

Cuban heel *n.* a moderately high straight heel of a man's or woman's shoe.

cubby *n.* (*pl.* **-ies**) (in full **cubby hole**) **1** a very small room. **2** a snug space. [from dialect *cub* 'stall, pen', of Low German origin]

cube ● *n.* **1** ▶ a solid contained by six equal squares. **2** a cube-shaped block. **3** *Math.* the product of a number multiplied by its square. ● *v.tr.* **1** find the cube of (a number). **2** cut (food for cooking etc.) into small cubes. [from Greek *kubos*]

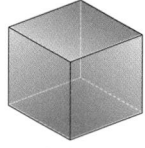

CUBE

cube root *n.* the number which produces a given number when cubed.

cubic *adj.* **1** cube-shaped. **2** of three dimensions. **3** involving the cube (and no higher power) of a number (*cubic equation*). **4** (*attrib.*) designating a unit of measure equal to the volume of a cube whose side is one of the linear unit specified (*cubic metre*).

cubical *adj.* cube-shaped. □ **cubically** *adv.*

cubicle *n.* **1** a small partitioned space, screened for privacy. **2** a small separate sleeping compartment. [from Latin *cubiculum*]

cubiform *adj.* cube-shaped.

cubism *n.* ▼ a style and movement in art, esp. painting, in which objects are represented as an assemblage of geometrical forms. □ **cubist** *n.* & *adj.*

CUBISM

Cubism was a movement originated by Picasso and Braque. Partly inspired by the late paintings of Cézanne, and also by African sculpture, cubists constructed paintings with multiple viewpoints, creating overlapping planes within the composition. This represented a significant break from the linear perspective that had prevailed since the Renaissance, and revealed an aim to represent objects as they are 'known', rather than as they appear momentarily from a single position. Stressing reality without recourse to traditional forms of illusion, cubists after 1912 incorporated into their paintings fragments of the 'real world', such as newsprint.

Violin and Guitar (1913), PABLO PICASSO

TIMELINE

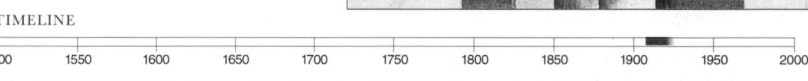

1500   1550   1600   1650   1700   1750   1800   1850   1900   1950   2000

C

cubit *n.* an ancient measure of length, approximately equal to the length of a forearm. [from Latin *cubitum* 'elbow']

cuboid ● *adj.* cube-shaped; like a cube. ● *n. Geom.* a rectangular parallelepiped. □ **cuboidal** *adj.*

cub reporter an inexperienced newspaper reporter.

Cub Scout see CUB *n.* 3.

cuckold ● *n.* the husband of an adulteress. ● *v.tr.* make a cuckold of. [based on Old French *cucu* 'cuckoo'] □ **cuckoldry** *n.*

cuckoo ● *n.* ◀ a long-tailed songbird of the family Cuculidae, having a characteristic call and laying its eggs in the nests of small birds. ● *predic.adj. colloq.* crazy, foolish. [from Old French *cucu*]

CUCKOO:
COMMON
CUCKOO
(*Cuculus
canorus*)

cuckoo clock *n.* a clock that strikes the hour with a sound like a cuckoo's call. ▷ CLOCK

cuckoo pint *n.* ▶ a wild arum, *Arum maculatum*, with arrow-shaped leaves and scarlet berries. [earlier *-pintle*, from *pintel* 'penis', with reference to the shape of the flower spike]

cuckoo spit *n.* froth exuded by larvae of insects of the family Cercopidae on leaves, stems, etc.

cucumber *n.* **1** a long green fleshy fruit, used in salads. **2** the climbing plant, *Cucumis sativus*, yielding this. [from Latin *cucumer*]

cud *n.* half-digested food returned to the mouth of ruminants for further chewing. [Old English]

cuddle ● *v.* **1** *tr.* hug, fondle. **2** *intr.* (often foll. by *up*) nestle together. ● *n.* a prolonged and fond hug. [16th-century coinage] □ **cuddlesome** *adj.*

spathe

berries

flower spike

CUCKOO PINT
(*Arum maculatum*)

cuddly *adj.* (**cuddlier**, **cuddliest**) tempting to cuddle; given to cuddling.

cudgel ● *n.* a short thick stick used as a weapon. ● *v.tr.* (**cudgelled**, **cudgelling**; *US* **cudgeled**, **cudgeling**) beat with a cudgel. □ **cudgel one's brains** think hard about a problem. **take up the cudgels** (often foll. by *for*) make a vigorous defence. [Old English]

cue[1] ● *n.* **1 a** the last words of an actor's speech serving as a signal to another actor to enter or speak. **b** a similar signal to a singer etc. **2 a** a stimulus to perception etc. **b** a signal for action. **c** a hint on appropriate behaviour. ● *v.tr.* (**cues, cued, cueing** or **cuing**) **1** give a cue to. **2** put (a piece of audio equipment, esp. a record player or tape recorder) in readiness to play a particular part of the recorded material. □ **cue in 1** insert a cue for. **2** give information to. **on cue** at the correct moment. **take one's cue from** follow the example or advice of. [16th-century coinage]

cue[2] *Billiards etc.* ● *n.* a long straight tapering rod for striking the ball. ▷ SNOOKER. ● *v.* (**cues, cued, cueing** or **cuing**) **1** *tr.* strike (a ball) with a cue. **2** *intr.* use a cue. [variant of QUEUE] □ **cueist** *n.*

cue ball *n. Billiards* the ball that is to be struck with the cue. ▷ SNOOKER

cuff[1] *n.* **1 a** the end part of a sleeve. **b** the part of a glove covering the wrist. **2** *N. Amer.* a trouser turn-up. **3** (in *pl.*) *colloq.* handcuffs. □ **off the cuff** *colloq.*

without preparation, extempore. [Middle English] □ **cuffed** *adj.* (also in *comb.*).

cuff[2] ● *v.tr.* strike with an open hand. ● *n.* such a blow. [16th-century coinage]

cuff link *n.* a device of two joined studs etc. to fasten the sides of a cuff together.

Cufic var. of KUFIC.

cui bono? /kwee-**bon**oh/ *int.* who stands, or stood, to gain? (with the implication that this person is responsible). [Latin, = to whom (is it) a benefit?]

cuirass /kwi-**ras**/ *n. hist.* ▼ a piece of armour consisting of breastplate and back-plate fastened together. [based on Latin *corium* 'leather']

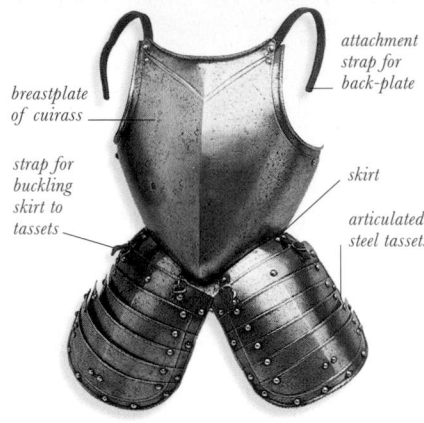

*breastplate
of cuirass*

*strap for
buckling
skirt to
tassets*

*attachment
strap for
back-plate*

skirt

*articulated
steel tassets*

CUIRASS: 16TH-CENTURY ITALIAN CUIRASS
BREASTPLATE, SKIRT, AND TASSETS

cuisine /kwi-**zeen**/ *n.* a style or method of cooking. [French]

cul-de-sac /**kul**-dĕ-sak/ *n.* (*pl.* **culs-de-sac** *pronunc.* same) **1** a street or passage closed at one end. **2** a futile course. [French, literally 'sack-bottom']

culinary *adj.* of or for cooking or the kitchen. [based on Latin *culina* 'kitchen'] □ **culinarily** *adv.*

cull ● *v.tr.* **1** select or gather (*knowledge culled from books*). **2** pick (flowers, fruit, etc.). **3** select (animals), esp. for killing. ● *n.* **1** an act of culling. **2** an animal or animals culled. [from Latin *colligere* 'to collect'] □ **culler** *n.*

cullet *n.* recycled waste or broken glass used in glass-making. [variant of earlier *collet*, in the obsolete sense 'glass left on the blowing-iron when the finished article is removed']

culminate *v.* **1** *intr.* (usu. foll. by *in*) reach its highest or final point. **2** *tr.* bring to its highest or final point. [based on Late Latin *culminatus* 'exalted'] □ **culmination** *n.*

culottes /kew-**lots**/ *n.pl.* women's (usu. short) trousers cut to resemble a skirt. [French, literally 'knee-breeches']

culpable *adj.* deserving blame. [based on Latin *culpa* 'blame'] □ **culpability** *n.* **culpably** *adv.*

culprit *n.* a person accused of or guilty of an offence. [17th-century coinage, originally from *Culprit, how will you be tried?*, said to a prisoner pleading Not Guilty]

cult *n.* **1** a system of religious worship esp. as expressed in ritual. **2 a** devotion to a person or thing (*the cult of aestheticism*). **b** a popular fashion. **3** (*attrib.*) denoting a person or thing popularized in this way (*cult film; cult figure*). [from Latin *cultus* 'worship'] □ **cultic** *adj.* **cultism** *n.* **cultist** *n.*

cultivar *n. Bot.* a cultivated plant variety produced by selective breeding.

cultivate *v.tr.* **1 a** prepare and use (soil etc.) for crops or gardening. **b** break up (the ground) with a cultivator. **2 a** raise or produce (crops). **b** culture (bacteria, cells, etc.). **3 a** (often as **cultivated** *adj.*) apply oneself to improving or developing (the mind etc.). **b** pay attention to or nurture; ingratiate oneself

with. [based on Latin *cultiva* (*terra*) 'arable (land)'] □ **cultivable** *adj.* **cultivatable** *adj.* **cultivation** *n.*

cultivator *n.* **1** ▼ a mechanical implement for breaking up the ground and uprooting weeds. **2** a person or thing that cultivates.

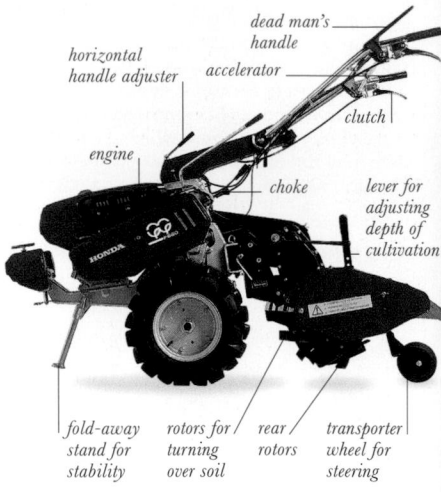

*horizontal
handle adjuster*

*dead man's
handle*

accelerator

clutch

engine

choke

*lever for
adjusting
depth of
cultivation*

*fold-away
stand for
stability*

*rotors for
turning
over soil*

*rear
rotors*

*transporter
wheel for
steering*

CULTIVATOR: FRONT-ENGINED
PETROL-DRIVEN CULTIVATOR

cultural *adj.* of or relating to the cultivation of the mind or manners, esp. through artistic or intellectual activity. □ **culturally** *adv.*

culture ● *n.* **1 a** the arts and other manifestations of human intellectual achievement regarded collectively. **b** a refined understanding of this. **2** the customs, civilization, and achievements of a particular time or people (*studied Chinese culture*). **3** improvement by mental or physical training. **4 a** the cultivation of plants; the rearing of bees etc. **b** the cultivation of the soil. **5 a** the cultivation of bacteria etc. in an artificial nutrient medium. **b** a growth so obtained. ● *v.tr.* maintain (cells etc.) in conditions suitable for growth. [from Latin *cultura*]

cultured *adj.* having refined taste and manners and a good education.

cultured pearl *n.* a pearl formed by an oyster after the insertion of a foreign body into its shell.

culture vulture *n. colloq.* a person eager to acquire culture.

culvert *n.* an underground channel carrying water across a road etc. or *Brit.* an electric cable. [18th-century coinage]

cum *prep.* (usu. in *comb.*) with, combined with, also used as (*a bedroom-cum-study*). [Latin]

cumber *v.tr. literary* hamper, hinder, inconvenience. [Middle English]

cumbersome *adj.* inconveniently bulky. □ **cumbersomely** *adv.* **cumbersomeness** *n.*

cumbia *n.* **1** a kind of dance music of Colombian origin, similar to salsa. **2** a dance performed to this. [from Colombian Spanish]

cumbrous *adj.* = CUMBERSOME. □ **cumbrously** *adv.* **cumbrousness** *n.*

cumin *n.* (also **cummin**) **1** ▶ an umbelliferous plant, *Cuminum cymium*, bearing aromatic seeds. **2** these seeds used as flavouring. ▷ SPICE. [from Greek *kuminon*]

ripening seeds

lax stems

CUMIN
(*Cuminum cymium*)

cummerbund *n.* a waist sash. [from Persian *kamarband* 'loin-band']

cummin var. of CUMIN.

cumquat var. of KUMQUAT.

cumulate ● *v.tr. & intr.* amass; combine. ● *adj.* massed. [based on Latin *cumulatus* 'heaped'] □ **cumulation** *n.*

cumulative *adj.* increasing, increased, or formed by successive additions. □ **cumulatively** *adv.* **cumulativeness** *n.*

cumulonimbus *n.* (*pl.* **cumulonimbuses** or **cumulonimbi**) *Meteorol.* a cloud like cumulus but formed in towering masses, as in thunderstorms. ▷ CLOUD, HURRICANE.

cumulus *n.* (*pl.* **cumuli**) *Meteorol.* clouds formed in rounded masses heaped on each other above a flat base. ▷ CLOUD, HURRICANE. [Latin, literally 'heap'] □ **cumulous** *adj.*

cuneiform /**kew**-ni-form/ ● *adj.* **1** wedge-shaped. **2** of, relating to, or using the wedge-shaped writing in ancient Babylonian etc. inscriptions. ● *n.* ▶ cuneiform writing. [based on Latin *cuneus* 'wedge']

cunnilingus *n.* (also **cunnilinctus**) oral stimulation of the female genitals. [Latin, based on *cunnus* 'vulva' + *lingere* 'to lick']

cunning ● *adj.* (**cunninger**, **cunningest**) **1 a** skilled in ingenuity or deceit. **b** selfishly clever or crafty. **2** ingenious (*a cunning device*). **3** *N. Amer.* attractive, quaint. ● *n.* **1** craftiness. **2** skill, ingenuity. [from Old Norse *kunnandi* 'knowing'] □ **cunningly** *adv.* **cunningness** *n.*

cunt *n. coarse slang* **1** the female genitals. **2** *offens.* a stupid person. [Middle English]

cup ● *n.* **1** a small bowl-shaped container for drinking from. **2 a** its contents (*a cup of tea*). **b** = CUPFUL. **3** a cup-shaped thing. **4** flavoured wine, cider, etc., usu. chilled. **5** an ornamental cup-shaped trophy. **6** one's fate or fortune (*a bitter cup*). ● *v.tr.* (**cupped**, **cupping**) **1** form (esp. one's hands) into the shape of a cup. **2** take or hold as in a cup. □ **one's cup of tea** *colloq.* what interests or suits one. **in one's cups** *colloq.* while drunk; drunk. [from medieval Latin *cuppa*]

cupboard *n.* a recess or piece of furniture with a door and (usu.) shelves.

cupboard love *n.* a display of affection meant to secure some gain.

Cup Final *n. Brit.* the final match in a competition for a cup.

cupful *n.* (*pl.* **-fuls**) **1** the amount held by a cup, esp. *N. Amer.* a half-pint or 8-ounce measure in cookery. **2** the contents of a full cup.

■ **Usage** A *cupful* is a measure, and so *three cupfuls* is a quantity regarded in terms of a cup; *three cups full* denotes the actual cups, as in *he brought us three cups full of water*.

Cupid *n.* **1** the Roman god of love represented as a naked winged boy archer. **2** (also **cupid**) a representation of Cupid. [from Latin *Cupido* 'desire']

cupidity *n.* greed for gain. [based on Latin *cupidus* 'desirous']

cupola /**kew**-pŏ-lă/ *n.* **1 a** a rounded dome forming a roof or ceiling. **b** a small rounded dome adorning a roof. **2** a revolving dome protecting mounted guns. **3** (in full **cupola furnace**) a furnace for melting metals. [from Late Latin *cupula* 'little cask'] □ **cupolaed** *adj.*

cuppa *n.* (also **cupper**) *Brit. colloq.* **1** a cup of. **2** a cup of tea.

cupreous *adj.* of or like copper. [related to CUPRIC]

cupric *adj. Chem.* of copper, esp. divalent copper. [based on Late Latin *cuprum* 'copper'] □ **cupriferous** *adj.*

cupro-nickel *n.* an alloy of copper and nickel, esp. in the proportions 3:1 as used in 'silver' coins.

cuprous *adj. Chem.* of copper, esp. monovalent copper. [based on Late Latin *cuprum* 'copper']

cup-tie *n. Brit.* a match in a competition for a cup.

cur *n.* **1** a worthless or snappy dog. **2** *colloq.* a contemptible man. [Middle English]

curable *adj.* that can be cured. □ **curability** *n.*

curaçao /kewr-ă-**soh**/ *n.* (*pl.* **-os**) an orange-flavoured liqueur. [from *Curaçao*, the name of the Caribbean island producing these oranges]

curacy *n.* (*pl.* **-ies**) a curate's office or the tenure of it.

curare /k'yuu-**rar**-i/ *n.* a resinous bitter substance prepared from S. American plants of the genera *Strychnos* and *Chondodendron*, paralysing the motor nerves. [Carib]

curate[1] *n.* a member of the clergy engaged as assistant to a parish priest. [from medieval Latin *curatus*]

curate[2] *v.* **1** *tr.* act as curator of (a museum, exhibits, etc.). **2** *intr.* perform the duties of a curator. [back-formation from CURATOR] □ **curation** *n.*

curate's egg *n.* esp. *Brit.* a thing that is partly good and partly bad. [from the story of a meek curate who, when given a stale egg, stated that 'parts of it' were 'excellent']

curator *n.* a keeper or custodian of a museum or other collection. [Latin] □ **curatorial** *adj.* **curatorship** *n.*

curb ● *n.* **1** a check or restraint. **2** ▶ a strap etc. fastened to the bit and passing under a horse's lower jaw, used as a check. **3** an enclosing border or edging. **4** = KERB. ● *v.tr.* **1** restrain. **2** put a curb on (a horse). [from Latin *curvare* 'to bend']

curd *n.* **1** (often in *pl.*) a coagulated substance formed by the action of acids on milk, which may be made into cheese or eaten as food. **2** the edible head of a cauliflower. [Middle English] □ **curdy** *adj.*

curd cheese *n.* a soft smooth cheese made from skimmed milk curds.

curdle *v.tr. & intr.* make into or become curds; coagulate. □ **make one's blood curdle** fill one with horror. [based on CURD] □ **curdler** *n.*

cure ● *v.* **1** *tr.* (often foll. by *of*) restore (a person or animal) to health (*was cured of pleurisy*). **2** *tr.* eliminate (a disease, evil, etc.). **3** *tr.* preserve by salting, drying, etc. **4** *tr.* **a** vulcanize (rubber). **b** harden (concrete or plastic). **5** *intr.* effect a cure. **6** *intr.* undergo a process of curing. ● *n.* **1** restoration to health. **2** a thing that effects a cure. **3** a course of healing treatment. [from Latin *curare* 'to take care of'] □ **curative** *adj. & n. Med.* **curer** *n.*

curé /**kewr**-ay/ *n.* a parish priest in France etc. [French]

cure-all *n.* a panacea.

curette ● *n.* a surgeon's small instrument for scraping. ● *v.tr. & intr.* clean or scrape with a curette. [French, based on *curer* 'to cleanse'] □ **curettage** *n.*

curfew *n.* **1 a** a regulation requiring people to remain indoors between specified hours. **b** the hour designated as the beginning of such a restriction. **c** a daily signal indicating this. **2** *hist.* a medieval regulation requiring people to extinguish fires at a fixed hour in the evening. **3** the ringing of a bell at a fixed evening hour. [from Old French *cuevrefeu*, based on *couvrir* 'to cover' + *feu* 'fire']

Curia *n.* (also **curia**) the papal court; the government departments of the Vatican. [Latin: originally a division of an ancient Roman tribe] □ **Curial** *adj.*

curie *n.* a unit of radioactivity. [named after Pierre Curie (see CURIUM)]

curio *n.* (*pl.* **-os**) a rare or unusual object or person. [19th-century abbreviation of CURIOSITY]

curiosity *n.* (*pl.* **-ies**) **1** inquisitiveness. **2** strangeness. **3** a strange, rare, or interesting object.

curious *adj.* **1** inquisitive. **2** strange, surprising. [from Latin *curiosus* 'careful'] □ **curiously** *adv.* **curiousness** *n.*

curium *n.* an artificially made transuranic radioactive metallic element. [named after Marie Curie, 1867–1934, and Pierre Curie, 1859–1906, French discoverers of radium]

curl ● *v.* **1** *tr. & intr.* (often foll. by *up*) bend or coil into a spiral. **2** *intr.* move in a spiral form. **3 a** *intr.* (of the upper lip) be raised slightly on one side in disapproval. **b** *tr.* cause (the lip) to do this. **4** *intr.* play curling. ● *n.* **1** a lock of curled hair. **2** anything spiral or curved inwards. **3 a** a curling movement or act. **b** the state of being curled. □ **curl up 1** lie or sit with the knees drawn up. **2** *colloq.* writhe with embarrassment or horror. [from Middle Dutch *krul*] □ **curly** *adj.* (**curlier**, **curliest**). **curliness** *n.*

curler *n.* **1** a roller etc. for curling the hair. **2** a player in the game of curling.

curlew *n.* (*pl.* same or **curlews**) a wading bird of the genus *Numenius*, with a long slender downcurved bill. ▷ WADING BIRD. [from Old French *courlieu*]

curlicue *n.* a decorative curl or twist. [from *curly* + CUE[2] in earlier sense 'plait' or Q]

curling *n.* **1** in senses of CURL *v.* **2** a game played on ice, in which large round flat stones are slid across the surface.

curling tongs *n.pl.* (also **curling iron**) a heated device for twisting the hair into curls.

curly endive see ENDIVE 1.

curmudgeon *n.* a bad-tempered or miserly person. [16th century coinage] □ **curmudgeonly** *adj.*

currant *n.* **1** a small seedless dried grape. **2 a** a shrub of the genus *Ribes* producing red, white, or black berries. **b** such a berry. [from Anglo-French *raisins de Coarantz* 'grapes of Corinth', the original source]

currency *n.* (*pl.* **-ies**) **1 a** the money in general use in a country. **b** any other commodity used as money. **2** the condition of being current (e.g. of words or ideas).

current ● *adj.* **1** belonging to the present time; happening now (*current events*; *the current week*). **2** (of money, opinion, a rumour, a word, etc.) in general circulation or use. ● *n.* **1** a body of water, air, etc., moving esp. through a stiller surrounding body. **2** a flow of electricity, i.e. an ordered movement of electrically charged particles. ▷ ALTERNATING CURRENT. **3** (usu. foll. by *of*) a general tendency or course (of events, opinions, etc.). [from Old French *corant* 'running']

current account *n. Brit.* a bank account from which money may be drawn without notice.

currently *adv.* at the present time; now.

curriculum *n.* (*pl.* **curricula**) **1** the subjects included in a course of study. **2** any programme of activities. [Latin, literally 'course'] □ **curricular** *adj.*

curriculum vitae /-**vee**-ty/ *n.* (*pl.* **curricula vitae** or **vitarum**) a brief account of one's education and previous occupations. [Latin, literally 'course of life']

curry[1] *n.* (*pl.* **-ies**) a dish of meat, vegetables, etc., cooked in a sauce of hot-tasting spices, usu. served with rice. ● *v.tr.* (**-ies**, **-ied**) prepare or flavour with a sauce of hot-tasting spices (*curried eggs*). [from Tamil *kaṟi*]

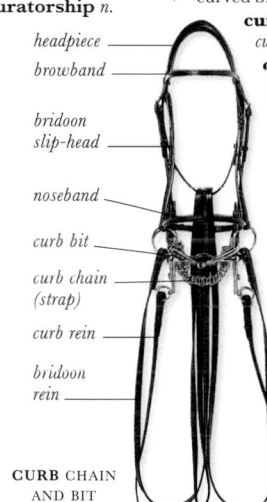

pictogram for beer   cuneiform wedge

CUNEIFORM: EXAMPLE OF SUMERIAN CUNEIFORM TEXT

headpiece
browband
bridoon slip-head
noseband
curb bit
curb chain (strap)
curb rein
bridoon rein

CURB CHAIN AND BIT OF A DOUBLE BRIDLE

C

curry[2] *v.tr.* (**-ies**, **-ied**) **1** groom (a horse) with a curry-comb. **2** treat (tanned leather) to improve its properties. □ **curry favour** ingratiate oneself. [from Old French *correier*]

curry-comb *n.* a hand-held serrated device used in grooming horses.

curry powder *n.* a preparation of spices for making curry.

curse ● *n.* **1** a solemn utterance intended to invoke the wrath of a supernatural power. **2** the evil supposedly resulting from a curse. **3** a violent exclamation of anger; a profane oath. **4** a thing that causes evil or harm. **5** (prec. by *the*) *colloq.* menstruation. ● *v.* **1** *tr.* utter a curse against. **2** *tr.* (usu. in *passive*; foll. by *with*) afflict with (*cursed with blindness*). **3** *intr.* utter expletive curses; swear. **4** *tr.* excommunicate. [Old English] □ **curser** *n.*

cursed *adj.* damnable, abominable. □ **cursedly** *adv.* **cursedness** *n.*

cursive ● *adj.* (of writing) done with joined characters. ● *n.* cursive writing. [from medieval Latin (*scriptura*) *cursiva*] □ **cursively** *adv.*

cursor *n.* **1** *Math.* etc. a transparent slide engraved with a hairline and forming part of a slide rule. **2** *Computing* a movable indicator on a VDU screen identifying a particular position in the display. [Latin, literally 'runner']

cursory *adj.* hasty, hurried. [from Latin *cursorius* 'of a runner'] □ **cursorily** *adv.* **cursoriness** *n.*

curt *adj.* noticeably or rudely brief. [from Latin *curtus* 'cut short'] □ **curtly** *adv.* **curtness** *n.*

curtail *v.tr.* cut short; reduce. [from obsolete *curtal* 'horse with docked tail'] □ **curtailment** *n.*

curtain ● *n.* **1** a piece of cloth etc. hung up as a screen, esp. at a window or between the stage and auditorium of a theatre. ▷ THEATRE. **2** *Theatr.* **a** the rise or fall of the stage curtain between acts or scenes. **b** = CURTAIN CALL. **3** a partition or cover. **4** (in *pl.*) *slang* the end. ● *v.tr.* **1** furnish or cover with a curtain or curtains. **2** (foll. by *off*) shut off with a curtain or curtains. [from Late Latin *cortina*]

curtain call *n.* an audience's summons to actor(s) to take a bow after the fall of the curtain.

curtain-raiser *n.* **1** *Theatr.* a piece prefaced to the main performance. **2** a preliminary event.

curtain wall *n.* **1** the plain wall of a fortified place, connecting two towers etc. ▷ CASTLE. **2** *Archit.* a piece of plain wall not supporting a roof.

curtsy (also **curtsey**) ● *n.* (*pl.* **-ies** or **-eys**) a woman's or girl's formal greeting made by bending the knees and lowering the body. ● *v.intr.* (**-ies**, **-ied** or **-eys**, **-eyed**) make a curtsy. [variant of COURTESY]

curvaceous *adj.* (esp. of a woman) having a shapely curved figure.

curvature *n.* **1** the act or state of curving. **2** a curved form. **3** *Geom.* **a** the deviation of a curved surface from a plane. **b** the quantity expressing this.

curve ● *n.* **1** a line or surface of which no part is straight or flat. **2** a curved form or thing. **3** a curved line on a graph. ● *v.tr. & intr.* bend or shape so as to form a curve. [based on Latin *curvus* 'bent'] □ **curved** *adj.*

curvet ● *n.* a horse's leap with the hind legs raised with a spring before the forelegs reach the ground. ● *v.intr.* (**curvetted**, **curvetting** or **curveted**, **curveting**) (of a horse or rider) make a curvet. [from Italian *corvetta* 'little curve']

curvi- *comb. form* curved.

curviform *adj.* having a curved shape.

curvilinear *adj.* contained by or consisting of curved lines. □ **curvilinearly** *adv.*

curvy *adj.* (**curvier**, **curviest**) **1** having many curves. **2** (of a woman's figure) shapely. □ **curviness** *n.*

cuscus *n.* any of several nocturnal arboreal marsupials of the genus *Phalanger*, native to New Guinea and northern Australia. [native name]

cushion ● *n.* **1** a bag stuffed with a mass of soft material for sitting or leaning on etc. **2** a means of

protection against shock. **3** the padded rim of a billiard table. ▷ POOL. **4** a body of air supporting a hovercraft etc. ● *v.tr.* **1** provide or protect with a cushion or cushions. **2** mitigate the adverse effects of. [from Latin *culcita*] □ **cushiony** *adj.*

cushy *adj.* (**cushier**, **cushiest**) *colloq.* (of a job etc.) easy and pleasant. [based on Persian *kuš* 'pleasure'] □ **cushiness** *n.*

cusp *n.* **1** an apex or peak. **2** the point at which two curves meet. **3** a cone-shaped prominence on the surface of a tooth. [from Latin *cuspis* 'point, apex'] □ **cuspate** *adj.* **cusped** *adj.* **cuspidal** *adj.*

cuspidor *n.* *N. Amer.* a spittoon. [Portuguese, literally 'spitter']

cuss *colloq.* ● *n.* **1** a curse. **2** usu. *derog.* a person; a creature. ● *v.tr. & intr.* curse.

cussed /kus-id/ *adj. colloq.* awkward and stubborn. □ **cussedly** *adv.* **cussedness** *n.*

cuss word *n. colloq.* a swear word.

custard *n.* **1** a sweet sauce made with milk and flavoured cornflour. **2** a dish made with milk and eggs, usu. sweetened. [originally an open pie of meat or fruit in a sauce: based on Old French *crouste* 'crust']

custard pie *n.* a pie containing custard or foam, commonly thrown in slapstick comedy.

custodian *n.* a guardian or keeper, esp. of a public building etc. □ **custodianship** *n.*

custody *n.* **1** guardianship; protective care. **2** imprisonment. □ **take into custody** arrest. [based on Latin *custos -odis* 'guardian'] □ **custodial** *adj.*

custom *n.* **1 a** the usual way of behaving or acting (*a slave to custom*). **b** a particular established way of behaving. **2** *Law* established usage having the force of law. **3** esp. *Brit.* business patronage (*lost custom*). **4** (in *pl.*; also treated as *sing.*) **a** a duty levied on certain imported and exported goods. **b** the official department that administers this. **c** the area at a port, frontier, etc., where customs officials deal with incoming goods etc. [from Latin *consuetudo*]

customary *adj.* **1** usual; in accordance with custom. **2** *Law* in accordance with custom. □ **customarily** *adv.*

custom-built *adj.* made to a customer's order.

customer *n.* **1** a person who buys goods or services from a shop or business. **2** a person one has to deal with (*an awkward customer*).

custom house *n.* (also **customs house**) the office at a port or frontier etc. at which customs duties are levied.

customize *v.tr.* (also **-ise**) make to order or modify according to individual requirements.

custom-made *adj.* = CUSTOM-BUILT.

cut ● *v.* (**cutting**; *past* and *past part.* **cut**) **1** *tr.* (also *absol.*) penetrate or wound with a sharp-edged instrument. **2** *tr. & intr.* (often foll. by *into*) divide or be divided with a knife etc. **3** *tr.* **a** trim (hair, a hedge, etc.) by cutting. **b** detach (flowers, corn, etc.) by cutting. **4** *tr.* (foll. by *loose, open*, etc.) make loose, open, etc. by cutting. **5** *tr.* (esp. as **cutting** *adj.*) cause sharp physical or mental pain to (*a cutting remark*; *a cutting wind*). **6** *tr.* (often foll. by *down*) **a** reduce (wages, prices, time, etc.). **b** reduce or cease (services etc.). **7** *tr.* **a** shape or fashion (a coat, gem, key, record, etc.) by cutting. **b** make (a path, tunnel, etc.) by removing material. **8** *tr.* perform, make (*cut a caper*; *cut a sorry figure*). **9** *tr.* (also *absol.*) cross, intersect (*the line cuts the circle at two points*). **10** *intr.* (foll. by *across, through*, etc.) traverse, esp. as a shorter way (*cut across the grass*). **11** *tr.* **a** ignore or refuse to recognize (a person). **b** renounce (a connection). **12** *tr.* esp. *N. Amer.* deliberately fail to attend (a class etc.). **13** *Cards* **a** divide (a pack) into two parts. **b** *intr.* select a dealer etc. by dividing the pack. **14** *Cinematog.* **a** *tr.* edit (a film or tape). **b** *intr.* (often in *imper.*) stop filming or recording. **c** *intr.* (foll. by *to*) go quickly to (another shot). **15** *tr.* switch off (an engine etc.). **16** *tr.* hit (a ball) with a chopping motion. **17** *tr. N. Amer.* dilute, adulterate. ● *n.* **1** an act of cutting. **2** a division or wound made by cutting. **3** a stroke with a knife, sword, whip, etc. **4 a** a reduction (in prices, wages, etc.). **b** *Brit.* a cessation (of a power supply etc.). **5** an excision of part of

CUT

The way in which a butcher cuts a carcass of meat is dictated by the animal's anatomy and breed, consumer requirements, and religious custom. Regional climates and local ingredients, such as herbs, fruit, and vegetables, influence cooking methods, and also therefore demand cuts of a certain kind. Butchering techniques also vary widely from country to country, and so cuts of meat differ equally. Their names vary almost as much, with national and regional terminologies sometimes conflicting.

EXAMPLES OF CUTS OF MEAT

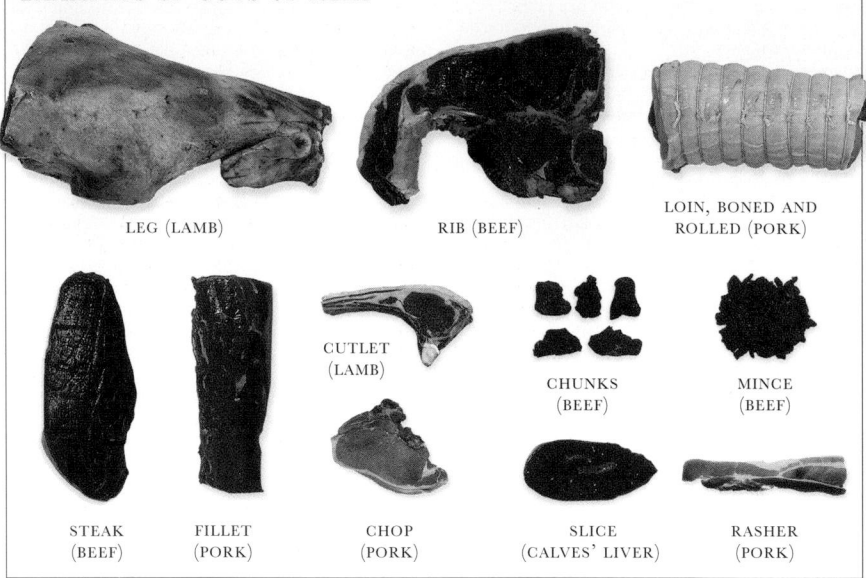

LEG (LAMB)　　RIB (BEEF)　　LOIN, BONED AND ROLLED (PORK)

CUTLET (LAMB)　　CHUNKS (BEEF)　　MINCE (BEEF)

STEAK (BEEF)　　FILLET (PORK)　　CHOP (PORK)　　SLICE (CALVES' LIVER)　　RASHER (PORK)

a play, film, book, etc. **6** a wounding remark or act. **7** the way or style in which a garment, the hair, etc., is cut. **8** ◀ a piece of meat etc. cut from a carcass. **9** *colloq.* commission; a share of profits. **10** *Tennis & Cricket* etc. a stroke made by cutting. **11** ignoring or refusal to recognize a person. □ **a cut above** *colloq.* noticeably superior to. **be cut out** (foll. by *for*, or *to* + infin.) be suited (*was not cut out to be a teacher*). **cut and dried 1** completely decided; pre-arranged; inflexible. **2** (of opinions etc.) ready-made, lacking freshness. **cut and run** *colloq.* run away. **cut and thrust 1** a lively interchange of argument etc. **2** the use of both the edge and the point of a sword. **cut back 1** reduce (expenditure etc.). **2** prune (a tree etc.). **cut both ways 1** serve both sides of an argument etc. **2** (of an action) have both good and bad effects. **cut a corner** go across and not round it. **cut corners** do a task etc. perfunctorily or incompletely, esp. to save time. **cut dead** completely refuse to recognize (a person). **cut down 1 a** bring or throw down by cutting. **b** kill by means of a sword or disease. **2** see sense 6 of *v.* **3** reduce the length of (*cut down the trousers to make shorts*). **4** (often foll. by *on*) reduce one's consumption (*cut down on beer*). **cut in 1** interrupt. **2** pull in too closely in front of another vehicle (esp. having overtaken it). **3** give a share of profits etc. to (a person). **cut into 1** make a cut in. **2** interfere with and reduce (*travelling cuts into my free time*). **cut it fine** see FINE[1]. **cut it out** (usu. in *imper.*) *colloq.* stop doing that (esp. quarrelling). **cut loose 1** begin to act freely. **2** see sense 4 of *v.* **cut one's losses** (or **a loss**) abandon an unprofitable enterprise before losses become too great. **cut the mustard** *N. Amer. slang* reach the required standard. **cut no ice** *colloq.* **1** have no influence or importance. **2** achieve little or nothing. **cut off 1** remove by cutting. **2 a** (often in *passive*) bring to an abrupt end or (esp. early) death. **b** intercept, interrupt; prevent from continuing (*cut off supplies; cut off the gas*). **c** disconnect (a person engaged in a telephone conversation) (*was suddenly cut off*). **3 a** prevent from travelling or going out (*cut off by the snow*). **b** (as **cut off** *adj.*) isolated, remote (*felt cut off in the country*). **4** disinherit (*was cut off without a penny*). **cut out 1** remove from the inside by cutting. **2** make by cutting from a larger whole. **3** omit; leave out. **4** *colloq.* stop doing or using (*cut out chocolate; cut out the arguing*). **5** cease or cause to cease functioning (*the engine cut out*). **cut short** interrupt; terminate prematurely (*cut short his visit*). **cut one's teeth on** acquire initial practice or experience from (something). **cut a tooth** have it appear through the gum. **cut up 1** cut into pieces. **2** destroy utterly. **3** (usu. in *passive*) *Brit. colloq.* distress greatly (*was very cut up about it*). **4** criticize severely. **cut up rough** *Brit. colloq.* show anger or resentment. [Middle English]

cutaneous *adj.* of the skin. [based on Latin *cutis* 'skin']

cutaway *adj.* **1** (of a diagram etc.) with some parts left out to reveal the interior. **2** (of a coat) with the front below the waist cut away.

cutback *n.* an instance or the act of cutting back, esp. a reduction in expenditure.

cute *adj. colloq.* **1 a** attractive, pretty; quaint. **b** affectedly attractive. **2** clever, ingenious. [shortening of ACUTE] □ **cutely** *adv.* **cuteness** *n.*

CUT GLASS
TUMBLER

cutesy *adj. colloq.* dainty or quaint to an affected degree.

cut glass *n.* ◀ glass with patterns and designs cut on it.

cuticle *n.* the dead skin at the base of a fingernail or toenail. ▷ NAIL. [from Latin *cuticula* 'little skin'] □ **cuticular** *adj.*

cutis *n. Anat.* the true skin or dermis, underlying the epidermis. [Latin, literally 'skin']

cutlass *n.* a short sword with a slightly curved blade, formerly used by sailors. [from Latin *cultellus* 'little coulter']

cutler *n.* a person who makes or deals in cutlery. [based on Latin *cultellus* 'knife']

cutlery *n.* knives, forks, and spoons for use at table.

cutlet *n.* **1** *Brit.* a neck-chop of mutton or lamb. ▷ CUT. **2** a small piece of veal etc. for frying. **3** a flat cake of minced meat or nuts and breadcrumbs etc. [from Old French *costelet* 'little rib']

cut-off *n.* **1** the point at which something is cut off. **2** a device for stopping a flow. **3** *US* a short cut. **4** (in *pl.*) shorts, esp. made by cutting the legs off jeans.

cut-out *n.* **1** a figure cut out of paper etc. **2** a device for automatic disconnection.

cut-out box *n. US* = FUSE BOX.

cut-price *adj.* (also **cut-rate**) selling or sold at a reduced price.

cutter *n.* **1** a person or thing that cuts. **2** a tailor etc. who takes measurements and cuts cloth. **3** *Naut.* **a** a small fast sailing ship. **b** a small boat carried by a large ship.

cut-throat ● *n.* **1** a murderer. **2** (in full **cut-throat razor**) *Brit.* a long-bladed usu. folding razor. ● *adj.* (of competition) ruthless and intense.

cutting ● *n.* **1** *Brit.* a piece cut from a newspaper etc. **2** a piece cut from a plant for propagation. **3** an excavated channel through high ground for a railway or road. ● *adj.* in senses of CUT *v.* 5. □ **cuttingly** *adv.*

cutting edge ● *n.* **1** an edge that cuts. **2** the forefront of a movement etc. **3** the most significant factor. ● *attrib.adj.* (**cutting-edge**) pioneering, innovative.

cuttle-bone *n.* the internal shell of the cuttlefish.

cuttlefish *n.* (*pl.* usu. same) any marine cephalopod mollusc of the genera *Sepia* and *Sepiola*, having ten arms and ejecting a black fluid when threatened or pursued. ▷ CEPHALOPOD. [Old English, related to obsolete *cod* 'bag', with reference to its ink-bag]

cutwater *n.* **1** the forward edge of a ship's prow. **2** a wedge-shaped projection from the pier of a bridge.

cutworm *n.* any of various caterpillars that eat through the stems of young plants level with the ground.

CV *abbr.* curriculum vitae.

cwm *n.* **1** (in Wales) = COOMB. **2** *Geog.* a cirque. [Welsh]

cwt. *abbr.* hundredweight.

cyanide *n.* any of the highly poisonous salts or esters of hydrocyanic acid, esp. potassium cyanide.

cyanobacterium *n.* any prokaryotic organism of the division Cyanobacteria, capable of photosynthesizing.

cyanocobalamin *n.* a vitamin of the B complex, found in foods of animal origin such as liver, fish, and eggs. [blend of CYANOGEN and COBALT and VITAMIN]

cyanogen *n. Chem.* a colourless highly poisonous gas intermediate in the preparation of many fertilizers. [based on Greek *kuanos* 'dark blue mineral', as being a constituent of Prussian blue]

cyanosis *n. Med.* a bluish discoloration of the skin due to the presence of oxygen-deficient blood. [from Greek *kuanōsis* 'blueness'] □ **cyanotic** *adj.*

cyber- *prefix* forming words relating to electronic communication networks and virtual reality.

cybernetics *n.* the science of communications and automatic control systems in both machines and living things. [based on Greek *kubernētēs* 'steersman'] □ **cybernetic** *adj.* **cybernetician** *n.* **cyberneticist** *n.*

cyberpunk *n.* a style of science fiction featuring urban counter-culture in a world of high technology and virtual reality.

cyberspace *n.* the notional environment in which electronic communication occurs; virtual reality.

cycad *n.* ▶ a palmlike plant of the order Cycadales (including fossil forms). [from supposed Greek *kukas*, scribal error for *koikas* 'Egyptian palms']

CYCAD:
SAGO PALM
(*Cycas revoluta*)

cyclamate *n.* any of various compounds related to sulphamic acid and formerly used as artificial sweetening agents. [contraction of chemical name *cyclohexylsulphamate*]

cyclamen *n.* (*pl.* same or **cyclamens**) ▶ any plant of the genus *Cyclamen*, originating in Europe, having pink, red, or white flowers with reflexed petals. [from Greek *kuklaminos*]

CYCLAMEN
(*Cyclamen repandum*)

cycle ● *n.* **1 a** a recurrent round or period (of events, phenomena, etc.). **b** the time needed for one such round or period. **2 a** *Physics* etc. a recurrent series of operations or states. **b** *Electr.* = HERTZ. **3** a series of songs, poems, etc., usu. on a single theme. **4** a bicycle, tricycle, or similar machine. ● *v.intr.* **1** ride a bicycle etc. **2** move in cycles. [from Greek *kuklos* 'circle']

cycle track *n.* (also **cycleway**) *Brit.* a path or road for bicycles.

cyclic *adj.* **1 a** recurring in cycles. **b** belonging to a chronological cycle. **2** *Chem.* with constituent atoms forming a ring.

cyclical *adj.* = CYCLIC 1. □ **cyclically** *adv.*

cyclist *n.* a rider of a cycle, esp. of a bicycle.

cyclo- *comb. form* circle, cycle, or cyclic. [from Greek *kuklos* 'circle']

cyclo-cross *n.* cross-country racing on bicycles.

cycloid *n. Math.* a curve traced by a point on a circle when the circle is rolled along a straight line. □ **cycloidal** *adj.*

cyclometer /sy-**klom**-i-ter/ *n.* **1** an instrument for measuring circular arcs. **2** an instrument for measuring the distance traversed by a vehicle.

cyclone *n.* **1** a system of winds rotating inwards to an area of low barometric pressure; a depression. ▷ DEPRESSION. **2** (in full **tropical cyclone**) a violent wind system of this kind in a small area. □ **cyclonic** *adj.* **cyclonically** *adv.*

cyclopedia *n.* (also **cyclopaedia**) an encyclopedia. □ **cyclopedic** *adj.*

cyclosporin *n. Med.* a peptide drug used to prevent the rejection of grafts and transplants. [based on *-sporum*, part of the name of a fungus which produces it]

cyclotron *n. Physics* an apparatus in which charged atomic and subatomic particles are accelerated by an alternating electric field while following an outward spiral or circular path in a magnetic field.

cyder *Brit.* var. of CIDER.

cygnet *n.* a young swan. [from Greek *kuknos* 'swan']

cylinder *n.* **1 a** ▶ a uniform solid or hollow body with straight sides and a circular section. **b** a thing of this shape, e.g. a container for liquefied gas. **2** a cylinder-shaped part of various machines, esp. a piston-chamber in an engine. ▷ INTERNAL-COMBUSTION ENGINE. **3** *Printing* a metal roller. ▷ PRINTING. [based on Greek *kulindein* 'to roll'] □ **cylindrical** *adj.* **cylindrically** *adv.*

CYLINDER

cylinder seal *n. Antiq.* a small barrel-shaped object of stone or baked clay bearing a cuneiform inscription, esp. for use as a seal.

C

cymbal *n.* ▶ a musical instrument consisting of a concave brass or bronze plate, struck with another or with a stick etc. to make a ringing sound. ▷ DRUM KIT, ORCHESTRA, PERCUSSION. [based on Greek *kumbē* 'cup'] □ **cymbalist** *n.*

cynic ● *n.* **1** a person who has little faith in human sincerity and integrity. **2** (**Cynic**) one of a school of ancient Greek philosophers founded by Antisthenes, marked by ostentatious contempt for ease and pleasure. ● *adj.* **1** (**Cynic**) of the Cynics. **2** = CYNICAL. [from Greek *kuōn kunos* 'dog', nickname for a Cynic] □ **cynicism** *n.*

cynical *adj.* **1** incredulous of human sincerity or integrity. **2** disregarding accepted or appropriate standards (*a cynical attempt to secure votes*). **3** sneering, mocking. □ **cynically** *adv.*

cynosure *n.* a centre of attraction or admiration. [from Greek *kunosoura* 'dog's tail, Ursa Minor']

cypher var. of CIPHER.

cypress /**sy**-prĕs/ *n.* (also **cypress tree**) ▶ any evergreen coniferous tree of the genus *Cupressus* or *Chamaecyparis*, esp. *Cupressus sempervirens*, with hard wood and dark foliage. ▷ CONIFER. [from Greek *kuparissos*]

Cypriot (also **Cypriote**) ● *n.* a native or national of Cyprus. ● *adj.* of Cyprus.

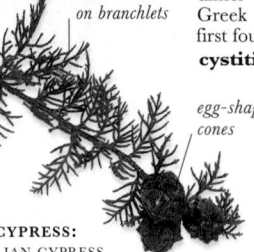

leather
handles

CYMBALS

blunt leaves
on branchlets

egg-shaped
cones

CYPRESS:
ITALIAN CYPRESS
(*Cupressus sempervirens*)

Cyrillic ● *adj.* denoting the alphabet used esp. for Russian and Bulgarian ● *n.* this alphabet. [named after St *Cyril*, 826–69, its reputed inventor]

cyst *n. Med.* a sac or cavity of abnormal character containing fluid. [from Greek *kustis* 'bladder']

cysteine *n. Biochem.* a sulphur-containing amino acid, essential in the human diet and a constituent of many enzymes.

cystic *adj.* **1** of the urinary bladder. **2** of the gall bladder. **3** of the nature of a cyst.

cystic fibrosis *n.* a hereditary disease affecting the exocrine glands and usu. resulting in respiratory infections.

cystine *n. Biochem.* an organic base which is a naturally occurring dimer of cysteine. [based on Greek *kustis* 'bladder', because first found in urinary calculi]

cystitis *n.* inflammation of the urinary bladder, usu. accompanied by frequent painful urination.

cysto- *comb. form* the urinary bladder. [from Greek *kustē, kustis* 'bladder']

cystoscope *n.* an instrument inserted in the urethra for examining the urinary bladder. [based on Greek *kustē kustis* 'bladder'] □ **cystoscopy** *n.*

-cyte *comb. form Biol.* a mature cell (*leucocyte*) (cf. -BLAST). [from Greek *kutos* 'vessel']

cyto- *comb. form Biol.* cells or a cell. [from Greek *kutos* 'vessel']

cytogenetics *n.* the study of inheritance in relation to the structure and function of cells. □ **cytogenetic** *adj.* **cytogenetical** *adj.* **cytogenetically** *adv.* **cytogeneticist** *n.*

cytology *n.* the study of cells. □ **cytological** *adj.* **cytologically** *adv.* **cytologist** *n.*

cytoplasm *n.* the protoplasmic content of a cell excluding its nucleus. ▷ CELL. □ **cytoplasmic** *adj.*

cytosine *n. Biochem.* a pyrimidine derivative found in all living tissue as a component base of DNA and RNA. ▷ DNA

cytotoxic *adj.* toxic to cells.

czar etc. var. of TSAR etc.

Czech /chek/ ● *n.* **1** a native or national of the Czech Republic, Bohemia, or (*hist*) Czechoslovakia. **2** the West Slavonic language of the Czech people (cf. SLOVAK). ● *adj.* of or relating to the Czechs or their language. [Polish spelling of Bohemian *Čech*]

Czechoslovak /chek-ŏ-**sloh**-vak/ (also **Czechoslovakian**) ● *n.* a native or national of the former state of Czechoslovakia. ● *adj.* of or relating to Czechoslovaks or the former state of Czechoslovakia.

D¹ *n.* (also **d**) (*pl.* **Ds** or **D's**) **1 a** the fourth letter of the alphabet. **b** a thing shaped like this. **2** *Mus.* the second note of the diatonic scale of C major. ▷ NOTATION. **3** (as a Roman numeral) 500. **4** the fourth highest class or category (of academic marks etc.).

D² *symb.* **1** *Chem.* the isotope deuterium. **2** electric flux density.

d *abbr.* (also **d.**) **1** died. **2** departs. **3** delete. **4** daughter. **5** diameter. **6** depth.

'd *abbr. colloq.* (usu. after pronouns) had, would (*I'd*; *he'd*). [abbreviation]

DA *abbr. US* district attorney.

da *abbr.* deca-.

dab¹ ● *v.* (**dabbed**, **dabbing**) **1** *tr.* press (a surface) briefly with a cloth etc., without rubbing. **2** *tr.* press (a sponge etc.) lightly on a surface. **3** *tr.* (foll. by *on*) apply (a substance) by dabbing a surface. **4** *intr.* (usu. foll. by *at*) aim a feeble blow; tap. **5** *tr.* strike lightly; tap. ● *n.* **1** a brief application of a cloth etc. to a surface without rubbing. **2** a small amount applied in this way (*a dab of paint*). **3** a light blow. **4** (in *pl.*) *Brit. slang* fingerprints. [Middle English] □ **dabber** *n.*

dab² *n.* a small flatfish of the genus *Limanda*. [Middle English]

dabble *v.* **1** *intr.* (usu. foll. by *in*, *at*) take a superficial interest (in a subject or activity). **2** *intr.* move the feet, hands, etc. about in esp. shallow liquid. **3** *tr.* wet partly, stain, splash. [from Dutch *dabbelen* or from DAB¹] □ **dabbler** *n.*

dabchick *n.* = LITTLE GREBE.

dab hand *n.* (usu. foll. by *at*) an expert.

dace *n.* (*pl.* same) any of several small freshwater fishes related to the carp, esp. *Leuciscus leuciscus*. [from Old French *darz*, *dars* 'dart']

dacha *n.* a Russian country cottage. [Russian, literally 'gift (of land)']

dachshund /daks-huund/ *n.* a dog of a short-legged long-bodied breed. [German, literally 'badger-dog']

dactyl *n.* a metrical foot (‒‿‿) consisting of one long syllable followed by two short. [from Greek *daktulos* 'finger', the three bones corresponding to the three syllables] □ **dactylic** *adj.*

dad *n. colloq.* father.

Dada *n.* an early 20th-c. movement in art, literature, music, and film, repudiating conventions. [French] □ **Dadaism** *n.* **Dadaist** *n. & adj.* **Dadaistic** *adj.*

daddy *n.* (*pl.* **-ies**) *colloq.* father.

daddy-long-legs *n. Brit.* a crane-fly.

dado *n.* (*pl.* **-os**) **1** the lower part of the wall of a room when visually distinct from the upper part. **2** the plinth of a column. ▷ PEDESTAL. **3** the cube of a pedestal between the base and the cornice. [Italian]

daemon var. of DEMON 4.

daemonic var. of DEMONIC.

daffodil ● *n.* **1 a** a bulbous plant, *Narcissus pseudonarcissus*, with a yellow trumpet-shaped corona. **b** any of various other plants of the genus *Narcissus*. **2** (in full **daffodil yellow**) a pale yellow colour. ● *adj.* (in full **daffodil yellow**; hyphenated when *attrib.*) pale yellow. [from Greek *asphodelos*]

daffy *adj.* (**daffier**, **daffiest**) *colloq.* = DAFT. [from obsolete *daff* 'simpleton'] □ **daffily** *adv.* **daffiness** *n.*

daft *adj. esp. Brit.* silly, foolish, crazy. [Old English]

dag *n. Austral. & NZ slang* an eccentric or noteworthy person (*he's a bit of a dag*). [obsolete dialect word]

dagger *n.* **1** a short pointed stabbing weapon. **2** *Printing* = OBELUS 1. □ **at daggers drawn** in bitter enmity. **look daggers at** glare angrily at.

daggy *adj.* (**daggier**, **daggiest**) *Austral. & NZ slang* **1** dowdy, scruffy. **2** unfashionable.

dago *n.* (*pl.* **-os** or **-oes**) *slang offens.* a foreigner, esp. a Spaniard, Portuguese, or Italian. [from *Diego*, Spanish equivalent of 'James']

daguerreotype /da-ge-rŏ-typ/ *n.* ► an early photograph using a silvered plate and mercury vapour. [named after L. *Daguerre*, French inventor, 1789–1851]

DAGUERREOTYPE

dahlia /day-liǎ/ *n.* any garden plant of the genus *Dahlia*, cultivated for its many-coloured flowers. [named after A. Dahl, Swedish botanist, 1751–1789]

Dáil /doil/ *n.* (in full **Dáil Éireann** /air-ěn/) the lower House of Parliament in the Republic of Ireland. [Irish]

daily ● *adj.* done, produced, or occurring every day or every weekday. ● *adv.* **1** every day. **2** constantly. ● *n.* (*pl.* **-ies**) *colloq.* **1** a daily newspaper. **2** *Brit.* a charwoman.

daily bread *n.* necessary food; a livelihood.

dainty ● *adj.* (**daintier**, **daintiest**) **1** delicately pretty. **2** delicate or small. **3** (of food) choice. **4** fastidious. ● *n.* (*pl.* **-ies**) a choice delicacy. [based on Latin *dignus* 'worthy'] □ **daintily** *adv.* **daintiness** *n.*

daiquiri /dak-i-ri/ *n.* (*pl.* **daiquiris**) a cocktail of rum, lime juice, etc. [from *Daiquiri*, a rum-producing district in Cuba]

dairy *n.* (*pl.* **-ies**) **1** a place for the storage, processing, and distribution of milk and its products. **2** a shop where milk and milk products are sold. **3** (*attrib.*) of, containing, or concerning milk and its products (and sometimes eggs). [Middle English, based on earlier *dæge* 'maidservant']

dairymaid *n.* a woman employed in a dairy.

dairyman *n.* (*pl.* **-men**) **1** a man dealing in dairy products. **2** a man employed in a dairy.

dais /day-iss/ *n.* a low platform, usu. at the upper end of a hall. [from medieval Latin *discus* 'table']

daisy *n.* (*pl.* **-ies**) **1** a small plant, *Bellis perennis*, with white-petalled flowers. **2** a plant with similar flowers. □ **pushing up the daisies** *slang* dead and buried. [Old English *dæges ēage* 'day's eye', the flower opening in the morning]

daisy chain *n.* a string of daisies threaded together.

daisy wheel *n.* a spoked disc bearing printed characters, used in word processors and typewriters.

dal var. of DHAL.

Dalai Lama *n.* the spiritual head of Tibetan Buddhism.

dale *n.* a valley. [Old English]

dalesman *n.* (*pl.* **-men**) an inhabitant of the dales in northern England.

dalliance *n.* **1** a leisurely or frivolous passing of time. **2** an instance of light-hearted flirting; a casual love affair. [based on DALLY]

dally *v.intr.* (**-ies**, **-ied**) **1** delay; waste time, esp. frivolously. **2** (often foll. by *with*) play about; flirt, treat frivolously. [from Old French *dalier* 'to chat']

Dalmatian *n.* a dog of a large white short-haired breed with dark spots. [from *Dalmatia*, a region in Croatia]

dam¹ ● *n.* **1** ▼ a barrier across a river etc., forming a reservoir or preventing flooding. **2** a barrier made by a beaver. ● *v.tr.* (**dammed**, **damming**) **1** provide or confine with a dam. **2** (often foll. by *up*) block up; obstruct. [from Middle Dutch]

DAM

A dam is a structure built to hold back water in order to prevent flooding, to store water for domestic and industrial use, or to provide hydroelectric power. Most dams are built across river valleys. The design of a dam depends on factors such as the size and shape of the valley, and the type of rock and soil occurring there.

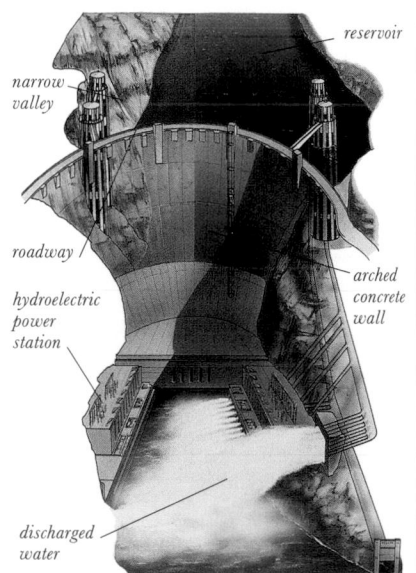

FEATURES OF AN ARCH DAM

reservoir
narrow valley
roadway
hydroelectric power station
arched concrete wall
discharged water

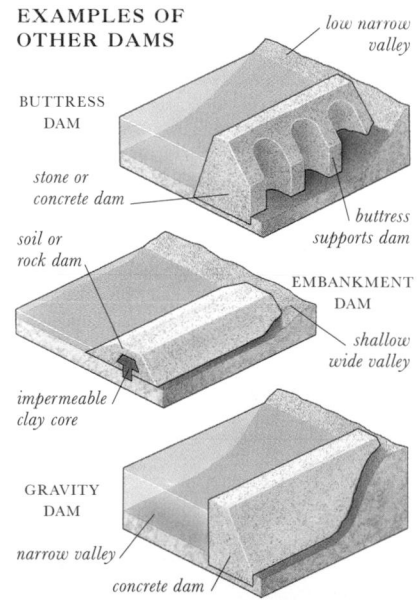

EXAMPLES OF OTHER DAMS

BUTTRESS DAM
stone or concrete dam
low narrow valley
buttress supports dam

EMBANKMENT DAM
soil or rock dam
impermeable clay core
shallow wide valley

GRAVITY DAM
narrow valley
concrete dam

D

dam² *n.* the mother of esp. a mammal. [variant of DAME]

damage ● *n.* **1** harm or injury. **2** (in *pl.*) *Law* financial compensation for a loss or an injury. **3** (prec. by *the*) *slang* cost. ● *v.tr.* inflict damage on. [from Latin *damnum* 'loss, damage'] □ **damagingly** *adv.*

damascene /dam-ă-seen/ *v.tr.* decorate (metal) by etching or inlaying esp. with gold or silver. [from *Damascene* 'of Damascus']

damask ● *n.* **1** a figured woven fabric (esp. silk or linen) with a pattern visible on both sides. **2** twilled table linen with woven designs shown by the reflection of light. ● *adj.* **1** made of or resembling damask. **2** velvety pink or vivid red. ● *v.tr.* weave with figured designs. [from Latin *Damascus*, proper name of the city]

damask rose *n.* ◄ an old sweet-scented variety of rose used to make attar.

dame *n.* **1** (**Dame**) **a** (in the UK) the title given to a woman with the rank of Knight Commander or holder of the Grand Cross in the Orders of Chivalry. **b** a woman holding this title. **2** *Brit.* a comic middle-aged female character in modern pantomime, usu. played by a man. **3** *N. Amer. slang* a woman. [from Latin *domina* 'mistress']

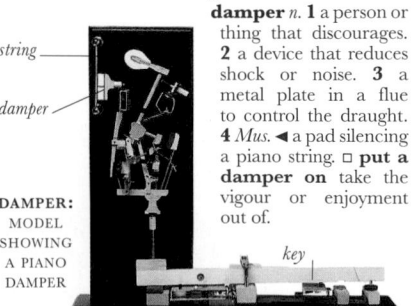

DAMASK ROSE
(*Rosa damascena*)

dammit *int.* damn it.

damn ● *v.tr.* **1** (often *absol.* or as *int.* of anger or annoyance, = *may God damn*) curse (a person or thing). **2** doom to hell; cause the damnation of. **3** condemn, censure (*a review damning the book*). **4** (often as **damning** *adj.*) (of a circumstance, evidence, etc.) show or prove to be guilty. ● *n.* **1** an uttered curse. **2** *colloq.* a negligible amount (*not worth a damn*). ● *adj. & adv. colloq.* = DAMNED. □ **damn all** *Brit. colloq.* nothing at all. **not give a damn** see GIVE. [from Latin *damnare* 'to inflict loss on'] □ **damningly** *adv.*

damnable *adj.* hateful, annoying. □ **damnably** *adv.*

damnation ● *n.* eternal punishment in hell. ● *int.* expressing anger.

damned *colloq.* ● *adj.* damnable. ● *adv.* extremely (*damned hot*). □ **do one's damnedest** do one's utmost.

damp ● *adj.* slightly wet. ● *n.* diffused moisture in the air, on a surface, or in a solid. ● *v.tr.* **1** make damp; moisten. **2** (often foll. by *down*) **a** take the force out of (*damp one's enthusiasm*). **b** make spiritless. **c** make (a fire) burn less strongly by reducing the flow of air to it. **3** reduce or stop the vibration of (esp. the strings of a musical instrument). **4** quieten. [from Old High German *dampf* 'steam'] □ **dampish** *adj.* **damply** *adv.* **dampness** *n.*

damp course *n.* a layer of waterproof material in the wall of a building near the ground, to prevent rising damp.

dampen *v.* **1** *tr. & intr.* make or become damp. **2** *tr.* make less forceful. □ **dampener** *n.*

damper *n.* **1** a person or thing that discourages. **2** a device that reduces shock or noise. **3** a metal plate in a flue to control the draught. **4** *Mus.* ◄ a pad silencing a piano string. □ **put a damper on** take the vigour or enjoyment out of.

string
damper

DAMPER: MODEL SHOWING A PIANO DAMPER

key

damp-proof ● *adj.* impervious to damp. ● *v.tr.* make damp-proof.

damp-proof course *n.* = DAMP COURSE.

damp squib *n. Brit.* an unsuccessful attempt to impress etc.

damsel *n. archaic* or *literary* a young unmarried woman. [from Old French, based on Latin *domina* 'mistress']

damselfly *n.* (*pl.* **-flies**) ► an insect of the order Odonata, like a dragonfly but with its wings folded over the body when resting.

DAMSELFLY: BEAUTIFUL DEMOISELLE (*Agrion virgo*)

damson ● *n.* **1** **a** a small dark purple plumlike fruit. **b** (also **damson tree**) the tree, *Prunus institia*, bearing this. **2** a dark purple colour. ● *adj.* damson-coloured. [from Latin *damascenum (prunum)* '(plum) of Damascus']

damson cheese *n.* a solid preserve of damsons and sugar.

dan *n.* **1** any of ten degrees of advanced proficiency in judo or karate. **2** a holder of any of these. [Japanese]

dance ● *v.* **1** *intr.* move rhythmically to music. **2** *intr.* skip or jump about. **3** *tr.* **a** perform (a specified dance). **b** perform (a specified role) in a ballet etc. **4** *intr.* bob up and down. **5** *tr.* dandle (a child). ● *n.* **1 a** a piece of dancing; a sequence of steps in dancing. **b** a special form of this. **2** a single round or turn of a dance. **3** a social gathering for dancing. **4** a piece of music for dancing to or in a dance rhythm. **5** a dancing or lively motion. □ **dance attendance on** follow or wait on (a person) obsequiously. **lead a person a dance** (or **merry dance**) *Brit.* cause a person much trouble. [from Old French] □ **danceable** *adj.* **dancer** *n.*

dance hall *n.* a public hall for dancing.

d. and c. *n.* dilatation (of the cervix) and curettage (of the uterus), performed after a miscarriage or for the removal of cysts, tumours, etc.

dandelion *n.* a plant of the genus *Taraxacum* (daisy family), with jagged leaves and a large bright yellow flower on a hollow stalk. [from French *dent-de-lion* 'lion's tooth', from the shape of the leaves]

dandelion clock *n.* the downy seed-head of a dandelion.

dander *n. colloq.* temper, indignation. □ **get one's dander up** become angry.

dandify *v.tr.* (**-ies**, **-ied**) (usu. as **dandified** *adj.*) cause to resemble a dandy.

dandle *v.tr.* dance (a child) on one's knees or in one's arms. [16th-century coinage]

dandruff *n.* flakes of dead skin in the hair. [16th-century coinage]

dandy ● *n.* (*pl.* **-ies**) **1** a man unduly devoted to style, smartness, and fashion in dress and appearance. **2** *colloq.* an excellent thing. ● *adj.* (**dandier, dandiest**) esp. *N. Amer. colloq.* splendid. [18th-century coinage] □ **dandyish** *adj.* **dandyism** *n.*

Dane *n.* **1** a native or national of Denmark. **2** *hist.* a Viking invader of England in the 9th–11th c. [from Old Norse]

danger *n.* **1** liability or exposure to harm. **2** a thing that causes or may cause harm. □ **in danger of** likely to incur or to suffer from. [earlier in sense 'power': based on Latin *dominus* 'lord']

danger list *n. Brit.* a list of those dangerously ill.

danger money *n. Brit.* extra payment for dangerous work.

dangerous *adj.* involving or causing danger. □ **dangerously** *adv.* **dangerousness** *n.*

dangle *v.* **1** *intr.* be loosely suspended and able to sway. **2** *tr.* hold or carry loosely suspended. **3** *tr.* hold out (a hope, temptation, etc.) enticingly. □ **dangler** *n.* **dangly** *adj.*

Danish ● *adj.* of Denmark or the Danes. ● *n.* **1** the Danish language. **2** (prec. by *the*; treated as *pl.*) the Danish people.

Danish blue *n.* a white blue-veined cheese. ▷ CHEESE

Danish pastry *n.* a yeast cake topped with icing, fruit, nuts, etc.

dank *adj.* disagreeably damp and cold. [Middle English] □ **dankly** *adv.* **dankness** *n.*

daphne *n.* any flowering shrub of the genus *Daphne*. [from *Daphnē*, a Greek nymph changed into a laurel to escape Apollo's advances]

daphnia *n.* a minute freshwater crustacean of the genus *Daphnia*, enclosed in a transparent carapace and with long antennae and prominent eyes. [modern Latin]

dapper *adj.* **1** neat and precise, esp. in dress or movement. **2** sprightly. [from Middle Dutch] □ **dapperly** *adv.* **dapperness** *n.*

dapple ● *v. tr. & intr.* mark or become marked with spots of colour or shade. ● *n.* a dappled effect.

dapple grey ● *adj.* (hyphenated when *attrib.*) ▼ (of an animal's coat) grey or white with darker spots. ● *n.* a dapple-grey horse.

DAPPLE-GREY ORLOV TROTTER

Darby and Joan *n.* esp. *Brit.* a devoted old married couple. [characters in a poem (1735) in the *Gentleman's Magazine*]

Darby and Joan club *n. Brit.* a club for people over 60.

dare ● *v.tr.* (*3rd sing. present* usu. **dare** before an expressed or implied infinitive without *to*) **1** (foll. by infin. with or without *to*) venture (to); have the courage or impudence (to) (*dare he do it?; if they dare to come; how dare you?*). **2** (usu. foll. by *to* + infin.) defy or challenge (a person) (*I dare you to own up*). ● *n.* **1** an act of daring. **2** a challenge, esp. to prove courage. □ **I dare say 1** it is probable. **2** probably; I grant that much. [Old English] □ **darer** *n.*

daredevil ● *n.* a recklessly daring person. ● *adj.* recklessly daring. □ **daredevilry** *n.*

daring ● *n.* adventurous courage. ● *adj.* adventurous, bold; prepared to take risks. □ **daringly** *adv.*

dariole *n.* a dish cooked and served in a small mould. [from Old French]

dark ● *adj.* **1** with little or no light. **2** of a deep or sombre colour. **3** (of a person) with deep brown or black hair or skin. **4** gloomy, depressing, dismal (*dark thoughts*). **5** evil, sinister (*dark deeds*). **6** sullen, angry (*a dark mood*). **7** secret, mysterious (*the dark and distant past; keep it dark*). **8** ignorant, unenlightened (*dark ages*). ● *n.* **1** absence of light. **2** nightfall (*don't go out after dark*). **3** a lack of knowledge. **4** a dark area or colour, esp. in painting. □ **in the dark 1** with little or no light. **2** lacking information. [Old English] □ **darkish** *adj.* **darkly** *adv.* **darkness** *n.* **darksome** *adj. poet.*

Dark Ages *n.pl.* (also **Dark Age**) (prec. by *the*) **1** the period of European history preceding the Middle Ages, esp. the 5th–10th c. **2** (often **dark ages**) any period of supposed unenlightenment.

Dark Continent *n.* (prec. by *the*) a name for Africa, esp. when little known to Europeans.

darken *v.* **1** *tr.* make dark or darker. **2** *intr.* become dark or darker. □ **never darken a person's door** keep away from a person permanently.

dark glasses *n.pl.* spectacles with dark-tinted lenses.

dark horse *n.* a little-known person who unexpectedly becomes successful.

dark matter *n. Astron.* hypothetical non-luminous material in space, not detected, but predicted by many cosmological theories.

darkroom *n.* a room for photographic work, with normal light excluded.

darling ● *n.* **1** a beloved or lovable person or thing. **2** a favourite. **3** *colloq.* a pretty or endearing person or thing. ● *adj.* **1** beloved, lovable. **2** favourite. **3** *colloq.* charming or pretty. [Old English]

darn[1] ● *v.tr.* **1** mend by interweaving yarn across a hole with a needle. **2** embroider with a large running stitch. ● *n.* a darned area in material. [17th-century coinage]

darn[2] *v.tr., int., adj., & adv. colloq.* = DAMN (in imprecatory senses).

darned *adj. & adv. colloq.* = DAMNED.

darnel *n.* any of several grasses of the genus *Lolium*, esp. *L. temulentum*, a weed of cereal crops. [Middle English]

darning *n.* **1** the action of a person who darns. **2** things to be darned.

dart ● *n.* **1** a small pointed missile thrown or fired as a weapon. **2 a** ▶ a small pointed missile with a feather or plastic flight, used in the game of darts. **b** (in *pl.*; usu. treated as *sing.*) an indoor game in which such darts are thrown at a circular target to score points. **3** a sudden rapid movement. **4** *Zool.* a dartlike structure, such as an insect's sting. **5** a tapering tuck stitched in a garment. ● *v.* **1** *intr.* move or go suddenly or rapidly (*darted into the shop*). **2** *tr.* throw (a missile). **3** *tr.* direct suddenly (*a glance etc.*). [from Old French *darz, dars*]

flight

DARTS

dartboard *n.* a circular board marked with numbered segments, used as a target in darts.

Darwinian ● *adj.* of or relating to Darwin's theory of the evolution of species by the action of natural selection. ● *n.* an adherent of this theory. [from C. *Darwin*, English naturalist, 1809–1882] □ **Darwinism** *n.* **Darwinist** *n. & adj.*

dash ● *v.* **1** *intr.* rush hastily or forcefully (*dashed up the stairs*). **2** *tr.* strike or fling with great force (*dashed it to the ground*). **3** *tr.* frustrate, daunt, dispirit (*dashed their hopes*). **4** *tr. Brit. colloq.* (**dash it** or **dash it all**) = DAMN *v.* 1. ● *n.* **1** a rush or onset; a sudden advance (*made a dash for shelter*). **2** a horizontal stroke in writing or printing to mark a pause or break in sense or to represent omitted letters or words. **3** impetuous vigour or the capacity for this. **4** showy appearance or behaviour; stylishness. **5** *N. Amer.* a sprinting race. **6** the longer signal of the two used in Morse code (cf. DOT *n.* 2). **7** a slight admixture, esp. of a liquid. **8** = DASHBOARD. □ **cut a dash** make a brilliant show. **dash down** (or **off**) write or finish hurriedly. [Middle English]

dashboard *n.* the surface below the windscreen of a motor vehicle or aircraft, containing instruments and controls. ▷ INSTRUMENT PANEL

dashiki /dah-shi-ki/ *n.* a loose brightly coloured shirt worn by American blacks. [West African]

dashing *adj.* **1** spirited, lively. **2** stylish. □ **dashingly** *adv.*

dastardly *adj.* cowardly, despicable. [from earlier *dastard* 'base coward']

DAT *abbr.* digital audio tape.

data *n.pl.* (also treated as *sing.*, although the singular form is strictly *datum*) **1** known facts or things used as a basis for inference or reckoning. **2** quantities or characters operated on by a computer etc. [plural of DATUM]

■ **Usage** (1) In scientific, philosophical, and general use, this word is usually considered to denote a number of items and is thus treated as plural with *datum* as the singular. (2) In computing and allied subjects (and sometimes in general use), it is treated as a mass (or collective) noun and used with words like *this*, *that*, and *much*, with singular verbs, e.g. *useful data has been collected*. Some people consider use (2) to be incorrect but it is more common than use (1). However, *data* is not a singular countable noun.

data bank *n.* **1** a store or source of data. **2** = DATABASE.

database *n.* a structured set of data held in a computer.

datable *adj.* (often foll. by *to*) capable of being dated (to a particular time).

data capture *n.* the action or process of entering data into a computer.

data processing *n.* a series of operations on data, esp. by a computer. □ **data processor** *n.*

data protection *n. Brit.* legal control over access to data stored in computers.

date[1] ● *n.* **1** a day of the month. **2** a particular day or year, esp. when a given event occurred. **3** a statement (usu. giving the day, month, and year) in a document or inscription etc., of the time of composition or publication. **4** the period to which a work of art etc. belongs. **5** the time when an event happens or is to happen. **6** *colloq.* **a** an appointment or social engagement, esp. with a person of the opposite sex. **b** esp. *N. Amer.* a person with whom one has a social engagement. ● *v.* **1** *tr.* mark with a date. **2** *tr.* **a** assign a date to (an object, event, etc.). **b** (foll. by *to*) assign to a particular time, period, etc. **3** *intr.* have its origins at a particular time. **4** *intr.* become evidently out of date (*a design that dates and dates*). **5** *tr.* indicate or expose as being out of date (*that hat really dates you*). **6** *colloq.* **a** *tr.* make an arrangement with (a person) to meet socially. **b** *intr.* meet socially by agreement (*they are now dating regularly*). □ **to date** until now. [from the Latin formula *data (epistola)* '(letter) given', used in dating letters]

date[2] *n.* **1** a dark oval single-stoned fruit. **2** (in full **date palm**) the tall tree *Phoenix dactylifera*, native to W. Asia and N. Africa, bearing this fruit. [based on Greek *daktulos* 'finger', from the leaf shape]

date line *n.* **1** (**Date Line**) (in full **International Date Line**) an imaginary north-south line through the Pacific Ocean, to the east of which the date is a day earlier than it is to the west. **2** a line at the head of a dispatch or special article in a newspaper showing the date and place of writing.

date rape *n.* rape by a person with whom one is on a date.

date stamp ● *n.* **1** an adjustable rubber stamp etc. used to record a date. **2** the impression made by this. ● *v.tr.* (**date-stamp**) mark with a date stamp.

dative *Gram.* ● *n.* the case of nouns and pronouns (and words in grammatical agreement with them) indicating an indirect object or recipient. ● *adj.* of or in the dative. [based on Latin *dare* 'to give']

datum *n.* (*pl.* **data**: see DATA) **1** a piece of information. **2** a thing known or granted; an assumption or premiss from which inferences may be drawn. **3** a fixed starting point of a scale etc. (*datum line*). [Latin, literally 'thing given']

datura *n.* any poisonous plant of the genus *Datura*, e.g. the thorn apple. [from Hindi]

daub ● *v.tr.* **1** spread (paint, plaster, or some other thick substance) crudely or roughly. **2** coat or smear (a surface) with paint etc. **3 a** (also *absol.*) paint crudely or unskilfully. **b** lay (colours) on crudely and clumsily. ● *n.* **1** paint or other substance daubed on a surface. **2** plaster, clay, etc., for coating a surface, esp. mixed with straw and applied to laths or wattles to form a wall. ▷ WATTLE AND DAUB. **3** a crude painting. [from Latin *dealbare* 'to whitewash'] □ **dauber** *n.*

daube /dohb/ *n.* a stew of braised meat with wine etc. [French]

daughter *n.* **1** a girl or woman in relation to either or both of her parents. **2** a female descendant. **3** (foll. by *of*) a female member of a family, nation, etc. **4** (foll. by *of*) a woman who is regarded as the spiritual descendant of, or as spiritually attached to, a person or thing. [Old English] □ **daughterly** *adj.*

daughter-in-law *n.* (*pl.* **daughters-in-law**) the wife of one's son.

daunt *v.tr.* discourage, intimidate. [based on Latin *domare* 'to tame'] □ **daunting** *adj.* **dauntingly** *adv.*

dauntless *adj.* intrepid, persevering.

dauphin *n. hist.* the eldest son of the King of France. [French]

Davenport *n.* **1** *Brit.* an ornamental writing desk with drawers and a sloping surface for writing. **2** *US* a large heavily upholstered sofa. [probably from Captain *Davenport*, for whom early examples of the desk were made (18th c.)]

davit *n.* a small crane on board a ship. [from Old French, based on the name *David*]

Davy *n.* (*pl.* **-ies**) ▶ (in full **Davy lamp**) a miner's safety lamp with the flame enclosed by wire gauze. [named after Sir H. *Davy*, English chemist, 1778–1829, who invented it]

Davy Jones *n. slang* (in full **Davy Jones's locker**) the bottom of the sea, esp. regarded as the grave of those drowned at sea.

dawdle *v.* **1** *intr.* **a** walk slowly and idly. **b** delay; waste time. **2** *tr.* (foll. by *away*) waste (time).

dawn ● *n.* **1** daybreak. **2** the beginning of something. ● *v.intr.* **1** (of a day) begin; grow light. **2** (often foll. by *on*, *upon*) begin to become evident or understood (by a person). [from earlier *dawning*, related to DAY] □ **dawning** *n.*

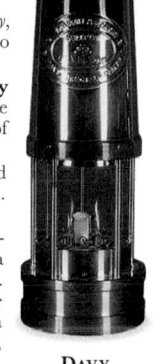

DAVY LAMP

dawn chorus *n.* the singing of many birds at the break of day.

day *n.* **1** the time between sunrise and sunset. **2** a period of 24 hours as a unit of time. **3** daylight (*clear as day*). **4** the time in a day during which work is normally done (*an eight-hour day*). **5 a** (also *pl.*) a period of the past or present (*the modern day; the old days*). **b** (prec. by *the*) the present time (*the issues of the day*). **6** the prime of a person's life (*have had my day; in my day things were different*). **7** a point of time (*will do it one day*). **8** the date of a particular festival or event (*graduation day; pay day; Christmas Day*). **9** a particular date; a date agreed on. **10** a day's endeavour, or the period of an endeavour, esp. as bringing success (*win the day*). □ **call it a day** end a period of activity, esp. satisfied that enough has been done. **day by day** gradually. **day in, day out** routinely, constantly. **day of rest** the sabbath. **from day one** from the beginning. **one of these days** before very long. **one of those days** a day when things go badly. **that will be the day** *colloq.* that will never happen. **this day and age** the present time or period. [Old English]

daybed *n.* a bed for daytime rest.

day-boy *n.* (*fem.* **day-girl**) *Brit.* a boy or girl educated at a boarding school whilst living at home.

daybreak *n.* the first appearance of light in the morning.

day care *n.* (often hyphenated when *attrib.*) **1** the supervision of young children during the working day. **2** the care provided by a day centre.

day centre *n.* (also **day care centre**) a place providing care for the elderly or handicapped during the day.

D

daydream ● *n.* a pleasant fantasy or reverie. ● *v.intr.* indulge in this.

Day-Glo ● *n. propr.* a make of fluorescent paint or other colouring. ● *adj.* coloured with or like this.

daylight *n.* **1** the light of day. **2** dawn (*before daylight*). **3 a** openness, publicity. **b** open knowledge. **4** a visible gap or interval. **5** (in *pl.*) *colloq.* one's life or consciousness (*beat the living daylights out of them*). □ **see daylight** begin to understand what was previously obscure.

daylight robbery *n. Brit. colloq.* a blatantly excessive charge.

daylight saving *n.* the achieving of longer evening daylight, esp. in summer, by setting the time an hour ahead of the standard time.

day nursery *n.* a nursery where children are looked after during the working day.

day off *n.* a day's holiday.

Day of Judgement *n.* = JUDGEMENT DAY.

day of reckoning *n.* the time when something must be atoned for or avenged.

day out *n. Brit.* an excursion for a day.

day release *n. Brit.* a system of allowing employees days off work for education.

day return *n. Brit.* a fare or ticket at a reduced rate for a journey out and back in one day.

day room *n.* a room, esp. a communal room in an institution, used during the day.

day school *n.* a school for pupils living at home.

daytime *n.* the part of the day when there is natural light.

day-to-day *adj.* mundane, routine.

day trip *n.* a trip or excursion completed in one day. □ **day tripper** *n. Brit.*

daze ● *v.tr.* stupefy, bewilder. ● *n.* a state of confusion or bewilderment (*in a daze*). [based on Old Norse *dasathr* 'weary'] □ **dazedly** *adv.*

dazzle ● *v.tr.* **1** blind temporarily or confuse the sight of by an excess of light. **2** impress or overpower (a person) with knowledge, ability, or any brilliant display or prospect. ● *n.* bright confusing light. [related to DAZE] □ **dazzlement** *n.* **dazzler** *n.* **dazzling** *adj.* **dazzlingly** *adv.*

dB *abbr.* decibel(s).

DC *abbr.* **1** (also **dc**) direct current. **2** District of Columbia.

DCL *abbr.* Doctor of Civil Law.

DD *abbr.* Doctor of Divinity.

D-Day *n.* **1** the day (6 June 1944) on which Allied forces invaded northern France. **2** the day on which an important operation is to begin or a change to take effect. [D: abbreviation of *day*]

DDT *abbr.* dichlorodiphenyltrichloroethane, a synthetic organic compound used as an insecticide, but now widely banned for its damaging effects on wildlife.

de- *prefix* **1** forming verbs and their derivatives: **a** down, away (*descend*). **b** completely (*declare*; *denude*). **2** added to verbs and their derivatives to form verbs and nouns implying removal or reversal (*decentralize*; *de-ice*).

deacon *n.* **1** (in episcopal Churches) a minister of the third order, below bishop and priest. **2** (in Nonconformist Churches) a lay officer attending to a congregation's secular affairs. **3** (in the early Church) an appointed minister of charity. [from Greek *diakonos* 'servant']

deaconess *n.* a woman in the early Church and in some modern Churches with functions analogous to a deacon's.

deactivate *v.tr.* make inactive or less reactive. □ **deactivation** *n.*

dead ● *adj.* **1** no longer alive. **2** *colloq.* extremely tired or unwell. **3** benumbed (*my fingers are dead*). **4** (foll. by *to*) insensitive to. **5** no longer effective or in use; extinct. **6** (of a match, of coal, etc.) no longer burning; extinguished. **7** inanimate.

8 a lacking force or vigour. **b** (of sound) not resonant. **9 a** quiet; lacking activity (*the dead season*). **b** motionless, idle. **10 a** (of a microphone, telephone, etc.) not transmitting any sound. **b** (of a circuit, conductor, etc.) carrying or transmitting no current (*a dead battery*). **11** (of the ball in a game) out of play. **12** abrupt, complete (*come to a dead stop*; *a dead faint*; *in dead silence*). ● *adv.* **1** absolutely, exactly, completely (*dead on target*; *dead level*; *dead tired*). **2** *Brit. colloq.* very, extremely (*dead easy*). ● *n.* (prec. by *the*) **1** (treated as *pl.*) those who have died. **2** a time of silence or inactivity (*the dead of night*). □ **dead to the world** *colloq.* fast asleep; unconscious. [Old English] □ **deadness** *n.*

deadbeat ● *adj.* (usu. **dead beat** when *predic.*) *colloq.* exhausted. ● *n.* **1** *colloq.* an idle, feckless, or disreputable person. **2** *US slang* a person constantly in debt.

deadbolt *n. esp. US* a bolt engaged by turning a knob or key, rather than by spring action.

dead cert *Brit.* see CERT.

dead duck *n. colloq.* an unsuccessful or useless person or thing.

deaden *v.* **1** *tr. & intr.* deprive of or lose vitality, force, brightness, sound, feeling, etc. **2** *tr.* (foll. by *to*) make insensitive.

dead end *n.* **1** a closed end of a road, passage, etc. **2** (often, with hyphen, *attrib.*) a situation offering no prospects of progress.

dead hand *n.* an oppressive persisting influence.

dead-head ● *n.* **1** *Brit.* a faded flower head. **2** *colloq.* a passenger or member of an audience who has made use of a free ticket. **3** *colloq.* a useless person. ● *v.tr.* remove dead-heads from (a plant).

dead heat *n.* **1** a race in which two or more competitors finish exactly level. **2** the result of such a race.

dead language *n.* a language no longer spoken.

dead letter *n.* **1** a law or practice no longer observed or recognized. **2** an unclaimed or undelivered letter.

deadline *n.* a time limit for the completion of an activity etc.

deadlock ● *n.* **1** a situation, esp. one involving opposing parties, in which no progress can be made. **2** a type of lock requiring a key to open or close it. ● *v.tr. & intr.* bring or come to a standstill.

dead loss *n.* **1** *colloq.* a useless person or thing. **2** a complete loss.

deadly ● *adj.* (**deadlier**, **deadliest**) **1 a** causing or able to cause fatal injury or serious damage. **b** poisonous (*deadly snake*). **2** intense, extreme (*deadly dullness*). **3** (of an aim etc.) extremely accurate or effective. **4** deathlike (*deadly pallor*). **5** *colloq.* dreary, dull. **6** implacable. ● *adv.* **1** like death; as if dead (*deadly faint*). **2** extremely, intensely (*deadly serious*). □ **deadliness** *n.*

deadly nightshade *n.* ◄ a highly poisonous plant, *Atropa belladonna*, with drooping purple flowers and black cherry-like fruit.

DEADLY NIGHTSHADE
(*Atropa belladonna*)

deadly sin *n.* a sin regarded as leading to damnation, esp. pride, covetousness, lust, gluttony, envy, anger, or sloth.

dead man's handle *n.* (also **dead man's pedal**) a controlling device on an electric train allowing power to be connected only as long as the operator presses on it.

dead march *n.* a funeral march.

dead nettle *n.* a plant of the genus *Lamium* or a related genus of the mint family, having nettle-like leaves but without stinging hairs.

dead on *adj.* exactly right.

deadpan *adj. & adv.* lacking expression or emotion.

dead reckoning *n.* calculation of a ship's position from the log, compass, etc., when observations are impossible.

dead ringer see RINGER.

dead set *n.* a determined attack or attempt.

dead shot *n.* person who shoots extremely accurately.

dead weight *n.* (also **dead-weight**) **1 a** an inert mass. **b** a heavy burden. **2** a debt not covered by assets. **3** the total weight carried on a ship.

dead wood *n. colloq.* one or more useless people or things.

deaf *adj.* **1** wholly or partly without hearing (*deaf in one ear*). **2** (foll. by *to*) refusing to listen or comply. **3** insensitive to harmony, rhythm, etc. (*tone-deaf*). □ **fall on deaf ears** be ignored. **turn a deaf ear** be unresponsive. [Old English] □ **deafness** *n.*

deaf aid *n. Brit.* a hearing aid.

deaf-blind *adj.* (of a person) both deaf and blind.

deafen *v.tr.* **1** (often as **deafening** *adj.*) overpower with sound. **2** deprive of hearing by noise, esp. temporarily. □ **deafeningly** *adv.*

deaf mute *n.* a person who is both deaf and dumb.

■ **Usage** The term *deaf mute* is now generally avoided in favour of the term *profoundly deaf*. If complete unambiguity is needed, *deaf without speech* can be used.

deal[1] ● *v.* (*past* and *past part.* **dealt**) **1** *intr.* **a** (foll. by *with*) take measures concerning (a problem, person, etc.), esp. in order to put something right. **b** (foll. by *with*) do business with; associate with. **c** (foll. by *with*) discuss or treat (a subject). **d** (often foll. by *by*) behave in a specified way towards a person (*dealt honourably by them*). **2** *intr.* (foll. by *in*) sell or be concerned with commercially (*deals in insurance*). **3** *tr.* distribute or apportion to several people etc. **4** *tr.* (also *absol.*) distribute (cards) to players. **5** *tr.* cause to be received; administer (*deal a heavy blow*). **6** *tr.* assign as a share or deserts to a person (*Providence dealt them much happiness*). ● *n.* **1** (usu. **a good** or **great deal**) **a** a large amount (*a good deal of trouble*). **b** to a considerable extent (*is a great deal better*). **2** a business arrangement; a transaction. **3** a specified form of treatment (*gave them a rough deal*; *got a fair deal*). **4 a** the distribution of cards by dealing. **b** a player's turn to do this (*it's my deal*). **c** the round of play following this. **d** a set of hands dealt to players. □ **it's a deal** *colloq.* expressing assent to an agreement. [Old English]

deal[2] *n.* **1** fir or pine timber. **2** a board of this timber. [from Middle Dutch *dele* 'plank']

dealer *n.* **1** a person or business dealing in (esp. retail) goods (*contact your dealer*; *car-dealer*). **2** the player dealing at cards. **3** a jobber on the Stock Exchange. □ **dealership** *n.* (in sense 1).

■ **Usage** The term *dealer* in sense 3 was officially replaced by *broker-dealer* in 1986 (see Usage Note at BROKER).

dealings *n.pl.* contacts or transactions. □ **have dealings with** associate with.

dealt *past* and *past part.* of DEAL[1].

dean[1] *n.* **1 a** the head of the chapter of a cathedral or collegiate church. **b** (usu. **rural dean**) *Brit.* a member of the clergy exercising supervision over a group of parochial clergy within a division of an archdeaconry. **2 a** a college or university official with disciplinary and advisory functions. **b** the head of a university faculty or department or of a medical school. [based on Late Latin *decanus* 'chief of a group of ten']

dean[2] var. of DENE.

deanery *n.* (*pl.* **-ies**) **1** a dean's house or office. **2** *Brit.* the group of parishes presided over by a rural dean.

dear ● *adj.* **1 a** beloved or much esteemed. **b** as a merely polite or ironic form (*my dear man*). **2** used as a formula of address, esp. at the beginning of letters (*Dear Sir*). **3** (often foll. by *to*) precious; much cherished. **4** (usu. in *superl.*) earnest (*my dearest wish*). **5 a** high-priced relative to its value. **b** having high prices. ● *n.* (esp. as a form of address) dear person.

● *adv.* at great cost (*buy cheap and sell dear; will pay dear*). ● *int.* expressing surprise, dismay, pity, etc. (*dear me!; oh dear!; dear, dear!*). [Old English]

dearie *n.* (esp. as a form of address) usu. *joc.* or *iron.* my dear. □ **dearie me!** *int.* expressing surprise, dismay, etc.

Dear John *n.* (often *attrib.*) *colloq.* a letter terminating a personal relationship.

dearly *adv.* **1** affectionately, fondly (*loved him dearly*). **2 a** earnestly; keenly. **b** very much, greatly (*would dearly love to go*). **3** at great cost.

dearth *n.* scarcity or lack. [Middle English]

death *n.* **1** the ending of life. **2** the event that terminates life. **3 a** the fact or process of being killed or killing (*stone to death*). **b** the fact or state of being dead (*eyes closed in death; their deaths caused rioting*). **4** the destruction or permanent cessation of something (*the death of our hopes*). **5** (usu. **Death**) a personification of death, usu. represented by a skeleton. **6** a lack of religious faith or spiritual life. □ **at death's door** close to death. **be the death of 1** cause the death of. **2** be very harmful to. **catch one's death of cold** *colloq.* catch a serious chill etc. **do to death 1** overdo. **2** kill. **fate worse than death** *colloq.* a disastrous misfortune or experience. **like death warmed up** (or *US* **over**) *colloq.* very tired or ill. **put to death** kill; execute. **to death** to the utmost, extremely (*bored to death*). [Old English] □ **deathless** *adj.* **deathlike** *adj.*

deathbed *n.* a bed as the place where a person is dying or has died.

death blow *n.* **1** a blow or other action that causes death. **2** an event or circumstance that abruptly ends an activity, enterprise, etc.

death camp *n.* a prison camp in which many people die or are put to death.

death certificate *n.* an official statement of the cause and date and place of a person's death.

death duty *n. Brit. hist.* a tax levied on property after the owner's death.

deathly ● *adj.* (**deathlier, deathliest**) suggestive of death (*deathly silence*). ● *adv.* in a deathly way (*deathly pale*).

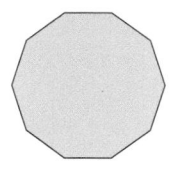

death mask *n.* ◄ a cast taken of a dead person's face.

death penalty *n.* punishment by being put to death.

death rate *n.* the number of deaths per thousand of population per year.

death rattle *n.* a gurgling sound sometimes heard in a dying person's throat.

death row *n.* (esp. with reference to the US) a prison block or section for prisoners sentenced to death.

death squad *n.* an armed paramilitary group formed to kill political enemies etc.

DEATH MASK OF HEINRICH HEINE (1797–1856), GERMAN POET AND WRITER

death tax *n. US* a tax on property payable on the owner's death.

death toll *n.* the number of people killed in an accident, battle, etc.

death trap *n. colloq.* a dangerous building, vehicle, etc.

death warrant *n.* **1** an order for the execution of a condemned person. **2** anything that causes the end of an established practice etc.

death-watch *n.* (in full **death-watch beetle**) ► a small beetle, *Xestobium rufovillosum*, which makes a sound like a watch ticking, once supposed to portend death.

DEATH-WATCH BEETLE (*Xestobium rufovillosum*)

death wish *n.* a desire (usu. unconscious) for the death of oneself or another.

deb *n. colloq.* a debutante.

debacle /day-bah-kl/ *n.* (also **débâcle**) **1 a** an utter defeat or failure. **b** a sudden collapse or downfall. **2** a confused rush or rout; a stampede. **3 a** a break-up of ice in a river, with resultant flooding. **b** a sudden rush of water carrying along blocks of stone and other debris. [French]

debag *v.tr.* (**debagged, debagging**) *Brit. slang* remove the trousers of (a person), esp. as a joke.

debar *v.tr.* (**debarred, debarring**) (foll. by *from*) exclude from admission or from a right; prohibit from an action (*was debarred from entering*). [from French *débarrer*]

debark[1] *v.tr. & intr.* land from a ship. [from French *débarquer*]

debark[2] *v.tr.* remove the bark from (a tree).

debase *v.tr.* **1** lower in quality, value, or character. **2** depreciate (coin) by alloying etc. □ **debasement** *n.* **debaser** *n.*

debatable *adj.* **1** questionable; subject to dispute. **2** capable of being debated. □ **debatably** *adv.*

debate ● *v.* **1** *tr.* (also *absol.*) discuss or dispute about (an issue, proposal, etc.), esp. formally in a legislative assembly, public meeting, etc. **2** *tr.* consider or ponder (a matter). **b** *intr.* consider different sides of a question. ● *n.* **1** a formal discussion on a particular matter, esp. in a legislative assembly etc. **2** debating, discussion (*open to debate*). [from Old French] □ **debater** *n.*

debauch ● *v.tr.* **1** corrupt morally. **2** make intemperate or sensually indulgent. **3** deprave or debase (taste or judgement). **4** (as **debauched** *adj.*) dissolute. ● *n.* **1** a bout of sensual indulgence. **2** debauchery. [from Old French *deshaucher*]

debauchee *n.* a person given to excessive sensual indulgence.

debauchery *n.* excessive sensual indulgence; licentiousness.

debenture *n.* **1** *Brit.* an acknowledgement of indebtedness, esp. a bond of a company or corporation acknowledging a debt and providing for payment of interest at fixed intervals. **2** (in full **debenture bond**) *US* a fixed-interest bond of a company or corporation, backed by general credit rather than specified assets. [based on Latin *debēre* 'to owe']

debilitate *v.tr.* enfeeble, enervate. □ **debilitation** *n.*

debility *n.* feebleness, esp. of health. [based on Latin *debilis* 'weak']

debit ● *n.* **1** (in bookkeeping) **a** an entry recording a sum owed. **b** the sum recorded. **c** the total of such sums. **2** the debit side of an account. ● *v.tr.* (**debited, debiting**) **1** (foll. by *against, to*) enter (an amount) on the debit side of an account (*debited £500 against me*). **2** (foll. by *with*) enter (a person) on the debit side of an account (*debited me with £500*). [from Latin *debitum* 'debt']

debit card *n.* a card allowing the holder to transfer money from one bank account to another via a computer terminal when making a purchase etc.

debonair /deb-on-**air**/ *adj.* carefree, cheerful, self-assured. [from Old French *debonaire*, from *de bon aire* 'of good disposition']

debouch *v.intr.* **1** (of troops or a stream) issue from a ravine, wood, etc., into open ground. **2** (of a river, road, etc.) merge into a larger body or area. [from French *déboucher*]

debridement *Med.* the removal of damaged tissue or foreign matter from a wound etc. [F, lit. 'unbridling']

debrief *v.tr. colloq.* interrogate (a person) about a completed mission or undertaking. □ **debriefing** *n.*

debris /**deb**-ree/ *n.* scattered fragments, esp. of something wrecked or destroyed. **2** *Geol.* an accumulation of loose material, e.g. from rocks or plants. [from obsolete French *débriser* 'to break down']

debt *n.* **1** something that is owed, esp. money. **2** a state of obligation to pay something owed (*in debt*). □ **in a person's debt** under an obligation to a person. [based on Latin *debēre* 'to owe']

debt of honour *n.* a debt not legally recoverable, esp. a sum lost in gambling.

debtor *n.* a person who owes a debt.

debug *v.tr.* (**debugged, debugging**) **1** remove concealed listening devices from (a room etc.). **2** identify and remove defects from (a machine, computer program, etc.). **3** delouse.

debugger *n. Computing* a program for debugging other programs.

debunk *v.tr. colloq.* **1** show the good reputation of (a person, institution, etc.) to be spurious. **2** expose the falseness of (a claim etc.). □ **debunker** *n.*

debut /**day**-bew/ *n.* (also **début**) **1** the first public appearance of a performer on stage etc.; the opening performance of a show etc. **2** the first appearance of a debutante in society. [from French *débuter* 'to lead off']

debutant /**deb**-yoo-tahng/ *n.* (also **débutant**) a male performer making his first public appearance. [related to DEBUT]

debutante /**deb**-yoo-tahnt/ *n.* (also **débutante**) **1** a (usu. wealthy) young woman making her social debut. **2** a female performer making her first public appearance. [related to DEBUT]

Dec. *abbr.* December.

deca- *comb. form* (also **dec-** before a vowel) **1** having ten. **2** tenfold. **3** ten (*decagram; decalitre*). [from Greek *deka* 'ten']

decade *n.* **1** a period of ten years. **2** a series or group of ten. [based on Greek *deka* 'ten']

decadence /**dek**-ă-děnss/ *n.* **1** moral or cultural deterioration, esp. after a peak or culmination of achievement. **2** decadent behaviour; a state of decadence. [from French, related to DECAY]

decadent /**dek**-ă-děnt/ ● *adj.* **1 a** in a state of moral or cultural deterioration; showing or characterized by decadence. **b** of a period of decadence. **2** self-indulgent. ● *n.* a decadent person. □ **decadently** *adv.*

decaf (also **decaff**) ● *n. propr.* decaffeinated coffee. ● *adj.* decaffeinated.

decaffeinate *v.tr.* **1** remove the caffeine from. **2** reduce the quantity of caffeine in.

decagon *n.* ▼ a plane figure with ten sides and angles.

decahedron *n.* (*pl.* **decahedra** or **decahedrons**) ▼ a solid figure with ten faces.

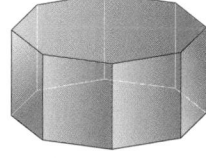

DECAGON　　　　　　**DECAHEDRON**

decal *n. colloq.* = DECALCOMANIA 2.

decalcify *v.tr.* (**-ies, -ied**) remove lime or calcareous matter from (a bone, tooth, etc.). □ **decalcification** *n.*

decalcomania *n. US* **1** a process of transferring designs from specially prepared paper to the surface of glass, porcelain, etc. **2** a picture or design used in or made by this process. [based on French *décalquer* 'to transfer']

decalitre *n.* (*US* **decaliter**) a metric unit of capacity, equal to 10 litres.

Decalogue *n.* the Ten Commandments (given by God to Moses on Mount Sinai (Exod. 20: 1–17)). [from Greek phrase *hoi deka logoi* 'the Ten Commandments']

D

D

decametre *n.* (*US* **decameter**) a metric unit of length, equal to 10 metres.

decamp *v.intr.* **1** break up or leave a camp. **2** depart suddenly; abscond. [from French *décamper*]

decanal *adj.* **1** of a dean or deanery. **2** of the south side of a choir, the side on which the dean sits. [based on Late Latin *decanus* (see DEAN)]

decant *v.tr.* **1** gradually pour off (liquid) from one container to another, esp. without disturbing the sediment. **2** *colloq.* transfer as if by pouring. [based on Greek *kanthos* 'corner of the eye', used of the lip of a beaker]

decanter *n.* a stoppered glass container into which wine or spirit is decanted.

decapitate *v.tr.* **1** behead. **2** cut the head or end from. [based on Latin *caput* 'head'] □ **decapitation** *n.*

decapod *n.* **1** ▼ any crustacean of the order Decapoda, characterized by five pairs of walking legs. **2** any of various cephalopod molluscs having ten tentacles. [from Greek *deka* 'ten' + *pous podos* 'foot']

DECAPOD: FURROWED CRAB (*Xantho incisus*)

decarbonize *v.tr.* (also **-ise**) remove carbon or carbonaceous deposits from (an internal-combustion engine etc.).

decathlon *n.* an athletic contest in which each competitor takes part in ten events. [from Greek *deka* 'ten' + *athlon* 'contest'] □ **decathlete** *n.*

decay ● *v.* **1 a** *intr.* rot, decompose. **b** *tr.* cause to rot or decompose. **2** *intr.* & *tr.* decline or cause to decline in quality, power, wealth, energy, beauty, etc. **3** *intr. Physics* (usu. foll. by *to*) (of a substance etc.) undergo change by radioactivity. ● *n.* **1** a rotten state; a process of wasting away. **2** a decline in health, quality, etc. **3** *Physics* a change into another substance etc. by radioactivity. **4** decayed tissue. [based on Latin *cadere* 'to fall']

decease *formal* esp. *Law* ● *n.* death. ● *v.intr.* die. [based on Latin *decessus* 'gone away']

deceased *formal* ● *adj.* dead. ● *n.* (usu. prec. by *the*) a person who has died, esp. recently.

deceit *n.* **1** the act or process of deceiving. **2** a dishonest trick or stratagem. **3** a tendency to deceive.

deceitful *adj.* **1** (of a person) using deceit. **2** (of an act, practice, etc.) intended to deceive. □ **deceitfully** *adv.* **deceitfulness** *n.*

deceive *v.* **1** *tr.* make (a person) believe what is false, mislead purposely. **2** *tr.* be unfaithful to, esp. sexually. **3** *intr.* use deceit. □ **be deceived** be mistaken or deluded. **deceive oneself** persist in a mistaken belief. [from Latin *decipere* 'to catch by guile'] □ **deceiver** *n.*

decelerate *v.* **1** *intr.* & *tr.* begin or cause to begin to reduce speed. **2** *tr.* make slower (*decelerated motion*). [based on ACCELERATE] □ **deceleration** *n.*

December *n.* the twelfth month of the year. [originally the tenth month of the Roman year: Latin, based on *decem* 'ten']

decency *n.* (*pl.* **-ies**) **1** generally accepted standards of behaviour or propriety. **2** avoidance of obscenity. **3** (in *pl.*) the requirements of correct behaviour. [from Latin *decentia* 'appropriateness']

decennial *adj.* **1** lasting ten years. **2** recurring every ten years. [based on Latin *decem* 'ten' + *annus* 'year']

decent *adj.* **1 a** conforming with generally accepted standards of behaviour or propriety. **b** avoiding obscenity. **2** respectable. **3** acceptable; good enough. **4** *Brit.* kind, obliging (*was decent enough to apologize*). [from Latin *decent-* 'being fitting'] □ **decently** *adv.*

decentralize *v.tr.* (also **-ise**) **1** transfer (powers etc.) from a central to a local authority. **2** reorganize on the basis of greater local autonomy. □ **decentralist** *n.* & *adj.* **decentralization** *n.*

decentre *v.tr.* (*US* **decenter**) remove the centre from.

deception *n.* **1** the act or an instance of deceiving; the process of being deceived. **2** a thing that deceives.

deceptive *adj.* apt to deceive; easily mistaken for something else or as having a different quality. □ **deceptively** *adv.*

deci- *comb. form* one-tenth (*decilitre*; *decimetre*). [from Latin *decimus* 'tenth']

decibel *n.* a unit (one-tenth of a bel) used in the comparison of two power levels relating to electrical signals or sound intensities.

decide *v.* **1 a** *intr.* come to a resolution as a result of consideration. **b** *tr.* have or reach as one's resolution about something (*decided to stay*; *decided that we should leave*). **2** *tr.* **a** cause (a person) to reach a resolution (*was unsure about going but the weather decided me*). **b** resolve or settle (a question, dispute, etc.). **3** *intr.* give a judgement. [from Latin *decidere* 'to cut off']

decided *adj.* **1** (usu. *attrib.*) definite, unquestionable (*a decided difference*). **2** having clear opinions; resolute, not vacillating.

decidedly *adv.* undoubtedly, undeniably.

decider *n.* **1** a game, race, etc., to decide between competitors finishing equal in a previous contest. **2** any person or thing that decides.

deciduous *adj.* **1** ▼ (of a tree) shedding its leaves annually. ▷ TREE. **2** (of leaves, horns, teeth, etc.) shed periodically. [based on Latin *cadere* 'to fall']

oak in winter   *oak in full summer foliage*

DECIDUOUS OAK IN WINTER AND SUMMER

decigram *n.* (also **decigramme**) a metric unit of mass, equal to 0.1 gram.

decilitre *n.* (*US* **deciliter**) a metric unit of capacity, equal to 0.1 litre.

decimal ● *adj.* **1** (of a system of numbers, weights, measures, etc.) based on the number ten, in which the smaller units are related to the principal units as powers of ten (units, tens, hundreds, thousands, etc.). **2** of tenths or ten; reckoning or proceeding by tens. ● *n.* a decimal fraction. [from Latin *decimus* 'tenth']

decimal fraction *n.* a fraction whose denominator is a power of ten, esp. when expressed positionally by units to the right of a decimal point.

decimalize *v.tr.* (also **-ise**) **1** express as a decimal. **2** convert to a decimal system. □ **decimalization** *n.*

decimal place *n.* the position of a digit to the right of a decimal point.

decimal point *n.* a full point or dot placed before the numerator in a decimal fraction.

decimate *v.tr.* **1** *disp.* kill or remove a large proportion of. **2** *orig. Mil.* kill or remove one in every ten of. [from Latin *decimare* 'to take the tenth man'] □ **decimation** *n.*

■ **Usage** Sense 1 is now the usual sense of *decimate* although it is often deplored as an inappropriate use. This word should not be used to mean 'defeat utterly'.

decimetre *n.* (*US* **decimeter**) a metric unit of length, equal to 0.1 metre.

decipher *v.tr.* **1** convert (a text written in cipher) into an intelligible script or language. **2** determine the meaning of (anything obscure or unclear). □ **decipherable** *adj.* **decipherment** *n.*

decision *n.* **1** the act or process of deciding. **2** a conclusion or resolution reached after consideration (*have made my decision*). **3 a** the settlement of a question. **b** a formal judgement. **4** resoluteness. [from Latin *decisio*]

decisive *adj.* **1** that decides an issue; conclusive. **2** able to decide quickly and effectively. □ **decisively** *adv.* **decisiveness** *n.*

deck ● *n.* **1 a** a platform in a ship covering all or part of the hull's area at any level and serving as a floor. ▷ FERRY, HOVERCRAFT, SAILING BOAT. **b** the accommodation on a particular deck of a ship. **2** a floor or compartment of a bus. **3** a component or unit in sound-reproduction equipment that incorporates a playing or recording mechanism for discs, tapes, etc. **4** *N. Amer.* a pack of cards. **5** *slang* the ground. **6** any floor or platform, esp. the floor of a pier or a platform for sunbathing. ● *v.tr.* **1** decorate, adorn. **2** furnish with or cover as a deck. **3** *slang* knock (a person) to the ground; floor. □ **below deck** (or **decks**) in or into the space below the main deck. **on deck 1** in the open air on a ship's main deck. **2** esp. *US* ready for action, work, etc. [from Middle Dutch *dec* 'roof, cloak']

deckchair *n.* a folding chair of wood and canvas.

-decker *comb. form* having a specified number of decks or layers (*double-decker*).

deckhand *n.* a person employed in cleaning and odd jobs on a ship's deck.

deckle edge *n.* the rough uncut edge of (esp. handmade) paper. □ **deckle-edged** *adj.*

declaim *v.* **1** *intr.* & *tr.* speak or utter rhetorically or affectedly. **2** *intr.* practise oratory or recitation. **3** *intr.* (foll. by *against*) protest forcefully. [from Latin *declamare*] □ **declamation** *n.* **declamatory** *adj.*

declaration *n.* **1** the act or process of declaring. **2** a formal, emphatic, or deliberate statement or announcement.

declarative ● *adj.* **1 a** of the nature of, or making, a declaration. **b** *Gram.* (of a sentence) that takes the form of a simple statement. **2** *Computing* designating high-level programming languages which can be used to solve problems without requiring the programmer to specify an exact procedure to be followed. ● *n.* **1** a declaratory statement or act. **2** *Gram.* a declarative sentence. □ **declaratively** *adv.*

declare *v.* **1** *tr.* announce openly or formally (*declare war*). **2** *tr.* pronounce to be something (*declared it invalid*). **3** *tr.* (usu. foll. by *that* + clause) assert emphatically. **4** *tr.* acknowledge possession of (dutiable goods, income, etc.). **5** *tr.* (as **declared** *adj.*) who admits to being such (*a declared atheist*). **6** *tr.* (also *absol.*) *Cricket* close (an innings) voluntarily before all the wickets have fallen. **7** *tr.* (also *absol.*) *Cards* name (the trump suit). **8** *intr.* (foll. by *for*, *against*) take the side of one party or another. □ **declare oneself** reveal one's intentions or identity. [based on Latin *clarus* 'clear'] □ **declaratory** *adj.* **declarer** *n.*

declassify *v.tr.* (**-ies**, **-ied**) declare (information etc.) to be no longer secret. □ **declassification** *n.*

declension *n.* **1** *Gram.* **a** the variation of the form of a noun, pronoun, or adjective, by which its grammatical case, number, and gender are identified. **b** the class in which a noun etc. is put according to the exact form of this variation. **2** deterioration, declining. [related to DECLINE] □ **declensional** *adj.*

declination *n.* **1** a downward bend or turn. **2** *Astron.* the angular distance of a star etc. north or south of the celestial equator. **3** the angular deviation of a compass needle from true north. □ **declinational** *adj.*

decline ● *v.* **1** *intr.* lose strength or vigour; decrease. **2** *tr.* (also *absol.*) **a** reply with formal courtesy that one will not accept (an invitation etc.). **b** refuse, esp. formally and courteously (*declined to do anything*). **3** *intr.* slope downwards. **4** *intr.* bend down, droop. **5** *tr. Gram.* state the forms of (a noun, pronoun, or adjective) corresponding to cases, number, and gender. **6** *intr.* (of a day, life, etc.) draw to a close. **7** *tr.* bend down. ● *n.* **1** gradual loss of vigour or excellence (*on the decline*). **2** decay, deterioration. **3** the Sun's gradual setting; the last part of the course (of the Sun, of life, etc.). **4** a fall in price. [based on Latin *clinare* 'to bend'] □ **declinable** *adj.* **decliner** *n.*

declining years *n.pl.* old age.

declivity *n.* (*pl.* **-ies**) a downward slope. [based on Latin *clivus* 'slope'] □ **declivitous** *adj.*

declutch *v.intr.* disengage the clutch of a motor vehicle.

decoction *n.* **1** concentration of, or extraction of the essence of, a substance by boiling in water etc. **2** the extracted liquor. [based on Latin *coquere* 'to boil']

decode *v.tr.* convert (a coded message) into intelligible language. □ **decodable** *adj.*

decoder *n.* **1** ▼ a person or thing that decodes. **2** an electronic device for analysing signals and feeding separate amplifier channels.

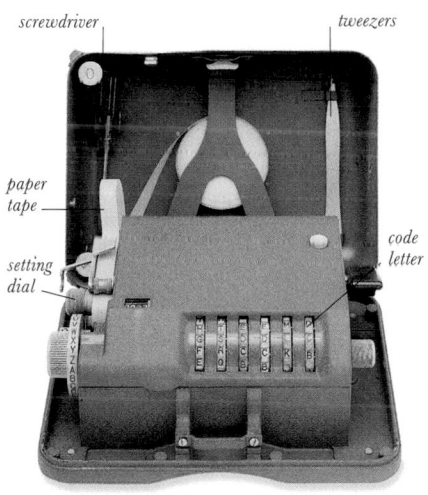

screwdriver   *tweezers*

paper tape

setting dial

code letter

DECODER: SECOND WORLD WAR US CIPHER MACHINE

decoke *Brit. colloq.* ● *v.tr.* remove carbon or carbonaceous material from (an internal-combustion engine). ● *n.* the process of decoking.

décolletage /day-kol-**tah**zh/ *n.* a low neckline of a woman's dress etc. [French]

décolleté /day-kol-ĕ-tay/ ● *adj.* (also **décolletée**) **1** (of a dress etc.) having a low neckline. **2** (of a woman) wearing a dress with a low neckline. ● *n.* a low neckline. [French]

decolonize *v.tr.* (also **-ise**) (of a state) withdraw from (a colony), leaving it independent. □ **decolonization** *n.*

decommission *v.tr.* **1** close down (a nuclear reactor etc.). **2** take (a ship) out of service.

decompose *v.* **1** *intr.* decay, rot; disintegrate. **2** *tr.* separate into elements or simpler constituents; cause to decay or rot. [from French *décomposer*] □ **decomposition** *n.*

decompress *v.tr.* subject to decompression; relieve or reduce the compression on.

decompression *n.* **1** release from compression. **2** a gradual reduction of air pressure on a person who has been subjected to high pressure (esp. underwater).

decompression chamber *n.* ▼ an enclosed space for subjecting a person to decompression.

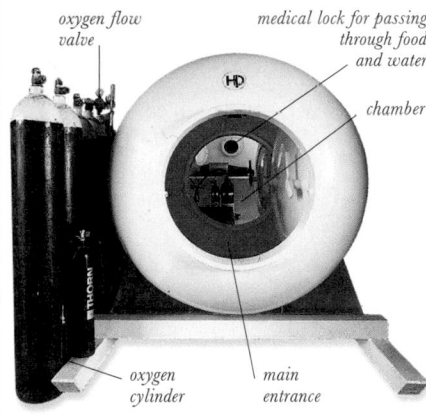

oxygen flow valve

medical lock for passing through food and water

chamber

oxygen cylinder

main entrance

DECOMPRESSION CHAMBER

decompression sickness *n.* a condition caused by too rapid decompression, resulting in the formation of nitrogen bubbles in the tissues.

decompressor *n. Brit.* a device for reducing pressure in the engine of a motor vehicle.

decongestant ● *adj.* that relieves (esp. nasal) congestion. ● *n.* a medicinal agent that relieves nasal congestion.

deconsecrate *v.tr.* transfer (esp. a building) from sacred to secular use. □ **deconsecration** *n.*

deconstruction *n.* a method of critical analysis of philosophical and literary language. [from French] □ **deconstruct** *v.tr.* **deconstructionism** *n.* **deconstructionist** *adj. & n.* **deconstructive** *adj.*

decontaminate *v.tr.* remove contamination from. □ **decontamination** *n.*

decontextualize *v.tr.* (also **-ise**) study or treat in isolation from its context. □ **decontextualization** *n.*

decontrol ● *v.tr.* (**decontrolled**, **decontrolling**) release (a commodity etc.) from controls or restrictions, esp. those imposed by the State. ● *n.* the act of decontrolling.

decor /**day**-kor/ *n.* (also **décor**) **1** the furnishing and decoration of a room etc. **2** the decoration and scenery of a stage. [related to DECORATE]

decorate *v.tr.* **1** provide with adornments. **2** esp. *Brit.* provide (a room etc.) with new paint, wallpaper, etc. **3** serve as an adornment to. **4** confer an award or distinction on. [based on Latin *decus -oris* 'beauty']

decoration *n.* **1** the process or art of decorating. **2** a thing that decorates or serves as an ornament. **3** a medal etc. conferred as an honour. **4** (in *pl.*) flags etc. put up on an occasion of public celebration.

decorative *adj.* serving to decorate. □ **decoratively** *adv.* **decorativeness** *n.*

decorator *n.* a person who decorates, esp. *Brit.* one who paints or papers houses professionally.

decorum /di-**kor**-ŭm/ *n.* polite dignified behaviour. □ **decorous** *adj.*

découpage *n.* the decoration of surfaces with paper cut-outs. [French, literally 'cutting out']

decouple *v.tr.* separate, disengage, dissociate.

decoy /**dee**-koy/ ● *n.* **1** ► a person or thing used to lure an animal or person into a trap or danger. **2** a bait or enticement. ● *v.tr.* (often foll. by *into, out of*) allure or entice, esp. using a decoy. [17th-century coinage]

decrease ● *v.tr. & intr.* make or become smaller or fewer. ● *n.* **1** the act or an instance of decreasing. **2** the amount by which a thing decreases. [based on Latin *crescere* 'to grow'] □ **decreasingly** *adv.*

decree ● *n.* **1** an official order issued by a legal authority. **2** a judgement or decision of certain law courts. ● *v.tr.* (**decrees**, **decreed**, **decreeing**) ordain by decree. [based on Latin *decernere* 'to decide']

decree absolute *n. Brit.* a final order for divorce, enabling either party to remarry.

decree nisi /-**ny**-sy/ *n. Brit.* a provisional order for divorce, made absolute within a fixed period. [nisi: Latin, literally 'unless']

decrement *n.* **1** *Physics* the ratio of the amplitudes in successive cycles of a damped oscillation. **2** the amount lost by diminution or waste. **3** the act of decreasing. [related to DECREASE]

decrepit *adj.* weakened or worn out by age, infirmity or long use. [based on Latin *crepare* 'to creak'] □ **decrepitude** *n.*

decretal /di-**kree**-tăl/ *n.* **1** a papal decree. **2** (in *pl.*) a collection of these, forming part of canon law. [from Late Latin (*epistola*) *decretalis* '(letter) of decree']

decriminalize *v.tr.* (also **-ise**) cease to treat as criminal. □ **decriminalization** *n.*

decry *v.tr.* (**-ies**, **-ied**) disparage, belittle. [from French *décrier*] □ **decrier** *n.*

decrypt *v.tr.* decipher (a cryptogram). □ **decryption** *n.*

dedicate *v.tr.* **1** (foll. by *to*) devote (esp. oneself) to a special task or purpose. **2** (foll. by *to*) address (a book etc.) as a compliment to a friend, patron, etc. **3** (often foll. by *to*) devote (a building etc.) to a deity or purpose. **4** (as **dedicated** *adj.*) **a** (of a person) devoted to an aim or vocation. **b** (of equipment, esp. a computer) designed for a specific purpose. [based on Latin *dicare* 'to declare'] □ **dedicatee** *n.* **dedicative** *adj.* **dedicator** *n.* **dedicatory** *adj.*

dedication *n.* **1** the act or an instance of dedicating; the process or quality of being dedicated. **2** a dedicatory inscription.

deduce *v.tr.* (often foll. by *from*) infer; draw as a logical conclusion. [based on Latin *ducere* 'to lead'] □ **deducible** *adj.*

deduct *v.tr.* (often foll. by *from*) subtract, take away (an amount, portion, etc.) [based on Latin *deductus* 'led away, withdrawn']

deductible ● *adj.* that may be deducted, esp. from tax to be paid or taxable income. ● *n. US* = EXCESS *n.* 4. □ **deductibility** *n.*

deduction *n.* **1 a** the act of deducting. **b** an amount deducted. **2 a** the inferring of particular instances from a general law. **b** a conclusion deduced.

deductive *adj.* of or reasoning by deduction. □ **deductively** *adv.*

dee *n.* **1** the letter D. **2** a thing shaped like this.

deed ● *n.* **1** a thing done intentionally or consciously. **2** a brave, skilful, or conspicuous act. **3** actual fact or performance (*kind in word and deed*). **4** *Law* a written or printed document often used for a legal transfer of ownership and bearing the disposer's signature. ● *v.tr. US* convey or transfer by legal deed. [Old English]

deed of covenant *n. Brit.* an agreement to pay a specified amount regularly to a charity etc., enabling the recipient to recover the tax paid by the donor on an equivalent amount of income.

deed poll *n.* esp. *Brit.* a deed made and executed by one party only, esp. to change one's name.

deejay *n. colloq.* a disc jockey.

deem *v.tr. formal* regard, consider, judge. [Old English]

DECOY DUCKS

D

de-emphasize *v.tr.* (also **-ise**) **1** remove emphasis from. **2** reduce emphasis on.

deemster *n.* a judge in the Isle of Man.

deep ● *adj.* **1 a** extending far down from the top (*deep hole*). **b** extending far in from the surface or edge (*deep border*). **2** (*predic.*) **a** extending to a specified depth (*water six feet deep*; *ankle-deep in mud*). **b** in a specified number of ranks one behind another (*soldiers six deep*). **3** situated far down or back (*hands deep in his pockets*). **4** coming or brought from far down or in (*deep sigh*). **5** low-pitched, full-toned, not shrill (*deep voice*). **6** intense, vivid, extreme (*deep disgrace*). **7** heartfelt, absorbing (*deep affection*). **8** (*predic.*) fully absorbed or overwhelmed (*deep in a book*). **9** profound, penetrating, not superficial (*deep thinker*; *deep insight*). **10** *colloq.* cunning or secretive (*a deep one*). ● *n.* **1** (prec. by *the*) *poet.* the sea. **2** a deep part of the sea. **3** an abyss, pit, or cavity. **4** a deep state (*deep of the night*). **5** *poet.* a mysterious region of thought or feeling. ● *adv.* **1** deeply; far down or in (*dig deep*). **2** *Sport* at a distance from the batsman or other focus of play. □ **go off** (or **go in off**) **the deep end** *colloq.* give way to anger or emotion. **in deep water** (or **waters**) in trouble or difficulty. **jump** (or **be thrown**) **in at the deep end** face a difficult problem, undertaking, etc., with little experience of it. [Old English] □ **deeply** *adv.* **deepness** *n.*

deepen *v.tr. & intr.* make or become deep or deeper.

deep-freeze ● *n.* **1** a refrigerator in which food can be quickly frozen and kept at a very low temperature. **2** a suspension of activity. ● *v.tr.* (**-froze**, **-frozen**) freeze or store (food) in a deep-freeze.

deep-fry *v.tr.* (**-fries**, **-fried**) fry (food) in an amount of fat or oil sufficient to cover it.

deep-laid *adj.* (of a scheme) secret and elaborate.

deep-rooted *adj.* (esp. of convictions) firmly established.

deep sea *n.* the deeper parts of the ocean (often hyphenated when *attrib.*: *deep-sea diving*).

deep-seated *adj.* (of emotion, disease, etc.) firmly established, profound.

deep space *n.* the regions beyond the solar system or the Earth's atmosphere.

deer *n.* (*pl.* same) ▼ any hoofed grazing or browsing animal of the family Cervidae, the males of which usu. have deciduous branching antlers. [Old English]

deerstalker *n.* **1** ▶ a soft cloth cap with peaks in front and behind and ear-flaps. **2** *Brit.* a person who stalks deer.

DEERSTALKER

de-escalate *v.tr.* reduce the level or intensity of. □ **de-escalation** *n.*

deface *v.tr.* **1** spoil the appearance of. **2** make illegible. [from Old French] □ **defaceable** *adj.* **defacement** *n.* **defacer** *n.*

de facto ● *adv.* in fact, whether by right or not. ● *adj.* that exists or is such in fact (*a de facto ruler*). [Latin]

defalcate /dee-făl-kayt/ *v.intr. formal* misappropriate property in one's charge, esp. money. [from medieval Latin *defalcare* 'to lop'] □ **defalcator** *n.*

defalcation *n. formal* **1** *Law* **a** a misappropriation of money. **b** an amount misappropriated. **2** a shortcoming.

defame *v.tr.* attack the good reputation of. [based on Latin *fama* 'report'] □ **defamation** *n.* **defamatory** *adj.*

default ● *n.* **1** failure to fulfil an obligation. **2** lack, absence. **3** a pre-selected option adopted by a computer program until an alternative is specified. ● *v.* **1** *intr.* fail to fulfil an obligation. **2** *tr.* declare (a party) in default and give judgement against that party. □ **by default 1** because of inaction. **2** because of a lack of opposition. **go by default** fail by default. [from Old French *defaillir* 'to fail']

defaulter *n.* a person who defaults, esp. *Brit.* a soldier guilty of a military offence.

defeat ● *v.tr.* **1** overcome in a battle or other contest. **2** frustrate, baffle. **3** reject (a motion etc.) by voting. ● *n.* the act or an instance of defeating or being defeated. [based on Latin *facere* 'to do']

defeatism *n.* **1** an excessive readiness to accept defeat. **2** conduct conducive to this. □ **defeatist** *n. & adj.*

defecate /def-ĕ-kayt/ *v.intr.* discharge faeces from the body. [based on Latin *faex faecis* 'dregs'] □ **defecation** *n.*

defect ● *n.* /dee-fekt/ lack of something essential; imperfection. **2** a shortcoming. **3** a blemish. ● *v.intr.* /di-fekt/ abandon one's country, cause, etc. in favour of another. [from Latin *deficere* 'to desert, fail'] □ **defection** *n.* **defector** *n.*

defective ● *adj.* **1** having a defect or defects; incomplete, faulty. **2** *archaic* or *offens.* mentally handicapped. **3** (usu. foll. by *in*) lacking, deficient. ● *n. archaic* or *offens.* a mentally handicapped person. □ **defectively** *adv.* **defectiveness** *n.*

defence *n.* (*US* **defense**) **1** the act of defending from or resisting attack. **2 a** a means of resisting attack. **b** a thing that protects. **c** the military resources of a country. **3** (in *pl.*) fortifications. **4 a** justification, vindication. **b** a speech or piece of writing used to this end. **5 a** the defendant's case in a lawsuit. **b** *colloq.* the counsel for the defendant. **6 a** the action or role of defending one's goal etc. against attack. **b** the players in a team who perform this role. [from Latin *defensum* 'thing defended'] □ **defenceless** *adj.* **defencelessly** *adv.* **defencelessness** *n.*

defenceman *n.* (*US* **defenseman**) (*pl.* **-men**) (in ice hockey and lacrosse) a player in a defensive position.

defend *v.tr.* (also *absol.*) **1** (often foll. by *against, from*) resist an attack made on; protect. **2** uphold by argument. **3** conduct the case for (a defendant in a lawsuit). **4** compete to retain (a title) in a contest. **5** *absol.* (in various sports and games) resist attacks, scoring, etc. [from Latin *defendere*] □ **defender** *n.*

defendant *n.* a person etc. sued or accused in a court of law.

defenestration *n. formal* or *joc.* the action of throwing (esp. a person) out of a window. [based on Latin *fenestra* 'window'] □ **defenestrate** *v.tr.*

defense *US* var. of DEFENCE.

defenseman *US* var. of DEFENCEMAN.

defensible *adj.* **1** supportable by argument. **2** that can be easily defended militarily. □ **defensibility** *n.* **defensibly** *adv.*

defensive *adj.* **1** done or intended for defence or to defend. **2** (of a person or attitude) concerned to challenge criticism. □ **on the defensive 1** expecting criticism. **2** in an attitude or position of defence. □ **defensively** *adv.* **defensiveness** *n.*

defer[1] *v.tr.* (**deferred**, **deferring**) postpone. [related to DIFFER] □ **deferment** *n.* **deferrable** *adj.* **deferral** *n.*

defer[2] *v.intr.* (**deferred**, **deferring**) (foll. by *to*) yield or make concessions. [based on Latin *ferre* 'to bring'] □ **deferrer** *n.*

deference *n.* **1** courteous regard, respect. **2** compliance with the advice or wishes of another.

deferential *adj.* showing deference; respectful. □ **deferentially** *adv.*

defiance *n.* open disobedience; bold resistance. □ **in defiance of** disregarding; in conflict with. [from Old French *defiance*]

defiant *adj.* showing defiance; openly disobedient. □ **defiantly** *adv.*

defibrillation *n. Med.* the stopping of fibrillation of the heart. □ **defibrillator** *n.*

deficiency *n.* (*pl.* **-ies**) **1** the state or condition of being deficient. **2** (usu. foll. by *of*) a lack or shortage. **3** a thing lacking. **4** the amount by which a thing, esp. revenue, falls short.

deficiency disease *n.* a disease caused by the lack of some essential element in the diet.

deficient *adj.* **1** (usu. foll. by *in*) incomplete; insufficient in a quality. **2** insufficient in quantity, force, etc. **3** (in full **mentally deficient**) *archaic* or *offens.* having a mental handicap. [from Latin *deficient-* 'forsaking, failing'] □ **deficiently** *adv.*

deficit *n.* **1** the amount by which a thing (esp. a sum

DEER

Deer are ruminant, even-toed, hoofed mammals, found throughout Europe, Asia, and North and South America. With the exception of reindeer, only male deer bear antlers. During the breeding season, bucks use their antlers as weapons in fights for the favour of females. Most species are gregarious, living in herds with elaborate social organization.

RED DEER
(*Cervus elaphus*)

FALLOW DEER
(*Cervus dama*)

REINDEER
(*Rangifer tarandus*)

MOOSE
(*Alces alces*)

of money) is too small. **2** an excess of liabilities over assets. [from Latin, literally 'it is wanting']

defile[1] *v.tr.* **1** make dirty; pollute. **2** corrupt. **3** desecrate. [from Old French *defouler* 'to trample down'] □ **defilement** *n.* **defiler** *n.*

defile[2] ● *n.* **1** a narrow way. **2** a gorge. ● *v.intr.* march in file. [from French]

define *v.tr.* **1** give the exact meaning of (a word etc.). **2** describe or explain the scope of (*define one's position*). **3** make clear, esp. in outline (*well-defined image*). **4** mark out the limits of. **5** (of properties) make up the total character of. [based on Latin *finis* 'end'] □ **definable** *adj.* **definer** *n.*

definite ● *adj.* **1** having exact and discernible limits. **2** clear and distinct; not vague. **3** certain, sure (*a definite offer; is it definite that he was there?*). ● *n.* a definite thing or object. □ **definiteness** *n.*

■ **Usage** See Usage Note at DEFINITIVE.

definite article *n. Gram.* the word (*the* in English) preceding a noun and implying a specific or previously mentioned instance (as in *the book on the table*; *the art of government*).

definite integral *n. Math.* an integral expressed as the difference between the values of the integral at specified upper and lower limits of the independent variable.

definitely ● *adv.* **1** in a definite manner. **2** certainly; without doubt. ● *int. colloq.* yes, certainly.

definition *n.* **1 a** the act or process of defining. **b** a statement of the meaning of a word or the nature of a thing. **2 a** the degree of distinctness in outline of an object or image (esp. of an image produced by a lens or shown in a photograph or on a cinema or television screen). **b** making or being distinct in outline. □ **definitional** *adj.*

definitive *adj.* **1** (of an answer, treaty, etc.) decisive, final. **2** (of an edition of a book etc.) most authoritative. **3** (of a postage stamp) for permanent use, not special or commemorative etc. □ **definitively** *adv.*

■ **Usage** In sense 1, *definitive* is often confused with *definite*, which does not have connotations of authority and conclusiveness: *a definite no* is a firm refusal, whereas *a definitive no* is an authoritative judgement or decision that something is not the case.

deflagrate *v.tr. & intr.* burn away with sudden flame. □ **deflagration** *n.*

deflate *v.* **1 a** *tr.* let air or gas out of. **b** *intr.* be emptied of air or gas. **2 a** *tr.* cause to lose confidence or conceit. **b** *intr.* lose confidence. **3** *Econ.* **a** *tr.* subject (a currency or economy) to deflation. **b** *intr.* pursue a policy of deflation. **4** *tr.* reduce the importance of, depreciate. □ **deflator** *n.*

deflation *n.* **1** the act or process of deflating or being deflated. **2** *Econ.* reduction of the amount of money in circulation to increase its value as a measure against inflation. **3** *Geol.* the removal of particles of rock etc. by the wind. □ **deflationary** *adj.* **deflationist** *n. & adj.*

deflect *v.* **1** *tr. & intr.* bend or turn aside from a straight course or intended purpose. **2** (often foll. by *from*) **a** *tr.* cause to deviate. **b** *intr.* deviate. [based on Latin *flectere* 'to bend']

deflection *n.* (also **deflexion**) **1** the act or process of deflecting or being deflected. **2** a lateral bend or turn; a deviation. **3** *Physics* the displacement of a pointer on a measuring instrument from its zero position.

deflector *n.* a thing that deflects, esp. a device for deflecting a flow of air etc.

deflower *v.tr.* **1** deprive (esp. a woman) of virginity. **2** ravage, spoil. **3** strip of flowers. [based on Latin *flos floris* 'flower']

defoliate *v.tr.* remove leaves from. [based on Latin *folium* 'leaf'] □ **defoliant** *n. & adj.* **defoliation** *n.* **defoliator** *n.*

DEFOREST: RECENTLY DEFORESTED HILLSIDE

deforest *v.tr.* ▲ clear of forests or trees. □ **deforestation** *n.*

deform *v.* **1** *tr.* make ugly, deface. **2** *tr.* put out of shape. **3** *intr.* undergo deformation; be deformed. [based on Latin *forma* 'shape'] □ **deformable** *adj.* **deformation** *n.*

deformed *adj.* (of a person or limb) misshapen.

deformity *n.* (*pl.* **-ies**) **1** the state of being deformed; ugliness, disfigurement. **2** a malformation, esp. of body or limb.

defraud *v.tr.* (often foll. by *of*) cheat by fraud. [from Latin *defraudare*] □ **defrauder** *n.*

defray *v.tr.* provide money to pay (a cost). [based on medieval Latin *fredum* 'fine for breach of the peace'] □ **defrayable** *adj.* **defrayal** *n.* **defrayment** *n.*

defrock *v.tr.* deprive (a person) of ecclesiastical status. [from French *défroquer*]

defrost *v.* **1** *tr.* remove frost or ice from (a refrigerator, windscreen, etc.). **2** *tr.* unfreeze (frozen food). **3** *intr.* become unfrozen. □ **defroster** *n.*

deft *adj.* neatly skilful or dexterous; adroit. [Middle English, in obsolete sense 'meek'] □ **deftly** *adv.* **deftness** *n.*

defunct *adj.* **1** no longer existing. **2** no longer used or in fashion. [from Latin *defunctus* 'dead']

defuse *v.tr.* **1** remove the fuse from (an explosive device). **2** reduce the tension or potential danger in (a crisis, difficulty, etc.).

defy *v.tr.* (**-ies**, **-ied**) **1** resist openly; refuse to obey. **2** present insuperable obstacles to (*defies solution*). **3** (foll. by *to* + infin.) challenge (a person) to do something. [based on Latin *fidus* 'faithful']

degenerate ● *adj.* having lost the qualities that are normal and desirable or proper to its kind. ● *n.* a degenerate person or animal. ● *v.intr.* become degenerate. [based on Latin *genus -eris* 'race'] □ **degeneracy** *n.* **degenerately** *adv.* **degeneration** *n.*

degenerative *adj.* **1** of or tending to degeneration. **2** (of disease) characterized by progressive, often irreversible, deterioration.

degrade *v.tr.* **1** reduce to a lower rank, esp. as a punishment. **2** bring into dishonour or contempt. **3** debase (*degraded water quality*). **4** *Chem.* reduce to a simpler molecular structure. **5** *Physics* reduce (energy) to a less convertible form. [based on Latin *gradus* 'step'] □ **degradable** *adj.* **degradation** *n.* **degradative** *adj.*

degrading *adj.* humiliating. □ **degradingly** *adv.*

degrease *v.tr.* remove unwanted grease or fat from. □ **degreaser** *n.*

degree *n.* **1** a stage in an ascending or descending scale or process. **2** a stage in intensity or amount (*in some degree*). **3** relative condition (*each is good in its degree*). **4** *Math.* a unit of measurement of angles. **5** *Physics* a unit in a scale of temperature, hardness, etc. **6** *Med.* each of a set of grades (usu. three) used to classify burns (often *attrib.*: *third-degree burns*). **7** an academic rank conferred usu. after examination or on completion of a course. **8** a grade of criminality (*murder in the first degree*). **9** a step in direct genealogical descent. **10** social or official rank. □ **by degrees** a little at a time; gradually. **to a degree** *colloq.* considerably. [based on Latin *gradus* 'step']

degrees of comparison see COMPARISON.

degrees of frost see FROST.

dehorn *v.tr.* remove the horns from (an animal).

dehumanize *v.tr.* (also **-ise**) **1** deprive of human characteristics. **2** make impersonal or machine-like. □ **dehumanization** *n.*

dehumidify *v.tr.* (**-ies**, **-ied**) reduce the degree of humidity of; remove moisture from (esp. air). □ **dehumidification** *n.* **dehumidifier** *n.*

dehydrate *v.* **1** *tr.* **a** remove water from (esp. foods for preservation). **b** make dry, esp. make (the body) deficient in water. **c** render lifeless or uninteresting. **2** *intr.* lose water. □ **dehydration** *n.* **dehydrator** *n.*

de-ice *v.tr.* remove ice from, or prevent its formation on. □ **de-icer** *n.*

deify /dee-i-fy, day-i-fy/ *v.tr.* (**-ies**, **-ied**) **1** make a god of. **2** regard or worship as a god. [based on Latin *deus* 'god'] □ **deification** *n.*

deign /dayn/ *v.intr.* (foll. by *to* + infin.) think fit, condescend. [based on Latin *dignus* 'worthy']

deinstitutionalize *v.tr.* (also **-ise**) (usu. as **deinstitutionalized** *adj.*) remove from an institution or from the effects of institutional life. □ **deinstitutionalization** *n.*

deism /dee-izm, day-izm/ *n.* reasoned belief in the existence of a supreme being. [based on Latin *deus* 'god'] □ **deist** *n.* **deistic** *adj.* **deistical** *adj.*

deity /dee-iti, day-i-tee/ *n.* (*pl.* **-ies**) **1** ▶ a god or goddess. **2** divine status, quality, or nature. **3** (**the Deity**) God. [from ecclesiastical Latin *deitas*]

déjà vu /day-zhah voo/ *n.* (also **déjà vu**) **1** *Psychol.* an illusory feeling of having already experienced a present situation. **2** tedious familiarity. [French, literally 'already seen']

deject *v.tr.* (usu. as **dejected** *adj.*) make sad or dispirited; depress. [based on Latin *dejectus* 'thrown down'] □ **dejectedly** *adv.* **dejection** *n.*

DEITY: PAINTING DEPICTING THE HINDU DEITY GANESH

de jure /dee **joor**-i/ ● *adj.* rightful. ● *adv.* rightfully; by right. [Latin]

delay ● *v.* **1** *tr.* postpone; defer. **2** *tr.* make late (*was delayed at the traffic lights*). **3** *intr.* loiter; be late (*don't delay!*). ● *n.* **1** the act or an instance of delaying; the process of being delayed. **2** time lost by this. **3** a hindrance. [from Old French] □ **delayer** *n.*

delayed action *n.* (hyphenated when *attrib.*) the operation of something, esp. a bomb or camera, some time after being primed or set.

delectable *adj.* esp. *literary* or *joc.* delightful, delicious. [based on Latin *delectare* 'to delight'] □ **delectably** *adv.*

delectation *n. literary* pleasure, enjoyment (*sang for his delectation*).

D

215

D

delegate ● *n.* **1** an elected representative sent to a conference. **2** a member of a committee or deputation. ● *v.tr.* **1** (often foll. by *to*) **a** commit (authority etc.) to an agent or deputy. **b** entrust (a task) to another person. **2** send or authorize (a person) as a representative. [from Latin *delegatus* 'sent, assigned'] □ **delegable** *adj.* **delegator** *n.*

delegation *n.* **1** a body of delegates. **2** the act or process of delegating or being delegated.

delete *v.tr.* remove or obliterate (written or printed matter), esp. by striking out. [from Latin *delēre*] □ **deletion** *n.*

deleterious *adj.* harmful (to the mind or body). [from Greek *delētērios* 'noxious'] □ **deleteriously** *adv.*

delft *n.* (also **delftware**) **1** ▶ glazed, usu. blue and white, earthenware, made in Delft in Holland. **2** similar earthenware made in England.

deli *n.* (*pl.* **delis**) *colloq.* = DELICATESSEN.

deliberate ● *adj.* **1 a** intentional. **b** fully considered; not impulsive. **2** (of movement etc.) unhurried. ● *v.* **1** *intr.* think carefully; take counsel (*the jury deliberated for an hour*). **2** *tr.* consider, discuss carefully. [based on Latin *libra* 'balance'] □ **deliberately** *adv.* **deliberateness** *n.*

deliberation *n.* **1** careful consideration. **2** a debate; discussion. **3 a** caution and care. **b** (of movement) slowness or ponderousness.

deliberative *adj.* of, or appointed for the purpose of, deliberation or debate (*a deliberative assembly*).

delicacy *n.* (*pl.* **-ies**) **1** the quality of being delicate. **2** a choice or expensive food.

delicate *adj.* **1 a** fine in texture or structure; soft, slender, or slight. **b** (of colour, flavour, etc.) subtle or subdued. **2** (of a person) easily injured; susceptible to illness. **3 a** requiring sensitive handling; tricky (*a delicate situation*). **b** (of an instrument) highly sensitive. **4** deft (*a delicate touch*). **5** (of a person) avoiding the vulgar or offensive. **6** (esp. of actions) considerate. [Middle English] □ **delicately** *adv.* **delicateness** *n.*

delicatessen *n.* **1** a shop selling esp. exotic cooked meats, cheeses, etc. **2** (often *attrib.*) such foods. [based on French *délicat* 'delicate']

delicious *adj.* **1** highly delightful and enjoyable to the sense of taste or smell. **2** (of a joke etc.) very witty or much appreciated. [based on Latin *deliciae* 'delight'] □ **deliciously** *adv.* **deliciousness** *n.*

delight ● *v.* **1** *tr.* (often foll. by *with*, or *that* + clause, or *to* + infin.) please greatly. **2** *intr.* (often foll. by *in*, or *to* + infin.) take great pleasure; be highly pleased.

● *n.* **1** great pleasure. **2** something giving pleasure. [from Latin *delectare*] □ **delighted** *adj.* **delightedly** *adv.*

delightful *adj.* causing delight; very pleasant, charming. □ **delightfully** *adv.* **delightfulness** *n.*

delimit *v.tr.* (**delimited**, **delimiting**) determine the limits or boundary of. [based on Latin *limes -itis* 'boundary'] □ **delimitation** *n.*

delineate *v.tr.* portray by drawing etc. or in words. [based on Latin *linea* 'line'] □ **delineation** *n.*

delinquent ● *n.* an offender (*juvenile delinquent*). ● *adj.* **1** guilty of a minor crime or a misdeed. **2** failing in one's duty. **3** *US* in arrears. [from Latin *delinquent-* 'offending'] □ **delinquency** *n.* (*pl.* **-ies**). **delinquently** *adv.*

deliquesce *v.intr.* **1** become liquid, melt. **2** *Chem.* dissolve in water absorbed from the air. [from Latin *deliquescere* 'to melt away'] □ **deliquescence** *n.* **deliquescent** *adj.*

delirious *adj.* **1** affected with delirium; temporarily or apparently mad; raving. **2** wildly excited, ecstatic. □ **deliriously** *adv.*

delirium *n.* **1** an acutely disordered state of mind involving incoherent speech, hallucinations, and frenzied excitement. **2** great excitement, ecstasy. [Latin, based on *delirare* 'to bederanged']

delirium tremens *n.* a psychosis of chronic alcoholism involving tremors and hallucinations. [Latin]

deliver *v.tr.* **1 a** convey and hand over (mail, ordered goods, etc.) to the addressee or the purchaser. **b** (often foll. by *to*) hand over (*delivered the boy safely to his teacher*). **2** (often foll. by *from*) save, rescue, or set free (*delivered him from his enemies*). **3 a** give birth to (*delivered a girl*). **b** (in *passive*; often foll. by *of*) give birth (*was delivered of a child*). **c** assist at the birth of (*delivered six babies that week*). **d** assist in giving birth (*delivered the patient successfully*). **4** (often *refl.*) utter or recite (an opinion, a speech, a judgement, etc.) (*delivered himself of the observation*; *delivered the sermon well*). **5** (often foll. by *up*, *over*) abandon; surrender; hand over (*delivered his soul up to God*). **6** launch or aim (a blow, a ball, or an attack). **7** (*absol.*) *colloq.* = deliver the goods. □ **deliver the goods** *colloq.* carry out one's part of an agreement. [from Old French *delivrer*, related to LIBERATE] □ **deliverable** *adj.* & *n.* **deliverer** *n.*

deliverance *n.* **1** the act or an instance of rescuing; the process of being rescued. **2** a rescue.

delivery *n.* (*pl.* **-ies**) **1 a** the delivering of letters etc. **b** something delivered. **2 a** the process of childbirth. **b** an act of this. **3** deliverance. **4** an act of pitching, esp. of a cricket ball. **5** the act of giving or

surrendering (*delivery of the town to the enemy*). **6** the manner or style of. uttering a speech etc. □ **take delivery of** receive (something purchased).

dell *n.* a small usu. wooded hollow or valley. [Old English]

delouse *v.tr.* rid (a person or animal) of lice.

Delphic *adj.* (also **Delphian**) **1** (of an utterance, prophecy, etc.) obscure, ambiguous, or enigmatic. **2** of or concerning the ancient Greek oracle at Delphi.

delphinium *n.* (*pl.* **delphiniums**) any garden plant of the genus *Delphinium* (buttercup family), with tall spikes of usu. blue flowers. [based on Greek *delphin* 'dolphin', from the shape of the spur]

delta *n.* **1** ▼ a triangular tract of deposited earth, alluvium, etc., at the mouth of a river, formed by its diverging outlets. ▷ SEDIMENT. **2** the fourth letter of the Greek alphabet (Δ, δ). [from Phoenician] □ **deltaic** *adj.*

delta wing *n.* ▼ the triangular sweptback wing of an aircraft. ▷ FIGHTER

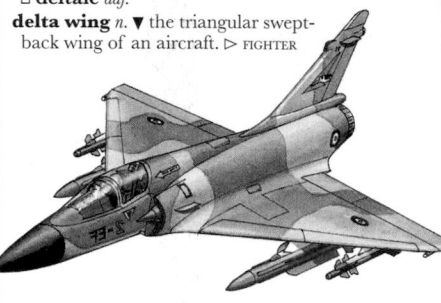

DELTA WING: MIRAGE 2000C JET FIGHTER WITH DELTA WINGS

deltoid *n.* (in full **deltoid muscle**) a thick triangular muscle covering the shoulder joint and used for raising the arm away from the body. ▷ MUSCULATURE

delude *v.tr.* deceive or mislead. [based on Latin *ludere* 'to play']

deluge ● *n.* **1** a great flood. **2** (**the Deluge**) the biblical Flood (Gen. 6-8). **3** a great outpouring of words, paper, etc.). **4** a heavy fall of rain. ● *v.tr.* **1** flood. **2** inundate with a great number or amount (*deluged with complaints*). [from Latin, related to *lavare* 'to wash']

delusion *n.* **1** a false belief or impression. **2** *Psychol.* this as a symptom or form of mental disorder. [from Late Latin *delusio*] □ **delusional** *adj.*

delusions of grandeur *n.pl.* a false idea of oneself as being important, noble, famous, etc.

delusive *adj.* deceptive or unreal. □ **delusively** *adv.* **delusiveness** *n.*

de luxe *adj.* **1** luxurious or sumptuous. **2** of a superior kind. [French]

delve *v.* **1** *intr.* (often foll. by *in*, *into*) **a** search energetically (*delved into his pocket*). **b** research (*delved into his family history*). **2** *tr.* & *intr.* *poet.* dig. [Old English] □ **delver** *n.*

demagnetize *v.tr.* (also **-ise**) remove the magnetic properties of. □ **demagnetization** *n.* **demagnetizer** *n.*

demagogue *n.* (*US* **-gog**) a political agitator appealing to the basest instincts of a mob. [from Greek *dēmos* 'the people' + *agōgos* 'leading'] □ **demagogic** *adj.* **demagoguery** *n.* **demagogy** *n.*

demand ● *n.* **1** an insistent and peremptory request, made as of right. **2** *Econ.* the requirement of purchasers or consumers for a commodity (*no demand for solid tyres these days*). **3** an urgent claim (*care of her mother makes demands on her*). ● *v.tr.* **1** (often foll. by *of*, *from*, or *to* + infin., or *that* + clause) ask for (something) insistently and urgently, as of right. **2** require or need (*a task demanding skill*). **3** insist on being told (*demanded her business*). **4** (as **demanding** *adj.*) making demands; requiring skill, effort, etc. (*a demanding job*). □ **in demand** sought after. **on demand** as soon as a demand is made (*a cheque payable on demand*). [based on Latin *mandare* 'to order'] □ **demandingly** *adv.*

DELFT: DELFTWARE TILE

DELTA

As a river enters the sea it suddenly slows down. Its capacity for carrying sediment decreases and it may drop part of its sediment load in a huge fan of alluvial deposits called a delta. Often the river splits up into many smaller branches called distributaries.

TYPES OF DELTA

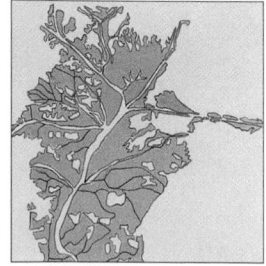

BIRD'S-FOOT (MISSISSIPPI)

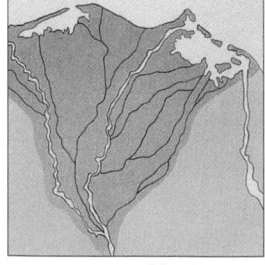

ARCUATE (NILE)

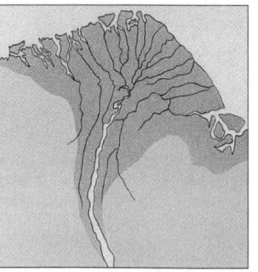

MODIFIED CUSPATE (NIGER)

demarcation *n.* **1** the act of marking a boundary or limits. **2** *Brit.* the trade-union practice of strictly assigning specific jobs to different unions. [based on Spanish *demarcar* 'to mark the bounds of'] □ **demarcate** *v.tr.*

dematerialize *v.tr. & intr.* (also **-ise**) make or become non-material or spiritual (esp. of psychic phenomena etc.). □ **dematerialization** *n.*

demean *v.tr.* (often. *refl.*) lower the dignity or status of. [related to MEAN²]

demeanour *n.* (*US* **demeanor**) outward behaviour or bearing. [related to MEAN²]

demented *adj.* mad; crazy. [based on Latin *mens mentis* 'mind'] □ **dementedly** *adv.* **dementedness** *n.*

dementia /di-**men**-shă/ *n. Med.* a chronic or persistent disorder of the mental processes due to brain disease or injury. [Latin]

dementia praecox /**pree**-koks/ *n.* schizophrenia.

demerara *n.* (in full **demerara sugar**) light brown cane sugar coming originally and chiefly from Demerara. [from *Demerara*, a region of Guyana]

demerge *v.tr.* separate (a business) from another.

demerger *n.* the act of demerging a business.

demerit *n.* **1** a quality or action deserving blame; a fault. **2** *N. Amer.* a mark awarded against an offender.

demesne /di-**mayn**/ *n.* **1 a** a sovereign's or state's territory; a domain. **b** land attached to a mansion etc. **c** landed property; an estate. **2** (usu. foll. by *of*) a region or sphere. [based on Latin *dominus* 'lord']

demi- *prefix* **1** half; half-size. **2** partially or imperfectly such (*demigod*). [from Latin *dimidius* 'half']

demigod *n.* (*fem.* **-goddess**) **1** a partly divine being. **2** the offspring of a god or goddess and a mortal.

demijohn *n.* a large bulbous bottle usu. in a wicker cover. ▷ FERMENTATION

demilitarize *v.tr.* (also **-ise**) remove a military organization or forces from (a frontier, a zone, etc.). □ **demilitarization** *n.*

demi-monde *n.* **1** a class of women considered to be of doubtful social standing and morality. **2** any group considered to be on the fringes of respectable society. [French, literally 'half-world']

demineralize *v.tr.* (also **-ise**) remove salts from (sea water etc.). □ **demineralization** *n.*

demise /di-**myz**/ *n.* **1** death. **2** termination (*demise of the agreement*). [from Anglo-French, related to DISMISS]

demisemiquaver *n. Brit. Mus.* a note having the time value of half a semiquaver and represented by a large dot with a three-hooked stem.

demist *v.tr.* clear mist from (a windscreen etc.). □ **demister** *n.*

demo *n.* (*pl.* **-os**) *colloq.* **1** = DEMONSTRATION 2, 3. **2** (*attrib.*) demonstrating the capabilities of computer software, a group of musicians, etc. (*demo software; demo tape*).

demob *Brit. colloq.* ● *v.tr.* (**demobbed**, **demobbing**) demobilize. ● *n.* demobilization.

demobilize *v.tr.* (also **-ise**) disband (troops). □ **demobilization** *n.*

democracy *n.* (*pl.* **-ies**) **1 a** a system of government by the whole population, usu. through elected representatives. **b** a state so governed. **c** any organization governed on democratic principles. **2** an egalitarian and tolerant form of society. [based on Greek *dēmos* 'the people']

democrat *n.* **1** an advocate of democracy. **2** (**Democrat**) (in the US) a member of the Democratic Party.

democratic *adj.* **1** of, like, practising, advocating, or constituting democracy or a democracy. **2** favouring social equality. □ **democratically** *adv.*

democratize *v.tr.* (also **-ise**) make (a state, institution, etc.) democratic. □ **democratization** *n.*

demodulate *v.tr. Physics* **1** extract (a modulating

signal) from its carrier. **2** separate a modulating signal from. □ **demodulation** *n.* **demodulator** *n.*

demography *n.* the study of the statistics of births, deaths, disease, etc. [based on Greek *dēmos* 'the people'] □ **demographer** *n.* **demographic** *adj.* **demographically** *adv.*

demolish *v.tr.* **1 a** pull down (a building). **b** completely destroy or break. **2** refute (an argument, theory, etc.). **3** *joc.* eat up completely and quickly. [based on Latin *moliri* 'to construct'] □ **demolisher** *n.* **demolition** *n.*

demon *n.* **1 a** an evil spirit or devil, esp. one thought to possess a person. **b** the personification of evil passion. **2** (often *attrib.*) a forceful, fierce, or skilful performer (*a demon player*). **3** a cruel or destructive person. **4** (also **daemon**) a divinity or supernatural being in ancient Greece. [from Greek *daimōn* 'deity']

demonetize *v.tr.* (also **-ise**) withdraw (a coin etc.) from use as money. [based on Latin *moneta* 'money'] □ **demonetization** *n.*

demoniac /di-**moh**-ni-ak/ ● *adj.* = DEMONIC. ● *n.* a person supposedly possessed by an evil spirit. □ **demoniacal** *adj.* **demoniacally** *adv.*

demonic *adj.* (also **daemonic**) **1** fiercely energetic or frenzied. **2 a** supposedly possessed by an evil spirit. **b** of or concerning such possession. **3** having or seeming to have supernatural genius or power.

demonism *n.* belief in the power of demons.

demonize *v.tr.* (also **-ise**) **1** make into or like a demon. **2** represent as a demon. □ **demonization** *n.*

demonolatry *n.* the worship of demons.

demonology *n.* the study of demons etc. □ **demonologist** *n.*

demonstrable *adj.* capable of being shown or logically proved. □ **demonstrably** *adv.*

demonstrate *v.* **1** *tr.* show evidence of (feelings etc.). **2** *tr.* describe and explain (a scientific proposition, machine, etc.) by experiment, practical use, etc. **3** *tr.* **a** logically prove the truth of. **b** be proof of the existence of. **4** *intr.* take part in or organize a public demonstration. [based on Latin *monstrare* 'to show']

demonstration *n.* **1** (foll. by *of*) **a** the outward showing of feeling etc. **b** an instance of this. **2** a public meeting, march, etc., for a political or moral purpose. **3 a** a practical exhibition or explanation of something, designed to teach or inform. **b** a practical display of a piece of equipment to show its capabilities. **4** proof provided by logic, argument, etc. **5** *Mil.* a show of military force. □ **demonstrational** *adj.*

demonstrative ● *adj.* **1** given to or marked by an open expression of feeling, esp. of affection. **2** (usu. foll. by *of*) logically conclusive; giving proof (*the work is demonstrative of their skill*). **3** *Gram.* (of an adjective or pronoun) indicating the person or thing referred to (e.g. *this*, *that*, *those*). ● *n. Gram.* a demonstrative adjective or pronoun. □ **demonstratively** *adv.*

demonstrator *n.* **1** a person who takes part in a political demonstration etc. **2 a** a person who demonstrates, esp. machines, equipment, etc., to prospective customers. **b** a machine, etc., esp. a car, used for such demonstrations. **3** a person who teaches by demonstration, esp. in a laboratory etc.

demoralize *v.tr.* (also **-ise**) destroy the morale of; make hopeless. [from French *démoraliser*] □ **demoralization** *n.* **demoralizing** *adj.* **demoralizingly** *adv.*

demote *v.tr.* reduce to a lower rank or class. □ **demotion** *n.*

demotic ● *n.* the popular colloquial form of modern Greek. ● *adj.* (esp. of language) popular, colloquial, or vulgar. [based on Greek *dēmos* 'the people']

demotivate *v.tr.* (also *absol.*) cause to lose motivation; discourage. □ **demotivation** *n.*

demur /di-**mer**/ ● *v.intr.* (**demurred**, **demurring**) **1** (often foll. by *to*, *at*) raise scruples or objections. **2** *Law* put in a demurrer. ● *n.* (also **demurral**) (usu. in *neg.*) **1** an objection (*agreed without demur*). **2** the act or process of objecting. [based on Latin *morari* 'to delay']

demure *adj.* (**demurer**, **demurest**) **1** quiet and reserved; modest. **2** affectedly shy and quiet; coy. [Middle English] □ **demurely** *adv.* **demureness** *n.*

demurrer *n.* an objection, esp. *Law* a pleading that an opponent's point is irrelevant.

demystify *v.tr.* (**-ies**, **-ied**) clarify or remove the mystery from (obscure beliefs or subjects etc.). □ **demystification** *n.*

demythologize *v.tr.* (also **-ise**) remove mythical elements from (a legend, famous person's life, etc.).

den ● *n.* **1** a wild animal's lair. **2** a place of crime or vice (*den of iniquity; opium den*). **3 a** a small private room or place for pursuing a hobby etc. **b** a hideout or secret place for children. ● *v.intr.* (**denned**, **denning**) live in or retreat to a den. [Old English]

denarius *n.* (*pl.* **denarii**) ◀ an ancient Roman silver coin. [Latin, literally '(coin) of ten asses']

DENARIUS: SILVER DENARIUS OF JULIUS CAESAR, 44 BC

denary *adj.* of ten; decimal. [based on Latin *deni* 'by tens']

denationalize *v.tr.* (also **-ise**) transfer (a nationalized industry or institution etc.) from public to private ownership. [from French *dénationaliser*] □ **denationalization** *n.*

denature *v.tr.* **1** change the properties of (a protein etc.) by heat, acidity, etc. **2** make (alcohol) unfit for drinking, esp. by the addition of another substance. [from French *dénaturer*] □ **denaturation** *n.*

dendrochronology *n.* ▼ a system of dating using the annual growth rings of trees. [based on Greek *dendron* 'tree'] □ **dendrochronological** *adj.* **dendrochronologist** *n.*

DENDROCHRONOLOGY: CROSS-SECTION THROUGH BISHOP PINE SHOWING GROWTH RINGS

period of rapid growth   period of slow growth

dendrology *n.* the scientific study of trees. [based on Greek *dendron* 'tree'] □ **dendrological** *adj.* **dendrologist** *n.*

dene *n.* (also **dean**) *Brit.* a narrow wooded valley. [Old English]

dengue /**deng**-gi/ *n.* an infectious viral disease transmitted by mosquitoes. [W. Indian Spanish, from Swahili]

deniable *adj.* that may be denied. □ **deniability** *n.*

denial *n.* **1** the act or an instance of denying. **2** a refusal of a request or wish.

denier /**den**-yer/ *n.* a unit of weight by which the fineness of silk, rayon, or nylon yarn is measured. [originally the name of a small coin, from Latin *denarius*]

D

D

denigrate *v.tr.* disparage the reputation of (a person). [based on Latin *niger* 'black'] □ **denigration** *n.* **denigrator** *n.* **denigratory** *adj.*

denim *n.* **1** (often *attrib.*) a usu. blue hard-wearing cotton twill fabric used for jeans, overalls, etc. **2** (in *pl.*) *colloq.* jeans, overalls, etc. made of this. [from French *serge de Nîmes* 'serge of *Nîmes*', a city in S. France]

denizen *n.* **1** (usu. foll. by *of*) an inhabitant or occupant. **2** *Brit.* a foreigner having certain rights in his or her adopted country. **3** a naturalized foreign word, animal, or plant. [from Old French *deinz* 'within']

denominate *v.tr.* **1** give a name to. **2** call or describe (a person or thing) as. [based on Latin *denominatus* 'named']

denomination *n.* **1** a Church or religious sect. **2** a class of units within a range or sequence of numbers, weights, money, etc. (*money of small denominations*). ▷ BANKNOTE. **3** a name or designation, esp. a characteristic or class name.

denominational *adj.* of or relating to a particular denomination. □ **denominationalism** *n.*

denominator *n. Math.* the number below the line in a vulgar fraction; a divisor.

denote *v.tr.* **1** be a sign of; indicate (*the arrow denotes direction*). **2** (usu. foll. by *that* + clause) mean, convey. **3** stand as a name for; signify. [based on Latin *nota* 'note'] □ **denotation** *n.* **denotative** *adj.*

■ **Usage** See Usage Note at CONNOTE.

denouement /day-**noo**-mahn/ *n.* (also **dénouement**) the final unravelling of a plot or complicated situation. [from French *dénouement*, literally 'unknotting']

denounce *v.tr.* **1** accuse publicly; condemn. **2** inform against. [based on Latin *nuntiare* 'to make known'] □ **denouncement** *n.* **denouncer** *n.*

dense *adj.* **1** closely compacted in substance; thick (*dense fog*). **2** crowded together (*the population is less dense on the outskirts*). **3** *colloq.* stupid. [from Latin *densus* 'thick, dense'] □ **densely** *adv.* **denseness** *n.*

density *n.* (*pl.* **-ies**) **1** the degree of compactness of a substance. **2** *Physics* degree of consistency measured by the quantity of mass per unit volume. **3** the opacity of a photographic image. **4** a crowded state.

dent ● *n.* **1** a slight mark or hollow in a surface. **2** a noticeable effect (*the lavish lunch made a dent in our funds*). ● *v.tr.* **1** mark with a dent. **2** have (esp. an adverse) effect on (*the news dented our hopes*). [Middle English]

dental *adj.* **1** of the teeth; of or relating to dentistry. **2** *Phonet.* (of a consonant) produced with the tongue-tip against the upper front teeth (as *th*) or the ridge of the teeth (as *n, d, t*). [based on Latin *dens dentis* 'tooth']

dental floss *n.* a type of thread used to clean between the teeth.

dental surgeon *n.* a dentist.

dentate *adj. Bot. & Zool.* toothed; serrated.

dentifrice *n.* a paste or powder for cleaning the teeth. [based on Latin *dens dentis* 'tooth' + *fricare* 'to rub']

dentil *n. Archit.* ▼ any of a series of small rectangular blocks as a decoration under the moulding of a cornice in classical architecture.

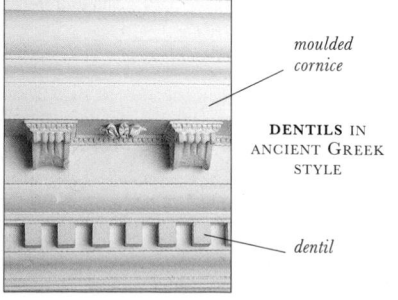

moulded cornice

DENTILS IN ANCIENT GREEK STYLE

dentil

dentine *n.* (*US* **dentin**) a hard dense bony tissue forming the bulk of a tooth. ▷ TOOTH

dentist *n.* a person who is qualified to treat the diseases and conditions that affect the mouth, jaws, teeth etc. □ **dentistry** *n.*

dentition *n.* **1** ▼ the type, number, and arrangement of teeth in a species etc. **2** the cutting of teeth; teething.

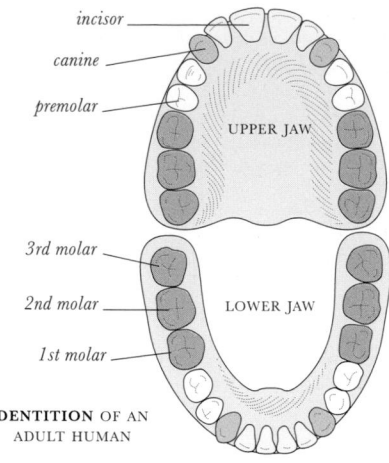

incisor
canine
premolar

UPPER JAW

3rd molar
2nd molar
1st molar

LOWER JAW

DENTITION OF AN
ADULT HUMAN

denture *n.* (usu. in *pl.*) a removable artificial replacement for one or more teeth, fixed to a removable plate or frame.

denuclearize *v.tr.* (also **-ise**) remove nuclear armaments from (a country etc.). □ **denuclearization** *n.*

denude *v.tr.* **1** make naked or bare. **2** (foll. by *of*) **a** strip of clothing, a covering, etc. **b** deprive of a possession or attribute. [based on Latin *nudus* 'naked'] □ **denudation** *n.*

denunciation *n.* the act or an instance of denouncing. □ **denunciate** *v.tr.* **denunciatory** *adj.*

deny /di-**ny**/ *v.tr.* (**-ies**, **-ied**) **1** declare untrue or non-existent (*denied the charge; denied that it is so*). **2** repudiate or disclaim (*denied his faith; denied his signature*). **3** (often foll. by *to*) refuse (a person or thing, or something to a person) (*this was denied to me; denied him the satisfaction*). □ **deny oneself** be abstinent. [based on Latin *negare* 'to say no'] □ **denier** *n.*

deodorant *n.* (often *attrib.*) a substance applied to the body or sprayed into the air to remove or conceal unpleasant smells (*a roll-on deodorant; has a deodorant effect*).

deodorize *v.tr.* (also **-ise**) remove or destroy the (usu. unpleasant) smell of. [based on Latin *odor* 'smell'] □ **deodorization** *n.* **deodorizer** *n.*

deoxygenate *v.tr.* remove oxygen, esp. free oxygen, from. □ **deoxygenation** *n.*

deoxyribonucleic acid /dee-ok-si-ry-boh-new-**klay**-ik/ *n.* see DNA.

dep. *abbr.* **1** departs. **2** deputy.

depart *v.* **1** *intr.* (usu. foll. by *from*) go away; leave (*the train departs from this platform*). **2** *intr.* (usu. foll. by *from*) diverge; deviate (*departs from standard practice*). **3** **a** *intr.* die. **b** *tr. formal* or *literary* leave by death (*departed this life*). [from Latin *dispertire* 'to divide']

departed *n.* (prec. by *the*) *euphem.* a particular dead person or dead people (*we are here to mourn the departed*).

department *n.* **1** a separate part of a complex whole, esp.: **a** a branch of municipal or state administration (*Department of Social Security*). **b** a branch of study and its administration at a university, school, etc. (*the physics department*). **c** a section of a large store (*hardware department*). **2** *colloq.* an area of special expertise. **3** an administrative district in France and other countries.

departmental *adj.* of or belonging to a department. □ **departmentalize** *v.tr.* (also **-ise**). **departmentalization** *n.* **departmentally** *adv.*

department store *n.* a large shop stocking many categories of goods in different departments.

departure *n.* **1** the act or an instance of departing. **2** a new course of action or thought (*driving a car is rather a departure for him*).

depend *v.intr.* **1** (often foll. by *on, upon*) be controlled or determined by (*success depends on hard work; it depends how you tackle the problem*). **2** (foll. by *on, upon*) **a** be unable to do without (*depends on her mother*). **b** rely on (*I'm depending on you to come*). □ **it** (or **it all** or **that**) **depends** expressing uncertainty or qualification in answering a question (*Will they come? It depends*). [based on Latin *pendēre* 'to hang']

dependable *adj.* reliable. □ **dependability** *n.* **dependably** *adv.*

dependant *n.* (*US* **dependent**) a person who relies on another esp. for financial support.

dependence *n.* **1** the state of being dependent (see DEPENDENT 1, 2, 3). **2** reliance; trust (*shows great dependence on his judgement*).

dependency *n.* (*pl.* **-ies**) **1** a country or province controlled by another. **2** anything subordinate or dependent. **3** = DEPENDENCE.

dependent ● *adj.* **1** (usu. foll. by *on*) depending, conditional, or subordinate. **2** unable to do without (esp. a drug). **3** maintained at another's cost. **4** *Gram.* (of a clause, phrase, or word) subordinate to a sentence or word. ● *n. US* var. of DEPENDANT. □ **dependently** *adv.*

depersonalize *v.tr.* (also **-ise**) **1** make impersonal. **2** deprive of personality. □ **depersonalization** *n.*

depict *v.tr.* **1** represent in a drawing or painting etc. **2** portray in words; describe (*the play depicts him as vain and petty*). [based on Latin *pingere* 'to paint'] □ **depiction** *n.*

depilate *v.tr.* remove the hair from. [based on Latin *pilus* 'hair'] □ **depilation** *n.*

depilatory /di-**pil**-ă-tŏri/ ● *adj.* that removes unwanted hair. ● *n.* (*pl.* **-ies**) a depilatory substance.

deplete *v.tr.* (esp. in *passive*) **1** reduce in numbers or quantity (*depleted forces*). **2** empty out; exhaust (*their energies were depleted*). [based on Latin *plēre* plet- 'to fill'] □ **depletion** *n.*

deplorable *adj.* exceedingly bad (*a deplorable meal*). □ **deplorably** *adv.*

deplore *v.tr.* feel or express strong disapproval of. [based on Latin *plorare* 'to bewail'] □ **deploringly** *adv.*

deploy *v.* **1** *Mil.* **a** *tr.* cause (troops) to spread out from a column into a line. **b** *intr.* (of troops) spread out in this way. **2** *tr.* bring (arguments, forces, etc.) into effective action. [from Latin *displicare* 'to unfold'] □ **deployment** *n.*

depoliticize *v.tr.* (also **-ise**) make (a person, an organization, etc.) non-political. □ **depoliticization** *n.*

deponent *n.* **1** *Law* a person making a deposition under oath. **2** a witness giving written testimony for use in court etc. [based on Latin *ponere* 'to place']

depopulate *v.tr.* reduce the population of. [based on Latin *populus* 'people'] □ **depopulation** *n.*

deport *v.tr.* **1** remove (a person) forcibly to another country; banish; exile. **2** *refl. literary* or *archaic* behave (in a specified manner) (*deported himself well*). [based on Latin *portare* 'to carry'] □ **deportation** *n.*

deportee *n.* a person who has been or is being deported.

deportment *n.* demeanour or manners, esp. of a cultivated kind.

depose *v.* **1** *tr.* remove from office, esp. dethrone. **2** *intr.* (usu. foll. by *to*, or *that* + clause) *Law* bear witness, esp. on oath in court. [based on Latin *ponere posit*- 'to place']

deposit ● *n.* **1 a** a sum of money in a bank account. **b** anything stored or entrusted for safe keeping, usu. in a bank. **2 a** a sum paid towards the price of a house prior to a mortgage loan, or as a first instalment on an item bought on hire purchase, or as a pledge for a contract. **b** a returnable sum payable on the short-term hire of a car, boat, etc. **3 a** a natural layer of sand, rock, coal, etc. **b** a layer of accumulated matter on a surface, e.g. fur on a kettle. ● *v.tr.* (**deposited, depositing**) **1 a** put or lay down in a (usu. specified) place (*deposited the book on the floor*). **b** (of water, wind, etc.) leave (matter etc.) lying in a displaced position. **2 a** store or entrust for keeping. **b** pay (a sum of money) into a bank account, esp. a deposit account. **3** pay (a sum) as a deposit. □ **on deposit** (of money) placed in a deposit account. [based on Latin *ponere posit-* 'to place']

deposit account *n. Brit.* a bank account that pays interest and from which money cannot usu. be withdrawn without notice or loss of interest.

depositary *n.* (*pl.* **-ies**) a person to whom something is entrusted.

deposition *n.* **1** the act or an instance of deposing, esp. a monarch. **2** *Law* **a** the process of giving sworn evidence; allegation. **b** an instance of this. **c** evidence given under oath. **3** (**the Deposition**) the taking down of the body of Christ from the Cross.

depositor *n.* a person who deposits money, property, etc.

depository *n.* (*pl.* **-ies**) **1 a** a storehouse. **b** a store (of wisdom, knowledge, etc.). **2** = DEPOSITARY.

depot /**dep**-oh/ *n.* **1** a storehouse. **2** *Mil.* **a** a storehouse for equipment etc. **b** the headquarters of a regiment. **3 a** a building for the servicing, parking, etc. of esp. buses, trains, or goods vehicles. **b** *N. Amer.* a railway or bus station. [from French *dépôt*, related to DEPOSIT]

deprave *v.tr.* pervert or corrupt, esp. morally. [based on Latin *pravus* 'crooked'] □ **depravation** *n.*

depravity *n.* moral corruption; wickedness.

deprecate *v.tr.* **1** express disapproval of or a wish against (a plan, proceeding, purpose, etc.). **2 a** express disapproval of (a person); reprove. **b** = DEPRECIATE 2. [based on Latin *precari* 'to pray'] □ **deprecatingly** *adv.* **deprecation** *n.* **deprecatory** *adj.*

■ **Usage** Although frequently encountered, the use of *deprecate* in sense 2b is widely regarded as incorrect. It is especially common, however, and no longer considered incorrect, in combination with *self-*, with *self-deprecation*, *self-deprecating*, and *self-deprecatory* being used far more often than *self-depreciation*, *self-depreciating*, and *self-depreciatory*.

DEPRESSION

Spiralling low-pressure areas, known as depressions or cyclones, often form in temperate latitudes where tropical and polar air masses meet. The cold air undercuts the warm air, and the fronts may merge to form an occluded front.

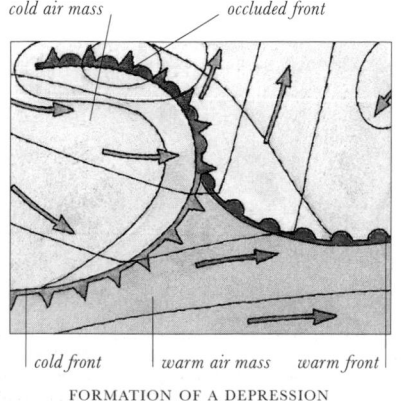

cold air mass   *occluded front*

cold front   *warm air mass*   *warm front*

FORMATION OF A DEPRESSION

DERAILLEUR

Derailleur gears switch a bicycle chain between different-sized sprockets on the front and rear hubs, thereby permitting several gear ratios, or speeds. Adjusting a shift lever, usually mounted on the handlebars, pulls on the gear cable, which moves the derailleurs laterally, guiding the chain between the sprockets.

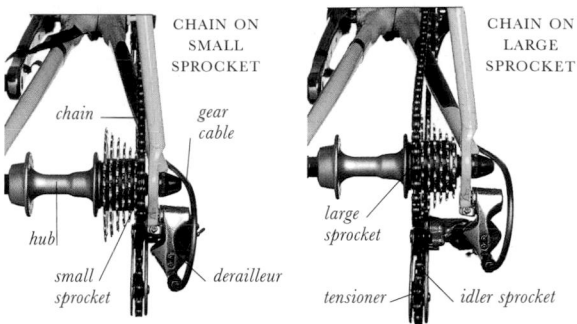

CHAIN ON SMALL SPROCKET

CHAIN ON LARGE SPROCKET

chain   *gear cable*

hub   *large sprocket*

small sprocket   *derailleur*   *tensioner*   *idler sprocket*

BICYCLE WHEEL HUB AND DERAILLEUR GEAR

depreciate *v.* **1** *tr. & intr.* diminish in value (*the pound is still depreciating*). **2** *tr.* disparage; belittle (*they are always depreciating his taste*). **3** *tr.* reduce the purchasing power of (money). [based on Latin *pretium* 'price'] □ **depreciatory** *adj.*

■ **Usage** See Usage Note at DEPRECATE.

depreciation *n.* **1** the amount of wear and tear (of a property etc.) for which a reduction may be made in a valuation or a balance sheet. **2** *Econ.* **a** the decrease in the value of a currency. **b** an instance of this. **3** an instance of disparagement; belittlement.

depredation *n.* (usu. in *pl.*) **1** ravaging, or plundering. **2** an instance or instances of this. [based on Latin *praedari* 'to plunder']

depress *v.tr.* **1** push or pull down; lower (*depressed the lever*). **2** make dispirited or dejected. **3** *Econ.* reduce the activity of (esp. trade). **4** (as **depressed** *adj.*) **a** dispirited or miserable. **b** *Psychol.* suffering from depression. [based on Latin *pressare* 'to keep pressing'] □ **depressing** *adj.* **depressingly** *adv.*

depressant *Med.* ● *adj.* sedative. ● *n.* an agent, esp. a drug, that sedates.

depressed area *n.* an area suffering from economic depression.

depression *n.* **1 a** *Med.* a pathological state of extreme dejection or melancholy, often with physical symptoms. **b** a reduction in vitality, vigour, or spirits. **2** a long period of financial and industrial decline; a slump. **3** *Meteorol.* ◄ a region or weather system marked by low barometric pressure. ▷ WEATHER CHART. **4** a sunken place or hollow on a surface. **5** pressing down.

depressive ● *adj.* **1** tending to depress. **2** *Psychol.* involving or characterized by depression. ● *n.* *Psychol.* a person suffering or with a tendency to suffer from depression.

depressurize *v.tr.* (also **-ise**) cause a drop in the pressure of the gas inside (a container), esp. to the ambient level. □ **depressurization** *n.*

deprivation *n.* (usu. foll. by *of*) the act or an instance of depriving; the state of being deprived (*deprivation of liberty*; *suffered many deprivations*).

deprive *v.tr.* **1** (usu. foll. by *of*) strip, dispossess; debar from enjoying (*illness deprived him of success*). **2** (as **deprived** *adj.*) **a** (of a child etc.) suffering from the effects of a poor or loveless home. **b** (of an area) with inadequate housing, facilities, employment, etc. [based on Latin *privare* 'to deprive'] □ **deprival** *n.*

Dept. *abbr.* Department.

depth *n.* **1 a** deepness (*the depth is not great at the edge*). **b** the measurement from the top down, from the surface inwards, or from the front to the back (*depth of the drawer is 12 inches*). **2** difficulty; abstruseness. **3 a** sagacity; wisdom. **b** intensity of emotion etc. (*the poem has little depth*). **4** an intensity of colour, darkness, etc. **5** (in *pl.*) **a** deep water, a deep place; an abyss. **b** a low, depressed state. **c** the lowest or inmost part (*the depths of the country*). **6** the middle (*in the depth of winter*). □ **in depth** comprehensively, thoroughly, or profoundly (cf. IN-DEPTH). **out of**

one's depth 1 in water over one's head. **2** engaged in a task or on a subject too difficult for one. [Middle English]

depth charge *n.* a bomb capable of exploding under water, esp. for dropping on a submerged submarine etc.

deputation *n.* a group of people appointed to represent others.

depute ● *v.tr.* /di-**pewt**/ (often foll. by *to*) **1** appoint as a deputy. **2** delegate (a task, authority, etc.) (*deputed the leadership to her*). ● *n.* /**dep**-yoot/ *Sc.* a deputy. [from Latin *deputare* 'to regard as, allot']

deputize *v.intr.* (also **-ise**) (usu. foll. by *for*) act as a deputy or understudy.

deputy *n.* (*pl.* **-ies**) **1** a person appointed or delegated to act for another or others (also *attrib.*: *deputy manager*). **2** *Polit.* a parliamentary representative in certain countries, e.g. France. □ **by deputy** by proxy. [Middle English variant of DEPUTE *n.*]

deracinate *v.tr.* *literary* **1** tear up by the roots. **2** obliterate, expunge. [from French, based on Late Latin *radicina* 'little root'] □ **deracination** *n.*

derail *v.tr.* (usu. in *passive*) cause (a train etc.) to leave the rails. [from French *dérailler*] □ **derailment** *n.*

derailleur /di-**ray**-ler/ *n.* ▲ a bicycle gear in which the ratio is changed by switching the line of the chain while pedalling so that it jumps to a different sprocket. ▷ BICYCLE. [from French *dérailleur*]

derange *v.tr.* **1** throw into confusion; disorganize. **2** (as **deranged** *adj.*) make insane (*deranged by the tragic events*). [from French *déranger*] □ **derangement** *n.*

Derby *n.* (*pl.* **-ies**) **1 a** an annual horse race run on the flat at Epsom. **b** a similar race elsewhere (*Kentucky Derby*). **2** (also **derby**) any important sporting contest. **3** (**derby**) *N. Amer.* a bowler hat. [named after the 12th Earl of *Derby*, founder of the horse race]

derecognize *v.tr.* (also **-ise**) cease to recognize the status of (esp. a trade union). □ **derecognition** *n.*

deregulate *v.tr.* remove regulations or restrictions from. □ **deregulation** *n.*

derelict ● *adj.* **1** abandoned, ownerless (esp. of a ship at sea or an empty decrepit property). **2** (esp. of property) ruined; dilapidated. **3** *N. Amer.* negligent (of duty etc.). ● *n.* **1** a person without a home, a job, or property. **2** abandoned property, esp. a ship. [based on Latin *relinquere* 'to leave']

dereliction *n.* **1** (usu. foll. by *of*) **a** neglect; failure to carry out one's obligations (*dereliction of duty*). **b** an instance of this. **2** the act or an instance of abandoning; the fact or process of being abandoned.

derestrict *v.tr.* **1** remove restrictions from. **2** *Brit.* remove speed restrictions from (a road, area, etc.). □ **derestriction** *n.*

deride *v.tr.* laugh scornfully at; ridicule. [based on Latin *ridere* 'to laugh'] □ **derider** *n.* **deridingly** *adv.*

de rigueur /dĕ rig-**er**/ *predic.adj.* required by custom or etiquette (*evening dress is de rigueur*). [French, literally 'of strictness']

derision *n.* ridicule; mockery (*bring into derision*). [from Late Latin *derisio*]

derisive *adj.* scoffing; ironical; scornful (*derisive cheers*). □ **derisively** *adv.* **derisiveness** *n.*

■ **Usage** See Usage Note at DERISORY.

derisory *adj.* **1** so small or unimportant as to be ridiculous (*derisory offer, derisory costs*). **2** = DERISIVE.

■ **Usage** Note the difference between *derisory* and *derisive*. Both words mean 'scoffing', but *derisory* also means 'ridiculously small', which is now its more usual sense.

derivation *n.* **1** the act or an instance of deriving or obtaining from a source; the fact or process of being derived. **2 a** the formation of a word from another word or from a root. **b** the tracing of the origin of a word. **3** extraction; descent. □ **derivational** *adj.*

derivative ● *adj.* derived from another source; not original (*his music is derivative and uninteresting*). ● *n.* **1** something derived from another, esp.: **a** a word derived from another or from a root (e.g. *quickly* from *quick*). **b** *Chem.* a chemical compound derived from another. **2** *Math.* a quantity measuring the rate of change of another. □ **derivatively** *adv.*

derive *v.* **1** *tr.* **a** (usu. foll. by *from*) get, obtain, or form (*derived satisfaction from work*). **b** (in *passive*; foll. by *from*) (of a word etc.) originate, be formed from. **2** *intr.* (foll. by *from*) **a** arise from, originate in, be descended or obtained from (*happiness derives from many things*). **b** = sense 1b. **3** *tr.* (usu. foll. by *from*) show or state the origin or formation of (a word etc.) (*derived the word from Latin*). **4** *tr.* *Math.* obtain (a function) by differentiation. [from Latin *derivare* 'to divert, derive'] □ **derivable** *adj.*

dermatitis *n.* inflammation of the skin. [based on Greek *derma -atos* 'skin']

dermatology *n.* the study of skin disorders. □ **dermatological** *adj.* **dermatologist** *n.*

dermis *n.* (also **derm** or **derma**) **1** (in general use) the skin. **2** *Anat.* the true skin, the layer of living tissue below the epidermis. ▷ SKIN. [modern Latin] □ **dermal** *adj.*

derogate *v.intr.* (foll. by *from*) *formal* **1** take away a part from; detract from (a merit, a right, etc.). **2** deviate from (correct behaviour etc.). [based on Latin *rogare* 'to ask']

derogation *n.* **1** (foll. by *of*) a lessening or impairment of (a law, authority, etc.). **2** deterioration; debasement.

derogatory *adj.* (often foll. by *to*) involving disparagement or discredit; insulting, depreciatory (*made a derogatory remark*). □ **derogatorily** *adv.*

derrick *n.* **1** a kind of crane for moving or lifting heavy weights, with a movable pivoted arm. **2** ▼ the framework over an oil well etc., holding the drilling machinery. ▷ OIL PLATFORM. [from the name of a London hangman *c.*1600]

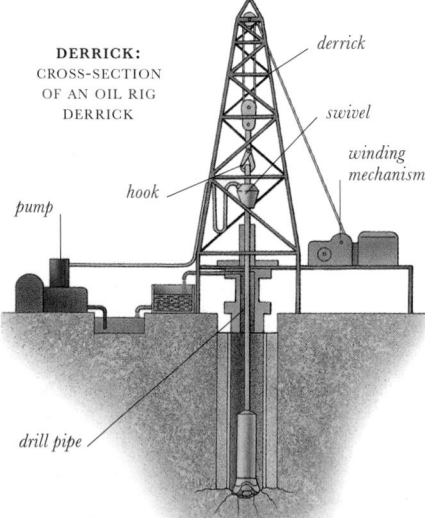

DERRICK:
CROSS-SECTION
OF AN OIL RIG
DERRICK

derrick
swivel
winding mechanism
hook
pump
drill pipe

DESERT

A desert is an arid area of land where vegetation is scarce, and which is characterized by extremely high or low temperatures, or by the evaporation of more water from the Earth's surface than is precipitated in the form of rain. Deserts cover about 33 per cent of the Earth's land surface, and this ratio is increasing through desertification.

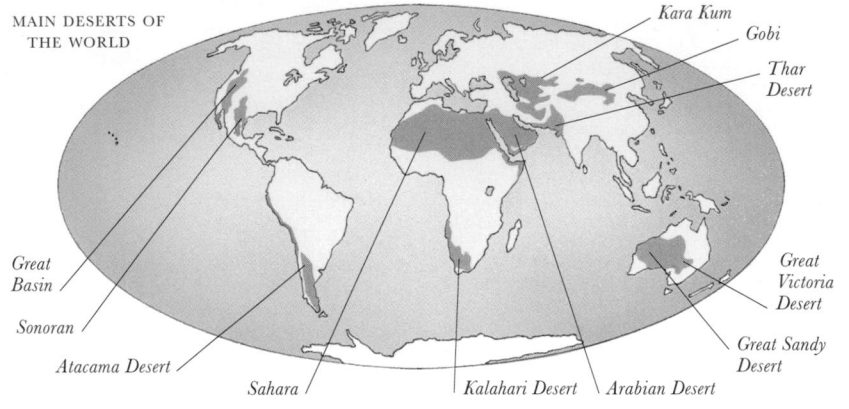

MAIN DESERTS OF THE WORLD

Kara Kum · Gobi · Thar Desert · Great Victoria Desert · Great Sandy Desert · Arabian Desert · Kalahari Desert · Sahara · Atacama Desert · Sonoran · Great Basin

---

derrière *n.* *colloq.* *euphem.* the buttocks. [French, literally 'behind']

derring-do *n.* *literary* or *joc.* heroic courage or action. [Middle English, a misinterpretation of *daring to do*]

derris *n.* **1** any woody tropical climbing leguminous plant of the genus *Derris*, bearing leathery pods. **2** an insecticide made from the root of some kinds of derris. [from Greek, literally 'leather covering', with reference to its pod]

derv *n.* *Brit.* diesel oil for road vehicles. [acronym from *d*iesel-*e*ngined *r*oad-*v*ehicle]

dervish *n.* a member of any of several Muslim fraternities vowed to poverty and austerity. [from Persian *darvēsh* 'a mendicant']

desalinate *v.tr.* remove salt from (esp. sea water). □ **desalination** *n.*

descale *v.tr.* remove the scale from.

descant ● *n.* /des-kant/ *Mus.* an independent treble melody above a basic melody, esp. of a hymn tune. ● *v.intr.* /dis-**kant**/ (foll. by *on*, *upon*) talk lengthily and tediously, esp. in praise of. [based on Latin *cantus* 'song']

descant recorder *n.* *Brit.* the most common size of recorder, with a range of two octaves.

descend *v.* **1** *tr. & intr.* go or come down (a hill, stairs, etc.). **2** *intr.* (of a thing) sink, fall (*rain descended heavily*). **3** *intr.* slope downwards, lie along a descending slope (*fields descended to the beach*). **4** *intr.* (usu. foll. by *on*) **a** make a sudden attack. **b** make an unexpected and usu. unwelcome visit. **5** *intr.* (usu. foll. by *from*, *to*) (of property, qualities, rights, etc.) be passed by inheritance. **6** *intr.* (foll. by *to*) stoop to (an unworthy act) (*descend to violence*). □ **be descended from** have as an ancestor. [based on Latin *scandere* 'to climb'] □ **descendent** *adj.*

descendant *n.* (often foll. by *of*) a person or thing descended from another (*a descendant of Charles I*).

descent *n.* **1 a** the act of descending. **b** an instance of this. **2 a** a way or path etc. by which one may descend. **b** a downward slope. **3** being descended; lineage, family origin. **4** a decline; a fall. **5** a sudden violent attack.

descramble *v.tr.* **1** convert or restore (a signal) to intelligible form. **2** counteract the effects of (a scrambling device). **3** recover an original signal from (a scrambled signal). □ **descrambler** *n.*

describe *v.tr.* **1 a** state the characteristics, appearance, etc. of, in spoken or written form (*described the landscape*). **b** (foll. by *as*) assert to be; call (*described him as a habitual liar*). **2 a** mark out or draw (esp. a geometrical figure). **b** move in (a specified way, esp.

---

a curve) (*described a parabola through the air*). [based on Latin *scribere* 'to write'] □ **describable** *adj.* **describer** *n.*

description *n.* **1 a** the act or an instance of describing; the process of being described. **b** a spoken or written representation (of a person, object, or event). **2** a sort, kind, or class (*no food of any description*).

descriptive *adj.* **1** serving or seeking to describe (*a descriptive writer*). **2** describing or classifying without expressing feelings or judging (*a purely descriptive account*). □ **descriptively** *adv.* **descriptiveness** *n.*

descry *v.tr.* (**-ies**, **-ied**) *literary* catch sight of; discern. [from Old French]

desecrate *v.tr.* violate (a sacred place or thing) with violence, profanity, etc. [based on Latin *sacer* 'sacred'] □ **desecration** *n.* **desecrator** *n.*

deseed *v.tr.* *Brit.* remove the seeds from (a plant, vegetable, etc.).

desegregate *v.tr.* abolish racial segregation in (schools etc.) or of (people etc.). □ **desegregation** *n.*

deselect *v.tr.* *Brit.* *Polit.* decline to select or retain as a constituency candidate in an election. □ **deselection** *n.*

desensitize *v.tr.* (also **-ise**) reduce or destroy the sensitiveness of (photographic materials to light, a person to an allergen, etc.). □ **desensitization** *n.* **desensitizer** *n.*

desert[1] /di-**zert**/ *v.* **1** *tr.* abandon, give up, leave (*deserted the sinking ship*). **2** *tr.* forsake or abandon (a cause, a person, etc.). **3** *tr.* fail (*his presence of mind deserted him*). **4** *intr.* *Mil.* run away (esp. from military service). **5** *tr.* (as **deserted** *adj.*) empty, abandoned (*a deserted house*). [related to DESERT[2]] □ **deserter** *n.* (in sense 4). **desertion** *n.*

desert[2] /**dez**-ert/ ● *n.* ▲ a dry barren often sand-covered area of land. ● *adj.* **1** uninhabited, desolate. **2** uncultivated, barren. [from Latin *desertus* 'left, forsaken']

desert[3] /di-**zert**/ *n.* **1** (in *pl.*) deserved reward or punishment (esp. in phr. **get one's just deserts**). **2** the fact of being worthy of reward or punishment; deservingness.

desert boot *n.* ▶ a suede etc. boot reaching to or extending just above the ankle. ▷ INFANTRY-MAN

DESERT BOOTS

desertification *n.* the process of making or becoming a desert.

deserve *v.tr.* (often foll. by *to* + infin.) show conduct or qualities worthy of (reward, punishment, etc.). [from Latin *deservire* 'to serve well'] □ **deservedly** *adv.*

deserving *adj.* meritorious. □ **deservingly** *adv.*

desexualize *v.tr.* (also **-ise**) deprive of sexual character or of the distinctive qualities of a sex.

déshabillé /day-za-**bee**-ay/ *n.* (also **déshabille** /day-za-**beel**/, **dishabille** /dis-a-**beel**/) a state of being only partly or carelessly clothed. [French, literally 'undressed']

desiccate *v.tr.* remove the moisture from (esp. food for preservation). [based on Latin *siccus* 'dry'] □ **desiccation** *n.* **desiccative** *adj.*

desiccator *n.* **1** an apparatus for desiccating. **2** *Chem.* ▼ an apparatus containing a drying agent to remove the moisture from specimens.

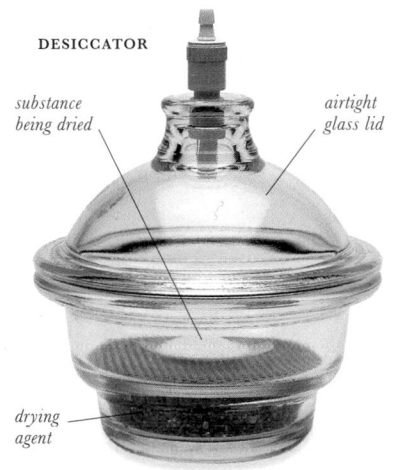

DESICCATOR

substance being dried

airtight glass lid

drying agent

desideratum *n.* (*pl.* **desiderata**) something desirable. [Latin]

design ● *n.* **1 a** a preliminary plan or sketch for making something. **b** the art of producing these. **2** a scheme of lines or shapes forming a pattern or decoration. **3** a plan, purpose, or intention. **4 a** a completed version of a sketch, concept, or pattern. **b** an established version of a product (*our most popular designs*). ● *v.tr.* **1** produce a design for (a thing). **2** intend or plan (*designed to offend*). **3** (*absol.*) be a designer. □ **by design** on purpose. **have designs on** have one's sights set on. [related to DESIGNATE]

designate ● *v.tr.* **1** (often foll. by *as*) appoint to an office or function (*designated him as official receiver*). **2** specify (*at designated times*). **3** (often foll. by *as*) describe as; entitle, style. **4** serve as the name or distinctive mark of (*English uses French words to designate ballet steps*). ● *adj.* (placed after noun) appointed to an office but not yet installed (*bishop designate*). [based on Latin *signum* 'mark'] □ **designator** *n.*

designation *n.* **1** a name, description, or title. **2** the act or process of designating.

designedly *adv.* by design; on purpose.

designer *n.* **1** a person who makes artistic designs or plans for construction, e.g. for clothing, theatre sets. **2** (*attrib.*) (of clothing etc.) bearing the name or label of a famous designer.

designer drug *n.* a synthetic analogue of an illegal drug, esp. one not itself illegal.

designing *adj.* crafty, artful, or scheming. □ **designingly** *adv.*

desirable *adj.* **1** worth having or wishing for (*it is desirable that nobody should smoke*). **2** arousing sexual desire. □ **desirability** *n.* **desirableness** *n.* **desirably** *adv.*

desire ● *n.* **1 a** a longing or craving. **b** a request (*your desire to remain anonymous is granted*). **2** sexual appetite; lust. **3** something desired (*his heart's desire*). ● *v.tr.* **1 a** (often foll. by *to* + infin., or *that* + clause)

long for; crave. **b** feel sexual desire for. **2** request. **3** *archaic* pray, entreat, or command. [from Latin *desiderare* 'to long for']

desirous *predic.adj.* **1** (usu. foll. by *of*) ambitious, desiring (*desirous of stardom*). **2** (usu. foll. by *to* + infin., or *that* + clause) hoping (*desirous to do the right thing*).

desist *v.intr.* (often foll. by *from*) *literary* abstain; cease. [based on Latin *sistere* 'to stop']

desk *n.* **1** a piece of furniture with a flat or sloped surface for writing on, and often drawers. **2** a counter which separates a customer from an assistant. **3** a section of a newspaper office, radio station, etc., dealing with a specified topic (*the sports desk*). **4** *Mus.* a music stand in an orchestra regarded as a unit of two players. [from medieval Latin *discus* 'table']

deskill *v.tr.* **1** render (a skilled worker) unskilled. **2** remove the need for skill from (a job, production, etc.).

desktop *n.* **1** the working surface of a desk. **2** (*attrib.*) (esp. of a microcomputer) suitable for use at an ordinary desk.

desktop publishing *n.* the production of printed matter with a desktop computer and printer.

desolate ● *adj.* **1** left alone; solitary. **2** (of a building or place) uninhabited, neglected, barren, dreary, empty (*a desolate moor*). **3** forlorn; miserable (*was left desolate and weeping*). ● *v.tr.* **1** depopulate or devastate; lay waste to. **2** (esp. as **desolated** *adj.*) make forlorn (*desolated by grief*). [based on Latin *solus* 'alone'] □ **desolately** *adv.* **desolateness** *n.* **desolation** *n.*

despair ● *n.* the complete loss or absence of hope. ● *v.intr.* **1** (often foll. by *of*) lose or be without hope. **2** (foll. by *of*) lose hope about (*his life is despaired of*). [based on Latin *sperare* 'to hope'] □ **despairingly** *adv.*

despatch var. of DISPATCH.

desperado *n.* (*pl.* **-oes** or *US* **-os**) a desperate or reckless person, esp. a criminal. [pseudo-Spanish, from obsolete English noun *desperate*]

desperate *adj.* **1** reckless from despair. **2 a** extremely dangerous or serious (*a desperate situation*). **b** staking all on a small chance (*a desperate remedy*). **3** very bad (*desperate poverty*). **4** (usu. foll. by *for*) needing or desiring very much (*desperate for recognition*). [based on Latin *sperare* 'to hope'] □ **desperately** *adv.* **desperateness** *n.* **desperation** *n.*

despicable *adj.* vile; contemptible, esp. morally. [based on Latin *despicari* 'to look down upon'] □ **despicably** *adv.*

despise *v.tr.* look down on as inferior, worthless, or contemptible. [based on Latin *specere* 'to look at'] □ **despiser** *n.*

despite *prep.* in spite of. [Middle English, related to DESPISE]

despoil *v.tr.* (often foll. by *of*) *literary* plunder; deprive. [based on Latin *spoliare* 'to spoil'] □ **despoilment** *n.* **despoliation** *n.*

despond ● *v.intr.* lose heart or hope; be dejected. ● *n. archaic* despondency. [from Latin *despondere* 'to give up']

despondent *adj.* in low spirits, dejected. □ **despondence** *n.* **despondency** *n.* **despondently** *adv.*

despot *n.* **1** an absolute ruler. **2** a tyrant. [from Greek *despotēs* 'master, lord'] □ **despotic** *adj.* **despotically** *adv.* **despotism** *n.*

des res *n. Brit. colloq.* a desirable residence.

dessert *n.* the sweet course of a meal, served at or near the end. [French, based on *desservir* 'to clear the table']

dessertspoon *n.* **1** a spoon used for dessert, smaller than a tablespoon and larger than a teaspoon. **2** the amount held by this. □ **dessertspoonful** *n.* (*pl.* **-fuls**).

dessert wine *n.* usu. sweet wine drunk with or following dessert.

destabilize *v.tr.* (also **-ise**) **1** render unstable. **2** subvert (esp. a foreign government). □ **destabilization** *n.*

destination *n.* a place to which a person or thing is going.

destine *v.tr.* (often foll. by *to*, *for*, or *to* + infin.) appoint; preordain; intend. □ **be destined to** be fated to. [from Latin *destinare* 'to make fast']

destiny *n.* (*pl.* **-ies**) **1 a** fate. **b** this regarded as a power. **2** what is destined to happen to a particular person etc. (*it was their destiny*).

destitute *adj.* **1** without food, shelter, etc.; completely impoverished. **2** (usu. foll. by *of*) lacking. [based on Latin *statuere* 'to place'] □ **destitution** *n.*

destock *v.intr.* reduce the stock or quantity held.

destroy *v.tr.* **1** pull or break down. **2** put an end to (*destroyed her confidence*). **3** kill (esp. a sick or savage animal) by humane means. **4** make useless. **5** ruin financially, professionally, or in reputation. [based on Latin *struere* 'to build']

destroyer *n.* **1** a person or thing that destroys. **2** *Naut.* a fast warship with guns and torpedoes to protect other ships.

destruct ● *v.* **1** *tr.* destroy (esp. one's own rocket) deliberately, esp. for safety reasons. **2** *intr.* be destroyed in this way. ● *n.* an act of destructing a rocket etc.

destructible *adj.* able to be destroyed.

destruction *n.* **1** the act or an instance of destroying; the process of being destroyed. **2** a cause of ruin (*greed was their destruction*). [from Latin *destructio*]

destructive *adj.* **1** (often foll. by *to*, *of*) destroying or tending to destroy (*a destructive child*). **2** negative in attitude or criticism. □ **destructively** *adv.* **destructiveness** *n.*

desuetude /dis-**yoo**-i-tewd/ *n.* a state of disuse. [based on Latin *desuetus* 'unaccustomed']

desulphurize *v.tr.* (also **-ise**, *US* **desulfurize**) remove sulphur or sulphur compounds from. □ **desulphurization** *n.*

desultory /**des**-ŭl-tŏri/ *adj.* **1** going constantly from one subject to another, esp. in a half-hearted way. **2** disconnected; unmethodical; superficial. [based on Latin *salire* 'to leap'] □ **desultorily** *adv.* **desultoriness** *n.*

detach *v.tr.* **1** (often foll. by *from*) unfasten or disengage and remove. **2** *Mil.* send (a ship, officer etc.) on a separate mission. **3** (as **detached** *adj.*) **a** impartial; unemotional (*a detached viewpoint*). **b** esp. *Brit.* (esp. of a house) not joined to another or others. [from French *détacher*] □ **detachable** *adj.* **detachedly** *adv.*

detachment *n.* **1 a** a state of aloofness or indifference. **b** impartiality. **2 a** the act or process of detaching or being detached. **b** an instance of this. **3** *Mil.* a separate group or unit used for a specific purpose.

detail ● *n.* **1** a small or subordinate particular. **2** small items or particulars regarded collectively (*has an eye for detail*). **3** (often in *pl.*) a number of particulars (*filled in the details*). **4 a** a minor decoration on a building, in a picture, etc. **b** a small part of a picture etc. shown alone. **5** *Mil.* **a** the distribution of orders for the day. **b** a small detachment of soldiers etc. for special duty. ● *v.tr.* **1** give particulars of. **2** relate circumstantially. **3** *Mil.* assign for special duty. **4** (as **detailed** *adj.*) **a** (of a picture, story, etc.) having many details. **b** itemized (*a detailed list*). □ **in detail** minutely. [based on French *tailler* 'to cut']

detain *v.tr.* **1** keep in confinement or under restraint. **2** delay. [based on Latin *tenēre* 'to hold'] □ **detainment** *n.*

detainee *n.* a person detained in custody.

detect *v.tr.* **1 a** (often foll. by *in*) reveal the guilt of. **b** discover (a crime). **2** perceive the existence of (*detected a smell of burning*). [based on Latin *tegere* 'to cover'] □ **detectable** *adj.* **detector** *n.*

detection *n.* **1** the act or an instance of detecting; the process or an instance of being detected. **2** the work of a detective.

detective ● *n.* (often *attrib.*) a person, esp. a member of a police force, employed to investigate crimes. ● *adj.* serving to detect.

D

détente /day-**tahnt**/ *n.* (also **detente**) an easing of strained relations esp. between states. [French, literally 'relaxation']

detention *n.* **1** detaining or being detained. **2 a** being kept in school after hours as a punishment. **b** an instance of this. **3** custody; confinement.

detention centre *n.* an institution for the brief detention of esp. young offenders.

deter *v.tr.* (**deterred**, **deterring**) **1** (often foll. by *from*) discourage or prevent (a person) through fear or dislike of the consequences. **2** check or prevent (a thing, process, etc.). [based on Latin *terrēre* 'to frighten']

detergent • *n.* **1** a water-soluble cleansing agent which combines with impurities and dirt to make them more soluble. **2** any additive with a similar action. • *adj.* cleansing, esp. in the manner of a detergent. [based on Latin *tergēre* 'to wipe']

deteriorate *v.tr.* & *intr.* make or become bad or worse. [based on Late Latin *deterior* 'worse'] □ **deterioration** *n.* **deteriorative** *adj.*

determinant • *adj.* serving to determine or define. • *n.* **1** a determining factor, element, word, etc. **2** *Math.* a quantity obtained by the addition of products of the elements of a square matrix according to a given rule.

determinate *adj.* **1** limited in time, space, or character. **2** of definite scope or nature. [from Latin *determinatus* 'determined'] □ **determinacy** *n.* **determinately** *adv.*

determination *n.* **1** firmness of purpose; resoluteness. **2** the process of deciding, determining, or calculating.

determine *v.* **1** *tr.* find out or establish precisely. **2** *tr.* decide or settle. **3** *tr.* be a decisive factor in regard to. **4** *intr.* & *tr.* make or cause (a person) to make a decision (*what determined you to do it?*). [from Latin *determinare*] □ **determinable** *adj.*

determined *adj.* showing determination. □ **determinedly** *adv.* **determinedness** *n.*

determiner *n.* **1** a person or thing that determines. **2** *Gram.* any of a class of words (e.g. *a*, *the*, *every*) that determine the kind of reference a noun or noun group has.

determinism *n.* *Philos.* the doctrine that all events, including human action, are determined by causes regarded as external to the will. □ **determinist** *n.* **deterministic** *adj.*

deterrent • *adj.* that deters. • *n.* a deterrent thing or factor. □ **deterrence** *n.*

detest *v.tr.* hate, loathe. [from Latin *detestari* 'to denounce, renounce'] □ **detestation** *n.*

detestable *adj.* intensely disliked; very unpleasant. □ **detestably** *adv.*

dethrone *v.tr.* **1** remove from the throne, depose. **2** remove from a position of authority. □ **dethronement** *n.*

detonate *v.* **1** *tr.* set off (an explosive charge). **2** *intr.* explode, esp. loudly. [based on Latin *tonare* 'to thunder'] □ **detonation** *n.* **detonative** *adj.*

detonator *n.* a device or charge used to detonate an explosive.

detour *n.* a divergence from a direct or intended route. [from French *détour* 'change of direction']

detox *n.* esp. *US colloq.* = DETOXIFICATION (see DETOXIFY).

detoxify *v.tr.* (**-ies**, **-ied**) remove the poison from. □ **detoxification** *n.*

detract *v.* **1** *intr.* (foll. by *from*) **a** reduce. **b** diminish, belittle. **2** *tr.* (usu. foll. by *from*) take away (a part of something). [based on Latin *detractus* 'taken away'] □ **detraction** *n.* **detractor** *n.*

detriment *n.* **1** harm, damage. **2** something causing this. [from Latin *detrimentum*, based on *terere* 'to impair'] □ **detrimental** *adj.* **detrimentally** *adv.*

detritus /di-**try**-tŭs/ *n.* **1** matter produced by erosion, such as gravel, sand, etc. **2** debris. [Latin, literally 'wearing down'] □ **detrital** *adj.*

de trop /dĕ **troh**/ *predic.adj.* not wanted, unwelcome. [French, literally 'excessive']

deuce[1] *n.* **1** the two on dice or playing cards. **2** *Tennis* the score at which two consecutive points are needed to win. [from Latin accusative *duos* 'two']

deuce[2] *n.* *colloq.* the Devil, used to express surprise or annoyance (*who the deuce are you?*). [formed as DEUCE[1], two aces at dice being the worst throw]

deuced *adj.* & *adv.* *archaic* damned, confounded (*a deuced liar*). □ **deucedly** *adv.*

deus ex machina *n.* an unexpected power or event saving a seemingly hopeless situation, esp. in a play or novel. [modern Latin translation of Greek *theos ek mēkhanēs* 'god from the machinery', with reference to the gods of Greek theatre]

deuterium *n.* *Chem.* a stable isotope of hydrogen with a mass about double that of the usual isotope.

deuteron *n.* *Physics* the nucleus of a deuterium atom, consisting of a proton and a neutron.

Deutschmark /**doich**-mark/ *n.* (also **Deutsche Mark** /**doi**-chĕ/) the chief monetary unit of Germany. [German, literally 'German mark']

devalue *v.tr.* (**devalues**, **devalued**, **devaluing**) reduce the value of. □ **devaluation** *n.*

devastate *v.tr.* **1** cause great destruction to. **2** (often in *passive*) overwhelm with shock or grief. [based on Latin *vastare* 'to lay waste'] □ **devastation** *n.* **devastator** *n.*

devastating *adj.* crushingly effective; overwhelming. □ **devastatingly** *adv.*

devein *v.tr.* remove the main central vein from (a shrimp or prawn).

develop *v.* (**developed**, **developing**) **1** *tr.* & *intr.* **a** make or become bigger, fuller, more elaborate, etc. **b** bring or come to an active, visible or mature state. **c** bring or come into existence (*an argument developed*). **2** *tr.* begin to suffer from (*developed a rattle*). **3** *tr.* **a** construct on (land). **b** convert (land) to a new purpose. **4** *tr.* treat (photographic film etc.) to make the image visible. [based on Latin *volupare* 'to wrap'] □ **developable** *adj.* **developer** *n.*

developing country *n.* a poor or undeveloped country that is becoming more advanced.

development *n.* **1** the act or an instance of developing; the process of being developed. **2 a** a stage of growth or advancement. **b** a thing that has developed (*the latest developments*). **3** a full-grown state. **4** the process of developing a photograph. **5** a developed area of land. **6** advancement of a country or an area.

developmental *adj.* **1** incidental to growth (*developmental diseases*). **2** evolutionary. □ **developmentally** *adv.*

deviant • *adj.* that deviates from the normal. • *n.* a deviant person or thing. [from Latin *deviant-* 'turning aside'] □ **deviance** *n.* **deviancy** *n.*

deviate *v.intr.* (often foll. by *from*) turn aside or diverge (from a course of action, truth, etc.); digress. [based on Late Latin *deviatus* 'turned out of the way'] □ **deviator** *n.* **deviatory** *adj.*

deviation *n.* **1 a** a deviating, digressing. **b** an instance of this. **2** *Statistics* the amount by which a single measurement differs from the mean.

device *n.* **1 a** a thing made or adapted for a particular purpose. **b** an explosive contrivance. **2** a plan, scheme, or trick. **3** an emblematic or heraldic design. □ **leave a person to his or her own devices** leave a person to do as he or she wishes. [from Old French *devis*]

devil • *n.* **1** (usu. **the Devil**) (in Christian and Jewish belief) the supreme spirit of evil; Satan. **2 a** an evil spirit; a demon. **b** a personified evil force or attribute. **3 a** a wicked or cruel person. **b** a mischievously energetic, clever, or self-willed person. **4** *colloq.* a person, a fellow (*lucky devil*). **5** fighting spirit, mischievousness (*the devil is in him tonight*). **6** *colloq.* something awkward (*this door is a devil to open*). **7** (**the devil** or **the Devil**) *colloq.* used to express surprise or annoyance (*who the devil are you?*). **8** *Brit.* a literary hack exploited by an employer. **9** a junior legal counsel. • *v.* (**devilled**, **devilling**; *US* **deviled**, **deviling**) **1** *tr.* cook (food) with hot seasoning. **2** *intr. Brit.* act as a devil for an author or barrister. **3** *tr. US* harass, worry. □ **devil-may-care** cheerful and reckless. **a devil of a** *colloq.* a considerable, difficult, or remarkable. **the devil's own** *colloq.* very difficult or unusual (*the devil's own job*). **the devil to pay** trouble to be expected. **like the devil** with great energy. **play the devil with** cause severe damage to. **speak** (or **talk**) **of the devil** said when a person appears just after being mentioned. **the very devil** (*predic.*) *colloq.* a great difficulty or nuisance. [from Greek *diabolos* 'accuser, slanderer']

devilish • *adj.* **1** of or like a devil; evil. **2** mischievous. • *adv. colloq.* very, extremely. □ **devilishly** *adv.* **devilishness** *n.*

devilment *n.* mischief, wild spirits.

devilry *n.* (also **deviltry**) **1** reckless mischief. **2** black magic.

devil's advocate *n.* a person who argues against a proposition to test it.

devious *adj.* **1** (of a person etc.) not straightforward. **2** circuitous. **3** erring. [based on Latin *via* 'way'] □ **deviously** *adv.* **deviousness** *n.*

devise *v.tr.* **1** plan or invent by careful thought. **2** *Law* leave (real estate) by will. [from Old French *deviser*] □ **devisable** *adj.* **devisee** *n.* (in sense 2). **deviser** *n.* **devisor** *n.* (in sense 2).

devitalize *v.tr.* (also **-ise**) take away strength and vigour from. □ **devitalization** *n.*

devoid *predic.adj.* (foll. by *of*) quite lacking or free from. [from Old French *devoidier*, related to VOID]

devolution *n.* **1** the delegation of power, esp. by central government to local or regional administration. **2** descent or passing on through a series of stages. [from Late Latin *devolutio*, related to DEVOLVE] □ **devolutionary** *adj.* **devolutionist** *n.*

devolve *v.* **1** (foll. by *on*, *upon*, etc.) **a** *tr.* pass (work or duties) to (a deputy etc.). **b** *intr.* (of work or duties) pass to (a deputy etc.). **2** *intr.* (foll. by *on*, *to*, *upon*) *Law* (of property etc.) fall by succession to. [based on Latin *volvere* 'to roll'] □ **devolvement** *n.*

Devonian • *adj.* **1** of or relating to Devon in SW England. **2** *Geol.* of the fourth period of the Palaeozoic era. • *n.* **1** this period or system. **2** a native of Devon. [from medieval Latin *Devonia* 'Devonshire']

devote *v.tr.* & *refl.* (foll. by *to*) apply or give over to (a particular activity or purpose or person). [based on Latin *devotus* 'dedicated by vow']

devoted *adj.* very loving or loyal. □ **devotedly** *adv.* **devotedness** *n.*

devotee *n.* **1** (usu. foll. by *of*) a zealous enthusiast or supporter. **2** a zealously pious person.

devotion *n.* **1** (usu. foll. by *to*) enthusiastic attachment or loyalty (to a person or cause); great love. **2 a** religious worship. **b** (in *pl.*) prayers. □ **devotional** *adj.*

devour *v.tr.* **1** eat hungrily or greedily. **2** (of fire etc.) engulf, destroy. **3** take in eagerly. **4** absorb the attention of (*devoured by anxiety*). [from Latin *devorare* 'to swallow down']

devout *adj.* **1** earnestly religious. **2** earnestly sincere (*devout hope*). [from Latin *devotus* 'dedicated by vow'] □ **devoutly** *adv.* **devoutness** *n.*

dew • *n.* **1** atmospheric vapour condensing in small drops on cool surfaces at night. **2** similar glistening moisture. **3** freshness, refreshing quality. • *v.tr.* wet with or as with dew. [Old English] □ **dewy** *adj.*

dewberry *n.* (*pl.* **-ies**) **1** a bluish fruit like the blackberry. **2** the shrub, *Rubus caesius*, bearing this.

dewdrop *n.* a drop of dew.

dewfall *n.* **1** the time when dew begins to form. **2** evening.

dewlap *n.* ► a loose fold of skin hanging from the throat of cattle, dogs, etc. [Middle English]

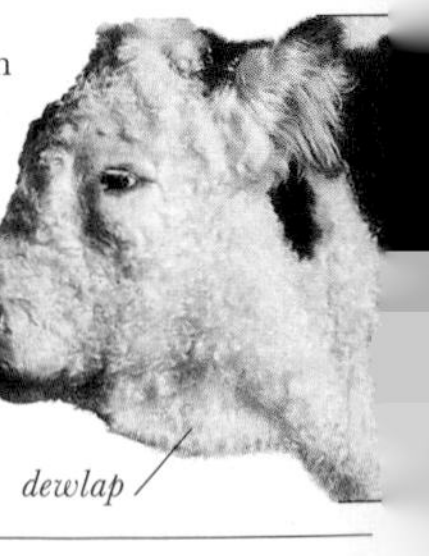

DEWLAP OF A HEREFORD BULL

dew point *n.* the temperature at which dew forms.

dewy-eyed *adj.* naively sentimental.

Dexedrine *n. Pharm. propr.* the more active isomer of amphetamine.

dexter *adj.* esp. *Heraldry* on or of the right-hand side (the observer's left) of a shield etc. [Latin, literally 'on the right']

dexterity *n.* **1** skill in handling. **2** mental adroitness. **3** right-handedness.

dexterous *adj.* (also **dextrous**) having or showing dexterity. □ **dexterously** *adv.* **dexterousness** *n.*

dextrose *n. Chem.* a form of glucose.

DFC *abbr. Brit.* Distinguished Flying Cross.

DFM *abbr. Brit.* Distinguished Flying Medal.

dhal *n.* (also **dal**) **1** split pulses, a common foodstuff in India. **2** a dish made with these. [Hindi]

dharma *n.* **1** esp. *Hinduism* **a** the eternal law of the cosmos. **b** moral or social custom; right behaviour. **2** *Buddhism* universal truth. [Sanskrit, literally 'decree, custom']

dhoti *n.* (*pl.* **dhotis**) the loincloth worn by male Hindus. [from Hindi *dhotī*]

dhow *n.* ▼ a lateen-rigged ship used on the Arabian sea. [from Arabic *dāwa*]

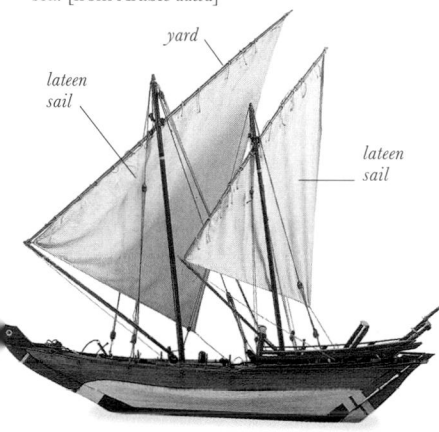

DHOW: PEARLING DHOW FROM KUWAIT

di- *comb. form* **1** twice, two-, double. **2** *Chem.* containing two atoms, molecules, or groups of a specified kind (*dichromate, dioxide*). [Greek]

dia. *abbr.* diameter.

dia- *prefix* (also **di-** before a vowel) **1** through (*diaphanous*). **2** apart (*diacritical*). **3** across (*diameter*).

diabetes /dy-ă-**bee**-teez/ *n.* any disorder of the metabolism with excessive thirst and the production of large amounts of urine, esp. diabetes mellitus. [from Greek, literally 'syphon']

diabetes mellitus *n.* the commonest form of diabetes, caused by a deficiency of insulin, in which sugar and starch are not properly metabolized. [Latin *mellitus* 'sweet']

diabetic ● *adj.* **1** of or relating to or having diabetes. **2** for use by diabetics. ● *n.* a person suffering from diabetes.

diabolic *adj.* **1** of the Devil. **2** devilish; inhumanly cruel or wicked. [from Latin *diabolus*, related to DEVIL] □ **diabolically** *adv.*

diabolical *adj.* **1** = DIABOLIC 1. **2** = DIABOLIC 2. **3** *colloq.* outrageous; disgracefully bad.

diachronic *adj. Linguistics* etc. concerned with the historical development of a subject. [based on Greek *khronos* 'time'] □ **diachronically** *adv.* **diachronism** *n.* **diachronous** *adj.* **diachrony** *n.*

diaconal /dy-**ak**-ŏn-ăl/ *adj.* of a deacon. [based on ecclesiastical Latin *diaconus* (see DEACON)]

diaconate /dy-**ak**-ŏn-ăt/ *n.* **1 a** the office of deacon. **b** a person's time as deacon. **2** a body of deacons.

diacritic ● *n.* a sign used to indicate different

sounds or values of a letter. ● *adj.* = DIACRITICAL *adj.* [based on Greek *diakrinein* 'to distinguish']

diacritical ● *adj.* distinguishing, distinctive. ● *n.* (in full **diacritical mark** or **sign**) = DIACRITIC *n.*

diadem *n.* **1** a crown or headband worn as a sign of sovereignty. **2** a wreath worn round the head. **3** sovereignty. **4** a crowning distinction. [from Greek *diadēma*]

diaeresis /dy-**eer**-i-sis/ *n.* (*US* **dieresis**) (*pl.* **-ses**) a mark over a vowel (as in *naïve*) to indicate that it is sounded separately. [from Greek, literally 'separation']

diagnose *v.tr.* make a diagnosis of (a disease, a mechanical fault, etc.). □ **diagnosable** *adj.*

diagnosis *n.* (*pl.* **diagnoses**) **1 a** the identification of a disease by means of a patient's symptoms. **b** an instance or formal statement of this. **2 a** the identification of the cause of a mechanical fault etc. **b** an instance of this. [based on Greek *diagignōskein* 'to discern']

diagnostic ● *adj.* of or assisting diagnosis. ● *n.* a symptom. □ **diagnostically** *adv.* **diagnostician** *n.*

diagnostics *n.* **1** (treated as *pl.*) *Computing* mechanisms used to identify faults in hardware or software. **2** (treated as *sing.*) the science of diagnosing disease.

diagonal ● *adj.* **1** crossing a straight-sided figure from corner to corner. **2** slanting, oblique. ● *n.* a straight line joining two non-adjacent corners. [based on Greek *gōnia* 'angle'] □ **diagonally** *adv.*

diagram ● *n.* **1** a drawing showing the general scheme or outline of an object and its parts. **2** a graphic representation of the course or results of an action or process. ● *v.tr.* (**diagrammed**, **diagramming**; *US* **diagramed**, **diagraming**) represent by means of a diagram. [from Greek *diagramma*] □ **diagrammatic** *adj.* **diagrammatically** *adv.*

dial ● *n.* **1** the face of a clock or watch. **2** a plate with a scale for measuring weight, volume, etc., indicated by a pointer. **3** a movable disc on a telephone, with finger-holes and numbers for making a connection. **4 a** a plate or disc etc. on a radio or television set for selecting wavelength or channel. **b** a similar selecting device on other equipment. **5** *Brit. slang* a person's face. ● *v.tr.* (**dialled**, **dialling**; *US* **dialed**, **dialing**) **1** (also *absol.*) select (a telephone number) by means of a dial or set of buttons (*dialled 999*). **2** measure, indicate, or regulate by means of a dial. [from medieval Latin *diale* 'clock-dial'] □ **dialler** *n.*

dialect *n.* **1** a form of speech peculiar to a particular region. **2** a subordinate variety of a language with non-standard vocabulary, pronunciation, or grammar. [from Greek *dialektos* 'discourse'] □ **dialectal** *adj.* **dialectologist** *n.* **dialectology** *n.*

dialectic *n. Philos.* **1** (often in *pl.*, usu. treated as *sing.*) **a** the art of investigating the truth of opinions. **b** logical disputation. **2 a** enquiry into metaphysical contradictions and their solutions. **b** the existence or action of opposing social forces etc. [from Greek *dialektikē (tekhnē)* '(art) of debate']

dialectical *adj.* of dialectic or dialectics. □ **dialectically** *adv.*

dialectical materialism *n.* the Marxist theory that political and historical events are due to a conflict of social forces caused by man's material needs.

dialectician *n.* a person skilled in dialectic.

dialectics *n.* (treated as *sing.* or *pl.*) = DIALECTIC *n.* 1.

dialling code *n. Brit.* a sequence of numbers dialled to connect a telephone with the exchange of the telephone being called.

dialling tone *n.* (*N. Amer.* **dial tone**) a sound indicating that a caller may start to dial.

dialogue *n.* (*US* **dialog**) **1 a** conversation. **b** conversation in written form. **2 a** a discussion, esp. one between representatives of two groups. **b** a conversation, a talk (*long dialogues between the two main characters*). [based on Greek *dialegesthai* 'to converse']

dialogue box *n.* (*US* **dialog box**) *Computing* a small area on-screen in which the user is prompted to provide information, select commands, etc.

dial tone *N. Amer.* var. of DIALLING TONE.

dialyse *v.tr.* (*US* **dialyze**) separate by means of dialysis.

dialysis /dy-**al**-i-sis/ *n.* (*pl.* **dialyses**) **1** *Chem.* the separation of particles in a liquid by differences in their ability to pass through a membrane into another liquid. **2** *Med.* ▼ the clinical purification of blood by this technique, as a substitute for the normal function of the kidney. [from Greek *dialusis*]

DIALYSIS

Dialysis is often used in cases of kidney failure to remove waste products from blood by diffusion through a semi-permeable membrane. Smaller waste-product molecules pass through the membrane into a solution, called dialysate, for disposal; larger molecules, such as those of red blood cells and proteins, are retained. In haemodialysis, blood from an artery passes through a coiled tube and back into a vein.

FILTERING ACTION OF A SEMI-PERMEABLE MEMBRANE

dialysate

waste products

semi-permeable membrane

red blood cell

DEMONSTRATION OF HAEMODIALYSIS

blood pump

coiled membrane tube

tank with dialysate

tube from artery

tube to vein

warming solution

compressed air

dialysate

used dialysate

D

diamanté /dee-ă-**mon**-tay/ ● *adj.* decorated with powdered crystal or another sparkling substance. ● *n.* fabric or costume jewellery so decorated. [French, literally 'set with diamonds']

diameter /dy-**am**-i-ter/ *n.* **1 a** ▶ a straight line passing from side to side through the centre of a circle or sphere. **b** the length of this line. **2** a transverse measurement; width, thickness. **3** a unit of linear measurement of magnifying power (*a lens magnifying 2,000 diameters*). [from Greek *diametros* (*grammē*) '(line) measuring across']

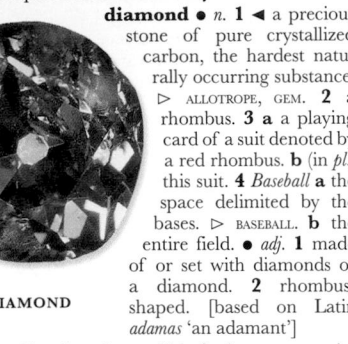

diameter

DIAMETER

diametrical *adj.* (also **diametric**) **1** of or along a diameter. **2** (of opposition, difference, etc.) complete. □ **diametrically** *adv.*

diamond ● *n.* **1** ◀ a precious stone of pure crystallized carbon, the hardest naturally occurring substance. ▷ ALLOTROPE, GEM. **2 a** rhombus. **3 a** a playing card of a suit denoted by a red rhombus. **b** (in *pl.*) this suit. **4** *Baseball* **a** the space delimited by the bases. ▷ BASEBALL. **b** the entire field. ● *adj.* **1** made of or set with diamonds or a diamond. **2** rhombus-shaped. [based on Latin *adamas* 'an adamant']

DIAMOND

diamondback *n.* **1** an edible freshwater terrapin, *Malaclemys terrapin*, native to N. America, with lozenge-shaped markings on its shell. **2** any rattlesnake of the genus *Crotalus*, native to N. America, with diamond-shaped markings. ▷ SNAKE

diamond jubilee *n.* the 60th (or 75th) anniversary of an event.

diamond wedding *n.* a 60th (or 75th) wedding anniversary.

dianthus *n.* any flowering plant of the genus *Dianthus*, e.g. a carnation or pink. [from Greek *Dios anthos* 'flower of Zeus']

diapason /dy-ă-**pay**-zŏn/ *n.* **1** the compass of a voice or musical instrument. **2** a fixed standard of musical pitch. **3** (in full **open** or **stopped diapason**) either of two main organ stops extending through the organ's whole compass. [from Greek *dia pasōn (khordōn)* 'through all (notes)']

diaper *n.* **1** *N. Amer.* a baby's nappy. **2 a** a fabric with a small diamond pattern. **b** this pattern. [based on medieval Greek *aspros* 'white']

diaphanous *adj.* (of fabric etc.) light and delicate, and almost transparent. [from Greek *diaphanes*, based on *phainein* 'to show']

diaphragm /dy-ă-fram/ *n.* **1** a muscular partition separating the thorax from the abdomen in mammals. ▷ RESPIRATION. **2** a partition in animal and plant tissues. **3** a disc pierced by one or more holes in optical and acoustic systems etc. ▷ RECEIVER. **4** a device for varying the effective aperture of the lens in a camera etc. **5** a thin contraceptive cap fitting over the cervix. **6** a thin sheet used as a partition etc. [from Greek *diaphragma* 'partition-wall'] □ **diaphragmatic** *adj.*

diarist *n.* a person who keeps a diary.

diarize *v.* (also **-ise**) **1** *intr.* keep a diary. **2** *tr.* enter in a diary.

diarrhoea /dy-ă-**ree**-ă/ *n.* (*US* **diarrhea**) a condition of excessively frequent and loose bowel movements. [based on Greek *diarrhein* 'to flow through'] □ **diarrhoeal** *adj.*

diary *n.* (*pl.* **-ies**) **1** a daily record of events or thoughts. **2** a book for this or for noting future engagements. [based on Latin *dies* 'day']

Diaspora /dy-**ass**-pŏ-ră/ *n.* **1** (prec. by *the*) **a** the dispersion of the Jews among the Gentiles mainly in the 8th–6th c. BC. **b** Jews dispersed in this way.

2 (also **diaspora**) **a** any group of people similarly dispersed. **b** their dispersion. [Greek]

diastase *n. Biochem.* = AMYLASE. [from Greek *diastasis* 'separation']

diastole *n. Physiol.* the period between two contractions of the heart when the heart muscle relaxes and allows the chambers to fill with blood (cf. SYSTOLE). [from Greek, literally 'a separating'] □ **diastolic** *adj.*

diathermy *n.* the application of high-frequency electric currents to produce heat in the deeper tissues of the body. [based on Greek *thermon* 'heat']

diatom *n.* ▼ a unicellular alga found as plankton and forming fossil deposits. [based on Greek *diatomos* 'cut in two'] □ **diatomaceous** *adj.*

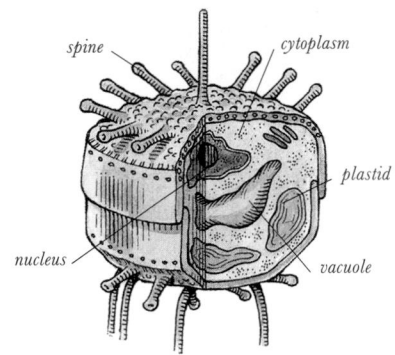

spine   *cytoplasm*

plastid

nucleus   *vacuole*

DIATOM (*Thalassiosira* species)

diatomic *adj.* consisting of two atoms.

diatonic *adj. Mus.* **1** (of a scale, interval, etc.) involving only notes proper to the prevailing key without chromatic alteration. **2** (of a melody or harmony) constructed from such a scale. [from Greek *diatonikos* 'at intervals of a tone']

diatribe *n.* a forceful verbal attack. [from Greek *diatribē* 'discourse']

diazepam /dy-**az**-i-pam/ *n.* a tranquillizing muscle-relaxant drug with anticonvulsant properties used to relieve anxiety, tension, etc., e.g. Valium. [from benzo*diazepine* + *am*]

dibber *n.* = DIBBLE.

dibble ● *n.* ▶ a hand tool for making holes in the ground for seeds or young plants. ● *v.* **1** *tr.* sow or plant with a dibble. **2** *tr.* prepare (soil) with a dibble. **3** *intr.* use a dibble. [Middle English]

DIBBLE

dice ● *n.pl.* **1 a** small cubes with faces bearing one to six spots used in games of chance. **b** (treated as *sing.*) one of these cubes (see DIE[2]). **2** a game played with one or more such cubes. **3** food cut into small cubes for cooking. ● *v.* **1 a** *intr.* play dice. **b** *intr.* take great risks, gamble (*dicing with death*). **c** *tr.* (foll. by *away*) gamble away. **2** *tr.* cut (food) into small cubes. □ **no dice** *colloq.* (there is) no chance of success, cooperation, etc. [Middle English]

■ **Usage** See Usage Note at DIE[2].

dicey *adj.* (**dicier, diciest**) *slang* risky, unreliable.

dichotomy /dy-**kot**-ŏmi/ *n.* (*pl.* **-ies**) **1** a division into two classes, parts, etc. **2** a sharp or paradoxical contrast. [from Greek *dikhotomia*, based on *dikho-* 'apart'] □ **dichotomize** *v.tr. & intr.* (also **-ise**). **dichotomous** *adj.*

■ **Usage** The use of *dichotomy* to mean 'dilemma' or 'ambivalence', as in *I was faced with the dichotomy of wanting to pass the exam but not wanting to please my teacher*; *She alone in the book conveys the dichotomy of the white immigrants towards blacks*, is considered incorrect in standard English.

dichromatic *adj.* **1** two-coloured. **2 a** (of animal species) having individuals that show different colorations. **b** having vision sensitive to only two of the three primary colours. [based on Greek *khrōmatikos* 'relating to colour']

dick[1] *n. coarse slang* the penis. [pet form of the name *Richard*]

dick[2] *n. slang* a detective.

dicken *int. Austral. slang* an expression of disgust or disbelief. [usu. associated with DICKENS or the name *Dickens*]

dickens *n.* (usu. prec. by *how, what, why*, etc., *the*) *colloq.* (esp. in exclamations) deuce; the Devil (*what the dickens are you doing here?*). [16th-century coinage]

Dickensian ● *adj.* **1** of or relating to Charles Dickens, English novelist d. 1870, or his work. **2** resembling or reminiscent of the situations, poor social conditions, or comically repulsive characters described in Dickens's work. ● *n.* an admirer or student of Dickens or his work.

dicker *esp. US* ● *v.* **1 a** *intr.* bargain, haggle. **b** *tr.* barter, exchange. **2** *intr.* dither, hesitate. ● *n.* a deal, a barter.

dickhead *n. coarse slang* an idiot. [based on DICK[1]]

dicky[1] *n.* (also **dickey**) (*pl.* **-ies** or **-eys**) *colloq.* **1** a false shirt-front. **2** (in full **dicky bird**) a child's word for a little bird. [partly from *Dicky*, pet form of *Richard*]

dicky[2] *adj.* (**dickier, dickiest**) *Brit. slang* unsound; likely to collapse or fail. [18th-century coinage]

dicotyledon /dy-kot-i-**lee**-dŏn/ *n.* any flowering plant with an embryo which bears two cotyledons. ▷ ANGIOSPERM, COTYLEDON, FLOWER. [modern Latin *dicotyledones*] □ **dicotyledonous** *adj.*

dicta *pl.* of DICTUM.

Dictaphone *n. propr.* a machine for recording and playing back dictated letters etc.

dictate ● *v.* **1** *tr.* say or read aloud (words to be written down or recorded). **2 a** *tr.* prescribe or lay down authoritatively. **b** *intr.* give orders. ● *n.* (usu. in *pl.*) an authoritative instruction (*dictates of conscience*). [from Latin *dictare* 'to say often']

dictation *n.* **1 a** the saying of words to be written down or recorded. **b** an instance of this. **c** the material that is dictated. **2 a** authoritative prescription. **b** an instance of this. **c** a command.

dictator *n.* **1** a ruler with unrestricted authority. **2** a person with supreme authority in any sphere. **3** a domineering person.

dictatorial *adj.* **1** of or like a dictator. **2** imperious, overbearing. □ **dictatorially** *adv.*

dictatorship *n.* **1** a state ruled by a dictator. **2 a** the position, rule, or period of rule of a dictator. **b** rule by a dictator. **3** absolute authority in any sphere.

diction *n.* **1** the manner of enunciation in speaking or singing. **2** the choice of words or phrases. [based on Latin *dicere dict-* 'to say']

dictionary *n.* (*pl.* **-ies**) **1** a book that lists and explains the words of a language or gives equivalent words in another language. **2** a reference book on any subject, the items of which are arranged in alphabetical order. [from medieval Latin *dictionarium* 'a repertory of words']

dictum *n.* (*pl.* **dicta** or **dictums**) **1** a formal utterance or pronouncement. **2** a saying or maxim. [Latin, literally 'thing said']

did *past* of DO[1].

didactic *adj.* **1** meant to instruct. **2** (of a person) tediously pedantic. [based on Greek *didaskein* 'to teach'] □ **didactically** *adv.* **didacticism** *n.*

diddle *v. colloq.* **1** *tr.* cheat, swindle. **2** *intr. US* waste time. [probably from Jeremy *Diddler*, a character in Kenney's *Raising the Wind* (1803), who constantly borrowed money which he did not repay]

diddums *int. Brit.* expressing commiseration esp. to a child. [from *did 'em*, i.e. 'did they (tease you etc.)?']

didgeridoo n. (also **didjeridoo**) ◄ an Australian Aboriginal wind instrument of long tubular shape.

didn't contr. did not.

die[1] v. (**dies**, **died**, **dying**) **1** intr. cease to live (*died of hunger*). **2** intr. **a** come to an end, fade away (*the project died within six months*). **b** cease to function (*the engine died*). **c** (of a flame) go out. **3** intr. (foll. by *on*) die or cease to function while in the presence or charge of (a person). **4** intr. be exhausted or tormented (*nearly died of boredom*). **5** tr. suffer (a specified death) (*died a natural death*). □ **be dying** (foll. by *for*, or *to* + infin.) wish for longingly or intently (*was dying for a drink; am dying to see you*). **die away** become weaker or fainter to the point of extinction. **die back** (of a plant) decay from the tip towards the root. **die down** become less loud or strong. **die hard** be slow to disappear; persist obdurately (*old habits die hard*). **die off** die one after another. **die out** become extinct. **never say die** keep up one's courage, not give in. [Middle English]

die[2] n. **1** sing. of DICE n. 1a. **2** (pl. **dies**) **a** an engraved device for stamping a design on coins, medals, etc. **b** a device for stamping, cutting, or moulding material into a particular shape. □ **as straight** (or **true**) **as a die 1** quite straight. **2** entirely honest or loyal. **the die is cast** an irrevocable step has been taken. [based on Latin *datum*, literally 'thing given']

DIDGERIDOO

■ **Usage** *Dice*, rather than *die*, is now the standard singular as well as plural form in the games sense (sense 1 above), e.g. *one dice, two dice*.

die-casting n. the process or product of casting from metal moulds. □ **die-cast** v.tr.

diehard n. a conservative or stubborn person.

dielectric Electr. ● adj. insulating. ● n. an insulating medium or substance.

dieresis US var. of DIAERESIS.

diesel n. **1** (in full **diesel engine**) an internal combustion engine in which the heat produced by the compression of air in the cylinder ignites the fuel. **2** a vehicle driven by a diesel engine. **3** fuel for a diesel engine. [named after R. *Diesel*, German engineer, 1858–1913]

diesel-electric ● n. a vehicle driven by the electric current produced by a diesel-engined generator. ▷ TRAIN. ● adj. of or powered by this means.

diesel oil n. a heavy petroleum fraction used as fuel in diesel engines. ▷ FRACTIONAL DISTILLATION

die-stamping n. embossing paper etc. with a die.

diet[1] ● n. **1** the kinds of food that a person or animal habitually eats. **2** a special course of food to which a person is restricted. ● v.intr. (**dieted**, **dieting**) restrict oneself to small amounts or special kinds of food, esp. to control one's weight. ● attrib.adj. with reduced fat or sugar content. [from Greek *diaita* 'a way of life'] □ **dieter** n.

diet[2] n. **1** a legislative assembly in certain countries. **2** hist. a national or international conference. [from medieval Latin *dieta* 'day's work, wages, etc.']

dietary adj. of or relating to a diet.

dietetic adj. of or relating to diet.

dietetics n.pl. (usu. treated as sing.) the scientific study of diet and nutrition.

dietitian n. (also **dietician**) an expert in dietetics.

differ v.intr. **1** (often foll. by *from*) be unlike or distinguishable. **2** (often foll. by *with*) disagree. [from Latin *differre* 'to bear in different directions']

difference n. **1** the state or condition of being different or unlike. **2** a point in which things differ. **3** a degree of unlikeness. **4 a** the quantity by which amounts differ; a deficit (*will have to make up the difference*). **b** the remainder left after subtraction. **5 a** a disagreement, quarrel, or dispute. **b** the grounds of disagreement (*put aside their differences*). □ **make a** (or **all the** etc.) **difference** have a significant effect or influence. **make no difference** have no effect.

different adj. **1** unlike, distinguishable in nature, form, or quality. **2** distinct, separate; not the same. **3** colloq. unusual (*wanted to do something different*). [from Latin *different-* 'differing'] □ **differently** adv. **differentness** n.

■ **Usage** In sense 1 *different from* is generally regarded as the most acceptable collocation; *to* is common in less formal British use; *than* is established in US use and also found in British use, esp. when followed by a clause, e.g. *I am a different person than I was a year ago*.

differential ● adj. **1 a** of, exhibiting, or depending on a difference. **b** varying according to circumstances. **2** Math. relating to infinitesimal differences. **3** constituting a specific difference; distinctive; relating to specific differences (*differential diagnosis*). **4** Physics & Mech. concerning the difference of two or more motions, pressures, etc. ● n. **1** a difference between individuals of the same kind. **2** a difference in wage between industries or categories of employees in the same industry. **3** a difference between rates of interest etc. **4** Math. **a** an infinitesimal difference between successive values of a variable. **b** a function expressing this as a rate of change with respect to another variable. **5** (in full **differential gear**) a gear allowing a vehicle's driven wheels to revolve at different speeds in cornering. □ **differentially** adv.

differential calculus n. a method of calculating rates of change, maximum or minimum values, etc.

differentiate v. **1** tr. constitute a difference between or in. **2** tr. & (often foll. by *between*) intr. find differences (between); discriminate. **3** tr. & intr. make or become different in the process of development. **4** tr. Math. transform (a function) into its derivative. □ **differentiation** n. **differentiator** n.

differently abled adj. euphem. disabled.

difficult adj. **1 a** needing much effort or skill. **b** troublesome, perplexing. **2** (of a person): **a** not easy to please or satisfy. **b** uncooperative, troublesome. **3** characterized by hardships or problems (*a difficult period in his life*).

difficulty n. (pl. **-ies**) **1** the state or condition of being difficult. **2 a** a difficult thing; a problem or hindrance. **b** (often in pl.) a cause of distress or hardship (*in financial difficulties*). □ **with difficulty** not easily. [Middle English, from Latin *difficultas*]

diffident adj. **1** shy, lacking self-confidence. **2** excessively reticent. [from Latin *diffident-* 'mistrusting'] □ **diffidence** n. **diffidently** adv.

diffract v.tr. cause to undergo diffraction.

diffraction n. Physics ▼ the process by which a beam of light or other system of waves is spread out as a result of passing through a narrow aperture or across an edge, often accompanied by interference between the waveforms produced. ▷ INTERFERENCE. [based on Latin *diffractus* 'broken into pieces']

diffuse ● adj. /di-**fewss**/ **1** spread out, not concentrated. **2** not concise; long-winded, verbose. ● v.tr. & intr. /di-**fewz**/ **1** disperse or be dispersed from a centre. **2** spread or be spread widely. **3** Physics intermingle by diffusion. [from Latin *diffusus* 'extensive'] □ **diffusely** adv. **diffuseness** n. **diffusible** adj. **diffusive** adj.

diffuser n. (also **diffusor**) **1** a person or thing that diffuses. **2** Engin. a duct for broadening an airflow and reducing its speed.

diffusion n. **1** the act or an instance of diffusing; the process of being diffused. **2** Physics & Chem. ▼ the interpenetration of substances by the natural movement of their particles.

DIFFUSION OF POTASSIUM PERMANGANATE IN WATER

dig ● v. (**digging**; past and past part. **dug**) **1** intr. break up and remove or turn over soil, ground, etc. **2** tr. **a** break up and displace (the ground etc.) in this way. **b** (foll. by *up*) break up the soil of (fallow land). **3** tr. make (a hole, grave, tunnel, etc.) by digging. **4** tr. (often foll. by *up*, *out*) **a** obtain or remove by digging. **b** find or discover after searching. **5** tr. (also *absol.*) excavate (an archaeological site). **6** tr. slang like, appreciate, or understand. **7** tr. & intr. (foll. by *in*, *into*) thrust or poke into. **8** intr. make one's way by digging (*dug through the mountainside*). ● n. **1** a piece of digging. **2** a thrust or poke (*a dig in the ribs*). **3** colloq.

D

DIFFRACTION

Diffraction is the bending or spreading out of waves, such as the water waves shown here in a ripple tank, as they pass the edge of a barrier. When waves pass through a small gap, which consists of two edges, they spread out in concentric semicircles.

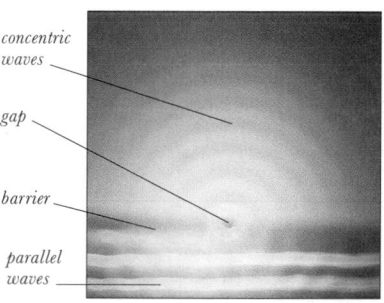

diffracted waves

barrier

parallel waves

concentric waves

gap

barrier

parallel waves

DEMONSTRATION OF EDGE DIFFRACTION

DEMONSTRATION OF DIFFRACTION THROUGH A SMALL GAP

D

DIGESTION

The digestive system comprises a group of organs that break down food into particles that can be absorbed by the body, and eliminate waste products. In humans, the digestive tract begins at the mouth and includes the oesophagus, stomach, small and large intestines, rectum, and anus. It is connected, via ducts, to salivary glands, the gall bladder, and the pancreas, which provide bile and enzymes to aid digestion, and to the liver, which helps to metabolize food products into a form that can be stored (e.g. fat and protein). Undigested food is solidified into faeces in the large intestine, ready for excretion via the anus.

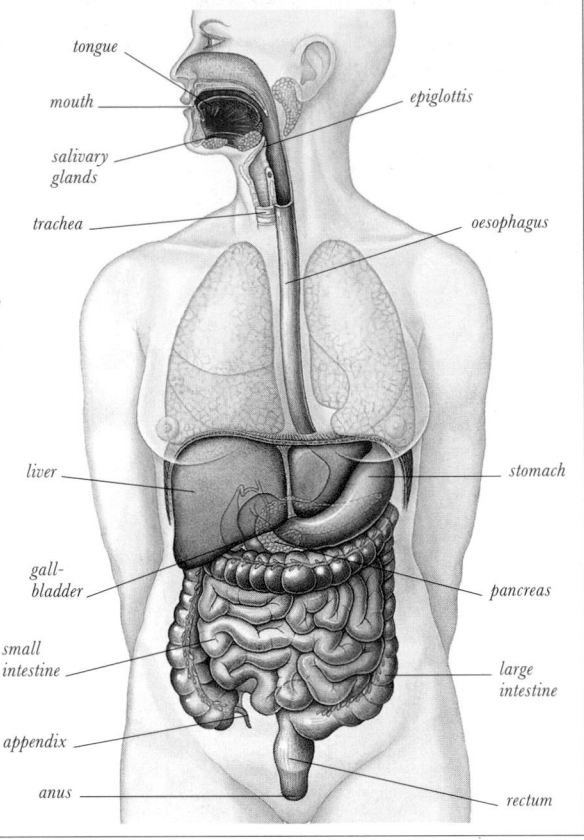

HUMAN DIGESTIVE SYSTEM

tongue
mouth
salivary glands
trachea
epiglottis
oesophagus
liver
stomach
gall-bladder
pancreas
small intestine
large intestine
appendix
anus
rectum

---

a pointed remark. **4** an archaeological excavation. **5** (in *pl.*) esp. *Brit. colloq.* lodgings. □ **dig one's heels** (or **feet** or **toes**) **in** be obstinate. **dig in** *colloq.* begin eating. **dig oneself in 1** prepare a defensive trench or pit. **2** establish one's position. [Middle English]

digest ● *v.tr.* /dy-**jest**/ **1** break down (food) in the stomach and bowels into simpler molecules that can be assimilated by the body. **2** understand and assimilate mentally. **3** *Chem.* treat (a substance) with heat, enzymes, or a solvent in order to decompose it, extract the essence, etc. **4 a** reduce to a systematic or convenient form; summarize. **b** think over; arrange in the mind. ● *n.* /**dy**-jest/ **1** a methodical summary esp. of a body of laws. **2** a regular or occasional synopsis of current literature or news. [from Latin *digerere digest-* 'to distribute'] □ **digester** *n.* **digestibility** *n.* **digestible** *adj.*

digestion *n.* **1** ▲ the process of digesting. **2** the capacity to digest food (*has a weak digestion*). **3** digesting a substance by means of heat, enzymes, or a solvent.

digestive ● *adj.* **1** of or relating to digestion. **2** aiding or promoting digestion. ● *n.* **1** a substance that aids digestion. **2** (in full **digestive biscuit**) *Brit.* a semi-sweet wholemeal biscuit.

digger *n.* **1** a person or machine that digs, esp. a mechanical excavator. **2** a miner. **3** *colloq.* an Australian or New Zealander.

digit *n.* **1** any numeral from 0 to 9. **2** *Anat. & Zool.* a finger, thumb, or toe. [from Latin *digitus*]

digital *adj.* **1** designating, relating to, operating with, or created using, signals or information represented by digits (*a digital recording*). ▷ RECORD. **2** (of a clock, watch, etc.) giving a reading by means of displayed digits as opposed to hands (cf. ANALOGUE *adj.* 2). ▷ CLOCK. □ **digitalize** *v.tr.* (also **-ise**). **digitally** *adv.*

digital audio tape *n.* magnetic tape on which sound is recorded digitally.

digitalin /di-ji-**tay**-lin/ *n.* the pharmacologically

active constituent(s) of the foxglove. [based on DIGI-TALIS]

digitalis /di-ji-**tay**-lis/ *n.* a drug prepared from the dried leaves of foxgloves and containing substances that stimulate the heart muscle. [modern Latin genus name of the foxglove, literally 'relating to the finger']

digitize *v.tr.* (also **-ise**) ▼ convert (data etc.) into digital form, esp. for a computer. □ **digitization** *n.*

dignified *adj.* having or expressing dignity.

dignify *v.tr.* (**-ies, -ied**) **1** give dignity to. **2** ennoble; make worthy or illustrious. **3** give the form or appearance of dignity to (*dignified the house with the name of mansion*). [based on Latin *dignus* 'worthy']

dignitary *n.* (*pl.* **-ies**) a person holding high rank or office.

dignity *n.* (*pl.* **-ies**) **1** a composed and serious manner. **2** the state of being worthy of honour or respect. **3** worthiness, excellence (*the dignity of work*). **4** a high rank or position. □ **beneath one's dignity** not worthy enough for one. **stand on one's dignity** insist on being treated with respect. [from Latin *dignitas*]

digraph *n.* a group of two letters representing one sound, as in *ph* and *ey*.

■ **Usage** *Digraph* is sometimes confused with *ligature* which means 'two or more letters joined together'.

digress *v.intr.* depart from the main subject. [from Latin *digredi digress-* 'to go aside'] □ **digression** *n.* **digressive** *adj.*

digs see DIG *n.* 5.

dike[1] var. of DYKE[1].

dike[2] var. of DYKE[2].

diktat *n.* a categorical statement or decree. [German, literally 'a dictate']

dilapidated *adj.* in a state of disrepair or ruin. [from Latin *dilapidatus* 'demolished']

dilapidation *n.* **1 a** the process of bringing into disrepair or ruin. **b** a state of disrepair. **2** (in *pl.*) repairs required at the end of a tenancy or lease.

dilatation *n.* **1** the widening or expansion of a hollow organ or cavity. **2** the process of dilating.

dilatation and curettage see D. AND C.

dilate *v.* **1** *tr. & intr.* make or become wider or larger. **2** *intr.* speak or write at length. [from Latin *dilatare* 'to spread out'] □ **dilation** *n.*

dilatory /**dil**-ă-tŏri/ *adj.* given to or causing delay. [from Late Latin *dilatorius*] □ **dilatoriness** *n.*

dildo *n.* (*pl.* **-os** or **-oes**) an object shaped like an erect penis and used for sexual stimulation. [16th-century coinage]

dilemma *n.* **1** a situation in which a choice has to be made between two equally undesirable alternatives. **2** a state of indecision between two alternatives. **3** *disp.* a difficult situation; a problem. [Greek, literally 'double premiss']

■ **Usage** The use of *dilemma* in sense 3 is considered incorrect by some people.

dilettante /dil-i-**tan**-ti/ *n.* (*pl.* **dilettanti** or **dilettantes**) a person who studies a subject superficially. [Italian, literally 'delighting'] □ **dilettantism** *n.*

diligence *n.* **1** careful and persistent application or effort. **2** industriousness. [from Latin *diligentia*, related to DILIGENT]

diligent *adj.* **1** careful and steady in application

DIGITIZE

Digitizing involves converting a continuously varying signal, known as an analogue signal, into one composed of discrete units, known as a digital signal. In the digitizing process, the analogue waveform is measured many times every second, and each part of the measured wave is broken down into units. Each unit is given a binary number related to the height of the wave at that point.

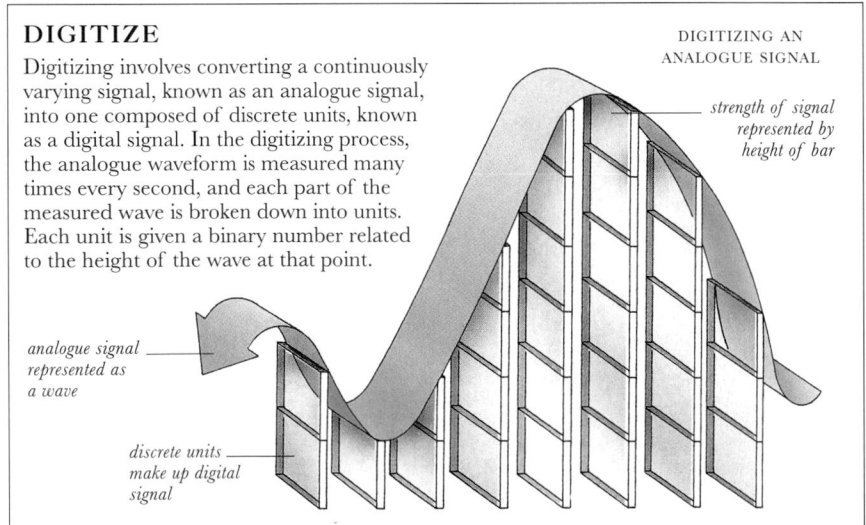

DIGITIZING AN ANALOGUE SIGNAL

strength of signal represented by height of bar

analogue signal represented as a wave

discrete units make up digital signal

to one's work or duties. **2** showing care and effort. [from Latin *diligent-* 'delighting in'] □ **diligently** *adv.*

DILL
(*Anethum graveolens*)

dill[1] *n.* **1** ◀ an umbelliferous herb, *Anethum graveolens*, with yellow flowers and aromatic seeds. **2** the leaves (in full **dill weed**) or seeds of this plant used for flavouring and medicinal purposes. [Old English]

dill[2] *n. Austral. & NZ slang* **1** a fool or simpleton. **2** the victim of a trickster.

dill pickle *n.* pickled cucumber etc. flavoured with dill.

dilly *n.* (*pl.* **-ies**) esp. *US slang* a remarkable or excellent person or thing. [originally as adj. in sense 'delightful, delicious']

dilly-dally *v.intr.* (**-ies**, **-ied**) *colloq.* **1** dawdle, loiter. **2** vacillate.

dilute ● *v.tr.* **1** reduce the strength of (a fluid) by adding water or another solvent. **2** weaken or reduce the strength or forcefulness of. ● *adj.* diluted. [based on Latin *luere* 'to wash'] □ **dilution** *n.*

dim ● *adj.* (**dimmer**, **dimmest**) **1 a** only faintly luminous or visible; not bright. **b** obscure; ill-defined. **2** not clearly perceived or remembered. **3** *colloq.* stupid. **4** (of the eyes) not seeing clearly. ● *v.* (**dimmed**, **dimming**) **1** *tr. & intr.* make or become dim. **2** *tr. US* dip (headlights). □ **take a dim view of** *colloq.* **1** disapprove of. **2** feel gloomy about. [Old English] □ **dimly** *adv.* **dimness** *n.*

dime *n. N. Amer.* **1** a ten-cent coin. **2** *colloq.* a small amount of money. [based on Latin *decima pars* 'tenth part']

dimension *n.* **1** a measurable extent of any kind, as length, breadth, depth. **2** (in *pl.*) size, scope, extent. **3** an aspect or facet. [from Latin *dimensio*, based on *mensus* 'measured'] □ **dimensional** *adj.* (also in *comb.*). **dimensionless** *adj.*

dimer *n. Chem.* a compound consisting of two identical molecules linked together. □ **dimeric** *adj.*

diminish *v.* **1** *tr. & intr.* make or become smaller or less. **2** *tr.* lessen the reputation of. [from Latin *diminuere* 'to break up small']

diminished *adj.* **1** reduced; made smaller or less. **2** *Mus.* (of an interval) less by a semitone than the corresponding minor or perfect interval.

diminished responsibility *n. Brit.* the limitation of criminal responsibility on the ground of mental abnormality.

diminuendo *Mus.* ● *n.* (*pl.* **-os** or **diminuendi**) **1** a gradual decrease in loudness. **2** a passage to be performed with such a decrease. ● *adv. & adj.* with a gradual decrease in loudness. [Italian, literally 'diminishing']

diminution *n.* **1** the act or an instance of diminishing. **2** the amount by which something diminishes. [from Latin *diminutio*, related to DIMINISH]

diminutive ● *adj.* **1** tiny. **2** *Gram.* (of a word or suffix) implying smallness, either actual or imputed in token of affection, scorn, etc. (e.g. *-let*, *-ling*). ● *n. Gram.* a diminutive word or suffix.

dimmer *n.* **1** (in full **dimmer switch**) a device for varying the brightness of an electric light. **2** *US* **a** (in *pl.*) small parking lights on a motor vehicle. **b** a headlight on low beam.

dimorphic *adj.* (also **dimorphous**) *Biol., Chem., & Mineral.* exhibiting or occurring in, two distinct forms. [based on Greek *morphē* 'form'] □ **dimorphism** *n.*

dimple ● *n.* a small hollow in the flesh, esp. in the cheeks or chin. ● *v.* **1** *intr.* produce or show dimples. **2** *tr.* produce dimples in (a cheek etc.). [Middle English] □ **dimply** *adj.*

dim sum *n.* (also **dim sim**) a Chinese dish of small steamed or fried savoury dumplings containing various fillings, served as a snack or course.

dimwit *n. colloq.* a stupid person. □ **dim-witted** *adj.*

DIN *n.* any of a series of technical standards originating in Germany and used internationally, esp. to designate electrical connections, film speeds, and paper sizes. [from German *Deutsche Industrie-Norm*]

din ● *n.* a prolonged loud and distracting noise. ● *v.* (**dinned**, **dinning**) **1** *tr.* (foll. by *into*) instil (something to be learnt) by constant repetition. **2** *intr.* make a din. [Old English]

dinar /dee-nar/ *n.* the chief monetary unit of the states of the former Yugoslavia and certain countries of the Middle East and N. Africa. [from Latin *denarius*, a small coin]

dine *v.* **1** *intr.* **a** eat dinner. **b** (foll. by *on*, *upon*) eat for dinner. **2** *tr.* give dinner to. □ **dine out 1** dine away from home. **2** (foll. by *on*) be entertained to dinner etc. on account of (one's ability to relate an interesting event, story, etc.). [from Old French *diner*]

diner *n.* **1** a person who dines. **2** a railway dining car. **3** *N. Amer.* a small restaurant. **4** a small dining room.

dinette *n.* **1** a small room or part of a room used for eating meals. **2** *N. Amer.* a set of table and chairs for this.

dingbat *n. slang* **1** *N. Amer. & Austral.* a stupid or eccentric person. **2** (in *pl.*) *Austral. & NZ* **a** madness. **b** discomfort, unease (*gives me the dingbats*). [19th-century coinage, in early use applied to various vaguely specified objects]

ding-dong ● *n.* **1** the sound of alternate chimes. **2** *Brit. colloq.* an intense argument or fight. **3** *Brit. colloq.* a riotous party. ● *adj.* (of a contest etc.) evenly matched and intensely waged; thoroughgoing. [16th-century coinage]

dinghy /ding-gi/ *n.* (*pl.* **-ies**) **1** a small boat carried by a ship. **2** ▼ a small pleasure boat. **3** a small inflatable rubber boat. ▷ BOAT. [from Hindi *ḍiṅgī*]

DINGO
(*Canis dingo*)

dingle *n.* a deep wooded valley or dell. [Middle English]

dingo *n.* (*pl.* **-oes** or **-os**) ▼ a wild Australian dog, *Canis dingo*. [from Aboriginal *din-gu* 'domesticated dingo']

dingy /din-ji/ *adj.* (**dingier**, **dingiest**) dirty-looking, drab, dull-coloured. □ **dinginess** *n.*

dining car *n.* a railway carriage equipped as a restaurant.

dining room *n.* a room in which meals are eaten.

dinkum *adj. Austral. & NZ colloq.* genuine, right. □ **fair dinkum 1** fair play. **2** genuine(ly), honest(ly), true, truly. [19th-century coinage]

dinkum oil *n. Austral. & NZ colloq.* the honest truth.

dinky *adj.* (**dinkier**, **dinkiest**) *colloq.* **1** *Brit.* neat and attractive; small, dainty. **2** *N. Amer.* trifling, insignificant. [from Scots *dink* 'neat']

dinner *n.* **1** the main meal of the day, taken either at midday or in the evening. **2** a formal evening meal. [from Old French *diner*]

dinner jacket *n.* a man's short usu. black formal jacket for evening wear.

D

DINGHY

The term dinghy is applied to different types of small pleasure boat, but is most commonly used to refer to a sailing dinghy, which is a small open boat powered by sail. Although there are numerous classes of sailing dinghy, ranging from ones suitable for novice sailors to competitive racing dinghies, the basic parts, as shown here, are common to most sailing dinghies.

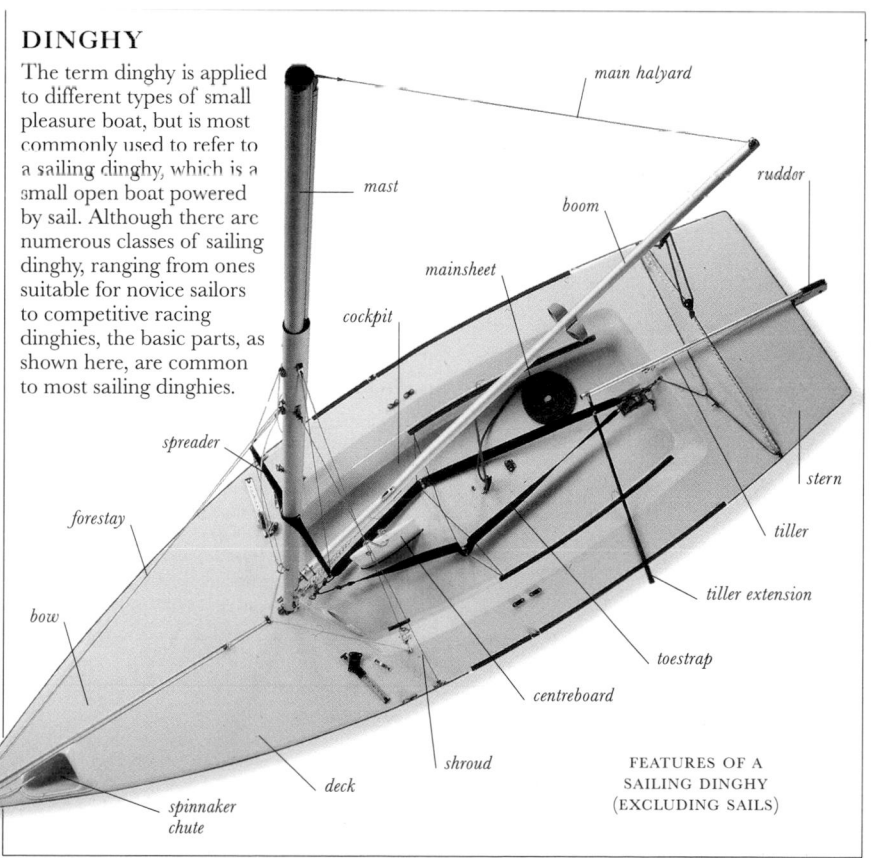

main halyard
rudder
mast
boom
mainsheet
cockpit
stern
spreader
tiller
forestay
tiller extension
bow
toestrap
centreboard
shroud
deck
spinnaker chute

FEATURES OF A
SAILING DINGHY
(EXCLUDING SAILS)

D

dinner lady *n. Brit.* a woman who supervises children's lunch in a school.

dinner party *n.* a party to which guests are invited to eat dinner together.

dinner service *n.* a set of usu. matching crockery for serving a meal.

dinner time *n.* the time at which dinner is customarily eaten.

dinosaur *n.* **1 ▶** an extinct reptile of the Mesozoic era. **2** a large unwieldy system or organization. [from Greek *deinos* 'terrible' + *sauros* 'lizard'] □ **dinosaurian** *adj. & n.*

dint ● *n.* a dent. ● *v.tr.* mark with dints. □ **by dint of** by force or means of. [Old English]

diocesan ● *adj.* of or concerning a diocese. ● *n.* the bishop of a diocese.

diocese *n.* a district under the pastoral care of a bishop. [from Greek *dioikēsis* 'administration']

diode *n. Electronics* **1 ▼** a semiconductor allowing the flow of current in one direction only and having two terminals. ▷ RADIO. **2** a thermionic valve having two electrodes. [based on ELECTRODE]

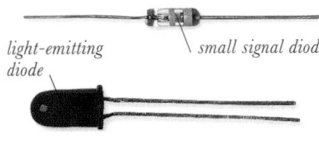

light-emitting diode   small signal diode

DIODES

dioecious /dy-ee-shŭs/ *adj.* **1** *Bot.* having male and female organs on separate plants. **2** *Zool.* having the two sexes in separate individuals (cf. MONOECIOUS). [from Greek *di-* 'two-' + *-oikos* '-housed']

Dionysiac /dy-ŏ-niz-i-ak/ *adj.* (also **Dionysian**) **1** wildly sensual; unrestrained. **2** (in Greek mythology) of or relating to Dionysus, the Greek god of wine, or his worship. [from Greek *Dionusos*]

dioptre /dy-op-ter/ *n.* (*US* **diopter**) *Optics* a unit of refractive power of a lens, equal to the reciprocal of its focal length in metres. [from Greek *dioptra*, a kind of theodolite]

diorama *n.* **1** a scenic painting in which changes in colour and direction of illumination simulate a sunrise etc. **2** a small representation of a scene with three-dimensional figures, viewed through a window etc. **3** a small-scale model or film set. [based on Greek *horama* 'a sight']

diorite *n. Geol.* **▶** a coarse-grained plutonic igneous rock containing quartz. [based on Greek *diorizein* 'to distinguish'] □ **dioritic** *adj.*

dioxide *n. Chem.* an oxide containing two atoms of oxygen (*carbon dioxide*).

dioxin *n. Chem.* any of a class of cyclic compounds produced as chemical by-products.

Dip. *abbr.* Diploma.

dip ● *v.* (**dipped**, **dipping**) **1** *tr.* put or let down briefly into liquid etc. **2** *intr.* **a** go below a surface or level (*the sun dipped below the horizon*). **b** (of a level of income, activity, etc.) decline slightly (*profits dipped in May*). **3** *intr.* extend downwards; take or have a downward slope (*the road dips after the bend*). **4** *intr.* go under water and emerge quickly. **5** *intr.* (foll. by *into*) **a** read briefly from (a book etc.). **b** take a cursory interest in (a subject). **6** (foll. by *into*) **a** *intr.* put a hand, ladle, etc., into a container to take something out. **b** *tr.* put (a hand etc.) into a container to do this. **c** *intr.* spend from or make use of one's resources (*dipped into our savings*). **7** *tr. & intr.* lower or be lowered, esp. in salute. **8** *tr. Brit.* lower the beam of (a vehicle's headlights) to reduce dazzle. **9** *tr.* colour (a fabric) by immersing it in dye. **10** *tr.* wash (sheep) by immersion in a vermin-killing liquid. ● *n.* **1** an act of

DIORITE SEEN THROUGH A MICROSCOPE

quartz

dipping or being dipped. **2** a liquid into which something is dipped. **3** a brief bathe in the sea, a river, etc. **4** a brief downward slope in a road etc. **5** a sauce or dressing into which food is dipped before eating. [Old English]

Dip. A.D. *abbr. Brit.* Diploma in Art and Design.

Dip. Ed. *abbr. Brit.* Diploma in Education.

Dip. H.E. *abbr. Brit.* Diploma of Higher Education.

diphosphate *n. Chem.* a compound with two phosphate groups in the molecule, or a salt with two phosphate anions per cation.

diphtheria *n.* an acute infectious bacterial disease with inflammation of a mucous membrane esp. of the throat. [based on Greek *diphthera* 'skin']

diphthong *n.* **1** a speech sound in one syllable in which the articulation begins as for one vowel and moves towards another (as in *coin*, *loud*, and *side*). **2** a digraph representing the sound of a diphthong or single vowel (as in *feat*). [from Greek *diphthoggos* 'having two sounds']

diplodocus /di-plod-ŏ-kŭs/ *n.* a huge planteating dinosaur of the genus *Diplodocus*, of the Jurassic period, with a long neck and long slender tail. [from Greek *diplous* 'double' + *dokos* 'wooden beam']

diploid *Biol.* ● *adj.* (of an organism or cell) having two complete sets of chromosomes per cell. ● *n.* a diploid cell or organism. ▷ MEIOSIS. [based on Greek *diplous* 'double']

diploma *n.* **1** a certificate of qualification awarded by a college etc. **2** a document conferring an honour or privilege. [from Greek *diplōma* 'folded paper']

diplomacy *n.* **1 a** the management of international relations. **b** expertise in this. **2** tact. [from French *diplomatie*]

diplomat *n.* **1** a member of a diplomatic service. **2** a tactful person.

diplomate *n.* esp. *US* a person who holds a diploma.

diplomatic *adj.* **1 a** of or involved in diplomacy. **b** skilled in diplomacy. **2** tactful. [related to DIPLOMA] □ **diplomatically** *adv.*

diplomatic bag *n. Brit.* a container in which official mail etc. is dispatched to or from an embassy, not usu. subject to customs inspection.

diplomatic corps *n.* the body of diplomats representing other countries at a seat of government.

diplomatic immunity *n.* the exemption of diplomatic staff abroad from arrest, taxation, etc.

diplomatic service *n. Brit.* the branch of public service concerned with the representation of a country abroad.

diplomatist *n.* = DIPLOMAT.

dipole *n.* **1** *Physics* two equal and oppositely charged or magnetized poles separated by a distance. **2** *Chem.* a molecule in which a concentration of positive charges is separated from a concentration of negative charges. **3** an aerial consisting of a horizontal metal rod with a connecting wire at its centre.

dipper *n.* **1** a diving bird, *Cinclus cinclus*. **2** a ladle.

dippy *adj.* (**dippier**, **dippiest**) *slang* crazy, silly.

dipshit *n.* esp. *N. Amer. slang* a contemptible or inept person.

dipso *n.* (*pl.* **-os**) *colloq.* a dipsomaniac.

dipsomania *n.* an abnormal craving for alcohol. [from Greek *dipsa* 'a thirst' + *mania* 'madness'] □ **dipsomaniac** *n.*

dipstick *n.* **1** a graduated rod for measuring the depth of a liquid, esp. in a vehicle's engine. **2** *slang* a foolish or inept person; an idiot.

dipterous *adj.* of or relating to the insect order Diptera, whose members have two membranous wings. [based on Greek *pteron* 'wing']

DIPTYCH: INTERIOR OF THE WILTON DIPTYCH (*c.*1395)

diptych /dip-tik/ *n.* **▲** a painting on two hinged panels which may be closed like a book. [from Greek *diptukha* '(folding) pair of writing tablets']

dire *adj.* **1 a** calamitous, dreadful (*in dire straits*). **b** ominous (*dire warnings*). **c** (*predic.*) *Brit. colloq.* very bad. **2** urgent (*in dire need*). [from Latin *dirus*] □ **direly** *adv.*

direct ● *adj.* **1** extending or moving in a straight line or by the shortest route; not crooked or circuitous. **2 a** straightforward; going straight to the point. **b** frank. **3** without intermediaries or the intervention of other factors (*direct rule; made a direct approach*). **4** (*of descent*) lineal, not collateral. **5** complete, greatest possible (*the direct opposite*). ● *adv.* **1** without an intermediary or intervening factor (*dealt with them direct*). **2** by a direct route (*send it direct to London*). ● *v.tr.* **1** control, guide; govern the movements of. **2** (foll. by *to* + infin., or *that* + clause) give a formal order or command to. **3** (foll. by *to*) **a** address (a letter etc.). **b** tell or show (a person) the way to a destination. **4** (foll. by *at, to, towards*) **a** point, aim, or cause (a blow or missile) to move in a certain direction. **b** point or address (one's attention, a remark, etc.). **5** guide as an adviser, as a principle, etc. (*I do as duty directs me*). **6 a** (also *absol.*) supervise the performing, staging, etc., of (a film, play, etc.). **b** supervise the performance of (an actor etc.). **7** (also *absol.*) guide the performance of (a group of musicians). [from Latin *directus* 'directed, guided'] □ **directness** *n.*

direct action *n.* action such as a strike or sabotage directly affecting the public and meant to reinforce demands on a government, employer, etc.

direct current *n.* an electric current flowing in one direction only. ▷ CIRCUIT

direct debit *n. Brit.* an arrangement for the regular debiting of a bank account at the request of the payee.

direct dialling *n.* the facility of dialling a telephone number without making use of the operator. □ **direct dial** *attrib.adj.*

direct-grant school *n. hist.* (in the UK) a school receiving funds from the Government and not from a local authority.

direction *n.* **1** the act or process of directing; supervision. **2** (usu. in *pl.*) an order or instruction. **3 a** the course or line along which a person or thing moves or looks, or which must be taken to reach a destination. **b** (in *pl.*) guidance on how to reach a destination. **c** the point to or from which a person or thing moves or looks. **4** the tendency or scope of a theme, subject, or inquiry. □ **directionless** *adj.*

directional *adj.* **1** of or indicating direction. **2** *Electronics* **a** concerned with the transmission of radio or sound waves in a particular direction. **b** (of equipment) designed to receive radio or sound waves most effectively from a particular direction or directions. □ **directionality** *n.* **directionally** *adv.*

DINOSAUR

Dinosaurs were the dominant land vertebrates for most of the Mesozoic era (248–65 million years ago). They are separated into two groups according to the structure of the pelvis: ornithischian (bird-hipped) dinosaurs had a pubis that slanted backwards; most saurischian (lizard-hipped) dinosaurs had a forward-slanting pubis. Examples of dinosaurs from sub-groups within these two main groups are shown below.

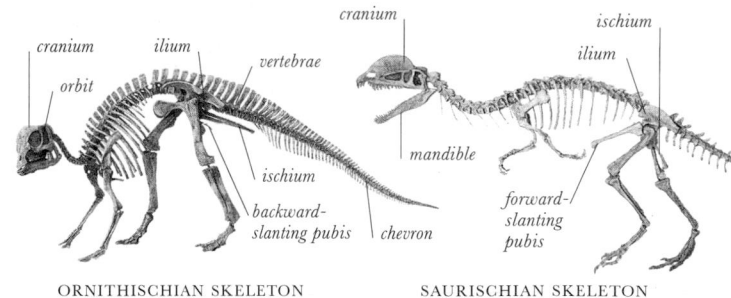

cranium
orbit
ilium
vertebrae
ischium
backward-slanting pubis
chevron
ORNITHISCHIAN SKELETON

cranium
ischium
ilium
mandible
forward-slanting pubis
SAURISCHIAN SKELETON

D

EXAMPLES OF DINOSAURS

ORNITHISCHIANS

PACHYCEPHALOSAURIA
(*Stegoceras*)

CERATOPSIA
(*Triceratops*)

STEGOSAURIA
(*Stegosaurus*)

ANKYLOSAURIA
(*Euoplocephalus*)

ORNITHOPODA
(*Iguanadon*)

SAURISCHIANS

COELUROSAURIA
(*Compsognathus*)

ORNITHOMIMOSAURIA
(*Gallimimus*)

CARNOSAURIA
(*Tyrannosaurus*)

SAUROPODA
(*Barosaurus*)

DEINONYCHOSAURIA
(*Deinonychus*)

D

direction-finder *n.* a device for determining the source of radio waves, esp. as an aid in navigation.

directive ● *n.* a general instruction from one in authority. ● *adj.* serving to direct.

directly ● *adv.* **1 a** at once; without delay. **b** presently, shortly. **2** exactly, immediately (*directly opposite; directly after lunch*). **3** in a direct manner. ● *conj. Brit. colloq.* as soon as (*will tell you directly they come*).

direct mail *n.* advertising sent unsolicited through the post to prospective customers. □ **direct mailing** *n.*

direct object *n.* the primary object of the action of a transitive verb.

director *n.* **1** a person who directs or controls something. **2** a member of the managing board of a commercial company. **3** a person who directs a film etc. [from Late Latin *director* 'governor'] □ **directorial** *adj.* **directorship** *n.* (esp. in sense 2).

directorate *n.* **1** a board of directors. **2** the office of director.

director-general *n.* (*pl.* **director-generals**) esp. *Brit.* the chief executive of a large organization.

director of public prosecutions *n. Brit.* = PUBLIC PROSECUTOR.

directory *n.* (*pl.* **-ies**) **1** a book listing a particular group of individuals or organizations with various details. **2** a computer file listing other files or programs etc.

directory enquiries *n.pl.* (*N. Amer.* **directory assistance**) a telephone service providing a subscriber's number on request.

direct proportion *n.* a relation between quantities whose ratio is constant.

direct speech *n.* words as actually spoken, not reported.

direct tax *n.* a tax levied on the person who ultimately bears the burden of it, esp. on income.

dirge *n.* **1** a lament for the dead. **2** any mournful song or lament. [Middle English, from Latin imperative *dirige* 'direct', first word of Psalm 5:8, used in the Latin Office for the Dead]

dirigible /di-rij-ibŭl/ ● *adj.* capable of being guided. ● *n.* a dirigible balloon or airship. [from Latin *dirigibilis* 'that can be directed']

diriment impediment *n.* a factor (e.g. the existence of a prior marriage) rendering a marriage null and void from the beginning.

dirk *n.* a short dagger, esp. as formerly worn by Scottish Highlanders. [16th-century coinage]

dirndl *n.* **1** ▼ a woman's dress styled in imitation of Alpine peasant costume, with close-fitting bodice, tight waistband, and full skirt. **2** (in full **dirndl skirt**) a full skirt of this kind. [German dialect word, literally 'little girl']

close-fitting bodice

full skirt

DIRNDL DRESSES

dirt *n.* **1** unclean matter that soils. **2 a** earth, soil. **b** earth, cinders, etc., used to make a surface for a road etc. (usu. *attrib.*: *dirt track*). **3** foul or malicious words or talk. **4** excrement. **5** a dirty condition. **6** a person or thing considered worthless. □ **treat like dirt** treat (a person) contemptuously. [from Old Norse *drit* 'excrement']

dirt bike *n.* a motorcycle designed for use on unmade roads and tracks, esp. in scrambling.

dirt cheap *adj. & adv. colloq.* extremely cheap.

dirt track *n.* a course made of rolled cinders, soil, etc., for motorcycle racing or flat racing (often hyphenated when *attrib.*: *dirt-track race*).

dirty ● *adj.* (**dirtier**, **dirtiest**) **1** soiled, unclean. **2** causing one to become dirty (*a dirty job*). **3** sordid, lewd; morally illicit or questionable (*dirty joke*). **4** unpleasant, nasty. **5** dishonourable, unfair (*dirty play*). **6** (of weather) rough, squally. **7** (of a colour) not pure or clear, dingy. **8** *colloq.* (of a nuclear weapon) producing considerable radioactive fallout ● *adv. slang* (with adjectives expressing magnitude) very (*a dirty great diamond*). **2** dirtily; unfairly (*play dirty*). ● *v.tr. & intr.* (**-ies, -ied**) make or become dirty. □ **do the dirty on** *Brit. colloq.* play a mean trick on. □ **dirtiness** *n.*

dirty dog *n. colloq.* a scoundrel; a despicable person.

dirty linen *n. colloq.* intimate secrets, esp. of a scandalous nature.

dirty look *n. colloq.* a look of disapproval, anger, or disgust.

dirty money *n.* **1** money obtained unlawfully or immorally. **2** *Brit.* extra money paid to those who handle dirty materials.

dirty old man *n. colloq.* a lecherous man.

dirty trick *n.* **1** a dishonourable and deceitful act. **2** (in *pl.*) underhand political activity, esp. to discredit an opponent.

dirty weekend *n. Brit. colloq.* a weekend spent clandestinely with a lover.

dirty word *n.* **1** an offensive or indecent word. **2** a word for something which is disapproved of (*profit is a dirty word*).

dirty work *n.* dishonourable or illegal activity.

dis (also **diss**) *US slang* ● *v.tr.* (**dissed, dissing**) put a person down; bad-mouth. ● *n.* disrespect.

dis- *prefix* forming nouns, adjectives, and verbs: **1** expressing negation (*dishonest*). **2** indicating reversal or absence of an action or state (*disengage; disbelieve*). **3** indicating removal of a thing or quality (*dismember; disable*). **4** indicating separation (*distinguish; disperse*). **5** indicating completeness or intensification of the action (*disembowel; disgruntled*). **6** indicating expulsion from (*disbar*).

disability *n.* (*pl.* **-ies**) **1** a physical incapacity, either congenital or caused by injury, disease, etc., esp. when limiting a person's ability to work. **2** a lack of some asset, quality, or attribute, that prevents a person from doing something. **3** a legal disqualification.

disable *v.tr.* **1** render unable to function. **2** (often as **disabled** *adj.*) deprive of physical or mental ability. □ **disablement** *n.*

disablist *adj.* discriminating or prejudiced against disabled people.

disabuse *v.tr.* **1** (foll. by *of*) free from a mistaken idea. **2** disillusion, undeceive.

disaccharide /dy-**sak**-ă-ryd/ *n. Chem.* a sugar whose molecule contains two linked monosaccharides.

disaccord ● *n.* disagreement, disharmony. ● *v.intr.* (usu. foll. by *with*) disagree; be at odds.

disadvantage ● *n.* **1** an unfavourable circumstance or condition. **2** damage to one's interest or reputation. ● *v.tr.* cause disadvantage to. □ **at a disadvantage** in an unfavourable position or aspect.

disadvantaged *adj.* placed in unfavourable circumstances (esp. of a person lacking the normal social opportunities).

disadvantageous *adj.* **1** involving disadvantage. **2** derogatory; discreditable.

disaffected *adj.* **1** disloyal, esp. to one's superiors. **2** estranged; no longer friendly; discontented. [originally in sense 'disliked']

disaffection *n.* **1** disloyalty. **2** political discontent.

disaffiliate *v.* **1** *tr.* end the affiliation of. **2** *intr.* end one's affiliation. **3** *tr. & intr.* detach. □ **disaffiliation** *n.*

disafforest *v.tr. Brit.* clear of forests or trees.

disagree *v.intr.* (**disagrees, disagreed, disagreeing**) (often foll. by *with*) **1** hold a different opinion. **2** quarrel. **3** (of factors or circumstances) not correspond. **4** have an adverse effect upon (a person's health, digestion, etc.). □ **disagreement** *n.*

disagreeable *adj.* **1** unpleasant. **2** bad-tempered. □ **disagreeably** *adv.*

disallow *v.tr.* refuse to allow or accept as valid; prohibit. □ **disallowance** *n.*

disambiguate *v.tr.* remove ambiguity from. □ **disambiguation** *n.*

disappear *v.intr.* **1** cease to be visible; pass from sight. **2** cease to exist or be in circulation or use (*trams had all but disappeared*). **3** (of a person or thing) go missing. □ **disappearance** *n.*

disappoint *v.tr.* (also *absol.*) fail to fulfil a desire or expectation of (a person). **2** frustrate (hopes etc.). □ **be disappointed** fail to have one's expectation etc. fulfilled in some regard (*was disappointed with you; am disappointed to be last*). [from French *désappointer*] □ **disappointedly** *adv.* **disappointing** *adj.* **disappointingly** *adv.*

disappointment *n.* **1** an event, thing, or person that disappoints. **2** a feeling of distress, vexation, etc., resulting from this (*I cannot hide my disappointment*).

disapprobation *n.* strong disapproval.

disapprove *v.* **1** *intr.* (usu. foll. by *of*) have or express an unfavourable opinion. **2** *tr.* be displeased with. □ **disapproval** *n.* **disapproving** *adj.* **disapprovingly** *adv.*

disarm *v.* **1** *tr.* take weapons away from (often foll. by *of*: *were disarmed of their rifles*). **2** *intr.* (of a state etc.) disband or reduce its armed forces. **3** *tr.* remove the fuse from (a bomb etc.). **4** *tr.* deprive of the power to injure. **5** *tr.* pacify or allay the hostility or suspicions of; mollify; placate. □ **disarmer** *n.* **disarming** *adj.* (esp. in sense 5). **disarmingly** *adv.*

disarmament *n.* the reduction by a state of its military forces and weapons.

disarrange *v.tr.* bring into disorder.

disarray ● *n.* (often prec. by *in, into*) disorder, confusion. ● *v.tr.* throw into disorder.

disassemble *v.tr.* take (a machine etc.) to pieces. □ **disassembly** *n.*

disassociate *v.tr. & intr.* = DISSOCIATE. □ **disassociation** *n.*

disaster *n.* **1** a great or sudden misfortune. **2 a** complete failure. **b** a person or enterprise ending in failure. [originally in sense 'unfavourable aspect of a star': based on Latin *astrum* 'star'] □ **disastrous** *adj.* **disastrously** *adv.*

disavow *v.tr.* disclaim knowledge of, responsibility for, or belief in. □ **disavowal** *n.*

disband *v.* **1** *intr.* (of an organized group etc.) cease to work or act together; disperse. **2** *tr.* cause (such a group) to disband. □ **disbandment** *n.*

disbar *v.tr.* (**disbarred, disbarring**) deprive (a barrister) of the right to practise. □ **disbarment** *n.*

disbelieve *v.* **1** *tr.* be unable or unwilling to believe (a person or statement). **2** *intr.* have no faith. □ **disbelief** *n.* **disbeliever** *n.* **disbelievingly** *adv.*

disbud *v.tr.* (**disbudded, disbudding**) remove buds from.

disburse *v.* **1** *tr.* expend (money). **2** *tr.* defray (a cost). **3** *intr.* pay money. [from Old French *desbourser*, based on medieval Latin *bursa* 'purse'] □ **disbursement** *n.*

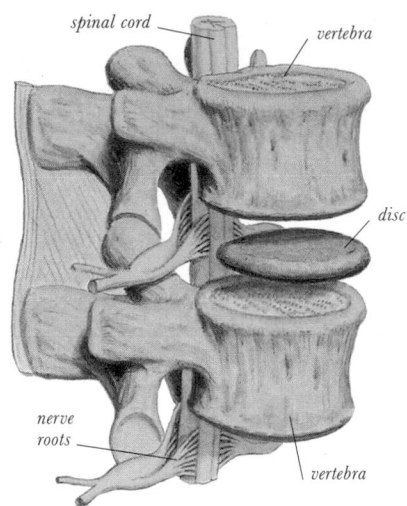

DISC: SECTION OF THE HUMAN SPINE
SHOWING AN INTERVERTEBRAL DISC

disc *n.* (also **disk** esp. *US* and in sense 4a) **1 a** a flat thin circular object. **b** a round flat or apparently flat surface (*the sun's disc*). **c** a mark of this shape. **2** ▲ a layer of cartilage between vertebrae. **3** a gramophone record. **4 a** (usu. **disk**; in full **magnetic disk**) a computer storage device consisting of a rotatable disc or discs with a magnetic coating. ▷ COMPUTER, HARD DISK. **b** (in full **optical disc**) a smooth non-magnetic disc for data recorded and read by laser. [from Latin *discus*] □ **diskless** *adj. Computing.*

discard ● *v.tr.* /dis-**kard**/ reject as unwanted. ● *n.* /**dis**-kard/ a discarded item. [based on CARD¹]

discarnate *adj.* having no physical body; separated from the flesh. [based on Latin *caro carnis* 'flesh']

disc brake *n.* a brake employing the friction of pads against a disc.

discern *v.tr.* **1** perceive clearly with the mind or the senses. **2** make out by thought or by gazing, listening, etc. [based on Latin *cernere* 'to separate'] □ **discernible** *adj.* **discernibly** *adv.*

discerning *adj.* having or showing good judgement or insight.

discernment *n.* good judgement or insight.

discerptible *adj. literary* able to be plucked apart; divisible.

discharge ● *v.* **1** *tr.* **a** let go, release, esp. from a duty, commitment, or period of confinement. **b** relieve (a bankrupt) of residual liability. **2** *tr.* dismiss from office, employment, etc. **3** *tr.* **a** fire (a gun etc.). **b** (of a gun etc.) fire (a bullet etc.). **4 a** *tr.* (also *absol.*) pour out or cause to pour out (pus, liquid, etc.) (*the wound was discharging*). **b** *intr.* (foll. by *into*) (of a river etc.) flow into. **5** *tr.* **a** carry out, perform (a duty or obligation). **b** relieve oneself of (a financial commitment) (*discharged his debt*). **6** *tr. Law* cancel (an order of court). **7** *tr. Physics* release an electrical charge from. **8** *tr.* **a** relieve (a ship etc.) of its cargo. **b** unload (a cargo). ● *n.* **1** the act or an instance of discharging; the process of being discharged. **2** a dismissal. **3 a** a release, exemption, acquittal, etc. **b** a written certificate of release etc. **4** an act of firing a gun etc. **5 a** an emission (of pus, liquid, etc.). **b** the liquid or matter so discharged. **6** (usu. foll. by *of*) **a** the payment (of a debt). **b** the performance (of a duty etc.). **7** *Physics* **a** the release of a quantity of electric charge from an object. **b** a flow of electricity through the air or other gas, esp. when accompanied by the emission of light. **8** the unloading (of a ship or a cargo). [from Old French *descharger*] □ **discharger** *n.* (in sense 7 of *v.*)

disc harrow *n.* ► a harrow with cutting edges consisting of a row of concave discs set at an oblique angle.

disciple *n.* **1** a follower or pupil of a leader, teacher, philosophy, etc. (*a disciple of Zen Buddhism*). **2 a** a personal follower of Christ, esp. one of the twelve Apostles. **b** any early believer in Christ. [from Latin *discipulus*, based on *discere* 'to learn'] □ **discipleship** *n.*

disciplinarian *n.* a person who upholds or practises firm discipline (*a strict disciplinarian*).

disciplinary *adj.* of, promoting, or enforcing discipline.

discipline ● *n.* **1 a** a control or order exercised over people or animals. **b** the system of rules used to maintain this control. **c** the behaviour of groups subjected to such rules (*poor discipline in the ranks*). **2** mental, moral, or physical training. **3** a branch of instruction or learning. **4** punishment. **5** *Eccl.* mortification by physical self-punishment, esp. scourging. ● *v.tr.* **1** punish, chastise. **2** bring under control by training in obedience. [related to DISCIPLE]

disc jockey *n.* the presenter of a selection of usu. recorded popular music.

disclaim *v.tr.* **1** deny or disown (*disclaim all responsibility*). **2** (often *absol.*) *Law* renounce a legal claim to (property etc.).

disclaimer *n.* **1** a renunciation or disavowal, esp. of responsibility. **2** *Law* an act of repudiating another's claim or renouncing one's own.

disclose *v.tr.* **1** make known (*disclosed the truth*). **2** expose to view. [from medieval Latin *disclaudere disclaus-* 'to unclose']

disclosure *n.* **1** the act or an instance of disclosing; the process of being disclosed. **2** something disclosed; a revelation.

disco *colloq.* ● *n.* (*pl.* **-os**) **1** = DISCOTHEQUE. **2** = DISCO MUSIC. ● *v.intr.* (**-oes**, **-oed**) **1** attend a discotheque. **2** dance to disco music (*discoed the night away*).

discography *n.* (*pl.* **-ies**) **1** a descriptive catalogue of gramophone records. **2** the study of gramophone records.

discoid *adj.* disc-shaped. [based on Greek *diskos* 'discus']

discolour *v.tr. & intr.* (*US* **discolor**) spoil the colour of; stain; tarnish. □ **discoloration** *n.* (also **discolouration**).

discombobulate *v.tr. N. Amer. slang* disturb; disconcert.

discomfit *v.tr.* (**discomfited**, **discomfiting**) **1** disconcert or baffle. **2** thwart. [based on Latin *conficere* 'to put together'] □ **discomfiture** *n.*

■ **Usage** Care should be taken not to confuse *discomfit* with *discomfort*. Examples of each are: *We were discomfited by his request to walk through the pouring rain rather than take a taxi*, and *He was by nature a recluse, discomforted by every encounter.*

discomfort ● *n.* **1 a** a lack of ease; slight pain (*tight collar caused discomfort*). **b** mental uneasiness (*his presence caused her discomfort*). **2** a lack of comfort. ● *v.tr.* make uneasy; distress.

■ **Usage** See Usage Note at DISCOMFIT.

discommode *v.tr.* inconvenience (a person etc.). [from obsolete French *discommoder*]

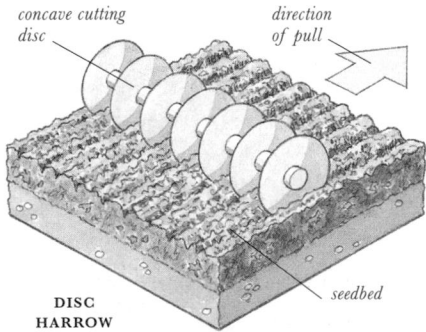

DISC
HARROW

discompose *v.tr.* disturb the composure of. □ **discomposure** *n.*

disco music *n.* popular dance music characterized by a heavy bass rhythm.

disconcert *v.tr.* **1** disturb the composure of; fluster (*disconcerted by his expression*). **2** spoil or upset (plans etc.). □ **disconcerting** *adj.* **disconcertingly** *adv.*

disconnect *v.tr.* **1** break the connection of (things, ideas, etc.). **2** put (an electrical device) out of action by disconnecting the parts, esp. by pulling out the plug.

disconnected *adj.* incoherent and illogical.

disconnection *n.* (also **disconnexion**) the act or an instance of disconnecting; the state of being disconnected.

disconsolate *adj.* **1** forlorn or inconsolable. **2** unhappy or disappointed. [based on Latin *consolatus* 'consoled'] □ **disconsolately** *adv.*

discontent ● *n.* lack of contentment; restlessness, dissatisfaction. ● *adj.* dissatisfied (*was discontent with his lot*). ● *v.tr.* (esp. as **discontented** *adj.*) make dissatisfied. □ **discontentedly** *adv.* **discontentment** *n.*

discontinue *v.* (**discontinues**, **discontinued**, **discontinuing**) **1** *intr. & tr.* cease or cause to cease to exist or be made (*a discontinued line*). **2** give up, cease from (*discontinued his visits*). **3** *tr.* cease taking or paying (a newspaper, a subscription, etc.). □ **discontinuance** *n.* **discontinuation** *n.*

discontinuous *adj.* lacking continuity in space or time; intermittent. □ **discontinuity** *n.* **discontinuously** *adv.*

discord *n.* **1** disagreement; strife. **2** harsh clashing noise; clangour. **3** *Mus.* **a** a lack of harmony between notes sounding together. **b** an unpleasing or unfinished chord needing to be completed by another. [from Latin *discordare* 'to be at variance']

discordant *adj.* **1** disagreeing; at variance. **2** (of sounds) not in harmony; dissonant. □ **discordance** *n.* **discordantly** *adv.*

discotheque *n.* **1** a club etc. for dancing to recorded popular music. **2** *Brit.* **a** the professional lighting and sound equipment used at a discotheque. **b** a business that provides this. **3** *Brit.* a party with dancing to popular music, esp. using such equipment. [from French, literally 'record library']

discount ● *n.* /**dis**-kownt/ **1** a deduction from a bill or amount due. **2** a deduction from the amount of a bill of exchange etc. by a person who gives value for it before it is due. **3** the act or an instance of discounting. ● *v.tr.* /dis-**kownt**/ **1** disregard as unreliable or unimportant (*discounted his story*). **2** reduce the effect of (an event etc.) by previous action. **3 a** deduct (esp. an amount from a bill etc.). **b** reduce in price. **4** give or get the present worth of (a bill not yet due). □ **at a discount 1** below the nominal or usual price. **2** not in demand; depreciated. [from obsolete French *descompte* (n.), *descompter* (v.)] □ **discounter** *n.*

discountenance *v.tr.* **1** disconcert. **2** refuse to countenance; show disapproval of.

discourage *v.tr.* **1** deprive of courage, confidence, or energy. **2** dissuade (*discouraged him from going*). **3** inhibit or seek to prevent (an action etc.) by showing disapproval (*smoking is discouraged*). [from Old French *descouragier*] □ **discouragement** *n.* **discouragingly** *adv.*

discourse ● *n.* /**dis**-korss/ **1** *literary* **a** a conversation; talk. **b** a dissertation or treatise on an academic subject. **c** a lecture or sermon. **2** *Linguistics* a connected series of utterances; a text. ● *v.intr.* /dis-**korss**/ **1** talk; converse. **2** speak or write at length. [from Latin *discursus* 'running to and fro']

discourteous *adj.* impolite; rude. □ **discourteously** *adv.*

discourtesy *n.* (*pl.* **-ies**) **1** bad manners; rudeness. **2** an impolite act or remark.

discover *v.tr.* **1 a** find out or become aware of. **b** be the first to find or find out (*who discovered America?*).

D

2 (in show business) find and promote as a new singer, actor, etc. [from Late Latin *discooperire* 'to uncover'] □ **discoverable** *adj*. **discoverer** *n*.

discovery *n*. (*pl*. **-ies**) **1 a** the act or process of discovering or being discovered. **b** an instance of this (*the discovery of a new planet*). **2** a person or thing discovered.

discredit ● *n*. **1** harm to reputation (*brought discredit on the enterprise*). **2** a person or thing causing this (*he is a discredit to his family*). **3** lack of credibility (*throws discredit on her story*). ● *v.tr*. (**discredited, discrediting**) **1** harm the good reputation of. **2** cause to be disbelieved. **3** refuse to believe.

discreditable *adj*. bringing discredit; shameful. □ **discreditably** *adv*.

discreet *adj*. (**discreeter, discreetest**) **1 a** circumspect. **b** tactful; trustworthy. **2** unobtrusive (*a discreet touch of rouge*). [from Latin *discretus* 'separate' with Late Latin sense from its derivative *discretio* 'discernment'] □ **discreetly** *adv*.

discrepancy *n*. (*pl*. **-ies**) **1** difference; inconsistency. **2** an instance of this. [based on Latin *discrepare* 'to be discordant'] □ **discrepant** *adj*.

discrete *adj*. individually distinct; separate, discontinuous. [related to DISCREET] □ **discretely** *adv*. **discreteness** *n*.

discretion *n*. **1** being discreet; discreet behaviour (*treats confidences with discretion*). **2** prudence; self-preservation. **3** the freedom to act and think as one wishes (*it is within his discretion to leave*). **4** *Law* a court's freedom to decide a sentence etc. □ **age** (or **years**) **of discretion** the age at which a person is able to manage his or her own affairs. **at the discretion of** to be settled or disposed of according to the judgement or choice of. **use one's discretion** act according to one's judgement. □ **discretionary** *adj*.

discriminate *v*. **1** *intr*. make or see a distinction; differentiate. **2** *intr*. make a distinction, esp. unjustly. **3** *intr*. (foll. by *against*) select for unfavourable treatment. **4** *tr*. (usu. foll. by *from*) make or see or constitute a difference in or between (*many things discriminate one person from another*). **5** *intr*. observe distinctions carefully; have good judgement. **6** *tr*. mark as distinctive; be a distinguishing feature of. [based on Latin *discrimen* 'distinction'] □ **discriminative** *adj*. **discriminator** *n*. **discriminatory** *adj*.

discriminating *adj*. **1** able to discern distinctions. **2** having good taste.

discrimination *n*. **1** unfavourable treatment based on prejudice. **2** good taste or judgement in artistic matters etc. **3** the power of discriminating or observing differences. **4** a distinction made with the mind or in action.

discursive *adj*. rambling or digressive. [based on Latin *discurrere discurs-* 'to run to and fro'] □ **discursively** *adv*. **discursiveness** *n*.

discus *n*. (*pl*. **discuses**) **1** a heavy thick-centred disc thrown in ancient Greek games. **2** ▶ a similar disc thrown in modern field events. [from Greek *diskos*]

discuss *v.tr*. **1** hold a conversation about. **2** examine by argument. [from Latin *discutere discuss-* 'to shake apart'] □ **discussant** *n*.

discussion *n*. **1** a conversation, esp. on specific subjects; a debate (*had a discussion about what they should do*). **2** an examination by argument.

disdain ● *n*. scorn; contempt. ● *v.tr*. **1** regard with disdain. **2** think oneself superior to; reject (*disdained his offer, disdained to enter, disdained answering*). [from Latin *dedignari* 'to reject as unworthy']

disdainful *adj*. showing disdain or contempt. □ **disdainfully** *adv*.

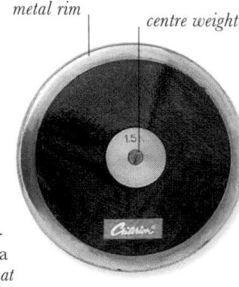

metal rim

centre weight

DISCUS

disease *n*. **1** an unhealthy condition of the body or the mind. **2** a corresponding physical condition of plants. **3** a particular kind of disease with special symptoms or location. [from Old French *desaise*]

diseased *adj*. **1** affected with disease. **2** abnormal, disordered.

disembark *v.tr. & intr*. put or go ashore or land from a ship; remove from or leave an aircraft, train, etc. □ **disembarkation** *n*.

disembarrass *v.tr*. **1** (usu. foll. by *of*) relieve (of a load etc.). **2** free from embarrassment.

disembody *v.tr*. (**-ies, -ied**) (esp. as **disembodied** *adj*.) separate or free from the body or a concrete form (*disembodied spirit; disembodied voice*).

disembowel *v.tr*. (**disembowelled, disembowelling**; *US* **disemboweled, disemboweling**) remove the bowels or entrails of.

disempower *v.tr*. remove the power to act from (a person, group, etc.). □ **disempowerment** *n*.

disenchant *v.tr*. free from enchantment; disillusion. □ **disenchantment** *n*.

disencumber *v.tr*. free from encumbrances.

disenfranchise *v.tr*. (also **disfranchise**) **1 a** deprive (a person) of the right to vote. **b** deprive (a place) of the right to send a representative to Parliament. **2** deprive (a person) of rights as a citizen or of a franchise held. □ **disenfranchisement** *n*.

disengage *v*. **1** *tr*. detach, free, loosen, or separate (parts etc.) (*disengaged the clutch*). **2** *tr*. *Mil*. remove (troops) from a battle or a battle area. **3** *intr*. become detached. **4** *intr*. (as **disengaged** *adj*.) **a** unoccupied; free; vacant. **b** uncommitted.

disengagement *n*. **1 a** the act of disengaging. **b** an instance of this. **2** freedom from ties; detachment.

disentangle *v*. **1** *tr*. **a** unravel, untwist. **b** (often *refl*.) free from complications; extricate (*disentangled herself from the difficulty*). **2** *intr*. become disentangled. □ **disentanglement** *n*.

disentitle *v.tr*. (usu. foll. by *to*) deprive of any rightful claim. □ **disentitlement** *n*.

disequilibrium *n*. a lack or loss of equilibrium; instability.

disestablish *v.tr*. **1** deprive (a church) of state support. **2** depose from an official position. **3** terminate the establishment of. □ **disestablishment** *n*.

disfavour (*US* **disfavor**) ● *n*. **1** disapproval or dislike. **2** the state of being disliked (*fell into disfavour*). ● *v.tr*. regard or treat with disfavour.

disfigure *v.tr*. spoil the beauty of; deform; deface. [from Old French *desfigurer*] □ **disfigurement** *n*.

disfranchise var. of DISENFRANCHISE.

disgorge *v.tr*. **1** eject from the throat or stomach. **2** pour forth, discharge. [from Old French *desgorger*, based on *gorge* 'throat'] □ **disgorgement** *n*.

disgrace ● *n*. **1** shame; ignominy (*brought disgrace on his family*). **2** a dishonourable, inefficient, or shameful person, thing, state of affairs, etc. (*the bus service is a disgrace*). ● *v.tr*. **1** bring shame or discredit on. **2** degrade from a position of honour; dismiss from favour. □ **in disgrace** out of favour. [from Italian *disgrazia* (n.), *disgraziare* (v.)]

disgraceful *adj*. shameful; dishonourable; degrading. □ **disgracefully** *adv*.

disgruntled *adj*. discontented; sulky. [from obsolete *gruntle* 'to grumble'] □ **disgruntlement** *n*.

disguise ● *v.tr*. **1** alter the appearance, sound, smell, etc., of so as to conceal the identity; make unrecognizable. **2** misrepresent or cover up (*disguised their intentions*). ● *n*. **1 a** a costume, false beard, make-up, etc., used to alter the appearance so as to conceal or deceive. **b** any action, manner, etc., used for deception. **2 a** the act or practice of disguising; the concealment of reality. **b** an instance of this. □ **in disguise** **1** wearing a concealing costume etc. **2** appearing to be the opposite (*a blessing in disguise*).

disgust ● *n*. **1** strong aversion; repugnance. **2** a strong distaste for a food, drink, medicine, etc.; nausea. ● *v.tr*. cause disgust in (*their behaviour disgusts me; was disgusted to find a slug*). □ **in disgust** as a result of disgust (*left in disgust*). [from Italian *disgusto*, based on Latin *gustus* 'taste'] □ **disgustedly** *adv*.

disgusting *adj*. arousing aversion or indignation (*disgusting behaviour*). □ **disgustingly** *adv*.

dish ● *n*. **1 a** a shallow container for cooking or serving food. **b** the food served in a dish (*all the dishes were delicious*). **c** a particular kind of food (*a meat dish*). **2** (in *pl*.) dirty plates, cutlery, cooking pots, etc. after a meal. **3 a** a dish-shaped object or cavity. **b** = SATELLITE DISH. **4** *slang* a sexually attractive person. ● *v.tr*. **1** put (food) into a dish ready for serving. **2** *Brit. colloq*. **a** outmanoeuvre. **b** destroy (one's hopes, chances, etc.). **3** make concave or dish-shaped. □ **dish out** *slang* distribute. **dish up** **1** serve or prepare to serve (food). **2** *colloq*. seek to present (facts, arguments, etc.) attractively. [from Latin *discus* 'disc'] □ **dishful** *n*. (*pl*. **-fuls**).

dishabille var. of DÉSHABILLÉ.

disharmony *n*. a lack of harmony; discord. □ **disharmonious** *adj*.

dishcloth *n*. a usu. open-weave cloth for washing dishes.

dishearten *v.tr*. cause to lose courage or confidence; make despondent. □ **dishearteningly** *adv*. **disheartenment** *n*.

dishevelled /dish-ev-ĕld/ *adj*. (*US* **disheveled**) untidy; ruffled; disordered. [from Old French *deschevelé*] □ **dishevel** *v.tr*. (**dishevelled, dishevelling**; *US* **disheveled, disheveling**). **dishevelment** *n*.

dishonest *adj*. fraudulent or insincere. □ **dishonesty** *n*. **dishonestly** *adv*.

dishonour (*US* **dishonor**) ● *n*. **1** a state of shame or disgrace. **2** something that causes dishonour. ● *v.tr*. **1** treat without honour or respect. **2** disgrace (*dishonoured his name*). **3** refuse to accept or pay (a cheque or bill of exchange).

dishonourable *adj*. (*US* **dishonorable**) **1** causing disgrace; ignominious. **2** unprincipled. □ **dishonourably** *adv*.

dishwasher *n*. **1** a machine for automatically washing dishes. **2** a person employed to wash dishes.

dishwater *n*. water in which dishes have been washed.

dishy *adj*. (**dishier, dishiest**) *Brit. slang* sexually attractive.

disillusion ● *n*. freedom from illusions. ● *v.tr*. disenchant. □ **disillusionment** *n*.

disincentive ● *n*. something that tends to discourage a particular action, progress, etc. ● *adj*. tending to discourage.

disincline *v.tr*. (usu. foll. by *to* + infin. or *for*) make unwilling or reluctant. □ **disinclination** *n*.

disinfect *v.tr*. cleanse of infection, esp. with a disinfectant. □ **disinfection** *n*.

disinfectant ● *n*. a usu. commercially produced chemical liquid that destroys germs etc. ● *adj*. causing disinfection.

disinfest *v.tr*. rid of vermin, infesting insects, etc.

disinflation *n*. *Econ*. a policy designed to counteract inflation without causing deflation. □ **disinflationary** *adj*.

disinformation *n*. false information, intended to mislead.

disingenuous *adj*. having secret motives; insincere. □ **disingenuously** *adv*. **disingenuousness** *n*.

disinherit *v.tr*. (**disinherited, disinheriting**) reject as one's heir; deprive of the right of inheritance. [based on obsolete *inherit* 'to make heir'] □ **disinheritance** *n*.

disintegrate *v*. **1** *tr. & intr*. **a** separate into component parts or fragments; crumble. **b** lose or cause to lose cohesion. **2** *intr. colloq*. deteriorate mentally or physically. **3** *intr. & tr. Physics* undergo or cause to undergo disintegration. □ **disintegrative** *adj.* **disintegrator** *n.*

disintegration *n.* **1** the act or an instance of disintegrating. **2** *Physics* any process in which a nucleus emits a particle or particles or divides into smaller nuclei.

disinter /dis-in-ter/ *v.tr.* (**disinterred**, **disinterring**) remove (esp. a corpse) from the ground; unearth. □ **disinterment** *n.*

disinterest *n.* **1** *disp.* lack of interest; unconcern. **2** impartiality.

■ **Usage** The use of *disinterest* in sense 1 to mean 'lack of interest' is sometimes objected to, but it is in this sense that is is most commonly found and the alternative *uninterest* is rare. The phrase *lack of interest* avoids both ambiguity and accusations of incorrect usage.

disinterested *adj.* **1** not influenced by one's own advantage. **2** *disp.* uninterested. [from obsolete *disinteress* 'to rid of interest'] □ **disinterestedly** *adv.* **disinterestedness** *n.*

■ **Usage** *Disinterested* is commonly used informally to mean 'uninterested', but this is widely regarded as incorrect.

disinvest *v.intr.* (foll. by *from*, or *absol.*) reduce or dispose of one's investment (in a place, company, etc.). □ **disinvestment** *n.*

disjoin *v.tr.* separate or disunite. [from Latin *disjungere* 'to disunite']

disjoint *v.tr.* **1** take apart at the joints. **2** (as **disjointed** *adj.*) (esp. of conversation) incoherent. **3** disturb the working or connection of. □ **disjointedly** *adv.* **disjointedness** *n.*

disjunction *n.* **1** the process of disjoining; separation. **2** an instance of this.

disjunctive ● *adj.* **1** involving separation. **2** *Gram.* (esp. of a conjunction) expressing a choice between two words etc. ● *n. Gram.* a disjunctive conjunction or other word. □ **disjunctively** *adv.*

disk var. of DISC (esp. *US & Computing*).

disk drive *n.* a mechanism for rotating a disk and reading or writing data from or to it. ▷ COMPUTER

diskette *n. Computing* = FLOPPY *n.*

dislike ● *v.tr.* have an aversion or objection to; not like ● *n.* **1** a feeling of repugnance or not liking. **2** an object of dislike. □ **dislikable** *adj.* (also **dislikeable**).

dislocate *v.tr.* **1** disturb the normal connection of (esp. a joint in the body). **2** disrupt. **3** displace. □ **dislocation** *n.*

dislodge *v.tr.* remove from an established or fixed position. □ **dislodgement** *n.* (also **dislodgment**).

disloyal *adj.* (often foll. by *to*) **1** not loyal; unfaithful. **2** untrue to one's allegiance. □ **disloyally** *adv.* **disloyalty** *n.*

dismal *adj.* **1** causing or showing gloom; miserable. **2** dreary or sombre. **3** *colloq.* feeble or inept (*a dismal performance*). [originally noun, literally 'unlucky days', from medieval Latin *dies mali*, two days in each month held to be unpropitious] □ **dismally** *adv.*

dismantle *v.tr.* **1** take to pieces; pull down. **2** deprive of defences or equipment. [from Old French *desmanteler* 'to divest of a mantle'] □ **dismantlement** *n.* **dismantler** *n.*

dismast *v.tr.* deprive (a ship) of masts; break down the mast or masts of.

dismay ● *v.tr.* fill with consternation or anxiety; reduce to despair. ● *n.* **1** consternation or anxiety. **2** depression or despair. [from Old French, literally 'to deprive of power']

dismember *v.tr.* **1** tear or cut the limbs from. **2** divide up (a country etc.). [based on Latin *membrum* 'limb'] □ **dismemberment** *n.*

dismiss *v.* **1 a** *tr.* cause to leave one's presence; disperse (an assembly or army). **b** *intr.* (of an assem-

bly etc.) break ranks. **2** *tr.* discharge from employment, office, etc., esp. dishonourably. **3** *tr.* put out of one's thoughts (*dismissed him from memory*). **4** *tr.* treat summarily (*dismissed his application*). **5** *tr. Law* refuse further hearing to (a case). **6** *tr. Cricket* put (a batsman or a side) out. [based on Latin *mittere miss-* 'to send'] □ **dismissal** *n.* **dismissible** *adj.*

dismissive *adj.* tending to dismiss from consideration. □ **dismissively** *adv.* **dismissiveness** *n.*

dismount *v.* **1 a** *intr.* alight from a horse, bicycle, etc. **b** *tr.* (usu. in *passive*) throw from a horse, unseat. **2** *tr.* remove (a thing, esp. a gun) from its mounting.

disobedient *adj.* disobeying; rebellious. [alteration of Late Latin *inobedient-* 'not obeying'] □ **disobedience** *n.* **disobediently** *adv.*

disobey *v.tr.* (also *absol.*) fail or refuse to obey; disregard (orders); break (rules).

disoblige *v.tr.* **1** refuse to consider the convenience or wishes of. **2** (as **disobliging** *adj.*) uncooperative.

disorder ● *n.* **1** a lack of order; confusion. **2** a riot; a commotion. **3** *Med.* a usu. minor ailment or disease. ● *v.tr.* **1** throw into confusion; disarrange. **2** *Med.* upset. [alteration of earlier *disordain*] □ **disordered** *adj.*

disorderly *adj.* **1** untidy; confused. **2** unruly; riotous. **3** *Law* contrary to public order or morality. □ **disorderliness** *n.*

disorderly house *n.* a brothel.

disorganize *v.tr.* (also **-ise**) **1** destroy the system or order of. **2** (as **disorganized** *adj.*) lacking organization or system. □ **disorganization** *n.*

disorient *v.tr.* = DISORIENTATE.

disorientate *v.tr.* **1** confuse (a person) as to his or her bearings. **2** confuse (a person). □ **disorientation** *n.*

disown *v.tr.* refuse to recognize; repudiate; disclaim.

disparage *v.tr.* **1** speak slightingly of; depreciate. **2** bring discredit on. [from Old French *desparagier* 'to marry unequally'] □ **disparagement** *n.* **disparagingly** *adv.*

disparate /dis-pă-răt/ *adj.* essentially different in kind; without comparison or relation. [from Latin *disparatus* 'separated'] □ **disparity** *n.* (*pl.* **-ies**) **disparately** *adv.* **disparateness** *n.*

dispassionate *adj.* free from passion; calm; impartial. □ **dispassionately** *adv.* **dispassionateness** *n.*

dispatch (also **despatch**) ● *v.tr.* **1** send off to a destination or for a purpose. **2** perform (business, a task, etc.) promptly. **3** kill, execute. **4** *colloq.* eat (food, a meal, etc.) quickly. ● *n.* **1** the act or an instance of sending. **2** the act or an instance of killing. **3 a** an official written message on state or esp. military affairs. **b** a report sent in by a newspaper's correspondent. **c** any written message requiring fast delivery. **4** promptness (*done with dispatch*). [from Spanish *despachar* 'to expedite'] □ **dispatcher** *n.*

dispatch box *n.* (also **dispatch case**) a container for esp. official state or military documents or dispatches.

dispatch rider *n.* a motorcyclist or rider on horseback carrying dispatches.

dispel *v.tr.* (**dispelled**, **dispelling**) dissipate; disperse; scatter. [from Latin *dispellere* 'to drive apart']

dispensable *adj.* able to be done without; unnecessary. □ **dispensability** *n.*

dispensary *n.* (*pl.* **-ies**) a place where medicines etc. are dispensed.

dispensation *n.* **1 a** the act or an instance of dispensing or distributing. **b** something distributed. **2** (usu. foll. by *from*) exemption from a penalty, duty, or religious observance; an instance of this. **3** a religious or political system obtaining in a nation etc. **4** the ordering or management of the world by Providence. □ **dispensational** *adj.*

dispense *v.* **1** *tr.* distribute; deal out. **2** *tr.* administer (a sacrament, justice, etc.). **3** *tr.* make up and give

out (medicine etc.) according to a doctor's prescription. **4** *intr.* (foll. by *with*) **a** do without; render needless. **b** give exemption from (a rule). [from Latin *dispensare* 'to weigh or pay out']

dispenser *n.* a person or thing that dispenses something, e.g. medicine, good advice, cash.

disperse *v.* **1** *intr. & tr.* go, send, drive, or distribute in different directions or over a wide area. **2 a** *intr.* (of people at a meeting etc.) leave and go their various ways. **b** *tr.* cause to do this. **3** *tr.* send to or station at separate points. **4** *tr.* disseminate. [based on Latin *dispersus* 'scattered'] □ **dispersal** *n.* **disperser** *n.* **dispersible** *adj.* **dispersive** *adj.*

dispersion *n.* **1** the act or an instance of dispersing; the process of being dispersed. **2** *Chem.* a mixture of particles of one substance distributed uniformly in another. **3** *Statistics* the extent to which values of a variable differ from the mean. **4** *Ecol.* the pattern of distribution of individuals within the habitat.

dispirit *v.tr.* **1** (esp. as **dispiriting** *adj.*) make despondent; discourage. **2** (as **dispirited** *adj.*) dejected; discouraged. □ **dispiritedly** *adv.* **dispiritedness** *n.* **dispiritingly** *adv.*

displace *v.tr.* **1** shift from its accustomed place. **2** remove from office. **3** take the place of; oust.

displaced person *n.* a refugee.

displacement *n.* **1** the act or an instance of displacing; the process or an instance of being displaced. **2** *Physics* the amount of a fluid displaced by a solid floating or immersed in it. **3** *Psychol.* **a** the substitution of one idea or impulse for another. **b** the unconscious transfer of strong unacceptable emotions from one object to another. **4** the amount by which a thing is moved from a position.

displacement ton see TON 4.

display ● *v.tr.* **1** expose to view; exhibit. **2** show ostentatiously. **3** reveal (*displayed his ignorance*). ● *n.* **1** the act or an instance of displaying. **2 a** an exhibition or show. **b** a thing or things intended to be looked at. **3** ostentation; flashiness. **4 ▼** the distinct behaviour of some animals used to attract a mate. **5 a** the presentation of signals or data on a visual display unit etc. **b** the information so presented. [from Latin *displicare* 'to scatter', later 'to unfold'] □ **displayer** *n.*

puffed out throat feathers

fanned tail

DISPLAY: COURTSHIP DISPLAY OF A MALE CAPERCAILLIE (*Tetrao urogallus*)

displease *v.tr.* make indignant or angry; offend; annoy. [from Old French *desplaisir*] □ **displeasing** *adj.* **displeasingly** *adv.*

displeasure *n.* disapproval; anger; dissatisfaction.

disport *v.intr. & refl.* frolic; gambol; enjoy oneself. [from Old French *desporter*]

D

disposable ● *adj.* **1** intended to be used once and then thrown away. **2** that can be got rid of, made over, or used. **3** (esp. of assets) at the owner's disposal. ● *n.* a thing designed to be thrown away after one use. □ **disposability** *n.*

disposable income *n.* **1** income after tax and other necessary expenditure. **2** the total amount of money at the disposal of consumers in a country etc.

disposal *n.* (usu. foll. by *of*) the act or an instance of disposing of something. □ **at one's disposal 1** available for one's use. **2** subject to one's orders or decisions.

■ **Usage** *Disposal* is the noun corresponding to the verb *dispose of* 'get rid of, deal with, etc.'. *Disposition* is the noun corresponding to *dispose* 'arrange, incline'.

dispose *v.* **1** *tr.* (usu. foll. by *to*, or *to* + *infin.*) **a** make willing; incline (*disposed him to the idea*). **b** have a tendency to (*disposed to buckle*). **2** *tr.* place suitably (*disposed the chairs*). **3** *tr.* (as **disposed** *adj.*) having a specified mental inclination (usu. in *comb.*: *ill-disposed*). **4** *intr.* determine the course of events (*man proposes, God disposes*). □ **dispose of 1 a** deal with. **b** get rid of. **c** finish. **d** kill. **2** sell. **3** prove (a claim, an argument, an opponent, etc.) to be incorrect. **4** consume (food). [from Latin *disponere disposit-* 'to place separately'] □ **disposer** *n.*

disposition *n.* **1** (often foll. by *to*) a natural tendency; an inclination; a person's temperament. **2 a** setting in order; arranging. **b** the relative position of parts; an arrangement. **3** (usu. in *pl.*) preparations; plans. [from Latin *dispositio*, related to DISPOSE]

■ **Usage** See Usage Note at DISPOSAL.

dispossess *v.tr.* **1** oust (a person). **2** (usu. foll. by *of*) deprive. □ **dispossession** *n.*

disproof *n.* **1** refutation. **2** an instance of this.

disproportion *n.* **1** a lack of proportion. **2** an instance of this. □ **disproportional** *adj.* **disproportionally** *adv.*

disproportionate *adj.* **1** lacking proportion. **2** relatively too large, long etc. □ **disproportionately** *adv.* **disproportionateness** *n.*

disprove *v.tr.* prove false. □ **disprovable** *adj.*

disputable *adj.* open to question; uncertain. □ **disputably** *adv.*

disputation *n.* **1 a** disputing, debating. **b** an argument; a controversy. **2** a formal debate.

disputatious *adj.* argumentative. □ **disputatiously** *adv.* **disputatiousness** *n.*

dispute ● *v.* **1** *intr.* (usu. foll. by *with*, *against*) **a** debate, argue. **b** quarrel. **2** *tr.* discuss, esp. heatedly (*disputed whether it was true*). **3** *tr.* question the truth or correctness or validity of (a statement, alleged fact, etc.). **4** *tr.* contend for; strive to win (*disputed the crown*). **5** *tr.* resist (a landing, advance, etc.). ● *n.* **1** a controversy; a debate. **2** a quarrel. **3** a disagreement leading to industrial action. □ **in dispute 1** being argued about. **2** *Brit.* (of a workforce) involved in industrial action. [from Latin *disputare* 'to estimate'] □ **disputant** *n.* **disputer** *n.*

disqualify *v.tr.* (**-ies**, **-ied**) **1** (often foll. by *from*) debar from a competition or pronounce ineligible as a winner. **2** (often foll. by *for*, *from*) make or pronounce ineligible or unsuitable (*his age disqualifies him for the job*). □ **disqualification** *n.*

disquiet ● *v.tr.* worry. ● *n.* anxiety; unrest. □ **disquieting** *adj.* **disquietingly** *adv.*

disquietude *n.* a state of uneasiness; anxiety.

disquisition *n.* a long or elaborate treatise or discourse. [from Latin *disquisitio* 'investigation']

disregard ● *v.tr.* **1** pay no attention to; ignore. **2** treat as of no importance; neglect. ● *n.* (often foll. by *of*, *for*) indifference; neglect.

disrepair *n.* poor condition due to neglect.

disreputable *adj.* **1** of bad reputation; discred-

itable. **2** not respectable in appearance; dirty, untidy. □ **disreputableness** *n.* **disreputably** *adv.*

disrepute *n.* a lack of good reputation or respectability; discredit.

disrespect *n.* a lack of respect; discourtesy. □ **disrespectful** *adj.* **disrespectfully** *adv.*

disrobe *v.tr.* & *refl.* (also *absol.*) undress.

disrupt *v.tr.* **1** interrupt the flow or continuity of. **2** separate forcibly; shatter. [based on Latin *disruptus* 'broken into pieces'] □ **disrupter** *n.* (also **disruptor**). **disruption** *n.* **disruptive** *adj.* **disruptively** *adv.* **disruptiveness** *n.*

diss var. of DIS.

dissatisfy *v.tr.* (**-ies**, **-ied**) make discontented; fail to satisfy. □ **dissatisfaction** *n.* **dissatisfiedly** *adv.*

dissect /di-**sekt**/ *v.tr.* **1** cut into pieces. **2** cut up (a plant or animal) to examine its structure etc., or (a corpse) for a post-mortem. **3** analyse. [based on Latin *dissectus* 'cut in pieces'] □ **dissection** *n.* **dissector** *n.*

dissemble *v.* **1** *intr.* talk or act hypocritically. **2** *tr.* **a** disguise or conceal (a feeling, intention, act, etc.). **b** (as **dissembled** *adj.*) simulated, pretended. [based on Latin *dissimulare*] □ **dissemblance** *n.* **dissembler** *n.*

disseminate *v.tr.* scatter about, spread (esp. ideas) widely. [based on Latin *semen* 'seed'] □ **dissemination** *n.* **disseminator** *n.*

disseminated sclerosis see SCLEROSIS 2.

dissension *n.* disagreement giving rise to discord. [from Latin *dissensio* 'differing in feeling']

dissent ● *v.intr.* (often foll. by *from*) **1** feel or express disagreement. **2** differ in religious opinion, esp. from the doctrine of an established or orthodox Church. ● *n.* **1 a** a difference of opinion. **b** an expression of this. **2** nonconformity. [from Latin *dissentire*] □ **dissenting** *adj.*

dissenter *n.* **1** a person who dissents. **2** (**Dissenter**) *Brit.* a member of a non-established Church.

dissentient ● *adj.* disagreeing with a majority or official view. ● *n.* a person who dissents. [from Latin *dissentient-* 'dissenting']

dissertation *n.* a detailed discourse on a subject, esp. one submitted for an academic degree or diploma. [based on Latin *dissertare* 'to discuss']

disservice *n.* an ill turn.

dissident ● *adj.* disagreeing, esp. with an established government, system, etc. ● *n.* a dissident person. [from Latin *dissident-* 'disagreeing'] □ **dissidence** *n.*

dissimilar *adj.* (often foll. by *to*) unlike, not similar. □ **dissimilarity** *n.* (*pl.* **-ies**).

dissimulate *v.tr.* & *intr.* dissemble. [based on Latin *dissimulatus* 'concealed, disguised'] □ **dissimulation** *n.*

dissipate *v.* **1 a** *tr.* cause to disappear or disperse. **b** *intr.* disperse, disappear. **2** *tr.* squander (money, energy, etc.). **3** *intr.* (as **dissipated** *adj.*) dissolute. [based on Latin *dissipatus* 'scattered'] □ **dissipative** *adj.* **dissipator** *n.*

dissipation *n.* **1** dissolute or debauched living. **2** (usu. foll. by *of*) wasteful expenditure (*dissipation of resources*). **3** dispersion or disintegration. **4** a frivolous amusement.

dissociate *v.tr.* & *intr.* (usu. foll. by *from*) disconnect or become disconnected. □ **dissociate oneself from** declare oneself unconnected with. [based on Latin *socius* 'companion'] □ **dissociation** *n.* **dissociative** *adj.*

dissoluble *adj.* able to be disintegrated, loosened, or disconnected; soluble. [from Latin *dissolubilis*] □ **dissolubility** *n.* **dissolubly** *adv.*

dissolute *adj.* lax in morals; licentious. [from Latin *dissolutus* 'loose'] □ **dissolutely** *adv.* **dissoluteness** *n.*

dissolution *n.* **1** disintegration; decomposition. **2** (usu. foll. by *of*) the undoing or relaxing of a bond, esp. a partnership or an alliance. **3** the

dismissal or dispersal of an assembly, esp. of a parliament at the end of its term. **4** death.

dissolve *v.* **1** *tr.* & *intr.* incorporate or become incorporated into a liquid so as to form a solution. **2** *intr.* & *tr.* disappear or cause to disappear gradually. **3 a** *tr.* dismiss (an assembly, esp. Parliament). **b** *intr.* (of an assembly) be dissolved. **4** *tr.* annul (a partnership, marriage, etc.). **5** *intr.* (of a person) become emotionally overcome. [from Latin *dissolvere* 'to disunite'] □ **dissolvable** *adj.*

dissonant *adj.* **1** *Mus.* harsh-toned; inharmonious. **2** incongruous. [from Latin *dissonant-* 'disagreeing in sound'] □ **dissonance** *n.* **dissonantly** *adv.*

dissuade *v.tr.* (often foll. by *from*) discourage (a person); persuade against. [from Latin *dissuadēre*] □ **dissuasion** *n.* **dissuasive** *adj.*

distaff *n.* ▼ a cleft stick holding wool or flax wound for spinning by hand. [Old English, the first element being apparently related to Low German *diesse* 'bunch of flax']

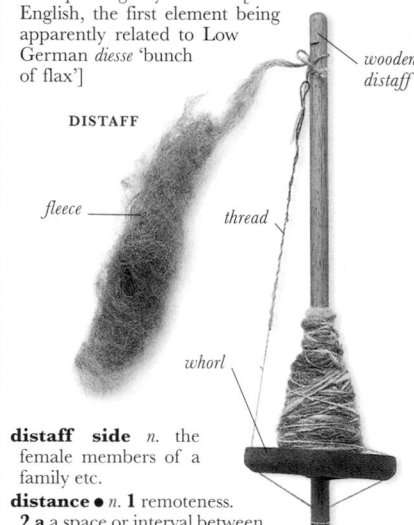

DISTAFF

wooden distaff

fleece

thread

whorl

distaff side *n.* the female members of a family etc.

distance ● *n.* **1** remoteness. **2 a** a space or interval between two things. **b** the length of this (*a distance of twenty miles*). **3** a distant point or place. **4** aloofness; reserve. **5** a remoter field of vision (*in the distance*). **6** an interval of time (*can't remember at this distance*). ● *v.tr.* (often *refl.*) **1** place far off (*distanced herself from them*). **2** leave far behind in a race or competition. □ **at a distance** far off. **go the distance 1** *Boxing* complete a fight without being knocked out. **2** complete a hard task; endure an ordeal. **keep one's distance** maintain one's reserve. [from Latin *distantia* 'a standing apart']

distance learning *n.* education by correspondence course or from broadcasts, telephone tutorials, etc.

distant *adj.* **1 a** far away in space or time. **b** (usu. *predic.*; often foll. by *from*) at a specified distance (*three miles distant*). **2** remote in position, time, etc. (*distant prospect*; *distant relation*). **3** reserved; cool (*a distant nod*). **4** abstracted (*a distant stare*). **5** faint, vague (*a distant memory*). [from Latin *distant-* 'standing apart'] □ **distantly** *adv.*

distaste *n.* (usu. foll. by *for*) dislike; aversion. □ **distasteful** *adj.* **distastefully** *adv.* **distastefulness** *n.*

distemper[1] ● *n.* **1** *Brit.* a kind of paint using glue or size instead of an oil-base. **2** a method of mural and poster painting using this. ● *v.tr. Brit.* paint with distemper. [from Late Latin *distemperare* 'to soak, macerate']

distemper[2] *n.* a viral disease of esp. dogs, causing fever, coughing, and catarrh.

distend *v.tr.* & *intr.* swell out by pressure from within (*distended stomach*). [from Latin *distendere* 'to stretch apart'] □ **distensible** *adj.* **distensibility** *n.* **distension** *n.*

distich /**dis**-tik/ *n. Prosody* a verse couplet. [from Greek *distikhon*, based on *stikhos* 'line']

distil *v.* (*US* **distill**) (**distilled**, **distilling**) **1** *tr.* *Chem* ▶ purify (a liquid) by vaporizing then condensing it and collecting the resulting liquid. **2** *tr.* extract the essential meaning of (an idea etc.). **3** *tr.* make (whisky, essence, etc.) by distilling raw materials. **4** *tr. & intr.* come as or give forth in drops; exude. [from Latin *destillare* 'to drip down'] □ **distillate** *n.* **distillation** *n.* **distillatory** *adj.*

distiller *n.* a person who distils, esp. a manufacturer of alcoholic liquor.

distillery *n.* (*pl.* **-ies**) a place where alcoholic liquor is distilled.

distinct *adj.* **1** (often foll. by *from*) **a** not identical; separate; individual. **b** different in kind or quality; unlike. **2 a** clearly perceptible. **b** clearly understandable. **3** unmistakable (*a distinct impression of being watched*). [from Latin *distinctus* 'distinguished'] □ **distinctly** *adv.* **distinctness** *n.*

■ **Usage** *Distinct* is sometimes confused with *distinctive*. Note the difference in sense between *There was a distinct smell of soap in the bathroom* (an unmistakable, clearly perceptible smell), and *The hall had its own distinctive smell of polish* (a characteristic smell).

distinction *n.* **1 a** the act or an instance of discriminating or distinguishing. **b** the difference made by distinguishing. **2 a** something that differentiates, e.g. a mark, name, or title. **b** the fact of being different. **3** special consideration or honour. **4** excellence; eminence.

distinctive *adj.* distinguishing, characteristic. □ **distinctively** *adv.* **distinctiveness** *n.*

■ **Usage** See Usage Note at DISTINCT.

distingué /di-**stang**-gay/ *adj.* (*fem.* **distinguée** *pronunc.* same) having a distinguished air, features, manner, etc. [French]

distinguish *v.* **1** *tr.* (often foll. by *from*) **a** see or point out the difference of (*cannot distinguish one from the other*). **b** constitute such a difference (*the mole distinguishes him from his twin*). **c** treat as different (*do not distinguish the mind from the body*). **2** *tr.* characterize (*distinguished by his greed*). **3** *tr.* discover by listening, looking, etc. (*could distinguish two voices*). **4** *tr.* (usu. *refl.*; often foll. by *by*) make prominent or noteworthy. **5** *intr.* (foll. by *between*) make or point out a difference between. [from Latin *distinguere*] □ **distinguishable** *adj.*

distinguished *adj.* **1** (often foll. by *for, by*) of high standing; eminent; famous. **2** = DISTINGUÉ.

distort *v.tr.* **1** put out of shape. **2** misrepresent. [based on Latin *distortus* 'twisted in different ways'] □ **distortedly** *adv.* **distortedness** *n.* **distortion** *n.*

distract *v.tr.* **1** (often foll. by *from*) draw away the attention of. **2** bewilder, perplex. **3** (as **distracted** *adj.*) troubled or distraught. **4** amuse, esp. in order to take the attention from pain. [based on Latin *distractus* 'drawn asunder'] □ **distractedly** *adv.*

distraction *n.* **1 a** the act of distracting, esp. the mind. **b** something that distracts. **2** a relaxation; an amusement. **3** a lack of concentration. **4** confusion; perplexity. **5** frenzy; madness. □ **to distraction** almost to a state of madness.

distrain *v.intr.* (usu. foll. by *upon*) *Law* impose distraint (on a person, goods, etc.). [based on Latin *stringere* 'to draw tight'] □ **distrainer** *n.* **distrainment** *n.* **distrainor** *n.*

distraint *n.* *Law* the seizure of chattels to enforce payment.

distrait *adj.* (*fem.* **distraite**) not paying attention; distraught. [from Old French *destrait* 'distracted']

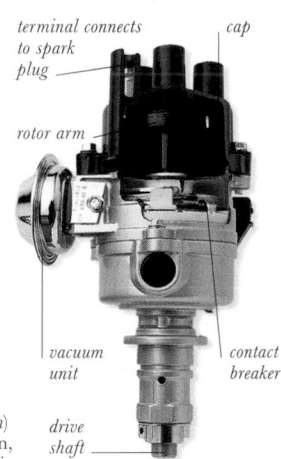

terminal connects to spark plug

cap

rotor arm

vacuum unit

contact breaker

drive shaft

DISTRIBUTOR WITH CUTAWAY CAP

DISTIL

To distil a liquid it must be heated to boiling point. In the demonstration shown here, a solution of sodium dichromate is heated in a flask. The solvent, in this case water, boils away from the solution leaving sodium dichromate crystals. The water vapour passes into a condenser where it is cooled and becomes liquid again. The distillation is continued until the components of the mixture have been completely separated. The purified liquid is known as the distillate.

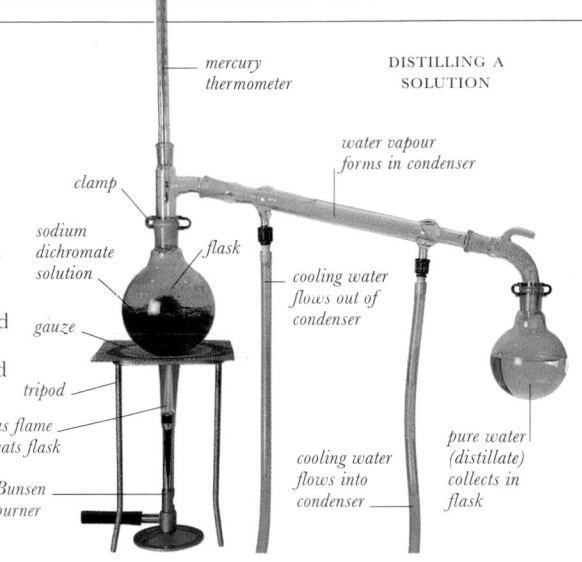

mercury thermometer

DISTILLING A SOLUTION

clamp

water vapour forms in condenser

sodium dichromate solution

flask

cooling water flows out of condenser

gauze

tripod

gas flame heats flask

Bunsen burner

cooling water flows into condenser

pure water (distillate) collects in flask

---

distraught *adj.* distracted with worry, fear, etc. [related to DISTRACT]

distress ● *n.* **1** severe pain, sorrow, anguish, etc. **2** the lack of money or comforts. **3** *Law* = DISTRAINT. **4** breathlessness; exhaustion. ● *v.tr.* **1** subject to distress. **2** cause anxiety to; make unhappy. □ **in distress** suffering or in danger. [from Old French *destresse*] □ **distressful** *adj.* **distressingly** *adv.*

distressed *adj.* **1** suffering from distress. **2** impoverished (*distressed gentlefolk; in distressed circumstances*).

distributary *n.* (*pl.* **-ies**) a branch of a river or glacier that does not return to the main stream after leaving it (as in a delta). ▷ DELTA

distribute /dis-**trib**-yoot/ *v.tr.* **1** give shares of; deal out. **2** spread about; scatter. **3** divide into parts; arrange; classify. [based on Latin *distributus* 'assigned separately'] □ **distributable** *adj.*

distribution *n.* **1** the act or an instance of distributing; the process of being distributed. **2** *Econ.* **a** the dispersal of goods etc. among consumers, brought about by commerce. **b** the extent to which different groups, classes, or individuals share in the total production or wealth of a community. **3** *Statistics* the way in which a characteristic is spread over members of a class. □ **distributional** *adj.*

distributive *adj.* of, concerned with, or produced by distribution. □ **distributively** *adv.*

distributor *n.* **1** a person or thing that distributes. **2** an agent who supplies goods. **3** *Electr.* ◀ a device in an internal-combustion engine for passing current to each spark plug in turn.

district *n.* **1 a** (often *attrib.*) a territory marked off for special administrative etc. purposes. **b** *Brit.* a division of a county or region electing its own councillors. **2** an area which has specified characteristics; a region (*the wine-growing district*). [from medieval Latin *districtus* '(territory of) jurisdiction']

district attorney *n.* (in the US) the prosecuting officer of a district.

district nurse *n.* *Brit.* a peripatetic nurse serving a rural or urban area.

distrust ● *n.* a lack of trust; doubt; suspicion. ● *v.tr.* have no trust or confidence in; doubt. □ **distrustful** *adj.* **distrustfully** *adv.*

disturb *v.tr.* **1** break the rest, calm, or quiet of; interrupt. **2** agitate; worry (*your story disturbs me*). **3** move

---

from a settled position (*the papers had been disturbed*). **4** (as **disturbed** *adj.*) *Psychol.* emotionally or mentally unstable or abnormal. [based on Latin *turba* 'tumult'] □ **disturber** *n.* **disturbing** *adj.* **disturbingly** *adv.*

disturbance *n.* **1** the act or an instance of disturbing; the process of being disturbed. **2** a tumult; an uproar. **3** agitation; worry.

disulphide *n.* (*US* **disulfide**) *Chem.* a binary chemical containing two atoms of sulphur in each molecule.

disunion *n.* a lack of union; separation; dissension. □ **disunite** *v.tr. & intr.* **disunity** *n.*

disuse ● *n.* /dis-**yooss**/ lack of use or practice; discontinuance. **2** a disused state. ● *v.tr.* /dis-**yooz**/ cease to use. □ **fall into disuse** cease to be used.

disyllable *n.* *Prosody* a word or metrical foot of two syllables. [from Greek *disullabos*] □ **disyllabic** *adj.*

ditch ● *n.* a long narrow excavated channel esp. for drainage or to mark a boundary. ● *v.* **1** *intr.* make or repair ditches. **2** *tr. colloq.* leave in the lurch; abandon. **3** *colloq.* **a** *tr.* bring (an aircraft) down on the sea in an emergency. **b** *intr.* (of an aircraft) make a forced landing on the sea. [Old English] □ **ditcher** *n.*

ditchwater *n.* stagnant water in a ditch.

dither ● *v.intr.* hesitate; be indecisive. ● *n. colloq.* **1** a state of agitation or apprehension. **2** a state of hesitation; indecisiveness. [variant of dialect *didder*] □ **ditherer** *n.* **dithery** *adj.*

dithyramb /**dith**-i-ram/ *n.* **1** a wild choral hymn in ancient Greece. **2** a passionate or inflated poem etc. [from Greek *dithurambos*] □ **dithyrambic** *adj.*

dittany *n.* (*pl.* **-ies**) **1 a** (in full **dittany of Crete**) a dwarf shrub, *Origanum dictamnus* (mint family), with woolly leaves. **b** *US* a similar herb, *Cunila origanoides*. **2** = FRAXINELLA. [from Greek *diktamnon*]

ditto *n.* (*pl.* **-os**) **1** (in accounts, lists, etc.) the aforesaid, the same. **2** *colloq.* (replacing a word or phrase to avoid repetition) the same (*came in late last night and ditto the night before*). [Italian dialect, based on Latin *dictus* 'said']

■ **Usage** In sense 1, the word *ditto* is often replaced by ditto marks under the word or sum to be repeated.

ditto marks *n.pl.* two commas (,,) etc. representing 'ditto'.

ditty *n.* (*pl.* **-ies**) a short simple song. [from Latin *dictatum* 'thing dictated']

diuretic /dy-yoor-**et**-ik/ ● *adj.* causing increased output of urine. ● *n.* a diuretic drug. [based on Greek *diourein* 'to urinate']

D

diurnal *adj.* **1** of or during the day; not nocturnal. **2** daily; of each day. **3** *Astron.* occupying one day. [from Latin *diurnus*, based on *dies* 'day'] □ **diurnally** *adv.*

diva /**dee**-vă/ *n.* (*pl.* **divas**) a great or famous woman singer; a prima donna. [Italian, literally 'goddess']

divalent *adj. Chem.* having a valency of two. □ **divalency** *n.*

divan *n.* **1** a long, low, backless sofa. **2** a bed consisting of a base and mattress. [from Persian *dīvān* 'anthology, register, court, bench']

dive ● *v.intr.* (*past* and *past part.* **dived** or *US* also **dove**) **1** plunge head first into water, esp. as a sport. **2 a** *Aeron.* (of an aircraft) plunge steeply downwards at speed. **b** *Naut.* (of a submarine) submerge. **c** (of a person) plunge downwards. **3** (foll. by *into*) *colloq.* put one's hand into (a pocket, handbag, container, etc.) quickly and deeply. ● *n.* **1** an act of diving; a plunge. **2 a** the steep descent of an aircraft. **b** the submerging of a submarine. **3** *colloq.* a disreputable nightclub etc. **4** *Boxing slang* a pretended knockout (*took a dive in the second round*). □ **dive in** *colloq.* help oneself (to food). [Old English, related to DEEP, DIP]

dive-bomb *v.tr.* bomb (a target) while diving in an aircraft. □ **dive-bomber** *n.*

umbilical supplies air and electricity

helmet

weight belt

wetsuit

DIVER: OIL-RIG DIVER

diver *n.* **1** a person who dives. ▷ SCUBA-DIVING. **2** ◀ a person who wears a diving suit to work under water for long periods. **3** any large waterbird of the family Gaviidae, with a straight, sharply pointed bill.

diverge *v.intr.* **1 a** proceed in a different direction or in different directions from a point. **b** take a different course or different courses (*their interests diverged*). **2 a** (often foll. by *from*) depart from a set course. **b** differ markedly. [from medieval Latin *divergere*] □ **divergence** *n.* **divergency** *n.* **divergent** *adj.* **divergently** *adv.*

divers *adj. archaic* or *literary* more than one; sundry; several. [from Latin *diversus* 'turned different ways']

diverse *adj.* unlike in nature or qualities; varied. [Middle English] □ **diversely** *adv.*

diversify *v.* (**-ies, -ied**) **1** *tr.* make diverse; vary. **2** *tr. Commerce* spread (investment) over several enterprises or products, esp. to reduce the risk of loss. **3** *intr.* (often foll. by *into*) esp. *Commerce* (of a firm etc.) expand the range of products handled. □ **diversification** *n.*

diversion *n.* **1 a** the act of diverting. **b** an instance of this. **2 a** the diverting of attention deliberately. **b** a stratagem for this purpose (*created a diversion*). **3** a recreation or pastime. **4** *Brit.* an alternative route when a road is closed. [from Late Latin *diversio*] □ **diversionary** *adj.*

diversity *n.* (*pl.* **-ies**) being diverse; variety.

divert /dy-**vert**/ *v.tr.* **1** (often foll. by *from*, *to*) **a** deflect. **b** distract. **2** (often as **diverting** *adj.*) entertain; amuse. [from Latin *divertere*] □ **divertingly** *adv.*

diverticular disease *n.* a condition with abdominal pain as a result of muscle spasms in the presence of diverticula.

diverticulum /dy-ver-**tik**-yoo-lŭm/ *n.* (*pl.* **diverticula**) *Anat.* a blind tube formed in a cavity or passage, esp. an abnormal one in the alimentary tract. [later variant of Latin *deverticulum* 'byway'] □ **diverticulosis** *n.*

divertimento /di-ver-ti-**men**-toh/ *n.* (*pl.* **divertimenti** or **-os**) *Mus.* a light and entertaining composition. [Italian, literally 'diversion']

divest *v.tr.* (usu. foll. by *of*; often *refl.*) **1** unclothe; strip (*divested himself of his jacket*). **2** deprive, dispossess; free, rid. [based on Latin *vestire* 'to clothe'] □ **divestment** *n.*

divi var. of DIVVY.

divide ● *v.* **1** *tr. & intr.* (often foll. by *in, into*) separate or be separated into parts; break up; split. **2** *tr. & intr.* (often foll. by *out*) distribute; deal; share. **3** *tr.* **a** cut off; separate; part. **b** mark out into parts (*a ruler divided into inches*). **c** specify different kinds of, classify (*people can be divided into two types*). **4** *tr.* cause to disagree (*religion divided them*). **5** *Math.* **a** *tr.* find how many times (a number) contains another (*divide 20 by 4*). **b** *tr.* (of a number) be contained in (a number) without a remainder (*4 divides into 20*). **c** *intr.* be susceptible of division (*10 divides by 2 and 5*). **d** *tr.* find how many times (a number) is contained in another (*divide 4 into 20*). **6** *Parl.* **a** *intr.* (of a legislative assembly etc.) part into two groups for voting (*the House divided*). **b** so divide (a Parliament etc.) for voting. ● *n.* **1** a dividing or boundary line (*the divide between rich and poor*). **2** *Geog.* a watershed. [from Latin *dividere* 'to separate']

dividend *n.* **1 a** a sum of money paid by a company to shareholders. **b** a similar sum payable to winners in a football pool or to members of a cooperative. **2** *Math.* a number to be divided. **3** a benefit from any action (*their long training paid dividends*). [from Latin *dividendum*]

divider *n.* **1** a screen etc. dividing a room into two parts. **2** (in *pl.*) a measuring compass.

divination /div-in-**ay**-shŏn/ *n.* supposed insight into the future or the unknown gained by supernatural means. □ **divinatory** *adj.*

divine ● *adj.* (**diviner, divinest**) **1 a** of, from, or like God or a god. **b** sacred (*divine service*). **2** *colloq.* excellent; delightful. ● *v.* **1** *tr.* discover by guessing, intuition, inspiration, or magic. **2** *tr.* foresee, predict, conjecture. **3** *intr.* practise divination. ● *n.* a cleric, usu. an expert in theology. [from Latin *divus* 'godlike'] □ **divinely** *adv.* **diviner** *n.* **divinize** *v.tr.* (also **-ise**).

divine office see OFFICE 9b.

chamber at normal air pressure

diving bell *n.* ◀ an open-bottomed box or bell, supplied with air, in which a person can descend into deep water.

diving board *n.* an elevated board used for diving from.

diving suit *n.* a watertight suit usu. with a helmet and an air supply, worn for working under water.

divining rod *n.* = DOWSING ROD.

divinity *n.* (*pl.* **-ies**) **1** the state or quality of being divine. **2 a** a god; a divine being. **b** (as **the Divinity**) God. **3** the study of religion.

divisible *adj.* capable of being divided, esp. without a remainder (*15 is divisible by 3*). [related to DIVIDE] □ **divisibility** *n.*

decompression chamber

entry hatch

division *n.* **1** the act or an instance of dividing; the process of being divided. **2** *Math.* the process of dividing one number by another. **3** disagreement or discord (*division of opinion*). **4** *Parl.* the separation of members of a legislative body into two sets for counting votes.

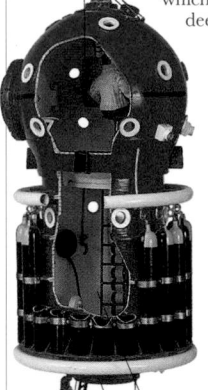

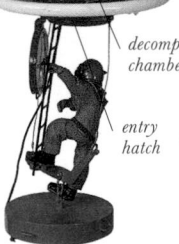

DIVING BELL: CUTAWAY MODEL OF A 1965 SEATASK DIVING BELL

5 one of two or more parts into which a thing is divided. **6** a major unit of administration or organization, esp.: **a** a group of army brigades or regiments. **b** *Sport* a grouping of teams within a league. [from Latin *divisio*, related to DIVIDE] □ **divisional** *adj.* **divisionally** *adv.*

division sign *n.* the sign (÷) indicating that one quantity is to be divided by another.

divisive *adj.* tending to divide, esp. in opinion; causing disagreement. □ **divisively** *adv.* **divisiveness** *n.*

divisor *n. Math.* a number by which another is to be divided.

divorce ● *n.* **1** the legal dissolution of a marriage. **2** a severance or separation (*a divorce between thought and feeling*). ● *v.* **1 a** *tr.* (usu. as **divorced** *adj.*) (often foll. by *from*) legally dissolve the marriage of (*a divorced couple; he wants to get divorced from her*). **b** *intr.* separate by divorce (*they divorced*). **c** *tr.* end one's marriage with (*divorced him*). **2** *tr.* (often foll. by *from*) detach, separate (*divorced from reality*). [from Latin *divortere* 'to turn aside']

divorcee (*US masc.* **divorcé** /div-or-**say**/, *fem.* **divorcée** /div-or-**say**/) a divorced person.

divot *n.* a piece of turf cut out by a golf club in making a stroke. [16th-century coinage]

divulge *v.tr.* disclose; reveal (a secret etc.). [from Latin *divulgare* 'to spread abroad among the people'] □ **divulgation** *n.* **divulgement** *n.* **divulgence** *n.*

divvy (also **divi**) *colloq.* ● *n.* (*pl.* **-ies**) *Brit.* a dividend. ● *v.tr.* (**-ies, -ied**) (often foll. by *up*) share out. [20th-century coinage]

Diwali *n.* a Hindu festival with lights, held in the period October to November. [from Sanskrit *dīpavalī* 'row of lights']

Dixie *n.* the southern states of the US. [19th-century coinage]

dixie *n.* a large iron cooking pot used by campers etc. [from Persian *degcha* 'little pot']

Dixieland *n.* **1** = DIXIE. **2** a kind of jazz with a strong two-beat rhythm and collective improvisation.

DIY *abbr.* esp. *Brit.* do-it-yourself.

dizzy ● *adj.* (**dizzier, dizziest**) **1 a** giddy, unsteady. **b** lacking mental stability; confused. **c** *colloq.* scatterbrained. **2** causing giddiness. ● *v.tr.* (**-ies, -ied**) **1** make dizzy. **2** bewilder. [Old English] □ **dizzily** *adv.* **dizziness** *n.*

DJ *abbr.* **1** *Brit.* dinner jacket. **2** disc jockey.

djellaba /**jel**-ă-bă/ *n.* (also **djellabah, jellaba**) ► a loose hooded woollen cloak worn or as worn by Arab men. [from Arabic *jallaba*]

djinn var. of JINNEE.

dl *abbr.* decilitre(s).

D-layer *n.* the lowest layer of the ionosphere able to reflect low-frequency radio waves.

D.Litt. *abbr.* Doctor of Letters. [Latin *Doctor Litterarum*]

DM *abbr.* (also **D-mark**) Deutschmark.

dm *abbr.* decimetre(s).

D.Mus. *abbr.* Doctor of Music.

DJELLABA

DNA *abbr.* ▲ deoxyribonucleic acid, a self-replicating material which carries the genetic information in chromosomes.

D-notice *n. Brit.* a government notice to news editors not to publish items on specified subjects, for reasons of security. [D: from *defence*]

do[1] ● *v.* (*3rd sing. present* **does**; *past* **did**; *past part.* **done**) **1** *tr.* perform, carry out, achieve, complete (work etc.) (*did his homework; there's a lot to do*). **2** *tr.* **a** produce, make (*she was doing a painting; I did a translation*). **b** provide (*do you do lunches?*). **3** *tr.* bestow,

---

DNA

DNA is a nucleic acid that constitutes the genes in virtually all living organisms. It governs cell growth and is responsible for the transmission of genetic information from one generation to the next. A DNA molecule consists of two strands that spiral around each other to form a double helix. The strands are held together by subunits called bases, which always pair in specific ways: adenine with thymine and cytosine with guanine.

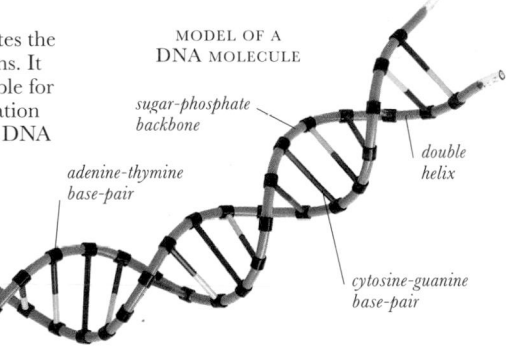

MODEL OF A DNA MOLECULE

sugar-phosphate backbone

adenine-thymine base-pair

double helix

cytosine-guanine base-pair

D

---

grant; have a specified effect on (*a walk would do you good*; *do me a favour*). **4** *intr.* act, behave, proceed (*do as I do*; *she would do well to accept the offer*). **5** *tr.* **a** work at for a living, be occupied with (*what does your father do?*). **b** work at, study (*he did chemistry at university*; *we're doing Chaucer next term*). **6 a** *intr.* be suitable or acceptable; suffice (*a sandwich will do until we get home*; *that will never do*). **b** *tr.* satisfy; be suitable for (*that hotel will do me nicely*). **7** *tr.* deal with; put in order (*the garden needs doing*; *the barber will do you next*; *I must do my hair before we go*). **8** *intr.* **a** fare; get on (*the patients were doing excellently*; *he did badly in the test*). **b** perform, work (*could do better*). **9** *tr.* **a** solve; work out (*we did the puzzle*). **b** (prec. by *can* or *be able to*) be competent at (*can you do cartwheels?*; *I never could do maths*). **10** *tr.* **a** traverse (a certain distance) (*we did fifty miles today*). **b** travel at a specified speed (*he overtook us doing about eighty*). **11** *tr. colloq.* act or behave like (*did a Houdini*). **12** *intr.* **a** *colloq.* finish (*I've done in the bathroom*). **b** (as **done** *adj.*) be over (*the day is done*). **13** *tr.* produce or give a performance of (*we've never done 'Pygmalion'*). **14** *tr.* cook, esp. to the right degree (*do it in the oven*; *the potatoes aren't done yet*). **15** *intr.* be in progress (*what's doing?*). **16** *tr. colloq.* visit; see the sights of (*we did all the art galleries*). **17** *tr. colloq.* **a** (often as **done** *adj.*) exhaust; tire out (*the climb has completely done me*). **b** beat up, defeat, kill. **c** ruin (*now you've done it*). **18** *tr. slang* **a** rob (*they did a shop in Soho*). **b** swindle (*I was done at the market*). **19** *tr. Brit. slang* prosecute, convict (*they were done for shoplifting*). **20** *tr. slang* undergo (a specified term of imprisonment) (*he did two years for fraud*). **21** *tr. slang* take (a drug). • *v.aux.* **1 a** (except with *be*, *can*, *may*, *ought*, *shall*, *will*) in questions and negative statements (*do you understand?*; *I don't smoke*). **b** (except with *can*, *may*, *ought*, *shall*, *will*) in negative commands (*don't be silly*; *do not come tomorrow*). **2** *ellipt.* or in place of verb or verb and object (*you know her better than I do*; *I wanted to go and I did so*; *tell me, do!*). **3** forming emphatic present and past tenses (*I do want to*; *do tell me*; *they did go but she was out*). **4** in inversion for emphasis (*rarely does it happen*; *did he but know it*). • *n.* (*pl.* **dos** or **do's**) *colloq.* an elaborate social event, party, or operation. □ **be done with** see DONE. **be to do with** be concerned or connected with (*the argument was to do with money*). **do away with** *colloq.* **1** abolish. **2** kill. **do battle** enter in combat. **do down** *Brit. colloq.* **1** cheat, swindle. **2** get the better of; overcome. **3** criticize, put down. **do for 1** be satisfactory or sufficient for. **2** *colloq.* (esp. as **done for** *adj.*) destroy, ruin, kill (*he knew he was done for*). **do in 1** *slang* **a** kill. **b** ruin, do injury to. **2** *colloq.* exhaust, tire out. **do nothing for** (or **to**) *colloq.* detract from the appearance or quality of. **do one's nut** *Brit. slang* be extremely angry or agitated. **do out** *Brit. colloq.* clean or redecorate (a room). **do a person out of** *colloq.* unjustly deprive a person of; swindle out of (*he was done out of his holiday*). **do over 1** *slang* attack; beat up. **2** *N. Amer. colloq.* do again. **do proud** see PROUD. **dos and**

don'ts rules of behaviour. **do something for** (or **to**) *colloq.* enhance the appearance or quality of (*that carpet does something for the room*). **do to** (*archaic* **unto**) treat in a specified way. **do to death** see DEATH. **do the trick** see TRICK. **do up 1** fasten, secure. **2** *colloq.* **a** refurbish, renovate. **b** adorn, dress up. **do well for oneself** prosper. **do well out of** profit by. **do with** (prec. by *could*) would be glad to have; would profit by (*I could do with a rest*). **do without** manage without; forgo (also *absol.*: *we shall just have to do without*). [Old English]

do² var. of DOH.

do. *abbr.* ditto.

DOA *abbr.* dead on arrival (at hospital etc.).

doable *adj.* that can be done.

Dobermann *n.* (in full **Dobermann pinscher**) a large dog of a German breed with a smooth coat. ▷ DOG. [named after L. *Dobermann*, 19th-century German dog-breeder, + German *Pinscher* 'terrier']

doc *n. colloq.* doctor.

docile *adj.* submissive, easily managed. [from Latin *docilis* 'teachable'] □ **docilely** *adv.* **docility** *n.*

dock¹ • *n.* **1** an artificially enclosed body of water for the loading, unloading, and repair of ships. **2** (in *pl.*) a range of docks with wharves and offices; a dockyard. **3** *US* a ship's berth, a wharf. • *v.* **1** *tr. & intr.* bring or come into a dock. **2 a** *tr.* join (spacecraft) together in space. **b** *intr.* (of spacecraft) be joined. □ **in dock** *colloq.* in hospital or (of a vehicle) laid up for repairs. [from Middle Dutch *docke*]

dock² *n.* the enclosure in a criminal court for the accused. □ **in the dock** *Brit.* on trial. [16th-century coinage]

dock³ *n.* any coarse, broadleaved weed of the genus *Rumex*. [Old English]

dock⁴ *v.tr.* **1** cut short (an animal's tail). **2 a** (often foll. by *from*) deduct (a part) from wages, supplies, etc. **b** reduce (wages etc.) in this way. [Middle English]

docker *n.* a person employed to load and unload ships.

docket • *n. Brit.* **1** a document or label listing goods delivered or the contents of a package. **2** a voucher; an order form. • *v.tr.* (**docketed**, **docketing**) label with a docket. [15th-century coinage]

dockland *n.* a district near docks.

dockside *n.* (often *attrib.*) the area immediately adjacent to a dock.

dock-tailed *adj.* having a docked tail.

dockyard *n.* an area with docks and equipment for building and repairing ships, esp. *Brit.* for naval use.

Doc Martens var. of DR MARTENS.

doctor • *n.* **1 a** a qualified practitioner of medicine; a physician. **b** *N. Amer.* a qualified dentist or veterinary surgeon. **2** a person who holds a doctorate (*Doctor of Civil Law*). • *v.tr. colloq.* **1** *Brit.* castrate or spay. **2** adulterate. **3** tamper with, falsify. □ **what the doctor ordered** *colloq.* something

beneficial or desirable. [Latin, literally 'teacher'] □ **doctorly** *adj.*

doctoral *adj.* of or for a degree of doctor.

doctorate *n.* the highest university degree in any faculty, sometimes honorary.

Doctor Martens var. of DR MARTENS.

Doctor of Philosophy *n.* **1** a doctorate in any faculty except law, medicine, or sometimes theology. **2** a person holding such a degree.

doctrinaire • *adj.* seeking to apply a theory or doctrine dogmatically. • *n.* a doctrinaire person. [French] □ **doctrinairism** *n.*

doctrinal *adj.* of or inculcating a doctrine or doctrines. □ **doctrinally** *adv.*

doctrine *n.* **1** what is taught; a body of instruction. **2 a** a principle of religious or political etc. belief. **b** a set of such principles; dogma. [from Latin *doctrina* 'teaching'] □ **doctrinism** *n.* **doctrinist** *n.*

docudrama *n.* a dramatized television film based on real events.

document • *n.* a piece of written or printed matter that provides a record or evidence of events, an agreement, ownership, identification, etc. • *v.tr.* **1** prove by or provide with documents or evidence. **2** record in a document. [from Latin *documentum* 'proof']

documentary • *adj.* **1** consisting of documents (*documentary evidence*). **2** providing a factual record or report. • *n.* (*pl.* **-ies**) a documentary film etc.

documentation *n.* **1** the accumulation, classification, and dissemination of information. **2** the material collected or disseminated. **3** the collection of documents relating to a process or event.

dodder *v.intr.* tremble or totter, esp. from age. [17th-century coinage] □ **dodderer** *n.*

doddery *adj.* tending to tremble or totter, esp. from age.

doddle *n. Brit. colloq.* an easy task.

dodeca- *comb. form* twelve. [from Greek]

dodecagon *n.* ▼ a plane figure with twelve sides.

dodecahedron *n.* (*pl.* **dodecahedra** or **dodecahedrons**) ▼ a solid figure with twelve faces. □ **dodecahedral** *adj.*

DODECAGON   DODECAHEDRON

dodge • *v.* **1** *intr.* (often foll. by *about*, *behind*, *round*) move quickly to one side or quickly change position, to elude a pursuer, blow, etc. (*dodged behind the chair*). **2** *tr.* **a** evade by cunning or trickery (*dodged paying the fare*). **b** elude (a pursuer, opponent, blow, etc.) by a sideward movement etc. • *n.* **1** a quick movement to avoid or evade something. **2** a clever trick or expedient. [16th-century coinage] □ **dodger** *n.*

dodgem *n.* (in full **dodgem car**) a small electrically powered car, driven in an enclosure at a funfair with the aim of bumping or avoiding other such cars. [US proprietary name]

dodgy *adj.* (**dodgier**, **dodgiest**) **1** *colloq.* awkward, unreliable, tricky. **2** *Brit.* cunning, artful.

dodo *n.* (*pl.* **-os** or **-oes**) ◄ a large extinct flightless bird, *Raphus cucullatus*, formerly native to Mauritius. [from Portuguese *doudo* 'simpleton']

doe *n.* a female fallow deer, reindeer, hare, rabbit, etc. [Old English]

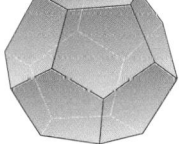

DODO (*Raphus cucullatus*)

D

doer *n.* **1** a person who does something. **2** a person who acts rather than merely talking or thinking.

does *3rd sing. present* of DO[1].

doesn't *contr.* does not.

doff *v.tr.* esp. *literary* take off (one's hat, clothing). [Middle English, literally 'do off']

dog ● *n.* **1 a** ▶ a domesticated carnivorous mammal, *Canis familiaris*, occurring in many different breeds kept as pets or for work or sport. **b** a wild animal of the genus *Canis*, including wolves, jackals, and coyotes, or of the family Canidae. **2** the male of the dog, or of the fox (also **dog-fox**) or wolf (also **dog-wolf**). **3** *colloq.* **a** a despicable person. **b** a person of a specified kind (*a lucky dog*). **4** a mechanical device for gripping. **5** *N. Amer. slang* something poor; a failure. **6** = FIREDOG. **7** (in *pl.*; prec. by *the*) *Brit. colloq.* greyhound racing. ● *v.tr.* (**dogged**, **dogging**) follow closely and persistently; pursue, track. □ **dog's breakfast** (or *Brit.* **dinner**) *colloq.* a mess. **go to the dogs** *slang* deteriorate, be ruined. [Old English] □ **doglike** *adj.*

dog biscuit *n.* a hard thick biscuit for feeding dogs.

dog collar *n.* **1** a collar for a dog. **2** *colloq.* a clerical collar.

dog days *n.pl.* the hottest period of the year.

doge *n.* *hist.* the chief magistrate of Venice or Genoa. [from Venetian Italian *doze*]

dog-eared *adj.* (of a book etc.) with the corners worn or battered with use.

dog-end *n.* *slang* a cigarette end.

dogfight ● *n.* **1** a close combat between fighter aircraft. **2** uproar; a fight like that between dogs. ● *v.intr.* take part in a dogfight. □ **dogfighter** *n.*

dogfish *n.* (*pl.* usu. same) ◀ any of various small sharks, esp. of the families Scyliorhinidae and Squalidae. ▷ EGG, SHARK

dogged /dog-id/ *adj.* tenacious; grimly persistent. [Middle English, based on DOG] □ **doggedly** *adv.* **doggedness** *n.*

doggerel *n.* poor or trivial verse. [Middle English]

doggie var. of DOGGY *n.*

doggo *adv.* □ **lie doggo** *Brit. slang* lie motionless or hidden, making no sign.

doggone esp. *N. Amer. slang* ● *adj. & adv.* damned. ● *int.* expressing annoyance.

doggy ● *adj.* **1** of or like a dog. **2** devoted to dogs. ● *n.* (also **doggie**) (*pl.* **-ies**) a little dog; a pet name for a dog. □ **dogginess** *n.*

doggy bag *n.* a bag given to a customer in a restaurant or to a guest at a party etc. for putting leftovers in to take home.

doggy-paddle var. of DOG-PADDLE.

dog handler *n.* a person, esp. a police officer, in charge of a dog or dogs. □ **dog-handling** *n.*

doghouse *n.* *N. Amer.* a dog's kennel. □ **in the doghouse** *slang* in disgrace or disfavour.

DOGFISH: LESSER-SPOTTED DOGFISH (*Scyliorhinus canicula*)

dog in the manger *n.* a person who prevents others from using something, although that person has no use for it.

dog-leg *n.* a sharp bend like that in a dog's hind leg.

dogma *n.* **1** a principle, tenet, or system of these, esp. as laid down by the authority of a Church. **2** an arrogant declaration of opinion. [from Greek *dogma* 'opinion']

dogmatic *adj.* **1** (of a person) given to asserting or imposing personal opinions; arrogant. **2** intolerantly authoritative. □ **dogmatically** *adv.*

dogmatism *n.* a tendency to be dogmatic. □ **dogmatist** *n.*

do-gooder *n.* a well-meaning but unrealistic philanthropist or reformer.

dog-paddle *n.* (also **doggy-paddle**) an elementary swimming stroke like that of a dog.

dog rose *n.* ◀ a wild hedge-rose, *Rosa canina*.

dogsbody *n.* (*pl.* **-ies**) *Brit. colloq.* a drudge.

dog sled *n.* a sled designed to be pulled by dogs.

dog's life *n.* a life of misery or harassment.

dogs of war *n.pl. poet.* the havoc accompanying war.

dog-star *n.* Sirius, the brightest star in the sky. [so called as it appears to follow at the heels of Orion the hunter]

dog-tired *adj.* tired out.

DOG ROSE (*Rosa canina*)

dog-tooth *n.* **1** ▼ a small pointed ornament or moulding, esp. in Norman and Early English architecture. **2** a broken check pattern used esp. in cloth for suits.

DOG-TOOTH ORNAMENT IN ROMANESQUE-STYLE ARCH

dog-tooth ornament

dog trials *n.pl. Austral. & NZ* a public competitive display of the skills of sheepdogs.

dog trot *n.* a gentle easy trot.

dog-violet *n.* any of various scentless wild violets, esp. *Viola riviniana*.

dogwatch *n. Naut.* either of two short watches (4–6 or 6–8 p.m.).

DOGWOOD (*Cornus alba*)

dogwood *n.* ◀ any of various shrubs of the genus *Cornus*, with dark red branches, greenish-white flowers, and purple berries.

DoH *abbr.* (in the UK) Department of Health.

doh *n.* (also **do**) *Mus.* **1** (in tonic sol-fa) the first and eighth note of a major scale. **2** the note C in the fixed-doh system. [18th-century coinage: from Italian *do*, an arbitrarily chosen syllable]

doily *n.* (also **doyley**) (*pl.* **-ies** or **-eys**) a small ornamental mat of paper, lace, etc., on a plate for cakes etc. [originally the name of a fabric: from *Doiley*, a 17th-century London draper]

doing *n.* **1 a** an action; the performance of a deed (*famous for his doings*). **b** activity, effort (*it takes a lot of doing*). **2** *colloq.* a scolding; a beating. **3** (in *pl.*) esp. *Brit. slang* things needed; adjuncts; things whose names are not known (*have we got all the doings?*).

do-it-yourself ● *adj.* (of work, esp. building, painting, decorating, etc.) done or to be done by an amateur at home. ● *n.* such work.

dojo *n.* (*pl.* **-os**) **1** a room or hall in which judo and other martial arts are practised. **2** a mat on which judo etc. is practised. [Japanese]

Dolby *n. propr.* an electronic noise-reduction system used esp. in tape-recording to reduce hiss. [named after R. M. *Dolby*, US inventor, born 1933]

dolce *adv. & adj. Mus.* ● *adv.* sweetly and softly. ● *adj.* performed in this manner. [Italian]

doldrums *n.pl.* (usu. prec. by *the*) **1** low spirits; a feeling of boredom or depression. **2** a period of inactivity or state of stagnation. **3** an equatorial ocean region of calms, sudden storms, and light unpredictable winds. ▷ TRADE WIND

dole *n.* **1** (usu. prec. by *the*) *Brit. colloq.* benefit claimable by the unemployed from the State. **2 a** charitable distribution. **b** a charitable (esp. sparing, niggardly) gift of food, clothes, or money. ● *v.tr.* (usu. foll. by *out*) deal out sparingly. □ **on the dole** *colloq.* receiving state benefit for the unemployed. [Old English]

doleful *adj.* **1** mournful, sad. **2** dreary, dismal. [Middle English] □ **dolefully** *adv.* **dolefulness** *n.*

doll ● *n.* **1** a small model of a human figure as a child's toy. **2** *slang* a young woman (or also *US* a young man), esp. an attractive one. **3** a ventriloquist's dummy. ● *v.tr. & intr.* (foll. by *up*; often *refl.*) dress up smartly. [pet form of the name *Dorothy*]

dollar *n.* **1** the chief monetary unit of the US, Canada, and Australia. **2** the chief monetary unit of certain countries in the Pacific, West Indies, SE Asia, Africa, and S. America. [from German *Taler*, short for *Joachimstaler*, a coin from the *Joachimstal* silver-mine]

dollar mark *n.* (also **dollar sign**) the sign $, representing a dollar.

dollop ● *n.* a shapeless lump of food etc. ● *v.tr.* (**dolloped**, **dolloping**) (usu. foll. by *out*) serve out in large shapeless quantities.

doll's house *n.* (*N. Amer.* **dollhouse**) a miniature toy house for dolls.

dolly *n.* (*pl.* **-ies**) **1** a child's name for a doll. **2** a movable platform for a cine-camera. **3** *Cricket colloq.* an easy catch or hit. **4** a stick for stirring clothes in a washtub.

dolly-bird *n. Brit. colloq.* an attractive and stylish young woman.

dolly mixture *n. Brit.* any of a mixture of small variously shaped and coloured sweets.

dolman sleeve *n.* a loose sleeve cut in one piece with the body of a garment. [based on Turkish *dolama* 'robe']

dolmen *n.* a megalithic tomb with a large flat stone laid on upright ones. ▷ QUOIT. [French]

dolomite *n.* ▼ a mineral or rock of calcium magnesium carbonate. [named after D. de *Dolomieu*, French geologist, 1750–1801] □ **dolomitic** *adj.*

DOLOMITE

quartz matrix

curved crystal faces

dolomite crystals

dolorous *adj. literary* or *joc.* **1** distressing, painful; doleful, dismal. **2** distressed, sad. □ **dolorously** *adv.*

dolour /dol-er/ *n.* (*US* **dolor**) *literary* sorrow, distress. [from Latin *dolor* 'pain, grief']

DOG

Dogs belong to the family Canidae, which includes wolves, jackals, and foxes. All modern domestic dogs (*Canis familiaris*) are descended from the grey wolf (*Canis lupus*). There are now more than 300 different breeds of domestic dog and these are often classified into various types, according to the task for which they were originally bred. These tasks included herding, hunting, and guarding. However, many breeds are now kept mainly or exclusively as pets, irrespective of their original function.

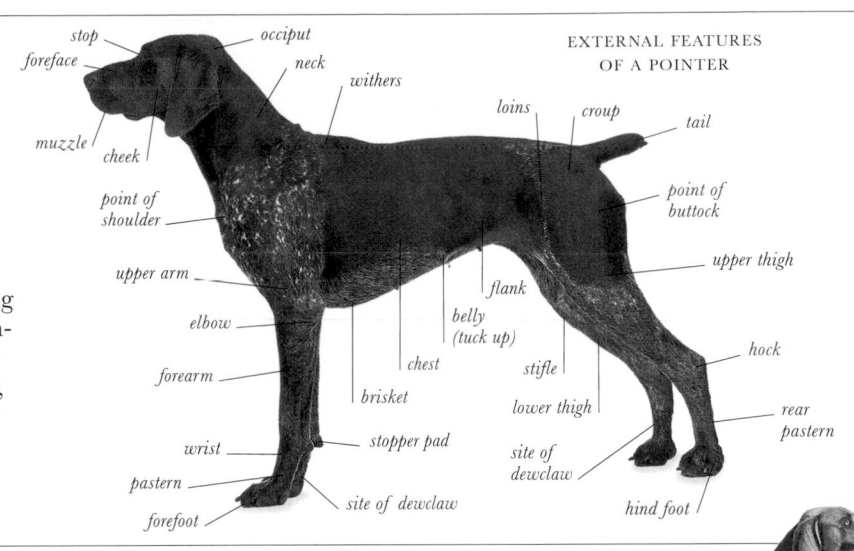

EXTERNAL FEATURES OF A POINTER

stop · occiput · foreface · neck · withers · muzzle · cheek · loins · croup · tail · point of shoulder · point of buttock · upper arm · upper thigh · elbow · flank · belly (tuck up) · hock · forearm · chest · stifle · brisket · lower thigh · rear pastern · wrist · stopper pad · site of dewclaw · pastern · site of dewclaw · forefoot · hind foot

TYPES OF DOG

WORKING DOGS

ALASKAN MALAMUTE

DOBERMANN

HOUNDS

BEAGLE

AFGHAN HOUND

HERDING DOGS

ROUGH COLLIE

CARDIGAN WELSH CORGI

OLD ENGLISH SHEEPDOG

SPORTING DOGS

STANDARD POODLE

WEIMARANER

GOLDEN RETRIEVER

TERRIERS

KERRY BLUE

AIREDALE

COMPANION DOGS

GERMAN SPITZ

PEKINGESE

SHIH TZU

D

DOLPHIN

Dolphins are aquatic mammals belonging to the order Cetacea, and generally have beak-like snouts and streamlined bodies. They can be broadly divided into oceanic and river dolphins. Oceanic dolphins, which belong to the family Delphinidae, are distributed throughout all oceans; some species are coastal or partly river-ine. River dolphins, which belong to the family Platanistidae, are found in the largest rivers of Asia and South America. One species of dolphin, the franciscana, is closely related to the river dolphins but lives in coastal waters.

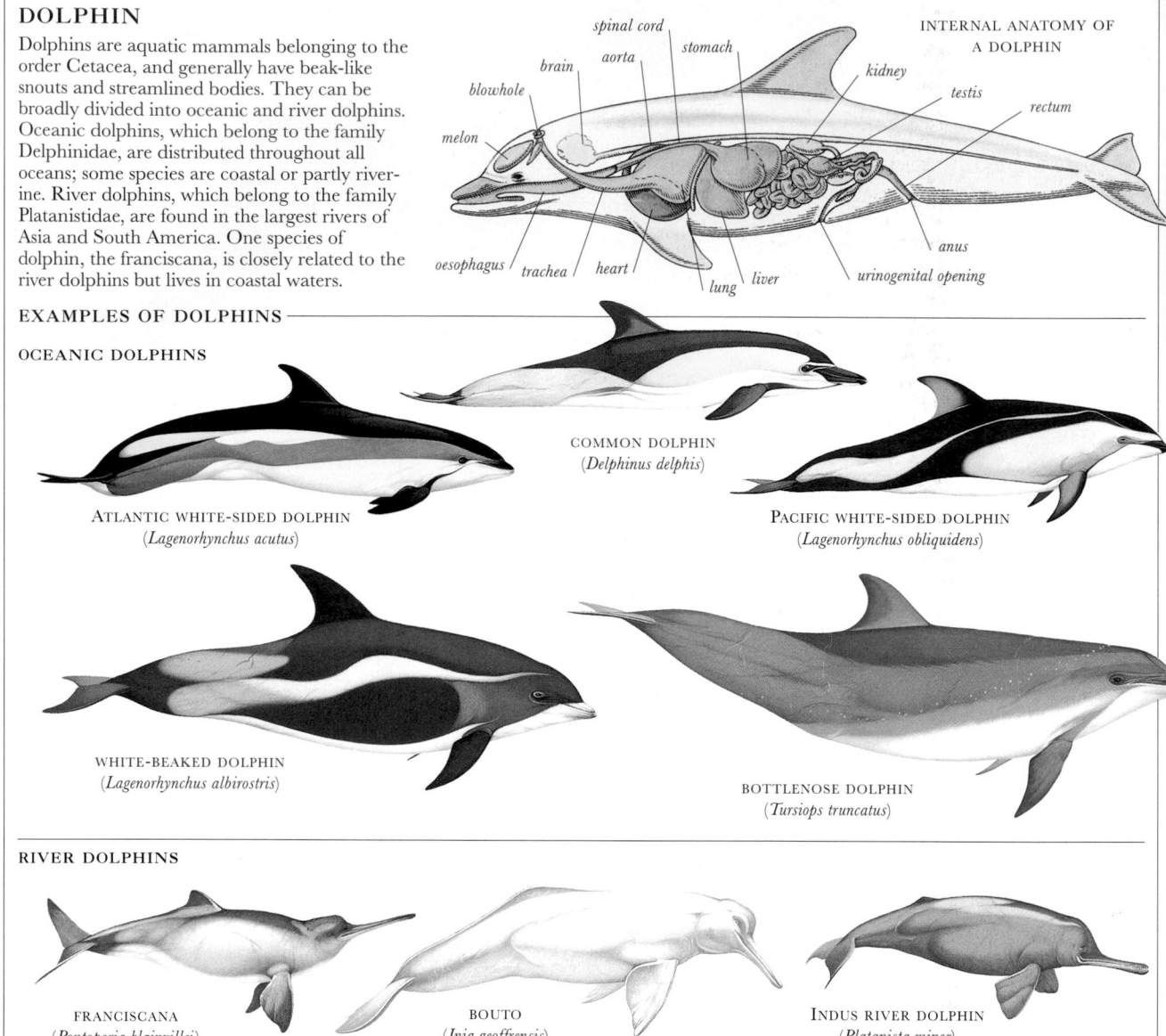

INTERNAL ANATOMY OF A DOLPHIN

spinal cord, brain, aorta, stomach, kidney, testis, rectum, blowhole, melon, oesophagus, trachea, heart, lung, liver, anus, urinogenital opening

EXAMPLES OF DOLPHINS

OCEANIC DOLPHINS

COMMON DOLPHIN
(*Delphinus delphis*)

ATLANTIC WHITE-SIDED DOLPHIN
(*Lagenorhynchus acutus*)

PACIFIC WHITE-SIDED DOLPHIN
(*Lagenorhynchus obliquidens*)

WHITE-BEAKED DOLPHIN
(*Lagenorhynchus albirostris*)

BOTTLENOSE DOLPHIN
(*Tursiops truncatus*)

RIVER DOLPHINS

FRANCISCANA
(*Pontoporia blainvillei*)

BOUTO
(*Inia geoffrensis*)

INDUS RIVER DOLPHIN
(*Platanista minor*)

dolphin *n.* **1** ▲ any of various porpoise-like aquatic mammals. ▷ CETACEAN. **2** (also **dolphinfish**) = DORADO 1. **3** a bollard, pile, or buoy for mooring. **4** a structure for protecting the pier of a bridge.

dolphinarium *n.* (*pl.* **dolphinariums**) *Brit.* an aquarium for dolphins, esp. one open to the public.

dolt *n.* a stupid person. □ **doltish** *adj.* **doltishness** *n.*

Dom *n.* **1** a title prefixed to the names of some Roman Catholic dignitaries, and Benedictine and Carthusian monks. **2** the Portuguese equivalent of *Don* (see DON¹ 2a, b). [sense 1: Latin *dominus* 'master']

domain *n.* **1** an area under one rule; a realm. **2** an estate or lands under one control. **3** a sphere of control or influence. [from Old French *demeine*]

dome ● *n.* **1** ▶ a rounded vault as a roof, with a circular, elliptical, or polygonal base. **2** a dome-shaped thing. **3** *slang* the head. ● *v.tr.* (usu. as **domed** *adj.*) cover with or shape as a dome. [from Latin *domus* 'house'] □ **domelike** *adj.*

domestic ● *adj.* **1** of the home, household, or family affairs. **2** of one's own country, not foreign or international. **3** (of an animal) kept by or living with humans. **4** fond of home life. ● *n.* a household

servant. [based on Latin *domus* 'home'] □ **domestically** *adv.*

domesticate *v.tr.* **1** tame (an animal) to live with humans. **2** accustom to home life and management. **3** naturalize (a plant or animal). □ **domesticable** *adj.* **domestication** *n.*

domesticity *n.* **1** the state of being domestic. **2** domestic or home life.

domestic science *n.* the study of household management.

domicile (also **domicil**) ● *n.* **1** a dwelling place; one's home. **2** *Law* **a** a place of permanent residence. **b** the fact of residing. ● *v.tr.* (usu. as **domiciled** *adj.*) (usu. foll. by *at, in*) establish or settle in a place. [from Latin *domicilium*]

domiciliary *adj.* of a dwelling place (esp. *Brit.* of a doctor's, official's, etc., visit to a person's home).

dominant ● *adj.* **1** dominating, prevailing, most influential. **2 a** (of an allele) expressed even when inherited from only one parent. **b** (of an inherited characteristic) appearing in an individual even when its allelic counterpart is also inherited (cf. RECESSIVE 2). ▷ MENDELISM. ● *n.* *Mus.* the fifth note of

the diatonic scale of any key. [from Latin *dominant-* 'dominating'] □ **dominance** *n.* **dominantly** *adv.*

dominate *v.* **1** *tr.* & (foll. by *over*) *intr.* exercise control over (*fear dominated them for years; dominates over his friends*). **2** *intr.* (of a person, sound, feature of a scene, etc.) be the most influential or conspicuous. **3** *tr.* & (foll. by *over*) *intr.* (of a building etc.) overlook. [from Latin *dominari dominat-*] □ **domination** *n.* **dominator** *n.*

domineer *v.intr.* (often as **domineering** *adj.*) behave in an arrogant and overbearing way. [from Dutch *domineren* 'to rule'] □ **domineeringly** *adv.*

Dominican ● *adj.* of or relating to St Dominic or the order of preaching friars which he founded. ● *n.* a Dominican friar, nun, or sister (see also BLACK FRIAR). [from *Dominicus*, Latin name of *Domingo* de Guzmán (St Dominic)]

dominion *n.* **1** sovereignty, control. **2** the territory of a sovereign or government. **3** *hist.* a self-governing territory of the British Commonwealth. [based on Latin *dominus* 'lord']

domino *n.* (*pl.* **-oes**) **1 a** any of 28 small oblong pieces marked with 0–6 pips in each half. **b** (in *pl.*;

usu. treated as *sing.*) a game played with these. **2** a loose cloak with a mask for the upper part of the face. [French]

domino effect *n.* (also **domino theory**) the effect whereby (or the theory that) one event will cause a sequence of similar events, like a row of falling dominoes.

don[1] *n.* **1** a university teacher, esp. a senior member of a college at Oxford or Cambridge. **2 (Don) a** a Spanish title prefixed to a male forename. **b** a Spanish gentleman; a Spaniard. **c** *N. Amer. slang* a high-ranking member of the Mafia. [Spanish, from Latin *dominus* 'lord']

don[2] *v.tr.* (**donned**, **donning**) put on (clothing). [literally, 'do on']

donate *v.tr.* give or contribute (money etc.), esp. to a charity. □ **donator** *n.*

donation *n.* **1** the act or an instance of donating. **2** something, esp. money, donated. [based on Latin *donum* 'gift']

done *past part.* of DO[1]. ● *adj.* **1** *colloq.* socially acceptable (*the done thing*). **2** (often with *in, up*) *colloq.* tired out. **3** (esp. as *int.* in reply to an offer etc.) accepted. □ **be done with** have finished with, be finished with. **done for** *colloq.* in serious trouble. **have done** have ceased or finished. **have done with** be rid of; have finished dealing with.

doner kebab /don-er/ *n.* spiced lamb cooked on a spit and served in slices, often with pitta bread. [from Turkish, literally 'rotating kebab']

donjon *n.* the great tower or innermost keep of a castle. [archaic spelling of DUNGEON]

donkey *n.* (*pl.* **-eys**) **1** a domestic ass. **2** *colloq.* a stupid or foolish person.

donkey engine *n.* a small auxiliary engine.

donkey jacket *n. Brit.* a thick weatherproof jacket worn by workers and as a fashion garment.

donkey's years *n.pl. colloq.* a very long time.

donkey work *n.* the laborious part of a job; drudgery.

donna *n.* **1** an Italian, Spanish, or Portuguese woman. **2 (Donna)** a title prefixed to the forename of such a woman. [Italian, from Latin *domina* 'mistress']

donnish *adj.* like or resembling a college don, esp. in supposed pedantry. □ **donnishly** *adv.* **donnishness** *n.*

donor *n.* **1** a person who gives or donates something (e.g. to a charity). **2** a person who provides blood for a transfusion, semen for insemination, or an organ or tissue for transplantation. [based on Latin *donare* 'to give']

donor card *n.* an official card authorizing use of organs for transplant, carried by the donor.

donor fatigue *n.* apathy in the general public to requests for donations to charitable causes, as a result of repeated appeals for money, overexposure to media portrayal of suffering, or a feeling that no change can be achieved.

don't ● *contr.* do not. ● *n.* a prohibition (*dos and don'ts*).

donut *US* var. of DOUGHNUT.

doodah *n. colloq.* a gadget or 'thingummy'. [from the refrain of the song *Camptown Races*]

doodle ● *v.intr.* scribble or draw, esp. absentmindedly. ● *n.* a scrawl or drawing so made. [originally in sense 'foolish person': from Low German *dudelkopf*] □ **doodler** *n.*

doodlebug *n.* **1** *US* any of various insects.

2 *US* an unscientific device for locating minerals. **3** *Brit. colloq.* a flying bomb.

doom ● *n.* **1 a** a grim fate or destiny. **b** death or ruin. **2** a condemnation. ● *v.tr.* **1** condemn or destine (*doomed to destruction*). **2** (esp. as **doomed** *adj.*) consign to misfortune or destruction. [Old English *dōm* 'statute, judgement']

doom-laden *adj.* portending, suggesting, or predicting doom.

doomsday *n.* the day of the Last Judgement. □ **till doomsday** for ever.

doomwatch *n.* organized vigilance or observation to avert danger, esp. from environmental pollution. □ **doomwatcher** *n.*

door *n.* **1 ▼** a hinged, sliding, or revolving barrier for closing and opening an entrance to a building, room, cupboard, etc. **2 a** an entrance or exit; a doorway. **b** a means of access or approach. □ **lay** (or **lie**) **at the door of** impute (or be imputable) to. [Old English] □ **doored** *adj.* (also in *comb.*).

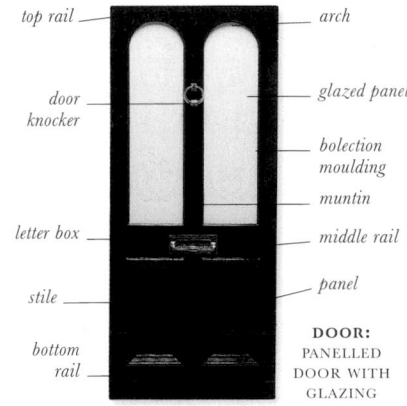

top rail   arch

door knocker   glazed panel

bolection moulding

muntin

letter box   middle rail

stile   panel

bottom rail

DOOR: PANELLED DOOR WITH GLAZING

doorbell *n.* a bell in a house etc. rung by visitors outside to signal their arrival.

doorframe *n.* the structure into which a door is fitted.

doorkeeper *n.* = DOORMAN.

doorknob *n.* a knob for turning to release the latch of a door.

door knocker *n.* a handle of metal or wood fixed to a door by a hinge to allow visitors to signal their arrival by knocking. ▷ DOOR

doorman *n.* (*pl.* **-men**) a person on duty at the door to a large building; a janitor or porter.

doormat *n.* **1** a mat at an entrance for wiping mud etc. from the shoes. **2** a feebly submissive person.

doornail *n.* a nail with which doors were studded for strength or ornament. □ **dead as a doornail** completely or unmistakably dead.

doorpost *n.* each of the uprights of a door frame.

doorstep ● *n.* **1** a step leading up to the outer door of a house etc. **2** *Brit. slang* a thick slice of bread. ● *v.intr.* (**-stepped**, **-stepping**) *Brit.* go from door to door selling, canvassing, etc. □ **on one's** (or **the**) **doorstep** very close.

doorstop *n.* a device for keeping a door open or to prevent it from striking a wall etc. when opened.

door-to-door *adj.* (of selling etc.) done at each house in turn.

doorway *n.* an opening filled by a door.

dopamine *n. Biochem.* an amine present in the body as a neurotransmitter and a precursor of other substances including adrenalin.

dope ● *n.* **1** a varnish applied to the cloth surface of aeroplane parts. **2** a thick liquid used as a lubricant etc. **3 a** *slang* a narcotic; a stupefying drug. **b** a drug etc. given to a horse or greyhound, or taken by an athlete, to affect performance. **4** *slang* a stupid person. **5** *slang* information about a subject, esp. if not generally known. ● *v.* **1** *tr.* administer dope to, drug. **2** *tr.* apply dope to. **3** *intr.* take addictive drugs.

DOME

Domes are curved roofs that were first built on palaces and religious buildings as striking symbols of the building's status. They can be categorized according to the shape of the dome. The framework of the dome, such as the one shown here, often has very complex bracing systems. The shape of the base depends on the plan of the walls on which the dome is constructed, known as the drum.

ogee-curved dome

MODEL SHOWING THE FRAMEWORK OF A SAUCER DOME

straight brace

volute

lantern

cornice

pedestal

projecting pier buttress

vertical post

floor joist

circular window

floorboard

principal rafter

strut

shaft connecting lantern and church interior

oval window

straight brace

circular baseplate

TYPES OF DOME

HEMISPHERICAL   POLYHEDRAL   SAUCER   ONION

D

DOPPLER EFFECT

The changing pitch of the siren of a passing police car is an example of the Doppler effect on sound waves. As the car moves towards an observer, the sound waves are short and reach the observer more frequently, and so the pitch rises. As the car moves away, the waves are longer and reach the observer less frequently, and so the pitch drops. The siren is in fact constantly producing sound of the same frequency.

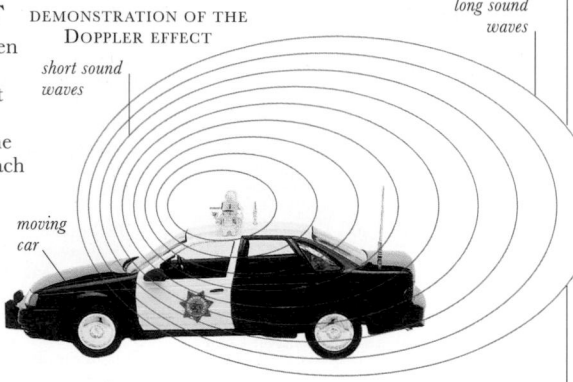

DEMONSTRATION OF THE DOPPLER EFFECT

long sound waves

short sound waves

moving car

□ **dope out** *slang* discover. [from Dutch *doop* 'sauce'] □ **doper** *n.*

dopey *adj.* (also **dopy**) (**dopier**, **dopiest**) *colloq.* **1 a** half asleep. **b** stupefied by or as if by a drug. **2** stupid, silly. □ **dopily** *adv.* **dopiness** *n.*

doppelgänger /dop-ĕl-geng-er/ *n.* an apparition or double of a living person. [German, literally 'double-goer']

Doppler effect *n.* (also **Doppler shift**) *Physics* ▲ an increase (or decrease) in the frequency of sound, light, or other waves as the source and observer move towards (or away) from each other. [named after C. J. *Doppler*, Austrian physicist, 1803–53]

dopy var. of DOPEY.

dorado *n.* (*pl.* **-os**) **1** ▼ a blue and silver marine fish, *Coryphaena hippurus*. **2** a gold-coloured freshwater fish, *Salminus maxillosus*, native to S. America. [based on Late Latin *deauratus* 'gilt']

DORADO (*Coryphaena hippurus*)

Doric /do-rik/ *Archit.* ● *adj.* of the oldest, sturdiest, and simplest of the Greek orders. ▷ COLUMN. ● *n.* ▼ the Doric order. [from Greek *Dōrikos*]

dork *n. slang* **1** the penis. **2** a stupid or contemptible person. [20th-century coinage]

dorm *n. colloq.* dormitory.

dormant *adj.* **1** lying inactive; sleeping. **2 a** (of a volcano etc.) temporarily inactive. **b** (of potential faculties etc.) in abeyance. **3** (of plants) alive but not actively growing. [from (Old) French, literally 'sleeping'] □ **dormancy** *n.*

dormer *n.* (in full **dormer window**) a projecting upright window in a sloping roof. ▷ CHATEAU. [originally in sense 'bedroom window': based on Latin *dormire* 'to sleep']

dormitory *n.* (*pl.* **-ies**) **1** a sleeping room with several beds, esp. in a school or institution. ▷ MONASTERY. **2** (in full **dormitory town** etc.) a small town or suburb from which people travel to work in a city etc. **3** *US* a university or college hall of residence or hostel. [based on Latin *dormire dormit-* 'to sleep']

dormouse *n.* (*pl.* **dormice**) ▶ any mouselike rodent of the family Gliridae, esp. *Muscardinus avellanarius*, noted for its long hibernation. [Middle English, associated with Latin *dormire* 'to sleep']

dorsal *adj. Anat., Zool.,* & *Bot.* **1** of, on, or near the back (cf. VENTRAL). ▷ FISH. **2** ridge-shaped. [based on Latin *dorsum* 'back'] □ **dorsally** *adv.*

dory[1] *n.* (*pl.* **-ies**) a marine fish of the family Zeidae, with a thin deep body, esp. the John Dory. ▷ JOHN DORY. [from French *dorée* (fem.) 'gilded']

dory[2] *n.* (*pl.* **-ies**) *N. Amer.* & *W.Ind.* a flat-bottomed fishing boat with high sides.

DOS *n. Computing* a program for manipulating information on a disk. [abbreviation of *d*isk *o*perating *s*ystem]

dosage *n.* **1** the size of a dose of medicine, radiation, etc. **2** the giving of medicine in doses.

dose ● *n.* **1** an amount of a medicine or drug taken at one time. **2** a quantity of something adminis-

tered or allocated (e.g. work, praise, punishment, etc.). **3** the amount of ionizing radiation received by a person or thing. **4** *slang* a venereal infection. ● *v.tr.* give a dose or doses to. □ **like a dose of salts** *Brit. colloq.* very fast and efficiently. [from Greek *dosis* 'gift']

dosh *n. Brit. slang* money. [20th-century coinage]

dosimeter /doh-sim-i-ter/ *n.* (also **dosemeter**) a device used to measure an absorbed dose of ionizing radiation. □ **dosimetric** *adj.* **dosimetry** *n.*

doss *v.intr. Brit. slang* **1** (often foll. by *down*) sleep, esp. roughly or in cheap lodgings. **2** (often foll. by *about, around*) spend time idly. **3** a thing perceived as fun or a soft option, requiring little effort. [18th-century coinage]

dosser *n. Brit. slang* **1** a person who dosses. **2** = DOSS-HOUSE.

doss-house *n. Brit.* a cheap lodging house, esp. for vagrants.

dossier *n.* a set of documents, esp. about a person, event, or subject. [based on French *dos*, so called from the label on the back]

dot ● *n.* **1 a** a small spot, speck, or mark. **b** such a mark as part of an *i* or *j*, as a full stop, etc. **c** a decimal point. **2** the shorter signal of the two used in Morse code (cf. DASH n. 6). ● *v.tr.* (**dotted**, **dotting**) **1 a** mark with a dot or dots. **b** place a dot over (a letter). **2** (often foll. by *about*) scatter like dots. **3** partly cover as with dots (*a sea dotted with ships*). □ **dot the i's and cross the t's** *colloq.* **1** minutely accurate, emphasize details. **2** add the final touches to a task. **on the dot** exactly on time. **the year dot** *Brit. colloq.* a time far in the past. [Old English *dott* 'head of a boil']

dotage *n.* feeble-minded senility (*in his dotage*). [based on French *radoter* 'to ramble on']

DORMOUSE: COMMON DORMOUSE (*Muscardinus avellanarius*)

dotard *n.* a person who is feeble-minded, esp. from senility. [related to DOTE]

dote *v.intr.* (foll. by *on, upon*) be foolishly or excessively fond of. [Middle English, corresponding to Middle Dutch *doten* 'to be silly']

dot matrix printer *n.* ▲ a printer with characters formed from dots printed by configurations of the tips of small pins or wires.

dotted line *n.* a line of dots on a document.

dotterel *n.* a small migratory plover, *Eudromias morinellus*. [based on DOTE, named from the ease with which it is caught, taken to indicate stupidity]

dottle *n.* a remnant of unburnt tobacco in a pipe.

dotty *adj.* (**dottier**, **dottiest**) esp. *Brit. colloq.* **1** feeble-minded, silly. **2** eccentric. **3** absurd. **4** (foll. by *about, on*) infatuated with; obsessed by. [19th-century coinage] □ **dottily** *adv.* **dottiness** *n.*

double ● *adj.* **1 a** consisting of two parts or things. **b** consisting of two identical parts. **2** twice as much or many (*double the amount*; *double the number*; *double thickness*). **3** having twice the usual size, quantity, strength, etc. (*double whisky*). **4** designed for two people (*double bed*). **5 a** having some part double. **b** (of a flower) having more than one circle of petals. **c** (of a domino) having the same number of pips on each half. **6** having two different roles or interpretations, esp. implying confusion or deceit (*double meaning*; *leads a double life*). ● *adv.* **1** at or to twice the amount etc. (*counts double*). **2** two together (*sleep double*). ● *n.* **1 a** a double quantity or thing; twice as much or many. **b** *colloq.* a double measure of spirits. **2 a** a person who looks exactly like another. **b** an understudy. **3** (in *pl.*) *Sport* (in tennis, badminton, etc.) a game between two pairs of players. **4** *Sport* a pair of victories over the same team, a pair of championships at the same game, etc. **5** a system of betting in which the winnings and stake from the first bet are transferred to a second. **6** *Bridge* the doubling of an opponent's bid. **7** *Darts*

DORIC

The Doric order, which dates from the 7th century BC, is the oldest of the three main ancient Greek architectural orders. Doric temples have fluted columns with plain capitals and no bases. The friezes are decorated with carved panels called metopes, which are separated by plainer panels called triglyphs.

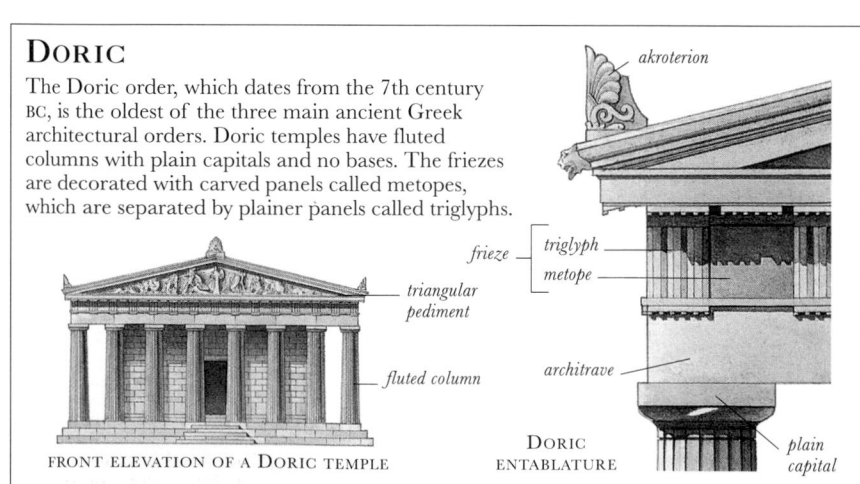

akroterion

triglyph

metope

frieze

triangular pediment

architrave

fluted column

FRONT ELEVATION OF A DORIC TEMPLE

DORIC ENTABLATURE

plain capital

DOT MATRIX PRINTER

A dot matrix printer is a computer printer that uses an arrangement of pins or wires from a matrix to form printed characters. A signal from an electromagnet causes the hammer to hit a pin. The pin strikes an inked-up ribbon making a dot on the paper. The pins are activated in different combinations so that each character is made up of several vertical dot patterns.

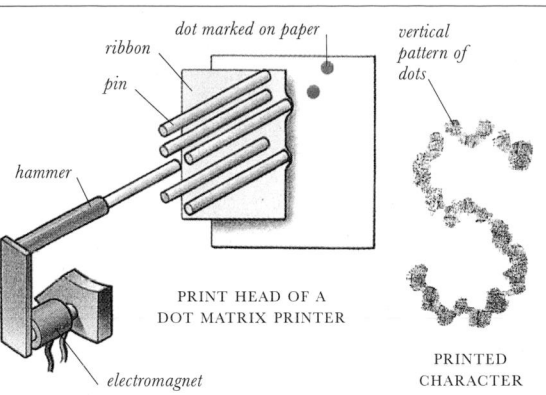

dot marked on paper
ribbon
pin
hammer
vertical pattern of dots
PRINT HEAD OF A DOT MATRIX PRINTER
electromagnet
PRINTED CHARACTER

D

---

a hit on the narrow ring enclosed by the two outer circles of a dartboard. ● *v.* **1** *tr. & intr.* make or become twice as much or many; increase twofold; multiply by two. **2** *tr.* amount to twice as much as. **3 a** *tr.* fold or bend (paper, cloth, etc.) over on itself. **b** *intr.* become folded. **4 a** *tr.* (of an actor) play (two parts) in the same piece. **b** *intr.* be understudy etc. **5** *intr.* (usu. foll. by *as*) play a twofold role. **6** *intr.* turn sharply in flight or pursuit. **7** *tr. Naut.* sail round (a headland). **8** *tr. Bridge* make a call increasing the value of the points to be won or lost on (an opponent's bid). **9** *intr. Mus.* play two or more musical instruments (*the clarinettist doubles on tenor sax*). □ **at** (or *US* **on**) **the double** running, hurrying. **bent double** folded, stooping. **double back** take a new direction opposite to the previous one. **double or nothing** (or *Brit.* **quits**) a gamble to decide whether a player's loss or debt be doubled or cancelled. **double up 1 a** bend or curl up. **b** cause to do this. **2** be overcome with pain or laughter. **3** share or assign to a room, quarters, etc., with another or others. **4** fold or become folded. **5** use winnings from a bet as stake for another. [from Latin *duplus*] □ **doubler** *n.* **doubly** *adv.*

double act *n.* an act involving two people.

double agent *n.* an agent who purports to spy for one country while working for another.

double-barrelled *adj.* **1** (of a gun) having two barrels. ▷ SHOTGUN. **2** *Brit.* (of a surname) having two parts joined by a hyphen. **3** twofold.

double bass *n.* ▼ the largest and lowest-pitched instrument of the violin family. ▷ ORCHESTRA, STRINGED

scroll
fingerboard
shoulder
bridge
soundhole
soundboard
tailpiece
DOUBLE BASS

double bill *n.* a programme with two principal items.

double bind *n.* a dilemma.

double-blind *adj.* (of a test or experiment) in which neither the tester nor the subject has knowledge of identities etc. that might lead to bias.

double bluff *n.* an action or statement intended to appear as a bluff, but in fact genuine.

double boiler *n.* a saucepan with a detachable upper compartment heated by boiling water in the lower one.

double bond *n.* a pair of bonds between two atoms in a molecule.

double-breasted *adj.* (of a coat etc.) having two fronts overlapping across the body.

double-check *v.tr.* verify twice.

double chin *n.* a chin with a fold of loose flesh below it.

double cream *n. Brit.* thick cream with a high fat content.

double-cross ● *v.tr.* deceive or betray (a person one is supposedly helping). ● *n.* an act of doing this. □ **double-crosser** *n.*

double-dealing ● *n.* deceit. ● *adj.* practising deceit. □ **double-dealer** *n.*

double-decker *n.* **1** a bus having an upper and lower deck. **2** *colloq.* anything consisting of two layers.

double Dutch *n. Brit. colloq.* incomprehensible talk.

double-edged *adj.* **1** having two functions or (often contradictory) applications. **2** (of a knife etc.) having two cutting edges.

double entendre /doobl ahn-**tahndr**/ *n.* **1** a word or phrase open to two interpretations, one usu. risqué or indecent. **2** humour using such words or phrases. [obsolete French, literally 'double understanding']

double entry *n.* a system of bookkeeping in which each transaction is entered as a debit in one account and a credit in another.

double exposure *n.* the accidental or deliberate repeated exposure of a plate, film, etc.

double fault *Tennis* ● *n.* two consecutive faults in serving. ● *v.intr.* (**double-fault**) serve a double fault.

double feature *n.* a cinema programme with two full-length films.

double figures *n.pl.* the numbers from 10 to 99.

double first *n. Brit.* **1** first-class honours in two subjects or examinations at a university. **2** a person achieving this.

double-fronted *adj.* (of a house) with principal windows on either side of the front door.

double glazing *n.* **1** glazing consisting of two layers of glass with a space between them, designed to reduce loss of heat and exclude noise. **2** the provision of this. □ **double-glazed** *adj.*

double Gloucester *n.* a kind of hard cheese originally made in Gloucestershire. ▷ CHEESE

double-headed *adj.* **1** having a double head or two heads. **2** (of a train) pulled by two locomotives.

double helix *n.* a pair of parallel helices with a common axis, esp. in the structure of the DNA molecule. ▷ DNA

double-jointed *adj.* having joints that allow unusual bending of the fingers, limbs, etc.p

double knitting *n.* a grade of yarn that is double the usual thickness.

double-lock *v.tr.* lock by a double turn of the key.

double negative *n.* a negative statement containing two negative elements (e.g. *didn't say nothing*).

■ **Usage** The use of the double negative as exemplified above is considered ungrammatical in standard English. However, two negatives are acceptable in instances such as *a not ungenerous sum* (meaning 'quite a generous sum').

double-park *v.tr. & intr.* park (a vehicle) alongside one that is already parked at the roadside.

double play *n. Baseball* putting out two runners.

double pneumonia *n.* pneumonia affecting both lungs.

double quick *adj. & adv.* very quick or quickly.

double saucepan *n. Brit.* = DOUBLE BOILER.

doublespeak *n.* language or talk that is ambiguous or obscure.

double standard *n.* a rule or principle applied more strictly to some people than to others.

double-stopping *n. Mus.* the sounding of two strings at once on a violin etc. □ **double stop** *n.*

doublet *n.* **1** either of a pair of similar things. **2** *hist.* a man's short close-fitting jacket. [from French, literally 'something folded']

double take *n.* a delayed reaction to a situation etc. immediately after one's first reaction.

double-talk *n.* = DOUBLESPEAK.

doublethink *n.* the capacity to accept contrary opinions at the same time. [coined by George Orwell in *Nineteen Eighty-Four* (1949)]

double time *n.* **1** payment of an employee at twice the normal rate. **2** *Mil.* the regulation running pace.

double whammy *n. colloq.* a twofold blow or setback.

doubloon *n.* **1** *hist.* ◀ a Spanish gold coin. **2** (in *pl.*) *slang* money. [from Spanish *doblón*]

DOUBLOONS

doubt ● *n.* **1** a feeling of uncertainty; an undecided state of mind (*be in no doubt about*; *have no doubt that*). **2** an inclination to disbelieve. **3** an uncertain state of things. **4** a lack of full proof or clear indication (*benefit of the doubt*). ● *v.* **1** *tr.* feel uncertain or undecided about (*I doubt that you are right*; *I do not doubt but that you are wrong*). **2** *tr.* hesitate to believe. **3** *intr.* feel uncertain or undecided; have doubts (*never doubted of success*). **4** *tr.* call in question. □ **in doubt** open to question. **no doubt** certainly; probably; admittedly. **without doubt** (or **a doubt**) certainly. [from Latin *dubitare* 'to hesitate'] □ **doubter** *n.*

doubtful *adj.* **1** feeling doubt. **2** causing doubt. **3** unreliable (*a doubtful ally*). □ **doubtfully** *adv.*

doubting Thomas *n.* an incredulous or sceptical person (after John 20:24-29).

doubtless *adv.* **1** certainly; no doubt. **2** probably. □ **doubtlessly** *adv.*

douche /doosh/ ● *n.* **1** a jet of liquid applied to part of the body for cleansing or medicinal purposes. **2** a device for producing such a jet. ● *v.* **1** *tr.* treat with a douche. **2** *intr.* use a douche. [French, based on Italian *doccia* 'pipe']

dough *n.* **1** a thick mixture of flour etc. and liquid, for baking into bread, pastry, etc. **2** *slang* money. [Old English]

doughnut *n.* (*US* **donut**) a small fried cake of sweetened dough.

doughty /dow-ti/ *adj.* (**doughtier**, **doughtiest**) *archaic* or *joc.* valiant. [Old English]

doughy *adj.* (**doughier**, **doughiest**) having the form or consistency of dough. □ **doughiness** *n.*

D

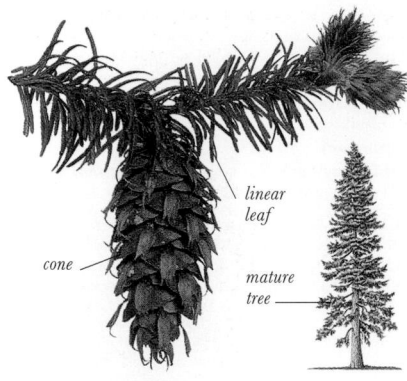

DOUGLAS FIR (*Pseudotsuga menziesii*)

linear leaf

cone

mature tree

Douglas fir *n.* (also **Douglas pine** or **Douglas spruce**) ▲ any large conifer of the genus *Pseudotsuga*, of western N. America. [named after D. Douglas, Scots botanist, 1798–1834]

dour /rhymes with poor/ *adj.* severe, stern, obstinate. [Middle English (originally Scots)] □ **dourly** *adv.*

douse /dowss/ *v.tr.* (also **dowse**) **1 a** throw water over. **b** plunge into water. **2** extinguish (a light). [16th-century coinage]

dove[1] *n.* **1** any bird of the family Columbidae, with short legs, small head, and large breast. **2** a gentle or innocent person. **3** *Polit.* an advocate of peace or peaceful policies. **4** a soft grey colour. [from Old Norse *dúfa*]

dove[2] *US past* and *past part.* of DIVE.

dovecote *n.* (also **dovecot**) a shelter with nesting-holes for domesticated pigeons.

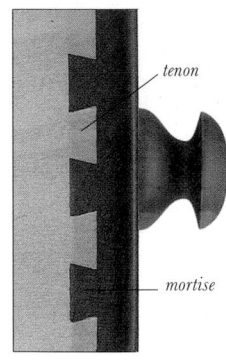

tenon

mortise

DOVETAIL JOINTS IN A DRAWER SIDE

dovetail ● *n.* **1** ◄ a joint formed by a mortise with a tenon shaped like a dove's spread tail. **2** such a tenon. ● *v.* **1** *tr.* join together by means of a dovetail. **2** *tr. & intr.* fit readily together; combine neatly or compactly.

dowager *n.* **1** a widow with a title or property derived from her late husband (*Queen dowager; dowager duchess*). **2** *colloq.* a dignified elderly woman. [from Old French *douag(i)ere*]

dowdy *adj.* (**dowdier, dowdiest**) **1** (of clothes) unattractively dull. **2** dressed in dowdy clothes. [from Middle English *dowd* 'slut'] □ **dowdily** *adv.* **dowdiness** *n.*

dowel ● *n.* a headless peg for holding together components of a structure. ● *v.tr.* (**dowelled, dowelling**; *US* **doweled, doweling**) fasten with a dowel. [from Middle Low German *dovel*]

dowelling *n.* (*US* **doweling**) rods for cutting into dowels.

dower *n.* **1** a widow's share for life of her husband's estate. **2** *archaic* a dowry. **3** a natural gift or talent. [based on Latin *dotare* 'to endow']

dower house *n. Brit.* a smaller house near a big one, forming part of a widow's dower.

Dow–Jones index *n.* (also **Dow–Jones average**) a figure indicating the relative price of shares on the New York Stock Exchange. [named after C. H. Dow, 1851–1902, & E. D. Jones, 1856–1920, American economists]

down[1] ● *adv.* **1** into or towards a lower place (*fall down; knelt down*). **2** in a lower place or position

(*blinds were down*). **3** to or in a place regarded as lower, esp.: **a** southwards. **b** *Brit.* away from a major city or a university. **4 a** in or into a low or weaker position, mood, or condition (*hit a man when he's down; many down with colds*). **b** in a position of lagging behind or losing (*our team was three goals down; £5 down on the transaction*). **c** (of a computer system) out of action. **5** from an earlier to a later time (*customs handed down; down to 1600*). **6** to a finer or thinner consistency or a smaller amount or size (*grind down; water down; boil down*). **7** cheaper (*bread is down; shares are down*). **8** into a more settled state (*calm down*). **9** in writing; in or into recorded or listed form (*copy it down; I got it down on tape; you are down to speak next*). **10** (of part of a larger whole) paid, dealt with (*£5 down, £20 to pay; three down, six to go*). **11** *Naut.* with the current or wind. **12** inclusively of the lower limit in a series (*read down to the third paragraph*). **13** (as *int.*) lie down, put (something) down, etc. **14** downstairs, esp. after rising (*is not down yet*). **15** swallowed (*could not get the pill down*). **16** *Amer. Football* (of the ball) out of play. ● *prep.* **1** downwards along, through, or into. **2** from top to bottom of. **3** along (*walk down the road; cut down the middle*). **4** at or in a lower part of (*situated down the river*). ● *adj.* **1** directed downwards. **2** *Brit.* of travel away from a capital or centre (*the down train; the down platform*). ● *v.tr. colloq.* **1** knock or bring down. **2** swallow. ● *n.* **1 a** *Sport* an act of putting down. **b** *Amer. Football* any of a series of chances to advance the ball for a score. **2** a reverse of fortune (*ups and downs*). **3** *colloq.* a period of depression. □ **be** (or **have a**) **down on** *colloq.* disapprove of; show animosity towards. **be down to 1** be attributable to. **2** be the responsibility of. **3** have used up everything except (*down to their last tin of rations*). **down on one's luck** *colloq.* **1** temporarily unfortunate. **2** dispirited by misfortune. **down to the ground** *colloq.* completely. **down tools** *Brit. colloq.* cease work, esp. to go on strike. **down with** *int.* expressing rejection of a specified person or thing. [Old English]

down[2] *n.* **1 a** the first covering of young birds. **b** ► a bird's under-plumage. **c** a layer of fine soft feathers. **2** fine soft hair esp. on the face. **3** short soft hairs on some leaves, fruit, seeds, etc. **4** a fluffy substance, e.g. thistledown. [from Old Norse *dúnn*]

down[3] *n.* **1** an area of open rolling land. **2** (in *pl.*; usu. prec. by *the*) undulating chalk and limestone uplands esp. in southern England. [Old English]

down and out ● *adj.* (hyphenated when *attrib.*) **1** penniless, destitute. **2** *Boxing* unable to resume the fight. ● *n.* (**down-and-out**) a destitute person.

down at heel *adj.* esp. *Brit.* **1** (of a shoe) with the heel worn down. **2** impoverished; shabby, slovenly.

downbeat ● *n. Mus.* an accented beat, usu. the first of the bar. ● *adj.* **1** pessimistic, gloomy. **2** relaxed.

downcast *adj.* **1** (of eyes) looking downwards. **2** dejected.

down draught *n.* a downward draught, esp. one down a chimney into a room.

downer *n. slang* **1** a depressant or tranquillizing drug. **2** a depressing person or experience; a failure. **3** = DOWNTURN.

downfall *n.* **1 a** a fall from prosperity or power. **b** the cause of this. **2** a sudden heavy fall of rain etc.

downgrade ● *v.tr.* **1** make lower in rank or status. **2** speak disparagingly of. ● *n.* esp. *US* an instance of downgrading or being downgraded (in sense 1 of *v.*). □ **on the downgrade** *US* in decline.

downhearted *adj.* dejected; in low spirits.

downhill ● *adv.* in a descending direction, esp. towards the bottom of an incline. ● *adj.* **1** sloping down, descending. **2** declining; deteriorating. ● *n.* **1** *Skiing* a downhill race with few turns. ▷ SKI. **2 a**

downward slope. **3** a decline. □ **go downhill** *colloq.* decline, deteriorate. □ **downhiller** *n. Skiing.*

down in the mouth *adj. colloq.* looking unhappy.

downland *n.* = DOWN[3].

downlink *n.* a telecommunications link for receiving signals from a satellite, spacecraft, or aircraft (also *attrib:* the *downlink wavelength*). ● *v.tr.* relay (such signals) to Earth.

download *Computing* ● *v.tr.* transfer (data) from one storage device or system to another. ● *n.* (often *attrib.*) a transfer of this type (*download utilities*).

downmarket *adj. & adv.* esp. *Brit. colloq.* towards or relating to the cheaper sector of the market.

down payment *n.* a partial payment made at the time of purchase.

downpipe *n. Brit.* a pipe to carry rainwater from a roof. ▷ HOUSE

downplay *v.tr.* play down; minimize the importance of.

downpour *n.* a heavy fall of rain.

downrate *v.tr.* make lower in value, standard, importance, etc.

downright ● *adj.* **1** plain, straightforward. **2** utter (*a downright lie; downright nonsense*). ● *adv.* thoroughly (*downright inconsiderate*).

downscale *US* ● *v.tr.* reduce or restrict in size, scale, or extent. ● *adj.* at the lower end of a scale; inferior.

downside *n.* **1** the negative aspect of something; a disadvantage or drawback. **2** a downward movement of share prices etc.

downsize *v.tr. & intr.* esp. *US* reduce in size.

downspout *n. US* = DOWNPIPE.

Down's syndrome *n. Med.* a congenital disorder due to a chromosome defect, characterized by diminished intelligence and physical abnormalities including short stature and a broad facial profile (cf. MONGOLISM). [named after J. L. H. *Down*, English physician, 1828–96]

downstage *adj. & adv.* at or to the front of the stage. ▷ THEATRE

downstairs ● *adv.* **1** down a flight of stairs. **2** to or on a lower floor. ● *adj.* (also **downstair**) situated downstairs. ● *n.* the lower floor.

downstream ● *adv.* in the direction of the flow of a stream etc. ● *adj.* moving downstream.

down time *n.* time during which a machine, esp. a computer, is out of action or unavailable for use.

down-to-earth *adj.* practical, realistic.

downtown esp. *N. Amer.* ● *adj.* of or in the more central or lower part of a town or city. ● *n.* a downtown area. ● *adv.* in or into a downtown area.

DOWN FEATHERS FROM A DUCK

down town *adv.* **1** into a town from a higher or outlying part. **2** esp. *N. Amer.* to or in the business part of a city (see also DOWNTOWN).

downtrodden *adj.* oppressed; badly treated.

downturn *n.* a decline, esp. in economic activity.

down under *adv. colloq.* in or to the antipodes, i.e. to Australia or New Zealand.

downward ● *adv.* (also **downwards**) towards what is lower, inferior, less important, or later. ● *adj.* moving, extending, pointing, or leading downward. □ **downwardly** *adv.*

downwind *adj. & adv.* in the direction in which the wind is blowing.

downy *adj.* (**downier, downiest**) **1 a** of, like, or covered with down. **b** soft and fluffy. **2** *Brit. slang* aware, knowing.

dowry *n.* (*pl.* **-ies**) property or money brought by a bride to her husband. [from Old French *douaire* 'dower']

dowse[1] /dowz/ *v.intr.* search for underground water or minerals by holding a stick or rod which dips abruptly when over the right spot. [17th-century coinage] □ **dowser** *n.*

dowse[2] var. of DOUSE.

dowsing rod *n.* a stick or rod used in dowsing.

doxology *n.* (*pl.* **-ies**) a liturgical formula of praise to God. [based on Greek *doxa* 'glory']

doyen *n.* (*fem.* **doyenne**) the most senior of a particular category or body of people. [French, related to DEAN[1]]

doyley var. of DOILY.

doz. *abbr.* dozen.

doze ● *v.intr.* sleep lightly; be half asleep. ● *n.* a short light sleep. □ **doze off** fall lightly asleep. [17th-century coinage]

dozen *n.* **1** (prec. by *a* or a number) (*pl.* **dozen**) twelve (*a dozen eggs; two dozen packets; ordered three dozen*). **2** a set or group of twelve (*packed in dozens*). **3** *colloq.* about twelve, a fairly large indefinite number. **4** (in *pl.*; usu. foll. by *of*) *colloq.* very many (*made dozens of mistakes*). □ **talk nineteen to the dozen** *Brit.* talk incessantly. [from Latin *duodecim* 'twelve']

dozy *adj.* (**dozier**, **doziest**) **1** drowsy; tending to doze. **2** *Brit. colloq.* stupid or lazy. □ **dozily** *adv.* **doziness** *n.*

D.Phil. *abbr.* Doctor of Philosophy.

DPP *abbr.* (in the UK) Director of Public Prosecutions.

Dr *abbr.* **1** Doctor. **2** Drive. **3** debtor; debit.

dr. *abbr.* **1** drachm(s). **2** drachma(s). **3** dram(s).

drab[1] ● *adj.* (**drabber**, **drabbest**) **1** dull, uninteresting. **2** of a dull brownish colour. ● *n.* **1** this colour. **2** monotony. □ **drably** *adv.* **drabness** *n.*

drab[2] see DRIBS AND DRABS.

drachm /dram/ *n.* a weight or measure formerly used by apothecaries, equivalent to 60 grains or one-eighth of an ounce, or (in full **fluid drachm**) 60 minims, one-eighth of a fluid ounce. [from Greek *drakhmē*, an Attic weight and coin]

drachma /ˈdrakmă/ *n.* (*pl.* **drachmas** or **drachmae** /-mee/) **1** the chief monetary unit of Greece. **2** a silver coin of ancient Greece. [from Greek *drakhmē*]

drack *adj. Austral. slang* **1** (esp. of a woman) unattractive. **2** dismal, dull. [20th-century coinage]

draconian *adj.* (also **draconic**) (esp. of laws) very harsh or severe. [from *Drakōn*, 7th-century BC Greek legislator]

draft ● *n.* **1 a** a preliminary written version of a speech, document, etc. **b** a rough preliminary outline of a scheme. **c** a sketch of work to be carried out. **2 a** a written order for payment of money by a bank. **b** the drawing of money by means of this. **3** (foll. by *on*) a demand made on a person's confidence, friendship, etc. **4 a** a party detached from a larger group for a special purpose. **b** the selection of this. **5** *US* compulsory military service. **6** a reinforcement. **7** *US* = DRAUGHT. ● *v.tr.* **1** prepare a draft of (a document, scheme, etc.). **2** select for a special purpose. **3** *US* conscript. [phonetic spelling of DRAUGHT] □ **draftee** *n.* **drafter** *n.*

draftsman *n.* (*pl.* **-men**) **1** a person who drafts documents. **2** = DRAUGHTSMAN 1.

drafty *US* var. of DRAUGHTY.

drag ● *v.* (**dragged**, **dragging**) **1** *tr.* pull along with effort. **2 a** *tr.* allow (one's feet, tail, etc.) to trail along the ground. **b** *intr.* trail along the ground. **c** *intr.* (of time etc.) go or pass slowly or tediously. **3 a** *intr.* (usu. foll. by *for*) use a grapnel or drag to find a drowned person or lost object. **b** *tr.* search the bottom of (a river etc.) with grapnels, nets, or drags. **4** *tr. colloq.* take (a person) to a place etc., esp. against his or her will. **5** *intr.* (foll. by *on*, *at*) *colloq.* draw on (a cigarette etc.). **6** *intr.* continue at tedious length. ● *n.* **1** an obstruction to progress. **2** *colloq.* a boring or dreary person, duty, performance, etc. **3 a** a lure drawn before hounds as a substitute for a fox. **b** a hunt using this. **4** an apparatus for dredging or recovering drowned persons etc. from under water. **5** = DRAGNET 1. **6** *slang* a draw on a cigarette etc. **7** *slang* **a** women's clothes worn by men. **b** a party at which these are worn. **c** clothes in general. **8** an act of dragging. **9 a** *Brit. slang* a motor car. **b** (in full **drag race**) an acceleration race between cars. **10** *slang* a street or road (*the main drag*). □ **drag one's feet** (or **heels**) be deliberately slow or reluctant to act. **drag in** introduce (a subject) irrelevantly. **drag out** protract. **drag up** *colloq.* **1** deliberately mention (an unwelcome subject). **2** *Brit.* rear (a child) without proper training. [Old English]

draggle ● *v.* **1** *tr.* make dirty or wet or limp by trailing. **2** *intr.* hang trailing. **3** *intr.* lag; straggle in the rear.

draggy *adj.* (**draggier**, **draggiest**) *colloq.* **1** tedious. **2** unpleasant.

dragnet *n.* **1** a net drawn through a river or across ground to trap fish or game. **2** a systematic hunt for criminals etc.

dragoman *n.* (*pl.* **dragomans** or **dragomen**) an interpreter or guide. [from Semitic *targumānu*]

dragon *n.* **1** a mythical monster like a reptile, usu. with wings and able to breathe out fire. **2** a fierce woman. [from Greek *drakōn* 'serpent']

dragonfly *n.* (*pl.* **-flies**) ▼ any of various predatory insects of the order Odonata, having a long slender body with two pairs of large transparent wings.

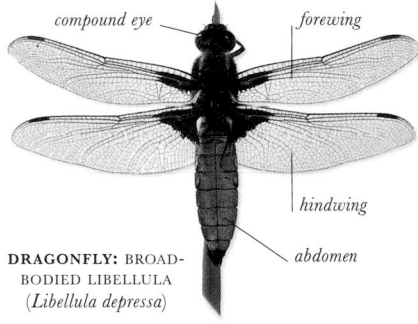

compound eye   forewing

hindwing

abdomen

DRAGONFLY: BROAD-BODIED LIBELLULA (*Libellula depressa*)

dragoon ● *n.* **1** a cavalryman. **2** a rough fierce man. **3** a variety of pigeon. ● *v.tr.* (foll. by *into*) coerce into doing something. [originally in sense 'carbine' (thought of as breathing fire) from French *dragon* 'dragon']

drag queen *n. slang* a male homosexual transvestite.

drag race see DRAG *n.* 9b.

dragster *n.* ▼ a car built or modified to take part in drag races.

drain ● *v.* **1** *tr.* draw off liquid from, esp.: **a** make (land etc.) dry by providing an outflow for moisture. **b** (of a river) carry off the superfluous water of (a district). **c** remove purulent matter from (an abscess). **2** *tr.* (foll. by *off*, *away*) draw off (liquid). **3** *intr.* (foll. by *away*, *off*, *through*) flow or trickle away. **4** *intr.* become dry as liquid flows away (*put it there to drain*). **5** *tr.* exhaust or deprive (a person or thing) of strength, resources, etc. **6** *tr.* **a** empty (liquid) to the dregs. **b** empty (a container) by drinking the contents. ● *n.* **1 a** a channel, conduit, or pipe carrying off liquid, esp. an artificial conduit for water or sewage. **b** a tube for drawing off the discharge from an abscess etc. **2** a constant outflow, withdrawal, or expenditure (*a great drain on my resources*). □ **down the drain** *colloq.* lost, wasted. **laugh like a drain** *Brit.* laugh copiously; guffaw. [Old English]

drainage *n.* **1** the process or means of draining (*the land has poor drainage*). **2** a system of drains. **3** what is drained off.

drainboard *n. N. Amer.* = DRAINING BOARD.

draincock *n.* a cock for draining the water out of a boiler etc.

drainer *n.* **1** a device for draining; anything on which things are put to drain. **2** a person who drains.

draining board *n.* a sloping surface beside a sink, on which washed dishes etc. are left to drain.

drainpipe *n.* **1** a pipe for carrying off water, sewage, etc. from a building. ▷ HOUSE. **2** (*attrib.*) (of trousers etc.) very narrow. **3** (in *pl.*) very narrow trousers.

drake *n.* a male duck. ▷ DUCK. [Middle English]

dram *n.* **1** a small drink of spirits. **2** = DRACHM. [from medieval Latin *drama*]

drama *n.* **1** a play for acting on stage or for broadcasting. **2 a** the art of writing and presenting plays. **b** the art of acting. **3** an exciting or emotional event, set of circumstances, etc. **4** dramatic quality (*the drama of the situation*). [from Greek]

dramatic *adj.* **1** of drama. **2** sudden and exciting or unexpected. **3** vividly striking. **4** (of a gesture etc.) theatrical, overdone, absurd. □ **dramatically** *adv.*

dramatic irony *n.* = TRAGIC IRONY.

dramatics *n.pl.* (often treated as *sing.*) **1** the production and performance of plays. **2** exaggerated or showy behaviour.

dramatis personae *n.pl.* (often treated as *sing.*) **1** the characters in a play. **2** a list of these. [Latin, literally 'persons of the drama']

DRAGSTER

A dragster is a high-powered, single-seat car that is raced on a straight quarter-mile (400 m) track. There are several classes of design, engine, and fuel. The fastest, known as 'top-fuellers', run on rocket fuel, and can complete the course in less than five seconds.

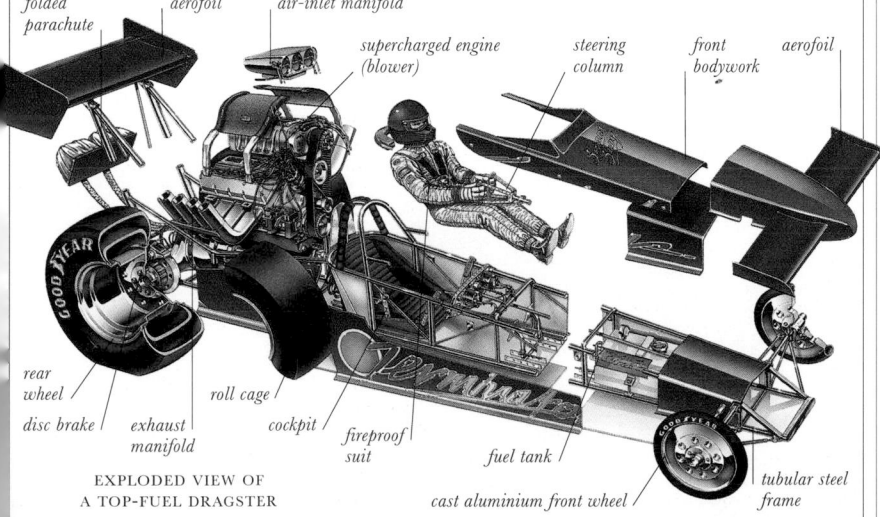

folded parachute   aerofoil   air-inlet manifold   supercharged engine (blower)   steering column   front bodywork   aerofoil

rear wheel   disc brake   exhaust manifold   roll cage   cockpit   fireproof suit   fuel tank   cast aluminium front wheel   tubular steel frame

EXPLODED VIEW OF A TOP-FUEL DRAGSTER

D

D

dramatist *n.* a writer of dramas.

dramatize *v.* (also **-ise**) **1 a** *tr.* adapt (a novel etc.) to form a play. **b** *intr.* admit of such adaptation. **2** *tr.* make a dramatic scene of. **3** *tr.* (also *absol.*) express or react to in a dramatic way. □ **dramatization** *n.*

drank *past* of DRINK.

drape ● *v.tr.* **1** hang, cover loosely, or adorn with cloth etc. **2** arrange (clothes or hangings) in folds. ● *n.* **1** (often in *pl.*) a curtain or drapery. **2** a piece of drapery. [from Late Latin *drappus* 'cloth']

draper *n. Brit.* a retailer of textile fabrics.

drapery *n.* (*pl.* **-ies**) **1** clothing or hangings arranged in folds. **2** (often in *pl.*) a curtain or hanging. **3** *Brit.* cloth; textile fabrics. **4** *Brit.* the trade of a draper.

drastic *adj.* having a far-reaching effect; severe. [from Greek *drastikos*] □ **drastically** *adv.*

drat *colloq.* ● *v.tr.* (**dratted, dratting**) (usu. as an exclamation) curse, confound (*drat the thing!*). ● *int.* expressing anger or annoyance. [from *God* (as '*od*) *rot*] □ **dratted** *adj.*

draught (*US* **draft**) ● *n.* **1** a current of air in a confined space. **2** pulling, traction. **3** *Naut.* the depth of water needed to float a ship. **4** the drawing of liquor from a cask etc. **5 a** a single act of drinking. **b** the amount drunk in this. **c** a dose of liquid medicine. **6** (in *pl.*; usu. treated as *sing.*) *Brit.* a game for two played with twelve pieces each on a draughtboard. ● *v.tr.* = DRAFT. □ **feel the draught** *colloq.* suffer from adverse conditions. [from Old Norse *drahtr*]

draught beer *n.* beer drawn from a cask.

draughtboard *n. Brit.* a chequered board, identical to a chessboard, used in draughts.

draught horse *n.* ▼ a horse used for pulling heavy loads. ▷ HORSE

DRAUGHT HORSE:
SHIRE-HORSES
PULLING A PLOUGH

draught-proof ● *adj.* proof against draughts. ● *v.tr.* make draught-proof.

draughtsman *n.* (*pl.* **-men**) **1** a person who makes drawings, plans, or sketches. **2** a piece in draughts. **3** = DRAFTSMAN 1. □ **draughtsmanship** *n.*

draughty *adj.* (*US* **drafty**) (**-ier, -iest**) (of a room etc.) letting in sharp currents of air.

draw ● *v.* (*past* **drew**; *past part.* **drawn**) **1** *tr.* pull or cause to move towards or after one. **2** *tr.* pull (a thing) up, over, or across. **3** *tr.* pull (curtains etc.) open or shut. **4** *tr.* take (a person) aside. **5** *tr.* attract; bring; take in (*drew a deep breath; I felt drawn to her; drew my attention to the matter*). **6** *intr.* (foll. by *at, on*) suck smoke from (a cigarette, pipe, etc.). **7** *tr.* (also *absol.*) take out; remove (a tooth, a gun from a holster, etc.). **8** *tr.* obtain or take from a source (*draw a salary; draw inspiration; drew £100 from my account*). **9** *tr.* trace (a line, mark, furrow, or figure). **10 a** *tr.* produce (a picture) by tracing lines and marks. **b** *tr.* represent (a thing) by this means. **c** *absol.* make a drawing. **11** *tr.* (also *absol.*) finish (a contest or game) with neither side winning. **12** *intr.* proceed, move, come (*drew near the bridge; draw to a close*). **13** *tr.* infer (a conclusion). **14** *tr.* **a** elicit, evoke (*draw criticism;*

draw ruin upon oneself). **b** bring about, entail. **c** induce (a person) to reveal facts, feelings, or talent (*refused to be drawn*). **d** (foll. by *to* + infin.) induce (a person) to do something. **e** *Cards* cause to be played (*drew all the trumps*). **15** *tr.* haul up (water) from a well. **16** *tr.* bring out (liquid from a container or blood from a wound). **17** *tr.* extract a liquid essence from. **18** *tr.* (of a chimney or pipe) promote or allow a draught. **19** *intr.* (of tea) infuse. **20 a** *tr.* obtain by lot (*drew the winner*). **b** *absol.* draw lots. **21** *intr.* (foll. by *on*) make a demand on a person, a person's skill, memory, imagination, etc. **22** *tr.* write out (a bill, cheque, or draft) (*drew a cheque on the bank*). **23** *tr.* frame (a document) in due form, compose. **24** *tr.* formulate or perceive (a comparison or distinction). **25** *tr.* (of a ship) require (a specified depth of water) to float in. **26** *tr.* disembowel (*hang, draw, and quarter*). **27** *tr. Hunting* search (cover) for game. **28** *tr.* drag (a badger or fox) from a hole. **29** *tr.* a protract, stretch, elongate (*long-drawn agony*). **b** make (wire) by pulling a piece of metal through successively smaller holes. ● *n.* **1** an act of drawing. **2 a** a person or thing that draws custom, attention, etc. **b** the power to attract attention. **3** the drawing of lots. **4** a drawn game. **5** a suck on a cigarette etc. **6** the act of removing a gun from its holster in order to shoot (*quick on the draw*). **7** strain, pull. □ **draw back** withdraw from an undertaking. **draw a blank** see BLANK. **draw a person's fire** attract hostility, criticism, etc., away from a more important target. **draw in 1 a** (of successive days) become shorter. **b** (of a day) approach its end. **c** (of successive evenings or nights) start earlier. **2** persuade to join. **3** (of a train etc.) arrive at a station. **draw in one's horns** become less assertive or ambitious. **draw the line at** set a limit of tolerance etc. at. **draw lots** see LOT. **draw off** withdraw (troops). **draw on 1** approach, come near. **2** lead to, bring about. **3** allure. **4** put (gloves, boots, etc.) on. **draw out 1** prolong. **2** elicit. **3** induce to talk. **4** (of successive days) become longer. **5** (of a train etc.) leave a station etc. **6** write out in proper form. **7** lead out, detach, or array (troops). **draw up 1** draft (a document etc.). **2** bring or come into regular order. **3** come to a halt. **4** make (oneself) erect. **5** (foll. by *with, to*) gain on or overtake. **quick on the draw** quick to act or react. [Old English]

drawback *n.* a disadvantage.

drawbridge *n.* a bridge hinged at one end so that it may be raised. ▷ CASTLE

drawcord *n.* a cord on clothing etc. that can be drawn up tight.

drawer *n.* **1** a person or thing that draws, esp. a person who draws a cheque etc. **2** a boxlike storage compartment without a lid, sliding in and out of a frame, table, etc. (*chest of drawers*). **3** (in *pl.*) *archaic* or *joc.* knickers or underpants. □ **drawerful** *n.* (*pl.* **-fuls**).

drawing *n.* **1 a** the art of representing by line. **b** delineation without colour or with a single colour. **c** the art of representing with pencils, pens, crayons, etc., rather than paint. **2** ▶ a picture produced in this way.

drawing board *n.* a board for spreading drawing paper on. □ **back to the drawing board** back to begin afresh (after the failure of an enterprise).

drawing pin *n. Brit.* a flat-headed pin for fastening paper etc. to a surface.

drawing room *n.* **1** a room for comfortable sitting or entertaining in. **2** *US* a private compartment in a train. [earlier *withdrawing-room*, to which women withdrew after dinner]

DRAWING OF QUEEN JANE
SEYMOUR (1536) BY HANS
HOLBEIN THE YOUNGER

drawl ● *v.* **1** *intr.* speak with drawn-out vowel sounds. **2** *tr.* utter in this way. ● *n.* a drawling utterance or way of speaking. [16th-century coinage]

drawn *past part.* of DRAW. ● *adj.* looking strained from fear, anxiety, or pain.

drawn-out *adj.* = LONG-DRAWN.

drawstring *n.* a string that can be pulled to tighten the mouth of a bag, the waist of a garment, etc.

dray[1] *n.* **1** a low cart without sides for heavy loads. **2** *Austral.* & *NZ* a two-wheeled cart. [Old English]

dray[2] var. of DREY.

dray horse *n.* a large, powerful horse.

dread ● *v.tr.* **1** (foll. by *that*, or *to* + infin.) fear greatly. **2** shrink from; look forward to with great apprehension. **3** be in great fear of. ● *n.* **1** great fear, apprehension, awe. **2** an object of fear or awe. ● *adj.* **1** dreaded. **2** *archaic* awe-inspiring, revered. [Old English]

dreadful *adj.* **1** terrible; inspiring fear or awe. **2** *colloq.* troublesome, disagreeable; very bad. □ **dreadfully** *adv.* **dreadfulness** *n.*

dreadlocks *n.pl.* a Rastafarian hairstyle in which the hair is twisted into tight braids or ringlets hanging down on all sides. □ **dreadlocked** *adj.*

dream ● *n.* **1 a** a series of pictures or events in the mind of a sleeping person. **b** the act or time of seeing this. **2** a daydream or fantasy. **3** an ideal, aspiration, or ambition. **4** a beautiful or ideal person or thing. **5** a state of mind without proper perception of reality (*goes about in a dream*). ● *v.* (*past* and *past part.* **dreamed** or **dreamt** /dremt/) **1** *intr.* experience a dream. **2** *tr.* imagine in or as if in a dream. **3** (usu. with *neg.*) **a** *intr.* (foll. by *of*) have any conception or intention of (*would not dream of upsetting them*). **b** *tr.* think of as a possibility (*never dreamt that he would come*). **4** *tr.* (foll. by *away*) spend (time) unprofitably. **5** *intr.* be inactive or unpractical. □ **dream up** imagine, invent. **like a dream** *colloq.* easily, effortlessly. [Old English *drēam* 'joy, music'] □ **dreamless** *adj.* **dreamlike** *adj.*

dreamboat *n. colloq.* **1** a very attractive or ideal person. **2** a very desirable or ideal thing.

dreamer *n.* **1** a person who dreams. **2** a romantic or unpractical person.

dreamland *n.* an ideal or imaginary land.

dream ticket *n.* an ideal pair of candidates standing together.

dream-world *n.* a state of mind distanced from reality.

dreamy *adj.* (**dreamier, dreamiest**) **1** given to daydreaming; fanciful; unpractical. **2** dreamlike; vague. **3** *colloq.* delightful. □ **dreamily** *adv.* **dreaminess** *n.*

drear *adj. poet.* = DREARY.

dreary *adj.* (**drearier, dreariest**) dismal, dull, gloomy. [Old English] □ **drearily** *adv.* **dreariness** *n.*

dredge[1] ● *v.* **1** *tr.* bring up as if with a dredge (*don't dredge all that up again*). **b** bring up or clear (mud etc.) from a river, harbour, etc. with a dredge. **2** *tr.* clean (a harbour, river, etc.) with a dredge. **3** *intr.* use a dredge. ● *n.* an apparatus used to scoop up objects or to clear mud etc. from a river or seabed. [form of 15th-century Scots *dreg*]

dredge[2] *v.tr.* **1** sprinkle with flour, sugar, etc. **2** (foll. by *over*) sprinkle (flour, sugar, etc.). [earlier in sense 'sweetmeat': from Old French *dragie, dragee*]

dredger[1] *n.* **1** a dredge. **2** a boat containing this.

dredger[2] *n.* a container with a perforated lid used for sprinkling flour, sugar, etc.

dreg *n.* **1** (usu. in *pl.*) **a** a sediment; grounds, lees, etc. **b** a worthless part (*the dregs of humanity*). **2** a small remnant (*not a dreg*). □ **drain** (or **drink**) **to the dregs** consume leaving nothing (*drained life to the dregs*). [Middle English]

drench ● *v.tr.* **1 a** wet thoroughly. **b** saturate; soak (in liquid). **2** force (an animal) to take medicine. ● *n.* **1** a soaking; a downpour. **2** medicine administered to an animal. [Old English]

dress ● *v.* **1 a** *tr.* clothe; array (*dressed in rags*; *dressed her quickly*). **b** *intr.* wear clothes of a specified kind or in a specified way (*dresses well*). **2** *intr.* **a** put on clothes. **b** put on formal or evening clothes. **3** *tr.* decorate or adorn. **4** *tr. Med.* **a** treat (a wound) with ointment etc. **b** apply a dressing to (a wound). **5** *tr.* trim, comb, brush, or smooth (the hair). **6** *tr.* **a** clean and prepare (poultry, a crab, etc.) for cooking or eating. **b** add a dressing to (a salad etc.). **7** *tr.* apply manure etc. to. **8** *tr.* finish the surface of (fabric, building stone, etc.). ● *n.* **1** a woman's garment consisting of a bodice and skirt. **2** a whole outfit (*wore the dress of a highlander*). **3** formal or ceremonial attire (*evening dress*). **4** an external covering; the outward form (*birds in their winter dress*). □ **dress down** *colloq.* **1** reprimand or scold. **2** dress informally. **dress out** attire conspicuously. **dress up 1** dress (oneself or another) elaborately for a special occasion. **2** dress in fancy dress. **3** disguise (unwelcome facts) by embellishment. [from (Old) French *dresser* 'to prepare']

dressage /dress-ah*zh*/ *n.* the training of a horse in obedience and deportment. [French, literally 'training']

dress circle *n.* the first gallery in a theatre, in which evening dress was formerly required.

dresser[1] *n.* **1** a kitchen sideboard with shelves above for displaying plates etc. **2** *N. Amer.* a dressing table or chest of drawers. [based on (Old) French *dresser* 'to prepare']

dresser[2] *n.* **1** a person who assists actors to dress, takes care of costumes, etc. **2** *Brit. Med.* a surgeon's assistant in operations. **3** a person who dresses in a specified way (*a snappy dresser*).

dressing *n.* **1** in senses of DRESS *v.* **2 a** a sauce, esp. of oil, vinegar, etc., for salads (*French dressing*). **b** *N. Amer.* stuffing. **3** a bandage or ointment for a wound. **4** size or stiffening used to finish fabrics. **5** compost etc. spread over land (*a top dressing of peat*).

dressing down *n. colloq.* a scolding.

dressing gown *n.* a loose usu. belted robe worn over nightwear or while resting.

dressing room *n.* **1** a room for changing the clothes etc. in a theatre, sports ground, etc. **2** a small room attached to a bedroom, containing clothes.

dressing station *n.* a place for giving emergency treatment to wounded people.

dressing table *n.* a table with a mirror, drawers, etc., used while applying make-up etc.

dressmaker *n. Brit.* a person, esp. a woman, who makes clothes professionally. □ **dressmaking** *n.*

dress rehearsal *n.* the final rehearsal of a play etc., in costume.

dress shirt *n.* **1** a man's usu. starched white shirt worn with evening dress. **2** *US* any man's long-sleeved shirt, usu. worn with a tie.

dressy *adj.* (**dressier**, **dressiest**) (of clothes or a person) smart, elegant. □ **dressiness** *n.*

drew *past* of DRAW.

drey *n.* (also **dray**) ◀ a squirrel's nest. [17th-century coinage]

dribble ● *v.* **1** *intr.* allow saliva to flow from the mouth. **2** *intr. & tr.* flow or allow to flow in drops. **3** *tr.* (also *absol.*) *Sport* move (a ball) forward with light touches of the feet, a stick, etc., or by continuous bouncing. ● *n.* **1** the act or an instance of dribbling. **2** a small trickling stream. [originally in sense 'to keep dripping'] □ **dribbler** *n.* **dribbly** *adj.*

driblet *n.* **1 a** a small quantity. **b** a petty sum. **2** a thin stream; a dribble.

dribs and drabs *n.pl. colloq.* small scattered amounts. [based on DRIBBLE]

dried *past* and *past part.* of DRY.

drier[1] *compar.* of DRY.

drier[2] var. of DRYER.

driest *superl.* of DRY.

grey squirrel

inner lining

tree fork

DREY: CROSS-SECTION OF A GREY SQUIRREL'S DREY

drift ● *n.* **1 a** a slow movement or variation. **b** such movement caused by a slow current. **2** the intention, meaning, scope, etc. of what is said etc. (*didn't understand his drift*). **3** a large mass of snow etc. accumulated by the wind. **4** esp. *derog.* a state of inaction. **5** slow deviation of a ship, aircraft, etc. from its course. **6** a large mass of esp. flowering plants (*a drift of bluebells*). **7** *Geol.* material deposited by the wind, a current of water, etc. **8** *S.Afr.* a ford. ● *v.* **1** *intr.* be carried by or as if by a current of air or water. **2** *intr.* move passively, casually, or aimlessly (*drifted into teaching*). **3** *tr. & intr.* pile up or be piled by the wind into drifts. [from Middle High German *trift* 'movement of cattle'] □ **driftage** *n.*

drifter *n.* **1** an aimless or rootless person. **2** a boat used for drift-net fishing.

drift-net *n.* a large net allowed to drift with the tide. □ **drift-netter** *n.* **drift-netting** *n.*

driftwood *n.* wood floating on or washed ashore by water.

drill[1] ● *n.* **1 a** ▼ a steel tool or machine used for boring cylindrical holes, sinking wells, etc. ▷ OIL PLATFORM, PNEUMATIC. **b** a dentist's rotary tool for cutting away part of a tooth etc. **2 a** esp. *Mil.* instruction or training in military exercises. **b** methodical training, esp. by repetition. **c** routine procedure to be followed in an emergency (*fire drill*). **3** *colloq.* a recognized procedure (*I expect you know the drill*). ● *v.* **1** *tr.* (also *absol.*) **a** (of a person or a tool) make a hole with a drill through or into. **b** make (a hole) with a drill. **2** *tr. & intr.* esp. *Mil.* subject to or undergo discipline by drill. **3** *tr.* impart (knowledge etc.) by a strict method. [from Middle Dutch *drillen* 'to bore'] □ **driller** *n.*

drill[2] ● *n.* **1** ▼ a machine used for making furrows and sowing seed. **2** a small furrow for sowing seed in. **3** a ridge with such furrows on top. **4** a row of plants so sown. ● *v.tr.* **1** sow (seed) with a drill. **2** plant (the ground) in drills. [18th-century coinage]

handle

seed hopper

harness link to horse

blade

furrow blade

shaft

DRILL: MODEL OF AN EARLY 19TH-CENTURY SEED DRILL

drill[3] *n.* a W. African baboon, *Mandrillus leucophaeus*, related to the mandrill.

drill[4] *n.* a coarse twilled cotton or linen fabric. [based on Latin *trilix* 'three-threaded']

drilling rig *n.* a structure with equipment for drilling an oil well etc. ▷ OIL PLATFORM

drily *adv.* (also **dryly**) in a dry manner.

drink ● *v.* (*past* **drank**; *past part.* **drunk**) **1 a** *tr.* swallow (a liquid). **b** *tr.* swallow the liquid contents of (a container). **c** *intr.* swallow liquid, take draughts. **2** *intr.* take alcohol, esp. to excess. **3** *tr.* (of a plant, porous material, etc.) absorb (moisture). **4** *refl.* bring (oneself etc.) to a specified condition by drinking. **5** *tr.* (usu. foll. by *away*) spend (wages etc.) on drink. **6** *tr.* wish (a person's good health, luck, etc.) by drinking (*drank his health*). ● *n.* **1 a** a liquid for drinking. **b** a draught or specified amount of this. **2 a** alcoholic liquor. **b** a portion, glass, etc. of this. **c** excessive indulgence in alcohol. **3** (as **the drink**) *colloq.* the sea. □ **drink in** listen to closely or eagerly (*drank in his every word*). **drink to** toast; wish success to. **drink up** drink the whole of; empty. [Old English] □ **drinkable** *adj.*

DRILL

An electric power drill can bore a hole in most materials by rapidly rotating a sharp bit or by pounding a bit in and out using a hammer mechanism. The hand drill and brace and bit are used mainly for woodwork.

OTHER TYPES OF DRILL

jaw   pinion   side handle

bit   chuck   drive wheel   main handle   turning handle

HAND DRILL

bit   jaw   chuck   quill   ratchet   handle   head   crank

BRACE AND BIT

hammer mechanism actuator

exhaust vent

jaw

chuck

air inlet

on/off trigger

ELECTRIC POWER DRILL

chuck key holder

DRILL BIT

screw-shaped groove   shaft

drink-driving *n. Brit.* the act of driving a vehicle with an excess of alcohol in the blood. □ **drink-driver** *n.*

drinker *n.* **1** a person who drinks (something). **2** a person who drinks alcohol, esp. to excess.

drip ● *v.* (**dripped**, **dripping**) **1** *intr. & tr.* fall or let fall in drops. **2** *intr.* (often foll. by *with*) be so wet as to shed drops. ● *n.* **1 a** the act or an instance of dripping (*the steady drip of rain*). **b** a drop of liquid (*a drip of paint*). **c** a sound of dripping. **2** *colloq.* a stupid, dull, or ineffective person. **3** *Med.* = DRIP-FEED *n.* □ **dripping wet** very wet. [from Middle Danish *drippe*]

drip-dry ● *v.* (**-dries**, **-dried**) **1** *intr.* (of fabric etc.) dry crease-free when hung up to drip. **2** *tr.* leave (a garment etc.) hanging up to dry. ● *adj.* able to be drip-dried.

drip-feed ● *v.tr.* feed intravenously in drops. ● *n.* **1** the continuous intravenous introduction of fluid into the body. **2** the fluid so introduced. **3** the apparatus used to do this.

drip-moulding *n.* a stone or other projection that deflects rain etc. from walls.

dripping *n.* **1** fat melted from roasted meat and used esp. for cooking. **2** (in *pl.*) water, grease, etc., dripping from anything.

drippy *adj.* (**drippier**, **drippiest**) **1** tending to drip. **2** *colloq.* ineffectual; sloppily sentimental. □ **drippily** *adv.* **drippiness** *n.*

dripstone *n.* **1** = DRIP-MOULDING. **2** a stone formation made by dripping water, e.g. a stalactite. ▷ CAVE

drive ● *v.* (*past* **drove**; *past part.* **driven**) **1** *tr.* (usu. foll. by *away*, *back*, *in*, *out*, *to*, etc.) urge in some direction, esp. forcibly. **2** *tr.* **a** (usu. foll. by *to* + infin., or *to* + verbal noun) compel or constrain forcibly. **b** (often foll. by *to*) force into a specified state (*drove him mad*). **c** (often *refl.*) urge to overwork. **3 a** *tr.* (also *absol.*) operate and direct the course of (a vehicle, a locomotive, etc.). **b** *tr. & intr.* convey or be conveyed in a vehicle, esp. a private car (cf. RIDE). **c** *tr.* (also *absol.*) urge and direct the course of (an animal drawing a vehicle or plough). **4** *tr.* (of wind, water, etc.) propel, send, or cause to go in some direction. **5** *tr.* **a** (often foll. by *into*) force (a stake, nail, etc.) into place by blows. **b** *Mining* bore (a tunnel etc.). **6** *tr.* effect or conclude forcibly (*drove a hard bargain*). **7** *tr.* (of steam or other power) set or keep (machinery) going. **8** *intr.* (usu. foll. by *at*) work hard; dash, rush. **9** *tr.* hit (a ball) hard from a freely swung bat etc. **10** *tr.* chase or frighten (game, an enemy in warfare, etc.) to an area where they may be killed or captured. ● *n.* **1** an act of driving in a motor vehicle; a journey or excursion in such a vehicle. **2 a** a motivation and energy (*lacks the drive needed to succeed*). **b** *Psychol.* an inner urge to attain a goal or satisfy a need. **3 a** a usu. landscaped street or road. **b** a usu. private road through a garden or park to a house. **4** *Cricket*, *Golf*, & *Tennis* a driving stroke of the bat etc. **5** an organized effort (*a famine-relief drive*). **6 a** the transmission of power to machinery (*front-wheel drive*). **b** the position of a steering wheel in a motor vehicle (*left-hand drive*). **c** *Computing* = DISK DRIVE. **7** *Brit.* an organized competition, for many players, of whist etc. **8** an act of driving game or an enemy. □ **drive at** seek or mean (*what is he driving at?*). **drive out** take the place of; oust; exorcize (evil spirits etc.). **driving rain** an excessive windblown downpour. [Old English] □ **drivable** *adj.* (also **driveable**).

drive-by *attrib.adj.* (of a crime etc.) carried out from a moving vehicle.

drive-in ● *attrib.adj.* (of a bank, cinema, etc.) able to be used while sitting in one's car. ● *n.* such a bank, cinema, etc.

drivel ● *n.* silly nonsense; twaddle. ● *v.intr.* (**drivelled**, **drivelling**; *US* **driveled**, **driveling**) **1** run at the mouth or nose. **2** talk childishly or idiotically. [Old English] **3** *tr.* (foll. by *away*) fritter; squander away. □ **driveller** *n.* (*US* **driveler**).

driven *past part.* of DRIVE.

drive-on *attrib.adj.* (also **drive-on/drive-off**) (of a ship) on to and from which motor vehicles may be driven.

driver *n.* **1** (often in *comb.*) a person who drives a vehicle. **2** *Golf* a club with a flat face and wooden head, used for driving from the tee. ▷ GOLF. □ **in the driver's seat** in charge. □ **driverless** *adj.*

driver's license *N. Amer.* var. of DRIVING LICENCE.

driver's test *N. Amer.* var. of DRIVING TEST.

driveway *n.* = DRIVE *n.* 3b.

driving licence *n.* (*N. Amer.* **driver's license**) a licence permitting a person to drive a motor vehicle.

driving range *n. Golf* an area for practising drives.

driving test *n.* (*N. Amer.* **driver's test**) an official test of competence to drive.

driving wheel *n.* a wheel of a car, locomotive, etc. transmitting motive power to the road or track.

drizzle ● *n.* **1** very fine rain. **2** esp. *Cookery* fine drops; a fine trickle. ● **1** *v.intr.* (esp. of rain) fall in very fine drops (*it's drizzling again*). **2** *v.tr.* esp. *Cookery* sprinkle in fine drops or a thin trickle. □ **drizzly** *adj.*

Dr Martens *n.pl.* (also **Doc Martens**, **Doctor Martens**) *propr.* ► a type of heavy usu. laced boot or shoe with a cushioned sole. [named after *Dr* K. *Maertens*, German inventor of the sole]

DR MARTENS

drogue *n.* **1** *Naut.* **a** a buoy at the end of a harpoon line. **b** a sea anchor. **2** *Aeron.* a truncated cone of fabric used as a brake, a target for gunnery, a windsock, etc. [18th-century coinage]

droll *adj.* **1** quaintly amusing. **2** strange; odd; surprising. [from French *drôle*] □ **drollery** *n.* (*pl.* **-ies**). **drolly** *adv.* **drollness** *n.*

dromedary /drom-i-dă-ri/ *n.* (*pl.* **-ies**) = ARABIAN CAMEL. [from Late Latin *dromedarius*]

drone ● *n.* **1** a non-working male of the honey bee. **2** an idler. **3** a deep humming sound. **4** a monotonous speech or speaker. **5 a** a pipe, esp. of a bagpipe, sounding a continuous note of fixed low pitch. ▷ BAGPIPE. **b** (on a stringed instrument) a string used to produce a continuous droning sound. **6** a remote-controlled pilotless aircraft or missile. ● *v.* **1** *intr.* make a deep humming sound. **2** *intr. & tr.* utter monotonously. **3 a** *intr.* be idle. **b** *tr.* (often foll. by *away*) idle away. [Old English]

drongo *n.* (*pl.* **-os** or **-oes**) **1** any black bird of the family Dicruridae, native to Asia, Africa, and Australia, having a long forked tail. **2** *Austral.* & *NZ slang derog.* a simpleton. [Malagasy (language of Madagascar)]

drool ● *v.intr.* **1** drivel; slobber. **2** (often foll. by *over*) show much pleasure or infatuation. ● *n.* slobbering; drivelling. [contraction of DRIVEL]

droop ● *v.* **1** *intr. & tr.* hang or allow to hang down; languish or sag, esp. from weariness. **2** *intr.* (of the eyes) look downwards. **3** *intr.* lose heart; flag. ● *n.* **1** a drooping attitude. **2** a loss of spirit or enthusiasm. [from Old Norse *drúpa* 'to hang the head'] □ **droopy** *adj.* (**droopier**, **droopiest**). **droopily** *adv.*

drop ● *n.* **1 a** a small round or pear-shaped portion of liquid that hangs or falls or adheres to a surface. **b** a very small amount of usu. drinkable liquid. **c** a glass etc. of alcoholic liquor (*take a drop with us*). **2 a** an abrupt slope. **b** the amount of this (*a drop of fifteen feet*). **c** a reduction in prices, temperature, etc. **d** a worsening (*a drop in status*). **3** something resembling a drop of liquid, esp.: **a** a pendant or earring. **b** a crystal ornament on a chandelier etc. **c** (often in *comb.*) a sweet or lozenge (*pear drop*). **4** something that drops or is dropped, esp.: **a** *Theatr.* scenery let down on to the stage. **b** a trapdoor on a gallows. **c** (in *comb.*) = sense 10 of *v.* (*drop handlebars*). **5** *Med.* **a** the smallest separable quantity of a liquid. **b** (in *pl.*) liquid medicine measured in drops (*eye drops*). **6** a minute quantity (*not a drop of pity*). **7** *slang* **a** a hiding place for illicit goods. **b** a secret place where documents etc. may be left or passed on in espionage. **8** *slang* a bribe. **9** *US* a letter box. ● *v.* (**dropped**, **dropping**) **1** *intr. & tr.* fall or let fall in drops. **2** *intr. & tr.* fall or allow to fall; relinquish; let go. **3 a** *intr. & tr.* sink or cause to sink or fall to the ground from exhaustion, a blow, a wound, etc. **b** *intr.* die. **4 a** *intr. & tr.* cease or cause to cease; abandon (*dropped the friendship*). **b** *tr. colloq.* cease to associate with. **5** *tr.* set down (a passenger etc.). **6** *tr. & intr.* utter or be uttered casually (*dropped a hint*). **7** *tr.* send casually (*drop me a postcard*). **8 a** *intr. & tr.* fall or allow to fall in direction, amount, condition, degree, pitch, etc. (*the wind dropped*; *we dropped the price*). **b** *intr.* let oneself fall. **9** *tr.* omit (a letter, esp. *h*, a syllable etc.) in speech. **10** *tr.* (as **dropped** *adj.*) in a lower position than usual (*dropped waist*). **11** *tr.* give birth to (esp. a lamb, a kitten, etc.). **12** *tr. Sport* lose (a game, a point, etc.). **13** *tr. Aeron.* deliver (supplies etc.) by parachute. **14** *tr. Rugby* **a** send (a ball) by a drop kick. **b** score (a goal) by a drop kick. **15** *tr. colloq.* dismiss or omit (*dropped from the team*). □ **at the drop of a hat** given the slightest excuse. **drop away** decrease or depart gradually. **drop back** (or **behind** or **to the rear**) fall back; get left behind. **drop back into** return to (a habit etc.). **drop a brick** esp. *Brit. colloq.* make an indiscreet or embarrassing remark. **drop a curtsy** *Brit.* make a curtsy. **drop down** descend a hill etc. **drop in** (or **by**) *colloq.* call casually as a visitor. **drop into** *colloq.* **1** call casually at (a place). **2** fall into (a habit etc.). **drop it!** *slang* stop that! **drop off 1** decline gradually. **2** *colloq.* fall asleep. **3** = sense 5 of *v.* **drop out** *colloq.* cease to participate. [Old English] □ **droplet** *n.*

drop curtain *n.* = DROP *n.* 4a.

drop-dead *attrib.adj. slang* stunningly beautiful; brilliant, excellent.

drophead *n. Brit.* the adjustable fabric roof of a car.

drop kick *n. Rugby* a kick made by dropping the ball and kicking it on the bounce.

drop-leaf *attrib.adj.* (of a table etc.) having a hinged flap.

drop-off *n.* **1** an act of dropping off or delivering something or someone. **2** a decline, a decrease (*a drop-off in sales*). **3** *N. Amer.* a sheer downward slope, a cliff.

drop-out *n.* **1** *colloq.* a person who has dropped out. **2** *Rugby* the restarting of a game by a drop kick.

dropper *n.* a device for administering liquid, esp. medicine, in drops. ▷ DRUG

droppings *n.pl.* **1** the dung of animals or birds. **2** something that falls or has fallen in drops.

drop scene *n.* = DROP *n.* 4a.

drop scone *n. Brit.* a small thick pancake made by dropping batter into a frying pan etc.

drop shot *n.* (in tennis, badminton, etc.) a shot dropping abruptly over the net.

dropsy *n.* (*pl.* **-ies**) = OEDEMA. [from Greek *hudrōps*] □ **dropsical** *adj.*

drosophila /drŏ-sof-i-lă/ *n.* a small fruit fly of the genus *Drosophila*, used extensively in genetic research because of its large chromosomes, numerous varieties, and rapid rate of reproduction. [from Greek *drosos* 'dew' + *philos* 'loving']

dross *n.* **1** rubbish. **2 a** the scum separated from metals in melting. **b** impurities. [Old English] □ **drossy** *adj.*

drought /drowt/ *n.* the continuous absence of rain; dry weather. [Old English] □ **droughty** *adj.*

drove[1] *past* of DRIVE.

drove[2] *n.* **1 a** a large number (of people etc.) moving together. **b** (in *pl.*) *colloq.* a great number (*arrived in droves*). **2** a herd or flock being driven or moving together. [Old English]

drover *n.* a person who drives herds to market. □ **drove** *v.tr.* **droving** *n.*

drown *v.* **1** *tr. & intr.* kill or be killed by submersion in liquid. **2** *tr.* flood; drench. **3** *tr.* (often foll. by *in*) deaden (grief etc.) with drink. **4** *tr.* (often foll. by *out*) make (a sound) inaudible by means of a louder sound. [Middle English (originally northern)]

drowned valley *n.* a valley partly or wholly submerged by a change in land levels.

drowse *v.intr.* be dull and sleepy or half asleep.

drowsy *adj.* (**drowsier**, **drowsiest**) **1** half asleep. **2** lulling. **3** sluggish. □ **drowsily** *adv.* **drowsiness** *n.*

drub *v.tr.* (**drubbed**, **drubbing**) **1** thump; belabour. **2** beat in a fight. [from Arabic *ḍaraba* 'to beat'] □ **drubbing** *n.*

drudge ● *n.* a servile worker, esp. at menial tasks. ● *v.intr.* (often foll. by *at*) work slavishly. [Middle English] □ **drudgery** *n.*

drug ● *n.* **1** ▶ a medicinal substance. **2** a narcotic, hallucinogen, or stimulant. ● *v.* (**drugged**, **drugging**) **1** *tr.* add a drug to (food or drink). **2** *tr.* **a** administer a drug to. **b** stupefy with a drug. **3** *intr. Brit.* take drugs as an addict. [from (Old) French *drogue*]

drugget *n.* **1** a coarse woven fabric used as a floor or table covering. **2** such a covering. [from French *droguet*]

druggist *n.* esp. *N. Amer.* a pharmacist.

drug peddler *n.* (also *colloq.* **drug pusher**) a person who sells esp. addictive drugs illegally.

drug squad *n. Brit.* a division of a police force investigating crimes involving illegal drugs.

drugstore *n. N. Amer.* a chemist's shop also selling light refreshments and other articles.

Druid *n.* (*fem.* **Druidess**) **1** an ancient Celtic priest, magician, or soothsayer of Gaul, Britain, or Ireland. **2** a member of a Welsh etc. Druidic order. [from Gaulish *druides*] □ **Druidic** *adj.* **Druidism** *n.*

drum ● *n.* **1 a** a percussion instrument or toy made of a hollow cylinder or hemisphere covered at the ends with stretched skin or parchment and sounded by striking. ▷ PERCUSSION. **b** (often in *pl.*) a drummer or a percussion section (*the drums are playing too loud*). **c** a sound made by or resembling that of a drum. **2** something resembling a drum in shape, esp.: **a** a cylindrical container or receptacle for oil etc. **b** a cylinder or barrel in machinery on which something is wound etc. **c** *Archit.* a stone block forming a section of a shaft. **3** *Zool. & Anat.* the eardrum. ● *v.* (**drummed**, **drumming**) **1** *intr. & tr.* play on a drum. **2** *tr. & intr.* beat or tap (knuckles, feet, etc.) continuously (on something). **3** *intr.* (of a bird or an insect) make a loud, hollow noise with quivering wings. □ **drum into** drive (a lesson) into (a person) by persistence. **drum out** *Mil.* dismiss with ignominy. **drum up** summon or call up (*drum up support*). [based on Low German *trommel* 'drum']

drumbeat *n.* a stroke or the sound of a stroke on a drum.

drum brake *n.* a brake in which shoes on a vehicle press against the drum on a wheel. ▷ BRAKE

drumhead *n.* **1** the skin of a drum. **2** an eardrum. **3** (*attrib.*) improvised (*drumhead court martial*).

drum kit *n.* ▶ a set of drums, cymbals, and brushes.

drum machine *n.* an electronic device that simulates percussion.

drum major *n.* the leader of a marching band.

drum majorette *n.* esp. *US* a member of a female baton-twirling parading group.

drummer *n.* a person who plays a drum or drums.

drumstick *n.* **1** a stick used for beating a drum. **2** the lower joint of the leg of a cooked chicken, turkey, etc.

drunk ● *adj.* **1** deprived of normal bodily and mental control by alcohol. **2** (often foll. by *with*) overcome with joy, success, etc. ● *n.* a habitually drunk person.

drunkard *n.* a person who is drunk, esp. habitually.

drunken *adj.* (usu. *attrib.*) **1** caused by or exhibiting drunkenness (*a drunken brawl*). **2** often drunk. □ **drunkenly** *adv.* **drunkenness** *n.*

drupe *n.* any fleshy or pulpy fruit enclosing a stone, e.g. an olive, plum, or peach. ▷ FRUIT. [from Greek *druppa* 'olive']

dry ● *adj.* (**drier**, **driest**) **1** free from moisture esp.: **a** with any moisture having evaporated, drained away, etc. (*clothes are not dry yet*). **b** (of the eyes) free from tears. **c** (of a climate etc.) not rainy (*dry spell*). **d** (of a river, well, etc.) not yielding water. **e** for use without moisture (*dry shampoo*). **f** (of a shave) with an electric razor. **2** (of wine etc.) not sweet (*dry sherry*). **3 a** plain or bare (*dry facts*). **b** dull (*dry as dust*). **4** (of a sense of humour, a joke, etc.) subtle, ironic, and quietly expressed. **5** (of a country, of legislation, etc.) prohibiting the sale of alcoholic drink. **6** (of toast, bread, etc.) without butter etc. **7** *Brit.* (of groceries etc.) solid, not liquid. **8** impassive, unsympathetic. **9** (of a cow etc.) not yielding milk. **10** *colloq.* thirsty or thirst-making. **11** *Brit. Polit. colloq.* of or being a political 'dry' (see sense 3 of *n.*). ● *v.* (**dries**, **dried**) **1** *tr. & intr.* make or become dry by wiping, evaporation, etc. **2** *tr.* (usu. as **dried** *adj.*) preserve (food etc.) by removing the moisture. **3** *intr.* (often foll. by *up*) *Theatr. colloq.* forget one's lines. ● *n.* (*pl.* **dries**) **1** the process or an instance of drying. **2** (prec. by *the*) a dry place (*come into the dry*). **3** *Brit. colloq.* a politician who advocates individual responsibility, free trade, and economic stringency, and opposes high government spending. □ **dry out 1** become fully dry. **2** (of an alcoholic etc.) undergo treatment to cure addiction. **dry up 1** make utterly dry. **2** *Brit.* dry dishes. **3** (of moisture) disappear utterly. **4** (of a well etc.) cease to yield water. **5** (esp. in *imper.*) *colloq.* cease talking. [Old English] □ **dryness** *n.*

DRUG

The most widely used drugs are medicines, taken for the prevention, treatment, or diagnosis of illness. Medicinal drugs can be taken in many forms. They are most commonly administered through ingestion, but can also be injected into a muscle, a vein, or under the skin. Inhalers deliver a drug through the nose or mouth to the lungs. Topical applications are applied to the surfaces of the body. Suppositories are inserted in the rectum or vagina, and droppers introduce drugs into the eye or the ear.

DRUG APPLICATIONS

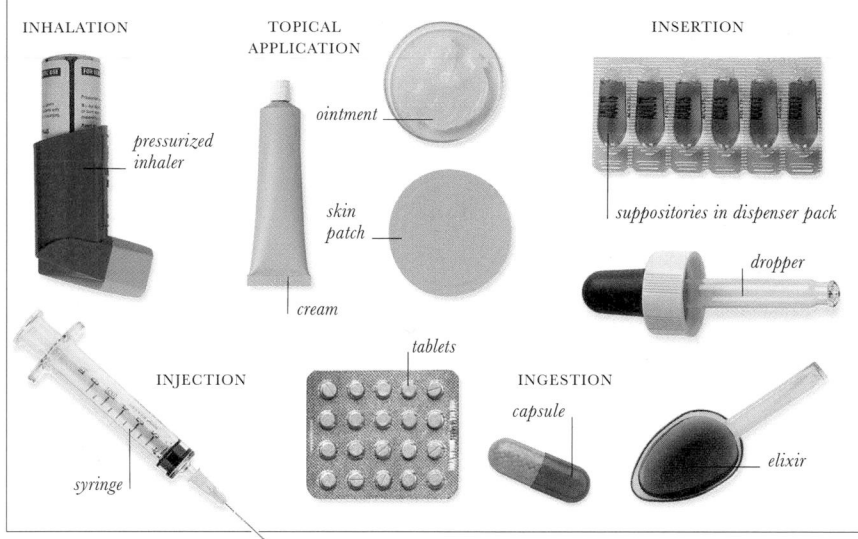

INHALATION
pressurized inhaler

TOPICAL APPLICATION
ointment
skin patch
cream

INSERTION
suppositories in dispenser pack
dropper

INJECTION
syringe

tablets

INGESTION
capsule
elixir

crash cymbal
tom-tom
ride cymbal
snare drum
floor tom
high-hat cymbal
tripod
bass drum
beater
pedal
lug

DRUM KIT

D

D

dryad *n. Mythol.* a nymph inhabiting a tree; a wood nymph. [based on Greek *drus* 'tree']

dry battery *n.* an electric battery consisting of dry cells. ▷ BATTERY

dry cell *n.* a cell in which the electrolyte is absorbed in a solid and cannot be spilled. ▷ BATTERY.

dry-clean *v.tr. & intr.* clean (clothes etc.), or be cleanable, with organic solvents without using water.

dry dock *n.* an enclosure for the building or repairing of ships, from which water can be pumped out.

dryer *n.* (also **drier**) an appliance for drying the hair, laundry, etc.

dry-eyed *adj.* not weeping.

dry fly *n.* ▼ an artificial fly which floats on the water (often hyphenated when *attrib.*: *dry-fly anglers*).

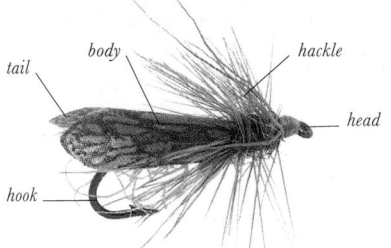

tail   *body*   *hackle*   *head*   *hook*

DRY FLY: GREY WULFF
DRY FLY REPRESENTING A MAYFLY

dry goods *n.pl.* **1** *Brit.* solid as opposed to liquid foodstuffs. **2** *US* fabrics, clothing, etc.

dry ice *n.* solid carbon dioxide.

dry land *n.* land as opposed to the sea etc.

dryly var. of DRILY.

dry measure *n.* a measure of capacity for dry goods.

dry rot *n.* **1** a type of decay affecting poorly ventilated wood. **2** fungi causing this.

dry run *n. colloq.* a rehearsal.

dry-shod *adj. & adv.* without wetting the shoes.

dry slope *n.* a ski slope covered with a plastic material which simulates snow.

drystone *attrib.adj. Brit.* (of a wall etc.) built without mortar.

drywall *n.* esp. *N. Amer.* = PLASTERBOARD.

DSC *abbr.* Distinguished Service Cross.

D.Sc. *abbr.* Doctor of Science.

DSM *abbr.* Distinguished Service Medal.

DSO *abbr.* (in the UK) Distinguished Service Order.

DSS *abbr.* (in the UK) Department of Social Security.

DT *abbr.* (also **DT's**) delirium tremens.

DTI *abbr.* (in the UK) Department of Trade and Industry.

DTP *abbr.* desktop publishing.

dual ● *adj.* **1** of two; twofold. **2** double (*dual ownership*). **3** *Gram.* (in some languages) denoting two persons or things. ● *n.* (also **dual number**) *Gram.* a dual form of a noun, verb, etc. [based on Latin *duo* 'two'] □ **duality** *n.* **dualize** *v.tr.* (also **-ise**). **dually** *adv.*

dual carriageway *n. Brit.* a road with a dividing strip between the traffic in opposite directions.

dual control *adj.* (of a vehicle or an aircraft) having two sets of controls, one for use by an instructor.

dualism *n.* being twofold; duality. □ **dualist** *n.* **dualistic** *adj.*

dual-purpose *adj.* (of a vehicle) usable for passengers or goods.

dub[1] *v.tr.* (**dubbed, dubbing**) **1** make (a person) a knight by the ritual touching of the shoulder with a sword. **2** give (a person) a nickname or title (*dubbed him a crank*). **3** *Brit.* dress (an artificial fishing-fly). **4** smear (leather) with grease. [from Old French *adober* 'to equip with armour, repair']

dub[2] *v.tr.* (**dubbed, dubbing**) **1** provide (a film etc.)

DUCK

More than 100 species of duck are found throughout the world. Most ducks nest on or beside fresh water, but some species spend much of their life on estuaries or shallow seas. Many ducks dive underwater to feed on molluscs or plant material. Surface-feeding ducks, including the mallard, sieve food from mud or water, or immerse only the front part of their body to reach food.

broad flat bill
EXTERNAL FEATURES OF A MALE MALLARD (*Anas platyrhynchos*)
white-bordered speculum (wing-patch)
waterproof plumage
webbed front toes
hind toe

EXAMPLES OF OTHER DUCKS

EIDER DUCK (*Somateria mollissima*)

HARLEQUIN DUCK (*Histrionicus histrionicus*)

NORTHERN SHOVELER (*Anas clypeata*)

WOOD DUCK (*Aix sponsa*)

TORRENT DUCK (*Merganetta armata*)

LONG-TAILED DUCK (*Clangula hyemalis*)

with an alternative soundtrack. **2** add (sound effects or music) to a film etc. **3** combine (soundtracks) into one. **4** transfer or make a copy of (recorded sound or images). [abbreviation of DOUBLE]

dubbin *n.* (also **dubbing**) prepared grease for softening and waterproofing leather. [based on DUB[1] 3]

dubiety /dew-by-iti/ *n.* (*pl.* **-ies**) *literary* doubt.

dubious *adj.* **1** hesitating (*dubious about going*). **2** of questionable value or truth (*a dubious claim*). **3** unreliable; suspicious (*dubious company*). [based on Latin *dubium* 'doubt'] □ **dubiously** *adv.* **dubiousness** *n.*

Dublin Bay prawn *n.* **1** = NORWAY LOBSTER. **2** (in *pl.*) scampi.

ducal *adj.* of, like, or bearing the title of a duke. [based on French *duc* 'duke']

ducat /duk-ăt/ *n. hist.* a gold coin, formerly current in most European countries. [from medieval Latin *ducatus* 'duchy']

duchess *n.* (as a title usu. **Duchess**) **1** a duke's wife or widow. **2** a woman holding the rank of duke. [from medieval Latin *ducissa*]

duchy *n.* (*pl.* **-ies**) **1** the territory of a duke or duchess. **2** (often as **the Duchy**) the royal dukedom of Cornwall or Lancaster. [related to DUKE]

duck[1] *n.* (*pl.* same or **ducks**) **1 a** ▲ any waterbird of the family Anatidae, with a broad flat bill and large webbed feet, esp. the domesticated form of the mallard. **b** the female of this. **c** the flesh of a duck as food. **2** (in full **duck's-egg**) *Cricket* the score of nought. **3** (also **ducks**) *Brit. colloq.* (esp. as a form of address) dear, darling. □ **like water off a duck's back** *colloq.* (of remonstrances etc.) producing no effect. [Old English]

duck[2] *v.intr. & tr.* **1** plunge or dip under water and emerge. **2** bend (the head or the body) quickly to avoid a blow or being seen, or as a bow or curtsy. **3** *colloq.* dodge (a task etc.). [Middle English] □ **ducker** *n.*

duck[3] *n.* **1** a strong untwilled linen or cotton fabric used for small sails and sailors' clothing. **2** (in *pl.*) trousers made of this (*white ducks*). [from Middle Dutch *doek*]

duckboard *n.* (usu. in *pl.*) a path of wooden slats placed over muddy ground or in a trench.

ducking-stool *n. hist.* a chair fastened to the end of a pole, which could be plunged into a pond.

duckling *n.* a young duck.

ducks and drakes *n.* a game of making a flat stone skim along the surface of water.

duckweed *n.* ▼ a tiny aquatic plant of the family Lemnaceae, esp. of the genus *Lemna*, growing on the surface of still water.

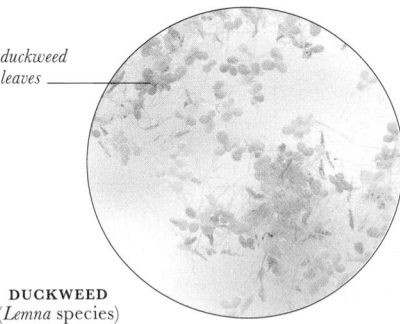

duckweed leaves

DUCKWEED (*Lemna* species)

ducky *n.* (*pl.* **-ies**) *Brit. colloq.* darling, dear. ● *adj.* sweet, pretty; splendid.

duct ● *n.* **1** a channel or tube for conveying fluid, cable, etc. **2 a** a tube in the body conveying lymph or glandular secretions such as tears, bile, etc. **b** *Bot.* a tube formed by cells that have lost their intervening end walls, holding air, water, etc. ● *v.tr.* convey through a duct. [from Latin *ductus* 'leading, aqueduct']

ductile *adj.* **1** (of a metal) capable of being drawn into wire; pliable, not brittle. **2** (of a substance) easily moulded. [from Latin *ductilis* 'that may be drawn'] □ **ductility** *n.*

ducting *n.* **1** a system of ducts. **2** material in the form of a duct or ducts.

ductless gland *n.* a gland secreting directly into the bloodstream; an endocrine gland.

dud *slang* ● *n.* **1** a useless or broken thing. **2** a counterfeit article. **3** (in *pl.*) clothes. ● *adj.* **1** useless or broken. **2** counterfeit. [Middle English]

dude *n. slang* **1** a fastidious aesthetic person, usu. male; a dandy. **2** a fellow; a guy. [19th-century coinage] □ **dudish** *adj.*

dude ranch *n.* (in the western US) a cattle ranch converted to a holiday centre for tourists etc.

dudgeon *n.* a feeling of offence; resentment. □ **in high dudgeon** very angry or angrily. [16th-century coinage]

due ● *adj.* **1** (*predic.*) owing or payable as a debt or an obligation (*our thanks are due to him; £500 was due on the 15th*). **2** (often foll. by *to*) merited; appropriate; fitting (*his due reward; received the applause due to a hero*). **3** (*attrib.*) rightful; proper; adequate. **4** (*predic.*) intended to arrive at a certain time (*a train is due at 7.30*). **5** (foll. by *to* + infin.) under an obligation or agreement to do something (*due to speak tonight*). ● *n.* **1** a person's right; what is owed to a person (*a fair hearing is my due*). **2** (in *pl.*) **a** what one owes (*pays his dues*). **b** *Brit.* an obligatory payment; a fee; a legal charge (*harbour dues; university dues*). ● *adv.* (of a point of the compass) exactly, directly (*went due east; a due north wind*). □ **due to** *disp.* because of, owing to (*he was late due to an accident*) (cf. sense 2 of *adj.*). **fall** (or **become**) **due** (of a bill etc.) be immediately payable. **in due course** at about the appropriate time. **2** in the natural order. [from Latin *debitus* 'owed']

▪ **Usage** The use of *due to* to mean 'because of' as in the example *He was late due to an accident* is regarded as unacceptable by some people. It can be avoided by substituting *His lateness was due to an accident*, *It was due to an accident that he was late*, or *He was late owing to/because of an accident*.

due date *n.* the date on which payment of a bill etc. falls due.

duel ● *n.* **1** *hist.* a contest with deadly weapons between two people to settle a point of honour. **2** any contest between two people, causes, animals, etc. ● *v.intr.* (**duelled, duelling**; *US* **dueled, dueling**) fight a duel or duels. [from Latin *duellum*, archaic form of *bellum* 'war'] □ **dueller** (*US* **dueler**). **duellist** *n.* (*US* **duelist**).

duende *n.* **1** an evil spirit. **2** inspiration. [Spanish]

duenna *n.* an older woman acting as a governess and companion to girls, esp. in a Spanish family. [from Spanish *dueña*, from Latin *domina* 'mistress']

duet *n. Mus.* a composition for two performers. [based on Latin *duo* 'two'] □ **duettist** *n.*

duff[1] *n.* a boiled pudding. [northern English form of DOUGH]

duff[2] *adj. Brit. slang* **1** worthless, counterfeit. **2** useless, broken.

duff[3] *v.tr slang* **1** *Brit. Golf* mishit (a shot, a ball); bungle. **2** *Austral.* steal and alter brands on (cattle). □ **duff up** *Brit.* beat; thrash.

duffel *n.* (also **duffle**) a coarse woollen cloth with a thick nap. [from *Duffel*, a town in Belgium]

duffel bag *n.* a cylindrical canvas bag closed by a drawstring.

duffel coat *n.* ▶ a hooded overcoat made of duffel and usu. fastened with toggles.

duffer *n. slang* **1** an inefficient, useless, or stupid person. **2** *Austral.* a person who duffs cattle. **3** *Austral.* an unproductive mine. [perhaps from Scots *dowfart* 'stupid person' from *douf* 'spiritless']

dug[1] *past* and *past part.* of DIG.

dug[2] *n.* the udder, breast, teat, or nipple of a female animal. [16th-century coinage]

dugong /dew-gong/ *n.* (*pl.* same or **dugongs**) ▼ a marine mammal (sirenian), *Dugong dugon*, of Asian seas and coasts. [from Malay *dūyong*]

hood

wooden toggle

DUFFEL COAT

DUGONG
(*Dugong dugon*)

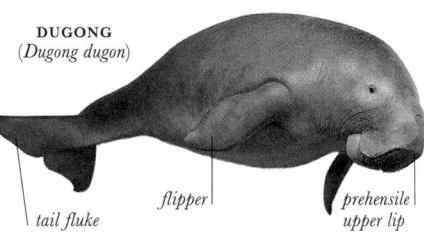

tail fluke   *flipper*   *prehensile upper lip*

dugout *n.* **1 a** a hollowed-out roofed shelter esp. for troops in trenches. **b** an underground air-raid or nuclear shelter. **c** *N. Amer. Sport* = BENCH *n.* 4. **2** a canoe made from a hollowed tree trunk.

duiker *n.* **1** any African antelope of the genus *Cephalophus*, usu. having a crest of long hair between its horns. **2** *S. Afr.* the long-tailed cormorant, *Phalacrocorax africanus*.

duke *n.* (as a title usu. **Duke**) **1** a person holding the highest hereditary title of the nobility. **2** a sovereign prince ruling a duchy or small state. [from Latin *dux ducis* 'leader']

dukedom *n.* **1** a territory ruled by a duke. **2** the rank of duke.

dulcet *adj.* (esp. of sound) sweet and soothing. [from Latin *dulcis* 'sweet']

dulcimer *n.* a musical instrument with strings of graduated length stretched over a sounding board or box, played by being struck with hammers. [from Old French *doulcemer*]

dulcitone *n.* a keyboard musical instrument with steel tuning forks which are struck by hammers. [from Latin *dulcis* 'sweet' + TONE]

dull ● *adj.* **1** slow to understand; stupid. **2** tedious; boring. **3** (of the weather) overcast; gloomy. **4 a** (esp. of a knife-edge etc.) blunt. **b** (of colour, light, sound, or taste) not bright, shining, vivid, or keen. **5** (of a pain etc.) indistinct and usu. prolonged (*a dull ache*). **6** sluggish, slow-moving (*dull trading*). **7** (of the ears, eyes, etc.) without keen perception. ● *v.tr. & intr.* make or become dull. [from Middle Dutch *dul* 'stupid'] □ **dullish** *adj.* **dullness** *n.* **dully** *adv.*

dullard *n.* a stupid person.

duly *adv.* **1** in due time or manner. **2** rightly, properly, fitly.

dumb *adj.* **1 a** (of a person) unable to speak. **b** (of an animal) naturally unable to speak (*our dumb friends*). **2** silenced by surprise, shyness, etc. **3** taciturn or reticent, esp. insultingly (*dumb insolence*). **4** (of an action etc.) performed without speech. **5** esp. *US colloq.* stupid; ignorant. **6** having no voice in government; inarticulate (*the dumb masses*). **7** (of a computer terminal etc.) able only to transmit or receive data; not programmable (opp. INTELLIGENT

3b). [Old English: sense 5 from German *dumm*] □ **dumbly** *adv.* **dumbness** *n.*

dumb-bell *n.* a short bar with a weight at each end, used for exercise. [from an 18th-century apparatus like that for ringing a church bell (but without the bell) used for exercise]

dumbfound *v.tr.* strike dumb; confound; nonplus. [blend of DUMB and CONFOUND]

dumb-iron *n.* the curved side piece of a motor vehicle chassis, joining it to the front springs.

dumbo *n.* (*pl.* **-os**) *slang* a stupid person; a fool.

dumbshow *n.* **1** significant gestures or mime. **2** a part of a play in early drama, acted in mime.

dumbsize *v.tr.* (also *absol.*) esp. *US* (of a company) reduce staff numbers to unreasonably low levels, with the result that work can no longer be carried out effectively. [humorously on the pattern of *downsize*]. **dumbsizing** *n.*

dumbstruck *adj.* greatly shocked or surprised and so lost for words.

dumb waiter *n.* **1** a small lift for carrying food, plates, etc., between floors. **2** *Brit.* a movable table, esp. with revolving shelves, used in a dining room.

dumdum *n.* (in full **dumdum bullet**) a kind of soft-nosed bullet that expands on impact and inflicts laceration. [named after *Dum-Dum*, a town and arsenal in India]

dummy ● *n.* (*pl.* **-ies**) **1** a model of a human being, esp.: **a** a ventriloquist's doll. **b** a figure used to model clothes in a shop window etc. **c** a target used for firearms practice. **2** (often *attrib.*) a counterfeit object used to replace or resemble a real or normal one. **3** *Rugby & Football* a pretended pass. **4** *colloq.* a stupid person. **5** a person taking no significant part; a figurehead. **6** *Brit.* a rubber or plastic teat for a baby to suck on. **7** *Bridge* the partner of the declarer, whose cards are exposed after the first lead. ● *adj.* sham; counterfeit. ● *v.tr.* (**-ies, -ied**) (usu. *absol.*) *Rugby & Football* pretend to pass (the ball). □ **dummy up** *US slang* keep quiet; give no information. **sell a person the** (or **a**) **dummy** *Rugby colloq.* deceive (an opponent) by pretending to pass the ball.

dummy run *n.* **1** a practice attack etc.; a trial run. **2** a rehearsal.

dump ● *n.* **1 a** a place for depositing rubbish. **b** a heap of rubbish. **2** *colloq.* an unpleasant or dreary place. **3** *Mil.* a temporary store of ammunition, provisions, etc. **4** an accumulated pile of ore, earth, etc. **5** *Computing* **a** a printout of stored data. **b** the process or result of dumping data. ● *v.tr.* **1** put down firmly or clumsily (*dumped the shopping on the table*). **2** deposit or dispose of (rubbish etc.). **3** *colloq.* abandon, desert. **4** *Mil.* leave (ammunition etc.) in a dump. **5** *Econ.* send (goods) to a foreign market for sale at a low price. **6** *Computing* **a** copy (stored data) to a different location. **b** reproduce the contents of (a store) externally. [Middle English]

dumper *n.* **1** a person or thing that dumps. **2** (in full **dumper truck**) a truck with a body that tilts or opens at the back for unloading.

dumpling *n.* **1 a** a small savoury ball of usu. suet, flour, and water, boiled in stew or water. **b** an apple or other fruit enclosed in dough and baked. **2** a small fat person.

dumps *n.pl. colloq.* depression; melancholy (*down in the dumps*).

dump truck *n. N. Amer.* = DUMPER 2.

dumpy *adj.* (**dumpier, dumpiest**) short and stout. □ **dumpily** *adv.*

dun[1] *adj.* of a dull greyish-brown colour. ● *n.* **1** a dun colour. **2** a dun horse. [Old English]

dun[2] *v.tr.* (**dunned, dunning**) importune for payment of a debt; pester. [abbreviation of obsolete *dunkirk* 'a privateer vessel', from *Dunkirk*, a sea port in France]

dunce *n.* a person slow at learning; a dullard. [from John *Duns* Scotus, scholastic theologian, 1265–1308, whose followers were ridiculed (16th c.) as enemies of learning]

D

D

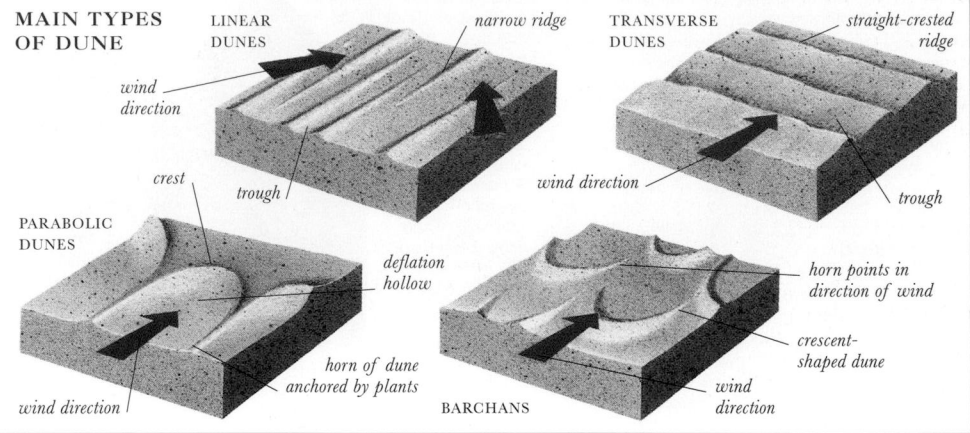

DUNE

Dunes form in different ways depending on the amount of sand available, the variability of wind direction, and the amount of vegetation cover. Linear dunes form where sand is scarce and the wind variable. Transverse dunes form at right angles to the wind in areas where there is abundant sand. Parabolic dunes are common on coasts, where there is abundant sand and the wind is strong. Barchans form on hard flat plains with little sand.

MAIN TYPES OF DUNE

LINEAR DUNES — wind direction — narrow ridge

TRANSVERSE DUNES — straight-crested ridge

crest — trough — wind direction — trough

PARABOLIC DUNES — deflation hollow — horn points in direction of wind

wind direction — horn of dune anchored by plants — BARCHANS — crescent-shaped dune — wind direction

---

dunce's cap *n.* a paper cone formerly put on the head of a dunce at school.

dunderhead *n.* a stupid person. [17th-century coinage] □ **dunderheaded** *adj.*

dune *n.* ▲ a mound or ridge of loose sand etc. formed by the wind. ▷ ERODE. [from Middle Dutch *dūne*]

dung ● *n.* the excrement of animals; manure. ● *v.tr.* apply dung to; manure (land). [Old English]

dungaree *n.* **1** a coarse Indian calico. **2** (in *pl.*) **a** overalls etc. made of dungaree or similar material. **b** *Brit.* trousers with a bib. [from Hindi *dungrī*]

dung-beetle *n.* ◀ a beetle whose larvae develop in dung, esp. one of the family Scarabaeidae.

dungeon *n.* a strong underground cell for prisoners. [originally DONJON, based on Latin *dominus* 'lord']

dunghill *n.* a heap of dung or refuse, esp. in a farmyard.

dunk *v.tr.* **1** dip (bread, a biscuit, etc.) into soup, coffee, etc. just before eating it. **2** immerse, dip (*was dunked in the river*). [from German *tunken* 'to dip']

DUNG-BEETLE

dunlin *n.* a long-billed sandpiper, *Calidris alpina*.

dunnock *n.* ▶ a small European songbird, *Prunella modularis*.

duo *n.* (*pl.* **-os**) **1** a pair of actors, entertainers, singers, etc. **2** *Mus.* a duet. [from Latin, literally 'two']

duodecimal ● *adj.* relating to or using a system of numerical notation that has twelve as a base. ● *n.* **1** the duodecimal system. **2** duodecimal notation. [based on Latin *duodecim* 'twelve'] □ **duodecimally** *adv.*

duodenum *n.* ▶ the first part of the small intestine immediately beyond the stomach. ▷ DIGESTION. [from medieval Latin *duodenum digitorum* 'length of 12 fingers' breadth'] □ **duodenal** *adj.* **duodenitis** *n.*

DUNNOCK
(*Prunella modularis*)

duologue *n.* a conversation between two people, esp. in a play. [based on Greek *duo* 'two']

duopoly /dew-op-ŏ-li/ *n.* (*pl.* **-ies**) *Econ.* the possession of trade in a commodity etc. by only two sellers. [based on Greek *duo* 'two' + *pōlein* 'to sell']

dupe ● *n.* a victim of deception. ● *v.tr.* make a fool of; cheat. [from dialect French *dupe* 'hoopoe', from the bird's supposedly stupid appearance] □ **dupery** *n.*

dupion *n.* **1** a rough silk fabric woven from the threads of double cocoons. **2** an imitation of this with other fibres. [based on Italian *doppio* 'double']

duple *adj.* of two parts. [from Latin *duplus*]

duple time *n.* rhythm consisting of two beats to the bar.

duplex ● *n.* esp. *N. Amer.* **1** a flat or maisonette on two levels. **2** a house subdivided for two families. ● *adj.* **1** having two elements; twofold. **2** esp. *US* **a** (of a flat) two-storeyed. **b** (of a house) for two families. [Latin, from *duo* 'two' + *plic-* 'fold']

duplicate ● *adj.* **1** exactly like something already existing; copied (esp. in large numbers). **2 a** having two corresponding parts. **b** existing in two examples; paired. **c** doubled. ● *n.* one of two or more identical things, esp. a copy of an original. ● *v.tr.* **1** multiply by two; double. **2** make or be an exact copy of. **3** repeat (an action etc.), esp. unnecessarily. □ **in duplicate** consisting of two exact copies. [from Latin *duplicatus* 'doubled'] □ **duplicable** *adj.* **duplication** *n.*

duplicator *n.* **1** a machine for making copies of a document, drawing, etc. **2** a person or thing that duplicates.

duplicity *n.* double-dealing; deceitfulness. [related to DUPLEX] □ **duplicitous** *adj.*

durable ● *adj.* **1** capable of lasting; hard-wearing. **2** (of goods) not for immediate consumption; able to be kept. ● *n.* (in *pl.*) durable goods. [from Latin *durabilis*] □ **durability** *n.* **durably** *adv.*

dura mater *n.* *Anat.* the tough outermost membrane enveloping the brain and spinal cord. ▷ EYE, HEAD. [literally 'hard mother', medieval Latin translation of Arabic *al-'umm al-jāfiya*, 'mother' indicating relationship]

duration *n.* the length of time for which something continues. □ **for the duration 1** for a very long time. **2** until the end of the war. [from medieval Latin *duratio*] □ **durational** *adj.*

durbar *n. hist.* **1** the court of an Indian ruler. **2** a public levee of an Indian prince or an Anglo-Indian governor or viceroy.

duress *n.* **1** compulsion, esp. illegal threats or violence (*under duress*). **2** imprisonment. [based on Latin *durus* 'hard']

during *prep.* **1** throughout (*read during the meal*). **2** at some point in (*came in during the evening*). [based on Latin *durare* 'to last, continue']

durum *n.* a kind of wheat, *Triticum durum*, yielding flour used for spaghetti etc. [Latin, literally 'hard thing']

dusk *n.* **1** the darker stage of twilight. **2** shade; gloom. [Old English *dox* 'dark, swarthy']

dusky *adj.* (**duskier, duskiest**) **1** shadowy; dim. **2** dark-coloured, darkish. □ **duskily** *adv.* **duskiness** *n.*

dust ● *n.* **1** finely powdered earth, dirt, etc. **2** fine powder of any material (*pollen dust; gold dust*). ● *v.tr.* **1** (also *absol.*) clear (furniture etc.) of dust etc. by wiping, brushing, etc. **2 a** sprinkle (esp. a cake) with powder, dust, sugar, etc. **b** sprinkle or strew (sugar, powder, etc.). □ **dust down** *Brit.* **1** wipe or brush the dust from. **2** *colloq.* reprimand. **3** = *dust off*. **dust off 1** remove the dust from. **2** use and enjoy again after long neglect. [Old English] □ **dustless** *adj.*

dust-bath *n.* a bird's rolling in dust to freshen its feathers.

dustbin *n. Brit.* a container for household refuse, esp. one kept outside.

dust bowl *n.* an area denuded of vegetation by drought or erosion and reduced to desert.

dustcart *n. Brit.* a vehicle used for collecting household refuse.

dust cover *n.* **1** = DUST SHEET. **2** = DUST JACKET.

duster *n. Brit.* a cloth for dusting furniture etc.

DUODENUM

The duodenum digests food that enters it from the stomach; this flow is controlled by the pyloric sphincter. Pancreatic juice containing enzymes breaks down the food and neutralizes stomach acids. Bile from the liver emulsifies fats for later digestion. Ducts running from the pancreas and liver to the duodenum unite to form a passageway called the ampulla of Vater.

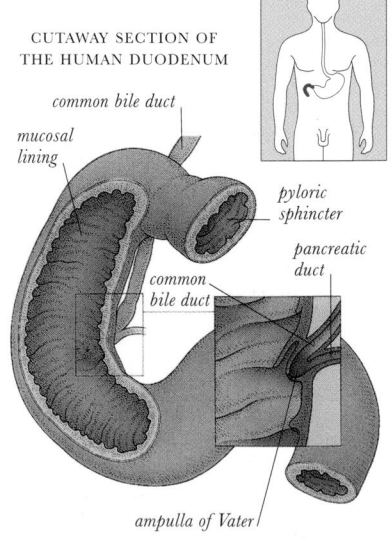

CUTAWAY SECTION OF THE HUMAN DUODENUM

common bile duct — mucosal lining — pyloric sphincter — pancreatic duct — common bile duct — ampulla of Vater

D

dust jacket *n.* a usu. decorated paper cover used to protect a book from dirt etc.

dustman *n.* (*pl.* **-men**) *Brit.* a man employed to clear household refuse.

dustpan *n.* a small pan into which dust etc. is brushed from the floor.

dust sheet *n. Brit.* a cloth put over furniture to protect it from dust.

dust-up *n. colloq.* a fight.

dust-wrapper *n.* = DUST JACKET.

dusty *adj.* (**dustier, dustiest**) **1** full of, covered with, or resembling dust. **2** uninteresting; dry. **3** (of a colour) dull or muted. □ **dustily** *adv.* **dustiness** *n.*

dusty answer *n. Brit.* a curt rejection of a request.

Dutch ● *adj.* of, relating to, or associated with the Netherlands. **●** *n.* **1** the language of the Netherlands. **2** (prec. by *the*; treated as *pl.*) the people of the Netherlands. □ **go Dutch** share expenses equally. [from Old High German *diutisc* 'national']

Dutch auction *n.* a sale of goods in which the price is reduced by the auctioneer until a buyer is found.

Dutch barn *n. Brit.* a barn roof over hay etc., set on poles and having no walls.

Dutch cap *n.* **1** *Brit.* a contraceptive diaphragm. **2** a woman's lace cap with triangular flaps on each side.

Dutch courage *n.* false courage gained from alcohol.

Dutch elm disease *n.* a disease of elms, often fatal, caused by the fungus *Ceratocystis ulmi* and spread by wood-boring beetles.

Dutch hoe *n.* a hoe used with a pushing action.

Dutchman *n.* (*pl.* **-men**; *fem.* **Dutchwoman**, *pl.* **-women**) **1** a native or national of the Netherlands. **2** a person of Dutch descent.

Dutch oven *n.* **1** a metal box the open side of which is turned towards a fire. **2** a covered cooking pot for braising etc.

Dutch treat *n.* a party, outing, etc. to which each person makes a contribution.

Dutch uncle *n.* a person giving advice with benevolent firmness.

Dutchwoman see DUTCHMAN.

dutiable *adj.* liable to customs or other duties.

dutiful *adj.* doing or observant of one's duty; obedient. □ **dutifully** *adv.* **dutifulness** *n.*

duty *n.* (*pl.* **-ies**) **1 a** a moral or legal obligation; a responsibility (*his duty to report it*). **b** the binding force of what is right (*strong sense of duty*). **2** payment to the public revenue, esp.: **a** levied on the import of goods (*customs duty*). **b** levied on the transfer of property, licences, etc. (*death duty*). **3** (often in *pl.*) a job or function (*his duties as caretaker*). □ **do duty for** serve as or pass for (something else). **on** (or **off**) **duty** engaged (or not engaged) in one's work. [related to DUE]

duty-bound *adj.* obliged by duty.

duty-free *adj.* (of goods) on which duty is not leviable.

duty-free shop *n.* a shop at an airport etc. at which duty-free goods can be bought.

duty officer *n.* the officer currently on duty.

duty-paid *adj.* (of goods) on which duty has been paid.

duvet /doo-vay/ *n. esp. Brit.* a thick soft quilt used instead of an upper sheet and blankets. [French, literally 'down']

Dvr. *abbr. Brit.* Driver.

dwarf ● *n.* (*pl.* **dwarfs** or **dwarves**) **1 a** a person of abnormally small stature. **b** an animal or plant much below the ordinary size. **2** a small mythological being with supernatural powers. **3** (in full **dwarf star**) a small usu. dense star. ▷ STAR. **4** (*attrib.*) of a kind very small in size (*dwarf bean*). **●** *v.tr.* **1** stunt in growth. **2** cause (something similar or comparable) to seem small or insignificant (*efforts dwarfed by their rivals' achievements*). [Old English] □ **dwarfish** *adj.*

■ **Usage** In sense 1, alternative terms such as *person of restricted growth* are now sometimes preferred.

DYE

A dye is a substance that is used to give colour to another material. Synthetic dyes are made by adding sulphur or chlorine to the colourless chemicals derived from distilling petroleum or coal tar. Natural dyes, as shown below, are produced by grinding down vegetable or animal material and mixing the resulting powder with water.

EXAMPLES OF NATURAL DYES

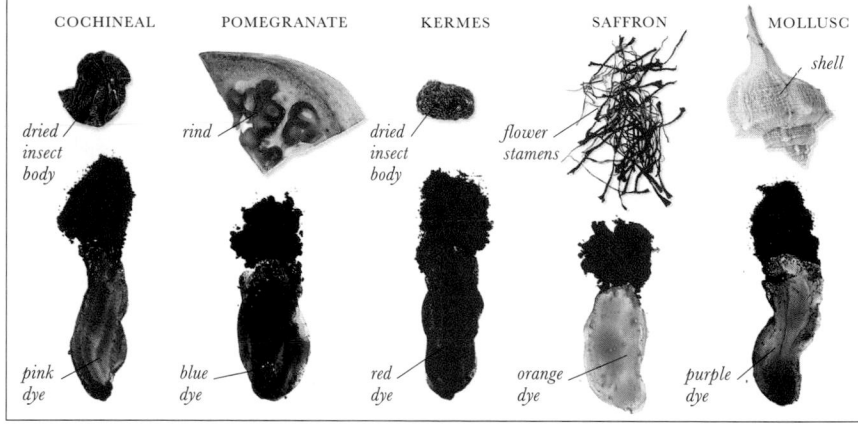

COCHINEAL   POMEGRANATE   KERMES   SAFFRON   MOLLUSC

dried insect body   *rind*   *dried insect body*   *flower stamens*   *shell*

pink dye   *blue dye*   *red dye*   *orange dye*   *purple dye*

dweeb *n. US slang* a studious or boring person; a nerd. [20th-century coinage]

dwell *v.intr.* (*past* and *past part.* **dwelt** or **dwelled**) (usu. foll. by *in, at, near, on,* etc.) *literary* live, reside (*dwelt in the forest*). □ **dwell on** (or **upon**) write, brood, or speak at length on. [Old English, originally 'to hinder, delay', later 'to continue in a place'] □ **dweller** *n.*

dwelling *n.* (also **dwelling place**) *formal* a house; a residence; an abode.

dwelling house *n.* a house used as a residence, not as an office etc.

dwindle *v.intr.* **1** become gradually smaller; shrink. **2** lose importance; decline. [from Old Norse *dvina*]

Dy *symb. Chem.* the element dysprosium.

dye ● *n.* **1 ▲** a substance used to change the colour of hair, fabric, wood, etc. **2** (in full **dyestuff**) a substance yielding a dye, esp. when in solution. **●** *v.tr.* (**dyeing**) **1** impregnate with dye. **2** make (a thing) a specified colour with dye (*dyed it yellow*). □ **dyed in the wool** (or *Brit.* **grain**) out and out; unchangeable, inveterate. [Old English] □ **dyeable** *adj.*

dyer *n.* a person who dyes cloth etc.

dyestuff see DYE 2.

dying *attrib.adj.* connected with, or at the time of, death (*his dying words*).

dyke[1] (also **dike**) **●** *n.* **1** a long wall or embankment built to prevent flooding, esp. from the sea. **2** a ditch. **3 a** a low wall, esp. of turf. **b** a causeway. **●** *v.tr.* provide or defend with a dyke or dykes. [from Middle Dutch *dijc* 'ditch, dam']

dyke[2] *n.* (also **dike**) *slang* a lesbian. [20th-century coinage]

dyn *abbr.* dyne.

dynamic ● *adj.* (also **dynamical**) **1** energetic; active; potent. **2** *Physics* **a** concerning motive force (opp. STATIC *adj.* 2a). **b** concerning force in actual operation. **3** of or concerning dynamics. **4** *Mus.* relating to the volume of sound. **●** *n.* **1** an energizing or motive force. **2** *Mus.* = DYNAMICS 3. □ **dynamically** *adv.*

dynamics *n.pl.* **1** (usu. treated as *sing.*) **a** the branch of mechanics concerned with the motion of bodies under the action of forces. ▷ GRAVITY. **b** the branch of any science in which forces or changes are considered (*aerodynamics*; *population dynamics*). **2** the motive forces, physical or moral, affecting behaviour and change in any sphere (*group dynamics*). **3** *Mus.* variation in loudness. □ **dynamicist** *n.* (in sense 1a).

dynamism *n.* energizing or dynamic action or power. [based on Greek *dunamis* 'power']

dynamite ● *n.* **1** a high explosive containing nitroglycerine. **2** a potentially dangerous person, thing, or situation. **●** *v.tr.* charge or shatter with dynamite. [based on Greek *dunamis* 'power'] □ **dynamiter** *n.*

dynamo *n.* (*pl.* **-os**) **1** esp. *Brit.* a machine converting mechanical energy into electrical energy, esp. by rotating coils of copper wire in a magnetic field. **2** *colloq.* an energetic person. [from Greek *dunamis* 'power']

dynamometer *n.* an instrument measuring energy expended by a mechanism, vehicle, etc.

dynast *n.* **1** a ruler. **2** a member of a dynasty. [from Greek *dunastēs*]

dynasty *n.* (*pl.* **-ies**) **1** a line of hereditary rulers. **2** a succession of leaders in any field. □ **dynastic** *adj.* **dynastically** *adv.*

dyne *n. Physics* a unit of force that, acting on a mass of one gram, increases its velocity by one centimetre per second every second along the direction that it acts. [related to DYNAMO]

dysentery /dis-ĕn-tri/ *n.* a disease with inflammation of the intestines, causing severe diarrhoea with blood and mucus. [based on Greek *entera* 'bowels'] □ **dysenteric** *adj.*

dysfunction *n.* an abnormality or impairment of function. □ **dysfunctional** *adj.*

dyslexia *n.* a disorder marked esp. by severe difficulty in reading and spelling. [based on Greek *lexis* 'speech', apparently by confusion of Greek *legein* 'to speak' and Latin *legere* 'to read'] □ **dyslectic** *adj.* & *n.* **dyslexic** *adj.* & *n.*

dysmenorrhoea /dis-men-ŏ-**ree**-ă/ *n.* painful or difficult menstruation.

dyspepsia *n.* indigestion. [from Greek *duspepsia*]

dyspeptic ● *adj.* of or relating to dyspepsia or the resulting depression. **●** *n.* a person suffering from dyspepsia.

dysphasia *n. Med.* lack of coordination in speech, owing to brain damage. [based on Greek *dusphatos* 'hard to utter'] □ **dysphasic** *adj.*

dysplasia *n. Med.* abnormal growth of tissues etc. [based on Greek *plasis* 'formation'] □ **dysplastic** *adj.*

dysprosium *n. Chem.* a naturally occurring soft metallic element of the lanthanide series. [based on Greek *dusprositos* 'hard to get at']

dystrophy /dis-trŏ-fi/ *n.* impaired nourishment of an organ or part of the body. See also MUSCULAR DYSTROPHY. [based on Greek *-trophia* 'nourishment'] □ **dystrophic** *adj.*

E

E¹ *n.* (also **e**) (*pl.* **Es** or **E's**) **1** the fifth letter of the alphabet. **2** *Mus.* the third note of the diatonic scale of C major. ▷ NOTATION

E² *abbr.* (also **E.**) **1** East; Eastern. **2** see E-NUMBER.

E³ *symb. Physics* energy ($E = mc^2$).

e *symb.* used on packaging (in conjunction with specification of weight, size, etc.) to indicate compliance with EU regulations.

e- *prefix* form of EX- 1 before some consonants.

each ● *det.* every one of two or more persons or things, regarded and identified separately (*each person*; *five in each class*). ● *pron.* each person or thing (*each of us*). [Old English *ǣlc* 'ever alike']

each other *pron.* one another.

each way *adj. & adv. Brit.* (of a bet) backing a horse etc. for either a win or a place.

eager *adj.* **1 a** full of keen desire. **b** (of passions etc.) keen, impatient. **2** (often foll. by *for*, or *to* + infin.) strongly desirous (*eager to learn*). [based on Latin *acer acris* 'sharp, swift'] □ **eagerly** *adv.* **eagerness** *n.*

eager beaver *n. colloq.* a very diligent person.

eagle *n.* **1 a** ▼ any of various large birds of prey of the family Accipitridae, with keen vision and powerful flight. ▷ RAPTOR. **b** a figure of an eagle, esp. as a symbol of the US. **2** *Golf* a score of two strokes under par at any hole. [from Latin *aquila*]

eagle eye *n.* keen sight, watchfulness. □ **eagle-eyed** *adj.*

eagle owl *n.* any large owl of the genus *Bubo*, with long ear-tufts. ▷ OWL

eaglet *n.* a young eagle.

ear¹ *n.* **1 ▲** the organ of hearing and balance, esp. the external part of this. ▷ INNER EAR. **2** the faculty for discriminating sounds (*an ear for music*). **3** listening, attention. □ **all ears** listening attentively. **have a person's ear** receive a favourable hearing. **out on one's ear** dismissed ignominiously. **up to one's ears** (often foll. by *in*) *colloq.* deeply involved or occupied. [Old English] □ **eared** *adj.* (also in *comb.*). **earless** *adj.*

ear² *n.* the seed-bearing head of a cereal plant. [Old English]

earache *n.* a pain in the ear.

earbash *v.tr.* esp. *Austral. slang* talk inordinately to; harangue. □ **earbasher** *n.* **earbashing** *n.*

eardrum *n.* the membrane of the middle ear. ▷ EAR

earful *n.* (*pl.* **-fuls**) *colloq.* **1** a copious or prolonged amount of talking. **2** a strong reprimand.

earl *n.* a British nobleman ranking between a marquess and a viscount. [Old English] □ **earldom** *n.*

Earl Marshal *n.* (in the UK) the officer presiding over the College of Heralds, with ceremonial duties on royal occasions.

ear lobe *n.* the lower soft pendulous external part of the ear.

early ● *adj. & adv.* (**earlier**, **earliest**) **1** before the due, usual, or expected time (*arrived early*). **2 a** not far on in the day or night, or in time (*early evening*). **b** prompt; promptly (*early payment appreciated*; *reply early for a reduction*). **3 a** not far on in a process (*Early English architecture*). **b** of the distant past (*early man*). **c** not far on in a sequence (*the early chapters*). **4 a** of childhood, esp. the pre-school years (*early learning*). **b** (of a creative work) immature, youthful. **5** flowering etc., before other varieties. ● *n.* (*pl.* **-ies**) (usu. in *pl.*) an early fruit or vegetable, esp. potatoes. □ **early** (or **earlier**) **on** at an early (or earlier) stage. [Old English] □ **earliness** *n.*

early bird *n. colloq.* a person who arrives, gets up, etc. early.

early days *n.pl. Brit.* early in time for something to happen etc.

early hours *n.pl.* the very early morning, usu. before dawn.

early music *n.* medieval, Renaissance, and baroque music, esp. as revived and played on period instruments. □ **early musician** *n.*

earmark ● *n.* **1** an identifying mark. **2** an owner's mark on the ear of an animal. ● *v.tr.* **1** (usu. foll. by *for*) set aside (money etc.) for a special purpose. **2** mark (sheep etc.) with an identifying mark.

earn *v.tr.* **1** (also *absol.*) **a** (of a person) obtain (income) in return for labour or services. **b** (of capital invested) bring in as interest or profit. **2 a** obtain as the reward for hard work or merit. **b** incur (a reproach, reputation, etc.). [Old English] □ **earner** *n.*

earned income *n.* income derived from wages etc.

earnest¹ ● *adj.* intensely serious. ● *n.* seriousness. □ **in** (or **in real**) **earnest** serious(ly), not joking(ly); with determination. [Old English] □ **earnestly** *adv.* **earnestness** *n.*

earnest² *n.* **1** money paid as an instalment, esp. to confirm a contract etc. **2** a foretaste (*in earnest of what is to come*). [Middle English]

earnings *n.pl.* money earned.

earnings-related *adj.* (of benefit, a pension, etc.) calculated on the basis of past or present income.

earphone *n.* a device applied to the ear to aid hearing or receive radio or telephone communications.

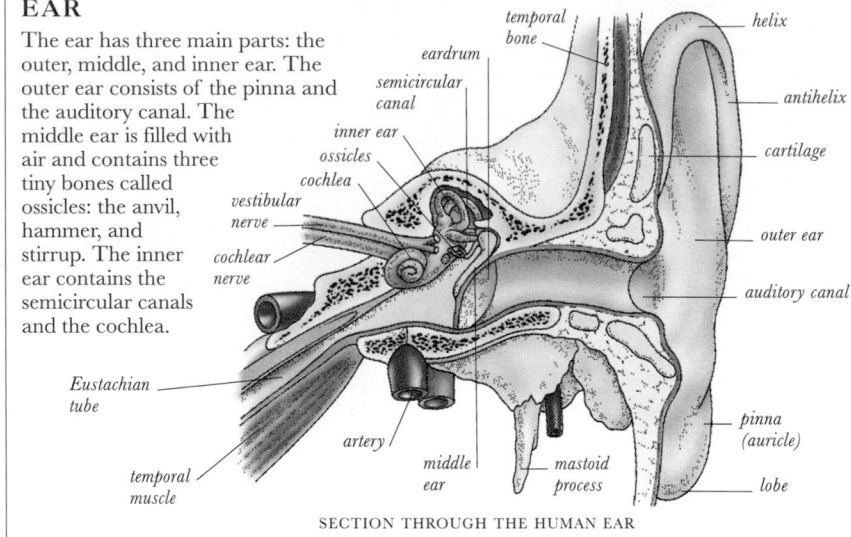

EAR

The ear has three main parts: the outer, middle, and inner ear. The outer ear consists of the pinna and the auditory canal. The middle ear is filled with air and contains three tiny bones called ossicles: the anvil, hammer, and stirrup. The inner ear contains the semicircular canals and the cochlea.

temporal bone · *helix* · *eardrum* · *semicircular canal* · *antihelix* · *inner ear* · *ossicles* · *cochlea* · *cartilage* · *vestibular nerve* · *cochlear nerve* · *outer ear* · *auditory canal* · *Eustachian tube* · *pinna (auricle)* · *artery* · *middle ear* · *mastoid process* · *lobe* · *temporal muscle*

SECTION THROUGH THE HUMAN EAR

EAGLE

Eagles are the most powerful of the birds of prey. Like other raptors, eagles grasp and kill prey with their huge talons, and use their hooked bills to tear through and eat flesh. There are more than 50 species of eagle, found all over the world.

binocular vision · *hooked bill* · *powerful wings* · *talon*

EXTERNAL FEATURES OF A BALD EAGLE (*Haliaeetus leucocephalus*)

EXAMPLES OF OTHER EAGLES

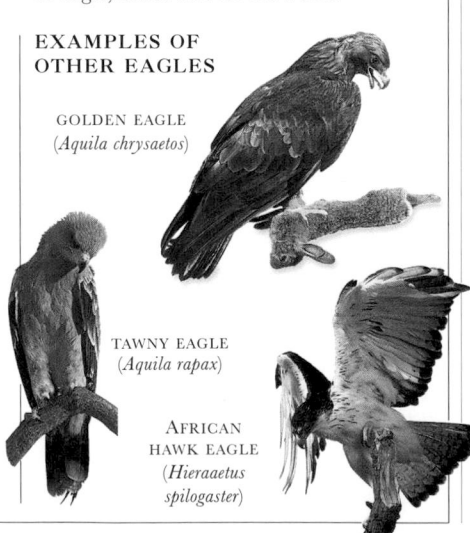

GOLDEN EAGLE (*Aquila chrysaetos*)

TAWNY EAGLE (*Aquila rapax*)

AFRICAN HAWK EAGLE (*Hieraaetus spilogaster*)

earpiece *n.* the part of a telephone etc. applied to the ear during use. ▷ RECEIVER

ear-piercing *adj.* loud and shrill.

earplug *n.* a piece of wax etc. placed in the ear to protect against cold air, water, or noise.

earring *n.* a piece of jewellery worn in or on (esp. the lobe of) the ear.

earshot *n.* the distance over which something can be heard (esp. *within* or *out of earshot*).

ear-splitting *adj.* excessively loud.

earth ● *n.* **1 a** (also **Earth**; often prec. by *the*) ► one of the planets of the solar system, orbiting about the Sun between Venus and Mars; the planet on which we live. ▷ SOLAR SYSTEM. **b** (prec. by *the*) land and sea, as distinct from sky. **2 a** dry land; the ground (*fell to earth*). **b** soil, clay, mould. **3** *Relig.* the present abode of humankind, as distinct from heaven or hell. **4** *Brit. Electr.* the connection to the earth as an arbitrary reference voltage in an electrical circuit. **5** the hole of a badger, fox, etc. **6** (prec. by *the*) *colloq.* a huge amount (*cost the earth*; *want the earth*). ● *v.* **1** *tr.* (foll. by *up*) *Brit.* cover (the roots and lower stems of plants) with heaped-up earth. **2 a** *tr.* drive (a fox) to its earth. **b** *intr.* (of a fox etc.) run to its earth. **3** *tr. Brit. Electr.* connect to the earth. □ **come back** (or **down**) **to earth** return to realities. **gone to earth** in hiding. **on earth** *colloq.* **1** existing anywhere (*happiest man on earth*). **2** as an intensifier (*what on earth?*). [Old English] □ **earthward** *adj. & adv.* **earthwards** *adv.*

earthbound *adj.* **1** attached to the Earth or earthly things. **2** moving towards the Earth.

earth closet *n. Brit.* a lavatory with dry earth used to cover excreta.

earthen *adj.* **1** made of earth. **2** made of baked clay.

earthenware ● *n.* ◄ pottery, vessels, etc. made of clay fired to a porous state which can be made impervious to liquids by the use of a glaze. ● *adj.* made of fired clay.

earthling *n.* an inhabitant of the Earth, esp. as regarded in science fiction by aliens.

earthly *adj.* **1** of the Earth or human life on it; terrestrial. **2** (usu. with *neg.*) *colloq.* remotely possible (*is no earthly use*). □ **not an earthly** *Brit. colloq.* no chance whatever. □ **earthliness** *n.*

earthly paradise see PARADISE 3.

earth-pig *n.* = AARDVARK.

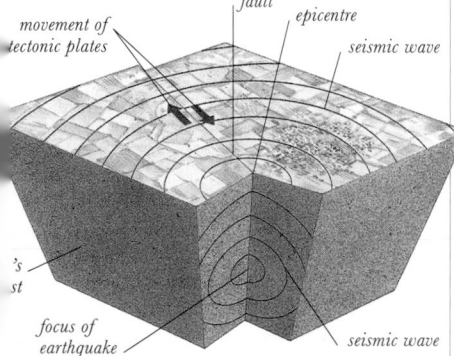

EARTHENWARE: TRADITIONAL GREEK EARTHENWARE POT

earthquake *n.* **1** ▼ a convulsion of the Earth's crust due to the release of accumulated stress as a result of faults in strata or volcanic action. **2** a social etc. disturbance.

EARTHQUAKE: CROSS-SECTION OF THE EARTH'S CRUST DURING AN EARTHQUAKE

movement of tectonic plates · *fault* · *epicentre* · *seismic wave* · *focus of earthquake* · *seismic wave*

Earth sciences *n.pl.* the sciences concerned with the Earth or part of it, or its atmosphere (e.g. geology, oceanography, meteorology).

earth-shattering *adj.* (also **earth-shaking**) *colloq.*

EARTH

The fifth largest planet in the solar system, the Earth is the only planet known to support life. The Earth has four main layers: a solid metal inner core with a temperature of about 4,000 °C (7,200 °F); a molten metal outer core; a mantle composed largely of a rock called peridotite; and the crust, of which there are two different types, continental and oceanic.

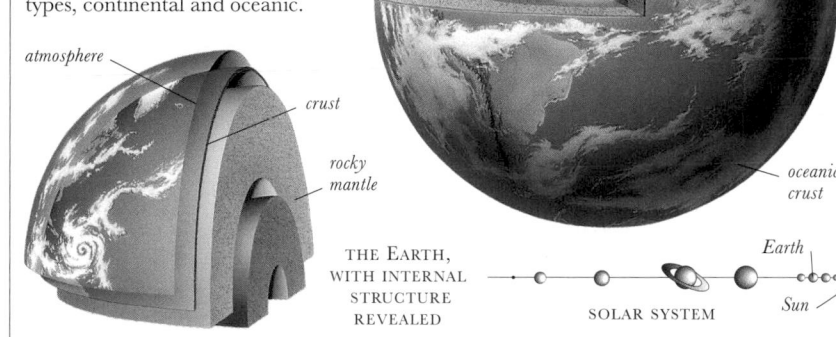

continental crust · *molten outer core* · *solid inner core* · *atmosphere* · *crust* · *rocky mantle* · *oceanic crust*

THE EARTH, WITH INTERNAL STRUCTURE REVEALED

SOLAR SYSTEM · *Earth* · *Sun*

---

having a traumatic or devastating effect. □ **earth-shatteringly** *adv.*

earth tremor see TREMOR *n.* 3.

earthwork *n.* **1** an embankment, fortification, etc. made of earth. **2** the process of excavating soil in civil engineering work.

earthworm *n.* any of various annelid worms, esp. of the genus *Lumbricus* or *Allolobophora*, living and burrowing in the ground. ▷ ANNELID

earthy *adj.* (**earthier**, **earthiest**) **1** of or like earth or soil. **2** somewhat coarse or crude (*earthy humour*). □ **earthily** *adv.* **earthiness** *n.*

ear-trumpet *n.* a trumpet-shaped device formerly used as a hearing aid.

earwax *n.* a yellow waxy secretion produced by the ear.

earwig *n.* **1** any small elongate insect of the order Dermaptera, with a pair of terminal appendages in the shape of forceps. ▷ INSECT. **2** *US* a small centipede. [Old English]

ease ● *n.* **1** absence of difficulty (*did it with ease*). **2** freedom or relief from pain, embarrassment, or constraint. ● *v.* **1** *tr.* relieve from pain or anxiety etc. **2** *intr.* (often foll. by *off*, *up*) **a** become less painful or burdensome. **b** begin to take it easy. **c** moderate one's behaviour, habits, etc. **3** *intr. Meteorol.* become less severe. **4 a** *tr.* slacken. **b** *tr. & intr.* (foll. by *through*, *into*, etc.) move or be moved carefully into place. **5** *intr.* (often foll. by *off*) *Stock Exch.* (of shares etc.) descend in price or value. □ **at ease 1** free from constraint. **2** *Mil.* in a relaxed attitude while on parade, with the feet apart. [from Old French *eise*] □ **easer** *n.*

easel *n.* ► a standing frame for supporting an artist's work, a blackboard, etc. [from Dutch *ezel*]

easement *n. Law* a right of way or a similar right over another's land. [from Old French *aisement*]

easily *adv.* **1** without difficulty. **2** by far (*easily the best*). **3** very probably (*it could easily snow*).

east ● *n.* **1 a** the point of the horizon where the Sun rises at the equinoxes. **b** the compass point corresponding to this. **c** the direction in which this lies. ▷ COMPASS. **2** (usu. **the East**) **a** *Brit.* the regions or countries lying to the east of Europe. **b** *hist.* the former

EASEL: ARTIST'S STUDIO EASEL

Communist states of eastern Europe. **3** the eastern part of a country, town, etc. ● *adj.* **1** towards, at, near, or facing east. **2** coming from the east (*east wind*). ● *adv.* **1** towards, at, or near the east. **2** (foll. by *of*) further east than. □ **to the east** (often foll. by *of*) in an easterly direction. [Old English]

eastbound *adj.* travelling or leading eastwards.

Easter *n.* (also **Easter Day** or **Easter Sunday**) the festival (held on a variable Sunday in March or April) commemorating Christ's resurrection. [Old English, apparently from *Ēostre*, a goddess associated with spring]

Easter egg *n.* an artificial usu. chocolate egg given at Easter.

easterly ● *adj. & adv.* **1** in an eastern position or direction. **2** (of a wind) blowing from the east. ● *n.* (*pl.* **-ies**) a wind blowing from the east. ▷ TRADE WIND

eastern *adj.* **1** of, in, or towards, the east. **2** (**Eastern**) of or in the Far, Middle, or Near East. □ **easterner** *n.* **easternmost** *adj.*

Eastern Church *n.* any of the Christian Churches originating in eastern Europe and the Middle East, esp. (in full **Eastern Orthodox Church**) the Orthodox Church.

Easter week *n.* the week beginning on Easter Sunday.

East Indian *adj.* of or relating to the islands etc. east of India, esp. the Malay archipelago.

east-north-east *n.* the direction or compass point midway between east and north-east.

east-south-east *n.* the direction or compass point midway between east and south-east.

eastward ● *adj. & adv.* (also **eastwards**) towards the east. ● *n.* an eastward direction or region.

easy ● *adj.* (**easier**, **easiest**) **1** not difficult. **2 a** free from pain or discomfort. **b** comfortably off (*easy circumstances*). **3** free from awkwardness or constraint (*an easy manner*). **4** compliant, obliging (*an easy touch*). ● *adv.* (**easier**, **easiest**) with ease; in an effortless or relaxed manner. ● *int.* go carefully; move gently. □ **easy as pie** see PIE¹. **easy does it** *colloq.* go carefully. **easy on the eye** (or **ear** etc.) *colloq.* pleasant to look at (or listen to etc.). **go easy** (usu. foll. by *with*, *on*) be sparing or cautious. **I'm easy** *colloq.* I have no preference. **of easy virtue** (of a woman) sexually promiscuous. **stand easy!** *Brit. Mil.* permission to a squad standing at ease to relax their attitude further. **take it easy 1** proceed gently or carefully. **2** relax; avoid overwork. [from Old French *aisié* 'eased'] □ **easiness** *n.*

E

ECHINODERM

Starfishes and their relatives make up a group of sea-dwelling invertebrates known as echinoderms. Their bodies are usually divided into five equal parts, and most have small, sucker-tipped tube feet. They have no head, no specialized excretory organs, and no central nervous system.

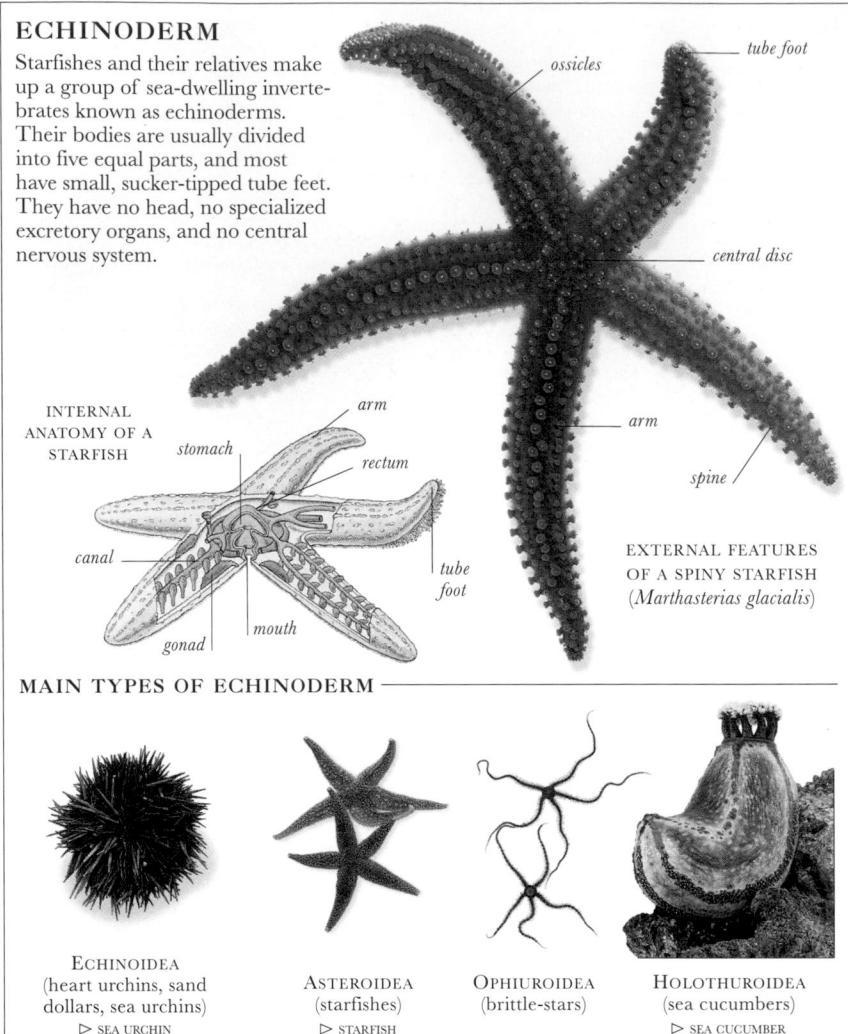

INTERNAL ANATOMY OF A STARFISH

arm
ossicles
tube foot
central disc
arm
spine
stomach
rectum
canal
tube foot
gonad
mouth

EXTERNAL FEATURES OF A SPINY STARFISH (*Marthasterias glacialis*)

MAIN TYPES OF ECHINODERM

ECHINOIDEA
(heart urchins, sand dollars, sea urchins)
▷ SEA URCHIN

ASTEROIDEA
(starfishes)
▷ STARFISH

OPHIUROIDEA
(brittle-stars)

HOLOTHUROIDEA
(sea cucumbers)
▷ SEA CUCUMBER

easy chair *n.* a large comfortable chair, usu. an armchair.

easygoing *adj.* **1** placid and tolerant; relaxed in manner. **2** (of a horse) having an easy gait.

easy money *n.* money got without effort (esp. of dubious legality).

easy-peasy *adj. Brit. slang* very simple.

Easy Street *n. colloq.* affluence.

easy terms *n.pl.* payment by instalments.

easy touch *n. slang* a gullible person, esp. one easily induced to part with money.

eat *v.* (*past* **ate**; *past part.* **eaten**) **1 a** *tr.* take into the mouth, chew, and swallow (food). **b** *intr.* consume food. **c** *tr.* devour (*eaten by a lion*). **2** *intr.* (foll. by *(away)* *at, into*) **a** destroy gradually. **b** begin to consume or diminish (resources etc.). **3** *tr. colloq.* trouble, vex (*what's eating you?*). □ **eat one's heart out** suffer from excessive longing. **eat humble pie** see HUMBLE. **eat out** have a meal away from home, esp. in a restaurant. **eat up 1** (also *absol.*) eat or consume completely. **2** use or deal with rapidly or wastefully (*eats up petrol*). **3** encroach upon (*eating up the neighbouring states*). **4** preoccupy (*eaten up with pride*). **eat one's words** admit that one was wrong. [Old English]

eatable ● *adj.* that is in a condition to be eaten. ● *n.* (usu. in *pl.*) food.

eater *n.* **1** a person who eats (*a big eater*). **2** *Brit.* an eating apple etc.

eating *adj.* **1** suitable for eating (*eating apple*). **2** used for eating (*eating house*). **3** of or relating to the process of eating (*eating disorders*).

eats *n.pl. colloq.* food.

eau de Cologne /oh dě kŏ-**lohn**/ *n.* an alcohol-based perfume originally from Cologne. [French, literally 'water of Cologne']

eaves *n.pl.* the underside of a projecting roof. ▷ ROOF. [Old English]

eavesdrop *v.intr.* (**-dropped**, **-dropping**) listen secretly to a private conversation. □ **eavesdropper** *n.*

ebb ● *n.* the movement of the tide out to sea (also *attrib.*: *ebb tide*). ● *v.intr.* (often foll. by *away*) **1** (of tide-water) recede. **2** decline (*his life was ebbing away*). □ **at a low ebb** in a poor condition or state of decline. [Old English]

ebonite *n.* = VULCANITE.

ebony ● *n.* (*pl.* **-ies**) **1** a heavy hard dark wood. **2** a tropical tree of the genus *Diospyros* producing this. ● *adj.* **1** made of ebony. **2** black like ebony. [from Greek *ebenos* 'ebony tree']

ebullient *adj.* exuberant, high-spirited. [from Latin *ebullient-* 'bubbling out'] □ **ebullience** *n.* **ebulliency** *n.* **ebulliently** *adv.*

EC *abbr.* **1** East Central. **2 a** European Community. **b** European Commission.

■ **Usage** The term *EC* meaning 'European Community' was replaced by *EU* 'European Union' in November 1993.

ecad /**ee**-kad/ *n. Ecol.* an organism modified by its environment. [from Greek *oikos* 'house']

eccentric ● *adj.* **1** odd or capricious in behaviour or appearance. **2** (also **excentric**) **a** not placed, or not having its axis etc. placed, centrally (cf. CONCENTRIC). **b** (often foll. by *to*) (of a circle) not concentric (with another). **c** (of an orbit) not circular. ▷ ORBIT. ● *n.* **1** an eccentric person. **2** (also **excentric**) *Mech.* an eccentric contrivance for changing rotatory into backward-and-forward motion. [from Greek *ekkentros*, literally 'out of centre'] □ **eccentrically** *adv.* **eccentricity** *n.* (*pl.* **-ies**).

ecclesiastic ● *n.* a clergyman. ● *adj.* = ECCLESIASTICAL. [based on Greek *ekklēsia* 'assembly, church']

ecclesiastical *adj.* of or relating to the Church or the clergy. □ **ecclesiastically** *adv.*

eccrine *adj.* (of a gland, e.g. a sweat gland) secreting without loss of cell material.

ECG *abbr.* electrocardiogram.

echelon /**esh**-ě-lon/ *n.* **1** a level in an organization, in society, etc.; those occupying it (often in *pl.*: *the upper echelons*). **2** *Mil.* a wedge-shaped formation (*in echelon*). [from French *échelon*]

echidna /i-**kid**-nă/ *n.* an Australian egg-laying insectivorous mammal, with a covering of spines. [from Greek *ekhidna* 'viper']

echinoderm /i-**ky**-nŏ-derm/ *n.* ◄ any marine invertebrate of the phylum Echinodermata, which includes starfishes and sea urchins. [from Greek *exhinos* 'hedgehog' + *derma* 'skin']

echinoid /**ek**-in-oyd/ *n.* a sea urchin. ▷ SEA URCHIN

echo ● *n.* (*pl.* **-oes**) **1 a** the repetition of a sound by the reflection of sound waves. **b** the secondary sound produced. **2** a reflected radio or radar beam. ▷ RADAR. **3** a close imitation or imitator. **4** (often in *pl.*) circumstances or events reminiscent of earlier ones. ● *v.* (**-oes**, **-oed**) **1** *intr.* **a** (of a place) resound with an echo. **b** (of a sound) resound. **2** *tr.* repeat (a sound) by an echo. **3** *tr.* **a** repeat (another's words). **b** imitate the opinions or actions of (a person). [from Greek *ēkhō*] □ **echoer** *n.* **echoey** *adj.* **echoless** *adj.*

echocardiography *n. Med.* the use of ultrasound waves to investigate the action of the heart. □ **echocardiogram** *n.* **echocardiograph** *n.* **echocardiographer** *n.*

echo chamber *n.* an enclosure with sound-reflecting walls.

echogram *n.* a record made by an echo sounder.

echograph *n.* a device for automatically recording echograms.

echoic /e-**koh**-ik/ *adj.* (of a word) onomatopoeic. □ **echoically** *adv.*

echolocation *n.* ▼ the location of objects by reflected sound, esp. ultrasound.

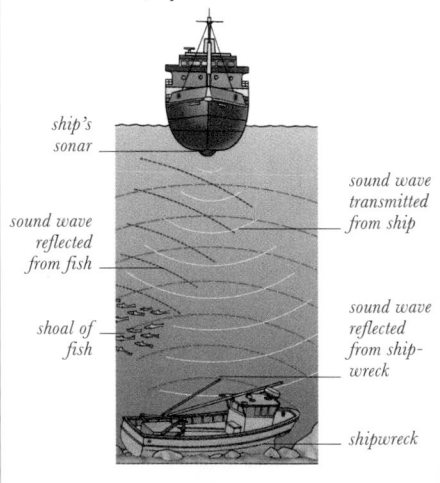

ship's sonar

sound wave reflected from fish

shoal of fish

sound wave transmitted from ship

sound wave reflected from ship-wreck

shipwreck

ECHOLOCATION: SHIP DETECTING UNDERWATER OBJECTS BY ECHOLOCATION

echo sounder *n.* a depth-sounding apparatus using timed echos. □ **echo-sounding** *n.* (often *attrib.*).

echt /ekht/ *adj.* authentic, typical. [German]

éclair *n.* a small elongated iced cake of choux pastry filled with cream. [French, literally 'lightning']

eclampsia *n.* a convulsive condition occurring esp. in pregnant women. [based on Greek *eklampsis* 'sudden development'] □ **eclamptic** *adj.*

éclat /e-klah/ *n.* **1** brilliant display; dazzling effect. **2** conspicuous success. [French]

eclectic ● *adj.* deriving ideas, style, etc. from various sources. ● *n.* an eclectic person. [based on Greek *eklegein* 'to select'] □ **eclectically** *adv.* **eclecticism** *n.*

eclipse ● *n.* **1** ▼ the obscuring of the light from one celestial body by another. **2** a deprivation of light or the period of this. **3** a rapid or sudden loss of importance or prominence. ● *v.tr.* **1** (of a celestial body) obscure the light from or to (another). **2** intercept (light, esp. of a lighthouse). **3** outshine, surpass. [based on Greek *ekleipein* 'to leave its place'] □ **eclipser** *n.*

ecliptic ● *n.* the Sun's apparent path among the stars during the year. ● *adj.* of an eclipse or the ecliptic.

eclogue *n.* a short poem, esp. a pastoral dialogue. [from Greek *eklogē* 'selection']

eco- *comb. form* ecology, ecological.

ecocide *n.* destruction of the natural environment.

ecoclimate *n.* climate considered as an ecological factor.

eco-friendly *adj.* not harmful to the environment.

eco-label *n.* a label identifying manufactured products that satisfy certain environmental conditions. □ **eco-labelling** *n.*

ecology *n.* **1** the branch of biology dealing with the relations of organisms to one another and to their physical surroundings. **2** (in full **human ecology**) the study of the interaction of people with their environment. [based on Greek *oikos* 'house'] □ **ecological** *adj.* **ecologically** *adv.* **ecologist** *n.*

economic *adj.* **1** of or relating to economics. **2** maintained for profit. **3** adequate to repay or recoup expenditure with some profit (*an economic rent*). **4** considered or studied with regard to human needs (*economic geography*). □ **economically** *adv.*

economical *adj.* sparing in the use of resources; avoiding waste. □ **economically** *adv.*

economics *n.pl.* (often treated as *sing.*) **1 a** the science of the production and distribution of wealth. **b** the application of this to a particular subject (*the economics of publishing*). **2** the condition of a country etc. as regards material prosperity.

economist *n.* **1** an expert in or student of economics. **2** a person who manages financial or economic matters.

economize *v.intr.* (also **-ise**) **1** be economical; make economies. **2** (foll. by *on*) use sparingly; spend less on. □ **economization** *n.* **economizer** *n.*

economy *n.* (*pl.* **-ies**) **1 a** the wealth and resources of a community. **b** a particular kind of this (*a capitalist economy*). **c** the administration or condition of an economy. **2 a** the careful management of (esp. financial) resources; frugality. **b** (often in *pl.*) an instance of this (*made many economies*). **3** sparing use (*economy of language*). **4** (also **economy class**) the cheapest class of air travel. **5** (also **economy-size**) (*attrib.*) (of goods) consisting of a large quantity for a proportionally lower cost. [from Greek *oikonomia* 'household management']

ecosphere *n.* **1** the region of space including planets where conditions are such that living things can exist. **2** = BIOSPHERE.

ecosystem *n.* a biological community of interacting organisms and their physical environment. ▷ SOIL

ecotourism *n.* tourism directed towards exotic natural environments, esp. intended to support conservation efforts. □ **ecotourist** *n.*

ecru ● *n.* the colour of unbleached linen; light fawn. ● *adj.* of this colour. [from French *écru* 'unbleached']

ecstasy *n.* (*pl.* **-ies**) **1** an overwhelming feeling of rapture. **2** (usu. **Ecstasy**) *slang* a powerful stimulant and hallucinogenic drug. [from Greek *ekstasis* 'standing outside oneself'] □ **ecstatic** *adj. & n.* **ecstatically** *adv.*

ECT *abbr.* electroconvulsive therapy.

ectogenesis *n.* *Biol.* the production of structures outside the organism. [modern Latin] □ **ectogenetic** *adj.* **ectogenic** *adj.* **ectogenous** *adj.*

ectomorph *n.* a person with a lean and delicate build of body (cf. ENDOMORPH, MESOMORPH). ▷ MESOMORPH. [based on Greek *morphē* 'form'] □ **ectomorphic** *adj.* **ectomorphy** *n.*

-ectomy *comb. form* denoting a surgical operation in which a part of the body is removed (*appendectomy*). [from Greek *ektomē* 'excision']

ectopic *adj.* *Med.* in an abnormal place or position. [from Greek *ektopos* 'out of place']

ectopic pregnancy *n.* ▼ a pregnancy occurring outside the womb.

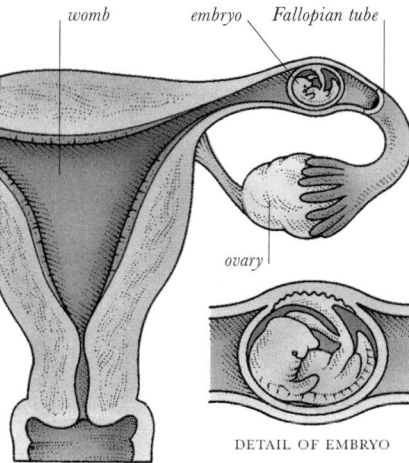

ectoplasm *n.* **1** the dense outer layer of the cytoplasm. **2** a supposed viscous substance exuding from the body of a medium during a spiritualistic trance. □ **ectoplasmic** *adj.*

ecu *n.* (*pl.* same or **ecus**) (also **Ecu, ECU**) European Currency Unit. [acronym]

ecumenical *adj.* of or representing the whole Christian world, esp. seeking or promoting worldwide Christian unity. [from Greek *oikoumenikos* 'of the inhabited Earth'] □ **ecumenically** *adv.* **ecumenism** *n.*

eczema *n.* inflammation of the skin, with itching and discharge from blisters. [from Greek] □ **eczematous** *adj.*

ed. *abbr.* **1** edited by. **2** edition. **3** editor. **4** educated; education.

Edam *n.* a round Dutch cheese, usu. pale yellow with a red wax coating. [from *Edam*, a town in the Netherlands]

edaphic /i-daf-ik/ *adj.* **1** *Bot.* of or relating to the soil. **2** *Ecol.* produced or influenced by the soil. [based on Greek *edaphos* 'floor']

eddy ● *n.* (*pl.* **-ies**) **1** a circular movement of water causing a small whirlpool. **2** a movement of wind, smoke, etc. resembling this. ● *v.tr. & intr.* (**-ies, -ied**) whirl round in eddies.

edelweiss /ay-děl-vys/ *n.* an Alpine plant, *Leontopodium alpinum*, with woolly white bracts around the flower heads. [German, from *edel* 'noble' + *weiss* 'white']

edema *US* var. of OEDEMA.

Eden *n.* (also **Garden of Eden**) a place or state of great happiness, with reference to the abode of Adam and Eve at the Creation. [from Hebrew *'ēden*, originally in sense 'delight']

ECLIPSE

A lunar eclipse occurs when the Earth passes between the Sun and the full Moon, so that the Earth's shadow is cast on the Moon. This darkens the Moon for the duration of the eclipse. A solar eclipse occurs when a new Moon passes directly between the Earth and the Sun. A solar eclipse is said to be total or partial depending on whether the observer is in the umbra or penumbra of the Moon's shadow.

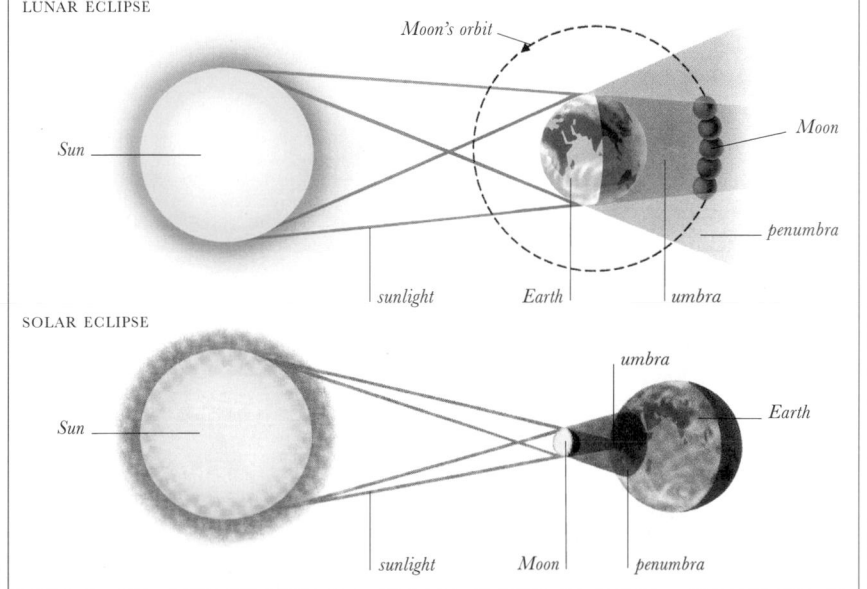

LUNAR ECLIPSE

Moon's orbit

Sun

Moon

penumbra

sunlight   *Earth*   *umbra*

SOLAR ECLIPSE

umbra

Sun

Earth

penumbra

sunlight   *Moon*   *penumbra*

E

edentate ● *adj.* **1** having no or few teeth. **2** *Zool.* ▼ of or belonging to the order Edentata (or Xenarthra) of mammals lacking incisor and canine teeth. ● *n.* *Zool.* an edentate mammal. [from Latin *edentatus*]

edge ● *n.* **1** a boundary line or margin of an area or surface. **2** a narrow surface of a thin object. **3** the meeting-line of two surfaces of a solid. **4 a** the sharpened side of the blade of a cutting instrument or weapon. **b** the sharpness of this (*the knife has lost its edge*). **5** the area close to a steep drop. **6** anything compared to an edge, esp. the crest of a ridge. **7 a** (as a personal attribute) incisiveness. **b** keenness, excitement (esp. as an element in an otherwise routine situation). ● *v.* **1** *tr. & intr.* (often foll. by *in, into, out,* etc.) move gradually or furtively towards an objective. **2** *tr.* **a** provide with an edge or border. **b** form a border. **c** trim the edge of. **3** *tr.* sharpen (a knife, tool, etc.). **4** *tr.* *Cricket* strike (the ball) with the edge of the bat. □ **have the edge on** (or **over**) have a slight advantage over. **on edge 1** tense and restless or irritable. **2** eager, excited. **on the edge of** almost involved in or affected by. **set a person's teeth on edge** (of a taste or sound) cause an unpleasant nervous sensation. **take the edge off** make less effective or intense. [Old English]

edgeways *adv.* (also **edgewise**) **1** with the edge uppermost or towards the viewer. **2** edge to edge. □ **get a word in edgeways** contribute to a conversation when the dominant speaker pauses briefly.

edging *n.* **1** something forming an edge or border. **2** the process of making an edge.

edgy *adj.* (**edgier, edgiest**) irritable; nervously anxious. □ **edgily** *adv.* **edginess** *n.*

edible ● *adj.* fit or suitable to be eaten. ● *n.* (in *pl.*) food. [based on Latin *edere* 'to eat'] □ **edibility** *n.*

edict *n.* an order proclaimed by authority. [from Latin *edictum*]

edifice *n.* a building, esp. a large imposing one. [from Latin *aedificium*]

edify *v.tr.* (**-ies, -ied**) (of an experience etc.) improve morally or intellectually. [from Latin *aedificare* 'to build up'] □ **edification** *n.* **edifying** *adj.* **edifyingly** *adv.*

edit ● *v.tr.* (**edited, editing**) **1 a** assemble, prepare, modify, or condense (written material) for publication. **b** prepare an edition of (an author's work). **2** be in overall charge of (a newspaper etc.). **3** take extracts from and collate (films etc.) to form a unified sequence. **4 a** prepare (data) for processing by a computer. **b** alter (a text entered in a word processor etc.). **5 a** reword to correct, or to alter the emphasis. **b** (foll. by *out*) remove (part) from a text etc. ● *n.* **1 a** piece of editing. **2** an edited item. [from French *éditer*]

edition *n.* **1 a** one of the particular forms in which a text is published (*pocket edition*). **b** a copy of a book in a particular form (*a first edition*). **2** a whole number of copies of a book, newspaper, etc. issued at one time. **3** a particular version or instance of a regular broadcast. **4** a person or thing similar to or resembling another (*a miniature edition of her mother*). [from Latin *editio* 'putting out']

editor *n.* **1** a person who edits material for publication or broadcasting. **2** a person who directs the preparation of a newspaper etc., or a particular section of one (*sports editor*). **3** a person who selects or commissions material for publication. **4** a person who edits film etc. **5** a program enabling the user to alter text held in a computer. □ **editorship** *n.*

editorial ● *adj.* of or concerned with editing or editors. ● *n.* an article giving a newspaper editor's opinion on a topical issue. □ **editorialist** *n.* **editorialize** *v.intr.* (also **-ise**). **editorially** *adv.*

educate *v.tr.* (also *absol.*) **1** give intellectual, moral, and social instruction to. **2** provide education for. **3** (often foll. by *in,* or *to* + infin.) train or instruct for a particular purpose. [based on Latin *educatus* 'reared'] □ **educable** *adj.* **educability** *n.* **educative** *adj.* **educator** *n.*

educated *adj.* **1** having had an education, esp. to a higher level than average. **2** resulting from a (good) education (*an educated accent*). **3** based on experience or study (*an educated guess*).

education *n.* **1** systematic instruction. **2** a particular kind of or stage in education (*further education*). **3** development of character or mental powers. □ **educational** *adj.* **educationalist** *n.* **educationally** *adv.* **educationist** *n.*

educe *v.tr.* bring out or develop from latent or potential existence. [from Latin *educere* 'to lead out'] □ **eduction** *n.*

edutainment *n.* entertainment with an educational aspect; infotainment.

Edwardian ● *adj.* of, characteristic of, or associated with the reign of King Edward VII (1901–10). ● *n.* a person belonging to this period.

-ee *suffix* forming nouns denoting: **1** the person affected by the verbal action (*addressee; employee*). **2** a person concerned with or described as (*absentee; bargee*). **3** an object of smaller size (*bootee*).

EEC *abbr.* European Economic Community.

■ **Usage** See Usage Note at EUROPEAN COMMUNITY.

EEG *abbr.* electroencephalogram.

eel *n.* **1** ▼ any of various snakelike fish, with a slender body and poorly developed fins, esp. one of the genus *Anguilla*. ▷ FISH. **2** a slippery or evasive person or thing. [Old English] □ **eel-like** *adj.* **eely** *adj.*

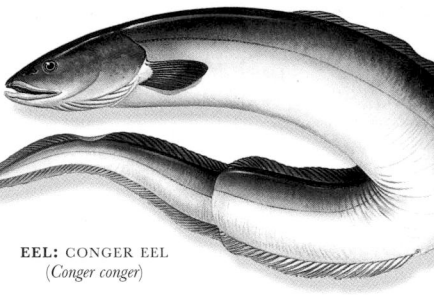

EEL: CONGER EEL
(*Conger conger*)

eelgrass *n.* **1** any marine plant of the genus *Zostera,* with long ribbon-like leaves. **2** any submerged freshwater plant of the genus *Vallisneria.*

eerie *adj.* (**eerier, eeriest**) gloomy and strange; weird, frightening (*an eerie silence*). [originally northern English and Scots *eri*] □ **eerily** *adv.* **eeriness** *n.*

ef- *prefix* assim. form of EX- 1 before *f.*

efface *v.* **1** *tr.* rub or wipe out (a mark etc.). **2** *tr.* (in abstract senses) obliterate; wipe out (*effaced it from his memory*). **3** *tr.* utterly surpass; eclipse (*success has effaced all previous attempts*). **4** *refl.* make oneself insignificant or inconspicuous. [from French *effacer*] □ **effacement** *n.*

effect ● *n.* **1** the result or consequence of an action etc. **2** efficacy (*had little effect*). **3** an impression produced on a spectator, hearer, etc. (*lights had a pretty effect*). **4** (in *pl.*) property. **5** (in *pl.*) the lighting, sound, etc. used to accompany a play, film, broadcast, etc. **6** *Physics* a physical phenomenon (*Doppler effect*). **7** the state of being operative. ● *v.tr.* bring about. □ **bring** (or **carry**) **into effect** accomplish. **for effect** to create an impression. **give effect to** make operative. **in effect** for practical purposes. **take effect** become operative. **to the effect that** the gist being. **to that effect** having that result or implication. **with effect from** coming into operation at or on (a stated time). [from Latin *effectus*]

■ **Usage** See Usage Note at AFFECT[1].

effective ● *adj.* **1 a** having a definite or desired effect. **b** efficient. **2** impressive. **3 a** actual; existing in fact rather than officially or theoretically (*took effective control in their absence*). **b** actually usable; realizable; equivalent in its effect (*effective money; effective demand*). **4** coming into operation (*effective as from 1 May*). ● *n.* a soldier available for service. □ **effectively** *adv.* **effectiveness** *n.* **effectivity** *n.*

effectual *adj.* **1** capable of producing the required effect. **2** valid. □ **effectually** *adv.* **effectuality** *n.* **effectualness** *n.*

effeminate *adj.* (of a man) feminine in appearance

EDENTATE

Although the word edentate means 'without teeth', the only members of the scientific order Edentata that do not have teeth are the anteaters. Other edentates lack incisors and canines, but have peg-like molars and premolars.

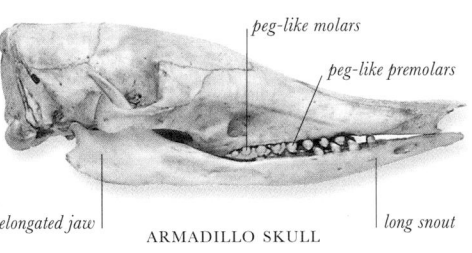

peg-like molars
peg-like premolars
elongated jaw
ARMADILLO SKULL
long snout

EXAMPLES OF EDENTATES

GIANT ARMADILLO
(*Priodontes maximus*)

SOUTHERN TAMANDUA
(*Tamandua tetradactyla*)

THREE-TOED SLOTH
(*Bradypus tridactylus*)

GIANT ANTEATER
(*Myrmecophaga tridactyla*)

or manner. [from Latin *effeminatus* 'having become a woman'] □ **effeminacy** *n.* **effeminately** *adv.*

efferent /ˈef-er-ĕnt/ *adj. Physiol.* conducting outwards (*efferent nerves; efferent vessels*) (opp. AFFERENT). [from Latin *efferent-* 'carrying out']

effervesce *v.intr.* **1** give off bubbles of gas. **2** be lively. [from Latin *effervescere* 'to begin to boil'] □ **effervescence** *n.* **effervescent** *adj.*

effete *adj.* **1** feeble and incapable, ineffectual. **2** worn out. [from Latin *effetus* 'worn out by bearing young'] □ **effeteness** *n.*

efficacious *adj.* (of a thing) producing or sure to produce the desired effect. [from Latin *efficax*, related to EFFICIENT] □ **efficaciously** *adv.* **efficacy** *n.*

efficiency *n.* (*pl.* **-ies**) **1** the state or quality of being efficient. **2** *Mech. & Physics* the ratio of useful work performed to the total energy expended or heat taken in.

efficient *adj.* **1** productive with minimum waste or effort. **2** (of a person) capable; acting effectively. [from Latin *efficient-* 'accomplishing'] □ **efficiently** *adv.*

effigy *n.* (*pl.* **-ies**) a sculpture or model of a person. □ **in effigy** in the form of a (usu. crude) representation of a person. [from Latin *effigies*]

effloresce *v.intr.* **1** burst out into flower. **2** *Chem.* **a** (of a substance) turn to a fine powder on exposure to air. **b** (of salts) come to the surface and crystallize on it. **c** (of a surface) become covered with salt particles. [from Latin *efflorescere*] □ **efflorescence** *n.*

effluence *n.* **1** a flowing out (of light, electricity, etc.). **2** that which flows out. [from medieval Latin *effluentia*]

effluent ● *adj.* flowing out. ● *n.* **1** sewage or industrial waste discharged into a river, the sea, etc. **2** a stream or lake flowing from a larger body of water.

effluvium *n.* (*pl.* **effluvia**) an unpleasant or noxious odour or exhaled substance affecting the lungs or the sense of smell etc. [based on Latin *effluere* 'to flow out']

efflux *n.* = EFFLUENCE. □ **effluxion** *n.*

effort *n.* **1** strenuous physical or mental exertion. **2** a determined attempt. **3** *Mech.* a force exerted. ▷ LEVER. **4** *colloq.* something accomplished (*not bad for a first effort*). [based on Latin *fortis* 'strong'] □ **effortful** *adj.* **effortfully** *adv.*

effortless *adj.* **1** requiring no effort (*effortless methods of cookery*). **2** natural, easy (*effortless grace*). □ **effortlessly** *adv.* **effortlessness** *n.*

effrontery *n.* (*pl.* **-ies**) **1** impudent audacity (esp. *have the effrontery to*). **2** an instance of this. [based on Late Latin *effrons -ontis* 'shameless']

effulgent *adj. literary* radiant; shining brilliantly. [from Latin *effulgere* 'shining forth'] □ **effulgence** *n.*

effuse ● *adj.* /i-fewss/ *Bot.* (of an inflorescence etc.) spreading loosely. ● *v.tr.* /i-fewz/ **1** pour forth (liquid, light, etc.). **2** give out (ideas etc.). [from Latin *effusus* 'poured out']

effusion *n.* **1** a copious outpouring. **2** usu. *derog.* an unrestrained flow of words.

effusive *adj.* gushing, demonstrative (*effusive praise*). □ **effusively** *adv.* **effusiveness** *n.*

EFL *abbr.* English as a foreign language.

Efta /ef-ta/ *abbr.* (also **EFTA**) European Free Trade Association.

EFTPOS /eft-poss/ *abbr.* electronic funds transfer at point of sale.

e.g. *abbr.* for example. [Latin *exempli gratia*]

egalitarian ● *adj.* **1** of or relating to the principle of equal rights for all (*an egalitarian society*). **2** advocating this principle. ● *n.* a person who advocates egalitarian principles. [from French *égalitaire*] □ **egalitarianism** *n.*

egg[1] *n.* **1 a** ▲ the reproductive body produced by females of animals such as birds, reptiles, fish, etc., enclosed in a protective layer and capable of developing into a new individual. **b** the egg of the domestic hen, used for food. **2** *Biol.* the female reproductive cell in animals and plants. **3** *colloq.* a

EGG

An egg is a single cell with the capacity to develop into a new individual. Development may take place inside the mother's body (as in most mammals) or outside, in which case the egg has a protective covering such as a shell. The shelled eggs of birds and reptiles contain enough yolk to sustain the developing embryo until it hatches. Pores in the shell allow the embryo to exchange oxygen and carbon dioxide with the atmosphere.

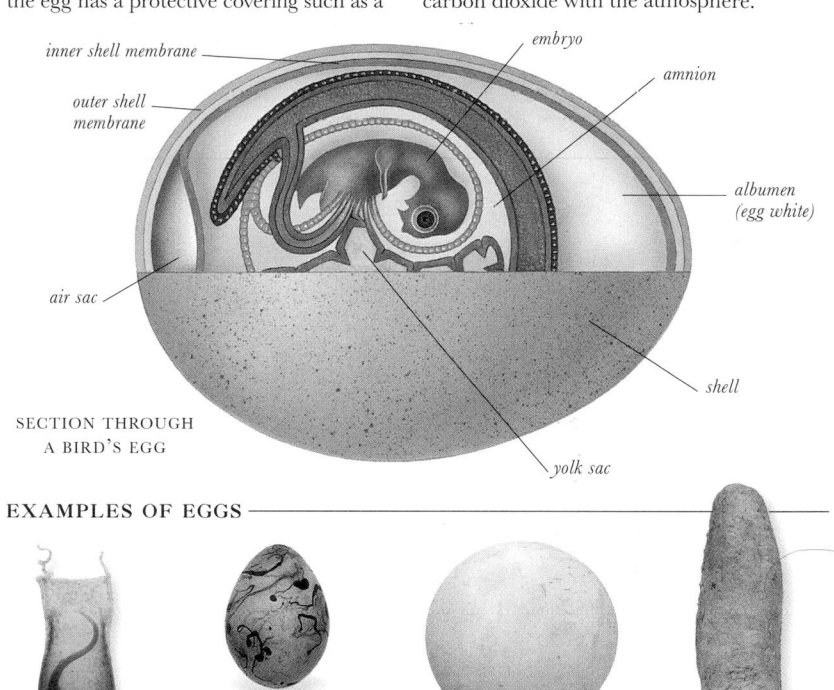

SECTION THROUGH A BIRD'S EGG

inner shell membrane · *outer shell membrane* · *air sac* · *embryo* · *amnion* · *albumen (egg white)* · *shell* · *yolk sac*

EXAMPLES OF EGGS

DOGFISH EGG (MERMAID'S PURSE)

BALTIMORE ORIOLE EGG

TOAD EGGS

GALAPAGOS TORTOISE EGG

LADYBIRD EGGS

GROUND PYTHON EGG

E

person or thing qualified in some way (*a tough egg*). □ **have** (or **put**) **all one's eggs in one basket** *colloq.* risk everything on a single venture. **with egg on one's face** *colloq.* made to look foolish. [from Old Norse] □ **eggy** *adj.* (**eggier, eggiest**).

egg[2] *v.tr.* (foll. by *on*) urge (*egged them on to do it*). [from Old Norse *eggja* 'to edge']

eggcup *n.* a cup for holding a boiled egg.

egghead *n. colloq.* an intellectual; an expert.

egg-nog *n.* (also *Brit.* **egg-flip**) a drink of alcoholic spirit with beaten egg, milk, etc.

eggplant *n.* esp. *N. Amer.* = AUBERGINE *n.* 1, 2.

eggshell ● *n.* **1** the shell of an egg. **2** anything very fragile. ● *adj.* **1** (of china) thin and fragile. **2** (of paint) with a slight gloss finish.

egg white *n.* the white of an egg.

ego *n.* (*pl.* **-os**) **1** *Metaphysics* a conscious thinking subject. **2** *Psychol.* the part of the mind that reacts to reality and has a sense of individuality. **3** a sense of self-esteem. [Latin, literally 'I']

egocentric *adj.* **1** centred in the ego. **2** self-centred, egoistic. □ **egocentrically** *adv.* **egocentricity** *n.* **egocentrism** *n.*

egoism *n.* **1** an ethical theory that treats self-interest as the foundation of morality. **2** = EGOTISM. □ **egoist** *n.* **egoistic** *adj.* **egoistical** *adj.* **egoistically** *adv.*

■ **Usage** The senses of *egoism* and *egotism* overlap, but *egoism* alone is a term used in philosophy and

psychology to mean 'self-interest' (often contrasted with *altruism*).

egomania *n.* morbid egotism. □ **egomaniac** *n.* **egomaniacal** *adj.*

egotism *n.* **1** the practice of continually talking about oneself; self-centredness. **2** an exaggerated opinion of oneself; conceit. **3** selfishness. □ **egotist** *n.* **egotistic** *adj.* **egotistical** *adj.*

■ **Usage** See Usage Note at EGOISM.

ego trip *n. colloq.* activity etc. devoted entirely to one's own interests or feelings.

egregious /i-gree-jŭs/ *adj.* **1** outstandingly bad (*egregious folly; an egregious ass*). **2** *archaic* or *joc.* remarkable. [from Latin *egregius* 'illustrious', literally 'standing out from the flock'] □ **egregiously** *adv.*

egress /ee-gres/ *n.* **1 a** a going out. **b** the right of going out. **2** an exit; a way out. [from Latin *egressus*]

egret *n.* any of various herons of the genus *Egretta* or *Bulbulcus*, usu. having long white feathers in the breeding season. [from Provençal *aigreta*]

Egyptian ● *adj.* **1** of or relating to Egypt in NE Africa. **2** of or for Egyptian antiquities (*Egyptian room*). ● *n.* **1** a native of ancient or modern Egypt; a national of the Arab Republic of Egypt. **2** the Hamitic language used in ancient Egypt until the 3rd c. AD.

Egyptology *n.* the study of the language, history, and culture of ancient Egypt. □ **Egyptologist** *n.*

E

eh *int. colloq.* **1** expressing enquiry or surprise. **2** inviting assent. **3** asking for something to be repeated or explained. [Middle English, instinctive exclamation]

eider *n.* **1** (in full **eider duck**) any of several large northern ducks, esp. *Somateria mollissima*. ▷ DUCK. **2** (in full **eider-down**) small soft feathers from the breast of the eider duck. [from Icelandic *aethr*]

eiderdown *n. Brit.* a quilt stuffed with down (originally from the eider) or some other soft material.

eight ● *n.* **1** one more than seven. **2** a symbol for this (8, viii, VIII). **3** (in full **figure of eight**) (in ice-skating, country dancing, etc.) a figure resembling the form of 8. **4** a size etc. denoted by eight. **5** an eight-oared rowing boat or its crew. **6** eight o'clock. ● *adj.* that amount to eight. □ **have one over the eight** *Brit. slang* have one drink too many. [Old English]

eighteen ● *n.* **1** one more than seventeen. **2** a symbol for this (18, xviii, XVIII). **3** a size etc. denoted by eighteen. **4** a set or team of eighteen individuals. **5** (**18**) *Brit.* (of films) classified as suitable for persons of 18 years and over. ● *adj.* that amount to eighteen. [Old English] □ **eighteenth** *adj. & n.*

eightfold *adj. & adv.* **1** eight times as much or as many. **2** consisting of eight parts. **3** amounting to eight.

eighth ● *n.* **1** the position in a sequence corresponding to the number 8 in the sequence 1–8. **2** something occupying this position. **3** one of eight equal parts of a thing. ● *adj.* that is the eighth. □ **eighthly** *adv.*

eightsome *n.* **1** (in full **eightsome reel**) a lively Scottish reel for eight dancers. **2** the music for this.

eighty ● *n.* (*pl.* **-ies**) **1** the product of eight and ten. **2** a symbol for this (80, lxxx, LXXX). **3** (in *pl.*) the numbers from 80 to 89, esp. the years of a century or of a person's life. ● *adj.* that amount to eighty. [Old English] □ **eightieth** *adj. & n.* **eightyfold** *adj. & adv.*

einsteinium *n. Chem.* a transuranic radioactive metallic element produced artificially. [named after A. *Einstein*, German-American physicist, 1879–1955]

eisteddfod /I-s*teth*-vod, I-s*ted*-vŏd/ *n.* (*pl.* **eisteddfods** or **eisteddfodau** /I-s*teth*-vod-I/) a congress of Welsh bards; a festival for musical competitions etc. [Welsh, literally 'session'] □ **eisteddfodic** *adj.*

either ● *conj.* as one of two mutually exclusive possibilities (*either come in or go out*; *is either black or white*). ● *adv.* (after a neg. sentence) **1** any more than the person or thing just mentioned (*Tim didn't like it and Patrick didn't either*). **2** moreover, indeed (*there is no time to lose, either*). ● *pron.* one or the other of two (*either of you can go*; *I like both twins but Jeremy doesn't like either*). ● *det.* **1** one or the other of two (*you may have either book*). **2** each of two (*either side of the road*). □ **either way** in either case or event. [Old English]

ejaculate ● *v.tr.* (also *absol.*) **1** utter suddenly. **2** eject (fluid etc., esp. semen) from the body. ● *n.* semen that has been ejaculated from the body. [based on Latin *ejaculatus* 'darted out'] □ **ejaculation** *n.* **ejaculator** *n.* **ejaculatory** *adj.*

eject *v.tr.* **1** send or drive out precipitately or by force. **2 a** cause (the pilot etc.) to be propelled from an aircraft in an emergency. **b** (*absol.*) (of the pilot etc.) be ejected in this way (*they both ejected at 1,000 feet*). **3** cause to be removed or drop out. **4** dispossess (a tenant etc.). **5** dart forth; emit. [based on Latin *ejectus* 'thrown out'] □ **ejection** *n.* **ejectment** *n.*

ejector *n.* a device for ejecting.

ejector seat *n.* a device for the automatic ejection of the pilot etc. of an aircraft in an emergency.

eke *v.tr.* □ **eke out 1** (foll. by *with*, *by*) supplement; make the best use of (defective means etc.). **2** contrive to make (a livelihood) or support (an existence). [Old English]

ELASMOBRANCH

The elasmobranchs form the main group of cartilaginous fish. They have five to seven prominent gill slits that open directly into the water, instead of being protected by a gill cover as in the bony fish. They have tough, usually grey skin covered in denticles (small tooth-like scales). Elasmobranchs have numerous teeth that can be lost during feeding, but which are continually replaced (as often as once a week).

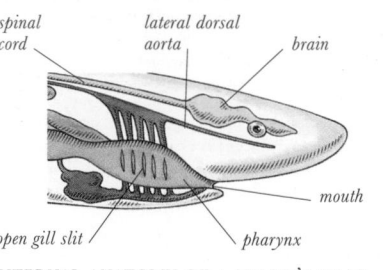

spinal cord | lateral dorsal aorta | brain | mouth | pharynx | open gill slit

INTERNAL ANATOMY OF A SHARK'S HEAD

MAIN TYPES OF ELASMOBRANCH

SHARKS
great white shark
(*Carcharodon carcharias*)

RAYS
thornback ray
(*Raja clavata*)

elaborate ● *adj.* **1** minutely worked out. **2** complicated. ● *v.* **1** *tr.* **a** work out or explain in detail. **b** (*absol.*) go into details (*I need not elaborate*). **2** *tr.* produce by labour. **3** *intr.* (foll. by *on*) explain in detail. [from Latin *elaboratus* 'extensively worked'] □ **elaborately** *adv.* **elaborateness** *n.* **elaboration** *n.*

élan /ay-*lan*/ *n.* (also **elan**) vivacity, dash. [French]

eland *n.* any antelope of the genus *Tragelaphus*, native to Africa, having spirally twisted horns, esp. the largest of living antelopes, *T. derbianus*. [Dutch, literally 'elk']

elapse *v.intr.* (of time) pass by. [based on Latin *elapsus* 'slipped away']

elasmobranch /i-*laz*-mŏ-brank/ *n. Zool.* ▲ a cartilaginous fish of the subclass Elasmobranchii, including sharks, skates, and rays. ▷ CARTILAGINOUS FISH, RAY, SHARK. [modern Latin *elasmobranchii*, from Greek *elasmos* 'beaten metal' + *bragkhia* 'gills']

elasmosaurus *n.* ▼ a large extinct marine reptile with paddle-like limbs and tough crocodile-like skin. [from Greek *elasmos* 'beaten metal' + *sauros* 'lizard']

ELASMOSAURUS:
A CRETACEOUS
PLESIOSAUR

elastane *n.* an elastic polyurethane, used esp. for hosiery, underwear, and other close-fitting clothing.

elastic ● *adj.* **1** able to resume its normal bulk or shape spontaneously after contraction, dilatation, or distortion. **2** springy. **3** (of a person or feelings) buoyant. **4** flexible, adaptable (*elastic conscience*). ● *n.* elastic cord or fabric, usu. woven with strips of rubber. [from Greek *elastikos* 'propulsive'] □ **elastically** *adv.* **elasticity** *n.* **elasticize** *v.tr.* (also **-ise**).

elasticated *adj. Brit.* (of a fabric) made elastic by weaving with rubber thread.

elastic band *n.* = RUBBER BAND.

elastin *n.* an elastic fibrous glycoprotein found in connective tissue.

elastomer *n.* a natural or synthetic rubber or rubber-like plastic. □ **elastomeric** *adj.*

elate *v.tr.* **1** (esp. as **elated** *adj.*) inspirit, stimulate. **2** make proud. [based on Latin *elatus* 'raised'] □ **elatedly** *adv.* **elatedness** *n.* **elation** *n.*

elbow ● *n.* **1 a** the joint between the forearm and the upper arm. ▷ JOINT. **b** the part of the sleeve of a garment covering the elbow. **2** an elbow-shaped bend or corner; a short piece of piping bent through a right angle. ● *v.tr.* **1** (foll. by *in*, *out*, *aside*, etc.) thrust or jostle (a person or oneself). **2** (foll. by *in*, *out*, *through*, etc.) make (one's way) by thrusting or jostling. □ **at one's elbow** close at hand. **give a person the elbow** *colloq.* dismiss or reject a person. [Old English]

elbow grease *n. colloq.* vigorous polishing; hard work.

elbow room *n. colloq.* adequate space to move or work in.

elder[1] ● *attrib.adj.* (of a person) of a greater age. ● *n.* **1** the older of two persons (*which is the elder?*). **2** (in *pl.*) **a** persons of greater age or seniority (*respect your elders*). **b** persons venerable because of age. **3** a person advanced in life. **4** an official in the early Christian, Presbyterian, or Mormon Churches. [Old English, related to OLD] □ **eldership** *n.*

elder² *n.* any shrub or tree of the genus *Sambucus*, with white flowers and usu. blue-black or red berries. [Old English]

elderberry *n.* (*pl.* **-ies**) ► the berry of the elder, esp. the common elder (*Sambucus nigra*) used for making jelly, wine, etc.

elderly *adj.* **1** somewhat old. **2** past middle age.

elder statesman *n.* an influential experienced person, esp. a politician, of advanced age.

eldest ● *adj.* first-born or oldest surviving. **●** *n.* the eldest of three or more indicated (*who is the eldest?*).

eldorado *n.* (*pl.* **-os**) **1** any imaginary country or city abounding in gold. **2** a place of great abundance. [from Spanish *el dorado* 'the gilded']

eldritch *adj.* *Sc.* & *N. Amer.* **1** weird. **2** hideous. [16th-century coinage]

elecampane /el-i-kam-**payn**/ *n.* a sunflower-like plant, *Inula helenium*, with bitter aromatic leaves and roots. [from medieval Latin *enula campana*]

elect ● *v.tr.* **1** choose (*the principles they elected to follow*). **2** choose (a person) by vote (*elected a new chairman*). **●** *adj.* **1** chosen. **2** select, choice. **3** (in *comb.*, after a noun designating office) chosen but not yet in office (*president-elect*). [from Latin *electus* 'picked'] □ **electable** *adj.*

election *n.* **1** the process of electing or being elected. **2** the act or an instance of electing.

electioneer ● *v.intr.* **1** take part in an election campaign. **2** *derog.* seek election by currying favour with voters. **●** *n.* a person who electioneers.

elective ● *adj.* **1 a** (of an office or its holder) filled or appointed by election. **b** (of authority) derived from election. **2** (of a body) having the power to elect. **3** having a tendency to act on or be concerned with some things rather than others (*elective affinity*). **4** (of a course of study) chosen by the student. **5** (of a surgical operation etc.) not urgently necessary. **●** *n.* *US* an elective course of study. □ **electively** *adv.*

elector *n.* **1** a person who has the right of voting to elect an MP etc. **2** *US* a member of an electoral college.

electoral *adj.* relating to or ranking as electors. □ **electorally** *adv.*

electoral college *n.* **1** a body of persons representing the states of the US, who cast votes for the election of the President. **2** a body of electors.

electorate *n.* **1** a body of electors. **2** *Austral.* & *NZ* an area represented by one Member of Parliament.

electric ● *adj.* **1** of, worked by, or charged with electricity; producing or capable of generating electricity. ▷ CIRCUIT. **2** causing or charged with sudden and dramatic excitement (*the atmosphere was electric*). **●** *n.* **1** an electric light, vehicle, etc. **2** (in *pl.*) electrical equipment. [based on Greek *ēlektron* 'amber', the rubbing of which causes electrostatic phenomena] □ **electrically** *adv.*

---

electrical *adj.* **1** of or concerned with or of the nature of electricity. **2** operating by electricity. **3** = ELECTRIC *adj.* 2.

electric blanket *n.* an electrically wired blanket used for heating a bed.

    electric blue ● *n.* a steely or brilliant light blue. **●** *adj.* (hyphenated when *attrib.*) of this colour.

    electric chair *n.* a chair used for capital punishment by electrocution.

    electric eel *n.* an eel-like freshwater fish, *Electrophorus electricus*, native to S. America, that kills its prey by electric shock.

    electric eye *n.* *colloq.* a photoelectric cell operating a relay when the beam of light illuminating it is obscured.

electric field *n.* a region of electrical influence.

electric fire *n.* *Brit.* an electrically operated incandescent or convector heater, usu. portable and for domestic use.

electric hare see HARE *n.* 2.

electrician *n.* a person who installs or maintains electrical equipment, esp. professionally.

electricity *n.* **1** a form of energy resulting from the existence of charged particles (electrons, protons, etc.), either statically as an accumulation of charge or dynamically as a current. **2** the branch of physics dealing with electricity. **3** a supply of electric current for heating, lighting, etc. **4** a state of heightened emotion; excitement, tension.

electric ray *n.* any of several fish of the ray family Torpedinidae which can give an electric shock (see RAY²).

electric shock *n.* the effect of a sudden discharge of electricity on a person or animal.

electric storm *n.* a violent disturbance of the electrical condition of the atmosphere.

electrify *v.tr.* (**-ies**, **-ied**) **1** charge (a body) with electricity. **2** convert to the use of electric power. **3** cause sudden excitement in. □ **electrification** *n.*

electro- *comb. form* of, relating to, or caused by electricity (*electrocute*; *electromagnet*).

electrocardiogram *n.* a record traced by an electrocardiograph.

electrocardiograph *n.* an instrument recording the electric currents generated by a heartbeat. □ **electrocardiographic** *adj.* **electrocardiography** *n.*

electroconvulsive *adj.* (of a therapy) employing the application of electric shocks to the brain, which induces a convulsion, as in some treatments for mental illness.

electrocute *v.tr.* **1** kill by electricity (as a form of capital punishment). **2** cause the death of by electric shock. □ **electrocution** *n.*

electrode *n.* a conductor through which electricity enters or leaves an electrolyte, gas, vacuum, etc. ▷ BATTERY, ELECTROPLATE. [based on Greek *hodos* 'way']

electrodynamics *n.pl.* (usu. treated as *sing.*) the study of electricity in motion. □ **electrodynamic** *adj.*

---

electroencephalogram *n.* a record traced by an electroencephalograph.

electroencephalograph *n.* an instrument recording the electrical activity of the brain. □ **electroencephalography** *n.*

electrolyse *v.tr.* (*US* **-yze**) subject to or treat by electrolysis. □ **electrolyser** *n.*

electrolysis *n.* **1** *Chem.* the decomposition of a substance by the application of an electric current. ▷ ELECTROPLATE. **2** *Surgery* this process applied to the destruction of tumours, hair-roots, etc. □ **electrolytic** *adj.* **electrolytically** *adv.*

electrolyte *n.* **1** a liquid which contains ions and can be decomposed by electrolysis, esp. that present in a battery. ▷ BATTERY, ELECTROPLATE. **2** (usu. in *pl.*) *Physiol.* the ionized or ionizable constituents of a living cell, blood, etc. [based on Greek *lutos* 'released']

electromagnet *n.* a soft metal core made into a magnet by the passage of electric current through a coil surrounding it. ▷ MRI, RECEIVER

electromagnetic *adj.* having both an electrical and a magnetic character or properties. □ **electromagnetically** *adv.*

electromagnetic radiation *n.* ▼ a kind of radiation including visible light, radio waves, gamma rays, X-rays, etc., in which electric and magnetic fields vary simultaneously.

electromagnetism *n.* **1** ▼ the magnetic forces produced by electricity. **2** the study of this.

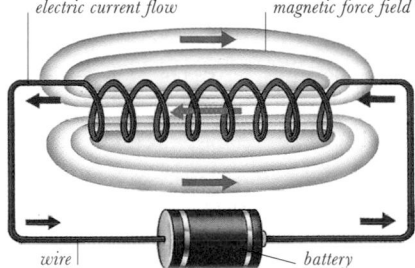

electric current flow   *magnetic force field*

wire   *battery*

ELECTROMAGNETISM: DEMONSTRATION OF MAGNETISM PRODUCED BY ELECTRIC CURRENT

electromechanical *adj.* relating to the application of electricity to mechanical processes, devices, etc.

electrometer /i-lek-**trom**-i-ter/ *n.* an instrument for measuring electrical potential without drawing any current from the circuit. □ **electrometric** *adj.* **electrometry** *n.*

electromotive *adj.* producing or tending to produce an electric current.

electromotive force *n.* a difference in potential that tends to give rise to an electric current.

electron *n.* a stable subatomic particle with a charge of negative electricity, found in all atoms and acting as the primary carrier of electricity in solids. ▷ ATOM

electron beam *n.* a stream of electrons in a gas or vacuum. ▷ MONITOR

ELDERBERRY: COMMON ELDER (*Sambucus nigra*)

ELECTROMAGNETIC RADIATION

Electromagnetic radiation is a form of energy that travels through space and matter. There are many types of radiation, all of which are identical except for their wavelengths and energy. Radio waves, for example, have long wavelengths and low energy, while X-rays have shorter wavelengths and higher energy.

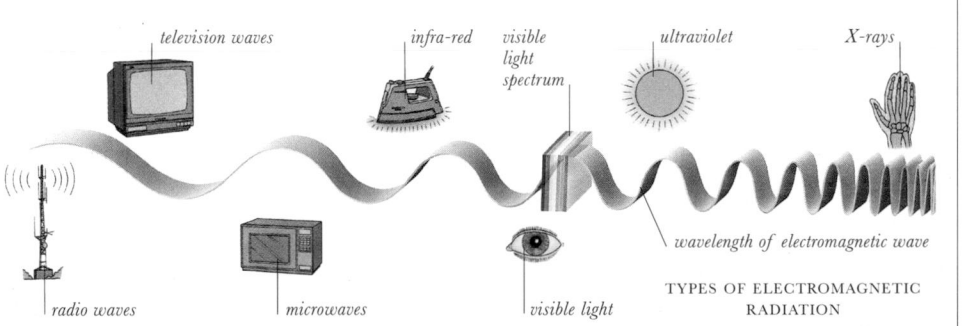

television waves   *infra-red*   *visible light spectrum*   *ultraviolet*   *X-rays*

radio waves   *microwaves*   *visible light*

wavelength of electromagnetic wave

TYPES OF ELECTROMAGNETIC RADIATION

E

E

electron gun *n.* a device for producing a narrow stream of electrons from a heated cathode. ▷ TELEVISION

electronic *adj.* **1 a** produced by or involving the flow of electrons. **b** of or relating to electrons or electronics. **2** (of a device) using electronic components. **3 a** (of music) produced by electronic means and usu. recorded on tape. **b** (of a musical instrument) producing sounds by electronic means. □ **electronically** *adv.*

electronic mail *n.* **1** messages distributed by electronic means esp. from one computer system to one or more recipients. **2** the electronic mail system.

electronic publishing *n.* the publishing of books etc. in machine-readable form rather than on paper.

electronics *n.pl.* **1** (treated as *sing.*) the branch of physics and technology concerned with the behaviour and movement of electrons in a vacuum, gas, semiconductor, etc. **2** (treated as *pl.*) the circuits used in this.

electronic tagging *n.* the attaching of electronic markers to people, goods, etc., enabling them to be traced.

electron lens *n.* a device for focusing a stream of electrons by means of electric or magnetic fields.

electron microscope *n.* a microscope with high magnification and resolution, employing electron beams in place of light.

electron pair *n.* **1** *Chem.* two electrons in the same orbital in an atom or molecule. **2** *Physics* an electron and a positron produced in a high-energy reaction.

electronvolt *n.* a unit of energy equal to the work done on an electron in accelerating it through a potential difference of one volt.

electrophoresis /i-lek-troh-fŏ-ree-sis/ *n. Physics* & *Chem.* the movement of charged particles in a fluid or gel under the influence of an electric field. [based on Greek *phorēsis* 'being carried'] □ **electrophoretic** *adj.*

electroplate ● *v.tr.* ▼ coat by electrolytic deposition with chromium, silver, etc. ● *n.* electroplated articles. □ **electroplater** *n.*

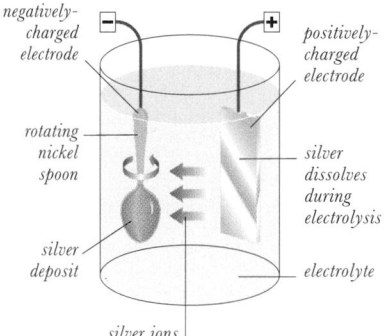

ELECTROPLATE: ELECTROPLATING A SPOON WITH SILVER

electroporation *n. Biol.* the action or process of introducing DNA or chromosomes into the cells of bacteria etc. using a pulse of electricity to open the pores in the cell membranes briefly. [based on Greek *poros* 'passage, pore']

electroscope *n.* an instrument for detecting and measuring electricity, esp. as an indication of the ionization of air by radioactivity. ▷ STATIC ELECTRICITY

electro-shock *attrib.adj.* (of medical treatment) by means of electric shocks.

electrostatic *adj.* of or relating to stationary electric charges or electrostatics.

electrostatics *n.* the study of stationary electric charges or fields as opposed to electric currents.

electrostatic units *n.pl.* a system of units based primarily on the forces between electric charges.

ELEPHANT

The Indian and African elephants are the only two surviving species of the order Proboscidea (meaning animals with a proboscis or trunk). Elephants are herbivorous, highly intelligent, and extremely social, living in matriarchal herds.

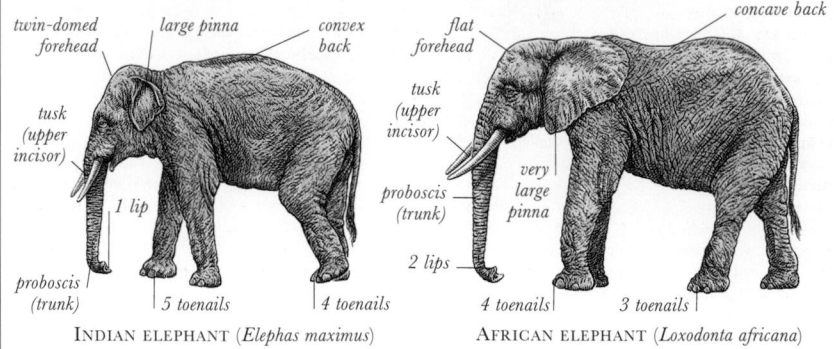

INDIAN ELEPHANT (*Elephas maximus*)

AFRICAN ELEPHANT (*Loxodonta africana*)

electrotechnology *n.* the science of the application of electricity in technology. □ **electrotechnical** *adj.*

electrotherapy *n.* the treatment of diseases by the use of electricity.

electrotype ● *v.tr.* copy by the electrolytic deposition of copper on a mould, esp. for printing. ● *n.* a copy so formed.

elegant *adj.* **1** graceful. **2** tasteful, refined. **3** (of a mode of life etc.) of refined luxury. **4** ingeniously simple and pleasing. **5** *US* excellent. [from Latin *elegant-* 'discriminating'] □ **elegance** *n.* **elegantly** *adv.*

elegiac ● *adj.* **1** (of a metre) used for elegies. **2** mournful. ● *n.* (in *pl.*) verses in an elegiac metre. □ **elegiacally** *adv.*

elegize *v.* (also **-ise**) **1** *intr.* (often foll. by *upon*) write an elegy. **2** *intr.* write in a mournful strain. **3** *tr.* write an elegy upon. □ **elegist** *n.*

elegy *n.* (*pl.* **-ies**) **1** a song of lament, esp. for the dead. **2** a poem in elegiac metre. [from Greek *elegos* 'mournful poem']

element *n.* **1** a component part; a contributing factor. **2** *Chem.* & *Physics* any of the substances that cannot be resolved by chemical means into simpler substances. **3 a** any of the four substances (earth, water, air, and fire) in ancient and medieval philosophy. **b** a being's natural abode or environment. **4** a resistance wire that heats up in an electric heater, cooker, etc. **5** (in *pl.*) atmospheric agencies, esp. wind and storm. **6** (in *pl.*) the rudiments of learning or of a branch of knowledge. **7** (in *pl.*) the bread and wine of the Eucharist. **8** *Math.* & *Logic* an entity that is a single member of a set. □ **in** (or **out of**) **one's element** in (or out of) one's accustomed or preferred surroundings. [from Latin *elementum*]

elemental *adj.* **1** of the four elements. **2** of the powers of nature (*elemental worship*). **3** comparable to a force of nature (*elemental grandeur*; *elemental tumult*). **4** uncompounded (*elemental oxygen*). **5** essential.

elementary *adj.* **1 a** dealing with the simplest facts of a subject. **b** simple. **2** *Chem.* not decomposable.

elementary particle *n.* a subatomic particle, esp. one not known to be decomposable into simpler particles.

elementary school *n.* **1** *Brit. hist.* a school in which primary instruction is given. **2** *N. Amer.* a primary school for usu. the first six or eight grades.

elephant *n.* (*pl.* same or **elephants**) ▲ the largest living land animal, of which two species survive, the larger African (*Loxodonta africana*) and the smaller Indian (*Elephas maximus*), both with a trunk and long curved ivory tusks. [from Greek *elephas -antos* 'ivory, elephant'] □ **elephantoid** *adj.*

elephantiasis *n.* gross enlargement of the body,

esp. the limbs, due to lymphatic obstruction by a nematode parasite transmitted by mosquitoes.

elephantine *adj.* **1** of elephants. **2 a** huge. **b** clumsy, unwieldy.

elevate *v.tr.* **1** bring to a higher position. **2** raise, lift. **3** exalt in rank etc. **4** (usu. as **elevated** *adj.*) raise morally or intellectually (*elevated style*). [based on Latin *elevatus* 'raised']

elevation *n.* **1 a** the process of elevating or being elevated. **b** the angle with the horizontal, esp. of a gun or of the direction of a celestial object. **c** the height above a given level, esp. sea level. **d** a high position. **2 a** a drawing or diagram made by projection on a vertical plane (cf. PLAN *n.* 2). **b** a flat drawing of the front, side, or back of a house etc. **3** *Ballet* **a** the capacity of a dancer to attain height in springing movements. **b** the action of tightening the muscles and uplifting the body. □ **elevational** *adj.* (in sense 2).

elevator *n.* **1** a hoisting machine. **2** *Aeron.* the movable part of a tailplane for changing the pitch of an aircraft. ▷ AIRCRAFT. **3** *N. Amer.* **a** = LIFT *n.* 3a. **b** a place for lifting and storing quantities of grain.

eleven ● *n.* **1** one more than ten. **2** a symbol for this (11, xi, XI). **3** a size etc. denoted by eleven. **4** eleven o'clock. **5** a set or team of eleven individuals. ● *adj.* that amount to eleven. [Old English]

elevenfold *adj.* & *adv.* **1** eleven times as much or as many. **2** consisting of eleven parts.

elevenses *n.* (usu. treated as *pl.*) *Brit. colloq.* light refreshment taken about 11 a.m.

eleventh ● *n.* **1** the position in a sequence corresponding to the number 11 in the sequence 1–11. **2** something occupying this position. **3** one of eleven equal parts of a thing. ● *adj.* that is the eleventh. □ **the eleventh hour** the last possible moment.

elf *n.* (*pl.* **elves**) **1** a mythological being, esp. one that is small and mischievous. **2** a sprite or little creature. [Old English] □ **elfish** *adj.* **elvish** *adj.*

elfin *adj.* of elves; elflike.

elf-lock *n.* a tangled mass of hair.

elicit *v.tr.* (**elicited, eliciting**) **1** draw out, evoke (an admission, response, etc.). **2** draw forth (what is latent). [based on Latin *elicitus* 'drawn forth'] □ **elicitation** *n.* **elicitor** *n.*

elide *v.tr.* omit (a vowel or syllable) by elision. [from Latin *elidere* 'to crush']

eligible *adj.* **1** fit or entitled to be chosen (*eligible for a rebate*). **2** desirable or suitable, esp. as a partner in marriage. [from Late Latin *eligibilis*] □ **eligibility** *n.*

eliminate *v.tr.* **1** remove, get rid of. **2** exclude from consideration; ignore as irrelevant. **3** exclude from further participation in a competition etc. on defeat. [based on Latin *limen* 'threshold'] □ **eliminable** *adj.* **elimination** *n.* **eliminator** *n.* **eliminatory** *adj.*

elision *n.* **1** the omission of a vowel or syllable in pronouncing (as in *I'm, let's, e'en*). **2** the omission of a passage in a book etc. [related to ELIDE]

elite *n.* (also **élite**) **1** (prec. by *the*) the best of a group. **2** a select group or class. [from French]

elitism *n.* (also **élitism**) **1** advocacy of or reliance on leadership or dominance by a select group. **2** a sense of belonging to an elite. □ **elitist** *n. & adj.* (also **élitist**).

elixir *n.* **1 a** a preparation supposedly able to change metals into gold. **b** (in full **elixir of life**) a preparation supposedly able to prolong life indefinitely. **c** a supposed remedy for all ills. **2** *Pharm.* an aromatic solution used as a medicine or flavouring. [from Arabic *al-iksīr*]

Elizabethan ● *adj.* of the time of Queen Elizabeth I (1558–1603) or of Queen Elizabeth II (1952–). ● *n.* a person of the time of Queen Elizabeth I or II.

elk *n.* (*pl.* same or **elks**) **1** a large deer, *Alces alces*, of northern Eurasia and N. America. **2** *N. Amer.* a wapiti. [Middle English]

ell *n. hist.* a former measure of length, about 45 inches. [Old English]

ellipse *n.* ► a regular oval, traced by a point moving in a plane so that the sum of its distances from two other points is constant, or resulting when a cone is cut by an oblique plane which does not intersect the base. [from Greek *elleipsis* 'defect']

ellipsis *n.* (also **ellipse**) (*pl.* **ellipses** /-seez/) **1** the omission from a sentence of words needed to complete the construction or sense. **2** a set of three dots etc. indicating an omission.

ellipsoid *n.* a solid of which all the plane sections normal to one axis are circles and all the other plane sections are ellipses. □ **ellipsoidal** *adj.*

elliptic *adj.* (also **elliptical**) of, relating to, or having the form of an ellipse or ellipsis. [from Greek *elleiptikos* 'defective'] □ **elliptically** *adv.* **ellipticity** *n.*

elm *n.* **1** (also **elm tree**) ◄ any tree of the genus *Ulmus*, with rough serrated leaves. **2** (in full **elmwood**) the wood of the elm. [Old English] □ **elmy** *adj.*

elocution *n.* **1** the art of clear and expressive speech, esp. of distinct pronunciation and articulation. **2** a particular style of speaking. [from Latin *elocutio* 'speaking out'] □ **elocutionary** *adj.* **elocutionist** *n.*

elongate *v.tr.* lengthen, prolong. [based on Late Latin *elongatus* 'removed to a distance'] □ **elongation** *n.*

elongated *adj.* **1** long in relation to its width. **2** that has been made longer.

elope *v.intr.* **1** run away to marry secretly. **2** run away with a lover. [from Anglo-French *aloper*] □ **elopement** *n.*

eloquence *n.* **1** fluent and effective use of language. **2** rhetoric.

eloquent *adj.* **1** possessing or showing eloquence. **2** (often foll. by *of*) clearly expressive or indicative. [from Latin *eloquent-* 'speaking out'] □ **eloquently** *adv.*

Elsan *n. Brit. propr.* a type of transportable chemical lavatory. [apparently from *E. L.* Jackson (its manufacturer) + *sanitation*]

else *adv.* **1** besides (*nowhere else; who else*). **2** instead (*what else could I say?*). **3** otherwise; if not (*run, (or) else you will be late*). [Old English]

elsewhere *adv.* in or to some other place.

elucidate *v.tr.* throw light on; explain. [based on Late Latin *elucidatus* 'made bright'] □ **elucidation** *n.* **elucidatory** *adj.*

elude *v.tr.* **1** escape adroitly from (a danger, difficulty,

ELLIPSE

pursuer, etc.); dodge. **2** avoid compliance with (a law, request, etc.) or fulfilment of (an obligation). **3** (of a fact, solution, etc.) escape from or baffle (a person's memory or understanding). [from Latin *eludere*]

elusive *adj.* **1** difficult to find or catch. **2** difficult to remember or recall. **3** (of an answer etc.) avoiding the point raised. □ **elusively** *adv.* **elusiveness** *n.*

elver *n.* a young eel. [variant of *eel-fare* 'a brood of young eels']

elves *pl.* of ELF.

elvish see ELF.

Elysium *n.* **1** (also **Elysian Fields**) (in Greek mythology) the abode of the blessed after death. **2** a place or state of ideal happiness. [from Greek *Elusion (pedion)* 'abode of the blessed'] □ **Elysian** *adj.*

elytron /el-i-tron/ *n.* (*pl.* **elytra**) each of the two wing-cases of a beetle. ▷ BEETLE. [from Greek *elutron* 'sheath']

em *n. Printing* **1** a unit for measuring the amount of printed matter in a line, usually equal to the nominal width of capital M. **2** a unit of measurement equal to 12 points. [name of the letter *M*]

'em *pron. colloq.* them (*let 'em all come*). [originally a form of Middle English *hem* '(to) them']

emaciate *v.tr.* (esp. as **emaciated** *adj.*) make abnormally thin or feeble. [based on Latin *macies* 'leanness'] □ **emaciation** *n.*

e-mail (also **email**) ● *n.* = ELECTRONIC MAIL. ● *v.tr.* **1** send e-mail to (a person). **2** send by e-mail.

emanate *v.* **1** *intr.* (of an idea, rumour, etc.) issue, originate. **2** *intr.* (of gas, light, etc.) proceed, issue. **3** *tr.* emit; send forth. [based on Latin *emanatus* 'flowed out']

emanation *n.* **1** the act or process of emanating. **2** something that emanates from a source.

emancipate *v.tr.* **1** free from restraint, esp. legal, social, or political. **2** (usu. as **emancipated** *adj.*) cause to be less inhibited by moral or social convention. **3** free from slavery. [based on Latin *emancipatus* 'released (from control)'] □ **emancipation** *n.* **emancipator** *n.* **emancipatory** *adj.*

emasculate ● *v.tr.* **1** deprive of force or vigour, make feeble or ineffective. **2** castrate. ● *adj.* **1** deprived of force or vigour. **2** castrated. **3** effeminate. [from Latin *emasculatus* 'castrated'] □ **emasculation** *n.*

embalm *v.tr.* **1** preserve (a corpse) from decay. **2** preserve from oblivion. **3** give balmy fragrance to. [from Old French *embaumer*] □ **embalmer** *n.* **embalmment** *n.*

embank *v.tr.* shut in or confine (a river etc.) with an artificial bank.

embankment *n.* an earth or stone bank for keeping back water, or for carrying a road or railway.

embargo ● *n.* (*pl.* **-oes**) **1** an order of a state forbidding foreign ships to enter, or any ships to leave, its ports. **2** an official suspension of commerce or other activity (*be under an embargo*). **3** an impediment. ● *v.tr.* (**-oes**, **-oed**) **1** place under an embargo. **2** seize (a ship, goods) for state service. [Spanish, from *embargar* 'to arrest']

embark *v.* **1** *tr. & intr.* put or go on board a ship or aircraft. **2** *intr.* (foll. by *on, upon*) engage in an activity or undertaking. [from French *embarquer*] □ **embarkation** *n.* (in sense 1).

embarrass *v.tr.* **1** cause (a person) to feel awkward or ashamed. **2** (as **embarrassed** *adj.*) encumbered with debts. **3** hamper, impede. [from Italian *imbarrare* 'to bar in'] □ **embarrassedly** *adv.* **embarrassingly** *adv.* **embarrassment** *n.*

embassy *n.* (*pl.* **-ies**) **1 a** the residence or offices of an ambassador. **b** the ambassador and staff attached to an embassy. **2** a deputation to a foreign country. [from medieval Latin *ambasciata*]

embattle *v.tr.* **1 a** set in battle array. **b** fortify against attack. **2** provide with battlements. **3** (as **embattled** *adj.*) **a** prepared or arrayed for battle. **b** involved in a conflict or difficult undertaking.

embed *v.tr.* (also **imbed**) (**-bedded**, **-bedding**) **1** (esp. as **embedded** *adj.*) fix firmly in a surrounding mass (*embedded in concrete*). **2** (of a mass) surround so as to fix firmly. □ **embedment** *n.*

embellish *v.tr.* **1** beautify, adorn. **2** add interest to (a narrative) with fictitious additions. [from Old French *embellir*] □ **embellishment** *n.*

ember *n.* (usu. in *pl.*) a small piece of glowing coal or wood in a dying fire. [Old English]

Ember days *n.pl.* any of the days traditionally reserved for fasting and prayer in the Christian Church, now associated with ordinations. [Old English]

embezzle *v.tr.* (also *absol.*) divert (funds) fraudulently to one's own use. [based on Old French *besiller* 'to maltreat'] □ **embezzlement** *n.* **embezzler** *n.*

embitter *v.tr.* **1** arouse bitter feelings in (a person). **2** make more bitter or painful. **3** render (a person or feelings) hostile. □ **embitterment** *n.*

emblazon *v.tr.* **1 a** portray conspicuously. **b** adorn (a shield) with heraldic devices. **2** adorn brightly and conspicuously. **3** celebrate, extol.

emblem *n.* **1** a symbol or representation typifying or identifying an institution, quality, etc. **2** (foll. by *of*) (of a person) the type (*the very emblem of courage*). **3** a heraldic device or symbolic object as a distinctive badge. ▷ INSIGNIA. [from Greek *emblēma* 'insertion'] □ **emblematic** *adj.* **emblematical** *adj.* **emblematically** *adv.*

emblematize *v.tr.* (also **-ise**) **1** serve as an emblem of. **2** represent by an emblem.

embody *v.tr.* (**-ies**, **-ied**) **1** give a concrete or discernible form to (an idea etc.). **2** (of a thing or person) be an expression of (an idea etc.). **3** express tangibly (*courage embodied in heroic actions*). **4** include, comprise. □ **embodiment** *n.*

embolden *v.tr.* make bold; encourage.

embolism *n. Med.* an obstruction of an artery by a clot of blood, air bubble, etc. [Middle English in sense 'intercalation', from Greek]

embolus *n.* (*pl.* **emboli**) an object causing an embolism. [Latin, literally 'piston']

emboss *v.tr.* **1** ▼ carve or mould in relief. **2** form figures etc. so that they stand out on (a surface). **3** make protuberant. [from Old French]

EMBOSS: EMBOSSED TUDOR ROSE

embrace ● *v.tr.* **1 a** hold (a person) closely in the arms. **b** (*absol.*, of two people) hold each other closely. **2** clasp, enclose. **3** accept eagerly (an offer, opportunity, etc.). **4** adopt (a course of action, doctrine, cause, etc.). **5** include, comprise. **6** take in with the eye or mind. ● *n.* an act of embracing; holding in the arms. [from Old French *embracer*] □ **embraceable** *adj.* **embracement** *n.* **embracer** *n.*

embrasure *n.* **1** the bevelling of a wall at the sides of a door or window. **2** a small opening in a parapet of a fortified building. [French] □ **embrasured** *adj.*

E

E

embrocation n. a liquid rubbed on the body to relieve muscular pain etc. [based on Greek *embrokhē* 'lotion']

embroider v.tr. **1** (also *absol.*) **a** decorate (cloth etc.) with needlework. **b** create (a design) in this way. **2** add interest to (a narrative) with fictitious additions. [based on Old French *brouder*] □ **embroiderer** n.

embroidery n. (*pl.* **-ies**) **1** the art of embroidering. **2** embroidered work. **3** unnecessary or extravagant ornament; elaboration.

embroil v.tr. (often foll. by *with*) involve (a person) in conflict or difficulties. [from French *embrouiller*] □ **embroilment** n.

embryo n. (*pl.* **-os**) **1 a** an unborn or unhatched offspring. ▷ EGG. **b** ▼ a human offspring in the first eight weeks from conception. **2** a rudimentary plant in a seed. **3** a thing in a rudimentary stage. **4** (*attrib.*) undeveloped, immature. □ **in embryo** undeveloped. [from Greek *embruon* 'foetus'] □ **embryonal** adj. **embryonic** adj. **embryonically** adv.

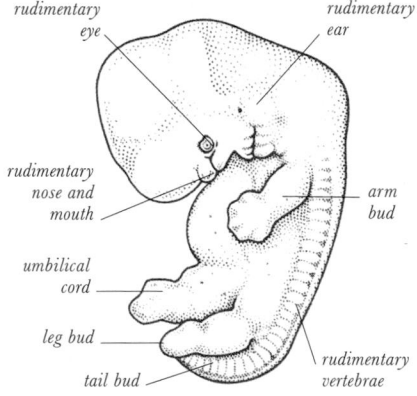

EMBRYO: SIX-WEEK-OLD HUMAN EMBRYO

rudimentary eye

rudimentary ear

rudimentary nose and mouth

arm bud

umbilical cord

leg bud

tail bud

rudimentary vertebrae

embryology n. the study of embryos. □ **embryologic** adj. **embryological** adj. **embryologically** adv. **embryologist** n.

emcee colloq. ● n. a master of ceremonies or compère. ● v.tr. & intr. (**emcees**, **emceed**) compère. [the letters *MC*]

emend v.tr. edit (a text etc.) to remove errors and corruptions. [from Latin *emendare*] □ **emendation** n. **emendatory** adj.

emerald ● n. **1** a bright green precious stone. ▷ GEM, MATRIX. **2** (in full **emerald green**) the colour of this. ● adj. (in full **emerald green**; hyphenated when *attrib.*) bright green. [from Greek *smaragdos*]

Emerald Isle n. literary Ireland.

emerge v.intr. (often foll. by *from*) **1** come up or out into view. **2** (of facts, circumstances, etc.) become known. **3** become recognized or prominent (*emerged as a leading contender*). **4** (of a question, difficulty, etc.) become apparent. [from Latin *emergere*] □ **emergence** n.

emergency n. (*pl.* **-ies**) **1** a sudden state of danger, conflict, etc., requiring immediate action. **2** a medical condition or patient requiring immediate treatment. **3** (*attrib.*) for use in an emergency (*emergency exit*). [from medieval Latin *emergentia*]

emergent adj. **1** becoming apparent; emerging. **2** (of a nation) newly formed or made independent.

emeritus adj. retired and retaining one's title as an honour (*emeritus professor*). [Latin, literally 'deserved']

emery n. a coarse corundum used for polishing metal etc. [from Greek *smēris* 'polishing powder']

emery board n. a strip of thin wood or board coated with emery or another abrasive, used as a nail file.

emery paper n. (also **emery cloth**) paper or cloth covered with emery, used for polishing or cleaning metals etc.

emetic /i-met-ik/ ● adj. that causes vomiting. ● n. an emetic medicine. [from Greek *emetikos*]

EMF abbr. **1** (usu. **emf**) electromotive force. **2** electromagnetic field(s).

emigrant ● n. a person who emigrates. ● adj. emigrating.

emigrate v.intr. leave one's own country to settle in another. [based on Latin *emigratus* 'migrated out'] □ **emigration** n.

émigré /em-i-gray/ n. (also **emigre**) an emigrant, esp. a political exile. [French]

eminence n. **1** distinction; recognized superiority. **2** a piece of rising ground. **3** (**Eminence**) a title of a cardinal (*Your Eminence*; *His Eminence*).

éminence grise /em-i-nahnss greez/ n. (*pl.* **éminences grises** *pronunc.* same) a person who exercises power or influence without holding office. [French, literally 'grey eminence': originally applied to Cardinal Richelieu's grey-cloaked private secretary, Père Joseph, 1577–1638]

eminent adj. **1** distinguished, notable. **2** (of qualities) remarkable in degree. [from Latin *eminent-* 'jutting'] □ **eminently** adv.

emir /em-eer/ n. a title of various Muslim rulers. [from Arabic *'amīr*]

emirate n. the rank, domain, or reign of an emir.

emissary n. (*pl.* **-ies**) a person sent on a diplomatic mission. [from Latin *emissarius* 'scout']

emission n. **1** (often foll. by *of*) the process or an act of emitting. **2** a thing emitted. [from Latin *emissio*]

emissive adj. having the power to radiate light, heat, etc. □ **emissivity** n.

emit v.tr. (**emitted**, **emitting**) **1** send out (heat, light, vapour, etc.). **2** utter (a cry etc.). [from Latin *emittere*]

Emmental /em-ĕn-tahl/ n. (also **Emmenthal**) a kind of hard Swiss cheese with many holes in it, similar to Gruyère. ▷ CHEESE. [from *Emmental*, a valley in Switzerland]

emmer n. ▶ a kind of wheat, *Triticum dicoccum*, grown mainly for fodder. [from Old High German *amer* 'spelt']

emollient ● adj. that softens or soothes the skin. ● n. an emollient substance. [from Latin *emollient-* 'softening'] □ **emollience** n.

EMMER
(*Triticum dicoccum*)

emolument n. a salary or fee from employment or office. [from Latin *emolumentum*]

emote v.intr. colloq. show excessive emotion.

emotion n. **1** a strong mental or instinctive feeling such as love or fear. **2** emotional intensity or sensibility (*he spoke with emotion*). [earlier in sense 'agitation of the mind', from French] □ **emotionless** adj.

emotional adj. **1** of or relating to the emotions. **2** (of a person) easily affected by or readily displaying emotion. **3** expressing or based on emotion (*an emotional appeal*). **4** arousing emotion (*an emotional issue*). □ **emotionalism** n. **emotionality** n. **emotionalize** v.tr. (also **-ise**). **emotionally** adv.

■ **Usage** See Usage Note at EMOTIVE.

emotive adj. **1** of or characterized by emotion. **2** arousing emotion. **3** arousing feeling; not purely descriptive. □ **emotively** adv. **emotiveness** n. **emotivity** n.

■ **Usage** Although the senses of *emotive* and *emotional* overlap, e.g. both *an emotive issue* and *an emotional issue* are common, *emotive* should not be used of people to mean 'emotional'. It is wrong to say *He is an emotive person* unless what is meant is that he arouses emotion in others, and it is similarly incorrect to say *They reacted emotively*.

empanel v.tr. (also **impanel**) (**-panelled**, **-panelling**; *US* **-paneled**, **-paneling**) enrol or enter on a panel (those eligible for jury service). □ **empanelment** n.

empathize v.intr. (also **-ise**) *Psychol.* (usu. foll. by *with*) exercise empathy.

empathy n. *Psychol.* the power of identifying oneself mentally with a person or object. [translation of German *Einfühlung*] □ **empathetic** adj. **empathetically** adv. **empathic** adj. **empathically** adv.

emperor n. the sovereign of an empire. [from Latin *imperator*] □ **emperorship** n.

emperor penguin n. ▶ the largest kind of penguin, *Aptenodytes forsteri*, of the Antarctic. ▷ PENGUIN

emphasis n. (*pl.* **emphases**) **1** special importance or prominence attached to a thing, fact, idea, etc. (*emphasis on economy*). **2** stress laid on a word or words to indicate special meaning or importance. **3** vigour or intensity of expression, feeling, action, etc. [based on Greek *emphainein* 'to exhibit']

emphasize v.tr. (also **-ise**) **1** bring (a thing, fact, etc.) into special prominence. **2** lay stress on (a word in speaking).

EMPEROR PENGU(IN)
(*Aptenodytes forsteri*)

emphatic adj. **1** (of language, tone, or gesture) forcibly expressive. **2** (of words): **a** bearing the stress. **b** used to give emphasis. **3** expressing oneself with emphasis. □ **emphatically** adv.

emphysema /em-fi-see-mă/ n. enlargement of the air sacs of the lungs causing breathlessness. [from Greek *emphusēma*]

empire n. **1** an extensive group of states or countries under a single authority. **2** supreme dominion. **3** a large commercial organization etc. owned or directed by one person or group. [from Latin *imperium*]

empire builder n. a person who deliberately acquires extra territory, authority, etc. □ **empire building** n.

empirical adj. based or acting on observation or experiment, not on theory. □ **empirically** adv.

emplacement n. **1** the act or an instance of putting in position. **2** a platform or defended position for a gun.

employ v.tr. **1** use the services of (a person) in return for payment. **2** (often foll. by *for, in, on*) use (a thing, time, energy, etc.) esp. to good effect. **3** (often foll. by *in*) keep (a person) occupied. □ **in the employ of** employed by. [based on Latin *implicari* 'to be involved'] □ **employable** adj. **employability** n. **employer** n.

employee n. (*US* also **employe**) a person employed for wages or salary.

employment n. **1** the act of employing or the state of being employed. **2** a person's regular trade or profession.

employment office n. (formerly **employment exchange**) esp. *Brit.* a government office finding work for the unemployed.

emporium n. (*pl.* **emporia** or **-ums**) **1** a large shop selling a wide variety of goods. **2** a centre of commerce, a market. [from Greek *emporion*]

empower v.tr. (foll. by *to* + infin.) **1** authorize, license. **2** give power to; make able. □ **empowerment** n.

empress n. **1** the wife or widow of an emperor. **2** a woman emperor.

empty ● adj. (**emptier**, **emptiest**) **1** containing nothing. **2** (of a house etc.) unoccupied or unfurnished. **3** (of a transport vehicle etc.) without a load, passengers, etc. **4 a** meaningless, hollow.

insincere (*empty threats*). **b** without substance or purpose (*an empty existence*). **5** *colloq.* hungry. ● *v.* (**-ies, -ied**) **1** *tr.* remove the contents of. **2** *tr.* (often foll. by *into*) transfer (the contents of a container). **3** *intr.* become empty. **4** *intr.* (usu. foll. by *into*) (of a river) discharge itself. ● *n.* (*pl.* **-ies**) *colloq.* an empty container. [Old English] □ **emptily** *adv.* **emptiness** *n.*

empty-handed *adj.* (usu. *predic.*) **1** bringing or taking nothing. **2** having achieved or obtained nothing.

empty-headed *adj.* foolish; lacking common sense.

empurple *v.tr.* **1** make purple or red. **2** make angry.

em rule *n. Brit.* a long dash used in punctuation.

EMS *abbr.* European Monetary System.

EMU *abbr.* economic and monetary union (of the EC); European monetary union.

emu *n.* a large flightless bird, *Dromaius novaehollandiae*, native to Australia. [from Portuguese *ema*]

emulate *v.tr.* **1** try to equal or excel. **2** imitate zealously. **3** *Computing* reproduce the function or action of (a different computer or software system). [based on Latin *aemulatus* 'rivalled'] □ **emulation** *n.* **emulative** *adj.* **emulator** *n.*

emulsifier *n.* any substance that stabilizes an emulsion, esp. one added to processed foods.

emulsify *v.tr.* (**-ies, -ied**) convert into an emulsion. □ **emulsifiable** *adj.* **emulsification** *n.*

emulsion ● *n.* **1** a fine dispersion of one liquid in another, esp. as paint, medicine, etc. **2** a mixture of a silver compound suspended in gelatin etc. for coating photographic plates or films. **3** *Brit.* = EMULSION PAINT. ● *v.tr. Brit.* paint with emulsion paint. [from modern Latin *emulsio*]

emulsion paint *n.* a paint consisting of an emulsion of resin in water.

en *n. Printing* a unit of measurement equal to half an em. [name of the letter *N*]

enable *v.tr.* **1** (foll. by *to* + infin.) give (a person etc.) the means or authority to do something. **2** make possible. **3** esp. *Computing* make (a device) operational; switch on. □ **enablement** *n.* **enabler** *n.*

enact *v.tr.* **1 a** (often foll. by *that* + clause) ordain, decree. **b** make (a bill etc.) law. **2** play (a part or scene on stage or in life). □ **enactive** *adj.*

enactment *n.* **1** a law enacted. **2** the process of enacting.

enamel ● *n.* **1** ▼ a glasslike opaque ornamental or preservative coating on metal etc. **2 a** a smooth hard coating. **b** = ENAMEL PAINT. **c** a cosmetic simulating this. **3** the hard coating of a tooth. ▷ TOOTH. **4** a work of art done in enamel. ● *v.tr.* (**enamelled, enamelling**; *US* **enameled, enameling**) inlay or encrust (a metal etc.) with enamel. [from Anglo-French *enameler*] □ **enameller** *n.* **enamelwork** *n.*

ENAMEL: 13TH-CENTURY
ENAMELLED PORCELAIN MOSQUE LAMP

enamel paint *n.* a paint that dries to give a smooth hard coat.

enamour /i-**nam**-er/ *v.tr.* (*US* **enamor**) (usu. in *passive*; foll. by *of*) **1** inspire with love or liking. **2** charm, delight. [from Old French *enamourer*]

enantiomer *n. Chem.* a molecule that is the mirror image of another. □ **enantiomeric** *adj.*

en bloc /ahn **blok**/ *adv.* in a block; all at the same time; wholesale. [French]

enc. var. of ENCL.

encamp *v.tr.* & *intr.* **1** settle in a military camp. **2** lodge in the open in tents.

encampment *n.* a place where troops etc. are encamped.

encapsulate *v.tr.* **1** enclose in or as in a capsule. **2** summarize; express the essential features of. □ **encapsulation** *n.*

encase *v.tr.* **1** put into a case. **2** surround as with a case. □ **encasement** *n.*

encash *v.tr. Brit.* convert (bills etc.) into cash. □ **encashable** *adj.* **encashment** *n.*

encaustic ● *adj.* **1** (in painting, ceramics, etc.) using pigments mixed with hot wax, which are burned in as an inlay. **2** (of bricks and tiles) inlaid with differently coloured clays burnt in. ● *n.* **1** the art of encaustic painting. **2** a painting done with this technique. [from Greek *egkaustikos*]

encephalitis *n.* inflammation of the brain. □ **encephalitic** *adj.*

encephalo- *comb. form* brain. [from Greek *egkephalos* 'brain']

encephalogram *n.* an X-ray photograph of the brain.

encephalograph *n.* an instrument for recording the electrical activity of the brain.

encephalopathy *n.* (*pl.* **-ies**) a disease of the brain.

enchain *v.tr.* **1** fetter. **2** hold fast (the attention etc.). [from French *enchaîner*] □ **enchainment** *n.*

enchant *v.tr.* **1** charm, delight. **2** bewitch. [from Latin *incantare* 'to chant, charm'] □ **enchantedly** *adv.* **enchanting** *adj.* **enchantingly** *adv.* **enchantment** *n.*

enchanter *n.* (*fem.* **enchantress**) a person who enchants, esp. by supposed use of magic.

enchilada /en-chi-**lah**-dă/ *n.* a tortilla with chilli sauce and usu. a filling, esp. meat. [Latin American Spanish, literally 'seasoned with chilli']

encipher *v.tr.* convert into coded form using a cipher. □ **encipherment** *n.*

encircle *v.tr.* **1** (usu. foll. by *with*) surround, encompass. **2** form a circle round. □ **encirclement** *n.*

encl. *abbr.* (also **enc.**) **1** enclosed. **2** enclosure.

enclave *n.* a portion of territory of one state surrounded by territory of another or others, as viewed by the surrounding territory. [based on Latin *clavis* 'key']

enclose *v.tr.* **1** (often foll. by *with*, *in*) **a** surround with a wall, fence, etc. **b** shut in on all sides. **2** put in a receptacle (esp. in an envelope together with a letter). **3** (usu. as **enclosed** *adj.*) seclude (a religious community) from the outside world. [based on Old French *enclos* 'enclosed']

enclosure *n.* **1** the act of enclosing. **2** *Brit.* an enclosed space or area, esp. at a sporting event. **3** a thing enclosed with a letter.

encode *v.tr.* put (a message etc.) into code or cipher. □ **encoder** *n.*

encomium *n.* (*pl.* **encomiums** or **encomia**) a formal or high-flown expression of praise. [based on Greek *kōmos* 'revelry']

encompass *v.tr.* **1** surround or form a circle about, esp. to protect or attack. **2** contain. □ **encompassment** *n.*

encore /ong-kor/ ● *n.* **1** a call by an audience or spectators for the repetition of an item, or for a further item. **2** such an item. ● *v.tr.* **1** call for the repetition of (an item). **2** call back (a performer) for this. ● *int.* again, once more. [French, literally 'again']

encounter ● *v.tr.* **1** meet by chance or unexpectedly. **2** meet as an adversary. ● *n.* **1** a meeting by chance. **2** a meeting in conflict. [from Old French *encontre* (n.), *encontrer* (v.)]

encourage *v.tr.* **1** give courage, confidence, or hope to. **2** (foll. by *to* + infin.) urge. **3** stimulate by help, reward, etc. **4** promote or assist (an enterprise, opinion, etc.). □ **encouragement** *n.* **encourager** *n.* **encouraging** *adj.*

encroach *v.intr.* (often foll. by *on*, *upon*) intrude, esp. on another's territory or rights. [from Old French *encrochier* 'to fasten upon'] □ **encroachment** *n.*

encrust *v.tr.* (also **incrust**) **1** cover with a crust. **2** overlay with an ornamental crust of precious material. [from Latin *incrustare*] □ **encrustment** *n.*

encrustation var. of INCRUSTATION.

encrypt *v.tr.* convert (data) into code, esp. to prevent unauthorized access. [based on Greek *kruptos* 'hidden'] □ **encryption** *n.*

encumber *v.tr.* be a burden to; hamper, impede. [from Old French *encombrer* 'to block up']

encumbrance *n.* a burden; an impediment; an annoyance.

encyclical ● *n.* a papal letter sent to all bishops of the Roman Catholic Church. ● *adj.* (of a letter) for wide circulation. [from Greek *egkuklios*]

encyclopedia *n.* (also **encyclopaedia**) a book, often in several volumes, giving information on many subjects, or on many aspects of one subject, usu. arranged alphabetically. [based on Greek *egkuklios paideia* 'all-round education']

encyclopedic *adj.* (also **encyclopaedic**) (of knowledge or information) comprehensive.

encyst *v.tr.* & *intr. Biol.* enclose or become enclosed in a cyst. □ **encystation** *n.* **encystment** *n.*

end ● *n.* **1 a** the extreme limit. **b** an extremity of a line, or of the greatest dimension of an object. **c** the furthest point (*to the ends of the Earth*). **2** the surface bounding a thing at either extremity; an extreme part. **3 a** conclusion, finish (*no end to his misery*). **b** the latter or final part. **c** death, destruction, downfall (*met an untimely end*). **d** result, outcome. **e** an ultimate state or condition. **4 a** a thing one seeks to attain, a purpose (*will do anything to achieve his ends; to what end?*). **b** the object for which a thing exists. **5** a remnant, a piece left over (*cigarette end*). **6** (prec. by *the*) *colloq.* the limit of endurability. **7** the half of a sports pitch or court occupied by one team or player. ● *v.* **1** *tr.* & *intr.* bring or come to an end. **2** *tr.* put an end to; destroy. **3** *intr.* (foll. by *in*) have as its result (*will end in tears*). **4** *intr.* (foll. by *by*) do or achieve eventually (*ended by marrying an heiress*). □ **at an end** exhausted or completed. **come to an end 1** be completed or finished. **2** become exhausted. **end on** with the end facing one, or with the end adjoining the end of the next object. **end to end** with the end of each of a series adjoining the end of the next. **end up** reach a specified state, action, or place eventually (*ended up a drunkard; ended up making a fortune*). **in the end** finally; after all. **keep one's end up** do one's part despite difficulties. **make ends meet** live within one's income. **no end** *colloq.* to a great extent, very much. **no end of** *colloq.* much or many of. **on end 1** upright (*hair stood on end*). **2** continuously (*for three weeks on end*). **put an end to 1** stop (an activity etc.). **2** abolish, destroy. [Old English]

endanger *v.tr.* place in danger. □ **endangerment** *n.*

endangered species *n.* a species in danger of extinction.

endear *v.tr.* (usu. foll. by *to*) make dear to or beloved by.

endearing *adj.* inspiring affection. □ **endearingly** *adv.*

endearment *n.* **1** an expression of affection. **2** liking, affection.

endeavour (*US* **endeavor**) ● *v.intr.* (foll. by *to* + infin.) try earnestly. ● *n.* (often foll. by *at*, or *to* + infin.) effort directed towards a goal; an earnest attempt. [Middle English, from *to put oneself in devoir* 'to do one's utmost']

endemic *adj.* (often foll. by *to*) regularly or only found among a particular people or in a certain region. [from Greek *endēmos* 'native'] □ **endemically** *adv.* **endemicity** *n.* **endemism** *n.*

endgame *n.* the final stage of a game (esp. chess), when few pieces remain.

ending *n.* **1** an end or final part, esp. of a story. **2** an inflected final part of a word.

endive *n.* **1** (in full **curly endive**) ▶ a curly-leaved plant, *Cichorium endivia*, used in salads. **2** *N. Amer.* a chicory crown. [from Greek *entubon*]

endless *adj.* **1** infinite; without end; eternal. **2** continual, incessant. **3** *colloq.* innumerable. **4** (of a belt, chain, etc.) made as a loop for continuous action over wheels etc. □ **endlessly** *adv.* **endlessness** *n.*

endmost *adj.* nearest the end.

endocarditis *n.* inflammation of the lining of the heart.

endocrine *adj.* ▼ (of a gland) secreting directly into the blood. [based on Greek *krinein* 'to sift']

endocrinology *n.* the study of the structure and physiology of endocrine glands. □ **endocrinological** *adj.* **endocrinologist** *n.*

endogamy *n.* **1** *Anthropol.* marrying within the same tribe. **2** *Bot.* pollination from the same plant. [based on Greek *gamos* 'marriage'] □ **endogamous** *adj.*

endogenous *adj.* growing or originating from within. □ **endogenesis** *n.* **endogeny** *n.*

endometriosis /en-doh-mee-tri-oh-sis/ *n.* the appearance of endometrial tissue outside the womb.

ENDIVE
(*Cichorium endivia*)

ENDOCRINE

Endocrine glands produce hormones that the body needs in order to grow properly and work smoothly. The hormones are secreted directly into the circulatory system, and carried in the bloodstream towards target tissues.

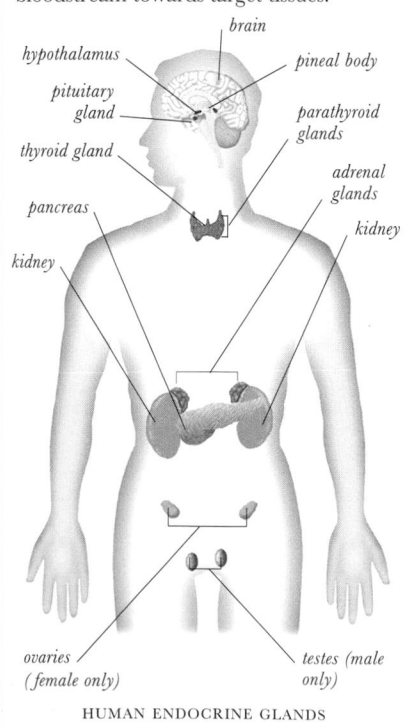

hypothalamus
brain
pituitary gland
pineal body
parathyroid glands
thyroid gland
pancreas
adrenal glands
kidney
kidney
ovaries (female only)
testes (male only)

HUMAN ENDOCRINE GLANDS

endometrium *n. Anat.* the membrane lining the womb. [based on Greek *mētra* 'womb'] □ **endometrial** *adj.*

endomorph *n.* a person with a soft round build of body and a high proportion of fat tissue (cf. ECTOMORPH, MESOMORPH). ▷ MESOMORPH. [based on Greek *morphē* 'form'] □ **endomorphic** *adj.* **endomorphy** *n.*

endorphin *n. Biochem.* any of a group of peptide neurotransmitters occurring naturally in the brain and having pain-relieving properties. [from French *endorphine*]

endorse *v.tr.* (also **indorse**) **1** declare one's approval of. **2** sign or write on the back of (a document), esp. the back of (a bill, cheque, etc.) as the payee. **3** *Brit.* enter details of a conviction for a motoring offence on (a driving licence). [based on Latin *dorsum* 'back'] □ **endorsable** *adj.* **endorsee** *n.* **endorser** *n.*

endorsement *n.* (also **indorsement**) **1** the act or an instance of endorsing. **2** something with which a document etc. is endorsed, esp. a signature. **3** a record in a driving licence of a conviction for a motoring offence.

endoscope *n. Surgery* ▼ an instrument for viewing the internal parts of the body. □ **endoscopic** *adj.* **endoscopy** *n.*

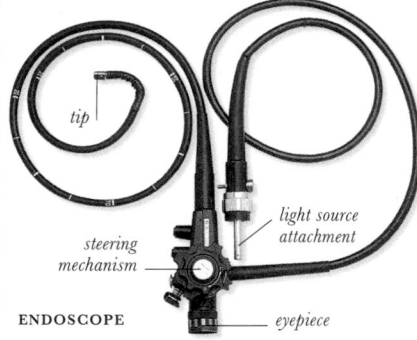

tip
steering mechanism
light source attachment
eyepiece

ENDOSCOPE

endoskeleton *n.* an internal skeleton, as found in vertebrates, echinoderms, etc.

endosperm *n.* albumen enclosed with the germ in seeds.

endotoxin *n.* a toxin present inside a bacterial cell and released when it disintegrates.

endow *v.tr.* **1** bequeath or give a permanent income to (a person, institution, etc.). **2** (esp. as **endowed** *adj.*) (usu. foll. by *with*) invest or provide (a person or thing) with a talent, ability, etc. [from Anglo-French *endouer*]

endowment *n.* **1** the act or an instance of endowing. **2** assets, esp. property or income with which a person or body is endowed. **3** (usu. in *pl.*) skill, talent, etc., with which a person is endowed. **4** (*attrib.*) denoting forms of insurance involving payment by the insurer of a sum on a specified date, or on the death of the insured person if earlier.

endowment mortgage *n. Brit.* a mortgage linked to endowment insurance of the mortgagor's life, the capital being repaid from the sum insured.

endpaper *n.* a usu. blank leaf of paper at the beginning and end of a book, fixed to the inside of the cover. ▷ BOOK

end product *n.* the final product of manufacture, radioactive decay, etc.

end result *n.* final outcome.

endue *v.tr.* (**-dues, -dued, -duing**) (foll. by *with*) *literary* invest or provide (a person or thing) with qualities, powers, etc. [earlier in sense 'to induct, put on clothes': from Latin *induere*]

endurance *n.* **1** the power or habit of enduring (*beyond endurance*). **2** the ability to withstand prolonged strain (*endurance test*).

endure *v.* **1** *tr.* undergo (a difficulty, hardship, etc.). **2** *tr.* **a** tolerate (a person) (*cannot endure him*). **b** (esp. with *neg.*; foll. by *to* + infin.) bear. **3** *intr.* remain in existence; last. **4** *tr.* submit to. [from Latin *indurare* 'to harden'] □ **endurability** *n.* **endurable** *adj.* **enduringly** *adv.*

end-user *n.* the person, customer, etc., who is the ultimate user of a product.

end zone *n. Amer. Football* the rectangular area at the end of the field into which the ball must be carried or passed to score a touchdown. ▷ FOOTBALL

enema *n.* (*pl.* **enemas** or **enemata**) **1** the injection of liquid or gas into the rectum, esp. to expel its contents. **2** a fluid used for this. [Greek]

enemy *n.* (*pl.* **-ies**) **1** a person or group actively opposing or hostile to another, or to a cause etc. **2** (often *attrib.*) **a** a hostile nation or army, esp. in war. **b** a member of this. **c** a hostile ship or aircraft. **3** (usu. foll. by *of*, *to*) an adversary or opponent. [from Latin *inimicus*]

energetic *adj.* **1** strenuously active. **2** forcible, vigorous. □ **energetically** *adv.*

energize *v.* (also **-ise**) **1** infuse energy into (a person or work). **2** provide energy for the operation of (a device). □ **energizer** *n.*

energy *n.* (*pl.* **-ies**) **1** force, vigour; capacity for activity. **2** (in *pl.*) individual powers in use (*devote your energies to this*). **3** *Physics* the capacity of matter or radiation to do work. **4** the means of doing work as provided by the utilization of physical or chemical resources (*nuclear energy*). [from Greek *energeia*]

enervate ● *v.tr.* /en-er-vayt/ deprive of vigour or vitality. ● *adj.* /i-ner-văt/ enervated. [from Latin *enervatus* 'weakened'] □ **enervation** *n.*

enfant terrible /ahn-fahn te-reebl/ *n.* (*pl.* **enfants terribles** *pronunc.* same) a person who causes embarrassment by indiscreet or unruly behaviour. [French, literally 'terrible child']

enfeeble *v.tr.* make feeble. □ **enfeeblement** *n.*

enfilade ● *n.* gunfire directed along a line from end to end. ● *v.tr.* direct an enfilade at (troops, a road, etc.). [French]

enfold *v.tr.* **1** (usu. foll. by *in*, *with*) wrap up; envelop. **2** clasp, embrace.

enforce *v.tr.* **1** compel observance of (a law etc.). **2** (foll. by *on*, *upon*) impose (an action, conduct, one's will). **3** persist in (a demand or argument). □ **enforceable** *adj.* **enforceability** *n.* **enforcement** *n.* **enforcer** *n.*

enfranchise *v.tr.* **1** give (a person) the right to vote. **2** *hist.* free (a slave, villein, etc.). □ **enfranchisement** *n.*

ENG *abbr.* electronic news-gathering.

engage *v.* **1** *tr.* esp. *Brit.* employ or hire (a person). **2** *tr.* **a** (usu. in *passive*) employ busily; occupy (*are you engaged tomorrow?*). **b** hold fast (a person's attention). **3** *tr.* (usu. in *passive*) bind by a promise, esp. of marriage. **4** *tr.* (usu. foll. by *to* + infin.) bind by a contract. **5** (usu. foll. by *with*) *Mech.* **a** *tr.* interlock (parts of a gear etc.); cause (a part) to interlock. **b** *intr.* (of a part, gear, etc.) interlock. **6 a** *intr.* (usu. foll. by *with*) (of troops etc.) come into battle. **b** *tr.* bring (troops) into battle. **c** *tr.* come into battle with (an enemy etc.). **7** *intr.* take part (*engage in politics*). **8** *intr.* (foll. by *that* + clause or *to* + infin.) pledge oneself. [from French *engager*]

engagé /ong-gazh-ay/ *adj.* (of a writer etc.) morally committed. [French]

engaged *adj.* **1** under a promise to marry. **2 a** occupied, busy. **b** reserved, booked. **3** *Brit.* (of a telephone line) unavailable because already in use.

engagement *n.* **1** the act or state of engaging or being engaged. **2** an appointment with another person. **3** a betrothal. **4** an encounter between hostile forces.

engaging *adj.* attractive, charming. □ **engagingly** *adv.*

engender *v.tr.* give rise to; bring about (a feeling etc.). [from Latin *ingenerare*]

engine *n.* **1** a mechanical contrivance consisting of

E

several parts working together, esp. as a source of power. ▷ INTERNAL-COMBUSTION ENGINE, JET ENGINE, STEAM ENGINE. **2 a** a railway locomotive. **b** = FIRE ENGINE. **c** = STEAM ENGINE. □ **engined** *adj.* (also in *comb.*). **engineless** *adj.*

engineer ● *n.* **1** a person qualified in a branch of engineering, esp. as a professional. **2** = CIVIL ENGINEER. **3 a** a person who makes or is in charge of engines. **b** a person who maintains machines; a mechanic; a technician. **4** *N. Amer.* the driver of a locomotive. **5** a person, esp. a soldier, who designs and constructs military works. **6** (foll. by *of*) a skilful or artful contriver. ● *v.tr.* **1** arrange, contrive, or bring about, esp. artfully. **2** construct or manage as an engineer.

engineering *n.* the application of science to the design, building, and use of machines, constructions, etc.

engine house *n.* a building where an engine is housed.

engine room *n.* a room containing engines (esp. in a ship).

English ● *adj.* of or relating to England or its people or language. ● *n.* **1** the language of England, now used in the British Isles, the United States, and most Commonwealth or ex-Commonwealth countries. **2** (prec. by *the*; treated as *pl.*) the people of England. [Old English] □ **Englishness** *n.*

English horn *n.* = COR ANGLAIS.

Englishman *n.* (*pl.* **-men**) a man who is English by birth or descent.

Englishwoman *n.* (*pl.* **-women**) a woman who is English by birth or descent.

engorged *adj.* **1** crammed. **2** *Med.* congested with blood. [from French *engorgé*] □ **engorgement** *n.*

engrain *var.* of INGRAIN.

engrave *v.tr.* **1** (often foll. by *on*) carve (a text or design) on a hard surface. **2** (often foll. by *with*) inscribe or ornament (a surface) in this way. **3** (often foll. by *on*) impress deeply on a person's memory etc. □ **engraver** *n.*

engraving *n.* **1** ▶ a print made from an engraved plate, block, or other surface. **2** the process or art of cutting a design etc. on a hard surface.

engross *v.tr.* **1** absorb the attention of; occupy fully (*engrossed in studying*). **2** make a fair copy of (a legal document). [from Anglo-French *engrosser*] □ **engrossing** *adj.* (in sense 1). **engrossment** *n.*

engulf *v.tr.* flow over and swamp; overwhelm. □ **engulfment** *n.*

enhance *v.tr.* heighten or intensify (qualities, powers, value, etc.); improve (something already of good quality). [from Anglo-French *enhauncer*] □ **enhancement** *n.* **enhancer** *n.*

enharmonic *adj.* *Mus.* of or having intervals smaller than a semitone. [from Greek *enarmonikos*] □ **enharmonically** *adv.*

enigma *n.* **1** a puzzling thing or person. **2** a riddle or paradox. [from Greek *ainigma*] □ **enigmatic** *adj.* **enigmatical** *adj.* **enigmatically** *adv.*

enjoin *v.tr.* **1** (foll. by *to* + infin. or by *that* + clause) command or order (a person). **2** (usu. foll. by *from*) *Law* prohibit (a person) by order. [from Latin *injungere*] □ **enjoinment** *n.*

enjoy *v.tr.* **1** take delight or pleasure in. **2** have the use or benefit of. **3** *Brit.* experience (*enjoy poor health*). □ **enjoy oneself** experience pleasure. [from Old French] □ **enjoyer** *n.* **enjoyment** *n.*

ENGRAVING: DETAIL FROM METAL PLATE ENGRAVING OF ST SIMON (1523) BY ALBRECHT DÜRER

enjoyable *adj.* pleasant; giving enjoyment. □ **enjoyability** *n.* **enjoyableness** *n.* **enjoyably** *adv.*

enkephalin *n.* *Biochem.* either of two morphine-like peptides (endorphins) occurring naturally in the brain and thought to control levels of pain. [based on Greek *egkephalos* 'brain']

enkindle *v.tr. literary* **1 a** cause (flames) to flare up. **b** stimulate (feeling, passion, etc.). **2** inflame with passion.

enlarge *v.* **1** *tr. & intr.* make or become larger or wider. **2** *intr.* (usu. foll. by *upon*) expatiate. **3** *tr. Photog.* produce an enlargement of (a negative). [from Old French *enlarger*]

enlargement *n.* **1** the act or an instance of enlarging; the state of being enlarged. **2** *Photog.* a print that is larger than the negative from which it is produced, or larger than an enprint.

enlarger *n.* *Photog.* an apparatus for making enlargements.

enlighten *v.tr.* **1** (often foll. by *on*) instruct or inform (about a subject). **2** (esp. as **enlightened** *adj.*) free from prejudice or superstition.

enlightenment *n.* **1** the act or an instance of enlightening; the state of being enlightened. **2** (**the Enlightenment**) the 18th-c. philosophy emphasizing reason and individualism rather than tradition.

enlist *v.* **1** *intr. & tr.* enrol in the armed services. **2** *tr.* secure as a means of help or support. □ **enlister** *n.* **enlistment** *n.*

enlisted man *n.* *US* a soldier or sailor below the rank of officer.

enliven *v.tr.* **1** give life or spirit to. **2** make cheerful, brighten (a picture or scene). □ **enlivener** *n.* **enlivenment** *n.*

en masse /ahn **mass**/ *adv.* **1** all together. **2** in a mass. [French]

enmesh *v.tr.* entangle in or as in a net. □ **enmeshment** *n.*

enmity *n.* (*pl.* **-ies**) **1** the state of being an enemy. **2** a feeling of hostility. [based on Latin *inimicus* 'enemy']

ennoble *v.tr.* **1** make (a person) a noble. **2** make noble; elevate. □ **ennoblement** *n.*

ennui /ahn-**wee**/ *n.* mental weariness from lack of occupation or interest; boredom. [based on Latin *in odio* 'in hatred']

enology *US var.* of OENOLOGY.

enormity *n.* (*pl.* **-ies**) **1** extreme wickedness. **2** a serious error. **3** *disp.* great size; enormousness.

■ **Usage** The use of *enormity* in sense 3 is often found, e.g. *the enormity of the problem*, but is regarded as incorrect by many people.

enormous *adj.* very large; huge. [from Latin *enormis*] □ **enormously** *adv.* **enormousness** *n.*

enough ● *det. & predic.adj.* as much or as many as required (*we have enough apples*). ● *pron.* an amount or quantity that is enough (*we have enough of everything now*). ● *adv.* (after an adj. or adv.) **1** to the required degree, adequately (*are you warm enough?*). **2** fairly (*she sings well enough*). **3** very, quite (*you know well enough what I mean*). ● *int.* that is enough. □ **have had enough of** want no more of; be satiated with or tired of. [Old English]

en passant /ahn pas-**ahnt**/ *adv.* by the way. [French, literally 'in passing']

enprint *n.* *Brit.* a standard-sized photographic print.

enquire *v.* **1** *intr.* (often foll. by *of*) seek information; ask a question (of a person). **2** *intr.* (foll. by *after*, *for*) ask about a person, a person's health, etc. **3** *tr.* ask for information as to (*enquired my name*; *enquired whether we were coming*). **4** *intr.* = INQUIRE 1. [from Latin

inquirere] □ **enquirer** *n.* **enquiring** *adj.* **enquiringly** *adv.*

■ **Usage** A useful distinction exists between *enquire* and *inquire*, although some people use these two words interchangeably. *Enquire* is best used to mean 'to ask' in general contexts, while *inquire* is best reserved to mean 'to make a formal investigation'. In cases of academic investigation, *enquire* tends to be preferred e.g. *enquire into the nature of happiness*. The same distinction exists between *enquiry* and *inquiry*.

enquiry *n.* (*pl.* **-ies**) **1** the act or an instance of asking or seeking information. **2** = INQUIRY.

■ **Usage** See Usage Note at ENQUIRE.

enrage *v.tr.* (esp. as **enraged** *adj.*) (often foll. by *at*, *by*, *with*) make furious. □ **enragement** *n.*

enrapture *v.tr.* give intense delight to.

enrich *v.tr.* **1** make rich or richer. **2** make richer in quality, flavour, nutritive value, etc. **3** add to the contents of (a collection, museum, or book). **4** increase the content of an isotope in (a material), esp. that of isotope U-235 in uranium. □ **enrichment** *n.*

enrobe *v.intr.* put on a robe, vestment, etc.

enrol *v.* (*US* **enroll**) (**enrolled**, **enrolling**) **1** *intr.* join a society etc. **2** *tr.* (usu. foll. by *in*) incorporate (a person) as a member of a society etc. [from Old French *enroller*] □ **enrollee** *n.*

enrolment *n.* (*US* **enrollment**) **1** the act or an instance of enrolling; the state of being enrolled. **2** *US* the number of persons enrolled, esp. at a school or college.

en route /ahn **root**/ *adv.* (often foll. by *to*, *for*) on the way. [French]

en rule *n.* *Brit.* a short dash used in punctuation.

ensconce *v.tr.* (usu. *refl.* or in *passive*) establish or settle comfortably, safely, or secretly.

ensemble /ahn-**sahmbl**/ *n.* **1 a** a thing viewed as the sum of its parts. **b** the general effect of this. **2** a set of clothes worn together. **3** a group of actors, dancers, musicians, etc., performing together. **4** *Mus.* a concerted passage for an ensemble. [based on Latin *simul* 'at the same time']

enshrine *v.tr.* **1** enclose in or as in a shrine. **2** preserve or cherish. □ **enshrinement** *n.*

enshroud *v.tr. literary* cover with or as with a shroud.

ensign *n.* **1 a** a banner or flag, esp. the military or naval flag of a nation. ▷ SHIP. **b** *Brit.* ▼ each of three flags, the blue, red, and white ensigns, with the union flag in the corner. **2** a standard-bearer. **3 a** *hist.* the lowest commissioned infantry officer. **b** *US* the lowest commissioned officer in the navy. [from Latin *insignia* 'distinguished things']

ENSIGN: BRITISH RED ENSIGN

ensile *v.tr.* put (fodder) into a silo. □ **ensilage** *n.*

enslave *v.tr.* make (a person) a slave. □ **enslavement** *n.* **enslaver** *n.*

ensnare *v.tr.* catch in or as in a snare; entrap. □ **ensnarement** *n.*

ensue *v.intr.* (**ensues**, **ensued**, **ensuing**) **1** happen afterwards. **2** (often foll. by *from*, *on*) occur as a result. [based on Latin *sequi* 'to follow']

en suite /ahn **sweet**/ ● *adv.* forming a single unit (*bedroom with bathroom en suite*). ● *adj.* **1** forming a single unit (*en suite bathroom*). **2** with a bathroom attached (*seven en suite bedrooms*). [French, literally 'in sequence']

E

ensure *v.tr.* **1** (often foll. by *that* + clause) make certain. **2** (usu. foll. by *against*) make safe.

ENT *abbr.* ear, nose, and throat.

entablature *n. Archit.* ▼ the upper part of a classical building supported by columns, comprising architrave, frieze, and cornice. ▷ COLUMN, DORIC. [from Italian *intavolatura* 'boarding up']

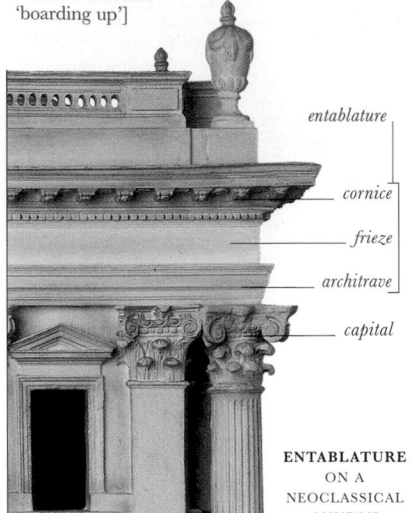

entablature

cornice

frieze

architrave

capital

ENTABLATURE
ON A
NEOCLASSICAL
CHURCH

entail *v.tr.* **1** necessitate or involve unavoidably (*the work entails much effort*). **2** *Law* bequeath (property etc.) so that it remains within a family. [Middle English] □ **entailment** *n.*

entangle *v.tr.* **1** cause to get caught in a snare or among obstacles. **2** involve in difficulties or illicit activities.

entanglement *n.* **1** the act or condition of entangling or being entangled. **2 a** a thing that entangles. **b** *Mil.* an extensive barrier erected to obstruct an enemy's movements.

entente /on-tont/ *n.* **1** = ENTENTE CORDIALE. **2** a group of states in such a relation. [French, literally 'understanding']

entente cordiale /ahn-tahnt cor-di-**ahl**/ *n.* a friendly understanding between states, esp. (often **Entente Cordiale**) that reached in 1904 between Britain and France. [French, literally 'cordial understanding']

enter *v.* **1 a** *intr.* (often foll. by *into*) go or come in. **b** *tr.* go or come into. **c** *intr.* come on stage (as a direction: *enter Macbeth*). **2** *tr.* penetrate (*a bullet entered his chest*). **3** *tr.* (often foll. by *up*) write (a name, details, etc.) in a list, book, etc. **4 a** *intr.* become a competitor (*entered for the long jump*). **b** *tr.* become a competitor in (an event). **c** *tr.* record the name of (a person etc.) as a competitor (*entered two horses for the Derby*). **5** *tr.* **a** become a member of (a society etc.). **b** enrol (a person) as a member or prospective member of a society, school, etc. **6** *tr.* make known; present for consideration (*entered a protest*). **7** *tr.* put into an official record. **8** *intr.* (foll. by *into*) **a** engage in (conversation, relations, an undertaking, etc.). **b** subscribe to; bind oneself by (an agreement etc.). **c** form part of (one's calculations, plans, etc.). **9** *intr.* (foll. by *on, upon*) **a** begin; undertake; begin to deal with (a subject). **b** assume the functions of (an office). [from Latin *intrare*]

enteric /en-**te**-rik/ *adj.* of the intestines. [from Greek *enterikos*]

enteritis *n.* inflammation of the (small) intestine, often causing diarrhoea.

enterprise *n.* **1** an undertaking, esp. a bold or difficult one. **2** readiness to engage in such undertakings. **3** a business firm. [from Old French *entreprise* (fem.) 'undertaken']

enterprising *adj.* **1** ready to engage in enterprises. **2** resourceful, imaginative, energetic. □ **enterprisingly** *adv.*

entertain *v.tr.* **1** amuse; occupy agreeably. **2 a** receive or treat as a guest. **b** (*absol.*) receive guests (*they entertain a great deal*). **3** give attention or consideration to (an idea, feeling, or proposal). [earlier in sense 'to keep up, maintain': from French *entretenir*]

entertainer *n.* a person who entertains, esp. professionally on stage etc.

entertaining *adj.* amusing, diverting. □ **entertainingly** *adv.*

entertainment *n.* **1** the act or an instance of entertaining; the process of being entertained. **2** a performance or show.

enthral *v.tr.* (*US* **enthrall**, **inthrall**) (**-thralled**, **-thralling**) **1** captivate, please greatly. **2** enslave. [based on THRALL] □ **enthralment** *n.* (*US* **enthrallment**).

enthrone *v.tr.* install (a king, bishop, etc.) on a throne, esp. ceremonially. □ **enthronement** *n.*

enthuse *v.intr. & tr. colloq.* be or make enthusiastic.

enthusiasm *n.* **1** (often foll. by *for, about*) **a** strong interest or admiration. **b** great eagerness. **2** an object of enthusiasm. [from Greek *enthousiasmos* 'possession by a god']

enthusiast *n.* (often foll. by *for*) a person who is full of enthusiasm.

enthusiastic *adj.* having or showing enthusiasm. □ **enthusiastically** *adv.*

entice *v.tr.* (often foll. by *from, into, or to* + infin.) persuade by the offer of pleasure or reward. [from Old French *enticier*] □ **enticement** *n.* **enticer** *n.* **enticing** *adj.* **enticingly** *adv.*

entire *adj.* **1** whole, complete. **2** not broken or decayed. **3** unqualified, absolute (*an entire success*). **4** in one piece; continuous. [from Latin *integer* 'untouched, whole']

entirely *adv.* **1** wholly, completely. **2** solely, exclusively.

entirety *n.* (*pl.* **-ies**) **1** completeness. **2** (usu. foll. by *of*) the sum total. □ **in its entirety** in its complete form; completely.

entitle *v.tr.* **1 a** (usu. foll. by *to*) give (a person etc.) a just claim. **b** (foll. by *to* + infin.) give (a person etc.) a right. **2** give (a book etc.) the title of. □ **entitlement** *n.*

entity *n.* (*pl.* **-ies**) **1** a thing with distinct existence. **2** a thing's existence regarded distinctly. [based on Late Latin *ent*- 'being'] □ **entitative** *adj.*

entomb *v.tr.* **1** place in or as in a tomb. **2** serve as a tomb for. □ **entombment** *n.*

entomology *n.* the study of insects. [from modern Latin *entomologia*] □ **entomological** *adj.* **entomologist** *n.*

entourage /on-toor-ah*zh*/ *n.* a group of people attending an important person. [French]

entr'acte /on-trakt/ *n.* **1** an interval between two acts of a play. **2** a piece of music or a dance performed during this. [French, literally 'between act']

entrails *n.pl.* **1** the intestines. ▷ INTESTINE. **2** the innermost parts (*entrails of the Earth*). [from medieval Latin *intralia*]

entrance[1] /en-trănss/ *n.* **1** the act or an instance of going or coming in. **2** a door, passage, etc., by which one enters. **3** right of admission. **4** the coming of an actor on stage. [from Old French]

entrance[2] /en-trahnss/ *v.tr.* **1** enchant, delight. **2** put into a trance. □ **entrancement** *n.* **entrancing** *adj.* **entrancingly** *adv.*

entrant *n.* a person who enters an examination, profession, etc.

entrap *v.tr.* (**entrapped**, **entrapping**) **1** catch in or as in a trap. **2** (often foll. by *into* + verbal noun) beguile or trick (a person). □ **entrapment** *n.*

entreat *v.tr.* **1** (foll. by *to* + infin. or *that* + clause) ask (a person) earnestly. **2** ask earnestly for (a thing). [from Old French *entraiter*] □ **entreatingly** *adv.*

entreaty *n.* (*pl.* **-ies**) an earnest request; a supplication.

entrecôte /on-trĕ-koht/ *n.* a boned steak cut off the sirloin. [French]

entrée /on-tray/ *n.* **1 a** *Brit.* a dish served between the fish and meat courses. **b** esp. *N. Amer.* the main dish of a meal. **2** the right or privilege of admission, esp. at Court. [French]

entrench *v.tr.* **1 a** establish firmly (in a defensible position, in office, etc.). **b** (as **entrenched** *adj.*) (of an attitude etc.) not easily modified. **2** apply extra safeguards to (rights etc. guaranteed by legislation). □ **entrench oneself** adopt a well-defended position. □ **entrenchment** *n.*

entrepôt /on-trĕ-poh/ *n.* a commercial centre for import and export, and for collection and distribution. [French]

entrepreneur /on-trĕ-prĕn-**er**/ *n.* a person who undertakes a commercial venture. [French] □ **entrepreneurial** *adj.* **entrepreneurialism** *n.* (also **entrepreneurism**). **entrepreneurially** *adv.* **entrepreneurship** *n.*

entropy *n. Physics* a measure of the unavailability of a system's thermal energy for conversion into mechanical work, in some contexts interpreted as a measure of the degree of disorder or randomness in the system. [from German *Entropie*] □ **entropic** *adj.* **entropically** *adv.*

entrust *v.tr.* **1** (foll. by *to*) give responsibility for (a person or a thing) to a person. **2** (foll. by *with*) assign responsibility for a thing to (a person). □ **entrustment** *n.*

entry *n.* (*pl.* **-ies**) **1 a** the act or an instance of going or coming in. **b** the coming of an actor on stage. **c** ceremonial entrance. **2** liberty to go or come in. **3 a** a place of entrance; a door, gate, etc. **b** *Brit.* a lobby. **4** *Brit.* a passage between buildings. **5 a** an item entered in a diary, list, account book, etc. **b** the recording of this. **6** a person or thing competing in a race, contest, etc. **7** the start or resumption of music for a particular instrument in an ensemble. [based on Latin *intrare* 'to enter']

entryism *n.* infiltration into a political organization to change or subvert it. □ **entrist** *n.* **entryist** *n.*

entryphone *n. Brit. propr.* an intercom device at an entrance to a building by which callers may identify themselves to gain admission.

entwine *v.tr.* **1** (foll. by *with, about, round*) twine together (a thing with or round another). **2** interweave. □ **entwinement** *n.*

E-number *n. Brit.* a code number preceded by the letter E, denoting a food additive according to EC directives.

enumerate *v.tr.* **1** specify (items); mention one by one. **2** count; establish the number of. □ **enumerable** *adj.* **enumeration** *n.* **enumerative** *adj.*

enumerator *n.* a person employed in census-taking.

enunciate *v.tr.* **1** pronounce (words) clearly. **2** express (a proposition or theory) in definite terms. **3** proclaim. [based on Latin *enuntiatus* 'stated clearly'] □ **enunciation** *n.* **enunciative** *adj.* **enunciator** *n.*

enuresis *n. Med.* involuntary urination. [modern Latin] □ **enuretic** *adj. & n.*

envelop *v.tr.* (**enveloped**, **enveloping**) (often foll. by *in*) **1** wrap up or cover completely. **2** make obscure; conceal (*was enveloped in mystery*). [from Old French *envoluper*] □ **envelopment** *n.*

envelope *n.* **1** a folded paper container, usu. with a sealable flap, for a letter etc. **2** a wrapper or covering. **3** the structure within a balloon or airship containing the gas. ▷ HOT-AIR BALLOON, ZEPPELIN. **4** the outer metal or glass housing of a vacuum tube, electric light, etc.

envenom *v.tr.* **1** put poison on or into; make poisonous. **2** infuse venom or bitterness into (feelings, words, or actions).

enviable *adj.* (of a person or thing) exciting or likely to excite envy. □ **enviably** *adv.*

envious *adj.* (often foll. by *of*) feeling or showing envy. □ **enviously** *adv.*

environment *n.* **1** the physical surroundings, conditions, circumstances, etc., in which a person lives (*poor home environment*). **2** the area surrounding a place. **3 a** external conditions as affecting plant and animal life. **b** (**the environment**) the totality of the physical conditions on the Earth or a part of it. **4** *Computing* the overall structure within which a user, computer, or program operates. □ **environmental** *adj.* **environmentally** *adv.*

environmentalist *n.* a person who is concerned with or advocates the protection of the environment. □ **environmentalism** *n.*

environment-friendly *adj.* not harmful to the environment.

environs *n.pl.* a surrounding district, esp. round an urban area.

envisage *v.tr.* **1** have a mental picture of (a thing not yet existing). **2** contemplate or conceive, esp. as a possibility or desirable future event. [from French *envisager*] □ **envisagement** *n.*

envision *v.tr.* envisage, visualize.

envoy *n.* **1** a messenger or representative, esp. on a diplomatic mission. **2** (in full **envoy extraordinary**) a minister plenipotentiary, ranking below ambassador. [from French *envoyé* 'sent']

envy ● *n.* (*pl.* **-ies**) **1** discontent aroused by another's better fortune etc. **2** the object of this feeling. ● *v.tr.* (**-ies**, **-ied**) feel envy of (a person, circumstances, etc.). [from Latin *invidēre* 'to envy'] □ **envier** *n.*

enwrap *v.tr.* (also **inwrap**) (**-wrapped**, **-wrapping**) (often foll. by *in*) *literary* wrap or enfold.

enzyme *n.* *Biochem.* a protein acting as a catalyst in a specific biochemical reaction. [from medieval Greek *enzumos*] □ **enzymatic** *adj.* **enzymic** *adj.* **enzymology** *n.*

EOC *abbr.* Equal Opportunities Commission.

Eocene *Geol.* ● *adj.* of or relating to the second epoch of the Tertiary period. ● *n.* this epoch or system. [from Greek *ēōs* 'dawn' + *kainos* 'new']

eolian *US* var. of AEOLIAN.

eolithic *adj.* *Archaeol.* of the period preceding the palaeolithic age. [from French *éolithique*]

eon var. of AEON.

eosin *n.* a red fluorescent dye used esp. as a stain in optical microscopy.

EP *abbr.* **1** electroplate. **2** (esp. of a gramophone record) extended-play. **3** extreme pressure (used in grading lubricants).

epact *n.* the number of days by which the solar year exceeds the lunar year.

epaulette /ep-ă-let/ *n.* (*US* **epaulet**) ◄ an ornamental shoulder-piece on a coat etc., esp. on a uniform. [from French *épaulette* 'little shoulder']

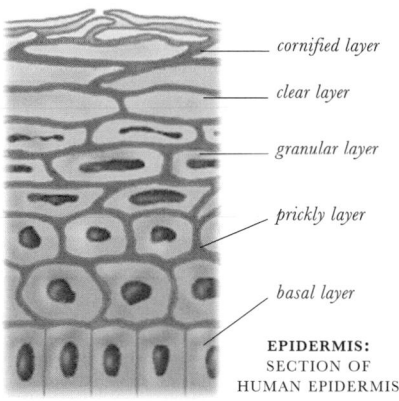

fringed epaulette

EPAULETTE ON A GRENADIER OFFICER'S COAT

épée /ay-pay/ *n.* a sharp-pointed duelling-sword, used (with the end blunted) in fencing. ▷ FENCING. [French] □ **épéeist** *n.*

ephedrine /ef-ĕ-drin/ *n.* an alkaloid drug.

ephemera[1] /i-fem-ĕ-ră/ *n.* (*pl.* **ephemeras** or **ephemerae** /-ree/) **1** an insect living only a day or a few days. **2** = EPHEMERON 1. [from Greek *ephēmeros* 'lasting only a day']

ephemera[2] *pl.* of EPHEMERON 1.

ephemeral *adj.* lasting or of use for only a short time; transitory. □ **ephemerality** *n.* **ephemerally** *adv.*

ephemerist *n.* a collector of ephemera.

ephemeron *n.* **1** (*pl.* **ephemera**) (usu. in *pl.*) **a** a thing (esp. a printed item) of short-lived interest. **b** a short-lived thing. **2** (*pl.* **ephemerons**) = EPHEMERA[1] 1.

epic ● *n.* **1** a long poem narrating the deeds of one or more heroic or legendary figures. **2** a book or film based on an epic narrative or heroic in type. ● *adj.* **1** of or like an epic. **2** grand, heroic. [based on Greek *epos* 'song, word'] □ **epical** *adj.* **epically** *adv.*

epicene ● *adj.* **1** *Gram.* denoting either sex without change of gender. **2** of, for, or used by both sexes. **3** having characteristics of both sexes or of neither sex. **4** effete, effeminate. ● *n.* an epicene person. [based on Greek *koinos* 'common']

epicentre *n.* (*US* **epicenter**) **1** *Geol.* the point at which an earthquake reaches the Earth's surface. ▷ EARTHQUAKE. **2** the central point of a difficulty. □ **epicentral** *adj.*

epicure *n.* a person with refined tastes, esp. in food and drink. [from medieval Latin *epicurus* 'one preferring sensual enjoyment'] □ **epicurism** *n.*

Epicurean ● *n.* **1** a disciple or student of the Greek philosopher Epicurus. **2** (**epicurean**) a person devoted to (esp. sensual) enjoyment. ● *adj.* **1** of or concerning Epicurus or his ideas. **2** (**epicurean**) characteristic of an epicurean. [from Greek name *Epikouros*] □ **Epicureanism** *n.*

epidemic ● *n.* **1** a widespread occurrence of a disease in a community at a particular time. **2** such a disease. **3** (foll. by *of*) a wide prevalence of something. ● *adj.*

in the nature of an epidemic. [from Greek *epidēmia* 'prevalence of disease'] □ **epidemically** *adv.*

epidemiology *n.* the study of the incidence and distribution of diseases. □ **epidemiological** *adj.* **epidemiologist** *n.*

epidermis *n.* **1** ▼ the outer cellular layer of the skin. ▷ SKIN. **2** *Bot.* the outer layer of cells of leaves, stems, roots, etc. [based on Greek *derma* 'skin'] □ **epidermal** *adj.* **epidermic** *adj.* **epidermoid** *adj.*

cornified layer

clear layer

granular layer

prickly layer

basal layer

EPIDERMIS: SECTION OF HUMAN EPIDERMIS

epidiascope *n.* an optical projector capable of giving images of both opaque and transparent objects.

epididymis /ep-i-did-i-mŭs/ *n.* (*pl.* **epididymides** /ep-i-di-dim-i-deez/) *Anat.* a convoluted duct behind the testis, along which sperm passes to the vas deferens. ▷ REPRODUCTIVE ORGANS. [based on Greek *didumoi* 'testicles']

epidural ● *adj.* **1** *Anat.* on or around the dura mater. **2** (of an anaesthetic) introduced into the space around the dura mater of the spinal cord. ● *n.* an epidural anaesthetic, used esp. in childbirth. [based on DURA MATER]

epifauna *n.* *Zool.* the animal life which lives on the surface of the seabed etc., or attached to submerged objects or to aquatic animals or plants. □ **epifaunal** *adj.*

epigenetic *adj.* *Biol.* due to external, not genetic, influences.

epiglottis *n.* *Anat.* a flap of cartilage at the root of the tongue, depressed during swallowing to cover the windpipe. ▷ HEAD, TONGUE. [based on Greek *glōtta* 'tongue'] □ **epiglottal** *adj.* **epiglottic** *adj.*

epigram *n.* **1** a short witty poem. **2** a pointed saying. **3** the use of concise witty remarks. [from Greek *epigramma*] □ **epigrammatic** *adj.* **epigrammatically** *adv.* **epigrammatist** *n.*

epigraph *n.* an inscription. [from Greek *epigraphē*]

epigraphy *n.* the study of (esp. ancient) inscriptions. □ **epigraphic** *adj.* **epigraphically** *adv.* **epigraphist** *n.*

epilate *v.tr.* *Med.* remove hair by the roots from. [from French *épiler*] □ **epilation** *n.*

epilepsy *n.* a neurological disorder marked by episodes of sensory disturbance, loss of consciousness, or convulsions. [from Greek *epilēpsia* 'taking hold of'] □ **epileptic** *n. & adj.*

epilogue *n.* (*US* also **epilog**) **1 a** the concluding part of a literary work. **b** an appendix. **2** a speech or short poem addressed to the audience by an actor at the end of a play (cf. PROLOGUE *n.* 1a). **3** *Brit.* a short piece at the end of a day's broadcasting. [from Greek *epilogos*] □ **epilogist** *n.*

epiphany /i-pif-ă-ni/ *n.* (*pl.* **-ies**) **1** (**Epiphany**) **a** the manifestation of Christ to the Magi. **b** the festival commemorating this on 6 January. **2** any manifestation of a god or demigod. [from Greek *epiphaneia* 'manifestation'] □ **epiphanic** *adj.*

epiphyte *n.* ◄ a plant growing on another but not parasitic. [based on Greek *phuton* 'plant'] □ **epiphytic** *adj.*

EPIPHYTE

Epiphytes, such as bromeliads and orchids, live above ground on other plants. However, they are not parasitic, obtaining their nutrients from rainwater and organic debris such as leaf litter.

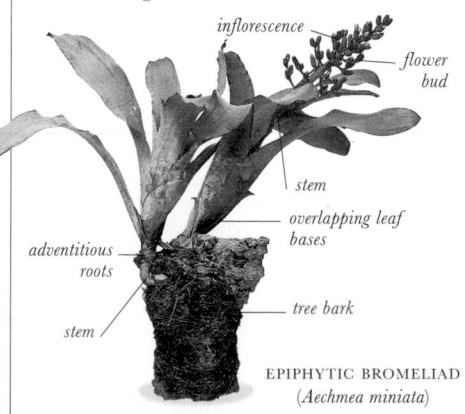

inflorescence

flower bud

stem

overlapping leaf bases

adventitious roots

stem

tree bark

EPIPHYTIC BROMELIAD
(*Aechmea miniata*)

EPIPHYTIC ORCHID
(*Brassavola nodosa*)

leaf

peduncle

flower

tree bark

aerial root

E

episcopacy *n.* (*pl.* **-ies**) **1** government of a Church by bishops. **2** (prec. by *the*) the bishops.

episcopal *adj.* **1** of a bishop or bishops. **2** (of a Church) constituted on the principle of government by bishops. [based on ecclesiastical Latin *episcopus* 'bishop'] □ **episcopally** *adv.*

Episcopal Church *n.* the Anglican Church in Scotland and the US, with elected bishops.

episcopalian ● *adj.* **1** of episcopacy. **2** of an episcopal Church or (**Episcopalian**) the Episcopal Church. ● *n.* **1** an adherent of episcopacy. **2** (**Episcopalian**) a member of the Episcopal Church. □ **episcopalianism** *n.*

episcopate *n.* **1** the office or tenure of a bishop. **2** (prec. by *the*) the bishops collectively.

episiotomy *n.* (*pl.* **-ies**) a surgical cut made at the opening of the vagina during childbirth. [based on Greek *epision* 'pubic region']

episode *n.* **1** one event or a group of events as part of a sequence. **2** each of the parts of a serial story or broadcast. **3** an incident or set of incidents in a narrative. [from Greek *epeisodion*] □ **episodic** *adj.* **episodical** *adj.* **episodically** *adv.*

epistemology *n.* the theory of knowledge, esp. with regard to its methods and validation. □ **epistemological** *adj.* **epistemologically** *adv.* **epistemologist** *n.*

epistle *n.* **1** *formal* or *joc.* a letter, esp. a long one on a serious subject. **2** (also **Epistle**) any of the letters of the Apostles in the New Testament. **3** a poem etc. in the form of a letter. [based on Greek *epistellein* 'to send news']

epistolary *adj.* of or in the form of a letter or letters.

epistyle *n. Archit.* = ARCHITRAVE. [from Greek *epi* 'above' + *stulos* 'pillar']

epitaph *n.* words written in memory of a person who has died, esp. as a tomb inscription. [from Greek *epitaphion* 'funeral oration']

epithelium *n.* (*pl.* **epitheliums** or **epithelia**) *Anat.* the tissue forming the outer layer of the body surface and lining many hollow structures. ▷ NOSE, SKIN. [modern Latin] □ **epithelial** *adj.*

epithet *n.* **1** an adjective or other descriptive word expressing a quality or attribute. **2** such a word as a term of abuse. [based on Greek *epitithenai* 'to add'] □ **epithetic** *adj.*

epitome /i-pit-ōmi/ *n.* **1** a person or thing embodying a quality, class, etc. **2** a thing representing another in miniature. **3** a summary of a written work. [based on Greek *epitemnein* 'to cut short'] □ **epitomist** *n.*

epitomize *v.tr.* (also **-ise**) **1** be a perfect example of (a quality etc.). **2** make an epitome of (a work). □ **epitomization** *n.*

EPNS *abbr.* electroplated nickel silver.

epoch /ee-pok/ *n.* **1** a period of history or of a person's life marked by notable events. **2** the beginning of an era. **3** *Geol.* a division of a period, corresponding to a set of strata. [from Greek *epokhē* 'fixed point of time'] □ **epochal** *adj.*

epoch-making *adj.* remarkable, historic; of major importance.

eponym *n.* **1** a person (real or imaginary) after whom a discovery, place, etc., is named or thought to be named. **2** the name given. [based on Greek *onoma* 'name'] □ **eponymous** *adj.*

EPOS *abbr.* electronic point-of-sale (of retail outlets recording information electronically).

epoxide *n. Chem.* a compound containing an oxygen atom bonded in a triangular arrangement to two carbon atoms.

epoxy *adj. Chem.* relating to or derived from an epoxide.

epoxy resin *n.* a synthetic thermosetting resin containing epoxy groups.

EPROM *n. Computing* a read-only memory whose contents can be erased and replaced by a special process. [from *e*rasable *p*rogrammable *ROM*]

eps *abbr.* earnings per share.

epsilon *n.* the fifth letter of the Greek alphabet (E, ε). [from Greek, literally 'bare or simple E']

Epsom salts *n.pl.* a preparation of magnesium sulphate used as a purgative etc. [named after *Epsom*, a town in Surrey]

equable *adj.* **1** even; not varying. **2** uniform and moderate (*an equable climate*). **3** (of a person) not easily angered. [from Latin *aequabilis*] □ **equability** *n.* **equably** *adv.*

equal ● *adj.* **1** (often foll. by *to*, *with*) the same in quantity, quality, size, rank, etc. **2** evenly balanced (*an equal contest*). **3** having the same rights (*human beings are essentially equal*). **4** uniform in application or effect. ● *n.* a person or thing equal to another, esp. in rank, status, or characteristic quality. ● *v.tr.* (**equalled**, **equalling**; *US* **equaled**, **equaling**) **1** be equal to in number, quality, etc. **2** achieve something that is equal to. □ **be equal to** have the ability or resources for. [based on Latin *aequus* 'even'] □ **equality** *n.*

equalize *v.* (also **-ise**) **1** *tr.* & *intr.* make or become equal. **2** *intr.* level the score in a match. □ **equalizer** *n.* (also **-iser**). **equalization** *n.*

equally *adv.* **1** in an equal manner (*treated them all equally*). **2** to an equal degree (*is equally important*).

■ **Usage** In sense 2, construction with *as* (e.g. *equally as important*) is often found, but is considered incorrect by some people.

equal opportunity *n.* (often in *pl.*) the opportunity or right to be employed, paid, etc., without discrimination on grounds of sex, race, etc.

equal sign *n.* (also **equals sign**) the symbol =.

equanimity *n.* mental composure, evenness of temper, esp. in misfortune. [based on Latin *aequus* 'even' + *animus* 'mind'] □ **equanimous** *adj.*

equate *v.* **1** *tr.* (usu. foll. by *to*, *with*) regard as equal or equivalent. **2** *intr.* (foll. by *with*) **a** be equal or equivalent to. **b** agree or correspond. [based on Latin *aequatus* 'made even'] □ **equatable** *adj.*

equation /i-kway-zhŏn/ *n.* **1** the process of equating or making equal; the state of being equal. **2** *Math.* a statement that two mathematical expressions are equal (indicated by the sign =). **3** *Chem.* a formula representing a chemical reaction. □ **equational** *adj.*

equator *n.* **1** ▼ an imaginary line around the Earth or other body, equidistant from the poles. **2** *Astron.* = CELESTIAL EQUATOR. [from medieval Latin *aequator*] □ **equatorial** *adj.* **equatorially** *adv.*

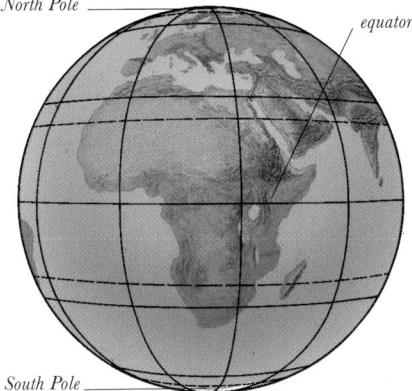

North Pole ———

equator

South Pole ———

EQUATOR

equerry *n.* (*pl.* **-ies**) an officer of the British royal household attending members of the royal family. [from Old French *esquier* 'esquire']

equestrian ● *adj.* **1** of or relating to horses and horse-riding. **2** on horseback. ● *n.* (*fem.* **equestrienne**) a rider or performer on horseback. [based on Latin *eques* 'horseman'] □ **equestrianism** *n.*

equi- *comb. form* equal. [from Latin *aequus* 'equal']

equiangular *adj.* having equal angles.

equidistant *adj.* at equal distances. □ **equidistantly** *adv.*

equilateral *adj.* having all its sides equal in length.

equilibrist *n.* an acrobat, esp. on a high rope.

equilibrium *n.* (*pl.* **equilibria** or **equilibriums**) **1** a state of physical balance. **2** a state of mental or emotional equanimity. [based on Latin *libra* 'balance']

equine /ek-wyn/ *adj.* of or like a horse. [based on Latin *equus* 'horse']

equinoctial ● *adj.* **1** happening at or near the time of an equinox. **2** of or relating to equal day and night. **3** at or near the (terrestrial) equator. ● *n.* (in full **equinoctial line**) = CELESTIAL EQUATOR.

equinoctial point *n.* the point at which the ecliptic cuts the celestial equator (twice each year at an equinox).

equinoctial year see YEAR 1.

equinox *n.* the time or date (twice each year) at which the Sun crosses the celestial equator (about 22 Sept. and 20 Mar.). [from medieval Latin *equinoxium*]

equip *v.tr.* (**equipped**, **equipping**) supply with what is needed. [from French *équiper*] □ **equipper** *n.*

equipage /ek-wi-pij/ *n.* **1 a** requisites for an undertaking. **b** an outfit for a special purpose. **2** a carriage and horses with attendants.

equipment *n.* **1** the necessary articles, clothing, etc., for a purpose. **2** the process of equipping or being equipped.

equipoise ● *n.* **1** equilibrium; a balanced state. **2** a counterbalancing thing. ● *v.tr.* counterbalance.

equitable /ek-wit-ăbŭl/ *adj.* **1** fair, just. **2** *Law* valid in equity as distinct from law. [based on Latin *aequus* 'fair'] □ **equitableness** *n.* **equitably** *adv.*

equitation *n.* the art and practice of horsemanship and horse-riding. [from Latin *equitatio*]

equity *n.* (*pl.* **-ies**) **1** fairness. **2** the application of general principles of justice to correct or supplement the law. **3 a** the value of the shares issued by a company. **b** (in *pl.*) stocks and shares not bearing fixed interest. **4** the net value of a mortgaged property after deduction of charges. [from Latin *aequitas*]

equivalent ● *adj.* **1** (often foll. by *to*) equal in value, amount, etc. **2** corresponding. **3** (of words) having the same meaning. **4** having the same result. ● *n.* an equivalent thing, amount, word, etc. [from Late Latin *aequivalent-* 'being of equal worth'] □ **equivalence** *n.* **equivalency** *n.* **equivalently** *adv.*

equivocal *adj.* **1** of double or doubtful meaning. **2** of uncertain nature. **3** (of a person, character, etc.) suspect. [based on Late Latin *aequivocare* 'to call by the same name'] □ **equivocality** *n.* **equivocally** *adv.* **equivocalness** *n.*

equivocate *v.intr.* use ambiguity to conceal the truth. [related to EQUIVOCAL] □ **equivocation** *n.* **equivocator** *n.* **equivocatory** *adj.*

ER *abbr.* Queen Elizabeth. [Latin *Elizabetha Regina*]

Er *symb. Chem.* the element erbium.

er *int.* expressing hesitation or a pause in speech.

era *n.* **1** a system of chronology reckoning from a noteworthy event (*the Christian era*). **2** a distinct period, esp. regarded historically (*the pre-Roman era*). **3** a date at which an era begins. **4** *Geol.* a major division of time. [from Late Latin *aera* 'number expressed in figures']

eradicate *v.tr.* root out; destroy completely. [based on Latin *eradicatus* 'rooted out'] □ **eradicable** *adj.* **eradication** *n.* **eradicator** *n.*

erase *v.tr.* **1** rub out. **2** remove all traces of (*erased it from my memory*). **3** remove recorded material from (a magnetic medium). [based on Latin *erasus* 'scraped out'] □ **erasable** *adj.* **erasure** *n.*

eraser *n.* a thing that erases, esp. a piece of rubber etc. used for removing pencil etc. marks.

erbium *n. Chem.* a soft silvery metallic element of the lanthanide series. [modern Latin, from *Ytterby* in Sweden, where first found]

ere *prep. & conj. poet.* or *archaic* before (of time) (*ere they come*). [Old English]

erect ● *adj.* **1** upright, vertical. **2** (of the penis etc.) enlarged and rigid, esp. in sexual excitement. **3** (of hair) bristling, standing up from the skin. ● *v.tr.* **1** raise; set upright. **2** build. **3** establish (*erect a theory*). [from Latin *erectus* 'set up'] □ **erectable** *adj.* **erection** *n.* **erectly** *adv.* **erectness** *n.* **erector** *n.*

erectile *adj.* that can be erected or become erect.

eremite *n.* a hermit or recluse (esp. Christian). [from Old French] □ **eremitic** *adj.* **eremitical** *adj.*

erg *n. Physics* a unit of work or energy. [from Greek *ergon* 'work']

ergo *adv.* therefore. [Latin]

ergocalciferol *n.* = CALCIFEROL.

ergonomics *n.* the study of the efficiency of persons in their working environment. [based on Greek *ergon* 'work'] □ **ergonomic** *adj.* **ergonomist** *n.*

ergot *n.* **1** a disease of rye and other cereals caused by the fungus *Claviceps purpurea*. **2 a** this fungus. **b** the dried spore-containing structures of this, used to aid childbirth. [from Old French *argot* 'cock's spur']

erica *n.* ◀ any shrub of the genus *Erica*, with small leathery leaves and bell-like flowers. [from Greek *ereikē* 'heath']

ericaceous *adj.* **1** of or relating to the plant family Ericaceae, which includes heathers, azaleas, and rhododendrons. **2** (of compost) suitable for ericaceous and other lime-hating plants.

ERM *abbr.* exchange-rate mechanism.

ermine *n.* (*pl.* same or **ermines**) **1** the stoat, esp. when in its white winter fur. **2** its white fur, used to trim robes etc. [from Old French *(h)ermine*] □ **ermined** *adj.*

Ernie *n.* (in the UK) a device for drawing prizewinning numbers of Premium Bonds. [acronym from *e*lectronic *r*andom *n*umber *i*ndicator *e*quipment]

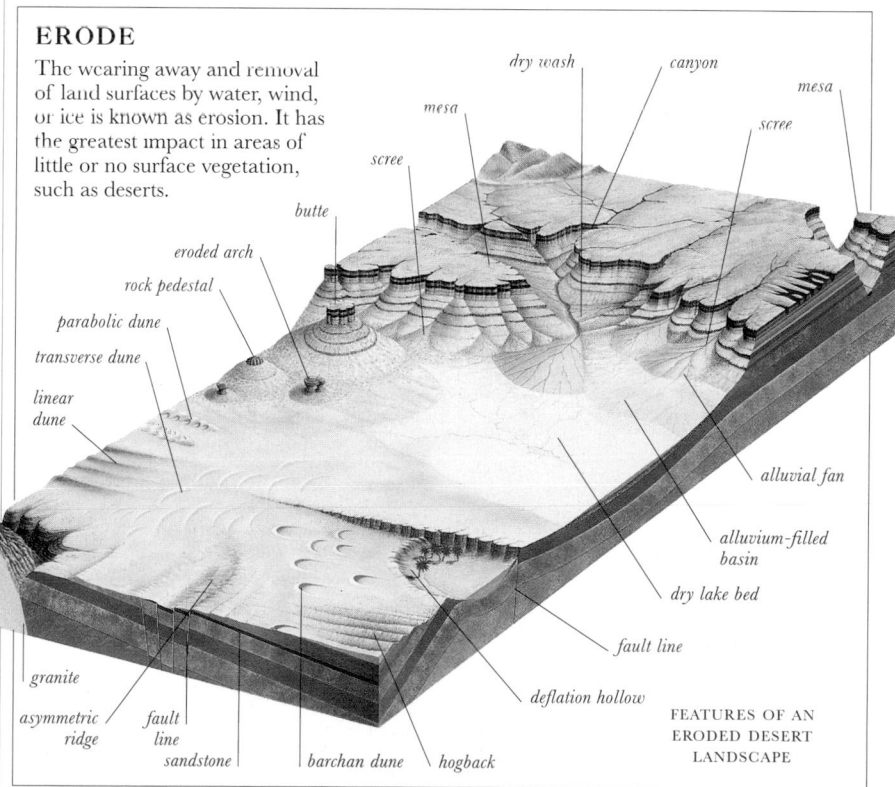

ERICA:
DORSET HEATH
(*Erica ciliaris*)

erode *v.tr. & intr.* ▶ wear away, destroy or be destroyed gradually. [based on Latin *rodere* 'to gnaw'] □ **erodible** *adj.* **erosion** *n.* **erosive** *adj.*

erogenous *adj.* **1** (esp. of a part of the body) sensitive to sexual stimulation. **2** giving rise to sexual desire or excitement.

erotic *adj.* of or causing sexual love, esp. tending to arouse sexual desire or excitement. [based on Greek *erōs erōtos* 'sexual love'] □ **erotically** *adv.*

erotica *n.pl.* erotic literature or art.

eroticism *n.* **1** erotic nature or character. **2** the use of or response to erotic images or stimulation.

erotism *n.* = EROTICISM.

eroto- *comb. form* erotic, eroticism.

erotogenic *adj.* (also **erotogenous**) = EROGENOUS.

erotomania *n.* **1** excessive or abnormal erotic desire. **2** a preoccupation with sexual passion. □ **erotomaniac** *n.*

err *v.intr.* **1** be mistaken or incorrect. **2** do wrong; sin. □ **err on the side of** act with a specified bias. [from Latin *errare* 'to stray']

errand *n.* **1** a short journey, esp. on another's behalf, to take a message, collect goods, etc. **2** the object of such a journey. [Old English]

errand of mercy *n.* a journey or mission to relieve suffering etc.

errant *adj.* **1** deviating from an accepted standard. **2** *literary* or *archaic* travelling in search of adventure (*knight errant*). [Middle English] □ **errancy** *n.* (in sense 1). **errantry** *n.* (in sense 2).

erratic *adj.* **1** inconsistently variable in conduct, opinions, etc. **2** uncertain in movement. [related to ERR] □ **erratically** *adv.* **erraticism** *n.*

erratic block *n.* a large rock carried from a distance by glacial action.

erratum *n.* (*pl.* **errata**) an error in printing or writing. [Latin, literally 'thing that has strayed']

erroneous *adj.* incorrect; arising from error. [based on Latin *erro -onis* 'vagabond'] □ **erroneously** *adv.* **erroneousness** *n.*

error *n.* **1** a mistake. **2** the condition of being wrong in conduct or judgement (*led into error*). **3** a wrong opinion or judgement. **4** the degree of inaccuracy in a calculation etc. [from Latin] □ **errorless** *adj.*

ersatz ● *adj.* substitute, imitation (esp. of inferior quality). ● *n.* an ersatz thing. [German, literally 'replacement']

Erse *archaic* or *derog.* ● *adj.* of or relating to Highland or Irish Gaelic. ● *n.* the Gaelic language. [early Scots form of IRISH]

erst *adv. archaic* formerly; of old. [Old English]

erstwhile ● *adj.* former, previous. ● *adv. archaic* = ERST.

eructation *n.* the act or an instance of belching. [from Latin *eructatio*]

erudite *adj.* learned. [from Latin *eruditus* 'trained'] □ **eruditely** *adv.* **erudition** *n.*

erupt *v.intr.* **1** break out suddenly or dramatically. **2** (of a volcano) become active and eject lava etc. **3** (of a rash, boil, etc.) appear on the skin. **4** (of the teeth) break through the gums. [based on Latin *eruptus* 'broken out'] □ **eruption** *n.* **eruptive** *adj.*

erysipelas /e-ri-sip-i-lăs/ *n. Med.* a streptococcal infection producing inflammation and a deep red colour on the skin. [from Greek *erusipelas*]

erythema /e-ri-th'ee-mă/ *n.* a superficial reddening of the skin, usu. in patches. [modern Latin]

erythro- *comb. form* red. [from Greek *eruthros* 'red']

erythrocyte *n.* a red blood cell. ▷ BLOOD. □ **erythrocytic** *adj.*

Es *symb. Chem.* the element einsteinium.

-es[1] *suffix* forming plurals of nouns ending in sibilant sounds (such words in *-e* dropping the *e*) (*kisses*; *cases*; *boxes*) and of a few ending in *-o* (*potatoes*; *heroes*).

-es[2] *suffix* forming the 3rd person sing. present of verbs ending in sibilant sounds (such words in *-e* dropping the *e*) and ending in *-o* (but not *-oo*) (*goes*; *places*; *pushes*).

escalate *v.* **1** *intr. & tr.* increase or develop (usu. rapidly) by stages. **2** *tr.* cause to become more intense. □ **escalation** *n.*

escalator *n.* a moving staircase consisting of a circulating belt forming steps. [based on French *escalade* 'climbing by ladder']

escallonia *n.* an evergreen shrub of the S. American genus *Escallonia*, bearing pink or white flowers. [named after *Escallon*, 18th-century Spanish traveller]

escalope *n.* a thin slice of meat without any bone, esp. veal. [from Old French, literally 'shell']

escapade *n.* a piece of reckless behaviour.

escape ● *v.* **1** *intr.* (often foll. by *from*) get free of the restriction or control of. **2** *intr.* (of a gas, liquid, etc.) leak. **3** *intr.* succeed in avoiding danger, punishment, etc. **4** *tr.* get completely free of (a person, grasp, etc.). **5** *tr.* elude (a commitment, danger, etc.). **6** *tr.* elude the notice or memory of (*nothing escapes you*). **7** *tr.* (of words etc.) issue unawares from (a person's lips). ● *n.* **1** the act or an instance of escaping; avoidance of danger, injury, etc. **2** the state of having escaped (*a narrow escape*). **3** a means of escaping (often *attrib.*: *escape hatch*). **4** a leakage of gas etc. **5** a temporary relief from reality or worry. **6** a garden plant running wild. **7** (in full **escape key**) *Computing* a key which either ends the current operation, or converts subsequent characters to a control sequence (*escape routine*; *escape sequence*). [from Anglo-French *escaper*] □ **escapable** *adj.* **escaper** *n.*

escape clause *n.* a clause specifying the conditions under which a contracting party is free from an obligation.

escapee *n.* a person, esp. a prisoner, who has escaped.

E

ERODE

The wearing away and removal of land surfaces by water, wind, or ice is known as erosion. It has the greatest impact in areas of little or no surface vegetation, such as deserts.

dry wash · canyon · mesa · mesa · scree · scree · butte · eroded arch · rock pedestal · parabolic dune · transverse dune · linear dune · alluvial fan · alluvium-filled basin · dry lake bed · fault line · granite · asymmetric ridge · fault line · sandstone · barchan dune · hogback · deflation hollow

FEATURES OF AN ERODED DESERT LANDSCAPE

escapement *n.* the part of a clock or watch that connects and regulates the motive power.

escapism *n.* the tendency to seek distraction and relief from reality. □ **escapist** *n. & adj.*

escapology *n.* the techniques of escaping from confinement, esp. as entertainment. □ **escapologist** *n.*

escarpment *n.* (also **escarp**) *Geol.* a long steep slope at the edge of a plateau etc. [from French *escarpement*]

eschatology *n.* **1** the part of theology concerned with death and final destiny. **2** a belief or beliefs about the destiny of mankind and the world. [based on Greek *eskhatos* 'last'] □ **eschatological** *adj.* **eschatologist** *n.*

escheat ● *n.* **1** the reversion of property to the state, or (in feudal law) to a lord, on the owner's dying without legal heirs. **2** property affected by this. ● *v.* **1** *tr.* hand over (property) as an escheat. **2** *tr.* confiscate. **3** *intr.* revert by escheat. [based on Latin *excidere* 'to fall to a person's share']

eschew *v.tr. literary* avoid; abstain from. [from Old French *eschiver*] □ **eschewal** *n.*

eschscholtzia /i-sholt-siǎ/ *n.* a yellow- or orange-flowered plant of the genus *Eschscholtzia*. [named after J. F. von *Eschscholtz*, German botanist, 1793–1831]

escort ● *n.* /ess-kort/ **1** one or more persons, vehicles, ships, etc., accompanying a person, vehicle, etc., esp. for protection or security or as a mark of rank or status. **2** a person accompanying a person of the opposite sex socially. ● *v.tr.* /i-skort/ act as an escort to. [from Italian *scorta* (fem.) 'conducted']

escritoire /ess-kree-twah/ *n.* a writing desk with drawers etc. [French]

escrow *n. Law* **1** money, property, or a written bond, kept in the custody of a third party until a specified condition has been fulfilled. **2** the status of this (*in escrow*). [from Old French *escroe* 'scrap, scroll']

escudo *n.* (*pl.* **-os**) the chief monetary unit of Portugal and Cape Verde. [based on Latin *scutum* 'shield']

escutcheon *n.* **1** a shield or emblem bearing a coat of arms. **2** the middle part of a ship's stern where the name is placed. **3** the protective plate around a keyhole or door handle. [based on Latin *scutum* 'shield']

Esd. *abbr.* Esdras (Apocrypha).

ESE *abbr.* east-south-east.

-ese *suffix* forming adjectives and nouns denoting: **1** an inhabitant or language of a country or city (*Japanese*; *Milanese*; *Viennese*). **2** often *derog.* character or style, esp. of language (*officialese*).

esker *n.* (also **eskar**) *Geol.* a long ridge of post-glacial gravel in river valleys. ▷ VALLEY. [from Irish *eiscir*]

Eskimo (also **Esquimau**) often *offens.* ● *n.* (*pl.* same or **-os** or **Esquimaux** *pronunc.* same or /-mohz/) **1** a member of a people inhabiting northern Canada, Alaska, Greenland, and eastern Siberia. **2** any of the languages of this people. ● *adj.* of or relating to the Eskimos or their language. [from Algonquian, literally 'eaters of raw flesh']

■ **Usage** In Canada and, increasingly, elsewhere the term *Inuit* is used to refer to Canadian Eskimos and also to Eskimos generally. The term *Eskimo* may offend some people.

ESL *abbr.* English as a second language.

ESN *abbr. hist.* educationally subnormal.

esophagus *US var. of* OESOPHAGUS.

esoteric *adj.* (of a doctrine, mode of speech, etc.) intelligible only to the initiated. [from Greek *esōterikos*] □ **esoterically** *adv.* **esotericist** *n.* **esotericism** *n.*

ESP *abbr.* extrasensory perception.

espadrille *n.* a light canvas shoe with a plaited fibre sole. [from Provençal *espardillo*]

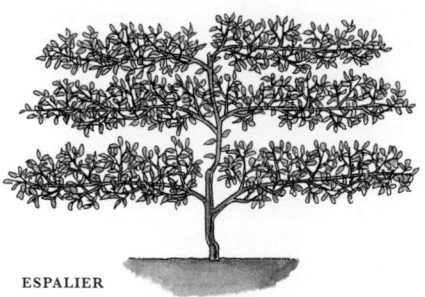

ESPALIER

espalier /iss-**pal**-i-er/ ● *n.* **1** a lattice along which the branches of a tree or shrub are trained. **2** ▲ a tree or shrub trained in this way. ● *v.tr.* train in this way. [French, from Italian *spalliera*]

esparto *n.* (*pl.* **-os**) (in full **esparto grass**) a coarse grass, *Stipa tenacissima*, native to Spain and N. Africa, used to make good-quality paper. [Spanish, based on Greek *sparton* 'rope']

especial *adj.* **1** notable. **2** attributed or belonging chiefly to one person or thing (*your especial charm*). [from Latin *specialis* 'special']

especially *adv.* chiefly; much more than in other cases.

Esperanto *n.* an artificial universal language devised in 1887. [pen-name of its inventor, L. L. Zamenhof, Polish physician, 1859–1917]

espionage /**ess**-pi-ŏn-ahzh/ *n.* the practice of spying or of using spies. [from French *espionnage*]

esplanade *n.* **1** a long open level area for walking on, esp. beside the sea. **2** a level space separating a fortress from a town. [from Spanish *esplanada*]

espousal *n.* **1** (foll. by *of*) the espousing of a cause etc. **2** *archaic* a marriage or betrothal.

espouse *v.tr.* **1** adopt or support (a cause, doctrine, etc.). **2** *archaic* **a** (usu. of a man) marry. **b** (usu. foll. by *to*) give (a woman) in marriage. [based on Latin *sponsus* 'betrothed']

espresso *n.* (also **expresso**) (*pl.* **-os**) **1** strong concentrated black coffee made under steam pressure. **2** a machine for making this. [Italian, literally 'pressed out']

esprit /ess-**pree**/ *n.* **1** wit. **2** spirit, liveliness. [French]

esprit de corps /ess-pree dĕ **kor**/ *n.* a feeling of devotion to and pride in the group one belongs to. [French, literally 'spirit of the body']

espy *v.tr.* (**-ies**, **-ied**) *literary* catch sight of. [from Old French *espier*]

Esq. *abbr.* Esquire.

-esque /esk/ *suffix* forming adjectives meaning 'in the style of' or 'resembling' (*romanesque*; *Schumannesque*; *statuesque*).

Esquimau *var. of* ESKIMO.

esquire *n.* **1** (usu. as abbr. **Esq.**) **a** *Brit.* a title appended to a man's surname when no other form of address is used. **b** *US* a title appended to a lawyer's surname. **2** *archaic* = SQUIRE *n.* 2. [from Latin *scutarius* 'shield-bearer']

-ess *suffix* forming nouns denoting females (*actress*; *lioness*; *mayoress*).

essay ● *n.* /**ess**-ay/ **1** a composition, usu. short and in prose, on any subject. **2** *formal* an attempt. ● *v.tr.* /e-**say**/ *formal* attempt, try. [based on Latin *exigere* 'to weigh'] □ **essayist** *n.*

essence *n.* **1** fundamental nature or inherent characteristics. **2 a** an extract obtained by distillation etc. **b** a perfume. **3** the constituent of a plant that determines its chemical properties. □ **in essence** fundamentally. **of the essence** indispensable. [based on Latin *esse* 'to be']

essential ● *adj.* **1** absolutely necessary; indispensable. **2** fundamental, basic. **3** of or constituting the essence of a person or thing. ● *n.* (esp. in *pl.*) a basic or indispensable element or thing. □ **essentiality** *n.* **essentially** *adv.*

essential element *n.* any of various elements required by living organisms for normal growth.

essential oil *n.* a volatile oil derived from a plant etc. with its characteristic odour.

establish *v.tr.* **1** set up or consolidate (a business, system, etc.) on a permanent basis. **2** (foll. by *in*) settle (a person or oneself) in some capacity. **3** (esp. as **established** *adj.*) achieve permanent acceptance for (a custom, belief, practice, institution, etc.). **4 a** place beyond dispute (a fact etc.). **b** find out, ascertain. [based on Latin *stabilis* 'stable'] □ **establisher** *n.*

established Church *n.* a Church recognized by the state as the national Church.

establishment *n.* **1** the act or an instance of establishing; the process of being established. **2 a** a business organization or public institution. **b** a place of business. **c** a residence. **3 a** the staff of an organization. **b** a household. **4** any organized body permanently maintained. **5** a Church system organized by law. **6 a** (**the Establishment**) the group in a society exercising authority or influence, and seen as resisting change. **b** any influential or controlling group (*the literary establishment*).

estate *n.* **1** a property consisting of an extensive area of land usu. with a large house. **2** *Brit.* a modern residential or industrial area with integrated design or purpose. **3** all of a person's assets and liabilities. **4** a property where rubber, tea, grapes, etc., are cultivated. **5** (in full **estate of the realm**) esp. *hist.* an order or class forming (or regarded as) a part of the body politic. **6** *archaic* or *literary* a state or position in life (*the estate of holy matrimony*). **7** *Brit. colloq.* = ESTATE CAR. □ **the Three Estates** Lords Spiritual (the heads of the Church), Lords Temporal (the peerage), and the Commons. [from Old French *estat*]

estate agent *n. Brit.* **1** a person whose business is the sale or lease of buildings and land on behalf of others. **2** the steward of an estate.

estate car *n. Brit.* a car with the passenger area extended and combined with space for luggage. ▷ CAR

estate duty *n. Brit. hist.* death duty levied on property.

estate of the realm see ESTATE 5.

esteem ● *v.tr.* **1** (usu. in *passive*) have a high regard for. **2** *formal* consider (*esteemed it an honour*). ● *n.* high regard; favour (*held them in esteem*). [from Latin *aestimare* 'to fix the price of']

ester *n. Chem.* any of a class of organic compounds produced by replacing the hydrogen of an acid by an alkyl etc. radical, many of which occur naturally as oils and fats. [German] □ **esterify** *v.tr.* (**-ies**, **-ied**)

esthete *US var. of* AESTHETE.

esthetic *US var. of* AESTHETIC.

estimable *adj.* worthy of esteem. [related to ESTEEM]

estimate ● *n.* **1** an approximate judgement. **2** a price specified as that likely to be charged for work to be undertaken. ● *v.tr.* (also *absol.*) **1** form an estimate of. **2** (foll. by *that* + clause) make a rough calculation. **3** value or measure by estimation; adjudge. [based on Latin *aestimatus* 'appraised'] □ **estimator** *n.*

estimation *n.* **1** the process or result of estimating. **2** judgement of worth (*in my estimation*).

estival *US var. of* AESTIVAL.

estivate *US var. of* AESTIVATE.

Estonian ● *n.* **1 a** a native of Estonia, a Baltic republic. **b** a person of Estonian descent. **2** the language of Estonia. ● *adj.* of or relating to Estonia or its people or language.

estrange *v.tr.* **1** (usu. in *passive*) cause to turn away in feeling or affection; alienate. **2** (as **estranged** *adj.*) (of a husband or wife) no longer living with his or her spouse. [from Latin *extraneare* 'to treat as a stranger'] □ **estrangement** *n.*

estrogen *US var. of* OESTROGEN.

estrus etc. *US var. of* OESTRUS etc.

estuary *n.* (*pl.* **-ies**) a wide tidal mouth of a river. ▷ COASTLINE. [from Latin *aestuarium* 'tidal channel'] □ **estuarine** *adj.*

ETA[1] *abbr.* estimated time of arrival.

ETA[2] /et-ă/ *n.* a Basque separatist movement in Spain. [from Basque *Euzkadi ta Azkatasuna* 'Basque homeland and liberty']

eta /ee-tă/ *n.* the seventh letter of the Greek alphabet (H, η). [Greek]

et al. *abbr.* and others. [Latin *et alii, et alia*, etc.]

etc. *abbr.* = ET CETERA.

et cetera (also **etcetera**) ● *adv.* **1 a** and the rest; and similar things or people. **b** or similar things or people. **2** and so on. ● *n.* (in *pl.*) the usual sundries or extras. [Latin]

etch *v.* **1** *tr.* **a** reproduce (a picture etc.) by engraving a design on a metal plate with acid. **b** engrave (a plate) in this way. **2** *intr.* practise this craft. **3** *tr.* (foll. by *on, upon*) impress deeply (esp. on the mind). [from Old High German *azzen* 'to cause to eat or to be eaten'] □ **etcher** *n.*

etching *n.* **1** a print made from an etched plate. **2** the art of producing these plates

eternal *adj.* **1** existing always; without an end or (usu.) beginning in time. **2** essentially unchanging (*eternal truths*). **3** *colloq.* constant; seeming not to cease (*your eternal nagging*). □ **the Eternal** God. [from Latin *aeternus*] □ **eternality** *n.* **eternalize** *v.tr.* (also **-ise**). **eternally** *adv.*

Eternal City *n.* (prec. by *the*) Rome.

eternal triangle *n.* a relationship between three people, usu. two of one sex and one of the other, involving sexual rivalry.

eternity *n.* (*pl.* **-ies**) **1** infinite or unending (esp. future) time. **2** *Theol.* endless life after death. **3** the state of being eternal. **4** (often prec. by *an*) *colloq.* a very long time. [from Latin *aeternitas*, based on *aevum* 'age']

eternity ring *n.* a finger ring set with gems all round.

ethane *n.* *Chem.* a gaseous hydrocarbon of the alkane series, occurring in natural gas.

ethanol *n.* *Chem.* = ALCOHOL 1.

ethene *n.* *Chem.* = ETHYLENE.

ether *n.* **1** *Chem.* **a** a colourless volatile organic liquid used as an anaesthetic or solvent. **b** any of a class of organic compounds with a similar structure to this, having an oxygen joined to two alkyl etc. groups. **2** (also **aether**) the clear sky; the upper regions of air. **3** (also **aether**) *hist.* **a** a medium formerly assumed to permeate space. **b** a medium through which electromagnetic waves were formerly thought to be transmitted. [from Greek *aithēr*] □ **etheric** *adj.*

ethereal *adj.* (also **etherial**) **1** light, airy. **2** highly delicate, esp. in appearance. **3** heavenly, celestial. □ **ethereality** *n.* **ethereally** *adv.*

Ethernet *n.* *Computing* a system of communication for local area networks by coaxial cable that prevents simultaneous transmission by more than one station.

ethic *n.* a set of moral principles (*the Quaker ethic*). [from Greek *ēthikos*]

ethical *adj.* **1** relating to morals. **2** morally correct. **3** (of a medicine or drug) not advertised to the general public, and usu. available only on a doctor's prescription. □ **ethicality** *n.* **ethically** *adv.*

ethical investment *n.* investment in companies that meet ethical criteria specified by the investor.

ethics *n.pl.* **1** (usu. treated as *sing.*) moral philosophy. **2 a** (treated as *pl.*) moral principles. **b** (often treated as *pl.*) a set of these (*medical ethics*). □ **ethicist** *n.*

Ethiopian ● *n.* **1** a native or national of Ethiopia in NE Africa. **2** a person of Ethiopian descent. ● *adj.* of or relating to Ethiopia. [from Greek *Aithiops*]

ethnic ● *adj.* **1 a** (of a social group) having a common national or cultural tradition. **b** (of clothes, music, etc.) characteristic of or influenced by the traditions of a particular people or culture, esp. one regarded as exotic. **2** denoting origin by birth or descent rather than nationality (*ethnic Turks*). **3** relating to race or culture (*ethnic group*; *ethnic origins*). ● *n.* **1** *N. Amer.* & *Austral.* a member of an (esp. minority) ethnic group. **2** (in *pl.*; usu. treated as *sing.*) = ETHNOLOGY. [from Greek *ethnikos* 'heathen'] □ **ethnically** *adv.* **ethnicity** *n.*

ethnic cleansing *n.* *euphem.* the mass expulsion or extermination of members of a particular ethnic or religious group in a certain area.

ethno- *comb. form* ethnic, ethnological. [from Greek *ethnos* 'nation']

ethnobotany *n.* **1** the traditional knowledge of a people concerning plants and their uses. **2** the study of such knowledge.

ethnocentric *adj.* evaluating other races and cultures by criteria specific to one's own. □ **ethnocentrically** *adv.* **ethnocentricity** *n.* **ethnocentrism** *n.*

ethnography *n.* the scientific description of races and cultures of humankind. □ **ethnographer** *n.* **ethnographic** *adj.* **ethnographical** *adj.*

ethnology *n.* the comparative scientific study of human peoples. □ **ethnological** *adj.* **ethnologist** *n.*

ethology *n.* **1** the science of animal behaviour. **2** the science of character-formation in human behaviour. □ **ethological** *adj.* **ethologist** *n.*

ethos *n.* the characteristic spirit or attitudes of a community, people, or system, or of a literary work etc. [from Greek *ēthos* 'nature, disposition']

ethyl *n.* (*attrib.*) *Chem.* a monovalent radical derived from ethane by removal of a hydrogen atom (*ethyl alcohol*). [German]

ethylene *n.* *Chem.* a gaseous hydrocarbon of the alkene series, occurring in natural gas and used in the manufacture of polythene.

ethylene glycol *n.* a colourless viscous hygroscopic liquid used as an antifreeze and in the manufacture of polyesters.

etiolate *v.tr.* **1** make (a plant) pale by excluding light. **2** give a sickly hue to (a person). [from Norman French *étieuler* 'to make into haulm'] □ **etiolation** *n.*

etiology *US* var. of AETIOLOGY.

etiquette *n.* **1** the conventional rules of social behaviour. **2 a** the customary behaviour of members of a profession towards each other. **b** the unwritten code governing this (*medical etiquette*). [from French]

Etruscan ● *adj.* of or relating to ancient Etruria in Italy. ● *n.* **1** a native of Etruria. **2** the language of Etruria. [from Latin *Etruscus*]

et seq. *abbr.* (also **et seqq.**) and the following (pages etc.). [Latin *et sequentia*]

-ette *suffix* forming nouns meaning: **1** small (*kitchenette*; *cigarette*). **2** imitation or substitute (*leatherette*; *flannelette*). **3** female (*usherette*; *suffragette*).

étude /ay-tewd/ *n.* a short musical composition designed to improve the technique of the player. [French, literally 'study']

etymology *n.* (*pl.* **-ies**) **1 a** the sources of the formation of a word and the development of its meaning. **b** an account of these. **2** the branch of linguistics concerned with etymologies. [from Greek *etumologia*] □ **etymological** *adj.* **etymologically** *adv.* **etymologist** *n.*

EU *abbr.* European Union.

■ **Usage** See Usage Note at EUROPEAN COMMUNITY.

Eu *symb.* *Chem.* the element europium.

eu- *comb. form* well, easily.

eucalyptus *n.* (also **eucalypt**) (*pl.* **eucalyptuses**, **eucalypti** /-ty/, or **eucalypts**) **1** ◄ any tree of the genus *Eucalyptus*, native to Australasia, many being cultivated for their timber, for the oil from their leaves, for gums and resins, or as ornamental trees. **2** (in full **eucalyptus oil**) the oil from eucalyptus leaves used as an antiseptic etc. [based on Greek *kaluptos* 'covered', the unopened flower being protected by a cap]

Eucharist *n.* **1** the Christian sacrament commemorating the Last Supper, in which bread and wine are consecrated and consumed. **2** the consecrated elements, esp. the bread (*receive the Eucharist*). [based on Greek *eukharistos* 'grateful'] □ **Eucharistic** *adj.*

euchre /yoo-ker/ ● *n.* an American card game for two, three, or four players. ● *v.tr.* **1** (in euchre) gain the advantage over (another player) when that player fails to take three tricks. **2** deceive, outwit. **3** *Austral.* exhaust, ruin. [from German dialect *Jucker(spiel)*]

Euclidean *adj.* of or relating to Euclid, 3rd-c. BC Alexandrian geometrician. [from Greek *Eukleideios*]

Euclidean geometry *n.* the geometry of ordinary experience, in which the postulates of Euclid are valid.

Euclidean space *n.* space for which Euclidean geometry is valid.

eugenics *n.* the science of improving the population by controlled breeding for desirable inherited characteristics. □ **eugenic** *adj.* **eugenically** *adv.* **eugenicist** *n.* **eugenist** *n.*

eukaryote /yoo-kă-ri-oht/ *n.* *Biol.* an organism consisting of a cell or cells in which the genetic material is DNA in the form of chromosomes contained within a distinct nucleus (cf. PROKARYOTE). □ **eukaryotic** *adj.*

eulogize *v.tr.* (also **-ise**) praise in speech or writing. □ **eulogist** *n.* **eulogistic** *adj.*

eulogy *n.* (*pl.* **-ies**) **1 a** a speech or writing in praise of a person. **b** an expression of praise. **2** *US* a funeral oration in praise of a person. [from Late Latin *eulogia* 'praise']

eunuch /yoo-nŭk/ *n.* a castrated man. [from Greek *eunoukhos*, literally 'bedchamber attendant']

euonymus /yoo-on-i-mŭs/ *n.* any tree or shrub of the genus *Euonymus*, e.g. the spindle tree. [from Greek *euōnumos* 'of lucky name']

euphemism *n.* **1** a mild or vague expression substituted for one thought to be too harsh or direct (e.g. *pass over* for *die*). **2** the use of such expressions. [based on Greek *euphēmos* 'fair of speech'] □ **euphemistic** *adj.* **euphemistically** *adv.* **euphemize** *v.tr.* & *intr.* (also **-ise**).

euphonious *adj.* **1** sounding pleasant, harmonious. **2** concerning euphony. □ **euphoniously** *adv.*

euphonium *n.* ▼ a brass instrument of the tuba family. ▷ BRASS. [modern Latin]

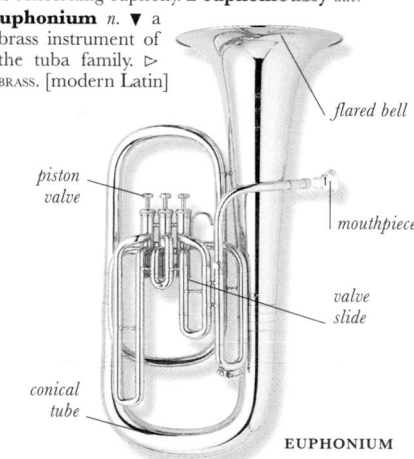

flared bell

piston valve

mouthpiece

valve slide

conical tube

EUPHONIUM

euphony *n.* (*pl.* **-ies**) **1 a** pleasantness of sound, esp. of a word or phrase. **b** a pleasant sound. **2** the tendency to make a phonetic change for ease of pronunciation. [from Greek *euphōnia*] □ **euphonic** *adj.*

euphorbia *n.* any plant of the genus *Euphorbia*, including spurges. ▷ SUCCULENT. [based on *Euphorbus*, 1st-century Greek physician]

EUCALYPTUS:
MOUNT WELLINGTON
PEPPERMINT
(*Eucalyptus coccifera*)

E

E

euphoria *n.* a feeling of well-being. [Greek, based on *euphoros* 'borne well'] □ **euphoric** *adj.* **euphorically** *adv.*

euphoriant ● *adj.* inducing euphoria. ● *n.* a euphoriant drug.

Eurasian ● *adj.* **1** of mixed European and Asian parentage. **2** of Europe and Asia. ● *n.* a Eurasian person.

Euratom *n.* European Atomic Energy Community.

eureka /yoor-**eek**-ă/ ● *int.* I have found it! (expressing joy at a discovery etc.). ● *n.* an exultant cry of 'eureka'. [from Greek *heurēka* 'I have found it', attributed to Archimedes, Greek mathematician, died 212 BC]

Euro ● *adj.* European. ● *n.* (*pl.* **-os**) **1** a European. **2** a Eurodollar. **3** (also **euro**) the name agreed for the future European currency unit, to replace the ecu after monetary union.

Euro- *comb. form* Europe, European.

Eurobond *n.* an international bond issued outside the country in whose currency its value is stated.

Eurocheque *n.* **1** a cheque issued under a banking arrangement enabling account-holders from one European country to use their cheques in another. **2** this arrangement.

Eurocrat *n.* usu. *derog.* a bureaucrat in the administration of the European Union.

Eurodollar *n.* a dollar held outside the US (not necessarily in Europe).

Euro-MP *n.* a member of the European Parliament.

European ● *adj.* **1** of or in Europe. **2 a** descended from natives of Europe. **b** originating in or characteristic of Europe. **3 a** happening in or extending over Europe. **b** concerning Europe as a whole rather than its individual countries. **4** of or relating to the European Union. ● *n.* **1 a** a native or inhabitant of Europe. **b** a person descended from natives of Europe. **c** a white person. **2** a person concerned with European matters. □ **Europeanism** *n.* **Europeanize** *v.tr. & intr.* (also **-ise**). **Europeanization** *n.*

European Community *n.* an economic and political association of certain European countries as a unit with internal free trade and common external tariffs.

■ **Usage** The European Community (EC) was formed in 1967 from the European Coal and Steel Community (ECSC), the European Economic Community (EEC), and the European Atomic Energy Community (Euratom). The name 'European Communities' is used in legal contexts where the three distinct organizations are recognized. The name 'European Economic Community' (EEC) is sometimes used loosely for the merged organization. In November 1993 the EC became known as the European Union (EU).

European Economic Community see note at EUROPEAN COMMUNITY.

europium *n. Chem.* a soft silvery metallic element of the lanthanide series, occurring naturally in small quantities. [modern Latin]

Euro-rebel *n.* a person who does not share his or her political party's enthusiasm for the European Union.

Euro-sceptic *n.* a person who is not enthusiastic about increasing the powers of the European Union.

Eurovision *n.* a network of European television production administered by the European Broadcasting Union.

Eustachian tube /yoo-**stay**-shăn/ *n. Anat.* a tube leading from the pharynx to the cavity of the middle ear. ▷ EAR. [named after B. *Eustachio*, Italian anatomist, 1520–74]

eustasy *n.* a change in sea level throughout the world caused by tectonic movements, melting of glaciers, etc. [based on German *eustatisch* (adj.)] □ **eustatic** *adj.*

eutectic *Chem.* ● *adj.* (of a mixture, alloy, etc.) having the lowest freezing point of any possible proportions of its constituents. ● *n.* a eutectic mixture. [from Greek *eutēktos* 'easily melting']

euthanasia *n.* **1** the painless killing of a patient suffering from an incurable and painful disease. **2** such a death. [Greek]

eutherian *n. & adj. Zool.* ● *n.* a mammal of the infraclass Eutheria, giving nourishment to its unborn young through a placenta (as in humans). ▷ MAMMALS. ● *adj.* of or relating to this infraclass, which includes all mammals except marsupials and monotremes. [EU- + Greek *thēr* 'wild beast']

eutrophic *adj.* (of a lake etc.) rich in nutrients and so supporting a dense plant population, the decomposition of which kills animal life by depriving it of oxygen. [based on Greek *trephein* 'to nourish'] □ **eutrophicate** *v.tr.* **eutrophication** *n.*

eV *abbr.* electronvolt.

evacuate *v.tr.* **1 a** remove (people) from a place of danger. **b** empty (a place) in this way. **2** make empty (a vessel of air etc.). **3** (of troops) withdraw from (a place). **4 a** empty (the bowels or other bodily organ). **b** discharge (faeces etc.). [based on Latin *evacuatus* 'emptied'] □ **evacuation** *n.*

evacuee *n.* a person evacuated from a place of danger.

evade *v.tr.* **1 a** escape from, avoid, esp. by guile or trickery. **b** avoid doing (one's duty etc.). **c** avoid answering (a question). **2 a** avoid paying (tax) by illegitimate presentation of one's finances. **b** defeat the intention of (a law etc.). **3** (of a thing) elude or baffle (a person). [from Latin *evadere*] □ **evader** *n.*

evaluate *v.tr.* **1** assess, appraise. **2 a** find or state the number or amount of. **b** find a numerical expression for. □ **evaluation** *n.* **evaluative** *adj.* **evaluator** *n.*

evanesce *v.intr.* **1** fade from sight. **2** become effaced. [from Latin *evanescere*]

evanescent *adj.* quickly fading. □ **evanescence** *n.*

evangelical ● *adj.* **1** of or according to the teaching of the gospel or the Christian religion. **2** of a branch of Protestant Christianity emphasizing the authority of Scripture, personal conversion, and the doctrine of salvation by faith in the Atonement. **3** zealously advocating a cause. ● *n.* a member of the evangelical tradition. [from ecclesiastical Greek *euaggelikos*] □ **evangelicalism** *n.* **evangelically** *adv.*

evangelism *n.* **1** the preaching of the gospel. **2** zealous advocacy of a cause or doctrine.

evangelist *n.* **1** any of the writers of the four Gospels. **2** a preacher of the gospel. **3** a lay person doing missionary work.

evangelistic *adj.* **1** of or relating to evangelism. **2** of the four evangelists.

evangelize *v.tr.* (also **-ise**) **1** (also *absol.*) preach the gospel to. **2** convert (a person) to Christianity. □ **evangelization** *n.* **evangelizer** *n.*

evaporate *v.* **1** *intr.* turn from solid or liquid into vapour. ▷ MATTER. **2** *intr. & tr.* lose or cause to lose moisture as vapour. **3** *intr. & tr.* disappear or cause to disappear (*our courage evaporated*). [based on Latin *vapor* 'steam'] □ **evaporation** *n.* **evaporative** *adj.* **evaporator** *n.*

evaporated milk *n.* milk concentrated by partial evaporation.

evasion *n.* **1** the act of evading. **2 a** a subterfuge or prevaricating excuse. **b** an evasive answer. [from Latin *evasio*]

evasive *adj.* **1** seeking to evade something. **2** not direct in one's answers etc. **3** enabling or effecting evasion (*evasive action*). **4** (of a person) habitually practising evasion. □ **evasively** *adv.* **evasiveness** *n.*

eve *n.* **1** the evening or day before a church festival or any date or event (*Christmas Eve; the eve of the funeral*). **2** the time just before anything (*the eve of the election*). **3** *archaic* evening. [Middle English]

even[1] ● *adj.* (**evener**, **evenest**) **1** level. **2 a** uniform in quality; constant. **b** equal in number, amount, value, score, etc. **c** equally balanced. **3** (usu. foll. by *with*) in the same plane or line. **4** (of a person's temper etc.) equable, calm. **5 a** (of a number) divisible by two without a remainder. **b** bearing such a number (*no parking on even dates*). **c** not involving fractions; exact (*in even dozens*). ● *adv.* **1** used to invite comparison of the stated assertion, negation, etc., with an implied one that is less strong or remarkable (*never even opened* [let alone read] *the letter; does he even suspect* [not to say realize] *the danger?*). **2** used to introduce an extreme case (*even you must realize it; it might even cost £100*). ● *v.tr. & intr.* make or become even. □ **even as** at the very moment that. **even now 1** now as well as before. **2** at this very moment. **even so 1** notwithstanding that; nevertheless. **2** quite so. **3** in that case as well as in others. **even though** despite the fact that. **get** (or **be**) **even with** have one's revenge on. [Old English] □ **evenly** *adv.* **evenness** *n.*

even[2] *n. poet.* evening. [Old English]

even break *n. colloq.* an equal chance.

even chance *n.* an equal chance of success or failure.

even-handed *adj.* impartial. □ **even-handedly** *adv.* **even-handedness** *n.*

evening ● *n.* the end part of the day, esp. from about 6 p.m., or sunset if earlier, to bedtime (*this evening; during the evening; evening meal; had a lively evening*). ● *int. colloq.* = good evening (see GOOD *adj.* 14). [Old English]

evening dress *n.* formal dress for evening wear.

evening primrose *n.* ◄ any plant of the genus *Oenothera* with pale yellow flowers that open in the evening, and from whose seeds an oil is extracted for medicinal use.

evening star *n.* a planet, esp. Venus, when visible in the west after sunset.

even money *n.* betting odds offering the gambler the chance of winning the amount he or she staked.

evens *n.pl. Brit.* = EVEN MONEY.

evensong *n.* a service of evening prayer, esp. that of Anglican churches.

event *n.* **1** a thing that happens. **2 a** the fact of a thing's occurring. **b** a result or outcome. **3** an item in a sports programme, or the programme as a whole. □ **at all events** (or **in any event**) whatever happens. **in the event** as it turns (or turned) out. **in the event of** if (a specified thing) happens (*in the event of his death; in the event of our losing*). **in the event that** *disp.* if it happens that. [from Latin *eventus* 'having happened']

EVENING PRIMROSE (*Oenothera biennis*)

■ **Usage** *In the event that* is considered awkward by some people. It can usually be avoided by rephrasing, e.g. *in the event that it rains* can be replaced by *in the event of rain.*

eventer *n. Brit.* a horse or rider who takes part in horse trials.

eventful *adj.* marked by noteworthy events. □ **eventfulness** *n.*

eventide *n. archaic* or *poet.* = EVENING.

eventing *n. Brit.* participation in horse trials, esp. cross-country, dressage, and showjumping.

eventual *adj.* occurring or existing in due course or at last. [related to EVENT] □ **eventually** *adv.*

eventuality *n.* (*pl.* **-ies**) a possible event or outcome.

eventuate *v.intr. formal* **1** turn out in a specified way as the result. **2** (often foll. by *in*) result.

ever *adv.* **1** at all times; always (*ever hopeful; ever after*). **2** at any time (*have you ever been to Paris?; as good as* *ever*). **3** as an emphatic word: **a** in any way; at all (*how ever did you do it?*). **b** (prec. by *as*) in any manner possible (*be as quick as ever you can*). **4** (often in *comb.*) constantly (*ever-present*). **5** (foll. by *so, such*) *Brit. colloq.* very; very much (*is ever so easy; was ever such a nice man*). **6** (foll. by *compar.*) constantly, continually; increasingly (*grew ever larger; ever more sophisticated*). □ **ever since** throughout the period since. **for ever 1** for all future time. **2** *colloq.* for a long time (cf. FOREVER). [Old English]

■ **Usage** When *ever* is used with a question word for emphasis it is written separately (see sense 3). When used with a relative pronoun or adverb to give it indefinite or general force, *ever* is written as one word with the relative pronoun or adverb, e.g. *However it's done, it's difficult.*

evergreen ● *adj.* **1** always green or fresh. **2** (of a plant) retaining green leaves throughout the year. **●** *n.* an evergreen plant. ▷ TREE

everlasting ● *adj.* **1** lasting for ever. **2** lasting for a long time, esp. so as to become unwelcome. **3** (of flowers) keeping their shape and colour when dried. **●** *n.* **1** eternity. **2** = IMMORTELLE. □ **everlastingly** *adv.* **everlastingness** *n.*

evermore *adv.* for ever; always.

every *det.* **1** each without exception (*heard every word; watched her every movement*). **2** each at a specified interval in a series (*comes every four days*). **3** all possible (*there is every prospect of success*). □ **every bit as** *colloq.* (in comparisons) quite as (*every bit as good*). **every now and again** (or **now and then**) from time to time. **every other** each second in a series (*every other day*). **every so often** occasionally. **every which way** *N. Amer. colloq.* **1** in all directions. **2** in a disorderly manner. [Old English, from *æfre ælc* 'ever each']

everybody *pron.* every person.

everyday *adj.* **1** occurring every day. **2** suitable for or used on ordinary days. **3** commonplace, usual.

Everyman *n.* the ordinary or typical human being. [name of the principal character in a 15th-century morality play]

everyone *pron.* everybody.

every one *n.* each one (see also EVERYONE).

everything *pron.* **1** all things; all the things of a group or class. **2** *colloq.* **a** a great deal (*he owes her everything*). **b** the essential consideration (*speed is everything*).

everywhere *adv.* **1** in every place. **2** *colloq.* in many places.

evict *v.tr.* expel (a tenant) from a property by legal process. [based on Latin *evictus* 'conquered completely'] □ **eviction** *n.*

evidence ● *n.* **1** the available facts, circumstances, etc. indicating whether or not a thing is true or valid. **2** *Law* **a** information tending to prove a fact or proposition. **b** statements or proofs admissible as testimony in a law court. **3** clearness, obviousness. **●** *v.tr.* be evidence of. □ **in evidence** noticeable, conspicuous.

evident *adj.* plain or obvious; manifest. [from Latin *evident-* 'seeing plainly']

evidential *adj.* of or providing evidence. □ **evidentially** *adv.*

evidently *adv.* **1** plainly, obviously. **2** (qualifying a whole sentence) it is plain that; it would seem that (*evidently, we're too late*). **3** (said in reply) so it appears.

evil ● *adj.* **1** morally bad; wicked. **2** harmful or tending to harm. **3** disagreeable (*has an evil temper*). **4** unlucky; causing misfortune (*evil days*). **●** *n.* **1** an evil thing; an instance of something evil. **2** wickedness. □ **speak evil of** slander. [Old English] □ **evilly** *adv.* **evilness** *n.*

evil eye *n.* a gaze superstitiously believed to be able to cause harm.

evince *v.tr.* **1** indicate or make evident. **2** show that one has (a quality). [from Latin *evincere* 'to prove']

eviscerate /i-**vis**-er-ayt/ *v.tr. formal* **1** disembowel. **2** empty or deprive of essential contents. [based on Latin *evisceratus* 'disembowelled'] □ **evisceration** *n.*

evocative *adj.* tending to evoke (esp. feelings or memories). □ **evocatively** *adv.*

evoke *v.tr.* **1** inspire or draw forth (memories, feelings, a response, etc.). **2** = INVOKE 3. [from Latin *evocare*] □ **evocation** *n.* **evoker** *n.*

evolution *n.* **1** gradual development. **2** ▼ a process by which species develop from earlier forms, as an explanation of their origins. **3** the appearance or presentation of events etc. in due succession (*the evolution of the plot*). **4** a change in the disposition of troops or ships. **5** the giving off or evolving of gas, heat, etc. **6** an opening out. [from Latin *evolutio* 'unrolling'] □ **evolutional** *adj.* **evolutionary** *adj.* **evolutionarily** *adv.*

evolutionist *n.* a person who believes in evolution as explaining the origin of species. □ **evolutionism** *n.*

evolve *v.* **1** *intr. & tr.* develop gradually by a natural process. **2** *tr.* devise (a theory, plan, etc.). **3** *intr. & tr.* unfold; open out. **4** *tr.* give off (gas, heat, etc.). [from Latin *evolvere* 'to unroll'] □ **evolvement** *n.*

ewe *n.* a female sheep. [Old English]

ewer *n.* a large water jug with a wide mouth. [based on Latin *aquarius* 'of water']

ex¹ *prep.* **1** (of goods) sold from (*ex-works*). **2** (of stocks or shares) without, excluding.

ex² *n. colloq.* a former husband or wife.

ex- *prefix* (also **e-** before some consonants, **ef-** before *f*) **1** forming verbs meaning: **a** out, forth (*exclude; exit*). **b** upward (*extol*). **c** thoroughly (*excruciate*). **d** bring into a state (*exasperate*). **e** remove or free from (*expatriate; exonerate*). **2** forming nouns from titles of office, status, etc., meaning 'formerly' (*ex-president; ex-wife*).

exacerbate /ig-**zass**-er-bayt/ *v.tr.* **1** make (pain, anger, etc.) worse. **2** irritate (a person). [based on Latin *acerbus* 'bitter'] □ **exacerbation** *n.*

exact ● *adj.* **1** accurate; correct in all details (*an exact description*). **2 a** precise. **b** (of a person) tending to precision. **●** *v.tr.* **1** demand and enforce payment of (money etc.). **2 a** demand; insist on. **b** (of circumstances) require urgently. [from Latin *exactus*] □ **exactitude** *n.* **exactness** *n.*

exacting *adj.* **1** making great demands. **2** calling for much effort. □ **exactingly** *adv.*

exaction *n.* **1** the act or an instance of exacting; the process of being exacted. **2 a** an illegal or exorbitant demand; an extortion. **b** a sum or thing exacted.

exactly *adv.* **1** accurately, precisely; in an exact manner (*worked it out exactly*). **2** in exact terms (*exactly when did it happen?*). **3** (said in reply) quite so; I quite agree.

exact science *n.* a science admitting of absolute or quantitative precision.

exaggerate *v.tr.* **1** (also *absol.*) give an impression of (a thing) that makes it seem larger or greater etc. than it really is. **2** enlarge or alter beyond normal or due proportions (*spoke with exaggerated politeness*). [based on Latin *exaggeratus* 'heaped up'] □ **exaggeratedly** *adv.* **exaggeration** *n.* **exaggerator** *n.*

exalt *v.tr.* **1** raise in rank or power etc. **2** praise highly. **3** (usu. as **exalted** *adj.*) make lofty or noble (*exalted aims; an exalted style*). [from Latin *exaltare*] □ **exaltedness** *n.*

exaltation *n.* **1** the act or an instance of exalting; the state of being exalted. **2** elation; rapturous emotion.

exam *n. colloq.* = EXAMINATION 3b.

examination *n.* **1** the act or an instance of examining; the state of being examined. **2** a detailed inspection. **3 a** the testing of the proficiency or knowledge of candidates for a qualification by questions. **b** a test of this kind. **4** an instance of examining or being examined medically. **5** *Law* the formal questioning of the accused or of a witness in court.

examine *v.tr.* **1** enquire into the nature or condition etc. of. **2** look closely at. **3** test the proficiency of. **4** check the health of (a patient). **5** *Law* formally question (the accused or a witness) in court. [from Latin *examinare* 'to weigh, test'] □ **examinable** *adj.* **examinee** *n.* **examiner** *n.*

example *n.* **1** a thing characteristic of its kind or illustrating a general rule. **2** a person, thing, or piece of conduct, regarded in terms of its fitness to be imitated or likelihood of being imitated (*must set him an example; you are a bad example*). **3** a circumstance or treatment seen as a warning to others, a person so treated (*shall make an example of you*). **4** a problem or exercise designed to illustrate a rule. □ **for example** by way of illustration. [from Latin *exemplum*]

ex ante *adj. Econ.* based on expected results, forecast. [modern Latin, = 'from before']

exarch *n.* in the Orthodox Church, a bishop lower in rank than a patriarch and having jurisdiction wider than the metropolitan of a diocese. [ecclesiastical Latin from Greek *exarkhos*] □ **exarchate** *n.*

exasperate *v.tr.* irritate intensely. [based on Latin *exasperatus* 'roughened'] □ **exasperatedly** *adv.* **exasperatingly** *adv.* **exasperation** *n.*

ex cathedra /eks kă-**th'ee**-dră/ *adj. & adv.* with full authority (esp. of a papal pronouncement). [Latin, literally 'from the (teacher's) chair']

EVOLUTION

Evolution is a process by which living things change over time, and adapt to the conditions of their environment. For example, fossils reveal that the modern horse evolved from smaller ancestors; the earliest horse, *Hyracotherium*, was about the size of a small dog. Evolution can also bring about a reduction in size, and a loss of redundant features, such as wings.

EVOLUTION OF THE HORSE

HYRACOTHERIUM
(50 million years ago)

MESOHIPPUS
(30 million years ago)

MERYCHIPPUS
(20 million years ago)

EQUUS
(modern horse)

E

EXCAVATE

Excavating machinery, such as the excavator shown here, is used for digging holes or trenches and earth-moving. A variety of tools, such as a clamshell grab, can be attached to the excavator's head to perform different tasks.

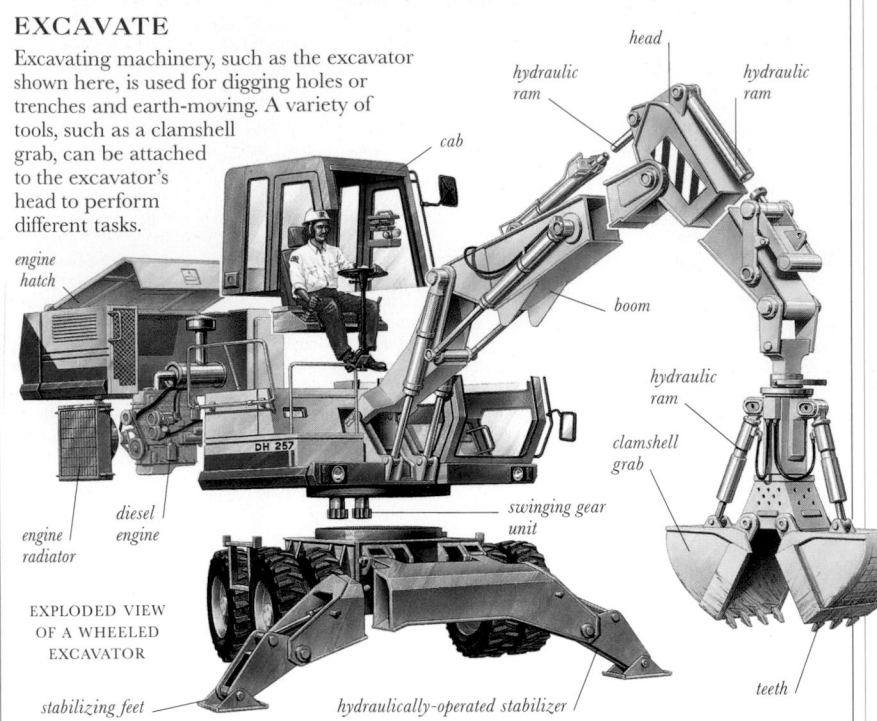

EXPLODED VIEW
OF A WHEELED
EXCAVATOR

head · *hydraulic ram* · *hydraulic ram* · *cab* · *boom* · *hydraulic ram* · *clamshell grab* · *engine hatch* · *engine radiator* · *diesel engine* · *engine radiator* · *swinging gear unit* · *stabilizing feet* · *hydraulically-operated stabilizer* · *teeth*

excavate *v.tr.* **1 a** ▲ make (a hole or channel) by digging. **b** dig out material from (the ground). **2** reveal or extract by digging. **3** (also *absol.*) *Archaeol.* dig systematically to explore (a site). [based on Latin *cavus* 'hollow'] □ **excavation** *n.* **excavator** *n.*

exceed *v.tr.* **1** be more or greater than. **2** go beyond or do more than is warranted by (a set limit, esp. of one's instructions or rights). **3** surpass. [from Latin *excedere* 'to go out']

exceeding *adj.* **1** surpassing in amount or degree. **2** pre-eminent.

exceedingly *adv.* very; to a great extent.

excel *v.* (**excelled**, **excelling**) (often foll. by *in*, *at*) **1** *tr.* be superior to. **2** *intr.* be pre-eminent (*excels at games*). □ **excel oneself** surpass one's previous performance. [from Latin *excellere* 'to be eminent']

excellence *n.* the state of excelling; surpassing merit or quality. [related to EXCEL]

Excellency *n.* (*pl.* **-ies**) (usu. prec. by *Your*, *His*, *Her*, *Their*) a title of ambassadors, governors, etc.

excellent *adj.* extremely good. □ **excellently** *adv.*

eccentric var. of ECCENTRIC (in technical senses).

except ● *v.tr.* (often as **excepted** *adj.* placed after object) exclude from a general statement, condition, etc. (*excepted him from the amnesty*; *present company excepted*). ● *prep.* (often foll. by *for*, or *that* + clause) not including; other than (*all failed except him*; *is all right except that it is too long*). ● *conj.* archaic unless (*except he be born again*). [from Latin *exceptus* 'taken out']

excepting *prep.* = EXCEPT *prep.*

■ **Usage** *Excepting* should be used only after *not* and *always*; otherwise, *except* should be used.

exception *n.* **1** the act or an instance of excepting; the state of being excepted. **2** a thing that has been or will be excepted. **3** an instance that does not follow a rule. □ **take exception** (often foll. by *to*) object; be resentful (about). **with the exception of** except; not including.

exceptionable *adj.* open to objection.

■ **Usage** *Exceptionable* should not be confused with *exceptional*. Note the difference in meaning between *Her new book was unexceptionable* (i.e. it contained nothing that would cause objections) and *Her new book was unexceptional* (i.e. it was mediocre).

exceptional *adj.* **1** forming an exception. **2** unusual; not typical (*exceptional circumstances*). **3** unusually good; outstanding. □ **exceptionality** *n.* **exceptionally** *adv.*

■ **Usage** See Usage Note at EXCEPTIONABLE.

excerpt ● *n.* /ek-serpt/ a short extract from a book, film, piece of music, etc. ● *v.tr.* /ik-serpt/ (also *absol.*) take (an extract) from a book etc. [from Latin *excerptum* 'thing plucked out'] □ **excerptible** *adj.* **excerption** *n.*

excess ● *n.* **1** the state or an instance of exceeding. **2** the amount by which one quantity or number exceeds another. **3 a** the overstepping of the accepted limits of moderation, esp. intemperance in eating or drinking. **b** (in *pl.*) outrageous or immoderate behaviour. **4** *Brit.* part of an insurance claim to be paid by the insured. ● *attrib.adj.* **1** that exceeds a limited or prescribed amount (*excess weight*). **2** *Brit.* required as extra payment (*excess postage*). □ **in** (or **to**) **excess** exceeding the proper amount or degree. **in excess of** more than; exceeding. [from Latin *excessus*]

excessive *adj.* too much or too great. □ **excessively** *adv.* **excessiveness** *n.*

exchange ● *n.* **1** the act or an instance of giving one thing and receiving another in its place. **2** the giving of money for its equivalent in the money of the same or esp. another country. **3** a place or installation containing the apparatus for connecting telephone calls. **4** a place where merchants, bankers, etc. gather to transact business. **5 a** an office where certain information is given or a service provided, usu. involving two parties. **b** an employment office. **6** a system of settling debts without the use of money, by bills of exchange (see BILL OF EXCHANGE). **7 a** a short conversation, esp. a disagreement or quarrel. **b** a sequence of letters between correspondents. ● *v.* **1** *tr.* (often foll. by *for*) give or receive (one thing) in place of another. **2** *tr.* give and receive as equivalents (e.g. things or people, blows, information, etc.). **3** *intr.* (often foll.

by *with*) make an exchange. □ **in exchange** (often foll. by *for*) as a thing exchanged (for). [from Old French *eschangier*] □ **exchangeable** *adj.* **exchangeability** *n.* **exchanger** *n.*

exchange rate *n.* the value of one currency in terms of another.

exchequer *n.* **1** *Brit.* the former government department in charge of national revenue. **2** a royal or national treasury. **3** the money of a private individual or group. [based on medieval Latin *scaccarium* 'chessboard', its original sense (with reference to accounts kept by counters on a chequered cloth)]

■ **Usage** With reference to sense 1, the functions of this department now belong to the Treasury, although the name formally survives, esp. in the title *Chancellor of the Exchequer*.

excise¹ /ek-syz/ ● *n.* **1** a duty or tax on goods and commodities produced or sold within the country of origin. **2** a tax levied on certain licences. ● *v.tr.* charge excise on (goods). [from Middle Dutch *excijs*]

excise² /ik-syz/ *v.tr.* **1** remove (a passage of a book etc.). **2** cut out (an organ etc.) by surgery. [from Latin *excidere excis*-] □ **excision** *n.*

excitable *adj.* (esp. of a person) easily excited. □ **excitability** *n.* **excitably** *adv.*

excitation *n.* **1** the act or an instance of exciting. **2** the state of being excited; excitement.

excite *v.tr.* **1 a** rouse the feelings or emotions of (a person). **b** bring into play; rouse up (feelings, faculties, etc.). **c** arouse sexually. **2** provoke; bring about (an action or active condition). **3** promote the activity of (an organism, tissue, etc.) by stimulus. [from Latin *excitare*] □ **excitant** *adj.* & *n.* **excitatory** *adj.* **excitedly** *adv.* **excitedness** *n.* **excitement** *n.* **exciter** *n.*

exciting *adj.* arousing great interest or enthusiasm; stirring. □ **excitingly** *adv.*

exclaim *v.* **1** *intr.* cry out suddenly, esp. in anger, surprise, pain, etc. **2** *tr.* (foll. by *that*) utter by exclaiming. [from Latin *exclamare*]

exclamation *n.* **1** the act or an instance of exclaiming. **2** words exclaimed.

exclamation mark *n.* (*US* also **exclamation point**) a punctuation mark (!) indicating an exclamation.

exclamatory *adj.* of or serving as an exclamation.

exclude *v.tr.* **1** shut or keep out (a person or thing) from a place, group, privilege, etc. **2** remove from consideration. **3** prevent the occurrence of; make impossible (*excluded all doubt*). [from Latin *excludere*] □ **excludable** *adj.* **excluder** *n.*

exclusion *n.* the act or an instance of excluding; the state of being excluded. □ **to the exclusion of** so as to exclude. □ **exclusionary** *adj.*

exclusive ● *adj.* **1** excluding other things. **2** (*predic.*; foll. by *of*) not including; except for. **3** tending to exclude others, esp. socially; select. **4** catering for few or select customers; high-class. **5 a** (of a commodity) not obtainable elsewhere. **b** (of a newspaper article) not published elsewhere. **6** (*predic.*; foll. by *to*) restricted or limited to; existing or available only in. **7** employed or followed or held to the exclusion of all else (*my exclusive occupation*; *exclusive rights*). ● *n.* an article or story published by only one newspaper or periodical. □ **exclusively** *adv.* **exclusiveness** *n.* **exclusivity** *n.*

excogitate *v.tr.* think out; contrive. [based on Latin *excogitatus* 'found out by thought'] □ **excogitation** *n.*

excommunicate *Eccl.* ● *v.tr.* officially exclude (a person) from participation in the sacraments, or from formal communion with the Church. ● *adj.* excommunicated. ● *n.* an excommunicated person. [from Latin *excommunicatus*] □ **excommunication** *n.*

excoriate *v.tr.* **1 a** remove part of the skin of (a person etc.) by abrasion. **b** strip or peel off (skin). **2** censure severely. [based on Latin *corium* 'hide'] □ **excoriation** *n.*

excrement *n.* (in *sing.* or *pl.*) faeces. [related to EXCRETE] □ **excremental** *adj.*

excrescence *n.* **1** an abnormal or morbid outgrowth on the body or a plant. **2** an ugly addition. [from Latin *excrescentia*] □ **excrescent** *adj.*

excreta *n.pl.* waste discharged from the body, esp. faeces and urine.

excrete *v.tr.* (also *absol.*) (of an animal or plant) separate and expel (waste matter). [based on Latin *excretus* 'sifted out'] □ **excretion** *n.* **excretory** *adj.*

excruciating *adj.* causing acute mental or physical pain. [based on Latin *excruciatus* 'tortured'] □ **excruciatingly** *adv.* **excruciation** *n.*

exculpate *v.tr. formal* **1** free from blame. **2** (foll. by *from*) clear (a person) of a charge. [based on Latin *culpa* 'blame'] □ **exculpation** *n.* **exculpatory** *adj.*

excursion *n.* a short journey for pleasure, with return to the starting point. [from Latin *excursio*] □ **excursionist** *n.*

excuse ● *v.tr.* /ik-**skewz**/ **1** try to lessen the blame attaching to (a person, act, or fault). **2** (of a fact) serve in mitigation of (a person or act). **3** obtain exemption for (a person or oneself). **4** (foll. by *from*, or with double object) release (a person) from a duty etc. (*excused from supervision duties; excused him the fee*). **5** overlook or forgive (a fault or offence). **6** *refl.* apologize for leaving. ● *n.* /ik-**skewss**/ **1** a reason put forward to mitigate or justify an offence, fault, etc. **2** an apology (*made my excuses*). □ **be excused** be allowed to leave a room etc., e.g. to go to the lavatory. **excuse me** a polite apology for an interruption etc., or for disagreeing. [from Latin *excusare*] □ **excusable** *adj.* **excusably** *adv.* **excusatory** *adj.*

ex-directory *adj. Brit.* not listed in a telephone directory, at the wish of the subscriber.

ex dividend *adj. & adv.* (of stocks or shares) not including the next dividend.

execrable *adj.* abominable, detestable. [related to EXECRATE] □ **execrably** *adv.*

execrate *v.* **1** *tr.* express or feel abhorrence for. **2** *tr.* curse (a person or thing). **3** *intr.* utter curses. [based on Latin *exsecratus* 'cursed'] □ **execration** *n.* **execratory** *adj.*

execute *v.tr.* **1** carry out a sentence of death on (a condemned person). **2** carry into effect, perform (a plan, duty, command, operation, etc.). **3** carry out a design for (a product of art or skill). **4** make (a legal instrument) valid by signing, sealing, etc. **5** put into effect (a judicial sentence, the terms of a will, etc.). [based on Latin *exsecutus* 'followed out'] □ **executable** *adj.*

execution *n.* **1** the carrying out of a sentence of death. **2** the act or an instance of carrying out or performing something. **3** technique or style of performance in the arts, esp. music. □ **executionary** *adj.*

executioner *n.* an official who carries out a sentence of death.

executive ● *n.* **1** a person or body with managerial or administrative responsibility in a business organization etc. **2** a branch of a government or organization concerned with executing laws, agreements, etc., or with other administration or management. ● *adj.* concerned with executing laws, agreements, etc., or with other administration or management. □ **executively** *adv.*

executor *n.* (*fem.* **executrix**) a person appointed by a testator to carry out the terms of his or her will. □ **executorship** *n.* **executory** *adj.*

exegesis /eks-i-**jee**-sis/ *n.* (*pl.* **exegeses**) critical explanation of a text, esp. of Scripture. [from Greek *exēgēsis*] □ **exegete** *n.* **exegetic** *adj.* **exegetical** *adj.*

exemplar *n.* **1** a model or pattern. **2** a typical or parallel instance. [from Old French *exemplaire*]

exemplary *adj.* **1** fit to be imitated; outstandingly good. **2** serving as a warning. □ **exemplarily** *adv.*

exemplify *v.tr.* (**-ies, -ied**) **1** illustrate by example. **2** be an example of. □ **exemplification** *n.*

exempt ● *adj.* **1** free from an obligation or liability etc. imposed on others. **2** (foll. by *from*) not liable to. ● *v.tr.* (usu. foll. by *from*) make exempt. [from Latin *exemptus* 'taken out'] □ **exemption** *n.*

exercise ● *n.* **1** activity requiring physical effort, done esp. as training or to sustain or improve health. **2** mental or spiritual activity, esp. as practice to develop a faculty. **3** (often in *pl.*) a particular task or set of tasks devised as practice in a technique etc. **4 a** the use or application of a mental faculty, right, etc. **b** practice of an ability, quality, etc. **5** (often in *pl.*) military drill or manoeuvres. **6** (foll. by *in*) a process directed at or concerned with something specified (*was an exercise in public relations*). ● *v.* **1** *tr.* use or apply (a faculty, right, influence, restraint, etc.). **2** *tr.* perform (a function). **3 a** *intr.* take (esp. physical) exercise; do exercises. **b** *tr.* provide (an animal) with exercise. **4** *tr.* **a** tax the powers of. **b** perplex, worry. [from Latin *exercitium*] □ **exercisable** *adj.* **exerciser** *n.*

exercise book *n.* **1** a book containing exercises. **2** *Brit.* a book for writing school work, notes, etc., in.

exert *v.tr.* **1** exercise, bring to bear (a quality, influence, etc.). **2** *refl.* (often foll. by *for*, or *to* + infin.) use one's efforts or endeavours; strive. [based on Latin *exsertus* 'put forth'] □ **exertion** *n.*

exeunt /**eks**-iunt/ *v.intr.* (as a stage direction) (actors) leave the stage. □ ***exeunt omnes*** all leave the stage. [Latin, literally 'they go out']

exfoliate *v.* **1** *intr.* (of bone, the skin, a mineral, etc.) come off in scales or layers. **2** *tr.* **a** shed (material) in scales or layers. **b** (also *absol.*) cause (the skin etc.) to shed flakes or scales. **3** *intr.* ► (of a tree) throw off layers of bark. [based on Late Latin *exfoliatus* 'stripped of leaves'] □ **exfoliation** *n.* **exfoliative** *adj.*

EXFOLIATE: PEELING BIRCH BARK

ex gratia /eks **gray**-shă/ ● *adv.* as a favour rather than from an (esp. legal) obligation. ● *adj.* granted on this basis. [Latin, literally 'from favour']

exhalation *n.* **1 a** an expiration of air. **b** a puff of breath. **2** a mist, vapour.

exhale *v.* **1** *tr.* (also *absol.*) breathe out (esp. air or smoke) from the lungs. **2** *tr.* & *intr.* give off or be given off in vapour. [from Latin *exhalare*]

exhaust ● *v.tr.* **1** consume or use up the whole of. **2** (often as **exhausted** *adj.* or **exhausting** *adj.*) tire out. **3** study or expound on (a subject) completely. **4** (often foll. by *of*) empty (a container etc.) of its contents. ● *n.* **1** waste gases etc. expelled from an engine after combustion. **2** (also **exhaust pipe**) the pipe or system by which these are expelled. ▷ CAR, OFF-ROAD. [from Latin *exhaustus* 'drawn out'] □ **exhauster** *n.* **exhaustible** *adj.*

exhaustion *n.* **1** the act or an instance of exhausting a thing; the state of being exhausted. **2** a total loss of strength or vitality.

exhaustive *adj.* thorough, comprehensive. □ **exhaustively** *adv.* **exhaustiveness** *n.*

exhibit ● *v.tr.* (**exhibited, exhibiting**) **1** show or reveal publicly (for interest or amusement, in competition, etc.). **2 a** show, display. **b** manifest (a quality). ● *n.* **1** a thing or collection of things in an exhibition. **2** a document or other item produced in a law court as evidence. [from Latin *exhibēre exhibit-* 'to hold out'] □ **exhibitory** *adj.*

exhibition *n.* **1** a display (esp. public) of works of art etc. **2** the act or an instance of exhibiting; the state of being exhibited. **3** *Brit.* a scholarship, esp. from the funds of a school, college, etc.

exhibitioner *n. Brit.* a student who has been awarded an exhibition.

exhibitionism *n.* **1** a tendency towards display or extravagant behaviour. **2** *Psychol.* a mental condition characterized by the compulsion to display one's genitals in public. □ **exhibitionist** *n.* **exhibitionistic** *adj.* **exhibitionistically** *adv.*

exhibitor *n.* a person who provides an item or items for an exhibition.

exhilarate *v.tr.* (often as **exhilarating** *adj.* or **exhilarated** *adj.*) affect with great liveliness or joy; raise the spirits of. [based on Latin *exhilaratus* 'made cheerful'] □ **exhilaratingly** *adv.* **exhilaration** *n.*

exhort *v.tr.* (often foll. by *to* + infin.) urge or advise strongly or earnestly. [from Latin *exhortari*] □ **exhortation** *n.* **exhortatory** *adj.* **exhorter** *n.*

exhume *v.tr.* dig out, unearth (esp. a buried corpse). [based on Latin *humus* 'ground'] □ **exhumation** *n.*

ex hypothesi /eks hy-**poth**-ĕ-sy/ *adv.* according to the hypothesis proposed. [modern Latin]

exigency /**eks**-i-jĕn-si/ *n.* (*pl.* **-ies**) (also **exigence**) **1** an urgent need or demand. **2** an emergency. □ **exigent** *adj.*

exiguous /ig-**zig**-yoo-ŭs/ *adj.* scanty, small. [from Latin *exiguus* 'scanty'] □ **exiguity** *n.*

exile ● *n.* **1** expulsion from one's native land or (**internal exile**) native town etc. **2** long absence abroad, esp. enforced. **3** a person expelled or long absent from his or her native country. ● *v.tr.* (foll. by *from*) officially expel (a person) from his or her native country or town etc. [from Latin *exilium*] □ **exilic** *adj.*

exist *v.intr.* **1** have a place as part of objective reality. **2 a** have being under specified conditions. **b** (foll. by *as*) exist in the form of. **3** (of circumstances etc.) occur; be found. **4** be alive, live.

existence *n.* **1** the fact or condition of being or existing. **2** continued being, esp. the manner of one's existing or living under adverse conditions (*a wretched existence*). **3** all that exists. [based on Latin *exsistent-* 'coming into being']

existent *adj.* existing, actual, current.

existential *adj.* **1** of or relating to existence. **2** *Philos.* concerned with existence, esp. with human existence as viewed by existentialism. □ **existentially** *adv.*

existentialism *n.* a philosophical theory emphasizing the existence of the individual person as a free and responsible agent determining his or her own development. □ **existentialist** *n.*

exit ● *n.* **1** a passage or door by which to leave a room, building, etc. **2 a** the act of going out. **b** the right or freedom to go out. **3** a place where vehicles can leave a motorway or major road. **4** the departure of an actor from the stage. ● *v.intr.* (**exited, exiting**) **1** go out of a room, building, etc. **2** (as a stage direction) (an actor) leaves the stage (*exit Macbeth*). [Latin, literally 'he or she goes out']

exit poll *n.* a poll of people leaving a polling station, asking how they voted.

exocrine *adj.* (of a gland) secreting through a duct. [based on Greek *krinein* 'to sift']

exodus *n.* **1** a mass departure of people. **2** (**Exodus**) *Bibl.* the departure of the Israelites from Egypt. [from Greek *exodos*]

ex officio /eks ŏ-**fish**-ioh/ *adv. & adj.* by virtue of one's office or status. [Latin]

exogamy *n.* **1** *Anthropol.* marriage of a man outside his own tribe. **2** *Biol.* the fusion of reproductive cells from distantly related or unrelated individuals. □ **exogamous** *adj.*

exogenous *adj.* growing or originating from outside. □ **exogenously** *adv.*

exonerate *v.tr.* (often foll. by *from*) **1** free or declare free from blame etc. **2** release from a duty etc. [based on Latin *exoneratus* 'unburdened'] □ **exoneration** *n.*

exorbitant *adj.* (of a price, demand, etc.) grossly excessive. [from Late Latin *exorbitant-* 'leaving the track'] □ **exorbitance** *n.* **exorbitantly** *adv.*

exorcize *v.tr.* (also **-ise**) **1** expel (a supposed evil spirit) by invocation etc. **2** (often foll. by *of*) free (a person or place) of a supposed evil spirit. [from Greek *exorkizein*] □ **exorcism** *n.* **exorcist** *n.*

E

exoskeleton *n.* ▶ a rigid external covering for the body in certain animals, esp. arthropods. ▷ ARTHRO-POD. □ **exoskeletal** *adj.*

exosphere *n.* the layer of atmosphere furthest from the Earth. ▷ ATMOSPHERE

exothermic *adj.* esp. *Chem.* occurring or formed with the evolution of heat.

exotic ● *adj.* **1** introduced from a foreign (esp. tropical) country (*exotic fruits*). **2** attractively or remarkably strange or unusual; bizarre. ● *n.* an exotic person or thing. [based on Greek *exō* 'outside'] □ **exotically** *adv.* **exoticism** *n.*

exotica *n.pl.* remarkably strange or rare objects.

expand *v.* **1** *tr. & intr.* increase in size or importance. **2** *intr.* (often foll. by *on*) give a fuller description or account. **3** *intr.* become more genial or effusive. **4** *tr.* set or write out in full. **5** *tr. & intr.* spread out flat. [from Latin *expandere* 'to spread out'] □ **expandable** *adj.* **expander** *n.*

expanse *n.* a wide continuous area or extent of land, space, etc. [related to EXPAND]

expansion *n.* **1** the act or an instance of expanding; the state of being expanded. **2** enlargement of the scale or scope of (esp. commercial) operations. **3** increase in the amount of a state's territory or area of control. □ **expansionary** *adj.* **expansionism** *n.* **expansionist** *n.* **expansionistic** *adj.* (all in senses 2, 3).

expansive *adj.* **1** able or tending to expand. **2** extensive, wide-ranging. **3** (of a person, feelings, or speech) effusive, open. □ **expansively** *adv.* **expansiveness** *n.* **expansivity** *n.*

expat *n. & adj. colloq.* = EXPATRIATE.

expatiate /eks-**pay**-shi-ayt/ *v.intr.* (usu. foll. by *on, upon*) speak or write at length or in detail. [from Latin *expatiari* 'to digress'] □ **expatiation** *n.*

expatriate ● *adj.* **1** living abroad. **2** exiled. ● *n.* an expatriate person. ● *v.tr.* expel (a person) from his or her native country. [based on Latin *patria* 'native land'] □ **expatriation** *n.*

expect *v.tr.* **1** (often foll. by *to* + infin., or *that* + clause) **a** regard as likely. **b** (often foll. by *of*) look for as appropriate or one's due (from a person) (*I expect cooperation*). **2** (often foll. by *that* + clause) *colloq.* think, suppose. **3** be shortly to have (a baby). [from Latin *exspectare*] □ **expectable** *adj.*

expectancy *n.* (*pl.* **-ies**) **1** a state of expectation. **2** a prospect, esp. of future possession.

expectant *adj.* **1** (often foll. by *of*) expecting. **2** having the expectation of possession, status, etc. **3** (*attrib.*) expecting a baby (said of the mother or father). □ **expectantly** *adv.*

expectation *n.* **1** the act or an instance of expecting or looking forward. **2** something expected or hoped for. **3** (foll. by *of*) the probability of an event. **4** (in *pl.*) one's prospects of inheritance.

expectorant ● *adj.* causing expectoration. ● *n.* an expectorant medicine.

expectorate *v.tr.* (also *absol.*) cough or spit out (phlegm etc.) from the throat or lungs. [based on Latin *pector-* 'breast'] □ **expectoration** *n.*

expedient ● *adj.* advantageous; advisable on practical rather than moral grounds. ● *n.* a means of attaining an end. [from Latin *expedient-* 'forwarding matters'] □ **expedience** *n.* **expediency** *n.* **expediently** *adv.*

expedite *v.tr.* **1** assist the progress of; hasten (an action, process, etc.). **2** accomplish (business) quickly. [based on Latin *expeditus*, literally 'with feet freed'] □ **expediter** *n.*

expedition *n.* **1** a journey or voyage for a particular purpose, esp. exploration, scientific research, or war. **2** the personnel or ships etc. undertaking this. [from Latin *expeditio*]

expeditionary *adj.* of or used in an expedition, esp. military.

expeditious *adj.* acting or done with speed and efficiency. □ **expeditiously** *adv.*

expel *v.tr.* (**expelled**, **expelling**) (often foll. by *from*)

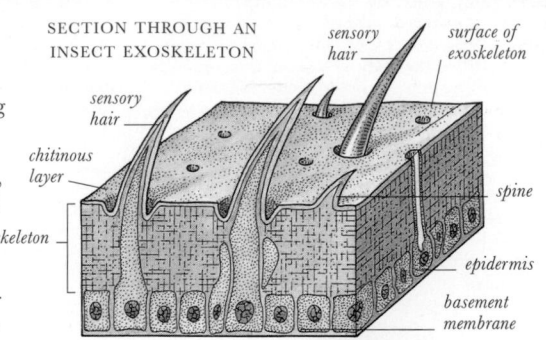

EXOSKELETON

Many animals do not have a bony internal skeleton, but instead have a hard outer casing called an exoskeleton. The exoskeleton has the same function as an internal skeleton, providing strength and support; it also protects the soft, inner organs. To permit growth, some animals periodically shed their exoskeleton and form a new, larger one.

SECTION THROUGH AN INSECT EXOSKELETON

sensory hair   *surface of exoskeleton*   *sensory hair*   *chitinous layer*   *exoskeleton*   *spine*   *epidermis*   *basement membrane*

EXAMPLES OF ANIMALS WITH EXOSKELETONS

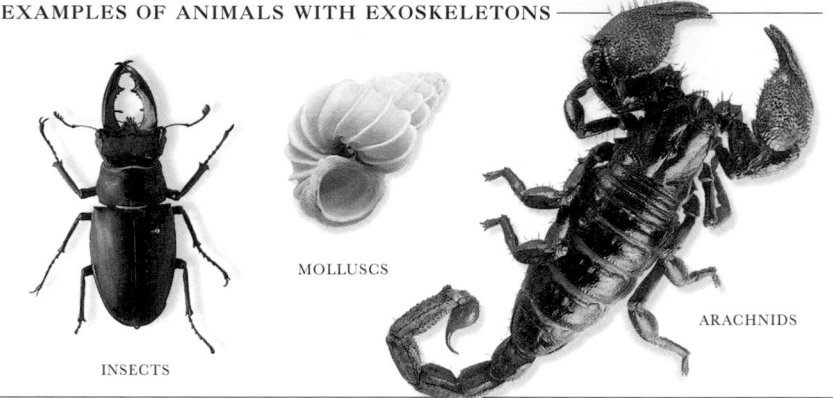

MOLLUSCS

INSECTS

ARACHNIDS

1 deprive (a person) of the membership of or involvement in (a school, society, etc.). **2** force out or eject (a thing from its container etc.). **3** order or force to leave a building etc. [from Latin *expellere*] □ **expellee** *n.* **expeller** *n.*

expend *v.tr.* spend or use up (money, time, etc.). [from Latin *expendere*]

expendable *adj.* **1** that may be sacrificed or dispensed with, esp. to achieve a purpose. **2** not regarded as worth preserving or saving. □ **expendability** *n.*

expenditure *n.* **1** the process or an instance of spending or using up. **2** a thing (esp. a sum of money) expended.

expense *n.* **1** cost incurred; payment of money. **2** (usu. in *pl.*) **a** the cost incurred in doing a particular job etc. **b** an amount paid to reimburse this. **3** a thing that is a cause of much expense. □ **at the expense of** so as to cause loss, deprivation, or harm to. [from Late Latin *expensa* '(money) spent']

expense account *n.* a list of an employee's expenses to be reimbursed by the employer.

expensive *adj.* **1** costing much. **2** making a high charge. □ **expensively** *adv.* **expensiveness** *n.*

experience ● *n.* **1** actual observation of or practical acquaintance with facts or events. **2** knowledge or skill resulting from this. **3 a** an event regarded as affecting one (*an unpleasant experience*). **b** the fact or process of being so affected (*learnt by experience*). ● *v.tr.* **1** have experience of; undergo. **2** feel (an emotion etc.). [based on Latin *experiri* 'to try'] □ **experienceable** *adj.*

experienced *adj.* **1** having had much experience. **2** skilled from experience (*an experienced driver*).

experiential *adj.* involving or based on experience. □ **experientially** *adv.*

experiment ● *n.* a procedure undertaken to make a discovery, test a hypothesis, or demonstrate a known fact. ● *v.intr.* (often foll. by *on, with*) make an experiment. [from Latin *experimentum*] □ **experimentation** *n.* **experimenter** *n.*

experimental *adj.* **1** based on or making use of experiment (*experimental psychology*). **2 a** used in

experiments. **b** serving or resulting from (esp. incomplete) experiment; tentative, provisional. □ **experimentalism** *n.* **experimentalist** *n.* **experimentally** *adv.*

expert ● *adj.* **1** (often foll. by *at, in*) having special skill at a task or knowledge in a subject. **2** (*attrib.*) involving or resulting from this (*expert evidence*; *an expert piece of work*). ● *n.* (often foll. by *at, in*) an expert person. [from Latin *expertus* 'tried'] □ **expertly** *adv.* **expertness** *n.*

expertise *n.* expert skill, knowledge, or judgement.

expiate *v.tr.* **1** pay the penalty for (wrongdoing). **2** make amends for. [based on Latin *expiatus* 'appeased'] □ **expiation** *n.* **expiatory** *adj.*

expire *v.* **1** *intr.* (of a period of time, validity, etc.) come to an end. **2** *intr.* (of a document, authorization, etc.) cease to be valid. **3** *intr.* (of a person) die. **4** *tr.* (usu. foll. by *from*; also *absol.*) exhale (air etc.) from the lungs. [from Latin *exspirare*] □ **expiration** *n.* **expiratory** *adj.* (in sense 4).

expiry *n.* the end of the validity or duration of something.

explain *v.tr.* **1 a** (also *absol.*) make clear or intelligible. **b** make known in detail. **2** (foll. by *that* + clause) say by way of explanation. **3** account for (one's conduct etc.). □ **explain away** minimize the significance of (a difficulty or mistake) by explanation. **explain oneself 1** make one's meaning clear. **2** give an account of one's motives or conduct. [from Latin *explanare* 'to smooth out'] □ **explainable** *adj.* **explainer** *n.*

explanation *n.* **1** the act or an instance of explaining. **2** a statement or circumstance that explains something. [related to EXPLAIN]

explanatory *adj.* serving or intended to serve to explain. □ **explanatorily** *adv.*

expletive *n.* a swear word or other expression, used in an exclamation. [from Late Latin *expletivus*]

explicable *adj.* that can be explained.

explicate *v.tr.* **1** develop the meaning of (an idea etc.). **2** explain (esp. a literary text). [based on Latin *explicatus* 'unfolded'] □ **explication** *n.* **explicative** *adj.* **explicator** *n.* **explicatory** *adj.*

explicit *adj.* **1 a** expressly stated, leaving nothing merely implied. **b** describing or representing nudity or intimate sexual activity. **2** (of knowledge, a notion, etc.) definite, clear. **3** (of a person, book, etc.) outspoken. [from Latin *explicitus*] □ **explicitly** *adv.* **explicitness** *n.*

explode *v.* **1 a** *intr.* (of gas, gunpowder, a bomb, a boiler, etc.) expand suddenly with a loud noise owing to a release of internal energy. **b** *tr.* cause (a bomb etc.) to explode. **2** *intr.* give vent suddenly to emotion, esp. anger. **3** *intr.* increase suddenly or rapidly. **4** *tr.* show (a theory etc.) to be baseless. **5** *tr.* (as **exploded** *adj.*) (of a drawing etc.) showing the components of a mechanism separated but in the normal relative positions. [earlier in sense 'to hiss off the stage': from Latin *explodere*] □ **exploder** *n.*

exploit ● *n.* /**eks**-ploit/ a daring feat. ● *v.tr.* /ik-**sploit**/ **1** make use of (a resource etc.); derive benefit from. **2** usu. *derog.* utilize or take advantage of (esp. a person) for one's own ends. [from Old French *esploit*] □ **exploitable** *adj.* **exploitation** *n.* **exploitative** *adj.* **exploiter** *n.* **exploitive** *adj.*

exploration *n.* **1** an act or instance of exploring. **2** the process of exploring. □ **explorational** *adj.*

exploratory *adj.* **1** (of discussion etc.) preliminary. **2** involving exploration or investigation (*exploratory surgery*).

explore *v.tr.* **1** travel through (a country etc.) in order to learn about it. **2** inquire into. [from Latin *explorare*] □ **explorative** *adj.* **explorer** *n.*

explosion *n.* **1** the act or an instance of exploding. **2** a sudden outburst of noise. **3** a sudden outbreak of feeling, esp. anger. **4** a rapid or sudden increase. [from Latin *explosio* 'scornful rejection' (see EXPLODE)]

explosive ● *adj.* **1** able or tending or likely to explode. **2** likely to cause a violent outburst etc.; (of a situation etc.) dangerously tense. ● *n.* an explosive substance. □ **explosively** *adv.* **explosiveness** *n.*

Expo *n.* (also **expo**) (*pl.* **-os**) a large international exhibition. [abbreviation of EXPOSITION 4]

exponent *n.* **1** a person who favours or promotes an idea etc. **2** a representative or practitioner of an activity, profession, etc. **3** a person who explains or interprets something. **4** *Math.* a raised symbol or expression beside a numeral indicating how many times it is to be multiplied by itself (e.g. $2^3 = 2 \times 2 \times 2$). [from Latin *exponent-* 'setting forth']

exponential *adj.* **1** *Math.* of or indicated by a mathematical exponent. **2** (of an increase etc.) more and more rapid. □ **exponentially** *adv.*

export ● *v.tr.* /ik-**sport**/ send out (goods or services) esp. for sale in another country. ● *n.* /**ek**-sport/ **1** the process of exporting. **2 a** an exported article or service. **b** (in *pl.*) the amount or value of goods exported (*exports exceeded £50m*). [from Latin *exportare*] □ **exportable** *adj.* **exportability** *n.* **exportation** *n.* **exporter** *n.*

expose *v.tr.* **1** leave uncovered or unprotected, esp. from the weather. **2** (foll. by *to*) **a** put at risk of (*exposed to danger*). **b** lay open, subject, or introduce to (an influence etc.). **3** *Photog.* subject (a film) to light, esp. in a camera. **4** reveal the identity or fact of (esp. a person or thing disapproved of or guilty of crime etc.). **5** exhibit, display. □ **expose oneself** display one's body, esp. the genitals, publicly and indecently. [from Old French *exposer*] □ **exposer** *n.*

exposé /ik-**spoh**-zay/ *n.* **1** an orderly statement of facts. **2** the act or an instance of revealing something discreditable. [French, literally 'exposed']

exposition *n.* **1** an explanatory statement or account. **2** an explanation or commentary. **3** *Mus.* the part of a movement in which the principal themes are first presented. **4** a large public exhibition. □ **expositional** *adj.*

expositor *n.* an expounder or interpreter. □ **expository** *adj.*

ex post facto *adj. & adv.* with retrospective action or force. [from Latin *ex postfacto* 'in the light of subsequent events']

expostulate *v.intr.* (often foll. by *with* a person) make a protest; remonstrate. [based on Latin *postulare* 'to demand'] □ **expostulation** *n.* **expostulatory** *adj.*

exposure *n.* (foll. by *to*) **1** the act or condition of exposing or being exposed. **2** a physical condition resulting from being exposed to the elements. **3** *Photog.* **a** the action of exposing a film etc. to the light. **b** the duration of this action. **c** the area of film etc. affected by it.

expound *v.tr.* **1** set out in detail (a doctrine etc.). **2** explain or interpret. [from Old French *espondre*] □ **expounder** *n.*

express[1] *v.tr.* **1** represent or make known (thought, feelings, etc.) in words or by gestures, conduct, etc. **2** *refl.* say what one thinks or means. **3** esp. *Math.* represent by symbols. **4** squeeze out (liquid or air). [from Old French *expresser*] □ **expresser** *n.* **expressible** *adj.*

express[2] ● *adj.* **1** operating at high speed. **2** definitely stated, not merely implied. **3 a** done, made, or sent for a special purpose. **b** (of messages or goods) delivered by a special fast service. ● *adv.* **1** at high speed. **2** by express train or delivery service. ● *n.* **1** an express train or delivery service. **2** *US* a company undertaking the transport of parcels etc. [from Latin *expressus* 'distinctly shown'] □ **expressly** *adv.* (in senses 2 and 3a of *adj.*).

expression *n.* **1** the act or an instance of expressing. **2** a word or phrase expressed. **3** *Math.* a collection of symbols expressing a quantity. **4** a person's facial appearance or intonation of voice, esp. as indicating feeling. **5** the depiction of feeling, movement, etc., in art. **6** the conveying of feeling in the performance of a piece of music. □ **expressional** *adj.* **expressionless** *adj.* **expressionlessly** *adv.* **expressionlessness** *n.*

expressionism *n.* ▼ a style of painting, music, drama, etc., in which an artist or writer seeks to express emotional experience rather than impressions of the external world. □ **expressionist** *n. & adj.* **expressionistic** *adj.* **expressionistically** *adv.*

expressive *adj.* **1** full of expression (*an expressive look*). **2** (foll. by *of*) serving to express (*words expressive of contempt*). □ **expressively** *adv.* **expressiveness** *n.* **expressivity** *n.*

expresso var. of ESPRESSO.

express train *n.* a fast train, stopping at few intermediate stations.

expressway *n. N. Amer. & Austral.* an urban motorway.

expropriate *v.tr.* **1** take away (property) from its owner. **2** (foll. by *from*) dispossess. [based on Latin *proprium* 'property'] □ **expropriation** *n.* **expropriator** *n.*

expulsion *n.* the act or an instance of expelling; the process of being expelled. [from Latin *expulsio*] □ **expulsive** *adj.*

expunge *v.tr.* (often foll. by *from*) erase, remove (esp. a passage from a book or a name from a list). [from Latin *expungere* 'to mark for deletion by means of points'] □ **expunger** *n.*

expurgate *v.tr.* remove matter thought to be objectionable from (a book etc.). [based on Latin *purgare* 'to cleanse'] □ **expurgation** *n.* **expurgator** *n.*

exquisite *adj.* **1** extremely beautiful or delicate. **2** acute; keenly felt (*exquisite pleasure*). **3** keen; highly sensitive or discriminating (*exquisite taste*). [earlier in sense 'carefully ascertained': from Latin *exquisitus* 'sought out'] □ **exquisitely** *adv.* **exquisiteness** *n.*

ex-service *adj. Brit.* **1** having formerly been a member of the armed forces. **2** relating to ex-service personnel.

ex-serviceman *n.* (*pl.* **-men**) esp. *Brit.* a former male member of the armed forces.

ex-servicewoman *n.* (*pl.* **-women**) esp. *Brit.* a former female member of the armed forces.

extant *adj.* (esp. of a document etc.) still existing, surviving. [from Latin *extant-* 'standing out']

extemporaneous *adj.* spoken or done without preparation. □ **extemporaneously** *adv.*

extemporary *adj.* — EXTEMPORANEOUS. □ **extemporarily** *adv.*

extempore /ik-**stem**-per-i/ *adj. & adv.* without preparation. [from Latin *ex tempore*, literally 'out of the time']

E

EXPRESSIONISM

Expressionism is an artistic concept that distorts the representation of reality to express an inner vision. This approach is the direct opposite of that adopted by the Impressionists, who placed a strong emphasis on imitating nature. Expressionism is particularly associated with an early 20th-century artistic movement in northern and central Europe. Germany became the centre of expressionism, and one of the leading expressionist groups, Der Blaue Reiter ('The Blue Rider'), whose leaders included Wassily Kandinsky and Paul Klee, was formed there. In literature, expressionism is seen as a revolt against realism and naturalism, and writers such as August Strindberg, Franz Kafka, and James Joyce were associated with the movement.

Self Portrait Screaming (1910), EGON SCHIELE

TIMELINE

1500   1550   1600   1650   1700   1750   1800   1850   1900   1950   2000

E

extemporize *v.tr.* (also **-ise**) (also *absol.*) compose or produce (music, a speech, etc.) without preparation; improvise. □ **extemporization** *n.*

extend *v.* **1** *tr. & intr.* lengthen or make larger in space or time. **2** *tr.* stretch or lay out at full length. **3** *intr. & tr.* (foll. by *to, over*) reach or be or make continuous over a certain area. **4** *intr.* (foll. by *to*) have a certain scope (*the permit does not extend to camping*). **5** *tr.* offer or accord (an invitation, hospitality, kindness, etc.). [from Latin *extendere*] □ **extendable** *adj.* **extendability** *n.* **extender** *n.* **extendible** *adj.* **extendibility** *n.* **extensible** *adj.* **extensibility** *n.*

extended family *n.* a family including relatives living near.

extended-play *attrib.adj.* (of a gramophone record) playing for longer than most singles, usu. at 45 r.p.m.

extension *n.* **1** the act or an instance of extending; the process of being extended. **2** prolongation; enlargement. **3** a part enlarging or added on to a main structure or building. **4** an additional part of anything. **5** a subsidiary telephone on the same line as the main one. **6** an additional period of time. □ **extensional** *adj.*

extensive *adj.* **1** covering a large area in space or time. **2** having a wide scope; far-reaching. □ **extensively** *adv.* **extensiveness** *n.*

extent *n.* **1** the space over which a thing extends. **2** the width or limits of application; scope. [from medieval Latin *extenta*]

extenuate *v.tr.* (often as **extenuating** *adj.*) lessen the seeming seriousness of (guilt or an offence) by reference to some mitigating factor. [based on Latin *extenuatus* 'made thin'] □ **extenuation** *n.* **extenuatory** *adj.*

exterior ● *adj.* **1 a** of or on the outer side. **b** (foll. by *to*) situated on the outside of (a building etc.). **c** coming from outside. **2** *Cinematog.* outdoor. ● *n.* **1** the outward aspect or surface of a building etc. **2** the apparent behaviour or demeanour of a person. **3** *Cinematog.* an outdoor scene. [Latin, literally 'outer'] □ **exteriority** *n.* **exteriorize** *v.tr.* (also **-ise**) **exteriorly** *adv.*

exterminate *v.tr.* destroy utterly (esp. something living). [based on Latin *exterminatus* 'driven beyond boundaries'] □ **extermination** *n.* **exterminator** *n.* **exterminatory** *adj.*

external ● *adj.* **1 a** of or situated on the outside or visible part. **b** coming or derived from the outside or an outside source. **2** relating to a country's foreign affairs. **3** (of medicine etc.) for use on the outside of the body. **4** for or concerning students taking the examinations of a university without attending it. ● *n.* (in *pl.*) **1** the outward features or aspect. **2** external circumstances. **3** inessentials. [based on Latin *exterus* 'outside'] □ **externality** *n.* (*pl.* **-ies**). **externally** *adv.*

externalize *v.tr.* (also **-ise**) give or attribute external existence to. □ **externalization** *n.*

extinct *adj.* **1** (of a family, class, or species) that has died out. **2** (of a volcano) that no longer erupts. [from Latin *exstinctus* 'extinguished']

extinction *n.* the act of making extinct; the state of being or process of becoming extinct. □ **extinctive** *adj.*

extinguish *v.tr.* **1** cause (a flame, light, etc.) to die out; put out. **2** put an end to; terminate; obscure utterly (a feeling, quality, etc.). [formed irregularly from Latin *extinguere*] □ **extinguishment** *n.*

extinguisher *n.* a person or thing that extinguishes, esp. = FIRE EXTINGUISHER.

extirpate *v.tr.* root out; destroy completely. [based on Latin *stirps* 'stem'] □ **extirpation** *n.* **extirpator** *n.*

extol *v.tr.* (**extolled, extolling**) praise enthusiastically. [from Latin *extollere*]

extort *v.tr.* obtain by force, threats, persistent demands, etc. [based on Latin *extortus* 'twisted out']

extortion *n.* **1** the act or an instance of extorting, esp. money. **2** illegal exaction. □ **extortioner** *n.* **extortionist** *n.*

extortionate *adj.* (of a price etc.) exorbitant. □ **extortionately** *adv.*

extra ● *adj.* additional; more than is usual or necessary or expected. ● *adv.* **1** more than usually. **2** additionally (*was charged extra*). ● *n.* **1** an extra thing. **2** a thing for which an extra charge is made. **3** a person engaged temporarily in a film or play, esp. as one of a crowd. **4** a special issue of a newspaper etc. **5** *Cricket* a run scored other than from a hit with the bat.

extra- *prefix* **1** outside, beyond (*extraterrestrial*). **2** beyond the scope of (*extra-curricular*).

extract ● *v.tr.* /ik-**strakt**/ **1** remove or take out, esp. by effort or force (anything firmly rooted). **2** obtain (money, an admission, etc.) with difficulty or against a person's will. **3** obtain (a natural resource) from the earth. **4** select or reproduce for quotation or performance (a passage of writing, music, etc.). **5** obtain (juice etc.) by suction, pressure, distillation, etc. **6** derive (pleasure etc.). **7** *Math.* find (the root of a number). ● *n.* /**ek**-strakt/ **1** a short passage taken from a book, piece of music, etc.; an excerpt. **2** a preparation containing the active principle of a substance in concentrated form (*malt extract*). [from Latin *extractus* 'drawn out'] □ **extractable** *adj.*

extraction *n.* **1** the act or an instance of extracting; the process of being extracted. **2** origin, lineage, descent (*of Indian extraction*).

extractive *adj.* of or involving extraction, esp. extensive extracting of natural resources without provision for their renewal.

extractor *n.* **1** a person or machine that extracts. **2** (*attrib.*) *Brit.* (of a device) that extracts stale air etc. (*extractor fan*).

extra-curricular *adj.* (of an activity at school, college, etc.) not included in the normal curriculum.

extraditable *adj.* **1** liable to extradition. **2** (of a crime) warranting extradition.

extradite *v.tr.* hand over (a person accused or convicted of a crime) to the foreign state etc. in which the crime was committed. □ **extradition** *n.*

extrados *n.* *Archit.* the upper or outer curve of an arch (opp. INTRADOS). ▷ WINDOW. [as EXTRA- + French *dos* 'back' from Latin *dorsum*]

extramarital *adj.* (esp. of sexual relations) occurring outside marriage. □ **extramaritally** *adv.*

extramural *adj.* **1** taught or conducted off the premises of a university, college, or school. **2** *Brit.* additional to normal teaching or studies, esp. for non-resident students. [based on Latin *extra muros* 'outside the walls'] □ **extramurally** *adv.*

extraneous /ik-**stray**-ni-ŭs/ *adj.* **1** of external origin. **2** (often foll. by *to*) **a** separate from the object to which it is attached etc. **b** external to; irrelevant or unrelated to. [from Latin *extraneus*] □ **extraneously** *adv.*

extraordinary *adj.* **1** unusual or remarkable; out of the usual course. **2** unusually great (*an extraordinary talent*). **3 a** (of an official etc.) additional; specially employed (*envoy extraordinary*). **b** (of a meeting) specially convened. [from Latin *extraordinarius*] □ **extraordinarily** *adv.* **extraordinariness** *n.*

extrapolate /ik-**strap**-ŏ-layt/ *v.tr.* (also *absol.*) **1** *Math.* extend (a range of values or a curve) or calculate (unknown values etc.) by extension of trends in a known range of values etc. **2** infer more widely from a limited range of known facts. □ **extrapolation** *n.* **extrapolative** *adj.*

extrasensory *adj.* derived by means other than the known senses, e.g. by telepathy, clairvoyance, etc. (*extrasensory perception*).

extraterrestrial ● *adj.* outside the Earth or its atmosphere. ● *n.* (in science fiction) a being from outer space.

extravagant *adj.* **1** spending (esp. money) excessively; immoderate or wasteful in use of resources. **2** exorbitant; costing much. **3** exceeding normal restraint or sense; unreasonable, absurd (*extravagant claims*). [from medieval Latin *extravagant-* 'wandering from the normal path'] □ **extravagance** *n.* **extravagantly** *adv.*

extravaganza *n.* **1** a fanciful literary, musical, or dramatic composition. **2** a spectacular theatrical or television production. [from Italian *estravaganza* 'extravagance']

extravert var. of EXTROVERT.

extreme ● *adj.* **1** reaching a high or the highest degree; exceedingly great or intense (*extreme old age*; *in extreme danger*). **2** severe, stringent; lacking restraint or moderation (*take extreme measures*; *an extreme reaction*). **3** outermost (*the extreme edge*). **4** *Polit.* on the far left or right of a party. **5** utmost; last. ● *n.* **1** (often in *pl.*) one or other of two things as remote or as different as possible. **2** a thing at either end of anything. **3** the highest or most extreme degree of anything. **4** *Math.* the first or the last term of a ratio or series. □ **go to extremes** take an extreme course of action. **go to the other extreme** take a diametrically opposite course of action. **in the extreme** to an extreme degree. [from Latin *extremus* 'most outward'] □ **extremely** *adv.* **extremeness** *n.*

extreme unction *n.* *RC Ch.* (former name for) the sacrament of Anointing of the Sick, esp. when administered to the dying.

extremist *n.* (also *attrib.*) a person who holds extreme or fanatical political or religious views. □ **extremism** *n.*

extremity *n.* (*pl.* **-ies**) **1** the extreme point; the very

---

EYE

The human eye is contained in a bony socket in the skull. Light rays that enter the pupil are focused by the cornea and lens to form an image on the retina. These images are converted into electrical impulses, which are transmitted along the optic nerve to the brain.

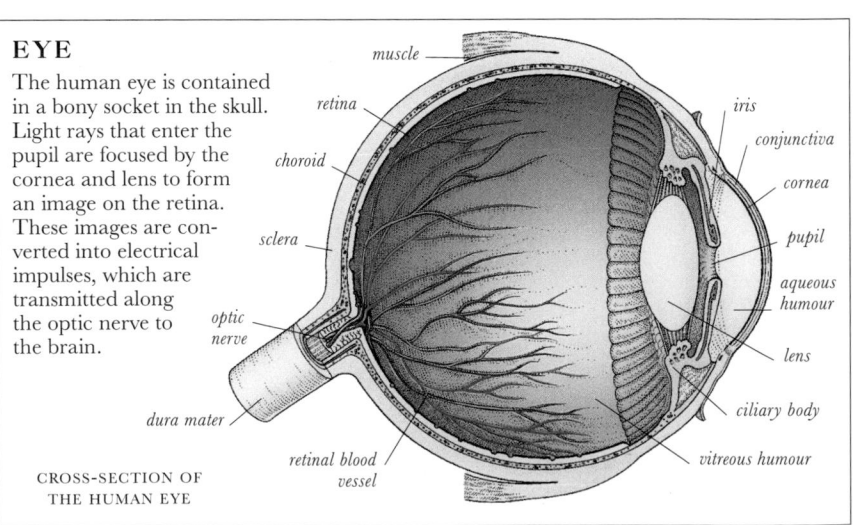

CROSS-SECTION OF THE HUMAN EYE

muscle · *retina* · *iris* · *choroid* · *conjunctiva* · *cornea* · *sclera* · *pupil* · *optic nerve* · *aqueous humour* · *lens* · *dura mater* · *retinal blood vessel* · *ciliary body* · *vitreous humour*

end. **2** (in *pl.*) the hands and feet. **3** a condition of extreme adversity.

extricate *v.tr.* (often foll. by *from*) free or disentangle from a constraint or difficulty. [based on Latin *extricatus* 'disentangled'] □ **extricable** *adj.* **extrication** *n.*

extrinsic *adj.* **1** not inherent or intrinsic. **2** (often foll. by *to*) extraneous; not belonging (to). [from Late Latin *extrinsicus* 'outward'] □ **extrinsically** *adv.*

extrovert (also **extravert**) ● *n.* **1** an outgoing or sociable person. **2** *Psychol.* a person predominantly concerned with external things or objective considerations. ● *adj.* typical or characteristic of an extrovert. [based on Latin *(extra) vertere* 'to turn (to the outside)'] □ **extroversion** *n.* **extroverted** *adj.*

■ **Usage** The original spelling, *extravert*, is often preferred in technical use.

extrude *v.tr.* **1** (foll. by *from*) thrust or force out. **2** shape metal, plastic, etc., by forcing it through a die. [from Latin *extrudere*] □ **extrusion** *n.* **extrusive** *adj.*

exuberant *adj.* **1** lively, high-spirited. **2** (of a plant etc.) prolific. **3** (of feelings etc.) abounding, lavish, effusive. [from Latin *exuberant-* 'being fruitful'] □ **exuberance** *n.* **exuberantly** *adv.*

exude *v.* **1** *tr.* & *intr.* (of a liquid, moisture, etc.) escape or cause to escape gradually. **2** *tr.* emit (a smell). **3** *tr.* display (an emotion etc.) freely or abundantly (*exuded displeasure*). [from Latin *exsudare*] □ **exudate** *n.* **exudation** *n.* **exudative** *adj.*

exult *v.intr.* (often foll. by *at, in, over,* or *to* + infin.) **1** be greatly joyful. **2** (often foll. by *over*) have a feeling of triumph (over a person). [from Latin *exsultare* 'to leap for joy'] □ **exultancy** *n.* **exultant** *adj.* **exultantly** *adv.* **exultation** *n.* **exultingly** *adv.*

eye ● *n.* **1 a** ◄ the organ of sight in humans and other animals. ▷ HEAD, SIGHT. **b** the light-detecting organ in some invertebrates. **2** the region round the eye (*eyes swollen from weeping*). **3** (in *sing.* or *pl.*) sight. **4** a particular visual faculty or talent; visual appreciation (*cast an expert eye over*). **5** (in *sing.* or *pl.*) a look, gaze, or glance (*a friendly eye*). **6** a thing like an eye, esp.: **a** a spot on a peacock's tail. **b** the leaf bud of a potato. **7** the centre of something circular, e.g. a flower or target. **8** the centre of a storm or hurricane. ▷ HURRICANE. **9** an aperture in a needle for the thread. **10** a ring or loop for a bolt or hook etc. to pass through. ● *v.tr.* (**eyes, eyed, eyeing** or **eying**) (often foll. by *up*) watch or observe closely.

□ **all eyes** watching intently. **an eye for an eye** retaliation in kind (Exod. 21:24). **get** (or **keep**) **one's eye in** *Brit. Sport* accustom oneself (or keep oneself accustomed) to the conditions of play so as to judge speed, distance, etc. **have an eye for** be capable of perceiving or appreciating. **have one's eye on** wish or plan to procure. **have eyes for** be interested in; wish to acquire. **have an eye to** have as one's objective; prudently consider. **keep an eye on 1** pay attention to. **2** look after; take care of. **keep an eye open** (or **out**) (often foll. by *for*) watch out carefully. **keep one's eyes open** (or **peeled** or *Brit.* **skinned**) watch out; be on the alert. **make eyes** (or **sheep's eyes**) (foll. by *at*) look amorously or flirtatiously at. **my** (or **all my**) **eye** *slang* nonsense. **one in the eye** (foll. by *for*) a disappointment or setback. **see eye to eye** (often foll. by *with*) be in full agreement. **set eyes on** catch sight of. **take one's eyes off** (usu. in *neg.*) stop watching; stop paying attention to. **under the eye of** under the supervision or observation of. **up to the** (or **one's**) **eyes in 1** deeply engaged or involved in; inundated with. **2** to the utmost limit (*mortgaged up to the eyes*). **with one's eyes open** deliberately; with full awareness. **with one's eyes shut** (or **closed**) **1** easily; with little effort. **2** without awareness; unobservantly. **with an eye to** with a view to; prudently considering. **with one eye on** directing one's attention partly to. [Old English] □ **eyed** *adj.* (also in *comb.*). **eyeless** *adj.*

eyeball ● *n.* the ball of the eye within the lids and socket. ● *v. N. Amer. slang* **1** *tr.* look or stare at. **2** *intr.* look or stare. □ **eyeball to eyeball** confronting closely.

eyebath *n.* a small glass or vessel for applying lotion etc. to the eye.

eye bolt *n.* a bolt or bar with an eye at the end for a hook etc.

eyebright *n.* ◄ any plant of the genus *Euphrasia,* traditionally used as a remedy for weak eyes.

eyebrow *n.* the line of hair growing on the ridge above the eye socket. □ **raise one's eyebrows** (or **an eyebrow**) show surprise, disbelief, or disapproval.

eye-catching *adj.* striking, attractive.

EYEBRIGHT
(*Euphrasia* species)

eye contact *n.* looking directly into another person's eyes.

eyeful *n.* (*pl.* **-fuls**) *colloq.* **1** a long steady look. **2** a visually striking person or thing. **3** anything thrown or blown into the eye.

eyeglass *n.* **1 a** a lens for correcting or assisting defective sight. **b** (in *pl.*) a pair of these held in the hand or kept in position on the nose by means of a frame or a spring. **2** (in *pl.*) esp. *N. Amer.* = SPECTACLES.

eyehole *n.* a hole to look through.

eyelash *n.* each of the hairs growing on the edges of the eyelids. □ **by an eyelash** by a very small margin.

eyelet *n.* **1** a small hole in paper, leather, cloth, etc., for string or rope etc. to pass through. **2** a metal ring reinforcement for this. [from Old French *oillet* 'little eye']

eyelid *n.* the upper or lower fold of skin closing to cover the eye.

eyeliner *n.* a cosmetic applied as a line round the eye. ▷ MAKE-UP

eye-opener *n. colloq.* an enlightening experience; an unexpected revelation. □ **eye-opening** *adj.*

eyepatch *n.* a patch worn to protect an injured eye.

eyepiece *n.* the lens or lenses to which the eye is applied at the end of a microscope, telescope, etc. ▷ CAMCORDER, TELESCOPE

eye-rhyme *n.* a correspondence of words in spelling but not in pronunciation.

eye-shade *n.* a device to protect the eyes, esp. from strong light.

eyeshadow *n.* a coloured cosmetic applied to the skin round the eyes. ▷ MAKE-UP

eyesight *n.* the faculty or power of seeing.

eyesore *n.* a visually offensive or ugly thing, esp. a building.

eye strain *n.* fatigue of the (internal or external) muscles of the eye.

eye-tooth *n.* a canine tooth just under or next to the eye, esp. one in the upper jaw.

eyewash *n. slang* nonsense, bunkum; pretentious or insincere talk.

eyewitness *n.* a person who has seen a thing happen and can give evidence of it.

eyrie /eer-i/ *n.* (also **aerie**) **1** a nest of a bird of prey, esp. an eagle, built high up. **2** a house etc. perched high up. [from medieval Latin *aeria*]

E

F

F¹ *n.* (also **f**) (*pl.* **Fs** or **F's**) **1** the sixth letter of the alphabet. **2** *Mus.* the fourth note of the diatonic scale of C major. ▷ NOTATION

F² *abbr.* (also **F.**) **1** Fahrenheit. **2** female. **3** *Brit.* fine (pencil lead). **4** *Biol.* filial generation.

F³ *symb.* **1** *Chem.* the element fluorine. **2** farad(s). **3** force.

f¹ *abbr.* (also **f.**) **1** female. **2** feminine. **3** following page etc. **4** (*f*) *Mus.* forte. **5** folio.

f² *symb.* **1** focal length (cf. F-NUMBER). **2** femto-. **3** frequency.

FA *abbr.* **1** (in the UK) Football Association. **2** = FANNY ADAMS.

fa var. of FAH.

fab *adj. colloq.* fabulous, marvellous.

fable ● *n.* **1 a** a story, esp. a supernatural one, not based on fact. **b** a tale, esp. with animals as characters, conveying a moral. **2** (*collect.*) myths and legendary tales (*in fable*). **3 a** a false statement; a lie. **b** a thing only supposed to exist. ● *v.tr.* (as **fabled** *adj.*) celebrated in fable; famous, legendary. [from Latin *fabula* 'discourse']

fabric *n.* **1 a** a woven material; a textile. **b** other material resembling woven cloth. **2** a structure or framework, esp. the walls, floor, and roof of a building. **3** (in abstract senses) the essential structure of a thing (*the fabric of society*). [from Latin *fabrica* 'craft']

fabricate *v.tr.* **1** construct esp. from prepared components. **2** invent or concoct (a story etc.). **3** forge (a document). [based on Latin *fabricatus* 'fashioned'] □ **fabrication** *n.* **fabricator** *n.*

fabulist *n.* **1** a composer of fables. **2** a liar.

fabulous *adj.* **1** incredible, exaggerated, (*fabulous wealth*). **2** *colloq.* marvellous (*looking fabulous*). **3 a** celebrated in fable. **b** legendary, mythical. [from Latin *fabulosus*] □ **fabulously** *adv.* **fabulousness** *n.*

façade /fă-**sahd**/ *n.* (also **facade**) **1** ▲ the face of a building, esp. its principal front. **2** an outward esp. deceptive appearance. [French]

face ● *n.* **1** ▼ the front of the head from the forehead to the chin. **2** facial expression (*had a happy face*). **3** coolness, effrontery. **4** the surface of a thing esp.: **a** the visible part of a celestial body. **b** a side of a mountain etc. (*the north face*). **c** the (usu. vertical)

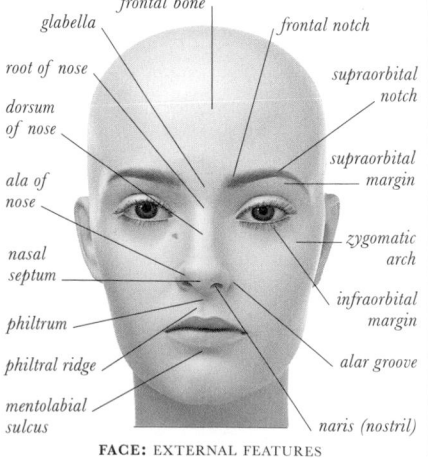

FRONTAL BONE
glabella
root of nose
dorsum of nose
ala of nose
nasal septum
philtrum
philtral ridge
mentolabial sulcus
frontal notch
supraorbital notch
supraorbital margin
zygomatic arch
infraorbital margin
alar groove
naris (nostril)

FACE: EXTERNAL FEATURES

FAÇADE

A building's façade offers a unified face to the world, while providing an opportunity for architectural expression. Types of façade vary greatly among building styles, from the formal ordering of classical architecture to the intricate detailing of Gothic buildings or the theatricality of the baroque. The dramatic interest of the façade shown here is achieved by the use of classical motifs, such as the dome, pediment, and columns, which are drawn together symmetrically around the grand entrance.

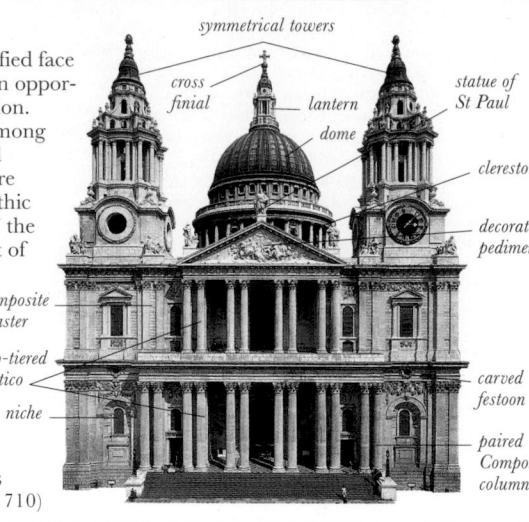

symmetrical towers
cross finial
lantern
dome
statue of St Paul
clerestory
decorated pediment
Composite pilaster
two-tiered portico
niche
carved festoon
paired Composite columns

WEST FAÇADE OF ST PAUL'S CATHEDRAL, ENGLAND (1675–1710)

surface of a coal-seam. **d** *Geom.* each surface of a solid. **e** the façade of a building. **f** the dial of a clock etc. **5 a** the functional side of a tool etc. **b** the distinctive side of a playing card. **c** the obverse of a coin. **6** = TYPEFACE. **7** the outward appearance or aspect (*the unacceptable face of capitalism*). ● *v.* **1** *tr. & intr.* look or be positioned towards or in a certain direction (*facing the window; the room faces north*). **2** *tr.* be opposite (*facing page 20*). **3** *tr.* **a** (often foll. by *down, out*) meet resolutely or defiantly (*face one's critics*). **b** not shrink from (*face the facts*). **4** *tr.* present itself to (*the problem that faces us*). **5** *tr.* **a** cover the surface of (a thing) with a coating etc. **b** put a facing on (a garment). **6** *intr. & tr.* turn or cause to turn in a certain direction. □ **face down** (or **downwards**) with the face or surface turned towards the ground, floor, etc. (see also sense 3a of *v.*). **face off** take up an attitude of confrontation, esp. at the start of a fight etc. **face the music** stand up to unpleasant consequences, esp. criticism. **face to face** (often foll. by *with*) confronting each other. **face up** (or **upwards**) with the face or surface turned upwards to view. **face up to** accept bravely; confront. **have the face** be shameless enough. **in face** (or **the face**) of **1** despite. **2** confronted by. **in your face** see IN-YOUR-FACE. **on the face of it** as it would appear. **put a bold** (or **brave**) **face on it** accept difficulty etc. cheerfully or with courage. **put one's face on** *colloq.* apply make-up to one's face. **put a new face on** alter the aspect of. **save face** preserve esteem. **set one's face against** oppose with determination. **show one's face** see SHOW. **to a person's face** openly in a person's presence. [from Latin *facies*] □ **faced** *adj.* (also in *comb.*). **facing** *adj.* (also in *comb.*).

face card *n.* = COURT CARD.

facecloth *n.* **1** a cloth for washing one's face. **2** a smooth-surfaced woollen cloth.

face flannel *n. Brit.* = FACECLOTH 1.

faceless *adj.* **1** without identity. **2** lacking character. **3** without a face. □ **facelessness** *n.*

facelift *n.* **1** cosmetic surgery to remove wrinkles etc. **2** a procedure to improve the appearance of a thing.

face-off *n.* a direct confrontation.

face pack *n. Brit.* a preparation applied to the face and beneficial to the complexion.

face paint *n.* paint for applying to the face. □ **face-painter** *n.* **face-painting** *n.*

facer *n. colloq.* **1** *Brit.* a sudden difficulty. **2** a blow in the face.

face-saving *n.* (usu. *attrib.*) the preserving of one's reputation, credibility, etc. □ **face-saver** *n.*

facet *n.* **1** a particular aspect of a thing. **2** ◀ one side of a many-sided body, esp. a cut gem. **3** one segment of a compound eye. ▷ COMPOUND EYE. [from French *facette* 'little face'] □ **faceted** *adj.* (also in *comb.*).

facet

FACET: MANY-FACETED CUT DIAMOND

facetious *adj.* intending or intended to be amusing, esp. inopportunely. [based on Latin *facetia* 'jest'] □ **facetiously** *adv.* **facetiousness** *n.*

face-to-face *attrib.adj.* with the people involved facing each other or in each other's presence (*face-to-face discussions*).

face value *n.* **1** the nominal value as printed or stamped on money. **2** the superficial appearance or implication of a thing.

facia /**fay**-shă/ *n.* (also **fascia**) **1** *Brit.* **a** the instrument panel of a motor vehicle. **b** any similar panel for operating machinery. **2** the upper part of a shopfront with the proprietor's name etc.

facial ● *adj.* of or for the face. ● *n.* a beauty treatment for the face. □ **facially** *adv.*

facile /**fa**-syl/ *adj.* usu. *derog.* **1** easily achieved but of little value. **2** (of speech etc.) fluent, glib. [from Latin *facilis* 'easy'] □ **facilely** *adv.* **facileness** *n.*

facilitate *v.tr.* make easy, less difficult or more easily achieved. [based on Latin *facilis* 'easy'] □ **facilitation** *n.* **facilitative** *adj.* **facilitator** *n.*

facility *n.* (*pl.* **-ies**) **1** ease; absence of difficulty. **2** dexterity, aptitude (*facility of expression*). **3** (esp. in *pl.*) an opportunity, the equipment, or the resources for doing something. **4** *US* a plant, installation, or establishment. [from Latin *facilitas* 'easiness']

facing *n.* **1 a** a layer of material covering part of a garment etc. for contrast or strength. **b** (in *pl.*) ▼ the cuffs, collar, etc., of a military jacket. **2** an outer layer covering the surface of a wall etc.

collar facing
breast facing
cuff facing

FACINGS ON A MILITARY JACKET

facsimile /fak-**sim**-ili/ *n.* **1** an exact copy, esp. of writing, a picture, etc. (often *attrib.: facsimile edition*). **2 a** production of an exact copy of a document etc. by electronic scanning and transmission (see also FAX). **b** a copy produced in this way. □ **in facsimile** as an exact copy. [modern Latin, from *fac* 'make' + *simile* (neut.) 'same']

fact *n.* **1** a thing that is known to have occurred, to exist, or to be true. **2** a datum of experience (often foll. by an explanatory clause or phrase: *the fact that fire burns*). **3** (usu. in *pl.*) a piece of evidence. **4** truth, reality. **5** a thing assumed as the basis for argument or inference. □ **before** (or **after**) **the fact** before (or after) the committing of a crime. **a fact of life** something that must be accepted. **facts and figures** precise details. **in** (or **in point of**) **fact 1** as a matter of fact. **2** (in summarizing) in short. [from Latin *factum* 'thing done']

factice *n. Chem.* a rubber-like substance obtained by vulcanizing unsaturated vegetable oils. [German *Faktis* from Latin *facticius* 'artificial']

faction[1] *n.* **1** a small organized dissentient group within a larger one, esp. in politics. **2** a state of dissension within an organization. [French from Latin *factio*] □ **factional** *adj.* **factionalize** *v.tr.* & *intr.* (also **-ise**).

faction[2] *n.* a book, film, etc., using real events as a basis for a fictional narrative or dramatization. [blend of FACT and FICTION]

factious *adj.* of, characterized by, or inclined to faction. □ **factiously** *adv.* **factiousness** *n.*

■ **Usage** The similarity in sense between *faction* (see FACTION[1] 1) and *fraction* (see FRACTION 4) may lead to confusion between the adjectives *factious* and *fractious*. *Fractious*, however, is now only used to mean 'unruly' or 'peevish'.

factitious *adj.* **1** specially contrived (*factitious value*). **2** not natural (*factitious joy*). [from Latin *facticius*, based on *facere* 'to make'] □ **factitiously** *adv.* **factitiousness** *n.*

factoid *n.* **1** an assumption or speculation that is reported and repeated so often that it becomes accepted as fact. **2** *US* a brief or trivial item of news or information.

factor *n.* **1** a circumstance, fact, or influence contributing to a result. **2** *Math.* a whole number etc. that when multiplied with another produces a given number. **3** *Biol.* a gene etc. determining hereditary character. **4** (foll. by identifying number) *Med.* any of a group of substances in the blood contributing to coagulation. **5 a** a merchant buying and selling on commission. **b** *Sc.* a land agent or steward. **c** an agent or deputy. [from Latin *factor* 'maker, doer'] □ **factorize** *v.tr.* & *intr.* (also **-ise**) *Math.*

factor VIII *n.* (also **factor eight**) *Med.* a blood protein involved in clotting, whose deficiency causes haemophilia.

factorial *Math.* ● *n.* the product of a number and all the whole numbers below it. ● *adj.* of a factor or factorial. □ **factorially** *adv.*

factory *n.* (*pl.* **-ies**) a building or buildings where manufacturing processes are carried out. [based on Latin *factor* 'maker']

factory farming *n.* a system of rearing livestock using intensive methods. □ **factory farm** *n.*

factory floor *n.* workers in industry as distinct from management.

factory ship *n.* ▼ a fishing ship with processing facilities.

factory shop *n.* (also **factory outlet**) a shop in which goods are sold directly by the manufacturers at a discount.

factotum *n.* (*pl.* **factotums**) an employee who does all kinds of work. [medieval Latin, from *fac* 'do' + *totum* (neut.) 'whole']

fact sheet *n.* a paper setting out relevant information.

facts of life *n.pl.* (prec. by *the*) information about sexual functions and practices.

factual *adj.* **1** based on or concerned with fact. **2** actual, true. □ **factuality** *n.* **factually** *adv.* **factualness** *n.*

faculty *n.* (*pl.* **-ies**) **1** an aptitude or ability for a particular activity. **2** an inherent mental or physical power. **3 a** *Brit.* a group of related university departments (*faculty of modern languages*). **b** *N. Amer.* the teaching staff of a university or college. [from Latin *facultas* 'ability']

fad *n.* **1** a craze. **2** a peculiar notion or idiosyncrasy. [19th-century coinage] □ **faddish** *adj.* **faddishly** *adv.* **faddishness** *n.* **faddism** *n.* **faddist** *n.*

faddy *adj.* (**faddier, faddiest**) *Brit.* having arbitrary likes and dislikes, esp. about food. □ **faddily** *adv.* **faddiness** *n.*

fade ● *v.* **1** *intr.* & *tr.* lose or cause to lose colour. **2** *intr.* lose freshness or strength. **3** *intr.* **a** (of light etc.) grow pale or dim. **b** (of sound) grow faint. **4** *intr.* (of a feeling etc.) diminish. **5** *tr.* (foll. by *in, out*) *Cinematog.* & *Broadcasting* cause (a picture or sound) to appear or disappear, increase or decrease, gradually. ● *n.* the action or an instance of fading. □ **do a fade** *slang* depart. **fade away** languish, grow thin. [from Old French *fade* 'dull, insipid'] □ **fadeless** *adj.* **fader** *n.* (in sense 6 of *v.*).

fado *n.* (*pl.* **-os**) a type of (esp. plaintive) popular Portuguese song. [Portuguese, literally 'fate']

faeces /fee-seez/ *n.pl.* (*US* **feces**) waste matter discharged from the bowels. [Latin] □ **faecal** *adj.*

faff *Brit. colloq.* ● *v.intr.* (often foll. by *about, around*) fuss, dither. ● *n.* a fuss.

fag[1] *n.* **1** esp. *Brit. colloq.* a piece of drudgery. **2** esp. *Brit. colloq.* a cigarette. **3** *Brit.* (at public schools) a junior pupil who runs errands for a senior. ● *v.* (**fagged, fagging**) **1** *colloq.* **a** *tr.* (often foll. by *out*) tire out; exhaust. **b** *intr. Brit.* toil. **2** *intr. Brit.* (at public schools) act as a fag. [16th-century coinage]

fag[2] *n. N. Amer. slang offens.* a male homosexual. [abbreviation of FAGGOT]

fag end *n. colloq. Brit.* a cigarette end.

faggot *n.* **1** (usu. in *pl.*) *Brit.* a ball or roll of seasoned chopped liver etc., baked or fried. **2** (*US* **fagot**) a bundle of sticks or twigs bound together as fuel. **3** *slang* **a** *Brit. derog.* an unpleasant woman. **b** *N. Amer. offens.* a male homosexual. [from Old French *fagot*] □ **faggoty** *adj.*

fah *n.* (also **fa**) *Mus.* **1** (in tonic sol-fa) the fourth note of a major scale. **2** the note F in the fixed-doh system. [Middle English]

Fahrenheit /fa-ren-hyt/ *adj.* of a scale of temperature on which water freezes at 32° and boils at 212° under standard conditions. [named after G. *Fahrenheit*, German physicist, 1686–1736]

F

FACTORY SHIP

Factory ships are equipped not just for catching fish but also for the immediate processing and freezing of the catch. The fish are gutted and cleaned in the factory area, and then stored in ice. The freshness of the fish is secured by this immediate freezing, and so the vessel can stay out at sea for many weeks, trawling for more catches.

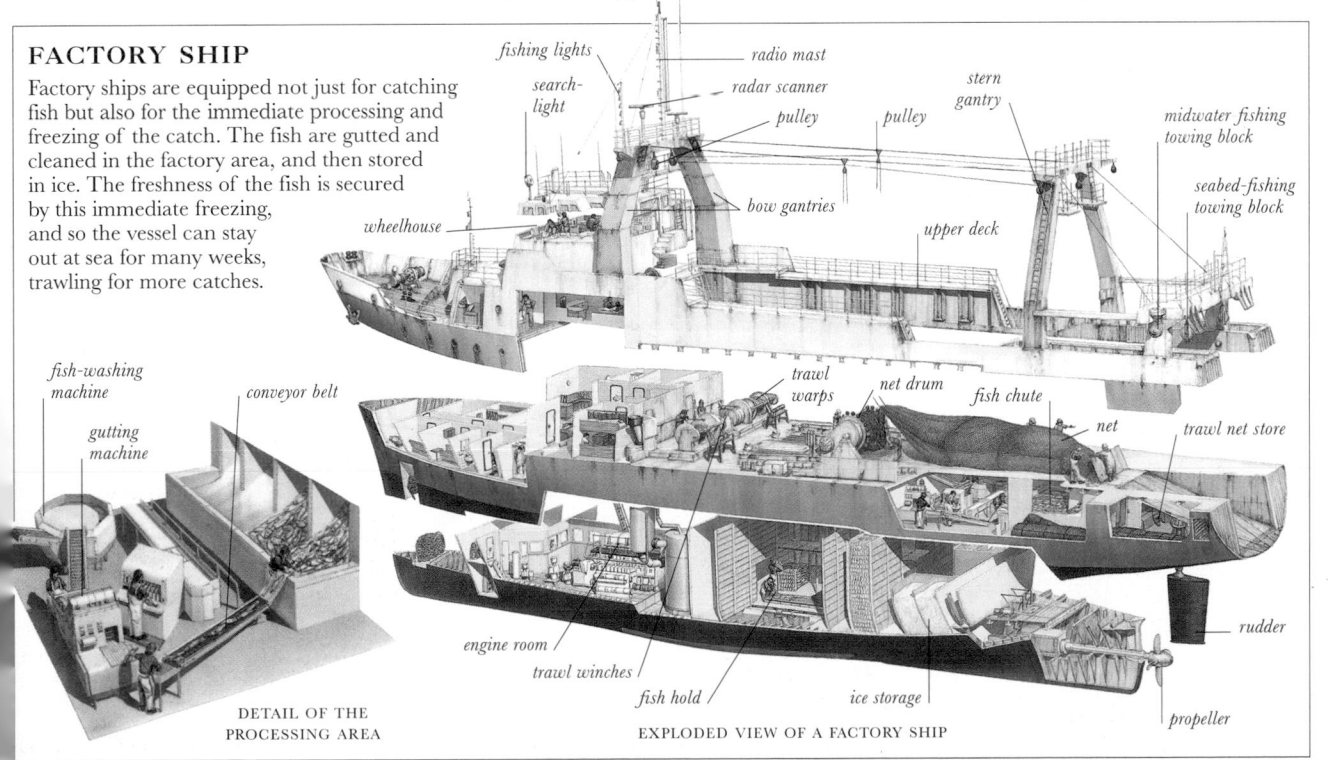

fishing lights · radio mast · search-light · radar scanner · stern gantry · pulley · pulley · midwater fishing towing block · bow gantries · seabed-fishing towing block · wheelhouse · upper deck · fish-washing machine · conveyor belt · trawl warps · net drum · fish chute · net · trawl net store · gutting machine · rudder · engine room · trawl winches · fish hold · ice storage · propeller

DETAIL OF THE PROCESSING AREA

EXPLODED VIEW OF A FACTORY SHIP

F

faience /**fy**-ahnss/ *n.* decorated and glazed earthenware and porcelain. [from *Faenza*, a city in Italy where pottery was made]

fail ● *v.* **1** *intr.* not succeed. **2 a** *tr. & intr.* be or judge to be unsuccessful in (an examination etc.). **b** *tr.* (of a commodity etc.) not pass (a test of quality). **3** *intr.* be unable to; neglect to (*failed to appear*). **4** *tr.* disappoint; let down. **5** *intr.* (of supplies, crops, etc.) be or become insufficient. **6** *intr.* become weaker; cease functioning (*the engine has failed*). **7** *intr.* **a** (of an enterprise) collapse. **b** become bankrupt. ● *n.* a failure in a test. □ **without fail** for certain, whatever happens. [based on Latin *fallere* 'to deceive']

failed *adj.* **1** not good enough (*a failed actor*). **2** deficient; broken-down (*a failed crop; a failed battery*).

failing ● *n.* a fault or shortcoming; a weakness, esp. in character. ● *prep.* in default of; if not.

fail-safe *adj.* reverting to a safe condition in the event of a breakdown etc.

failure *n.* **1** lack of success. **2** an unsuccessful person, thing, or attempt. **3** non-performance, non-occurrence. **4** breaking down or ceasing to function (*heart failure*). **5** bankruptcy. [from Anglo-French *failer*]

fain *archaic* ● *predic.adj.* (foll. by *to* + infin.) **1** willing under the circumstances to. **2** left with no alternative but to. ● *adv.* gladly (esp. *would fain*). [Old English]

faint ● *adj.* **1** indistinct, pale, dim; not clearly perceived. **2** (of a person) weak or giddy. **3** slight, remote (*a faint chance*). **4** half-hearted (*faint praise*). **5** = FEINT². ● *v.intr.* **1** lose consciousness from a drop in blood pressure. **2** become faint. ● *n.* a sudden loss of consciousness. [from Old French *faint, feint* 'feigned, sluggish'] □ **faintness** *n.*

faint-hearted *adj.* cowardly, timid. □ **faint-heartedness** *n.*

faintly *adv.* **1** very slightly (*faintly amused*). **2** indistinctly, feebly.

fair¹ ● *adj.* **1** just, equitable; in accordance with the rules. **2** blond; light or pale in colour or complexion. **3 a** of (only) moderate quality or amount; average. **b** considerable, satisfactory (*a fair chance of success*). **4** (of weather) fine and dry; (of the wind) favourable. **5** clean, clear, unblemished (*fair copy*). **6** beautiful, attractive. **7** *Austral. & NZ* complete, unquestionable. ● *adv.* **1** in a fair manner (*play fair*). **2** *Brit.* exactly, completely (*was hit fair on the jaw*). □ **fair and square** *adv. & adj.* **1** exactly. **2** straightforward, honest, above board. **a fair deal** equitable treatment. **fair dinkum** see DINKUM. **fair dos** *Brit. colloq.* fair shares. **fair enough** *colloq.* that is reasonable. **fair's fair** *colloq.* all involved should act fairly. **for fair** *US slang* completely. **in a fair way to** likely to. [Old English] □ **fairish** *adj.* **fairness** *n.*

fair² *n.* (also *pseudo-archaic* **fayre**) **1** a gathering of stalls, amusements, etc., for public entertainment. **2** a periodic market, often with entertainments. **3** an exhibition to promote particular products. [from Latin *feriae* 'holiday']

fair game *n.* a legitimate target or object.

fairground *n.* an outdoor area where a fair is held.

Fair Isle *n.* (also *attrib.*) ▼ a piece of knitwear knitted in a characteristic particoloured design. [from *Fair Isle* in the Shetlands, where the design was first devised]

FAIR ISLE KNITWEAR

fairly *adv.* **1** in a fair manner; justly. **2** moderately, acceptably (*fairly good*). **3** to a noticeable degree (*fairly narrow*). **4** utterly (*fairly beside himself*). **5** actually (*fairly jumped for joy*). □ **fairly and squarely** = *fair and square* (see FAIR¹).

fair-minded *adj.* just, impartial. □ **fair-mindedly** *adv.* **fair-mindedness** *n.*

fair play *n.* reasonable treatment or behaviour.

fair sex *n.* (prec. by *the*) women.

fairway *n.* **1** a navigable channel. **2** ▼ the part of a golf course between a tee and its green, kept free of rough grass. ▷ GOLF

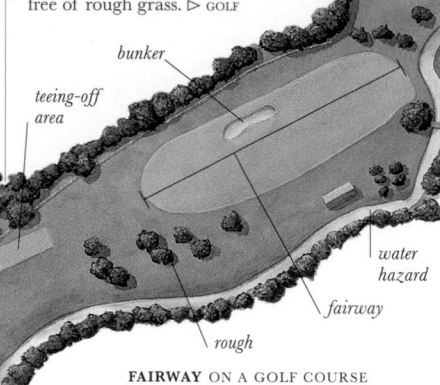

FAIRWAY ON A GOLF COURSE

fair-weather friend *n.* a friend or ally who is unreliable in times of difficulty.

fairy *n.* (*pl.* **-ies**) **1** a small, winged, imaginary being of human form, believed magical. **2** *slang offens.* a male homosexual. [from Old French *faerie*] □ **fairy-like** *adj.*

fairy cake *n. Brit.* a small individual usu. iced sponge cake.

fairy godmother *n.* a benefactress.

fairyland *n.* **1** the imaginary home of fairies. **2** an enchanted region.

fairy lights *n.pl.* esp. *Brit.* small decorative coloured lights.

fairy ring *n.* a ring of darker grass caused by fungi.

fairy story *n.* (also **fairy tale**) **1** a children's tale about fairies. **2** an incredible story; a fabrication.

fait accompli /fayt ă-**kom**-pli/ *n.* (*pl.* **faits accomplis** *pronunc.* same) a thing that has been done and is past altering. [French, literally 'accomplished fact']

faith *n.* **1** complete trust or confidence. **2** firm belief, esp. without logical proof. **3** religious belief. **4** duty or commitment to fulfil a trust, promise, etc. (*keep faith*). [based on Latin *fides*]

faithful *adj.* **1** showing faith. **2** (often foll. by *to*) loyal, trustworthy. **3** accurate; true to fact (*a faithful account*). **4 a** (**the Faithful**) the believers in a religion. **b** (**the faithful**) the loyal adherents of a political party. □ **faithfulness** *n.*

faithfully *adv.* in a faithful manner. □ **yours faithfully** esp. *Brit.* a formula for ending a business or formal letter.

faith healing *n.* healing achieved by faith and prayer as opposed to conventional medicine. □ **faith healer** *n.*

faithless *adj.* **1** false, unreliable, disloyal. **2** without religious faith. □ **faithlessly** *adv.* **faithlessness** *n.*

fake ● *n.* **1** a thing or person that is not genuine. **2** a trick. ● *adj.* counterfeit; not genuine. ● *v.tr.* **1** make (a false thing) appear genuine; forge, counterfeit. **2** make a pretence of having (a feeling, illness, etc.). □ **faker** *n.* **fakery** *n.*

fakir /**fay**-keer/ *n.* (also **faquir**) a Muslim or (rarely) Hindu religious mendicant or ascetic. [from Arabic *fakīr* 'needy man']

falafel var. of FELAFEL.

falciform *adj. Anat.* curved like a sickle.

falcon *n.* ▶ any diurnal bird of prey of the family Falconidae, having long pointed wings, and sometimes trained to hunt small game for sport. ▷ RAPTOR. [from Late Latin *falco -onis*]

falconry *n.* the breeding and training of hawks; the sport of hawking. □ **falconer** *n.*

falderal *n.* (also **folderol**) **1** a gewgaw or trifle. **2** a nonsensical refrain in a song. **3** esp. *N. Amer.* nonsense; trivial display. [perhaps from *falbala* 'trimming on a dress']

fall ● *v.intr.* (*past* **fell**; *past part.* **fallen**) **1 a** descend rapidly from a higher to a lower level (*fell from the top floor*). **b** drop or be dropped (*supplies fell by parachute*). **2 a** (often foll. by *over*) cease to stand upright. **b** come suddenly to the ground. **3** (foll. by *into*) stumble or be drawn into (a trap etc.). **4** become detached and descend or disappear. **5** take a downward direction: **a** (of hair, clothing, etc.) hang down. **b** (of ground etc.) slope. **6 a** find a lower level; sink lower. **b** subside, abate. **7** (of a barometer etc.) show a lower reading. **8** occur (*darkness fell*). **9** decline (*demand is falling; standards have fallen*). **10 a** (of the face) show dismay. **b** (of the eyes or a glance) look downwards. **11 a** lose power or status (*the government will fall*). **b** lose esteem, moral integrity, etc. **12** commit sin. **13** take or have a particular direction or place (*his eye fell on me*). **14 a** be naturally divisible (*the subject falls into three parts*). **b** (foll. by *under, within*) be classed among. **15** occur at a specified time (*Easter fell early*). **16** come by chance or duty (*it fell to me to answer*). **17** pass into a specified condition (*fall into decay*). **18 a** (of a position etc.) be overthrown or captured; be defeated; fail. **19** die (*fall in battle*). **20** (foll. by *on, upon*) **a** attack. **b** meet with. **c** embrace or embark on avidly. **21** (foll. by *to* + verbal noun) begin (*fell to wondering*). **22** (foll. by *to*) revert (*revenues fall to the Crown*). ● *n.* **1** the act or an instance of falling; a sudden rapid descent. **2** that which falls or has fallen, e.g. snow etc. **3** the recorded amount of rainfall etc. **4** a decline or diminution. **5** downfall (*the fall of Rome*). **6 a** succumbing to temptation. **b** (**the Fall**) *Bibl.* the sin of Adam and its consequences. **7 a** (of material, land, light, etc.) a downward direction; a slope. **b** a downward difference in height (*a fall of 3 inches*). **8** (also **Fall**) *N. Amer.* autumn. **9** (esp. in *pl.*) a waterfall, cataract, or cascade. **10 a** a throw in wrestling which keeps the opponent on the ground for a specified time. **b** a controlled act of falling in judo etc. □ **fall about** *Brit. colloq.* be helpless, esp. with laughter. **fall apart** (or **to pieces**) **1** break into pieces. **2** (of a situation etc.) be reduced to chaos. **3** lose one's capacity to cope. **fall away 1** (of a surface) incline abruptly. **2** gradually vanish. **3** desert, revolt. **fall back** retreat. **fall back on** have recourse to in difficulty. **fall behind 1** lag. **2** be in arrears. **fall down** (often foll. by *on*) fail; fail to deliver (payment etc.). **fall for** *colloq.* **1** be captivated or deceived by. **2** yield to the charms or merits of. **fall foul** (*N. Amer.* also **afoul**) **of** come into conflict with. **fall in 1 a** take one's place in military formation. **b** (as *int.*) the order to do this. **2** collapse inwards. **fall in love** see LOVE. **fall into line** take one's place in the ranks. **b** conform with others. **fall into place** begin to make sense or cohere. **fall in with 1** meet by chance.

FALCON: LANNER FALCON (*Falco biarmicus*)

2 agree with; accede to; humour. **3** coincide with. **fall off 1** (of demand etc.) decrease. **2** withdraw. **fall out 1** quarrel. **2** (of the hair etc.) become detached. **3** *Mil.* come out of formation. **4** result; come to pass; occur. **fall over oneself** *colloq.* **1** be eager or competitive. **2** stumble through haste, confusion, etc. **fall short 1** be or become inadequate. **2** (of a missile etc.) not reach its target. **fall short of** fail to reach or obtain. **fall through** come to nothing; miscarry. **fall to** begin an activity. [Old English]

fallacy *n.* (*pl.* **-ies**) **1** a mistaken belief, esp. based on unsound argument. **2** misleading or unsound argument. [from Latin *fallacia* 'deception'] □ **fallacious** *adj.* **fallaciously** *adv.* **fallaciousness** *n.*

fallen *past part.* of FALL *v.* ● *adj.* **1** (*attrib.*) having lost one's honour or reputation. **2** killed in war.

faller *n.* a person, animal, or thing that falls, esp. a person or animal in a race, or the value of shares on the stock market.

fall guy *n. slang* **1** an easy victim. **2** a scapegoat.

fallible *adj.* **1** capable of making mistakes. **2** liable to be erroneous. [based on Latin *fallere* 'to deceive'] □ **fallibility** *n.* **fallibly** *adv.*

falling-out *n.* a quarrel.

falling star *n.* a meteor.

fall-off *n.* a decrease, deterioration, withdrawal, etc.

Fallopian tube *n. Anat.* ▼ either of two tubes in female mammals along which ova travel to the uterus. ▷ OVARY, REPRODUCTIVE ORGANS. [named after G. *Fallopio*, Italian anatomist, 1523–1562]

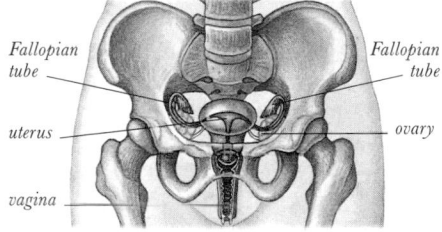

FALLOPIAN TUBES IN THE FEMALE HUMAN BODY

fallout *n.* **1** radioactive nuclear debris. **2** the adverse side effects of a situation etc.

fallow[1] ● *adj.* **1 a** (of land) ploughed and harrowed but left unsown. **b** uncultivated. **2** (of an idea etc.) potentially useful but not yet in use. **3** inactive. ● *n.* fallow or uncultivated land. [Middle English] □ **fallowness** *n.*

fallow[2] *adj.* of a pale brownish or reddish yellow. [Old English]

fallow deer *n.* a small deer, *Cervus dama*, having a white-spotted reddish-brown coat in the summer. ▷ DEER

false ● *adj.* **1** not according with fact; incorrect. **2 a** artificial, spurious (*false teeth*). **b** acting as such, esp. deceptively (*a false lining*). **3** illusory (*a false economy*). **4** improperly so called (*false acacia*). **5** deceptive. **6** (foll. by *to*) deceitful, treacherous, or unfaithful. **7** illegal (*false imprisonment*). ● *adv.* in a false manner (esp. *play false*). [from Latin *falsus*] □ **falsely** *adv.* **falseness** *n.* **falsity** *n.* (*pl.* **-ies**).

false acacia see ACACIA 2.

false alarm *n.* an alarm given needlessly.

false colour *n.* colour introduced during the production of an image to aid interpretation and not present in the object.

false colours *n.pl. Brit.* deceitful pretence.

false dawn *n.* **1** a transient light in the east before dawn. **2** a promising sign which comes to nothing.

false god *n.* a god that is falsely claimed to exist.

falsehood *n.* **1** the state of being false, esp. untrue. **2** a false or untrue thing. **3 a** the act of lying. **b** a lie or lies.

false move *n.* an imprudent or careless act.

false pretences *n.pl.* misrepresentations made with intent to deceive (esp. *under false pretences*).

false start *n.* **1** an invalid start in a race. **2** an unsuccessful attempt to begin something.

false step *n.* a slip; a mistake.

falsetto *n.* (*pl.* **-os**) **1** a method of voice production used by male singers, esp. tenors, to sing notes higher than their normal range. **2** a singer using this method. [Italian, diminutive of *falso* 'false']

falsework *n.* a temporary framework or support used during building to form arches etc.

falsies *n.pl. colloq.* pads of material used to increase the apparent size of the breasts.

falsify *v.tr.* (**-ies**, **-ied**) **1** fraudulently alter or make false (a document, evidence, etc.). **2** misrepresent. **3** make wrong; pervert. □ **falsifiable** *adj.* **falsification** *n.*

falter *v.* **1** *intr.* stumble; stagger; go unsteadily. **2** *intr.* waver; lose courage. **3** *tr. & intr.* stammer; speak hesitatingly. [Middle English] □ **falterer** *n.* **falteringly** *adv.*

fame *n.* **1** renown; the state of being famous. **2** *archaic* reputation. [from Latin *fama*]

famed *adj.* (foll. by *for*) famous; much spoken of (*famed for its good food*).

familiar ● *adj.* **1 a** (often foll. by *to*) well known; no longer novel. **b** often encountered or experienced. **2** (foll. by *with*) knowing a thing well or in detail. **3** (often foll. by *with*) well acquainted (with a person); intimate. **4** excessively informal. **5** unceremonious. ● *n.* **1** a close friend or associate. **2** (in full **familiar spirit**) a demon supposedly attending and obeying a witch etc. [Middle English, related to FAMILY] □ **familiarly** *adv.*

familiarity *n.* (*pl.* **-ies**) **1** the state of being well known. **2** (foll. by *with*) close acquaintance. **3** a close relationship. **4** behaviour that is informal, esp. excessively so. [from Latin *familiaritas*]

familiarize *v.tr.* (also **-ise**) **1** (foll. by *with*) make (a person) conversant or well acquainted. **2** make (a thing) well known. [based on French *familiare* 'familiar'] □ **familiarization** *n.*

family *n.* (*pl.* **-ies**) **1** a set of relations, living together or not. **2 a** the members of a household. **b** a person's children. **c** (*attrib.*) serving the needs of families (*family butcher*). **3 a** all the descendants of a common ancestor. **b** a group of peoples from a common stock. **4** a group of languages derived from a particular early language. **5** a group of objects distinguished by common features. **6** *Biol.* a group of related genera of animals or plants. **7** (**in the family way**) *colloq.* pregnant. [from Latin *familia* 'household'] □ **familial** *adj.*

family credit *n.* (in the UK) a regular payment by the state to a low-income family.

Family Division *n.* (in the UK) a division of the High Court dealing with adoption, divorce, etc.

family man *n.* a man having a wife and children, esp. one fond of family life.

family name *n.* a surname.

family planning *n.* birth control.

family tree *n.* a genealogical chart.

famine *n.* extreme scarcity, esp. of food. [from Latin *fames* 'hunger']

famish *v.* **1** *v.tr. & intr.* (usu. in *passive*) reduce or be reduced to extreme hunger. **2** *intr. colloq.* feel very hungry. [related to FAMINE]

famous *adj.* (often foll. by *for*) celebrated; well known. [based on Latin *fama* 'fame'] □ **famousness** *n.*

famously *adv.* **1** *colloq.* excellently (*got on famously*). **2** notably.

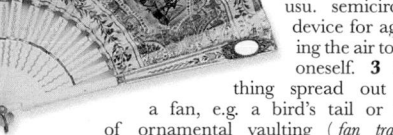

FAN: 19TH-CENTURY EUROPEAN FAN

fan[1] ● *n.* **1** an apparatus, usu. with rotating blades, giving a current of air for ventilation etc. **2** ◀ a folding, usu. semicircular device for agitating the air to cool oneself. **3** anything spread out like a fan, e.g. a bird's tail or kind of ornamental vaulting (*fan tracery*). ▷ VAULT. ● *v.* (**fanned**, **fanning**) **1** *tr.* **a** blow a current of air on, with, or as with a fan. **b** agitate (the air) with a fan. **2** *tr.* (of a breeze) blow gently on. **3** *intr. & tr.* (usu. foll. by *out*) spread out in the shape of a fan. [from Latin *vannus* 'winnowing-fan'] □ **fanlike** *adj.*

fan[2] *n.* a devotee of a particular activity, performer, etc. [abbreviation of FANATIC]

fanatic ● *n.* a person filled with excessive and often misguided enthusiasm for something. ● *adj.* excessively enthusiastic. [originally in religious sense: based on Latin *fanum* 'temple'] □ **fanatical** *adj.* **fanatically** *adv.* **fanaticism** *n.* **fanaticize** *v.intr. & tr.* (also **-ise**).

fan belt *n.* ▼ a belt that drives a fan to cool the radiator in a motor vehicle.

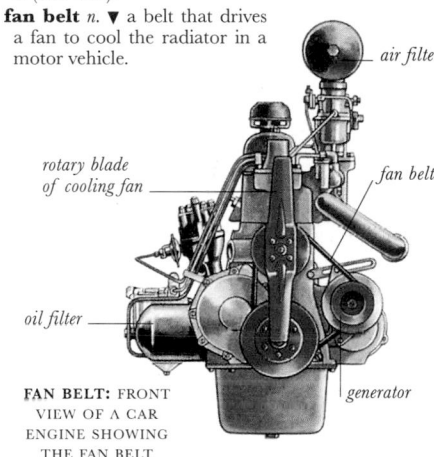

FAN BELT: FRONT VIEW OF A CAR ENGINE SHOWING THE FAN BELT

air filter

fan belt

rotary blade of cooling fan

oil filter

generator

fancier *n.* a connoisseur or follower of some activity or thing (*pigeon fancier*).

fanciful *adj.* **1** existing only in the imagination or fancy. **2** whimsical, capricious. **3** fantastically designed, ornamented, etc., odd-looking. □ **fancifully** *adv.* **fancifulness** *n.*

fancy ● *n.* (*pl.* **-ies**) **1** an individual taste or inclination. **2** a caprice or whim. **3** a thing favoured, e.g. a horse to win a race. **4** an arbitrary supposition. **5 a** the faculty of using imagination or of inventing imagery. **b** a mental image. **6** unfounded belief. ● *adj.* (usu. *attrib.*) (**fancier**, **fanciest**) **1** ornamental; not plain. **2** whimsical, extravagant (*at a fancy price*). **3** based on imagination, not fact. **4** (of foods etc.) of fine quality. ● *v.tr.* (**-ies**, **-ied**) **1** (foll. by *that* + clause) be inclined to suppose. **2** *Brit. colloq.* feel a desire for (*do you fancy a drink?*). **3** *Brit. colloq.* find sexually attractive. **4** *colloq.* have an unduly high opinion of (oneself etc.). **5** select (a horse etc.) as the likely winner. **6** (in *imper.*) expressing surprise (*fancy that!*). **7** picture to oneself. □ **catch** (or **take**) **a person's fancy** please or appeal to a person. **take a fancy to** become (esp. inexplicably) fond of. [contraction of FANTASY] □ **fanciable** *adj.* (in sense 3 of *v.*). **fancily** *adv.* **fanciness** *n.*

fancy dress *n.* fanciful costume, esp. for masquerading as a different person or as an animal etc. at a party.

fancy-free *adj.* (often in phr. **footloose and fancy-free**) without (esp. emotional) commitments.

fancy goods *n.pl.* ornamental novelties etc.

F

FANG

In venomous snakes, the fangs are usually folded back against the roof of the mouth, only swinging forward when needed to attack prey. Venom stored in a sac at the back of the mouth passes along a tube to be released through a tiny hole close to the fang's point.

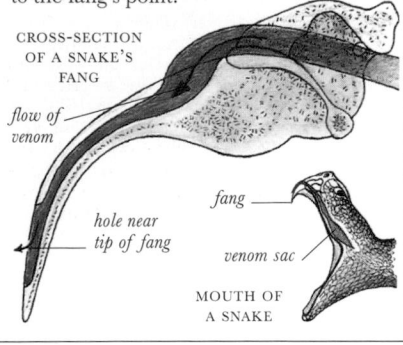

CROSS-SECTION OF A SNAKE'S FANG

flow of venom

hole near tip of fang

fang

venom sac

MOUTH OF A SNAKE

fancy man n. slang derog. **1** a woman's lover. **2** a pimp.

fancy woman n. slang derog. a mistress.

fandango n. (pl. **-oes** or **-os**) **1** a lively Spanish dance for two. **2** nonsense, tomfoolery. [Spanish]

fandom n. the world of fans and enthusiasts, esp. of fans of science fiction magazines.

fanfare n. a short showy or ceremonious sounding of trumpets etc. [French]

fanfaronade n. **1** arrogant talk; brag. **2** a fanfare. [French *fanfaronnade* from *fanfaron* 'braggart']

fang n. **1** a large sharp tooth, esp. a canine tooth of a dog or wolf. ▷ CARNIVORE. **2** (usu. in *pl.*) **a** ▲ the tooth of a venomous snake, by which poison is injected. **b** the biting mouthpart of a spider. ▷ SPIDER. **3** the root of a tooth or its prong. [from Old Norse] □ **fanged** adj. (also in *comb.*).

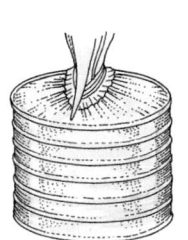

FANLIGHT ABOVE A GEORGIAN FRONT DOOR

fan heater n. an electric heater in which a fan drives air over an element.

fanlight n. ◀ a small originally semicircular window over a door or another window.

fan mail n. letters from fans.

fanny n. (pl. **-ies**) **1** Brit. coarse slang the female genitals. **2** N. Amer. slang the buttocks. [20th century coinage]

Fanny Adams n. Brit. slang **1** (also **sweet Fanny Adams**) nothing at all. **2** Naut. **a** canned meat. **b** stew. [name of a murder victim c.1870]

■ **Usage** *Fanny Adams*, or its abbreviated form *FA*, is sometimes understood as a euphemism for *fuck all*.

fan palm n. a palm tree with fan-shaped leaves.

fantail n. **1** a pigeon with a broad tail. **2** a fan-shaped tail or end. □ **fantailed** adj.

fantasia /fan-**tay**-ziă/ n. a musical or other composition free in form and often in improvisatory style; a composition based on several familiar tunes. [Italian, literally 'fantasy']

fantasize v. (also **phantasize**, **-ise**) **1** intr. have a fantasy or fanciful vision. **2** tr. imagine; create a fantasy about. □ **fantasist** n.

fantastic adj. (also **fantastical**) **1** colloq. excellent, extraordinary. **2** extravagantly fanciful. **3** grotesque or quaint. [Middle English, related to FANTASY] □ **fantasticality** n. **fantastically** adv.

fantasy n. (also **phantasy**) (pl. **-ies**) **1** the faculty of inventing images, esp. extravagant or visionary ones. **2** a fanciful mental image; a daydream. **3** a whimsical speculation. **4** a fantastic invention or composition. [from Latin *phantasia* 'appearance', based on Greek]

fantasy football n. (also **fantasy cricket** etc.) a competition in which participants select imaginary teams from among the players in a league etc. and score points according to the actual performance of their players.

fanzine n. a magazine for fans, esp. those of science fiction, sport, or popular music. [blend of FANATIC and MAGAZINE]

far (**further**, **furthest** or **farther**, **farthest**) ● adv. **1** at or to or by a great distance (*far away; far off; far out*). **2** a long way (off) in space or time (*are you travelling far?; we talked far into the night*). **3** to a great extent or degree; by much (*far better; far too early*). ● adj. **1** situated at or extending over a great distance in space or time; remote (*a far country*). **2** more distant (*the far end of the hall*). □ **as far as 1** to the distance of (a place). **2** to the extent that (*travel as far as you like*). **by far** by a great amount. **far and away** by a very large amount. **far and near** everywhere. **far and wide** over a large area. **far from** very different from being; tending to the opposite of (*the problem is far from being solved*). **go far 1** achieve much. **2** contribute greatly. **3** be adequate. **go too far** go beyond the limits of what is reasonable, polite, etc. **how far** to what extent. **so far 1** to such an extent or distance; to this point. **2** until now. **so** (or **in so**) **far as** (or **that**) to the extent that. **so far so good** progress has been satisfactory up to now. [Old English]

farad n. Electr. the SI unit of capacitance, such that one coulomb of charge causes a potential difference of one volt. [shortening of *faraday*, named after M. *Faraday*, English physicist, 1791–1867]

faraway attrib.adj. **1** remote; long-past. **2** (of a look) dreamy. **3** (of a voice) sounding as if from a distance.

farce n. **1** a **a** low comic dramatic work based on ludicrously improbable events. **b** this branch of drama. **2** absurdly futile proceedings. [based on Latin *farcire* 'to stuff', used metaphorically of interludes etc.]

farceur n. **1** a joker. **2** an actor or writer of farces. [French]

farcical adj. **1** extremely ludicrous or futile. **2** of or like farce. □ **farcically** adv.

far cry n. (usu. foll. by *from*) a long way; a very different experience.

fare ● n. **1** a **a** the price a passenger has to pay to be conveyed by bus, train, etc. **b** a fare-paying passenger. **2** a range of food. ● v.intr. literary progress; get on (*how did you fare?*). [Old English]

Far East n. (prec. by *the*) China, Japan, and other countries of E. Asia. □ **Far Eastern** adj.

fare stage n. Brit. **1** a section of a bus etc. route for which a fixed fare is charged. **2** a stop marking this.

farewell ● int. goodbye, adieu. ● n. leave-taking; departure (also attrib.: *a farewell kiss*). [Middle English]

far-fetched adj. (of an explanation etc.) strained, unconvincing.

far-flung adj. extending far; widely distributed.

far gone adj. **1** advanced in time. **2** colloq. in an advanced state of illness, drunkenness, etc.

farina n. the flour or meal of cereal, nuts, or starchy roots. [Latin] □ **farinaceous** adj.

farm ● n. **1** an area of land and its buildings used under one management for growing crops, rearing animals, etc. **2** a place or establishment for breeding a particular type of animal, growing fruit, etc.

(*trout farm; mink farm*). **3** = FARMHOUSE. ● v. **1** a tr. use (land) for growing crops, rearing animals, etc. **b** intr. be a farmer; work on a farm. **2** tr. breed (fish etc.) commercially. **3** tr. **a** delegate or subcontract (work) to others. **b** contract (the collection of taxes) to another for a fee. **c** arrange for (a person, esp. a child) to be looked after by another, with payment. [originally applied only to leased land: from medieval Latin *firma* 'fixed payment'] □ **farming** n.

farmer n. **1** a person who runs a farm. **2** a person to whom the collection of taxes is contracted for a fee. [from medieval Latin *firmarius, firmator*]

farmhand n. a worker on a farm.

farmhouse n. a dwelling place attached to a farm.

farmstead n. a farm and its buildings.

farmyard n. a yard attached to a farmhouse.

faro /**fair**-oh/ n. a gambling card game in which bets are placed on the order of appearance of the cards. [from French *pharaon* 'Pharaoh', reputedly the name of the king of hearts]

far-off attrib.adj. remote.

far out adj. (hyphenated when attrib.) slang **1** avant-garde, unconventional. **2** excellent.

farrago /fă-**rah**-goh/ n. (pl. **-os** or US **-oes**) a medley or hotchpotch. [Latin, literally 'mixed fodder'] □ **farraginous** adj.

far-reaching adj. **1** widely applicable. **2** having important consequences or implications.

farrier n. **1** a smith who shoes horses. **2** a person who treats the disease and injuries of horses. [based on Latin *ferrum* 'iron, horseshoe'] □ **farriery** n.

farrow ● n. **1** a litter of pigs. **2** the birth of a litter. ● v.tr. (also absol.) (of a sow) produce (pigs). [Old English]

far-seeing adj. shrewd in judgement; prescient.

Farsi n. the modern Persian language, the official language of Iran. [Persian: cf. PARSEE]

far-sighted adj. **1** having foresight, prudent. **2** esp. N. Amer. = LONG-SIGHTED. □ **far-sightedly** adv. **far-sightedness** n.

fart coarse slang ● v.intr. **1** emit wind from the anus. **2** (foll. by *about, around*) behave foolishly. ● n. **1** an emission of wind from the anus. **2** an unpleasant person. [Old English]

farther var. of FURTHER adv. & adj.

farthest var. of FURTHEST.

farthing n. **1** hist. ◀ (in the UK) a former coin and monetary unit equal to a quarter of an old penny (withdrawn in 1961). **2** the least possible amount (*it doesn't matter a farthing*). [Old English, literally 'fourth part']

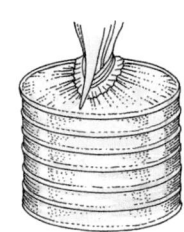

FARTHING

farthingale n. hist. ▼ a hooped petticoat or a stiff curved roll to extend a woman's skirt. [based on Spanish *verdugo* 'rod']

WHEEL-SHAPED FARTHINGALE

BELL-SHAPED FARTHINGALE

FARTHINGALES

fartlek n. Athletics a method of training for middle- and long-distance running, mixing fast with slow work. [Swedish, from *fart* 'speed' + *lek* 'play']

fasces n.pl. **1** Rom.Hist. a bundle of rods with a projecting axe-blade, as a symbol of a magistrate's power. **2** (in Fascist Italy) a bundle of rods as an emblem of authority. [Latin pl. of *fascis* 'bundle']

fascia /**fash**-iă/ n. (pl. **fasciae** /-i-ee/ or **fascias**) **1** Archit. **a** a long flat surface between mouldings on the architrave in classical architecture. **b** a flat board, usu. of wood, covering the ends of rafters. **2** a stripe or band. **3** /fash-ă/ *Anat.* a thin sheath of fibrous tissue, esp. that enclosing a muscle or other organ. □ **fascial** *adj.*

fascicle /fas-i-kŭl/ *n.* (also **fascicule**) a separately published instalment of a book. [from Latin *fasciculus* 'little bundle']

fascinate *v.tr.* **1** capture the interest of; attract. **2** paralyse (a victim) with fear. [based on Latin *fascinatus* 'enchanted'] □ **fascinated** *adj.* **fascinating** *adj.* **fascinatingly** *adv.* **fascination** *n.* **fascinator** *n.*

Fascism /fash-izm/ *n.* **1** the totalitarian principles and organization of the extreme right-wing nationalist movement in Italy (1922–43). **2** (also **fascism**) **a** any similar nationalist and authoritarian movement. **b** (loosely) any system of extreme right-wing or authoritarian views. [from Italian, based on Latin *fascis* 'bundle, group'] □ **Fascist** *n. & adj.* (also **fascist**). **Fascistic** *adj.* (also **fascistic**).

■ **Usage** Some people find the use of *Fascism* in sense 2b unacceptable.

fashion ● *n.* **1** ▼ the current popular custom or style, esp. in dress. **2** a manner of doing something (*in a peculiar fashion*). **3** (in *comb.*) in a specified manner (*walk crab-fashion*). **4** fashionable society (*a woman of fashion*). ● *v.tr.* (often foll. by *into*) make into a particular or the required form. □ **after** (or **in**) **a fashion** as well as is practicable, though not satisfactorily. **in** (or **out of**) **fashion** fashionable (or not fashionable). [based on Latin *facere* 'to do, make']

fashionable *adj.* **1** following, suited to, or influenced by the current fashion. **2** characteristic of or favoured by those who are leaders of social fashion. □ **fashionableness** *n.* **fashionably** *adv.*

fast[1] ● *adj.* **1** rapid, quick-moving. **2** capable of high speed (*a fast car*). **3** enabling or causing or intended for high speed (*a fast road*; *fast bowler*). **4** (of a clock etc.) showing a time ahead of the correct time. **5 a** (of a photographic film) needing only a short exposure. **b** (of a lens) having a large aperture. **6 a** firmly fixed or attached. **b** secure; firmly established (*a fast friendship*). **7** (of a colour) not fading. **8** (of a person) immoral, dissipated. ● *adv.* **1** quickly;

in quick succession. **2** firmly, tightly (*stand fast*; *eyes fast shut*). **3** soundly, completely (*fast asleep*). □ **pull a fast one** *colloq.* try to deceive or gain an unfair advantage. [Old English]

fast[2] ● *v.intr.* abstain from all or some kinds of food or drink. ● *n.* an act or period of fasting. [from Old Norse]

fastback *n.* **1** a motor car with the rear sloping continuously down to the bumper. **2** such a rear.

fast breeder *n.* (also **fast breeder reactor**) a reactor using fast neutrons to produce the same fissile material as it uses.

fast buck see BUCK[2].

fasten *v.* **1** *tr.* make or become fixed or secure. **2** *tr.* (foll. by *in*, *up*) lock securely; shut in. **3** *tr.* **a** (foll. by *on*, *upon*) direct (a look, thoughts, etc.) fixedly or intently. **b** focus or direct the attention fixedly upon (*fastened him with her eyes*). **4** *intr.* (foll. by *on*, *upon*) **a** take hold of. **b** single out. **5** *tr.* (foll. by *off*) fix with stitches or a knot. [Old English] □ **fastener** *n.*

fastening *n.* a device that fastens something; a fastener.

F

FASHION

In Western countries, styles of clothing, or 'fashions', are continually evolving, often reflecting broader shifts in mores, customs, and attitudes. This can clearly be seen in the changes in fashion during the 20th century. The formal clothing of the 1900s gave way to more relaxed, practical attire as many rigid social conventions disappeared.

Women's clothing, in particular, once restrictive and designed to preserve female modesty, became freer and more revealing – first in the 1920s and then in the decades following the Second World War (1939–1945). New fabrics, such as nylon and Lycra, and improved technologies contributed to the speed of transition.

WOMEN'S FASHION IN THE **20**TH CENTURY

| 1900s | 1910s | 1920s | 1930s | 1940s | 1950s | 1960s | 1970s | 1980s | 1990s |

MEN'S FASHION IN THE **20**TH CENTURY

| 1900s | 1910s | 1920s | 1930s | 1940s | 1950s | 1960s | 1970s | 1980s | 1990s |

F

fast food *n.* food that can be prepared and served quickly and easily, esp. in a snack bar or restaurant.

fast forward ● *n.* a control on a tape or video player for advancing the tape rapidly. ● *adj.* (**fast-forward**) designating such a control. ● *v.tr.* (**fast-forward**) advance (a tape) rapidly, sometimes while simultaneously playing it at high speed.

fastidious *adj.* **1** very careful in matters of choice or taste; fussy. **2** easily disgusted; squeamish. [Middle English from Latin *fastidium* 'loathing'] □ **fastidiously** *adv.* **fastidiousness** *n.*

fastigiate *adj. Bot.* **1** ◄ having a conical or tapering outline. **2** having parallel upright branches. [based on Latin *fastigium* 'gable-top']

fastness *n.* **1** a stronghold or fortress. **2** the state of being secure. [related to FAST¹]

fast neutron *n.* a neutron with high kinetic energy.

fast reactor *n.* a nuclear reactor using mainly fast neutrons.

fast-talk *v.tr. N. Amer. colloq.* persuade by rapid or deceitful talk.

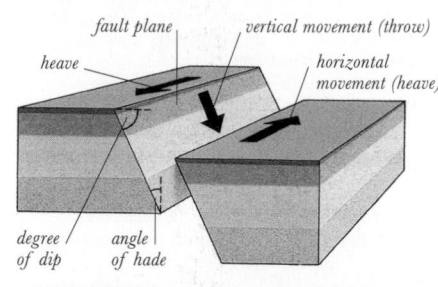

FASTIGIATE OUTLINE OF A SPANISH FIR TREE

fast track ● *n.* a route or method providing more rapid results than would normally be expected. ● *v.tr.* (**fast-track**) **1** accelerate the development of (a product or project). **2** promote (a person) rapidly.

fat ● *n.* **1** ▼ a natural oily or greasy substance occurring esp. in animal bodies. **2** the part of anything containing this. **3** excessive presence of fat in a person or animal. **4** *Chem.* any of a group of natural esters of glycerol and various fatty acids existing as solids at room temperature. ● *adj.* (**fatter, fattest**) **1** (of a person or animal) having excessive fat. **2** (of an animal) made plump for slaughter; fatted. **3** containing much fat. **4** greasy, oily, unctuous. **5** (of land or resources) fertile, rich; yielding abundantly. **6 a** thick, substantial in content (*a fat book*). **b** substantial as an asset or opportunity (*a fat cheque; was given a fat part in the play*). **7** *colloq. iron.* very little; not much (*a fat chance; a fat lot*). ● *v.tr. & intr.* (**fatted, fatting**) make or become fat. □ **kill the fatted calf** celebrate, esp. at a prodigal's return (Luke 15). **live off** (or **on**) **the fat of the land** have the best of everything. [Old English] □ **fatless** *adj.* **fatly** *adv.* **fatness** *n.* **fattish** *adj.*

fatal *adj.* **1** causing or ending in death (*a fatal accident*). **2** destructive; ruinous; ending in disaster (*was fatal to their chances; made a fatal mistake*). **3** fateful. [from Latin *fatalis*, related to FATE] □ **fatally** *adv.*

FAULT

A fault is the result of a fracture in the Earth's crust, in which different forces acting upon the rock layers on either side of the fracture cause movement between them. Different combinations of forces at work and angles of fracture (measured by the degree of dip and angle of hade) give rise to a series of fault descriptions. The principal types are shown here.

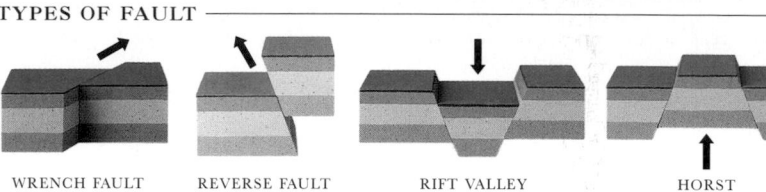

MOVEMENT OF AN OBLIQUE-SLIP FAULT

TYPES OF FAULT

WRENCH FAULT   REVERSE FAULT   RIFT VALLEY   HORST

fatalism *n.* **1** the belief that all events are predetermined and therefore inevitable. **2** a submissive attitude to events as being inevitable. □ **fatalist** *n.* **fatalistic** *adj.* **fatalistically** *adv.*

fatality *n.* (*pl.* **-ies**) **1 a** an occurrence of death by accident or in war etc. **b** a person killed in this way. **2** a fatal influence. **3** a predestined liability to disaster. [from Late Latin *fatalitas*, related to FATE]

fate ● *n.* **1** a power regarded as predetermining events unalterably. **2 a** the future regarded as determined by such a power. **b** an individual's appointed lot. **3** death, destruction. **4** (usu. **Fate**) a goddess of destiny. ● *v.tr.* **1** (usu. in *passive*) preordain (*was fated to win*). **2** (as **fated** *adj.*) doomed to destruction. [from Latin *fatum* 'that which is spoken']

fateful *adj.* **1** important, decisive; having far-reaching consequences. **2** controlled as if by fate. **3** causing or likely to cause disaster. □ **fatefully** *adv.*

fat-head *n. colloq.* a stupid person. □ **fat-headed** *adj.*

fat hen *n.* the white goosefoot, *Chenopodium album.*

father ● *n.* **1 a** a man in relation to a child born from his fertilization of an ovum. **b** (in full **adoptive father**) a man who has continuous care of a child, esp. by adoption. **2** any male animal in relation to its offspring. **3** (usu. in *pl.*) a forefather. **4** an originator or early leader. **5** a person who deserves special respect (*the father of his country*). **6** (**Fathers** or **Fathers of the Church**) early Christian theologians. **7** (also **Father**) **a** (often as a title or form of address) a priest. **b** a religious leader. **8** (**the Father**) (in Christian belief) the first person of the Trinity. **9** (**Father**) a venerable person, esp. as a title in personifications (*Father Time*). **10** the oldest member or doyen (*Father of the House*). **11** (usu. in *pl.*) the leading men or elders in a city or state (*city fathers*). ● *v.tr.* **1** beget; be the father of. **2** behave as a father towards. **3** originate (a scheme etc.). **4** (foll. by *on*) assign the paternity of (a child, book) to a person. [Old English] □ **fatherhood** *n.* **fatherless** *adj.*

Father Christmas *n.* = SANTA CLAUS.

father figure *n.* an older man who is respected like a father.

father-in-law *n.* (*pl.* **fathers-in-law**) the father of one's husband or wife.

fatherland *n.* one's native country.

fatherly *adj.* **1** like or characteristic of a father in affection, care, etc. (*fatherly concern*). **2** of or proper to a father.

Father's Day *n.* a day (usu. the third Sunday in June) established for a special tribute to fathers.

fathom ● *n.* (*pl.* often **fathom** when prec. by a number) a measure of six feet, esp. used in taking depth soundings. ● *v.tr.* **1** grasp or comprehend (a problem or difficulty). **2** measure the depth of (water). [Old English *fæthm* 'outstretched arms'] □ **fathomable** *adj.* **fathomless** *adj.*

fatigue ● *n.* **1** extreme tiredness. **2** weakness in materials, esp. metal, caused by repeated variations of stress. **3** a reduction in the efficiency of a muscle, organ, etc., after prolonged activity. **4** (in *pl.*) esp. *N. Amer.* clothing of various types worn by military personnel (*camouflage fatigues; combat fatigues*). **5** *archaic* **a** a non-military duty in the army, often as a punishment. **b** (in full **fatigue-party**) a group of soldiers ordered to do such a duty. **c** (in *pl.*) clothing worn for such a duty ● *v.tr.* (**fatigues, fatigued, fatiguing**) cause fatigue in; tire, exhaust. [from Latin *fatigare* 'to tire out']

fatism var. of FATTISM.

fatist var. of FATTIST (see FATTISM).

fatso *n.* (*pl.* **-oes**) *slang offens.* a fat person. [probably from FAT or the designation *Fats*]

fatstock *n. Brit.* livestock fattened for slaughter.

fatten *v.tr. & intr.* make or become fat.

fattening *adj.* (of foods) easily causing an increase in weight.

fattism *n.* (also **fatism**) prejudice or discrimination against fat people. □ **fattist** *n. & adj.* (also **fatist**).

fatty ● *adj.* (**fattier, fattiest**) **1** like fat; oily, greasy. **2** consisting of or containing fat; adipose. **3** marked by abnormal deposition of fat. ● *n.* (*pl.* **-ies**) *colloq.* a fat person. □ **fattiness** *n.*

FAT

Fat – also known as adipose tissue – is an important component of all animal bodies. Most fat is stored just beneath the skin, although various internal organs, such as the kidneys, heart, and liver, are also protected by a surrounding layer of fat. The purpose of fat is threefold: it is a highly concentrated reserve of energy; it acts as insulation against the loss of body heat; and it provides a buffer to absorb shock in areas of the body that experience frequent impact or pressure, such as the buttocks.

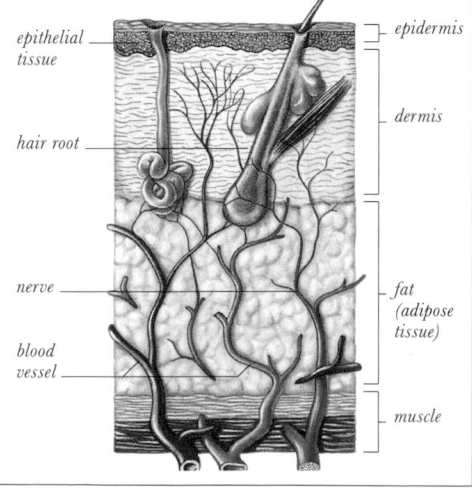

CROSS-SECTION OF HUMAN SKIN WITH HEAVY CONCENTRATION OF FAT

epithelial tissue / epidermis / hair root / dermis / nerve / fat (adipose tissue) / blood vessel / muscle

fatty acid *n.* any of a class of organic compounds consisting of a hydrocarbon chain and a terminal carboxyl group.

fatuous *adj.* vacantly silly; purposeless, idiotic. [from Latin *fatuus* 'foolish'] □ **fatuity** *n.* (*pl.* **-ies**). **fatuously** *adv.* **fatuousness** *n.*

fatwa *n.* (in Islamic countries) an authoritative ruling on a religious matter. [Arabic]

faucet *n.* esp. *US* a tap. [from Old French *fausset* 'vent-peg']

fault ● *n.* **1** a defect or imperfection of character or of structure, appearance, etc. **2** a break in an electric circuit. **3** a transgression, offence, or thing wrongly done. **4 a** *Tennis* etc. a service of the ball not in accordance with the rules. **b** (in show-jumping) a penalty for an error. **5** responsibility for wrongdoing, error, etc. (*it will be your own fault*). **6** a defect regarded as the cause of something wrong (*the fault lies in the teaching methods*). **7** *Geol.* ◄ an extended break in the continuity of strata. ▷ EARTHQUAKE, MOUNTAIN. ● *v.* **1** *tr.* find fault with; blame. **2** *tr.* declare to be faulty. **3** *tr.* *Geol.* break the continuity of (strata). **4** *intr.* commit a fault. **5** *intr.* *Geol.* show a fault. □ **at fault** guilty; to blame. **find fault** (often foll. by *with*) make an adverse criticism; complain. **to a fault** (usu. of a commendable quality etc.) excessively (*generous to a fault*). [based on Latin *fallere* 'to fail']

faultless *adj.* without fault; free from defect or error. □ **faultlessly** *adv.* **faultlessness** *n.*

faulty *adj.* (**faultier**, **faultiest**) having faults; imperfect.

faun *n.* ▼ one of a class of Latin rural deities with a human face and torso and a goat's horns, legs, and tail. [from Latin *Faunus*, name identified with the Greek god Pan]

fauna *n.* (*pl.* **faunas**) **1** the animal life of a region or geological period (cf. FLORA). **2** a treatise on or list of this. [modern Latin, from the name of a rural goddess, sister of Faunus: see FAUN] □ **faunal** *adj.*

faute de mieux /foht de m'yer/ *adv.* for want of a better alternative. [French]

fauvism *n.* ▲ a style of painting with vivid use of colour. □ **fauvist** *n.* [French *fauve* 'wild beast', applied to painters of the school of Matisse]

faux /foh/ *adj.* false, imitation (*a faux fur hood*). [French, literally 'false']

faux pas /foh pah/ *n.* (*pl.* same) **1** a tactless mistake; a blunder. **2** a social indiscretion. [French, literally 'false step']

FAUN: ANCIENT ROMAN FIGURE OF A FAUN

fave *n. & adj.* slang = FAVOURITE (esp. in show business).

favour (*US* **favor**) ● *n.* **1** an act of kindness (*did it as a favour*). **2** approval, goodwill; friendly regard (*gained their favour*; *look with favour on*). **3** partiality; too lenient or generous treatment. **4** aid, support (*under favour of night*). **5** a thing given or worn as a mark of favour or support, e.g. a badge or a knot of ribbons. ● *v.tr.* **1** regard or treat with favour or partiality. **2** give support or approval to; promote, prefer. **3 a** be to the advantage of (a person). **b** facilitate (a process etc.). **4** tend to confirm (an idea or theory). **5** (foll. by *with*) oblige (*favour me with a reply*). **6** (as **favoured** *adj.*) having special advantages. **7** *colloq.* resemble in features. □ **in favour 1** meeting with approval. **2** (foll. by *of*) **a** in support of. **b** to the advantage of. **out of favour** lacking approval. [from Latin *favor*]

favourable *adj.* (*US* **favorable**) **1 a** well disposed; propitious. **b** approving. **2** giving consent (*a favourable answer*). **3** promising, auspicious (*a favourable*

aspect). **4** helpful, suitable. [from Latin *favorabilis*, related to FAVOUR] □ **favourableness** *n.* **favourably** *adv.*

favourite (*US* **favorite**) ● *adj.* preferred to all others (*my favourite book*). ● *n.* **1** a specially favoured or preferred person or thing. **2** *Sport* a competitor thought most likely to win. [from Italian *favorito* 'favoured']

favouritism *n.* (*US* **favoritism**) the unfair favouring of one person or group at the expense of another.

fawn[1] ● *n.* **1** a deer in its first year. **2** a light yellowish brown. ● *adj.* of a light yellowish-brown colour. ● *v.tr.* (also *absol.*) (of a deer) bring forth (young). [based on Latin *fetus* 'offspring']

fawn[2] *v.intr.* **1** (often foll. by *on*, *upon*) (of a person) behave servilely, show cringing affection. **2** (of an animal, esp. a dog) show extreme affection. [Old English] □ **fawning** *adj.* **fawningly** *adv.*

fax ● *n.* **1** facsimile transmission (see FACSIMILE *n.* 2). **2 a** a copy produced or message sent by this. **b** ▼ a machine for transmitting and receiving these. ● *v.tr.* transmit in this way.

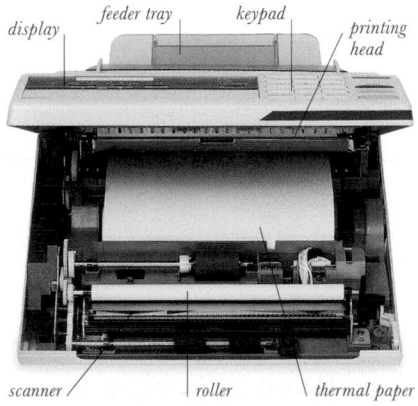

display | feeder tray | keypad | printing head

scanner | roller | thermal paper

FAX MACHINE WITH INTERNAL MECHANISM REVEALED

FAUVISM

Fauvism was a short-lived but influential movement that developed from post-Impressionism. Whereas painters before the fauvists had used colour primarily to imitate visual appearance, Henri Matisse, André Derain, and Maurice de Vlaminck (the main exponents of fauvism) attempted to free colour from its representational purpose, and use it instead as an expression of feeling. In this painting by Matisse, the green of the shadows in the interior and the red of the masts in the background are based not on observation but on emotional response to the moment. The fauvists' approach to colour had a profound effect upon expressionism and the development of abstractionism.

The Open Window (1905), HENRI MATISSE

TIMELINE

| 1500 | 1550 | 1600 | 1650 | 1700 | 1750 | 1800 | 1850 | 1900 | 1950 | 2000 |

F

fay *n.* *literary* a fairy. [based on Latin *fata* 'the Fates']

fayre see FAIR[2].

faze *v.tr.* (often as **fazed** *adj.*) *colloq.* disconcert, disorientate. [Old English]

FBA *abbr.* Fellow of the British Academy.

FBI *abbr.* (in the US) Federal Bureau of Investigation.

Fe *symb. Chem.* the element iron. [Latin *ferrum*]

fealty *n.* (*pl.* **-ies**) **1** *hist.* **a** a feudal tenant's or vassal's fidelity to a lord. **b** an acknowledgement of this. **2** allegiance. [from Latin *fidelitas*]

fear ● *n.* **1 a** an unpleasant emotion caused by exposure to danger, expectation of pain, etc. **b** a state of alarm (*he in fear*). **2** a cause of fear (*all fears removed*). **3** (often foll. by *of*) dread or fearful respect (towards) (*fear of heights*; *fear of one's elders*). **4** anxiety for the safety of (*in fear of their lives*). **5** danger; likelihood (of something unwelcome) (*there is little fear of failure*). ● *v.* **1 a** *tr.* feel fear about or towards. **b** *intr.* feel fear. **2** *intr.* (foll. by *for*) feel anxiety about (*feared for my life*). **3** *tr.* have uneasy expectation of (*fear the worst*). **4** *tr.* (usu. foll. by *that* + clause) apprehend with fear or regret (*I fear that you are wrong*). **5** *tr.* **a** (foll. by *to* + infin.) hesitate. **b** (foll. by verbal noun) shrink from (*he feared meeting his ex-wife*). **6** *tr.* show reverence towards. □ **for fear of** (or **that**) to avoid the risk of (or that). **never fear** there is no danger of that. **no fear** *Brit. colloq.* expressing strong denial or refusal. **without fear or favour** impartially. [Old English]

fearful *adj.* **1** (usu. foll. by *of*, or *that* + clause) afraid. **2** awful. **3** *colloq.* extremely unwelcome or unpleasant (*a fearful row*). □ **fearfully** *adv.* **fearfulness** *n.*

fearless *adj.* **1** courageous, brave. **2** (foll. by *of*) without fear. □ **fearlessly** *adv.* **fearlessness** *n.*

fearsome *adj.* appalling or frightening. □ **fearsomely** *adv.* **fearsomeness** *n.*

feasible *adj.* **1** practicable, possible. **2** *disp.* likely, probable (*it is feasible that it will rain*). [based on Latin *facere* 'to do, make'] □ **feasibility** *n.* **feasibly** *adv.*

■ **Usage** The use of *feasible* in sense 2 to mean 'possible' or 'probable' in the sense 'likely' is considered incorrect by many people. *Possible* or *probable* should be used instead.

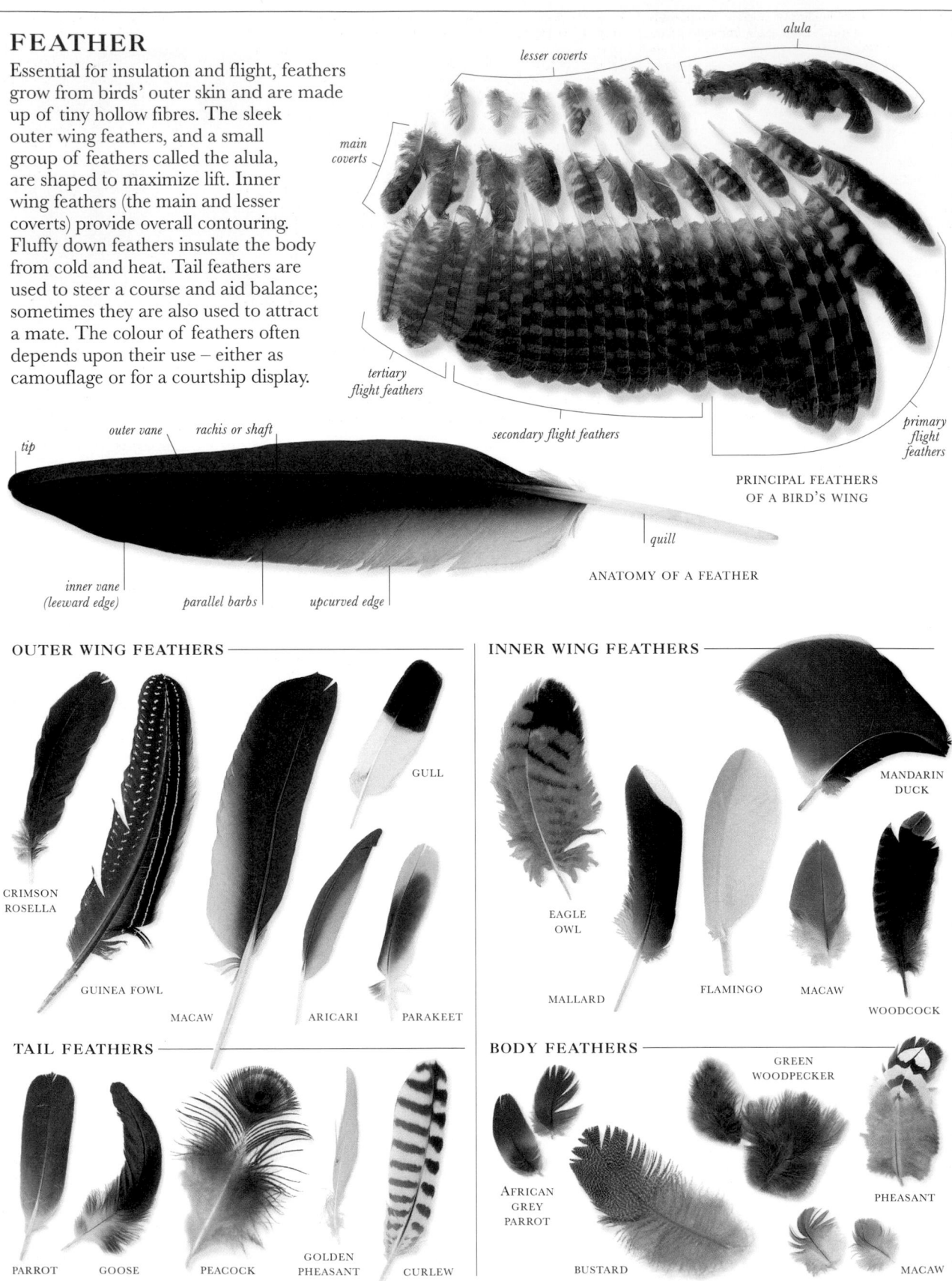

FEATHER

Essential for insulation and flight, feathers grow from birds' outer skin and are made up of tiny hollow fibres. The sleek outer wing feathers, and a small group of feathers called the alula, are shaped to maximize lift. Inner wing feathers (the main and lesser coverts) provide overall contouring. Fluffy down feathers insulate the body from cold and heat. Tail feathers are used to steer a course and aid balance; sometimes they are also used to attract a mate. The colour of feathers often depends upon their use – either as camouflage or for a courtship display.

F

alula

lesser coverts

main coverts

tertiary flight feathers

secondary flight feathers

primary flight feathers

PRINCIPAL FEATHERS OF A BIRD'S WING

tip

outer vane

rachis or shaft

inner vane (leeward edge)

parallel barbs

upcurved edge

quill

ANATOMY OF A FEATHER

OUTER WING FEATHERS

CRIMSON ROSELLA

GUINEA FOWL

MACAW

GULL

ARICARI

PARAKEET

INNER WING FEATHERS

EAGLE OWL

MALLARD

FLAMINGO

MANDARIN DUCK

MACAW

WOODCOCK

TAIL FEATHERS

PARROT

GOOSE

PEACOCK

GOLDEN PHEASANT

CURLEW

BODY FEATHERS

GREEN WOODPECKER

AFRICAN GREY PARROT

BUSTARD

PHEASANT

MACAW

feast ● *n.* **1** a large or sumptuous meal. **2** a gratification to the senses or mind. **3** a religious celebration. ● *v.* **1** *intr.* partake of a feast; eat and drink sumptuously. **2** *tr.* regale. □ **feast one's eyes on** take pleasure in beholding. [based on Latin *festus* 'joyous'] □ **feaster** *n.*

feast of Tabernacles *n.* = SUCCOTH.

feat *n.* a noteworthy act or achievement. [from Old French *fait, fet*, related to FACT]

feather ● *n.* **1** ◄ any of the appendages growing from a bird's skin, with a horny hollow stem and fine strands. **2** one or more of these as decoration etc. **3** (*collect.*) **a** plumage. **b** game birds. ● *v.tr.* **1** cover or line with feathers. **2** *Rowing* turn (an oar) so that it passes through the air edgeways. **3** *Aeron.* & *Naut.* cause (blades) to rotate in such a way as to lessen the air or water resistance. □ **a feather in one's cap** an achievement to one's credit. **feather one's nest** enrich oneself. **in fine** (or **high**) **feather** in good spirits. [Old English] □ **feathered** *adj.* (also in *comb.*). **featheriness** *n.* **featherless** *adj.* **feathery** *adj.*

feather bed ● *n.* a bed with a mattress stuffed with feathers. ● *v.tr.* (**feather-bed**) (**-bedded, -bedding**) provide with (esp. financial) advantages.

feather-bedding *n.* making or being made comfortable by favourable economic treatment.

feather-brain *n.* (also **feather-head**) a silly or absent-minded person. □ **feather-brained** *adj.* (also **feather-headed**).

feathering *n.* **1** bird's plumage. **2** the feathers of an arrow. **3** a feather-like structure in an animal's coat. **4** *Archit.* cusps in tracery.

featherweight *n.* **1 a** a weight in certain sports intermediate between bantamweight and lightweight. **b** a boxer etc. of this weight. **2** a very light person or thing. **3** (usu. *attrib.*) an unimportant thing.

feature ● *n.* **1** a distinctive or characteristic part of a thing. **2** (usu. in *pl.*) a distinctive part of the face. **3** a distinctive or regular article in a newspaper or magazine. **4 a** (in full **feature film**) a full-length film intended as the main item in a cinema programme. **b** (in full **feature programme**) a broadcast devoted to a particular topic. ● *v.* **1** *tr.* make a special display or attraction of; give special prominence to. **2** *tr.* & *intr.* have as or be an important actor, participant, or topic in a film, broadcast, etc. **3** *intr.* be a feature. [from Latin *factura* 'formation'] □ **featured** *adj.* (also in *comb.*). **featureless** *adj.*

Feb. *abbr.* February.

febrifuge /**feb**-ri-fewj/ *n.* a medicine or treatment that reduces fever; a cooling drink. [based on Latin *febris* 'fever']

febrile /**fee**-bryl/ *adj.* of or relating to fever; feverish. [based on Latin *febris* 'fever'] □ **febrility** *n.*

February *n.* (*pl.* **-ies**) the second month of the year. [based on Latin *februa*, name of a purification feast held in this month]

feces *US* var. of FAECES.

feckless *adj.* **1** feeble, ineffective. **2** unthinking, irresponsible (*feckless gaiety*). [Scots *feck* from *effeck*, variant of EFFECT] □ **fecklessly** *adv.* **fecklessness** *n.*

fecund *adj.* **1** prolific, fertile. **2** fertilizing. [from Latin *fecundus*] □ **fecundity** *n.*

fecundate *v.tr.* **1** make fruitful. **2** = FERTILIZE 2. □ **fecundation** *n.*

fed *past* and *past part.* of FEED.

federal *adj.* **1** of a system of government in which several states form a unity but remain independent in internal affairs. **2** relating to or affecting such a federation. **3** of or relating to the central government (*federal laws*). **4** (also **Federal**) favouring centralized government. **5** (**Federal**) *US* of the Northern States in the Civil War. [based on Latin *foedus -eris* 'league, covenant'] □ **federalism** *n.* **federalist** *n.* **federalize** *v.tr.* (also **-ise**). **federalization** *n.* **federally** *adv.*

federate ● *v.tr.* & *intr.* organize or be organized on a federal basis. ● *adj.* having a federal organization. □ **federative** *adj.*

federation *n.* **1** a federal group of states. **2** a federated society or group. **3** the act or an instance of federating.

fedora /fi-**dor**-ă/ *n.* a low soft felt hat with a crown creased lengthways. [from *Fédora*, title of a drama by V. Sardou]

fed up *adj.* (also **fed to death**) (often foll. by *with*; hyphenated when *attrib.*) discontented or bored, esp. from a surfeit of something (*am fed up with the rain*; *fed-up commuters*).

fee *n.* **1** a payment made to a professional person or to a professional or public body in exchange for advice or services. **2** money paid as part of a special transaction, for a privilege, admission to a society, etc. (*enrolment fee*). **3** (in *pl.*) money regularly paid for continuing services. **4** *Law* an inherited estate, unlimited (**fee simple**) or limited (**fee tail**) as to the category of heir. [from medieval Latin *feodum, feudum*]

feeble *adj.* (**feebler, feeblest**) **1** weak, infirm. **2** lacking energy, force, or effectiveness. **3** dim, indistinct. **4** deficient in character or intelligence. [from Latin *flebilis* 'lamentable'] □ **feebleness** *n.* **feebly** *adv.*

feeble-minded *adj.* **1** unintelligent. **2** mentally deficient. □ **feeble-mindedly** *adv.* **feeble-mindedness** *n.*

feed ● *v.* (*past* and *past part.* **fed**) **1** *tr.* **a** supply with food. **b** put food into the mouth of. **2** *tr.* **a** give as food, esp. to animals. **b** graze (cattle). **3** *tr.* serve as food for. **4** *intr.* (usu. foll. by *on*) take food; eat. **5** *tr.* nourish; make grow. **6 a** *tr.* maintain supply of raw material, fuel, etc., to (a fire, machine, etc.). **b** *tr.* (foll. by *into*) supply (material) to a machine etc. **c** *intr.* (of a river etc.) flow into another body of water. **d** *tr.* insert further coins into (a meter) to continue its function, validity, etc. **7** *intr.* (foll. by *on*) **a** be nourished by. **b** derive benefit from. **8** *tr.* use (land) as pasture. **9** *tr.* *Theatr. slang* supply (an actor etc.) with cues. **10** *tr.* *Sport* send passes to (a player) in a ball game. **11** *tr.* provide (advice, information, etc.) to. ● *n.* **1** an amount of food, esp. for animals or *Brit.* infants. **2** the act or an instance of feeding; the giving of food. **3** *colloq.* a meal. **4** pasturage; green crops. **5 a** a supply of raw material to a machine etc. **b** the provision of this or a device for it. **6** the charge of a gun. **7** *Theatr. slang* an actor who supplies another with cues. □ **feed back** produce feedback. **feed up 1** fatten. **2** satiate (cf. FED UP). [Old English]

feedback *n.* **1** information about the result of an experiment etc.; response. **2** *Electronics* **a** the return of a fraction of the output signal from one stage of a circuit, amplifier, etc., to the input of the same or a preceding stage. **b** a signal so returned. **3** *Biol.* etc. the modification or control of a process or system by its results or effects.

feeder *n.* **1** a person or thing that feeds. **2** a person who eats in a specified manner. **3** *Brit.* a feeding bottle. **4** *Brit.* a bib. **5** a tributary stream. **6** a branch road, railway line, etc., linking outlying districts with a main communication system. **7** *Electr.* a main carrying electricity to a distribution point. **8** a feeding apparatus in a machine.

feeding bottle *n.* *Brit.* a bottle with a teat for feeding infants.

feedstuff *n.* fodder.

feel ● *v.* (*past* and *past part.* **felt**) **1** *tr.* **a** examine or search by touch. **b** (*absol.*) have the sensation of touch (*was unable to feel*). **2** *tr.* perceive or ascertain by touch (*could feel the warmth*; *felt that it was cold*). **3** *tr.* **a** undergo, experience (*shall feel my anger*). **b** exhibit or be conscious of (an emotion, sensation, conviction, etc.). **4 a** *intr.* have a specified feeling or reaction (*felt strongly about it*). **b** *tr.* be emotionally affected by (*felt the rebuke deeply*). **5** *tr.* (foll. by *that* + clause) have a vague or unreasoned impression (*I feel that I am right*). **6** *tr.* consider, think (*I feel it useful to go*). **7** *intr.* seem (*the air feels chilly*). **8** *intr.* be consciously; consider oneself (*I feel happy*; *do not feel well*). **9** *intr.* **a** (foll. by *with*) *Brit.* have sympathy with. **b** (foll. by *for*) have pity or compassion for. **10** *tr.* (often foll. by *up*) *slang* fondle clumsily for sexual gratification. ● *n.* **1** the act or an instance of feeling; testing by touch. **2** the sensation characterizing a material, situation, etc. **3** the sense of touch. □ **feel like** have a wish for; be inclined towards. **feel oneself** be fit or confident etc. **feel out** investigate cautiously. **feel strange** see STRANGE. **feel up to** be ready to face or deal with. **feel one's way** proceed carefully; act cautiously. **get the feel of** become accustomed to using. **make one's influence** (or **presence etc.**) **felt** assert one's influence; make others aware of one's presence etc. [Old English]

feeler *n.* **1** an organ in certain animals for touching or searching for food. **2** a tentative proposal (*put out feelers*). **3** a person or thing that feels.

feel-good *attrib.adj.* that creates a feeling of well-being in people (*a feel-good film*).

feeling ● *n.* **1 a** the capacity to feel; a sense of touch (*lost all feeling in his arm*). **b** a physical sensation. **2 a** a particular emotional reaction (*a feeling of despair*). **b** (in *pl.*) emotional susceptibilities (*hurt my feelings*; *had strong feelings about it*). **3** a particular sensitivity (*had a feeling for literature*). **4 a** an opinion or notion, esp. a vague or irrational one (*had a feeling she would be there*). **b** vague awareness (*had a feeling of safety*). **c** sentiment (*the general feeling was against it*). **5** readiness to feel sympathy or compassion. **6 a** the general emotional response produced by a work of art, piece of music, etc. **b** emotional commitment or sensibility in artistic execution (*played with feeling*). ● *adj.* **1** sensitive, sympathetic. **2** showing emotion or sensitivity. □ **feelingless** *adj.* **feelingly** *adv.*

F

feet *pl.* of FOOT.

feign /fayn/ *v.* **1** *tr.* simulate; pretend to be affected by (*feign madness*). **2** *intr.* indulge in pretence. [from Latin *fingere* 'to mould, contrive']

feint[1] /faynt/ ● *n.* **1** a sham attack or blow etc. **2** pretence. ● *v.intr.* make a feint. [from French *feinte* (fem.) 'feigned']

feint[2] /faynt/ *adj.* esp. *Printing* designating faint lines ruled on paper as a guide for handwriting. [from Old French, literally 'feigned']

feisty /**fys**-ti/ *adj.* (**feistier, feistiest**) *N. Amer. colloq.* **1** aggressive, spirited, exuberant. **2** touchy. [from obsolete *feist* 'small dog'] □ **feistily** *adv.* **feistiness** *n.*

felafel /fel-**ah**-fĕl/ *n.* (also **falafel**) a spicy Middle Eastern dish of fried rissoles made from mashed chickpeas or beans. [from Arabic *falāfil*]

feldspar *n.* (also **felspar**) *Mineral.* ▼ any of a group of aluminosilicates of potassium, sodium, or calcium. ▷ AGGREGATE. [from German *Feldspat, -spath*, literally 'field spar'] □ **feldspathic** *adj.* **feldspathoid** *adj.*

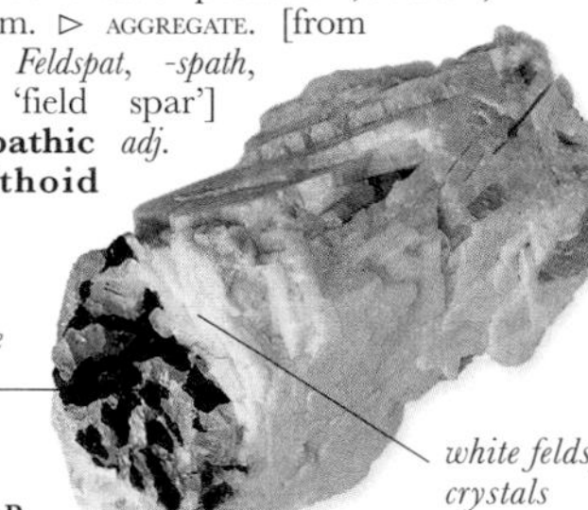

amphibole crystals

white feldspar crystals

FELDSPAR

felicitate *v.tr.* congratulate. [based on Latin *felicitatus* 'made happy'] □ **felicitation** *n.* (usu. in *pl.*).

felicitous *adj.* strikingly apt; pleasantly ingenious. □ **felicitously** *adv.*

felicity *n.* (*pl.* **-ies**) **1** intense happiness. **2** a cause of happiness. **3 a** a capacity for apt expression. **b** a well-chosen phrase. [from Latin *felicitas* 'happiness']

feline ● *adj.* **1** of or relating to the cat family. **2** catlike. ● *n.* an animal of the cat family Felidae. [from Latin *felinus*] □ **felinity** *n.*

fell[1] *past* of FALL *v.*

fell[2] *v.tr.* **1** cut down (esp. a tree). **2** strike or knock down (a person or animal). **3** stitch down (the edge of a seam) to lie flat. [Old English] □ **feller** *n.*

F

fell[3] *n. N.Engl.* **1** a hill. **2** a stretch of hills or moorland. [from Old Norse]

fell[4] *adj. poet.* or *literary* **1** fierce, ruthless. **2** terrible, destructive. □ **at** (or **in**) **one fell swoop** in a single action. [from Old French, related to FELON]

fell[5] *n.* an animal's hide or skin with its hair.

fellatio /fi-**lay**-shee-oh/ *n.* oral stimulation of the penis. [based on Latin *fellare* 'to suck'] □ **fellate** *v.tr.*

feller *n. colloq.* = FELLOW 1, 2 (see also FELL[2].)

fellow *n.* **1** *colloq.* a man or boy (*poor fellow!; my dear fellow*). **2** *derog.* a person regarded with contempt. **3** (usu. in *pl.*) a comrade (*were separated from their fellows*). **4** a counterpart; the other of a pair. **5** an equal; one of the same class. **6** a contemporary. **7 a** *Brit.* an incorporated senior member of a college. **b** an elected graduate receiving a stipend for a period of research. **c** a member of the governing body in some universities. **8** a member of a learned society. **9** (*attrib.*) belonging to the same class or activity (*fellow soldier*). [based on Old Norse, originally one who laid out money in a partnership]

fellow feeling *n.* sympathy from common experience.

fellowship *n.* **1** companionship, friendliness. **2** participation, sharing; community of interest. **3** a body of associates. **4** a brotherhood or fraternity. **5** the status or emoluments of a fellow of a college or society.

fellow-traveller *n.* **1** a person who travels with another. **2** a sympathizer with the Communist Party.

felon *n.* a person who has committed a felony. [from medieval Latin *felo -onis*]

felonious *adj.* **1** criminal. **2** *Law* **a** of or involving felony. **b** who has committed felony. □ **feloniously** *adv.*

felony *n.* (*pl.* **-ies**) a serious crime.

felspar var. of FELDSPAR.

felt[1] ● *n.* **1** a kind of cloth made by rolling and pressing wool etc., or by weaving and shrinking it. **2** a similar material made from other fibres. ● *v.* **1** *tr.* make into felt; mat together. **2** *tr.* cover with felt. **3** *intr.* become matted. [Old English] □ **felty** *adj.*

felt[2] *past* and *past part.* of FEEL.

felt-tip pen *n.* (also **felt-tipped pen, felt tip**) a pen with a writing point made of felt or fibre.

felucca *n.* a small Mediterranean coasting vessel with oars or lateen sails or both. [from Arabic]

female ● *adj.* **1** of the sex that can bear offspring or produce eggs. **2** (of plants or their parts) fruit-bearing. **3** of or consisting of women or female animals or female plants. **4** (of a screw, socket, etc.) hollow to receive a corresponding inserted part. *n.* a female person, animal, or plant. [from Latin *femella*] □ **femaleness** *n.*

female condom see CONDOM.

feminine ● *adj.* **1** of or characteristic of women. **2** having qualities associated with women. **3** womanly, effeminate. **4** *Gram.* of or denoting the gender proper to words or grammatical forms classified as female. ● *n. Gram.* a feminine gender or word. [based on Latin *femina* 'woman'] □ **femininely** *adv.* **feminineness** *n.* **femininity** *n.*

feminism *n.* the advocacy of women's rights on the ground of the equality of the sexes. □ **feminist** *n. & adj.*

feminity *n.* = FEMININITY (see FEMININE).

feminize *v.tr. & intr.* (also **-ise**) make or become feminine or female. □ **feminization** *n.*

femme fatale /fam fă-**tahl**/ *n.* (*pl.* **femmes fatales** *pronunc.* same) a seductively attractive woman. [French, literally 'deadly woman']

femto- *comb. form* denoting a factor of 10^{-15} (*femtometre*).

femur /**fee**-mer/ *n.* (*pl.* **femurs** or **femora** /**fem**-ŏ-ră/) *Anat.* ◄ the thigh bone, the thick bone between the hip and the knee. ▷ HIP JOINT, SKELETON. [Latin, literally 'thigh'] □ **femoral** *adj.*

fen *n.* **1** a low marshy area of land. **2** (**the Fens**) flat low-lying areas in and around Cambridgeshire. [Old English]

fence ● *n.* **1** a barrier or railing or other upright structure enclosing an area of ground, esp. to prevent or control access. **2** a large upright obstacle in steeplechasing or showjumping. ▷ SHOW-JUMPING. **3** *slang* a receiver of stolen goods. **4** a guard or guide in machinery. ● *v.* **1** *tr.* surround with or as with a fence. **2** *tr.* **a** (foll. by *in, off*) enclose or separate with or as with a fence. **b** (foll. by *up*) seal with or as with a fence. **3** *tr.* (foll. by *from, against*) screen, shield, protect. **4** *tr.* (foll. by *out*) exclude with or as with a fence. **5** *tr.* (also *absol.*) *slang* deal in (stolen goods). **6** *intr.* practise the sport of fencing. **7** *intr.* (foll. by *with*) evade answering (a person or question). **8** *intr.* (of a horse etc.) leap fences. □ **sit on the fence** remain neutral or undecided in a dispute etc. [Middle English from DEFENCE] □ **fencer** *n.*

FEMUR:
HUMAN UPPER
LEG SHOWING
THE FEMUR

femur

FERMENTATION

Food and drinks such as bread, soy sauce, beer, and wine are produced by the process of fermentation. Yeasts are used as biological catalysts to break down starch or sugar in the ingredients to produce carbon dioxide and ethanol. Carbon dioxide makes bread rise while ethanol forms part of beer and wine.

airlock

demijohn

fermenting mixture of grape juice, sugar, and yeast

FERMENTATION
OF WINE

fencing *n.* **1** a set or extent of fences. **2** material for making fences. **3** ▼ the art or sport of swordplay.

fend *v.* **1** *intr.* (foll. by *for*) look after (esp. oneself). **2** *tr.* (usu. foll. by *off*) ward off. [from DEFEND]

fender *n.* **1** a low frame bordering a fireplace. **2** *Naut.* padding protecting a ship against impact. **3** *N. Amer.* a vehicle's bumper.

fenestration *n.* **1** *Archit.* ◄ the arrangement of windows in a building. **2** *Surgery* an operation in which a new opening is formed, esp. in the bony labyrinth of the inner ear, as a form of treatment in some cases of deafness. [based on Latin *fenestra* 'window']

feng shui *n.* (in Chinese thought) a system of good and evil influences in the natural surroundings, considered when siting and designing buildings etc. [Chinese, from *feng* 'wind' + *shui* 'water']

FENESTRATION: TIERED FENESTRATION IN A GERMAN TOWN HOUSE

fennec *n.* ▼ a small fox, *Vulpes zerda*, native to N. Africa and Arabia, having large pointed ears. [from Arabic *fanak*]

fennel *n.* **1** a yellow-flowered herb, *Foeniculum vulgare*, with fragrant seeds and fine leaves used as flavourings. ▷ HERB. **2** the seeds of this. **3** (in full **Florence** or **sweet fennel**) a variety of this with swollen leaf-bases eaten as a vegetable. [based on Latin *fenum* 'hay']

FENNEC
(*Vulpes zerda*)

fenugreek *n.* **1** a leguminous plant, *Trigonella foenum-graecum*, with aromatic seeds. **2** these seeds used as flavouring, esp. ground and used in curry powder. [from Latin *fenum graecum* 'Greek hay']

feral *adj.* **1** (esp. of an animal or animal population) in a wild state after escape from captivity or domestication. **2** savage, brutal. **3** untamed, uncultivated. [from Latin *ferus* 'wild']

ferment ● *n.* /**fer**-ment/ **1** agitation, excitement, tumult. **2 a** fermenting, fermentation. **b** a fermenting agent. ● *v.* /fer-**ment**/ **1** *intr. & tr.* undergo or subject to fermentation. **2** *intr. & tr.* effervesce or

FENCING

The sport of fencing developed from traditional swordsmanship, and was one of the events included in the first modern Olympic Games in 1896. Competition bouts take place within a restricted area 14 m (46 ft) long by 2 m (6 ft) wide, using three types of regulation-length sword: the sabre, the foil, and the épée. Points are awarded for hits to specific target areas on the body. In the modern sport, these are registered electronically. Protective jackets, masks, and gloves are essential for the competitors' safety.

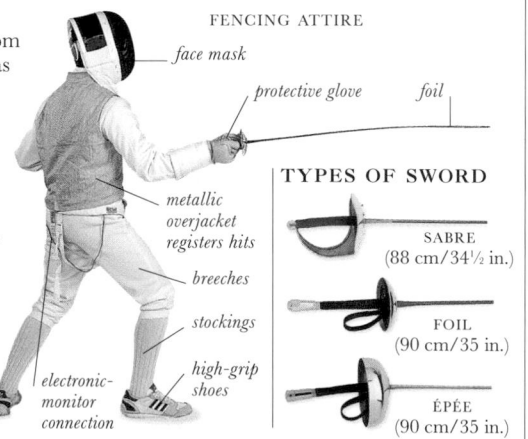

FENCING ATTIRE

face mask

protective glove

foil

metallic overjacket registers hits

breeches

stockings

high-grip shoes

electronic-monitor connection

TYPES OF SWORD

SABRE
(88 cm/34½ in.)

FOIL
(90 cm/35 in.)

ÉPÉE
(90 cm/35 in.)

cause to effervesce. **3** *tr.* excite; stir up. [from Latin *fermentum*] □ **fermentable** *adj.* **fermenter** *n.*

fermentation *n.* **1** ◀ the breakdown of a substance by micro-organisms, such as yeasts and bacteria, esp. of sugar to ethyl alcohol in making beers, wines, and spirits. **2** agitation, excitement. □ **fermentative** *adj.*

fermium *n. Chem.* an artificially produced transuranic radioactive metallic element. [named after E. *Fermi*, Italian-American physicist, 1901–54]

fern *n.* (*pl.* same or **ferns**) ▶ any flowerless plant of the order Filicopsida, usu. having feathery fronds. [Old English] □ **fernery** *n.* (*pl.* **-ies**) **ferny** *adj.*

ferocious *adj.* fierce, savage; wildly cruel. [from Latin *ferox -ocis*] □ **ferociously** *adv.* **ferociousness** *n.*

ferocity *n.* (*pl.* **-ies**) **1** ferocious nature; the state of being ferocious. **2** a ferocious act.

-ferous *comb. form* (usu. **-iferous**) forming adjectives with the sense 'bearing', 'having' (*auriferous*; *odoriferous*). [based on Latin *ferre* 'to bear'] □ **-ferously** *comb. form* forming adverbs. **-ferousness** *comb. form* forming nouns.

ferrate *n. Chem.* a salt in which the anion contains both iron (esp. in the trivalent form) and oxygen. [based on Latin *ferrum* 'iron']

ferrel var. of FERRULE.

ferret ● *n.* a small polecat, *Mustela putorius furo*, used in catching rabbits, rats, etc. ● *v.* (**ferreted**, **ferreting**) **1** *intr.* hunt with ferrets. **2** *intr.* rummage; search about. **3** *tr.* **a** clear out (holes or an area of ground) with ferrets. **b** take or drive away (rabbits etc.) with ferrets. **4** *tr.* (foll. by *out*) search out (secrets etc.). [based on Latin *fur* 'thief'] □ **ferreter** *n.* **ferrety** *adj.*

ferric *adj.* **1** of iron. **2** *Chem.* containing iron in a trivalent form (cf. FERROUS *adj.* 2).

Ferris wheel *n.* ▶ a fairground ride consisting of a giant revolving vertical wheel with passenger cars suspended on its outer edge. [named after G. W. G. *Ferris*, American engineer, 1859–96]

ferrite *n. Chem.* **1** a salt in which the anion contains both divalent iron and oxygen. **2** an allotrope of pure iron occurring in low-carbon steel. □ **ferritic** *adj.*

ferro- *comb. form Chem.* **1** iron, esp. in ferrous compounds (*ferrocyanide*). **2** (of alloys) containing iron (*ferromanganese*). [from Latin *ferrum* 'iron']

ferroconcrete ● *n.* concrete reinforced with steel ● *adj.* made of reinforced concrete.

ferroelectric *Physics* ● *adj.* exhibiting permanent electric polarization which varies in strength with the applied electric field. ● *n.* a ferroelectric substance. □ **ferroelectricity** *n.*

ferromagnetism *n. Physics* a phenomenon in which a material has a high susceptibility to magnetization, the strength of which varies with the applied magnetizing field, and which may persist after removal of the applied field. □ **ferromagnetic** *adj.*

ferrous *adj.* **1** containing iron. **2** *Chem.* containing iron in a divalent form (cf. FERRIC *adj.* 2). [based on Latin *ferrum* 'iron']

ferrule *n.* (also **ferrel**) a ring or cap strengthening the end of a stick or tube. [from Latin *viriola* 'little bracelet', assimilated to *ferrum* 'iron']

ferry ● *n.* (*pl.* **-ies**) **1** ▼ a boat or aircraft etc. for conveying passengers and goods as a regular service. **2** the service itself or the place where it

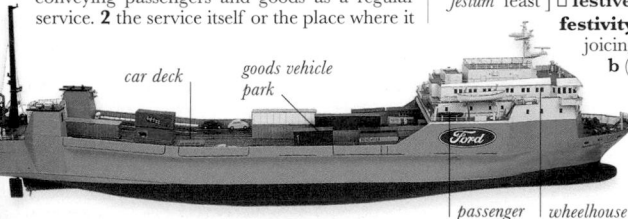

FERRY: MODERN CARGO AND PASSENGER FERRY

car deck / *goods vehicle park* / *passenger lounge* / *wheelhouse*

FERN

A mature fern plant, or sporophyte, typically has divided fronds. Reproductive structures (sori) form on the fronds' undersides and liberate spores into the air. The shed spores develop into gametophytes – simplified plants that produce male and female cells. Following fertilization, these give rise to new sporophytes.

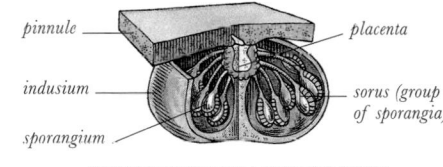
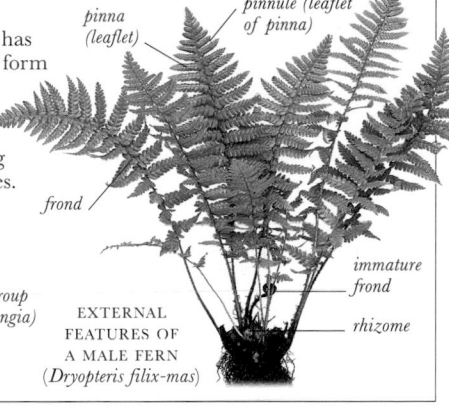

pinna (leaflet) · *pinnule (leaflet of pinna)* · *frond* · *immature frond* · *rhizome*

pinnule · *placenta* · *indusium* · *sorus (group of sporangia)* · *sporangium*

SECTION THROUGH A MATURE SORUS

EXTERNAL FEATURES OF A MALE FERN (*Dryopteris filix-mas*)

F

---

operates. ● *v.tr.* (**-ies**, **-ied**) **1** convey in a boat etc. across water. **2** transport from one place to another, esp. as a regular service. [from Old Norse *ferja*] □ **ferryman** *n.* (*pl.* **-men**)

fertile *adj.* **1 a** (of soil) producing abundant vegetation or crops. **b** fruitful. **2 a** (of a seed, egg, etc.) capable of becoming a new individual. **b** (of animals and plants) able to conceive young or produce fruit. **3** (of the mind) inventive. **4** (of nuclear material) able to become fissile by the capture of neutrons. [from Latin *fertilis*] □ **fertility** *n.*

fertilization *n.* (also **-isation**) **1** *Biol.* the fusion of male and female gametes during sexual reproduction to form a zygote. **2 a** ▼ the act or an instance of fertilizing. **b** the process of being fertilized.

fertilize *v.tr.* (also **-ise**) **1** make (soil etc.) fertile or productive. **2** cause (an egg, female animal, or plant) to develop a new individual by introducing male reproductive material.

fertilizer *n.* (also **-iser**) a chemical or natural substance added to soil to make it more fertile.

fervent *adj.* ardent, impassioned, intense. [from Latin *fervent-* 'boiling'] □ **fervency** *n.* **fervently** *adv.*

fervid *adj.* ardent, intense. □ **fervidly** *adv.*

fervour *n.* (*US* **fervor**) vehemence, passion, zeal. [Middle English, related to FERVENT]

fescue *n.* any fine-leaved grass of the genus *Festuca*, valuable for pasture and fodder. [from Latin *festuca* 'stalk, straw']

festal *adj.* **1** joyous, merry. **2** of a feast. □ **festally** *adv.*

fester *v.* **1** *tr. & intr.* make or become septic. **2** *intr.* cause continuing annoyance. **3** *intr.* rot, stagnate. [based on Latin *fistula* 'pipe, canal']

festival *n.* (also *attrib.*) **1** a day or period of celebration. **2** a concentrated series of concerts, plays, etc., held regularly in a town etc. [related to FEAST]

festival of lights *n.* **1** = HANUKKAH. **2** = DIWALI.

festive *adj.* **1** of or characteristic of a festival. **2** cheerful, joyous, celebratory. [based on Latin *festum* 'feast'] □ **festively** *adv.* **festiveness** *n.*

festivity *n.* (*pl.* **-ies**) **1** gaiety, rejoicing. **2 a** a festive celebration. **b** (in *pl.*) festive proceedings.

festoon ● *n.* **1** a chain of flowers, leaves, ribbons, etc., hung in a curve as a decoration. **2** a carved or moulded ornament representing this. ▷ FAÇADE, SHAKO. ● *v.tr.* (often foll. by *with*) adorn with or form into festoons; decorate elaborately. [from Italian *festone* 'festal ornament'] □ **festoonery** *n.*

Festschrift *n.* (also **festschrift**) (*pl.* **-schriften** or **-schrifts**) a collection of writings published in honour of a scholar. [German, literally 'celebration writing']

feta /fet-ă/ *n.* (also **fetta**) a white ewe's-milk or goat's-milk cheese made esp. in Greece. ▷ CHEESE. [modern Greek]

fetch ● *v.tr.* **1** go for and bring back (a person or thing) (*fetch a doctor*). **2** cause to come (*the thought of food fetched him*). **3** cause (blood, tears, a sigh) to come out. **4** draw (breath). **5** *colloq.* give (a blow, slap, etc.) (usu. with recipient stated: *fetched him a slap on the face*). **6** be sold for; realize (a price) (*fetched £10*). ● *n.* an act of fetching. □ **fetch and carry** run backwards and forwards with things, be a mere servant. **fetch up 1** arrive, come to rest. **2** *Brit.* vomit. [Old English]

fetching *adj.* attractive. □ **fetchingly** *adv.*

fête /fayt/ ● *n.* **1** *Brit.* an outdoor function with the sale of goods, amusements, etc., esp. to raise funds for a charity or cause. **2** a festival. ● *v.tr.* honour or entertain lavishly. [French]

fetid *adj.* (also **foetid**) stinking. [from Latin *fetidus*] □ **fetidly** *adv.* **fetidness** *n.*

fetish *n.* **1** *Psychol.* a thing abnormally stimulating or attracting sexual desire. **2 a** an object worshipped by primitive peoples. **b** a thing evoking irrational devotion or respect. [based on Latin *factitius* 'factitious'] □ **fetishism** *n.* **fetishist** *n.* **fetishistic** *adj.*

FERTILIZATION

Human fertilization begins when a sperm penetrates the corona radiata surrounding the ovum. A chemical change is then triggered, preventing the entry of other sperms. The sperm's flagellum is discarded, while its head, containing the nucleus and genetic material, continues towards the centre of the ovum.

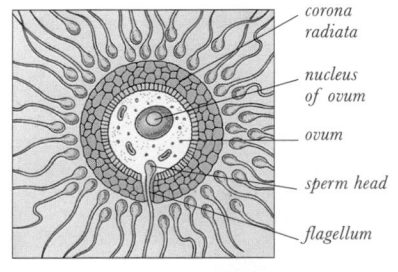

corona radiata · *nucleus of ovum* · *ovum* · *sperm head* · *flagellum*

HUMAN SPERM ENTERING THE OVUM

F

cannon-bone

fetlock

pastern

FETLOCK

fetlock *n.* ◄ the part of a horse's leg between the cannonbone and the pastern, where a tuft of hair often grows. ▷ HORSE. [related to German *Fessel* 'fetlock']

fetor *n.* a stench. [Latin (as FETID)]

fetta var. of FETA.

fetter ● *n.* **1** ▶ a shackle for holding a prisoner by the ankles. **2** (in *pl.*) captivity. **3** a restraint. ● *v.tr.* **1** put into fetters. **2** restrict, impede. [Old English]

fettle *n.* condition or trim (*in fine fettle*). [Old English]

fettuccine /fet-oo-**chee**-ni/ *n.* (also **fettucini**) pasta made in ribbons. [Italian, literally 'little ribbons']

fetus *US & Med.* var. of FOETUS.

feu /few/ *Sc.* ● *n.* **1** a perpetual lease at a fixed rent. **2** a piece of land so held. ● *v.tr.* (**feus, feued, feuing**) grant (land) on feu. [from Old French, variant of *fee* 'fief']

feud ● *n.* **1** a state of prolonged mutual hostility, esp. between two families, tribes, etc. **2** a prolonged or bitter quarrel or dispute. ● *v.intr.* conduct a feud. [from Old French, related to FOE] □ **feudist** *n. US.*

feudal *adj.* of, according to, or resembling the feudal system. □ **feudalism** *n.* **feudalistic** *adj.*

feudal system *n. hist.* the social system in medieval Europe whereby a vassal held land from a superior in exchange for allegiance and service.

fever ● *n.* **1 a** an abnormally high body temperature, often with delirium etc. **b** a disease characterized by this (*scarlet fever; typhoid fever*). **2** nervous excitement; agitation. ● *v.tr.* (esp. as **fevered** *adj.*) affect with fever or excitement. [from Latin *febris*]

feverfew *n.* ▶ an aromatic bushy plant, *Tanacetum parthenium* (daisy family), with feathery leaves and white daisy-like flowers. [based on Latin *febris fugare* 'to put fever to flight']

feverish *adj.* **1** having the symptoms of a fever. **2** excited, fitful, restless. □ **feverishly** *adv.* **feverishness** *n.* **feverous** *adj.*

fever pitch *n.* a state of extreme excitement.

few ● *adj. & det.* **1** not many (*few people came*). **2** (prec. by *a*) a small number of (*a few good restaurants*). ● *pron.* (treated as *pl.*) **1** (prec. by *a*) some but not many (*a few of his friends were there*). **2** a small number, not many (*many are called but few are chosen*). **3** (prec. by *the*) **a** the minority. **b** the elect. □ **every few** once in every small group of (*every few days*). **few and far between** scarce. **no fewer than** as many as (a specified number). [Old English]

■ **Usage** See Usage Note at LESS.

fey /fay/ *adj.* **1 a** strange, other-worldly; whimsical. **b** clairvoyant. **2** *Sc.* fated to die soon. [Old English] □ **feyly** *adv.* **feyness** *n.*

FEZ

fez *n.* (*pl.* **fezzes**) ◄ a flat-topped conical red cap with a tassel, worn by men in some Muslim countries. [Turkish] □ **fezzed** *adj.*

ff *abbr. Mus.* fortissimo.

ff. *abbr.* **1** following pages etc. **2** folios.

fiancé /fee-**ahn**-say/ *n.* (*fem.* **fiancée** *pronunc.* same) a person to whom another is engaged to be married. [French]

fiasco *n.* (*pl.* **-os**) a ludicrous or humiliating failure or breakdown. [Italian, literally 'bottle' (with unexplained allusion)]

fiat /**fy**-at/ *n.* **1** an authorization. **2** a decree. [Latin, literally 'let it be done']

fib ● *n.* a trivial or venial lie. ● *v.intr.* (**fibbed, fibbing**) tell a fib. □ **fibber** *n.*

fiber *US* var. of FIBRE.

fiberboard *US* var. of FIBREBOARD.

fiberglass *US* var. of FIBREGLASS.

Fibonacci series /fib-ŏn-**ah**-chi/ *n. Math.* a series of numbers in which each number (**Fibonacci number**) is the sum of the two preceding numbers, esp. 1, 1, 2, 3, 5, 8, etc. [named after L. *Fibonacci*, Italian mathematician]

fibre *n.* (*US* **fiber**) **1** any of the threads or filaments forming animal or vegetable tissue and textile substances. **2** a piece of glass in the form of a thread. **3 a** a substance formed of fibres. **b** a substance that can be spun, woven, or felted. **4** the structure or character of something (*lacks moral fibre*). **5** roughage in food. [from Latin *fibra*] □ **fibred** *adj.* (also in *comb.*). **fibreless** *adj.* **fibriform** *adj.*

fibreboard *n.* (*US* **fiberboard**) a building material made of wood or other plant fibres compressed into boards.

fibreglass *n.* (*US* **fiberglass**) **1** a textile fabric made from woven glass fibres. **2** ▶ a plastic reinforced by glass fibres.

fibre optics *n.* (treated as *sing.*) the use of thin flexible fibres of glass or other transparent solids to transmit light signals, e.g. for telecommunications or internal inspection of the body. □ **fibre-optic** *adj.*

fibril /**fy**-bril/ *n.* **1** a small fibre. **2** a subdivision of a fibre. [from modern Latin *fibrilla* 'little fibre'] □ **fibrillar** *adj.* **fibrillary** *adj.*

fibroblast *n. Anat.* a cell producing collagen fibres in connective tissue.

fibroid *adj.* **1** of or characterized by fibrous tissue. **2** resembling or containing fibres. ● *n.* a benign tumour in the wall of the womb.

fibrosis *n. Med.* a thickening and scarring of connective tissue, usu. as a result of injury. [modern Latin, based on *fibra* 'fibre'] □ **fibrotic** *adj.*

fibrositis *n.* inflammation of fibrous connective tissue, usu. rheumatic and painful. □ **fibrositic** *adj.*

fibrous *adj.* consisting of or like fibres. □ **fibrousness** *n.*

fibula *n.* (*pl.* **fibulae** /-lee/ or **fibulas**) *Anat.* ▶ the smaller and outer of the two bones between the knee and the ankle in terrestrial vertebrates. ▷ SKELETON. [Latin, perhaps related to *figere* 'fix'] □ **fibular** *adj.*

fiche /feesh/ *n.* (*pl.* same or **fiches**) a microfiche. [French, literally 'slip of paper']

fickle *adj.* inconstant, changeable, esp. in loyalty. [Old English] □ **fickleness** *n.* **fickly** *adv.*

fiction *n.* **1** an invented idea or statement or narrative. **2** literature, esp. novels, describing imaginary events and people. **3** a conventionally accepted falsehood (*polite fiction*). [from Latin *fictio*] □ **fictional** *adj.* **fictionality** *n.* **fictionalize** *v.tr.* (also **-ise**). **fictionalization** *n.* **fictionally** *adv.* **fictionist** *n.*

fictitious *adj.* **1** imaginary, unreal. **2** counterfeit; not genuine. [based on Latin *fingere fict-* 'to fashion'] □ **fictitiously** *adv.* **fictitiousness** *n.*

fictive *adj.* **1** creating or created by imagination. **2** not genuine. □ **fictiveness** *n.*

ficus *n.* a tree or shrub of the large genus *Ficus* (mulberry family), including the fig and the rubber plant. [Latin, literally 'fig, fig tree']

fiddle ● *n.* **1** *colloq.* or *derog.* a stringed instrument played with a bow, esp. a violin. **2** *Brit. colloq.* an instance of cheating or fraud. **3** a fiddly task. ● *v.* **1** *intr.* **a** (often foll. by *with, at*) play restlessly. **b** (often foll. by *about*) move aimlessly. **c** act idly or frivolously. **d** (usu. foll. by *with*) make minor adjustments; tinker. **2** *tr. Brit. slang* **a** cheat, swindle. **b** falsify. **c** get by cheating. **3** *intr.* play the fiddle. □ **as fit as a fiddle** in very good health. **on the fiddle** engaged in cheating or swindling. **play second fiddle** take a subordinate role. [Old English]

fiddle-faddle ● *n.* trivial matters. ● *v.intr.* fuss, trifle. ● *int.* nonsense! ● *adj.* (of a person or thing) petty, fussy.

fiddler *n.* **1** a fiddle-player. **2** *Brit. slang* a swindler, a cheat. [Old English]

fiddlesticks *int.* nonsense!

fiddling *adj.* **1 a** petty, trivial. **b** contemptible, futile. **2** *Brit.* = FIDDLY. **3** that fiddles.

fiddly *adj.* (**fiddlier, fiddliest**) *Brit.* intricate, awkward, or tiresome to do or use.

fideism *n.* the doctrine that all or some knowledge depends on faith or revelation. [based on Latin *fides* 'faith'] □ **fideist** *n.* **fideistic** *adj.*

fidelity *n.* **1** (often foll. by *to*) faithfulness, loyalty. **2** strict conformity to truth or fact. **3** exact correspondence to the original. **4** precision in reproduction of sound (*high fidelity*). [from Latin *fidelitas*]

fidget ● *v.intr.* (**fidgeted, fidgeting**) **1** move or act restlessly or nervously, usu. while maintaining basically the same posture. **2** be uneasy, worry. ● *n.* **1** a person who fidgets. **2** (usu. in *pl.*) **a** bodily uneasiness seeking relief in spasmodic movements; such movements. **b** a restless mood. [from obsolete or dialect *fidge* 'to twitch'] □ **fidgety** *adj.* **fidgetiness** *n.*

fiduciary ● *adj.* **1 a** of a trust, trustee, or trusteeship. **b** held or given in trust. **2** (of a paper currency) depending for its value on public confidence or securities. ● *n.* (*pl.* **-ies**) a trustee. [from Latin *fiduciarius*]

fie *int. archaic* expressing disgust, shame, etc. [from Latin *fi*, an exclamation of disgust at a stench]

fief *n.* **1** a piece of land held under the feudal system or in fee. **2** a person's sphere of operation or control. [from (Old) French]

fiefdom *n.* a fief.

field ● *n.* **1** an area of open land, esp. one enclosed and used for pasture or crops. **2** an area rich in some natural product (*gas field; diamond field*). **3** a piece of land used for games etc. (*football field*). **4 a** the participants in a contest or sport. **b** all the competitors in a race or all except those specified. **5** *Cricket* the side fielding. **6** an expanse of ice, snow, sea, sky, etc. **7 a** a battlefield. **b** (*attrib.*) (of artillery etc.) light and mobile for use on campaign. **8** an area of operation or activity; a subject of study. **9 a** the region in which a force is effective (*gravitational field; magnetic field*). **b** the force exerted in such an area. **10** a range of perception (*field of view; filled the field of the telescope*). **11** (*attrib.*) **a** (of an animal or plant) found in the countryside, wild (*field mouse*).

FETTER: 18TH-CENTURY ANKLE FETTERS

FEVERFEW (*Tanacetum parthenium*)

FIBREGLASS: 1950s FIBREGLASS CHAIR

FIBULA: HUMAN LOWER LEG SHOWING THE FIBULA

fibula

b carried out or working in the natural environment, not in a laboratory etc. (*field test*). **12** the background of a picture, coin, flag, etc. **13** *Computing* a part of a record, representing an item of data. ● *v.* **1** *Cricket, Baseball* etc. **a** *intr.* act as a fielder. **b** *tr.* stop (and return) (the ball). **2** *tr.* select (a team or individual) to play in a game. **3** *tr.* deal with (a succession of questions etc.). □ **in the field 1** campaigning. **2** working etc. away from one's laboratory, headquarters, etc. **play the field** *colloq.* avoid exclusive attachment to one person or activity etc. **take the field 1** begin a campaign. **2** (of a sports team) go on to a pitch to begin a game. [Old English]

field day *n.* **1** a successful or exciting time (*when crowds form, pickpockets have a field day*). **2** *Mil.* an exercise, esp. in manoeuvring.

fielder *n. Cricket, Baseball,* etc. a member (other than the bowler or pitcher) of the side that is fielding. ▷ BASEBALL

field events *n.pl.* athletic sports other than races (e.g. shot-putting, jumping). ▷ TRACK

fieldfare *n.* a thrush, *Turdus pilaris,* having grey plumage with a speckled breast.

field glasses *n.pl.* binoculars for outdoor use.

field hockey *n. N. Amer.* = HOCKEY¹ 1. ▷ HOCKEY

field hospital *n.* a temporary hospital near a battlefield.

field marshal *n.* (in the British army) an officer of the highest rank.

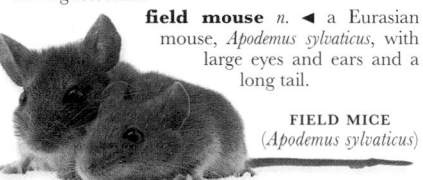

field mouse *n.* ◄ a Eurasian mouse, *Apodemus sylvaticus,* with large eyes and ears and a long tail.

FIELD MICE
(*Apodemus sylvaticus*)

field officer *n.* an army officer of field rank.

field of vision *n.* all that comes into view when the eyes are turned in some direction.

field rank *n.* esp. *Brit.* any rank in an army above captain and below general.

fieldsman *n.* (*pl.* **-men**) *Cricket* = FIELDER.

field sports *n.pl.* outdoor sports, esp. hunting, shooting, and fishing.

fieldwork *n.* the practical work of a surveyor, collector of scientific data, sociologist, etc., conducted in the natural environment rather than a laboratory, office, etc. □ **fieldworker** *n.*

fiend *n.* **1 a** an evil spirit, a demon. **b** (prec. by *the*) the Devil. **2 a** a very wicked or cruel person. **b** a mischievous or annoying person. **3** (with a qualifying word) *colloq.* a devotee or addict (*a fitness fiend*). [Old English] □ **fiendlike** *adj.*

fiendish *adj.* **1** like a fiend; extremely cruel or unpleasant. **2** extremely difficult. □ **fiendishly** *adv.* **fiendishness** *n.*

fierce *adj.* (**fiercer, fiercest**) **1** vehemently aggressive or frightening in temper or action, violent. **2** intense, ardent. **3** unpleasantly strong or intense; (*fierce heat*). [from Latin *ferus* 'savage'] □ **fiercely** *adv.* **fierceness** *n.*

fiery *adj.* (**fierier, fieriest**) **1 a** consisting of or flaming with fire. **b** (of an arrow etc.) fire-bearing. **2** bright red. **3** hot as fire. **4 a** flashing, ardent (*fiery eyes*). **b** spirited, irritable (*fiery temper*). **c** (of a horse) mettlesome. □ **fierily** *adv.* **fieriness** *n.*

fiesta *n.* **1** a holiday or festivity. **2** a religious festival in Spanish-speaking countries. [Spanish, literally 'feast']

fife ● *n.* **1** a kind of small shrill flute used in military music. **2** its player. ● *v.* **1** *intr.* play the fife. **2** *tr.* play (an air etc.) on the fife. [from German *Pfeife* 'pipe'] □ **fifer** *n.*

fifteen ● *n.* **1** one more than fourteen. **2** a symbol for this (15, xv, XV). **3** a size etc. denoted by fifteen. **4** a team of fifteen players, esp. in rugby. ● *adj.* that amount to fifteen. [Old English] □ **fifteenth** *adj.* & *n.*

Fighters are fast and highly manoeuvrable aircraft. On-board computers help the pilot to control and navigate the plane and launch its weaponry. Fighters are capable of carrying air-to-air and air-to-ground missiles for airborne, land, and sea targets. Their defensive systems include electronic beams and flares for confusing enemy fire.

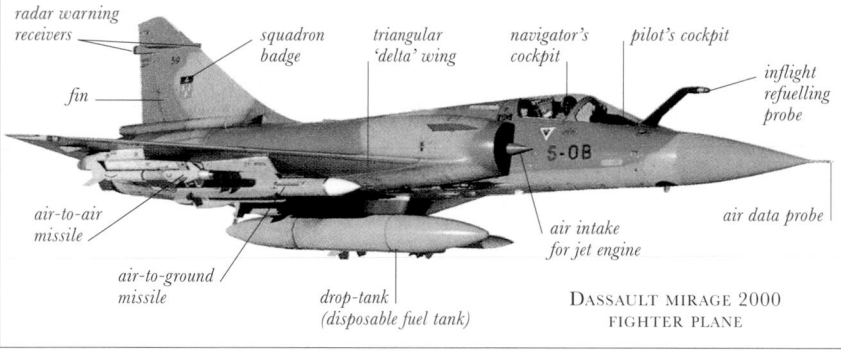

radar warning receivers　squadron badge　triangular 'delta' wing　navigator's cockpit　pilot's cockpit　inflight refuelling probe　fin　5-OB　air-to-air missile　air-to-ground missile　drop-tank (disposable fuel tank)　air intake for jet engine　air data probe

DASSAULT MIRAGE 2000
FIGHTER PLANE

fifth ● *n.* **1** the position in a sequence corresponding to that of the number 5 in the sequence 1–5. **2** something occupying this position. **3** the fifth person etc. in a race or competition. **4** any of five equal parts of a thing. **5** *Mus.* **a** an interval or chord spanning five consecutive notes in the diatonic scale (e.g. C to G). **b** a note separated from another by this interval. ● *adj.* that is the fifth. [Old English] □ **fifthly** *adv.*

fifth column *n.* a group working for an enemy within a country at war etc. □ **fifth columnist** *n.*

fifth-generation *adj.* denoting a proposed new class of computer employing artificial intelligence.

fifty ● *n.* (*pl.* **-ies**) **1** the product of five and ten. **2** a symbol for this (50, l, L). **3** (in *pl.*) the numbers from 50 to 59, esp. the years of a century or of a person's life. **4** a set of fifty persons or things. ● *adj.* that amount to fifty. [Old English] □ **fiftieth** *adj.* & *n.* **fiftyfold** *adj.* & *adv.*

fifty-fifty ● *adj.* equal, with equal shares or chances (*on a fifty-fifty basis*). ● *adv.* equally, half-and-half (*go fifty-fifty*).

fig¹ *n.* **1** ► a soft pear-shaped fruit with many seeds, eaten fresh or dried. ▷ FRUIT. **2** (in full **fig tree**) any deciduous tree or shrub of the genus *Ficus,* esp. *F. carica,* which has broad leaves and bears figs. □ **not care** (or **give**) **a fig** not care at all. [from Latin *ficus*]

fig² *n.* **1** dress or equipment (*in full fig*). **2** condition or form (*in good fig*). [based on German *fegen* 'to furbish']

fig. *abbr.* figure.

fight ● *v.* (*past* and *past part.* **fought**) **1** *intr.* contend or struggle in war, battle, single combat, etc. **2** *tr.* contend with (an opponent) in this way. **3** *tr.* take part or engage in (a battle etc.). **4** *tr.* contend about (an issue, an election); maintain (a lawsuit, cause, etc.) against an opponent. **5** *intr.* campaign or strive determinedly to achieve something. **6** *tr.* strive to overcome (disease, fire, fear, etc.). **7** *tr.* make (one's) way by fighting. ● *n.* **1 a** a combat, esp. unpremeditated, between two or more persons, animals, or parties. **b** a boxing match. **c** a battle. **2** a conflict; a vigorous effort in the face of difficulty. **3** power or inclination to fight (*has no fight left*). □ **fight back 1** counter-attack. **2** suppress (one's feelings, tears, etc.). **fight down** suppress (one's feelings, tears, etc.). **fight for 1** fight on behalf of. **2** fight to secure (a thing). **fight off** repel with effort. **fight out** (usu. **fight it out**) settle (a dispute etc.) by fighting. **fight shy of** avoid; be unwilling to approach (a task etc.). [Old English]

fightback *n. Brit.* an act of retaliation; a rally or recovery.

fighter *n.* **1** a person or animal that fights. **2** ▲ a fast military aircraft designed for attacking other aircraft.

fighting chance *n.* an opportunity of succeeding by great effort.

fighting fit *adj.* fit enough to fight; at the peak of fitness.

fighting fund *n. Brit.* money raised to support a campaign.

fighting words *n.pl. colloq.* words indicating a willingness to fight.

fig leaf *n.* **1** a leaf of a fig tree. **2** a device for concealing something, esp. the genitals (Gen. 3:7).

figment *n.* a thing invented or existing only in the imagination. [from Latin *figmentum*]

figuration *n.* **1 a** the act of formation. **b** a mode of formation; a form. **c** a shape or outline. **2 a** ornamentation by designs. **b** *Mus.* ornamental patterns of scales, arpeggios, etc. **3** allegorical representation. [Middle English, related to FIGURE]

figurative *adj.* **1 a** metaphorical, not literal. **b** metaphorically so called. **2** characterized by or addicted to figures of speech. **3** of pictorial or sculptural representation. **4** emblematic, serving as a type. [Middle English, related to FIGURE] □ **figuratively** *adv.* **figurativeness** *n.*

figure ● *n.* **1** the external form or shape of a thing. **b** bodily shape. **2 a** a person as seen in outline but not identified. **b** a person as contemplated mentally (*a public figure*). **3 a** a representation of the human form in drawing, sculpture, etc. **b** an image or likeness. **c** an emblem or type. **4** *Geom.* a two-dimensional space enclosed by a line or lines, or a three-dimensional space enclosed by a surface or surfaces. **5 a** a numerical symbol, esp. any of the ten in Arabic notation. **b** a number so expressed. **c** an amount of money, a value (*cannot put a figure on it*). **d** (in *pl.*) arithmetical calculations. **6** a diagram or illustrative drawing. **7** a decorative pattern. **8 a** a division of a set dance. **b** (in skating) a prescribed pattern of movements from a stationary position. **9** *Mus.* a short succession of notes producing a single impression. **10** (in full **figure of speech**) a recognized form of rhetorical expression, esp. metaphor or hyperbole. ● *v.* **1** *intr.* appear or be mentioned, esp. prominently. **2** *tr.* represent in a diagram or picture. **3** *tr.* **a** embellish with a pattern (*figured satin*). **b** *Mus.* embellish with figures. **4** *tr.* mark with numbers or prices. **5 a** *tr.* calculate. **b** *intr.* do arithmetic. **6** esp. *N. Amer.* **a** *tr.* understand, ascertain, consider. **b** *intr. colloq.* be likely or understandable (*that figures*). □ **figure on** *US* count on, expect. **figure out 1** work out by arithmetic or

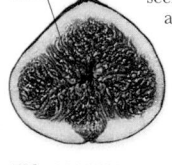

seeds

FIG: COMMON FIG
(*Ficus carica*)

F

logic. **2** estimate. **3** understand. [from Latin *figura* (n.), *figurare* (v.)] □ **figureless** *adj.*

figurehead *n.* **1** a nominal leader or head without real power. **2** ▼ a carving, usu. a bust or a full-length figure, at a ship's prow.

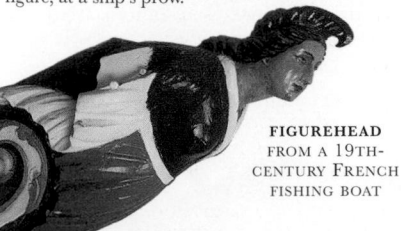

FIGUREHEAD
FROM A 19TH-
CENTURY FRENCH
FISHING BOAT

figure of eight *n.* (usu. hyphenated when *attrib.*) **1** the shape of the number eight. **2** something that has this shape.

figure of fun *n.* a ridiculous person.

figure of speech see FIGURE *n.* 10.

figure skating *n.* skating in prescribed patterns from a stationary position. □ **figure skater** *n.*

figurine *n.* a statuette. [from Italian *figurina*]

figwort *n.* ▶ any plant of the genus *Scrophularia* (family Scrophulariaceae), with dull purplish-brown flowers, once believed to be useful against scrofula.

Fijian ● *adj.* of or relating to Fiji, its people, or language. ● *n.* **1** a native or national of Fiji. **2** the language of this people.

filament *n.* **1** a slender threadlike body or fibre (esp. in animal or vegetable structures). **2** a wire or thread in an electric bulb or thermionic valve, heated or made incandescent by an electric current. ▷ LIGHT BULB. [based on Latin *filum* 'thread'] □ **filamentary** *adj.* **filamented** *adj.* **filamentous** *adj.*

filariasis *n. pl.* **filariases**) a tropical disease caused by the presence of parasitic nematode worms esp. in the lymph vessels and transmitted by biting insects.

FIGWORT:
VARIEGATED WATER
FIGWORT (*Scrophularia
auriculata* 'Variegata')

filbert *n.* **1** a cultivated hazel, esp. *Corylus maxima*, bearing longish edible nuts. **2** this nut. [from dialect French *noix de filbert*, a nut ripe about St Philibert's day (20 Aug.)]

filch *v.tr.* pilfer, steal. [Middle English]

file[1] ● *n.* **1** a folder, box, etc., for holding loose papers. **2** a set of papers kept in this. **3** *Computing* a collection of (usu. related) data stored under one name. ● *v.tr.* **1** place (papers) in a file or among (esp. public) records. **2** submit (a petition for divorce, an application for a patent, etc.). **3** (of a reporter) send (a story, information, etc.) to a newspaper. □ **file away** place in a file, or make a mental note of, for future reference. **on file** in a file or filing system. [from Latin *filum* 'thread'] □ **filer** *n.*

file[2] ● *n.* a line of persons or things one behind another. ● *v.intr.* walk in a file. [related to FILE[1]]

file[3] ● *n.* a tool with a roughened surface for smoothing or shaping wood, fingernails, etc. ● *v.tr.* smooth or shape with a file. □ **file away** remove (roughness etc.) with a file. [Old English] □ **filer** *n.*

file server *n. Computing* a device which controls access to one or more separately stored files.

filet *n.* **1** a kind of net or lace with a square mesh. **2** a fillet of meat. [French, literally 'thread']

filial *adj.* of or due from a son or daughter. [from Latin *filialis*] □ **filially** *adv.*

filibuster ● *n.* **1** the obstruction of progress in a legislative assembly, esp. by prolonged speaking. **2** esp. *N. Amer.* a person who engages in a filibuster. ● *v.intr.* act as a filibuster.

filigree *n.* **1** fine metal openwork. **2** anything delicate resembling this. [from Latin *filum* 'thread' + *granum* 'seed'] □ **filigreed** *adj.*

filing *n.* (usu. in *pl.*) a particle rubbed off by a file.

filing cabinet *n.* a case with drawers for storing documents.

Filipino ● *n.* (*pl.* **-os**; *fem.* **Filipina**) a native or national of the Philippines, a group of islands in the SW Pacific. ● *adj.* of or relating to the Philippines or the Filipinos. [Spanish]

fill ● *v.* **1** *tr.* & *intr.* (often foll. by *with*) make or become full. **2** *tr.* occupy completely; spread over or through; pervade. **3** *tr.* block up (a cavity or hole in a tooth) with cement, amalgam, gold, etc. **4** *tr.* appoint a person to hold (a vacant post). **5** *tr.* occupy (vacant time). **6** *intr.* (of a sail) be distended by wind. **7** *tr.* (usu. as **filling** *adj.*) (esp. of food) satisfy, satiate. ● *n.* **1** (prec. by possessive) as much as one wants or can bear (*eat your fill*). **2** enough to fill something (*a fill of tobacco*). □ **fill the bill** be suitable or adequate. **fill in 1** *Brit.* add information to complete (a form etc.). **2 a** complete (a drawing etc.) within an outline. **b** fill (an outline) in this way. **3** fill (a hole etc.) completely. **4** (often foll. by *for*) act as a substitute. **5** occupy oneself during (time between other activities). **6** *colloq.* inform (a person) more fully. **fill out 1** enlarge to the required size. **2** become enlarged or plump. **3** *US* fill in (a form etc.). **fill up 1** make or become completely full. **2** *Brit.* fill in (a form etc.). **3** fill the petrol tank of (a car etc.). [Old English]

filler *n.* **1** material or an object used to fill a cavity or increase bulk. **2** an item filling space in a newspaper etc.

filler cap *n.* a cap closing the pipe leading to the petrol tank of a motor vehicle.

fillet ● *n.* **1 a** a fleshy piece of meat from near the loins or the ribs. ▷ CUT. **b** (in full **fillet steak**) the undercut of a sirloin. **c** a boned longitudinal section of a fish. **2** a headband, ribbon, string, or narrow band, for binding the hair or worn round the head. **3 a** a thin narrow strip. **b** a raised rim or ridge. **4** *Archit.* a narrow flat band separating two mouldings. ▷ WINDOW. ● *v.tr.* (**filleted**, **filleting**) **1 a** remove bones from (fish). **b** divide (fish or meat) into fillets. **2** bind or provide with a fillet or fillets. [from Latin *filum* 'thread'] □ **filleter** *n.*

filling *n.* **1** material that is used to fill, esp.: **a** a piece of material used to fill a cavity in a tooth. **b** the edible substance between the bread in a sandwich or between the pastry in a pie. **2** *US* weft.

filling station *n.* an establishment selling petrol etc. to motorists.

fillip *n.* a stimulus or incentive.

filly *n.* (*pl.* **-ies**) **1** a young female horse, usu. under four years old. **2** *colloq.* a girl or young woman. [related to FOAL]

film ● *n.* **1** a thin coating or covering layer. **2** *Photog.* ▼ a strip or sheet of plastic or other flexible base coated with light-sensitive emulsion for exposure in a camera. ▷ CAMERA. **3 a** a representation of a story, episode, etc., on a film or videotape, with the illusion of movement. **b** a story represented in this way. **c** (in *pl.*) the cinema industry. **4** a slight veil or haze etc. **5** a dimness or abnormal opacity affecting

the eyes. ● *v.tr.* **1** make a photographic or videotape film of (a scene, person, etc.). **2** (also *absol.*) make a cinema or television film of (a book etc.). [Old English *filmen* 'membrane']

film clip *n.* = CLIP[2] *n.* 3.

filmic *adj.* of or relating to films or cinematography.

film-maker *n.* a person who makes films. □ **film-making** *n.*

filmset *v.tr.* (**-setting**; *past* and *past part.* **-set**) *Printing* set (material for printing) by filmsetting. □ **film-setter** *n.*

filmsetting *n. Printing* typesetting using characters on photographic film.

film star *n.* a celebrated actor or actress in films.

filmstrip *n.* a series of transparencies in a strip for projection. ▷ PROJECTOR.

filmy *adj.* (**filmier**, **filmiest**) thin and translucent. □ **filmily** *adv.* **filminess** *n.*

filo /fee-loh/ *n.* (also **phyllo**) (usu. *attrib.*) a kind of dough usually layered in thin leaves to make sweet and savoury pastries (*filo pastry*). [from modern Greek *phullo* 'leaf']

Filofax *n. propr.* a portable loose-leaf filing system for personal or office use. [FILE[1] + *facts*]

filter ● *n.* **1** ▼ a porous device for removing impurities or solid particles from a liquid or gas passed through it. **2** = FILTER TIP. **3** ▶ a screen or attachment for absorbing or modifying light, X-rays, etc. ▷ POLARIZE. **4** a device for suppressing electrical or sound waves of frequencies not required. **5** *Brit.* **a** an arrangement for filtering traffic. **b** a traffic light signalling this. ● *v.* **1** *intr.* & *tr.* **1** pass or cause to pass through a filter. **2** (foll. by *through*, *into*, etc.) make way gradually. **3** (foll. by *out*) leak or cause to leak. **4** *Brit.* allow (traffic) or (of traffic) be allowed to pass to the left or right at a junction while traffic going straight ahead is halted (esp. at traffic lights). □ **filter out** remove (impurities etc.) by means of a filter. [from medieval Latin *filtrum* 'felt used as a filter']

*filter
paper*

*solid (coffee)
particle*

*liquid passes
through*

*filtered
coffee*

dissolved coffee

FILTER (*n.*1): COFFEE FILTER   *filter paper*

filterable *adj.* (also **filtrable**) **1** *Med.* (of a virus) able to pass through a filter that retains bacteria. **2** that can be filtered.

filter-feeding *n. Zool.* ▶ feeding by filtering out plankton or nutrients suspended in water. ▷ WHALE. □ **filter-feeder** *n.*

filter-paper *n.* porous paper for filtering.

filter tip *n.* **1** a filter on a cigarette removing some impurities. **2** a cigarette with this. □ **filter-tipped** *adj.*

filth *n.* **1** repugnant or extreme dirt. **2** vileness, corruption, obscenity. [Old English]

filthy ● *adj.* (**filthier**, **filthiest**) **1** extremely or disgustingly dirty. **2** obscene. **3** *Brit. colloq.* (of weather) very unpleasant. **4** vile; disgraceful. ● *adv.* **1** filthily (*filthy dirty*). **2** *colloq.* extremely (*filthy rich*). □ **filthily** *adv.* **filthiness** *n.*

filthy lucre *n.* **1** dishonourable gain (Tit. 1:11). **2** *joc.* money.

filtrable var. of FILTERABLE.

filtrate *n.* filtered liquid. □ **filtration** *n.*

fin *n.* **1** a flattened appendage on various parts of the body of many aquatic vertebrates and some invertebrates, including fish and

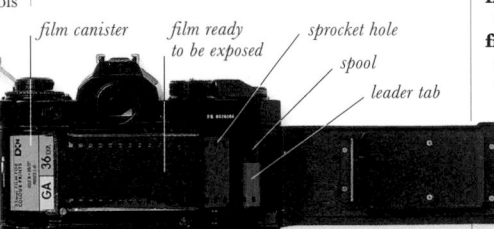

film canister   *film ready
to be exposed*   *sprocket hole*   *spool*   *leader tab*

FILM: 35MM PHOTOGRAPHIC FILM
LOADED IN A CAMERA

FILTER (n.3)

Photographic filters are used to modify the light passing through a lens. In the examples below, each colour filter allows light of predominantly the same colour through the lens, distorting the film's hues.

PICTURE TAKEN WITHOUT A FILTER

YELLOW FILTER

ORANGE FILTER

BLUE FILTER

cetaceans, for propelling, steering, and balancing (*dorsal fin, anal fin*). ▷ CETACEAN, FISH. **2** a small projecting surface or attachment on an aircraft, rocket, or motor car for ensuring aerodynamic stability. ▷ AIRCRAFT, SPACECRAFT. **3** an underwater swimmer's flipper. **4** a sharp lateral projection on the share or coulter of a plough. **5** a finlike projection on any device, for improving heat transfer etc. [Old English] □ **finless** *adj.* **finned** *adj.* (also in *comb.*).

finagle /fin-ay-gŭl/ *v.intr. & tr. colloq.* act or obtain dishonestly. [from dialect *fainaigue* 'to cheat'] □ **finagler** *n.*

final ● *adj.* **1** situated at the end, coming last. **2** conclusive, decisive, unalterable, putting an end to doubt. **3** concerned with the purpose or end aimed at. ● *n.* **1** the last or deciding heat or game in sports or in a competition (*Cup Final*). **2** the edition of a newspaper published latest in the day. **3 a** (usu. in *pl.*) *Brit.* the series of examinations at the end of a degree course. **b** *N. Amer.* an examination at the end of a term. **4** *Mus.* the principal note in any mode. [based on Latin *finis* 'end'] □ **finally** *adv.*

final clause *n. Gram.* a clause expressing purpose, introduced by *in order that, lest,* etc.

finale /fi-nah-li/ ● *n.* **1 a** the last movement of an instrumental composition. **b** a piece of music closing an act in an opera. **2** a conclusion. [Italian, related to FINAL]

finalist *n.* a competitor in the final of a competition etc.

finality *n.* (*pl.* -**ies**) the quality or fact of being final.

finalize *v.tr.* (also -**ise**) **1** put into final form. **2** complete; bring to an end. □ **finalization** *n.*

finance ● *n.* **1** the management of (esp. public) money. **2** monetary support for an enterprise. **3** (in *pl.*) the money resources of a state, company, or person. ● *v.tr.* provide capital for (a person or enterprise). [from Old French, related to FINE²]

finance company *n.* (also **finance house**) a company mainly providing money for hire purchase transactions.

financial *adj.* **1** of finance. **2** *Austral. & NZ slang* possessing money. □ **financially** *adv.*

financial year *n. Brit.* a year as reckoned for taxing or accounting.

financier *n.* a person engaged in large-scale finance. [French]

fin-back *n.* = FIN WHALE.

finch *n.* ▶ any small seed-eating songbird esp. of the family Fringillidae, including crossbills, canaries, and chaffinches. ▷ SONGBIRD. [Old English]

find ● *v.tr.* (*past* and *past part.* **found**) **1 a** discover by chance or effort (*found a key*). **b** become aware of. **2 a** get possession of by chance (*found a treasure*). **b** obtain, receive (*idea found acceptance*). **c** succeed in obtaining (*cannot find the money*). **d** summon up (*found courage to protest*). **3 a** seek out and provide (*will find you a book*). **b** supply, furnish (*each finds his own equipment*). **4** ascertain by study or calculation or inquiry (*could not find the answer*). **5 a** perceive or experience (*find no sense in it; find difficulty in breathing*). **b** (often in *passive*) recognize or discover to be present (*the word is not found in Shakespeare*). **c** regard or discover from experience (*finds England too cold; find it impossible to reply*). **6** *Law* (of a jury, judge, etc.) decide and declare (*found him guilty*). **7** reach by a natural or normal process (*water finds its own level*). ● *n.* **1** a discovery of treasure, minerals, etc. **2** a thing or person discovered, esp. when of value. □ **all found** *Brit.* (of an employee's wages) with board and lodging provided free. **find against** *Law* decide against (a person), judge to be guilty. **find fault** see FAULT. **find favour** prove acceptable. **find one's feet 1** become able to walk. **2** develop one's independent ability. **find out 1** discover or detect (a wrongdoer etc.). **2** (often foll. by *about*) get information. **3** discover (*find out where we are*). **4** (often foll. by

about) discover the truth, a fact, etc. (*he never found out*). **find one's way 1** (often foll. by *to*) manage to reach a place. **2** (often foll. by *into*) be brought or get. [Old English] □ **findable** *adj.*

finder *n.* **1** a person who finds. **2** a small telescope attached to a large one to locate an object for observation. **3** the viewfinder of a camera.

finding *n.* (often in *pl.*) a conclusion reached by an inquiry.

fine¹ ● *adj.* **1** of high quality. **2 a** excellent; of notable merit (*a fine painting*). **b** good, satisfactory (*that will be fine*). **3 a** pure, refined. **b** (of gold or silver) containing a specified proportion of pure metal. **4** of handsome appearance or size; imposing, dignified (*fine buildings; a person of fine presence*). **5** in good health (*I'm fine, thank you*). **6** (of weather etc.) bright and clear with sunshine; free from rain. **7 a** thin; sharp. **b** in small particles. **c** worked in slender thread. **d** (esp. of print) small. **e** (of a pen) narrow-pointed. **8** ornate, showy, smart. **9** fastidious, dainty, pretending refinement; (of speech or writing) affectedly ornate. **10 a** capable of delicate perception or discrimination. **b** perceptible only with difficulty (*a fine distinction*). **11** delicate, subtle, exquisitely fashioned. **12** (of wine or other goods) of a high standard; conforming to a specified grade. ● *n.* **1** fine weather (*in rain or fine*). **2** (in *pl.*) very small particles in mining, milling, etc. ● *adv.* **1** finely. **2** *colloq.* very well (*suits me fine*). ● *v.* (often foll. by *down*) **a** *tr.* make (beer or wine) clear. **b** *intr.* (of liquid) become clear. **2** *tr. & intr.* (often foll. by *away, down, off*) make or become finer, thinner, or less coarse; dwindle or taper, or cause to do so. □ **cut** (or **run**) **it fine** allow very little margin of time etc. **fine up** *Austral. colloq.* (of the weather) become fine. **not to put too fine a point on it** (as a parenthetic remark) to speak bluntly. [based on Latin *finire* 'to finish'] □ **finely** *adv.* **fineness** *n.*

fine² ● *n.* a sum of money exacted as a penalty. ● *v.tr.* punish by a fine (*fined him £5*). □ **in fine** to sum up; in short. [from medieval Latin *finis*] □ **finable** *adj.*

fine arts *n.pl.* those appealing to the mind or to the sense of beauty, as poetry, music, and esp. painting, sculpture, and architecture.

fine-drawn *adj.* **1** extremely thin. **2** subtle.

fine-grained *adj.* having a fine grain; consisting of small particles.

fine print *n.* detailed printed information, esp. in legal documents.

finery *n.* showy dress or decoration.

fine-spun *adj.* **1** delicate. **2** (of a theory etc.) too subtle, unpractical.

finesse /fin-ess/ ● *n.* **1** refinement. **2** subtle or delicate manipulation. **3** artfulness, esp. in handling a difficulty tactfully. **4** *Cards* an attempt to win a trick with a card that is not the highest held. ● *v.* **1** *intr. & tr.* use or achieve by finesse. **2** *intr. Cards* make a finesse. [French, related to FINE¹]

fine-tooth comb *n.* a comb with narrow close-set teeth. □ **go over with a fine-tooth comb** check or search thoroughly.

fine-tune *v.tr.* make small adjustments to (a mechanism etc.) in order to obtain the best possible results. □ **fine tuning** *n.*

finger ● *n.* **1** any of the terminal projections of the hand (including or excluding the thumb). ▷ HAND. **2** the part of a glove etc. covering a finger. **3 a** a finger-like object (*fish finger*). **b** a long narrow structure. **4** *colloq.* a measure of liquor in a glass, based on the breadth of a finger. ● *v.tr.* **1** touch, feel, or turn about with the fingers. **2** *Mus.* play (a passage) with fingers used in a particular way. **3** *N. Amer. slang* indicate (a victim, or a criminal to the police). □ **all fingers and thumbs** *Brit.* clumsy. **get** (or **pull**) **one's finger out** *Brit. slang* cease

FINCH: ZEBRA FINCHES (*Poephia guttata*)

F

FILTER-FEEDING

Baleen whales are the largest filter-feeders. They have modified mucous membrane plates (baleen) in their mouths, which look like huge fringed brushes. The whale draws seawater into its mouth and then expels it through the baleen, keeping food such as fish or krill trapped inside. The whale then wipes the plates clean with its tongue.

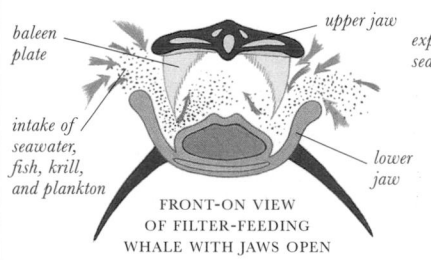

baleen plate
upper jaw
intake of seawater, fish, krill, and plankton
lower jaw

FRONT-ON VIEW OF FILTER-FEEDING WHALE WITH JAWS OPEN

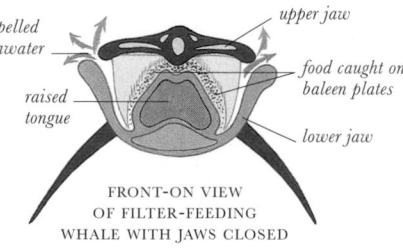

expelled seawater
upper jaw
food caught on baleen plates
raised tongue
lower jaw

FRONT-ON VIEW OF FILTER-FEEDING WHALE WITH JAWS CLOSED

F

procrastinating and start to act. **have a finger in the pie** be (esp. officiously) concerned in the matter. **lay a finger on** touch however slightly. **put one's finger on** locate or identify exactly. **put the finger on** *slang* **1** inform against. **2** identify (an intended victim). [Old English] □ **fingered** *adj.* (also in *comb.*). **fingerless** *adj.*

fingerboard *n.* a flat strip on the neck of a stringed instrument, against which the strings are pressed to vary their pitch. ▷ SITAR, STRINGED

finger bowl *n.* a small bowl for rinsing the fingers during a meal.

fingering *n.* **1** a manner or technique of using the fingers, esp. to play an instrument. **2** an indication of this in a musical score.

fingernail *n.* the nail at the tip of each finger. ▷ NAIL.

finger-paint ● *n.* paint that can be applied with the fingers. ● *v.intr.* apply paint with the fingers.

finger-plate *n.* a plate fixed to a door above the handle to prevent fingermarks.

finger-post *n.* a signpost at a road junction.

fingerprint ● *n.* **1** an impression made on a surface by the fingertips. **2** a distinctive characteristic. ● *v.tr.* record the fingerprints of (a person).

fingertip *n.* the tip of a finger. ▷ NAIL. □ **have at one's fingertips** be thoroughly familiar with (a subject etc.).

finial *n. Archit.* **1** ▼ an ornament finishing off the apex of a roof, pediment, gable, tower-corner, canopy, etc. ▷ CHURCH. **2** the topmost part of a pinnacle. [from Latin *finis* 'end']

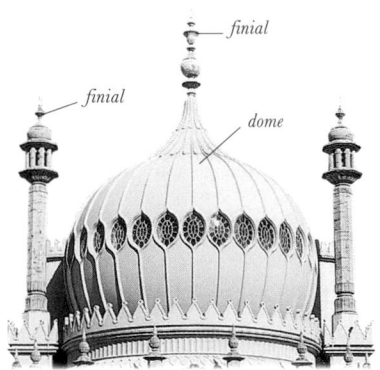

finial

finial

dome

FINIALS ON A REGENCY PAVILION

finical *adj.* = FINICKY. [16th-century coinage] □ **finicalness** *n.*

finicky *adj.* **1** over-particular, fastidious. **2** needing much attention to detail; fiddly. □ **finickiness** *n.*

finis *n.* **1** (at the end of a book) the end. **2** the end of anything, esp. of life. [Latin]

finish ● *v.* **1** *tr.* **a** (often foll. by *off*) bring to an end; come to the end of; complete. **b** (usu. foll. by *off*) *colloq.* kill; overcome completely. **c** (often foll. by *off*, *up*) consume the whole or the remainder of (food or drink) (*finish up your dinner*). **2** *intr.* **a** come to an end, cease. **b** reach the end, esp. of a race. **c** = *finish up*. **3** *tr.* **a** complete the manufacture of (cloth, woodwork, etc.) by surface treatment. **b** put the final touches to; make perfect or highly accomplished (*finished manners*). ● *n.* **1 a** the end, the last stage. **b** the point at which a race etc. ends. **2** a method, material, or texture used for surface treatment of wood, cloth, etc. (*mahogany finish*). **3** what serves to give completeness. **4** an accomplished or completed state. □ **fight to the finish** fight till one party is completely beaten. **finish off** provide with an ending. **finish up** (often foll. by *in*, *by*) esp. *Brit.* end in something, end by doing something (*the plan finished up in the waste-paper basket; finished up by apologizing*). **finish with** have no more to do with, complete one's use of or association with. [from Latin *finire*] □ **finisher** *n.*

finishing school *n.* a private college where girls are prepared for entry into fashionable society.

finishing touch *n.* (also **finishing touches** *pl.*) the final details completing and enhancing a piece of work etc.

finite *adj.* **1** limited, bounded; not infinite. **2** *Gram.* (of a part of a verb) having a specific number and person. [from Latin *finitus* 'finished'] □ **finitely** *adv.* **finiteness** *n.* **finitude** *n.*

Finn *n.* a native or national of Finland; a person of Finnish descent. [Old English]

finnan *n.* (in full **finnan haddock**) a haddock cured with the smoke of green wood, turf, or peat. [from *Findhorn* in Scotland]

Finnish ● *adj.* of the Finns or their language. ● *n.* the language of the Finns.

finny *adj.* **1** having fins; like a fin. **2** *poet.* of or teeming with fish.

fino *n.* (*pl.* **-os**) a light-coloured dry sherry. [Spanish, literally 'fine']

fin whale *n.* ▼ a large rorqual, *Balaenoptera physalus*, with a prominent dorsal fin.

dorsal fin

FIN WHALE (*Balaenoptera physalus*)

fiord var. of FJORD.

fir *n.* **1** (in full **fir tree**) any evergreen coniferous tree, esp. of the genus *Abies*, with needles borne singly on the stems (cf. PINE[1]). ▷ CONIFER. **2** the wood of the fir. [Middle English]

fir cone *n. Brit.* the fruit of the fir.

fire ● *n.* **1 a** the state or process of combustion, in which substances combine chemically with oxygen from the air and usu. give out bright light and heat. **b** flame or incandescence. **2** a conflagration, a destructive burning (*forest fire*). **3 a** burning fuel in a grate, furnace, etc. **b** *Brit.* = ELECTRIC FIRE. **c** = GAS FIRE. **4** firing of guns. **5 a** fervour, spirit, vivacity. **b** poetic inspiration, lively imagination. **c** vehement emotion. **6** burning heat, fever. ● *v.* **1 a** *tr.* (also *absol.*) discharge (a gun etc.). **b** *tr.* propel (a missile) from a gun etc. **c** *intr.* (of a gun etc.) be discharged. **2** *tr.* cause (explosive) to explode. **3** *tr.* deliver or utter in rapid succession (*fired insults at us*). **4** *tr. slang* dismiss (an employee) from a job. **5** *tr.* **a** set fire to with the intention of destroying. **b** kindle (explo-

sives). **6** *intr.* (of an internal-combustion engine, or a cylinder in one) undergo ignition of its fuel. **7** *tr.* supply (a furnace, engine, boiler, or power station) with fuel. **8** *tr.* **a** stimulate (the imagination or an emotion). **b** fill (a person) with enthusiasm. **9** *tr.* bake or dry (pottery, bricks, etc.). **10** *intr.* become heated or excited. □ **catch fire** begin to burn. **fire and brimstone** the supposed torments of hell. **fire away** *colloq.* begin; go ahead. **fire up** *colloq.* **1** stimulate, fill with enthusiasm, excite. **2** start up (an engine etc.). **go on fire** *Sc. & Ir.* catch fire. **on fire 1** burning. **2** excited. **set fire to** (or **set on fire**) ignite, kindle, cause to burn. **under fire** (often prec. by *come*) **1** being shot at. **2** being rigorously criticized or questioned. [Old English] □ **fireless** *adj.* **firer** *n.*

fire alarm *n.* a device for giving warning of fire.

firearm *n.* (usu. in *pl.*) a gun, esp. a pistol or rifle.

fireball *n.* **1** a large meteor. **2** a ball of flame, esp. from a nuclear explosion.

firebomb ● *n.* an incendiary bomb. ● *v.tr.* attack or destroy with a firebomb.

firebox *n.* the fuel-chamber of a steam engine or boiler. ▷ STEAM ENGINE

firebrand *n.* **1** a piece of burning wood. **2** a cause of trouble, esp. a person causing unrest.

firebreak *n.* an obstacle to the spread of fire in a forest etc., esp. an open space.

firebrick *n.* a fireproof brick used in a grate.

fire brigade *n.* esp. *Brit.* an organized body of firemen trained and employed to extinguish fires.

firebug *n. colloq.* a pyromaniac (see PYROMANIA).

fireclay *n.* clay capable of withstanding high temperatures, often used to make firebricks.

firecracker *n.* esp. *N. Amer.* an explosive firework; a banger.

firedamp *n.* a miners' name for methane, which is explosive when mixed in certain proportions with air.

fire department *n. US* = FIRE BRIGADE.

firedog *n.* a metal support for burning wood or for a grate or fire-irons.

fire door *n.* a fire-resistant door to prevent the spread of fire.

fire drill *n.* **1** a rehearsal of the procedures to be used in case of fire. **2** a primitive device for kindling fire with a stick and wood.

fire-eater *n.* **1** a conjuror who appears to swallow fire. **2** a person fond of quarrelling or fighting.

fire engine *n.* ▼ a vehicle carrying equipment for fighting large fires.

FIRE ENGINE

Fire engines transport a fire crew and their equipment to the scene of a blaze quickly. Modern engines are equipped with a water tank, pumps, and ladders, as well as a hydraulic boom and platform that enables firefighters to rescue people trapped in tall buildings. Compartments on the vehicle's sides contain hoses, oxygen tanks, and tools.

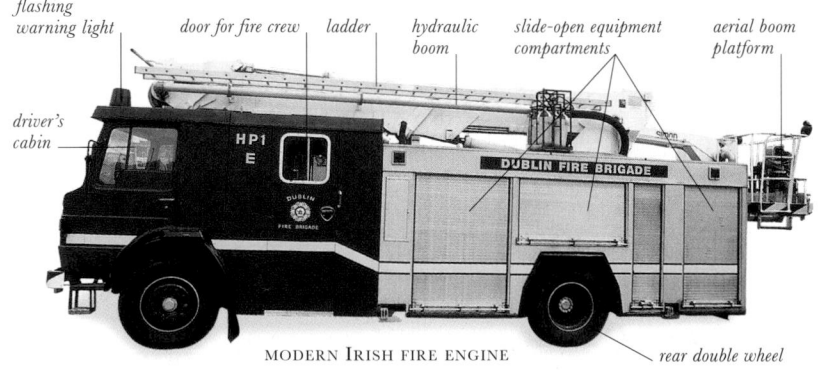

flashing warning light   *door for fire crew*   *ladder*   *hydraulic boom*   *slide-open equipment compartments*   *aerial boom platform*

driver's cabin

HP1 E

DUBLIN FIRE BRIGADE

MODERN IRISH FIRE ENGINE   *rear double wheel*

FIRE EXTINGUISHER

The water-filled fire extinguisher shown contains a canister of high-pressure gas. When the operating lever is depressed, a pin punctures the canister, releasing gas into the main cylinder. The pressure of the gas forces the water through the discharge tube and out of the nozzle.

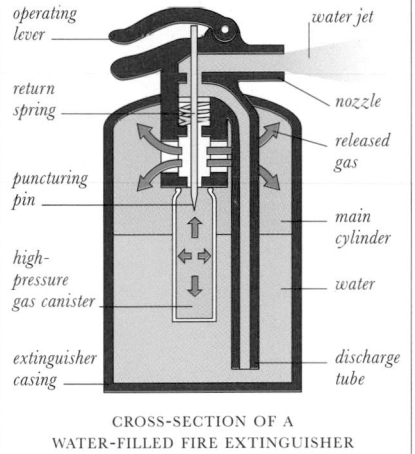

operating lever
water jet
return spring
nozzle
released gas
puncturing pin
main cylinder
high-pressure gas canister
water
extinguisher casing
discharge tube

CROSS-SECTION OF A
WATER-FILLED FIRE EXTINGUISHER

fire escape *n.* an emergency staircase or apparatus for escape from a building on fire.

fire extinguisher *n.* ▲ an apparatus for discharging gas, powder, water, or foam to extinguish a fire.

firefighter *n.* a person whose task is to extinguish fires. □ **fire-fighting** *n. & attrib.adj.*

firefly *n.* (*pl.* **-flies**) any soft-bodied beetle of the glow-worm family Lampyridae, emitting phosphorescent light, usu. in flashes.

fireguard *n.* **1** a protective screen or grid placed in front of a fireplace. **2** *N. Amer.* a fire-watcher. **3** *N. Amer.* a firebreak.

fire hose *n.* a hosepipe used in extinguishing fires.

fire-irons *n.pl.* tongs, poker, and shovel, for tending a domestic fire.

firelight *n.* light from a fire in a fireplace.

firelighter *n. Brit.* a piece of inflammable material to help start a fire in a grate.

firelock *n. hist.* a musket in which the priming was ignited by sparks.

fireman *n.* (*pl.* **-men**) **1** a member of a fire brigade. **2** a person who tends a furnace or the fire of a steam engine or steamship.

fireplace *n.* **1** a place for a domestic fire. **2** ▼ structure surrounding this.

mantelpiece or surround
mantelshelf
chimney
grate
ashpan
hearth

FIREPLACE

firepower *n.* **1** the destructive capacity of guns etc. **2** financial, intellectual, or emotional strength.

fire practice *n. Brit.* a fire drill.

fireproof ● *adj.* able to resist fire or great heat. ● *v.tr.* make fireproof.

fire-raiser *n. Brit.* an arsonist.

fire screen *n.* **1** a screen to keep off the direct heat of a fire. **2** a fireguard.

fireside *n.* **1** the area round a fireplace. **2** a person's home or home life.

fireside chat *n.* an informal talk.

fire station *n.* the headquarters of a fire brigade.

firestorm *n.* a very intense and destructive fire (usu. one caused by bombing) in which strong currents of air are drawn into the blaze from the surrounding area.

firethorn *n.* = PYRACANTHA.

fire-tongs *n.pl.* tongs for picking up pieces of coal etc. in tending a fire.

fire trap *n.* a building without proper provision for escape in case of fire.

fire-walking *n.* the (often ceremonial) practice of walking barefoot over hot stones, wood ashes, etc. □ **fire-walker** *n.*

fire-watcher *n.* a person keeping watch for fires, esp. those caused by bombs.

firewater *n. colloq.* strong alcoholic liquor.

fireweed *n.* ► any of several plants that spring up on burnt land, esp. the rosebay willowherb.

firewood *n.* wood for use as fuel.

firework *n.* **1** a device containing combustible chemicals that cause explosions or spectacular effects. **2** (in *pl.*) **a** an outburst of passion, esp. anger. **b** a display of wit or brilliance.

firing line *n.* **1** the front line in a battle. **2** the leading part in an activity etc.

firing party *n.* a group detailed to fire the salute at a military funeral.

firing squad *n.* **1** a group detailed to shoot a condemned person. **2** a firing party.

firkin *n.* **1** a small cask for liquids, butter, fish, etc. **2** *Brit.* (as a measure of beer etc.) half a kilderkin (usu. 9 imperial gallons or about 41 litres). [Middle English]

firm[1] ● *adj.* **1 a** of solid or compact structure. **b** fixed, stable. **c** steady; not shaking. **2 a** resolute, determined. **b** not easily shaken (*firm belief*). **c** steadfast, constant (*a firm friend*). **3** (of an offer etc.) not liable to cancellation after acceptance. ● *adv.* firmly (*stand firm*; *hold firm to*). ● *v.* **1** *tr. & intr.* (often foll. by *up*) make or become firm, secure, compact, or solid. **2** *tr.* (often foll. by *in*) fix (plants) firmly in the soil. [from Latin *firmus*] □ **firmly** *adv.* **firmness** *n.*

firm[2] *n.* a business concern. [based on Latin *firmare* 'to confirm by signature']

firmament *n. literary* the sky regarded as a vault or arch. [from Latin *firmamentum*] □ **firmamental** *adj.*

firmware *n. Computing* a permanent kind of software programmed into a read-only memory.

first ● *adj.* **1 a** earliest in time or order. **b** coming next after a specified or implied time (*shall take the first train*; *the first cuckoo*). **2** foremost in position, rank, or importance (*First Lord of the Treasury*; *first mate*). **3** *Mus.* performing the highest or chief of two or more parts for the same instrument or voice. **4** most willing or likely (*should be the first to admit the difficulty*). **5** basic or evident (*first principles*). ● *n.* **1** (prec. by *the*) the person or thing first mentioned or occurring. **2** the first occurrence of something notable. **3** *Brit.* a place in the first class in an examination. **4** the first day of a month. **5** first gear. **6** first place in a race. ● *adv.* **1** before any other person or thing (*first of all*; *first and foremost*; *first come first served*). **2** before someone or something else

FIREWEED:
ROSEBAY
WILLOWHERB
(*Chamerion
angustifolium*)

(*must get this done first*). **3** for the first time (*when did you first see her?*). **4** in preference; rather (*will see him damned first*). **5** *Brit.* first-class (*usually travels first*). □ **at first** at the beginning. **at first hand** directly from the original source. **first off** esp. *US colloq.* at first, first of all. **first up 1** first of all. **2** *Austral.* at the first attempt. **from the first** from the beginning. **from first to last** throughout. **get to first base** *US* achieve the first step towards an objective. **in the first place** as the first consideration. **of the first water** see WATER. [Old English]

first aid *n.* (hyphenated when *attrib.*) help given to an injured person until medical treatment is available. □ **first aider** *n.*

first blood see BLOOD.

first-born ● *adj.* eldest. ● *n.* the eldest child of a person.

first-class ● *adj.* **1** belonging to or travelling by the first class. **2** of the best quality; very good. ● *adv.* by first class (*travels first-class*).

first class *n.* **1** a set of persons or things grouped together as the best. **2** the best accommodation in a train, ship, etc. **3** the class of mail given priority in handling. **4** *Brit.* **a** the highest division in an examination list. **b** a place in this.

first cousin see COUSIN 1.

first-day cover *n.* an envelope with stamps postmarked on their first day of issue.

first-degree *adj. Med.* denoting burns that affect only the surface of the skin, causing reddening.

first finger *n.* the finger next to the thumb.

first floor *n.* (*N. Amer.* **second floor**) the floor above the ground floor.

first-foot *Sc.* ● *n.* the first person to cross a threshold in the New Year. ● *v.intr.* be a first-foot.

first-fruit *n.* (usu. in *pl.*) **1** the first agricultural produce of a season, esp. as offered to God. **2** the first results of work etc.

first gear *n.* the lowest in a set of gears.

first-hand *adj. & adv.* from the original source.

First Lady *n.* (in the US) the wife of the President.

first lieutenant *n. US* an army or air force officer next below captain.

first light *n.* the time when light first appears in the morning.

firstly *adv.* (in enumerating topics, arguments, etc.) in the first place, first (cf. FIRST *adv.*).

first mate *n.* (on a merchant ship) the officer second in command to the master.

first name *n.* a personal or Christian name.

first night *n.* the first public performance of a play etc.

first offender *n.* a criminal against whom no previous conviction is recorded.

first officer *n.* the mate on a merchant ship.

first past the post *adj.* **1** winning a race etc. by being the first to reach the finishing line. **2** *Brit.* (of an electoral system) selecting a candidate or party by simple majority.

first person see PERSON 3.

first post *n. Brit.* the first of several bugle calls giving notice of the hour of retiring at night.

first-rate *adj.* **1** of the highest class, excellent. **2** *colloq.* very well (*feeling first-rate*).

first refusal see REFUSAL 2.

first school *n. Brit.* a school for children from 5 to 9 years old.

first sergeant *n. US* the highest-ranking non-commissioned officer in a company.

first strike *adj.* an aggressive attack with nuclear weapons before their use by the enemy.

first thing *colloq.* ● *adv.* before anything else; very early in the morning (*shall do it first thing*). ● *n.* (prec. by *the*) even the most elementary fact or principle (*does not know the first thing about it*).

F

FISH

There are over 20,000 species of fish, divided into three groups: bony fish, cartilaginous fish, and jawless fish. Bony fish, which are the most numerous, have skeletons of bone, and swimbladders (gas-filled organs) to keep them afloat. Cartilaginous fish, such as sharks, rays, and ratfish, are mostly marine hunters; they have skeletons made of cartilage, and sandpaper-like skin. The primitive jawless fish have sucker-like mouths, and include lampreys and hagfish.

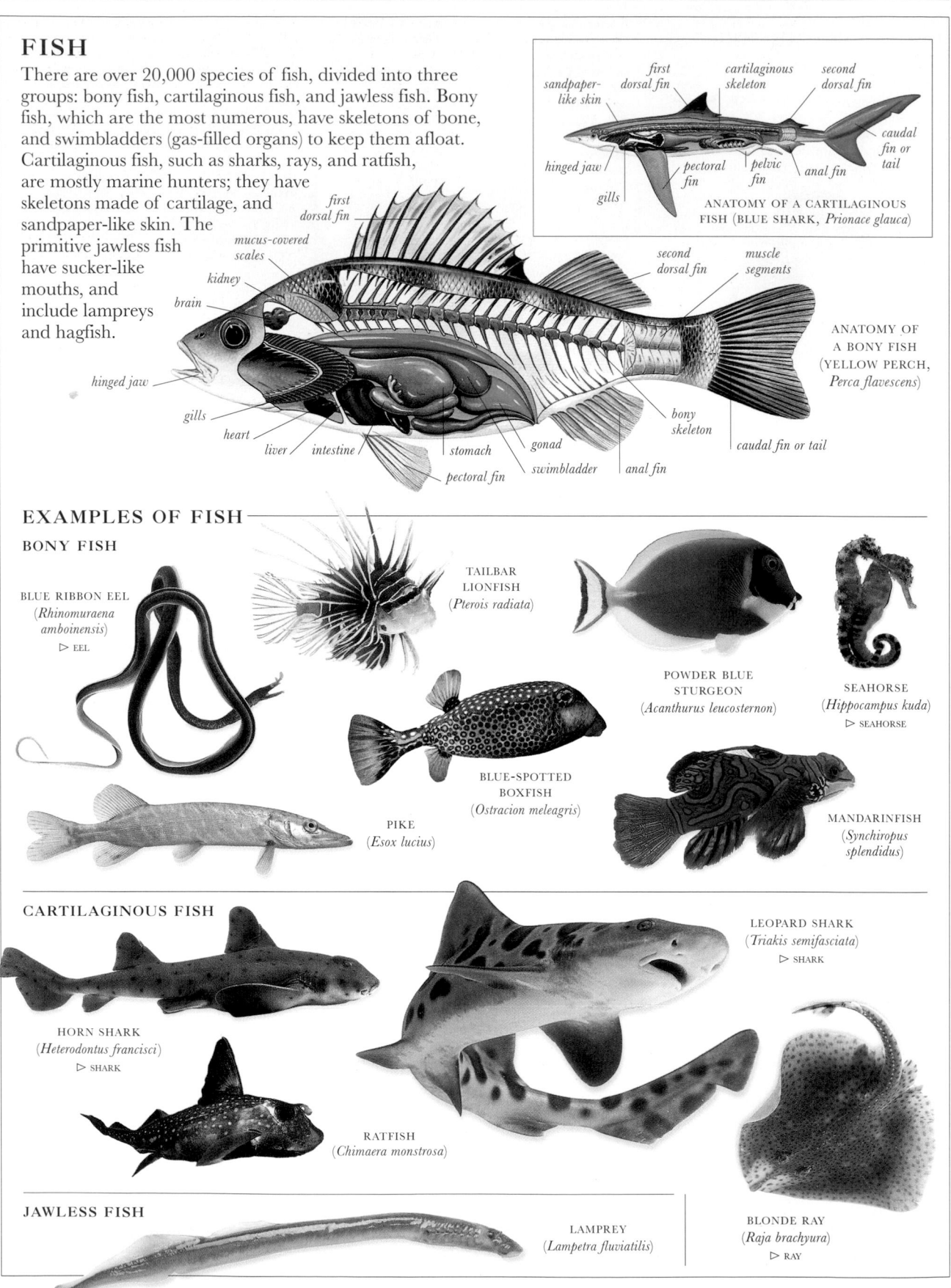

sandpaper-like skin

first dorsal fin

cartilaginous skeleton

second dorsal fin

caudal fin or tail

hinged jaw

pectoral fin

pelvic fin

anal fin

gills

ANATOMY OF A CARTILAGINOUS FISH (BLUE SHARK, *Prionace glauca*)

first dorsal fin

mucus-covered scales

kidney

brain

hinged jaw

gills

heart

liver

intestine

stomach

pectoral fin

swimbladder

gonad

anal fin

second dorsal fin

muscle segments

bony skeleton

caudal fin or tail

ANATOMY OF A BONY FISH (YELLOW PERCH, *Perca flavescens*)

EXAMPLES OF FISH

BONY FISH

BLUE RIBBON EEL
(*Rhinomuraena amboinensis*)
▷ EEL

TAILBAR LIONFISH
(*Pterois radiata*)

POWDER BLUE STURGEON
(*Acanthurus leucosternon*)

SEAHORSE
(*Hippocampus kuda*)
▷ SEAHORSE

BLUE-SPOTTED BOXFISH
(*Ostracion meleagris*)

PIKE
(*Esox lucius*)

MANDARINFISH
(*Synchiropus splendidus*)

CARTILAGINOUS FISH

LEOPARD SHARK
(*Triakis semifasciata*)
▷ SHARK

HORN SHARK
(*Heterodontus francisci*)
▷ SHARK

RATFISH
(*Chimaera monstrosa*)

BLONDE RAY
(*Raja brachyura*)
▷ RAY

JAWLESS FISH

LAMPREY
(*Lampetra fluviatilis*)

F

firth *n.* (also **frith**) **1** a narrow inlet of the sea. **2** an estuary. [from Old Norse *fjörthr* 'fjord']

fir tree see FIR 1.

fiscal ● *adj.* of public revenue. **●** *n.* **1** a legal official in some countries. **2** *Sc.* = PROCURATOR FISCAL. [based on Latin *fiscus* 'purse, treasury'] □ **fiscally** *adv.*

fiscal year *n.* = FINANCIAL YEAR.

fish[1] *n.* (*pl.* same or **fishes**) **1 ◀** a vertebrate cold-blooded animal with gills and fins living wholly in water. **2** an invertebrate animal living wholly in water, e.g. cuttlefish, shellfish, jellyfish. **3** the flesh of fish as food. **4** *colloq.* a person remarkable in some way (*an odd fish*). **5** (**the Fish** or **Fishes**) the zodiacal sign or constellation Pisces. **●** *v.* **1** *intr.* try to catch fish. **2** *tr.* fish for (a certain kind of fish) or in (a certain stretch of water). **3** *intr.* (foll. by *for*) **a** search for in water or a concealed place. **b** seek by indirect means (*fishing for compliments*). **4** *tr.* (foll. by *up*, *out*, etc.) retrieve with careful or awkward searching. □ **fish out of water** a person in an unsuitable or unwelcome environment or situation. **other fish to fry** other matters to attend to. [Old English] □ **fishlike** *adj.*

■ **Usage** The collective plural *fish* is now usual, but the older form *fishes* is still used, especially in technical writing, when referring to different kinds of fish (e.g. *the freshwater fishes of Europe*), and in biblical allusions etc. (e.g. *five loaves and two small fishes*).

fish[2] *n.* **1** a flat plate of iron, wood, etc., to strengthen a beam or joint. **2** *Naut.* a piece of wood, convex and concave, used to strengthen a mast etc. [based on French *ficher* 'to fix']

fishbowl *n.* a usu. round glass bowl for keeping pet fish in.

fish cake *n.* a cake of shredded fish and mashed potato, usu. eaten fried.

fisher *n.* **1** an animal that catches fish, esp. the pekan, a tree-living N. American marten, *Martes pennanti*, valued for its fur. ▷ MUSTELID. **2** *archaic* a fisherman.

fisherman *n.* (*pl.* **-men**) a person who catches fish.

fishery *n.* (*pl.* **-ies**) **1** a place where fish are caught or reared. **2** the industry of catching or rearing fish.

fish-eye lens *n.* a very wide-angle lens with a field of vision covering up to 180°, the scale being reduced towards the edges.

fish farm *n.* a place where fish are bred for food.

fish finger *n.* *Brit.* a small oblong piece of fish in batter or breadcrumbs.

fish-hook see HOOK *n.* 1b.

fishing *n.* **▶** the activity of catching fish, esp. for food or as a sport.

fishing line *n.* a long thread with a baited hook, sinker, float, etc., used for catching fish. ▷ FISHING

fishing rod *n.* a long tapering usu. jointed rod to which a fishing line is attached. ▷ FISHING

fish kettle *n.* an oval pan for boiling fish.

fishmeal *n.* ground dried fish used as fertilizer or animal feed.

fishmonger *n.* esp. *Brit.* a dealer in fish for food.

fishnet *n.* (often *attrib.*) an open-meshed fabric (*fishnet stockings*).

fish-plate *n.* **1** a flat piece of iron etc. connecting railway rails. **2** a flat piece of metal with ends like a fish's tail, used to position masonry.

fish slice *n.* *Brit.* a flat utensil for lifting fish and fried foods during and after cooking.

fishtail ● *n.* anything resembling a fish's tail in shape or movement. **●** *v.intr.* move the tail of a vehicle from side to side.

fishwife *n.* (*pl.* **-wives**) **1** a coarse-mannered or noisy woman. **2** a woman who sells fish.

fishy *adj.* (**fishier**, **fishiest**) **1 a** of or like (a) fish. **b** *joc.* or *poet.* abounding in fish. **2** *slang* arousing suspicion, questionable, mysterious (*something fishy going on*). □ **fishiness** *n.*

fissile *adj.* **1** capable of undergoing nuclear fission. **2** tending to split.

fission ● *n.* **1** the action of dividing or splitting into two or more parts. **2** *Physics* = NUCLEAR FISSION. **3** *Biol.* the division of a cell into new cells as a mode of reproduction. **●** *v.intr. & tr.* undergo or cause to undergo fission. [from Latin *fissio*, related to FISSURE] □ **fissionable** *adj.*

fission bomb *n.* an atom bomb.

fissure ● *n.* **1** an opening, usu. long and narrow, made by cracking, splitting, or separation of parts. **2** *Bot. & Anat.* a narrow opening in an organ etc., esp. a depression between convolutions of the brain. **3** a cleavage. **●** *v.tr. & intr.* split or crack. [based on Latin *findere fiss-* 'to cleave']

fist *n.* a tightly closed hand. □ **make a good** (or **poor** etc.) **fist** (foll. by *at, of*) *colloq.* make a good (or poor etc.) attempt at. [Old English] □ **fisted** *adj.* (also in *comb.*). **fistful** *n.* (*pl.* **-fuls**)

fisticuffs *n.pl.* fighting with the fists.

fistula *n.* (*pl.* **fistulas** or **fistulae** /-lee/) *Med.* an abnormal or surgically made passage between a hollow organ and the body surface or between two hollow organs. [Latin, literally 'pipe, flute'] □ **fistulous** *adj.*

fit[1] **●** *adj.* (**fitter**, **fittest**) **1 a** well suited. **b** (foll. by *to* + infin.) qualified, competent, worthy. **c** (foll. by *for*, or *to* + infin.) in a suitable condition, ready. **d** (foll. by *for*) good enough (*fit for a king*). **e** (foll. by *to* + infin.) sufficiently exhausted, troubled, or angry (*fit to drop*). **2** in good health or athletic condition. **3** proper, becoming, right (*it is fit that*). **●** *v.* (**fitted**, **fitting**) **1 a** *tr.* (also *absol.*) be of the right shape and size for (*the key doesn't fit the lock*; *these shoes don't fit*). **b** *tr.* make, fix, or insert (a thing) so that it is of the right size or shape (*fitted shelves in the alcoves*). **c** *intr.* (of a component) be correctly positioned (*that bit fits here*). **d** *tr.* find room for (*can't fit another person on the bench*). **2** *tr.* (foll. by *for*, or *to* + infin.) **a** make suitable; adapt. **b** make competent (*fitted him to be a priest*). **3** *tr.* supply, furnish (*fitted the boat with a new rudder*). **4** *tr.* fix in place (*fit a lock on the door*). **5** *tr.* = fit on. **6** *tr.* befit, become (*the punishment fits the crime*).

7 *tr.* (often foll. by *up*) esp. *Austral.* secure enough (genuine or false) evidence to convict; frame. **●** *n.* the way in which a garment, component, etc., fits (*a bad fit*; *a tight fit*). **●** *adv.* (foll. by *to* + infin.) *colloq.* in a suitable manner, appropriately (*was laughing fit to bust*). □ **fit the bill** = *fill the bill*. **fit in 1** be compatible or accommodating (*tried to fit in with their plans*). **2** find space or time for (*the dentist fitted me in at the last minute*). **fit on** *Brit.* try on (a garment). **fit out** (or **up**) equip. **see** (or **think**) **fit** decide or choose (a specified course of action). [Middle English] □ **fitly** *adv.* **fitness** *n.*

fit[2] *n.* **1** a sudden seizure of epilepsy, hysteria, apoplexy, fainting, or paralysis, with unconsciousness or convulsions. **2** a sudden brief attack of an illness or of symptoms (*fit of coughing*). **3** a sudden short bout or burst (*fit of energy*; *fit of giggles*). **4** *colloq.* an attack of strong feeling (*fit of rage*). **5** a capricious impulse; a mood (*when the fit was on him*). □ **by** (or **in**) **fits and starts** spasmodically. **give a person a fit** *colloq.* surprise or outrage him or her. **have a fit** *colloq.* be greatly surprised or outraged. **in fits** laughing uncontrollably. [Old English *fitt* 'conflict']

fitful *adj.* spasmodic or intermittent. □ **fitfully** *adv.* **fitfulness** *n.*

fitment *n.* (usu. in *pl.*) esp. *Brit.* a fixed item of furniture.

fitted *adj.* **1** made to fill a space or cover something closely or exactly (*a fitted carpet*). **2** esp. *Brit.* provided with appropriate equipment, fittings, etc. (*a fitted kitchen*). **3** esp. *Brit.* built-in; filling an alcove etc. (*fitted cupboards*).

fitter *n.* **1** a person who supervises the cutting, fitting, altering, etc. of garments. **2** a mechanic who fits together and adjusts machinery.

fitting ● *n.* **1** the process or an instance of having a garment etc. fitted (*needed several fittings*). **2 a** (in *pl.*) *Brit.* the fixtures and fitments of a building. **b** a piece of apparatus or furniture. **●** *adj.* proper, becoming, right. □ **fittingly** *adv.* **fittingness** *n.*

F

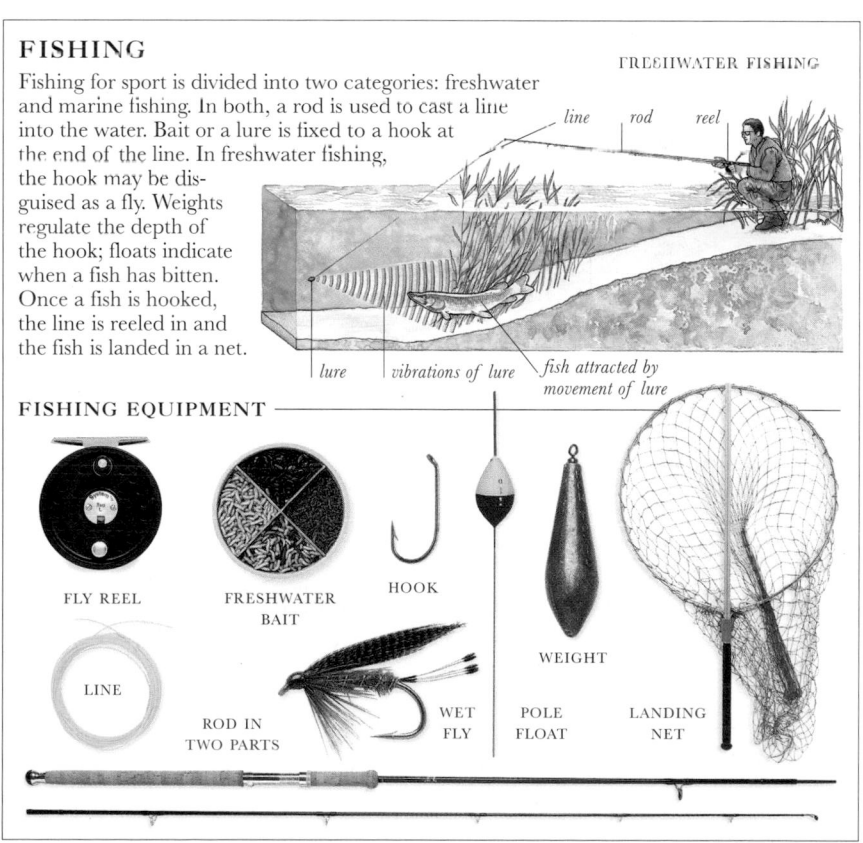

FISHING

Fishing for sport is divided into two categories: freshwater and marine fishing. In both, a rod is used to cast a line into the water. Bait or a lure is fixed to a hook at the end of the line. In freshwater fishing, the hook may be disguised as a fly. Weights regulate the depth of the hook; floats indicate when a fish has bitten. Once a fish is hooked, the line is reeled in and the fish is landed in a net.

FRESHWATER FISHING

line   rod   reel

lure   vibrations of lure

fish attracted by movement of lure

FISHING EQUIPMENT

FLY REEL

FRESHWATER BAIT

HOOK

POLE FLOAT

LANDING NET

WEIGHT

LINE

ROD IN TWO PARTS

WET FLY

FLAG

For centuries flags have been used as patriotic rallying points, as emblems, or as signals. All countries have their own flag, as do many organizations. Flags are usually made from strongly coloured fabric and are mostly rectangular or square. A flag is divided into four quarters, called cantons: those near the flagstaff are the hoist cantons; those furthest away are the fly cantons. Ships use flags to communicate at sea via the international code of signals (shown below). Flags that represent a letter of the alphabet also convey a specific message.

truck *becket* *toggle* *upper hoist canton* *upper fly canton* *chief mullet* *bunting cloth* *mullet (five-pointed star)* *roundel* *base mullet* *tack line* *canvas sleeve* *flagstaff* *halyard* *lower hoist canton* *lower fly canton*

PARTS OF A FLAG (NATIONAL FLAG OF GRENADA)

F

INTERNATIONAL CODE OF SIGNALS

ALPHABET / MESSAGE FLAGS

A / DIVER DOWN –
KEEP WELL CLEAR
AT LOW SPEED

B / I AM LOADING
AND DISCHARGING
DANGEROUS GOODS

C / YES
(AFFIRMATIVE)

D / KEEP CLEAR –
I AM MANOEUVRING
WITH DIFFICULTY

E / I AM DIRECTING
MY COURSE TO
STARBOARD

F / I AM DISABLED –
COMMUNICATE
WITH ME

G / I REQUIRE
A PILOT

H / I HAVE A
PILOT ON BOARD

I / I AM DIRECTING
MY COURSE TO
PORT

J / I AM ON FIRE –
KEEP CLEAR
OF ME

K / I WISH TO
COMMUNICATE

L / YOU SHOULD
STOP YOUR VESSEL
INSTANTLY

M / MY VESSEL IS
STOPPED, MAKING
NO WAY

N / NO
(NEGATIVE)

O / MAN
OVERBOARD

P / ALL PERSONS
REPAIR ON BOARD

Q / MY VESSEL IS
HEALTHY; I REQUEST
FREE PRATIQUE

R / NO MEANING

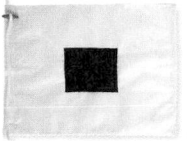

S / MY ENGINES
ARE GOING FULL
SPEED ASTERN

T / KEEP CLEAR
OF ME

U / YOU ARE
RUNNING INTO
DANGER

V / I REQUIRE
ASSISTANCE

W / I REQUIRE
MEDICAL
ASSISTANCE

X / STOP CARRYING
OUT YOUR
INTENTIONS

Y / I AM
DRAGGING
MY ANCHOR

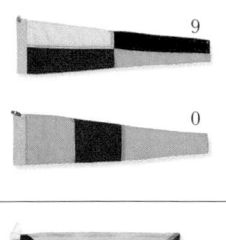

Z / I REQUIRE
A TUG

NUMBER FLAGS

1

2

3

4

5

6

7

8

9

0

five ● *n.* **1** one more than four. **2** a symbol for this (5, v, V). **3** a size etc. denoted by five. **4** a set or team of five individuals. **5** five o'clock. ● *adj.* that amount to five. [Old English]

five-a-side ● *adj.* designating football played with five players in each team. ● *n.* a game of five-a-side football.

five-eighth *n. Austral. & NZ Rugby* either of two players between the scrum-half and the centre three-quarter.

fivefold *adj. & adv.* **1** five times as much or as many. **2** consisting of five parts. **3** amounting to five.

five o'clock shadow *n.* beard-growth visible on a man's face in the latter part of the day.

fiver *n. colloq.* **1** *Brit.* a five-pound note. **2** *N. Amer.* a five-dollar bill.

fives *n.* a game played esp. in the UK, in which a ball is hit with a gloved hand or a bat against the walls of a court with three walls (**Eton fives**) or four walls (**Rugby fives**).

five senses *n.pl.* (prec. by *the*) sight, hearing, smell, taste, and touch.

five-star *adj.* of the highest class.

fix ● *v.* **1** *tr.* make firm or stable; fasten, secure (*fixed a picture to the wall*). **2** *tr.* decide, settle, specify (a price, date, etc.). **3** *tr.* mend, repair. **4** *tr.* implant in the mind (*couldn't get the rules fixed in his head*). **5** *tr.* **a** (foll. by *on*, *upon*) direct steadily, set (one's eyes, gaze, attention, or affection). **b** attract and hold (a person's attention, eyes, etc.). **c** (foll. by *with*) single out with one's eyes etc. **6** *tr.* place definitely, establish. **7** *tr.* determine the exact nature, position, etc., of; refer (a thing or person) to a definite place or time; identify, locate. **8 a** *tr.* make (eyes, features, etc.) rigid. **b** *intr.* (of eyes, features, etc.) become rigid. **9** *tr.* esp. *N. Amer. colloq.* prepare (food or drink). **10 a** *tr.* congeal. **b** *intr.* become congealed. **11** *tr. colloq.* punish, kill, silence, deal with (a person). **12** *tr. colloq.* **a** secure the support of (a person) fraudulently, esp. by bribery. **b** arrange the result of (a race, match, etc.) fraudulently. **13** *slang* **a** *tr.* inject (a person, esp. oneself) with a narcotic. **b** *intr.* take an injection of a narcotic. **14** *tr.* **a** make (a pigment, photographic image, etc.) fast or permanent. **b** *Biol.* preserve or stabilize (a specimen) prior to treatment or microscopic examination. **15** *tr.* (of a plant or micro-organism) assimilate (nitrogen or carbon dioxide). ● *n.* **1** *colloq.* a dilemma or predicament. **2 a** the act of finding one's position by bearings or astronomical observations. **b** a position found in this way. **3** *slang* a dose of a narcotic drug to which one is addicted. **4** *slang* bribery; an illicit arrangement. □ **be fixed** (usu. foll. by *for*) be disposed or affected (regarding) (*how are you fixed for Friday?*). **fix on** (or **upon**) choose, decide on. **fix up** **1** arrange, organize, prepare. **2** accommodate. **3** provide (a person) (*fixed me up with a job*). [based on Latin *fixus* 'fixed, fastened'] □ **fixable** *adj.* **fixedly** *adv.* **fixedness** *n.*

fixate *v.tr.* **1** direct one's gaze on. **2** *Psychol.* (usu. in *passive*) cause (a person) to acquire an abnormal attachment to persons or things (*was fixated on his son*).

fixation *n.* **1** the act or an instance of being fixated. **2** an obsession, concentration on a single idea. **3** fixing or being fixed. **4** coagulation. **5** the process of assimilating a gas to form a solid compound.

fixative ● *adj.* tending to fix or secure. ● *n.* a substance used to fix colours, hair, biological specimens, etc.

fixed-doh *attrib.adj.* (also **fixed-do**) applied to a system of sight-singing in which C is called 'doh', D is called 'ray', etc., irrespective of the key in which they occur (cf. MOVABLE-DOH).

fixed point *n. Physics* a well-defined reproducible temperature.

fixed star see STAR *n.* 2.

fixer *n.* **1** a person or thing that fixes. **2** *Photog.* a substance used for fixing a photographic image etc.

3 *colloq.* a person who makes arrangements, esp. of an illicit kind.

fixing *n.* **1** a method or means of fixing. **2** (in *pl.*) **a** *US* apparatus or equipment. **b** *N. Amer.* the trimmings or ingredients for a dish.

fixity *n.* **1** a fixed state. **2** permanence.

fixture *n.* **1 a** something fixed in position. **b** (usu. *predic.*) *colloq.* a person or thing confined to or established in one place (*he seems to be a fixture*). **2** *Brit.* **a** a sporting event. **b** the date agreed for this. **3** (in *pl.*) *Law* articles attached to a house or land and regarded as legally part of it. [based on Latin *figere fix-* 'to fix']

fizz ● *v.intr.* **1** make a hissing or spluttering sound. **2** (of a drink) effervesce. ● *n.* **1** effervescence. **2** *colloq.* an effervescent drink, esp. champagne.

fizzle ● *v.intr.* make a feeble hiss. ● *n.* such a sound. □ **fizzle out** end feebly.

fizzy *adj.* (**fizzier**, **fizziest**) effervescent. □ **fizziness** *n.*

fjord /fi-ord/ *n.* (also **fiord**) a long narrow inlet of sea between high cliffs. ▷ COASTLINE. [Norwegian]

fl. *abbr.* **1** floor. **2** floruit. **3** fluid.

flab *n. colloq.* fat; flabbiness.

flabbergast *v.tr.* (esp. as **flabbergasted** *adj.*) *colloq.* overwhelm with astonishment; dumbfound. [18th-century coinage]

flabby *adj.* (**flabbier**, **flabbiest**) **1** (of flesh etc.) hanging down; limp; flaccid. **2** (of language or character) feeble. [based on FLAP] □ **flabbily** *adv.* **flabbiness** *n.*

flaccid /flak-sid/ *adj.* **1 a** (of flesh etc.) hanging loose or wrinkled; limp, flabby. **b** (of plant tissue) soft; less rigid. **2** relaxed, drooping. **3** lacking vigour; feeble. [from Latin *flaccidus*] □ **flaccidity** *n.* **flaccidly** *adv.*

flack var. of FLAK. [20th-century coinage]

flag[1] ● *n.* **1 a** ◀ a piece of cloth attachable by one edge to a pole or rope and used as a country's emblem or as a standard, signal, etc. **b** a small toy, device, etc., resembling a flag. **2** a device that is raised to indicate that a taxi is for hire. ● *v.* (**flagged**, **flagging**) **1** *intr.* **a** grow tired; lose vigour; lag (*his energy flagged after the first lap*). **b** hang down; droop. **2** *tr.* **a** place a flag on or over. **b** mark out with or as if with a flag or flags. **3** *tr.* **a** inform (a person) by flag signals. **b** communicate (information) by flagging. □ **flag down** signal to (a vehicle or driver) to stop. **keep the flag flying** continue the fight. [16th-century coinage] □ **flagger** *n.*

flag[2] ● *n.* **1** a flat usu. rectangular stone slab used for paving. **2** (in *pl.*) a pavement made of these. ● *v.tr.* (**flagged**, **flagging**) pave with flags. [from Old Norse *flaga* 'slab of stone']

flag[3] *n.* ◀ any of various plants with sword-shaped leaves, esp. the yellow flag *Iris pseudacorus*.

> **Flag Day** *n. US* 14 June, the anniversary of the adoption of the Stars and Stripes in 1777.

> **flag day** *n. Brit.* a day on which money is raised for a charity by the sale of small paper flags etc. in the street.

flagellant ● *n.* **1** a person who scourges himself or herself or others as a religious discipline. **2** a person who engages in flogging as a sexual stimulus. ● *adj.* of or concerning flagellation. [from Latin *flagellant-* 'whipping']

flagellate[1] *v.tr.* scourge, flog (cf. FLAGELLANT).

FLAG:
YELLOW FLAG
(*Iris pseudacorus*)

flagellate[2] *adj.* having flagella. ● *n.* a protozoan having one or more flagella.

flagellation *n.* the act or practice of flagellating others or (esp.) oneself, as a sexual stimulus or religious discipline.

flagellum /fla-jel-ŭm/ *n.* (*pl.* **flagella**) **1** *Biol.* a long lashlike appendage found esp. on microscopic organisms. ▷ ALGA, BACTERIUM, SPERMATOZOON. **2** *Bot.* a runner; a creeping shoot. [Latin, literally 'whip'] □ **flagellar** *adj.*

FLAGEOLET:
CARVED NATIVE AMERICAN FLAGEOLET

mouthpiece   *finger hole*   *blowhole*

flageolet[1] *n.* ▲ a small flute blown at the end, like a recorder but with two thumb holes. [French]

flageolet[2] *n.* a kind of French kidney bean. ▷ PULSE. [from Latin *phaseolus* 'bean']

flag of convenience *n.* a foreign flag under which a ship is registered.

flag-officer *n.* an admiral, vice admiral, or rear admiral, or the commodore of a yacht club.

flag of truce *n.* a white flag indicating a desire for a truce.

flagon *n.* **1** a large bottle in which wine, cider, etc., is sold, usu. holding 1.13 litres (about 2 pints). **2** a large vessel usu. with a handle, spout, and lid, to hold wine etc. [from Late Latin *flasco -onis* 'flask']

flagpole *n.* = FLAGSTAFF.

flagrant *adj.* (of an offence or an offender) glaring; notorious; scandalous. [from Latin *flagrant-* 'blazing'] □ **flagrancy** *n.* **flagrantly** *adv.*

flagship *n.* **1** a ship having an admiral on board. **2** something that is held to be the best or most important of its kind.

flagstaff *n.* a pole on which a flag may be hoisted.

flagstone *n.* = FLAG[2] *n.*

flail *n.* ▲ a threshing tool consisting of a wooden staff with a short heavy stick swinging from it. ● *v.* **1** *tr.* beat or strike with or as if with a flail. **2** *intr.* wave or swing wildly. [Old English]

flair *n.* **1** an instinct for selecting or performing what is excellent, useful, etc. **2** talent or ability, esp. artistic or stylistic. [based on French *flairer* 'to smell']

flak *n.* (also **flack**) **1** anti-aircraft fire. **2** adverse criticism; abuse. [German, abbreviation of *Flug-(zeug)abwehrkanone* 'anti-aircraft gun']

flake ● *n.* **1 a** a small thin light piece of snow. **b** a similar piece of another material. **2** a thin broad piece of material peeled or split off. **3** *Archaeol.* a piece of hard stone chipped off and used as a tool. **4** a natural division of the flesh of some fish. **5** the dogfish or other shark as food. **6** *N. Amer. slang* a crazy, eccentric, or dim person. ● *v.tr. & intr.* **1** take off or come away in flakes. **2** sprinkle with or fall in snowlike flakes. □ **flake out** *colloq.* fall asleep or drop from exhaustion; faint. [Middle English]

flak jacket *n.* ▼ a protective jacket of heavy camouflage fabric reinforced with metal, worn by soldiers etc.

flaky *adj.* (**flakier**, **flakiest**) **1** of or like flakes; separating easily into flakes. **2** esp. *N. Amer. slang* crazy, eccentric. □ **flakiness** *n.*

flaky pastry *n.* pastry consisting of thin light layers.

flambé /flom-bay/ *adj.* (of food) covered with alcohol and set alight briefly. [French]

FLAK JACKET

flamboyant *adj.* **1** ostentatious; showy. **2** floridly decorated. **3** gorgeously coloured. [French, literally 'blazing'] □ **flamboyance** *n.* **flamboyantly** *adv.*

flame ● *n.* **1 a** ignited gas (*the fire burnt with a steady flame*). **b** one portion of this (*the flame flickered and died*). **c** (usu. in *pl.*) visible combustion (*burst into flames*). **2 a** a bright light; brilliant colouring. **b** a brilliant orange-red colour. **3 a** a strong passion, esp. love (*fan the flame*). **b** *colloq.* a boyfriend or

F

girlfriend. ● *v.* **1** *intr.* & *tr.* emit or cause to emit flames. **2** *intr.* **a** (of passion) break out. **b** (of a person) become angry. **3** *intr.* shine or glow like flame (*leaves flamed in the autumn Sun*). **4** *tr.* subject to the action of flame. □ **go up in flames** be consumed by fire. [from Latin *flamma*] □ **flameless** *adj.* **flamelike** *adj.*

flamenco *n.* (*pl.* **-os**) **1** a style of music played (esp. on the guitar) and sung by Spanish gypsies. **2** a dance performed to this music. [Spanish, literally 'Flemish']

flameproof *adj.* treated so as to be non-flammable.

flame-thrower *n.* (also **flame-projector**) a weapon for throwing a spray of flame.

flaming *attrib.adj.* **1** emitting flames. **2** very hot (*flaming June*). **3** *colloq.* **a** passionate (*a flaming row*). **b** expressing annoyance (*that flaming dog*). **4** brightly coloured (*flaming red hair*).

F

FLAMINGO: LESSER FLAMINGO (*Phoenicoaias minor*)

flamingo *n.* ◄ (*pl.* **-os** or **-oes**) any tall long-necked web-footed wading bird of the family Phoenicopteridae, with crooked bill and pink, scarlet, and black plumage. [from Provençal *flamenc* 'flaming one']

flammable *adj.* inflammable. [related to FLAME] □ **flammability** *n.*

■ **Usage** *Flammable* is used because *inflammable* can be mistaken for a negative (the true negative being *non-flammable*).

flan *n.* **1** a pastry case with a savoury or sweet filling. **2** a sponge base with a sweet topping. [via Old French *flaon* and medieval Latin *flado -onis* from Frankish]

flange *Engin.* ● *n.* a projecting flat rim, collar, or rib, used for strengthening or attachment. ● *v.tr.* provide with a flange. [17th-century coinage]

flank ● *n.* **1 a** the side of the body between the ribs and the hip. **b** the side of an animal carved as meat (*flank of beef*). **2** the side of a mountain, building, etc. **3** the right or left side of an army or other body of persons. ● *v.tr.* **1** (often in *passive*) be situated at both sides of (*a road flanked by mountains*). **2** *Mil.* **a** guard or strengthen on the flank. **b** menace the flank of. [middle English via Old French *flanc* from Frankish]

flannel ● *n.* **1 a** a kind of woven woollen fabric, usu. without a nap. **b** (in *pl.*) flannel garments, esp. trousers. **2** *Brit.* a small usu. towelling cloth, used for washing oneself. **3** *Brit. slang* nonsense; flattery. ● *v.* (**flannelled**, **flannelling**; *US* **flanneled**, **flanneling**) **1** *Brit. slang* **a** *tr.* flatter. **b** *intr.* use flattery. **2** *tr.* wash or clean with a flannel.

flannelette *n.* a napped cotton fabric imitating flannel.

flap ● *v.* (**flapped**, **flapping**) **1 a** *tr.* move (wings, the arms, etc.) up and down when flying, or as if flying. **b** *intr.* (of wings, the arms, etc.) move up and down. **2** *intr. colloq.* be agitated or panicky. **3** *intr.* swing or sway about; flutter. **4** *tr.* (usu. foll. by *away*, *off*) strike (flies etc.) with something broad; drive. **5** *intr. colloq.* (of ears) listen intently. ● *n.* **1** a piece of cloth, wood, paper, etc. hinged or attached by one side only and often used to cover a gap. **2** one up-and-down motion of a wing, an arm, etc. **3** *colloq.* a state of agitation; panic (*don't get into a flap*). **4** a hinged or sliding section of a wing used to control lift. **5** a light blow with something broad. [Middle English] □ **flappy** *adj.*

flapdoodle *n. colloq.* nonsense. [19th-century coinage]

flapjack *n.* **1** a cake made from oats and golden syrup etc. **2** *N. Amer.* a pancake.

flapper *n.* **1** a person or thing that flaps. **2** an instrument that is flapped to kill flies, scare birds, etc. **3** a person who panics easily. **4** *slang* (in the 1920s) a young unconventional or lively woman.

flare ● *v.* **1** *intr.* & *tr.* widen or cause to widen gradually (*flared trousers*). **2** *intr.* & *tr.* burn or cause to burn suddenly with a bright unsteady flame. **3** *intr.* burst into anger; burst forth. ● *n.* **1 a** a dazzling irregular flame or light. **b** a sudden outburst of flame. **2 a** ▶ a signal light used at sea. **b** a bright light used as a signal. **c** a flame dropped from an aircraft to illuminate a target etc. **3** *Astron.* a sudden burst of radiation from a star. ▷ SUN. **4 a** a gradual widening, esp. of a skirt or trousers. **b** (in *pl.*) wide-bottomed trousers. ● **flare up 1** burst into a sudden blaze. **2** become suddenly angry or active. [16th-century coinage]

FLARE WITH FIRING MECHANISM

flare · *firing pin* · *case containing firing mechanism*

flare-path *n.* an area illuminated to enable an aircraft to land or take off.

flare-up *n.* an outburst of flame, anger, activity, etc.

flash ● *v.* **1** *intr.* & *tr.* emit or reflect or cause to emit or reflect light briefly, suddenly, or intermittently; gleam or cause to gleam. **2** *intr.* break suddenly into flame; give out flame or sparks. **3** *tr.* send or reflect like a sudden flame (*his eyes flashed fire*). **4** *intr.* **a** burst suddenly into view or perception (*the explanation flashed upon me*). **b** move swiftly (*the train flashed through the station*). **5** *tr.* **a** send (news etc.) by radio, telegraph, etc. (*flashed a message to her*). **b** signal to (a person) by shining lights or headlights briefly. **6** *tr. colloq.* show ostentatiously (*flashed her wedding ring*). **7** *intr. slang* indecently expose oneself. ● *n.* **1** a sudden bright light or flame. **2** a very brief time; an instant (*all over in a flash*). **3 a** a brief, sudden burst of feeling (*a flash of hope*). **b** a sudden display (of wit, understanding, etc.). **4** = NEWSFLASH. **5** *Photog.* = FLASH-GUN. **6** *Brit. Mil.* a coloured patch of cloth on a uniform etc. as a distinguishing emblem. **7** vulgar display, ostentation. **8** a bright patch of colour. ● *adj. Brit. colloq.* **1** gaudy; showy (*a flash car*). **2** connected with thieves, the underworld, etc. □ **flash in the pan** a promising start followed by failure (from the priming of old guns). [Middle English, originally with reference to the rushing of water]

flashback *n.* a scene in a film, novel, etc. set in a time earlier than the main action.

flashbulb *n. Photog.* a bulb for a flashgun.

flash burn *n.* a burn caused by sudden intense heat, esp. from a nuclear explosion.

flash-cube *n.* a set of four flashbulbs arranged as a cube and operated in turn.

flasher *n.* **1** *slang* a man who indecently exposes himself. **2 a** an automatic device for switching lights rapidly on and off. **b** a sign or signal using this. **3** a person or thing that flashes.

flash flood *n.* a sudden local flood due to heavy rain etc.

flashgun *n.* ◄ a device producing a flash of intense light, used for photographing by night, indoors, etc.

flashing *n.* a usu. metallic strip used to prevent water penetration at the junction of a roof with a wall etc.

flash lamp *n.* a portable flashing electric lamp.

flashlight *n.* an electric torch.

flash memory *n.* *Computing* a type of memory device that retains data in the absence of a power supply.

flashpoint *n.* **1** the temperature at which vapour from oil etc. will ignite in air. **2** the point at which anger, indignation, etc. becomes uncontrollable.

flash unit *n.* = FLASHGUN.

flashy *adj.* (**flashier**, **flashiest**) showy; gaudy; cheaply attractive. □ **flashily** *adv.* **flashiness** *n.*

flask *n.* **1** ▶ a narrow-necked bulbous bottle for wine etc. or as used in chemistry. **2** = HIP FLASK. **3** *Brit.* = VACUUM FLASK. [from medieval Latin, related to FLAGON]

FLASK USED FOR CHEMICAL EXPERIMENT

flat[1] ● *adj.* (**flatter**, **flattest**) **1 a** horizontally level (*a flat roof*). **b** even; smooth; unbroken; without projection or indentation (*a flat stomach*). **c** with a level surface and little depth; shallow (*a flat cap*; *a flat heel*). **2** unqualified; downright (*a flat refusal*). **3 a** dull; lifeless; monotonous (*spoke in a flat tone*). **b** dejected. **4** (of a fizzy drink) having lost its effervescence. **5** *Brit.* (of an accumulator, a battery, etc.) having exhausted its charge. **6** *Mus.* **a** below true or normal pitch (*the violins are flat*). **b** (of a key) having a flat or flats in the signature. **c** (as **B flat**, **E flat**, etc.), a semitone lower than B, E, etc. ▷ NOTATION. **7** (of paint etc.) not glossy; matt. **8** (of a tyre) punctured; deflated. **9** (of a market, prices, etc.) inactive; sluggish. **10** of or relating to flat racing. ● *adv.* **1** lying at full length; spread out (*lay flat on the floor*; *flat against the wall*). **2** *colloq.* **a** completely, absolutely (*flat broke*). **b** exactly (*in five minutes flat*). **3** *Mus.* below the true or normal pitch (*always sings flat*). ● *n.* **1** the flat part of anything (*the flat of the hand*). **2** level ground, esp. a plain or swamp. **3** *Mus.* **a** a note lowered a semitone below natural pitch. **b** the sign (♭) indicating this. **4** (as **the flat**) *Brit.* a flat racing. **b** the flat racing season. **5** *Theatr.* a flat section of scenery mounted on a frame. **6** *colloq.* a flat tyre, a puncture. ● *v.tr.* (**flatted**, **flatting**) **1** make flat, flatten (esp. in technical use). **2** *US Mus.* make (a note) flat. □ **fall flat** fail to live up to expectations; not win applause. **flat out 1** at top speed. **2** using all one's strength, energy, or resources. **that's flat** *colloq.* let there be no doubt about it. [from Old Norse *flatr*] □ **flatly** *adv.* **flatness** *n.* **flattish** *adj.*

flat[2] *n.* a set of rooms, usu. on one floor, used as a residence. [alteration of obsolete *flet* 'floor, dwelling'] □ **flatlet** *n.*

flatfish *n.* (*pl.* usu. same) ▼ any marine fish of various families having an asymmetrical appearance with both eyes on one side of a flattened body, including halibut, plaice sole, flounders, etc.

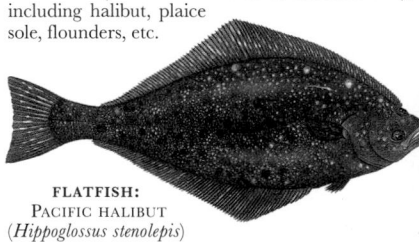

FLATFISH: PACIFIC HALIBUT (*Hippoglossus stenolepis*)

flat foot *n.* a foot with an arch that is lower than normal.

flat-footed *adj.* **1** having flat feet. **2** *colloq.* downright, positive. **3** *colloq.* unprepared; off guard (*was caught flat-footed*). □ **flat-footedly** *adv.* **flat-footedness** *n.*

flat iron *n. hist.* an iron heated externally and used for pressing clothes etc.

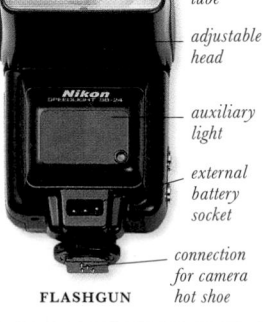

main flash tube · *adjustable head* · *auxiliary light* · *external battery socket* · *connection for camera hot shoe*

FLASHGUN

Nikon

flatmate *n. Brit.* a person in relation to one or more others living in the same flat.

flat race *n.* a horse race over level ground, as opposed to a steeplechase or hurdles. □ **flat racing** *n.*

flat rate *n.* a rate that is the same in all cases.

flat spin *n.* **1** *Aeron.* a nearly horizontal spin. **2** *Brit. colloq.* a state of panic.

flatten *v.* **1** *tr. & intr.* make or become flat. **2** *tr. colloq.* **a** humiliate. **b** knock down. □ **flattener** *n.*

flatter *v.tr.* **1** compliment unduly esp. for gain or advantage. **2** (usu. *refl.*; usu. foll. by *that* + clause) congratulate or delude (oneself etc.) (*I flatter myself that I can sing*). **3 a** (of a colour, a style, etc.) make (a person) appear to the best advantage. **b** (esp. of a portrait, a painter, etc.) represent too favourably. **4** make (a person) feel honoured. [Middle English] □ **flatterer** *n.* **flattering** *adj.* **flatteringly** *adv.*

flattery *n.* (*pl.* **-ies**) **1** exaggerated or insincere praise. **2** the act or an instance of flattering.

flatulent *adj.* **1 a** causing formation of gas in the alimentary canal. **b** caused by or suffering from this. **2** (of speech etc.) inflated, pretentious. [French] □ **flatulence** *n.*

flatus /flay-tŭs/ *n.* wind in or from the stomach or bowels. [Latin, literally 'a breath']

flatware *n.* **1** esp. *Brit.* plates, saucers, etc. **2** *N. Amer.* domestic cutlery.

flatworm *n.* any worm of the phylum Platyhelminthes, having a flattened body and no body cavity or blood vessels.

flaunt *v.tr. & intr.* **1** display ostentatiously (oneself or one's finery); show off; parade (*liked to flaunt his gold cuff-links; flaunted themselves before the crowd*). **2** wave or cause to wave proudly (*flaunted the banner*). [16th-century coinage]

■ **Usage** *Flaunt* should not be confused with *flout*, which means 'to disobey contemptuously'.

flautist *n.* a flute-player. [from Italian *flautista*]

flavour (*US* **flavor**) ● *n.* **1** a distinctive mingled sensation of smell and taste (*a cheesy flavour*). **2** an indefinable characteristic quality (*music with a romantic flavour*). **3** (usu. foll. by *of*) a slight admixture of a quality (*the flavour of failure hangs over the enterprise*). **4** esp. *US* = FLAVOURING. ● *v.tr.* give flavour to; season. □ **flavour of the month** (or **week**) a temporary trend or fashion. [from Old French *flaor*] □ **flavourful** *adj.* **flavourless** *adj.* **flavoursome** *adj.*

flavouring *n.* (*US* **flavoring**) a substance used to flavour food or drink.

flaw¹ ● *n.* **1** an imperfection; a blemish (*has a character without a flaw*). **2** a crack or similar fault (*the cup has a flaw*). **3** *Law* an invalidating defect in a legal matter. ● *v.tr. & intr.* crack; damage; spoil. [Middle English] □ **flawless** *adj.* **flawlessly** *adv.* **flawlessness** *n.*

flaw² *n.* a squall of wind.

flax *n.* **1 a** a blue-flowered plant, *Linum usitatissimum*, cultivated for its textile fibre and its seeds (see LINSEED). **b** a plant resembling this. **2** ◄ flax fibres. [Old English]

flaxen *adj.* **1** of flax. **2** (of hair) coloured like dressed flax; pale yellow.

flaxseed *n.* linseed.

FLAX FIBRES   **flay** *v.tr.* **1** strip the skin or hide off, esp. by beating. **2** criticize severely. **3** peel off (skin, bark, etc.). [Old English]

flea *n.* ► a small wingless jumping insect of the order Siphonaptera, feeding on blood. ▷ INSECT. □ **a flea in one's ear** a sharp reproof. [Old English]

fleabag *n.* *slang* a shabby or unattractive person or thing.

fleabane *n.* any of various plants of the genus *Inula* or *Pulicaria* (daisy family), formerly thought to repel fleas.

strong rear legs

laterally compressed body

FLEA

flea bite *n.* **1** the bite of a flea. **2** a trivial injury or inconvenience.

flea-bitten *adj.* **1** bitten by or infested with fleas. **2** shabby.

flea circus *n.* a show of performing fleas.

flea market *n.* a street market selling second-hand goods etc.

fleapit *n.* *Brit.* a dingy dirty place, esp. a run-down cinema.

fleck ● *n.* **1** a small patch of colour or light (*eyes with green flecks*). **2** a small particle or speck. **3** a spot on the skin; a freckle. ● *v.tr.* mark with flecks.

flection var. of FLEXION.

fled *past and past part.* of FLEE.

fledge *v.* **1** *intr.* (of a bird) grow feathers. **2** *tr.* provide (an arrow) with feathers. **3** *tr.* bring up (a young bird) until it can fly. **4** *tr.* (as **fledged** *adj.*) **a** able to fly. **b** independent; mature. **5** *tr.* deck or provide with feathers or down. [Old English]

fledgling *n.* (also **fledgeling**) **1** a young bird. **2** an inexperienced person.

flee *v.* (*past and past part.* **fled**) **1** *intr.* **a** run away. **b** seek safety by fleeing. **2** *tr.* run away from; leave abruptly; shun (*fled the room; fled his attentions*). **3** *intr.* vanish. [Old English]

fleece ● *n.* **1 ▼ a** the woolly covering of a sheep or a similar animal. **b** the amount of wool sheared from a sheep at one time. **2** something resembling a fleece, esp. a soft warm fabric with a pile, used esp. as a lining. ● *v.tr.* **1** (often foll. by *of*) strip (a person) of money, valuables, etc.; swindle. **2** remove the fleece from (a sheep etc.); shear. **3** cover as if with a fleece (*a sky fleeced with clouds*). [Old English] □ **fleeced** *adj.* (also in *comb.*).

FLEECE BEING SHEARED FROM A SHEEP

fleecy *adj.* (**fleecier**, **fleeciest**) **1** of or like a fleece. **2** covered with a fleece. □ **fleeciness** *n.*

fleet¹ *n.* **1 a** a number of warships under one commander-in-chief. **b** (prec. by *the*) all the warships and merchant ships of a nation. **2 a** number of ships, aircraft, buses, lorries, taxis, etc. operating together or owned by one proprietor. [Old English *flēot* 'ship, shipping']

fleet² *adj.* *poet.* or *literary* swift; nimble. [probably from Old Norse] □ **fleetly** *adv.* **fleetness** *n.*

Fleet Admiral *n.* *US* = ADMIRAL OF THE FLEET.

Fleet Air Arm *n.* *hist.* the aviation service of the Royal Navy.

fleet-footed *adj.* nimble; fast on one's feet.

fleeting *adj.* transitory; brief. □ **fleetingly** *adv.*

Fleet Street *n.* **1** the London press. **2** British journalism or journalists.

Fleming *n.* **1** a native of medieval Flanders in the Low Countries. **2** a member of a Flemish-speaking people inhabiting N. and W. Belgium. [Old English]

Flemish ● *adj.* of or relating to Flanders. ● *n.* the language of the Flemings. [from Middle Dutch]

flesh ● *n.* **1 a** the soft substance between the skin and bones of an animal or a human. **b** plumpness; fat (*has put on flesh*). **c** *archaic* meat, esp. excluding poultry, game, and offal. **2** the body as opposed to the mind or the soul, esp. considered as sinful. **3** the pulpy substance of a fruit or a plant. **4 a** the visible surface of the human body. **b** = FLESH COLOUR. **5** animal or human life. ● *v.tr.* embody in flesh. □ **flesh out** make or become substantial. **in the flesh** in bodily form, in person. **sins of the flesh** unchastity. **the way of all flesh** experience common to all humankind. [Old English] □ **fleshless** *adj.*

flesh and blood ● *n.* **1** the body or its substance. **2** humankind. **3** human nature, esp. as being fallible. ● *adj.* actually living, not imaginary or supernatural. □ **one's own flesh and blood** near relatives; descendants.

flesh colour *n.* a light brownish pink. □ **flesh-coloured** *adj.*

fleshly *adj.* (**fleshlier**, **fleshliest**) **1** (of desire etc.) bodily; sensual. **2** mortal, not divine. **3** worldly.

fleshpots *n.pl.* luxurious living (Exod. 16:3).

flesh tints *n.pl.* flesh colours as rendered by a painter.

flesh wound *n.* a wound not reaching to a bone or a vital organ.

fleshy *adj.* (**fleshier**, **fleshiest**) **1** plump, fat. **2** of flesh, without bone. **3** (of plant or fruit tissue) pulpy. **4** like flesh. □ **fleshiness** *n.*

fleur-de-lis /fler dĕ lee/ *n.* (also **fleur-de-lys**) (*pl.* **fleurs-** *pronunc.* same) **1** the iris flower. **2** *Heraldry* **a ►** a lily composed of three petals bound together near their bases. **b** the former royal arms of France. [from Old French *flour de lys* 'flower of the lily']

flew *past* of FLY¹.

flex¹ *v.tr. & intr.* **1** bend (a joint, limb, etc.) or be bent. **2** move (a muscle) or (of a muscle) be moved to bend a joint. [from Latin *flectere flex-* 'to bend']

flex² *n.* *Brit.* a flexible insulated cable used for carrying electric current to an appliance.

FLEUR-DE-LIS

flexible *adj.* **1** able to bend without breaking; pliable. **2** manageable. **3** adaptable; variable (*works flexible hours*). [from Latin *flexibilis*] □ **flexibility** *n.* **flexibly** *adv.*

flexion *n.* (also **flection**) **1** the act of bending or the condition of being bent, esp. of a limb or joint. **2** a bent part; a curve. [from Latin *flexio*, related to FLEX¹]

flexitime *n.* (*N. Amer.* also **flextime**) **1** a system of working a set number of hours with the starting and finishing times chosen within agreed limits by the employee. **2** the hours worked in this way.

flexor *n.* (in full **flexor muscle**) a muscle that bends part of the body. [modern Latin, related to FLEX¹]

flibbertigibbet *n.* a gossiping, frivolous, or restless person.

flick ● *n.* **1 a** a light sharp blow with a whip etc. **b** the sudden release of a bent finger or thumb, esp. to propel a small object. **2** a sudden movement or jerk. **3** a quick turn of the wrist in playing games, esp. in throwing or striking a ball. **4** a slight, sharp sound. **5** *colloq.* **a** a cinema film. **b** (in *pl.*; prec. by *the*) *Brit.* the cinema. ● *v.* **1** *tr.* strike or move with a flick (*flicked the ash off his cigar*). **2** *tr.* give a flick with (a whip, towel, etc.). **3** *intr.* make a flicking movement or sound. □ **flick through 1** turn over (cards, pages, etc.). **2 a** turn over the pages etc. of, by a rapid movement of the fingers. **b** look cursorily through (a book etc.). [Middle English]

flicker ● *v.intr.* **1** (of light) shine unsteadily. **2** (of a flame) burn unsteadily, alternately flaring and dying down. **3 a** (of a flag, a reptile's tongue, an eyelid, etc.) move or wave to and fro; quiver. **b** (of the wind) blow lightly and unsteadily. **4** (of hope etc.) waver. ● *n.* **1** a flickering movement or light. **2** a brief spell of hope, recognition, etc. □ **flicker out** die away after a final flicker. [Old English]

F

blade

*lock and
release
catch*

grip

spike

F

**FLICK
KNIFE**

flick knife *n. Brit.* ◀ a weapon with a blade that springs out from the handle when a button is pressed.

flier var. of FLYER.

flight[1] *n.* **1 a** the act or manner of flying through the air (*studied swallows' flight*). **b** the movement or passage of a projectile etc. through the air (*the flight of an arrow*). **2 a** a journey made through the air or in space. **b** a time-tabled journey made by an airline. **c** an RAF or USAF unit of about six aircraft. **3 a** a flock of birds, insects, etc. **b** a migration. **4** (usu. foll. by *of*) a series, esp. of stairs between floors, or of hurdles across a racetrack. **5** a mental or verbal excursion or sally (*a flight of fancy*). **6** the trajectory and pace of a ball in games. **7** the distance that a bird, aircraft, or missile can fly. **8** (usu. foll. by *of*) a volley (*a flight of arrows*). **9** the tail of a dart. ▷ DART. □ **in the first** (or **top**) **flight** taking a leading place. [Old English, related to FLY[1]]

flight[2] *n.* **1** the act or manner of fleeing. **2** a hasty retreat. □ **put to flight** cause to flee. **take** (or **take to**) **flight** flee. [Old English, related to FLEE]

flight attendant *n.* a steward or stewardess on an aeroplane.

flight bag *n.* a small zipped shoulder bag carried by air travellers.

flight control *n.* an internal or external system directing the movement of aircraft.

flight deck *n.* **1** the deck of an aircraft carrier used for take-off and landing. **2** the accommodation for the pilot, navigator, etc. in an aircraft.

flight feather *n.* any of the large primary or secondary feathers of a bird's wing, supporting it in flight. ▷ FEATHER, OWL

flightless *adj.* ◀ (of a bird etc.) naturally unable to fly.

flight lieutenant *n.* an RAF officer next in rank below squadron leader.

flight path *n.* the planned course of an aircraft or spacecraft.

flight recorder *n.* ▶ a device in an aircraft to record technical details during a flight.

flight sergeant *n.* a non-commissioned officer in the RAF ranking above chief technician.

flighty *adj.* (**flightier**, **flightiest**) **1** (usu. of a girl) frivolous, fickle, changeable. **2** crazy. □ **flightily** *adv.* **flightiness** *n.*

flimflam *n.* **1** a trifle; nonsense; idle talk. **2** humbug; deception. □ **flimflammery** *n.*

flimsy ● *adj.* (**flimsier**, **flimsiest**) **1** insubstantial, easily damaged (*a flimsy structure*). **2** (of an excuse etc.) unconvincing (*a flimsy pretext*). **3** paltry; trivial; superficial (*a flimsy play*). **4** (of clothing) thin (*a flimsy blouse*). ● *n.* (*pl.* **-ies**) *Brit.* **1 a** a very thin paper. **b** a document, esp. a copy, made on this. **2** a flimsy thing, esp. women's underwear. [18th-century coinage] □ **flimsily** *adv.* **flimsiness** *n.*

flinch *v.intr.* **1** draw back in pain or expectation of a blow etc.; wince. **2** (often followed by *from*) give way; shrink, turn aside (*flinched from his duty*). [from Old French *flenchir*]

fling ● *v.* (*past* and *past part.* **flung**) **1** *tr.* throw or hurl (an object) forcefully. **2** *refl.* **a** (usu. foll. by *into*) rush headlong (into a person's arms, a train, etc.). **b** (usu. foll. by *into*) embark wholeheartedly (on an enterprise). **3** *tr.* utter (words) forcefully. **4** *tr.* (usu. foll. by *out*) suddenly spread (the arms). **5** *tr.* (foll. by *on*, *off*)

**FLIGHTLESS
BIRD: OSTRICH**
(*Struthio camelus*)

put on or take off (clothes) carelessly or rapidly. **6** *intr.* go angrily or violently; rush (*flung out of the room*). **7** *tr.* put or send suddenly or violently (*was flung into jail*). **8** *tr.* (foll. by *away*) discard thoughtlessly (*flung away their reputation*). ● *n.* **1** an act or instance of flinging; a throw; a plunge. **2** a spell of indulgence or wild behaviour (*he's had his fling*). **3** an impetuous, whirling Scottish dance, esp. the Highland fling. [Middle English perhaps from Old Norse] □ **flinger** *n.*

flint *n.* **1 a** a hard grey stone of nearly pure silica occurring naturally as nodules or bands in chalk. **b** ◀ a piece of this esp. as flaked or ground to form a primitive tool or weapon. **2** a piece of hard alloy of rare-earth metals used to give an igniting spark in a cigarette lighter etc. **3** a piece of flint used with steel to produce fire. **4** anything hard and unyielding. [Old English] □ **flinty** *adj.* (**flintier**, **flintiest**)

**FLINT
BLADE**

flintlock *n. hist.* **1** ▼ an old type of gun fired by a spark from a flint. ▷ BLUNDERBUSS. **2** the lock producing such a spark.

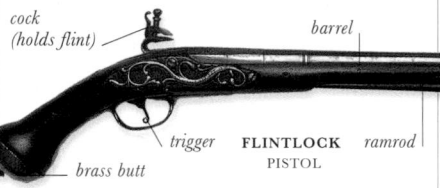

*cock
(holds flint)*   *barrel*

trigger **FLINTLOCK** *ramrod*
brass butt **PISTOL**

flip[1] ● *v.* (**flipped**, **flipping**) **1** *tr.* flick (a coin, pellet, etc.) with a quick movement so that it spins in the air. **2** *tr.* strike or flick (a person's ear, cheek, etc.) lightly or smartly. **b** move (a fan, whip etc.) with a sudden jerk. **3** *tr.* turn (a small object) over. **4** *intr.* **a** make a flicking noise with the fingers. **b** (foll. by *at*) strike smartly at. **5** *intr. slang* become suddenly angry, excited, or enthusiastic. ● *n.* **1** a smart light blow; a flick. **2** *Brit. colloq.* **a** a short pleasure flight in an aircraft. **b** a quick tour etc. ● *adj. colloq.* glib; flippant. □ **flip one's lid** *slang* **1** lose self-control. **2** go mad. **flip through** = *flick through*.

flip[2] *n.* **1** a drink of heated beer and spirit. **2** = EGG-NOG.

flip chart *n.* a large pad erected on a stand and bound so that one page can be turned over at the top to reveal the next.

thong **flip-flop** *n.* **1** ◀ a usu. plastic or rubber sandal with a thong between the big and second toe. **2** an electronic switching circuit changed from one stable state to another, or through an unstable state back to its stable state, by a triggering pulse.

**FLIP-FLOP:
PAIR OF RUBBER
FLIP-FLOPS**

flippant *adj.* treating serious things lightly; disrespectful. □ **flippancy** *n.* **flippantly** *adv.*

flipper *n.* **1** a broadened limb of a turtle, penguin, etc., used in swimming. ▷ CETACEAN. **2** ▶ a flat rubber etc. attachment worn on the foot for underwater swimming. **3** *slang* a hand.

flipping *adj. & adv. Brit. slang* expressing annoyance, or as an intensifier (*he flipping beat me*).

flip side *n. colloq.* **1** the less important side of a gramophone record. **2** the reverse or a concomitant of a thing.

flirt ● *v.intr.* **1** (usu. foll. by *with*) behave in a frivolously amorous or sexually enticing manner. **2** (usu. foll. by *with*) **a** superficially interest oneself (with an idea etc.). **b** trifle (with danger etc.). ● *n.* a person who indulges in flirting. □ **flirtation** *n.* **flirtatious** *adj.* **flirtatiously** *adv.* **flirtatiousness** *n.* **flirty** *adj.* (**flirtier**, **flirtiest**).

FLIPPER

flit ● *v.intr.* (**flitted**, **flitting**) **1** move lightly, softly, or rapidly (*flitted from one room to another*). **2** make short flights (*flitted from branch to branch*). **3** *Brit. colloq.* leave one's house etc. secretly to escape creditors etc. **4** *esp. Sc. & N.Engl.* change one's home. ● *n.* **1** an act of flitting. **2** (also **moonlight flit**) a secret change of abode in order to escape creditors etc. [from Old Norse *flytja*] □ **flitter** *n.*

flitch *n.* **1** a side of bacon. **2** a slab of outer timber from a tree trunk. [Old English]

flitch beam *n.* a compound beam, esp. of an iron plate between two slabs of wood.

flitter *v.intr.* flit about; flutter. [related to FLIT]

flitter-mouse *n.* = BAT[2].

float ● *v.* **1** *intr. & tr.* rest or move or cause (a buoyant object) to rest or move on the surface of a liquid without sinking. **b** get afloat or set (a stranded ship) afloat. **2** *intr.* drift (*the clouds floated high up*).

FLIGHT RECORDER

Most modern aircraft, whether military or civilian, carry a flight data recorder, often known as a 'black box'. The box records data from the main operating systems of the aircraft, and tapes conversations inside the flight deck. Data is stored on magnetic tape inside a strong titanium case, which protects it from impact and fire damage.

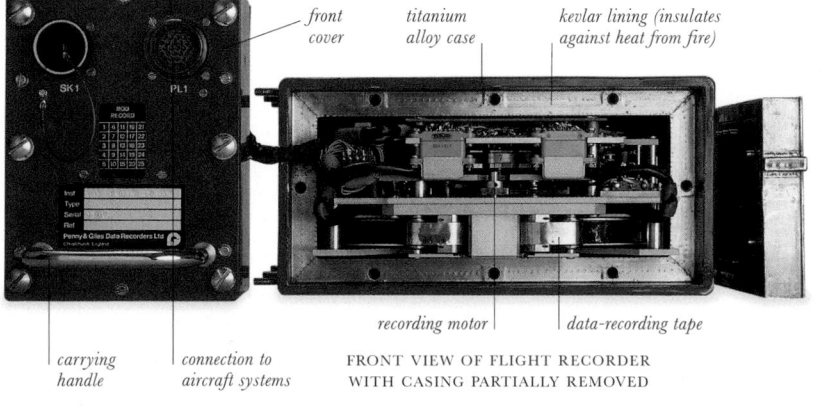

*front
cover*   *titanium
alloy case*   *kevlar lining (insulates
against heat from fire)*

recording motor   *data-recording tape*

*carrying
handle*   *connection to
aircraft systems*

**FRONT VIEW OF FLIGHT RECORDER
WITH CASING PARTIALLY REMOVED**

3 *intr. colloq.* move in a leisurely or casual way. **4** *intr.* (often foll. by *in*) move or be suspended freely in a liquid or a gas. **5** *tr.* **a** bring (a company etc.) into being. **b** offer (stock, shares, etc.) on the stock market. **6** *Commerce* **a** *intr.* (of currency) be allowed to have a fluctuating exchange rate. **b** *tr.* cause (currency) to float. **7** *intr. & tr.* circulate or cause (a rumour or idea) to circulate. **8** *tr.* waft (a buoyant object) through the air. ● *n.* **1** a thing that floats, esp.: **a** a raft. **b** a cork or quill on a fishing line as an indicator of a fish biting. **c** a cork supporting the edge of a fishing net. **d** a hollow or inflated part or organ supporting an organism in the water. **e** a hollow structure fixed underneath an aircraft enabling it to float on water. **f** a floating device on the surface of water, petrol, etc., controlling the flow. **2** *Brit.* a small usu. electrically powered vehicle (*milk float*). **3** a platform mounted on a lorry and carrying a display in a procession etc. **4 a** *Brit.* a sum of money used at the beginning of a period of selling in a shop, a fête, etc. to provide change. **b** petty cash. **5** (in *sing.* or *pl.*) *Brit. Theatr.* footlights. **6** a tool used for smoothing plaster. [Old English] □ **floatable** *adj.* **floatability** *n.* **floater** *n.*

floatation var. of FLOTATION.

floating *adj.* not settled in a definite place; variable (*the floating population*).

floating anchor *n.* a sea anchor.

floating bridge *n.* **1** a bridge on pontoons etc. **2** a ferry working on chains.

floating dock *n.* a floating structure usable as a dry dock.

floating kidney *n.* **1** an abnormal condition in which the kidneys are unusually movable. **2** such a kidney.

floating point *n. Computing* a decimal point that does not occupy a fixed position in the numbers processed.

floating rib *n.* any of the lower ribs, which are not attached to the breastbone.

floating voter *n.* a voter without allegiance to any political party.

floaty *adj. esp. Brit.* (esp. of a woman's garment or a fabric) light and airy.

flocculent *adj.* **1** like tufts of wool. **2** downy. [based on Latin *floccus* 'flock'] □ **flocculence** *n.*

flock[1] ● *n.* **1 a** a number of animals of one kind, esp. birds, feeding, resting, or travelling together. **b** a number of domestic animals kept together. **2** a large crowd of people. **3** people in the care of a minister, teacher, etc. ● *v.intr.* **1** congregate; mass. **2** (usu. foll. by *to, in, out, together*) go together in a crowd. [Old English]

flock[2] *n.* **1** a lock or tuft of wool, cotton, etc. **2 a** (also in *pl.*; often *attrib.*) material for quilting and stuffing made of wool refuse or torn-up cloth (*a flock pillow*). **b** powdered wool or cloth. [from Latin *floccus*]

flock paper *n.* (also **flock wallpaper**) wallpaper with a raised flock pattern.

floe *n.* a sheet of floating ice.

flog *v.* (**flogged**, **flogging**) **1** *tr.* **a** beat with a whip, stick, etc. **b** make work through violent effort (*flogged the engine*). **2** *tr. slang* **a** (often foll. by *off*) *Brit.* sell. **b** offer for sale. **3** *intr. & refl. Brit. slang* proceed by violent or painful effort. □ **flog a dead horse** waste energy on something unalterable. **flog to death** *colloq.* talk about at tedious length. [17th-century coinage] □ **flogger** *n.*

flood ● *n.* **1 a** an overflowing of water beyond its normal confines, over land. **b** the water that overflows. **2 a** a torrent (*a flood of rain*). **b** something resembling a torrent (*a flood of tears*). **3** the inflow of the tide (also in *comb.: flood tide*). **4** *colloq.* a floodlight. ● *v.* **1** *tr.* **a** cover with or overflow in a flood (*rain flooded the cellar*). **b** overflow as if with a flood (*the market was flooded with foreign goods*). **2** *tr.* irrigate (*flooded the paddy fields*). **3** *tr.* deluge with water.

4 *intr.* (often foll. by *in, through*) arrive in great quantities. **5** *intr.* become inundated (*the bathroom flooded*). **6** *tr.* overfill (a carburettor) with petrol. **7** *intr.* experience a uterine haemorrhage. **8** *tr.* (of rain etc.) fill (a river) to overflowing. □ **flood out** drive out (of one's home etc.) with a flood. [Old English]

flood and field *n.* sea and land.

floodgate *n.* **1** ▼ a gate opened or closed to admit or exclude water, esp. the lower gate of a lock. **2** (usu. in *pl.*) a last restraint holding back tears etc.

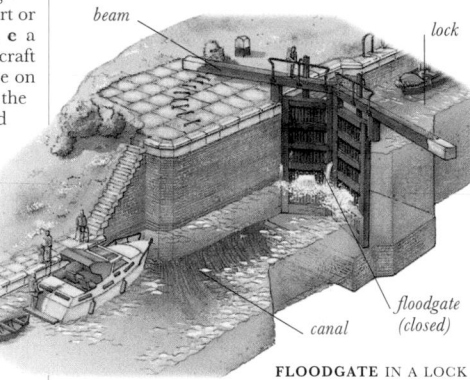

FLOODGATE IN A LOCK

floodlight ● *n.* **1** a large powerful light (usu. one of several) to illuminate a building, stage, etc. **2** the illumination so provided. ● *v.tr.* (*past* and *past part.* **floodlit**) illuminate with floodlights.

flood tide *n.* the periodical exceptional rise of the tide because of lunar or solar attraction.

flood water *n.* the water left by flooding.

floor ● *n.* **1 a** the lower surface of a room. **b** the boards etc. of which it is made. **2 a** the bottom of the sea, a cave, etc. **b** any level area. **3** a storey. **4 a** (in a legislative assembly) the part of the house where members sit and speak. **b** the right to speak next in debate (*gave him the floor*). **5** *Stock Exch.* the large central trading hall. **6** the minimum of prices, wages, etc. **7** *colloq.* the ground. ● *v.tr.* **1** provide with a floor; pave. **2** knock (a person) down. **3** *colloq.* confound, baffle. **4** *colloq.* get the better of. **5** cover the floor of (*leopard skins floored the hall*). □ **take the floor 1** begin to dance. **2** speak in a debate. [Old English] □ **floorless** *adj.*

floorboard *n.* a long wooden board used for flooring.

floorcloth *n. Brit.* a cloth for washing the floor.

floor exercises *n.pl.* (in gymnastics) a routine of exercises without equipment.

flooring *n.* the boards etc. of which a floor is made.

floor-length *adj.* (esp. of clothing) reaching to the floor.

floor manager *n.* **1** the stage manager of a television production. **2** a shopwalker.

floor show *n.* an entertainment presented on the floor (as opposed to the stage) of a nightclub etc.

floorwalker *n. US* = SHOPWALKER.

floozie *n.* (also **floozy**) (*pl.* **-ies**) *colloq.* a girl or a woman, esp. a disreputable one. [20th-century coinage]

flop ● *v.intr.* (**flopped**, **flopping**) **1** sway about heavily or loosely (*hair flopped over his face*). **2** move in an ungainly way (*flopped along in flippers*). **3** (often foll. by *down, on, into*) sit, kneel, lie, or fall awkwardly or suddenly. **4** *slang* (esp. of a play, film, etc.) fail; collapse (*flopped on Broadway*). **5** make a dull sound of a soft body landing, or of a flat thing slapping water. ● *n.* **1 a** a flopping movement. **b** the sound made by it. **2** *slang* a failure. ● *adv.* with a flop. [variant of FLAP]

flophouse *n. slang esp. US* a doss-house.

floppy ● *adj.* (**floppier**, **floppiest**) tending to flop; not firm or rigid. ● *n.* (*pl.* **-ies**) (in full **floppy disk**) *Computing* a flexible removable magnetic disc for data storage. □ **floppily** *adv.* **floppiness** *n.*

floptical *adj. Computing propr.* of, involving, or designed for a type of floppy disk drive using a laser to position the read-write head. [blend of FLOPPY and OPTICAL]

flora *n.* (*pl.* **floras** or **florae** /-ree/) the plants of a region or period (cf. FAUNA 1). [modern Latin, based on *flos floris* 'flower']

floral *adj.* **1** of flowers. **2** decorated with or depicting flowers. [based on Latin *flos floris* 'flower'] □ **florally** *adv.*

Florentine ● *adj.* **1** of or relating to Florence in Italy. **2** (**florentine**) (of a dish) served on a bed of spinach. ● *n.* a native or citizen of Florence. [from Latin *Florentia* 'Florence']

florescence *n.* flowering. [based on Latin *florescent-* 'beginning to bloom']

floret *n. Bot.* ▼ **1** each of the small flowers making up a composite flower head. ▷ INFLORESCENCE. **2** each stem of a head of cauliflower, broccoli, etc. **3** a small flower.

floriate *v.tr.* decorate with flower-designs etc.

floribunda *n.* a plant, esp. a rose, bearing dense clusters of flowers. [modern Latin, based on *flos floris* 'flower', influenced by *abundus* 'copious']

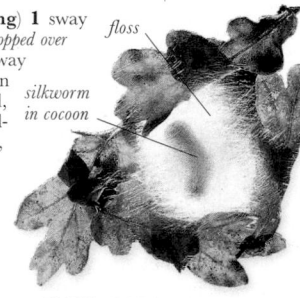

ray floret

disc florets

FLORET: COMPOSITE FLOWER HEAD (SUNFLOWER) SHOWING FLORETS

florid *adj.* **1** ruddy (*a florid complexion*). **2** (of a book, music, etc.) elaborately ornate. **3** flowery. [based on Latin *flos floris* 'flower'] □ **floridity** *n.* **floridly** *adv.* **floridness** *n.*

florin *n. hist.* **1 a** ▼ a former British coin worth two shillings. **b** an English gold coin of the 14th c., worth 6s. 8d. **2** a foreign coin of gold or silver, esp. a Dutch guilder. [from Italian *fiorino* 'little flower', the original coin bearing a fleur-de-lis]

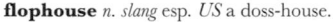

FLORIN: BRITISH FLORIN (1849)

florist *n.* a person who deals in or grows flowers. □ **floristry** *n.*

floristic *adj.* relating to the study of the distribution of plants. □ **floristically** *adv.* **floristics** *n.*

floruit ● *v.intr.* (he or she) was alive and working; flourished (of a painter, a writer, etc., whose exact dates are unknown). ● *n.* the period or date at which a person lived or worked. [Latin, literally 'he or she flourished']

floss ● *n.* **1** ▼ the rough silk enveloping a silkworm's cocoon. **2** untwisted silk thread used in embroidery. **3** = DENTAL FLOSS. ● *v.tr.* (also *absol.*) clean (the teeth) with dental floss. [from Old French *flosche* 'nap of velvet']

floss silk *n.* a rough silk used in cheap goods.

flossy *adj.* (**flossier**, **flossiest**) **1** of or like floss. **2** *colloq.* fancy, showy.

flotation *n.* (also **floatation**) the process of launching or financing a commercial enterprise.

flotilla *n.* **1** a small fleet. **2** a fleet of small ships. [Spanish, literally 'little fleet']

flotsam *n.* wreckage found floating. [based on Anglo-French *floter* 'to float']

floss

silkworm in cocoon

FLOSS AROUND A COCOON

F

flotsam and jetsam *n.* **1** odds and ends; rubbish. **2** vagrants etc.

flounce[1] ● *v.intr.* (often foll. by *away, about, off, out*) go or move with an agitated or impatient motion. ● *n.* a flouncing movement. [16th-century coinage]

flounce[2] ● *n.* a wide frill. ● *v.tr.* trim with a flounce or flounces. [based on Old French *froncir* 'to wrinkle']

flounder[1] ● *v.intr.* **1** struggle in mud, or as if in mud, or when wading. **2** perform a task badly or without knowledge. ● *n.* an act of floundering. □ **flounderer** *n.*

flounder[2] ● *n.* **1** a small edible flatfish, *Pleuronectes flesus*, of European coastal waters. **2** any small flatfish of the family Pleuronectidae or Bothidae. [from Old French *flondre*]

flour ● *n.* **1** ▼ a meal or powder obtained from ground wheat etc. **2** any fine powder. ● *v.tr.* sprinkle or coat with flour. [Middle English variant of FLOWER, signifying 'finest part'] □ **floury** *adj.* (**flourier, flouriest**). **flouriness** *n.*

wheat flour　　　*wholemeal flour*　　　*rye flour*

FLOUR: COMMON FLOUR TYPES

flourish ● *v.* **1** *intr.* **a** grow vigorously; thrive. **b** prosper. **c** be in one's prime. **d** be in good health. **2** *intr.* spend one's life; be active (at a specified time) (*flourished in the Middle Ages*) (cf. FLORUIT). **3** *tr.* show ostentatiously (*flourished his chequebook*). **4** *tr.* wave (a weapon etc.) vigorously. ● *n.* **1** an ostentatious gesture with a weapon, a hand, etc. **2** an ornamental curving decoration of handwriting. **3** a rhetorical embellishment. **4** *Mus.* an ornate passage or fanfare. [based on Latin *flos floris* 'flower'] □ **flourisher** *n.*

flout ● *v.* **1** *tr.* express contempt for (the law, rules, etc.) by word or action; mock. **2** *intr.* (often foll. by *at*) mock or scoff. ● *n.* a flouting speech or act.

■ **Usage** *Flout* should not be confused with *flaunt*, which means 'to display proudly, show off'.

flow ● *v.intr.* **1** glide along as a stream. **2 a** (of a liquid, esp. water) gush out; spring. **b** (of blood, liquid, etc.) be spilt. **3** (of money, electric current, etc.) circulate. **4** (of people or things) come or go in large numbers or smoothly (*traffic flowed down the hill*). **5** (of literary style etc.) proceed easily and smoothly. **6** (of a garment, hair, etc.) hang easily or gracefully. **7** (often foll. by *from*) result from (*his failure flows from his diffidence*). **8** (esp. of the tide) be in flood. **9** (of wine) be poured out copiously. **10** (of a rock or metal) undergo a permanent change of shape under stress. **11** (foll. by *with*) *archaic* be plentifully supplied with (*flow-ing with milk and honey*). ● *n.* **1 a** a flowing movement in a stream. **b** the manner in which a thing flows (*a sluggish flow*). **c** a flowing liquid (*couldn't stop the flow*). **d** a copious outpouring (*a continuous flow of complaints*). **2** the rise of a tide or a river (*ebb and flow*). **3** the gradual deformation of a rock or metal under stress. **4** *Sc.* a bog or morass. □ **go with the flow** be relaxed and not resist the tide of events. [Old English]

flow chart *n.* a diagram of the movement or action in a complex activity.

flow diagram *n.* = FLOW CHART.

flower ● *n.* **1** *Bot.* **a** ▶ the reproductive organ in a plant from which the fruit or seed develops. ▷ ANGIOSPERM, INFLORESCENCE. **b** a bloom. **c** a blossom on a cut stem, used in bunches for decoration. **2** a plant cultivated or noted for its flowers. ● *v.* **1** *intr.* (of a plant) produce flowers; bloom or blossom. **2** *intr.* reach a peak. **3** *tr.* cause or allow (a plant) to flower. **4** *tr.* decorate with worked flowers or a floral design. □ **the flower of** the best of. **in flower** with the flowers out. [from Latin *flos floris*] □ **flowered** *adj.* (also in *comb.*). **flowerless** *adj.* **flower-like** *adj.*

flower bed *n.* a garden bed in which flowers are grown.

flower head *n.* = HEAD *n.* 4d.

flowering *adj.* **1** (of a plant) in bloom. **2** capable of producing flowers.

flowerpot *n.* a pot in which a plant may be grown.

flowers of sulphur *n.pl. Chem.* a fine powder produced when sulphur evaporates and condenses.

flowery *adj.* **1** decorated with flowers or floral designs. **2** (of literary style etc.) high-flown; ornate. **3** full of flowers (*a flowery meadow*). □ **floweriness** *n.*

flowing *adj.* **1** (of literary style etc.) fluent; easy. **2** (of a line or contour) smoothly continuous, not abrupt. **3** (of hair, a garment, etc.) unconfined. □ **flowingly** *adv.*

flown *past part.* of FLY[1].

flowsheet *n.* = FLOW CHART.

Flt. Lt. *abbr.* (in the UK) Flight Lieutenant.

flu *n. colloq.* influenza.

fluctuate *v.intr.* vary irregularly; vacillate; rise and fall. [based on Latin *fluctuatus* 'undulated'] □ **fluctuation** *n.*

flue *n.* **1** a smoke-duct in a chimney. **2** a channel for conveying heat. [Middle English]

fluence *n. Brit. colloq.* influence. □ **put the fluence on** apply hypnotic etc. power to (a person).

fluent *adj.* **1 a** (of speech or literary style) flowing, natural. **b** having command of a foreign language (*is fluent in German*). **2** flowing easily or gracefully (*the fluent line of her arabesque*). [from Latin *fluent-* 'flowing'] □ **fluency** *n.* **fluently** *adv.*

fluff ● *n.* **1** soft, light, feathery material coming off blankets etc. **2** soft fur or feathers. **3** *slang* a mistake in a performance etc. **4** something insubstantial or trifling, esp. sentimental writing. ● *v.tr* & *intr.* **1** (often foll. by *up*) shake into or become a soft mass. **2** *colloq.* make a mistake in (a game, playing music, etc.); blunder (*fluffed his opening line*).

fluffy *adj.* (**fluffier, fluffiest**) **1** of or like fluff. **2** covered in fluff. □ **fluffily** *adv.* **fluffiness** *n.*

flugelhorn *n.* ▼ a valved brass wind instrument like a cornet but with a broader tone. ▷ BRASS. [from German *Flügel* 'wing' + *Horn* 'horn']

little-finger rest

flared bell

valves

mouthpiece

water key

FLUGELHORN

fluid ● *n.* **1** a substance, esp. a gas or liquid, whose shape is determined by its confines. **2** a fluid part or secretion. ● *adj.* **1** able to flow and alter shape freely. **2** constantly changing or fluctuating. (*the situation is fluid*). [from Latin *fluidus*] □ **fluidify** *v.tr.* (**-ies, -ied**). **fluidity** *n.* **fluidly** *adv.* **fluidness** *n.*

fluid drachm *see* DRACHM.

fluid mechanics *n.* the study of forces and flow within fluids.

fluid ounce *n.* one-twentieth or *US* one-sixteenth of a pint.

fluidram *n. US* a fluid drachm.

fluke[1] ● *n.* **1** a lucky accident (*won by a fluke*). **2** a chance breeze. ● *v.tr.* achieve by a fluke. [19th-century coinage]

fluke[2] *n.* **1** any parasitic flatworm of the class Trematoda, including liver flukes and blood flukes. **2** a flatfish, esp. a flounder. [Old English]

fluke[3] *n.* **1** *Naut.* a broad triangular plate on the arm of an anchor. **2** ▼ the barbed head of a lance, harpoon, etc. **3** either of the lobes of a whale's tail. ▷ CETACEAN. [16th-century coinage]

barb

FLUKE OF A HARPOON

fluky *adj.* (**flukier, flukiest**) obtained more by chance than skill. □ **flukily** *adv.* **flukiness** *n.*

flummery *n.* (*pl.* **-ies**) **1** empty compliments; trifles. **2** a sweet dish made with beaten eggs, sugar, etc. [from Welsh *llymru*]

flummox *v.tr. colloq.* confound, disconcert. [19th-century coinage]

flump ● *v.* (often foll. by *down*) **1** *intr.* fall or move heavily. **2** *tr.* set or throw down with a heavy thud. ● *n.* the action or sound of flumping.

flung *past* and *past part.* of FLING.

flunk *colloq.* ● *v.* **1** *tr.* **a** fail (an examination etc.). **b** fail (an examination candidate). **2** *intr.* (often foll. by *out*) fail utterly; give up. ● *n.* an instance of flunking.

flunkey *n.* (also **flunky**) (*pl.* **-eys** or **-ies**) usu. *derog.* **1** a liveried servant; a footman. **2** a toady; a snob. **3** *US* a person who does menial work. [18th-century coinage] □ **flunkeyism** *n.*

fluoresce *v.intr.* be or become fluorescent.

fluorescence *n.* **1** ▼ the visible or invisible radiation produced from certain substances as a result of incident radiation of a shorter wavelength as X-rays, ultraviolet light, etc. **2** the property of absorbing invisible light and emitting visible light. [from FLUORSPAR (which fluoresces), after *opalescence*]

fluorescent *adj.* (of a substance) having or showing fluorescence.

fluorescent lamp *n.* (also **fluorescent bulb**) a lamp or bulb radiating largely by fluorescence.

fluorescent screen *n.* a screen coated with fluorescent material to show images from X-rays etc.

FLUORESCENCE

Fluorescence is a type of luminescence. In the demonstration shown here, a bright light is shined into a test tube containing sodium fluorescein, which appears red in ambient light conditions. The fluorescein in the solution transforms energy from the torch light, emitting it as a bright green fluorescent light.

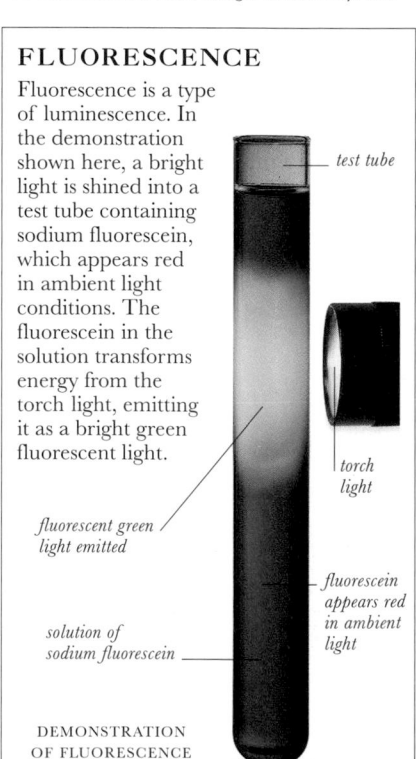

test tube

torch light

fluorescent green light emitted

fluorescein appears red in ambient light

solution of sodium fluorescein

DEMONSTRATION OF FLUORESCENCE

FLOWER

Flowers are the sites of sexual reproduction in flowering plants (angiosperms). The male reproductive organ is the stamen; the female structure consists of the ovary, style, and stigma. Flowering plants fall into two categories: dicotyledons and monocotyledons (known as dicots and monocots). In dicot flowers, there is a distinction between the outer sepals, which are typically green, and the petals, which are usually larger and colourful. In monocot flowers, the petals and sepals are similar, and are known collectively as tepals. Flowers also vary in their shape, growth habit, coloration, and petal arrangements.

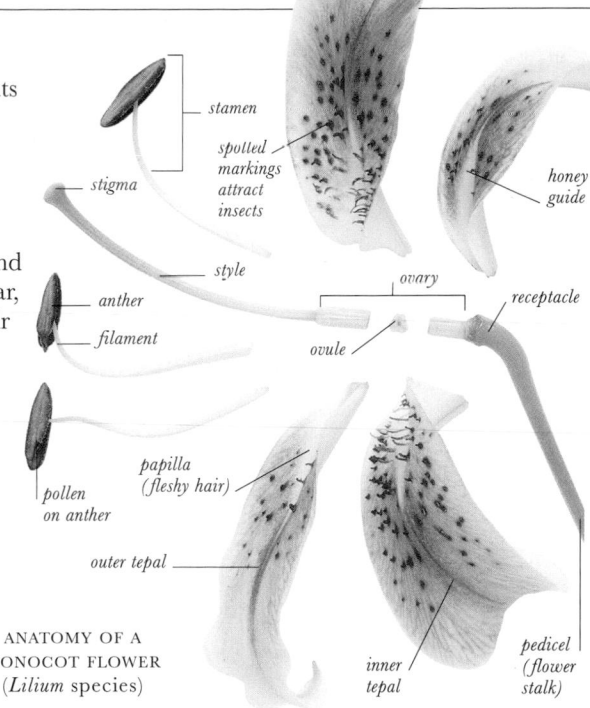

ANATOMY OF A
MONOCOT FLOWER
(*Lilium* species)

stamen · spotted markings attract insects · stigma · style · anther · filament · pollen on anther · ovary · ovule · receptacle · honey guide · papilla (fleshy hair) · outer tepal · inner tepal · pedicel (flower stalk)

DICOT AND MONOCOT FLOWER FEATURES

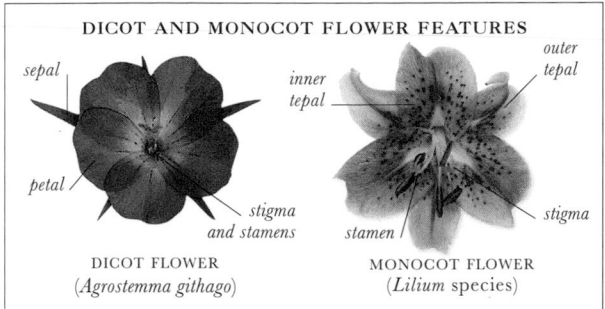

sepal · inner tepal · outer tepal · petal · stigma and stamens · stamen · stigma

DICOT FLOWER
(*Agrostemma githago*)

MONOCOT FLOWER
(*Lilium* species)

FLOWER HABITS

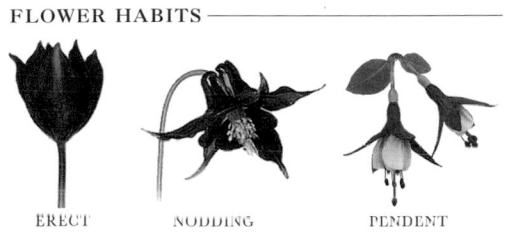

ERECT NODDING PENDENT

FLOWER COLORATION

SELF-COLOURED BICOLOURED PICOTEE STRIPED

PETAL ARRANGEMENTS

RECURVED REFLEXED SINGLE SEMI-DOUBLE DOUBLE FULLY DOUBLE

FLOWER SHAPES

CRUCIFORM STELLATE SAUCER-SHAPED CUP-SHAPED BELL-SHAPED TUBULAR FUNNEL-SHAPED

SALVERFORM TRUMPET-SHAPED ROSETTE POMPON PEA-LIKE PITCHER-SHAPED SLIPPER-SHAPED

F

fluoridate *v.tr.* add traces of fluoride to (drinking water etc.). □ **fluoridation** *n.* (also **fluoridization**).

fluoride *n.* any binary compound of fluorine.

fluorinate *v.tr.* **1** = FLUORIDATE. **2** introduce fluorine into (*fluorinated hydrocarbons*). □ **fluorination** *n.*

fluorine *n.* a poisonous pale yellow gaseous element of the halogen group. [French]

fluorite *n.* ◄ a mineral form of calcium fluoride. [Italian]

fluoro- *comb. form* **1** fluorine (*fluorocarbon*). **2** fluorescence (*fluoroscope*).

fluorocarbon *n.* a compound formed by replacing one or more hydrogen atoms in a hydrocarbon with fluorine atoms.

fluoroscope *n.* an instrument with a fluorescent screen on which X-ray images may be viewed without taking and developing X-ray photographs.

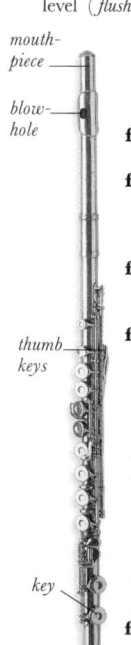

FLUORITE

fluorspar *n.* = FLUORITE. [based on Latin *fluere* 'to flow' + SPAR³]

flurry ● *n.* (*pl.* **-ies**) **1** a gust or squall (of snow or *Brit.* rain etc.). **2** a sudden burst of activity. **3** nervous agitation (*a flurry of speculation*). ● *v.tr.* (**-ies, -ied**) confuse by haste or noise; agitate.

flush¹ ● *v.* **1** *intr.* **a** blush, redden (*he flushed with embarrassment*). **b** glow with a warm colour (*sky flushed pink*). **2** *tr.* (usu. as **flushed** *adj.*) cause to glow or blush (*flushed with pride*). **3** *tr.* **a** cleanse (a drain etc.) by a rushing flow of water. **b** (often foll. by *away, down*) dispose of (an object) in this way. **4** *intr.* rush out, spurt. ● *n.* **1 a** a blush. **b** a glow of light or colour. **2 a** a rush of water. **b** the cleansing of a drain etc. by flushing. **3 a** a rush of emotion. **b** the elation produced by a victory etc. (*the flush of triumph*). **4** sudden abundance. **5** freshness; vigour (*in the first flush of womanhood*). **6 a** (in full **hot flush**) a sudden feeling of heat during the menopause. **b** a feverish temperature. **c** facial redness, esp. caused by fever, alcohol, etc. [Middle English] □ **flusher** *n.*

flush² ● *adj.* **1** (often foll. by *with*) in the same plane; level (*flush with the cooker*). **2** (usu. *predic.*) *colloq.* **a** having plenty of money. **b** (of money) abundant, plentiful. **3** full to overflowing; in flood. ● *v.tr.* **1** make (surfaces) level. **2** fill in (a joint) level with a surface. □ **flushness** *n.*

flush³ *n.* a hand of cards all of one suit. [from Latin *fluxus* 'flux']

flush⁴ ● *v.* **1** *tr.* cause (esp. a game bird) to fly up from cover. **2** *intr.* (of a bird) fly up and away. □ **flush out 1** reveal. **2** drive out. [Middle English]

fluster ● *v.tr.* & *intr.* make or become nervous or confused. ● *n.* a confused or agitated state. [17th-century coinage]

flute ● *n.* **1** ◄ a high-pitched wind instrument with holes along it stopped by the fingers or keys, esp. (in full **transverse flute**) the modern orchestral instrument, with a mouthpiece on the side near one end. ▷ ORCHESTRA, WOODWIND. **2 a** *Archit.* an ornamental vertical groove in a column. **b** any similar cylindrical groove. **3** a tall narrow wine glass. ● *v.* **1** *intr.* play the flute. **2** *intr.* speak, sing, or whistle in a fluting way. [from Old French] □ **flutelike** *adj.* **fluting** *n.* **flutist** *n.* *US* (cf. FLAUTIST). **fluty** *adj.* (in sense 1a of *n.*).

flutter ● *v.* **1 a** *intr.* flap the wings in flying or trying to fly. **b** *tr.* flap (the wings). **2** *intr.* fall with a quivering motion. **3** *intr.* & *tr.* move or cause

mouth-piece

blow-hole

thumb keys

key

to move irregularly (*fluttered the flag*). **4** *intr.* go about restlessly. **5** *tr.* agitate, confuse. **6** *intr.* (of a pulse or heartbeat) beat irregularly. **7** *intr.* tremble with excitement. ● *n.* **1 a** the act of fluttering. **b** an instance of this. **2** a state of tremulous excitement (*was in a flutter*; *caused a flutter with his behaviour*). **3** *Brit. colloq.* a small bet, esp. on a horse. **4** an abnormally rapid but regular heartbeat. **5** *Electronics* a rapid variation of pitch, esp. of recorded sound. **6** a vibration. [Old English] □ **fluttery** *adj.*

fluvial *adj.* of or found in a river or rivers. [from Latin *fluvialis*]

fluviatile *adj.* of, found in, or produced by a river or rivers [from Latin *fluvialis*]

fluvioglacial *adj.* *Geol.* of or caused by streams from glacial ice, or the combined action of rivers and glaciers.

flux ● *n.* **1** a process of flowing or flowing out. **2** an issue or discharge. **3** continuous change (*a state of flux*). **4** *Metallurgy* a substance mixed with a metal etc. to promote fusion. **5** *Electr.* the total electric or magnetic field passing through a surface. ● *v.* **1** *tr.* & *intr.* make or become fluid. **2** *tr.* **a** fuse. **b** treat with a fusing flux. [from Latin *fluxus*]

fly¹ ● *v.* (**flies**; *past* **flew**; *past part.* **flown**) **1** *intr.* move through the air under control, esp. with wings. **2** (of an aircraft or its occupants): **a** *intr.* travel through the air or through space. **b** *tr.* traverse (*flew the Channel*). **3** *tr.* **a** control the flight of (esp. an aircraft). **b** transport in an aircraft. **4 a** *tr.* cause to fly or remain aloft. **b** *intr.* (of a flag, hair, etc.) wave or flutter. **5** *intr.* pass or rise quickly through the air or over an obstacle. **6** *intr.* pass swiftly (*time flies*). **7** *intr.* **a** flee. **b** *colloq.* depart hastily. **8** *intr.* be forced off suddenly (*sent me flying*). **9** *intr.* (foll. by *at, upon*) **a** hasten or spring violently. **b** attack or criticize fiercely. **10** *tr.* flee from. ● *n.* (*pl.* **-ies**) **1** (*Brit.* usu. in *pl.*) **a** a flap on a garment, esp. trousers, to cover a fastening. **b** this fastening. **2** a flap at the entrance of a tent. **3** (in *pl.*) the space over the proscenium in a theatre. **4** the act or an instance of flying. □ **fly high 1** pursue a high ambition. **2** excel, prosper. **fly in the face of** openly disregard or disobey. **fly into a rage** (or **temper** etc.) become suddenly or violently angry. **fly a kite** test public opinion. **fly off the handle** *colloq.* lose one's temper suddenly. [Old English] □ **flyable** *adj.*

fly² *n.* (*pl.* **flies**) **1** ▲ any insect of the order Diptera, with one pair of usu. transparent wings. **2** any other winged insect. **3** a disease of plants or animals caused by flies (*potato-fly*). **4** a natural or artificial fly used as bait in fishing. ▷ DRY FLY. □ **fly in the ointment** a minor irritation that spoils enjoyment. **fly on the wall** an unnoticed observer. **like flies** in large numbers. **no flies on** *colloq.* nothing to diminish (a person's) astuteness. [Old English]

fly³ *adj.* (**flyer, flyest**) **1** *Brit. slang* knowing, clever, alert. **2** *N. Amer. slang* stylish; good-looking. [19th-century coinage] □ **flyness** *n.*

fly agaric *n.* a poisonous fungus, *Amanita muscaria*, forming bright red mushrooms with white flecks. ▷ TOADSTOOL.

flyaway *adj.* (of hair etc.) tending to fly out or up; streaming.

flyblown *adj.* tainted, esp. by flies.

fly-by-night ● *adj.* unreliable. ● *n.* an unreliable person.

flycatcher *n.* ▼ any of various passerine birds catching flying insects, esp. of the family Muscicapidae, Tyrannidae (**tyrant flycatcher**), and Monarchidae (**monarch flycatcher**).

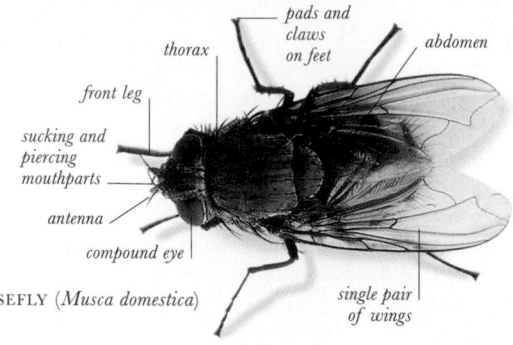

FLYCATCHER: SPOTTED FLYCATCHER (*Muscicapa striata*)

fly-drive ● *attrib.adj.* designating a holiday which combines the cost of the flight and car rental. ● *n.* such a holiday. ● *v.intr.* take such a holiday.

flyer *n.* (also **flier**) **1** an airman or airwoman. **2** a thing that flies in a specified way (*a poor flyer*). **3** *colloq.* a fast-moving animal or vehicle. **4** an ambitious or outstanding person; an outstanding thing. **5** a small handbill. **6** *US* a speculative investment.

fly-fish *v.intr.* fish with a fly.

fly-half *n.* *Rugby* a stand-off half. ▷ RUGBY

flying ● *adj.* **1** fluttering or waving in the air; hanging loose. **2** hasty, brief (*a flying visit*). **3** designed for rapid movement. **4** (of an animal) able to make very long leaps by using winglike membranes etc. ● *n.* flight, esp. in an aircraft. □ **with flying colours** with distinction.

flying boat *n.* a large seaplane with a fuselage that resembles a boat.

FLY

Unlike other flying insects, the 90,000 species of fly have two wings instead of four. They also have large compound eyes, and sticky pads and claws on their feet that allow them to walk on any surface. Flies develop by metamorphosis, their larvae being commonly known as maggots.

pads and claws on feet

thorax

abdomen

front leg

sucking and piercing mouthparts

antenna

compound eye

single pair of wings

EXTERNAL FEATURES OF A HOUSEFLY (*Musca domestica*)

EXAMPLES OF FLIES

SOUTH AMERICAN FLY (*Pantophthalmus bellardii*)

CRANE FLY (*Holorusia* species)

AFRICAN BEE FLY (*Ligyra venus*)

ROBBER FLY (*Mallophora atra*)

flying bomb *n.* a pilotless aircraft with an explosive warhead.

flying buttress *n. Archit.* ▼ a buttress slanting from a separate column, usu. forming an arch with the wall it supports. ▷ GOTHIC

flying buttress   *flying buttress*

FLYING BUTTRESS: ELEVATION OF WESTMINSTER ABBEY, ENGLAND, SHOWING FLYING BUTTRESSES

flying doctor *n.* a doctor (esp. in a large sparsely populated area) who visits distant patients by aircraft.

Flying Dutchman *n.* **1** a ghostly ship supposedly doomed to sail the seas forever. **2** its captain.

flying fish *n.* ▼ any tropical fish of the family Exocoetidae, with wing-like pectoral fins for gliding through the air.

FLYING FISH
(*Exocetus volitans*)   *pectoral fin*

flying fox *n.* a large fruitbat, esp. of the genus *Pteropus*, with a foxlike head. ▷ FRUITBAT

flying lemur *n.* either of two lemur-like mammals of the genus *Cynocephalus*, of SE Asia, having a membrane between the fore and hind limbs for gliding from tree to tree. Also called *colugo*. ▷ MAMMAL

flying officer *n.* the RAF rank next below flight lieutenant.

flying picket *n. Brit.* an industrial picket that can be moved rapidly from one site to another, esp. to reinforce local pickets.

flying saucer *n.* any unidentified, esp. circular, flying object, popularly supposed to be extraterrestrial.

flying squad *n. Brit.* a rapidly mobile police detachment.

flying start *n.* **1** a start (of a race etc.) in which the starting point is passed at full speed. **2** a vigorous start giving an initial advantage.

flyleaf *n.* (*pl.* **-leaves**) a blank leaf at the beginning or end of a book.

flyover *n.* **1** *Brit.* a bridge carrying one road or railway over another. **2** *US* = FLY-PAST.

fly-paper *n.* sticky treated paper for catching flies.

fly-past *n. Brit.* a ceremonial flight of aircraft.

fly-pitcher *n. Brit. slang* a street trader. □ **fly-pitching** *n.*

fly-post *v.tr. Brit.* display (posters etc.) rapidly in unauthorized places.

flysheet *n.* **1** a tract or circular of two or four pages. **2** *Brit.* a fabric cover over a tent for extra protection. ▷ TENT

fly-tip *v.tr. Brit.* illegally dump (waste). □ **fly-tipper** *n.* **fly-tipping** *n.*

flytrap *n.* any of various plants that catch flies, esp. the Venus flytrap.

flyweight *n.* **1** a weight in certain sports intermediate between light flyweight and bantamweight, in the amateur boxing scale 48–51 kg but differing for professionals, wrestlers, and weightlifters. **2** a boxer etc. of this weight.

flywheel *n.* ▶ a heavy wheel on a revolving shaft used to regulate machinery or accumulate power. ▷ INTERNAL-COMBUSTION ENGINE

FM *abbr.* **1** Field Marshal. **2** frequency modulation.

Fm *symb. Chem.* the element fermium.

f-number *n. Photog.* the ratio of the focal length to the effective diameter of a lens. ▷ APERTURE

foal ● *n.* the young of a horse or related animal. ● *v.tr.* give birth to (a foal). □ **in** (or **with**) **foal** (of a mare etc.) pregnant. [Old English]

foam ● *n.* **1** a mass of small bubbles formed on or in liquid by agitation, fermentation, etc. **2** a froth of saliva or sweat. **3** a substance resembling these, e.g. foam rubber, foam plastic. ● *v.intr.* **1** emit foam; froth. **2** run with foam. **3** (of a vessel) be filled and overflow with foam. □ **foam at the mouth** be very angry. [Old English] □ **foamless** *adj.* **foamy** *adj.* (**foamier, foamiest**).

fob[1] *n.* **1** (in full **fob-chain**) a chain of a pocket watch. **2** a small pocket for carrying a watch. **3** a tab on a keyring.

fob[2] *v.tr.* (**fobbed, fobbing**) □ **fob off 1** (often foll. by *with* a thing) deceive into accepting something inferior. **2** (often foll. by *on to* a person) palm or pass off (an inferior thing). [Middle English]

f.o.b. *abbr.* free on board (see FREE).

focaccia /fŏ-kach-ă/ *n.* (*pl.* **focaccias**) a type of flat Italian bread made with yeast and olive oil and often flavoured with herbs etc. [Italian]

focal length *n.* (also **focal distance**) the distance between the centre of a lens or curved mirror and its focus. ▷ LENS

focal point *n.* **1** = FOCUS *n.* 1. **2** = FOCUS *n.* 3.

fo'c'sle *var.* of FORECASTLE.

focus ● *n.* (*pl.* **focuses** or **foci** /foh sy/) **1** *Physics* **a** the point at which rays or waves meet after reflection or refraction. ▷ SIGHT. **b** the point from which diverging rays or waves appear to proceed. **2 a** *Optics* the point at which an object must be situated for a lens or mirror to give a well-defined image. **b** the adjustment of the eye or a lens necessary to produce a clear image. **c** a state of clear definition (*out of focus*). **3** the centre of interest or activity (*focus of attention*). **4** *Med.* the principal site of an infection or other disease. ● *v.* (**focused, focusing** or **focussed, focussing**) **1** *tr.* bring into focus. **2** *tr.* adjust the focus of (a lens, the eye, etc.). **3** *tr. & intr.* (often foll. by *on*) concentrate or be concentrated on. **4** *intr. & tr.* converge or make converge to a focus. [Latin, literally 'hearth'] □ **focal** *adj.* **focuser** *n.*

fodder ● *n.* dried hay or straw etc. for cattle etc. ● *v.tr.* give fodder to. [Old English]

foe *n.* esp. *poet.* or *formal* an enemy or opponent. [Old English *fāh* 'hostile']

foetid *var.* of FETID.

foetus /fee-tŭs/ *n.* (*US & Med.* **fetus**) (*pl.* **-tuses**) ▼ an unborn mammalian offspring, esp. an unborn human of more than eight weeks. [from Latin *fetus* 'offspring'] □ **foetal** *adj.*

foeticide *n.*

fog ● *n.* **1** ▼ a thick cloud of water droplets or smoke suspended at or near the Earth's surface. **2** *Photog.* cloudiness on a developed negative etc. **3** an uncertain or confused position or state. ● *v.* (**fogged, fogging**) **1** *tr.* **a** (often foll. by *up*) cover with fog or condensed vapour. **b** bewilder or confuse. **2** *intr.* (often foll. by *up*) become covered with fog or condensed vapour. □ **in a fog** puzzled; at a loss.

fog bank *n.* a mass of fog at sea.

fogbound *adj.* unable to proceed because of fog.

fogey *n.* (also **fogy**) (*pl.* **-eys** or **-ies**) a dull old-fashioned person (esp. *old fogey*). [18th-century coinage] □ **fogeydom** *n.* **fogeyish** *adj.*

foggy *adj.* (**foggier, foggiest**) **1** (of the atmosphere) thick or obscure with fog. **2** vague, confused, unclear. □ **not have the foggiest** esp. *Brit. colloq.* have no idea at all. □ **fogginess** *n.*

foghorn *n.* a deep-sounding instrument for warning ships in fog.

fog lamp *n.* a lamp, esp. on a motor vehicle, used to improve visibility in fog.

fogy *var.* of FOGEY.

foible *n.* a minor weakness or idiosyncrasy.

foil[1] *v.tr.* frustrate, baffle, defeat. [Middle English in sense 'to trample down']

tip of revolving shaft

gas

flywheel   *piston*

drive belt

generator

FLYWHEEL IN A GENERATOR

umbilical cord

foetus

placenta

amniotic fluid

womb

vagina

FOETUS: NINE-WEEK-OLD HUMAN FOETUS IN THE WOMB

F

FOG

There are two main types of fog. Advection fog occurs at sea when warm, moist air flows over cold sea water. The water vapour in the air condenses to form a layer of fog.

Radiation fog occurs on land on cool, clear nights. As the ground loses its heat, it may cool the air nearby, creating fog. Mist is a light fog, while smog is fog with pollutants.

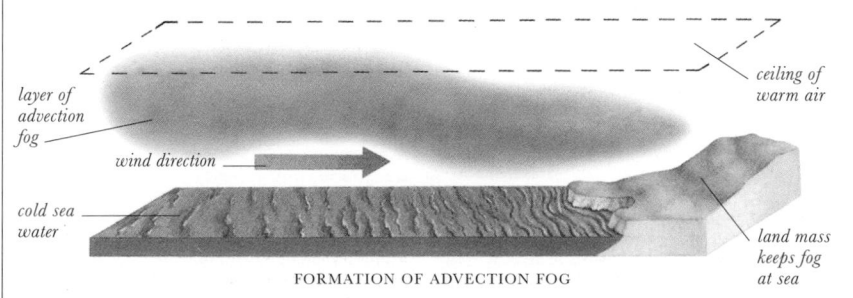

ceiling of warm air

layer of advection fog

wind direction

cold sea water

land mass keeps fog at sea

FORMATION OF ADVECTION FOG

FOLD

Folds in the Earth's surface occur when the tectonic plates of the Earth's crust collide, causing the rock strata to deform. The strata are squeezed horizontally and vertically, and the scale and severity of folding can vary greatly. The type of fold produced depends on the strength of the forces, the rock's resilience, and the arrangement of the strata. Various characteristic fold types are shown here.

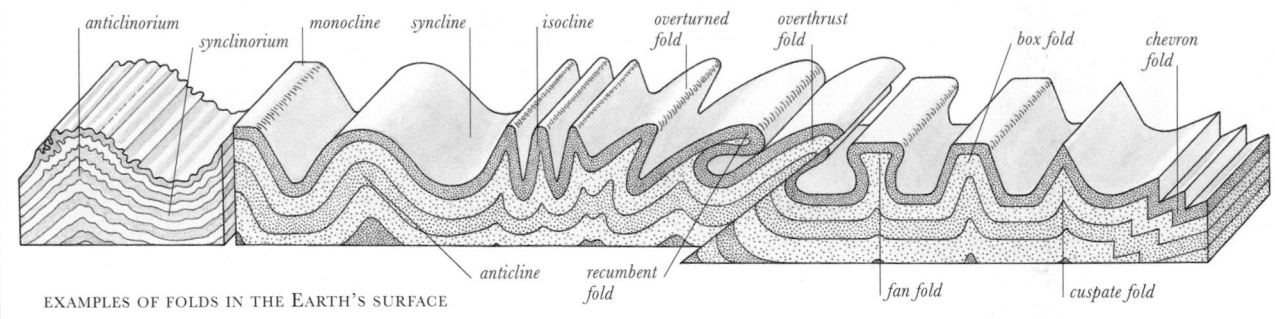

anticlinorium *synclinorium* *monocline* *syncline* *isocline* *overturned fold* *overthrust fold* *box fold* *chevron fold*

anticline *recumbent fold* *fan fold* *cuspate fold*

EXAMPLES OF FOLDS IN THE EARTH'S SURFACE

F

foil² *n.* **1** metal hammered or rolled into a thin sheet (*aluminium foil*). **2** a person or thing that enhances the qualities of another by contrast. [from Latin *folium* 'leaf']

foil³ *n.* ◄ a light blunt-edged sword with a button on its point used in fencing. ▷ FENCING. [16th-century coinage]

foist *v.tr.* (foll. by *on*, *upon*) impose (an unwelcome person or thing) on. [originally of palming a false die: from Dutch dialect *vuisten* 'to take in the hand']

fol. *abbr.* folio.

fold¹ ● *v.* **1** *tr.* **a** bend or close (a thing) over upon itself. **b** (foll. by *back*, *over*, *down*) bend a part of (a thing) in the manner specified (*fold down the flap*). **2** *intr.* become or be able to be folded. **3** *tr.* (foll. by *away*, *up*) make compact by folding. **4** *intr.* (often foll. by *up*) *colloq.* **a** collapse, disintegrate. **b** (of an enterprise) fail; go bankrupt. **5** *tr. poet.* embrace (esp. *fold in the arms* or *to the breast*). **6** *tr.* (foll. by *about*, *round*) clasp (the arms); wrap, envelop. **7** *tr.* (foll. by *in*) mix (an ingredient with others) by gently cutting and turning. ● *n.* **1** the act or an instance of folding. **2** a line made by or for folding. **3** a folded part. **4** *Brit.* a hollow among hills. **5** *Geol.* ▲ a curvature of strata. ▷ MOUNTAIN. □ **fold one's arms** place one's arms across the chest, side by side or entwined. [Old English] □ **foldable** *adj.*

fold² *n.* **1** = SHEEPFOLD. **2** a body of believers or members of a Church. [Old English]

folder *n.* a folding cover or holder for loose papers.

folding door *n.* a door with jointed sections, folding on itself when opened.

folding money *n.* esp. *US colloq.* banknotes.

fold-out *n.* an oversize page in a book etc. to be unfolded by the reader.

foliage *n.* leaves, leafage. [based on Latin *folium* 'leaf']

foliar *adj.* of or relating to leaves.

foliar feed *n.* feed supplied to leaves of plants.

foliate ● *adj.* **1** leaflike. **2** having leaves. ● *v.intr.* split into laminae. [from Latin *foliatus* 'leaved'] □ **foliation** *n.*

folic acid *n.* a vitamin of the B complex, found in leafy green vegetables, liver, and kidney. [based on Latin *folium* 'leaf', because found esp. in green leaves]

folio ● *n.* (*pl.* **-os**) **1** a leaf of paper etc., esp. one numbered only on the front. **2** a sheet of paper folded once making two leaves of a book. **3** a book made of such sheets. ● *adj.* (of a book) made of folios, of the largest size. □ **in folio** made of folios. [Latin, literally 'on leaf' (as specified)]

folk *n.* (*pl.* **folk** or **folks**) **1** (treated as *pl.*) people in general or of a specified class (*few folk about*; *townsfolk*). **2** (in *pl.*) (usu. **folks**) one's parents or relatives. **3** (treated as *sing.*) a people. **4** (treated as *sing.*) *colloq.* = FOLK MUSIC. **5** (*attrib.*) of popular origin; traditional (*folk art*, *folk hero*). [Old English]

folk dance *n.* **1** a dance of popular origin. **2** the music for such a dance. □ **folk dancer** *n.* **folk dancing** *n.*

folklore *n.* the traditional beliefs and stories of a people; the study of these. □ **folkloric** *adj.* **folklorist** *n.* **folkloristic** *adj.*

folk music *n.* traditional music or modern music in this style.

folk singer *n.* a singer of folk songs.

folk song *n.* a song of popular or traditional origin or style.

folksy *adj.* (**folksier**, **folksiest**) **1** friendly, sociable, informal. **2** having the characteristics of folk art, culture, etc. □ **folksiness** *n.*

folk tale *n.* a popular or traditional story.

folkweave *n. Brit.* a rough loosely woven fabric.

follicle *n. Anat.* ◄ a small secretory cavity, sac, or gland. ▷ OVARY, SKIN. [from Latin *folliculus* 'little bellows'] □ **follicular** *adj.*

follicle-stimulating hormone *n. Physiol.* a pituitary hormone which promotes the formation of ova or sperm.

follow *v.* **1** *tr.* or (foll. by *after*) *intr.* go or come after (a person or thing proceeding ahead). **2** *tr.* go along (a route, path, etc.). **3** *tr.* & *intr.* come after in order or time. **4** *tr.* take as a guide or leader. **5** *tr.* conform to (*follow your example*). **6** *tr.* practise (a trade or profession). **7** *tr.* undertake (a course of study etc.). **8** *tr.* understand the meaning or tendency of (a speaker or argument). **9** *tr.* maintain awareness of the current state or progress of (events etc. in a particular sphere). **10** *tr.* (foll. by *with*) provide with a sequel or successor. **11** *intr.* be necessarily true as a result of something else. **b** (foll. by *from*) be a result of. □ **follow one's nose** trust to instinct. **follow on 1** continue. **2** (of a cricket team) have to bat again immediately after the first innings. **follow out** carry out; adhere precisely to (instructions etc.). **follow suit 1** *Cards* play a card of the suit led. **2** conform to another person's actions. **follow through 1** continue (an action etc.) to its conclusion. **2** *Sport* continue the movement of a stroke after the ball has been struck. **follow up 1** (foll. by *with*) pursue, develop, supplement. **2** make further investigation of. [Old English]

follower *n.* **1** an adherent or devotee. **2** a person or thing that follows.

following ● *prep.* coming after in time; as a sequel to. ● *n.* **1** a body of adherents or devotees. **2** (**the following**) (treated as *sing.* or *pl.*) the person(s) or thing(s) now to be mentioned. ● *adj.* that follows or comes after.

follow-the-leader *n.* (also *Brit.* **follow-my-leader**) a game in which players must do as the leader does.

follow-up *n.* a subsequent or continued action, measure, experience, etc.

folly *n.* (*pl.* **-ies**) **1** foolishness; lack of good sense. **2** a foolish act, behaviour, idea, etc. **3** ▼ a costly ornamental building. [based on Old French *fol* 'mad']

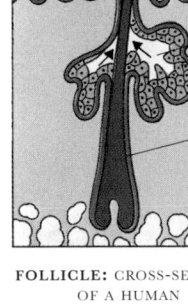

sebum secretion *hair*

sebum

sebaceous gland

follicle

FOLLICLE: CROSS-SECTION OF A HUMAN HAIR FOLLICLE

button

FOIL

FOLLY: 18TH-CENTURY ENGLISH GARDEN FOLLY

foment *v.tr.* **1** instigate or stir up (trouble, sedition, etc.). **2 a** bathe with warm or medicated liquid. **b** apply warmth to. [based on Latin *fomentum* 'poultice'] □ **fomenter** *n.*

fomentation *n.* **1** the act or an instance of fomenting. **2** materials prepared for application to a wound etc.

fond *adj.* **1** (*predic.*; foll. by *of*) having affection or a liking for. **2** (*attrib.*) affectionate, loving, doting. **3** (*attrib.*) (of beliefs etc.) foolishly optimistic or credulous; naive. [Middle English, from obsolete *fon* 'to be foolish'] □ **fondly** *adv.* **fondness** *n.*

fondant *n.* a soft sweet of flavoured sugar. [French, literally 'melting']

fondle *v.tr.* touch or stroke lovingly; caress. [back-formation from *fondling* 'fondled person'] □ **fondler** *n.*

fondue *n.* **1** a dish of flavoured melted cheese into which pieces of bread are dipped. **2** any other dish in which small pieces of food are dipped into hot oil or sauce. [French, literally 'melted']

font[1] *n.* **1** a receptacle in a church for baptismal water. ▷ CHURCH. **2** the reservoir for oil in a lamp. [Old English *font, fant* via Old Irish *fant, font* from Latin *fons fontis* 'fountain, baptismal water']

font[2] *n.* (also *Brit.* **fount**) *Printing* a set of type of one face or size. [from Old French *fonte* 'a melting']

fontanelle *n.* (*US* **fontanel**) ▼ a membranous space in an infant's skull at the angles of the parietal bones. [earlier in sense 'outlet for bodily secretions': from Old French *fontenelle* 'little fountain']

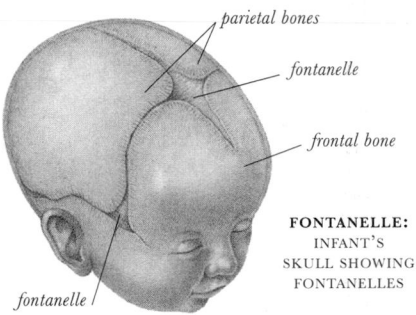

FONTANELLE:
INFANT'S
SKULL SHOWING
FONTANELLES

parietal bones
fontanelle
frontal bone
fontanelle

food *n.* **1** a nutritious substance, esp. solid in form, taken into an animal or a plant to maintain life and growth. **2** mental stimulus (*food for thought*). [Old English]

food additive *n.* a non-nutritional substance added to food as a colouring, flavouring, etc.

food chain *n.* ▼ a series of organisms each dependent on the next as a source of food.

foodie *n.* (also **foody**) (*pl.* **-ies**) *colloq.* a person with a particular interest in food; a gourmet.

food poisoning *n.* illness due to bacteria or toxins in food.

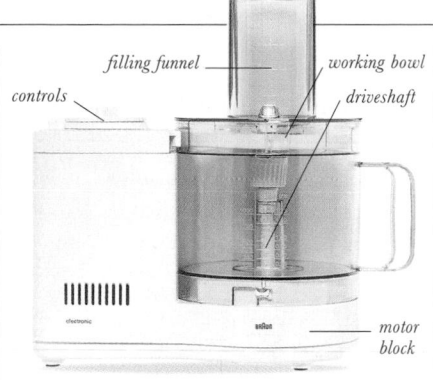

FOOD PROCESSOR

filling funnel
working bowl
driveshaft
controls
motor block

food processor *n.* ▲ a machine for chopping and mixing food materials.

foodstuff *n.* any substance suitable as food.

food value *n.* the relative nourishing power of a food.

fool[1] ● *n.* **1** a person who acts unwisely or imprudently; a stupid person. **2** *hist.* a jester; a clown. **3** a dupe. ● *v.* **1** *tr.* deceive so as to cause to appear foolish. **2** *tr.* (foll. by *into* + verbal noun, or *out of*) trick; cause to do something foolish. **3** *tr.* play tricks on; dupe. **4** *intr.* act in a joking, frivolous, or teasing way. **5** *intr.* (foll. by *about, around*) **a** behave in a playful or silly way. **b** engage in sexual (esp. adulterous) activity. ● *adj. N. Amer. colloq.* foolish, silly. □ **act** (or **play**) **the fool** behave in a silly way. **make a fool of** make (a person or oneself) look foolish; trick or deceive. **no** (or **nobody's**) **fool** a shrewd or prudent person. [from Latin *follis* 'bellows, empty-headed person']

fool[2] *n.* esp. *Brit.* a dessert of usu. stewed fruit crushed and mixed with cream, custard, etc. [16th-century coinage]

foolery *n.* foolish behaviour.

foolhardy *adj.* (**foolhardier**, **foolhardiest**) rashly or foolishly bold; reckless. [from Old French *fol* 'foolish' + *hardi* 'bold'] □ **foolhardily** *adv.* **foolhardiness** *n.*

foolish *adj.* (of a person, action, etc.) lacking good sense or judgement; unwise. □ **foolishly** *adv.* **foolishness** *n.*

foolproof *adj.* (of a procedure, mechanism, etc.) so straightforward or simple as to be incapable of misuse or mistake.

foolscap *n. Brit.* a size of paper, about 330 × 200 (or 400) mm. [named from the former water-mark representing a fool's cap]

fool's errand *n.* a fruitless venture.

fool's gold *n.* ▶ iron pyrites.

fool's paradise *n.* happiness founded on an illusion.

fool's parsley *n.* a highly poisonous plant, *Aethusa cynapium*, resembling parsley.

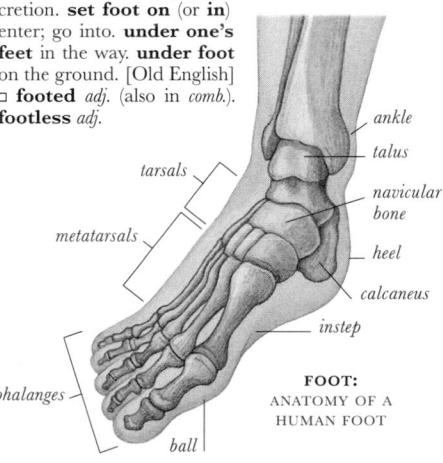

iron pyrites

FOOL'S GOLD

foot ● *n.* (*pl.* **feet**) **1 a** ▼ the lower extremity of the leg below the ankle. ▷ ANKLE. **b** the part of a sock etc. covering the foot. **2 a** the lower or lowest part of a page, stairs, etc. **b** the lower end of a table. **c** the end of a bed where the user's feet normally rest. **d** a part of a chair, appliance, etc. on which it rests. **3** the base, often projecting, of anything extending vertically. **4** a step, place, or tread; a manner of walking (*fleet of foot*). **5** (*pl.* **feet** or **foot**) a unit of linear measure equal to 12 inches (30.48 cm). **6** *Prosody* a group of syllables (one usu. stressed) constituting a metrical unit. **7** *Brit. hist.* infantry (*a regiment of foot*). **8** *Zool.* the locomotive or adhesive organ of invertebrates. ▷ GASTROPOD, RAZOR-SHELL. **9** *Bot.* the part by which a petal is attached. **10** a device on a sewing machine for holding the material steady as it is sewn. ● *v.tr.* **1** (usu. as **foot it**) **a** traverse (esp. a long distance) by foot. **b** dance. **2** pay (a bill, esp. one considered large). □ **at a person's feet** as a person's disciple or subject. **feet of clay** a fundamental weakness in a person otherwise revered. **get one's feet wet** begin to participate. **have one's** (or **both**) **feet on the ground** be practical. **have a foot in the door** have a prospect of success. **have one foot in the grave** be near death or very old. **my foot!** *int. colloq.* expressing strong contradiction. **not put a foot wrong** make no mistakes. **on foot** walking, not riding etc. **put one's feet up** *colloq.* take a rest. **put one's foot down** *colloq.* **1** be firmly insistent or repressive. **2** *Brit.* accelerate a motor vehicle. **put one's foot in it** *colloq.* commit a blunder or indiscretion. **set foot on** (or **in**) enter; go into. **under one's feet** in the way. **under foot** on the ground. [Old English] □ **footed** *adj.* (also in *comb.*). **footless** *adj.*

FOOD CHAIN

A food chain is a pathway that shows how energy and nutrients pass between living things. Each chain links a single series of species, with different food chains interconnecting to form food webs. In a food chain, each species occupies a particular position, known as a trophic level. The marine food web here shows a number of separate food chains, with a maximum of five trophic levels. In each chain, the first level is occupied by plant-like planktonic organisms, which make food by photosynthesis. These 'producers' supply food that can then be passed on to 'consumers' – animals that either eat the producers or each other. Few food chains have more than five trophic levels, because a large amount of energy is lost each time that food is passed on.

killer whale (highest trophic level)
seabird
seal
minke whale
fish
squid
movement of food and energy
krill
plankton (lowest trophic level)

MARINE FOOD CHAINS

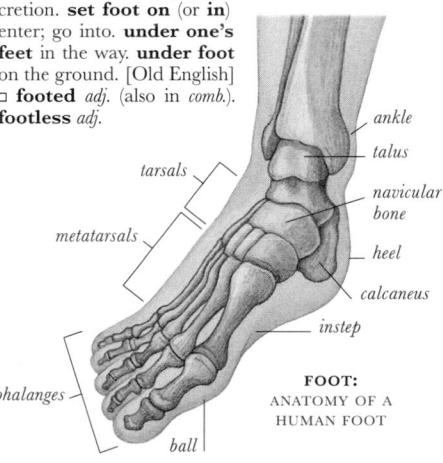

FOOT:
ANATOMY OF A
HUMAN FOOT

ankle
talus
navicular bone
heel
calcaneus
instep
tarsals
metatarsals
phalanges
ball

footage *n.* **1** length or distance in feet. **2** an amount of film made for showing, broadcasting, etc.

foot-and-mouth disease *n.* a contagious viral disease of cattle etc.

FOOTBALL

The term football is applied to various games around the world. Association Football (soccer) is played by two teams, each of 11 players, who attempt to get the ball into the opponent's goal, usually by kicking it. In American football, two teams with 11 players on the field – up to 40 players can appear in a game for each side – score points by crossing the opponent's goal line, either by passing the ball or carrying it across (a touchdown), or by kicking it between the goalposts (a field goal). In Australian Rules football, 18 players on each side score goals (six points) through the inner goalposts, or 'behinds' (one point) between the inner and outer goalposts.

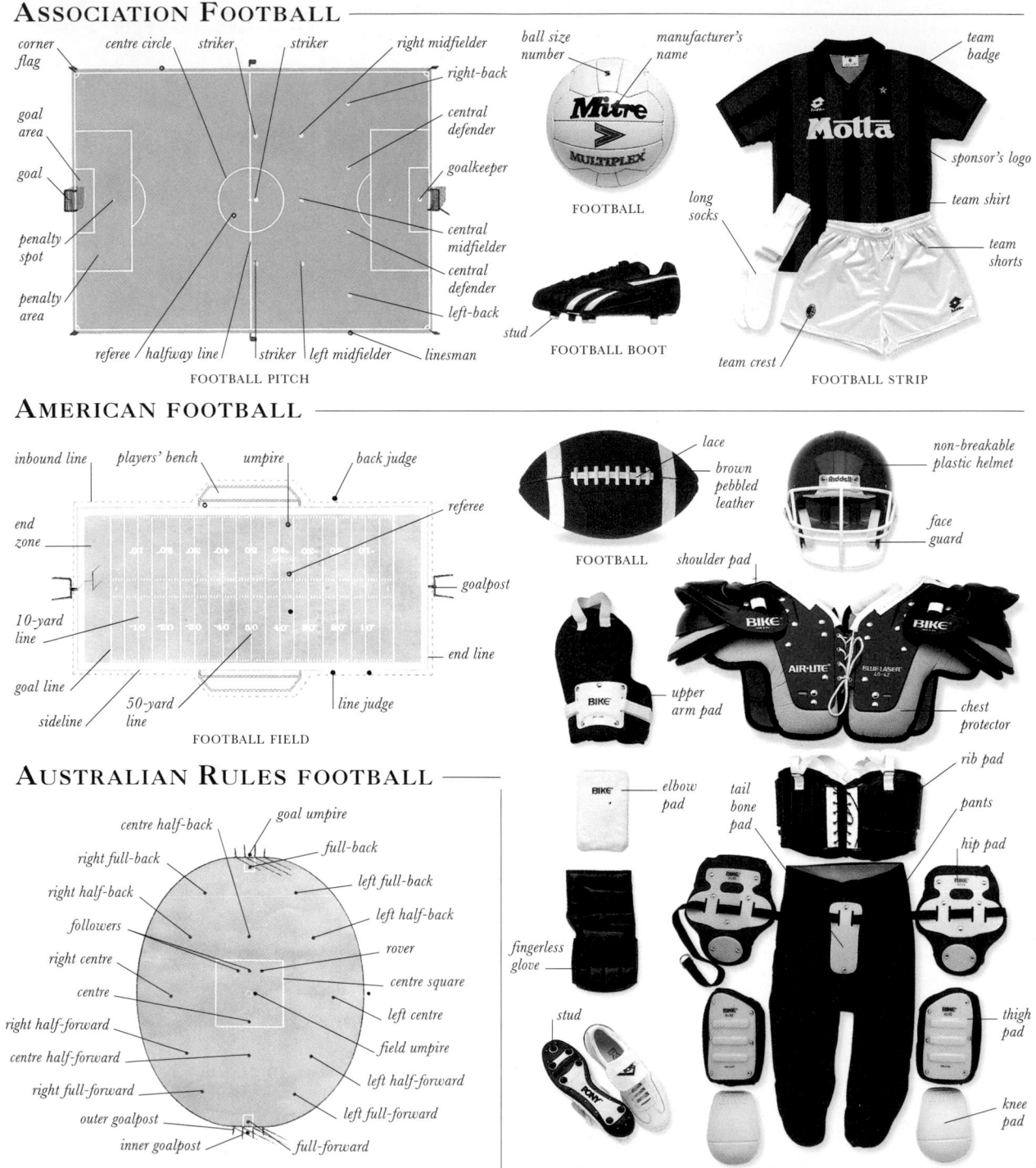

ASSOCIATION FOOTBALL

corner flag · centre circle · striker · striker · right midfielder · right-back · central defender · goalkeeper · central midfielder · central defender · left-back · linesman

goal area · goal · penalty spot · penalty area · referee · halfway line · striker · left midfielder

FOOTBALL PITCH

ball size number · manufacturer's name

FOOTBALL

stud

FOOTBALL BOOT

team badge · sponsor's logo · team shirt · team shorts · long socks · team crest

FOOTBALL STRIP

AMERICAN FOOTBALL

inbound line · players' bench · umpire · back judge · referee · goalpost · end line

end zone · 10-yard line · goal line · sideline · 50-yard line · line judge

FOOTBALL FIELD

lace · brown pebbled leather

FOOTBALL

non-breakable plastic helmet · face guard

shoulder pad · rib pad · pants · hip pad

upper arm pad · chest protector

elbow pad · tail bone pad

fingerless glove · stud · thigh pad · knee pad

AUSTRALIAN RULES FOOTBALL

centre half-back · goal umpire · full-back · left full-back · left half-back · rover · centre square · left centre · field umpire · left half-forward · left full-forward · full-forward

right full-back · right half-back · followers · right centre · centre · right half-forward · centre half-forward · right full-forward · outer goalpost · inner goalpost

FOOTBALL PITCH

FOOTBALL BOOTS

PROTECTIVE EQUIPMENT

F

football *n.* **1** ◄ any of several esp. outdoor games between two teams played with a ball on a pitch with goals at each end, esp. *Brit.* = ASSOCIATION FOOTBALL. **2** ◄ a large inflated ball of a kind used in these games. □ **footballer** *n.*

football pool *n.* (also **football pools** *pl.*) a form of gambling on the results of football matches.

footboard *n.* **1** a board to support the feet or a foot. **2** an upright board at the foot of a bed.

footbrake *n.* a brake operated by the foot in a motor vehicle.

footbridge *n.* a bridge for use by pedestrians.

footer[1] *n.* **1** (in *comb.*) a person or thing of so many feet in length or height (*six-footer*). **2** a line or block of text appearing at the foot of each page of a document etc.

footer[2] var. of FOOTY.

footfall *n.* the sound of a footstep.

foothill *n.* (often in *pl.*) any of the low hills around the base of a mountain.

foothold *n.* **1** a place, esp. in climbing, where a foot can be supported securely. **2** a secure initial position or advantage.

footie var. of FOOTY.

footing *n.* **1** a foothold; a secure position (*lost his footing*). **2** the basis on which an enterprise is established or operates; the position or status of a person in relation to others (*on an equal footing*).

footlights *n.pl.* a row of lights along the front of a stage. ▷ THEATRE

footling *adj. colloq.* trivial, silly.

footloose *adj.* (often in phr. **footloose and fancy-free**) free to go where or act as one pleases.

footman *n.* (*pl.* **-men**) a liveried servant.

footmark *n.* a footprint.

footnote *n.* a note printed at the foot of a page.

footpad *n. hist.* an unmounted highwayman.

footpath *n.* **1** *Brit.* a path for pedestrians, esp. a pavement at the side of a road. **2** a path for walking along through woods, fields, etc.

footplate *n.* esp. *Brit.* the platform in the cab of a locomotive for the crew.

footprint *n.* **1** the impression left by a foot or shoe. **2** the area over which an aircraft is audible, a broadcast can be received, etc.

footrest *n.* a support for the feet or a foot.

foot soldier *n.* a soldier who fights on foot.

footsore *adj.* having sore feet, esp. from walking.

footstep *n.* **1** a step taken in walking. **2** the sound of this. □ **follow** (or **tread**) **in a person's footsteps** do as another person did before.

footstool *n.* a low stool for resting the feet on when sitting.

footway *n. Brit.* a path or way for pedestrians.

footwear *n.* shoes, socks, etc.

footwork *n.* the use of the feet, esp. skilfully, in sports, dancing, etc.

footy *n.* (also **footie**, **footer**) *colloq.* = FOOTBALL 1.

fop *n.* an affectedly elegant or fashionable man; a dandy. [17th-century coinage] □ **foppery** *n.* **foppish** *adj.* **foppishly** *adv.* **foppishness** *n.*

for ● *prep.* **1** in the interest or to the benefit of; intended to go to (*these flowers are for you; wish to see it for myself*). **2** in defence, support, or favour of (*fight for one's rights*). **3** suitable or appropriate to (*a dance for beginners; not for me to say*). **4** in respect of or with reference to; regarding (*usual for ties to be worn; don't care for him at all; MP for Lincoln*). **5** representing or in place of (*here for my uncle*). **6** in exchange against (*swopped it for a bigger one*). **7 a** as the price of (*give me £5 for it*). **b** at the price of (*bought it for £5*). **c** to the amount of (*a bill for £100*). **8** as the penalty of (*fined them heavily for it*). **9** in requital of (*that's for upsetting my sister*). **10** as a reward for (*here's £5 for your trouble*). **11** with a view to; in the hope or quest of; in order to get (*go for a walk; did it for the money*). **12** corresponding to (*word for word*). **13** to reach; in the direction of; towards (*left for Rome*). **14** con-

-ducive or conducively to; in order to achieve (*take the pills for a sound night's sleep*). **15** so as to start promptly at (*arrive at seven-thirty for eight*). **16** through or over (a distance or period); during (*walked for miles; sang for two hours*). **17** in the character of; as being (*for the last time; know it for a lie*). **18** because of; on account of (*could not see for tears*). **19** in spite of; notwithstanding (*for all your fine words*). **20** considering or making due allowance in respect of (*good for a beginner*). ● *conj.* because, since, seeing that. □ **be for it** *Brit. colloq.* be in imminent danger of punishment or other trouble. **for ever** see EVER (cf. FOREVER). **o** (or **oh**) **for** (as *int.*) expressing longing for a thing. [Old English]

forage ● *n.* **1** food for horses and cattle. **2** the act or an instance of searching for food. ● *v.* **1** *intr.* (often foll. by *for*) go searching; rummage (esp. for food). **2** *tr.* get by foraging. [from Old French *fourrage*] □ **forager** *n.*

forage cap *n.* an infantry undress cap.

foramen *n.* (*pl.* **foramina**) *Anat.* an opening, hole, or passage, esp. in a bone. [Latin]

forasmuch as *conj. archaic* because, since.

foray ● *n.* a sudden attack; a raid. ● *v.intr.* make or go on a foray. [from Old French *forager*, related to FODDER]

forbade (also **forbad**) past of FORBID.

forbear[1] *v.intr. & tr.* (past **forbore**; past part. **forborne**) *literary* abstain or desist (from) (*could not forbear (from) speaking out; forbore to mention it*). [Old English]

forbear[2] var. of FOREBEAR.

forbearance *n.* patient self-control; tolerance.

forbid *v.tr.* (**forbidding**; past **forbade** or **forbad**; past part. **forbidden**) **1** (foll. by *to* + infin.) order not (*I forbid you to go*). **2** refuse to allow (a thing, or a person to have a thing) (*I forbid it; was forbidden any wine*). **3** refuse a person entry to (*the gardens are forbidden to children*). [Old English]

forbidden fruit *n.* something desired or enjoyed all the more because not allowed.

forbidding *adj.* uninviting, repellent, stern. □ **forbiddingly** *adv.*

forbore past of FORBEAR[1].

forborne past part. of FORBEAR[1].

force ● *n.* **1** power; exerted strength or impetus; intense effort. **2** coercion or compulsion, esp. with the use or threat of violence. **3 a** military strength. **b** (in *pl.*) troops; fighting resources. **c** an organized body of people, esp. soldiers, police, or workers. **4** binding power; validity. **5** effect; precise significance (*the force of their words*). **6** mental or moral strength; influence, efficacy (*force of habit*). **7** *Physics* **a** an influence tending to change the motion of a body or produce motion or stress in a stationary body. **b** the intensity of this. **8** a person or thing regarded as exerting influence (*is a force for good*). ● *v.tr.* **1** constrain (a person) by force. **2** make a way through or into by force. **3** (usu. with prep. or adv.) drive or propel violently or against resistance (*the wind forced them back*). **4** (foll. by *on, upon*) impose or press (on a person) (*forced their views on us*). **5 a** cause or produce by effort (*forced a smile*). **b** attain by strength or effort (*forced an entry; must force a decision*). **c** make (a way) by force. **6** strain or increase to the utmost; overstrain. **7** artificially hasten the growth of (a plant). **8** seek or demand quick results from; accelerate the process of (*force the pace*). □ **by force of** by means of. **force a person's hand** make a person act prematurely or unwillingly. **force the issue** render an immediate decision necessary. **in force 1** valid, effective. **2** in great strength or numbers. **join forces** combine efforts. [based on Latin *fortis* 'strong'] □ **forceable** *adj.* **forceably** *adv.* **forcer** *n.*

forced labour *n.* compulsory labour, esp. under harsh conditions.

forced landing *n.* the unavoidable landing of an aircraft in an emergency.

forced march *n.* a long and vigorous march esp. by troops.

force-feed *n.* force (esp. a prisoner) to take food.

force field *n.* (in science fiction) an invisible barrier of force.

forceful *adj.* **1** vigorous, powerful. **2** (of speech) compelling, impressive. □ **forcefully** *adv.* **forcefulness** *n.*

force majeure /torss ma-**zher**/ *n.* **1** irresistible compulsion or coercion. **2** unforeseeable events excusing a person from the fulfilment of a contract. [French, literally 'superior strength']

forcemeat *n.* meat or vegetables etc. chopped and seasoned for use as a stuffing or a garnish. [based on Old French *farsir* 'to stuff']

forceps *n.* (*pl.* same) ▼ surgical pincers. [Latin]

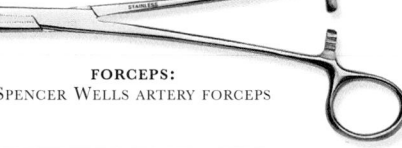

FORCEPS:
SPENCER WELLS ARTERY FORCEPS

forcible *adj.* done by or involving force; forceful. □ **forcibleness** *n.* **forcibly** *adv.*

ford ● *n.* a shallow place where a river or stream may be crossed by wading or in a vehicle. ● *v.tr.* cross (water) at a ford. [Old English] □ **fordable** *adj.* **fordless** *adj.*

fore ● *adj.* situated in front. ● *int. Golf* a warning to a person in the path of a ball. □ **to the fore** in front; conspicuous.

fore and aft ● *adv.* at bow and stern; all over the ship. ● *adj.* (**fore-and-aft**) **1** (of a sail or rigging) set lengthwise. **2** *Naut. & Aeron.* longitudinal (*fore-and-aft line*).

forearm[1] /**for**-arm/ *n.* the part of the arm from the elbow to the wrist or the fingertips. ▷ RADIUS

forearm[2] /for-**arm**/ *v.tr.* prepare or arm beforehand.

forebear *n.* (also **forbear**) (usu. in *pl.*) an ancestor. [FORE + *beer* 'one who exists before']

foreboding *n.* an expectation of trouble or evil; a presage or omen.

forebrain *n. Anat.* the anterior part of the brain.

forecast ● *v.tr.* (past and past part. **-cast** or **-casted**) predict; estimate or calculate beforehand. ● *n.* a calculation or estimate of something future, esp. coming weather. □ **forecaster** *n.*

forecastle /**fohk**-sŭl/ *n.* (also **fo'c'sle**) *Naut.* ▼ the forward part of a ship.

foremast

FORECASTLE OF
AN EARLY
19TH-CENTURY
74-GUN SHIP

bowsprit

forecastle

F

F

foreclose *v.tr.* **1** (also *absol.*; foll. by *on*) stop (a mortgage) from being redeemable or (a mortgager) from redeeming, esp. as a result of defaults in payment. **2** exclude, prevent. [based on Old French *forclos* 'closed out'] □ **foreclosure** *n.*

forecourt *n.* **1** an enclosed space in front of a building. **2** *Brit.* the part of a filling station where petrol is supplied.

forefather *n.* (usu. in *pl.*) **1** an ancestor. **2** a member of a past generation of a family or people.

forefinger *n.* the finger next to the thumb.

forefoot *n.* (*pl.* **-feet**) either of the front feet of a four-footed animal.

forefront *n.* **1** the foremost part. **2** the leading position.

foregather *v.intr.* (also **forgather**) assemble; meet together; associate. [from Dutch *vergaderen*]

forego[1] *v.tr.* & *intr.* (**-goes**; *past* **-went**; *past part.* **-gone**) precede in place or time. [Old English] □ **foregoer** *n.*

forego[2] var. of FORGO.

foregoing *adj.* preceding; previously mentioned.

foregone conclusion *n.* an easily foreseen or predictable result.

foreground *n.* **1** the part of a view that is nearest the observer. **2** the most conspicuous position. [from Dutch *voorgrond*]

forehand *n. Tennis* etc. **1 a** ◀ a stroke played with the palm of the hand facing the opponent. **2 b** (*attrib.*) (also **forehanded**) of or made with a forehand.

FOREHAND TENNIS STROKE

forehead *n.* the part of the face above the eyebrows. [Old English]

foreign *adj.* **1** of, from, in, or characteristic of a country or a language other than one's own. **2** dealing with other countries (*foreign service*). **3** (often foll. by *to*) unfamiliar, strange, alien (*his behaviour is foreign to me*). **4** coming from outside (*foreign matter in the mechanism*). [based on Latin *foras* 'outside'] □ **foreignness** *n.*

Foreign and Commonwealth Office *n.* the British government department dealing with foreign affairs.

foreign body *n.* an extraneous material object, esp. one ingested, introduced, etc., into the body.

foreigner *n.* a person born in or coming from a foreign country.

foreign exchange *n.* **1** the currency of other countries. **2** dealings in these.

foreign legion *n.* a body of foreign volunteers in a modern, esp. the French, army.

foreign minister *n.* (also **foreign secretary**) *Brit.* a government minister in charge of his or her country's relations with other countries.

Foreign Office *n. Brit. hist.* or *colloq.* = FOREIGN AND COMMONWEALTH OFFICE.

foreign service *n. N. Amer.* = DIPLOMATIC SERVICE.

foreknowledge *n.* prior knowledge of an event etc.

foreland *n.* a cape or promontory.

foreleg *n.* either of the front legs of a quadruped.

forelimb *n.* either of the front limbs of an animal.

forelock *n.* ▶ a lock of hair growing just above the forehead.

forelock

FORELOCK
ON A HORSE

FORESHORTEN

In this diagram, the figure on the right is foreshortened, appearing to recede towards the horizon. This effect can be achieved by dividing up the side-on view of the figure at the left edge of the picture plane. The divisions are joined to the vanishing point on the horizon. Where these lines intersect with the picture plane, horizontal lines can be plotted, providing the divisions for foreshortening the figure.

DEMONSTRATION OF FORESHORTENING

picture plane (edge-on) — *horizon line* — *vanishing point*

plotted horizontal lines

foreshortened figure

side-on view of figure

---

foreman *n.* (*pl.* **-men**) **1** a worker with supervisory responsibilities. **2** the member of a jury who presides over its deliberations and speaks on its behalf.

foremast *n.* the forward mast of a ship. ▷ MAN-OF-WAR, SCHOONER

foremost ● *adj.* **1** the chief or most notable. **2** the most advanced in position; the front. ● *adv.* before anything else in position; in the first place (*first and foremost*). [Old English superlative of *forma* 'first']

forename *n.* a first or Christian name.

forenoon *n. archaic* except *Law* & *Naut.* the part of the day before noon.

forensic *adj.* **1** of or used in connection with courts of law, esp. in relation to crime detection. **2** of or employing forensic science. [from Latin *forensis*] □ **forensically** *adv.*

■ **Usage** The use of *forensic* in sense 2 is common, but it is considered an illogical extension of sense 1 by some people.

forensic science *n.* the application of biochemical and other scientific techniques to the investigation of crime.

foreordain *v.tr.* predestine; ordain beforehand. □ **foreordination** *n.*

forepaw *n.* either of the front paws of a quadruped.

foreplay *n.* stimulation preceding sexual intercourse.

forerunner *n.* **1** a predecessor. **2** an advance messenger.

foresail *n. Naut.* the principal sail on a foremast. ▷ MAN-OF-WAR, SCHOONER

foresee *v.tr.* (*past* **-saw**; *past part.* **-seen**) (often foll. by *that* + clause) see or be aware of beforehand. [Old English] □ **foreseeable** *adj.* **foreseeably** *adv.* **foreseeability** *n.*

foreshadow *v.tr.* be a warning or indication of (a future event).

foreshore *n.* the part of the shore between high and low water marks.

foreshorten *v.tr.* ▲ show or portray (an object) with the apparent shortening due to visual perspective.

foresight *n.* **1** regard or provision for the future. **2** the process of foreseeing. **3** the front sight of a gun. ▷ GUN. **4** *Surveying* a sight taken forwards. [Middle English] □ **foresighted** *adj.* **foresightedly** *adv.* **foresightedness** *n.*

foreskin *n.* the fold of skin covering the end of the penis.

forest ● *n.* **1** (often *attrib.*) a large area of trees and undergrowth. **2** the trees growing in it. **3** a large number or dense mass of vertical objects (*a forest of masts*). ● *v.tr.* **1** plant with trees. **2** convert into a forest. [from Late Latin *forestis silva* 'wood outside the walls of a park']

forestall *v.tr.* **1** act in advance of in order to prevent. **2** anticipate (the action of another, or an event). **3** anticipate the action of. [Middle English]

forestay *n. Naut.* a stay from the head of the foremast to a ship's deck or bowsprit. ▷ DINGHY, RIGGING

forester *n.* **1** a person in charge of a forest or skilled in forestry. **2** a person or animal living in a forest.

forestry *n.* the science or management of forests.

foretaste *n.* partial enjoyment or suffering in advance; anticipation.

foretell *v.tr.* (*past* and *past part.* **-told**) tell of or presage (an event etc.) before it takes place; predict, prophesy. □ **foreteller** *n.*

forethought *n.* **1** care or provision for the future. **2** previous thinking or devising. **3** deliberate intention.

foretold *past* and *past part.* of FORETELL.

forever *adv.* continually, persistently (*is forever complaining*) (cf. *for ever* (see EVER)).

forewarn *v.tr.* warn beforehand.

forewent *past* of FOREGO[1], FOREGO[2].

forewoman *n.* (*pl.* **-women**) **1** a female worker with supervisory responsibilities. **2** a woman who presides over a jury's deliberations and speaks on its behalf.

foreword *n.* introductory remarks at the beginning of a book, often by a person other than the author.

forfeit /for-fit/ ● *n.* **1** a penalty for a breach of contract or neglect; a fine. **2** a trivial fine for a breach of rules in clubs etc. or in games. **3** something surrendered as a penalty. **4** the process of forfeiting. ● *adj.* lost or surrendered as a penalty. ● *v.tr.* (**forfeited**, **forfeiting**) lose the right to, be deprived of, or have to pay as a penalty. [from Old French *forfet*, *forfait* 'transgression'] □ **forfeitable** *adj.*

forfend *v.tr.* **1** *US* protect by precautions. **2** *archaic* avert; keep off.

forgather var. of FOREGATHER.

forgave *past* of FORGIVE.

forge[1] ● *v.tr.* **1 a** *Brit.* make (money etc.) in fraudulent imitation. **b** write (a document or signature) in order to pass it as written by another. **2** ▼ shape (esp. metal) by heating and hammering. ● *n.* **1** a blacksmith's workshop; a smithy.

FORGE: BLACKSMITH FORGING METAL ON AN ANVIL

2 a a furnace or hearth for melting or refining metal. **b** a workshop containing this. [from Latin *fabricare* 'to fabricate'.] □ **forgeable** *adj.* **forger** *n.*

forge² *v.intr.* move forward gradually or steadily. □ **forge ahead 1** take the lead in a race. **2** progress rapidly. [18th-century coinage]

forgery *n.* (*pl.* **-ies**) **1** the act or an instance of forging a document etc. **2** a forged document etc.

forget *v.* (**forgetting**; *past* **forgot**; *past part.* **forgotten** or esp. *US* **forgot**) **1** *tr.* & (often foll. by *about*) *intr.* lose the remembrance of; not remember (a person or thing). **2** *tr.* (often foll. by clause or *to* + infin.) not remember; neglect (*forgot to come; forgot how to do it*). **3** *tr.* (also *absol.*) put out of mind; cease to think of (*forgive and forget*). □ **forget oneself 1** neglect one's own interests. **2** act unbecomingly or unworthily. [Old English] □ **forgettable** *adj.*

forgetful *adj.* **1** apt to forget, absent-minded. **2** (often foll. by *of*) forgetting, neglectful. □ **forgetfully** *adv.* **forgetfulness** *n.*

forget-me-not *n.* ▶ any plant of the genus *Myosotis*, esp. *M. scorpioides* with small yellow-eyed bright blue flowers.

forgive *v.tr.* (also *absol.* or with double object) (*past* **forgave**; *past part.* **forgiven**) **1** cease to feel angry or resentful towards; pardon (an offender or offence). **2** remit or let off (a debt or debtor). [Old English] □ **forgivable** *adj.* **forgivably** *adv.* **forgiver** *n.*

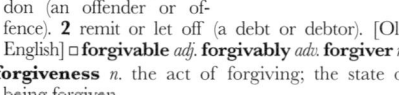

FORGET-ME-NOT: WOOD FORGET-ME-NOT (*Myosotis sylvatica*)

forgiveness *n.* the act of forgiving; the state of being forgiven.

forgiving *adj.* inclined readily to forgive. □ **forgivingly** *adv.*

forgo *v.tr.* (also **forego**) (**-goes**; *past* **-went**; *past part.* **-gone**) abstain from; go without; relinquish. [Old English]

forgot *past* of FORGET.

forgotten *past part.* of FORGET.

fork ● *n.* **1** an instrument with two or more prongs used in eating or cooking. **2** a similar much larger instrument used for digging, lifting, etc. **3** any pronged device or component (*tuning fork*). ▷ TUNING FORK. **4** a forked support for a bicycle wheel. ▷ OFF-ROAD. **5 a** a divergence of anything, e.g. a stick or road, or *N. Amer.* a river, into two parts. **b** either of the two parts (*take the left fork*). ● *v.* **1** *intr.* form a fork or branch by separating into two parts. **2** *intr.* take one or other road etc. at a fork (*fork left for Banbury*). **3** *tr.* dig or lift etc. with a fork. □ **fork out** *colloq.* hand over or pay, usu. reluctantly. **fork over** turn over (soil etc.) with a fork. [from Latin *furca*]

forked *adj.* **1** having a fork or forklike end or branches. **2** divergent, cleft.

fork-lift truck *n.* a vehicle with a horizontal fork in front for lifting and carrying loads.

forlorn *adj.* **1** sad and abandoned or lonely. **2** in a pitiful state; of wretched appearance. [from obsolete *forlese* 'to lose'] □ **forlornly** *adv.* **forlornness** *n.*

forlorn hope *n.* a faint remaining hope or chance. [from Dutch *verloren hoop* 'lost troop', originally of a detachment of assault troops etc.]

form ● *n.* **1 a** a shape; an arrangement of parts. **b** the outward aspect (esp. apart from colour) or shape of a body. **2** a person or animal as visible or tangible (*the familiar form of the postman*). **3** the mode in which a thing exists or manifests itself (*took the form of a book*). **4** a species, kind, or variety. **5** a printed document with blank spaces for information to be inserted. **6** esp. *Brit.* a class in a school. **7** a customary method; what is usually done (*common form*). **8** a set order of words; a formula. **9** behaviour according to a rule or custom. **10** (prec. by *the*) correct procedure (*knows the form*). **11 a** (of an athlete, horse, etc.) condition of health and training (*is in top form*). **b** *Racing* details of previ-

ous performances. **12** general state or disposition (*was in great form*). **13** *Brit. slang* a criminal record. **14** formality or mere ceremony. **15** *Gram.* one of the ways in which a word may be spelt or pronounced or inflected. **16** arrangement and style in literary or musical composition. **17** *Philos.* the essential nature of a species or thing. **18** *Brit.* a long bench without a back. **19** a hare's lair. ● *v.* **1** *tr.* make or fashion into a certain shape or form. **2** *intr.* take a certain shape; be formed. **3** *tr.* be the material of; make up or constitute (*together form a unit; forms part of the structure*). **4** *tr.* develop or establish as a concept, institution, or practice (*form an idea; formed an alliance*). **5** *tr.* (foll. by *into*) embody, organize. **6** *tr.* & *intr.* (often foll. by *up*) esp. *Mil.* bring or be brought into a certain arrangement or formation. □ **in form** fit for racing etc. **off form** esp. *Brit.* not playing or performing well. **on form** esp. *Brit.* playing or performing well. **out of form** not fit for racing etc. [from Latin *forma* 'mould, form']

formal *adj.* **1** in accordance with rules, convention, or ceremony (*formal dress; a formal occasion*). **2** precise or symmetrical (*a formal garden*). **3** prim or stiff in manner. **4** perfunctory, having the form without the spirit. **5** valid or correctly so called because of its form; explicit (*a formal agreement*). **6** in accordance with recognized forms or rules. **7** of or concerned with (outward) form or appearance, esp. as distinct from content or matter. □ **formally** *adv.*

formaldehyde /for-mal-di-hyd/ *n.* a colourless pungent gas used as a disinfectant and preservative and in the manufacture of synthetic resins.

formalin *n.* a colourless solution of formaldehyde in water used as a preservative for biological specimens etc.

formalism *n.* **1** excessive adherence to prescribed forms. **2** *derog.* an artist's concentration on form at the expense of content. □ **formalist** *n.* **formalistic** *adj.*

formality *n.* (*pl.* **-ies**) **1 a** a formal, esp. meaningless, act, regulation, or custom. **b** a thing done simply to comply with a rule. **2** the rigid observance of rules or convention. **3** ceremony; elaborate procedure. **4** being formal; precision of manners.

formalize *v.tr.* (also **-ise**) **1** give definite shape or legal formality to. **2** make ceremonious, precise, or rigid. □ **formalization** *n.*

format ● *n.* **1** the shape and size of a book, periodical, etc. **2** the style or manner of an arrangement or procedure. **3** *Computing* a defined structure for holding data etc. in a record. ● *v.tr.* (**formatted, formatting**) **1** arrange or put into a format. **2** *Computing* prepare (a storage medium) to receive data. [from Latin *formatus* (*liber*) 'shaped (book)']

formate *n.* *Chem.* a salt or ester of formic acid.

formation *n.* **1** the act or an instance of forming; the process of being formed. **2** a thing formed. **3** a structure or arrangement of parts. **4** a particular arrangement, e.g. of troops, aircraft in flight, etc. **5** *Geol.* an assemblage of rocks or series of strata having some common characteristic. □ **formational** *adj.*

formative *adj.* serving to form or fashion; of formation. [Middle English, related to FORM] □ **formatively** *adv.*

former¹ *attrib.adj.* **1** of or occurring in the past or an earlier period (*in former times*). **2** having been previously (*her former husband*). **3** (prec. by *the*; often *absol.*) the first or first mentioned of two. [Middle English, from *forme* 'first']

former² *n.* **1** a person or thing that forms. **2** (in *comb.*) *Brit.* a pupil of a specified form in a school (*fourth-former*).

formerly *adv.* in the past; in former times.

Formica *n. propr.* a hard durable plastic laminate used for working surfaces, cupboard doors, etc. [20th-century coinage]

formic acid *n.* a colourless irritant volatile acid contained in the fluid emitted by some ants. [based on Latin *formica* 'ant']

formidable *adj.* **1** inspiring fear or dread. **2** inspiring respect or awe. **3** likely to be hard to overcome, resist, or deal with. [Latin *formidabilis*] □ **formidableness** *n.* **formidably** *adv.*

formless *adj.* shapeless; without determinate or regular form. □ **formlessly** *adv.* **formlessness** *n.*

formula *n.* (*pl.* **formulas** or (esp. in senses 1, 2) **formulae** /-lee/) **1** *Chem.* a set of chemical symbols showing the constituents of a substance and their relative proportions. **2** *Math.* a mathematical rule expressed in symbols. **3 a** a fixed form of words, esp. one used on social or ceremonial occasions. **b** a rule unintelligently or slavishly followed. **c** a form of words embodying agreement etc. **4 a** a list of ingredients; a recipe. **b** esp. *N. Amer.* an infant's liquid food preparation. **5** a classification of racing car, esp. by the engine capacity. [Latin, literally 'little form'] □ **formulaic** *adj.* **formularize** *v.tr.* (also **-ise**) **formulize** *v.tr.* (also **-ise**)

formulary *n.* (*pl.* **-ies**) a collection of formulas or set forms, esp. for religious use. [from Latin *formularius* (*liber*) '(book) of formulae']

formulate *v.tr.* **1** express in a formula. **2** express clearly and precisely. □ **formulation** *n.*

fornicate *v.intr. archaic* or *joc.* (of people not married or not married to each other) have sexual intercourse voluntarily. [based on Latin *fornix -icis* 'brothel'] □ **fornication** *n.* **fornicator** *n.*

forsake *v.tr.* (*past* **forsook**; *past part.* **forsaken**) **1** give up; renounce. **2** desert, abandon. [Old English *forsacan* 'to deny, renounce, refuse'] □ **forsakenness** *n.* **forsaker** *n.*

forsooth *adv. archaic* or *joc.* truly; no doubt. [Old English]

forswear *v.tr.* (*past* **forswore**; *past part.* **forsworn**) **1** abjure; renounce on oath. **2** (*refl.* or in *passive*) swear falsely; commit perjury. [Old English]

forsythia /for-syth-iă/ *n.* ◀ any ornamental shrub of the genus *Forsythia*, with bright yellow flowers. [modern Latin, named after W. *Forsyth*, English botanist, 1737–1804]

FORSYTHIA (*Forsythia intermedia* 'Lynwood')

fort *n.* ▼ a fortified building or position. [from Latin *fortis* 'strong']

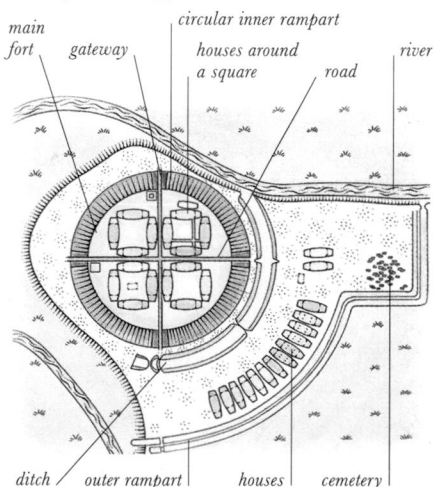

main fort   gateway   circular inner rampart   houses around a square   road   river

ditch   outer rampart   houses   cemetery

FORT: LAYOUT OF A CIRCULAR VIKING FORT

F

F

FOSSIL

For an organism's remains to be fossilized, the natural process of decay must be arrested. Rapid burial is essential to isolate the remains from air and water. If the organism's cavities are filled with hard minerals, the dead organism becomes more resistant than the sediment around it and is said to be fossilized. Fossilization may also occur through refrigeration (organisms in ice) or carbonization (e.g. leaves in coal). Organisms sometimes leave cast-type fossils (e.g. footprints in mud) or become preserved in amber (the fossilized resin of a plant).

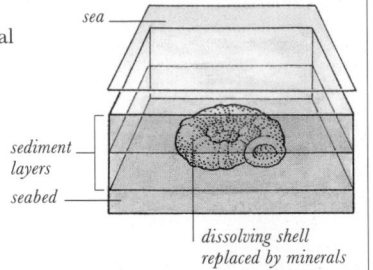

sea
sediment layers
seabed
dissolving shell replaced by minerals

FORMATION OF A SHELL FOSSIL

EXAMPLES OF FOSSILS

  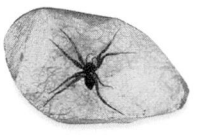  

CLYPEASTER IN SAND   *DICROIDIUM* LEAF IN MUDSTONE   SPIDER TRAPPED IN AMBER   BEETLE IN TAR AND SAND   AMMONITE IN IRON PYRITES

forte[1] /for-tay/ n. **1** a thing in which a person excels. **2** *Fencing* the part of a sword blade from the hilt to the middle. [from Latin *fortis* 'strong']

forte[2] /for-tay/ *Mus.* ● *adj.* performed loudly. ● *adv.* loudly. ● *n.* a passage to be performed loudly. [Italian, literally 'strong, loud']

forth *adv. archaic* except in set phrases and after certain verbs, esp. *bring, come, go,* and *set.* **1** forward; into view. **2** onwards in time (*from this time forth; henceforth*). **3** forwards. **4** out from a starting point (*set forth*). □ **and so forth** and so on; and the like. [Old English]

forthcoming *adj.* **1** about or likely to appear or become available. **2** produced when wanted (*no reply was forthcoming*). **3** (of a person) informative, responsive. □ **forthcomingness** *n.*

forthright *adj.* **1** direct and outspoken. **2** decisive. [Old English] □ **forthrightly** *adv.* **forthrightness** *n.*

forthwith *adv.* immediately; without delay. [Middle English]

fortification *n.* **1** the act or an instance of fortifying; the process of being fortified. **2** *Mil.* (usu. in *pl.*) defensive works fortifying a position.

fortify *v.tr.* (**-ies, -ied**) **1** provide or equip with defensive works. **2** strengthen or invigorate mentally or morally. **3** strengthen the structure of. **4** strengthen (wine) with alcohol. **5** increase the nutritive value of (food, esp. with vitamins). [based on Latin *fortis* 'strong'] □ **fortifiable** *adj.* **fortifier** *n.*

fortissimo *Mus.* ● *adj.* performed very loudly. ● *adv.* very loudly. ● *n.* (*pl.* **-os** or **fortissimi**) a passage to be performed very loudly. [Italian, literally 'loudest']

fortitude *n.* courage in pain or adversity. [from Latin *fortitudo*]

fortnight *n.* a period of two weeks. [Old English *fēowertīene niht* 'fourteen nights']

fortnightly esp. *Brit.* ● *adj.* done, produced, or occurring once a fortnight. ● *adv.* every fortnight. ● *n.* (*pl.* **-ies**) a magazine etc. issued every fortnight.

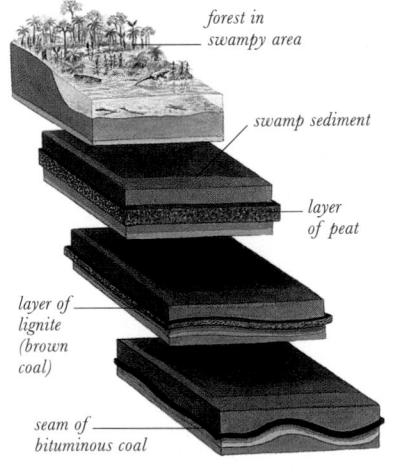

town hall and justice courts
forum
market stalls

FORUM: ROMAN LONDON'S FORUM, *c.*3RD CENTURY BC

Fortran *n.* (also **FORTRAN**) *Computing* a high-level programming language used esp. for scientific calculations. [from *for*mula *tran*slation]

fortress *n.* a military stronghold, esp. a strongly fortified town. [related to FORT]

fortuitous *adj.* due to or characterized by chance. [from Latin *fortuitus*] □ **fortuitously** *adv.* **fortuitousness** *n.*

fortunate *adj.* **1** lucky, prosperous. **2** auspicious, favourable. [based on Latin *fortuna* 'luck']

fortunately *adv.* **1** luckily, successfully. **2** (qualifying a whole sentence) it is fortunate that.

fortune *n.* **1 a** chance or luck as a force in human affairs. **b** a person's destiny. **2** (in *sing.* or *pl.*) the good or bad luck that befalls a person or an enterprise. **3** good luck. **4** prosperity. **5** (also *colloq.* **small fortune**) great wealth; a huge sum of money. [from Latin *fortuna* 'luck, chance']

fortune hunter *n. colloq.* a person seeking wealth by marriage.

fortune-teller *n.* a person who claims to predict future events in a person's life. □ **fortune-telling** *n.*

forty ● *n.* (*pl.* **-ies**) **1** the product of four and ten. **2** a symbol for this (40, xl, XL). **3** (in *pl.*) the numbers from 40 to 49, esp. the years of a century or of a person's life. ● *adj.* that amount to forty. [Old English] □ **fortieth** *adj. & n.* **fortyfold** *adj. & adv.*

forty winks *n.pl. colloq.* a short sleep.

forum *n.* **1** a place of or meeting for public discussion. **2** a periodical etc. giving an opportunity for discussion. **3** a court or tribunal. **4** *hist.* ◄ a public square or market place in an ancient Roman city. [Latin, in sense 4]

forward ● *adj.* **1** lying in one's line of motion. **2** onward or towards the front. **3** precocious; bold in manner; presumptuous. **4 a** *Commerce* relating to future produce, delivery, etc. (*forward contract*). **b** prospective; advanced; with a view to the future (*forward planning*). **5** advanced; progressing towards or approaching maturity or completion. ● *n.* an attacking player in football, hockey, etc. ● *adv.* **1** to the front; into prominence. **2** in advance; ahead. **3** onward so as

to make progress (*not getting any further forward*). **4** towards the future; continuously onwards (*from this time forward*). **5** (also **forwards**) **a** in the direction one is facing. **b** in the normal direction of motion or of traversal. **c** with continuous forward motion (*rushing forward*). ● *v.tr.* **1 a** send (a letter etc.) on to a further destination. **b** esp. *Brit.* dispatch (goods etc.). **2** help to advance; promote. [Old English] □ **forwarder** *n.* **forwardly** *adv.* **forwardness** *n.* (esp. in sense 3 of *adj.*).

forward-looking *adj.* progressive; favouring change.

forwards var. of FORWARD *adv.* 5.

forwent *past* of FORGO.

fossil ● *n.* **1** ◄ the remains or impression of a prehistoric plant or animal in rock, amber, etc. (often *attrib.: fossil shells*). ▷ ARCHAEOPTERYX. **2** *colloq.* an antiquated or unchanging person or thing. ● *adj.* **1** of or like a fossil. **2** antiquated. [based on Latin *fodere foss-* 'to dig'] □ **fossiliferous** *adj.* **fossilize** *v.tr. & intr.* (also **-ise**). **fossilization** *n.*

fossil fuel *n.* ▼ a natural fuel such as coal or gas formed from the remains of living organisms.

foster ● *v.tr.* **1 a** promote the growth or development of. **b** encourage or harbour (a feeling). **2** (of circumstances) be favourable to. **3 a** bring up (another's child). **b** (often foll. by *out*) *Brit.* (of a local authority etc.) assign (a child) to be fostered. ● *adj.* **1** having a family connection by fostering (*foster brother; foster parent*). **2** concerned with fostering a child (*foster care; foster home*). [Old English] □ **fosterage** *n.* (esp. in sense 3 of *v.*). **fosterer** *n.*

fought *past* and *past part.* of FIGHT.

foul ● *adj.* **1** offensive to the senses; loathsome, stinking. **2** dirty, soiled, filthy. **3** *colloq.* revolting, disgusting. **4 a** containing or charged with noxious matter (*foul air*). **b** clogged, choked. **5** disgustingly abusive or offensive (*foul language; foul deeds*). **6** unfair; against the rules of a game etc. (*by fair means or foul*). **7** (of the weather) wet, rough, stormy. **8** (of a rope etc.) entangled. ● *n.* **1** *Sport* an unfair or invalid

FOSSIL FUEL

Decaying organic matter produces gases that are usually lost to the atmosphere. If plant and animal remains are trapped in sediment, however, they may form fossil fuels. Land plants buried in mud may form a layer of peat, which over millions of years is compressed to form coal. Oil and natural gas can be produced by marine life decaying under sediment.

forest in swampy area
swamp sediment
layer of peat
layer of lignite (brown coal)
seam of bituminous coal

FORMATION OF COAL

stroke or piece of play. **2** a collision or entanglement. ● *adv.* unfairly. ● *v.* **1** *tr. & intr.* make or become foul or dirty. **2** *tr.* (of an animal) make dirty with excrement. **3** *Sport* **a** *tr.* commit a foul against (a player). **b** *intr.* commit a foul. **4 a** *tr.* (often foll. by *up*) cause (an anchor, cable, etc.) to become entangled or muddled. **b** *intr.* become entangled. **5** *tr.* (usu. foll. by *up*) *colloq.* spoil or bungle. [Old English] □ **foully** *adv.* **foulness** *n.*

foul mouth *n.* a person who uses foul language. □ **foul-mouthed** *adj.*

foul play *n.* **1** unfair play in games. **2** treacherous or violent activity, esp. murder.

foul-up *n.* a muddled or bungled situation.

found[1] *past* and *past part.* of FIND.

found[2] *v.tr.* **1 a** establish (esp. with an endowment). **b** originate or initiate (an institution). **2** be the original builder or begin the building of (a town etc.). **3** lay the base of (a building etc.). **4** (foll. by *on*, *upon*) construct or base (a story, theory, rule, etc.) according to a specified principle or ground. [from Latin *fundare*, based on *fundus* 'bottom']

found[3] *v.tr.* **1 a** melt and mould (metal). **b** fuse (materials for glass). **2** make by founding. [from Latin *fundere* 'to pour'] □ **founder** *n.*

foundation *n.* **1 a** the solid ground or base on which a building rests. **b** (usu. in *pl.*) the lowest load-bearing part of a building, usu. below ground level. ▷ HOUSE. **2** a body or ground on which other parts are overlaid. **3** a basis or underlying principle (*the report has no foundation*). **4 a** the act or an instance of establishing or constituting esp. an endowed institution. **b** such an institution, e.g. a monastery, college, or hospital. **5** (in full **foundation garment**) a woman's supporting undergarment, e.g. a corset. [from Latin *fundatio*, related to FOUND[2]] □ **foundational** *adj.*

foundation course *n.* a preliminary basic course of study.

foundation cream *n.* a cream used as a base for applying cosmetics. ▷ MAKE-UP

foundation stone *n.* a stone laid with ceremony to celebrate the founding of a building.

founder[1] *n.* a person who founds an institution.

founder[2] *v.intr.* **1** (of a ship) fill with water and sink. **2** (of a plan etc.) fail. **3** (of earth, a building, etc.) fall down or in. **4** (of a horse or its rider) fall to the ground, fall from lameness, stick fast in mud etc. [based on Latin *fundus* 'bottom']

foundling *n.* an abandoned infant of unknown parentage. [Middle English]

foundry *n.* (*pl.* -**ies**) a workshop for or a business of casting metal.

fount[1] *n. poet.* a spring or fountain; a source.

fount[2] *Brit.* var. of FONT[2].

fountain *n.* **1 a** a jet or jets of water made to spout for ornamental purposes or for drinking. **b** a structure provided for this. **2** a structure for the constant public supply of drinking water. **3** a source (in physical or abstract senses). [from Latin *fons fontis* 'a spring'] □ **fountained** *adj.* (also in *comb.*).

fountainhead *n.* an original source.

fountain pen *n.* a pen with a reservoir or cartridge holding ink. ▷ PEN

four ● *n.* **1** one more than three. **2** a symbol for this (4, iv, IV). **3** a size etc. denoted by four. **4** a four-oared rowing boat or its crew. **5** four o'clock. **6** a hit at cricket scoring four runs. ● *adj.* that amount to four. □ **on all fours** on hands and knees. [Old English]

fourfold *adj. & adv.* **1** four times as much or as many. **2** consisting of four parts. **3** amounting to four.

four-in-hand *n.* a vehicle with four horses driven by one person.

four-letter word *n.* a short obscene word.

fourpenny *adj. Brit.* costing four pence, esp. before decimalization.

fourpenny one *n. Brit. colloq.* a hit or blow.

four-poster *n.* a bed with a post at each corner supporting a canopy.

fourscore *n. archaic* eighty.

foursome *n.* **1** a group of four persons. **2** *Brit.* a golf match between two pairs with partners playing the same ball.

four-square ● *adj.* **1** solidly based. **2** steady, resolute. ● *adv.* steadily, resolutely.

four-stroke *attrib.adj.* (of an internal-combustion engine) having a cycle of four strokes (intake, compression, combustion, and exhaust). ▷ INTERNAL-COMBUSTION ENGINE

fourteen ● *n.* **1** one more than thirteen. **2** a symbol for this (14, xiv, XIV). **3** a size etc. denoted by fourteen. ● *adj.* that amount to fourteen. [Old English] □ **fourteenth** *adj. & n.*

fourth ● *n.* **1** the position in a sequence corresponding to that of the number 4 in the sequence 1–4. **2** something occupying this position. **3** the fourth person etc. in a race or competition. **4** each of four equal parts of a thing; a quarter. **5** fourth gear. **6** *Mus.* **a** an interval or chord spanning four consecutive notes in the diatonic scale (e.g. C to F). **b** a note separated from another by this interval. ● *adj.* that is the fourth. [Old English] □ **fourthly** *adv.*

fourth dimension *n.* **1** a postulated dimension additional to those determining area and volume. **2** time regarded as equivalent to linear dimensions.

fourth estate *n. joc.* the press; journalism.

four-wheel drive *n.* drive acting on all four wheels of a vehicle (see DRIVE *n.* 6a). ▷ CAR

fovea /foh-vi-ă/ *n.* (*pl.* **foveae** /-vi-ee/) *Anat.* a small depression or pit, esp. the pit in the retina of the eye for focusing images. [Latin] □ **foveal** *adj.* **foveate** *adj.*

fowl (*pl.* same or **fowls**) ● *n.* **1 a** (in full **domestic fowl**) a domestic cock or hen kept chiefly for its eggs and flesh. ▷ BANTAM. **b** any other domesticated bird kept for its eggs or flesh, e.g. the turkey, duck, goose, and guinea fowl. **2** the flesh of these birds as food. ● *v.intr.* catch or hunt wildfowl. [Old English] □ **fowler** *n.* **fowling** *n.*

fowl pest *n.* an infectious virus disease of fowls.

fox ● *n.* **1 a** ▼ any of various doglike mammals of the genus *Vulpes* or a related genus, with a bushy tail, esp. the reddish *V. vulpes*. **b** the fur of a fox. **2 a** cunning or sly person. **3** *N. Amer. slang* an attractive woman. ● *v.tr.* **1** deceive, baffle, trick. **2** (usu. as **foxed** *adj.*) discolour (the leaves of a book, engraving, etc.) with brownish marks. [Old English] □ **foxing** *n.* (in sense 2 of *v.*). **foxlike** *adj.*

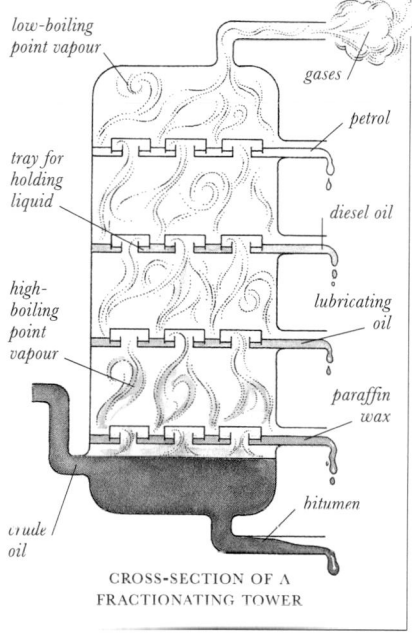

FOX: RED FOX
(*Vulpes vulpes*)

foxglove *n.* ▶ any tall plant of the genus *Digitalis*, esp. *D. purpurea*, with erect spikes of purple or white bell-shaped flowers.

foxhole *n. Mil.* a hole in the ground used as a shelter.

foxhound *n.* a kind of hound bred and trained to hunt foxes.

fox-hunt ● *n.* a hunt for a fox with hounds. ● *v.intr.* engage in a fox-hunt. □ **fox-hunter** *n.* **fox-hunting** *n. & adj.*

fox terrier *n.* a kind of short-haired terrier.

foxtrot ● *n.* **1** a ballroom dance with slow and quick steps. **2** the music for this. ● *v.intr.* (**foxtrotted**, **foxtrotting**) perform this dance.

foxy *adj.* (**foxier**, **foxiest**) **1** of or like a fox.

FOXGLOVE
(*Digitalis purpurea*)

FRACTIONAL

Fractional distillation is the process used to separate complex mixtures, such as crude oil, into their component parts. In the diagram below, crude oil is heated and pumped into a fractionating tower. Vapours from the oil cool as they rise. At each tier, a different compound of the crude oil reaches the temperature at which it condenses, and so collects on trays. The resultant liquids are then drained off through pipes.

low-boiling point vapour

gases

petrol

tray for holding liquid

diesel oil

high-boiling point vapour

lubricating oil

paraffin wax

bitumen

crude oil

CROSS-SECTION OF A
FRACTIONATING TOWER

2 sly or cunning. **3** reddish brown. **4** (of paper) damaged, esp. by mildew. **5** *N. Amer. slang* (of a woman) sexually attractive. □ **foxily** *adv.* **foxiness** *n.*

foyer /foy-ay/ *n.* the entrance hall or other large area in a hotel, theatre, etc. [French, literally 'hearth']

Fr *symb. Chem.* the element francium.

Fr. *abbr.* (also **Fr**) Father.

fr. *abbr.* franc(s).

fracas /frak-ah/ *n.* (*pl.* same) a noisy disturbance or quarrel. [based on Italian *fracassare* 'to make an uproar']

fraction *n.* **1** a numerical quantity that is not a whole number (e.g. ½, 0.5). **2** a small, esp. very small, part, piece, or amount. **3** a portion of a mixture separated by distillation etc. **4** *Polit.* an organized dissentient group. [based on Latin *frangere fract-* 'to break'] □ **fractionary** *adj.* **fractionize** *v.tr.* (also **-ise**).

fractional *adj.* **1** of or relating to being a fraction. **2** very slight; incomplete. **3** *Chem.* ▲ relating to the separation of parts of a mixture by making use of their different physical properties (*fractional crystallization*; *fractional distillation*). □ **fractionalize** *v.tr.* (also **-ise**). **fractionally** *adv.* (esp. in sense 2).

fractionate *v.tr.* **1** break up into parts. **2** separate by fractional distillation etc. □ **fractionation** *n.*

fractious *adj.* irritable, peevish. [related to obsolete *fraction* 'disruption of peace'] □ **fractiously** *adv.* **fractiousness** *n.*

■ **Usage** See Usage Note at FACTIOUS.

F

FRACTURE

There are several types of bone fracture, determined by the degree and direction of the force applied. A straight-on force may cause a different break from an oblique one; more than one break may occur; or only one side of the bone may be broken.

TYPES OF FRACTURE

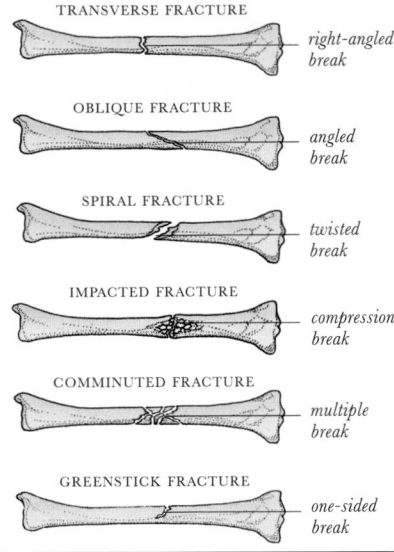

TRANSVERSE FRACTURE — *right-angled break*

OBLIQUE FRACTURE — *angled break*

SPIRAL FRACTURE — *twisted break*

IMPACTED FRACTURE — *compression break*

COMMINUTED FRACTURE — *multiple break*

GREENSTICK FRACTURE — *one-sided break*

fracture ● *n.* **1** ▲ breakage or breaking, esp. of a bone or cartilage. **2** the result of breaking; a crack or split. ● *v.intr. & tr.* **1** *Med.* undergo or cause to undergo a fracture.

fragile *adj.* **1** easily broken; weak. **2** of delicate frame or constitution; not strong. [from Latin *fragilis*] □ **fragilely** *adv.* **fragility** *n.*

fragment ● *n.* /*frag*-měnt/ **1** a part broken off; a detached piece. **2** an isolated or incomplete part. **3** the remains of an otherwise lost or destroyed book or work of art. ● *v.tr. & intr.* /frag-**ment**/ break or separate into fragments. [from Latin *fragmentum*] □ **fragmental** *adj.* **fragmentize** *v.tr.* (also -**ise**).

fragmentary *adj.* **1** consisting of fragments. **2** disconnected. □ **fragmentarily** *adv.*

fragmentation *n.* the process or an instance of breaking into fragments.

fragmentation bomb *n.* a bomb designed to break up into small rapidly-moving fragments when exploded.

fragrance *n.* **1** sweetness of smell. **2** a sweet scent. [from (Old) French, based on Latin *fragrare* 'to smell sweet']

fragrant *adj.* sweet-smelling. [from Latin *fragrant-* 'smelling sweet'] □ **fragrantly** *adv.*

frail *adj.* **1** fragile, delicate. **2** in weak health. **3** morally weak. [from Latin *fragilis* 'fragile'] □ **frailly** *adv.* **frailness** *n.*

frailty *n.* (*pl.* -**ies**) **1** the condition of being frail. **2** a fault, weakness, or foible.

frame ● *n.* **1** a case or border enclosing a picture, window, door, etc. **2** the basic rigid supporting structure of anything, e.g. of a building, motor vehicle, or aircraft. **3** (in *pl.*) the structure of spectacles holding the lenses. **4** a human or animal body, esp. with reference to its size or structure. **5 a** an established order, plan, or system (*the frame of society*). **b** construction, constitution, build. **6** a temporary state (esp. in **frame of mind**). **7** a single complete image or picture on a cinema film

or transmitted in a series of lines by television. **8 a** a triangular structure for positioning the balls in snooker etc. **b** a round of play in snooker etc. **9** a boxlike structure of glass etc. for protecting plants. **10** *N. Amer. slang* = FRAME-UP. ● *v.tr.* **1 a** set in or provide with a frame. **b** serve as a frame for. **2** construct by a combination of parts or in accordance with a design or plan. **3** formulate the essentials of (a complex thing, idea, etc.). **4** (foll. by *to*, *into*) adapt or fit. **5** *colloq.* concoct a false charge or evidence against; devise a plot with regard to. **6** articulate (words). [Old English *framian* 'to be of service'] □ **framable** *adj.* **frameless** *adj.* **framer** *n.*

frame of reference *n.* **1** a set of standards or principles governing behaviour, thought, etc. **2** *Geom.* a system of geometrical axes for defining position.

frame-up *n. colloq.* a conspiracy, esp. to make an innocent person appear guilty.

framework *n.* **1** an essential supporting structure. **2** a basic system.

franc *n.* the chief monetary unit of France, Belgium, Switzerland, Luxembourg, etc. [from Latin *Francorum Rex* 'king of the Franks', written on the earliest (French) gold coins so called]

franchise ● *n.* **1** the right to vote at state (esp. parliamentary) elections. **2** full membership of a corporation or state; citizenship. **3** authorization granted by a company to sell its goods or services in a particular way. **4** a right or privilege granted to a person or corporation. ● *v.tr.* grant a franchise to. [based on Old French *franc*, *franche* 'free'] □ **franchisee** *n.* **franchiser** *n.* (also **franchisor**).

Franciscan ● *n.* a friar, sister, or lay member of an order founded by St Francis of Assisi (see also GREY FRIAR). ● *adj.* of St Francis or his order. [from medieval Latin name *Franciscus*]

francium *n. Chem.* a radioactive metallic element occurring naturally in uranium and thorium ores. [modern Latin, based on *France*, the discoverer's country]

Franco- *comb. form* (also **franco-**) **1** French; French and (*Franco-German*). **2** regarding France or the French (*Francophile*).

Francophile *n.* a person who is fond of France or the French.

francophone ● *n.* a French-speaking person. ● *adj.* French-speaking.

frangible *adj.* breakable, fragile. [based on Latin *frangere* 'to break']

frangipani /fran-ji-**pan**-i/ *n.* (*pl.* **frangipanis**) **1** ◄ any tropical tree or shrub of the genus *Plumeria*, esp. *P. rubra* with clusters of fragrant white, pink, or yellow flowers. **2** the perfume from this plant. [named after M. *Frangipani*, 16th-century Italian marquis, inventor of a perfume for scenting gloves]

FRANGIPANI (*Plumeria rubra*)

franglais /frahng-glay/ *n.* a corrupt version of French using many words and idioms borrowed from English. [French, blend of *français* 'French' and *anglais* 'English']

Frank *n.* a member of the Germanic nation or coalition that conquered Gaul in the 6th c. [Old English] □ **Frankish** *adj. & n.*

frank ● *adj.* **1** candid, outspoken (*a frank opinion*). **2** undisguised, avowed (*frank admiration*). **3** ingenuous, open (*a frank face*). ● *v.tr.* imprint (a letter) with an official mark to record the payment of postage. ● *n.* a franking mark. [from medieval Latin *francus* 'free', from FRANK (since only Franks had full freedom in Frankish Gaul)] □ **franker** *n.* **frankness** *n.*

Frankenstein *n.* (in full **Frankenstein's monster**) a thing that becomes terrifying to its maker. [from Baron *Frankenstein*, a character in and the title of a novel (1818) by Mary Shelley]

frankfurter *n.* a seasoned smoked sausage made of beef and pork. [from German *Frankfurter Wurst* 'Frankfurt sausage']

frankincense *n.* an aromatic gum resin used for burning as incense. [from Old French *franc encens* 'pure incense']

frankly *adv.* **1** in a frank manner. **2** (qualifying a whole sentence) to be frank.

frantic *adj.* **1** wildly excited; frenzied. **2** characterized by great hurry or anxiety; desperate, violent. [from Latin *phreneticus* 'delirious'] □ **frantically** *adv.* **franticness** *n.*

frappé /frap-ay/ ● *adj.* (esp. of wine) iced, cooled. ● *n.* **1** an iced drink. **2** a soft water ice. [French, literally 'iced, chilled']

fraternal *adj.* **1** of or suitable to a brother; brotherly. **2** (of twins) developed from separate ova and not necessarily similar. **3** *N. Amer.* of or concerning a fraternity (see FRATERNITY 3). [based on Latin *frater* 'brother'] □ **fraternalism** *n.* **fraternally** *adv.*

fraternity *n.* (*pl.* -**ies**) **1** a religious brotherhood. **2** a group or company with common interests, or of the same professional class. **3** *N. Amer.* a male students' society in a university or college. **4** brotherliness.

fraternize *v.intr.* (also -**ise**) (often foll. by *with*) **1** associate; make friends. **2** (of troops) enter into friendly relations with enemy troops or the inhabitants of an occupied country. □ **fraternization** *n.*

fratricide *n.* **1** the killing of one's brother or sister. **2** a person who does this. □ **fratricidal** *adj.*

Frau /frow/ *n.* (*pl.* **Frauen**) (often as a title) a German-speaking woman. [German]

fraud *n.* **1** criminal deception. **2** a dishonest artifice or trick. **3** a person or thing not fulfilling what is claimed or expected of him, her, or it. [from Latin *fraus fraudis*]

fraudster *n.* a person who commits fraud, esp. in business dealings.

fraudulent *adj.* **1** characterized or achieved by fraud. **2** guilty of fraud. □ **fraudulence** *n.* **fraudulently** *adv.*

fraught *adj.* **1** (foll. by *with*) filled or attended with (*fraught with danger*). **2** tense, distressing. [based on Middle Dutch *vrachten* 'to load with cargo']

Fräulein /froi-lyn/ *n. offens.* (often as a title or form of address) an unmarried (esp. young) German-speaking woman. [German]

■ **Usage** *Fräulein* is now considered insulting by many German-speaking women, and *Frau* is the preferred term for all such women.

fraxinella *n.* ► an aromatic plant, *Dictamnus albus* (rue family), having foliage that emits an ethereal inflammable oil.

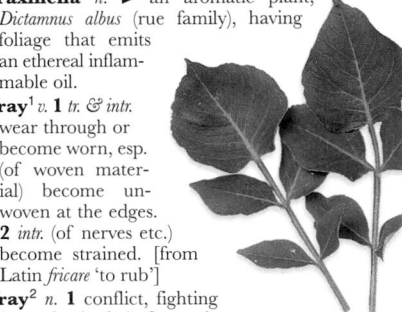

FRAXINELLA: WHITE DITTANY (*Dictamnus albus*)

fray[1] *v.* **1** *tr. & intr.* wear through or become worn, esp. (of woven material) become unwoven at the edges. **2** *intr.* (of nerves etc.) become strained. [from Latin *fricare* 'to rub']

fray[2] *n.* **1** conflict, fighting (*eager for the fray*). **2** a noisy quarrel. [Middle English, related to AFFRAY]

frazzle *colloq.* ● *n.* a worn, charred, or exhausted state (esp. in phr. **worn**, **burnt**, etc. **to a frazzle**). ● *v.tr.* (esp. as **frazzled** *adj.*) **1** wear out; exhaust. **2** char. [19th-century coinage]

freak ● *n.* **1** (also **freak of nature**) a monstrosity; an abnormally developed individual or thing. **2** (often *attrib.*) an abnormal, irregular, or bizarre occurrence (*a freak storm*). **3** *colloq.* **a** an unconventional person. **b** a person with a specified enthusiasm (*health freak*). **4** a caprice or vagary. ● *v.* (often foll. by *out*) *colloq.* **1** *intr. & tr.* become or make very angry. **2** *intr. & tr.* undergo or cause to undergo hallucinations etc., esp. from use of narcotics. **3** *intr.* adopt a wildly unconventional lifestyle. [16th-century coinage] □ **freaky** *adj.* (**freakier, freakiest**).

freakish *adj.* **1** of or like a freak. **2** bizarre, unconventional. □ **freakishly** *adv.* **freakishness** *n.*

freckle ● *n.* (often in *pl.*) a small light brown patch on the skin, usu. caused by exposure to the sun. ● *v.* **1** (usu. as **freckled** *adj.*) mark with freckles. **2** *intr.* be marked with freckles. [Middle English, from Old Norse] □ **freckly** *adj.*

freckle-faced *adj.* having a freckled face.

free ● *adj.* (**freer, freest**) **1** not in bondage to or under the control of another; having personal rights and social and political liberty. **2** (of a state, its citizens etc.) autonomous, democratic. **3 a** unrestricted; not restrained or fixed. **b** not confined or imprisoned. **c** released from ties or duties. **d** unrestrained as to action; independent. **4** (foll. by *of*, *from*) **a** exempt from (*free of tax*). **b** not containing or subject to a specified (usu. undesirable) thing (*free of preservatives*; *free from disease*). **5** (foll. by *to* + infin.) able to take a specified action (*free to choose*). **6** unconstrained (*free gestures*). **7 a** costing nothing. **b** not subject to tax, duty, etc. **8 a** clear of engagements (*are you free tomorrow?*). **b** not occupied or in use (*the bathroom is free now*). **c** clear of obstructions. **9** spontaneous, unforced (*free compliments*). **10** open to all comers. **11** lavish, profuse (*free with their money*). **12** frank, unreserved. **13** (of a literary style) not observing the strict laws of form. **14** (of a translation) conveying the broad sense. **15** forward, impudent. **16** (of talk, stories, etc.) slightly indecent. **17** *Physics* **a** not modified by an external force. **b** not bound in an atom or molecule. **18** *Chem.* not combined (*free oxygen*). ● *adv.* **1** in a free manner. **2** without cost or payment. ● *v.tr.* **1** make free; set at liberty. **2** (foll. by *of*, *from*) relieve from (something undesirable). **3** disengage, disentangle. □ **for free** *colloq.* free of charge, gratis. **free and easy** informal, unceremonious. **free on board** (or **rail**) without charge for delivery to a ship or railway wagon. **free up** *colloq.* **1** make available. **2** make less restricted. [Old English] □ **freely** *adv.* **freeness** *n.*

-free *comb. form* free of or from (*duty-free*; *trouble-free*).

free agent *n.* a person with freedom of action.

freebase *n. slang* cocaine that has been purified by heating with ether, and is inhaled or smoked.

freebie *n. colloq.* a thing provided free of charge.

freeboard *n.* ▶ the part of a ship's side between the waterline and the deck.

freebooter *n.* a pirate or lawless adventurer. [from Dutch *vrijbuiter*]

freeborn *adj.* inheriting a citizen's rights and liberty.

Free Church *n.* a Church dissenting or seceding from an established Church.

freedman *n.* (*pl.* **-men**) an emancipated slave.

freedom *n.* **1** the condition of being free or unrestricted. **2** personal or civic liberty. **3** the power of self-determination. **4** the state of being free to act (often foll. by *to* + infin.: *we have the freedom to leave*). **5** frankness, outspokenness. **6** (foll. by *from*) the condition of being exempt from or not subject to (a defect, burden, etc.). **7** (foll. by *of*) **a** full or honorary participation in (membership, privileges, etc.). **b** unrestricted use of (facilities etc.). **8** a privilege possessed by a city or corporation. **9** facility or ease in action. **10** boldness of conception. [Old English]

freedom fighter *n.* a person who takes part in resistance to an established political system etc.

free enterprise *n.* a system in which private business operates in competition and largely free of state control.

free fall ● *n.* (usu. hyphenated when *attrib.*) movement under the force of gravity only. ● *v.intr.* (**free-fall**) move in a free fall.

free fight *n.* a general fight in which all present join.

Freefone *n.* (also **Freephone, free-**) *Brit.* a telephone service by means of which an organization pays for certain incoming calls.

free-for-all *n.* a free fight, unrestricted discussion, etc.

free-form *attrib.adj.* of an irregular shape or structure.

freehand ● *adj.* (of a drawing or plan etc.) done by hand without special instruments. ● *adv.* in a freehand manner.

free hand *n.* freedom to act at one's own discretion (see also FREEHAND).

free-handed *adj.* generous. □ **free-handedly** *adv.* **free-handedness** *n.*

freehold ● *n.* **1** tenure of land or property in fee simple or fee tail or for life. **2** esp. *Brit.* land, property, or an office held by such tenure. ● *adj.* held by or having the status of freehold. □ **freeholder** *n.*

free house *n. Brit.* an inn or public house not controlled by a brewery.

free-kick *n. Football* a set kick allowed to be taken by one side without interference from the other.

freelance ● *n.* (also **freelancer**) a person, usu. self-employed, offering services on a temporary basis (often *attrib.*: *a freelance editor*). ● *v.intr.* act as a freelance. ● *adv.* as a freelance. [19th-century coinage]

freeloader *n.* esp. *N. Amer. slang* a person who eats or drinks at others' expense; a sponger. □ **freeload** *v.intr.*

free love *n.* sexual relations according to choice and unrestricted by marriage.

freeman *n.* (*pl.* **-men**) **1** a person who has the freedom of a city, company, etc. **2** a person who is not a slave.

free market *n.* a market in which prices are determined by unrestricted competition (usu. hyphenated when *attrib.*: *a free-market economy*).

Freemason *n.* a member of an international fraternity for mutual help, with elaborate secret rituals. □ **Freemasonry** *n.*

free pardon see PARDON *n.* 2.

Freephone *var.* of FREEFONE.

free port *n.* **1** a port area where goods in transit are exempt from customs duty. **2** a port open to all traders.

Freepost *n.* esp. *Brit.* a postal service whereby postage is paid by the addressee.

freer *compar.* of FREE.

free radical *n.* an uncharged atom or group of atoms with one or more unpaired electrons.

free-range *adj.* **1** (of hens etc.) kept in natural conditions with freedom of movement. **2** (of eggs) produced by such birds.

free sheet *n.* a free newspaper.

freesia *n.* ▼ any bulbous plant of the genus *Freesia*, native to Africa, having fragrant coloured flowers. [modern Latin, named after F. H. T. *Freese*, German physician, died 1876]

free speech *n.* the right to express opinions freely.

free spirit *n.* an independent or uninhibited person.

free-spoken *adj.* speaking candidly; not concealing one's opinions.

freest *superl.* of FREE.

free-standing *adj.* not supported by or adjoining another structure.

freestyle ● *adj.* (of a contest) in which all styles are allowed, esp.: **1** *Swimming* in which any style of stroke may be used. **2** *Wrestling* with few restrictions on the holds permitted. ● *n.* freestyle swimming or wrestling. □ **freestyler** *n.*

freethinker *n.* a person who rejects dogma or authority. □ **freethinking** *n.* & *adj.*

free throw *n.* **1** an unimpeded throw awarded to a player following a foul etc. **2** *Basketball* such a throw allowing a shot at the basket, taken from behind a marked line.

free trade *n.* international trade left to its natural course without restriction on imports or exports.

free verse *n.* = VERS LIBRE.

free vote *n.* a parliamentary vote not subject to party discipline.

freeway *n.* esp. *US* **1** an express highway, esp. with controlled access. **2** a toll-free highway.

freewheel *v.intr.* **1** ride a bicycle with the pedals at rest. **2** move or act without constraint or effort.

free wheel *n.* the driving wheel of a bicycle, able to revolve with the pedals at rest.

free will *n.* **1** the power of acting without the constraint of necessity or fate. **2** the ability to act at one's own discretion (*of my own free will*).

freeze ● *v.* (*past* **froze**; *past part.* **frozen**) **1** *tr.* & *intr.* **a** turn or be turned into ice or another solid by cold. **b** (often foll. by *over*, *up*) make or become rigid as a result of the cold. **2** *intr.* be or feel very cold. **3** *tr.* & *intr.* cover or become covered with ice. **4** *intr.* (foll. by *to*, *together*) adhere by frost. **5** *tr.* preserve (food) by refrigeration below freezing point. **6** *tr.* & *intr.* **a** make or become motionless or powerless through fear etc. **b** react or cause to react with sudden detachment. **7** *tr.* stiffen or harden, injure or kill, by chilling (*frozen to death*). **8** *tr.* make (assets etc.) unrealizable. **9** *tr.* fix or stabilize (prices etc.) at a certain level. **10** *tr.* arrest (an action) at a stage of development. **11** *tr.* = FREEZE-FRAME *v.* ● *n.* **1** a state of frost; a period of very cold weather. **2** the fixing or stabilization of prices etc. **3** = FREEZE-FRAME *n.* □ **freeze out** esp. *US colloq.* exclude by competition or boycott etc. **freeze up** obstruct or be obstructed by the formation of ice. [Old English] □ **freezable** *adj.* **frozenly** *adv.*

freeze-dry *v.tr.* (**-dries, -dried**) freeze and dry by the sublimation of ice in a high vacuum.

freeze-frame ● *n.* (also *attrib.*) the facility of stopping a videotape etc. in order to view a motionless image. ● *v.tr.* use freeze-frame on (an image etc.).

freezer *n.* a refrigerated cabinet or room for preserving food at very low temperatures; = DEEP-FREEZE *n.*

freeze-up *n.* a period or conditions of extreme cold.

freezing *adj.* (also **freezing cold**) *colloq.* very cold.

freezing-mixture *n.* salt and snow or some other mixture used to freeze liquids.

freezing point *n.* the temperature at which a liquid, esp. water, freezes.

freight ● *n.* **1** the transport of goods more slowly and cheaply than by express delivery. **2** goods transported; cargo. **3** a charge for such transportation. ● *v.tr.* **1** transport (goods) as freight. **2** load with freight. [from Middle Dutch *vrecht*]

freight car *n.* a railway wagon for carrying freight.

freighter *n.* a ship or aircraft designed to carry freight.

Freightliner *n. Brit. propr.* a train carrying goods in containers.

French ● *adj.* **1** of or relating to France or its people or language. **2** having French characteristics. ● *n.* **1** the language of France. **2** (prec. by *the*; treated as *pl.*) the people of France. **3** *colloq.* bad language (*excuse my French*). **4** *colloq.* dry vermouth (*gin and French*). [Old English] □ **Frenchify** *v.tr.* (**-ies, -ied**). **Frenchness** *n.*

FREEBOARD ON A LONGBOAT

FREESIA
(*Freesia* 'Everett')

F

French bean *n. Brit.* **1** a bean plant, *Phaseolus vulgaris*, cultivated for its pods and seeds. **2 a** the pod used as food. **b** the seed used as food.

French bread *n.* white bread in a long crisp loaf.

French Canadian ● *n.* a Canadian whose principal language is French. ● *adj.* (**French-Canadian**) of or relating to French-speaking Canadians.

French chalk *n.* a kind of steatite used for marking cloth, as a dry lubricant, etc.

French door *n.* = FRENCH WINDOW.

French dressing *n.* **1** esp. *Brit.* a salad dressing of vinegar and oil, usu. seasoned. **2** *US* a salad dressing made with mayonnaise and ketchup.

French fried potatoes *n.pl.* (*N. Amer.* **French fries**) potato chips.

French horn *n.* ▼ a coiled brass wind instrument with a wide bell. ▷ BRASS

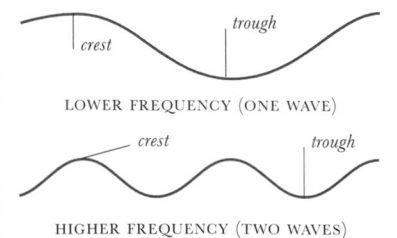

mouth-piece

finger keys

valves

coiled tubing

wide bell

FRENCH HORN

French kiss *n.* a kiss with one partner's tongue inserted in the other's mouth.

French knickers *n.pl.* wide-legged knickers.

French leave *n.* absence without permission.

French letter *n. Brit. colloq.* a condom.

Frenchman *n.* (*pl.* **-men**) a man who is French by birth or descent.

French polish ● *n.* shellac polish for wood. ● *v.tr.* polish with this.

French seam *n.* a seam with the raw edges enclosed.

French window *n.* (usu. in *pl.*) a glazed door in an outside wall, serving as a window and door.

Frenchwoman *n.* (*pl.* **-women**) a woman who is French by birth or descent.

frenetic *adj.* **1** frantic, frenzied. **2** fanatic. [from Greek *phrenitikos*] □ **frenetically** *adv.*

frenzy ● *n.* (*pl.* **-ies**) **1** mental derangement; wild excitement or agitation. **2** delirious fury. ● *v.tr.* (**-ies, -ied**) (usu. as **frenzied** *adj.*) drive to frenzy; infuriate. [based on Greek *phrēn* 'mind'] □ **frenziedly** *adv.*

frequency *n.* (*pl.* **-ies**) **1** commonness of occurrence. **2 a** the state of being frequent; frequent occurrence. **b** the process of being repeated at short intervals. **3** *Physics* ▼ the rate of recurrence of a vibration, cycle, etc.; the number of repetitions in a given time, esp. per second (abbr.: *f*) **4** *Statistics* the ratio of the number of actual to possible occurrences of an event.

FREQUENCY

In physics, frequency refers to the number of periodic vibrations, oscillations, or waves that occur per unit of time. The unit of frequency is the hertz (Hz); one hertz is equivalent to one cycle per second. The human ear can hear sounds from vibrations in the range 20–20,000 Hz.

crest   trough

LOWER FREQUENCY (ONE WAVE)

crest   trough

HIGHER FREQUENCY (TWO WAVES)

FRESCO

A fresco is a form of wall painting in which pigments mixed with water are applied to a layer of fresh, damp plaster known as an intonaco. As the intonaco dries, it absorbs the pigments, and so the painting becomes part of the wall. The earliest frescoes were found in Knossos, Crete (*c.*1750–1400 BC), but the art form reached its greatest heights under the Italian Renaissance masters.

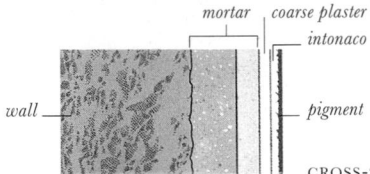

mortar   coarse plaster

intonaco

wall   pigment

CROSS-SECTION OF A FRESCO

The Angel Appearing to Zacharias (detail), (1485–90)
DOMENICO GHIRLANDAIO

frequency band *n. Electronics* = BAND¹ *n.* 4a.

frequency modulation *n. Electronics* the modulation of a radio wave etc. by variation of its frequency, esp. to carry an audio signal. ▷ WAVELENGTH

frequent ● *adj.* /**free**-kwĕnt/ **1** occurring often or in close succession. **2** habitual (*a frequent caller*). **3** found near together; abundant. ● *v.tr.* /fri-**kwent**/ attend or go to habitually. [from Latin *frequens -entis* 'crowded'] □ **frequentation** *n.* **frequenter** *n.* **frequently** *adv.*

frequentative *Gram.* ● *adj.* expressing frequent repetition or intensity of action. ● *n.* a verb or verbal form or conjugation expressing this (e.g. *chatter, twinkle*).

fresco *n.* (*pl.* **-os** or **-oes**) **1** ▲ a painting done in watercolour on a wall or ceiling while the plaster is still wet. **2** this method of painting (esp. *in fresco*). [Italian, literally 'cool, fresh'] □ **frescoed** *adj.*

fresh ● *adj.* **1** newly made or obtained (*fresh sandwiches*). **2 a** other, different; not previously known or used (*start a fresh page*). **b** additional (*fresh supplies*). **3** (foll. by *from*) lately arrived from. **4** not stale or faded (*fresh memories*). **5** (of food) not preserved by salting, freezing, etc. **6** not salty (*fresh water*). **7 a** pure, untainted, invigorating (*fresh air*). **b** bright and pure in colour (*a fresh complexion*). **8** (of the wind) brisk. **9** alert, vigorous (*never felt fresher*). **10** *colloq.* **a** cheeky. **b** amorously impudent. **11** young and inexperienced. ● *adv.* newly, recently (esp. in *comb.*: *fresh-baked*). ● *n.* esp. *literary* the fresh part of the day etc. (*in the fresh of the morning*). [from Old French *freis fresche*] □ **freshly** *adv.* **freshness** *n.*

freshen *v.* **1** *tr. & intr.* make or become fresh or fresher. **2** *intr. & tr.* (foll. by *up*) **a** wash, change one's clothes, etc. **b** revive, refresh, renew.

fresher *n. Brit. colloq.* = FRESHMAN.

freshet *n.* **1** a rush of fresh water flowing into the sea. **2** the flood of a river.

fresh-faced *adj.* having a clear and young-looking complexion.

freshman *n.* (*pl.* **-men**; *fem.* **woman**, *pl.* **-women**) a first-year student at university or *N. Amer.* at high school.

freshwater *adj.* of or found in fresh water; not of the sea.

fret¹ ● *v.* (**fretted, fretting**) **1** *intr.* **a** be greatly and visibly worried or distressed. **b** be irritated or resentful. **2** *tr.* **a** cause anxiety or distress to. **b** irritate, annoy. **3** *tr.* wear or consume by gnawing or rubbing. ● *n.* esp. *Brit.* irritation, vexation, querulousness (esp. *in a fret*). [Old English, related to EAT]

fret² ● *n.* an ornamental pattern made of continuous combinations of straight lines joined usu. at right angles. ● *v.tr.* (**fretted, fretting**) **1** embellish or decorate with a fret. **2** adorn (esp. a ceiling) with carved or embossed work. [from Old French *frete* 'trellis-work']

fret³ *n.* each of a sequence of bars or ridges on the fingerboard of a guitar etc., to guide fingering. ▷ GUITAR, SITAR. [16th-century coinage] □ **fretless** *adj.* **fretted** *adj.*

fretboard *n.* a fretted fingerboard.

fretful *adj.* visibly anxious or distressed. □ **fretfully** *adv.* **fretfulness** *n.*

fretsaw *n.* a narrow saw on a frame, for cutting thin wood in patterns. ▷ SAW

fretwork *n.* ornamental work in wood, done with a fretsaw.

Freudian *Psychol.* ● *adj.* of or relating to the Austrian psychologist Sigmund Freud (d. 1939) or his methods of psychoanalysis. ● *n.* a follower of Freud or his methods. □ **Freudianism** *n.*

Freudian slip *n.* an unintentional error regarded as revealing subconscious feelings.

Fri. *abbr.* Friday.

friable *adj.* easily crumbled. [from Latin *friabilis*] □ **friability** *n.* **friableness** *n.*

friar *n.* a member of certain male religious orders, esp. the four mendicant orders (Augustinians, Carmelites, Dominicans, and Franciscans). [from Latin *frater* 'brother'] □ **friarly** *adj.*

friar's balsam *n.* (also **friars' balsam**) a tincture of benzoin etc. used esp. as an inhalant.

friary *n.* (*pl.* **-ies**) a convent of friars.

fricassee ● *n.* a dish of stewed or fried pieces of meat served in a thick white sauce. ● *v.tr.* (**fricassees, fricasseed**) make a fricassee of. [French *fricassée* (fem.) 'cut up and cooked in sauce']

fricative *Phonet.* ● *adj.* made by the friction of breath in a narrow opening. ● *n.* a consonant made in this way, e.g. *f* and *th*. [based on Latin *fricare* 'to rub']

friction *n.* **1** the action of one object rubbing against another. **2** the resistance an object encounters in moving over another. **3** a clash of wills, temperaments, or opinions. [related to FRICATIVE] □ **frictional** *adj.* **frictionless** *adj.*

Friday ● *n.* the sixth day of the week, following Thursday. ● *adv. colloq.* **1** on Friday. **2** (**Fridays**) on Fridays; each Friday. [Old English, named after *Frigg*, wife of Odin]

fridge *n. colloq.* = REFRIGERATOR. [abbreviation]

fridge-freezer *n.* esp. *Brit.* an upright unit comprising a refrigerator and a freezer, each self-contained.

friend *n.* **1** a person with whom one enjoys mutual affection and regard (usu. exclusive of sexual or family bonds). **2** a sympathizer, helper, or patron (*no friend to virtue*). **3** an ally or neutral person (*friend or foe?*). **4 a** a person already mentioned (*my friend at the next table*). **b** used as a polite or ironic form of address. **5** a regular contributor to an institution. **6** (**Friend**) a member of the Society of Friends, a Quaker. □ **be** (or **keep**) **friends with** be friendly with. **my learned friend** used by a lawyer in court to refer to another. [Old English] □ **friended** *adj.* **friendless** *adj.*

friendly ● *adj.* (**friendlier, friendliest**) **1** acting as or like a friend, well disposed, kindly. **2 a** (often foll. by *with*) on amicable terms. **b** not hostile. **3 a** (of a thing) serviceable, convenient, opportune. **b** = USER-FRIENDLY. **4** (esp. in *comb.*) not harming; helping (*reader-friendly*). ● *n.* (*pl.* **-ies**) *Brit.* = FRIENDLY MATCH. ● *adv.* in a friendly manner. □ **friendlily** *adv.* **friendliness** *n.*

friendly fire *n. Mil.* gunfire coming from one's own side, esp. as the cause of accidental injury to one's own forces.

friendly match *n. Brit. Sport.* a match not played in competition for a cup etc.

Friendly Society *n. Brit.* a mutual association providing sickness benefits, life assurance, and pensions.

friendship *n.* **1** being friends, the relationship between friends. **2** a friendly disposition felt or shown.

frier var. of FRYER.

Friesian *Brit.* ● *n.* a large animal of a usu. black and white breed of dairy cattle originally from Friesland. ● *adj.* of or concerning Friesians. [variant of FRISIAN]

frieze *n.* **1** *Archit.* **a** ▼ the part of an entablature between the architrave and the cornice. ▷ ENTABLATURE. **b** a horizontal band of sculpture filling this. **2** a band of decoration elsewhere, esp. along a wall near the ceiling. [based on Latin *Phrygium* (*opus*) '(work) of Phrygia']

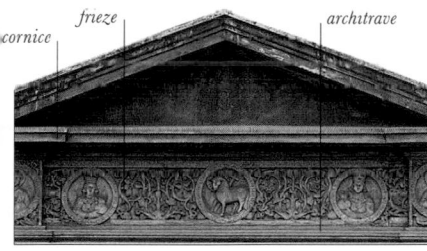

FRIEZE: 8TH-CENTURY ROMAN FRIEZE

frig *coarse slang* ● *vtr. & intr.* (**frigged, frigging**) **1** = FUCK *v.* **2** masturbate. ● *n.* = FUCK *n.* 1a, 2.

frigate *n.* **1** *Brit.* a naval escort vessel. **2** *hist.* a warship. [from French *frégate*]

frigate bird *n.* any seabird of the family Fregatidae, found in tropical seas, with a wide wingspan and deeply forked tail. ▷ SEABIRD

fright *n.* **1 a** a sudden and extreme fear. **b** an instance of this (*gave me a fright*). **2** a person or thing looking grotesque or ridiculous. □ **take fright** become frightened. [Old English]

frighten *v.tr.* **1** fill with fright; terrify. **2** (foll. by *away*, *off*, *out of*, *into*) drive or force by fright. □ **frightening** *adj.* **frighteningly** *adv.*

frightener *n.* a person or thing that frightens. □ **put the frighteners on** *Brit. slang* intimidate.

frightful *adj.* **1 a** dreadful, shocking. **b** ugly. **2** *colloq.* extremely bad (*a frightful idea*). **3** *colloq.* very great, extreme. □ **frightfully** *adv.* **frightfulness** *n.*

frigid *adj.* **1 a** lacking friendliness or enthusiasm. **b** dull, insipid. **2** (of a woman) sexually unresponsive. **3** (esp. of climate or air) cold. [from Latin *frigidus* 'cold'] □ **frigidity** *n.* **frigidly** *adv.* **frigidness** *n.*

frijoles /fri-hoh-les/ *n.pl.* beans. [Spanish]

frill ● *n.* **1 a** a strip of gathered or fluted material, used as an ornamental edging. **b** a similar paper ornament on a ham-knuckle etc. **c** a natural fringe of feathers, hair, etc., on esp. a bird or a plant. **2** (in *pl.*) unnecessary embellishments or accomplishments. ● *v.tr.* **1** decorate with a frill. **2** form into a frill. [16th-century coinage] □ **frilled** *adj.* **frilly** *adj.* (**frillier, frilliest**). **frilliness** *n.*

frill lizard *n.* (also **frilled lizard** or **frill-necked lizard**) ► a large N. Australian lizard, *Chlamydosaurus kingii*, with an erectile membrane round the neck.

fringe ● *n.* **1 a** an ornamental bordering of threads left loose or formed into tassels. **b** such a bordering made separately. **c** any border or edging. **2 a** esp. *Brit.* a portion of the front hair hanging over the forehead. **b** a natural border of hair etc. in an animal or plant. **3 a** an outer edge, margin, or limit. **b** (*attrib.*) taking place on the periphery (*fringe group*). **c** (*attrib.*) unconventional (*fringe theatre*). **4** a thing, part, or area of minor importance. ● *v.tr.* **1** adorn or encircle with a fringe. **2** serve as a fringe to. [from Late Latin *fimbria*] □ **fringeless** *adj.*

fringe benefit *n.* an employee's benefit supplementing a money wage or salary.

fringe medicine *n.* systems of treatment of disease etc. not regarded as orthodox.

frippery *n.* (*pl.* **-ies**) **1** showy, tawdry, or unnecessary ornament, esp. in dress. **2** empty display in literary style etc. **3 a** knick-knacks, trifles. **b** a knick-knack or trifle. [based on Old French *frepe* 'rag']

frisbee *n. propr.* a concave plastic disc designed for skimming through the air as an outdoor game.

frisée *n.* = ENDIVE 1. [French]

Frisian ● *n.* **1** a native or inhabitant of Friesland (comprising parts of NW Netherlands and NW Germany). **2** the language of Friesland. ● *adj.* of or relating to Friesland, its people, or language. [from Old Frisian *Frīsa*]

frisk ● *v.* **1** *intr.* leap or skip playfully. **2** *tr.* feel over or search (a person) for a weapon etc. (usu. rapidly). ● *n.* **1** a playful leap or skip. **2** the frisking of a person. [based on Old French *frisque* 'lively']

frisky *adj.* (**friskier, friskiest**) lively, playful. □ **friskily** *adv.* **friskiness** *n.*

frisson /free-son/ *n.* an emotional thrill. [French, literally 'a shiver']

frit *adj. dial. & colloq.* frightened.

frith var. of FIRTH.

fritillary *n.* (*pl.* **-ies**) **1** any plant of the genus *Fritillaria* (lily family), having pendent bell-like flowers. **2** any of various butterflies, esp. of the genus *Argynnis*, having red-brown wings chequered with black. [based on Latin *fritillus* 'dicebox']

erect frill

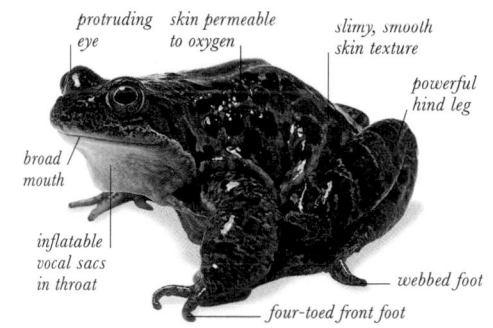

FRILL LIZARD
(*Chlamydosaurus kingii*)

fritter[1] *v.tr.* (usu. foll. by *away*) waste (money, energy, etc.) triflingly. [from obsolete *fritters* 'fragments']

fritter[2] *n.* a piece of fruit, meat, etc., coated in batter and deep-fried. [based on Latin *frigere* frict- 'to fry']

frivolous *adj.* **1** trifling. **2** lacking seriousness; silly. [from Latin *frivolus*] □ **frivolity** *n.* (*pl.* **-ies**). **frivolously** *adv.* **frivolousness** *n.*

frizz ● *v.* **1** *tr.* form (hair) into a mass of small curls. **2** *intr.* (of hair) form itself into small curls. ● *n.* **1** frizzed hair. **2** a row of curls. [from French *friser* 'to curl'] □ **frizzy** *adj.* (**frizzier, frizziest**). **frizziness** *n.*

frizzle[1] *v.intr. & tr.* **1** fry, toast, or grill, with a sputtering noise. **2** (often foll. by *up*) burn or shrivel. [based on Latin *frigere* 'to fry']

frizzle[2] ● *v.* **1** *tr.* form (hair) into tight curls. **2** *intr.* (often foll. by *up*) (of hair etc.) curl tightly. ● *n.* frizzled hair. [16th-century coinage] □ **frizzly** *adj.*

fro *adv.* back (now only in *to and fro*: see TO). [from Old Norse *frá* 'from']

frock ● *n.* **1** *Brit.* a woman's or girl's dress. **2 a** a monk's or priest's long gown with loose sleeves. **b** priestly office. **3** a smock. ● *v.tr.* invest with priestly office. [from Old French *froc*]

frock coat *n.* a man's long-skirted coat not cut away in front.

frog[1] *n.* **1** ▼ any of various small tailless amphibians of the order Anura, having a moist smooth skin and legs developed for jumping. ▷ SPAWN, TOAD. **2** (**Frog**) *slang offens.* a French person. □ **frog in the** (or **one's**) **throat** *colloq.* an irritation in the throat; hoarseness. [Old English] □ **froggy** *adj.*

frog[2] *n.* an elastic horny substance in the sole of a horse's foot. [17th-century coinage]

FROG

Frogs are amphibians of the order Anura, which includes toads and consists of about 2,500 species. Frogs characteristically have squat bodies, smooth skin, strong hind legs for leaping, and webbed feet. Most reproduce in water, laying eggs that develop into larvae (tadpoles). They are the most widespread amphibians, with habitats ranging from lakes, marshes, and rainforests to mountains and even deserts.

protruding eye   skin permeable to oxygen   slimy, smooth skin texture   powerful hind leg   broad mouth   inflatable vocal sacs in throat   webbed foot   four-toed front foot

EXTERNAL FEATURES OF A COMMON FROG (*Rana temporaria*)

EXAMPLES OF OTHER FROGS

TOMATO FROG
(*Dyscophus antongilii*)

WHITE'S TREEFROG
(*Litoria caerulea*)

POISON DART FROG
(*Dendrobates* species)

F

F

frog[3] *n.* an ornamental coat-fastening of a spindle-shaped button and loop. [18th-century coinage] □ **frogged** *adj.* **frogging** *n.*

froghopper *n.* ▶ any jumping plant-sucking bug of the family Cercopidae, whose larvae produce a protective mass of froth.

frogman *n.* (*pl.* **-men**) a person equipped with a rubber suit, flippers, and an oxygen supply for underwater swimming.

frogmarch ● *v.tr.* **1** hustle (a person) forward holding and pinning the arms from behind. **2** carry (a person) in a frogmarch. ● *n.* the carrying of a person face downwards by four others each holding a limb.

frogspawn *n.* the eggs of a frog, usu. surrounded by transparent jelly. ▷ SPAWN

frolic ● *v.intr.* (**frolicked**, **frolicking**) play about cheerfully, gambol. ● *n.* **1** cheerful play. **2** a prank. **3** a merry party. ● *adj. archaic* **1** full of pranks, sportive. **2** joyous, mirthful. [based on Dutch *vrolijk* 'glad'] □ **frolicker** *n.*

frolicsome *adj.* merry, playful. □ **frolicsomely** *adv.* **frolicsomeness** *n.*

from *prep.* expressing separation or origin, followed by: **1** a person, place, time, etc., that is the starting point of motion or action, or of extent in place or time (*rain comes from the clouds; dinner is served from 8*). **2** a place, object, etc. whose distance or remoteness is reckoned (*ten miles from Rome; apart from its moral aspect*). **3 a** a source (*a man from Italy; a conclusion from data*). **b** a giver or sender (*from Father Christmas*). **4 a** a thing or person avoided, escaped, lost, etc. (*released him from prison*). **b** a person or thing deprived (*took his gun from him*). **5** a reason, cause, or motive (*died from fatigue*). **6** a thing distinguished or unlike (*know black from white*). **7** a lower limit (*tickets from £5*). **8** a state changed for another (*raised the penalty from a fine to imprisonment*). **9** an adverb or preposition of time or place (*from long ago; from abroad*). **10** the position of a person who observes or considers (*saw it from the roof*). **11** a model (*painted it from nature*). □ **from a child** since childhood. **from now on** henceforward. **from time to time** occasionally. [Old English]

fromage frais /from-a*zh* fray/ *n.* a type of smooth soft fresh cheese. [French, literally 'fresh cheese']

frond *n. Bot.* ▼ a large usu. divided leaf in esp. ferns and palms. ▷ FERN. [from Latin *frons frondis* 'leaf']

FROND OF THE
MALE FERN
(*Dryopteris filix-mas*)

front ● *n.* **1** the side or part normally nearer or towards the spectator or the direction of motion (*the front of the car*). **2** any face of a building, esp. that of the main entrance. **3** *Mil.* **a** the foremost line or part of an army etc. **b** line of battle. **c** a scene of actual fighting. **e** the direction in which a formed line faces (*change front*). **4 a** a sector of activity regarded as resembling a military front. **b** an organized political group. **5 a** demeanour, bearing. **b** outward appearance. **6** a forward or conspicuous position (*come to the front*). **7 a** a bluff. **b** a pretext. **8** a person etc. serving to cover subversive or illegal activities. **9** (prec. by *the*) esp. *Brit.* the promenade of a seaside resort. **10** *Meteorol.* ▶ the forward edge of an advancing mass of cold or warm air. ▷ WEATHER CHART. **11** impudence. ● *attrib.adj.* **1** of the front. **2** situated in front. ● *v.* **1** *intr.* (foll. by *on, to, towards, upon*) have the front facing or directed. **2** *intr.* (foll. by *for*) *colloq.* act as a front or cover for. **3** *tr.* furnish with a front (*fronted with stone*). **4** *tr.* lead (a band etc.). **5** *tr.* front. **6** *tr. Broadcasting* act as presenter

or host of (a programme). □ **in front 1** in an advanced position. **2** facing the spectator. **in front of 1** ahead of. **2** in the presence of, confronting. **on the front burner** see BURNER. [from Latin *frons frontis*] □ **frontless** *adj.* **frontward** *adj. & adv.* **frontwards** *adv.*

frontage *n.* **1** the front of a building. **2 a** land abutting on a street or on water. **b** the land between the front of a building and the road. **3** extent of front (*with little frontage*). **4 a** the way a thing faces. **b** outlook.

frontal[1] *adj.* **1** of, at, or on the front (*a frontal attack; a frontal view*). **2** of the forehead (*frontal bone*). [from modern Latin *frontalis*] □ **frontally** *adv.*

frontal[2] *n. Eccl.* **1** a covering for the front of an altar. **2** the façade of a building. [from Latin *frontale*]

frontal lobe *n.* each of the paired lobes of the brain lying immediately behind the forehead, including areas concerned with behaviour, learning, and voluntary movement. ▷ BRAIN

front bench *n. Brit.* the foremost seats in the House of Commons. □ **frontbencher** *n.*

front door *n.* **1** the chief entrance of a building. **2** a chief means of approach or access.

frontier *n.* **1 a** the border between two countries. **b** the district on each side of this. **2** the limits of attainment or knowledge in a subject. **3** (in the US) the borders between settled and unsettled country. [from Latin *frons frontis* 'front']

frontiersman *n.* (*pl.* **-men**; *fem.* **frontierswoman**, *pl.* **-women**) a person living in the region of a frontier, esp. between settled and unsettled country.

frontispiece *n.* an illustration facing the title-page of a book or of one of its divisions. [based on Latin *frons frontis* 'front' + *specere* 'to look' (assimilated to PIECE)]

front line *n.* the foremost part of an army or a group under attack.

frontman *n.* **1** a person acting as a front or cover (see FRONT *n.* 8). **2** *Broadcasting* a programme's presenter or host. **3** the leader of a group of musicians etc.

front office *n.* a main office, esp. *Brit.* police headquarters.

front page *n.* the first page of a newspaper, esp. as containing important or remarkable news.

front runner *n.* **1** the contestant most likely to succeed. **2** an athlete or horse running best when in the lead.

front-wheel drive *n.* drive acting on the front wheels of a motor vehicle (see DRIVE *n.* 6a).

frost ● *n.* **1 a** white frozen dew. **b** a consistent temperature below freezing point causing frost to

form. **2** a chilling dispiriting atmosphere. ● *v.* **1** *intr.* (usu. foll. by *over, up*) become covered with frost. **2** *tr.* **a** cover with or as if with frost, powder, etc. **b** injure (a plant etc.) with frost. **3** *tr.* give a roughened or finely granulated surface to (*frosted glass*). **4** *tr. US* cover or decorate (a cake etc.) with icing. □ **degrees of frost** *Brit.* degrees below freezing point. [Old English] □ **frostless** *adj.*

frostbite *n.* injury to body tissues, esp. the nose, fingers, or toes, due to freezing.

frosting *n.* **1** *US* icing. **2** a rough surface on glass etc.

frosty *adj.* (**frostier**, **frostiest**) **1** cold with frost. **2** covered with or as with hoar frost. **3** unfriendly in manner. □ **frostily** *adv.* **frostiness** *n.*

froth ● *n.* **1 a** a collection of small bubbles; foam. **b** scum. **2 a** idle talk or ideas. **b** anything insubstantial or of little worth. ● *v.* **1** *intr.* emit or gather froth. **2** *tr.* cause (beer etc.) to foam. [from Old Norse *frotha*] □ **frothily** *adv.* **frothiness** *n.* **frothy** *adj.* (**frothier**, **frothiest**).

frou-frou /froo-froo/ *n.* **1** a rustling, esp. of a dress. **2** frills, frippery. [French]

frown ● *v.intr.* **1** wrinkle one's brows, esp. in displeasure or deep thought. **2** (foll. by *at, on, upon*) express disapproval. **3** (of a thing) present a gloomy aspect. ● *n.* **1** an action of frowning. **2** a look expressing severity, disapproval, or deep thought. [from Old French *froigne* 'surly look'] □ **frowningly** *adv.*

frowsty *adj.* (**frowstier**, **frowstiest**) *Brit.* fusty, stuffy. [variant of FROWZY] □ **frowstiness** *n.*

frowzy *adj.* (also **frowsy**) (**-ier**, **-iest**) **1** fusty. **2** slatternly, dingy. [17th-century coinage] □ **frowziness** *n.*

froze *past* of FREEZE.

frozen *past part.* of FREEZE.

frozen shoulder *n. Med.* a shoulder joint which is painfully stiff.

FRS *abbr.* (in the UK) Fellow of the Royal Society.

fructiferous *adj.* bearing fruit. [from Latin *fructifer*, based on *fructus* 'fruit']

fructify *v.* (**-ies**, **-ied**) **1** *intr.* bear fruit. **2** *tr.* make fruitful. [based on Latin *fructus* 'fruit'] □ **fructification** *n.*

fructose *n. Chem.* a simple sugar found in honey and fruits. [based on Latin *fructus* 'fruit']

frugal *adj.* **1** sparing or economical, esp. as regards food. **2** sparingly used or supplied, meagre, costing little. [from Latin *frugalis*] □ **frugality** *n.* **frugally** *adv.*

frugivorous *adj.* feeding on fruit. [based on Latin *frux frugis* 'fruit']

fruit ● *n.* **1 a** ▶ the usu. sweet and fleshy edible product of a plant or tree, containing seed. **b** (in *sing.*) these in quantity (*eats fruit*). **2** the seed of a plant or tree with its covering, e.g. an acorn, pea pod, cherry, etc. **3** (usu. in *pl.*) vegetables, grains,

---

FRONT

In meteorology, a front is the meeting point between two air masses of different temperature. In a warm front, warm air gradually rises over cold air, bringing steady rain.

In a cold front, a mass of cold air undercuts warm air, forcing it to rise sharply. Short, heavy rain showers occur, followed by lowered temperatures and light showers.

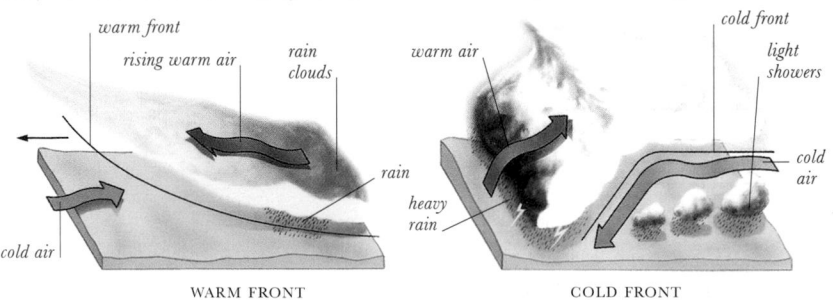

WARM FRONT   COLD FRONT

FRUIT

A fruit is the part of a plant that holds the seeds and aids in their dispersal. It develops from the ovary of a flower that has been pollinated, and can be juicy and colourful or hard and dry. There are two broad categories: succulent and dry fruits. Of the succulent fruits, berries typically have a combined mesocarp and endocarp layer, and many seeds; drupes usually have a fleshy mesocarp and one seed surrounded by a woody endocarp. Aggregate fruits such as blackberries are made up of small drupes. False fruits develop from parts of the flower as well as the ovary. Dry fruits may be dehiscent (splitting open to scatter seeds) or indehiscent (falling without breaking apart).

DEVELOPMENT OF A FRUIT (MELON)

insect pollinates flower

flower shrivels and dies

remains of flower

ovary begins to swell

fruit grows and ripens

combined mesocarp and endocarp layer

seeds

cortex

exocarp

pedicel (remains of flower stalk)

exocarp

FEATURES OF A BERRY FRUIT (KIWI FRUIT, *Actinidia chinensis*)

SUCCULENT FRUITS

EXAMPLES OF BERRIES

GRAPES
(*Vitis vinifera*)

MELON
(*Cucumis melo*)

GOOSEBERRY
(*Ribes grossularia*)

LEMON
(*Citrus limon*)

TOMATO
(*Lycopersicon esculentum*)

CAPE GOOSEBERRY
(*Physalis peruviana*)

EXAMPLES OF DRUPES AND AGGREGATE FRUITS

PEACH (DRUPE)
(*Prunus persica*)

MANGO (DRUPE)
(*Mangifera indica*)

BLACKBERRY (AGGREGATE FRUIT)
(*Rubus fruticosus*)

FALSE FRUITS

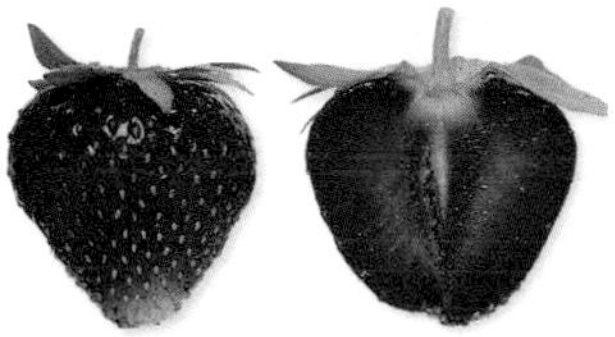

PSEUDOCARP
strawberry
(*Fragaria × ananassa*)

SYCONIUM
fig
(*Ficus carica*)

POME
apple
(*Malus sylvestris*)

DRY FRUITS

DEHISCENT FRUITS

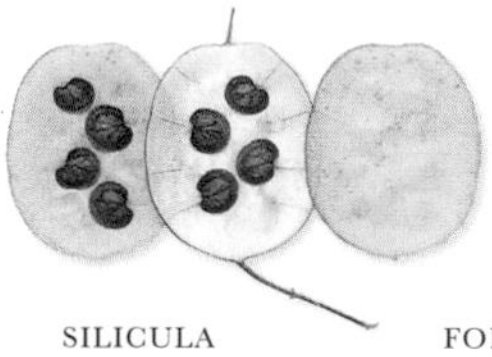

SILICULA
honesty
(*Lunaria annua*)

FOLLICLE
larkspur
(*Delphinium* species)

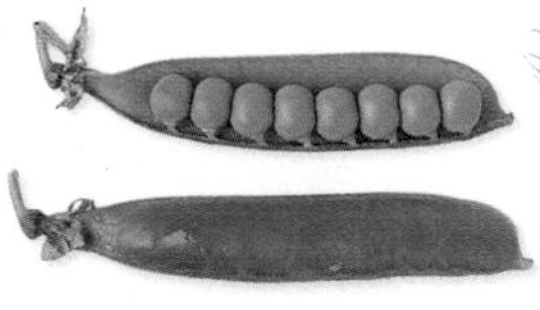

POD OR LEGUME
pea
(*Pisum sativum*)

CAPSULE
love-in-a-mist
(*Nigella damascena*)

INDEHISCENT FRUITS

ACHENE (CLUSTER)
field marigold
(*Calendula arvensis*)

NUT
acorn
(*Quercus* species)

etc. used for food (*fruits of the Earth*). **4** (usu. in *pl.*) the result of action etc. (*fruits of his labours*). **5** *slang* esp. *US* a male homosexual. **6** *Bibl.* an offspring (*the fruit of the womb*). ● *v.intr. & tr.* bear or cause to bear fruit. [from Latin *fructus* 'fruit, enjoyment'] □ **fruited** *adj.* (also in *comb.*). **fruiter** *n.*

fruitarian *n.* a person who eats only fruit.

fruitbat *n.* ▼ any large bat of the suborder Megachiroptera, feeding on fruit. ▷ BAT

fruit cake *n.* **1** a cake containing dried fruit. **2** (**fruitcake**) *slang* an eccentric or mad person.

fruit cocktail *n.* a finely chopped fruit salad.

fruiterer *n.* esp. *Brit.* a dealer in fruit.

fruit fly *n.* (*pl.* **flies**) any of various flies, esp. of the genus *Drosophila*, having larvae that feed on fruit.

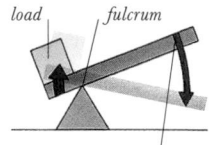

FRUITBAT
(*Pteropus* species)

fruitful *adj.* **1** producing much fruit. **2** successful; beneficial, remunerative. **3** producing offspring, esp. prolifically. □ **fruitfully** *adv.* **fruitfulness** *n.*

fruiting body *n.* the spore-bearing part of a fungus. ▷ MUSHROOM

fruition /froo-ish-ŏn/ *n.* **1 a** the bearing of fruit. **b** the production of results. **2** the realization of aims or hopes. **3** enjoyment. [based on Latin *frui* 'to enjoy', erroneously associated with *fruit*]

fruitless *adj.* **1** not bearing fruit. **2** useless, unsuccessful. □ **fruitlessly** *adv.* **fruitlessness** *n.*

fruit machine *n. Brit.* a coin-operated gaming machine giving random combinations of symbols often representing fruit.

fruit salad *n.* various fruits cut up and served in syrup, juice, etc.

fruit sugar *n.* fructose.

fruity *adj.* (**fruitier**, **fruitiest**) **1 a** of fruit. **b** tasting or smelling like fruit. **2** (of a voice etc.) of full rich quality. **3** *Brit. colloq.* full of rough humour or (usu. scandalous) interest; suggestive. □ **fruitily** *adv.* **fruitiness** *n.*

frump *n.* a dowdy unattractive old-fashioned woman. [16th-century coinage] □ **frumpish** *adj.* **frumpishly** *adv.*

frumpy *adj.* (**frumpier**, **frumpiest**) dowdy, unattractive, and old-fashioned. □ **frumpily** *adv.* **frumpiness** *n.*

frustrate *v.tr.* **1** make (efforts) ineffective. **2** prevent (a person) from achieving a purpose. **3** (as **frustrated** *adj.*) **a** discontented because unable to achieve one's desire. **b** sexually unfulfilled. **4** disappoint (a hope). [based on Latin *frustratus* 'disappointed'] □ **frustratedly** *adv.* **frustrating** *adj.* **frustratingly** *adv.* **frustration** *n.*

fry[1] ● *v.tr. & intr.* (**fries**, **fried**) **1** cook or be cooked in hot fat. **2** burn or overheat; frizzle, scorch. **3** *slang* electrocute or be electrocuted. ● *n.* (*pl.* **fries**) **1** *Brit.* various internal parts of animals usu. eaten fried (*lamb's fry*). **2 a** a dish of fried food, esp. meat. **b** (in *pl.*) *N. Amer.* = FRENCH FRIED POTATOES. **3** *US* a social gathering where fried food is served. □ **fry up** heat or reheat (food) in a frying pan. [from Latin *frigere*]

fry[2] *n.pl.* young or newly hatched fishes. [from Old Norse *frjó*]

fryer *n.* (also **frier**) **1** a person who fries. **2** a vessel for frying esp. fish. **3** *US* a young chicken suitable for frying.

frying pan *n.* (*N. Amer.* **frypan**) a shallow pan used in frying.

fry-up *n. Brit. colloq.* a dish of miscellaneous fried food.

f-stop *n. Photog.* a camera setting corresponding to a particular f-number.

ft *abbr.* foot, feet.

fuchsia /few-shă/ *n.* ▶ any shrub of the genus *Fuchsia*, with drooping red, purple, or white flowers. [modern Latin, named after L. *Fuchs*, German botanist, 1501–66]

fuck *coarse slang* ● *v.* **1** *tr. & intr.* have sexual intercourse (with). **2** *intr.* (foll. by *about*, *around*) mess about; fool around. **3** *tr.* (usu. as an exclamation) curse, confound (*fuck the thing!*). **4** *intr.* (as **fucking** *adj.*, *adv.*) used as an intensive to express annoyance etc. ● *int.* expressing anger or annoyance. ● *n.* **1 a** an act of sexual intercourse. **b** a partner in sexual intercourse. **2** the slightest amount (*don't give a fuck*). □ **fuck all** *Brit.* nothing. **fuck off** go away. **fuck up 1** make a mess of. **2** disturb emotionally. **3** make a blunder. [16th-century coinage] □ **fucker** *n.* (often as a term of abuse).

■ **Usage** Although widely used in many sections of society, *fuck* is still generally considered to be one of the most offensive words in English.

fuck-up *n. coarse slang* a mess or muddle.

fucus /few-kŭs/ *n.* (*pl.* **fuci** /few-sy/) ◀ any seaweed of the genus *Fucus*, with flat leathery fronds. [Latin, literally 'rock-lichen'] □ **fucoid** *adj.*

fuddle ● *v.tr.* confuse or stupefy, esp. with alcoholic liquor. ● *n.* **1** confusion. **2** intoxication. [16th-century coinage]

fuddy-duddy *colloq.* ● *adj.* old-fashioned or quaintly fussy. ● *n.* (*pl.* **-ies**) a fuddy-duddy person. [20th-century coinage]

FUCUS: SERRATED WRACK FUCUS (*Fucus serratus*)

fudge ● *n.* **1** a soft toffee-like sweet made with milk, sugar, butter, etc. **2** nonsense. **3** a piece of dishonesty or faking. ● *v.* **1** *tr.* put together in a makeshift or dishonest way; fake. **2** *tr.* deal with incompetently. **3** *intr.* practise such methods.

fuehrer var. of FÜHRER.

fuel ● *n.* **1** material burnt or used as a source of heat or power or nuclear energy. **2** food as a source of energy. **3** anything that sustains or inflames emotion or passion. ● *v.* (**fuelled**, **fuelling**; *US* **fueled**, **fueling**) **1** *tr.* supply with fuel. **2** *tr.* inflame (an argument, feeling, etc.) (*drink fuelled his anger*). **3** *intr.* take in or get fuel. [based on Latin *focus* 'hearth']

FUCHSIA
(*Fuchsia* 'Love's Reward')

fuel cell *n.* a cell producing an electric current direct from a chemical reaction.

fuel element *n.* an element of nuclear fuel etc. for use in a reactor.

fuel injection *n.* ▼ the direct introduction of fuel under pressure into the combustion units of an internal-combustion engine. □ **fuel-injected** *adj.*

fuel oil *n.* oil used as fuel in an engine or furnace.

fuel rod *n.* a rod-shaped fuel element.

fug *n. Brit. colloq.* stuffiness or fustiness of the air in a room. [19th-century coinage] □ **fuggy** *adj.*

fugal *adj.* of the nature of a fugue.

-fuge *comb. form* forming adjectives and nouns denoting expelling or dispelling (*febrifuge*; *vermifuge*). [based on Latin *fugare* 'to put to flight']

fugitive ● *adj.* **1** fleeing. **2** transient, fleeting. **3** (of literature) of passing interest, ephemeral. **4** flitting, shifting. ● *n.* **1** a person who flees. **2** an exile or refugee. [from Latin *fugitivus*]

fugue *n.* **1** *Mus.* a contrapuntal composition in which a short melody or phrase is introduced by one part and successively taken up by others and developed by interweaving the parts. **2** *Psychol.* loss of awareness of one's identity, often coupled with flight from one's usual environment. [from Latin *fuga* 'flight']

fugued *adj.* in the form of a fugue.

führer /fewr-er/ *n.* (also **fuehrer**) a leader, esp. a tyrannical one. [German, literally 'leader']

fulcrum *n.* (*pl.* **fulcra** or **fulcrums**) ▶ the point against which a lever is placed to get a purchase or on which it turns or is supported. ▷ LEVER, SCALE. [Latin, literally 'post of a couch']

FULCRUM

fulfil *v.tr.* (*US* **fulfill**) (**fulfilled**, **fulfilling**) **1** carry out (a prophecy or promise). **2 a** satisfy (a desire or prayer). **b** (as **fulfilled** *adj.*) completely happy. **3 a** execute, obey (a command or law). **b** perform, carry out (a task). **4** comply with (conditions). **5** answer (a purpose). **6** bring to an end, finish, complete (a period or piece of work). □ **fulfil oneself** develop one's gifts and character to the full. [Old English] □ **fulfilment** *n.* (*US* **fulfillment**).

full[1] ● *adj.* **1** holding all its limits will allow (*the bucket is full*; *full of water*). **2** having eaten to one's limits or satisfaction. **3** abundant, copious, satisfying (*led a full life*; *give full details*; *the book is very full on this point*). **4** (foll. by *of*) having or holding an abundance of; showing marked signs of (*full of interest*; *full of*

FUEL INJECTION

In some vehicles, fuel injectors have replaced the carburettor as a means of introducing fuel directly into the cylinders of an internal-combustion engine. A computer-controlled pump squirts tiny, exact amounts of fuel directly into the cylinders. In petrol engines, the fuel is injected at the start of the first induction stroke of the four-stroke cycle. Fuel injection is standard in diesel engines, and where a catalytic converter is fitted.

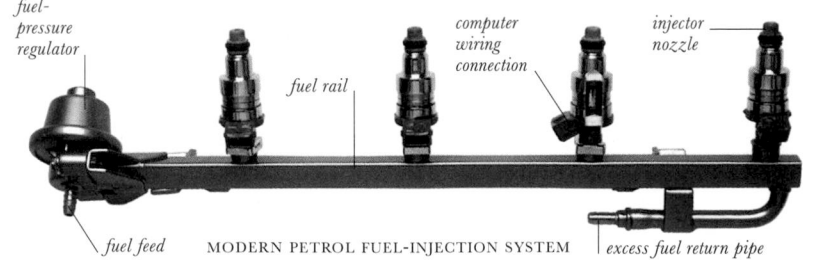

fuel-pressure regulator — fuel rail — computer wiring connection — injector nozzle — fuel feed — MODERN PETROL FUEL-INJECTION SYSTEM — excess fuel return pipe

mistakes). **5** (foll. by *of*) **a** engrossed in thinking about (*full of himself*). **b** unable to refrain from talking about (*full of the news*). **6** complete, perfect (*full membership; full daylight; waited a full hour*). **7 a** (of tone or colour) deep and clear. **b** (of light) intense. **c** (of motion etc.) vigorous (*a full pulse; at full gallop*). **8** plump, rounded (*a full figure*). **9** (of clothes) made of much material arranged in folds. **10** (of the heart etc.) overcharged with emotion. ● *adv.* **1** very (*you know full well*). **2** quite, fully (*full six miles; full ripe*). **3** exactly (*hit him full on the nose*). **4** more than sufficiently (*full early*). □ **at full length 1** lying stretched out. **2** without abridgement. **come full circle** see CIRCLE. **full speed** (or **steam**) **ahead!** an order to proceed at maximum speed or to pursue a course of action energetically. **full up** completely full. **in full 1** without abridgement. **2** to or for the full amount (*paid in full*). **in full swing** at the height of activity. **in full view** entirely visible. **to the full** to the utmost extent. [Old English]

full² *v.tr.* cleanse and thicken (cloth). [Middle English, back-formation from FULLER]

full-back *n.* a defensive player, or a position near the goal, in football, hockey, etc. ▷ FOOTBALL, RUGBY

full beam *n.* the brightest setting of a vehicle's headlights.

full-blooded *adj.* **1** vigorous, hearty, sensual. **2** not hybrid. □ **full-bloodedly** *adv.* **full-bloodedness** *n.*

full-blown *adj.* fully developed.

full board *n.* provision of accommodation and all meals at a hotel etc.

full-bodied *adj.* rich in quality, tone, etc.

full brother *n.* a brother born of the same parents.

full-cream *adj.* of or made from unskimmed milk.

full dress ● *n.* formal clothes worn on great occasions. ● *attrib.adj.* (**full-dress**) (of a debate etc.) of major importance.

fuller *n.* a person who fulls cloth. [from Latin *fullo*]

fuller's earth *n.* a type of clay used in fulling cloth.

full face ● *adv.* (also **in full face**) with all the face visible to the observer. ● *adj.* (**full-face**) with all the face visible to the observer.

full-frontal *attrib.adj.* **1** (of nudity or a nude figure) with full exposure at the front. **2** unrestrained, explicit.

full-grown *adj.* having reached maturity.

full house *n.* **1** a maximum attendance at a theatre, in Parliament, etc. **2** *Poker* a hand with three of a kind and a pair.

full-length *adj.* **1** not shortened. **2** (of a mirror, portrait, etc.) showing the whole height of the human figure.

full lock see LOCK¹ *n.* 3b.

full marks *n.pl.* (*US* **high marks**) the maximum award in an examination, in assessment of a person, etc.

full moon *n.* **1** the Moon with its whole disc illuminated. **2** the time when this occurs.

fullness *n.* (also **fulness**) **1** being full. **2** (of sound, colour, etc.) richness, volume, body. **3** all that is contained (in the world etc.). □ **in the fullness of time** at the appropriate or destined time.

full point *n.* = FULL STOP 1.

full professor *n.* a professor of the highest grade in a university etc.

full-scale *adj.* not reduced in size, complete.

full sister *n.* a sister born of the same parents.

full stop *n.* **1** a punctuation mark (.) used at the end of a sentence or an abbreviation. **2** a complete cessation.

full term *n.* the completion of a normal pregnancy.

full tilt see TILT.

full-time ● *adj.* occupying or using the whole of the available working time (*a full-time job*). ● *adv.* on a full-time basis (*works full-time*).

full time *n.* **1** the total normal duration of work etc. **2** the end of a football etc. match.

full-timer *n.* a person who does a full-time job.

fully *adv.* **1** completely, entirely (*am fully aware*). **2** no less or fewer than (*fully 60*).

fully-fashioned *adj.* (of women's clothing) shaped to fit the body.

fully-fledged *adj. Brit.* (or **fully fledged** *predic.*) mature.

fulmar *n.* any medium-sized seabird of the genus *Fulmarus*, with stout body, robust bill, and rounded tail. [from Old Norse *fúll már* 'foul gull', referring to its habit of regurgitating its stomach contents]

fulminant *adj.* **1** fulminating. **2** *Med.* (of a disease or symptom) developing suddenly. [from Latin *fulminant-* 'striking with lightning']

fulminate *v.intr.* **1** express censure loudly and forcefully. **2** explode violently; flash like lightning (*fulminating mercury*). **3** *Med.* (of a disease or symptom) develop suddenly. [based on Latin *fulmen -minis* 'lightning'] □ **fulmination** *n.*

fulness var. of FULLNESS.

fulsome *adj.* **1** disgusting by excess of flattery, servility, or expressions of affection; excessive, cloying. **2** *disp.* copious. [Middle English] □ **fulsomely** *adv.* **fulsomeness** *n.*

■ **Usage** The original meaning of *fulsome* was 'copious' (see sense 2 above). However, this usage is now considered incorrect, and *fulsome* is used only as a pejorative term, applied to nouns such as *flattery*, *praise*, and *tribute*, meaning 'excessive' or 'cloying'.

fumble ● *v.* **1** *intr.* use the hands awkwardly, grope about. **2** *tr.* **a** handle clumsily or nervously. **b** *Sport* fail to stop (a ball) cleanly. ● *n.* an act of fumbling. [from Dutch *fommelen*] □ **fumbler** *n.* **fumblingly** *adv.*

fume ● *n.* (usu. in *pl.*) exuded gas or smoke or vapour, esp. when harmful or unpleasant. ● *v.* **1 a** *intr.* emit fumes. **b** *tr.* give off as fumes. **2** *tr.* be affected by (esp. suppressed) anger (*was fuming at their inefficiency*). **3** *tr.* **a** fumigate. **b** subject to fumes (to darken tints in oak, photographic film, etc.). [from Latin *fumus* 'smoke'] □ **fumy** *adj.*

fumigate *v.tr.* **1** disinfect or purify with fumes. **2** apply fumes to. [based on Latin *fumus* 'smoke'] □ **fumigant** *n.* **fumigation** *n.* **fumigator** *n.*

fun ● *n.* **1** amusement, esp. lively or playful. **2** a source of this. **3** (in full **fun and games**) exciting or amusing goings-on. ● *attrib.adj. disp. colloq.* amusing, enjoyable (*a fun thing to do*) □ **be great** (or **good**) **fun** be very amusing **for fun** (or **for the fun of it**) not for a serious purpose. **have fun** enjoy oneself. **in fun** as a joke, not seriously. **make fun of** mock; ridicule. **what fun!** how amusing! [from obsolete *fun*, variant of *fon* 'to make a fool of']

■ **Usage** The use of *fun* as an attributive adjective is common in informal use, but is considered incorrect by some people.

funboard *n.* ▼ a type of windsurfing board that is less stable but faster than a standard board.

function ● *n.* **1 a** an activity proper to a person or institution. **b** a mode of action or activity by which a thing fulfils its purpose. **c** an official or professional duty. **2 a** a public ceremony or occasion. **b** a social gathering, esp. a large, formal, or important one. **3** *Math.* a variable quantity regarded in relation to another or others in terms of which it may be expressed or on which its value depends (*x is a function of y and z*). ● *v.intr.* fulfil a function, operate; be in working order. [from Latin *functio*] □ **functionless** *adj.*

FUNBOARD

functional *adj.* **1** of or serving a function. **2** (esp. of buildings) designed or intended to be practical rather than attractive; utilitarian. **3** *Physiol.* **a** (esp. of disease) of or affecting only the functions of an organ etc., not structural or organic. **b** (of mental disorder) having no discernible organic cause. **c** (of an organ) having a function, not functionless or rudimentary. **4** *Math.* of a function. □ **functionality** *n.* **functionally** *adv.*

functional food *n.* a food containing health-giving additives.

functional group *n. Chem.* a group of atoms that determine the reactions of a compound containing the group.

functionalism *n.* belief in or stress on the practical application of a thing. □ **functionalist** *n.*

functionary *n.* (*pl.* **-ies**) a person who has to perform official functions or duties; an official.

function key *n. Computing* a key which is used to generate instructions.

fund ● *n.* **1** a permanent stock of something ready to be drawn upon (*a fund of knowledge; a fund of tenderness*). **2** a stock of money, esp. one set apart for a purpose. **3** (in *pl.*) money resources. ● *v.tr.* **1** provide with money. **2** convert (a debt repayable on demand or at a stated time) into a more or less permanent debt at fixed interest. □ **in funds** *Brit. colloq.* having money to spend. [from Latin *fundus* 'bottom, piece of land']

fundament *n. joc.* the buttocks. [from Latin *fundamentum*]

fundamental ● *adj.* of, affecting, or serving as a base or foundation, essential, primary (*a fundamental change; the fundamental form*). ● *n.* **1** (usu. in *pl.*) a fundamental principle. **2** *Mus.* a fundamental note. □ **fundamentally** *adv.*

fundamentalism *n.* **1** strict maintenance of traditional Protestant beliefs. **2** strict maintenance of ancient or fundamental doctrines of any religion. □ **fundamentalist** *n. & adj.*

fundamental note *n. Mus.* the lowest note of a chord.

fundamental particle *n.* a subatomic particle.

fundamental tone *n. Mus.* the tone produced by vibration of the whole of a sonorous body (opp. HARMONIC).

fundholder *n. Brit.* a GP who is provided with and controls his or her own budget. □ **fundholding** *n. & adj.*

fund-raiser *n.* a person who seeks financial support for a cause, enterprise, etc. □ **fund-raising** *n.*

funeral ● *n.* **1 a** the burial or cremation of a dead person with its ceremonies. **b** a burial or cremation procession. **2** *colloq.* one's (usu. unpleasant) concern (*that's your funeral*). ● *attrib.adj.* of or used etc. at a funeral (*funeral oration*). [from Latin *funus -eris*]

funeral director *n.* an undertaker.

funeral parlour *n.* (*N. Amer.* also **funeral home**) an establishment where the dead are prepared for burial or cremation.

funeral pile *n.* (also **funeral pyre**) a pile of wood etc. on which a corpse is burnt.

funerary *adj.* of or used at a funeral or funerals.

funereal *adj.* **1** of or appropriate to a funeral. **2** dismal, dark. □ **funereally** *adv.*

funfair *n. Brit.* a fair, or part of one, consisting of amusements and sideshows.

fungi *pl.* of FUNGUS.

fungicide *n.* a fungus-destroying substance. □ **fungicidal** *adj.*

fungoid ● *adj.* **1** resembling a fungus in texture or in rapid growth. **2** of a fungus or fungi. ● *n.* a fungoid plant.

fungous *adj.* **1** having the nature of a fungus. **2** springing up like a mushroom; transitory. [Middle English, from Latin *fungosus*]

F

fungus /fung-gŭs/ *n.* (*pl.* **fungi** /fung-gy/ or **funguses**) **1** ▶ any of a group of spore-producing organisms feeding on organic matter, including moulds, yeast, mushrooms, and toadstools. **2** anything similar usu. growing suddenly and rapidly. **3** *Med.* a spongy morbid growth. **4** *slang* a beard. [Latin] □ **fungal** *adj.* **fungiform** *adj.* **fungivorous** *adj.*

weight of descending car helps pull up ascending car

cable

FUNICULAR RAILWAY IN OPERATION

funicular /few-nik-yoo-ler/ ● *adj.* ◀ (of a railway, esp. on a mountainside) operating by cable with ascending and descending cars counterbalanced. ● *n.* a funicular railway. [based on Latin *funis* 'rope']

funk[1] *slang* ● *n.* **1** fear, panic. **2** *Brit.* a coward. ● *v. Brit.* **1** *intr.* flinch, shrink, show cowardice. **2** *tr.* try to evade (an undertaking), shirk. **3** *tr.* be afraid of. [18th-century Oxford slang]

funk[2] *n. slang* **1** funky music. **2** *US* a strong smell.

funky *adj.* (**funkier**, **funkiest**) *slang* **1** (esp. of jazz or rock music) earthy, bluesy, with a heavy rhythmical beat. **2** fashionable. **3** unconventional; striking. **4** *US* having a strong smell. □ **funkily** *adv.* **funkiness** *n.*

funnel ● *n.* **1** a tube or pipe widening at the top, for pouring liquid, powder, etc., into a small opening. **2** a metal chimney on a steam engine or ship. ● *v.tr. & intr.* (**funnelled**, **funnelling**; *US* **funneled**, **funneling**) guide or move through or as through a funnel. [based on Latin *infundere* 'to pour in'] □ **funnel-like** *adj.*

funny ● *adj.* (**funnier**, **funniest**) **1** amusing, comical. **2** strange, perplexing, hard to account for. **3** *colloq.* slightly unwell, eccentric, etc. ● *n.* (*pl.* **-ies**) (usu. in *pl.*) *colloq.* **1** a comic strip in a newspaper. **2** a joke. [related to FUN] □ **funnily** *adv.* **funniness** *n.*

funny bone *n.* the part of the elbow over which the ulnar nerve passes.

funny business *n.* **1** *slang* misbehaviour or deception. **2** comic behaviour, comedy.

fun run *n. colloq.* an uncompetitive run, esp. for sponsored runners in support of a charity.

fur ● *n.* **1 a** the short fine soft hair of certain animals, distinguished from the longer hair. **b** the skin of such an animal with the fur on it. **2 a** the coat of certain animals as material for making, trimming, or lining clothes. **b** a trimming or lining made of the dressed coat of such animals, or of material imitating this. **c** a garment made of or trimmed or lined with fur. **3** (*collect.*) furred animals. **4 a** a coating formed on the tongue in sickness. **b** *Brit.* a coating formed on the inside surface of a pipe, kettle, etc., by hard water. ● *v.* (**furred**, **furring**) **1** *tr.* (esp. as **furred** *adj.*) **a** line or trim with fur. **b** provide (an animal) with fur. **c** clothe (a person) with fur. **d** coat (a tongue, the inside of a kettle) with fur. **2** *intr. Brit.* (of a kettle etc.) become coated with fur. [from Old French *fuerre* 'sheath'] □ **furless** *adj.*

furbelow

FURBELOW ON AN EDWARDIAN PETTICOAT

furbelow ● *n.* **1** ◀ a gathered strip or pleated border of a skirt or petticoat. **2** (in *pl.*; esp. in phr. **frills and furbelows**) *derog.* showy ornaments. ● *v.tr* adorn with furbelows. [18th-century variant of *falbala* 'flounce, trimming']

furbish *v.tr.* **1** remove rust from, polish, burnish. **2** give a new look to, renovate, revive (something antiquated). [from Old French *forbir*]

furcate ● *adj.* forked, branched. ● *v.intr.* form a fork, divide. [based on Latin *furca* 'fork'] □ **furcation** *n.*

furious *adj.* **1** extremely angry. **2** full of fury. **3** raging, violent, intense. [from Latin *furiosus*] □ **furiously** *adv.*

furl *v.* **1** *tr.* roll up and secure (a sail, umbrella, flag, etc.). **2** *intr.* become furled. **3** *tr.* **a** close (a fan). **b** fold up (wings). [from Old French *fer(m)* 'firm' + *lier* 'to bind']

furlong *n.* an eighth of a mile, 220 yards. [Old English, from *furh lang* 'long furrow']

furlough /fer-loh/ ● *n.* leave of absence, esp. granted to a member of the services or to a missionary. ● *v. US* **1** *tr.* grant furlough to. **2** *intr.* spend furlough. [from Dutch *verlof*]

furnace *n.* **1** an enclosed structure for intense heating by fire. **2** a very hot place. [from Latin *fornax -acis*]

furnish *v.tr.* **1** provide (a house etc.) with all necessary contents, esp. movable furniture. **2** (foll. by *with*) cause to have possession or use of. **3** provide, afford, yield. [from Old French *furnir*]

furnished *adj.* (of a house etc.) let with furniture.

furnisher *n.* **1** a person who sells furniture. **2** a person who furnishes.

furnishings *n.pl.* the furniture and fitments in a house, room, etc.

furniture *n.* **1** the movable equipment of a house, room, etc., e.g. tables, beds. **2** *Naut.* a ship's equipment. **3** accessories, e.g. the handles and lock of a door. □ **part of the furniture** *colloq.* a person or thing taken for granted. [from French *fourniture*]

furniture beetle *n.* a beetle, *Anobium punctatum*, the larvae of which bore into wood (see WOODWORM).

furore /fewr-or-i/ *n.* (*US* **furor** /fewr-or/) **1** an uproar; an outbreak of fury. **2** a wave of enthusiastic admiration, a craze. [from Latin *furor*]

furrier /fu-ri-er/ *n.* a dealer in furs. [based on Old French *forrer* 'to trim with fur']

furrow ● *n.* **1** a narrow trench made by a plough. **2** a rut, groove, or deep wrinkle. **3** a ship's track. ● *v.* **1** *tr.* plough. **2** *tr.* **a** make furrows, grooves, etc. in. **b** mark with wrinkles. **3** *intr.* (esp. of the brow) become furrowed. [Old English]

furry *adj.* (**furrier**, **furriest**) like or covered with fur. □ **furriness** *n.*

fur seal *n.* ▼ any of several related seals with thick fur on the underside used commercially as sealskin.

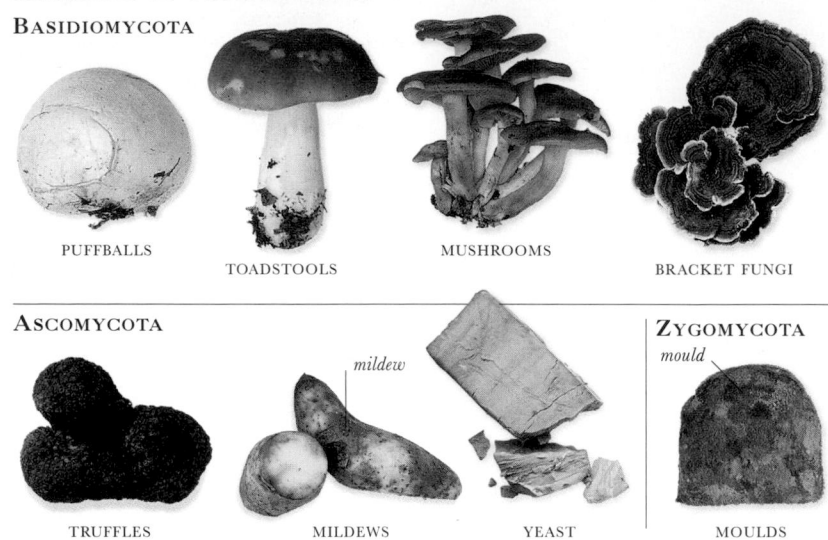

FUR SEAL: GALÁPAGOS FUR SEAL (*Arctocephalus galapagoensis*)

further ● *adv.* (also **farther**) **1** more distant in space or time (*unsafe to proceed further*). **2** at a greater distance (*nothing was further from his thoughts*). **3** to a greater extent, more (*will enquire further*). **4** in addition (*I may add further*). ● *adj.* (also **farther**) **1** more distant or advanced (*on the further side*). **2** more, additional (*threats of further punishment*). ● *v.tr.* promote, favour (a scheme etc.). □ **further to** *formal* following on from (esp. an earlier letter etc.). **till further notice** (or **orders**) to continue until explicitly changed. [Old English] □ **furthermost** *adj.*

■ **Usage** The form *farther* is used especially with reference to physical distance, although *further* is preferred by many people even in this sense.

FUNGUS

Neither plants nor animals, fungi form a separate kingdom. They absorb food from living or dead organic matter, and reproduce by spores. There are three main divisions. Basidiomycota, which includes mushrooms and toadstools, embraces species that form spores in microscopic structures called basidia. Ascomycota is a varied division of some 30,000 species, which form spores in microscopic structures called asci. Zygomycota includes mould-like fungi that live on decaying plant and animal matter.

EXAMPLES OF FUNGUS TYPES

BASIDIOMYCOTA

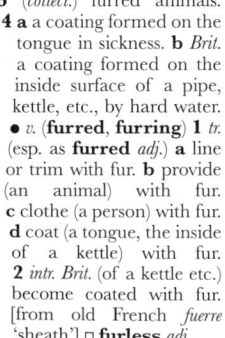

PUFFBALLS   TOADSTOOLS   MUSHROOMS   BRACKET FUNGI

ASCOMYCOTA   **ZYGOMYCOTA**

mildew   *mould*

TRUFFLES   MILDEWS   YEAST   MOULDS

furtherance *n.* furthering or being furthered; the advancement of a scheme etc.

further education *n.* *Brit.* education for persons above school age but usu. below degree level.

furthermore *adv.* in addition, besides.

furthest (also **farthest**) ● *adj.* most distant. ● *adv.* to or at the greatest distance. [Middle English]

■ **Usage** The form *farthest* is used especially with reference to physical distance, although *furthest* is preferred by many people even in this sense.

furtive *adj.* **1** done by stealth, clandestine, meant to escape notice. **2** sly, stealthy. **3** stolen, taken secretly. [from Latin *furtivus*] □ **furtively** *adv.* **furtiveness** *n.*

fury *n.* (*pl.* **-ies**) **1 a** wild and passionate anger. **b** a fit of rage (*in a blind fury*). **c** impetuosity in battle etc. **2** violence of a storm, disease, etc. **3** (**Fury**) (usu. in *pl.*) (in Greek mythology) each of usu. three goddesses sent from the underworld to avenge crime. **4** an avenging spirit. **5** an angry or malignant woman. □ **like fury** *colloq.* with great force or effect. [from Latin *furia*]

furze *n.* = GORSE. [Old English]

fuse[1] ● *v.* **1** *tr.* & *intr.* melt with intense heat. **2** *tr.* & *intr.* blend or amalgamate into one whole by or as by melting. **3** *tr.* provide (a circuit, plug, etc.) with a fuse. **4** *Brit.* **a** *intr.* (of an appliance) cease to function when a fuse blows. **b** *tr.* cause (an appliance) to do this. ● *n.* ◀ a device or component for protecting an electric circuit, containing a strip or wire of easily melted metal and placed in the circuit so as to break it by melting when an excessive current passes through. □ **blow a fuse** lose one's temper. [from Latin *fundere fus-* 'to melt']

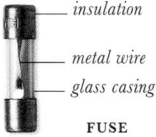

insulation

metal wire

glass casing

FUSE

fuse[2] (also **fuze**) ● *n.* **1** a device for igniting a bomb or explosive charge, consisting of a tube or cord etc. filled or saturated with combustible matter. **2** a component in a shell, mine, etc., designed to detonate an explosive charge. ● *v.tr.* fit a fuse to. [from Latin *fusus* 'spindle' (from the shape of the tube in sense 1)] □ **fuseless** *adj.*

fuse box *n.* a box housing the fuses for circuits in a building.

fuselage /few-zĕ-lah*zh*/ *n.* the body of an aeroplane. ▷ SPACECRAFT. [based on French *fuseler* 'to cut into a spindle']

fusible *adj.* that can be easily fused or melted.

fusil *n.* *hist.* a light musket. [based on Latin *focus* 'hearth, fire']

fusilier *n.* (*US* also **fusileer**) **1** a member of any of several British regiments formerly armed with fusils. **2** *Hist.* ▶ a soldier armed with a fusil. [French (as FUSIL)]

fusillade *n.* **1** a continuous discharge of firearms. **2** a sustained outburst of criticism etc. [French]

fusion *n.* **1** the act or an instance of fusing or melting. **2** a fused mass. **3** the blending of different things into one. **4** a coalition. **5** *Physics* = NUCLEAR FUSION.

fusion bomb *n.* a bomb involving nuclear fusion, esp. a hydrogen bomb.

fuss ● *n.* **1** excited commotion, bustle. **2 a** excessive concern about a trivial thing. **b** abundance of petty detail. **3** a sustained protest or dispute. **4** a person who fusses. ● *v.* **1** *intr.* **a** make a fuss. **b** busy oneself restlessly with trivial things. **c** move fussily. **2** *tr.* *Brit.* agitate, worry. □ **make a fuss** complain vigorously. **make a fuss over** (or *Brit.* **of**) treat (a person or animal) with great or excessive attention. [18th-century coinage] □ **fusser** *n.*

fusspot *n.* *colloq.* a person given to fussing.

fussy *adj.* (**fussier**, **fussiest**) **1** inclined to fuss. **2** full of unnecessary detail or decoration. **3** fastidious. □ **fussily** *adv.* **fussiness** *n.*

fustian *n.* **1** thick twilled cotton cloth with a short nap, usu. dyed in dark colours. **2** bombast. ● *adj.* **1** made of fustian. **2** bombastic. **3** worthless. [from medieval Latin *fustaneus* 'relating to cloth from Fostat', a suburb of Cairo]

fusty *adj.* (**fustier**, **fustiest**) **1** musty. **2** stuffy. **3** antiquated, old-fashioned. [from Old French *fusté* 'smelling of the cask'] □ **fustily** *adv.* **fustiness** *n.*

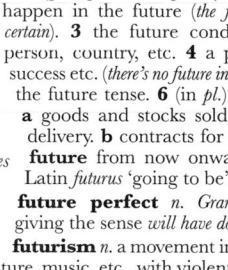

shako

cockade

bayonet

coat
(habit)

fusil
(flintlock
musket)

breeches

gaiter

FUSILIER:
FRENCH FUSILIER
(1807–12)

futile *adj.* **1** useless, ineffectual, vain. **2** frivolous, trifling. [from Latin *futilis*, related to *fundere* 'pour'] □ **futilely** *adv.* **futility** *n.*

futon /foo-ton/ *n.* **1** a Japanese quilted mattress used as a bed. **2** a type of low wooden sofa bed having such a mattress. [Japanese]

future ● *adj.* **1 a** going or expected to happen or be or become (*his future career*). **b** that will be something specified (*my future wife*). **c** that will be after death (*a future life*). **2 a** of time to come (*future years*). **b** *Gram.* (of a tense or participle) describing an event yet to happen. ● *n.* **1** time to come (*past, present, and future*). **2** what will happen in the future (*the future is uncertain*). **3** the future condition of a person, country, etc. **4** a prospect of success etc. (*there's no future in it*). **5** *Gram.* the future tense. **6** (in *pl.*) *Stock Exch.* **a** goods and stocks sold for future delivery. **b** contracts for these. □ **in future** from now onwards. [from Latin *futurus* 'going to be']

future perfect *n.* *Gram.* a tense giving the sense *will have done*.

futurism *n.* a movement in art, literature, music, etc., with violent departure from traditional forms so as to express movement and growth. □ **futurist** *n.*

futuristic *adj.* **1** suitable for the future; ultra-modern. **2** of futurism. **3** relating to the future. □ **futuristically** *adv.*

futurity *n.* (*pl.* **-ies**) **1** future time. **2** (in *sing.* or *pl.*) future events.

futurology *n.* systematic forecasting of the future. □ **futurological** *adj.* **futurologist** *n.*

fuze var. of FUSE[2].

fuzz ● *n.* **1** fluff. **2** fluffy or frizzled hair. **3** *slang* **a** the police. **b** a police officer. ● *v.tr.* & *intr.* make or become fluffy or blurred. [16th-century coinage]

fuzzy *adj.* (**fuzzier**, **fuzziest**) **1 a** like fuzz. **b** fluffy. **c** frizzy. **2** blurred, indistinct. **3** *Computing* & *Logic* (of a set) of which membership is determined imprecisely according to probability functions, of or relating to such sets (*fuzzy logic*). □ **fuzzily** *adv.* **fuzziness** *n.*

G

G

GALAXY

Galaxies are classed as spiral, irregular, or elliptical. Spiral galaxies vary in the size and structure of the central hub and spiral arms; of these, barred spiral galaxies – to which our galaxy, the Milky Way, may belong – have a central bar consisting of millions of stars, which rotate in unity. Spiral and irregular galaxies hold quantities of gas from which new stars are created. Elliptical galaxies contain old red stars and practically no gas.

MAIN TYPES OF GALAXY

SPIRAL GALAXY   BARRED SPIRAL GALAXY   IRREGULAR GALAXY   ELLIPTICAL GALAXY

G[1] *n.* (also **g**) (*pl.* **Gs** or **G's**) **1** the seventh letter of the alphabet. **2** *Mus.* the fifth note in the diatonic scale of C major. ▷ NOTATION

G[2] *abbr.* (also **G.**) *N. Amer. colloq.* = GRAND *n.* 2.

G[3] *symb.* **1** gauss. **2** giga-. **3** gravitational constant.

g[1] *abbr.* (also **g.**) gelding.

g[2] *symb.* **1** gram(s). **2** gravity.

G7 *attrib.adj.* relating to or designating a group of seven leading industrialized nations.

Ga *symb. Chem.* the element gallium.

gab *colloq.* ● *n.* talk, chatter. ● *v.intr.* (**gabbed**, **gabbing**) talk, chatter. □ **gift of the gab** the facility of speaking eloquently or profusely. [18th-century variant of GOB[1]]

gabardine *n.* (also **gaberdine**) **1** a smooth durable twill-woven cloth esp. of worsted or cotton. **2** *Brit.* a garment made of this, esp. a raincoat.

gabble ● *v.tr. & intr.* talk or utter too fast or unintelligibly. ● *n.* fast unintelligible talk. [from Middle Dutch *gabbelen*] □ **gabbler** *n.*

gabby *adj.* (**gabbier**, **gabbiest**) *colloq.* talkative.

gaberdine var. of GABARDINE. [from Old French *gauvardine*]

gable *n.* **1 a** the triangular upper part of a wall at the end of a ridged roof. ▷ HALF-TIMBERED, ROOF. **b** (in full **gable-end**) a gable-topped wall. **2** a gable-shaped canopy over a window or door. [from Old Norse *gafl*] □ **gabled** *adj.* (also in *comb.*).

gad *v.intr.* (**gadded**, **gadding**) (foll. by *about*, *abroad*, *around*) go about idly or in search of pleasure. [back-formation from obsolete *gadling* 'companion']

gadabout *n.* a person who gads about.

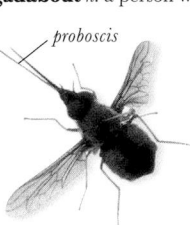

proboscis

gadfly *n.* (*pl.* **-flies**) **1** ◀ a cattle-biting fly, esp. a warble fly, horsefly, or botfly. **2** an irritating or harassing person. [based on obsolete *gad* 'goad, spike']

GADFLY: ORIENTAL HORSEFLY

gadget *n.* any small and usu. ingenious mechanical device or tool. [19th-century nautical coinage] □ **gadgeteer** *n.* **gadgetry** *n.* **gadgety** *adj.*

gadolinium *n. Chem.* a soft silvery metallic element of the lanthanide series. [modern Latin]

gadwall *n.* a brownish-grey freshwater duck, *Anas strepera*. [17th-century coinage]

gadzooks *int. archaic* an expression of asseveration etc. [alteration of *God* + *zooks* of unknown origin]

Gael /gayl/ *n.* **1** a Scottish Celt. **2** a Gaelic-speaking Celt. [from Gaelic *Gaidheal*]

Gaelic /gay-lik/ ● *n.* a Celtic language spoken in Ireland and Scotland. ● *adj.* of or relating to the Gaels or Gaelic.

gaff[1] *n.* **1 a** ▶ a stick with an iron hook for landing large fish. **b** a barbed fishing spear. **2** *Naut.* a spar to which the head of a fore-and-aft sail is bent. ▷ SCHOONER, SHIP. ● *v.tr.* seize (a fish) with a gaff. [from Provençal *gaf* 'hook']

gaff[2] *n. Brit. slang* □ **blow the gaff** let out a plot or secret. [19th-century coinage]

GAFF: TELESCOPIC GAFF (EXTENDED)

gaffe *n.* a blunder; an indiscreet act or remark. [French]

gaffer *n.* **1** an old fellow. **2** *Brit. colloq.* a foreman or boss. **3** *colloq.* the chief electrician in a film or television production unit.

gag ● *n.* **1** a piece of cloth etc. thrust into or held over the mouth, esp. to prevent speaking or crying out. **2** a joke, comic scene, or humorous action. **3** an actor's interpolation in a dramatic dialogue. **4** a thing or circumstance restricting free speech. **5** *Parl.* a closure or guillotine. ● *v.* (**gagged**, **gagging**) **1** *tr.* apply a gag to. **2** *tr.* deprive of free speech. **3 a** *intr.* choke or retch. **b** *tr.* cause to do this. **4** *intr. Theatr.* make gags. [Middle English]

gaga *adj. slang* **1** senile. **2** fatuous; slightly crazy. [French, literally 'senile']

gage[1] *n.* **1** a pledge; a thing deposited as security. **2** *archaic* **a** a challenge to fight. **b** a symbol of this, esp. a glove thrown down. [from French *gage*]

gage[2] *US* var. of GAUGE.

gaggle *n.* **1** a flock of geese. **2** *colloq.* a disorderly group of people. [Middle English]

Gaia /gy-ă/ *n.* the Earth viewed as a vast self-regulating organism (*Gaia hypothesis*; *Gaia theory*). [Greek, literally 'Earth'] □ **Gaian** *n. & adj.*

hook

gaiety *n.* **1** the state of being merry; mirth. **2** merrymaking. **3** a bright appearance. [from French *gaieté*]

gaillardia /gay-**lar**-diă/ *n.* ▶ any plant of the genus *Gaillardia* (daisy family), with showy flowers. [named after *Gaillard* de Marentonneau, 18th-century French botanist]

gaily *adv.* **1** in a gay or light-hearted manner. **2** with a bright or colourful appearance.

gain ● *v.* **1** *tr.* obtain or secure (usu. something desired or favourable) (*gain an advantage*). **2** *tr.* acquire (a sum) as profits; earn. **3** *tr.* obtain as an increment or addition (*gain momentum*; *gain weight*). **4** *intr.* (foll. by *in*) make a specified advance or improvement (*gained in stature*). **5** (of a clock etc.) **a** *intr.* have the fault of becoming fast. **b** *tr.* become fast by (a specific amount of time). **6** *intr.* (often foll. by *on*, *upon*) come closer to a person or thing pursued. **7** *tr.* **a** bring over to one's views. **b** (foll. by *over*) win by persuasion etc. **8** *tr.* reach or arrive at (a desired place). ● *n.* **1** something gained, achieved, etc. **2** an increase of possessions etc.; a profit, advance, or improvement. **3** the acquisition of wealth. **4** (in *pl.*) sums of money acquired by trade etc., winnings. **5** an increase in amount. □ **gain ground** see GROUND[1]. **gain time** improve one's chances by causing or accepting delay. [from Old French *gaigner* 'to till, acquire'] □ **gainer** *n.*

gainful *adj.* **1** (of employment) paid. **2** lucrative. □ **gainfully** *adv.* **gainfulness** *n.*

gainsay *v.tr.* (*past* and *past part.* **gainsaid**) *archaic* or *literary* deny, contradict. [Middle English, based on obsolete *gain-* 'against']

gait *n.* a manner of walking or forward motion. [from Old Norse]

gaiter *n.* ▶ a covering of cloth, leather, etc. for the leg below the knee, for the ankle, for part of a machine, etc. [from French *guêtre*] □ **gaitered** *adj.*

Gal. *abbr.* Galatians (New Testament).

gal *n. slang* a girl. [representing variant pronunciation]

GAILLARDIA
(*Gaillardia* × *grandiflora* 'Kobold')

MUD GAITER

GAITERS USED FOR LEG PROTECTION

SNOW GAITER

gal. *abbr.* gallon(s).

gala *n.* **1** (often *attrib.*) a festive or special occasion (*a gala performance*). **2** *Brit.* a festive gathering for sports, esp. swimming. [from Old French *gale* 'rejoicing']

galactose *n.* a simple sugar present in many polysaccharides.

galago /gă-**lay**-goh/ *n.* (*pl.* **-os**) = BUSHBABY. [modern Latin genus name]

galantine *n.* white meat or fish boned, cooked, pressed, and served cold in aspic etc. [alteration of Old French *galatine*]

galaxy *n.* (*pl.* **-ies**) **1** ▲ any of many independent systems of stars, dust, etc. held together by gravitational attraction. **2 a** (**the Galaxy**) the galaxy of which the solar system is a part. **b** = MILKY WAY. **3** (foll. by *of*) a brilliant gathering. [originally in sense 'the Milky Way': based on Greek *gala galaktos* 'milk'] □ **galactic** *adj.*

galbanum *n.* a bitter aromatic gum resin produced from kinds of ferula. [Middle English]

gale *n.* **1** a very strong wind. **2** a storm or an outburst, esp. of laughter. [16th-century coinage]

galena *n.* ◄ a bluish, grey or black mineral ore of lead sulphide. ▷ ORE. [Latin, literally 'lead at a certain stage of smelting']

galenic *adj.* (also **galenical**) **1** of or relating to Galen, a Greek physician of the 2nd c. AD, or his methods. **2** made of natural as opposed to synthetic components.

GALENA: CUBIC CRYSTALS

galia melon *n.* a small roundish variety of melon with rough skin and orange flesh.

Galilean¹ /gal-i-**lee**-an/ *adj.* of or relating to Galileo, Italian astronomer d. 1642, or his methods.

Galilean² /gal-i-**lee**-an/ ● *adj.* **1** of Galilee in Palestine. **2** Christian. ● *n.* **1** a native of Galilee. **2** a Christian. **3** (prec. by *the*) *derog.* Christ.

gall¹ *n.* **1** impudence. **2** rancour. **3** bitterness; anything bitter (*gall and wormwood*). **4** the bile of animals. **5** the gall bladder and its contents. [from Old Norse]

gall² ● *n.* **1** a sore on the skin made by chafing. **2 a** vexation. **b** a cause of this. **3** a place rubbed bare. ● *v.tr.* **1** rub sore. **2** vex, annoy. [Old English *gealla* 'sore on a horse'] □ **gallingly** *adv.*

gall³ *n.* **1** ▼ a growth produced by insects or fungus etc. on plants and trees, esp. on oak. **2** (*attrib.*) of insects producing galls (*gall-fly*). [from Latin *galla*]

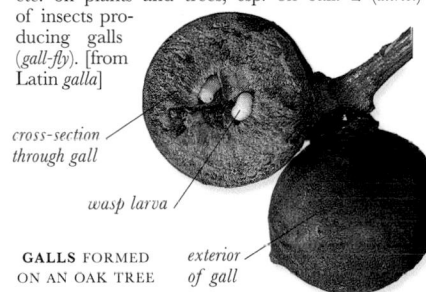

cross-section through gall

wasp larva

exterior of gall

GALLS FORMED ON AN OAK TREE

gall. *abbr.* gallon(s).

gallant ● *adj.* /**gal**-ănt/ **1** brave, chivalrous. **2 a** (of a ship, horse, etc.) grand, stately. **b** *archaic* finely dressed. **3** /gal-**ănt**, gă-**lant**/ **a** markedly attentive to women. **b** amatory. ● *n.* /**gal**-ănt, gă-**lant**/ **1** a ladies' man; a paramour. **2** *archaic* a man of fashion; a fine gentleman. [from Old French *galant* 'making merry'] □ **gallantly** *adv.* **gallantry** *n.*

gall bladder *n.* ▲ the vessel storing bile after its secretion by the liver and before release into the intestine. ▷ DIGESTION

galleon *n. hist.* **1** a ship of war (usu. Spanish). **2 a** large Spanish ship used in American trade. **3** a vessel shorter and higher than a galley. [from Spanish *galeón*]

galleria /gal-ĕ-**ree**-ă/ *n.* a collection of small shops under a single roof; an arcade. [Italian]

gallery *n.* (*pl.* **-ies**) **1** a room or building for showing works of art. **2** a balcony, esp. a platform projecting from the inner wall of a church etc. (*minstrels' gallery*). ▷ ROMANESQUE. **3 a** the highest balcony in a theatre. **b** its occupants. **4 a** a covered space for walking in, partly open at the side. **b** a long narrow passage in the thickness of a wall or supported on corbels, open towards the interior of the building. **5** a long narrow room, passage, or corridor. **6** *Mil. & Mining* a horizontal underground passage. **7** a group of spectators at a golf match etc. □ **play to the gallery** seek to win approval by appealing to popular taste. [from medieval Latin *galeria*] □ **galleried** *adj.*

galley *n.* (*pl.* **-eys**) **1** *hist.* **a** a low flat single-decked vessel using sails and oars, and usu. rowed by slaves or criminals. **b** an ancient Greek or Roman warship with one or more banks of oars. **c** a large open rowing boat, e.g. that used by the captain of a man-of-war. **2** a ship's or aircraft's kitchen. **3** (in full

GALL BLADDER

Together with the hepatic ducts and the bile ducts, the gall bladder forms part of the human biliary system. Bile, an alkaline fluid secreted by the liver, drains through the hepatic ducts to the gall bladder, where it is stored in concentrated form. When food is consumed, the gall bladder releases bile via the cystic duct and common bile duct to the stomach, where the bile aids digestion of fats.

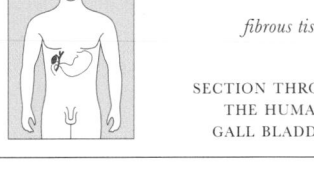

gall bladder

right and left hepatic ducts

common hepatic duct

cystic duct from gall bladder

muscle

mucous membrane

fibrous tissue

common bile duct

SECTION THROUGH THE HUMAN GALL BLADDER

galley proof) *Printing* a proof in the form of long single-column strips, not in sheets or pages. [from medieval Greek *galaia*]

galley slave *n.* **1** *hist.* a person condemned to row in a galley. **2** a drudge.

galliard *n. hist.* **1** a lively dance usu. in triple time for two persons. **2** the music for this. [earlier as *adj.*: from Old French *gaillard* 'valiant']

Gallic *adj.* **1** French or typically French. **2** of the Gauls. [from Latin *Gallicus*] □ **Gallicize** *v.tr. & intr.* (also **-ise**).

gallice /**gal**-i-si/ *adv.* in French. [Latin, literally 'in Gaulish']

Gallicism *n.* a French idiom, esp. one adopted in another language.

gallimaufry *n.* (*pl.* **-ies**) a heterogeneous mixture. [from French *galimafrée*]

gallinaceous *adj.* of or relating to the order Galliformes, which includes domestic poultry, pheasants, etc. [based on Latin *gallus* 'cock']

gallium *n. Chem.* a soft bluish-white metallic element occurring naturally in zinc blende, bauxite, and kaolin. [based on Latin *Gallia* 'France', named patriotically by its discoverer Lecoq de Boisbaudran, 1838–1912]

gallivant *v.intr. colloq.* **1** gad about. **2** flirt. [19th-century coinage]

Gallo- *comb. form* **1** French; French and. **2** Gallic; Gallic and (*Gallo-Roman*).

gallon *n.* **1 a** *Brit.* a measure of capacity equal to eight pints and equivalent to 4.55 litres, used for liquids and corn etc. **b** *US* a measure of capacity equivalent to 3.79 litres, used for liquids. **2** (usu. in *pl.*) *colloq.* a large amount. [based on medieval Latin *galléta*, a measure for wine] □ **gallonage** *n.*

gallop ● *n.* **1** the fastest pace of a horse or other quadruped, with all the feet off the ground together in each stride. **2** a ride at this pace. **3** *Brit.* a track or ground for this. ● *v.* (**galloped, galloping**) **1 a** *intr.* (of a horse etc. or its rider) go at the pace of a gallop. **b** *tr.* make (a horse etc.) gallop. **2** *intr.* (foll. by *through, over*) read, recite, or talk at great speed. **3** *intr.* progress rapidly (*galloping inflation*). [from Old French *galop*] □ **galloper** *n.*

gallows *n.pl.* (usu. treated as *sing.*) **1** a structure, usu. of two uprights and a crosspiece, for the hanging of criminals. **2** (prec. by *the*) execution by hanging. [Old English]

gallows humour *n.* grim and ironical humour.

gallstone *n.* a small hard mass formed in the gall bladder or bile ducts.

Gallup poll *n.* an assessment of public opinion by questioning a representative sample. [named after G. H. *Gallup*, American statistician, 1901–84]

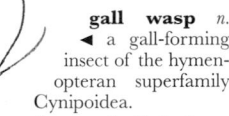

gall wasp *n.* ◄ a gall-forming insect of the hymenopteran superfamily Cynipoidea.

GALL WASP: MARBLE GALL WASP (*Andricus kollari*)

galop ● *n.* **1** a lively dance in duple time. **2** the music for this. ● *v.intr.* (**galoped, galoping**) perform this dance. [French]

galore *adv.* in abundance (placed after noun: *flowers galore*). [from Irish *go leór* 'to sufficiency']

galosh *n.* (usu. in *pl.*) a waterproof overshoe, usu. of rubber. [from Late Latin *gallicula* 'small Gallic shoe']

galumph *v.intr. colloq.* **1** move noisily or clumsily. **2** go prancing in triumph. [sense 2: coined by Lewis Carroll]

galvanic *adj.* **1 a** sudden and remarkable (*a galvanic effect*). **b** stimulating; full of energy. **2** involving electricity produced by chemical action. □ **galvanically** *adv.*

galvanize *v.tr.* (also **-ise**) **1** (often foll. by *into*) rouse forcefully, esp. by shock or excitement (*was galvanized into action*). **2** stimulate by or as if by electricity. **3** coat (iron) with zinc (usu. without the use of electricity) as a protection against rust. [from L. *Galvani*, Italian physiologist, 1737–98] □ **galvanization** *n.* **galvanizer** *n.*

galvanometer *n.* ▼ an instrument for detecting and measuring small electric currents. □ **galvanometric** *adj.*

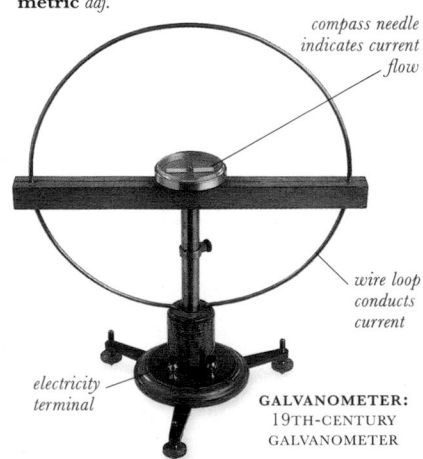

compass needle indicates current flow

wire loop conducts current

electricity terminal

GALVANOMETER: 19TH-CENTURY GALVANOMETER

G

G

gambit n. **1** a chess opening in which a player sacrifices a piece or pawn to secure an advantage. **2** an opening move in a discussion etc. **3** a trick or device. [from Italian *gambetto* 'tripping up']

gamble ● v. **1** intr. play games of chance for money. **2** tr. **a** bet (a sum of money) in gambling. **b** (often foll. by *away*) lose (assets) by gambling. **3** intr. take great risks in the hope of substantial gain. **4** intr. (foll. by *on*) act in the hope of (*gambled on fine weather*). ● n. **1** a risky undertaking or attempt. **2** a spell or an act of gambling. [from obsolete *gamel* 'to sport'] □ **gambler** n.

gamboge /gam-**boh**zh/ n. ▶ a gum resin used as a yellow pigment and as a purgative. [from modern Latin *gambaugium*, based on *Cambodia* (now Kampuchea)]

GAMBOGE: ARTISTS' PIGMENT

gambol ● v.intr. (**gambolled**, **gambolling**; US **gamboled**, **gamboling**) skip or frolic playfully. ● n. a playful frolic. [from Spanish *gambado*]

game¹ ● n. **1** a form or spell of play or sport, esp. a competitive one played according to rules. **2** a single portion of play forming a scoring unit in some contests. **3** (in *pl.*) **a** Brit. athletics or sports as organized in a school etc. **b** a meeting for athletic etc. contests (*Olympic Games*). **4** a winning score in a game; the state of the score in a game. **5** the equipment for a game. **6** one's level of achievement in a game, as specified (*played a good game*). **7 a** a piece of fun (*was only playing a game with you*). **b** (in *pl.*) tricks (*none of your games!*). **8** a scheme etc. regarded as a game (*so that's your game*). **9** a policy or line of action. **10** (*collect.*) **a** wild animals or birds hunted for sport or food. **b** the flesh of these. **11** a hunted animal; a quarry or object of pursuit or attack. ● adj. **1** spirited; eager and willing. **2** (foll. by *for*, or *to* + infin.) having the spirit or energy. ● v.intr. play at games of chance for money; gamble. □ **the game is up** the scheme is revealed. **off** (or **on**) **one's game** playing badly (or well). **on the game** Brit. slang involved in prostitution or thieving. **play the game** behave fairly. [Old English] □ **gamely** adv. **gameness** n. **gamester** n.

game² adj. (of a leg, arm, etc.) lame, crippled. [18th-century word]

game bird n. a bird shot for sport or food.

gamekeeper n. a person employed to breed and protect game. □ **gamekeeping** n.

gamelan /gam-ĕ-lan/ n. ▼ a type of orchestra found in Java and Bali, with a wide range of bronze percussion instruments. [native name in Java]

gong-chime

GAMELAN: GONG-CHIMES USED IN AN INDONESIAN GAMELAN ORCHESTRA

game of chance n. a game decided by luck, not skill.

game plan n. **1** a winning strategy worked out in advance for a particular match. **2** a plan of campaign, esp. in politics.

game point n. Tennis etc. a point which, if won, would win the game.

gamer n. a person who plays a game or games.

gamesmanship n. the art or practice of winning games or other contests by gaining a psychological advantage over an opponent.

gamete n. Biol. a mature germ cell able to unite with another in sexual reproduction. [from Greek *gametē* 'wife'] □ **gametic** adj.

game theory n. (also **games theory**) the mathematical analysis of competitive strategies where choices depend on the actions of others.

gameto- /gă-mee-toh/ comb. form Biol. gamete.

gametogenesis n. Biol. the process by which cells undergo meiosis to form gametes. ▷ MEIOSIS

gametophyte n. the gamete-producing form of a plant that has alternation of generations between this and the asexual form (sporophyte). ▷ BRYOPHYTE. □ **gametophytic** adj.

game warden n. an official locally supervising game and hunting.

gamin /gam-in/ n. **1** a street urchin. **2** an impudent child. [French]

gamine /gam-een/ n. **1** a girl gamin. **2** a girl with mischievous or boyish charm. [French]

gaming house n. a place frequented for gambling.

gaming table n. a table used for gambling.

gamma n. **1** the third letter of the Greek alphabet (Γ, γ). **2** Brit. a third-class mark given for a piece of work or in an examination. **3** the third member of a series. [from Greek]

gamma globulin n. a mixture of blood plasma proteins, mainly immunoglobulins, of relatively low electrophoretic mobility, often given to boost immunity.

gamma radiation n. (also **gamma rays**) electromagnetic radiation of very short wavelength.

gammon ● n. **1** the bottom piece of a flitch of bacon including a hind leg. **2** the ham of a pig cured like bacon. ● v.tr. cure (bacon). [from Old Northern French *gambon*]

gammy adj. (**gammier**, **gammiest**) Brit. colloq. (esp. of a leg) lame; permanently injured. [dialect form of GAME²]

gamut n. **1** the whole range or scope of anything (*the whole gamut of crime*). **2** Mus. **a** the whole series of notes used in medieval or modern music. **b** a major diatonic scale. □ **run the gamut of** experience or perform the complete range of. [from medieval Latin *gamma* + *ut*, arbitrarily named notes]

gamy adj. (**gamier**, **gamiest**) **1** having the flavour or scent of game kept till it is high. **2** N. Amer. scandalous, sensational. **3** = GAME¹ adj. □ **gamily** adv. **gaminess** n.

gander n. **1** a male goose. **2** slang a look, a glance (*take a gander*). [Old English]

gang¹ n. **1 a** a band of persons acting or going about together. **b** colloq. such a band pursuing a purpose causing disapproval. **2** a set of workers, slaves, or prisoners. □ **gang up** colloq. **1** (often foll. by *with*) act in concert. **2** (foll. by *on*) combine against. [from Old Norse *gangr* 'going']

gang² v.intr. Sc. go. [Old English]

gang-bang n. slang an occasion on which several men successively have sexual intercourse with one woman.

ganger n. Brit. the foreman of a gang of workers, esp. navvies.

gangland n. the world of gangs and gangsters.

gangle v.intr. move ungracefully. [back-formation from GANGLING]

gangling adj. (of a person) loosely built; lanky. [literally 'going about', related to GANG²]

ganglion n. (*pl.* **ganglia** or **ganglions**) **1 a** an enlargement or knot on a nerve etc. containing an assemblage of nerve cells. **b** a mass of grey matter in the central nervous system forming a nerve-nucleus. ▷ NERVOUS SYSTEM. **2** Med. a cyst, esp. on a tendon sheath. [from Greek *gagglion*] □ **ganglionated** adj. **ganglionic** adj.

gangly adj. (**ganglier**, **gangliest**) = GANGLING.

gangplank n. a movable plank for boarding or disembarking from a ship etc.

gang rape n. the successive rape of a person by a group of people.

gangrene Med. ● n. death of a part of the body tissue, usually resulting from obstructed circulation. ● v.tr. & intr. affect or become affected with gangrene. [from Greek *gaggraina*] □ **gangrenous** adj.

gangster n. a member of a gang of violent criminals. □ **gangsterism** n.

gangue /gang/ n. valueless earth etc. in which ore is found. [from German *Gang* 'course, lode']

gangway ● n. **1** Brit. a passage, esp. between rows of seats. **2 a** an opening in a ship's bulwarks. **b** a bridge laid from ship to shore. **c** a passage on a ship. **3** a temporary bridge on a building site etc. ● int. make way!

ganja n. the flowering tops of Indian hemp used as a narcotic. [from Hindi *gānjhā*]

gannet n. **1** a large seabird of the genus *Sula*, which catches fish by plunge-diving. ▷ SEABIRD. **2** Brit. colloq. a greedy person. [Old English] □ **gannetry** n. (*pl.* **-ies**).

gantry n. (*pl.* **-ies**) **1** an overhead structure supporting a travelling crane or railway or road signals. ▷ FACTORY SHIP. **2** a structure supporting a space rocket prior to launching.

gaol Brit. var. of JAIL.

gaoler Brit. var. of JAILER.

gap n. **1** an unfilled space or interval; a blank; a break in continuity. **2** a wide (usu. undesirable) divergence in views etc. (*generation gap*). **3** a gorge or pass. [from Old Norse, related to GAPE] □ **gappy** adj.

gape ● v.intr. **1 a** open one's mouth wide, esp. in amazement or wonder. **b** be or become wide open. **2** (foll. by *at*) gaze curiously or wondrously. **3** split. ● n. **1** an open-mouthed stare. **2** a rent or opening. [from Old Norse *gapa*] □ **gapingly** adv.

gap-toothed adj. having gaps between the teeth.

garage ● n. **1** a building or shed for housing a motor vehicle or vehicles. **2** an establishment which sells petrol etc., or repairs and sells motor vehicles, or both. ● v.tr. put or keep (a motor vehicle) in a garage. [French, literally 'sheltering']

garage sale n. esp. N. Amer. a sale of miscellaneous household goods, usu. for charity, held in the garage of a private house.

garam masala /gurăm mă-sah-lă/ n. ▶ a spice mixture used in Indian cookery. [from Urdu *garam maṣālah*]

GARAM MASALA

garb ● n. **1** clothing, esp. of a distinctive kind. **2** the way a person is dressed. ● v.tr. (usu. in passive or refl.) put (esp. distinctive) clothes on (a person). [from Italian *garbo*]

garbage n. **1** refuse. **2** foul or rubbishy literature etc. **3 a** nonsense. **b** Computing incorrect or useless data (*garbage in, garbage out*). [from Anglo-French]

garble v.tr. **1** unintentionally distort or confuse (messages etc.). **2 a** mutilate in order to misrepresent. **b** make (usu. unfair or malicious) selections from (statements etc.). [from Arabic *garbala* 'to sift'] □ **garbler** n.

Garda n. **1** the state police force of the Irish Republic. **2** (also **garda**) (*pl.* **-dai** /-dee/) a member of this. [Irish *Garda Síochána* 'Civic Guard']

garden ● n. **1** esp. Brit. a piece of ground, usu. adjoining a private house, used for growing flowers etc. and as a place of recreation. **2** (esp. in *pl.*) ornamental grounds laid out for public enjoyment. **3** (*attrib.*) **a** (of plants) cultivated, not wild. **b** for use in a garden (*garden seat*). **4** (usu. in *pl.* prec. by a name) Brit. a street, square, etc. (*Onslow Gardens*). **5** an especially fertile region. **6** US a large public hall. ● v.intr. cultivate or work in a garden. [from Old French *jardin*] □ **gardener** n. **gardening** n.

garden centre *n.* an establishment where plants and garden equipment etc. are sold.

garden city *n.* an industrial or other town laid out systematically with spacious surroundings, parks, etc.

gardenia *n.* ▶ any tree or shrub of the genus *Gardenia*, with large white or yellow flowers and usu. a fragrant scent. [named after Dr A. *Garden*, Scots naturalist, 1730–91]

GARDENIA
(*Gardenia augusta* 'Veitchii')

gardening leave *Brit. euphem.* suspension of an employee on full pay, usu. to prevent his or her re-employment by a competitor before the contractual period of notice has been served.

garden party *n.* a social event held on a lawn or in a garden.

garden suburb *n. Brit.* a suburb laid out spaciously with open spaces, parks, etc.

garfish *n.* (*pl.* usu. same) **1** any mainly marine fish of the family Belonidae, having long beaklike jaws. **2** *US* ▼ any similar freshwater fish of the genus *Lepisosteus*. **3** *NZ* & *Austral.* either of two marine fish of the genus *Hemiramphus*.

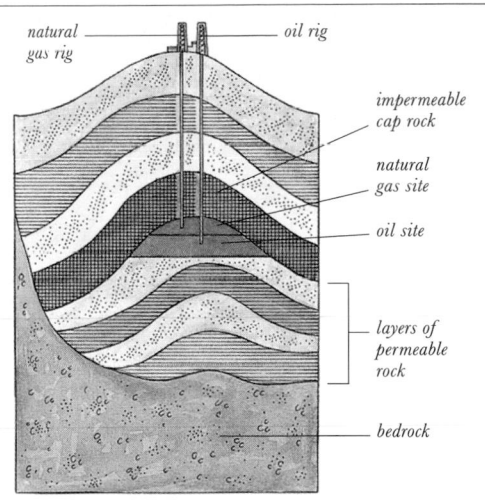

GAS FIELD

Natural gas (largely methane) and oil are normally found together. Both derive from microscopic marine organisms buried in layers of sediment and broken down over millions of years. Less dense than water, the two fuels may rise through permeable rocks to collect beneath a stratum of cap rock, often in folds created by movements in the Earth's crust. The site of natural gas and oil can thus be accurately predicted by studying rock formations.

CROSS-SECTION SHOWING
THE GEOLOGICAL
FORMATION OF A GAS FIELD

natural gas rig — *oil rig* — *impermeable cap rock* — *natural gas site* — *oil site* — *layers of permeable rock* — *bedrock*

G

GARFISH: GARPIKE
(*Lepisosteus osseus*)

garganey /gar-gă-nı/ *n.* (*pl.* **-eys**) a small duck, *Anas querquedula*, the drake of which has a white stripe from eye to neck. [from Italian dialect *garganei*]

gargantuan *adj.* enormous, gigantic. [from the name of a giant in Rabelais' book *Gargantua* (1534)]

gargle ● *v.* **1** *tr.* (also *absol.*) wash (one's mouth and throat) with a liquid kept in motion by breathing through it. **2** *intr.* make a sound as when doing this. ● *n.* a liquid used for gargling [based on French *gargouille* 'throat']

gargoyle *n.* ▶ a grotesque carved human or animal face or figure projecting from the gutter of a building as a spout. ▷ CHURCH. [from Old French *gargouille* 'throat, gargoyle']

garibaldi *n.* (*pl.* **garibaldis**) **1** *hist.* a kind of loose blouse worn by women and children. **2** *Brit.* a biscuit containing a layer of currants. [named after G. *Garibaldi*, Italian patriot, 1807–82]

spout

GARGOYLE: REPLICA OF A GOTHIC-STYLE GARGOYLE

garish /gair-ish/ *adj.* **1** obtrusively bright; showy. **2** gaudy; over-decorated. [16th-century coinage] □ **garishly** *adv.* **garishness** *n.*

garland ● *n.* **1** a wreath of flowers, leaves, etc., worn on the head or hung as a decoration. **2** a prize or distinction. ● *v.tr.* **1** adorn with garlands. **2** crown with a garland. [from Old French *garlande*]

garlic *n.* **1** ◀ any of various alliums, esp. *Allium sativum*. **2** the strong-smelling pungent-tasting bulb of this plant, used as a flavouring in cookery.

garlic bulb

GARLIC
(*Allium sativum*)

[Old English, from *gār* 'spear' + *lēac* 'leek'] □ **garlicky** *adj.*

garment *n.* **1 a** an article of dress. **b** (in *pl.*) clothes. **2** the outward and visible covering of anything. [from Old French *garnement*]

garner ● *v.tr.* **1** collect. **2** store, deposit. ● *n. literary* a storehouse or granary. [from Latin *granarium* 'granary']

garnet *n.* ▶ a vitreous silicate mineral, esp. a transparent deep red kind used as a gem. [from medieval Latin *granatum* 'pomegranate', from its resemblance to the fruit's pulp]

garnish ● *v.tr.* decorate or embellish (esp. food). ● *n.* (also **garnishing**) a decoration or embellishment, esp. to food. [earlier in sense 'to equip or arm': from Old French *garnir*]

garniture *n.* **1** decoration or trimmings, esp. of food. **2** accessories, appurtenances. [French, related to GARNISH]

garotte var. of GARROTTE.

garret *n.* **1** a top-floor or attic room, esp. a dismal one. **2** an attic. [from Old French *garite* 'watchtower']

garrison ● *n.* **1** the troops stationed in a fortress etc. to defend it. **2** the building occupied by them. ● *v.tr.* **1** provide (a place) with or occupy as a garrison. **2** place on garrison duty. [based on Old French *garir* 'to defend, furnish']

garrotte (also **garotte**; *US* **garrote**) ● *v.tr.* execute or kill by strangulation, esp. with a length of wire etc. ● *n. hist.* **1** a Spanish method of execution by garrotting. **2** the apparatus used for this. [from French *garrotter*]

garrulous *adj.* talkative, loquacious. [based on Latin *garrire* 'to chatter'] □ **garrulity** *n.* **garrulously** *adv.* **garrulousness** *n.*

garter ● *n.* **1** a band worn to keep a sock or stocking up. **2** *N. Amer.* a suspender for a sock or stocking. ● *v.tr.* fasten (a stocking) or encircle (a leg) with a garter. [based on Old French *garet* 'bend of the knee']

garter snake *n.* ▶ any water snake of the genus *Thamnophis*, native to N. America, having lengthwise stripes.

garter stitch *n.* a plain knitting stitch or pattern, forming ridges in alternate rows. ▷ KNITTING

GARTER SNAKE
(*Thamnophis* species)

garth *n. Brit.* an open space within cloisters. [from Old Norse *garthr*]

gas ● *n.* (*pl.* **gases** or, esp. *US*, **gasses**) **1** any airlike substance which moves freely to fill any space available, irrespective of its quantity. ▷ MATTER. **2** such a substance used as a domestic or industrial fuel (also *attrib.*: *gas cooker*). **3** nitrous oxide or another gas used as an anaesthetic (esp. in dentistry). **4** a gas or vapour used in warfare. **5** *N. Amer. colloq.* petrol. **6** *slang* pointless idle talk. **7** *slang* an amusing thing or person. ● *v.* (**gases, gassed, gassing**) **1** *tr.* expose to gas, esp. to kill or make unconscious. **2** *intr.* give off gas. **3** *tr.* (usu. foll. by *up*) *N. Amer. colloq.* fill the tank of (a motor vehicle) with petrol. **4** *intr. colloq.* talk idly or boastfully. [word invented by J. B. van Helmont, Belgian chemist, 1577–1644] □ **gaseous** *adj.* **gaseousness** *n.*

gasbag *n.* **1** a container of gas for a balloon or airship. **2** *slang* an idle talker.

gas chamber *n.* an airtight chamber that can be filled with poisonous gas to kill people or animals.

gas-cooled *adj.* (of a nuclear reactor etc.) cooled by a current of gas.

gas field *n.* ▲ an area yielding natural gas.

gas fire *n.* a domestic fire using gas as its fuel.

gas-fired *adj.* (of a power station etc.) using gas as its fuel.

gash ● *n.* **1** a long and deep slash, cut, or wound. **2 a** a cleft such as might be made by a slashing cut. **b** the act of making such a cut. ● *v.tr.* make a gash in. [from Old French *garcer* 'to scarify']

gasholder *n.* a large receptacle for storing gas; a gasometer.

gasify *v.tr.* & *intr.* (**-ies, -ied**) convert or be converted into gas. □ **gasification** *n.*

gasket *n.* **1** a sheet or ring of rubber etc. shaped to seal the junction of metal surfaces. **2** *Naut.* a small cord securing a furled sail to a yard. □ **blow a gasket** *slang* lose one's temper. [perhaps from French *garcette* 'thin rope']

gaskin *n.* the hinder part of a horse's thigh. ▷ HORSE

gaslight *n.* **1** a jet of burning gas, usu. heating a mantle, to provide light. **2** light emanating from this. □ **gaslit** *adj.*

GARNET

G

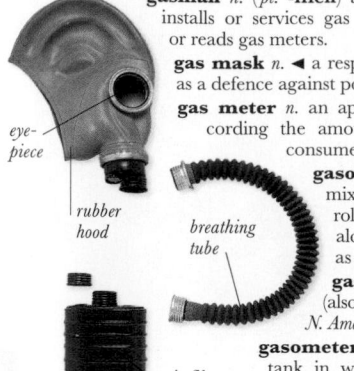

GAS MASK
(*c.*1990)

gasman *n.* (*pl.* **-men**) a man who installs or services gas appliances, or reads gas meters.

gas mask *n.* ◀ a respirator used as a defence against poison gas.

gas meter *n.* an apparatus recording the amount of gas consumed.

gasohol *n.* a mixture of petrol and ethyl alcohol used as fuel.

gasoline *n.* (also **gasolene**) *N. Amer.* petrol.

gasometer *n.* a large tank in which gas is stored for distribution by pipes to users.

gasp ● *v.* **1** *intr.* catch one's breath with an open mouth as in exhaustion or astonishment. **2** *intr.* (foll. by *for*) strain to obtain by gasping (*gasped for air*). **3** *tr.* (often foll. by *out*) utter with gasps. ● *n.* a convulsive catching of breath. [from Old Norse *geispa* 'to yawn']

gas-permeable *adj.* (esp. of a contact lens) allowing the diffusion of gases into and out of the cornea.

gas ring *n.* a hollow ring perforated with gas jets, used esp. for cooking.

gas station *n. N. Amer.* a filling station.

gassy *adj.* (**gassier**, **gassiest**) **1 a** of or like gas. **b** full of gas. **2** *colloq.* (of talk etc.) pointless, verbose. □ **gassiness** *n.*

gastrectomy *n.* (*pl.* **-ies**) a surgical operation in which all or part of the stomach is removed.

gastric *adj.* of the stomach. [based on Greek *gastēr* 'stomach']

gastric flu *n.* a popular name for an intestinal disorder of unknown cause.

gastric juice *n.* a thin clear virtually colourless acid fluid secreted by the stomach glands and active in promoting digestion.

gastritis *n.* inflammation of the lining of the stomach.

gastroenteric *adj.* of or relating to the stomach and intestines.

gastroenteritis *n.* inflammation of the stomach and intestines.

gastroenterology *n.* the branch of medicine which deals with disorders of the stomach and intestines. □ **gastroenterological** *adj.* **gastroenterologist** *n.*

gastrointestinal *adj.* of or relating to the stomach and the intestines.

gastronome *n.* a gourmet.

gastronomy *n.* the practice, study, or art of eating and drinking well. [from Greek *gastronomia*] □ **gastronomic** *adj.* **gastronomical** *adj.* **gastronomically** *adv.*

gastropod *n.* ▼ any mollusc of the class Gastropoda, most often moving by means of a large muscular foot, e.g. a snail, slug, whelk, etc. [from French *gastéropode*]

gastroscope *n.* an optical instrument used for inspecting the interior of the stomach.

gas turbine *n.* a turbine driven by a flow of gas or by gas from combustion.

gasworks *n. pl.* a place where gas is manufactured and processed.

gate ● *n.* **1** a barrier, usu. hinged, used to close an opening made for entrance and exit through a wall, fence, etc. **2** such an opening. **3** a means of entrance or exit. **4** a numbered place of access to aircraft at an airport. **5 a** an electrical signal that causes or controls the passage of other signals. **b** an electrical circuit with an output that depends on the combination of several inputs. **6** a device holding back water in a lock etc. **7 a** the number of people entering by payment at the gates of a sports ground etc. **b** (in full **gate money**) the proceeds taken for admission. **8** = STARTING GATE. ● *v.tr.* **1** *Brit.* confine to college or school as a punishment. **2** (as **gated** *adj.*) (of a road) having a gate or gates to control the movement of traffic or animals. [Old English]

-gate *comb. form* forming nouns denoting a scandal comparable in some way to the Watergate scandal of 1972 (*Irangate*).

gateau /gat-oh/ *n.* (*pl.* **gateaus** or **gateaux** /-tohz/) esp. *Brit.* a rich cake, usu. containing cream or fruit. [from French *gâteau* 'cake']

gatecrasher *n.* an uninvited guest at a party etc. □ **gatecrash** *v.tr. & intr.*

gatefold *n.* a page in a book or magazine etc. that folds out to be larger than the page-format.

gatehouse *n.* **1** a house standing by a gateway, esp. to a large house or park. ▷ MONASTERY. **2** *hist.* a room over a city gate, often used as a prison.

gateleg *n.* (in full **gateleg table**) a table with folding flaps supported by legs swung open like gates. □ **gatelegged** *adj.*

gate money see GATE[1] *n.* 7b.

gatepost *n.* a post on which a gate is hung or against which it shuts.

gate valve *n.* a valve in which a sliding part controls the extent of the aperture.

gateway *n.* **1** an entrance with or opening for a gate. **2** a frame or structure built over a gate. **3** a means of access or entry (*gateway to Scotland*; *gateway to success*). **4** *Computing* a device used to connect two different networks.

gather ● *v.* **1** *tr. & intr.* bring or come together; assemble. **2** *tr.* (usu. foll. by *up*) **a** bring together from scattered places or sources. **b** take up together from the ground etc. **c** draw into a smaller compass. **3** *tr.* acquire by gradually collecting. **4** *tr.* **a** pick a quantity of (flowers etc.). **b** collect (grain etc.) as a harvest. **5** *tr.* (often foll. by *that* + clause) infer or understand. **6** *tr.* be subjected to or affected by the accumulation or increase of (*unread books gathering dust*; *gather speed*). **7** *tr.* (often foll. by *up*) summon up (one's thoughts, energy, etc.) for a purpose. **8** *tr.* gain or recover (one's breath). **9** *tr.* **a** draw (material, or one's brow) together in folds or wrinkles. **b** pucker or draw together (fabric, a garment, etc.) by running a thread through. **10** *intr.* come to a head; develop a purulent swelling. ● *n.* (in *pl.*) a part of a garment that is gathered or drawn in. □ **gather way** (of a ship) begin to move. [Old English] □ **gatherer** *n.*

gathering *n.* **1** an assembly or meeting. **2** a purulent swelling. **3** a group of leaves taken together in bookbinding.

gauche /gohsh/ *adj.* **1** lacking ease or grace; socially awkward. **2** tactless. [French, 'left-handed, awkward'] □ **gauchely** *adv.* **gaucheness** *n.*

gaucherie /goh-shĕ-ri/ *n.* **1** gauche manners. **2** a gauche action.

gaucho /gow-choh/ *n.* (*pl.* **-os**) ▼ a cowboy from the S. American pampas. [Latin American Spanish]

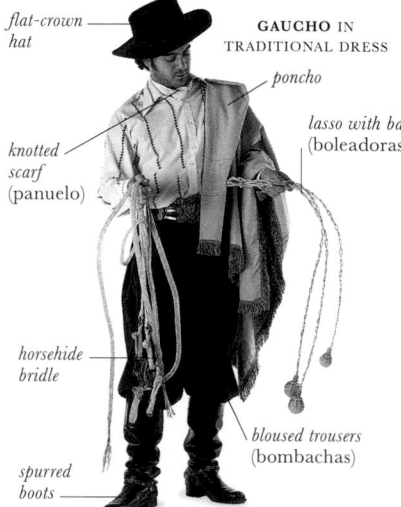

GAUCHO IN TRADITIONAL DRESS

flat-crown hat

poncho

knotted scarf (panuelo)

lasso with balls (boleadoras)

horsehide bridle

bloused trousers (bombachas)

spurred boots

gaud *n.* a gaudy thing; a showy ornament.

gaudy[1] *adj.* (**gaudier**, **gaudiest**) tastelessly showy. □ **gaudily** *adv.* **gaudiness** *n.*

gaudy[2] *n.* (*pl.* **-ies**) *Brit.* an annual feast or entertainment, esp. a college dinner for old members etc. [from Latin *gaudium* 'joy' or *gaude* 'rejoice!']

gauge /gayj/ (*US* also **gage**: see also sense 6) ● *n.* **1** a standard measure, esp.: **a** the capacity of a barrel. **b** the fineness of a textile. **c** the diameter of a bullet. **d** the thickness of sheet metal. **2** any of various measuring instruments. **3** the distance between rails or opposite wheels. **4** the capacity,

---

GASTROPOD

All gastropods, whether marine or land-dwelling, move on a single flat, muscular foot and are equipped with tentacles and a radula – a rasping, tongue-like organ. Marine gastropods respire through gills, while many freshwater and land gastropods have lungs. Most are cased within a protective shell.

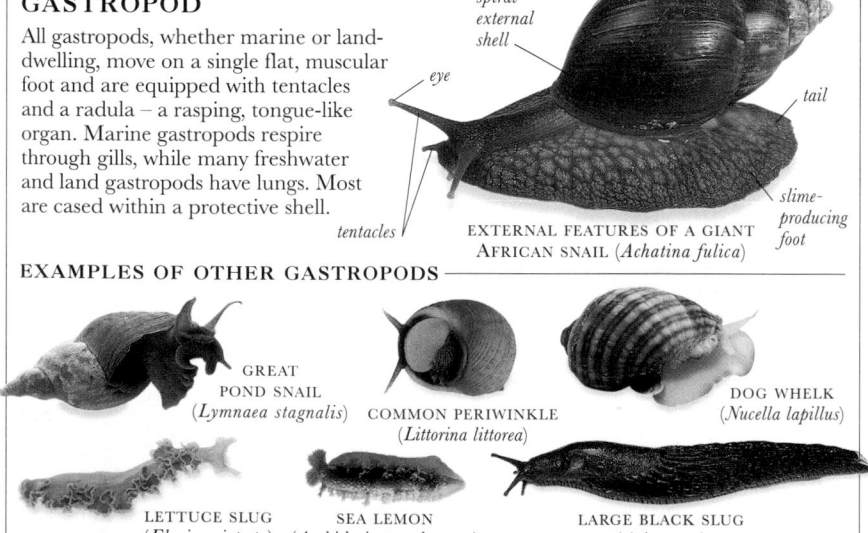

spiral external shell

eye

tail

slime-producing foot

tentacles

EXTERNAL FEATURES OF A GIANT AFRICAN SNAIL (*Achatina fulica*)

EXAMPLES OF OTHER GASTROPODS

GREAT POND SNAIL (*Lymnaea stagnalis*)

COMMON PERIWINKLE (*Littorina littorea*)

DOG WHELK (*Nucella lapillus*)

LETTUCE SLUG (*Elysia crispata*)

SEA LEMON (*Archidoris pseudoargus*)

LARGE BLACK SLUG (*Arion ater*)

extent, or scope of something. **5** a means of estimating; a criterion or test. **6** (usu. **gage**) *Naut.* a relative position with respect to the wind. ● *v.tr.* **1** measure exactly (esp. objects of standard size). **2** determine the capacity or content of. **3** estimate or form a judgement of (a person, situation, etc.). [from Old Northern French] □ **gauger** *n.*

Gaul *n.* a native or inhabitant of ancient Gaul. [from French *Gaule*, name of the country]

gauleiter / **gow**-ly-ter/ *n.* **1** *hist.* an official governing a district under Nazi rule. **2** a local or petty tyrant. [German, from *Gau* 'administrative district' + *Leiter* 'leader']

Gaulish ● *adj.* of or relating to the ancient Gauls. ● *n.* the language of the ancient Gauls.

gault *n. Geol.* **1** a series of clay and marl beds between the upper and lower greensand in southern England. **2** clay obtained from these beds. [16th-century coinage]

gaunt *adj.* **1** lean, haggard. **2** grim or desolate in appearance. [Middle English] □ **gauntly** *adv.* **gauntness** *n.*

gauntlet[1] *n.* **1** a stout glove with a long loose wrist. **2** *hist.* ◄ an armoured glove. **3** the part of the glove covering the wrist. ▷ ARMOUR □ **take up the gauntlet** see TAKE. **throw down the gauntlet** see THROW. [from Old French *gantelet* 'little glove']

GAUNTLETS FROM A 16TH-CENTURY ITALIAN SUIT OF ARMOUR

gauntlet[2] *n.* □ **run the gauntlet** **1** receive harsh criticism. **2** pass between two rows of people and receive blows from them, as a punishment or ordeal. [earlier *gantlope*, from Swedish *gata* 'lane' + *lopp* 'course']

gauss /gowss/ *n.* (*pl.* same or **gausses**) a unit of magnetic induction, equal to one ten-thousandth of a tesla. [named after K. *Gauss*, German mathematician, 1777–1855]

gauze *n.* **1** a thin transparent fabric of silk, cotton, etc. **2** a fine mesh of wire etc. [from French *gaze*]

gauzy *adj.* (**gauzier**, **gauziest**) **1** like gauze; thin and translucent. **2** flimsy, delicate. □ **gauzily** *adv.*

gave *past of* GIVE.

gavel *n.* a small hammer used by an auctioneer, or for calling a meeting to order. [19th-century coinage]

gavotte *n.* **1** a French dance popular in the eighteenth century. **2** a piece of music for this. [from *Gavot*, native of an Alpine region]

Gawd *n. slang* (esp. as *int.*) God.

gawk ● *v.intr. colloq.* stare stupidly. ● *n.* an awkward or bashful person. [from Old Norse *gá* 'to heed'] □ **gawkish** *adj.*

gawky *adj.* (**gawkier**, **gawkiest**) awkward or ungainly. □ **gawkily** *adv.* **gawkiness** *n.*

gawp *v.intr. Brit. colloq.* stare stupidly or obtrusively. [from Middle English *galpen* 'to yawn'] □ **gawper** *n.*

gay ● *adj.* (**gayer**, **gayest**) **1** light-hearted and carefree. **2** brightly coloured; showy (*a gay scarf*). **3** *colloq.* **a** homosexual. **b** intended for or used by homosexuals (*a gay bar*). ● *n. colloq.* a homosexual, esp. male. [from Old French *gai*] □ **gayness** *n.*

■ **Usage** The use of *gay* to mean 'homosexual' is favoured by homosexuals with reference to themselves. It still has an informal feel to it but is now well established and in widespread general use.

GEARBOX

The gearbox, or manual transmission, of a car applies the engine's turning force (torque) to the wheels, and also allows the wheels to turn at a different rate to the engine. To engage the gears, clutch plates connecting the engine and gearbox are clamped together by a spring. To disengage the gears, pressure on this spring is released by pressing down the clutch pedal.

CUTAWAY VIEW OF THE 5-SPEED MANUAL GEARBOX OF A CAR

gear knob · gear lever · remote linkage · rubber bush · 5th gear · reverse gear · 1st gear · shift rail · 2nd gear · 3rd gear · site of 4th gear (hidden by casing) · clutch release rod · torque input · clutch bell-housing · clutch slave cylinder · gearbox casing · sound-deadening rib · oil drain plug · layshaft gear · gear selector fork · synchronizer ring · tail housing · torque output

---

gazania *n.* any herbaceous plant of the genus *Gazania*, with showy yellow or orange daisy-shaped flowers. [named after Theodore of *Gaza*, Greek scholar, 1398–1478]

gaze ● *v.intr.* (foll. by *at, into, on, upon*, etc.) look fixedly. ● *n.* a fixed or intent look. [Middle English] □ **gazer** *n.*

gazebo /gă-**zee**-boh/ *n.* (*pl.* **-os** or **-oes**) a summer house or turret designed to give a wide view.

gazelle *n.* ◄ any of various small graceful soft-eyed antelopes of Asia or Africa, esp. of the genus *Gazella*. [French]

gazette ● *n.* **1** a newspaper. **2** *Brit.* an official journal containing public notices. ● *v.tr. Brit.* announce or publish in an official gazette. [originally in sense 'news-sheet': from Venetian *gazeta de la novita* 'a halfpenny-worth of news']

gazetteer *n.* a geographical index or dictionary. [earlier in sense 'journalist', for whom such an index was provided: from Italian *gazzettiere*]

gazpacho *n.* (*pl.* **-os**) a Spanish soup made with tomatoes, peppers, cucumber, garlic, etc., and served cold. [Spanish]

gazump *v.tr.* (also *absol.*) *Brit. colloq.* **1** (of a seller) raise the price of a property after accepting an offer from (a buyer). **2** swindle. [20th-century coinage] □ **gazumper** *n.*

gazunder *v.tr.* (also *absol.*) *Brit. colloq.* (of a buyer) lower the amount of an offer made to (the seller) for a property, esp. just before exchange of contracts.

GB *abbr.* Great Britain.

GBH *abbr. Brit.* grievous bodily harm.

GC *abbr.* (in the UK) George Cross.

GCE *abbr.* (in England, Wales, and Northern Ireland) General Certificate of Education.

GCHQ *abbr.* (in the UK) Government Communications Headquarters.

GCSE *abbr.* (in England, Wales, and Northern Ireland) General Certificate of Secondary Education.

Gd *symb. Chem.* the element gadolinium.

GDP *abbr.* gross domestic product.

Ge *symb. Chem.* the element germanium.

GAZELLE: THOMSON'S GAZELLE (*Gazella thomsoni*)

---

gean /geen/ *n.* **1** ► the wild sweet cherry, *Prunus avium*. **2** the fruit of this. [from Old French *guine*]

gear ● *n.* **1** (often in *pl.*) a set of toothed wheels that work together to transmit and control motion from an engine, esp. to the road wheels of a vehicle. ▷ DERAILLEUR, GEARBOX. **2** a particular function or state of adjustment of engaged gears (*low gear; second gear*). **3** a mechanism, apparatus, or tackle for a special purpose (*winding gear; landing gear*). **4** *colloq.* clothing, esp. when modern or fashionable. ● *v.* **1** *tr.* (foll. by *to*) adjust or adapt to suit a special purpose or need. **2** *tr.* (often foll. by *up*) equip with gears. **3** *tr.* (foll. by *up*) make ready or prepared. **4** *intr.* (foll. by *with*) work smoothly with. □ **in gear** with a gear engaged. **out of gear 1** with no gear engaged. **2** out of order. [from Old Norse *gervi*]

GEAN (*Prunus avium*)

gearbox *n.* **1** the casing that encloses a set of gears. **2** ▲ a set of gears with its casing, esp. in a motor vehicle. ▷ CLUTCH, SYNCHROMESH.

gearing *n.* **1** a set or arrangement of gears in a machine. **2** *Finance* the ratio of a company's loan capital (debt) to the value of its ordinary shares (equity).

gear lever *n. Brit.* a lever used to engage or change gear, esp. in a motor vehicle. ▷ GEARBOX

gear shift *n.* esp. *N. Amer.* = GEAR LEVER.

gearstick *n. Brit.* = GEAR LEVER.

gearwheel *n.* **1** a toothed wheel in a set of gears. ▷ OBSERVATORY. **2** (in a bicycle) the cogwheel driven directly by the chain. ▷ BICYCLE

GEC *abbr.* General Electric Company.

gecko *n.* (*pl.* **-os** or **-oes**) ▼ any of various mainly nocturnal lizards found in warm climates, with adhesive feet for climbing vertical surfaces. ▷ LIZARD. [from Malay *geko(k)*]

GECKO: TOKAY GECKO (*Gekko gecko*)

G

gee[1] *int.* (also **gee whiz**) *N. Amer. colloq.* a mild expression of surprise, discovery, etc.

gee[2] (often foll. by *up*) ● *int.* a command to a horse etc. to go faster. ● *v.tr.* (**geed, geeing**) command (a horse etc.) to go faster. [17th-century coinage]

gee-gee *n. Brit. colloq.* a horse. [originally a child's word, from GEE[2]]

geese *pl.* of GOOSE.

geezer *n. slang* a person, esp. an old man. [dialect pronunciation of *guiser* 'mummer']

Geiger counter /**gy**-ger/ *n.* ▼ a device for measuring radioactivity by detecting and counting ionizing particles. [named after H. *Geiger*, German physicist, 1882–1945]

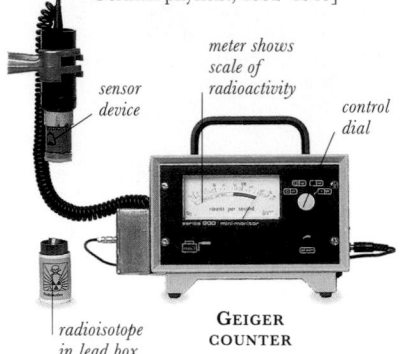

meter shows scale of radioactivity

sensor device

control dial

GEIGER COUNTER

radioisotope in lead box

geisha /**gay**-shă/ *n.* (*pl.* same or **geishas**) (also **geisha girl**) **1** a Japanese hostess trained in entertaining men with dance and song. **2** a Japanese prostitute. [Japanese, literally 'entertainer']

gel ● *n.* **1** a semi-solid colloidal suspension or jelly, of a solid dispersed in a liquid. **2** a jelly-like substance used for setting the hair. ● *v.intr.* (**gelled, gelling**) **1** form a gel. **2** = JELL *v.* 1b. **3** = JELL *v.* 2.

gelada /jĕ-**lah**-dă/ *n.* (*pl.* same or **geladas**) a brownish gregarious baboon, *Theropithecus gelada*, with a bare red patch on its chest, native to Ethiopia. [from native name *č'ällada*]

gelatin *n.* (also **gelatine**) a virtually colourless tasteless transparent water-soluble protein derived from collagen and used in food, photography, etc. [from Italian *gelatina*]

gelatinous *adj.* **1** of or like gelatin. **2** of a jelly-like consistency. □ **gelatinize** *v.tr. & intr.* (also **-ise**). **gelatinization** *n.* **gelatinously** *adv.*

geld *v.tr.* castrate or spay. [based on Old Norse *geldr* 'barren']

gelding *n.* a gelded animal, esp. a male horse.

gelid /**jel**-id/ *adj.* **1** icy, ice-cold. **2** chilly, cool. [from Latin *gelidus*]

gelignite *n.* a high explosive made with a gel of nitroglycerine and nitrocellulose. [based on GELATIN + Latin *ignis* 'fire']

gelly *n. Brit. slang* gelignite.

gelsemium /jel-**see**-mi-ŭm/ *n.* a preparation of the rhizome of *Gelsemium sempervivens*, a twining shrub of southern N. America, used medicinally esp. to treat neuralgia.

gem ● *n.* **1** ▶ a precious or semi-precious stone, esp. when cut and polished or engraved. **2** an object or person of great beauty or worth. ● *v.tr.* (**gemmed, gemming**) adorn with or as with gems. [from Latin *gemma* 'bud, jewel'] □ **gemlike** *adj.*

geminate ● *adj.* combined in pairs. ● *v.tr.* **1** double, repeat. **2** arrange in pairs. [from Latin *geminatus* 'doubled'] □ **gemination** *n.*

Gemini *n.* **1** *Astron.* ▶ a northern constellation (the Twins), said to represent the twins Castor and Pollux, whose names are given to its two brightest stars. **2** *Astrol.* **a** the third sign of the zodiac, which the Sun enters about 21 May. ▷ ZODIAC. **b** a person born

when the Sun is in this sign. [Latin, literally 'twins'] □ **Geminian** *n. & adj.*

gemsbok /**gemz**-bok/ *n.* a large antelope, *Oryx gazella*, of SW and E. Africa. [from Dutch, literally 'chamois']

gemstone *n.* a precious stone used as a gem.

gemütlich /gĕ-**moot**-likh/ *adj.* **1** pleasant and comfortable. **2** genial, agreeable. [German]

Gen. *abbr.* General.

gen *Brit. slang* ● *n.* information. ● *v.tr. & intr.* (**genned, genning**) (foll. by *up*) provide with or obtain information.

-gen *comb. form Chem.* that which produces (*hydrogen*; *antigen*). [from root of Greek *gignesthai* 'to be born, become']

genco *n. Brit.* a power-generating company, esp. a private company selling electricity. [*gen*erating + *co*mpany]

gendarme /**zhon**-darm/ *n.* a soldier employed in specific public police duties in French-speaking countries. [French, from *gens d'armes* 'men of arms']

gendarmerie /zhon-**dar**-mĕ-ri/ *n.* **1** a force of gendarmes. **2** the headquarters of such a force.

gender *n.* **1 a** the grammatical classification of nouns and related words, roughly corresponding to the two sexes and sexlessness. **b** each of the classes of nouns (see MASCULINE, FEMININE, NEUTER *n.* 1, COMMON *adj.* 6). **2** esp. *colloq.* or *euphem.* **a** = SEX *n.* 1. **b** = SEX *n.* 2 (often *attrib.*: *gender issues*). **c** = SEX *n.* 3. [based on Latin *genus* 'race, stock']

gender bender *adj.* a person or thing not conforming to sexual stereotypes.

gendered *adj.* of or specific to the male or female sex.

gene *n.* ▲ a unit of heredity composed of DNA or RNA in a chromosome etc., that determines a particular characteristic of an individual. ▷ DNA. [from German *Gen*]

genealogy *n.* (*pl.* **-ies**) **1 a** a line of descent traced continuously from an ancestor. **b** an account or exposition of this. **2** the study and investigation of lines of descent. **3** a plant's or animal's line of development from earlier forms. [based on Greek *genea* 'race'] □ **genealogical**

adj. **genealogically** *adv.* **genealogist** *n.* **genealogize** *v.tr. & intr.* (also **-ise**).

genera *pl.* of GENUS.

general ● *adj.* **1** completely or almost universal. **2** prevalent, widespread, usual. **3** not partial, particular, local, or sectional. **4** relating to whole classes or all cases. **5** including points common to the individuals of a class and neglecting the differences (*a general term*). **6** not restricted or specialized (*general knowledge*). **7 a** roughly corresponding or adequate. **b** sufficient for practical purposes. **8** not detailed (*a general resemblance*). **9** vague (*spoke only in general terms*). **10** chief, head; having overall authority (*general manager*; *Secretary-General*). ● *n.* **1 a** an army officer ranking next below field marshal or above lieutenant general. **b** a commander of an army. **2** *US* **a** = LIEUTENANT GENERAL, MAJOR GENERAL. **b** an officer of the army or air force ranking below field marshal. **3** a strategist (*a great general*). **4** the head of a religious order, e.g. of the Jesuits or the Salvation Army. □ **in general 1** as a normal rule; usually. **2** for the most part. [from Latin *generalis*]

General American *n.* a form of US speech not markedly dialectal or regional.

general anaesthetic *n.* an anaesthetic that affects the whole body, usu. with loss of consciousness.

General Assembly *n.* the highest ecclesiastical court of various national churches, esp. the Church of Scotland.

General Certificate of Education *n.* (in England, Wales, and Northern Ireland) an examination set esp. for secondary-school pupils at advanced level and, formerly, at ordinary level.

General Certificate of Secondary Education *n.* (in England, Wales, and Northern Ireland) an examination replacing and combining the GCE ordinary level and CSE examinations.

general delivery *n. N. Amer.* = POSTE RESTANTE.

general election *n.* the national election of representatives to a legislature (esp. in the UK to the House of Commons).

general headquarters *n.* (treated as *sing.* or *pl.*) the headquarters of a military commander.

generalissimo *n.* (*pl.* **-os**) the commander of a combined military force consisting of army, navy, and air force units. [Italian]

generalist *n.* a person competent in several different fields or activities (opp. SPECIALIST).

generality *n.* (*pl.* **-ies**) **1** a statement or principle etc. having general validity or force. **2** applicability to a whole class of instances. **3** vagueness; lack of detail. **4** (foll. by *of*) the main body or majority.

generalization *n.* (also **-isation**) **1** a general notion or proposition obtained by inference from particular cases. **2** the act or an instance of generalizing.

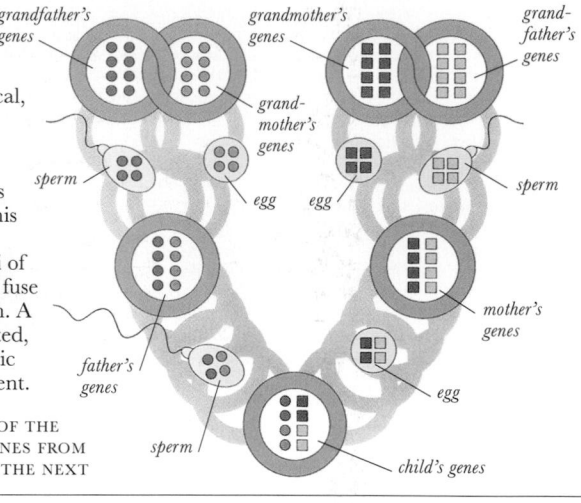

GENE

Genes, inherited from parents and previous forebears, determine the physical, intellectual, and emotional characteristics of a person. The genetic coding that governs such characteristics is transmitted via DNA. This is borne on chromosomes contained within the nuclei of sperm and egg cells, which fuse together during fertilization. A new individual is thus created, possessing a blend of genetic information from each parent.

grandfather's genes

grandmother's genes

grandfather's genes

grandmother's genes

sperm

egg egg

sperm

mother's genes

father's genes

egg

sperm

child's genes

DEMONSTRATION OF THE TRANSMISSION OF GENES FROM ONE GENERATION TO THE NEXT

Castor

Pollux

GEMINI: FIGURE OF TWINS FORMED FROM THE STARS OF GEMINI

GEM

Some 50 minerals are commonly used as gems. Normally, the surface of a gem is cut into flat faces, known as facets. The lapidary who cuts the stone aims to display its best features, most notably its colour, clarity, and weight. However, some aspects may be compromised to preserve the weight – and thus the value – of the gem.

MAIN TYPES OF CUT

BRILLIANT-CUTS
ROUND
OVAL

STEP-CUTS
TABLE
SQUARE
OCTAGONAL
BAGUETTE
OVAL

SIMPLE-CUT
CABOCHON

MIXED-CUTS
CUSHION
MIXED

FANCY-CUTS
PENDELOQUE
SCISSORS
MARQUISE

YELLOW/BROWN GEMS

CORNELIAN

SARDONYX

CITRINE

HESSONITE

CASSITERITE

AMBER

FIRE OPAL

HYPERSTHENE

GREEN GEMS

JADEITE

EMERALD

HIDDENITE

MALACHITE

PERIDOT

MOLDAVITE

BLUE/VIOLET GEMS

SAPPHIRE

LAPIS LAZULI

AMETHYST

TURQUOISE

AQUAMARINE

SODALITE

RED/PINK GEMS

RUBY

RHODONITE

KUNZITE

PYROPE

COLOURLESS GEMS

DIAMOND

ROCK CRYSTAL

SCHEELITE

PETALITE

WHITE GEMS

PEARL

MILKY QUARTZ

BLACK GEMS

JET

SCHORL

IRIDESCENT GEMS

FIRE AGATE

OPAL

LABRADORITE

G

generalize v. (also **-ise**) **1** intr. **a** speak in general or indefinite terms. **b** form general principles or notions. **2** tr. reduce to a general statement, principle, or notion. **3** tr. give a general character to. **4** tr. infer (a law or conclusion) by induction. **5** tr. Math. & Philos. express in a general form; extend the application of. **6** tr. bring into general use. □ **generalizability** n. **generalizer** n. **generalizable** adj.

generally adv. **1** usually; in most cases. **2** in a general sense; without regard to particulars or exceptions (generally speaking). **3** for the most part; extensively (not generally known). **4** in most respects (they were generally well-behaved).

general meeting n. a meeting open to all the members of a society etc.

General National Vocational Qualification n. (in the UK) a general qualification for students preparing for specific training or higher education, set at various levels and (at Intermediate and Advanced levels) corresponding in standard to GCSE and GCE A levels.

general practitioner n. a doctor working in the community and treating cases of all kinds in the first instance. □ **general practice** n.

general-purpose adj. having a range of potential uses or functions.

generalship n. **1** the art or practice of exercising military command. **2** military skill; strategy. **3** skilful management; tact, diplomacy.

general staff n. the staff assisting a military commander in planning and administration.

general strike n. a strike of workers in all or most trades.

General Synod n. the highest governing body in the Church of England.

general theory of relativity see RELATIVITY 2b.

generate v.tr. **1** bring into existence; produce, evolve. **2** produce (electricity). [based on Latin generatus 'begotten'] □ **generable** adj.

generation n. **1** all the people born at a particular time, regarded collectively (my generation; the rising generation). **2** a single step in descent or pedigree (have known them for three generations). **3** a stage in (esp. technological) development (fourth-generation computers). **4** the average time in which children are ready to take the place of their parents (usu. reckoned at about 30 years). **5** production by natural or artificial process, esp. the production of electricity or heat. **6** procreation. □ **generational** adj.

generation gap n. differences of outlook or opinion between people of different generations.

generative adj. **1** of or concerning procreation. **2** able to produce, productive.

generator n. **1** a machine for converting mechanical into electrical energy. ▷ HYDROELECTRIC, NUCLEAR POWER. **2** an apparatus for producing gas, steam, etc.

generic adj. **1** characteristic of or relating to a class; general. **2** Biol. characteristic of or belonging to a genus. **3** (of goods, esp. a drug) having no brand name. [from French générique] □ **generically** adv.

generous adj. **1** giving or given freely. **2** magnanimous, noble-minded, unprejudiced. **3** ample, abundant, copious (a generous portion). [from Latin generosus 'noble, magnanimous'] □ **generosity** n. **generously** adv.

genesis n. **1** the origin, or mode of formation or generation, of a thing. **2** (**Genesis**) the first book of the Old Testament. [from Greek]

genet /jen-it/ n. **1** ▶ any cat-like mammal of the genus Genetta, native to Africa and S. Europe, with spotted fur and a long ringed bushy tail. **2** the fur of the genet. [from Arabic jarnait]

gene therapy n. Med. the introduction of normal genes into cells in place of missing or defective ones in order to correct genetic disorders.

genetic adj. **1** of genetics or genes; inherited. **2** of, in, or concerning origin; causal. [related to GENESIS] □ **genetically** adv.

genetic code n. Biochem. the system of correspondence between triplets of bases in DNA and specific amino acids, by which a gene sequence embodies the instructions for synthesis of a specific protein.

genetic engineering n. the deliberate modification of the characters of an organism by the manipulation of the genetic material.

genetic fingerprinting n. (also **genetic profiling**) the analysis of characteristic patterns in DNA as a means of identifying individuals.

genetics n. (usu. treated as sing.) the study of heredity and the variation of inherited characteristics. □ **geneticist** n.

genial adj. **1** jovial, sociable, kindly, cheerful. **2** (of the climate) mild and warm; conducive to growth. **3** cheering, enlivening. [from Latin genialis] □ **geniality** n. **genially** adv.

-genic comb. form forming adjectives meaning: **1** producing (carcinogenic; pathogenic). **2** well suited to (photogenic; radiogenic). **3** produced by. [based on -GEN] □ **-genically** comb. form forming adverbs.

genie n. (pl. usu. **genii** /-ni-I/) a jinnee or spirit of Arabian folklore, esp. one contained within a bottle, lamp, etc. and capable of granting wishes. [from Latin genius]

genii pl. of GENIE, GENIUS.

genital ● adj. of or relating to the reproductive organs. ● n. (in pl.) the external organ or organs of reproduction. ▷ REPRODUCTIVE ORGANS. [from Latin genitalis]

genitalia n.pl. the genitals.

genitive Gram. ● n. the case of nouns and pronouns (and words in grammatical agreement with them) indicating possession or close association. ● adj. of or in the genitive. [from Latin genitivus]

genito-urinary adj. of the genital and urinary organs. ▷ REPRODUCTIVE ORGANS, URINARY SYSTEM

genius n. **1** (pl. **geniuses**) an exceptional intellectual or creative power. **2** (pl. **geniuses** or **genii** /-ni-I/) a person having this. [Latin, based on gignere 'to beget']

genoa n. **1** (in full **genoa jib**) a large jib or foresail used esp. on racing yachts. **2** (in full **Genoa cake**) a rich fruit cake with almonds on top. [from Genoa, a city in Italy]

genocide n. the mass extermination of human beings, esp. of a particular race or nation. [based on Greek genos 'race'] □ **genocidal** adj.

genome /jeen-ohm/ n. **1** the haploid set of chromosomes of an organism. **2** the genetic material of an organism. [blend of GENE and CHROMOSOME]

genotype n. Biol. the genetic constitution of an individual. [from German] □ **genotypic** adj.

genre /zhahnr/ n. **1** a kind or style, esp. of art or literature (e.g. Romantic, drama, satire). **2** (in full **genre painting**) the painting of scenes from ordinary life. [French]

gent n. colloq. **1** a gentleman. **2** (**the Gents**) Brit. a men's public lavatory.

genteel adj. **1** affectedly or ostentatiously refined or stylish. **2** often iron. of or appropriate to the upper classes. [earlier gentile, readoption of French gentil 'gentle'] □ **genteelly** adv.

genteelism n. a word used because it is thought to be less vulgar than the commoner word (e.g. perspire for sweat).

gentian /jen-shăn/ n. ◀ any plant of the genus Gentiana or Gentianella, found esp. in mountainous regions, and usu. having violet or vivid blue trumpet-shaped flowers. [from Latin gentiana, named after Gentius, king of Illyria]

gentian violet n. a violet dye used as an antiseptic, esp. in the treatment of burns.

gentile ● adj. **1** (**Gentile**) **a** not Jewish. **b** (of a person) not belonging to one's religious community. **2** of or relating to a nation or tribe. ● n. (**Gentile**) a person who is not Jewish. [based on Latin gens gentis 'family']

gentility n. **1** social superiority. **2** good manners; habits associated with the nobility. [related to GENTLE]

gentle adj. (**gentler**, **gentlest**) **1** mild or kind in temperament. **2 a** moderate; not harsh (a gentle rebuke; a gentle breeze). **b** gradual (gentle progression; gentle slope). **3** archaic noble (of gentle birth). **4** quiet; requiring patience (gentle art). [from Latin gentilis, based on gens 'family'] □ **gentleness** n. **gently** adv.

gentlefolk n.pl. literary people of good family.

gentleman n. (pl. **-men**) **1** a man (in polite or formal use). **2** a chivalrous, courteous, or well-educated man. **3** a man of good social position or of wealth and leisure (country gentleman). **4** a man of noble birth attached to a royal household (gentleman in waiting). **5** (in pl. as a form of address) a male audience or the male part of an audience. [translating Old French gentilz hom]

gentlemanly adj. like or befitting a gentleman. □ **gentlemanliness** n.

gentleman's agreement n. (also **gentlemen's agreement**) one which is binding in honour but not legally enforceable.

gentlewoman n. (pl. **-women**) archaic a woman of good birth or breeding.

gentoo n. a penguin, Pygoscelis papua, esp. abundant in the Falkland Islands.

gentrify v.tr. (**-ies**, **-ied**) convert (a working-class or inner-city district etc.) into an area of middle-class residence. □ **gentrification** n. **gentrifier** n.

gentry n.pl. the class of people next below the nobility in position and birth.

genuflect v.intr. bend the knee, esp. in worship or as a sign of respect. [from ecclesiastical Latin genuflectere] □ **genuflection** n. (also **genuflexion**). **genuflector** n.

genuine adj. **1** really coming from its stated, advertised, or reputed source. **2** properly so called; not sham. **3** pure-bred. [based on Latin genu 'knee', with reference to a father's acknowledging a newborn child by placing it on his knee] □ **genuinely** adv. **genuineness** n.

genus n. (pl. **genera**) **1** Biol. a taxonomic grouping of organisms having common characteristics distinct from those of other genera, usu. containing several or many species and being one of a series constituting a taxonomic family. **2** a kind or class having common characteristics. [Latin, literally 'race, stock, kind']

geo- comb. form earth. [from Greek]

geocentric adj. **1** considered as viewed from the centre of the Earth. **2** having or representing the Earth as the centre; not heliocentric. □ **geocentrically** adv.

geochemistry n. the chemistry of the Earth and its rocks, minerals, etc. □ **geochemical** adj. **geochemist** n.

geochronology n. **1** the study and measurement of geological time by means of geological events. **2** the ordering of geological events. □ **geochronological** adj. **geochronologist** n.

GENTIAN: SPRING GENTIAN (Gentiana verna)

GENET: COMMON GENET (Genetta genetta)

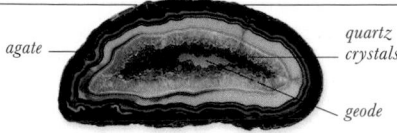

GEODE FORMED WITHIN AGATE
(BANDED CHALCEDONY)

geode *n.* **1** ▲ a small cavity lined with crystals or other mineral matter. **2** a rock containing such a cavity. [from Greek *geōdēs* 'earthy'] □ **geodic** *adj.*

geodesic *adj.* **1** of or relating to geodesy. Cf. GEODETIC. **2** designating, or designed according to, constructional principles based on spheres and geodesic lines.

geodesic dome *n.* ► a dome constructed of short struts along geodesic lines.

geodesic line *n.* the shortest possible line between two points on a curved surface.

geodesy *n.* the branch of mathematics dealing with the shape and area of the Earth. □ **geodesist** *n.*

geodetic *adj.* of or relating to geodesy, esp. as applied to land surveying.

geography *n.* **1** the study of the Earth's physical features, climate, population, etc. **2** the main physical features of an area. **3** the layout or arrangement of rooms in a building. [from Greek *geōgraphia*] □ **geographer** *n.* **geographic** *adj.* **geographical** *adj.* **geographically** *adv.*

geology *n.* **1** the science of the Earth, including the composition, structure, and origin of its rocks. ▷ ROCK CYCLE. **2** this science applied to any other planet or celestial body. **3** the geological features of a district. □ **geologic** *adj.* **geological** *adj.* **geologically** *adv.* **geologist** *n.*

geomagnetic *adj.* of or relating to the magnetic properties of the Earth. □ **geomagnetism** *n.*

geometric *adj.* (also **geometrical**) **1** of, according to, or like geometry. **2** (of a design, architectural feature, etc.) characterized by or decorated with regular lines and shapes. □ **geometrically** *adv.*

geometrical series *n.* a series in geometrical progression.

geometric mean *n.* the central number in a geometric progression, also calculable as the nth root of a product of n numbers (as 9 from 3 and 27).

geometric progression *n.* a progression of numbers with a constant ratio between each number and the one before (as 1, 3, 9, 27, 81).

geometry *n.* **1** the branch of mathematics concerned with the properties and relations of points, lines, surfaces, and solids. **2** the relative arrangement of objects or parts. □ **geometrician** *n.*

geomorphology *n.* the study of the physical features of the surface of the Earth and their relation to its geological structures. □ **geomorphological** *adj.* **geomorphologist** *n.*

geophysics *n.* the physics of the Earth. □ **geophysical** *adj.* **geophysicist** *n.*

geopolitics *n.* **1** the politics of a country as determined by its geographical features. **2** the study of this. □ **geopolitical** *adj.* **geopolitically** *adv.* **geopolitician** *n.*

Geordie *Brit. colloq.* ● *n.* **1** a native of Tyneside. **2** the dialect spoken on Tyneside. ● *adj.* of or relating to Tyneside, its people, or its dialect. [from the name *George*]

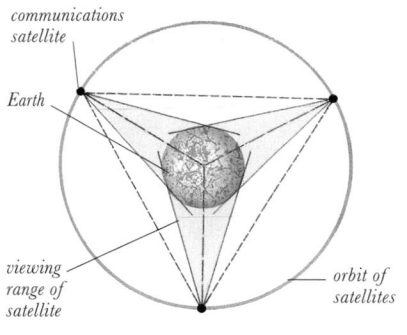

GEODESIC DOME:
DOME-SHAPED GREENHOUSE

GERANIUM: HEDGEROW
CRANESBILL
(*Geranium pyrenaicum*)

George Cross *n.* (also **George Medal**) (in the UK) each of two (different) decorations for bravery awarded esp. to civilians, instituted in 1940 by King George VI.

georgette *n.* a thin silk or crêpe dress material. [named (*c.*1900) after *Georgette* de la Plante, French dressmaker]

Georgian[1] *adj.* **1** of or characteristic of the time of Kings George I–IV (1714–1830), esp. of architecture of this period. **2** of or characteristic of the time of Kings George V and VI (1910–52), esp. of the literature of 1910–20.

Georgian[2] ● *adj.* of or relating to Georgia, a country of SE Europe. ● *n.* **1** a native of Georgia; a person of Georgian descent. **2** the language of Georgia.

Georgian[3] ● *adj.* of or relating to Georgia in the US. ● *n.* a native of Georgia.

geoscience *n.* Earth sciences, esp. geology. □ **geoscientist** *n.*

geosphere *n.* **1** the solid surface of the Earth. ▷ EARTH. **2** any of the almost spherical concentric regions of the Earth and its atmosphere.

geostationary *adj.* ► (of an artificial satellite of the Earth) moving in such an orbit as to remain above the same point on the Earth's surface (cf. GEOSYNCHRONOUS).

geosynchronous *adj.* (of an artificial satellite of the Earth) moving in an orbit equal to the Earth's period of rotation (cf. GEOSTATIONARY).

geothermal *adj.* relating to, originating from, or produced by the internal heat of the Earth.

geranium *n.* **1** ◄ any herbaceous plant or shrub of the genus *Geranium* bearing fruit shaped like the bill of a crane, e.g. cranesbill. **2** (in general use) a cultivated pelargonium. [from Greek *geranion*]

gerbera *n.* any plant of the genus *Gerbera* (daisy family) of Africa or Asia. [named after T. *Gerber*, 18th-century German naturalist]

gerbil *n.* ► a mouselike desert rodent of the subfamily Gerbillinae, esp. *Meriones unguiculatus*, kept as a pet. [from modern Latin *gerbillus* 'little jerboa']

geriatric ● *adj.* **1** of or relating to old people. **2** *colloq.* old, outdated. ● *n.* an old person, esp. one receiving special care. [based on Greek *gēras* 'old age' + *iatros* 'doctor']

■ **Usage** *Geriatric* may cause offence when used in sense 2 of the adjective.

geriatrics *n.pl.* (treated as *sing.*) a branch of medicine or social science dealing with the health and care of old people. □ **geriatrician** *n.*

germ *n.* **1** a micro-organism, esp. one which causes disease. **2 a** a portion of an organism capable of developing into a new one; the rudiment of an animal or plant. **b** an embryo of a seed (*wheatgerm*). **3** an original idea etc. from which something may develop; an elementary principle. [from Latin *germen* 'sprout'] □ **in germ** not yet developed. □ **germy** *adj.*

German ● *n.* **1** a native or national of Germany; a person of German descent. **2** the language of Germany, also used in Austria and Switzerland. ● *adj.* of or relating to Germany or its people or language. [from Latin *Germanus*, with reference to related peoples of central and northern Europe, a name perhaps given by Celts to their neighbours]

german *adj.* (placed after *brother*, *sister*, or *cousin*) **1** having both parents the same (*brother german*). **2** having both grandparents the same on one side

GERBIL: PALLID GERBIL
(*Meriones unguiculatus*)

GEOSTATIONARY

A satellite placed 35,880 km (22,296 miles) above the equator takes 24 hours to travel its orbit – the time it takes the Earth to spin on its axis – and so seems to hover over the Earth's surface. Three evenly spaced satellites can thus view the entire globe.

communications satellite

Earth

viewing range of satellite

orbit of satellites

VIEWING RANGE OF SATELLITES IN
GEOSTATIONARY ORBIT (NOT TO SCALE)

(*cousin german*). **3** *archaic* germane. [from Latin *germanus* 'of the same parents']

germane *adj.* (usu. foll. by *to*) relevant (to a subject under consideration). [variant of GERMAN] □ **germanely** *adv.* **germaneness** *n.*

Germanic ● *adj.* **1** having German characteristics. **2** *hist.* of the Germans. **3** of the Scandinavians, Anglo-Saxons, or Germans. **4** of the languages or language group called Germanic. ● *n.* **1** the branch of Indo-European languages including English, German, Dutch, and the Scandinavian languages. **2** the language of early Germanic peoples.

Germanist *n.* an expert in or student of the language, literature, and civilization of Germany, or Germanic languages.

germanium *n.* *Chem.* a lustrous brittle semi-metallic element occurring naturally in sulphide ores and used in semi-conductors. [based on Latin *Germanus* 'German']

Germanize *v.tr. & intr.* (also **-ise**) make or become German; adopt or cause to adopt German customs etc. □ **Germanization** *n.* **Germanizer** *n.*

German measles *n.pl.* (also treated as *sing.*) a contagious disease, rubella, with symptoms like mild measles.

German shepherd *n.* (also **German shepherd dog**) ▼ an Alsatian.

GERMAN SHEPHERD

German silver *n.* a white alloy of nickel, zinc, and copper.

germ cell *n.* **1** a cell containing half the number of chromosomes of a somatic cell and able to unite with one from the opposite sex to form a new individual; a gamete. **2** any embryonic cell with the potential of developing into a gamete.

GERMINATE

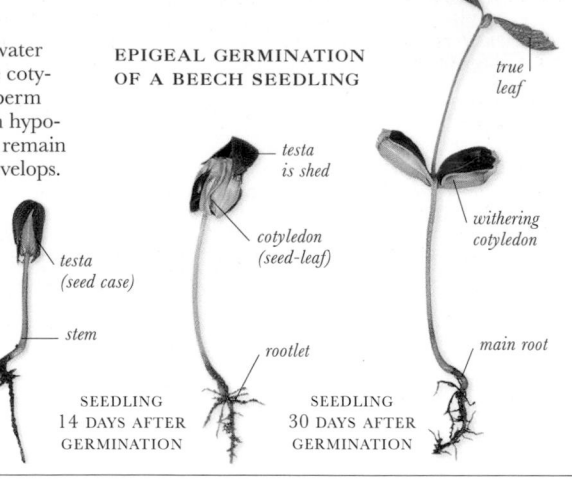

A germinating seed absorbs water and swells. Food stored in the cotyledons (seed-leaves) or endosperm allows the embryo to grow. In hypogeal germination, cotyledons remain below ground as the shoot develops. In epigeal germination (right), cotyledons are borne above the soil on a stem. As the cotyledons turn green, they begin to produce food through photosynthesis, withering as the true leaves unfurl.

EPIGEAL GERMINATION
OF A BEECH SEEDLING

true leaf

testa
is shed

cotyledon
(seed-leaf)

withering
cotyledon

testa
(seed case)

stem

rootlet

main root

GERMINATING
SEEDLING

SEEDLING
14 DAYS AFTER
GERMINATION

SEEDLING
30 DAYS AFTER
GERMINATION

germicide *n.* a substance destroying germs, esp. those causing disease. □ **germicidal** *adj.*

germinal *adj.* **1** relating to or of the nature of a germ or germs (see GERM 1). **2** in the earliest stage of development. **3** productive of new ideas. [based on Latin *germen germin-* 'sprout'] □ **germinally** *adv.*

germinate *v.* **1 a** *intr.* ▲ sprout, bud, or put forth shoots. **b** *tr.* cause to sprout or shoot. **2 a** *tr.* cause (ideas etc.) to originate or develop. **b** *intr.* come into existence. □ **germination** *n.*

germ warfare *n.* the systematic spreading of micro-organisms to cause disease in an enemy population.

gerontocracy *n.* **1** government by old people. **2** a state or society so governed. [based on Greek *gerōn -ontos* 'old man'] □ **gerontocrat** *n.*

gerontology *n.* the scientific study of old age, the process of ageing, and the special problems of old people. □ **gerontological** *adj.* **gerontologist** *n.*

gerrymander *v.tr.* (also *Brit.* **jerrymander**) **1** manipulate the boundaries of (a constituency etc.) so as to give undue influence to some party or class. **2** manipulate (a situation etc.) to gain advantage. [from the name of Governor *Gerry* of Massachusetts + *salamander*, referring to the redrawn shape of a political district (1812)] □ **gerrymanderer** *n.*

gerund *n. Gram.* a form of a verb functioning as a noun, originally in Latin ending in *-ndum* (declinable), in English ending in *-ing* and used distinctly as a part of a verb (e.g. *do you mind my asking you?*). [from Late Latin *gerundum* 'that which is to be carried out']

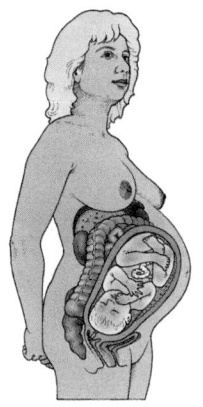

GESSO: DESIGN
DRAWN INTO GESSO

gesso /jes-oh/ *n.* (*pl.* **-oes**) ◄ gypsum as used in painting or sculpture. [from Latin *gypsum*]

gestalt *n. Psychol.* an organized whole that is perceived as more than the sum of its parts. [German, literally 'form, shape'] □ **gestaltism** *n.* **gestaltist** *n.*

gestalt psychology *n.* a system maintaining that perceptions, reactions, etc. are gestalts.

Gestapo *n.* the German secret police under Nazi rule. [German, from *Geheime Staatspolizei*]

gestate *v.tr.* **1** carry (a foetus) in gestation. **2** develop (an idea etc.).

gestation *n.* **1 a** ► the process of carrying or being carried in the womb between conception and birth. **b** this period. **2** the private development of a plan, idea, etc. [from Latin *gestatio*]

gesticulate *v.* **1** *intr.* use gestures instead of or in addition to speech. **2** *tr.* express with gestures. [from Latin *gesticulari*] □ **gesticulation** *n.* **gesticulative** *adj.* **gesticulatory** *adj.*

gesture ● *n.* **1** a movement of a limb or the body as an expression of thought or feeling. **2** the use of such movements, esp. as a rhetorical device. **3** an action to evoke a response or convey intention, usu. friendly (*goodwill gesture*). ● *v.tr. & intr.* gesticulate. [from medieval Latin *gestura*] □ **gestural** *adj.*

get *v.* (**getting**; *past* **got** or *archaic* **gat**; *past part.* **got** or *N. Amer.* (and in *comb.*) **gotten**) **1** *tr.* come into the possession of; receive or earn (*get a job*; *got £200 a week*). **2** *tr.* fetch, obtain, procure, purchase (*get my book for me*; *got a new car*). **3** *tr.* go to reach or catch (a bus, train, etc.). **4** *tr.* prepare (a meal etc.). **5** *intr. & tr.* reach or cause to reach a certain state or condition; become or cause to become (*get rich*; *get one's feet wet*; *get to be famous*; *got them ready*; *got him into trouble*). **6** *tr.* obtain as a result of calculation. **7** *tr.* contract (a disease etc.). **8** *tr.* establish or be in communication with via telephone or radio; receive (a radio signal). **9** *tr.* experience or suffer; have inflicted on one; receive as one's lot or penalty (*got four years in prison*). **10 a** *tr.* succeed in bringing, placing, etc. (*cannot get the key into the lock*; *flattery will get you nowhere*). **b** *intr. & tr.* succeed or cause to succeed in coming or going (*will get you there somehow*; *got absolutely nowhere*). **11** *tr.* (*prec. by* **have**) **a** possess (*have not got a penny*). **b** (foll. by *to* + infin.) be bound or obliged (*have got to see you*). **12** *tr.* (foll. by *to* + infin.) induce; prevail upon (*got them to help me*). **13** *tr. colloq.* understand (a person or an argument) (*have you got that?*; *do you get me?*). **14** *tr. colloq.* inflict punishment or retribution on, esp. in retaliation (*I'll get you for that*). **15** *tr. colloq.* **a** annoy. **b** move; affect emotionally. **c** attract, obsess. **d** amuse. **16** *intr.* (foll. by *to* + infin.) develop an inclination as specified (*am getting to like it*). **17** *intr.* (foll. by pres. part.) begin (*get going*). **18** *tr.* (esp. in *past* or *perfect*) catch in an argument; corner, puzzle. **19** *tr.* establish (an idea etc.) in one's mind. □ **be getting on for** be approaching (a specified time, age, etc.). **get about** (or **around**) **1** travel extensively or fast; go from place to place. **2** manage to walk, move about, etc., esp. after illness. **3** (of news) be circulated, esp. orally. **get across 1** manage to communicate (an idea etc.). **2** (of an idea etc.) be communicated successfully. **3** *Brit. colloq.* annoy, irritate. **get along** (or **on**) **1** (foll. by *together*, *with*) live harmoniously, accord. **2** *Brit. colloq.* **a** (as *imper.*) be off! **b** (as *int.*) nonsense! (expressing scepticism). **get at 1** reach; get hold of. **2** *colloq.* imply (*what are you getting at?*). **3** *colloq.* nag, criticize, bully. **get away 1** escape. **2** (foll. by *with*) escape blame or punishment for. **get back 1** move back or away. **2** return, arrive home. **3** recover (something lost). **4** (usu. foll. by *to*) contact later (*I'll get back to you*). **get back at** *colloq.* retaliate against. **get by** *colloq.* **1** just manage, even with difficulty. **2** be acceptable. **get down 1** alight, descend (from a vehicle, ladder, etc.). **2** record in writing. **get a person down** depress or deject him or her. **get down to** begin working on or studying; turn one's attention seriously to. **get even** (often foll. by *with*) achieve revenge; act in retaliation. **get hold of 1** grasp (physically). **2** make contact with (a person). **3** acquire. **get in 1** enter; gain entrance. **2** arrive. **3** be elected. **get into** become interested or involved in. **get it** *slang* be punished or in trouble. **get it into one's head** (foll. by *that* + clause) firmly believe or maintain; realize. **get off 1** *colloq.* be acquitted; escape with little or no punishment. **2** start. **3** alight; alight from (a bus etc.). **4** go, or cause to go, to sleep. **5** (foll. by *with*, *together*) *Brit. colloq.* form an amorous or sexual relationship, esp. abruptly or quickly. **get a person off** *colloq.* cause a person to be acquitted. **get on 1** make progress; manage. **2** enter (a bus etc.). **3** esp. *Brit.* = get along 1. **get on to 1** make contact with. **2** understand; become aware of. **get out 1** leave or escape. **2** manage to go outdoors. **3** alight from a vehicle. **4** become known. **5** succeed in uttering, publishing, etc. **6** *Brit.* solve or finish (a puzzle etc.). **get out of 1** avoid or escape (a duty etc.). **2** abandon (a habit) gradually. **get over 1** recover from (an illness,

GESTATION

Length of gestation bears some relation to the adult size of an animal. While human gestation lasts 40 weeks, an elephant's gestation period is 22 months. Human gestation is divided into trimesters. By the end of the first trimester, the body systems, organs, nerves, and muscles of the foetus are well developed. During the second trimester, the foetus grows hair, sucks its thumb, and coughs. In the third trimester, most babies lie head down, awaiting birth.

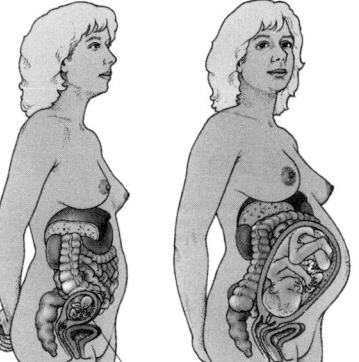

STAGES OF HUMAN GESTATION

foetus

FIRST TRIMESTER   SECOND TRIMESTER   THIRD TRIMESTER

upset, etc.). **2** overcome (a difficulty). **3** manage to communicate (an idea etc.). **get a thing over** (or **over with**) complete (a tedious task) promptly. **get one's own back** *Brit.* have one's revenge. **get rid of** see RID. **get round** (*US* **around**) **1** successfully coax or cajole (a person) esp. to secure a favour. **get round to** deal with (a task etc.) in due course. **get somewhere** make progress; be initially successful. **get there** *colloq.* **1** succeed. **2** understand what is meant. **get through 1** pass or assist in passing (an examination, an ordeal, etc.). **2** finish or use up (esp. resources). **3** (often foll. by *to*) make contact by telephone. **4** (foll. by *to*) succeed in making (a person) listen or understand. **get to 1** reach. **2** = *get down to*. **get together** gather, assemble. **get up 1** rise or cause to rise from sitting etc., or from bed after sleeping or an illness. **2** ascend or mount, e.g. on horseback. **3** (of fire, wind, or the sea) begin to be strong or agitated. **4** prepare or organize. **5** enhance or refine one's knowledge of (a subject). **6** produce or stimulate (*get up steam; get up speed*). **7** (often *refl.*) dress or arrange elaborately; make presentable; arrange the appearance of. **8** (foll. by *to*) *Brit. colloq.* indulge or be involved in (*always getting up to mischief*). **get-up-and-go** *colloq.* energy, enthusiasm. **get the wind up** see WIND[1]. [from Old Norse *geta* 'to obtain, beget, guess'] □ **gettable** *adj.* **getter** *n.*

getaway *n.* an escape, esp. after committing a crime.

get-out *n. Brit.* a means of avoiding something.

get-together *n. colloq.* a social gathering.

get-up *n. colloq.* a style or arrangement of dress etc., esp. an elaborate one.

gewgaw *n.* a gaudy plaything or ornament; a bauble. [Middle English]

geyser /ˈgeez-er/ *n.* **1** ▼ an intermittently gushing hot spring that throws up a tall column of water. **2** *Brit.* an apparatus for heating water. [from Icelandic *Geysir*, name of a particular spring]

Ghanaian /gah-**nay**-ăn/ ● *adj.* of or relating to Ghana in W. Africa. ● *n.* a native or national of Ghana; a person of Ghanaian descent.

ghastly *adj.* (**ghastlier, ghastliest**) **1** horrible, frightful. **2** *colloq.* objectionable, unpleasant. **3** deathlike, pallid. [Middle English, based on obsolete *gast* 'to terrify'] □ **ghastlily** *adv.* **ghastliness** *n.*

ghat /gaht/ *n.* in India: **1** steps leading down to a river. **2** a landing place. [Hindi]

ghee *n.* Indian clarified butter esp. from the milk of a buffalo or cow. [from Sanskrit *ghṛtá-* 'sprinkled']

gherkin *n.* a small variety of cucumber, or a young green cucumber, used for pickling. [from medieval Greek *aggourion*]

ghetto *n.* (*pl.* **-os** or **-oes**) **1** a part of a city, esp. a slum area, occupied by a minority group or groups. **2** *hist.* the Jewish quarter in a city. **3** a segregated group or area. □ **ghettoize** *v.tr.* (also **ghettoise**).

ghetto blaster *n. slang* a large portable radio and cassette player, esp. one used to play loud pop music.

ghillie var. of GILLIE.

ghost ● *n.* **1** a supposed apparition of a dead person or animal; a disembodied spirit. **2** a mere semblance (*not a ghost of a chance*). **3** a secondary image produced by defective television reception or by a telescope. ● *v.* **1** *intr.* (often foll. by *for*) act as ghost writer. **2** *tr.* act as ghost writer of (a work). [Old English] □ **ghost-like** *adj.*

ghostbuster *n. colloq.* a person who professes to banish ghosts, poltergeists, etc.

ghosting *n.* the appearance of a 'ghost' (see GHOST *n.* 3) in a television picture.

ghostly *adj.* (**ghostlier, ghostliest**) like a ghost. □ **ghostliness** *n.*

ghost town *n.* a deserted town with few or no remaining inhabitants.

ghost train *n.* (at a funfair) an open-topped miniature railway in which the rider experiences ghoulish sights, sounds, etc.

ghost writer *n.* a person who writes on behalf of the credited author of a work. □ **ghost-write** *v.tr. & intr.*

ghoul /gool/ *n.* **1** a person morbidly interested in death etc. **2** an evil spirit or phantom. **3** a spirit in Arabic folklore preying on travellers. [from Arabic *ġūl*, a protean desert demon] □ **ghoulish** *adj.* **ghoulishly** *adv.* **ghoulishness** *n.*

GHQ *abbr.* General Headquarters.

ghyll *Brit.* var. of GILL[3].

GI ● *n.* (*pl.* **GIs**) a private soldier in the US Army. ● *adj.* of or for US servicemen. ▷ INFANTRYMAN. [abbreviation of *government* (or *general*) *issue*]

giant ● *n.* **1** (*fem.* **giantess**) an imaginary or mythical being of human form but superhuman size. **2** an abnormally tall or large person, animal, or plant. **3** a person of exceptional ability, integrity, courage, etc. **4** a very large, bright star. ● *attrib.adj.* **1** gigantic; monstrous. **2** of a very large kind. [from Greek *gigas gigant-*] □ **giantism** *n.* **giant-like** *adj.*

criminal's skull

giant-killer *n.* a person who defeats a seemingly much more powerful opponent.

giant sequoia see SEQUOIA.

gibber ● *v.intr.* speak fast and inarticulately; chatter incoherently. ● *n.* such speech or sound.

gibberish *n.* unintelligible or meaningless speech; nonsense.

gibbet *n. hist.* **1** a gallows. **2** ◄ an upright post with an arm from which the bodies of executed criminals were left hanging in chains, irons, or an iron cage as a warning or deterrent to others. [from Old French *gibet*]

gibbon *n.* any small ape of the genus *Hylobates*, native to SE Asia. [French, from a native name]

gibbous /ˈgib-ŭs/ *adj.* **1** convex or protuberant. **2** (of a moon or planet) having the bright part greater than a semicircle and less than a circle. ▷ LUNAR MONTH. [based on Late Latin *gibbus* 'hump']

gibe (also **jibe**) ● *v.intr.* (often foll. by *at*) jeer, mock. ● *n.* an instance of gibing; a taunt. □ **giber** *n.*

giblets *n.pl.* the liver, gizzard, neck, etc. of a bird, usu. removed and cooked separately. [from Old French *gibelet* 'game stew']

giddy ● *adj.* (**giddier, giddiest**) **1** having a sensation of whirling and a tendency to fall, stagger, or spin round. **2 a** overexcited. **b** excitable, frivolous. **3** tending to make one giddy. ● *v.tr. & intr.* (**-ies, -ied**) make or become giddy. [Old English *gidig* 'insane', literally 'possessed by a god'] □ **giddily** *adv.* **giddiness** *n.*

giddy-up ● *int.* commanding a horse to go or go faster. ● *v.tr.* urge to go or go faster.

gift ● *n.* **1** a thing given; a present. **2** a natural ability or talent. **3** the power to give (*in his gift*). **4** the act or an instance of giving. **5** *colloq.* an easy task. ● *v.tr.* bestow as a gift. □ **look a gift-horse in the mouth** (usu. *neg.*) find fault with what has been given. [Middle English from Old Norse *gipt*]

gifted *adj.* exceptionally talented or intelligent. □ **giftedness** *n.*

gift of the gab see GAB.

gift of tongues see TONGUE.

gift token *n.* (also **gift voucher**) *Brit.* a voucher used as a gift and exchangeable for goods.

giftware *n.* goods sold as being suitable as gifts.

gift-wrap ● *v.tr.* (**-wrapped, -wrapping**) wrap attractively as a gift. ● *n.* (**giftwrap**) decorative paper etc. for wrapping gifts.

gig[1] *n.* **1** a light two-wheeled one-horse carriage. **2** a light boat for rowing or sailing. [Middle English]

gig[2] *colloq.* ● *n.* **1** an engagement of an entertainer, esp. of musicians to play jazz, pop, or dance music, usu. for a single appearance. **2** a performance of this kind. ● *v.intr.* (**gigged, gigging**) perform a gig. [20th-century coinage]

giga- *comb. form* denoting a factor of 10^9 (*gigawatt*) or (in *Computing*) a factor of 2^{30} (*gigabyte*). [from Greek *gigas* 'giant']

gigaflop *n. Computing* a unit of computing speed equal to one thousand million floating-point operations per second.

gigantic *adj.* **1** very large; enormous. **2** like or suited to a giant. [based on Latin *gigas gigantis* 'giant'] □ **gigantesque** *adj.* **gigantically** *adv.*

gigantism *n.* abnormal largeness.

giggle ● *v.intr.* laugh in half-suppressed spasms, esp. in an affected or silly manner. ● *n.* **1** such a laugh. **2** *colloq.* an amusing person or thing. □ **giggler** *n.* **giggly** *adj.* (**gigglier, giggliest**)

gigolo /ˈjig-ŏ-loh/ *n.* (*pl.* **-os**) **1** a young man paid by an older woman to be her escort or lover. **2** a professional male dancing partner or escort. [French, formed as masculine of *gigole* 'dance hall woman']

gigot /ˈjig-ŏt/ *n.* a leg of mutton or lamb. [French dialect, literally 'little leg']

gigot sleeve *n.* a leg-of-mutton sleeve.

G

GIBBET: 18TH-CENTURY GIBBET CAGE

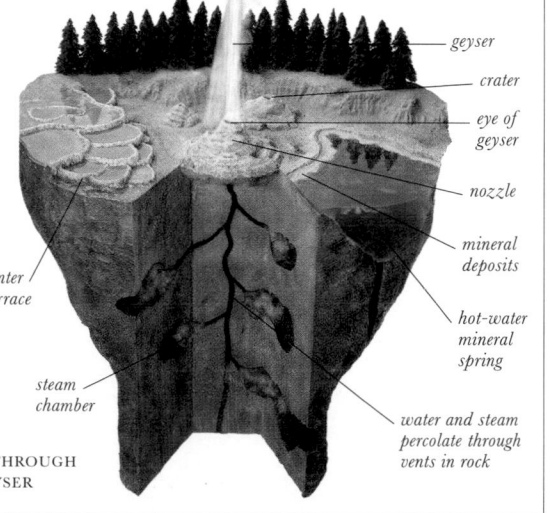

GEYSER

A geyser field occurs in a geothermal area, where trapped water is heated by energy within subterranean volcanic rocks. The eruption cycle begins as water seeps into caverns corroded into the rock. Intense heat causes the water in each chamber to boil and vaporize. Rising pressure then forces overlying water upwards through vents to the eye of the geyser, followed by steam. As pressure drops, the eruption dies, recommencing as the chambers refill.

geyser
crater
eye of geyser
nozzle
mineral deposits
hot-water mineral spring
water and steam percolate through vents in rock
sinter terrace
steam chamber

SECTION THROUGH A GEYSER

gild[1] *v.tr.* (*past part.* **gilded** or as adj. in sense 1 **gilt**) **1** cover thinly with gold. **2** tinge with a golden colour or light. **3** give a specious or false brilliance to. □ **gild the lily** try to improve what is already beautiful or excellent. [Old English] □ **gilder** *n.*

gild[2] var. of GUILD.

gilded cage *n.* a luxurious but restrictive environment.

gilded youth *n.pl.* young people of wealth, fashion, and flair.

gilding *n.* **1** the act or art of applying gilt. **2 ▶** material used in applying gilt.

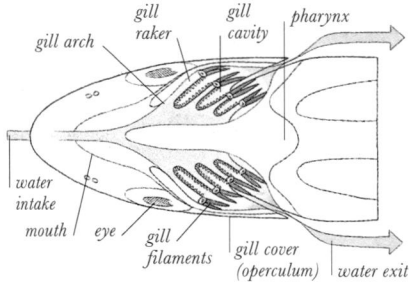

GILDING: MATERIALS REQUIRED FOR GILDING

protective parchment
gilt (gold leaf)
gilding tip
gilt applied to plaster ground
round-bladed knife

gilet /*zhee*-lay/ *n. Brit.* **1** a woman's light garment resembling a waistcoat. **2** a sleeveless padded jacket. [French, literally 'waistcoat']

gill[1] /gil/ *n.* (usu. in *pl.*) **1 ▼** the respiratory organ in fishes and other aquatic animals. **2** the vertical radial plates on the underside of mushrooms and other fungi. ▷ MUSHROOM. **3** the flesh below a person's jaws and ears (*green about the gills*). [from Old Norse] □ **gilled** *adj.* (also in *comb.*).

GILL: INTERNAL ANATOMY OF A FISH'S HEAD AND GILLS

gill raker *gill cavity* *pharynx* *gill arch* *water intake* *mouth* *eye* *gill filaments* *gill cover (operculum)* *water exit*

gill[2] /jil/ *n.* a unit of liquid measure, equal to a quarter of a pint. [from Late Latin *gillo* 'water pot']

gill[3] /gil/ *n.* (also **ghyll**) *Brit.* **1** a deep usu. wooded ravine. **2** a narrow mountain torrent. [from Old Norse *gil* 'glen']

gillie /gil-i/ *n.* (also **ghillie**) *Sc.* **1** a man or boy attending a person hunting or fishing. **2** *hist.* a Highland chief's attendant. [from Gaelic *gille* 'lad, servant']

gill-net *n.* a net for entangling fish by the gills.

gillyflower /jil-i-/ *n.* **1** (in full **clove gillyflower**) a clove-scented pink. **2** any of various similarly scented flowers such as the wallflower or white stock. [based on Greek *karuophullon* 'clove']

gilt[1] • *adj.* **1** covered thinly with gold. **2** gold-coloured. • *n.* **1** gold or a goldlike substance applied in a thin layer to a surface. **2** (often in *pl.*) *Brit.* a gilt-edged security. [variant of *gilded*]

gilt[2] *n.* a young sow. [from Old Norse *gyltr*]

gilt-edged *adj.* **1** (of securities, stocks, etc.) having a high degree of reliability as an investment. **2** having a gilded edge.

giltwood *adj.* made of wood and gilded.

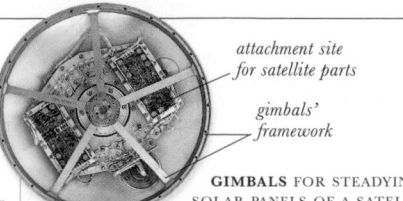

attachment site for satellite parts
gimbals' framework

GIMBALS FOR STEADYING SOLAR PANELS OF A SATELLITE

gimbals *n.pl.* ▲ a contrivance, usu. of rings and pivots, for keeping instruments horizontal in ships, aircraft, etc. [from Latin *gemellus* 'little twin']

gimcrack /jim-krak/ *adj.* showy but flimsy and worthless. [Middle English *gibecrake*, a kind of ornament] □ **gimcrackery** *n.*

gimlet *n.* a small tool with a screw-tip for boring holes. [from Old French *guimbelet*]

gimmick *n. colloq.* a trick or device, esp. to attract publicity or trade. [20th-century US coinage] □ **gimmickry** *n.* **gimmicky** *adj.*

gimp[1] /gimp/ *n.* (also **guimp**, **gymp**) **1** a twist of silk etc. with cord or wire running through it. **2** fishing line of silk etc. bound with wire. [Dutch]

gimp[2] /gimp/ *slang* • *n.* **1** a lame person or leg. **2** a stupid or contemptible person. • *v.intr.* limp, hobble. [20th-century US coinage]

gin[1] *n.* a spirit made from grain or malt and flavoured with juniper berries. [abbreviation of *geneva* 'genever']

gin[2] *n.* **1** a snare or trap. **2** a machine for separating cotton from its seeds. [from Old French *engin* 'engine'] □ **ginner** *n.*

ginger • *n.* **1 a** a hot spicy root usu. powdered for use in cooking, or preserved in syrup, or candied. ▷ SPICE. **b** the plant, *Zingiber officinale*, of SE Asia, having this root. **2** a light reddish-yellow. • *adj.* of a ginger colour. • *v.tr.* **1** flavour with ginger. **2** (foll. by *up*) enliven. [from Sanskrit *śṛṅgaveram*] □ **gingery** *adj.*

ginger ale *n.* an effervescent non-alcoholic clear drink flavoured with ginger extract.

ginger beer *n.* an effervescent mildly alcoholic or non-alcoholic cloudy drink made by fermenting a mixture of ginger and syrup.

gingerbread *n.* a cake made with treacle or syrup and flavoured with ginger.

ginger group *n. Brit.* a group within a party or movement that presses for stronger policy or action.

gingerly • *adv.* in a cautious manner. • *adj.* showing great caution.

ginger nut *n. Brit.* a ginger-flavoured biscuit.

ginger snap *n.* a thin brittle biscuit flavoured with ginger.

ginger wine *n.* a drink of fermented sugar, water, and bruised ginger.

gingham /ging-ăm/ *n.* a plain-woven cotton cloth, esp. striped or checked. [based on Malay *ginggang* 'striped']

gingivitis /jin-ji-vy-tis/ *n.* inflammation of the gums. [based on Latin *gingiva* 'gum']

ginkgo /gink-goh/ *n.* (also **gingko**) (*pl.* **-os** or **-oes**) ◀ an originally Chinese and Japanese tree, *Ginkgo biloba*, with fan-shaped leaves and yellow flowers. [Japanese *ginkyo* from Chinese *yinxing* 'silver apricot']

ginormous *adj. Brit. slang* very large; enormous. [blend of GIANT and ENORMOUS]

gin rummy *n.* a form of the card game rummy.

ginseng /jin-seng/ *n.* **1** any of several medicinal plants of the genus *Panax*, found in E. Asia and N. America. **2 ▶** the root of this. [from Chinese *renshen*, perhaps = man-image, with allusion to its forked root]

GINKGO: MAIDENHAIR TREE (*Ginkgo biloba*)

GINSENG ROOT (*Panax ginseng*)

GIRAFFE

The world's tallest animal, giraffes live among the acacias of the African savannah. The sole giraffe species contains eight subspecies, differing in their coat markings.

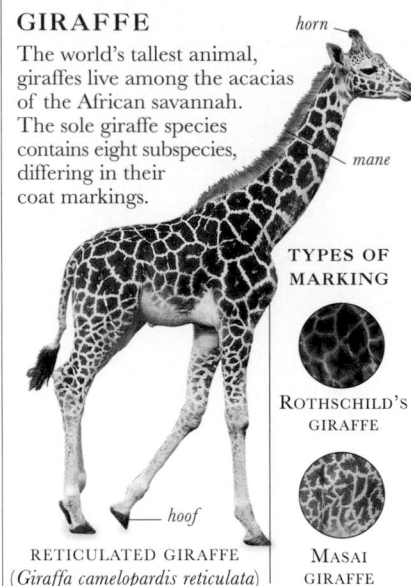

horn
mane
hoof

TYPES OF MARKING

ROTHSCHILD'S GIRAFFE

MASAI GIRAFFE

RETICULATED GIRAFFE (*Giraffa camelopardis reticulata*)

gippy tummy /jip-i/ *n.* (also **gyppy tummy**) *Brit. colloq.* diarrhoea affecting visitors to hot countries. [gippy: abbreviation of EGYPTIAN]

gipsy var. of GYPSY.

giraffe *n.* (*pl.* same or **giraffes**) ▲ a ruminant mammal, *Giraffa camelopardalis* of Africa, the tallest living animal, with a long neck and forelegs. [from Arabic *zarāfa*]

gird *v.tr.* (*past* and *past part.* **girded** or **girt**) *literary* **1** encircle, attach, or secure with a belt or band. **2** enclose or encircle. **3** (foll. by *round*) place (cord etc.) round. □ **gird** (or **gird up**) **one's loins** prepare for action. [Old English, related to GIRTH]

girder *n.* an iron or steel beam or compound structure for bearing loads.

girdle[1] • *n.* **1** a belt or cord worn round the waist. **2** a woman's corset extending from waist to thigh. **3** the bony support for a limb (*pelvic girdle*). • *v.tr.* surround with a girdle. [Old English, related to GIRD]

girdle[2] *n. Sc.* & *N.Engl.* = GRIDDLE.

girl *n.* **1** a female child. **2** *colloq.* a young woman. **3** *colloq.* a girlfriend. **4** a female servant. [Middle English] □ **girlhood** *n.*

girl Friday *n.* a female helper or follower. [after MAN FRIDAY]

girlfriend *n.* **1** a regular female companion or lover. **2** a female friend.

Girl Guide *n.* = GUIDE *n.* 9.

girlie (also **girly**) *colloq.* • *n.* (*pl.* **-ies**) a girl (esp. as a term of endearment). • *adj.* **1** girlish. **2** (of a magazine etc.) depicting young women in erotic poses.

girlish *adj.* of or like a girl. □ **girlishly** *adv.*

Girl Scout *n.* a girl belonging to the Scout Association.

giro /jy-roh/ *Brit.* • *n.* (*pl.* **-os**) **1** a system of credit transfer between banks, post offices, etc. **2** a cheque or payment by giro. • *v.tr.* (**-oes**, **-oed**) pay by giro. [from Italian, literally 'circulation (of money)']

girt[1] *past part.* of GIRD.

girt[2] var. of GIRTH.

girth *n.* (also **girt**) **1** the measurement around the waist, a tree trunk, or a thing of similar shape. **2** a band round the body of a horse to secure the saddle etc. ▷ SHOW-JUMPING. [from Gothic *gairda*]

gismo var. of GIZMO.

gist /jist/ *n.* the substance or essence of a matter. [based on Latin *jacēre* 'to lie, consist in']

G

gîte /zheet/ *n.* a furnished holiday house in France, usu. small and in a rural district. [originally in sense 'lodging': from Old French *gîste*]

give ● *v.* (*past* **gave**; *past part.* **given**) **1** *tr.* (also *absol.*) hand over as a present (*gave them her old curtains; gives to cancer research*). **2** *tr.* **a** transfer the ownership of; bequeath (*gave him £200 in her will*). **b** transfer, esp. temporarily or for safe keeping; hand over; provide with (*gave him the dog to look after; gave them a drink*). **c** administer (medicine). **d** communicate or impart (a message, compliments, etc.) (*give her my best wishes*). **3** *tr.* (usu. foll. by *for*) make over in exchange or payment (*gave him £30 for the bicycle*). **4** *tr.* **a** confer; grant (a benefit, an honour, etc.). **b** accord; bestow (one's affections, confidence, etc.). **c** award; administer (one's approval, blame, etc.); tell, offer (esp. something unpleasant) (*gave him my blessing; gave him the sack*). **d** pledge (*gave his word*). **5** *tr.* **a** perform (an action etc.) (*gave him a kiss; gave a jump*). **b** utter (*gave a shriek*). **6** *tr.* allot; assign; grant (*was given the contract*). **7** *tr.* (in *passive*; foll. by *to*) be inclined to or fond of (*is given to speculation*). **8** *tr.* yield as a product or result (*the lamp gives a bad light*). **9** *intr.* **a** yield to pressure; lose firmness (*they pushed hard but the door wouldn't give; old elastic gives too much*). **b** collapse (*the roof gave under the pressure*). **10** *intr.* (usu. foll. by *of*) grant; bestow (*gave freely of his time*). **11** *tr.* **a** commit, consign, or entrust (*give her into your care*). **b** sanction the marriage of (a daughter etc.). **12** *tr.* devote; dedicate (*gave his life to music*). **13** *tr.* (usu. *absol.*) *colloq.* tell what one knows (*What happened? Come on, give!*). **14** *tr.* present; offer; show; hold out (*gives no sign of life; gave her his arm*). **15** *tr. Theatr.* read, recite, perform, act, etc. (*gave them Hamlet's soliloquy*). **16** *tr.* impart; be a source of (*gave its name to the battle; gives him a right to complain*). **17** *tr.* allow (esp. a fixed amount of time) (*can give you five minutes*). **18** *tr.* (usu. foll. by *for*) value (something) (*gives nothing for their opinions*). **19** *tr.* concede (*I give you the victory*). **20** *tr.* deliver (a judgement etc.) authoritatively (*gave his verdict*). **21** *tr. Cricket* (of an umpire) declare (a batsman) out or not out. **22** *tr.* toast (a person, cause, etc.) (*I give you our President*). **23** *tr.* provide (a party, meal, etc.) as host (*gave a banquet*). ● *n.* **1** capacity to yield or bend under pressure; elasticity (*there is no give in a stone floor*). **2** ability to adapt or comply (*no give in his attitudes*). □ **give and take** *v.tr.* exchange (words, blows, or concessions). ● *n.* an exchange of words etc.; a compromise. **give as good as one gets** retort adequately in words or blows. **give away 1** transfer as a gift. **2** hand over (a bride) ceremonially to a bridegroom. **3** betray or expose to ridicule or detection. **4** esp. *Sport* give inadvertently to the opposition (*gave away a penalty*). **5** *Austral.* abandon, desist from, lose faith or interest in. **give back** return (something) to its previous owner or in exchange. **give birth** (**to**) see BIRTH. **give chase** pursue a person, animal, etc.; hunt. **give the game** (or **show**) **away** reveal a secret or intention. **give a hand** see HAND. **give a person his** or **her due** acknowledge, esp. grudgingly, a person's rights, abilities, etc. **give in 1** cease fighting or arguing; yield. **2** *Brit.* hand in (a document etc.) to an official etc. **give me** I prefer (*give me the Greek islands any day*). **give off** emit (vapour etc.). **give oneself** (of a woman) yield sexually. **give oneself airs** act pretentiously. **give oneself up to 1** abandon oneself to (an emotion). **2** addict oneself to. **give on to** (or **into**) (of a window, corridor, etc.) overlook or lead into. **give or take** *colloq.* add or subtract (a specified amount or number) in estimating. **give out 1** announce; emit; distribute. **2** cease or break down from exhaustion etc. **3** run short. **give over** *Brit.* **1** *colloq.* cease from doing; abandon (a habit etc.); desist (*give over sniffing*). **2** hand over. **3** devote. **give rise to** cause. **give a person to understand** inform authoritatively. **give up 1** resign; surrender. **2** part with. **3** deliver (a wanted person etc.). **4** pronounce incurable or insoluble; renounce hope of. **5** renounce or cease (an activity). **give up the ghost** *archaic* or *colloq.* die. **give way** see WAY. **give a person what for**

colloq. punish or scold severely. **not give a damn** (or *Brit.* **monkey's** or **toss** etc.) *colloq.* not care at all. **what gives?** *colloq.* what is the news?; what's happening? [Old English] □ **giver** *n.*

give-away *n. colloq.* **1** an inadvertent revelation. **2** an act of giving away. **3** a free gift; a low price.

given ● *adj.* **1** as previously stated or assumed; granted; specified (*given that he is a liar, we cannot trust him; a given number*). **2** *Law* (of a document) signed and dated (*given this day the 30th June*). ● *n.* a known fact or situation.

given name *n. US* = FORENAME.

gizmo /giz-moh/ *n.* (also **gismo**) (*pl.* **-os**) *slang* a gadget. [20th-century coinage]

gizzard *n.* **1** a muscular thick-walled part of a bird's stomach, for grinding food usu. with grit. ▷ BIRD. **2** a similar organ in some fish, insects, molluscs, and other invertebrates. [from Latin *gigeria* 'cooked entrails of fowl']

glacé /gla-say/ *adj.* **1** (of fruit, esp. cherries) preserved in sugar. **2** (of leather etc.) smooth; polished. [French, literally 'iced']

glacé icing *n.* icing made with icing sugar and water.

glacial *adj.* **1** of ice. **2** *Geol.* characterized or produced by ice. [from Latin *glacialis* 'icy'] □ **glacially** *adv.*

glacial period *n.* (also **glacial epoch**) a period in the Earth's history when ice sheets were exceptionally extensive.

glaciated *adj.* **1** marked or polished by the action of ice. **2** covered or having been covered by glaciers or ice sheets. □ **glaciation** *n.*

glacier *n.* ▼ a slowly-moving mass or river of ice formed by the accumulation and compaction of snow on mountains or near the poles. ▷ CIRQUE, OUTWASH, VALLEY. [from French, based on Latin *glacies* 'ice']

glaciology *n.* the science of the internal dynamics and effects of glaciers. □ **glaciological** *adj.* **glaciologist** *n.*

glad *adj.* (**gladder**, **gladdest**) **1** (*predic.*) pleased; willing (*shall be glad to come; would be glad of a chance to talk about it*). **2 a** marked by, filled with, or expressing joy (*a glad expression*). **b** (of news, events, etc.) giving joy (*glad tidings*). [Old English] □ **gladly** *adv.* **gladness** *n.* **gladsome** *adj. poet.*

gladden *v.tr.* make glad.

glade *n.* an open space in a forest. [Middle English]

GLADIOLUS
(*Gladiolus*
'Beau Rivage')

glad eye *n.* (prec. by *the*) *colloq.* an amorous glance.

glad hand ● *n.* a warm greeting or welcome. ● *v.tr.* (**glad-hand**) greet or welcome warmly. □ **glad-hander** *n.*

gladiator *n. hist.* a man trained to fight at ancient Roman shows. [Latin, based on *gladius* 'sword'] □ **gladiatorial** *adj.*

gladiolus *n.* (*pl.* **gladioli** /-ly/ or **gladioluses**) ◄ a plant of the genus *Gladiolus* (iris family), with sword-shaped leaves and usu. brightly coloured flower spikes. [Latin, literally 'little sword']

glad rags *n.pl. colloq.* best clothes.

Gladstone bag *n.* a bag like a briefcase having two equal compartments joined by a hinge. [named after W. E. *Gladstone*, English statesman, 1809–98]

glam *colloq.* ● *adj.* glamorous. ● *n.* glamour. [abbrev.]

glamorize *v.tr.* (also **glamourize**, **-ise**) make glamorous or attractive. □ **glamorization** *n.*

glamour *n.* (*US* also **glamor**) **1** physical attractiveness, esp. when achieved by make-up etc. **2** alluring or exciting beauty or charm (*the glamour of New York*). [variant of GRAMMAR, from the medieval association of learning with occult practices] □ **glamorous** *adj.* **glamorously** *adv.*

glamour girl *n.* (also **glamour boy**) an attractive young woman (or man).

glance ● *v.* **1** *intr.* cast a momentary look (*glanced up at the sky*). **2** *intr.* (of a bullet, ball, etc.) bounce (off an object) obliquely. **3** *intr.* (of talk or a talker) pass quickly over a subject or subjects (*glanced over the question of payment*). **4** *intr.* (of a bright object or light) flash, dart, or gleam (*the sun glanced off the knife*). **5** *tr.* (esp. of a weapon) strike (an object) obliquely. **6** *tr. Cricket* deflect (the ball) with an oblique stroke. ● *n.* **1** a brief look. **2** a flash or gleam (*a glance of sunlight*). **3** *Cricket* a stroke with the bat's face turned slantwise to deflect the ball. □ **at a glance** immediately upon looking. **glance over** (or **through**) read cursorily. [from Old French *glacier* 'to slip'] □ **glancingly** *adv.*

gland[1] *n.* **1 a** an organ in an animal body secreting substances for use in the body or for ejection. **b** a structure resembling this, such as a lymph gland. ▷ ENDOCRINE, LYMPHATIC SYSTEM. **2** *Bot.* a secreting cell or group of cells on the surface of a plant structure. [from Latin *glandulae* 'throat-glands']

G

GLACIER

A valley glacier forms from snow collected in cirques. The snow compresses into ice, which slowly creeps downhill under its own weight, gathering moraine (rocky debris) in its path, and gradually eroding a U-shaped valley. If ice at the snout melts faster than the overall creep of the glacier, then the glacier retreats. Meltwater streams deposit banks of sand and gravel, but flush finer sediment on to an outwash plain.

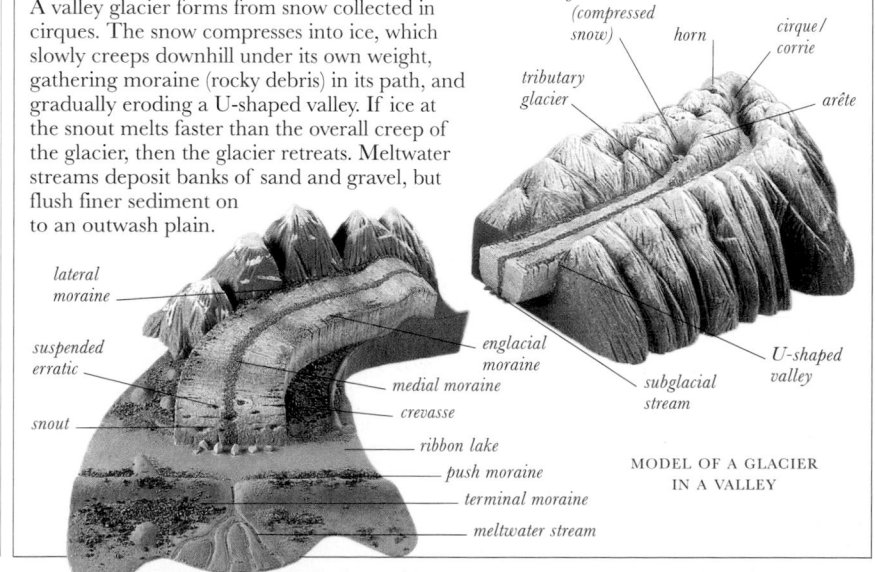

firn (compressed snow)
horn
cirque/corrie
tributary glacier
arête
lateral moraine
suspended erratic
englacial moraine
medial moraine
snout
crevasse
subglacial stream
U-shaped valley
ribbon lake
push moraine
terminal moraine
meltwater stream

MODEL OF A GLACIER IN A VALLEY

G

GLASS

A supercooled liquid made mainly from sand, glass is easily shaped, and forms clear, hard objects that remain untainted by chemicals. Glass objects are often mass-produced by the moulding process, in which jets of compressed air force molten glass into the shape of a mould. Sheet glass is made by the float-glass process, in which molten glass is floated on the surface of liquid tin and cut into lengths when cool.

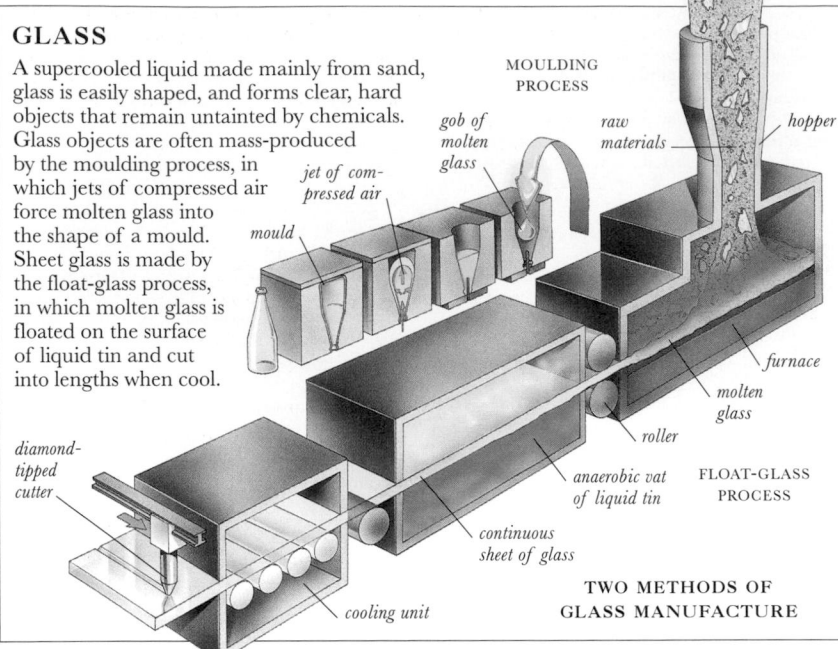

MOULDING PROCESS

gob of molten glass

jet of compressed air

mould

raw materials

hopper

furnace

molten glass

roller

anaerobic vat of liquid tin

FLOAT-GLASS PROCESS

diamond-tipped cutter

continuous sheet of glass

cooling unit

TWO METHODS OF GLASS MANUFACTURE

---

gland[2] *n.* a sleeve used to produce a seal round a piston rod or other shaft. [19th-century coinage]

glanders *n.pl.* (also treated as *sing.*) a contagious disease of horses. [from Old French *glandre*]

glandular *adj.* of or relating to a gland or glands.

glandular fever *n.* an infectious viral disease characterized by swelling of the lymph glands and prolonged lassitude; infectious mononucleosis.

glans *n.* (*pl.* **glandes**) the rounded part forming the end of the penis or clitoris. ▷ REPRODUCTIVE ORGANS. [Latin, literally 'acorn']

glare ● *v.* **1** *intr.* look fiercely or fixedly. **2** *intr.* shine dazzlingly or disagreeably. **3** *tr.* express (hatred, defiance, etc.) by a look. ● *n.* **1 a** strong fierce light, esp. sunshine. **b** oppressive public attention (*the glare of fame*). **2** a fierce or fixed look. [from Middle Dutch *glaren* 'to gleam, glare'] □ **glary** *adj.*

glaring *adj.* **1** obvious, conspicuous (*a glaring error*). **2** shining oppressively. **3** staring fiercely. □ **glaringly** *adv.*

glasnost /glaz-nost/ *n.* (in the former Soviet Union) the policy or practice of more open consultative government and wider dissemination of information. [Russian *glasnost'*, literally 'publicity, openness']

glass ● *n.* **1 a** (often *attrib.*) ▲ a hard, brittle, usu. transparent, translucent, or shiny substance, made by fusing sand with soda and lime and sometimes other ingredients. **b** any similar substance which has solidified from a molten state without crystallizing (*volcanic glass*). **2** (often *collect.*) an object or objects made from glass, esp.: **a** esp. *Brit.* a drinking vessel. **b** esp. *Brit.* a mirror. **c** an hourglass. **d** a window. **e** a greenhouse (*rows of lettuce under glass*). **f** glass ornaments. **g** a barometer. **h** *Brit.* a glass disc covering a watch face. **i** a magnifying lens. **j** a monocle. **3** (in *pl.*) **a** spectacles. **b** field glasses; opera glasses. **4** the amount of liquid contained in a glass; a drink (*he likes a glass*). ● *v.tr.* (usu. as **glassed** *adj.*) fit with glass. ● *adj.* of or made from glass. [Old English] □ **glassful** *n.* (*pl.* **-fuls**). **glasslike** *adj.*

glass-blowing *n.* the blowing of semi-molten glass to make glassware. □ **glass-blower** *n.*

glass case *n.* an exhibition display case made mostly from glass.

glass ceiling *n.* an unacknowledged barrier to personal advancement.

glass cutter *n.* **1** a worker who cuts glass. **2** a tool used for cutting glass.

glass eye *n.* a false eye made from glass.

glass fibre *n. Brit.* **1** filaments of glass made into fabric. **2** such filaments embedded in plastic as reinforcement (often *attrib.*: *glass-fibre gliders*).

glasshouse *n. Brit.* **1** a greenhouse. **2** *slang* a military prison.

glasspaper *n.* paper covered with powdered glass and used for smoothing and polishing.

glassware *n.* articles made from glass.

glass wool *n.* glass in the form of fine fibres used for packing and insulation.

glasswort *n.* a salt-marsh plant of the genus *Salicornia* or *Salsola*, formerly burnt for use in glass-making. ▷ HALOPHYTE

glassy *adj.* (**glassier**, **glassiest**) **1** of or resembling glass, esp. in smoothness. **2** (of the eye, the expression, etc.) abstracted; dull; fixed (*fixed her with a glassy stare*). □ **glassily** *adv.*

Glaswegian ● *adj.* of or relating to Glasgow in Scotland. ● *n.* a native of Glasgow. [from *Glasgow*, on the pattern of *Norwegian* etc.]

glaucoma *n.* an eye-condition with increased pressure within the eyeball, causing gradual loss of sight. [based on Greek *glaukos* 'glaucous', from the grey-green haze in the pupil]

glaucous *adj.* **1** ◄ of a dull greyish-green or blue colour. **2** covered with a powdery bloom as of grapes. [from Greek *glaukos*]

glaze ● *v.* **1** *tr.* **a** fit (a window, picture, etc.) with glass. **b** provide (a building) with glass windows. **2** *tr.* **a** cover (pottery etc.) with a glaze. **b** fix (paint) on pottery with a glaze. **3** *tr.* cover (pastry, meat, etc.) with a glaze. **4** *intr.* (often foll. by *over*) (of the eyes) become fixed or glassy. **5** *tr.* cover (cloth, paper, leather, a painted surface, etc.) with a glaze or other similar finish. **6** *tr.* give a glassy surface to, e.g. by rubbing. ● *n.* **1** a vitreous substance used to glaze pottery. **2** a smooth shiny coating on food. **3** a thin topcoat of transparent paint used to modify the tone of the underlying colour. **4** a smooth surface formed by glazing. [Middle English]

GLAUCOUS
FOLIAGE OF A
EUCALYPTUS TREE

glazier *n.* a person whose trade is glazing windows etc. □ **glaziery** *n.*

glazing *n.* **1** the act or an instance of glazing. **2** windows (see also DOUBLE GLAZING). **3** material used to produce a glaze.

gleam ● *n.* **1** a faint or brief light (*a gleam of sunlight*). **2** a faint, sudden, or temporary show (*not a gleam of hope*). ● *v.intr.* **1** emit gleams. **2** shine with a faint or intermittent brightness. **3** (of a quality) be indicated (*fear gleamed in his eyes*). [Old English]

glean *v.tr.* **1** collect or scrape together (news, facts, gossip, etc.) in small quantities. **2 a** (also *absol.*) gather (ears of corn etc.) after the harvest. **b** strip (a field etc.) after a harvest. [from Late Latin *glennare*] □ **gleaner** *n.*

gleanings *n.pl.* things gleaned, esp. facts.

glebe *n.* **1** a piece of land serving as part of a clergyman's benefice and providing income. **2** *poet.* earth; land; a field. [from Latin *gl(a)eba* 'clod, soil']

glee *n.* **1** mirth; delight. **2** a song for three or more voices, singing different parts simultaneously. [Old English *glēo* 'minstrelsy, jest']

glee club *n.* a society for singing part-songs.

gleeful *adj.* exuberantly or triumphantly joyful. □ **gleefully** *adv.*

glen *n.* a narrow valley. [from Gaelic & Irish *gleann*]

glengarry *n.* (*pl.* **-ies**) ► a brimless Scottish hat with a cleft down the centre and usu. two ribbons hanging at the back. [named after *Glengarry* in Scotland]

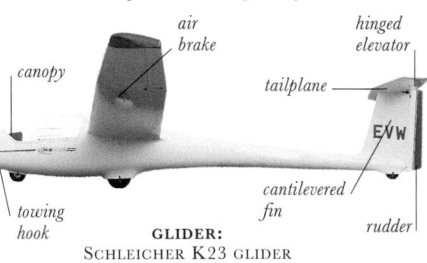

ribbon

GLENGARRY:
WORLD WAR I SCOTTISH
BATTALION GLENGARRY

glib *adj.* (**glibber**, **glibbest**) fluent and voluble but insincere and shallow. [related to obsolete *glibbery* 'slippery'] □ **glibly** *adv.* **glibness** *n.*

glide ● *v.* **1** *intr.* (of a stream, bird, snake, ship, train, skater, etc.) move with a smooth continuous motion. **2** *intr.* (of an aircraft) fly without engine power. **3** *intr.* of time etc.: **a** pass gently and imperceptibly. **b** pass and change gradually and imperceptibly (*night glided into day*). **4** *intr.* move stealthily. **5** *tr.* cause to glide (*breezes glided the ship on its course*). ● *n.* **1** the act of gliding. **2** an instance of this. [Old English]

glide path *n.* an aircraft's line of descent to land.

glider *n.* **1** ▼ an aircraft that flies without an engine. ▷ AIRCRAFT. **2** a person or thing that glides.

air brake

hinged elevator

canopy

tailplane

EVW

cantilevered fin

towing hook

rudder

GLIDER:
SCHLEICHER K23 GLIDER

gliding *n.* the sport of flying in a glider.

glimmer ● *v.intr.* shine faintly or intermittently. ● *n.* **1** a feeble or wavering light. **2** (usu. foll. by *of*) a faint gleam (of hope, understanding, etc.). **3** a glimpse. [Middle English]

glimmering *n.* **1** = GLIMMER *n.* **2** an act of glimmering.

glimpse ● *n.* **1** a momentary or partial view (*caught a glimpse of her*). **2** a faint and transient appearance (*glimpses of the truth*). ● *v.tr.* see faintly or partly (*glimpsed his face in the crowd*). [Middle English]

glint ● *v.intr. & tr.* flash or cause to flash; glitter; sparkle; reflect (*eyes glinted with amusement; the sword glinted fire*). ● *n.* a brief flash of light; a sparkle. [alteration of Middle English *glent*]

glissade /gli-sahd/ ● *n.* **1** an act of sliding down a steep slope of snow or ice, usu. on the feet with the support of an ice axe etc. **2** a gliding step in ballet. ● *v.intr.* perform a glissade. [French]

glissando *n.* (*pl.* **glissandi** or **-os**) *Mus.* a continuous slide of adjacent notes upwards or downwards. [Italian, from French *glissant* 'sliding']

glisten ● *v.intr.* shine, esp. like a wet object, snow, etc. ● *n.* a glitter; a sparkle. [Old English]

glister *archaic* ● *v.intr.* sparkle; glitter. ● *n.* a sparkle; a gleam. [Middle English]

glitch *n. colloq.* a sudden irregularity or malfunction. [20th-century coinage]

glitter ● *v.intr.* **1** shine, esp. with a bright reflected light; sparkle. **2** (usu. foll. by *with*) **a** be showy or splendid (*glittered with diamonds*). **b** be ostentatious or flashily brilliant (*glittering rhetoric*). ● *n.* **1** a sparkle. **2** showiness. **3** tiny pieces of sparkling material. [from Old Norse *glitra*] □ **glittery** *adj.*

glitterati *n.pl. slang* the fashionable set of literary or show-business people.

glitz *n. slang* extravagant but superficial display.

glitzy *adj.* (**glitzier**, **glitziest**) *slang* extravagant, ostentatious; tawdry, gaudy. [based on GLITTER, suggested by RITZY]

gloaming *n. poet.* twilight; dusk. [Old English]

gloat ● *v.intr.* (often foll. by *on, upon, over*) consider or contemplate with lust, greed, malice, triumph, etc. (*gloated over his collection*). ● *n.* **1** the act of gloating. **2** a look or expression of triumphant satisfaction. [16th-century coinage]

glob *n.* a mass or lump of semi-liquid substance, e.g. mud. [20th-century coinage]

global *adj.* **1** worldwide (*global conflict*). **2 a** relating to or embracing a group of items etc.; total. **b** *Computing* operating or applying through the whole of a file, program, etc. □ **globally** *adv.*

globalize *v.tr.* (also **-ise**) make global. □ **globalization** *n.*

global village *n.* the world considered as a single community linked by telecommunications.

global warming *n.* ▼ a potential increase in temperature of the Earth's atmosphere caused by the greenhouse effect

globe *n.* **1 a** (prec. by *the*) the planet Earth. **b** a planet, star, or sun. **c** any spherical body, a ball. **2** a spherical representation of the Earth or of the constellations with a map on the surface. **3** a golden

GLOBAL WARMING

For millions of years, gases in the Earth's atmosphere have trapped sufficient heat from solar radiation to sustain life. However, an increase in human activity may now be raising levels of 'greenhouse gases' such as carbon dioxide, so that excess heat is trapped in the atmosphere.

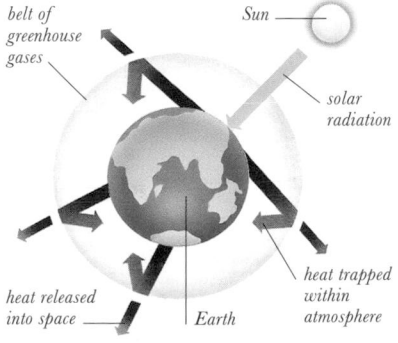

belt of greenhouse gases
Sun
solar radiation
heat released into space
Earth
heat trapped within atmosphere

DEMONSTRATION OF GLOBAL WARMING

sphere as an emblem of sovereignty; an orb. **4** any spherical glass vessel, esp. a fishbowl, a lamp, etc. [from Latin *globus*] □ **globose** *adj.*

globe artichoke *n.* ◄ the head of the artichoke plant.

globe-trotter *n.* a person who travels widely. □ **globe-trotting** *n. & attrib.adj.*

globular *adj.* **1** globe-shaped, spherical. **2** composed of globules.

globule *n.* a small globe or round particle; a drop. [from Latin *globulus*]

globulin *n.* any of a group of single proteins characterized by solubility only in salt solutions and esp. forming a large fraction of blood serum protein.

glockenspiel /**glok**-ĕn-speel/ *n.* a musical instrument with bells or metal bars or tubes struck by hammers. [German, literally 'bell-play']

gloom ● *n.* **1** darkness; obscurity. **2** melancholy; despondency. **3** *poet.* a dark place. ● *v.* **1** *intr.* be gloomy or melancholy; frown. **2** *intr.* (of the sky etc.) be dull or threatening; lour. **3** *intr.* appear darkly or obscurely. **4** *tr.* cover with gloom; make dark or dismal. [Middle English]

gloomy *adj.* (**gloomier**, **gloomiest**) **1** dark; unlighted. **2** depressed; sullen. **3** dismal; depressing. □ **gloomily** *adv.* **gloominess** *n.*

glop *n. US slang* a liquid or sticky mess, esp. inedible food.

glorify *v.tr.* (**-ies**, **-ied**) **1** make glorious. **2** transform into something more splendid. **3** extol; praise. **4** (as **glorified** *adj.*) seeming or pretending to be more splendid than in reality (*a glorified office boy*). [from ecclesiastical Latin *glorificare*] □ **glorification** *n.*

glorious *adj.* **1** possessing glory; illustrious. **2** conferring glory; honourable. **3** *colloq.* splendid; magnificent; delightful (*a glorious day*). **4** *iron.* intense; unmitigated (*a glorious muddle*). □ **gloriously** *adv.*

glory ● *n.* (*pl.* **-ies**) **1** high renown or fame; honour. **2** adoring praise (*Glory to the Lord*). **3** resplendent majesty or magnificence; great beauty (*the glory of Versailles*; *the glory of the rose*). **4** a thing that brings renown or praise; a distinction. **5** the bliss and splendour of heaven. **6** an aureole, a halo. ● *v.intr.* (**-ies**, **-ied**) pride oneself; exult (*glory in their skill*). □ **glory be!** **1** expressing enthusiastic piety. **2** *colloq.* an exclamation of surprise or delight. [from Latin *gloria*]

glory-box *n. Austral. & NZ* a box for women's clothes etc., stored in preparation for marriage.

glory-hole *n.* **1** *colloq.* an untidy room, drawer, or receptacle. **2** *N. Amer.* an open quarry.

glory-of-the-snow *n.* – CHIONODOXA.

gloss¹ ● *n.* **1 a** a surface shine or lustre. **b** an instance of this; a smooth finish. **2 a** a deceptively attractive appearance. **b** an instance of this. **3** (in full **gloss paint**) paint formulated to give a hard glossy finish (cf. MATT *n.*). ● *v.tr.* make glossy. □ **gloss over 1** seek to conceal beneath a false appearance. **2** conceal or evade by mentioning briefly or misleadingly. [16th-century coinage]

gloss² ● *n.* **1 a** an explanatory word or phrase inserted between the lines or in the margin of a text. **b** a comment, explanation, interpretation, or paraphrase. **2** a misrepresentation of another's words. **3 a** a glossary. **b** an interlinear translation or annotation. ● *v.tr.* **1** write a gloss or glosses to (a text, word, etc.). **2** read a different sense into; explain away. [alteration of GLOZE]

glossary *n.* (*pl.* **-ies**) (also **gloss**) an alphabetical list of terms or words found in or relating to a specific subject or text; a brief dictionary. [from Latin *glossarium*]

glossolalia *n.* = *gift of tongues* (see TONGUE). [from Greek *glōssa* 'tongue' + *-lalia* 'speaking']

glossy ● *adj.* (**glossier**, **glossiest**) **1** having a shine; smooth. **2** (of paper etc.) smooth and shiny. **3** (of a magazine etc.) printed on such paper. ● *n.* (*pl.* **-ies**) *colloq.* **1** a glossy magazine. **2** a photograph with a glossy surface. □ **glossily** *adv.* **glossiness** *n.*

glottal stop *n.* a sound produced by the sudden opening or shutting of the glottis.

glottis *n.* ▼ the part of the larynx that consists of the vocal cords and the slit-like opening between them. [based on Greek *glōtta*, variant of *glōssa* 'tongue']

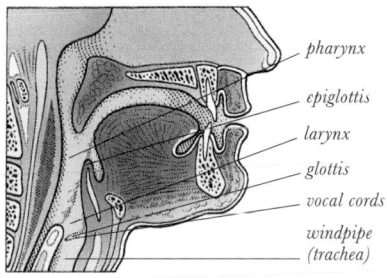

pharynx
epiglottis
larynx
glottis
vocal cords
windpipe (trachea)

GLOTTIS: INTERNAL FEATURES OF THE HUMAN HEAD SHOWING THE GLOTTIS

glove ● *n.* **1** a covering for the hand, worn esp. for protection against cold or dirt, and usu. having separate fingers. **2** a padded protective glove, esp.: **a** a boxing glove. **b** a glove worn by a wicketkeeper or baseball catcher. ● *v.tr.* cover or provide with a glove or gloves. [Old English] □ **glover** *n.*

glovebox *n.* **1** a box for gloves. **2** a closed chamber with sealed-in gloves for handling radioactive material etc. **3** = GLOVE COMPARTMENT.

glove compartment *n.* a recess for small articles in the dashboard of a motor vehicle.

glove puppet *n.* esp. *Brit.* a small cloth puppet fitted on the hand and worked by the fingers.

glow ● *v.intr.* **1 a** throw out light and heat without flame. **b** shine like something heated in this way. **2** (of the cheeks) redden, esp. from cold or exercise. **3 a** (of the body) be heated. **b** express or experience strong emotion (*glowing with indignation*). **4** show a warm colour (*the painting glows with warmth*). **5** (as **glowing** *adj.*) expressing pride or satisfaction (*a glowing report*). ● *n.* **1** a glowing state. **2** a bright warm colour, esp. the red of cheeks. **3** ardour; passion. **4** a feeling induced by good health, exercise, etc.; well-being. [Old English] □ **glowingly** *adv.*

glower ● *v.intr.* stare or scowl, esp. angrily. ● *n.* a glowering look. □ **gloweringly** *adv.*

glow-worm *n.* a soft-bodied beetle of the genus *Lampyris* whose wingless female emits light from the end of the abdomen.

gloxinia *n.* any tropical plant of the genus *Gloxinia*, native to S. America, with large bell flowers. [named after B. P. *Gloxin*, 18th-century German botanist]

gloze *v.tr.* (also **gloze over**) explain away; extenuate; palliate. [based on Latin *glossa* 'tongue']

glucose *n.* a simple sugar containing six carbon atoms, found in fruit juice etc., which is an important energy source in living organisms. [from Greek *gleukos* 'sweet wine']

glue ● *n.* an adhesive substance used for sticking objects or materials together. ● *v.tr.* (**glues**, **glued**, **gluing** or **glueing**) **1** fasten or join with glue. **2** keep or put very close (*an eye glued to the keyhole*). [from Latin *gluten*] □ **gluey** *adj.* (**gluier**, **gluiest**).

glue ear *n.* blocking of the Eustachian tube, esp. in children.

glue-sniffing *n.* the inhalation of intoxicating fumes from the solvents in adhesives etc. □ **glue-sniffer** *n.*

glühwein /**gloo**-vyn/ *n.* mulled wine. [German]

glum *adj.* (**glummer**, **glummest**) looking or feeling dejected; sullen. [related to dialect *glum* 'to frown'] □ **glumly** *adv.* **glumness** *n.*

glut ● *v.tr.* (**glutted**, **glutting**) **1** feed (a person, one's stomach, etc.) or indulge (an appetite, a desire, etc.) to the full; satiate. **2** fill to excess. **3** *Econ.* overstock (a market). ● *n.* **1** *Econ.* supply exceeding demand. **2** full indulgence. [Middle English]

GLOBE ARTICHOKE (*Cynara scolymus*)

G

glutamate *n.* any salt or ester of glutamic acid, esp. a sodium salt used to enhance the flavour of food.

glutamic acid *n. Biochem.* a naturally occurring amino acid, a constituent of many proteins.

gluten *n.* a mixture of two proteins present in flour. [from Latin *gluten* 'glue']

gluteus *n.* (*pl.* **glutei**) ▼ any of the three muscles in each buttock. [from Greek *gloutos* 'buttock'] □ **gluteal** *adj.*

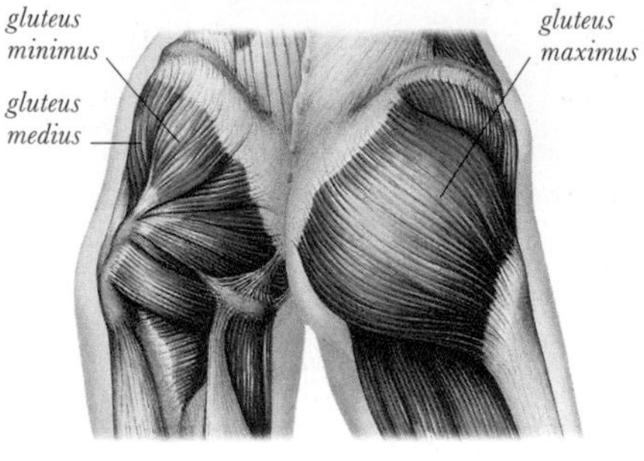

GLUTEUS MUSCLES IN THE HUMAN BUTTOCKS

glutinous *adj.* sticky; like glue. [from Latin *glutinosus*] □ **glutinously** *adv.* **glutinousness** *n.*

glutton *n.* **1** a greedy eater. **2** *colloq.* a person insatiably eager (*a glutton for work*). **3** a voracious animal, *Gulo gulo*, of the weasel family. □ **glutton for punishment** a person eager to take on hard or unpleasant tasks. [based on Latin *gluttus* 'greedy'] □ **gluttonous** *adj.* **gluttonously** *adv.*

gluttony *n.* greed or excess in eating.

glycerine /**gliss**-er-een/ *n.* (*US* **glycerin**) = GLYCEROL. [based on Greek *glukeros* 'sweet']

glycerol /**gliss**-er-ol/ *n.* a colourless sweet viscous liquid formed as a by-product in the manufacture of soap, used as an emollient and laxative, and in explosives, antifreeze, etc.

glyco- /**gly**-koh/ *comb. form* sugar. [from Greek *glukus* 'sweet']

glycogen *n. Biochem.* a polysaccharide serving as a store of carbohydrates, esp. in animal tissues.

glycolysis *n. Biochem.* the breakdown of glucose by enzymes.

glycoprotein *n.* any of a class of compounds consisting of a protein combined with a carbohydrate.

glycosuria *n.* a condition characterized by an excess of sugar in the urine, associated with diabetes, kidney disease, etc. □ **glycosuric** *adj.*

glyph *n.* **1** a sculptured character or symbol. **2** a vertical groove, esp. that on a Greek frieze. [from Greek *gluphē* 'carving'] □ **glyphic** *adj.*

GM *abbr.* **1** (in the UK) George Medal. **2** (in the US) General Motors. **3** general manager. **4** *Brit.* grant-maintained.

gm *abbr.* gram(s).

G-man *n.* (*pl.* **G-men**) **1** *US colloq.* an FBI agent. **2** *Ir.* a political detective. [G: abbreviation of *government*]

GMT *abbr.* Greenwich Mean Time.

gnarled *adj.* (also **gnarly**) (of a tree, hands, etc.) knobbly, twisted, rugged. [variant of *knarled*, related to KNURL] □ **gnarl** *n.*

gnash ● *v.* **1** *tr.* grind (the teeth). **2** *intr.* (of the teeth) strike together; grind. ● *n.* an act of grinding the teeth. [variant of obsolete *gnacche* or *gnast*]

gnashers *n.pl. slang* teeth, esp. false teeth.

gnat *n.* **1** any small two-winged biting fly of the genus *Culex*, esp. *C. pipiens*. **2** an insignificant annoyance. **3** a tiny thing. [Old English]

gnaw *v.* (*past part.* **gnawed** or **gnawn**) **1 a** *tr.* bite persistently; wear away by biting. **b** *intr.* bite, nibble. **2 a** *intr.* (foll. by *at*, *into*) (of a destructive agent, pain, fear, etc.) corrode; waste away; consume; torture. **b** *tr.* corrode, consume, torture, etc. with pain, fear, etc. (*was gnawed by doubt*). **3** *tr.* (as **gnawing** *adj.*) persistent; worrying. [Old English]

gneiss /nyss/ *n.* ► a usu. coarse-grained metamorphic rock principally of feldspar, quartz, and ferromagnesian minerals. ▷ METAMORPHIC, ROCK CYCLE. [German]

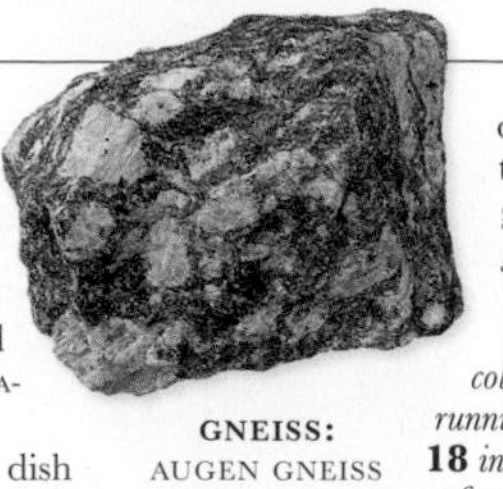

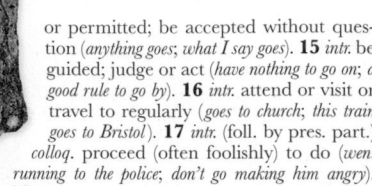

GNEISS: AUGEN GNEISS

gnocchi /**n'yok**-i/ *n.pl.* an Italian dish of small dumplings usu. made from potato, semolina flour, etc., and often flavoured with spinach and cheese. [Italian, based on *nocchio* 'knot in wood']

gnome *n.* **1 a** a dwarfish legendary creature supposed to guard the Earth's treasures underground. **b** a figure of a gnome, esp. as a garden ornament. **2** (esp. in *pl.*) *colloq.* a person with sinister influence, esp. financial (*gnomes of Zurich*). [from modern Latin *gnomus*, word invented by Paracelsus] □ **gnomish** *adj.*

gnomic *adj.* of, consisting of, or using aphorisms; sententious. [based on Greek *gnōmē* 'opinion']

gnomon *n.* **1** ► the rod or pin etc. on a sundial that shows the time by the position of its shadow. **2** *Astron.* a column etc. used in observing the Sun's meridian altitude. [from Greek *gnōmōn* 'indicator'] □ **gnomonic** *adj.*

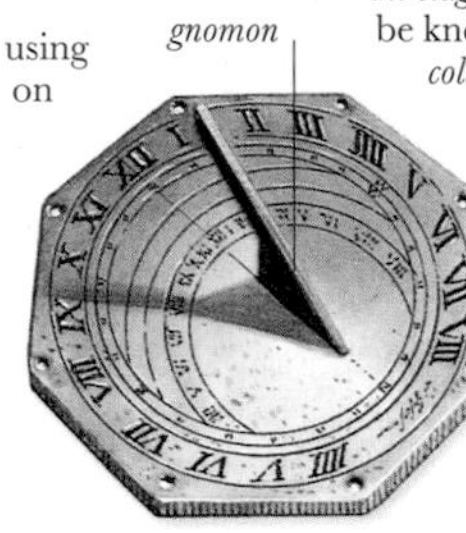

GNOMON ON AN 18TH-CENTURY SUNDIAL

gnostic ● *adj.* **1** relating to knowledge, esp. esoteric mystical knowledge. **2** (**Gnostic**) concerning the Gnostics; occult; mystic. ● *n.* (**Gnostic**) (usu. in *pl.*) a Christian heretic of the 1st–3rd c. claiming mystical knowledge. [from Greek *gnōstikos*] □ **Gnosticism** *n.*

GNP *abbr.* gross national product.

gnu *n.* any antelope of the genus *Connochaetes*, native to S. Africa, with a large erect head. [from Aboriginal *nqu*]

GNVQ *abbr.* General National Vocational Qualification.

go[1] ● *v.* (*3rd sing. present* **goes**; *past* **went**; *past part.* **gone**) **1** *intr.* **a** start moving or be moving from one place or point in time to another; travel, proceed. **b** (foll. by *to* + infin., or *and* + verb) proceed in order to (*went to find him*; *go and buy some bread*). **c** (foll. by *and* + verb) *colloq.* expressing annoyance (*you went and told him*; *they've gone and broken it*). **2** *intr.* (foll. by verbal noun) make a special trip for; participate in; proceed to do (*went skiing*; *then went shopping*; *often goes running*). **3** *intr.* lie or extend in a certain direction (*the road goes to London*). **4** *intr.* leave; depart (*they had to go*). **5** *intr.* move, act, work, etc. (*the clock doesn't go*; *his brain is going all the time*). **6** *intr.* **a** make a specified movement (*go like this*). **b** make a sound (of a specified kind) (*the gun went bang*; *the cow went 'moo'*). **c** (of a bell etc.) make a sound in functioning (*with its sirens going*). **d** *colloq.* say (*so he goes to me 'Why didn't you like it?'*). **7** *intr.* be in a specified state (*go hungry*; *went in fear of his life*). **8** *intr.* **a** pass into a specified condition (*gone bad*; *went to sleep*). **b** *colloq.* die. **c** proceed or escape in a specified condition (*the poet went unrecognized*; *the crime went unnoticed*). **9** *intr.* (of time or distance) pass, elapse; be traversed (*ten days to go before Easter*; *the last mile went quickly*). **10** *intr.* **a** have a specified content or wording (*the tune goes like this*). **b** be current or accepted (*so the story goes*). **c** be suitable; fit; match (*the shoes don't go with the hat*). **d** be regularly kept or put (*the forks go here*). **e** fit; be accommodated (*this won't go into the cupboard*). **11** *intr.* **a** turn out, proceed; take a course or view (*things went well*; *Liverpool went Labour*). **b** be successful (*make the party go*; *went like a bomb*). **c** progress (*we've still a long way to go*). **12** *intr.* **a** be sold (*went for £1*). **b** (of money) be spent (*£200 went on a new jacket*). **13** *intr.* **a** be relinquished, dismissed, or abolished (*the car will have to go*). **b** fail, decline; give way, collapse (*his sight is going*; *the bulb has gone*). **14** *intr.* be acceptable or permitted; be accepted without question (*anything goes*; *what I say goes*). **15** *intr.* be guided; judge or act (*have nothing to go on*; *a good rule to go by*). **16** *intr.* attend or visit or travel to regularly (*goes to church*; *this train goes to Bristol*). **17** *intr.* (foll. by pres. part.) *colloq.* proceed (often foolishly) to do (*went running to the police*; *don't go making him angry*). **18** *intr.* act or proceed to a certain point (*will go so far and no further*; *went as high as £100*). **19** *intr. colloq.* (of a number) be capable of being contained in another (*6 into 5 won't go*). **20** *tr. Cards* bid; declare (*go nap*; *has gone two spades*). **21** *intr.* be allotted or awarded; pass (*the job went to his rival*). **22** *intr.* (foll. by *to*, *towards*) amount to; contribute to (*12 inches go to make a foot*; *this will go towards your holiday*). **23** *intr.* (in *imper.*) begin motion (a starter's order in a race) (*ready, steady, go!*). **24** *intr.* refer or appeal (*go to him for help*). **25** *intr.* take up a specified profession (*went on the stage*; *gone soldiering*). **26** *intr.* (usu. foll. by *by*, *under*) be known or called (*goes by the name of Droopy*). **27** *tr. colloq.* proceed to (*go jump in the lake*). **28** *intr.* (foll. by *for*) apply to; have relevance for (*that goes for me too*). ● *n.* (*pl.* **goes**) **1** the act or an instance of going. **2** mettle; spirit; dash; animation (*she has a lot of go in her*). **3** vigorous activity (*it's all go*). **4** *colloq.* a success (*made a go of it*). **5** *colloq.* a turn; an attempt (*I'll have a go*; *it's my go*). **6** esp. *Brit. colloq.* a state of affairs (*a rum go*). **7** esp. *Brit. colloq.* an attack of illness (*a bad go of flu*). **8** esp. *Brit. colloq.* a quantity of liquor, food, etc. served at one time. ● *adj. colloq.* functioning properly (*all systems are go*). □ **from the word go** *colloq.* from the very beginning. **go about 1** busy oneself with; set to work at. **2** be socially active. **3** (foll. by pres. part.) make a habit of doing (*goes about telling lies*). **4** *Naut.* change to an opposite tack. **go against 1** be contrary to (*goes against my principles*). **2** have an unfavourable result for (*decision went against them*). **go ahead** proceed without hesitation. **go along with** agree to; take the same view as. **go around 1** (foll. by *with*) be regularly in the company of. **2** = *go about* 3. **go at** take in hand energetically; attack. **go away** depart, esp. from home for a holiday etc. **go back 1** return (to). **2** extend backwards in space or time. **3** (of the hour, a clock, etc.) be set to an earlier standard time (*the clocks go back in the autumn*). **go back on** fail to keep (one's word, promise, etc.). **go bail** see BAIL[1]. **go begging** see BEG. **go by 1** pass. **2** be dependent on; be guided by. **go by default** see DEFAULT. **go down 1 a** (of an amount) become less (*the coffee has gone down a lot*). **b** subside (*the flood went down*). **c** decrease in price; lose value. **2 a** (of a ship) sink. **b** (of the Sun) set. **3** (usu. foll. by *to*) be continued to a specified point. **4** deteriorate; fail; (of a computer network etc.) cease to function. **5** be recorded in writing. **6** be swallowed. **7** (often foll. by *with*) find acceptance. **8** *Brit. colloq.* leave university. **9** *Brit. colloq.* be sent to prison (*went down for ten years*). **10** fall (before a conqueror). **go down with** *Brit.* begin to suffer from (a disease). **go Dutch** see DUTCH. **go far** be very successful. **go for 1** go to fetch. **2** be accounted as or achieve (*went for nothing*). **3** prefer; choose (*that's the one I go for*). **4** *colloq.* strive to attain (*go for it!*). **5** *colloq.* attack (*the dog went for him*). **go forward 1** proceed, progress (*go forward into the next round*). **2** (of the hour, a clock, etc.) be altered to a later time, esp. summer time. **go great guns** see GUN. **go halves** (or **shares**) share equally. **go in 1** enter a room, house, etc. **2** (usu. foll. by *for*) enter as a competitor. **3** (of the Sun etc.) become obscured by cloud. **go in for** take as one's object, style, pursuit, principle, etc. **going!, gone!** an auctioneer's announcement that bidding is closing or closed. **go into 1** enter (a place); go to stay in (hospital etc.). **2** pass into (a state or condition) (*he has gone into hiding*; *the company went into liquidation*). **3** investigate or discuss. **4** (of resources etc.) be invested in (*a lot of effort went into this*). **5** start a career or interest in. **6** dress oneself in (mourning etc.).

go it *Brit. colloq.* **1** act vigorously, furiously, etc. **2** indulge in dissipation. **go a long way 1** have a great effect; contribute or progress significantly. **2** (of food, money, etc.) last a long time, buy much. **3** = *go far.* **go off 1** explode. **2** leave the stage. **3** gradually cease to be felt. **4** (esp. of foodstuffs) deteriorate; decompose. **5** go to sleep; become unconscious. **6** begin. **7** (of an alarm) begin to sound. **8** die. **9** be got rid of by sale etc. **10** *Brit. colloq.* begin to dislike (*I've gone off him*). **go off at** *Austral.* & *NZ slang* reprimand, scold. **go off well** (or **badly** etc.) (of an enterprise etc.) be received or accomplished well (or badly etc.). **go on 1** continue, persevere (*decided to go on with it; went on trying; unable to go on*). **2** *colloq.* **a** talk at great length. **b** (foll. by *at*) admonish (*went on and on at him*). **3** (foll. by *to* + infin.) proceed (*went on to become a star*). **4** happen. **5** conduct oneself (*shameful, the way they went on*). **6** *Theatr.* appear on stage. **7** *Cricket* begin bowling. **8** (of a garment) be large enough for its wearer. **9** take one's turn to do something. **10** (also **go upon**) *Brit. colloq.* use as evidence (*police don't have anything to go on*). **11** (esp. in *neg.*) *colloq.* **a** concern oneself about. **b** care for (*don't go much on red hair*). **go out 1** leave a room, house, etc. **2** be broadcast. **3** be extinguished. **4** have a sexual relationship. **5** (of a government) leave office. **6** cease to be fashionable. **7** (usu. foll. by *to*) depart, esp. to a colony etc. **8** *colloq.* lose consciousness. **9** (of workers) strike. **10** (usu. foll. by *to*) (of the heart etc.) expand with sympathy etc. towards (*my heart goes out to them*). **11** *Golf* play the first nine holes in a round. **12** *Cards* be the first to dispose of one's hand. **13** (of a tide) ebb; recede to low tide. **go over 1** inspect the details of; rehearse; retouch. **2** change one's allegiance or religion. **3** (of a play etc.) be received, esp. favourably (*went over well in Dundee*). **go round** (or *US* **around**) **1** spin, revolve. **2** be long enough to encompass. **3** (of food etc.) suffice for everybody. **4** (usu. foll. by *to*) visit informally. **5** = *go around.* **go slow** *Brit.* deliberately work slowly, as a form of industrial action (cf. GO-SLOW). **go through 1** be dealt with or completed. **2** discuss in detail; scrutinize in sequence. **3** perform (a ceremony, a recitation, etc.). **4** undergo. **5** *colloq.* use up; spend (money etc.). **6** make holes in. **7** (of a book) be successively published in (so many editions). **8** *Austral. slang* abscond. **go through with** not leave unfinished; complete. **go to the bar** become a barrister. **go to blazes** (or **hell** or **Jericho** etc.) *slang* an exclamation of dismissal, contempt, etc. **go to the country** see COUNTRY. **go together 1** match; fit. **2** have a sexual relationship. **go to it!** *colloq.* begin work! **go to show** (or **prove**) serve as evidence (or proof) (also *absol.*). **go under** sink; fail; succumb. **go up 1** increase in price. **2** *Brit. colloq.* enter university. **3** be consumed (in flames etc.); explode. **go well** (or **ill** etc.) (often foll. by *with*) turn out well (or ill etc.). **go with 1** be harmonious with; match. **2** agree to; take the same view as. **3 a** be a pair with. **b** have a sexual relationship with. **4** follow the drift of. **go without** manage without; forgo (also *absol.*: *we shall just have to go without*). **go with the tide** (or **times**) do as others do. **have a go at 1** esp. *Brit.* attack, criticize. **2** attempt, try. **on the go** *colloq.* **1** in constant motion. **2** constantly working. **to go 1** still to be dealt with. **2** *N. Amer.* (of refreshments etc.) to be eaten or drunk off the premises. **who goes there?** a sentry's challenge. [Old English; *went:* originally the past tense of WEND]

go[2] *n.* a Japanese board game of territorial possession and capture. [Japanese]

goad ● *n.* **1** a spiked stick used for urging cattle forward. **2** anything that torments or incites. ● *v.tr.* **1** urge on with a goad. **2** (usu. foll. by *on, into*) irritate; stimulate (*goaded me on to win*). [Old English, related to Lombard (Italian) *gaida* 'arrowhead']

go-ahead ● *n.* permission to proceed. ● *adj.* enterprising.

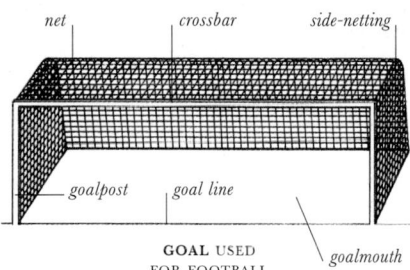

net   *crossbar*   *side-netting*

goalpost   *goal line*

GOAL USED FOR FOOTBALL.   *goalmouth*

goal *n.* **1** the object of a person's ambition or effort; a destination (*fame is his goal; London was our goal*). **2 a** *Football* ▲ a pair of posts linked by a crossbar, forming a space into which the ball has to be sent to score. ▷ FOOTBALL. **b** a cage or basket used similarly in other games. **c** a successful attempt to score (*it's a goal!*). **d** a point won (*scored 3 goals*). **3** a point marking the end of a race. □ **in goal** in the position of goalkeeper. [Middle English in sense 'limit, boundary'] □ **goalless** *adj.*

goal average *n. Football* the ratio of the numbers of goals scored for and against a team in a series of matches.

goal difference *n. Football* the difference of goals scored for and against a team.

goalie *n. colloq.* = GOALKEEPER.

goalkeeper *n.* a player stationed to protect the goal in various sports. ▷ FOOTBALL, HOCKEY. □ **goalkeeping** *n.*

goal kick *n.* **1** *Football* a kick by the defending side after attackers send the ball over the goal line without scoring. **2** *Rugby* an attempt to kick a goal. □ **goal-kicker** *n. Rugby.* **goal-kicking** *n. Rugby.*

goal line *n.* a line between the posts of a goal, extended to form the end boundary of a field of play or the boundary beyond which a try or touchdown may be scored (cf. TOUCHLINE). ▷ GOAL, RUGBY

goalmouth *n.* the space between or near the posts of a goal in football, hockey, etc. ▷ GOAL

goalpost *n.* either of the two upright posts of a goal. ▷ GOAL □ **move the goalposts** alter the basis or scope of a procedure during its course.

goalscorer *n.* a player who scores a goal. □ **goalscoring** *n. & adj.*

goanna *n. Austral.* a monitor lizard. [corruption of IGUANA]

goat *n.* **1 a** ▼ a hardy lively frisky short-haired domesticated mammal, *Capra aegagrus*, having horns and (in the male) a beard, and kept for its milk and meat. ▷ UNGULATE. **b** either of two similar mammals, the mountain goat and the Spanish goat. **2** any other mammal of the genus *Capra*, including the ibex. **3** a lecherous man. **4** *Brit. colloq.* a foolish person. **5** (**the Goat**) the zodiacal sign Capricorn or the constellation Capricornus. ▷ CAPRICORN. **6** *US* a scapegoat. □ **get a person's goat** *colloq.* irritate a person. [Old English] □ **goatish** *adj.* **goaty** *adj.*

GOAT: MALE BAGOT GOAT   *beard*

goat-antelope *n.* a ruminant mammal of the subfamily Caprinae, esp. of the tribe Rupicaprini, which includes the chamois, and Rocky Mountain goat.

goatee *n.* (in full **goatee beard**) a small pointed beard like a goat's.

goatherd *n.* a person who tends goats.

goatskin *n.* **1** the skin of a goat. **2** a garment or bottle made out of goatskin.

gob[1] *n.* esp. *Brit. slang* the mouth. [perhaps from Gaelic & Irish, = beak, mouth]

gob[2] *slang* ● *n.* **1** *Brit.* a clot of slimy matter. **2** *N. Amer.* a small lump. **3** (in *pl.*; foll. by *of*) *N. Amer.* lots of. ● *v.intr.* (**gobbed, gobbing**) *Brit.* spit. [Middle English from Old French *go(u)be* 'mouthful']

gobbet *n.* **1** a piece or lump of flesh, food, slime, etc. **2** an extract from a text, esp. one set for translation or comment in an examination. [from Old French *gobet*]

gobble[1] *v.tr. & intr.* eat hurriedly and noisily. □ **gobbler** *n.*

gobble[2] *v.intr.* **1** (of a turkeycock) make a characteristic swallowing sound in the throat. **2** make such a sound when speaking.

gobbledegook *n.* (also **gobbledygook**) *colloq.* pompous or unintelligible jargon.

go-between *n.* an intermediary.

goblet *n.* **1** ▶ a drinking vessel with a foot and a stem. **2** *archaic* a metal or glass bowl-shaped drinking cup without handles. **3** a goblet-shaped receptacle forming part of a liquidizer. [from Old French *gobelet* 'little cup']

goblin *n.* a mischievous ugly dwarf-like creature of folklore. [Middle English]

gobsmacked *adj. Brit. slang* utterly astonished. [with reference to clapping a hand to one's mouth in astonishment] □ **gobsmacking** *adj.*

GOBLET

gobstopper *n.* a very large hard sweet.

goby *n.* (*pl.* **-ies**) ▼ having ventral fins joined to form a sucker or disc. [from Greek *kōbios* 'gudgeon']

GOBY: BUMBLEBEE FISH (*Brachygobius doriae*)   *sucker*

go-by *n. colloq.* a snub; a slight (*gave him the go-by*).

go-cart *n.* **1** a handcart. **2** a pushchair. **3** var. of GO-KART. **4** *archaic* a baby walker.

god *n.* **1 a** (in many religions) a superhuman being or spirit worshipped as having power over nature, human fortunes, etc. **b** an image, idol, animal, or other object worshipped as divine or symbolizing a god. **2** (**God**) (in Christian and other monotheistic religions) the creator and ruler of the universe. **3 a** an adored, admired, or influential person. **b** something worshipped like a god (*makes a god of success*). **4** (in *pl.*; prec. by *the*) *Theatr.* **a** the gallery. **b** the people sitting in it. □ **for God's sake!** see SAKE[1]. **God the Father, Son, and Holy Ghost** (in the Christian tradition) the persons of the Trinity. [Old English] □ **godhood** *n.*

God-awful *adj. slang* extremely unpleasant, nasty, etc.

godchild *n.* (*pl.* **-children**) a person in relation to a godparent.

goddam *adj.* (also **goddamned**) *slang* accursed, damnable.

god-daughter *n.* a female godchild.

goddess *n.* **1** a female deity. **2** a woman who is adored.

godetia *n.* any plant of the genus *Clarkia* (or *Godetia*), having showy rose-purple or reddish flowers. [named after C. H. *Godet*, Swiss botanist, 1797–1879]

godfather *n.* **1** a male godparent. **2** a person directing an illegal organization, esp. a leader of the American Mafia.

G

G

God-fearing *adj.* earnestly religious.

godforsaken *adj.* devoid of all merit; dismal; dreary.

God-given *adj.* received as from God; possessed from birth or by divine authority.

godhead *n.* (also **Godhead**) **1 a** the state of being God or a god. **b** divine nature. **2** a deity. **3** (**the Godhead**) God.

godless *adj.* **1** impious; wicked. **2** without a god. **3** not recognizing God. □ **godlessness** *n.*

godlike *adj.* **1** resembling God or a god. **2** befitting or appropriate to a god.

godly *adj.* (**-ier, -iest**) religious, pious, devout. □ **godliness** *n.*

godmother *n.* a female godparent.

godown *n.* a warehouse in parts of E. Asia. [from Malay *godong*]

godparent *n.* a person who presents a child at baptism and responds on the child's behalf.

godsend *n.* an unexpected but welcome event or acquisition.

godson *n.* a male godchild.

God squad *n. slang* **1** a religious organization, esp. an evangelical Christian group. **2** its members.

godwit *n.* any wading bird of the genus *Limosa*, with long legs and a long straight or slightly upcurved bill. [16th-century coinage]

goer *n.* **1** a person or thing that goes (*a slow goer*). **2** (often in *comb.*) a person who attends (*a churchgoer*). **3** *Brit. colloq.* **a** a lively or persevering person or animal. **b** a sexually promiscuous person. **4** *colloq.* a project likely to be accepted or to succeed.

goes *3rd sing. present of* GO[1].

go-faster stripes *n.pl.* striped stickers for a motor car, usu. placed along the sides of the bodywork to give a sporty appearance.

gofer *n.* esp. *N. Amer. slang* a person who runs errands.

goffer ● *v.tr.* make wavy, flute, or crimp (a lace edge, a trimming, etc.) with heated irons. ● *n.* an iron used for goffering. [from French *gaufrer* 'to stamp with a patterned tool']

go-getter *n. colloq.* an aggressively enterprising person.

goggle ● *v.* **1** *intr.* **a** look with wide-open eyes. **b** (of the eyes) be rolled about; protrude. **2** *tr.* turn (the eyes) sideways or from side to side. ● *adj.* (usu. *attrib.*) (of the eyes) protuberant or rolling. ● *n.* **1** (in *pl.*) **a** spectacles for protecting the eyes from glare, dust, water, etc. **b** *colloq.* spectacles. **2** a goggling expression. [Middle English]

goggle-box *n. Brit. colloq.* a television set.

goggle-eyed *adj.* having staring or protuberant eyes, esp. through astonishment or disbelief.

go-go *adj. colloq.* **1** (of a dancer, music, etc.) in modern style; lively and rhythmic. **2** unrestrained; energetic. **3** (of investment) speculative.

going ● *n.* **1 a** the act or process of going. **b** an instance of this. **2 a** the condition of the ground for walking, riding, etc. **b** progress affected by this (*found the going hard*). ● *adj.* **1** in or into action (*set the clock going*). **2** esp. *Brit.* existing, available (*there's cold beef going*). **3** current, prevalent (*the going rate*). □ **get going** start steadily talking, working, etc. **going for one** *colloq.* acting in one's favour (*he has got a lot going for him*). **going on fifteen** etc. esp. *US* approaching one's fifteenth etc. birthday. **going on for** *Brit.* approaching (a time, an age, etc.) (*must be going on for 6 years*). **going to** intending or intended to; about to (*it's going to sink!*). **to be going on with** to start with; for the time being. **while the going is good** while conditions are favourable.

going away *n.* a departure, esp. on a honeymoon (often, with hyphen, *attrib.*: *going-away outfit*).

going concern *n.* a thriving business.

going-over *n.* (*pl.* **goings-over**) **1** *colloq.* an inspec-

tion or overhaul. **2** *slang* a thrashing. **3** *US colloq.* a scolding.

goings-on *n.pl.* behaviour, esp. of a morally suspect nature.

goitre /goi-ter/ *n.* (*US* **goiter**) *Med.* a swelling of the neck resulting from enlargement of the thyroid gland. [based on Latin *guttur* 'throat'] □ **goitred** *adj.* **goitrous** *adj.*

go-kart *n.* (also **go-cart**) a miniature racing car with a skeleton body.

gold

quartz crystals

GOLD IN QUARTZ MATRIX

gold ● *n.* **1** ◄ a yellow malleable ductile high-density metallic element resistant to chemical reaction, occurring naturally in quartz veins and gravel, and precious as a monetary medium, in jewellery, etc. ▷ METAL. **2** the colour of gold. **3 a** coins or articles made of gold. **b** wealth. **4** something precious, beautiful, or brilliant (*all that glitters is not gold*). **5** = GOLD MEDAL. **6** the bull's-eye of an archery target (usu. gilt). ● *adj.* **1** made wholly or chiefly of gold. **2** coloured like gold. [Old English]

gold brick *slang* ● *n.* **1** a thing with only a surface appearance of value. **2** *US* a lazy person. ● *v.intr.* (**gold-brick**) *US* shirk.

gold card *n.* a charge card issued only to very creditworthy people and giving benefits not available to holders of the standard card.

goldcrest *n.* a very small warbler, *Regulus regulus*, with a golden crest.

gold-digger *n.* **1** *slang* a woman who wheedles money out of men. **2** a person who digs for gold.

gold disc *n. Brit.* an award given to a recording artist or group for sales of a record etc. exceeding a specified high figure.

gold dust *n.* **1** gold in fine particles as often found naturally. **2** ◄ a plant, *Alyssum saxatile*, with many small yellow flowers.

golden *adj.* **1 a** made or consisting of gold. **b** yielding gold. **2** coloured or shining like gold (*golden hair*). **3** precious; valuable; excellent; important (*a golden memory*; *a golden opportunity*).

golden age *n.* **1** a supposed past age when people were happy and innocent. **2** the period of a nation's greatest prosperity, literary merit, etc.

golden boy *n.* (*fem.* **golden girl**) *colloq.* a popular or successful person.

golden delicious *n.* a greenish-yellow variety of dessert apple.

golden eagle *n.* a large eagle, *Aquila chrysaetos*, with yellow-tipped head-feathers. ▷ EAGLE.

Golden Fleece *n.* (in Greek mythology) a fleece of gold sought and won by Jason.

golden girl SEE GOLDEN BOY.

golden goose *n.* a continuing source of wealth or profit.

golden hamster SEE HAMSTER.

golden handcuffs *n.pl. colloq.* a promise of future benefits, e.g. pensions or share options, for those who stay with a company.

golden handshake *n. colloq.* a payment given on redundancy or early retirement.

golden hello *n. Brit. colloq.* a payment made by an employer to a keenly-sought recruit.

golden jubilee *n.* **1** the fiftieth anniversary of a sovereign's accession. **2** any other fiftieth anniversary.

golden mean *n.* the principle of moderation.

golden oldie *n. colloq.* **1** an old hit record or film etc. that is still well known and popular. **2** a person who is no longer young but is still successful in his or her field.

GOLD DUST
(*Alyssum saxatile*)

golden orfe *n.* a yellow variety of orfe, kept in aquaria.

golden parachute *n. colloq.* financial compensation guaranteed to executives dismissed as a result of a merger or takeover.

golden retriever *n.* a retriever with a thick golden-coloured coat. ▷ DOG

golden rod *n.* any plant of the genus *Solidago* with a rodlike stem and a spike of small bright yellow flowers.

golden rule *n.* a basic principle of action, esp. 'do as you would be done by'.

golden share *n.* a share in a company that controls at least 51 per cent of the voting rights (esp. held by a government in a privatized industry in order to prevent undesirable takeovers).

golden syrup *n. Brit.* a pale treacle.

golden wedding *n.* the fiftieth anniversary of a wedding.

goldfield *n.* a district in which gold is found as a mineral.

goldfinch *n.* ◄ any of various brightly coloured songbirds of the genus *Carduelis*, esp. the Eurasian *C. carduelis*, with a yellow band across each wing.

GOLDFINCH
(*Carduelis carduelis*)

goldfish *n.* (*pl.* usu. same) ▼ a small reddish-golden Chinese carp, *Carassius auratus*, kept for ornament.

GOLDFISH:
FANTAIL GOLDFISH
(*Carassius auratus*)

goldfish bowl *n.* **1** a globular glass container for goldfish. **2** a place or situation lacking privacy.

gold foil *n.* gold beaten into a thin sheet.

gold leaf *n.* gold beaten into a very thin sheet. ▷ GILDING

gold medal *n.* a gold-coloured medal, usu. awarded as first prize.

gold mine *n.* **1** a place where gold is mined. **2** *colloq.* a source of wealth.

gold plate ● *n.* **1** vessels made of gold. **2** material plated with gold. ● *v.tr.* (**gold-plate**) plate with gold.

gold record *n. US* = GOLD DISC.

gold reserve *n.* a reserve of gold coins or bullion held by a central bank etc.

gold rush *n.* a rush to a newly discovered goldfield.

goldsmith *n.* a worker in gold.

gold standard *n. Econ.* a system by which the value of a currency is defined in terms of gold.

golf ● *n.* ▲ a game in which a small hard ball is struck with clubs into a series of 18 or 9 holes with the fewest possible strokes. ▷ FAIRWAY. ● *v.intr.* play golf. [Middle English]

golf bag *n.* a bag used for carrying clubs and balls.

golf ball *n.* **1** a ball used in golf. ▷ GOLF. **2** a small ball used in some electric typewriters to carry the type.

golf cart *n.* **1** a trolley used for carrying clubs in golf. **2** a motorized cart for golfers and equipment.

golf club *n.* **1** a club used in golf. ▷ GOLF. **2** an association for playing golf. **3** the premises used by a golf club.

golf course *n.* the course on which golf is played. ▷ GOLF

GOLF

Now a popular international sport, golf was established in Scotland by the 16th century. Players use wooden or metal clubs, each with a different function, to hit a ball from a level teeing ground, down a fairway – marked with hazards such as bunkers (sandpits) and rough (uncut grass) – on to a putting green and into a target hole. Competing singly or in teams, players move from one hole to the next on the course, trying to advance the ball using as few strokes as possible.

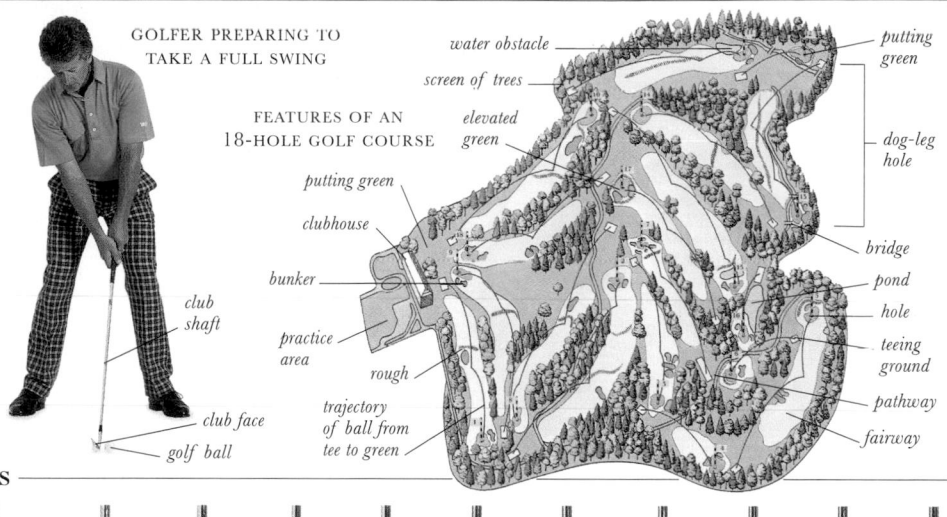

GOLFER PREPARING TO
TAKE A FULL SWING

FEATURES OF AN
18-HOLE GOLF COURSE

water obstacle
screen of trees
elevated green
putting green
clubhouse
bunker
practice area
rough
trajectory of ball from tee to green
putting green
dog-leg hole
bridge
pond
hole
teeing ground
pathway
fairway

club shaft
club face
golf ball

EXAMPLES OF GOLF CLUBS

 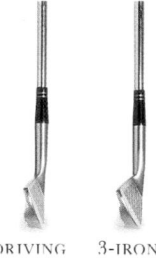    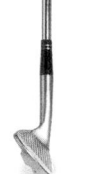 

PUTTER   1-WOOD (DRIVER)   5-WOOD   DRIVING IRON   3-IRON   4-IRON   5-IRON   6-IRON   7-IRON   8-IRON   9-IRON   PITCHING WEDGE   SAND WEDGE

golfer *n.* a golf player.

golf links *n.pl.* = LINKS.

golliwog *n.* a black-faced brightly dressed soft doll with fuzzy hair. [from *Golliwogg*, a doll character in books by B. Upton, US writer, died 1912]

golly[1] *int.* expressing surprise. [euphemism for GOD]

golly[2] *n.* (*pl.* -**ics**) *Brit. colloq.* = GOLLIWOG.

gonad *n.* an animal organ producing gametes, e.g. the testis or ovary. ▷ REPRODUCTIVE ORGANS. [based on Greek *gonē gonos* 'generation, seed'] □ **gonadal** *adj.*

gondola *n.* **1** ▼ a light flat-bottomed boat used on Venetian canals. **2** a car suspended from an airship or balloon, or attached to a ski lift. [Venetian Italian]

gondolier *n.* the oarsman on a gondola. ▷ GONDOLA

gone *past part.* of GO[1]. ● *adj.* **1** *Brit.* (of time) past (*not until gone nine*). **2 a** lost; hopeless. **b** dead. **3** *colloq.* pregnant for a specified time (*already three months gone*). **4** *slang* completely enthralled or entranced.

□ **be gone** depart (cf. BEGONE). **gone on** *slang* infatuated with.

goner /gon-er/ *n.* *slang* a person or thing that is doomed, ended, irrevocably lost, etc.; a dead person.

gong *n.* **1** ▶ a metal disc with a turned rim, giving a resonant note when struck. ▷ ORCHESTRA. **2** a saucer-shaped bell. **3** *Brit. slang* a medal. [Malay]

gonorrhoea /gon-ŏ-ree-ă/ (*US* **gonorrhea**) a venereal disease with inflammatory discharge from the urethra or vagina. [from Greek *gonorrhoia*]

gonzo *adj.* esp. *US* **1** of or associated with journalistic writing of an exaggerated, subjective, and fictionalized style. **2** *colloq.* bizarre; crazy. [20th-century coinage]

central boss

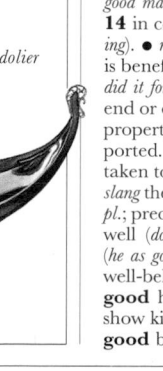

beater

GONG: TRADITIONAL GONG FROM BORNEO

goo *n.* *colloq.* **1** a sticky or slimy substance. **2** sickly sentiment. [20th-century coinage]

good ● *adj.* (**better**, **best**) **1** having the right or desired qualities; adequate. **2 a** (of a person) efficient, competent (*good at French*; *a good driver*). **b** (of a thing) reliable, efficient (*good brakes*). **c** (of health etc.) strong (*good eyesight*). **3 a** kind (*good of you to come*). **b** morally excellent; virtuous (*a good deed*). **c** charitable (*good works*). **d** well-behaved (*a good child*). **4** enjoyable, agreeable (*a good party*; *good news*). **5** thorough, considerable (*a good wash*). **6 a** not less than (*waited a good hour*). **b** considerable in number, quality, etc. (*a good many people*). **7** beneficial (*good for you*). **8 a** valid, sound (*a good reason*). **b** financially sound (*his credit is good*). **c** (usu. foll. by *for*) *US* (of a ticket) valid. **9** in exclamations of surprise (*good heavens!*). **10** right, proper, expedient (*thought it good to have a try*). **11** fresh, eatable, untainted. **12** (sometimes patronizing) commendable, worthy (*your good lady wife*; *good men and true*; *my good man*). **13** well-shaped, attractive (*has good legs*). **14** in courteous greetings and farewells (*good morning*). ● *n.* **1** (only in *sing.*) that which is good; what is beneficial or morally right (*only good can come of it*; *did it for your own good*). **2** (only in *sing.*) a desirable end or object (*a future good*). **3** (in *pl.*) **a** *Law* movable property or merchandise. **b** *Brit.* things to be transported. **c** (prec. by *the*) *colloq.* what one has undertaken to supply (esp. *deliver the goods*). **d** (prec. by *the*) *slang* the real thing; the genuine article. **4** (treated as *pl.*; prec. by *the*) virtuous people. ● *adv.* N. *Amer. colloq.* well (*doing pretty good*). □ **as good as** practically (*he as good as told me*). **as good as gold** extremely well-behaved. **be (a certain amount) to the good** have as net profit or advantage. **do good** show kindness, act philanthropically. **do a person good** be beneficial to. **for good (and all)** finally,

GONDOLA

Gondolas, handbuilt from nine different woods, have plied the canals of Venice, Italy, for over 1,000 years. Once used to transport goods from markets to the residences (*palazzi*), gondolas now serve largely as pleasurecraft for tourists, or to ferry Venetians to events such as weddings and funerals.

TRADITIONAL VENETIAN GONDOLA

ferro (symbol of 6 city districts below a doge's cap)
black lacquer finish
passenger seat
rowlock (forcola)
gondolier
oak frame
hippocampus (sea horse) ornament
carved trim
oar

G

permanently. **good and** *colloq.* used as an intensifier before an adj. or adv. (*raining good and hard*). **good for 1** able to perform; inclined for (*good for a ten-mile walk*). **2** able to be trusted to pay (*is good for £10*). **good for you!** (or **him!**, **her!**, etc.) an exclamation of approval towards a person. **good on you!** (or **him!** etc.) esp. *Austral. & NZ = good for you!* **have a good mind** see MIND. **have the goods on a person** *slang* have information about a person which may be used to his or her detriment. **have a good time** enjoy oneself. **in a person's good books** see BOOK. **in good faith** with honest or sincere intentions. **in** (or **on**) **good form** see GOOD FORM. **in good time 1** with no risk of being late. **2** (also **all in good time**) in due course but without haste. **make good 1** make up for, compensate for, pay (an expense). **2** fulfil (a promise); effect (a purpose or an intended action). **3** demonstrate the truth of (a statement). **4** gain and hold (a position). **5** replace or restore (a thing lost or damaged). **6** (*absol.*) accomplish what one intended. **to the good** having as profit or benefit. [Old English *gōd*, from Germanic] □ **goodish** *adj.*

Good Book *n.* (prec. by *the*) the Bible.

good breeding *n.* correct manners.

goodbye (*US* also **goodby**) ● *int.* expressing good wishes on parting, ending a telephone conversation, etc., or said with reference to a thing discarded or irrevocably lost. ● *n.* (*pl.* **goodbyes** or *US* also **goodbys**) the saying of 'goodbye'; a parting; a farewell. [contraction of *God be with you!*]

good company *n.* **1** a pleasant companion. **2** a suitable associate or group of friends.

good faith *n.* sincerity of intention.

good form *n.* □ what complies with current social conventions. □ **in good form** in a state of good health or training. **on good form** playing or performing well; in good spirits.

good-for-nothing ● *adj.* worthless. ● *n.* a worthless person.

Good Friday *n.* the Friday before Easter Sunday, commemorating the Crucifixion.

good-hearted *n.* kindly, well-meaning.

good humour *n.* a genial mood.

good-humoured *adj.* genial, cheerful, amiable. □ **good-humouredly** *adv.*

goodie var. of GOODY *n.*

good job *n. Brit.* a fortunate state of affairs (*it's a good job you came early*).

good-looker *n.* a handsome or attractive person.

good-looking *adj.* handsome; attractive.

good luck ● *n.* **1** good fortune. **2** an omen of this. ● *int.* an exclamation of well-wishing.

goodly *adj.* (**goodlier**, **goodliest**) **1** *archaic* comely, handsome. **2** considerable in size or quantity.

good money *n.* **1** money that might usefully have been spent elsewhere. **2** *colloq.* high wages.

good nature *n.* a friendly disposition.

good-natured *adj.* kind, patient; easygoing. □ **good-naturedly** *adv.*

goodness ● *n.* **1** virtue; excellence, esp. moral. **2** kindness (*had the goodness to wait*). **3** what is beneficial in a thing (*vegetables with all the goodness boiled out*). ● *int.* (as a substitution for 'God') expressing surprise, anger, etc.

goodnight *int.* expressing good wishes on parting at night or at bedtime.

goodo *adj. Austral. & NZ = GOOD adj.* 10.

goods and chattels *n.pl.* all kinds of personal property.

good-tempered *adj.* having a good temper; not easily annoyed. □ **good-temperedly** *adv.*

good-time *attrib.adj.* recklessly pursuing pleasure. □ **good-timer** *n.*

good times *n.pl.* a period of prosperity.

goodwill *n.* **1** kindly feeling. **2** the established reputation of a business etc. as enhancing its value. **3** cheerful consent or acquiescence; readiness, zeal. **4** (**good will**) the intention and hope that good will result.

good word *n.* (often in phr. **put in a good word for**) words in recommendation or defence.

good works *n.pl.* charitable acts.

goody ● *n.* (also **goodie**) (*pl.* **-ies**) **1** *Brit. colloq.* a good or favoured person, esp. a hero in a story, film, etc. **2** (usu. in *pl.*) something good or attractive, esp. to eat. **3** = GOODY-GOODY. ● *int.* expressing childish delight.

goody-goody *colloq.* ● *n.* (*pl.* **-ies**) a smug or obtrusively virtuous person. ● *adj.* obtrusively or smugly virtuous.

gooey *adj.* (**gooier**, **gooiest**) *colloq.* **1** viscous, sticky. **2** sickly, sentimental.

goof *slang* ● *n.* **1** a foolish or stupid person. **2** a mistake. ● *v.* **1** *tr.* bungle. **2** *intr.* blunder. **3** (often foll. by *off*) idle. [from medieval Latin *gufus* 'coarse']

goofy *adj.* (**goofier**, **goofiest**) *slang* **1** stupid, silly, daft. **2** having or displaying protruding or crooked front teeth. □ **goofily** *adv.* **goofiness** *n.*

googly *n.* (*pl.* **-ies**) *Cricket* an off-break ball bowled with apparent leg-break action. [20th-century coinage]

goolie *n.* (also **gooly**) (*pl.* **-ies**) (usu. in *pl.*) *Brit. slang* a testicle.

goon *n. slang* **1** a stupid or playful person. **2** esp. *N. Amer.* a ruffian hired by racketeers etc. to terrorize political or industrial opponents.

goop *n. Brit. slang* a stupid or fatuous person. [20th-century coinage] □ **goopy** *adj.* (**goopier**, **goopiest**) **goopiness** *n.*

goosander *n.* a large diving duck, *Mergus merganser*, with a narrow serrated bill.

goose ● *n.* (*pl.* **geese**) **1 a** ◀ any of various large waterbirds of the family Anatidae, with short legs, webbed feet, and a broad bill. ▷ WATERFOWL. **b** the female of this (opp. GANDER *n.* 1). **c** the flesh of a goose as food. **2** *colloq.* a simpleton. **3** (*pl.* **gooses**) a tailor's smoothing iron, having a handle like a goose's neck. ● *v.tr. slang* poke (a person) in the bottom. [Old English *gōs*, from Germanic]

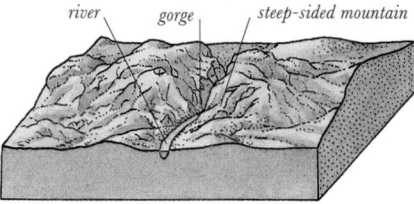

GOOSE: CHINESE GANDER

gooseberry *n.* (*pl.* **-ies**) **1** a round edible yellowish-green berry with a thin usu. translucent skin enclosing seeds in a juicy flesh. ▷ FRUIT. **2** the thorny shrub, *Ribes grossularia*, bearing this fruit. **3** *Brit. colloq.* an unwanted extra person (esp. in phr. **play gooseberry**).

goose bumps *n.pl. N. Amer.* = GOOSE-FLESH.

goose egg *n. N. Amer.* a zero score in a game.

goose-flesh *n.* (also **goose pimples** *n.pl.* or **goose-skin**) a pimply state of the skin with the hairs erect, produced by cold, fright, etc.

goosefoot *n.* (*pl.* **-foots**) any plant of the genus *Chenopodium*, having leaves shaped like the foot of a goose.

goose pimples see GOOSE-FLESH.

goose-skin see GOOSE-FLESH.

goose-step ● *n.* a military marching step in which the knees are kept stiff. ● *v.intr.* march in this way.

gopher /goh-fer/ *n.* **1** (in full **pocket gopher**) any burrowing rodent of the family Geomyidae, native to N. America, having food-pouches on the cheeks. **2** *N. Amer.* a ground squirrel. **3** (in full **gopher tortoise**) a tortoise, *Gopherus polyphemus*, native to the southern US. [18th-century coinage]

Gordian knot *n.* **1** an intricate knot. **2** a difficult problem or task. □ **cut the Gordian knot** solve a problem by force or by evasion. [named after *Gordius*, king of Phrygia, who tied an intricate knot finally cut by Alexander the Great]

gore[1] *n.* blood that has been shed, esp. when clotted. [Old English *gor* 'dung, dirt']

gore[2] *v.tr.* pierce with a horn, tusk, etc. [Middle English]

gore[3] ● *n.* **1** a wedge-shaped piece in a garment. **2** a triangular or tapering piece in an umbrella etc. ● *v.tr.* shape (a garment) with a gore. [Old English *gāra* 'triangular piece of land']

Gore-Tex *n. propr.* a synthetic breathable waterproof fabric used for outdoor clothing.

gorge ● *n.* **1** ▼ a narrow opening between hills. ▷ RIVER. **2** an act of gorging. **3** the contents of the stomach. ● *v.* **1** *intr.* feed greedily. **2** *tr.* **a** (often *refl.*) satiate. **b** devour greedily. □ **one's gorge rises at** one is sickened by. [from Latin *gurges* 'whirlpool']

river   *gorge*   *steep-sided mountain*

GORGE: SECTION THROUGH A GORGE CUT BY A RIVER

gorgeous *adj.* **1** richly coloured, sumptuous. **2** *colloq.* very pleasant, splendid (*gorgeous weather*). **3** *colloq.* strikingly beautiful. [from Old French *gorgias* 'fine, elegant'] □ **gorgeously** *adv.*

gorget *n.* **1** *hist.* **a** a piece of armour for the throat. ▷ ARMOUR. **b** a woman's wimple. **2** ▶ a patch of colour on the throat of a bird, insect, etc. [from Old French *gorgete*]

gorgon *n.* **1** (in Greek mythology) each of three snake-haired sisters (esp. Medusa) with the power to turn anyone who looked at them to stone. **2** a frightening or repulsive person, esp. a woman.

gorget

GORGET OF A CONGO PEAFOWL (*Afropavo congensis*)

Gorgonzola *n.* a type of rich cheese with bluish-green veins. ▷ CHEESE. [from *Gorgonzola*, a village in Italy, where it was originally made]

gorilla *n.* **1** the largest anthropoid ape, *Gorilla gorilla*, native to central Africa, having a large head, short neck, and prominent mouth. ▷ PRIMATE. **2** *colloq.* a heavily built man of aggressive demeanour. [name adopted (1847) from *Gorillai*, the Greek name of an African tribe noted for hairiness]

gormless *adj.* esp. *Brit. colloq.* foolish, lacking sense. [based on dialect *gaum* 'understanding'] □ **gormlessly** *adv.* **gormlessness** *n.*

gorse *n.* ◀ any spiny yellow-flowered shrub of the genus *Ulex*. [Old English *gors(t)*] □ **gorsy** *adj.*

gory *adj.* (**gorier**, **goriest**) **1** involving bloodshed; bloodthirsty (*a gory film*). **2** covered in gore. □ **gory details** *joc.* explicit details. □ **gorily** *adv.* **goriness** *n.*

gosh *int.* expressing surprise. [euphemism for GOD]

goshawk *n.* a large short-winged hawk, *Accipiter gentilis*. [Old English]

gosling *n.* a young goose. [from Old Norse *gǽslingr*]

go-slow *n. Brit.* a form of industrial action in which employees deliberately work slowly.

GORSE (*Ulex parviflorus*)

GOTHIC

Gothic architecture flourished from the mid-12th century into the 16th century, when many of Europe's greatest cathedrals were under construction. Gothic buildings are characterized by pointed arches, flying buttresses, rib vaults, and ornamental stone tracery. Such features are often complemented by high-quality stained glass and sculpture.

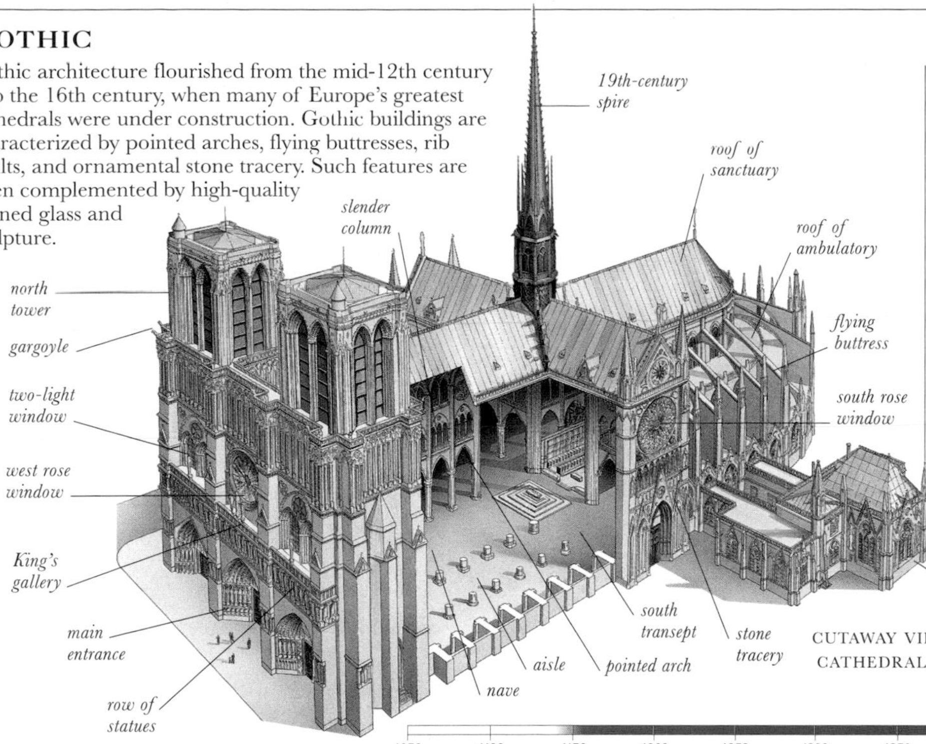

19th-century spire
roof of sanctuary
roof of ambulatory
flying buttress
south rose window
slender column
north tower
gargoyle
two-light window
west rose window
King's gallery
main entrance
row of statues
nave
aisle
pointed arch
south transept
stone tracery
treasury

CUTAWAY VIEW OF A 13TH-CENTURY GOTHIC CATHEDRAL (NOTRE DAME, PARIS, FRANCE)

TIMELINE
1050 1100 1150 1200 1250 1300 1350 1400 1450 1500 1550

GOTHIC WINDOWS

LANCET   TWO-LIGHT WINDOW

GEOMETRIC TRACERY   PERPENDICULAR TRACERY

G

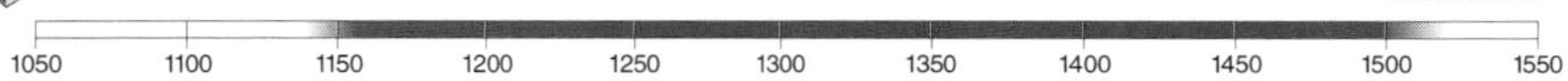

gospel *n.* **1** the teaching or revelation of Christ. **2** (**Gospel**) **a** the record of Christ's life and teaching in the first four books of the New Testament. **b** each of these books. **c** a portion from one of these read at a service. **3** (also **gospel truth**) a thing regarded as absolutely true (*take my word as gospel*). **4** a principle one acts on or advocates. **5** (in full **gospel music**) black American evangelical religious singing. [Old English *gōdspel* 'good news']

gospeller *n.* (*US* **gospeler**) the reader of the Gospel in a Communion service.

gossamer ● *n.* **1** a filmy substance of small spiders' webs. **2** delicate filmy material. **3** a thread of gossamer. ● *adj.* light and flimsy as gossamer. [Middle English] □ **gossamered** *adj.*

gossip ● *n.* **1 a** unconstrained talk or writing esp. about persons or social incidents. **b** idle talk; groundless rumour. **2** an informal chat, esp. about persons or social incidents. **3** a person who indulges in gossip. ● *v.intr.* (**gossiped**, **gossiping**) talk or write gossip. [earlier in sense 'godparent': from Old English *godsibb* 'person related to one in God'] □ **gossiper** *n.* **gossipy** *adj.*

gossip column *n.* a section of a newspaper devoted to gossip about well-known people. □ **gossip columnist** *n.*

gossip monger *n.* a perpetrator of gossip.

got *past* and *past part.* of GET.

Goth *n.* **1** a member of a Germanic tribe that invaded the Roman Empire in the 3rd–5th c. **2** (**goth**) **a** a style of rock music derived from punk, often with apocalyptic or mystical lyrics. **b** a member of a subculture favouring black clothing, white and black make-up, metal jewellery, and goth music. [from Greek *Go(t)thoi*, from Gothic]

Gothic ● *adj.* **1** of the Goths or their language. **2** ▲ in the style of architecture prevalent in W. Europe in the 12th–16th c., characterized by pointed arches. **3** (of a novel etc.) in a style popular in the 18th–19th c., with supernatural or horrifying events. **4** barbarous, un-couth. **5** *Printing* (of type) old-fashioned German, black letter, or sans serif. ● *n.* **1** the Gothic language. **2** Gothic architecture. **3** *Printing* ▼ Gothic type. □ **Gothically** *adv.* **Gothicism** *n.* **Gothicize** *v.tr. & intr.* (also **-ise**).

*Incipit liber Brelith quez
A principio creauit deus*

GOTHIC TYPE FROM A 15TH-CENTURY GERMAN BIBLE

gotten *US past part.* of GET.

gouache /goo-**ahsh**/ *n.* **1** ▼ a method of painting in opaque pigments ground in water and thickened with a glue-like substance. **2** these pigments. **3** a picture painted in this way. [from Italian *guazzo*]

white gouache

GOUACHE USED TO EMPHASIZE FORM IN A WATERCOLOUR PAINTING

Gouda *n.* a flat round usu. Dutch cheese with a yellow rind. [from *Gouda*, a town in the Netherlands, where it was originally made]

gouge ● *n.* **1** ◄ a chisel with a concave blade, used in carpentry, sculpture, and surgery. **2** an indentation or groove made with or as with this. ● *v.tr.* **1** cut with or as with a gouge.

concave blade

GOUGE: CARPENTER'S GOUGE

2 a (foll. by *out*) force out (esp. an eye with the thumb) with or as with a gouge. **b** force out the eye of (a person). [from Late Latin *gubia*] □ **gouger** *n.*

goujons /goo-**jonz**/ *n.pl. Brit.* deep-fried strips of chicken or fish. [French]

goulash *n.* a highly-seasoned Hungarian soup or stew of meat and vegetables, flavoured with paprika. [from Hungarian *gulyás* 'herdsman' + *hús* 'meat']

gourd *n.* **1 a** a fleshy usu. large fruit with a hard skin. **b** any of various climbing or trailing plants of the family Cucurbitaceae bearing such a fruit. **2** ► the hollow hard skin of a gourd, dried and used as a drinking vessel, water container, ornament, etc. [from Latin *cucurbita*]

gourmand /goor-**mănd**/ *n.* **1** a glutton. **2** *disp.* a gourmet. [from Old French]

■ **Usage** The use of *gourmand* in sense 2 is considered incorrect by some people; it is therefore preferable to use *gourmet*.

GOURD: TRADITIONAL AFRICAN WATER CONTAINER

gourmandise /goor-mahn-**deez**/ *n.* gluttony.

gourmet /goor-**may**/ ● *n.* a connoisseur of good food, having a discerning palate. ● *attrib.adj.* **1** of a kind or standard suitable for gourmets. **2** of or relating to a gourmet. [French, literally 'wine-taster']

gout *n.* **1** a disease with inflammation of the smaller joints, esp. the toe, as a result of excess uric acid salts in the blood. **2 a** a drop, esp. of blood. **b** a splash or spot. [from Latin *gutta* 'drop', with reference to the medieval theory of the flowing down of humours] □ **gouty** *adj.*

govern *v.* **1** *tr.* rule or control with authority; conduct the policy and affairs of. **2 a** *tr.* influence or determine (a person or a course of action). **b** *intr.* be the predominating influence. **3** *tr.* be a standard or principle for; constitute a law for; serve to decide a case (a case). **4** *tr.* check or control (esp. passions). **5** *tr. Gram.* (esp. of a verb or preposition) have (a noun or pronoun or the case of these) depending on it. [from Latin *gubernare* 'to steer, rule'] □ **governable** *adj.* **governability** *n.*

governance *n.* **1** the act or manner of governing. **2** the office or function of governing. **3** sway, control.

governess *n.* a woman employed to teach children in a private household.

governessy *adj.* characteristic of a governess; prim.

governing body *n.* the body of managers of an institution.

government *n.* **1** the act or manner of governing. **2** the system by which a state or community is governed. **3 a** a body of persons governing a state. **b** (usu. **Government**) a particular ministry in office. **4** the State as an agent. □ **governmental** *adj.* **governmentally** *adv.*

government issue *adj. US* (of equipment) provided by the government.

government pension see PENSION[1] *n.* 1a.

government surplus *n.* unused equipment sold by the government.

governor *n.* **1** a ruler. **2 a** an official governing a province, town, etc. **b** *Brit.* a representative of the Crown in a colony. **3** the executive head of each state of the US. **4** an officer commanding a fortress or garrison. **5** the head or a member of a governing body of an institution. **6** *Brit.* the official in charge of a prison. **7** *Brit. slang* **a** one's employer. **b** one's father. **c** *colloq.* (as a form of address) sir. **8** *Mech.* an automatic regulator controlling the speed of an engine etc. □ **governorate** *n.* **governorship** *n.*

Governor-General *n.* (*pl.* **Governors-General**) the representative of the Crown in a Commonwealth country that regards the British Monarch as head of state.

gown ● *n.* **1** a loose flowing garment, esp. a long dress worn by a woman. **2** the official robe of an alderman, judge, cleric, member of a university, etc. **3** a protective overall worn by a surgeon, a hospital patient, etc. **4** the members of a university as distinct from the permanent residents of the university town. ● *v.tr.* (usu. as **gowned** *adj.*) attire in a gown. [from Late Latin *gunna* 'fur garment']

goy *n.* (*pl.* **goyim** or **goys**) *slang offens.* a Jewish name for a non-Jew. [from Hebrew *gōy* 'people, nation'] □ **goyish** *adj.* (also **goyish**).

GP *abbr.* **1** general practitioner. **2** Grand Prix.

Gp. Capt. *abbr.* (in the RAF) Group Captain.

GPO *abbr.* **1** *Brit.* General Post Office. **2** *US* Government Printing Office.

GPS *abbr.* Global Positioning System, an accurate worldwide navigational and surveying facility based on the reception of signals from an array of orbiting satellites.

gr *abbr.* (also **gr.**) **1** gram(s). **2** grain(s). **3** gross. **4** grey.

grab ● *v.* (**grabbed**, **grabbing**) **1** *tr.* **a** seize suddenly. **b** capture, arrest. **2** *tr.* take greedily or unfairly. **3** *tr. slang* attract the attention of, impress. **4** *intr.* (foll. by *at*) snatch at. **5** *intr.* (of brakes) act harshly or jerkily. ● *n.* **1** a sudden clutch or attempt to seize. **2** a mechanical device for clutching. ▷ EXCAVATE. **3** the practice of grabbing. □ **up for grabs** *slang* readily obtainable or available; on offer. [from Middle Dutch *grabben*] □ **grabber** *n.*

grab bag *n. N. Amer.* a lucky dip.

grabby *adj. colloq.* tending to grab; greedy, grasping.

grab handle *n.* (also **grab rail** etc.) a handle or rail etc. to steady passengers in a moving vehicle.

grace ● *n.* **1** attractiveness, esp. in elegance of proportion or manner or movement; gracefulness. **2** courteous good will (*had the grace to apologize*). **3** an attractive feature; an accomplishment (*social graces*). **4 a** (in Christian belief) the unmerited favour of God; a divine saving and strengthening influence. **b** the state of receiving this. **c** a divinely given talent. **5** goodwill, favour (*fall from grace*). **6** delay granted as a favour (*a year's grace*). **7** a short thanksgiving before or after a meal. **8** (**Grace**) (in Greek mythology) each of three beautiful sister goddesses, bestowers of beauty and charm. **9** (**Grace**) (prec. by *His, Her, Your*) forms of description or address for a duke, duchess, or archbishop. ● *v.tr.* add grace to; enhance or embellish; confer honour on (*a vase graced the table; graced us with his presence*). □ **with good** (or **bad**) **grace** as if willingly (or reluctantly). [based on Latin *gratus* 'pleasing']

grace and favour *attrib.adj. Brit.* designating a house etc. occupied by permission of a sovereign etc.

graceful *adj.* having or showing grace or elegance. □ **gracefully** *adv.* **gracefulness** *n.*

graceless *adj.* lacking grace or elegance or charm. □ **gracelessly** *adv.*

grace note *n.* an extra note as an embellishment.

gracile *adj.* slender; esp. *Anthropol.* (of hominid species) of slender build. [from Latin *gracilis* 'slender']

gracious ● *adj.* **1** indulgent and beneficent to inferiors. **2** (of God) merciful, benign. **3** characterized by elegance and usu. wealth (*gracious grandeur; gracious rooms*). ● *int.* expressing surprise. □ **graciously** *adv.* **graciousness** *n.*

gracious living *n.* an elegant way of life.

grackle *n.* **1** ◄ any of various orioles, esp. of the genus *Quiscalus*, native to America. **2** any of various mynahs, esp. of the genus *Gracula*, native to Asia. [from Latin *graculus* 'jackdaw']

GRACKLE: COMMON GRACKLE (*Quiscalus quiscula*)

gradate *v.* **1** *v.intr. & tr.* pass or cause to pass by gradations from one shade to another. **2** *tr.* arrange in steps or grades of size etc.

gradation *n.* (usu. in *pl.*) **1** a stage of transition or advance. **2 a** a certain degree in rank, intensity, merit, divergence, etc. **b** arrangement in such degrees. **3** (of paint etc.) the gradual passing from one shade, tone, etc. to another. **4** *Philol.* ablaut. [from Latin *gradatio*]

grade ● *n.* **1 a** a certain degree in rank, merit, proficiency, quality, etc. **b** a class of persons or things of the same grade. **2 a** a mark indicating the quality of a student's work. **b** *Brit.* an examination, esp. in music. **3** *N. Amer.* a class in school. **4 a** a gradient or slope. **b** the rate of ascent or descent. ● *v.* **1** *tr.* arrange in grades. **2** *intr.* pass gradually between grades, or into a grade. **3** *tr.* give a grade to (a student). **4** *tr.* blend so as to affect the grade of colour with tints passing into each other. □ **make the grade** *colloq.* succeed; reach the desired standard. [from Latin *gradus* 'step']

grader *n.* **1** a person or thing that grades. **2** (in *comb.*) *N. Amer.* a pupil of a specified grade in a school (*sixth-grader*).

grade school *n. US* elementary school.

gradient *n.* **1** esp. *Brit.* **a** a stretch of road, railway, etc. that slopes. **b** the amount of such a slope. **2** the rate of rise or fall of temperature, pressure, etc. in passing from one region to another.

gradual *adj.* **1** taking place or progressing slowly or by degrees. **2** not rapid or steep or abrupt. [based on Latin *gradus* 'step'] □ **gradually** *adv.* **gradualness** *n.*

gradualism *n.* a policy of gradual reform rather than sudden change or revolution. □ **gradualist** *n.*

graduand *n. Brit.* a person about to receive an academic degree.

graduate ● *n.* **1** a person who has been awarded an academic degree (also *attrib.: graduate student*). **2** *N. Amer.* a person who has completed a course of study. ● *v.* **1** *intr.* **a** take an academic degree or (*N. Amer.*) a high school diploma. **b** (foll. by *from*) be awarded a degree of a specified university. **c** (foll. by *in*) be awarded a degree in a specified subject. **2** *tr. N. Amer.* confer a degree, diploma, etc. upon; send out as a graduate from a university etc. **3** *intr.* **a** (foll. by *to*) move up to (a higher grade of activity etc.). **b** (foll. by *as, in*) gain specified qualifications. **4** *tr.* mark out in degrees or parts. **5** *tr.* arrange in gradations; apportion according to a scale. **6** *intr.* (foll. by *into, away*) pass by degrees. [from medieval Latin *graduari* 'to take a degree']

graduated pension *n.* (in the UK) a system of pension contributions by employees in proportion to their wages or salary.

graduate school *n. N. Amer.* a department of a university for advanced work by graduates.

graduation *n.* **1** the act or an instance of graduating or being graduated. **2** a ceremony at which degrees are conferred. **3** each or all of the marks on a vessel or instrument indicating degrees of quantity etc.

Graeco- /greek-oh/ *comb. form* (also **Greco-**) Greek; Greek and.

graffiti ● *n.pl.* (*sing.* **graffito**) inscriptions or drawings scribbled, scratched, or sprayed on a surface. ● *v.tr.* (**graffitied**) **1** cover (a surface) with graffiti. **2** write as graffiti (*graffitied initials*). [Italian, literally 'scratches'] □ **graffitist** *n.*

■ **Usage** *Graffiti* is, in formal terms, a plural noun and as such should be used with a plural verb. This rule is straightforward when referring to individual inscriptions, e.g. *The graffiti were aggressive and insulting.* The singular form in such examples is *graffito*, e.g. *The graffito on the tombstone said simply 'Jim'.* It is wrong to use the plural form *graffiti* as a singular in such contexts, e.g. *The most common graffiti is 'Vive le roi'.* An alternative to *graffito* is *piece of graffiti*, e.g. *We saw an amusing piece of graffiti.* However, the most common use of *graffiti* is as a collective or mass noun, referring to inscriptions in general or en masse. As such, this word is usually found with a singular verb, e.g. *Graffiti is an increasing problem.* Most people find this use natural and acceptable.

graft[1] ● *n.* **1** *Bot.* **a** ▼ a shoot or scion inserted into a slit in a stock, from which it receives sap. **b** the place where a graft is inserted. **c** an instance or the process of inserting a shoot or scion. **2** *Surgery* **a** a piece of living tissue, organ, etc., transplanted surgically. **b** an instance or the process of doing this. **3** *Brit. slang* work (esp. in phr. **hard graft**). ● *v.* **1** *tr.* **a** insert (a scion) as a graft. **b** insert a graft on (a stock). **2** *intr.* insert a graft. **3** *tr. Surgery* transplant (living tissue). **4** *tr.* (foll. by *in, on*) insert or fix (a thing) permanently to another. **5** *intr. Brit. slang* work hard. [from Greek *graphion* 'stylus'] □ **grafter** *n.*

GRAFT

In many woody and herbaceous plants, a budded stem (scion) may be grafted on to a rootstock (stock) of another species or cultivar. Cells in the cambial layers of the two plants bond, creating a composite plant with more desirable characteristics.

WHIP-AND-TONGUE GRAFT

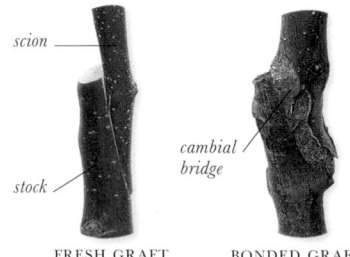

scion

stock

cambial bridge

FRESH GRAFT   BONDED GRAFT

GRAIN

Grain crops (cereals) are the most important of all the world's foods and have been cultivated since earliest times. Grain kernels are typically rich in starch, protein, and oil, while the husk contains vitamins and fibre. If kept dry, grains can be stored for months or years.

EXAMPLES OF DRIED GRAINS

WILD RICE
(*Zizania aquatica*)

OATS
(*Avena sativa*)

WHEAT
(*Triticum vulgare*)

POT BARLEY
(*Hordeum vulgare*)

MAIZE (CORN)
(*Zea mays*)

MILLET
(*Panicum miliaceum*)

graft[2] *colloq.* ● *n.* **1** practices, esp. bribery, used to secure illicit gains in politics or business. **2** such gains. ● *v.intr.* seek or make such gains. [19th-century coinage] □ **grafter** *n.*

Grail *n.* (in full **Holy Grail**) (in medieval legend) the cup or platter used by Christ at the Last Supper, and in which Joseph of Arimathea received Christ's blood at the Cross, esp. as the object of quests by medieval knights. [from medieval Latin *gradalis* 'dish']

grain ● *n.* **1** ▲ a fruit or seed of a cereal. **2 a** (*collect.*) wheat or any allied grass used as food. ▷ GRASS. **b** (*collect.*) their fruit. **c** any particular species of corn. **3 a** a small hard particle of salt, sand, etc. **b** a discrete particle or crystal, usu. small, in a rock or metal. **4** the smallest unit of weight in the troy and avoirdupois systems, equal to $^1/_{5760}$ of a pound troy and $^1/_{7000}$ of a pound avoirdupois (approx. 0.0648 grams). **5** the smallest possible quantity (*not a grain of truth in it*). **6 a** roughness of surface. **b** *Photog.* a granular appearance on a photograph or negative. **7** the texture of skin, wood, stone, fabric, etc. **8 a** a pattern of lines of fibre in wood or paper. **b** lamination or planes of cleavage in stone, coal, etc. **9** nature, temper, tendency. ● *v.* **1** *tr.* paint in imitation of the grain of wood or marble. **2** *tr.* give a granular surface to. **3** *tr. & intr.* form into grains. □ **against the grain** (often in phr. **go against the grain**) contrary to one's natural inclination or feeling. [from Latin *granum*] □ **grained** *adj.* (also in *comb.*).

grainy *adj.* (**grainier**, **grainiest**) **1** granular. **2** resembling the grain of wood. **3** *Photog.* having a granular appearance. □ **graininess** *n.*

grallatorial *adj. Zool.* of or relating to long-legged wading birds. [based on Latin *grallator* 'stilt-walker']

gram *n.* (also *Brit.* **gramme**) a metric unit of mass equal to one-thousandth of a kilogram. [from Greek *gramma* 'small weight']

-gram *comb. form* forming nouns denoting a thing written or recorded (*anagram*; *epigram*). [from or suggested by Greek *gramma* 'thing written'] □ **-grammatic** *comb. form* forming adjectives.

graminaceous *adj.* of or like grass; grassy. [based on Latin *gramen -inis* 'grass']

graminivorous *adj.* feeding on grass, cereals, etc.

grammar *n.* **1** the study or rules of a language's inflections or other means of showing the relation between words. **2** application of the rules of grammar (*bad grammar*). **3** a book on grammar. **4** the elements or rudiments of an art or science. **5** *Brit. colloq.* = GRAMMAR SCHOOL. [from Greek *grammatikē (tekhnē)* '(art) of letters']

grammarian *n.* an expert in grammar or linguistics; a philologist.

grammar school *n. Brit.* esp. *hist.* a selective state secondary school with a mainly academic curriculum.

grammatical *adj.* of or conforming to the rules of grammar, or to the formal principles of an art, science, etc. [from Greek *grammatikos*] □ **grammaticality** *n.* **grammatically** *adv.*

gramme *Brit.* var. of GRAM.

gramophone *n.* = RECORD PLAYER. [formed by inversion of *phonogram*, a sound recording] □ **gramophonic** *adj.*

gramophone record see RECORD *n.* 3.

grampus *n.* (*pl.* **grampuses**) **1** ▼ a dolphin, *Grampus griseus*, with a blunt snout and long pointed black flippers. **2** the killer whale. [from Latin *crassus piscis* 'fat fish']

pointed flippers

GRAMPUS
(*Grampus griseus*)

gran *n. colloq.* grandmother.

granadilla var. of GRENADILLA.

granary *n.* (*pl.* **-ies**) **1** a storehouse for threshed grain. **2** a region producing, and esp. exporting, much corn. **3** *propr.* a type of brown bread or flour containing whole grains of wheat. [from Latin *granarium*]

grand ● *adj.* **1 a** splendid, imposing, dignified. **b** solemn or lofty in conception or expression; noble. **2** main (*grand staircase*). **3** (**Grand**) of the highest rank (*Grand Vizier*). **4** *colloq.* excellent, enjoyable (*had a grand time*). **5** displaying opulence (*the grand folk at the manor*). **6** (in *comb.*) in family relationships, denoting the second degree of ascent or descent (*granddaughter*). ● *n.* **1** = GRAND PIANO. **2** (*pl.* same) (usu. in *pl.*) *slang* a thousand dollars or pounds. [from Latin *grandis* 'full-grown'] □ **grandly** *adv.* **grandness** *n.*

grandad *n.* (also **granddad**) *colloq.* **1** grandfather. **2** an elderly man.

grandchild *n.* (*pl.* **-children**) a child of one's son or daughter.

granddaughter *n.* a female grandchild.

grand duchy *n.* a state ruled by a grand duke or duchess.

grand duke *n.* (also **grand duchess**) a prince (or princess) or noble person ruling over a territory.

grandee *n.* **1** a Spanish or Portuguese nobleman of the highest rank. **2** a person of high rank or eminence. [from Spanish & Portuguese *grande*]

grandeur /grand-yer/ *n.* **1** majesty, splendour; dignity of appearance or bearing. **2** high rank, eminence. **3** nobility of character. [French, literally 'greatness']

grandfather *n.* a male grandparent. □ **grandfatherly** *adj.*

grandfather clock *n.* a clock in a tall free-standing wooden case, driven by weights. ▷ CLOCK

grandiflora *adj.* bearing large flowers. [modern Latin]

grandiloquent *adj.* **1** pompous or inflated in language. **2** given to boastful talk. [alteration of Latin *grandiloquus*] □ **grandiloquence** *n.* **grandiloquently** *adv.*

grandiose *adj.* **1** producing or meant to produce an imposing effect. **2** planned on an ambitious or magnificent scale. [French from Italian *grandioso*] □ **grandiosely** *adv.* **grandiosity** *n.*

grand jury *n.* esp. *US Law* a jury selected to examine the validity of an accusation prior to trial.

grandma *n. colloq.* grandmother.

grand mal /gron **mal**/ *n.* a serious form of epilepsy with loss of consciousness (often *attrib.*: *grand mal seizure*). [French, literally 'great sickness']

grandmama *n. archaic colloq.* = GRANDMA.

grand master *n.* **1** a chess player of the highest class. **2** (**Grand Master**) the head of a military order of knighthood, of Freemasons, etc.

grandmother *n.* a female grandparent. □ **grandmotherly** *adj.*

grandmother clock *n.* a clock like a grandfather clock but in a smaller case.

Grand National *n.* a steeplechase held annually at Aintree, Liverpool, UK.

grand opera *n.* opera on a serious theme, or in which the entire libretto is sung.

grandpa *n. colloq.* grandfather.

grandpapa *n. archaic colloq.* = GRANDPA.

grandparent *n.* a parent of one's father or mother.

grand piano *n.* a large full-toned piano with horizontal strings. ▷ PIANO

Grand Prix /grahn **pree**/ *n.* (*pl.* **Grands Prix** *pronunc.* same) any of several important international motor or motorcycle racing events. [French, literally 'great or chief prize']

grandsire *n. archaic* **1** grandfather. **2** (in bell-ringing) a method of change-ringing.

grand slam *n.* **1** *Bridge* the winning of 13 tricks. **2** the winning of all of a group of major championships or matches in a sport.

grandson *n.* a male grandchild.

grandstand *n.* the main stand for spectators at a racecourse etc. ▷ RACECOURSE

grand total *n.* the final amount after everything is added up; the sum of other totals.

grand unified theory *n. Physics* a theory attempting to give a single explanation of the strong, weak, and electromagnetic interactions between subatomic particles.

grange *n.* **1** *Brit.* a country house with farm buildings. **2** *archaic* a barn. [from medieval Latin *granica (villa)* 'granary']

graniferous *adj.* producing grain or a grainlike seed. [based on Latin *granum* 'grain'] □ **graniform** *adj.*

granite *n.* **1** ▶ a granular crystalline igneous rock of quartz, mica, feldspar, etc., used for building. ▷ IGNEOUS. **2** a determined or resolute quality, attitude, etc. [from Italian *granito*, literally 'grained'] □ **granitic** *adj.* **granitoid** *adj. & n.*

GRANITE:
PORPHYRITIC
GRANITE

granivorous *adj.* feeding on grain. □ **granivore** *n.*

granny *n.* (also **grannie**) (*pl.* **-ies**) *colloq.* grandmother.

granny flat *n.* (also **granny annexe**) *Brit.* part of a house made into self-contained accommodation for an elderly relative.

G

**GRANNY
KNOT**

granny knot *n.* ◄ a reef knot crossed the wrong way and therefore insecure. ▷ KNOT

grant ● *v.tr.* **1 a** consent to fulfil (a request etc.) (*granted all he asked*). **b** allow (a person) to have (a thing). **c** (as **granted** *adj.*) *Brit. colloq.* apology accepted. **2** give formally; transfer legally. **3** (often foll. by *that* + clause) concede, esp. as a basis for argument. ● *n.* **1** the process of granting or a thing granted. **2** a sum of money given by the State. **3** *Law* a legal conveyance by written instrument. □ **take for granted 1** assume something to be true or valid. **2** cease to appreciate through familiarity. [from Old French *gr(e)anter*] □ **grantee** *n.* (esp. in sense 2 of *v.*). **granter** *n.* **grantor** *n.* (esp. in sense 2 of *v.*).

grant aid *n.* a grant by central government to local government or an institution.

Granth /grunt/ *n.* (in full **Granth Sahib**) ▼ the sacred scriptures of the Sikhs. [Hindi, literally 'book, code']

G

GRANTH: 20TH-CENTURY INDIAN
GURU GRANTH SAHIB

grant-in-aid *n.* (*pl.* **grants-in-aid**) = GRANT AID.

grant-maintained *adj.* (of a school) funded by central rather than local government, and self-governing.

gran turismo *n.* = GT.

granular *adj.* **1** of or like grains or granules. **2** having a granulated surface or structure. □ **granularity** *n.*

granulate *v.* **1** *tr. & intr.* form into grains (*granulated sugar*). **2** *tr.* roughen the surface of. **3** *intr.* (of a wound etc.) heal, join. □ **granulation** *n.* **granulator** *n.*

granule *n.* a small grain. [from Late Latin *granulum*]

grape *n.* **1** a berry growing in clusters on a vine, used as fruit and in making wine. **2** (prec. by *the*) *colloq.* wine. [from Old French *grape* 'bunch of grapes'] □ **grapey** *adj.* (also **grapy**).

grapefruit *n.* (*pl.* same) a large round yellow citrus fruit with an acid juicy pulp. ▷ CITRUS FRUIT. [from GRAPE + FRUIT, probably because the fruits grow in clusters]

grape hyacinth *n.* ▼ a plant of the genus *Muscari* (lily family), with clusters of usu. blue flowers.

GRAPE HYACINTH (*Muscari armeniacum*)

GRASS

The grass family contains some 9,000 species, including both terrestrial and aquatic species. No other plant family has been so successful in colonizing a broad range of habitats across the world. Most grasses have inconspicuous flowers that are wind-pollinated. Certain species (the cereals) are cultivated as food crops; others are employed in horticulture.

EXTERNAL
FEATURES OF
COUCH GRASS
(*Agropyron repens*)

*caryopsis
(dry fruit)*

*culm
(jointed
stem)*

node

*sheathing
leaf base*

roots

*round,
hollow stem*

*lamina
(blade)*

MAIN TYPES OF GRASS

CEREALS
bread wheat
(*Triticum aestivum*)

GRASSES
winter wild oat
(*Avena sterilis*)

BAMBOOS
(*Arundinaria
nitida*)

REEDS
giant reed
(*Arundo donax*)

grapeseed oil *n.* oil extracted from the residue of grapes.

grapeshot *n.* *hist.* small balls used as charge in a cannon and scattering when fired.

grapevine *n.* **1** any of various vines of the genus *Vitis*. **2** *colloq.* the means of transmission of a rumour.

graph ● *n.* a diagram showing the relation between usu. two variable quantities, each measured along one of a pair of axes. ● *v.tr.* plot or trace on a graph. [abbreviation of *graphic formula*]

-graph *comb. form* forming nouns meaning: **1** a thing written or drawn etc. in a specified way (*autograph*). **2** an instrument that records (*seismograph*).

graphic ● *adj.* **1** of or relating to the visual or descriptive arts, esp. writing and drawing. **2** vividly descriptive. **3** = GRAPHICAL. ● *n.* a product of the graphic arts (cf. GRAPHICS 1, 3b). [from Greek *graphikos*] □ **graphically** *adv.* **graphicness** *n.*

graphical *adj.* **1** of or in the form of graphs (see GRAPH). **2** graphic. □ **graphically** *adv.*

graphical user interface *n.* a visual means of interacting with a computer, using items such as windows and icons.

graphic arts *n.pl.* the visual and technical arts involving design, writing, drawing, printing, etc. □ **graphic artist** *n.*

graphic equalizer *n.* a device for the separate control of the strength and quality of selected frequency bands.

graphic novel *n.* an adult novel published in comic-strip format.

graphics *n.pl.* (usu. treated as *sing.* except in sense 3b) **1** the products of the graphic arts. **2** the use of diagrams in calculation and design. **3** (in full **computer graphics**) *Computing* **a** the use of computers linked to monitors to generate and manipulate visual images. **b** the visual images produced.

graphite *n.* ▶ a grey crystalline allotropic form of carbon used as a lubricant, in pencils, etc. ▷ ALLOTROPE. [based on Greek *graphein* 'to write']

graphology *n.* the study of handwriting, esp. as a supposed guide to character. □ **graphological** *adj.* **graphologist** *n.*

GRAPHITE

graph paper *n.* paper printed with a network of lines as a basis for drawing graphs.

grapnel *n.* **1** a device with iron claws, attached to a rope and used for dragging or grasping. **2** a small anchor with several flukes. [from Old French *grapon*]

grapple ● *v.* **1** *intr.* (often foll. by *with*) fight at close quarters or in close combat. **2** *intr.* (foll. by *with*) try to manage a difficult problem etc. **3** *tr.* **a** grip with the hands; come to close quarters with. **b** seize with or as with a grapnel. ● *n.* **1 a** a hold or grip in or as in wrestling. **b** a contest at close quarters. **2** a clutching-instrument. [from Old French *grapil* 'little hook'] □ **grappler** *n.*

grappling hook *n.* = GRAPNEL 1.

grappling iron *n.* = GRAPNEL 1.

grasp ● *v.* **1** *tr.* **a** clutch at; seize greedily. **b** hold firmly; grip. **2** *intr.* (foll. by *at*) try to seize; accept avidly. **3** *tr.* understand or realize (a fact or meaning). ● *n.* **1 a** a firm hold; grip. **2** (foll. by *of*) **a** mastery (*a grasp of the situation*). **b** a mental hold (*a grasp of the facts*). □ **grasp at a straw** (or **at straws**) see STRAW. **grasp the nettle** *Brit.* tackle a difficulty boldly. [Middle English] □ **graspable** *adj.* **grasper** *n.*

grasping *adj.* avaricious, greedy. □ **graspingly** *adv.* **graspingness** *n.*

grass ● *n.* **1 a** ▲ a plant of the family Gramineae, with long narrow leaves, jointed stems, and spikes of small wind-pollinated flowers, including cereals, reeds, and bamboos. **b** vegetation consisting of usu. short plants of this family. **2** pastureland. **3** a lawn. **4** *slang* marijuana. **5** *Brit. slang* an informer. ● *v.* **1** *tr.* cover with turf. **2** *tr.* *US* provide with pasture. **3** *Brit. slang* **a** *tr.* betray, esp. to the police. **b** *intr.* inform the police. □ **at grass 1** grazing. **2** out of work, on holiday, etc. **out to grass 1** out to graze. **2** in retirement. [Old English] □ **grassy** *adj.* (**grassier**, **grassiest**).

grass box *n. Brit.* a receptacle for cut grass on a lawnmower.

grass court *n.* a grass-covered tennis court.

grasshopper *n.* a jumping and chirping plant-eating insect of the order Orthoptera. ▷ ORTHOPTERAN

grassland *n.* a large open area of country covered with grass, esp. one used for grazing.

GRAVITY

In 1687 Sir Isaac Newton postulated his theory that a gravitational force acts upon all matter that has mass. Furthermore, the force between two objects depends not only upon their physical mass but also upon the distance between them. Thus, if the Moon had twice its actual mass (as shown below), the gravitational force between the Earth and the Moon would be twice as large as at present. If the Moon were also half its actual distance from the Earth, the force of gravity would be four times as large.

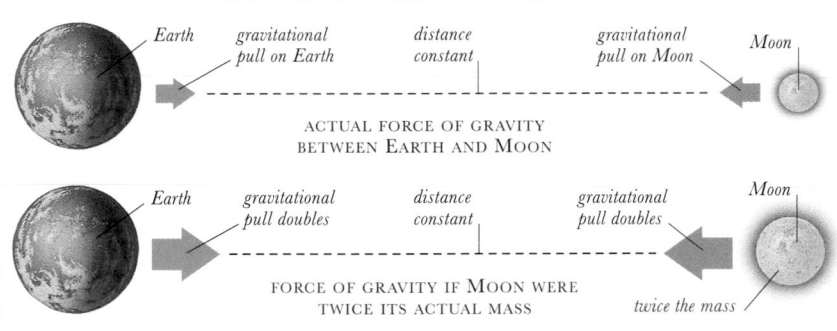

HOW GRAVITY CHANGES WITH MASS

Earth   *gravitational pull on Earth*   *distance constant*   *gravitational pull on Moon*   *Moon*

ACTUAL FORCE OF GRAVITY
BETWEEN EARTH AND MOON

Earth   *gravitational pull doubles*   *distance constant*   *gravitational pull doubles*   *Moon*

FORCE OF GRAVITY IF MOON WERE
TWICE ITS ACTUAL MASS   *twice the mass*

---

grass roots *n.pl.* **1** a fundamental level or source. **2** ordinary people; the rank and file of an organization, esp. a political party.

grass skirt *n.* a skirt made of long grass and leaves fastened to a waistband.

grass snake *n.* **1** *Brit.* a common Eurasian snake, *Natrix natrix*, greenish-brown or greenish-grey with a yellow band around the neck. **2** *N. Amer.* the common greensnake, *Opheodrys vernalis*.

grass widow *n.* (*masc.* **grass widower**) a person whose husband (or wife) is away for a prolonged period.

grate[1] *v.* **1** *tr.* reduce to small shreds by rubbing on a serrated surface. **2** *intr.* (often foll. by *against, on*) rub with a harsh scraping sound. **3** *tr.* utter in a harsh tone. **4** *intr.* **a** sound harshly. **b** (often foll. by *on*) have an irritating effect. **5** *tr.* grind (one's teeth). **6** *intr.* (of a hinge etc.) creak. [from Old French *grater*]

grate[2] *n.* **1** the recess of a fireplace or furnace. **2** a metal frame confining fuel in a fireplace etc. ▷ FIRE-PLACE. [from Latin *cratis* 'hurdle']

grateful *adj.* **1** feeling or showing gratitude. **2** pleasant, acceptable. [based on obsolete *grate* 'pleasing', from Latin *gratus*] □ **gratefully** *adv.* **gratefulness** *n.*

grater *n.* a device for reducing cheese or other food to small shreds.

graticule *n.* a series of fine lines or fibres incorporated in an optical instrument as a measuring scale or as an aid in locating objects. [from Latin *craticula* 'gridiron']

gratify *v.tr.* (**-fies, -fied**) **1 a** please, delight. **b** please by compliance; assent to the wish of. **2** yield to (a feeling or desire). [from Latin *gratificari* 'to do a favour to'] □ **gratification** *n.* **gratifier** *n.* **gratifying** *adj.* **gratifyingly** *adv.*

gratin *n. Cookery* **1** a light browned crust usu. of breadcrumbs or melted cheese. **2** a dish cooked with this (cf. AU GRATIN).

grating[1] *adj.* **1** sounding harsh or discordant. **2** having an irritating effect. □ **gratingly** *adv.*

grating[2] *n.* **1** a framework of parallel or crossed metal bars. **2** *Optics* a set of parallel wires, lines ruled on glass, etc., for producing spectra by diffraction.

gratis *adv. & adj.* without charge. [Latin, literally 'by favour']

gratitude *n.* being thankful; readiness to return kindness. [based on Latin *gratus* 'thankful']

gratuitous *adj.* **1** given or done free of charge. **2** uncalled for; lacking good reason. [from Latin *gratuitus* 'spontaneous'] □ **gratuitously** *adv.* **gratuitousness** *n.*

gratuity *n.* (*pl.* **-ies**) a tip. [from medieval Latin *gratuitas* 'gift']

graunch *v.intr. & tr. Brit. colloq.* make or cause to make a crunching or grinding sound.

gravadlax var. of GRAVLAX.

gravamen *n.* (*pl.* **gravamens** or **gravamina**) **1** the essence or most serious part of an argument. **2** a grievance. [Late Latin, literally 'inconvenience']

grave[1] /grayv/ *n.* **1 a** a trench dug in the ground to receive a coffin on burial. **b** the place where someone is buried. **2** (prec. by *the*) death. □ **turn in one's grave** (of a dead person) be likely to have been shocked or angry if still alive. [Old English]

grave[2] ● *adj.* /grayv/ **1 a** serious, weighty (*a grave matter*). **b** dignified, solemn, sombre (*a grave look*). **2** extremely threatening (*grave danger*). **3** /grahv/ (of sound) low-pitched, not acute. ● *n.* /grahv/ = GRAVE ACCENT. [from Latin *gravis* 'heavy, serious'] □ **gravely** *adv.* **graveness** *n.*

grave[3] /grayv/ *v.tr.* (*past part.* **graven** or **graved**) **1** (foll. by *in, on*) fix indelibly (on one's memory). **2** *archaic* engrave. [Old English *grafan* 'to dig, engrave']

grave accent /grahv/ *n.* a mark (`) placed over a vowel in some languages to denote pronunciation, length, etc., originally indicating low or falling pitch.

gravedigger *n.* a person who digs graves.

gravel ● *n.* **1 a** a mixture of coarse sand and small water-worn or pounded stones, used for paths and roads and as an aggregate. **b** *Geol.* a stratum of this. **2** *Med.* aggregations of crystals formed in the urinary tract. ● *v.tr.* (**gravelled, gravelling**; *US* **graveled, graveling**) **1** lay or strew with gravel. **2** perplex, puzzle, nonplus. [from Old French *gravel(e)* 'little shore']

gravelly *adj.* **1** of, like, or containing gravel. **2** (of a voice) deep and rough-sounding.

graven *past part.* of GRAVE[3].

graven image *n.* an idol.

graveside *n.* the ground at the edge of a grave.

gravestone *n.* a stone marking a grave.

graveyard *n.* a burial ground.

gravid *adj. literary* or *Zool.* pregnant; carrying eggs or young. [from Latin *gravidus*]

gravimeter *n.* an instrument for measuring the difference in the force of gravity from one place to another.

gravimetry *n.* the measurement of weight. □ **gravimetric** *adj.*

graving dock *n.* = DRY DOCK.

gravitas *n.* solemn demeanour; seriousness. [Latin]

gravitate *v.intr.* **1** (foll. by *to, towards*) move or be attracted to (some source of influence). **2 a** move or tend by force of gravity towards. **b** sink by or as if by gravity. [from modern Latin *gravitare*]

gravitation *n. Physics* **1** a force of attraction between any particle of matter in the universe and any other. **2** the effect of this, esp. the falling of bodies to the Earth. □ **gravitational** *adj.* **gravitationally** *adv.*

gravitational constant *n.* the constant in Newton's law of gravitation relating gravity to the masses and separation of bodies (symbol **G**).

gravitational field *n.* the region of space surrounding a body in which another body experiences a force of attraction.

gravity *n.* **1 a** ◀ the force that attracts a body towards the centre of the Earth or towards any other physical body having mass. **b** the degree of intensity of this measured by acceleration. **c** gravitational force. **2** the property of having weight. **3 a** importance, seriousness. **b** solemnity, sobriety; serious demeanour. [from Latin *gravitas* 'weightiness']

gravity feed *n.* the supply of material by its fall under gravity.

gravlax *n.* (also **gravadlax**) a Scandinavian dish of dry-cured salmon marinated in herbs. [Swedish, from *grav* 'trench' + *lax* 'salmon', from the former practice of marinating salmon in a hole in the ground]

gravure *n.* = PHOTOGRAVURE.

gravy *n.* (*pl.* **-ies**) **1** the juices exuding from meat during and after cooking. **2** sauce for food, made from these etc. [Middle English]

gravy boat *n.* a boat-shaped vessel for serving gravy.

gravy train *n. slang* a source of easy financial benefit.

gray[1] *n. Physics* the SI unit of the absorbed dose of ionizing radiation, corresponding to one joule per kilogram. [named after L. H. *Gray*, English radiobiologist, 1905–65]

gray[2] *US* var. of GREY.

graybeard *US* var. of GREYBEARD.

grayling *n.* **1** ▼ any silver-grey freshwater fish of the genus *Thymallus*, with a long high dorsal fin. **2** a butterfly, *Hipparchia semele*, having wings with grey undersides and bright eye-spots on the upper side.

high dorsal fin

GRAYLING (*Thymallus thymallus*)

graze[1] *v.* **1** *intr.* (of cattle etc.) eat growing grass. **2** *tr.* **a** feed (cattle etc.) on growing grass. **b** feed on (grass). **3** *intr.* pasture cattle. **4** *intr. colloq.* **a** eat snacks or small meals throughout the day. **b** flick rapidly between television channels. **c** casually sample something. [Old English] □ **grazer** *n.*

graze[2] ● *v.* **1** *tr.* scrape (the skin) so as to break the surface but cause little bleeding. **2 a** *tr.* touch lightly in passing. **b** *intr.* (foll. by *against, along*, etc.) move with a light passing contact. ● *n.* an act or instance of grazing; the result of grazing.

grazier *n.* **1** a person who feeds cattle for market. **2** *Austral.* a large-scale sheep farmer or cattle farmer. □ **graziery** *n.*

grazing *n.* **1** in senses of GRAZE[1, 2]. **2** grassland suitable for pasturage.

grease ● *n.* **1** oily or fatty matter, esp. as a lubricant. **2** the melted fat of a dead animal. ● *v.tr.* smear or lubricate with grease. □ **grease the palm of** *colloq.* bribe. **like greased lightning** *colloq.* very fast. [based on Latin *crassus* 'fat, thick']

G

grease gun *n.* ► a device for pumping grease under pressure to a particular point.

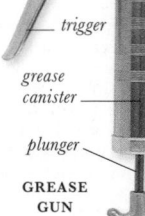

trigger

grease canister

plunger

GREASE GUN

greasepaint *n.* a waxy composition used as make-up for actors.

greaseproof *adj.* (esp. of paper) impervious to the penetration of grease.

greaser *n.* **1** *slang* a member of a gang of youths with long hair and riding motorcycles. **2** *US slang offens.* a Mexican or Spanish American.

greasy *adj.* (**greasier**, **greasiest**) **1 a** of or like grease. **b** smeared with grease. **c** containing or having too much grease. **2 a** slippery. **b** (of a person or manner) smarmy. **c** objectionable. □ **greasily** *adv.* **greasiness** *n.*

greasy pole *n. colloq.* a difficult pathway to success.

great ● *adj.* **1 a** of a size, amount, extent, or intensity considerably above the average (*made a great hole*). **b** also with implied surprise, contempt, etc. (*you great idiot!*; *look at that great wasp*). **c** reinforcing other words denoting size etc. (*a great many*). **2** pre-eminent; worthy or most worthy of consideration (*the great thing is not to get caught*). **3** grand, imposing (*a great occasion*). **4 a** (esp. of a public or historic figure) distinguished. **b** (**the Great**) as a title denoting the most important (*Alfred the Great*). **5 a** (of a person) remarkable in ability, character, etc. (*a great thinker*). **b** (of a thing) outstanding of its kind (*the Great Fire*). **6** (foll. by *at*, *on*) skilled, well informed. **7** doing a thing habitually or extensively (*a great reader*). **8** (also **greater**) the larger of the species etc. (*great auk*). **9** (**Greater**) (of a city etc.) including adjacent urban areas (*Greater Manchester*). **10** *colloq.* **a** very enjoyable or satisfactory (*had a great time*). **b** (as an exclamation) fine, very good. **11** (in *comb.*) denoting one degree further removed upwards or downwards (*great-uncle*). ● *n.* a great or outstanding person or thing. ● *adv. colloq.* excellently, well, successfully. □ **great and small** all classes or types. **the great and the good** often *iron.* distinguished and worthy people. **to a great extent** largely. [Old English] □ **greatness** *n.*

great ape *n.* any of the large apes of the family Pongidae, closely related to humans.

Great Britain *n.* England, Wales, and Scotland.

great circle *n.* any circle on the surface of a sphere which lies in a plane passing through the sphere's centre and represents the shortest distance between any two points on the circle.

greatcoat *n.* a long heavy overcoat.

Great Dane *n.* ▼ a dog of a very large short-haired breed.

GREAT DANE

greatly *adv.* by a considerable amount; much.

Great Russian *hist.* ● *n.* **1** a Russian. **2** the Russian language. ● *adj.* Russian.

great tit *n.* a Eurasian songbird, *Parus major*, with black and white head markings.

Great War *n.* the First World War (1914–18).

greave *n.* (usu. in *pl.*) a piece of armour for the shin. ▷ ARMOUR. [from Old French *greve* 'shin, greave']

grebe *n.* any diving bird of the family Podicipedidae, with a long neck, lobed toes, and almost no tail. [from French]

Grecian /gree-shăn/ *adj.* (of architecture or facial outline) following Greek models or ideals. [based on Latin *Graecia* 'Greece']

Greco- var. of GRAECO-.

greed *n.* intense or excessive desire, esp. for food or wealth.

greedy *adj.* (**greedier**, **greediest**) **1** having or showing greed. **2** (foll. by *for*, or *to* + infin.) very keen or eager. [Old English] □ **greedily** *adv.* **greediness** *n.*

Greek ● *n.* **1 a** a native or national of modern Greece; a person of Greek descent. **b** a native or citizen of any of the ancient states of Greece. **2** the Indo-European language of Greece. ● *adj.* of Greece or its people or language. [from Greek *Graikoi*, according to Aristotle the prehistoric name of the Hellenes] □ **Greekness** *n.*

Greek cross *n.* a cross with four equal arms.

green ● *adj.* **1** of the colour between blue and yellow in the spectrum; coloured like grass etc. **2 a** covered with leaves or grass. **b** mild and without snow (*a green Christmas*). **3** (of fruit etc. or wood) unripe or unseasoned. **4** not dried, smoked, or tanned. **5** inexperienced, gullible. **6 a** (of the complexion) sickly-hued. **b** jealous, envious. **7** young, flourishing. **8** not withered or worn out (*a green old age*). **9** (also **Green**) concerned with or supporting protection of the environment as a political principle. ● *n.* **1** a green colour or pigment. **2** green clothes or material. **3 a** a piece of common grassy land (*village green*). **b** a grassy area used for a special purpose (*putting green*). **c** *Golf* a fairway. ▷ GOLF. **4** (in *pl.*) green vegetables. **5** (also **Green**) a member or supporter of an environmental group or party. **6** (in *pl.*) *Brit. slang* sexual intercourse. **7** *slang* low-grade marijuana. **8** *slang* money. **9** green foliage or growing plants. ● *v.tr.* & *intr.* make or become green. □ **green in a person's eye** a sign of gullibility (*do you see any green in my eye?*). [Old English] □ **greenish** *adj.* **greenness** *n.*

greenback *n.* **1** *US* a US legal-tender note; the US dollar. **2** any of various green-backed animals.

green belt *n.* an area of open land round a city, on which building is restricted.

green card *n.* **1** *Brit.* an international insurance document for motorists. **2** *US* a permit allowing a foreign national to live and work permanently in the US.

green crop *n. Brit.* a crop used as fodder in a green state rather than as hay etc.

green drake *n. Brit.* the common mayfly.

greenery *n.* green foliage or growing plants.

green-eyed *adj.* jealous.

green-eyed monster *n.* (prec. by *the*) jealousy.

green fee *n. Golf* (*US* also **greens fee**) a charge for playing one round or session on a course.

greenfield *n.* (*attrib.*) (of a site) having no previous building development on it.

greenfinch *n.* ► a finch, *Carduelis chloris*, with green and yellow plumage.

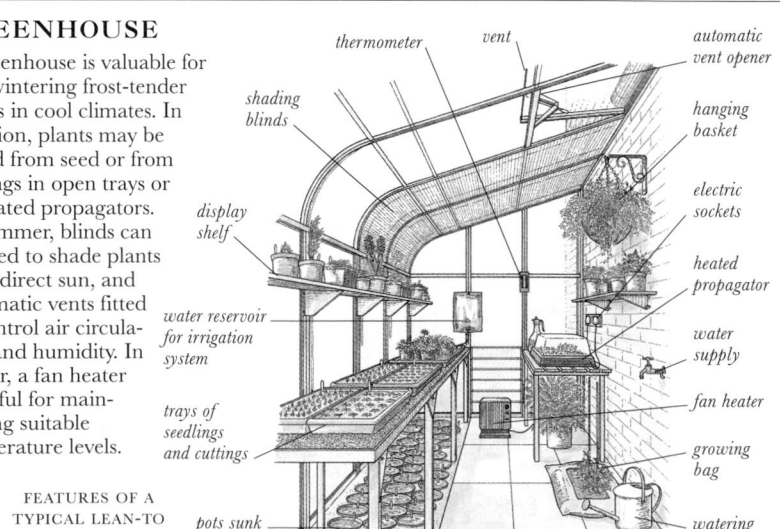

GREENFINCH
(*Carduelis chloris*)

green fingers *n.pl. Brit.* skill in growing plants.

greenfly *n.* (*pl.* same or **-flies**) *Brit.* a green aphid.

greengage *n.* a roundish green fine-flavoured variety of plum. [named after Sir W. Gage, 1657–1727]

greengrocer *n. Brit.* a retailer of fruit and vegetables. □ **greengrocery** *n.* (*pl.* **-ies**).

greenhorn *n.* an inexperienced or foolish person; a new recruit.

greenhouse *n.* ▼ a light structure with the sides and roof mainly of glass, for rearing plants.

greenhouse effect *n.* the trapping of the Sun's warmth in the lower atmosphere caused by high levels of carbon dioxide and other gases. ▷ GLOBAL WARMING

greenhouse gas *n.* any of various gases, esp. carbon dioxide, that contribute to the greenhouse effect.

greening *n.* **1** the process or result of making something green or becoming green. **2** the planting of trees etc. in urban or desert areas. **3** the process of becoming or making aware of or sensitive to ecological issues.

greenkeeper *n.* (*US* also **greenskeeper**) the keeper of a golf course.

green light *n.* **1** a green light used as a signal to proceed on a road etc. **2** *colloq.* permission to go ahead with a project.

greenmail *n. Stock Exch.* the practice of buying enough shares in a company to threaten a takeover, thereby forcing its owners to buy them back at a

---

GREENHOUSE

A greenhouse is valuable for overwintering frost-tender plants in cool climates. In addition, plants may be raised from seed or from cuttings in open trays or in heated propagators. In summer, blinds can be used to shade plants from direct sun, and automatic vents fitted to control air circulation and humidity. In winter, a fan heater is useful for maintaining suitable temperature levels.

FEATURES OF A TYPICAL LEAN-TO GREENHOUSE

thermometer   *vent*   *automatic vent opener*

shading blinds   *hanging basket*

display shelf   *electric sockets*

water reservoir for irrigation system   *heated propagator*

trays of seedlings and cuttings   *water supply*

fan heater

growing bag

pots sunk into sand   *watering can*

higher price in order to retain control of the business. [on the pattern of *blackmail*] □ **greenmailer** *n.*

green manure *n.* growing plants ploughed into the soil as fertilizer.

Green Paper *n.* (in the UK) a preliminary report of Government proposals, for discussion.

green pepper *n.* the unripe fruit of *Capsicum annuum*.

green pound *n.* the exchange rate for the pound used in payments for agricultural produce in the EU.

green revolution *n.* 1 an increase in crop production in developing countries. 2 a rise of environmental concern in industrialized countries.

green room *n.* a room in a theatre, etc. in which performers may relax when they are not on stage, etc.

greensand *n.* 1 ▶ a greenish kind of sandstone, often imperfectly consolidated. 2 a stratum largely formed of this sandstone.

greens fee *US* var. of GREEN FEE.

greensick *adj.* affected with chlorosis. □ **greensickness** *n.*

greenskeeper *US* var. of GREEN-KEEPER.

GREENSAND

green-stick fracture *n.* a bone-fracture, esp. in children, in which one side of the bone is broken and one only bent. ▷ FRACTURE

greenstone *n.* 1 a greenish igneous rock containing feldspar and hornblende. 2 a variety of jade found in New Zealand.

greenstuff *n.* vegetation; green vegetables.

greensward *n. archaic* or *literary* 1 grassy turf. 2 an expanse of this.

green tea *n.* tea made from steam-dried, not fermented, leaves.

green thumb *n.* = GREEN FINGERS.

Greenwich Mean Time /gren-ich/ *n.* (also **Greenwich Time**) the local time on the meridian of Greenwich, used as an international basis of time-reckoning. [from *Greenwich* in London, former site of the Royal Observatory]

greenwood *n.* a woodland in summer.

greeny *adj.* greenish (*greeny-yellow*).

greet[1] *v.tr.* 1 address politely or welcomingly on meeting or arrival. 2 receive or acknowledge in a specified way. 3 (of a sight etc.) become apparent to or noticed by. [Old English *grētan* 'to handle, attack, salute'] □ **greeter** *n.*

greet[2] *v.intr. Sc.* weep. [Old English]

greeting *n.* 1 the act or an instance of welcoming or addressing politely. 2 words, gestures, etc., used to greet a person. 3 (often in *pl.*) an expression of goodwill.

greetings card *n.* (*US* **greeting card**) a decorative card sent to convey greetings.

gregarious *adj.* 1 fond of company. 2 living in flocks or communities. [based on Latin *grex gregis* 'flock'] □ **gregariously** *adv.* **gregariousness** *n.*

Gregorian calendar *n.* the calendar introduced in 1582 by Pope Gregory XIII.

Gregorian chant *n.* plainsong church music, named after Pope Gregory I.

gremlin *n. colloq.* an imaginary mischievous sprite regarded as responsible for mechanical faults. [20th-century coinage]

grenade *n.* ▶ 1 a small bomb thrown by hand (in full **hand grenade**) or launched mechanically. 2 a glass receptacle containing chemicals which disperse on impact, for testing drains, extinguishing fires, etc. [from Spanish *granada* 'pomegranate']

GRENADE: CROSS-SECTION OF WORLD WAR II BRITISH 'MILLS BOMB'

striker
explosive chamber
safety-pin
body
detonator
percussion cap
fuse

grenadier *n.* 1 *Brit.* (**Grenadiers** or **Grenadier Guards**) the first regiment of the royal household infantry. 2 *hist.* a soldier armed with grenades.

grenadilla *n.* (also **granadilla**) ▶ a passion fruit. [from Spanish *granadilla* 'little pomegranate']

grew *past* of GROW.

grey (*US* **gray**) ● *adj.* 1 of a colour intermediate between black and white. 2 a (of the weather etc.) dull, dismal. b bleak; (of a person) depressed. 3 a (of hair) turning white with age etc. b (of a person) having grey hair. 4 anonymous, unidentifiable. ● *n.* 1 a a grey colour or pigment. b grey clothes or material (*dressed in grey*). 2 a grey or white horse. ● *v.tr.* & *intr.* make or become grey. [Old English] □ **greyish** *adj.* **greyly** *adv.* **greyness** *n.*

grey area *n.* a situation or topic not readily conforming to an existing set of rules.

greybeard *n.* (*US* **graybeard**) 1 an old man. 2 *dial.* = OLD MAN'S BEARD.

Grey Friar *n.* a Franciscan friar.

grey goose *n.* any goose of the genus *Anser*, with mainly grey plumage.

greyhound *n.* a dog of a tall slender breed capable of high speed. [Old English]

greylag *n.* (in full **greylag goose**) a wild goose, *Anser anser*, native to Europe. [18th-century coinage]

grey market *n.* unofficial trade esp. in unissued shares or in scarce goods.

grey matter *n.* 1 the darker tissues of the brain and spinal cord. ▷ MENINX. 2 *colloq.* intelligence.

grey seal *n.* a common large seal, *Halichoerus grypus*, of the N. Atlantic. ▷ PINNIPED

grey squirrel *n.* an American squirrel, *Sciurus carolinensis*, introduced into Europe in the 19th c. ▷ DREY, RODENT

grey water *n.* household waste water from baths, sinks, washing machines, etc. (cf. BLACK WATER).

grid *n.* 1 a framework of spaced parallel bars; a grating. 2 a system of numbered squares printed on a map and forming the basis of map references. 3 a network of lines, electric power connections, etc. 4 a pattern of lines marking the starting places on a motor racing track. 5 an arrangement of town streets in a rectangular pattern. [back-formation from GRIDIRON] □ **gridded** *adj.*

griddle ● *n.* a circular iron plate placed over a fire or otherwise heated for baking etc. ● *v.tr.* cook with a griddle. [from Latin *craticula* 'gridiron']

gridiron *n.* 1 a cooking utensil of metal bars for broiling or grilling. 2 = GRID 5. [Middle English]

gridlock *n.* 1 a traffic jam affecting a whole network of intersecting streets. 2 = DEADLOCK *n.* 1. □ **gridlocked** *adj.*

grief *n.* 1 deep or intense sorrow or mourning. 2 the cause of this. 3 *colloq.* trouble; annoyance. □ **come to grief** meet with disaster. **good** (or **great**) **grief!** an exclamation of surprise etc. [from Old French]

grievance *n.* a real or fancied cause for complaint. [from Old French *grevance* 'injury']

grieve *v.* 1 *tr.* cause grief or great distress to. 2 *intr.* suffer grief, esp. at another's death. [based on Latin *gravis* 'heavy']

grievous *adj.* 1 (of pain etc.) severe. 2 causing grief. 3 injurious. 4 flagrant, heinous. □ **grievously** *adv.* **grievousness** *n.*

grievous bodily harm *n. Law* serious injury inflicted intentionally.

griffin *n.* (also **gryphon**) a fabulous creature with an eagle's head and wings and a lion's body. ▷ CORINTHIAN. [from Greek *grups*]

griffon *n.* 1 a dog of a small terrier-like breed with coarse or smooth hair. 2 (in full **griffon vulture**) a large vulture, *Gyps fulvus* of Eurasia and N. Africa. [sense 1: French]

grig *n.* 1 a small eel. 2 a grasshopper or cricket. [Middle English] □ **merry** (or **lively**) **as a grig** full of fun; extravagantly lively.

grill[1] ● *n.* 1 a *Brit.* a device on a cooker for radiating heat downwards. b = GRIDIRON 1. 2 food cooked on a grill. 3 (in full **grill room**) a restaurant serving grilled food. ● *v.* 1 *tr.* & *intr. Brit.* cook or be cooked under a grill or on a gridiron. 2 *tr.* & *intr.* subject or be subjected to extreme heat, esp. from the Sun. 3 *tr.* subject to severe questioning or interrogation. [from Old French] □ **grilling** *n.* (in sense 3 of *v.*).

grill[2] var. of GRILLE.

grille *n.* (also **grill**) 1 a grating or latticed screen, used as a partition or to allow discreet vision. 2 = RADIATOR GRILL. [from medieval Latin *graticula, craticula* 'gridiron']

grilse *n.* a salmon that has returned to fresh water after a single winter at sea. [Middle English]

grim *adj.* (**grimmer**, **grimmest**) 1 of a stern or forbidding appearance. 2 harsh, merciless, severe. 3 ghastly, joyless (*has a grim truth in it*). 4 unpleasant, unattractive. □ **like grim death** with great determination. [Old English] □ **grimly** *adv.* **grimness** *n.*

grimace ● *n.* a distortion of the face made in disgust etc. or to amuse. ● *v.intr.* make a grimace. [based on Spanish *grima* 'fright']

grime ● *n.* soot or dirt ingrained in a surface. ● *v.tr.* blacken with grime. [originally as a verb: from Middle Dutch] □ **grimy** *adj.* (**grimier**, **grimiest**). **griminess** *n.*

grin ● *v.* (**grinned**, **grinning**) 1 *intr.* smile broadly showing the teeth. 2 *tr.* express by grinning. ● *n.* the act or action of grinning. □ **grin and bear it** take pain or misfortune stoically. [Old English] □ **grinningly** *adv.*

grind ● *v.* (*past* and *past part.* **ground**) 1 a *tr.* reduce to small particles or powder by crushing. b *intr.* (of a machine etc.) move with a crushing action. 2 a *tr.* reduce, sharpen, or smooth by friction. b *tr.* & *intr.* rub or rub together gratingly. 3 *tr.* (often foll. by *down*) oppress, wear down (*grinding poverty*). 4 *intr.* a (often foll. by *away*) work or study hard. b (foll. by *out*) produce with effort. c (foll. by *on*) (of a sound) continue gratingly. 5 *tr.* turn the handle of (a barrel organ etc.). 6 *intr. slang* (of a dancer) rotate the hips. ● *n.* 1 the act or an instance of grinding. 2 *colloq.* hard dull work (*the daily grind*). 3 the size of ground particles. □ **grind to a halt** stop laboriously. [Old English] □ **grindingly** *adv.*

grinder *n.* 1 a person or thing that grinds, esp. a machine (*coffee grinder*). 2 a molar tooth.

grindstone *n.* 1 ▶ a thick revolving disc used for grinding, sharpening, and polishing. 2 a kind of stone used for this. □ **keep one's nose to the grindstone** work hard and continuously.

'eye' to hold shaft

GRINDSTONE FOR MILLING FLOUR

gringo *n.* (*pl.* **-os**) *colloq.* a foreigner, esp. a British or N. American person, in a Spanish-speaking country. [Spanish, literally 'gibberish']

grip ● *v.* (**gripped**, **gripping**) 1 a *tr.* grasp tightly. b *intr.* take a firm hold, esp. by friction. 2 *tr.* (of a feeling or emotion) deeply affect (a person). 3 *tr.* compel the attention or interest of (*a gripping story*).

GRENADILLA: PURPLE PASSION FRUIT (*Passiflora edulis*)

● *n.* **1 a** a firm hold; a tight grasp or clasp. **b** a manner of grasping or holding. **2** the power of holding attention. **3 a** a mental or intellectual understanding or mastery. **b** effective control of a situation (*lose one's grip*). **4 a** a part of a machine that grips or holds something. **b** a part by which a tool, weapon, etc., is held in the hand. **5** = HAIRGRIP. **6** a travelling bag. **7** an assistant in a theatre, film studio, etc. □ **come** (or **get**) **to grips with** begin to deal with or understand. **get a grip 1** (foll. by *on*) = *come to grips with*. **2** (in full **get a grip on oneself**) control or discipline oneself. [Old English *gripe* 'handful'] □ **grippingly** *adv.*

gripe ● *v.* **1** *intr. colloq.* complain. **2** *tr.* affect with gastric or intestinal pain. ● *n.* **1** (usu. in *pl.*) gastric or intestinal pain; colic. **2** *colloq.* **a** a complaint. **b** the act of griping. [Old English] □ **griper** *n.*

gripe water *n. Brit. propr.* a solution to relieve colic etc. in infants.

grisaille /griz-**ayl**/ *n.* a method of painting in grey monochrome, often to imitate sculpture. [French, based on *gris* 'grey']

grisly *adj.* (**grislier**, **grisliest**) causing horror, disgust, or fear. [Old English *grislic* 'terrifying'] □ **grisliness** *n.*

grist *n.* **1** corn to grind. **2** malt crushed for brewing. □ **grist to the** (or **a person's**) **mill** a source of profit or advantage. [Old English]

gristle *n.* tough cartilaginous animal tissue. [Old English] □ **gristly** *adj.*

grit ● *n.* **1** particles of stone or sand, esp. as causing discomfort, clogging machinery, etc. **2** coarse sandstone. **3** *colloq.* pluck, endurance. ● *v.* (**gritted**, **gritting**) **1** *tr.* spread grit on (icy roads etc.). **2** *tr.* clench (the teeth). **3** *intr.* make a grating sound. [Old English] □ **gritter** *n.* **grittiness** *n.* **gritty** *adj.* (**grittier**, **grittiest**).

grits *n.pl.* **1** (treated as *sing.* or *pl.*) esp. *US* **a** coarsely ground grain, esp. corn. **b** = HOMINY. **2** oats that have been husked but not ground (or only coarsely). [Old English]

grizzle *v.intr. Brit. colloq.* **1** (esp. of a child) cry fretfully. **2** complain whiningly. [18th-century coinage] □ **grizzler** *n.* **grizzly** *adj.*

grizzled *adj.* having, or streaked with, grey hair. [from earlier *grizzle* 'grey': from Old French *gris* 'grey']

grizzly ● *adj.* (**grizzlier**, **grizzliest**) grey, greyish, grey-haired. ● *n.* (*pl.* **-ies**) (in full **grizzly bear**) ◄ a large variety of brown bear, found in N. America.

GRIZZLY BEAR
(*Ursus arctos horribilis*)

groan ● *v.* **1 a** *intr.* make a deep sound expressing pain, grief, or disapproval. **b** *tr.* utter with groans. **2** *intr.* (usu. foll. by *under, beneath, with*) be loaded or oppressed. ● *n.* the sound made in groaning. [Old English, related to GRIN] □ **groaner** *n.*

groat *n.* **1** *hist.* a silver coin worth four old pence. **2** *archaic* a small sum (*don't care a groat*). [originally in sense 'great, i.e. thick (penny)': from Middle Dutch *groot*]

groats *n.pl.* hulled or crushed grain, esp. oats. [Old English]

Gro-bag see GROWBAG.

grocer *n.* a dealer in food and household provisions. [Middle English and Anglo-French *grosser* 'a person who sells in the gross']

grocery *n.* (*pl.* **-ies**) **1** a grocer's trade or shop. **2** (in *pl.*) provisions, esp. food, sold by a grocer.

grockle *n. Brit. dial.* & *slang* a visitor or holidaymaker, esp. from the North or Midlands to SW England. [20th-century coinage]

grog *n.* a drink of spirit (originally rum) and water.

groggy *adj.* (**groggier**, **groggiest**) muzzy or unsteady from being semi-conscious, hungover, etc. □ **groggily** *adv.* **grogginess** *n.*

groin[1] ● *n.* **1** the depression between the belly and the thigh. **2** *Archit.* **a** an edge formed by intersecting vaults. ▷ VAULT. **b** an arch supporting a vault. ● *v.tr. Archit.* build with groins. [Middle English]

groin[2] *US* var. of GROYNE.

grommet ● *n.* **1** a metal, plastic, or rubber eyelet placed in a hole to protect or insulate a rope or cable etc. passed through it. **2** ▼ a tube surgically implanted in the eardrum to make a communication with the middle ear. [from archaic French *gromette* 'curb chain']

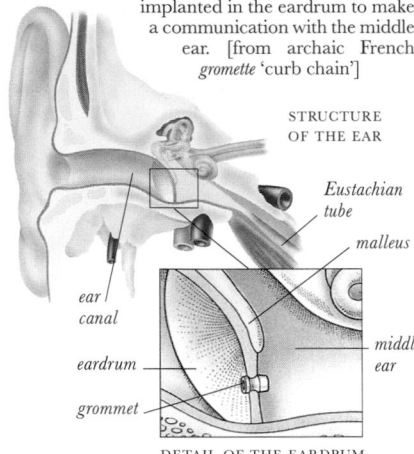

STRUCTURE OF THE EAR

Eustachian tube

malleus

ear canal

middle ear

eardrum

grommet

DETAIL OF THE EARDRUM

GROMMET: LOCATION OF A GROMMET IN THE HUMAN EAR

groom ● *n.* **1** a person employed to take care of horses. **2** = BRIDEGROOM. **3** *Brit. Mil.* any of certain officers of the Royal Household. ● *v.tr.* **1 a** tend to, esp. brush the coat of (a horse, dog, etc.). **b** (of an animal) clean and comb the fur of (another) (also *refl.*). **2 a** give a neat or tidy appearance to (a person, etc.). **b** carefully attend to (a lawn, ski slope, etc.). **3** prepare or train (a person) for a particular purpose or activity. [Middle English]

groove ● *n.* **1 a** a channel or hollow, esp. one made to guide motion or receive a corresponding ridge. **b** a spiral track cut in a gramophone record. **2 a** an established routine or habit. **b** a monotonous routine, a rut. **3** *slang* an established rhythmic pattern (*got a groove going*). ● *v.* **1** *tr.* make a groove or grooves in. **2** *slang* **a** play music (esp. jazz or dance music) rhythmically. **b** dance or move rhythmically to music. **c** enjoy oneself. □ **in the groove** *slang* **1** doing or performing well. **2** fashionable. [from obsolete Dutch *groeve* 'furrow']

groovy *adj.* (**groovier**, **grooviest**) **1** *slang* (often *joc.*) fashionable and exciting; enjoyable, excellent. **2** of or like a groove. □ **groovily** *adv.*

grope ● *v.* **1** *intr.* (usu. foll. by *for*) feel about or search blindly. **2** *intr.* (foll. by *for, after*) search mentally. **3** *tr.* feel (one's way) towards something. **4** *tr. slang* fondle clumsily for sexual pleasure. ● *n.* the process or an instance of groping. [Old English] □ **groper** *n.* **gropingly** *adv.*

grosbeak /**grohss**-beek/ *n.* ► any of various finches and cardinals having stout conical bills. [from French *grosbec*]

grosgrain /**groh**-grayn/ *n.* a corded fabric of silk etc. [French, literally 'coarse grain']

gros point /groh **pwahng**/ *n.* cross stitch embroidery on canvas. [French, literally 'large stitch']

gross ● *adj.* **1** overfed; repulsively fat. **2** (of a person, manners, or morals) noticeably coarse, unre-

fined, or indecent. **3** *slang* disgusting. **4** flagrant (*gross negligence*). **5** total; without deductions (*gross income*). **6 a** luxuriant, rank. **b** thick, solid, dense. **7** (of the senses etc.) dull. ● *v.tr.* produce or earn as gross profit or income. ● *n.* (*pl.* same) an amount equal to twelve dozen. □ **gross up** increase (a net amount) to its value before deductions. [*adj.*: from Late Latin *grossus*; *n.*: from French *grosse douzaine* 'large dozen'] □ **grossly** *adv.* **grossness** *n.*

gross domestic product *n.* the total value of goods produced and services provided in a country in one year.

gross national product *n.* the gross domestic product plus the total of net income from abroad.

grot *Brit. slang* ● *n.* rubbish, junk. ● *adj.* dirty.

grotesque ● *adj.* **1** comically or repulsively distorted. **2** incongruous, absurd. ● *n.* **1** a decorative form interweaving human and animal features. **2** a comically distorted figure or design. [from Italian *grottesca* 'grotto-like (painting etc.)'] □ **grotesquely** *adv.* **grotesqueness** *n.* **grotesquerie** *n.*

grotto *n.* (*pl.* **-oes** or **-os**) **1** a small picturesque cave. **2** an artificial ornamental cave. [from Greek *kruptē* 'crypt'] □ **grottoed** *adj.*

grotty *adj.* (**grottier**, **grottiest**) *Brit. slang* unpleasant, dirty, shabby, unattractive. □ **grottiness** *n.*

grouch *colloq.* ● *v.intr.* grumble. ● *n.* **1** a discontented or grumpy person. **2** a fit of grumbling or the sulks; a complaint. [variant of Middle English *grutch* 'grudge'] □ **grouchy** *adj.* (**grouchier**, **grouchiest**). **grouchily** *adv.* **grouchiness** *n.*

ground[1] ● *n.* **1 a** the surface of the Earth, esp. as contrasted with the air around it. **b** a part of this qualified in some way (*low ground*). **2** soil, earth (*stony ground*). **3 a** a limited or defined area (*the ground beyond the farm*). **b** the extent of a subject dealt with (*the book covers a lot of ground*). **4** (often in *pl.*) a motive or reason (*ground for concern*). **5** an area of a special kind or for special use (often in *comb.*: *cricket ground*). **6** (in *pl.*) an area of usu. enclosed land attached to a house etc. **7** an area or basis for agreement etc. (*common ground*). **8 a** (in painting) the prepared surface giving the predominant colour or tone. **b** (in embroidery etc.) the undecorated surface. **9** (in *pl.*) solid particles, esp. of coffee, forming a residue. **10** *Electr.* = EARTH *n.* 4. **11** the bottom of the sea. **12** *Brit.* the floor of a room etc. **13** (*attrib.*) **a** (of animals) living on or in the ground; (of fish) living at the bottom of water; (of plants) dwarfish or trailing. **b** relating to or concerned with the ground (*ground staff*). ● *v.* **1** *tr.* refuse authority for (a pilot or an aircraft) to fly. **2 a** *tr.* run (a ship) aground; strand. **b** *intr.* (of a ship) run aground. **3** *tr.* (foll. by *in*) instruct thoroughly (in a subject). **4** *tr.* (often as **grounded** *adj.*) (foll. by *on*) base (a conclusion etc.) on. **5** *tr. Electr.* = EARTH *v.* 3. **6** *intr.* alight on the ground. **7** *tr.* place or lay (esp. weapons) on the ground. □ **break new** (or **fresh**) **ground** treat a subject previously not dealt with. **gain** (or **make**) **ground 1** advance steadily; make progress. **2** (foll. by *on*) catch (a person) up. **get off the ground** *colloq.* make a successful start. **give** (or **lose**) **ground** retreat, decline; lose the advantage. **go to ground 1** (of a fox etc.) enter its earth etc. **2** (of a person) become inaccessible for a prolonged period. **hold one's ground** not retreat or give way. **on the ground** at the point of production or operation. **thin on the ground** not numerous. [Old English]

ground[2] *past* and *past part.* of GRIND.

groundbait *n.* bait thrown to the bottom of a fishing ground.

ground control *n.* the personnel and equipment that monitor and direct the landing etc. of aircraft or spacecraft.

ground cover *n.* plants covering the surface of the earth, esp. low-growing spreading plants that inhibit the growth of weeds.

ground crew *n.* the people who maintain and service an aircraft on the ground.

GROSBEAK: JAPANESE GROSBEAK FINCH (*Eophona personata*)

G

ground elder *n.* ◀ an umbelliferous plant, *Aegopodium podagraria*, with spreading underground stems, common as a weed.

grounder *n.* (esp in baseball) a ball that is hit or passed along the ground.

ground floor *n.* the floor of a building at ground level.

ground frost *n.* frost on the surface of the ground or in the top layer of soil.

GROUND ELDER
(Aegopodium podagraria)

ground glass *n.* **1** glass made non-transparent by grinding etc. **2** glass ground to a powder.

groundhog *n.* = WOODCHUCK.

grounding *n.* basic training or instruction.

ground ivy *n.* a common Eurasian hedge-plant, *Glechoma hederacea*, with bluish-purple flowers.

groundless *adj.* without motive or foundation.

groundnut *n.* **1** *Brit.* = PEANUT 1, 2. **2 a** a N. American wild bean. **b** its edible tuber.

ground plan *n.* **1** the plan of a building at ground level. **2** the general outline of a scheme.

ground rent *n.* esp. *Brit.* rent for land leased for building.

ground rule *n.* a basic principle.

groundsel *n.* any plant of the genus *Senecio* (daisy family), with yellow rayless flowers, esp. *S. vulgaris*, common as a weed. [Old English]

groundsheet *n.* a waterproof sheet for spreading on the ground.

groundsman *n.* (*pl.* **-men**) *Brit.* a person who maintains a sports ground.

ground speed *n.* an aircraft's speed relative to the ground.

ground squirrel *n.* any ground-dwelling rodent resembling a squirrel, esp. one of the genus *Spermophilus*.

groundswell *n.* a heavy sea caused by a distant or past storm or an earthquake.

groundwater *n.* water found in soil or in crevices etc. in rock.

groundwork *n.* **1** preliminary or basic work. **2** a foundation or basis.

ground zero *n.* the point on the ground under an exploding bomb.

group ● *n.* **1** a number of persons or things located close together, or considered or classed together. **2** a number of people working together or sharing beliefs. **3** a number of commercial companies under common ownership. **4** an ensemble playing popular music. **5** a division of an air force or air-fleet. ● *v.* **1** *tr. & intr.* form or be formed into a group. **2** *tr.* (often foll. by *with*) place in a group or groups. **3** *tr.* form (colours, figures, etc.) into a well-arranged and harmonious whole. **4** *tr.* classify. [from Italian *gruppo*] □ **groupage** *n.*

group captain *n.* an RAF officer next below air commodore.

group dynamics *n.pl.* (also treated as *sing.*) *Psychol.* **1** the interaction of people in groups. **2** the principles perceived as underlying such interaction.

grouper *n.* ▶ any marine fish of the family Serranidae, with heavy body, big head, and wide mouth. [from Portuguese *garupa*]

groupie *n. colloq.* **1** an ardent follower of touring pop groups. **2** a fan, enthusiast, or follower (*chess groupie*).

grouping *n.* **1** a process or system of allocation to groups. **2** a formation or arrangement in a group or groups.

group practice *n.* a medical practice in which several doctors are associated.

group therapy *n.* therapy in which patients are brought together to assist one another psychologically.

groupware *n. Computing* software designed to facilitate collective working.

grouse[1] *n.* (*pl.* same) **1** ▼ any of various game birds of the family Tetraonidae, with a plump body and feathered legs. **2** the flesh of a grouse used as food. [16th-century coinage]

GROUSE: HAZEL GROUSE
(Bonasa bonasia)

grouse[2] *colloq.* ● *v.intr.* grumble or complain pettily. ● *n.* a complaint. [19th-century coinage] □ **grouser** *n.*

grout ● *n.* a thin fluid mortar for filling gaps in tiling etc. ● *v.tr.* provide or fill with grout. □ **grouter** *n.*

grove *n.* a small wood or group of trees. [related to Old English *grǣfa* 'brushwood']

grovel *v.intr.* (**grovelled**, **grovelling**; *US* **groveled**, **groveling**) **1** behave obsequiously in seeking favour or forgiveness. **2** lie prone in abject humility. [based on obsolete *grufe* 'face down'] □ **groveller** *n.* **grovelling** *adj.* **grovellingly** *adv.*

grow *v.* (*past* **grew**; *past part.* **grown**) **1** *intr.* increase in size, height, quantity, degree, etc. **2** *intr.* **a** develop or exist as a living plant or natural product. **b** germinate, sprout. **3** *intr.* be produced; come naturally into existence. **4** *intr.* (as **grown** *adj.*) fully matured. **5** *intr.* **a** become gradually (*grow rich*). **b** (foll. by *to* + infin.) come by degrees (*grew to like it*). **6** *intr.* (foll. by *into*) **a** become, having grown or developed (*will grow into a fine athlete*). **b** become large enough for or suited to (*grew into her new job*). **7** *intr.* (foll. by *on*) become gradually more appealing to. **8** *tr.* **a** produce (plants, etc.) by cultivation. **b** bring forth. **c** allow (a beard etc.) to increase in length. **9** *tr.* (in *passive*, foll. by *over*, *up*) be covered with a growth. □ **grow out of 1** become too large to wear (a garment). **2** become too mature to retain (a childish habit etc.). **3** develop from. **grow up 1** advance to maturity. **2** (of a custom) arise. [Old English] □ **growable** *adj.*

growbag *n.* (also **Gro-bag** *propr.*) = GROWING BAG.

grower *n.* **1** (often in *comb.*) a person growing produce (*fruit-grower*). **2** a plant that grows in a specified way (*a fast grower*).

growing bag *n. Brit.* a bag containing potting compost, in which plants, e.g. tomatoes, may be grown.

growing pains *n.pl.* **1** early difficulties in the development of an enterprise etc. **2** neuralgic pain in children's legs due to fatigue etc.

growl ● *v.intr.* **1 a** (often foll. by *at*) (esp. of a dog) make a low guttural sound, usu. of anger. **b** murmur angrily. **2** rumble. ● *n.* **1** a growling sound, esp. made by a dog. **2** an angry murmur. **3** a rumble.

growler *n.* **1** a person or thing that growls, esp. *slang* a dog. **2** a small iceberg.

grown *past part.* of GROW.

grown-up ● *adj.* adult. ● *n.* an adult person.

growth *n.* **1** the act or process of growing. **2** an increase in size or value. **3** something that has grown or is growing. **4** *Med.* an abnormal formation. **5** the cultivation of produce.

growth hormone *n.* a substance which stimulates the growth of a plant or animal.

growth industry *n.* an industry that is developing rapidly.

growth ring *n.* a concentric layer of wood, shell, etc., developed during a period of growth. ▷ DENDROCHRONOLOGY

growth stock *n.* stock that tends to increase in capital value rather than yield high income.

groyne *n.* (*US* **groin**) a timber framework or low broad wall built out from a shore to check erosion of a beach. ▷ LONGSHORE DRIFT. [from Late Latin *grunium* 'pig's snout']

grub ● *n.* **1** the larva of an insect. **2** *colloq.* food. ● *v.* (**grubbed**, **grubbing**) **1** *tr. & intr.* dig superficially. **2** *tr.* clear (ground, roots, etc.). **3** *tr.* (foll. by *up*, *out*) **a** extract by digging (*grubbing up weeds*). **b** extract (information etc.) by searching in books etc. **4** *intr.* search, rummage. [Middle English] □ **grubber** *n.*

grubby *adj.* (**grubbier**, **grubbiest**) **1** dirty, grimy, slovenly. **2** of or infested with grubs. □ **grubbily** *adv.* **grubbiness** *n.*

grub-screw *n.* a small headless screw.

grudge ● *n.* a persistent feeling of resentment (*bears a grudge against me*). ● *v.tr.* **1** be resentfully unwilling to give or allow (a thing). **2** be reluctant to do (a thing) (*grudged paying so much*). [from Old French *grouchier* 'to murmur']

grudging *adj.* reluctant; not willing (*grudging approval*). □ **grudgingly** *adv.* **grudgingness** *n.*

gruel *n.* a liquid food of oatmeal etc. boiled in milk or water. [Middle English]

gruelling *adj.* (*US* **grueling**) extremely demanding, severe, or tiring. [from archaic verb *gruel* 'to exhaust, punish'] □ **gruellingly** *adv.*

gruesome *adj.* horrible, grisly. [based on Scots *grue* 'to shudder'] □ **gruesomely** *adv.* **gruesomeness** *n.*

gruff *adj.* **1 a** (of a voice) low and harsh. **b** (of a person) having a gruff voice. **2** surly, rough-mannered. [from Dutch *grof* 'coarse'] □ **gruffly** *adv.* **gruffness** *n.*

grumble ● *v.* **1** *intr.* **a** (often foll. by *at*, *about*, *over*) complain peevishly. **b** be discontented. **2** *intr.* **a** utter a dull inarticulate sound; murmur. **b** rumble. **3** *tr.* (often foll. by *out*) utter complainingly. **4** *intr.* (as **grumbling** *adj.*) *colloq.* causing intermittent discomfort without causing illness (*a grumbling appendix*). ● *n.* **1** a complaint. **2 a** a dull inarticulate sound; a murmur. **b** a rumble. □ **grumbler** *n.* **grumbling** *adj.* **grumblingly** *adv.* **grumbly** *adj.*

grump *n. colloq.* **1** a grumpy person. **2** (in *pl.*) a fit of sulks. □ **grumpish** *adj.* **grumpishly** *adv.*

grumpy *adj.* (**grumpier**, **grumpiest**) morosely irritable; surly. □ **grumpily** *adv.* **grumpiness** *n.*

grunge *n.* **1** esp. *N. Amer.* grime, dirt. **2** (in full **grunge rock**) a relaxed style of rock music characterized by a raucous guitar sound. **3** the fashion associated with this music, including unkempt hair, flannel shirts, and ripped jeans. □ **grungy** *adj.*

grunt ● *n.* **1** a low guttural sound made by a pig. **2** a sound resembling this. ● *v.* **1** *intr.* (of a pig) make a grunt or grunts. **2** *intr.* (of a person) make a low inarticulate sound resembling this, esp. to express effort, assent, etc. **3** *tr.* utter with a grunt. [Old English] □ **grunter** *n.*

Gruyère *n.* a firm pale cheese made from cow's milk. ▷ CHEESE. [from *Gruyère*, district in Switzerland]

gryphon var. of GRIFFIN.

G-string *n.* **1** *Mus.* a string sounding the note G. **2** a narrow strip of cloth etc. covering only the genitals and attached to a string round the waist.

GROUPER: NASSAU GROUPER
(Epinephelus striatus)

G-suit *n.* a garment with inflatable pressurized pouches, worn to withstand high acceleration. [G: abbreviation of *gravity*]

GT *adj.* designating a high-performance car. [Italian *gran turismo*, literally 'great touring']

GTi *adj.* designating a high-performance car with a fuel-injected engine. [GT + *i*njection]

guacamole /gwah-kǎ-**moh**-li/ *n.* a dish of mashed avocado pears. [from Aztec *ahuacatl* 'avocado' + *molli* 'sauce']

guanaco /gwǎ-**nah**-koh/ *n.* (*pl.* **-os**) ◀ a S. American mammal, *Lama guanicoe*, related to the llama. [from Quechua *huanacu*]

guanine /**gwah**-neen/ *n. Biochem.* a purine found in all living organisms as a component base of DNA and RNA. ▷ DNA. [based on GUANO]

guano /**gwan**-noh/ ● *n.* (*pl.* **-os**) **1** the excrement of seabirds used as manure. **2** artificial manure. ● *v.tr.* (**-oes**, **-oed**) fertilize with guano. [Spanish]

GUANACO
(Lama guanicoe)

guarantee ● *n.* **1 a** a formal promise or assurance, esp. of a specified quality and durability. **b** a document giving such an undertaking. **2** = GUARANTY. **3** a person making a guaranty or giving a security. ● *v.tr.* (**guarantees**, **guaranteed**) **1 a** give or serve as a guarantee for. **b** assure the permanence etc. of. **c** provide with a guarantee. **2** (foll. by *that* + clause, or *to* + infin.) give a promise or assurance. **3 a** (foll. by *to*) secure the possession of (a thing) for a person. **b** make (a person) secure against a risk or in possession of a thing.

guarantor *n.* a person who gives a guarantee or guaranty.

guaranty *n.* (*pl.* **-ies**) **1** a written or other undertaking to answer for the payment of a debt or for the performance of an obligation by another person liable in the first instance. **2** a thing serving as security for a guaranty.

guard ● *v.* **1** *tr.* (often foll. by *from*, *against*) watch over and defend or protect from harm. **2** *tr.* keep watch by (a door etc.) to control entry or exit. **3** *tr.* supervise (prisoners etc.). **4** *tr.* keep (thoughts or speech) in check. **5** *tr.* provide with safeguards. **6** *intr.* (foll. by *against*) take precautions. ● *n.* **1** a state of vigilance or watchfulness. **2** a person who protects or keeps watch. **3** a body of soldiers etc. serving to protect a place or person. **4** *Brit.* an official who rides with and is in general charge of a train. **5** a part of an army detached for some purpose (*advance guard*). **6** (in *pl.*) (usu. **Guards**) any of various bodies of troops nominally employed to guard a monarch. **7** a thing that protects or defends. **8** (often in *comb.*) a device fitted to a machine etc., to prevent injury (*fireguard*). □ **be on** (or **keep** or **stand**) **guard** (of a sentry etc.) keep watch. **lower one's guard** reduce vigilance against attack. **off** (or **off one's**) **guard** unprepared for some surprise or difficulty. **on** (or **on one's**) **guard** prepared for all contingencies; vigilant. [from Old French *garde*]

guarded *adj.* (of a remark etc.) cautious, avoiding commitment. □ **guardedly** *adv.*

guardhouse *n.* a building used to accommodate a military guard or to detain prisoners.

guardian *n.* **1** a protector or keeper. **2** a person having legal custody of another, esp. a minor. □ **guardianship** *n.*

guardian angel *n.* a spirit conceived as watching over a person or place.

guardroom *n.* a room with the same purpose as a guardhouse.

guardsman *n.* (*pl.* **-men**) **1** a soldier belonging to a body of guards. **2** (in the UK) a soldier of a regiment of Guards.

guard's van *n. Brit.* a railway coach or compartment occupied by a guard.

guava /**gwah**-vǎ/ *n.* **1** a small tropical American tree, *Psidium guajava*, bearing an edible pale orange fruit. **2** ▶ this fruit. [from Spanish *guayaba*]

gubbins *n. Brit.* **1** *colloq.* paraphernalia. **2** a gadget. **3** something of little value; rubbish. [originally in sense 'fragments': from obsolete *gobbon*]

gubernatorial *adj.* esp. *US* of or relating to a governor. [based on Latin *gubernator* 'governor']

gudgeon¹ *n.* ▼ a small European freshwater fish, *Gobio gobio*, often used as bait. [from Latin *gobio -onis* 'goby']

GUAVA
(Psidium guajava)

GUDGEON
(Gobio gobio)

gudgeon² *n.* **1** any of various kinds of pivot. **2** the tubular part of a hinge. **3** a socket at the stern of a boat, into which a rudder is fitted. **4** a pin holding two blocks of stone etc. together. [from Old French *goujon* 'little gouge']

gudgeon pin *n. Brit.* a pin holding a piston rod and a connecting rod together.

guelder rose *n.* ◀ a deciduous shrub, *Viburnum opulus*, with round bunches of creamy-white flowers. [from Dutch *geldersche roos* 'rose from *Gelderland*', a Dutch province']

Guernsey *n.* (*pl.* **-eys**) **1** an animal of a breed of dairy cattle from Guernsey in the Channel Islands. **2** (**guernsey**) **a** a thick (originally fisherman's) sweater of esp. oiled dark blue wool. **b** *Austral.* a football shirt.

guerrilla *n.* (also **guerilla**) a member of a small independently acting group taking part in irregular fighting. [Spanish, literally 'little war']

GUELDER ROSE
(Viburnum opulus 'Roseum')

guess ● *v.* **1** *tr.* (often *absol.*) estimate without calculation or measurement. **2** *tr.* form a hypothesis or opinion about; conjecture; think likely (*cannot guess how you did it; guess them to be Italian*). **3** *tr.* conjecture or estimate correctly (*you have to guess the weight*). **4** *intr.* (foll. by *at*) make a conjecture about. ● *n.* an estimate or conjecture. □ **I guess** *colloq.* I think it likely; I suppose. [Middle English] □ **guesser** *n.*

guesstimate (also **guestimate**) *colloq.* ● *n.* an estimate based more on guesswork than calculation. ● *v.tr.* (also *absol.*) form a guesstimate of.

guesswork *n.* the process of, or results achieved by, guessing.

guest ● *n.* **1** a person invited to visit another's house or have a meal etc. at the expense of the inviter. **2** a person lodging at a hotel, boarding house, etc. **3 a** an outside performer invited to take part with a regular body of performers. **b** a person who takes part by invitation in a radio or television programme (often *attrib.*: *guest artist*). **4** (*attrib.*) **a** serving or set

aside for guests (*guest room*; *guest night*). **b** acting as a guest (*guest speaker*). **5** an organism living in close association with another. ● *v.intr.* be a guest on a radio or television show or in a theatrical performance etc. □ **be my guest** make what use you wish of the available facilities. [from Old Norse *gestr*]

guest beer *n. Brit.* **1** (in a tied public house) a beer offered in addition to those produced by the brewery. **2** (in a free house) a beer available only temporarily.

guest house *n.* a private house offering paid accommodation.

guestimate var. of GUESSTIMATE.

guff *n. slang* empty talk. [19th-century coinage, originally in sense 'puff']

guffaw ● *n.* a boisterous laugh. ● *v.* **1** *intr.* utter a guffaw. **2** *tr.* say with a guffaw. [originally Scots]

guidance *n.* **1** advice or information aimed at resolving a problem, difficulty, etc. **2** the action or process of guiding or being guided (*missile guidance*).

guide ● *n.* **1** a person who leads or shows the way, or directs the movements of a person or group. **2** a person who conducts tours. **3** a professional mountain climber in charge of a group. **4** an adviser. **5** a directing principle (*one's feelings are a bad guide*). **6** a book with essential information on a subject, esp. = GUIDEBOOK. **7** a thing marking a position or guiding the eye. **8** *Mech.* **a** a bar, rod, etc., directing the motion of something. **b** a gauge etc. controlling a tool. **9** (**Guide**) *Brit.* a member of the Guides Association, an organization similar to the Scouts. ● *v.tr.* **1 a** act as guide to. **b** arrange the course of (events). **2** be the principle, motive, or ground of (an action, judgement, etc.). **3** direct the affairs of (a state etc.). [from Old French *guide* (n.), *guider* (v.)]

guidebook *n.* a book of information about a place for visitors, tourists, etc.

guided missile *n.* a missile directed to its target by remote control or by equipment within itself.

guide dog *n.* a dog trained to guide a blind person.

guideline *n.* a principle directing action.

Guider *n. Brit.* an adult leader in the Guides Association.

guild *n.* (also **gild**) **1** an association of people for mutual aid or the pursuit of a common goal. **2** a medieval association of craftsmen or merchants. [Middle English, related to earlier *gild* 'payment, sacrifice']

guilder *n.* the chief monetary unit of the Netherlands. [alteration of Dutch *gulden*]

guildhall *n.* **1 a** the meeting place of a guild or corporation. **b** *Brit.* a town hall. **2** (**Guildhall**) the hall of the Corporation of the City of London, used for ceremonial occasions.

guile *n.* treachery, deceit; cunning or sly behaviour. [Middle English] □ **guileful** *adj.* **guileless** *adj.* **guilelessly** *adv.*

guillemot /**gil**-i-mot/ *n.* any narrow-billed auk of the genus *Uria* or *Cepphus*, nesting on cliffs or islands. [French, diminutive of *Guillaume* 'William']

guillotine ● *n.* **1** esp. *hist.* ◀ a machine with a heavy knife blade sliding vertically in grooves, used for beheading. **2** a device for cutting paper, metal, etc., by means of a descending blade. **3** *Brit. Parl.* a method of preventing delay in the discussion of a bill by fixing times at which various parts of it must be voted on. ● *v.tr.* use a guillotine on. [French, named after J.-I. *Guillotin*, French physician, 1738–1814, who recommended its use (1789)]

guillotine blade

wooden frame

bench for victim to lie on

hole for victim's head

GUILLOTINE: REPLICA OF LATE 18TH-CENTURY FRENCH GUILLOTINE

GUITAR

The first narrow-waisted guitars appeared in 15th-century Italy and Spain, and were derived from stringed instruments of the ancient world. Modern steel-string, flat-top and archtop acoustic guitars, however, originated in 19th-century North America, at a similar time to the development of classical guitars in Spain. Electric guitars were the result of research into the artificial amplification of sound from musical instruments in the 1930s.

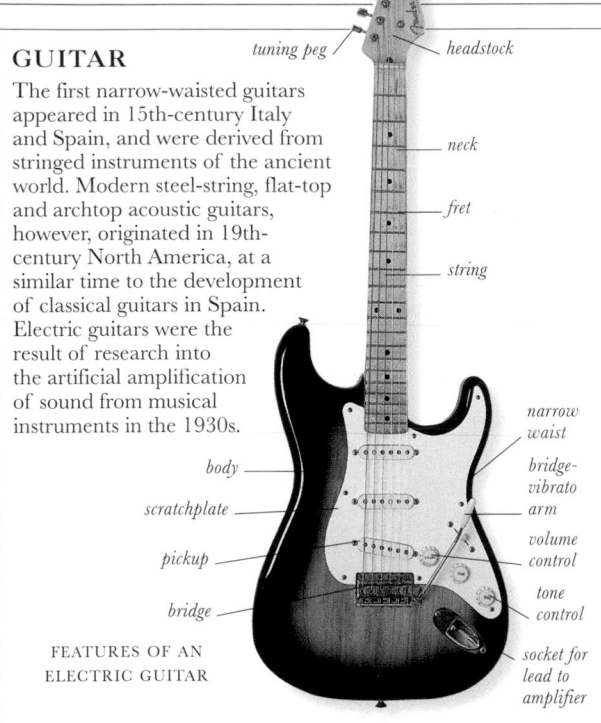

tuning peg   headstock   neck   fret   string   narrow waist   bridge-vibrato arm   volume control   tone control   body   scratchplate   pickup   bridge   socket for lead to amplifier

FEATURES OF AN ELECTRIC GUITAR

MAIN TYPES OF GUITAR

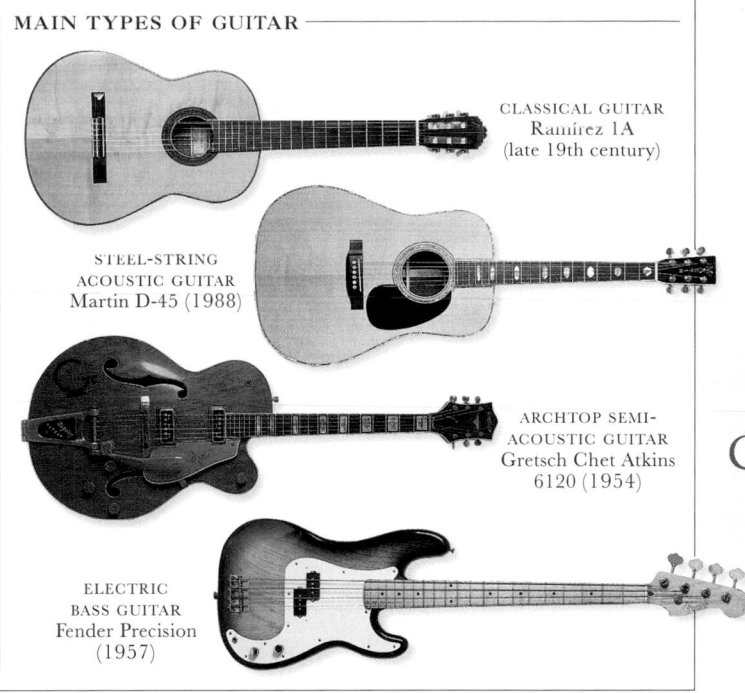

CLASSICAL GUITAR
Ramírez 1A
(late 19th century)

STEEL-STRING ACOUSTIC GUITAR
Martin D-45 (1988)

ARCHTOP SEMI-ACOUSTIC GUITAR
Gretsch Chet Atkins 6120 (1954)

ELECTRIC BASS GUITAR
Fender Precision (1957)

G

guilt *n.* **1** the fact of having committed a specified or implied offence. **2 a** culpability. **b** the feeling of this. [Old English]

guiltless *adj.* **1** (often foll. by *of* an offence) innocent. **2** (foll. by *of*) not having knowledge or possession of. □ **guiltlessly** *adv.*

guilty *adj.* (**guiltier, guiltiest**) **1** culpable of or responsible for a wrong. **2** conscious of or affected by guilt (*a guilty conscience; a guilty look*). **3** concerning guilt (*a guilty secret*). **4** (often foll. by *of*) **a** having committed a (specified) offence. **b** *Law* adjudged to have committed a specified offence. □ **guiltily** *adv.*

guimp var. of GIMP[1].

guinea *n.* **1** *Brit.* the sum of 21 shillings (£1.05), used especially in determining professional fees and auction prices. **2** *hist.* a former British gold coin worth 21 shillings, first coined for the African trade. [from *Guinea* in W. Africa]

guinea fowl *n.* any African fowl of the family Numididae, esp. *Numida meleagris*, with slate-coloured white-spotted plumage.

guinea pig *n.* **1** a domesticated S. American rodent, *Cavia porcellus*, having a sturdy body and vestigial tail, kept as a pet or for research in biology etc. ▷ RODENT. **2** a person or thing used as a subject for experiment.

guipure /g'ip-yoor/ *n.* a heavy lace of linen pieces joined by embroidery. [French]

guise *n.* **1** an assumed appearance; a pretence (*in the guise of; under the guise of*). **2** external appearance. **3** *archaic* style of attire, garb. [Middle English]

guitar *n.* ▲ a usu. six-stringed musical instrument with a fretted fingerboard, played by plucking with the fingers or a plectrum. ▷ STRINGED. [from Greek *kithara*] □ **guitarist** *n.*

Gujarati (also **Gujerati**) ● *n.* (*pl.* **Gujaratis**) **1** the language of Gujarat in W. India. **2** a native of Gujarat. ● *adj.* of or relating to Gujarat or its language. [Hindi]

gulch *n. N. Amer.* a ravine, esp. one in which a torrent flows.

gulf *n.* **1** ▶ a stretch of sea consisting of a deep inlet with a narrow mouth. **2** (**the Gulf**) **a** the Persian Gulf. **b** the Gulf of Mexico. **3** a deep hollow; a chasm or abyss. **4** a wide difference of feelings, opinion, etc. [from Greek *kolpos* 'bosom, gulf']

Gulf Stream *n.* a warm current flowing from the Gulf of Mexico to Newfoundland, across the North Atlantic Ocean, and along the coast of NW Europe.

Gulf War syndrome *n.* a range of symptoms affecting veterans of the 1991 Gulf War, including skin disorders, headaches, and congenital defects in their children, attributed to vaccinations, drugs taken to protect against chemical warfare, toxins released from burning oil fields, etc.

gull[1] *n.* any of various long-winged web-footed seabirds of the family Laridae, typically having white plumage with a grey or black mantle, and a bright bill. ▷ SEABIRD. [from Celtic]

gull[2] *v.tr.* dupe, fool.

gullet *n.* **1** the food-passage extending from the mouth to the stomach. **2** the throat. [from Old French, literally 'little throat']

gullible *adj.* easily persuaded or deceived. □ **gullibility** *n.*

gully *n.* (also **gulley**) (*pl.* **-ies** or **-eys**) **1** a water-worn ravine. **2** a gutter or drain. **3** *Austral. & NZ* a river valley. **4** *Cricket* **a** the fielding position between point and slips. ▷ CRICKET. **b** a fielder in this position. [from French *goulet* 'bottle-neck']

gulp ● *v.* **1** *tr.* swallow hastily, greedily, or with effort. **2** *intr.* swallow with difficulty; choke. **3** *tr.* (foll. by *down, back*) stifle, suppress (esp. tears). ● *n.* **1** an act of gulping (*drained it in one gulp*). **2** an effort to swallow. **3** a large mouthful of a drink. [Middle English]

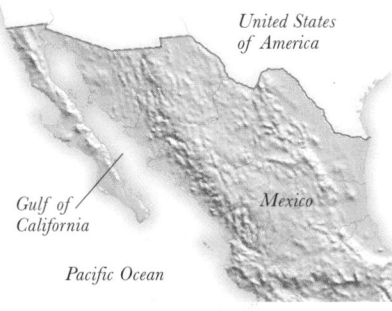

United States of America

Gulf of California

Mexico

Pacific Ocean

GULF OF CALIFORNIA, MEXICO

gum[1] ● *n.* **1 a** a viscous secretion of some trees and shrubs that hardens on drying but is soluble in water. **b** *Brit.* an adhesive substance made from this. **2** *N. Amer.* chewing gum. **3** = GUMDROP. **4** = GUM ARABIC. **5** = GUM TREE. **6** a secretion collecting in the corner of the eye. ● *v.tr.* (**gummed, gumming**) **1** smear or cover with gum. **2** fasten with gum. □ **gum up 1** (of a mechanism etc.) become clogged or obstructed with stickiness. **2** *colloq.* interfere with the smooth running of (*gum up the works*). [from Egyptian *kemui*]

gum[2] *n.* (usu. in *pl.*) the firm flesh around the roots of the teeth. ▷ TOOTH. [Old English]

gum[3] *n. colloq.* □ **by gum!** a mild oath. [corruption of *God*]

gum arabic *n.* a gum exuded by some kinds of acacia and used as glue and in incense.

gumbo *n.* (*pl.* **-os**) *N. Amer.* **1** okra. **2** a spicy chicken or seafood soup thickened with okra, rice, etc. **3** (**Gumbo**) a patois of blacks and Creoles spoken esp. in Louisiana. [of African origin]

gumboil *n.* a small abscess on the gums.

gumboot *n.* a rubber boot; a wellington.

gumdrop *n.* a soft coloured sweet made with gelatin or gum arabic.

gumma *n.* (*pl.* **gummas** or **gummata**) *Med.* a small soft swelling occurring in the connective tissue of the liver, brain, testes, and heart, and characteristic of the late stages of syphilis. [from Latin *gummi* 'gum'] □ **gummatous** *adj.*

gummy[1] *adj.* (**gummier, gummiest**) **1** sticky. **2** suffused with or exuding gum. □ **gumminess** *n.*

gummy[2] *adj.* (**gummier, gummiest**) toothless.

gumption *n. colloq.* **1** resourcefulness, initiative. **2** common sense. [18th-century Scots coinage]

gum resin *n.* a vegetable secretion of resin mixed with gum, e.g. gamboge.

gumshield *n.* ▶ a pad protecting a boxer's teeth and gums.

gumshoe *n.* **1** a galosh. **2** *N. Amer. slang* a detective.

gum tree *n.* a tree exuding gum, esp. a eucalyptus. □ **up a gum tree** *Brit. colloq.* in great difficulties.

GUMSHIELD

GUN

From small arms such as handguns to heavy artillery such as howitzers, all guns are classed by the width (calibre) of the barrel. Whatever the type, an explosion in one area propels a bullet or shell from the barrel towards its target. While many guns are destined for military action, others are used by police, or by civilians in sport, for hunting game, or for self-defence.

foresight *slide catch* *safety catch* *rear sight*
muzzle
slide
barrel clamp
trigger guard *trigger* *cocking lever* *pistol grip* *magazine release catch*

FEATURES OF A MODERN AUTOMATIC PISTOL

EXAMPLES OF GUNS

REVOLVER
US .44 in. Smith & Wesson (1873)

SHORT-MAGAZINE RIFLE
British .303 in. Lee Enfield (1902)

SNIPER'S RIFLE
Japanese 6.5 mm type 97 (c.1937)

SILENCED AUTOMATIC PISTOL
British .22 in. (c.1939–45)

CARBINE
US 5.56 mm Colt Commando (1960s–90s)

SUB-MACHINE GUN
German 9 mm Heckler and Koch (1990s)

G

gum turpentine see TURPENTINE *n.* 1.

gun ● *n.* **1** ▲ a kind of weapon consisting of a metal tube from which bullets or other missiles are propelled by explosive force. **2** a starting pistol. **3** a device for discharging insecticide, grease, electrons, etc., in the required direction (often in *comb.*: *grease gun*). **4** *Brit.* a member of a shooting party. **5** *N. Amer.* a gunman. **6** the firing of a gun. ● *v.* (**gunned**, **gunning**) **1** *tr.* (usu. foll. by *down*) shoot (a person) with a gun. **2** *tr. colloq.* accelerate (an engine or vehicle). **3** *intr.* go shooting. **4** *intr.* (foll. by *for*) seek out determinedly to attack or rebuke. □ **go great guns** *colloq.* proceed vigorously or successfully. **jump the gun** *colloq.* start before a signal is given, or before an agreed time. **stick to one's guns** *colloq.* maintain one's position under attack. [Middle English]

gunboat *n.* a small vessel with heavy guns.

gunboat diplomacy *n.* political negotiation supported by the threat of military force.

gun carriage *n.* a wheeled support for a gun.

gun cotton *n.* an explosive used for blasting, made by steeping cotton in nitric and sulphuric acids.

gun dog *n.* a dog trained to follow sportsmen using guns and to retrieve game.

gunfight *n.* a fight with firearms. □ **gunfighter** *n.*

gunfire *n.* **1** the firing of a gun or guns, esp. repeatedly. **2** the noise from this.

gunge *Brit. colloq.* ● *n.* sticky or viscous matter. ● *v.tr.* (usu. foll. by *up*) clog or obstruct with gunge. [20th-century coinage]

gung-ho *adj.* **1** enthusiastic. **2** uninhibited; quick to take action. [based on Chinese *gonghe* 'to work together', slogan adopted by US Marines (1942)]

gunk *n. slang* viscous or liquid material. [20th-century coinage, originally the proprietary name of a detergent]

gunman *n.* (*pl.* **-men**) a man armed with a gun, esp. in committing a crime.

gunmetal ● *n.* **1** (in full **gunmetal grey**, **gunmetal blue**) a dull bluish-grey colour. **2** an alloy of copper and tin or zinc (formerly used for guns).

● *adj.* (in full **gunmetal grey**, **gunmetal blue**; hyphenated when *attrib.*) dull bluish grey (*gunmetal-grey wings*).

gunnel var. of GUNWALE.

gunner *n.* **1** *Brit.* an artillery soldier (esp. as an official term for a private). **2** *Naut.* a warrant officer in charge of a battery, magazine, etc. **3** a member of an aircraft crew who operates a gun. **4** a person who hunts game with a gun.

gunnery *n.* **1** the construction and management of large guns. **2** the firing of guns.

gunpoint *n.* □ **at gunpoint** threatened with a gun or an ultimatum etc.

gunpowder *n.* **1** ▶ an explosive made of saltpetre, sulphur, and charcoal. **2** a fine green tea of granular appearance.

gunroom *n.* **1** a room in a house for storing sporting guns. **2** *Brit.* quarters for junior officers (originally for gunners) in a warship.

GUNPOWDER

gun-runner *n.* a person engaged in the illegal sale or importing of firearms. □ **gun-running** *n.*

gunship *n.* a heavily armed helicopter or other aircraft. ▷ HELICOPTER

gunshot *n.* **1** a shot fired from a gun. **2** the range of a gun (*within gunshot*).

gunslinger *n. slang* a gunman.

gunsmith *n.* a person who makes, sells, and repairs small firearms.

gunwale /gun-ăl/ *n.* (also **gunnel**) the upper edge of the side of a boat or ship. ▷ SHIP, TRIREME. [formerly used to support guns]

guppy *n.* (*pl.* **-ies**) ▶ a freshwater fish, *Poecilia reticulata*, of the W. Indies and S. America. [named after R. J. L. *Guppy*, 19th-century Trinidadian clergyman who sent the first specimen to the British Museum]

gurdwara /gerd-**wah**-ră/ *n.* a Sikh temple. [from Sanskrit *guru* 'teacher' + *dvāra* 'door']

gurgle ● *v.* **1** *intr.* make a bubbling sound as of water from a bottle. **2** *tr.* utter with such a sound. ● *n.* a gurgling sound.

Gurkha *n.* **1** a member of the dominant Hindu race in Nepal. **2** a Nepalese soldier serving in the British army. [native name, from Sanskrit *go* 'cow' + *rakṣ* 'to protect']

gurnard *n.* (also **gurnet**) any marine fish of the family Triglidae, having a large spiny head with mailed sides, and three finger-like pectoral rays used for walking on the seabed etc. [based on Latin *grunnire* 'to grunt']

guru *n.* **1** a Hindu or Sikh spiritual teacher or head of a religious sect. **2** an influential teacher. [Hindi, from Sanskrit]

gush ● *v.* **1** *tr. & intr.* emit or flow in a sudden and copious stream. **2** *intr.* speak or behave with effusiveness. ● *n.* **1** a sudden or copious stream. **2** an effusive manner. [Middle English] □ **gushing** *adj.* **gushingly** *adv.*

gusher *n.* **1** an oil well from which oil flows without being pumped. **2** an effusive person.

gushy *adj.* (**gushier**, **gushiest**) extremely effusive.

gusset *n.* **1** a piece let into a garment etc. to strengthen or enlarge a part. **2** a bracket strengthening an angle of a structure. [from Old French *gousset* 'flexible joint in armour'] □ **gusseted** *adj.*

gust ● *n.* **1** a sudden strong rush of wind. **2** a burst of rain, fire, smoke, or sound. **3** a passionate or emotional outburst. ● *v.intr.* blow in gusts. [from Old Norse *gustr*]

gustation *n.* the act or capacity of tasting. [based on Latin *gustus* 'taste'] □ **gustatory** *adj.*

gusto *n.* (*pl.* **-os** or **-oes**) zest; enjoyment. [Italian]

gusty *adj.* (**gustier**, **gustiest**) **1** characterized by or blowing in gusts. **2** characterized by gusto. □ **gustily** *adv.* **gustiness** *n.*

gut ● *n.* **1** the lower alimentary canal or a part of this; the intestine. ▷ INTESTINE. **2** (in *pl.*) the bowel or entrails. **3** (in *pl.*) *colloq.* personal courage and determination; perseverance. **4** (in *pl.*) *colloq.* the belly as the source of appetite. **5** (in *pl.*) **a** the contents of anything. **b** the essence of a thing. **6 a** material for violin or racket strings or surgical use made from the intestines of animals. **b** material for fishing lines made from the silk-glands of silkworms. **7** (*attrib.*) **a** instinctive (*a gut reaction*). **b** fundamental (*a gut issue*). ● *v.tr.* (**gutted**, **gutting**) **1** remove or destroy the internal fittings of (a house etc.). **2** take out the guts of (a fish). **3** (as **gutted** *adj.*) *slang* bitterly disappointed; deeply upset. **4** extract the essence of (a book etc.). □ **hate a person's guts** *colloq.* dislike a person intensely. **sweat** (or **work**) **one's guts out** *colloq.* work extremely hard. [Old English]

gut flora *n.pl.* = INTESTINAL FLORA.

gutless *adj. colloq.* lacking courage or determination; feeble. □ **gutlessness** *n.*

gutsy *adj.* (**gutsier**, **gutsiest**) *colloq.* **1** courageous. **2** greedy. □ **gutsily** *adv.* **gutsiness** *n.*

gutta-percha *n.* a tough plastic substance obtained from the latex of various Malaysian trees. [from Malay *getah* 'gum' + *percha*, name of a tree]

gutter ● *n.* **1** a shallow trough below the eaves of a house, or a channel at the side of a street, to carry off rainwater. ▷ HOUSE. **2** (prec. by *the*) a poor or degraded background or environment. **3** an open conduit along which water flows out. **4** a groove. ● *v.intr.* **1** flow in streams. **2** (of a candle) burn unsteadily and melt away rapidly forming channels in the sides. [based on Latin *gutta* 'drop']

GUPPY:
BLONDE GUPPY
(*Poecilia reticulata*)

guttering n. **1 a** the gutters of a building etc. **b** a section or length of a gutter. **2** material for gutters.

gutter press n. Brit. sensational journalism concerned esp. with the private lives of public figures.

guttersnipe n. a street urchin.

guttural ● adj. **1** throaty, harsh-sounding. **2 a** Phonet. (of a consonant) produced in the throat or by the back of the tongue and palate. **b** (of a sound) coming from the throat. **c** of the throat. ● n. Phonet. a guttural consonant (e.g. k, g). [based on Latin guttur 'throat']

guv n. Brit. slang = GOVERNOR 7c.

guy[1] ● n. **1** colloq. a man; a fellow. **2** (usu. in pl.) N. Amer. a person of either sex. **3** Brit. an effigy of Guy Fawkes burnt on a bonfire on 5 Nov. **4** Brit. a grotesquely dressed person. ● v.tr. **1** ridicule. **2** Brit. exhibit in effigy. [earliest in sense 3, from Guy Fawkes, conspirator in the Gunpowder Plot (1605)]

guy[2] ● n. a rope or chain to secure a tent or steady a crane-load etc. ▷ TENT. ● v.tr. secure with a guy or guys.

guzzle v.tr. & intr. eat, drink, or consume greedily. □ **guzzler** n.

Gy abbr. = GRAY[1].

gybe (US **jibe**) ● v. **1** intr. (of a fore-and-aft sail or boom) swing across. **2** tr. cause (a sail) to do this. **3** intr. (of a ship or its crew) change course so that this happens. ● n. a change of course causing gybing. [from obsolete Dutch gijben]

gym n. colloq. **1** a gymnasium. **2** gymnastics.

gymkhana n. a meeting for competition or display in sport, esp. horse-riding. [from Hindi gendkhāna 'ball-house, racket court']

gymnasium n. (pl. **gymnasiums** or **gymnasia**) a room or building equipped for gymnastics. [based on Greek gumnazein 'to exercise naked']

gymnast n. an expert in gymnastics.

gymnastic adj. of or involving gymnastics. [from Greek gumnastikos]

gymnastics n.pl. (also treated as sing.) **1 ▼** exercises developing or displaying physical agility and coordination, usu. in competition. **2** other physical or mental agility of a specified kind (verbal gymnastics; pianistic gymnastics).

G

GYMNASTICS

While forms of gymnastics were popular in the ancient world, modern gymnastics date only from the early 19th century but are now practised up to Olympic level. A gymnast combines set patterns of movement to display technique, as well as flexibility, strength, and agility. In artistic gymnastics, women perform exercises on the floor, beam, vault, and asymmetric bars; men perform on the floor, pommel horse, vault, rings, parallel bars, and horizontal bar. Rhythmic gymnastics are executed to music by women using ribbons, balls, hoops, ropes, or clubs. Sports acrobatics, evolved from acrobatic circus acts, feature balance work and tumbling.

swivel

ribbon
wand

raised arm

flexed hand

pointed toes

leotard

DEMONSTRATION
OF AN ARABESQUE IN
RHYTHMIC GYMNASTICS

EXAMPLES OF GYMNASTIC MOVEMENTS

BALANCES

V-SIT BALANCE

SHOULDER STAND BALANCE

ARABESQUE

TURNING MOVES

CARTWHEEL

HOOP WORK

HOOP JUMP

SHAPES

ARCH

BOX SPLITS

BRIDGE

BALL WORK

BALL BALANCE

JUMPS AND LEAPS

STAG LEAP

TUCK JUMP

STRADDLE PIKE JUMP

STAR JUMP

SPORTS ACROBATICS

STAG BALANCE

STRADDLE LEVER BALANCE

COUNTER-BALANCE

SHOULDER BALANCE

G

GYMNOSPERM

Mostly trees and shrubs, gymnosperms comprise four phyla: conifers (by far the largest phylum), cycads, gnetophytes, and the ginkgo. Unlike angiosperms, gymnosperms produce their seeds on the surface of specialized scales, which are often arranged in cones. Because their seeds do not develop inside a protective ovary, gymnosperms do not form fruits.

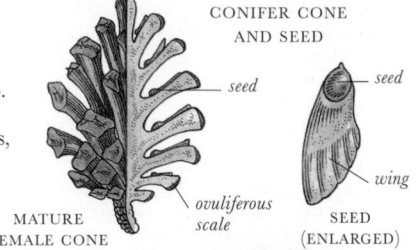

CONIFER CONE
AND SEED

seed

seed

wing

ovuliferous
scale

MATURE
FEMALE CONE

SEED
(ENLARGED)

MAIN TYPES OF GYMNOSPERM

CONIFERS
bishop pine
(*Pinus muricata*) ▷ CONIFER

GINKGO
(*Ginkgo biloba*)

CYCADS
sago palm
(*Cycas revoluta*)

GNETOPHYTES
(*Welwitschia
mirabilis*)

gymnosperm *n.* ▲ any of various plants having seeds unprotected by an ovary, including the conifers, cycads, and ginkgo. [based on Greek *gumnos* 'naked'] □ **gymnospermous** *adj.*

gymp var. of GIMP[1].

gymslip *n. Brit.* a sleeveless tunic, usu. belted, worn by schoolgirls.

gynaecology /gy-ni-**kol**-ŏji/ *n.* (*US* **gynecology**) the science of the physiological functions and diseases of women. [based on Greek *gunē gunaikos* 'woman'] □ **gynaecological** *adj.* **gynaecologist** *n.*

gyp[1] *n. Brit. colloq.* pain or severe discomfort. [19th-century coinage]

gyp[2] *slang* ● *v.tr.* (**gypped, gypping**) cheat, swindle. ● *n.* an act of cheating; a swindle.

GYPSUM: DESERT
ROSE FORMATION

gyppy tummy var. of GIPPY TUMMY.

gypsophila *n.* any plant of the genus *Gypsophila* (daisy family), with a profusion of small flowers. [from Greek *gupsos* 'chalk' + *philos* 'loving']

gypsum *n.* ▼ a hydrated form of calcium sulphate occurring naturally and used to make plaster of Paris and in the building industry. [from Greek *gupsos*]

gypsy *n.* (also **gipsy**) (*pl.* **-ies**) **1** (also **Gypsy**) a member of a nomadic people of Europe and N. America, of Hindu origin with dark skin and hair, and speaking a language (Romany) related to Hindi. **2** a person resembling or living like this people. [from EGYPTIAN, denoting the supposed origin of gypsies when they appeared in England in the early 16th c.]

gypsy moth *n.* a kind of tussock moth, *Lymantria dispar*, whose larvae are very destructive to foliage.

gyrate ● *v.intr.* go in a circle or spiral; revolve, whirl. ● *adj. Bot.* arranged in rings or convolutions. [based on Greek *guros* 'ring'] □ **gyration** *n.* **gyrator** *n.* **gyratory** *adj.*

gyrfalcon /**jer**-fawl-kŏn/ *n.* ▶ a large falcon, *Falco rusticolus*, of cold northern regions. [from Old Norse *geirfálki*]

gyro *n.* (*pl.* **-os**) *colloq.* **1** = GYROSCOPE. **2** = GYROCOMPASS.

gyro- *comb. form* **1** rotation. **2** gyroscopic. [from Greek *guros* 'ring']

gyrocompass *n.* a non-magnetic compass giving true north and bearings from it by means of a gyroscope.

gyroscope *n.* ▼ a wheel or disc mounted so as to spin rapidly about an axis whose orientation is not fixed but is unperturbed by tilting of the mount, esp. used in stabilizers, gyrocompasses, navigation systems, etc. □ **gyroscopic** *adj.*

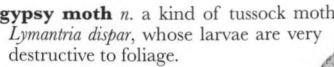

GYRFALCON
(*Falco rusticolus*)

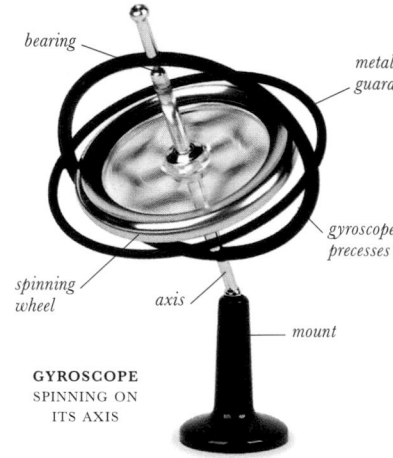

bearing

metal
guard

gyroscope
precesses

spinning
wheel

axis

mount

GYROSCOPE
SPINNING ON
ITS AXIS

H

H¹ *n.* (also **h**) (*pl.* **Hs** or **H's**) **1** the eighth letter of the alphabet. **2** anything having the form of an H (esp. in *comb.*: H-*girder*).

H² *abbr.* (also **H.**) **1** (of a pencil lead) hard. **2** hydrant. **3** *slang* heroin.

H³ *symb.* **1** *Chem.* the element hydrogen. **2** henry(s). **3** magnetic field strength.

h¹ *abbr.* (also **h.**) **1** height. **2** hour(s). **3** hot.

h² *symb.* hecto-.

Ha *symb. Chem.* the element hahnium.

ha¹ (also **hah**) ● *int.* expressing surprise, suspicion, triumph, etc. (cf. HA HA). ● *v.intr.* (in **hum and ha**): see HUM¹. [Middle English]

ha² *abbr.* hectare(s).

habeas corpus /hay-bi-ăs kor-pŭs/ *n.* a writ requiring a person to be brought before a judge or into court, esp. to investigate the lawfulness of his or her detention. [Latin, literally 'you must have the body']

haberdasher *n.* **1** *Brit.* a dealer in dress accessories and sewing goods. **2** *N. Amer.* a dealer in men's clothing. [Middle English] □ **haberdashery** *n.* (*pl.* **-ies**).

habiliment *n.* (usu. in *pl.*) clothes suited to a particular purpose. [from Old French *habillement*]

habit *n.* **1** a settled or regular tendency or practice (*has a habit of ignoring me*). **2** a practice that is hard to give up. **3** a mental constitution or attitude. **4** *colloq.* an addictive practice, esp. of taking drugs. **5** ▼ **a** the dress of a particular class, esp. of a religious order. **b** (in full **riding habit**) a woman's riding dress. **6** *Biol.* & *Crystallog.* a mode of growth. □ **make a habit of** do regularly. [from Latin *habitus* 'condition']

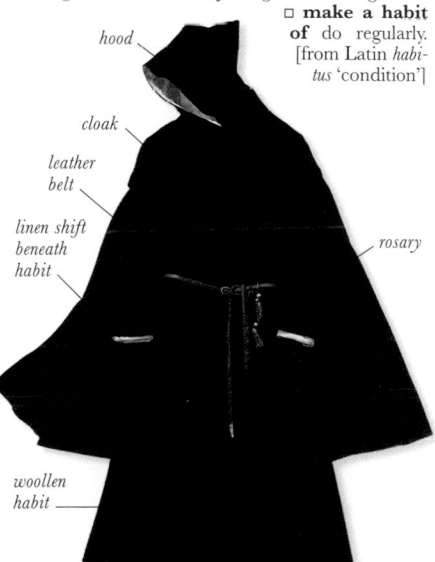

hood
cloak
leather belt
linen shift beneath habit
rosary
woollen habit

HABIT: BENEDICTINE MONK'S HABIT

habitable *adj.* that can be inhabited. [from Latin *habitabilis*] □ **habitability** *n.*

habitant *n.* **1** an inhabitant. **2 a** an early French settler in Canada or Louisiana. **b** a descendant of these settlers. [from Latin *habitant-* 'inhabiting']

habitat *n.* the natural home of an organism. [Latin, literally 'it dwells']

habitation *n.* **1** the process of inhabiting (*fit for human habitation*). **2** a house or home.

habit-forming *adj.* causing addiction.

habitual *adj.* **1** done constantly or as a habit. **2** regular, usual. **3** given to a (specified) habit (*a habitual smoker*). □ **habitually** *adv.* **habitualness** *n.*

habituate *v.tr.* accustom. [based on Late Latin *habituatus* 'brought into a condition'] □ **habituation** *n.*

habitué /hă-bit-yoo-ay/ *n.* a habitual visitor or resident. [French, literally 'accustomed']

háček /hach-ek/ *n.* a diacritic mark (ˇ) placed over letters to modify the sound in some Slavonic and Baltic languages. [Czech, literally 'little hook']

hachures /hash-yoorz/ *n.pl.* parallel lines used in hill-shading on maps, their closeness indicating the steepness of gradient. [French] □ **hachure** *v.tr.*

hacienda /ha-si-en-dă/ *n.* in Spanish-speaking countries: **1** an estate or plantation with a dwelling house. **2** a factory. [Spanish, based on Latin *facienda* 'things to be done']

hack¹ ● *v.* **1** *tr.* cut or chop roughly. **2** *tr.* kick the shin of (an opponent at football). **3** *intr.* deliver cutting blows. **4** *tr.* cut (one's way) through thick foliage etc. **5 a** *intr.* (usu. foll. by *into*) use a computer to gain unauthorized access to data in a system. **b** *tr.* gain unauthorized access to (data in a computer). **6** *tr. slang* **a** manage, cope with. **b** tolerate. ● *n.* **1** a kick with the toe of a boot. **2** a gash or wound, esp. from a kick. **3 a** a mattock. **b** a miner's pick. □ **hacking cough** a short dry frequent cough. [Old English *haccian* 'to cut in pieces']

hack² ● *n.* **1 a** a horse for ordinary riding. **b** a horse let out for hire. **c** = JADE² 1. **2** a dull, uninspired writer. **3** a person hired to do dull routine work. **4** *N. Amer.* a taxi. ● *attrib.adj.* **1** used as a hack. **2** typical of a hack; commonplace (*hack work*). ● *v.* **1** *intr.* use a horse for ordinary riding. **2** *tr.* ride (a horse) in this way. [abbreviation of HACKNEY]

hacker *n.* **1** a person or thing that hacks or cuts roughly. **2** a person who uses computers for a hobby, esp. to gain unauthorized access to data.

hackette *n. colloq. usu. derog.* a female journalist.

hackle *n.* **1** a long feather or series of feathers on the neck or saddle of a domestic cock and other birds. **2** (in *pl.*) the erectile hairs along the back of a dog, which rise when it is angry or alarmed. □ **make a person's hackles rise** cause a person to be angry or indignant. [Middle English, related to HOOK]

hackney *n.* (*pl.* **-eys**) **1** a light horse with a high-stepping trot. **2** (*attrib.*) designating any of various vehicles kept for hire. [Middle English]

■ **Usage** *Hackney* is no longer used except in *hackney carriage*, still in official use as a term for 'taxi'.

hackneyed *adj.* (of a phrase etc.) made trite by overuse.

hacksaw *n.* a saw with a narrow blade set in a frame, for cutting metal. ▷ SAW

had *past* and *past part.* of HAVE.

haddock *n.* (*pl.* same) ▶ an edible marine fish, *Melanogrammus aeglefinus*, of the N. Atlantic. [Middle English]

Hades /hay-deez/ *n.* (in Greek mythology) the underworld. [from Greek *haidēs*, originally a name of Pluto, god of the dead]

hadn't *contr.* had not.

hadron *n. Physics* any strongly interacting subatomic particle. □ **hadronic** *adj.* [based on Greek *hadros* 'bulky']

haemal /hee-măl/ *adj.* (*US* **hemal**) *Anat.* **1** of or concerning the blood. **2** situated on the same side of the body as the heart and major blood vessels. [based on Greek *haima* 'blood']

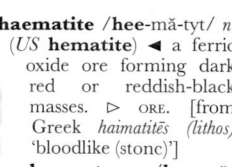

haematite /hee-mă-tyt/ *n.* (*US* **hematite**) ◄ a ferric oxide ore forming dark red or reddish-black masses. ▷ ORE. [from Greek *haimatitēs (lithos)* 'bloodlike (stone)']

HAEMATITE

haemato- /hee-mă-toh/ *comb. form* (*US* **hemato-**) blood. [from Greek *haima haimat-* 'blood']

haematology /hee-mă-tol-ŏji/ *n.* (*US* **hematology**) the study of the physiology of the blood. □ **haematological** *adj.* **haematologist** *n.*

haemo- /hee-moh/ *comb. form* (*US* **hemo-**) = HAEMATO-. [abbr.]

haemodialysis /hee-moh-/ *n.* (*US* **hemodialysis**) = DIALYSIS 2.

haemoglobin /hee-mŏ-gloh-bin/ *n.* (*US* **hemoglobin**) a red oxygen-carrying protein containing iron, present in the red blood cells of vertebrates. [shortened from HAEMATO- + GLOBULIN]

haemophilia /hee-mŏ-/ *n.* (*US* **hemophilia**) *Med.* a usu. hereditary disorder with a tendency to bleed severely from even a slight injury, through the failure of the blood to clot normally. □ **haemophilic** *adj.*

haemophiliac /hee-mŏ-/ *n.* (*US* **hemophiliac**) a person suffering from haemophilia.

haemorrhage /hem-ŏ-rij/ *n.* (*US* **hemorrhage**) ● *n.* **1** an escape of blood from a ruptured blood vessel, esp. when profuse. **2** an extensive damaging loss suffered by a state, organization, etc., esp. of people or assets. ● *v.* **1** *intr.* suffer a haemorrhage. **2** *tr.* lose or dissipate, esp. wastefully. [from Greek *haimorrhagia*, literally 'bursting of blood'] □ **haemorrhagic** *adj.*

haemorrhoid /hem-ŏ-roid/ *n.* (*US* **hemorrhoid**) (usu. in *pl.*) swollen veins at or near the anus; piles. [from Greek *haimorrhoides (phlebes)* 'bleeding (veins)']

haemostasis /hee-mŏ-stay-sis/ *n.* (*US* **hemostasis**) the stopping of the flow of blood from a wound etc. □ **haemostatic** *adj.*

haere mai /hy-rĕ my/ *int. NZ* welcome. [Maori, literally 'come hither']

hafnium *n. Chem.* a silvery lustrous metallic element occurring naturally with zirconium, used in tungsten alloys for filaments and electrodes. [based on Latin *Hafnia* 'Havn', former name of Copenhagen, Denmark]

haft ● *n.* the handle of a dagger or knife etc. ● *v.tr.* provide with a haft. [Old English]

hag *n.* **1** an ugly old woman. **2** a witch. [Middle English] □ **haggish** *adj.*

haggard *adj.* looking exhausted and distraught, esp. from fatigue, worry, privation, etc. [from French *hagard*] □ **haggardly** *adv.* **haggardness** *n.*

HADDOCK
(*Melanogrammus aeglefinus*)

haggis *n.* a Scottish dish consisting of a sheep's or calf's offal mixed with suet, oatmeal, etc., and boiled in a bag made from the animal's stomach or in an artificial bag. [Middle English]

haggle ● *v.intr.* dispute or bargain persistently. ● *n.* a dispute or wrangle. [earlier in sense 'to hack': from Old Norse *höggva* 'to hew'] □ **haggler** *n.*

H

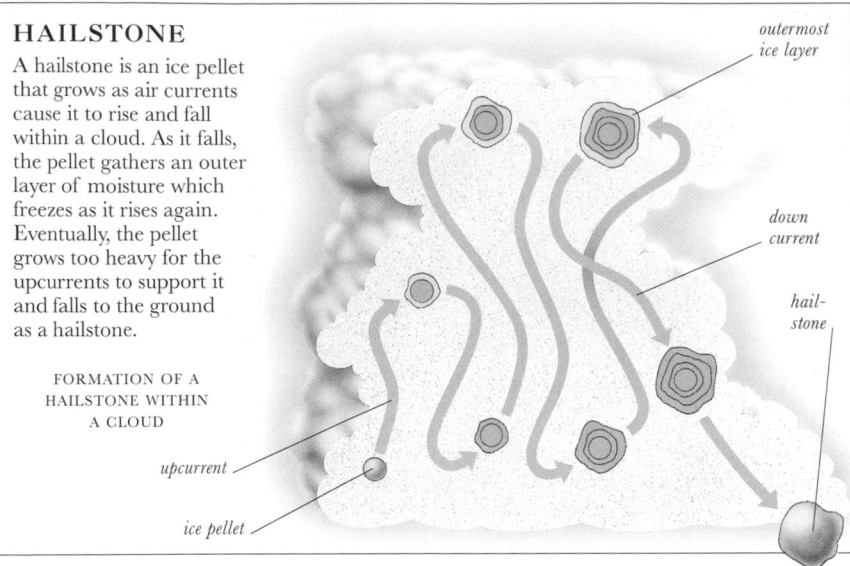

HAILSTONE

A hailstone is an ice pellet that grows as air currents cause it to rise and fall within a cloud. As it falls, the pellet gathers an outer layer of moisture which freezes as it rises again. Eventually, the pellet grows too heavy for the upcurrents to support it and falls to the ground as a hailstone.

FORMATION OF A
HAILSTONE WITHIN
A CLOUD

outermost
ice layer

down
current

hail-
stone

upcurrent

ice pellet

hagio- *comb. form* of saints or holiness. [from Greek *hagios* 'holy']

hagiographer *n.* a writer of the lives of saints.

hagiography *n.* **1** the writing of the lives of saints. **2** an idealized biography of any person. □ **hagiographic** *adj.* **hagiographical** *adj.*

hagiolatry *n.* the worship of saints.

hagiology *n.* literature dealing with the lives and legends of saints. □ **hagiological** *adj.* **hagiologist** *n.*

hag-ridden *adj.* afflicted by nightmares or anxieties.

hah var. of HA[1].

ha-ha *n.* a ditch with a wall on its inner side below ground level, forming a boundary without interrupting the view. [French]

ha ha *int.* representing laughter. [Old English]

hahnium *n. Chem.* the artificial radioactive element of atomic number 105. [named after O. *Hahn*, German chemist, 1879–1968]

haiku /**hy**-koo/ *n.* (*pl.* same) a Japanese three-part poem of usu. 17 syllables. [Japanese]

hail[1] ● *n.* **1** pellets of frozen rain falling in showers. **2** (foll. by *of*) a barrage or onslaught. ● *v.* **1** *intr.* (prec. by *it* as subject) hail falls (*it is hailing*; *if it hails*). **2 a** *tr.* pour down (blows, words, etc.). **b** *intr.* come down forcefully. [Old English]

hail[2] ● *v.* **1** *tr.* greet enthusiastically. **2** *tr.* signal to (*hailed a taxi*). **3** *tr.* (often foll. by *as*) acclaim (*hailed him king*). **4** *intr.* (foll. by *from*) have one's home or origins in (*hails from Mauritius*). ● *int. archaic* or *literary* expressing greeting. ● *n.* **1** a greeting or act of hailing. **2** distance as affecting the possibility of hailing (*was within hail*). [from Old Norse *heill* 'sound, whole']

hail-fellow-well-met *adj.* informal; showing usu. excessive familiarity.

Hail Mary *n.* the Ave Maria (see AVE *n.* 1).

hailstone *n.* ▲ a pellet of hail.

hailstorm *n.* a period of heavy hail.

hair *n.* **1** ▶ **a** any of the fine threadlike strands growing from the skin of mammals, esp. from the human head. **b** these collectively (*his hair is falling out*). **2 a** an artificially produced hairlike strand, e.g. in a brush. **b** a mass of such hairs. **3** an elongated cell growing from the epidermis of a plant. **4** a very small quantity or extent (also *attrib.*: *a hair crack*). □ **get in a person's hair** *colloq.* encumber or annoy a person. **keep one's hair on** *Brit. colloq.* remain calm; not get angry. **let one's hair down** *colloq.* abandon restraint. **make one's hair stand on end** horrify one. **not turn a hair**

remain unmoved or unaffected. [Old English] □ **haired** *adj.* (also in *comb.*). **hairless** *adj.* **hairlike** *adj.*

hairbreadth *n.* = HAIR'S BREADTH (esp. *attrib.*: *a hairbreadth escape*).

hairbrush *n.* a brush for arranging or smoothing the hair.

haircare *n.* the care of the hair.

haircloth *n.* stiff cloth woven from hair.

haircut *n.* **1** a cutting of the hair. **2** the style in which the hair is cut.

hairdo *n.* (*pl.* **-dos**) *colloq.* the style of or an act of styling a woman's hair.

hairdresser *n.* **1** a person who cuts and styles hair, esp. professionally. **2** the business or establishment of a hairdresser. □ **hairdressing** *n.*

hairdryer *n.* (also **hairdrier**) an electrical device for drying the hair by blowing warm air over it.

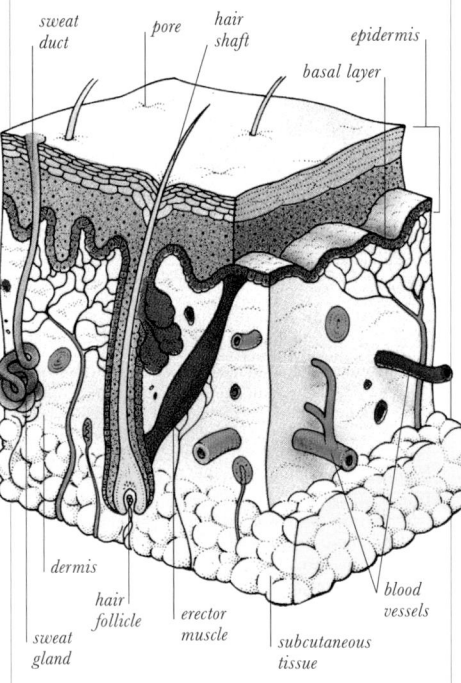

sweat
duct

pore

hair
shaft

epidermis

basal layer

dermis

hair
follicle

erector
muscle

subcutaneous
tissue

sweat
gland

blood
vessels

HAIR: SECTION THROUGH HUMAN
SKIN SHOWING HAIR

hairgrip *n. Brit.* a flat hairpin with the ends close together.

hairline *n.* **1** the edge of a person's hair, esp. on the forehead. **2** (usu. *attrib.*) a very thin line or crack etc.

hairnet *n.* a piece of fine mesh-work for confining the hair.

hair of the dog *n.* alcoholic drink to cure the effects of alcoholic drink.

hairpiece *n.* a quantity of hair used to augment a person's natural hair.

hairpin *n.* a U-shaped pin for fastening the hair.

hairpin bend *n.* a sharp U-shaped bend in a road.

hair-raising *adj.* terrifying.

hair's breadth *n.* a very small amount or margin.

hair shirt ● *n.* a shirt of haircloth, worn formerly by penitents and ascetics. ● *attrib.adj.* (**hair-shirt**) austere, harsh, self-sacrificing.

hairslide *n. Brit.* a clip for keeping the hair in position.

hair-splitting *adj. & n.* making excessively fine distinctions. □ **hair-splitter** *n.*

hairspray *n.* a solution sprayed on to the hair to keep it in place.

hairspring *n.* a fine spring regulating the balance wheel in a watch.

hairstyle *n.* a particular way of arranging the hair. □ **hairstyling** *n.* **hairstylist** *n.*

hair-trigger *n.* a trigger of a firearm set for release at the slightest pressure.

hairy *adj.* (**hairier**, **hairiest**) **1** covered with hair. **2** having the feel of hair. **3** *slang* alarmingly unpleasant or difficult. □ **hairily** *adv.* **hairiness** *n.*

haj *n.* (also **hajj**) the Muslim pilgrimage to Mecca. [from Arabic *ḥāǧǧ* 'pilgrimage']

haji *n.* (also **hajji**) (*pl.* **-s**) **1** a Muslim who has been to Mecca as a pilgrim. **2** (**Haji**) a title given to such a pilgrim. [related to HAJ]

haka *n.* **1** a Maori ceremonial war dance accompanied by chanting. **2** an imitation of this by members of a New Zealand sports team before a match. [Maori]

hake *n.* any edible marine fish of the genus *Merluccius*, esp. *M. merluccius* with an elongated body and large head. [Middle English]

halal /hă-**lahl**/ ● *v.tr.* (**halalled**, **halalling**) kill (an animal) as prescribed by Muslim law. ● *n.* (often *attrib.*) meat prepared in this way. [from Arabic *ḥalāl* 'lawful']

halberd *n.* (also **halbert**) *hist.* a combined spear and battleaxe. ▷ ROUNDHEAD. [from Middle High German *helmbarde*]

halcyon /**hal**-si-ŏn/ *adj.* **1** calm, peaceful (*halcyon days*). **2** (of a period) happy, prosperous. [from Greek *(h)alkuōn* 'kingfisher']

hale[1] *adj.* strong and healthy (esp. in **hale and hearty**). [Old English *hāl* 'whole'] □ **haleness** *n.*

hale[2] *v.tr.* drag or draw forcibly. [from Old Norse *hala*]

half ● *n.* (*pl.* **halves**) **1** either of two equal or corresponding parts or groups into which a thing, number, or quantity, is or might be divided. **2** *colloq.* = HALF-BACK. **3** *Brit. colloq.* half a pint, esp. of beer. **4** either of two equal periods of play in sports. **5** *colloq.* a half-price fare or ticket, esp. for a child. ● *predet.* of an amount or quantity equal to a half, or loosely to a part thought of as roughly a half (*take half the men*; *spent half the time reading*; *half a pint*). ● *adj.* forming a half (*a half share*). ● *adv.* **1** (often in *comb.*) to the extent of half; partly (*only half-cooked*; *half-frozen*; *half-laughing*). **2** to a certain extent; somewhat (esp. in idiomatic phrases: *half dead*; *am half inclined to agree*). **3** (in reckoning time) by the amount of half (*half past two*). □ **half cock** see COCK[1]. **by half** (prec. by *too* + adj.) excessively (*too clever by half*). **by halves** imperfectly or incompletely (*never does things by halves*). **half a chance** *colloq.* the slightest opportunity (esp. *given half a chance*). **half an eye** the slightest degree of perceptiveness. **have half a mind** see MIND. **the**

half of it *colloq.* the rest or more important part of something (usu. after *neg.*: *you don't know the half of it*). **not half 1** not nearly (*not half long enough*). **2** *colloq.* not at all (*not half bad*). **3** *Brit. slang* to an extreme degree (*he didn't half get angry*). [Old English]

■ **Usage** In sense 3 of the adverb, the word *past* is often omitted in colloquial usage, e.g. *She came at half two*. In some parts of Scotland and Ireland this means 'half past one'.

half a crown var. of HALF-CROWN.

half a dozen var. of HALF-DOZEN.

half-and-half ● *adv.* in equal parts. ● *adj.* that is half one thing and half another.

half-back *n.* (in some sports) a player between the forwards and full-backs. ▷ FOOTBALL

half-baked *adj.* **1** incompletely considered or planned. **2** (of enthusiasm etc.) only partly committed. **3** foolish.

half-blood *n.* **1** a person having one parent in common with another. **2** this relationship. **3** = HALF-BREED.

half board *n. Brit.* provision of bed, breakfast, and one main meal at a hotel etc.

half-breed *n. offens.* a person of mixed race.

half-brother *n.* a brother with whom one has only one parent in common.

half-caste *offens.* ● *n.* a person whose parents are of different races. ● *adj.* of or relating to such a person.

half-crown *n.* (also **half a crown**) *hist.* (in the UK) a former coin and monetary unit equal to 2s. 6d. (12½p).

half-cut *adj. Brit. slang* fairly drunk.

half-dozen *n.* (also **half a dozen**) *colloq.* six, or about six.

half-hardy *adj.* (of a plant) able to grow in the open air at all times except in severe frost.

half-hear *v.tr.* (*past.* and *past part.* **half-heard**) hear (a thing) incompletely (*she only half-heard their shouts above the sound of the television*).

half-hearted *adj.* lacking enthusiasm; feeble. □ **half-heartedly** *adv.* **half-heartedness** *n.*

half hitch *n.* ▶ a noose or knot formed by passing the end of a rope round its standing part and then through the loop.

half holiday *n.* a day of which half is taken as a holiday.

HALF HITCH

half-hour *n.* **1** (also **half an hour**) a period of 30 minutes. **2** a point of time 30 minutes after any hour o'clock. □ **half-hourly** *adj. & adv.*

half-landing *n.* a landing part of the way up a flight of stairs, whose length is twice the width of the flight plus the width of the well.

half-life *n.* the time taken for the radioactivity or some other property of a substance to fall to half its original value.

half-light *n.* a dim imperfect light.

half-marathon *n.* a long-distance running race, usu. of 13 miles 352 yards (21.243 km).

half mast *n.* the position of a flag halfway down the mast, as a mark of respect for a person who has died. □ **at half mast** often *joc.* (esp. of a garment) having slipped down.

half measures *n.pl.* an unsatisfactory compromise or inadequate policy.

half-moon *n.* **1** the Moon when only half its illuminated surface is visible from Earth. **2** the time when this occurs. **3** a semicircular object.

half nelson see NELSON.

half note *n.* esp. *N. Amer. Mus.* = MINIM 1.

half pay *n.* reduced income, esp. on retirement.

halfpenny /ˈhaypni/ *n.* (also **ha'penny**) (*pl.* **-pennies** or **-pence**) (in the UK) a former bronze coin worth half a penny (withdrawn in 1984).

half-sister *n.* a sister with whom one has only one parent in common.

half-sole *n.* the sole of a boot or shoe from the shank to the toe.

half-term *n. Brit.* a period about halfway through a school term, when a short holiday is usually taken.

half-timbered *adj. Archit.* ▼ having walls with a timber frame and a brick or plaster filling. □ **half-timbering** *n.*

plaster infill   timber frame   pointed gable

HALF-TIMBERED: 17TH-CENTURY HALF-TIMBERED ENGLISH HOUSE

half-time *n.* **1** the time at which half of a game or contest is completed. **2** a short interval occurring at this time.

half-title *n.* **1** the title or abbreviated title of a book, printed on the recto of the leaf preceding the title-page. **2** the title of a section of a book printed on the recto of the leaf preceding it.

half-tone *n.* **1** a reproduction printed from a block (produced by photographic means) in which the various tones of grey are produced from small and large black dots. **2** esp. *US Mus.* a semitone.

half-track *n.* **1** a propulsion system for land vehicles with wheels at the front and an endless driven belt at the back. **2** a vehicle equipped with this.

half-truth *n.* a statement that conveys only part of the truth.

half-volley *n.* (*pl.* **-eys**) (in ball games) the playing of a ball as soon as it bounces off the ground.

halfway ● *adv.* **1** at a point equidistant between two others (*halfway to Rome*). **2** to some extent; more or less (*halfway decent*). ● *adj.* situated halfway (*a halfway point*).

halfway house *n.* **1** a compromise. **2** the halfway point in a progression. **3** a centre for rehabilitating ex-prisoners, mental patients, or others unused to normal life. **4** an inn midway between two towns.

halfwit *n.* **1** *colloq.* a foolish or stupid person. **2** a person who is mentally deficient. □ **half-witted** *adj.* **half-wittedly** *adv.* **half-wittedness** *n.*

half-yearly *adj. & adv.* esp. *Brit.* at intervals of six months.

halibut *n.* (*pl.* same) ▶ any of various large marine flatfishes, esp. *Hippoglossus hippoglossus* of the N. Atlantic, used as food. [Middle English, from *haly* 'holy' + *butt* 'flatfish']

halide /ˈhaylyd/ *n. Chem.* a binary compound of a halogen with another element or group.

haliotis *n.* ▶ any edible gastropod mollusc of the genus *Haliotis* with an ear-shaped shell lined with mother-of-pearl. [from Greek *hals hali-* 'sea' + *ous ōt-* 'ear']

halite /ˈhalyt/ It/ *n.* rock salt. [based on Greek *hals* 'salt']

halitosis *n.* = BAD BREATH. [based on Latin *halitus* 'breath']

hall *n.* **1 a** a space or passage into which the front entrance of a house etc. opens. **b** *N. Amer.* a corridor or passage in a building. **2** a large room or building for meetings, meals, concerts, etc. **3** *Brit.* a large country house, esp. with a landed estate. **4** (*Brit.* in full **hall of residence**) a university residence for students. **5 a** (in a college etc.) a common dining room. **b** *Brit.* dinner in this. **6** the building of a guild (*Fishmongers' Hall*). **7** a large public room in a palace etc. [Old English]

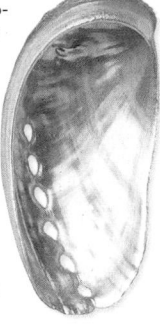

HALIOTIS: INNER SURFACE OF HALIOTIS SHELL

hallelujah /hal-i-loo-yă/ var. of ALLELUIA.

hallmark ● *n.* **1** a mark used by the British assay offices indicating the standard of gold, silver, and platinum. **2** any distinctive feature. ● *v.tr.* **1** stamp with a hallmark. **2** designate as excellent. [from Goldsmiths' *Hall* in London, where articles are tested and stamped]

hallo esp. *Brit.* var. of HELLO.

Hall of Fame *n.* **1** esp. *N. Amer.* a building with memorials of people who have excelled, esp. in a particular sport. **2** a group of people famous in a particular sphere.

hall of residence see HALL 4.

halloo ● *int.* **1** inciting dogs to the chase. **2** calling attention. **3** expressing surprise. ● *n.* the cry 'halloo'. ● *v.* (**halloos, hallooed**) **1** *intr.* cry 'halloo', esp. to dogs. **2** *intr.* shout to attract attention. **3** *tr.* urge on (dogs etc.) with shouts.

hallow *v.tr.* **1** make holy, consecrate. **2** honour as holy. [Old English]

Hallowe'en *n.* the eve of All Saints' Day, 31 Oct.

hall porter *n. Brit.* a porter who carries baggage etc. in a hotel.

hallstand *n.* a stand in the hall of a house, with a mirror, pegs, etc.

hallucinate *v.* **1** *tr.* produce illusions in the mind of (a person). **2** *intr.* experience hallucinations. [from Latin (*h*)*allucinari* 'to wander in mind'] □ **hallucinator** *n.*

hallucination *n.* the apparent perception of an object not actually present. □ **hallucinatory** *adj.*

hallucinogen *n.* a drug causing hallucinations. □ **hallucinogenic** *adj.*

hallway *n.* an entrance hall or corridor.

halm var. of HAULM.

halo ● *n.* (*pl.* **-oes** or **-os**) **1** a disc or circle of light shown surrounding the head of a sacred person. **2** the glory associated with an idealized person etc. **3** a circle of white or coloured light round a lumi-

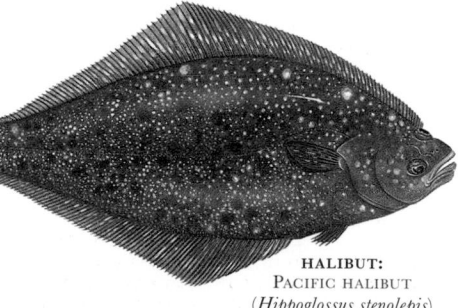

HALIBUT: PACIFIC HALIBUT (*Hippoglossus stenolepis*)

H

H

nous body, esp. the Sun or Moon. **4** a circle or ring. ● *v.tr.* (**-oes, -oed**) surround with a halo. [from Greek *halōs* 'disc of the Sun or Moon']

halogen /hal-ŏ-jĕn/ *n.* **1** *Chem.* any of a group of reactive non-metallic elements (fluorine, chlorine, bromine, iodine, and astatine) which form strongly acidic compounds with hydrogen from which simple salts can be made. **2** (*attrib.*) (of lamps and radiant heat sources) using a filament surrounded by a halogen, usu. iodine vapour. [based on Greek *hals halos* 'salt'] □ **halogenic** *adj.*

halon /hay-lon/ *n. Chem.* any of various gaseous compounds of carbon, bromine, and other halogens, used to extinguish fires.

halophyte /hal-ŏ-fyt/ *n.* ▶ a plant adapted to saline conditions. [based on Greek *hals halos* 'salt']

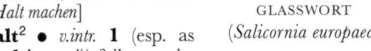

halt[1] ● *n.* **1** a stop (usu. temporary) (*come to a halt*). **2** a temporary stoppage on a march or journey. **3** *Brit.* a minor stopping place on a local railway line. ● *v.intr. & tr.* stop; come or bring to a halt. □ **call a halt** (**to**) decide to stop. [originally in phrase *make halt*, from German *Halt machen*]

HALOPHYTE:
GLASSWORT
(*Salicornia europaea*)

halt[2] ● *v.intr.* **1** (esp. as **halting** *adj.*) fail to make smooth progress. **2** hesitate (*halt between two opinions*). **3** walk hesitatingly. **4** *archaic* be lame. ● *adj. archaic* lame. [Old English] □ **haltingly** *adv.*

halter *n.* **1** a rope or strap with a headstall for horses or cattle. **2 a** a strap round the back of a woman's neck holding her dress-top and leaving her shoulders and back bare. **b** a dress-top held by this. [Old English]

halter-neck *attrib.adj.* (of a garment) held up by a strap around the neck.

halva *n.* (also **halvah**) a sweet confection of sesame flour and honey. [from Arabic *ḥalwa*]

halve *v.tr.* **1** divide into two halves or parts. **2** reduce by half. **3** share equally. **4** *Golf* use the same number of strokes as one's opponent in (a hole or match).

halves *pl.* of HALF.

halyard *n. Naut.* a rope or tackle for raising or lowering a sail or yard etc. ▷ DINGHY, FLAG. [Middle English *halier*, related to HALE[2]]

ham ● *n.* **1 a** the upper part of a pig's leg salted and dried or smoked for food. **b** the meat from this. **2** the back of the thigh; the thigh and buttock. **3** (often *attrib.*) *slang* an inexpert or unsubtle actor or piece of acting. **4** (in full **radio ham**) *colloq.* the operator of an amateur radio station. ● *v.intr. & tr.* (often foll. by *up*) (**hammed, hamming**) *slang* overact; act or treat emotionally or sentimentally. [Old English]

hamburger *n.* a beefburger. [German, literally 'of Hamburg', in Germany]

ham-fisted *adj. colloq.* clumsy. □ **ham-fistedly** *adv.* **ham-fistedness** *n.*

ham-handed *adj. colloq.* = HAM-FISTED.

Hamitic ● *n.* a group of African languages including ancient Egyptian and Berber. ● *adj.* **1** of or relating to this group of languages. **2** of or relating to the Hamites, a group of peoples in Egypt and N. Africa, by tradition descended from Noah's son Ham (Gen. 10:6 ff.).

hamlet *n.* a small village. [based on Middle Low German *hamm* 'village']

hammer ● *n.* **1 a** a tool with a heavy metal head at right angles to the handle, used for breaking, driving nails, etc. **b** a machine with a metal block serving the same purpose. **c** a similar contrivance, as for exploding the charge in a gun, striking the

strings of a piano, etc. ▷ PIANO. **2** an auctioneer's mallet for indicating by a sharp tap that an article is sold. **3 a** a metal ball attached to a wire for throwing in an athletic contest. **b** the sport of throwing the hammer. ● *v.* **1 a** *tr. & intr.* hit or beat with or as with a hammer. **b** *intr.* strike loudly. **2** *tr.* **a** drive in (nails) with a hammer. **b** fasten or secure by hammering (*hammered the lid down*). **3** *tr.* (often foll. by *in*) inculcate (ideas, knowledge, etc.) forcefully or repeatedly. **4** *tr. colloq.* utterly defeat; inflict heavy damage on. **5** *intr.* (foll. by *at, away at*) work hard or persistently at. □ **come under the hammer** be sold at an auction. **hammer out 1** make flat or smooth by hammering. **2** work out the details of laboriously. **3** play (a tune, esp. on the piano) loudly or clumsily. [Old English] □ **hammering** *n.* (esp. in sense 4 of *v.*). **hammerless** *adj.*

hammer and sickle *n.* ▶ the symbols of the industrial worker and the peasant used as the emblem of the former USSR and of international communism.

hammer and tongs *adv. colloq.* with great vigour and commotion.

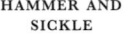

HAMMER AND
SICKLE

hammer drill *n.* a drill with a bit that moves backwards and forwards while rotating.

hammerhead *n.* (also **hammerhead shark**) any shark of the family Sphyrnidae, with a flattened head and eyes in lateral extensions of it. ▷ SHARK.

hammer-toe *n.* a deformity in which the toe is bent permanently downwards.

hammock *n.* a bed of canvas or rope network, suspended by cords at the ends. [from Spanish *hamaca*]

hammy *adj.* (**hammier, hammiest**) **1** of or like ham. **2** *colloq.* over-theatrical.

hamper[1] ● *n.* **1** a large basket usu. with a hinged lid and containing food (*picnic hamper*) or *US* laundry. **2** *Brit.* a selection of food, drink, etc., for an occasion. [from Old French *hanapier* 'case for a goblet']

hamper[2] *v.tr.* **1** prevent the free movement or activity of. **2** impede, hinder. [Middle English]

hamster *n.* a Eurasian rodent of the subfamily Cricetinae, having a short tail and large cheek pouches for storing food, esp. (in full **common hamster**) *Cricetus cricetus* and (in full **golden hamster**) *Mesocricetus auratus*, often kept as a pet or as a laboratory animal. ▷ RODENT. [from Old High German *hamustro* 'corn-weevil']

hamstring *Anat.* ● *n.* **1** ▼ each of five tendons at the back of the knee in humans. ▷ KNEE. **2** the great tendon at the back of the hock in quadrupeds.

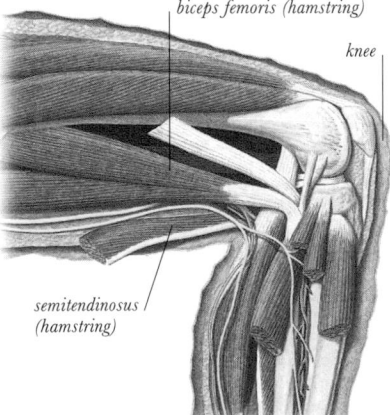

biceps femoris (hamstring)

knee

semitendinosus (hamstring)

HAMSTRING: TWO OF THE HAMSTRING
TENDONS IN THE HUMAN LEG

● *v.tr.* (*past* and *past part.* **hamstrung** or **hamstringed**) **1** cripple by cutting the hamstrings of (a person or animal). **2** prevent the activity or efficiency of.

hand ● *n.* **1 a** ▶ the end of the human arm beyond the wrist. **b** in other primates, the end part of a forelimb, also used as a foot. **2 a** (often in *pl.*) control, management, custody, disposal (*is in good hands*). **b** agency or influence (*suffered at their hands*). **c** a share in an action; active support. **3** the pointer of a clock or watch. **4** the right or left side or direction relative to a person or thing. **5 a** a skill (*a hand for making pastry*). **b** a person skilful in some respect. **6** a person who does or makes something, esp. distinctively (*a picture by the same hand*). **7** an individual's writing or the style of this; a signature. **8** a person etc. as the source of information etc. (*at first hand*). **9** a pledge of marriage. **10** a manual worker esp. in a factory, on a farm, or on board ship. **11 a** the playing cards dealt to a player. **b** the player holding these. **c** a round of play. **12** *colloq.* applause (*got a big hand*). **13** the unit of measure of a horse's height, equal to 4 inches (10.16 cm). **14** *Brit.* a foreleg cut of pork. **15** a bunch of bananas. **16** (*attrib.*) **a** operated or held in the hand (*hand drill, hand luggage*). **b** done by hand and not by machine (*hand-knitted*). ● *v.tr.* **1** deliver; transfer by hand or otherwise. **2** convey verbally (*handed me a lot of abuse*). **3** *colloq.* give away too readily (*handed them the advantage*). □ **all hands 1** the entire crew of a ship. **2** the entire workforce. **at hand 1** close by. **2** about to happen. **by hand 1** by a person and not a machine. **2** delivered privately and not by post. **from hand to mouth** satisfying only one's immediate needs (also *attrib.*: *a hand-to-mouth existence*). **get** (or **have** or **keep**) **one's hand in** become (or be or remain) practised in something. **give** (or **lend**) **a hand** assist in an action or enterprise. **hand down 1** pass the ownership or use of to another, esp. a descendant. **2 a** transmit (a decision) from a higher court etc. **b** *US* express (an opinion or verdict). **hand in glove** in collusion or association. **hand in hand** in close association. **hand it to** *colloq.* acknowledge the merit of. **hand on** pass (a thing) to the next in a series. **hand out 1** distribute. **2** award, allocate (*the judges handed out stiff sentences*). **hand over** deliver; surrender possession of. **hand over fist** *colloq.* with rapid progress. **hand round** (or *US* **around**) distribute. **hands down** with no difficulty. **hands off** a warning not to touch or interfere with something. ● *adj.* (**hands-off**) not involving or requiring direct control or intervention. **hands-on 1** *Computing* of or requiring personal operation at a keyboard. **2** involving or offering active participation rather than theory. **hands up!** an instruction to raise one's hands in surrender or to signify assent or participation. **have** (or **take**) **a hand in** share or take part in. **have one's hands full** be fully occupied. **have one's hands tied** *colloq.* be unable to act. **in hand 1** receiving attention. **2** in reserve. **3** under one's control. **lay** (or **put**) **one's hands on** see LAY[1]. **off one's hands** no longer one's responsibility. **on every hand** (or **all hands**) to or from all directions. **on hand 1** available. **2** present, in attendance. **on one's hands 1** resting on one as a responsibility. **2** at one's disposal; available (*with time on his hands*). **on the one** (or **the other**) **hand** from one (or another) point of view. **out of hand 1** out of control. **2** peremptorily (*refused out of hand*). **put** (or **set**) **one's hand to** start work on; engage in. **to hand 1** within easy reach. **2** (of a letter) received. **turn one's hand to** undertake (as a new activity). [Old English] □ **handless** *adj.*

handbag *n.* a small bag for a purse etc., carried esp. by a woman.

handball *n.* **1 a** *Brit.* a game similar to football in which the ball is thrown rather than kicked. **b** a game in which a ball is hit with the hand in a walled court. **2** *Football* intentional touching of the ball with the hand or arm by a player other than the goalkeeper in the penalty area, constituting a foul.

HAND

The human hand is a sensitive tool with opposable fingers and thumb. A system of muscles and tendons in the forearm and hand flex and extend a framework of 27 bones, allowing a wide range of precise movements.

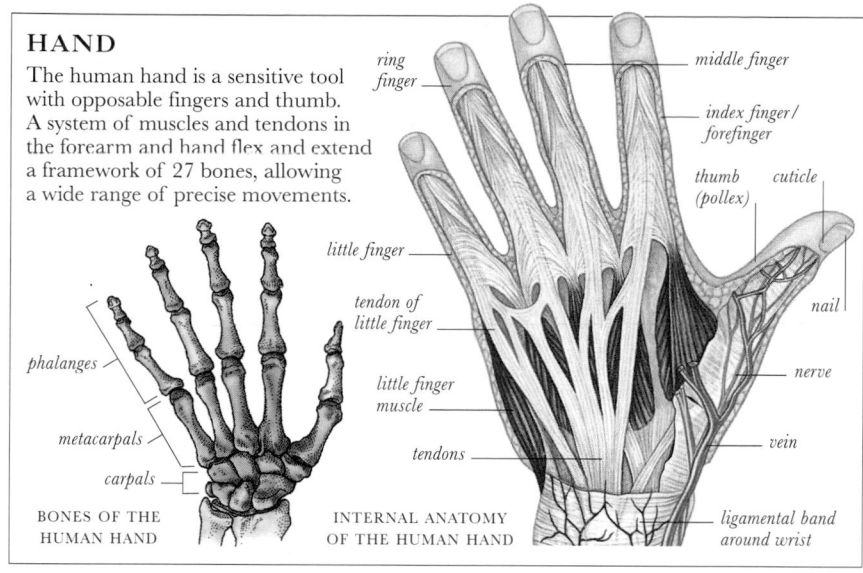

ring finger

middle finger

index finger/forefinger

thumb (pollex)

cuticle

little finger

tendon of little finger

nail

little finger muscle

nerve

phalanges

vein

metacarpals

tendons

carpals

ligamental band around wrist

BONES OF THE HUMAN HAND

INTERNAL ANATOMY OF THE HUMAN HAND

handbasin *n.* a small washbasin.

handbell *n.* a small bell rung by hand, esp. one of a set giving a range of notes.

handbill *n.* a printed notice distributed by hand.

handbook *n.* a short manual or guidebook.

handbrake *n.* a brake operated by hand.

h. & c. *abbr. Brit.* hot and cold (water).

handcart *n.* a small cart pushed or drawn by hand.

handclap *n.* a clapping of the hands.

handcraft ● *n.* = HANDICRAFT. ● *v.tr.* make by handicraft.

handcuff ● *n.* (in *pl.*) ▶ a pair of lockable linked metal rings for securing a prisoner's wrists. ● *v.tr.* put handcuffs on.

-handed *adj.* (in *comb.*) **1** for or involving a specified number of hands (in various senses) (*two handed*). **2** using chiefly the hand specified (*left-handed*). □ **-handedly** *adv.* **-handedness** *n.* (both in sense 2).

handful *n.* (*pl.* **-fuls**) **1** a quantity that fills the hand. **2** a small number or amount. **3** *colloq.* a troublesome person or task.

hand grenade see GRENADE.

handgrip *n.* **1** a grasp with the hand. **2** a handle designed for easy holding.

handgun *n.* a small firearm held in and fired with one hand. ▷ GUN

hand-held ● *adj.* designed to be held in the hand. ● *n.* a small hand-held computer.

handhold *n.* something for the hands to grip on (in climbing, sailing, etc.).

handicap ● *n.* **1 a** a disadvantage imposed on a superior competitor in order to make the chances more equal. **b** a race or contest in which this is imposed. **2** the number of strokes by which a golfer normally exceeds par for the course. **3** a thing that makes progress or success difficult. **4** a condition that markedly restricts a person's ability to function physically, mentally, or socially. ● *v.tr.* (**handicapped, handicapping**) **1** impose a handicap on. **2** place at a disadvantage. [probably from phrase *hand in cap*: the cap held forfeit money in a game of chance (17th c.)] □ **handicapper** *n.*

handicapped *adj.* suffering from a physical or mental disability.

handicraft *n.* work that requires both manual and artistic skill. [Middle English]

HANDCUFF: 19TH-CENTURY BRITISH HANDCUFFS

handiwork *n.* work done or a thing made by hand, or by a particular person. [Old English]

handkerchief *n.* (*pl.* **handkerchiefs** or **-chieves**) a square of cloth for wiping one's nose, etc.

handle ● *n.* **1** the part by which a thing is held, carried, or controlled. **2** a fact that may be taken advantage of (*gave a handle to his critics*). **3** *colloq.* a personal title. **4** the feel of goods when handled. ● *v.tr.* **1** touch, feel, operate, or move with the hands. **2** manage or deal with (*knows how to handle people*). **3** deal in (goods). **4** discuss or write about (a subject). [Old English] □ **handleable** *adj.* **handleability** *n.* **handled** *adj.* (also in *comb.*).

handlebar *n.* (often in *pl.*) the steering bar of a bicycle etc. ▷ BICYCLE

handlebar moustache *n.* a thick moustache extended sideways with curved ends.

handler *n.* **1** a person who handles or deals in certain commodities. **2** a person who trains and looks after an animal (esp. a police dog).

handmade *adj.* made by hand and not by machine.

handmaid *n.* (also **handmaiden**) *archaic* a female servant.

hand-me-down *n.* an article of clothing etc. passed on from another person.

handout *n.* **1** something given free to a needy person. **2** a statement given to the press etc.

handover *n.* esp. *Brit.* the act or an instance of handing over.

hand-pick *v.tr.* (usu. as **handpicked** *adj.*) choose carefully or personally.

handpump *n.* a pump operated by hand.

handrail *n.* a narrow rail for holding as a support.

handsaw *n.* a saw worked by one hand. ▷ SAW

handset *n.* a telephone mouthpiece and earpiece forming one unit. ▷ TELEPHONE

handshake *n.* the shaking of a person's hand with one's own as a greeting etc.

handsome *adj.* (**handsomer, handsomest**) **1** (esp. of a man) good-looking. **2** imposing, fine (*handsome building*; *handsome stallion*). **3 a** generous, liberal (*a handsome present*). **b** (of a price, fortune, etc., as assets gained) considerable. [Middle English in sense 'easily handled, suitable'] □ **handsomeness** *n.*

handsomely *adv.* **1** generously, liberally. **2** finely, beautifully. **3** *Naut.* carefully.

handspike *n.* a wooden rod shod with iron, used as a lever on board ship and by artillery soldiers.

handspring *n.* a somersault in which one lands first on the hands and then on the feet.

handstand *n.* an act of balancing on one's hands with the feet in the air or against a wall.

hand-to-hand *adj.* (of fighting) at close quarters.

hand tool *n.* a tool operated by hand without electricity.

handwork *n.* work done with the hands. □ **handworked** *adj.*

handwriting *n.* **1** writing with a pen, pencil, etc. ▷ CALLIGRAPHY. **2** a person's particular style of writing. □ **handwritten** *adj.*

handy *adj.* (**handier, handiest**) **1** convenient to handle or use. **2** ready to hand. **3** clever with the hands. □ **handily** *adv.* **handiness** *n.*

handyman *n.* (*pl.* **-men**) a person able or employed to do occasional domestic repairs and minor renovations.

hang ● *v.* (*past* and *past part.* **hung** except in sense 7) **1** *tr.* **a** secure or cause to be supported from above, esp. with the lower part free. **b** (foll. by *up, on, on to*, etc.) attach loosely by suspending from the top. **2** *tr.* set up (a door, gate, etc.) on its hinges. **3** *tr.* place (a picture) on a wall or in an exhibition. **4** *tr.* attach (wallpaper) to a wall. **5** *tr.* (foll. by *on*) *colloq.* attach the blame for (a thing) to (a person) (*you can't hang that on me*). **6** *tr.* (foll. by *with*) decorate by hanging pictures or decorations etc. (*a hall hung with tapestries*). **7** *tr.* & *intr.* (*past* and *past part.* **hanged**) **a** suspend or be suspended by the neck until dead, esp. as a form of capital punishment. **b** as a mild oath (*hang the expense*; *let everything go hang*). **8** *tr.* let droop (*hang one's head*). **9** *tr.* suspend (meat or game) from a hook and leave it until dry or tender or high. **10** *intr.* be or remain hung (in various senses). **11** *intr.* remain static in the air. **12** *intr.* be present or imminent, esp. oppressively or threateningly (*a hush hung over the room*). **13** *intr.* (foll. by *on*) **a** be dependent on (*everything hangs on the discussions*). **b** listen closely to (*hangs on their every word*). ● *n.* **1** the way a thing hangs or falls. **2** a downward droop or bend. □ **be hung up on** *slang* have a psychological obsession or problem about (*is hung up on her father*). **get the hang of** *colloq.* understand the technique or meaning of. **hang around** (also *Brit.* **about**) **1 a** loiter or dally; not move away. **b** linger near (a person or place). **c** wait. **2** (foll. by *with*) associate with (a person etc.). **hang back 1** show reluctance to act or move. **2** remain behind. **hang fire** be slow in taking action or in progressing. **hang heavily** (or **heavy**) (of time) pass slowly. **hang in** esp. *N. Amer. colloq.* **1** persist, persevere. **2** linger. **hang on 1** (foll. by *to*) continue or persevere. **2** (often foll. by *to*) continue to hold or grasp. **3** (foll. by *to*) retain; fail to give back. **4 a** *colloq.* wait for a short time. **b** (in telephoning) continue to listen during a pause in the conversation. **hang out 1** hang from a window, clothes line, etc. **2** protrude or cause to protrude downwards. **3** (foll. by *of*) lean out of (a window etc.). **4** *slang* reside or be often present. **hang together 1** make sense. **2** remain associated. **hang up 1** hang from a hook, peg, etc. **2** end a telephone conversation, esp. (foll. by *on*) abruptly (*then he hung up on me*). **not care** (or **give**) **a hang** *colloq.* not care at all. [Old English, partly from Old Norse]

hangar *n.* a building for housing aircraft etc. [French] □ **hangarage** *n.*

hangdog *adj.* shamefaced.

hanger *n.* **1** a person or thing that hangs. **2** (in full **coat-hanger**) a shaped piece of wood or plastic etc. from which clothes may be hung.

hanger-on *n.* (*pl.* **hangers-on**) a follower or dependant.

hang-glider *n.* a frame with a fabric aerofoil stretched over it, from which the pilot is suspended, controlling its flight by body movement. □ **hang-glide** *v.intr.* **hang-gliding** *n.*

hanging ● *n.* **1 a** the practice or an act of executing by hanging a person. **b** (*attrib.*) meriting or causing this (*a hanging offence*). **2** (usu. in *pl.*) draperies hung on a wall etc. ● *adj.* **1** that hangs or is hung; suspended. **2** situated on a steep slope (*hanging gardens*; *hanging glacier*).

H

H

hangman *n.* (*pl.* **-men**) **1** an ´executioner who hangs condemned persons. **2** a game for two in which failed attempts to guess the letters of a word are recorded by drawing a gallows and someone hanging on it.

hangnail *n.* = AGNAIL. [alteration of AGNAIL]

hang-out *n. slang* a place one lives in or frequently visits.

hangover *n.* **1** a severe headache or other after-effects caused by drinking an excess of alcohol. **2** a survival from the past.

Hang Seng index *n.* a figure indicating the relative price of representative shares on the Hong Kong Stock Exchange. [from *Hang Seng*, name of a Hong Kong bank]

hang-up *n. slang* an emotional problem or inhibition.

hank *n.* a coil or skein of wool or thread etc. [from Old Norse *hönk*]

hanker *v.intr.* (foll. by *for, after,* or *to* + infin.) long for; crave. □ **hankerer** *n.* **hankering** *n.*

hanky *n.* (also **hankie**) (*pl.* **-ies**) *colloq.* a handkerchief.

hanky-panky *n. slang* **1** naughtiness, esp. sexual. **2** dishonest dealing; trickery. [19th-century coinage]

Hanoverian /han-ŏ-veer-iăn/ *adj.* of or relating to the British sovereigns from George I to Victoria (1714–1901). [from *Hanover* in Germany, whose Elector became George I in 1714]

Hansard *n.* the official verbatim record of debates in the British Parliament. [named after T. C. *Hansard*, English printer, died 1833, who first printed it]

Hansen's disease *n.* = LEPROSY 1. [named after G. H. A. *Hansen*, Norwegian physician, 1841–1912]

hansom *n.* (in full **hansom cab**) *hist.* ▼ a two-wheeled horse-drawn cab accommodating two inside, with the driver seated behind. [named after J. A. *Hansom*, English architect, 1803–82, who designed it]

HANSOM:
19TH-CENTURY
BRITISH HANSOM CAB

Hanukkah /han-uu-kă/ *n.* (also **Chanukkah**) the Jewish festival of lights, commemorating the purification of the Temple in 165 BC. [from Hebrew *ḥā nukkāh* 'consecration']

hap *n. archaic* **1** chance, luck. **2** a chance occurrence. [from Old Norse *happ*]

ha'penny var. of HALFPENNY.

haphazard ● *adj.* done etc. by chance; random. ● *adv.* at random. □ **haphazardly** *adv.* **haphazardness** *n.*

hapless *adj.* unfortunate. □ **haplessly** *adv.* **haplessness** *n.*

haploid *adj. Biol.* **1** (of a cell) having a single set of unpaired chromosomes. ▷ MEIOSIS. **2** (of an organism) composed of haploid cells. [from Greek *haplous* 'single' + *eidos* 'form']

happen ● *v.intr.* **1** occur. **2** (foll. by *to* + infin.) have the (good or bad) fortune to (*I happened to meet her*). **3** (foll. by *to*) be the (esp. unwelcome) fate or experience of (*I hope nothing happens to them*). **4** (foll. by *on*) encounter or discover by chance. ● *adv. N.Engl. dial.*

perhaps, maybe (*happen it'll rain*). □ **as it happens** in fact (*as it happens, it turned out well*). [Middle English]

happening ● *n.* **1** an event or occurrence. **2** an improvised or spontaneous theatrical etc. performance. ● *adj. slang* exciting, fashionable, trendy.

happenstance *n. esp. N. Amer.* a thing that happens by chance.

happy *adj.* (**happier, happiest**) **1** feeling or showing pleasure or contentment. **2 a** fortunate; characterized by happiness. **b** (of words, behaviour, etc.) apt, pleasing. **3** *colloq.* slightly drunk. **4** (in *comb.*) *colloq.* inclined to use excessively or at random (*trigger-happy*). □ **happy as a sandboy** see SANDBOY. [Middle English] □ **happily** *adv.* **happiness** *n.*

happy event *n. colloq.* the birth of a child.

happy families *n. Brit.* a card game the object of which is to acquire four members of the same 'family'.

happy-go-lucky *adj.* cheerfully casual.

happy hour *n.* a period of the day when drinks are sold at reduced prices.

happy hunting ground *n.* a place where success or enjoyment is obtained.

happy medium *n.* a satisfactory compromise; the avoidance of extremes.

hara-kiri *n.* ritual suicide by disembowelment with a sword, formerly practised by Samurai to avoid dishonour. [colloquial Japanese, from *hara* 'belly' + *kiri* 'cutting']

harangue /hă-rang/ ● *n.* a lengthy and earnest speech. ● *v.tr.* lecture or make a harangue to. [from medieval Latin *harenga*]

harass /ha-răs/ *v.tr.* **1** trouble and annoy continually or repeatedly. **2** make repeated attacks on. [from Old French *harer* 'to set a dog on'] □ **harasser** *n.* **harassment** *n.*

■ **Usage** This word is also often pronounced with the stress on the second syllable, but this is considered incorrect by some people.

harbinger /har-bin-jer/ *n.* **1** a person or thing that announces or signals the approach of another. **2** a forerunner. [originally in sense 'a person who provides lodging': based on Old French *herberge* 'lodging']

harbour (*US* **harbor**) ● *n.* **1** a place of shelter for ships. **2** a shelter; a place of refuge or protection. ● *v.* **1** *tr.* give shelter to (esp. a criminal or wanted person). **2** *tr.* keep in one's mind, esp. resentfully (*harbour a grudge*). **3** *intr.* come to anchor in a harbour. [Old English]

harbour master *n.* (*US* **harbormaster**) an official in charge of a harbour.

hard ● *adj.* **1** (of a substance, material, etc.) firm and solid. **2 a** difficult to understand or explain (*a hard problem*). **b** difficult to accomplish (*a hard decision*). **c** (foll. by *to* + infin.) not easy to (*hard to believe; hard to please*). **3** difficult to bear (*a hard life*). **4** unfeeling; severely critical. **5** (of a season or the weather) severe (*a hard winter; a hard frost*). **6** harsh or unpleasant to the senses (*hard colours*). **7 a** strenuous, enthusiastic, intense (*a hard worker; a hard fight*). **b** severe, uncompromising (*a hard bargain; hard words*). **c** *Polit.* extreme; most radical (*the hard right*). **8 a** (of liquor) strongly alcoholic. **b** (of drugs) potent and addictive. **c** (of radiation) highly penetrating. **d** (of pornography) highly obscene. **9** (of water) containing mineral salts that make lathering difficult. **10** established; not disputable (*hard facts*). **11** *Stock Exch.* (of currency, prices, etc.) high; not likely to fall in value. **12** (of a consonant) guttural (as *c* in *cat, g* in *go*). ● *adv.* **1** strenuously, intensely, copiously (*try hard; look hard at; is raining hard*). **2** with difficulty or effort (*hard-earned*). **3** so as to be hard or firm (*the jelly set hard*). ● *n. Brit.* **1** a sloping roadway across a foreshore. **2** *slang* = HARD LABOUR (*got two years' hard*). □ **be hard on 1** be difficult for. **2** be severe in one's treatment or criticism of. **3** be unpleasant to (the

senses). **be hard put to it** (usu. foll. by *to* + infin.) find it difficult. **hard at it** *colloq.* busily working or occupied. **hard by** near; close by. **a hard case 1** *colloq.* **a** an intractable person. **b** *Austral.* & *NZ* an amusing or eccentric person. **2** a case of hardship. **hard on** (or **upon**) close to in pursuit etc. **put the hard word on** *Austral.* & *NZ slang* ask a favour of. [Old English] □ **hardish** *adj.* **hardness** *n.*

hard and fast *adj.* (of a rule or a distinction made) definite, unalterable, strict.

hardback ● *adj.* (of a book) bound in stiff covers. ● *n.* a hardback book.

hardball *n. N. Amer.* **1** = BASEBALL. **2** *slang* uncompromising methods or dealings, esp. in politics (*play hardball*).

hardbitten *adj. colloq.* tough and cynical.

hardboard *n.* stiff board made of compressed and treated wood pulp.

hard-boiled *adj.* **1** (of an egg) boiled until the white and the yolk are solid. **2** (of a person) tough, shrewd.

hard cash *n.* negotiable coins and banknotes.

hard cheese see CHEESE[1].

hard copy *n.* printed material produced by computer.

hard-core *adj.* **1** forming a nucleus or centre. **2** blatant, uncompromising. **3** (of pornography) explicit, obscene. **4** (of drug addiction) relating to 'hard' drugs.

hard core *n.* **1** an irreducible nucleus. **2** *colloq.* **a** the most committed members of a society etc. **b** a conservative or reactionary minority. **3** (usu. **hard-core**) *Brit.* solid material forming the foundation of a road etc. **4** (usu. **hardcore**) popular music that is experimental in nature and usu. characterized by high volume and aggressive presentation.

hardcover *adj.* & *n. esp. N. Amer.* = HARDBACK.

hard disk *n. Computing* ▼ a rigid usu. magnetic disk, having a large data storage capacity. ▷ COMPUTER

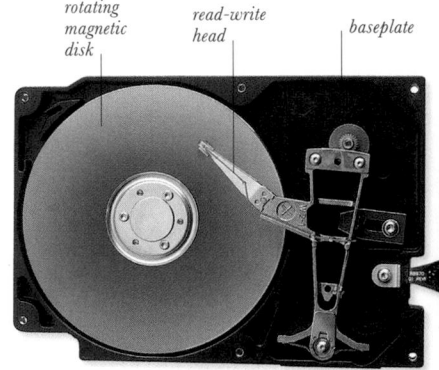

rotating magnetic disk   *read-write head*   *baseplate*

HARD DISK

hard-done-by *adj. Brit.* unfairly treated.

hard-earned *adj.* that has taken a great deal of effort to earn or acquire.

harden *v.* **1** *tr.* & *intr.* make or become hard or harder. **2** *intr.* & *tr.* become, or make (one's attitude etc.), less sympathetic. **3** *intr.* (of prices etc.) cease to fall or fluctuate. □ **harden off** inure (a plant) to cold by gradual increase of its exposure. □ **hardener** *n.*

hardening *n.* **1** the process or an instance of becoming hard. **2** (in full **hardening of the arteries**) *Med.* = ARTERIOSCLEROSIS.

hard feelings *n.pl.* feelings of resentment.

hard hat *n.* **1** protective headgear worn on building sites etc. **2** *colloq.* a reactionary person.

hard-headed *adj.* practical, realistic; not sentimental. □ **hard-headedly** *adv.* **hard-headedness** *n.*

hard-hearted *adj.* unfeeling, unsympathetic. □ **hard-heartedly** *adv.* **hard-heartedness** *n.*

hardihood *n.* boldness, daring.

hard labour *n.* heavy manual work as a punishment, esp. in a prison.

hard line ● *n.* unyielding adherence to a firm policy. ● *attrib.adj.* (**hardline**) unyielding, strict, firm. □ **hardliner** *n.*

hard lines *n.pl. Brit. colloq.* = HARD LUCK.

hard luck *n.* worse fortune than one deserves.

hardly *adv.* **1** scarcely; only just (*we hardly knew them*). **2** only with difficulty (*could hardly speak*). **3** harshly. □ **hardly any** almost no; almost none. **hardly ever** very rarely.

■ **Usage** *Hardly* should not be used with negative constructions. Expressions such as *I couldn't hardly see* are non-standard; the correct form is *I could hardly see.*

hard-nosed *adj. colloq.* realistic, uncompromising.

hard nut *n. slang* a tough, aggressive person.

hard of hearing *adj.* somewhat deaf.

hard-on *n. coarse slang* an erection of the penis.

hard pad *n.* a form of distemper in dogs etc.

hard palate *n.* the front part of the palate. ▷ HEAD

hardpan *n. Geol.* a hardened layer of clay occurring in or below the soil profile.

hard-pressed *adj.* **1** closely pursued. **2** burdened with urgent business.

hard roe see ROE[1] 1.

hard sell *n.* aggressive salesmanship.

hardship *n.* **1** severe suffering or privation. **2** the circumstance causing this.

hard shoulder *n. Brit.* a hardened strip alongside a motorway for stopping on in an emergency.

hardstanding *n.* an area of hard material for a vehicle to stand on when not in use.

hard stuff *n. colloq.* strong alcoholic drink, esp. whisky.

hard tack *n.* a ship's biscuit.

hard up *adj.* **1** short of money. **2** (foll. by *for*) at a loss for; lacking.

hardware *n.* **1** tools and household articles of metal etc. **2** heavy machinery or armaments. **3** the mechanical and electronic components of a computer etc.

hard-wearing *adj.* able to stand much wear.

hard-wired *adj.* involving or achieved by permanently connected circuits designed to perform a specific function.

hardwood *n.* the wood from a deciduous broadleaved tree. ▷ WOOD

hard-working *adj.* diligent.

hardy *adj.* (**hardier**, **hardiest**) **1** robust; capable of enduring difficult conditions. **2** (of a plant) able to grow in the open air all the year. [from Old French *hardi* 'emboldened'] □ **hardiness** *n.*

hardy annual *n.* **1** an annual plant that may be sown in the open. **2** *Brit. joc.* a subject that comes up at regular intervals.

hare ● *n.* **1** any of various mammals esp. of the genus *Lepus* resembling a large rabbit. ▷ LAGOMORPH. **2** (in full **electric hare**) a dummy hare propelled by electricity, used in greyhound racing. ● *v.intr.* run with great speed. □ **start a hare** *Brit.* raise a topic of conversation. [Old English]

harebell *n.* ▶ a plant, *Campanula rotundifolia*, with slender stems and pale blue bell-shaped flowers. Also (esp. *Sc.*) called *bluebell.*

hare-brained *adj.* rash, wild.

harelip *n.* often *offens.* = CLEFT LIP. □ **harelipped** *adj.*

■ **Usage** *Harelip* is now usually regarded as offensive; *cleft lip* is the preferred term.

HAREBELL
(*Campanula rotundifolia*)

HARNESS

A harness consists of three or more main elements. The bridle and reins are used by the driver to control the horse. The collar around its neck enables the horse to draw its load. Breeching straps allow it to brake or to reverse the load.

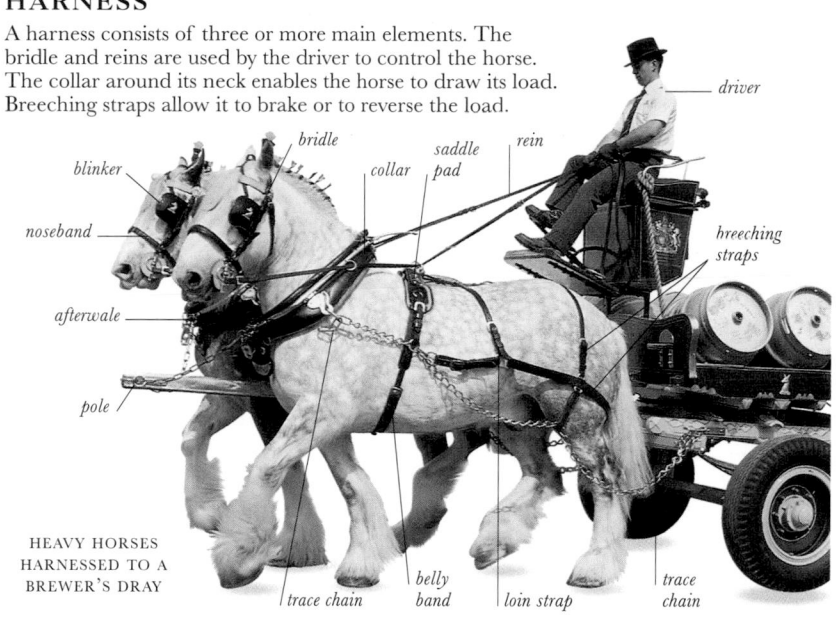

HEAVY HORSES
HARNESSED TO A
BREWER'S DRAY

driver
rein
saddle pad
collar
bridle
blinker
breeching straps
noseband
afterwale
pole
trace chain
belly band
loin strap
trace chain

---

harem /har-*eem*/ *n.* **1** the women of a Muslim household, living in a separate part of the house. **2** their quarters. [from Arabic *ḥarām*, literally 'prohibited place']

haricot /*ha*-ri-koh/ *n.* (in full **haricot bean**) a variety of French bean with small white seeds dried and used as a vegetable. ▷ PULSE. [French]

hark *v.intr.* (usu. in *imper.*) *archaic* listen attentively. □ **hark back** revert to a topic discussed earlier. [Old English]

harken var. of HEARKEN.

harlequin ● *n.* (**Harlequin**) a mute character in pantomime, usu. masked and dressed in a diamond-patterned costume. ● *adj.* in varied colours. [French, from earlier *Herlequin*, leader of a legendary troop of horsemen]

harlequinade *n.* **1** the part of a pantomime featuring Harlequin. **2** a piece of buffoonery.

harlot *n. archaic* a prostitute. [Middle English in sense 'lad, knave': from Old French *harlot*] □ **harlotry** *n.*

harm ● *n.* hurt, damage. ● *v.tr.* cause harm to. □ **out of harm's way** in safety. [Old English]

harmful *adj.* causing or likely to cause harm. □ **harmfulness** *n.* **harmfully** *adv.*

harmless *adj.* **1** not able or likely to cause harm. **2** inoffensive. □ **harmlessly** *adv.* **harmlessness** *n.*

harmonic ● *adj.* **1** of or characterized by harmony; harmonious. **2** *Mus.* **a** of or relating to harmony. **b** (of a tone) produced by vibration of a string etc. in an exact fraction of its length. ● *n. Mus.* an overtone accompanying at a fixed interval (and forming a note with) a fundamental tone. [from Greek *harmonikos*] □ **harmonically** *adv.*

harmonica *n.* ▶ a small rectangular wind instrument played by blowing or sucking air through it.

reed chamber

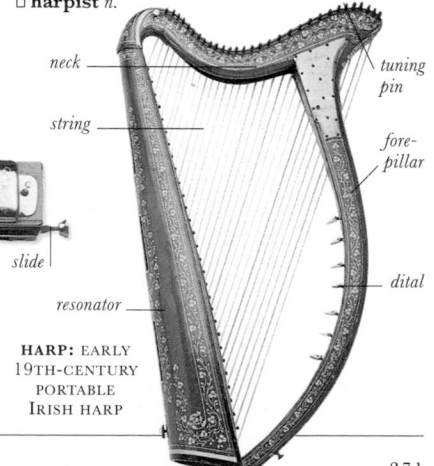

HARMONICA

slide

harmonious *adj.* **1** sweet-sounding, tuneful. **2** forming a pleasing or consistent whole. **3** free from disagreement or dissent. □ **harmoniously** *adv.* **harmoniousness** *n.*

harmonium *n.* a keyboard instrument in which air is driven through metal reeds by bellows operated by the feet. [based on Latin *harmonia* 'harmony']

harmonize *v.* (also **-ise**) **1** *tr.* add notes to (a melody) to produce harmony. **2** *tr. & intr.* (often followed by *with*) bring into or be in harmony. **3** *intr.* make or form a pleasing or consistent whole. □ **harmonization** *n.*

harmony *n.* (*pl.* **-ies**) **1 a** a combination of simultaneously sounded musical notes to produce chords and chord progressions, esp. as having a pleasing effect. **b** the study of this. **2 a** an apt or aesthetic arrangement of parts. **b** the pleasing effect of this. **3** agreement, concord. **4** a collation of parallel narratives, esp. of the Gospels. □ **in harmony 1** (of singing etc.) producing chords; not discordant. **2** in agreement, concord. **harmony of the spheres** see SPHERE. [from Greek *harmonia* 'concord']

harness ● *n.* **1** ▲ the equipment of straps and fittings by which an animal is fastened to a cart etc. and controlled. **2** a similar arrangement for fastening a thing to a person's body, for restraining a young child, etc. ● *v.tr.* **1 a** put a harness on. **b** (foll. by *to*) attach by a harness. **2** make use of (natural resources) esp. to produce energy. □ **in harness** in the routine of daily work. [from Old Norse *herr* 'army' + *nest* 'provisions']

harp ● *n.* ▼ a large upright roughly triangular musical instrument consisting of a frame housing a series of strings, played by plucking with the fingers. ▷ ORCHESTRA, STRINGED. ● *v.intr.* (foll. by *on*, *on about*) talk repeatedly and tediously about. [Old English] □ **harpist** *n.*

neck
tuning pin
string
fore-pillar
slide
dital
resonator

HARP: EARLY
19TH-CENTURY
PORTABLE
IRISH HARP

harpoon ● *n.* a barbed spearlike missile with a rope attached, for catching whales etc. ● *v.tr.* spear with a harpoon. [from Greek *harpē* 'sickle'] □ **harpooner** *n.*

harpsichord *n.* a keyboard instrument with horizontal strings which are plucked mechanically. [from Late Latin *harpa* 'harp' + *chorda* 'string'] □ **harpsichordist** *n.*

harpy *n.* (*pl.* **-ies**) **1** (in Greek and Roman mythology) a monster with a woman's head and body and bird's wings and claws. **2** a grasping unscrupulous person. [from Greek *harpuiai* 'snatchers']

harquebus /har-kwi-bŭs/ *n.* (also **arquebus**) *hist.* an early type of portable gun supported on a tripod or on a forked rest. [from French *(h)arquebuse*]

harridan *n.* a bad-tempered old woman. [17th-century slang]

harrier[1] *n.* a person who harries or lays waste.

harrier[2] *n.* **1** a hound used for hunting hares. **2** (in *pl.*) (usu. **Harriers** as part of a club's name) cross-country runners as a group or club. [based on HARE]

harrier[3] *n.* ▼ any bird of prey of the genus *Circus*, with long wings for swooping over the ground. [earlier *harrower*, from *harrow* 'to harry, rob']

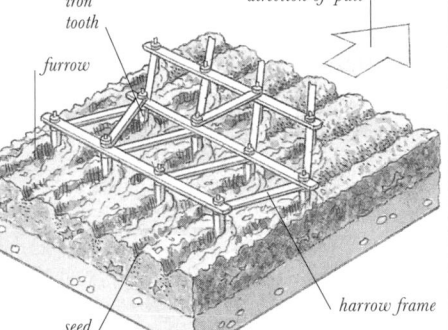

HARRIER:
MARSH HARRIER
(*Circus aeruginosus*)

harrow ● *n.* ▼ a heavy frame with iron teeth dragged over ploughed land to break up clods, remove weeds, cover seed, etc. ● *v.tr.* **1** draw a harrow over (land). **2** (usu. as **harrowing** *adj.*) distress greatly. [from Old Norse *hervi*] □ **harrowingly** *adv.*

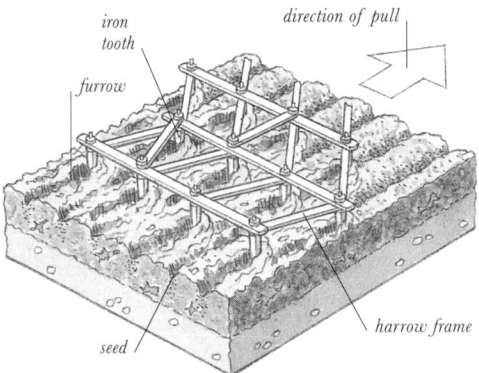

direction of pull

iron tooth

furrow

seed

harrow frame

HARROW: ACTION OF A HARROW

harry *v.tr.* (**-ies**, **-ied**) **1** ravage or despoil. **2** harass. [related to Old English *here* 'army']

harsh *adj.* **1** unpleasantly rough or sharp, esp. to the senses. **2** severe, cruel. [from Middle Low German *harsch* 'rough'] □ **harshen** *v.tr. & intr.* **harshly** *adv.* **harshness** *n.*

harslet var. of HASLET.

hart *n.* the male of the deer (esp. the red deer) usu. over five years old. [Old English]

hartebeest /har-ti-beest/ *n.* any large African antelope of the genus *Alcelaphus*, with ringed horns bent back at the tips. [from Dutch *hert* 'hart' + *beest* 'beast']

harum-scarum /hair-ŭm-**skair**-ŭm/ *colloq.* ● *adj.* wild and reckless. ● *n.* such a person. [based on HARE and SCARE]

harvest ● *n.* **1 a** the process of gathering in crops etc. **b** the season when this takes place. **2** the season's yield. **3** the product of any action. ● *v.tr.* **1** gather as a harvest, reap. **2** experience (consequences). [Old English] □ **harvestable** *adj.*

harvester *n.* **1** a reaper. **2** a reaping machine.

harvest festival *n.* a thanksgiving festival for the harvest, esp. *Brit.* a church service.

harvestman *n.* (*pl.* **-men**) any of various arachnids of the order Opiliones, with very long thin legs. ▷ ARACHNID

harvest moon *n.* the full moon nearest to the autumn equinox.

harvest mouse *n.* ▶ a small mouse, *Micromys minutus*, that nests in the stalks of growing grain.

has *3rd sing. present* of HAVE.

has-been *n. colloq.* a person or thing that has lost a former importance.

hash[1] ● *n.* **1** a dish of cooked meat cut into small pieces and recooked. **2 a** a mixture; a jumble. **b** a mess. **3** reused or recycled material. ● *v.tr.* (often foll. by *up*) **1** make (meat etc.) into a hash. **2** recycle (old material). □ **make a hash of** *colloq.* make a mess of; bungle. **settle a person's hash** *colloq.* deal with and subdue a person. [based on French *hache* 'hatchet']

hash[2] *n. colloq.* hashish.

hash[3] *n.* (also **hash sign**) the symbol #.

hashish /hash-eesh/ *n.* a resinous product of the top leaves and tender parts of hemp, smoked or chewed for its narcotic effects. [from Arabic *ḥašīš* 'dry herb, powdered hemp leaves']

haslet *n.* (also **harslet**) pieces of offal cooked together and usu. compressed into a meat loaf. [from Old French *hastelet* 'little (piece of) roast meat']

hasn't *contr.* has not.

hasp *n.* a hinged metal clasp that fits over a staple and can be secured by a padlock. [Old English]

hassle *colloq.* ● *n.* **1** a prolonged trouble or inconvenience. **2** an argument. ● *v.* **1** *tr.* harass, annoy. **2** *intr.* argue, quarrel. [20th-century coinage, originally dialect]

hassock *n.* a thick firm cushion for kneeling on, esp. in church. [Old English]

haste ● *n.* **1** urgency of movement or action. **2** excessive hurry. ● *v.intr. archaic* = HASTEN. □ **in haste** quickly; hurriedly. **make haste** hurry; be quick. [from Old French]

hasten *v.* **1** *intr.* make haste; hurry. **2** *tr.* cause to occur or be ready or be done sooner.

hasty *adj.* (**hastier**, **hastiest**) **1** hurried; acting too quickly or hurriedly. **2** said, made, or done too quickly or too soon; rash. **3** quick-tempered. □ **hastily** *adv.* **hastiness** *n.*

hat *n.* **1** ▼ a covering for the head, often with a brim and worn out of doors. **2** *colloq.* a person's occupation or capacity, esp. one of several (*wearing his managerial hat*). □ **hats off** (as *int.*; foll. by *to*) expressing admiration or appreciation. **keep it under one's hat** *colloq.* keep it secret. **out of a hat** by random selection. **pass the hat** (or *Brit.* **the hat round**) collect contributions of money. **take off one's hat to** *colloq.* acknowledge admiration for. **throw one's hat in the ring** take up a challenge. □ **hatful** *n.* (*pl.* **-fuls**). **hatless** *adj.* [Old English]

hatband *n.* a band of ribbon etc. round a hat above the brim. ▷ HAT

hatbox *n.* a box to hold a hat, esp. for travelling.

hatch[1] *n.* **1** an opening between two rooms, e.g. between a kitchen and a dining room for serving food. **2** an opening or door in an aircraft, spacecraft, etc. **3** *Naut.* **a** = HATCHWAY. **b** a trapdoor or cover for this (often in *pl.*: *batten the hatches*). [Old English]

hatch[2] ● *v.* **1** *intr.* **a** (often foll. by *out*) (of a young bird or fish etc.) emerge from the egg. **b** (of an egg) produce a young animal. **2** *tr.* incubate (an egg). **3** *tr.* (also foll. by *up*) devise (a plot etc.). ● *n.* **1** the act or an instance of hatching. **2** a brood hatched. [Middle English]

hatch[3] *v.tr.* mark (a surface) with close parallel lines. [from French *hacher* 'to draw lines upon'] □ **hatching** *n.*

HARVEST MOUSE
(*Micromys minutus*)

HAT

Hats may be worn to provide protection from extremes of the weather or to signify the social status of the wearer. In addition to these functions, hats are viewed as fashion accessories.

brim

crease

crown

hatband

trimming

STETSON
(10X Beaver Stetson™)

EXAMPLES OF OTHER HATS

STRAW BOATER

BERET

TOP HAT

PANAMA

BASEBALL CAP

BOWLER

hatchback *n.* a car with a sloping back hinged at the top to form a door. ▷ CAR

hatchery *n.* (*pl.* **-ies**) a place for hatching eggs, esp. of fish or poultry.

hatchet *n.* a light short-handled axe. [from Old French *hachette* 'little axe']

hatchet job *n. colloq.* a fierce verbal attack on a person, esp. in print.

hatchet man *n. colloq.* **1** a hired killer. **2** a person employed to carry out a hatchet job.

hatchway *n.* an opening in a ship's deck for lowering cargo into the hold. ▷ SHIP

hate ● *v.tr.* **1** feel intense dislike towards. **2 a** dislike. **b** (foll. by verbal noun or *to* + infin.) be reluctant (to do something). ● *n.* **1** hatred. **2** *colloq.* a hated person or thing (esp. in phr. **pet hate**). [Old English] □ **hatable** *adj.* (also **hateable**). **hater** *n.*

hateful *adj.* arousing hatred. □ **hatefully** *adv.* **hatefulness** *n.*

hate mail *n.* usu. anonymous letters of hostility towards the recipient.

hatpin *n.* a long pin, often decorative, for securing a hat to the hair.

hatred *n.* intense dislike or ill will.

hatstand *n.* a stand with hooks on which to hang hats.

hatter *n.* a maker or seller of hats.

hat-trick *n.* **1** *Cricket* the taking of three wickets by the same bowler with three successive balls. **2** three goals, points, (esp. consecutive) successes, etc.

haughty *adj.* (**haughtier**, **haughtiest**) arrogantly self-admiring and disdainful. [from Latin *altus* 'high'] □ **haughtily** *adv.* **haughtiness** *n.*

haul ● *v.* **1** *tr.* pull or drag forcibly. **2** *tr.* transport by lorry, cart, etc. **3** *intr.* turn a ship's course. **4** *tr.* (usu. foll. by *up*) *colloq.* bring for reprimand or trial. ● *n.* **1** the act or an instance of hauling. **2** an amount gained or acquired. **3** a distance to be traversed (*a short haul*). □ **haul over the coals** see COAL. [variant of HALE²] □ **hauler** *n.*

haulage *n.* **1** the commercial transport of goods. **2** a charge for this.

haulier *n. Brit.* a person or firm engaged in the transport of goods.

haulm *n.* (also **halm**) **1** a stalk or stem. **2** the stalks or stems collectively of peas, beans, potatoes, etc. [Old English]

haunch *n.* **1** the fleshy part of the buttock with the thigh, esp. in animals. **2** the leg and loin of a deer etc. as food. [from Old French *hanche*]

haunt ● *v.tr.* **1** *tr.* **a** (of a ghost) visit (a place) regularly. **b** (as **haunted** *adj.*) frequented by a ghost. **2** frequent (a place). **3** (of a memory etc.) be persistently in the mind of. ● *n.* **1** (often in *pl.*) a place frequented by a person. **2** a place frequented by animals, esp. for food and drink. [from Old French *hanter*] □ **haunter** *n.*

haunting *adj.* (of a melody etc.) wistful, evocative. □ **hauntingly** *adv.*

Hausa /how-să/ ● *n.* (*pl.* same or **Hausas**) **1** a member of a people of W. Africa and Sudan. **2** the Hamitic language of this people, widely used in W. Africa. ● *adj.* of or relating to this people or language. [native name]

haute couture /oht koo-tewr/ *n.* high fashion; the leading fashion houses. [French, literally 'high dressmaking']

haute cuisine /oht kwi-zeen/ *n.* cookery of a high standard. [French, literally 'high cookery']

hauteur /oh-ter/ *n.* haughtiness of manner. [French]

have (3rd *sing. present* **has**; *past and past part.* **had**) ● *v.tr.* **1** hold in possession as one's property or at one's disposal (*has a car*). **2** hold in a certain relationship (*has a sister*). **3** contain as a part or quality (*house has two floors*). **4 a** undergo, experience (*had a shock*). **b** be subjected to a specified state (*had my car stolen*). **c** cause, instruct, or invite (a person or thing) to be in a particular state or take a particular action (*had him dismissed*; *had them to stay*). **5 a** engage in (an

activity) (*had an argument*). **b** hold (a meeting, party, etc.). **6** eat or drink (*had a beer*). **7** (usu. in *neg.*) accept or tolerate; permit to (*I won't have it*). **8 a** let (a feeling etc.) be present (*have nothing against them*). **b** show or feel (mercy, pity, etc.) towards another person (*have mercy!*). **c** (foll. by *to* + infin.) show by action that one is influenced by (a feeling etc.) (*have the goodness to leave*). **9 a** give birth to (offspring). **b** conceive mentally (an idea etc.). **10** receive, obtain (*had a letter from him*). **11** be burdened with or committed to (*has a job to do*). **12 a** have obtained (a qualification) (*has six O levels*). **b** know (a language) (*has no Latin*). **13** *colloq.* **a** get the better of (*I had him there*). **b** (usu. in *passive*) cheat (*you were had*). **14** *coarse slang* have sexual intercourse with. ● *v.aux.* (with *past part.* or *ellipt.*, to form the perfect, pluperfect, and future perfect tenses, and the conditional mood) (*have worked*; *had seen*; *will have been*; *had I known, I would have gone*; *have you met her? yes, I have*). ● *n.* (usu. in *pl.*) *colloq.* a person who has wealth or resources. □ **had best** see BEST. **had better** would find it prudent to. **had rather** see RATHER. **have done**, **have done with** see DONE. **have an eye for**, **have eyes for**, **have an eye to** see EYE. **have a good mind to** see MIND. **have got to** *colloq.* = *have to*. **have had it** *colloq.* **1** have missed one's chance. **2** have been killed, defeated, etc. **have it 1** (foll. by *that* + clause) express the view that. **2** win a decision in a vote etc. **3** have found the answer etc. **have it away** (or **off**) *Brit. coarse slang* have sexual intercourse. **have it in for** *colloq.* be hostile towards. **have it out** (often foll. by *with*) *colloq.* attempt to settle a dispute by discussion. **have it one's own way** see WAY. **have on 1** be wearing (clothes). **2** be committed to (an engagement). **3** *Brit. colloq.* tease; play a trick on. **have out** get (a tooth etc.) extracted (*had her tonsils out*). **have to** be obliged to, must. **have up** *colloq.* bring (a person) before a court of justice, interviewer, etc. [Old English]

■ **Usage** See Usage Note at OF.

haven *n.* **1** a harbour or port. **2** a place of refuge. [from Old Norse *höfn*]

have-not *n.* (usu. in *pl.*) *colloq.* a person lacking wealth or resources.

haven't *contr.* have not.

haver /hay-ver/ ● *v.intr. Brit.* **1** talk foolishly; babble. **2** vacillate, hesitate. ● *n.* (usu. in *pl.*) *Sc.* foolish talk; nonsense. [18th-century coinage]

haversack *n.* a stout bag carried on the back or over the shoulder. [from German *Haber* 'oats' + *Sack* 'sack']

havoc *n.* widespread destruction; great confusion or disorder. □ **play havoc with** *colloq.* cause great confusion or difficulty to. [from Old French *havo(t)*]

haw¹ *n.* the fruit of the hawthorn. [Old English]

haw² ● *int.* expressing hesitation. ● *v.intr.* (in **hum and haw**): see HUM¹.

Hawaiian ● *n.* **1 a** a native of Hawaii, an island or island group in the N. Pacific. **b** a person of Hawaiian descent. **2** the language of Hawaii. ● *adj.* of or relating to Hawaii or its people or language.

hawfinch *n.* any large stout finch of the genus *Coccothraustes*, with a heavy beak for cracking seeds.

hawk¹ ● *n.* **1** ▶ any of various birds of prey of the family Accipitridae, having a characteristic curved beak, rounded short wings, and a long

HAWK:
HARRIS'S HAWK
(*Parabuteo unicinctus*)

tail. ▷ RAPTOR. **2** *Polit.* a person who advocates an aggressive or warlike policy, esp. in foreign affairs. **3** a rapacious person. ● *v.intr.* hunt game with a hawk. [Old English] □ **hawkish** *adj.* **hawkishness** *n.* **hawklike** *adj.*

hawk² *v.* **1** *intr.* clear the throat noisily. **2** *tr.* (foll. by *up*) bring (phlegm etc.) up from the throat.

hawker *n.* a person who travels about selling goods. [16th-century coinage] □ **hawk** *v.tr.*

hawk-eyed *adj.* keen-sighted.

hawkmoth *n.* ▼ any large darting and hovering moth of the family Sphingidae, having narrow front wings and a stout body. ▷ MOTH

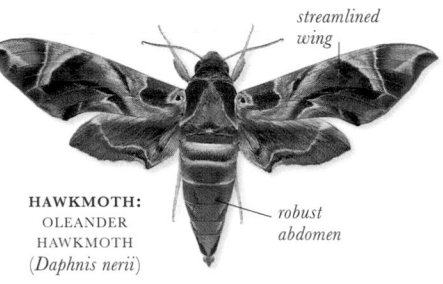

streamlined wing

HAWKMOTH:
OLEANDER
HAWKMOTH
(*Daphnis nerii*)

robust abdomen

hawkweed *n.* ◀ any plant of the genus *Hieracium* (daisy family), with yellow flowers.

hawser *n. Naut.* a thick rope or cable for mooring or towing a ship. ▷ ROPE. [based on Old French *haucier* 'to hoist']

hawthorn *n.* any thorny shrub or tree of the genus *Crataegus* (rose family), esp. *C. monogyna*, with small dark red berries. [Old English]

HAWKWEED:
COMMON
HAWKWEED
(*Hieracium vulgatum*)

hay *n.* grass mown and dried for fodder. □ **make hay (while the sun shines)** seize opportunities for profit or enjoyment. [Old English]

hay fever *n.* an allergy with catarrhal and asthmatic symptoms, caused by pollen or dust.

haymaker *n.* **1** a person who tosses and spreads hay to dry after mowing. **2** an apparatus for shaking and drying hay. **3** *slang* a forceful punch. □ **haymaking** *n.*

hayrick *n.* = HAYSTACK.

hayseed *n.* **1** grass seed obtained from hay. **2** *N. Amer., Austral., & NZ colloq.* a rustic or yokel.

haystack *n.* a packed pile of hay with a pointed or ridged top.

haywire *adj. colloq.* **1** badly disorganized, out of control. **2** (of a person) erratic. [from the use of hay-baling wire in makeshift repairs]

hazard ● *n.* **1** a danger or risk. **2** a source of this. **3** chance. **4** *Golf* an obstruction in playing a shot, e.g. a bunker, water, etc. ● *v.tr.* **1** venture on (*hazard a guess*). **2** run the risk of. **3** expose to hazard. [from Arabic *az-zahr* 'chance, luck'] □ **hazardous** *adj.* **hazardously** *adv.*

haze *n.* **1** obscuration of the atmosphere near the Earth by fine particles of water, smoke, or dust. **2** mental obscurity or confusion.

hazel ● *n.* **1** any shrub or small tree of the genus *Corylus*, esp. *C. avellana* bearing round brown edible nuts. **2** wood from the hazel. **3** a reddish-brown or greenish-brown colour (esp. of the eyes). ● *adj.* (esp. of the eyes) of a reddish- or greenish-brown colour. [Old English]

hazelnut *n.* the fruit of the hazel, a round brown hard-shelled nut. ▷ NUT

hazy *adj.* (**hazier**, **haziest**) **1** misty. **2** vague, indistinct.

H

H

3 confused, uncertain. [17th-century coinage, originally nautical] □ **hazily** *adv.* **haziness** *n.*

HB *abbr.* hard black (pencil lead).

H-bomb *n.* = HYDROGEN BOMB.

HDTV *abbr.* high-definition television.

HE *abbr.* **1** His or Her Excellency. **2** His Eminence. **3** high explosive.

He *symb. Chem.* the element helium.

he ● *pron.* (*obj.* **him**; *poss.* **his**; *pl.* **they**) **1** the man or boy or male animal previously named or in question. **2** a person etc. of unspecified sex, esp. referring to one already named or identified (*if anyone comes he will have to wait*). ● *n.* **1** a male; a man. **2** (in *comb.*) male (*he-goat*). **3** *Brit.* a children's chasing game, with the chaser designated 'he'. [Old English]

head ● *n.***1** ▼ the upper part of the human body, or the foremost or upper part of an animal's body, containing the brain, mouth, and sense organs. ▷ FACE. **2 a** the head regarded as the seat of intellect. **b** intelligence (*use your head*). **c** mental aptitude or tolerance (usu. foll. by *for*: *a good head for business*). **3** *colloq.* a headache. **4** a thing like a head in form or position, esp.: **a** the operative part of a tool. **b** the flattened top of a nail. **c** the ornamented top of a pillar. **d** a mass of flowers etc. at the top of a stem. **e** the flat end of a drum. **f** the foam on top of a glass of beer etc. **g** the upper horizontal part of a window frame etc. **5** life when regarded as vulnerable (*it cost him his head*). **6 a** a person in charge (esp. *Brit.* the principal teacher at a school or college). **b** a position of leadership. **7** the forward part of something, e.g. a queue. **8** the upper end of something, e.g. a bed. **9** the top or highest part of something, e.g. a page. **10** a person regarded as a numerical unit (*£10 per head*). **11** (*pl.* same) **a** an individual animal as a unit. **b** (treated as *pl.*) a number of cattle etc. (*20 head*). **12 a** the side of a coin bearing the image of a head. **b** (usu. in *pl.*) this side as a choice when tossing a coin. **13 a** the source of a river etc. **b** the end of a lake etc. at which a river enters. **14** the height or length of a head as a measure. **15** the component of a machine that is in contact with or very close to what is being worked on, esp.: **a** the component on a tape recorder that touches the moving tape and converts the signals. **b** the part of a record player that holds the playing cartridge and stylus. **c** = PRINTHEAD. **16 a** a confined body of water or steam in an engine etc. **b** the pressure exerted by this. **17** a promontory (esp. in place names: *Beachy Head*). **18** *Naut.* **a** the bows of a ship. **b** (often in *pl.*) a ship's latrine. **19** a main topic or category for

consideration. **20** *Journalism* = HEADLINE *n.* 1. **21** a culmination, climax, or crisis. **22** the fully developed top of a boil etc. ● *attrib.adj.* chief (*head gardener; head office*). ● *v.* **1** *tr.* be at the head or front of. **2** *tr.* be in charge of (*headed a small team*). **3** *tr.* a provide with a head or heading. **b** (of an inscription etc.) serve as a heading for. **4 a** *intr.* face or move in a specified direction (often foll. by *for*: *is heading for trouble*). **b** *tr.* direct in a specified direction. **5** *tr. Football* strike (the ball) with the head. **6 a** *tr.* (often foll. by *down*) cut the head off (a plant etc.). **b** *intr.* (of a plant etc.) form a head. □ **above one's head** beyond one's ability to understand. **come to a head** reach a crisis. **enter** (or **come into**) **one's head** *colloq.* occur to one. **from head to toe** (or **foot**) all over a person's body. **get** (or **take**) **it into one's head** (foll. by *that* + clause or *to* + infin.) form a definite idea, esp. mistakenly or impetuously. **get one's head down** *Brit. slang* **1** go to bed. **2** concentrate on the task in hand. **give a person his** or **her head** allow a person to act freely. **go out of one's head** go mad. **go to one's head 1** (of liquor) make one slightly drunk. **2** (of success) make one conceited. **head and shoulders** *colloq.* by a considerable amount. **head off 1** get ahead of so as to intercept and turn aside. **2** forestall. **head over heels 1** turning over completely in forward motion as in a somersault etc. **2** topsy-turvy. **3** completely (*head over heels in love*). **hold up one's head** be confident or unashamed. **in one's head 1** in one's thoughts or imagination. **2** by mental process. **keep one's head** remain calm. **keep one's head down** *colloq.* remain inconspicuous in difficult or dangerous times. **lose one's head** lose self-control; panic. **make head or tail of** (usu. with *neg.* or *interrog.*) understand at all. **off one's head** *colloq.* crazy. **off the top of one's head** *colloq.* impromptu. **on one's** (or **one's own**) **head** as one's sole responsibility. **out of one's head** *colloq.* crazy. **over one's head 1** beyond one's ability to understand. **2** without one's knowledge or involvement. **3** with disregard for one's own (stronger) claim (*was promoted over their heads*). **put heads together** consult together. **put into a person's head** suggest to a person. **turn a person's head** make a person conceited. **with one's head in the**

clouds see CLOUD. [Old English] □ **headed** *adj.* (also in *comb.*). **headless** *adj.* **headward** *adj. & adv.*

headache *n.* **1** a continuous pain in the head. **2** *colloq.* a worrying problem. □ **headachy** *adj.*

headband *n.* a band worn round the head as decoration or to keep the hair off the face.

headbanger *n. slang* **1** a young person shaking violently to the rhythm of pop music. **2** a crazy or eccentric person.

headboard *n.* an upright panel forming or placed behind the head of a bed.

head-butt ● *n.* a forceful thrust with the top of the head into the head, chin, or body of another person. ● *v.tr.* attack with a head-butt.

headcount *n.* **1** a counting of individual people. **2** a total number of people, esp. in a particular organization.

headdress *n.* ◄ an ornamental covering or band for the head.

header *n.* **1** *Football* a shot or pass made with the head. **2** *colloq.* a headlong fall or dive. **3** a brick or stone laid at right angles to the face of a wall. ▷ BRICK. **4** (in full **header-tank**) a tank of water etc. maintaining pressure in a plumbing system. **5** a line or block of text appearing at the top of each page of a document etc. (cf. FOOTER[1] 2).

head first *adv.* **1** with the head foremost. **2** precipitately.

headgear *n.* a hat or headdress.

headhunting *n.* **1** the practice among some peoples of collecting the heads of dead enemies as trophies. **2** the practice of filling a (usu. senior) business position by approaching a suitable person employed elsewhere. □ **headhunt** *v.tr.* (also *absol.*). **headhunter** *n.*

heading *n.* **1 a** a title at the head of a page. **b** a division or section of a subject of discourse etc. **2** a horizontal passage made in preparation for building a tunnel.

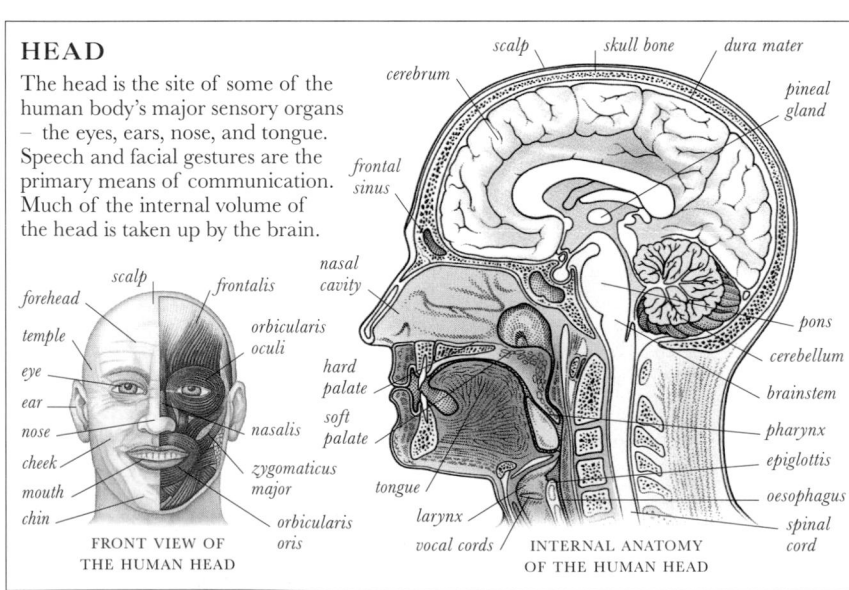

HEADDRESS: NATIVE AMERICAN WAR BONNET

headlamp *n.* = HEADLIGHT.

headland *n.* a promontory. ▷ COASTLINE

headlight *n.* **1** a strong light at the front of a motor vehicle or railway engine. **2** the beam from this.

headline ● *n.* **1** a heading at the top of an article or page, esp. in a newspaper. **2** (in *pl.*) the most important items of news in a newspaper or news bulletin. ● *v.* **1** *tr.* give a headline to. **2** *intr.* appear as the star performer.

headlock *n. Wrestling* a hold with an arm round the opponent's head.

headlong *adv. & adj.* **1** with head foremost. **2** in a rush. [Middle English]

headman *n.* (*pl.* **-men**) the chief man of a tribe etc.

headmaster *n.* (*fem.* **headmistress**) the principal teacher in charge of a school. □ **headmasterly** *adj.*

head of state *n.* (*pl.* **heads of state**) the title of the head of a state, usu. the leader of the ruling party or a monarch.

head-on *adj. & adv.* **1** with the front foremost (*a head-on crash*). **2** in direct confrontation.

headphone *n.* (usu. in *pl.*) a pair of earphones joined by a band placed over the head, for listening to audio equipment etc.

headquarters *n.* (treated as *sing.* or *pl.*) the administrative centre of an organization etc.

HEAD

The head is the site of some of the human body's major sensory organs – the eyes, ears, nose, and tongue. Speech and facial gestures are the primary means of communication. Much of the internal volume of the head is taken up by the brain.

scalp · forehead · temple · eye · ear · nose · cheek · mouth · chin · frontalis · orbicularis oculi · nasalis · zygomaticus major · orbicularis oris

FRONT VIEW OF THE HUMAN HEAD

scalp · skull bone · dura mater · cerebrum · pineal gland · frontal sinus · nasal cavity · hard palate · soft palate · tongue · larynx · vocal cords · pons · cerebellum · brainstem · pharynx · epiglottis · oesophagus · spinal cord

INTERNAL ANATOMY OF THE HUMAN HEAD

headrest *n.* a support for the head, esp. on a seat or chair.

headroom *n.* **1** the space or clearance between the top of a vehicle and the underside of a bridge etc. **2** the space above a driver's or passenger's head in a vehicle.

headsail *n.* a sail on a ship's foremast or bowsprit.

headscarf *n.* a scarf worn round the head and tied under the chin.

headset *n.* a set of headphones, often with a microphone attached.

headship *n.* the position of chief or leader, esp. *Brit.* of a headmaster or headmistress.

headshrinker *n. slang* a psychiatrist.

headsquare *n. Brit.* a rectangular scarf for wearing on the head.

headstall *n.* the part of a halter or bridle that fits round a horse's head.

head start *n.* an advantage granted or gained at an early stage.

headstone *n.* a (usu. inscribed) stone set up at the head of a grave.

headstrong *adj.* self-willed and obstinate.

head teacher *n.* the teacher in charge of a school.

head-to-head ● *n.* a conversation, confrontation, or contest between two parties. ● *attrib.adj.* involving two parties confronting each other. ● *adv.* confronting another party. [translation of French *tête-à-tête*]

headwater *n.* (in *sing.* or *pl.*) streams flowing from the sources of a river.

headway *n.* **1** progress. **2** the rate of progress of a ship. **3** = HEADROOM 1.

headwind *n.* a wind blowing from directly in front.

headword *n.* a word forming a heading.

headwork *n.* mental work or effort.

heady *adj.* (**headier**, **headiest**) **1** (of liquor) potent, intoxicating. **2** (of success etc.) likely to cause conceit. **3** impetuous, violent. □ **headily** *adv.* **headiness** *n.*

heal *v.* **1** *intr.* (often foll. by *up*) (of a wound or injury) become sound or healthy again. **2** *tr.* cause to heal or be cured, or be made sound again. **3** *tr.* put right (differences etc.). **4** *tr.* alleviate (sorrow etc.). [Old English] □ **healable** *adj.* **healer** *n.*

health *n.* **1** the state of being well in body or mind. **2** a person's mental or physical condition. **3** soundness (*the health of the nation*). [Old English] □ **healthful** *adj.*

health centre *n. Brit.* the headquarters of a group of local medical services.

health farm *n.* a residential establishment where people seek improved health by a regimen of dieting, exercise, etc.

health food *n.* natural food thought to have health-giving qualities.

health service *n. Brit.* a public service providing medical care.

health visitor *n. Brit.* a trained nurse who visits those in need of medical attention in their homes.

healthy *adj.* (**healthier**, **healthiest**) **1** having, showing, or promoting good health. **2** beneficial, helpful. □ **healthily** *adv.* **healthiness** *n.*

heap ● *n.* **1** a collection of things lying haphazardly one on another. **2** (esp. in *pl.*) *colloq.* a large number or amount (*heaps of time*). **3** *colloq.* an old or dilapidated thing, esp. a motor vehicle. ● *v.* **1** *tr. & intr.* (foll. by *up*, *together*, etc.) collect or be collected in a heap. **2** *tr.* (foll. by *with*) load copiously. **3** *tr.* (foll. by *on*, *upon*) accord or offer copiously to. **4** *tr.* (as **heaped** *adj.*) *Brit.* (of a spoonful etc.) with the contents piled above the brim. [Old English]

hear *v.* (*past* and *past part.* **heard**) **1** *tr.* (also *absol.*) perceive (sound etc.) with the ear. **2** *tr.* listen to (*heard them on the radio*). **3** *tr.* listen judicially to and judge. **4** *intr.* (foll. by *about*, *of*, or *that* + clause) be told or informed. **5** *intr.* (foll. by *from*) be contacted by. **6** *tr.* be ready to obey (an order). **7** *tr.* grant (a prayer). □ **have heard of** be aware of. **hear! hear!** *int.*

HEART

The human heart is a muscular organ that pumps blood around the body. The constant circulation supplies oxygen and nutrients to all organs and tissues, as well as carrying waste away. The heart has two chambers, divided by a muscular septum. One-way blood flow between the upper atrium and the lower ventricle is controlled by valves.

CROSS-SECTION THROUGH THE HUMAN HEART

superior vena cava
arch of aorta
pulmonary artery
pulmonary valve
pulmonary veins
left atrium
endocardium (membrane)
mitral valve
aortic valve
left ventricle
myocardium
pericardium
septum
descending aorta
inferior vena cava
right ventricle
tricuspid valve
right atrium

H

expressing agreement (esp. with something said in a speech). **hear a person out** listen to all that a person says. **hear say** (or **tell**) (usu. foll. by *of*, or *that* + clause) be informed. **will not hear of** will not allow or agree to. [Old English] □ **hearer** *n.*

hearing *n.* **1** the faculty of perceiving sounds. **2** earshot (*within hearing*). **3** an opportunity to state one's case (*give them a fair hearing*). **4** the listening to evidence in a law court.

hearing aid *n.* ▶ a small device to amplify sound, worn by a partially deaf person.

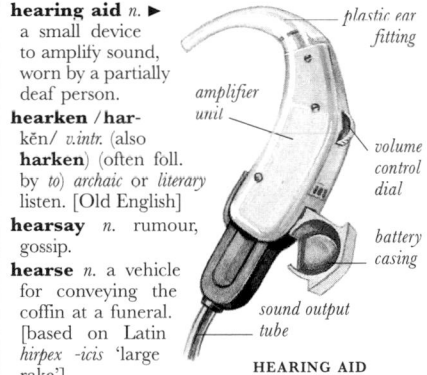

plastic ear fitting
amplifier unit
volume control dial
battery casing
sound output tube

HEARING AID

hearken /har-kĕn/ *v.intr.* (also **harken**) (often foll. by *to*) *archaic* or *literary* listen. [Old English]

hearsay *n.* rumour, gossip.

hearse *n.* a vehicle for conveying the coffin at a funeral. [based on Latin *hirpex -icis* 'large rake']

heart *n.* **1** ▲ a hollow muscular organ maintaining the circulation of blood by rhythmic contraction and dilation. ▷ CARDIOVASCULAR. **2** the region of the heart; the breast. **3 a** the heart regarded as the centre of thought and emotion. **b** a person's capacity for feeling emotion (*has no heart*). **4 a** courage (*take heart*). **b** one's mood (*change of heart*). **5 a** the central or innermost part of something. **b** the vital part (*the heart of the matter*). **6** the close compact head of a cabbage etc. **7 a** a heart-shaped thing. **b** a conventional representation of a heart. **8 a** a playing card of a suit denoted by a red figure of a heart. **b** (in *pl.*) this suit. □ **at heart 1** in one's inmost feelings. **2** basically, essentially. **break a person's heart** overwhelm a person with sorrow. **by heart** from memory. **give** (or **lose**) **one's heart** (often foll. by *to*) fall in love (with). **have the heart** (usu. with *neg.*; foll. by *to* + infin.) be insensitive or hard-hearted enough. **in heart** *Brit.* in good spirits. **in one's heart of hearts** in one's inmost feelings. **take to heart** be much affected by. **to one's heart's content** see CONTENT¹. **with all one's**

heart sincerely; with all goodwill. [Old English] □ **-hearted** *adj.* (in *comb.*).

heartache *n.* mental anguish or grief.

heart attack *n.* a sudden occurrence of coronary thrombosis.

heartbeat *n.* a pulsation of the heart.

heartbreak *n.* overwhelming distress. □ **heartbreaker** *n.* **heartbreaking** *adj.* **heartbreakingly** *adv.* **heartbroken** *adj.*

heartburn *n.* a burning sensation in the chest resulting from indigestion.

hearten *v.tr. & intr.* make or become more cheerful. □ **heartening** *adj.* **hearteningly** *adv.*

heart failure *n.* severe failure of the heart to function properly, esp. as a cause of death.

heartfelt *adj.* sincere; deeply felt.

hearth *n.* **1 a** the floor of a fireplace. **b** the area in front of a fireplace. **2** this symbolizing the home. **3** the bottom of a blast furnace where molten metal collects. ▷ BLAST FURNACE. [Old English]

heartily *adv.* **1** in a hearty manner; with goodwill, appetite, or vigour. **2** to a great degree (*am heartily sick of it*).

heartland *n.* the central or most important part of an area.

heartless *adj.* unfeeling, pitiless. □ **heartlessly** *adv.* **heartlessness** *n.*

heart-lung machine *n.* a machine that temporarily takes over the functions of the heart and lungs.

heart-rending *adj.* very distressing. □ **heart-rendingly** *adv.*

heart's-blood *n. Brit.* lifeblood, life.

heart-searching *n.* the thorough examination of one's own feelings and motives.

heartsease *n.* (also **heart's-ease**) ▶ a pansy, esp. the wild pansy, *Viola tricolor.*

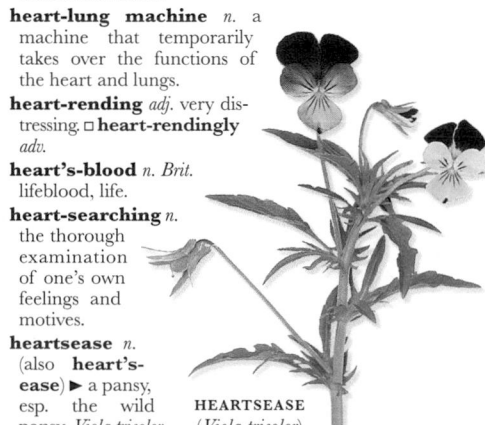

HEARTSEASE
(*Viola tricolor*)

H

heartsick *adj.* despondent. □ **heartsickness** *n.*

heartstrings *n.pl.* one's deepest emotions.

heart-throb *n.* **1** beating of the heart. **2** *colloq.* a person, usu. a celebrity, for whom one has (esp. immature) romantic feelings.

heart-to-heart ● *adj.* (of a conversation etc.) candid, intimate. ● *n.* a candid or personal conversation.

heart-warming *adj.* emotionally rewarding.

heartwood *n.* the dense inner part of a tree trunk yielding the hardest timber. ▷ WOOD

hearty *adj.* (**heartier**, **heartiest**) **1** strong, vigorous. **2** spirited. **3** (of a meal or appetite) large. **4** warm, friendly. □ **heartiness** *n.*

heat ● *n.* **1 a** the condition of being hot. **b** the sensation or perception of this. **2** *Physics* a form of energy arising from the random motion of the molecules of bodies, which may be transferred by conduction, convection, or radiation. **3** hot weather. **4 a** warmth of feeling. **b** anger or excitement. **5** (foll. by *of*) the most intense period of an activity (*the heat of the battle*). **6 a** (usu. preliminary or trial) round in a race or contest. **7** the receptive period of the sexual cycle, esp. in female mammals. **8** pungency of flavour; the quality (of food) of producing a burning sensation. ● *v.* **1** *tr. & intr.* make or become hot or warm. **2** *tr.* inflame; excite or intensify. □ **in the heat of the moment** during or resulting from intense activity, without pause for thought. **on heat** (of mammals, esp. females) sexually receptive. **turn the heat on** *colloq.* concentrate an attack or criticism on (a person). [Old English]

heated *adj.* **1** angry; inflamed with passion or excitement. **2** made hot. □ **heatedly** *adv.*

heater *n.* **1** a device for warming the air in a room etc. **2** a container with an element etc. for heating the contents (*water heater*). **3** *US slang* a gun.

heath *n.* **1 a** esp. *Brit.* an area of open uncultivated land with heather, coarse grasses, etc. **b** *Bot.* an area dominated by dwarf ericaceous shrubs. **2** a plant growing on a heath, esp. of the genus *Erica* or *Calluna*. [Old English] □ **heathy** *adj.*

heathen ● *n.* **1** a person who does not belong to a widely held religion as regarded by those that do. **2** a person regarded as lacking culture or moral principles. **3** *Bibl.* a Gentile. ● *adj.* **1** of or relating to heathens. **2** having no religion. [Old English] □ **heathendom** *n.* **heathenism** *n.*

heather *n.* **1** an evergreen shrub, *Calluna vulgaris* (family Ericaceae), with purple bell-shaped flowers. **2** any of various related shrubs growing esp. on moors and heaths. [Middle English] □ **heathery** *adj.*

Heath Robinson *adj.* *Brit.* absurdly ingenious and impractical in design or construction. [named after W. *Heath Robinson*, English cartoonist, 1872–1944, who drew such contrivances]

heating *n.* **1** the imparting or generation of heat. **2** equipment or devices used to provide heat.

heat lamp *n.* a lamp used for its heat as well as its light.

heatproof ● *adj.* able to resist great heat. ● *v.tr.* make heatproof.

heat-seeking *adj.* (of a missile etc.) able to detect infra-red radiation to guide it to its target.

heatstroke *n.* a feverish condition caused by excessive exposure to high temperature.

heatwave *n.* a prolonged period of abnormally hot weather.

heave ● *v.* (*past* and *past part.* **heaved** or esp. *Naut.* **hove**) **1** *tr.* lift or haul with great effort. **2** *tr.* utter with effort or resignation. **3** *tr. colloq.* throw. **4** *intr.* rise and fall rhythmically or spasmodically. **5** *intr. colloq.* retch. ● *n.* an instance of heaving. □ **heave in sight** *Naut.* or *colloq.* come into view. **heave to** esp. *Naut.* bring or be brought to a standstill. [Old English, related to Latin *capere* 'to take']

heave-ho *int.* a sailors' cry, esp. on raising the anchor. □ **give the heave-ho to** *slang* dismiss, reject.

heaven *n.* **1** (also **Heaven**) a place regarded in some religions as the abode of God and the angels, and of the good after death. **2** a place or state of supreme bliss. **3** *colloq.* something delightful. **4** (usu. **Heaven**) God, Providence. **5** (**the heavens**) esp. *poet.* the sky. [Old English] □ **heavenward** *adj. & adv.* **heavenwards** *adv.*

heavenly *adj.* **1** of heaven; divine. **2** of the heavens or sky. **3** *colloq.* very pleasing. □ **heavenliness** *n.*

heavenly body *n.* a natural object in outer space, e.g. a planet etc.; a celestial object.

heaven-sent *adj.* providential; wonderfully opportune.

heavy ● *adj.* (**heavier**, **heaviest**) **1** of great weight; difficult to lift. **2** of great density. **3** abundant (*a heavy crop*). **4** severe, intense (*heavy fighting*). **5** doing something to excess (*a heavy drinker*). **6 a** striking with force (*heavy blows*). **b** (of the sea) having large powerful waves. **7** (of rock music etc.) highly amplified with a strong beat. **8** (of machinery etc.) very large of its kind. **9** causing a strong impact (*a heavy fall*). **10** needing much physical effort (*heavy work*). **11** (foll. by *with*) laden. **12** carrying heavy weapons (*the heavy brigade*). **13 a** (of a speech etc.) serious or sombre in tone or attitude. **b** (of a person) sternly repressive (*heavy father*). **14 a** (of food) hard to digest. **b** (of a literary work etc.) hard to understand. **15** (of bread etc.) too dense from not having risen. **16** (of ground) difficult to traverse or work. **17** hard to endure (*heavy demands*). **18 a** coarse, ungraceful (*heavy features*). **b** unwieldy. ● *n.* (*pl.* **-ies**) **1** *colloq.* a large violent person; a thug. **2** a villainous or tragic role in a play etc. **3** (usu. in *pl.*) *Brit. colloq.* a serious newspaper. ● *adv.* heavily (esp. in *comb.*: *heavy-laden*). □ **heavy on** using a lot of (*heavy on petrol*). **make heavy weather of** see WEATHER. [Old English] □ **heavily** *adv.* **heaviness** *n.* **heavyish** *adj.*

heavy breathing *n.* breathing that is audible through being deep or laboured.

heavy-duty *adj.* **1** intended to withstand hard use. **2** *US colloq.* significant in size, amount, etc.

heavy-footed *adj.* awkward, ponderous.

heavy going *adj.* slow or difficult to progress with.

heavy-handed *adj.* **1** clumsy. **2** oppressive. □ **heavy-handedly** *adv.* **heavy-handedness** *n.*

heavy-hearted *adj.* sad, doleful.

heavy hydrogen *n.* = DEUTERIUM.

heavy industry *n.* industry producing machinery etc.

heavy metal *n.* **1** heavy guns. **2** metal of high density. **3** (often *attrib.*) *colloq.* a type of highly amplified harsh-sounding rock music with a strong beat.

heavy sleeper *n.* a person who sleeps deeply.

heavy water *n.* a substance composed entirely or mainly of deuterium oxide.

heavyweight *n.* **1 a** a weight in certain sports, e.g. in amateur boxing over 81 kg. **b** a boxer etc. of this weight. **2** a person, animal, or thing of above average weight. **3** *colloq.* a person of influence or importance.

hebe *n.* ▶ any flowering shrub of the genus *Hebe*. [named after the Greek goddess *Hēbē*]

Hebraic /hib-**ray**-ik/ *adj.* of Hebrew or the Hebrews. □ **Hebraically** *adv.*

Hebrew ● *n.* **1** a member of a Semitic people originally centred in ancient Palestine. **2 a** the language of this people. **b** a modern form of this. ● *adj.* **1** of or in Hebrew. **2** of the Hebrews or the Jews. [from Hebrew *'ibrî* 'one from the other side (of the river)']

heck *int. colloq.* a mild exclamation of surprise or dismay. [alteration of HELL]

heckle ● *v.tr.* **1** interrupt and harass (a public speaker). **2** dress (flax or hemp). ● *n.* an act of heckling. [Middle English] □ **heckler** *n.*

hectare *n.* a metric unit of square measure, equal to 100 ares (2.471 acres or 10,000 square metres). [French] □ **hectarage** *n.*

hectic *adj.* busy and confused. [from Greek *hektikos* 'habitual'] □ **hectically** *adv.*

hecto- *comb. form* a hundred, esp. of a unit in the metric system. [formed irregularly from Greek *hekaton* 'hundred']

hectogram *n.* (also **hectogramme**) a metric unit of mass, equal to one hundred grams.

hectolitre *n.* (*US* **hectoliter**) a metric unit of capacity, equal to one hundred litres.

hectometre *n.* (*US* **hectometer**) a metric unit of length, equal to one hundred metres.

hector *v.tr.* bully, intimidate. [earlier in sense 'a swaggering fellow': from Greek *Hektōr*, a Trojan hero] □ **hectoringly** *adv.*

he'd *contr.* **1** he had. **2** he would.

hedge ● *n.* **1** a fence or boundary formed by dense bushes or shrubs. **2** a protection against possible loss or diminution. ● *v.* **1** *tr.* surround or bound with a hedge. **2** *tr.* (foll. by *in*) enclose. **3 a** *tr.* reduce one's risk of loss on (a bet or speculation) by compensating transactions on the other side. **b** *intr.* avoid a definite decision or commitment. **4** *intr.* make or trim hedges. [Old English] □ **hedger** *n.*

hedgehog *n.* a small nocturnal mammal of the family Erinaceidae, esp. *Erinaceus europaeus*, having a piglike snout and a coat of spines and rolling itself up into a ball for defence.

hedge-hop *v.intr.* fly at a very low altitude.

hedgerow *n.* a row of bushes etc. forming a hedge.

hedge sparrow *n.* = DUNNOCK.

hedge trimmer *n.* an electric device for trimming hedges.

hedonism *n.* **1** belief in pleasure as the highest good and humankind's proper aim. **2** behaviour based on this. [based on Greek *hēdonē* 'pleasure'] □ **hedonist** *n.* **hedonistic** *adj.*

-hedron /hee-drŏn/ *comb. form* (*pl.* **-hedra** or **-hedrons**) forming nouns denoting geometrical solids with various numbers or shapes of faces (*dodecahedron*; *rhombohedron*). [from Greek *hedra* 'seat, base'] □ **-hedral** *comb. form* forming adjectives.

heebie-jeebies *n.pl.* (prec. by *the*) *slang* a state of nervous depression or anxiety (*it gave me the heebie-jeebies*). [20th-century coinage]

heed ● *v.tr.* attend to; take notice of. ● *n.* careful attention. [Old English]

heedful *adj.* (often foll. by *of*) mindful, attentive; careful, cautious. □ **heedfully** *adv.* **heedfulness** *n.*

heedless *adj.* (often foll. by *of*) inattentive, regardless; careless (*went out, heedless of the rain*). □ **heedlessly** *adv.* **heedlessness** *n.*

hee-haw ● *n.* the bray of a donkey. ● *v.intr.* emit a braying sound.

HEBE (*Hebe* 'Bowles' Variety')

heel[1] ● *n.* **1** the back part of the foot below the ankle. ▷ ACHILLES HEEL. **2** the corresponding part in vertebrate animals. ▷ HORSE. **3 a** the part of a sock etc. covering the heel. **b** the part of a shoe or boot supporting the heel. ▷ SHOE. **4** a thing like a heel in form or position, e.g. on the hand or a golf club. **5** *colloq.* a person regarded with contempt or disapproval. ● *v.* **1** *tr.* fit or renew a heel on (a shoe or boot). **2** *intr.* touch the ground with the heel as in dancing. **3** *intr.* (foll. by *out*) *Rugby* pass the ball with the heel. □ **at heel 1** (of a dog) close behind. **2** (of a person etc.) under control. **at (or on) the heels of** following

HELICOPTER

Helicopters are lifted, propelled, and steered by powerful rotating blades (rotors). Able to take off vertically, hover, and fly in any direction, these versatile machines are held stable in flight by the balancing action of their tail rotor. First developed in the 1920s, modern helicopters date from the advent of turbojet engines in 1955. They are now used for such diverse purposes as military gunships, air ambulances, and air taxis; for spraying crops; and for aerial survey and observation, particularly of road traffic conditions.

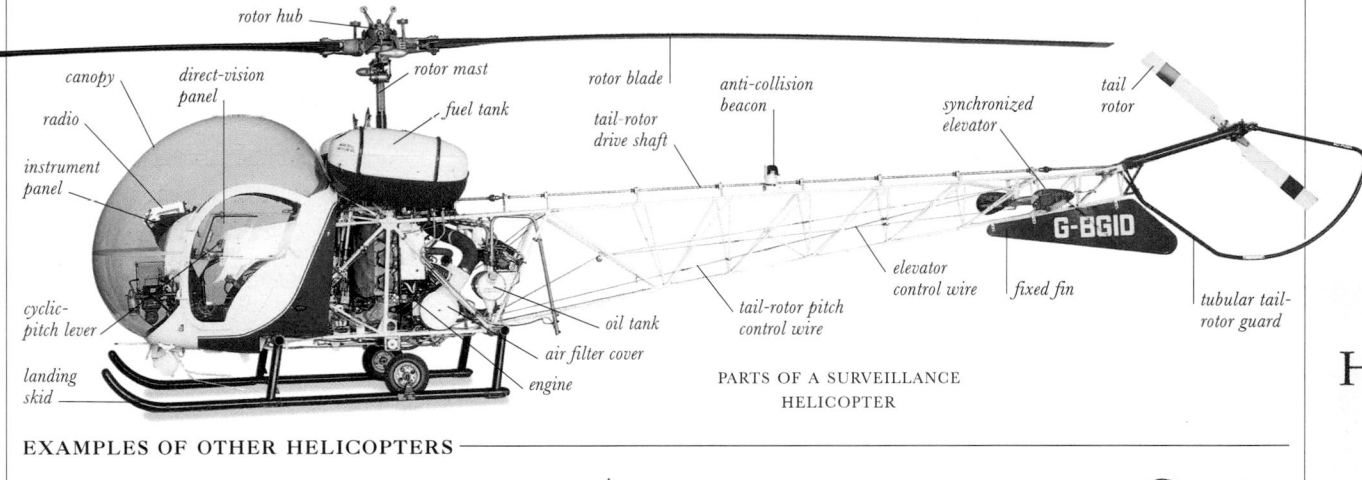

PARTS OF A SURVEILLANCE HELICOPTER

EXAMPLES OF OTHER HELICOPTERS

MULTI-PURPOSE HELICOPTER   MILITARY GUNSHIP   PERSONNEL CARRIER

H

---

closely after (a person or event). **cool** (or *Brit.* **kick**) **one's heels** be kept waiting. **down at heel 1** (of a shoe) with the heel worn down. **2** (of a person) shabby. **take to one's heels** run away. **to heel 1** (of a dog) close behind. **2** (of a person etc.) under control. **turn on one's heel** turn sharply round. [Old English] □ **heelless** *adj.*

heel² ● *v.* **1** *intr.* (of a ship etc.) lean over owing to the pressure of wind or an uneven load (cf. LIST² *v.*). **2** *tr.* cause (a ship etc.) to do this. ● *n.* the act or amount of heeling.

heel³ *v.tr.* (toll. by *in*) set (a plant) in the ground and cover its roots. [Old English]

heelball *n.* **1** a mixture of hard wax and lampblack used by shoemakers for polishing. **2** this or a similar mixture used in brass rubbing.

heft *v.tr.* lift (something heavy), esp. to judge its weight.

hefty *adj.* (**heftier**, **heftiest**) **1** (of a person) big and strong. **2** (of a thing) large, heavy, powerful. □ **heftily** *adv.* **heftiness** *n.*

hegemony /hi-jem-ŏni/ *n.* leadership or dominance, esp. by one state of a confederacy. [from Greek *hēgemonia*]

Hegira /hej-i-ră, hij-ră/ *n.* (also **Hejira**, **Hijra**) **1** Muhammad's departure from Mecca to Medina in AD 622. **2** the Muslim era reckoned from this date. [from Arabic *hijra* 'departure from one's country']

heifer /hef-er/ *n.* a cow that has not borne a calf, or has borne only one calf. [Old English]

heigh *int.* expressing encouragement or enquiry.

heigh-ho *int.* expressing boredom, resignation, etc.

height *n.* **1** the measurement from base to top or (of a person) from head to foot. **2** the elevation above ground or a recognized level (usu. sea level). **3** any considerable elevation (*situated at a height*). **4 a** a high place or area. **b** rising ground. **5** the top of something. **6 a** the most intense part or period of anything (*the battle was at its height*). **b** an extreme example (*the height of fashion*). [Old English]

heighten *v.tr. & intr.* make or become higher or more intense.

heinous /hay-nŭs, hee-nŭs/ *adj.* (of a crime or criminal) utterly odious or wicked. [from Old French *haïneus*] □ **heinously** *adv.* **heinousness** *n.*

heir air *n.* **1** a person entitled to property or rank as the legal successor of its former owner. **2** a person deriving or morally entitled to some thing, quality, etc. from a predecessor. [from Latin *heres -edis*] □ **heirdom** *n.* **heirless** *adj.* **heirship** *n.*

heir apparent *n.* (*pl.* **heirs apparent**) an heir whose claim cannot be set aside by the birth of another heir.

■ **Usage** Note that *heir apparent* does not mean 'seeming heir'.

heiress /air-ess/ *n.* a female heir, esp. to wealth or high title.

heirloom /air-loom/ *n.* **1** a piece of personal property that has been in a family for several generations. **2** a piece of property received as part of an inheritance. [based on LOOM¹]

heist /hyst/ *N. Amer. slang* ● *n.* a robbery. ● *v.tr.* rob. [representing a local pronunciation of HOIST]

Hejira var. of HEGIRA.

held *past* and *past part.* of HOLD¹.

heli- *comb. form* helicopter (*heliport*).

helical *adj.* having the form of a helix. □ **helically** *adv.* **helicoid** *adj. & n.*

helices *pl.* of HELIX.

helicopter *n.* ▲ a type of aircraft obtaining lift and propulsion from horizontally revolving overhead blades. ▷ AIRCRAFT. [from Greek *helix* 'helix' + *pteron* 'wing']

helio- *comb. form* the Sun. [from Greek *hēlios* 'sun']

heliocentric *adj.* **1** regarding the Sun as centre. **2** considered as viewed from the Sun's centre. □ **heliocentrically** *adv.*

heliogram *n.* a message sent by heliograph.

heliograph ● *n.* ▶ a signalling apparatus reflecting sunlight in flashes from a movable mirror. ● *v.tr.* send (a message) by heliograph. □ **heliography** *n.*

heliotrope ● *n.* **1 a** any plant of the genus *Heliotropium* (borage family), with fragrant purple flowers. **b** the scent of these. **2** (**winter heliotrope**) a plant of the daisy family, *Petasites fragrans*, which produces fragrant lilac flowers in winter. **3** a light purple colour. ● *adj.* light purple. [from Greek *hēliotropion* 'plant turning to the sun']

helipad *n.* a landing pad for helicopters.

heliport *n.* a place where helicopters take off and land.

heli-skiing *n.* skiing for which transport up the mountain is by helicopter.

helium *n. Chem.* a colourless light inert gaseous element occurring in deposits of natural gas, used in airships and as a refrigerant. [based on Greek *hēlios* 'sun', as first identified in the Sun's atmosphere]

helix *n.* (*pl.* **helices** /hel-i-seez/) ▶ an object having a three-dimensional shape like that of a wire wound round a cylinder or cone, as in a corkscrew or spiral staircase. [from Greek]

HELIX

hell ● *n.* **1** the abode of the dead; in Christian, Jewish, and Islamic belief, the place of punishment or torment for the souls of the damned. **2** a place or state of misery or wickedness. ● *int.* an exclamation of surprise or annoyance. □ **beat** (or **knock** etc.) **the hell out of** *colloq.* beat etc. without restraint. **for the hell of it** *colloq.* for fun. **give a person hell** *colloq.* scold or punish or make things difficult for a person. **the hell** (usu. prec. by *what*, *where*, *who*, etc.) expressing anger, disbelief, etc. (*who the hell is this?*; *the hell you are!*). **hell for leather**

HELIOGRAPH: LATE 19TH-CENTURY BRITISH ARMY HELIOGRAPH

H

at full speed. **hell to pay** great trouble, resulting from a previous action. **like hell** *colloq.* **1** not at all. **2** recklessly, exceedingly. **play hell** (or *Brit.* **merry hell**) **with** *colloq.* be upsetting or disruptive to. **what the hell** *colloq.* it is of no importance. [Old English] □ **hell-like** *adj.* **hellward** *adv. & adj.*

he'll *contr.* he will; he shall.

hell-bent *adj.* (foll. by *on*) recklessly determined.

hell-cat *n.* a spiteful violent woman.

hellebore /hel-i-bor/ *n.* ▼ any evergreen plant of the genus *Helleborus* (buttercup family), having large white, cream, green, or purplish flowers, e.g. the Christmas rose. [from Greek *(h)elleboros*]

HELLEBORE
(*Helleborus lividus*)

Hellene *n.* **1** a native of modern Greece. **2** an ancient Greek. [from Greek *Hellēn* 'a Greek'] □ **Hellenic** *adj.*

Hellenism *n.* Greek character or culture (esp. that of ancient Greece). □ **Hellenize** *v.tr. & intr.* (also **-ise**). **Hellenization** *n.*

Hellenist *n.* an expert on or admirer of Greek language or culture.

Hellenistic *adj.* of or relating to Greek history, language, and culture of the period 4th–1st c. BC.

hellfire *n.* the fire or fires regarded as existing in hell.

hell-hole *n.* an oppressive or unbearable place.

hell-hound *n.* a fiend.

hellish ● *adj.* **1** of or like hell. **2** *colloq.* extremely difficult or unpleasant. ● *adv. Brit. colloq.* (as an intensifier) extremely (*hellish expensive*). □ **hellishly** *adv.* **hellishness** *n.*

hello (also **hullo**, esp. *Brit.* **hallo**) ● *int.* **1** an expression of informal greeting, or esp. *Brit.* of surprise. **2** a cry used to call attention. ● *n.* (*pl.* **-os**) a cry of 'hello'. ● *v.intr.* (**-oes**, **-oed**) cry 'hello'. [variant of earlier *hollo*]

hellraiser *n.* a person who causes trouble or creates chaos. □ **hellraising** *adj. & n.*

Hell's Angel *n.* a member of a gang of male motorcycle enthusiasts notorious for outrageous and violent behaviour.

helm *n.* a tiller or wheel by which a ship's rudder is controlled. ▷ BOAT. □ **at the helm** in control; at the head (of an organization etc.). [Old English]

helmet *n.* ▶ any of various protective head coverings worn by soldiers, police officers, divers, motorcyclists, etc. [from Old French] □ **helmeted** *adj.*

helmsman *n.* (*pl.* **-men**) a steersman.

helot *n.* a serf, esp. (**Helot**) of a class in ancient Sparta. [from Greek *heilōtes*, erroneously taken as 'inhabitants of *Helos*', an ancient Greek town] □ **helotism** *adj.* **helotry** *n.*

help ● *v.tr.* **1** provide (a person etc.) with the means towards what is needed or sought (*helped me with my work*). **2** (foll. by *up*, *down*, etc.) assist

or give support to (a person) in moving etc. as specified (*helped her into the chair*). **3** (often *absol.*) be of use or service to (a person) (*does that help?*). **4** contribute to alleviating (a pain or difficulty). **5** prevent or remedy (*it can't be helped*). **6** (usu. with *neg.*) **a** refrain from (*could not help laughing*). **b** *refl.* refrain from acting (*couldn't help himself*). **7** (often foll. by *to*) serve (a person with food) (*shall I help you to greens?*). ● *n.* **1** the act of helping or being helped (*we need your help*; *came to our help*). **2** a person or thing that helps. **3** a domestic assistant. □ **help oneself** (often foll. by *to*) **1** serve oneself (with food etc.). **2** take without seeking help or permission. **help a person out** give a person help, esp. in difficulty. [Old English] □ **helper** *n.*

helpful *adj.* **1** giving help; useful. **2** obliging. □ **helpfully** *adv.* **helpfulness** *n.*

helping *n.* a portion of food, esp. at a meal.

helping hand *n.* assistance.

helpless *adj.* **1** lacking help or protection; defenceless. **2** unable to act without help. □ **helplessly** *adv.* **helplessness** *n.*

helpline *n.* a telephone service providing help with problems.

helpmate *n.* a helpful companion or partner (usu. a husband or wife).

helter-skelter ● *adv.* in disorderly haste. ● *adj.* characterized by disorderly haste. ● *n. Brit.* a tall spiral slide round a tower, at a fairground.

hem¹ ● *n.* the edge of a piece of cloth, turned under and sewn down. ● *v.tr.* (**hemmed**, **hemming**) turn down and sew in the edge of (a piece of cloth etc.). □ **hem in** confine; restrict the movement of. [Old English]

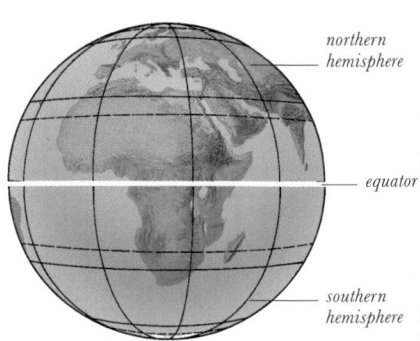

HELMET OF AN AMERICAN FOOTBALL PLAYER

HEMIPTERA

Hemipterans form a hugely varied group of insects, the 'true bugs'. All possess biting and sucking mouthparts, used to draw fluids from plant or animal tissues (most species are herbivorous). While the majority of hemipterans are terrestrial, the group also includes all aquatic bugs.

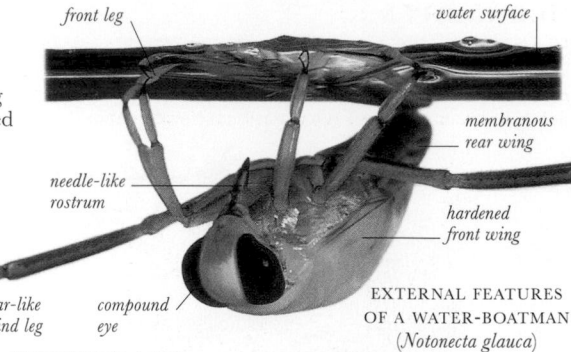

front leg · water surface · membranous rear wing · hardened front wing · needle-like rostrum · oar-like hind leg · compound eye

EXTERNAL FEATURES OF A WATER-BOATMAN
(*Notonecta glauca*)

EXAMPLES OF OTHER HEMIPTERANS

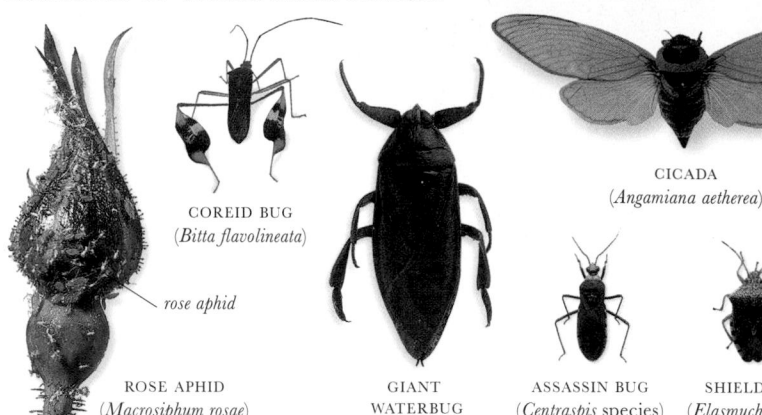

COREID BUG
(*Bitta flavolineata*)

rose aphid

ROSE APHID
(*Macrosiphum rosae*)

GIANT WATERBUG
(*Lethocerus grandis*)

CICADA
(*Angamiana aetherea*)

ASSASSIN BUG
(*Centraspis* species)

SHIELD BUG
(*Elasmucha grisea*)

hem² ● *int.* attracting attention or expressing hesitation by a slight cough. ● *n.* an utterance of this. ● *v.intr.* (**hemmed**, **hemming**) say *hem*; hesitate in speech. □ **hem and haw** = *hum and haw* (see HUM¹).

hemal etc. *US* var. of HAEMAL etc.

he-man *n.* (*pl.* **-men**) a masterful or virile man.

hemato- etc. *US* var. of HAEMATO- etc.

hemi- *comb. form* half. [from Greek]

hemiplegia *n. Med.* paralysis of one side of the body. [modern Latin] □ **hemiplegic** *n. & adj.*

Hemiptera *n. pl.* ▲ an order of insects comprising the 'true' bugs, which have mouthparts adapted for piercing and sucking. [from Greek *hemi-* + *pteron* 'wing'] □ **hemipteran** *n. & adj.* **hemipterous** *adj.*

hemisphere *n.* **1** half of a sphere. **2** ▼ a half of the Earth, esp. as divided by the equator (into *northern* and *southern hemisphere*) or by a line passing through the poles (into *eastern* and *western hemisphere*). □ **hemispheric** *adj.* **hemispherical** *adj.*

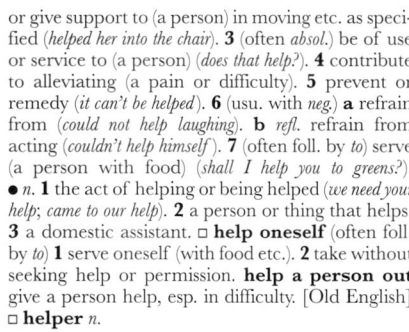

northern hemisphere · equator · southern hemisphere

HEMISPHERE: GLOBE DIVIDED INTO NORTHERN AND SOUTHERN HEMISPHERES

HERALDRY

Charges, or heraldic devices, were first used during the 12th century to identify armour-clad knights in battle. Knights wore their coat of arms, passed down from father to son, on their shield, armour, and surcoat.

Modern heraldry uses the blazon system to describe and record both existing and newly created coats of arms, which symbolize the power and authority invested in a particular town, city, nation, or family.

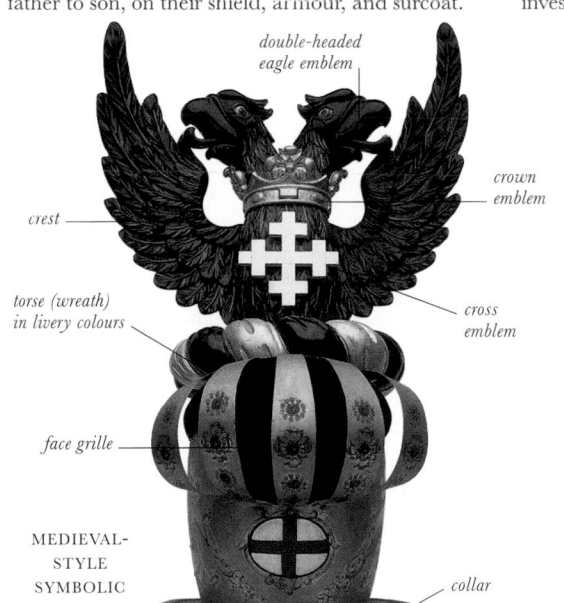

double-headed eagle emblem

crest

crown emblem

torse (wreath) in livery colours

cross emblem

face grille

MEDIEVAL-STYLE SYMBOLIC HELMET

collar

CHARGES

DOUBLE-HEADED EAGLE

LION

DOG

BEAR

HERALDIC STANDARD

H

---

hemline *n.* the line or level of the lower edge of a skirt, dress, or coat.

hemlock *n.* **1** a poisonous umbelliferous plant, *Conium maculatum*, with fernlike leaves and small white flowers. **2** a poison obtained from this. [Old English]

hemo- *comb. form US* var. of HAEMO-.

hemp *n.* **1** (in full **Indian hemp**) a herbaceous plant, *Cannabis sativa*, native to Asia. **2** its fibre extracted from the stem and used to make rope and stout fabrics. ▷ ROPE. **3** any of several narcotic drugs made from the hemp plant, esp. marijuana or cannabis. [Old English, related to Greek *kannabis*]

hempen *adj.* made from hemp.

hemstitch ● *n.* ▼ a decorative stitch used in sewing hems. ▷ STITCH. ● *v.tr.* hem with this stitch.

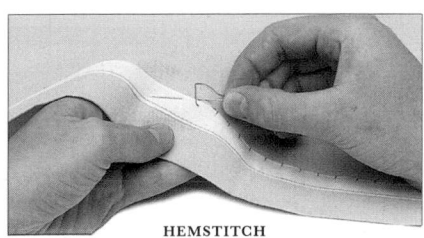

HEMSTITCH

hen *n.* **1** a female bird, esp. of a domestic fowl. **2** (in *pl.*) domestic fowls of either sex. [Old English]

hence *adv.* **1** from this time (*two years hence*). **2** for this reason (*hence we seem to be wrong*). **3** *archaic* from here; from this place. [Old English]

henceforth *adv.* (also **henceforward**) from this time onwards.

henchman *n.* (*pl.* **-men**) often *derog.* a trusted supporter. [Old English *hengst* 'male horse' + MAN]

hen-coop *n.* a coop for keeping fowls in.

henge *n.* ▶ a prehistoric monument consisting of a circle of stone or wood uprights. [back-formation from *Stonehenge*, such a monument in S. England]

hen harrier *n.* a common harrier, *Circus cyaneus*, of open country and moorland.

henna ● *n.* **1** a tropical shrub, *Lawsonia inermis*, having small pink, red, or white flowers. **2** the reddish dye from its shoots and leaves, esp. used to colour hair. ● *v.tr.* (**hennaed**, **hennaing**) dye (hair) with henna. [from Arabic *ḥinnā'*]

hen-party *n. colloq.* often *derog.* a social gathering of women.

henpeck *v.tr.* (usu. as **henpecked** *adj.*) (of a woman) constantly harass (a man, esp. her husband).

henry *n.* (*pl.* **-ies** or **henrys**) *Electr.* the SI unit of inductance which gives an electromotive force of one volt in a closed circuit with a uniform rate of change of current of one ampere per second. [named after J. *Henry*, American physicist, 1797–1878]

hep var. of HIP³.

heparin *n. Biochem.* a sulphur-containing polysaccharide used as an anticoagulant in the treatment of thrombosis. [based on Greek *hēpar* 'liver'] □ **heparinize** *v. tr.* (also **-ise**).

hepatic /hip-at-ik/ *adj.* **1** of or relating to the liver. ▷ CARDIOVASCULAR, LIVER. **2** dark brownish red; liver-coloured. [based on Greek *hēpar -atos* 'liver']

HENGE: STONEHENGE, ENGLAND, *c.*2,000 BC

hepatitis *n.* inflammation of the liver; a disease in which this occurs. [Modern Latin]

hepatitis A *n.* a form of viral hepatitis transmitted in food, causing fever and jaundice.

hepatitis B *n.* a severe form of viral hepatitis transmitted in infected blood, causing fever, debility, and jaundice.

hepta- *comb. form* seven. [from Greek]

heptagon *n.* ▶ a plane figure with seven sides and angles. □ **heptagonal** *adj.*

heptathlon *n.* an athletic contest, usu. for women, in which each competitor takes part in seven events. □ **heptathlete** *n.*

heptavalent *adj. Chem.* having a valency of seven.

HEPTAGON

her ● *pron.* objective case of SHE (*I like her*). ● *poss.det.* of or belonging to her (*her house*; *her own business*).

■ **Usage** The use of *her* instead of *she* after the verb 'to be' (as in *It's her all right*; *I am older than her*) is considered by some to be grammatically incorrect but is normal in ordinary usage. *Him, me, them,* and *us* are used similarly, e.g. *It's them on the phone again*; *It's us who will have to pay for it*. See also Usage Note at THAN.

herald ● *n.* **1** an official messenger bringing news. **2** a forerunner (*spring is the herald of summer*). **3 a** *hist.* an officer responsible for State ceremonial and etiquette. **b** (in the UK) an official of the Heralds' College, concerned with recording lineage and granting arms. ● *v.tr.* proclaim the approach of; usher in. [from Old French *herau(l)t*]

heraldic *adj.* of or concerning heraldry. □ **heraldically** *adv.*

heraldist *n.* an expert in heraldry.

heraldry *n.* **1** the science or art of a herald, esp. in dealing with armorial bearings. **2** ▲ armorial bearings.

HERB

Plants have been exploited since ancient times both as a source of food and medicine, and to scent or cleanse the home. Many herbs are traditionally used to alleviate the symptoms of disease, either through orally or locally applied herbal treatments, or through aromatherapy or homoeopathy. In the domestic environment, fresh or dried herbs are used to flavour culinary dishes, while herbal extracts provide a base for many household compounds for cleaning, polishing, sterilizing, and laundering. Shown here are some of the more familiar herbs.

CULINARY HERBS

THYME
garden thyme
(*Thymus vulgaris*)

ROSEMARY
(*Rosmarinus officinalis*)

MINT
basil mint
(*Mentha aquatica*)

CORIANDER
(*Coriandrum sativum*)

PARSLEY
curled parsley
(*Petroselinum crispum*)

BASIL
sweet basil
(*Ocimum basilicum*)

BORAGE
(*Borago officinalis*)

MARIGOLD
(*Calendula officinalis*)

SAGE
common sage
(*Salvia officinalis*)

MARJORAM (OREGANO)
compact marjoram
(*Origanum vulgare compactum*)

FENNEL
(*Foeniculum vulgare*)

BAY
(*Laurus nobilis*)

MEDICINAL HERBS

SCENTED MAYWEED
(*Chamomilla recutita*)

TEA TREE
(*Melaleuca alternifolia*)

OPIUM POPPY
(*Papaver somniferum*)

AROMATIC HERBS

WORMWOOD
(*Artemisia absinthium*)

HYSSOP
(*Hyssopus officinalis*)

LAVENDER
(*Lavandula angustifolia*)

herb *n.* **1** any non-woody seed-bearing plant. **2** ◀ any plant with leaves, seeds, or flowers used for flavouring, medicine, scent, etc. [from Latin *herba* 'green crops, herb'] □ **herb-like** *adj.* **herby** *adj.* (**herbier, herbiest**).

herbaceous *adj.* of, designating, or relating to herbs (see HERB 1).

herbaceous border *n.* a garden border containing esp. perennial flowering plants.

herbage *n.* **1** herbaceous vegetation. **2** the succulent part of this, esp. as pasture.

herbal ● *adj.* of herbs in medicinal and culinary use. ● *n.* a book with descriptions and accounts of the properties of these.

herbalist *n.* **1** a practitioner of herbal medicine; a dealer in medicinal herbs. **2** a collector of or writer on plants, esp. an early botanical writer. □ **herbalism** *n.*

herbarium *n.* (*pl.* **herbaria**) **1** a systematically arranged collection of dried plants. **2** a book, room, or building for these. [Late Latin]

herbicide *n.* a toxic substance used to destroy unwanted vegetation.

herbivore *n.* an animal that feeds on plants. □ **herbivorous** *adj.*

herb tea *n.* an infusion of herbs.

herb tobacco *n.* a mixture of herbs smoked as a substitute for tobacco.

Herculean /her-kew-**lee**-ăn/ *adj.* having or requiring great strength or effort. [from Latin name *Herculeus*]

herd ● *n.* **1** a large number of animals, esp. cattle, feeding or travelling or kept together. **2** (prec. by *the*) *derog.* a large number of people; a mob (*prefers not to follow the herd*). ● *v.* **1** *intr. & tr.* go or cause to go in a herd (*herded together for warmth; herded the cattle into the field*). **2** *tr.* tend (sheep, cattle, etc.). [Old English] □ **herder** *n.*

herdsman *n.* (*pl.* **-men**) the owner or keeper of a herd of domesticated animals.

here ● *adv.* **1** in or at or to this place or position. **2** indicating a person's presence or a thing offered (*here is your coat; my son here will show you*). **3** at this point in the argument, situation, etc. ● *n.* this place. ● *int.* **1** calling attention: short for *come here, look here,* etc. (*here, where are you going with that?*). **2** indicating one's presence in a roll-call: short for *I am here.* □ **here and there** in various places. **here goes!** *colloq.* an expression indicating the start of a bold act. **here's to** I drink to the health of. **neither here nor there** of no importance or relevance. [Old English]

hereabouts *adv.* (also **hereabout**) near this place.

hereafter ● *adv.* **1** from now on; in the future. **2** in the world to come (after death). ● *n.* **1** the future. **2** life after death.

hereby *adv.* by this means; as a result of this.

hereditable *adj.* that can be inherited.

hereditary *adj.* **1** (of disease, instinct, etc.) able to be passed down from one generation to another. **2 a** descending by inheritance. **b** holding a position by inheritance. □ **hereditarily** *adv.*

heredity *n.* **1 a** the passing on of physical or mental characteristics genetically from one generation to another. **b** these characteristics. **2** the genetic constitution of an individual. [from Latin *hereditas* 'heirship']

Hereford *n.* an animal of a breed of red and white beef cattle. [from *Hereford,* a city and county in England]

herein *adv. formal* in this matter, book, etc.

hereinafter *adv.* esp. *Law formal* **1** from this point on. **2** in a later part of this document etc.

hereof *adv. formal* of this.

heresy /**he**-ri-si/ *n.* (*pl.* **-ies**) **1** esp. *RC Ch.* **a** belief or practice contrary to orthodox doctrine. **b** an instance of this. **2 a** opinion contrary to what is normally accepted or maintained. **b** an instance of this. [from Greek *hairesis* 'choice, sect']

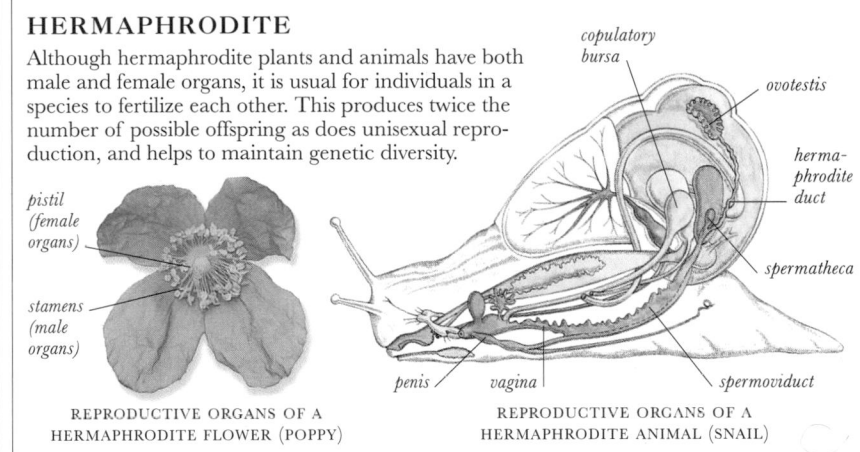

HERMAPHRODITE

Although hermaphrodite plants and animals have both male and female organs, it is usual for individuals in a species to fertilize each other. This produces twice the number of possible offspring as does unisexual reproduction, and helps to maintain genetic diversity.

pistil (female organs)

stamens (male organs)

REPRODUCTIVE ORGANS OF A
HERMAPHRODITE FLOWER (POPPY)

copulatory bursa

ovotestis

hermaphrodite duct

spermatheca

penis

vagina

spermoviduct

REPRODUCTIVE ORGANS OF A
HERMAPHRODITE ANIMAL (SNAIL)

heretic /**he**-ri-tik/ *n.* **1** the holder of an unorthodox opinion. **2** a person believing in or practising religious heresy. [from Greek *hairetikos* 'able to choose'] □ **heretical** *adj.* **heretically** *adv.*

hereto *adv. formal* to this matter.

heretofore *adv. formal* before this time.

hereunto *adv. archaic* to this.

hereupon *adv.* after this; in consequence of this.

herewith *adv.* with this (esp. of an enclosure in a letter etc.).

heritable *adj.* **1** *Law* **a** (of property) capable of being inherited by heirs-at-law (cf. MOVABLE *adj.* 2). **b** capable of inheriting. **2** *Biol.* (of a characteristic) transmissible from parent to offspring. [based on ecclesiastical Latin *hereditare* 'to inherit'] □ **heritability** *n.* **heritably** *adv.*

heritage *n.* **1** anything that is or may be inherited. **2** inherited circumstances, benefits, etc. (*a heritage of confusion*). **3** a nation's historic buildings, monuments, countryside, etc. [from Old French]

hermaphrodite ● *n.* **1** *Anat. & Zool.* ▲ a person or animal having both male and female sexual organs. **2** *Bot.* ▲ a plant having stamens and pistils in the same flower. ● *adj.* combining both sexes. [from *Hermaphroditus,* a son of Hermes and Aphrodite, who merged with the nymph Salmacis in one body] □ **hermaphroditic** *adj.* **hermaphroditism** *n.*

hermetic *adj.* (also **hermetical**) **1** with an airtight closure. **2** protected from outside agencies. [from *Hermes (Trismegistus)* '(thrice-greatest) Hermes'] □ **hermetically** *adv.* **hermetism** *n.*

hermetic seal *n.* an airtight seal.

hermit *n.* **1** an early Christian recluse. **2** any person living in solitude. [based on Greek *eremos* 'solitary'] □ **hermitic** *adj.*

hermitage *n.* **1** a hermit's dwelling. **2** a monastery.

hermit crab *n.* ▼ a crab of the family Paguridae, living in a cast-off mollusc shell for protection.

discarded mollusc shell

HERMIT CRAB
(*Dardanus megistos*)

hernia *n.* (*pl.* **hernias** or **herniae** /-ni-ee/) the displacement and protrusion of part of an organ through the wall of the cavity containing it, esp. of the abdomen. [Latin] □ **hernial** *adj.* **herniated** *adj.*

hero *n.* (*pl.* **-oes**) **1** a person noted or admired for courage, outstanding achievements, etc. (*Newton, a hero of science*). **2** the chief male character in a play, story, etc. [from Greek *heros*]

heroic ● *adj.* **1** of, like, or fit for a hero. **2 a** (of language) grand, high-flown, dramatic. **b** (of a work of art) ambitious in scale or subject. ● *n.* (in *pl.*) **1** high-flown language or sentiments. **2** unduly bold behaviour. □ **heroically** *adv.*

heroic couplet *n.* two lines of rhyming iambic pentameters.

heroin *n.* a highly addictive crystalline analgesic drug derived from morphine, often used as a narcotic.

heroine *n.* **1** a woman noted or admired for courage, outstanding achievements, etc. **2** the chief female character in a poem, play, story, etc. **3** *Gk Antiq.* a demigoddess.

heroism *n.* heroic conduct or qualities.

heron *n.* ▶ any of various large wading birds of the family Ardeidae, esp. *Ardea cinerea,* with long legs and a long S-shaped neck. [from Old French *hairon*] □ **heronry** *n.* (*pl.* **-ies**)

hero's welcome *n.* a rapturous welcome, like that given to a successful warrior.

hero-worship ● *n.* idealization of an admired man. ● *v.tr.* (**-wor-shipped, -wor-shipping**; *US* **-worshiped, -worshiping**) worship as a hero; idolize. □ **hero-worshipper** *n.*

HERON: PURPLE HERON
(*Ardea purpurea*)

herpes /**her**-peez/ *n.* a virus disease with outbreaks of blisters on the skin etc. [from Greek *herpes* *-etos* 'shingles'] □ **herpetic** *adj.*

herpes simplex *n.* a viral infection which may produce cold sores, genital inflammation, or conjunctivitis.

herpes zoster *n.* = SHINGLES. [based on Greek *zoster* 'belt, girdle']

herpetology *n.* the study of reptiles. [based on Greek *herpeton* 'reptile'] □ **herpetological** *adj.* **herpetologist** *n.*

Herr /hair/ *n.* (*pl.* **Herren** /**he**-rĕn/) **1** the title of a German man; Mr. **2** a German man. [from Old High German *herro* 'more exalted']

herring *n.* a N. Atlantic fish, *Clupea harengus,* coming near the coast in large shoals to spawn. [Old English]

H

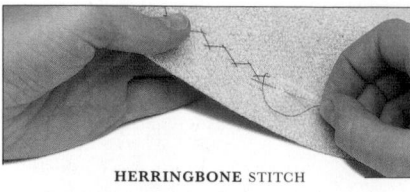

HERRINGBONE STITCH

herringbone n. ▲ a stitch with a zigzag pattern.

herring gull n. a large gull, *Larus argentatus*, with dark wing-tips.

hers poss.pron. the one or ones belonging to or associated with her. □ **of hers** of or belonging to her (*a friend of hers*).

herself pron. **1 a** emphat. form of SHE or HER (*she herself will do it*). **b** refl. form of HER (*she has hurt herself*). **2** in her normal state of body or mind (*does not feel quite herself today*). □ **be herself** act in her normal unconstrained manner. **by herself** see *by oneself*.

hertz n. (*pl.* same) the SI unit of frequency, equal to one cycle per second. [named after H. R. *Hertz*, German physicist, 1857–94]

he's contr. **1** he is. **2** he has.

hesitant adj. hesitating; irresolute. □ **hesitance** n. **hesitancy** n. **hesitantly** adv.

hesitate v.intr. **1** (often foll. by *about*, *over*) show or feel indecision or uncertainty; pause in doubt (*hesitated over her choice*). **2** (often foll. by *to* + infin.) be reluctant (*I hesitate to inform against him*). [from Latin *haesitare*] □ **hesitatingly** adv. **hesitation** n.

hessian n. a strong coarse sacking made of hemp or jute. [from *Hesse*, a state in Germany]

hetero n. (*pl.* -os) colloq. a heterosexual.

hetero- comb. form other, different (often opp. HOMO-). [from Greek *heteros* 'other']

heterocyclic adj. Chem. (of a compound) with a bonded ring of atoms of more than one kind.

heterodox adj. (of a person, opinion, etc.) not orthodox. [based on Greek *doxa* 'opinion'] □ **heterodoxy** n.

heterodyne Radio ● adj. relating to the production of a lower frequency from the combination of two almost equal high frequencies. ● v.intr. produce a lower frequency in this way. [based on Greek *dunamis* 'power']

heterogeneous adj. (also disp. **heterogenous**) **1** diverse in character. **2** varied in content. [based on Greek *genos* 'kind'] □ **heterogeneity** n. **heterogeneously** adv.

▪**Usage** The less common form *heterogenous* is considered incorrect by some people and best avoided. Cf. *homogeneous* and *homogenous* which have quite different senses but are often confused: see Usage Note at HOMOGENEOUS.

heterologous adj. not homologous. □ **heterology** n.

heteromorphic adj. (also **heteromorphous**) Biol. **1** of dissimilar forms. **2** (of insects) existing in different forms at different stages in their life cycle. □ **heteromorphism** n.

heterosexual ● adj. **1** feeling or involving sexual attraction to persons of the opposite sex. **2** concerning heterosexual relations or people. **3** relating to the opposite sex. ● n. a heterosexual person. □ **heterosexuality** n. **heterosexually** adv.

het up adj. colloq. excited, overwrought. [from dialect *het* 'heated']

heuristic /hewr-**iss**-tik/ ● adj. **1** allowing or assisting to discover. **2** Computing proceeding to a solution by trial and error. ● n. (in *pl.*; usu. treated as *sing.*) Computing the study and use of heuristic techniques in data processing. [based on Greek *heuriskein* 'to find'] □ **heuristically** adv.

hew v.tr. (past part. **hewn** or **hewed**) **1** (often foll. by *down, away, off*) chop or cut (a thing) with an axe, a sword, etc. **2** cut (a block of wood etc.) into shape. □ **hew one's way** make a way for oneself by hewing. [Old English] □ **hewer** n.

hex[1] ● v. **1** intr. practise witchcraft. **2** tr. cast a spell on; bewitch. ● n. **1** a magic spell. **2** a witch. [from German *Hexe*]

hex[2] adj. & n. esp. Computing = HEXADECIMAL. [abbreviation]

hexa- comb. form six. [from Greek *hex* 'six']

hexad n. a group of six.

hexadecimal esp. Computing ● adj. relating to or using a system of numerical notation that has 16 rather than 10 as a base. ● n. the hexadecimal system; hexadecimal notation. □ **hexadecimally** adv.

hexagon n. a plane figure with six sides and angles. □ **hexagonal** adj.

hexagram n. **1** ► a figure formed by two intersecting equilateral triangles. **2** a figure of six lines. [based on Greek *gramma* 'line']

HEXAGRAM

hexahedron n. (*pl.* **hexahedra** or **hexahedrons**) ▼ a solid figure with six faces. □ **hexahedral** adj.

HEXAHEDRON

hexameter /hek-**sam**-i-ter/ n. a line or verse of six metrical feet. □ **hexametric** adj.

hexane n. Chem. a liquid hydrocarbon of the alkane series.

hexavalent adj. having a valency of six.

hey int. calling attention or expressing joy, surprise, enquiry, enthusiasm, etc. [Middle English]

heyday n. the flush or full bloom of youth, vigour, prosperity, etc. [earlier an exclamation of joy, surprise, etc.]

hey presto! int. Brit. a phrase announcing the successful completion of a trick or other surprising achievement.

HF abbr. high frequency.

Hf symb. Chem. the element hafnium.

hf. abbr. half.

Hg symb. Chem. the element mercury. [modern Latin *hydrargyrum*]

hg abbr. hectogram(s).

HGV abbr. Brit. heavy goods vehicle.

HH abbr. **1** Brit. Her or His Highness. **2** His Holiness. **3** double-hard (pencil lead).

hi int. calling attention or as a greeting. [parallel form to HEY]

hiatus /hy-**ay**-tŭs/ n. (*pl.* **hiatuses**) **1** a break or gap, esp. in a series, account, or chain of proof. **2** Prosody & Gram. a break between two vowels coming together but not in the same syllable, as in *though hid the ear*. [Latin, literally 'gaping', from *hiare* 'gape'] □ **hiatal** adj.

hiatus hernia n. Med. the protrusion of an organ, esp. the stomach, through the oesophageal opening in the diaphragm.

Hib n. Med. a bacterium, *Haemophilus influenzae* type B, causing infant meningitis (often attrib.: *Hib vaccine*).

hibernate v.intr. **1** (of some animals) spend the winter in a dormant state. **2** remain inactive. [based on Latin *hibernatus* 'wintered'] □ **hibernation** n. **hibernator** n.

Hibernian archaic poet. ● adj. of or concerning Ireland. ● n. a native of Ireland. [from Latin *Hibernia*, based on Celtic]

hibiscus n. (*pl.* **hibiscuses**) ► any tree or shrub of the genus *Hibiscus*, cultivated for its large brightly coloured flowers. [from Greek *hibiskos* 'marsh mallow']

hic int. expressing the sound of a hiccup, esp. a drunken hiccup.

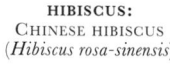

HIBISCUS:
CHINESE HIBISCUS
(*Hibiscus rosa-sinensis*)

hiccup (also **hiccough** pronunc. same) ● n. **1** an involuntary spasm of the diaphragm and respiratory organs, with sudden closure of the glottis and characteristic coughlike sound. **2** a temporary or minor fault or setback. ● v.intr. (**hiccuped**, **hiccuping**) make a hiccup or series of hiccups. □ **hiccupy** adj.

hick n. colloq. a country dweller; a provincial. [pet form of the name *Richard*]

hickory n. (*pl.* -ies) **1** ▼ any N. American tree of the genus *Carya*, yielding tough heavy wood and bearing nutlike edible fruits (see PECAN). **2 a** the wood of these trees. **b** a stick made of this. [from Algonquian *pawcohiccora*]

male catkins

HICKORY:
SHAGBARK HICKORY
(*Carya ovata*)

hid past of HIDE[1].

hidden past part. of HIDE[1].

hidden agenda n. a secret or ulterior motive behind an action, statement, etc.

hide[1] ● v. (past **hid**; past part. **hidden** or archaic **hid**) **1** tr. put or keep out of sight. **2** intr. conceal oneself. **3** tr. (usu. foll. by *from*) keep (a fact) secret (*hid his real motive from her*). **4** tr. conceal (a thing) from sight intentionally or not (*trees hid the house*). ● n. Brit. a camouflaged shelter used for observing wildlife or hunting animals. □ **hide one's head** keep out of sight, esp. from shame. **hide out** (or **up**) remain in concealment. [Old English] □ **hider** n.

hide[2] ● n. **1** the skin of an animal, esp. when tanned or dressed. **2** joc. the human skin, esp. on the buttocks (*I'll tan your hide*). [Old English] □ **hided** adj. (also in comb.).

hide-and-seek n. a children's game in which one or more players seek a child or children hiding.

hideaway n. a hiding place or place of retreat.

hidebound adj. **1** narrow-minded; bigoted. **2** (of the law, rules, etc.) constricted by tradition.

hideous adj. **1** frightful, repulsive, or revolting, to the senses or the mind. **2** colloq. unpleasant. [based on Old French *hide* 'fear'] □ **hideously** adv. **hideousness** n.

hideout n. a hiding place.

hidey-hole n. Brit. colloq. a hiding place.

hiding[1] n. colloq. a thrashing. □ **on a hiding to nothing** Brit. in a position from which there can be no successful outcome.

hiding[2] n. **1** the act or an instance of hiding. **2** the state of remaining hidden (*go into hiding*).

hie v.intr. & refl. (**hies**, **hied**, **hieing** or **hying**) archaic or poet. go quickly (*hie to your chamber*; *hied him to the chase*). [Old English *higian* 'to strive, pant']

hierarchy /**hyr**-ar-ki/ n. (*pl.* -ies) **1 a** a system in which grades or classes of status or authority are ranked one above the other. **b** a hierarchical system (of government, management, etc.). **c** (foll. by *of*) a range in order of importance (*hierarchy of values*). **2 a** a priestly government. **b** a priesthood organized in grades. □ **hierarchic** adj. **hierarchical** adj.

hieratic /hyr-**at**-ik/ adj. **1** of or concerning priests; priestly. **2** of the ancient Egyptian writing of abridged hieroglyphics as used by priests. [based on Greek *hierasthai* 'to be a priest'] □ **hieratically** *adv.*

hiero- /hyr-oh/ *comb. form* sacred, holy. [from Greek *hieros* 'sacred']

hieroglyph /hyr-ŏ-glif/ *n.* ▶ a picture of an object representing a word, syllable, or sound, as used in ancient Egyptian and other writing.

hieroglyphic /hyr-ŏ-glif-ik/ ● *adj.* **1** of or written in hieroglyphs. **2** symbolical. ● *n.* (in *pl.*) hieroglyphs; hieroglyphic writing. [based on Greek *gluphē* 'carving']

hi-fi *colloq.* ● *adj.* of high fidelity. ● *n.* (*pl.* **hi-fis**) a set of equipment for high-fidelity sound reproduction.

higgledy-piggledy *adv. & adj.* in confusion or disorder.

high ● *adj.* **1 a** of great vertical extent (*a high building*). **b** (*predic.*; often in *comb.*) of a specified height (*one inch high*; *water was waist-high*). **2** far above ground or sea level etc. (*a high altitude*). **3** extending above the normal or average level (*high boots*; *jersey with a high neck*). **4** of exalted, esp. spiritual, quality (*high principles*). **5** of exalted rank (*in high society*). **6 a** great; intense; extreme; powerful (*high praise*; *high temperature*). **b** greater than normal (*high prices*). **c** extreme in religious or political opinion (*high Tory*). **7** (often foll. by *on*) *colloq.* intoxicated by alcohol or esp. drugs. **8** (of a sound or note) of high frequency; shrill. **9** (of a period, an age, a time, etc.) at its peak (*high summer*; *High Renaissance*). **10 a** (of meat etc.) beginning to go bad; off. **b** (of game) well-hung and slightly decomposed. ● *n.* **1** a high, or the highest, level or figure. **2** an area of high barometric pressure; an anticyclone. **3** *slang* a euphoric state, esp. drug-induced (*I'm on a high at the moment*). **4** *N. Amer. colloq.* high school. ● *adv.* **1** far up; aloft (*flew the flag high*). **2** in or to a high degree. **3** at a high price. **4** (of a sound) at or to a high pitch (*sang high*). □ **from on high** from heaven or a high place. **high old** (*attrib.*) *colloq.* most enjoyable. **high opinion of** a favourable opinion of it. **in high feather** see FEATHER. **on high** in or to heaven or a high place. **on one's high horse** *colloq.* behaving superciliously or arrogantly. **run high 1** (of the sea) have a strong current with high tide. **2** (of feelings) be strong. [Old English]

high altar *n.* the chief altar of a church. ▷ CATHEDRAL

high and dry *adv.* (usu. in phr. **left high and dry**) **1** stranded without resources. **2** (of a ship) out of the water, esp. stranded.

high and low *adv.* (esp. in phr. **search high and low**) everywhere.

high and mighty *adj. colloq.* arrogant.

highball *n. N. Amer.* a drink of spirits and soda etc., served with ice in a tall glass.

highbrow *colloq.* ● *adj.* intellectual; cultural. ● *n.* an intellectual or cultured person.

high chair *n.* an infant's chair with long legs and a tray, for use at meals.

High Church ● *n.* a tradition within the Anglican Church emphasizing ritual, priestly authority, sacraments, and historical continuity with Catholic Christianity. ● *adj.* of or relating to this tradition.

high-class *adj.* of high quality.

high colour *n.* a flushed complexion.

high command *n.* an army commander-in-chief and associated staff.

High Commission *n.* an embassy from one Commonwealth country to another. □ **High Commissioner** *n.*

High Court *n.* **1** a supreme court of justice, esp. in England (in full **High Court of Justice**) the court of unlimited civil jurisdiction forming part of the Supreme Court. **2** (often **high court**) (in the US) a supreme court in a state.

high day *n.* a festal day.

Higher *n.* (usu. in *pl.*) (in Scotland) an examination leading to the Scottish Certificate of Education, Higher Grade.

higher animal *n.* an animal showing relatively advanced characteristics, e.g. a placental mammal.

higher court *n.* a court that can overrule the decision of another.

higher education *n.* education at university etc., esp. to degree level.

higher mathematics *n.pl.* (usu. treated as *sing.*) advanced mathematics as taught at university etc.

higher plant *n.* a plant showing relatively advanced characteristics, e.g. a flowering plant.

highest common factor *n.* the highest number that can be divided exactly into each of two or more numbers.

high explosive *n.* an extremely explosive substance used in shells, bombs, etc.

highfalutin /hy-fă-**loo**-tin/ *adj.* (also **highfaluting**) *colloq.* absurdly pompous or pretentious.

high fashion *n.* = HAUTE COUTURE.

high fidelity *n.* the reproduction of sound with little distortion, giving a result very similar to the original.

high finance *n.* financial transactions involving large sums.

high-five *n. N. Amer. slang* a gesture of celebration or greeting in which two people slap each other's palms with their arms outstretched over their heads.

high-flown *adj.* (of language etc.) extravagant, bombastic.

high-flyer *n.* (also **high-flier**) **1** a person with the potential and usu. ambition to succeed, esp. academically or in business. **2** a thing with potential for exceptional, usu. commercial, achievement (*high-flyer of the sports car range*). □ **high-flying** *adj.*

high frequency *n.* a frequency, esp. in radio, of 3–30 megahertz

high gear *n.* a gear of a vehicle providing a high ratio between the speed of the driven wheels and that of the driving mechanism and so a high speed to the vehicle itself.

high-grade *adj.* of high quality.

high-handed *adj.* disregarding others' feelings; overbearing. □ **high-handedly** *adv.* **high-handedness** *n.*

high heels *n.pl.* women's shoes with high heels. □ **high-heeled** *adj.*

high jinks *n.pl.* boisterous joking or merrymaking.

high jump *n.* **1** an athletic event consisting of jumping as high as possible over a bar of adjustable height. **2** *Brit. colloq.* a drastic punishment (*he's for the high jump*). □ **high-jumper** *n.*

high kick *n.* a dancer's kick high in the air. □ **high-kicking** *attrib.adj.*

highland ● *n.* (usu. in *pl.*) **1** an area of high or mountainous land. **2** (**the Highlands**) the mountainous part of Scotland. ● *adj.* **1** relating to high or mountainous land. **2** (**Highland**) of or relating to the Highlands. □ **highlander** *n.* (also **Highlander**). **Highlandman** *n.* (*pl.* **-men**).

Highland cattle *n.* ▶ cattle of a shaggy-haired breed with long curved widely spaced horns.

Highland dress *n.* the Scottish kilt etc.

Highland fling see FLING *n.* 3.

high-level *adj.* **1** (of negotiations etc.) conducted by high-ranking people. **2** *Computing* (of a programming language) not machine-dependent and usu. at a level of abstraction close to natural language.

---

high life *n.* (also **high living**) a luxurious existence ascribed to the upper classes.

highlight ● *n.* **1** (in a painting etc.) a light area, or one seeming to reflect light. **2** a moment or detail of vivid interest; an outstanding feature. **3** (usu. in *pl.*) a light streak in the hair, esp. one produced by bleaching or dyeing. ● *v.tr.* **1 a** bring into prominence; draw attention to. **b** mark with a highlighter. **2** create highlights in (the hair).

highlighter *n.* a marker pen which overlays colour on a printed word etc., leaving it legible and emphasized.

high-lows *n. pl. archaic* boots reaching over the ankles.

highly *adv.* **1** in a high degree (*highly amusing*; *commend it highly*). **2** honourably; favourably (*think highly of him*).

highly strung *adj.* (hyphenated when *attrib.*) very sensitive or nervous.

high marks *US var.* of FULL MARKS.

high-minded *adj.* **1** having high moral principles. **2** *archaic* proud. □ **high-mindedly** *adv.* **high-mindedness** *n.*

highness *n.* **1** the state of being high (*highness of taxation*) (cf. HEIGHT). **2** (**Highness**) a title of a prince or princess (*Her Highness*; *Your Royal Highness*).

high-octane *adj.* (of fuel used in internal-combustion engines) having good antiknock properties, not detonating readily during the power stroke.

high-pitched *adj.* **1** (of a sound) high. **2** (of a roof) steep.

high places *n.pl.* the upper ranks of an organization etc.

high point *n.* the maximum or best state reached.

high-powered *adj.* **1** having great power or energy. **2** important or influential.

high pressure *n.* **1** a high degree of activity or exertion. **2** a condition of the atmosphere with the pressure above average, e.g. in an anticyclone.

high priest *n.* **1** a chief priest, esp. *hist.* Jewish. **2** (*fem.* **high priestess**) the head of any cult.

high profile *n.* exposure to attention or publicity (usu. hyphenated when *attrib.*: *high-profile event*).

high-quality *adj.* of high quality.

high-ranking *adj.* of high rank, senior.

high relief see RELIEF 6.

high-rise ● *attrib.adj.* (of a building) having many storeys. ● *n.* such a building.

high-risk *attrib.adj.* involving or exposed to danger (*high risk sports*).

high road *n.* **1** *Brit.* a main road. **2** (usu. foll. by *to*) a direct route (*on the high road to success*).

high roller *n. N. Amer. slang* a person who gambles large sums or spends freely.

high school *n.* **1** *Brit.* a grammar school. **2** *N. Amer. & Sc.* a secondary school.

high sea *n.* (also **high seas** *pl.*) open seas not within any country's jurisdiction.

high season *n.* the period of the greatest number of visitors at a resort etc.

HIGHLAND CATTLE: COW

HIEROGLYPHS ON AN ANCIENT EGYPTIAN SCARAB, *c.*1350 BC

H

H

high-security *attrib.adj.* **1** (of a prison, lock, etc.) extremely secure. **2** (of a prisoner) kept in a high-security prison.

High Sheriff see SHERIFF 1a.

high-sounding *adj.* pretentious, bombastic.

high-speed *attrib.adj.* operating at great speed.

high-spirited *adj.* vivacious; cheerful.

high spirits *n.pl.* vivacity; cheerfulness. □ **in high spirits** very cheerful; in a very good mood.

high spot *n. colloq.* the most enjoyable feature, moment, or experience.

High Steward see STEWARD *n.* 6.

high street *n. Brit.* a main road, esp. the principal shopping street of a town (usu. hyphenated when *attrib.*: *high-street bank*).

high table *n. Brit.* a table on a platform at a public dinner or for the fellows of a college.

hightail *v.intr. N. Amer. colloq.* move at high speed.

high tea *n. Brit.* a main evening meal usu. consisting of a cooked dish, bread and butter, tea, etc.

high-tech ● *adj.* **1** (of interior design etc.) imitating styles more usual in industry etc., esp. using steel, glass, or plastic in a functional way. **2** employing, requiring, or involved in high technology. ● *n.* (**high tech**) = HIGH TECHNOLOGY.

high technology *n.* advanced technological development, esp. in electronics.

high tension *n.* = HIGH VOLTAGE.

high tide *n.* **1** the state of the tide when at its highest or fullest level. **2** the time of this.

high time *n.* a time when something is late or overdue (*it is high time they arrived*).

high-toned *adj.* stylish; dignified; superior.

high treason see TREASON 1.

high-up *n. colloq.* a person of high rank.

high voltage *n.* electrical potential large enough to cause injury or damage if diverted, as in power transmission cables.

high water *n.* = HIGH TIDE.

high water mark *n.* the level reached by the sea etc. at high tide.

highway *n.* **1 a** a public road. **b** a main route (by land or water). **2** a direct course of action (*on the highway to success*).

Highway Code *n.* (in the UK) the official booklet of guidance for road users.

highwayman *n.* (*pl.* **-men**; *fem.* **highwaywoman**, *pl.* **-women**) *hist.* a robber of passengers, travellers, etc., usu. mounted.

high wire *n.* a high tightrope.

high words *n.pl.* angry talk.

hijack ● *v.tr.* **1** seize control of (a loaded lorry, an aircraft in flight, etc.), esp. to force it to a different destination. **2** seize (goods) in transit. **3** take over (an organization etc.) by force or subterfuge in order to redirect it. ● *n.* an instance of hijacking. [20th-century coinage] □ **hijacker** *n.*

Hijra var. of HEGIRA.

hike ● *n.* **1** a long country walk, esp. with a rucksack etc. **2** an increase (of prices etc.). ● *v.* **1** *intr.* walk for a long distance, esp. across country with boots, rucksack, etc. **2** *tr.* (usu. foll. by *up*) hitch up (clothing etc.). **3** *tr.* increase (prices etc.). [19th-century dialect word] □ **hiker** *n.*

hilarious *adj.* **1** exceedingly funny. **2** boisterously merry. [from Greek *hilaros* 'cheerful'] □ **hilariously** *adv.* **hilariousness** *n.* **hilarity** *n.*

hill *n.* **1** a naturally raised area of land, not as high as a mountain. **2** (often in *comb.*) a heap; a mound (*anthill; dunghill*). **3** a sloping piece of road. □ **old as the hills** very ancient. **over the hill** *colloq.* **1** past the prime of life; declining. **2** past the crisis. [Old English]

hill-billy *n.* (*pl.* **-ies**) *US colloq.*, often *derog.* a person from a remote or mountainous area, esp. in the Appalachians (cf. HICK).

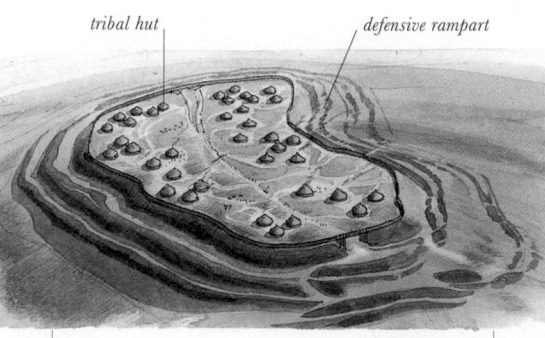

tribal hut   *defensive rampart*

HILL FORT: IRON AGE HILLFORT, ENGLAND, *c.*300 BC

hill fort *n.* ▲ a fort built on a hill.

hillock *n.* a small hill or mound. □ **hillocky** *adj.*

hillside *n.* the sloping side of a hill.

hilltop *n.* the summit of a hill.

hillwalking *n.* the pastime of walking in hilly country. □ **hillwalker** *n.*

hilly *adj.* (**hillier**, **hilliest**) having many hills. □ **hilliness** *n.*

hilt *n.* the handle of a sword, dagger, etc. ▷ SWORD. □ **up to the hilt** completely. [Old English]

him *pron.* **1** *objective case* of HE (*I saw him*). **2** *archaic* himself (*fell and hurt him*).

■ **Usage** See Usage Note at HER.

himself *pron.* **1 a** *emphat. form* of HE or HIM (*he himself will do it*). **b** *refl. form* of HIM (*he has hurt himself*). **2** in his normal state of body or mind (*does not feel quite himself today*). □ **be himself** act in his normal unconstrained manner. **by himself** see *by oneself*.

hind[1] *adj.* (esp. of parts of the body) situated at the back (*hind leg*) (opp. FORE *adj.*). [Middle English]

hind[2] *n.* a female deer (esp. a red deer), esp. in and after the third year. [Old English]

hindbrain *n. Anat.* the lower part of the brainstem.

hinder[1] *v.tr.* (also *absol.*) impede; delay; prevent (*you will hinder him; hindered me from working*). [Old English]

hinder[2] *adj.* rear, hind (*the hinder part*). [Middle English]

Hindi ● *n.* **1** a group of spoken dialects of northern India. **2** a literary form of Hindustani, an official language of India. ● *adj.* of or concerning Hindi. [Urdu, from *Hindi* 'India']

hindmost *adj.* furthest behind; most remote.

hindquarters *n.pl.* the hind legs and adjoining parts of a quadruped.

hindrance *n.* **1** the act or an instance of hindering; the state of being hindered. **2** a thing that hinders.

hindsight *n.* wisdom after the event (*realized with hindsight that they were wrong*).

Hindu ● *n.* (*pl.* **Hindus**) a follower of Hinduism. ● *adj.* of or concerning Hindus or Hinduism.

Hinduism *n.* the main religious and social system of India, including belief in reincarnation, the worship of several gods, and a caste system. □ **Hinduize** *v.tr.* (also **-ise**).

Hindustani ● *n. hist.* **1** a group of mutually intelligible languages and dialects spoken in north-west India, principally Hindi and Urdu. **2** the Delhi dialect of Hindi, widely used throughout India as a lingua franca. ● *adj.* of or relating to the culture of north-west India. [Urdu, from Persian]

■ **Usage** *Hindustani* was the usual term in the 18th and 19th centuries for the native language of north-west India. The usual modern term is *Hindi*, although *Hindustani* is still sometimes used to refer to the lingua franca.

hinge ● *n.* **1 a** a movable joint on which a door, lid, etc. swings. **b** *Biol.* a natural joint performing a similar function, e.g. that of a bivalve shell. **2** a point or principle on which everything depends.

● *v.* (**hingeing** or **hinging**) **1** *intr.* (foll. by *on*) depend (on a principle, an event, etc.) (*all hinges on his acceptance*). **2** *tr.* attach with or as if with a hinge. [Middle English] □ **hinged** *adj.* **hingeless** *adj.*

hinny *n.* (*pl.* **-ies**) the offspring of a female donkey and a male horse. [from Greek *hinnos*]

hint ● *n.* **1** a slight or indirect indication or suggestion (*took the hint and left*). **2** a small piece of practical information. **3** a very small trace; a suggestion. ● *v.tr.* (often foll. by *that* + clause) suggest slightly (*hinted the contrary; hinted that they were wrong*). □ **hint at** give a hint of; refer indirectly to.

hinterland *n.* **1** the areas beyond a coastal district or a river's banks. **2** an area served by a port or other centre. [German, from *hinter* 'behind' + *Land* 'land']

hip[1] *n.* a projection of the pelvis and upper thigh bone on each side of the body. ▷ HIP JOINT. [Old English] □ **hipped** *adj.* (also in *comb.*).

hip[2] *n.* ▶ the fruit of a rose, esp. a wild kind. [Old English]

hip[3] *adj.* (also **hep**) (**hipper**, **hippest** or **hepper**, **heppest**) *slang* following the latest fashion in music, clothes, etc. [20th-century coinage] □ **hipness** *n.*

hip[4] *int.* introducing a united cheer (*hip, hip, hooray*). [19th-century coinage]

HIP: ROSE HIPS (*Rosa rugosa*)

hip bath *n.* a portable bath in which a person sits.

hip bone *n.* a bone forming the hip, esp. the ilium.

hip flask *n.* a flask for spirits etc., carried in a hip pocket.

hip hop *n.* **1** a style of popular music of US black and Hispanic origin, featuring rap with an electronic backing. **2** the subculture associated with this, including graffiti art, break-dancing, etc. [20th-century coinage]

hip joint *n.* ▼ the articulation of the head of the thigh bone with the ilium. ▷ JOINT

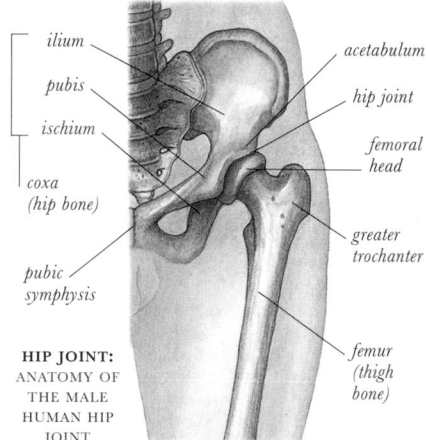

ilium
pubis
ischium
coxa (hip bone)
pubic symphysis

acetabulum
hip joint
femoral head
greater trochanter
femur (thigh bone)

HIP JOINT: ANATOMY OF THE MALE HUMAN HIP JOINT

hipped roof var. of HIP ROOF.

hippie var. of HIPPY[1].

hippo *n.* (*pl.* **-os**) *colloq.* a hippopotamus.

hip pocket *n.* a trouser pocket just behind the hip. □ **in one's hip pocket** *N. Amer.* completely under control.

Hippocratic oath *n.* (*hist.* except in revised form in certain medical schools) an oath taken by doctors prior to beginning medical practice, affirming their obligations and proper conduct. [from *Hippocrates*, Greek physician, 5th century BC]

hippodrome n. **1** a music hall, theatre, or dance hall. **2** Antiq. a course for chariot races etc. [from Greek hippos 'horse' + dromos 'race, course']

hippopotamus n. (pl. **hippopotamuses** or **hippopotami** /-my/) a large thick-skinned four-legged mammal, Hippopotamus amphibius, native to Africa, inhabiting rivers, lakes, etc. [from Greek hippos 'horse' + potamos 'river']

hippy[1] n. (also **hippie**) (pl. **-ies**) (esp. in the 1960s) a person of unconventional appearance, typically with long hair, jeans, beads, etc., often associated with hallucinogenic drugs and a rejection of conventional values.

hippy[2] adj. having large hips.

hip roof n. (also **hipped roof**) ▶ a roof with the sides and the ends inclined.

hipster[1] Brit. ● adj. (of a garment) hanging from the hips rather than the waist. ● n. (in pl.) such trousers.

hipster[2] n. slang a person who is hip. □ **hipsterism** n.

hire ● v.tr. **1** (often foll. by from) procure the temporary use of (a thing) for an agreed payment (hired a van from them). **2** esp. US employ (a person). ● n. **1** hiring or being hired. **2** payment for this. □ **for hire** ready to be hired. **hire out** grant the temporary use of (a thing) for an agreed payment. [Old English] □ **hireable** adj. (US **hirable**). **hirer** n.

hire car n. Brit. a car available for hire.

hired girl n. (also **hired man**) N. Amer. a domestic servant, esp. on a farm.

hireling n. usu. derog. a person who works for hire.

hire purchase n. Brit. a system by which a person may purchase a thing by regular payments while having the use of it.

hirsute /herss-yoot/ adj. hairy, shaggy. [from Latin hirsutus] □ **hirsuteness** n.

his ● poss.det. of or belonging to him (his house; his own business). ● poss.pron. the one or ones belonging to or associated with him (it is his; his are over there). □ **of his** of or belonging to him (a friend of his).

Hispanic ● adj. **1** of or relating to Spain or to Spain and Portugal. **2** of Spain and other Spanish-speaking countries. ● n. a Spanish-speaking person, esp. one of Latin American descent, living in the US. [based on Latin Hispanica 'Spain'] □ **Hispanicize** v.tr. (also **-ise**)

hiss ● v. **1** intr. (of a person, snake, goose, etc.) make a sharp sibilant sound, esp. as a sign of disapproval (the water hissed on the hotplate; audience booed and hissed). **2** tr. express disapproval of (a person etc.) by hisses. **3** tr. whisper (a threat etc.) urgently or angrily ('Get back!' he hissed). ● n. **1** a sharp sibilant sound as of the letter s, esp. as an expression of disapproval. **2** Electronics unwanted interference at audio frequencies. [Middle English]

histamine n. Biochem. an amine causing contraction of muscle in hollow organs and dilation of capillaries, released by cells in response to injury and in allergic and inflammatory reactions. □ **histaminic** adj.

histo- comb. form (also **hist-** before a vowel) Biol. tissue. [from Greek histos 'web, tissue']

histogram n. Statistics ▶ a chart consisting of rectangles (usu. drawn vertically from a baseline) whose areas and positions are proportional to the value or range of a number of variables.

histology n. the study of the microscopic structure of tissues. □ **histological** adj. **histologist** n.

historian n. **1** a writer of history. **2** a person learned in or studying history.

historic adj. **1** famous or important in history or potentially so (a historic moment). **2** Gram. (of a tense) normally used to narrate past events.

■ **Usage** Note the relatively limited scope of usage of historic as compared with historical. Apart from

the specialist use in grammatical terminology, historic is confined to meaning 'famous or important with regards to history', as in a historic event.

historical adj. **1** of or concerning history (historical evidence). **2** belonging to history, not to prehistory or legend. **3** (of the study of a subject) based on an analysis of its development over a period. **4** belonging to the past, not the present. **5** (of a novel, a film, etc.) dealing or professing to deal with historical events. **6** in connection with history, from the historian's point of view (of purely historical interest). □ **historically** adv.

■ **Usage** See Usage Note at HISTORIC.

historicism n. **1** the theory that social and cultural phenomena are determined by history. **2** the belief that historical events are governed by laws. □ **historicist** n.

historicity n. the historical genuineness of an event etc.

historic present n. the present tense used instead of the past in vivid narration.

historiography n. **1** the writing of history. **2** the study of history-writing. [from medieval Latin historiographia] □ **historiographer** n. **historiographic** adj. **historiographical** adj.

history n. (pl. **-ies**) **1** a continuous, usu. chronological, record of important or public events. **2 a** the study of past events, esp. human affairs. **b** the total accumulation of past events, esp. relating to human affairs or to the accumulation of developments connected with a particular nation, person, thing, etc. (our island history; the history of astronomy; he has a history of illness). **3** an eventful past (this house has a history). **4 a** a systematic or critical account of or research into a past event or events etc. **b** a similar record or account of natural phenomena. **5** a historical play. □ **make history 1** influence the course of history. **2** do something memorable. [Middle English via Latin historia from Greek historia 'finding out, narrative']

histrionic ● adj. (of behaviour) theatrical, dramatic. ● n. (in pl.) insincere and dramatic behaviour designed to impress. [based on Latin histrio -onis 'actor'] □ **histrionically** adv.

hit ● v. (**hitting**; past and past part. **hit**) **1** tr. **a** strike with a blow or a missile. **b** (of a moving body) strike (the plane hit the ground). **c** reach (a target, a person, etc.) with a directed missile (hit the window with the ball). **2** tr. cause to suffer or affect adversely; wound. **3** intr. (often foll. by at, against, upon) direct a blow. **4** tr. (often foll. by against, on) knock (a part of the body) (hit his head on the door frame). **5** tr. light upon; get at (a thing aimed at) (he's hit the truth at last; tried to hit the right tone in his apology) (see hit on). **6** tr. colloq. **a** encounter (hit a snag). **b** arrive at (hit an all-time low; hit the town). **c** indulge in, esp. liquor etc. (hit the bottle). **7** tr. esp. US slang rob or kill. **8** tr. occur force-

fully to (the seriousness of the situation only hit him later). **9** tr. Sport **a** propel (a ball etc.) with a bat etc. to score runs or points. **b** score (runs etc.) in this way. **10** tr. represent exactly. ● n. **1** a blow; a stroke. **b** a collision. **2** a shot etc. that hits its target. **3** colloq. a popular success, esp. in entertainment. **4** esp. US slang **a** a murder or other violent crime. **b** a drug injection etc. □ **hit-and-miss** aimed or done carelessly or at random. **hit-and-run** attrib.adj. **1** relating to an act of accidental or wilful damage committed by a person who leaves the scene before being discovered. **2** (of a person) committing an act of this kind. **hit back** retaliate. **hit below the belt 1** esp. Boxing give a foul blow. **2** treat or behave unfairly. **hit it off** (often foll. by with, together) agree or be congenial. **hit the nail on the head** state the truth exactly. **hit on** (or **upon**) find (what is sought), esp. by chance. **hit out** deal vigorous physical or verbal blows (hit out at her enemies). **hit the road** (US **trail**) slang depart. **hit the roof** see ROOF. **hit the sack** see SACK[1]. **make a hit** (usu. foll. by with) be successful or popular. [from Old Norse hitta 'to meet with'] □ **hitter** n.

hitch ● v. **1 a** tr. fasten with a loop, hook, etc.; tether (hitched the horse to the cart). **b** intr. (often foll. by in, on to, etc.) become fastened in this way (the rod hitched in to the bracket). **2** tr. move (a thing) with a jerk; shift slightly (hitched the pillow to a comfortable position). **3** colloq. **a** intr. = HITCH-HIKE. **b** tr. obtain (a lift) by hitch-hiking. ● n. **1** an impediment; a temporary obstacle. **2** an abrupt pull or push; a jerk. **3** a noose or knot of various kinds. ▷ KNOT. **4** colloq. a free ride in a vehicle. □ **get hitched** colloq. marry. **hitch up** lift (esp. clothing) with a jerk. [Middle English] □ **hitcher** n.

hitch-hike ● v.intr. travel by seeking free lifts in passing vehicles. ● n. a journey made by hitch-hiking. □ **hitch-hiker** n.

hi-tech adj. = HIGH-TECH.

hither usu. formal or literary ● adv. to or towards this place. ● adj. situated on this side; the nearer (of two). [Old English]

hither and thither adv. (also **hither and yon**) in various directions; to and fro.

hitherto adv. until this time, up to now.

hit list n. slang a list of prospective victims.

hit man n. (pl. **hit men**) slang a male hired assassin.

hit-out n. Austral. slang a brisk gallop.

hit parade n. colloq. a list of the current best-selling records of popular music.

Hittite ● n. a member or the language of an ancient people of Asia Minor and Syria. ● adj. of or relating to the Hittites or their language. [from Hebrew Hittīm]

HIV abbr. human immunodeficiency virus, a retrovirus which causes Aids.

HIV-positive adj. diagnosed as testing positive for HIV.

hive n. **1** a beehive. **2** a busy swarming place. **3** a swarming multitude. □ **hive off** esp. Brit. **1** separate from a larger group. **2** form into or assign (work) to a subsidiary department or company. [Old English]

hives n.pl. **1** a skin eruption, esp. nettle-rash. **2** Brit. inflammation of the larynx etc. [16th-century coinage, originally Scots]

hiya int. colloq. a word used in greeting. [corruption of how are you?]

hl abbr. hectolitre(s).

HM abbr. Brit. **1** Her (or His) Majesty('s). **2** Mus. heavy metal.

hm abbr. hectometre(s).

h'm int. & n. (also **hmm**) = HEM[2], HUM[2].

HMG abbr. (in the UK) Her or His Majesty's Government.

HMI abbr. (in the UK) Her or His Majesty's Inspector (of Schools).

HMS abbr. (in the UK) Her or His Majesty's Ship.

HMSO abbr. (in the UK) Her or His Majesty's Stationery Office.

HNC abbr. (in the UK) Higher National Certificate.

inclined end

HIP ROOF

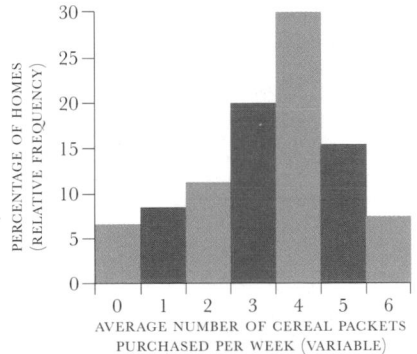

y-axis: PERCENTAGE OF HOMES (RELATIVE FREQUENCY)
x-axis: AVERAGE NUMBER OF CEREAL PACKETS PURCHASED PER WEEK (VARIABLE)

HISTOGRAM SHOWING RATE OF CEREAL PURCHASE PER HOUSEHOLD

H

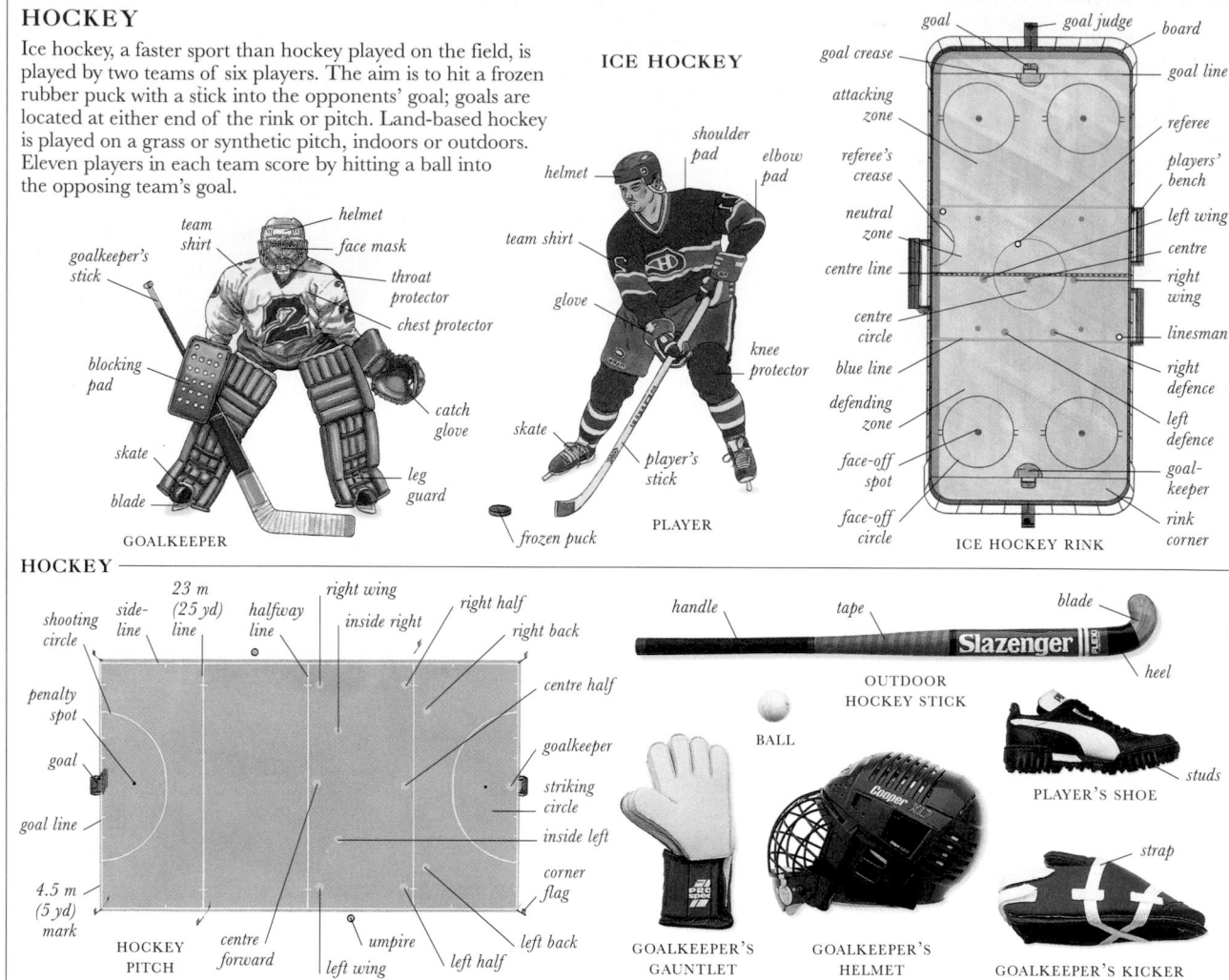

HOCKEY

Ice hockey, a faster sport than hockey played on the field, is played by two teams of six players. The aim is to hit a frozen rubber puck with a stick into the opponents' goal; goals are located at either end of the rink or pitch. Land-based hockey is played on a grass or synthetic pitch, indoors or outdoors. Eleven players in each team score by hitting a ball into the opposing team's goal.

ICE HOCKEY

shoulder pad · elbow pad · helmet · team shirt · glove · knee protector · skate · player's stick · frozen puck

PLAYER

team shirt · helmet · goalkeeper's stick · face mask · throat protector · chest protector · blocking pad · catch glove · skate · blade · leg guard

GOALKEEPER

goal · goal judge · board · goal crease · goal line · attacking zone · referee · referee's crease · players' bench · neutral zone · left wing · centre · centre line · right wing · centre circle · linesman · blue line · right defence · defending zone · left defence · face-off spot · goalkeeper · face-off circle · rink corner

ICE HOCKEY RINK

HOCKEY

shooting circle · side-line · 23 m (25 yd) line · halfway line · right wing · inside right · right half · right back · penalty spot · centre half · goal · goalkeeper · goal line · striking circle · inside left · 4.5 m (5 yd) mark · corner flag · centre forward · umpire · left back · left wing · left half

HOCKEY PITCH

handle · tape · blade · heel

OUTDOOR HOCKEY STICK

BALL

studs

PLAYER'S SHOE

GOALKEEPER'S GAUNTLET

strap

GOALKEEPER'S HELMET

GOALKEEPER'S KICKER

HND *abbr.* (in the UK) Higher National Diploma.

Ho *symb. Chem.* the element holmium.

ho *int.* **1 a** an expression of admiration or (often repeated as **ho! ho!** etc.) derision, surprise, or triumph. **b** (in *comb.*) the second element of various exclamations (*heigh-ho*; *what ho*). **2** a call for attention. [Middle English]

hoard ● *n.* **1** a stock or store (esp. of money) laid by. **2** an amassed store of facts etc. **3** *Archaeol.* an ancient store of treasure etc. ● *v.* **1** *tr.* (often *absol.*; often foll. by *up*) amass (money etc.) and put away; store. **2** *intr.* accumulate more than one's current requirements of food etc. in a time of scarcity. [Old English] □ **hoarder** *n.*

hoarding *n.* **1** *Brit.* a large, usu. wooden, structure used to carry advertisements etc. **2** a board fence erected round a building site etc. [from Old French *hourd*, related to HURDLE]

hoar frost *n.* frozen water vapour deposited in clear still weather on vegetation etc.

hoarse *adj.* **1** (of the voice) rough and deep; husky; croaking. **2** having such a voice. [Old English] □ **hoarsely** *adv.* **hoarsen** *v.tr. & intr.* **hoarseness** *n.*

hoary *adj.* (**hoarier, hoariest**) **1 a** (of hair) grey or white with age. **b** having such hair; aged. **2** old and trite (*a hoary joke*). □ **hoarily** *adv.* **hoariness** *n.*

hoax ● *n.* a humorous or malicious deception; a practical joke. ● *v.tr.* deceive (a person) with a hoax. [18th-century coinage] □ **hoaxer** *n.*

hob *n.* **1 a** *Brit.* a cooking appliance or the flat top part of a cooker, with hotplates or burners. **b** a flat metal shelf at the side of a fireplace, used esp. for heating a pan etc. **2** = HOBNAIL.

hobbit *n.* a member of an imaginary race similar to humans, of small size and with hairy feet, in stories by J.R.R. Tolkien. [described as 'a hole-dweller' by its inventor Tolkien, English writer, 1892–1973]

hobble ● *v.* **1** *intr.* walk lamely; limp. **2** *tr.* tie together the legs of (a horse etc.) to prevent it from straying. ● *n.* **1** an uneven or infirm gait. **2** a rope, clog, etc. used for hobbling a horse etc. ▷ TROTTING. [Middle English] □ **hobbler** *n.*

hobbledehoy *n. colloq.* **1** a clumsy or awkward youth. **2** a hooligan. [16th-century coinage]

hobby[1] *n.* (*pl.* **-ies**) a favourite leisure-time activity or occupation. [Middle English *hobyn, hoby*, pet forms of *Robin*] □ **hobbyist** *n.*

hobby[2] *n.* (*pl.* **-ies**) any of several small long-winged falcons, esp. *Falco subbuteo*. [from Old French *hobé* 'little falcon']

hobby horse *n.* **1** a child's toy consisting of a stick with a horse's head. **2** a preoccupation; a favourite topic of conversation.

hobgoblin *n.* a mischievous imp.

hobnail *n.* a heavy-headed nail used for boot-soles. □ **hobnailed** *adj.*

hobnob *v.intr.* (**hobnobbed, hobnobbing**) (usu. foll. by *with*) mix socially or informally. [from phrase *hob or nob* 'give or take', referring to alternate drinking]

hobo *n.* (*pl.* **-oes** or **-os**) *N. Amer.* a wandering worker; a tramp. [19th-century coinage]

Hobson's choice *n.* a choice of taking the thing offered or nothing. [from T. *Hobson*, Cambridge carrier, 1554–1631, who offered such a choice of horses]

hock[1] *n.* **1** the joint of a quadruped's hind leg between the knee and the fetlock. ▷ HORSE. **2** a knuckle of pork; the lower joint of a ham. [Old English]

hock[2] *n. Brit.* a German white wine from the Rhineland. [based on German *Hochheimer*]

hock[3] *esp. N. Amer. slang* ● *v.tr.* pawn; pledge. ● *n.* a pawnbroker's pledge. □ **in hock 1** in pawn. **2** in debt. **3** in prison. [from Dutch *hok* 'hutch, debt']

hockey[1] *n.* **1** *Brit.* ▲ a game played between two teams on a field with curved sticks and a small hard ball. **2** *N. Amer.* = ▲ ICE HOCKEY. [16th-century coinage] □ **hockeyist** *n. N. Amer.* (in sense 2).

hockey[2] var. of OCHE.

hocus-pocus *n.* deception; trickery. [17th-century sham Latin]

hod *n.* **1** a V-shaped open trough on a pole used for carrying bricks, mortar, etc. **2** a portable receptacle for coal.

hodgepodge *n.* = HOTCHPOTCH 1, 2. [Middle English]

Hodgkin's disease *n.* a malignant disease of lymphatic tissues usu. characterized by enlargement of the lymph nodes. [named after T. *Hodgkin*, English physician, 1798–1866]

hodman *n.* (*pl.* **-men**) *Brit.* **1** a labourer who carries a hod. **2** a literary hack.

hoe ● *n.* ▼ a long-handled tool with a thin metal blade, used for weeding etc. ● *v.* (**hoes**, **hoed**, **hoeing**) **1** *tr.* weed (crops); loosen (earth); dig up or cut down with a hoe. **2** *intr.* use a hoe. □ **hoe in** *Austral.* & *NZ slang* eat eagerly. **hoe into** *Austral.* & *NZ slang* attack (food, a person, a task). [from Old French *houe*] □ **hoer** *n.*

hoecake *n.* *US* a coarse cake of maize flour originally baked on the blade of a hoe.

hoedown *n.* *N. Amer.* **1 a** a lively folk dance. **b** the music for this. **2** a party at which such dancing takes place.

hog ● *n.* **1 a** a domesticated pig, esp. a castrated male reared for slaughter. **b** any of several other pigs of the family Suidae, e.g. a warthog. **2** *colloq.* a greedy person. ● *v.tr.* (**hogged**, **hogging**) *colloq.* take greedily; hoard selfishly; monopolize. □ **go the whole hog** *colloq.* do something completely or thoroughly. **hog-tie** *N. Amer.* **1** secure by fastening the hands and feet or all four feet together. **2** restrain, impede. [Old English] □ **hogger** *n.* **hoggish** *adj.* **hoggishly** *adv.* **hoggishness** *n.* **hoglike** *adj.*

hogback *n.* (also **hog's back**) a steep-sided ridge of a hill. ▷ ERODE

hogmanay *n.* *Sc.* **1** New Year's Eve. **2** a celebration on this day. [17th-century coinage]

hog's back var. of HOGBACK.

hogshead *n.* **1** a large cask. **2** a liquid or dry measure, usu. about 50 imperial gallons. [Middle English]

hogwash *n.* *colloq.* nonsense, rubbish.

hogweed *n.* ▶ any of various coarse weeds of the genus *Heracleum*, esp. *H. sphondylium*.

ho ho *int.* **1** representing deep jolly laughter. **2** expressing surprise, triumph, or derision.

ho-hum *int.* expressing boredom. [imitative of a yawn]

hoick *Brit. colloq.* ● *v.tr.* (often foll. by *out*) lift or pull, esp. with a jerk. ● *n.* a jerky pull; a jerk.

hoi polloi *n.* (often prec. by *the* : see note below) the masses; the common people. [Greek, literally 'the many (people)']

■ **Usage** The use of *hoi polloi* with *the* is strictly unnecessary, since *hoi* = 'the', but this construction is very common.

HOGWEED
(*Heracleum sphondylium*)

hoist ● *v.tr.* **1** raise or haul up. **2** raise by means of ropes and pulleys etc. ● *n.* **1** an act of hoisting, a lift. **2** ▶ an apparatus for hoisting. **3** the part of a flag nearest the staff. □ **hoist with one's own petard** see PETARD. [Middle English] □ **hoister** *n.*

hoity-toity *adj.* haughty; petulant; snobbish. [based on obsolete *hoit* 'to indulge in riotous mirth']

hokey *adj.* (also **hoky**) (**hokier**, **hokiest**) *N. Amer. slang* sentimental, melodramatic, artificial. [based on HOKUM] □ **hokeyness** *n.*

hokey-cokey *n.* *Brit.* a communal dance performed in a circle with synchronized shaking of the limbs in turn.

hoki *n.* an edible marine fish, *Macruronus novaezelandiae*, related to the hake and native to the southern coasts of New Zealand. [Maori]

hokum *n.* esp. *US slang* **1** sentimental, popular, sensational, or unreal situations, dialogue, etc., in a film or play etc. **2** bunkum; rubbish. [20th-century coinage]

hoky var. of HOKEY.

hold[1] ● *v.* (*past* and *past part.* **held**) **1** *tr.* **a** keep fast; grasp (esp. in the hands or arms). **b** (also *refl.*) keep or sustain (a thing, oneself, one's head, etc.) in a particular position (*hold it to the light*; *held himself erect*). **c** grasp so as to control (*hold the reins*). **2** *tr.* (of a vessel etc.) contain or be capable of containing (*the jug holds two pints*; *the hall holds 900*). **3** *tr.* possess, gain, or have, esp.: **a** be the owner or tenant of (land, property, stocks, etc.) (*holds the farm from the trust*). **b** gain or have gained (a degree, record, etc.) (*holds the long jump record*). **c** have the position of (a job or office). **d** have (a specified playing card) in one's hand. **e** keep possession of (a person's thoughts, etc.), esp. against attack (*held the fort against the enemy*; *held his place in her estimation*). **4** *intr.* remain unbroken; not give way (*the roof held under the storm*). **5** *tr.* observe; celebrate; conduct (a meeting, festival, conversation, etc.). **6** *tr.* **a** keep (a person etc.) in a specified condition, place, etc. (*held him prisoner*; *held him at arm's length*). **b** detain, esp. in custody (*hold him until I arrive*). **7** *tr.* **a** engross (a person's or a person's attention) (*the book held him for hours*). **b** dominate (*held the stage*). **8** *tr.* (foll. by *to*) make (a person etc.) adhere to (terms, a promise, etc.). **9** *intr.* (of weather) continue fine. **10** *tr.* (often foll. by *to* + infin., or *that* + clause) think; believe (*held it to be self-evident*; *held that the Earth was flat*). **11** *tr.* regard with a specified feeling (*held him in contempt*). **12** *tr.* **a** cease; restrain (*hold your fire*). **b** *US colloq.* withhold; not use (*a burger please, and hold the onions!*). **13** *tr.* keep or reserve (*will you hold our seats please?*). **14** *tr.* be able to drink (liquor) without effect (*can't hold his drink*). **15** *tr.* (usu. foll. by *that* + clause) (of a judge, a court, etc.) lay down; decide. **16** *tr. Mus.* sustain (a note). **17** *intr.* = *hold the line* 2. ● *n.* **1** a grasp (*catch hold of him*; *keep a hold on him*). **2** (often in *comb.*) a thing to hold by (*seized the hand-hold*). **3** (foll. by *over*) influence over (*has a strange hold over them*). **4** a manner of holding in wrestling etc. □ **hold (a thing) against (a person)** resent or regard as discreditable to (a person). **hold aloof** avoid communication with people etc. **hold back 1** impede the progress of; restrain. **2** keep (a thing) to or for oneself. **3** (often foll. by *from*) hesitate; refrain. **hold one's breath** see BREATH. **hold by** (or **to**) adhere to (a choice, purpose, etc.). **hold court** preside over one's admirers etc., like a sovereign. **hold dear** regard with affection. **hold down 1** repress. **2** *colloq.* be competent enough to keep (one's job etc.). **hold everything!** (or **it!**) cease action or movement. **hold the fort 1** act as a temporary substitute. **2** cope in an emergency. **hold forth** (an inducement etc.). **2** usu. *derog.* speak at length or tediously. **hold good** (or **true**) be valid; apply. **hold one's ground** see GROUND[1]. **hold a person's hand** give a person guidance or moral support. **hold hands** grasp one another by the hand as a sign of affection or for support or guidance. **hold hard!** *Brit.* stop!; wait! **hold one's head high** behave proudly and confidently. **hold one's horses** *colloq.* stop; slow down. **hold in** keep in check, confine. **hold the line 1** not yield. **2** maintain a telephone connection. **hold off 1** delay; not begin. **2** keep one's distance. **hold on 1** keep one's grasp on something. **2** wait a moment. **3** (when telephoning) not ring off. **hold out 1** stretch forth (a hand etc.). **2** offer (an inducement etc.). **3** maintain resistance. **4** persist or last. **hold out for** continue to demand. **hold out on** *colloq.* refuse something to (a person). **hold over** postpone. **hold something over** threaten (a person) constantly with something. **hold one's own** see OWN. **hold together 1** cohere. **2** cause to cohere. **hold one's tongue** *colloq.* be silent. **hold to ransom** *Brit.* **1** keep (a person) prisoner until a ransom is paid. **2** demand concessions from by threats of damaging action. **hold up 1 a** support; sustain. **b** maintain (the head etc.) erect. **2** exhibit, display. **3** arrest the progress of; obstruct. **4** stop and rob by violence or threats. **hold water** (of reasoning) be sound; bear examination. **hold with** (usu. with *neg.*) *colloq.* approve of (*don't hold with motorbikes*). **on hold 1** (when telephoning) holding the line. **2** (esp. in phr. **put on hold**) temporarily inactive or receiving little attention. **take hold** (of a custom or habit) become established. **there is no holding him** (or **her** etc.) he (or she etc.) is restive, high-spirited, determined, etc. **with no holds barred** with no restrictions, all methods being permitted. [Old English] □ **holdable** *adj.*

hold[2] *n.* a cavity in the lower part of a ship or aircraft in which the cargo is stowed. ▷ FACTORY SHIP. [alteration of Old English *hol* 'hollow']

holdall *n.* *Brit.* a portable case or bag for miscellaneous articles.

holdback *n.* **1** something serving to hold a thing in place. **2** a hindrance.

holder *n.* **1** (often in *comb.*) a device or implement for holding something (*cigarette-holder*). **2 a** the possessor of a title etc. **b** the occupant of an office etc.

holding *n.* **1 a** a land held by lease (cf. SMALLHOLDING). **b** the tenure of land. **2** stocks, property, etc. held.

holding company *n.* a company created to hold the shares of other companies, which it then controls.

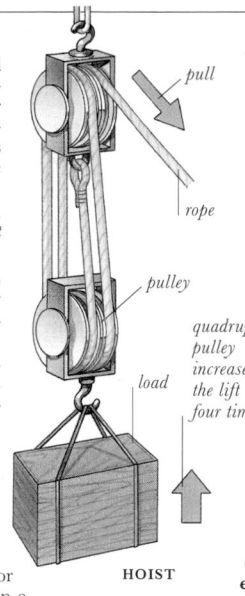

pull

rope

pulley

load

quadruple pulley increases the lift four times

HOIST

H

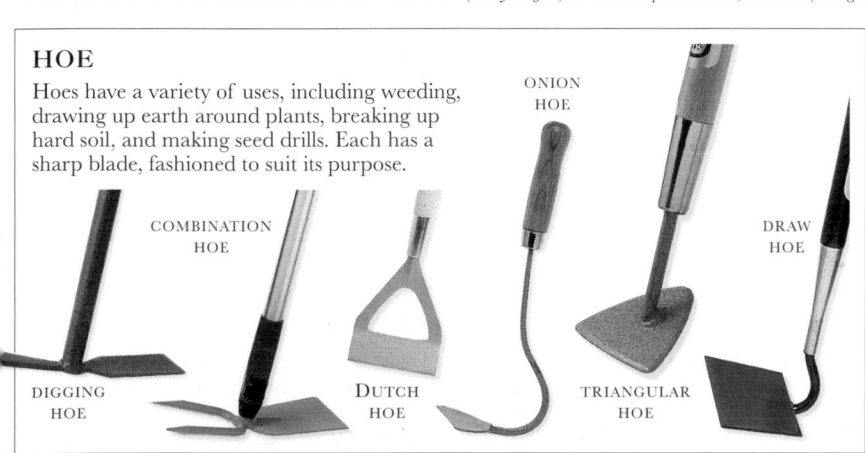

HOE

Hoes have a variety of uses, including weeding, drawing up earth around plants, breaking up hard soil, and making seed drills. Each has a sharp blade, fashioned to suit its purpose.

COMBINATION HOE

ONION HOE

DRAW HOE

DIGGING HOE

DUTCH HOE

TRIANGULAR HOE

H

holding operation *n.* a manoeuvre designed to maintain the status quo.

hold-up *n.* **1** a stoppage or delay by traffic, fog, etc. **2** a robbery, esp. by the use of threats or violence. **3** each of a pair of stockings held up by elasticated tops rather than by suspenders.

hole ● *n.* **1 a** an empty space in a solid body. **b** an aperture in or through something. **2** an animal's burrow. **3** a cavity or receptacle into which the ball must be propelled in various sports or games, e.g. golf. ▷ GOLE. **4** *colloq.* a small, mean, or dingy abode. **5** *colloq.* an awkward situation. **6** *Golf* **a** a point scored by a player who gets the ball from tee to hole with the fewest strokes. **b** the terrain or distance from tee to hole. ● *v.* **1** *tr.* make a hole or holes in. **2** *tr.* pierce the side of (a ship). **3 a** *tr. Golf* send (the ball) into a hole. **b** *intr.* (usu. foll. by *out*) *Golf* send the ball into a hole. □ **hole up** *N. Amer. colloq.* hide oneself. **make a hole in** use a large amount of. [Old English] □ **holey** *adj.*

hole-and-corner *adj.* secret; underhand.

hole-in-one *n.* (*pl.* **holes-in-one**) *Golf* a shot that enters the hole from the tee.

hole in the heart *n.* a congenital defect in the heart septum.

hole in the wall *n. Brit. colloq.* an automatic cash dispenser installed in the outside wall of a bank etc.

holiday ● *n.* **1** (often in *pl.*) esp. *Brit.* an extended period of recreation, esp. away from home or in travelling; a break from work (cf. VACATION *n.* 1, 2). **2** a day of festivity or recreation when no work is done, esp. a religious festival etc. **3** (*attrib.*) (of clothes etc.) festive. ● *v.intr.* esp. *Brit.* spend a holiday. □ **on holiday** (or **one's holidays**) *Brit.* in the course of one's holiday; having a break from work. **take a holiday** have a break from work. [Old English *hāligdæg* 'holy day']

holiday camp *n. Brit.* a camp for holidaymakers with accommodation, entertainment, and facilities on site.

holidaymaker *n.* esp. *Brit.* a person on holiday.

holier-than-thou *adj. colloq.* self-righteous.

holiness *n.* **1** sanctity; the state of being holy. **2** (**Holiness**) a title used when referring to or addressing the pope.

holism *n.* (also **wholism**) **1** *Philos.* the theory that certain wholes are greater than the sum of their parts (cf. REDUCTIONISM 2). **2** *Med.* the treating of the whole person including mental and social factors rather than just the symptoms of a disease. □ **holist** *adj. & n.* **holistic** *adj.* **holistically** *adv.*

holland *n.* a smooth hard-wearing linen fabric. [from Dutch *Holtlant*, literally 'woodland', describing the area of manufacture]

hollandaise sauce /hol-ăn-**dayz**/ *n.* a creamy sauce of melted butter, egg yolks, vinegar, etc., served esp. with fish. [from French fem. of *hollandais* 'Dutch']

holler *dial.* or *N. Amer. colloq.* ● *v.* **1** *intr.* make a loud cry or noise. **2** *tr.* express with a loud cry or shout. ● *n.* a loud cry, noise, or shout. [variant of late Middle English *hollo*]

hollow ● *adj.* **1 a** having a hole or cavity inside; not solid throughout. **b** having a depression; sunken (*hollow cheeks*). **2** (of a sound) echoing, as though made in or on a hollow container. **3** empty; hungry. **4** without significance; meaningless (*a hollow triumph*). **5** insincere; cynical; false (*a hollow laugh*; *hollow promises*). ● *n.* **1** a hollow place; a hole. **2** a valley; a basin. ● *v.tr.* (often foll. by *out*) make hollow; excavate. ● *adv. colloq.* completely (*beaten hollow*). [Old English *holh* 'cave'] □ **hollowly** *adv.* **hollowness** *n.*

hollow-cheeked *adj.* with sunken cheeks.

hollow-eyed *adj.* with eyes deep sunk.

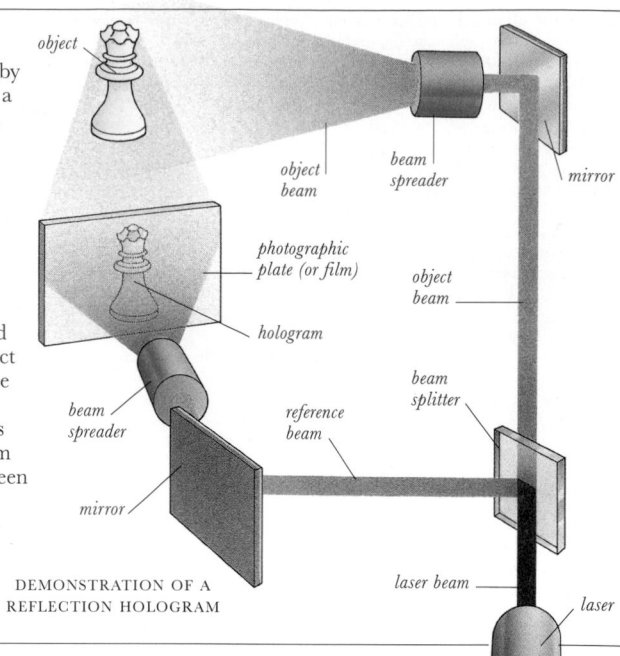

HOLOGRAM

A hologram is created by lighting an object with a laser beam split in two. The reference beam is directed towards a photographic plate or film, while the object beam is aimed at the object itself. The plate is thus struck simultaneously by light from the reference beam and by the light of the object beam reflected from the object. Interference between the two beams causes a pattern to form on the plate, which is seen as a three-dimensional hologram when illuminated by laser light of matching wavelength.

object · *object beam* · *beam spreader* · *mirror* · *photographic plate (or film)* · *object beam* · *hologram* · *beam splitter* · *beam spreader* · *reference beam* · *mirror* · *laser beam* · *laser*

DEMONSTRATION OF A
REFLECTION HOLOGRAM

---

hollow-hearted *adj.* insincere.

holly *n.* (*pl.* **-ies**) an evergreen shrub, *Ilex aquifolium*, with prickly usu. dark green leaves and red berries. [Old English]

hollyhock *n.* ◀ a tall plant, *Alcea rosea* (mallow family), with large showy flowers of various colours. [Middle English, from HOLLY + obsolete *hock* 'mallow']

holm /hohm/ *n.* (in full **holm-oak**) an evergreen oak, *Quercus ilex*, with holly-like young leaves. [Middle English]

holmium /**hohl**-mi-ŭm/ *n. Chem.* a soft silvery metallic element of the lanthanide series. [modern Latin, based on *Holmia* 'Stockholm', in Sweden]

holo- *comb. form* whole. [from Greek *holos* 'whole']

holocaust *n.* **1** a case of large-scale destruction, esp. by fire or nuclear war. **2** (**the Holocaust**) the mass murder of the Jews by the Nazis 1941–5. [based on Greek *kaustos* 'burnt']

Holocene *Geol.* ● *adj.* of or relating to the most recent epoch of the Quaternary period, marked by the development of human culture. ● *n.* this period or system. [based on Greek *kainos* 'new']

hologram *n. Physics* **1** ▲ a three-dimensional image formed by the interference of light beams from a coherent light source. **2** a photograph of the interference pattern, which when suitably illuminated produces a three-dimensional image.

holograph ● *adj.* wholly written by hand by the person named as the author. ● *n.* a holograph document.

holography *n. Physics* the study or production of holograms. □ **holographic** *adj.* **holographically** *adv.*

hols *n.pl. Brit. colloq.* holidays.

holster *n.* a leather case for a pistol or revolver. [17th-century coinage]

holt *n. Brit.* an animal's (esp. an otter's) lair. [variant of HOLD[1]]

holy *adj.* (**holier**, **holiest**) **1** morally and spiritually excellent or perfect, and to be revered. **2** belonging to, devoted to, or empowered by,

HOLLYHOCK
(*Alcea rosea* 'Nigra')

God. **3** consecrated; sacred. **4** used in trivial exclamations (*holy mackerel!*). [Old English] □ **holily** *adv.*

Holy Communion see COMMUNION 3.

holy day *n.* a religious festival.

Holy Family *n.* the young Jesus with his mother and St Joseph.

Holy Father *n.* the Pope.

Holy Ghost *n.* = HOLY SPIRIT.

Holy Grail see GRAIL.

Holy Land *n.* **1** W. Palestine, esp. Judaea. **2** a region similarly revered in non-Christian religions.

holy of holies *n.* **1** the inner chamber of the sanctuary in the Jewish Temple in Jerusalem, separated by a veil from the outer chamber. **2** an innermost shrine. **3** a thing regarded as most sacred.

holy orders *n.pl.* the status of a member of the clergy, esp. the grades of bishop, priest, and deacon.

Holy Sacrament see SACRAMENT 3.

Holy Saturday *n.* Saturday in Holy Week.

Holy Scripture *n.* the Bible.

Holy See *n.* the papacy or the papal court.

Holy Spirit *n.* the third person of the Trinity, God as spiritually acting.

holy terror see TERROR 2b.

Holy Trinity see TRINITY 3.

holy war *n.* a war waged in support of a religious cause.

holy water *n.* water dedicated to holy uses, or blessed by a priest.

Holy Week *n.* the week before Easter.

Holy Writ *n.* holy writings collectively, esp. the Bible.

homage *n.* acknowledgement of superiority, dutiful reverence (*pay homage to*). [based on Latin *homo -minis* 'man']

hombre /**om**-bray/ *n. US slang* a man. [Spanish]

Homburg *n.* ▼ a man's felt hat with a narrow curled brim and a lengthwise dent in the crown. [from *Homburg* in Germany]

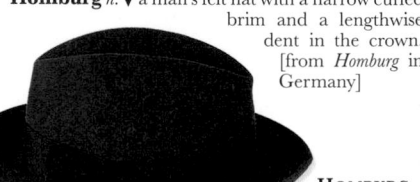

HOMBURG

home ● *n.* **1 a** the place where one lives; a fixed residence. **b** a dwelling house. **2** family circumstances (*comes from a good home*). **3** the native land of a person or of a person's ancestors. **4** an institution for persons needing care, rest, or refuge (*nursing home*). **5** the place where a thing originates, is kept, or is native or most common. **6 a** the finishing point in a race. **b** (in games) the place where one is free from attack; the goal. ● *attrib.adj.* **1 a** of or connected with one's home. **b** carried on, done, or made at home. **2 a** in one's own country (*home industries*; *the home market*). **b** dealing with the domestic affairs of a country. **3** *Sport* played on one's own ground etc. (*home match*). ● *adv.* **1 a** to one's home or country (*go home*). **b** arrived at home (*is he home yet?*). **c** *N. Amer.* at home (*stay home*). **2** to the point aimed at; completely (*drove the nail home*). ● *v.* **1** *intr.* (esp. of a trained pigeon) return home (cf. HOMING 1). **2** *intr.* (often foll. by *on*, *in on*) (of a vessel, missile, etc.) be guided by a landmark, radio beam, etc. **3** *tr.* provide with a home. □ **at home 1** in one's own house or native land. **2** at ease (*make yourself at home*). **3** (usu. foll. by *in*, *on*, *with*) familiar or well informed. **4** available to callers. **close to home** affecting one closely. **come home to** become fully realized by. **come home to roost** see ROOST. **home and dry** *Brit.* having achieved one's purpose. **home, James!** *joc.* drive home quickly! **home from home** a place other than one's home where one feels at home. [Old English] □ **homelike** *adj.*

home banking *n.* the use of any of various telecommunications systems in which a customer may carry out banking transactions via a home computer, a cable television network, or by telephone.

home-brew *n.* beer or other alcoholic drink brewed at home. □ **home-brewed** *adj.*

homecoming *n.* arrival at home.

Home Counties *n.pl.* (in the UK) the counties closest to London.

home farm *n. Brit.* a farm (one of several on an estate) set aside to provide produce for the owner.

home-grown *adj.* grown or produced at home.

Home Guard *n. hist.* the British citizen army organized in 1940 to defend the UK against invasion.

home help *n. Brit.* a person employed to help in another's home, esp. one provided by a local authority.

homeland *n.* **1** one's native land. **2** *hist.* a partially self-governing area in S. Africa set aside for a particular indigenous African people or peoples (the official name for a Bantustan).

homeless *adj.* lacking a home. □ **homelessness** *n.*

home loan *n.* a loan advanced to a person to assist in buying a house, flat, etc.

homely *adj.* (**homelier**, **homeliest**) **1** *Brit.* **a** simple, plain. **b** unpretentious. **c** primitive. **2** *N. Amer.* (of a person) unattractive, ugly. **3** comfortable in the manner of a home, cosy. □ **homeliness** *n.*

home-made *adj.* made at home.

home movie *n.* a film made at home or of one's own activities.

Home Office *n.* the British government department dealing with law and order, immigration, etc., in England and Wales.

homeopath esp. *US* var. of HOMOEOPATH.

homeopathy etc. esp. *US* var. of HOMOEOPATHY etc.

homeotherm *n.* an organism that maintains its body temperature at a constant level, usu. above that of the environment, by its metabolic activity; a warm-blooded organism. [from Greek *homoios* 'like' + *thermē* 'heat'] □ **homeothermal** *adj.* **homeothermic** *adj.* **homeothermy** *n.*

homeowner *n.* a person who owns his or her own home.

home page *n.* a hypertext document on the World Wide Web, serving as an introductory focus of information relating to an organization or individual.

home plate *n. Baseball* ▶ a plate beside which the batter stands.

home port *n.* the port from which a ship originates.

homer *n.* **1** a homing pigeon. **2** *Baseball* a home run.

home rule *n.* the government of a country or region by its own citizens.

home run *n. Baseball* a hit that allows the batter to make a complete circuit of the bases.

Home Secretary *n.* (in the UK) the Secretary of State in charge of the Home Office.

home shopping *n.* shopping carried out from home using catalogues, satellite TV channels, etc.

homesick *adj.* depressed by longing for one's home during absence from it. □ **homesickness** *n.*

homespun ● *adj.* **1 a** (of cloth) made of yarn spun at home. **b** (of yarn) spun at home. **2** plain, simple, unsophisticated, homely. ● *n.* **1** homespun cloth. **2** anything plain or homely.

homestead *n.* **1** a house, esp. a farmhouse, and outbuildings. **2** *Austral. & NZ* the owner's residence on a sheep or cattle station. **3** *N. Amer.* an area of land (usu. 160 acres) granted to a settler as a home. □ **homesteader** *n.* **homesteading** *n.*

home straight *n.* (also **home stretch**) the concluding stretch of a racecourse. ▷ RACECOURSE

homestyle *adj. N. Amer.* (esp. of food) of a kind made or done at home, homely.

home town *n.* the town of one's birth or early life or present fixed residence.

home truth *n.* basic but unwelcome information concerning oneself.

homeward ● *adv.* (also **homewards**) towards home. ● *adj.* going or leading towards home.

homeward-bound *adv. & adj.* (esp. of a ship) preparing to go, or on the way, home.

homework *n.* **1** work to be done at home, esp. by a school pupil. **2** preparatory work or study.

homeworker *n.* a person who works from home, esp. doing low-paid piecework.

homey *adj.* (also **homy**) (**homier**, **homiest**) suggesting home; cosy. □ **homeyness** *n.*

homicide *n.* **1** the killing of a human being by another. **2** a person who kills a human being. [from Latin] □ **homicidal** *adj.*

homily *n.* (*pl.* **-ies**) **1** a sermon. **2** a tedious moralizing discourse. [based on Greek *homilos* 'crowd'] □ **homiletic** *adj.* **homilist** *n.*

homing *attrib.adj.* **1** (of a pigeon) trained to fly home, bred for long-distance racing. **2** (of a device) for guiding to a target etc.

hominid ● *n.* ◀ any member of the primate family Hominidae, including humans and their fossil ancestors. ● *adj.* of or relating to this family. [based on Latin *homo hominis* 'man']

hominoid ● *adj.* like a human. ● *n.* an animal resembling a human.

hominy *n.* (esp. in the US) coarsely ground maize kernels boiled with water or milk. [Algonquian]

homo *n.* (*pl.* **-os**) *colloq.* a homosexual.

homo- *comb. form* same (often opp. HETERO-). [from Greek *homos* 'same']

Homo *n.* any primate of the genus *Homo*, including modern humans and various extinct species.

homoeopath *n.* (also esp. *US* **homeopath**) a person who practises homoeopathy.

homoeopathy /hohm-i-op-ăthi/ *n.* (also esp. *US* **homeopathy**) the treatment of disease by minute doses of drugs that in a healthy person would produce symptoms of the disease (cf. ALLOPATHY). [from Greek *homoios* 'like' + *patheia* 'feeling'] □ **homoeopathic** *adj.* **homoeopathically** *adv.*

homoerotic *adj.* homosexual.

homogeneous *adj.* (also *disp.* **homogenous**) **1** of the same kind. **2** consisting of parts all of the same kind; uniform. **3** *Math.* containing terms all of the same degree. [based on Greek *genos* 'kind'] □ **homogeneity** *n.*

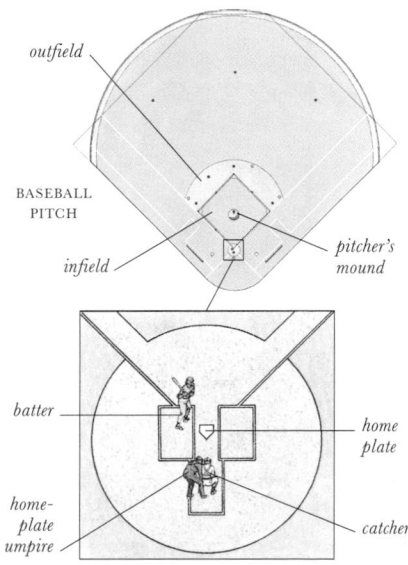

HOMINID: MODEL OF AN AUSTRALOPITHECINE HOMINID

■ **Usage** The variant *homogenous* is considered incorrect by many people and is best avoided. It is found especially in spoken English and arose perhaps under the influence of the verb *homogenize*

homogenize *v.* (also **-ise**) **1** *tr. & intr.* make or become homogeneous. **2** *tr.* treat (milk) so that the fat droplets are emulsified and the cream does not separate. □ **homogenization** *n.*

homogenous *adj.* see HOMOGENEOUS.

homogeny *n. Biol.* similarity due to common descent.

homograft *n.* a tissue graft from a donor of the same species as the recipient.

homograph *n.* a word spelt like another but of different meaning or origin (e.g. POLE[1], POLE[2]).

homolog *US* var. of HOMOLOGUE.

homologous *adj.* **1 a** having the same relation, relative position, etc. **b** corresponding. **2** *Biol.* (of organs etc.) similar in position, structure, and evolutionary origin but not necessarily in function (opp. ANALOGOUS 2). **3** *Biol.* (of chromosomes) pairing at meiosis and having the same structural features and pattern of genes. [based on Greek *logos* 'ratio, proportion']

homologue *n.* (*US* **homolog**) a homologous thing.

homology *n.* a homologous state or relation; correspondence.

homomorphic *adj.* of the same or similar form. □ **homomorphism** *n.*

homonym *n.* **1** a word of the same spelling or sound as another but of different meaning; a homograph or homophone. **2** a namesake. [based on Greek *onoma* 'name'] □ **homonymous** *adj.*

homophobia *n.* a hatred or fear of homosexuals. □ **homophobe** *n.* **homophobic** *adj.*

homophone *n.* **1** a word having the same sound as another but of different meaning, origin, or spelling (e.g. *pair*, *pear*). **2** a symbol denoting the same sound as another.

H

outfield

BASEBALL PITCH

infield

pitcher's mound

batter

home plate

home-plate umpire

catcher

HOME PLATE

H

homophonic *adj. Mus.* in unison; characterized by movement of all parts to the same melody. □ **homophonically** *adv.*

homophonous *adj.* **1** (of music) homophonic. **2** (of a word or symbol) that is a homophone. □ **homophony** *n.*

homopteran *n.* any insect of the suborder Homoptera, including true bugs with wings of a uniform texture, e.g. aphids and cicadas. [based on Greek *pteron* 'wing'] □ **homopterous** *adj.*

Homo sapiens /**sap**-i-enz/ *n.* modern humans regarded as a species. [Latin, literally 'wise man']

homosexual ● *adj.* **1** feeling or involving sexual attraction to persons of the same sex. **2** concerning homosexual relations or people. ● *n.* a homosexual person. □ **homosexuality** *n.* **homosexually** *adv.*

homosocial *adj.* restricting social intercourse to members of one's own sex. □ **homosociality** *n.*

homunculus *n.* (*pl.* **homunculi** /-ly/) a little man, a manikin. [Latin]

homy var. of HOMEY.

Hon. *abbr.* **1** Honorary. **2** Honourable.

hon *n. colloq.* = HONEY 3.

honcho *n.* (*pl.* **-os**) *N. Amer. slang* **1** a leader or manager, the person in charge. **2** an admirable man. [from Japanese *han'chō* 'group leader']

hone ● *n.* a whetstone, esp. for razors. ● *v.tr.* sharpen on or as on a hone. [Old English *hān* 'stone']

honest ● *adj.* **1** fair and just, not cheating or stealing. **2** free of deceit and untruthfulness, sincere. **3** fairly earned (*an honest living*). **4** (of an act or feeling) showing fairness. **5** (of a thing) unadulterated, unsophisticated. ● *adv. colloq.* genuinely, really. □ **make an honest woman of** *colloq.* or *joc.* marry (esp. a pregnant woman). [from Latin *honestus*]

honest broker *n.* a mediator in international, industrial, etc., disputes.

honestly *adv.* **1** in an honest way. **2** really (*I don't honestly know; honestly, the cheek of it!*).

honest-to-God (also **honest-to-goodness**) *colloq.* ● *adj.* genuine, real. ● *adv.* genuinely, really.

honesty *n.* **1** being honest. **2** truthfulness. **3** ► a plant of the genus *Lunaria* with purple or white flowers. ▷ SEED

honey *n.* (*pl.* **-eys**) **1** a sweet sticky yellowish fluid made by bees from nectar. **2** esp. *N. Amer.* (usu. as a form of address) darling, sweetheart. [Old English]

honey bee *n.* see BEE 1a.

honeybun *n.* (also **honeybunch**) (esp. as a form of address) darling.

honeycomb ● *n.* **1** ▼ a structure of hexagonal cells of wax, made by bees to store honey and eggs. **2 a** a pattern arranged hexagonally. **b** fabric made with a pattern of raised hexagons etc. ● *v.tr.* **1** fill with cavities or tunnels, undermine. **2** mark with a honeycomb pattern.

HONESTY
(*Lunaria annua*)

HONEYCOMB AND WORKER BEES

honeydew *n.* **1** a sweet sticky substance found on leaves and stems, excreted by aphids. **2** a variety of melon with smooth pale skin and sweet green flesh.

honeyed *adj.* **1** of or containing honey. **2** (of words, flattery, etc.) sweet; sweet-sounding.

honey fungus *n.* ► a parasitic fungus, *Armillaria mellea*, with honey-coloured edible toadstools.

honeymoon ● *n.* **1** a holiday taken by a newly married couple. **2** an initial period of enthusiasm or goodwill. ● *v.intr.* (usu. foll. by *in*, *at*) spend a honeymoon. [originally with reference to waning affection, compared to the changing moon] □ **honeymooner** *n.*

honeysuckle *n.* any climbing shrub of the genus *Lonicera* with fragrant yellow and pink flowers. [Middle English extension of *honeysuck*]

honey-sweet *adj.* sweet as honey.

honk ● *n.* **1** the cry of a wild goose. **2** the harsh sound of a car horn. ● *v.* **1** *intr.* emit or give a honk. **2** *tr.* cause to do this.

honky *n.* (*pl.* **-ies**) *US black slang offens.* a white person. [20th-century coinage]

honky-tonk *n. colloq.* **1** ragtime piano music. **2** a cheap or disreputable nightclub, dance hall, etc. [19th-century coinage]

honor *US* var. of HONOUR.

honorable *US* var. of HONOURABLE.

honorarium *n.* (*pl.* **honorariums** or **honoraria**) a fee, esp. a voluntary payment for professional services rendered without the normal fee. [Latin]

honorary *adj.* **1 a** conferred as an honour, without the usual requirements, functions, etc. (*honorary degree*). **b** holding such a title or position (*honorary colonel*). **2** (of an office or its holder) unpaid (*honorary treasurer*).

honorific ● *adj.* **1** conferring honour. **2** (esp. of oriental forms of speech) implying respect. ● *n.* an honorific form of words. □ **honorifically** *adv.*

honour (*US* **honor**) ● *n.* **1** high respect; glory; credit, reputation. **2** adherence to what is right or to a conventional standard of conduct. **3** nobleness of mind, magnanimity (*honour among thieves*). **4** a thing conferred as a distinction, esp. an official award for bravery or achievement. **5** (foll. by *of* + verbal noun, or *to* + infin.) privilege, special right (*had the honour of being invited*). **6 a** exalted position. **b** (**Honour**) (prec. by *your*, *his*, etc.) a title of a circuit judge or *US* a mayor. **7** (foll. by *to*) a person or thing that brings honour (*she is an honour to her profession*). **8 a** a woman's chastity. **b** the reputation for this. **9** (in *pl.*) **a** a special distinction for proficiency in an examination. **b** a course of degree studies more specialized than for an ordinary pass. **10 a** *Bridge* the ace, king, queen, jack, and ten, esp. of trumps, or the four aces at no trumps. **b** *Whist* the ace, king, queen, and jack, esp. of trumps. **11** *Golf* the right of driving off first as having won the last hole (*it is my honour*). ● *v.tr.* **1** respect highly. **2** confer honour on. **3** accept (a bill) or pay (a cheque) when due. **4** acknowledge. □ **do the honours** perform the duties of a host to guests etc. **honours are even** *Brit.* there is equality in the contest. **in honour of** as a celebration of. **on one's honour** (usu. foll. by *to* + infin.) under a moral obligation. [from Latin *honor*]

honourable *adj.* (*US* **honorable**) **1 a** worthy of honour. **b** bringing honour to its possessor. **c** showing honour, not base. **d** consistent with honour. **e** *colloq.* or *joc.* (of the intentions of a man courting a woman) directed towards marriage. **2** (**Honourable**) a title, given to certain high offi-

HONEY FUNGUS
(*Armillaria mellea*)

cials, the children of certain ranks of the nobility, and MPs. □ **honourably** *adv.*

honourable mention *n.* an award of merit to a candidate in an examination, a work of art, etc., not awarded a prize.

honours list *n.* a list of persons awarded honours.

hooch *n.* (also **hootch**) *N. Amer. colloq.* alcoholic liquor, esp. inferior or illicit whisky. [abbreviation of *hoochinoo*, name of a liquor-making Alaskan tribe]

hood[1] ● *n.* **1 a** a covering for the head and neck, whether part of a cloak etc. or separate. **b** a separate hoodlike garment worn over a university gown or a surplice to indicate the wearer's degree. **2** *Brit.* a folding waterproof top of a motor car, pram, etc. **3** *N. Amer.* the bonnet of a motor vehicle. **4** a canopy to protect users of machinery or to remove fumes etc. **5** a hoodlike structure or marking on the head or neck of a cobra, seal, etc. **6** a leather covering for a hawk's head. ● *v.tr.* cover with a hood. [Old English] □ **hooded** *adj.* **hoodless** *adj.* **hoodlike** *adj.*

hood[2] *n.* esp. *US slang* a gangster or gunman. [abbreviation of HOODLUM]

hooded crow *n.* a piebald grey and black crow, of a northern race of the carrion crow.

hoodlum *n.* **1** a street hooligan, a young thug. **2** a gangster. [19th-century coinage]

hoodoo esp. *US* ● *n.* **1 a** bad luck. **b** a thing or person that brings or causes this. **2** voodoo. ● *v.tr.* (**hoodoos**, **hoodooed**) **1** make unlucky. **2** bewitch. [alteration of VOODOO]

hoodwink *v.tr.* deceive, delude. [earlier in sense 'blindfold']

hooey *n.* & *int. colloq.* nonsense, humbug. [20th-century coinage]

hoof *n.* (*pl.* **hoofs** or **hooves**) the horny part of the foot of a horse, antelope, and other ungulates. ▷ HORSE, UNGULATE. □ **hoof it** *slang* go on foot. **on the hoof** (of cattle) not yet slaughtered. [Old English] □ **hoofed** *adj.* (also in *comb.*).

hoofer *n. slang* a professional dancer.

hoo-ha *n. colloq.* a commotion, a row; uproar, trouble. [20th-century coinage]

hook ● *n.* **1 a** a piece of metal or other material bent back at an angle or with a round bend, for catching hold or for hanging things on. **b** (in full **fish-hook**) ▼ a bent piece of wire, usu. barbed and baited, for catching fish. **2** a curved cutting instrument (*reaping-hook*). **3 a** a sharp bend, e.g. in a river. **b** a projecting point of land (*Hook of Holland*). **4 a** *Cricket* & *Golf* a hooking stroke (see sense 5 of *v.*). **b** *Boxing* a short swinging blow with the elbow bent and rigid. ● *v.* **1** *tr.* **a** grasp with a hook. **b** secure with a hook or hooks. **2** (often foll. by *on*, *up*) **a** *tr.* attach with or as with a hook. **b** *intr.* be or become attached with a hook. **3** *tr.* catch with or as with a hook. **4** *tr. slang* steal. **5** *tr.* **a** *Cricket* play (the ball) round from the off to the on side with an upward stroke. **b** (also *absol.*) *Golf* strike (the ball) so that it deviates towards the striker. **6** *tr. Rugby* secure (the ball) and pass it backward with the foot in the scrum. **7** *tr. Boxing* strike (one's opponent) with the

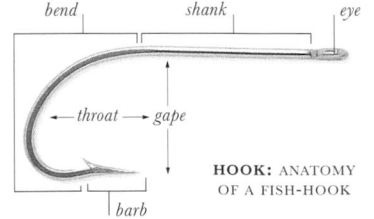

HOOK: ANATOMY OF A FISH-HOOK

elbow bent and rigid. □ **by hook or by crook** by one means or another, by fair means or foul. **hook, line, and sinker** entirely. **off the hook 1** *colloq.* no longer in difficulty or trouble. **2** (of a telephone receiver) not on its rest, so preventing incoming calls. **sling** (or **take**) **one's hook** *Brit. slang* make off, run away. [Old English] □ **hookless** *adj.* **hooklet** *n.* **hooklike** *adj.*

hookah *n.* an oriental tobacco pipe with a long tube passing through water for cooling the smoke as it is drawn through. [from Arabic *ḥukkah* 'casket, jar']

hook and eye *n.* ► a small metal hook and loop as a fastener on a garment.

HOOK AND EYE

hooked *adj.* **1** hook-shaped (*hooked nose*). **2** furnished with a hook or hooks. **3** in senses of HOOK *v.* □ **hooked on** *slang* addicted to; captivated by.

hooker *n.* **1** *Rugby* the player in the middle of the front row of the scrum who tries to hook the ball. ▷ RUGBY. **2** *slang* a prostitute.

hookey *n.* (also **hooky**) *N. Amer.* □ **play hookey** *colloq.* play truant. [19th-century coinage]

hook-nose *n.* an aquiline nose. □ **hook-nosed** *adj.*

hook-up *n.* a connection, esp. an interconnection of broadcasting equipment for special transmissions.

hookworm *n.* **1** any of various parasitic nematode worms with hooklike mouthparts for attachment and feeding, infesting the gut of humans and animals. **2** a disease caused by an infestation of these, often resulting in severe anaemia.

hooligan *n.* a young ruffian, esp. a member of a gang. [19th-century coinage] □ **hooliganism** *n.*

hoop[1] ● *n.* **1** a circular band of metal, wood, etc., esp. as part of a framework. **2 a** a ring bowled along by a child. **b** a large ring, usu. with paper stretched over it, for circus performers to jump through. **3** esp. *Brit.* an arch through which the balls are hit in croquet. **4** a band in contrasting colour on a sports shirt, jockey's cap, etc. ● *v.tr.* **1** bind with a hoop or hoops. **2** encircle with or as with a hoop. □ **be put** (or **go**) **through the hoop** (or **hoops**) undergo an ordeal. [Old English]

hoop[2] var. of WHOOP.

hoopla *n.* **1** *Brit.* a game in which rings are thrown in an attempt to encircle one of various prizes. **2** *colloq.* commotion. **3** *colloq.* pretentious nonsense.

hoopoe /hoo-poo/ *n.* ◄ a salmon-pink bird, *Upupa epops*, with black and white wings and tail, a large erectile crest, and a long downward-curving bill. [from Latin *upupa*, imitative of its cry]

HOOPOE
(*Upupa epops*)

hooray *int.* **1** = HURRAH. **2** *Austral.* & *NZ* goodbye. [variant of HURRAH]

Hooray Henry *n. Brit. colloq.* a rich ineffectual young man.

hoot ● *n.* **1** an owl's cry. **2** the sound made by a motor horn or a steam whistle. **3** a shout expressing scorn or disapproval. **4 a** a short outburst (of laughter). **b** *colloq.* a cause of this (*the escapade was a hoot*). ● *v.* **1** *intr.* **a** (of an owl) utter its cry. **b** (of a motor horn or steam whistle) make a hoot. **c** (often foll. by *at*) make loud sounds, esp. of scorn or merriment. **2** *tr.* **a** assail with scornful shouts.

b (often foll. by *out, away*) drive away by hooting. **3** *tr.* sound (a motor horn or steam whistle). [Middle English]

hootch var. of HOOCH.

hooter *n.* **1** *Brit.* a siren or steam whistle, esp. as a signal for work to begin or cease. **2** *Brit.* the horn of a motor vehicle. **3** *slang* a nose.

hoots *int. Sc.* & *N.Engl.* expressing dissatisfaction or impatience. [a natural exclamation]

Hoover *Brit.* ● *n. propr.* a vacuum cleaner (properly one made by the Hoover company). ● *v.* (**hoover**) **1** *tr.* (also *absol.*) clean (a carpet etc.) with a vacuum cleaner. **2** (foll. by *up*) **a** *tr.* suck up with or as with a vacuum cleaner (*hoovered up the crumbs*). **b** *absol.* clean a room etc. with a vacuum cleaner. [named after W. H. *Hoover*, American manufacturer, 1849–1932]

hooves *pl.* of HOOF.

hop[1] ● *v.* (**hopped, hopping**) **1** *intr.* (of a bird etc.) spring with two or all feet at once. **2** *intr.* (of a person) jump on one foot. **3** *intr.* move or go quickly (*hopped over the fence*). **4** *tr.* cross (a ditch etc.) by hopping. **5** *tr. colloq.* a jump into (a vehicle). **b** obtain (a ride) in this way. **6** *tr.* (usu. as **hopping** *n.*) (esp. of aircraft) pass quickly from one (place of a specified type) to another (*hedge-hopping*). ● *n.* **1** a hopping movement. **2** *colloq.* an informal dance. **3** a short journey, esp. a flight. □ **hop in** (or **out**) *colloq.* get into (or out of) a car etc. **hop it** *Brit. slang* go away. **hopping mad** very angry **on the hop** *Brit. colloq.* **1** unprepared (*caught on the hop*). **2** bustling about. [Old English]

hop[2] ● *n.* **1** ► a climbing plant, *Humulus lupulus*, cultivated for the cones borne by the female. **2** (in *pl.*) **a** the ripe cones of this, used to give a bitter flavour to beer. **b** *Austral.* & *NZ colloq.* beer. ● *v.* (**hopped, hopping**) **1** *tr.* flavour with hops. **2** *intr.* produce or pick hops. [from Middle Dutch *hoppe*]

hop-bind *n.* (also **hop-bine**) the climbing stem of the hop.

cone

HOP[1]: COMMON HOP
(*Humulus lupulus*)

hope ● *n.* **1** (in *sing.* or *pl.*, often foll. by *of, that*) expectation and desire combined (*hope of getting the job*). **2 a** a person, thing, or circumstance that gives cause for hope. **b** ground of hope, promise. **3** what is hoped for. ● *v.* **1** *intr.* (often foll. by *for*) feel hope. **2** *tr.* expect and desire. **3** *tr.* feel fairly confident. □ **hope against hope** cling to a mere possibility. **not a** (or **some**) **hope!** *colloq.* no chance at all. [Old English] □ **hoper** *n.*

hope chest *n. N. Amer.* = BOTTOM DRAWER.

hopeful ● *adj.* **1** feeling hope. **2** causing or inspiring hope. **3** likely to succeed, promising. ● *n.* (in full **young hopeful**) **1** a person likely to succeed. **2** *iron.* a person likely to be disappointed. □ **hopefulness** *n.*

hopefully *adv.* **1** in a hopeful manner. **2** (qualifying a whole sentence) *disp.* it is to be hoped.

■ **Usage** The use of *hopefully* in sense 2 is extremely common, but it is still considered incorrect by some people. The main reason is that other such adverbs, e.g. *regrettably*, *fortunately*, etc., can be converted to the form *it is regrettable*, *it is fortunate*, etc., but *hopefully* converts to *it is to be hoped*. This use of *hopefully* probably arose as a translation of German *hoffentlich*, used in the same way. Its use is best restricted to informal contexts.

hopeless *adj.* **1** feeling no hope. **2** admitting no hope (*a hopeless case*). **3** inadequate, incompetent (*am hopeless at tennis*). □ **hopelessly** *adv.* **hopelessness** *n.*

hoplite *n.* ► a heavily armed foot soldier of ancient Greece.

HOPLITE: ANCIENT GREEK FOOT SOLDIER, *c.*200 BC

hopper[1] *n.* **1** a person who hops. **2** a hopping arthropod, e.g. a flea or young locust. **3** a container tapering downward to an opening for discharging its contents. ▷ DRILL

hopper[2] *n.* a hop-picker.

hopsack *n.* **1 a** a coarse material made from hemp etc. **b** sacking for hops made from this. **2** a coarse clothing fabric of a loose plain weave.

hopscotch *n.* a children's game of hopping over squares or oblongs marked on the ground to retrieve a flat stone etc.

hop, skip, and jump *n.* (also **hop, step, and jump**) = TRIPLE JUMP.

horde *n.* **1 a** usu. *derog.* a large group, a gang. **b** a moving swarm or pack (of insects, wolves etc.). **2** a troop of nomads. [from Turkic *ordī* 'camp']

horehound *n.* a herbaceous plant of the mint family. [Old English, from *hār* 'hoar' + *hūne*, name of a plant]

horizon *n.* **1** the line at which the earth and sky appear to meet. **2** limit of mental perception, experience, interest, etc. □ **on the horizon** (of an event) just imminent or becoming apparent. [from Greek *horizōn (kuklos)* 'limiting (circle)']

horizontal ● *adj.* **1 a** parallel to the plane of the horizon, at right angles to the vertical (*horizontal plane*). **b** (of machinery etc.) having its parts working in a horizontal direction. **2 a** combining firms engaged in the same stage of production (*horizontal integration*). **b** involving social groups of equal status etc. **3** of or at the horizon. ● *n.* a horizontal line, plane, etc. □ **horizontality** *n.* **horizontally** *adv.*

hormone *n.* **1** *Physiol.* a regulatory substance produced in an organism and transported in tissue fluids to stimulate specific cells or tissues into action. ▷ ENDOCRINE. **2** a synthetic substance with a similar effect. [based on Greek *horman* 'to set in motion'] □ **hormonal** *adj.*

hormone replacement therapy *n.* treatment with oestrogens to alleviate menopausal symptoms.

horn ● *n.* **1** a hard permanent outgrowth, often curved and pointed, on the head of esp. hoofed mammals. ▷ RHINOCEROS. **2** each of two deciduous branched appendages on the head of (esp. male) deer. **3** a hornlike projection on the head of other animals, e.g. a snail's tentacle. **4** the substance of which horns are composed. **5** anything resembling or compared to a horn in shape. **6** *Mus.* **a** = FRENCH HORN. **b** a wind instrument played by lip vibration, originally made of horn, now usu. of brass. ▷ BRASS, ORCHESTRA. **7** an instrument sounding a warning or other signal. **8** a receptacle or instrument made of horn. **9** a horn-shaped projection. **10** *US colloq.* a telephone. **11** the extremity of the Moon or other crescent. **12** an arm or branch of a river, bay, etc. ● *v.tr.* **1** (esp. as **horned** *adj.*) provide with horns. **2** gore with the horns. □ **horn in** *slang* **1** (usu. foll. by *on*) intrude. **2** interfere. **horn of plenty** a cornucopia. **on the horns of a dilemma** faced with a decision involving equally unfavourable alternatives. [Old English] □ **horned** *adj.* **hornist** *n.* (in senses 6a and b of *n.*). **hornless** *adj.* **hornlike** *adj.*

hornbeam *n.* any tree of the genus *Carpinus*, with a smooth bark and a hard tough wood.

HORSE

Horses are ungulate mammals, descended from the first equine (*Eohippus*) over a period of 50 million years. While all modern horses belong to one species (*Equus caballus*), domestic forms are selectively bred for specific purposes such as riding, racing, or harness work.

H

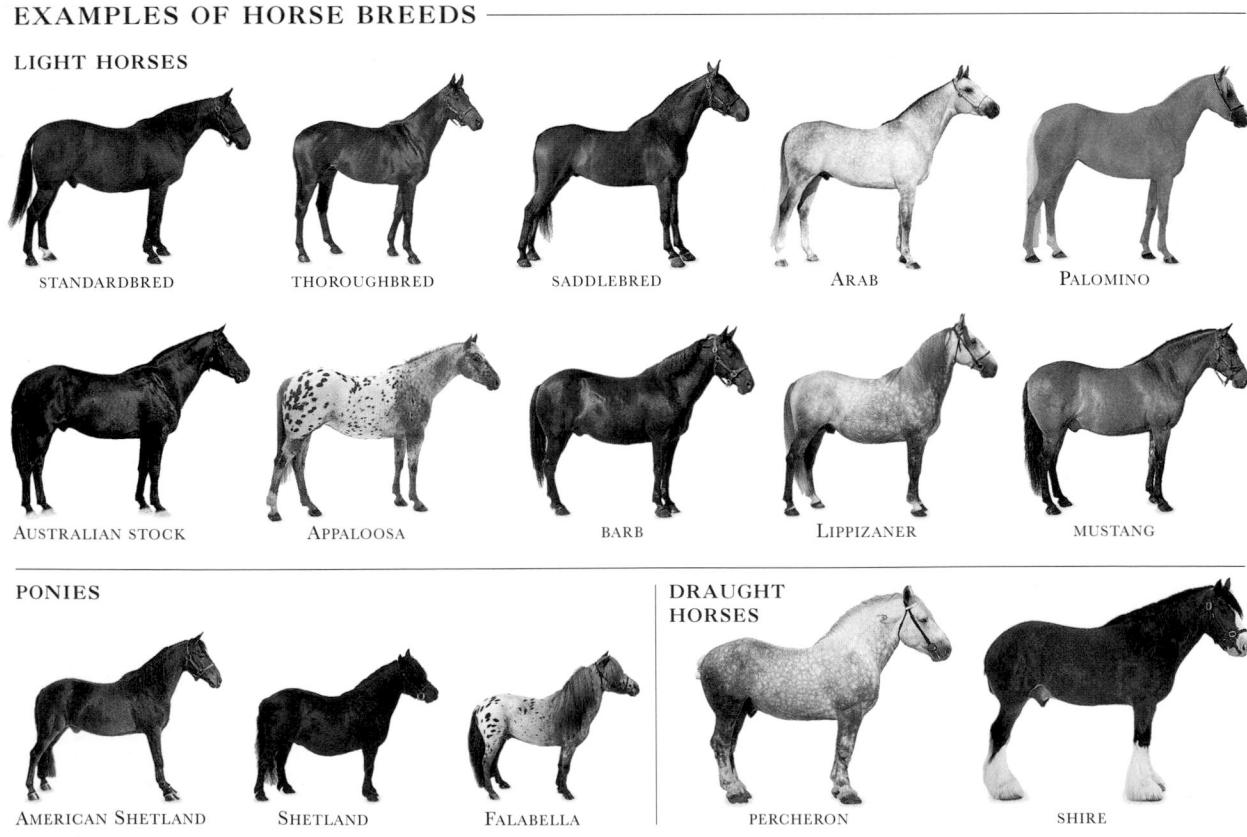

mane
crest
ear
forelock
forehead
eye
nose
croup
loin
back
withers
dock
throat-latch
cheek
chin groove
mouth
muzzle
buttock
neck
shoulder
breast
thigh
tail
stifle
flank
belly
chest
elbow
gaskin
foreleg
hock
chestnut
knee
cannon-bone
fetlock
coronet
ergot
pastern
heel
hoof

EXTERNAL FEATURES OF
THE DOMESTIC HORSE
(*Equus caballus*)

EXAMPLES OF HORSE BREEDS

LIGHT HORSES

STANDARDBRED   THOROUGHBRED   SADDLEBRED   ARAB   PALOMINO

AUSTRALIAN STOCK   APPALOOSA   BARB   LIPPIZANER   MUSTANG

PONIES

AMERICAN SHETLAND   SHETLAND   FALABELLA

DRAUGHT HORSES

PERCHERON   SHIRE

hornbill *n.* any bird of the tropical family Bucerotidae, with a hornlike excrescence on its large red or yellow curved bill.

hornblende *n.* ▶ a dark brown, black, or green mineral occurring in many igneous and metamorphic rocks. [German]

HORNBLENDE

horned toad *n.* **1** ▼ an American lizard, *Phrynosoma cornutum*, covered with spiny scales. **2** any SE Asian toad of the family Pelobatidae, with horn-shaped extensions over the eyes.

spiny scales *horn*

HORNED TOAD
(*Phrynosoma cornutum*)

hornet *n.* a large wasp, *Vespa crabro*. ▷ MIMESIS. □ **stir up a hornets' nest** provoke or cause trouble or opposition. [Old English]

hornpipe *n.* **1** a lively dance (esp. associated with sailors). **2** the music for this. [Middle English: originally the name of a wind instrument partly of horn]

horn-rimmed *adj.* (esp. of spectacles) having rims made of horn or a substance resembling it.

hornwort *n.* any aquatic rootless plant of the genus *Ceratophyllum*, with forked leaves.

horny *adj.* (**hornier**, **horniest**) **1** of or like horn. **2** hard like horn, callous. **3** *slang* sexually excited. □ **horniness** *n.*

horology *n.* the art of measuring time, making clocks, watches, etc.; the study of this. [based on Greek *hōra* 'time'] □ **horologer** *n.* **horological** *adj.* **horologist** *n.*

horoscope *n. Astrol.* **1** a forecast of a person's future based on a diagram showing the relative positions of the stars and planets at that person's birth. **2** such a diagram (*cast a horoscope*). [from Greek *hōra* 'time' + *skopos* 'observer'] □ **horoscopic** *adj.* **horoscopy** *n.*

horrendous *adj.* horrifying; awful. [from Latin *horrendus* 'to be shuddered at'] □ **horrendously** *adv.*

horrible *adj.* **1** causing or likely to cause horror; hideous, shocking. **2** *colloq.* unpleasant, excessive (*horrible noise*). [from Latin *horribilis*] □ **horribleness** *n.* **horribly** *adv.*

horrid *adj.* **1** horrible, revolting. **2** *colloq.* unpleasant, disagreeable (*horrid weather*). **3** *poet.* rough, bristling. [from Latin *horridus*] □ **horridly** *adv.* **horridness** *n.*

horrific *adj.* horrifying. [from Latin *horrificus*] □ **horrifically** *adv.*

horrify *v.tr.* (**-ies**, **-ied**) arouse horror in; shock, scandalize. □ **horrification** *n.* **horrifying** *adj.* **horrifyingly** *adv.*

horripilation *n. literary* = GOOSE-FLESH. [based on Latin *horrēre* 'to bristle' + *pilus* 'hair']

horror ● *n.* **1** an intense feeling of loathing and fear. **2 a** (often foll. by *of*) intense dislike. **b** (often foll. by *at*) *colloq.* intense dismay. **3 a** a person or thing causing horror. **b** *colloq.* a bad or mischievous person etc. **4** (in *pl.*; prec. by *the*) a fit of horror, depression, or nervousness. **5** (in *pl.*) an exclamation of dismay. ● *attrib.adj.* (of films etc.) designed to arouse pleasurable feelings of horror. [from Latin]

horror-struck *adj.* (also **horror-stricken**) horrified, shocked.

hors de combat /or dĕ **com**-bah/ *adj.* out of the fight or the running.

hors d'oeuvre /or dervr/ *n.* (*pl.* same or **hors d'oeuvres** *pronunc.* same or /or **dervz**/) an appe-

tizer served usu. at the beginning of a meal. [French, literally 'outside the work']

horse ● *n.* **1 a** ◀ a solid-hoofed plant-eating quadruped, *Equus caballus*, with flowing mane and tail, used for riding and to carry and pull loads. ▷ SHOWJUMPING. **b** an adult male horse; a stallion or gelding. **c** any other four-legged mammal of the genus *Equus*, including asses and zebras. ▷ EVOLUTION. **d** (*collect.*; treated as *sing.*) cavalry. **2** = VAULTING HORSE. **3 a** a frame or structure on which something is mounted or supported. **b** = SAWHORSE. **c** = CLOTHES HORSE 1. **4** *slang* heroin. ● *v.* **1** *intr.* (foll. by *around*) fool about. **2** *tr.* provide (a person or vehicle) with a horse or horses. **3** *intr.* mount or go on horseback. □ **from the horse's mouth** (of information etc.) from the person directly concerned or another authoritative source. **horses for courses** *Brit.* the matching of tasks and talents. [Old English] □ **horselike** *adj.*

horseback *n.* the back of a horse, esp. as sat on in riding. □ **on horseback** mounted on a horse.

horsebox *n. Brit.* a closed vehicle for transporting a horse or horses.

horse brass see BRASS *n.* 5.

horse chestnut *n.* **1** (also **horse chestnut tree**) any large tree of the genus *Aesculus*, with upright conical clusters of white or pink or red flowers. **2** the smooth dark brown inedible nut of this.

horseflesh *n.* **1** the flesh of a horse, esp. as food. **2** horses collectively.

horsefly *n.* (*pl.* **-flies**) any of various biting dipterous insects of the family Tabanidae, troublesome esp. to horses.

Horse Guards *n.pl.* (in the UK) **1** ◀ a cavalry brigade of the household troops, now an armoured-car regiment. **2** the headquarters of this brigade in Whitehall.

HORSE GUARDS: MOUNTED SENTRY OF THE HORSE GUARDS, LONDON, ENGLAND

horsehair *n.* hair from the mane or tail of a horse, used for padding etc.

horse latitudes *n.pl.* a belt of calms in each hemisphere between the trade winds and the westerlies. ▷ TRADE WIND

horseless *adj.* without a horse.

horseless carriage *n. archaic* a motor car.

horseman *n.* (*pl.* **-men**) **1** a rider on horseback. **2** a skilled rider. □ **horsemanship** *n.*

horse opera *n. N. Amer. slang* a western film.

horseplay *n.* boisterous play.

horsepower *n.* (*pl.* same) **1** an imperial unit of power (about 750 watts). **2** the power of an engine etc. measured in terms of this.

horse race *n.* a race between horses with riders. □ **horse racing** *n.*

horseradish *n.* **1** a cruciferous plant, *Armoracia rusticana*, with long lobed leaves. **2** the pungent root of this scraped or grated as a condiment, often made into a sauce.

horse sense *n. colloq.* plain common sense.

horseshoe *n.* **1** a U-shaped iron shoe for a horse. **2** a thing of this shape (e.g. a magnet).

horseshoe bat *n.* a bat of the Old World family Rhinolophidae, usu. with a horseshoe-shaped ridge on the nose. ▷ BAT

horseshoe crab *n.* ▶ a large marine arthropod, *Limulus polyphemus*, with a horseshoe-shaped shell and a long tail-spine.

horsetail *n.* **1** the tail of a horse (formerly used in Turkey as a standard, or as an ensign denoting the rank of pasha). **2** any cryptogamous plant of the genus *Equisetum*, like a horse's tail, with a hollow jointed stem and scalelike leaves.

strobilus *sterile shoot* *scalelike leaf* *joint* *photosynthetic stem* *fertile stem* *rhizome*

HORSETAIL:
COMMON HORSETAIL
(*Equisetum arvense*)

horse-trading *n.* **1** *N. Amer.* dealing in horses. **2** shrewd bargaining.

horsewhip ● *n.* a whip for driving horses. ● *v.tr.* (**-whipped, -whipping**) beat with a horsewhip.

horsewoman *n.* (*pl.* **-women**) **1** a woman who rides on horseback. **2** a skilled woman rider.

horsy *adj.* (also **horsey**) (**horsier, horsiest**) **1** of or like a horse. **2** concerned with or devoted to horses or horse racing. □ **horsily** *adv.* **horsiness** *n.*

hortatory *adj.* (also **hortative**) tending or serving to exhort. [based on Latin *hortari* 'to exhort'] □ **hortation** *n.*

horticulture *n.* the art of garden cultivation. [based on Latin *hortus* 'garden'] □ **horticultural** *adj.* **horticulturalist** *n.* **horticulturist** *n.*

hosanna *n. & int.* a shout of adoration (Matt. 21:9, 15, etc.). [from Hebrew *hôša 'nā*, for *hôšî'a-nnā* 'save now!']

hose ● *n.* **1** a flexible tube for conveying water. **2 a** (*collect.*; treated as *pl.*) stockings and socks (esp. in trade use). **b** *hist.* ▶ breeches (*doublet and hose*). ● *v.tr.* **1** (often foll. by *down*) water or spray or drench with a hose. **2** provide with hose. [Old English]

hosepipe *n. Brit.* = HOSE *n.* 1.

hosier *n.* a dealer in hosiery.

hosiery *n.* **1** stockings and socks. **2** *Brit.* knitted or woven underwear.

doublet *hose*

hospice *n.* **1** a home for people who are ill (esp. terminally) or *Brit.* destitute. **2** a lodging for travellers, esp. one kept by a religious order. [from Latin *hospitium*]

hospitable *adj.* giving hospitality. [based on medieval Latin *hospitare* 'to entertain'] □ **hospitably** *adv.*

hospital *n.* **1** an institution providing medical and surgical treatment and nursing care for ill or injured people. **2** *hist.* **a** a hospice. **b** an establishment of the Knights Hospitallers. **3** *Brit. Law* a charitable institution. [from medieval Latin *hospitale*, literally 'hospitable (place)'] □ **hospitalize** *v.tr.* (also **-ise**). **hospitalization** *n.*

HOSE: 14TH-CENTURY ITALIAN DOUBLET AND HOSE

hospitaler *US* var. of HOSPITALLER.

hospitality *n.* the friendly and generous reception and entertainment of guests or strangers.

hospitaller *n.* (*US* **hospitaler**) (also **Hospitaller**) a member of a charitable religious order.

hospital trust *n.* (in the UK) a trust consisting of a National Health Service hospital or hospitals no longer under local authority control.

HORSESHOE CRAB
(*Limulus polyphemus*)

H

H

host[1] *n.* **1** (usu. foll. by *of*) a large number of people or things. **2** *archaic* an army. [from Latin *hostis* 'stranger, enemy']

host[2] ● *n.* **1** a person who receives or entertains another as a guest. **2** the landlord of an inn (*mine host*). **3** *Biol.* an organism having a parasite or commensal. **4** an animal or person that has received a transplanted organ etc. **5** the compère of a show. ● *v.tr.* act as host at (an event) or to (a person). [from Latin *hospes -pitis* 'host, guest']

host[3] *n.* the bread consecrated in the Eucharist. [from Latin *hostia* 'victim']

hosta *n.* ▼ any perennial garden plant of the genus *Hosta* with green or variegated leaves and clusters of tubular mauve or white flowers. [named after N. T. *Host*, Austrian physician, 1761–1834]

HOSTA (*Hosta* 'Tall Boy')

hostage *n.* **1** a person seized or held as security for the fulfilment of a condition. **2** a pledge or security. [from Old French, based on Latin *obses obsidis* 'hostage']

hostage to fortune *n.* an acquisition, commitment, etc., regarded as endangered by unforeseen circumstances.

hostel *n.* **1** *Brit.* a house of residence or lodging for students etc. **2** = YOUTH HOSTEL. **3** *archaic* an inn. [from medieval Latin]

hostelling *n.* (*US* **hosteling**) the practice of staying in youth hostels, esp. while travelling. □ **hosteller** *n.*

hostelry *n.* (*pl.* **-ies**) *archaic* or *literary* an inn.

hostess *n.* **1** a woman who receives or entertains a guest. **2** a woman employed to welcome and entertain customers at a nightclub etc. **3** a stewardess on an aircraft, train, etc.

hostile *adj.* **1** of an enemy. **2** (often foll. by *to*) unfriendly, opposed. [based on Latin *hostis* 'stranger'] □ **hostilely** *adv.*

hostility *n.* (*pl.* **-ies**) **1** being hostile, enmity. **2** a state of warfare. **3** (in *pl.*) acts of warfare. **4** opposition (in thought etc.).

hot ● *adj.* (**hotter**, **hottest**) **1 a** having a relatively or noticeably high temperature. **b** (of food or drink) prepared by heating and served without cooling. **2** producing the sensation of heat (*hot flush*). **3** (of spices etc.) pungent. **4** (of a person) feeling heat. **5 a** (often foll. by *for, on*) eager, keen (*in hot pursuit*). **b** (foll. by *on*) *colloq.* strict with. **c** (foll. by *on*) *colloq.* knowledgeable about. **6 a** ardent, passionate, excited. **b** angry or upset. **c** lustful. **d** exciting. **7 a** (of news etc.) fresh, recent. **b** *Brit. colloq.* (of Treasury bills) newly issued. **8** *Hunting* (of the scent) fresh and strong. **9 a** (of a player) very skilful. **b** (of a competitor) strongly fancied to win (*a hot favourite*). **c** (of a hit etc. in ball games) difficult for an opponent to deal with. **10** (of music, esp. jazz) strongly rhythmical and emotional. **11** *slang*

a (of goods) stolen. **b** (of a person) wanted by the police. **12** *slang* radioactive. **13** *colloq.* (of information) unusually reliable (*hot tip*). ● *v.tr. & intr.* (**hotted**, **hotting**) (usu. foll. by *up*) *Brit. colloq.* **1** make or become hot. **2** make or become active, lively, exciting, or dangerous. ● *adv.* **1** *Brit.* angrily, severely (*give it him hot*). **2** eagerly. □ **have the hots for** *slang* be sexually attracted to. **hot under the collar** angry, resentful, or embarrassed. **make it** (or **things**) **hot for a person** persecute a person. **not so hot** *colloq.* only mediocre. **sell** (or **go**) **like hot cakes** see CAKE. [Old English] □ **hotly** *adv.* **hotness** *n.* **hottish** *adj.*

hot air *n. colloq.* empty, boastful, or excited talk.

hot-air balloon *n.* ▶ a balloon consisting of a bag in which air is heated by burners located below it, causing it to rise. ▷ AIRCRAFT

hotbed *n.* **1** a bed of earth heated by fermenting manure, for raising or forcing plants. **2** (foll. by *of*) an environment promoting the growth of something, esp. something unwelcome (*hotbed of vice*).

hot-blooded *adj.* ardent, passionate.

hotchpotch *n.* **1** a confused mixture, a jumble. **2** a dish of many mixed ingredients, esp. a stew with vegetables. [from Old French *hocher* 'to shake' + *pot* 'pot']

hot cross bun *n.* a bun marked with a cross, traditionally eaten on Good Friday.

hot dog *n.* a hot sausage sandwiched in a soft roll.

hotel *n.* **1** an establishment providing accommodation and meals for payment. **2** *Austral.* & *NZ* a public house. [from French *hôtel*, later form of HOSTEL]

hotelier /hoh-**tel**-i-ay/ *n.* a hotel-keeper.

hot flush see FLUSH[1] *n.* 6a.

hotfoot ● *adv.* in eager haste. ● *v.tr.* hurry eagerly (esp. *hotfoot it*). ● *adj.* acting quickly.

hothead *n.* an impetuous person.

hot-headed *adj.* impetuous, excitable. □ **hot-headedness** *adj.* **hot-headedness** *n.*

hothouse ● *n.* **1** a heated building, usu. largely of glass, for rearing plants out of season or in a climate colder than is natural for them (often attrib.: *hothouse flowers*). **2** an environment that encourages the rapid growth or development of something. ● *v.tr.* raise in or as if in a hothouse; force the development of.

hotline *n.* a direct exclusive line of communication, esp. for emergencies.

hot metal *n. Printing* using type made from molten metal.

hot money *n.* capital transferred at frequent intervals.

hot pants *n.pl.* very brief shorts, usu. with a bib top, worn as a fashion garment.

hotplate *n.* a heated metal plate etc. (or a set of these) for cooking food or keeping it hot.

hotpot *n. Brit.* a casserole of meat and vegetables, usu. with a layer of potato on top.

hot potato *n. colloq.* a controversial or awkward matter or situation.

hot rod *n.* a motor vehicle modified to have extra power and speed.

hot seat *n. slang* **1** a position of difficult responsibility. **2** the electric chair.

hot shoe *n. Photog.* a socket on a camera with electrical contacts for a flashgun etc.

envelope

cable

burner

basket

HOT-AIR BALLOON

hotshot esp. *US colloq.* ● *n.* an important or exceptionally able person. ● *attrib.adj.* important, able, expert, suddenly prominent.

hot spot *n.* **1** a small region that is relatively hot. **2** a lively or dangerous place.

hot spring *n.* a spring of naturally hot water.

hot stuff *n. colloq.* **1** a formidably capable person. **2** an important person or thing. **3** a sexually attractive person. **4** a spirited, strong-willed, or passionate person. **5** a book, film, etc. with a strongly erotic content.

hot-tempered *adj.* impulsively angry.

Hottentot often *offens.* ● *n.* (*pl.* same or **Hottentots**) = NAMA *n.* 1, 2. ● *adj.* = NAMA *adj.* [Dutch]

> ■ **Usage** *Nama* is now the preferred name for this people and their language.

hotting *n. slang* the practice of driving recklessly in a stolen car. □ **hotter** *n.*

hot tub *n.* a large tub filled with hot aerated water and used by one or several people for recreation or physical therapy.

hot war *n.* an open war, with active hostilities.

hot water *n. colloq.* difficulty, trouble, or disgrace (*be in hot water*).

hot-water bottle *n.* (*US* **hot-water bag**) a container, usu. made of rubber, filled with hot water, esp. to warm a bed.

hot-wire *v.tr.* esp. *N. Amer. slang* start the engine of (a car etc.) by bypassing the ignition switch.

hough *Brit.* ● *n.* **1** = HOCK[1] 1. **2** a cut of beef etc. from this and the leg above it. ● *v.tr.* hamstring. [Old English *hōh* 'heel']

hoummos var. of HUMMUS.

hound ● *n.* **1** a dog used for hunting, esp. one able to track by scent. **2** *colloq.* a despicable man. **3** a person keen in pursuit of something (usu. in *comb.*: *news-hound*). ● *v.tr.* **1** harass or pursue relentlessly. **2** chase or pursue with a hound. **3** (foll. by *at*) set (a dog or person) on (a quarry). **4** urge on or nag (a person). □ **ride to hounds** go fox-hunting on horseback. [Old English]

houndstooth *n.* a check pattern with notched corners suggestive of canine teeth.

hour *n.* **1** a twenty-fourth part of a day and night, 60 minutes. **2** a time of day, a point in time (*a late hour*). **3** (in *pl.*) this number of hours and minutes past midnight on the 24-hour clock (*assemble at 20.00 hours*). **4** a period set aside for some purpose (*lunch hour*). **b** (in *pl.*) a fixed period of time for work etc. (*office hours*). **5** a short indefinite period of time (*an idle hour*). **6** the present time (*question of the hour*). **7** a time for action etc. (*the hour has come*). **8** the distance travelled in one hour (*we are an hour from London*). **9** *RC Ch.* **a** prayers to be said at one of seven fixed times of day (*book of hours*). **b** any of these times. **10** (prec. by *the*) each time o'clock of a whole number of hours (*buses leave on the hour*). □ **after hours** after closing time. **till all hours** till very late. [from Greek *hōra* 'season, hour']

hourglass *n.* ▶ a reversible device with two connected glass bulbs containing sand that takes an hour to pass from the upper to the lower bulb.

houri /**hoor**-i/ *n.* (*pl.* **houris**) a beautiful young woman, esp. in the Muslim Paradise. [based on Arabic *ḥawrā'* 'gazelle-like' (of the eyes)]

HOURGLASS

HOUSE

Most Western houses are built from materials such as timber, stone, brick, and concrete. Foundations, walls, and roof spaces are usually constructed to provide insulation and conceal pipes and cables for gas, electricity, water, drainage, and heating. In houses of the future, solar panels may be a regular energy-saving feature.

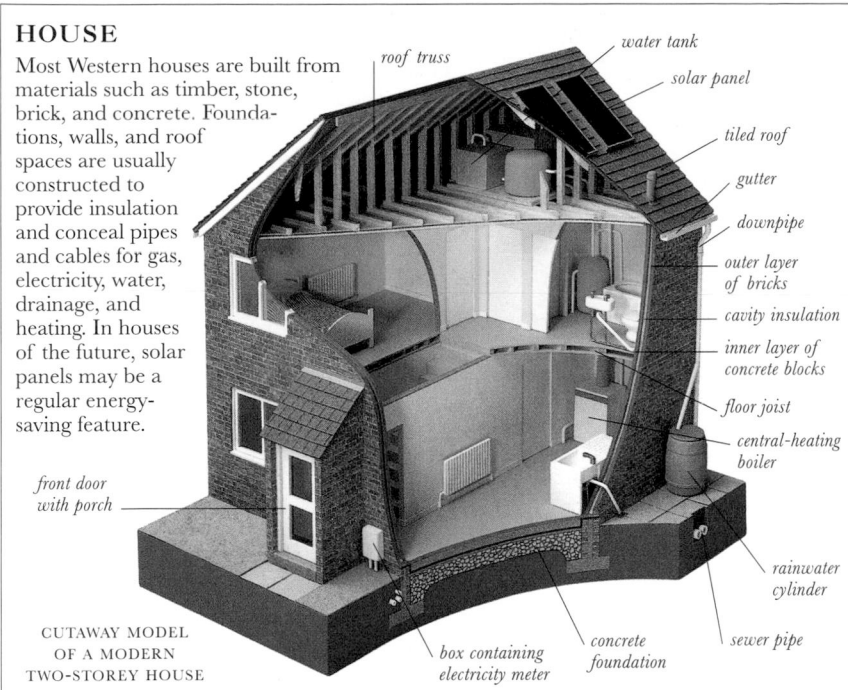

roof truss
water tank
solar panel
tiled roof
gutter
downpipe
outer layer of bricks
cavity insulation
inner layer of concrete blocks
floor joist
central-heating boiler
rainwater cylinder
sewer pipe
concrete foundation
box containing electricity meter
front door with porch

CUTAWAY MODEL OF A MODERN TWO-STOREY HOUSE

---

hourly ● *adj.* **1** done or occurring every hour. **2** frequent, continual. **3** reckoned hour by hour (*hourly wage*). ● *adv.* **1** every hour. **2** frequently, continually.

house ● *n.* /howss/ **1 a** ▲ a building for human habitation. **b** (*attrib.*) kept in, frequenting, or infesting houses (*house plant*). **2** a building for a special purpose (*opera house*). **3** a building for keeping animals or goods (*hen house*). **4 a** a religious community. **b** the buildings occupied by it. **5** *Brit.* **a** a body of pupils living in the same building at a boarding school. **b** such a building. **c** a division of a day school for games, competitions, etc. **6** (usu. **House**) a family, esp. a royal family; a dynasty (*House of York*). **7 a** a firm or institution. **b** *Brit.* its place of business. **c** (**the House**) *Brit. colloq.* the Stock Exchange. **8 a** a legislative or deliberative assembly. **b** the building where it meets. **c** (**the House**) (in the UK) the House of Commons or Lords; (in the US) the House of Representatives. **9 a** an audience in a theatre etc. **b** *Brit.* a performance in a theatre or cinema. **c** a theatre. **10** *Astrol.* a twelfth part of the heavens. **11** (*attrib.*) living in a hospital as a member of staff (*house surgeon*). **12 a** a place of public refreshment (*coffee house*; *public house*). **b** (*attrib.*) (of wine) selected by the management of a hotel etc. to be offered at a special price. **13** *Sc.* a dwelling that is one of several in a building. **14** (in full **house music**) a style of popular dance music typically using drum machines, synthesized bass lines, sparse repetitive vocals, and a fast beat. ● *v.tr.* /howz/ **1** provide (a person etc.) with a house or houses or other accommodation. **2** store (goods etc.). **3** enclose or encase (a part or fitting). **4** fix in a socket etc. □ **keep house** provide for or manage a household. **like a house on fire 1** vigorously, fast. **2** successfully. **on the house** at the management's expense, free. **play house** play at being a family in its home. **put** (or **set**) **one's house in order** make necessary reforms. **set up house** begin to live in a separate dwelling. [Old English] □ **houseful** *n.* (*pl.* **-fuls**). **houseless** *adj.*

house agent *n. Brit.* an agent for the sale and letting of houses.

house arrest *n.* detention in one's own house etc., not in prison.

houseboat *n.* a boat fitted up for living in.

housebound *adj.* unable to leave one's house through illness etc.

housebreaker *n.* **1** a person guilty of housebreaking. **2** *Brit.* a person who is employed to demolish houses.

housebreaking *n.* the act of breaking into a building, esp. in daytime, to commit a crime (in 1968 replaced as a statutory crime in English law by BURGLARY).

housebuilding *n.* the activity of building houses. □ **housebuilder** *n.*

housebuyer *n.* a person who buys a house. □ **house-buying** *n. & adj.*

housecoat *n.* a woman's garment for informal wear in the house, usu. a long dresslike coat.

house-father *n.* a man in charge of a house, esp. of a home for children.

housefinch *n.* a red-breasted finch, *Carpodacus mexicanus*, common in western N. America.

housefly *n.* (*pl.* **-flies**) ▼ any fly of the family Muscidae, esp. *Musca domestica*, breeding in decaying organic matter and often entering houses.

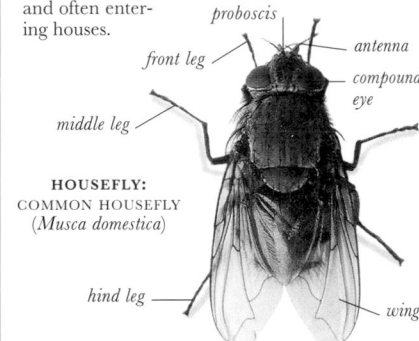

proboscis
antenna
compound eye
front leg
middle leg
HOUSEFLY: COMMON HOUSEFLY (*Musca domestica*)
hind leg
wing

house guest *n.* a guest staying for some days in a private house.

household *n.* **1** the occupants of a house regarded as a unit. **2** a house and its affairs. **3** (prec. by *the*) (in the UK) the royal household.

householder *n.* **1** a person who owns or rents a house. **2** the head of a household.

---

household troops *n.pl.* (in the UK) troops nominally employed to guard the sovereign.

household word *n.* (also **household name**) **1** a familiar name or saying. **2** a familiar person or thing.

house-hunting *n.* the process of seeking a house to live in. □ **house-hunter** *n.*

house-husband *n.* a husband who carries out the household duties traditionally carried out by a housewife.

housekeeper *n.* a person, esp. a woman, employed to manage a household.

housekeeping *n.* **1** the management of household affairs. **2** money allowed for this. **3** the operations of maintenance, record-keeping, etc. in an organization.

houseleek *n.* ► a succulent plant, *Sempervivum tectorum*, with pink flowers, growing on walls and roofs.

house lights *n.pl.* the lights in the auditorium of a theatre.

house magazine *n.* a magazine published by a firm and dealing mainly with its own activities.

HOUSELEEK
(*Sempervivum tectorum*)

housemaid *n.* a female servant in a house, esp. *Brit.* in charge of reception rooms and bedrooms.

housemaid's knee *n.* inflammation of the kneecap.

houseman *n.* (*pl.* **-men**) *Brit.* a resident doctor at a hospital etc.

house martin *n.* a black and white swallow-like bird, *Delichon urbica*, which builds a mud nest on house walls etc.

housemaster *n.* (*fem.* **housemistress**) the teacher in charge of a house at a boarding school.

house-mother *n.* a woman in charge of a house, esp. of a home for children.

house mouse *n.* a usu. grey mouse, *Mus musculus*, very common as a scavenger around human dwellings, and bred as a pet and experimental animal.

house music see HOUSE *n.* 14.

house of cards *n.* **1** an insecure scheme etc. **2** a structure built (usu. by a child) out of playing cards.

House of Commons *n.* (in the UK) the elected chamber of Parliament.

house of God *n.* a church, a place of worship.

house of ill fame *n. archaic* a brothel.

House of Keys *n.* (in the Isle of Man) the elected chamber of Tynwald.

House of Lords *n.* **1** (in the UK) the chamber of Parliament composed of peers and bishops. **2** a committee of specially qualified members of this appointed as the ultimate judicial appeal court.

House of Representatives *n.* the lower house of the US Congress and other legislatures.

house-parent *n.* a house-mother or house-father.

house plant *n.* a plant grown indoors.

house-proud *adj.* attentive to, or unduly preoccupied with, the care and appearance of the home.

houseroom *n.* space or accommodation in one's house. □ **not give houseroom to** *Brit.* not have in any circumstances.

house-sit *v.intr.* live in and look after a house while its owner is away. □ **housesitter** *n.*

Houses of Parliament *n.pl.* **1** the Houses of Lords and Commons regarded together. **2** the buildings where they meet.

house sparrow *n.* a common brown and grey sparrow, *Passer domesticus*, which nests in the eaves and roofs of houses.

house style *n.* a particular printer's or publisher's etc. preferred way of presentation.

H

HOVERCRAFT

Mostly used for passenger transport, a hover-craft skims over land or water, propelled on a cushion of air. The air is sucked into inlets and pumped by fans beneath the hull, where it is contained by an inflatable flexible skirt. The fastest models can travel at a speed of 120 k.p.h. (75 m.p.h.).

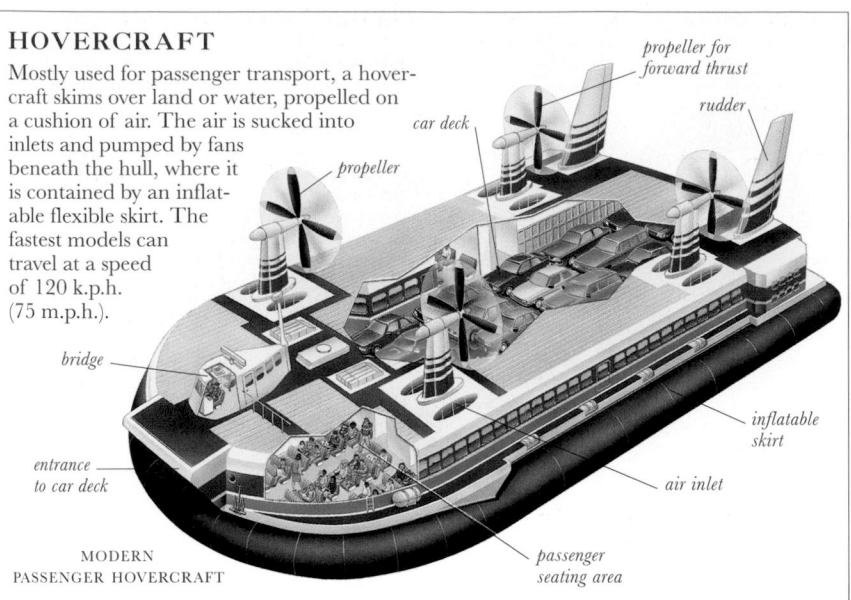

propeller for forward thrust

car deck

rudder

propeller

bridge

entrance to car deck

inflatable skirt

air inlet

passenger seating area

MODERN
PASSENGER HOVERCRAFT

H

house-to-house ● *adj. & adv.* performed at or carried to each house in turn. ● *n.* a house-to-house collection, search, etc.

housetop *n.* the roof of a house. □ **proclaim** (or **shout** etc.) **from the housetops** announce publicly.

house-train *v.tr.* (often as **house-trained** *adj.*) *Brit.* train (an animal) to be clean in the house.

house-warming *n.* a party celebrating a move to a new home.

housewife *n.* (*pl.* **-wives**) **1** a woman (usu. married) managing a household. **2** *Brit.* a case for needles, thread, etc. □ **housewifely** *adj.*

housewifery *n.* **1** housekeeping. **2** skill in this.

housework *n.* regular work done in housekeeping, e.g. cleaning and cooking.

housing *n.* **1 a** dwelling houses collectively. **b** the provision of these. **2** shelter, lodging. **3** a rigid casing, esp. for moving or sensitive parts of a machine. **4** the hole or niche cut in one piece of wood to receive some part of another in order to join them.

housing estate *n. Brit.* a residential area planned as a unit.

hove *past* of HEAVE.

hovel *n.* a small miserable dwelling. [Middle English]

hover ● *v.intr.* **1** (of a bird etc.) remain in one place in the air. **2** (often foll. by *about, round*) wait close at hand. **3** remain undecided. ● *n.* **1** hovering. **2** a state of suspense. [Middle English, from obsolete *hove* 'to linger'] □ **hoverer** *n.*

hovercraft *n.* (*pl.* same) ▲ a vehicle or craft that travels over land or water on a cushion of air provided by a downward blast.

hoverfly *n.* (*pl.* **-flies**) ◄ any fly of the family Syrphidae, hovering with rapidly beating wings.

hoverport *n.* a terminal for hovercraft.

how ● *interrog.adv.* **1** by what means, in what way (*how do you do it?*; *but how to bridge the gap?*). **2** in what condition, esp. of health (*how is the patient?*). **3 a** to what extent (*how far is it?*). **b** to what extent good or well, what ... like (*how was the film?*). ● *rel.adv.* in whatever way, as (*do it how you can*). ● *conj. colloq.* that (*told us how he'd been in India*). ● *n.* the way a thing is done (*the how and why of it*).

HOVERFLY
(*Syrphus ribesii*)

□ **how about 1** would you like. **2** what is to be done about. **3** what is the news about. **how are you? 1** what is your state of health? **2** = *how do you do?* **how come?** see COME. **how do you do?** a formal greeting. **how many** what number. **how much 1** what amount (*how much do I owe you?*). **2** what price (*how much is it?*). **how's that? 1** what is your explanation of that? **2** *Cricket* (said to an umpire) is the batsman out or not? [Old English]

howbeit *adv. archaic* nevertheless.

howdah *n.* a seat for two or more, usu. with a canopy, for riding on the back of an elephant or camel. [from Arabic *hawdaj* 'litter']

how-do-you-do (or **how-d'ye-do**) *n.* (*pl.* **-dos**) *colloq.* an awkward situation.

howdy *int. US* = *how do you do?* (see HOW). [corruption]

however *adv.* **1 a** in whatever way (*do it however you want*). **b** to whatever extent, no matter how (*must go however inconvenient*). **2** nevertheless. **3** *colloq.* (as an emphatic) in what way, by what means (*however did that happen?*).

howitzer *n.* a short gun for high-angle firing of shells at low velocities. [from Czech *houfnice* 'catapult']

howl ● *n.* **1** a long loud doleful cry uttered by a dog, wolf, etc. **2** a prolonged wailing noise, e.g. as made by a strong wind. **3** a loud cry of pain or rage. **4** a yell of derision or merriment. **5** *Electronics* a howling noise in a loudspeaker due to electrical or acoustic feedback. ● *v.* **1** *intr.* make a howl. **2** *intr.* weep loudly. **3** *tr.* utter (words) with a howl. □ **howl down** prevent (a speaker) from being heard by howls of derision. [Middle English]

howler *n.* **1** *colloq.* a glaring mistake. **2** ► a S. American monkey of the genus *Alouatta*. **3** a person or animal that howls.

howling *adj.* **1** that howls. **2** *colloq.* extreme (*a howling shame*). **3** *archaic* dreary (*howling wilderness*).

howling dervish see WHIRLING DERVISH.

HOWLER: RED HOWLER
(*Alouatta seniculus*)

howsoever *adv.* **1** in whatsoever way. **2** to whatsoever extent.

hoy *int.* used to call attention, drive animals, or *Naut.* hail or call aloft. [Middle English: a natural cry]

hoyden *n.* a boisterous girl. [originally in sense 'rude fellow'] □ **hoydenish** *adj.*

h.p. *abbr.* (also **HP**) **1** horsepower. **2** *Brit.* hire purchase. **3** high pressure.

HQ *abbr.* headquarters.

hr. *abbr.* hour.

HRH *abbr. Brit.* Her or His Royal Highness.

hrs. *abbr.* hours.

HRT *abbr.* hormone replacement therapy.

HT *abbr.* high tension.

hub *n.* **1** the central part of a wheel, rotating on or with the axle. ▷ DERAILLEUR. **2** a central point of interest, activity, etc. [16th-century coinage]

hubble-bubble *n.* **1** a rudimentary form of hookah. **2** a bubbling sound. **3** confused talk.

hubbub *n.* **1** a confused din. **2** a disturbance or riot.

hubby *n.* (*pl.* **-ies**) *colloq.* a husband.

hubcap *n.* a cover for the hub of a vehicle's wheel. ▷ CAR

hubris /hew-bris/ *n.* arrogant pride or presumption. [Greek] □ **hubristic** *adj.*

huckleberry *n.* (*pl.* **-ies**) **1** any low-growing N. American shrub of the genus *Gaylussacia*. **2** the soft fruit of this plant.

huckster ● *n.* **1** a mercenary person. **2** *US* a publicity agent, esp. for broadcast material. **3** a pedlar or hawker. ● *v.* **1** *intr.* bargain, haggle. **2** *tr.* carry on a petty traffic in. **3** *tr.* adulterate. [Middle English] □ **hucksterism** *n.*

huddle ● *v.* **1** *tr. & intr.* (often foll. by *up*) crowd together; nestle closely. **2** *intr. & refl.* (often foll. by *up*) coil one's body into a small space. ● *n.* **1** a confused or crowded mass of people or things. **2** *colloq.* a close or secret conference (esp. in **go into a huddle**). [16th-century coinage]

hue *n.* **1** a colour or tint. **2** a variety or shade of colour. [Old English *hēw* 'form, beauty'] □ **-hued** *adj.* (in *comb.*). **hueless** *adj.*

hue and cry *n.* a loud outcry. [from Anglo-French *hu e cri*, literally 'outcry and cry']

huff ● *v.* **1** *intr.* give out loud puffs of air, steam, etc. **2** *intr.* bluster loudly or threateningly (*huffing and puffing*). **3** *tr.* (in draughts) remove (an opponent's man that could have made a capture) from the board as a forfeit. ● *n.* a fit of petty annoyance. □ **in a huff** annoyed and offended.

huffy *adj.* (**huffier**, **huffiest**) **1** apt to take offence. **2** offended. □ **huffily** *adv.* **huffiness** *n.*

hug ● *v.tr.* (**hugged**, **hugging**) **1** squeeze tightly in one's arms, esp. with affection. **2** (of a bear) squeeze (a person) between its forelegs. **3** keep close to (the kerb etc.). **4** cherish or cling to (prejudices etc.). ● *n.* **1** a strong esp. affectionate clasp with the arms. **2** a squeezing grip in wrestling. [16th-century coinage] □ **huggable** *adj.*

huge *adj.* **1** extremely large; enormous. **2** (of immaterial things) very great (*a huge success*). [from Old French *ahuge*] □ **hugeness** *n.*

hugely *adv.* **1** enormously (*hugely successful*). **2** very much (*enjoyed it hugely*).

hugger-mugger ● *adj. & adv.* **1** in secret. **2** confused; in confusion. ● *n.* **1** secrecy. **2** confusion.

Huguenot /hew-gĕ-noh/ *n. hist.* a French Protestant. [French]

huh *int.* expressing disgust, surprise, etc. [imitative]

hula *n.* (also **hula-hula**) a dance performed by Hawaiian women, characterized by flowing arm movements. [Hawaiian]

hula hoop *n.* a large hoop for spinning round the body with hula-like movements.

hula skirt *n.* a long grass skirt.

hulk *n.* **1 a** the body of a dismantled ship, used as a store vessel etc. **b** (in *pl.*) *hist.* this used as a prison. **2** *colloq.* a large clumsy-looking person or thing. [from Middle Dutch]

hulking *adj. colloq.* bulky; large and clumsy.

hull¹ ● *n.* the body or frame of a ship, airship, etc. ▷ AIRCRAFT, BOAT. ● *v.tr.* pierce the hull of (a ship) with gunshot etc. [Middle English]

hull² ● *n.* **1** the outer covering of a fruit, esp. the pod of peas and beans, the husk of grain, or the green calyx of a strawberry. **2** a covering. ● *v.tr.* remove the hulls from (fruit etc.). [Old English *hulu* 'husk']

hullabaloo *n.* (*pl.* **hullabaloos**) an uproar or clamour. [18th-century coinage]

hullo var. of HELLO.

hum¹ ● *v.* (**hummed, humming**) **1** *intr.* make a low steady continuous sound like that of a bee. **2** *tr.* (also *absol.*) sing (a wordless tune) with closed lips. **3** *intr.* utter a slight inarticulate sound. **4** *intr. colloq.* be in an active state (*really made things hum*). **5** *intr. Brit. colloq.* smell unpleasantly. ● *n.* **1** a humming sound. **2** *Brit. colloq.* a bad smell. □ **hum and haw** (or **ha**) *Brit.* hesitate, esp. in speaking. [Middle English] □ **hummable** *adj.* **hummer** *n.*

hum² *int.* expressing hesitation or dissent.

human ● *adj.* **1** of, relating to, or characteristic of humankind or people; of or belonging to the genus *Homo*. ▷ BODY. **2** consisting of human beings (*the human race*). **3** of or characteristic of humankind esp. as being weak, fallible, etc. (*is only human*). **4** showing (esp. the better) qualities of humankind (*proved to be very human*). ● *n.* a human being. [from Latin *humanus*] □ **humanness** *n.*

human being *n.* any man or woman or child of the species *Homo sapiens*.

human chain *n.* a line of people formed for passing things along.

humane *adj.* **1** benevolent, compassionate. **2** inflicting the minimum of pain. **3** (of a branch of learning) tending to civilize or confer refinement. □ **humanely** *adv.* **humaneness** *n.*

human ecology see ECOLOGY 2.

humanism *n.* **1** a system of thought concerned with human rather than divine or supernatural matters. **2** an outlook emphasizing common human needs and concerned with humankind as responsible and progressive intellectual beings. **3** (often **Humanism**) literary culture, esp. that of the Renaissance humanists.

humanist *n.* **1** an adherent of humanism. **2** a humanitarian. □ **humanistic** *adj.* **humanistically** *adv.*

humanitarian ● *n.* **1** a person who seeks to promote human welfare. **2** a philanthropist. ● *adj.* **1** of, relating to, or holding the views of humanitarians. **2** of or relating to human welfare (*on humanitarian grounds*). □ **humanitarianism** *n.*

■ **Usage** The adjective *humanitarian* is often used inaccurately by reporters, e.g. *This is the worst humanitarian disaster within living memory*, as if *humanitarian* meant 'of or relating to humanity'. Such use can be avoided by using the adjective *human* instead.

humanity *n.* (*pl.* **-ies**) **1 a** the human race. **b** human beings collectively. **c** the fact or condition of being human. **2** humaneness. **3** (in *pl.*) human attributes. **4** (in *pl.*) learning or literature concerned with human culture.

humanize *v.tr.* (also **-ise**) **1** make human; give a human character to. **2** make humane. □ **humanization** *n.*

humankind *n.* human beings collectively.

humanly *adv.* **1** by human means (*if humanly possible*). **2** in a human manner. **3** from a human point of view. **4** with human feelings.

humanoid ● *adj.* having human form or character. ● *n.* a humanoid animal or thing.

human rights *n.pl.* rights held to be justifiably belonging to any person.

human shield *n.* a person or group of persons placed near a potential target to deter attack.

humble ● *adj.* (**humbler, humblest**) **1** having or showing a low estimate of one's own importance. **2** of low social or political rank (*humble origins*). **3** of modest pretensions, dimensions, etc. ● *v.tr.* **1** make humble; abase. **2** lower the rank or status of. □ **eat humble pie** make a humble apology; accept humiliation. [from Latin *humilis* 'lowly'; *humble pie*: from *umbles* 'edible offal'] □ **humbleness** *n.* **humbly** *adv.*

humble-bee *n.* = BUMBLE-BEE. [Middle English]

humbug ● *n.* **1** deceptive or false talk or behaviour. **2** an impostor. **3** *Brit.* a boiled sweet usu. flavoured with peppermint. ● *v.* (**humbugged, humbugging**) **1** *intr.* be or behave like an impostor. **2** *tr.* deceive, hoax. [18th-century coinage] □ **humbuggery** *n.*

humdinger *n. slang* an excellent or remarkable person or thing. [20th-century coinage]

humdrum *adj.* **1** commonplace, dull. **2** monotonous. [16th-century coinage]

humerus *n.* (*pl.* **humeri** /-ry/) **1** ▼ the bone of the upper arm in man. ▷ SKELETON. **2** the corresponding bone in other vertebrates. [Latin, literally 'shoulder'] □ **humeral** *adj.*

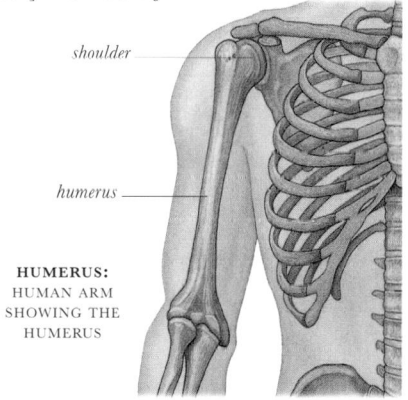

shoulder

humerus

HUMERUS:
HUMAN ARM
SHOWING THE
HUMERUS

humid *adj.* (of the air or climate) warm and damp. [from French *humide* or Latin *humidus* 'moist'] □ **humidly** *adv.*

humidify *v.tr.* (**-ies, -ied**) make (air etc.) humid or damp. □ **humidifier** *n.* **humidification** *n.*

humidity *n.* (*pl.* **-ies**) **1** a humid state. **2** moisture. **3** the degree of moisture esp. in the atmosphere.

humiliate *v.tr.* make humble; injure the dignity or self-respect of. [based on Late Latin *humiliatus* 'made lowly'] □ **humiliating** *adj.* **humiliatingly** *adv.* **humiliation** *n.* **humiliator** *n.*

humility *n.* **1** humbleness, meekness. **2** a humble condition. [from Latin *humilitas*]

hummingbird *n.* ▼ any small nectar-feeding tropical American bird of the family Trochilidae, that makes a humming sound with its wings when it hovers.

HUMMINGBIRD:
FORK-TAILED
WOODNYMPH
(*Thalurania furcata*)

hummock *n.* **1** a hillock or knoll. **2** *US* a piece of forested ground rising above a marsh. **3** a hump or ridge in an ice field. [16th-century coinage] □ **hummocky** *adj.*

hummus *n.* (also **hoummos**) a thick sauce or spread made from ground chickpeas. [from Turkish *humus* 'mashed chickpeas']

humongous *adj.* (also **humungous**) *slang* huge, enormous. [20th-century coinage]

humor *US* var. of HUMOUR.

humoresque *n.* a short lively piece of music.

humorist *n.* **1** a facetious person. **2** a humorous talker, actor, or writer. □ **humoristic** *adj.*

humorous *adj.* **1** showing humour or a sense of humour. **2** facetious, comic. □ **humorously** *adv.* **humorousness** *n.*

humour (*US* **humor**) ● *n.* **1 a** the quality of being amusing or comic. **b** the expression of humour in literature, speech, etc. **2** (in full **sense of humour**) the ability to perceive or express humour or take a joke. **3** (a mood or state of mind (*bad humour*). **4** (in full **cardinal humour**) *hist.* each of the four chief fluids of the body (blood, phlegm, yellow bile, black bile), thought to determine a person's physical and mental qualities. ● *v.tr.* **1** gratify or indulge (a person or taste etc.). **2** adapt oneself to. □ **out of humour** displeased. [from Latin *humor* 'moisture'] □ **-humoured** *adj.* (in *comb.*). **humourless** *adj.* **humourlessly** *adv.* **humourlessness** *n.*

hump ● *n.* **1** a rounded protuberance on the back of a camel etc., or as an abnormality on a person's back. **2** a rounded raised mass of earth etc. **3** a critical point in an undertaking, ordeal, etc. **4** (prec. by *the*) *Brit. slang* a fit of depression or vexation (*it gives me the hump*). ● *v.tr.* **1 a** (often foll. by *about*) *colloq.* lift or carry (heavy objects etc.) with difficulty. **b** esp. *Austral.* hoist up, shoulder (one's pack etc.). **2** make hump-shaped. **3** *coarse slang* have sexual intercourse with. □ **over the hump** over the worst. [17th-century coinage] □ **humped** *adj.* **humpless** *adj.*

humpback *n.* **1 a** a back deformed by a hump. **b** a person having this. **2** ▼ a baleen whale, *Megaptera novaeangliae*, with a dorsal fin forming a hump. □ **humpbacked** *adj.*

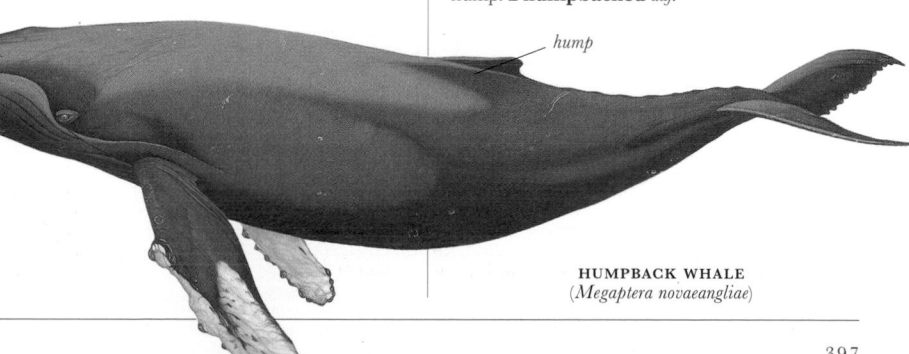

hump

HUMPBACK WHALE
(*Megaptera novaeangliae*)

H

H

HURRICANE

A typical hurricane is some 1,500 km (1,000 miles) across, and consists of bands of cumulonimbus cloud arranged in spirals around the eye of the storm. Within these bands, warm air rises quickly, causing torrential rain and drawing in winds that may gust at up to 360 k.p.h. (220 m.p.h.). Hurricanes form over tropical oceans and die out over land.

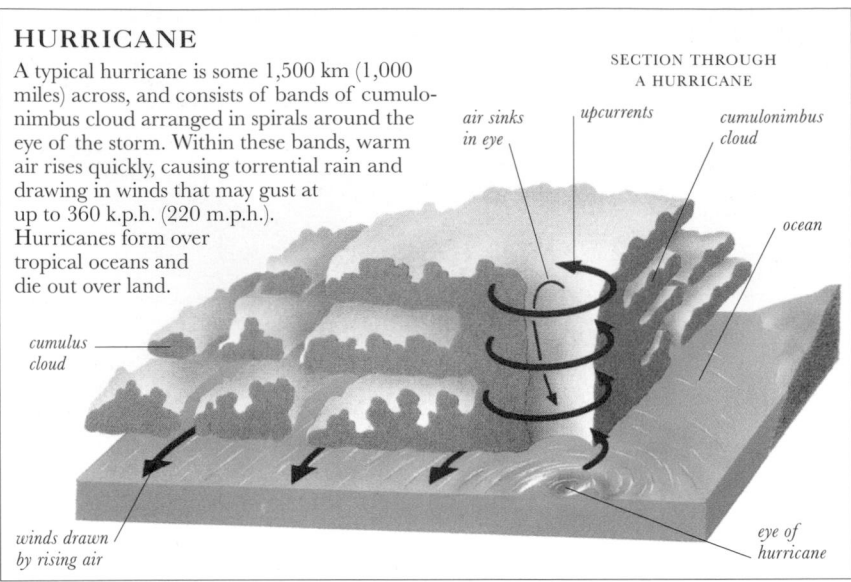

SECTION THROUGH A HURRICANE

air sinks in eye

upcurrents

cumulonimbus cloud

ocean

cumulus cloud

winds drawn by rising air

eye of hurricane

---

humpback bridge *n. Brit.* a small bridge with a steep ascent and descent.

humph *int. & n.* an inarticulate sound expressing doubt or dissatisfaction.

humpy *adj.* (**humpier**, **humpiest**) **1** having a hump or humps. **2** humplike.

humungous var. of HUMONGOUS.

humus *n.* the organic constituent of soil, usu. formed by the decomposition of plants and leaves. ▷ SOIL. [Latin, literally 'soil']

Hun *n.* **1** a member of a warlike Asiatic nomadic people who invaded and ravaged Europe in the 4th–5th c. **2** *offens.* a German (esp. in military contexts). [from Turkic *Hun-yü*] □ **Hunnish** *adj.*

hunch ● *v.tr.* **1** bend or arch into a hump. **2** thrust out or up to form a hump. ● *n.* **1** an intuitive feeling or conjecture. **2** *US colloq.* a hint. **3** a hump. **4** a thick piece. [Middle English]

hunchback *n.* = HUMPBACK 1. □ **hunchbacked** *adj.*

hundred ● *n.* (*pl.* **hundreds** or (in sense 1) **hundred**) (in *sing.*, prec. by *a* or *one*) **1** the product of ten and ten. **2** a symbol for this (100, c, C). **3** a set of a hundred things. **4** (in *sing.* or *pl.*) *colloq.* a large number. **5** (in *pl.*) the years of a specified century (*the seventeen hundreds*). **6** *Brit. hist.* a subdivision of a county or shire, having its own court. ● *adj.* **1** that amount to a hundred. **2** used to express whole hours in the 24-hour system (*thirteen hundred hours*). □ **a** (or **one**) **hundred per cent** ● *adv.* entirely, completely. ● *adj.* **1** entire, complete. **2** fully recovered. [Old English] □ **hundredfold** *adj. & adv.* **hundredth** *adj. & n.*

hundreds and thousands *n.pl. Brit.* tiny coloured sweets used chiefly for decorating cakes etc.

hundredweight *n.* (*pl.* same or **-weights**) **1** (in full **long hundredweight**) *Brit.* a unit of weight equal to 112 lb avoirdupois (about 50.8 kg). **2** (in full **metric hundredweight**) a unit of weight equal to 50 kg.

hung *past* and *past part.* of HANG.

Hungarian ● *n.* **1 a** a native or national of Hungary in central Europe. **b** a person of Hungarian descent. **2** the language of Hungary. ● *adj.* of or relating to Hungary or its people or language. [from *Hungari* 'Magyar nation']

hunger ● *n.* **1** a feeling of pain or discomfort, or (in extremes) an exhausted condition, caused by lack of food. **2** (often foll. by *for*, *after*) a strong desire. ● *v.intr.* **1** (often foll. by *for*, *after*) have a craving or strong desire. **2** feel hunger. [Old English]

hunger strike *n.* the refusal of food as a form of protest. □ **hunger striker** *n.*

hung-over *adj. colloq.* suffering from a hangover.

hung parliament *n.* a parliament in which no party has a clear majority.

hungry *adj.* (**hungrier**, **hungriest**) **1** feeling or showing hunger; needing food. **2** characterized by hunger (*those were hungry days*). **3** (often foll. by *for*) eager, craving. □ **hungrily** *adv.* **hungriness** *n.*

hunk *n.* **1 a** a large piece cut off (*a hunk of bread*). **b** a thick or clumsy piece. **2** *colloq.* **a** a very large person. **b** a sexually attractive, ruggedly handsome man. [19th-century coinage] □ **hunky** *adj.* (**hunkier**, **hunkiest**).

hunkers *n.pl.* the haunches.

hunky-dory *adj. colloq.* excellent. [19th-century coinage]

hunt ● *v.* **1** *tr.* (also *absol.*) **a** pursue and kill (wild animals or game) for sport or food. **b** *Brit.* pursue on horseback and usu. kill (a fox) using hounds. **c** *Brit.* use (hounds or a horse) for hunting. **d** (of an animal) chase (its prey). **2** *intr.* (foll. by *after*, *for*) seek, search (*hunting for a pen*). **3** *intr.* **a** oscillate. **b** *Brit.* (of an engine etc.) run alternately too fast and too slow. **4** *tr.* **a** (foll. by *away* etc.) drive off by pursuit. **b** pursue with hostility. **5** *tr.* scour (a district) in pursuit of game. **6** *tr.* (as **hunted** *adj.*) (of a look etc.) expressing alarm or terror as of one being hunted. ● *n.* **1** the practice of hunting or an instance of this. **2 a** an association of people engaged in hunting with hounds. **b** an area where hunting takes place. □ **hunt down** pursue and capture. **hunt out** find by searching; track down. [Old English, from *hentan* 'to seize'] □ **hunting** *n.*

hunter *n.* **1 a** (*fem.* **huntress**) a person or animal that hunts. **b** a horse used in hunting. **2** a person who seeks something. **3** a watch with a hinged cover protecting the glass.

hunter-gatherer *n.* a member of a people whose mode of subsistence is based on hunting animals and gathering plants etc.

hunting crop see CROP *n.* 3.

hunting horn *n.* a straight horn used in hunting.

hunting pink see PINK[1] *n.* 4.

Huntington's chorea *n.* chorea accompanied by a progressive dementia. [named after G. *Huntington*, American neurologist, 1851–1916]

huntress see HUNTER 1a.

huntsman *n.* (*pl.* **-men**) **1** a hunter. **2** a hunt official in charge of hounds.

hurdle ● *n.* **1 a** each of a series of light frames to be cleared by athletes in a race. **b** (in *pl.*) a hurdle race. **2** an obstacle or difficulty. **3** a portable rectangular frame used as a tem-

porary fence etc. ● *v.* **1 a** *intr.* run in a hurdle race. **b** *tr.* clear (a hurdle). **2** *tr.* fence off etc. with hurdles. [Old English] □ **hurdler** *n.*

hurdy-gurdy *n.* (*pl.* **-ies**) **1** a musical instrument with a droning sound, played by turning a handle. **2** *colloq.* a barrel organ.

hurl ● *v.tr.* **1** throw with great force. **2** utter (abuse etc.) vehemently. **3** *intr.* play hurley. ● *n.* **1** a forceful throw. **2** the act of hurling. [Middle English]

hurly-burly *n.* boisterous activity; commotion.

hurrah (also **hurray**) ● *int. & n.* an exclamation of joy or approval. ● *v.intr.* cry or shout 'hurrah' or 'hurray'.

hurricane *n.* ◀ a storm with a violent wind, esp. a tropical cyclone. [from Spanish *huracan* & Portuguese *furacão*]

hurricane lamp *n.* an oil lamp designed to resist a high wind.

hurry ● *n.* **1 a** great haste. **b** (with *neg.* or *interrog.*) a need for haste (*what's the hurry?*). **2** (often foll. by *for*, or *to* + infin.) eagerness to get a thing done quickly. ● *v.* (**-ies**, **-ied**) **1** *intr.* move or act with great or undue haste. **2** *tr.* (often foll. by *away*, *along*) cause to move or proceed in this way. **3** *tr.* (as **hurried** *adj.*) done rapidly owing to lack of time. □ **in a hurry 1** hurrying. **2** *colloq.* easily or readily (*shall not ask again in a hurry*). [16th-century coinage] □ **hurriedly** *adv.* **hurriedness** *n.*

hurt ● *v.* (*past* and *past part.* **hurt**) **1** *tr.* (also *absol.*) cause pain, injury, or harm to. **2** *tr.* cause mental distress to. **3** *intr.* suffer pain or harm (*my arm hurts*). ● *n.* **1** bodily or material injury. **2** harm, wrong. [from Old French *hurter*]

hurtful *adj.* causing (esp. mental) hurt. □ **hurtfully** *adv.* **hurtfulness** *n.*

hurtle *v.* **1** *intr. & tr.* move or hurl rapidly or with a clattering sound. **2** *intr.* come with a crash. [from obsolete *hurt* 'to strike forcibly']

husband ● *n.* a married man esp. in relation to his wife. ● *v.tr.* manage thriftily. [from Old Norse *húsbóndi*] □ **husbander** *n.* **husbandhood** *n.* **husbandless** *adj.* **husbandly** *adj.*

husbandman *n.* (*pl.* **-men**) a man who cultivates the ground; a farmer.

husbandry *n.* **1** farming. **2 a** management of resources. **b** careful management.

hush ● *v.tr. & intr.* make or become silent or quiet. ● *int.* calling for silence. ● *n.* an expectant stillness or silence. □ **hush up** suppress public mention of (an affair). [back-formation from obsolete interjection *husht* 'quiet!']

hush-hush *adj. colloq.* highly secret or confidential.

hush money *n.* money paid to prevent the disclosure of a discreditable matter.

husk ● *n.* **1** the dry outer covering of some fruits or seeds. ▷ MAST. **2** the worthless outside part of a thing. ● *v.tr.* remove a husk or husks from. [Middle English]

husky[1] *adj.* (**huskier**, **huskiest**) **1** (of a person or voice) dry in the throat; hoarse. **2** of or full of husks. **3** dry as a husk. **4** tough, strong, hefty. □ **huskily** *adv.* **huskiness** *n.*

husky[2] *n.* (*pl.* **-ies**) ▼ a dog of a powerful breed used in the Arctic for pulling sledges.

HUSKY

huss *n.* dogfish as food. [Middle English]

hussar /huu-**zar**/ *n.* **1** ◀ a soldier of a light cavalry regiment. **2** a Hungarian light horseman of the 15th c. [based on Italian *corsaro* 'corsair']

   hussy *n.* (*pl.* **-ies**) *derog.* an impudent or immoral girl or woman. [phonetic reduction of HOUSE-WIFE, the original sense]

    hustings *n.* parliamentary election proceedings. [from Old Norse *histhing* 'house of assembly']

hustle ● *v.* **1** *tr.* push roughly; jostle. **2** *tr.* **a** (foll. by *into, out of,* etc.) force or deal with hurriedly or unceremoniously (*hustled them out of the room*). **b** (foll. by *into*) coerce (*was hustled into agreeing*). **3** *intr.* push one's way; bustle. **4** *tr. colloq.* **a** obtain by forceful action. **b** swindle. **5** *intr. US slang* engage in prostitution. ● *n.* **1** an act or instance of hustling. **2** *colloq.* a fraud or swindle. [from Middle Dutch *husselen* 'to shake, toss']

HUSSAR: 19TH-CENTURY FRENCH HUSSAR OFFICER

   hustler *n. slang* **1** an active, enterprising, or unscrupulous individual. **2** *US* a prostitute.

hut *n.* **1** a small simple or crude house or shelter. **2** *Mil.* a temporary wooden etc. house for troops. [from Middle High German *hütte*] □ **hut-like** *adj.*

hutch *n.* a box or cage, usu. with a wire mesh front, for keeping rabbits etc. [from medieval Latin *hutica*]

Hutu ● *n.* (*pl.* same, **Hutus**, or **Bahutu**) a member of a Bantu-speaking people forming the majority population in Rwanda and Burundi. ● *adj.* of or relating to the Hutu people. [Bantu]

hyacinth ● *n.* **1** any bulbous plant of the genus *Hyacinthus* with racemes of usu. purplish-blue, pink, or white bell-shaped fragrant flowers. **2** = GRAPE HYACINTH. **3** the purplish-blue colour of some hyacinth flowers. ● *adj.* purplish blue. [from Greek *huakinthos*, flower and gem; also the name of a youth loved by Apollo] □ **hyacinthine** *adj.*

hyaena var. of HYENA.

hyalite *n.* a colourless variety of opal. [based on Greek *hualos* 'glass']

hyaluronic acid *n. Biochem.* a viscous fluid carbohydrate found in synovial fluid, the vitreous humour of the eye, etc. [from *hyaloid* 'glassy' + *-uronic,* chemical suffix]

hybrid ● *n.* **1** *Biol.* the offspring of two plants or animals of different species or varieties. **2** *offens.* a person of mixed racial or cultural origin. **3** a thing composed of incongruous elements, e.g. a word with parts taken from different languages. ● *adj.* **1** bred as a hybrid from different species or varieties. **2** *Biol.* heterogeneous. [from Latin *hybrida* 'offspring of a tame sow and wild boar, child of a freeman and slave, etc.'] □ **hybridism** *n.* **hybridity** *n.* **hybridize** *v.tr. & intr.* (also **-ise**). **hybridizable** *adj.* **hybridization** *n.*

hydra *n.* **1** a freshwater polyp of the genus *Hydra* with a tubular body and tentacles around the mouth. **2** any water snake. **3** something which is hard to destroy. [from Greek *hudra* 'water snake', esp. a fabulous one with many heads]

   hydrangea /hy-**drayn**-jă/ *n.* ◀ any shrub of the genus *Hydrangea* with large white, pink, or blue flowers. [from Greek *hudōr* 'water' + *aggos* 'vessel', from the cup shape of its seed capsule]

HYDRANGEA (*Hydrangea macrophylla* 'Altona')

HYDRAULIC

A hydraulic system uses fluid to convert a small force to a large one, as in the brakes of a car. A long, weak push on the master piston displaces liquid within the system. As the master piston is narrower than the slave, this produces a short, strong push on the slave.

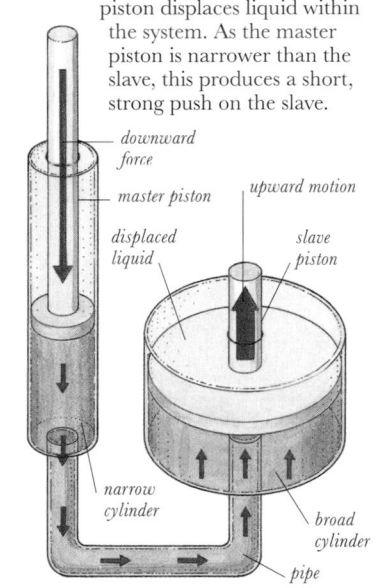

- downward force
- master piston
- displaced liquid
- upward motion
- slave piston
- narrow cylinder
- broad cylinder
- pipe

DEMONSTRATION OF A HYDRAULIC SYSTEM

---

hydrant *n.* a pipe (esp. in a street) with a nozzle to which a hose can be attached for drawing water from the main.

hydrate *Chem.* ● *n.* a compound of water combined with another compound or with an element. ● *v.tr.* **1 a** combine chemically with water. **b** (as **hydrated** *adj.*) chemically bonded to water. **2** cause to absorb water. [based on Greek *hudōr* 'water'] □ **hydration** *n.* **hydrator** *n.*

hydraulic *adj.* **1** (of water, oil, etc.) conveyed through pipes or channels usu. by pressure. **2** ▲ (of a mechanism etc.) operated by liquid moving in this manner (*hydraulic brakes*). ▷ SIMULATOR. [based on Greek *hudōr* 'water' + *aulos* 'pipe'] □ **hydraulically** *adv.*

---

hydraulics *n.pl.* (usu. treated as *sing.*) the science of the conveyance of liquids through pipes etc. esp. as motive power.

hydride *n. Chem.* a binary compound of hydrogen with an element, esp. with a metal.

hydro *n.* (*pl.* **-os**) *colloq.* **1** a hotel or clinic etc. originally providing hydropathic treatment. **2** a hydroelectric power plant.

hydro- *comb. form* (also **hydr-** before a vowel) **1** having to do with water or a fluid (*hydroelectric*). **2** *Med.* affected with an accumulation of serous fluid (*hydrocephalus*). **3** *Chem.* combined with hydrogen (*hydrochloric*). [from Greek]

hydrocarbon *n. Chem.* a compound of hydrogen and carbon. ▷ ALKANE, ALKENE, ALKYNE

hydrocephalus *n. Med.* an accumulation of fluid in the brain, esp. in young children. □ **hydrocephalic** *adj.*

hydrochloric acid *n. Chem.* a solution of the colourless gas hydrogen chloride in water.

hydrochloride *n. Chem.* a compound of an organic base with hydrochloric acid.

hydrocortisone *n. Biochem.* a steroid hormone produced by the adrenal cortex, used medicinally to treat inflammation and rheumatism.

hydrocyanic acid *n. Chem.* a highly poisonous volatile liquid with a characteristic odour of bitter almonds.

hydrodynamics *n.* the science of forces acting on or exerted by fluids (esp. liquids). □ **hydrodynamic** *adj.* **hydrodynamical** *adj.* **hydrodynamicist** *n.*

hydroelectric *adj.* **1** ▼ generating electricity by utilization of water-power. **2** (of electricity) generated in this way. □ **hydroelectricity** *n.*

hydrofoil *n.* **1** a boat equipped with a device consisting of planes for lifting its hull out of the water to increase its speed. **2** this device.

hydrogel *n.* a gel in which the liquid component is water.

hydrogen *n. Chem.* a colourless gaseous element, without taste or odour, the lightest of the elements and occurring in water and all organic compounds. [from French *hydrogène*] □ **hydrogenous** *adj.*

hydrogenate *v.tr.* charge with or cause to combine with hydrogen. □ **hydrogenation** *n.*

hydrogen bomb *n.* an immensely powerful nuclear bomb utilizing the explosive fusion of hydrogen nuclei.

hydrogen peroxide *n.* a colourless viscous unstable liquid with strong oxidizing properties.

H

HYDROELECTRIC

In a hydroelectric power station, gravity forces water between two reservoirs via a turbine. The momentum of the surging water turns the turbine, which powers a generator to produce electricity.

CROSS-SECTION OF A HYDROELECTRIC POWER STATION

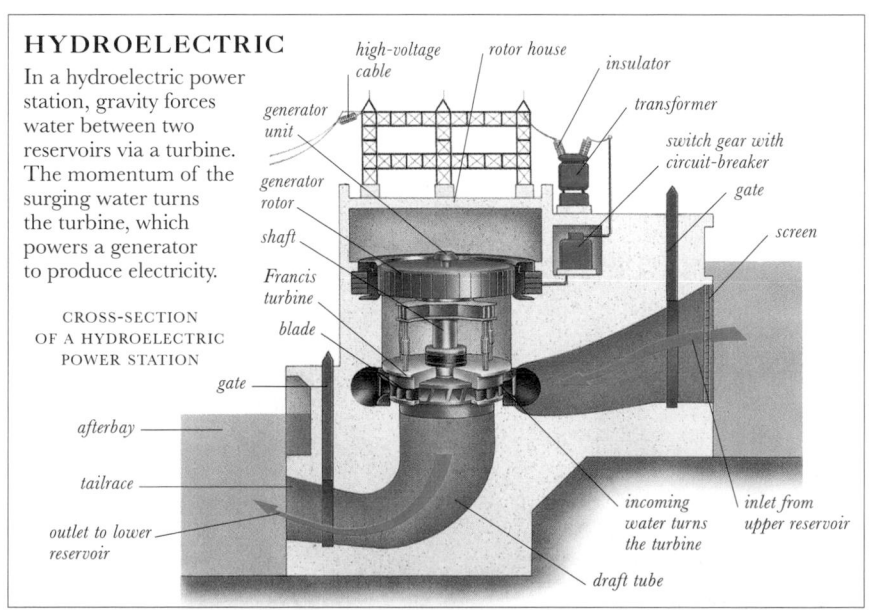

- high-voltage cable
- rotor house
- insulator
- generator unit
- transformer
- generator rotor
- switch gear with circuit-breaker
- shaft
- gate
- Francis turbine
- screen
- blade
- gate
- afterbay
- tailrace
- incoming water turns the turbine
- inlet from upper reservoir
- outlet to lower reservoir
- draft tube

H

hydrogen sulphide *n.* a colourless poisonous gas with a disagreeable smell, formed by rotting animal matter.

hydrogeology *n.* the branch of geology dealing with underground and surface water. □ **hydrogeological** *adj.* **hydrogeologist** *n.*

hydrography *n.* the science of surveying and charting seas, lakes, rivers, etc. □ **hydrographer** *n.* **hydrographic** *adj.* **hydrographical** *adj.* **hydrographically** *adv.*

hydroid *Zool.* ● *n.* ◄ a cnidarian of the order Hydroida, in which the polyp phase is predominant, e.g. sea anemones, corals, hydras. ▷ CNIDARIAN, CORAL. ● *adj.* of or relating to this order.

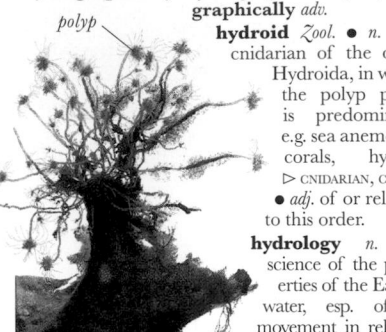

polyp

HYDROID
(*Tubularia indivisa*)

hydrology *n.* the science of the properties of the Earth's water, esp. of its movement in relation to land. □ **hydrologic** *adj.* **hydrological** *adj.* **hydrologically** *adv.* **hydrologist** *n.*

hydrolyse *v.tr. & intr.* (also **hydrolyze**) subject to or undergo the chemical action of water. □ **hydrolysis** *n.* **hydrolytic** *adj.*

hydromechanics *n.* the mechanics of liquids; hydrodynamics.

hydrometer /hy-**drom**-i-ter/ *n.* an instrument for measuring the density of liquids. □ **hydrometric** *adj.* **hydrometry** *n.*

hydropathy *n.* the treatment of disorders by external and internal application of water. □ **hydropathic** *adj.* **hydropathist** *n.*

hydrophilic *adj.* **1** having an affinity for water. **2** readily mixing with or wetted by water. [based on Greek *philos* 'loving']

hydrophobia *n.* **1** a morbid aversion to water, esp. as a symptom of rabies in humans. **2** rabies, esp. in humans. □ **hydrophobic** *adj.*

hydroplane *n.* **1** a light fast motor boat designed to skim over water. **2** a finlike attachment which enables a submarine to rise and fall in water.

hydroponics *n.* the process of growing plants in sand, gravel, or liquid, without soil and with added nutrients. [based on Greek *ponos* 'labour'] □ **hydroponic** *adj.* **hydroponically** *adv.*

hydrosphere *n.* the waters of the Earth's surface.

hydrostatic *adj.* of the equilibrium of liquids and the pressure exerted by liquid at rest. □ **hydrostatically** *adv.*

hydrostatics *n.* the branch of mechanics concerned with the hydrostatic properties of liquids.

hydrotherapy *n.* the use of water in treating disorders, usu. by means of exercises in swimming pools. □ **hydrotherapist** *n.*

hydrothermal *adj.* of the action of heated water on the Earth's crust. □ **hydrothermally** *adv.*

hydrous *adj. Chem. & Mineral.* containing water. [based on Greek *hudōr hudro-* 'water']

hydroxide *n. Chem.* a metallic compound containing oxygen and hydrogen either as a hydroxide ion or a hydroxyl group.

hydroxy- *comb. form Chem.* having a hydroxide ion or a hydroxyl group.

hydroxyl *n. Chem.* the monovalent group containing hydrogen and oxygen, as -OH.

hyena /hy-**ee**-nă/ *n.* (also **hyaena**) ▶ any flesh-eating mammal of the family Hyaenidae. [from Greek *huaina*, fem. of *hus* 'pig']

HYENA:
STRIPED HYENA
(*Hyaena hyaena*)

HYMENOPTERAN

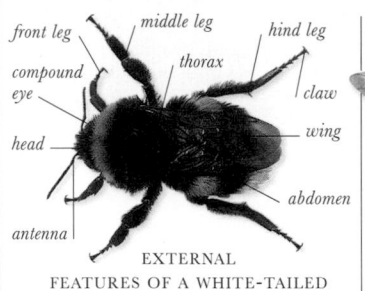

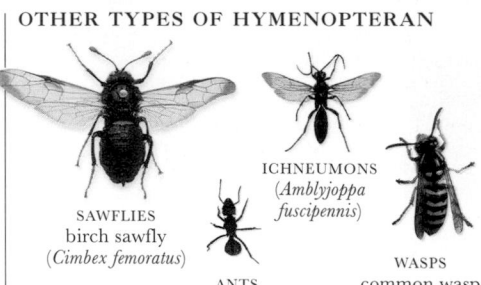

Hymenopterans are a huge group of insects comprising ants, bees, and wasps, together with sawflies, gall wasps, ichneumon wasps, and other parasites. Most (except worker ants) have two pairs of membranous wings joined by tiny hooks, with veins forming largish cells. Many species live in social groups, each rank fulfilling specific functions.

front leg *middle leg* *hind leg*

compound eye *thorax* *claw*

head *wing*

abdomen

antenna

EXTERNAL FEATURES OF A WHITE-TAILED BUMBLEBEE (*Bombus lucorum*)

OTHER TYPES OF HYMENOPTERAN

SAWFLIES
birch sawfly
(*Cimbex femoratus*)

ICHNEUMONS
(*Amblyjoppa fuscipennis*)

ANTS
(unidentified species)

WASPS
common wasp
(*Vespula vulgaris*)

---

hygiene *n.* **1 a** a study, or set of principles, for maintaining health. **b** conditions or practices conducive to maintaining health. **2** sanitary science. [from Greek *hugieinē (tekhnē)* '(art) of health']

hygienic *adj.* conducive to hygiene; clean and sanitary. □ **hygienically** *adv.*

hygienist *n.* a specialist in the promotion and practice of cleanliness for the preservation of health.

hygro- *comb. form* moisture. [from Greek]

hygrometer /hy-**grom**-i-ter/ *n.* ▶ an instrument for measuring the humidity of the air or a gas. □ **hygrometric** *adj.* **hygrometry** *n.*

hygroscope *n.* an instrument which indicates but does not measure the humidity of the air.

hygroscopic *adj.* **1** of the hygroscope. **2** (of a substance) tending to absorb moisture from the air.

hying *pres. part.* of HIE.

hymen *n. Anat.* a membrane at the opening of the vagina that is usu. broken at the first occurrence of sexual intercourse. [from Greek *humēn* 'membrane']

hymenopteran *n.* ▲ any insect of the order Hymenoptera having four transparent wings, including bees, wasps, and ants. [from Greek *humenopteros* 'membrane winged'] □ **hymenopterous** *adj.*

hymn ● *n.* a song of esp. Christian praise. ● *v. tr.* praise or celebrate in hymns. [from Greek *humnos*]

hymnal /**him**-năl/ *n.* a hymn book.

hymn book *n.* a book of hymns.

hyoscine *n.* a poisonous alkaloid found in plants of the nightshade family, and used as an anti-emetic in motion sickness and a preoperative medication for examination of the eye.

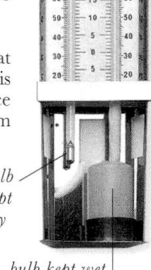

thermometers

bulb kept dry

bulb kept wet

HYGROMETER:
WET AND DRY HYGROMETER

hype[1] *slang* ● *n.* extravagant or intensive publicity promotion. ● *v.tr.* promote (a product) with extravagant publicity. [20th-century coinage]

hype[2] *n. slang* **1** a drug addict. **2** a hypodermic needle or injection. □ **hyped up** stimulated by or as if by a hypodermic injection.

hyper *adj. slang* hyperactive, highly strung.

hyper- *prefix* meaning: **1** over, beyond, above (*hyperphysical*). **2** exceeding (*hypersonic*). **3** excessively; above normal (*hyperbole; hypersensitive; hyperinflation*).

hyperactive *adj.* (of a person, esp. a child) abnormally active. □ **hyperactivity** *n.*

hyperbola /hy-**per**-bŏ-lă/ *n.* (*pl.* **hyperbolas** or **hyperbolae** /-lee/) *Geom.* the plane curve of two equal branches, produced when a cone is cut by a plane that makes a larger angle with the base than the side of the cone. ▷ CONIC SECTION. [from Greek *huperbolē* 'excess']

hyperbole /hy-**per**-bŏ-li/ *n. Rhet.* an exaggerated statement not meant to be taken literally. □ **hyperbolical** *adj.* **hyperbolically** *adv.*

hyperbolic *adj.* **1** *Geom.* of or relating to a hyperbola. **2** *Math.* (of a function, e.g. a cosine) having the same relation to a rectangular hyperbola as the trigonometric functions do to a circle.

hypercritical *adj.* excessively critical.

hypercube *n.* a geometrical figure in four or more dimensions, analogous to a cube in three dimensions.

hyperglycaemia /hy-per-gly-**see**-miă/ *n.* (*US* **hyperglycemia**) an excess of glucose in the bloodstream, often associated with diabetes mellitus. □ **hyperglycaemic** *adj.*

hypericum *n.* any shrub of the genus *Hypericum* with five-petalled yellow flowers. [from Greek *hupereikon*]

hyperinflation *n.* monetary inflation at a very high rate.

hyperkinesis *n. Med.* **1** muscle spasm. **2** a disorder of children marked by hyperactivity and inability to attend. [based on Greek *kinēsis* 'motion'] □ **hyperkinetic** *adj.*

hyperlink *n.* ● *n.* a link from a hypertext document to another location, usu. activated by clicking on a highlighted word or image on the screen. ● *v.tr.* link (data) in this way.

hypermarket *n. Brit.* a very large self-service store.

hypermedia *n.* = MULTIMEDIA.

hyperphysical *adj.* supernatural.

hypersensitive *adj.* excessively sensitive. □ **hypersensitivity** *n.*

hypersonic *adj.* **1** relating to speeds of more than five times the speed of sound. **2** relating to sound frequencies above about a thousand million hertz. [on the pattern of *supersonic, ultrasonic*] □ **hypersonically** *adv.*

hyperspace *n.* space of more than three dimensions, esp. (in science fiction) a notional space-time continuum in which motion and communication at speeds greater than that of light are supposedly possible.

hypertension *n.* **1** abnormally high blood pressure. **2** a state of great emotional tension. □ **hypertensive** *adj.*

hypertext *n. Computing* a software system allowing extensive cross-referencing between related sections of text and associated graphic material.

hyperthermia *n. Med.* the condition of having a body temperature greatly above normal. [based on Greek *thermē* 'heat']

hyperthyroidism *n. Med.* overactivity of the thyroid gland, resulting in an increased rate of metabolism. □ **hyperthyroid** *adj.*

hypertonic *adj.* **1** (of muscles) having high tension. **2** (of a solution) having a greater osmotic pressure than another solution. □ **hypertonia** *n.* (in sense 1). **hypertonicity** *n.*

hypertrophy *n.* the enlargement of an organ or tissue from the increase in size of its cells. [based on Greek *-trophia* 'nourishment'] □ **hypertrophic** *adj.* **hypertrophied** *adj.*

hyperventilation *n.* breathing at an abnormally rapid rate. □ **hyperventilate** *v.intr.*

hypha *n.* (*pl.* **hyphae** /-fee/) a filament in the mycelium of a fungus. [from Greek *huphē* 'web'] □ **hyphal** *adj.*

hyphen ● *n.* the sign (-) used to join words semantically or syntactically (as in *pick-me-up, rock-forming*), to indicate the division of a word at the end of a line, or to indicate a missing or implied element (as in *man-* and *womankind*). ● *v.tr.* **1** write (a compound word) with a hyphen. **2** join (words) with a hyphen. [from Greek *huphen* 'together']

hyphenate *v.tr.* = HYPHEN *v.* □ **hyphenation** *n.*

hypno- *comb. form* sleep, hypnosis. [from Greek *hupnos* 'sleep']

hypnosis *n.* **1** a state like sleep in which the subject acts only on external suggestion. **2** artificially produced sleep. [based on Greek *hupnos* 'sleep']

hypnotherapy *n.* the treatment of disease by hypnosis. □ **hypnotherapist** *n.*

hypnotic ● *adj.* **1** of or producing hypnosis. **2** soporific. ● *n.* **1** a thing that produces sleep. **2** a person under or open to the influence of hypnotism. [based on Greek *hupnoun* 'to put to sleep'] □ **hypnotically** *adv.*

hypnotism *n.* the study or practice of hypnosis. □ **hypnotist** *n.*

hypnotize *v.tr.* (also **-ise**) **1** produce hypnosis in. **2** fascinate; capture the mind of. □ **hypnotizable** *adj.*

hypo[1] *n. Photog.* the chemical sodium thiosulphate (incorrectly called hyposulphite) used as a photographic fixer.

hypo[2] *n.* (*pl.* **-os**) *colloq.* = HYPODERMIC *n.*

hypo- *prefix* (before a vowel or h usu. **hyp-**) **1** under (*hypodermic*). **2** below normal (*hypoxia*). **3** slightly (*hypomania*). **4** *Chem.* containing an element combined in low valence (*hypochlorous*).

hypo-allergenic *adj.* having little tendency, or a specially reduced tendency, to cause an allergic reaction.

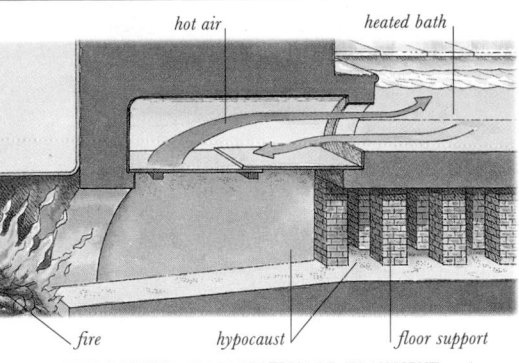

HYPOCAUST: CROSS-SECTION OF AN ANCIENT ROMAN HYPOCAUST

hot air   *heated bath*   *fire*   *hypocaust*   *floor support*

hypocaust *n.* ▲ a hollow space under the floor in ancient Roman houses, into which hot air was sent for heating a room or bath. [from Greek *hupokauston* 'place heated from below']

hypochlorite *n. Chem.* a salt of hypochlorous acid.

hypochlorous acid *n. Chem.* an unstable acid existing only in dilute solution and used in bleaching and water treatment.

hypochondria *n.* **1** abnormal anxiety about one's health. **2** morbid depression without cause. [from Greek *hupokhondria*, the soft area below the ribs, supposed seat of melancholy]

hypochondriac ● *n.* a person suffering from hypochondria. ● *adj.* (also **hypochondriacal**) of or affected by hypochondria.

hypocrisy *n.* (*pl.* **-ies**) **1** the making of false claims to virtue. **2** an instance of this. [from Greek *hupokrisis* 'acting of a part']

hypocrite /**hip**-ŏ-krit/ *n.* a person given to hypocrisy. [from Greek *hupokritēs* 'actor'] □ **hypocritical** *adj.* **hypocritically** *adv.*

hypodermic ● *adj. Med.* **1** of or relating to the area beneath the skin. **2 a** (of a drug etc. or its application) injected beneath the skin. **b** (of a needle, syringe, etc.) used to do this. ● *n.* a hypodermic injection or syringe. [based on Greek *derma* 'skin'] □ **hypodermically** *adv.*

hypoglycaemia /hy-poh-gly-**see**-miǎ/ *n.* (*US* **hypoglycemia**) a deficiency of glucose in the bloodstream. □ **hypoglycaemic** *adj.*

hypomania *n.* a minor form of mania. □ **hypomanic** *adj.*

hypotension *n.* abnormally low blood pressure. □ **hypotensive** *adj.*

hypotenuse /hy-**pot**-i-newz/ *n.* ◄ the side opposite the right angle of a right-angled triangle. [from Greek *hupoteinousa (grammē)* 'subtending (line)']

hypotenuse   *right angle*   HYPOTENUSE

hypothalamus *n.* (*pl.* **-mi** /-my/) *Anat.* ► the region of the brain which controls body temperature, thirst, hunger, etc. ▷ BRAIN, ENDOCRINE. □ **hypothalamic** *adj.*

hypothermia *n. Med.* the condition of having an abnormally low body temperature. [based on Greek *thermē* 'heat']

hypothesis /hy-**poth**-i-sis/ *n.* (*pl.* **hypotheses**) a proposition or supposition made as the basis for reasoning or investigation. [from Greek *hupothesis* 'foundation']

hypothesize /hy-**poth**-i-syz/ *v.* (also **-ise**) **1** *intr.* frame a hypothesis. **2** *tr.* assume as a hypothesis. □ **hypothesizer** *n.*

hypothetical *adj.* **1** of or based on or serving as a hypothesis. **2** supposed but not necessarily real or true. □ **hypothetically** *adv.*

hypothyroidism *n. Med.* subnormal activity of the thyroid gland, resulting in cretinism. □ **hypothyroid** *n. & adj.*

hypoventilation *n.* breathing at an abnormally slow rate.

hypoxia *n. Med.* a deficiency of oxygen reaching the tissues. □ **hypoxic** *adj.*

hyrax *n.* ▼ any small mammal of the order Hyracoidea. [from Greek *hurax* 'shrew-mouse']

HYRAX: ROCK HYRAX
(*Procavia capensis*)

hyssop *n.* any small bushy aromatic herb of the genus *Hyssopus*, esp. *H. officinalis*, formerly used medicinally. ▷ HERB. [from Greek *hyssōpos*]

hysterectomy *n.* (*pl.* **-ies**) the surgical removal of the womb. [based on Greek *hustera* 'womb'] □ **hysterectomize** *v.tr.* (also **-ise**).

hysteresis *n. Physics* a phenomenon whereby changes in an effect lag behind changes in its cause. [from Greek *husterēsis* 'being behind']

hysteria *n.* **1** a wild uncontrollable emotion or excitement. **2** a functional disturbance of the nervous system, of psychoneurotic origin.

hysteric *n.* **1** (in *pl.*) **a** a fit of hysteria. **b** *colloq.* overwhelming laughter (*we were in hysterics*). **2** a hysterical person. [from Greek *husterikos* 'of the womb']

hysterical *adj.* **1** of or affected with hysteria. **2** morbidly or uncontrolledly emotional. **3** *colloq.* extremely funny or amusing. □ **hysterically** *adv.*

Hz *abbr.* hertz.

brain   *hypothalamus*   *cerebellum*

HYPOTHALAMUS: THE HUMAN BRAIN SHOWING THE HYPOTHALAMUS

H

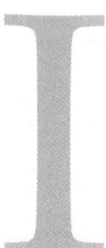

I[1] *n.* (also **i**) (*pl.* **Is** or **I's**) **1** the ninth letter of the alphabet. **2** (as a Roman numeral) one.

I[2] *pron.* (*obj.* **me**; *poss.* **my, mine**; *pl.* **we**) used by a speaker or writer to refer to himself or herself. [Old English]

I[3] *abbr.* (also **I.**) Island(s), Isle(s).

I[4] *symb.* **1** *Chem.* the element iodine. **2** electric current.

i *symb. Math.* the imaginary square root of minus one.

iambic *Prosody* ● *adj.* of or using iambuses. ● *n.* (usu. in *pl.*) iambic verse.

iambus *n.* (*pl.* **iambuses** or **-bi** /-by/) *Prosody* a foot consisting of one short (or unstressed) followed by one long (or stressed) syllable. [from Greek *iambos*]

ib. var. of IBID.

IBA *abbr.* (in the UK) Independent Broadcasting Authority.

I-beam *n.* a girder of I-shaped section.

Iberian ● *adj.* of ancient Iberia, the peninsula now comprising Spain and Portugal; of Spain and Portugal. ● *n.* **1** a native of ancient Iberia. **2** any of the languages of ancient Iberia. [based on Greek *Ibēres* 'Spaniards']

ibex *n.* (*pl.* **ibexes**) a wild goat, *Capra ibex*, esp. of mountainous areas of Europe, N. Africa, and Asia, with thick curved ridged horns. [Latin]

ibid. *abbr.* (also **ib.**) in the same book or passage etc. [Latin *ibidem* 'in the same place']

ibis *n.* (*pl.* **ibises**) ▼ any wading bird of the family Threskiornithidae with a long down-curved bill. [from Greek]

IBIS:
SCARLET IBIS
(*Eudocimus ruber*)

ibuprofen /I-bew-**proh**-fĕn/ *n.* an analgesic and anti-inflammatory drug used esp. as a stronger alternative to aspirin.

i/c *abbr.* **1** in charge. **2** in command.

ice ● *n.* **1 a** frozen water, a brittle transparent crystalline solid. **b** a sheet of this on the surface of water (*fell through the ice*). **2** *Brit.* a portion of ice cream or water ice (*would you like an ice?*). **3** *slang* diamonds. ● *v.* **1** *tr.* mix with or cool in ice (*iced drinks*). **2** *tr. & intr.* **a** cover or become covered with ice. **b** freeze. **3** *tr.* cover (a cake etc.) with icing. □ **on ice 1** performed by skaters. **2** *colloq.* held in reserve. **on thin ice** in a risky situation. [Old English]

ice age *n.* a glacial period.

ice axe *n.* a tool used by mountain climbers for cutting footholds.

ICEBERG

In the southern hemisphere, broad, tabular icebergs are formed when sections detach themselves from the floating edges of the ice sheets that extend from Antarctica. In the northern hemisphere, icebergs form when wind and tidal action cause large chunks of ice to break away from glaciers. All icebergs are made up of frozen fresh water, as opposed to sea water, and only the top 12 per cent is visible above sea level.

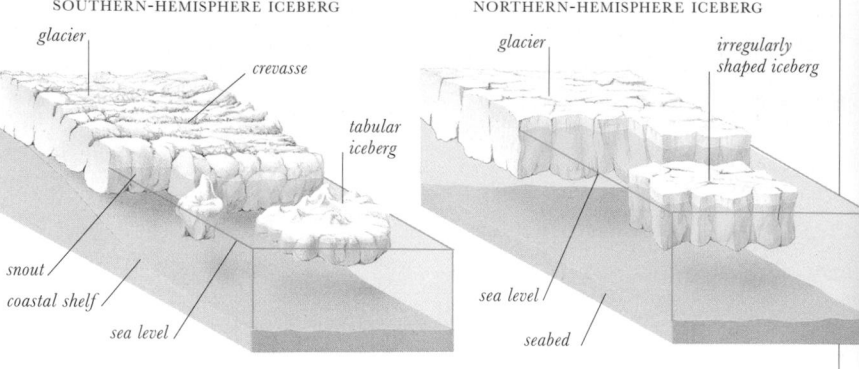

SOUTHERN-HEMISPHERE ICEBERG

glacier
crevasse
tabular iceberg
snout
coastal shelf
sea level

NORTHERN-HEMISPHERE ICEBERG

glacier
irregularly shaped iceberg
sea level
seabed

---

iceberg *n.* ▲ a large floating mass of ice detached from a glacier or ice sheet and carried out to sea. □ **the tip of the iceberg** a small perceptible part of something, the greater part of which is hidden.

iceberg lettuce *n.* any of various crisp lettuces with a freely blanching head.

iceblock *n.* *Austral.* & *NZ* = ICE LOLLY.

ice blue ● *n.* a very pale blue colour. ● *adj.* (hyphenated when *attrib.*) of this colour.

ice-boat *n.* **1** a boat mounted on runners for travelling on ice. **2** a boat used for breaking ice on a river etc.

ice-bound *adj.* confined by ice.

icebox *n.* a compartment in a refrigerator for making and storing ice.

ice-breaker *n.* **1** = ICE-BOAT 2. **2** something that serves to relieve inhibitions, start a conversation, etc.

ice bucket *n.* a bucket-like container with chunks of ice, used either to keep a bottle of wine chilled or to hold ice for drinks.

ice cap *n.* a permanent covering of ice.

ice-cold *adj.* as cold as ice.

ice cream *n.* a sweet creamy frozen food.

ice cube *n.* a small block of ice made in a refrigerator.

ice dancing *n.* ice-skating to choreographed dance moves, esp. competitively and in pairs.

iced lolly var. of ICE LOLLY.

ice floe *n.* = FLOE.

ice hockey *n.* a form of hockey played on ice with a puck. ▷ HOCKEY

Icelander *n.* **1** a native or national of Iceland, an island in the N. Atlantic. **2** a person of Icelandic descent.

Icelandic ● *adj.* of or relating to Iceland. ● *n.* the language of Iceland.

ice lolly *n.* (also **iced lolly**) *Brit.* a piece of flavoured ice on a stick.

iceman *n.* (*pl.* **-men**) **1** a man skilled in crossing ice. **2** esp. *N. Amer.* a man who sells or delivers ice.

ice pack *n.* a quantity of ice applied to the body for medical etc. purposes.

ice pick *n.* a needle-like implement with a handle for splitting up small pieces of ice.

ice rink *n.* = RINK 1.

ice sheet *n.* a permanent layer of ice covering an extensive tract of land.

ice-skate ● *n.* a skate consisting of a boot with a blade beneath, for skating on ice. ● *v.intr.* skate on ice. □ **ice-skater** *n.* **ice-skating** *n.*

ice station *n.* a meteorological research centre in polar regions.

ice water *n.* water from, or cooled by the addition of, ice.

I Ching *n.* an ancient Chinese manual of divination based on symbolic trigrams and hexagrams. [from Chinese *yijing* 'book of changes']

ichneumon /ik-**new**-mŏn/ *n.* **1** (in full **ichneumon wasp**) any small hymenopterous insect of the family Ichneumonidae, depositing eggs in or on the larva of another insect as food for its own larva. ▷ OVIPOSITOR. **2** a mongoose of N. Africa, *Herpestes ichneumon*, noted for destroying crocodile eggs. [from Greek *ikhneumōn*, literally 'tracker', a spider-hunting wasp]

ichthyo- /**ik**-thi-oh/ *comb. form* fish. [from Greek *ikhthus* 'fish']

ichthyology /ik-thi-**ol**-ŏji/ *n.* the study of fishes. □ **ichthyological** *adj.* **ichthyologist** *n.*

ichthyosaurus /ik-thi-ŏ-**sor**-ŭs/ *n.* (also **ichthyosaur**) ▼ any extinct marine reptile of the order Ichthyosauria, with four flippers. [from Greek *ikhthus* 'fish' + *sauros* 'lizard']

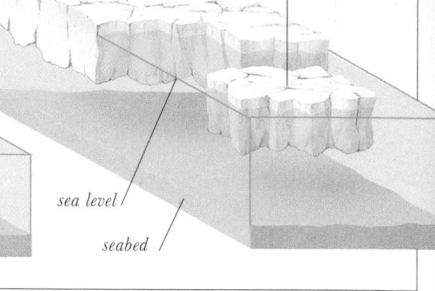

ICHTHYOSAURUS: FOSSILIZED ICHTHYOSAURUS
SKELETON (*Ichthyosaurus megacephalus*)

icicle *n.* a hanging tapering piece of ice, formed by the freezing of dripping water. [Middle English]

icing *n.* **1** a coating of a sugar mixture on a cake or biscuit. **2** the formation of ice on a ship or aircraft. □ **icing on the cake** an attractive though inessential addition or enhancement.

icing sugar *n.* *Brit.* finely powdered sugar.

icon *n.* (also **ikon**) **1** a devotional painting or carving of Christ or another holy figure, esp. in the Eastern Church. ▷ ICONOSTASIS. **2** an image or statue. **3** *Computing* a symbol or graphic representation on a VDU screen of a program, option, or window. **4** an object of particular admiration, esp.

as a representative symbol of something (*a literary icon of the 1970s*). [from Greek *eikōn* 'image']

iconic *adj.* **1** of or having the nature of an image or portrait. **2** (of a statue) following a conventional type. □ **iconicity** *n.*

icono- *comb. form* an image or likeness. [from Greek *eikōn*]

iconoclasm *n.* **1** the breaking of images. **2** the assailing of cherished beliefs.

iconoclast *n.* **1** a person who attacks cherished beliefs. **2** a person who destroys images used in religious worship. [from ecclesiastical Greek *eikonoklastēs*, literally 'icon breaker'] □ **iconoclastic** *adj.*

iconography *n.* (*pl.* **-ies**) **1** the illustration of a subject by drawings or figures. **2 a** the study of portraits, esp. of an individual. **b** the study of artistic images or symbols. [from Greek *eikonographia* 'sketch'] □ **iconographer** *n.* **iconographic** *adj.* **iconographical** *adj.* **iconographically** *adv.*

iconostasis *n.* (*pl.* **iconostases**) ▼ (in the Eastern Church) a screen bearing icons and separating the sanctuary from the nave.

ICONOSTASIS IN A 19TH-CENTURY GREEK CHURCH

Labels: doorway to sanctuary; icon; iconostasis

icosahedron *n.* (*pl.* **icosahedra** or **icosahedrons**) ◄ a solid figure with twenty faces. [based on Greek *eikosi* 'twenty'] □ **icosahedral** *adj.*

icy *adj.* (**icier**, **iciest**) **1** very cold. **2** covered with or abounding in ice. **3** unfriendly, hostile. □ **icily** *adv.* **iciness** *n.*

ID *abbr.* identification, identity (*ID card*).

I'd *contr.* **1** I had. **2** I should; I would.

ICOSAHEDRON

id *n. Psychol.* the inherited instinctive impulses of the individual as part of the unconscious. [Latin, literally 'that']

idea *n.* **1** a plan formed by mental effort (*have you any ideas?; had the idea of writing a book*). **2 a** a mental impression; a concept. **b** a vague belief (*had an idea you were married; had no idea where you were*). **3** an intention, purpose, or essential feature (*the idea is to make money*). **4** an archetype or pattern. □ **have no idea** *colloq.* **1** not know at all. **2** be completely incompetent. [Greek, literally 'form, pattern']

ideal ● *adj.* **1 a** answering to one's highest conception. **b** perfect. **2 a** existing only in idea. **b** visionary. **3** embodying an idea. **4** relating to or consisting of ideas; dependent on the mind. ● *n.* **1** a perfect type, or a conception of this. **2** an actual thing as a standard for imitation. [from Late Latin *idealis*] □ **ideality** *n.* (*pl.* **-ies**). **ideally** *adv.*

idealism *n.* **1** the practice of forming or following after ideals, esp. unrealistically. **2** the representation

of things in ideal form. **3** imaginative treatment. □ **idealist** *n.* **idealistic** *adj.* **idealistically** *adv.*

idealize *v.tr.* (also **-ise**) **1** regard or represent in ideal form or character. **2** exalt in thought to ideal perfection. □ **idealization** *n.* **idealizer** *n.*

idée fixe /ee-day feeks/ *n.* (*pl.* **idées fixes** *pronunc.* same) an idea that dominates the mind; an obsession. [French, literally 'fixed idea']

identical *adj.* **1** (of different things) agreeing in every detail. **2** (of one thing viewed at different times) one and the same. **3** (of twins) developed from a single fertilized ovum, therefore of the same sex and usu. very similar in appearance. [from medieval Latin *identicus*] □ **identically** *adv.*

identification *n.* **1** the act or an instance of identifying. **2** a means of identifying a person. **3** (*attrib.*) serving to identify (*identification card*).

identification parade *n. Brit.* an assembly of persons from whom a suspect is to be identified.

identify *v.* (**-ies**, **-ied**) **1** *tr.* establish the identity of; recognize. **2** *tr.* establish or select by consideration (*identify the best method of solving the problem*). **3** *tr.* (foll. by *with*) associate (a person or oneself) inseparably or very closely (*with a party, policy, etc.*). **4** *tr.* treat (a thing) as identical. **5** *intr.* (foll. by *with*) **a** regard oneself as sharing characteristics of (another person). **b** associate oneself. [from medieval Latin *identificare*] □ **identifiable** *adj.* **identifiably** *adv.* **identifier** *n.*

identikit *n.* (often *attrib.*) *propr.* a reconstructed picture of a person (esp. one sought by the police) assembled from transparent strips showing typical facial features according to witnesses' descriptions.

identity *n.* (*pl.* **-ies**) **1 a** the quality or condition of being a specified person or thing. **b** individuality, personality (*felt he had lost his identity*). **2** identification or the result of it (*a case of mistaken identity; identity card*). **3** absolute sameness (*no identity of interests between them*). **4** *Algebra* **a** the equality of two expressions for all values of the quantities expressed by letters. **b** an equation expressing this. **5** *Math.* **a** (in full **identity element**) an element in a set, left unchanged by any operation to it. **b** a transformation that leaves an object unchanged. [based on Latin *idem* 'same']

identity crisis *n.* a period during which an individual experiences a feeling of loss or breakdown of his or her identity.

identity parade *n. Brit.* = IDENTIFICATION PARADE.

ideogram *n.* ▼ a character symbolizing the idea of a thing without indicating the sequence of sounds in its name (e.g. a numeral, and many Chinese characters). [based on Greek *idea* 'form']

CHINESE CHARACTER FOR TREE   ROMAN NUMERAL TWO

WHEELCHAIR ACCESS SIGN   AIRPORT SYMBOL

IDEOGRAMS

ideograph *n.* = IDEOGRAM. □ **ideographic** *adj.* **ideography** *n.*

ideologue *n.* **1** a theorist; a visionary. **2** an adherent of an ideology.

ideology *n.* (*pl.* **-ies**) **1** the system of ideas at the basis of an economic or political theory (*Marxist ideology*). **2** the manner of thinking characteristic

of a class or individual (*bourgeois ideology*). [based on Greek *idea* 'form'] □ **ideological** *adj.* **ideologically** *adv.* **ideologist** *n.*

ides *n.pl.* the eighth day after the nones in the ancient Roman calendar (the 15th day of March, May, July, October, the 13th of other months). [from Latin *idus*]

idiocy *n.* (*pl.* **-ies**) **1** utter foolishness; idiotic behaviour or action. **2** extremely low intelligence.

idiom *n.* **1** a group of words established by usage and having a meaning not deducible from those of the individual words (as in *over the Moon, see the light*). **2** a form of expression peculiar to a language, person, or group of people. **3 a** the language of a people or country. **b** the specific character of this. **4** a characteristic mode of expression in music, art, etc. [from Greek *idiōma* 'private property']

idiomatic *adj.* **1** relating to or conforming to idiom. **2** characteristic of a particular language. □ **idiomatically** *adv.*

idiosyncrasy *n.* (*pl.* **-ies**) **1** a mental constitution, view, or feeling, or mode of behaviour, peculiar to a person. **2** anything highly individualized or eccentric. **3** a mode of expression peculiar to an author. [from Greek *idios* 'own' + *sun* 'together' + *krasis* 'mixture'] □ **idiosyncratic** *adj.* **idiosyncratically** *adv.*

idiot *n.* **1** *colloq.* a stupid person. **2** a person of extremely low intelligence. [from Greek *idiōtēs* 'layman, ignorant person'] □ **idiotic** *adj.* **idiotically** *adv.*

idle ● *adj.* (**idler**, **idlest**) **1** lazy, indolent. **2** not in use; not working. **3** (of time etc.) unoccupied. **4** having no special basis or purpose (*idle rumour; idle curiosity*). **5** useless. **6** (of an action, thought, or word) ineffective, worthless, vain. ● *v.* **1 a** *intr.* (of an engine) run slowly without doing any work. **b** *tr.* cause (an engine) to idle. **2** *intr.* be idle. **3** *tr.* (foll. by *away*) pass (time etc.) in idleness. [Old English *īdel* 'empty, useless'] □ **idleness** *n.* **idler** *n.* **idly** *adv.*

idol *n.* **1** an image of a deity etc. used as an object of worship. **2** *Bibl.* a false god. **3** an object of excessive or supreme adulation (*cinema idol*). [from Greek *eidōlon* 'phantom']

idolater *n.* (*fem.* **idolatress**) **1** a worshipper of idols. **2** a devoted admirer. [from Greek *eidōlolatrēs*] □ **idolatrous** *adj.*

idolatry *n.* **1** the worship of idols. **2** great adulation.

idolize *v.tr.* (also **-ise**) **1** venerate or love excessively. **2** make an idol of. □ **idolization** *n.* **idolizer** *n.*

idyll /id-il/ *n.* (also **idyl**) **1** a short description in verse or prose of a picturesque scene or incident, esp. in rustic life. **2** an episode suitable for such treatment, usu. a love story. **3** a blissful period or scene. [from Greek *eidullion* 'little form']

idyllic *adj.* **1** blissfully peaceful and happy. **2** of or like an idyll. □ **idyllically** *adv.*

i.e. *abbr.* that is to say. [Latin *id est*]

if ● *conj.* **1** introducing a conditional clause: **a** on the condition or supposition that; in the event that (*if he comes I will tell him; if you are tired we will rest*). **b** (with past tense) implying that the condition is not fulfilled (*if I were you; if I knew I would say*). **2** even though (*I'll finish it, if it takes me all day*). **3** whenever (*if I am not sure I ask*). **4** whether (*see if you can find it*). **5 a** expressing wish or surprise (*if I could just try!; if it isn't my old hat!*). **b** expressing a request (*if you wouldn't mind opening the door?*). **6** and perhaps not (*very rarely if at all*). **7** (with reduction of a conditional clause to its significant word) if there is or it is etc. (*took little if any*). **8** despite being (*a useful if cumbersome device*). ● *n.* a condition or supposition (*too many ifs about it*). □ **if anything** perhaps even (*if anything, it's too large; if anything, he finds maths easier*). **if only 1** even if for no other reason than (*I'll come if only to see her*). **2** (often *ellipt.*) an expression of regret (*if only I had thought of it; if only I could swim!*). **if so** if that is the case. [Old English]

iffy *adj.* (**iffier**, **iffiest**) *colloq.* **1** uncertain, doubtful. **2** of questionable quality.

igloo n. an Eskimo dome-shaped dwelling, esp. one built of blocks of snow. [Eskimo, literally 'house']

igneous adj. **1** of fire; fiery. **2** Geol. ▶ (esp. of rocks) volcanic. ▷ ROCK CYCLE. [based on Latin ignis 'fire']

ignite v. **1** tr. set fire to. **2** intr. catch fire. **3** tr. Chem. heat to the point of combustion or chemical change. **4** tr. provoke or excite (feelings etc.). [based on Latin ignitus 'on fire'] □ **ignitability** n. **ignitable** adj.

igniter n. **1** a device for igniting a fuel mixture in an engine. ▷ ROCKET. **2** a device for causing an electric arc.

ignition n. **1** a mechanism for, or the action of, starting the combustion of mixture in the cylinder of an internal-combustion engine. **2** the act or an instance of igniting or being ignited.

ignition key n. a key to operate the ignition of a motor vehicle.

ignoble adj. (**ignobler**, **ignoblest**) **1** dishonourable. **2** of low birth, position, or reputation. [from Latin ignobilis] □ **ignobleness** n. **ignobly** adv.

ignominious adj. **1** causing or deserving ignominy. **2** humiliating. □ **ignominiously** adv. **ignominiousness** n.

ignominy n. dishonour, infamy. [from Latin ignominia]

ignoramus n. (pl. **ignoramuses**) an ignorant person. [Latin, literally 'we do not know': earlier in legal use]

ignorance n. lack of knowledge.

ignorant adj. **1 a** lacking knowledge or experience. **b** (foll. by of, in) uninformed (about a fact or subject). **2** colloq. uncouth. [from Latin ignorant- 'not knowing'] □ **ignorantly** adv.

■ **Usage** It is better to follow ignorant by of (a fact etc.) or in (a subject etc.) than about, e.g. I was ignorant of my rights; I am ignorant in these matters.

ignore v.tr. **1** refuse to take notice of. **2** intentionally disregard. [from Latin ignorare 'to ignore, not know'] □ **ignorable** adj.

iguana n. ▼ any of various large lizards of the family Iguanidae, having a spiny crest along the back. ▷ LIZARD. [from Carib iwana]

IGUANA:
COMMON
IGUANA
(Iguana iguana)

iguanodon n. a large, partly bipedal herbivorous dinosaur of the Cretaceous period, with a broad stiff tail and a spike on each thumb. ▷ DINOSAUR. [based on Greek odous odontos 'tooth', its teeth resembling those of the iguana]

ikebana /i-ki-**bah**-nă/ n. the art of Japanese flower arrangement, with formal display according to strict rules. [Japanese, literally 'living flowers']

ikon var. of ICON.

il- prefix assim. form of IN- before l.

ilang-ilang var. of YLANG-YLANG.

ilea pl. of ILEUM.

ileum n. (pl. **ilea**) Anat. ▶ the third and last portion of the small intestine. ▷ INTESTINE.

ilex n. **1** any tree or shrub of the genus Ilex, esp. the common holly. **2** the holm-oak. [Latin]

ilia pl. of ILIUM.

IGNEOUS

Molten magma cooling slowly within batholiths and other intrusions creates coarse- and intermediate-grained igneous rocks, such as granite and dolerite. The finer-grained basalt is commonly formed by volcanic lava cooling more quickly on the Earth's surface. Lava that is subject to a very rapid chilling gives rise to obsidian, which is composed of crystals so small that the rock's appearance is of smooth glass.

SECTION OF THE EARTH'S CRUST SHOWING VOLCANIC FEATURES

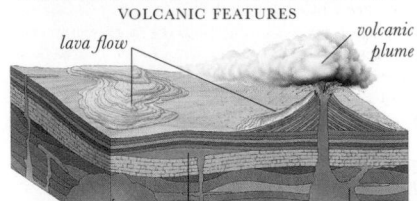

lava flow • volcanic plume • batholith • laccolith • magma chamber

EXAMPLES OF IGNEOUS ROCKS

DOLERITE   PINK GRANITE   BASALT   SNOWFLAKE OBSIDIAN

iliac adj. of the lower body or ilium (iliac artery). ▷ CARDIOVASCULAR. [from Late Latin iliacus]

ilium n. (pl. **ilia**) **1** the bone forming the upper part of each half of the human pelvis. ▷ HIP JOINT, SKELETON. **2** the corresponding bone in animals. [Latin]

ilk n. **1** colloq., usu. derog. a family, class, sort, or kind (for John and his ilk there is only one kind of music). **2** (in **of that ilk**) Sc. of the same place, estate, or name (Guthrie of that ilk = of Guthrie). [Old English ilca 'same']

■ **Usage** Of that ilk is a Scots term meaning 'of the same place, estate, or name'. By misunderstanding ilk has come to mean 'family' or 'sort'. This should be avoided in formal English.

I'll contr. I shall; I will.

ill ● adj. (attrib. except in sense 1) **1** (usu. predic.) out of health; sick (is ill; was taken ill with pneumonia; mentally ill people). **2** wretched, unfavourable (ill fortune; ill luck). **3** harmful (ill effects). **4** hostile, unkind (ill feeling). **5** faulty, unskilful (ill taste; ill management). **6** (of manners or conduct) improper. ● adv. **1** badly, wrongly (ill-matched). **2 a** imperfectly (ill-provided). **b** scarcely (can ill afford to do it). **3** unfavourably (it would have gone ill with them). ● n. **1** injury, harm. **2** evil. □ **ill at ease** embarrassed, uneasy. **speak ill of** say something unfavourable about. [from Old Norse illr]

■ **Usage** The use of ill to mean 'vomiting' or 'tending to vomit', as in He was outside being ill is nonstandard. See also Usage Note at SICK¹.

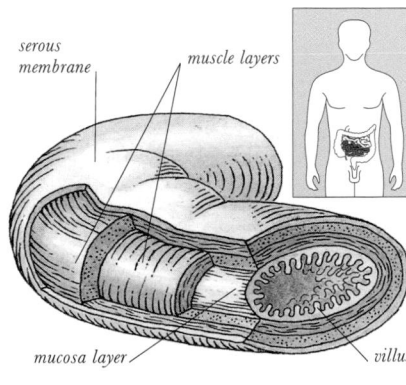

serous membrane • muscle layers • mucosa layer • villus

ILEUM: CUTAWAY SECTION OF THE HUMAN ILEUM

ill-advised adj. **1** (of a person) foolish or imprudent. **2** (of a plan etc.) not well formed or considered.

ill-assorted adj. not well matched.

ill-behaved adj. having bad manners or conduct.

ill-bred adj. badly brought up; rude.

ill-conceived adj. badly planned or conceived.

ill-considered adj. = ILL-ADVISED 2.

ill-defined adj. not clearly defined.

ill-disposed adj. **1** unfavourably disposed. **2** malevolent.

illegal adj. **1** not legal. **2** contrary to law. □ **illegality** n. (pl. **-ies**). **illegally** adv.

illegible adj. not legible. □ **illegibility** n. **illegibly** adv.

illegitimate adj. **1** (of a child) born of parents not married to each other. **2 a** unlawful. **b** abnormal. **3** improper. **4** wrongly inferred. □ **illegitimacy** n. **illegitimately** adv.

ill-equipped adj. not adequately equipped or qualified.

ill-fated adj. destined to or bringing bad fortune.

ill-favoured adj. (US **ill-favored**) unattractive.

ill feeling n. bad feeling; animosity.

ill-fitting adj. fitting badly.

ill-founded adj. (of an idea etc.) baseless.

ill-gotten adj. gained by wicked or unlawful means.

ill health n. poor physical or mental condition.

ill humour n. irritability. □ **ill-humoured** adj.

illiberal adj. **1** intolerant, narrow-minded. **2** without liberal culture. **3** not generous; stingy. **4** vulgar, sordid. □ **illiberality** n. (pl. **-ies**). **illiberally** adv. [from Latin illiberalis 'mean, sordid']

illicit adj. unlawful, forbidden (illicit dealings). □ **illicitly** adv. **illicitness** n.

illimitable adj. limitless.

ill-informed adj. inadequately informed.

illiterate ● adj. **1** unable to read. **2** uneducated. ● n. an illiterate person. □ **illiteracy** n.

ill-judged adj. unwise; badly considered.

ill-mannered adj. having bad manners; rude.

ill-matched adj. badly matched; unsuited.

ill nature n. churlishness, unkindness. □ **ill-natured** adj.

illness n. **1** a disease. **2** the state of being ill.

illogical adj. devoid of or contrary to logic. □ **illogicality** n. (pl. **-ies**). **illogically** adv.

ill-omened adj. attended by bad omens.

ill-prepared adj. badly or inadequately prepared.

I

ill-starred *adj.* unlucky; destined to failure.

ill-suited *adj.* **1** not suited to doing something; unsuitable. **2** inappropriate.

ill temper *n.* moroseness. □ **ill-tempered** *adj.*

ill-timed *adj.* done or occurring at an inappropriate time.

ill-treat *v.tr.* treat badly; abuse. □ **ill-treatment** *n.*

illuminance *n. Physics* the amount of luminous flux per unit area.

illuminate *v.tr.* **1** light up; make bright. **2** decorate (buildings etc.) with lights. **3** ▼ decorate (an initial letter, a manuscript, etc.) with gold, silver, or brilliant colours. **4** help to explain (a subject etc.) **5** enlighten spiritually or intellectually. **6** shed lustre on. [based on Latin *illuminatus* 'brightened'] □ **illuminating** *adj.* **illuminatingly** *adv.* **illuminative** *adj.* **illuminator** *n.*

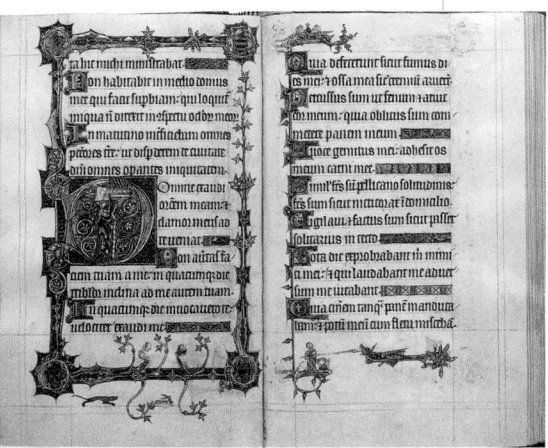

ILLUMINATE: 14TH-CENTURY ILLUMINATED MANUSCRIPT

illuminati *n.pl.* persons claiming to possess special knowledge or enlightenment.

illumination *n.* **1** the act or process of illuminating. **2** (in *pl.*) lights used in decorating a street, building, etc.

illumine *v.tr. literary* **1** light up; make bright. **2** enlighten spiritually. [from Latin (as ILLUMINATE)]

ill use *n.* ill-treatment. □ **ill-use** *v.tr.*

illusion *n.* **1** deception, delusion. **2** a misapprehension of the true state of affairs. **3 a** the faulty perception of an object. **b** an instance of this. **4** a figment of the imagination. **5** = OPTICAL ILLUSION. □ **be under the illusion** (foll. by *that* + clause) believe mistakenly. [from Latin *illusio* 'mockery'] □ **illusional** *adj.*

illusionist *n.* a conjuror. □ **illusionism** *n.* **illusionistic** *adj.*

illusive *adj.* = ILLUSORY.

illusory *adj.* **1** deceptive (esp. as regards value or content). **2** having the character of an illusion. □ **illusorily** *adv.*

illustrate *v.tr.* **1 a** provide (a book, newspaper, etc.) with pictures. **b** elucidate (a description etc.) by drawings or pictures. **2** serve as an example of. **3** explain or make clear, esp. by examples. [originally in sense 'to light up': from Latin *illustrare*]

illustration *n.* **1** a drawing or picture illustrating a book, magazine article, etc. **2** an example serving to elucidate. **3** the act or an instance of illustrating. □ **illustrational** *adj.*

illustrative *adj.* serving as an explanation or example.

illustrator *n.* a person who makes illustrations, esp. for magazines, books, advertising copy, etc.

illustrious *adj.* distinguished, renowned. [from Latin *illustris*]

ill will *n.* bad feeling; animosity.

ill wind *n.* an unfavourable or untoward circumstance (with reference to the proverb *it's an ill wind that blows nobody good*).

im- *prefix* assim. form of IN- before *b, m, p.*

image ● *n.* **1** a representation of the external form of a person or thing in sculpture, painting, etc. **2** the character or reputation of a person or thing as generally perceived. **3** an optical appearance or counterpart produced by light or other radiation from an object reflected in a mirror, refracted through a lens, etc. **4** semblance, likeness (*God created man in His own image*). **5** a person or thing that closely resembles another (*is the image of his father*). **6** a typical example. **7** a simile or metaphor. **8 a** mental representation. **b** an idea or conception. **9** *Math.* a set formed by mapping from another set. ● *v.tr.* **1** make an image of; portray. **2** reflect, mirror. **3** describe or imagine vividly. **4** typify. [from Latin *imago*]

image-maker *n.* a person employed to create a public image for a politician, product, etc.

image processing *n.* the analysis and manipulation of an image. □ **image processor** *n.*

imagery *n.* **1** figurative illustration, esp. as used by an author. **2** images collectively. **3** statuary, carving. **4** mental images collectively.

imaginable *adj.* that can be imagined (*the greatest difficulty imaginable*).

imaginary *adj.* **1** existing only in the imagination. **2** *Math.* being the square root of a negative quantity.

imagination *n.* **1** a mental faculty forming images or concepts of objects not present to the senses. **2** the ability of the mind to be creative or resourceful. **3** the process of imagining.

imaginative *adj.* **1** having or showing imagination. **2** given to using the imagination. □ **imaginatively** *adv.*

imagine *v.tr.* **1 a** form a mental image or concept of. **b** picture to oneself. **2** think or conceive (*imagined them to be soldiers*). **3** guess (*cannot imagine what they are doing*). **4** suppose; be of the opinion (*I imagine you will need help*). [from Latin *imaginari*] □ **imaginer** *n.*

imagines *pl.* of IMAGO.

imaginings *n.pl.* fancies, fantasies.

imago /i-**may**-goh/ *n.* (*pl.* **-os** or **imagines** /i-**maj**-i-neez/) *Zool.* the fully developed stage of an insect after all metamorphoses, e.g. a butterfly or beetle. ▷ METAMORPHOSIS. [Latin, literally 'image']

imam /im-**ahm**/ *n.* **1** a leader of prayers in a mosque. **2** a title of various Muslim leaders. [from Arabic] □ **imamate** *n.*

imbalance *n.* **1** lack of balance. **2** disproportion.

imbecile ● *n.* **1** an adult with a mental age of about five. **2** *colloq.* a stupid person. ● *adj.* mentally weak; idiotic. [earlier in sense 'physically weak': from Latin *imbecillus* 'without a staff'] □ **imbecilic** *adj.* **imbecility** *n.* (*pl.* **-ies**).

imbed var. of EMBED.

imbibe *v.tr.* **1** (also *absol.*) drink (esp. alcoholic liquor). **2 a** assimilate (ideas etc.). **b** absorb (moisture etc.). **3** inhale (air etc.). [from Latin *imbibere*] □ **imbiber** *n.* **imbibition** *n.*

imbroglio /im-**broh**-li-oh/ *n.* (*pl.* **-os**) **1** a confused situation. **2** a confused heap. [Italian, literally 'an entangling']

imbue *v.tr.* (**imbues, imbued, imbuing**) **1** inspire or permeate (with feelings, qualities, etc.). **2** saturate. **3** dye. [based on Latin *imbutus* 'moistened']

IMF *abbr.* International Monetary Fund.

imitate *v.tr.* **1** follow the example of; copy the action(s) of. **2** mimic. **3** make a copy of; reproduce. [based on Latin *imitatus* 'copied'] □ **imitator** *n.*

imitation *n.* **1** the act or an instance of imitating or being imitated. **2** a copy. **3** counterfeit (often *attrib.*: *imitation leather*).

imitative *adj.* **1** (often foll. by *of*) imitating; following a model or example. **2** counterfeit. **3** (of a word) **a** that reproduces a natural sound (e.g. *fizz*). **b** whose sound is thought to correspond to the appearance etc. of the object or action described (e.g. *blob*).

immaculate *adj.* **1** perfectly clean and tidy. **2** perfectly executed (*an immaculate performance*). **3** free from fault; innocent. [from Latin *immaculatus*] □ **immaculately** *adv.*

Immaculate Conception *n. RC Ch.* the doctrine that God preserved the Virgin Mary from the taint of original sin from the moment she was conceived.

immanent *adj.* **1** present within, inherent. **2** (of the supreme being) permanently pervading the universe. [from Late Latin *immanent-* 'remaining within'] □ **immanence** *n.*

immaterial *adj.* **1** of no essential consequence; unimportant. **2** not material; incorporeal.

immature *adj.* **1** not mature or fully developed. **2** lacking emotional or intellectual development. **3** unripe. □ **immaturely** *adv.* **immaturity** *n.*

immeasurable *adj.* not measurable; immense. □ **immeasurably** *adv.*

immediate *adj.* **1** occurring or done at once (*an immediate reply*). **2** nearest, next; not separated by others (*the immediate vicinity; the immediate future; my immediate neighbour*). **3** most pressing or urgent (*our immediate concern was to get him to hospital*). **4** having direct effect; without an intervening medium or agency (*the immediate cause of death*). [from Late Latin *immediatus*] □ **immediacy** *n.*

immediately ● *adv.* **1** without pause or delay. **2** without intermediary. ● *conj.* esp. *Brit.* as soon as.

immemorial *adj.* **1** ancient beyond memory or record. **2** very old. □ **immemorially** *adv.*

immense *adj.* **1** immeasurably large; huge. **2** considerable (*made an immense difference*). **3** *colloq.* very good. [from Latin *immensus* 'unmeasured'] □ **immenseness** *n.* **immensity** *n.*

immensely *adv.* **1** very much (*enjoyed myself immensely*). **2** to an immense degree.

immerse *v.tr.* **1 a** dip, plunge. **b** cause (a person) to be completely under water. **2** absorb or involve deeply. **3** bury, embed. [based on Latin *immersus* 'immersed']

immersion *n.* **1** immersing or being immersed. **2** baptism by immersing the whole person in water. **3** mental absorption.

immersion heater *n.* an electric heater designed for direct immersion in a liquid to be heated, esp. as a fixture in a hot water tank.

immigrant ● *n.* a person who immigrates. ● *adj.* **1** immigrating. **2** of or concerning immigrants.

immigrate *v.* **1** *intr.* come as a permanent resident to a country other than one's native land. **2** *tr.* bring in (a person) as an immigrant. □ **immigration** *n.*

imminent *adj.* impending; about to happen. [from Latin *imminent-* 'overhanging'] □ **imminence** *n.* **imminently** *adv.*

immiscible *adj.* (often foll. by *with*) that cannot be mixed.

immobile *adj.* **1** not moving. **2** not able to move or be moved. □ **immobility** *n.*

immobilize *v.tr.* (also **-ise**) **1** make or keep immobile. **2** make (esp. a vehicle or troops) incapable of being moved. **3** keep (a limb or patient) restricted in movement for healing purposes. **4** restrict the free movement of. **5** withdraw (coins) from circulation to support banknotes. □ **immobilization** *n.* **immobilizer** *n.*

immoderate *adj.* excessive; lacking moderation. □ **immoderately** *adv.* **immoderation** *n.*

immodest *adj.* **1** lacking modesty; forward, impudent. **2** lacking due decency. □ **immodestly** *adv.* **immodesty** *n.*

immolate *v.tr.* **1** kill or offer as a sacrifice. **2** *literary* sacrifice (a valued thing). [based on Latin *immolatus* 'sprinkled with sacrificial meal'] □ **immolation** *n.*

immoral *adj.* **1** not conforming to accepted standards of morality (cf. AMORAL). **2** morally wrong (esp. in sexual matters). **3** depraved, dissolute. □ **immorality** *n.* (*pl.* **-ies**). **immorally** *adv.*

immortal ● *adj.* **1 a** living for ever; not mortal. **b** divine. **2** unfading. **3** likely or worthy to be famous for all time. ● *n.* **1 a** an immortal being. **b** (in *pl.*) the gods of antiquity. **2** a person of enduring fame. □ **immortality** *n.* **immortalize** *v.tr.* (also **-ise**). **immortalization** *n.*

immortelle *n.* a flower of the daisy family with papery texture, retaining its shape and colour after being dried. [French]

immovable *adj.* (also **immoveable**) **1** that cannot be moved. **2** steadfast, unyielding. **3** emotionless. **4** not subject to change (*immovable law*). **5** motionless. **6** *Law* (of property) consisting of land, houses, etc. □ **immovability** *n.* **immovably** *adv.*

immune *adj.* **1 a** *Biol.* resistant to a particular infection, toxin, etc., owing to the presence of specific antibodies or sensitized white blood cells. **b** relating to immunity (*immune mechanism*). **2** (foll. by *from*, *to*) free or exempt from or not subject to. [from Latin *immunis* 'exempt from public service or charge']

immune response *n.* the reaction of the body to the introduction into it of an antigen. ▷ INFLAMMATION

immunity *n.* (*pl.* **-ies**) **1** *Biol.* the ability of an organism to resist a specific infection, toxin, etc. **2** freedom or exemption.

immunize *v.tr.* (also **-ise**) make immune, usu. by inoculation. □ **immunization** *n.*

immuno- *comb. form* immunity to infection.

immunodeficiency *n.* a reduction in a person's normal immune defences.

immunogenic *adj.* *Biochem.* of, relating to, or possessing the ability to elicit an immune response.

immunoglobulin *n.* *Biochem.* any of a group of structurally related blood proteins which function as antibodies.

immunology *n.* the scientific study of immunity. □ **immunologic** *adj.* **immunological** *adj.* **immunologically** *adv.* **immunologist** *n.*

immunosuppression *n.* *Biochem.* the partial or complete suppression of the immune response of an individual. □ **immunosuppressant** *n.*

immunosuppressive ● *adj.* partially or completely suppressing the immune response of an individual. ● *n.* an immunosuppressive drug.

immure *v.tr.* **1** imprison. **2** *refl.* shut oneself away. [from medieval Latin *immurare*] □ **immurement** *n.*

immutable *adj.* **1** unchangeable. **2** not subject to variation in different cases. □ **immutability** *n.* **immutably** *adv.*

imp *n.* **1** a mischievous child. **2** a small mischievous devil or sprite. [Old English *impe* 'young shoot, scion']

impact ● *n.* **1** the action of one body coming forcibly into contact with another. **2** an effect or influence. ● *v.* **1** *tr.* press or fix firmly. **2** *tr.* (as **impacted** *adj.*) **a** (of a tooth) wedged between another tooth and the jaw. **b** (of a fractured bone) with the parts crushed together. ▷ FRACTURE. **3 a** *intr.* have an impact. **b** *tr.* have an impact on. [from Latin *impactus* 'impinged'] □ **impaction** *n.*

impair *v.tr.* damage or weaken. [based on Late Latin *pejorare* 'to make worse'] □ **impairment** *n.*

impala *n.* (*pl.* same) a medium-sized antelope, *Aepyceros melampus*, of S. and E. Africa. [Zulu]

impale *v.tr.* (foll. by *on*, *upon*, *with*) transfix or pierce with a sharp instrument. [from medieval Latin *impalare*] □ **impalement** *n.*

impalpable *adj.* **1** not easily grasped by the mind; intangible. **2** imperceptible to the touch. **3** (of powder) very fine. □ **impalpably** *adv.*

impanel var. of EMPANEL.

impart *v.tr.* **1** communicate (news etc.). **2** give a share of (a thing). [from Latin *impartire*]

impartial *adj.* treating all sides in a dispute etc.

equally; unprejudiced, fair. □ **impartiality** *n.* **impartially** *adv.*

impassable *adj.* that cannot be traversed.

impasse /**am**-pahss/ *n.* a position from which progress is impossible; deadlock. [French]

impassible *adj.* **1** impassive. **2** incapable of feeling or emotion. **3** incapable of suffering injury. □ **impassibly** *adv.*

impassioned *adj.* deeply felt; ardent (*an impassioned plea*).

impassive *adj.* **1 a** deficient in or incapable of feeling emotion. **b** undisturbed by passion. **2** without sensation. **3** not subject to suffering. □ **impassively** *adv.* **impassiveness** *n.* **impassivity** *n.*

impasto *n.* *Art* **1** the process of laying on paint thickly. **2** this technique of painting. [Italian, literally 'coating with paste']

impatiens *n.* any plant of the genus *Impatiens*, including busy Lizzie and balsam. [modern Latin]

impatient *adj.* **1 a** lacking patience or tolerance. **b** (of an action) showing a lack of patience. **2** restlessly eager. **3** (foll. by *of*) intolerant. □ **impatience** *n.* **impatiently** *adv.*

impeach *v.tr.* **1** *Brit.* charge with a crime against the State, esp. treason. **2** esp. *US* charge (the holder of a public office) with misconduct. **3** call in question, disparage (a person's integrity etc.). [from Late Latin *impedicare* 'to entangle'] □ **impeachable** *adj.* **impeachment** *n.*

impeccable *adj.* **1** (of behaviour, performance, etc.) faultless, exemplary. **2** not liable to sin. [based on Latin *peccare* 'to sin'] □ **impeccability** *n.* **impeccably** *adv.*

impecunious *adj.* having little or no money. [based on Latin *pecuniosus* 'having money'] □ **impecuniosity** *n.*

impedance *n.* *Electr.* the total effective resistance of an electric circuit etc. to alternating current. ▷ CIRCUIT

■ **Usage** *Impedance*, a technical term, is sometimes confused with *impediment*, which means 'a hindrance' or 'a speech defect'.

impede *v.tr.* retard by obstructing; hinder. [from Latin *impedire* 'to shackle the feet of']

impediment *n.* **1** a hindrance or obstruction. **2** a defect in speech, e.g. a lisp or stammer.

■ **Usage** See Usage Note at IMPEDANCE.

impedimenta *n.pl.* **1** encumbrances. **2** travelling equipment, esp. of an army.

impel *v.tr.* (**impelled**, **impelling**) **1** drive, force, or urge. **2** propel. [from Latin *impellere*] □ **impeller** *n.*

impend *v.intr.* **1** be about to happen. **2 a** (of a danger) be threatening. **b** hang; be suspended. [from Latin *impendēre*] □ **impending** *adj.*

impenetrable *adj.* **1** that cannot be penetrated. **2** inscrutable, unfathomable. **3** inaccessible to ideas, influences, etc. □ **impenetrability** *n.* **impenetrably** *adv.*

impenitent *adj.* not repentant or penitent.

imperative ● *adj.* **1** urgent. **2** obligatory. **3** commanding, peremptory. **4** *Gram.* (of a mood) expressing a command (e.g. *come here!*). ● *n.* **1** *Gram.* the imperative mood. **2** a command. **3** an essential or urgent thing. [based on Late Latin *imperare* 'to command'] □ **imperatively** *adv.*

imperceptible *adj.* **1** that cannot be perceived. **2** very slight, gradual, or subtle. □ **imperceptibly** *adv.*

imperfect ● *adj.* **1** not fully formed or done; faulty, incomplete. **2** *Gram.* (of a tense) denoting a (usu. past) action in progress but not completed at the time in question (e.g. *they were singing*). ● *n.* the imperfect tense. □ **imperfectly** *adv.*

imperfection *n.* **1** incompleteness. **2 a** faultiness. **b** a fault or blemish.

imperial *adj.* **1** of or characteristic of an empire. **2 a** of or characteristic of an emperor. **b** supreme

in authority. **c** majestic, august. **d** magnificent. **3** (of non-metric weights and measures) used or formerly used by statute in the UK (*imperial gallon*). [from Latin *imperialis*] □ **imperially** *adv.*

imperialism *n.* **1** an imperial rule or system. **2** usu. *derog.* a policy of acquiring dependent territories or of extending a country's influence through trade, diplomacy, etc. □ **imperialistic** *adj.*

imperialist ● *n.* usu. *derog.* an advocate or agent of imperial rule or of imperialism. ● *adj.* of or relating to imperialism or imperialists.

imperil *v.tr.* (**imperilled**, **imperilling**; *US* **imperiled**, **imperiling**) bring or put into danger.

imperious *adj.* **1** overbearing, domineering. **2** urgent, imperative. [based on Latin *imperium* 'command'] □ **imperiously** *adv.* **imperiousness** *n.*

imperishable *adj.* that cannot perish.

impermanent *adj.* not permanent. □ **impermanence** *n.*

impermeable *adj.* **1** that cannot be penetrated. **2** that does not permit the passage of fluids. □ **impermeability** *n.*

impermissible *adj.* not allowable.

impersonal *adj.* **1** having no personal feeling or reference. **2** having no personality. **3** *Gram.* **a** (of a verb) used only with a formal subject (usu. *it*) and expressing an action not attributable to a definite subject (e.g. *it is snowing*). **b** (of a pronoun) = INDEFINITE 3. □ **impersonality** *n.* **impersonally** *adv.*

impersonate *v.tr.* **1** pretend to be (another person) for the purpose of entertainment or fraud. **2** act (a character). [based on Latin *persona* 'person'] □ **impersonation** *n.* **impersonator** *n.*

impertinent *adj.* **1** rude or insolent; lacking proper respect. **2** out of place; absurd. □ **impertinence** *n.* **impertinently** *adv.*

imperturbable *adj.* not excitable; calm. □ **imperturbability** *n.* **imperturbably** *adv.*

impervious *adj.* (usu. foll. by *to*) **1** not responsive (to an argument, outside influence, etc.). **2** not affording passage to a fluid etc. □ **imperviously** *adv.* **imperviousness** *n.*

impetigo /im-pi-**ty**-goh/ *n.* a contagious skin infection forming pustules and yellow crusty sores. [Latin]

impetuous *adj.* **1** acting or done rashly or with sudden energy. **2** moving forcefully or rapidly. [from Late Latin *impetuosus*] □ **impetuosity** *n.* **impetuously** *adv.* **impetuousness** *n.*

impetus *n.* **1** the force with which a body moves. **2** a driving force or impulse. [Latin, literally 'assault']

impiety /im-**py**-iti/ *n.* (*pl.* **-ies**) **1** a lack of piety or reverence. **2** an act etc. showing this.

impinge *v.tr.* (**impinging**) **1** make an impact; have an effect. **2** encroach. [from Latin *impingere* 'to drive (a thing) at'] □ **impingement** *n.*

impious /im-pi-ŭs/ *adj.* **1** not pious. **2** wicked, profane. □ **impiously** *adv.*

impish *adj.* of or like an imp; mischievous. □ **impishly** *adv.* **impishness** *n.*

implacable *adj.* that cannot be appeased. [from French] □ **implacability** *n.* **implacably** *adv.*

implant ● *v.tr.* **1** insert or fix. **2** instil (a principle, idea, etc.) in a person's mind. **3** plant. **4** *Med.* **a** insert (tissue, a substance, a device, etc.) into the body. **b** (in *passive*) (of a fertilized ovum) become attached to the wall of the womb. ● *n.* **1** a thing implanted. **2** a thing implanted in the body, e.g. a piece of tissue or a capsule containing therapeutic radioactive material. □ **implantation** *n.*

implausible *adj.* not plausible. □ **implausibility** *n.* **implausibly** *adv.*

implement ● *n.* **1** a tool, instrument, or utensil. **2** *Law* performance of an obligation. ● *v.tr.* **1 a** put (a decision, plan, etc.) into effect. **b** fulfil (an undertaking). **2** complete (a contract etc.). [from medieval Latin *implementa* (pl.)] □ **implementation** *n.* **implementer** *n.*

implicate *v.tr.* **1** (often foll. by *in*) show (a person) to be concerned or involved (in a charge, crime, etc.).

2 (in *passive*; often foll. by *in*) be affected or involved. **3** lead to as a consequence or inference. [based on Latin *implicatus* 'entangled, closely connected']

implication *n.* **1** what is involved in or implied by something else. **2** the act of implicating or implying. □ **by implication** by what is implied or suggested rather than by formal expression.

implicit *adj.* **1** implied though not plainly expressed. **2** virtually contained. **3** absolute, unquestioning, unreserved (*implicit obedience*). [from Latin *implicitus*] □ **implicitly** *adv.*

implode *v.intr. & tr.* burst or cause to burst inwards. [based on Latin *plodere* 'to clap', on the pattern of *explode*] □ **implosion** *n.* **implosive** *adj.*

implore *v.tr.* **1** entreat (a person). **2** beg earnestly for. [from Latin *implorare* 'to invoke with tears'] □ **imploringly** *adv.*

imply *v.tr.* (**-ies**, **-ied**) **1** (often foll. by *that* + clause) strongly suggest the truth or existence of (a thing not expressly asserted). **2** insinuate, hint (*what are you implying?*). **3** signify. [from Latin *implicare* 'to fold in'] □ **implied** *adj.* **impliedly** *adv.*

■ **Usage** See Usage Note at INFER.

impolite *adj.* ill-mannered, uncivil, rude. □ **impolitely** *adv.* **impoliteness** *n.*

impolitic *adj.* **1** inexpedient, unwise. **2** not politic.

imponderable ● *adj.* that cannot be estimated. ● *n.* (usu. in *pl.*) something difficult or impossible to assess. □ **imponderably** *adv.*

import ● *v.tr.* **1** bring in (esp. foreign goods) to a country. **2 a** imply, indicate, signify. **b** express, make known. ● *n.* **1** the process of importing. **2 a** an imported article or service. **b** (in *pl.*) an amount imported (*imports exceeded £50m*). **3** what is implied; meaning. **4** importance. [from Latin *importare* 'to bring in'] □ **importation** *n.* **importer** *n.* (both in sense 1 of *v.*).

importance *n.* **1** the state of being important. **2** import, significance. **3** personal consequence.

important *adj.* **1** of great effect or consequence; momentous. **2** (of a person) having high rank or authority. **3** pompous. □ **importantly** *adv.*

importunate *adj.* **1** making persistent or pressing requests. **2** (of affairs) urgent. □ **importunity** *n.*

importune *v.tr.* **1** solicit (a person) pressingly. **2** solicit for an immoral purpose. [from medieval Latin *importunari*]

impose *v.* **1** *tr.* (often foll. by *on*, *upon*) require (a tax, duty, charge, or obligation) to be paid or undertaken (by a person etc.). **2** *tr.* enforce compliance with. **3** *intr. & refl.* (foll. by *on*, *upon*, or *absol.*) demand the attention or commitment of (a person) (*I do not want to impose on you any longer*). **4** *tr.* (often foll. by *on*, *upon*) palm (a thing) off on (a person). [from Latin *imponere imposit-* 'to inflict, deceive']

imposing *adj.* impressive, formidable, esp. in appearance. □ **imposingly** *adv.* **imposingness** *n.*

imposition *n.* **1** the act or an instance of imposing; the process of being imposed. **2** an unfair demand or burden. **3** a tax or duty.

impossibility *n.* (*pl.* **-ies**) **1** the fact or condition of being impossible. **2** an impossible thing or circumstance.

impossible *adj.* **1** not possible; that cannot occur, exist, or be done (*such a thing is impossible; it is impossible to alter them*). **2** (loosely) not easy; not convenient; not easily believable. **3** *colloq.* (of a person or thing) outrageous, intolerable. □ **impossibly** *adv.*

impost *n.* a tax, duty, or tribute. [from Latin *impostus* 'imposed']

impostor *n.* (also **imposter**) **1** a person who assumes a false character or pretends to be someone else. **2** a swindler. [Late Latin]

imposture *n.* the act or an instance of fraudulent deception.

impotent *adj.* **1 a** powerless; lacking all strength. **b** helpless, decrepit. **2** (esp. of a male) unable to achieve a sexual erection or orgasm. □ **impotence** *n.* **impotency** *n.* **impotently** *adv.*

impound *v.tr.* **1** confiscate. **2** take possession of. **3** shut up in a pound. □ **impoundment** *n.*

impoverish *v.tr.* **1** make poor. **2** exhaust the strength or natural fertility of. [from Old French *empoverir*] □ **impoverishment** *n.*

impracticable *adj.* impossible in practice. □ **impracticability** *n.*

impractical *adj.* **1** not practical. **2** esp. *US* not practicable. □ **impracticality** *n.* **impractically** *adv.*

imprecation *n.* **1** a spoken curse. **2** the act of uttering an imprecation. [based on Latin *precari* 'to pray'] □ **imprecatory** *adj.*

imprecise *adj.* not precise. □ **imprecisely** *adv.* **imprecision** *n.*

impregnable *adj.* **1** (of a fortified position) that cannot be taken by force. **2** resistant to attack or criticism. [from Old French *imprenable* 'untakeable'] □ **impregnability** *n.* **impregnable** *adj.*

impregnate *v.tr.* **1** fill or saturate. **2** imbue, fill (with feelings, moral qualities, etc.). **3** make pregnant. [based on Late Latin *impregnat-* 'made pregnant'] □ **impregnation** *n.*

impresario *n.* (*pl.* **-os**) an organizer of public entertainments. [Italian, based on *impresa* 'undertaking']

impress[1] ● *v.tr.* **1 a** affect or influence deeply. **b** (also *absol.*) affect (a person) favourably (*was most impressed*). **2** emphasize (an idea etc.) (*must impress on you the need to be prompt*). **3 a** imprint or stamp. **b** apply (a mark etc.) with pressure. **4** make a mark or design on (a thing) with a stamp, seal, etc. ● *n.* **1** the act or an instance of impressing. **2** a mark made by a seal, stamp, etc. **3** a characteristic mark or quality. **4** = IMPRESSION 1. [from Old French *empresser*]

impress[2] *v.tr. hist.* force (men) to serve in the army or navy. □ **impressment** *n.*

impression *n.* **1** an effect produced (esp. on the mind or feelings). **2** a notion or belief (esp. a vague or mistaken one) (*my impression is they are afraid*). **3** an imitation of a person or sound, esp. done to entertain. **4 a** the impressing of a mark. **b** a mark impressed. **5** esp. *Brit.* an unaltered reprint from standing type or plates (esp. as distinct from *edition*). **6** the number of copies of a book, newspaper, etc., issued at one time. **7** *Dentistry* a negative copy of the teeth or mouth made by pressing them into a soft substance.

impressionable *adj.* easily influenced. □ **impressionability** *n.*

Impressionism *n.* ▼ a style or movement in art concerned with the effect of light on objects. [from French *impressionnisme*, after *Impression: Soleil levant*, title of a painting by Monet (1872)]

impressionist *n.* **1** an entertainer who impersonates famous people etc. **2** (**Impressionist**) an adherent or practitioner of Impressionism.

I

IMPRESSIONISM

Emerging in Paris during the 1860s, Impressionism was an artistic movement that drew inspiration from the simplicity of everyday life. Many of the movement's leading artists, such as Monet, Cézanne, Pissarro, and Renoir, painted in the open air, working quickly to create an 'impression' of what they saw. These artists attempted to capture with paint the natural, transient effects of light and colour.

The Waterlily Pond (1899), CLAUDE MONET

TIMELINE

| 1500 | 1550 | 1600 | 1650 | 1700 | 1750 | 1800 | 1850 | 1900 | 1950 | 2000 |

• *adj.* (**Impressionist**) of or relating to Impressionism or Impressionists.

impressionistic *adj.* **1** in the style of Impressionism. **2** subjective, unsystematic. □ **impressionistically** *adv.*

impressive *adj.* **1** impressing the mind or senses, esp. so as to cause approval or admiration. **2** (of language, a scene, etc.) tending to excite deep feeling. □ **impressively** *adv.* **impressiveness** *n.*

imprimatur *n.* **1** *RC Ch.* an official licence to print (an ecclesiastical or religious book etc.). **2** official approval. [Latin, literally 'let it be printed']

■ **Usage** *Imprimatur* meaning 'an official licence to print' is sometimes confused with *imprint* 'the name of the publisher or printer etc. printed in a book'.

imprint • *v.tr.* **1** impress or establish firmly, esp. on the mind. **2 a** make a stamp or impression of (a figure etc.) on a thing. **b** make an impression on (a thing) with a stamp etc. **3** (usu. in *passive*; often foll. by *on* or *to*) *Biol.* cause (a young animal etc.) to recognize another as a parent or object of habitual trust. • *n.* **1** an impression or stamp. **2** the printer's or publisher's name and other details printed in a book. [from Latin *imprimere*]

■ **Usage** See Usage Note at IMPRIMATUR.

imprison *v.tr.* **1** put into prison. **2** confine. [from Old French *emprisoner*] □ **imprisonment** *n.*

impro *n.* (*pl.* **-os**) *colloq.* **1** (often *attrib.*) improvisation, esp. as a theatrical technique. **2** an instance of this.

improbable *adj.* **1** not likely to be true or to happen. **2** difficult to believe. □ **improbability** *n.* **improbably** *adv.*

improbity *n.* (*pl.* **-ies**) **1** wickedness. **2** dishonesty. **3** a wicked or dishonest act.

impromptu • *adj.* & *adv.* extempore, unrehearsed. • *n.* (*pl.* **impromptus**) **1** an extempore performance or speech. **2** a short piece of usu. solo instrumental music. [from Latin *in promptu* 'in readiness']

improper *adj.* **1 a** unseemly; indecent. **b** not in accordance with accepted rules of behaviour. **2** inaccurate, wrong. **3** not properly so called. □ **improperly** *adv.*

improper fraction *n.* a fraction in which the numerator is greater than or equal to the denominator.

impropriety *n.* (*pl.* **-ies**) **1** lack of propriety; indecency. **2** an instance of improper conduct etc. **3** incorrectness. **4** unfitness.

improve *v.* **1 a** *tr.* & *intr.* make or become better. **b** *intr.* (foll. by *on*, *upon*) produce something better than. **2** *absol.* (as **improving** *adj.*) giving moral benefit (*improving literature*). [based on Old French *emprou*, literally 'into profit'] □ **improver** *n.*

improvement *n.* **1** the act or an instance of improving or being improved. **2** something that improves, esp. an addition or alteration that adds to value. **3** something that has been improved.

improvident *adj.* **1** lacking foresight or care for the future. **2** not frugal; thriftless. □ **improvidence** *n.*

improvise *v.tr.* (also *absol.*) **1** compose or perform (music, verse, etc.) extempore. **2** provide or construct (a thing) extempore. [based on Latin *improvisus* 'unforeseen'] □ **improvisation** *n.* **improvisational** *adj.* **improvisatory** *adj.* **improviser** *n.*

imprudent *adj.* rash, indiscreet. □ **imprudence** *n.* **imprudently** *adv.*

impudent *adj.* **1** insolently disrespectful; impertinent. **2** shamelessly presumptuous. **3** unblushing. [from Latin *impudens impudent-* 'shameless'] □ **impudence** *n.* **impudently** *adv.*

impugn /im-pewn/ *v.tr.* challenge or call in question. [from Latin *impugnare* 'to assail'] □ **impugnment** *n.*

impulse *n.* **1** the act or an instance of impelling; a push. **2** an impetus. **3** *Physics* **a** an indefinitely large force acting for a very short time but producing a finite change of momentum (e.g. the blow of a hammer). **b** the change of momentum produced by this or any force. **4** a wave of excitation in a nerve. **5** a sudden desire or tendency to act without reflection (*did it on impulse*). [from Latin *impulsus* 'a push']

impulsion *n.* **1** the act or an instance of impelling. **2** a mental impulse. **3** impetus.

impulsive *adj.* **1** (of a person or conduct etc.) apt to be affected or determined by sudden impulse. **2** tending to impel. **3** *Physics* acting as an impulse. □ **impulsively** *adv.* **impulsiveness** *n.*

impunity *n.* exemption from punishment or from the injurious consequences of an action. □ **with impunity** without having to suffer the normal injurious consequences. [from Latin *impunitas*]

impure *adj.* **1** adulterated. **2** dirty. **3** unchaste. **4** (of a colour) mixed with another colour.

impurity *n.* (*pl.* **-ies**) **1** the quality or condition of being impure. **2 a** a thing or constituent which impairs the purity of something. **b** *Electronics* a trace element deliberately added to a semiconductor.

impute *v.tr.* (foll. by *to*) regard as being done or caused or possessed by. [from Latin *imputare* 'to enter in the account'] □ **imputable** *adj.* **imputation** *n.*

In *symb. Chem.* the element indium.

in • *prep.* **1** expressing inclusion or position within limits of space, time, circumstance, etc. (*in England*; *in bed*; *in the rain*). **2** during the time of (*in the night*; *in 1995*). **3** within the time of (*will be back in two hours*). **4 a** with respect to (*blind in one eye*; *good in parts*). **b** as a kind of (*the latest thing in luxury*). **5** as a proportionate part of (*one in three failed*; *a gradient of one in six*). **6** with the form or arrangement of (*packed in tens*; *falling in folds*). **7** as a member of (*in the army*). **8** concerned with (*is in politics*). **9** as or regarding the content of (*there is something in what you say*). **10** within the ability of (*does he have it in him?*). **11** having the condition of; affected by (*in bad health*; *in danger*). **12** having as a purpose (*in search of*; *in reply to*). **13** by means of or using as material (*drawn in pencil*; *modelled in bronze*). **14 a** using as the language of expression (*written in French*). **b** (of music) having as its key (*symphony in C*). **15** (of a word) having as a beginning or ending (*words in un-*). **16** wearing (*in blue*; *in a suit*). **17** with the identity of (*found a friend in Mary*). **18** (of an animal) pregnant with (*in calf*). **19** into (with a verb of motion or change: *put it in the box*; *cut it in two*). **20** introducing an indirect object after a verb (*believe in*; *engage in*; *share in*). **21** forming adverbial phrases (*in any case*; *in reality*; *in short*). • *adv.* expressing position within limits, or motion to such a position: **1** into a room, house, etc. (*come in*). **2** at home, in one's office, etc. (*is not in*). **3** so as to be enclosed (*locked in*). **4** in a publication (*is the advertisement in?*). **5** in or to the inward side (*rub it in*). **6 a** in fashion, season, or office (*long skirts are in*; *strawberries are not yet in*). **b** elected (*the Democrat got in*). **7** exerting favourable action or influence (*their luck was in*). **8** *Sport* **a** (of a shot, serve, etc.) within the boundary of the playing area. **b** *Cricket* (of a player or side) batting. **9** (of transport) at the platform etc. (*the train is in*). **10** (of a season, harvest, order, etc.) having arrived or been received. **11** *Brit.* (of a fire) continuing to burn. **12** denoting effective action (*join in*). **13** (of the tide) at the highest point. **14** (in *comb.*) *colloq.* denoting prolonged or concerted action, esp. by large numbers (*sit-in*; *teach-in*). • *adj.* **1** internal; living in; inside (*in-patient*). **2** fashionable (*the in thing to do*). **3** confined to or shared by a group of people (*in-joke*). □ **in all** see ALL. **in at** present at; contributing to (*in at the kill*). **in between** see BETWEEN *adv.* **in for 1** about to undergo. **2** competing in or for. **3** involved in; committed to. **in on** sharing in; privy to. **ins and outs** (often foll. by *of*) all the details. **in so far as** see FAR. **in that** because; in so far as. **in with** on good terms with. [Old English]

in. *abbr.* inch(es).

in-[1] *prefix* (also **il-** before *l*, **im-** before *b*, *m*, *p*, **ir-** before *r*) added to: **1** adjectives, meaning 'not' (*inedible*; *insane*). **2** nouns, meaning 'without, lacking' (*inaction*).

in-[2] *prefix* (also **il-** before *l*, **im-** before *b*, *m*, *p*, **ir-** before *r*) in, on, into, towards, within (*induce*; *influx*; *insight*; *intrude*). [IN, or from or suggested by Latin *in* IN *prep.*]

inability *n.* **1** the state of being unable. **2** a lack of means.

in absentia *adv.* in (his, her, or their) absence. [Latin]

inaccessible *adj.* **1** not accessible. **2** (of a person) unapproachable. □ **inaccessibility** *n.* **inaccessibly** *adv.*

inaccurate *adj.* not accurate. □ **inaccuracy** *n.* (*pl.* **-ies**). **inaccurately** *adv.*

inaction *n.* **1** lack of action. **2** sluggishness.

inactive *adj.* **1** not active or inclined to act. **2** passive. **3** indolent. □ **inactivate** *v.tr.* **inactivation** *n.* **inactivity** *n.*

inadequate *adj.* (often foll. by *to*) **1** not adequate. **2** (of a person) unable to deal with a situation. □ **inadequacy** *n.* (*pl.* **-ies**). **inadequately** *adv.*

inadmissible *adj.* that cannot be admitted or allowed. □ **inadmissibility** *n.* **inadmissibly** *adv.*

inadvertent *adj.* **1** (of an action) unintentional. **2 a** not properly attentive. **b** negligent. [based on obsolete *advertent* 'attentive'] □ **inadvertence** *n.* **inadvertency** *n.* **inadvertently** *adv.*

inadvisable *adj.* not advisable. □ **inadvisability** *n.*

inalienable *adj.* that cannot be transferred to another. □ **inalienability** *n.* **inalienably** *adv.*

inane *adj.* **1** silly, senseless. **2** empty. [from Latin *inanis* 'empty, vain'] □ **inanely** *adv.* **inaneness** *n.* **inanity** *n.* (*pl.* **-ies**).

inanimate *adj.* **1** not animate; not endowed with (esp. animal) life. **2** lifeless. **3** spiritless, dull. □ **inanimately** *adv.* **inanimation** *n.*

inanimate nature *n.* everything other than the animal world.

inanition *n.* emptiness, esp. exhaustion from lack of nourishment. [based on Late Latin *inanire* 'to make empty']

inapplicable *adj.* (often foll. by *to*) not applicable; unsuitable. □ **inapplicability** *n.* **inapplicably** *adv.*

inapposite *adj.* not apposite; out of place. □ **inappositely** *adv.* **inappositeness** *n.*

inappropriate *adj.* not appropriate. □ **inappropriately** *adv.* **inappropriateness** *n.*

inapt *adj.* **1** not apt or suitable. **2** unskilful. □ **inaptitude** *n.* **inaptly** *adv.*

■ **Usage** See Usage Note at INEPT.

inarch *v.tr.* graft (a plant) by connecting a growing branch without separation from the parent stock.

inarticulate *adj.* **1** unable to speak distinctly or express oneself clearly. **2** (of speech) indistinctly pronounced. **3** dumb. **4** esp. *Anat.* not jointed. □ **inarticulacy** *n.* **inarticulately** *adv.* **inarticulateness** *n.*

inasmuch *adv.* (foll. by *as*) **1** since, because. **2** to the extent that. [Middle English]

inattentive *adj.* **1** heedless. **2** neglecting to show courtesy. □ **inattention** *n.* **inattentively** *adv.* **inattentiveness** *n.*

inaudible *adj.* that cannot be heard. □ **inaudibility** *n.* **inaudibly** *adv.*

inaugurate *v.tr.* **1** admit (a person) formally to office. **2** initiate the public use of (a building etc.). **3** begin, introduce. **4** enter with ceremony upon (an undertaking etc.). [based on Latin *inauguratus* 'consecrated after taking omens'] □ **inaugural** *adj.* **inauguration** *n.* **inaugurator** *n.*

inauspicious *adj.* **1** ill-omened, unpropitious. **2** unlucky. □ **inauspiciously** *adv.* **inauspiciousness** *n.*

INCANDESCENT

Heat produces the illumination in an incandescent light source. For example, in a light bulb an electrical current runs through a fine filament, heating it greatly. The heat caused by the current makes the metal filament glow white-hot, producing a strong source of light.

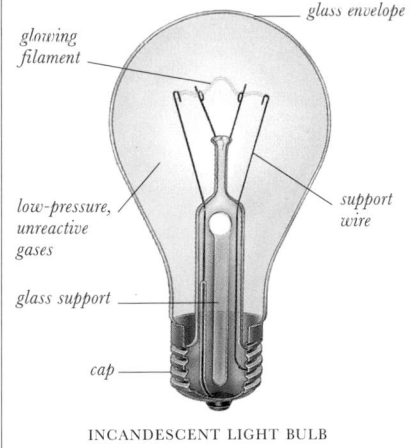

glass envelope

glowing filament

low-pressure, unreactive gases

support wire

glass support

cap

INCANDESCENT LIGHT BULB

inauthentic *n.* not authentic; not genuine. □ **inauthenticity** *n.*

inboard ● *adv.* within the sides of or towards the centre of a ship, aircraft, or vehicle. ● *adj.* situated inboard.

inborn *adj.* existing from birth; implanted by nature.

inbred *adj.* 1 inborn. 2 produced by inbreeding.

inbreeding *n.* breeding from closely related animals or persons. □ **inbreed** *v.tr. & intr.* (past and past part. **inbred**).

inbuilt *adj.* incorporated as part of a structure.

Inc. *abbr.* N. Amer. Incorporated.

Inca *n.* a member of an American Indian people in Peru before the Spanish conquest. [Peruvian, literally 'lord, royal person'] □ **Incan** *adj.*

incalculable *adj.* 1 too great for calculation. 2 that cannot be reckoned beforehand. 3 (of a person etc.) uncertain. □ **incalculability** *n.* **incalculably** *adv.*

in camera see CAMERA.

incandescent *adj.* 1 glowing with heat. 2 shining brightly. 3 ▲ (of a light) produced by a glowing white-hot filament. [from Latin *incandescent-* 'becoming white'] □ **incandesce** *v.intr. & tr.* **incandescence** *n.* **incandescently** *adv.*

incantation *n.* 1 a a magical formula. b the use of this. 2 a spell or charm. [from Late Latin *incantatio* 'chant'] □ **incantational** *adj.* **incantatory** *adj.*

incapable *adj.* 1 (often foll. by *of*) a not capable. b lacking the required quality or characteristic (*incapable of hurting anyone*). 2 not capable of rational conduct (*drunk and incapable*). □ **incapability** *n.* **incapably** *adv.*

incapacitate *v.tr.* 1 render incapable or unfit. 2 disqualify. □ **incapacitant** *n.* **incapacitation** *n.*

incapacity *n.* (*pl.* **-ies**) 1 inability; lack of the necessary power. 2 legal disqualification. 3 an instance of incapacity.

in-car *attrib.adj.* occurring, situated, or carried in a car.

incarcerate *v.tr.* imprison or confine. [based on medieval Latin *incarceratus* 'put in prison'] □ **incarceration** *n.*

incarnadine *poet.* ● *n.* flesh colour; crimson. ● *adj.*

flesh-coloured; crimson. ● *v.tr.* dye incarnadine. [French *incarnadin -ine* from Italian *incarnadino* (for *-tino*), from *incarnato* INCARNATE *adj.*]

incarnate ● *adj.* 1 embodied in flesh, esp. in human form (*the devil incarnate*). 2 represented in a recognizable or typical form (*folly incarnate*). ● *v.tr.* 1 embody in flesh. 2 put (an idea etc.) into concrete form. 3 be the living embodiment of (a quality). [from ecclesiastical Latin *incarnatus* 'made flesh']

incarnation *n.* 1 a embodiment in (esp. human) flesh. b (**the Incarnation**) the embodiment of God in Christ. 2 (often foll. by *of*) a living type (of a quality etc.).

incase var. of ENCASE.

incautious *adj.* heedless, rash. □ **incaution** *n.* **incautiously** *adv.* **incautiousness** *n.*

incendiary ● *adj.* 1 (of a bomb) designed to cause fires. 2 a of or relating to the malicious setting on fire of property. b guilty of this. 3 inflammatory. ● *n.* (*pl.* **-ies**) 1 an incendiary device. 2 an incendiary person. [based on Latin *incendium* 'conflagration'] □ **incendiarism** *n.*

incense[1] /in-senss/ ● *n.* 1 a gum or spice producing a sweet smell when burned. 2 the smoke of this. ● *v.tr.* 1 treat or perfume with incense. 2 burn incense to (a deity etc.). [from ecclesiastical Latin *incensum* 'a thing burnt']

incense[2] /in-senss/ *v.tr.* (often foll. by *at*, *with*, *against*) enrage. [from Old French *incenser*]

incentive ● *n.* 1 (often foll. by *to*) a motive or incitement, esp. to action. 2 a payment or concession to stimulate greater output by workers. ● *adj.* serving to motivate or incite. [from Latin *incentivus* 'setting the tune']

inception *n.* a beginning. [from Latin *inceptio*]

incertitude *n.* uncertainty, doubt.

incessant *adj.* unceasing, repeated. [from Late Latin *incessant-* 'not ceasing'] □ **incessancy** *n.* **incessantly** *adv.* **incessantness** *n.*

incest *n.* sexual intercourse between persons too closely related to marry. [based on Latin *castus* 'chaste']

incestuous *adj.* 1 involving or guilty of incest. 2 (of human relationships generally) excessively restricted. □ **incestuously** *adv.* **incestuousness** *n.*

inch ● *n.* 1 a unit of linear measure equal to one-twelfth of a foot (2.54 cm). 2 a (as a unit of rainfall) a quantity that would cover a horizontal surface to a depth of 1 inch. b (of atmospheric or other pressure) an amount that balances the weight of a column of mercury 1 inch high. 3 (as a unit of map-scale) so many inches representing 1 mile on the ground. 4 a small amount (usu. with *neg.*: *would not yield an inch*). ● *v.tr. & intr.* move gradually in a specified way (*inched forward*). □ **every inch** 1 entirely (*looked every inch a queen*). 2 the whole distance (*every inch of the way*). **inch by inch** bit by bit. **within an inch of** almost to the point of. [Old English *ynce* from Latin *uncia* 'twelfth part']

-in-chief *comb. form* (as second element) supreme (*commander-in-chief*).

inchoate /in-**koh**-ayt/ *adj.* 1 just begun. 2 undeveloped. [from Latin *inchoatus* 'begun'] □ **inchoative** *adj.*

■ **Usage** *Inchoate*, meaning 'just begun' or 'undeveloped', should not be confused with *incoherent* or *chaotic*, although all these words can often be found in similar contexts. *Inchoate scribbles* thus means 'undeveloped' rather than 'incoherent' pieces of writing.

incidence *n.* 1 (often foll. by *of*) the fact, manner, or rate, of occurrence or action. 2 the extent of influence of a thing. 3 *Physics* the falling of a line, or of a thing moving in a line, upon a surface. 4 the act or an instance of coming into contact with a thing.

incident ● *n.* 1 a an event or occurrence, esp. a minor one. b a minor or detached event attracting general attention or noteworthy in some way. 2 a hostile clash, esp. of troops of countries at war (*a frontier incident*). 3 a distinct piece of action in a play or a poem. 4 *Law* a privilege, burden, etc., attaching to an obligation or right. ● *adj.* 1 (often foll. by *to*) apt or liable to happen; naturally attaching or dependent. 2 (often foll. by *on*, *upon*) (of light etc.) falling or striking. [from Latin *incident-* 'happening to']

incidental ● *adj.* 1 (often foll. by *to*) a having a minor role in relation to a more important thing, event, etc. b not essential. 2 (foll. by *to*) liable to happen. 3 (foll. by *on*, *upon*) following as a subordinate event. ● *n.* (usu. in *pl.*) a minor detail, expense, event, etc.

incidentally *adv.* 1 by the way; as an unconnected remark. 2 in an incidental way.

incidental music *n.* music used as a background to the action of a film, broadcast, etc.

incinerate *v.tr.* 1 consume (a body etc.) by fire. 2 reduce to ashes. [based on medieval Latin *incineratus* 'reduced to ashes'] □ **incineration** *n.*

incinerator *n.* a furnace or apparatus for burning esp. refuse to ashes.

incipient *adj.* 1 beginning. 2 in an initial stage. [from Latin *incipient-* 'beginning'] □ **incipience** *n.* **incipiency** *n.* **incipiently** *adv.*

incise *v.tr.* 1 make a cut in. 2 engrave. [based on Latin *incisus* 'cut into']

incision *n.* 1 a cut; a division produced by cutting; a notch. 2 the act of cutting into a thing. [from Old French *incision* or Late Latin *incisio*]

incisive *adj.* 1 mentally sharp; acute. 2 clear and effective. 3 cutting, penetrating. □ **incisively** *adv.* **incisiveness** *n.*

incisor *n.* ► a narrow-edged cutting-tooth at the front of the mouth ▷ DENTITION, TOOTH

incite *v.tr.* (often foll. by *to*, or *to* + infin.) urge or stir up. [from Latin *incitare*] □ **incitation** *n.* **incitement** *n.* **inciter** *n.*

incivility *n.* (*pl.* **-ies**) 1 discourtesy, rudeness. 2 a discourteous or rude act.

incl. *abbr.* including.

inclement *adj.* (of the weather or climate) severe; cold or stormy. □ **inclemency** *n.* (*pl.* **-ies**). **inclemently** *adv.*

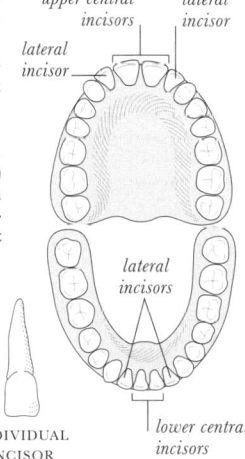

upper central incisors

lateral incisor

lateral incisor

lateral incisor

lateral incisors

INDIVIDUAL INCISOR

lower central incisors

INCISOR

PLAN OF HUMAN DENTITION

inclination *n.* 1 (often foll. by *to*) a disposition or propensity. 2 (often foll. by *for*) a liking or affection. 3 a a leaning, slope, or slant. b a bending of the body or head in a bow. 4 the difference of direction of two lines or planes, esp. as measured by the angle between them. 5 the dip of a magnetic needle. [from Old French *inclination* or Latin *inclinatio*]

incline ● *v.* 1 *tr.* (usu. in *passive*; often foll. by *to*, *for*, or *to* + infin.) a make (a person, feelings, etc.) willing or favourably disposed (*am inclined to think so*; *does not incline me to agree*). b give a specified tendency to (a thing) (*the door is inclined to bang*). 2 *intr.* a be disposed (*I incline to think so*). b (often foll. by *to*, *towards*) tend. 3 *intr. & tr.* lean or turn away from a given direction, esp. the vertical. 4 *tr.* bend (the head, body, or oneself) forward or downward. ● *n.* 1 a slope. 2 an inclined plane. □ **incline one's ear** (often foll. by *to*) listen favourably. [from Latin *inclinare*] □ **incliner** *n.*

INCLINED PLANE

An inclined plane reduces the effort needed to raise an object by supporting part of its weight. The lower the gradient of the plane, the more weight it supports, and the less effort is needed to raise an object. However, a low gradient also means that an object, such as this car, must be pulled a greater distance along the plane to reach the desired height.

DEMONSTRATION OF THE EFFECT OF AN INCLINED PLANE

car is gradually raised along inclined plane

pulley supports cable

effort exerted via winch

weight of car partially supported by plane

I

inclined plane *n.* ▲ a sloping plane (esp. as a means of reducing the force needed to raise a load).

include *v.tr.* **1** comprise or reckon in as part of a whole. **2** (as **including** *prep.*) counting in the reckoning (*six members, including the chairman*). **3** treat or regard as so included. [from Latin *includere* 'to enclose'] □ **inclusion** *n.*

inclusive *adj.* **1** (foll. by *of*) including, comprising. **2** with the inclusion of the limits stated (*pages 7 to 26 inclusive*). **3** including all the normal services etc. (*a hotel offering inclusive terms*). **4 a** not excluding any section of society. **b** (of language) deliberately non-sexist. [from medieval Latin *inclusivus*] □ **inclusively** *adv.* **inclusiveness** *n.*

incognito ● *adj. & adv.* with one's name or identity kept secret. ● *n.* (*pl.* **-os**) **1** a person who is incognito. **2** the pretended identity of such a person. [Italian, from Latin *incognitus* 'unknown']

incoherent *adj.* **1** (of a person) unable to speak intelligibly. **2** (of speech etc.) lacking logic or consistency. □ **incoherence** *n.* **incoherency** *n.* (*pl.* **-ies**). **incoherently** *adv.*

incombustible *adj.* that cannot be burnt. □ **incombustibility** *n.*

income *n.* the money or other assets received, esp. periodically or in a year, from one's business, lands, work, investments, etc. [Middle English in sense 'arrival']

income group *n.* a section of the population determined by income.

income support *n.* a system by which people on low incomes can, according to their circumstances, claim a payment from the State.

income tax *n.* a tax levied on income.

incoming ● *adj.* **1** coming in (*the incoming tide; incoming telephone calls*). **2** succeeding another person or persons (*the incoming tenant*). **3** (of profit) accruing. ● *n.* **1** (usu. in *pl.*) revenue, income. **2** the act of arriving or entering.

incommensurable ● *adj.* **1** not comparable in respect of magnitude or value. **2** (foll. by *with*) utterly disproportionate to. **3** *Math.* (often foll. by *with*) (of a magnitude or magnitudes) having no common factor, integral, or fractional. ● *n.* (usu. in *pl.*) an incommensurable quantity. □ **incommensurability** *n.* **incommensurably** *adv.*

incommensurate *adj.* **1** (often foll. by *with, to*) out of proportion; inadequate. **2** = INCOMMENSURABLE *adj.* 1. □ **incommensurately** *adv.* **incommensurateness** *n.*

incommode *v.tr.* **1** hinder, inconvenience. **2** trouble, annoy. [based on Latin *incommodare* 'to inconvenience']

incommodious *adj.* not affording good accommodation; uncomfortable. □ **incommodiously** *adv.* **incommodiousness** *n.*

incommunicable *adj.* that cannot be communicated. □ **incommunicability** *n.* **incommunicably** *adv.*

incommunicado *adj.* without means of communication with others. [Spanish]

incommunicative *adj.* not communicative; taciturn. □ **incommunicatively** *adv.* **incommunicativeness** *n.*

incomparable *adj.* **1** without an equal. **2** (often foll. by *with, to*) not to be compared. □ **incomparability** *n.* **incomparably** *adv.*

incompatible *adj.* **1** opposed in character; discordant. **2** (often foll. by *with*) inconsistent. **3** (of persons) unable to live etc. together in harmony. **4** (of equipment etc.) not capable of being used in combination. □ **incompatibility** *n.* **incompatibly** *adv.*

incompetent ● *adj.* **1 a** (often foll. by *to* + infin.) not qualified or able to perform a particular function. **b** (of a witness etc.) not legally qualified. **2** showing a lack of skill (*an incompetent performance*). ● *n.* an incompetent person. □ **incompetence** *n.* **incompetency** *n.* **incompetently** *adv.*

incomplete *adj.* not complete. □ **incompletely** *adv.* **incompleteness** *n.*

incomprehensible *adj.* (often foll. by *to*) that cannot be understood. □ **incomprehensibility** *n.* **incomprehensibly** *adv.*

incomprehension *n.* failure to understand.

inconceivable *adj.* **1** that cannot be imagined. **2** *colloq.* unbelievable. □ **inconceivability** *n.* **inconceivably** *adv.*

inconclusive *adj.* (of an argument, evidence, or action) not decisive or convincing. □ **inconclusively** *adv.* **inconclusiveness** *n.*

incongruous *adj.* **1** out of place; absurd. **2** (often foll. by *with*) out of keeping. □ **incongruity** *n.* (*pl.* **-ies**). **incongruously** *adv.*

inconsequent *adj.* **1** irrelevant. **2** lacking logical sequence. **3** disconnected. □ **inconsequence** *n.* **inconsequently** *adv.*

inconsequential *adj.* **1** unimportant. **2** = INCONSEQUENT. □ **inconsequentiality** *n.* (*pl.* **-ies**). **inconsequentially** *adv.* **inconsequentialness** *n.*

inconsiderable *adj.* **1** of small size, value, etc. **2** not worth considering. □ **inconsiderably** *adv.*

inconsiderate *adj.* thoughtless, rash; lacking regard for the feelings of others. □ **inconsiderately** *adv.* **inconsiderateness** *n.* **inconsideration** *n.*

inconsistent *adj.* **1** acting at variance with one's own principles or former conduct. **2** (often foll. by *with*) not in keeping; discordant. □ **inconsistency** *n.* (*pl.* **-ies**). **inconsistently** *adv.*

inconsolable *adj.* that cannot be consoled. □ **inconsolability** *n.* **inconsolably** *adv.*

inconsonant *adj.* (often foll. by *with, to*) not harmonious; not compatible. □ **inconsonance** *n.* **inconsonantly** *adv.*

inconspicuous *adj.* not easily noticed. □ **inconspicuously** *adv.* **inconspicuousness** *n.*

inconstant *adj.* **1** (of a person) fickle. **2** frequently changing; irregular. □ **inconstancy** *n.* (*pl.* **-ies**). **inconstantly** *adv.*

incontestable *adj.* that cannot be disputed. □ **incontestability** *n.* **incontestably** *adv.*

incontinent *adj.* **1** unable to control movements of the bowels or bladder or both. **2** lacking self-restraint (esp. in regard to sexual desire). □ **incontinence** *n.* **incontinently** *adv.*

incontrovertible *adj.* indisputable. □ **incontrovertibility** *n.* **incontrovertibly** *adv.*

inconvenience ● *n.* **1** lack of suitability to personal requirements or ease. **2** a cause or instance of this. ● *v.tr.* cause inconvenience to. □ **inconvenient** *adj.* **inconveniently** *adv.*

incorporate *v.* **1** *tr.* (often foll. by *in, with*) form into one body or whole. **2** *intr.* become incorporated. **3** *tr.* combine (ingredients) into one substance. **4** *tr.* admit as a member. **5** *tr.* **a** constitute as a legal corporation. **b** (as **incorporated** *adj.*) forming a legal corporation. [based on Late Latin *incorporatus* 'embodied'] □ **incorporation** *n.* **incorporator** *n.*

incorporeal *adj.* **1** not composed of matter. **2** of immaterial beings. □ **incorporeally** *adv.* **incorporeity** *n.*

incorrect *adj.* **1** not in accordance with fact. **2** improper. □ **incorrectly** *adv.* **incorrectness** *n.*

incorrigible *adj.* **1** (of a person or habit) incurably bad. **2** not readily improved. □ **incorrigibility** *n.* **incorrigibly** *adv.*

incorruptible *adj.* **1** that cannot be corrupted, esp. by bribery. **2** that cannot decay. □ **incorruptibility** *n.* **incorruptibly** *adv.*

increase ● *v.* **1** *tr. & intr.* make or become greater or more numerous. **2** *intr.* advance (in quality, attainment, etc.). **3** *tr.* intensify (a quality). ● *n.* **1** growth, enlargement. **2** (of people, animals, or plants) multiplication. **3** the amount or extent of an increase. □ **on the increase** increasing, esp. in frequency. [from Latin *increscere*] □ **increasable** *adj.* **increaser** *n.* **increasingly** *adv.*

incredible *adj.* **1** that cannot be believed. **2** *colloq.* amazing. □ **incredibility** *n.* **incredibly** *adv.*

incredulous *adj.* (often foll. by *of*) unwilling to believe. □ **incredulity** *n.* **incredulously** *adv.*

increment *n.* an increase or addition, esp. one of a series on a fixed scale. [from Latin *incrementum*] □ **incremental** *adj.* **incrementally** *adv.*

incriminate *v.tr.* **1** (often as **incriminating** *adj.*) tend to prove the guilt of (*incriminating evidence*). **2** involve in an accusation. **3** charge with a crime. [based on Late Latin *incriminatus* 'accused'] □ **incrimination** *n.* **incriminatory** *adj.*

incrust var. of ENCRUST.

incrustation *n.* (also **encrustation**) **1** the process of encrusting or state of being encrusted. **2** a crust or hard coating. **3** a deposit on a surface. [from Late Latin *incrustatio*]

incubate *v.* **1** *tr.* (also *absol.*) sit on or artificially heat (eggs) in order to bring forth young birds etc. **2** *tr.* cause the development of (bacteria etc.). **3** *tr. & intr.* develop slowly. [based on Latin *incubatus* 'lain upon']

incubation *n.* **1 a** the act of incubating. **b** brooding. **2** *Med.* (in full **incubation period**) the period between exposure to an infection and the appearance of the first symptoms. □ **incubative** *adj.* **incubatory** *adj.*

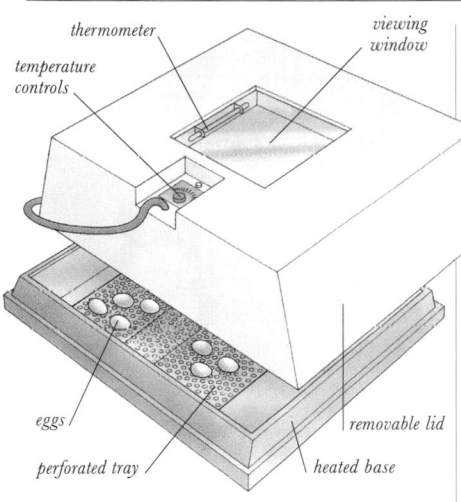

INCUBATOR FOR HATCHING BIRDS' EGGS

incubator *n.* ▲ an apparatus used to provide a suitable temperature and environment for incubation.

incubus /ing-kew-bŭs/ *n.* (*pl.* **incubi** /-by/) **1** a male demon believed to have sexual intercourse with sleeping women. **2** a nightmare. **3** a person or thing that oppresses like a nightmare. [based on Latin *incubo* 'nightmare']

inculcate *v.tr.* (often foll. by *upon*, *in*) urge or impress (a fact, habit, or idea) persistently. [based on Latin *inculcatus* 'trodden in'] □ **inculcation** *n.*

inculpate /in-kul-payt/ *v.tr.* **1** involve in a charge. **2** accuse, blame. [based on Latin *culpa* 'blame'] □ **inculpation** *n.* **inculpative** *adj.* **inculpatory** *adj.*

incumbent ● *adj.* **1** (foll. by *on*, *upon*) resting as a duty (*it is incumbent on you to warn them*). **2** currently holding office (*the incumbent president*). ● *n.* the holder of an office or post. [from Latin *incumbent-* 'lying upon'] □ **incumbency** *n.*

incunabulum *n.* (*pl.* **incunabula**) ▼ a book printed at an early date, esp. before 1501. [from Latin *incunabula* 'swaddling-clothes, cradle']

INCUNABULUM: 15TH-CENTURY
ENGLISH INCUNABULUM

incur *v.tr.* (**incurred**, **incurring**) suffer, experience, or become subject to (something unpleasant) as a result of one's own behaviour etc. (*incurred huge debts*). [Middle English from Latin *incurrere*] □ **incurrable** *adj.*

incurable ● *adj.* that cannot be cured. ● *n.* a person who cannot be cured. □ **incurability** *n.* **incurably** *adv.*

incurious *adj.* **1** lacking curiosity. **2** heedless, careless. □ **incuriosity** *n.* **incuriously** *adv.*

incursion *n.* an invasion or attack, esp. when sudden or brief. [related to INCUR] □ **incursive** *adj.*

incurve *v.tr.* **1** bend into a curve. **2** (as **incurved** *adj.*) curved inwards. □ **incurvation** *n.*

Ind. *abbr.* **1** Independent. **2 a** India. **b** Indian.

indebted *adj.* (usu. foll. by *to*) **1** owing gratitude or obligation. **2** owing money. □ **indebtedness** *n.*

indecent *adj.* offending against recognized standards of decency. □ **indecency** *n.* (*pl.* **-ies**). **indecently** *adv.*

indecent assault *n.* a sexual attack not involving rape.

indecent exposure *n.* the intentional act of publicly and indecently exposing one's body, esp. the genitals.

indecision *n.* lack of decision; hesitation. □ **indecisive** *adj.* **indecisively** *adv.* **indecisiveness** *n.*

indeclinable *adj.* Gram. **1** that cannot be declined. **2** having no inflections.

indecorous *adj.* **1** improper. **2** in bad taste. □ **indecorously** *adv.* **indecorousness** *n.*

indeed ● *adv.* **1** in truth (*they are, indeed, a remarkable family*). **2** expressing emphasis or intensification (*indeed it is*). **3** admittedly (*there are indeed exceptions*). **4** in point of fact (*if indeed such a thing is possible*). ● *int.* expressing irony, contempt, incredulity, etc.

indefatigable *adj.* unwearying, unremitting. [from Latin *indefatigabilis*] □ **indefatigability** *n.* **indefatigably** *adv.*

indefensible *adj.* that cannot be defended or justified. □ **indefensibility** *n.* **indefensibly** *adv.*

indefinable *adj.* that cannot be defined or exactly described. □ **indefinably** *adv.*

indefinite *adj.* **1** vague, undefined. **2** unlimited. **3** Gram. not determining the person, thing, time, etc., referred to. □ **indefiniteness** *n.*

indefinite article *n.* Gram. a word (*a* and *an* in English) preceding a noun and implying lack of specificity.

indefinitely *adv.* **1** for an unlimited time. **2** in an indefinite manner.

indefinite pronoun *n.* a pronoun indicating a person, amount, etc., without being definite or particular, e.g. *any, some, anyone*.

indelible *adj.* that cannot be rubbed out or (in abstract senses) removed. [based on Latin *delere* 'to efface'] □ **indelibility** *n.* **indelibly** *adv.*

indelicate *adj.* **1** coarse, unrefined. **2** tactless. **3** tending to indecency. □ **indelicacy** *n.* (*pl.* **-ies**). **indelicately** *adv.*

indemnify *v.tr.* (**-ies**, **-ied**) **1** (often foll. by *from*, *against*) protect or secure in respect of a loss etc. **2** (often foll. by *for*) secure (a person) against legal responsibility for actions. **3** (often foll. by *for*) compensate for expenses etc. [based on Latin *indemnis* 'unhurt'] □ **indemnification** *n.*

indemnity *n.* (*pl.* **-ies**) **1 a** compensation for loss incurred. **b** a sum paid for this. **2** security against loss. **3** legal exemption from penalties etc. incurred. [from Late Latin *indemnitas*]

indent[1] ● *v.* **1** *tr.* start (a line of print or writing) further from the margin than other lines. **2** Brit. **a** *intr.* (often foll. by *on*, *upon* a person, *for* a thing) make a requisition. **b** *tr.* order (goods) by requisition. **3** *tr.* make toothlike notches in. **4** *tr.* form deep recesses in (a coastline etc.). ● *n.* **1** Brit. **a** an order (esp. from abroad) for goods. **b** an official requisition for stores. **2** an indented line. **3** indentation. **4** an indenture. [based on Latin *dens dentis* 'tooth'] □ **indentation** *n.* **indentor** *n.*

indent[2] *v.tr.* **1** make a dent in. **2** impress (a mark etc.). [Middle English]

indention *n.* (an) indentation, esp. in printing or writing.

indenture ● *n.* **1** (usu. in *pl.*) a sealed agreement or contract. **2** a formal list, certificate, etc. ● *v.tr. hist.* bind (a person) by indentures. [from Anglo-French *endenture*] □ **indentureship** *n.*

independence *n.* (often foll. by *of*, *from*) the fact or process of being independent.

independent ● *adj.* **1 a** (often foll. by *of*) not depending on authority or control. **b** self-governing. **2 a** not depending on another person for one's opinion or livelihood. **b** (of income or resources) making it unnecessary to earn one's living. **3** unwilling to be under an obligation to others. **4** Polit. acting independently of any party. **5** not depending on something else for its validity etc. (*independent proof*). **6** (of broadcasting, a school, etc.) not supported by public funds. ● *n.* a person who is politically independent. □ **independently** *adv.*

in-depth *attrib.adj.* thorough; done in depth.

indescribable *adj.* **1** too unusual or extreme to be described. **2** vague, indefinite. □ **indescribability** *n.* **indescribably** *adv.*

indestructible *adj.* that cannot be destroyed. □ **indestructibility** *n.* **indestructibly** *adv.*

indeterminable *adj.* **1** that cannot be ascertained. **2** (of a dispute etc.) that cannot be settled. □ **indeterminably** *adv.*

indeterminate *adj.* **1** not fixed in extent, character, etc. **2** left doubtful; vague. **3** Math. (of a quantity) not limited to a fixed value by the value of another quantity. □ **indeterminacy** *n.* **indeterminately** *adv.* **indeterminateness** *n.*

indetermination *n.* **1** lack of determination. **2** the state of being indeterminate.

index ● *n.* (*pl.* **indexes** or esp. in technical use **indices**) **1** an alphabetical list with references, usu. at the end of a book. **2** = CARD INDEX. **3** (in full **index number**) a number showing the variation of prices or wages as compared with a chosen base period (*retail price index*). **4** Math. **a** the exponent of a number. **b** the power to which it is raised. **5 a** a pointer, esp. on an instrument. ▷ SEXTANT. **b** an indicator of a trend, direction, etc. **c** (usu. foll. by *of*) a sign, token, or indication of something. ● *v.tr.* **1** provide (a book etc.) with an index. **2** enter in an index. **3** relate (wages etc.) to the value of a price index. [from Latin *index* 'forefinger, informer, sign'] □ **indexation** *n.* **indexer** *n.* **indexical** *adj.*

index finger *n.* the forefinger.

index-linked *adj.* related to the value of a retail price index. □ **index-linking** *n.*

Indian ● *n.* **1 a** a native or national of India. **b** a person of Indian descent. **2** an American Indian. ● *adj.* **1** of or relating to India, or to the Indian subcontinent. **2** of or relating to the aboriginal peoples of America. [from Greek *Indos*, the River Indus]

■ **Usage** *Indian* is a misnomer for the native peoples of America, having arisen from the mistaken belief of Christopher Columbus and other Europeans in the 15th–16th centuries that they had reached part of India by a new route. The term is considered to convey an offensive stereotype by some. However, it is used by many Native Americans in the US as a term of pride and respect. The full forms *American Indian* (and in Canada, *Canadian Indian*) are unambiguous alternatives. See also Usage Note at NATIVE AMERICAN.

Indian club *n.* ◀ each of a pair of bottle-shaped clubs swung to exercise the arms in gymnastics.

Indian corn *n.* maize.

Indian file *n.* = SINGLE FILE.

Indian hemp see HEMP 1.

Indian ink *n.* Brit. **1** a black pigment made originally in China and Japan. **2** a dark ink made from this.

Indian Ocean *n.* the ocean between Africa to the west, and Australia to the east. ▷ OCEAN

INDIAN
CLUBS

Indian summer *n.* **1** a period of unusually dry warm weather sometimes occurring in late autumn. **2** a late period of life characterized by comparative calm.

India paper *n.* **1** a soft absorbent kind of paper used for proofs of engravings. **2** a very thin tough opaque printing paper.

India rubber *n.* = RUBBER[1] 2.

indicate *v.* (often foll. by *that* + clause) **1** *tr.* point out; make known. **2** *tr.* be a sign or symptom of; express the presence of. **3** *tr.* (often in *passive*) suggest; call for; require (*stronger measures are indicated*). **4** *tr.* admit to or state briefly (*indicated his disapproval*). **5** *tr.* (of a gauge etc.) give as a reading. **6** *intr.* signal one's intention to turn etc. using an indicator. [based on Latin *indicatus* 'made known'] □ **indication** *n.*

indicative ● *adj.* **1** (foll. by *of*) serving as an indication. **2** *Gram.* (of a mood) denoting simple statement of a fact. ● *n. Gram.* **1** the indicative mood. **2** a verb in this mood. □ **indicatively** *adv.*

indicator *n.* **1** a person or thing that indicates esp. performance, change, etc. **2** a device indicating the condition of a machine etc. **3** *Brit.* a board in a railway station etc. giving current information. **4** a device (esp. a flashing light) on a vehicle to show that it is about to change direction.

indicatory *adj.* = INDICATIVE *adj.* 1.

indices *pl.* of INDEX.

indict /in-**dyt**/ *v.tr.* accuse (a person) formally by legal process. [from Old French *enditier*] □ **indictee** *n.* **indicter** *n.*

indictable /in-**dyt**-ăbŭl/ *adj.* **1** (of an offence) rendering the person who commits it liable to be charged with a crime. **2** (of a person) so liable.

indictment /in-**dyt**-měnt/ *n.* **1** the act of indicting. **2 a** a formal accusation. **b** a document containing a charge. **3** something that serves to condemn or censure.

indie *colloq.* ● *adj.* (of a pop group or record label) not belonging to one of the major record companies. ● *n.* **1** such a group or label. **2** an independent film company.

indifference *n.* **1** lack of interest or attention. **2** unimportance. **3** neutrality.

indifferent *adj.* **1** neither good nor bad; mediocre. **2 a** not especially good. **b** fairly bad. **3** (foll. by *to*) having no interest in or sympathy for. [from Latin *indifferent*- 'making no difference'] □ **indifferently** *adv.*

indigenize *v.tr.* (also **-ise**) make indigenous. □ **indigenization** *n.*

indigenous *adj.* **1** native to a region. **2** (foll. by *to*) belonging naturally to a place. [based on Latin *indigena* 'a native'] □ **indigenously** *adv.*

indigent *adj.* needy, poor. [from Late Latin *indigent*- 'lacking'] □ **indigence** *n.*

indigestible *adj.* **1** difficult or impossible to digest. **2** too complex to read or comprehend easily. □ **indigestibility** *n.*

indigestion *n.* **1** difficulty in digesting food. **2** pain or discomfort caused by this.

indignant *adj.* feeling or showing indignation. [from Latin *indignant*- 'regarding as unworthy'] □ **indignantly** *adv.*

indignation *n.* scornful anger at supposed unjust or unfair conduct or treatment.

indignity *n.* (*pl.* **-ies**) **1** a slight or insult. **2** the humiliating quality of something. [from Latin *indignitas*]

indigo ● *n.*(*pl.* **-os**) **1** a blue dye obtained from the indigo plant. **2** ▶ any plant of the genus *Indigofera*. **3** (in full **indigo blue**) a colour between blue and violet in the spectrum. ● *adj.* (in full **indigo blue**; hyphenated when *attrib.*) of this colour. [from Greek *indikon* 'Indian (dye)']

INDIGO
(*Indigofera decora*)

INDUCTION

Electromagnetic induction occurs when a magnet moves near a coil of wire. The effect of the induction is to produce an electric current whose strength depends upon the speed of motion and the strength of the magnet, as well as upon the number of turns of the coil.

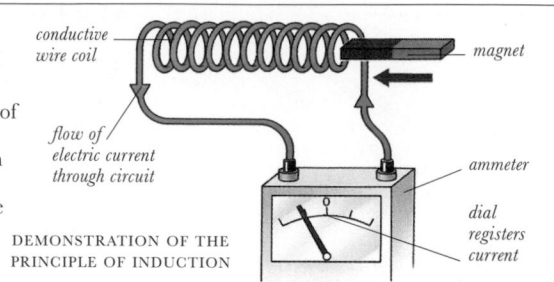

conductive wire coil

magnet

flow of electric current through circuit

ammeter

dial registers current

DEMONSTRATION OF THE PRINCIPLE OF INDUCTION

indirect *adj.* **1** not going straight to the point. **2** (of a route etc.) not straight. **3** not directly sought or aimed at (*an indirect result*). □ **indirectly** *adv.* **indirectness** *n.*

indirect object *n. Gram.* a person or thing affected by a verbal action but not primarily acted on (e.g. *him* in *give him the book*).

indirect question *n. Gram.* a question in reported speech (e.g. *they asked who I was*).

indirect speech *n.* = REPORTED SPEECH.

indirect tax *n.* a tax levied on goods and services and not on income or profits.

indiscernible *adj.* that cannot be discerned or distinguished from another. □ **indiscernibly** *adv.*

indiscipline *n.* lack of discipline.

indiscreet *adj.* **1** not discreet; revealing secrets. **2** injudicious, unwary. □ **indiscreetly** *adv.*

indiscretion *n.* **1** lack of discretion. **2** an indiscreet action, remark, etc.

indiscriminate *adj.* **1** making no distinctions. **2** confused, promiscuous. □ **indiscriminately** *adv.* **indiscriminateness** *n.* **indiscrimination** *n.*

indispensable *adj.* (often foll. by *to, for*) that cannot be dispensed with; necessary. □ **indispensability** *n.* **indispensably** *adv.*

indisposed *adj.* **1** slightly unwell. **2** averse or unwilling. □ **indisposition** *n.*

indisputable *adj.* that cannot be disputed. □ **indisputability** *n.* **indisputably** *adv.*

indissoluble *adj.* **1** that cannot be dissolved or decomposed. **2** lasting, stable. □ **indissolubility** *n.* **indissolubly** *adv.*

indistinct *adj.* **1** not distinct. **2** confused, obscure. □ **indistinctly** *adv.* **indistinctness** *n.*

indistinguishable *adj.* (often foll. by *from*) not distinguishable. □ **indistinguishably** *adv.*

indite *v.tr. formal* or *joc.* **1** put (a speech etc.) into words. **2** write (a letter etc.). [from Old French *enditier*]

indium *n. Chem.* a soft silvery-white metallic element used for electroplating and in semiconductors. [from Latin *indicum* 'indigo', with reference to its spectral lines]

individual ● *adj.* **1** single. **2** particular, special; not general. **3** having a distinct character. **4** characteristic of a particular person. **5** designed for use by one person. ● *n.* **1** a single member of a class. **2** a single human being. **3** *colloq.* a person (*a most unpleasant individual*). **4** a distinctive person. [Middle English in sense 'indivisible': from medieval Latin *individualis*]

individualism *n.* **1** the habit or principle of being self-reliant. **2** a social theory favouring the free action of individuals. □ **individualist** *n.* **individualistic** *adj.*

individuality *n.* (*pl.* **-ies**) **1** individual character, esp. when strongly marked. **2** separate existence.

individualize *v.tr.* (also **-ise**) **1** give an individual character to. **2** (esp.

as **individualized** *adj.*) personalize or tailor to suit the individual (*individualized notepaper*; *individualized training course*). □ **individualization** *n.*

individually *adv.* **1** personally; in an individual capacity. **2** in a distinctive manner. **3** one by one; not collectively.

individuate *v.tr.* individualize; form into an individual. □ **individuation** *n.*

indivisible *adj.* not divisible. □ **indivisibility** *n.* **indivisibly** *adv.*

Indo- *comb. form* Indian; Indian and.

indoctrinate *v.tr.* teach (a person or group) systematically or for a long period to accept ideas uncritically. □ **indoctrination** *n.* **indoctrinator** *n.*

Indo-European ● *adj.* **1** of or relating to the family of languages spoken over most of Europe and Asia as far as N. India. **2** of or relating to the hypothetical parent language of this family. ● *n.* **1** the Indo-European family of languages. **2** the hypothetical parent language of these.

indolent *adj.* lazy; wishing to avoid activity or exertion. [from Late Latin *indolent*- 'not causing pain'] □ **indolence** *n.* **indolently** *adv.*

indomitable *adj.* **1** that cannot be subdued; unyielding. **2** stubbornly persistent. [based on Latin *domitare* 'to tame'] □ **indomitability** *n.* **indomitably** *adv.*

Indonesian ● *n.* **1** a native or national of Indonesia in SE Asia. **2** a person of Indonesian descent. ● *adj.* of or relating to Indonesia or its people or language(s). [based on Greek *Indos* 'Indian' + *nēsos* 'island']

indoor *adj.* situated, carried on, or used within a building or under cover (*indoor aerial*; *indoor games*).

indoors *adv.* into or within a building.

indorse var. of ENDORSE.

indorsement var. of ENDORSEMENT.

indrawn *adj.* **1** (of breath etc.) drawn in. **2** aloof.

indubitable *adj.* that cannot be doubted. [from Latin *indubitabilis*] □ **indubitably** *adv.*

induce *v.tr.* **1** (often foll. by *to* + infin.) prevail on; persuade. **2** bring about. **3** *Med.* bring on (labour) artificially. **4** *Electr.* produce (a current) by induction. **5** infer; derive as a deduction. [from Latin *inducere*] □ **inducer** *n.* **inducible** *adj.*

inducement *n.* **1** (often foll. by *to*) an attraction that leads one on. **2** a thing that induces.

induct *v.tr.* (often foll. by *to, into*) **1 a** introduce into office. **b** introduce (a member of the clergy) into possession of a benefice. **2** introduce, initiate. [based on Latin *inductus* 'led in'] □ **inductee** *n.*

inductance *n. Electr.* the property of an electric circuit that causes an electromotive force to be generated by a change in the current flowing.

induction *n.* **1** the act of inducting or inducing. **2** *Med.* the act of bringing on (esp. labour) by artificial means. **3** *Logic* the inference of a general law from particular instances. **4** (often *attrib.*) a formal introduction to a new job etc. (*attended an induction course*). **5** *Electr.* **a** ▲ the production of an electric or magnetic state by the proximity (without contact) of an electrified or magnetized body. **b** the production of an electric current in a conductor by a change of magnetic field. ▷ ELECTROMAGNETISM. **6** the drawing of a fuel mixture into the cylinders of an internal-combustion engine. **7** *US* enlistment for military service.

induction coil *n.* a coil for generating intermittent high voltage from a direct current.

induction loop *n.* a loop of wire around an area in a building etc., producing an electromagnetic signal received directly by hearing aids.

inductive *adj.* **1** (of reasoning etc.) of or based on induction. **2** of electric or magnetic induction. □ **inductively** *adv.*

inductor *n.* **1** *Electr.* a component (in a circuit) which possesses inductance. **2** a person who inducts a member of the clergy.

indulge *v.* **1** *intr.* (often foll. by *in*) take pleasure freely. **2** *tr.* yield freely to (a desire etc.). **3** *tr.* gratify the wishes of; favour. [from Latin *indulgēre* 'to give free rein to'] □ **indulger** *n.*

indulgence *n.* **1 a** the act of indulging. **b** the state of being indulgent. **2** something indulged in. **3** *RC Ch.* the remission of temporal punishment in purgatory, still due for sins after absolution.

indulgent *adj.* **1** lenient; ready to overlook faults etc. **2** indulging. □ **indulgently** *adv.*

industrial *adj.* **1** of or relating to industry or industries. **2** for use in industry (*industrial alcohol*). **3** characterized by highly developed industries (*the industrial nations*). □ **industrially** *adv.*

industrial action *n. Brit.* any action, esp. a strike or work to rule, taken by employees as a protest.

industrial archaeology *n.* the study of machines, factories, bridges, etc., formerly used in industry.

industrial estate *n. Brit.* an area of land developed for the siting of industrial enterprises.

industrialism *n.* a social or economic system in which manufacturing industries are prevalent.

industrialist *n.* a person engaged in the management of industry.

industrialize *v.* (also **-ise**) **1** *tr.* introduce industries to (a country or region etc.). **2** *intr.* become industrialized. □ **industrialization** *n.*

industrial relations *n.pl.* the relations between management and workers in industries.

industrial-strength *adj.* (often *attrib.*) often *joc.* strong, powerful.

industrious *adj.* diligent, hard-working. □ **industriously** *adv.* **industriousness** *n.*

industry *n.* (*pl.* **-ies**) **1 a** a branch of trade or manufacture. **b** trade and manufacture collectively. **2** concerted or copious activity. **3** diligence. [from Latin *industria* 'diligence']

Indy *n.* a chiefly American form of motor racing, usu. at very high speeds on oval circuits (often *attrib.*: *Indy racing*). [from *Indianapolis* in the US, where the principal Indy race is held]

Indycar *n.* **1** ▼ a car used in Indy racing. **2** (*attrib.*) = INDY (*Indycar champion*; *Indycar team*).

inebriate ● *v.tr.* **1** make drunk. **2** excite. ● *adj.* drunken. ● *n.* a drunkard. [from Latin *inebriatus* 'drunk'] □ **inebriation** *n.* **inebriety** *n.*

inedible *adj.* not edible, esp. not suitable for eating (cf. UNEATABLE). □ **inedibility** *n.*

ineducable *adj.* incapable of being educated. □ **ineducability** *n.*

ineffable *adj.* **1** unutterable; too great for description in words. **2** that must not be uttered. [from Latin *ineffabilis*] □ **ineffability** *n.* **ineffably** *adv.*

ineffaceable *adj.* that cannot be effaced.

ineffective *adj.* **1** not producing any effect or the desired effect. **2** (of a person) inefficient; not achieving results. **3** lacking artistic effect. □ **ineffectively** *adv.* **ineffectiveness** *n.*

ineffectual *adj.* **1 a** without effect. **b** not producing the desired or expected effect. **2** (of a person) lacking the ability to achieve results (*an ineffectual leader*). □ **ineffectuality** *n.* **ineffectually** *adv.* **ineffectualness** *n.*

inefficacious *adj.* (of a remedy etc.) not producing the desired effect. □ **inefficaciously** *adv.* **inefficacy** *n.*

inefficient *adj.* **1** not efficient or fully capable; incompetent. **2** (of a person) not fully capable; incompetent. □ **inefficiency** *n.* **inefficiently** *adv.*

inelastic *adj.* **1** not elastic. **2** unadaptable, inflexible, unyielding. □ **inelasticity** *n.*

inelegant *adj.* **1** ungraceful. **2 a** unrefined. **b** (of a style) unpolished. □ **inelegance** *n.* **inelegantly** *adv.*

ineligible *adj.* not eligible. □ **ineligibility** *n.* **ineligibly** *adv.*

ineluctable *adj.* **1** irresistible. **2** inescapable. [from Latin *ineluctabilis*] □ **ineluctability** *n.* **ineluctably** *adv.*

inept *adj.* **1 a** clumsy, unskilful. **b** absurd, silly. **2** inappropriate. [from Latin *ineptus*] □ **ineptitude** *n.* **ineptly** *adv.* **ineptness** *n.*

■ **Usage** *Inept* and *inapt* are easily confused because they have virtually the same meanings. However, *inept* is a far commoner word than *inapt* and is usually used in sense 1a, 'clumsy, unskilful'. *Inapt* is more often used to mean 'unsuitable, inappropriate'. This difference is illustrated by the example *His after-dinner speech was both inept and inapt*, i.e. it was both clumsy and inappropriate.

inequable *adj.* **1** not fairly distributed. **2** not uniform.

inequality *n.* (*pl.* **-ies**) **1 a** lack of equality. **b** an instance of this. **2** the state of being variable.

inequitable /in-**ek**-wit-ăbŭl/ *adj.* unfair, unjust. □ **inequitably** *adv.*

inequity *n.* (*pl.* **-ies**) unfairness, bias.

ineradicable *adj.* that cannot be eradicated. □ **ineradicably** *adv.*

inert *adj.* **1** without inherent power of action, motion, or resistance. **2** without active chemical or other properties. **3** sluggish, slow. [from Latin *iners inert-* 'unskilled, inactive'] □ **inertly** *adv.* **inertness** *n.*

inert gas *n.* = NOBLE GAS.

inertia *n.* **1** *Physics* a property of matter by which it continues in its existing state of rest or uniform motion in a straight line, unless that state is changed by an external force. **2 a** inertness, sloth. **b** a tendency to remain unchanged. [Latin] □ **inertial** *adj.* **inertialess** *adj.*

inertia reel *n.* a reel device which allows a vehicle seat belt to unwind freely but which locks under force of impact or rapid deceleration.

inertia selling *n. Brit.* the sending of unsolicited goods in the hope of making a sale.

I

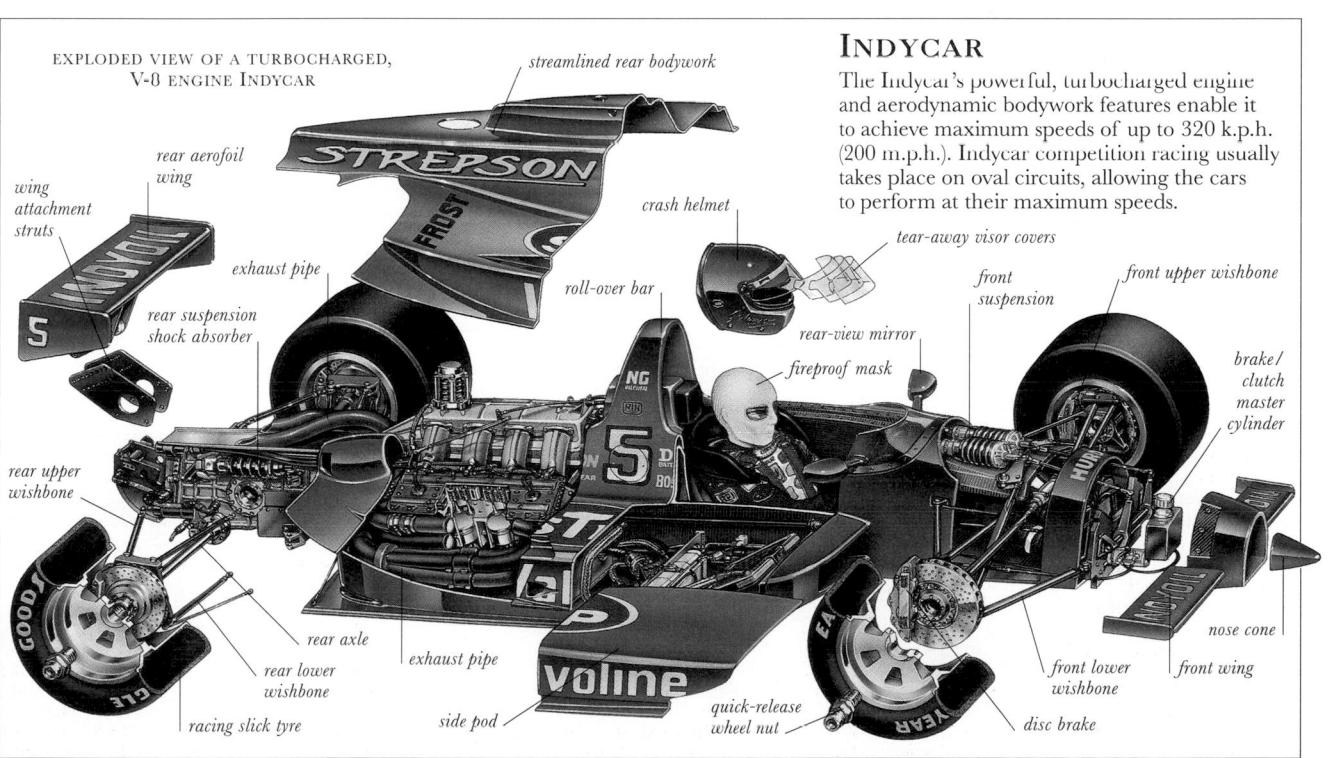

INDYCAR

The Indycar's powerful, turbocharged engine and aerodynamic bodywork features enable it to achieve maximum speeds of up to 320 k.p.h. (200 m.p.h.). Indycar competition racing usually takes place on oval circuits, allowing the cars to perform at their maximum speeds.

EXPLODED VIEW OF A TURBOCHARGED, V-8 ENGINE INDYCAR

streamlined rear bodywork
rear aerofoil wing
wing attachment struts
exhaust pipe
rear suspension shock absorber
crash helmet
tear-away visor covers
roll-over bar
front suspension
front upper wishbone
rear-view mirror
fireproof mask
brake/ clutch master cylinder
rear upper wishbone
rear axle
exhaust pipe
rear lower wishbone
racing slick tyre
side pod
quick-release wheel nut
front lower wishbone
disc brake
nose cone
front wing

I

inescapable *adj.* that cannot be escaped or avoided. □ **inescapability** *n.* **inescapably** *adv.*

inessential ● *adj.* **1** not necessary. **2** dispensable. ● *n.* an inessential thing.

inestimable *adj.* too great, intense, precious, etc., to be estimated. □ **inestimably** *adv.*

inevitable ● *adj.* **1 a** unavoidable. **b** that is bound to occur or appear. **2** *colloq.* tiresomely predictable. ● *n.* (prec. by *the*) that which is inevitable. [from Latin *inevitabilis*] □ **inevitability** *n.* **inevitableness** *n.* **inevitably** *adv.*

inexact *adj.* not exact. □ **inexactitude** *n.* **inexactly** *adv.* **inexactness** *n.*

inexcusable *adj.* (of a person, action, etc.) that cannot be excused or justified. □ **inexcusably** *adv.*

inexhaustible *adj.* that cannot be exhausted or used up. □ **inexhaustibility** *n.* **inexhaustibly** *adv.*

inexorable /in-**eks**-er-ăbŭl/ *adj.* **1** relentless. **2** that cannot be persuaded by request or entreaty. [from Latin *inexorabilis*] □ **inexorability** *n.* **inexorably** *adv.*

inexpedient *adj.* not expedient. □ **inexpediency** *n.*

inexpensive *adj.* not expensive, cheap. □ **inexpensively** *adv.* **inexpensiveness** *n.*

inexperience *n.* lack of experience, or of the resulting knowledge or skill. □ **inexperienced** *adj.*

inexpert *adj.* unskilful; lacking expertise. □ **inexpertly** *adv.* **inexpertness** *n.*

inexplicable *adj.* that cannot be explained or accounted for. □ **inexplicability** *n.* **inexplicably** *adv.*

inexplicit *adj.* not definitely or clearly expressed.

inexpressible *adj.* that cannot be expressed. □ **inexpressibly** *adv.*

inexpressive *adj.* not expressive. □ **inexpressively** *adv.* **inexpressiveness** *n.*

inextinguishable *adj.* **1** not quenchable. **2** indestructible. **3** (of laughter etc.) irrepressible.

in extremis **1** at the point of death. **2** in great difficulties. [Latin]

inextricable *adj.* **1** (of a circumstance) that cannot be escaped from. **2** (of a knot, problem, etc.) that cannot be unravelled or solved. [from Latin *inextricabilis*] □ **inextricably** *adv.*

infallible *adj.* **1** incapable of error. **2** (of a method, test, proof, etc.) unfailing; sure to succeed. □ **infallibility** *n.* **infallibly** *adv.*

infamous /**in**-fă-mŭs/ *adj.* **1** notoriously bad; having a bad reputation. **2** abominable. [from Latin *infamis*] □ **infamously** *adv.* **infamy** *n.* (*pl.* **-ies**).

infancy *n.* (*pl.* **-ies**) **1** early childhood; babyhood. **2** an early state in the development of an idea, undertaking, etc. [related to INFANT]

infant *n.* **1 a** a child during the earliest period of its life. **b** *Brit.* a schoolchild below the age of seven years. **2** (esp. *attrib.*) a thing in an early stage of its development. [from Latin *infans infant-* 'unable to speak']

infanticide *n.* **1** the killing of an infant soon after birth. **2** a person who kills an infant. [from Late Latin *infanticidium*] □ **infanticidal** *adj.*

infantile *adj.* **1** like or characteristic of a child. **2** childish, immature (*infantile humour*).

infantile paralysis *n.* poliomyelitis.

infant mortality *n.* death before the age of one.

infantry *n.* (*pl.* **-ies**) a body of soldiers who march and fight on foot; foot soldiers collectively.

infantryman *n.* (*pl.* **-men**) ► a soldier of an infantry regiment.

infarct *n.* *Med.* a small localized area of dead tissue caused by an inadequate blood supply. [based on Latin *farctus* 'stuffed']

infatuate *v.tr.* (usu. as **infatuated** *adj.*) **1** (often foll. by *with*) inspire with intense usu. transitory fondness or admiration. **2** affect with extreme folly. [based on Latin *infatuatus* 'made a fool of'] □ **infatuation** *n.*

infect *v.tr.* **1** contaminate (air, water, etc.) with harmful organisms or noxious matter. **2 a** affect (a person) with disease etc. **b** affect (a computer system) with a virus. [based on Latin *infectus* 'tainted'] □ **infector** *n.*

infection *n.* **1 a** the process of infecting or state of being infected. **b** an instance of this; an infectious disease. **c** the presence of a virus in, or its entry into, a computer system. **2** communication of disease, esp. by the agency of air, water, etc.

infectious *adj.* **1** infecting with disease. **2** (of a disease) liable to be transmitted by air, water, etc. **3** (of emotions etc.) quickly affecting others. □ **infectiously** *adv.* **infectiousness** *n.*

infelicitous *adj.* not felicitous; unfortunate. □ **infelicitously** *adv.*

infelicity *n.* (*pl.* **-ies**) **1 a** inaptness of expression etc. **b** an instance of this. **2** unhappiness.

infer *v.tr.* (**inferred**, **inferring**) (often foll. by *that* + clause) **1** deduce or conclude from facts and reasoning. **2** *disp.* imply, suggest. [from Latin *inferre*] □ **inferable** *adj.* (also **inferrable**).

■ **Usage** The use of *infer* in sense 2 is considered incorrect by many people since it is the reverse of the primary sense of the verb. It should be avoided by using *imply* or *suggest*.

inference *n.* **1** the act or an instance of inferring. **2** *Logic* **a** the forming of a conclusion from premisses. **b** a thing inferred. □ **inferential** *adj.* **inferentially** *adv.*

inferior ● *adj.* **1** (often foll. by *to*) lower in rank, quality, etc. **2** poor in quality. **3** (of figures or letters) written or printed below the line. ● *n.* a person inferior to another, esp. in rank. [Latin, literally 'that is further below'] □ **inferiorly** *adv.*

inferiority *n.* the state of being inferior.

inferiority complex *n.* an unrealistic feeling of general inadequacy, sometimes marked by aggressive behaviour in compensation.

infernal *adj.* **1 a** of hell or the underworld. **b** hellish, fiendish. **2** *colloq.* detestable, tiresome. [from Latin *infernus* 'situated below'] □ **infernally** *adv.*

inferno *n.* (*pl.* **-os**) **1** a raging fire. **2** a scene of horror or distress. **3** hell. [Italian]

infertile *adj.* not fertile. □ **infertility** *n.*

infest *v.tr.* (esp. of vermin) overrun (a place). [from Latin *infestare* 'to assail'] □ **infestation** *n.*

infidel ● *n.* a person who does not believe in religion or in a particular religion; an unbeliever. ● *adj.* **1** that is an infidel. **2** of unbelievers. [from Latin *infidelis*]

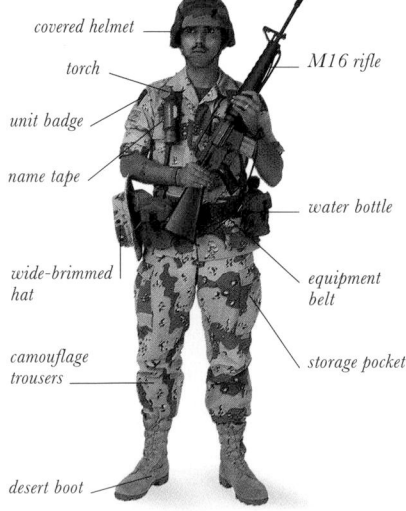

covered helmet
torch
unit badge
name tape
wide-brimmed hat
camouflage trousers
desert boot
M16 rifle
water bottle
equipment belt
storage pocket

INFANTRYMAN IN US
DESERT COMBAT UNIFORM

INFLAMMATION

Damage to the skin, or a localized infection, induces an influx of phagocytic blood cells and proteins to the affected area to fight bacteria or repair tissue damage. The increased supply of blood causes the redness and swelling of inflammation.

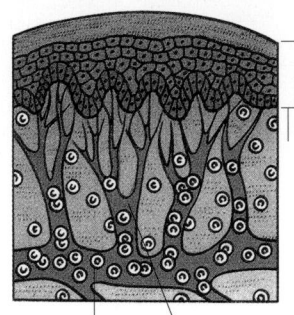

swollen skin tissue

phagocytic cells   enlarged blood vessels

CROSS-SECTION OF INFLAMED HUMAN SKIN

infidelity *n.* (*pl.* **-ies**) **1** disloyalty, or esp. unfaithfulness to a sexual partner. **2** an instance of this.

infield *n.* **1** *Cricket* the part of the ground near the wicket. **2** *Baseball* **a** the area within the four bases. **b** the defensive positions near the bases. ▷ BASEBALL. □ **infielder** *n.*

infighting *n.* **1** hidden conflict or competitiveness within an organization. **2** boxing at closer quarters than arm's length. □ **infighter** *n.*

infill ● *n.* **1** material used to fill a hole, gap, etc. **2** the placing of buildings to occupy the space between existing ones. ● *v.tr.* fill in (a cavity etc.).

infilling *n.* = INFILL *n.*

infiltrate *v.* **1 a** *tr.* & *intr.* penetrate, gain entrance or access (to) surreptitiously and by degrees (as spies etc.). **b** *tr.* cause to do this. **2** *tr.* & *intr.* permeate by filtration. **3** *tr.* & *intr.* (often foll. by *into*, *through*) introduce (fluid) by filtration. □ **infiltration** *n.* **infiltrator** *n.*

infinite ● *adj.* **1** boundless, endless. **2** very great or many (*infinite resources*). ● *n.* **1** (**the Infinite**) God. **2** (**the infinite**) infinite space. □ **infinitely** *adv.*

infinitesimal ● *adj.* infinitely or very small. ● *n.* an infinitesimal amount. [from modern Latin *infinitesimus*] □ **infinitesimally** *adv.*

infinitive *n.* a form of a verb expressing the verbal notion without a particular subject, tense, etc. (e.g. *see* in *we came to see*, *let him see*). [from Latin *infinitivus*] □ **infinitival** *adj.*

infinity *n.* (*pl.* **-ies**) **1** the state of being infinite. **2** an infinite number or extent. **3** *Math.* infinite quantity.

infirm *adj.* physically weak, esp. through age. □ **infirmity** *n.* (*pl.* **-ies**). **infirmly** *adv.*

infirmary *n.* (*pl.* **-ies**) **1** a hospital. **2** a place for the ill in a monastery, school, etc. ▷ MONASTERY

infix *v.tr.* (often foll. by *in*) **1** fix (a thing in another). **2** impress (a fact etc. in the mind).

in flagrante delicto /in flă-**gran**-ti di-**lik**-toh/ *adv.* in the very act of committing an offence. [Latin, literally 'in blazing crime']

inflame *v.* **1** *tr.* & *intr.* (often foll. by *with*, *by*) provoke or become provoked to strong feeling, esp. anger. **2** *Med.* **a** *intr.* become hot, reddened, and sore. **b** *tr.* cause inflammation or fever in (a body etc.). **3** *tr.* aggravate. **4** *intr.* & *tr.* catch or set on fire. **5** *tr.* light up with or as if with flames.

inflammable *adj.* **1** easily set on fire; flammable. **2** easily excited. □ **inflammability** *n.* **inflammableness** *n.*

■ **Usage** See Usage Note at FLAMMABLE.

inflammation *n.* **1** the act or an instance of inflaming. **2** *Med.* ◄ a localized physical condition with heat, swelling, redness, and usu. pain.

inflammatory *adj.* **1** (esp. of speeches etc.) tending to cause anger etc. **2** of or tending to cause inflammation of the body.

inflatable ● *adj.* that can be inflated. ● *n.* an inflatable object.

inflate *v.tr.* **1** distend (a balloon etc.) with air or gas. **2** (usu. foll. by *with*; usu. in *passive*) puff up (a person with pride etc.). **3 a** (often *absol.*) bring about inflation of (a currency). **b** raise (prices) artificially. **4** exaggerate or embellish. **5** (as **inflated** *adj.*) (esp. of language, sentiments, etc.) bombastic. [based on Latin *inflatus* 'blown into'] □ **inflatedly** *adv.* **inflatedness** *n.* **inflator** *n.*

inflation *n.* **1** the act of inflating. **2** *Econ.* **a** a general increase in prices. **b** an increase in available currency regarded as causing this. □ **inflationary** *adj.* **inflationist** *n. & adj.*

inflect *v.* **1** *tr.* change the pitch of (the voice, a musical note, etc.). **2** *Gram.* **a** *tr.* change the form of (a word) to express tense, gender, number, mood, etc. **b** *intr.* undergo such change. **3** *tr.* bend inwards; curve. [from Latin *inflectere*] □ **inflective** *adj.*

inflection *n.* (also **inflexion**) **1 a** the act or condition of inflecting or being inflected. **2** *Gram.* **a** the process or practice of inflecting words. **b** an inflected form of a word. **c** a suffix etc. used to inflect, e.g. *-ed.* **3** a modulation of the voice. **4** *Geom.* a change of curvature from convex to concave at a particular point on a curve. □ **inflectional** *adj.* **inflectionally** *adv.* **inflectionless** *adj.*

inflexible *adj.* **1** unbendable. **2** stiff; immovable; obstinate. □ **inflexibility** *n.* **inflexibly** *adv.*

inflict *v.tr.* (usu. foll. by *on, upon*) **1** administer, deal (a stroke, wound, defeat, etc.). **2** (also *refl.*) often *joc.* impose (suffering, a penalty, oneself, one's company, etc.) on (*shall not inflict myself on you any longer*). [based on Latin *inflictus* 'struck against'] □ **inflicter** *n.* **inflictor** *n.*

■ **Usage** Care should be taken not to confuse *inflict* with *afflict*. One *inflicts* something *on* or *upon* someone, or one is *afflicted with* or *by* something, e.g. *They were afflicted by a virus* is correct, as is *A virus was inflicted upon them.*

infliction *n.* **1** the act or an instance of inflicting. **2** something inflicted, esp. a troublesome or boring experience. [Late Latin *inflictio*]

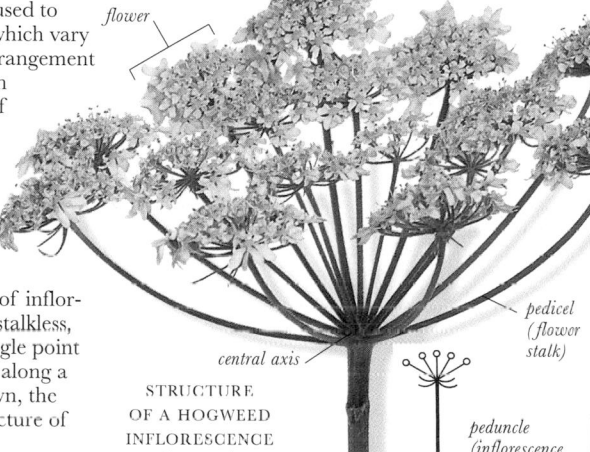

INFLORESCENCE

The term inflorescence is used to describe all flower heads, which vary greatly according to the arrangement of individual flowers within them. The simplest form of inflorescence is a solitary flower borne on a single stem. A capitulum often looks similar, but consists of a disc-like pad supporting a number of densely packed florets. The flowers in other types of inflorescence may be stalked or stalkless, and may radiate from a single point or be arranged at intervals along a stem. In the examples shown, the diagrams illustrate the structure of each type of inflorescence.

flower

pedicel (flower stalk)

central axis

STRUCTURE OF A HOGWEED INFLORESCENCE (UMBEL)

peduncle (inflorescence stalk)

EXAMPLES OF OTHER INFLORESCENCES

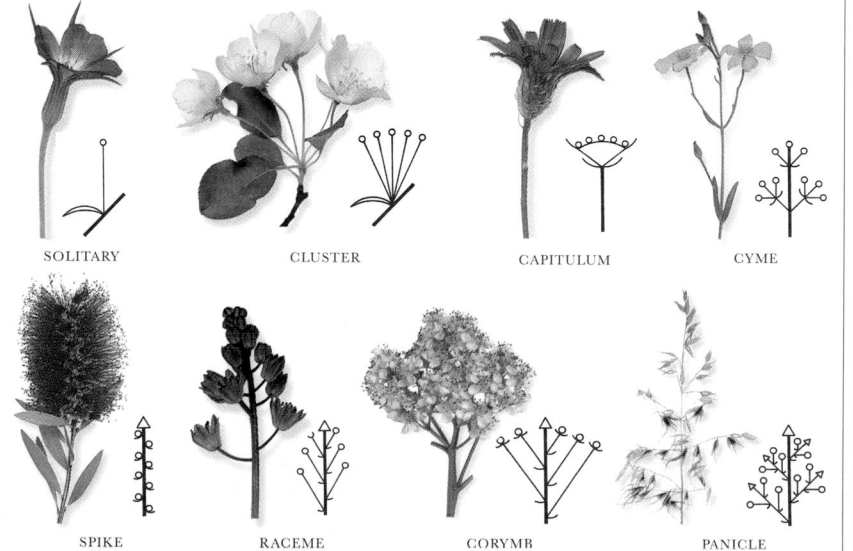

SOLITARY   CLUSTER   CAPITULUM   CYME

SPIKE   RACEME   CORYMB   PANICLE

in-flight *attrib.adj.* occurring or provided during an aircraft flight.

inflorescence *n.* **1** *Bot.* **a** ▼ the complete flower head of a plant including stems, stalks, bracts, and flowers. **b** the arrangement of this. **2** the process of flowering. [based on Late Latin *inflorescere* 'to come into flower']

inflow *n.* **1** a flowing in. **2** something that flows in. □ **inflowing** *n. & adj.*

influence ● *n.* **1** (usu. foll. by *on, upon*) the effect a person or thing has on another. **2** (usu. foll. by *over, with*) moral ascendancy or power. **3** a thing or person exercising such power (*is a good influence on them*). ● *v.tr.* exert influence on; have an effect on. □ **under the influence** *colloq.* drunk. [based on Latin *influent-* 'flowing in'] □ **influenceable** *adj.* **influencer** *n.*

influent ● *adj.* flowing in. ● *n.* a tributary stream.

influential *adj.* having a great influence or power. □ **influentially** *adv.*

influenza *n.* a highly contagious virus infection causing fever, severe aching, and catarrh, often occurring in epidemics. [from medieval Latin *influentia* 'influence'] □ **influenzal** *adj.*

influx *n.* (often foll. by *into*) **1** a continual stream of people or things (*an influx of complaints*). **2** (usu. foll. by *into*) a flowing in, esp. of a stream etc. [French *influx* or Late Latin *influxus*]

info *n. colloq.* information.

infomercial *n.* (also **informercial**) esp. *US* an advertising film, esp. on television, which promotes a product in an informative and purportedly objective style.

inform *v.* **1** *tr.* (usu. foll. by *of, about, on,* or *that, how* + clause) tell. **2** *intr.* (usu. foll. by *against, on*) give incriminating information about a person to the authorities. **3** *tr.* impart its quality to. [from Latin *informare* 'to give shape to, describe'] □ **informant** *n.*

informal *adj.* **1** without ceremony or formality (*just an informal chat*). **2** (of language, clothing, etc.) everyday; normal. □ **informality** *n.* (*pl.* **-ies**). **informally** *adv.*

information *n.* **1 a** something told; knowledge. **b** (usu. foll. by *on, about*) items of knowledge; news. **2** (usu. foll. by *against*) *Law* a charge or complaint lodged with a court or magistrate. **3 a** the act of informing or telling. **b** an instance of this. □ **informational** *adj.* **informationally** *adv.*

information retrieval *n.* the tracing and recovery of information stored in books, computers, etc.

information science *n.* the study of processes for storing and retrieving (esp. scientific or technical) information.

information superhighway see SUPERHIGHWAY.

information technology *n.* the study or use of systems (esp. computers, telecommunications, etc.) for storing, retrieving, and sending information.

informative *adj.* giving information; instructive. □ **informatively** *adv.* **informativeness** *n.*

informed *adj.* **1** with knowledge of the facts (*take an informed decision*). **2** educated; knowledgeable (*informed readers*).

informer *n.* **1** a person who informs against another. **2** a person who informs or advises.

informercial var. of INFOMERCIAL.

infotainment *n.* broadcast material intended both to entertain and to inform.

infra- *comb. form* **1** below (opp. SUPRA-). **2** *Anat.* below or under a part of the body. [from or suggested by Latin *infra* 'below, beneath']

infra *adv.* below, further on (in a book).

infraction *n.* esp. *Law* a violation or infringement. [from Latin *infractio,* related to INFRINGE]

infra dig *predic.adj. colloq.* beneath one's dignity; unbecoming. [abbreviation of Latin *infra dignitatem*]

infrangible *adj.* **1** unbreakable. **2** inviolable. □ **infrangibility** *n.* **infrangibly** *adv.* [obsolete French *infrangible* or medieval Latin *infrangibilis*]

I

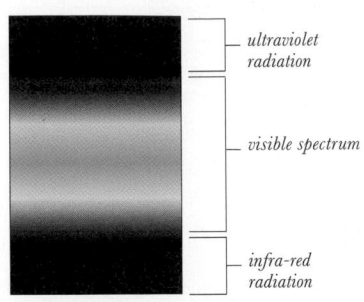

INFRA-RED RADIATION WITHIN
THE ELECTROMAGNETIC SPECTRUM

I

infra-red *adj.* (*US & Sci.* **infrared**) ▲ of or using electromagnetic radiation having a wavelength just greater than the red end of the visible spectrum. ▷ ELECTROMAGNETIC RADIATION, THERMOGRAPH

infrastructure *n.* **1 a** the basic structural foundations of a society or enterprise. **b** roads, bridges, sewers, etc., regarded as a country's economic foundation. **2** permanent installations as a basis for military etc. operations. □ **infrastructural** *adj.*

infrequent *adj.* not frequent. □ **infrequency** *n.* **infrequently** *adv.*

infringe *v.* **1** *tr.* **a** act contrary to; violate (a law, an oath, etc.). **b** act in defiance of (another's rights etc.). **2** *intr.* (usu. foll. by *on, upon*) encroach; trespass. [from Latin *infringere*] □ **infringement** *n.* **infringer** *n.*

infuriate *v.tr.* fill with fury; enrage. □ **infuriating** *adj.* **infuriatingly** *adv.*

infuse *v.* **1** *tr.* (usu. foll. by *with*) imbue; pervade (*anger infused with resentment*). **2** *tr.* steep (herbs, tea, etc.) in liquid to extract the content. **3** *tr.* (usu. foll. by *into*) instil (grace, spirit, life, etc.). **4** *intr.* undergo infusion (*let it infuse for five minutes*). [based on Latin *infusus* 'poured in'] □ **infusable** *adj.* **infuser** *n.*

infusible *adj.* not able to be fused or melted.

infusion *n.* **1** a liquid obtained by infusing. **2** an infused element; an admixture. **3** *Med.* a slow injection of a substance into a vein or tissue. **4 a** the act of infusing. **b** an instance of this.

ingenious *adj.* **1** clever at inventing, constructing, organizing, etc. **2** (of a machine, theory, etc.) cleverly contrived. [from Latin *ingeniosus*] □ **ingeniously** *adv.* **ingeniousness** *n.*

■ **Usage** See Usage Note at INGENUOUS.

ingénue /an-*zhay*-**new**/ *n.* **1** an innocent or unsophisticated young woman. **2** *Theatr.* such a part in a play. [French, literally 'ingenuous female']

ingenuity *n.* skill in devising or contriving. [from Latin *ingenuitas* 'ingenuousness': English sense by confusion of *ingenious* with *ingenuous*]

ingenuous *adj.* **1** innocent; artless. **2** open; frank. [from Latin *ingenuus* 'freeborn, frank'] □ **ingenuously** *adv.* **ingenuousness** *n.*

■ **Usage** *Ingenuous*, meaning 'open, frank, innocent', is sometimes confused with *ingenious*, which means 'clever at inventing'.

ingest *v.tr.* **1** take in (food etc.); eat. **2** absorb (facts, knowledge, etc.). [based on Latin *ingestus* 'carried in'] □ **ingestion** *n.* **ingestive** *adj.*

inglenook *n.* a space within the opening on either side of a large fireplace. [based on dialect (originally Scots) *ingle* 'fire burning on a hearth']

inglorious *adj.* **1** shameful; ignominious. **2** not famous. □ **ingloriously** *adv.* **ingloriousness** *n.*

ingoing *adj.* going in; entering.

ingot *n.* a usu. oblong piece of cast metal, esp. of gold, silver, or steel. [Middle English]

ingrain *v.tr.* (also **engrain**) **1** (esp. as **ingrained** *adj.*) implant (a habit, belief, or attitude) ineradicably in a person. **2** (as **ingrained** *adj.*) (of dirt etc.)

deeply embedded. [from Old French *engrainer* 'to dye in grain']

ingratiate *v.refl.* (usu. foll. by *with*) bring oneself into favour. [based on Latin *in gratiam* 'into favour'] □ **ingratiation** *n.*

ingratiating *adj.* intended to gain grace or favour. □ **ingratiatingly** *adv.*

ingratitude *n.* a lack of due gratitude.

ingredient *n.* a component part in a recipe, mixture, or combination. [from Latin *ingredient-* 'entering']

ingress *n.* the act or right of going in or entering. [from Latin *ingressus* 'entrance'] □ **ingression** *n.*

ingrowing *adj.* growing inwards, esp. (of a toenail) growing into the flesh. □ **ingrown** *adj.* **ingrowth** *n.*

inguinal /*ing*-gwin-ăl/ *adj.* of the groin. [based on Latin *inguen -inis* 'groin']

inhabit *v.tr.* (**inhabited**, **inhabiting**) (of a person or animal) dwell in; occupy. [from Latin *inhabitare*] □ **inhabitable** *adj.* **inhabitability** *n.* **inhabitant** *n.*

inhalant *n.* a medicine for inhaling.

inhale *v.tr.* (often *absol.*) breathe in (air, gas, tobacco smoke, etc.). [from Latin *inhalare* 'to breathe in'] □ **inhalation** *n.*

inhaler *n.* ▶ a device for administering an inhalant, esp. to relieve asthma. ▷ DRUG

inharmonious *adj.* esp. *Mus.* not harmonious. □ **inharmoniously** *adv.*

inhere *v.intr.* (often foll. by *in*) *formal* be inherent. [from Latin *inhaerēre*]

inherent *adj.* (often foll. by *in*) existing in something, esp. as a permanent or characteristic attribute. □ **inherently** *adv.*

inherit *v.tr.* (**inherited**, **inheriting**) **1** receive (property, rank, title, etc.) by legal descent or succession. **2** derive (a quality or characteristic) genetically from one's parents or ancestors. [based on Latin *heres* 'heir'] □ **inheritable** *adj.* **inheritability** *n.* **inheritor** *n.* (*fem.* **inheritrix**).

inheritance *n.* **1** something that is inherited. **2** the act of inheriting.

inheritance tax *n.* a tax levied on property etc. acquired by gift or inheritance.

inhibit *v.tr.* (**inhibited**, **inhibiting**) **1** hinder, restrain, or prevent (an action or progress). **2** (as **inhibited** *adj.*) subject to inhibition. **3** (usu. foll. by *from* + verbal noun) forbid or prohibit (a person etc.). [based on Latin *inhibitus* 'held in'] □ **inhibitor** *n.* **inhibitory** *adj.*

inhibition *n.* **1** *Psychol.* a restraint on the direct expression of an instinct. **2** *colloq.* an emotional resistance to a thought, an action, etc. (*no inhibitions about singing in public*). **3 a** the act of inhibiting. **b** the process of being inhibited.

inhospitable *adj.* **1** not hospitable. **2** (of a region,

canister

plastic outer casing

nozzle

mouthpiece

INHALER

coast, etc.) not affording shelter etc. □ **inhospitableness** *n.* **inhospitably** *adv.*

inhospitality *n.* the act or process of being inhospitable.

in-house ● *adj.* done or existing within an institution, company, etc. (*an in-house project*). ● *adv.* internally, without outside assistance.

inhuman *adj.* brutal; unfeeling; barbarous. □ **inhumanly** *adv.*

inhumane *adj.* not humane. □ **inhumanely** *adv.*

inhumanity *n.* (*pl.* **-ies**) **1** brutality; barbarousness; callousness. **2** an inhumane act.

inimical *adj.* (usu. foll. by *to*) **1** hostile. **2** harmful. [from Late Latin *inimicalis*] □ **inimically** *adv.*

inimitable *adj.* impossible to imitate. [from Latin *inimitabilis*] □ **inimitability** *n.* **inimitably** *adv.*

iniquity *n.* (*pl.* **-ies**) **1** wickedness; unrighteousness. **2** a gross injustice. [from Latin *iniquitas*] □ **iniquitous** *adj.* **iniquitously** *adv.*

initial ● *adj.* of, existing, or occurring at the beginning (*initial stage; initial expenses*). ● *n.* **1** = INITIAL LETTER. **2** the first letter of a name (esp. in *pl.*: *whose initials are JDP?*). ● *v.tr.* (**initialled**, **initialling**; *US* **initialed**, **initialing**) mark or sign with one's initials. [from Latin *initialis*] □ **initially** *adv.*

initialize *v.tr.* (also **-ise**) (often foll. by *to*) *Computing* set to the value or put in the condition appropriate to the start of an operation. □ **initialization** *n.*

initial letter *n.* a letter at the beginning of a word.

initiate ● *v.tr.* **1** begin; set going; originate. **2 a** (usu. foll. by *into*) admit (a person) into a society, an office etc., esp. with a ritual. **b** (usu. foll. by *in, into*) instruct (a person) in a science, art, etc. ● *n.* a person who has been newly initiated. ● *adj.* (of a person) newly initiated (*an initiate member*). [from Latin *initiatus* 'initiated'] □ **initiation** *n.* **initiator** *n.* **initiatory** *adj.*

initiative *n.* **1** the ability to initiate things; enterprise (*he lacks initiative*). **2** a first step; origination (*a peace initiative*). **3** the power or right to begin something. □ **on one's own initiative** without being prompted by others. **take the initiative** (often foll. by *in* + verbal noun) be the first to take action.

inject *v.tr.* **1** *Med.* **a** (usu. foll. by *into*) drive or force (a solution, medicine, etc.) by or as if by a syringe. **b** (usu. foll. by *with*) fill (a cavity etc.) by injecting. **c** administer medicine etc. to (a person) by injection. **2** insert or introduce by way of interruption or as a boost (*may I inject a note of realism?*). [based on Latin *injectus* 'thrown in'] □ **injectable** *adj. & n.* **injection** *n.* **injector** *n.*

injection moulding *n.* ▼ the shaping of rubber or plastic articles by injecting heated material into a mould. □ **injection-moulded** *adj.*

in-joke *n.* a joke that is shared exclusively by a group of people.

injudicious *adj.* unwise; ill-judged. □ **injudiciously** *adv.* **injudiciousness** *n.*

injunction *n.* **1** an authoritative warning or order. **2** *Law* a judicial order restraining a person from an act or compelling redress to an injured party. [from Late Latin *injunctio*] □ **injunctive** *adj.*

INJECTION MOULDING

INJECTION MOULDING PROCESS

In the process of injection moulding, plastic granules are fed through a hopper to be heated in a chamber. A screw in the chamber rotates, forcing the molten plastic into a mould, where it quickly cools and solidifies into the shape required.

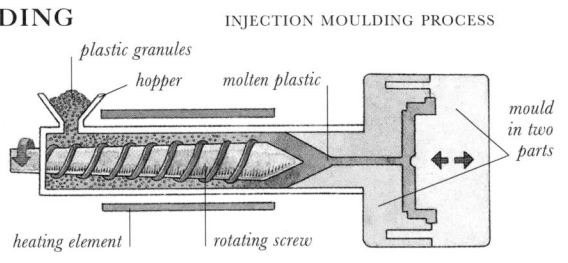

plastic granules

hopper

molten plastic

mould in two parts

heating element

rotating screw

injure *v.tr.* **1** hurt or damage. **2** harm or impair (*illness might injure her chances*). **3** do wrong to. □ **injurer** *n.*

injured *adj.* **1** harmed or hurt. **2** offended; wronged (*in an injured tone*).

injurious *adj.* **1** hurtful. **2** (of language) insulting; libellous. □ **injuriously** *adv.*

injury *n.* (*pl.* **-ies**) **1 a** physical harm or damage. **b** an instance of this (*head injuries*). **2** *esp. Law* wrongful action or treatment. [from Latin *injuria* 'a wrong']

injury time *n. Brit. Football* extra playing time allowed by a referee to compensate for time lost in dealing with injuries.

injustice *n.* **1** a lack of fairness or justice. **2** an unjust act. □ **do a person an injustice** judge a person unfairly.

ink ● *n.* **1** a coloured fluid or paste used for writing, printing, duplicating, etc. **2** *Zool.* a black liquid ejected by a cuttlefish, octopus, etc. ● *v.tr.* **1** (usu. foll. by *in*, *over*, etc.) mark with ink. **2** apply ink to. [from Greek *egkauston*, purple ink used by Roman emperors for signatures]

ink-blot test *n.* = RORSCHACH TEST.

ink-jet printer *n. Computing* a printer in which the characters are formed by minute jets of ink.

inkling *n.* (often foll. by *of*) a slight knowledge or suspicion; a hint. [from Middle English *inkle* 'to utter in an undertone']

inkwell *n.* a pot for ink usu. housed in a hole in a desk.

inky *adj.* (**inkier**, **inkiest**) of, as black as, or stained with ink. □ **inkiness** *n.*

inlaid *past* and *past part.* of INLAY.

inland ● *adj.* **1** situated in the interior of a country. **2** *esp. Brit.* carried on within the limits of a country; domestic (*inland trade*). ● *adv.* in or towards the interior of a country. □ **inlander** *n.*

inland navigation *n.* communication by canals and rivers.

Inland Revenue *n.* (in the UK) the government department responsible for assessing and collecting taxes and inland duties.

in-law *n.* (often in *pl.*) a relative by marriage.

inlay ● *v.tr.* (*past* and *past part.* **inlaid**) **1** (usu. foll. by *in*) embed (a thing in another) so that the surfaces are even. **2** (usu. foll. by *with*; often as **inlaid** *adj.*) ▼ ornament (a thing with inlaid work). ● *n.* **1** inlaid work. **2** material inlaid. □ **inlayer** *n.*

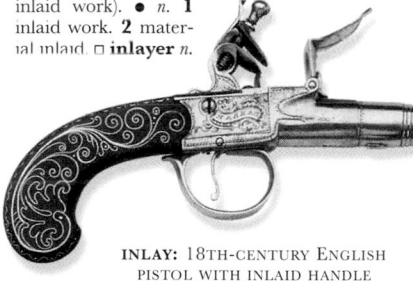

INLAY: 18TH-CENTURY ENGLISH PISTOL WITH INLAID HANDLE

inlet *n.* **1** a small arm of the sea, a lake, or a river. **2** a piece inserted, *esp.* in dressmaking etc. **3** a way of entry. [Middle English]

in-line *adj.* **1** having parts arranged in a line. **2** constituting an integral part of a continuous sequence of operations or machines.

in loco parentis /pă-ren-tis/ *adv.* in the place or position of a parent (used of a teacher etc. responsible for children). [Latin]

inmate *n.* (often foll. by *of*) an occupant of a hospital, prison, institution, etc.

in memoriam *prep.* in memory of (a dead person). [Latin]

inmost *adj.* **1** most inward. **2** most intimate.

inn *n.* **1** a public house providing alcoholic liquor for consumption on the premises, and sometimes accommodation etc. **2** *hist.* a house providing accommodation, *esp.* for travellers. [Old English]

INNER EAR

Inside the human inner ear the cochlea, a fluid-filled spiral, converts sound waves into electrical impulses, which are transmitted via the cochlear nerve to the brain. Three semicircular canals, also containing fluid, maintain our sense of balance. The canals are connected to the brain via the vestibular nerve.

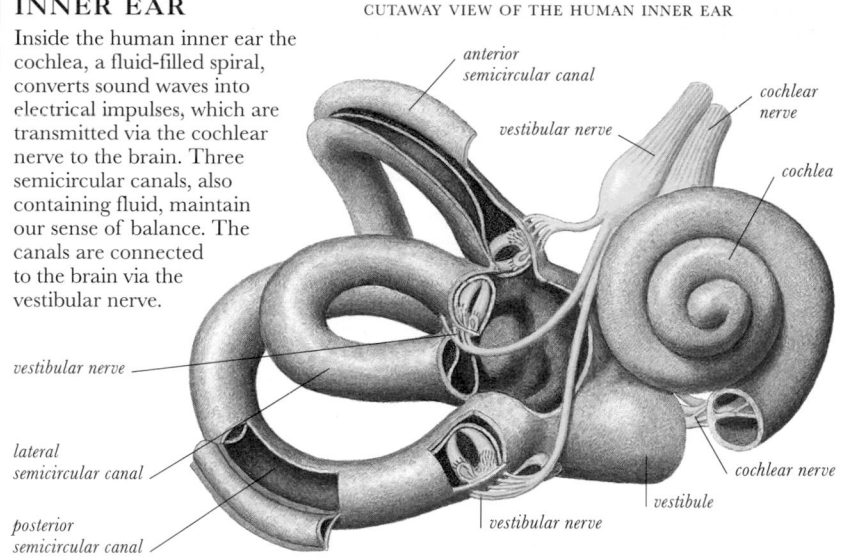

CUTAWAY VIEW OF THE HUMAN INNER EAR

anterior semicircular canal

cochlear nerve

vestibular nerve

cochlea

vestibular nerve

lateral semicircular canal

posterior semicircular canal

vestibular nerve

cochlear nerve

vestibule

innards *n.pl. colloq.* **1** entrails. **2** internal works (of an engine etc.).

innate *adj.* **1** inborn; natural. **2** *Philos.* originating in the mind. [Middle English from Latin *innatus*] □ **innately** *adv.* **innateness** *n.*

inner ● *adj.* (usu. *attrib.*) **1** further in; inside; interior (*the inner compartment*). **2** (of thoughts, feelings, etc.) deeper; more secret. ● *n. Brit.* the division of a target next to the bull's-eye. [Old English] □ **innerly** *adv.* **innermost** *adj.*

inner bar *n. Brit. Law* Queen's or King's Counsel collectively.

inner circle *n.* an exclusive group of friends or associates within a larger group.

inner city *n.* the area near the centre of a city, *esp.* when densely populated (also, with hyphen, *attrib.*: *inner-city housing*).

inner ear *n.* ▲ the semicircular canals and cochlea, which form the organs of balance and hearing. ▷ EAR

inner man *n.* (also **inner woman**) **1** the soul or mind. **2** *joc.* the stomach.

    inner tube *n.* a separate inflatable tube inside the cover of a pneumatic tyre.

    inner woman *n.* see INNER MAN.

inning *n. N. Amer.* each division of a game of baseball during which both sides have a turn at batting. [from earlier verb *in* 'to go in']

innings *n.* (*pl.* same or *colloq.* **inningses**) **1** *esp. Cricket* **a** the part of a game during which a side is in or batting. **b** the play or score of a player during a turn at batting. **2** a period during which a government, party, cause, etc. is in office or effective. **3** a period during which a person can achieve something.

innkeeper *n.* a person who keeps an inn.

innocent ● *adj.* **1** free from moral wrong; sinless. **2** (usu. foll. by *of*) not guilty (of a crime etc.). **3** free from responsibility for an event yet suffering its consequences (*innocent bystanders*). **4** simple; guileless; naive. **5** harmless. ● *n.* an innocent person, *esp.* a young child. [from Latin *innocent-* 'not hurting'] □ **innocence** *n.* **innocently** *adv.*

innocuous *adj.* **1** not injurious; harmless. **2** inoffensive. [from Latin *innocuus*] □ **innocuously** *adv.* **innocuousness** *n.*

Inn of Court *n. Brit. Law* each of the four legal societies having the exclusive right of admitting people to the English bar.

innovate *v.intr.* **1** bring in new methods, ideas, etc.

2 (often foll. by *in*) make changes. [based on Latin *innovatus* 'altered'] □ **innovation** *n.* **innovative** *adj.* **innovator** *n.* **innovatory** *adj.*

innuendo *n.* (*pl.* **-oes** or **-os**) **1** an allusive or oblique remark or hint, usu. disparaging. **2** a remark with a double meaning, usu. suggestive. [Latin, literally 'by nodding at, by pointing to']

innumerable *adj.* too many to be counted. □ **innumerably** *adv.*

innumerate *adj.* having no knowledge of or feeling for mathematical operations; not numerate. □ **innumeracy** *n.*

inoculate *v.tr.* treat (a person or animal) with a vaccine, usu. by injection, to promote immunity against a disease. [originally in sense 'to insert (a bud) into a plant': from Latin *inocular*] □ **inoculable** *adj.* **inoculation** *n.* **inoculator** *n.*

inoffensive *adj.* not objectionable; harmless. □ **inoffensively** *adv.* **inoffensiveness** *n.*

inoperable *adj.* **1** *Surgery* that cannot suitably be operated on (*inoperable cancer*). **2** that cannot be operated; inoperative. □ **inoperability** *n.* **inoperably** *adv.*

inoperative *adj.* not working or taking effect.

inopportune *adj.* not appropriate, *esp.* as regards time. □ **inopportunely** *adv.* **inopportuneness** *n.*

inordinate *adj.* immoderate; excessive. □ **inordinately** *adv.*

inorganic *adj.* **1** *Chem.* (of a compound) not organic, usu. of mineral origin (opp. ORGANIC 4). **2** without organized physical structure. **3** not arising by natural growth; extraneous. □ **inorganically** *adv.*

inorganic chemistry *n.* the chemistry of inorganic compounds.

in-patient *n.* a patient who lives in hospital while under treatment.

input ● *n.* **1** what is put in or taken in. **2** *Electronics* **a** a place where, or a device through which, energy, information, etc., enters a system (*a tape recorder with inputs for microphone and radio*). **b** energy supplied to a device or system; an electrical signal. **3** the action or process of putting in or feeding in. **4** a contribution of information etc. ● *v.tr.* (**inputting**; *past* and *past part.* **input** or **inputted**) (often foll. by *into*) **1** put in. **2** *Computing* supply (data, programs, etc., to a computer, program, etc.). □ **inputter** *n.*

inquest *n.* **1** *Law* **a** *Brit.* an inquiry by a coroner's court into the cause of a death. **b** a judicial inquiry to ascertain the facts relating to an incident etc. **2** *colloq.* a discussion analysing the outcome of a game, an election, etc. [from Old French *enqueste*]

inquietude *n.* uneasiness.

inquire *v.* **1** *intr.* seek information formally; make a formal investigation. **2** *intr. & tr.* = ENQUIRE. □ **inquirer** *n.*

■ **Usage** See Usage Note at ENQUIRE.

inquiry *n.* (*pl.* **-ies**) **1** an investigation, esp. an official one. **2** = ENQUIRY.

inquiry agent *n. Brit.* a private detective.

inquisition *n.* **1** usu. *derog.* an intensive search or investigation. **2** a judicial or official inquiry. **3** (**the Inquisition**) *RC Ch. hist.* an ecclesiastical tribunal for the suppression of heresy, esp. in Spain, using torture and execution. [from Latin *inquisitio* 'examination']

inquisitive *adj.* **1** unduly curious; prying. **2** seeking knowledge; inquiring. □ **inquisitively** *adv.* **inquisitiveness** *n.*

inquisitor *n.* **1** an official investigator. **2** *hist.* an officer of the Inquisition.

inquisitorial *adj.* **1** of or like an inquisitor. **2** offensively prying. **3** *Law* (of a trial etc.) in which the judge has a prosecuting role (opp. ACCUSATORIAL). □ **inquisitorially** *adv.*

inquorate *adj. Brit.* not constituting a quorum.

in re /**ray**/ *prep.* = RE¹ 1. [Latin, literally 'in the matter (of)']

inroad *n.* **1** (often in *pl.*; usu. foll. by *on, into*) an encroachment; a using up of resources etc. (*makes inroads on my time*). **2** a hostile attack.

inrush *n.* a rushing in; an influx. □ **inrushing** *adj. & n.*

insalubrious *adj.* (of a climate or place) unhealthy. □ **insalubrity** *n.*

insane *adj.* **1** not of sound mind; mad. **2** *colloq.* extremely foolish. □ **insanely** *adv.* **insanity** *n.* (*pl.* **-ies**).

insanitary *adj.* not sanitary; dirty.

insatiable *adj.* **1** unable to be satisfied. **2** (usu. foll. by *of*) extremely greedy. [from Latin *insatiabilis*] □ **insatiability** *n.* **insatiably** *adv.*

inscribe *v.tr.* **1 a** (usu. foll. by *in, on*) write or carve (words etc.) on stone, metal, a book, etc. **b** (usu. foll. by *with*) mark (a surface) with characters. **2** (usu. foll. by *to*) write an informal dedication (to a person) in or on (a book etc.). **3** enter the name of (a person) on a list or in a book. [from Latin *inscribere*]

inscription *n.* **1** words inscribed, esp. on a stone, monument, coin, in a book, etc. **2** the act of inscribing. [from Latin *inscriptio*] □ **inscriptional** *adj.*

inscrutable *adj.* wholly mysterious, impenetrable. [based on Latin *scrutari* 'to search thoroughly'] □ **inscrutability** *n.* **inscrutably** *adv.*

insect *n.* **1** ▶ any arthropod of the class Insecta, having a head, thorax, abdomen, two antennae, three pairs of thoracic legs, and usu. one or two pairs of thoracic wings. ▷ EXOSKELETON. **2** (loosely) any other small invertebrate animal esp. with several pairs of legs. [from Latin *insectum (animal)* 'notched (animal)']

insecticide *n.* a substance used for killing insects. □ **insecticidal** *adj.*

insectivore *n.* **1** ▶ any animal that feeds on insects, esp. a mammal of the order Insectivora, including shrews, hedgehogs, and moles. **2** any plant which captures and absorbs insects. [French] □ **insectivorous** *adj.*

insecure *adj.* **1** (of a person or state of mind) uncertain; lacking confidence. **2 a** unsafe; not firm or fixed. **b** (of ice, ground, etc.) liable to give way. □ **insecurely** *adv.* **insecurity** *n.*

inseminate *v.tr.* **1** introduce semen into (a female) by natural or artificial means. **2** sow (seed etc.). [based on Latin *inseminatus* 'sown in'] □ **insemination** *n.* **inseminator** *n.*

insensate *adj.* **1** without physical sensation; unconscious. **2** without sensibility; unfeeling. **3** stupid. [from ecclesiastical Latin *insensatus*] □ **insensately** *adv.*

insensible *adj.* **1** unconscious. **2** (usu. foll. by *of, to*) unaware; indifferent (*insensible of her needs*). **3** without emotion; callous. □ **insensibility** *n.* **insensibly** *adv.*

insensitive *adj.* (often foll. by *to*) **1** showing or feeling no sympathetic or emotional response. **2** not sensitive to physical stimuli. □ **insensitively** *adv.* **insensitiveness** *n.* **insensitivity** *n.*

insentient *adj.* not sentient; inanimate. □ **insentience** *n.*

inseparable *adj.* (esp. of friends) unable or unwilling to be separated. □ **inseparability** *n.* **inseparably** *adv.*

insert ● *v.tr.* **1** (usu. foll. by *in, into, between*, etc.) place, fit, or thrust (a thing) into another. **2** (usu. foll. by *in, into*) introduce (a letter, word, article, advertisement, etc.) into a newspaper etc. ● *n.* something inserted, e.g. a loose page in a magazine. [from Latin *insertus* 'put into'] □ **inserter** *n.*

insertion *n.* **1** the act or an instance of inserting. **2** an amendment etc. inserted in writing or printing. **3** each appearance of an advertisement in a newspaper etc. **4** an ornamental section of needlework inserted into plain material (*lace insertions*).

in-service *attrib.adj.* (of training) intended for those actively engaged in the profession or activity concerned.

INSET /**in**-set/ *n.* (often *attrib.*) training during term-time for teachers in British state schools. [acronym from *in*-service *e*ducation and *t*raining]

inset ● *n.* **1 a** an extra page or pages inserted in a folded sheet or in a book; an insert. **b** a small map, photograph, etc., inserted within the border of a larger one. **2** a piece let into a dress etc. ● *v.tr.* (**insetting**; *past* and *past part.* **inset** or **insetted**) **1** put in as an inset. **2** decorate with an inset.

inshore *adv. & adj.* at sea but close to the shore. □ **inshore of** nearer to shore than.

inside ● *n.* **1 a** the inner side or surface of a thing. **b** the inner part; the interior. **2** the side of a path next to the wall or away from the road. **3** (usu. in *pl.*) *colloq.* the stomach and bowels (*something wrong with my insides*). **4** *colloq.* a position affording inside information (*knows someone on the inside*). ● *adj.* **1** situated on or in, or derived from, the inside. **2** *Hockey* & (now less often) *Football* nearer to the centre of the field (*inside forward; inside left; inside right*). ● *adv.* **1** on, in, or to the inside. **2** *slang* in prison. ● *prep.* **1** on the inner side of; within (*inside the house*). **2** in less than (*inside an hour*). □ **inside of** *colloq.* in less than (a week etc.).

inside information *n.* information not accessible to outsiders.

inside job *n. colloq.* a crime committed by a person living or working on the premises burgled etc.

inside out ● *adv.* with the inner surface turned outwards. ● *attrib.adj.* (**inside-out**) in this condition (*an inside-out building with lifts on the outside*). □ **know a thing inside out** know a thing thoroughly. **turn inside out 1** turn the inner surface outwards. **2** *colloq.* cause confusion or a mess in.

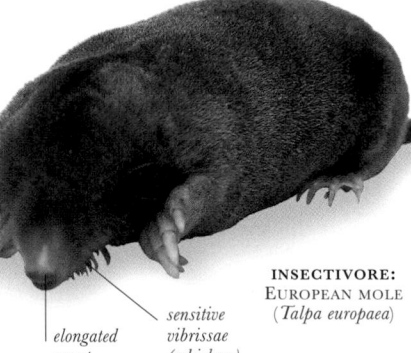

INSECTIVORE:
EUROPEAN MOLE
(*Talpa europaea*)

elongated snout   *sensitive vibrissae (whiskers)*

insider *n.* **1** a person who is within a society, organization, etc. **2** a person privy to a secret.

insider dealing *n.* (also **insider trading**) *Stock Exch.* the illegal practice of trading to one's own advantage through having access to confidential information.

inside track *n.* **1** the track which is shorter, because of the curve. **2** a position of advantage.

insidious *adj.* **1** proceeding or progressing inconspicuously but harmfully (*an insidious disease*). **2** treacherous; crafty. [from Latin *insidiosus* 'cunning'] □ **insidiously** *adv.*

insight *n.* (usu. foll. by *into*) **1** the capacity of understanding hidden truths etc., esp. of character or situation. **2** an instance of this. □ **insightful** *adj.* **insightfully** *adv.*

insignia /in-**sig**-niǎ/ *n.* (treated as *sing.* or *pl.*; usu. foll. by *of*) **1** ▼ badges (*wore his insignia of office*). **2** distinguishing marks. [Latin, literally 'distinguished (things)']

eagle emblem

battle honour commemoration

INSIGNIA: FIRST WORLD WAR PRUSSIAN
MILITARY INSIGNIA

■ **Usage** *Insignia* is, in origin, a plural noun; its singular form *insigne* is rarely encountered. *Insignia* can be treated as a singular or plural, e.g. *He was wearing camouflage dress, and no rank insignia was/were visible*, but should not be used as a countable noun.

insignificant *adj.* **1** unimportant. **2** (of a person) undistinguished. **3** meaningless. □ **insignificance** *n.* **insignificantly** *adv.*

insincere *adj.* not sincere. □ **insincerely** *adv.* **insincerity** *n.* (*pl.* **-ies**).

insinuate *v.tr.* **1** convey indirectly or obliquely; hint (*insinuated that she was lying*). **2** (often *refl.*; usu. foll. by *into*) **a** introduce (oneself, a person, etc.) into favour, office, etc., by subtle manipulation. **b** introduce (a thing, an idea, oneself, etc.) deviously into a place (*insinuated himself into the Royal Box*). [based on Latin *insinuatus* 'curved in'] □ **insinuatingly** *adv.* **insinuation** *n.*

insipid *adj.* **1** lacking vigour or interest; dull. **2** lacking flavour; tasteless. [from Late Latin *insipidus*] □ **insipidity** *n.* **insipidly** *adv.* **insipidness** *n.*

insist *v.tr.* (usu. foll. by *that* + clause; also *absol.*) maintain or demand assertively (*insisted that he was innocent; give me the bag! I insist!*). □ **insist on** demand or maintain (*I insist on being present; insists on his suitability*). [from Latin *insistere* 'to stand on, persist']

insistent *adj.* **1** (often foll. by *on*) insisting; demanding positively or continually (*is insistent on taking me with him*). **2** obtruding itself on the attention (*the insistent rattle of the window frame*). □ **insistence** *n.* **insistently** *adv.*

in situ /**sit**-yoo/ *adv.* **1** in its place. **2** in its original place. [Latin]

insobriety *n.* intemperance, esp. in drinking.

insofar *adv.* = in so far (see FAR).

insolation *n.* exposure to the Sun's rays, esp. for bleaching. [based on Latin *sol* 'sun']

insole *n.* **1** a removable sole worn in a boot or shoe for warmth etc. **2** the fixed inner sole of a boot or shoe. ▷ SHOE

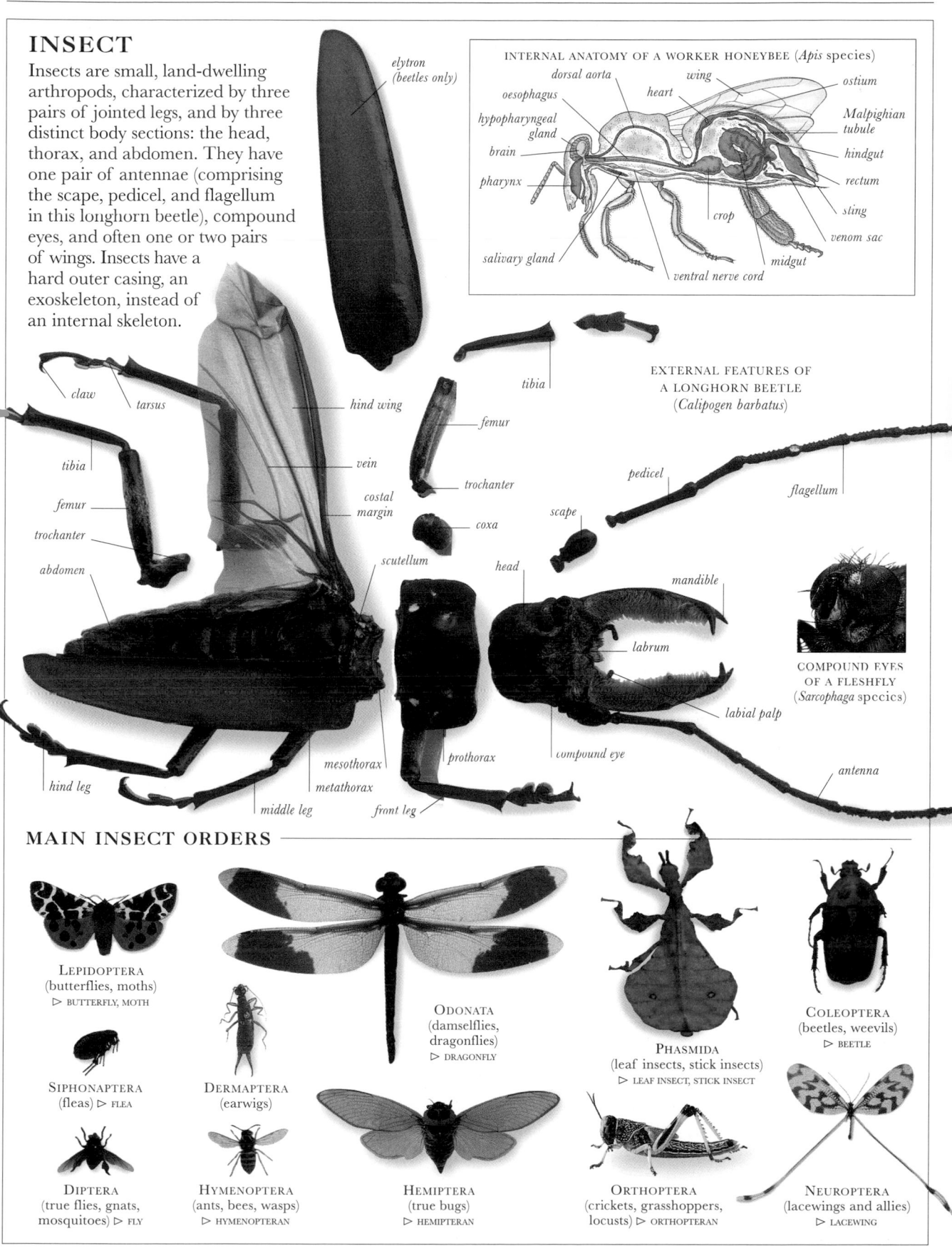

INSECT

Insects are small, land-dwelling arthropods, characterized by three pairs of jointed legs, and by three distinct body sections: the head, thorax, and abdomen. They have one pair of antennae (comprising the scape, pedicel, and flagellum in this longhorn beetle), compound eyes, and often one or two pairs of wings. Insects have a hard outer casing, an exoskeleton, instead of an internal skeleton.

elytron (beetles only)

INTERNAL ANATOMY OF A WORKER HONEYBEE (*Apis* species)

dorsal aorta
oesophagus
heart
wing
ostium
hypopharyngeal gland
brain
Malpighian tubule
pharynx
hindgut
rectum
salivary gland
crop
sling
venom sac
ventral nerve cord
midgut

EXTERNAL FEATURES OF A LONGHORN BEETLE (*Calipogen barbatus*)

claw
tarsus
tibia
hind wing
femur
tibia
femur
vein
trochanter
costal margin
coxa
scape
pedicel
flagellum
trochanter
abdomen
scutellum
head
mandible
labrum

COMPOUND EYES OF A FLESHFLY (*Sarcophaga* species)

labial palp
hind leg
mesothorax
metathorax
prothorax
compound eye
middle leg
front leg
antenna

MAIN INSECT ORDERS

LEPIDOPTERA
(butterflies, moths)
▷ BUTTERFLY, MOTH

SIPHONAPTERA
(fleas) ▷ FLEA

DERMAPTERA
(earwigs)

ODONATA
(damselflies, dragonflies)
▷ DRAGONFLY

PHASMIDA
(leaf insects, stick insects)
▷ LEAF INSECT, STICK INSECT

COLEOPTERA
(beetles, weevils)
▷ BEETLE

DIPTERA
(true flies, gnats, mosquitoes) ▷ FLY

HYMENOPTERA
(ants, bees, wasps)
▷ HYMENOPTERAN

HEMIPTERA
(true bugs)
▷ HEMIPTERAN

ORTHOPTERA
(crickets, grasshoppers, locusts) ▷ ORTHOPTERAN

NEUROPTERA
(lacewings and allies)
▷ LACEWING

419

insolent *adj.* offensively contemptuous or arrogant; insulting. [from Latin *insolent-* 'being unaccustomed'] □ **insolence** *n.* **insolently** *adv.*

insoluble *adj.* **1** incapable of being solved. **2** incapable of being dissolved. □ **insolubility** *n.* **insolubly** *adv.*

insolvent ● *adj.* **1** unable to pay one's debts. **2** relating to insolvency (*insolvent laws*). ● *n.* an insolvent person. □ **insolvency** *n.*

insomnia *n.* habitual sleeplessness; inability to sleep. [Latin] □ **insomniac** *n. & adj.*

insomuch *adv.* **1** (foll. by *that* + clause) to such an extent. **2** (foll. by *as*) inasmuch.

insouciant /in-soo-si-ănt/ *adj.* carefree; unconcerned. [French] □ **insouciance** *n.* **insouciantly** *adv.*

inspect *v.tr.* **1** look closely at or into. **2** examine officially. [from Latin *inspicere* 'to look into' or *inspectare* 'to view'] □ **inspection** *n.*

inspector *n.* **1** a person who inspects. **2** an official employed to supervise. **3** a police officer below a superintendent and (*Brit.*) above a sergeant in rank. □ **inspectorate** *n.* **inspectorial** *adj.*

inspiration *n.* **1 a** a supposed force or influence on poets, artists, musicians, etc., stimulating creativity, ideas, etc. **b** a person, principle, faith, etc. as a source of creativity or moral fervour. **c** a similar divine influence supposed to have led to the writing of Scripture etc. **2** a sudden brilliant idea. **3** a drawing in of breath; inhalation. □ **inspirational** *adj.*

inspire *v.tr.* **1** stimulate (a person) to esp. creative activity or moral fervour (*inspired her to write; inspired by God*). **2 a** (usu. foll. by *with*) animate (a person) with a feeling. **b** (usu. foll. by *into*) instil (a feeling) into a person etc. **c** (usu. foll. by *in*) create (a feeling) in a person. **3** prompt; give rise to (*the poem was inspired by the autumn*). **4** (as **inspired** *adj.*) **a** (of a work of art etc.) as if prompted by or emanating from a supernatural source; characterized by inspiration (*an inspired speech*). **b** (of a guess) intuitive but accurate. **5** (also *absol.*) breathe in (air etc.); inhale. [from Latin *inspirare* 'to breathe into'] □ **inspiratory** *adj.* **inspiredly** *adv.* **inspirer** *n.* **inspiring** *adj.* **inspiringly** *adv.*

inspirit *v.tr.* (**inspirited**, **inspiriting**) **1** put life into; animate. **2** (usu. foll. by *to*, or *to* + infin.) encourage (a person). □ **inspiriting** *adj.* **inspiritingly** *adv.*

inst. *abbr.* **1** = INSTANT *adj.* 4 (*the 6th inst.*). **2** institute. **3** institution.

instability *n.* (*pl.* **-ies**) **1** a lack of stability. **2** *Psychol.* unpredictability in behaviour etc. **3** an instance of instability.

install *v.tr.* (also **instal**) (**installed**, **installing**) **1** place in position ready for use. **2** place in an office or rank with ceremony (*installed in the office of chancellor*). **3** establish (oneself, a person, etc.) in a place, condition, etc. (*installed herself at the head of the table*). [from medieval Latin *installare*] □ **installer** *n.*

installation *n.* **1 a** the act or an instance of installing. **b** the process or an instance of being installed. **2 a** a large piece of equipment etc. installed for use. **b** a subsidiary military or industrial establishment.

instalment *n.* (*US* **installment**) **1** a sum of money due as one of several usu. equal payments for something. **2** any of several parts, esp. of a television or radio serial or a magazine story. [from Anglo-French *estalement* 'a fixing']

instance ● *n.* **1** an example or illustration (*just another instance of his lack of determination*). **2** a particular case (*that's not true in this instance*). ● *v.tr.* cite as an instance. □ **at the instance of** at the request or suggestion of. **for instance** as an example. **in the first** (or **second** etc.) **instance** in the first (or second etc.) place; at the first (or second etc.) stage of a proceeding. [from Latin *instantia*]

instant ● *adj.* **1** occurring immediately (*an instant result*). **2 a** (of food etc.) processed to allow quick

preparation. **b** prepared with little effort (*I have no instant solution*). **3** urgent; pressing. **4** *Commerce* of the current month (*the 6th instant*). ● *n.* **1** a precise moment (*come here this instant; told you the instant I heard*). **2** a short space of time (*was there in an instant*). [from Latin *instant-* 'being present, pressing upon']

instantaneous *adj.* **1** occurring or done in an instant. **2** *Physics* existing at a particular instant. [from medieval Latin *instantaneus*] □ **instantaneity** *n.* **instantaneously** *adv.*

instantiate *v.tr.* represent by an instance. □ **instantiation** *n.*

instantly *adv.* **1** immediately; at once. **2** *archaic* urgently; pressingly.

instead *adv.* **1** (foll. by *of*) as a substitute or alternative to; in place of (*instead of this one; stayed instead of going*). **2** as an alternative (*took me instead*) (cf. STEAD).

instep *n.* **1** the inner arch of the foot between the toes and the ankle. **2** the part of a shoe etc. fitting over or under this.

instigate *v.tr.* **1** bring about by incitement or persuasion (*who instigated the inquiry?*). **2** (usu. foll. by *to*) urge on, incite. [based on Latin *instigatus* 'urged'] □ **instigation** *n.* **instigator** *n.*

instil *v.tr.* (*US* **instill**) (**instilled**, **instilling**) **1** introduce (a feeling, idea, etc.) into a person's mind etc. gradually. **2** put (a liquid) into something in drops. [from Latin *instillare* 'to put in by drops'] □ **instillation** *n.*

instinct ● *n.* **1 a** an innate pattern of behaviour in most animals in response to certain stimuli. **b** a similar propensity in human beings to act without conscious intention; innate impulsion. **2** (usu. foll. by *for*) unconscious skill; intuition. ● *predic.adj.* (foll. by *with*) imbued, filled (with life, beauty, force, etc.). [Middle English in sense 'impulse'] □ **instinctual** *adj.* **instinctually** *adv.*

instinctive *adj.* **1** relating to or prompted by instinct. **2** apparently unconscious or automatic (*an instinctive reaction*). □ **instinctively** *adv.*

institute ● *n.* **1** a society or organization for the promotion of science, education, etc. **2** a building used by an institute. ● *v.tr.* **1** establish; found. **2 a** initiate (an inquiry etc.). **b** begin (proceedings) in a court. **3** (usu. foll. by *to*, *into*) appoint (a person) as a cleric in a church etc. [from Latin *institutum*, literally 'established (thing)']

institution *n.* **1** the act or an instance of instituting. **2 a** a society or organization founded esp. for charitable, religious, educational, or social purposes. **b** a building used by an institution. **3** an established law, practice, or custom. **4** *colloq.* (of a person, a custom, etc.) a familiar object. **5** the establishment of a cleric etc. in a church, parish, etc.

institutional *adj.* **1** of or like an institution. **2** typical of institutions, esp. in being regimented or unimaginative (*the food was dreadfully institutional*). **3** (of religion) expressed or organized through institutions (Churches etc.). □ **institutionalism** *n.* **institutionally** *adv.*

institutionalize *v.tr.* (also **-ise**) **1** (as **institutionalized** *adj.*) **a** made dependent after a long period in an institution. **b** established in practice or custom (*institutionalized secrecy*). **2** place or keep (a person) in an institution. **3** convert into an institution; make institutional. □ **institutionalization** *n.*

in-store *adj. & adv.* within a store (*in-store bakery*).

instruct *v.tr.* **1** teach (a person) a subject etc. (*instructed her in French*). **2** (usu. foll. by *to* + infin.) direct; command (*instructed him to fill in the hole*). **3** inform (a person) of a fact etc. **4** *Brit.* **a** (of a client or solicitor) give information to (a solicitor or counsel). **b** authorize (a solicitor or counsel) to act for one. [based on Latin *instructus* 'built, taught']

instruction *n.* **1** (often in *pl.*) a direction; an order (*gave him his instructions*). **2** teaching; education (*took a course of instruction*). **3** *Brit. Law* (in *pl.*) directions to a solicitor or counsel. **4** *Computing* a direction in a

computer program defining and effecting an operation. □ **instructional** *adj.*

instructive *adj.* tending to instruct; enlightening (*found the experience instructive*). □ **instructively** *adv.*

instructor *n.* (*fem.* **instructress**) **1** a person who instructs; a teacher, demonstrator, etc. **2** *N. Amer.* a university teacher ranking below assistant professor.

instrument ● *n.* **1** a tool or implement, esp. for delicate or scientific work. **2** (in full **musical instrument**) a device for producing musical sounds. ▷ ORCHESTRA. **3 a** a thing used in performing an action (*the meeting was an instrument in his success*). **b** a person made use of (*is merely their instrument*). **4** a measuring device, esp. in a car or aircraft. **5** a formal, esp. legal, document. ● *v.tr.* **1** arrange (music) for instruments. **2** equip with instruments (for measuring, recording, controlling, etc.). [from Latin *instrumentum*]

instrumental ● *adj.* **1** serving as an instrument or means (*was instrumental in finding the money*). **2** (of music) performed on instruments, without singing (cf. VOCAL *adj.* 4). **3** of, or arising from, an instrument (*instrumental error*). ● *n.* a piece of music performed by instruments, not by the voice. □ **instrumentalist** *n.* **instrumentality** *n.* **instrumentally** *adv.*

instrumentation *n.* **1 a** the arrangement or composition of music for a particular group of musical instruments. **b** the instruments used in any one piece of music. **2 a** the design, provision, or use of instruments in industry, science, etc. **b** such instruments collectively.

instrument panel *n.* (also **instrument board**) ▼ a surface, esp. in a car or aeroplane, containing the dials etc. of measuring devices.

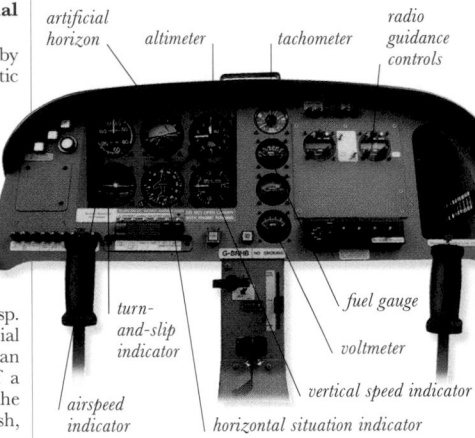

INSTRUMENT PANEL OF A LIGHT AIRCRAFT

Labels: artificial horizon · altimeter · tachometer · radio guidance controls · turn-and-slip indicator · fuel gauge · voltmeter · airspeed indicator · horizontal situation indicator · vertical speed indicator

insubordinate *adj.* disobedient; rebellious. □ **insubordination** *n.*

insubstantial *adj.* **1** lacking solidity or substance. **2** not real. □ **insubstantiality** *n.*

insufferable *adj.* **1** intolerable. **2** unbearably conceited etc. □ **insufferably** *adv.*

insufficient *adj.* not sufficient; inadequate. □ **insufficiency** *n.* **insufficiently** *adv.*

insular *adj.* **1 a** of or like an island. **b** separated or remote. **2** ignorant of or indifferent to cultures, peoples, etc., outside one's own experience; narrow-minded. [from Late Latin *insularis*] □ **insularity** *n.*

insulate *v.tr.* **1** prevent the passage of electricity, heat, or sound from (a thing, room, etc.) by interposing non-conductors. **2** detach (a person or thing) from their surroundings; isolate. [based on Latin *insula* 'island'] □ **insulation** *n.* ▷ FLEX, HOUSE, SOLAR PANEL.

insulator *n.* **1** a thing or substance used for insulation against electricity, heat, or sound. **2** an insulating device to support telegraph wires etc.

3 a device preventing contact between electrical conductors.

insulin *n. Biochem.* a polypeptide hormone produced in the pancreas, which regulates the amount of glucose in the blood, and the lack of which causes diabetes. [based on Latin *insula* 'island']

insult ● *v.tr.* **1** speak to or treat with scornful abuse. **2** offend the self-respect or modesty of. ● *n.* **1** an insulting remark or action. **2** something so worthless or contemptible as to be offensive (*an insult to his intelligence*). [from Latin *insultare*] □ **insulting** *adj.* **insultingly** *adv.*

insuperable *adj.* **1** (of a barrier) impossible to surmount. **2** (of a difficulty etc.) impossible to overcome. □ **insuperability** *n.* **insuperably** *adv.*

insupportable *adj.* **1** unable to be endured. **2** unjustifiable. □ **insupportably** *adv.*

insurance *n.* **1** the act or an instance of insuring. **2 a** a sum paid for this; a premium. **b** a sum paid out as compensation for theft, damage, loss, etc. **3** the business of providing insurance policies. **4** = INSURANCE POLICY. **5** a measure taken to provide for a possible contingency (*take an umbrella as insurance*). [from Old French *enseürance*]

insurance policy *n.* **1** a contract of insurance. **2** a document detailing such a policy and constituting a contract.

insure *v.tr.* **1** (often foll. by *against*; also *absol.*) secure the payment of a sum of money in the event of loss or damage to (property, life, a person, etc.) by regular payments or premiums (*insured the house for £100,000; we have insured against flood damage*). **2** (of the owner of a property, an insurance company, etc.) secure the payment of (a sum of money) in this way. **3** (usu. foll. by *against*) provide for (a possible contingency) (*insured themselves against the rain by taking umbrellas*). **4** *US* = ENSURE. [Middle English variant of ENSURE] □ **insurable** *adj.*

insured ● *adj.* covered by insurance. ● *n.* (usu. prec. by *the*) a person etc. covered by insurance.

insurer *n.* **1** a person or company offering insurance policies for premiums; an underwriter. **2** a person who takes out insurance.

insurgent ● *adj.* in active revolt. ● *n.* a rebel; a revolutionary. [from Latin *insurgent-* 'rising up'] □ **insurgence** *n.* **insurgency** *n.* (*pl.* **-ies**).

insurmountable *adj.* unable to be surmounted or overcome. □ **insurmountably** *adv.*

insurrection *n.* a rebellion. [from Late Latin *insurrectio*] □ **insurrectionary** *adj.* **insurrectionist** *n.*

insusceptible *adj.* (usu. foll. by *to*) not susceptible (to treatment, an influence, etc.).

intact *adj.* **1** entire; unimpaired. **2** untouched. [from Latin *intactus* 'untouched'] □ **intactness** *n.*

intaglio /in-tal-yoh/ *n.* (*pl.* **-os**) **1** ► a gem with an incised design. **2** an engraved design. **3** a carving, esp. incised, in hard material. **4** a process of printing from an engraved design. [Italian] ▷ PRINTING

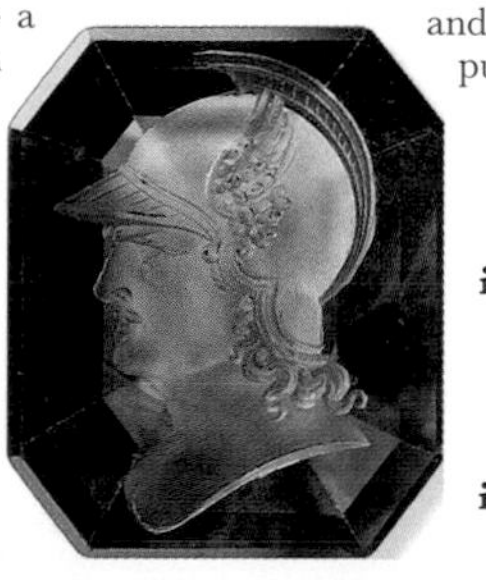

INTAGLIO: REPRODUCTION ROMAN INTAGLIO SEAL

intake *n.* **1 a** the action of taking in. **b** an instance of this. **2 a** a number (of people etc.) or the amount taken in or received (*this year's intake of students*). **b** such people etc. **3** a place where water is taken into a channel or pipe from a river, or fuel or air enters an engine etc.

intangible ● *adj.* **1** unable to be touched. **2** unable to be grasped mentally. ● *n.* something that cannot be precisely measured or assessed. □ **intangibility** *n.* **intangibly** *adv.*

integer /in-ti-jer/ *n.* **1** a whole number. **2** a thing complete in itself. [from Latin adj., literally 'untouched, whole']

integral ● *adj.* **1 a** of a whole or necessary to the completeness of a whole. **b** forming a whole (*integral design*). **c** complete. **2** *Math.* **a** of or denoted by an integer. **b** involving only integers, esp. as coefficients of a function. ● *n. Math.* a quantity of which a given function is the derivative, i.e. which yields that function when differentiated, and which may express the area under the curve of a graph of the function. [from Late Latin *integralis*] □ **integrality** *n.* **integrally** *adv.*

integral calculus *n.* mathematics concerned with finding integrals, their properties and application, etc. (cf. DIFFERENTIAL CALCULUS).

integrate *v.* **1** *tr.* **a** combine (parts) into a whole. **b** complete (an imperfect thing) by the addition of parts. **2** *tr.* & *intr.* bring or come into equal participation in or membership of society, a school, etc. **3** *tr.* desegregate, esp. racially. **4** *tr. Math.* find the integral of. [based on Latin *integratus* 'made whole'] □ **integrable** *adj.* **integrative** *adj.* **integrator** *n.*

integrated circuit *n.* a small chip etc. of material incorporating the functions of several separate components of a conventional electrical circuit.

integration *n.* **1** the act or an instance of integrating. **2** the intermixing of persons previously segregated. □ **integrationist** *n.* & *adj.*

integrity *n.* **1** moral uprightness; honesty. **2** wholeness; soundness. [from Latin *integritas* 'wholeness']

integument *n.* a natural outer covering, as a skin, husk, rind, etc. [from Latin *integumentum*] □ **integumentary** *adj.*

intellect *n.* **1 a** the faculty of reasoning, knowing, and thinking, as distinct from feeling. **b** the understanding or mental powers (of a particular person etc.) (*his intellect is not great*). **2** a clever or knowledgeable person. [from Latin *intellectus* 'understanding']

intellectual ● *adj.* **1** of or relating to the intellect. **2** possessing a high level of understanding or intelligence. **3** requiring, or appealing to, the intellect. ● *n.* a person possessing a highly developed intellect. □ **intellectuality** *n.* **intellectualize** *v.tr.* & *intr.* (also **-ise**). **intellectually** *adv.*

intellectualism *n.* the exercise of the intellect at the expense of the emotions.

intelligence *n.* **1 a** the intellect; the understanding. **b** quickness of understanding. **2 a** the collection of information, esp. of military or political value. **b** people employed in this. **c** information so collected. **3** an intelligent or rational being.

intelligence quotient *n.* a number denoting the ratio of a person's intelligence to the statistical norm, 100 being average.

intelligence test *n.* a test designed to measure intelligence rather than acquired knowledge.

intelligent *adj.* **1** having or showing intelligence, esp. of a high level. **2** clever. **3 a** (of a device or machine) able to vary its behaviour in response to varying situations and requirements and past experience. **b** (esp. of a computer terminal) having its own data-processing capability; incorporating a microprocessor (opp. DUMB 7). [from Latin *intelligent-* 'understanding'] □ **intelligently** *adv.*

intelligentsia *n.* **1** the class of intellectuals regarded as possessing culture and political initiative. **2** people doing intellectual work; intellectuals. [Russian]

intelligible *adj.* able to be understood. [from Latin *intelligibilis*] □ **intelligibility** *n.* **intelligibly** *adv.*

intemperate *adj.* **1** (of a person, conduct, or speech) immoderate, unbridled (*used intemperate language*). **2 a** given to excessive indulgence in alcohol. **b** excessively indulgent in one's appetites. □ **intemperance** *n.* **intemperately** *adv.* **intemperateness** *n.*

intend *v.tr.* **1** have as one's purpose (*we intend to go; we intend going; we intend that it shall be done*). **2** (usu. foll. by *for*, or *to* + infin.) design or destine (a person or a thing) (*I intend him to go; intended him for an academic career*). **3** (often foll. by *as*) mean (*what does he intend by that?; intended it as a warning*). **4** (in *passive*; foll. by *for*) **a** be meant for a person to have or use etc. (*they are intended for the children*). **b** be designed for (*intended for a small child's hand*). [from Latin *intendere* 'to direct, purpose']

intended ● *adj.* **1** done on purpose. **2** designed, meant. ● *n. colloq.* one's fiancé or fiancée.

intense *adj.* (**intenser**, **intensest**) **1** existing in a high degree; extreme, forceful (*intense joy; intense cold*). **2 a** feeling, or apt to feel, strong emotion (*very intense about her music*). **b** expressing strong emotion (*a deeply intense poem*). **3** (of a colour) very strong or deep. **4** (of an action etc.) highly concentrated (*intense thought*). [from Latin *intensus* 'directed'] □ **intensely** *adv.*

■ **Usage** *Intense* is sometimes confused with *intensive* and wrongly used to describe a course of study etc.

intensifier *n.* **1** a person or thing that intensifies. **2** *Gram.* a word or prefix used to give force or emphasis.

intensify *v.tr.* & *intr.* (**-ies**, **-ied**) make or become intense or more intense. □ **intensification** *n.*

intensity *n.* (*pl.* **-ies**) **1** the quality or an instance of being intense. **2** esp. *Physics* the measurable amount of some quality, e.g. force, brightness, a magnetic field, etc.

intensive *adj.* **1** thorough, vigorous; directed to a single point, area, or subject (*intensive study; intensive bombardment*). **2** of or relating to intensity as opposed to extent; producing intensity. **3** serving to increase production in relation to costs (*intensive farming methods*). **4** (usu. in *comb.*) *Econ.* making much use of (*a labour-intensive industry*). **5** *Gram.* (of an adjective, adverb, etc.) expressing intensity; giving force or emphasis, as *really* in *my feet are really cold.* □ **intensively** *adv.* **intensiveness** *n.*

■ **Usage** See Usage Note at INTENSE.

intensive care *n.* medical treatment with constant monitoring etc. of a dangerously ill patient (also, with hyphen, *attrib.*: *intensive-care unit*).

intent ● *n.* (usu. without article) intention; a purpose (*with intent to defraud; my intent to reach the top; with evil intent*). ● *adj.* **1** (usu. foll. by *on*) **a** resolved; bent; determined (*was intent on succeeding*). **b** attentively occupied (*intent on his books*). **2** (esp. of a look) earnest; eager. □ **to all intents and purposes** practically; virtually. [from Latin *intentus*] □ **intently** *adv.* **intentness** *n.*

intention *n.* **1** a thing intended; an aim or purpose (*it was not his intention to interfere; have no intention of staying*). **2** the act of intending (*done without intention*). **3** (usu. in *pl.*) *colloq.* a person's designs in respect to marriage (*are his intentions strictly honourable?*). □ **intentioned** *adj.* (usu. in *comb.*).

intentional *adj.* done on purpose. □ **intentionality** *n.* **intentionally** *adv.*

inter /in-ter/ *v.tr.* (**interred**, **interring**) deposit (a corpse etc.) in the earth, a tomb, etc.; bury. [from Old French *enterrer*]

inter- *prefix* **1** between, among (*intercontinental*). **2** mutually, reciprocally (*interbreed*).

interact *v.intr.* act reciprocally; act on each other. □ **interactant** *adj.* & *n.* **interaction** *n.* **interactional** *adj.*

interactive *adj.* **1** reciprocally active; acting upon or influencing each other. **2** (of a computer or other electronic device) allowing a two-way flow of information between it and a user. □ **interactively** *adv.* **interactivity** *n.*

inter alia *adv.* among other things. [Latin]

interbreed *v.intr.* & *tr.* (*past* and *past part.* **-bred**) breed or cause to breed with members of a different stock, race, or species to produce a hybrid.

intercalary *adj.* **1 a** (of a day or a month) inserted in the calendar to harmonize it with the solar year, e.g. 29 Feb. in leap years. **b** (of a year) having such an addition. **2** interpolated.

intercalate /in-ter-kă-layt/ *v.tr.* **1** (also *absol.*) insert (an intercalary day etc.). **2** interpose (anything out of the ordinary course). **3** (as **intercalated** *adj.*) (of strata etc.) interposed. [based on Latin *intercalatus* 'proclaimed as inserted in the calendar'] □ **intercalation** *n.*

intercede *v.intr.* (usu. foll. by *with*) intervene on behalf of another; plead (*they interceded with the king for his life*). [from Latin *intercedere* 'to intervene']

intercellular *adj. Biol.* located or occurring between cells.

intercept *v.tr.* **1** seize, catch, or stop (a person, message, vehicle, ball, etc.) going from one place to another. **2** (usu. foll. by *from*) cut off (light etc.). **3** check or stop (motion etc.). [based on Latin *interceptus* 'seized between (places)'] □ **interception** *n.* **interceptive** *adj.*

interceptor *n.* **1** an aircraft used to intercept enemy raiders. **2** a person or thing that intercepts.

intercession *n.* **1** the act of interceding, esp. by prayer. **2** an instance of this, esp. a prayer on behalf of another. [from Latin *intercessio*] □ **intercessor** *n.* **intercessory** *adj.*

interchange ● *v.tr.* **1** (of two people) exchange (things) with each other. **2** put each of (two things) in the other's place; alternate. ● *n.* **1** a reciprocal exchange between two people etc. **2** alternation (*the interchange of woods and fields*). **3** a road junction designed so that traffic streams do not intersect. □ **interchangeable** *adj.* **interchangeability** *n.* **interchangeably** *adv.*

intercity ● *adj.* existing or travelling between cities, esp. (**InterCity** *Brit. propr.*) with reference to train travel. ● *n.* (*pl.* **intercities**) a usu. fast train operating between cities.

intercom *n. colloq.* **1** a system of intercommunication by radio or telephone between or within offices, aircraft, etc. **2** an instrument used in this.

intercommunicate *v.intr.* **1** communicate reciprocally. **2** (of rooms etc.) have free passage into each other; have a connecting door. □ **intercommunication** *n.*

intercommunion *n.* **1** mutual fellowship, esp. mutual sharing of the Eucharist by Christian denominations. **2** mutual action or relationship.

interconnect *v.tr. & intr.* connect with each other. □ **interconnection** *n.*

intercontinental *adj.* connecting or travelling between continents.

interconvert *v.tr. & intr.* convert into each other. □ **interconversion** *n.*

intercooler *n.* an apparatus for cooling gas between successive compressions, esp. in a car or truck engine. □ **intercool** *v.tr.*

intercorrelate *v.tr. & intr.* correlate with one another. □ **intercorrelation** *n.*

intercostal *adj.* between the ribs (of the body or a ship). □ **intercostally** *adv.*

intercourse *n.* **1** communication or dealings between individuals, nations, etc. **2** = SEXUAL INTERCOURSE. [from Latin *intercursus*]

intercrop *v.tr.* (**-cropped**, **-cropping**) (also *absol.*) raise (a crop) among plants of a different kind. □ **intercropping** *n.*

intercut *v.tr.* (**-cutting**; *past* and *past part.* **-cut**) *Cinematog.* alternate (shots) with contrasting shots by cutting.

interdenominational *adj.* concerning more than one (religious) denomination. □ **interdenominationally** *adv.*

interdepartmental *adj.* concerning more than one department. □ **interdepartmentally** *adv.*

interdepend *v.intr.* depend on each other. □ **interdependence** *n.* **interdependency** *n.* **interdependent** *adj.*

interdict ● *n.* **1** an authoritative prohibition. **2** *RC Ch.* a sentence debarring a person, or esp. a place, from ecclesiastical functions and privileges. ● *v.tr.* **1** prohibit (an action). **2** forbid the use of.

3 (usu. foll. by *from* + verbal noun) restrain (a person). **4** (usu. foll. by *to*) forbid (a thing) to a person. [from Latin *interdictum* 'interposed, forbidden by decree'] □ **interdiction** *n.*

interdisciplinary *adj.* of or between more than one branch of learning.

interest ● *n.* **1 a** concern; curiosity (*have no interest in fishing*). **b** a quality exciting curiosity or holding the attention (*this magazine lacks interest*). **2** a subject, hobby, etc., in which one is concerned (*his interests are gardening and sport*). **3** advantage or profit (*it is in your interest to go*; *look after your own interests*). **4** money paid for the use of money lent. **5** (usu. foll. by *in*) **a** a financial stake (in an undertaking etc.). **b** a legal concern, title, or right (in property). **6 a** a party or group having a common concern (*the brewing interest*). **b** a principle in which a party or group is concerned. **7** the selfish pursuit of one's own welfare, self-interest. ● *v.tr.* **1** excite the curiosity or attention of (*your story interests me greatly*). **2** (usu. foll. by *in*) cause (a person) to take a personal interest or share (*can I interest you in a holiday abroad?*). **3** (as **interested** *adj.*) having a private interest; not impartial or disinterested (*an interested party*). □ **in the interest** (or **interests**) **of** as something that is advantageous to. [from Latin *interest* 'it matters, it makes a difference'] □ **interestedly** *adv.*

interesting *adj.* causing curiosity; holding the attention. □ **interestingly** *adv.*

interface ● *n.* **1** esp. *Physics* a surface forming a common boundary between two regions. **2** a point where interaction occurs between two systems, processes, subjects, etc. (*the interface between psychology and education*). **3** esp. *Computing* an apparatus for connecting two pieces of equipment so that they can be operated jointly. ● *v.* (often foll. by *with*) **1** *tr. & intr.* connect with (another piece of equipment etc.) by an interface. **2** *intr.* interact (with another person etc.).

■ **Usage** The use of the noun and the verb in sense 2 is deplored by some people, because it often reduces the word to a high-sounding synonym for *boundary*, *meeting point*, *link*, *liaison*, *interact*, etc.

interfacing *n.* a stiffish material between two layers of fabric in collars etc.

interfaith *adj.* of, relating to, or between different religions or members of different religions.

interfere *v.intr.* **1** (usu. foll. by *with*) **a** (of a person) meddle; obstruct a process etc. **b** (of a thing) be a hindrance. **2** (usu. foll. by *in*) take part or intervene, esp. without invitation or necessity. **3** (foll. by *with*) *Brit. euphem.* molest or assault sexually. **4** *Physics* (of light or other waves) combine so as to cause interference. [from Old French *s'entreferir* 'to strike each other'] □ **interferer** *n.* **interfering** *adj.* **interferingly** *adv.*

interference *n.* **1** (usu. foll. by *with*) **a** the act of

interfering. **b** an instance of this. **2** the fading or disturbance of received radio signals. **3** *Physics* ▼ the combination of two or more wave motions to form a resultant wave in which the displacement is reinforced or cancelled. □ **interferential** *adj.*

interferon *n. Biochem.* any of various proteins released by cells, usu. in response to a virus, and able to inhibit viral replication.

interfile *v.tr.* **1** file (two sequences) together. **2** file (one or more items) into an existing sequence.

interfuse *v.* **1** *tr.* **a** (usu. foll. by *with*) mix (a thing) with; intersperse. **b** blend (things) together. **2** *intr.* (of two things) blend with each other. [based on Latin *interfusus* 'poured between'] □ **interfusion** *n.*

intergalactic *adj.* of or situated between two or more galaxies.

interglacial ● *adj.* of or relating to a period of milder climate between glacial periods. ● *n.* such a period.

intergovernmental *adj.* concerning or conducted between two or more governments.

interim ● *n.* the intervening time (*in the interim he had died*). ● *adj.* provisional, temporary. [Latin, literally 'meanwhile']

interior ● *adj.* **1** inner. **2** inland. **3** internal; domestic. **4** (usu. foll. by *to*) situated further in or within. **5** existing in the mind. **6** drawn, photographed, etc. within a building. **7** coming from inside. ● *n.* **1** the interior part; the inside. **2** the interior part of a country or region. **3 a** the home affairs of a country. **b** a department dealing with these (*Minister of the Interior*). **4** a representation of the inside of a building or a room. [Latin, literally 'inner'] □ **interiorize** *v.tr.* (also **-ise**).

interior angle *n.* the angle between adjacent sides of a rectilinear figure.

interior monologue *n.* a form of writing expressing a character's inner thoughts.

interior-sprung *adj. Brit.* (of a mattress etc.) with internal springs.

interject *v.tr.* **1** utter (words) abruptly or parenthetically. **2** interrupt with. [based on Latin *interjectus* 'cast between']

interjection *n.* an exclamation, esp. as a part of speech (e.g. *ah!*, *dear me!*). □ **interjectional** *adj.*

interlace *v.* **1** *tr.* bind intricately together; interweave. **2** *tr.* mingle, intersperse. **3** *intr.* cross each other intricately. □ **interlacement** *n.*

interlard *v.tr.* (usu. foll. by *with*) mix (writing or speech) with different material, esp. with unusual words or phrases.

interleave *v.tr.* insert (usu. blank) leaves between the leaves of (a book etc.).

interline *v.tr.* put an extra lining between the ordinary lining and the fabric of (a garment etc.).

interlinear *adj.* written or printed between the lines of a text.

INTERFERENCE

Interference is caused by waves acting upon one another. In this demonstration, two waves on water radiate in a circular pattern. Their paths cross and cancel out in the central area, but further away from the epicentre, the waves interfere constructively, and combine to produce a new pattern.

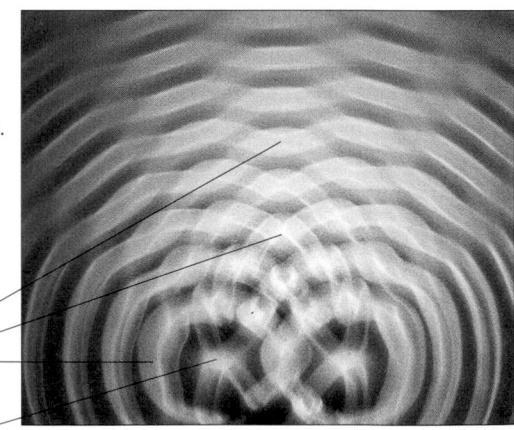

combined wave pattern

wave patterns cancel out

radiating wave pattern

DEMONSTRATION OF WAVE INTERFERENCE

epicentre of wave

interlining n. material used to interline a garment.

interlink v.tr. & intr. link or be linked together.

interlock ● v. **1** intr. engage with each other by overlapping or by the fitting together of projections and recesses. **2** tr. (usu. in passive) lock or clasp within each other. ● adj. (of a fabric) knitted with closely interlocking stitches. ● n. a device or mechanism for connecting or coordinating the function of different components. □ **interlocker** n.

interlocutor n. (fem. **interlocutrix**) a person who takes part in a conversation. [based on Latin interloqui interlocut- 'to interrupt in speaking'] □ **interlocution** n.

interlocutory adj. of dialogue or conversation.

interloper n. **1** an intruder. **2** a person who interferes in others' affairs, esp. for profit. [based on dialect loper, form of LEAP v.] □ **interlope** v.intr.

interlude n. **1 a** a pause between the acts of a play. **b** something performed during this pause. **2 a** an intervening time, space, or event that contrasts with what goes before or after. **b** a temporary amusement or entertaining episode. **c** a piece of music played between other pieces, the verses of a hymn, etc. [from medieval Latin interludium]

intermarriage n. **1** marriage between people of different races, castes, families, etc. **2** (loosely) marriage between near relations.

intermarry v.intr. (-ies, -ied) (foll. by with) (of races, castes, families, etc.) become connected by marriage.

intermediary ● n. (pl. -ies) an intermediate person or thing, esp. a mediator. ● adj. acting as mediator; intermediate. [from Latin intermedius]

intermediate ● adj. coming between two things in time, place, order, character, etc. ● n. an intermediate thing. ● v.intr. (foll. by between) act as intermediary; mediate. [based on Latin medius 'middle'] □ **intermediation** n.

intermediate technology n. technology suitable for use in developing countries.

interment /in-ter-měnt/ n. the burial of a corpse.

■ **Usage** Do not confuse interment meaning 'burial' with internment 'confinement' and internship 'period of serving as an intern'.

intermezzo /in-ter-**met**-soh/ n. (pl. **intermezzi** or **-os**) **1 a** a short connecting instrumental movement in a musical work. **b** a similar piece performed independently. **c** a short piece for a solo instrument. **2** a short light dramatic or other performance inserted between the acts of a play. [Italian]

interminable adj. **1** endless. **2** tediously long or habitual. **3** with no prospect of an end. [from Late Latin interminabilis] □ **interminableness** n. **interminably** adv.

intermingle v.tr. & intr. mix together; mingle.

intermission n. **1** a pause or cessation. **2** an interval between parts of a play, film, concert, etc. **3** a period of inactivity. [from Latin intermissio]

intermittent adj. occurring at intervals; not continuous. [from Latin intermittent- 'suspending, leaving off'] □ **intermittency** n. **intermittently** adv.

intermix v.tr. & intr. mix together. □ **intermixable** adj.

intermolecular adj. between molecules.

intern ● n. (also **interne**) esp. N. Amer. a recent graduate or advanced student receiving supervised training in a hospital and acting as an assistant physician or surgeon. ● v. **1** tr. oblige (a prisoner, alien, etc.) to reside within prescribed limits. **2** intr. esp. N. Amer. serve as an intern. [from Latin internus 'internal'] □ **internment** n. (in sense 1 of v.). **internship** n. esp. N. Amer. (in sense 2 of v.).

■ **Usage** See Usage Note at INTERMENT.

internal adj. **1** of or situated in the inside or invisible part. **2** relating or applied to the inside of the body (internal injuries). **3** of a nation's domestic affairs. **4** Brit. (of a student) attending a university etc. as well as taking its examinations. **5** used or applying within an organization. **6 a** intrinsic. **b** of the mind or soul. [from Latin internus] □ **internality** n. **internally** adv.

internal-combustion engine n. ▼ an engine in which motive power is generated by the expansion of exhaust gases from the burning of fuel with air inside the engine.

internal exile see EXILE n. 1.

internalize v.tr. (also **-ise**) Psychol. make (attitudes, behaviour, etc.) part of one's nature by learning or unconscious assimilation. □ **internalization** n.

internal market n. **1** = SINGLE MARKET. **2** (in the UK) a system of decentralized funding in the National Health Service whereby hospital departments purchase each other's services contractually.

international ● adj. **1** existing, involving, or carried on between two or more nations. **2** agreed on or used by all or many nations (international driving licence). ● n. **1** Brit. **a** a contest between teams representing different countries. **b** a member of such a team. **2** (**International**) any of four associations founded to promote socialist or communist action. □ **internationality** n. **internationally** adv.

International Date Line see DATE LINE 1.

internationalism n. the advocacy of a community of interests among nations. □ **internationalist** n.

internationalize v.tr. (also **-ise**) **1** make international. **2** bring under the protection or control of two or more nations. □ **internationalization** n.

interne var. of INTERN n.

internecine /in-ter-**nee**-syn/ adj. mutually destructive. [originally in sense 'deadly': from Latin internecinus]

internee n. a person interned.

Internet n. an international computer network linking computers from educational institutions, government agencies, industry, etc.

interoperable adj. able to operate in conjunction. □ **interoperability** n.

interpellate /in-ter-pĕ-layt/ v.tr. (in a parliament) interrupt the order of the day by demanding an explanation from (the minister concerned). [based on Latin interpellatus 'interrupted by speaking'] □ **interpellation** n. **interpellator** n.

interpenetrate v. **1** intr. (of two things) penetrate each other. **2** tr. pervade; penetrate thoroughly. □ **interpenetration** n. **interpenetrative** adj.

interpersonal adj. occurring between persons. □ **interpersonally** adv.

interplanetary adj. **1** between planets. **2** relating to travel between planets.

interplay n. **1** reciprocal action. **2** the operation of two things on each other.

Interpol n. the International Criminal Police Commission. [abbreviation of International police]

interpolate /in-ter-pŏ-layt/ v.tr. **1 a** insert (words) in a book etc., esp. to give false impressions. **b** make such insertions in (a book etc.). **2** interject (a remark) in a conversation. **3** estimate (intermediate values) from surrounding known values. [based on Latin interpolatus 'furnished up'] □ **interpolation** n. **interpolator** n.

interpose v. **1** tr. (often foll. by between) insert (a thing) between others. **2** tr. say (words) as an interruption. **3** tr. exercise or advance (a veto or objection) so as to interfere. **4** intr. (often foll. by between) intervene (between parties). [from French interposer] □ **interposition** n.

interpret v. (**interpreted, interpreting**) **1** tr. explain the meaning of (words, a dream, etc.). **2** tr. elucidate (creative work). **3** intr. act as an interpreter. **4** tr. explain or understand (behaviour etc.)

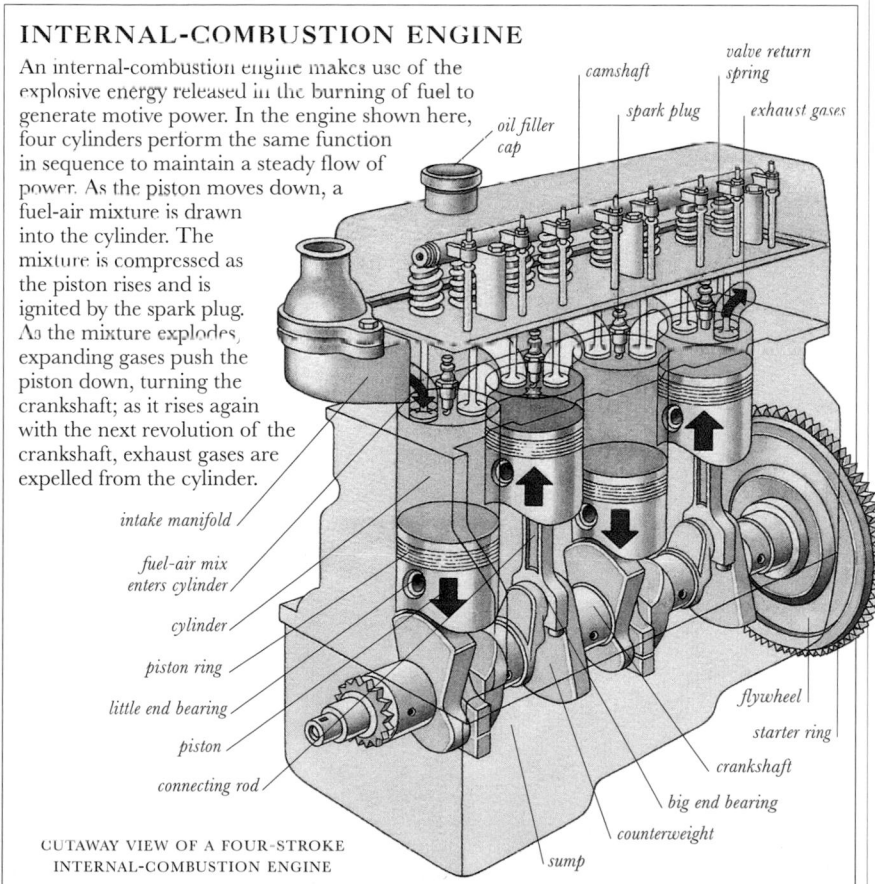

INTERNAL-COMBUSTION ENGINE

An internal-combustion engine makes use of the explosive energy released in the burning of fuel to generate motive power. In the engine shown here, four cylinders perform the same function in sequence to maintain a steady flow of power. As the piston moves down, a fuel-air mixture is drawn into the cylinder. The mixture is compressed as the piston rises and is ignited by the spark plug. As the mixture explodes, expanding gases push the piston down, turning the crankshaft; as it rises again with the next revolution of the crankshaft, exhaust gases are expelled from the cylinder.

oil filler cap
camshaft
spark plug
valve return spring
exhaust gases
intake manifold
fuel-air mix enters cylinder
cylinder
piston ring
little end bearing
piston
connecting rod
flywheel
starter ring
crankshaft
big end bearing
counterweight
sump

CUTAWAY VIEW OF A FOUR-STROKE
INTERNAL-COMBUSTION ENGINE

in a specified manner (*interpreted his gesture as mocking*). [from Latin *interpretari* 'to explain, translate']
□ **interpretable** *adj.* **interpretation** *n.* **interpretational** *adj.* **interpretative** *adj.* **interpretatively** *adv.* **interpretive** *adj.* **interpretively** *adv.*

interpreter *n.* a person who interprets, esp. one who translates speech orally.

interracial *adj.* existing between or affecting different races. □ **interracially** *adv.*

interregnum *n.* (*pl.* **interregnums** or **interregna**) **1** an interval when normal government is suspended, esp. between successive reigns or regimes. **2** an interval or pause. [Latin, based on *regnum* 'reign']

interrelate *v.* **1** *tr.* relate (two or more things) to each other. **2** *intr.* (of two or more things) relate to each other. □ **interrelation** *n.* **interrelationship** *n.*

interrogate *v.tr.* ask questions of (a person) esp. closely or formally. [based on Latin *interrogatus* 'asked at intervals'] □ **interrogation** *n.* **interrogator** *n.*

interrogative ● *adj.* **1 a** of or like a question; used in questions. **b** *Gram.* (of an adjective or pronoun) asking a question (e.g. *who?*, *which?*). **2** having the form or force of a question. **3** suggesting enquiry (*an interrogative tone*). ● *n.* an interrogative word (e.g. *what?*, *why?*). □ **interrogatively** *adv.*

interrogatory *adj.* questioning; of or suggesting enquiry.

interrupt *v.tr.* **1** act so as to break the continuous progress of (an action, speech, etc.). **2** obstruct (a person's view etc.). **3** break the continuity of. [based on Latin *interruptus* 'broken between'] □ **interrupter** *n.* **interruptible** *adj.* **interruption** *n.* **interruptive** *adj.* **interruptor** *n.*

intersect *v.* **1** *tr.* divide (a thing) by passing or lying across it. **2** *intr.* (of lines, roads, etc.) cross or cut each other. [based on Latin *intersectus* 'cut between'] □ **intersection** *n.* **intersectional** *adj.*

intersexual *adj.* existing between the sexes. □ **intersexuality** *n.*

interspace ● *n.* an interval of space or time. ● *v.tr.* put interspaces between.

interspecific *adj.* formed from or occurring between or among individuals of different species.

intersperse *v.tr.* **1** (often foll. by *between*, *among*) scatter; place here and there. **2** (foll. by *with*) diversify (a thing or things with others so scattered). [based on Latin *interspersus* 'sprinkled between'] □ **interspersion** *n.*

interstate ● *adj.* existing or carried on between states, esp. of the US. ● *n.* US each motorway of a system of motorways between states.

interstellar *adj.* occurring or situated between stars.

interstice /in-ter-stis/ *n.* **1** an intervening space. **2** a chink or crevice. [from Latin *interstitium*]

interstitial *adj.* of, forming, or occupying interstices. □ **interstitially** *adv.*

intertribal *adj.* existing or occurring between different tribes.

intertwine *v.* **1** *tr.* (often foll. by *with*) entwine (together). **2** *intr.* become entwined. □ **intertwinement** *n.*

interval *n.* **1** an intervening time or space. **2** *Brit.* a pause or break, esp. between the parts of a theatrical or musical performance. **3** the difference in pitch between two sounds. **4** the distance between persons or things in respect of qualities. □ **at intervals** here and there; now and then. [from Latin *intervallum* 'space between ramparts, interval'] □ **intervallic** *adj.*

intervene *v.intr.* (often foll. by *between*, *in*) **1** occur in time between events. **2** come between so as to prevent or modify the result or course of events. **3** be situated between things. **4** come in as an extraneous factor or thing. [from Latin *intervenire*] □ **intervener** *n.* **intervenor** *n.*

intervention *n.* **1** the act or an instance of intervening. **2** interference, esp. by a state in another's affairs. **3** mediation.

interventionist *n.* a person who favours intervention. □ **interventionism** *n.*

intervertebral *adj.* between vertebrae.

interview ● *n.* **1** an oral examination of an applicant for employment etc. **2** a conversation between a reporter etc. and a person of public interest, used for a broadcast or publication. **3** a meeting of persons face to face, esp. for consultation. **4** a session of formal questioning by the police. ● *v.* **1** *tr.* hold an interview with. **2** *intr.* participate in an interview; perform (well etc.) at interview. [from French *entrevue*] □ **interviewee** *n.* **interviewer** *n.*

inter-war *attrib.adj.* existing in the period between two wars.

interweave *v.tr.* (*past* **-wove**; *past part.* **-woven**) **1** (often foll. by *with*) weave together. **2** blend intimately.

interwork *v.* **1** *intr.* work together or interactively. **2** *tr.* interweave.

intestate ● *adj.* not having made a will before death. ● *n.* a person who has died intestate. [from Latin *intestatus*] □ **intestacy** *n.*

intestinal flora *n.pl.* the symbiotic bacteria naturally inhabiting the gut.

intestine *n.* (in *sing.* or *pl.*) ▼ the lower part of the alimentary canal from the end of the stomach to the anus. [from Latin *intestinum*] □ **intestinal** *adj.* ▷ DIGESTION

transverse colon (large intestine)
duodenum (small intestine)
stomach
descending colon (large intestine)
ascending colon (large intestine)
jejunum (small intestine)
appendix
rectum
ileum (small intestine)
anus

INTESTINE: STRUCTURE OF THE HUMAN INTESTINE

inthrall *US* var. of ENTHRAL.

intifada /in-ti-fah-dă/ *n.* a movement of Palestinian uprising. [Arabic, literally 'uprising']

intimacy *n.* (*pl.* **-ies**) **1** close familiarity or friendship; closeness. **2** an intimate act, esp. sexual intercourse. **3** a private cosy atmosphere. **4** an intimate remark; an endearment.

intimate[1] /in-ti-măt/ ● *adj.* **1** closely acquainted; familiar, close (*an intimate friend*). **2** private and personal (*intimate thoughts*). **3** (usu. foll. by *with*) having sexual relations. **4** (of knowledge) detailed. **5** (of a relationship between things) close. **6** (of mixing etc.) thorough. **7** (of a place etc.) promoting close personal relationships. ● *n.* a very close friend. [from Latin *intimus* 'inmost'] □ **intimately** *adv.*

intimate[2] /in-ti-mayt/ *v.tr.* **1** (often foll. by *that* + clause) state or make known. **2** imply, hint. [based on Late Latin *intimatus* 'made known'] □ **intimation** *n.*

intimidate *v.tr.* frighten or overawe, esp. to influence. [based on medieval Latin *intimidatus* 'rendered timid'] □ **intimidating** *adj.* **intimidation** *n.* **intimidator** *n.* **intimidatory** *adj.*

into *prep.* **1** expressing motion or direction to a point on or within (*ran into the house*). **2** expressing a change of state (*turned into a dragon; separated into groups*). **3** after the beginning of (*five minutes into the game*). **4** *colloq.* interested in; knowledgeable about (*into art*). [Old English]

intolerable *adj.* that cannot be endured. □ **intolerableness** *n.* **intolerably** *adv.*

intolerant *adj.* not tolerant, esp. of views or behaviour differing from one's own. □ **intolerance** *n.* **intolerantly** *adv.*

intonation *n.* **1** modulation of the voice; accent. **2** the act of intoning. **3** accuracy of musical pitch. □ **intonational** *adj.*

intone *v.tr.* **1** recite (prayers etc.) with prolonged sounds, esp. in a monotone. **2** utter with a particular tone. [from medieval Latin *intonare*] □ **intoner** *n.*

in toto *adv.* completely. [Latin]

intoxicate *v.tr.* **1** make drunk. **2** excite or elate beyond self-control. [based on medieval Latin *intoxicatus* 'filled with poison'] □ **intoxicant** *n. & adj.* **intoxicatingly** *adv.* **intoxication** *n.*

intra- *prefix* forming adjectives usu. from adjectives, meaning 'on the inside, within' (*intramural*).

intractable *adj.* **1** hard to control or deal with. **2** difficult, stubborn. □ **intractability** *n.* **intractably** *adv.*

intrados *n.* *Archit.* the lower or inner curve of an arch (opp. EXTRADOS). ▷ ARCH, WINDOW

intramural *adj.* **1** situated or done within walls. **2** forming part of normal university or college studies. □ **intramurally** *adv.*

intramuscular *adj.* in or into a muscle or muscles.

intransigent ● *adj.* uncompromising, stubborn. ● *n.* an intransigent person. [from Spanish *los intransigentes*, name adopted by extreme Spanish republicans] □ **intransigence** *n.* **intransigency** *n.* **intransigently** *adv.*

intransitive *adj.* (of a verb or sense of a verb) that does not take or require a direct object. □ **intransitively** *adv.* **intransitivity** *n.*

intrapreneur *n.* a company employee who develops innovative products etc.

intrauterine *adj.* within the womb.

intrauterine device *n.* a contraceptive device fitted inside the uterus and physically preventing the implantation of fertilized ova.

intravenous *adj.* in or into a vein or veins. □ **intravenously** *adv.*

in-tray *n.* esp. *Brit.* a tray for incoming documents, letters, etc.

intrepid *adj.* fearless; very brave. [from Latin *intrepidus* 'not alarmed'] □ **intrepidity** *n.* **intrepidly** *adv.*

intricate *adj.* very complicated; perplexingly detailed. [from Latin *intricatus* 'entangled'] □ **intricacy** *n.* (*pl.* **-ies**). **intricately** *adv.*

intrigue ● *v.* (**intrigues**, **intrigued**, **intriguing**) **1** *intr.* (foll. by *with*) **a** carry on an underhand plot. **b** use secret influence. **2** *tr.* fascinate. ● *n.* **1** an underhand plot or plotting. **2** *archaic* a secret love affair. [French] □ **intriguer** *n.* **intriguing** *adj.* (esp. in sense 2 of *v.*). **intriguingly** *adv.*

intrinsic *adj.* inherent, essential; belonging naturally. [originally in sense 'interior': from Latin *intrinsecus* 'inwardly'] □ **intrinsically** *adv.*

intro *n.* (*pl.* **-os**) *colloq.* an introduction.

intro- *comb. form* into (*introduce*). [from Latin *intro* 'to the inside']

introduce *v.tr.* **1** (foll. by *to*) make (a person or oneself) known by name to another. **2** announce or present to an audience. **3 a** bring into use. **b** put on sale for the first time. **4** bring (a piece of legislation) before a legislative assembly. **5** (foll. by *to*) draw the attention of (a person) to a subject. **6** (often foll. by *into*) **a** insert (*introduce into the tank*). **b** usher in; bring forward. **7** begin. [from Latin *introducere*] □ **introducer** *n.*

introduction *n.* **1** the act or an instance of introducing; the process of being introduced. **2** a formal presentation of one person to another. **3** a

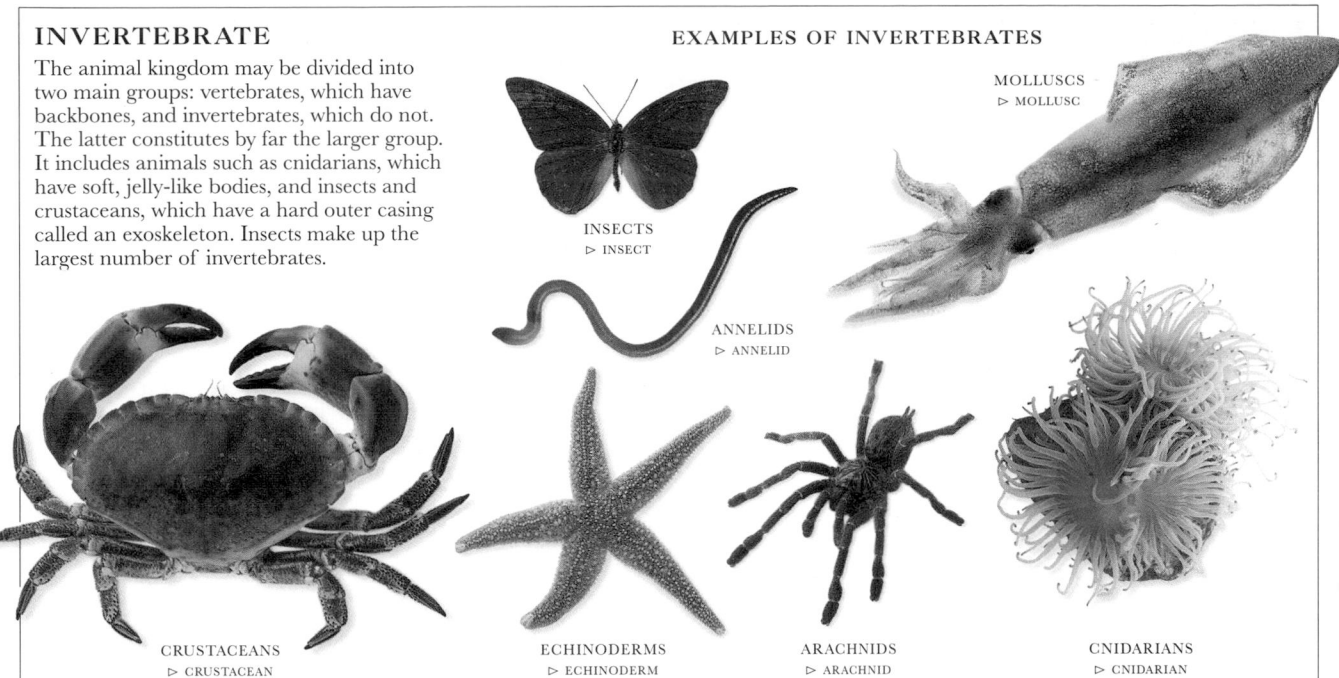

INVERTEBRATE

The animal kingdom may be divided into two main groups: vertebrates, which have backbones, and invertebrates, which do not. The latter constitutes by far the larger group. It includes animals such as cnidarians, which have soft, jelly-like bodies, and insects and crustaceans, which have a hard outer casing called an exoskeleton. Insects make up the largest number of invertebrates.

EXAMPLES OF INVERTEBRATES

MOLLUSCS
▷ MOLLUSC

INSECTS
▷ INSECT

ANNELIDS
▷ ANNELID

CRUSTACEANS
▷ CRUSTACEAN

ECHINODERMS
▷ ECHINODERM

ARACHNIDS
▷ ARACHNID

CNIDARIANS
▷ CNIDARIAN

preliminary section at the beginning of a book, piece of music, etc. **4** an introductory treatise. **5** a thing introduced. □ **introductory** *adj.*

introspection *n.* the examination of one's own mental and emotional processes etc. [based on Latin *introspicere introspect-* 'to look inwards'] □ **introspective** *adj.* **introspectively** *adv.*

introvert ● *n.* **1** *Psychol.* a person predominantly concerned with his or her own thoughts and feelings rather than with external things. **2** a shy inwardly thoughtful person. ● *adj.* (also **introverted**) typical or characteristic of an introvert. [based on modern Latin *introvertere* 'to turn inwards'] □ **introversion** *n.* **introverted** *adj.*

intrude *v.* (foll. by *on*, *upon*, *into*) **1** *intr.* come uninvited or unwanted; force oneself abruptly on others. **2** *tr.* thrust or force (something unwelcome) on a person. [from Latin *intrudere*] □ **intruder** *n.*

intrusion *n.* **1** the act or an instance of intruding. **2** an unwanted interruption etc. **3** *Geol.* ▼ an influx of molten rock between or through strata etc. but not reaching the surface. ▷ IGNEOUS. **4** the occupation of a vacant estate etc. to which one has no claim. [from medieval Latin *intrusio*] □ **intrusive** *adj.* **intrusively** *adv.*

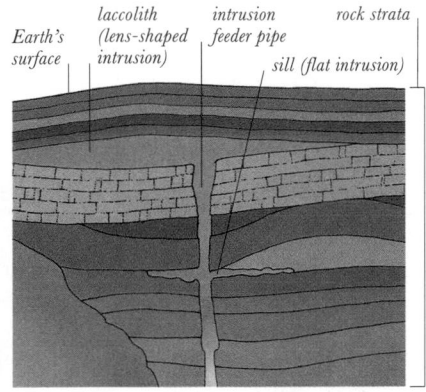

Earth's surface *laccolith (lens-shaped intrusion)* *intrusion feeder pipe* *rock strata* *sill (flat intrusion)*

INTRUSION: CROSS-SECTION OF THE EARTH'S CRUST SHOWING INTRUSIONS

intuit *v.* **1** *tr.* know by intuition. **2** *intr.* receive knowledge by direct perception. [from Latin *intueri intuit-* 'to consider'] □ **intuitable** *adj.*

intuition *n.* **1** immediate apprehension by the mind or by a sense. **2** immediate insight. □ **intuitional** *adj.*

intuitive *adj.* **1** of, characterized by, or possessing intuition. **2** perceived by intuition. □ **intuitively** *adv.* **intuitiveness** *n.*

Inuit ● *n.* **1** (*pl.* same) an Eskimo, esp. a Canadian Eskimo. **2** any of the languages spoken by these peoples. ● *adj.* of or relating to the Inuit or their languages. [Eskimo, literally 'people']

■ **Usage** See Usage Note at ESKIMO.

inundate *v.tr.* (often foll. by *with*) **1** flood. **2** overwhelm. [based on Latin *inundatus* 'flowed into'] □ **inundation** *n.*

inure *v.tr.* (often in *passive*; foll. by *to*) accustom (a person) to something esp. unpleasant. [Middle English] □ **inurement** *n.*

in utero /yoo-tĕ-roh/ *adv.* in the womb; before birth. [Latin]

invade *v.tr.* (often *absol.*) **1** enter (a country etc.) under arms. **2** swarm into or onto. **3** (of a disease) attack (a body etc.). **4** encroach upon (esp. privacy). [from Latin *invadere*] □ **invader** *n.*

invalid[1] /in-vă-lid/ ● *n.* **1** a person enfeebled or disabled by illness or injury. **2** (*attrib.*) **a** of or for invalids (*invalid car*). **b** being an invalid (*her invalid mother*). ● *v.tr.* (**invalided**, **invaliding**) **1** (often foll. by *out* etc.) esp. *Brit.* remove from active service (a person who has become an invalid). **2** (usu. in *passive*) disable (a person) by illness. □ **invalidism** *n.*

invalid[2] /in-**val**-id/ *adj.* not valid. □ **invalidly** *adv.*

invalidate *v.tr.* **1** make invalid. **2** remove the validity or force of (a contract etc.). □ **invalidation** *n.*

invalidity *n.* **1** lack of validity. **2** bodily infirmity.

invaluable *adj.* above valuation; inestimable. □ **invaluableness** *n.* **invaluably** *adv.*

invariable *adj.* **1** unchangeable; always the same. **2** *Math.* constant. □ **invariability** *n.* **invariably** *adv.*

invasion *n.* **1** the act of invading or process of being invaded. **2** an entry of a hostile army into a country. [from Latin *invasio*]

invasive *adj.* **1** (of weeds, cancer cells, etc.) tending to spread. **2** (of medical procedures etc.) involving

the introduction of instruments into the body. **3** tending to encroach on the privacy etc. of others.

invective *n.* a strong verbal attack. [from Late Latin *invectivus* 'abusive']

inveigh *v.intr.* (foll. by *against*) speak or write with strong hostility. [from Latin *invehi* 'to go into, assail']

inveigle *v.tr.* (foll. by *into*, or *to* + infin.) entice; persuade by guile. [earlier *enve(u)gle*, from Old French *aveugler* 'to blind'] □ **inveiglement** *n.*

invent *v.tr.* **1** create by thought; originate. **2** concoct (a false story etc.). [based on Latin *inventus* 'found out, contrived'] □ **inventable** *adj.* **invention** *n.* **inventor** *n.*

inventive *adj.* **1** able or inclined to invent. **2** showing ingenuity. □ **inventively** *adv.* **inventiveness** *n.*

inventory /in-věn-tri/ ● *n.* (*pl.* **-ies**) **1** a complete list of goods etc. **2** items listed in this. **3** *US* the total of a firm's commercial assets. ● *v.tr.* (**-ies**, **-ied**) **1** make an inventory of. **2** enter (items) in an inventory.

inverse ● *adj.* inverted in order or relation. ● *n.* **1** the state of being inverted. **2** (often foll. by *of*) a thing that is the opposite or reverse of another. [from Latin *inversus* 'inverted'] □ **inversely** *adv.*

inverse proportion *n.* (also **inverse ratio**) a relation between two quantities such that one increases in proportion as the other decreases.

inverse square law *n.* a law by which the intensity of an effect, such as gravitational force, illumination, etc., changes in inverse proportion to the square of the distance from the source.

inversion *n.* **1** the act of turning upside down or inside out. **2** the reversal of a normal order or relation. **3** (in full **temperature inversion**) the reversal of the normal variation of air temperature with altitude. **4** the process or result of inverting. □ **inversive** *adj.*

invert ● *v.tr.* **1** turn upside down. **2** reverse the order or relation of. ● *n.* a homosexual. [from Latin *invertere*] □ **inverter** *n.* **invertibility** *n.* **invertible** *adj.*

invertebrate ● *adj.* (of an animal) not having a backbone. ● *n.* ▲ an invertebrate animal.

inverted comma *n.* esp. *Brit.* = QUOTATION MARK.

invert sugar *n.* a mixture of glucose and fructose obtained by the hydrolysis of sucrose.

invest *v.* **1** *tr.* (often foll. by *in*) apply or use (money), esp. for profit. **2** *intr.* (often foll. by *in*) devote (time

I

IONIC

The term Ionic applies to one of the classical architectural orders. It is especially attributable to temple architecture, and is characterized by the use of fluted columns, volutes (spiral scrolls) on each capital, and a continuous, sculpted frieze. The triangular pediment on the main façade is generally simple and unadorned.

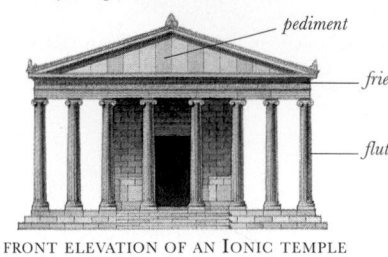

FRONT ELEVATION OF AN IONIC TEMPLE

pediment
frieze
fluted column

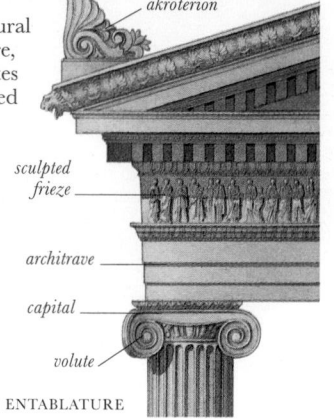

IONIC ENTABLATURE

akroterion
sculpted frieze
architrave
capital
volute

---

etc.) to an enterprise. **3** *intr.* (foll. by *in*) **a** put money for profit (into stocks etc.). **b** *colloq.* buy (*invested in a new car*). **4** *tr.* **a** (foll. by *with*) provide, endue, or credit (a person or thing with qualities, insignia, or rank). **b** (foll. by *in*) attribute or entrust (qualities or feelings). [from Latin *investire*] □ **investable** *adj.* **investor** *n.*

investigate *v.* **1** *tr.* inquire into; examine. **2** *intr.* make a systematic inquiry or search. [based on Latin *investigatus* 'searched into'] □ **investigation** *n.* **investigational** *adj.* **investigator** *n.* **investigatory** *adj.*

investigative *adj.* seeking or serving to investigate, esp. (of journalism) inquiring intensively into controversial issues.

investiture *n.* **1** the formal investing of a person with honours or rank, esp. by a sovereign. **2** (often foll. by *with*) the act of enduing (with attributes). [from medieval Latin *investitura*]

investment *n.* **1** the act or process of investing. **2** money invested. **3** property etc. in which money is invested.

investment trust *n.* a limited company whose business is the investment of its shareholders' funds.

inveterate *adj.* **1** (of a person) confirmed in an (esp. undesirable) habit etc. **2** (of a habit etc.) long established. [from Latin *inveteratus* 'made old'] □ **inveteracy** *n.* **inveterately** *adv.*

invidious *adj.* (of an action, attitude, etc.) likely to excite resentment or indignation against the person responsible (*an invidious task*). [based on Latin *invidia* 'envy'] □ **invidiously** *adv.* **invidiousness** *n.*

invigilate *v.intr.* *Brit.* supervise candidates at an examination. [originally in sense 'to keep watch': from Latin *invigilare*] □ **invigilation** *n.* **invigilator** *n.*

invigorate *v.tr.* give vigour or strength to. [based on medieval Latin *vigorare vigorat-* 'to make strong'] □ **invigorating** *adj.* **invigoratingly** *adv.* **invigoration** *n.*

invincible *adj.* unconquerable. □ **invincibility** *n.* **invincibly** *adv.*

inviolable *adj.* not to be violated or profaned. [from Latin *inviolabilis*] □ **inviolability** *n.* **inviolably** *adv.*

inviolate *adj.* **1** not violated or profaned. **2** safe from violation or harm. [from Latin *inviolatus*] □ **inviolately** *adv.*

invisible *adj.* **1** not visible to the eye. **2** too small to be seen or noticed. **3** artfully concealed (*invisible mending*). □ **invisibility** *n.* **invisibly** *adv.*

invisible exports *n.pl.* (also **invisible imports** etc.) items, esp. services, involving payment between countries but not constituting tangible commodities.

invitation *n.* **1** the process of inviting or fact of being invited, esp. to a social occasion. **2** a letter or card used to invite someone.

invite ● *v.* **1** *tr.* (often foll. by *to*, or *to* + infin.) ask (a person) courteously to come, or to do something (*were invited to lunch*). **2** *tr.* make a formal courteous request for (*invited comments*). **3** *tr.* tend to elicit (*invited abuse*). **4 a** *tr.* attract. **b** *intr.* be attractive. ● *n. colloq.* an invitation. [from Latin *invitare*] □ **invitee** *n.*

■ **Usage** Although over three centuries old, the use of *invite* as a noun meaning 'invitation' is still highly informal.

---

inviting *adj.* **1** attractive. **2** enticing, tempting. □ **invitingly** *adv.*

in vitro /**vee**-troh/ *adj. & adv. Biol.* (of processes or reactions) taking place in a test tube or other laboratory environment. [Latin, literally 'in glass']

in vivo /**vee**-voh/ *adj. & adv. Biol.* (of processes) taking place in a living organism. [Latin, literally 'in a living thing']

invocation *n.* **1** the act or an instance of invoking, esp. in prayer. **2** an appeal to a supernatural being for inspiration. [from Latin *invocatio*] □ **invocatory** *adj.*

invoice ● *n.* a list of goods or services rendered, with prices and charges; a bill. ● *v.tr.* **1** make an invoice of (goods and services). **2** send an invoice to (a person). [earlier *invoyes*, pl. of *invoy* 'dispatch']

invoke *v.tr.* **1** call on (a deity etc.) in prayer or as a witness. **2** appeal to (the law etc.). **3** summon (a spirit) by charms. **4** ask earnestly for. [from Latin *invocare*] □ **invoker** *n.*

involuntary *adj.* **1** done without conscious control; unintentional. **2** (of a muscle) not under the control of the will. □ **involuntarily** *adv.* **involuntariness** *n.*

involute *adj.* **1** involved, intricate. **2** ◀ curled spirally. **3** *Bot.* rolled inwards at the edges. [from Latin *involutus* 'wrapped up']

involuted *adj.* **1** complicated, abstruse. **2** = INVOLUTE *adj.* 2.

involution *n.* **1** the process of involving. **2** an entanglement. **3** intricacy. **4** curling inwards. **5** a part that curls inwards. □ **involutional** *adj.*

involve *v.tr.* **1** (often foll. by *in*) cause (a person or thing) to participate or share the experience (of a situation etc.). **2** imply, entail, make necessary. **3** (foll. by *in*) implicate (a person in a crime etc.). **4** include or affect in its operations. **5** (as **involved** *adj.*) **a** (often foll. by *in*) concerned or interested. **b** complicated in thought or form. **c** amorously associated. [from Latin *involvere*] □ **involvement** *n.*

INVOLUTE SHELL

---

invulnerable *adj.* that cannot be wounded or hurt. □ **invulnerability** *n.* **invulnerably** *adv.*

inward ● *adj.* **1** directed toward the inside; going in. **2** situated within. **3** mental, spiritual. ● *adv.* (also **inwards**) **1** (of motion or position) towards the inside. **2** in the mind or soul. [Old English *innanweard*]

inward-looking *adj.* introverted, insular.

inwardly *adv.* **1** on the inside. **2** in the mind or soul. **3** (of speaking) not aloud; inaudibly.

inwards var. of INWARD *adv.*

inwrap var. of ENWRAP.

inwrought *adj.* **1 a** (often foll. by *with*) (of a fabric) decorated (with a pattern). **b** (often foll. by *in, on*) (of a pattern) wrought (in or on a fabric). **2** closely blended.

in-your-face *adj.* (also **in your face** *predic.*) *slang* aggressively blatant or provocative. [from *in your face* used as a derisive insult]

IOC *abbr.* International Olympic Committee.

iodide *n. Chem.* any compound of iodine with another element or group.

iodine *n.* **1** *Chem.* a non-metallic element of the halogen group, forming a violet vapour. **2** a solution of this in alcohol used as a mild antiseptic. [based on Greek *iōdēs* 'violet-like']

iodize *v.tr.* (also **-ise**) treat or impregnate with iodine. □ **iodization** *n.*

ion *n.* an atom, molecule, or group that has lost one or more electrons (= CATION), or gained one or more electrons (= ANION). [Greek, literally 'going'] □ **ionic** *adj.* **ionically** *adv.*

ion exchange *n.* the exchange of ions of the same charge between a usu. aqueous solution and a solid, used in water-softening etc. □ **ion-exchanger** *n.*

Ionic ● *adj.* **1** ▲ of the order of Greek architecture characterized by a column with scroll-shapes on either side of the capital. ▷ COLUMN. **2** of the ancient Greek dialect used in Ionia. ● *n.* the Ionic dialect. [from Greek *Iōnikos*]

ionize *v.tr. & intr.* (also **-ise**) convert or be converted into an ion or ions. □ **ionizable** *adj.* **ionization** *n.*

ionizer *n.* (also **-iser**) any thing which produces ionization, esp. a device used to improve the quality of the air in a room etc.

ionizing radiation *n.* a radiation of sufficient energy to cause ionization in the medium through which it passes.

ionosphere *n.* ▼ an ionized region of the atmosphere above the mesosphere, able to reflect radio waves for long-distance transmission round the Earth (cf. TROPOSPHERE). ▷ ATMOSPHERE. □ **ionospheric** *adj.*

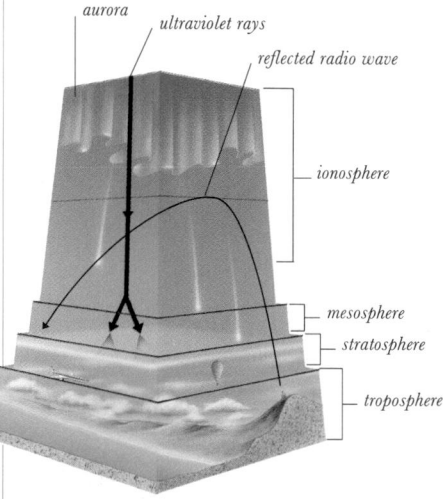

aurora
ultraviolet rays
reflected radio wave
ionosphere
mesosphere
stratosphere
troposphere

IONOSPHERE: SECTION THROUGH THE LOWER DIVISIONS OF THE EARTH'S ATMOSPHERE

iota *n.* **1** the ninth letter of the Greek alphabet (Ι, ι). **2** (usu. with *neg.*) the smallest possible amount. [Greek *iōta* (as the smallest letter)]

IOU *n.* a signed document acknowledging a debt. [representing pronunciation of *I owe you*]

ipecac *n. colloq.* ipecacuanha.

ipecacuanha /ip-i-kak-yoo-**ah**-nă/ *n.* the root of a S. American shrub, *Cephaelis ipecacuanha*, used as an emetic and expectorant. [Portuguese]

ipso facto *adv.* **1** by that very fact or act. **2** thereby. [Latin]

IQ *abbr.* = INTELLIGENCE QUOTIENT.

Ir *symb. Chem.* the element iridium.

ir- *prefix* assim. form of IN- before *r*.

IRA *abbr.* Irish Republican Army.

Iranian ● *adj.* **1** of or relating to Iran in the Middle East. **2** of or relating to the Indo-European group of languages including Persian and Kurdish. ● *n.* **1** a native or national of Iran. **2** a person of Iranian descent.

Iraqi ● *adj.* of or relating to Iraq in the Middle East. ● *n.* (*pl.* **Iraqis**) **1 a** a native or national of Iraq. **b** a person of Iraqi descent. **2** the form of Arabic spoken in Iraq.

irascible *adj.* irritable; hot-tempered. [based on Latin *irasci* 'to grow angry'] □ **irascibility** *n.* **irascibly** *adv.*

irate *adj.* angry, enraged. [from Latin *iratus*] □ **irately** *adv.* **irateness** *n.*

ire *n. literary* anger. [from Latin *ira*] □ **ireful** *adj.*

iridaceous *adj. Bot.* of or relating to the family Iridaceae of plants growing from bulbs, corms, or rhizomes. [from modern Latin *iridaceus*]

iridescent *adj.* **1** showing rainbow-like luminous colours. **2** changing colour with position. [related to IRIS] □ **iridescence** *n.* **iridescently** *adv.*

iridium *n. Chem.* a hard white metallic element of the transition series used esp. in alloys. [modern Latin]

iris *n.* **1** the flat circular coloured membrane behind the cornea of the eye, with a circular opening (pupil) in the centre. ▷ EYE. **2** ► any herbaceous plant of the genus *Iris* (family Iridaceae). **3** (in full **iris diaphragm**) an adjustable diaphragm for regulating the size of a central hole esp. for the admission of light to a lens. [from Greek, literally 'rainbow, iris']

standard (inner tepal)
beard
lip
stigma flap
fall (outer tepal)

IRIS
(*Iris* 'Banbury Beauty')

Irish ● *adj.* of or relating to Ireland, its people, or its Celtic language. ● *n.* **1** the Celtic language of Ireland. **2** (prec. by *the*; treated as *pl.*) the people of Ireland. [Middle English, from earlier *Iras* 'the Irish']

Irish bull *n.* = BULL³ 1.

Irishman *n.* (*pl.* **-men**) a man who is Irish by birth or descent.

Irish stew *n.* a stew of mutton, potato, and onion.

Irish wolfhound *n.* ► **1** a large, often greyish hound of a rough-coated breed. **2** this breed.

Irishwoman *n.* (*pl.* **-women**) a woman who is Irish by birth or descent.

irk *v.tr.* (often prec. by *it* as subject) bore, irritate, annoy. [Middle English]

irksome *adj.* tedious, **IRISH WOLFHOUND**

annoying, tiresome. □ **irksomely** *adv.* **irksomeness** *n.*

iroko *n.* (*pl.* **-os**) **1** either of two African trees, *Chlorophora excelsa* or *C. regia*. **2** the light-coloured hardwood from these trees. ▷ WOOD. [Ibo (a language of SE Nigeria)]

iron ● *n.* **1** *Chem.* a silver-white ductile metallic element much used for tools and implements. ▷ BLAST FURNACE, METALS. **2** this as a symbol of firmness (*will of iron*). **3** a tool or implement made of iron. **4** a household, now usu. electrical, implement with a flat base which is heated to smooth clothes etc. **5** a golf club with an iron or steel sloping head angled to loft the ball (*seven-iron*). ▷ GOLF. **6** (usu. in *pl.*) a fetter (*clapped in irons*). **7** (usu. in *pl.*) a stirrup. **8** (often in *pl.*) *Brit. archaic* an iron support for a malformed leg. **9** a preparation of iron as a tonic or dietary supplement. ● *adj.* **1** made of iron. **2** very robust. **3** unyielding (*iron determination*). ● *v.tr.* **1** smooth (clothes etc.) with an iron. **2** furnish or cover with iron. □ **iron out** remove or smooth over (difficulties etc.). [Old English] □ **ironer** *n.* **ironless** *adj.* **iron-like** *adj.*

Iron Age *n.* the period following the Bronze Age when iron replaced bronze in the making of implements and weapons.

ironclad ● *adj.* **1** clad or protected with iron. **2** impregnable; rigorous. ● *n. hist.* an early name for a 19th-c. warship protected by iron plates.

Iron Curtain *n. hist.* a notional barrier to the passage of people and information between the former Soviet bloc and the West.

ironic *adj.* (also **ironical**) **1** using or displaying irony. **2** in the nature of irony. [from Greek *eirōnikos* 'dissembling'] □ **ironically** *adv.*

ironing *n.* clothes etc. for ironing or just ironed.

ironing board *n.* a flat surface usu. on legs and of adjustable height on which clothes etc. are ironed.

ironist *n.* a person who uses irony. □ **ironize** *v.intr.* (also **-ise**)

ironmonger *n. Brit.* a dealer in hardware etc. □ **ironmongery** *n.* (*pl.* **-ies**).

iron-mould *n.* (*US* **iron-mold**) a spot caused by iron-rust or an ink-stain, esp. on fabric.

iron pyrites *see* PYRITES.

iron rations *n.pl.* a small emergency supply of food.

ironstone *n.* **1** ► any rock containing a substantial proportion of an iron compound. **2** a kind of hard white opaque stoneware.

ironware *n.* articles made of iron.

ironwork *n.* **1** things made of iron. **2** work in iron.

ironworks *n.* (treated as *sing.* or *pl.*) a place where iron is smelted or iron goods are made.

irony *n.* (*pl.* **-ies**) **1** an expression of meaning, often humorous or sarcastic, by the use of language of a different or opposite tendency. **2** an ill-timed or perverse arrival of an event or circumstance that is in itself desirable. **3** (also **dramatic irony**) a literary technique in which the audience can perceive hidden meanings unknown to the characters. [from Greek *eirōneia* 'simulated ignorance']

IRONSTONE:
HAEMATITE

Iroquoian /i-rŏ-**kwoi**-ăn/ ● *n.* **1** a language family of eastern N. America, including Cherokee and Mohawk. **2** a member of the Iroquois Indians. ● *adj.* of or relating to the Iroquois or the Iroquoian language family or one of its members.

Iroquois /i-rŏ-**kwoi**/ ● *n.* (*pl.* same) **1 a** a confederacy of six American Indian peoples (Mohawk, Oneida, Seneca,

Onondaga, Cayuga, and Tuscarora) formerly inhabiting New York State, now living mainly in Canada. **b** a member of any of these peoples. **2** any of the Iroquoian languages of these peoples. ● *adj.* of or relating to the Iroquois or their languages. [from Algonquian]

irradiant *adj. literary* shining brightly. □ **irradiance** *n.*

irradiate *v.tr.* **1** subject to radiation. **2** shine upon; light up. **3** throw light on (a subject). [based on Latin *irradiatus* 'shone out']

irradiation *n.* **1** the process of irradiating. **2** the process of exposing food to gamma rays to kill micro-organisms. **3** shining, illumination.

irrational *adj.* **1** illogical; unreasonable. **2** not endowed with reason. **3** *Math.* (of a root etc.) not rational; not commensurate with the natural numbers (e.g. a non-terminating decimal). □ **irrationality** *n.* **irrationally** *adv.*

irreconcilable *adj.* **1** implacably hostile. **2** (of ideas etc.) incompatible. □ **irreconcilability** *n.* **irreconcilably** *adv.*

irrecoverable *adj.* that cannot be recovered or remedied. □ **irrecoverably** *adv.*

irredeemable *adj.* **1** that cannot be redeemed. **2** hopeless, absolute. □ **irredeemably** *adv.*

irredentist *n.* a person advocating the restoration to his or her country of any territory formerly belonging to it. [based on Italian (*Italia*) *irredenta* 'unredeemed (Italy)'] □ **irredentism** *n.*

irreducible *adj.* **1** that cannot be reduced or simplified. **2** (often foll. by *to*) that cannot be brought to a desired condition. □ **irreducibility** *n.* **irreducibly** *adv.*

irrefutable *adj.* that cannot be refuted. □ **irrefutability** *n.* **irrefutably** *adv.*

irregular ● *adj.* **1** not regular in shape, unsymmetrical; varying in form. **2** (of a surface) uneven. **3** contrary to a rule, moral principle, or custom; abnormal. **4** not occurring at regular intervals. **5** (of troops) not belonging to the regular army. **6** *Gram.* (of a verb, noun, etc.) not inflected according to the usual rules. **7** disorderly. ● *n.* (in *pl.*) irregular troops. □ **irregularity** *n.* (*pl.* **-ies**). **irregularly** *adv.*

irrelevant *adj.* not relevant. □ **irrelevance** *n.* **irrelevancy** *n.* (*pl.* **-ies**). **irrelevantly** *adv.*

irreligion *n.* disregard of or hostility to religion.

irreligious *adj.* **1** indifferent or hostile to religion. **2** lacking a religion. □ **irreligiously** *adv.*

irremediable *adj.* that cannot be remedied. □ **irremediably** *adv.*

irremovable *adj.* that cannot be removed.

irremovable *adj.* that cannot be removed.

irreparable /i-**rep**-er-ăbŭl/ *adj.* (of an injury, loss, etc.) that cannot be rectified or made good. □ **irreparably** *adv.*

irreplaceable *adj.* **1** that cannot be replaced. **2** of which the loss cannot be made good.

irrepressible *adj.* that cannot be repressed or restrained. □ **irrepressibility** *n.* **irrepressibly** *adv.*

irreproachable *adj.* faultless, blameless. □ **irreproachably** *adv.*

irresistible *adj.* **1** too strong or convincing to be resisted. **2** delightful; alluring. □ **irresistibly** *adv.*

irresolute *adj.* **1** hesitant. **2** lacking in resoluteness. □ **irresolutely** *adv.* **irresolution** *n.*

irresolvable *adj.* **1** that cannot be resolved into its components. **2** (of a problem) that cannot be solved.

irrespective *adj.* (foll. by *of*) not taking into account; regardless of.

irresponsible *adj.* **1** acting or done without due sense of responsibility. **2** not responsible for one's conduct. □ **irresponsibility** *n.* **irresponsibly** *adv.*

irresponsive *adj.* (often foll. by *to*) not responsive. □ **irresponsiveness** *n.*

I

ISOMER

Compounds that have the same molecular formula, but a different configuration of atoms, are known as isomers. Butane and 2-methylpropane, for example, both have the chemical formula C_4H_{10}, but their atoms link up in different ways. As a result, each isomeric form has different physical and chemical properties.

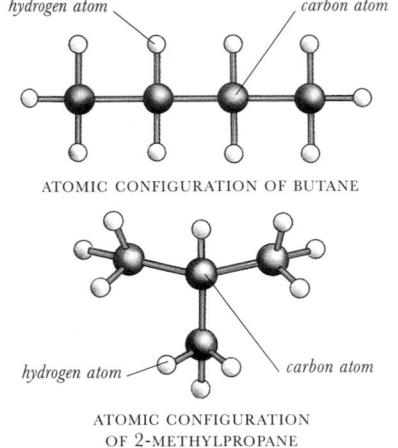

hydrogen atom   carbon atom

ATOMIC CONFIGURATION OF BUTANE

hydrogen atom   carbon atom

ATOMIC CONFIGURATION
OF 2-METHYLPROPANE

irretrievable *adj.* that cannot be retrieved or restored. □ **irretrievably** *adv.*

irreverent *adj.* lacking reverence. □ **irreverence** *n.* **irreverently** *adv.*

irreversible *adj.* not reversible. □ **irreversibility** *n.* **irreversibly** *adv.*

irrevocable *adj.* **1** unalterable. **2** gone beyond recall. □ **irrevocability** *n.* **irrevocably** *adv.*

irrigate *v.tr.* **1 a** supply water to (land) by means of channels. **b** (of a stream etc.) supply (land) with water. **2** *Med.* apply a flow of water or medication to (a wound etc.). [based on Latin *irrigatus* 'watered'] □ **irrigable** *adj.* **irrigation** *n.* **irrigator** *n.*

irritable *adj.* **1** easily annoyed. **2** (of an organ etc.) very sensitive to contact. [from Latin *irritabilis*] □ **irritability** *n.* **irritably** *adv.*

irritable bowel syndrome *n.* a condition involving abdominal pain and diarrhoea or constipation and associated with stress, depression, etc.

irritant ● *adj.* causing irritation. ● *n.* an irritant substance. □ **irritancy** *n.*

irritate *v.tr.* **1** excite to anger; annoy. **2** stimulate discomfort in (a part of the body). **3** *Biol.* stimulate (an organ) to an active response. [based on Latin *irritatus* 'provoked'] □ **irritatedly** *adv.* **irritating** *adj.* **irritatingly** *adv.* **irritation** *n.* **irritative** *adj.*

is *3rd sing. present of* BE.

ISBN *abbr.* international standard book number.

ischaemia /iss-kee-mĭă/ *n.* (*US* **ischemia**) *Med.* a reduction of the blood supply to part of the body. [from Greek *iskhaimos* 'keeping back'] □ **ischaemic** *adj.*

-ise *suffix* var. of -IZE.

■ **Usage** See Usage Note at -IZE.

-ish *suffix* forming adjectives: **1** from nouns, meaning: **a** having the qualities of (*boyish*). **b** of the nationality of (*Danish*). **2** from adjectives, meaning 'somewhat' (*thickish*). **3** *colloq.* denoting an approximate age or time of day (*fortyish*; *six-thirtyish*).

isinglass *n.* **1** a kind of gelatin obtained from fish and used in making jellies, glue, etc. **2** mica. [corruption of obsolete Dutch *huisenblas* 'sturgeon's bladder']

Islam *n.* **1** the religion of the Muslims, a monotheistic faith regarded as revealed through Muhammad as the Prophet of Allah. **2** the Muslim world. [from Arabic *islām* 'submission (to God)'] □ **Islamic** *adj.* **Islamism** *n.* **Islamist** *n.* **Islamize** *v.tr.* (also **-ise**). **Islamization** *n.*

island *n.* **1** a piece of land surrounded by water. **2** = TRAFFIC ISLAND. **3** a detached or isolated thing. [Old English]

islander *n.* a native or inhabitant of an island.

island-hop *v.intr.* move from one island to another.

isle *n. poet.* (and in place names) an island or peninsula. [from Latin *insula*]

islet *n.* **1** a small island. **2** *Anat.* a portion of tissue structurally distinct from surrounding tissues. [from Old French]

-ism *suffix* forming nouns, esp. denoting: **1** an action or its result (*baptism*; *organism*). **2** a system, principle, or ideological movement (*Conservatism*; *jingoism*; *feminism*). **3** a state or quality (*heroism*; *barbarism*). **4** a basis of prejudice or discrimination (*racism*; *sexism*). **5** a peculiarity in language (*Americanism*). **6** a pathological condition (*alcoholism*; *Parkinsonism*).

isn't *contr.* is not.

iso- *comb. form* **1** equal (*isometric*). **2** *Chem.* isomeric, esp. of a hydrocarbon with a branched chain of carbon atoms (*isobutane*). [from Greek *isos* 'equal']

isobar *n.* a line on a map connecting positions having the same atmospheric pressure. [from Greek *isobarēs* 'of equal weight'] □ **isobaric** *adj.*
▷ WEATHER CHART

isochronous /I-sok-rŏn-ŭs/ *adj.* **1** occurring at the same time. **2** occupying equal time. [based on Greek *khronos* 'time']

isolate *v.tr.* **1 a** place apart or alone. **b** place (a patient thought to be contagious or infectious) in quarantine. **2 a** identify and separate for attention (*isolated the problem*). **b** *Chem.* prepare (a substance) in a pure form. **3** insulate (electrical apparatus). [based on Latin *insula* 'island'] □ **isolable** *adj.* **isolatable** *adj.* **isolator** *n.*

isolated *adj.* **1** lonely; cut off from society or contact; remote (*feeling isolated*; *an isolated farmhouse*). **2** untypical, exceptional (*an isolated example*).

isolation *n.* **1** the act or an instance of isolating; the state of being isolated. **2** (*attrib.*) designating a hospital, ward, etc. for patients with contagious or infectious diseases. □ **in isolation** considered singly and not relatively.

isolationism *n.* the policy of holding aloof from the affairs of other countries or groups. □ **isolationist** *n.*

isomer *n.* **1** *Chem.* each of two or more compounds with the same molecular formula but a different arrangement of atoms and different properties. **2** *Physics* each of two or more atomic nuclei that have the same atomic number and the same

mass number but different energy states. [from Greek *isomerēs* 'sharing equally'] □ **isomeric** *adj.* **isomerism** *n.* **isomerize** *v.tr. & intr.* (also **-ise**).

isometric *adj.* **1** of equal measure. **2** *Physiol.* (of muscle action) developing tension while the muscle is prevented from contracting. **3** (of a drawing etc.) with the plane of projection at equal angles to the three principal axes of the object shown. **4** *Math.* (of a transformation) without change of shape or size. [based on Greek *isometria* 'equality of measure'] □ **isometrically** *adv.* **isometry** *n.* (in sense 4).

isometrics *n.pl.* a system of physical exercises in which muscles are caused to act against each other or against a fixed object.

isomorphic *adj.* (also **isomorphous**) **1** exactly corresponding in form and relations. **2** *Crystallog.* having the same form. □ **isomorph** *n.* **isomorphism** *n.*

isosceles /I-sos-i-leez/ *adj.* (of a triangle) having two sides equal. [from Greek *isoskelēs*]

isotherm *n.* **1** a line on a map connecting places having the same temperature. **2** a curve for changes in a physical system at a constant temperature. [based on Greek *thermē* 'heat'] □ **isothermal** *adj.* **isothermally** *adv.*

isotonic *adj.* **1** having the same osmotic pressure. **2** *Physiol.* (of muscle action) taking place with normal contraction. □ **isotonically** *adv.*

isotope *n. Chem.* ▼ each of two or more forms of an element differing from each other in relative atomic mass, and in nuclear but not chemical properties. [based on Greek *topos* 'place' (i.e. in the periodic table of elements)] □ **isotopic** *adj.* **isotopically** *adv.* **isotopy** *n.*

isotropic *adj.* having the same physical properties in all directions. [based on Greek *tropos* 'turn'] □ **isotropically** *adv.* **isotropy** *n.*

Israeli /iz-ray-li/ ● *adj.* of or relating to the modern state of Israel in the Middle East. ● *n.* (*pl.* **Israelis**) **1** a native or national of Israel. **2** a person of Israeli descent. [from Hebrew *yisrā'ēl* 'he that strives with God' (Gen. 32:28)]

Israelite /iz-ră-lyt/ ● *n.* a member of the ancient Hebrew nation or people, esp. an inhabitant of the northern kingdom of the Hebrews (*c.*930–721 BC). ● *adj.* of or relating to the Israelites.

issue ● *n.* **1 a** a giving out or circulation of shares, notes, stamps, etc. **b** a quantity of coins, supplies, copies of a newspaper or book etc., circulated at one time. **c** an item or amount given out or distributed. **d** each of a regular series of a magazine etc. (*the May issue*). **2 a** an outgoing, an outflow. **b** a way out or outlet, esp. the place of the emergence of a stream etc. **3** a point in question; an important subject of debate or litigation. **4** a result; an outcome. **5** *Law* children, progeny (*without male*

ISOTOPE

Isotopes are different forms of the same element. They have identical chemical properties and occupy the same place on the periodic table, but each isotopic form has a different number of neutrons in the nucleus of its atoms, giving each form a different mass. Hydrogen, for example, can exist in three isotopic forms (as below).

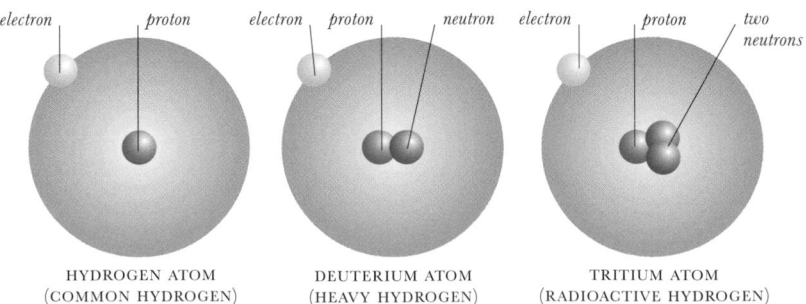

electron   proton   electron   proton   neutron   electron   proton   two neutrons

HYDROGEN ATOM
(COMMON HYDROGEN)   DEUTERIUM ATOM
(HEAVY HYDROGEN)   TRITIUM ATOM
(RADIOACTIVE HYDROGEN)

I

issue). ● *v.* (**issues, issued, issuing**) **1** *intr. literary* go or come out. **2** *tr.* **a** send forth; publish; put into circulation. **b** supply, esp. officially or authoritatively (foll. by *to, with: issued passports to them; issued them with passports*). **3** *intr.* **a** be derived or result. **b** (foll. by *in*) end, result. **4** *intr.* (foll. by *from*) emerge from a condition. □ **at issue 1** under discussion; in dispute. **2** at variance. **join** (or **take**) **issue** (foll. by *with, on*) identify an issue for argument. [based on Latin *exitus* 'having exited'] □ **issuable** *adj.* **issuance** *n.* **issueless** *adj.* **issuer** *n.*

-ist *suffix* forming personal nouns (and in some senses related adjectives) denoting: **1** an adherent of a system etc. in *-ism*: see -ISM 2 (*Marxist; fatalist*). **2 a** a member of a profession (*pathologist*). **b** a person concerned with something (*tobacconist*). **3** a person who uses a thing (*violinist; balloonist; motorist*). **4** a person who does something expressed by a verb in *-ize* (*plagiarist*). **5** a person who subscribes to a prejudice or practises discrimination (*racist; sexist*).

isthmus /issth-mŭs/ *n.* (*pl.* **isthmuses**) ▼ a narrow piece of land connecting two larger bodies of land. [from Greek *isthmos*] □ **isthmian** *adj.*

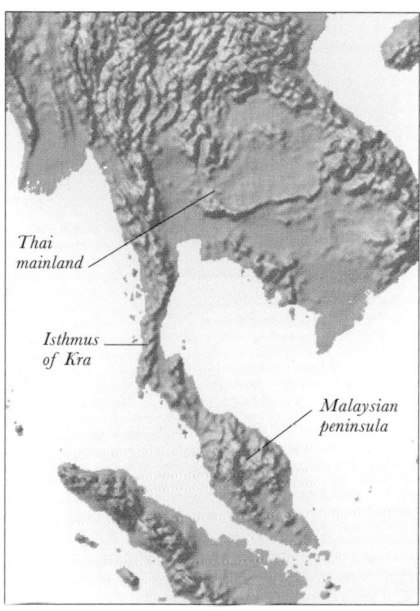

Thai mainland

Isthmus of Kra

Malaysian peninsula

ISTHMUS BETWEEN THAILAND AND MALAYSIA

IT *abbr. Computing* information technology.

it *pron.* (*poss.* **its**; *pl.* **they**) **1** the thing (or occasionally the animal or child) previously named or in question (*took a stone and threw it*). **2** the person in question (*Who is it? It is I; is it a boy or a girl?*). **3** as the subject of an impersonal verb (*it is raining; it is Tuesday; it is two miles to Bath*). **4** as a substitute for a deferred subject or object (*it is intolerable, this delay; I take it that you agree*). **5** as a substitute for a vague object (*brazen it out; run for it!*). **6** as the antecedent to

a relative word (*it was an owl (that) I heard*). **7** exactly what is needed (*absolutely it*). **8** the extreme limit of achievement. **9** *colloq.* sexual intercourse; sex appeal. **10** (in children's games) a player who has to perform a required feat, esp. to catch the others. □ **that's it** *colloq.* that is: **1** what is required. **2** the difficulty. **3** the end, enough. **this is it** *colloq.* **1** the expected event is at hand. **2** this is the difficulty. [Old English]

Italian ● *n.* **1 a** a native or national of Italy. **b** a person of Italian descent. **2** the Romance language used in Italy and parts of Switzerland. ● *adj.* of or relating to Italy or its people or language. [from Italian *Italiano* 'of Italy']

Italianate *adj.* of Italian style or appearance

italic ● *adj.* **1 a** *Printing* of the sloping kind of letters now used esp. for emphasis and in foreign words. **b** (of handwriting) compact and pointed like 16th-c. Italian handwriting. ▷ CALLIGRAPHY. **2** (**Italic**) of ancient Italy. ● *n.* **1** a letter in italic type. **2** this type. [from Greek *italikos* 'Italian', because introduced by Aldo Manuzio of Venice]

italicize *v.tr.* (also **-ise**) print in italics. □ **italicization** *n.*

itch ● *n.* **1** an irritation in the skin. **2** an impatient desire. ● *v.intr.* **1** feel an irritation in the skin. **2** feel a desire to do something (*I'm itching to tell you the news*). [Old English]

itchy *adj.* (**itchier, itchiest**) having or causing an itch. □ **have itchy feet** *colloq.* **1** be restless. **2** have a strong urge to travel. □ **itchiness** *n.*

it'd *contr. colloq.* **1** it had. **2** it would.

-ite *suffix* forming nouns meaning 'a person or thing connected with': **1** in names of persons: **a** as natives of a country (*Israelite*). **b** often *derog.* as followers of a movement etc. (*pre-Raphaelite; Trotskyite*). **2** in names of things: **a** fossil organisms (*ammonite*). **b** minerals (*graphite*). **c** constituent parts of a body or organ (*somite*). **d** explosives (*dynamite*). **e** commercial products (*ebonite; vulcanite*). **f** salts of acids having names in *-ous* (*nitrite; sulphite*).

item *n.* **1 a** any of a number of enumerated or listed things. **b** an entry in an account. **2** an article (*household items*). **3** a distinct piece of news, information, etc. **4** *colloq.* a couple in a romantic or sexual relationship. [Latin, literally 'in like manner, also']

itemize *v.tr.* (also **-ise**) state or list item by item. □ **itemization** *n.* **itemizer** *n.*

iterate *v.tr.* repeat; state repeatedly. [based on Latin *iteratus* 'done again'] □ **iteration** *n.* **iterative** *adj.* **iteratively** *adv.*

itinerant ● *adj.* travelling from place to place. ● *n.* an itinerant person. [from Late Latin *itinerant-* 'travelling'] □ **itinerancy** *n.*

itinerary *n.* (*pl.* **-ies**) **1** a detailed route. **2** a record of travel. **3** a guidebook. [from Late Latin *itinerarium*]

-itis *suffix* forming nouns, esp.: **1** names of inflammatory diseases (*appendicitis; bronchitis*). **2** *colloq.* in extended uses with reference to conditions compared to diseases (*electionitis*).

it'll *contr. colloq.* it will; it shall.

its *poss.det.* of or belonging to it or itself (*can see its advantages; the dog injured its paw*).

■ **Usage** Care should be taken not to confuse *its* with *it's*. *Its*, meaning 'of or belonging to it', does not have an apostrophe, e.g. *Its handle had fallen off*. The apostrophe is used only in the short form of *it is* or *it has*, e.g. *It's raining; It's been a long time since we met.*

it's *contr.* **1** it is. **2** it has.

■ **Usage** See Usage Note at ITS.

itself *pron.* emphatic and refl. form of IT. □ **by itself** apart from its surroundings, automatically, spontaneously. **in itself** viewed in its essential qualities (*not in itself a bad thing*).

itsy-bitsy *adj.* (also **itty-bitty**) *colloq. usu. derog.* tiny, insubstantial, slight.

ITV *abbr.* (in the UK) Independent Television.

IUD *abbr.* intrauterine device.

IV *abbr.* intravenous.

I've *contr.* I have.

IVF *abbr. in vitro* fertilization.

ivied *adj.* overgrown with ivy.

ivory ● *n.* (*pl.* **-ies**) **1** ◀ a hard creamy-white substance composing the main part of the tusks of an elephant, hippopotamus, walrus, and narwhal. ▷ ELEPHANT. **2** the colour of this. **3** (usu. in *pl.*) **a** an article made of ivory. **b** *slang* anything made of or resembling ivory, esp. a piano key or a tooth. ● *adj.* of the colour of ivory; creamy white. [from Latin *ebur eboris*]

ivory tower *n.* a state of seclusion from the ordinary world and the harsh realities of life.

ivy *n.* (*pl.* **-ies**) **1** a climbing evergreen shrub, *Hedera helix*, with usu. shiny dark green five-angled leaves. **2** any of various other climbing or trailing plants including ground ivy and poison ivy. [Old English]

IVORY: 20TH-CENTURY INDIAN IVORY BROOCH

Ivy League *n.* a group of universities in the eastern US.

-ize *suffix* (also **-ise**) forming verbs, meaning: **1** make or become such (*Americanize; realize*). **2** treat in such a way (*monopolize; pasteurize*). **3 a** follow a special practice (*economize*). **b** have a specified feeling (*sympathize*). **4** affect with, provide with, or subject to (*oxidize; hospitalize*). □ **-ization** *suffix* forming nouns. **-izer** *suffix* forming agent nouns.

■ **Usage** The form *-ize* has been in use in English since the 16th c., it is widely used in American English, but is not an Americanism. The alternative spelling *-ise* (reflecting a French influence) is in common use, especially in British English, and is obligatory in certain cases: (*a*) where it forms part of a larger word-element, such as *-mise* (= sending) in *compromise*, and *-prise* (= taking) in *surprise*; and (*b*) in verbs corresponding to nouns with *-s-* in the stem, such as *advertise* and *televise*.

I

J

J¹ *n.* (also **j**) (*pl.* **Js** or **J's**) the tenth letter of the alphabet.

J² *symb.* (also **J.**) joule(s).

jab ● *v.tr.* (**jabbed**, **jabbing**) **1 a** poke roughly. **b** stab. **2** (foll. by *into*) thrust (a thing) hard or abruptly. ● *n.* **1** an abrupt blow. **2** *colloq.* a hypodermic injection. **3** a cutting remark. [originally Scots]

jabber ● *v.* **1** *intr.* chatter volubly. **2** *tr.* utter (words) fast and indistinctly. ● *n.* meaningless jabbering; a gabble.

jabiru /**jab**-i-roo/ *n.* a large black-necked stork of the genus *Ephippiorhynchus*, esp. *E. mycteria* of Central and S. America, with mainly white plumage. [Tupi-Guarani (a S. American Indian language)]

jabot /*zhab*-oh/ *n.* ▶ an ornamental frill or ruffle of lace etc. on the front of a shirt or blouse. [French, originally in sense 'crop of a bird']

jabot

JABOT: 18TH-CENTURY
GENTLEMAN'S JABOT

jacana /jak-ă-nă/ *n.* (also **jaçana** /jas-ă-**nah**/) any of various small tropical wading birds of the family Jacanidae, with elongated toes and hind claws which enable them to walk on floating leaves etc. ▷ WADING BIRD. [Portuguese]

jacaranda *n.* a tropical American tree with fragrant wood, esp. one of the genus *Jacaranda*, with trumpet-shaped blue flowers. [Tupi-Guarani (a S. American Indian language)]

jacinth /jas-inth/ *n.* ▶ a reddish-orange variety of zircon used as a gem. [from Latin *hyacinthus* 'hyacinth']

jack ● *n.* **1** a device for lifting heavy objects, esp. the axle of a vehicle off the ground while changing a wheel etc. **2** ▼ a playing card with a picture of a man, page, or knave, etc. **3** a ship's flag, esp. one flown from the bow and showing nationality. **4** (in full **jack socket**) a socket designed to receive a jack plug. **5** a small white ball in bowls, at which the players aim. **6 a** = JACKSTONE 1. **b** (in *pl.*) = JACKSTONE 2. **7** (**Jack**) the familiar form of *John* esp. typifying the common man (*I'm all right, Jack*). **8** the figure of a man striking the bell on a clock. **9** *slang* a detective; a police officer. **10** *US slang* money. **11** the male of various animals (*jackass*). ● *v.tr.* (usu. foll. by *up*) **1** raise with or as with a jack (in sense 1). **2** *colloq.* raise e.g. prices. □ **every man jack** every person. **jack in** (or **up**) *slang* abandon (an attempt etc.). [Middle English *Iakke*, pet name for *John*]

JACKS ON
PLAYING CARDS

jackal *n.* **1** any of various wild doglike mammals of the genus *Canis*, esp. *C. aureus*, found in Africa and S. Asia, usu. hunting or scavenging for food in packs. **2** *colloq.* a person who does preliminary drudgery for another. [from Persian *šagāl*]

jackaroo *n.* (also **jackeroo**) *Austral. colloq.* a novice on a sheep station or cattle station.

jackass *n.* **1** a male ass. **2** a stupid person.

jackboot *n.* **1** a large boot reaching above the knee worn chiefly by soldiers. **2** this as a symbol of fascism or military oppression. □ **jackbooted** *adj.*

Jack-by-the-hedge *n.* a white-flowered cruciferous plant, *Alliaria petiolata*, of shady places.

jackdaw *n.* ▼ a small grey-headed crow, *Corvus monedula*.

JACKDAW
(*Corvus monedula*)

jackeroo var. of JACKAROO.

jacket ● *n.* **1 a** a sleeved short outer garment. **b** a thing worn for protection or support (*life jacket*). **2** a casing or covering. **3** = DUST JACKET. **4** the skin of a potato. **5** an animal's coat. ● *v.tr.* (**jacketed**, **jacketing**) cover with a jacket. [from Old French *ja(c)quet* 'small tunic']

jacket potato *n. Brit.* a baked potato served with the skin on.

Jack Frost *n.* frost personified.

jackfruit *n.* **1** an East Indian tree, *Artocarpus heterophyllus*, bearing fruit resembling breadfruit. **2** this fruit. [based on Portuguese *jaca*]

jackhammer *n.* esp. *N. Amer.* a portable pneumatic hammer or drill.

jack-in-the-box *n.* a toy figure that springs out of a box when it is opened.

jackknife ● *n.* (*pl.* **-knives**) **1** a large clasp-knife. **2** a dive in which the body is first bent at the waist and then straightened. ● *v.* (**-knifed**, **-knifing**) **1** *intr.* (of an articulated vehicle) fold against itself in an accident. **2** *intr. & tr.* fold like a jackknife.

jack of all trades *n.* a person who can do many different kinds of work.

jack-o'-lantern *n.* **1** a will-o'-the-wisp. **2** a pumpkin lantern.

jack plug *n.* a plug for use esp. in sound equipment, consisting of a single shaft.

jackpot *n.* a large prize or amount of winnings, esp. accumulated in a game or lottery etc. □ **hit the jackpot** *colloq.* **1** win a large prize. **2** have remarkable luck or success. [originally in a form of poker, with two jacks as minimum to open the pool]

jackrabbit *n.* any of various large N. American prairie hares of the genus *Lepus*, with very long ears and hind legs. [earlier *jackass-rabbit*, so called from the long ears]

Jack Russell *n.* (in full **Jack Russell terrier**) a terrier of a small working breed with short legs. [named after Revd John (*Jack*) *Russell*, English clergyman and dog-breeder, 1795–1883]

jackstone *n.* **1** a small piece of metal etc. used with others in tossing games. **2** (in *pl.*) such a tossing game.

Jack tar *n.* a sailor.

Jacobean ● *adj.* of or relating to the reign of James I of England. ● *n.* a person of the time of James I. [from ecclesiastical Latin *Jacobus* 'James']

Jacobite *n. hist.* a supporter of James II of England after his removal from the throne in 1688, or of the Stuarts. [from ecclesiastical Latin *Jacobus* 'James'] □ **Jacobitism** *n.*

Jacob's ladder *n.* ▶ a plant, *Polemonium caeruleum*, with corymbs of blue or white flowers, and leaves suggesting a ladder. [from Jacob's dream of a ladder reaching to heaven (Gen. 28:12)]

ladder-like leaves

JACOB'S LADDER
(*Polemonium caeruleum*)

jacquard /**jak**-ard/ *n.* **1** an apparatus with perforated cards, fitted to a loom to facilitate the weaving of figured fabrics. **2** (in full **jacquard loom**) a loom fitted with this. **3** a fabric or article made with this. [named after J. M. *Jacquard*, French inventor, 1752–1834]

jacuzzi /jă-**koo**-zi/ *n.* (*pl.* **jacuzzis**) *propr.* a large bath with underwater jets of water to massage the body. [named after C. *Jacuzzi*, US inventor, 1903–86]

jade¹ ● *n.* **1** ▶ a hard usu. green stone composed of silicates of calcium and magnesium, or of sodium and aluminium, used for ornaments and implements. **2** the green colour of jade. ● *adj.* of this colour. [from Spanish *piedra de ijada* 'stone of the flank', i.e. stone for colic (which it was believed to cure)]

jade² *n.* **1** an inferior or worn-out horse. **2** *derog.* a disreputable woman. [Middle English]

JADE: 18TH-CENTURY MEXICAN JADE MASK

jaded *adj.* tired or worn out; surfeited. □ **jadedly** *adv.* **jadedness** *n.*

jadeite *n.* a green, blue, or white sodium aluminium silicate form of jade. ▷ GEM

jag¹ ● *n.* a sharp projection of rock etc. ● *v.tr.* (**jagged**, **jagging**) **1** cut or tear unevenly. **2** make indentations in. [Middle English] □ **jagger** *n.*

jag² *n.* esp. *US colloq.* **1** a bout of drinking. **2** a period of indulgence in an activity, emotion, etc. **3** a bundle (of hay, logs, etc.). [16th-century coinage]

jagged *adj.* **1** with an unevenly cut or torn edge. **2** deeply indented. □ **jaggedly** *adv.* **jaggedness** *n.*

jaggy *adj.* (**jaggier**, **jaggiest**) **1** = JAGGED. **2** (also **jaggie**) *Sc.* prickly.

jaguar *n.* ▼ a large heavily built spotted feline, *Panthera onca*, of Central and S. America. [from Tupi-Guarani (a S. American Indian language)]

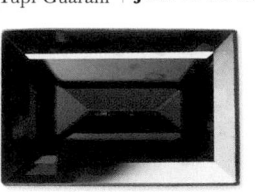

JACINTH

JAGUAR (*Panthera onca*)

jaguarundi *n.* (*pl.* **jaguarundis**) a long-tailed slender feline, *Felis yaguarondi*, of Central and S. America. [Tupi-Guarani (a S. American Indian language)]

jail (also *Brit.* **gaol**) ● *n.* **1** a place to which persons are committed by a court for detention. **2** confinement in a jail. ● *v.tr.* put in jail. [from Old Northern French *gaole*]

jailbait *n.* (*collect.*) *slang* a girl, or girls, under the age of consent.

jailbird *n.* (also *Brit.* **gaolbird**) a prisoner or habitual criminal.

jailbreak *n.* (also *Brit.* **gaolbreak**) an escape from jail.

jailer *n.* (also *Brit.* **gaoler**) a person in charge of a jail or of the prisoners in it.

jailhouse *n.* esp. *N. Amer.* a prison.

Jain /jyn/ ● *n.* an adherent of a non-theistic Indian religion. ● *adj.* of or relating to this religion. [from Sanskrit *jainas* 'saint, victor'] □ **Jainism** *n.*

jake *adj.* *N. Amer.*, *Austral.*, & *NZ slang* all right; satisfactory. [20th-century coinage]

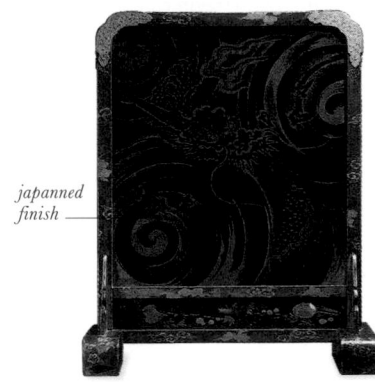
JALAPEÑO PEPPER

jalapeño /hal-ă-**payn**-yoh/ *n.* (*pl.* **-os**) (also **jalapeño pepper**) ◀ a very hot green chilli pepper, used esp. in Mexican-style cooking. [Mexican Spanish]

jalopy /jă-**lop**-i/ *n.* (*pl.* **-ies**) *colloq.* a dilapidated old motor vehicle. [20th-century coinage]

jalousie /*zh*al-oo-zee/ *n.* a blind or shutter made of a row of angled slats to keep out rain etc. and control the influx of light. [French]

jam[1] ● *v.* (**jammed**, **jamming**) **1 a** *tr.* squeeze or wedge into a space. **b** *intr.* become wedged. **2 a** *tr.* cause (machinery or a component) to become wedged or immovable so that it cannot work. **b** *intr.* become jammed in this way. **3** *tr.* cram together in a compact mass. **4** *intr.* (foll. by *in*, *on to*) push or crowd (*they jammed on to the bus*). **5** *tr.* **a** block (a passage, road, etc.) by crowding or obstructing. **b** (foll. by *in*) obstruct the exit of (*we were jammed in*). **6** *tr.* (usu. foll. by *on*) apply (brakes etc.) forcefully or abruptly. **7** *tr.* make (a radio transmission) unintelligible by causing interference. **8** *intr.* *colloq.* (in jazz etc.) extemporize with other musicians. ● *n.* **1** a squeeze or crush. **2** a crowded mass (*traffic jam*). **3** *colloq.* a predicament. **4** a stoppage (of a machine etc.) due to jamming. **5** (in full **jam session**) *colloq.* improvised playing by a group of usu. jazz musicians. □ **jammer** *n.*

jam[2] *n.* **1** a conserve of fruit and sugar boiled to a thick consistency. **2** *Brit.* *colloq.* something easy or pleasant (*money for jam*). □ **jam tomorrow** *Brit.* a pleasant thing often promised but never forthcoming.

jamb *n.* *Archit.* a side post or surface of a doorway, window, or fireplace. [from Late Latin *gamba* 'hoof']

jambalaya /jam-bă-**lyr**/ *n.* a Cajun dish of rice with shrimps, chicken, etc. [Louisiana French from modern Provençal *jambalaia*]

jamboree *n.* **1** a celebration. **2** a large rally of Scouts. [19th-century coinage]

jam jar *n.* **1** a glass jar for containing jam. **2** *Brit.* *rhyming slang* a car.

jammy *adj.* (**jammier**, **jammiest**) **1** covered with jam. **2** *Brit.* *colloq.* **a** lucky. **b** profitable.

jam-packed *adj.* *colloq.* full to capacity.

jam session see JAM[1] *n.* 5.

Jan. *abbr.* January.

jane *n.* □ **plain jane** an unattractive girl or woman.

jangle ● *v.* **1** *intr.* & *tr.* make, or cause (a bell etc.) to make, a harsh metallic sound. **2** *tr.* irritate (the nerves etc.) by discordant sound or speech etc. ● *n.* a harsh metallic sound. [from Old French *jangler*]

janitor *n.* **1** a doorkeeper. **2** a caretaker of a building. [Latin, based on *janua* 'door'] □ **janitorial** *adj.*

janizary *n.* (also **janissary**) (*pl.* **-ies**) **1** *hist.* a member of the Turkish infantry forming the Sultan's guard in the 14th–19th c. **2** a devoted follower. [based on Turkish *yeni* 'new' + *çeri* 'troops']

January *n.* (*pl.* **-ies**) the first month of the year. [from Latin *Januarius* (*mensis*) '(month) of' *Janus*, guardian god of doors and beginnings]

Jap *n.* & *adj.* *colloq.* *offens.* = JAPANESE.

japan ● *n.* ▼ a hard usu. black varnish, esp. of a kind brought originally from Japan. ● *v.tr.* (**japanned**, **japanning**) **1** varnish with japan. **2** make black and glossy.

japanned finish

JAPAN: JAPANNED AND LACQUERED ANTIQUE SCREEN

Japanese ● *n.* (*pl.* same) **1 a** a native or national of Japan. **b** a person of Japanese descent. **2** the language of Japan. ● *adj.* of or relating to Japan, its people, or its language.

Japanese quince *n.* = JAPONICA.

jape ● *n.* a practical joke. ● *v.intr.* play a joke. [Middle English] □ **japery** *n.*

Japlish *n.* a blend of Japanese and English, used in Japan.

japonica *n.* any flowering shrub of the genus *Chaenomeles*, esp. *C. speciosa*, with round white, green, or yellow edible fruits and bright red flowers. [modern Latin fem. of *japonicus* 'Japanese']

jar[1] *n.* **1 a** a container of glass, earthenware, plastic, etc., usu. cylindrical. **b** the contents of this. **2** *Brit.* *colloq.* a glass of beer. [from Arabic *jarra*] □ **jarful** *n.*

jar[2] ● *v.* (**jarred**, **jarring**) **1** *intr.* (of sound, words, manner, etc.) sound discordant or grating (on the nerves etc.). **2 a** *tr.* (foll. by *against*, *on*) strike or cause to strike with vibration or a grating sound. **b** *intr.* (of a body affected) vibrate gratingly. **3** *tr.* send a shock through (a part of the body) (*the fall jarred his neck*). **4** *intr.* (foll. by *with*) be at variance; be in conflict or in dispute. ● *n.* **1** a jarring sound or sensation. **2** a physical shock or jolt. **3** lack of harmony; disagreement. [Middle English]

jardinière /*zh*ar-din-**yair**/ *n.* **1** an ornamental pot or stand for the display of growing plants. **2** a dish of mixed vegetables. [French, literally 'female gardener']

jargon *n.* **1** words or expressions used by a particular group or profession (*medical jargon*). **2** barbarous or debased language. [from Old French]

jasmine *n.* (also **jasmin**, **jessamin**, **jessamine**) ▶ any of various ornamental shrubs of the genus *Jasminum* usu. with white or yellow flowers. [from Persian *yāsamīn*]

JASMINE: YELLOW JASMINE (*Jasminum humile*)

jasper *n.* ▶ an opaque variety of quartz, usu. red, yellow, or brown. [from Latin *iaspis*]

JASPER: RED JASPER

jaundice ● *n.* **1** *Med.* a condition with yellowing of the skin or whites of the eyes, often caused by obstruction of the bile duct or by liver disease. **2** disordered (esp. mental) vision. **3** envy. ● *v.tr.* **1** affect with jaundice. **2** (esp. as **jaundiced** *adj.*) affect (a person) with envy. [from Old French *jaunice* 'yellowness']

jaunt ● *n.* a short excursion for enjoyment. ● *v.intr.* take a jaunt. [16th-century coinage]

jaunty *adj.* (**jauntier**, **jauntiest**) **1** cheerful and self-confident. **2** dashing, pert (*jaunty hat*). [earlier *jentee*, from French *gentil* 'noble'] □ **jauntily** *adv.* **jauntiness** *n.*

Javanese *n.* (*pl.* same) **1 a** a native or inhabitant of Java in Indonesia. **b** a person of Javanese descent. **2** the Austronesian language of central Java. ● *adj.* of or relating to Java, its people, or its language.

javelin *n.* **1** a light spear thrown in a competitive sport or as a weapon. **2** the athletic event or sport of throwing the javelin. [from Gallo-Roman *gabalottus*]

jaw ● *n.* **1 a** each of the upper and lower bony structures in vertebrates forming the framework of the mouth and containing the teeth. **b** the parts of certain invertebrates used for the ingestion of food. **2 a** (in *pl.*) the mouth with its bones and teeth. **b** the narrow mouth of a valley, channel, etc. **c** the gripping parts of a tool or machine. **d** gripping-power (*jaws of death*). **3** *colloq.* **a** talkativeness (*hold your jaw*). **b** a sermonizing talk. ● *v.* *colloq.* **1** *intr.* speak esp. at tedious length. **2** *tr.* **a** persuade by talking. **b** admonish or lecture. [from Old French *joe* 'cheek, jaw'] □ **jawless** *adj.*

jawbone *n.* a bone of the jaw, esp. that of the lower jaw, or either half of this. ▷ VERTEBRATE

jawline *n.* the outline of the jaw.

jay *n.* **1** ▶ a noisy European bird, *Garrulus glandarius*, with vivid pinkish-brown, blue, black, and white plumage. ▷ PASSERINE. **2** any other bird of the subfamily Garrulinae. [from Late Latin *gaius*]

JAY (*Garrulus glandarius*)

jaywalk *v.intr.* cross or walk in the street or road without regard for traffic. □ **jaywalker** *n.*

jazz ● *n.* **1** music of African-American origin characterized by improvisation, syncopation, and usu. a forceful rhythm. **2** *colloq.* pretentious talk or behaviour (*all that jazz*). ● *v.intr.* play or dance to jazz. □ **jazz up** brighten or enliven. [20th-century coinage] □ **jazzer** *n.*

jazzman *n.* (*pl.* **-men**) a male jazz musician.

jazzy *adj.* (**jazzier**, **jazziest**) **1** of or like jazz. **2** vivid, showy. □ **jazzily** *adv.*

JCB *n.* *Brit.* *propr.* a type of mechanical excavator with a shovel at the front and a digging arm at the rear. [from *J. C. Bamford*, the makers]

J-cloth *n.* (also **J cloth** *propr.*) a type of cloth used esp. for household cleaning. [from *Johnson and Johnson*, original makers]

J

J

JEEP

The jeep was first designed in 1944 for military use on rough terrain. Now used also for civil purposes, this versatile vehicle is easily adapted or repaired by bolting new or replacement parts on to the solid metal framework.

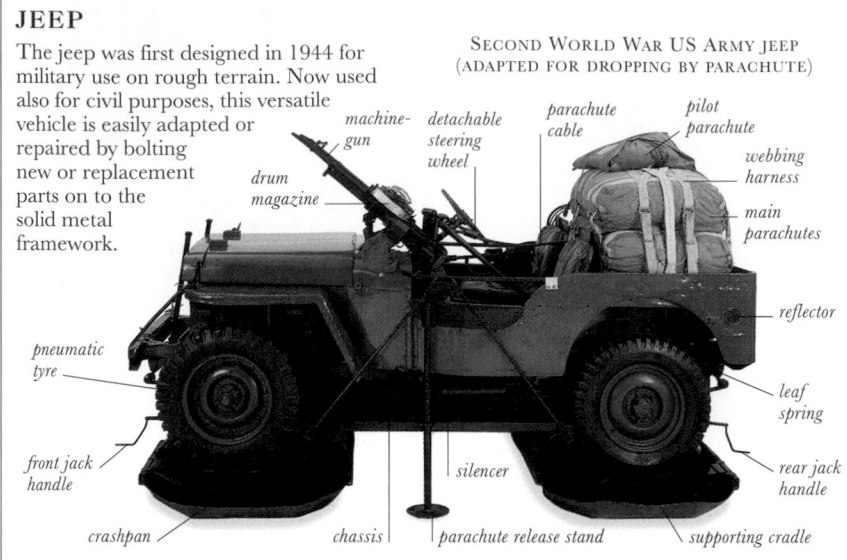

SECOND WORLD WAR US ARMY JEEP
(ADAPTED FOR DROPPING BY PARACHUTE)

machine-gun • detachable steering wheel • parachute cable • pilot parachute • drum magazine • webbing harness • main parachutes • reflector • pneumatic tyre • leaf spring • front jack handle • silencer • rear jack handle • crashpan • chassis • parachute release stand • supporting cradle

---

jealous *adj.* **1** fiercely protective (of rights etc.). **2** resentful of rivalry in love or affection. **3** envious (of a person or a person's advantages etc.). **4** (of God) intolerant of disloyalty. **5** (of inquiry, supervision, etc.) vigilant. [from medieval Latin *zelosus* 'zealous'] □ **jealously** *adv.*

jealousy *n.* (*pl.* **-ies**) **1** a jealous state or feeling. **2** an instance of this.

jeans *n.pl.* hard-wearing trousers made of denim or other cotton fabric, for informal wear. [Middle English *jean* 'twilled cotton cloth', from medieval Latin *Janua* 'Genoa']

jeep *n. propr.* ▲ a small sturdy motor vehicle with four-wheel drive. [from *GP*, literally 'general purposes', influenced by US comic strip animal 'Eugene the Jeep']

jeepers *int.* (also **jeepers creepers**) *N. Amer. slang* expressing surprise etc. [corruption of *Jesus*]

jeer ● *v.* **1** *intr.* (usu. foll. by *at*) scoff derisively. **2** *tr.* scoff at; deride. ● *n.* a scoff or taunt. [16th-century coinage] □ **jeeringly** *adv.*

jehad var. of JIHAD.

Jehovah *n.* the Hebrew name of God in the Old Testament. [from Hebrew *YHVH*, with the vowels of *adonai* 'my lord' included]

Jehovah's Witness *n.* a member of a millenarian Christian sect rejecting the supremacy of the State and religious institutions over personal conscience, faith, etc.

jejune /ji-joon/ *adj.* **1** intellectually unsatisfying; shallow. **2** puerile. **3** (of ideas, writings, etc.) meagre, scanty; dry and uninteresting. **4** (of land) barren. [originally in sense 'fasting': from Latin *jejunus*]

jejunum /ji-joon-üm/ *n. Anat.* the part of the small intestine between the duodenum and ileum. ▷ INTESTINE. [Latin, literally 'fasting thing']

Jekyll and Hyde /jek-il/ *n.* a person alternately displaying opposing good and evil personalities. [from R. L. Stevenson's story *The Strange Case of Dr Jekyll and Mr Hyde* (1886)]

jell *v.intr. colloq.* **1 a** set as a jelly. **b** (of ideas etc.) take a definite form. **2** (of people) readily cooperate or reach an understanding.

jellaba var. of DJELLABA.

jellify *v.tr. & intr.* (**-ies**, **-ied**) turn into jelly; make or become like jelly.

jello *n.* (also **Jell-O** *propr.*) esp. *N. Amer.* a fruit-flavoured gelatin dessert; jelly.

jelly ● *n.* (*pl.* **-ies**) **1 a** a semi-transparent preparation of boiled sugar and fruit juice or milk etc., set to a semi-solid consistency, eaten as a dessert. **b** a similar preparation for use as a jam or a condiment (*redcurrant jelly*). **c** a similar preparation derived from meat, bones, etc., and gelatin (*marrowbone jelly*). **2** any substance of a similar consistency. **3** *Brit. slang* gelignite. ● *v.* (**-ies**, **-ied**) **1** *intr. & tr.* set or cause to set as a jelly, congeal. **2** *tr.* set (food) in a jelly (*jellied eels*). [based on Latin *gelare* 'to freeze'] □ **jelly-like** *adj.*

jelly baby *n. Brit.* a jelly-like sweet in the stylized shape of a baby.

jelly bag *n.* a bag for straining juice for jelly.

jelly bean *n.* a bean-shaped sweet with a jelly-like centre and a hard sugar coating.

jellyfish *n.* (*pl.* usu. same) **1** ▼ a marine cnidarian of the class Scyphozoa having an umbrella-shaped jelly-like body and stinging tentacles. ▷ CNIDARIAN. **2** *colloq.* a feeble person.

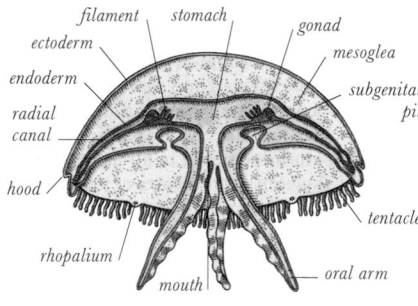

filament • stomach • gonad • ectoderm • mesoglea • endoderm • subgenital pit • radial canal • hood • tentacle • rhopalium • oral arm • mouth

JELLYFISH: CROSS-SECTION

jemmy (*N. Amer.* **jimmy**) ● *n.* (*pl.* **-ies**) a burglar's short crowbar. ● *v.tr.* (**-ies**, **-ied**) force open with a jemmy. [pet form of the name *James*]

je ne sais quoi /zhĕ nĕ say **kwah**/ *n.* an indefinable something. [French, literally 'I do not know what']

jenny *n.* (*pl.* **-ies**) **1** *hist.* = SPINNING JENNY. **2** a female donkey or ass. [pet form of the name *Janet*]

jenny-wren *n.* a popular name for a female wren.

jeopardize /jep-er-dyz/ *v.tr.* (also **-ise**) endanger.

jeopardy /jep-er-di/ *n.* danger, esp. of severe harm or loss. [from Latin *jocus* 'game' + *partitus* 'divided']

jerboa *n.* ▶ any small desert rodent of the family Dipodidae with long hind legs and the ability to make large jumps. [from Arabic *yarbū'*]

JERBOA (*Jaculus jaculus*)

jeremiad *n.* a doleful complaint or lamentation. [with reference to the Lamentations of Jeremiah (Old Testament)]

Jeremiah *n.* a dismal prophet; a denouncer of the times. [biblical reference (see JEREMIAH)]

jerk[1] ● *n.* **1** a sharp sudden pull, twitch, etc. **2** a spasmodic muscular twitch. **3** (in *pl.*) *Brit. colloq.* exercises (*physical jerks*). **4** *slang* a fool. ● *v.* **1** *intr.* move with a jerk. **2** *tr.* pull, twist, etc., with a jerk. **3** *tr.* throw with a suddenly arrested motion. **4** *tr. Sport* (in weightlifting) raise (a weight) from shoulder level to above the head. □ **jerk off** *coarse slang* masturbate. [16th-century coinage] □ **jerky** *adj.* (**jerkier**, **jerkiest**). **jerkily** *adv.*

jerk[2] *v.tr.* cure (beef) by cutting it in long slices and drying it in the sun. [from Latin American Spanish *charquear*]

jerkin *n.* **1** ▶ a sleeveless jacket. **2** *hist.* a man's close-fitting jacket, often of leather. [16th-century coinage]

punched design

JERKIN: 16TH-CENTURY LEATHER JERKIN

jeroboam /je-rŏ-**boh**-ăm/ *n.* a wine bottle of 4 times the ordinary size. [named after *Jeroboam*, King of Israel (1 Kings 11:28, 14:16)]

Jerry *n.* (*pl.* **-ies**) *Brit. slang* **1** a German (esp. in military contexts). **2** the Germans collectively.

jerry *n.* (*pl.* **-ies**) *Brit. slang* a chamber pot.

jerry-builder *n.* a builder of unsubstantial houses with poor-quality materials. [19th-century coinage] □ **jerry-building** *n.* **jerry-built** *adj.*

jerrycan *n.* (also **jerrican**) a kind of (originally German) petrol or water can.

jerrymander *Brit.* var. of GERRYMANDER.

jersey *n.* (*pl.* **-eys**) **1 a** a knitted usu. woollen pullover or similar garment. **b** a plain-knitted fabric. **2** (**Jersey**) a light brown dairy cow from Jersey. [from *Jersey*, largest of the Channel Islands]

Jerusalem artichoke *n.* **1** a species of sunflower, *Helianthus tuberosus*, with edible underground tubers. **2** ▶ this tuber used as a vegetable. [corruption of Italian *girasole* 'sunflower']

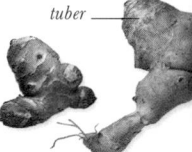

tuber

JERUSALEM ARTICHOKE (*Helianthus tuberosus*)

jess *n.* a short strap of leather, silk, etc., put round the leg of a hawk in falconry. [based on Latin *jactus* 'a throw']

jessamin (also **jessamine**) var. of JASMINE.

jest ● *n.* **1 a** a joke. **b** fun. **2 a** a raillery, banter. **b** an object of derision (*a standing jest*). ● *v.intr.* **1** joke; make jests. **2** fool about; play or act triflingly. □ **in jest** in fun. [originally in sense 'exploit': from Latin *gesta* 'done']

jester *n. hist.* a professional joker or 'fool' at a medieval court etc.

Jesuit *n.* a member of the Society of Jesus, a Roman Catholic order founded by St Ignatius Loyola and others in 1534. [based on *Jesus*]

Jesuitical *adj.* **1** of or concerning the Jesuits. **2** *offens.* dissembling or equivocating. □ **Jesuitically** *adv.*

jet[1] ● *n.* **1** a stream of liquid, gas, etc. shot out, esp. from a small opening. **2** a spout or nozzle for this purpose. **3** a jet engine or plane. ● *v.* (**jetted**, **jetting**) **1** *intr.* spurt out in jets. **2** *tr. & intr. colloq.* send or travel by jet plane. [from Latin *jactare* 'to throw repeatedly']

JET ENGINE

The turbojet, the simplest type of jet engine, produces thrust by burning a combination of fuel and air which releases a powerful stream of hot exhaust gases. This also turns a turbine, which runs an air compressor, which in turn forces more air into the combustion chamber. In a turbofan jet engine, a low-pressure turbine drives a fan, which forces air through bypass ducts to join the exhaust stream, producing dual thrust. A turboprop jet engine spins a propeller and expels exhaust gases, both producing thrust.

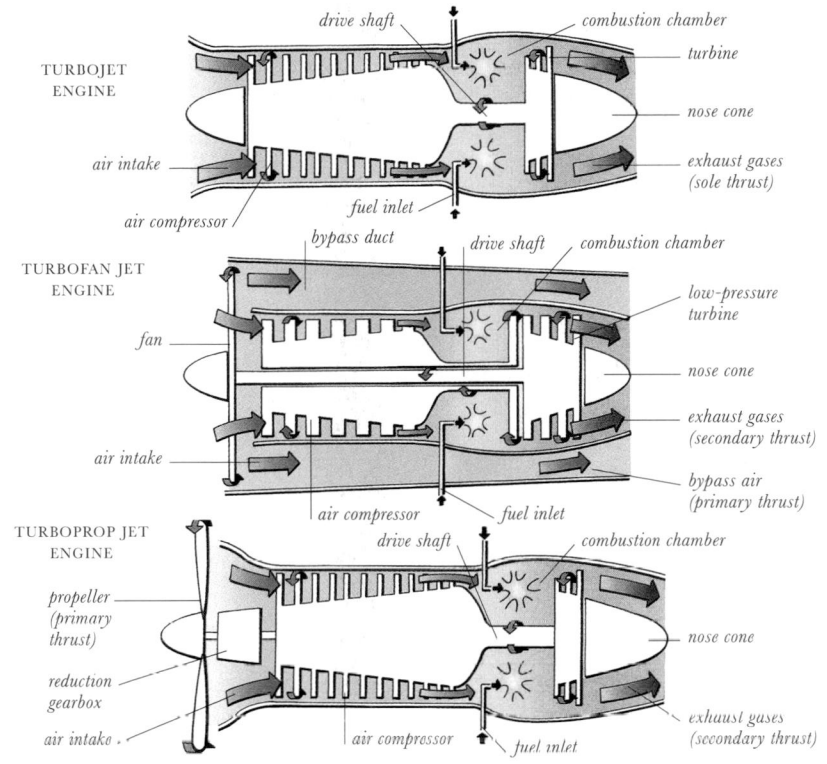

TURBOJET ENGINE — drive shaft, combustion chamber, turbine, nose cone, air intake, exhaust gases (sole thrust), fuel inlet, air compressor

TURBOFAN JET ENGINE — bypass duct, drive shaft, combustion chamber, low-pressure turbine, fan, nose cone, exhaust gases (secondary thrust), air intake, bypass air (primary thrust), air compressor, fuel inlet

TURBOPROP JET ENGINE — drive shaft, combustion chamber, propeller (primary thrust), nose cone, reduction gearbox, air intake, exhaust gases (secondary thrust), air compressor, fuel inlet

jet² *n.* **1 a** ▼ a hard black variety of lignite capable of being carved and highly polished. ▷ GEM. **b** (*attrib.*) made of this. **2** a deep glossy black. [from Greek *(lithos) gagatēs* '(stone) from *Gagai*', a town in Asia Minor]

jet engine *n.* ▲ an engine using jet propulsion for forward thrust, esp. of an aircraft.

jetfoil *n.* a type of passenger-carrying hydrofoil.

jet lag *n.* extreme tiredness etc. felt after a long flight across time zones. □ **jet-lagged** *adj.*

jet-propelled *adj.* **1** having jet propulsion. **2** very fast.

jet propulsion *n.* propulsion by the backward ejection of a high-speed jet of gas etc.

jetsam *n.* discarded material washed ashore, esp. that thrown overboard. [contraction of *jettison*]

jet set *n. colloq.* wealthy people frequently travelling by air, esp. for pleasure. □ **jet-setter** *n.* **jet-setting** *adj.*

jet ski ● *n. propr.* (*pl.* **skis**) ▶ a jet-propelled vehicle like a motorbike, for riding across water. ● *v.intr.* (**jet-ski**) (**-skies**, **-skied**, **-skiing**) ride on a jet ski.

jet stream *n.* **1** a narrow current of very strong winds encircling the globe several miles above the Earth. **2** the flow of vapour from a jet engine.

jettison ● *v.tr.* **1** throw (esp. heavy material) overboard to lighten a ship, aircraft, etc. **2** get rid of. ● *n.* the act of jettisoning. [based on Latin *jactatio -onis* 'act of throwing']

JET: MODERN TURKISH JET NECKLACE

jetty *n.* (*pl.* **-ies**) **1** a pier or breakwater constructed to protect or defend a harbour, coast, etc. **2** a landing pier. [from Old French *jetee* (fem.) 'thrown']

Jew *n.* a person of Hebrew descent or whose religion is Judaism. [from Hebrew *yᵉhûdî*]

jewel ● *n.* **1 a** a precious stone. **b** this as used for its hardness as a bearing in watchmaking. **2** a jewelled personal ornament. **3** a precious person or thing. ● *v.tr.* (**jewelled**, **jewelling**; *US* **jeweled**, **jeweling**) **1** (esp. as **jewelled** *adj.*) adorn or set with jewels. **2** (in watchmaking) set with jewels. [from Old French *joel*]

jeweller *n.* (*US* **jeweler**) a maker of or dealer in jewels or jewellery.

jeweller's rouge *n.* finely ground rouge for polishing metal.

jewellery *n.* (also **jewelry**) jewels or other items for personal adornment, regarded collectively.

Jewess *n. offens.* a female Jew.

Jewish *adj.* **1** of or relating to Jews. **2** of Judaism. □ **Jewishness** *n.*

Jewry *n.* (*pl.* **-ies**) **1** Jews collectively. **2** *hist.* a Jews' quarter in a town etc.

jew's harp *n.* a small musical instrument held between the teeth and struck with the finger.

Jezebel *n.* a shameless or immoral woman. [from *Jezebel*, wife of Ahab (1 Kings 16, 19, 21)]

jib¹ ● *n.* **1** a triangular staysail extending from the outer end of the jib-boom to the top of the fore-mast or from the bowsprit to the masthead. ▷ SCHOONER, SHIP. **2** the projecting arm of a crane. ● *v.tr. & intr.* (**jibbed**, **jibbing**) (of a sail etc.) pull or swing round; gybe. [17th-century coinage]

jib² *v.intr.* (**jibbed**, **jibbing**) **1 a** (of an animal, esp. a horse) stop and refuse to go on. **b** (of a person) refuse to continue. **2** (foll. by *at*) show aversion to. [19th-century coinage]

jibe¹ var. of GIBE.

jibe² *US* var. of GYBE.

jiff *n.* (also **jiffy**, *pl.* **-ies**) *colloq.* a short time; a moment (*in a jiffy*; *half a jiff*). [18th-century coinage]

Jiffy bag *n. propr.* a type of padded envelope for postal use.

jig ● *n.* **1 a** a lively dance with leaping movements. **b** the music for this, usu. in triple time. **2** a device that holds a piece of work and guides the tools operating on it. ● *v.* (**jigged**, **jigging**) **1** *intr.* dance a jig. **2** *tr. & intr.* move quickly and jerkily up and down. **3** *tr.* work on or equip with a jig or jigs. □ **jig about** fidget. [16th-century coinage]

jigger¹ ● *n.* **1 a** a measure of spirits etc. **b** a small glass holding this. **2** a person or thing that jigs. ● *v.tr.* (usu. in phr. **I'll be jiggered**) *slang* confound, damn. **2** *Brit.* exhaust; damage, break.

jigger² var. of CHIGGER.

jiggery-pokery *n.* esp. *Brit. colloq.* deceitful or dishonest dealing, trickery.

jiggle ● *v.* (often foll. by *about* etc.) **1** *tr.* shake lightly; rock jerkily. **2** *intr.* fidget. ● *n.* a light shake. □ **jiggly** *adj.*

J

JET SKI

For the rider, a jet ski combines the speed of a motorcycle with the skills of water-skiing. Since their first commercial production in 1973, jet skis have become a popular aquatic craft for sport and entertainment worldwide.

EXPLODED DIAGRAM OF A JET SKI

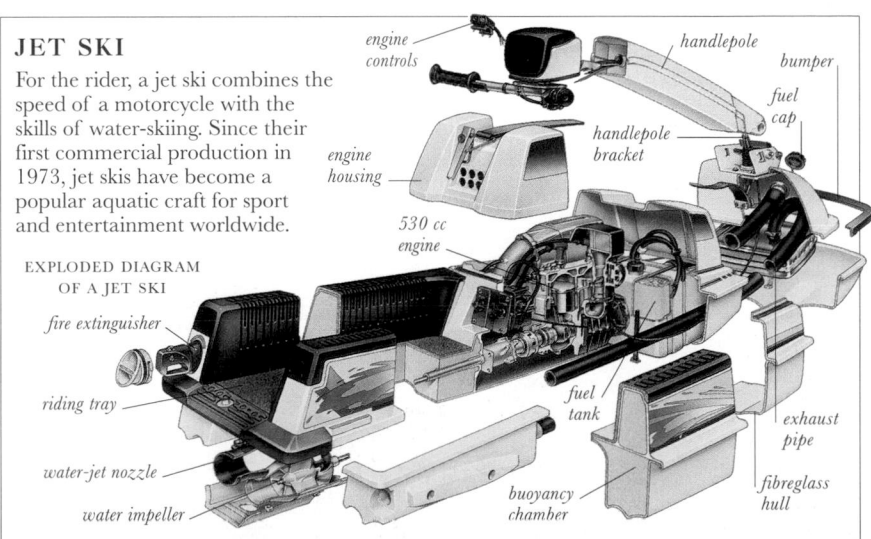

engine controls, handlepole, bumper, fuel cap, handlepole bracket, engine housing, 530 cc engine, fire extinguisher, riding tray, water-jet nozzle, water impeller, fuel tank, buoyancy chamber, exhaust pipe, fibreglass hull

J

jigsaw *n.* **1 a** (in full **jigsaw puzzle**) a picture on board or wood etc. cut into interlocking pieces to be reassembled. **b** a mental puzzle resolvable by assembling pieces of information. **2** ▶ a machine saw with a fine blade enabling it to cut curved lines. ▷ SAW

JIGSAW
fine blade

jihad /ji-hard/ *n.* (also **jehad**) a holy war undertaken by Muslims against unbelievers. [from Arabic]

jilt *v.tr.* abruptly reject or abandon (a lover etc.). [17th-century coinage]

Jim Crow *n. US* **1** the practice of segregating blacks. **2** *offens.* a black person. [name of a black character in a 19th-century plantation song]

jim-jams *n.pl.* **1** *slang* = DELIRIUM TREMENS. **2** *colloq.* a fit of depression or nervousness.

jimmy *N. Amer.* var. of JEMMY.

jingle ● *n.* **1** a mixed noise as of bells or light metal objects being shaken together. **2 a** a repetition of sound in a phrase etc. **b** a short verse of this kind used in advertising etc. ● *v.* **1** *intr. & tr.* to make a jingling sound. **2** *intr.* (of writing) be full of rhymes etc. [Middle English] □ **jingly** *adj.*

jingo *n.* (*pl.* **-oes**) a supporter of policies favouring war; a blustering patriot. [from use of *by jingo* in a popular song, associated with the sending of a British fleet to resist Russia in 1878] □ **jingoism** *n.* **jingoist** *n.* **jingoistic** *adj.*

jink ● *v.* **1** *intr.* move elusively; dodge. **2** *tr.* elude by dodging. ● *n.* dodging or eluding. [originally Scots]

jinnee *n.* (also **jinn, djinn**) (*pl.* **jinn** or **djinn**) (in Muslim mythology) a spirit in human or animal form, with power over people. [from plural of Arabic *jinn*]

jinx *colloq.* ● *n.* a person or thing that seems to cause bad luck. ● *v.tr.* (often in *passive*) subject (a person or thing) to bad luck.

jitter *colloq.* ● *n.* (**the jitters**) extreme nervousness. ● *v.intr.* be nervous; act nervously. [20th-century coinage] □ **jittery** *adj.* **jitteriness** *n.*

jitterbug ● *n.* **1** a nervous person. **2** *hist.* a fast dance popular in the 1940s. ● *v.intr.* (**-bugged, -bugging**) dance the jitterbug.

jiu-jitsu var. of JU-JITSU.

jive ● *n.* **1** a jerky lively style of dance performed to jazz or rock and roll music. **2** music for this. ● *v.intr.*

1 dance the jive. **2** play jive music. [20th-century coinage] □ **jiver** *n.*

Jnr. *abbr.* Junior.

jo *n.* (*pl.* **joes**) *Sc.* a sweetheart or beloved. [variant of JOY]

job ● *n.* **1** a piece of work, esp. one done for hire or profit. **2** a paid position of employment. **3** *colloq.* **a** anything one has to do. **b** a specified operation or other matter (*a nose job*; *a respray job*). **4** *colloq.* a difficult task (*had a job to find them*). **5** *slang* a crime, esp. a robbery. **6** esp. *Brit. colloq.* a state of affairs (*is a bad job*). ● *v.* (**jobbed, jobbing**) **1** *intr.* do jobs; do piecework. **2 a** *intr.* deal in stocks. **b** *tr.* buy and sell (stocks or goods) as a middleman. **3** *tr.* deal corruptly with (a matter). □ **just the job** *Brit. colloq.* exactly what is wanted. **on the job** *colloq.* at work; in the course of doing a piece of work. **out of a job** unemployed. [16th-century coinage]

jobber *n.* **1** (in the UK) a principal or wholesaler dealing on the Stock Exchange (permitted only to deal with brokers, not directly with the public). **2** *US* **a** a wholesaler. **b** *derog.* = BROKER 2. **3** a person who jobs.

■ **Usage** The term *jobber* in sense 1 was officially replaced by *broker-dealer* in 1986, broker-dealers being entitled to act as both agents and principals in share dealings.

jobbery *n.* corrupt dealing.

jobbing *adj.* working on separate or occasional jobs (esp. of computers, gardeners, printers, etc.).

jobcentre *n.* (in the UK) any of several government offices displaying information about available jobs.

job-hunt *v.intr. colloq.* seek employment.

jobless *adj.* without a job; unemployed. □ **joblessness** *n.*

job lot *n.* a miscellaneous group of articles, esp. sold or bought together.

Job's comforter *n.* a person who under the guise of comforting aggravates distress. [from the patriarch *Job* in the Old Testament (Job 16:2)]

job-sharing *n.* an arrangement by which a full-time job is done jointly by two or more part-time employees who share the remuneration etc. □ **job-share** *n. & v.intr.*

jobsworth *n. Brit. colloq.* an official who upholds petty rules. [contraction of 'it's more than my *job's worth* (not) to']

jobwork *n.* work done and paid for by the job.

Jock *n. colloq.* often *offens.* a Scotsman. [Scots form of the name *Jack*]

jock[1] *n. colloq.* **1** a jockey. **2** a disc jockey.

jock[2] *n. N. Amer. colloq.* **1** = JOCKSTRAP. **2** a well-built rugged man.

jockey ● *n.* (*pl.* **-eys**) ◀ a rider in horse races, esp. a professional one. ● *v.* (**-eys, -eyed**) **1** *tr.* **a** trick or cheat (a person). **b** outwit. **2** *tr.* (foll. by *away, out, in*, etc.) draw (a person) by trickery. **3** *intr.* cheat. □ **jockey for position** try to gain an advantageous position. [diminutive of JOCK] □ **jockeyship** *n.*

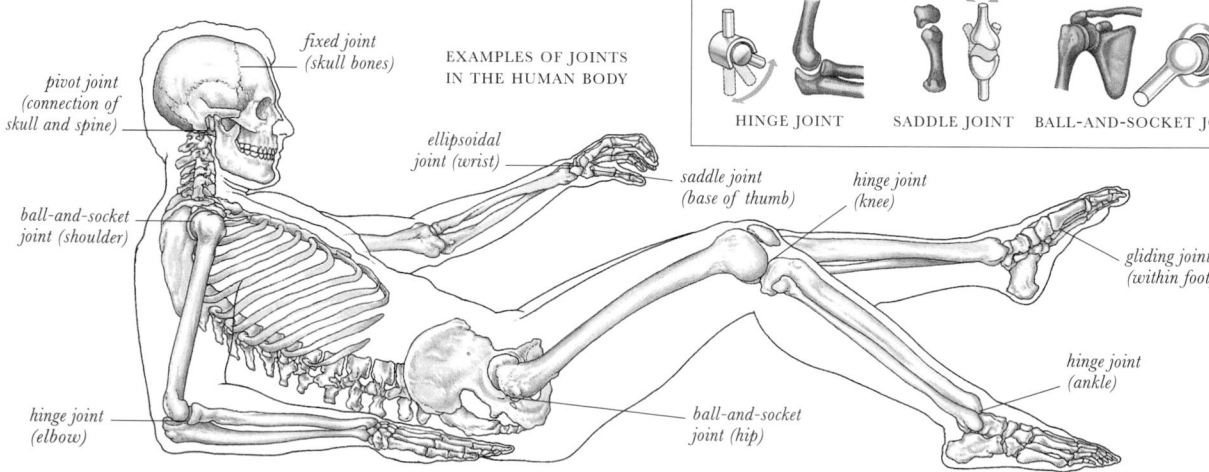

jockey cap

racing-silk jacket

whip

riding boot

JOCKEY

jockey cap *n.* a strengthened cap with a long peak, as worn by jockeys.

jockstrap *n.* **1** a support or protection for the male genitals, worn esp. by sportsmen. **2** *N. Amer. colloq.* an athletic person, esp. a student participant in sport. [based on slang *jock* 'male genitals']

jocose /jŏ-kohss/ *adj.* **1** playful in style. **2** fond of joking, jocular. [from Latin *jocosus*] □ **jocosely** *adv.* **jocosity** *n.* (*pl.* **-ies**).

jocular *adj.* **1** merry; fond of joking. **2** of the nature of a joke; humorous. [based on Latin *joculus* 'little jest'] □ **jocularity** *n.* (*pl.* **-ies**). **jocularly** *adv.*

jocund /jok-ŭnd/ *adj. literary* merry, cheerful, sprightly. [from

---

JOINT

Joints are classified by their structure and by the manner of articulation between the bones that they link. Fixed or slightly movable joints, such as between the vertebrae within the spine, are held in place by fibrous tissue (ligaments) or cartilage. In synovial joints, articulating bone surfaces are enclosed within a fibrous capsule, and covered with smooth cartilage, allowing more flexible movement.

ACTIONS OF HUMAN SYNOVIAL JOINTS

PIVOT JOINT   ELLIPSOIDAL JOINT   GLIDING JOINT

HINGE JOINT   SADDLE JOINT   BALL-AND-SOCKET JOINT

fixed joint (skull bones)

EXAMPLES OF JOINTS IN THE HUMAN BODY

pivot joint (connection of skull and spine)

ellipsoidal joint (wrist)

saddle joint (base of thumb)

hinge joint (knee)

ball-and-socket joint (shoulder)

gliding joint (within foot)

hinge joint (ankle)

hinge joint (elbow)

ball-and-socket joint (hip)

Latin *jocundus* 'agreeable'] □ **jocundity** *n.* (*pl.* **-ies**). **jocundly** *adv.*

jodhpurs /jod-perz/ *n.pl.* long breeches for riding etc., close-fitting below the knee. ▷ SHOWJUMPING. [from *Jodhpur*, a city in India]

Joe Bloggs *n. Brit. colloq.* a hypothetical average man.

joey *n.* (*pl.* **-eys**) *Austral.* **1** a young kangaroo. **2** a young animal. [from Aboriginal *joè*]

jog ● *v.* (**jogged, jogging**) **1** *intr.* run at a slow pace, esp. as exercise. **2** *intr.* (of a horse) move at a jogtrot. **3** *intr.* (often foll. by *on, along*) proceed laboriously. **4** *intr.* move up and down with an unsteady motion. **5** *tr.* nudge. **6** *tr.* shake with a push or jerk. **7** *tr.* stimulate (the memory). ● *n.* **1** a shake, push, or nudge. **2** a slow walk or trot. [Middle English] □ **jogger** *n.*

joggle ● *v.tr. & intr.* shake or move by or as if by repeated jerks. ● *n.* **1** a slight shake. **2** the act or action of joggling. [based on JOG]

jogtrot *n.* **1** a slow regular trot. **2** a monotonous progression.

john *n. esp. N. Amer. slang* **1** a lavatory. **2** a prostitute's client. [from the name *John*]

John Bull *n.* a personification of England or the typical Englishman. [name of a character in J. Arbuthnot's satire *Law is a Bottomless Pit* (1712)]

John Dory *n.* (*pl.* **-ies**) ► a European marine fish, *Zeus faber*, with a laterally flattened body and a black spot on each side.

johnny *n.* (*pl.* **-ies**) *Brit.* **1** *slang* a condom. **2** *colloq.* a fellow; a man. [familiar form of the name *John*]

johnny-come-lately *n. colloq.* a recently arrived person.

joie de vivre /zhwah dĕ **veevr**/ *n.* a feeling of exuberant enjoyment of life. [French, literally 'joy of living']

join ● *v.* **1** *tr.* (often foll. by *to, together*) put together; fasten, unite. **2** *tr.* connect (points) by a line etc. **3** *tr.* become a member of (an association etc.). **4** *tr.* take one's place with or in (a procession etc.). **5** *tr.* a come into the company of (a person). **b** (foll. by *in*) take part with (others) in an activity etc. **c** (foll. by *for*) share the company of for a specified occasion (*may I join you for lunch?*). **6** *intr.* (often foll. by *with, in*) come together; be united. **7** *tr.* be or become continuous with (*the Inn joins the Danube at Passau*). ● *n.* a point, line, or surface at which two or more things are joined. □ **join battle** begin fighting. **join forces** combine efforts. **join hands 1** clasp hands. **2** combine in an action or enterprise. **join in** (also *absol.*) take part in (an activity). **join up 1** enlist for military service. **2** (often foll. by *with*) unite, connect. [from Latin *jungere* 'to join']

joiner *n.* **1** a person who makes furniture and light woodwork (cf. CARPENTER). **2** *colloq.* a person who readily joins societies etc. □ **joinery** *n.* (in sense 1).

joint ● *n.* **1 a** a place at which two things or parts of a structure are joined. **b** a device for joining these. **2** ◄ a structure in an animal body by which two bones are fitted together. **3 a** a division of an animal carcass as meat. **b** any of the parts of which a body is made up. **4** *slang* a place of meeting for drinking etc. **5** *slang* a marijuana cigarette. **6** *Geol.* a fissure in rock. ● *adj.* **1** held, done by, or belonging to, two or more persons etc. (*a joint mortgage*). **2** sharing with another in some action etc. (*joint author*). ● *v.tr.* **1** connect by joints. **2** divide at a joint or into joints. □ **out of joint 1** (of a bone) dislocated. **2** out of order. [from Old French, literally 'joined'] □ **jointless** *adj.* **jointly** *adv.*

jointress *n.* a widow who holds a jointure. [from obsolete *jointer* 'joint possessor']

joint stock *n.* capital held jointly; a common fund.

joint-stock company *n.* a company formed on the basis of a joint stock.

jointure ● *n.* an estate settled on a wife for the period during which she survives her husband. ● *v.tr.* provide with a jointure.

joist *n.* each of a series of parallel supporting beams used in floors, ceilings, etc. ▷ HOUSE. [based on Latin *jacēre* 'to lie'] □ **joisted** *adj.*

jojoba /hŏ-**hoh**-bă/ *n.* ► a plant, *Simmondsia chinensis*, with seeds yielding an oily extract used in cosmetics etc. [Mexican Spanish]

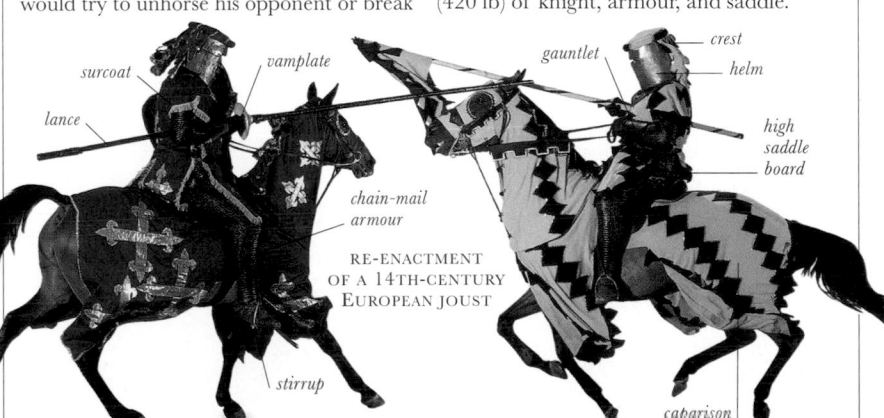

JOJOBA
(*Simmondsia chinensis*)

— *leaves*
— *seeds*

joke ● *n.* **1 a** a thing said or done to excite laughter. **b** a witticism or jest. **2** a ridiculous person or thing. ● *v.* **1** *intr.* make jokes; tease. **2** *tr.* poke fun at. [17th-century coinage, originally slang] □ **jokingly** *adv.* **joky** *adj.* (also **jokey**). **jokily** *adv.*

joker *n.* **1** a person who jokes. **2** *slang* a person. **3** a playing card used in some games.

jollify *v.tr. & intr.* (**-ies, -ied**) make or be merry. □ **jollification** *n.*

jollity *n.* (*pl.* **-ies**) **1** merrymaking; festiveness. **2** (in *pl.*) festivities.

jolly ● *adj.* (**jollier, jolliest**) **1** cheerful and good-humoured; merry. **2** festive, jovial. **3** slightly drunk. **4** *colloq.* (of a person or thing) very pleasant, delightful (often *iron.: a jolly shame*). ● *adv. colloq.* very (*jolly unlucky*). ● *v.tr.* (**-ies, -ied**) **1** (usu. foll. by *along*) *colloq.* coax or humour (a person) in a friendly way. **2** chaff, banter. ● *n.* (*pl.* **-ies**) *Brit. colloq.* a party or celebration. [from Old French *jolif* 'gay, pretty'] □ **jollily** *adv.* **jolliness** *n.*

Jolly Roger *n.* a pirates' black flag, usu. with the skull and crossbones.

jolt ● *v.* **1** *tr.* disturb or shake from the normal position (esp. in a moving vehicle) with a jerk. **2** *tr.* give a mental shock to. **3** *intr.* (of a vehicle) move along with jerks. ● *n.* **1** such a jerk. **2** a surprise or shock. [16th-century coinage] □ **jolty** *adj.*

Jonah *n.* a person who seems to bring bad luck. [from *Jonah* in the Old Testament]

jonquil *n.* a bulbous plant, *Narcissus jonquilla*, with clusters of small fragrant yellow flowers. [from Spanish *junquillo* 'little reed']

Jordanian ● *adj.* of or relating to the kingdom of Jordan in the Middle East. ● *n.* **1** a native or national

of Jordan. **2** a person of Jordanian descent. [from *Jordan*, a river flowing into the Dead Sea]

josh *colloq.* ● *n.* a good-natured or teasing joke. ● *v.* **1** *tr.* tease or banter. **2** *intr.* indulge in ridicule. [19th-century coinage] □ **josher** *n.*

joss *n.* a Chinese idol.

joss stick *n.* a stick of fragrant tinder mixed with clay, burnt as incense.

jostle ● *v.* **1** *tr.* push against; elbow. **2** *tr.* (often foll. by *away, from*, etc.) push (a person) abruptly or roughly. **3** *intr.* (foll. by *against*) knock or push, esp. in a crowd. **4** *intr.* (foll. by *with*) have a rough exchange. ● *n.* **1** the act or an instance of jostling. **2** a collision. [Middle English, based on JOUST]

jot ● *v.tr.* (**jotted, jotting**) (usu. foll. by *down*) write briefly or hastily. ● *n.* (usu. with *neg.* expressed or implied) a very small amount (*not one jot*). [from Greek *iōta* 'iota']

jotter *n. Brit.* a small pad or notebook for making notes etc.

jotting *n.* (usu. in *pl.*) a jotted note.

joule /jool/ *n.* the SI unit of work or energy. [named after J. P. *Joule*, English physicist, 1818–89]

journal *n.* **1** a newspaper or periodical. **2** a daily record of events. **3** *Naut.* a logbook. **4** the part of a shaft or axle that rests on bearings. [from Late Latin *diurnalis* 'diurnal']

journalese *n.* a hackneyed style of language characteristic of some newspaper writing.

journalist *n.* a person employed to write for, edit, or report for, a newspaper, journal, or newscast. □ **journalism** *n.* **journalistic** *adj.* **journalistically** *adv.*

journey ● *n.* (*pl.* **-eys**) **1** an act of going from one place to another, esp. at a long distance. **2** the distance travelled in a specified time (*a day's journey*). ● *v.intr.* (**-eys, -eyed**) make a journey. [from Old French *jornee* 'day's work or travel'] □ **journeyer** *n.*

journeyman *n.* (*pl.* **-men**) **1** a qualified mechanic or artisan who works for another. **2** *derog.* **a** a reliable but not outstanding worker. **b** a mere hireling. [based on obsolete *journey* 'a day's work']

joust *hist.* ● *n.* ▼ a combat between two knights on horseback with lances, esp. for sport. ● *v.intr.* engage in a joust. [from Old French *juster* 'to bring together'] □ **jouster** *n.*

Jove *n.* (in Roman mythology) Jupiter (king of the gods). □ **by Jove!** an exclamation of surprise or approval. [from oblique case of Old Latin *Jovis* 'Jupiter']

J

JOUST

In 15th-century Europe, knights practised the skills of battle by jousting. A knight would try to unhorse his opponent or break his lance against the other's shield. A jousting horse (destrier) carried some 190 kg (420 lb) of knight, armour, and saddle.

surcoat — *vamplate* — *gauntlet* — *crest* — *helm*
lance — *high saddle board*
chain-mail armour

RE-ENACTMENT OF A 14TH-CENTURY EUROPEAN JOUST

stirrup — *caparison*

jovial *adj.* **1** merry. **2** convivial. **3** hearty and good-humoured. [from Late Latin *jovialis* 'of Jupiter', planet reputed to influence those born under it] □ **joviality** *n.* **jovially** *adv.*

jowl[1] *n.* **1** the jaw or jawbone. **2** the cheek (*cheek by jowl*). [Old English] □ **-jowled** *adj.* (in *comb.*).

jowl[2] *n.* **1** the external loose skin on the throat or neck when prominent. **2** the dewlap of an ox, wattle of a bird, etc. [Old English] □ **jowly** *adj.*

joy *n.* **1** (often foll. by *at, in*) a vivid emotion of pleasure. **2** a thing that causes joy. **3** *Brit. colloq.* satisfaction, success (*got no joy*). [based on Latin *gaudēre* 'to rejoice'] □ **joyful** *adj.* **joyfully** *adv.* **joyfulness** *n.* **joyless** *adj.*

joyous *adj.* (of an occasion, circumstance, etc.) characterized by pleasure or joy; joyful. □ **joyously** *adv.* **joyousness** *n.*

joyride *colloq.* ● *n.* a ride for pleasure, esp. one in a stolen motor car. ● *v.intr.* (*past* **-rode**; *past part.* **-ridden**) go for a joyride. □ **joyrider** *n.*

joystick *n.* **1** *colloq.* the control column of an aircraft. **2** a lever to control the movement of an image on a VDU screen.

JP *abbr.* (in the UK) Justice of the Peace.

Jr. *abbr.* Junior.

jubilant *adj.* exultant, rejoicing. [from Latin *jubilant-* 'shouting for joy'] □ **jubilance** *n.* **jubilantly** *adv.*

jubilee *n.* **1** a time or season of rejoicing. **2** an anniversary of an event, esp. the 25th or 50th. **3** exultant joy. [based on Hebrew *yōbēl*, originally in sense 'ram's-horn trumpet', with which the jubilee year was proclaimed]

Jubilee clip *n. propr.* an adjustable steel band secured with a screw.

Judaeo- /joo-dee-oh/ *comb. form* (*US* **Judeo-**) Jewish; Jewish and.

Judaism /joo-day-izm/ *n.* **1** the religion of the Jews, with a belief in one God and a basis in Mosaic and rabbinical teachings. **2** the Jews collectively. □ **Judaic** *adj.* **Judaist** *n.*

Judas *n.* a person who betrays a friend. [from *Judas* Iscariot who betrayed Christ (Luke 22)]

judder ● *v.intr.* **1** (esp. of a mechanism) vibrate noisily or violently. **2** (of a singer's voice) oscillate in intensity. ● *n.* an instance of juddering.

Judeo- *US* var. of JUDAEO-.

judge ● *n.* **1** a public officer appointed to hear and try legal cases. **2** a person appointed to decide in a competition or dispute. **3 a** a person who decides a question. **b** a person regarded in terms of capacity to decide on the merits of a thing or question (*a good judge of art*). ● *v.* **1** *tr.* **a** try (a cause) in a court of justice. **b** pronounce sentence on (a person). **2** *tr.* estimate, appraise. **3** *tr.* act as a judge of (a dispute or contest). **4** *tr.* (often foll. by *to* + infin. or *that* + clause) conclude, consider, or suppose. **5** *intr.* **a** form a judgement. **b** act as judge. [from Latin *judex*] □ **judgeship** *n.*

judgement *n.* (also **judgment**) **1** the critical faculty; discernment (*an error of judgement*). **2** good sense. **3** an opinion or estimate (*in my judgement*). **4** the sentence of a court of justice. **5** often *joc.* a deserved misfortune (*it is a judgement on you*). **6** criticism. □ **against one's better judgement** contrary to what one really feels to be advisable.

judgemental *adj.* (also **judgmental**) **1** of or concerning or by way of judgement. **2** condemning, critical. □ **judgementally** *adv.*

Judgement Day *n.* the day on which the Last Judgement is believed to take place.

judicature *n.* **1** the administration of justice. **2** a judge's term of office. **3** judges collectively. **4** a court of justice. [based on Latin *judicare* 'to judge']

judicial *adj.* **1** of, done by, or proper to a court of law. **2** having the function of judgement (*a judicial assembly*). **3** of or proper to a judge. **4** expressing a judgement. [based on Latin *judex judic-* 'judge'] □ **judicially** *adv.*

judicial separation see SEPARATION 2.

J

JUDO

Judo is a system of unarmed combat developed in the East. Competitors attempt to throw, pin, or master their opponent during a controlled bout on a regulation mat. Coloured belts indicate the student's level of proficiency.

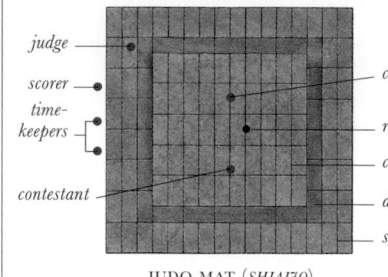

JUDO MAT (*SHIAIJO*)

judge
scorer
time-keepers
contestant
contestant
referee
contest area
danger area
safety area

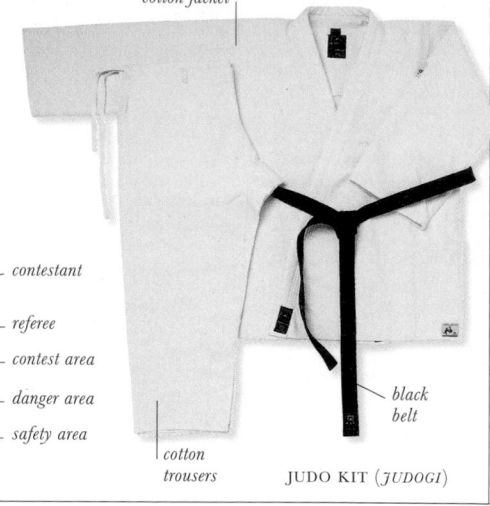

cotton jacket

black belt

cotton trousers

JUDO KIT (*JUDOGI*)

---

judiciary *n.* (*pl.* **-ies**) the judges of a state collectively.

judicious *adj.* **1** sensible, prudent. **2** sound in discernment and judgement. □ **judiciously** *adv.* **judiciousness** *n.*

judo *n.* ▲ a sport of unarmed combat derived from ju-jitsu. [Japanese, from *jū* 'gentle' + *dō* 'way'] □ **judoist** *n.*

jug ● *n.* **1** *Brit.* a deep vessel for holding liquids, with a handle and often with a spout or lip shaped for pouring. **2** *N. Amer.* a large vessel, esp. for liquids, with a narrow mouth. **3** a jugful. **4** *slang* prison. ● *v.tr.* (**jugged**, **jugging**) **1** (usu. as **jugged** *adj.*) stew or boil (a hare or rabbit) in a covered vessel. **2** *slang* imprison. □ **jugful** *n.* (*pl.* **-fuls**).

juggernaut *n.* **1** esp. *Brit.* a large heavy motor vehicle, esp. an articulated lorry. **2** a huge or overwhelming force or object. [from Sanskrit *Jagannātha* 'lord of the world': a title of Krishna, whose idol was carried in procession on a huge cart]

juggle ● *v.* **1 a** *intr.* (often foll. by *with*) keep several objects in the air at once by tossing and catching them. **b** *tr.* perform such feats with (balls etc.). **2** *tr.* deal with (several activities) at once. **3** *intr. & tr.* (foll. by *with*) **a** deceive or cheat. **b** misrepresent (facts). **c** rearrange adroitly. ● *n.* **1** a piece of juggling. **2** a fraud. [from Latin *joculari* 'to jest'] □ **juggler** *n.*

Jugoslav var. of YUGOSLAV.

jugular ● *adj.* **1** of the neck or throat. **2** (of fish) having ventral fins in front of the pectoral fins. ● *n.* = JUGULAR VEIN. [based on Latin *jugulum* 'collarbone, throat']

jugular vein *n.* ▼ any of several large veins of the neck which carry blood from the head. ▷ CARDIO-VASCULAR

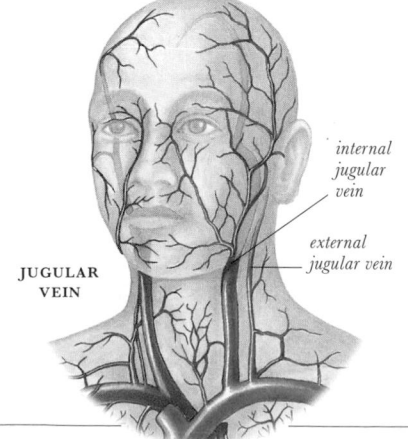

internal jugular vein

external jugular vein

JUGULAR VEIN

---

juice ● *n.* **1** the liquid part of vegetables or fruits. **2** animal fluid, esp. a secretion (*gastric juice*). **3** the essence or spirit of anything. **4** *colloq.* petrol or electricity as a source of power. ● *v.tr.* extract the juice from (a fruit etc.). [from Latin *jus* 'broth, juice'] □ **juiceless** *adj.*

juicy *adj.* (**juicier**, **juiciest**) **1** full of juice; succulent. **2** *colloq.* substantial or interesting; racy; scandalous. □ **juicily** *adv.* **juiciness** *n.*

ju-jitsu /joo-jit-soo/ *n.* (also **jiu-jitsu**, **ju-jutsu**) a Japanese system of unarmed combat and physical training. [from Japanese *jū* 'gentle' + *jutsu* 'skill']

ju-ju *n.* **1** ▶ a charm or fetish of some W. African peoples. **2** a supernatural power attributed to this. [perhaps from French *joujou* 'toy']

jujube /joo-joob/ *n.* **1 a** any plant of the genus *Ziziphus* bearing edible acidic berry-like fruits. **b** this fruit. **2** a flavoured jelly-like lozenge imitating this. [from Greek *zizuphon*]

jukebox *n.* a coin-operated machine that plays a selected musical recording. [based on Creole *juke* 'disorderly']

Jul. *abbr.* July.

julep /joo-lep/ *n.* **1 a** a sweet drink, esp. as a vehicle for medicine. **b** a medicated drink as a mild stimulant etc. **2** *US* iced and flavoured spirits and water (*mint julep*). [from Persian *gul* 'rose' + *āb* 'water']

JU-JU: MODERN WEST AFRICAN JU-JU

Julian *adj.* of or associated with Julius Caesar. [from Latin *Julianus*]

Julian calendar *n.* a calendar introduced by Julius Caesar, in which the year consisted of 365 days, every fourth year having 366.

julienne ● *n.* vegetables cut into short thin strips. ● *adj.* cut into thin strips. [French, from the name *Jules* or *Julien*]

Juliet cap *n.* a small net ornamental cap worn by brides etc. [from association with Shakespeare's heroine in *Romeo and Juliet*]

July *n.* (*pl.* **Julys**) the seventh month of the year. [from Latin *Julius*, named after Julius Caesar]

jumble ● *v.* **1** *tr.* (often foll. by *up*) confuse; mix up. **2** *intr.* move about in disorder. ● *n.* **1** a confused state or heap; a muddle. **2** *Brit.* articles collected for a jumble sale. □ **jumbly** *adj.*

jumble sale *n. Brit.* a sale of miscellaneous usu. second-hand articles, esp. for charity.

jumbo *colloq.* ● *n.* (*pl.* **-os**) **1** a large animal (esp. an elephant), person, or thing. **2** (in full **jumbo jet**) a large airliner with capacity for several hundred passengers (usu. applied specifically to the Boeing 747). ● *adj.* **1** very large of its kind. **2** extra large (*jumbo packet*). [19th-century coinage, originally of a person but popularized as the name of a zoo elephant sold in 1882]

jump ● *v.* **1** *intr.* rise off the ground etc. by sudden muscular effort in the legs. **2** *intr.* (often foll. by *up, from, in, out*, etc.) move suddenly or hastily (*we jumped into the car*). **3** *intr.* give a sudden bodily movement from shock etc. **4** *intr.* undergo a rapid change, esp. an advance in status. **5** *intr.* (often foll. by *about*) change the subject etc. rapidly. **6 a** *intr.* rise or increase suddenly (*prices jumped*). **b** *tr.* cause to do this. **7** *tr.* **a** pass over (an obstacle etc.) by jumping. **b** move or pass over (an intervening thing) to a point beyond. **8** *tr.* skip or pass over (a passage in a book etc.). **9** *tr.* cause (a horse, etc.) to jump. ▷ SHOWJUMPING. **10** *intr.* (foll. by *to, at*) reach a conclusion hastily. **11** *tr.* (of a train) leave (the rails) owing to a fault. **12** *tr.* ignore and pass (a red traffic light etc.). **13** *tr.* pounce on or attack (a person) unexpectedly. ● *n.* **1** the act or an instance of jumping. **2 a** a sudden bodily movement caused by shock or excitement. **b** (**the jumps**) *colloq.* extreme nervousness. **3** an abrupt rise in amount, status, etc. **4** an obstacle to be jumped, esp. by a horse. **5 a** a sudden transition. **b** a gap in a series etc. □ **jump at** accept eagerly. **jump bail** see BAIL[1]. **jump down a person's throat** *colloq.* reprimand or contradict a person fiercely. **jump the gun** see GUN. **jump on** *colloq.* attack or criticize severely and without warning. **jump the queue 1** push forward out of one's turn. **2** take unfair precedence over others. **jump ship** (of a sailor) desert. **jump to it** *Brit. colloq.* act promptly and energetically. [16th-century coinage]

jumped-up *adj. Brit. colloq.* presumptuously arrogant.

jumper[1] *n.* **1** *Brit.* a knitted pullover. **2** a loose outer jacket worn by sailors. **3** *N. Amer.* a pinafore dress.

jumper[2] *n.* **1** a person or animal that jumps. **2** *Electr.* a short wire used to shorten a circuit or close it temporarily.

jumping-off place *n.* (also **jumping-off point**) the place or point of starting.

jump jet *n.* a jet aircraft that can take off and land vertically.

jump lead *n. Brit.* each of a pair of cables for conveying current from the battery of a motor vehicle to that of another.

jump-off *n.* a deciding round in a showjumping competition.

jump rope *n. N. Amer.* a skipping rope.

jump-start ● *v.tr.* start (a motor vehicle) with jump leads. ● *n.* the action of jump-starting.

jumpsuit *n.* a one-piece garment for the whole body.

jumpy *adj.* (**jumpier, jumpiest**) **1** nervous; easily startled. **2** making sudden movements, esp. of nervous excitement. □ **jumpily** *adv.* **jumpiness** *n.*

Jun. *abbr.* **1** June. **2** Junior.

junction *n.* **1** a point at which two or more things are joined. **2** a place where railway lines or roads meet or cross. [from Latin *junctio*, related to JOIN]

junction box *n.* a box containing a junction of electric cables etc.

juncture *n.* **1** a critical convergence of events; a critical point of time (*at this juncture*). **2** a place where things join. **3** an act of joining.

June *n.* the sixth month of the year. [from Latin *Junius* 'sacred to Juno']

June bug *n.* ◄ any of various beetles, esp. N. American chafers, appearing in June.

JUNE BUG

jungle *n.* **1 a** land overgrown with tangled vegetation, esp. in the tropics. **b** an area of such land. **2** a wild tangled mass. **3** a place of bewildering complexity or confusion, or of a struggle for survival (*blackboard jungle*). [from Sanskrit *jangala* 'desert, forest'] □ **jungly** *adj.*

junior ● *adj.* **1** less advanced in age. **2** (foll. by *to*) inferior in age, standing, or position. **3** (placed after a person's name) junior to another of the same name. **4** of less or least standing (*junior partner*). **5** *Brit.* (of a school) having pupils in a younger age range, usu. 7–11. **6** *N. Amer.* of the year before the final year at university, high school, etc. ● *n.* **1** a junior person. **2** one's inferior in length of service etc. **3** a junior student. **4** *US colloq.* a young male child, esp. in relation to his family. [Latin, literally 'younger']

junior high school *n. N. Amer.* a school intermediate between elementary school and high school.

junior management *n.* **1** the lowest level of management in an organization. **2** the managers at this level usu. with supervisory rather than full management responsibility (cf. MIDDLE MANAGEMENT, SENIOR MANAGEMENT).

junior technician *n.* an RAF rank next above senior aircraftman.

juniper *n.* ◄ any evergreen shrub or tree of the genus *Juniperus*, esp. *J. communis* with prickly leaves and dark purple berries. [from Latin *juniperus*]

leaves

berries

JUNIPER (*Juniperus communis*)

junk[1] ● *n.* **1** discarded articles; rubbish. **2** anything regarded as of little value. **3** *slang* a narcotic drug, esp. heroin. **4** *Naut.* hard salt meat. **5** a lump of fibrous tissue in a sperm whale's head, containing spermaceti. ● *v.tr.* discard as junk. [Middle English]

junk[2] *n.* ► a flat-bottomed sailing vessel used in the China seas, with a prominent stern and lugsails. [of Oriental origin]

junk bond *n.* a high-yielding high-risk security, esp. one issued to finance a take-over.

junket ● *n.* **1** a dish of sweetened and flavoured milk curds, often served with fruit or cream. **2** a feast. **3** a pleasure outing. **4** *N. Amer.* an official's tour at public expense. ● *v.intr.* (**junketed, junketing**) feast, picnic. [from Old French *jonquette* 'rush-basket', used to carry junket]

junk food *n.* food with low nutritional value.

junkie *n. slang* a drug addict.

junk mail *n.* unsolicited advertising matter sent by post.

junk shop *n.* a shop selling cheap second-hand goods or antiques.

junta *n.* **1** a political or military clique or faction taking power after a revolution or *coup d'état*. **2** a deliberative or administrative council in Spain or Portugal. [from Latin *juncta* (fem.) 'joined']

Jupiter *n.* ▼ the largest planet of the solar system, orbiting the Sun between Mars and Saturn. ▷ SOLAR SYSTEM. [from Latin *Jovis pater*, literally 'Jove father']

JUNK: TRADITIONAL CHINESE JUNK

J

JUPITER

Jupiter is the largest, most massive planet in the solar system. Its rapid rate of rotation in 9 hours 55 minutes causes the clouds in its atmosphere to form dark, low-altitude 'belts' and bright, high altitude 'zones' – both with huge storm systems which encircle the planet parallel with the equator. Jupiter has two faint rings, and is orbited by 16 known moons, of which Ganymede, Callisto, Io, and Europa (the Galileans) are the largest.

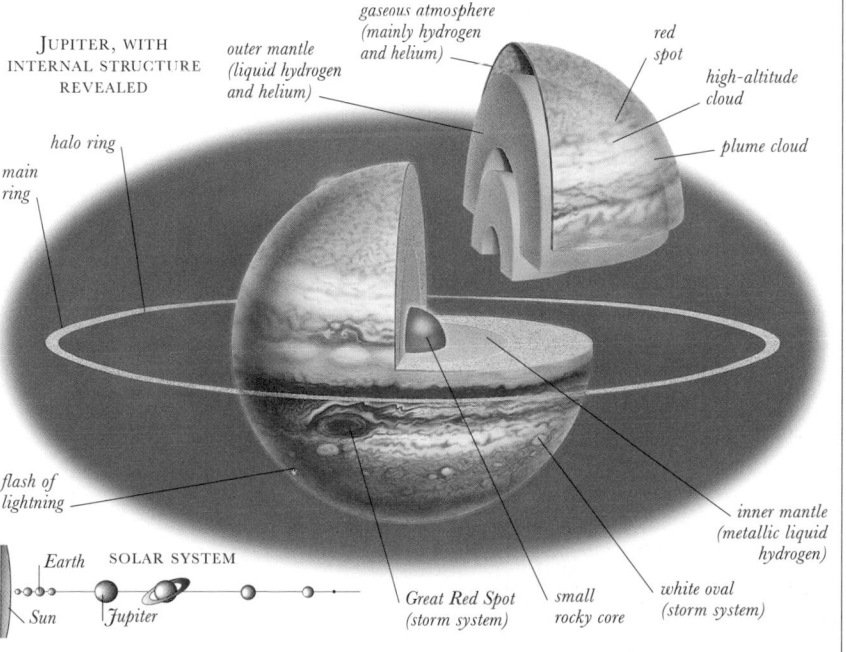

JUPITER, WITH INTERNAL STRUCTURE REVEALED

halo ring

main ring

gaseous atmosphere (mainly hydrogen and helium)

outer mantle (liquid hydrogen and helium)

red spot

high-altitude cloud

plume cloud

flash of lightning

inner mantle (metallic liquid hydrogen)

Earth SOLAR SYSTEM

Sun *Jupiter*

Great Red Spot (storm system)

small rocky core

white oval (storm system)

Jurassic *Geol.* ● *adj.* of or relating to the second period of the Mesozoic era. ● *n.* this era or system. [based on French *Jura*, a system of mountain ranges]

juridical *adj.* **1** of judicial proceedings. **2** relating to the law. [from Latin *juridicus*] □ **juridically** *adv.*

jurisdiction *n.* **1** (often foll. by *over, of*) the administration of justice. **2 a** legal or other authority. **b** the extent of this; the territory it extends over. [from Latin *jurisdictio*] □ **jurisdictional** *adj.*

jurisprudence *n.* the science or philosophy of law. [from Latin *jus juris* 'law' + *prudentia* 'knowledge'] □ **jurisprudential** *adj.*

jurist *n.* **1** an expert in law. **2** a legal writer. **3** *US* **a** a lawyer. **b** a judge. □ **juristic** *adj.*

juror *n.* **1** a member of a jury. **2** a person who takes an oath.

jury *n.* (*pl.* **-ies**) **1** a body of usu. twelve persons giving a verdict in a court of justice. **2** a body of persons awarding prizes in a competition. [based on Latin *jurare* 'to swear']

jury box *n.* the enclosure for the jury in a law court.

juryman *n.* (*pl.* **-men**) a member of a jury.

jury-rigged *adj.* **1** *Naut.* having temporary makeshift rigging. **2** makeshift, improvised.

jurywoman *n.* (*pl.* **-women**) a female member of a jury.

just ● *adj.* **1** morally right or fair. **2** (of treatment etc.) deserved (*a just reward*). **3** (of feelings, opinions, etc.) well-grounded (*just resentment*). **4** right in amount etc.; proper. ● *adv.* **1** exactly (*just what I need*). **2** exactly or nearly at this or that moment (*I have just seen them*). **3** *colloq.* simply, merely (*we were just good friends; it just doesn't make sense*). **4** barely; no more than (*I just managed it; just a minute*). **5** *colloq.* positively (*it is just splendid*). **6** quite (*not just yet*). □ **just about** *colloq.* almost exactly; almost completely. **just in case** as a precaution. **just now 1** at this moment. **2** a little time ago. **just so 1** exactly arranged (*they like everything just so*). **2** it is exactly as you say. [from Latin *justus*] □ **justly** *adv.* **justness** *n.*

justice *n.* **1** just conduct. **2** fairness. **3** the exercise of authority in the maintenance of right. **4** judicial proceedings (*was brought to justice; the Court of Justice*). **5 a** a magistrate. **b** a judge. □ **do justice to** treat fairly or appropriately; show due appreciation of. **do oneself justice** perform in a manner worthy of one's abilities. □ **justiceship** *n.* (in sense 5).

Justice of the Peace *n.* a lay magistrate appointed to preserve the peace in a county, town, etc., hear minor cases, grant licences, etc.

justiciary ● *n.* (*pl.* **-ies**) an administrator of justice. ● *adj.* of the administration of justice.

justifiable *adj.* that can be justified or defended. □ **justifiability** *n.* **justifiably** *adv.*

justify *v.tr.* (**-ies, -ied**) **1** show the justice or rightness of (a person, act, etc.). **2** demonstrate the correctness of (an assertion etc.). **3** adduce adequate grounds for (conduct, a claim, etc.). **4** (as **justified** *adj.*) just, right (*am justified in assuming*). **5** *Printing* adjust (a line of type) to fill a space evenly. [from Late Latin *justificare* 'to do justice to'] □ **justification** *n.* **justificatory** *adj.*

jut ● *v.intr.* (**jutted, jutting**) (often foll. by *out, into, through*, etc.) protrude, project. ● *n.* a projection; a protruding point. [variant of JET¹]

JUTE: HANK OF RAW JUTE FIBRES

jute *n.* **1** ◀ a rough fibre made from the bark of a jute plant, used for making twine and rope, and woven into sacking, mats, etc. **2** an Asian plant of the genus *Corchorus* yielding this fibre. [from Sanskrit *jūṭa* 'braid of hair']

juvenile ● *adj.* **1 a** young, youthful. **b** of or for young persons. **2** often *derog.* immature (*behaving in a very juvenile way*). ● *n.* **1** a young person. **2** an actor playing the part of a youthful person. [from Latin *juvenilis*] □ **juvenilely** *adv.* **juvenility** *n.*

juvenile court *n.* a court for the trial of children under 17 or (in the US) 18.

juvenile delinquency *n.* the committing of offences by persons below the age of legal responsibility. □ **juvenile delinquent** *n.*

juvenilia *n.pl.* works produced by an author or artist in youth. [Latin, literally 'juvenile things']

juxtapose *v.tr.* **1** place (things) side by side. **2** (foll. by *to, with*) place (a thing) beside another. [French *juxtaposer* from Latin *juxta* 'next'] □ **juxtaposition** *n.* **juxtapositional** *adj.*

J

K

K¹ *n.* (also **k**) (*pl.* **Ks** or **K's**) the eleventh letter of the alphabet.

K² *abbr.* (also **K.**) **1** King, King's. **2** Köchel (catalogue of Mozart's works). **3** (also **k**) (prec. by a numeral) **a** *Computing* a unit of 1,024 (i.e. 2¹⁰) bytes or bits, or loosely 1,000. **b** thousand. [sense 3: abbreviation of KILO-]

K³ *symb.* **1** *Chem.* the element potassium. **2** kelvin(s). [sense 1: from modern Latin *kalium*]

k¹ *abbr.* (also **k.**) knot(s) (see KNOT¹ *n.* 2a).

k² *symb.* **1** kilo-. **2** *Math.* a constant.

kabbala var. of CABBALA 1.

Kabbalah /kă-bah-lă/ *n.* (also **Kabbala**, **Cabbala**, **Cabala**) the Jewish mystical tradition. [from Rabbinical Hebrew *ḳabbālā* 'tradition'] □ **Kabbalism** *n.* **Kabbalist** *n.* **Kabbalistic** *adj.*

kabuki *n.* a form of popular traditional Japanese drama with highly stylized song, acted by males only. [Japanese, from *ka* 'song' + *bu* 'dance' + *ki* 'art']

Kaddish *n.* *Judaism* **1** a Jewish mourner's prayer. **2** a doxology in the synagogue service. [from Aramaic *ḳaddīš* 'holy']

kadi var. of CADI.

Kaffir /kaf-er/ *n.* **1 a** *hist.* a member of the Xhosa-speaking peoples of S. Africa. **b** the language of these peoples. **2** *S.Afr. offens.* any black African (now an actionable insult). [originally in sense 'a non-Muslim': from Arabic *kāfir* 'infidel']

kaffiyeh var. of KEFFIYEH.

Kafkaesque *adj.* impenetrably oppressive, nightmarish, as in the fiction of Franz Kafka. [German-speaking novelist, 1883–1924]

kaftan *n.* (also **caftan**) **1** a long usu. belted tunic worn by men in countries of the Near East. **2 a** a woman's long loose dress. **b** a loose shirt or top. [from Turkish *kaftān*]

kail var. of KALE.

kailyard var. of KALEYARD.

kaiser /ky-zer/ *n.* *hist.* an emperor, esp. of Germany or Austria. [German] □ **kaisership** *n.*

kalanchoe /kal-ăn-koh-i/ *n.* a succulent plant of the mainly African genus *Kalanchoe*, which includes several house plants, some producing miniature plants from the edges of the leaves. [from Chinese *gāláncài*]

Kalashnikov *n.* a type of rifle or submachine gun made in Russia. [named after M.T. *Kalashnikov*, born 1919, its Russian developer]

kale *n.* (also **kail**) ◄ a variety of cabbage which forms no compact head. [Middle English, northern form of COLE]

kaleidoscope *n.* **1** a tube containing mirrors and pieces of coloured glass or paper, whose reflections produce changing patterns when the tube is rotated. **2** a constantly changing group of bright or interesting

KALE (*Brassica oleracea acephala*)

objects. [based on Greek *kalos* 'beautiful' + *eidos* 'form'] □ **kaleidoscopic** *adj.* **kaleidoscopically** *adv.*

kalends var. of CALENDS.

kaleyard *n.* (also **kailyard**) *Sc.* a kitchen garden.

Kama Sutra /kah-mă soo-tră/ *n.* an ancient Sanskrit treatise on the art of erotic love.

kamikaze /kam-i-kah-zi/ ● *n. hist.* **1** a Japanese aircraft loaded with explosives and deliberately crashed by its pilot on its target. **2** the pilot of such an aircraft. ● *adj.* **1** of or relating to a kamikaze. **2** reckless, dangerous, potentially self-destructive. [Japanese, from *kami* 'divinity' + *kaze* 'wind']

kangaroo *n.* a plant-eating marsupial of the genus *Macropus*, native to Australia and New Guinea, with a long tail and strong hind quarters enabling it to travel by jumping. ▷ MARSUPIAL. [from Aboriginal *ganurru*, name of a specific kind of kangaroo]

kangaroo court *n.* an improperly constituted or illegal court held by strikers etc.

kangaroo rat *n.* any burrowing rodent of the genus *Dipodomys*, having elongated hind feet.

kaolin *n.* a fine soft white clay used esp. for making porcelain and in medicines. [from Chinese *Gaoling*, a mountain in Jiangxi province, where it is found]

kapellmeister /kă-pel-mys-ter/ *n.* (*pl.* same) the conductor of an orchestra, opera, choir, etc., esp. in German contexts. [German]

kapok

kapok /kay-pok/ *n.* ◄ a cotton-like substance found surrounding the seeds of a tropical tree, *Ceiba pentandra*, used for stuffing cushions, soft toys, etc. [from Malay *kāpoq*]

Kaposi's sarcoma *n.* *Med.* a form of cancer involving multiple tumours of the lymph nodes or skin, occurring esp. in people with depressed immune systems, e.g. as a result of Aids. [named after M.K. *Kaposi*, Hungarian dermatologist, 1837–1902]

kappa *n.* the tenth letter of the Greek alphabet (K, κ). [Greek]

kaput /kă-puut/ *predic.adj. colloq.* broken, ruined; done for. [from French (*être*) *capot* '(to be) without tricks in piquet etc.']

KAPOK SEED POD (*Ceiba pentandra*)

karabiner /ka-ră been-er/ *n.* ► a coupling link with safety closure, used by mountaineers. ▷ ROCK-CLIMBING. [from German *karabinerhaken* 'spring-hook']

karakul /ka-ră-kuul/ *n.* (also **caracul**) **1** a variety of Asian sheep with a dark curled fleece when young. **2** fur made from or resembling this. [Russian]

karaoke /ka-ri-oh-ki/ *n.* a form of entertainment in which people sing popular songs as soloists against a pre-recorded

backing (often *attrib.*: *karaoke bar*). [Japanese, literally 'empty orchestra']

karat *US* var. of CARAT 2.

karate /kă-rah-ti/ *n.* a Japanese form of kung fu, a system of combat using the hands and feet as weapons. [Japanese, from *kara* 'empty' + *te* 'hand']

karma *n.* *Buddhism* & *Hinduism* **1** the sum of a person's actions in previous states of existence, viewed as deciding his or her fate in future existences. **2** destiny. [Sanskrit, literally 'action, fate'] □ **karmic** *adj.*

karst *n.* a limestone region with underground drainage and many cavities and passages caused by the dissolution of the rock. [from German *der Karst*, a limestone region in Slovenia]

kasbah *n.* (also **casbah**) **1** the citadel of a N. African city. **2** an Arab quarter near this. [from Arabic *kas(a)ba* 'citadel']

Kashmiri ● *adj.* of or relating to Kashmir or its people or language. ● *n.* **1** a native or inhabitant of Kashmir. **2** the language of Kashmir. [from *Kashmir* in the western Himalayas]

katydid /kay-ti-did/ *n.* ▼ any of various green grasshoppers of the family Tettigoniidae, native to the US.

KATYDID: FALSE LEAF KATYDID (*Ommatopia pictifolia*)

kauri /kow-ri/ *n.* (*pl.* **kauris**) a coniferous New Zealand tree, *Agathis australis*, which produces valuable timber and a resin. [Maori]

kauri gum *n.* resin of the kauri tree.

kayak /ky-ak/ ● *n.* **1** ▼ an Inuit one-man canoe consisting of a light wooden frame covered with sealskins. **2** a small covered canoe. ● *v.intr.* (**kayaked**, **kayaking**) travel by kayak; paddle a kayak. [Inuit]

kayo *colloq.* ● *v.tr.* (**-oes**, **-oed**) knock out; stun by a blow. ● *n.* (*pl.* **-os**) a knockout. [representing pronunciation of *KO*]

kazoo *n.* a toy musical instrument into which the player sings or hums. [19th-century coinage]

KB *abbr.* kilobyte(s).

KARABINER: SNAP KARABINER

KBE *abbr.* (in the UK) Knight Commander of the Order of the British Empire.

KAYAK

The Inuit of northern Canada, Alaska, Russia, and Greenland traditionally used kayaks to hunt sea mammals such as seals and whales. Kayaks were completely enclosed with waterproof sealskin except for an opening for the hunter to climb in at the top.

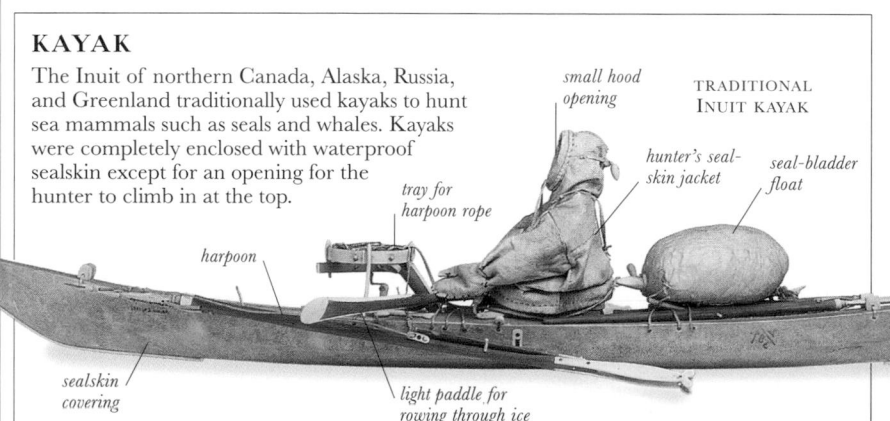

TRADITIONAL INUIT KAYAK

small hood opening

hunter's seal-skin jacket

seal-bladder float

tray for harpoon rope

harpoon

sealskin covering

light paddle for rowing through ice

KC *abbr.* King's Counsel.

kcal *abbr.* kilocalorie(s).

kea /kee-ă/ *n.* ▶ a parrot, *Nestor notabilis*, of New Zealand, with brownish-green and red plumage. [Maori]

kebab *n.* small pieces of meat, vegetables, etc., cooked on a skewer. [from Arabic *kabāb*]

kedge ● *v.* **1** *tr.* move (a ship) by means of a hawser attached to a small anchor. **2** *intr.* (of a ship) move in this way. ● *n.* (in full **kedge anchor**) a small anchor for this purpose.

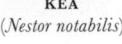

KEA
(*Nestor notabilis*)

kedgeree *n.* **1** an Indian dish of rice, split pulse, onions, eggs, etc. **2** a European dish of fish, rice, hard-boiled eggs, etc. [from Sanskrit *k'rsara*, a dish of rice and sesame]

keek *Sc.* ● *v.intr.* peep. ● *n.* a peep. [Middle English *kike* 'to peep']

keel ● *n.* the lengthwise timber or steel structure along the base of a ship or some aircraft. ▷ SAILING BOAT. ● *v.* **1** (often foll. by *over*) **a** *intr.* turn over or fall down. **b** *tr.* cause to do this. **2 a** *intr.* (of a boat) turn keel upwards. **b** *tr.* turn up the keel of (a boat). [from Old Norse *kjǫlr*] □ **keelless** *adj.*

keelboat *n.* **1** a yacht built with a permanent keel instead of a centreboard. **2** a large flat-bottomed boat used on American rivers.

keelhaul *v.tr.* **1** *hist.* drag (a person) through the water under the keel of a ship as a punishment. **2** scold or rebuke severely.

keelson *n.* (also **kelson**) a line of timber fastening a ship's floor-timbers to its keel. [Middle English]

keen[1] *adj.* **1** (of a person, desire, or interest) eager, ardent (*a keen sportsman*). **2** (foll. by *on*) much attracted by; enthusiastic about. **3** (of the senses) sharp; highly sensitive. **4** intellectually acute. **5** (of a knife etc.) sharp. **6** (of a sound, light, etc.) penetrating, vivid, strong. **7** (of a wind, frost, etc.) piercingly cold. **8** (of a pain etc.) acute, bitter. **9** *Brit.* (of a price) competitive. [Old English] □ **keenly** *adv.* **keenness** *n.*

keen[2] ● *n.* an Irish funeral song accompanied with wailing. ● *v.intr.* utter the keen. [from Irish *caoine*] □ **keener** *n.*

keep ● *v.* (*past* and *past part.* **kept**) **1** *tr.* have continuous charge of; retain possession of. **2** *tr.* (foll. by *for*) retain or reserve for a future occasion or time (*will keep it for tomorrow*). **3** *tr. & intr.* retain or remain in a specified condition, position, course, etc. (*keep cool*; *keep off the grass*; *keep them happy*). **4** *tr.* put or store in a regular place (*knives are kept in this drawer*). **5** *tr.* (foll. by *from*) cause to avoid or abstain from something (*will keep you from going too fast*). **6** *tr.* detain (*what kept you?*). **7** *tr.* **a** observe (a law, custom, etc.). **b** honour or fulfil (a commitment, undertaking, etc.) (*keep one's word*). **c** respect the commitment implied by (a secret etc.). **d** act fittingly on the occasion of (*keep the sabbath*). **8** *tr.* own and look after (animals) (*keeps bees*). **9** *tr.* **a** provide for the sustenance of (a person, family, etc.). **b** (foll. by *in*) maintain (a person) with a supply of. **10** *tr.* carry on; manage (a shop, business, etc.). **11 a** *tr.* maintain (accounts, a diary, etc.) by making the requisite entries. **b** *tr.* maintain (a house) in proper order. **12** *tr.* have (a commodity) regularly on sale (*do you keep buttons?*). **13** *tr.* guard or protect (a person or place, a goal in football, etc.). **14** *tr.* preserve (*keep order*). **15** *intr.* (foll. by verbal noun) continue or do repeatedly or habitually (*why do you keep saying that?*). **16** *tr.* continue to follow (a way or course). **17** *intr.* **a** (esp. of perishable commodities) remain in good condition. **b** (of news or information etc.) admit of being withheld for a time.

18 *tr.* *archaic* remain in (one's bed, room, house, etc.). **19** *tr.* retain one's place in (a seat or saddle, one's ground, etc.) against opposition or difficulty. **20** *tr.* maintain (a person) in return for sexual favours (*a kept woman*). ● *n.* **1** maintenance or the essentials for one's life (esp. food) (*hardly earn your keep*). **2** *hist.* ▼ a tower or stronghold. ▷ CASTLE. □ **for keeps** *colloq.* (esp. of something received or won) permanently, indefinitely. **how are you keeping?** *Brit.* how are you? **keep at** persist or cause to persist with. **keep away** (often foll. by *from*) **1** avoid being near. **2** prevent from being near. **keep back 1** remain or keep at a distance. **2** retard the progress of. **3** conceal; decline to disclose. **4** retain, withhold (*kept back £50*). **keep down 1** hold in subjection. **2** keep low in amount. **3** lie low; stay hidden. **4** manage not to vomit (food eaten). **keep one's feet** manage not to fall. **keep one's hair on** see HAIR. **keep in with** remain on good terms with. **keep off 1** stay or cause to stay away from. **2** ward off; avert. **3** abstain from. **4** avoid (a subject) (*let's keep off religion*). **keep on 1** continue to do something; do continually (*kept on laughing*). **2** continue to use or employ. **3** (foll. by *at*) pester or harass. **keep out 1** keep or remain outside. **2** exclude. **keep to 1** adhere to (a course, schedule, etc.). **2** observe (a promise). **3** confine oneself to. **keep to oneself 1** avoid contact with others. **2** refuse to disclose or share. **keep track of** see TRACK[1]. **keep under** hold in subjection. **keep up 1** maintain (progress etc.). **2** prevent (prices, one's spirits, etc.) from sinking. **3** keep in repair, in an efficient or proper state, etc. **4** carry on (a correspondence etc.). **5** prevent (a person) from going to bed, esp. when late. **6** (often foll. by *with*) manage not to fall behind. **keep up with the Joneses** strive to compete socially with one's neighbours. [Old English]

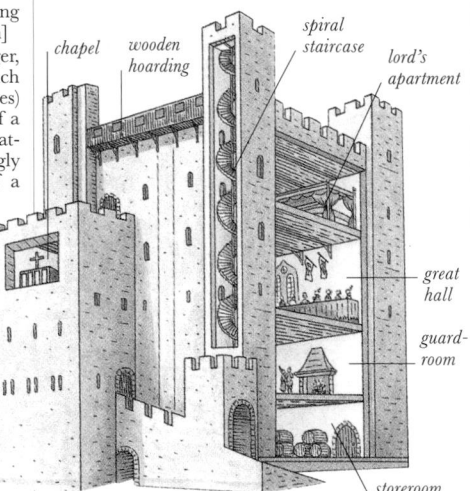

KEEP: 11TH-CENTURY ENGLISH CASTLE KEEP

(labels: chapel; wooden hoarding; spiral staircase; lord's apartment; great hall; guard-room; storeroom)

keeper *n.* **1** a person who keeps or looks after something or someone. **2** *Brit.* a custodian of a museum, art gallery, forest, etc. **3 a** = GAMEKEEPER. **b** a person in charge of animals in a zoo. **4 a** = WICKETKEEPER. **b** = GOALKEEPER. **5** a bar of soft iron placed across the poles of a horseshoe magnet to maintain its strength. **6 a** a plain ring to preserve a hole in a pierced ear lobe; a sleeper. **b** a ring worn to keep another on the finger.

keep-fit *n.* (often *attrib.*) esp. *Brit.* regular exercises to promote personal fitness and health.

keeping *n.* **1** custody, charge (*in safe keeping*). **2** agreement, harmony (esp. *in* or *out of keeping*).

keepnet *n.* a net for keeping fish alive until they are returned to the water.

keepsake *n.* a thing kept for the sake of or in remembrance of the giver or original owner.

keffiyeh /kĕ-fee-ĕ/ *n.* (also **kaffiyeh**) ▶ a Bedouin Arab's kerchief worn as a headdress. [from Arabic *keffiya*]

keg *n.* a small barrel. [from Old Norse *kaggi*]

keg beer *n.* *Brit.* beer to which carbon dioxide has been added in a sealed metal container, from which it is supplied.

KEFFIYEH

(labels: woollen coils; keffiyeh)

kelp *n.* **1** any of several large broad-fronded brown seaweeds esp. of the genus *Laminaria*, used as manure. **2** the calcined ashes of seaweed, formerly used in glass-making and soap manufacture. [Middle English]

kelpie *n.* **1** *Sc.* a water spirit, usu. in the form of a horse, reputed to delight in the drowning of travellers etc. **2** an Australian sheepdog originally bred from a Scottish collie. [17th-century coinage]

kelson var. of KEELSON.

kelt *n.* a salmon or sea trout after spawning. [Middle English]

kelter var. of KILTER.

kelvin *n.* the SI unit of thermodynamic temperature, equal in magnitude to the degree Celsius. [named after Lord *Kelvin*, British physicist, 1824–1907]

Kelvin scale *n.* a scale of temperature with absolute zero as zero.

kempt *adj.* combed; neatly kept. [past participle of (now dialect) *kemb* 'to comb']

ken ● *n.* range of sight or knowledge (*it's beyond my ken*). ● *v.tr.* (**kenning**; *past* and *past part.* **kenned** or **kent**) *Sc. & N.Engl.* **1** recognize at sight. **2** know. [Old English]

kendo *n.* ▲ Japanese fencing with two-handed bamboo swords. [Japanese, literally 'sword-way']

kennel ● *n.* **1** a small shelter for a dog. **2** (in *pl.*) a breeding or boarding establishment for dogs. ● *v.tr.* (**kennelled**, **kennelling**; *US* **kenneled**, **kenneling**) put into or keep in a kennel. [based on Latin *canis* 'dog']

kent *past* and *past part.* of KEN.

Kenyan ● *adj.* of or relating to Kenya in E. Africa. ● *n.* **1** a native or national of Kenya. **2** a person of Kenyan descent.

kepi *n.* (*pl.* **kepis**) ▶ a military cap with a horizontal peak. [from Swiss German *käppi* 'little cap']

kept *past* and *past part.* of KEEP.

keratin *n.* any of a group of fibrous proteins occurring in hair, feathers, hoofs, claws, horns, etc. [based on Greek *keras keratos* 'horn'] □ **keratinize** *v.tr. & intr.* (also **-ise**).

keratitis *n.* *Med.* inflammation of the cornea of the eye. [from Greek *kerat-* (denoting the cornea) + -ITIS]

keratotomy *n.* *Med.* a surgical operation involving cutting into the cornea of the eye, esp. (in full **radial keratotomy**) to correct myopia. [from Greek *kerat-* (denoting the cornea) + *-tomia* 'cutting']

KEPI OF A CONFEDERATE ARMY INFANTRYMAN

kerb *n.* *Brit.* a stone edging to a pavement or raised path.

kerb-crawler *n.* *Brit.* a (usu. male) person who drives slowly near the edge of the road in an attempt to engage a prostitute or harass esp. female passers-by. □ **kerb-crawling** *n.*

K

KENDO

Kendo, meaning 'way of the sword', derives from the art of kenjutsu, practised by Japanese warriors in the 14th century. Today it is an internationally recognized martial art, in which points are awarded for striking the opponent's body showing the correct technique and spiritual attitude. Bouts take place on a wooden square and last up to five minutes.

practice sword (shinai)

mask (men)

headcloth (hachimaki)

shoulder protector

throat protector

jacket (kendo-gi)

breastplate (do)

padded glove (kote)

apron (tare)

divided skirt (hakama)

DEMONSTRATION OF KENDO SWORDPLAY

kerb drill *n. Brit.* precautions, esp. looking to right and left, before crossing a road.

kerbside *n. Brit.* the side of a road or pavement nearer the kerb.

kerbstone *n. Brit.* each of a series of stones forming a kerb.

kerchief *n.* a cloth used to cover the head. [from Old French *couvrechief*, from *couvrir* 'to cover' + *chief* 'head']

kerfuffle *n.* esp. *Brit. colloq.* a fuss or commotion. [Scots *curfuffle*, from *fuffle* 'to disorder']

kermes /ˈker-miz/ *n.* **1** (in full **kermes oak**) a small evergreen oak, *Quercus coccifera*, of the Mediterranean region. **2 a** the female of a scale-insect, *Kermes ilicis*, which forms berry-like galls on the kermes oak. **b** a red dye made from the bodies of these insects. ▷ DYE. [from Arabic & Persian *ḳirmiz*]

kern *Printing* ● *n.* the part of a metal type projecting beyond its body or shank. ● *v.tr.* **1** provide (type) with kerns; make (letters) overlap. **2** adjust the spacing between (characters). □ **kerned** *adj.*

kernel *n.* **1** a central, softer, usu. edible part within a hard shell of a nut, fruit stone, seed, etc. ▷ NUT. **2** the whole seed of a cereal. **3** the nucleus or essential part of anything. [from Old English *cyrnel*]

kerosene *n.* (also **kerosine**) esp. *N. Amer.* a fuel oil obtained by distillation from petroleum or shale, suitable for use in jet engines and domestic heating boilers; paraffin oil. [based on Greek *kēros* 'wax']

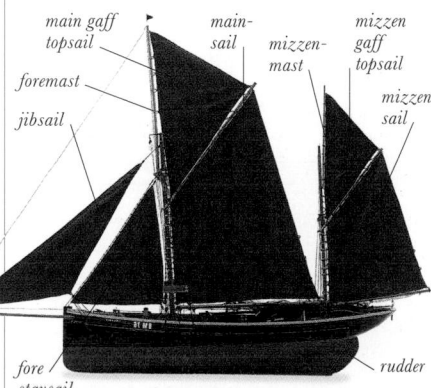

KESTREL (*Falco tinnunculus*)

kestrel *n.* ◀ any small falcon, esp. *Falco tinnunculus*, which hovers. ▷ NEST. [Middle English]

ketamine *n.* an anaesthetic and pain-killing drug, also used (illicitly) as a hallucinogen.

ketch *n.* ▶ a two-masted fore-and-aft rigged sailing boat with a mizzen-mast stepped forward of the rudder and smaller than its foremast. [Middle English]

ketchup *n.* (*US* also **catsup**) a spicy sauce made from tomatoes, mushrooms, vinegar, etc., used as a condiment.

ketone *n.* any of a class of organic compounds in which two hydrocarbon groups are linked by a carbonyl group, e.g. propanone (acetone). [from German *Keton*, alteration of *Aketon* 'acetone'] □ **ketonic** *adj.*

kettle *n.* a vessel, usu. of metal with a lid, spout, and handle, for boiling water in. □ **a different kettle of fish** a different matter altogether. **a pretty** (or **fine**) **kettle of fish** an awkward state of affairs. [from Latin *catillus* 'little pot'] □ **kettleful** *n.* (*pl.* **-fuls**)

kettledrum *n.* a large bowl-shaped drum with adjustable pitch. ▷ PERCUSSION

Kevlar *n. propr.* a synthetic fibre of high tensile strength used esp. as a reinforcing agent in the manufacture of rubber products, e.g. tyres.

key[1] ● *n.* (*pl.* **keys**) **1** an instrument, usu. of metal, for moving the bolt of a lock. **2** a similar implement for operating a switch. **3** an instrument for grasping screws, pegs, nuts, etc., esp. one for winding a clock etc. **4** a lever depressed by the finger in playing the organ, piano, flute, concertina, etc. ▷ PIANO. **5** each of several buttons for operating a typewriter, word processor, computer terminal, etc. **6** a means of access (*the key to success*). **7** (*attrib.*) essential; of vital importance (*the key element in the problem*). **8 a** a solution or explanation. **b** a word or system for solving a cipher or code. **c** an explanatory list of symbols used in a map, table, etc. **d** a book or part of a book containing solutions to mathematical problems etc. **9** *Mus.* a group of notes based on a particular note and comprising a scale, regarded as a unit forming the tonal basis of a piece of music (*a study in the key of C major*). **10** a tone or style of thought or expression. **11** the roughness of a surface, helping the adhesion of plaster etc. **12** the winged seed of a sycamore etc. **13** a mechanical device for making or breaking an electric circuit, e.g. in telegraphy. ● *v.tr.* (**keys**, **keyed**) **1** (foll. by *in*, *on*, etc.) fasten with a pin, wedge, bolt, etc. **2** (often foll. by *in*) enter (data) by means of a keyboard. ▷ COMPUTER, PIANO. **3** roughen (a surface) to help the adhesion of plaster etc. **4** (foll. by *to*) align or link (one thing to another). □ **key up** (often foll. by *to*, or *to* + infin.) make (a person) nervous or tense; excite. [Old English] □ **keyless** *adj.*

key[2] *n.* a low-lying island or reef, esp. in the W. Indies. [from Spanish *cayo* 'shoal, reef']

keyboard ● *n.* **1** a set of keys on a typewriter, computer, piano, etc. ▷ COMPUTER. **2** an electronic musical instrument with keys arranged as on a piano. ● *v.tr.* enter (data) by means of a keyboard. □ **keyboarder** *n.* (in sense 1 of *n.*). **keyboardist** *n.* (in sense 2 of *n.*).

keyholder *n.* a person who has a key to a place, esp. to an office or factory.

keyhole *n.* a hole by which a key is put into a lock.

keyhole surgery *n. Brit.* minimally invasive surgery carried out through a very small incision.

key money *n. Brit.* a payment required from an incoming tenant for the provision of a key to the premises.

Keynesian /ˈkaynz-iăn/ ● *adj.* of or relating to the economic theories of J. M. Keynes (d. 1946), esp. regarding state control of the economy through money and taxation. ● *n.* an adherent of these theories. □ **Keynesianism** *n.*

keynote *n.* **1** a prevailing tone or idea. **2** (*attrib.*) intended to set the prevailing tone at a meeting or conference (*keynote address*). **3** *Mus.* the note on which a key is based.

keypad *n.* a miniature keyboard or set of buttons for operating a portable electronic device, telephone, etc.

keyring *n.* a ring for keeping keys on.

key signature *n. Mus.* the combination of sharps or flats after the clef at the beginning of each staff indicating the key of a composition. ▷ NOTATION

keystone *n.* **1** the central principle of a system, policy, etc. **2** a central stone at the summit of an arch. ▷ ARCH

keystroke *n.* a single depression of a key on a keyboard.

keyword *n.* **1** the key to a cipher etc. **2 a** a word of great significance. **b** an informative word used in an information retrieval system to indicate the content of a document etc.

KG *abbr.* (in the UK) Knight of the Order of the Garter.

kg *abbr.* kilogram(s).

KGB *n.* the state security police of the former USSR from 1954. [from Russian *Komitet gosudarstvennoĭ bezopasnosti* 'committee of State security']

khaki ● *adj.* dull brownish yellow. ● *n.* (*pl.* **khakis**) **1** khaki fabric, used esp. in military dress. **2** dull brownish yellow. [from Urdu *k͟hākī* 'dust-coloured']

■ **Usage** In the military sense (see sense 1 of the noun above), this term has now been largely replaced by *olive drab*.

khan *n.* a title given to rulers and officials in central Asia, Afghanistan, etc. [from Turkic *k͟hān* 'lord'] □ **khanate** *n.*

khat /kaht/ *n.* **1** a shrub, *Catha edulis*, grown in Arabia. **2** the leaves of this shrub, chewed or infused as a stimulant. [from Arabic *k͟hāt*]

Khmer ● *n.* **1** a native of the ancient Khmer kingdom in SE Asia, or of modern Cambodia. **2** the language of the Khmers. ● *adj.* of the Khmers or their language. [native name]

kHz *abbr.* kilohertz.

kibble ● *v.tr.* grind or chop (dried corn, beans, etc.) coarsely. ● *n. N. Amer.* ground meal shaped into pellets esp. for pet food. [18th-century coinage]

kibbutz /ki-buuts/ *n.* (*pl.* **kibbutzim** /-eem/) a communal esp. farming settlement in Israel. [from modern Hebrew *ḳibbūṣ* 'gathering']

kibbutznik *n.* a member of a kibbutz. [Yiddish]

main gaff topsail

mainsail

mizzen gaff topsail

mizzen-mast

mizzen sail

foremast

jibsail

fore staysail

rudder

KETCH: EARLY 20TH-CENTURY BRITISH KETCH

K

kibitzer *n. esp. N. Amer. colloq.* **1** an onlooker at cards etc., esp. one who offers unwanted advice. **2** a busybody, a meddler. [from German *Kiebitz* 'lapwing, busybody']

kibosh /ky-bosh/ *n. slang* nonsense. □ **put the kibosh on** put an end to; finally dispose of. [19th-century coinage]

kick ● *v.* **1** *tr.* strike or propel forcibly with the foot or hoof etc. **2** *intr.* (usu. foll. by *at*, *against*) **a** strike out with the foot. **b** express annoyance at or dislike of (treatment, a proposal, etc.); rebel against. **3** *tr. colloq.* give up (a habit). **4** *tr.* (often foll. by *out* etc.) expel or dismiss forcibly. **5** *refl.* be annoyed with oneself (*I'll kick myself if I'm wrong*). **6** *tr. Football* score (a goal) by a kick. ● *n.* **1** a blow with the foot or hoof etc. **2** *colloq.* **a** a sharp stimulant effect, esp. of alcohol. **b** (often in *pl.*) a pleasurable thrill (*did it just for kicks; got a kick out of flying*). **3** the recoil of a gun when discharged. □ **kick about** (or **around**) *colloq.* **1 a** drift idly from place to place. **b** be unused or unwanted. **2 a** treat roughly or scornfully. **b** discuss (an idea) unsystematically. **kick against the pricks** see PRICK. **kick ass** (or **some ass**) *N. Amer. coarse slang* act forcefully or in a domineering manner (cf. KICK-ASS). **kick the bucket** *slang* die. **kick one's heels** see HEEL[1]. **kick in 1** knock down (a door etc.) by kicking. **2** esp. *US slang* contribute (esp. money); pay one's share. **3** become activated, start. **kick in the pants** (or **teeth**) *colloq.* a humiliating punishment or setback. **kick off 1 a** *Football* begin or resume a match. **b** *colloq.* begin. **2** remove (shoes etc.) by kicking. **kick over the traces** see TRACE[2]. **kick up** (or **kick up a fuss** etc.) *colloq.* create a disturbance; object or register strong disapproval. **kick up one's heels** frolic. **kick a person upstairs** *colloq.* shelve a person by giving him or her ostensible promotion or a title. [Middle English] □ **kicker** *n.*

kick-ass *adj. N. Amer. coarse slang* forceful, aggressive, domineering (cf. *kick ass* (KICK)).

kickback *n. colloq.* **1** the force of a recoil. **2** (usu. illegal) payment for help or favours, esp. in business.

kick-boxing *n.* a form of boxing characterized by the use of blows with the feet as well as with gloved fists.

kick-down *n. Brit.* a device for changing gear in a motor vehicle by full depression of the accelerator.

kick-off *n.* **1** *Football* the start or resumption of a match. **2** (in phr. **for a kick-off**) *Brit. colloq.* a start (*that's wrong for a kick-off*).

kickstand *n.* a rod attached to a bicycle or motorcycle and kicked into a vertical position to support the vehicle when stationary.

kick-start ● *n.* (also **kick-starter**) a device to start the engine of a motorcycle etc. by the downward thrust of a pedal. ● *v.tr.* **1** start (a motorcycle etc.) in this way. **2** start or restart (a process etc.) by providing some initial impetus.

kick-turn *n.* a standing turn in skiing.

kid[1] ● *n.* **1** a young goat. **2** the leather made from its skin. **3** *colloq.* a child or young person. ● *v.intr.* (**kidded**, **kidding**) (of a goat) give birth. □ **handle with kid gloves** handle in a gentle, delicate, or excessively tactful manner. **kids' stuff** *slang* something very simple. [from Old Norse *kith*]

kid[2] *v.* (**kidded**, **kidding**) *colloq.* **1** *tr. & refl.* deceive, trick. **2** *tr. & intr.* tease (*only kidding*). □ **no kidding** (or **kid**) *slang* that is the truth. □ **kidder** *n.* **kiddingly** *adv.*

kid brother *n.* (also **kid sister**) *colloq.* a younger brother or sister.

kiddie *n.* (also **kiddy**) (*pl.* **-ies**) *colloq.* = KID[1] *n.* 3.

kiddo *n.* (*pl.* **-os**) *colloq.* (esp. as a form of address) = KID[1] *n.* 3.

kidnap *v.tr.* (**kidnapped**, **kidnapping**; *US* **kidnaped**, **kidnaping**) carry off (a person etc.) by illegal force or deception, esp. to obtain a ransom. [based on archaic slang *nap* 'to nab, steal'] □ **kidnapper** *n.*

kidney *n.* (*pl.* **-eys**) **1** ▲ either of a pair of organs in the abdominal cavity of mammals, birds, and reptiles, which remove nitrogenous wastes from the blood and excrete urine. ▷ ENDOCRINE, URINARY SYSTEM. **2** the kidney of a sheep, ox, or pig as food. [Middle English]

kidney bean *n.* a kidney-shaped bean, esp. a dark red one from a dwarf French bean plant. ▷ PULSE

kidney dish *n.* a kidney-shaped dish, esp. one used in surgery.

kidney machine *n.* = ARTIFICIAL KIDNEY.

kid sister SEE KID BROTHER.

kieselguhr /kee-zĕl-goor/ *n.* a soft friable porous deposit formed of fossil diatoms, used as a filter, filler, insulator, etc., in various manufacturing processes. [German, from *Kiesel* 'gravel' + dialect *Guhr* 'earthy deposit']

Kikuyu ● *n.* (*pl.* same or **Kikuyus**) **1** a member of an agricultural people forming the largest Bantu-speaking group in Kenya. **2** the language of this people. ● *adj.* of or relating to this people or their language. [native name]

kilim ● *n.* ◀ a pileless woven carpet, rug, etc., made in Turkey, Kurdistan, and neighbouring areas. ● *attrib.adj.* designating such a carpet, rug, etc. [from Persian *gelīm*]

kill ● *v.tr.* **1 a** deprive of life or vitality; put to death; cause the death of. **b** (*absol.*) cause or bring about death (*must kill to survive*). **2** destroy; put an end to (feelings etc.). **3** *refl.* (often foll. by *pres. part.*) *colloq.* **a** overexert oneself. **b** laugh heartily. **4** *colloq.* overwhelm (a person) with amusement, delight, etc. **5** switch off (a spotlight, engine, etc.). **6** *colloq.* delete (a line, paragraph, etc.) from a computer file. **7** *colloq.* cause pain or discomfort to (*my feet are killing me*). **8** pass (time), usu. while waiting for a specific event (*had an hour to kill before the interview*). **9** defeat (a bill in Parliament). **10 a** *Tennis* etc. hit (the ball) so skilfully that it cannot be returned. **b** stop (the ball) dead. **11** neutralize or render ineffective (taste, sound, colour, etc.) (*thick carpet killed the sound of footsteps*). ● *n.* **1** an act of killing (esp. an animal). **2** an animal or animals killed, esp. by a hunter. **3** *colloq.* the destruction or disablement of an enemy aircraft, submarine, etc. □ **dressed to kill** dressed showily, seductively, or impressively. **in at the kill** present at or benefiting from the successful conclusion of an enterprise. **kill off 1** get rid of or destroy completely. **2** (of an author) bring about the death of (a fictional character). **kill two birds with one stone** achieve two aims at once. **kill with kindness** spoil (a person) with over-indulgence. [Middle English]

killer *n.* **1 a** a person, animal, or thing that kills. **b** a murderer. **2** *colloq.* **a** an impressive, formidable, or excellent person or thing. **b** a hilarious joke. **c** a decisive blow (*his brilliant header proved to be the killer*).

killer bee *n. colloq.* an Africanized honey bee.

killer cell *n. Physiol.* a white blood cell which destroys infected or cancerous cells.

killer instinct *n.* **1** an innate tendency to kill. **2** a ruthless streak.

killer whale *n.* a voracious cetacean, *Orcinus orca*, with a white belly and prominent dorsal fin.

killifish *n.* (*pl.* usu. same) ▼ any small freshwater or brackish-water fish of the family Cyprinodontidae or Poeciliidae, often brightly coloured and kept in aquaria.

KILLIFISH: STEEL-BLUE APHYOSEMION (*Aphyosemion gardneri*)

killing ● *n.* **1 a** the causing of death. **b** an instance of this. **2** a great (esp. financial) success (*make a killing*). ● *adj. colloq.* **1** overwhelmingly funny. **2** exhausting; very strenuous. □ **killingly** *adv.*

killing bottle *n.* a bottle containing poisonous vapour to kill insects collected as specimens.

killjoy *n.* a person who throws gloom over or prevents other people's enjoyment.

KIDNEY

In the human body, the two kidneys, each up to 12 cm (5 in) long, are located at the rear of the abdomen. They each contain some one million filtering units, which process the blood, regulating both the volume of water within the body and levels of salts within body fluids. Most water and virtually all nutrients are reabsorbed into the blood, while excess water and waste products are expelled from the body as urine.

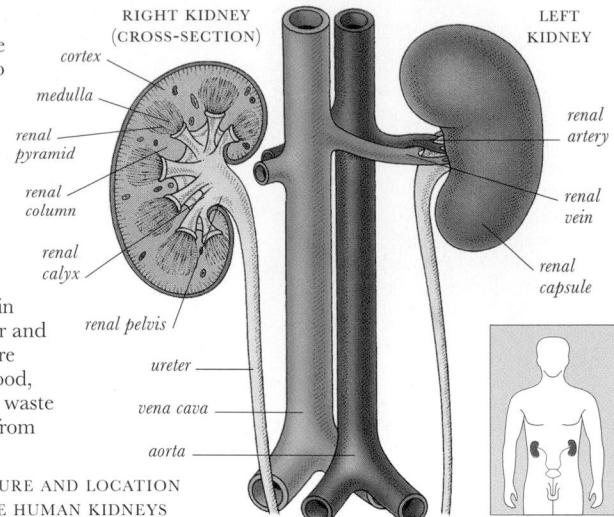

RIGHT KIDNEY (CROSS-SECTION)

LEFT KIDNEY

cortex
medulla
renal pyramid
renal column
renal calyx
renal pelvis
renal artery
renal vein
renal capsule
ureter
vena cava
aorta

STRUCTURE AND LOCATION OF THE HUMAN KIDNEYS

KILIM: MODERN TURKISH KILIM

K

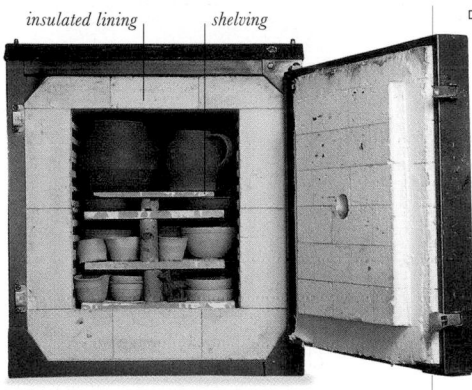

insulated lining   shelving

KILN STACKED WITH POTTERY FOR FIRING

kiln *n.* ▲ a furnace or oven for burning, baking, or drying, esp. for calcining lime or firing pottery etc. [from Latin *culina* 'kitchen']

kiln-dry *v.tr.* (**-ies**, **-ied**) dry in a kiln.

kilo /kee-loh/ *n.* (*pl.* **-os**) **1** a kilogram. **2** a kilometre. [French: abbreviation]

kilo- /kil-oh/ *comb. form* denoting a factor of 1,000 (esp. in metric units).

kilobyte *n. Computing* 1,024 (i.e. 2^{10}) bytes as a measure of memory size.

kilocalorie *n.* = CALORIE 2.

kilocycle *n.* a former measure of frequency, equivalent to 1 kilohertz.

kilogram *n.* (also **-gramme**) the SI unit of mass (approx. 2.205 lb).

kilohertz *n.* a measure of frequency equivalent to 1,000 cycles per second.

kilojoule /kil-ŏ-jool/ *n.* 1,000 joules, esp. as a measure of the energy value of foods.

kilolitre *n.* (*US* **-liter**) 1,000 litres (equivalent to 220 imperial gallons).

kilometre *n.* (*US* **kilometer**) a metric unit of measurement equal to 1,000 metres (approx. 0.62 miles).

kiloton *n.* (also **kilotonne**) a unit of explosive power equivalent to 1,000 tons of TNT.

kilovolt *n.* 1,000 volts.

kilowatt *n.* 1,000 watts.

kilowatt-hour *n.* a measure of electrical energy equivalent to a power consumption of 1,000 watts for one hour.

kilt *n.* **1** a skirtlike garment, usu. of pleated tartan cloth and reaching to the knees, traditionally worn by Highland men. **2** a similar garment worn by women and children. [from Scandinavian] □ **kilted** *adj.*

kilter *n.* (also **kelter**) good working order (esp. *out of kilter*). [17th-century coinage]

kimono *n.* (*pl.* **-os**) **1** ▶ a long loose Japanese robe worn with a sash. **2** a European dressing gown modelled on this. [Japanese, from *ki* 'wearing' + *mono* 'thing'] □ **kimonoed** *adj.*

kin ● *n.* one's relatives or family. ● *predic.adj.* (of a person) related (*we are kin; he is kin to me*). □ **kith and kin** see KITH. **next of kin** see NEXT OF KIN. [Old English]

kind[1] *n.* **1 a** a race or species (*human kind*). **b** a natural group of animals, plants, etc. (*the wolf kind*). **2** class, type, sort, variety. **3** the manner or fashion natural to a person etc. (*true to kind*).

KIMONO: TRADITIONAL JAPANESE KIMONO (SASH NOT SHOWN)

□ **in kind 1** in the same form, likewise (*was insulted and replied in kind*). **2** (of payment) in goods or labour not money (*received their wages in kind*). **3** in character or quality (*differ in degree but not in kind*). **kind of** *colloq.* to some extent (*I kind of expected it*). **a kind of** used to imply looseness, vagueness, exaggeration, etc., in the term used (*I suppose he's a kind of doctor*). **of a kind 1** *derog.* scarcely deserving the name (*a choir of a kind*). **2** similar in some important respect (*they're two of a kind*). **one's own kind** those with whom one has much in common. [Old English]

■ **Usage** In sense 2, *these* (or *those*) *kind* is often encountered when followed by a plural, as in *I don't like these kind of films*, but *this kind* or *these kinds* is usually preferable, e.g. *I don't like this* (or *that*) *kind of film, I don't like these* (or *those*) *kinds of films*.

kind[2] *adj.* **1** friendly, generous, benevolent, or gentle. **2** (usu. foll. by *to*) showing friendliness, affection, or consideration. **3** affectionate. [Old English, originally in sense 'natural, native']

kindergarten *n.* an establishment for pre-school learning. [German, literally 'children's garden']

kind-hearted *adj.* of a kind disposition. □ **kind-heartedly** *adv.* **kind-heartedness** *n.*

kindle *v.* **1** *tr.* light or set on fire (a flame, fire, substance, etc.). **2** *intr.* catch fire, burst into flame. **3** *tr.* arouse or inspire (enthusiasm, jealousy, etc.). **4** *intr.* become animated, glow with passion etc. (*her imagination kindled*). [from Old Norse *kynda*]

kindling *n.* small sticks etc. for lighting fires.

kindly[1] *adv.* **1** in a kind manner (*spoke to the child kindly*). **2** often *iron.* used in a polite request or demand (*kindly acknowledge this letter; kindly leave me alone*). □ **take a thing kindly** like or be pleased by it. **take kindly to** be pleased by or endeared to (a person or thing).

kindly[2] *adj.* (**kindlier**, **kindliest**) **1** kind, kind-hearted. **2** (of climate etc.) pleasant, genial. □ **kindlily** *adv.* **kindliness** *n.*

kindness *n.* **1** the state or quality of being kind. **2** a kind act.

kindred ● *n.* **1** one's relations, collectively. **2** a relationship by blood. **3** a resemblance or affinity in character. ● *adj.* **1** related by blood or marriage. **2** allied or similar in character (*other kindred symptoms*). [KIN + Old English *rǣden* 'condition']

kindred spirit *n.* a person whose character and outlook have much in common with one's own.

kine *archaic pl.* of COW[1].

kinematics *n.pl.* (usu. treated as *sing.*) the branch of mechanics concerned with the motion of objects without reference to the forces which cause the motion. [based on Greek *kinēma -matos* 'motion'] □ **kinematic** *adj.*

kinetic *adj.* of or due to motion. [from Greek *kinētikos*] □ **kinetically** *adv.*

kinetic art *n.* a form of art that depends on movement for its effect.

kinetic energy *n.* energy which a body possesses by virtue of being in motion.

kinetics *n.pl.* (usu. treated as *sing.*) **1** = DYNAMICS 1a. **2** the branch of physical chemistry or biochemistry concerned with measuring and studying the rates of chemical or biochemical reactions.

kinetic theory *n.* a theory which explains the physical properties of matter in terms of the motions of its constituent particles.

kinfolk *N. Amer.* var. of KINSFOLK.

king *n.* **1** (as a title usu. **King**) a male sovereign, esp. the hereditary ruler of an independent state. **2** a person or thing pre-eminent in a specified field or class (*railway king*). **3** (*attrib.*) a large (or the largest) kind of plant, animal, etc. (*king penguin*). **4** *Chess* the piece on each side which the opposing side has to checkmate to win. ▷ CHESS. **5** a piece in draughts with extra capacity for moving, made by crowning an ordinary piece that has reached the opponent's baseline. **6** ▶ a playing card bearing a representation of a king and usu. ranking next below an ace. [Old English] □ **kinglike** *adj.* **kingly** *adj.* **kingliness** *n.* **kingship** *n.*

kingbolt *n.* = KINGPIN.

King Charles spaniel *n.* ▼ a spaniel of a small black, tan, and white breed.

KING: PLAYING-CARD KING

KING CHARLES SPANIEL

king cobra *n.* a large and venomous hooded Indian snake, *Ophiophagus hannah*.

king crab *n.* **1** = HORSESHOE CRAB. **2** *US* any of various large edible spider crabs.

kingcup *n. Brit.* a marsh marigold.

kingdom *n.* **1** an organized community headed by a king. **2** the territory subject to a king. **3 a** the spiritual reign attributed to God (*Thy kingdom come*). **b** the sphere of this (*kingdom of heaven*). **4** a domain belonging to a person, animal, etc. **5** a province of nature (*the plant kingdom*). **6** a specified mental or emotional province (*kingdom of the heart*). □ **kingdom come** *colloq.* eternity; the next world. [Old English]

kingfisher *n.* any bird of the family Alcedinidae, with a long sharp beak, diving for fish in rivers etc., esp. *Alcedo atthis*, a small European bird with bright blue plumage.

King James Bible *n.* (also **King James Version**) = AUTHORIZED VERSION.

kingmaker *n.* a person who makes kings, leaders, etc., through the exercise of political influence.

king of beasts *n.* the lion.

king of birds *n.* the eagle.

kingpin *n.* **1 a** a main or large bolt in a central position. **b** a vertical bolt used as a pivot. **2** an essential person or thing, esp. in a complex system.

king post *n.* an upright post from the tie-beam of a roof to the apex of a truss.

king prawn *n.* a large edible prawn of the genus *Penaeus*, common esp. in Australasia.

King's Counsel *n.* (in the UK) = QUEEN'S COUNSEL.

King's English *n.* = QUEEN'S ENGLISH.

King's evidence *n. Brit. Law* = QUEEN'S EVIDENCE.

King's Guide *n.* (in the UK) = QUEEN'S GUIDE.

King's highway *n. Brit.* = QUEEN'S HIGHWAY.

king-size *adj.* (also **king-sized**) very large.

king's ransom *n.* a fortune.

King's Scout *n.* (in the UK) = QUEEN'S SCOUT.

King's Speech *n.* (in the UK) = QUEEN'S SPEECH.

kink ● *n.* **1 a** a short backward twist in wire or tubing etc. **b** a tight wave in hair. **2** a mental twist or quirk. ● *v.intr. & tr.* form or cause to form a kink. [from Middle Low German *kinke*]

K

KINKAJOU
(*Potos flavus*)

kinkajou /kink-ă-joo/ *n.* ◄ a Central and S. American nocturnal fruit-eating mammal, *Potos flavus*, with a prehensile tail and living in trees. [French *quin-cajou* from Algonquian]

kinky *adj.* (**kinkier**, **kinkiest**) **1** *colloq.* **a** given to or involving bizarre or unusual sexual behaviour. **b** (of clothing etc.) bizarre in a sexually provocative way. **2** strange, eccentric. **3** having kinks or twists. □ **kinkily** *adv.* **kinkiness** *n.*

kinsfolk *n.pl.* (also *N. Amer.* **kinfolk**) one's relations by blood.

kinship *n.* **1** blood relationship. **2** the sharing of characteristics or origins.

kinsman *n.* (*pl.* **-men**; *fem.* **kinswoman**, *pl.* **-women**) **1** a blood relation or (loosely) a relation by marriage. **2** a member of one's own tribe or people.

kiosk *n.* **1** a light open-fronted booth from which food, newspapers, tickets, etc., are sold. **2** a telephone box. **3** *Austral.* a building in which refreshments are served in a park, zoo, etc. [from Persian *guš*]

kip[1] *Brit. slang* ● *n.* **1** a sleep. **2** a bed or cheap lodging house. ● *v.intr.* (**kipped**, **kipping**) sleep. [18th-century coinage]

kip[2] *n. Austral. slang* a small piece of wood from which coins are spun in the game of two-up. [Middle English]

kipper ● *n.* a kippered fish, esp. herring. ● *v.tr.* cure (a herring etc.) by splitting open, salting, and drying in the open air or smoke. [Middle English]

Kir /keer/ *n. propr.* a drink made from dry white wine and blackcurrant liqueur. [named after Canon Felix *Kir*, 1876–1968, said to have invented the recipe]

kirby grip *n.* (also **Kirbigrip** *propr.*) *Brit.* a type of sprung hairgrip. [from *Kirby*, part of original manufacturer's name]

Kirghiz var. of KYRGYZ.

kirk *n. Sc. & N.Engl.* **1** a church. **2** (**the Kirk** or **the Kirk of Scotland**) the Church of Scotland. [Old English]

Kirk-session *n.* the lowest court in the Church of Scotland.

kirsch /keersh/ *n.* (also **kirschwasser** /keersh-vas-er/) a brandy distilled from the fermented juice of cherries. [from German *Kirsche* 'cherry' (*Wasser* 'water')]

kismet *n.* destiny, fate. [from Arabic *kisma(t)*]

kiss ● *v.tr.* **1** touch with the lips, esp. as a sign of love, affection, greeting, or reverence. **2** express (greeting or farewell) in this way. **3** *absol.* (of two persons) touch each other's lips in this way. **4** (also *absol.*) (of a snooker ball etc. in motion) lightly touch (another ball). ● *n.* **1** a touch with the lips. **2** the slight impact when one snooker ball etc. lightly touches another. **3** a small sweetmeat or piece of confectionery. □ **kiss and tell** recount one's sexual exploits. **kiss a person's arse** *coarse slang* act obsequiously towards a person. **kiss away** remove (tears etc.) by kissing. **kiss the dust** submit abjectly; be overthrown. **kiss goodbye to** *colloq.* accept the loss of. **kiss off** esp. *N. Amer. slang* **1** dismiss, get rid of. **2** go away, die. [Old English] □ **kissable** *adj.*

kiss-curl *n.* a small curl of hair on the forehead, at the nape, or in front of the ear.

kisser *n.* **1** a person who kisses. **2** *slang* the mouth; the face.

kissing cousin *n.* (also **kissing kin** or **kind**) a distant relative (given a formal kiss on occasional meetings).

kissing gate *n. Brit.* a gate hung in a V- or U-shaped enclosure, letting one person through at a time.

kiss of death *n.* an apparently friendly act which causes ruin.

kiss-off *n.* esp. *N. Amer. slang* an abrupt or rude dismissal.

kiss of life *n.* mouth-to-mouth resuscitation.

kiss of peace *n. Eccl.* a ceremonial kiss, esp. during the Eucharist, as a sign of unity.

kissogram *n.* (also **Kissagram** *propr.*) *Brit.* a novelty telegram or greetings message delivered with a kiss.

kit[1] ● *n.* **1** a set of articles, equipment, or clothing needed for a specific purpose (*first-aid kit*; *bicycle-repair kit*). **2** *Brit.* the clothing etc. needed for any activity, esp. sport (*football kit*). **3** a set of all the parts needed to assemble a piece of furniture, a model, etc. ● *v.tr.* (**kitted**, **kitting**) (often foll. by *out*, *up*) esp. *Brit.* equip with the appropriate clothing or tools. [from Middle Dutch *kitte* 'wooden vessel']

kit[2] *n.* **1** a kitten. **2** a young fox, badger, etc.

kitbag *n.* a large, usu. cylindrical bag used for carrying a soldier's, traveller's, or sportsman's equipment.

kitchen *n.* **1 a** the room or area where food is prepared and cooked. **b** kitchen fitments or units, esp. as sold together. **2** (*attrib.*) of or belonging to the kitchen (*kitchen knife*; *kitchen table*). [based on Latin *coquere* 'to cook']

kitchen cabinet *n.* a group of unofficial advisers.

kitchenette *n.* a small kitchen or part of a room fitted as a kitchen.

kitchen garden *n.* a garden where vegetables and sometimes fruit or herbs are grown.

kitchen midden *n.* a prehistoric refuse-heap which marks an ancient settlement.

kitchen roll *n. Brit.* a roll of absorbent paper for cleaning up spillages etc.

kitchen-sink *attrib.adj.* (in art forms) depicting extreme realism, esp. drabness or sordidness (*kitchen-sink school of painting*; *kitchen-sink drama*).

kitchen tea *n. Austral. & NZ* a party held before a wedding to which female guests bring items of kitchen equipment as presents.

kitchenware *n.* the utensils used in the kitchen.

kite ● *n.* **1** ▲ a toy consisting of a light framework with thin material stretched over it, flown in the wind at the end of a long string. **2** any of various soaring birds of prey esp. of the genus *Milvus* with long wings and usu. a forked tail. **3** *Brit. slang* an aeroplane. **4** *slang* a fraudulent cheque, bill, or receipt. **5** *Geom.* a quadrilateral figure symmetrical about one diagonal. ● *v.* **1** *intr.* soar like a kite. **2** *tr.* (also *absol.*) *slang* originate or pass (fraudulent cheques, bills, or receipts). **3** *tr.* (also *absol.*) *slang* raise (money) by dishonest means (*kite a loan*). [Old English]

Kitemark *n.* an official kite-shaped mark on goods approved by the British Standards Institution.

kith *n.* □ **kith and kin** friends and relations. [Old English]

kitsch /kich/ *n.* (often *attrib.*) garish, tasteless, or sentimental art (*kitsch plastic models of the royal family*). [German] □ **kitschiness** *n.* **kitschy** *adj.* (**kitschier**, **kitschiest**).

kitten ● *n.* **1** a young cat. **2** a young ferret etc. ● *v.intr. & tr.* (of a cat etc.) give birth or give birth to. □ **have kittens** *colloq.* be extremely upset, anxious, or nervous. [from Old French *chitoun*]

K

KITE

Kites were first developed more than 2,500 years ago by the ancient Chinese, who used them for aerial reconnaissance in battle and to bear archers aloft over the enemy. Today, kites are flown both as a pastime and as a sport. A basic kite consists of a nylon-covered frame supported by spars. Launched and held aloft by rising wind currents, the kite is controlled from the ground by a flying line.

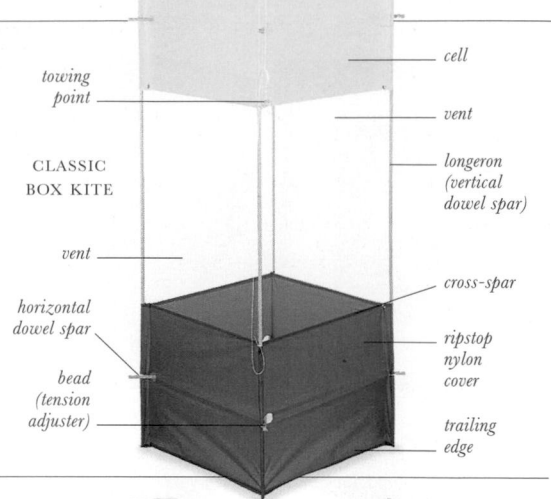

CLASSIC BOX KITE

towing point · *cell* · *vent* · *longeron (vertical dowel spar)* · *vent* · *cross-spar* · *horizontal dowel spar* · *ripstop nylon cover* · *bead (tension adjuster)* · *trailing edge*

OTHER TYPES OF KITE

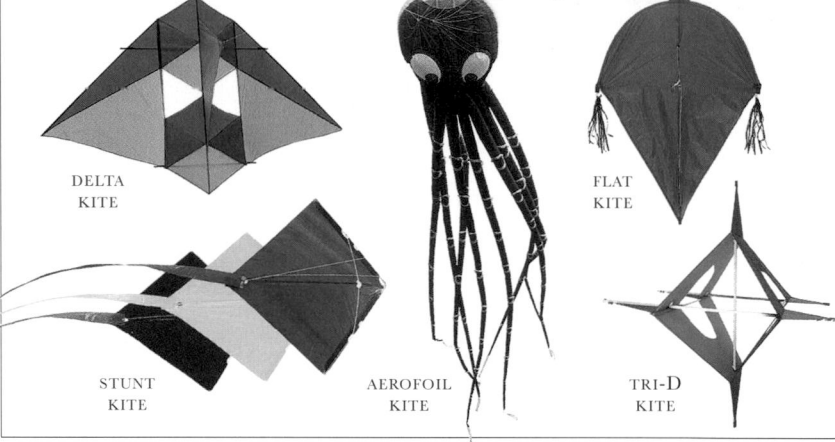

DELTA KITE · FLAT KITE · STUNT KITE · AEROFOIL KITE · TRI-D KITE

kittenish *adj.* **1** like a young cat; playful and lively. **2** flirtatious, coy. □ **kittenishly** *adv.* **kittenishness** *n.*

kittiwake *n.* a small gull of the genus *Rissa*, esp. *Rissa tridactyla* of the N. Atlantic and Arctic Oceans.

kitty[1] *n.* (*pl.* **-ies**) **1** a fund of money for communal use. **2** the pool in some card games. **3** the jack in bowls. [19th-century coinage]

kitty[2] *n.* (*pl.* **-ies**) a pet name or a child's name for a kitten or cat.

kitty-corner (also **kitty-cornered**, **cater-cornered**, **catty-corner(ed)**) *N. Amer.* ● *adj.* placed or situated diagonally. ● *adv.* diagonally. [based on dialect *cater* 'diagonally']

kiwi *n.* (*pl.* **kiwis**) **1** ▼ a flightless New Zealand bird of the genus *Apteryx* with hair-like feathers and a long bill. **2** (**Kiwi**) *colloq.* a New Zealander. [Maori]

KIWI:
BROWN KIWI
(*Apteryx australis*)

kiwi fruit *n.* ◀ the fruit of a climbing plant, *Actinidia chinensis*, having a thin hairy skin, green flesh, and black seeds.

kJ *abbr.* kilojoule(s).

KKK *abbr. US* Ku Klux Klan.

kl *abbr.* kilolitre(s).

Klansman *n.* (*pl.* **-men**; *fem.* **Klanswoman**, *pl.* **-women**) a member of the Ku Klux Klan.

klaxon *n. propr.* a horn or warning hooter. [name of the manufacturer]

Kleenex *n.* (*pl.* same or **Kleenexes**) *propr.* a disposable paper handkerchief.

KIWI FRUIT
(*Actinidia chinensis*)

kleptomania *n.* a recurrent urge to steal, usu. without regard for need or profit. [based on Greek *kleptēs* 'thief'] □ **kleptomaniac** *n. & adj.*

Klondike *n.* a source of valuable material. [from *Klondike* in Yukon, Canada, where gold was found (1896)]

klutz *n.* esp. *N. Amer. colloq.* **1** a clumsy, awkward person. **2** a fool. [from German *Klotz* 'wooden block'] □ **klutzy** *adj.*

km *abbr.* kilometre(s).

kn. *abbr. Naut.* knot(s) (see KNOT[1] *n.* 2a).

knack *n.* **1** a faculty of doing a thing adroitly. **2** a trick or habit (*has a knack of offending people*). [Middle English]

knacker *Brit.* ● *n.* **1** a buyer of horses, cattle, etc. for slaughter. **2** a buyer of old houses, ships, etc. for the materials. ● *v.tr. slang* **1** kill. **2** (esp. as **knackered** *adj.*) exhaust, wear out. [18th-century coinage, in sense 'old or worn out horse']

knap[1] *n.* chiefly *dial.* the crest of a hill or of rising ground. [Old English]

knap[2] *v.tr.* (**knapped**, **knapping**) break (stones for roads or building, flints, or *Austral.* ore) with a hammer. [Middle English] □ **knapper** *n.*

knapsack *n.* a soldier's or hiker's bag with shoulder straps, carried on the back. [Middle Low German]

knapweed *n.* ▶ any of various plants of the genus *Centaurea*, with thistle-like purple flowers. [Middle English, based on *knop* 'tuft']

KNAPWEED:
COMMON
KNAPWEED
(*Centaurea nigra*)

knave *n.* **1** a rogue, a scoundrel. **2** = JACK *n.* 2. [Old English *cnafa* 'boy, servant', from West Germanic] □ **knavery** *n.* (*pl.* **-ies**) **knavishness** *n.* **knavish** *adj.* **knavishly** *adv.*

knead *v.tr.* **1 a** work (a yeast mixture, clay, etc.) into dough, paste, etc., by pummelling and folding. **b** make (bread, pottery, etc.) in this way. **2** blend or weld together (*kneaded them into a unified group*). **3** massage (muscles etc.) as if kneading. [Old English] □ **kneader** *n.* **kneadable** *adj.*

knee ● *n.* **1 a** (often *attrib.*) ▼ the joint between the thigh and the lower leg in humans. ▷ JOINT. **b** the corresponding joint in other animals. **c** the area around this. **d** the upper surface of the thigh of a sitting person; the lap (*held her on his knee*). **2** the part of a garment covering the knee. **3** anything resembling a knee in shape or position, esp. a piece of wood or iron bent at an angle, a sharp turn in a graph, etc. ● *v.* (**knees**, **kneed**, **kneeing**) **1** *tr.* touch or strike with the knee (*kneed the ball past him; kneed him in the groin*). **2** *Brit. colloq.* **a** *tr.* cause (trousers etc.) to bulge at the knee. **b** *intr.* (of trousers etc.) bulge at the knee (*tend to knee*). □ **bend** (or **bow**) **the knee 1** kneel in submission, worship, or supplication. **2** submit. **bring to its** (or **his** or **her**) **knees** reduce (a thing or person) to a state of weakness or submission. **on** (or **on one's**) **bended knee** (or **knees**) kneeling, esp. in supplication, submission, or worship. [Old English]

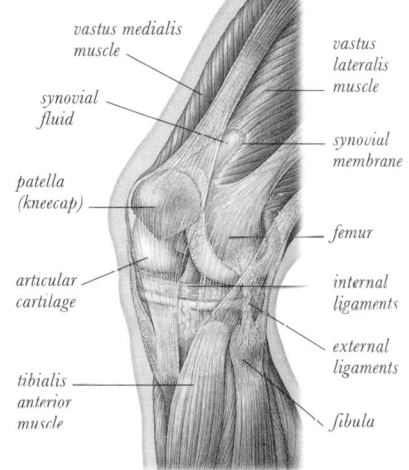

vastus medialis
muscle

synovial
fluid

patella
(kneecap)

articular
cartilage

tibialis
anterior
muscle

vastus
lateralis
muscle

synovial
membrane

femur

internal
ligaments

external
ligaments

fibula

KNEE: HUMAN LEG SHOWING THE KNEE

knee-bend *n.* the action of bending the knee, esp. as a physical exercise.

knee-breeches *n.pl.* close-fitting trousers reaching to or just below the knee.

kneecap ● *n.* **1** the convex bone in front of the knee joint. ▷ KNEE. **2** a protective covering for the knee. ● *v.tr.* (**-capped**, **-capping**) *colloq.* shoot (a person) in the knee or leg as a punishment. □ **kneecapping** *n.*

knee-deep *adj.* **1** (usu. foll. by *in*) **a** immersed up to the knees. **b** deeply involved. **2** so deep as to reach the knees.

knee-high *adj. & adv.* so high as to reach the knees. □ **knee-high to a grasshopper** very small or very young.

kneehole *n.* a space for the knees, esp. under a desk (often *attrib.*: *kneehole desk*).

knee-jerk ● *n.* a sudden involuntary kick caused by a blow on the tendon just below the knee. ● *attrib.adj.* predictable, automatic, stereotyped (*a knee-jerk reaction*).

knee joint *n.* **1** = KNEE *n.* 1a, b. **2** a joint made of two pieces hinged together.

kneel *v.intr.* (*past* and *past part.* **knelt** or esp. *US* **kneeled**) fall or rest on the knees or a knee. [Old English]

knee-length *adj.* reaching the knees.

kneeler *n.* **1** a hassock or cushion used for kneeling. **2** a person who kneels.

knees-up *n. Brit. colloq.* a lively party or gathering.

knell ● *n.* **1** the sound of a bell, esp. when rung solemnly for a death or funeral. **2** an announcement, event, etc., regarded as a solemn warning of disaster. ● *v.* **1** *intr.* **a** (of a bell) ring solemnly, esp. for a death or funeral. **b** make a doleful or ominous sound. **2** *tr.* proclaim by or as by a knell (*knelled the death of all their hopes*). □ **ring the knell of** announce or herald the end of. [Old English]

knelt *past* and *past part.* of KNEEL.

knew *past* of KNOW.

Knickerbocker Glory *n. Brit.* ice cream served with other ingredients in a tall glass.

knickerbockers *n.pl.* ▶ loose-fitting breeches gathered at the knee or calf. [named after Diedrich *Knickerbocker*, pretended author of W. Irving's *History of New York* (1809)]

knickers *n.pl.* **1** *Brit.* a woman's or girl's undergarment covering the body from the waist or hips to the top of the thighs and having leg-holes or separate legs. **2** *N. Amer.* **a** knickerbockers. **b** a boy's short trousers. **3** (as *int.*) *Brit. slang* an expression of contempt.

knick-knack *n.* (also **nick-nack**) **1** a useless and usually worthless ornament; a trinket. **2** a small, dainty article of furniture, dress, etc. [reduplication of archaic *knack* 'trinket'] □ **knick-knackery** *n.*

knife ● *n.* (*pl.* **knives**) **1 a** a metal blade used as a cutting tool with usu. one long sharp edge fixed rigidly in a handle or hinged (cf. PENKNIFE). **b** a similar tool used as a weapon. **2** a cutting blade forming part of a machine. **3** (as **the knife**) *colloq.* a surgical operation or operations. ● *v.* **1** *tr.* cut or stab with a knife. **2** *tr. slang* bring about the defeat of (a person) by underhand means. **3** *intr.* (usu. foll. by *through*) cut or cut its way like a knife. □ **get one's knife into** treat maliciously or vindictively. [from Old Norse *knífr*] □ **knifelike** *adj.*

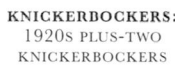

knicker-bockers

KNICKERBOCKERS:
1920s PLUS-TWO
KNICKERBOCKERS

K

knife-edge *n.* **1** the edge of a knife. **2** a position of extreme danger or uncertainty. **3** a steel wedge on which a pendulum etc. oscillates. **4** = ARÊTE.

knife-grinder *n.* a travelling sharpener of knives etc.

knife-pleat *n.* a narrow flat pleat on a skirt etc., usu. overlapping another.

knifepoint *n.* the pointed end of a knife. □ **at knifepoint** threatened with a knife or an ultimatum etc.

knight ● *n.* **1** a man awarded a non-hereditary title (*Sir*) by a sovereign. **2** *hist.* **a** a man, usu. noble, raised esp. by a sovereign to honourable military rank after service as a page and squire. ▷ JOUST, TABARD. **b** a military follower or attendant, esp. of a lady as her champion in a war or tournament. **3** *Chess* a piece usu. shaped like a horse's head. ▷ CHESS. ● *v.tr.* confer a knighthood on. [Old English *cniht* 'youth, hero'] □ **knighthood** *n.* **knightly** *adj. & adv. poet.*

knight commander see COMMANDER 2.

knight errant *n.* **1** a medieval knight wandering in search of chivalrous adventures. **2** a man of a chivalrous or quixotic nature. □ **knight-errantry** *n.*

Knight Hospitaller *n.* (*pl.* **Knights Hospitallers**) a member of an order of monks with a military history, founded at Jerusalem *c.*1050.

Knight Templar *n.* (*pl.* **Knights Templars**) *hist.* a member of a religious and military order for the protection of pilgrims to the Holy Land, suppressed in 1312.

KNIT

The earliest known samples of true knitting date from 7th-century Arabia. Modern knitting still consists of the creation of a continuous looped fabric using a length of yarn and two or more eyeless needles. The combination of knit, purl, and other stitches, together with coloured yarns and needles of varying size, can produce an enormous diversity of sophisticated effects and textures.

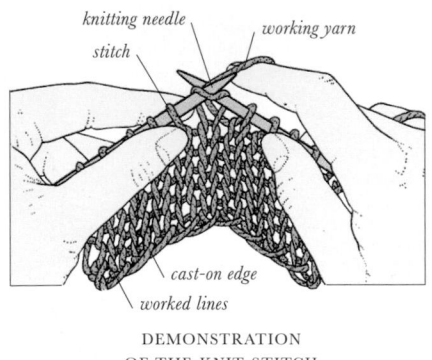

knitting needle
stitch
working yarn

cast-on edge
worked lines

DEMONSTRATION
OF THE KNIT STITCH

TYPES OF KNITTING STITCH

GARTER STITCH   STOCKING STITCH

BERRY STITCH   DOUBLE MOSS STITCH

BASKETWEAVE STITCH   SIX-STITCH CABLE

K

kniphofia /ni-**foh**-fiă/ n. a tall ornamental plant of the genus *Kniphofia* (lily family), with long spikes or dense racemes of red, yellow, or orange flowers, e.g. the red-hot poker. ▷ RED-HOT POKER. [named after J.H. *Kniphof*, German botanist, 1704–63]

knit ● v. (**knitting**; *past* and *past part.* **knitted** or (esp. in senses 2–4) **knit**) **1** *tr.* (also *absol.*) **a** ▲ make (a garment, blanket, etc.) by interlocking loops of esp. wool with knitting needles. **b** make (a garment etc.) with a knitting machine. **c** make (a plain stitch) in knitting (*knit one, purl one*). **2 a** *tr.* contract (the forehead) in vertical wrinkles. **b** *intr.* (of the forehead) contract; frown. **3** *tr. & intr.* make or become close or compact (*a close-knit group*). **4** *intr.* (of parts of a broken bone) become joined; heal. ● *n.* knitted material or a knitted garment. □ **knit up 1** make or repair by knitting. **2** conclude, finish, or end. [Old English] □ **knitter** *n.*

knitting *n.* **1** a garment etc. in the process of being knitted. **2 a** the act of knitting. **b** an instance of this.

knitting machine *n.* a machine used for knitting garments etc.

knitting needle *n.* a thin pointed rod used esp. in pairs for knitting. ▷ KNIT

knitwear *n.* knitted garments.

knives *pl.* of KNIFE.

knob ● *n.* **1 a** a rounded protuberance, esp. at the end or on the surface of a thing. **b** a handle of a door, drawer, etc., shaped like a knob. **c** a knob-shaped attachment for pulling, turning, etc. (*press the knob under the desk*). **2** a small piece (of butter, coal, sugar, etc.). **3** esp. *N. Amer.* a prominent round hill. **4** *coarse slang* the penis. ● *v.tr.* (**knobbed, knobbing**) provide with a knob or knobs. □ **with knobs on** *Brit. slang* that and more (used as a retort to an insult, in emphatic agreement, etc.) (*and the same to you with knobs on*). [from Middle Low German *knobbe* 'knot, knob, bud'] □ **knobby** *adj.*

knobble *n. Brit.* a small knob. [Middle English] □ **knobbly** *adj.* (also *N. Amer.*).

knobkerrie *n.* a short stick with a knobbed head used as a weapon, esp. in S. Africa. [suggested by Afrikaans *knopkierie*]

knock ● *v.* **1 a** *tr.* strike with an audible sharp blow (*knocked the table three times*). **b** *intr.* strike, esp. a door to gain admittance (*can you hear someone knocking?;*

knocked at the door). **2** *tr.* make (a hole, a dent, etc.) by knocking (*knock a hole in the fence*). **3** *tr.* (usu. foll. by *in, out, off*, etc.) drive (a thing, a person, etc.) by striking (*knocked the ball into the hole; knocked those ideas out of his head; knocked her hand away*). **4** *tr. colloq.* criticize. **5** *intr.* **a** (of a motor or other engine) make a thumping or rattling noise. **b** = PINK[3]. **6** *tr. Brit. slang* make a strong impression on, astonish. ● *n.* **1** an act of knocking. **2** a sharp rap, esp. at a door. **3** an audible sharp blow. **4** the sound of knocking in an engine. □ **knock about** (or **around**) **1** strike repeatedly; treat roughly (*knocked her about*). **2** lead a wandering adventurous life; wander aimlessly. **3** be present without design or volition (*there's a cup knocking about somewhere*). **4** (usu. foll. by *with*) *Brit.* be associated socially (*knocks about with his brother*). **knock against 1** collide with. **2** come across casually. **knock back 1** *colloq.* eat or drink, esp. quickly. **2** *Brit. colloq.* disconcert. **3** reverse the progress of. **4** *Austral. & NZ colloq.* refuse, rebuff. **knock the bottom out of** see BOTTOM. **knock down 1** strike (esp. a person) to the ground. **2** demolish. **3** (usu. foll. by *to*) (at an auction) dispose of (an article) to a bidder by a knock with a hammer (*knocked the Picasso down to him for a million*). **4** *colloq.* lower the price of (an article). **5** take (machinery, furniture, etc.) to pieces for transportation. **knock into a cocked hat** see COCKED HAT. **knock into shape** see SHAPE. **knock off 1** strike off with a blow. **2** *colloq.* **a** finish work (*knocked off at 5.30*). **b** finish (work) (*knocked off work early*). **3** *colloq.* dispatch (business). **4** *colloq.* rapidly produce (a work of art, verses, etc.). **5** deduct (a sum) from a price, bill, etc. **6** *slang* steal. **7** *Brit. coarse slang offens.* have sexual intercourse with (a woman). **8** *slang* kill. **knock on** *Rugby* drive (a ball) with the hand or arm towards the opponents' goal line. **knock on the head 1** stun or kill (a person) by a blow on the head. **2** put an end to (a scheme etc.). **knock on** (or **knock**) **wood** *N. Amer.* = touch wood. **knock out 1** make (a person) unconscious by a blow on the head. **2** knock down (a boxer) for a count of 10, thereby winning the contest. **3** defeat, esp. in a knockout competition. **4** *colloq.* astonish. **5** (*refl.*) *colloq.* exhaust (*knocked themselves out swimming*). **6** *colloq.* make or write (a plan etc.) hastily. **7** empty (a tobacco pipe) by tapping. **8** *Austral., NZ, & US slang* earn. **knock sideways** *colloq.* disconcert; astonish. **knock one's socks off** see SOCK[1]. **knock spots off** *Brit.* defeat easily.

knock together put together or assemble hastily or roughly. **knock up 1** *Brit.* make hastily. **2** drive upwards with a blow. **3 a** become exhausted or ill. **b** exhaust or make ill. **4** *Brit.* arouse (a person) by a knock at the door. **5** *Cricket* score (runs) rapidly. **6** esp. *US slang* make pregnant. **7** *Brit.* practise a ball game before formal play begins. **take a** (or **the**) **knock** be badly affected financially or emotionally. [Old English]

knockabout ● *attrib.adj.* **1** (of comedy) boisterous; slapstick. **2** (of clothes) suitable for rough use. **3** *Austral.* of a farm or station handyman. ● *n.* **1** *Austral.* a farm or station handyman. **2** a knockabout performer or performance.

knock-back *n. Austral. & NZ colloq.* a refusal; a rebuff.

knock-down ● *attrib.adj.* **1** (of a blow, misfortune, argument, etc.) overwhelming. **2** *colloq.* (of a price) very low. **3** (of a price at auction) reserve. **4** (of furniture etc.) easily dismantled and reassembled. **5** (of an insecticide) rapidly immobilizing. ● *n. Austral. & NZ slang* an introduction (to a person).

knocker *n.* **1** a metal or wooden instrument hinged to a door for knocking to call attention. **2** a person or thing that knocks. **3** (in *pl.*) *coarse slang* a woman's breasts. **4** a person who buys or sells door to door. □ **on the knocker 1** *Brit.* **a** (buying or selling) from door to door. **b** (obtained) on credit. **2** *Austral. & NZ colloq.* promptly.

knocker-up *n. Brit. hist.* a person employed to rouse early workers by knocking at their doors or windows.

knocking shop *n. Brit. slang* a brothel.

knock knees *n.pl.* an abnormal condition with the legs curved inwards at the knee. □ **knock-kneed** *adj.*

knock-off *n.* (often *attrib.*) *colloq.* a copy or imitation made esp. for commercial gain.

knock-on *n. Rugby* an act of knocking on.

knock-on effect *n.* esp. *Brit.* a secondary, indirect, or cumulative effect.

knockout *n.* **1** the act of making unconscious by a blow. **2** *Boxing* etc. a blow that knocks an opponent out. **3** *Brit.* a competition in which the loser in each round is eliminated (also *attrib.: a knockout round*). **4** *colloq.* an outstanding or irresistible person or thing.

knockout drops *n.pl.* a drug added to a drink to cause unconsciousness.

knock-up *n. Brit.* a warm-up at tennis etc.

knoll *n.* a small hill or mound. [Old English *cnoll* 'hilltop']

knot[1] ● *n.* **1 a** an intertwining of a rope, string, tress of hair, etc., with another, itself, or something else to join or fasten together. **b** ▶ a set method of tying a knot (*a reef knot*). **c** a ribbon etc. tied as an ornament and worn on a dress etc. **d** a tangle in hair, knitting, etc. **2 a** a unit of a ship's or aircraft's speed equivalent to one nautical mile per hour (see NAUTICAL MILE). **b** *colloq.* a nautical mile. **3** (usu. foll. by *of*) a group or cluster (*a small knot of journalists at the gate*). **4** a bond or tie, esp. of wedlock. **5** a hard lump of tissue in an animal or human body. **6 a** a knob or protuberance in a stem, branch, or root. **b** a hard mass formed in a tree trunk at the intersection with a branch. **c** a round cross-grained piece in timber where a branch has been cut through. **d** a node on the stem of a plant. **7** a difficulty; a problem. **8** a central point in a problem or the plot of a story etc. ● *v.* (**knotted, knotting**) **1** *tr.* tie in a knot. **2** *tr.* entangle. **3** *tr.* knit (the brows). **4** *tr.* unite closely or intricately (*knotted together in intrigue*). **5 a** *intr.* make knots for fringing. **b** *tr.* make (a fringe) with knots. □ **at a rate of knots** *Brit. colloq.* very fast. **get knotted!** *Brit. slang* an expression of disbelief, annoyance, etc. **tie in knots** *colloq.* baffle or confuse completely. [Old English] □ **knotting** *n.* (esp. in sense 5a of *v.*).

knot[2] *n.* a small sandpiper, *Calidris canutus.* [Middle English]

knot-garden *n.* an intricately designed formal garden.

KNOT

Early people first tied knots in single-strand fibres, and later in longer, thicker ropes. Modern knot types suit specific purposes. Stopper knots prevent lines sliding through the hands, and may add weight to the end of a throwing line. Binding knots are used to fasten tightly around an object or to tie sails. Bends join two ropes of similar or different weight, while quick-release hitches can secure rope to a pole or ring, or tether animals. Loop knots may be dropped over an object, threaded through a ring, or tied around the wrist or waist.

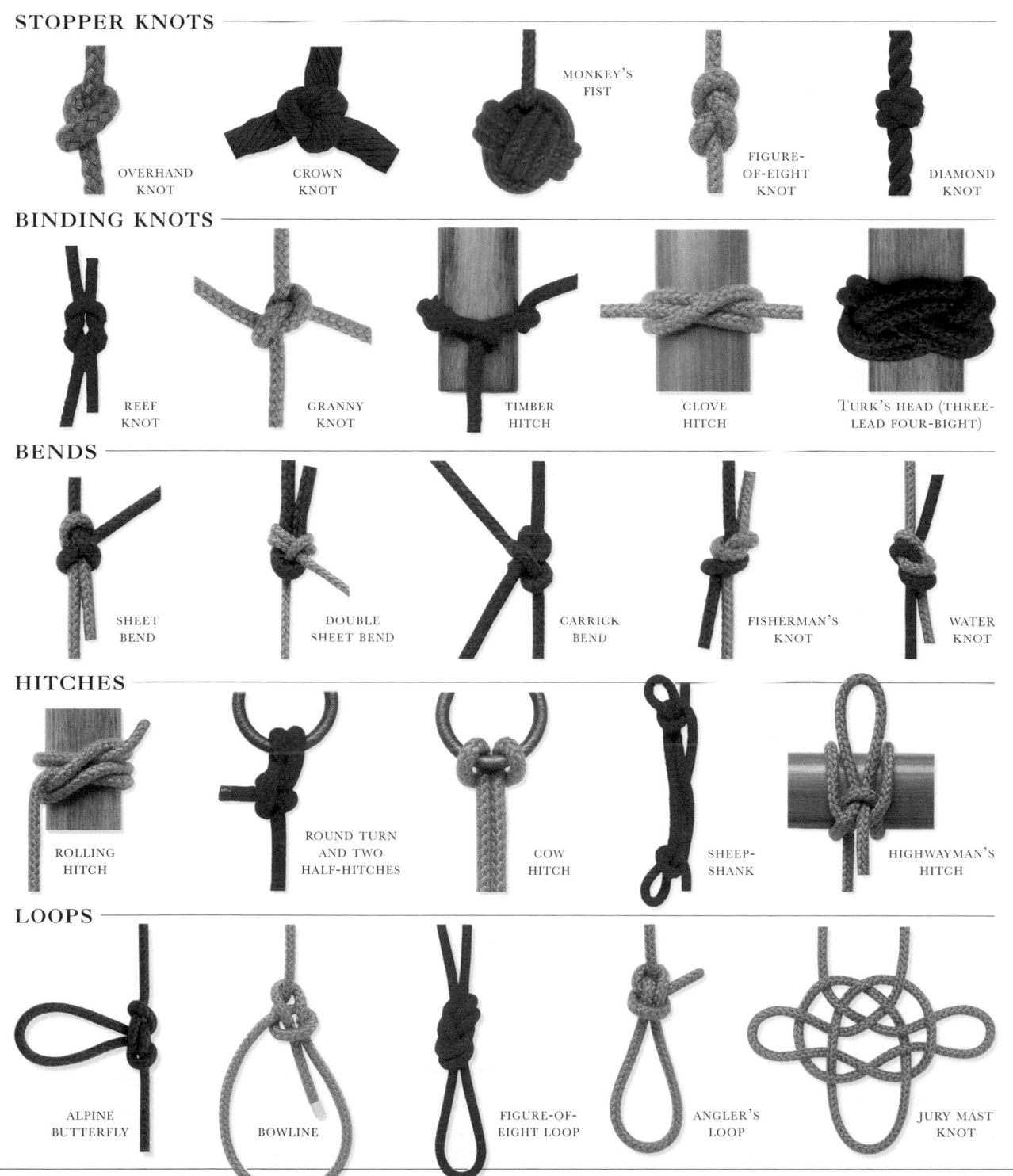

STOPPER KNOTS

OVERHAND KNOT

CROWN KNOT

MONKEY'S FIST

FIGURE-OF-EIGHT KNOT

DIAMOND KNOT

BINDING KNOTS

REEF KNOT

GRANNY KNOT

TIMBER HITCH

CLOVE HITCH

TURK'S HEAD (THREE-LEAD FOUR-BIGHT)

BENDS

SHEET BEND

DOUBLE SHEET BEND

CARRICK BEND

FISHERMAN'S KNOT

WATER KNOT

HITCHES

ROLLING HITCH

ROUND TURN AND TWO HALF-HITCHES

COW HITCH

SHEEP-SHANK

HIGHWAYMAN'S HITCH

LOOPS

ALPINE BUTTERFLY

BOWLINE

FIGURE-OF-EIGHT LOOP

ANGLER'S LOOP

JURY MAST KNOT

K

knotgrass *n.* **1** ▶ a common weed, *Polygonum aviculare*, with creeping stems and small pink flowers. **2** any of various other plants, esp. grasses, with jointed stems.

knot-hole *n.* a hole in a piece of timber where a knot has fallen out.

knotty *adj.* (**knottier, knottiest**) **1** full of knots. **2** puzzling (*a knotty problem*).

knotweed *n.* a plant of the family Polygonaceae, esp. *Reynoutria japonica*, a fast-growing Japanese plant, widely naturalized.

KNOTGRASS
(*Polygonum aviculare*)

know ● *v.* (*past* **knew**; *past part.* **known**) **1** *tr.* **a** have in the mind; have learnt; be able to recall (*knows a lot about cars; knows what to do*). **b** (also *absol.*) be aware of (a fact) (*he knows I am waiting; I think he knows*). **c** have a good command of (*knew German; knows his tables*). **2** *tr.* be acquainted or friendly with. **3** *tr.* **a** recognize; identify (*I knew him at once; knew him for an American*). **b** (foll. by *to* + infin.) be aware of (a person or thing) as being or doing what is specified (*knew them to be rogues*). **c** (foll. by *from*) be able to distinguish (*did not know him from Adam*). **4** *tr.* have experience of (*her joy knew no bounds*). **5** *tr.* have personal experience of (fear etc.). **6** *tr.* (as **known** *adj.*) **a** publicly acknowledged (*a known thief; a known fact*). **b** *Math.* (of a quantity etc.) having a value that can be stated. **7** *intr.* have understanding or knowledge. **8** *tr. archaic* have sexual intercourse with. ● *n.* (in phr. **in the know**) *colloq.* well informed; having special knowledge. □ **all one knows** (or **knows how**) **1** all one can (*did all he knew to stop it*). **2** *adv.* to the utmost of one's power (*tried all she knew*). **before one knows where one is** with baffling speed. **don't you know** *colloq.* or *joc.* an expression used for emphasis (*such a bore, don't you know*). **for all** (or **aught**) **I know** so far as my knowledge extends. **have been known to** have occasionally in the past (*they have been known to turn up late*). **know about** have information about. **know best** be or claim to be better informed etc. than others. **know better than** (foll. by *that*, or to + infin.) be wise, well informed, or well-mannered enough to avoid (specified behaviour etc.). **know by name 1** have heard the name of. **2** be able to give the name of. **know by sight** recognize the appearance (only) of. **know how** know the way to do something. **know of** be aware of; have heard of (*not that I know of*). **know one's own mind** be decisive, not vacillate. **know the ropes** (or **one's stuff**) be fully knowledgeable or experienced. **know a thing or two** be experienced or shrewd. **know what's what** have adequate knowledge of the world, life, etc. **know who's who** be aware of who or what each person is. **not know that …** *colloq.* be fairly sure that … not (*I don't know that I want to go*). **not know what hit one** be suddenly injured, killed, disconcerted, etc. **not want to know** refuse to take any notice of. **what do you know** (or **know about that**)? *colloq.* an expression of surprise. **you know something** (or **what**)? I am going to tell you something. **you never know** nothing in the future is certain. [Old English] □ **knowable** *adj.* **knower** *n.*

know-all *n. esp. Brit. colloq.* a person who seems to know everything.

know-how *n.* **1** practical knowledge. **2** natural skill.

knowing ● *n.* the state of being aware or informed of any thing. ● *adj.* **1** usu. *derog.* cunning; sly. **2** showing knowledge or awareness; shrewd. □ **there is no knowing** no one can tell. □ **knowingness** *n.*

knowingly *adv.* **1** consciously; intentionally (*had never knowingly injured him*). **2** in a knowing manner (*smiled knowingly*).

know-it-all *n. esp. N. Amer.* = KNOW-ALL.

knowledge *n.* **1 a** (usu. foll. by *of*) awareness or familiarity gained by experience (of a person, fact, or thing) (*have no knowledge of that*). **b** a person's

range of information (*is not within his knowledge*). **2 a** (usu. foll. by *of*) a theoretical or practical understanding of a subject, language, etc. (*has a good knowledge of Greek*). **b** the sum of what is known (*every branch of knowledge*). **3** *Philos.* true, justified belief; certain understanding, as opposed to opinion. **4** = CARNAL KNOWLEDGE. □ **come to one's knowledge** become known to one. **to my knowledge 1** so far as I know. **2** as I know for certain. [Middle English]

knowledgeable *adj.* (also **knowledgable**) well informed; intelligent. □ **knowledgeably** *adv.*

known *past part.* of KNOW.

know-nothing *n.* an ignorant person.

knuckle ● *n.* **1** the bone at a finger joint, esp. that adjoining the hand. **2 a** a projection of the carpal or tarsal joint of a quadruped. **b** a joint of meat consisting of this with the adjoining parts, esp. of bacon or pork. ● *v.tr.* strike, press, or rub with the knuckles. □ **knuckle down** (often foll. by *to*) **1** apply oneself seriously (to a task etc.). **2** (also **knuckle under**) give in; submit. **rap on** (or **over**) **the knuckles** see RAP[1]. [from Middle Dutch *knökel* 'little bone']

knuckle-bone *n.* **1** bone forming a knuckle. **2** the bone of a sheep or other animal corresponding to or resembling a knuckle. **3** a knuckle of meat. **4** (in *pl.*) **a** animal knuckle-bones used in the game of jacks. **b** the game of jacks.

knuckleduster *n.* a metal guard worn over the knuckles in fighting, esp. to increase the effect of blows.

knucklehead *n. colloq.* a stupid or dull-witted person.

knurl *n.* a small projecting knob, ridge, etc. □ **knurled** *adj.*

KO *abbr.* **1** knockout. **2** kick-off.

koala /koh-**ah**-lă/ *n.* an Australian bearlike marsupial, *Phascolarctos cinereus*, having thick grey fur and feeding on eucalyptus leaves. ▷ MARSUPIAL. [from Aboriginal *gula*]

■ **Usage** The embellished form, *koala bear*, is now considered incorrect.

kob *n.* (*pl.* same) (in full **kob antelope**) a grazing antelope, *Kobus kob*, native to African savannah. [from a native name]

Kodiak *n.* (in full **Kodiak bear**) a very large Alaskan race of the brown bear. [from *Kodiak Island, Alaska*]

kohl *n.* a black powder used as eye make-up esp. in Eastern countries. [from Arabic *kuḥl*]

kohlrabi /kohl-**rah**-bi/ *n.* (*pl.* **kohlrabies**) ▼ a variety of cabbage with an edible turnip-like swollen stem. [from medieval Latin *caulorapa*]

KOHLRABI STEMS
(*Brassica oleracea gongylodes*)

koi *n.* (also **koi carp**) (*pl.* same) a carp of a large ornamental variety bred in Japan. [Japanese]

kola var. of COLA.

Komodo dragon *n.* (also **Komodo monitor**) ▶ a large monitor lizard, *Varanus komodoensis*, native to the E. Indies. [from *Komodo Island in Indonesia*]

kook /kook/ *US slang* ● *n.* a crazy or eccentric person. ● *adj.* crazy; eccentric. [20th-century coinage]

kookaburra *n.* ▶ any Australian kingfisher of the genus *Dacelo*, esp. *D. novaeguineae*, which makes a strange laughing cry. [from Aboriginal *guguburra*]

kooky *adj.* (**kookier, kookiest**) *slang* crazy, eccentric, strange.

kopek (also **kopeck**) var. of COPECK.

kopi /koh-pi/ *n. Austral.* powdered gypsum. [from Aboriginal dialect *gabi*]

koppie *n.* (also **kopje**) *S.Afr.* a small hill. [Afrikaans, literally 'little head']

Koran *n.* (also **Quran, Qur'an**) ▼ the Islamic sacred book, believed to be the word of God as dictated to Muhammad and written down in Arabic. [from Arabic *ḳur'ān* 'recitation'] □ **Koranic** *adj.*

KOOKABURRA: LAUGHING KOOKABURRA (*Dacelo novaeguineae*)

KORAN: 15TH-CENTURY TURKISH KORAN

Korean ● *n.* **1** a native or national of N. or S. Korea in SE Asia. **2** the language of Korea. ● *adj.* of or relating to Korea or its people or language.

korma *n.* a mildly-spiced Indian curry dish of meat or fish marinaded in yogurt or curds. [from Turkish *kavurma*]

kosher /koh-sher/ ● *adj.* **1** (of food or premises in which food is sold, cooked, or eaten) fulfilling the requirements of Jewish law. **2** *colloq.* correct; genuine; legitimate. ● *n.* **1** kosher food. **2** a kosher shop. [from Hebrew *kāšēr* 'proper']

kotow var. of KOWTOW.

koumiss *n.* (also **kumiss, kumis**) a fermented liquor prepared from esp. mare's milk, used by Asian nomads and medicinally. [from Tartar *kumiz*]

kowhai /koh-wy/ *n.* any of several trees or shrubs of the genus *Sophora*, esp. *S. tetraptera* native to New Zealand and Chile with pendant clusters of yellow flowers. [Maori]

kowtow (also **kotow**) ● *n. hist.* the Chinese custom of kneeling and touching the ground with the forehead in worship or submission. ● *v.intr.* **1** (usu. foll. by *to*) act obsequiously. **2** *hist.* perform the kowtow.

KOMODO DRAGON
(*Varanus komodoensis*)

K

KRAAL

A typical kraal is composed of a meeting area, animal pens, and enclosures for the householder and each of his wives. Linked by passageways, each enclosure contains a sleeping hut, kitchen, granary, and storehouse. The kraal site is inhabited for some ten years.

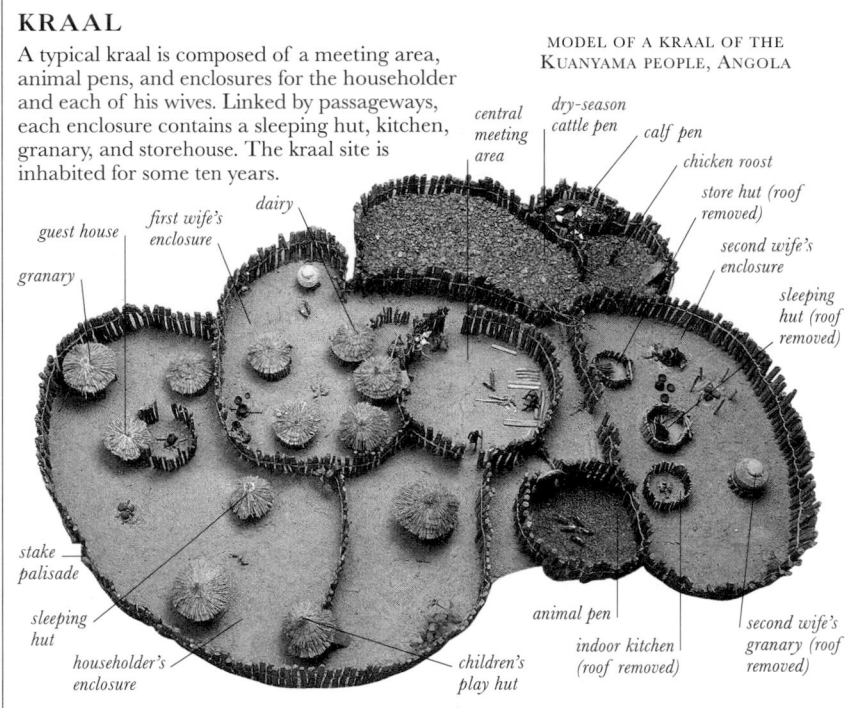

MODEL OF A KRAAL OF THE KUANYAMA PEOPLE, ANGOLA

guest house
granary
first wife's enclosure
dairy
central meeting area
dry-season cattle pen
calf pen
chicken roost
store hut (roof removed)
second wife's enclosure
sleeping hut (roof removed)
stake palisade
sleeping hut
householder's enclosure
children's play hut
animal pen
indoor kitchen (roof removed)
second wife's granary (roof removed)

KP *n. US Mil. colloq.* **1** enlisted men detailed to help the cooks. **2** kitchen duty. [abbreviation of *kitchen police*]

k.p.h. *abbr.* kilometres per hour.

Kr *symb. Chem.* the element krypton.

kraal *n. S.Afr.* **1** ▲ a village of huts enclosed by a fence. **2** an enclosure for cattle or sheep. [Afrikaans]

kraft *n* (in full **kraft paper**) a kind of strong smooth brown wrapping paper. [from Swedish, literally 'strength']

kraken /krah-kĕn/ *n.* a large mythical sea monster said to appear off the coast of Norway. [Norwegian]

Kraut *n. slang offens.* a German. [shortening of SAUERKRAUT]

kremlin *n.* **1** a citadel within a Russian town. **2** (**the Kremlin**) **a** the citadel in Moscow. **b** the Russian or (formerly) USSR Government housed within it. [from Russian *Kreml'*, of Tartar origin]

krill *n.* ▶ tiny planktonic crustaceans found in the seas around the Antarctic and eaten by fish and some seals and whales. [from Norwegian *kril* 'tiny fish']

KRILL:
ANTARCTIC KRILL
(*Euphausia superba*)

krona /kroh-nă/ *n.* **1** (*pl.* **kronor** *pronunc.* same) the chief monetary unit of Sweden. **2** (*pl.* **kronur** *pronunc.* same) the chief monetary unit of Iceland. [Swedish & Icelandic, literally 'crown']

krone /kroh-nĕ/ *n.* (*pl.* **kroner** *pronunc.* same) the chief monetary unit of Denmark and Norway. [Danish & Norwegian, literally 'crown']

krugerrand *n.* a S. African gold coin. [named after S. J. P. *Kruger*, S. African statesman, 1825–1904]

krummhorn *n.* (also **crumhorn**) a medieval wind instrument with a double reed and a curved end. [German, literally 'crooked horn']

krypton *n. Chem.* an inert gaseous element of the noble gas group used in fluorescent lamps etc. [from Greek *krupton* 'hidden thing']

KT *abbr.* **1** Knight Templar. **2** (in the UK) Knight of the Order of the Thistle.

Kt. *abbr.* Knight.

kt. *abbr.* knot (see KNOT[1] *n.* 2a).

Ku *symb. Chem.* the element kurchatovium.

kudos /kew-doss/ *n.* **1** glory; renown. **2** (often treated as *pl.*) *US disp.* praise, acclaim. [Greek]

■ **Usage** *Kudos* is not a plural noun and there is no singular *kudo*. Use in sense 2 should therefore be avoided.

kudu /koo-doo/ *n.* (*pl.* **-s** or same) either of two African antelopes, *Tragelaphus strepsiceros* or *T. imberbis*, with white stripes and corkscrew-shaped ridged horns. [from Xhosa *i-qudu*]

Kufic (also **Cufic**) ● *n.* an early angular form of the Arabic alphabet found chiefly in decorative inscriptions. ● *adj.* of or in this type of script. [attributed to the scholars of *Kufa*, a city S. of Baghdad in Iraq]

Ku Klux Klan *n.* a secret society of white people in the US, originally founded in the southern states after the Civil War to oppose social change and black emancipation by violence and terrorism.

kukri /kuuk-ri/ *n.* (*pl.* **kukris**) ▼ a curved knife broadening towards the point, used by Gurkhas. [from Hindi *kukrī*]

KUKRI: TRADITIONAL GURKHA KNIFE

kumara /koo-mă-ră/ *n. NZ* a sweet potato. [Maori]

kumis (also **kumiss**) var. of KOUMISS.

kümmel /kuum-ĕl/ *n.* a sweet liqueur flavoured with caraway and cumin seeds. [German]

kumquat /kum-kwot/ *n.* (also **cumquat**) **1** ▶ an orange-like fruit with a sweet rind and acid pulp, used in preserves. **2** any shrub or small tree of the genus *Fortunella* yielding this. [based on Chinese *kin kü* 'golden orange']

kung fu *n.* a Chinese martial art resembling karate. [from Chinese *gongfu*]

kurchatovium *n. Chem.* the artificial radioactive element of atomic number 104. [named after I. V. *Kurchatov*, Russian physicist, 1903–60]

KUMQUAT
(*Fortunella japonica*)

K

Kurd *n.* a member of a mainly pastoral Aryan Islamic people living in Kurdistan (contiguous areas of Iraq, Iran, and Turkey). [Kurdish]

Kurdish ● *adj.* of or relating to the Kurds or their language. ● *n.* the Iranian language of the Kurds.

kurta *n.* (also **kurtha**) a loose shirt or tunic worn by esp. Hindu men and women. [Hindi]

kV *abbr.* kilovolt(s).

kW *abbr.* kilowatt(s).

kWh *abbr.* kilowatt-hour(s).

KWIC *n.* esp. *Computing* keyword in context.

kyle *n.* (in Scotland) a narrow channel between islands or between an island and the mainland. [from Gaelic *caol* 'strait']

kylie *n. W. Austral.* a boomerang. [from Aboriginal *garli*]

Kyrgyz /keer-g'eez/ (also **Kirghiz**) ● *n.* (*pl.* same) **1** a member of a Mongol people living in central Asia between the Volga and the Irtysh rivers, chiefly in Kyrgyzstan. **2** the Turkic language of this people. ● *adj.* of or relating to this people or their language. [Kyrgyz]

L

L¹ *n.* (also **l**) (*pl.* **Ls** or **L's**) **1** the twelfth letter of the alphabet. **2** (as a Roman numeral) 50. **3** a thing shaped like an L.

L² *abbr.* (also **L.**) **1** Lake. **2** *Brit.* learner driver (cf. L-PLATE). **3** Liberal. **4** lire. **5** left.

l¹ *abbr.* (also **l.**) **1** left. **2** line. **3** liquid. **4** length.

l² *symb.* litre(s).

£ *abbr.* (preceding a numeral) pound or pounds (of money). [Latin *libra*]

La *symb. Chem.* the element lanthanum.

la var. of LAH.

laager *n.* **1** esp. *S.Afr.* a camp or encampment, esp. formed by a circle of wagons. **2** *Mil.* a park for armoured vehicles. [Afrikaans]

Lab. *abbr.* **1** Labour. **2** Labrador.

lab *n. colloq.* a laboratory.

label ● *n.* **1** a usu. small piece of paper, fabric, etc., for attaching to an object and giving information about it etc. **2** esp. *derog.* a short classifying phrase or name applied to a person etc. **3 a** the logo, title, or trade mark of a company. **b** a record-producing company or part of one. **4** an adhesive stamp on a parcel etc. **5** a word used in a dictionary entry to specify its register, nationality, etc. **6** *Biol.* & *Chem.* a radioactive isotope, fluorescent dye, etc., used to label another substance. ● *v.tr.* (**labelled, labelling**; *US* **labeled, labeling**) **1** attach a label to. **2** (usu. foll. by *as*) assign to a category (*labelled them as irresponsible*). **3** *Biol.* & *Chem.* make identifiable by replacing an atom with one of a distinctive radioactive isotope, or by attaching a fluorescent dye to the molecule. [originally in sense 'a strip, band', from Old French] □ **labeller** *n.*

labia *pl.* of LABIUM.

labial ● *adj.* **1 a** of the lips. **b** *Zool.* of, like, or serving as a lip, a liplike part, or a labium. **2** *Phonet.* **a** (of a consonant) requiring partial or complete closure of the lips (e.g. *p*, *b*, *f*, *v*, *m*, *w*). **b** (of a vowel) requiring rounded lips (e.g. *oo* in moon). ● *n. Phonet.* a labial sound. □ **labialize** *v.tr.* (also **-ise**). **labially** *adv.*

labiate ● *n.* any plant of the family Labiatae, including mint and rosemary. ● *adj.* **1** *Bot.* of or relating to the Labiatae. **2** *Bot.* & *Zool.* like a lip or labium.

labile *adj.* liable to undergo change; unstable. □ **lability** *n.*

labium *n.* (*pl.* **labia**) (usu. in *pl.*) *Anat.* each fold of skin of the two pairs that enclose the vulva. ▷ REPRODUCTIVE ORGANS. [Latin, literally 'lip']

labor etc. *US* & *Austral.* var. of LABOUR etc.

laboratory *n.* (*pl.* **-ies**) a room or building fitted out for scientific experiments, research, chemical manufacture, etc. [from medieval Latin *laboratorium*]

laborious *adj.* **1** needing hard work or toil (*a laborious task*). **2** (esp. of literary style) pedestrian; not fluent. [from Latin *laboriosus*] □ **laboriously** *adv.* **laboriousness** *n.*

labour (*US, Austral.* **labor**) ● *n.* **1** physical or mental work; exertion. **2 a** workers, esp. manual, considered as a social class or political force. **b** (**Labour**) the Labour Party. **3** the process of childbirth. **4** a particular task, esp. of a difficult nature. ● *v.* **1** *intr.* work hard; exert oneself. **2** *intr.* (usu. foll. by *for*, or *to* + infin.) strive for a purpose. **3** *tr.* **a** elaborate needlessly (*I will not labour the point*). **b** (as **laboured** *adj.*) not spontaneous or fluent. **4** *intr.*

(often foll. by *under*) suffer under (a disadvantage or delusion) (*laboured under universal disapproval*). **5** *intr.* proceed with trouble or difficulty (*laboured slowly up the hill*). □ **labour in vain** make a fruitless effort. **labour of love** a task done for pleasure, not reward. [from Latin *labor*]

labour camp *n.* a prison camp enforcing a regime of hard labour.

labourer *n.* (*US* **laborer**) **1** a person doing unskilled, usu. manual, work for wages. **2** a person who labours.

Labour Exchange *n. Brit. colloq.* or *hist.* an employment exchange.

labour force *n.* the body of workers employed, esp. at a single plant.

labour-intensive *adj.* (of a form of work) needing a large work force or a large amount of work in relation to output.

labourism *n.* (*US* **laborism**) the principles of a Labour Party or the Labour movement.

labour market *n.* the supply of labour with reference to the demand on it.

Labour Party *n.* **1** a British political party formed to represent the interests of ordinary working people. **2** any similar political party in other countries.

labour-saving *adj.* (of an appliance etc.) designed to reduce or eliminate work.

Labrador *n.* (in full **Labrador dog** or **retriever**) a retriever of a breed with a black or golden coat. [from *Labrador*, a large peninsula in NE Canada]

laburnum *n.* ▼ any small tree of the genus *Laburnum* with racemes of golden flowers yielding poisonous seeds. [Latin]

labyrinth *n.* **1** a complicated irregular network of passages etc.; a maze. **2** an intricate or tangled arrangement. [from Greek *laburinthos*, originally referring to the mythological maze which housed the Minotaur, a creature half-man half-bull] □ **labyrinthian** *adj.* **labyrinthine** *adj.*

LAC *abbr.* Leading Aircraftman.

lac¹ /lak/ *n.* a resinous substance secreted as a protective covering by the lac insect, and used to make varnish and shellac. [from Sanskrit *lākṣā*]

lac² var. of LAKH.

LABURNUM:
COMMON LABURNUM
(*Laburnum anagyroides*)

lace ● *n.* **1** ▼ a fine open fabric, esp. of cotton or silk, made by weaving thread in patterns and used esp. for trimming garments. **2** a cord or leather strip passed through eyelets or hooks on opposite sides of a shoe, garment, etc., pulled tight and fastened. ● *v.tr.* **1** (usu. foll. by *up*) **a** fasten or tighten with lace or laces. **b** compress the waist of (a person) with a laced corset. **2** (usu. foll. by *with*) **a** add an ingredient to (a drink, dish, etc.) to enhance or adulterate flavour, strength, effect, etc. (*laced with rum*). **b** intermingle (*ribaldry laced with philosophy*). **3** (usu. foll. by *with*) **a** streak (a sky etc.) with colour (*cheek laced with blood*). **b** interlace or embroider (fabric) with thread etc. **4** (often foll. by *through*) pass (a shoelace etc.) through. **5** trim with lace. [from Latin *laqueus* 'noose']

lace-pillow *n.* a cushion

placed on the lap and providing support in lace-making.

lacerate *v.tr.* **1** mangle or tear (esp. flesh or tissue). **2** cause pain to (the feelings etc.). [based on Latin *laceratus* 'torn up'] □ **lacerable** *adj.* **laceration** *n.*

lace-up *Brit.* ● *n.* a shoe fastened with a lace. ● *attrib.adj.* (of a shoe etc.) fastened by a lace or laces.

lacewing *n.* ▼ a neuropterous insect. ▷ INSECT

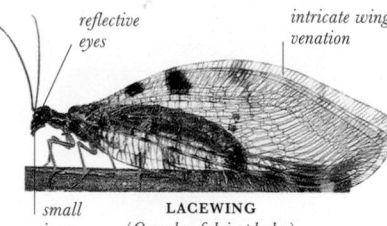

reflective eyes
intricate wing venation
small jaws
LACEWING
(*Osmylus fulvicephalus*)

lachrymal *adj.* (also **lacrimal, lacrymal**) **1** *formal* of or for tears. **2** (usu. as **lacrimal**) *Anat.* concerned in the secretion of tears (*lacrimal canal*). ▷ SKULL, TEAR DUCT. [based on Latin *lacrima* 'tear']

lachrymatory *adj. formal* of or causing tears.

lachrymose *adj. formal* **1** given to weeping; tearful. **2** melancholy; inducing tears. □ **lachrymosely** *adv.*

lacing *n.* **1** lace trimming, esp. on a uniform. **2** a laced fastening on a shoe or garment. **3** a dash of spirits in a beverage.

lac insect *n.* an Asian scale insect, *Laccifer lacca*, living in trees.

lack ● *n.* (usu. foll. by *of*) an absence, want, or deficiency. ● *v.tr.* be without or deficient in (*lacks courage*). □ **for lack of** owing to the absence of. **lack for** lack. [Middle English]

lackadaisical *adj.* **1** listless; idle. **2** feebly sentimental and affected. [based on archaic interjection *lackaday, -daisy*] □ **lackadaisically** *adv.*

lacker var. of LACQUER.

lackey *n.* (also **lacquey**) (*pl.* **-eys**) **1** *derog.* **a** a servile political follower. **b** an obsequious parasitical person. **2 a** (usu. liveried) footman or manservant. **b** a servant. [from Catalan *alacay* 'magistrate']

lacking *adj.* **1** absent or deficient. **2** *colloq.* deficient in intellect; mentally subnormal.

lacklustre *adj.* (*US* **lackluster**) **1** lacking in vitality, force, or conviction. **2** (of the eye) dull.

laconic *adj.* **1** (of a style of speech or writing) brief; concise; terse. **2** (of a person) laconic in speech etc. [based on Greek *Lakōn* 'Spartan', the Spartans being known for their terse speech] □ **laconically** *adv.* **laconicism** *n.* **laconism** *n.*

lacquer (also **lacker**) ● *n.* **1** a sometimes coloured liquid made of shellac dissolved in alcohol, or of synthetic substances, that dries to form a hard protective coating. **2** *Brit.* a chemical substance sprayed on hair to keep it in place. **3** the sap of the lacquer tree used to varnish wood etc. **4** *Art* decorative ware made of wood coated with lacquer. ● *v.tr.* coat with lacquer. [from obsolete French *lacre* 'sealing wax'] □ **lacquerer** *n.*

lacquer tree *n.* an E. Asian tree, *Rhus verniciflua*, the sap of which is used as a varnish for wood.

lacquerware *n.* decorative lacquered articles.

lacquey var. of LACKEY.

lacrimal var. of LACHRYMAL.

LACE: DETAIL OF 19TH-CENTURY ENGLISH LACE

lacrosse *n.* ▶ a game like hockey, but with a ball driven by, caught, and carried in a crosse. [French]

lacrymal var. of LACHRYMAL.

lactate[1] *v.intr.* (of mammals) secrete milk. [based on Latin *lactatus* 'suckled'] □ **lactation** *n.*

lactate[2] *n.* *Chem.* any salt or ester of lactic acid.

lacteal ● *adj.* **1** of milk. **2** *Anat.* (of a vessel) conveying milky fluid. ● *n.* (in *pl.*) *Anat.* the lymphatic vessels of the small intestine which absorb digested fats. [from Latin *lacteus*]

lactescent *adj.* **1** milky. **2** yielding a milky juice.

lactic *adj.* *Chem.* of, relating to, or obtained from milk. [based on Latin *lac lactis* 'milk']

lactic acid *n.* a carboxylic acid formed in sour milk, and produced in the muscle tissues during strenuous exercise.

lacto- *comb. form* milk. [from Latin *lac lactis* 'milk']

lactobacillus /lak-toh-bă-**sil**-ŭs/ *n.* (*pl.* **-bacilli**) *Biol.* any rod-shaped bacterium of the family Lactobacillaceae, producing lactic acid.

lactose *n.* *Chem.* a disaccharide sugar occurring in milk.

lacuna /lă-**koo**-nă/ *n.* (*pl.* **lacunae** /-nee/ or **lacunas**) **1** a hiatus, blank, or gap. **2** a missing portion or empty page, esp. in an ancient manuscript etc. [Latin, literally 'pool'] □ **lacunal** *adj.* **lacunar** *adj.* **lacunary** *adj.* **lacunose** *adj.*

LACW *abbr.* Leading Aircraftwoman.

lacy *adj.* (**lacier**, **laciest**) of or resembling lace fabric. □ **lacily** *adv.* **laciness** *n.*

lad *n.* **1 a** a boy or youth. **b** a young son. **2** (esp. in *pl.*) esp. *Brit. colloq.* a man; a fellow (*he's one of the lads*). **3** *Brit. colloq.* a high-spirited fellow; a rogue (*he's a bit of a lad*). **4** *Brit.* a stable worker (regardless of age or sex). [Middle English] □ **laddish** *adj.* **laddishness** *n.*

ladder ● *n.* **1** a set of horizontal bars of wood or metal fixed between two uprights and used for climbing up or down. **2** *Brit.* a vertical strip of unravelled fabric in a stocking etc. resembling a ladder. **3** a hierarchical structure. ● *v.* *Brit.* **1** *intr.* (of a stocking etc.) develop a ladder. **2** *tr.* cause a ladder in (a stocking etc.). [Old English]

ladder-back *n.* (in full **ladder-back chair**) an upright chair with a back resembling a ladder.

ladder stitch *n.* transverse bars in embroidery.

ladder tournament *n. Brit.* a sporting contest with each participant listed and entitled to a higher place by defeating the one above.

lade *v.* (*past part.* **laden**) **1** *tr.* **a** put cargo on board (a ship). **b** ship (goods) as cargo. **2** *intr.* (of a ship) take on cargo. **3** *tr.* (as **laden** *adj.*) (usu. foll. by *with*) **a** heavily loaded. **b** painfully burdened with sorrow etc. [Old English] □ **lading** *n.*

la-di-da *adj. colloq.* pretentious or snobbish, esp. in manner or speech.

ladies *pl.* of LADY.

ladies' fingers *n.pl. Brit.* = OKRA.

ladies' man *n.* (also **lady's man**) a man fond of female company; a seducer.

ladies' room *n.* a women's lavatory in a hotel etc.

ladle ● *n.* **1** a large long-handled spoon with a cup-shaped bowl used for serving esp. soups and gravy. ▷ UTENSIL. **2** a vessel for transporting molten metal in a foundry. ● *v.tr.* (often foll. by *out*) transfer (liquid) with a ladle. □ **ladleful** *n.* (*pl.* **-fuls**). [Old English]

lady *n.* (*pl.* **-ies**) **1 a** a woman regarded as being of superior social status or as having the refined manners associated with this. **b** (**Lady**) a title used by peeresses, wives and widows of knights, etc. **2** (often *attrib.*) a female person or animal (*lady butcher*; *lady dog*). **3** *colloq.* **a** a wife. **b** a man's girlfriend. **4** a ruling woman (*lady of the house*). □ **the Ladies** (or **Ladies'**) *Brit.* a women's public lavatory. [Old English, from *hlāf* 'loaf' + a Germanic base meaning 'to knead'] □ **ladyhood** *n.*

LACROSSE

Lacrosse is played as a 12-a-side game for women and a 10-a-side game for men. Each team aims to score goals by propelling the ball into their opponents' goal net. The women's pitch has no absolute boundaries, but the men's pitch has clearly defined sidelines and endlines. The ball is kept in play by being carried, thrown, or batted with the crosse, or rolled or kicked, in any direction. In both games, play can continue beyond the goal areas.

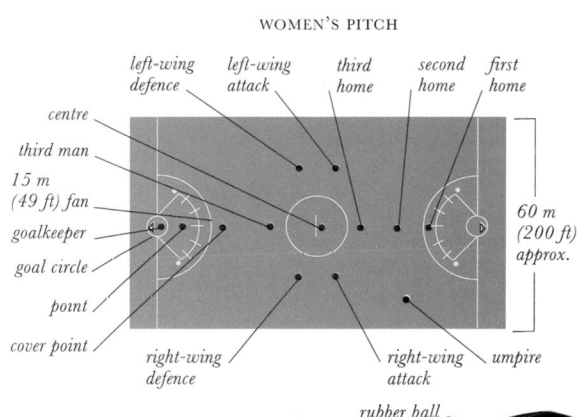

WOMEN'S PITCH

left-wing defence / left-wing attack / third home / second home / first home / centre / third man / 15 m (49 ft) fan / goalkeeper / goal circle / point / cover point / right-wing defence / right-wing attack / umpire / 60 m (200 ft) approx.

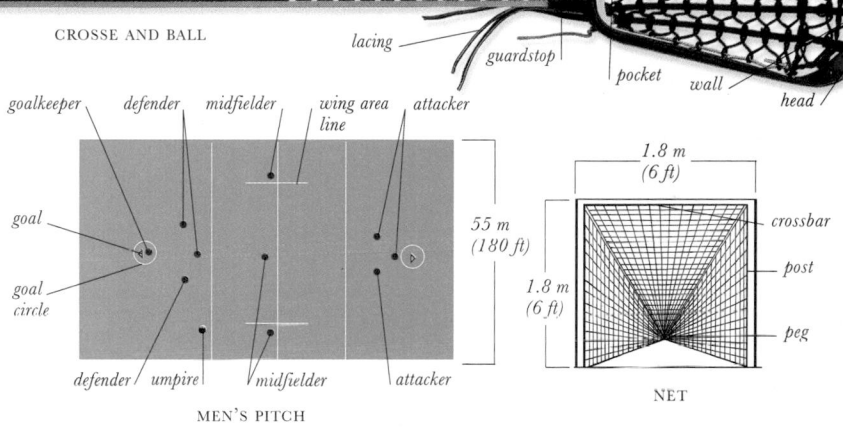

CROSSE AND BALL

handle / throat / net / rubber ball / lacing / guardstop / pocket / wall / head

goalkeeper / defender / midfielder / wing area line / attacker / goal / goal circle / defender / umpire / midfielder / attacker

MEN'S PITCH

55 m (180 ft)

NET

1.8 m (6 ft) / crossbar / post / peg / 1.8 m (6 ft)

L

---

ladybird *n.* ▼ a coleopterous insect of the family Coccinellidae, with wing-cases usu. of a reddish-brown colour with black spots. ▷ EGG

hardened forewing (elytron)

flexible hind wing

LADYBIRD
(*Anatis ocellata*)

ladybug *n. dial.* & *N. Amer.* = LADYBIRD.

Lady chapel *n.* a chapel in a church or cathedral dedicated to the Virgin Mary. ▷ CATHEDRAL

Lady Day *n.* esp. *Brit.* the feast of the Annunciation, 25 Mar.

lady-in-waiting *n.* (*pl.* **ladies-in-waiting**) a lady attending a queen or princess.

ladykiller *n.* a practised and habitual seducer.

ladylike *adj.* **1** with the modesty, manners, etc., of a lady. **2** (of a man) effeminate.

lady-love *n.* a man's sweetheart.

Lady Mayoress *n.* the wife of a Lord Mayor.

lady of the house *n.* the female head of a household.

lady's bedstraw see BEDSTRAW 2.

ladyship *n.* *archaic* the state of being a lady. □ **her** (or **your**) **Ladyship** (or **ladyship**) (*pl.* **their** (or **your**) **Ladyships**) a respectful form of reference or address to a Lady.

lady's maid *n.* a lady's personal maidservant.

lady's man var. of LADIES' MAN.

lady's mantle *n.* any plant of the genus *Alchemilla* (rose family), with yellowish-green clustered flowers.

lady's slipper *n.* ▶ any orchid of the genus *Cypripedium*, with a usu. yellow slipper-shaped lip on its flowers.

laevulose /**leev**-yoo-lohz/ *n.* (*US* **levu-lose**) = FRUCTOSE.

lag[1] ● *v.intr.* (**lagged**, **lagging**) (often foll. by *behind*) fall behind; not keep pace. ● *n.* a delay. [originally in sense 'hindmost person, to hang back']

lag[2] ● *v.tr.* (**lagged**, **lagging**) enclose or cover in lagging. ● *n.* the non-heat-conducting cover of a boiler etc.

lag[3] *Brit. slang* ● *n.* (esp. as **old lag**) a habitual convict. ● *v.tr.* (**lagged**, **lagging**) **1** send to prison. **2** apprehend; arrest. [19th-century coinage]

lagan *n.* goods or wreckage lying on the bed of the sea, sometimes with a marker buoy etc. for later retrieval. [Old French, perhaps of Scandinavian origin, from root of LIE[1], LAY[2]]

lager *n.* a kind of beer, effervescent and light in colour and body. [from German *Lagerbier* 'beer brewed for keeping']

lager lout *n. Brit. colloq.* a youth who behaves badly as a result of excessive drinking.

laggard ● *n.* a dawdler. ● *adj.* dawdling; slow. □ **laggardly** *adj. & adv.*

lagging *n.* material providing heat insulation for a boiler, pipes, etc.

LADY'S SLIPPER
(*Cypripedium calceolus*)

lip

LAGOMORPH

The order Lagomorpha includes rabbits, hares, and pikas. Lagomorphs have long ears, powerful hind legs for jumping, forelimbs adapted for burrowing, and a small tail. They are closely related to rodents and share many characteristics with them, including chisel-shaped incisors (four in the upper jaw and two in the lower) that grow continually; they also share the habit of eating their faeces to extract more nutrients from their plant diet.

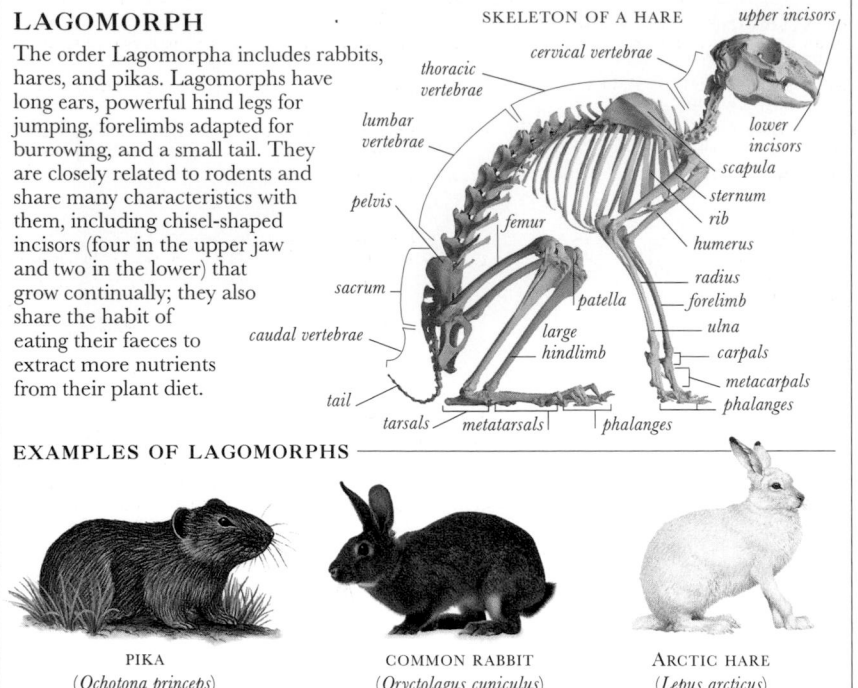

SKELETON OF A HARE

upper incisors, cervical vertebrae, thoracic vertebrae, lumbar vertebrae, pelvis, femur, sacrum, patella, caudal vertebrae, large hindlimb, tail, tarsals, metatarsals, phalanges, lower incisors, scapula, sternum, rib, humerus, radius, forelimb, ulna, carpals, metacarpals, phalanges

EXAMPLES OF LAGOMORPHS

PIKA
(*Ochotona princeps*)

COMMON RABBIT
(*Oryctolagus cuniculus*)

ARCTIC HARE
(*Lepus arcticus*)

L

lagomorph *n. Zool..* ▲ any mammal of the order Lagomorpha, including hares and rabbits.

lagoon *n.* **1** a stretch of salt water separated from the sea by a low sandbank, coral reef, etc. **2** the enclosed water of an atoll. ▷ ATOLL. **3** *US, Austral., & NZ* a small freshwater lake. [from Latin *lacuna*]

lah *n.* (also **la**) *Mus.* **1** (in tonic sol-fa) the sixth note of a major scale. **2** the note A in the fixed-doh system. [from Latin *la(bii)*, word arbitrarily chosen]

laid *past and past part.* of LAY[1].

laid-back *adj. colloq.* relaxed, unbothered, easygoing.

laid paper *n.* paper with the surface marked in fine ribs.

laid up *adj.* confined to bed or the house.

lain *past part.* of LIE[1].

lair *n.* **1 a** a wild animal's resting place. **b** a person's hiding place (*tracked him to his lair*). **2** a place where domestic animals lie down. **3** *Brit.* a shed or enclosure for cattle on the way to market. [Old English]

laird *n. Sc.* a landowner. [Scots form of LORD] □ **lairdship** *n.*

laissez-faire /less-ay-**fair**/ *n.* the theory or practice of governmental abstention from interference in the workings of the market etc. [French, literally 'let act']

laity /**lay**-iti/ *n.* (usu. prec. by *the*; usu. treated as *pl.*) lay people, as distinct from the clergy. [related to LAY[2]]

lake[1] *n.* **1** ▶ a large body of water surrounded by land. **2** (**the Lakes**) = LAKE DISTRICT. [from Latin *lacus* 'basin, pool, lake']

lake[2] *n.* **1** a reddish colouring originally made from lac (*crimson lake*). **2** a complex formed by the action of dye and mordants applied to fabric to fix colour. [variant of LAC[1]]

Lake District *n.* the region of the English lakes in Cumbria.

lake-dwelling *n.* a prehistoric hut built on piles driven into the bed or shore of a lake. □ **lake-dweller** *n.*

lakh *n.* (also **lac**) (usu. foll. by *of*) *Anglo-Ind.* a hundred thousand (rupees etc.). [from Sanskrit *lakṣa*]

Lallan *Sc.* ● *n.* (now usu. **Lallans**) a Lowland Scots dialect, esp. as a literary language. ● *adj.* of or concerning the Lowlands of Scotland. [variant of LOWLAND]

lam *v.* (**lammed, lamming**) *colloq.* **1** *tr.* thrash; hit. **2** *intr.* (foll. by *into*) hit (a person etc.) hard with a stick etc.

lama *n.* a Tibetan or Mongolian Buddhist monk. [from Tibetan *blama* (with silent *b*)]

lamasery *n.* (*pl.* **-ies**) a monastery of lamas. [from French *lamaserie*]

lamb ● *n.* **1** a young sheep. **2** the flesh of a lamb as food. ▷ CUT. **3** a mild or gentle person, esp. a young child. ● *v.* **1 a** *tr.* (in *passive*) (of a lamb) be born. **b** *intr.* (of a ewe) give birth to lambs. **2** *tr.* tend (lambing ewes). □ **the Lamb** (or **Lamb of God**) a name for Christ (see John 1:29). **like a lamb** meekly, obediently. [Old English] □ **lambkin** *n.* **lamblike** *adj.*

lambada /lam-**bah**-dǎ/ *n.* a fast erotic Brazilian dance which couples perform with their stomachs touching. [Portuguese, literally 'a beating']

lambaste *v.tr.* (also **lambast**) *colloq.* **1** thrash; beat. **2** criticize severely.

lambda *n.* **1** the eleventh letter of the Greek alphabet (Λ, λ). **2** (as λ) the symbol for wavelength. [Greek]

lambent *adj.* **1** (of a flame or a light) playing on a surface with a soft radiance. **2** (of the eyes, sky, etc.) softly radiant. **3** (of wit etc.) lightly brilliant. [from Latin *lambent-* 'licking'] □ **lambency** *n.*

lamb's ears *n.* a garden plant, *Stachys byzantina*, with whitish woolly leaves.

lambskin *n.* a prepared skin from a lamb with the wool on or as leather.

lamb's lettuce *n.* a plant, *Valerianella locusta*, used in salad.

lamb's-tails *n.pl. Brit.* catkins from the hazel tree.

lambswool (also **lamb's-wool**) ● *n.* soft fine wool from a young sheep used in knitted garments etc. ● *adj.* made of lambswool.

lame ● *adj.* **1** disabled, esp. in the foot or leg; limping. **2 a** (of an argument, excuse, etc.) unconvincing; unsatisfactory. **b** (of verse etc.) halting. ● *v.tr.* **1** make lame; disable. **2** harm permanently. [Old English] □ **lamely** *adv.* **lameness** *n.*

lamé /**lah**-may/ ● *n.* a fabric with gold or silver threads interwoven. ● *adj.* (of fabric etc.) having such threads. [from Latin *lamina*]

lamebrain *n. N. Amer. colloq.* a stupid person.

lame duck *n.* **1** a disabled or weak person. **2** *Brit.* a defaulter on the Stock Exchange. **3** *Brit.* a firm etc. in financial difficulties. **4** *US* an official (esp. the President) in the final period of office, after the election of a successor.

lamella *n.* (*pl.* **lamellae** /-lee/) **1** a thin layer, membrane, scale, or platelike tissue or part, esp. in bone tissue. **2** *Bot.* a membranous fold in a chloroplast. [Latin, literally 'little scale'] □ **lamellar** *adj.* **lamellate** *adj.*

lamellicorn ● *n.* any beetle of the superfamily Scarabaeoidea (formerly Lamellicornia), having lamelliform antennae, including the stag beetle, cockchafer, dung-beetle, etc. ● *adj.* of or relating to this superfamily. [from modern Latin *lamellicornis*, from Latin *lamella* (see LAMELLA) + *cornu* 'horn']

lament ● *n.* **1** a passionate expression of grief. **2** a song or poem of mourning or sorrow. ● *v.tr.* (also *absol.*) **1** express or feel grief for or about; regret (*lamented the closure of the school*). **2** (as **lamented** *adj.*) a conventional expression referring to a recently dead person (*your late lamented father*). □ **lament for** (or **over**) mourn or regret. [from Latin *lamentum*] □ **lamentation** *n.* **lamenter** *n.* **lamentingly** *adv.*

lamentable /**lam**-in-tǎ-bǔl/ *adj.* deplorable; regrettable. □ **lamentably** *adv.*

LAKE

Natural lakes are formed when the supply of water to a basin (for instance by rain or streams) is greater than the amount of water lost by evaporation and seepage. In some cases, the formation of natural barriers, such as glacial moraines or landslides, provides a dam, allowing water to accumulate. In others, seepage is reduced by the presence of impermeable rocks under the lake bed. Lakes tend to be classified according to the mode of origin of their basin; for example, glacial, alluvial, volcanic, or fault-related.

EXAMPLES OF LAKE TYPES

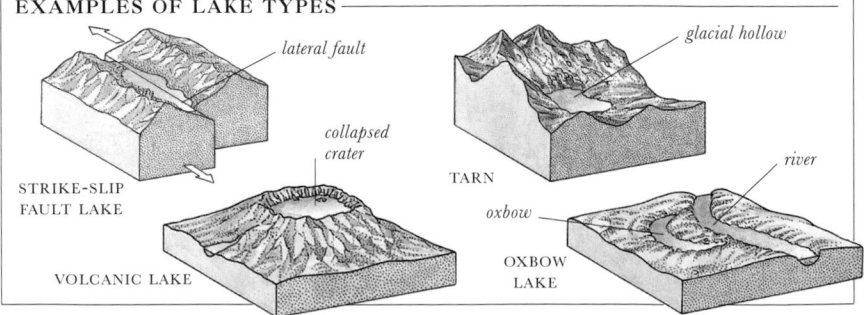

lateral fault, collapsed crater, STRIKE-SLIP FAULT LAKE, VOLCANIC LAKE, glacial hollow, TARN, oxbow, river, OXBOW LAKE

lamina n. (pl. **laminae** /-nee/) a thin plate, scale, or layer, e.g. of sedimentary rock or organic tissue. [Latin] □ **laminar** adj.

laminate ● v. 1 beat or roll (metal) into thin plates. 2 tr. overlay with metal plates, a plastic layer, etc. 3 tr. manufacture by placing layer on layer. 4 tr. & intr. split into layers or leaves. ● n. a laminated structure or material. ● adj. in the form of lamina or laminae. □ **lamination** n. **laminator** n.

laminitis n. inflammation of the laminae of the hoof in horses and other animals.

Lammas n. (in full **Lammas Day**) the first day of August, formerly observed as harvest festival. [Old English, literally 'loaf mass']

lammergeier /lam-er-gy-er/ n. (also **lammergeyer**) ▼ a large vulture, *Gypaetus barbatus*, with a very large wingspan – often of 3 m (40 in) – and dark beardlike feathers on either side of its beak. [from German *Lämmer* 'lambs' + *Geier* 'vulture']

beardlike feathers

LAMMERGEIER
(*Gypaetus barbatus*)

large wingspan

lamp n. 1 a device for producing a steady light, esp.: **a** an electric bulb, and usu. its holder (*bedside lamp*). **b** an oil lamp. **c** a usu. glass holder for a candle. **d** a gas jet and mantle. 2 a device producing esp. ultraviolet or infrared radiation as a treatment for various complaints. [from Late Latin *lampada*] □ **lampless** adj.

lampblack n. a pigment made from soot.

lamplight n. light given by a lamp or lamps. □ **lamplit** adj.

lamplighter n. hist. 1 a person who lights street lamps. 2 US a spill for lighting lamps.

lampoon ● n. a satirical attack on a person etc. ● v.tr. satirize. [from French *lampon*] □ **lampoonist** n.

lamp-post n. a tall post supporting a street light.

lamprey /lam-pri/ n.(pl. **-eys**) ▼ any eel-like fish of the family Petromyzonidae, without scales, paired fins, or jaws, but having a sucker mouth. ▷ FISH. [from medieval Latin *lampreda*]

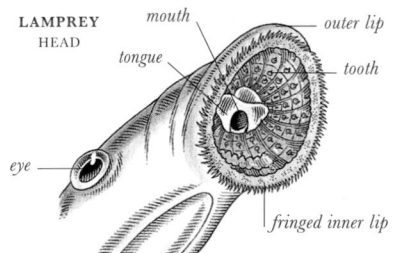

LAMPREY HEAD

mouth
outer lip
tongue
tooth
eye
fringed inner lip

lampshade n. a usu. translucent cover for a lamp used to soften or direct its light.

lamp standard n. = LAMP-POST.

LAN n. Computing local area network.

Lancastrian ● n. 1 a native of Lancashire or Lancaster in NW England. 2 hist. a follower of the House of Lancaster in the Wars of the Roses. ● adj. of or concerning Lancashire or Lancaster, or the House of Lancaster.

lance ● n. 1 **a** hist. a long weapon with a wooden shaft and a pointed steel head, used by a horseman in charging. ▷ JOUST. **b** a similar weapon used for spearing a fish. 2 a metal pipe supplying oxygen to burn metal. 3 = LANCER 1. ● v.tr. 1 Surgery prick or cut open with a lancet. 2 pierce with a lance. [from Latin *lancea*]

lance bombardier n. a rank in the Royal Artillery corresponding to lance corporal in the infantry.

lance corporal n. the lowest rank of NCO in the Army.

lanceolate adj. shaped like a lance-head, tapering to each end. ▷ LEAF. [based on Latin *lanceola* 'little lance']

lancer n. 1 hist. a soldier of a cavalry regiment armed with lances. 2 (in pl.) **a** a quadrille for 8 or 16 pairs. **b** the music for this.

lancet n. a small broad two-edged surgical knife with a sharp point. [from Old French *lancette*]

lancet arch n. (also **lancet light**, **lancet window**) ▶ a narrow arch or window with a pointed head. ▷ ARCH, CATHEDRAL.

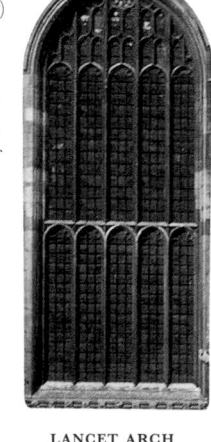

LANCET ARCH

land ● n. 1 the solid part of the Earth's surface, as opposed to the sea or air. 2 **a** an expanse of country; ground; soil. **b** such land in relation to its use etc., or as a basis for agriculture (*works on the land*). 3 a country, nation, or state (*land of hope and glory*). 4 **a** a landed property. **b** (in pl.) estates. ● v. 1 **a** tr. & intr. set or go ashore. **b** intr. (often foll. by at) disembark. 2 tr. bring (an aircraft etc.) to the ground or the surface of water. 3 intr. (of an aircraft, parachutist, etc.) alight on the ground or water. 4 tr. bring (a fish) to land, esp. with a hook or net. 5 tr. & intr. (also refl.) often foll. by up) colloq. bring to, reach, or find oneself in a certain situation, place, or state. 6 tr. colloq. **a** deal (a person etc. a blow etc.) (*landed him one in the eye*). **b** (full. by *with*) Brit. present (a person) with (a problem etc.). 7 tr. set down (a person, cargo, etc.) from a vehicle, ship, etc. 8 tr. colloq. win or obtain (a prize, job, etc.). □ **how the land lies** what the state of affairs is. **in the land of the living** joc. still alive. **land of Nod** sleep (with pun on the phr. in Gen. 4:16). **land on one's feet** attain a good position, job, etc., by luck. [Old English] □ **landless** adj. **landward** adj. & adv. **landwards** adv.

land agent n. Brit. 1 the steward of an estate. 2 an agent for the sale of estates.

landau /lan-daw/ n. ▼ a four-wheeled enclosed carriage with a removable front cover and a back cover that can be raised and lowered. [from *Landau*, near Karlsruhe in Germany]

land bridge n. a neck of land joining two large land masses.

landed adj. 1 owning land (*landed gentry*). 2 consisting of, including, or relating to land (*landed property*).

landfall n. the approach to land, esp. for the first time on a sea or air journey.

landfill n. 1 waste material etc. used to landscape or reclaim areas of ground. 2 the process of disposing of rubbish in this way.

land force n. (also **land forces**) armies, not naval or air forces.

landform n. a natural feature of the Earth's surface.

land girl n. Brit. a woman doing farm work, esp. in wartime.

landholder n. the proprietor or, esp., the tenant of land.

landing n. 1 **a** the act or process of coming to land. **b** an instance of this. **c** (also **landing place**) a place where ships etc. land. 2 **a** a platform between two flights of stairs. **b** a passage leading to upstairs rooms.

landing craft n. any of several types of craft esp. designed for putting troops and equipment ashore.

landing gear n. the undercarriage of an aircraft. ▷ AIRCRAFT

landing pad n. a small area designed for helicopters to land and take off from.

landing stage n. a platform, often floating, on which goods and passengers are disembarked.

landing strip n. an airstrip.

landlady n. (pl. **-ies**) 1 a woman who lets land, a building, etc., to a tenant. 2 a woman who keeps a boarding house, lodgings, or Brit. a public house.

landline n. a means of telecommunication over land.

landlocked adj. almost or entirely enclosed by land.

landlord n. 1 a man who lets land, a building, etc., to a tenant. 2 a man who keeps a boarding house, lodgings, or Brit. a public house.

landlubber n. a person unfamiliar with the sea or sailing.

landmark n. 1 **a** a conspicuous object in a district etc. **b** an object marking the boundary of an estate, country, etc. 2 an event, change, etc. marking a stage or turning point in history etc.

land mass n. a large area of land.

landmine n. 1 an explosive mine laid in or on the ground. 2 a parachute mine.

land-office business n. US colloq. enormous trade.

landowner n. an owner of land. □ **landownership** n. **landowning** adj. & n.

landrail n. = CORNCRAKE.

landscape ● n. 1 natural or imaginary scenery, as seen in a broad view. 2 (often attrib.) a picture representing this; the genre of landscape painting. 3 (in graphic design etc.) a format in which the width of an illustration etc. is greater than the height. ● v.tr. (also absol.) improve (a piece of land) by landscape gardening. [from Middle Dutch *landscap*] □ **landscapist** n.

landscape gardening n. the art or practice of laying out ornamental grounds or grounds imitating natural scenery. □ **landscape gardener** n.

landscape painter n. an artist who paints landscapes.

landslide n. 1 the sliding down of a mass of land from a mountain, cliff, etc. 2 an overwhelming majority for one side in an election.

L

LANDAU:
STEAM-DRIVEN LANDAU CARRIAGE, 1854

chimney *back cover* *landau body* *front cover* *driver's seat* *steering tiller* *brake lever*
coke hopper *water tank* *chauffeur's seat* *step* *iron rim* *wooden spoke* *steam chest* *twin-cylinder steam engine* *steam pipe* *wheel hub* *towing hook*

L

landslip *n. Brit.* = LANDSLIDE 1.

landsman *n.* (*pl.* **-men**) a non-sailor.

land tax *n. hist.* a tax assessed on landed property.

land yacht *n.* a vehicle with wheels and sails for recreational use on a beach etc.

lane *n.* **1** a narrow, often rural, road, street, or path. **2** a division of a road for a stream of traffic. **3** a strip of track or water for a runner, rower, or swimmer in a race. **4** a path or course prescribed for or regularly followed by a ship, aircraft, etc. **5** a gangway. [Old English]

langlauf /lang-lowf/ *n.* cross-country skiing; a cross-country skiing race. [German, literally 'long run']

langouste /long-**goost**/ *n.* a crayfish or spiny lobster. [French]

langoustine /long-**gooss**-teen/ *n.* = NORWAY LOBSTER. [French]

language *n.* **1** the method of human communication, either spoken or written, consisting of the use of words in an agreed way. **2** the language of a particular community or country etc. **3 a** the faculty of speech. **b** a style of expression; the use of words, etc. (*his language was poetic*). **c** (also **bad language**) coarse, crude, or abusive speech. **4** a system of symbols and rules for writing computer programs or algorithms. **5** any method of expression or communication (*the language of mime*). **6** a professional or specialized vocabulary. **7** literary style. [based on Latin *lingua* 'tongue']

language laboratory *n.* a room equipped with tape recorders etc. for learning a foreign language.

languid *adj.* lacking vigour; idle; inert. [from Latin *languidus*] □ **languidly** *adv.* **languidness** *n.*

languish *v.intr.* **1** be or grow feeble; lose or lack vitality. **2** put on a sentimentally tender or languid look. □ **languish for** droop or pine for. **languish under** suffer under (esp. depression, confinement, etc.). [from Latin *languēre*] □ **languishment** *n.*

languor /lang-ger/ *n.* **1** lack of energy or alertness; idleness. **2** faintness; fatigue. **3** a soft or tender mood or effect. **4** an oppressive stillness (of the air etc.). [Latin] □ **languorous** *adj.* **languorously** *adv.*

lank *adj.* **1** (of hair, grass, etc.) long, limp, and straight. **2** thin and tall. **3** shrunken; spare. [Old English] □ **lankly** *adv.* **lankness** *n.*

lanky *adj.* (**lankier**, **lankiest**) (of limbs, a person, etc.) ungracefully thin and long or tall. □ **lankily** *adv.* **lankiness** *n.*

lanolin *n.* a fat found naturally on sheep's wool and used as a base for ointments. [German]

lantern *n.* **1 a** a lamp with a transparent usu. glass case protecting a candle flame etc. **b** a similar electric etc. lamp. **c** its case. **2** a raised structure on a dome, room, etc., glazed to admit light or ventilation. ▷ DOME. **3** the light-chamber of a lighthouse. **4** = MAGIC LANTERN. [from Greek *lamptēr* 'torch, lamp']

lantern fish *n.* any marine fish of the family Myctophidae, having small light organs on the head and body.

lantern-fly *n.* (*pl.* **-flies**) any tropical homopterous insect of the family Fulgoridae, formerly thought to be luminous.

lantern jaws *n.pl.* long thin jaws and chin, giving a hollow look to the face.

lantern slide *n.* ▶ a slide for projection by a magic lantern etc.

deadeye

lanyard

deadeye

LANYARD
BETWEEN
DEADEYES

LANTERN
SLIDE IN A
MAGIC
LANTERN

chimney

magic lantern

slide

lens

lanthanide *n. Chem.* any of a series of fifteen metallic elements with similar chemical properties, from lanthanum to lutetium in the periodic table. [from German]

lanthanum *n. Chem.* a silvery metallic element of the lanthanide series which is used in the manufacture of alloys and catalysts. [based on Greek *lanthanein* 'to escape notice', from having remained undetected in cerium oxide]

lanyard *n.* **1** a cord hanging round the neck or looped round the shoulder, esp. of a Scout or sailor etc., to which a knife etc. may be attached. **2** *Naut.* ◀ a short rope or line used for securing, tightening, etc. **3** a cord attached to a breech mechanism for firing a gun. [from Old French *laniere*]

Laodicean /lay-oh-di-**see**-ăn/ *adj.* lukewarm or half-hearted, esp. in religion or politics. [from Latin *Laodicea* in Asia Minor, with reference to the early Christians there (see Rev. 3:16)]

Laotian /lay-oh-**shăn**/ ● *n.* **1 a** a native or national of Laos in SE Asia. **b** a person of Laotian descent. **2** the language of Laos. ● *adj.* of or relating to Laos or its people or language.

lap[1] *n.* **1 a** the front of the body from the waist to the knees of a sitting person. **b** the clothing, esp. a skirt, covering the lap. **2** a hollow among hills. **3** a hanging flap on a garment, a saddle, etc. □ **in** (or **on**) **a person's lap** as a person's responsibility. **in the lap of the gods** (of an event etc.) open to chance; beyond human control. **in the lap of luxury** in extremely luxurious surroundings. [Old English *læppa* 'fold, flap'] □ **lapful** *n.* (*pl.* **-fuls**)

lap[2] ● *n.* **1 a** one circuit of a racetrack etc. **b** a section of a journey etc. (*on the last lap*). **2 a** an amount of overlapping. **b** an overlapping part. **3** a single turn of thread, etc., round a reel etc. ● *v.* (**lapped**, **lapping**) **1** *tr.* lead or overtake (a competitor) by one or more laps. **2** *tr.* (often foll. by *about*, *round*) coil, fold, or wrap (a garment etc.) round. **3** *tr.* (usu. foll. by *in*) enfold in wraps etc. **4** *tr.* (as **lapped** *adj.*) (usu. foll. by *in*) enfolded caressingly. **5** *tr.* surround (a person) with an influence etc. **6** *intr.* (usu. foll. by *over*) project; overlap. **7** *tr.* cause to overlap. [Middle English]

lap[3] ● *v.* (**lapped**, **lapping**) **1** *tr.* **a** (also *absol.*) (usu. of an animal) drink (liquid) with the tongue. **b** (usu. foll. by *up*) consume greedily. **2 a** *tr.* (of water) move or beat upon (a shore) with a rippling sound as of lapping. **b** *intr.* (of waves etc.) move in ripples; make a lapping sound. ● *n.* **1 a** the process or an act of lapping. **b** the amount of liquid taken up. **2** the sound of wavelets on a beach. [Old English]

laparoscope *n. Surgery* a fibre-optic instrument for insertion through the abdominal wall. [based on Greek *lapara* 'flank'] □ **laparoscopy** *n.* (*pl.* **-ies**)

laparotomy *n.* (*pl.* **-ies**) a surgical incision into the abdominal cavity for exploration or diagnosis. [based on Greek *lapara* 'flank']

lapdog *n.* a small pet dog.

lapel *n.* the part of a coat, jacket, etc., folded back against the front part round the neck opening. [based on LAP[1]] □ **lapelled** *adj.*

lapidary ● *adj.* **1** concerned with stone or stones. **2** engraved upon stone. **3** (of writing style) dignified and concise, suitable for inscriptions. ● *n.* (*pl.* **-ies**) a cutter, polisher, or engraver of gems. [based on Latin *lapis -idis* 'stone']

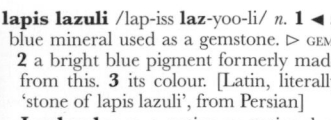

LAPIS LAZULI

lapis lazuli /lap-iss **laz**-yoo-li/ *n.* **1** ◀ a blue mineral used as a gemstone. ▷ GEM. **2** a bright blue pigment formerly made from this. **3** its colour. [Latin, literally 'stone of lapis lazuli', from Persian]

Laplander *n.* a native or national of Lapland. [from Swedish *Lappland*]

lap of honour *n. Brit.* a ceremonial circuit of a football pitch, a track, etc., by a winner or winners.

Lapp ● *n.* **1** a member of the indigenous population of the extreme north of Scandinavia. **2** the language of the Lapps. ● *adj.* of or relating to the Lapps or their language. [Swedish]

■ **Usage** The Lapps' own name for themselves, *Sami*, is now often preferred with reference to the people.

lappet *n.* **1** a small flap or fold of a garment etc. **2** a hanging or loose piece of flesh, such as a lobe or wattle. [based on LAP[1]]

lapse ● *n.* **1** a slight error; a slip of memory etc. **2** a weak or careless decline into an inferior state. **3** (foll. by *of*) an interval or passage of time. **4** *Law* the termination of a right or privilege through disuse etc. ● *v.intr.* **1** fail to maintain a position or standard. **2** (foll. by *into*) fall back into an inferior or previous state. **3** (of a right or privilege etc.) become invalid through disuse etc. **4** (as **lapsed** *adj.*) (of a person or thing) that has lapsed. [from Latin *lapsus* 'slipped']

laptop *n.* (often *attrib.*) ▼ a microcomputer that is portable and suitable for use while travelling.

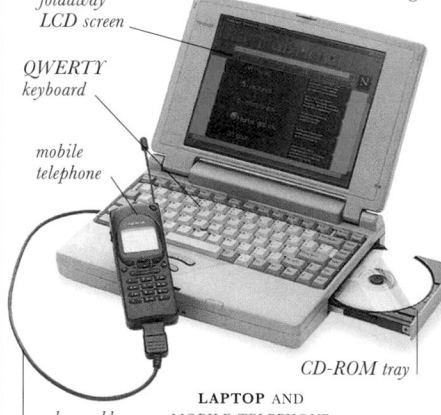

foldaway LCD screen

QWERTY keyboard

mobile telephone

CD-ROM tray

modem cable

LAPTOP AND
MOBILE TELEPHONE

lapwing *n.* a plover, *Vanellus vanellus*, with black and white plumage, crested head, and a shrill cry. [Old English *hléapewince*, from *hléapan* 'to leap' + base of *wink* 'to move from side to side']

larboard *n. & adj. Naut. archaic* = PORT[3]. [Middle English]

larceny *n.* (*pl.* **-ies**) *hist.* the theft of personal property (replaced in 1968 by *theft*). [based on Latin *latro* 'robber'] □ **larcenist** *n.* **larcenous** *adj.*

larch *n.* **1** ▶ a deciduous coniferous tree of the genus *Larix*, with bright foliage and producing tough timber. **2** (in full **larchwood**) its wood. ▷ WOOD. [from Latin *larix -icis*]

lard ● *n.* the internal fat of the abdomen of pigs, esp. when rendered for use esp. in cooking. ● *v.tr.* **1** insert strips of fat or bacon in(meat etc.) before

needles

cone

LARCH:
EUROPEAN LARCH
(*Larix decidua*)

LARVA

The larva represents the second stage in the life cycle of those insects, such as wasps, butterflies, beetles, and flies, that undergo complete metamorphosis. It follows the egg stage, and precedes the pupal and adult stages. A larva often has a different diet from that of the adult. It does not have wings, and may also lack legs. During the larval stage, which may last several years, the insect grows by periodically shedding its hard outer skin, or exoskeleton, and replacing it with a new, larger skin underneath.

EXAMPLES OF INSECT LARVAE

CADDIS-FLY LARVA
(*Glyphotaelius pellucidus*)

SWALLOWTAIL
LARVA
(*Papilio machaon*)

FLOUR BEETLE LARVA
(*Tenebrio molitor*)

LASER

A laser consists of a tube containing a substance known as a lasing medium, which may be solid, liquid, or gaseous. A power source, such as a flash tube, excites the atoms of the lasing medium, causing them to emit light in the form of photons. These photons are reflected backwards and forwards between mirrors at either end of the tube, colliding with other atoms and releasing more photons as they go. Some photons pass through the half-silvered mirror, emerging from the tube as a thin beam of coherent light, with waves all of the same colour.

CUTAWAY VIEW OF A
HELIUM-NEON LASER

waves of red light · *flash tube* · *photon* · *half-silvered mirror* · *gaseous lasing medium* · *mirror*

cooking. **2** (foll. by *with*) embellish with particular words or expressions. [from Latin *lardum*] □ **lardy** *adj.*

larder *n.* **1** a room or large cupboard for storing food. **2** a wild animal's store of food, esp. for winter. [from medieval Latin *lardarium*, related to LARD]

lardon *n.* (also **lardoon**) a strip of fat bacon used to lard meat. [French]

lardy-cake *n. Brit.* cake made with lard, currants, etc.

large ● *adj.* **1** of considerable or relatively great size or extent. **2** of the larger kind (*the large intestine*). **3** of wide range; comprehensive. **4** pursuing an activity on a large scale (*large farmer*). ● *n.* (**at large**) **1** at liberty. **2** as a body or whole (*the people at large*). **3** (of a narration etc.) at full length and with all details. **4** without a specific target (*scatters insults at large*). □ **in large** on a large scale. **large as life** see LIFE. **larger than life** see LIFE. [from Latin *larga* (fem.) 'copious'] □ **largeness** *n.* **largish** *adj.*

large intestine *n.* the caecum, colon, and rectum collectively. ▷ DIGESTION.

largely *adv.* to a great extent; principally (*is largely due to laziness*).

large-minded *adj.* liberal; not narrow-minded.

large-scale *adj.* made or occurring on a large scale or in large amounts.

largesse /lar-*zhess*/ *n.* (also **largess**) **1** money or gifts freely given, esp. on a special occasion, by a person in high position. **2** generosity, beneficence. [from (Old) French]

largo *Mus.* ● *adv. & adj.* in a slow tempo and dignified in style. ● *n.* (*pl.* **-os**) a largo passage or movement. [Italian, literally 'broad']

lariat *n.* **1** a lasso. **2** a tethering-rope, esp. used by cowboys. [based on Spanish *reatar* 'to tie again']

lark[1] *n.* **1** any small bird of the family Alaudidae with brown plumage, elongated hind claws, and tuneful song. **2** any of various similar birds. [Old English]

lark[2] *colloq.* ● *n.* **1** a frolic or spree; an amusing incident. **2** *Brit.* a type of activity, affair, etc. (*fed up with this digging lark*). ● *v.intr.* (foll. by *about*) play tricks; frolic. [19th-century coinage] □ **larky** *adj.*

larkspur *n.* **1** a plant of the genus *Consolida* (buttercup family), with spurred flowers. **2** a delphinium.

Larry *n.* □ **as happy as Larry** *Brit. colloq.* extremely happy.

larva *n.* (*pl.* **larvae** /-vee/) **1** ◄ the active immature form of an insect, forming the stage between egg and pupa. ▷ METAMORPHOSIS. **2** an immature form of other animals that undergo some metamorphosis [earlier in sense 'disembodied spirit': Latin, literally 'ghost, mask'] □ **larval** *adj.*

laryngeal /lă-**rin**-ji-ăl/ *adj.* of or relating to the larynx.

laryngitis /la-rin-**jy**-tiss/ *n.* inflammation of the larynx.

larynx *n.* (*pl.* **larynges** /lă-**rin**-jeez/) the hollow muscular organ forming an air passage to the lungs and holding the vocal cords. ▷ RESPIRATION. [from Greek *larugx*]

lasagne /lă-**zan**-yă/ *n.* pasta in the form of sheets. ▷ PASTA. [based on Latin *lasanum* 'cooking pot']

Lascar *n.* a sailor from India or SE Asia. [from Urdu & Persian *laškar* 'army']

lascivious *adj.* **1** lustful. **2** inciting to or evoking lust. [based on Latin *lascivia* 'lustfulness'] □ **lasciviously** *adv.* **lasciviousness** *n.*

lase *v.intr.* **1** function as or in a laser. **2** (of a substance) undergo the physical processes employed in a laser.

laser *n.* ▲ a device that generates an intense beam of coherent monochromatic radiation in the infrared, visible, or ultraviolet region of the electromagnetic spectrum. ▷ HOLOGRAM. [acronym from *light amplification by stimulated emission of radiation*]

laserdisc *n.* a disc on which signals and data are recorded to be reproduced by directing a laser beam on to the surface.

laser printer *n.* ▼ a printer in which a laser is used to form a pattern of dots on a photosensitive drum corresponding to the pattern of print required.

LaserVision *n. propr.* a system for the reproduction of video signals recorded on a disc with a laser.

lash ● *v.* **1** *tr. & intr.* make a sudden whip-like movement. **2** *tr.* beat with a whip etc. **3** *intr.* pour or rush with great force. **4** *intr.* (foll. by *at, against*) strike violently. **5** *tr.* castigate in words. **6** *tr.* urge on as with a lash. **7** *tr.* (foll. by *down, together*, etc.) fasten with a cord, rope, etc. **8** *tr.* (of rain, wind, etc.) beat forcefully upon. ● *n.* **1 a** a sharp blow made by a whip, rope, etc. **b** (prec. by *the*) punishment by beating with a whip etc. **2** the flexible end of a whip. **3** (usu. in *pl.*) an eyelash. □ **lash out 1** (often foll. by

L

LASER PRINTER

Laser printers produce permanent high-resolution images made up of tiny dots. The image to be printed is represented by a binary code signal which causes a laser beam to turn on and off intermittently. Guided by a spinning mirror, this on-off beam focuses via lenses on to a rotating drum. As the beam scans across the drum, it changes a negative charge of static electricity into a positive charge. Particles of ink adhere to the positively charged areas of the drum, building up a complete image that is transferred on to paper in the form of a printed document.

DEMONSTRATION OF HOW A LASER PRINTER WORKS

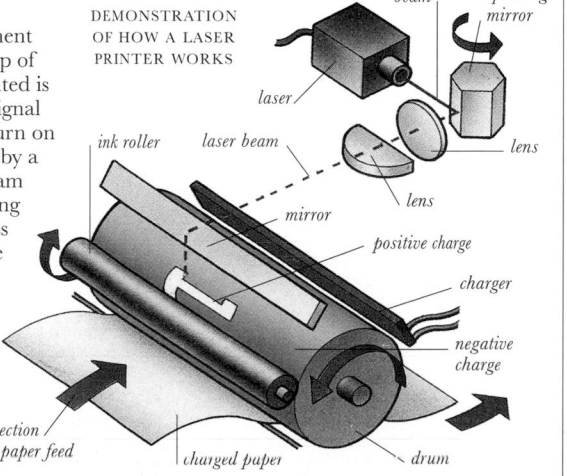

beam · *spinning mirror* · *laser* · *lens* · *lens* · *positive charge* · *charger* · *negative charge* · *drum* · *mirror* · *laser beam* · *ink roller* · *direction of paper feed* · *charged paper*

L

at) speak or hit out angrily. **2** (often foll. by *on*) *Brit.* spend money extravagantly. [Middle English] □ **lashless** *adj.*

lashing *n.* **1** a beating with a whip etc. **2** cord used for lashing.

lashings *n.pl.* (foll. by *of*) *Brit. colloq.* plenty; an abundance.

lass *n.* esp. *Sc.* & *N.Engl.* or *poet.* a girl or young woman. [from Old Norse *laskwa* (fem.) 'unmarried']

Lassa fever *n.* an acute and often fatal febrile viral disease of tropical Africa. [from *Lassa*, a village in Nigeria]

lassie *n. colloq.* = LASS.

lassitude *n.* **1** languor, weariness. **2** disinclination to exert or interest oneself. [from Latin *lassitudo*]

lasso ● *n.* (*pl.* **-os** or**-oes**) ◄ a rope with a noose at one end, used esp. in N. America for catching cattle etc. ● *v.tr.* (**-oes**, **-oed**) catch with a lasso. [from Spanish *lazo* 'lace'] □ **lassoer** *n.*

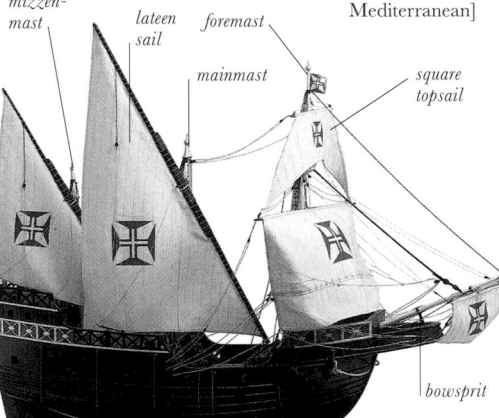

LASSO

last[1] ● *adj.* **1** after all others; coming at or belonging to the end. **2 a** most recent; next before a specified time (*last Christmas*). **b** preceding (*got on at the last station*). **3** only remaining (*the last biscuit*). **4** (prec. by *the*) least likely or suitable (*the last person I'd want*). **5** the lowest in rank (*the last place*). *adv.* **1** after all others (esp. in *comb.*: *last-mentioned*). **2** on the last occasion before the present (*when did you last see him?*). **3** (esp. in enumerating) lastly. ● *n.* **1** a person or thing that is last, last-mentioned, etc. **2** (prec. by *the*) the last mention or sight etc. (*shall never hear the last of it*). **3** the last performance of certain acts (*breathed his last*). **4** (prec. by *the*) **a** the end or last moment. **b** death. □ **at last** (or **long last**) in the end; after much delay. **on one's last legs** see LEG. **pay one's last respects** see PAY. **to** (or **till**) **the last** till the end; esp. till death. [Old English]

last[2] *v.intr.* **1** remain unexhausted or adequate or alive for a specified or considerable time (*enough to last us a week*). **2** continue for a specified time (*the journey lasts an hour*). □ **last out** remain adequate or in existence for the whole of a period previously stated or implied. [Old English]

last[3] *n.* a shoemaker's model for shaping or repairing a shoe or boot. [Old English *lǣste* 'last', *lēst* 'boot', *lāst* 'footprint']

last ditch *n.* a place of final desperate defence (often, with hyphen, *attrib.*: *last-ditch attempt*).

lasting *adj.* **1** continuing, permanent. **2** durable. □ **lastingly** *adv.*

lastly *adv.* finally; in the last place.

last minute *n.* (also **last moment**) the time just before an important event (often, with hyphen, *attrib.*: *last-minute rush*).

last name *n.* surname.

last post *n. Brit.* **1** the last of several bugle calls giving notice to retire at night. **2** this call at military funerals etc.

last rites *n.pl.* sacred rites for a person on the point of death.

last sleep *n.* death.

last straw *n.* (prec. by *the*) a slight addition to a burden or difficulty that makes it finally unbearable. [from the saying *it was the last straw that broke the camel's back*]

Last Supper *n.* the supper eaten by Christ and his disciples on the eve of the Crucifixion, as recorded in the New Testament.

last thing *adv.* very late, esp. as a final act before going to bed (*last thing at night*).

last word *n.* (prec. by *the*) **1** a final or definitive statement. **2** (often foll. by *in*) the latest fashion.

lat. *abbr.* latitude.

latch ● *n.* **1** a bar with a catch and lever used as a fastening for a gate etc. **2** a spring-lock preventing a door from being opened from the outside without a key after being shut. ● *v.tr.* & *intr.* fasten or be fastened with a latch. □ **latch on** (often foll. by *to*) *colloq.* **1** attach oneself (to). **2** understand. **on the latch** fastened by the latch only, not locked.

latchkey *n.* (*pl.* **-eys**) a key of an outer door.

latchkey child *n.* (also *colloq.* **latchkey kid**) a child who is alone at home after school until a parent returns from work.

late ● *adj.* **1** after the due or usual time; occurring or done after the proper time. **2 a** far on in the day or night or in a specified time or period. **b** far on in development. **3** flowering or ripening towards the end of the season. **4** (prec. by *the* or *my*, *his*, etc.) no longer alive or having the specified status (*the late president*). **5** (esp. in *superl.*) of recent date (*the latest songs*). ● *adv.* **1** after the due or usual time (*arrived late*). **2** far on in time (*this happened later on*). **3** at or till a late hour. **4** at a late stage of development. **5** formerly but not now (*late of the Scillies*). □ **at the latest** as the latest time envisaged (*by six at the latest*). **late in the day** at a late stage in the proceedings, esp. too late to be useful. **the latest** the most recent news, fashion, etc. [Old English] □ **lateness** *n.*

latecomer *n.* a person who arrives late.

lateen *adj.* ▼ (of a ship) rigged with a lateen sail. ▷ DHOW. [from French (*voile*) *latine* 'Latin (sail)', because common in the Mediterranean]

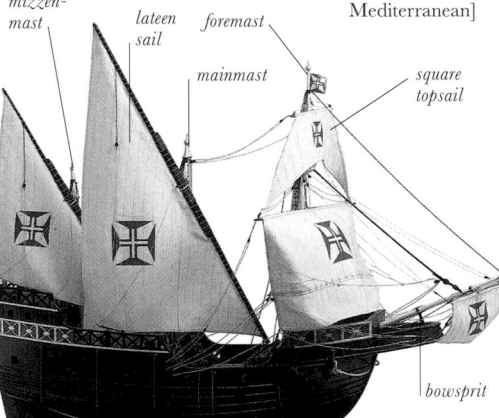

LATEEN: 15TH-CENTURY
PORTUGUESE LATEEN SHIP

labels: *mizzen-mast*, *lateen sail*, *foremast*, *mainmast*, *square topsail*, *bowsprit*

lateen sail *n.* a triangular sail on a long yard at an angle of 45° to the mast. ▷ LATEEN

Late Latin *n.* Latin of about AD 200–600.

lately *adv.* not long ago; recently; in recent times.

La Tène *Archaeol.* of or relating to the second cultural phase of the Iron Age in central and W. Europe, lasting from the 5th to the 1st centuries BC. [a district in Switzerland, where remains of it were first identified]

latent *adj.* **1** concealed, dormant. **2** existing but not developed or manifest. [from Latin *latent-* 'hiding'] □ **latency** *n.* **latently** *adv.*

latent heat *n. Physics* the heat required to convert a solid into a liquid or vapour, or a liquid into a vapour, without change of temperature.

latent image *n. Photog.* an image not yet made visible by developing.

lateral ● *adj.* **1** of, at, towards, or from the side or sides. **2** descended from a brother or sister of a person in direct line. ● *n.* a side part etc., esp. a lateral shoot or branch. [from Latin *lateralis*] □ **laterally** *adv.*

lateral line *n. Zool.* a visible line along the side of a fish consisting of a series of sense organs acting as vibration receptors.

lateral thinking *n. Brit.* a method of solving problems indirectly or by apparently illogical methods.

latex *n.* (*pl.* **latexes** or **latices** /**lay**-ti-seez/) **1** a milky fluid of mixed composition found in various plants and trees, esp. the rubber tree. **2** a synthetic product resembling this. [Latin, literally 'liquid']

lath *n.* (*pl.* **laths**) **1** a thin flat strip of wood, esp. as part of a framework or support for plaster etc. **2** (esp. in *phr.* **lath and plaster**) laths collectively as a building material, esp. as a foundation for supporting plaster. [Old English]

lathe *n.* a machine for shaping wood, metal, etc., by rotating the article against changeable cutting tools.

lather /**lah**-*ther*/ ● *n.* **1** a froth produced by agitating soap etc. and water. **2** frothy sweat, esp. of a horse. **3** a state of agitation. ● *v.* **1** *intr.* (of soap etc.) form a lather. **2** *tr.* cover with lather. **3** *intr.* (of a horse etc.) develop or become covered with lather. **4** *tr. colloq.* thrash. [Old English] □ **lathery** *adj.*

lathi *n.* (*pl.* **lathis**) (in India) a long heavy iron-bound bamboo stick used as a weapon, esp. by police. [Hindi *lāthī*]

latices *pl.* of LATEX.

Latin ● *n.* **1** the Italic language of ancient Rome and its empire, originating in Latium. **2** *Rom.Hist.* an inhabitant of ancient Latium in central Italy. ● *adj.* **1** of or in Latin. **2** of the countries or peoples using languages developed from Latin. **3** *Rom.Hist.* of or relating to ancient Latium or its inhabitants. **4** of the Roman Catholic Church. [based on *Latium* (see *n.* 2)] □ **Latinism** *n.* **Latinist** *n.*

Latina see LATINO *n.*

Latin America *n.* the parts of Central and S. America where Spanish or Portuguese is the main language. □ **Latin American** *n.* & *adj.*

Latinate *adj.* having the character of Latin.

Latin Church *n.* the Western Church.

Latin cross *n.* a plain cross with the lowest member longer than the other three.

Latinize *v.tr.* (also **-ise**) **1** give a Latin or Latinate form to. **2** translate into Latin. **3** make conformable to the ideas, customs, etc., of the ancient Romans, Latin peoples, or Latin Church. □ **Latinization** *n.* **Latinizer** *n.*

Latino /lă-**tee**-noh/ *N. Amer.* ● *n.* (*pl.* **-os**; *fem.* **Latina**) a Latin American inhabitant of the United States. ● *adj.* of or relating to these inhabitants. [Latin American Spanish]

latish *adj.* & *adv.* fairly late.

latitude *n.* **1** *Geog.* **a** the angular distance on a meridian north or south of the equator, expressed in degrees and minutes. ▷ LONGITUDE. **b** (usu. in *pl.*) regions or climes (*warm latitudes*). **2** freedom from narrowness; liberality of interpretation. **3** tolerated variety of action or opinion (*was allowed much latitude*). **4** *Astron.* the angular distance of a celestial object or point from the ecliptic. [from Latin *latitudo*] □ **latitudinal** *adj.* **latitudinally** *adv.*

latitudinarian ● *adj.* allowing latitude esp. in religion. ● *n.* a person with a latitudinarian attitude. □ **latitudinarianism** *n.*

latria *n. RC Ch.* supreme worship allowed to God alone. [Late Latin, from Greek *latreia* 'worship', from *latreuein* 'serve']

latrine *n.* a communal lavatory, esp. in a barracks etc. [from Latin *latrina* 'privy']

latter *adj.* **1** (prec. by *the*, *this*, etc.; usu. *absol.*) the second-mentioned or *disp.* last-mentioned person or thing. **2** nearer to the end (*the latter part of the year*). **3** recent. **4** belonging to the end of a period, of the world, etc. [Old English in sense 'later']

■ **Usage** The use of *latter* to mean 'last-mentioned of three or more' is considered incorrect by some people.

latter-day *attrib.adj.* modern, contemporary.

Latter-day Saints *n.pl.* the Mormons' name for themselves.

latterly *adv.* **1** in the latter part of life or of a period. **2** recently.

lattice *n.* **1** a structure of crossed laths or bars with spaces between, used as a fence etc. **2** *Crystallog.* a regular periodic arrangement of atoms, ions, or molecules. [from Old French *lattis*] □ **latticed** *adj.* **latticing** *n.*

lattice frame *n.* (also **lattice girder**) a girder or truss made of top and bottom members connected by struts usu. crossing diagonally.

lattice window *n.* ◄ a window with small panes set in diagonally crossing strips of lead.

Latvian ● *n.* **1 a** a native of Latvia, a Baltic republic. **b** a person of Latvian descent. **2** the language of Latvia. ● *adj.* of or relating to Latvia or its people or language.

laud ● *v.tr.* praise or extol, esp. in hymns. ● *n.* **1** *literary* praise; a hymn of praise. **2** (in *pl.*) the office of the first canonical hour of prayer. [based on Latin *laus laudis* 'praise']

LATTICE WINDOW

laudable *adj.* commendable, praiseworthy. □ **laudably** *adv.*

■ **Usage** *Laudable* 'praiseworthy' is sometimes confused with *laudatory* 'expressing praise'. The difference is illustrated by the sentence *Her laudable efforts were recognized in the mayor's laudatory speech.*

laudanum *n.* an opium preparation formerly used as a narcotic painkiller. [originally name given by Paracelsus to a costly medicament]

laudatory *adj.* expressing praise.

■ **Usage** See Usage Note at LAUDABLE.

lauds see LAUD *n.* 2.

laugh ● *v.* **1** *intr.* make the spontaneous sounds and movements usual in expressing lively amusement, scorn, derision, etc. **2** *tr.* express by laughing. **3** *intr.* (foll. by *at*) ridicule, make fun of. **4** *intr.* (in phr. **be laughing**) *colloq.* be in a fortunate or successful position. ● *n.* **1** the sound or act or manner of laughing. **2** *colloq.* a comical or ridiculous person or thing. □ **have the last laugh** be ultimately the winner. **laugh off** get rid of (embarrassment or humiliation) by joking. **laugh out of court** deprive of a hearing by ridicule. **laugh up one's sleeve** be secretly or inwardly amused. [Old English]

laughable *adj.* ludicrous; highly amusing. □ **laughably** *adv.*

laughing ● *n.* laughter. ● *adj.* in senses of LAUGH *v.* □ **no laughing matter** something serious. □ **laughingly** *adv.*

laughing gas *n.* nitrous oxide as an anaesthetic.

laughing hyena *n.* a hyena, *Crocuta crocuta*, whose howl is compared to a fiendish laugh.

laughing jackass *n.* = KOOKABURRA.

laughing stock *n.* a person or thing open to general ridicule.

laughter *n.* the act or sound of laughing.

launch[1] ● *v.* **1** *tr.* set (a vessel) afloat. **2** *tr.* hurl or send forth (a weapon, rocket, etc.). **3** *tr.* start or set in motion (an enterprise, a person on a course of action, etc.). **4** *tr.* formally introduce (a new product) with publicity etc. **5** *intr.* **a** (foll. by *out, into*) make a start, esp. on an ambitious enterprise. **b** (foll. by *into*)

LAVA

Magma (molten rock) emerging from a volcanic eruption is called lava. Magma bubbles up from a magma chamber deep under the ground and flows out through a vent. There are two main kinds of lava flow, both of which take their name from Hawaiian words. Aa (pronounced *ah-ah*) flows are viscous, and are covered in sharp angular blocks called scoria. Pahoehoe (*pa-hoy-hoy*) flows are less viscous and form a wrinkled skin with a rope-like appearance, caused by the lava flowing beneath.

EXAMPLES OF LAVA

AA LAVA

PAHOEHOE LAVA

CROSS-SECTION OF A VOLCANO, SHOWING LAVA FLOW

active juvenile volcano   *vent*   *main conduit*   *secondary conduit*   *lava flow*   *layers of volcanic ash*   *sagging older strata*   *magma chamber*

begin suddenly (a speech, song, etc.). ● *n.* the act or an instance of launching. [from Old French *lancier*]

launch[2] *n.* **1** a large motor boat. **2** *hist.* a man-of-war's largest boat. [from Spanish *lancha* 'pinnace']

launcher *n.* a structure or device to hold a rocket during launching.

launch pad *n.* (also **launching pad**) a platform from which rockets are launched.

launder *v.tr.* **1** wash and iron (clothes, linen, etc.). **2** *colloq.* transfer (funds) to conceal a dubious or illegal origin. [based on Latin *lavanda* 'things to be washed'] □ **launderer** *n.*

launderette *n.* (also **laundrette**) an establishment with coin-operated washing machines and dryers for public use.

laundress *n.* a woman who launders clothes, linen, etc., esp. professionally.

laundromat *n.* esp. *N. Amer.* a launderette.

laundry *n.* (*pl.* **-ies**) **1 a** a room or building for washing clothes etc. **b** a firm that washes clothes etc. commercially. **2** clothes or linen for laundering or newly laundered.

laureate ● *adj.* wreathed with laurel as a mark of honour. ● *n.* **1** a person who is honoured for outstanding achievement (*Nobel laureate*). **2** = POET LAUREATE. [based on Latin *laurea* 'laurel wreath'] □ **laureateship** *n.*

laurel ● *n.* **1** = BAY[2] 1. **2 a** (in *sing.* or *pl.*) ► a wreath of bay leaves, used as an emblem of victory or of distinction in poetry. **b** (in *pl.*) honour or distinction. **3** any plant with dark green glossy leaves like a bay tree. ● *v.tr.* (**laurelled**, **laurelling**; *US* **laureled**, **laureling**) wreathe with laurel. □ **look to one's laurels** beware of losing one's pre-eminence. **rest on one's laurels** be satisfied with what one has done and not seek further success. [from Latin *laurus*]

LAUREL

lav *n. colloq.* lavatory.

lava *n.* ▲ the matter which flows from a volcano and solidifies on cooling. ▷ VOLCANO. [Italian, originally applied to a stream of rain, from *lavare* 'to wash']

lavatorial *adj.* **1** of or relating to lavatories, esp. resembling the architecture or decoration of public lavatories. **2** (of humour etc.) scatological.

lavatory *n.* (*pl.* **-ies**) **1** a large receptacle for urinat-

ing or defecating into, usu. flushed by water. **2** a room or compartment containing one or more of these. [originally in sense 'washing-vessel': based on Latin *lavare* 'to wash']

lavatory paper *n. Brit.* = TOILET PAPER.

lavender ● *n.* **1 a** ▼ any small evergreen shrub of the genus *Lavandula*, with narrow leaves and blue, purple, or pink aromatic flowers. **b** its flowers and stalks dried and used for their scent. ▷ HERB. **2** a pale, slightly mauvish blue. ● *adj.* **1** pale, slightly mauvish blue. **2** having the fragrance of lavender flowers. [from medieval Latin *lavandula*]

lavender-water *n.* a perfume made from distilled lavender and alcohol.

LAVENDER (*Lavandula angustifolia* 'Munstead')

laver /lay-ver/ *n.* any of various edible seaweeds, esp. *Porphyra umbilicaulis*, having sheetlike fronds. [Latin]

laver bread *n.* a Welsh dish of laver which is boiled, dipped in oatmeal, and fried.

lavish ● *adj.* **1** giving or producing in large quantities; profuse. **2** generous, unstinting. **3** excessive, overabundant. ● *v.tr.* (often foll. by *on*) bestow or spend (money, praise, etc.) abundantly. [based on Old French *lavasse* 'deluge of rain'] □ **lavishly** *adv.* **lavishness** *n.*

law *n.* **1 a** a rule enacted or customary in a community and recognized as enjoining or prohibiting certain actions and enforced by the imposition of penalties. **b** a body of such rules (*the law of the land*; *forbidden under Scots law*). **2** the controlling influence of laws; respect for laws (*law and order*). **3** laws collectively as a social system or subject of study (*was reading law*). **4** binding force or effect (*their word is law*). **5** (prec. by *the*) **a** the legal profession. **b** *colloq.* the police. **6** the statute and common law (opp.

L

457

EQUITY 2). **7** (in *pl.*) jurisprudence. **8 a** the judicial remedy; litigation. **b** the law courts as providing this (*go to law*). **9** a rule of action or procedure, e.g. in a game, form of art, etc. **10** a regularity in natural occurrences, esp. as formulated or propounded in particular instances (*the law of gravity*; *Parkinson's law*). **11** divine commandments. □ **at** (or **in**) **law** according to the laws. **be a law unto oneself** do what one feels is right; disregard custom. **go to law** take legal action. **lay down the law** be dogmatic or authoritarian. **take the law into one's own hands** redress a grievance by one's own means, esp. by force. [from Old Norse *lag*, something 'laid down' or fixed]

law-abiding *adj.* obedient to the laws.

lawbreaker *n.* a person who breaks the law. □ **lawbreaking** *n. & adj.*

law centre *n. Brit.* an independent publicly-funded advisory service on legal matters.

law court *n.* a court of law.

lawful *adj.* conforming with, permitted by, or recognized by law. □ **lawfully** *adv.* **lawfulness** *n.*

lawgiver *n.* a person who lays down laws.

lawless *adj.* **1** having no laws or enforcement of them. **2** disregarding laws. □ **lawlessly** *adv.* **lawlessness** *n.*

Law Lord *n.* a member of the House of Lords qualified to perform its legal work.

lawmaker *n.* a legislator. □ **law-making** *adj. & n.*

lawman *n.* (*pl.* **-men**) *US* a law-enforcement officer, esp. a sheriff or police officer.

lawn[1] • *n.* a piece of grass kept mown and smooth. • *v.tr.* turn into lawn. [from Old French *launde* 'heath']

lawn[2] *n.* a fine linen or cotton fabric. [Middle English] □ **lawny** *adj.*

lawnmower *n.* ▼ a machine for cutting the grass on a lawn.

ROTARY BLADE

LAWNMOWER: PETROL-POWERED ROTARY LAWNMOWER

lawn tennis *n.* the usual form of tennis, played with a soft ball on an open grass or hard court (cf. REAL TENNIS).

■ **Usage** *Lawn Tennis* has been replaced by *Tennis* as the official international name of the sport.

law of succession *n.* the law regulating inheritance.

law of the jungle *n.* a state of ruthless competition.

lawrencium *n. Chem.* an artificially made transuranic radioactive metallic element. [named after E. O. *Lawrence*, American physicist, 1901–58]

lawsuit *n.* the process or an instance of making a claim in a law court.

law term *n. Brit.* a period appointed for the sitting of law courts.

lawyer *n.* a member of the legal profession, esp. a solicitor. □ **lawyerly** *adj.* [Middle English *law(i)er*, from LAW]

lax *adj.* **1** lacking care, concern, or firmness. **2** loose, relaxed; not compact. [from Latin *laxus* 'loose'] □ **laxity** *n.* **laxly** *adv.* **laxness** *n.*

laxative • *adj.* tending to stimulate or facilitate evacuation of the bowels. • *n.* a laxative medicine. [from Late Latin *laxativus*]

lay[1] • *v.* (*past* and *past part.* **laid**) **1** *tr.* place on a surface, esp. horizontally in a position of rest (*laid the book on the table*). **2** *tr.* put or bring into a certain or the required position or state (*lay a carpet, a cable*). **3** *intr. dial.* lie. **4** *tr.* make by laying (*lay the foundations*). **5** *tr.* (often *absol.*) (of a hen bird) produce (an egg). **6** *tr.* **a** cause to subside or lie flat. **b** deal with to remove (a ghost, fear, etc.). **7** *tr.* place or present for consideration (a case, proposal, etc.). **8** *tr.* set down as a basis or starting point. **9** *tr.* (usu. foll. by *on*) attribute or impute (blame etc.). **10** *tr.* locate (a scene etc.) in a certain place. **11** *tr.* prepare or make ready (a plan or a trap). **12** *tr.* prepare (a table) for a meal. **13** *tr.* place or arrange the material for (a fire). **14** *tr.* put down as a wager; stake. **15** *tr.* (foll. by *with*) coat or strew (a surface). **16** *tr. slang offens.* have sexual intercourse with (esp. a woman). • *n.* **1** the way, position, or direction in which something lies. **2** *slang offens.* **a** a partner (esp. female) in sexual intercourse. **b** an act of sexual intercourse. □ **in lay** (of a hen) laying eggs regularly. **lay about one 1** hit out on all sides. **2** criticize indiscriminately. **lay aside 1** put to one side. **2** cease to practise or consider. **3** save (money etc.) for future needs. **lay at the door of** see DOOR. **lay bare** expose, reveal. **lay a charge** make an accusation. **lay claim to** claim as one's own. **lay down 1** put on the ground or other surface. **2** relinquish; give up (an office). **3** formulate or insist on (a rule or principle). **4** begin to construct (a ship or railway). **5** store (wine) in a cellar. **6** sacrifice (one's life). **lay down the law** see LAW. **lay hands on 1** seize or attack. **2** place one's hands on or over, esp. in confirmation, ordination, or spiritual healing. **lay one's hands on** obtain, acquire, locate. **lay hold of** seize or grasp. **lay in** provide oneself with a stock of. **lay into** *colloq.* attack violently with words or blows. **lay it on thick** (or **with a trowel**) *colloq.* flatter or exaggerate grossly. **lay low** overthrow, kill, or humble. **lay off 1** discharge (workers) temporarily or permanently because of a shortage of work; make redundant. **2** *colloq.* desist. **lay on 1** esp. *Brit.* provide (a facility, amenity, etc.). **2** impose (a penalty, obligation, etc.). **3** inflict (blows). **4** spread on (paint etc.). **lay out 1** spread out. **2** expose to view. **3** prepare (a corpse) for burial. **4** *colloq.* knock unconscious. **5** arrange (grounds etc.) according to a plan. **6** expend (money). **lay store by** see STORE. **lay to rest** bury in a grave. **lay up 1** store, save. **2** put (a ship etc.) out of service. **lay waste** see WASTE. [Old English]

■ **Usage** The intransitive use of the verb *lay* in sense 3 to mean 'lie' is erroneous in standard English and arises probably as a result of confusion with *lay* as the past of *lie*, as in *The dog lay on the floor* which is correct.

lay[2] *adj.* **1 a** non-clerical. **b** not ordained into the clergy. **2 a** not professionally qualified, esp. in law or medicine. **b** of or done by such persons. [from Greek *laïkos*, from *laos* 'people']

lay[3] *n.* **1** a short lyric or narrative poem meant to be sung. **2** a song. [from Old French *lai*]

lay[4] *past* of LIE[1].

layabout *n.* a habitual loafer or idler.

lay-by *n.* (*pl.* **lay-bys**) **1** *Brit.* an area at the side of an open road where vehicles may stop. **2** a similar arrangement on a canal or railway. **3** *Austral. & NZ* a system of paying a deposit to secure an article for later purchase.

layer • *n.* **1** a thickness of matter, esp. one of several, covering a surface. **2** a person or thing that lays. **3** a hen that lays eggs (*a good layer*). **4** ◄ a shoot fastened down to take root while attached to the parent plant. • *v.tr.* **1 a** arrange in layers. **b** cut (hair) in layers. **2** propagate (a plant) as a layer. □ **layered** *adj.*

LAYER

layette *n.* a set of clothing, toilet articles, and bedclothes for a newborn child. [French, originally in sense 'little drawer']

layman *n.* (*pl.* **-men**; *fem.* **laywoman**, *pl.* **-women**) **1** any non-ordained member of a Church. **2** a person without professional or specialized knowledge in a particular subject.

lay-off *n.* **1** a temporary or permanent discharge of workers; a redundancy. **2** a period when this is in force.

lay open *v.tr.* **1** break the skin of. **2** (foll. by *to*) expose (to criticism etc.).

layout *n.* **1** the disposing or arrangement of a site, ground, etc. **2** the way in which plans, printed matter, etc., are arranged or set out. **3** something arranged or set out in a particular way.

layperson *n.* a layman or laywoman.

lay reader *n.* (in the Anglican Church) a lay person licensed to preach and to conduct some religious services.

laywoman see LAYMAN.

laze • *v.* **1** *intr.* spend time lazily or idly. **2** *tr.* (often foll. by *away*) pass (time) in this way. • *n.* a spell of lazing. [back-formation from LAZY]

lazy *adj.* (**lazier**, **laziest**) **1** disinclined to work, doing little work. **2** of or inducing idleness. **3** (of a river etc.) slow-moving. □ **lazily** *adv.* **laziness** *n.*

lazybones *n.* (*pl.* same) *colloq.* a lazy person.

lb *abbr.* a pound or pounds (weight). [Latin *libra*]

l.b.w. *abbr. Cricket* leg before wicket.

l.c. *abbr.* **1** in the passage cited. **2** lower case. [sense 1: Latin *loco citato*]

LCD *abbr.* **1** liquid crystal display. **2** lowest common denominator.

LCM *abbr.* lowest common multiple.

L/Cpl *abbr.* Lance Corporal.

Ld. *abbr.* Lord.

LEA *abbr.* (in the UK) Local Education Authority.

lea *n. poet.* a meadow or field. [Old English]

leach *v.* **1** *tr.* subject (bark, ore, ash, or soil) to the action of percolating fluid. **2** *tr. & intr.* (foll. by *away*, *out*) remove (soluble matter) or be removed in this way.

lead[1] /leed/ • *v.* (*past* and *past part.* **led**) **1** *tr.* cause to go with one, esp. by guiding or showing the way or by going in front. **2** *tr.* **a** direct the actions or opinions of. **b** (often foll. by *to*, or *to* + infin.) guide by persuasion or example or argument (*what led you to that conclusion?*; *was led to think you may be right*). **3** *tr.* (also *absol.*) provide access to; bring to a certain position or destination (*this door leads you into a small room*; *the path leads uphill*). **4** *tr.* pass or go through (a life etc. of a specified kind) (*led a miserable existence*). **5** *tr.* **a** have the first place in (*lead the dance*; *leads the world in sugar production*). **b** (also *absol.*) go first; be ahead in a race or game. **c** (also *absol.*) be pre-eminent in some field. **6** *tr.* be in charge of (*leads a team of researchers*). **7** *tr.* (also *absol.*) begin a round of play at cards by playing (a card) or a card of (a particular suit). **8** *intr.* (foll. by *to*) have as an end or outcome; result in (*what does all this lead to?*). **9** *intr.* (foll. by *with*) *Boxing* make an attack (with a particular blow). **10** *intr.* (foll. by *with*) (of a newspaper) use a particular item as the main story (*led with the Stock Market crash*). • *n.* **1** guidance given by going in front; example. **2 a** a leading place; the leadership (*is in the lead*; *take the lead*). **b** the amount by which a competitor is ahead of the next behind (*a lead of ten yards*). **3** a clue, esp. an important early one. **4** a strap or cord for leading a dog etc. **5 a** *Brit.* a conductor (usu. a wire) conveying electric current

L

from a source to an appliance. **b** *US* a conductor used in internal wiring. **6 a** the chief part in a play etc. **b** (*attrib.*) the chief instrument of a specified type (*lead guitar*). **7** (in full **lead story**) the item of news given the greatest prominence in a newspaper or magazine. **8 a** the act or right of playing first in a game or round of cards. **b** the card led. □ **lead by the nose** cajole (a person) into compliance. **lead a person a dance** see DANCE. **lead off** begin; make a start. **lead on 1** entice into going further than was intended. **2** mislead or deceive. **lead up** (or *N. Amer.* **down**) **the garden path** *colloq.* mislead. **lead the way** see WAY. [Old English] □ **leadable** *adj.*

lead² /led/ ● *n.* **1** *Chem.* a heavy bluish-grey soft ductile metallic element used in building and the manufacture of alloys. ▷ ORE. **2 a** graphite. **b** a thin length of this in a pencil. **3** a lump of lead used in sounding water. **4** (in *pl.*) lead frames holding the glass of a lattice or stained-glass window. **5** *Printing* **a** a metal strip used to create space between lines of type. **b** this space. ● *v.tr.* **1** cover, weight, or frame (a roof or window panes) with lead. **2** *Printing* space lines of (printed matter) with leads. **3** add a lead compound to (petrol etc.). □ **swing the lead** see SWING. [Old English] □ **leaded** *adj.* **leadless** *adj.*

leaden *adj.* **1** of or like lead. **2** heavy, slow, burdensome (*leaden limbs*). **3** inert, depressing (*leaden rule*). **4** lead-coloured (*leaden skies*). □ **leadenly** *adv.* **leadenness** *n.*

leader *n.* **1 a** a person or thing that leads. **b** a person followed by others. **2 a** the principal player or conductor in a music group. **b** *Brit.* the first violin in an orchestra. **3** *Brit.* = LEADING ARTICLE. **4** a short strip of non-functioning material at each end of a reel of film or recording tape for connection to the spool. **5** (in full **Leader of the House**) *Brit.* a member of the government officially responsible for initiating business in Parliament. **6** a shoot of a plant at the apex of a stem or of the main branch. □ **leaderless** *adj.* **leadership** *n.*

leader board *n.* a scoreboard, esp. at a golf course, showing the names etc. of the leading competitors.

lead-free *adj.* (of petrol) without added lead compounds.

lead-in *n.* an introduction, opening, etc.

leading¹ /lee-ding/ ● *adj.* chief; most important. ● *n.* guidance, leadership.

leading² /led-ing/ *n. Printing* ▼ the spacing of lines of type.

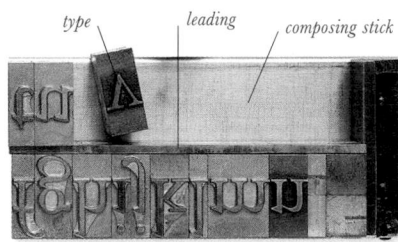

type   leading   composing stick

LEADING BETWEEN INVERTED METAL TYPE ON A COMPOSING STICK

leading aircraftman *n.* (*fem.* **leading aircraft-woman**) the rank above aircraftman in the RAF.

leading article *n. Brit.* a newspaper article giving the editorial opinion.

leading counsel *n.* the senior barrister of two or more in a case.

leading lady *n.* the actress playing the principal part in a play etc.

leading light *n.* a prominent and influential person.

leading man *n.* the actor playing the principal part in a play etc.

leading question *n.* a question that prompts the answer wanted, e.g. *So you never saw the accused hit the officer?*

■ **Usage** Note that *leading question* does not mean a 'principal' or 'loaded' or 'searching' question.

lead pencil *n.* a pencil of graphite enclosed in wood.

leaf ● *n.* (*pl.* **leaves**) **1** ▼ each of several flattened usu. green structures of a plant, usu. on the side of a stem or branch and the main organ of photosynthesis. ▷ SUCCULENT. **2 a** foliage regarded collectively. **b** the state of having leaves out (*a tree in leaf*). **3** a single thickness of paper, esp. in a book with each side forming a page. **4** a very thin sheet of metal, esp. gold or silver. **5 a** the hinged part or flap of a door, shutter, table, etc. **b** an extra section inserted to extend a table. ● *v.* **1** *intr.* put forth leaves. **2** *tr.* (foll. by *through*) turn over the pages of (a book etc.). [Old English] □ **leafage** *n.* **leafed** *adj.* (also

---

LEAF

A typical leaf consists of a thin flat lamina (blade) supported by a network of veins, a petiole (leaf-stalk), and a leaf base, where the petiole joins the stem. Leaves can be classified as simple, in which the lamina is a single unit, or compound, in which the lamina is divided into separate leaflets. Compound leaves may be pinnate, with pinnae (leaflets) on both sides of a rachis (main axis), or palmate, with leaflets arising from a single point at the tip of the petiole. Conifer leaves are usually simple and slender, and have a tough waxy surface. Unlike more delicate leaves, they often last for several years.

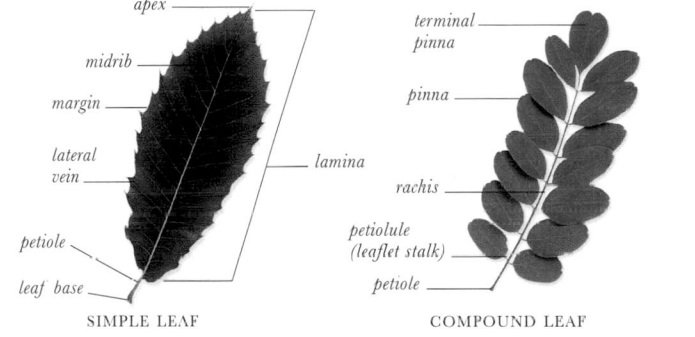

apex — midrib — margin — lateral vein — petiole — leaf base — lamina

terminal pinna — pinna — rachis — petiolule (leaflet stalk) — petiole

SIMPLE LEAF   COMPOUND LEAF

EXAMPLES OF LEAF TYPES AND SHAPES

CONIFEROUS

COMB-LIKE (pectinate)

NEEDLE-LIKE (acicular)

SCALE-LIKE

LOBED OR DIVIDED

PINNATIFID   PALMATELY LOBED

DIGITATE (5-palmate)   PINNATE

BIPINNATE (2-pinnate)   TRIPINNATE (3-pinnate)

SHAPES

LANCE-SHAPED (lanceolate)   HEART-SHAPED (cordate)   TRIANGULAR (deltoid)

SPOON-SHAPED (spathulate)   KIDNEY-SHAPED (reniform)   ARROW-SHAPED (sagittate)

ELLIPTIC   INVERSELY HEART-SHAPED (obcordate)   FAN-SHAPED (flabellate)

L

in *comb.*). **leafless** *adj.* **leaflike** *adj.* [Old English *lēaf*, from Germanic]

leaf insect *n.* ▼ any insect of the family Phylliidae, having a flattened body, leaflike in appearance.

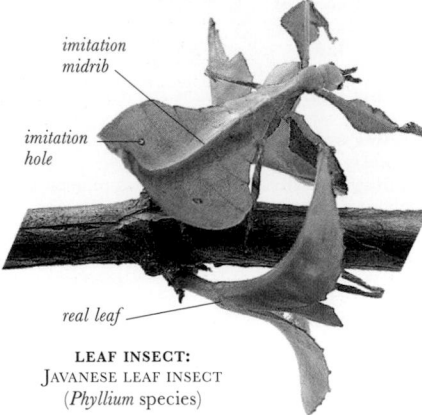

LEAF INSECT:
JAVANESE LEAF INSECT
(*Phyllium* species)

imitation midrib

imitation hole

real leaf

leaflet ● *n.* **1** a sheet of (usu. printed) paper (sometimes folded) giving information, esp. for free distribution. **2** a young leaf. **3** *Bot.* a division of a compound leaf. ● *v.tr.* (**leafleted**, **leafleting**) distribute leaflets to.

leaf mould *n.* soil consisting chiefly of decayed leaves.

leaf-stalk *n.* a petiole.

league[1] ● *n.* **1** a collection of people, countries, groups, etc., combining for a particular purpose, esp. mutual protection or cooperation. **2** an agreement to combine in this way. **3** a group of sports clubs which compete over a period for a championship. **4** a class of contestants etc. of comparable ability. ● *v.intr.* (**leagues**, **leagued**, **leaguing**) (often foll. by *together*) join in a league. □ **in league** allied, conspiring. [from Italian *liga*]

league[2] *n. archaic* a measure of distance, usu. about three miles. [from Late Latin *leuga*]

league table *n. Brit.* **1** a listing of competitors as a league, showing their ranking according to performance. **2** any list of ranking order.

leak ● *n.* **1** a hole in a pipe, container, etc. caused by wear or damage, through which matter, esp. liquid or gas, passes accidentally in or out. **c** the act or an instance of leaking. **2** a similar escape of electrical charge. **3** the intentional disclosure of secret information. ● *v.* **1 a** *intr.* (of liquid, gas, etc.) pass in or out through a leak. **b** *tr.* lose or admit (liquid, gas, etc.) through a leak. **2** *tr.* intentionally disclose (secret information). **3** *intr.* (often foll. by *out*) (of a secret, secret information) become known. □ **have** (or **take**) **a leak** *slang* urinate. [Middle English] □ **leaker** *n.*

leakage *n.* the action or result of leaking.

leaky *adj.* (**leakier**, **leakiest**) having a leak or leaks. □ **leakiness** *n.*

lean[1] ● *v.* (*past* and *past part.* **leaned** or esp. *Brit.* **leant**) **1** *intr. & tr.* (often foll. by *across, back, over*, etc.) be or place in a sloping position. **2** *intr. & tr.* (foll. by *against, on, upon*) rest or cause to rest for support against etc. **3** *intr.* (foll. by *on, upon*) rely on. **4** *intr.* (foll. by *to, towards*) be inclined or partial to. ● *n.* a deviation from the perpendicular; an inclination (*has a decided lean to the right*). □ **lean on** *colloq.* put pressure on (a person) to act in a certain way. **lean over backwards** see BACKWARDS. [Old English]

lean[2] ● *adj.* **1** (of a person or animal) thin; having no superfluous fat. **2** (of meat) containing little fat. **3** meagre (*lean crop*). **4** unremunerative. **5** (of a vaporized fuel mixture) having a high proportion of air. ● *n.* the lean part of meat. [Old English] □ **leanly** *adv.* **leanness** *n.*

lean-burn *adj.* designating an internal-combustion engine designed to run on a lean mixture to reduce pollution.

leaning *n.* a tendency or partiality.

lean-to *n.* (*pl.* **-tos**) a building with its roof leaning against a larger building or a wall.

lean years *n.pl.* years of scarcity.

leap ● *v.* (*past* and *past part.* **leaped** or **leapt**) **1** *intr.* jump or spring forcefully. **2** *tr.* jump across. **3** *intr.* (of prices etc.) increase dramatically. ● *n.* a forceful jump. □ **by leaps and bounds** with startlingly rapid progress. **leap in the dark** a daring step or enterprise whose consequences are unpredictable. **leap to the eye** be immediately apparent. [Old English] □ **leaper** *n.*

leapfrog ● *n.* a game in which players in turn vault with parted legs over others who are bending down. ● *v.* (**-frogged**, **-frogging**) **1** *intr.* (foll. by *over*) perform such a vault. **2** *tr.* vault over in this way. **3** *tr. & intr.* (of two or more people, vehicles, etc.) overtake alternately.

leap year *n.* a year, occurring once in four, with 366 days (including 29 Feb.).

learn *v.* (*past* and *past part.* **learned** or esp. *Brit.* **learnt**) **1** *tr.* gain knowledge of or skill in by study, experience, or being taught. **2** *tr.* (foll. by *to* + infin.) acquire or develop a particular ability (*learn to swim*). **3** *tr.* commit to memory (*will try to learn your names*). **4** *intr.* (foll. by *of*) be informed about. **5** *tr.* (foll. by *that, how*, etc. + clause) become aware of by information or from observation. **6** *tr. archaic* or *slang* teach. □ **learn one's lesson** see LESSON. [Old English] □ **learnable** *adj.* **learnability** *n.*

■ **Usage** The use of *learn* in sense 6 to mean 'teach', as in *I'll learn you*, is non-standard and to be avoided.

learned /ler-nid/ *adj.* **1** having much knowledge acquired by study. **2** showing or requiring learning (*a learned work*). **3** studied or pursued by learned persons. **4** scholarly (*a learned journal*). **5** *Brit.* as a courteous description of a lawyer in certain formal contexts (*my learned friend*). □ **learnedly** *adv.* **learnedness** *n.*

learner *n.* **1** a person who is learning a subject or skill. **2** (in full **learner driver**) a person who is learning to drive a motor vehicle and has not yet passed a driving test.

learning *n.* knowledge acquired by study.

learning curve *n.* **1** the rate of progress in learning or gaining experience. **2** a graph of this.

lease ● *n.* an agreement by which the owner of a building or land allows another to use it for a specified time, usu. in return for payment. ● *v.tr.* grant or take on lease. □ **a new lease of** (*N. Amer.* **on**) **life** a substantially improved prospect of living, or of use after repair. [based on Latin *laxus* 'loose'] □ **leasable** *adj.* **leaser** *n.*

leaseback *n.* the leasing of a property back to the vendor.

leasehold ● *n.* **1** the holding of property by lease. **2** property held by lease. ● *adj.* held by lease. □ **leaseholder** *n.*

leash ● *n.* a dog's lead or similar restraint. ● *v.tr.* **1** put a leash on. **2** restrain. □ **straining at the leash** eager to begin. [from a specific use of Old French *laisser* 'to let run on a slack lead']

least ● *det.* (usu. prec. by *the*; often with *neg.*) smallest, slightest, most insignificant (*it doesn't make the least difference*). ● *adj.* (of a species or variety) very small (*least tern*). ● *pron.* (prec. by *the*) the least amount. ● *adv.* in the slightest degree; very little (*this surprised her least*). □ **at least 1** at all events; anyway. **2** (also **at the least**) not less than. **in the least** (or **the least**) (usu. with *neg.*) in the smallest degree; at all (*not in the least offended*). **to say the least** (or **at the least**) used to imply the moderation of a statement (*that is doubtful to say the least*). [Old English]

leastways *adv.* (also **leastwise**) *dial.* or *colloq.* or at least, or rather.

leather ● *n.* **1** material made from the skin of an animal by tanning or a similar process. **2** a piece of

leather for polishing with. **3** (in *pl.*) leather clothes. ● *v.tr.* **1** cover with leather. **2** polish or wipe with a leather. **3** beat, thrash. [Old English]

leatherback *n.* ▼ a large marine turtle, *Dermochelys coriacea*, having a thick leathery carapace.

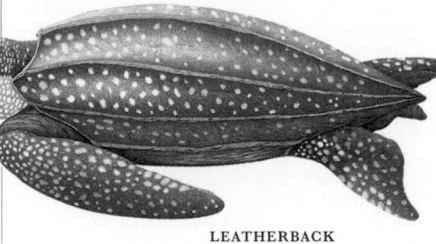

LEATHERBACK
(*Dermochelys coriacea*)

leatherette *n.* imitation leather.

leatherjacket *n. Brit.* ► a crane-fly larva with a tough skin.

leathern *n. archaic* made of leather.

leathery *adj.* **1** like leather. **2** (esp. of meat etc.) tough. □ **leatheriness** *n.*

leave[1] *v.* (*past* and *past part.* **left**) **1 a** *tr.* go away from. **b** *intr.* (often foll. by *for*) depart. **2** *tr.* cause to or let remain; depart without taking (*has left his gloves; left a slimy trail*). **3** *tr.* (also *absol.*) cease to reside at or attend or belong to or work for (*has left the school; I am leaving for another firm*). **4** *tr.* abandon, forsake, desert. **5** *tr.* have remaining after one's death (*leaves a wife and two children*). **6** *tr.* bequeath. **7** *tr.* (foll. by *to* + infin.) allow (a person or thing) to do something without interference or assistance (*leave the future to take care of itself*). **8** *tr.* (foll. by *to*) commit or refer to another person or agent (*leave that to me; nothing was left to chance*). **9** *tr.* **a** abstain from consuming or dealing with. **b** (in *passive*; often foll. by *over*) remain over. **10** *tr.* **a** deposit or entrust (a thing) to be attended to, collected, delivered, etc., in one's absence (*left a message with his secretary*). **b** depute (a person) to perform a function in one's absence (*leave you in charge*). **11** *tr.* allow to remain or cause to be in a specified state or position (*left the door open*). □ **be left with** retain or be burdened with. **have left** have remaining. **leave alone 1** refrain from disturbing, not interfere with. **2** not have dealings with. **leave be** *colloq.* refrain from disturbing, not interfere with. **leave behind 1** go away without. **2** leave as a consequence or a visible sign of passage. **3** pass. **leave a person cold** (or **cool**) not impress or excite a person. **leave go** *colloq.* relax one's hold. **leave hold of** cease holding. **leave it at that** abstain from comment or further action. **leave off 1** come to or make an end. **2** discontinue (*leave off work; leave off talking*). **3** not wear. **leave out** not include. **leave over** *Brit.* leave to be considered, settled, or used later. **left for dead** abandoned as being beyond rescue. [Old English] □ **leaver** *n.*

leave[2] *n.* **1** (often foll. by *to* + infin.) permission. **2 a** (in full **leave of absence**) permission to be absent from duty. **b** the period for which this lasts. □ **on leave** legitimately absent from duty. **take one's leave** (**of**) bid farewell to. **take leave of one's senses** see SENSE. **take leave to** venture or presume to. [Old English]

leaved *adj.* **1** having leaves. **2** (in *comb.*) having a leaf or leaves of a specified kind or number (*four-leaved clover*).

leaven /lev-ĕn/ ● *n.* **1** a substance added to dough to make it ferment and rise, esp. yeast. **2 a** a pervasive transforming influence. **b** (foll. by *of*) a tinge or admixture. ● *v.tr.* **1** ferment (dough) with leaven. **2** permeate and transform; modify with a tempering element. [from Latin *levamen* 'relief, alleviation']

LEATHERJACKET:
CRANE-FLY LARVA
(*Tipula* species)

leave of absence see LEAVE[2] 2a.

leaves *pl.* of LEAF.

leave-taking *n.* the act of taking one's leave.

leavings *n.pl.* things left over, esp. as worthless.

Lebanese ● *adj.* of or relating to Lebanon in the Middle East. ● *n.* (*pl.* same) **1** a native or national of Lebanon. **2** a person of Lebanese descent.

lech *colloq.* ● *v.intr.* behave lustfully. ● *n.* **1** a strong desire, esp. sexual. **2** a lecher.

lecher *n.* a lecherous man. [based on Old French *lechier* 'to live in debauchery']

lecherous *adj.* lustful, having strong or excessive sexual desire. □ **lecherously** *adv.* **lecherousness** *n.*

lechery *n.* unrestrained indulgence of sexual desire.

lecithin /less-i-thin/ *n.* **1** any of a group of phospholipids found naturally in animals, egg yolk, and some higher plants. **2** a preparation of this used to emulsify foods etc. [based on Greek *lekithos* 'egg yolk']

lectern *n.* **1** ▶ a stand for holding a book in a church or chapel. **2** a similar stand for a lecturer etc. [from medieval Latin *lectrum*]

lecture ● *n.* **1** a discourse giving information about a subject to a class etc. **2** a long serious speech esp. as a scolding or reprimand. ● *v.* **1** *intr.* (often foll. by *on*) deliver a lecture or lectures. **2** *tr.* talk seriously or reprovingly to (a person). **3** *tr.* instruct or entertain (a class or other audience) by a lecture. [from medieval Latin *lectura*]

lecturer *n.* a person who lectures, esp. as a teacher in higher education.

lectureship *n.* the office of lecturer.

lecture theatre see THEATRE 3.

LED *abbr.* ▼ light-emitting diode, a device used to display the time, meter readings, etc. ▷ DIODE

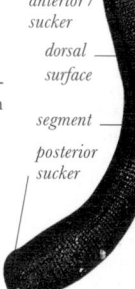

LECTERN

LED   *LED display*

LED AND LED DISPLAY
ON A STEREO SYSTEM

led *past* and *past part.* of LEAD[1].

ledge *n.* **1** a narrow horizontal surface projecting from a wall etc. **2** a shelf-like projection on the side of a rock or mountain. □ **ledged** *adj.* **ledgy** *adj.*

ledger *n.* the principal book containing a record of all the financial transactions of a company etc. **2** a flat gravestone. [based on Dutch *liggen* 'to lie' and *leggen* 'to lay']

lee *n.* **1** shelter given by a neighbouring object (*under the lee of*). **2** (in full **lee side**) the sheltered side, the side away from the wind (opp. WEATHER SIDE). [Old English]

leech[1] *n.* **1** ▶ any aquatic or terrestrial annelid worm of the class Hirudinea with suckers at both ends, esp. *Hirudo medicinalis*, a bloodsucking parasite of vertebrates formerly much used medically. **2** a person who extorts profit from or sponges on others. [Old English]

leech[2] *n.* archaic or joc. a physician; a healer. [Old English]

leek *n.* **1** an allium, *Allium porrum*, with flat overlapping leaves forming an elongated cylindrical bulb, used as food. **2** this as a Welsh national emblem. [Old English]

anterior sucker
dorsal surface
segment
posterior sucker

LEECH
(*Hirudo medicinalis*)

leer ● *v.intr.* look slyly or lasciviously or maliciously. ● *n.* a leering look. □ **leeringly** *adv.*

leery *adj.* (**leerier**, **leeriest**) *slang* **1** knowing, sly. **2** (foll. by *of*) wary. □ **leeriness** *n.*

lees *n.pl.* **1** the sediment of wine etc. **2** dregs, refuse. [pl. of Middle English *lie*, from medieval Latin *lia*]

lee shore *n.* the shore to leeward of a ship.

lee side see LEE 2.

leeward ● *adj.* & *adv.* on or towards the side sheltered from the wind (opp. WINDWARD). ● *n.* the leeward region, side, or direction (*to leeward*).

leeway *n.* **1** the sideways drift of a ship to leeward of the desired course. **2 a** a allowable deviation or freedom of action. **b** margin of safety. □ **make up leeway** recover lost time etc.

left[1] ● *adj.* **1** on or towards the side of the human body which is to the west when facing north. **2** on or towards the part of an object which is analogous to a person's left side or (with opposite sense) which is nearer to a spectator's left hand. **3** (also **Left**) *Polit.* of the Left. ● *adv.* on or to the left side. ● *n.* **1** the left-hand part or region or direction. **2** *Boxing* **a** the left hand. **b** a blow with this. **3** (often **Left**) *Polit.* a group or section favouring socialist or radical left-wing views. **4** (in full **stage left**) the side of a stage which is to the left of a person facing the audience. □ **have two left feet** be clumsy. **left and right** (or **left, right, and centre**) = *right and left*. [Old English in sense 'weak'] □ **leftish** *adj.*

left[2] *past* and *past part.* of LEAVE[1].

left-back *n.* (in football, hockey, etc.) a back who plays primarily on the left of the pitch.

left bank *n.* the bank of a river on the left facing downstream.

left-footed *adj.* **1** using the left foot by preference as more serviceable than the right. **2** (of a kick etc.) done or made with the left foot.

left-hand *adj.* **1** on or towards the left side of a person or thing (*left-hand drive*). **2** done with the left hand (*left-hand blow*). **3** (of a screw) = LEFT-HANDED 4b.

left hand *n.* **1** the hand of the left side. **2** (usu. prec. by *at*, *on*, *to*) the region or direction on the left side of a person.

left-handed *adj.* **1** using the left hand by preference as more serviceable than the right. **2** (of a tool etc.) made to be used with the left hand. **3** (of a blow etc.) done or made with the left hand. **4 a** turning to the left; towards the left. **b** (of a screw) advanced by turning to the left (anticlockwise). **5** (of a compliment) ambiguous. □ **left-handedly** *adv.* **left-handedness** *n.*

left-hander *n.* **1** a left-handed person. **2** a left-handed blow.

leftie var. of LEFTY.

leftism *n.* *Polit.* the principles or policy of the left. □ **leftist** *n.* & *adj.*

left luggage *n.* *Brit.* **1** luggage deposited for later retrieval. **2** (in full **left-luggage office**) a place for this, esp. at a railway station.

leftmost *adj.* furthest to the left.

leftover ● *n.* (usu. in *pl.*) an item (esp. of food) remaining after the rest has been used. ● *adj.* remaining over, surplus.

leftward ● *adv.* (also **leftwards**) towards the left. ● *adj.* going towards or facing the left.

left-wing *adj.* **1** socialist; radical. **2** of or relating to the left wing in football etc. ▷ RUGBY

left wing *n.* **1** the radical or socialist section of a political party or system. **2** the left side of a football etc. team on the field. **3** the left side of an army. □ **left-winger** *n.*

lefty *n.* (also **leftie**) (*pl.* **-ies**) *colloq.* **1** *Polit.* a left-winger. **2** a left-handed person.

leg *n.* **1 a** each of the limbs on which a person or animal walks and stands. **b** the part of this from the hip to the ankle. **2** a leg of an animal or bird as food. ▷ CUT. **3** a part of a garment covering a leg or part of a leg. **4 a** a support of a chair, table, bed,

etc. **b** a long thin support or prop, esp. a pole. **5** (in full **leg side**) *Cricket* the half of the field (as divided lengthways through the pitch) away from which the batsman's feet are pointed (opp. OFF n. 1). **6 a** a section of a journey. **b** a section of a relay race. **c** a stage in a competition. **d** one of two or more games constituting a round. □ **keep one's legs** not fall. **leg it** *colloq.* walk or run fast. **not have a leg to stand on** be unable to support one's argument by facts or sound reasons. **on one's last legs** near death or the end of one's usefulness etc. [from Old Norse *leggr*] □ **legged** *adj.* (also in comb.).

legacy *n.* (*pl.* **-ies**) **1** a gift left in a will. **2** something handed down by a predecessor (*legacy of corruption*). [based on Latin *legare* 'to bequeath']

legal *adj.* **1** of or based on law; concerned with law; falling within the province of law. **2** appointed or required by law. **3** permitted by law, lawful. [from Latin *legalis*] □ **legally** *adv.*

legal aid *n.* *Brit.* state assistance for legal advice or action.

legalese *n.* *colloq.* the technical language of legal documents.

legalism *n.* excessive adherence to law or formula. □ **legalist** *n.* & *adj.* **legalistic** *adj.* **legalistically** *adv.*

legality *n.* (*pl.* **-ies**) **1** lawfulness. **2** (in *pl.*) obligations imposed by law.

legalize *v.tr.* (also **-ise**) **1** make lawful. **2** bring into harmony with the law. □ **legalization** *n.*

legal proceedings see PROCEEDING 2.

legal separation see SEPARATION 2.

legal tender *n.* currency that cannot legally be refused in payment of a debt.

legate *n.* **1** a member of the clergy representing the Pope. **2** *Rom.Hist.* **a** a deputy of a general. **b** a governor or deputy governor of a province. [from Latin *legatus* 'delegated'] □ **legateship** *n.* **legatine** *adj.*

legatee *n.* the recipient of a legacy.

legation *n.* **1** a body of deputies. **2 a** the office and staff of a diplomatic minister. **b** the official residence of a diplomatic minister.

legato /li-gah-toh/ *Mus.* ● *adv.* & *adj.* in a smooth flowing manner (cf. STACCATO). ● *n.* (*pl.* **-os**) **1** a legato style of performance. **2** a legato passage. [Italian, literally 'bound']

legator *n.* the giver of a legacy.

leg before (in full **leg before wicket**) *Cricket* ● *adj.* & *adv.* (of a batsman) out because of illegally obstructing the ball with a part of the body. ● *n.* such a dismissal.

leg-break *n.* *Cricket* **1** a ball which deviates from the leg side after bouncing. **2** such deviation.

leg-bye *n.* a run scored from a ball that touches the batsman.

legend *n.* **1 a** a traditional story sometimes popularly regarded as historical but unauthenticated; a myth. **b** such stories collectively. **c** a popular but unfounded belief. **d** *colloq.* a person about whom unauthenticated tales are told; a famous or notorious person. **2 a** an inscription, esp. on a coin or medal. **b** *Printing* a caption. **c** wording on a map etc. explaining the symbols used. [from medieval Latin *legenda* 'what is to be read']

legendary *adj.* **1** of or connected with legends. **2** described in or based on a legend. **3** *colloq.* remarkable. □ **legendarily** *adv.*

legerdemain /lej-er-dĕ-mayn/ *n.* **1** sleight of hand. **2** trickery, sophistry. [from French *léger de main* 'light of hand']

leger line /lej-er/ *n.* *Mus.* ▼ a short line added for notes above or below the range of a staff. [leger: variant of LEDGER]

leger line

LEGER LINES BELOW A MUSICAL STAFF

legging *n.* (usu. in *pl.*) **1** close-fitting stretch trousers for women or children. **2** a stout protective outer covering for the leg from the knee to the ankle.

leggy *adj.* (**leggier**, **leggiest**) **1** long-legged. **2** long-stemmed. □ **legginess** *n.*

legible *adj.* (of handwriting, print, etc.) clear enough to read; readable. [from Late Latin *legibilis*] □ **legibility** *n.* **legibly** *adv.*

legion ● *n.* **1** a division of 3,000–6,000 men in the ancient Roman army. **2** a large organized body. ● *predic.adj.* great in number (*his good works were legion*). [from Latin *legio*] □ **legioned** *adj. poet.*

legionary ● *adj.* of a legion or legions. ● *n.* (*pl.* **-ies**) ▶ a member of a legion.

legionnaire *n.* **1** a member of a foreign legion. **2** a member of the American Legion or the Royal British Legion (associations for ex-service people).

legionnaires' disease *n.* a form of bacterial pneumonia spread esp. through air-conditioning systems etc.

leg-iron *n.* ◀ a shackle or fetter for the leg.

legislate *v.intr.* **1** make laws. **2** (foll. by *for*) make provision by law.

legislation *n.* **1** the process of making laws. **2** laws collectively. [from Late Latin *legis latio*, literally 'bringing of a law']

legislative *adj.* of or empowered to make laws. □ **legislatively** *adv.*

legislator *n.* **1** a member of a legislative body. **2** a lawgiver.

legislature *n.* the legislative body of a state.

legit *adj. colloq.* legitimate.

legitimate ● *adj.* **1** born of parents lawfully married to each other. **2** lawful, proper, regular. **3** logically admissible. ● *v.tr.* **1** make legitimate by decree, enactment, or proof. **2** justify. [from Latin *legitimus* 'lawful'] □ **legitimacy** *n.* **legitimately** *adv.* **legitimation** *n.*

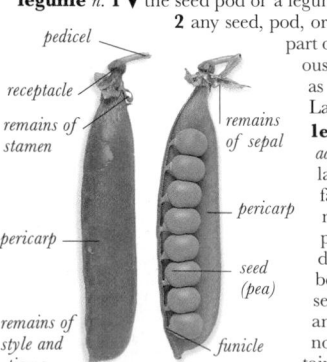

LEG-IRON

legitimatize *v.tr.* (also **-ise**) legitimize. □ **legitimatization** *n.*

legitimize *v.tr.* (also **-ise**) **1** make legitimate. **2** serve as a justification for. □ **legitimization** *n.*

legless *adj.* **1** having no legs. **2** *Brit. slang* drunk, esp. too drunk to stand.

Lego *n. propr.* a construction toy consisting of interlocking plastic building blocks. [from Danish *leg godt* 'play well']

leg-of-mutton sail *n.* a triangular mainsail.

leg-of-mutton sleeve *n.* a sleeve which is full and loose on the upper arm but close-fitting on the forearm.

leg-pull *n. colloq.* a hoax. □ **leg-pulling** *n.*

legroom *n.* space for the legs of a seated person.

leg side see LEG *n.* 5.

legume *n.* **1** ▼ the seed pod of a leguminous plant. **2** any seed, pod, or other edible part of a leguminous plant used as food. [from Latin *legumen*]

leguminous *adj.* of or relating to the family Leguminosae of plants, including peas and beans, having seeds in pods and usu. root nodules containing symbiotic bacteria.

LEGUME: PEA POD
(*Pisum sativum*)

pedicel
receptacle
remains of stamen
pericarp
remains of style and stigma
remains of sepal
pericarp
seed (pea)
funicle

LEGIONARY

Legionaries were Roman citizens who served as foot soldiers in the ancient Roman army. They enlisted voluntarily to serve in the legions for 20–25 years and their rigorous training made them the backbone of the army. Their distinctive uniform included the belt (*cingulum*), which was the legionary's badge of office, a segmented cuirass (*lorica segmentata*), a tunic, and a helmet (*cassis*). The *cingulum* consisted of decorated leather strips and gave protection to the groin in battle. Strong, well-ventilated military sandals (*caligae*) were patterned with iron hobnails, and were essential for long marches.

LEGIONARY'S UNIFORM

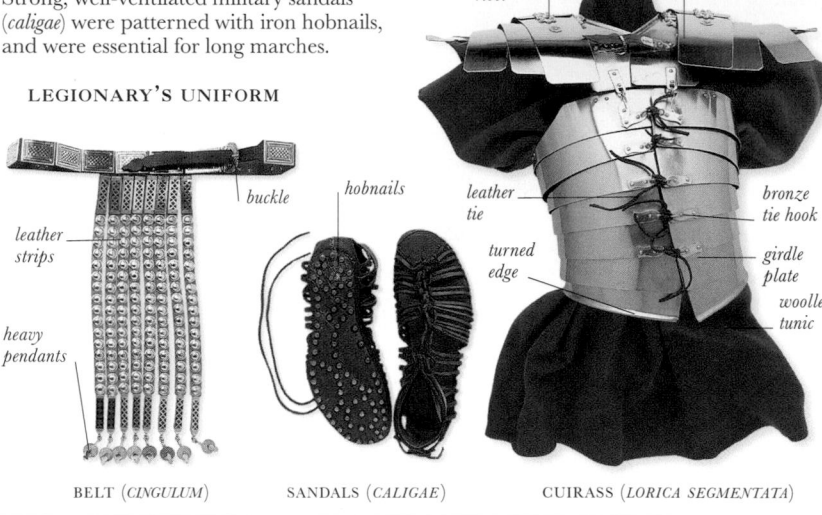

plume holder
brow guard
HELMET (*CASSIS*)
neck guard
boss
cheek guard
embossed rivet
shoulder plate
buckle
hobnails
leather tie
bronze tie hook
leather strips
turned edge
girdle plate
heavy pendants
woollen tunic

BELT (*CINGULUM*)   SANDALS (*CALIGAE*)   CUIRASS (*LORICA SEGMENTATA*)

mount a horse etc. **2** help to overcome a difficulty; a boost.

leg warmer *n.* either of a pair of tubular knitted garments covering the leg from ankle to thigh.

legwork *n.* work which involves a lot of walking, travelling, or physical activity.

lei /lay/ *n.* a Polynesian garland of flowers. [Hawaiian]

Leicester /less-ter/ *n.* (in full **Red Leicester**) a kind of mild firm cheese, usu. orange-coloured and originally made in Leicestershire.

leisure *n.* **1** free time; time at one's own disposal. **2** enjoyment of free time. □ **at leisure 1** not occupied. **2** in an unhurried manner. **at one's leisure** when one has time. [based on Latin *licēre* 'to be allowed']

leisure centre *n.* a large public building with sports facilities, bars, etc.

leisured *adj.* having ample leisure.

leisurely ● *adj.* having leisure; acting or done at leisure; unhurried, relaxed. ● *adv.* without hurry. □ **leisureliness** *n.*

leisurewear *n.* informal clothes, especially tracksuits and other sportswear.

leitmotif /lyt-moh-teef/ *n.* (also **leitmotiv**) a recurrent theme associated throughout a musical, literary, etc. composition with a particular person, idea, or situation. [from German *Leitmotiv* 'leading motif']

lemming *n.* **1** any small vole-like Arctic rodent of the genus *Lemmus* and related genera, including *L. lemmus* of Norway which is noted for mass migrations during which it attempts to cross large bodies of water. **2** a person who unthinkingly joins a mass movement, esp. a headlong rush to destruction. [Norwegian]

lemon ● *n.* **1 a** a pale yellow thick-skinned oval citrus fruit with acidic juice. ▷ BERRY. **b** (in full **lemon tree**) a tree of the species *Citrus limon* which produces this fruit. **2** a pale yellow colour. **3** *colloq.* a person or thing regarded as feeble or unsatisfactory or disappointing. ● *adj.* of or resembling the colour, flavour, or fragrance of a lemon. [from Arabic *līma*] □ **lemony** *adj.*

lemonade *n.* **1** an effervescent or still drink made from lemon juice. **2** *Brit.* a synthetic substitute for this.

lemon balm *n.* ▶ a bushy plant, *Melissa officinalis*, with leaves smelling and tasting of lemon.

lemon curd *n.* (also *Brit.* **lemon cheese**) a conserve made from lemons, butter, eggs, and sugar, with the consistency of cream cheese.

LEMON BALM:
GOLDEN LEMON BALM
(*Melissa officinalis* 'Aurea')

lemon drop *n.* a boiled sweet flavoured with lemon.

lemon geranium *n.* a lemon-scented pelargonium, *Pelargonium crispum*.

lemon grass *n.* any fragrant tropical grass of the genus *Cymbopogon*, yielding an oil smelling of lemon.

lemon plant *n.* = LEMON VERBENA.

lemon sole *n.* ▶ a flatfish, *Microstomus kitt*, of the plaice family. [from French *limande*]

lemon squash *n. Brit.* a soft drink made from lemons, sugar, and other ingredients, often sold in concentrated form.

LEMON SOLE
(*Microstomus kitt*)

leg-up *n.* **1** help to

L

LENS

Camera lenses can be divided into three broad groups: wide-angle, standard, and long-focus. Extreme wide-angle lenses of focal length 6–8 mm, known as fish-eyes, give a very distorted image, with vertical and horizontal lines bowed. A standard lens of 50 mm often has a wide maximum aperture. Its angle of view is similar to that of the human eye. Long-focus lenses of 80–1200 mm are useful for large images of distant subjects or when it is not possible to move close enough to use a shorter lens. The illustration and sequence of photographs below, which are all taken from the same viewpoint, show that, as the focal length of a lens increases, so the angle of view decreases.

STANDARD 50 MM CAMERA LENS

depth of field scale

lens mount

aperture ring

lens

focusing ring

FOCAL LENGTH AND ANGLE OF VIEW OF DIFFERENT CAMERA LENSES

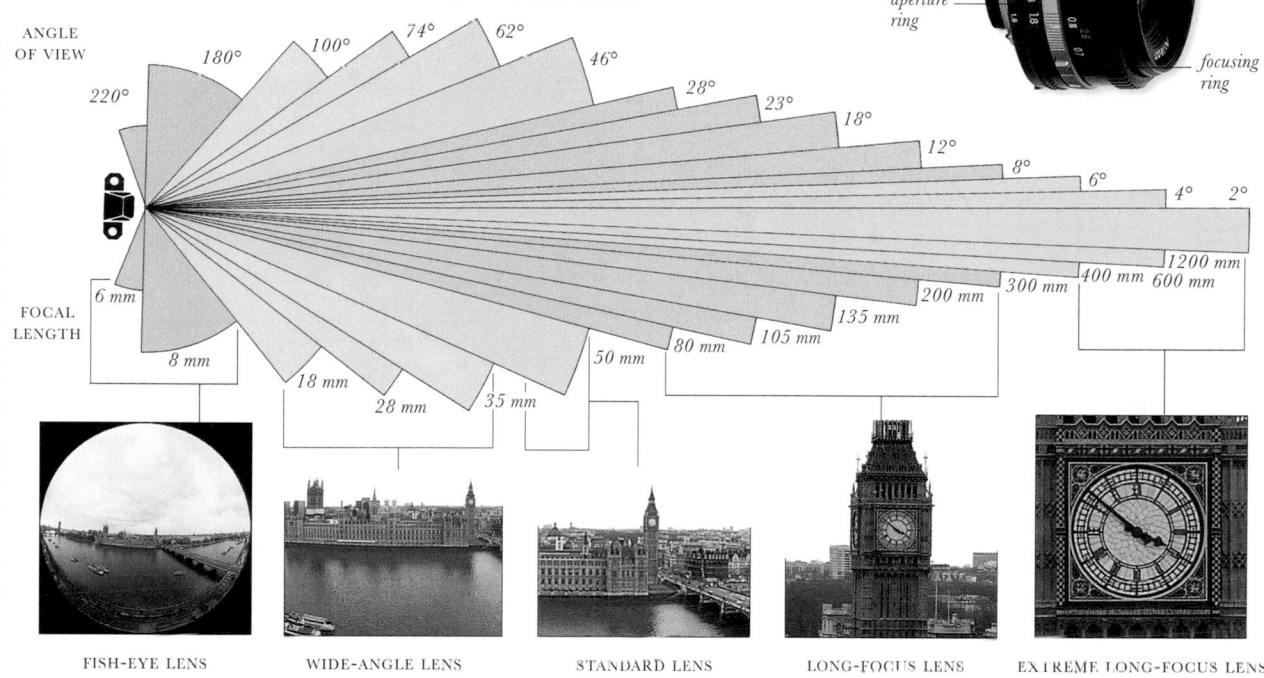

ANGLE OF VIEW

220° 180° 100° 74° 62° 46° 28° 23° 18° 12° 8° 6° 4° 2°

FOCAL LENGTH

6 mm 8 mm 18 mm 28 mm 35 mm 50 mm 80 mm 105 mm 135 mm 200 mm 300 mm 400 mm 600 mm 1200 mm

FISH-EYE LENS   WIDE-ANGLE LENS   STANDARD LENS   LONG-FOCUS LENS   EXTREME LONG-FOCUS LENS

---

lemon verbena n. a shrub, *Aloysia triphylla*, with lemon-scented leaves.

lemur /lee-mer/ n. ▼ any arboreal primate of the family Lemuridae native to Madagascar, with a pointed snout and long tail. [from Latin *lemures* 'spirits of the dead', from its spectre-like face]

lend v.tr. (*past* and *past part.* **lent**) **1** (usu. foll. by *to*) grant (to a person) the use of (a thing) on the understanding that it or its equivalent shall be returned. **2** allow the use of (money) at interest. **3** bestow or contribute (something temporary) (*lend assistance*; *lends a certain charm*). □ **lend an ear** listen. **lend a hand** = *give a hand* (see HAND). **lend itself to** be suitable for. [Old English] □ **lendable** adj. **lender** n. **lending** n.

lending library n. a library from which books may be borrowed.

length n. **1** measurement or extent from end to end. **2** extent in, of, or with regard to, time (*a stay of some length*; *the length of a speech*). **3 a** the distance a thing extends (*at arm's length*). **b** (in *comb.*) indicating a spec-

LEMUR: RING-TAILED LEMUR (*Lemur catta*)

ified limit of extent of a thing (*calf-length*; *book-length*). **c** the vertical extent of a garment when worn. **4** the length of a swimming pool as a measure of the distance swum. **5** the length of a horse, boat, etc., as a measure of the lead in a race. **6** a long stretch or extent (*a length of hair*). **7** a degree of thoroughness in action (*went to great lengths*). **8** a piece of material of a certain length (*a length of cloth*). **9** *Prosody* the quantity of a vowel or syllable. **10** *Cricket* **a** the distance from the batsman at which the ball pitches (*the bowler keeps a good length*). **b** the proper amount of this. □ **at length 1** (also **at great** etc. **length**) in detail. **2** after a long time, at last. [Old English]

lengthen v.tr. & intr. make or become longer. □ **lengthener** n.

lengthways adv. in a direction parallel with a thing's length.

lengthwise ● adv. lengthways. ● adj. lying or moving lengthways.

lengthy adj. (**lengthier**, **lengthiest**) of unusual or tedious length. □ **lengthily** adv. **lengthiness** n.

lenient adj. **1** merciful, tolerant. **2** (of punishment etc.) mild. [from Latin *lenient-* 'soothing'] □ **lenience** n. **leniency** n. **leniently** adv.

lenity n. (*pl.* **-ies**) *literary* **1** mercifulness. **2** an act of mercy. [based on Latin *lenis* 'gentle']

lens n. **1** a piece of a transparent substance with one or (usu.) both sides curved for concentrating or dispersing light rays esp. in optical instruments. ▷ EYE, TELESCOPE. **2** ▲ a combination of lenses used in photography. **3** = CONTACT LENS. [from Latin *lens lentis* 'lentil', from the similarity of shape] □ **lensed** adj. **lensless** adj.

lensman n. (*pl.* **-men**) = CAMERAMAN.

Lent n. *Eccl.* the period from Ash Wednesday to Holy Saturday, devoted to fasting and penitence in commemoration of Christ's fasting in the wilderness. [Middle English] □ **Lenten** adj.

lent past and past part. of LEND.

Lenten fare n. food without meat.

lenticular adj. **1** shaped like a lentil or a biconvex lens. **2** of the lens of the eye.

lentil n. **1** a leguminous plant, *Lens culinaris*, yielding edible biconvex seeds. **2** this seed, esp. used as food with the husk removed. ▷ PULSE. [from Latin *lenticula* 'little lentil']

Lent lily n. *Brit.* a daffodil, esp. a wild one.

lento *Mus.* ● adj. slow. ● adv. slowly. [Italian]

lentoid adj. = LENTICULAR 1.

Leo n. (*pl.* **-os**) **1** *Astron.* ▼ a large constellation (the Lion), said to represent the lion slain by Hercules. **2** *Astrol.* **a** the fifth sign of the zodiac, which the Sun enters about 21 July. ▷ ZODIAC. **b** a person born when the Sun is in this sign. [Latin, literally 'lion']

LEO: FIGURE OF A LION FORMED FROM THE STARS OF LEO

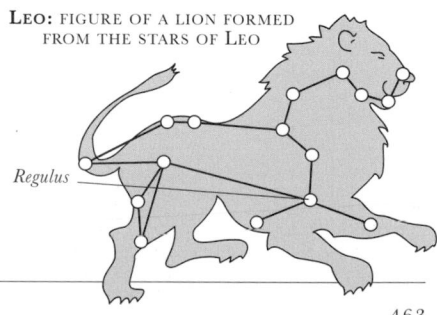

Regulus

leonine *adj.* **1** like a lion. **2** of or relating to lions. [from Latin *leoninus*]

leopard /lep-erd/ *n.* (*fem.* **leopardess**) **1** ▼ a large African or Asian feline mammal, *Panthera pardus*, with either a black-spotted yellowish-fawn or all-black coat; also called PANTHER. **2** *Heraldry* a lion passant guardant as in the arms of England. **3** (*attrib.*) spotted like a leopard (*leopard moth*). [from late Greek *leopardos*]

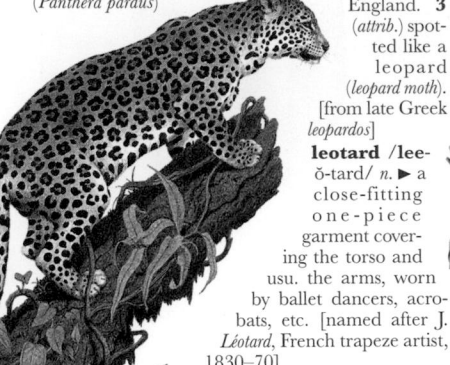

LEOPARD
(*Panthera pardus*)

leotard /lee-ŏ-tard/ *n.* ▶ a close-fitting one-piece garment covering the torso and usu. the arms, worn by ballet dancers, acrobats, etc. [named after J. *Léotard*, French trapeze artist, 1830–70]

leper *n.* **1** a person suffering from leprosy. **2** a person who is shunned for moral or social reasons. [Middle English]

lepidopterous *adj.* of the insect order Lepidoptera, comprising butterflies and moths, with four scale-covered wings. [based on Greek *lepis -idos* 'scale' + *pteron* 'wing'] □ **lepidopteran** *adj. & n.* **lepidopterist** *n.*

leprechaun *n.* a small mischievous sprite in Irish folklore. [from Old Irish *luchorpán*, from *lu* 'small' + *corp* 'body']

leprosarium *n.* a hospital for people with leprosy.

leprosy *n.* **1** a contagious bacterial disease that affects the skin, mucous membranes, and nerves, causing disfigurement. **2** moral corruption or contagion. □ **leprous** *adj.*

lesbian ● *n.* a homosexual woman. ● *adj.* **1** of homosexuality in women. **2** (**Lesbian**) of Lesbos. [based on Greek *Lesbos*, Aegean island and home of the poetess Sappho, from her alleged homosexuality] □ **lesbianism** *n.*

■ **Usage** See Usage Note at GAY.

lese-majesty /leez/ *n.* (also **lèse-majesté**) **1** treason. **2** an insult to a sovereign or ruler. **3** presumptuous conduct. [from Latin *laesa majestas* 'injured sovereignty']

lesion *n.* **1** damage. **2** injury. **3** *Med.* a morbid change in the functioning or texture of an organ etc. [from Latin *laesio*]

less ● *det.* **1** smaller in extent, quantity, degree, or duration (opp. MORE) (*of less importance*; *he eats less red meat than before*). **2** *disp.* fewer in number (*eat less biscuits*). ● *adv.* to a smaller extent, in a lower degree (*uses it less*; *goes less frequently than she did*; *a less popular book*). ● *pron.* **1** a smaller amount or quantity (*cannot take less*; *for less than £10*). **2** *disp.* fewer (*I don't have many friends, but he has even less*). ● *prep.* minus (*made £1,000 less tax*). □ **in less than no time** *joc.* very quickly or soon. **less and less** to an extent that is becoming continuously smaller. **much** (or **still**) **less** with even greater force of denial (*do not suspect him of negligence, much less of dishonesty*). [Old English]

■ **Usage** The use of *less* as a determiner with countable nouns, as in sense 2, or as a pronoun in sense 2, is regarded as incorrect in formal English, although it is frequent in informal usage. Strictly, *fewer* should be used instead.

-less *suffix* forming adjectives and adverbs: **1** from nouns, meaning 'not having, without, free from' (*doubtless*; *powerless*). **2** from verbs, meaning 'not affected by or doing the action of the verb' (*fathom-less*; *tireless*). □ **-lessly** *suffix* forming adverbs. **-lessness** *suffix* forming nouns.

lessee *n.* (often foll. by *of*) a person who holds a property by lease. [from Old French *lessé* 'leased']

lessen *v.tr. & intr.* make or become less, diminish.

lesser *adj.* (usu. *attrib.*) not so great as the other or the rest (*the lesser evil*; *the lesser celandine*).

lesson *n.* **1 a** an amount of teaching given at one time. **b** the time assigned to this. **2** (in *pl.*; foll. by *in*) systematic instruction (*gives lessons in dancing*). **3** a thing learnt or to be learnt by a pupil; an assignment. **4 a** an occurrence, example, rebuke, or punishment, that serves or should serve to warn or encourage (*let that be a lesson to you*). **b** a thing inculcated by experience or study. **5** a passage from the Bible read aloud during a church service. □ **learn one's lesson** profit from or bear in mind a particular (usu. unpleasant) experience. **teach a person a lesson** punish a person, esp. as a deterrent. [from Latin *lectio*]

lessor *n.* a person who lets a property by lease. [from Anglo-French]

lest *conj.* **1** in order that not, for fear that (*lest he forget*). **2** that (*afraid lest we should be late*). [Old English *thȳ lǣs* 'whereby less that']

■ **Usage** *Lest* is followed by the subjunctive or *should* (see examples above).

let[1] ● *v.tr.* (**letting**; *past* and *past part.* **let**) **1 a** allow to, not prevent or forbid (*we let them go*). **b** cause to (*let me know*; *let it be known*). **2** (foll. by *into*) **a** allow to enter. **b** make acquainted with (a secret etc.). **c** inlay in. **3** grant the use of (rooms, land, etc.) for rent or hire (*was let to the new tenant for a year*). **4** allow or cause (liquid or air) to escape (*let blood*). **5** award (a contract for work). ● *v.aux.* supplying the first and third persons of the imperative in exhortations (*let us pray*), commands (*let it be done at once*; *let there be light*), assumptions (*let AB be equal to CD*), and permission or challenge (*let him do his worst*). ● *n. Brit.* the act or an instance of letting a house, room, etc. (*a long let*). □ **let alone 1** not to mention, far less or more (*hasn't got a television, let alone a video*). **2** = *let be.* **let be** not interfere with, attend to, or do. **let down 1** lower. **2** fail to support or satisfy, disappoint. **3** lengthen (a garment). **4** *Brit.* deflate (a tyre). **let down gently** avoid humiliating abruptly. **let drop** (or **fall**) drop (esp. a word or hint) intentionally or by accident. **let fly 1** (often foll. by *at*) attack physically or verbally. **2** discharge (a missile). **let go 1** release. **2 a** (often foll. by *of*) lose or relinquish one's hold. **b** lose hold of. **3** cease to think or talk about. **let oneself go 1** give way to enthusiasm, impulse, etc. **2** neglect one's appearance or habits. **let in 1** allow to enter (*let the dog in*; *let in a flood of light*; *this would let in all sorts of evils*). **2** (usu. foll. by *for*) involve (a person, often oneself) in loss or difficulty. **3** (foll. by *on*) allow (a person) to share privileges, information, etc. **4** inlay (a thing) in another. **let oneself in** enter a building by means of a latchkey. **let loose 1** release from captivity or restraint. **2** (also foll. by *with*) emit abruptly (a scream, tirade, etc.). **let me see** see SEE[1]. **let off 1 a** fire (a gun). **b** explode (a bomb or firework). **2** allow or cause (steam, liquid, etc.) to escape. **3** allow to alight from a vehicle etc. **4 a** not punish or compel. **b** (foll. by *with*) punish lightly. **5** *Brit.* let (part of a house etc.). **let off steam** see STEAM. **let on** *colloq.* **1** reveal a secret. **2** pretend (*let on that he had succeeded*). **let out 1** allow to go out. **2** release from restraint. **3** reveal (a secret etc.). **4** make (a garment) looser. **5** put out to rent or to contract. **6** exculpate. **let rip** see RIP[1]. **let slip** see SLIP[1]. **let through** allow to pass. **let up** *colloq.* **1** become less intense or severe. **2** relax one's efforts. **to let** available for rent. [Old English]

let[2] ● *n.* **1** (in tennis, squash, etc.) an obstruction of a ball or a player, requiring the ball to be served again. **2** *archaic* (except in **without let or hindrance**) obstruction, hindrance. ● *v.tr.* (**letting**; *past* and *past part.* **letted** or **let**) *archaic* hinder, obstruct. [Old English]

-let *suffix* forming nouns, usu. diminutives (*flatlet*; *leaflet*) or denoting articles of ornament or dress (*anklet*).

let-down *n.* **1** a disappointment. **2** the release of milk from a mammary gland, esp. a cow's udder.

lethal *adj.* causing or sufficient to cause death. [based on Latin *letum* 'death'] □ **lethality** *n.* **lethally** *adv.*

lethargy *n.* **1** lack of energy. **2** *Med.* morbid drowsiness. [from Greek *lēthargia*] □ **lethargic** *adj.* **lethargically** *adv.*

let-off *n.* being allowed to escape something.

let-out *n. Brit. colloq.* an opportunity to escape from an awkward situation etc.

let's *contr.* let us (*let's go now*).

letter ● *n.* **1 a** a character representing one or more of the simple or compound sounds used in speech; any of the alphabetic symbols. **b** (in *pl.*) *Brit. colloq.* the initials of a degree etc. after the holder's name. **2 a** a written, typed, or printed communication, usu. sent by post or messenger. **b** (in *pl.*) an addressed legal or formal document for any of various purposes. **3** the precise terms of a statement, the strict verbal interpretation (*according to the letter of the law*). **4** (in *pl.*) **a** literature. **b** acquaintance with books, erudition. **c** authorship (*the profession of letters*). ● *v.tr.* **1 a** inscribe letters on. **b** impress a title etc. on (a book cover). **2** classify with letters. □ **to the letter** with adherence to every detail. [from Latin *littera* 'letter of alphabet', (in *pl.*) 'epistle, literature']

letter bomb *n.* a terrorist explosive device in the form of a postal packet.

letter box *n.* esp. *Brit.* a box or slot into which letters are posted or delivered. ▷ DOOR

letter-carrier *n. N. Amer.* a postman or postwoman.

lettered *adj.* well read or educated.

letterhead *n.* **1** a printed heading on stationery. **2** stationery with this.

letter-heading *n.* = LETTERHEAD 1.

lettering *n.* **1** the process of inscribing letters. **2** letters inscribed.

letter of comfort *n.* an assurance about a debt, short of a legal guarantee, given to a bank by a third party.

letter of credit *n.* a letter from a banker authorizing a person to draw money up to a specified amount, usu. from another bank.

letterpress *n.* **1** *Brit.* **a** the contents of an illustrated book other than the illustrations. **b** printed matter relating to illustrations. **2** ▼ printing from raised type.

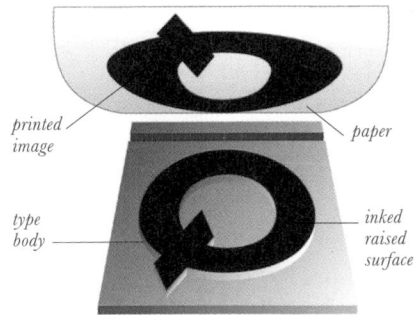

printed image   *paper*

type body   *inked raised surface*

LETTERPRESS

letters of administration *n.pl.* authority to administer the estate of an intestate.

lettuce *n.* **1** a plant of the daisy family, *Lactuca sativa*, with crisp edible leaves used esp. in salads. ▷ VEGETABLE. **2** any of various plants resembling this.

[based on Latin *lac lactis* 'milk', with reference to its milky juice]

let-up *n. colloq.* **1** a reduction in intensity. **2** a relaxation of effort.

leuco- /**loo**-koh/ *comb. form* white. [from Greek *leukos* 'white']

leucocyte /**loo**-kŏ-syt/ *n.* (also **leukocyte**) a colourless cell of blood, lymph, etc., important in fighting disease.

leucotomy /loo-**kot**-ŏ-mi/ *n.* (*pl.* **-ies**) the surgical cutting of white nerve fibres within the brain.

leukaemia /loo-**kee**-miă/ *n.* (*US* **leukemia**) *Med.* any of a group of malignant diseases in which the bone marrow and other blood-forming organs produce increased numbers of leucocytes. [based on Greek *leukos* 'white' + *haima* 'blood'] □ **leukaemic** *adj.*

leukocyte var. of LEUCOCYTE.

Levant *n.* (prec. by *the*) *archaic* the eastern part of the Mediterranean with its islands and neighbouring countries. [French, literally 'rising, point of sunrise']

levant *v.intr. Brit. slang* abscond, esp. with gaming losses unpaid.

Levantine ● *adj.* of or trading to the Levant. ● *n.* a native or inhabitant of the Levant.

levee[1] *n.* **1** *archaic* or *N. Amer.* an assembly of visitors or guests, esp. at a formal reception. **2** *hist.* (in the UK) an assembly held by the sovereign or sovereign's representative at which men only were received. **3** *hist.* a reception of visitors on rising from bed. [from French *levé*, variant of *lever* (n.) 'rising']

levee[2] *n. US* **1** an embankment against river floods. **2** ▼ a natural embankment built up by a river. **3** a landing place. [from French *levée*, literally 'raised']

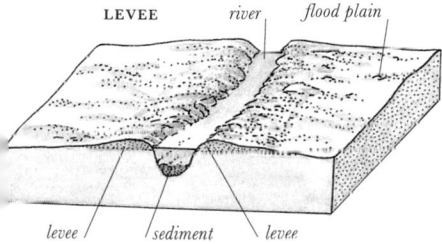

LEVEE   *river*   *flood plain*

levee   *sediment*   *levee*

level ● *n.* **1** a horizontal line or plane. **2** a height or value reached, a position on a scale (*sugar level in the blood; danger level*). **3** a social, moral, or intellectual standard. **4** a plane of rank or authority (*discussions at Cabinet level*). **5** an instrument giving a line parallel to the plane of the horizon. **6** a level surface. **7** a flat tract of land. ● *adj.* **1** flat and even; not bumpy. **2** horizontal. **3** (often foll. by *with*) **a** on the same horizontal plane as something else. **b** having equality with something else. **c** (of a spoonful etc.) with the contents flat with the brim. **4** even, uniform, equable, or well-balanced in quality, style, temper, judgement, etc. **5** esp. *Brit.* (of a race) having the leading competitors close together. ● *v.* (**levelled, levelling**; *US* **leveled, leveling**) **1** *tr.* make level, even, or uniform. **2** *tr.* (foll. by *to* (or *with*) the ground) raze or demolish. **3** *tr.* (also *absol.*) aim (a missile or gun). **4** *tr.* (also *absol.*; foll. by *at, against*) direct (an accusation, criticism, or satire). **5** *tr.* abolish (distinctions). **6** *intr.* (usu. foll. by *with*) *slang* be frank or honest. **7** *tr.* place on the same level. □ **do one's level best** *colloq.* do one's utmost. **find its level** (or **find its own level**) **1** (of a liquid) reach the same height in containers etc. which communicate with each other. **2** reach a stable level, value, position, etc. with respect to something else (*the pound found its level against the dollar*). **level down** *Brit.* bring down to a standard. **level off** make or become level. **level out** make or become level, remove differences from. **level up** *Brit.* bring up to a standard. **on the level** *colloq. adv.* honestly, without deception. ● *adj.*

LEVER

Levers multiply effort to give mechanical advantage. There are three classes of lever, each with a different arrangement of load, effort, and fulcrum. The force on the load is multiplied by the ratio of the distances of effort and load from the fulcrum. A class 1 lever has the fulcrum between load and effort. A class 2 lever has the load between fulcrum and the effort. A class 3 lever has the effort applied between load and fulcrum; it reduces the force on the load while increasing the distance it moves.

CLASSES OF LEVER

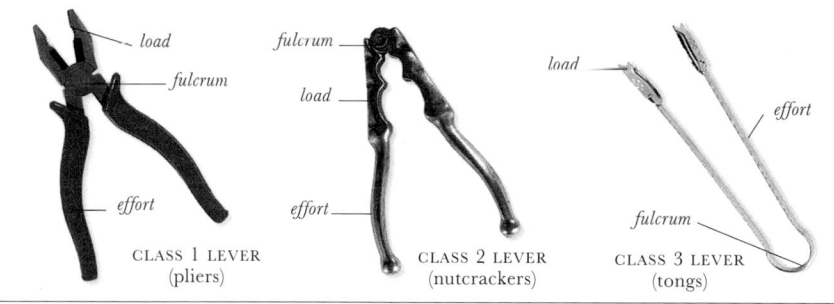

load   *fulcrum*   *fulcrum*   *load*   *effort*

load   *effort*   *effort*   *fulcrum*

CLASS 1 LEVER (pliers)   CLASS 2 LEVER (nutcrackers)   CLASS 3 LEVER (tongs)

---

honest, truthful. **on a level with 1** in the same horizontal plane as. **2** equal with. [from Latin *libella* 'little balance'] □ **levelly** *adv.* **levelness** *n.*

level crossing *n. Brit.* a crossing of a railway and a road, or two railways, at the same level.

level-headed *adj.* mentally well-balanced, sensible. □ **level-headedly** *adv.* **level-headedness** *n.*

leveller *n.* (*US* **leveler**) **1** a person who advocates the abolition of social distinctions. **2** a person or thing that levels.

level pegging *n. Brit.* equality of scores or achievements.

lever ● *n.* **1** a bar resting on a pivot, used to help lift a heavy or firmly fixed object. **2** *Mech.* ▲ a rigid bar pivoted about a fulcrum (fixed point) which can be acted upon by a force (effort) in order to move a load. **3** a projecting handle moved to operate a mechanism. **4** a means of exerting moral pressure. ● *v.* **1** *intr.* use a lever. **2** *tr.* lift, move, or act on with a lever. [from Old French *levier*]

leverage *n.* **1** the action of a lever; a way of applying a lever. **2** the power of a lever; the mechanical advantage gained by use of a lever. **3** a means of accomplishing a purpose; power, influence. **4** *US Commerce* = GEARING 2.

leveraged buyout *n.* the buyout of a company by its management using outside capital.

leveret /**lev**-er-it/ *n.* a young hare, esp. one in its first year. [from Anglo-French, literally 'little hare']

leviable see LEVY.

leviathan *n.* **1** *Bibl.* a sea monster. **2** anything very large or powerful. [from Hebrew *liwyāṯān*]

Levis *n.pl.* (also **Levi's** *propr.*) a type of denim jeans or overalls reinforced with rivets. [named after *Levi Strauss*, original US manufacturer]

levitate *v.* **1** *intr.* rise and float in the air (esp. with reference to spiritualism). **2** *tr.* cause to do this. [based on Latin *levis* 'light'] □ **levitation** *n.*

levity *n.* **1** lack of serious thought; frivolity. **2** inconstancy. **3** undignified behaviour. [from Latin *levitas*]

levulose *US* var. of LAEVULOSE.

levy ● *v.tr.* (**-ies, -ied**) **1 a** impose (a rate or toll). **b** raise (contributions or taxes). **c** (also *absol.*) raise a sum of money) by legal execution or process (*the debt was levied on the debtor's goods*). **d** seize (goods) in this way. **e** extort (*levy blackmail*). **2** enrol (troops etc.). **3** (usu. foll. by *upon, against*) wage (war). ● *n.* (*pl.* **-ies**) **1 a** the collecting of a contribution, tax, etc., or of property to satisfy a legal judgement. **b** a contribution, tax, etc., levied. **2 a** the act or an instance of enrolling troops etc. **b** (in *pl.*) troops enrolled. **c** a body of troops enrolled. **d** the number of troops enrolled. [from Latin *levare* 'to raise'] □ **leviable** *adj.*

---

lewd *adj.* **1** lascivious. **2** indecent, obscene. [Old English] □ **lewdly** *adv.* **lewdness** *n.*

lexical *adj.* **1** of the words of a language. **2** of or as of a lexicon. [from Greek *lexikos*] □ **lexically** *adv.*

lexicography *n.* the compiling of dictionaries. □ **lexicographer** *n.* **lexicographic** *adj.* **lexicographical** *adj.*

lexicology *n.* the study of the form, history, and meaning of words. □ **lexicological** *adj.* **lexicologist** *n.*

lexicon *n.* **1** a dictionary, esp. of Greek, Hebrew, Syriac, or Arabic. **2** the vocabulary of a person, language, branch of knowledge, etc. [from Greek *lexikon (biblion)* '(book) of words']

lexis *n.* **1** words, vocabulary. **2** the total stock of words in a language. [Greek]

ley[1] /lay/ *n.* a field temporarily under grass. [Middle English]

ley[2] /lay/ *n.* (in full **ley line**) a hypothetical straight line connecting prehistoric sites etc. [variant of LEA]

LF *abbr.* low frequency.

LH *abbr. Biochem.* luteinizing hormone.

l.h. *abbr.* left hand.

Li *symb. Chem.* the element lithium.

liability *n.* (*pl.* **-ies**) **1** the state of being liable. **2** a person or thing that is troublesome as an unwelcome responsibility; a handicap. **3** what a person is liable for, esp. (in *pl.*) debts.

liable *predic.adj.* **1** legally bound. **2** (foll. by *to*) subject to (a tax or penalty). **3** (foll. by *to* + infin.) under an obligation. **4** (foll. by *to*) exposed or open to (something undesirable). **5** (foll. by *to* + infin.) *disp.* apt, likely (*it is liable to rain*). **6** (foll. by *for*) answerable. [Middle English]

■ **Usage** The use of *liable* in sense 5, though common, is considered incorrect by some people.

liaise *v.intr.* (foll. by *with, between*) establish cooperation, act as a link. [back-formation from LIAISON]

liaison *n.* **1** communication or cooperation, esp. between military forces or units. **2** an illicit sexual relationship. [French]

liana *n.* (also **liane**) any of several climbing and twining plants of tropical forests. ▷ RAINFOREST. [from French *liane* 'clematis']

liar *n.* a person who tells a lie or lies.

lias *n.* **1** (**Lias**) *Geol.* the lower strata of the Jurassic system of rocks, consisting of shales and limestones rich in fossils. **2** a blue limestone rock found in SW England. [from Old French *lios* 'hard limestone'] □ **liassic** *adj.* (in sense 1).

Lib. *abbr.* Liberal.

lib *n. colloq.* (in names of political movements etc.) liberation (*women's lib*).

libation *n.* **1** the pouring out of a drink-offering to a god. **2** such a drink-offering. [from Latin *libatio*]

libber *n. colloq.* an advocate of women's liberation.

Lib Dem *n. Brit. colloq.* a Liberal Democrat.

libel ● *n.* **1** *Law* **a** a published false statement damaging to a person's reputation. **b** the act of publishing this. **2 a** a false and defamatory written statement. **b** (foll. by *on*) a thing that brings discredit by misrepresentation etc. (*the portrait is a libel on him*; *the book is a libel on human nature*). ● *v.tr.* (**libelled**, **libelling**; *US* **libeled**, **libeling**) **1** defame by libellous statements. **2** accuse falsely and maliciously. **3** *Law* publish a libel against. [originally in sense 'a formal document': from Latin *libellus* 'little book'] □ **libeller** *n.*

libellous *adj.* containing or constituting a libel. □ **libellously** *adv.*

liberal ● *adj.* **1** ample, abundant. **2** giving freely; generous. **3** open-minded. **4** not strict or rigorous; (of interpretation) not literal. **5** for general broadening of the mind, not professional or technical (*liberal studies*). **6 a** favouring individual liberty, free trade, and moderate political and social reform. **b** (**Liberal**) *Polit.* of or characteristic of Liberals or a Liberal Party. **7** *Theol.* regarding many traditional beliefs as dispensable, invalidated by modern thought, or liable to change (*liberal Protestant*; *liberal Judaism*). ● *n.* **1** a person of liberal views. **2** (**Liberal**) *Polit.* a supporter or member of a Liberal Party. [originally in sense 'befitting a free man': based on Latin *liber* 'free (man)'] □ **liberalism** *n.* **liberally** *adv.*

liberal arts *n.pl.* esp. *N. Amer.* the arts as distinct from science and technology.

Liberal Democrat *n.* (in the UK) a member of a party (formerly the *Social and Liberal Democrats*) formed from the Liberal Party and the Social Democratic Party.

liberality *n.* **1** free giving; munificence. **2** freedom from prejudice; breadth of mind.

liberalize *v.tr. & intr.* (also **-ise**) make or become more liberal or less strict. □ **liberalization** *n.*

Liberal Party *n.* **1** (in the UK) a political party advocating liberal policies (renamed in 1988 when it regrouped with others to form the Social and Liberal Democrats and known from 1989 as the Liberal Democrats). **2** a similar party elsewhere.

liberate *v.tr.* **1** set at liberty; set free. **2** free (a country etc.) from an oppressor or an enemy occupation. **3** (often as **liberated** *adj.*) free (a person) from rigid social conventions. **4** *slang* steal. **5** *Chem.* release (esp. a gas) from a state of combination. [based on Latin *liberatus* 'freed'] □ **liberator** *n.*

liberation *n.* the act or an instance of liberating; the state of being liberated. □ **liberationist** *n.*

liberation theology *n.* a theory which interprets liberation from social, political, and economic oppression as an anticipation of ultimate salvation.

libertarian *n.* an advocate of liberty. □ **libertarianism** *n.*

libertine ● *n.* a dissolute or licentious person. ● *adj.* licentious, dissolute. [from Latin *libertinus* 'freedman'] □ **libertinism** *n.*

liberty *n.* (*pl.* **-ies**) **1 a** freedom from captivity, imprisonment, slavery, or despotic control. **b** a personification of this. **2 a** the right or power to do as one pleases. **b** (foll. by *to* + infin.) right, power, opportunity, permission. **3** (usu. in *pl.*) a right, privilege, or immunity, enjoyed by prescription or grant. **4** setting aside of rules or convention. □ **at liberty 1** free, not imprisoned (*set at liberty*). **2** (foll. by *to* + infin.) entitled, permitted. **3** available, disengaged. **take liberties 1** (often foll. by *with*) behave in an unduly familiar manner. **2** (foll. by *with*) deal freely or superficially with rules or facts. **take the**

liberty (foll. by *to* + infin., or *of* + verbal noun) presume, venture. [from Latin *libertas*]

liberty bodice *n. Brit.* a close-fitting under-bodice with no stiffening.

liberty hall *n.* a place where one may do as one likes.

libidinous *adj.* lustful. [based on Latin *libido* 'lust']

libido /li-bee-doh/ *n.* (*pl.* **-os**) *Psychol.* psychic drive or energy, esp. that associated with sexual desire. [Latin] □ **libidinal** *adj.*

Lib-Lab *adj. Brit. hist.* Liberal and Labour.

Libra *n.* **1** *Astron.* ◀ a small constellation (the Scales or Balance), said to represent the pair of scales which is the symbol of justice. **2** *Astrol.* **a** the seventh sign of the zodiac, which the Sun enters at the northern autumnal equinox (about 22 Sept.). ▷ ZODIAC. **b** a person born when the Sun is in this sign. [originally in sense 'pound weight': Latin] □ **Libran** *n. & adj.*

LIBRA: FIGURE OF SCALES FORMED FROM THE STARS OF LIBRA

librarian *n.* a person in charge of, or an assistant in, a library. □ **librarianship** *n.*

library *n.* (*pl.* **-ies**) **1 a** a collection of books etc. for use by the public or by members of a group. **b** a person's collection of books. **2** a room or building containing a collection of books (for reading or reference rather than for sale). **3 a** a similar collection of films, records, computer routines, etc. **b** the place where these are kept. **4** a series of books issued by a publisher in similar bindings etc., usu. as a set.

library edition *n.* a strongly bound edition.

library science *n.* the study of librarianship.

libration *n.* an apparent oscillation of a celestial body, esp. the Moon, by which the parts near the edge of the disc are alternately in view and out of view. [from Latin *libratio*, based on *libra* 'balance']

libretto *n.* (*pl.* **libretti** or **-os**) the text of an opera. [Italian, literally 'little book'] □ **librettist** *n.*

Librium *n. propr.* a benzodiazepine drug used as a tranquillizer.

Libyan ● *adj.* **1** of or relating to modern Libya in N. Africa. **2** of ancient N. Africa west of Egypt. **3** of or relating to the Berber group of languages. ● *n.* **1 a** a native or national of modern Libya. **b** a person of Libyan descent. **2** an ancient language of the Berber group.

lice *pl.* of LOUSE.

licence *n.* (*US* **license**) **1** a permit from an authority to own or use something (esp. a dog, gun, television set, or vehicle), do something (esp. marry, print something, preach, or drive on a public road), or carry on a trade (esp. in alcoholic liquor). **2** permission (*have I your licence to remove the fence?*). **3 a** liberty of action, esp. when excessive; abuse of freedom. **b** licentiousness. **4** a writer's or artist's irregularity in grammar, metre, perspective, etc., or deviation from fact, esp. for effect (*poetic licence*). [based on Latin *licēre* 'to be lawful']

license *v.tr.* (also **licence**) **1** grant a licence to. **2** authorize the use of (premises) for a certain purpose, esp. the sale and consumption of alcoholic liquor. **3** authorize the publication of (a book etc.) or the performance of (a play). [Middle English] □ **licensable** *adj.* **licensor** *n.*

licensed victualler see VICTUALLER 2.

licensee *n.* the holder of a licence, esp. to sell alcoholic liquor.

license plate *n. US* the number plate of a licensed vehicle.

licentiate *n.* a holder of a certificate of competence to practise a certain profession, or of a university licence. [from medieval Latin *licentiatus* 'licensed']

licentious *adj.* **1** immoral, esp. in sexual relations. **2** *archaic* disregarding accepted rules or conventions. [from Latin *licentiosus*] □ **licentiously** *adv.* **licentiousness** *n.*

lichee var. of LYCHEE.

lichen /ly-kĕn/ *n.* ▼ any plant organism of the group Lichenes, composed of a fungus and an alga in symbiotic association growing on and colouring rocks, tree trunks, roofs, walls, etc. [from Greek *leikhēn*] □ **lichened** *adj.* **lichenology** *n.*

LICHEN

Lichens are symbiotic partnerships between algae and fungi: the algae live among the tiny threads formed by the fungus and supply it with food, which is produced by photosynthesis. Although they grow very slowly, lichens are extremely long-lived. They reproduce by means of spores or soredia (powdery vegetative fragments). Of the six forms of lichen, the three most common are foliose (leafy), crustose (flat and crusty), and fruticose (shrub-like). Some lichens, such as *Cladonia floerkeana*, are a combination of forms.

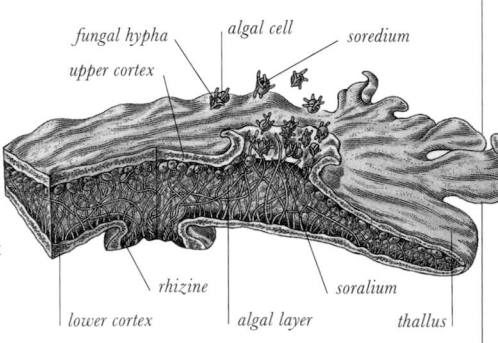

fungal hypha
algal cell
soredium
upper cortex
rhizine
soralium
lower cortex
algal layer
thallus

SECTION THROUGH FOLIOSE LICHEN

EXAMPLES OF LICHENS

CRUSTOSE
(*Caloplaca heppiana*)

FRUTICOSE
(*Cladonia portentosa*)

squamulose thallus
moss
fruticose thallus

SQUAMULOSE (SCALY) AND FRUTICOSE THALLUS
(*Cladonia floerkeana*)

L

LICH-GATE

lich-gate *n.* (also **lych-gate**) ▲ a roofed gateway to a churchyard, formerly used at burials for sheltering a coffin until the clergyman's arrival. ▷ CHURCH. [Old English *līc* 'corpse' + GATE]

licit *adj.* not forbidden; lawful. [from Latin *licitus*] □ **licitly** *adv.*

lick ● *v.* **1** *tr.* pass the tongue over. **2** *tr.* bring into a specified condition or position by licking (*licked it all up*; *licked it clean*). **3 a** *tr.* (of a flame, waves, etc.) play lightly over. **b** *intr.* move gently or caressingly (*flames licked at the staircase*). **4** *tr. colloq.* **a** defeat. **b** excel, surpass. **c** surpass the comprehension of (*has got me licked*). **5** *tr. colloq.* thrash. ● *n.* **1** an act of licking with the tongue. **2** = SALT LICK. **3** *colloq.* a fast pace (*at a lick*; *at full lick*). **4** *colloq.* a small amount; quick treatment with (foll. by *of*: *a lick of paint*). **5** a smart blow (*with a stick etc.*). □ **a lick and a promise** *colloq.* a hasty performance of a task, esp. of washing oneself. **lick a person's boots** (or **shoes**) be servile. **lick into shape** see SHAPE. **lick one's lips** (or *colloq.* **chops**) **1** look forward with relish. **2** show one's satisfaction. **lick one's wounds** be in retirement after defeat. [Old English] □ **licker** *n.* (also in *comb.*).

lickety-split *adv. colloq.* at full speed; headlong.

licking *n. colloq.* **1** a thrashing. **2** a defeat.

lickspittle *n.* a toady.

licorice var. of LIQUORICE.

lid *n.* **1** a hinged or removable cover, esp. for the top of a container. **2** = EYELID. **3** *slang* a hat. □ **put the lid** (or **tin lid**) **on** *Brit. colloq.* **1** be the culmination of. **2** put a stop to. **take** (or **blow** etc.) **the lid off** *colloq.* expose (a scandal etc.). [Old English] □ **lidded** *adj.* (also in *comb.*). **lidless** *adj.*

lido /lee-doh/ *n.* (*pl.* **-os**) *Brit.* a public open-air swimming pool or bathing beach. [Italian, from *Lido*, name of a bathing-beach near Venice]

lie¹ ● *v.intr.* (**lying**; *past* **lay**; *past part.* **lain**) **1** be in or assume a horizontal position on a supporting surface; be at rest on something. **2** (of a thing) rest flat on a surface (*snow lay on the ground*). **3** remain undisturbed or undiscussed etc. (*let matters lie*). **4 a** be kept or remain or be in a specified state or place (*lie hidden*; *lie in wait*; *malice lay behind those words*; *they lay dying*; *the books lay unread*; *the money is lying in the bank*). **b** (of abstract things) exist, reside; be in a certain position or relation (foll. by *in*, *with*, etc.: *the answer lies in education*; *my sympathies lie with the family*). **5 a** be situated or stationed (*the village lay to the east*; *the ships are lying off the coast*). **b** (of a road, route, etc.) lead (*the road lies over mountains*). **c** be spread out to view (*the desert lay before us*). **6** (of the dead) be buried in a grave. **7** (foll. by *with*) *archaic* have sexual intercourse. **8** *Law* be admissible or sustainable (*the objection will not lie*). ● *n.* the way or direction or position in which a thing lies. □ **let lie** not raise (a contro-

versial matter etc.) for discussion etc. **lie about** (or **around**) be left carelessly out of place. **lie ahead** be going to happen; be in store. **lie back** recline so as to rest. **lie down** assume a lying position; have a short rest. **lie down under** *Brit.* accept (an insult etc.) without protest. **lie heavy** cause discomfort or anxiety. **lie in** remain in bed in the morning. **lie in state** (of a deceased person of high rank) be laid in a public place of honour before burial. **lie low 1** keep quiet or unseen. **2** be discreet about one's intentions. **lie off** *Naut.* stand some distance from shore or from another ship. **lie over** be deferred. **lie to** *Naut.* come almost to a stop facing the wind. **lie up** (of a ship) go into dock or be out of commission. **lie with** be the responsibility of (a person) (*it lies with you to answer*). **take lying down** (usu. with *neg.*) accept (defeat, rebuke, etc.) without resistance or protest etc. [Old English]

■ **Usage** The transitive use of *lie*, meaning 'lay', as in *Lie him on the bed*, is incorrect.

lie² ● *n.* **1** an intentionally false statement (*tell a lie*; *pack of lies*). **2** imposture; false belief (*live a lie*). ● *v.* (**lies, lied, lying**) **1** *intr.* **a** tell a lie or lies (*they lied to me*). **b** (of a thing) be deceptive (*the camera cannot lie*). **2** *tr.* (usu. *refl.*; foll. by *into*, *out of*) get (oneself) into or out of a situation by lying (*lied themselves into trouble*; *lied my way out of danger*). □ **give the lie to** serve to show the falsity of (a supposition etc.). [Old English]

lied /leet/ *n.* (*pl.* **lieder** /lee-der/) a type of German song, esp. of the Romantic period, usu. for solo voice with piano accompaniment. [German]

lie detector *n.* an instrument for determining whether a person is telling the truth by testing for physiological changes considered to be symptomatic of lying.

lie-down *n. Brit.* a short rest.

liege /leej/ usu. *hist.* ● *adj.* (of a superior) entitled to receive or (of a vassal) bound to give feudal service or allegiance. ● *n.* **1** (in full **liege lord**) a feudal superior or sovereign. **2** (usu. in *pl.*) a vassal or subject. [from Old French]

liegeman *n.* (*pl.* **-men**) *hist.* a sworn vassal; a faithful follower.

lie-in *n. Brit.* a prolonged stay in bed in the morning.

lien /leen/ *n. Law* a right over another's property to protect a debt charged on that property. [from Latin *ligamen* 'bond']

lie of the land *n.* (prec. by *the*) esp. *Brit.* the current state of affairs.

lieu /lew/ *n.* □ **in lieu 1** instead. **2** (foll. by *of*) in the place of. [from Latin *locus* 'place']

Lieut. *abbr.* Lieutenant.

lieutenant /lef-ten-ănt/ *n.* **1** a deputy. **2 a** an army officer next in rank below captain. **b** a naval officer next in rank below lieutenant commander. **3** *US* a police officer next in rank below captain. [from Old French] □ **lieutenancy** *n.* (*pl.* **-ies**).

life *n.* (*pl.* **lives**) **1** the condition which distinguishes active animals and plants from inorganic matter, including the capacity for growth, functional activity, and continual change preceding death. **2 a** living things and their activity (*insect life*; *is there life on Mars?*). **b** human presence or activity (*no sign of life*). **3 a** the period during which life lasts, or the period from birth to the present time or from the present time to death (*have done it all my life*; *will regret it all my life*; *life membership*). **b** the duration of a thing's existence or of its ability to function (*the battery has a life of two years*). **4 a** a person's state of existence as a living individual (*sacrificed their lives*; *took many lives*). **b** a living person (*many lives were lost*). **5 a** an indi-

vidual's occupation, actions, or fortunes; the manner of one's existence (*that would make life easy*; *start a new life*). **b** a particular aspect of this (*love life*; *private life*). **6** the business and pleasures of the world (*travel is the best way to see life*). **7** man's earthly or supposed future existence (*this life and the next*). **8 a** energy, liveliness (*full of life*; *put some life into it!*). **b** an animating influence (*was the life of the party*). **9** the living form or model (*taken from the life*). **10** a biography. **11** *colloq.* a sentence of imprisonment for life (*they were all serving life*). **12** a chance; a fresh start (*cats have nine lives*; *gave the player three lives*). □ **come to life 1** emerge from unconsciousness or inactivity; begin operating. **2** (of an inanimate object) assume an imaginary animation. **for dear** (or **one's**) **life** as if or in order to escape death (*hanging on for dear life*; *run for your life*). **for life** for the rest of one's life. **for the life of** (foll. by personal pron.) even if (one's) life depended on it (*cannot for the life of me remember*). **give one's life 1** (foll. by *for*) die; sacrifice oneself. **2** (foll. by *to*) dedicate oneself. **large as life** *colloq.* in person, esp. prominently (*stood there large as life*). **larger than life 1** exaggerated. **2** (of a person) having an exuberant or striking personality. **lose one's life** be killed. **not on your life** *colloq.* most certainly not. **save a person's life 1** prevent a person's death. **2** save a person from serious difficulty. **take one's life in one's hands** take a crucial personal risk. **to the life** true to the original. [Old English]

life assurance *n.* = LIFE INSURANCE.

lifebelt *n. Brit.* a belt of buoyant or inflatable material for keeping a person afloat.

lifeblood *n.* **1** the blood, as being necessary to life. **2** the vital factor or influence.

lifeboat *n.* **1** ▼ a specially constructed boat launched from land to rescue those in distress at sea. ▷ BOAT. **2** a ship's small boat for use in emergency. ▷ SHIP

LIFEBOAT: SELF-RIGHTING ARUN CLASS LIFEBOAT

masthead light

life-raft   radar

rescue craft   davit

steering position

binnacle

wheelhouse

air-intake pipe

bollard

winch

anchor

5-4-04

rudder   propeller   sloping recovery deck   rubber fender   fast-planing hull

lifeboatman *n.* (*pl.* **-men**) a man who rescues people using a lifeboat.

lifebuoy *n.* a buoyant support for keeping a person afloat.

life cycle *n.* the series of changes in the life of an organism including reproduction.

life expectancy *n.* the average period that a person may expect to live.

life-force *n.* inspiration or a driving force or influence.

life-giving *adj.* sustaining life or uplifting and revitalizing.

lifeguard *n.* an expert swimmer employed to rescue bathers from drowning.

Life Guards *n.pl.* (in the UK) a regiment of the royal Household Cavalry.

life history *n.* the story of a person's life, esp. told at tedious length.

life insurance *n.* insurance for a sum to be paid on the death of the insured person.

life jacket *n.* ◄ a buoyant jacket for keeping a person afloat.

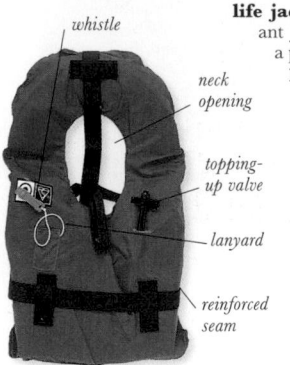

whistle
neck opening
topping-up valve
lanyard
reinforced seam

LIFE JACKET

lifeless *adj.* **1** lacking life; no longer living. **2** unconscious. **3** lacking movement or vitality. □ **lifelessly** *adv.* **lifelessness** *n.*

lifelike *adj.* closely resembling the person or thing represented.

lifeline *n.* **1 a** a rope etc. used for life-saving, e.g. that attached to a lifebuoy. **b** a diver's signalling line. **2** a sole means of communication or transport.

lifelong *adj.* lasting a lifetime.

life member *n.* a person who has lifelong membership of a society etc.

life peer *n. Brit.* a peer whose title lapses on death. □ **life peerage** *n.*

life-preserver *n.* **1** *Brit.* a short stick with a heavily loaded end. **2** a life jacket etc.

lifer *n.* **1** *slang* a person serving a life sentence. **2** *US* a person who serves in one of the armed services as a career.

life-raft *n.* ▼ an inflatable or timber etc. raft for use in an emergency instead of a boat.

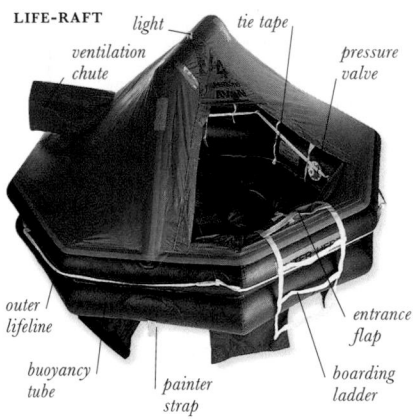

LIFE-RAFT
light
tie tape
ventilation chute
pressure valve
outer lifeline
buoyancy tube
painter strap
entrance flap
boarding ladder

life-saver *n. colloq.* **1** a thing that saves one from serious difficulty. **2** *Austral.* & *NZ* = LIFEGUARD.

life sciences *n.pl.* biology and related subjects.

life sentence *n.* **1** a sentence of imprisonment for life. **2** an illness or commitment etc. perceived as a continuing threat to one's freedom.

life-size (also **life-sized**) ● *adj.* of the same size as the person or thing represented. ● *n.* (**life size**) this size.

lifespan *n.* the length of time for which a person or creature lives, or for which a thing exists or is functional.

lifestyle *n.* the particular way of life of a person or group.

life-support *attrib.adj.* (of equipment) allowing vital functions to continue in an adverse environment or during severe disablement.

life-support machine *n. Med.* a ventilator or respirator.

life's work *n.* a task etc. pursued throughout one's lifetime.

LIGHT

Visible, or white, light is a form of electromagnetic radiation occurring between infra-red and ultraviolet waves in the electromagnetic spectrum. White light is a mixture of many different colours of light, each with its own wavelength. When white light passes through a prism it is refracted and split up into its various wavelengths, so that all the colours can be seen separately. These colours make up the visible spectrum. Our eyes detect colours by recognizing the different wavelengths of visible light.

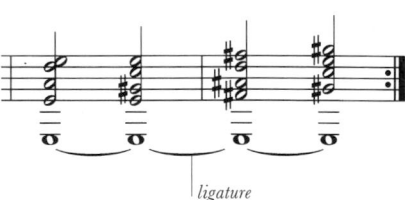

DETAIL FROM THE ELECTROMAGNETIC SPECTRUM

infra-red waves
visible light
ultraviolet waves
X-rays
visible spectrum
prism
white light

WHITE LIGHT REFRACTED BY A PRISM

---

life-threatening *adj.* (of an illness etc.) that endangers life.

lifetime *n.* **1** the duration of a person's life. **2** the duration of a thing or its usefulness. **3** *colloq.* an exceptionally long time. □ **of a lifetime** such as does not occur more than once in a person's life (*the chance of a lifetime; the journey of a lifetime*).

lift ● *v.* **1** *tr.* raise or remove to a higher position. **2** *intr.* go up; be raised; yield to an upward force (*the window will not lift*). **3** *tr.* give an upward direction to (the eyes or face). **4** *tr.* **a** elevate to a higher plane of thought or feeling (*the news lifted their spirits*). **b** make less heavy or dull; add interest to. **c** enhance, improve (*lifted their game after half-time*). **5** *intr.* (of a cloud, fog, etc.) rise, disperse. **6** *tr.* remove (a barrier or restriction). **7** *tr.* transport (supplies, troops, etc.) by air. **8** *tr. colloq.* **a** steal. **b** plagiarize (a passage of writing etc.). **9** *tr.* dig up (esp. potatoes etc. at harvest). **10** *tr.* hold or have on high (*the church lifts its spire*). **11** *tr.* hit (a cricket ball) into the air. **12** *tr.* (usu. in *passive*) perform cosmetic surgery on (esp. the face or breasts) to reduce sagging. ● *n.* **1** the act of lifting or process of being lifted. **2** a free ride in another person's vehicle (*gave them a lift*). **3 a** *Brit.* a platform or compartment housed in a shaft for raising and lowering persons or things to different floors of a building or different levels of a mine etc. **b** a similar apparatus for carrying persons up or down a mountain etc. (see SKI LIFT). **4 a** transport by air (see AIRLIFT *n.*). **b** a quantity of goods transported by air. **5** the upward pressure which air exerts on an aerofoil. ▷ AEROFOIL. **6** a supporting or elevating influence; a feeling of elation. **7** a layer of leather in the heel of a boot or shoe, esp. to correct shortening of a leg or increase height. **8** a rise in the level of the ground. **b** the extent to which water rises in a canal lock. □ **lift down** *Brit.* pick up and bring to a lower position. **lift a finger** (or **hand** etc.) (in *neg.*) make the slightest effort (*didn't lift a finger to help*). **lift up one's voice** sing out. [from Old Norse *lypta*] □ **liftable** *adj.* **lifter** *n.*

lift-off *n.* the vertical take-off of a spacecraft or rocket.

ligament *n.* **1** *Anat.* a short band of tough flexible fibrous connective tissue linking bones together. **2** any membranous fold keeping an organ in position. [from Latin *ligamentum* 'bond'] □ **ligamental** *adj.* **ligamentary** *adj.* **ligamentous** *adj.*

ligand *n.* **1** *Chem.* an ion or molecule attached to a metal atom by bonding in which both electrons are supplied by one atom. **2** *Biochem.* a molecule that binds to another (usu. larger) molecule. [from Latin *ligandus* 'to be bound']

ligate *v.tr. Surgery* tie up (a bleeding artery etc.). [based on Latin *ligatus* 'bound'] □ **ligation** *n.*

ligature ● *n.* **1** a tie or bandage. **2** *Mus.* ▼ a slur; a tie. **3** *Printing* two or more letters joined, e.g. æ. **4** a bond; a thing that unites. **5** the act of tying or binding. ● *v.tr.* bind or connect with a ligature.

■ **Usage** See Usage Note at DIGRAPH.

LIGATURES BELOW A MUSICAL STAFF

ligature

liger *n.* the offspring of a lion and a tigress. [portmanteau word from LION + TIGER]

light[1] ● *n.* **1** ▲ the natural agent (electromagnetic radiation of wavelength between about 390 and 740 nm) that stimulates sight and makes things visible. ▷ ELECTROMAGNETIC RADIATION. **2** the medium or condition of the space in which this is present. **3** an appearance of brightness (*saw a distant light*). **4 a** a source of light. **b** (in *pl.*) illuminations. **5** (often in *pl.*) a traffic light (*went through a red light; stop at the lights*). **6 a** the amount or quality of illumination in a place (*bad light stopped play*). **b** one's fair or usual share of this (*you are standing in my light*). **7 a** a flame or spark serving to ignite (*struck a light*). **b** a device producing this (*have you got a light?*). **8** the aspect in which a thing is regarded (*appeared in a new light*). **9 a** mental illumination; elucidation, enlightenment. **b** hope, happiness; a happy outcome. **c** spiritual illumination by divine truth. **10** vivacity, enthusiasm, or inspiration visible in a person's face, esp. in the eyes. **11** (in *pl.*) a person's mental powers or ability (*according to one's lights*). **12** an eminent person (*a leading light*). **13 a** the bright part of a thing; a highlight. **b** the bright parts of a picture etc. esp. suggesting illumination (*light and shade*). **14 a** a window or opening in a wall to let light in. **b** the perpendicular division of a mullioned window. ▷ WINDOW. **c** a pane of glass esp. in the side or roof of a greenhouse. **15** *Brit.* (in a crossword etc.) each of the items filling a space and to be deduced from the clues. **16** *Law* the light falling on windows, the obstruction of which by a neighbour is illegal. ● *v.* (*past* **lit**; *past part.* **lit** or (*attrib.*) **lighted**) **1** *tr.* & *intr.* set burning or begin to burn. **2** *tr.*

L

provide with light or lighting. **3** *tr.* show (a person) the way or surroundings with a light. **4** *intr.* (usu. foll. by *up*) (of the face or eyes) brighten with animation, pleasure, etc. ● *adj.* **1** well provided with light; not dark. **2** (of a colour) pale (*light blue; a light blue ribbon*). □ **bring** (or **come**) **to light** reveal or be revealed. **in a good** (or **bad**) **light** giving a favourable (or unfavourable) impression. **in (the) light of** having regard to; drawing information from. **light of one's life** usu. *joc.* a much loved person. **light up 1** *colloq.* begin to smoke a cigarette etc. **2** provide with lights or lighting; illuminate (a scene etc.). **lit up** *colloq.* drunk. **out like a light** deeply asleep or unconscious. **throw** (or **shed**) **light on** help to explain. [Old English] □ **lightish** *adj.* **lightless** *adj.* **lightness** *n.*

light[2] ● *adj.* **1** not heavy. **2 a** relatively low in weight, amount, density, intensity, etc. (*light arms; light traffic; light metal; light rain; a light breeze*). **b** deficient in weight (*light coin*). **3 a** carrying or suitable for small loads (*light aircraft*). **b** (of a ship) unladen. **c** carrying only light arms, armaments, etc. (*light brigade; light infantry*). **4 a** (of food, a meal, etc.) small in amount; easy to digest (*had a light lunch*). **b** (of a foodstuff) low in fat, cholesterol, or sugar, etc. **c** (of drink) not heavy on the stomach or not strongly alcoholic. **5 a** (of entertainment, music, etc.) intended for amusement, rather than edification; not profound. **b** frivolous, thoughtless, trivial (*a light remark*). **6** (of sleep or a sleeper) easily disturbed. **7** easily borne or done (*light duties*). **8** nimble; quick-moving (*a light step; light of foot; a light rhythm*). **9** (of a building etc.) graceful, elegant. **10** (of type) not heavy or bold. **11 a** free from sorrow; cheerful (*a light heart*). **b** giddy (*light in the head*). **12** (of soil) not dense; porous. **13** (of pastry, a sponge cake, etc.) fluffy and well-aerated during cooking and with the fat fully absorbed. **14** *archaic* (of a woman) unchaste or wanton; fickle. ● *adv.* **1** in a light manner (*tread light; sleep light*). **2** with a minimum load (*travel light*). ● *v.intr.* (*past* and *past part.* **lit** or **lighted**) (foll. by *on, upon*) come upon or find by chance. □ **light into** *colloq.* attack. **light out** *colloq.* depart. **make light of** treat as unimportant. **make light work of** do a thing quickly and easily. [Old English] □ **lightish** *adj.* **lightness** *n.*

light air *n.* a very light wind, force 1 on the Beaufort scale (1–3 m.p.h.).

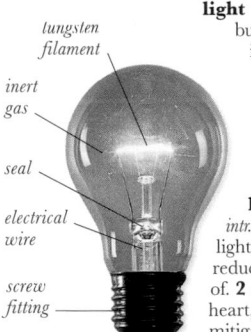

LIGHT BULB

tungsten filament
inert gas
seal
electrical wire
screw fitting
terminal

light bulb *n.* ◀ a glass bulb containing an inert gas and a metal filament, providing light when an electric current is passed through.

light-emitting diode see LED.

lighten[1] *v.* **1 a** *tr.* & *intr.* make or become lighter in weight. **b** *tr.* reduce the weight or load of. **2** *tr.* bring relief to (the heart, mind, etc.). **3** *tr.* mitigate (a penalty).

lighten[2] *v.* **1 a** *tr.* shed light on. **b** *tr.* & *intr.* make or grow lighter or brighter. **2** *intr.* **a** shine brightly; flash. **b** emit lightning (*it is lightening*).

lighter[1] *n.* a device for lighting cigarettes etc.

lighter[2] *n.* a boat, usu. flat-bottomed, for transferring goods from a ship to a wharf or another ship. [related to obsolete *light* 'to unload']

lighterman *n.* (*pl.* **-men**) a person who works on a lighter.

lighter-than-air *attrib.adj.* (of an aircraft) weighing less than the air it displaces.

lightfast *adj.* (of a dye, pigment, etc.) resistant to alteration on exposure to light. □ **lightfastness** *n.*

light-fingered *adj.* given to stealing.

light flyweight *n.* **1** a weight in amateur boxing up to 48 kg. **2** an amateur boxer of this weight.

light-footed *adj.* nimble.

light-headed *adj.* giddy, frivolous, delirious. □ **light-headedly** *adv.* **light-headedness** *n.*

light-hearted *adj.* **1** cheerful. **2** (unduly) casual, thoughtless. □ **light-heartedly** *adv.* **light-heartedness** *n.*

light heavyweight *n.* **1** the weight in some sports between middleweight and heavyweight. **2** a sportsman of this weight.

lighthouse *n.* ◀ a tower or other structure containing a beacon light to warn or guide ships at sea.

light industry *n.* the manufacture of small or light articles.

lighting *n.* **1** equipment in a room or street etc. for producing light. **2** the arrangement or effect of lights.

lighting-up time *n. Brit.* the time after which vehicles on the road must show the prescribed lights.

lightly *adv.* in a light (esp. frivolous or unserious) manner. □ **get off lightly** escape with little or no punishment. **take lightly** not be serious about (a thing).

light meter *n.* ▼ an instrument for measuring the intensity of the light, esp. to show the correct photographic exposure.

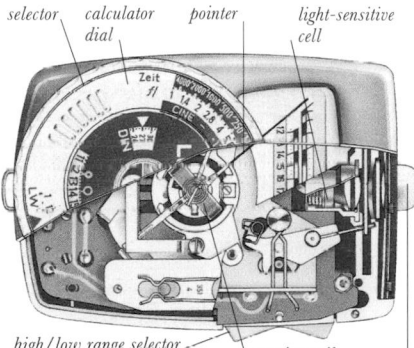

selector
calculator dial
pointer
light-sensitive cell
high/low range selector
moving coil
light integrator

LIGHT METER: CUTAWAY VIEW OF AN ANALOGUE LIGHT METER

lightning ● *n.* ▶ a flash of bright light produced by an electric discharge between clouds or between clouds and the ground. ● *attrib.adj.* very quick (*with lightning speed*). [Middle English]

lightning conductor *n.* (*US* **lightning rod**) a metal rod or wire fixed to an exposed part of a building or to a mast to divert lightning into the earth or sea.

lightning strike *n. Brit.* a strike by workers at short notice, esp. without official union backing.

light of day *n.* **1** daylight, sunlight. **2** general notice; public attention.

light-pen *n.* **1** a penlike photosensitive device held to the screen of a computer terminal for passing information on to it. **2** a light-emitting device used for reading bar codes.

light pollution *n.* excessive brightening of the night sky by street lights etc.

lightproof *adj.* able to resist the harmful effects of (esp. excessive) light.

light railway *n.* a railway constructed for light traffic.

lights *n.pl.* the lungs of sheep, pigs, bullocks, etc., used as a food esp. for pets. [Middle English, so named because of their lightness]

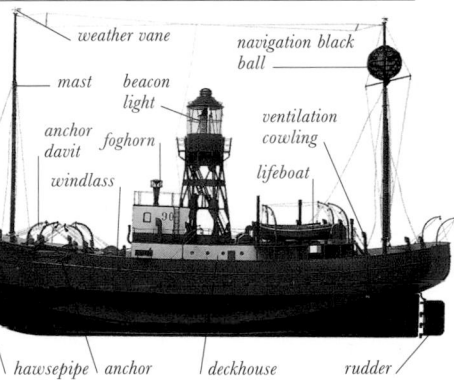

LIGHTSHIP: 1930s BRITISH LIGHTSHIP

weather vane
navigation black ball
mast
beacon light
ventilation cowling
anchor davit
foghorn
lifeboat
windlass
hawsepipe *anchor* *deckhouse* *rudder*

lightship *n.* ▲ a moored or anchored ship with a beacon light.

lightweight ● *adj.* **1** (of a person, animal, garment, etc.) of below average weight. **2** of little importance or influence. ● *n.* **1** a lightweight person, animal, or thing. **2 a** a weight in certain sports intermediate between featherweight and welterweight. **b** a boxer etc. of this weight.

lightwood *n.* **1** a tree with a light wood. **2** *US* wood or a tree with wood that burns with a bright flame.

light year *n.* **1** *Astron.* the distance light travels in one year, nearly 6 million million miles. **2** (in *pl.*) *colloq.* a long distance or great amount.

ligneous *adj.* **1** (of a plant) woody. **2** of the nature of wood. [based on Latin *lignum* 'wood']

lignin *n. Bot.* a complex organic polymer deposited in the cell walls of many plants.

lignite *n.* a soft brown coal showing traces of plant structure, intermediate between bituminous coal and peat. ▷ COAL. [French]

L

LIGHTNING

Lightning begins inside thunderclouds, when water and ice particles are thrown together by air currents, creating static electricity. Positive charges collect at the top of the cloud, negative at the bottom. Eventually the difference between the positive and negative charges is large enough to overcome the insulation of the air in between. A lightning bolt leaps between the two – or between the cloud and the positively charged ground – to neutralize the charge.

FORMATION OF LIGHTNING WITHIN A THUNDERCLOUD (CUMULONIMBUS)

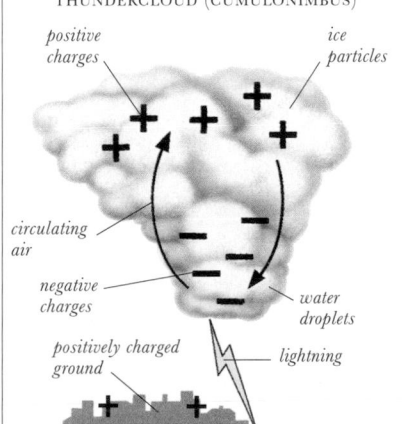

positive charges
ice particles
circulating air
negative charges
water droplets
positively charged ground
lightning

LIGHTHOUSE

weather vane
ventilation ball
beacon
guard rail
bedroom inside
winch room inside
entrance door

lignocaine *n. Pharm.* a local anaesthetic for the gums, mucous membranes, or skin, usu. given by injection.

ligustrum *n.* = PRIVET. [Latin]

likable var. of LIKEABLE.

like[1] ● *adj.* (often governing a noun as if a transitive participle such as *resembling*) (**more like**, **most like**) **1 a** having some or all of the qualities of another or each other or an original (*in like manner*; *as like as two peas*; *is very like her brother*). **b** resembling in some way, such as (*good writers like Dickens*). **c** (usu. in pairs correlatively) as one is so will the other be (*like mother, like daughter*). **2** characteristic of (*it is not like them to be late*). **3** in a suitable state or mood for (*felt like working*; *felt like a cup of tea*). ● *prep.* in the manner of; to the same degree as (*drink like a fish*; *sell like hot cakes*; *acted like an idiot*). ● *adv.* **1** *archaic* likely (*they will come, like enough*). **2** *slang* so to speak (*did a quick getaway, like*; *as I said, like, I'm no Shakespeare*). **3** *colloq.* likely (*as like as not*). ● *conj. colloq. disp.* **1** as (*cannot do it like you do*). **2** as if (*ate like they were starving*). ● *n.* **1** a counterpart; an equal; a similar person or thing (*shall not see its like again*). **2** (prec. by *the*) a thing or things of the same kind (*will never do the like again*). □ **and the like** and similar things (*music, painting, and the like*). **be nothing like** (usu. with compl.) be in no way similar or comparable or adequate. **like** (or **as like**) **as not** *colloq.* probably. **like so** *colloq.* like this; in this manner. **the likes of** *colloq.* a person such as. **what is he** (or **she** or **it** etc.) **like?** what sort of characteristics does he (or she, or it, etc.) have? [Middle English]

■ **Usage** When *like* means 'such as' (see sense 1b of the adjective), some people prefer *such as* to be used in formal contexts when more than one example is mentioned, e.g. *good writers such as Dickens, Shakespeare, and Hardy.* The use of *like* as a conjunction is often condemned and is therefore best avoided by using instead *as* or *as if* as appropriate.

like[2] ● *v.tr.* **1 a** find agreeable or enjoyable (*like reading*; *like the sea*; *like to dance*). **b** be fond of (a person). **2 a** choose to have; prefer (*like my coffee black*; *do not like such things discussed*). **b** wish for or be inclined to (*would like a cup of tea*; *should like to come*). **3** (usu. in *interrog.*; prec. by *how*) feel about; regard (*how would you like it if it happened to you?*). ● *n.* (in *pl.*) the things one likes or prefers. [Old English]

-like *comb. form* forming adjectives from nouns, meaning 'similar to, characteristic of' (*doglike*; *shell-like*; *tortoise-like*).

■ **Usage** In formations intended as nonce-words, or not generally current, the hyphen should be used. It may be omitted when the first element is of one syllable, but nouns in *-l* always require it.

likeable *adj.* (also **likable**) pleasant; easy to like. □ **likeability** *n.* **likeably** *adv.*

likelihood *n.* probability. □ **in all likelihood** very probably.

likely ● *adj.* (**likelier**, **likeliest**) **1** probable; such as well might happen or be true (*it is not likely that they will come*; *the most likely place is London*; *a likely story*). **2** (foll. by *to* + infin.) to be reasonably expected (*he is not likely to come now*). **3** promising; apparently suitable (*three likely lads*; *this is a likely spot*). ● *adv.* probably (*is very likely true*). □ **as likely as not** probably. **not likely!** *colloq.* certainly not; I refuse. [from Old Norse *líkligr*]

■ **Usage** When used as an adverb, *likely* must be preceded by *more*, *most*, or *very*. Use without the qualifying adverb is standard only in American English, e.g. *They'll likely not come.*

like-minded *adj.* having the same tastes, opinions, etc. □ **like-mindedness** *n.*

liken *v.tr.* (foll. by *to*) point out the resemblance of (a person or thing to another).

likeness *n.* **1** (usu. foll. by *between, to*) resemblance. **2** (foll. by *of*) a semblance or guise (*in the likeness of a ghost*). **3** a portrait or representation (*is a good likeness*).

likewise *adv.* **1** also, moreover. **2** similarly (*do likewise*).

liking *n.* **1** what one likes; one's taste (*is it to your liking?*). **2** (foll. by *for*) regard or fondness; taste or fancy (*had a liking for toffee*).

lilac ● *n.* **1** any shrub or small tree of the genus *Syringa*, esp. *S. vulgaris* with fragrant pale pinkish-violet or white blossoms. **2** a pale pinkish-violet colour. ● *adj.* of this colour. [from Persian *līlak* 'bluish']

liliaceous *adj.* **1** of or relating to the family Liliaceae of plants with elongated leaves growing from a corm, bulb, or rhizome. **2** lily-like. [based on Latin *lilium* 'lily']

lilliputian ● *n.* a diminutive person or thing. ● *adj.* diminutive. [from *Lilliput*, imaginary country in Swift's *Gulliver's Travels*, inhabited by tiny people]

Lilo *n.* (also **Li-lo** *propr.*) (*pl.* **-os**) *Brit.* a type of inflatable mattress. [alteration of *lie low*]

lilt ● *n.* **1 a** a light springing rhythm or step. **b** a song or tune marked by this. **2** (of the voice) a characteristic cadence or inflection. ● *v.intr.* (esp. as **lilting** *adj.*) move or speak etc. with a lilt. [Middle English]

lily *n.* (*pl.* **-ies**) **1 a** any bulbous plant of the genus *Lilium* (family Liliaceae), with large trumpet-shaped flowers on a tall slender stem. **b** any of various plants of similar appearance. **c** the water lily. **2** a heraldic fleur-de-lis. [from Latin *lilium*]

lily-livered *adj.* cowardly.

lily of the valley *n.* ◄ any plant of the genus *Convallaria* (lily family), with racemes of white bell-shaped fragrant flowers.

lily pad *n.* a floating leaf of a water lily.

lily white ● *n.* a pure white colour. ● *adj.* (hyphenated when *attrib.*) **1** of this colour. **2** faultless.

limb[1] ● *n.* **1** an arm, leg, or wing. **2** a large branch of a tree. **3** a branch of a cross. **4** a spur of a mountain. □ **out on a limb 1** isolated, stranded. **2** at a disadvantage. [Old English] □ **limbed** *adj.* (also in *comb.*).

limbless *adj.*

limb[2] *n. Astron.* a specified edge of the Sun, Moon, etc. [from Latin *limbus* 'hem, border']

limber[1] ● *adj.* **1** lithe, agile, nimble. **2** flexible. ● *v.* (usu. foll. by *up*) **1** *tr.* make (oneself or a part of the body etc.) supple. **2** *intr.* warm up in preparation for athletic etc. activity. [16th-century coinage] □ **limberness** *n.*

limber[2] ● *n.* ▼ the detachable front part of a gun carriage. ● *v.* **1** *tr.* attach a limber to (a gun etc.). **2** *intr.* fasten together the two parts of a gun carriage. [Middle English]

LIMBER OF A MID-19TH-CENTURY GUN CARRIAGE

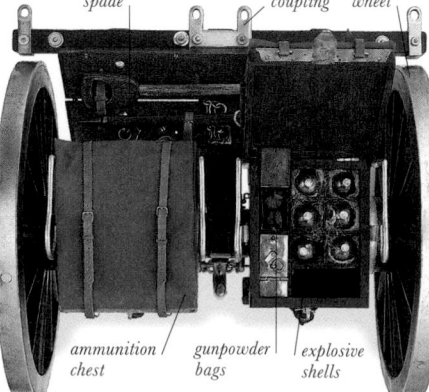

spade   coupling   wheel

ammunition chest   gunpowder bags   explosive shells

limbic *adj.* of or relating to a part of the brain concerned with basic emotions and instinctive actions. [based on Latin *limbus* 'edge']

limbo[1] *n.* (*pl.* **-os**) **1** (in some Christian beliefs) the supposed abode of the souls of unbaptized infants, and of the just who died before Christ. **2** an intermediate state or condition of awaiting a decision etc. **3** a state of neglect or oblivion. [from medieval Latin phrase *in limbo* 'on the edge']

limbo[2] *n.* (*pl.* **-os**) a W. Indian dance in which the dancer bends backwards to pass under a horizontal bar which is progressively lowered. [W. Indian]

lime[1] ● *n.* **1** (in full **quicklime**) a white caustic alkaline substance (calcium oxide) obtained by heating limestone. **2** (in full **slaked lime**) a white substance (calcium hydroxide) made by adding water to quicklime. **3** calcium or calcium salts. **4** *archaic* = BIRDLIME. ● *v.tr.* treat (wood, skins, land, etc.) with lime. [Old English, related to LOAM] □ **limeless** *adj.* **limy** *adj.* (**limier**, **limiest**).

lime[2] *n.* **1 a** a rounded citrus fruit like a lemon but greener, smaller, and more acid. ▷ CITRUS FRUIT. **b** (in full **lime tree**) the tree, *Citrus aurantifolia*, bearing this. **2** (in full **lime juice**) the juice of limes as a drink. **3** = LIME GREEN. [from Arabic *līma*]

lime[3] *n.* **1** (in full **lime tree**) any ornamental tree of the genus *Tilia*, esp. *T. europaea* with heart-shaped leaves and fragrant yellow blossom. ▷ TREE. **2** the wood of this. [Old English *lind* 'linden']

lime green ● *n.* a bright pale green colour like that of a lime (see LIME[2] 1a). ● *adj.* (hyphenated when *attrib.*) of this colour.

limekiln *n.* a kiln for heating limestone.

limelight *n.* **1** an intense white light used formerly in theatres. **2** (prec. by *the*) the focus of attention.

limerick *n.* a humorous or comic form of five-line poem with a rhyme scheme *aabba*. [from *Limerick*, a town and county in Ireland]

limestone *n. Geol.* ▶ a sedimentary rock composed mainly of calcium carbonate. ▷ SEDIMENT.

Limey *n.* (*pl.* **-eys**) *N. Amer. slang offens.* a British person (originally a sailor) or ship.

liminal *adj.* **1 a** of or relating to a transitional or initial stage. **b** marginal, insignificant. **2** occupying a position on, or on both sides of, a boundary or threshold. [based on Latin *limen limin-* 'threshold'] □ **liminality** *n.*

limit ● *n.* **1** a point, line, or level beyond which something does not or may not extend or pass. **2** (often in *pl.*) the boundary of an area. **3** the greatest or smallest amount permissible or possible. ● *v.tr.* (**limited**, **limiting**) **1** set or serve as a limit to. **2** (foll. by *to*) restrict. □ **be the limit** *colloq.* be intolerable or extremely irritating. **within limits** moderately; with some degree of freedom. [from Latin *limes limitis* 'boundary, frontier'] □ **limitable** *adj.* **limiter** *n.*

limitation *n.* **1** the act or an instance of limiting; the process of being limited. **2** (often in *pl.*) a condition of limited ability (*know one's limitations*). **3** (often in *pl.*) a limiting circumstance (*has its limitations*).

limited *adj.* **1** confined within limits. **2** not great in scope or talents (*has limited experience*). **3 a** few, scanty, restricted (*limited accommodation*). **b** restricted to a few examples (*limited edition*). **4** (after a company name) being a limited company. □ **limitedness** *n.*

limited company *n.* (also **limited liability company**) *Brit.* a company whose owners are legally responsible only to a limited amount for its debts.

limited liability *n. Brit.* the status of being legally responsible only to a limited amount for debts of a trading company.

limitless *adj.* **1** extending or going on indefinitely (*a limitless expanse*). **2** unlimited (*limitless generosity*). □ **limitlessly** *adv.* **limitlessness** *n.*

limnology *n.* the study of the physical phenomena of lakes and other fresh waters. [based on Greek *limnē* 'lake'] □ **limnological** *adj.* **limnologist** *n.*

limo /lim-oh/ *n.* (*pl.* **-os**) *colloq.* a limousine.

limousine *n.* a large luxurious motor car. [French, originally a caped cloak worn in *Limousin*, former French province]

limp[1] *v.intr.* **1** walk lamely. **2** (of a damaged ship, aircraft, etc.) proceed with difficulty. **3** (of verse) be defective. ● *n.* a lame walk. [related to obsolete *limphalt* 'lame'] □ **limpingly** *adv.*

limp[2] *adj.* **1** not stiff or firm; easily bent. **2** without energy or will. **3** (of a book) having a soft cover. [18th-century coinage] □ **limply** *adv.* **limpness** *n.*

limpet *n.* **1** ► any of various marine gastropod molluscs with a shallow conical shell and a broad muscular foot that sticks tightly to rocks. **2** a clinging person. [from medieval Latin *lampreda* 'limpet']

limpet mine *n.* a delayed-action mine designed to be attached to a ship's hull.

LIMPET

limpid *adj.* **1** (of water, eyes, etc.) clear, transparent. **2** (of writing) easily comprehended. [from Latin *limpidus*] □ **limpidity** *n.* **limpidly** *adv.* **limpidness** *n.*

limp-wristed *adj. colloq.* **1** effeminate. **2** ineffectual, feeble.

linage /lyn-ij/ *n.* **1** the number of lines in printed or written matter. **2** payment by the line.

linchpin *n.* (also **lynchpin**) **1** a pin passed through an axle-end to keep a wheel in position. **2** a person or thing vital to an enterprise, organization, etc. [Old English]

linctus *n. Brit.* a syrupy medicine, esp. a soothing cough mixture. [Latin, literally 'a licking']

lindane *n. Chem.* a toxic colourless isomer of benzene hexachloride used as an insecticide. [named after T. van der *Linden*, Dutch chemist, born 1884]

flower cluster

linden *n.* ◄ a lime tree. [Old English]

LINDEN:
LITTLELEAF LINDEN
(*Tilia cordata*)

line[1] ● *n.* **1** a continuous mark or band made on a surface (*drew a line*). **2** use of lines in art, esp. draughtsmanship or engraving. **3** a thing resembling such a mark esp. a furrow or wrinkle. **4** *Mus.* **a** each of (usu. five) horizontal marks forming a stave in musical notation. **b** a sequence of notes or tones forming a melody. **5 a** a straight or curved continuous extent of length without breadth. **b** the track of a moving point. **6** a contour or outline, esp. as a feature of design (*the yacht's clean lines*). **7 a** (on a map or graph) a curve connecting all points having a specified common property. **b** (**the Line**) the equator. **8 a** a limit or boundary. **b** a mark limiting the area of play, the starting or finishing point in a race, etc. **9 a** a row of persons or things. **b** a direction as indicated by them (*line of travel*). **c** *N. Amer.* a queue. **10 a** a row of printed or written words. **b** a portion of verse written in one line. **11** (in *pl.*) **a** a piece of poetry. **b** the words of an actor's part. **c** a specified amount of text etc. to be written out as a school punishment. **12** a short letter or note (*drop me a line*). **13** (in *pl.*) = MARRIAGE LINES. **14** a length of cord etc., usu. serving a specified purpose, esp. a fishing line or clothes line.

15 a a wire or cable for a telephone or telegraph. **b** a connection by means of this (*am trying to get a line*). **16 a** a single track of a railway. **b** one branch or route of a railway system. **17 a** a regular succession of buses, ships, etc., plying between certain places. **b** a company conducting this (*shipping line*). **18** a connected series of persons following one another in time (esp. several generations of a family) (*a long line of craftsmen*). **19 a** a course or manner of procedure, conduct, etc. (*along these lines*). **b** policy (*the party line*). **c** conformity (*bring them into line*). **20** a direction, course, or channel (*lines of communication*). **21** a department of activity; a branch of business (*not in my line*). **22** a range of commercial goods (*a new line in hats*). **23** *colloq.* a false or exaggerated account (*gave me a line about missing the bus*). **24 a** a connected series of military defences etc. (*behind enemy lines*). **b** an arrangement of soldiers or ships in a column or line formation (*ship of the line*). **c** (prec. by *the*) regular army regiments (not auxiliary forces or Guards). **25** each of the very narrow horizontal sections forming a television picture. **26** a narrow range of the spectrum that is noticeably brighter or darker than the adjacent parts. **27** the level of the base of most letters in printing and writing. **28** (as a measure) one-twelfth of an inch. ● *v.tr.* **1** mark with lines. **2** cover with lines (*a face lined with pain*). **3** position or stand at intervals along. □ **all along the line** at every point. **bring into line** make conform. **come into line** conform. **get a line on** *colloq.* learn something about. **in line for** likely to receive. **in the line of** in the course of (esp. duty). **in** (or **out of**) **line with** in (or not in) alignment or accordance with. **lay** (or **put**) **it on the line** speak frankly. **line up 1** arrange or be arranged in a line or lines. **2** organize (*had a job lined up*). **on the line 1** at risk (*put my reputation on the line*). **2** speaking on the telephone. **out of line 1** not in alignment; discordant. **2** behaving inappropriately. [Old English *līne* 'rope, series']

line[2] *v.tr.* **1 a** cover the inside surface of (a garment, box, etc.) with a layer of usu. different material. **b** serve as a lining for. **2** cover as if with a lining (*shelves lined with books*). **3** *colloq.* fill, esp. plentifully. □ **line one's pocket** (or **purse**) make money, usu. by corrupt means. [Middle English, from obsolete *line* 'flax', with reference to the use of linen for linings]

lineage /lin-i-ij/ *n.* lineal descent; ancestry, pedigree. [based on Latin *linea* 'line']

lineal *adj.* **1** in the direct line of descent or ancestry. **2** linear; of or in lines. □ **lineally** *adv.*

lineament *n.* (usu. in *pl.*) a distinctive feature or characteristic, esp. of the face. [from Latin *lineamentum*]

linear *adj.* **1 a** of or in lines. **b** of length (*linear extent*). **2** long and narrow and of uniform breadth. **3** involving one dimension only. **4** sequential. □ **linearity** *n.* **linearize** *v.tr.* (also **-ise**). **linearly** *adv.*

Linear B *n.* a form of Bronze Age writing found in Greece: an earlier undeciphered form (**Linear A**) also exists.

linear programming *n.* a mathematical technique for maximizing or minimizing a linear function of several variables, e.g. output or cost.

line drawing *n.* a drawing in which images are produced from variations of lines.

linefeed *n.* **1** the action of advancing paper in a printing machine by the space of one line. **2** the analogous movement of text on a VDU screen.

lineman *n.* (*pl.* **-men**) **1** a person who repairs and maintains telephone or electrical etc. lines. **2** a person who tests the safety of railway lines.

line manager *n.* a manager to whom an employee is directly responsible.

linen ● *n.* **1 a** a cloth woven from flax. **b** a particular kind of this. **2** (*collect.*) articles made, or originally made, of linen, e.g. sheets, undergarments, etc. ● *adj.* made of linen or flax. □ **wash one's dirty linen in public** be indiscreet about one's domestic quarrels etc. [Old English]

linen basket *n.* esp. *Brit.* a basket for soiled clothes.

line of credit *n.* an amount of credit extended to a borrower.

line of fire *n.* the expected path of gunfire, a missile, etc.

line of sight *n.* a straight line along which an observer has unobstructed vision.

line of vision *n.* the straight line along which an observer looks.

line-out *n.* (in rugby) parallel lines of opposing forwards at right angles to the touchline for the throwing in of the ball.

line printer *n.* a machine that prints output from a computer a line at a time.

liner[1] *n.* ▼ a ship or aircraft etc. carrying passengers on a regular line.

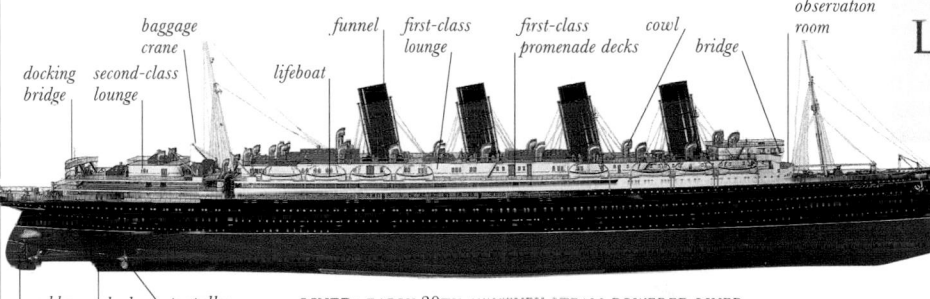

baggage crane *funnel* *first-class lounge* *first-class promenade decks* *cowl* *observation room*

docking bridge *second-class lounge* *lifeboat* *bridge*

rudder *keel* *propeller*

LINER: EARLY 20TH-CENTURY STEAM-POWERED LINER

liner[2] *n.* a removable lining.

liner train *n. Brit.* a fast goods train with detachable containers on permanently coupled wagons.

linesman *n.* (*pl.* **-men**) **1** (in games played on a pitch or court) an umpire's or referee's assistant who decides whether a ball falls within the playing area or not. **2** = LINEMAN 1.

line-up *n.* **1** a line of people for inspection. **2** an arrangement of persons in a team or nations etc. in an alliance.

ling[1] *n.* ▼ a long slender marine fish, *Molva molva*, of the E. Atlantic, related to the cod and used as food. [Middle English]

LING: COMMON LING
(*Molva molva*)

ling[2] *n.* any of various heathers, esp. *Calluna vulgaris*. [from Old Norse *lyng*]

-ling *suffix* **1** denoting a person or thing: **a** connected with (*hireling*). **b** having the property of being (*weakling*) or undergoing (*starveling*). **2** denoting a diminutive (*duckling*), often derogatory (*princeling*).

linger *v.intr.* **1 a** be slow or reluctant to depart. **b** stay about a place. **c** (foll. by *over*, *on*, etc.) dally.

2 (foll. by *on*) of an action or condition) be protracted; drag on. **3** (foll. by *on*) (of a dying person or custom) be slow in dying. [Middle English, related to LENGTHEN] □ **lingerer** *n.* **lingering** *adj.* **lingeringly** *adv.*

lingerie /*lahn-zh*er-i/ *n.* women's underwear and nightclothes. [French, from *linge* 'linen']

lingo *n.* (*pl.* **-os** or **-oes**) *colloq.* **1** a foreign language. **2** the vocabulary of a special subject or group of people. [from Latin *lingua* 'tongue']

lingua franca *n.* (*pl.* **lingua francas**) **1** a language adopted as a common language between speakers whose native languages are different. **2** a system for mutual understanding. [Italian, literally 'Frankish tongue']

lingual *adj.* **1** of or formed by the tongue. **2** of speech or languages. [based on Latin *lingua* 'tongue, language'] □ **lingually** *adv.*

linguist *n.* a person skilled in languages or linguistics.

linguistic *adj.* of or relating to language or the study of languages. □ **linguistically** *adv.*

linguistics *n.* the scientific study of language and its structure.

liniment *n.* an embrocation, usu. made with oil. [based on Latin *linire* 'to smear']

lining *n.* **1** a layer of material used to line a surface etc. **2** an inside layer or surface etc.

link ● *n.* **1** one loop or ring of a chain etc. **2 a** a connecting part; one in a series. **b** a state or means of connection. **3** a means of travel or transport between two places. ● *v.* **1** *tr.* (foll. by *together, to, with*) connect or join. **2** *tr.* clasp or intertwine (hands or arms). **3** *intr.* (foll. by *on, to, in to*) be joined; attach oneself to (a system, company, etc.). □ **link up** (foll. by *with*) connect or combine. [from Old Norse]

linkage *n.* **1** the action of linking; a link or system of links. **2 a** the linking of different issues in political negotiations. **b** *Genetics* the tendency of genes on the same chromosome to be inherited together.

linkman *n.* (*pl.* **-men**) **1** *Brit.* a person providing continuity in a broadcast programme. **2** a player between the forwards and backs in football etc.

links *n.pl.* (treated as *sing.* or *pl.*) a golf course, esp. one having undulating ground, coarse grass, etc. [from obsolete *link* 'rising ground']

link-up *n.* an act or result of linking up.

Linnaean /li-**nee**-ăn/ *adj.* of or relating to the Swedish naturalist Linnaeus or his system of classification of plants and animals.

design cut in linoleum

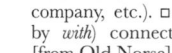

print

LINOCUT

■ **Usage** This word is spelt *Linnean* in *Linnean Society*.

linnet *n.* a finch, *Acanthis cannabina*, with brown and grey plumage. [from Old French *linette*]

lino *n.* (*pl.* **-os**) esp. *Brit.* linoleum.

linocut *n.* **1** ◄ a design carved in relief on a block of linoleum. **2** ◄ a print made from this. □ **linocutting** *n.*

linoleic acid *n. Chem.* a polyunsaturated fatty acid occurring in linseed and other oils and essential in the human diet. [based on Latin *linum* 'flax']

linolenic acid *n. Chem.* a polyunsaturated fatty acid (with one more double bond than linoleic acid) occurring in linseed and other oils and essential in the human diet. [based on German *Linolsäure* 'linoleic acid']

linoleum *n.* a material consisting of a canvas backing thickly coated with a preparation of linseed oil and powdered cork etc., used esp. as a floor covering. [from Latin *linum* 'flax' + *oleum* 'oil'] □ **linoleumed** *adj.*

linseed *n.* the seed of flax. [Old English]

linseed oil *n.* oil extracted from linseed and used in paint and varnish.

linsey-woolsey *n.* a fabric of coarse wool woven on a cotton warp. [Middle English, based on *linsey* 'coarse linen']

lint *n.* **1** *Brit.* a fabric, originally of linen, with a raised nap on one side, used for dressing wounds. **2** fluff. [Middle English] □ **linty** *adj.*

lintel *n. Archit.* ► a horizontal supporting piece of timber, stone, etc., across the top of a door or window. [from Old French, literally 'threshold'] □ **lintelled** *adj.* (*US* **linteled**)

lion *n.* **1** (*fem.* **lioness**) ▼ a large tawny flesh-eating cat, *Panthera leo*, of Africa and S. Asia. ▷ CARNIVORE. **2** (**the Lion**) the zodiacal sign or constellation Leo. ▷ LEO. **3** a brave or celebrated person. **4** the lion as a national emblem of Great Britain or as a representation in heraldry. [from Greek *leōn*] □ **lion-like** *adj.*

lion-heart *n.* a courageous person (esp. as a sobriquet of Richard I of England). □ **lion-hearted** *adj.*

canine teeth

mane (males only)

LION AND **LIONESS** (*Panthera leo*)

lionize *v.tr.* (also **-ise**) treat as a celebrity. □ **lionization** *n.* **lionizer** *n.*

lion's share *n.* (prec. by *the*) the largest or best part.

lip ● *n.* **1** either of the two fleshy parts forming the edges of the mouth-opening. **2** the edge of a cup, container, etc., esp. the part shaped for pouring from. **3** *colloq.* impudent talk. ● *v.tr.* (**lipped**, **lipping**) **1** touch with the lips; apply the lips to. **2** touch lightly. □ **hang on a person's lips** listen attentively to a person. **lick one's lips** see LICK. **smack one's lips** part the lips noisily in relish or anticipation, esp. of food. [Old English] □ **lipless** *adj.* **liplike** *adj.* **lipped** *adj.* (also in *comb.*).

lipase *n. Biochem.* any enzyme that catalyses the breakdown of fats. [based on Greek *lipos* 'fat']

lipid *n. Chem.* any of a class of organic compounds that are insoluble in water but soluble in organic solvents. [from French *lipide*]

lipoprotein *n. Biochem.* any of a group of soluble proteins that combine with and transport fat or other lipids in the blood plasma. [based on Greek *lipos* 'fat']

liposome *n. Biochem.* a minute artificial spherical sac usu. of a phospholipid membrane enclosing an aqueous core, esp. used to carry drugs to specific tissues. [from Greek *lipos* 'fat' + *sōma* 'body']

liposuction *n.* a technique in cosmetic surgery for removing excess fat from under the skin by suction. [based on Greek *lipos* 'fat']

lippy *adj.* (**lippier**, **lippiest**) *colloq.* **1** insolent, impertinent. **2** talkative.

lip-read *v.tr.* (*past* and *past part.* **-read**) (also *absol.*) (esp. of a deaf person) understand (speech) entirely from observing a speaker's lip movements.

lintel

LINTEL ON A GEORGIAN DOOR FRAME

lipsalve *n. Brit.* a preparation, usu. in stick form, to prevent or relieve sore lips.

lip-service *n.* an insincere expression of support etc.

lipstick *n.* a small stick of cosmetic for colouring the lips. ▷ MAKE-UP

lip-sync *n.* (also **-synch**) (in film acting etc.) the movement of a performer's lips in synchronization with a pre-recorded soundtrack.

liquefy *v.tr.* & *intr.* (also **liquify**) (**-ies**, **-ied**) *Chem.* make or become liquid. [from Latin *liquefacere*] □ **liquefacient** *adj.* & *n.* **liquefaction** *n.* **liquefiable** *adj.* **liquefier** *n.*

liqueur /lik-**yoor**/ *n.* any of several strong sweet alcoholic spirits, variously flavoured, usu. drunk after a meal. [French, literally 'liquor']

liquid ● *adj.* **1** having a consistency like that of water or oil, flowing freely but of constant volume. ▷ MATTER. **2** having the qualities of water in appearance (*liquid blue*). **3** (of sounds) clear and pure; fluent. **4 a** (of assets) easily converted into cash. **b** having ready cash or liquid assets. ● *n.* a liquid substance. [from Latin *liquidus*] □ **liquidly** *adv.* **liquidness** *n.*

liquidate *v.* **1 a** *tr.* wind up the affairs of (a company or firm) by ascertaining liabilities and apportioning assets. **b** *intr.* (of a company) be liquidated. **2** *tr.* clear or pay off (a debt). **3** *tr.* eliminate by killing; wipe out. □ **liquidation** *n.* **liquidator** *n.*

liquid crystal *n.* a turbid liquid with some order in its molecular arrangement.

liquid crystal display *n.* ► a form of visual display in electronic devices, in which the reflectivity of a matrix of liquid crystals changes as a signal is applied.

liquid crystal display

LIQUID CRYSTAL DISPLAY ON A CALCULATOR

liquidity *n.* (*pl.* **-ies**) **1** the state of being liquid. **2 a** availability of liquid assets. **b** (in *pl.*) liquid assets.

liquidize *v.tr.* (also **-ise**) reduce (esp. food) to a liquid or puréed state. □ **liquidizer** *n.*

liquid measure *n.* a unit for measuring the volume of liquids.

liquid paraffin *n.* esp. *Brit.* a colourless odourless oily liquid obtained from petroleum and used as a laxative.

liquify var. of LIQUEFY.

liquor *n.* **1** an alcoholic (esp. distilled) drink. **2** other liquid, esp. that produced in cooking. [from Latin *liquor*]

liquorice *n.* (esp. *US* **licorice**) **1** a black root extract used as a sweet and in medicine. **2** ◄ the leguminous plant from which it is obtained. [from Greek *glukurrhiza*, from *glukus* 'sweet' + *rhiza* 'root']

lira *n.* (*pl.* **lire**) **1** the chief monetary unit of Italy. **2** the chief monetary unit of Turkey. [from Latin *libra* 'pound (weight etc.)']

lisle *n.* (in full **lisle thread**) a fine smooth cotton thread for stockings etc. [from *Lisle*, former spelling of *Lille* in France]

LIQUORICE: WILD LIQUORICE (*Glycyrrhiza glabra*)

lisp ● *n.* a speech defect in which *s* is pronounced like *th* in *thick* and *z* is pronounced like *th* in *this*. ● *v.intr.* & *tr.* speak or utter with a lisp. [Old English] □ **lisper** *n.*

lissom *adj.* (also **lissome**) lithe, supple, agile. [based on LITHE] □ **lissomly** *adv.* **lissomness** *n.*

list[1] ● *n.* **1** a number of connected items, names, etc., written or printed together usu. consecutively to form a record or aid to memory. **2** (in *pl.*) *hist.* **a** palisades enclosing an area for a tournament.

b the scene of a contest. ● *v.* **1** *tr.* make a list of. **2** *tr.* enter in a list. **3** *tr.* (as **listed** *adj.*) **a** (of securities) approved for dealings on the Stock Exchange. **b** (of a building in the UK) officially designated as being of historical importance and officially protected. **4** *tr. & intr. archaic* enlist. □ **enter the lists** issue or accept a challenge. [Old English *liste* 'border, strip']

list² ● *v.intr.* (of a ship etc.) lean over to one side, esp. owing to a leak or shifting cargo. ● *n.* the process or an instance of listing. [17th-century coinage]

listen *v.intr.* **1 a** make an effort to hear something. **b** attentively hear a person speaking. **2** (often foll. by *to*) **a** give attention with the ear. **b** respond to advice or a request or to the person expressing it. **3** (also **listen out**) (often foll. by *for*) seek to hear by waiting alertly. □ **listen in 1** eavesdrop. **2** use a radio receiving set. [Old English]

listenable *adj.* easy or pleasant to listen to. □ **listenability** *n.*

listener *n.* **1** a person who listens. **2** a person receiving broadcast radio programmes.

listening post *n.* **1** a point near an enemy's lines for detecting movements by sound. **2** a station for intercepting electronic communications.

listeria *n.* any motile rodlike bacterium of the genus *Listeria*, esp. *L. monocytogenes* infecting humans and animals eating contaminated food. [named after J. *Lister*, English surgeon, 1827–1912]

listeriosis *n.* infection with listeria; a disease resulting from this.

listing *n.* **1** a list or catalogue. **2 a** the drawing up of a list. **b** an entry in a list or register.

listless *adj.* lacking energy or enthusiasm. [Middle English, based on obsolete *list* 'appetite, desire'] □ **listlessly** *adv.* **listlessness** *n.*

lit *past* and *past part.* of LIGHT¹, LIGHT².

litany *n.* (*pl.* **-ies**) **1 a** a series of petitions for use in church services or processions. **b** (**the Litany**) such petitions and responses contained in the Book of Common Prayer. **2** a tedious recital (*a litany of woes*). [from Greek *litaneia* 'prayer']

litchi var. of LYCHEE.

liter *US* var. of LITRE.

literacy *n.* the ability to read and write.

literal ● *adj.* **1** taking words in their usual or primary sense without metaphor or allegory **2** following the letter, text, or exact or original words (*literal translation*). **3** (in full **literal-minded**) (of a person) prosaic. **4 a** not exaggerated (*the literal truth*). **b** so called without exaggeration (*a literal extermination*). **5** *colloq. disp.* so called with some exaggeration or using metaphor (*a literal avalanche of mail*). **6** of, in, or expressed by a letter or the letters of the alphabet. ● *n. Brit. Printing* a misprint of a letter. [based on Latin *littera* 'letter'] □ **literalize** *v.tr.* (also **-ise**). **literally** *adv.* **literalness** *n.*

■ **Usage** The use of *literal* and *literally* simply as intensifiers (see sense 5 above) should be avoided in writing or formal speech.

literalism *n.* insistence on a literal interpretation. □ **literalist** *n.*

literary *adj.* **1** of, constituting, or occupied with books or written composition. **2** well informed about literature. **3** (of a word or idiom) used chiefly in literary works or other formal writing. [from Latin *litterarius*] □ **literarily** *adv.* **literariness** *n.*

literary criticism *n.* the art or practice of estimating the qualities and character of literary works. □ **literary critic** *n.*

literate ● *adj.* able to read and write; educated. ● *n.* a literate person. [from Latin *litteratus*] □ **literately** *adv.*

literati *n.pl.* **1** men or women of letters. **2** the learned class. [Latin]

literature *n.* **1** written works, esp. those whose value lies in beauty of language or in emotional effect. **2** the realm of letters. **3** the writings of a country or period. **4** literary production. **5** *colloq.* printed matter, leaflets, etc. **6** the material in print on a particular subject. [from Latin *litteratura*]

lithe *adj.* flexible, supple. [Old English] □ **lithely** *adv.* **litheness** *n.* **lithesome** *adj.*

lithium *n. Chem.* a soft silver-white metallic element. [based on Greek *lithos* 'stone']

litho *colloq.* ● *n.* = LITHOGRAPHY. ● *v.tr.* (**-oes**, **-oed**) produce by lithography.

litho- *comb. form* stone. [from Greek *lithos* 'stone']

lithograph ● *n.* a lithographic print. ● *v.tr.* **1** print by lithography. **2** write or engrave on stone.

lithography *n.* ▼ a process of printing from a plate so treated that ink adheres only to the design to be printed. ▷ PRINTING. □ **lithographer** *n.* **lithographic** *adj.* **lithographically** *adv.*

lithosphere *n. Geol.* ▼ the rigid outer part of the Earth consisting of the crust and upper mantle. ▷ EARTH. □ **lithospheric** *adj.*

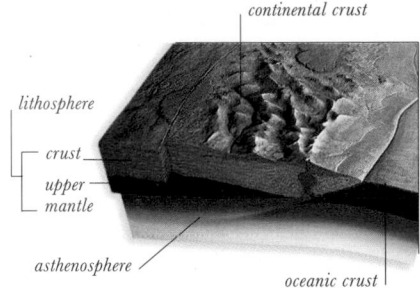

LITHOSPHERE: SECTION OF THE EARTH'S UPPER LAYERS SHOWING THE LITHOSPHERE

Lithuanian ● *n.* **1 a** a native of Lithuania, a Baltic republic. **b** a person of Lithuanian descent. **2** the language of Lithuania. ● *adj.* of or relating to Lithuania, its people, or its language.

litigant ● *n.* a party to a lawsuit. ● *adj.* engaged in a lawsuit. [French]

litigate *v.* **1** *intr.* go to law. **2** *tr.* contest (a point) in a lawsuit. [based on Latin *lis litis* 'lawsuit'] □ **litigable** *adj.* **litigation** *n.* **litigator** *n.*

litigious /li-tij-ŭs/ *adj.* **1** given to litigation. **2** of lawsuits. [from Latin *litigiosus*] □ **litigiously** *adv.* **litigiousness** *n.*

litmus *n.* a dye obtained from lichens that is red under acid conditions and blue under alkaline conditions. [from Old Norse *lit-mosi*, from *litr* 'dye' + *mosi* 'moss']

litmus paper *n.* a paper stained with litmus for use as a test for acids or alkalis.

litmus test *n. colloq.* a real or decisively indicative test.

litotes /ly-toh-teez/ *n.* ironical understatement, esp. using the negative (e.g. *I shan't be sorry* for *I shall be glad*). [from Greek *litotēs*]

litre *n.* (*US* **liter**) a metric unit of capacity, equal to 1,000 cubic centimetres (about 1.75 pints). [from Greek *litra*, a Sicilian monetary unit] □ **litreage** *n.*

Litt.D. *abbr.* Doctor of Letters. [Latin *Litterarum Doctor*]

litter ● *n.* **1 a** refuse, esp. paper, discarded in a public place. **b** odds and ends lying about. **2** disorderly accumulation of papers etc. **3** a number of young animals brought forth at a birth. **4** a vehicle containing a couch shut in by curtains and carried on men's shoulders or by beasts of burden. **5** a framework with a couch for transporting the sick and wounded. **6** straw, rushes, etc., as bedding, esp. for animals. **7** granular absorbent material for lining a box for a cat to urinate and defecate in indoors. ● *v.tr.* **1** make (a place) untidy with discarded refuse. **2** scatter untidily and leave lying about. **3** give birth to (whelps etc.). **4** (often foll. by *down*) **a** provide (a horse etc.) with litter as bedding. **b** spread litter or straw on (a floor) or in (a stable). [from Latin *lectus* 'bed']

litterbug *n. colloq.* = LITTER LOUT.

litter lout *n. Brit.* a person who carelessly drops litter in a public place.

little ● *adj.* (**littler**, **littlest**; **less** or **lesser**; **least**) **1** small in size, amount, degree, etc.; also used with affectionate or emotional overtones (*a friendly little chap*; *a silly little fool*). **2 a** short in stature (*a little man*). **b** of short distance or duration (*wait a little while*). **3** trivial (*exaggerates every little difficulty*). **4** operating on a small scale (*the little shopkeeper*). **5** as a distinctive epithet: **a** of a smaller or the smallest size etc. (*little finger*). **b** that is the smaller or smallest of the name (*little auk*). **6** young or younger (*my little sister*). **7** as of a child, evoking tenderness, amusement, etc. (*we know their little ways*). **8** mean, contemptible (*you little sneak*). ● *det.* **1** (prec. by *a*) a certain though small

LITHOGRAPHY

In traditional lithographic printing, an image is drawn on a stone plate with a greasy medium and fixed by applying an acidic solution. The plate is then dampened and rolled with ink, which adheres only to the greasy areas and is repelled by the water. Paper is laid on to the inked block and pressure is applied by a press, transferring the inked image to the paper. Today, most printed articles are produced by offset lithography, in which the image is transferred from a dampened and inked metal plate to an intermediate 'offset' roller, before being reproduced on paper.

IMAGE DRAWN ON STONE

LITHOGRAPHIC PRINT

TRADITIONAL LITHOGRAPHIC EQUIPMENT

CRAYON AND HOLDER

LITHOGRAPHIC PENCIL

TUSCHE PEN

ROLLER

ERASING STICK

L

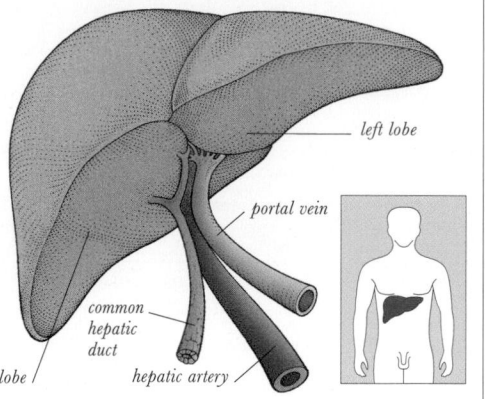

LIVER

Nutrients absorbed from the intestine reach the liver via the portal vein, and are processed and redistributed according to the body's requirements. Hence the liver regulates the levels of glucose, fats, and proteins in the blood. It also removes toxins, breaks down ageing red blood cells, and produces bile, which is stored in the gall bladder for discharge into the duodenum where it assists the absorption and digestion of fats.

STRUCTURE OF THE
HUMAN LIVER

left lobe

portal vein

common hepatic duct

right lobe

hepatic artery

---

amount of (*give me a little butter*). **2** inconsiderable (*gained little advantage from it*). ● *pron.* **1** only a small amount (*did what little I could*). **2** (usu. prec. by a determiner) a certain but no great amount (*every little helps*). ● *adv.* (**less**, **least**) **1** to a small extent only (*little-known authors*). **2** hardly (*they little thought*). **3** (prec. by *a*) somewhat (*is a little deaf*). □ **little by little** by degrees; gradually. **little or nothing** hardly anything. **no little** considerable. **not a little** much; a great deal. ● *adv.* extremely (*not a little concerned*). [Old English] □ **littleness** *n.*

Little Bear *n. Astron.* = URSA MINOR.

little end *n. Mech.* the smaller end of a connecting rod, attached to the piston.

little finger *n.* the smallest finger, at the outer end of the hand.

little grebe *n.* a small waterbird of the grebe family, *Tachybaptus ruficollis*.

little ones *n.pl.* young children or animals.

little people *n.pl.* (prec. by *the*) fairies.

little woman *n.* (prec. by *the*) *colloq.* often *derog.* one's wife.

littoral ● *adj.* of or on the shore. ● *n.* a region lying along a shore. [based on Latin *litus litoris* 'shore']

liturgical *adj.* of or related to liturgies or public worship. □ **liturgically** *adv.* **liturgist** *n.*

liturgy *n.* (*pl.* **-ies**) **1 a** a form of public worship, esp. in the Christian Church. **b** a set of formularies for this. **c** public worship in accordance with a prescribed form. **2** (**Liturgy**) the Communion office of the Orthodox Church. **3** (**the Liturgy**) the Book of Common Prayer. **4** *Gk Hist.* a public office or duty performed voluntarily by a rich Athenian. [from Greek *leitourgia* 'public service, worship of the gods']

livable var. of LIVEABLE.

live[1] /liv/ *v.* **1** *intr.* be or remain alive; have (esp. animal) life. **2** *intr.* (foll. by *on*) subsist or feed. **3** *intr.* (foll. by *on*, *off*) depend for subsistence (*lives off the family*). **4** *intr.* (foll. by *on*, *by*) sustain one's position or repute (*lives by his wits*). **5** *tr.* **a** (with compl.) spend, experience (*lived a happy life*). **b** express in one's life (*was living a lie*). **6** *intr.* conduct oneself in a specified way (*live quietly*). **7** *intr.* arrange one's expenditure etc. (*live modestly*). **8** *intr.* make or have one's abode. **9** *intr.* (foll. by *in*) spend the daytime (*the room does not seem to be lived in*). **10** *intr.* (of a person or thing) survive. □ **live and let live** condone others' failings so as to be similarly tolerated. **live down** (usu. with *neg.*) cause (past guilt etc.) to be forgotten. **live in** (of a student etc.) reside on the premises of one's college etc. **live it up** *colloq.* enjoy life in an active and extravagant way. **live out 1** survive (a danger, difficulty, etc.). **2** (of a student etc.) reside away from one's college etc. **live together** share a home and have a sexual relationship. **live up to** honour or fulfil. **live with 1** share a home with. **2** tolerate. **long live …!** an exclamation of loyalty (to a person etc. specified). [Old English]

live[2] /līv/ ● *adj.* **1** (*attrib.*) that is alive; living. **2 a** (of a performance) given in front of a public audience; heard or seen at the time of its occurrence, not from a recording. **b** (of a recording etc.) made of a live performance. **c** taking place concurrently (*live telephone bidding*). **3** not obsolete or exhausted (*disarmament is still a live issue*). **4** expending or still able to expend energy, esp.: **a** (of coals) glowing, burning. **b** (of a shell) unexploded. **c** (of a match) unkindled. **d** (of a wire, device, etc.) connected to a source of electrical power. **5** (of a wheel etc. in machinery) moving or imparting motion. ● *adv.* as a live performance (*the show went out live*). [form of ALIVE]

liveable *adj.* (also **livable**) **1** (of a house, climate, etc.) fit to live in. **2** (of a life) worth living. **3** (usu. **liveable with**) *colloq.* (of a person) easy to live with. □ **liveability** *n.*

lived-in *adj.* **1** (of a room etc.) showing signs of habitation. **2** *colloq.* (of a face) marked by experience.

live-in *attrib.adj.* **1** (of a sexual partner) cohabiting. **2** resident (*live-in nanny*).

livelihood *n.* a means of living; sustenance. [Old English]

livelong *adj. poet.* or *literary* in its entire length or apparently so (*the livelong day*). [Middle English *lefe longe* 'gladly long']

lively *adj.* (**livelier**, **liveliest**) **1** full of life; vigorous, energetic. **2** brisk (*a lively pace*). **3** stimulating (*a lively discussion*). □ **livelily** *adv.* **liveliness** *n.*

liven *v.tr. & intr.* (often foll. by *up*) *colloq.* make or become more lively.

liver[1] *n.* **1 a** ▲ a large lobed glandular organ in the abdomen of vertebrates, functioning in many metabolic processes. ▷ DIGESTION. **b** a similar organ in other animals. **2** the flesh of an animal's liver as food. ▷ CUT. **3** (in full **liver colour**) a dark reddish brown. [Old English]

liver[2] *n.* a person who lives in a specified way (*a clean liver*).

liver fluke *n.* either of two types of fluke, esp. *Fasciola hepatica*, the adults of which live within the liver tissues of vertebrates.

liverish *adj.* **1** suffering from a disorder of the liver. **2** peevish, glum. □ **liverishly** *adv.* **liverishness** *n.*

Liverpudlian ● *n.* a native of Liverpool in NW England. ● *adj.* of or relating to Liverpool. [jocular from *Liverpool* + PUDDLE]

liver salts *n.pl. Brit.* salts to cure dyspepsia or biliousness.

liver sausage *n.* esp. *Brit.* a sausage containing cooked liver etc.

liverwort *n.* any small leafy or thalloid bryophyte of the class Hepaticae, of which some have liver-shaped parts. ▷ BRYOPHYTE

livery *n.* (*pl.* **-ies**) **1 a** ▶ distinctive clothing worn by a member of a City Company, a servant, etc. **b** membership of a City livery company. **2** a distinctive colour scheme in which a company's vehicles are painted. **3** *US* = LIVERY STABLE. **4** *hist.* a provision of food or clothing for retainers etc. **5** *Law* **a** the legal delivery of property. **b** a writ allowing this. □ **at livery** (of a horse) kept for the owner and fed and groomed for a fixed charge. [from Old French *livrée* (fem.) 'delivered'] □ **liveried** *adj.* (esp. in senses 1a, 2).

livery company *n. Brit.* one of the London City Companies that formerly had a distinctive costume.

liveryman *n.* (*pl.* **-men**) **1** *Brit.* a member of a livery company. **2** a keeper of or attendant at a livery stable.

livery stable *n.* a stable where horses are kept at livery or let out for hire.

LIVERY:
FOOTMAN IN
19TH-CENTURY
LIVERY

lives *pl.* of LIFE.

livestock *n.* (usu. treated as *pl.*) animals, esp. on a farm, regarded as an asset.

live wire *n. colloq.* an energetic and forceful person.

livid *adj.* **1** *colloq.* furiously angry. **2** of a bluish leaden colour. [from Latin *lividus*] □ **lividity** *n.* **lividly** *adv.* **lividness** *n.*

living ● *n.* **1** a livelihood or means of maintenance (*made my living as a journalist*; *what does she do for a living?*). **2** *Brit. Eccl.* a position as a vicar or rector with an income or property. **3** (prec. by *the*; treated as *pl.*) those who are alive. ● *adj.* **1** now existent (*the greatest living poet*). **2** (of a likeness) exact. **3** (of a language) still in vernacular use. □ **within living memory** within the memory of people still living.

living death *n.* a state of hopeless misery.

living room *n.* a room for general day use.

living wage *n.* a wage that affords the means of normal subsistence.

living will *n.* a written statement (but not legally binding) of a person's desire not to be kept alive by artificial means in circumstances such as terminal illness.

lizard *n.* ▶ any reptile of the suborder Lacertilia or Sauria, having usu. a long body and tail and a rough or scaly hide. ▷ REPTILE. [from Latin *lacertus*]

LJ *abbr.* (*pl.* **L JJ**) *Brit.* Lord Justice.

'll *abbr. colloq.* (usu. after pronouns) shall, will (*I'll*; *that'll*).

LLAMA
(*Lama glama*)

llama *n.* **1** ◀ a S. American ruminant, *Lama glama*, kept as a beast of burden and for its soft woolly fleece. **2** the wool from this animal, or cloth made from it. [Spanish]

LL B *abbr.* Bachelor of Laws. [Latin *legum baccalaureus*]

LL D *abbr.* Doctor of Laws. [Latin *legum doctor*]

LL M *abbr.* Master of Laws. [Latin *legum magister*]

Lloyd's *n.* an incorporated society of insurance underwriters in London. [after the original meeting in a coffee house established (1688) by Edward *Lloyd*]

Lloyd's List *n.* a daily publication devoted to shipping news.

Lloyd's Register *n.* **1** an annual alphabetical list of ships assigned to various classes. **2** a society that produces this.

lm *abbr.* lumen(s).

lo *int. archaic* calling attention to an amazing sight. □ **lo and behold** *joc.* a formula introducing a

LIZARD

Numbering approximately 3,500 species, lizards make up over half of the world's reptiles. They are grouped into 17 families, with representatives of the ten principal families shown below. Most lizards have a long tail, a broad head, movable eyelids, a scaly skin, and four splayed legs, although in some species, such as the glass lizards, the legs are reduced or completely absent. Many are good climbers, and some – including chameleons and geckos – are specially adapted to life in trees. Most lizards also have special fracture points along their tails; if the lizard is attacked, the tail can be shed and then regenerated. Apart from some iguanas (which eat plants) and monitor lizards (which often eat carrion), the majority of lizards feed on small animals.

EXTERNAL FEATURES OF A
COMMON GREEN IGUANA
(*Iguana iguana*)

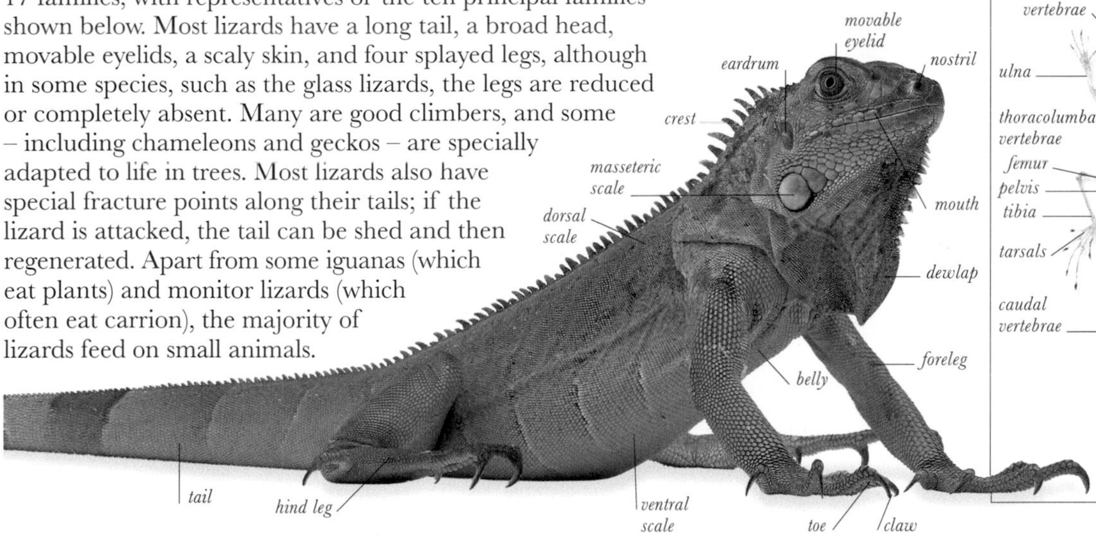

movable
eyelid
nostril
eardrum
crest
masseteric
scale
dorsal
scale
mouth
dewlap
belly
foreleg
tail
hind leg
ventral
scale
toe
claw

SKELETON OF A LIZARD

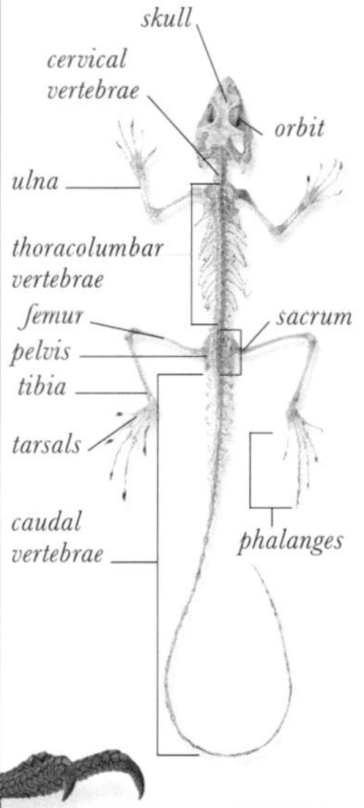

skull
cervical
vertebrae
orbit
ulna
thoracolumbar
vertebrae
femur
sacrum
pelvis
tibia
tarsals
caudal
vertebrae
phalanges

L

MAIN LIZARD FAMILIES

SCINCIDAE
eyed skink
(*Chalcides ocellatus*)

VARANIDAE
Bosc's monitor lizard
(*Varanus exanthematicus*)

AGAMIDAE
Thai water dragon
(*Physignathus concincinus*)

TEIIDAE
common tegu lizard
(*Tupinambis teguixin*)

PYGOPODIDAE
scaly-foot legless lizard
(*Pygopus lepidopodus*)

ANGUIDAE
European glass lizard
(*Ophisaurus apodus*)

IGUANIDAE
Texas horned lizard
(*Phrynosoma cornutum*)

LACERTIDAE
eyed lizard
(*Lacerta lepida*)

CHAMAELEONTIDAE
Jackson's chameleon
(*Chamaeleo jacksoni*)

GEKKONIDAE
leopard gecko
(*Eublepharus macularius*)

surprising or unexpected fact. [Middle English *lō* 'look']

loach *n.* ► any small edible freshwater fish of the family Cobitidae. [from Old French *loche*]

load ● *n.* **1** what is carried or is to be carried; a burden. **2** a unit of measure or weight of certain substances. **3** a commitment of work, responsibility, etc. **4** *colloq.* **a** (in *pl.*; often foll. by *of*) plenty; a lot. **b** (**a load of**) a quantity of (*a load of nonsense*). **5 a** *Electr.* the amount of power supplied by a generating system at any given time. **b** *Electronics* an impedance or circuit that receives or develops the output of a transistor or other device. **6** the weight or force borne by the supporting part of a structure. **7** a material object or force acting as a weight or clog. **8** the resistance of machinery to motive power. ● *v.* **1** *tr.* **a** put a load on or aboard (a person, ship, etc.). **b** place (a load or cargo) aboard a ship etc. **2** *intr.* (often foll. by *up*) (of a vehicle, or person) take a load aboard. **3** *tr.* (often foll. by *with*) oppress (*loaded with responsibilities*). **4** *tr.* add material weight to (*loaded the table with food*). **5** *tr.* (also **load up**) (foll. by *with*) **a** supply overwhelmingly (*loaded us with work*). **b** assail overwhelmingly (*loaded us with abuse*). **6** *tr.* charge (a firearm) with ammunition. **7** *tr.* insert (the required operating medium) in a device, e.g. film in a camera etc. □ **get a load of** *slang* listen attentively. [Old English *lād* 'journey, conveyance']

load displacement *n.* (also **load draught**) the displacement of a ship when laden.

loaded *adj.* **1** bearing or carrying a load. **2** *slang* **a** wealthy. **b** drunk. **c** *US* drugged. **3** (of dice etc.) weighted or given a bias. **4** (of a question or statement) charged with some hidden or improper implication.

loader *n.* **1** a loading machine. **2** (in *comb.*) a gun, machine, lorry, etc., loaded in a specified way (*breech-loader*). **3** an attendant who loads guns at a shoot. □ **-loading** *adj.* (in *comb.*) (in sense 2).

load line *n.* a Plimsoll line.

loadstar var. of LODESTAR.

loadstone var. of LODESTONE.

loaf[1] *n.* (*pl.* **loaves**) **1** a portion of baked bread, usu. of a standard size or shape. **2** other food formed into a particular shape (*meat loaf*). **3** *Brit. slang* the head, esp. as a source of common sense (*use your loaf*). [Old English]

loaf[2] *v.* **1** *intr.* (often foll. by *about*, *around*) spend time idly. **2** *tr.* (foll. by *away*) waste (time) idly. **3** *intr.* saunter.

loafer *n.* **1** an idle person. **2** *propr.* a leather shoe shaped like a moccasin with a flat heel.

loaf sugar *n.* a sugar loaf as a whole or cut into lumps.

loam *n.* **1** a fertile soil of clay and sand containing humus. **2** a clay-based paste used in making bricks etc. [Old English, related to LIME[1]] □ **loamy** *adj.* **loaminess** *n.*

loan ● *n.* **1** something lent, esp. a sum of money to be returned normally with interest. **2** the act of lending or state of being lent. ● *v.tr. disp.* lend (esp. money). □ **on loan** acquired or given as a loan. [from Old Norse *lán*] □ **loanable** *adj.* **loanee** *n.* **loaner** *n.*

■ **Usage** The use of the verb *loan* to mean 'lend' has some justification where a business loan is in question, e.g. *The gas industry is loaning money to the government*, but is considered incorrect by many people as a mere variant of *lend*.

loanholder *n.* **1** a person holding securities for a loan. **2** a mortgagee.

loan shark *n. colloq.* a person who lends money at exorbitant rates of interest.

loath *predic.adj.* (also **loth**) (usu. foll. by *to* + infin.) disinclined, reluctant (*loath to admit it*). [Old English]

loathe *v.tr.* regard with disgust; detest. [Old English] □ **loathing** *n.*

loathsome *adj.* arousing hatred or disgust. □ **loathsomeness** *n.*

loaves *pl.* of LOAF[1].

lob ● *v.tr.* (**lobbed**, **lobbing**) **1** hit or throw (a ball or missile etc.) slowly or in a high arc. **2** send (an opponent) a lobbed ball. ● *n.* **1 a** a ball struck in a high arc. **b** a stroke producing this result. **2** *Cricket* a slow underarm ball.

lobar *adj.* **1** of the lungs (*lobar pneumonia*). **2** of, relating to, or affecting a lobe.

lobate *adj. Biol.* having a lobe or lobes. □ **lobation** *n.*

lobby ● *n.* (*pl.* **-ies**) **1** a porch, ante-room, entrance hall, or corridor. **2 a** (in the House of Commons) a large hall used esp. for interviews between MPs and the public. **b** (also **division lobby**) each of two corridors to which MPs retire to vote. **3 a** a body of lobbyists (*the anti-abortion lobby*). **b** an organized attempt by members of the public to influence legislators. **4** (prec. by *the*) (in the UK) a group of journalists who receive unattributable briefings from the government (*lobby correspondent*). ● *v.* (**-ies**, **-ied**) **1** *tr.* solicit the support of (an influential person). **2** *tr.* (of members of the public) seek to influence (the members of a legislature). **3** *intr.* frequent a parliamentary lobby. [from medieval Latin *lobia* 'lodge'] □ **lobbyer** *n.* **lobbyism** *n.* **lobbyist** *n.*

lobe *n.* **1** a roundish and flattish projecting or pendulous part, often each of two or more such parts divided by a fissure (*lobes of the brain*). **2** = EAR LOBE. ▷ EAR. [from Greek *lobos* 'lobe, pod'] □ **lobed** *adj.* **lobeless** *adj.*

lobelia *n.* any plant of the genus *Lobelia*, with blue, scarlet, white, or purple flowers having a deeply cleft corolla. [named after M. de *Lobel*, Flemish botanist to James I, 1538–1616]

lobotomy *n.* (*pl.* **-ies**) *Med.* surgical incision into a lobe, esp. the frontal lobe of the brain. □ **lobotomize** *v.tr.* (also **-ise**).

lobscouse *n.* a sailor's dish of meat stewed with vegetables and ship's biscuit. [18th-century coinage]

lobster *n.* **1** ▼ any large marine crustacean of the family Nephropidae, with two pincer-like claws as the first pair of ten limbs. **2** its flesh as food. [from corruption of Latin *locusta* 'crustacean, locust']

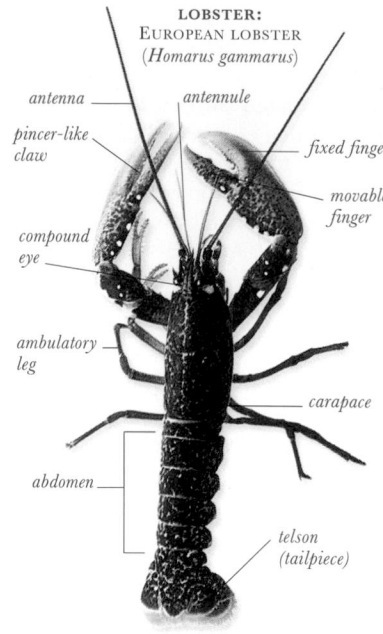

LOBSTER:
EUROPEAN LOBSTER
(*Homarus gammarus*)

antenna — *antennule* — *pincer-like claw* — *fixed finger* — *movable finger* — *compound eye* — *ambulatory leg* — *carapace* — *abdomen* — *telson (tailpiece)*

lobster pot *n.* a basket in which lobsters are trapped.

lobworm *n.* a large earthworm used as fishing bait. [based on obsolete *lob* 'pendulous object']

local ● *adj.* **1** belonging to or existing in a particular place or places. **2** peculiar to or only encountered in a particular place or places. **3** of or belonging to the neighbourhood (*the local doctor*). **4** of or affecting a part and not the whole (*local pain*). **5** (of a tele-

LOACH:
CLOWN LOACH
(*Botia macrantha*)

LOCK

Once a boat has passed into a lock, the rear gates are closed behind it. In a manually operated lock, this is done by pushing on the balance beams. A windlass is then turned to open the sluices in the front gates, raising or lowering the water level. The front gates are then opened, allowing the boat to exit. Locks can also be used to prevent flooding, by allowing excess water to pass from a higher to a lower reach of water. Many modern locks are hydraulically operated.

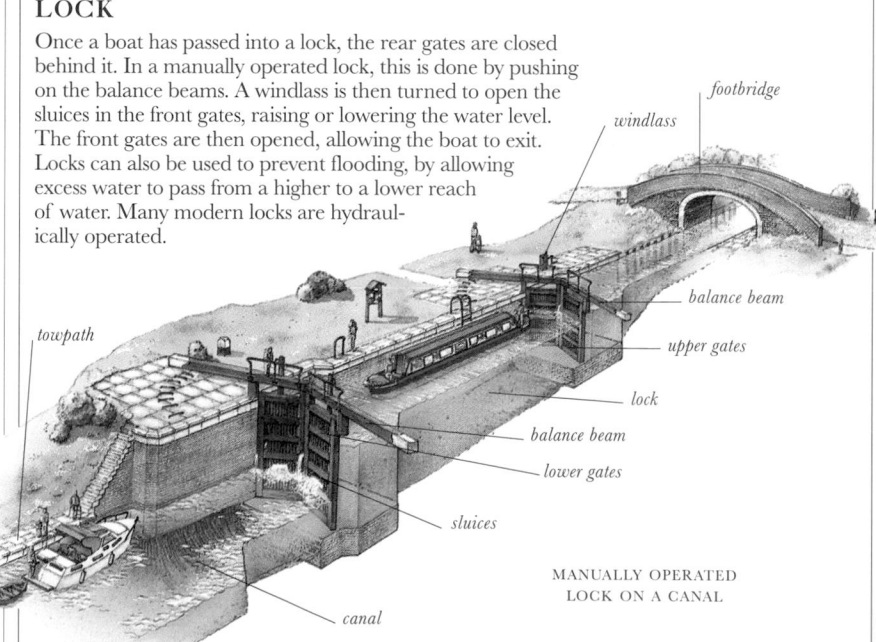

footbridge — *windlass* — *balance beam* — *upper gates* — *lock* — *balance beam* — *lower gates* — *sluices* — *towpath* — *canal*

MANUALLY OPERATED
LOCK ON A CANAL

phone call) to a nearby place and charged at a lower rate. **6** in regard to place. ● *n.* a local person or thing, esp.: **1** an inhabitant of a particular place regarded with reference to that place. **2** a local train, bus, etc. **3** (often prec. by *the*) *Brit. colloq.* a local public house. **4** a local anaesthetic. [based on Latin *locus* 'place'] □ **localize** *v.tr.* (also **-ise**). **locally** *adv.* **localness** *n.*

local anaesthetic *n.* an anaesthetic that affects a restricted area of the body.

local area network *n.* a computer network in which computers in close proximity are able to communicate and share resources.

local authority *n. Brit.* an administrative body in local government.

local bus *n.* a bus service operating over short distances.

local derby *n.* a match between two teams from the same district.

locale *n.* a scene or locality, esp. with reference to an event or occurrence taking place there. [from French *local*]

local government *n.* a system of administration of a county, parish, etc. by the elected representatives of those who live there.

locality *n.* (*pl.* **-ies**) **1** a district or neighbourhood. **2** the site or scene of something, esp. in relation to its surroundings. **3** the position of a thing; the place where it is.

local time *n.* **1** time measured from the Sun's transit over the meridian of a place. **2** time as reckoned in a particular region or time zone.

local train *n.* a train stopping at all the stations on its route.

local veto *n.* esp. *US* = LOCAL OPTION.

locate *v.tr.* **1** discover the exact place or position of (*locate the enemy's camp*). **2** establish or install in a place or in its proper place. **3** state the locality of. **4** (in *passive*) be situated. [based on Latin *locatus* 'placed'] □ **locatable** *adj.* **locator** *n.*

■ **Usage** In standard English, it is not acceptable to use *locate* to mean merely 'find', as in *I couldn't locate my key.*

location *n.* **1** a particular place. **2** the act of locating or process of being located. **3** an actual place or natural setting featured in a film or broadcast (*filmed on location*). □ **locational** *adj.*

locative *Gram.* ● *n.* the case of nouns, pronouns, and adjectives, expressing location. ● *adj.* of or in the locative.

loc. cit. *abbr.* in the passage already cited. [Latin *loco citato*]

loch /lok, lokh/ *n. Sc.* **1** a lake. **2** an arm of the sea, esp. when narrow or partially landlocked. [Middle English]

loci *pl.* of LOCUS.

loci classici *pl.* of LOCUS CLASSICUS.

lock[1] ● *n.* **1** a mechanism for fastening a door, lid, etc., with a bolt that requires a key or a combination of movements to work it. ▷ MORTISE LOCK, YALE LOCK. **2** ◀ a confined section of a canal or river where the level of the water can be changed by the use of gates and sluices. **3 a** the turning of a vehicle's front wheels. **b** (in full **full lock**) the maximum extent of this. **4** an interlocked or jammed state. **5** *Wrestling* a hold that prevents an opponent from moving a limb. **6** (in full **lock forward**) *Rugby* a player in the second row of a scrum. ▷ RUGBY. **7** a mechanism for exploding the charge of a gun. ● *v.* **1 a** *tr.* fasten with a lock. **b** *tr.* (foll. by *up*) shut and secure by locking. **c** *intr.* (of a door, window, etc.) have the means of being locked. **2** *tr.* **a** (foll. by *up, in, into*) enclose by locking or as if by locking. **b** (foll. by *up*) *colloq.* imprison (a person). **3** *tr.* (often foll. by *up, away*) allocate inaccessibly (*capital locked up in land*). **4** *tr. & intr.* make or become rigidly fixed or immovable. **5** *intr. & tr.* (often foll. by *into*) become or cause to become caught (*locked into a cycle of*

borrowing). **6** *tr.* (usu. in *passive*; foll. by *in*) entangle in an embrace or struggle. □ **lock on to** locate or cause to locate by radar etc. and then track. **lock out 1** keep (a person) out by locking the door. **2** (of an employer) submit (employees) to a lockout. **lock, stock, and barrel** *n.* the whole of a thing. ● *adv.* completely. **under lock and key** securely locked up. [Old English] □ **lockable** *adj.* **lockless** *adj.*

lock[2] *n.* **1** a portion of hair that coils or hangs together. **2** (in *pl.*) the hair of the head. [Old English] □ **-locked** *adj.* (in *comb.*).

locker *n.* **1** a small lockable cupboard or compartment, esp. each of several for public use. **2** *Naut.* a chest or compartment for clothes, ammunition, etc.

locker room *n.* a room containing small lockable cupboards in a sports centre etc.

locket *n.* ◀ a small ornamental case holding a portrait, lock of hair, etc., and usu. hung from the neck. [from Old French *locquet* 'little lock']

lock forward see LOCK[1] *n.* 6.

lockjaw *n.* = TRISMUS.

■ **Usage** The word *lockjaw* is not found in technical use.

lock-keeper *n.* a keeper of a lock on a river or canal.

lock-knit ● *adj.* (of a fabric) knitted with an interlocking stitch. ● *n.* such a fabric.

lockout *n.* the exclusion of employees by their employer from their place of work until certain terms are agreed to.

locksman *n.* (*pl.* **-men**) a lock-keeper.

locksmith *n.* a maker and mender of locks.

lock step *n.* marching with each person as close as possible to the one in front.

lock stitch *n.* a stitch made by a sewing machine by firmly locking together two threads or stitches. ▷ STITCH

lock-up ● *n.* **1** a house or room for the temporary detention of prisoners. **2** *Brit.* non-residential premises etc. that can be locked up, esp. a small shop or storehouse. **3** the locking up of premises for the night. ● *attrib.adj. Brit.* that can be locked up (*lock-up shop*).

loco[1] *n.* (*pl.* **-os**) *Brit. colloq.* a locomotive.

loco[2] ● *adj. slang* crazy. ● *n.* (*pl.* **-oes** or **-os**) (in full **loco-weed**) a poisonous leguminous plant of the US, esp. of the genus *Astragalus*, affecting the brains of cattle eating it. [Spanish, literally 'insane']

locomotion *n.* **1** motion or the power of motion from one place to another. **2** travel; a means of travelling, esp. an artificial one. [from Latin *loco* 'from a place' + *motio* 'motion']

locomotive ● *n.* (in full **locomotive engine**) ▲ an engine that travels under its own power, esp. one used for pulling trains. ▷ STEAM ENGINE, TRAIN. ● *adj.* **1** of or relating to or effecting locomotion (*locomotive power*). **2** having the power of or given to locomotion; not stationary.

locomotor *adj.* of or relating to locomotion.

loco-weed SEE LOCO[2].

locum /loh-kŭm/ *n. colloq.* = LOCUM TENENS.

locum tenens /teen-enz/ *n.* (*pl.* **locum tenentes** /ti-nen-teez/) a deputy acting esp. for a cleric or doctor. [medieval Latin, literally 'one holding a place'] □ **locum tenency** *n.*

locus *n.* (*pl.* **loci** /loh-sy/) **1** a position or point, esp. in a text, treatise, etc. **2** *Math.* a curve etc. formed by all the points satisfying a particular equation of the relation between coordinates, or by a point, line, or surface moving according to mathematically defined conditions. **3** *Biol.* the position of a gene, mutation, etc. on a chromosome. [Latin, literally 'place']

locus classicus *n.* (*pl.* **loci classici** /klas-i-sy/) the best known or most authoritative passage on a subject. [Latin, literally 'classical place']

locust *n.* **1** ▼ any of various African and Asian grasshoppers of the family Acrididae, migrating in swarms and destroying vegetation. ▷ ORTHOPTERAN.

LOCOMOTIVE

Trains are pulled by powerful engine units called locomotives. In a steam locomotive, pressure from the steam moves a piston back and forth, which turns the wheels via a connecting rod. In a diesel-electric locomotive, air is drawn into the engine cylinders and is compressed to increase its temperature; a small amount of diesel fuel is then injected into it. The resulting combustion drives the generator to produce electricity, which is fed to electric motors. In electric locomotives, electric current is picked up either from a catenary (overhead cable) via a pantograph, or from a third rail.

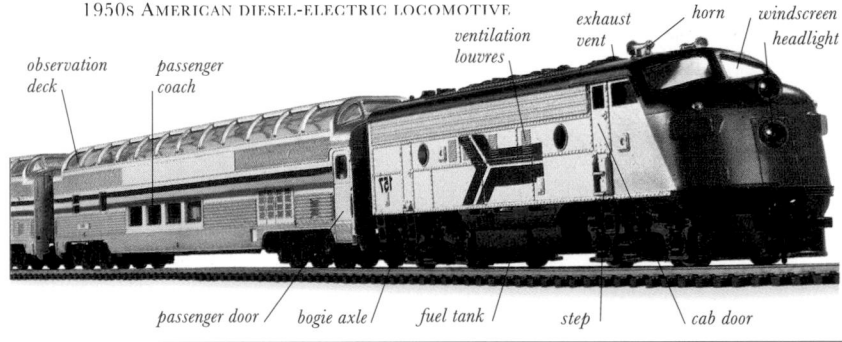

1950s AMERICAN DIESEL-ELECTRIC LOCOMOTIVE

observation deck — passenger coach — ventilation louvres — exhaust vent — horn — windscreen — headlight

passenger door — bogie axle — fuel tank — step — cab door

LOCKET: LATE 19TH-CENTURY ENGLISH LOCKET

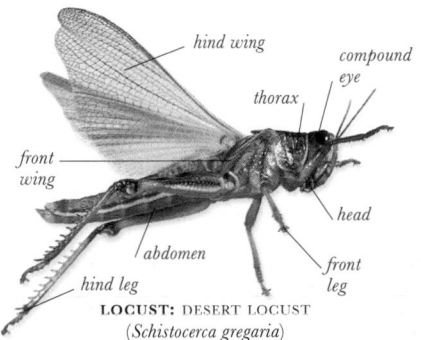

LOCUST: DESERT LOCUST (*Schistocerca gregaria*)

hind wing — compound eye — thorax — front wing — head — abdomen — front leg — hind leg

L

LODESTAR

In the northern hemisphere, the lodestar Polaris can be used to locate north, since it remains fixed almost directly above the North Pole. The stars Merak and Dubhe, in Ursa Major, act as pointers to Polaris.

POSITION OF THE LODESTAR Polaris

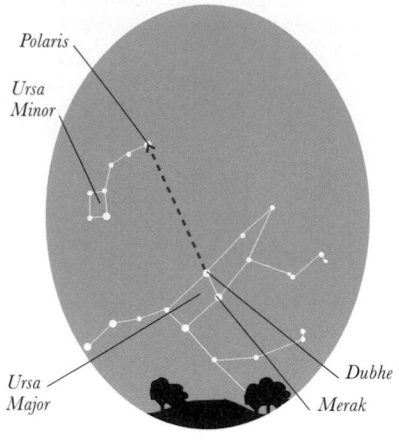

Polaris

Ursa Minor

Ursa Major

Dubhe

Merak

L

2 *US* a cicada. **3** (in full **locust bean**) a carob. **4** (in full **locust tree**) **a** a carob tree. **b** = ACACIA 2. **c** = KOWHAI. [from Latin *locusta* 'crustacean, locust']

locution *n.* **1** a word or phrase, esp. considered in regard to style or idiom. **2** style of speech. [from Latin *locutio*]

lode *n.* a vein of metal ore. [variant of LOAD]

loden *n.* a thick waterproof woollen cloth. [German]

lodestar *n.* (also **loadstar**) **1 ▲** a star that a ship etc. is steered by, esp. the pole star. **2 a** a guiding principle. **b** an object of pursuit. [based on obsolete *lode* 'way, journey']

iron filings

lodestone *n.* (also **loadstone**) **1** magnetic oxide of iron, magnetite. **2 a ◄** a piece of this used as a magnet. **b** a thing that attracts.

lodge ● *n.* **1** a small house at the gates of a park or in the grounds of a large house, occupied by a gatekeeper etc. **2** a large house or hotel, esp. in a resort. **3** a house occupied in the hunting or shooting season. **4** a porter's room or quarters at the gate of a college or other large building. **5** the members or the meeting place of a branch of a society such as the Freemasons. **6 ▼** a beaver's or otter's lair. ● *v.* **1** *tr.* bring forward or submit (a complaint). **2** *tr.* deposit (money etc.) for security. **3** *tr.* (foll.

LODESTONE WITH ATTRACTED IRON FILINGS

by *in, with*) place (power etc.) in a person or group. **4** *tr. & intr.* make or become fixed without further movement. **5** *tr.* **a** provide (a person) with sleeping quarters. **b** receive as a guest or inmate. **6** *intr.* reside or live, esp. as a paying guest. **7** *tr.* (in *passive*; foll. by *in*) be contained in. [from medieval Latin *laubia, lobia*]

lodger *n.* a person receiving accommodation in another's house for payment.

lodging *n.* **1** temporary accommodation. **2** (in *pl.*) a room or rooms (other than in a hotel) rented for lodging in. **3** a dwelling place.

lodging house *n.* a house in which lodgings are let.

loess /loh-iss/ *n.* a deposit of fine light-coloured wind-blown dust found esp. in the basins of large rivers. [from Swiss German *lösch* 'loose']

loft ● *n.* **1** the space under the roof of a house, above the ceiling of the top floor; an attic. **2** a room over a stable, esp. for hay and straw. **3** a gallery in a church or hall (*organ loft*). **4** a pigeon house. **5** *Golf* a backward slope in a club-head. ● *v.tr.* **1** send (a ball etc.) high up. **2** clear (an obstacle) in this way. [from Old Norse *lopt* 'air, sky, upper room']

lofty *adj.* (**loftier, loftiest**) **1** *literary* (of things) towering, soaring (*lofty heights*). **2** consciously haughty (*lofty contempt*). **3** sublime (*lofty ideals*). [related to LOFT] □ **loftily** *adv.* **loftiness** *n.*

log[1] ● *n.* **1** an unhewn piece of a felled tree, or a similar rough mass of wood, esp. cut for firewood. **2** a floating device for gauging the speed of a ship. **3** a record of events occurring during and affecting the voyage of a ship or aircraft. **4** any systematic record of things done, experienced, etc. **5** = LOGBOOK 1. ● *v.tr.* (**logged, logging**) **1 a** enter (details) in a logbook. **b** (of a ship) achieve (a certain distance). **2 a** enter (information) in a regular record. **b** attain (a cumulative total) (*logged 50 hours on the computer*). **3** cut into logs. □ **like a log 1** in a helpless or stunned state (*fell like a log*). **2** without stirring (*slept like a log*). **log in** = log on. **log on** (or **off**) go through the procedures to begin (or conclude) use of a computer system. [Middle English]

log[2] *n.* a logarithm (esp. prefixed to a number or algebraic symbol whose logarithm is to be indicated).

logan *n.* (in full **logan-stone**) = ROCKING-STONE.

loganberry *n.* (*pl.* **-ies**) **1 ▶** a dull red soft fruit, apparently a hybrid of a raspberry and a dewberry. **2** the plant bearing this, *Rubus loganobaccus*.

logarithm *n.* a figure representing the power to which a fixed number or base must be raised to produce a given number, used to simplify calculations as the addition and subtraction of logarithms is equivalent to multiplication and division. [from Greek *logos* 'reckoning, ratio' + *arithmos* 'number'] □ **logarithmic** *adj.* **logarithmically** *adv.*

logbook *n.* **1** a book containing a detailed record or log. **2** *Brit.* = REGISTRATION DOCUMENT.

log cabin *n.* a hut built of logs.

loge *n.* a private box or enclosure in a theatre. [French]

logger *n. N. Amer.* a lumberjack.

loggerhead *n.* (in full **loggerhead turtle**) **▶** a large-headed turtle, *Caretta caretta*, of warm seas. □ **at loggerheads** (often foll. by *with*) disagreeing or disputing.

logging *n.* the work of cutting and preparing forest timber.

logic *n.* **1 a** the science of reasoning, proof, thinking, or inference. **b** a particular scheme of or treatise on this. **2 a** a chain of reasoning (*I don't follow your logic*). **b** ability in reasoning (*argues with great learning and logic*). **c** reasoned argument (*is not governed by logic*). **3 a** the inexorable force or compulsion of a thing

(*the logic of events*). **b** the necessary consequence of (an argument, decision, etc.). **4 a** the principles underlying the arrangements of elements in a computer. **b** logical operations collectively. [from Greek *logikē* (*tekhnē*) 'art' of reason'] □ **logician** *n.*

logical *adj.* **1** of logic or formal argument. **2** not contravening the laws of thought, correctly reasoned. **3** deducible or defensible on the ground of consistency. **4** capable of correct reasoning. □ **logicality** *n.* **logically** *adv.*

logical positivism *n.* (also **logical empiricism**) a form of positivism in which symbolic logic is used and linguistic problems of meaning are emphasized.

logic bomb *n. Computing* a set of instructions secretly incorporated into a program so that if a particular logical condition is satisfied they will be carried out, usu. with harmful effects.

logistics *n.pl.* (often treated as *sing.*) **1** the organization of moving, lodging, and supplying troops and equipment. **2** the detailed organization and implementation of a plan or operation. [from French *logistique*] □ **logistic** *adj.* **logistical** *adj.* **logistically** *adv.*

logjam *n.* **1** a crowded mass of logs in a river. **2** a deadlock.

logo *n.* (*pl.* **-os**) an emblem or device used as the badge of an organization in display material. [abbreviation of LOGOTYPE]

logorrhoea /log-ŏ-ree-ă/ *n.* (*US* **logorrhea**) excessive flow of words, esp. in mental illness. [from Greek *logos* 'word' + *rhoia* 'flow']

logotype *n.* **1** *Printing* a single piece of type that prints a word or group of separate letters. **2 a** = LOGO. **b** *Printing* a single piece of type that prints this. [based on Greek *logos* 'word']

logrolling *n. US* **1** *colloq.* the practice of exchanging favours, esp. (in politics) of exchanging votes to mutual benefit. **2** a sport in which two contestants stand on a floating log and try to knock each other off. [political sense from phrase *you roll my log and I'll roll yours*] □ **logroller** *n.*

loin *n.* **1** (in *pl.*) the part of the body on both sides of the spine between the floating ribs and the hip bones. **2** a joint of meat that includes the loin vertebrae. ▷ CUT. [from Latin *lumbus*]

loincloth *n.* a cloth worn round the hips, esp. as a sole garment.

loiter *v.intr.* hang about; linger idly. □ **loiter with intent** *Brit.* hang about in order to commit a felony. [from Middle Dutch *loteren* 'to wag about'] □ **loiterer** *n.*

loll *v.intr.* **1** (often foll. by *about, around*) stand, sit, or recline in a lazy attitude. **2** hang loosely. [Middle English] □ **loller** *n.*

lollipop *n.* a large usu. flat rounded boiled sweet on a small stick.

lollipop man *n.* (*fem.* **lollipop lady**) *Brit. colloq.* an official using a circular sign on a stick to stop traffic for children to cross the road, esp. near a school.

lollop *v.intr.* (**lolloped, lolloping**) *colloq.* **1** flop about. **2** *Brit.* move or proceed in a lounging or ungainly way.

lolly *n.* (*pl.* **-ies**) **1** *colloq.* **a** esp. *Brit.* = LOLLIPOP. **b** esp.

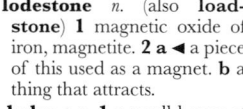

LOGANBERRY
(*Rubus loganobaccus*)

lodge chamber

platform

piled branches

underwater entrance

LODGE:
BEAVER'S LODGE

LOGGERHEAD TURTLE
(*Caretta caretta*)

Brit. = ICE LOLLY. **c** *Austral.* a sweet. **2** *Brit. slang* money.

Lombardy poplar *n.* a tall slender variety of poplar.

Londoner *n.* a native or inhabitant of London.

London pride *n.* a pink-flowered saxifrage, *Saxifraga × urbium*.

lone *attrib.adj.* **1** (of a person) solitary; without a companion or supporter. **2** (of a place) isolated. **3** unmarried or widowed (*lone parent*). [form of ALONE]

lone hand *n.* **1** *Cards* a hand played, or a player playing, against the rest at euchre. **2** a person or action without allies.

lonely *adj.* (**lonelier**, **loneliest**) **1** (of a person) solitary, companionless, isolated. **2** (of a place) unfrequented; (of a thing) standing apart; isolated. **3 a** sad because without friends or company. **b** imparting a sense of loneliness; dreary. □ **loneliness** *n.*

lonely heart *n.* a lonely person, esp. one seeking companionship by advertising in a newspaper etc.

loner *n.* a person or animal that prefers not to associate with others.

lonesome *adj.* **1** solitary, lonely. **2** feeling lonely or forlorn. **3** causing such a feeling. □ **by** (or **on**) **one's lonesome** *colloq.* all alone. □ **lonesomeness** *n.*

lone wolf *n.* a person who prefers to act alone.

long¹ ● *adj.* (**longer**, **longest**) **1** measuring much from end to end in space or time (*a long line; a long journey; a long time*). **2** (following a measurement) in length or duration (*2 metres long*). **3 a** consisting of a large number of items (*a long list*). **b** (seemingly more than the stated amount; tedious, lengthy (*ten long miles; tired after a long day*). **4** of elongated shape. **5 a** lasting or reaching far back or forward in time (*a long friendship*). **b** (of a person's memory) retaining things for a long time. **6** far-reaching; acting at a distance; involving a great interval or difference. **7** *Phonet.* & *Prosody* of a vowel or syllable: **a** having the greater of the two recognized durations. **b** (of a vowel)

LONGHORN COW

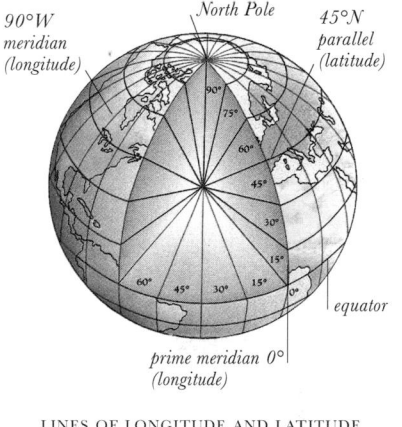

categorized as long with regard to quality and length (e.g. in standard British English the vowel in *food* is long as distinct from the short vowel in *good*) (cf. SHORT *adj.* 6). **8** (of odds or a chance) reflecting or representing a low level of probability. **9** (of a cold drink) large and refreshing. **10** *colloq.* (of a person) tall. **11** (foll. by *on*) *colloq.* well supplied with. ● *n.* a long interval or period (*it will not take long*). ● *adv.* (**longer**, **longest**) **1** by or for a long time (*long before; long ago; long live the king!*). **2** (following nouns of duration) throughout a specified time (*all day long*). **3** (in *compar.*; with *neg.*) after an implied point of time (*shall not wait any longer*). □ **as** (or **so**) **long as 1** during the whole time that. **2** provided that; only if. **at long last** see LAST¹. **before long** fairly soon (*shall see you before long*). **be long** (often foll. by *pres. part.* or *in* + verbal noun) take a long time; be slow (*I shan't be long*). **by a long chalk** see CHALK. **in the long run 1** over a long period. **2** eventually; finally. **long ago** in the distant past. **the long and the short of it 1** all that can or need be said. **2** the eventual outcome. **long in the tooth** rather old.

not by a long shot by no means. [Old English] □ **longish** *adj.*

long² *v.intr.* (foll. by *for*, or *to* + infin.) have a strong wish or desire for. [Old English *langian* 'to seem long, desire']

long. *abbr.* longitude.

long-awaited *adj.* that has been awaited for a long time.

longboat *n.* a sailing ship's largest boat.

longbow *n.* ◄ a bow drawn by hand and shooting a long feathered arrow.

long-case clock *n.* a grandfather clock.

long-dated *adj.* (of securities) not due for early payment or redemption.

long-dead *adj.* that has been dead for a long time.

long-distance ● *adj.* **1** (of a telephone call, road transport, etc.) between distant places. **2** *Brit.* (of a weather forecast) long-range. ● *adv.* (also **long distance**) between distant places (*phone long-distance*).

long division *n. Math.* division of numbers with details of the calculations written down.

long-drawn *adj.* (also **long-drawn-out**) prolonged, esp. unduly.

longe var. of LUNGE².

longevity /lon-jev-iti/ *n.* long life. [based on Latin *longus* 'long' + *aevum* 'age']

long face *n.* a dismal or disappointed expression. □ **long-faced** *adj.*

longhand *n.* ordinary handwriting (as opposed to shorthand or typing or printing).

long haul *n.* **1** the transport of goods or passengers over a long distance (hyphenated when *attrib.*: *long-haul flights*). **2** a prolonged effort or task.

long-headed *adj.* shrewd, far-seeing. □ **long-headedness** *n.*

longhorn *n.* **1** ◄ one of a breed of cattle with long horns. **2** any beetle of the family Cerambycidae with long antennae. ▷ BEETLE, INSECT

long hundredweight see HUNDREDWEIGHT 1.

longing ● *n.* a feeling of intense desire. ● *adj.* having or showing this feeling. □ **longingly** *adv.*

longitude /lon-ji-tewd/ *adj.* **1** *Geog.* ▲ the angular distance east or west from a standard meridian such as Greenwich to the meridian of any place. **2** *Astron.* the angular distance of a celestial object north or south of the ecliptic measured along a great circle through the object and the poles of the ecliptic. [Middle English, from Latin *longitudo -dinis*, from *longus* 'long']

longitudinal /lon-ji-tewd-in-ăl/ *adj.* **1** of or in length. **2** running lengthwise. **3** of longitude. □ **longitudinally** *adv.*

longitudinal wave *n. Physics* a wave vibrating in the direction of propagation.

long johns *n.pl. colloq.* underpants with full-length legs.

long jump *n.* an athletic contest of jumping as far as possible along the ground in one leap. □ **long-jumper** *n.*

long-lasting *adj.* that lasts, or has lasted, for a long time.

LONGBOW: 15TH-CENTURY ARCHER AND LONGBOW

LONGITUDE

Lines of longitude, or meridians, are imaginary lines drawn around the Earth from the North Pole to the South Pole. Positions of longitude are given in degrees east or west of the prime meridian, which passes through Greenwich, England. In contrast, lines of latitude, or parallels, are drawn around the Earth parallel to the equator. Positions of latitude are given in degrees north or south of the equator.

LINES OF LONGITUDE AND LATITUDE ON A GLOBE OF THE EARTH

L

long leg *n. Cricket* **1** a fielder far behind the batsman on the leg side. **2** this fielding position.

long-life *adj.* (of consumable goods) treated to preserve freshness.

long-lived *adj.* having a long life; durable.

long-lost *attrib.adj.* that has been lost or not seen for a long time.

long measure *n.* a measure of length (metres, miles, etc.).

long metre *n.* **1** a hymn stanza of four lines with eight syllables each. **2** a quatrain of iambic tetrameters with alternate lines rhyming.

long off *n.* (also **long on**) *Cricket* **1** a fielder far behind the bowler and towards the off (or on) side. **2** this fielding position.

long-playing *adj.* (of a gramophone record) playing for about 20–30 minutes on each side. □ **long-player** *n. Brit.*

long-range *adj.* **1** (of a missile etc.) having a long range of operation. **2** of or relating to a period of time far into the future.

long-running *adj.* continuing for a long time.

long ship *n. hist.* ▼ a long narrow warship with many rowers, used esp. by the Vikings.

LONG SHIP: VIKING COASTER

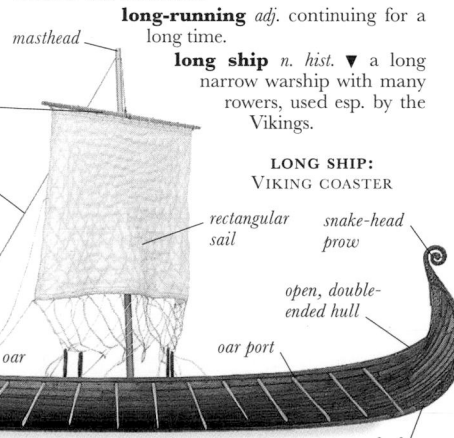

LONGSHORE DRIFT

Longshore drift is the movement of sand and shingle along the shoreline, caused by the ebb and flow of waves, and by the wind. This continual movement means a beach in winter may consist of coarse pebbles, while the same beach in the summer may be sandy. In places where longshore drift is strong, it can wash sand across a bay or river mouth, depositing it to form a spit. To reduce the beach matter being washed away in this manner, barriers, called groynes, are often built at right angles out into the sea.

river mouth
hook
sand spit
sand and shingle
beach matter build-up
groyne
receding wave
angled approaching wave

PROCESS OF LONGSHORE
DRIFT ON A BEACH

L

longshore *adj.* **1** existing on or frequenting the shore. **2** directed along the shore. [from *along shore*]

longshore drift *n.* ▲ the movement of material along a coast by waves which approach at an angle to the shore but recede directly away from it.

longshoreman *n.* (*pl.* **-men**) *US* a docker.

long shot *n.* **1** a wild guess or venture. **2** a bet at long odds. **3** *Cinematog.* a shot including objects at a distance.

long sight *n.* the ability to see clearly only what is comparatively distant. ▷ SIGHT

long-sighted *adj.* **1** having long sight. **2** having imagination or foresight. □ **long-sightedness** *n.*

long-sleeved *adj.* with sleeves reaching to the wrist.

longspur *n.* ▼ a N. American bunting of the genus *Calcarius*.

long-standing *adj.* that has long existed; not recent.

long-stay *attrib.adj.* **1** staying a long time (*long-stay patients*). **2** for people who are staying a long time (*long-stay car park*).

longstop *n.* **1** *Cricket* **a** a fielder directly behind the wicketkeeper. **b** this fielding position. **2** *Brit.* = BACKSTOP 2.

long-suffering *adj.* bearing provocation patiently. □ **long-sufferingly** *adv.*

long suit *n.* **1** ▼ many playing cards of one suit in a hand (esp. more than 3 or 4 in a hand of 13). **2** a thing at which one excels.

LONGSPUR:
LAPLAND BUNTING
(*Calcarius lapponicus*)

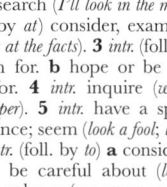

LONG SUIT OF HEARTS IN A MIXED HAND

long-term *adj.* occurring in or relating to a long period of time (*long-term plans*).

long-time *attrib.adj.* that has been such for a long time.

long ton see TON 1.

longueur /long-ger/ *n.* **1** a tedious passage in a book etc. **2** a tedious stretch of time. [French, literally 'length']

long vacation *n. Brit.* the summer vacation of law courts and universities.

long waist *n.* a low or deep waist of a dress or body. □ **long-waisted** *adj.*

long wave *n.* a radio wave of frequency less than 300 kHz.

longways *adv.* (also **longwise**) = LENGTHWAYS.

long-winded *adj.* **1** (of speech or writing) tediously lengthy. **2** able to run a long distance without rest. □ **long-windedly** *adv.* **long-windedness** *n.*

lonicera /lŏn-iss-er-ă/ *n.* **1** a dense evergreen shrub, *Lonicera nitidum*, much used as hedging. **2** = HONEYSUCKLE. [named after A. *Lonicerus*, German botanist, 1528–86]

loo[1] *n. Brit. colloq.* a lavatory. [20th-century coinage]

loo[2] *n.* **1** a round card game with penalties paid to the pool. **2** this penalty. [abbreviation of obsolete *lanterloo* from French *lanturlu*, meaningless refrain]

loofah *n.* (also **luffa**) **1** ▶ a climbing gourdlike plant, *Luffa cylindrica*, native to Asia, producing edible marrow-like fruits. **2** the dried fibrous vascular system of this fruit used to scrub the skin. [from Egyptian Arabic *lūfa*, the plant]

look ● *v.* **1 a** *intr.* (often foll. by *at*) use one's sight; turn one's eyes in some direction. **b** *tr.* turn one's eyes on; contemplate or examine (*looked me in the eyes*). **2** *intr.* **a** make a visual or mental search (*I'll look in the morning*). **b** (foll. by *at*) consider, examine (*we must look at the facts*). **3** (foll. by *for*) **a** search for. **b** hope or be on the watch for. **4** *intr.* inquire (*when one looks deeper*). **5** *intr.* have a specified appearance; seem (*look a fool*; *look foolish*). **6** *intr.* (foll. by *to*) **a** consider; take care of; be careful about (*look to the future*). **b** rely on (a person or thing) (*you can look to me for support*). **7** *intr.* (foll. by *into*) investigate or examine. **8** *tr.* (foll. by *what*, *where*, etc. + clause)

brown peel
fibrous fruit

LOOFAH:
SMOOTH LOOFAH
(*Luffa cylindrica*)

ascertain or observe by sight (*look where we are*). **9** *intr.* (of a thing) face or be turned, or have or afford an outlook, in a specified direction. **10** *tr.* express, threaten, or show (an emotion etc.) by one's looks. **11** *intr.* (foll. by *that* + clause) take care; make sure. **12** *intr.* (foll. by *to* + infin.) expect (*am looking to finish this today*). ● *n.* **1** an act of looking; a glance (*a scornful look*). **2** (in *sing.* or *pl.*) the appearance of a face; a person's expression or personal aspect. **3** the (esp. characteristic) appearance of a thing (*the place has a European look*). **4** style, fashion (*this year's look*; *the wet look*). ● *int.* (also **look here!**) calling attention, expressing a protest, etc. □ **look after 1** attend to; take care of. **2** follow with the eye. **3** seek for. **look one's age** appear to be as old as one really is. **look as if** suggest by appearance the belief that (*it looks as if he's gone*). **look back 1** (foll. by *on*, *upon*, *to*) turn one's thoughts to (something past). **2** (usu. with *neg.*) cease to progress (*since then we have never looked back*). **3** *Brit.* make a further visit later. **look before you leap** avoid precipitate action. **look daggers** see DAGGER. **look down on** (or **upon** or **look down one's nose at**) regard with contempt or a feeling of superiority. **look for trouble** see TROUBLE. **look forward to** await (an expected event) eagerly or with specified feelings. **look in** make a short visit or call. **look like 1** have the appearance of. **2** *Brit.* seem to be (*they look like winning*). **3** threaten or promise (*it looks like rain*). **4** indicate the presence of (*it looks like woodworm*). **look lively** (often in *imper.*) *colloq.* move (more) quickly or energetically. **look on 1** (often foll. by *as*) regard (*looks on you as a friend*). **2** be a spectator; avoid participation. **look out 1** direct one's sight out of a window etc. **2** (often foll. by *for*) be vigilant or prepared. **3** (foll. by *on*, *over*, etc.) have or afford a specified outlook. **4** *Brit.* search for and produce (*shall look one out for you*). **look over 1** inspect or survey (*looked over the house*). **2** examine (a document etc.) esp. cursorily (*shall look it over*). **look round** (*US* **around**) **1** look in every or another direction. **2** examine the objects of interest in a place. **3** examine the possibilities etc. with a view to deciding on a course of action. **look sharp** act promptly; make haste. **look through 1** examine the contents of, esp. cursorily. **2** penetrate (a pretence or pretender) with insight. **3** ignore by pretending not to see (*I waved, but you just looked through me*). **look up 1** search for (esp. information in a book). **2** *colloq.* go to visit (a person). **3** raise one's eyes. **4** improve, esp. in price, prosperity, or well-being (*things are looking up all round*). **look up to** respect or venerate. **not like the look of** find alarming or suspicious. [Old English] □ **-looking** *adj.* (in *comb.*).

lookalike *n.* a person or thing closely resembling another (*a Prince Charles lookalike*).

looker *n.* **1** a person having a specified appearance (*a great looker*). **2** *colloq.* a good-looking person, esp. a woman.

looker-on *n.* a person who is a mere spectator.

look-in *n. colloq.* **1** an informal call or visit. **2** a chance of participation or success (*never gets a look-in*).

looking-glass *n.* a mirror for looking at oneself.

lookout *n.* **1** a watch or looking out (*on the lookout for bargains*). **2 a** a post of observation. **b** a person or party or boat stationed to keep watch. **3** esp. *Brit.* a prospect of luck (*it's a bad lookout for them*). **4** *colloq.* a person's own concern.

look-see *n. colloq.* a survey or inspection. [from, or in imitation of, pidgin English]

loom[1] *n.* an apparatus for weaving yarn or thread into fabric. ▷ WEAVE. [Old English *gelōma* 'tool']

loom[2] *v.intr.* (often foll. by *up*) **1** come into sight dimly, esp. as a vague and often threatening shape. **2** (of an event or prospect) be ominously close.

loon *n.* **1** *N. Amer.* = DIVER 3. **2** *colloq.* a crazy person (cf. LOONY). [alteration of *loom* 'diver, guillemot', from Old Norse *lómr*]

loony *slang* ● *n.* (*pl.* **-ies**) a mad or silly person; a lunatic. ● *adj.* (**loonier, looniest**) crazy, silly. □ **looniness** *n.*

loony-bin *n. slang offens.* a mental home or hospital.

loop ● *n.* **1 a** a figure produced by a curve, or a doubled thread etc., that crosses itself. **b** anything forming this figure. ▷ KNOT. **2** a similarly shaped attachment or ornament formed of cord or thread etc. and fastened at the crossing. **3** a ring or curved piece of material as a handle etc. **4** a contraceptive coil. **5** (in full **loop line**) a railway or telegraph line that diverges from a main line and joins it again. **6** a manoeuvre in which an aeroplane describes a vertical loop. **7** *Skating* a manoeuvre describing a curve that crosses itself, made on a single edge. **8** *Electr.* a complete circuit for a current. **9** an endless strip of tape or film allowing continuous repetition. **10** *Computing* a programmed sequence of instructions that is repeated until or while a condition is satisfied. ● *v.* **1** *tr.* form (thread etc.) into a loop or loops. **2** *tr.* enclose with or as with a loop. **3** *tr.* (often foll. by *up, back, together*) fasten or join with a loop or loops. **4** *intr.* **a** form a loop. **b** move in looplike patterns. **5** *intr.* loop the loop (see LOOP-THE-LOOP). [Middle English]

loophole *n.* **1** a means of evading a rule etc. without infringing the letter of it. **2** ◀ a narrow vertical slit in a wall. ▷ NORMAN. [Middle English]

LOOPHOLE IN A CASTLE WALL

loop-the-loop *Aeron.* ● *n.* the feat of circling in a vertical loop. ● *v.intr.* (**loop the loop**) perform this feat.

loopy *adj.* (**loopier, loopiest**) *slang* crazy.

loose ● *adj.* **1 a** not or no longer held by bonds or restraint. **b** (of an animal) not confined or tethered etc. **2** detached or detachable from its place (*has come loose*). **3** not held together or contained or fixed (*loose papers; had her hair loose*). **4** hanging partly free (*a loose end*). **5** slack, relaxed; not tense or tight. **6** not compact or dense (*loose soil*). **7** (of language, concepts, etc.) inexact. **8** morally lax; dissolute (*loose living*). **9** (of the tongue) likely to speak indiscreetly. **10** (of the bowels) tending to diarrhoea. **11** *Sport* (of a ball) in play but not in any player's possession. **12** (in *comb.*) loosely (*loose-fitting*). ● *n. Brit.* a state of freedom or unrestrainedness. ● *v.tr.* **1** release; set free; free from constraint. **2** untie or undo (something that constrains). **3** relax (*loosed my hold on it*). **4** discharge (a gun or arrow etc.). □ **at a loose end** (or *N. Amer.* **at loose ends**) (of a person) unoccupied, esp. temporarily. **on the loose 1** escaped from captivity. **2** having a free enjoyable time. [from Old Norse *lauss*] □ **loosely** *adv.* **looseness** *n.* **loosish** *adj.*

loose box *n. Brit.* a compartment for a horse, in a stable or vehicle, in which it can move about.

loose cannon *n.* a person or thing causing unintentional or misdirected damage.

loose change *n.* money as coins in the pocket etc. for casual use.

loose cover *n. Brit.* a removable cover for a chair or sofa etc.

loose-leaf ● *adj.* (of a notebook, manual, etc.) with each leaf separate and removable. ● *n.* a loose-leaf notebook etc.

loose-limbed *adj.* having supple limbs.

loosen *v.tr. & intr.* make or become less tight or compact or firm. □ **loosen a person's tongue** make a person talk freely. **loosen up** = *limber up* (see LIMBER[1] *v.*). □ **loosener** *n.*

loosestrife *n.* **1** (in full **yellow loosestrife**) a tall

waterside plant, *Lysimachia vulgaris*, of the primrose family, with spikes of yellow flowers. **2** (in full **purple loosestrife**) a tall waterside plant, *Lythrum salicaria*, with spikes of star-shaped purple flowers. [translation based on Greek *lusimakhion*, confused with *Lusimakhos*, name of its discoverer]

loot ● *n.* **1** goods taken from an enemy; spoil. **2** *slang* money. ● *v.tr.* (also *absol.*) **1** rob (premises) or steal (goods) left unprotected, esp. after a riot. **2** plunder or sack (a city, premises, etc.). [from Hindi *lūṭ*] □ **looter** *n.*

lop[1] *v.tr.* (**lopped, lopping**) **1 a** (often foll. by *off, away*) cut or remove (a part or parts) from a whole, esp. branches from a tree. **b** remove branches from (a tree). **2** (often foll. by *off, away*) remove (items) as superfluous. [Old English] □ **lopper** *n.*

lop[2] *v.intr. & tr.* (**lopped, lopping**) hang limply.

lope ● *v.intr.* (esp. of animals) run with a long bounding stride. ● *n.* a long bounding stride. [from Old Norse *hlaupa* 'to leap']

lop-ears *n.pl.* drooping ears. □ **lop-eared** *adj.*

lopsided *adj.* with one side lower or smaller than the other. □ **lopsidedly** *adv.* **lopsidedness** *n.*

loquacious *adj.* talkative. [from Latin *loquax -acis*] □ **loquaciously** *adv.* **loquaciousness** *n.* **loquacity** *n.*

loquat /loh-kwot/ *n.* **1** a tree of the rose family, *Eriobotrya japonica*, bearing small yellow egg-shaped fruits. **2** this fruit. [from Chinese dialect *luh kwat* 'rush orange']

lord ● *n.* **1** a master or ruler. **2** *hist.* a feudal superior, esp. of a manor. **3** a peer of the realm or a person entitled to the title *Lord*. **4** (**Lord**) (often prec. by *the*) a name for God or Christ. **5** (**Lord**) a prefixed as the designation of a marquess, earl, viscount, or baron. **b** prefixed to the Christian name of the younger son of a duke or marquess. **c** (**the Lords**) = HOUSE OF LORDS. ● *int.* (**Lord**) expressing surprise, dismay, etc. □ **lord it over 1** domineer. **2** adopt an attitude of superiority over. [Old English, from *hlāfweard*, literally 'bread-keeper'] □ **lordlike** *adj.*

LORIS: SLENDER LORIS (*Loris tardigradus*)

Lord Advocate *n.* the principal law officer of the Crown in Scotland.

Lord Chamberlain *n.* (in full **Lord Chamberlain of the Household**) (in the UK) the official in charge of the Royal Household, formerly the licensor of plays.

Lord Chancellor *n.* (in the UK) the highest officer of the Crown, presiding in the House of Lords etc.

Lord Chief Justice *n.* (in the UK) the president of the Queen's Bench Division of the High Court.

Lord Lieutenant *n.* (in the UK) the chief executive authority and head of magistrates in each county.

lordly *adj.* (**lordlier, lordliest**) **1** haughty, imperious. **2** suitable for a lord. □ **lordliness** *n.*

Lord Mayor *n.* the title of the mayor in London and some other large cities.

Lord President of the Council *n.* (in the UK) the Cabinet minister presiding at the Privy Council.

Lord Privy Seal *n.* (in the UK) a senior Cabinet minister without specified official duties.

Lord Provost *n.* the head of a municipal corporation or borough in certain Scottish cities.

Lord's Day *n.* (prec. by *the*) Sunday.

lordship *n.* **1** (foll. by *of, over*) dominion, rule, or ownership. **2** *archaic* the state of being a lord. □ **his** (or **your**) **Lordship** (or **lordship**) (*pl.* **their** (or

your) **Lordships** or **lordships**) a respectful form of reference or address to a Lord, a judge, or a bishop.

Lord's Prayer *n.* the prayer taught by Christ to his disciples, beginning 'Our Father'.

Lords spiritual *n.pl.* the bishops in the House of Lords.

Lord's Supper *n.* the Eucharist.

Lords temporal *n.pl.* the members of the House of Lords other than the bishops.

Lordy *int.* = LORD *int.*

lore *n.* a body of traditions and knowledge on a subject or held by a particular group (*herbal lore; gypsy lore*). [Old English]

LORGNETTE: LATE-19TH-CENTURY TORTOISESHELL LORGNETTE

lorgnette /lorn-yet/ *n.* (in *sing.* or *pl.*) ▶ a pair of eyeglasses or opera glasses held by a long handle. [French, based on *lorgner* 'to squint']

lorikeet *n.* any of various small brightly coloured parrots of the subfamily Loriinae. ▷ PARROT. [diminutive of LORY, on the pattern of *parakeet*]

loris *n.* (*pl.* same) ◀ either of two small slow-moving nocturnal primates with small ears and a very short tail, *Loris tardigradus* of southern India (**slender loris**), and *Nycticebus coucang* of the E. Indies (**slow loris**). [French]

lorry *n. Brit.* (*pl.* **-ies**) a large motor vehicle for transporting goods etc. [19th-century coinage]

lory *n.* (*pl.* **-ies**) any of various brightly coloured Australasian and SE Asian parrots of the subfamily Loriinae. [from Malay *lūrī*]

Los Angeleno see ANGELENO.

lose *v.* (*past* and *past part.* **lost**) **1** *tr.* be deprived of or cease to have, esp. by negligence or misadventure. **2** *tr.* **a** be deprived of (a person, esp. a close relative) by death. **b** suffer the loss of (a baby) in childbirth. **3** *tr.* become unable to find; fail to keep in sight or follow or mentally grasp (*lose one's way*). **4** *tr.* let or have pass from one's control or reach (*lose one's chance*). **5** *tr.* be defeated in (a game, race, lawsuit, battle, etc.). **6** *tr.* **a** draw away from; evade (*lost our pursuers*). **b** *colloq.* get rid of, discard. **7** *tr.* forfeit (a stake, deposit, right to a thing, etc.). **8** *tr.* spend (time, efforts, etc.) to no purpose (*lost no time in raising the alarm*). **9** *intr.* **a** suffer loss or detriment. **b** be worse off, esp. financially. **10** *tr.* cause (a person) the loss of (*will lose you your job*). **11** *intr. & tr.* (of a timepiece) become slow; become slow by (a specified amount of time). **12** *tr.* (in *passive*) disappear, perish; be dead (*was lost in the war; is a lost art*). □ **be lost for words** not know what to say. **be lost** (or **lose oneself**) **in** be engrossed in. **be lost on** be wasted on, or not noticed or appreciated by. **be lost to** be no longer affected by or accessible to. **be lost without** have great difficulty if deprived of (*am lost without my diary*). **get lost** (usu. in *imper.*) *slang* go away. **lose one's balance 1** fail to remain stable; fall. **2** fail to retain one's composure. **lose one's cool** *colloq.* lose one's composure. **lose face** be humiliated; lose one's credibility. **lose ground** see GROUND[1]. **lose one's head** see HEAD. **lose heart** be discouraged. **lose one's heart** see HEART. **lose one's nerve** become timid or irresolute. **lose out** *colloq.* **1** (often foll. by *on*) be unsuccessful. **2** (foll. by *to*) not get a fair chance or advantage (in). **2** (foll. by *to*) be beaten in competition or replaced by. **lose one's temper** become angry. **lose time** allow time to pass with something unachieved etc. **lose touch** see TOUCH. **lose track of** see TRACK. [Old English *losian* 'to perish, destroy']

L

loser *n.* **1** a person or thing that loses or has lost (esp. a contest or game). **2** *colloq.* a person who regularly fails.

losing battle *n.* a contest or effort in which failure seems certain (*felt we were fighting a losing battle*).

loss *n.* **1** the act or an instance of losing; the state of being lost. **2** a person, thing, or amount lost. **3** the detriment or disadvantage resulting from losing (*that is no great loss*). □ **at a loss** (sold etc.) for less than was paid for it. **be at a loss** be puzzled or uncertain. **be at a loss for words** not know what to say. [Middle English]

loss adjuster *n. Insurance* an agent who assesses the amount of compensation arising from a loss.

loss-leader *n.* an item sold at a loss to attract customers.

loss-making *adj.* (of a business etc.) making a financial loss. □ **loss-maker** *n.*

lost *past* and *past part.* of LOSE.

lost cause *n.* an enterprise etc. with no chance of success.

lost soul *n.* **1** a soul that is damned. **2** a person who is unable to cope with everyday life; a bewildered or pitiful person.

lost wax *n.* ▼ a method of bronze-casting using a clay core and a wax coating placed in a mould.

lot ● *n.* **1** (prec. by *a* or in *pl.*) *colloq.* **a** a large number or amount. **b** much (*a lot warmer; smiles a lot; is lots better*). **2 a** each of a set of objects used in making a chance selection. **b** this method of deciding (*chosen by lot*). **3** a share, or the responsibility resulting from it. **4** a person's destiny, fortune, or condition. **5** esp. *N. Amer.* a plot of land (*parking lot*). **6** an article or set of articles for sale at an auction etc. **7** a number or quantity of associated persons or things. ● *v.tr.* (**lotted**, **lotting**) divide into lots. □ **cast** (or **draw**) **lots** decide by means of lots. **throw in one's lot with** decide to share the fortunes of. **the** (or **the whole**) **lot** esp. *Brit.* the whole number or quantity. **a whole lot** *colloq.* very much (*is a whole lot better*). [Old English *hlot* 'portion, choice']

■ **Usage** In sense 1a of the noun, *a lot of* is somewhat informal, but acceptable in serious writing, whereas *lots of* is not.

loth var. of LOATH.

lotion *n.* a medicinal or cosmetic liquid applied externally. [from Latin *lotio*]

lottery *n.* (*pl.* **-ies**) **1** a means of raising money by selling numbered tickets and giving prizes to the holders of numbers drawn at random. **2** an enterprise, process, etc., whose success is governed by chance (*life is a lottery*).

lotto *n.* **1** a game of chance like bingo, but with numbers drawn by the players instead of being called. **2** esp. *US* a lottery. [Italian]

lotus *n.* **1** (in Greek mythology) a legendary plant inducing luxurious languor when eaten. **2 a** ◄ any water lily of the genus *Nelumbo*, esp. *N. nucifera* of India, with large pink flowers. **b** this flower used symbolically in Hinduism and Buddhism. [from Greek *lōtos*]

lotus-eater *n.* a person given to indolent enjoyment.

LOTUS: RED LOTUS
(*Nelumbo nucifera*)

lotus position *n.* a cross-legged position of meditation with the feet resting on the thighs.

louche /loosh/ *adj.* disreputable, shifty. [French, literally 'squinting']

loud ● *adj.* **1** strongly audible, esp. noisily or oppressively so. **2** (of colours, design, etc.) gaudy, obtrusive. **3** (of behaviour) aggressive and noisy. ● *adv.* in a loud manner. □ **out loud 1** aloud. **2** loudly (*laughed out loud*). [Old English] □ **louden** *v.tr. & intr.* **loudish** *adj.* **loudly** *adv.* **loudness** *n.*

loud hailer *n. Brit.* an electronic device for amplifying the voice.

loudmouth *n. colloq.* a person who talks too much, esp. offensively or tactlessly. □ **loud-mouthed** *adj.*

loudspeaker *n.* ▲ an apparatus that converts electrical impulses into sound, esp. music and voice. ▷ RADIO

lough /lok, lokh/ *n. Ir.* = LOCH. [from Irish *loch*]

lounge ● *v.intr.* **1** recline comfortably and casually; loll. **2** stand or move about idly. ● *n.* **1** a place for lounging, esp.: **a** a public room (e.g. in a hotel). **b** a waiting room in an airport etc. **c** *Brit.* a sitting room in a house. **2** *Brit.* a spell of lounging.

lounge bar *n. Brit.* a more comfortable room for drinking in a public house.

lounge lizard *n. colloq.* an idler in fashionable society.

lounger *n.* **1** a person who lounges. **2** a piece of furniture for relaxing on.

lounge suit *n. Brit.* a man's formal suit for ordinary day wear.

loupe *n.* ▶ a small magnifying glass used by jewellers etc. [French]

lour *v.intr.* (also **lower**) **1** frown; look sullen. **2** (of the sky etc.) look dark and threatening. [Middle English] □ **loury** *adj.*

louse ● *n.* **1** (*pl.* **lice**) **a** a parasitic insect, *Pediculus humanus*, infesting the human hair and skin and transmitting various diseases (*head louse; body louse*). ▷ PARASITE. **b** any insect of the order Anoplura or Mallophaga, parasitic on mammals or birds. **c** any of several parasitic invertebrates. **2** (*pl.* **louses**) *slang* a contemptible or unpleasant person. ● *v.tr.* remove lice from. □ **louse up** *slang* make a mess of. [Old English]

lousy *adj.* (**lousier**, **lousiest**) **1** infested with lice. **2** *colloq.* very bad; disgusting (also as a term of general disparagement). **3** (often foll. by *with*) *colloq.* well supplied; teeming. □ **lousily** *adv.* **lousiness** *n.*

LOUDSPEAKER

A loudspeaker produces sound waves from electrical signals. The signals pass through a voice coil, which is attached to a cone-shaped diaphragm. The coil acts as an electromagnet, and around it is a strong permanent magnet. When the current flows one way, the magnetic forces push the electromagnet and the cone outwards. When the current flows the other way, the cone is pulled inwards. The vibrations of the cone produce sound waves.

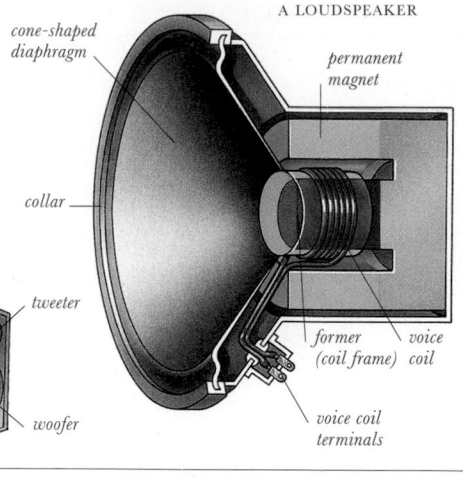

CUTAWAY VIEW OF
A LOUDSPEAKER

cone-shaped diaphragm

permanent magnet

collar

tweeter

LOUDSPEAKER
CABINET

cabinet

woofer

former
(coil frame)

voice
coil

voice coil
terminals

LOST WAX

In lost-wax casting, wax rods (runners and risers) are attached to a wax-covered clay model, creating channels for bronze to flow in. These are held in place with nails. The model is then encased in plaster and baked in a mould. The wax melts away through the channels and the molten bronze is poured in. When the bronze has cooled, the mould is broken open. The runners and risers are then sawn off, and the clay core removed.

STAGES IN THE LOST-WAX METHOD OF CASTING

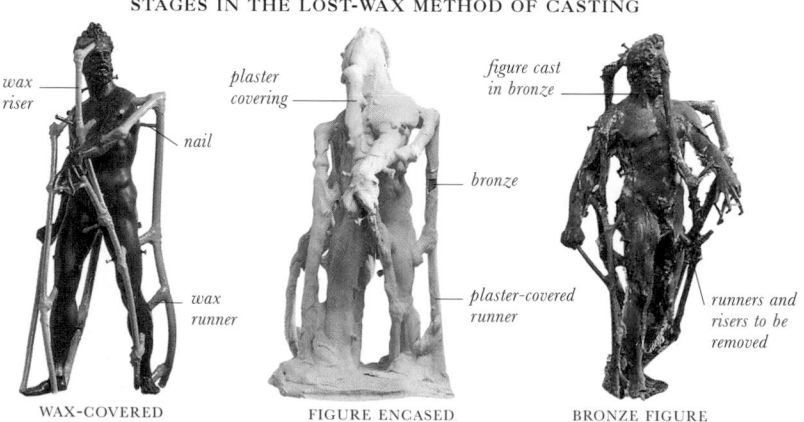

wax riser

nail

wax runner

plaster covering

bronze

plaster-covered runner

figure cast in bronze

runners and risers to be removed

WAX-COVERED
FIGURE

FIGURE ENCASED
IN PLASTER

BRONZE FIGURE
STRIPPED OF PLASTER

lens

protective case

LOUPE

L

lout *n.* a rough, crude, or ill-mannered person (usu. a man). □ **loutish** *adj.* **loutishly** *adv.* **loutishness** *n.*

louvre *n.* (also **louver**) **1** each of a set of overlapping slats designed to admit air and some light and exclude rain. **2** a domed structure on a roof with side openings for ventilation etc. [from Old French *lovier* 'skylight'] □ **louvred** *adj.*

lovable *adj.* (also **loveable**) inspiring or deserving love or affection. □ **lovableness** *n.* **lovably** *adv.*

LOVAGE
(*Levisticum officinale*)

lovage /luv-ij/ *n.* ◄ a S. European herb, *Levisticum officinale*, used for flavouring etc. [from Latin *ligusticum*, literally 'Ligurian (thing)']

lovat /luv-ăt/ ● *n.* (also **lovat green**) a muted green colour found esp. in tweed and woollen garments. ● *adj.* (also **lovat green**; hyphenated when *attrib.*) of this colour. [from *Lovat*, a place in Highland Scotland]

love ● *n.* **1** deep affection or fondness. **2** sexual passion. **3** sexual relations. **4 a** a beloved one; a sweetheart (often as a form of address). **b** *Brit. colloq.* a familiar form of address regardless of affection. **5** *colloq.* a person of whom one is fond. **6** affectionate greetings (*give him my love*). **7** (in some games) no score; nil. ● *v.tr.* **1** (also *absol.*) feel love or deep fondness for. **2** delight in; admire; greatly cherish. **3** *colloq.* like very much (*loves books*). **4** (foll. by verbal noun, or *to* + infin.) be inclined, esp. as a habit; greatly enjoy (*children love dressing up*). □ **fall in love** (often foll. by *with*) develop a great (esp. sexual) love (for). **for love** for pleasure not profit. **for the love of** for the sake of. **in love** (often foll. by *with*) deeply enamoured (of). **make love 1** (often foll. by *to*, *with*) have sexual intercourse (with). **2** (often foll. by *to*) *archaic* pay amorous attention (to). **out of love** no longer in love. [Old English]

loveable var. of LOVABLE.

love affair *n.* **1** a romantic or sexual relationship between two people in love. **2** an intense enthusiasm or liking for something.

love-apple *n.* *archaic* a tomato.

lovebird *n.* **1** ► any of various African and Madagascan parrots, esp. *Agapornis personata*. **2** (in *pl.*) *colloq.* an affectionate couple; lovers.

lovebite *n.* a red mark on the skin, caused by biting or sucking during sexual play.

love child *n.* an illegitimate child.

love game *n.* a game in which the loser makes no score.

love handles *n.pl.* esp. *N. Amer. slang* excess fat at the waist.

love-hate relationship *n.* an intensely emotional relationship involving ambivalent feelings.

love-in-a-mist *n.* a blue-flowered garden plant, *Nigella damascena*, with many delicate green bracts. ▷ SEED

LOVEBIRD:
MASKED LOVEBIRD
(*Agapornis personata*)

loveless *adj.* without love; unloving or unloved or both. □ **lovelessly** *adv.* **lovelessness** *n.*

love letter *n.* a letter expressing feelings of sexual love.

love life *n.* a person's life with regard to relationships with lovers.

lovelock *n.* a curl or lock of hair worn on the temple or forehead.

lovelorn *adj.* pining from unrequited love.

lovely ● *adj.* (**lovelier**, **loveliest**) **1** exquisitely beautiful. **2** *colloq.* pleasing, delightful. ● *n.* (*pl.* **-ies**) *colloq.* a pretty woman. □ **lovely and** *colloq.* delightfully (*lovely and warm*). □ **loveliness** *n.*

lovemaking *n.* **1** amorous sexual activity, esp. sexual intercourse. **2** *archaic* courtship.

love match *n.* a marriage made for love's sake.

love nest *n.* a secluded retreat for (esp. illicit) lovers.

lover *n.* **1** a person in love with another. **2** a person with whom another is having sexual relations. **3** (in *pl.*) a couple in love or having sexual relations. **4** a person who likes or enjoys something specified (*a music lover*, *a lover of words*).

love seat *n.* an armchair or small sofa for two.

lovesick *adj.* languishing with romantic love. □ **lovesickness** *n.*

lovey *n.* (*pl.* **-eys**) *Brit. colloq.* love, sweetheart (esp. as a form of address).

lovey-dovey *adj.* *colloq.* fondly affectionate, esp. in an unduly sentimental way.

loving ● *adj.* feeling or showing love; affectionate. ● *n.* affection; active love. □ **lovingly** *adv.* **lovingness** *n.*

loving cup *n.* a two-handled drinking cup passed round at banquets.

low[1] ● *adj.* **1** of less than average height; not high or tall or reaching far up (*a low wall*). **2 a** situated close to ground or sea level etc.; not elevated in position (*low altitude*). **b** (of the sun) near the horizon. **c** (of latitude) near the equator. **3** of or in humble rank or position (*of low birth*). **4** of small or less than normal amount or extent or intensity (*low price*; *low temperature*; *low in calories*). **5** small or reduced in quantity (*stocks are low*). **6** coming below the normal level (*a dress with a low neck*). **7** dejected; lacking vigour (*feeling low*; *in low spirits*). **8** (of a sound) not shrill or loud or high-pitched. **9** not exalted or sublime; commonplace. **10** unfavourable (*a low opinion*). **11** abject, mean, vulgar (*low cunning*; *low slang*). ● *n.* **1** a low or the lowest level or number (*the dollar has reached a new low*). **2** an area of low barometric pressure; a depression. ● *adv.* **1** in or to a low position or state. **2** in a low tone (*speak low*). **3** at or to a low pitch (*I can't sing so low*). [from Old Norse *lágr*] □ **lowish** *adj.* **lowness** *n.*

low[2] ● *n.* a sound made by cattle; a moo. ● *v.intr.* utter this sound. [Old English]

low-born *adj.* of humble birth.

lowbrow ● *adj.* not highly intellectual or cultured. ● *n.* a lowbrow person. □ **lowbrowed** *adj.*

Low Church *n.* a tradition within the Anglican Church giving little emphasis to ritual, priestly authority, and the sacraments.

low-class *adj.* of low quality or social class.

low comedy *n.* that in which the subject and the treatment border on farce.

Low Countries *n.pl.* the Netherlands, Belgium, and Luxembourg.

low-cut *adj.* (of a dress etc.) made with a low neckline.

low-density lipoprotein *n.* the form of lipoprotein in which cholesterol is transported in the blood.

low-down ● *adj.* abject, mean, dishonourable. ● *n.* (usu. foll. by *on*) *colloq.* the relevant information (about).

lower[1] ● *adj.* (*compar.* of LOW[1]). **1** less high in position or status. **2** situated to the south (*Lower California*). **3** (of an animal or plant) showing relatively primitive characteristics (e.g. a platypus or a fungus). **4** (often **Lower**) *Geol.* & *Archaeol.* designating an older, and hence usu. deeper, layer or the period in which it was formed or deposited. ● *adv.* in or to a lower position, status, etc. □ **lowermost** *adj.*

lower[2] *v.* **1** *tr.* let or haul down. **2** *tr.* & *intr.* make or become lower. **3** *tr.* degrade. □ **lower the tone** diminish the cultural content, prestige, or moral character (of a conversation, place, etc.).

lower[3] var. of LOUR.

lower case *n.* (hyphenated when *attrib.*) small letters.

lower class ● *n.* the members of the working class. ● *adj.* (**lower-class**) of the lower class.

Lower House *n.* the larger and usu. elected body in a legislature, esp. (in Britain) the House of Commons.

lower regions *n.pl.* (also **lower world**) hell; the realm of the dead.

lowest common denominator *n.* **1** the lowest common multiple of the denominators of several fractions. **2** the least desirable common feature of members of a group.

lowest common multiple *n.* the lowest quantity that is a multiple of two or more given quantities.

low frequency *n.* (in radio) 30–300 kilohertz.

low gear *n.* a gear of a vehicle providing a low ratio between the speed of the driven wheels and that of the driving mechanism and so a low speed to the vehicle itself.

low-grade *adj.* of low quality or strength.

low-impact *adj.* **1** (of exercise) not requiring energetic movement. **2** (of outdoor activity) undertaken with respect for the environment.

low-income *attrib.adj.* **1** of or relating to the income group comprising low-wage earners. **2** with a low national income (used esp. of poorer Third World countries).

low-key *adj.* lacking intensity or prominence; restrained.

lowland ● *n.* **1** (usu. in *pl.*) low-lying country. **2** (**Lowland**) (usu. in *pl.*) the region of Scotland lying south and east of the Highlands. ● *adj.* of or in lowland or (**Lowland**) the Scottish Lowlands. □ **lowlander** *n.* (also **Lowlander**).

low-level *adj.* *Computing* (of a programming language) close in form to machine language.

lowlight *n.* **1** *joc.* a monotonous or dull period; a feature of little prominence (*one of the lowlights of the evening*). **2** (usu. in *pl.*) a dark streak in the hair produced by dyeing. [on the pattern of *highlight*]

low-loader *n.* *Brit.* a lorry with a low floor and no sides, for heavy loads.

lowly *adj.* (**lowlier**, **lowliest**) **1** humble in feeling, behaviour, or status. **2** modest, unpretentious. **3** (of an organism) evolved to only a slight degree. □ **lowliness** *n.*

low-lying *adj.* at low altitude (above sea level etc.).

low-pitched *adj.* **1** (of a sound) low. **2** (of a roof) having only a slight slope.

low pressure *n.* an atmospheric condition with pressure below average, e.g. in a depression.

low profile ● *n.* avoidance of attention or publicity. ● *adj.* (**low-profile**) **1** (of a motor vehicle tyre) having a greater width than usual in relation to height. **2** (usu. *attrib.*) avoiding attention or publicity (*a low-profile manager*).

low relief see RELIEF 6.

low-rise *adj.* (of a building) having few storeys.

low season *n.* the period of fewest visitors at a resort etc.

low spirits *n.pl.* dejection, depression. □ **low-spirited** *adj.*

Low Sunday *n.* the Sunday after Easter.

low tide *n.* **1** the state of the tide when at its lowest level. **2** the time of this.

low water *n.* = LOW TIDE.

low water mark *n.* **1** the level reached by the sea etc. at low tide. **2** the minimum recorded level or value etc.

lox *n.* *N. Amer.* smoked salmon. [from Yiddish *laks*]

loyal *adj.* **1** (often foll. by *to*) true or faithful (to duty, love, or obligation). **2** steadfast in allegiance; devoted to one's sovereign or government. [from Latin *legalis* 'legal'] □ **loyally** *adv.*

loyalist *n.* (often *attrib.*) **1** a person who remains loyal to the legitimate sovereign etc. **2** (**Loyalist**) a supporter of union between Great Britain and Northern Ireland. □ **loyalism** *n.*

loyal toast *n.* a toast to the sovereign.

loyalty *n.* (*pl.* **-ies**) **1** the state of being loyal. **2** (often in *pl.*) a feeling or application of loyalty.

L

L

LOZENGE-SHAPED
GEMSTONE

lozenge *n.* **1** ◀ a rhombus or diamond figure. **2** a small sweet or medicinal tablet for dissolving in the mouth. [from Old French *losenge*]

LP *abbr.* long-playing (gramophone record).

L-plate *n. Brit.* a sign bearing the letter L, attached to the front and rear of a motor vehicle to indicate that it is being driven by a learner.

Lr *symb. Chem.* the element lawrencium.

LSD *abbr.* lysergic acid diethylamide.

Lt. *abbr.* **1** Lieutenant. **2** light.

Ltd. *abbr.* Limited.

Lu *symb. Chem.* the element lutetium.

lubricant ● *n.* a substance used to reduce friction. ● *adj.* lubricating.

lubricate *v.tr.* apply oil or grease etc. to (machinery etc.) in order to reduce friction. [based on Latin *lubricatus* 'made slippery'] □ **lubrication** *n.* **lubricative** *adj.* **lubricator** *n.*

lubricious *adj.* **1** slippery, smooth, oily. **2** lewd, prurient. **3** evasive. [from Latin *lubricus* 'slippery'] □ **lubricity** *n.*

lucerne *n.* (also **lucern**) *Brit.* = ALFALFA. [from modern Provençal *luzerno* 'glow-worm', with reference to its shiny seeds]

lucid *adj.* **1** expressing or expressed clearly; easy to understand. **2** of or denoting intervals of sanity between periods of insanity or dementia. [from Latin *lucidus*] □ **lucidity** *n.* **lucidly** *adv.*

Lucifer *n.* Satan. [Latin, literally 'light-bringing, morning star']

luck ● *n.* **1** chance regarded as the bringer of good or bad fortune. **2** circumstances of life (beneficial or not) brought by this. **3** good fortune; success due to chance (*in luck*; *out of luck*). ● *v.intr. colloq.* **1** (foll. by *upon, on*) chance to find or meet with. **2** (foll. by *into*) esp. *N. Amer.* acquire by good fortune. **3** (foll. by *out*) esp. *N. Amer.* achieve success or advantage by good luck. □ **for luck** to bring good fortune. **no such luck** *colloq.* unfortunately not. **try one's luck** make a venture. **with luck** if all goes well. **worse luck** *colloq.* unfortunately. [from Middle Low German *geluke*]

luckily *adv.* **1** (qualifying a whole sentence or clause) fortunately (*luckily there was enough food*). **2** in a lucky or fortunate manner.

luckless *adj.* having no luck; unfortunate. □ **lucklessness** *n.*

lucky *adj.* (**luckier, luckiest**) **1** having or resulting from good luck, esp. as distinct from skill or design or merit. **2** bringing good luck (*a lucky mascot*). **3** fortunate, appropriate (*a lucky guess*).

lucky dip *n. Brit.* a tub containing different articles concealed in wrapping or bran etc., and chosen at random by participants.

lucrative *adj.* profitable, yielding financial gain. [based on Latin *lucrari* 'to gain'] □ **lucratively** *adv.* **lucrativeness** *n.*

lucre /**loo**-ker/ *n. derog.* financial profit or gain. [from Latin *lucrum*]

lud *n. Brit.* □ **m'lud** (or **my lud**) a form of address to a judge in a court of law.

Luddite ● *n.* **1** *hist.* a member of any of the bands of English artisans who rioted against mechanization and destroyed machinery (1811–16). **2** a person opposed to increased industrialization or new technology. ● *adj.* of the Luddites or their beliefs. □ **Luddism** *n.* **Ludditism** *n.*

ludicrous *adj.* absurd or ridiculous; laughable. [from Latin *ludicrus*] □ **ludicrously** *adv.* **ludicrousness** *n.*

ludo *n. Brit.* a simple board game in which counters are moved round according to the throw of dice. [Latin, literally 'I play']

luff *v.tr.* (also *absol.*) **1** steer (a ship) nearer the wind.

LUNAR MONTH

As the Moon orbits the Earth, the amount of the sunlit side visible from the Earth changes, so that the Moon appears to take on different shapes, or phases. The time it takes for the Moon to go through all its different phases, from a new moon, when we see only a glimpse of the sunlit side, to a full moon, when we see all of its sunlit side, is called a lunar month. Although it takes the Moon 27.3 days to circle the Earth, a lunar month lasts 29.53 days, since the Earth moves as well as the Moon.

PHASES OF THE MOON

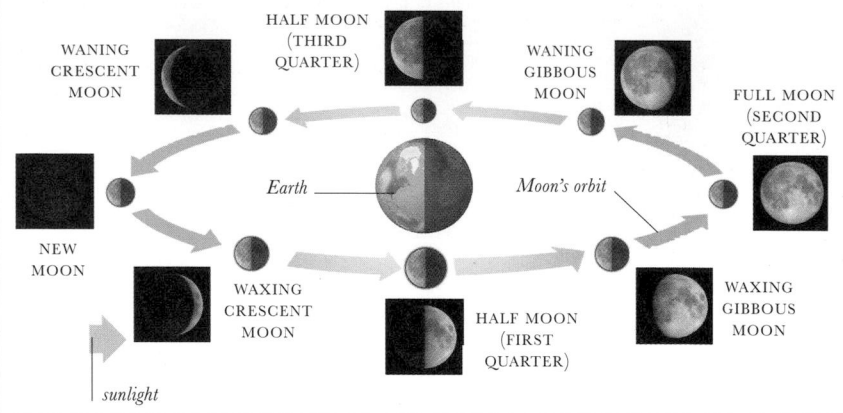

2 raise or lower (the jib of a crane or derrick). [from Old French *lof*]

luffa var. of LOOFAH.

lug[1] ● *v.* (**lugged, lugging**) **1** *tr.* drag or carry (a heavy object) with effort or violence. **2** *intr.* (usu. foll. by *at*) pull hard. ● *n.* a hard or rough pull. [Middle English]

lug[2] *n.* **1** *Sc.* or *colloq.* an ear. **2** a projection on an object by which it may be carried, fixed in place, etc.

luge /loozh/ ● *n.* a light toboggan for one or two people. ● *v.intr.* ride on a luge. [Swiss French]

luggage *n.* suitcases, bags, etc. to hold a traveller's belongings. [based on LUG[1]]

luggage van *n. Brit.* a railway carriage for travellers' luggage.

lugger *n.* ▼ a small ship carrying two or three masts with a lugsail on each. [based on LUGSAIL]

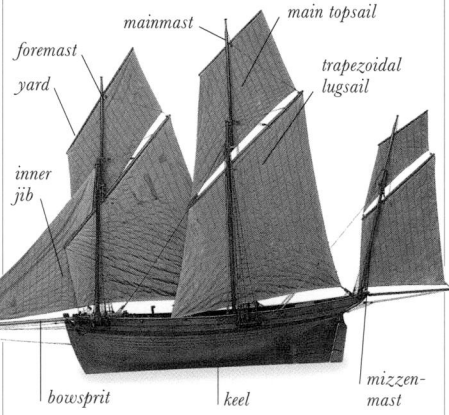

LUGGER: FRENCH LUGGER (*c.*1800)

lughole *n. Brit. colloq.* the ear orifice.

lugsail *n. Naut.* a quadrilateral sail which is bent on and hoisted from a yard.

lugubrious *adj.* doleful, mournful, dismal. [based on Latin *lugēre* 'to mourn'] □ **lugubriously** *adv.* **lugubriousness** *n.*

LUGWORM: BROWN LUGWORMS (*Arenicola* species)

lugworm *n.* ◀ any polychaete worm of the genus *Arenicola*, living in muddy sand and often used as bait by fishermen.

lukewarm *adj.* **1** moderately warm; tepid. **2** unenthusiastic, indifferent. [based on (now dialect) *luke, lew* 'mild, warm'] □ **lukewarmly** *adv.* **lukewarmness** *n.*

lull ● *v.* **1** *tr.* soothe or send to sleep gently. **2** *tr.* (usu. foll. by *into*) deceive (a person) into confidence (*lulled into a false sense of security*). **3** *tr.* allay (suspicions etc.) usu. by deception. **4** *intr.* (of noise, a storm, etc.) abate or fall quiet. ● *n.* a temporary quiet period in a storm or in any activity. [Middle English]

lullaby *n.* (*pl.* **-ies**) a soothing song to send a child to sleep.

lumbago *n.* rheumatic pain in the muscles of the lower back. [Latin]

lumbar *adj. Anat.* relating to the loin, esp. the lower back area. ▷ VERTEBRA. [based on Latin *lumbus* 'loin']

lumbar puncture *n.* the withdrawal of spinal fluid from the lower back with a hollow needle, usu. for diagnosis.

lumber[1] *v.intr.* (usu. foll. by *along, past, by*, etc.) move in a slow clumsy noisy way. [Middle English] □ **lumbering** *adj.*

lumber[2] ● *n.* **1** *Brit.* disused or useless cumbersome objects. **2** *N. Amer.* partly or fully prepared timber. ● *v.* **1** *tr. Brit.* **a** (usu. foll. by *with*) leave (a person etc.) with something unwanted or unpleasant (*always lumbering me with the cleaning*). **b** (as **lumbered** *adj.*) in an unwanted or inconvenient situation (*afraid of being lumbered*). **2** *tr.* (usu. foll. by *up*) *Brit.* obstruct. **3** *intr.* cut and prepare forest timber for transport. □ **lumberer** *n.* (in sense 3 of *v.*). **lumbering** *n.* (in sense 3 of *v.*).

lumberjack *n.* (also **lumberman**; *pl.* **-men**) esp. *N. Amer.* a person who fells, prepares, or conveys forest timber.

lumber-room *n. Brit.* a room where disused or cumbersome things are kept.

lumen *n. Physics* the SI unit of luminous flux. [Latin, literally 'a light, an opening']

luminaire *n.* a unit consisting of an electric light and its fittings. [French]

luminary n. (pl. **-ies**) **1** a person as a source of intellectual light or moral inspiration. **2** a prominent member of a group or gathering (a host of show-business luminaries).

luminescence n. the emission of light by a substance other than as a result of incandescence. □ **luminescent** adj.

luminous adj. **1** shedding light. **2** phosphorescent, visible in darkness (luminous paint). [from Latin luminosus] □ **luminosity** n. **luminously** adv.

lump[1] ● n. **1** a compact shapeless or unshapely mass. **2** a tumour, swelling, or bruise. **3** a heavy, dull, or ungainly person. **4** (prec. by the) Brit. casual workers in the building and other trades. ● v.tr. **1** (usu. foll. by together, with, in with, under, etc.) mass together or treat indiscriminately. **2** Brit. carry or throw carelessly (lumping crates round the yard). □ **lump in the throat** a feeling of pressure there, caused by emotion. [Middle English] □ **lumper** n.

lump[2] v.tr. colloq. endure or suffer (a situation) ungraciously. □ **like it or lump it** put up with something whether one likes it or not.

lumpectomy n. (pl. **-ies**) the surgical removal of a usu. cancerous lump from the breast.

lumpfish n. (pl. usu. same) ▼ a spiny-finned fish, Cyclopterus lumpus, of the N. Atlantic, with modified pelvic fins for clinging to objects. [based on Middle Dutch lumpe]

LUMPFISH
(Cyclopterus lumpus)
pelvic fins

lumpish adj. **1** heavy and clumsy. **2** stupid, lethargic. □ **lumpishly** adv. **lumpishness** n.

lump sugar n. sugar shaped into lumps or cubes.

lump sum n. **1** a sum covering a number of items. **2** money paid down at once (opp. INSTALMENT 1).

lumpy adj. (**lumpier**, **lumpiest**) **1** full of or covered with lumps. **2** (of water) cut up by the wind into small waves. □ **lumpily** adv. **lumpiness** n.

lunacy n. (pl. **-ies**) **1** insanity (originally of the intermittent kind attributed to changes of the Moon); the state of being a lunatic. **2** Law such mental unsoundness as interferes with civil rights or transactions. **3** great folly or eccentricity; a foolish act.

lunar adj. of, relating to, or determined by the Moon. [based on Latin luna 'month']

lunar eclipse n. an eclipse in which the Earth prevents sunlight from falling on the Moon. ▷ ECLIPSE

lunar module n. (also **lunar excursion module**) a small craft used for travelling between the Moon's surface and a spacecraft in orbit around the Moon. ▷ SPACECRAFT

lunar month n. **1** ◄ the period of the Moon's revolution, esp. a lunation. ▷ MOON. **2** (in general use) four weeks.

lunar year n. a period of 12 lunar months.

lunate adj. crescent-shaped. [from Latin lunatus]

lunatic ● n. **1** an insane person. **2** someone foolish or eccentric. ● adj. mad, foolish. [based on Latin luna 'moon', from the belief that changes of the Moon caused intermittent insanity]

lunatic asylum n. hist. a mental home or hospital.

lunatic fringe n. an extreme or eccentric minority group.

lunation n. the interval between new moons, about 29½ days. [based on Latin luna 'moon']

lunch ● n. the meal eaten in the middle of the day. ● v. **1** intr. eat one's lunch. **2** tr. provide lunch for. □ **luncher** n.

lunch box n. a container for a packed meal.

luncheon n. formal lunch. [16th-century coinage]

luncheon meat n. a block of ground meat ready to cut and eat.

luncheon voucher n. Brit. a voucher issued to employees and exchangeable for food at restaurants and shops.

lunchtime n. the time when lunch is eaten (often attrib.: lunchtime drinking).

LUNETTE

lunette n. **1** an arched aperture in a domed ceiling to admit light. **2** ► a crescent-shaped or semicircular space or alcove which contains a painting, statue, etc. **3** a watch-glass of flattened shape. [French, literally 'little crescent']

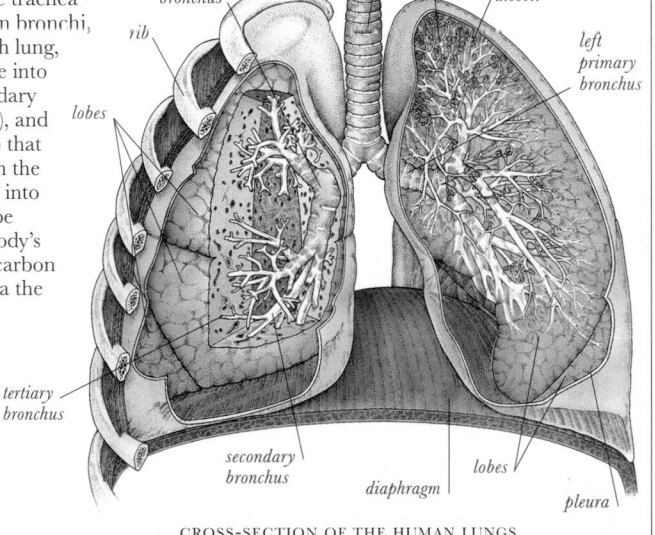

side reins
neckstrap
noseband (cavesson)
lunge rein
protective boots

LUNGE:
TROTTING ON
THE LUNGE

lung n. ▼ each of the pair of respiratory organs which bring air into contact with the blood in humans and many other vertebrates. ▷ RESPIRATION. [Old English] □ **lunged** adj. **lungful** n. (pl. **-fuls**). **lungless** adj.

lunge[1] ● n. **1** a sudden movement forward. **2** a thrust with a sword etc., esp. the basic attacking move in fencing. ● v.intr. make a lunge. [earlier allonge, from French allonger 'to lengthen']

lunge[2] n. (also **longe**) ◄ a long rope on which a horse is held and made to move in a circle round its trainer. [from (Old) French longe 'lengthening']

lungfish n. (pl. usu. same) ▼ any freshwater fish of the order Dipnoi, having gills and a modified swim-bladder used as lungs, and able to aestivate to survive drought.

LUNGFISH: AUSTRALIAN LUNGFISH
(Neoceratodus forsteri)

lung-power n. the power of one's voice.

lungwort n. **1** any herbaceous plant of the genus Pulmonaria, esp. P. officinalis with white-spotted leaves likened to a diseased lung. **2** a lichen, Lobaria pulmonaria, formerly believed to be a remedy for lung disease.

lupin n. (also **lupine**) ► any plant of the genus Lupinus, with long tapering spikes of blue, purple, pink, white, or yellow flowers. [from Latin lupinus]

lupine adj. of or like a wolf or wolves. [based on Latin lupus 'wolf']

lupus n. any of various ulcerous skin diseases, esp. tuberculosis of the skin. [Latin, literally 'wolf'] □ **lupoid** adj. **lupous** adj.

lurch[1] ● n. a sudden unsteady movement or leaning; a stagger. ● v.intr. stagger; move suddenly and unsteadily. [originally nautical lee-lurch, alteration of lee-latch 'drifting to leeward']

LUPIN
(Lupinus 'Chandelier')

L

LUNG

During inhalation, air enters the lungs via the trachea, and ultimately penetrates to microscopic thin-walled air sacs (alveoli). The trachea divides into two main bronchi, one feeding into each lung, where they subdivide into smaller tubes (secondary and tertiary bronchi), and tubules (bronchioles) that lead to the alveoli. In the lungs, oxygen passes into the bloodstream to be transported to the body's tissues, while waste carbon dioxide is exhaled via the alveoli.

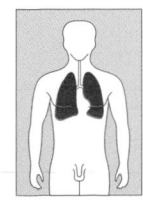

trachea (windpipe)
right primary bronchus
terminal bronchioles
alveoli
rib
left primary bronchus
lobes
tertiary bronchus
secondary bronchus
diaphragm
lobes
pleura

CROSS-SECTION OF THE HUMAN LUNGS

lurch[2] *n.* □ **leave in the lurch** desert (a friend etc.) in difficulties. [originally in sense 'a severe defeat in a game': from French *lourche*]

lurcher *n. Brit.* ◄ a cross-bred dog, usu. a retriever, collie, or sheepdog crossed with a greyhound.

lure ● *v.tr.* **1** (usu. foll. by *away, into*) entice (a person, an animal, etc.) usu. with some form of bait. **2** attract back again or recall (a person, animal, etc.) with the promise of a reward. ● *n.* **1** ▼ a thing used to entice. **2** (usu. foll. by *of*) the attractive or compelling qualities (of a pursuit etc.). **3** a falconer's apparatus for recalling a hawk, consisting of a bunch of feathers attached to a thong, within which the hawk finds food while being trained. [from Old French *luere*] □ **luring** *adj.* **luringly** *adv.*

LURCHER:
SHORT-HAIRED
LURCHER

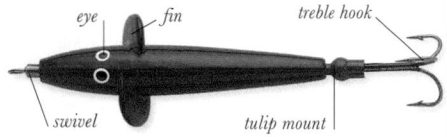

LURE:
DEVON MINNOW FISHING LURE

lurex *n. propr.* **1** a type of yarn which incorporates a glittering metallic thread. **2** fabric made from this yarn.

lurgy *n.* (*pl.* **-ies**) (esp. in phr. **the dreaded lurgy**) *Brit. joc.* an unspecified illness. [20th-century coinage, frequently used in *The Goon Show*, British radio series]

lurid *adj.* **1** vivid or glaring in colour (*lurid orange*). **2** sensational, horrifying, or terrible (*lurid details*). [from Latin *luridus*] □ **luridly** *adv.* **luridness** *n.*

lurk *v.intr.* **1** linger furtively or unobtrusively. **2** (usu. foll. by *in, under, about*, etc.) hide, esp. for sinister purposes. **3** (as **lurking** *adj.*) latent, semi-conscious (*a lurking suspicion*). [Middle English] □ **lurker** *n.*

luscious *adj.* **1 a** richly sweet in taste or smell. **b** *colloq.* delicious. **2** (of literary style, music, etc.) over-rich in sound, imagery, etc. **3** voluptuously attractive. [Middle English] □ **lusciously** *adv.* **lusciousness** *n.*

lush[1] *adj.* **1** (of vegetation, esp. grass) luxuriant and succulent. **2** luxurious. **3** (of colour, sound, etc.) rich, voluptuous. **4** *slang* good-looking, attractive. [Middle English] □ **lushly** *adv.* **lushness** *n.*

lush[2] esp. *N. Amer. slang* ● *n.* **1** alcohol, liquor. **2** an alcoholic; a drunkard. ● *v.* **1** *tr. & intr.* drink (alcohol). **2** *tr.* ply with alcohol. [18th-century coinage]

lust ● *n.* **1** strong sexual desire. **2 a** (usu. foll. by *for, of*) a passionate desire for (*a lust for power*). **b** (usu. foll. by *of*) a passionate enjoyment of (*the lust of battle*). **3** (usu. in *pl.*) a sensuous appetite regarded as sinful (*the lusts of the flesh*). ● *v.intr.* (usu. foll. by *after, for*) have a strong or excessive (esp. sexual) desire. [Old English] □ **lustful** *adj.* **lustfully** *adv.* **lustfulness** *n.*

luster *US* var. of LUSTRE.

lustre (*US* **luster**) ● *n.* **1** gloss, sheen. **2** a shiny or reflective surface. **3 a** a thin metallic coating giving an iridescent glaze to ceramics. **b** = LUSTREWARE. **4** a radiance or attractiveness; splendour, glory, distinction of achievements etc.) (*add lustre to; shed lustre on*). ● *v.tr.* put lustre on (pottery, a cloth,

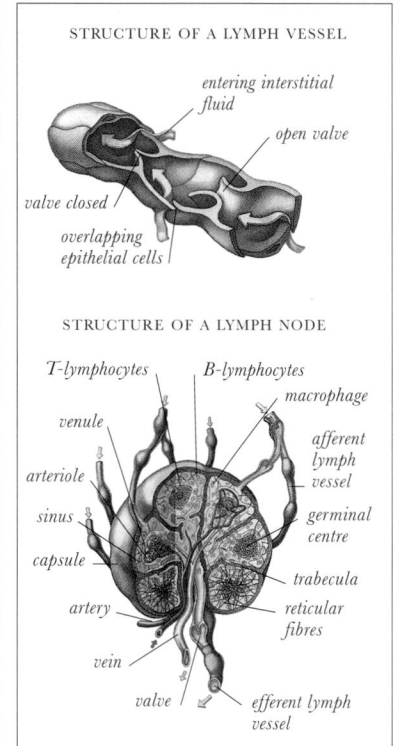

LYMPHATIC SYSTEM

The lymphatic system removes excess fluid from the body's tissues and returns it to the circulatory system. It also helps the body to fight infection. It consists of lymph vessels, lymph nodes, and associated lymphoid organs such as the spleen and tonsils. Lymph vessels form a network of tubes that extend all over the body. From lymph capillaries – the smallest vessels – lymph flows into larger vessels called lymphatics, which are studded with nodes. These nodes are collections of lymph tissue that act as filters and contain spaces (sinuses) where many scavenging white blood cells (macrophages) ingest bacteria and other foreign matter and debris. When an infection occurs, specialized white blood cells (lymphocytes) are released from the lymph nodes to fight infection.

STRUCTURE OF A LYMPH VESSEL

entering interstitial fluid
open valve
valve closed
overlapping epithelial cells

STRUCTURE OF A LYMPH NODE

T-lymphocytes
B-lymphocytes
macrophage
venule
afferent lymph vessel
arteriole
sinus
germinal centre
capsule
trabecula
artery
reticular fibres
vein
valve
efferent lymph vessel

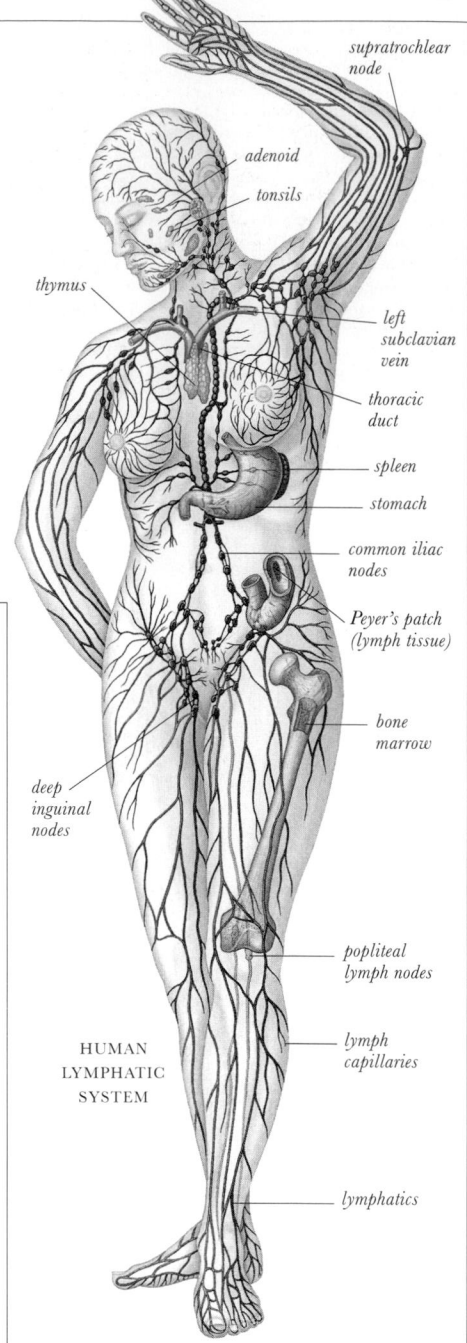

supratrochlear node
adenoid
tonsils
thymus
left subclavian vein
thoracic duct
spleen
stomach
common iliac nodes
Peyer's patch (lymph tissue)
deep inguinal nodes
bone marrow
popliteal lymph nodes
lymph capillaries
HUMAN LYMPHATIC SYSTEM
lymphatics

etc.). [from Latin *lustrare* 'to illuminate'] □ **lustreless** *adj.* (*US* **lusterless**). **lustrous** *adj.* **lustrously** *adv.* **lustrousness** *n.*

lustreware *n.* (*US* **lusterware**) ceramics with an iridescent glaze.

lusty *adj.* (**lustier**, **lustiest**) **1** healthy and strong. **2** vigorous or lively. □ **lustily** *adv.* **lustiness** *n.*

lutanist var. of LUTENIST.

lute[1] *n.* ◄ a guitar-like instrument with a long neck and a pear-shaped body. ▷ STRINGED. [from French *lut*]

lute[2] ● *n.* clay or cement used to stop a hole, make a joint airtight, etc. ● *v.tr.* apply lute to. [from Latin *lutum* 'mud, clay']

soundboard
bridge
soundhole
strings
bowl
tuning peg
scroll

LUTE:
16TH-CENTURY
ITALIAN LUTE

lutecium var. of LUTETIUM.

lutenist *n.* (also **lutanist**) a lute-player.

luteofulvous *adj.* orange-tawny.

lutetium *n.* (also **lutecium**) *Chem.* a silvery metallic element of the lanthanide series. [based on Latin *Lutetia*, ancient name of Paris, France, home of its discoverer]

Lutheran ● *n.* **1** a follower of Martin Luther, German religious reformer (d. 1546). **2** a member of the Church which accepts the Augsburg confession of 1530, with justification by faith alone as a cardinal doctrine. ● *adj.* of or characterized by the theology of Martin Luther. □ **Lutheranism** *n.*

luthier /loo-ti-er/ *n.* a maker of stringed instruments, esp. those of the violin family. [French]

luting *n.* = LUTE[2].

lutz *n. Sport* a jump in skating from the backward outside edge of one skate to the backward outside edge of the other, with a full turn in the air. [probably from the name of Gustave *Lussi* (b. 1898), who invented it]

luvvy *n.* (also **luvvie**) (*pl.* **-ies**) *Brit. colloq.* an actor or actress, esp. one who is particularly effusive or affected.

lux *n.* (*pl.* same) *Physics* the SI unit of illumination, equivalent to one lumen per square metre. [Latin, literally 'light']

luxe *n.* luxury (cf. DE LUXE). [from Latin *luxus* 'abundance']

luxuriant *adj.* **1** (of vegetation etc.) lush; profuse in growth. **2** exuberant (*luxuriant imagination*). **3** florid; richly ornate. [from Latin *luxuriant-* 'growing rank'] □ **luxuriance** *n.* **luxuriantly** *adv.*

■ **Usage** *Luxuriant*, meaning 'growing profusely, exuberant', is sometimes confused with *luxurious*, the adjective relating to *luxury*.

luxuriate *v.intr.* **1** (foll. by *in*) take self-indulgent delight in; enjoy in a luxurious manner. **2** relax in comfort.

luxurious *adj.* **1** supplied with luxuries. **2** extremely comfortable. **3** self-indulgent, voluptuous. □ **luxuriously** *adv.* **luxuriousness** *n.*

■ **Usage** See Usage Note at LUXURIANT.

luxury *n.* (*pl.* **-ies**) **1** choice or costly surroundings, possessions, food, etc. (*a life of luxury*). **2** something desirable for comfort or enjoyment, but not indispensable. **3** (*attrib.*) providing great comfort; expensive (*a luxury flat; a luxury holiday*). [from Latin *luxuria*]

LV *abbr. Brit.* luncheon voucher.

Lw *symb. Chem.* former symbol for the element lawrencium (now **Lr**).

lx *abbr.* lux.

lycanthropy *n.* the mythical transformation of a person into a wolf (cf. WEREWOLF). [based on Greek *lukos* 'wolf' + *anthrōpos* 'man'] □ **lycanthrope** *n.*

Lyceum *n.* **1 a** the garden at Athens in which Aristotle taught philosophy. **b** Aristotelian philosophy and its followers. **2** (**lyceum**) *US hist.* a literary institution, lecture hall, or teaching place. [Latin from Greek *Lukeion*, neut. of *Lukeios*, epithet of Apollo (from whose neighbouring temple the Lyceum was named)]

spiny skin

LYCHEE
(*Nephelium litchi*)

lychee *n.* (also **litchi**, **lichee**) **1** ◀ a sweet fleshy fruit with a thin spiny skin. **2** the tree, *Nephelium litchi*, originally from China, bearing this. [from Chinese *lìzhī*]

lych-gate var. of LICH-GATE.

Lycra *n. propr.* an elastic polyurethane fabric used esp. for close-fitting clothing.

lye *n.* **1** water made alkaline with vegetable ashes. **2** any strong alkaline solution, esp. of potassium hydroxide used for washing or cleansing. [Old English]

lying[1] *pres. part.* of LIE[1]. ● *n.* a place to lie (*a dry lying*).

lying[2] *pres. part.* of LIE[2]. ● *adj.* deceitful, false.

lymph *n.* **1** *Physiol.* a colourless fluid containing white blood cells, drained from the tissues and conveyed through the body in the lymphatic system. ▷ LYMPHATIC SYSTEM. **2** this fluid used as a vaccine. [from Latin *lympha* 'water'] □ **lymphoid** *adj.* **lymphous** *adj.*

lymphatic ● *adj.* **1** of or secreting or conveying lymph. **2** (of a person) pale, flabby, or sluggish. ● *n.* a veinlike vessel conveying lymph. [originally in sense 'frenzied': based on Greek *numpholēptos* 'seized by nymphs']

lymphatic system *n.* ◀ a network of vessels conveying lymph.

lymph gland *n.* (also **lymph node**) a small mass of tissue in the lymphatic system where lymph is purified and lymphocytes are formed. ▷ LYMPHATIC SYSTEM

lymphocyte *n.* a form of leucocyte occurring in the blood, in lymph, etc. ▷ BLOOD, LYMPHATIC SYSTEM. □ **lymphocytic** *adj.*

lymphoma *n.* (*pl.* **lymphomas**, **lymphomata**) any malignant tumour of the lymph nodes, excluding leukaemia.

lynch *v.tr.* (of a body of people) put (a person) to death for an alleged offence without a legal trial. [from *Lynch's law*, named after Capt. W. *Lynch*, head of a self-constituted judicial tribunal in Virginia *c*.1780] □ **lyncher** *n.* **lynching** *n.*

lynch law *n.* the procedure of a self-constituted illegal court that punishes or executes.

lynchpin var. of LINCHPIN.

lynx *n.* **1** ▼ a medium-sized cat, *Felis lynx*, with short tail, spotted fur, and tufted ear-tips. **2** its fur. [from Greek *lugx*] □ **lynxlike** *adj.*

LYNX
(*Felis lynx*)

lyre *n. Gk Antiq.* an ancient stringed instrument like a small U-shaped harp, played usu. with a plectrum. [from Greek *lura*]

lyre-bird *n.* any Australian bird of the family Menuridae, the male of which has a lyre-shaped tail.

lyric ● *adj.* **1** (of poetry) expressing the writer's emotions, usu. briefly and in stanzas. **2** (of a poet) writing in this manner. **3** of or for the lyre. **4** meant to be sung, fit to be expressed in song, songlike (*lyric drama; lyric opera*). ● *n.* **1** a lyric poem. **2** (in *pl.*) lyric verses. **3** (usu. in *pl.*) the words of a song.

lyrical *adj.* **1** = LYRIC *adj.*1, 2. **2** resembling, couched in, or using language appropriate to, lyric poetry. **3** *colloq.* highly enthusiastic (*wax lyrical about*). □ **lyrically** *adv.*

lyricism *n.* **1** the character or quality of being lyric or lyrical. **2** a lyrical expression. **3** high-flown sentiments.

lyricist *n.* a person who writes the words to a song.

lyse *v.tr. & intr. Biol.* bring about or undergo lysis. [back-formation from LYSIS]

lysergic acid diethylamide *n.* a powerful hallucinogenic drug. [lysergic: from hydro*lysis* + *ergot* + *-ic*]

lysin *n. Biol.* a substance, esp. an antibody, able to cause lysis of cells esp. bacteria. [from German *Lysine*]

lysine *n. Biochem.* an amino acid present in protein and essential in the diet of vertebrates. [from German *Lysin*]

lysis /ly-sis/ *n.* (*pl.* **lyses**) *Biol.* the disintegration of a cell. [from Greek *lusis* 'loosening']

lytic /lit-ik/ *adj.* of, relating to, or causing lysis.

-lytic *comb. form* forming adjectives corresponding to nouns in *-lysis*. [Greek *lutikos* (as LYSIS)]

L

M

M¹ *n.* (also **m**) (*pl.* **Ms** or **M's**) **1** the thirteenth letter of the alphabet. **2** (as a Roman numeral) 1,000.

M² *abbr.* (also **M.**) **1** *Monsieur.* **2** (in the UK in road designations) motorway.

M³ *symb.* mega-.

m¹ *abbr.* (also **m.**) **1 a** masculine. **b** male. **2** married. **3** mile(s). **4** million(s). **5** minute(s).

m² *symb.* **1** metre(s). **2** milli-. **3** *Physics* mass.

'm *abbr. colloq.* am (*I'm sorry*).

MA *abbr.* Master of Arts.

ma *n. colloq.* mother.

ma'am /mahm, mam/ *n.* madam (in the UK used esp. in addressing royalty).

Mac *n. colloq.* **1** a Scotsman. **2** *N. Amer.* a form of address to a male stranger. [from *Mac-* as a patronymic prefix in many Scottish and Irish surnames]

mac *n.* (also **mack**) *Brit. colloq.* mackintosh.

macabre /mă-**kahbr**/ *adj.* grim, gruesome. [from Old French *macabré*]

macadam *n.* **1** material for road-making with successive layers of compacted broken stone. **2** = TARMAC-ADAM. [named after J. L. *McAdam*, British surveyor, 1756–1836] □ **macadamize** *v.tr.* (also **-ise**)

macadamia *n.* any Australian evergreen tree of the genus *Macadamia*, esp. *M. integrifolia* and *M. tetraphylla*, bearing edible nutlike seeds. [named after J. *Macadam*, Australian chemist, 1827–65]

macaque /mă-**kahk**/ *n.* ► a medium-sized monkey of the Old World genus *Macaca*. [French, based on Bantu *makaku* 'some monkeys']

macaroni *n.* a tubular variety of pasta. [from late Greek *makaria* 'food made from barley']

macaroon *n.* a small light cake or biscuit made with white of egg, sugar, and ground almonds or coconut. [from French *macaron*]

macaw *n.* ▼ any long-tailed brightly coloured parrot of the genus *Ara* or *Anodorhynchus*, native to S. and Central America. ▷ PARROT. [from Portuguese *macao*, of unknown origin]

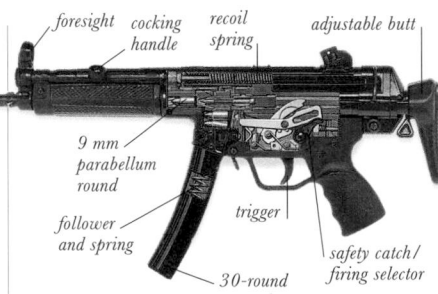

MACAW:
SCARLET MACAW
(*Ara macao*)

McCarthyism *n.* (esp. in the US) the policy of hunting out suspected or known Communists and removing them. [named after J. R. *McCarthy*, US senator (d. 1957), who instigated the policy (1950)]

McCoy *n. colloq.* □ **the** (or **the real**) **McCoy** the real thing; the genuine article. [19th-century coinage]

Mace *n.* an aerosol used to immobilize an assailant temporarily. ● *v.tr.* (also **mace**) spray with Mace. [US proprietary name]

mace¹ *n.* **1** a staff of office, esp. the symbol of the Speaker's authority in the House of Commons. **2** *hist.* ► a heavy club usu. having a metal head and spikes. **3** a stick used in the game of bagatelle. [from Old French *mace, masse* 'mallet']

mace² *n.* the dried outer covering of the nutmeg, used as a spice. ▷ SPICE. [from Latin *macir*, a red spicy bark]

macédoine /mas-i-**dwahn**/ *n.* mixed vegetables or fruit, esp. cut up small or in jelly. [French, literally 'Macedonia']

macerate *v.* **1** *tr. & intr.* make or become soft by soaking. **2** *intr.* waste away by fasting. [based on Latin *maceratus* 'made soft'] □ **maceration** *n.* **macerator** *n.*

Mach /mahk/ *n.* (in full **Mach number**) the ratio of the speed of a body to the speed of sound in the surrounding medium; often as **Mach 1**, **2**, etc., indicating the speed of sound, twice the speed of sound, etc. [named after E. *Mach*, Austrian physicist, 1838–1916]

machete /mă-**shet**-i/ *n.* a broad heavy knife used esp in Central America and the W. Indies as an implement and weapon. [Spanish, based on Latin *marcus* 'hammer']

machiavellian /mak-iă-**vel**-iăn/ *adj.* elaborately cunning; scheming, unscrupulous. [from N. *Machiavelli*, Florentine political writer, 1469–1527, who advocated morally questionable methods in the interests of the state]

machinable *adj.* capable of being cut by machine tools. □ **machinability** *n.*

machinate *v.intr.* lay plots; intrigue. [based on Latin *machinatus* 'contrived'] □ **machination** *n.*

machine ● *n.* **1** an apparatus applying mechanical power, having several parts each with a definite function. **2** a particular kind of machine, esp. a vehicle, a piece of electrical or electronic apparatus, etc. **3** an instrument that transmits a force or directs its application. **4** the controlling system of an organization etc. (*the party machine*). **5** a person who acts mechanically. **6** (esp. in *comb.*) a coin-operated dispenser (*cigarette machine*). ● *v.tr.* make or operate on with a machine. [from Greek *makhana*]

machine code *n.* (also **machine language**) a computer language that a particular computer can respond to directly.

machine-gun ● *n.* ▼ an automatic gun giving continuous fire. ▷ GUN. ● *v.tr.* (**-gunned, -gunning**) shoot at with a machine-gun. □ **machine-gunner** *n.*

MACE:
18TH-CENTURY
INDIAN SPIKED
MACE

MACAQUE
(*Macaca* species)

foresight · cocking handle · recoil spring · adjustable butt
9 mm parabellum round · follower and spring · trigger · safety catch / firing selector · 30-round magazine

MACHINE-GUN: GERMAN 9 MM SUB-MACHINE GUN WITH INNER MECHANISM REVEALED

machine-minder *n.* a person whose job is to attend to a machine.

machine-readable *adj.* in a form that a computer can process.

machinery *n.* (*pl.* **-ies**) **1** machines collectively. **2** the components of a machine; a mechanism. **3** (foll. by *of*) an organized system. **4** (foll. by *for*) the means devised or available (*the machinery for decision-making*).

machine tool *n.* a mechanically operated tool. □ **machine-tooled** *adj.*

machine translation *n.* translation carried out by a computer.

machine-washable *adj.* able to be washed in a washing machine without damage.

machinist *n.* **1** a person who operates a machine, esp. a machine tool or *Brit.* a sewing machine. **2** a person who makes machinery.

machismo *n.* exaggeratedly assertive manliness; a show of masculinity. [Spanish, based on *macho* 'male']

Mach number see MACH.

macho ● *adj.* showily manly or virile. ● *n.* (*pl.* **-os**) **1** a macho man. **2** = MACHISMO.

macintosh var. of MACKINTOSH.

mack var. of MAC.

mackerel *n.* (*pl.* same or **mackerels**) ▼ a N. Atlantic marine fish, *Scomber scombrus*, with a greenish-blue body, used for food. [from Old French *maquerel*]

MACKEREL: ATLANTIC MACKEREL
(*Scomber scombrus*)

mackerel sky *n.* a sky dappled with rows of small white fleecy clouds, like the pattern on a mackerel's back.

mackintosh *n.* (also **macintosh**) **1** *Brit.* a waterproof coat or cloak. **2** cloth waterproofed with rubber. [named after C. *Macintosh*, Scots inventor, 1766–1843]

macramé /mă-**krah**-mi/ *n.* **1** the art of knotting cord or string in patterns to make decorative articles. **2** ► articles made in this way. [from Arabic *mikrama*]

macro *n.* (also **macro-instruction**) *Computing* a single instruction that expands automatically into a set of instructions to perform a particular task.

macro- *comb. form* **1** long. **2** large; large-scale. [from Greek *makros* 'long, large']

macrobiotic ● *adj.* of a diet intended to prolong life, comprising pure vegetable foods, brown rice, etc. ● *n.* (in *pl.*; treated as *sing.*) the use or theory of such a dietary system.

MACRAMÉ:
DOUBLE-KNOTTED
MACRAMÉ CHAIN

macrocarpa *n.* an evergreen tree, *Cupressus macrocarpa*, often cultivated for hedges or windbreaks. [based on Greek *karpos* 'fruit']

macrocosm *n.* **1** the universe. **2** the whole of a complex structure. □ **macrocosmic** *adj.*

macroeconomics *n.* the study of large-scale or general economic factors. □ **macroeconomic** *adj.*

macromolecule *n. Biochem.* a molecule containing a very large number of atoms. □ **macromolecular** *adj.*

macron *n.* a mark (ˉ) over a long or stressed vowel. [Greek, literally 'long (thing)']

macronutrient *n.* a chemical required in relatively large amounts for the growth and development of living organisms.

macrophage *n.* a large phagocytic white blood cell usu. occurring at points of infection.

macrophotography *n.* photography producing photographs larger than life.

macroscopic *adj.* **1** visible to the naked eye. **2** regarded in terms of large units. □ **macroscopically** *adv.*

macula *n.* (*pl.* **maculae** /-lee/) **1** a dark spot, esp. a permanent one, in the skin. **2** (in full **macula lutea**) the region of greatest visual acuity in the retina. [Latin, literally 'spot, mesh'] □ **macular** *adj.*

mad ● *adj.* (**madder, maddest**) **1** insane; having a disordered mind. **2** wildly foolish. **3** (often foll. by *about* or *Brit.* on) wildly excited or infatuated (*mad about football; is chess-mad*). **4** *colloq.* angry. **5** (of an animal) rabid. **6** wildly light-hearted. ● *v.intr.* (**madded, madding**) *archaic* be mad; act madly (*the madding crowd*). □ **like mad** *colloq.* with great energy, intensity, or enthusiasm. **mad keen** *colloq.* extremely eager. [Old English *gemǣded* 'made insane'] □ **madness** *n.*

madam *n.* **1** a polite or respectful form of address or mode of reference to a woman. **2** *Brit. colloq.* a conceited or precocious girl or young woman. **3** a woman brothel-keeper. [from Old French *ma dame* 'my lady']

Madame /mǎ-**dahm**/ *n.* **1** (*pl.* **Mesdames** /may-**dahm**/) a title or form of address used of or to a French-speaking woman, corresponding to Mrs or madam. **2** (**madame**) = MADAM 1. [French, literally 'my lady']

madcap ● *adj.* **1** wildly impulsive. **2** undertaken without forethought. ● *n.* a wildly impulsive person.

mad cow disease *n. colloq.* = BSE.

madden *v.* **1** *tr. & intr.* make or become mad. **2** *tr.* irritate intensely. □ **maddening** *adj.* **maddeningly** *adv.*

madder *n.* **1** ▼ a herbaceous plant of the genus *Rubia*, with whorls of four to six leaves, including *R. tinctorum*, which was formerly cultivated as a source of red dye. **2** a red dye obtained from the root of the madder, or its synthetic substitute. [Old English]

made past and past part. of MAKE. ● *adj.* (usu. in *comb.*) **1** built or formed (*well-made; strongly-made*). **2** successful (*a self-made man*). □ **have** (or **have got**) **it made** *colloq.* be sure of success. **made for** ideally suited to.

Madeira *n.* **1** a fortified white wine from the island of Madeira off the coast of N. Africa. **2** (in full **Madeira cake**) a kind of rich sponge cake. □ **Madeiran** *n. & adj.*

madeleine /mad-**layn**/ *n.* a small fancy sponge cake. [French]

Mademoiselle /ma-dĕ-mwǎ-**zel**/ *n.* (*pl.* **Mesdemoiselles** /may-dĕ-mwǎ-**zel**/ **1** a title or form of address used of or to an unmarried French-speaking woman, corresponding to Miss or madam. **2** (**mademoiselle**) **a** a young Frenchwoman. **b** a French governess. [French, literally 'my damsel']

made to measure *adj.* (hyphenated when *attrib.*) (of clothes) made from measurements taken.

made to order *adj.* (hyphenated when *attrib.*) **1** made according to individual requirements. **2** exactly as wanted.

made up *adj.* (hyphenated when *attrib.*) **1** invented, not true. **2** wearing make-up. **3** (of a meal etc.) already prepared. **4** (of a road) surfaced, not rough.

MADDER: WILD MADDER (*Rubia peregrina*)

madhouse *n.* **1** *archaic* or *colloq.* a mental home or hospital. **2** *colloq.* a scene of confused uproar.

madly *adv.* **1** in a mad manner. **2** *colloq.* **a** passionately. **b** extremely.

madman *n.* (*pl.* **-men**) a man who is mad.

Madonna *n. Eccl.* **1** (prec. by *the*) a name for the Virgin Mary. **2** (usu. **madonna**) a picture or statue of the Madonna. [Italian, literally 'my lady']

madras *n.* **1** a strong cotton fabric with coloured or white stripes, checks, etc. **2** (**Madras**) a hot spiced curry dish usu. made with meat. [from *Madras*, a seaport in India]

madrigal *n.* **1** a usu. 16th-c. or 17th-c. part-song for several voices, usu. arranged in elaborate counterpoint and without instrumental accompaniment. **2** a short love poem. [from medieval Latin *carmen matricale* 'simple song'] □ **madrigalian** *adj.* **madrigalist** *n.*

madwoman *n.* (*pl.* **-women**) a woman who is mad.

maelstrom /**mayl**-strŏm/ *n.* **1** a great whirlpool. **2** a state of confusion. [early modern Dutch, the name of a mythical whirlpool]

maenad /**mee**-nad/ *n.* **1** a priestess or female follower of Bacchus. **2** a frenzied woman. [from Greek *Mainas -ados*]

maestro /**mys**-troh/ *n.* (*pl.* **maestri** or **-os**) **1** a distinguished musician, esp. a conductor. **2** a great performer in any sphere. [Italian, literally 'master']

Mae West *n. slang* an inflatable life jacket. [from the name of an American film actress, 1892–1980, noted for her large bust]

Mafia *n.* **1** an organized body of criminals, originally in Sicily and now esp. in Italy and the US. **2** (**mafia**) a group regarded as exerting a hidden sinister influence. [Italian (Sicilian) dialect, literally 'bragging']

Mafioso *n.* (*pl.* **Mafiosi**) **1** a member of the Mafia. **2** (**mafioso**) a member of a group regarded as exerting a hidden sinister influence. [Italian]

mag *n. colloq.* a magazine (periodical).

magazine *n.* **1** a periodical publication containing articles, stories, etc., usu. with illustrations. **2** a chamber for holding a supply of cartridges to be fed automatically to the breech of a gun. ▷ GUN, MACHINE-GUN. **3** a similar device feeding a camera, slide projector, etc. **4** a store for arms, ammunition, and provisions for use in war. **5** a store for explosives. [from Arabic *makāzin* 'storehouses']

magenta ● *n.* **1** a brilliant mauvish-crimson shade. **2** an aniline dye of this colour. ● *adj.* of or coloured

with magenta. [from *Magenta* in N. Italy, site of a battle (1859) fought shortly before the dye (of bloodlike colour) was discovered]

maggot *n.* a soft-bodied legless larva, esp. that of a blowfly etc. found in decaying matter. [from Old Norse *mathkr*] □ **maggoty** *adj.*

magi *pl.* of MAGUS.

magic ● *n.* **1 a** the supposed art of influencing the course of events by the occult control of nature or of spirits. **b** witchcraft. **2** conjuring tricks. **3** an inexplicable influence. **4** an enchanting quality or phenomenon. ● *adj.* **1** of or resulting from magic. **2** producing surprising results. **3** *colloq.* wonderful, exciting. ● *v.tr.* (**magicked, magicking**) change or create by magic, or apparently so. □ **like magic** very rapidly. **magic away** cause to disappear as if by magic. [from Greek *magikē (tekhnē)* '(art of) a magus']

magical *adj.* **1** of or relating to magic. **2** resembling magic; produced as if by magic. **3** wonderful, enchanting. □ **magically** *adv.*

magic bullet *n. colloq.* any highly specific medicine or other cure.

magic carpet *n.* a mythical carpet able to transport a person on it to any desired place.

magic eye *n.* a small cathode ray tube used to indicate the correct tuning of a radio receiver.

magician *n.* **1** a person skilled in or practising magic. **2** a conjuror. **3** a person with exceptional skill.

magic lantern *n.* a simple form of image-projector using photographic slides.

magic mushroom *n.* a mushroom producing psilocybin.

magic square *n.* a square divided into smaller squares each containing a number such that the sums of all vertical, horizontal, or diagonal rows are equal.

magisterial *adj.* **1** imperious. **2** invested with authority. **3** of or conducted by a magistrate. **4** highly authoritative. [based on Latin *magister* 'master'] □ **magisterially** *adv.*

magistracy *n.* (*pl.* **-ies**) **1** the office or authority of a magistrate. **2** magistrates collectively.

magistrate *n.* a civil officer administering the law, esp. an official conducting a court for minor cases and preliminary hearings (*magistrates' court*). [from Latin *magistratus* 'administrator']

maglev *n.* (usu. *attrib.*) ▼ a transport system in which trains glide above a track, supported by magnetic repulsion. [from *magnetic levitation*]

M

MAGLEV

Still at an experimental stage, maglev trains are propelled at speeds of up to 500 k.p.h. (311 m.p.h.) by superconducting electromagnets. In one system in Japan, coils in the track wall are fed an alternating electric current as the train passes. Each coil alternately attracts and repels the train coils, driving the vehicle forward. Other coils on the track wall and on the train interact to lift and guide it along the track.

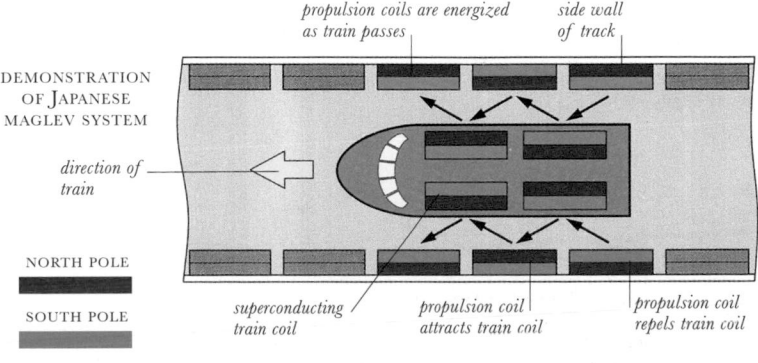

DEMONSTRATION OF JAPANESE MAGLEV SYSTEM

propulsion coils are energized as train passes

side wall of track

direction of train

NORTH POLE

SOUTH POLE

superconducting train coil

propulsion coil attracts train coil

propulsion coil repels train coil

MAGMA

Magma originates far beneath the surface of the Earth, where rocks are melted by intensely high temperatures. The molten magma may collect in a reservoir underground before emerging through a vent or fissure in the Earth's surface, in a volcanic eruption. When it reaches the surface, magma (now known as lava) cools and solidifies to form extrusive igneous rock. Magma does not always erupt on to the surface, but may solidify underground to form an intrusion of igneous rock, which appears on the surface only when overlying rocks are eroded. The fierce heat from rising magma is one of the forces that transforms other rocks by metamorphism.

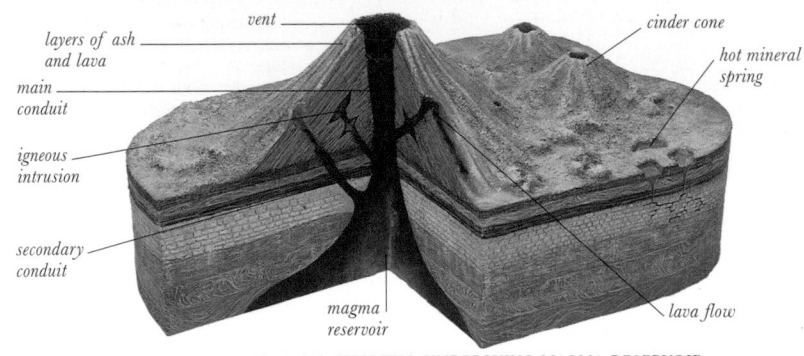

MODEL OF A VOLCANO SHOWING UNDERLYING MAGMA RESERVOIR

magma n. (pl. **magmas** or **magmata**) ▲ fluid or semi-fluid material under the Earth's surface from which igneous rock is formed by cooling. ▷ ROCK CYCLE, SEABED, VOLCANO. [Middle English in sense 'a solid residue': from Greek] □ **magmatic** adj.

Magna Carta n. (also **Magna Charta**) a charter of liberty obtained from King John of England in 1215. [medieval Latin, literally 'great charter']

magnanimous adj. nobly generous; not petty in feelings or conduct. [based on Latin magnus 'great' + animus 'soul'] □ **magnanimity** n. **magnanimously** adv.

magnate n. a wealthy and influential person (shipping magnate; financial magnate). [based on Latin magnus 'great']

magnesia n. 1 Chem. magnesium oxide. 2 (in general use) hydrated magnesium carbonate, a white powder used as an antacid and laxative. [from Greek Magnēsia (lithos) '(stone) of Magnesia', in Asia Minor] □ **magnesian** adj.

magnesium n. Chem. a silvery metallic element used for making light alloys and important as an essential element in living organisms.

magnet n. 1 a piece of iron, steel, alloy, ore, etc., having properties of attracting or repelling iron. 2 a lodestone. ▷ ALTERNATING CURRENT. 3 a person or thing that attracts. [from Greek Magnēs (lithos) 'Magnesian (stone)', originally referring to lodestone]

magnetic adj. 1 a having the properties of a magnet. b producing, produced by, or acting by magnetism. 2 capable of being attracted by or acquiring the properties of a magnet. 3 very attractive or alluring (a magnetic personality). □ **magnetically** adv.

magnetic compass n. = COMPASS n. 1.

magnetic disk see DISC n. 4a.

magnetic field n. ▶ a region of variable force around magnets, magnetic materials, or current-carrying conductors. ▷ ELECTROMAGNETISM

magnetic mine n. a submarine mine detonated by the proximity of a magnetized body.

magnetic needle n. a piece of magnetized steel used as an indicator on the dial of a compass and in magnetic and electrical apparatus. ▷ COMPASS, MAGNETIC FIELD

magnetic north n. the point indicated by the north end of a compass needle.

magnetic pole n. 1 each of the points near the extremities of the axis of rotation of the Earth or another body where a magnetic needle dips vertically. 2 each of the regions of a magnet, from which the magnetic forces appear to originate.

magnetic resonance imaging n. a form of medical imaging using the nuclear magnetic resonance of protons in the body.

magnetic storm n. a disturbance of the Earth's magnetic field caused by charged particles from the sun etc.

magnetic tape n. = TAPE n. 4a.

magnetism n. 1 a magnetic phenomena and their laws. b the property of producing these phenomena. 2 personal charm.

magnetite n. magnetic iron oxide. [from German Magnetit]

magnetize v.tr. (also **-ise**) 1 give magnetic properties to. 2 make into a magnet. 3 attract as or like a magnet. □ **magnetization** n.

magneto /mag-nee-toh/ n. (pl. **-os**) an electric generator using permanent magnets and producing high voltage, esp. for the ignition of an internal-combustion engine.

magnetometer n. an instrument measuring magnetic forces, esp. the Earth's magnetism. ▷ SPACECRAFT. □ **magnetometry** n.

magnetosphere n. the region surrounding a planet, star, etc., in which its magnetic field is effective.

magnetron n. an electron tube for amplifying or generating microwaves, with the flow of electrons controlled by an external magnetic field.

magnification n. 1 the act or an instance of magnifying; the process of being magnified. 2 the degree of magnification. 3 the apparent enlargement of an object by a lens.

magnificent adj. 1 splendid, stately. 2 sumptuously constructed or adorned. 3 colloq. fine, excellent. [from Latin magnificus] □ **magnificence** n. **magnificently** adv.

magnifico n. (pl. **-oes**) a magnate or grandee. [Italian, = MAGNIFICENT: originally with reference to Venice]

magnify v.tr. (**-ies**, **-ied**) 1 make (a thing) appear larger than it is, as with a lens. 2 exaggerate. 3 intensify. 4 archaic extol. [from Latin magnificare] □ **magnifier** n.

magnifying glass n. a lens used to produce an enlarged image.

magnitude n. 1 largeness. 2 a size. b a mathematical quantity. 3 importance. 4 a the degree of brightness of a star. b a class of stars arranged according to this (of the third magnitude). □ **of the first magnitude** very important. [from Latin magnitudo]

magnolia ● n. 1 ▶ any tree or shrub of the genus Magnolia, cultivated for its dark green foliage and large waxlike flowers in spring. 2 a pale creamy-white colour. ● adj. of this colour. [modern Latin, named after P. Magnol, French botanist, 1638–1715]

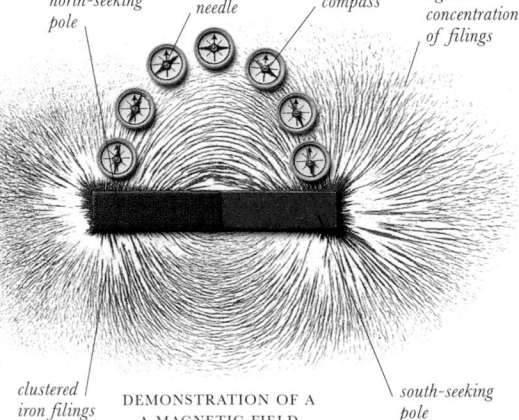

MAGNOLIA
(Magnolia × veitchii)

magnox n. a magnesium-based alloy used to enclose uranium fuel elements in a nuclear reactor. [from magnesium no oxidation]

magnum n. (pl. **magnums**) 1 a wine bottle of about twice the standard size. 2 a a cartridge or shell that is especially powerful or large. b (often attrib.) cartridge or gun adapted so as to be more powerful than its calibre suggests. [Latin, literally 'great (thing)']

magnum opus n. (pl. **magnum opuses** or **magna opera**) 1 a great work of art, literature, etc. 2 the most important work of an artist, writer, etc. [Latin, literally 'great work']

MAGNETIC FIELD

Magnetism is invisible, but lines of magnetic force around a magnet (the magnetic field) can be demonstrated. When unmagnetized magnetic material comes near a magnet, it becomes temporarily magnetized, with north and south poles that are attracted to the opposite poles of the magnet. Here, temporarily magnetized iron filings swivel to align with the magnet's field, with clusters around the poles where the force is strongest. The compass needles, which are already magnetized, show this effect in a similar way.

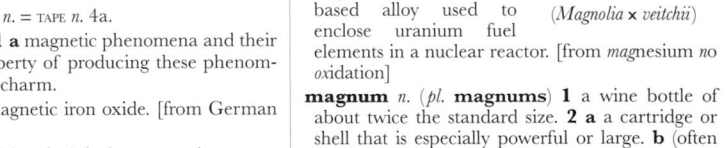

DEMONSTRATION OF A A MAGNETIC FIELD

magpie *n.* **1** ▶ a long-tailed crow, *Pica pica*, of Europe and N. America, with black and white plumage. **2** any of various birds with black and white plumage, esp. *Gymnorhina tibicen* of Australia. **3** a chatterer. **4** a person who collects things indiscriminately. [based on *Mag*, abbreviation of *Margaret*]

MAGPIE: BLACK-BILLED MAGPIE
(*Pica pica*)

magus /may-gŭs/ *n.* (*pl.* **magi** /may-jy/) **1** a priest of ancient Persia. **2** a sorcerer. **3** (**the** (**three**) **Magi**) the 'wise men' from the East who brought gifts to the infant Christ (Matt. 2:1–12). [from Old Persian]

Magyar ● *n.* **1** a member of a people now predominant in Hungary. **2** the language of this people; Hungarian. ● *adj.* of or relating to this people or language. [native name]

maharaja *n.* (also **maharajah**) *hist.* a title of some Indian princes. [from Hindi *mahā* 'great' + *rājā* 'king']

maharanee *n.* (also **maharani**) *hist.* a maharaja's wife or widow. [from Hindi *mahā* 'great' + *rānī* 'queen']

maharishi *n.* a great Hindu sage. [from Sanskrit *mahā* 'great' + *ŕishi* 'inspired sage']

mahatma *n.* **1 a** (in India etc.) a person regarded with reverence. **b** a sage. **2** each of a class of persons in India and Tibet supposed by some to have preternatural powers. [from Sanskrit *mahā* 'great' + *ātman* 'soul']

mah-jong *n.* (also **mah-jongg**) a Chinese game played with 136 or 144 pieces called tiles. [from Chinese dialect *ma-tsiang* 'sparrows']

mahlstick var. of MAULSTICK.

mahogany ● *n.* (*pl.* **-ies**) **1 a** a hard reddish-brown wood used esp. for furniture. ▷ WOOD. **b** the colour of this. **2** any tropical tree of the genus *Swietenia*, esp. *S. mahogoni*, yielding this wood. ● *adj.* of a rich reddish-brown colour. [17th-century coinage]

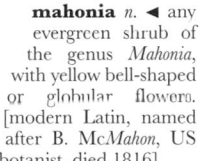

berries

MAHONIA: OREGON GRAPE
(*Mahonia aquifolium*)

mahonia *n.* ◀ any evergreen shrub of the genus *Mahonia*, with yellow bell-shaped or globular flowers. [modern Latin, named after B. McMahon, US botanist, died 1816]

mahout /mă-howt/ *n.* (in the Indian subcontinent) an elephant driver. [from Sanskrit *mahāmātra* 'high official']

maid *n.* **1** a female servant. **2** *Brit. archaic* or *poet.* a girl or young woman. [Middle English]

maiden *n.* **1 a** *archaic* or *poet.* a girl; a young unmarried woman. **b** (*attrib.*) unmarried (*maiden aunt*). **2** *Cricket* = MAIDEN OVER. **3** (*attrib.*) (of a female animal) unmated. **4** (often *attrib.*) **a** a horse that has never won a race. **b** a race open only to such horses. **5** (*attrib.*) being or involving the first attempt or occurrence (*maiden speech*; *maiden voyage*). [Old English] □ **maidenhood** *n.* **maidenly** *adj.*

maidenhair *n.* (in full **maidenhair fern**) a fern of the genus *Adiantum*, esp. *A. capillus-veneris*, with delicate fronds.

maidenhead *n.* **1** virginity. **2** the hymen.

maiden name *n.* a wife's surname before marriage.

maiden over *n.* *Cricket* an over in which no runs are scored off the bat.

maid of honour *n.* **1** an unmarried lady attending a queen or princess. **2** *Brit.* a kind of small custard tart. **3** *N. Amer.* a principal bridesmaid.

maidservant *n.* a female servant.

mail[1] ● *n.* **1 a** letters and parcels etc. conveyed by post. **b** the postal system. **c** one complete delivery or collection of mail. **d** one delivery of letters to one place, esp. to a business on one occasion. **2** = ELECTRONIC MAIL. **3** a vehicle carrying mail. ● *v.tr.* send by post. [from Old French *male* 'wallet']

mail[2] *n.* *hist.* armour made of rings, chains, or plates. ▷ VIKING. [based on Latin *macula* 'spot, mesh'] □ **mailed** *adj.*

mailbag *n.* a large sack for carrying mail.

mailboat *n.* a boat carrying mail.

mailbox *n.* *N. Amer.* a letter box.

mailed fist *n.* (prec. by *the*) physical force.

mailing *n.* **1** the action or process of sending something by mail. **2** something sent by mail.

mailing list *n.* a list of people to whom advertising matter, information, etc., is to be posted.

mailman *n.* (*pl.* **-men**) *N. Amer.* a postman.

mail order *n.* the ordering of goods by post (also, often with hyphen, *mail-order catalogue*).

mailshot *n.* a dispatch of mail, esp. advertising and promotional material, to a large number of addresses.

mail train *n.* a train carrying mail.

maim *v.tr.* **1** cripple, disable, mutilate. **2** harm, impair (*emotionally maimed by neglect*). [from Old French *mahaignier*]

main ● *adj.* **1** chief; principal (*the main part; the main point*). **2** exerted to the full (*by main force*). ● *n.* **1** a principal channel, duct, etc., for water, sewage, etc. (*water main*). **2** (usu. in *pl.*; prec. by *the*) *Brit.* **a** the central distribution network for electricity, gas, water, etc. **b** a domestic electricity supply as distinct from batteries. **3** *archaic* or *poet.* **a** the ocean or oceans (*the Spanish Main*). **b** the mainland for the most part. □ **in the main** for the most part. [partly from Old Norse *megenn* 'strong, powerful', partly from Old English *mægen* 'physical force']

main brace *n.* *Naut.* the brace attached to the main yard.

main chance *n.* (prec. by *the*) one's own interests.

main clause *n.* *Gram.* a clause that alone forms a complete sentence (cf. SUBORDINATE CLAUSE).

main course *n.* **1** the chief course of a meal. **2** *Naut.* the mainsail.

maincrop *attrib.adj.* (of a vegetable) produced by the main crop.

main drag *n.* *US colloq.* = MAIN STREET.

mainframe *n.* **1** the central processing unit of a computer. **2** (often *attrib.*) a large computer system.

mainland *n.* a large continuous extent of land, excluding neighbouring islands etc. □ **mainlander** *n.*

mainline *v.* *slang* **1** *intr.* take drugs intravenously. **2** *tr.* inject (drugs) intravenously. □ **mainliner** *n.*

main line *n.* **1** a chief railway line. **2** *slang* a principal vein (cf. MAINLINE). **3** *US* a chief road or street.

mainly *adv.* for the most part; chiefly.

mainmast *n.* *Naut.* the principal mast of a ship. ▷ RIGGING, SHIP

mainplane *n.* the principal supporting surface of an aircraft.

mainsail *n.* *Naut.* **1** (in a square-rigged vessel) the lowest sail on the mainmast. **2** (in a fore-and-aft rigged vessel) a sail set on the after part of the mainmast.

mainsheet *n.* *Naut.* the rope which controls the boom of the mainsail when set.

mainspring *n.* **1** the principal spring of a mechanical watch, clock, etc. **2** a chief motive power; an incentive.

mainstay *n.* **1** a chief support (*has been his mainstay since his trouble*). **2** *Naut.* a stay from the maintop to the foot of the foremast. ▷ RIGGING

mainstream *n.* **1** (often *attrib.*) the prevailing trend in opinion, fashion, etc. **2** a type of jazz based on the 1930s swing style and consisting esp. of solo improvisation on chord sequences. **3** the principal current of a river.

main street *n.* the principal street of a town.

maintain *v.tr.* **1** cause to continue; keep up, preserve (a state of affairs, an activity, etc.) (*maintained friendly relations*). **2** support by work, nourishment, expenditure, etc. (*maintained him in comfort; maintained themselves by fishing*). **3** assert as true (*maintained that she was the best; his story was true, he maintained*). **4** preserve (a building, machine, road, etc.) in good repair. **5** give aid to (a cause, party, etc.). **6** provide means for (a garrison etc. to be equipped) [from Latin *manu tenēre* 'to hold in the hand'] □ **maintainable** *adj.* **maintainability** *n.*

maintained school *n.* *Brit.* a school supported from public funds.

maintenance *n.* **1** the process of maintaining or being maintained. **2 a** the provision of the means to support life, esp. by work etc. **b** (also **separate maintenance**) a husband's or wife's provision for a spouse after separation or divorce; alimony. **3** *Law hist.* the offence of aiding a party in litigation without lawful cause. [Middle English, from Old French, from *maintenir*: see MAINTAIN]

maintop *n.* *Naut.* a platform above the head of the lower mainmast.

main yard *n.* *Naut.* the yard on which the mainsail is extended.

maiolica /mă-yol-i-kă/ *n.* (also **majolica**) **1** ◀ a white earthenware decorated with metallic colours, originally popular in the Mediterranean area during the Renaissance. **2** a modern imitation of this. [Italian, from the former name of Majorca]

MAIOLICA: 16TH-CENTURY ITALIAN MAIOLICA BOWL

maisonette *n.* (also **maisonnette**) **1** a part of a house, block of flats, etc., forming separate living accommodation, usu. on two floors and having a separate entrance. **2** a small house. [from French *maisonnette* 'little house']

maître d'hôtel /may-trĕ doh-tel/ *n.* (*pl.* **maîtres d'hôtel** *pronunc.* same) **1** the manager, head steward, etc., of a hotel. **2** a head waiter. [French, literally 'master of (the) house']

maize *n.* **1** ▶ a cereal plant, *Zea mays*, native to N. America, yielding large grains set in rows on a cob. **2** ▶ the cobs or grains of this. ▷ GRAIN. [from Spanish *maiz*]

Maj. *abbr.* Major.

majestic *adj.* stately and dignified; imposing. □ **majestically** *adv.*

MAIZE: CORN COBS
(*Zea mays*)

M

MAKE-UP

Since early times, people have used face and body paints for adornment and camouflage, and in religious ceremonies and rituals. Modern cosmetics provide a huge range of products designed specifically to enhance the colour and shape of the face, eyes, and lips.

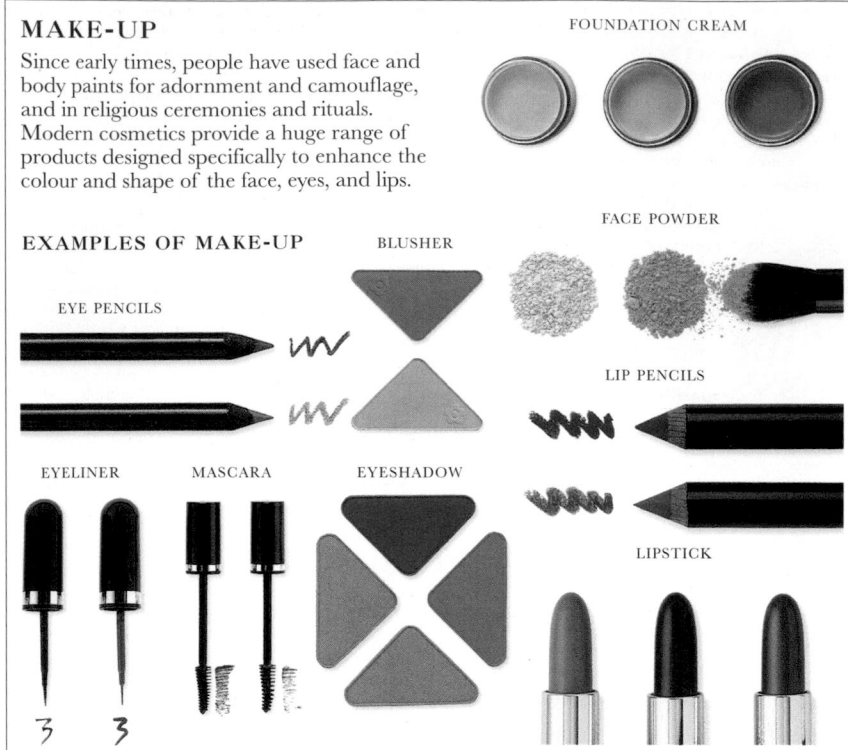

FOUNDATION CREAM

EXAMPLES OF MAKE-UP

BLUSHER

FACE POWDER

EYE PENCILS

LIP PENCILS

EYELINER   MASCARA   EYESHADOW

LIPSTICK

M

majesty *n.* (*pl.* **-ies**) **1** impressive stateliness, dignity, or authority. **2 a** royal power. **b** (**Majesty**) forming part of several titles given to a sovereign or a sovereign's wife or widow or used in addressing them (*Your Majesty; Her Majesty the Queen Mother*). [from Latin *majestas*]

major ● *adj.* **1** important, large, serious, significant (*a major road; the major consideration must be their health*). **2** (of an operation) serious. **3** *Mus.* **a** (of a scale) having intervals of a semitone between the third and fourth, and seventh and eighth degrees. **b** (of an interval) greater by a semitone than a minor interval (*major third*). **c** (of a key) based on a major scale. **4** of full legal age. **5** *Brit.* (appended to a surname, esp. in public schools) indicating the elder of two brothers (*Smith major*). ● *n.* **1** *Mil.* **a** an army officer next below lieutenant colonel and above captain. **b** an officer in charge of a section of band instruments (*drum major; pipe major*). **2** a person of full legal age. **3** *Mus.* a major key etc. **4** *N. Amer.* **a** a student's special subject or course. **b** a student specializing in a specified subject (*a philosophy major*). ● *v.intr.* (foll. by *in*) *N. Amer.* study or qualify in as a special subject (*majored in theology*). [Latin, literally 'greater']

major-domo *n.* (*pl.* **-os**) **1** the chief official of an Italian or Spanish princely household. **2** a house-steward; a butler. [from medieval Latin *major domus* 'chief of the house']

major general *n.* an officer next below a lieutenant general.

majority *n.* (*pl.* **-ies**) **1** the greater number or part. **2** *Polit.* **a** the number by which the votes cast for one party, candidate, etc. exceed those of the next (*won by a majority of 151*). **b** a party etc. receiving the greater number of votes. **3** full legal age (*attained his majority*). **4** the rank of major. [from medieval Latin *majoritas*]

■ **Usage** In sense 1, *majority* is strictly used only with countable nouns, e.g. *a majority of people*, and not with mass nouns, e.g. *a majority of the work*. When used with countable nouns, it is followed by a plural verb, e.g. *The majority of his books were failures*.

majority rule *n.* the principle that the greater number should exercise greater power.

majority verdict *n.* a verdict given by more than half of the jury, but not unanimous.

make ● *v.* (*past* and *past part.* **made**) **1** *tr.* construct; create; form from parts or other substances. **2** *tr.* (usu. foll. by *infin.* with or without *to*) cause or compel (*make him repeat it*). **3** *tr.* **a** cause to exist; bring about (*made a noise*). **b** cause to become or seem (*made him angry*). **4** *tr.* prepare; draw up (*made her will*). **5** *tr.* amount to (*makes a difference; 2 and 2 make 4*). **6** *tr.* **a** undertake or agree to (an aim or purpose) (*made a promise*). **b** execute or perform (a bodily movement, a speech, etc.) (*made a face*). **7** *tr.* gain, acquire, procure (money, a profit, etc.). **8** *tr.* prepare (tea, coffee, a dish, etc.) for consumption. **9** *tr.* **a** arrange bedclothes tidily on (a bed) ready for use. **b** arrange and light materials for (a fire). **10** *intr.* **a** proceed (*made towards the river*). **b** (foll. by *to* + infin.) begin an action (*he made to go*). **11** *tr. colloq.* **a** arrive at (a place) or in time for (a train etc.) (*made the six o'clock train*). **b** manage to attend (*couldn't make the concert; can make any day except Friday*). **c** achieve a place in (*made the first eleven*). **d** esp. *N. Amer.* achieve the rank of (*made colonel in three years*). **12** *tr.* establish or enact (a distinction, rule, law, etc.). **13** *tr.* estimate as (*what do you make the time?*). **14** *tr.* secure the success or advancement of (*it made my day*). **15** *tr.* accomplish (a distance, score, etc.) (*made 60 m.p.h. on the motorway*). **16** *tr.* **a** become by development or training (*made a great leader*). **b** serve as (*a log makes a useful seat*). **17** *tr.* (usu. foll. by *out*) cause to appear as (*makes him out a liar*). **18** *tr.* form in the mind (*I make no judgement*). **19** *tr.* (foll. by *it* + compl.) **a** determine, establish, or choose (*let's make it Tuesday*). **b** bring to (a chosen value etc.) (*decided to make it a dozen*). **20** *tr. slang* have sexual relations with. **21** *tr. Cards* **a** win (a trick). **b** play (a card) to advantage. **c** win the number of tricks that fulfils (a contract). **22** *tr. Cricket* score (runs). ● *n.* **1** (esp. of a product) a type, origin, brand, etc. of manufacture (*different make of car*). **2** a kind of mental, moral, or physical structure or composition. □ **make as if** (or **though**) (foll. by *to* + infin. or conditional) act as if (*made as if*

to leave). **make away** (or **off**) depart hastily. **make away with 1** get rid of; kill. **2** squander. **make believe** pretend. **make a clean breast of** see BREAST. **make conversation** talk politely. **make a day** (or **night** etc.) **of it** devote a whole day (or night etc.) to an activity. **make do 1** manage with the means available. **2** (foll. by *with*) manage with (something) as an inferior substitute. **make an example of** punish as a warning to others. **make a fool of** see FOOL[1]. **make for 1** tend to result in (happiness etc.). **2** proceed towards (a place). **3** assault; attack. **4** confirm (an opinion). **make friends** (often foll. by *with*) become friendly. **make fun of** see FUN. **make good** see GOOD. **make a habit of** see HABIT. **make a hash of** see HASH[1]. **make hay** see HAY. **make head or tail of** see HEAD. **make it 1** *colloq.* succeed in reaching, esp. in time. **2** *colloq.* be successful. **3** (usu. foll. by *with*) *slang* have sexual intercourse (with). **make it up 1** be reconciled, esp. after a quarrel. **2** fill in a deficit. **make it up to** remedy negligence, an injury, etc. to (a person). **make light of** see LIGHT[2]. **make love** see LOVE. **make a meal of** see MEAL[1]. **make merry** see MERRY. **make money** acquire wealth or an income. **make the most of** see MOST. **make much** (or **little** or **the best**) **of 1** derive much (or little etc.) advantage from. **2** give much (or little etc.) attention, importance, etc., to. **make a name for oneself** see NAME. **make no bones about** see BONE. **make nothing of 1** do without hesitation. **2** treat as a trifle. **3** be unable to understand, use, or deal with. **make of 1** construct from. **2** conclude to be the meaning or character of (*can you make anything of it?*). **make off** = *make away*. **make off with** carry away; steal. **make oneself scarce** see SCARCE. **make or break** (or esp. *Brit.* **mar**) cause the success or ruin of. **make out 1 a** distinguish by sight or hearing. **b** decipher (handwriting etc.). **2** understand (*can't make him out*). **3** assert; pretend (*made out he liked it*). **4** *colloq.* make progress; fare (*how did you make out?*). **5** (usu. foll. by *to, in favour of*) draw up; write out (*made out a cheque to her*). **6** *N. Amer. colloq.* indulge in sexual activity usu. stopping short of intercourse; neck, pet. **make over 1** transfer the possession of (a thing) to a person. **2** refashion (a garment etc.). **make a point of** see POINT. **make shift** see SHIFT. **make time** (usu. foll. by *for* or *to* + infin.) find an occasion when time is available. **make up 1** serve or act to overcome (a deficiency). **2** complete (an amount, a party, etc.). **3** compensate. **4** be reconciled. **5** put together; compound (*made up the medicine*). **6** sew together. **7** get (a sum of money, a company, etc.) together. **8** concoct (a story). **9** (of parts) compose (a whole). **10 a** apply cosmetics. **b** apply cosmetics to. **11** settle (a dispute). **12** prepare (a bed) for use with fresh sheets etc. **13** compile (a list, an account, etc.). **make up one's mind** decide, resolve. **make up to** curry favour with; court. **make water 1** urinate. **2** (of a ship) take in water. **make way 1** (often foll. by *for*) allow room for others to proceed. **2** achieve progress. **make one's way** proceed. **make with** *US colloq.* supply; perform; proceed with (*made with the feet and left in a hurry*). **on the make** *colloq.* **1** intent on gain. **2** looking for sexual partners. [Old English]

make-believe (also **make-belief**) ● *n.* pretence. ● *adj.* pretended.

make-over *n.* a complete transformation or remodelling.

maker *n.* **1** (often in *comb.*) a person or thing that makes. **2** (**our, the,** etc. **Maker**) God.

makeshift ● *adj.* temporary; serving for the time being. ● *n.* a temporary substitute or device.

make-up *n.* **1** ▲ cosmetics for the face etc., as used generally or by actors. **2** a person's character, temperament, etc. **3** the composition or constitution (of a thing).

makeweight *n.* **1** a small quantity or thing added to make up the full weight. **2** an unimportant extra person. **3** an unimportant point added to make an argument seem stronger.

making n. **1** in senses of MAKE v. **2** (in *pl.*) **a** earnings; profit. **b** (foll. by *of*) essential qualities or ingredients (*has the makings of a general*). □ **be the making of** ensure the success or favourable development of. **in the making** in the course of being made or formed.

mako n. (*pl.* **-os**) ▼ a large bluish shark of the genus *Isurus*, found worldwide. ▷ SHARK. [Maori]

mal- *comb. form* **1 a** bad, badly (*malpractice*; *maltreat*). **b** faulty, faultily (*malfunction*). **2** not (*maladroit*). [from French *mal* 'badly']

MAKO
(*Isurus oxyrinchus*)

malacca /mă-**lak**-ă/ n. (in full **malacca cane**) a rich-brown cane from the stem of the palm tree *Calamus scipionum*, used for walking sticks etc. [from *Malacca*, town and district on the Malay peninsula]

malachite /**mal**-ă-kyt/ n. ▶ a bright green mineral of hydrous copper carbonate, used for ornament. ▷ GEM. [from Greek *molokhitis*]

malacostracan ● n. any crustacean of the class Malacostraca, including crabs, shrimps, lobsters, and krill. ● adj. of or relating to this class. ▷ CRAB

MALACHITE:
BANDED VARIETY

maladaptive adj. (of an individual, species, etc.) failing to adjust adequately to the environment, and undergoing emotional, behavioural, physical, or mental repercussions. □ **maladaptation** n.

maladjusted adj. **1** not correctly adjusted. **2** (of a person) unable to adapt to or cope with the demands of a social environment. □ **maladjustment** n.

maladminister v.tr. manage or administer inefficiently, badly, or dishonestly. □ **maladministration** n.

maladroit adj. clumsy; bungling. □ **maladroitly** adv. **maladroitness** n.

malady n. (*pl.* **-ies**) **1** an ailment; a disease. **2** a morbid or depraved condition; something requiring a remedy. [from Old French *maladie*]

malaise n. **1** a non-specific bodily discomfort not associated with the development of a disease. **2** a feeling of uneasiness. [French]

malapropism n. (also **malaprop**) the use of a word in mistake for one sounding similar, to comic effect, e.g. dance a *flamingo* (for *flamenco*). [from Mrs *Malaprop* in Sheridan's play *The Rivals* (1775)]

malapropos /mal-ă-prŏ-**poh**/ ● adv. inopportunely; inappropriately. ● adj. inopportune; inappropriate. [from French *mal à propos*]

malaria n. an intermittent and remittent fever caused by a protozoan parasite of the genus *Plasmodium*, transmitted by a mosquito bite. [from Italian *mal 'aria* 'bad air'] □ **malarial** adj. **malarious** adj.

malarkey n. colloq. humbug; nonsense. [20th-century coinage]

malathion /mal-a-**th'y**-ŏn/ n. an insecticide containing phosphorus, with low toxicity to other animals.

Malay ● n. **1 a** a member of a people inhabiting Malaysia and Indonesia. **b** a person of Malay descent. **2** the Austronesian language of this people, the official language of Malaysia. ● adj. of or relating to this people or language. [from Malay *Melayu*] □ **Malayan** n. & adj.

Malaysian ● n. a native or inhabitant of Malaysia in SE Asia. ● adj. of or relating to Malaysia or its people.

malcontent ● n. a discontented person; a rebel. ● adj. discontented or rebellious.

male ● adj. **1** of the sex that can beget offspring by fertilization or insemination. **2** of men or male animals, plants, etc.; masculine (*the male sex*). **3** (of plants or their parts) containing only fertilizing organs. **4** (of parts of machinery etc.) designed to enter or fill the corresponding female part (*a male screw*). ● n. a male person or animal. [from Latin *masculus*] □ **maleness** n.

male chauvinist see CHAUVINIST 2.

malediction /mal-i-**dik**-shŏn/ n. **1** a curse. **2** the utterance of a curse. □ **maledictive** adj. **maledictory** adj. [based on Latin *maledicere* 'to speak evil of']

malefactor /**mal**-i-fak-ter/ n. a criminal; a person who does evil. [Latin]

malevolent /mă-**lev**-ŏ-lĕnt/ adj. wishing evil to others. [from Latin *malevolent*- 'wishing ill'] □ **malevolence** n. **malevolently** adv.

malfeasance n. Law evildoing. [based on Old French *malfaisant* 'doing evil'] □ **malfeasant** n. & adj.

malformation n. faulty formation. □ **malformed** adj.

malfunction ● n. a failure to function in a normal or satisfactory manner. ● v.intr. fail to function normally.

malice n. **1 a** the intention to do evil. **b** a desire to tease, esp. cruelly. **2** Law wrongful intention, esp. as increasing guilt. [from Latin *malitia*] □ **malicious** adj. **maliciously** adv. **maliciousness** n.

malice aforethought n. (also **malice prepense**) the intention to commit a crime, esp. murder.

malign /mă-**lyn**/ ● adj. **1** (of a thing) injurious. **2** (of a disease) malignant. **3** malevolent. ● v.tr. speak ill of; slander. [from Latin *malignus*] □ **malignity** n. (*pl.* **-ies**). **malignly** adv.

malignant adj. **1 a** (of a disease) very virulent or infectious (*malignant cholera*). **b** (of a tumour) tending to invade normal tissue and recur after removal; cancerous. **2** harmful; feeling or showing intense ill will. □ **malignancy** n. (*pl.* **-ies**). **malignantly** adv.

malignant pustule n. a form of anthrax.

malinger v.intr. feign illness to escape work etc. □ **malingerer** n.

mall /mal, mawl/ n. **1** a sheltered walk or promenade. **2** an enclosed shopping precinct. [applied to *The Mall* in London, originally an alley for *pall-mall*, a game]

mallard n. (*pl.* same or **mallards**) **1** ▼ a wild duck or drake, *Anas platyrhynchos*, of the northern hemisphere. **2** the flesh of the mallard. ▷ DUCK. [from Old French]

malleable adj. **1** (of metal etc.) able to be shaped by hammering. **2** adaptable; flexible. [based on Latin *malleare* 'to hammer'] □ **malleability** n. **malleably** adv.

mallee n. Austral. **1** any of several types of eucalyptus, esp. *Eucalyptus dumosa*, that flourish in arid areas. **2** an area of scrub formed by mallee. [Aboriginal]

mallet n. **1** ▶ a hammer, usu. of wood. **2** a long-handled wooden hammer for striking a croquet or polo ball. ▷ CROQUET. [from Latin *malleus*]

MALLET

mallow n. **1** any plant of the genus *Malva* (family Malvaceae), with hairy stems and leaves and pink or purple flowers. **2** any of several other plants of the family Malvaceae, including marsh mallow. [from Latin *malva*]

malmsey n. a strong sweet wine originally from Greece, now chiefly from Madeira. [from *Monemvasia*, a port in S. Greece]

malnourished adj. suffering from malnutrition. □ **malnourishment** n.

malnutrition n. a dietary condition resulting from the lack of foods necessary for health; insufficient nutrition.

malodorous adj. evil-smelling.

malpractice n. **1** improper or negligent professional treatment, esp. by a medical practitioner. **2 a** criminal wrongdoing. **b** an instance of this.

malt ● n. **1** barley or other grain that is steeped, germinated, and dried, for brewing etc. **2** esp. *Brit. colloq.* malt whisky; malt liquor. ● v.tr. convert (grain) into malt. [Old English] □ **malty** adj. (**maltier**, **maltiest**). **maltiness** n.

malted milk n. **1** a hot drink made from dried milk and a malt preparation. **2** the powdered mixture from which this is made.

Maltese ● n. (*pl.* same) **1 a** a native or national of Malta. **b** a person of Maltese descent. **2** the language of Malta. ● adj. of or relating to Malta or its people or language.

M

Maltese cross n. ◀ a cross with arms of equal length broadening from the centre, often indented at the ends.

Malthusian ● adj. of Malthus's doctrine that the uncontrolled increase of populations is checked only by the limits of their means of subsistence. ● n. a follower of Malthus. □ **Malthusianism** n.

MALTESE CROSS

malt liquor n. alcoholic liquor made from malt by fermentation, not distillation, e.g. beer, stout.

maltose n. Chem. a sugar produced by the hydrolysis of starch under the action of the enzymes in malt, saliva, etc.

maltreat v.tr. ill-treat. □ **maltreater** n. **maltreatment** n.

malt whisky n. whisky made from malted barley.

malversation n. formal **1** corrupt behaviour in a position of trust. **2** (often foll. by *of*) corrupt administration (of public money etc.). [French]

mama n. colloq. (esp. as a child's term) = MAMMA[1].

mamba n. any venomous African snake of the genus *Dendroaspis*, esp. the green and black mambas, which are varieties of *D. angusticeps*. [from Zulu *imamba*]

mambo n. (*pl.* **-os**) **1** a Latin American dance like the rumba. **2** the music for this. [Latin American Spanish]

mamma[1] n. (also **momma**) colloq. (esp. as a child's term) mother.

mamma[2] n. (*pl.* **mammae** /-mee/) **1** a milk-secreting organ of female mammals. **2** a corresponding non-secretory structure in male mammals. [Latin] □ **mammiform** adj.

MALLARD
(*Anas platyrhynchos*)

MALE

FEMALE

MAMMAL

Mammals, a group of about 4,000 species living in a variety of habitats, are unique in their possession of mammary glands, which produce milk to feed their young. Another distinctive feature is hair, which can be in the form of fur, wool, whiskers, prickles, or spines – although some species have lost their hair during the course of evolution. Mammals are divided into three unequal sub-groups. The largest of these is the placental mammals, whose young grow inside the mother's body where they are fed, via the placenta, from her blood. The young of marsupials leave the womb at an early stage, but continue to develop within the mother's pouch. Monotremes, comprising just three species, are the only egg-laying mammals.

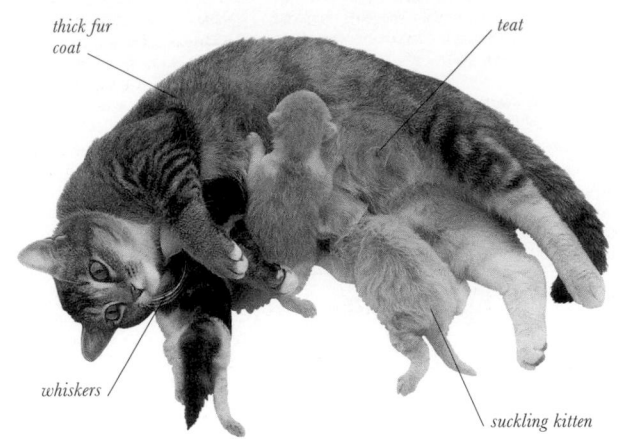

thick fur coat *teat* *whiskers* *suckling kitten*

DOMESTIC CAT AND SUCKLING KITTENS

MAMMAL ORDERS

PLACENTAL MAMMALS

PERISSODACTYLA
(horses, rhinos, tapirs)
▷ HORSE, RUMINANT, UNGULATE

PINNIPEDIA
(seals, sea lions, walruses)
▷ PINNIPED, SEAL

CETACEA
(dolphins, porpoises, whales)
▷ CETACEAN, DOLPHIN, PORPOISE, WHALE

PROBOSCIDEA
(elephants)
▷ ELEPHANT

TUBULIDENTATA
(aardvark)

PRIMATES
(apes, humans, monkeys)
▷ PRIMATE, PROSIMIAN

DERMOPTERA
(flying lemurs)

LAGOMORPHA
(hares, pikas, rabbits)
▷ LAGOMORPH

ARTIODACTYLA
(antelope, cattle, deer, goats)
▷ DEER, RUMINANT, UNGULATE

HYRACOIDEA
(hyraxes)
▷ HYRAX

SCANDENTIA
(tree shrews)

INSECTIVORA
(hedgehogs, moles, shrews)
▷ INSECTIVORE, SHREW

RODENTIA
(beavers, porcupines, rats, squirrels)
▷ RODENT

CHIROPTERA
(bats)
▷ BAT

MONOTREMES   **MARSUPIALS**

SIRENIA
(dugong, manatees)

XENARTHRA
(anteaters, armadillos, sloths)

PHOLIDOTA
(pangolins)

CARNIVORA
(bears, cats, dogs, hyenas, mustelids)
▷ BEAR, CARNIVORE, CAT, DOG, MUSTELID

MONOTREMATA
(platypus, spiny anteaters)
▷ PLATYPUS

MARSUPIALIA
(kangaroos, koalas, opossums, wombats)
▷ MARSUPIAL

M

mammal *n.* ◀ any vertebrate of the class Mammalia, usu. a warm-blooded quadruped with hair or fur, the females of which possess milk-secreting mammae for the nourishment of the young, and including human beings, dogs, cats, rodents, cattle, whales, bats, etc. [from Latin *mammalis*, related to MAMMA²] □ **mammalian** *adj. & n.*

mammary *adj. & n.* ● *adj.* of the human female breasts or milk-secreting organs of other mammals. ● *n.* (*pl.* **-ies**) *slang* a breast. ▷ BREAST

mammary gland *n.* the milk-producing gland of female mammals.

mammography *n. Med.* an X-ray technique of diagnosing and locating abnormalities of the breasts.

Mammon *n.* **1** wealth regarded as a god or as an evil influence. **2** the worldly rich. [from Aramaic *māmōn* 'riches' (see Matt. 6:24, Luke 16:9–13)]

mammoth ● *n.* ▶ any large extinct elephant of the genus *Mammuthus*, with a hairy coat and curved tusks. ● *adj.* huge. [from Russian *mamo(n)t*]

man ● *n.* (*pl.* **men**) **1** an adult human male, esp. as distinct from a woman or boy. **2 a** a person (*no man is perfect*). **b** the human race (*man is mortal*). **3** a person showing the characteristics associated with males (*she's more of a man than he is*). **4 a** a usu. male worker or employee (*the manager spoke to the men*). **b** esp. *Brit.* a manservant or valet. **5 a** (usu. in *pl.*) soldiers, sailors, etc., esp. non-officers (*was in command of 200 men*). **b** an individual (*fought to the last man*). **c** (usu. prec. by *the*, or *poss. pron.*) a person pursued (*I'm your man*). **6 a** a husband (*man and wife*). **b** *colloq.* a boyfriend or lover. **7 a** a human being of a specified historical period or character (*Renaissance man*). **b** a type of prehistoric human named after the place where remains were found (*Peking man*). **8** any one of a set of pieces used in playing chess etc. **9** (as second element in *comb.*) a man of a specified nationality, profession, etc. (*Dutchman*; *clergyman*). **10 a** an expression of impatience etc. used in addressing a male (*nonsense, man!*). **b** *colloq.* a general mode of address (*blew my mind, man!*). **11** (prec. by *a*) one (*what can a man do?*). **12** a person pursued (*the police have so far not caught their man*). **13** (**the Man**) *US slang* **a** the police. **b** *black slang* a person or group with power or authority. ● *v.tr.* (**manned**, **manning**) **1** supply (a ship, factory, etc.) with a person or people for work or defence etc. **2** work or service or defend (a specified piece of equipment, a fortification, etc.) (*man the pumps*). □ **as one man** in unison; in agreement. **be a man** be courageous. **be one's own man 1** be free to act; be independent. **2** be in full possession of one's faculties etc. **man and boy** from childhood. **man to man** with candour; honestly. **men's** (or **men's room**) a usu. public lavatory for men. **to a man** all without exception. [Old English]

man about town *n.* a fashionable man of leisure.

manacle ● *n.* (usu. in *pl.*) **1** a fetter or shackle for the hand. **2** a restraint. ● *v.tr.* fetter with manacles. [from Latin *manicula* 'little hand']

manage *v.* **1** *tr.* organize; regulate; be in charge of (a business, household, etc.). **2** *tr.* (often foll. by *to* + infin.) succeed in achieving (*managed a smile*). **3** *intr.* **a** (often foll. by *with*) succeed in one's aim, esp. against heavy odds (*managed with one assistant*). **b** meet one's needs with limited resources etc. (*manages on a pension*). **4** *tr.* maintain control over (*cannot manage their teenage son*). **5** *tr.* (often prec. by *can*, *be able to*) **a** (also *absol.*) cope with (*can you manage by yourself?*). **b** be free to attend on (a day) or at (a time) (*can you manage Thursday?*). **6** *tr.* handle or wield

(a tool, weapon, etc.). **7** *tr.* take or have charge or control of (an animal or animals, esp. cattle). [based on Latin *manus* 'hand']

manageable *adj.* able to be managed, controlled, or accomplished etc. without great difficulty. □ **manageability** *n.* **manageableness** *n.* **manageably** *adv.*

management *n.* **1** the process of managing or being managed; the action of managing. **2 a** the professional administration of business concerns, etc. **b** people engaged in this. **c** (prec. by *the*) governing body. **3** (usu. foll. by *of*) *Med.* the technique of treating a disease etc.

manager *n.* **1** a person controlling or administering a business or part of a business. **2** a person controlling the affairs, training, etc., of a person or team in sports etc. **3** *Brit. Parl.* a member of either House of Parliament appointed with others for some duty in which both Houses are concerned. **4** a person regarded in terms of skill in management (*a good business manager*). □ **managerial** *adj.* **managerially** *adv.* **managership** *n.*

manageress *n.* a woman manager, esp. of a shop, hotel, theatre, etc.

managing *adj.* (in *comb.*) esp. *Brit.* having executive authority (*managing director*).

mañana /man-**yah**-nă/ *adv.* in the indefinite future (esp. to indicate procrastination). [Spanish, literally 'tomorrow']

manatee *n.* a large aquatic plant-eating mammal [from Carib *manattoui*]

Mancunian ● *n.* a native or inhabitant of Manchester. ● *adj.* of or relating to Manchester. [from *Mancunium*, Latin name of Manchester]

mandala /man-dă-lă/ *n.* a symbolic circular figure representing the universe in various religions. [from Sanskrit *mandala* 'disc']

mandamus /man-**day**-mŭs/ *n. Law* a judicial writ issued as a command to an inferior court, or ordering a person to perform a public or statutory duty. [Latin, literally 'we command']

mandarin¹ *n.* **1** (**Mandarin**) the official language of China. **2** *hist.* a Chinese official. **3** a person of importance, esp. a government official. [from Sanskrit *mantrin* 'counsellor']

mandarin² *n.* (also **mandarine**) (in full **mandarin orange**) **1** a small flattish deep-coloured orange with a loose skin. ▷ CITRUS FRUIT. **2** the tree, *Citrus reticulata*, yielding this. [from French *mandarine*]

mandarin collar *n.* a small close-fitting upright collar.

mandarin duck *n.* a small Chinese duck, *Aix galericulata*, noted for its bright plumage.

mandate ● *n.* **1** an official command or instruction. **2** authority given by electors to a government, trade union, etc. **3** a commission to act for another. ● *v.tr.* instruct (a delegate) to act or vote in a certain way. [from Latin *mandatum* '(thing) commanded']

mandatory *adj.* **1** of or conveying a command. **2** compulsory. □ **mandatorily** *adv.*

mandible *n.* **1** ▶ the jaw, esp. the lower jaw in mammals and fishes. ▷ MAXILLA, SKULL. **2** the upper or lower part of a bird's beak. ▷ BIRD. **3** either half of the crushing organ in an arthropod's mouthparts.

▷ INSECT. [from Late Latin *mandibula*] □ **mandibular** *adj.*

mandolin *n.* (also **mandoline**) a musical instrument resembling a lute, having paired metal strings plucked with a plectrum. [from Italian *mandolino*] □ **mandolinist** *n.*

mandragora *n. hist.* the mandrake, esp. as a type of narcotic (Shakespeare's *Othello* III. iii. 334). [Old English, via medieval Latin and Latin from Greek *mandragoras*]

mandrake *n.* ▼ a poisonous plant, *Mandragora officinarum*, with white or purple flowers and large yellow fruit, having emetic and narcotic properties, and possessing a root once thought to resemble the human form and to shriek when plucked. [Middle English, from medieval Latin *mandragora*]

MANDRAKE
(*Mandragora officinarum*)

mandrel *n.* **1** a shaft in a lathe to which work is fixed while being turned. **2** a cylindrical rod round which metal or other material is forged or shaped. [16th-century coinage]

mandrill *n.* ◀ a large W. African baboon, *Mandrillus sphinx*, the adult of which has a brilliantly coloured face and blue-coloured buttocks.

mane *n.* **1** a growth of long hair on the neck of a horse, lion, etc. ▷ HORSE. **2** *colloq.* a person's long hair. [Old English] □ **maned** *adj.* (also in *comb.*). **maneless** *adj.*

man-eater *n. colloq.* a woman who has many men as lovers.

MANDRILL
(*Mandrillus sphinx*)

manège /man-**airzh**/ *n.* (also **manege**) **1** a riding school. **2** the movements of a trained horse. **3** horsemanship. [French, related to MANAGE]

manes *n.* **1** the deified souls of dead ancestors. **2** (treated as *sing.*) the revered ghost of a dead person. [Middle English, from Latin]

maneuver *US* var. of MANOEUVRE.

man Friday *n.* a male helper or follower. [from *Man Friday* in Defoe's novel *Robinson Crusoe* (1719)]

manful *adj.* brave; resolute. □ **manfully** *adv.* **manfulness** *n.*

mangabey *n.* any small long-tailed W. African monkey of the genus *Cercocebus*. [*Mangabey*, a region of Madagascar]

manganese *n.* **1** *Chem.* a grey brittle metallic transition element used with steel to make alloys (symbol **Mn**). **2** (in full **manganese oxide**) the black mineral oxide of this used in the manufacture of glass. [Italian, alteration of MAGNESIA] □ **manganic** *adj.* **manganous** *adj.*

mange *n.* a skin disease in hairy and woolly animals, caused by a parasitic mite. [based on Latin *manducare* 'to chew']

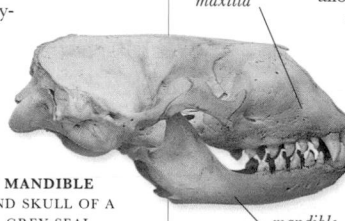

maxilla

MANDIBLE
AND SKULL OF A
GREY SEAL

mandible

M

mangel *n.* (also **mangold**) (in full **mangel-wurzel, mangold-wurzel**) a large kind of beet, *Beta vulgaris*, used as cattle food. [from German *Mangold* 'beet' (+ *Wurzel* 'root')]

manger *n.* a long open box or trough for horses or cattle to eat from. [based on Latin *mandere* 'to chew']

mangetout /monzh-too/ *n.* (*pl.* same or **-s** *pronunc.* same) a variety of pea eaten whole including the pod. ▷ VEGETABLE. [French, literally 'eat all']

mangle[1] ● *n.* esp. *Brit. hist.* a machine having two or more cylinders between which wet clothes etc. are squeezed and pressed. ● *v.tr.* press (clothes etc.) in a mangle. [based on Greek *magganon* 'axis of a pulley']

mangle[2] *v.tr.* **1** hack, cut about, or mutilate by blows etc. **2** spoil (a text etc.) by misquoting etc. **3** cut roughly so as to disfigure. [from Anglo-French]

mango *n.* (*pl.* **-oes** or **-os**) **1** a fleshy yellowish-red fruit, eaten ripe or used green for pickles etc. ▷ FRUIT. **2** (in full **mango tree**) the Indian evergreen tree, *Mangifera indica*, bearing this. [from Tamil *mān* 'mango tree' + *kāy* 'fruit']

mangrove *n.* ▼ any tropical tree or shrub of the genus *Rhizophora*, growing in shore-mud with many tangled roots above ground.

MANGROVE SWAMP

mangy /mayn-ji/ *adj.* (**mangier, mangiest**) **1** (esp. of a domestic animal) having mange. **2** squalid; shabby. □ **mangily** *adv.* **manginess** *n.*

manhandle *v.tr.* **1** move (heavy objects) by human effort. **2** *colloq.* handle (a person) roughly.

manhole *n.* a covered opening in a floor, pavement, sewer, etc. for workmen to gain access.

manhood *n.* **1** the state of being a man rather than a child or woman. **2 a** manliness; courage. **b** a man's sexual potency. **c** *colloq. euphem.* the penis. **3** the men of a country etc.

man-hour *n.* (also **man-day** etc.) an hour (or day etc.) regarded in terms of the amount of work that could be done by one person within this period.

manhunt *n.* an organized search for a person, esp. a criminal.

mania *n.* **1** *Psychol.* mental illness marked by periods of great excitement and violence. **2** (often foll. by *for*) excessive enthusiasm. [Greek, literally 'madness']

-mania *comb. form* **1** *Psychol.* denoting a special type of mental abnormality or obsession (*megalomania*). **2** denoting extreme enthusiasm or admiration (*bibliomania*).

maniac ● *n.* **1** *colloq.* a person exhibiting extreme symptoms of wild behaviour etc.; a madman. **2** *colloq.* an obsessive enthusiast. ● *adj.* of or behaving like a maniac. [from late Greek *maniakos*] □ **maniacal** *adj.* **maniacally** *adv.*

-maniac *comb. form* forming adjectives and nouns meaning 'affected with -mania' or 'a person affected with -mania'.

manic *adj.* of or affected by mania. □ **manically** *adv.*

manic-depressive *Psychol.* ● *adj.* affected by or relating to a mental disorder with alternating periods of elation and depression. ● *n.* a person having such a disorder. □ **manic depression** *n.*

manicure ● *n.* a usu. professional cosmetic treatment of the hands and fingernails. ● *v.tr.* apply a manicure to (the hands or a person). [from Latin *manus* 'hand' + *cura* 'care'] □ **manicurist** *n.*

manifest[1] ● *adj.* clear or obvious to the eye or mind. ● *v.* **1** *tr.* display or show (a quality, feeling, etc.) by one's acts etc. **2** *tr.* show plainly to the eye or mind. **3** *tr.* be evidence of. **4** *intr. & refl.* reveal itself. [from Latin *manus* 'hand' + *festus* (recorded in compounds) 'struck'] □ **manifestation** *n.* **manifestly** *adv.*

manifest[2] *n.* **1** a cargo-list for the use of customs officers. **2** a list of passengers in an aircraft or of trucks etc. in a goods train. [from Italian *manifesto*]

manifesto *n.* (*pl.* **-os**) a public declaration of policy and aims, esp. *Brit.* one issued before an election. [Italian]

manifold ● *adj.* *literary* **1** many and various (*manifold vexations*). **2** having various forms, parts, applications, etc. **3** performing several functions at once. ● *n.* **1** a manifold thing. **2** *Mech.* a pipe or chamber branching into several openings. [Old English] □ **manifoldly** *adv.* **manifoldness** *n.*

manikin *n.* (also **mannikin**) **1** a little man. **2** an anatomical model of the body. [from Dutch *manneken* 'little man']

Manila *n.* (also **Manilla**) **1** (in full **Manila hemp**) the strong fibre of a Philippine plant used for rope etc. **2** (also **manila**) a strong brown paper made from this. [from *Manila*, capital and chief port of the Philippines]

manilla *n.* a metal bracelet used by some African peoples as a medium of exchange. [Spanish, probably a diminutive of *mano* 'hand', from Latin *manus*]

man in the street *n.* (*US* also **man on the street**) an ordinary average person.

manioc *n.* **1** cassava. **2** the flour made from it. [from Tupi (Brazilian) *mandioca*]

manipulate *v.tr.* **1** handle, treat, or use, esp. skilfully **2** manage (a person, situation, etc.) to one's own advantage, esp. unfairly or unscrupulously. **3** manually examine and treat (a part of the body). **4** *Computing* alter, edit, or move (text, data, etc.). [influenced by French *manipuler*] □ **manipulable** *adj.* **manipulation** *n.* **manipulator** *n.* **manipulatory** *adj.*

manipulative *adj.* **1** characterized by unscrupulous exploitation for one's own ends. **2** of or concerning manipulation. □ **manipulatively** *adv.* **manipulativeness** *n.*

mankind *n.* **1** the human species. **2** male people, as distinct from female.

■ **Usage** Some people consider the use of *mankind* in sense 1 as sexist and prefer where possible to use *humankind* or *the human race* instead.

manky *adj.* (**mankier, mankiest**) *Brit. colloq.* **1** bad, inferior, defective. **2** dirty.

manly *adj.* (**manlier, manliest**) **1** having good qualities associated with men, such as courage, frankness, etc. **2** (of a woman) mannish. **3** (of things, qualities, etc.) befitting a man. □ **manliness** *n.*

man-made *adj.* (esp. of a textile fibre) made by man, artificial, synthetic.

MAN-OF-WAR

By the 18th century, large, heavily armed wooden sailing ships, known as 'men-of-war', were being built for northern European navies, who were engaged in the battle for control of the oceans and of the lucrative trade routes. The ships were classified according to how many guns they carried, the largest vessels being armed with more than 100 guns. The ships went into battle in single file so that broadsides from the multiple gun decks would have maximum effect.

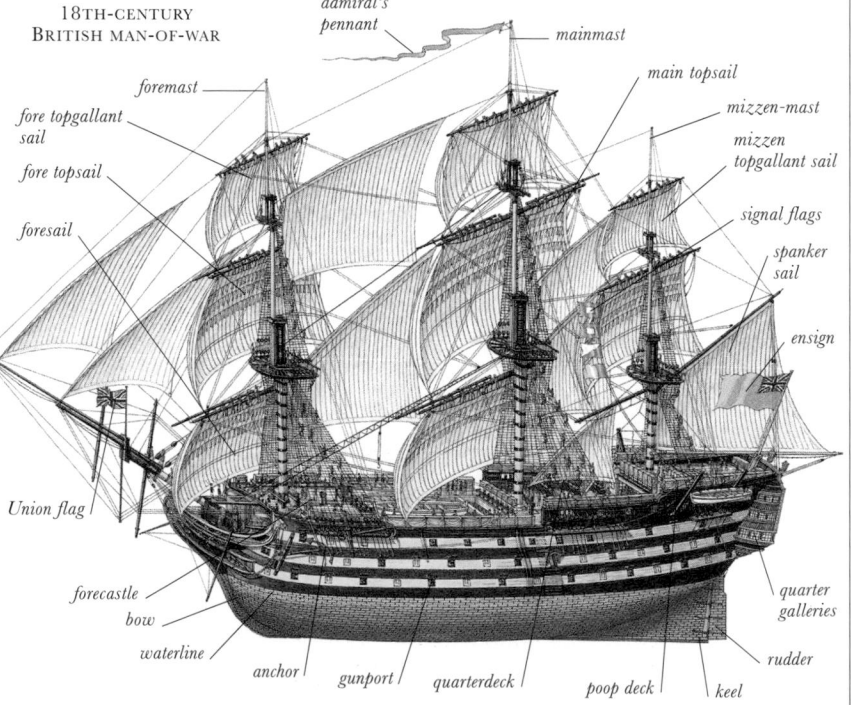

18TH-CENTURY BRITISH MAN-OF-WAR

manna *n.* **1** the substance miraculously supplied as food to the Israelites in the wilderness (Exod. 16). **2** an unexpected benefit (*manna from heaven*). **3** spiritual nourishment, esp. the Eucharist. **4** the sweet dried juice from the manna-ash and other plants, used as a mild laxative. [from Hebrew *mān*]

manned *adj.* (of an aircraft, spacecraft, etc.) having a human crew.

mannequin *n.* **1** a fashion model. **2** a window dummy. [French, literally 'manikin']

manner *n.* **1** a way a thing is done or happens. **2** (in *pl.*) social behaviour (*it is bad manners to stare*). **3** a person's outward bearing etc. (*has an imperious manner*). **4 a** a style in literature etc. (*in the manner of Rembrandt*). **b** = MANNERISM 2a. **5** *archaic* a kind or sort (*what manner of man is he?*). □ **all manner of** many different kinds of. **by all** (or **no**) **manner of means** see MEANS. **in a manner of speaking** in some sense; to some extent. **to the manner born** *colloq.* naturally at ease in a specified job etc. [based on Latin *manus* 'hand']

mannered *adj.* **1** (in *comb.*) behaving in a specified way (*ill-mannered*). **2** (of a style, artist, etc.) showing idiosyncratic mannerisms. **3** (of a person) eccentrically affected in behaviour.

mannerism *n.* **1** a habitual gesture or way of speaking etc. **2 a** excessive use of a distinctive style in art or literature. **b** a stylistic trick. □ **mannerist** *n.* **manneristic** *adj.*

mannerly *adj.* well-mannered; polite. □ **mannerliness** *n.*

mannikin var. of MANIKIN.

mannish *adj.* **1** usu. *derog.* (of a woman) masculine in appearance or manner. **2** characteristic of a man. □ **mannishly** *adv.* **mannishness** *n.*

manoeuvre (*US* **maneuver**) ● *n.* **1** a planned and controlled movement or series of moves. **2** (in *pl.*) a large-scale exercise of troops etc. **3** a skilful or artful plan. ● *v.* (**-ring**) **1** *intr. & tr.* perform or cause to perform a manoeuvre (*manoeuvred the car*). **2** *intr. & tr.* perform or cause (troops etc.) to perform military manoeuvres. **3 a** *tr.* (usu. foll. by *into, out, away*) force, drive, or manipulate (a person, thing, etc.) by scheming or adroitness. **b** *intr.* use artifice. [based on Latin *manus* 'hand' + *operari* 'to work'] □ **manoeuvrable** *adj.* **manoeuvrability** *n.*

man of God *n.* **1** a clergyman. **2** a male saint.

man of honour *n.* a man whose word can be trusted.

man of letters *n.* a scholar or author.

man of sense *n.* (*fem.* **woman of sense**) a sagacious person.

man of straw *n.* **1** an imaginary person set up as an opponent. **2** a stuffed effigy. **3** a person undertaking a financial commitment without adequate means. **4** a sham argument set up to be defeated.

man of the house *n.* the male head of a household.

man of the moment *n.* a man of importance at a particular time.

man of the world see WORLD.

man-of-war *n.* (*pl.* **men-of-war**) **1** esp. *hist.* ◀ an armed ship, esp. of a specified country. **2** a frigate bird.

manometer *n.* a pressure gauge for gases and liquids. [based on Greek *manos* 'thin'] □ **manometric** *adj.*

man on the street *US* var. of MAN IN THE STREET.

manor *n.* **1** (also **manor house**) a large country house with lands. **2** *Brit. hist.* a feudal lordship over lands. **3** *Brit. colloq.* the district covered by a police station. [from Old French *maneir* 'dwelling'] □ **manorial** *adj.*

manpower *n.* **1** the power generated by a man working. **2** the number of people available or required for work, service, etc.

manqué /**mong**-kay/ *adj.* (placed after noun) that might have been but is not (*a comic actor manqué*). [French, literally 'missed']

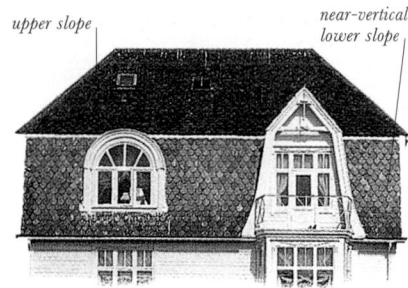

upper slope　　　　*near-vertical lower slope*

MANSARD ROOF

mansard *n.* ▲ a roof which has four sloping sides, each of which becomes steeper halfway down. [from French *mansarde*, named after F. Mansart, French architect, 1598–1666]

manse *n.* the house of a minister, esp. a Scottish Presbyterian. [from medieval Latin *mansus* 'house']

manservant *n.* (*pl.* **menservants**) a male servant.

mansion *n.* **1** a large house. **2** (usu. in *pl.*) *Brit.* a large building divided into flats. [from Latin *mansio* 'a staying', related to MANSE]

man-size *adj.* (also **man-sized**) **1** of the size of a man; very large. **2** big enough for a man.

manslaughter *n.* **1** the killing of a human being. **2** *Law* the unlawful killing of a human being without malice aforethought.

manta *n.* a large plankton-eating ray of the family Mobulidae, esp. *Manta birostris*, having winglike pectoral fins and a whip-like tail. ▷ RAY. [Latin American Spanish, literally 'large blanket']

mantel *n.* **1** = MANTELPIECE 1. **2** = MANTELSHELF.

mantelpiece *n.* **1** a structure of wood, marble, etc. above and around a fireplace. **2** = MANTELSHELF.

mantelshelf *n.* a shelf above a fireplace.

mantilla *n.* a lace scarf worn by Spanish women over the hair and shoulders. [Spanish, literally 'little cloak']

mantis *n.* (*pl.* same or **mantises**) a predatory insect of the family Mantidae, which waits for prey with its forelegs raised and folded like hands in prayer. [Greek, literally 'prophet']

mantle ● *n.* **1** a loose sleeveless cloak, esp. of a woman. **2** a covering (*a mantle of snow*). **3** a fragile lacelike tube fixed round a gas jet to give an incandescent light. **4** the region between the crust and the core of the Earth. ▷ EARTH. ● *v.tr.* clothe in or as if in a mantle; cover, envelop. [from Latin *mantellum* 'cloak']

mantra *n.* a word or sound repeated to aid concentration in meditation, originally in Hinduism and Buddhism. [Sanskrit, literally 'instrument of thought']

mantrap *n.* a trap for catching trespassers etc.

manual ● *adj.* **1** of or done with the hands (*manual labour*). **2** (of a machine etc.) worked by hand. ● *n.* **1 a** a book of instructions; a handbook. **b** any small book. **2** an organ keyboard played with the hands not the feet. ▷ ORGAN. [from Latin *manualis*] □ **manually** *adv.*

manufacture ● *n.* **1 a** the making of articles, esp. in a factory etc. **b** a branch of industry (*woollen manufacture*). **2** esp. *derog.* the merely mechanical production of literature etc. ● *v.tr.* **1** make (articles), esp. on an industrial scale. **2** invent or fabricate (evidence etc.). **3** esp. *derog.* make or produce in a mechanical way. [based on Latin *manufactum* 'made by hand'] □ **manufacturability** *n.* **manufacturable** *adj.* **manufacturer** *n.*

manumit *v.tr.* (**manumitted, manumitting**) *hist.* set (a slave) free. [from Latin *manumittere* 'to send forth from the hand'] □ **manumission** *n.*

manure ● *n.* **1** animal dung, esp. *Brit.* of horses, used for fertilizing land. **2** any compost or artificial fertilizer. ● *v.tr.* (also *absol.*) apply manure to (land etc.).

manuscript ● *n.* **1** text written by hand. **2** ▼ an author's handwritten or typed text. **3** handwritten form (*produced in manuscript*). ● *adj.* written by hand. [from medieval Latin *manuscriptus*, literally 'written by hand']

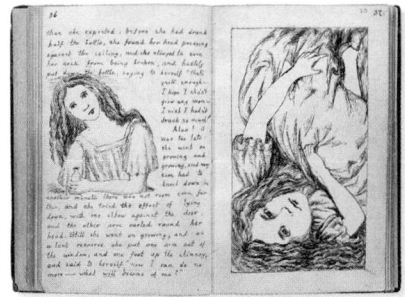

MANUSCRIPT OF *ALICE IN WONDERLAND* BY LEWIS CARROLL

Manx ● *adj.* of the Isle of Man. ● *n.* **1** *hist.* the former Celtic language of the Isle of Man. **2** (prec. by *the*; treated as *pl.*) the Manx people.

Manx cat *n.* a tailless variety of cat. ▷ CAT

Manx shearwater *n.* a brownish-black and white shearwater, *Puffinus puffinus*, of Atlantic and Mediterranean waters.

many (**more, most**) ● *det.* (used with countable nouns) great in number; numerous (*many times*). ● *pron.* (treated as *pl.*) **1** a large number (*many went*). **2** (prec. by *the*) the majority of people. □ **a good** (or **great**) **many** a large number. **as many** the same number of (*six mistakes in as many lines*). **many's the time** often. **many a time** many times. [Old English]

Maoism /*first part rhymes with* cow/ *n.* the Communist doctrines of Mao Zedong (d. 1976), Chinese statesman. □ **Maoist** *n. & adj.*

Maori /**mow**-ri; *first part rhymes with* cow/ ● *n.* (*pl.* same or **Maoris**) **1** a member of the Polynesian aboriginal people of New Zealand. **2** their language. [native name]

map ● *n.* **1 a** ▼ a usu. flat representation of the Earth's surface, or part of it. ▷ AZIMUTHAL PROJECTION, MERCATOR PROJECTION, RELIEF MAP. **b** a diagram of a route etc. **2** a two-dimensional representation of the stars etc. **3** a diagram showing the components of a thing. **4** *slang* the face. ● *v.tr.* (**mapped, mapping**) **1** represent on a map. **2** *Math.* associate each element of (a set) with an element of another set. **map out** arrange in detail; plan. **off the map** *colloq.* **1** of no account; obsolete. **2** very distant. **on the map** *colloq.* prominent, important. [based on medieval Latin *mappa mundi*, literally 'sheet of the world'] □ **mapper** *n.*

compass points　　*dwelling*　　*enlarged section*　　*woodland*

pond

road

river

contour line

MAP OF A VILLAGE AND SURROUNDING COUNTRYSIDE

M

maple *n.* **1** (also **maple tree**) any tree or shrub of the genus *Acer* grown for shade, ornament, wood, or its sugar. **2** the wood of the maple. [Old English *mapeltréow* 'maple tree']

maple leaf *n.* ▶ the leaf of the maple, used as an emblem of Canada.

maple sugar *n.* a sugar produced by evaporating the sap of the sugar maple etc.

MAPLE LEAF
(Acer saccharinum)

maple syrup *n.* a syrup produced from the sap of the sugar maple etc.

map-read *v.intr.* (esp. as **map-reading** *n.*) consult and interpret a map. □ **map-reader** *n.*

map reference *n.* a set of numbers and letters specifying a location as represented on a map.

maquette *n.* **1** a sculptor's small preliminary model in wax, clay, etc. **2** a preliminary sketch. [from Italian *machietta* 'little spot']

Maquis /ma-**kee**/ *n.* (*pl.* same) **1** the French resistance movement during the German occupation (1940–45). **2** a member of this. [French, literally 'brushwood']

Mar. *abbr.* March.

mar *v.tr.* (**marred**, **marring**) **1** impair the perfection of; spoil; disfigure. **2** *archaic* ruin. [Old English *merran* 'to hinder']

marabou *n.* (also **marabout**) **1** ▶ a large W. African stork, *Leptoptilos crumeniferus*. **2** a tuft of its down used as a trimming for hats etc. [from Arabic *murābiṭ* 'holy man', the stork being regarded as holy]

MARABOU
(Leptoptilos crumeniferus)

maraca *n.* a hollow clublike gourd or gourd-shaped container filled with beans etc. and usu. shaken in pairs as a percussion instrument. ▷ ORCHESTRA, PERCUSSION. [Portuguese]

maraschino /ma-rǎ-**skee**-noh/ *n.* (*pl.* **-os**) a strong sweet liqueur made from small black Dalmatian cherries. [Italian]

maraschino cherry *n.* a cherry preserved in maraschino and used to decorate cocktails etc.

marathon *n.* **1** a long-distance running race, usu. of 26 miles 385 yards (42.195 km). **2** a long-lasting or difficult task, operation, etc. [from *Marathon* in Greece, from where a messenger is said to have run to Athens with news of a military victory. (490 BC)]

maraud *v.* **1** *intr.* make a plundering raid. **2** *tr.* plunder (a place). [from French *marauder*, from *maraud* 'rogue'] □ **marauder** *n.*

marble ● *n.* **1** limestone in a metamorphic crystalline (or granular) state, and capable of taking a polish, used in sculpture and architecture. ▷ METAMORPHIC ROCKS. **2** (often *attrib.*) anything made of marble (*a marble clock*). **3 a** a small ball of glass etc., used as a toy. **b** (in *pl.*; treated as *sing.*) a game using these. **4** (in *pl.*) *slang* one's mental faculties (*he's lost his marbles*). **5** (in *pl.*) a collection of sculptures (*Elgin Marbles*). ● *v.tr.* (esp. as **marbled** *adj.*) stain or colour to look like variegated marble. [from Greek *marmaros* 'shining stone']

marble cake *n.* a cake with a mottled appearance, made of light and dark sponge.

marbling *n.* **1** colouring or marking like marble. **2** streaks of fat in lean meat.

marc *n.* **1** the refuse of pressed grapes etc. **2** a brandy made from this. [French]

marcasite *n.* ▶ a bronze-yellow crystalline iron sulphide mineral, used as a semi-precious stone. [from Persian]

marcasite crystals

chalk groundmass

MARCASITE

March *n.* the third month of the year. [from Latin *Martius (mensis)* '(month) of Mars']

march[1] ● *v.* **1** *intr.* (usu. foll. by *away*, *off*, *out*, etc.) walk in a military manner with a regular tread. **2** *tr.* (often foll. by *away*, *on*, *off*, etc.) cause to march or walk. **3** *intr.* **a** walk or proceed steadily, esp. across country. **b** continue unrelentingly (*time marches on*). **4** *intr.* take part in a protest march. ● *n.* **1 a** the act of marching. **b** the uniform step of troops etc. (*a slow march*). **2** a long difficult walk. **3** a procession as a demonstration. **4** (usu. foll. by *of*) progress or continuity (*the march of events*). **5** music to accompany a march. □ **march on 1** advance towards (a military objective). **2** proceed. **on the march 1** marching. **2** in steady progress. [based on Late Latin *marcus* 'hammer'] □ **marcher** *n.*

march[2] *n. hist.* **1** (usu. in *pl.*) a boundary, a frontier (esp. of the borderland between England and Scotland or Wales). **2** a tract of often disputed land between two countries. [from Old French *marche*, related to MARK[1]]

March hare *n.* a hare in the breeding season, characterized by exuberant behaviour, etc.

marching orders *n.pl.* **1** *Mil.* the direction for troops to depart for war etc. **2** a dismissal.

marchioness *n.* **1** the wife or widow of a marquess. **2** a woman holding the rank of marquess in her own right. [based on medieval Latin *marchio* 'captain of the marches']

march past ● *n.* the marching of troops past a saluting point at a review. ● *v.intr.* (of troops) carry out a march past.

Mardi Gras *n.* **1 a** Shrove Tuesday in some Catholic countries. **b** a carnival on this day. **2** the last day of a carnival etc. [French, literally 'fat Tuesday']

mare[1] *n.* the female of any equine animal, esp. the horse. [Old English *mearh* 'horse']

mare[2] *n.* (*pl.* **maria** or **mares**) **1** any of a number of large dark flat areas on the surface of the Moon, once thought to be seas. **2** a similar area on Mars. [Latin, literally 'sea']

mare's nest *n.* an illusory discovery.

mare's tail *n.* **1** a tall slender marsh plant, *Hippuris vulgaris*. **2** (in *pl.*) long straight streaks of cirrus cloud.

margarine *n.* a butter substitute made from vegetable oils or animal fats with milk etc. [based on Greek *margaron* 'pearl', from its lustre]

margay *n.* a small wild S. American cat, *Felis wiedii*. [from Tupi (Brazilian) *mbaracaìa*]

marge *n. Brit. colloq.* margarine.

margin ● *n.* **1** the edge or border of a surface. **2 a** the blank border on each side of the print on a page etc. **b** a line ruled esp. on exercise paper, marking off a margin. **3** an amount (of time, money, etc.) by which a thing exceeds, falls short, etc. **4** the lower limit (*his effort fell below the margin*). ● *v.tr.* (**margined**, **margining**) provide with a margin or marginal notes. [from Latin *margo -ginis*]

marginal ● *adj.* **1 a** of or written in a margin. **b** having marginal notes. **2 a** of or at the edge. **b** not significant or decisive (*of marginal interest*). **3** *Brit.* (esp. of a parliamentary seat) having a small

majority at risk in an election. **4** close to the limit, esp. of profitability. **5** barely adequate; unprovided for. ● *n. Brit.* a marginal constituency or seat. □ **marginality** *n.* **marginally** *adv.*

marginal cost *n.* the cost added by making one extra copy etc.

marginalia *n.pl.* marginal notes. [medieval Latin]

marginalize *v.tr.* (also **-ise**) make or treat as insignificant. □ **marginalization** *n.*

margin of error *n.* a usu. small difference allowed for miscalculation.

marguerite /mar-gě-**reet**/ *n.* an ox-eye daisy. [French, literally 'Margaret']

maria *pl.* of MARE[2].

marigold *n.* ▶ any plant of the genus *Calendula* or *Tagetes*, with golden or bright yellow flowers. ▷ HERB. [Middle English, from *Mary* + earlier dialect *gold*, the corn or garden marigold]

MARIGOLD
(Calendula officinalis)

marijuana /ma-ri-yoo**ah**-nǎ/ *n.* (also **marihuana**) **1** the dried leaves, flowering tops, and stems of the hemp, used as a drug and usu. smoked in cigarettes; cannabis. **2** the plant yielding these. [Latin American Spanish]

mallet

marimba *n.* **1** a kind of xylophone. **2** ▼ a modern orchestral instrument derived from this. [Congolese]

resonating metal tubes

MARIMBA

marina *n.* a specially designed harbour with moorings for pleasure yachts etc. [based on Latin *marinus* 'marine']

marinade ● *n.* **1** a mixture of wine, vinegar, oil, spices, etc. **2** meat, fish, etc., soaked in such a mixture. ● *v.tr.* = MARINATE. [from Spanish *marinada*]

marinate *v.tr.* soak in a marinade. [from French *mariner*] □ **marination** *n.*

marine ● *adj.* **1** of, found in, or produced by the sea. **2 a** of shipping or naval matters. **b** for use at sea. ● *n.* **1** a country's shipping, fleet, or navy. **2** a soldier trained to serve on land or sea. [Latin *mare* 'sea']

mariner *n.* a sailor.

marionette *n.* ▼ a puppet worked by strings. [from French, based on the name *Marion*]

MARIONETTES

M

marital *adj.* of marriage or the relations between husband and wife. [based on Latin *maritus* 'husband'] □ **maritally** *adv.*

maritime *adj.* **1** connected with the sea or seafaring. **2** living or found near the sea. [from Latin *maritimus*]

marjoram *n.* an aromatic herb used as a flavouring in cookery. ▷ HERB. [from medieval Latin *majorana*]

mark[1] ● *n.* **1** a trace, sign, stain, scar, etc., on a face, page, etc. **2** (esp. in *comb.*) **a** a written or printed symbol (*question mark*). **b** a numerical or alphabetical award denoting excellence, conduct, etc. (*a good mark for effort*). **3** (usu. foll. by *of*) a sign or indication of quality, character, etc. (*as a mark of respect*). **4** a sign, seal, etc., used for distinction or identification. **5 a** a target, object, goal, etc. (*missed the mark*). **b** a standard for attainment (*his work falls below the mark*). **6** a marker. **7** (usu. **Mark**) (followed by a numeral) a particular design etc., of a car etc. (*Mark 2 model*). **8** a runner's starting point in a race. ● *v.tr.* **1 a** make a mark on (a thing or person), esp. by writing, cutting, etc. **b** put a distinguishing or identifying mark, name, etc., on (*marked the tree with their initials*). **2 a** allot marks to (a student's work etc.). **b** record (the points gained in games etc.). **3** (often foll. by *by*) show or manifest (displeasure etc.) (*marked his anger by leaving early*). **4** notice or observe (*she marked his agitation*). **5 a** characterize or be a feature of (*a day marked by storms*). **b** celebrate (*marked the occasion with a toast*). **6** name or indicate by a sign or mark. **7 a** *Brit.* keep close to so as to prevent the free movement of (an opponent in sport). **b** *Austral. Rules* catch (the ball). **8** (as **marked** *adj.*) having natural marks (*marked with silver spots*). □ **beside** (or **off** or **wide of**) **the mark 1** irrelevant. **2** not accurate. **make one's mark** attain distinction. **mark down 1** mark (goods etc.) at a lower price. **2** make a written note of. **3** reduce the examination marks of. **mark off** (often foll. by *from*) separate (one thing from another) by a boundary etc. **mark out 1** plan (a course of action etc.). **2** destine (*marked out for success*). **3** trace out boundaries etc. **mark time 1** *Mil.* march on the spot, without moving forward. **2** act routinely. **3** await an opportunity to advance. **mark up 1** mark (goods etc.) at a higher price. **2** mark or correct (text etc.) for typesetting or alteration. **mark you** esp. *Brit.* please note (*without obligation, mark you*). **off the mark 1** having made a start. **2** = *beside the mark* (see MARK[1]). **of mark** noteworthy. **on the mark** ready to start. **on your mark** (or **marks**) (as an instruction) get ready to start (esp. a race). **up to the mark** reaching the usual or normal standard. [Old English]

mark[2] *n.* = DEUTSCHMARK. [Old English]

markdown *n.* a reduction in price.

marked *adj.* **1** having a visible mark. **2** clearly noticeable (*a marked difference*). **3** (of playing cards) having distinctive marks to assist cheating. □ **markedly** *adv.* **markedness** *n.*

marked man *n.* **1** a person whose conduct is watched with suspicion or hostility. **2** a person destined to succeed.

marker *n.* **1** a stone, post, etc., used to mark a place reached etc. **2** a person or thing that marks. **3** a felt-tipped pen with a broad tip. **4** a person who records a score, esp. in billiards.

market ● *n.* **1** the gathering of people for the purchase and sale of provisions, livestock, etc. **2** an open space or covered building used for this. **3 a** (often foll. by *for*) a demand for a commodity or service (*a ready market*). **b** a place or group providing such a demand (*UK market*). **4** conditions as regards, or opportunity for, buying or selling. **5** the rate of purchase and sale, market value (*the market fell*). **6** (prec. by *the*) the trade in a specified commodity (*the corn market*). ● *v.* (**marketed**, **marketing**) **1** *tr.* sell. **2** *tr.* offer for sale. **3** *intr.* buy or sell goods in a market. □ **be in the market for** wish to buy. **be on** (or **come into**) **the market** be offered for sale.

put on the market offer for sale. [based on Latin *mercatus* 'bought'] □ **marketing** *n.*

marketable *adj.* able or fit to be sold. □ **marketability** *n.*

market cross *n.* a structure erected in a market place, originally a stone cross, later an arcaded building.

marketeer *n.* **1** *Brit.* a supporter of the EEC and British membership of it. **2** a marketer.

market garden *n.* esp. *Brit.* a place where vegetables and fruit are grown for the market etc. □ **market gardener** *n.*

market maker *n.* *Brit.* a member of the Stock Exchange granted certain privileges and trading to prescribed regulations.

market place *n.* **1** an open space where a market is held in a town. **2** the arena of competitive or commercial dealings, bargaining, etc.

market price *n.* the price in current dealings.

market research *n.* the study of consumers' needs and preferences. □ **market researcher** *n.*

market town *n.* *Brit.* a town where a market is held.

market value *n.* value as a saleable thing.

marking *n.* (usu. in *pl.*) **1** an identification mark, esp. a symbol on an aircraft. **2** a mark or pattern of marks on an animal's fur, skin, etc.

marksman *n.* (*pl.* **-men**) a person skilled in shooting, esp. with a pistol or rifle. □ **marksmanship** *n.*

mark-up *n.* **1** the amount added to the cost price of goods to cover overhead charges etc. **2** the corrections made in marking up text.

marl ● *n.* soil consisting of clay and lime, with fertilizing properties. ● *v.tr.* apply marl to. [from Latin *marga*] □ **marly** *adj.*

marlin *n.* ▼ any of various large marine fish of the genera *Makaira* and *Tetrapterus*, with a long pointed upper jaw. [from MARLINSPIKE, with reference to its pointed snout]

MARLIN: STRIPED MARLIN
(*Tetrapterus audax*)

marlinspike *n.* (also **marline-spike**) *Naut.* a pointed iron tool used to separate strands of rope or wire. [originally apparently *marling-spike*, from *marl* 'fasten with marline']

marmalade *n.* a preserve of citrus fruit, usu. Seville oranges, made like jam. [from Portuguese *marmelada* 'quince jam']

marmalade cat *n.* a cat with mottled or striped orange fur.

Marmite *n.* *Brit. propr.* a preparation made from yeast extract and vegetable extract, used in sandwiches and for flavouring. [French, literally 'cooking pot']

marmoreal *adj. poet.* of or like marble. [related to MARBLE] □ **marmoreally** *adv.*

marmoset *n.* ▶ any of several small tropical American monkeys of the family Callithricidae, having a long silky coat and a bushy tail. [from Old French *marmouset* 'grotesque image', of unknown origin]

MARMOSET: COMMON MARMOSET
(*Callithrix jacchus*)

marmot *n.* ◀ any burrowing rodent of the genus *Marmota*, with a heavy-set body and short bushy tail, living in colonies. [from French *marmotte*]

Maronite ● *n.* a member of a Christian sect of Syrian origin, living chiefly in Lebanon. ● *adj.* of or relating to the Maronites. [from *Maro*, name of the 5th-century Syrian founder]

maroon[1] ● *adj.* brownish crimson. ● *n.* **1** this colour. **2** esp. an explosive device giving a loud report. [from French *marron* 'chestnut']

MARMOT: BOBAK MARMOT
(*Marmota bobak*)

maroon[2] *v.tr.* **1** leave (a person) isolated in a desolate place (esp. an island). **2** (of a person or a natural phenomenon) cause (a person) to be unable to leave a place. ● *n.* **1** a person descended from a group of fugitive slaves in the remoter parts of Surinam and the W. Indies. **2** a marooned person. [based on Spanish *cimarrón* 'wild']

marque *n.* a make of car, as distinct from a specific model (*the Jaguar marque*). [French, literally 'mark']

marquee /mar-kee/ *n.* **1** esp. *Brit.* a large tent used for social or commercial functions. **2** *N. Amer.* a rooflike projection over the entrance to a theatre, hotel, etc. [based on MARQUISE, taken as pl.]

marquess *n.* a British nobleman ranking between a duke and an earl (cf. MARQUIS). [variant of MARQUIS] □ **marquessate** *n.*

marquetry /mar-kit-ri/ *n.* inlaid work in wood, ivory, etc. [from French *marqueterie*]

marquis *n.* a foreign nobleman ranking between a duke and a count (cf. MARQUESS). [from Old French *marchis*] □ **marquisate** *n.*

marquise /mar-keez/ *n.* **1** the wife or widow of a marquis. **2** a woman holding the rank of marquis in her own right (cf. MARCHIONESS). [French fem. of MARQUIS]

marram *n.* ▶ a shore grass, *Ammophila arenaria*, that binds sand with its tough rhizomes. [from Old Norse *marálmr*]

marriage *n.* **1** the legal union of a man and a woman in order to live together and often to have children. **2** an act or ceremony establishing this union. **3** an intimate union (*the marriage of true minds*). □ **by marriage** as a result of a marriage (*related by marriage*). **in marriage** as husband or wife (*give in marriage; take in marriage*). [from Old French *mariage*]

MARRAM
(*Ammophila arenaria*)

marriageable *adj.* **1** fit for marriage, esp. old or rich enough to marry. **2** (of age) fit for marriage. □ **marriageability** *n.*

marriage bureau *n.* an establishment arranging introductions between persons wishing to marry.

marriage certificate *n.* a certificate certifying the completion of a marriage ceremony.

marriage guidance *n.* (in the UK) counselling of couples who have problems in married life.

marriage licence *n.* a licence to marry.

marriage lines *n.pl. Brit.* a marriage certificate.

marriage of convenience *n.* a marriage concluded to achieve some practical purpose, esp. financial or political.

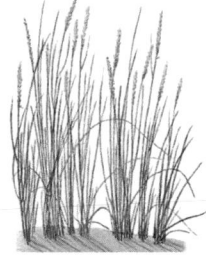

M

MARS

The fourth planet from the Sun, and the outermost rocky planet, Mars is known as the red planet because of the red iron-oxide dust that covers its surface. In its northern hemisphere are many vast plains formed of solidified lava. The southern hemisphere is pitted with craters and large impact basins. Mars' several huge, extinct volcanoes include Olympus Mons, the biggest known volcano in the solar system. The Martian atmosphere is much thinner than that of Earth, with only a few clouds and morning mists. Mars is orbited by two tiny moons, Phobos and Deimos.

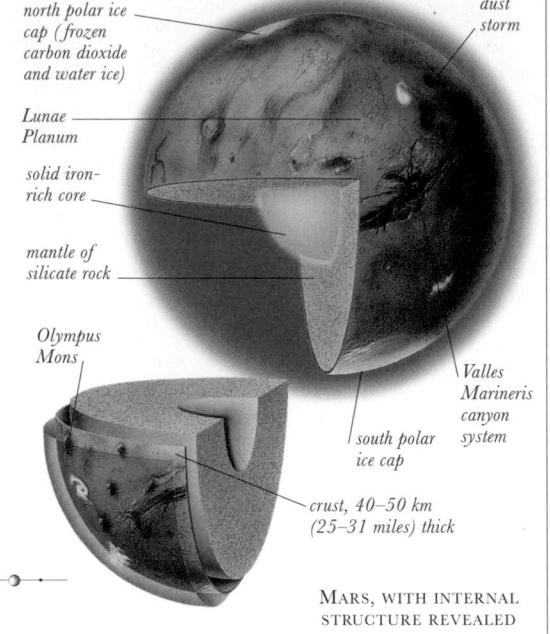

north polar ice cap (frozen carbon dioxide and water ice)

dust storm

Lunae Planum

solid iron-rich core

mantle of silicate rock

Olympus Mons

Valles Marineris canyon system

south polar ice cap

crust, 40–50 km (25–31 miles) thick

SOLAR SYSTEM

Earth

Sun

Mars

MARS, WITH INTERNAL STRUCTURE REVEALED

M

marriage settlement *n.* an arrangement securing property between spouses.

married ● *adj.* **1** united in marriage. **2** of or relating to marriage (*married name*; *married life*). ● *n.* (usu. in *pl.*) a married person (*young marrieds*).

marron glacé /mă-ron gla-say/ *n.* (*pl.* **marrons glacés** *pronunc.* same) a chestnut preserved in and coated with sugar. [French, literally 'iced chestnut']

marrow *n.* **1** *Brit.* (in full **vegetable marrow**) **a** a large usu. white-fleshed edible gourd. ▷ VEGETABLE. **b** the plant, *Cucurbita pepo*, yielding this. **2** (in full **bone marrow**) a soft fatty substance in the cavities of bones, in which blood cells are produced. **3** the essential part. □ **to the marrow** right through. [Old English]

marrowbone *n.* a bone containing edible marrow.

marrowfat *n.* a kind of large pea.

marry *v.* (**-ies, -ied**) **1** *tr.* **a** take as one's wife or husband in marriage. **b** (often foll. by *to*) (of a priest etc.) join (persons) in marriage. **c** (of a parent or guardian) give (a son, daughter, etc.) in marriage. **2** *intr.* **a** enter into marriage. **b** (foll. by *into*) become a member of (a family) by marriage. **3** *tr.* **a** unite intimately. **b** correlate (things) as a pair. □ **marry off** find a wife or husband for. **marry up** (often foll. by *with*) link or join up. [from Latin *maritare*]

marrying *adj.* likely or inclined to marry (*not a marrying man*).

Mars *n.* ▲ a reddish planet, fourth in order of distance from the Sun and next beyond the Earth. ▷ SOLAR SYSTEM

Marsala *n.* a dark sweet fortified dessert wine. [from *Marsala*, a town in Sicily]

Marseillaise /mar-say-**ayz**/ *n.* the national anthem of France. [French]

marsh *n.* (often *attrib.*) low land flooded in wet weather and usu. watery at all times. [Old English] □ **marshy** *adj.* (**marshier, marshiest**). **marshiness** *n.*

marshal ● *n.* **1 a** (in titles of ranks) a high-ranking officer in the armed forces (*Marshal of the Royal Air Force*). **b** a high-ranking officer of state (*Earl Marshal*). **2** an officer arranging ceremonies, controlling procedure at races, etc. **3** *US* **a** a federal or municipal law officer. **b** the head of a fire department. ● *v.tr.* (**marshalled, marshalling**; *US* **marshaled, marshaling**) arrange (soldiers,

facts, one's thoughts, etc.) in due order. [from Late Latin *mariscalcus*, literally 'horse-servant']

marshalling yard *n.* an area in which goods trains etc. are assembled.

Marshal of the Royal Air Force *n.* an officer of the highest rank in the Royal Air Force.

marsh gas *n.* methane.

marsh harrier *n.* a European harrier, *Circus aeruginosus* (see HARRIER³).

marsh hawk *n.* *N. Amer.* = HEN HARRIER.

marshland *n.* land consisting of marshes.

marshmallow *n.* a soft sweet made of sugar, albumen, gelatin, etc.

marsh mallow *n.* a shrubby herbaceous plant, *Althaea officinalis*, the roots of which were formerly used to make marshmallow.

marsh marigold *n.* ▶ a golden-flowered plant, *Caltha palustris* (buttercup family), growing in moist meadows etc.

marsupial ● *n.* ▼ any mammal of the order Marsupialia, usu. carrying and suckling its young in a pouch. ● *adj.* of or belonging to this order. [based on Greek *marsupion* 'pouch']

MARSH MARIGOLD (*Caltha palustris*)

mart *n.* **1** a trade centre. **2** an auction room. **3 a** a market. **b** a market place. [from obsolete Dutch variant of *markt* 'market']

Martello *n.* (*pl.* **-os**) (also **Martello tower**) a small circular fort, usu. on the coast. [alteration of Cape *Mortella* in Corsica, where such a tower proved difficult to capture (1794)]

marten *n.* any weasel-like carnivore of the genus *Martes*, having valuable fur. ▷ MUSTELID. [from Old French (*peau*) *martrine* 'marten (fur)']

martial *adj.* **1** of or appropriate to warfare. **2** warlike, brave; fond of fighting. [from Latin *martialis* 'of Mars'] □ **martially** *adv.*

martial arts *n.pl.* fighting sports such as judo and karate.

martial law *n.* military government, involving the suspension of ordinary law.

Martian ● *adj.* of the planet Mars. ● *n.* a hypothetical inhabitant of Mars. [from Latin *Martianus*]

martin *n.* a kind of swallow of the family Hirundinidae, esp. the house martin and sand martin. [late Middle English, from the forename *Martin*]

martinet *n.* a strict (esp. military or naval) disciplinarian. [named after J. *Martinet*, 17th-century French drill-master]

MARSUPIAL

Marsupials are distinguished by the way their offspring develop. Following a brief gestation period, the female gives birth to small, extremely immature young, which make their way into a pouch (marsupium) on the outside of the mother's abdomen. There they attach themselves to a nipple and continue to grow and develop. Found mainly in Australasia, this mammal order contains some 250 species.

EXAMPLES OF MARSUPIALS

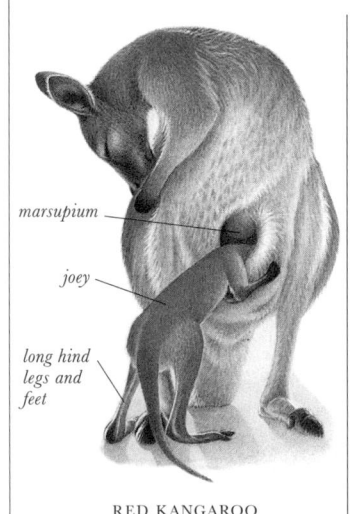

marsupium

joey

long hind legs and feet

RED KANGAROO (*Macropus rufus*)

KOALA (*Phascolarctos cinereus*)

VIRGINIA OPOSSUM (*Didelphis virginiana*)

WOMBAT (*Vombatidae ursinus*)

martingale n. ▶ a strap, or set of straps, fastened at one end to the noseband or reins of a horse and at the other end to the girth, to assist control. ▷ SHOW-JUMPING. [French]

martyr ● n. **1 a** a person who is put to death for refusing to renounce a faith or belief. **b** a person who suffers for adhering to a principle, cause, etc. **c** a person who suffers or pretends to suffer in order to obtain sympathy or pity. **2** (foll. by *to*) a constant sufferer from (an ailment). ● v.tr. **1** put to death as a martyr. **2** torment. [from Greek *martur* 'witness']

martyrdom n. **1** the sufferings and death of a martyr. **2** torment.

martyrology n. (pl. **-ies**) **1** a list or register of martyrs. **2** the history of martyrs. □ **martyrological** adj. **martyrologist** n.

marvel ● n. **1** a wonderful person or thing. **2** (foll. by *of*) a wonderful example of (a quality). ● v.intr. (**marvelled, marvelling**; US **marveled, marveling**) literary (foll. by *at*, or *that* + clause) feel surprise or wonder. [based on Late Latin *mirabilia* 'things to be wondered at']

marvellous adj. (US **marvelous**) **1** astonishing. **2** excellent. □ **marvellously** adv.

Marxism n. the political and economic theories of Karl Marx, predicting the revolutionary overthrow of capitalism by the proletariat and the eventual attainment of a classless communist society. □ **Marxist** n. & adj.

marzipan ● n. a paste of ground almonds, sugar, etc., used in confectionery and to coat cakes. ● v.tr. (**marzipanned, marzipanning**) cover with marzipan. [from Italian *marzapane*]

Masai /mass-I/ ● n. (pl. same or **Masais**) **1** ▼ a member of a pastoral people of mainly Hamitic stock living in Kenya and Tanzania. **2** the language of the Masai. ● adj. of or relating to the Masai or their language. [Bantu]

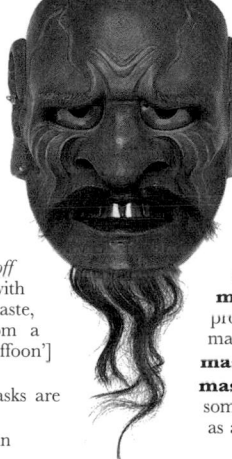
MARTINGALE: RUNNING MARTINGALE

noseband
neckstrap
rein
martingale
girth with martingale attached

elder's short staff
beaded necklace
-watting rush
traditional dress (rubeka)   **MASAI** FAMILY   *sandals* (namuka)

masala n. **1** any of various spice mixtures for use in Indian cookery. **2** a dish flavoured with this.

mascara n. a cosmetic for darkening the eyelashes. ▷ MAKE-UP. [Italian, literally 'mask']

mascarpone n. a soft mild Italian cream cheese.

mascot n. a person, animal, or thing that is supposed to bring good luck. [from modern Provençal *mascotto* 'little witch']

masculine ● adj. **1** of or characteristic of men. **2** manly, vigorous. **3** (of a woman) having qualities considered appropriate to a man. **4** *Gram.* of or denoting the gender proper to words or grammatical forms classified as male. ● n. *Gram.* the masculine gender; a masculine word. [from Latin *masculinus*] □ **masculinity** n. **masculinist** ● n. an advocate of the rights of men. ● adj. of or relating to the advocacy of the rights of men.

maser n. a device using the stimulated emission of radiation by excited atoms to amplify or generate coherent monochromatic electromagnetic radiation in the microwave range (cf. LASER). [from *m*icrowave *a*mplification by the *s*timulated *e*mission of *r*adiation]

mash ● n. **1** a soft mixture. **2** a mixture of boiled grain, bran, etc., given warm to horses etc. **3** *Brit. colloq.* mashed potatoes. **4** a mixture of malt grains and hot water used esp. to form wort for brewing. ● v.tr. **1** reduce (potatoes etc.) to a uniform mass by crushing. **2** crush or pound to a pulp. **3** mix (malt) with hot water to form wort. [Old English] □ **masher** n.

mask ● n. **1** ▶ a covering for all or part of the face worn as a disguise, for protection (e.g. by a fencer), or by a surgeon to prevent infection of a patient. ▷ FENCING. **2** a respirator used to filter inhaled air or to supply gas for inhalation. **3** a likeness of a person's face, esp. one made by taking a mould from the face (*death mask*). **4** a disguise or pretence (*throw off the mask*). ● v.tr. **1** cover (the face etc.) with a mask. **2** disguise or conceal (a taste, one's feelings, etc.). **3** protect from a process. [based on Arabic *maskara* 'buffoon'] □ **masked** adj. **masker** n.

masked ball n. a ball at which masks are worn.

masking tape n. adhesive tape used in painting to cover areas on which paint is not wanted.

masochism /mass-ŏ-kizm/ n. **1** a form of (esp. sexual) perversion characterized by gratification derived from one's own pain or humiliation (cf. SADISM 1). **2** *colloq.* the enjoyment of what appears to be painful or tiresome. [named after L. von Sacher-Masoch, Austrian novelist, 1835–95, who described cases of it]. □ **masochist** n. **masochistic** adj. **masochistically** adv.

mason n. **1** a person who builds with stone. **2** (**Mason**) a Freemason. [from Old Northern French *machun*]

Masonic adj. of Freemasons.

masonry n. **1 a** the work of a mason. **b** ▶ stonework. **2** (**Masonry**) Freemasonry.

masque n. a dramatic and musical entertainment esp. of the 16th–17th c. [variant of MASK]

masquerade ● n. **1** a false show or pretence. **2** a masked ball. ● v.intr. (often foll. by *as*) appear in disguise, assume a false appearance. [from Spanish *mascarada*] □ **masquerader** n.

MASK: JAPANESE NOH MASK FROM EDO PERIOD

MASONRY: MEDIEVAL WINDOW STONEWORK

Mass n. (also **mass**) **1** the Eucharist, esp. in the Roman Catholic Church. **2** a celebration of this. **3** the liturgy used in the Mass. **4** a musical setting of parts of this. [based on Latin *missa* 'dismissal']

mass ● n. **1** a body of matter of indefinite shape. **2** a dense aggregation of objects (*a mass of fibres*). **3** (in *sing.* or *pl.*; foll. by *of*) a large number or amount. **4** (usu. foll. by *of*) an unbroken expanse (of colour etc.). **5** (prec. by *the*) **a** the majority. **b** (in *pl.*) the ordinary people. **6** *Physics* the quantity of matter a body contains. **7** (*attrib.*) relating to, done by, or affecting large numbers of people or things; large-scale (*mass audience; mass action; mass murder*). ● v.tr. & intr. **1** assemble into a mass or as one body (*massed bands*). **2** *Mil.* (with reference to troops) concentrate or be concentrated. □ **in the mass** in the aggregate. [from Greek *maza* 'barley-cake']

massacre ● n. **1** a general slaughter (of persons, occasionally of animals). ● v.tr. **1** murder (esp. a large number of people) cruelly or violently. **2** *colloq.* defeat heavily; destroy. [from Old French *maçacre* 'slaughterhouse']

massage /mass-ahzh/ ● n. **1** the rubbing, kneading, etc., of muscles and joints with the hands, to stimulate their action, cure strains, etc. **2** an instance of this. ● v.tr. **1** apply massage to. **2** manipulate (statistics) to give an acceptable result. [French] □ **massager** n.

massage parlour n. **1** an establishment providing massage. **2** *euphem.* a brothel.

masseur n. (*fem.* **masseuse**) a person who gives massage professionally. [French]

massif n. a compact group of mountain heights. [French, literally 'massive']

massive adj. **1** large and heavy or solid. **2** (of the features, head, etc.) relatively large; of solid build. **3** exceptionally large (*took a massive overdose*). **4** substantial, impressive (*a massive reputation*). **5** *Mineral.* not visibly crystalline. [based on Latin *massa* 'mass'] □ **massively** adv. **massiveness** n.

mass market ● n. the market for mass-produced goods. ● v.tr. (**mass-market**) market (a product) on a large scale.

mass media n. = MEDIA 2.

mass noun n. *Gram.* **1** a noun denoting something which cannot be counted, such as a substance or quality, e.g. *luggage, china, happiness.* **2** a noun denoting something which usually cannot be counted, but is countable when it refers to units or types of something, e.g. *coffee, bread.*

mass number n. the total number of protons and neutrons in a nucleus.

mass production n. the production of large quantities of a standardized article by a standardized mechanical process. □ **mass-produce** v.tr.

mass spectrometer n. an apparatus separating isotopes, molecules, and molecular fragments according to mass by their passage in ionic form through electric and magnetic fields. □ **mass spectrometry** n.

mast¹ ● n. **1** a long upright post of timber, iron, etc., set up on a ship's keel, esp. to support sails. ▷ DINGHY, SAILING BOAT. **2** a post or lattice-work upright for supporting a radio or television aerial. **3** a flagpole (*half mast*). **4** (in full **mooring-mast**) a steel tower to the top of which an airship can be moored. ● v.tr. furnish (a ship) with masts. □ **before the mast** serving as an ordinary seaman (quartered in the forecastle). [Old English] □ **masted** adj. (also in *comb.*). **master** n. (also in *comb.*).

M

mast[2] *n.* ▶ the fruit of the beech, oak, etc., esp. as food for pigs, birds, etc. [Old English]

mastectomy *n.* (*pl.* **-ies**) the surgical removal of a breast. [based on Greek *mastos* 'breast']

master ● *n.* **1 a** a person having control of persons or things. **b** an employer. **c** a male head of a household (*master of the house*). **d** the owner of a horse, dog, etc. **e** the owner of a slave. **f** *Naut.* the captain of a merchant ship. **g** *Hunting* the person in control of a pack of hounds etc. **2** a male teacher. **3** the head of a college, school, etc. **4** a person who has or gets the upper hand. **5 a** a person skilled in a particular trade and able to teach others (often *attrib.*: *master carpenter*). **b** a skilled practitioner (*a master of innuendo*). **6** a holder of a usu. postgraduate university degree (*Master of Arts*). **7** a revered teacher in philosophy etc. **8** a great artist. **9** *Chess* etc. a player of proved ability at international level. **10** an original version (e.g. of a film or gramophone record) from which copies can be made. **11** (**Master**) a title prefixed to the name of a boy not old enough to be called *Mr* (*Master T. Jones*; *Master Tom*). ● *adj.* **1** commanding, superior (*a master spirit*). **2** main, principal (*master bedroom*). **3** controlling others (*master plan*). ● *v.tr.* **1** overcome, defeat. **2** acquire complete knowledge of (a subject) or facility in using (an instrument etc.). □ **be master of 1** have at one's disposal. **2** know how to control. **be one's own master** be independent or free to do as one wishes. **make oneself master of** acquire a thorough knowledge of or facility in using. [from Latin *magister*] □ **masterless** *adj.* **mastership** *n.*

Master Aircrew *n.* an RAF rank equivalent to warrant officer.

master-at-arms *n.* (*pl.* **masters-at-arms**) the chief police officer on a man-of-war or a merchant ship.

masterclass *n.* a class given by a person of distinguished skill, esp. in music.

masterful *adj.* **1** imperious, domineering. **2** masterly. □ **masterfully** *adv.* **masterfulness** *n.*

■ **Usage** *Masterful* is normally used of a person, whereas *masterly* is used of achievements, abilities, etc.

master key *n.* a key that opens several locks, each of which also has its own key.

masterly *adj.* worthy of a master; very skilful (*a masterly piece of work*). □ **masterliness** *n.*

■ **Usage** See Usage Note at MASTERFUL.

master mariner *n.* **1** the captain of a merchant ship. **2** a seaman certified competent to be captain.

master mason *n.* **1** a skilled mason, or one in business on his or her own account. **2** a fully qualified Freemason.

mastermind ● *n.* **1 a** a person with an outstanding intellect. **b** such an intellect. **2** the person directing an intricate operation. ● *v.tr.* plan and direct (a scheme or enterprise).

Master of Ceremonies *n.* **1** (also **MC**) a person introducing speakers at a banquet, or entertainers in a variety show. **2** a person in charge of ceremonies at a state or public occasion.

Master of the Rolls *n.* (in England and Wales) a judge who presides over the Court of Appeal.

masterpiece *n.* **1** an outstanding piece of artistry or workmanship. **2** a person's best work.

master stroke *n.* an outstandingly skilful act of policy etc.

MAST: BEECH MAST

nut

husk

M

---

master switch *n.* a switch controlling the supply of electricity etc. to an entire system.

masterwork *n.* a masterpiece.

mastery *n.* **1** dominion, sway. **2** masterly skill. **3** (often foll. by *of*) comprehensive knowledge or use of a subject or instrument. **4** (prec. by *the*) the upper hand.

masthead *n.* **1** the highest part of a ship's mast, esp. as a place of observation or punishment. **2 a** the title of a newspaper etc. at the head of the front or editorial page. **b** *N. Amer.* the listed details in a newspaper etc. referring to ownership, advertising rates, etc.

mastic *n.* **1** a gum or resin exuded from the bark of the mastic tree, used in making varnish. **2** (in full **mastic tree**) the evergreen tree, *Pistacia lentiscus*, yielding this. **3** a waterproof filler and sealant used in building. [from Greek *mastikhē*]

masticate *v.tr.* grind or chew (food) with one's teeth. [from Greek *mastikhan* 'to gnash the teeth'] □ **mastication** *n.* **masticatory** *adj.*

mastiff *n.* ▼ a dog of a large strong breed with drooping ears and pendulous lips. [based on Latin *mansuetus* 'tame']

mastitis *n.* inflammation of the breast or udder. [based on Greek *mastos* 'breast']

mastodon *n.* a large extinct mammal of the genus *Mammut*, resembling the elephant. [from Greek *mastos* 'breast' + *odous odontos* 'tooth' with reference to nipple-shaped tubercles on the crowns of its molar teeth] □ **mastodontic** *adj.*

mastoid *n.* **1** *Anat.* = MASTOID PROCESS. **2** *colloq.* mastoiditis. [from Greek *mastoeidēs*]

mastoiditis *n.* inflammation of the mastoid process.

MASTIFF

mastoid process *n.* a conical prominence on the temporal bone behind the ear, to which muscles are attached. ▷ EAR

masturbate *v.intr. & tr.* arouse oneself sexually or cause (another person) to be aroused by manual stimulation of the genitals. [based on Latin *masturbatus* 'masturbated'] □ **masturbation** *n.* **masturbator** *n.* **masturbatory** *adj.*

mat[1] ● *n.* **1** a piece of coarse material for wiping shoes on, esp. a doormat. **2** a piece of cork, rubber, plastic, etc., to protect a surface from the heat or moisture of an object placed on it. **3** a piece of resilient material for landing on in gymnastics, wrestling, etc. ● *v.* (**matted**, **matting**) **1** *tr.* (esp. as **matted** *adj.*) entangle in a thick mass (*matted hair*). **2** *intr.* become matted. □ **on the mat** *slang* being reprimanded. [from Late Latin *matta*]

mat[2] *n.* = MATRIX 1.

matador *n.* **1** ▼ a bullfighter whose task is to kill the bull. **2** a principal card in ombre, quadrille, etc. **3** a domino game in which the piece played must make a total of seven. [Spanish]

matador

silk outfit with gold sequins (traje de luces)

scarlet cape (muleta)

barbed darts (banderillas)

fighting bull (toro bravo)

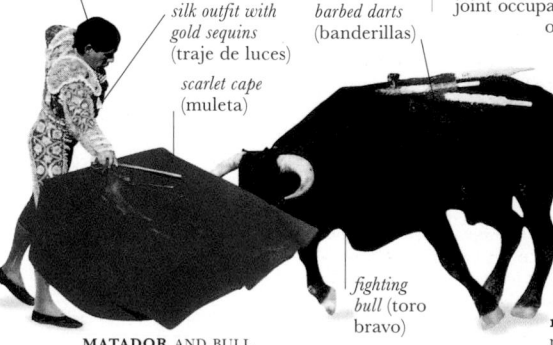

MATADOR AND BULL

---

match[1] ● *n.* **1** a contest or game in which persons or teams compete against each other. **2 a** a person able to contend with another as an equal (*meet one's match*). **b** a person or thing exactly like or corresponding to another. **3** a marriage. **4** a person viewed in regard to his or her eligibility for marriage (*an excellent match*). ● *v.* **1 a** *tr.* be equal to or harmonious with (*the curtains match the wallpaper*). **b** *intr.* (often foll. by *with*) correspond; harmonize (*his socks do not match*; *does the ribbon match with your hat?*). **2** *tr.* (foll. by *against*, *with*) place (a person etc.) in conflict, contest, or competition with (another). **3** *tr.* find material etc. that matches (another) (*can you match this silk?*). **4** *tr.* find (a person or thing) suitable for another (*matching unemployed workers with vacant posts*). □ **match up** (often foll. by *with*) fit to form a whole; tally. **match up to** be as good as or equal to. [Old English *gemæcca* 'mate, companion'] □ **matchable** *adj.*

match[2] *n.* **1** a short thin piece of wood etc., tipped with a composition that can be ignited by friction. **2** a slow-burning piece of wick, cord, etc., for firing a cannon etc. [from Old French *mesche*]

matchboard *n.* a board with a tongue cut along one edge and a groove along another, so as to fit with similar boards.

matchbox *n.* a box for holding matches.

matchless *adj.* without an equal, incomparable. □ **matchlessly** *adv.*

matchlock *n. hist.* **1** ▼ an old type of gun with a lock in which a match was placed for igniting the powder. **2** such a lock.

wooden stock

priming pan and cover

rope slow-match

barrel

trigger

trigger guard

lock

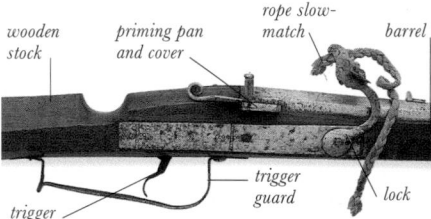

MATCHLOCK: 17TH-CENTURY GERMAN MATCHLOCK

matchmaker *n.* **1** a person who arranges marriages. **2** a person who schemes to bring couples together. □ **matchmaking** *n.*

matchplay *n. Golf* play in which the score is reckoned by counting the holes won by each side (cf. STROKE PLAY).

match point *n. Tennis* etc. **1** the state of a game when one side needs only one more point to win the match. **2** this point.

matchstick *n.* the stem of a match.

matchwood *n.* **1** wood suitable for matches. **2** minute splinters. □ **make matchwood of** smash utterly.

mate[1] ● *n.* **1** a friend or fellow worker. **2** *Brit. colloq.* a general form of address, esp. to another man. **3 a** each of a breeding pair, esp. of birds. **b** *colloq.* a partner in marriage. **c** (in *comb.*) a fellow member or joint occupant of (*team-mate*; *room-mate*). **4** *Naut.* an officer on a merchant ship subordinate to the master. **5** an assistant to a skilled worker (*plumber's mate*). ● *v.* (often foll. by *with*) **1 a** *tr.* bring (animals or birds) together for breeding. **b** *intr.* (of animals or birds) come together for breeding. **2** *intr. Mech.* fit well. [from Middle Low German *gemate* 'messmate'] □ **mateless** *adj.* **mate**[2] *n. & v.tr.* *Chess* = CHECKMATE. [from French *mat(er)*]

matelot /mat-loh/ *n.* (also **matlow**, **matlo**) *Brit. slang* a sailor. [French]

mater *n. Brit. archaic* or *joc. slang* mother. [Latin]

material ● *n.* **1** the matter from which a thing is made. **2** cloth, fabric. **3** (in *pl.*) things needed for an activity (*building materials; cleaning materials; writing materials*). **4** a person or thing of a specified kind or suitable for a purpose (*officer material*). **5** (in *sing.* or *pl.*) information etc. to be used in writing a book etc. **6** (in *sing.* or *pl.*, often foll. by *of*) the elements or constituent parts of a substance. ● *adj.* **1** of matter; corporeal. **2** concerned with bodily comfort etc. (*material well-being*). **3** (of conduct, points of view, etc.) not spiritual. **4** (often foll. by *to*) important, essential, relevant (*at the material time; material witness*). [from Late Latin *materialis*, related to MATTER] □ **materiality** *n.*

materialism *n.* a tendency to consider material possessions and physical comfort to be more important than spiritual values. □ **materialist** *n.* & *adj.* **materialistic** *adj.* **materialistically** *adv.*

materialize *v.* (also **-ise**) **1** *intr.* become actual fact. **2 a** *tr.* cause (a spirit) to appear in bodily form. **b** *intr.* (of a spirit) appear in this way. **3** *intr. colloq.* appear or be present when expected. **4** *tr.* represent or express in material form. □ **materialization** *n.*

materially *adv.* substantially, considerably.

matériel /mă-teer-i-**el**/ *n.* available means, esp. materials and equipment in warfare. [French]

maternal *adj.* **1** of or like a mother. **2** motherly. **3** related through the mother (*maternal uncle*). **4** of the mother in pregnancy and childbirth. [based on Latin *mater* 'mother'] □ **maternalism** *n.* **maternally** *adv.*

maternity *n.* **1** motherhood. **2** motherliness. **3** (*attrib.*) for women during pregnancy and just after childbirth (*maternity hospital; maternity dress*). [from medieval Latin *maternitas*]

matey (also **maty**) *Brit.* ● *adj.* (**matier, matiest**) (often foll. by *with*) sociable; familiar and friendly. ● *n.* (*pl.* **-eys**) *Brit. colloq.* (usu. as a form of address) mate, companion. □ **mateyness** *n.* (also **matiness**). **matily** *adv.*

math *n. N. Amer. colloq.* mathematics (cf. MATHS).

mathematical *adj.* **1** of mathematics. **2** (of a proof etc.) rigorously precise. [based on Greek *manthanein* 'to learn'] □ **mathematically** *adv.*

mathematics *n.pl.* **1** (usu. treated as *sing.*) the abstract science of number, quantity, and space studied in its own right (**pure mathematics**), or as applied to other disciplines such as physics, engineering, etc. (**applied mathematics**). **2** (often treated as *pl.*) the mathematical aspects of something. □ **mathematician** *n.*

maths *n. Brit. colloq.* mathematics (cf. MATH).

matinée /**mat**-in-ay/ *n.* (also **matinee**) an afternoon performance in the theatre, cinema, etc. [French, literally 'what occupies a morning']

matinée coat *n.* (also **matinée jacket**) *Brit.* a baby's short coat.

matinée idol *n.* a handsome actor admired chiefly by women.

matins *n.* (also **mattins**) (as *sing* or *pl.*) a service of morning prayer in the Anglican Church. [based on Latin *matutinus* 'of the morning']

matlo (also **matlow**) var. of MATELOT.

matriarch *n.* a woman who is the head of a family or tribe. [based on Latin *mater* 'mother'] □ **matriarchal** *adj.*

matriarchy *n.* (*pl.* **-ies**) a system of society, government, etc. ruled by a woman or women and with descent through the female line.

matrices *pl.* of MATRIX.

matricide *n.* **1** the killing of one's mother. **2** a person who commits matricide. [from Latin *matricida*] □ **matricidal** *adj.*

matriculate *v.tr.* & *intr.* admit to or be enrolled at a college or university. [based on Late Latin *matricula* 'register'] □ **matriculation** *n.*

matrimony *n.* (*pl.* **-ies**) **1** the rite of marriage. **2** the state of being married. [from Latin *matrimonium*] □ **matrimonial** *adj.* **matrimonially** *adv.*

matrix /**may**-tricks/ *n.* (*pl.* **matrices** /**may**-tri-seez/ or **matrixes**) **1** a mould in which a thing is cast or shaped, such as a gramophone record, printing type, etc. **2** an environment or substance in which a thing is developed. **3** ▶ a rock in which gems, fossils, etc., are embedded. **4** *Math.* a rectangular array of elements in rows and columns that is treated as a single entity. [Latin, literally 'breeding-female, womb, register']

matrix printer *n.* = DOT MATRIX PRINTER.

matron *n.* **1** a married woman, esp. a dignified and sober one. **2** a woman nurse and housekeeper in a school etc. **3** *Brit.* a woman in charge of the nursing in a hospital. [from Latin *matrona*] □ **matronhood** *n.*

■ **Usage** In sense 3, *senior nursing officer* is now the official term.

matronly *adj.* like or characteristic of a matron, esp. in respect of staidness or portliness.

matron of honour *n.* a married woman attending the bride at a wedding.

matt (also **matte**) ● *adj.* (of a colour, surface, etc.) dull, without lustre. ● *n.* (in full **matt paint**) paint formulated to give a dull flat finish (cf. GLOSS[1] *n.* 3). [from French *mat*]

matte *n. Cinematog.* a mask to obscure part of an image and allow another image to be superimposed, giving a combined effect. [French]

matter ● *n.* **1 a** a physical substance in general, as distinct from mind and spirit. **b** ▼ that which has mass and occupies space. **2** a particular substance (*colouring matter*). **3** (prec. by *the*; often foll. by *with*) the thing that is amiss (*what is the matter?*). **4 a** the substance of a book, speech, etc., as distinct from its manner or form. **b** *Logic* the particular content of a proposition, as distinct from its form. **5** a thing or things of a specified kind (*printed matter; reading matter*). **6** an affair or situation being considered, esp. in a specified way (*a serious matter; a matter for concern*). **7** *Physiol.* **a** any substance in or discharged from the body (*faecal matter; grey matter*). **b** pus. ● *v.intr.* (often foll. by *to*) be of importance; have

significance (*it does not matter to me when it happened*). □ **for that matter 1** as far as that is concerned. **2** and indeed also. **in the matter of** as regards. **a matter of 1** approximately (*for a matter of 40 years*). **2** a thing that relates to, depends on, or is determined by (*only a matter of time before they agree*). **no matter 1** (foll. by *when, how,* etc.) regardless of (*will do it no matter what the consequences*). **2** it is of no importance. [from Latin *materia* 'timber, substance, subject of discourse']

matter of course *n.* the natural or expected thing.

matter of fact ● *n.* what belongs to the sphere of fact as distinct from opinion etc. ● *adj.* (**matter-of-fact**) **1** unimaginative, prosaic. **2** unemotional. □ **as a matter of fact** in reality (esp. to correct a falsehood or misunderstanding). □ **matter-of-factly** *adv.* **matter-of-factness** *n.*

matter of form *n.* **1** a point of correct procedure. **2** *colloq.* mere routine.

matter of life and death *n.* a matter of vital importance.

matter of record see RECORD.

matting *n.* fabric of hemp, bast, grass, etc., for mats (*coconut matting*).

mattins var. of MATINS.

mattock *n.* ◀ an agricultural tool shaped like a pickaxe, with an adze and a chisel edge as the ends of the head. [Old English]

mattress *n.* a fabric case stuffed with soft, or springy material, or a similar case filled with air or water, used on or as a bed. [from Arabic *almaṭraḥ* 'the place, the cushion']

maturation *n.* **1** the act or an instance of maturing; the state of being matured. **2** the ripening of fruit. □ **maturational** *adj.*

mature ● *adj.* (**maturer, maturest**) **1 a** with fully developed powers of body and mind; adult. **b** sensible, wise. **2** complete in natural development; ripe. **3** (of a bill etc.) due for payment. ● *v.* **1 a** *tr.* & *intr.* develop fully. **b** *tr.* & *intr.* ripen. **c** *intr.* come to maturity. **2** *intr.* (of a bill etc.) become due for payment. [from Latin *maturus* 'timely, early'] □ **maturely** *adv.* **maturity** *n.*

mature student *n.* esp. *Brit.* an adult student who is older than most students.

MATRIX: EMERALD CRYSTAL IN MATRIX

emerald
calcite matrix

adze
chisel edge

MATTOCK

M

MATTER

The unique properties of the three states of matter – solid, gas, and liquid – are due to differences in the arrangement and movement of the particles that make them up. The particles of a solid are strongly attracted to each other, and are arranged in a regular repeating pattern, so maintaining a solid shape. Gas, however, expands in every direction as there are few bonds between its particles. Liquid flows because its particles are not held rigidly, but the attraction between the particles is sufficient to give a definite volume. Glass, a supercooled liquid, is rigid, although its particles are arranged randomly.

GAS

condensation
sublimation
supercooling
crystallization
evaporation

SUPERCOOLED LIQUID

SOLID   *freezing*   *melting*   LIQUID

ARRANGEMENT OF PARTICLES IN DIFFERENT STATES OF MATTER

M

matutinal *adj.* **1** of or occurring in the morning. **2** early. [from Latin *matutinus*]

maty var. of MATEY.

matzo *n.* (*pl.* **-os** or **matzoth**) **1** a wafer of unleavened bread for the Passover. **2** such bread collectively. [from Hebrew *maṣṣā h*]

maudlin *adj.* weakly or tearfully sentimental, esp. when drunk. [from ecclesiastical Latin *Magdalena* 'Magdalen', with reference to pictures of Mary Magdalen weeping]

maul ● *v.tr.* **1** (of an animal) tear and mutilate (prey etc.). **2** handle roughly or carelessly. **3** damage by criticism. ● *n.* **1** *Rugby* a loose scrum with the ball off the ground. **2** a brawl. **3** a heavy hammer, commonly of wood. [based on Latin *malleus* 'hammer'] □ **mauler** *n.*

maulstick *n.* (also **mahlstick**) a light stick with a padded leather ball at one end, held by a painter against the canvas etc. to support the hand using the brush. [from Dutch *maalstok*]

maunder *v.intr.* **1** talk in a dreamy or rambling manner. **2** move or act listlessly or idly.

Maundy *n.* (in the UK) the distribution of Maundy money. [from Latin *mandatum* 'mandate, commandment' (see John 13:34)]

Maundy money *n.* specially minted silver coins distributed by the British sovereign on Maundy Thursday.

Maundy Thursday *n.* the Thursday before Easter.

mausoleum *n.* (*pl.* **mausolea** or **mausoleums**) a large and grand tomb. [based on Greek *Mausōlos*, name of a king of Caria (4th c. BC)]

mauve /mohv/ ● *adj.* of a pale purple colour. ● *n.* this colour. [French, literally 'mallow'] □ **mauvish** *adj.*

maverick *n.* **1** *N. Amer.* an unbranded calf or yearling. **2** an unorthodox or independent-minded person. [named after S. A. *Maverick*, Texas rancher, 1803–70, who did not brand his cattle]

mavis *n.* *poet.* or *dial.* a song thrush. [Middle English from Old French *mauvis*, of uncertain origin]

maw *n.* **1 a** the stomach of an animal. **b** the jaws or throat of a voracious animal. **2** *colloq.* the stomach of a greedy person. [Old English]

mawkish *adj.* **1** sentimental in a feeble or sickly way. **2** having a faint sickly flavour. [from obsolete *mawk* 'maggot', from Old Norse *mathkr*] □ **mawkishly** *adv.* **mawkishness** *n.*

max *N. Amer. colloq.* ● *n.* (a) maximum. ● *adj.* maximal. ● *adv.* maximally. ● *v.* **1** *intr.* (foll. by *out*, and, often *at*) perform to the limit of one's ability (*the high-jumper maxed out at 6 foot*). **2** *tr.* (as **maxed out** *adj.*) having exhausted one's capabilities or capacity.

max. *abbr.* maximum.

maxi *n.* (*pl.* **maxis**) *colloq.* a maxi-coat, -skirt, etc.

maxi- *comb. form* very large or long (*maxi-coat*). [abbreviation of MAXIMUM]

maxilla *n.* (*pl.* **maxillae** /-lee/) **1** ▼ a jaw or jawbone, esp. the upper jaw in most vertebrates. ▷ SKELETON, SKULL. **2** the mouthpart of many arthropods used in chewing. [Latin, literally 'jaw'] □ **maxillary** *adj.*

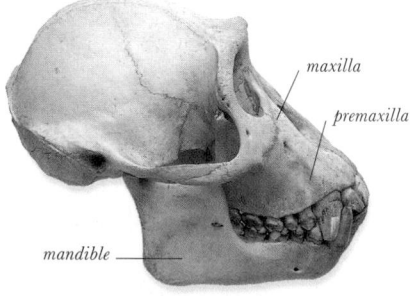

MAXILLA AND SKULL OF A CHIMPANZEE

maxilla
premaxilla
mandible

---

maxim *n.* a general truth or rule of conduct expressed in a sentence. [from medieval Latin *maxima (propositio)* 'maximum (proposition)']

maxima *pl.* of MAXIMUM.

maximal *adj.* being or relating to a maximum; the greatest possible in size, duration, etc. □ **maximally** *adv.*

maximize *v.tr.* (also **-ise**) make as large or great as possible. □ **maximization** *n.* **maximizer** *n.*

■ **Usage** *Maximize* should not be used in standard English to mean 'make as good as possible' or 'make the most of'.

maximum ● *n.* (*pl.* **maxima** or **maximums**) the highest possible or attainable amount. ● *adj.* that is a maximum. [Latin, literally 'greatest (thing)']

May *n.* **1** the fifth month of the year. **2** (**may**) *Brit.* the hawthorn or its blossom. [from Latin *Maius (mensis)* '(month) of the goddess Maia']

may *v.aux.* (*3rd sing. present* **may**; *past* **might**) **1** (often foll. by *well* for emphasis) expressing possibility (*it may be true; you may well lose your way*). **2** expressing permission (*you may not go; may I come in?*). **3** expressing a wish (*may he live to regret it*). **4** expressing uncertainty or irony in questions (*who may you be?; who are you, may I ask?*). □ **be that as it may** despite the fact that it may be so. **may as well** = *might as well* (see MIGHT¹). **that is as may be** that may or may not be so. [Old English]

■ **Usage** Both *can* and *may* are used to express permission (see sense 2). In more formal contexts *may* is usual since *can* also denotes capability (*can I move?* = am I physically able to move?; *may I move?* = am I allowed to move?).

Maya /my-ă/ ● *n.* **1** (*pl.* same or **Mayas**) a member of an ancient Indian people of Central America. **2** the language of this people. ● *adj.* of or relating to this people or language. [native name] □ **Mayan** *adj. & n.*

maybe *adv.* perhaps, possibly. [Middle English]

May Day *n.* 1 May esp. as a festival with dancing, or as an international holiday in honour of workers.

mayday *n.* an international radio distress signal used esp. by ships and aircraft. [representing pronunciation of French *m'aidez* 'help me']

mayflower *n.* any of various flowers that bloom in May, esp. the evergreen shrub *Epigaea repens*.

mayfly *n.* (*pl.* **-flies**) **1** ◄ any insect of the order Ephemeroptera, with an aquatic nymph and a fragile-winged adult which lives only briefly in spring. **2** an imitation mayfly used by anglers.

antenna
tail filament (cercus)

MAYFLY:
ADULT MAYFLY
(*Ephemera* species)

mayhem *n.* violent or damaging action; disruption, chaos. [from Old French *mayhem*, literally 'mutilation']

mayn't *contr.* may not.

maying *n. & adj.* participation in May Day festivities. [Middle English, from MAY]

mayonnaise *n.* **1** a thick creamy dressing made of egg yolks, oil, vinegar, etc. **2** a (usu. specified) dish dressed with this (*chicken mayonnaise*). [French]

mayor *n.* **1** the head of the municipal corporation of a city or borough. **2** (in England, Wales, and Northern Ireland) the head of a district council with the status of a borough. [from Latin, related to MAJOR] □ **mayoral** *adj.* **mayorship** *n.*

mayoralty *n.* (*pl.* **-ies**) **1** the office of mayor. **2** a mayor's period of office.

---

mayoress *n.* **1** a woman holding the office of mayor. **2** the wife of a mayor. **3** a woman fulfilling the ceremonial duties of a mayor's wife.

maypole *n.* a pole painted and decked with flowers and ribbons, for dancing round on May Day.

May queen *n.* a girl chosen to preside over celebrations on May Day.

maze *n.* **1** ◄ a network of paths and hedges designed as a puzzle for those who try to penetrate it. **2** a labyrinth. **3** (often foll. by *of*) a confused mass, network, etc. [Middle English, related to AMAZE] □ **mazy** *adj.*

MAZE

mazuma *n.* esp. *US & Austral. slang* money, cash. [Yiddish]

mazurka *n.* **1** a usu. lively Polish dance in triple time. **2** the music for this. [Polish, literally 'a woman of the province *Mazovia*']

MB *abbr.* **1** Bachelor of Medicine. **2** (also **Mb**) *Computing* megabyte. [sense 1: Latin *Medicinae Baccalaureus*]

MBA *abbr.* Master of Business Administration.

MBE *abbr.* Member of the Order of the British Empire.

MBO *abbr.* management buyout.

MC *abbr.* **1** Master of Ceremonies. **2** (in the UK) Military Cross. **3** (in the US) Member of Congress.

MCC *abbr.* Marylebone Cricket Club.

McCarthyism, McCoy see at MACC-.

M.Ch. *abbr.* (also **M.Chir.**) Master of Surgery. [Latin *Magister Chirurgiae*]

MCP *abbr.* *colloq.* male chauvinist pig.

MD *abbr.* **1** Doctor of Medicine. **2** Managing Director. **3** musical director. [sense 1: Latin *Medicinae Doctor*]

Md *symb.* *Chem.* the element mendelevium.

ME *abbr.* myalgic encephalomyelitis, a condition of unknown cause, with fever, aching, and prolonged tiredness, occurring esp. after a viral infection.

me¹ *pron.* **1** *objective case* of I² (*he saw me*). **2** *N. Amer. colloq.* myself; to or for myself (*I got me a gun*). **3** *colloq.* used in exclamations (*ah me!; dear me!; silly me!*). [Old English]

■ **Usage** See Usage Note at HER.

me² *n.* (also **mi**) *Mus.* **1** (in tonic sol-fa) the third note of a major scale. **2** the note E in the fixed-doh system. [from Latin *mira*]

mead *n.* an alcoholic drink of fermented honey and water. [Old English]

meadow *n.* **1** a piece of grassland, esp. one used for hay. **2** a piece of low well-watered ground, esp. near a river. [Old English] □ **meadowy** *adj.*

meadowland *n.* land used for the cultivation of grass, esp. for hay.

meadow saffron *n.* a meadow plant, *Colchicum autumnale*, resembling a crocus, and producing lilac flowers in the autumn while still leafless.

meadowsweet *n.* **1** ▶ a plant of the rose family, *Filipendula ulmaria*, common in meadows and damp places, with creamy-white fragrant flowers. **2** any of several plants of the genus *Spiraea* (rose family), native to N. America.

meagre *adj.* (*US* **meager**) **1** lacking in amount or quality. **2** (of a person or animal) lean, thin. [from Latin *macer*] □ **meagrely** *adv.* **meagreness** *n.*

MEADOWSWEET
(*Filipendula ulmaria*)

meal[1] *n.* **1** an occasion when food is eaten. **2** the food eaten on one occasion. □ **make a meal of 1** *Brit.* treat (a task etc.) too laboriously or fussily. **2** consume as a meal.[Old English *mǣl* 'mark, fixed time']

meal[2] *n.* **1** the edible part of any grain or pulse (usu. other than wheat) ground to powder. **2** *Sc.* oatmeal. **3** *US* maize flour. [Old English]

meal-beetle *n.* an insect, *Tenebrio molitor*, infesting granaries etc.

meals on wheels *n.pl.* (usu. treated as *sing.*) a service by which meals are delivered to old people, invalids, etc.

meal ticket *n.* a person or thing that is a source of food or income.

mealtime *n.* a time at which a meal is or is usually eaten.

mealworm *n.* the larva of the meal-beetle.

mealy *adj.* (**mealier, mealiest**) **1 a** of or like meal; soft and powdery. **b** containing meal. **2** (of a complexion) pale. **3** (in full **mealy-mouthed**) not outspoken; afraid to use plain expressions. □ **mealiness** *n.*

mean[1] *v.tr.* (*past* and *past part.* **meant**) **1 a** (often foll. by *to* + infin.) have as one's purpose or intention; have in mind (*they really mean mischief*; *I didn't mean to break it*). **b** (foll. by *by*) have as a motive in explanation (*what do you mean by that?*). **2** (often in *passive*) design or destine for a purpose (*mean it to be used*; *is meant to be a gift*). **3** intend to convey or indicate or refer to (a particular thing or notion) (*I mean we cannot go*; *I mean Richmond in Surrey*). **4** entail, involve (*it means catching the early train*). **5** (often foll. by *that* + clause) portend, signify (*this means trouble*; *your refusal means that we must look elsewhere*). **6** (of a word) have as its explanation in the same language or its equivalent in another language. **7** (foll. by *to*) be of some specified importance to (a person) (*that means a lot to me*). □ **mean business** be in earnest. **mean it** not be joking or exaggerating. **mean well** (often foll. by *to, towards, by*) have good intentions. [Old English, related to MIND]

mean[2] *adj.* **1** niggardly; not generous. **2** ignoble; uncooperative, unkind, or unfair. **3** (of a person's capacity, understanding, etc.) inferior, poor. **4** (of housing) not imposing in appearance; shabby. **5 a** malicious, ill-tempered. **b** *US* vicious or aggressive. **6** *colloq.* skilful, formidable (*is a mean fighter*). □ **no mean** a very good (*that is no mean achievement*). [Old English] □ **meanly** *adv.* **meanness** *n.*

mean[3] ● *n.* **1** a condition, quality, virtue, or course of action equally removed from two opposite (usu. unsatisfactory) extremes. **2** *Math.* **a** the term midway between the first and last terms of an arithmetical or geometrical etc. progression (*2 and 8 have the arithmetic mean 5 and the geometric mean 4*). **b** an average. ● *adj.* **1** (of a quantity) equally far from two extremes. **2** calculated as a mean. [from Latin *medianus* 'median']

meander ● *v.intr.* **1** wander at random. **2** (of a stream) wind about. ● *n.* **1** (in *pl.*) **a** the sinuous windings of a river. ▷ RIVER. **b** winding paths. **2** a circuitous journey. [based on Greek *Maiandros*, name of a winding river in Phrygia] □ **meandering** *adj. & n.*

meanie *n.* (also **meany**) (*pl.* **-ies**) *colloq.* a mean, niggardly, or small-minded person.

meaning ● *n.* **1** what is meant by a word, action, idea, etc. **2** significance. **3** importance. ● *adj.* expressive, significant (*a meaning glance*). □ **meaningly** *adv.*

meaningful *adj.* **1** full of meaning; significant. **2** *Logic* able to be interpreted. □ **meaningfully** *adv.* **meaningfulness** *n.*

meaningless *adj.* having no meaning or significance. □ **meaninglessly** *adv.* **meaninglessness** *n.*

means *n.pl.* **1** (often treated as *sing.*) that by which a result is brought about (*a means of quick travel*). **2 a** money resources (*live beyond one's means*). **b** wealth (*a man of means*). □ **by all means 1** certainly. **2** in every possible way. **3** at any cost. **by any means** in

any way (*not by any means obtrusive*). **by means of** by the agency or instrumentality of (a thing or action). **by no means** (or **no manner of means**) not at all; certainly not. [pl. of MEAN[3] in sense 'an intermediary']

mean sea level *n.* the sea level halfway between the mean levels of high and low water.

means test ● *n.* an inquiry into income as a basis for eligibility for State benefit etc. ● *v.tr.* (**means-test**) subject to or base on a means test.

meant *past* and *past part.* of MEAN[1].

meantime ● *adv.* = MEANWHILE. ● *n.* the intervening period (esp. *in the meantime*).

■ **Usage** As an adverb, *meantime* is less common than *meanwhile*.

meanwhile ● *adv.* **1** in the intervening period of time. **2** at the same time. ● *n.* the intervening period (esp. in phr. **in the meanwhile**).

meany var. of MEANIE.

measles *n.pl.* (also treated as *sing.*) an acute infectious viral disease marked by red spots on the skin. [Middle English]

measly *adj.* (**measlier, measliest**) *colloq.* inferior, contemptible, worthless.

measurable *adj.* that can be measured. □ **measurability** *n.* **measurably** *adv.*

measure ● *n.* **1** a size or quantity found by measuring. **2** a system of measuring (*liquid measure*; *linear measure*). **3** a rod, tape, vessel, etc. for measuring. **4 a** the degree, extent, or amount of a thing. **b** (foll. by *of*) some degree of (*there was a measure of wit in her remark*). **5** a unit of capacity, e.g. a bushel (*20 measures of wheat*). **6** a factor by which a person or thing is reckoned or evaluated (*their success is a measure of their determination*). **7** (usu. in *pl.*) suitable action to achieve some end (*took measures to ensure a good profit*). **8** a legislative enactment. **9** a prescribed extent or quantity. **10** *Printing* the width of a page or column of type. **11** poetical rhythm; metre. **12** *US Mus.* a bar or the time-content of a bar. ● *v.* **1** *tr.* ascertain the extent or quantity of (a thing) by comparison with a fixed unit or with an object of known size. **2** *intr.* be of a specified size (*it measures six inches*). **3** *tr.* ascertain the size and proportion of (a person) for clothes. **4** *tr.* estimate (a quality, person's character, etc.) by some standard or rule. **5** *tr.* (often foll. by *off*) mark (a line etc. of a given length). **6** *tr.* (foll. by *out*) distribute (a thing) in measured quantities. □ **beyond measure** excessively. **for good measure** as something beyond the minimum; as a finishing touch. **in some measure** partly. **measure up 1** (often *absol.*) take measurements of. **2** (often foll. by *to*) have the necessary qualifications (for). [from Latin *mensura*]

measured *adj.* **1** rhythmical; regular (*a measured tread*). **2** (of language) carefully considered.

measureless *adj.* not measurable; infinite.

measurement *n.* **1** the act or an instance of measuring. **2** an amount determined by measuring. **3** (in *pl.*) detailed dimensions.

measure of capacity *n.* a measure used for vessels and liquids or grains etc.

meat *n.* **1** the flesh of animals (esp. mammals) as food. ▷ CUT. **2** (foll. by *of*) the essence or chief part of. **3** esp. *US* the edible part of fruits, nuts, eggs, shellfish, etc. [Old English *mete* 'food'] □ **meatless** *adj.*

meatball *n.* small round ball of minced meat.

meat loaf *n.* minced or chopped meat moulded into the shape of a loaf and baked.

meat safe *n. Brit.* a cupboard for storing meat, usu. of wire gauze etc.

meaty *adj.* (**meatier, meatiest**) **1** full of meat; fleshy. **2** of or like meat. **3** full of substance. □ **meatily** *adv.* **meatiness** *n.*

Mecca *n.* a place which attracts people of a particular group. [*Mecca*, Muslim holy city in Arabia]

mechanic *n.* a skilled worker, esp. one who makes or uses or repairs machinery. [from Greek *mēkhanikos*]

mechanical *adj.* **1** of or relating to machines or mechanisms. **2** working or produced by machinery. **3** (of a person or action) automatic; lacking originality. **4** (of an agency, principle, etc.) belonging to mechanics. □ **mechanicalism** *n.* (in sense 4). **mechanically** *adv.* **mechanicalness** *n.*

mechanical advantage *n.* the ratio of exerted to applied force in a machine.

mechanical engineer *n.* an engineer dealing with the design, construction, and repair of machines. □ **mechanical engineering** *n.*

mechanical excavator *n.* a machine for removing soil from the ground by means of a crane to which a scoop is attached.

mechanics *n.pl.* **1** (treated as *sing.*) the branch of applied mathematics dealing with motion and tendencies to motion. **2** (treated as *sing.*) the science of machinery. **3** (usu. treated as *pl.*) **a** the construction, workings, or routine operation of a thing (*the mechanics of the cochlea*). **b** the practicalities or details of a thing (*the mechanics of how money is laundered*).

mechanism *n.* **1** the structure or adaptation of parts of a machine. **2** a system of parts working together in or as in a machine. **3** the mode of operation of a process. **4** a means (*control mechanism*; *no mechanism for complaints*).

mechanistic *adj.* of or connected with mechanics. □ **mechanistically** *adv.*

mechanize *v.tr.* (also **-ise**) **1** give a mechanical character to. **2** introduce machines in. **3** *Mil.* equip with tanks, armoured cars, etc. □ **mechanization** *n.* **mechanizer** *n.*

M.Ed. *abbr.* Master of Education.

Med *n. Brit. colloq.* the Mediterranean Sea.

medal *n.* ▼ a commemorative metal disc etc., esp. awarded for military or sporting achievement. [based on Latin *metallum* 'metal']

M

Korean action bar

ribbon

Olympic Games symbol

United Nations symbol

1996 OLYMPIAD GOLD MEDAL

UNITED NATIONS' KOREA MEDAL

MEDALS

medallion *n.* **1** a large medal. **2** a thing shaped like this, e.g. a decorative panel etc. [from Italian *medaglione*, related to MEDAL]

medallist *n.* (*US* **medalist**) a recipient of a (specified) medal (*gold medallist*).

medal play *n. Golf* = STROKE PLAY.

meddle *v.intr.* (often foll. by *with, in*) interfere in or busy oneself unduly with others' concerns. [based on Latin *miscēre* 'to mix'] □ **meddler** *n.*

meddlesome *adj.* fond of meddling; interfering.

media *n.pl.* **1** *pl.* of MEDIUM. **2** (usu. prec. by *the*) the main means of mass communication (esp. newspapers and broadcasting) regarded collectively.

■ **Usage** *Media* is commonly used as a mass noun with a singular verb (e.g. *The media is on our side*), but this is not generally accepted (cf. DATA, AGENDA).

mediaeval var. of MEDIEVAL.

medial *adj.* situated in the middle. [from Late Latin *medialis*] □ **medially** *adv.*

median ● *adj.* situated in the middle. **● n. 1** *Anat.* a median artery, vein, nerve, etc. **2** *Geom.* a straight line drawn from any vertex of a triangle to the middle of the opposite side. **3** *Math.* the middle value of a series of values arranged in order of size. [from Latin *medianus*]

mediate *v.* **1** *intr.* (often foll. by *between*) intervene (between parties in a dispute) to produce agreement or reconciliation. **2** *tr.* be the medium for bringing about (a result) or for conveying (a gift etc.). [based on Late Latin *mediatus* 'halved, gone between'] □ **mediation** *n.* **mediator** *n.* **mediatory** *adj.*

medic *n. colloq.* a medical practitioner or student. [from Latin *medicus*]

Medicaid *n.* (in the US) a federal system of health insurance for those requiring financial assistance. [MEDICAL + AID]

medical ● *adj.* **1** of or relating to the science of medicine in general. **2** of or relating to conditions requiring medical and not surgical treatment (*medical ward*). **● n.** *colloq.* a medical examination. [based on Latin *medicus* 'physician'] □ **medically** *adv.*

medical certificate *n.* a certificate of fitness or unfitness to work etc.

medical examination *n.* an examination to determine a person's physical fitness.

medical officer *n. Brit.* a person in charge of the health services of a local authority or other organization.

medical practitioner *n.* a physician or surgeon.

medicament *n.* a substance used for medical treatment. [from Latin *medicamentum*]

Medicare *n.* **1** (in the US) a federal system of health insurance for persons over 65 years of age. **2** (in Canada and Australia) a national health care scheme financed by taxation.

medicate *v.tr.* **1** treat medically. **2** impregnate with a medicinal substance. [based on Latin *medicatus* 'treated medically']

medication *n.* **1** a substance used for medical treatment. **2** treatment using drugs.

medicinal ● *adj.* (of a substance) having healing properties. **● n.** a medicinal substance. □ **medicinally** *adv.*

medicine *n.* **1** the science or practice of the diagnosis, treatment, and prevention of disease, esp. as distinct from surgical methods. **2** any drug or preparation used for the treatment or prevention of disease, esp. one taken by mouth. **3** a spell, charm, or fetish which is thought to cure afflictions. □ **a dose** (or **taste**) **of one's own medicine** treatment such as one is accustomed to giving others. **take one's medicine** submit to something disagreeable. [from Latin *medicina*]

medicine ball *n.* a large heavy stuffed usu. leather ball thrown and caught for exercise.

medicine chest *n.* a box containing medicines etc.

medicine man *n.* a person believed, esp. among N. American Indians, to have magical powers of healing.

medico *n.* (*pl.* **-os**) *colloq.* = MEDIC.

medieval *adj.* (also **mediaeval**) **1** of, or in the style of, the Middle Ages. **2** *colloq.* old-fashioned. [based on Latin *medius* 'middle' + *aevum* 'age'] □ **medievalism** *n.* **medievalist** *n.*

medieval history *n.* the history of the 5th–15th c.

medieval Latin *n.* Latin of about AD 600–1500.

medina *n.* the old Arab or non-European quarter of a N. African town. [Arabic, literally 'town']

mediocre *adj.* **1** of middling quality, neither good nor bad. **2** second-rate. [from Latin *mediocris* 'of middle height or degree']

mediocrity *n.* (*pl.* **-ies**) **1** the state of being mediocre. **2** a mediocre person or thing.

meditate *v.* **1** *intr.* **a** exercise the mind in (esp. religious) contemplation. **b** (usu. foll. by *on, upon*) focus on a subject in this manner. **2** *tr.* plan mentally. [from Latin *meditatus* 'mused over'] □ **meditation** *n.* **meditator** *n.*

meditative *adj.* **1** inclined to meditate. **2** indicative of meditation. □ **meditatively** *adv.* **meditativeness** *n.*

Mediterranean ● n. 1 a large landlocked sea bordered by southern Europe, SW Asia, and N. Africa. **2** a native of a country bordering on the Mediterranean. **● adj.** of or characteristic of the Mediterranean, countries bordering it, or their inhabitants (*Mediterranean climate*; *Mediterranean cookery*; *of Mediterranean appearance*). [from Latin *mediterraneus* 'inland']

medium ● n. (*pl.* **media** or **mediums**) **1** the middle quality, degree, etc. between extremes (*find a happy medium*). **2** the means by which something is communicated (*the medium of sound*; *the medium of television*). **3** the intervening substance through which impressions are conveyed to the senses etc. (*light passing from one medium into another*). **4** *Biol.* the physical environment or conditions of growth, storage, or transport of a living organism (*the shape of a fish is ideal for its fluid medium*; *growing mould on the surface of a medium*). **5** a means of doing something (*the medium through which money is raised*). **6** the material or form used by an artist, composer, etc. (*language as an artistic medium*). **7** the liquid (e.g. oil or gel) with which pigments are mixed for use in painting. **8** (*pl.* **mediums**) a person claiming to be in contact with the spirits of the dead and to communicate between the dead and the living. **● adj. 1** between two qualities, degrees, etc. **2** average; moderate (*of medium height*). [Latin, literally 'middle (thing)'] □ **mediumistic** *adj.* (in sense 8 of *n.*). **mediumship** *n.* (in sense 8 of *n.*).

medium dry *adj.* (of sherry, wine, etc.) having a flavour intermediate between dry and sweet.

medium-range *adj.* (of an aircraft, missile, etc.) able to travel a medium distance.

medium-sized *adj.* of average size.

medium wave *n.* esp. *Brit.* a radio frequency between 300 kHz and 3 MHz.

medlar *n.* **1** ▼ a tree of the rose family, *Mespilus germanica*, bearing small brown apple-like fruits. **2** the fruit of this tree which is eaten when decayed. [based on Greek *mespilē*]

fruit

MEDLAR
(*Mespilus germanica*)

medley *n.* (*pl.* **-eys**) **1** a varied mixture. **2** a collection of musical items from one work or various sources arranged as a continuous whole. [from Old French *medlee*, variant of *meslee*]

medulla *n. Anat.* the inner region of certain organs or tissues. [Latin, literally 'pith, marrow'] □ **medullary** *adj.*

medulla oblongata *n.* the continuation of the spinal cord within the skull, forming the lowest part of the brainstem. ▷ BRAINSTEM

medusa *n.* (*pl.* **medusae** /-zee/ or **medusas**) **1** a jellyfish. **2** *Zool.* a free-swimming sexual form of any coelenterate, having tentacles round the edge of a jelly-like body. [from Greek *Medousa*, name of one of three mythological snake-haired sisters]

meek *adj.* **1** humble and submissive. **2** piously gentle in nature. [from Old Norse *mjúkr* 'soft, gentle'] □ **meekly** *adv.* **meekness** *n.*

meerkat *n.* ▶ a small African mongoose, esp. (in full **grey meerkat**) *Suricata suricatta*, with grey and black stripes, living gregariously in burrows. Also called *suricate*. [Dutch, literally 'sea-cat']

MEERKAT: GREY MEERKAT
(*Suricata suricatta*)

bowl

MEERSCHAUM: MID-19TH-CENTURY MEERSCHAUM PIPE

meerschaum /meer-shăm/ *n.* **1** a soft white form of hydrated magnesium silicate, which resembles clay. **2** ◀ a tobacco pipe with the bowl made from this. [German translation of Persian *kef-i-daryā* 'sea-foam', with reference to its frothiness]

meet[1] ● *v.* (*past* and *past part.* **met**) **1 a** *tr.* encounter (a person or persons) by accident or design; come face to face with. **b** *intr.* (of two or more people) come into each other's company by accident or design (*decided to meet on the bridge*). **2** *tr.* go to a place to be present at the arrival of (a person, train, etc.). **3 a** *tr.* come together or into contact with (*where the road meets the flyover*). **b** *intr.* come together or into contact (*where the sea and the sky meet*). **4 a** *tr.* make the acquaintance of (*delighted to meet you*). **b** *intr.* (of two or more people) make each other's acquaintance. **5** *intr. & tr.* come together or come into contact with for the purposes of conference, business, worship, etc. (*the committee meets every week*; *the union met management yesterday*). **6** *tr.* **a** deal with or answer (a demand, objection, etc.) (*met the proposal with hostility*). **b** satisfy or conform with (proposals, deadlines, a person, etc.) (*agreed to meet the new terms*). **7** *tr.* pay (a bill etc.); provide the funds required by (a cheque etc.) (*meet the cost of the move*). **8** *tr. &* (foll. by *with*) *intr.* experience, encounter, or receive (success, disaster, a difficulty, etc.) (*met their death*; *met with many problems*). **9** *tr.* oppose in battle, contest, or confrontation. **10** *intr.* (of clothes, curtains, etc.) join or fasten correctly (*my jacket won't meet*). **● n. 1** the assembly of riders and hounds for a hunt. **2** the assembly of competitors for various sporting activities, esp. athletics. □ **make ends meet** see END. **meet the case** be adequate. **meet the eye** (or **the ear**) be visible (or audible). **meet a person's eye** look, in return, into the eyes of a person who is watching one. **meet a person halfway** make a compromise. **meet up** (often foll. by *with*) *colloq.* meet or make contact. **meet with 1** see sense 8 of *v.* **2** receive (a reaction) (*met with the committee's approval*). **3** esp. *US* = sense 1a of *v.* [Old English]

meet[2] *adj. archaic* suitable, fit, proper. [Old English]

meeting *n.* **1** in senses of MEET[1]. **2** an assembly of people, esp. the members of a society, committee, etc. **3** = RACE MEETING. **4** an assembly (esp. of Quakers) for worship. **5** the persons assembled (*address the meeting*).

meeting house *n.* a place of worship, esp. of Quakers etc.

mega *slang* **● adj. 1** excellent. **2** enormous. **● adv.** extremely (*mega famous*).

mega- *comb. form* **1** large. **2** denoting a factor of one million (10^6) in the metric system of measurement. [from Greek *megas* 'great']

megabuck *n. colloq.* **1** a million dollars. **2** (in *pl.*) a huge sum of money.

megabyte *n. Computing* 1,048,576 (i.e. 2^{20}) bytes as a measure of data capacity, or loosely 1,000,000.

megadeath *n.* the death of one million people (esp. as a unit in estimating the casualties of war).

megaflop *n.* **1** *Computing* a unit of computing speed equal to one million floating-point operations per second. **2** *slang* a complete failure.

megahertz *n.* (*pl.* same) one million hertz, esp. as a measure of frequency of radio transmissions.

megalith *n. Archaeol.* a large stone, esp. as a monument or part of one. [based on Greek *lithos* 'stone']

megalithic *adj. Archaeol.* made of or marked by the use of large stones.

megalo- *comb. form* great (*megalomania*). [Greek]

megalomania *n.* **1** a mental disorder producing delusions of grandeur. **2** a passion for grandiose schemes. □ **megalomaniac** *adj. & n.* **megalomaniacal** *adj.*

megalopolis *n.* **1** a great city or its way of life. **2** an urban complex consisting of a city and its environs. [based on Greek *polis* 'city']

megalosaurus *n.* (also **megalosaur**) ▼ a large flesh-eating dinosaur of the genus *Megalosaurus*, with stout hind legs and small forelimbs. [based on Greek *sauros* 'lizard']

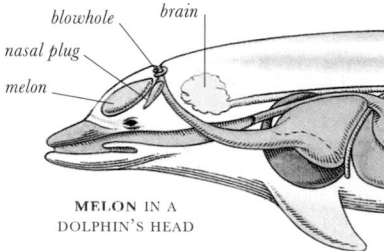

MEGALOSAURUS
(*Megalosaurus* species)

megaphone *n.* a large funnel-shaped device for amplifying the voice.

megastar *n.* a very famous person, esp. in the world of entertainment.

megastore *n.* a large shop selling many different types of goods.

megaton *n.* (also **megatonne**) a unit of explosive power equal to one million tons of TNT.

megawatt *n.* one million watts.

meiosis /my-**oh**-sis/ *n.* (*pl.* **meioses**) **1** *Biol.* ▼ a type of cell division that results in daughter cells with half the chromosome number of the parent cell. **2** = LITOTES. [based on Greek *meioun* 'to lessen'] □ **meiotic** *adj.*

melamine *n.* **1** a white crystalline compound used to make thermosetting resins. **2** (in full **melamine resin**) a plastic made from melamine and used esp. for laminated coatings. [from German *melam* (an arbitrary formation) + AMINE]

melancholia *n.* **1** a mental illness marked by depression and ill-founded fears. **2** = MELANCHOLY *n.* 1. [Late Latin]

melancholy ● *n.* (*pl.* **-ies**) **1 a** a pensive sadness. **b** a tendency to this. **2** *hist.* = BLACK BILE. **3** *Med archaic* = MELANCHOLIA ● *adj.* (of a person) sad, gloomy; (of a thing) saddening, depressing; (of words, a tune, etc.) expressing sadness. [from Greek *melas* 'black' + *khole* 'bile'] □ **melancholic** *adj.* **melancholically** *adv.*

Melanesian ● *n.* **1** a member of the dominant Negroid people of Melanesia, an island group in the W. Pacific. **2** any of the languages of this people. ● *adj.* of or relating to this people or their language. [based on Greek *melas* 'black' + *nēsos* 'island']

mélange /may-**lon**zh/ *n.* a mixture; a medley. [French]

melanin *n.* a dark pigment occurring in the hair, skin, and iris of the eye, that is responsible for tanning of the skin when exposed to sunlight. [based on Greek *melas melanos* 'black']

melanoma *n.* a usu. malignant tumour of melanin-forming cells in the skin.

Melba sauce *n.* a sauce made from puréed raspberries thickened with icing sugar. [named after Dame Nellie *Melba*, Australian operatic soprano, 1861–1931]

Melba toast *n.* very thin crisp toast.

meld *v.tr. & intr.* orig. *US* merge, blend. [from German *melden* 'to announce']

mêlée /**mel**-ay/ *n.* (*US* **melee**) **1** a confused fight, skirmish, or scuffle. **2** a muddle. [French]

melilot *n.* ◄ a leguminous plant of the genus *Melilotus*, with trifoliate leaves, small flowers, and a scent of hay when dried. [from Greek *melilōtos* 'honey lotus']

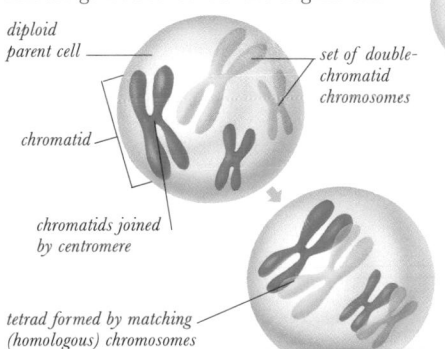

MELILOT: WHITE MELILOT
(*Melilotus alba*)

mellifluous *adj.* (of a voice or words) pleasing, musical, flowing. [based on Latin *mel* 'honey' + *fluere* 'to flow'] □ **mellifluously** *adv.*

mellow ● *adj.* **1** (of sound, colour, light) soft and rich; free from harshness. **2** (of character) softened or matured by age or experience. **3** genial, jovial. **4** slightly drunk. **5** (of fruit) soft, sweet, and juicy. **6** (of wine) well-matured, smooth. **7** (of earth) rich, loamy. ● *v.tr. & intr.* make or become mellow. [Middle English] □ **mellowness** *n.*

mclodeon *n.* (also **melodion**) **1** a small organ popular in the 19th c., similar to the harmonium. **2** a small German accordion, played esp. by folk musicians. [sense 1: alteration of *melodium*, blend of MELODY and HARMONIUM]

melodic *adj.* **1** of or relating to melody. **2** having or producing melody. □ **melodically** *adv.*

melodious *adj.* **1** of, producing, or having melody. **2** sweet-sounding. □ **melodiously** *adv.* **melodiousness** *n.*

melodrama *n.* **1** a sensational dramatic piece with crude appeals to the emotions. **2** the genre of drama of this type. **3** language, behaviour, or an occurrence suggestive of this. **4** *hist.* a play with songs interspersed and with music accompanying the action. [based on Greek *melos* 'music' + French *drame* 'drama'] □ **melodramatic** *adj.* **melodramatically** *adv.* **melodramatize** *v.tr.* (also **-ise**)

melody *n.* (*pl.* **-ies**) **1** an arrangement of single notes in a musically expressive succession. **2** the principal part in harmonized music. **3** a musical arrangement of words. **4** sweet music; tunefulness. [from Greek *melōidia*]

melon *n.* **1** the large round fruit of various plants of the gourd family, with sweet pulpy flesh and many seeds (*honeydew melon*; *watermelon*). ▷ FRUIT. **2** the plant producing this. **3** *Zool.* ▼ a mass of waxy material in the head of some toothed whales, thought to focus acoustic signals. [from Greek *mēlopepōn*, from *mēlon* 'apple' + *pepōn* 'gourd']

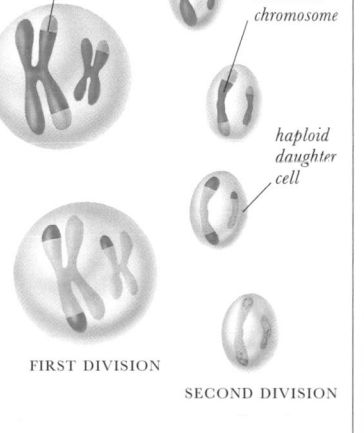

MELON IN A
DOLPHIN'S HEAD

M

melt ● *v.* **1** *intr.* become liquefied by heat. **2** *tr.* change to a liquid condition by heat (see also MOLTEN). **3** *intr. & tr.* soften or liquefy by the action of moisture; dissolve. **4** *intr.* **a** (of a person, feelings, the heart, etc.) be softened as a result of pity, love, etc. **b** dissolve into tears. **5** *tr.* soften (a person, feelings, the heart, etc.) (*a look to melt a heart of stone*). **6** *intr.* (usu. foll. by *into*) change or merge imperceptibly into another form or state (*night melted into dawn*). **7** *intr.* (of a person) leave or disappear unobtrusively (*melted into the background*; *melted away into the crowd*). **8** *intr.* (usu. as **melting** *adj.*) (of sound) be soft and liquid (*melting chords*). **9** *intr. colloq.* (of a person) suffer extreme heat (*I'm melting in this thick jumper*). ● *n.* **1** liquid metal etc. **2** an amount melted at any one time. **3** the process or an instance of melting. □ **melt away** disappear or make disappear by liquefaction. **melt down 1** melt (esp. metal articles) in order to reuse the raw material. **2** become liquid and lose structure (cf. MELTDOWN). **melt in the mouth** (of food) be delicious and esp. very light. [Old English] □ **melter** *n.* **meltingly** *adv.*

meltdown *n.* **1** the melting of a structure, esp. the overheated core of a nuclear reactor. **2** a disastrous event, esp. a rapid fall in share prices.

melting point *n.* the temperature at which a solid will melt.

melting pot *n.* **1** a pot in which metals etc. are melted and mixed. **2** a place where races, theories, etc. are mixed, or an imaginary pool where ideas are mixed together.

melt water *n.* water formed by the melting of snow and ice, esp. from a glacier.

member *n.* **1** a person belonging to a society, team, etc. **2** (**Member**) a person formally elected to take part in the proceedings of certain organizations (*Member of Parliament*; *Member of Congress*). **3** (also *attrib.*) a part or branch of a political body (*member state*; *a member of the Commonwealth*). **4** a constituent portion of a complex structure (*load-bearing member*). **5** a part of a sentence, equation, group of figures, mathematical set, etc. **6 a** any part or organ of the

---

MEIOSIS

Before a cell divides by meiosis, it contains one set of chromosomes from each parent. Matching chromosomes, each with two chromatids, then line up to form tetrads, and the chromatids overlap and swap pieces. In the first division, matching chromosomes separate, forming two new cells, each with a single pair of chromosomes. In the second division, the chromatids in each chromosome separate, forming four new, daughter cells, each with half the genetic content of the original cell.

DEMONSTRATION OF MEIOTIC
CELL DIVISION

crossed-over
chromatids

single-
chromatid
chromosome

haploid
daughter
cell

FIRST DIVISION

SECOND DIVISION

diploid
parent cell

set of double-
chromatid
chromosomes

chromatid

chromatids joined
by centromere

tetrad formed by matching
(homologous) chromosomes

body, esp. a limb. **b** the penis. **7** used in the title awarded to a person admitted to certain honours (*Member of the British Empire*). [from Latin *membrum* 'limb'] □ **membered** *adj.* (also in *comb.*).

membership *n.* **1** being a member. **2** the number of members. **3** the body of members.

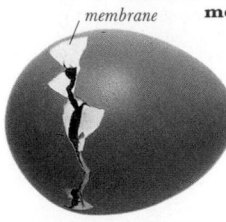
membrane

MEMBRANE LINING AN EGGSHELL

membrane *n.* **1** ◄ any pliable sheetlike structure acting as a boundary, lining, or partition in an organism. **2** a thin pliable sheet or skin. [from Latin *membrana* 'skin covering part of the body, parchment'] □ **membranous** *adj.*

memento *n.* (*pl.* **-oes** or **-os**) an object kept as a reminder of a person or an event. [Latin, literally 'remember']

memento mori *n.* a warning or reminder of death. [Latin, literally 'remember you must die']

memo *n.* (*pl.* **-os**) *colloq.* a memorandum.

memoir /**mem**-wah/ *n.* **1** a historical account or biography written from personal knowledge or special sources. **2** (in *pl.*) an autobiography or a written account of one's memory of certain events or people. **3** an essay on a learned subject specially studied by the writer. [from special use of French *mémoire* 'memory'] □ **memoirist** *n.*

memorabilia *n.pl.* souvenirs of memorable events, people, etc. [Latin]

memorable *adj.* **1** worth remembering. **2** easily remembered. □ **memorability** *n.* **memorably** *adv.*

memorandum *n.* (*pl.* **memoranda** or **memorandums**) **1** a note or record made for future use. **2** an informal written message, esp. in business, diplomacy, etc. [Latin, literally 'thing to be called to mind']

memorial ● *n.* **1** an object, institution, or custom established in memory of a person or event (*the Albert Memorial*). **2** (often in *pl.*) *hist.* a statement of facts as the basis of a petition etc.; a record; an informal diplomatic paper. ● *adj.* intending to commemorate a person or thing (*memorial service*). [from Latin *memorialis*] □ **memorialist** *n.*

Memorial Day *n.* (in the US) a day on which those who died on active service are remembered, usu. the last Monday in May.

memorialize *v.tr.* (also **-ise**) **1** commemorate. **2** address a memorial to.

memorize *v.tr.* (also **-ise**) commit to memory. □ **memorization** *n.*

memory *n.* (*pl.* **-ies**) **1** the faculty by which things are recalled to or kept in the mind. **2 a** this faculty in an individual (*my memory is beginning to fail*). **b** one's store of things remembered (*buried deep in my memory*). **3** a recollection or remembrance (*the memory of better times*). **4 a** the part of a computer etc. in which data or instructions can be stored for retrieval. **b** capacity for storing information in this way. **5** the remembrance of a person or thing (*his mother's memory haunted him*). **6** the reputation of a dead person (*his memory lives on*). **7** the length of time over which the memory or memories of any given person or group extends (*within living memory*). □ **from memory** without verification in books etc. **in memory of** to keep alive the remembrance of. [based on Latin *memor* 'mindful, remembering']

memory bank *n.* **1** the memory device of a computer etc. **2** the store of memories of an individual or group.

memory board *n.* a detachable storage device which can be connected to a computer.

memory lane *n.* (usu. prec. by *down, along*) an imaginary and sentimental journey into the past.

memsahib /**mem**-sahb/ *n. Anglo-Ind. hist.* a European married woman in India, as spoken of or to by Indians.

men *pl.* of MAN.

menace ● *n.* **1** a threat. **2** a dangerous or obnoxious thing or person. **3** *joc.* a pest; a nuisance. ● *v.tr.* & *intr.* threaten. [based on Latin *minax -acis* 'threatening'] □ **menacingly** *adv.*

ménage /**may**-nah*zh*/ *n.* the members of a household. [from Old French]

ménage à trois /ah **trwah**/ *n.* (*pl.* **ménages à trois** *pronunc.* same) an arrangement in which three people live together, usu. a married couple and the lover of one of them. [French, literally 'household of three']

menagerie *n.* **1** a collection of wild animals in captivity for exhibition etc. **2** the place where these are housed. [from French *ménagerie*]

menaquinone *n.* one of the K vitamins, produced by bacteria found in the large intestine and essential for the blood-clotting process. [from chemical name *methyl-naphthoquinone*]

menarche *n.* the onset of first menstruation. [based on Greek *arkhē* 'beginning']

mend ● *v.* **1** *tr.* restore to a sound condition; repair. **2** *intr.* heal. ● *n.* a darn or repair in material etc. (*a mend in my shirt*) □ **mend one's fences** make peace with a person. **mend one's ways** reform, improve one's habits. **on the mend** improving in health or condition. [from Anglo-French *mender*] □ **mender** *n.*

mendacious *adj.* lying, untruthful. [from Latin *mendax -dacis*] □ **mendaciously** *adv.* **mendacity** *n.* (*pl.* **-ies**).

mendelevium *n. Chem.* an artificially made transuranic radioactive metallic element. [named after D. I. *Mendeleev*, Russian chemist, 1834–1907]

Mendelism *n.* ▼ the theory of heredity based on the recurrence of certain inherited characteristics transmitted by genes. [from G. J. *Mendel*, Austrian botanist, 1822–84] □ **Mendelian** *adj.* & *n.*

mendicant ● *adj.* **1** begging. **2** (of a friar) living solely on alms. ● *n.* **1** a beggar. **2** a mendicant friar. [from Latin *mendicant-* 'begging']

mending *n.* **1** the action of a person who mends. **2** things, esp. clothes, to be mended.

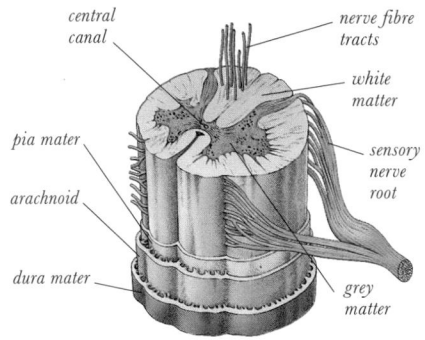
MENHIR: PREHISTORIC MENHIRS NEAR CARNAC, FRANCE

menfolk *n.pl.* **1** men in general. **2** the men of one's family.

menhaden *n.* any large herring-like fish of the genus *Brevoortia*, of the east coast of N. America, yielding valuable oil and used for fertilizer.

menhir /**men**-heer/ *n.* ◄ a tall upright usu. prehistoric monumental stone. [from Breton *men* 'stone' + *hir* 'long']

menial ● *adj.* **1** (esp. of unskilled domestic work) degrading, servile. **2** usu. *derog.* (of a servant) domestic. ● *n.* **1** a menial servant. **2** a servile person. [based on Old French *meinee* 'household'] □ **menially** *adv.*

meningitis /men-in-**jy**-tis/ *n.* inflammation of the meninges due to infection by viruses or bacteria.

meninx *n.* (*pl.* **meninges** /mi-**nin**-jeez/) (usu. in *pl.*) *Anat.* ▼ each of three membranes (the dura mater, arachnoid, and pia mater) that line the skull and vertebral canal and enclose the brain and spinal cord. [from Greek *mēninx* 'membrane'] □ **meningeal** *adj.*

central canal

nerve fibre tracts

white matter

pia mater

sensory nerve root

arachnoid

dura mater

grey matter

MENINX: SECTION THROUGH THE HUMAN SPINAL CORD SHOWING MENINGES

MENDELISM

Certain basic principles of genetics were established by the Austrian botanist Gregor Mendel, who found that the inheritance of characteristics follows predictable mathematical patterns. The expression of inherited characteristics depends on whether the genes are dominant (*R* below) or recessive (*r*) in form. A recessive gene is expressed only if it is partnered by an identical recessive gene. If paired with a dominant gene the effect is masked, but it still forms part of the genetic information passed to the next generation.

DEMONSTRATION OF MENDELISM IN A PLANT

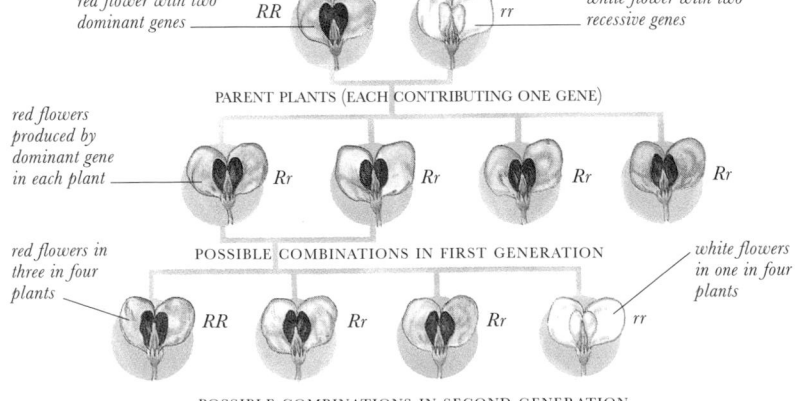

red flower with two dominant genes — *RR*

rr — *white flower with two recessive genes*

PARENT PLANTS (EACH CONTRIBUTING ONE GENE)

red flowers produced by dominant gene in each plant — *Rr* *Rr* *Rr* *Rr*

POSSIBLE COMBINATIONS IN FIRST GENERATION

red flowers in three in four plants — *RR* *Rr* *Rr* *rr* — *white flowers in one in four plants*

POSSIBLE COMBINATIONS IN SECOND GENERATION

M

meniscus *n.* (*pl.* **menisci** /mi-**nis**-I/) **1** *Physics* ▼ the curved upper surface of a liquid in a tube. **2** a lens that is convex on one side and concave on the other. **3** *Anat.* a thin fibrous cartilage between the surfaces of some joints, e.g. the knee. ▷ KNEE. **4** *Math.* a crescent-shaped figure. [from Greek *mēniskos* 'crescent']

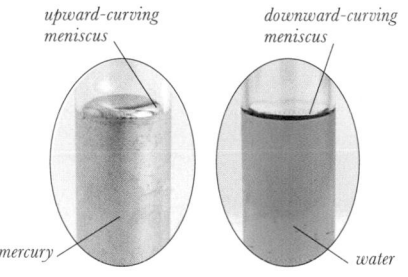

upward-curving meniscus   *downward-curving meniscus*

mercury   *water*

MENISCUS: MERCURY AND WATER MENISCI

Mennonite *n.* a member of a Protestant sect originating in Friesland in the 16th c. [from the name of its founder, *Menno* Simons, 1496–1561]

menopause *n.* **1** the ceasing of menstruation. **2** the period in a woman's life (usu. between 45 and 50) when this occurs. □ **menopausal** *adj*

menorah /mi-**nor**-ă/ *n.* ▶ a candelabrum used in Jewish worship, originally one with seven branches which stood in the Temple, now often one with eight branches used at Hanukkah, with a ninth candle used to light the rest. [Hebrew, literally 'candlestick']

menses *n.pl.* **1** blood and other materials discharged from the uterus at menstruation. **2** the time of menstruation. [Latin, literally 'months']

menstrual *adj.* of or relating to the menses or menstruation. [from Latin *menstrualis*]

menstrual cycle *n.* the process of ovulation and menstruation in female primates.

menstruate *v.intr.* undergo menstruation. [based on Latin *menstrua* 'monthly courses']

menstruation *n.* the process of discharging blood and other materials from the lining of the uterus in sexually mature non-pregnant women at intervals of about one lunar month until the menopause.

mensuration *n.* **1** measuring. **2** *Math.* the measuring of geometric magnitudes such as lengths, areas, and volumes. [from Late Latin *mensuratio*]

menswear *n.* clothes for men.

mental *adj.* **1** of or in the mind. **2** done by the mind. **3** *colloq.* **a** insane. **b** mad, crazy, angry, fanatical (*is mental about pop music*). **4** (*attrib.*) of or relating to disorders or illnesses of the mind (*mental hospital*). [based on Latin *mens mentis* 'mind'] □ **mentally** *adv.*

■ **Usage** In sense 4, *psychiatric* is now often preferred to *mental* as it is regarded as a less stigmatizing term.

mental age *n.* the degree of a person's mental development expressed as an age at which the same degree is attained by an average person.

mental block *n.* a particular mental inability due to subconscious emotional factors.

mental defective *n. archaic* or *offens.* a person with a mental handicap.

mental handicap *n.* a condition in which the intellectual capacity of a person is permanently so much lowered or underdeveloped as to prevent normal function in society. □ **mentally handicapped** *adj.*

MERCATOR PROJECTION

The most common type of world map was devised by the Dutch map-maker Gerardus Mercator in 1569. In the projection on which the map is based, the Earth's sphere is 'unwrapped' from a cylinder on to a flat rectangular surface, with the lines of longitude and latitude shown as a regular grid of straight lines. In a cylindrical projection such as this, the Earth's surface becomes visually more distorted towards the poles.

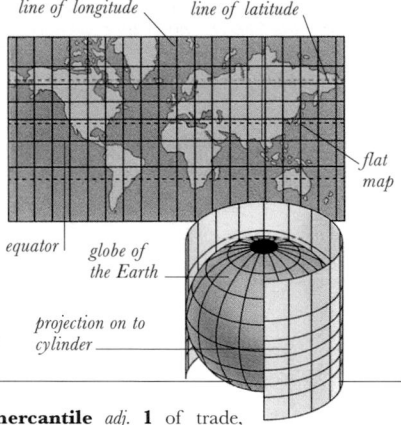

line of longitude   *line of latitude*

flat map

equator   *globe of the Earth*

projection on to cylinder

DEMONSTRATION OF A CYLINDRICAL (MERCATOR) PROJECTION

■ **Usage** The term *learning difficulties*, which strictly applies to educational problems, is sometimes preferred for or by people with certain mental handicaps.

mental illness *n.* a condition which causes serious abnormality or disorder in a person's behaviour or thinking capacity, esp. irrespective of intelligence; a disorder of the mind.

mentality *n.* (*pl.* **-ies**) **1** mental character or disposition. **2** kind or degree of intelligence. **3** what is in or of the mind.

mental nurse *n. Brit.* = PSYCHIATRIC NURSE.

mental patient *n. Brit.* = PSYCHIATRIC PATIENT.

mental reservation *n.* a qualification tacitly added in making a statement etc.

menthol *n.* a mint-tasting organic alcohol found in oil of peppermint etc., used as a flavouring and to relieve local pain. [based on Latin *mentha* 'mint']

mentholated *adj.* treated with or containing menthol.

mention • *v.tr.* **1** refer to briefly. **2** specify by name. **3** reveal or disclose (*do not mention this to anyone*). **4** *Brit.* (in dispatches) award (a person) a minor honour for meritorious military service • *n.* **1** a reference, esp. by name, to a person or thing. **2** *Brit.* (in dispatches) a military honour awarded for outstanding conduct. □ **don't mention it** said in polite dismissal of an apology or thanks. **make mention** (or **no mention**) **of** refer (or not refer) to. **not to mention** introducing a fact or thing of secondary or (as a rhetorical device) of primary importance. [from Latin *mentio*, based on *mens* 'mind'] □ **mentionable** *adj.*

mentor *n.* an experienced and trusted adviser. [from Greek *Mentōr*, adviser of the young Telemachus in Homer's *Odyssey* and Fénelon's *Télémaque*]

menu *n.* **1 a** a list of dishes available in a restaurant etc. **b** a list of items to be served at a meal. **2** *Computing* a list of options usu. displayed on-screen showing the commands or facilities available. [French, literally 'detailed list']

menu-driven *adj.* (of a program or computer) used by making selections from menus.

meow var. of MIAOW.

MEP *abbr.* Member of the European Parliament.

meperidine *n.* esp. *US* = PETHIDINE.

mephitic *adj.* **1** foul-smelling. **2** (of a vapour etc.) noxious, poisonous. [from Latin]

meranti *n.* a white, red, or yellow hardwood timber from a Malaysian or Indonesian tree of the genus *Shorea*. [Malay]

---

mercantile *adj.* **1** of trade, trading. **2** commercial. **3** mercenary; fond of bargaining. [based on Italian *mercante* 'merchant']

mercantile marine *n.* shipping employed in commerce not war.

Mercator projection /mer-**kay**-ter/ *n.* (also **Mercator's projection**) ▲ a projection of a map of the world on to a cylinder so that all the parallels of latitude have the same length as the equator. [from *Mercator*, Latinized name of G. Kremer, Flemish-born geographer, 1512–94]

mercenary • *adj.* primarily concerned with money or other reward (*mercenary motives*). • *n.* (*pl.* **-ies**) **1** a hired soldier in foreign service. **2** a person available for paid hire (*cricket mercenaries playing abroad*). [based on Latin *merces* 'reward']

mercer *n. Brit.* a dealer in textile fabrics. [based on Latin *merx mercis* 'goods']

mercerize *v.tr.* (also **-ise**) treat (cotton fabric or thread) under tension with caustic alkali to give greater strength and impart lustre. [from J. *Mercer*, 1791–1866, alleged inventor of the process]

merchandise • *n.* goods for sale. • *v.* **1** *intr.* trade, traffic. **2** *tr.* trade or traffic in. **3** *tr.* **a** promote the sale of (goods etc.). **b** advertise or publicize (an idea or person). [from Old French *marchandise*] □ **merchandiser** *n.*

merchant *n.* **1** a wholesale trader, esp. *Brit.* with foreign countries. **2** esp. *US* & *Sc.* a retail trader. **3** *colloq.* usu. *derog.* a person showing a partiality for a specified activity or practice (*speed merchant*). [based on *merx mercis* 'merchandise']

merchantable *adj.* saleable, marketable.

merchant bank *n.* esp. *Brit.* a bank dealing in commercial loans and finance. □ **merchant banker** *n.*

merchantman *n.* (*pl.* **-men**) a ship conveying merchandise.

merchant marine *n. US* = MERCHANT NAVY.

merchant navy *n. Brit.* a nation's commercial shipping.

merchant prince *n.* a wealthy merchant.

merchant ship *n.* = MERCHANTMAN.

merciful *adj.* having or showing or feeling mercy.

mercifully *adv.* **1** in a merciful manner. **2** (qualifying a whole sentence) fortunately (*mercifully, the sun came out*).

merciless *adj.* **1** pitiless. **2** showing no mercy. □ **mercilessly** *adv.*

mercurial • *adj.* **1** (of a person) sprightly, ready-witted, volatile. **2** of or containing mercury. • *n.* a drug containing mercury. □ **mercurially** *adv.*

mercury *n.* **1** *Chem.* ◄ a silvery-white heavy liquid metallic element used in barometers, thermometers, and amalgams; also called *quicksilver*. ▷ METALS, SPHYGMOMANOMETER.

mercury

MERCURY IN 18TH-CENTURY THERMOMETER

M

2 (**Mercury**) ▶ the planet nearest to the Sun. ▷ SOLAR SYSTEM. [from Latin name *Mercurius*, messenger of the gods and god of traders] □ **mercuric** *adj.*

mercy ● *n.* (*pl.* **-ies**) **1** compassion or forbearance shown to enemies or offenders in one's power. **2** the quality of compassion. **3** an act of mercy. **4** (*attrib.*) administered or performed out of compassion for a suffering person (*mercy killing*). **5** something to be thankful for (*small mercies*). ● *int.* expressing surprise or fear. □ **at the mercy of 1** in the power of. **2** liable to danger or harm from. **have mercy on** (or **upon**) show mercy to. [from Latin *merces* 'reward']

mere[1] *attrib.adj.* (**merest**) that is solely or no more or better than what is specified (*a mere boy; no mere theory*). [from Latin *merus* 'unmixed'] □ **merely** *adv.*

mere[2] *n. archaic* or *poet.* a lake. [Old English]

mere[3] *n.* a Maori war club. [Maori]

meretricious /me-ri-**trish**-ŭs/ *adj.* showily but falsely attractive. [from Latin *meretricius*]

merganser *n.* any of various diving fish-eating northern ducks of the genus *Mergus*, with a long narrow serrated hooked bill (cf. GOOSANDER). [from Latin *mergus* 'diver' + *anser* 'goose']

merge *v.* **1** *tr.* & *intr.* **a** combine or be combined. **b** join or blend gradually. **2** *intr.* & *tr.* (foll. by *in*) lose or cause to lose character and identity in (something else). [earlier in sense 'to immerse (oneself)': from Latin *mergere* 'to dip, plunge']

merger *n.* **1** the combining of two commercial companies etc. into one. **2** a merging.

meridian ● *n.* **1** a circle passing through the celestial poles and the zenith of a given place on the Earth's surface. **2 a** a circle of constant longitude, passing through a given place and the terrestrial poles. **b** the corresponding line on a map. **3** *archaic* the point at which a sun or star attains its highest altitude. **4** prime; full splendour. ● *adj.* **1** of noon. **2** of the period of greatest splendour, vigour, etc. [from Latin *meridies* 'midday']

meridional *adj.* **1** of or in the south (esp. of Europe). **2** of or relating to a meridian.

meringue /mĕ-**rang**/ *n.* **1** a confection of sugar, the white of eggs, etc., baked crisp. **2** a small cake or shell of this, usu. decorated or filled with whipped cream etc. [French]

merino *n.* (*pl.* **-os**) **1** (in full **merino sheep**) a variety of sheep with long fine wool. **2** a soft woollen or wool-and-cotton material like cashmere, originally of merino wool. **3** a fine woollen yarn. [Spanish]

merit ● *n.* **1** the quality of deserving well. **2** excellence, worth. **3** (usu. in *pl.*) **a** a thing that entitles one to reward or gratitude. **b** esp. *Law* intrinsic rights and wrongs (*the merits of a case*). ● *v.tr.* (**merited**, **meriting**) deserve. □ **on its merits** with regard only to its intrinsic worth. [from Latin *meritum* 'price, value']

meritocracy *n.* (*pl.* **-ies**) **1** government by persons selected according to merit. **2** a group of persons selected in this way. **3** a society governed by meritocracy. □ **meritocratic** *adj.*

meritorious *adj.* deserving reward, praise, or gratitude.

merlin *n.* a small European or N. American falcon, *Falco columbarius*. [from Old French *esmerillon*]

mermaid *n.* an imaginary sea creature, with the head and trunk of a woman and the tail of a fish. [Middle English]

mermaid's purse *n.* the horny egg-case of a skate, ray, or shark.

merman *n.* (*pl.* **-men**) the male equivalent of a mermaid.

merriment *n.* **1** exuberant enjoyment; being merry. **2** mirth, fun.

merry *adj.* (**merrier**, **merriest**) **1 a** joyous. **b** full of laughter or gaiety. **2** *Brit. colloq.* slightly drunk. □ **make merry 1** be festive; enjoy oneself. **2** (foll. by *over*) make fun of. **play merry hell with** see HELL. [Old English] □ **merrily** *adv.*

MERCURY

Mercury is a small, rocky planet whose surface has been heavily cratered by meteorites. The surface also has many ridges, called rupes, that are believed to have formed as the core of the young planet cooled and shrank. Mercury moves faster than any other planet, completing its orbit of the Sun in 88 Earth days, but its axial rotation is very slow, taking nearly 59 days. As a result, a solar day (from sunrise to sunrise) on Mercury lasts twice as long as the Mercurean year. Surface temperature on the planet varies from 430 °C (806 °F) on the sunlit side to -170 °C (-338 °F) on the dark side.

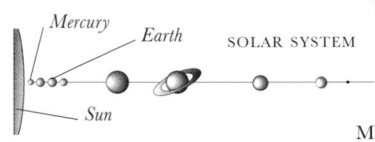

MERCURY, WITH INTERNAL STRUCTURE REVEALED

merry-go-round *n.* **1** a revolving machine with wooden horses or cars for riding on at a fair etc. **2** a cycle of bustling activities.

merrymaking *n.* revelling, fun.

mesa /**may**-să/ *n.* an isolated flat-topped hill with steep sides. ▷ ERODE. [Spanish, literally 'table']

mésalliance /mez-**al**-i-ănss/ *n.* a marriage with a person of a lower social position. [French]

mescal *n.* a peyote cactus. [from Aztec *mexcalli*]

mescal buttons *n.pl.* disc-shaped dried tops from the peyote cactus, eaten or chewed as an intoxicant.

mescaline *n.* (also **mescalin**) a hallucinogenic alkaloid present in mescal buttons.

Mesdames *pl.* of MADAME.

Mesdemoiselles *pl.* of MADEMOISELLE.

mesembryanthemum *n.* any of various succulent plants of the genus *Mesembryanthemum* of S. Africa, or related genera, having brightly coloured daisy-like flowers that fully open in sunlight. [from Greek *mesēmbria* 'noon' + *anthemon* 'flower']

mesh ● *n.* **1** a network fabric or structure. **2** each of the open spaces between the strands of a net or sieve etc. **3** (in *pl.*) **a** a network. **b** a snare. **4** (in *pl.*) *Physiol.* an interlaced structure. ● *v.* **1** *intr.* (of the teeth of a wheel) be engaged. **2** *intr.* be harmonious. **3** *tr.* catch in or as in a net. □ **in mesh** (of the teeth of wheels) engaged. [from Middle Dutch *maesche*]

mesmerism *n.* **1** *Psychol.* **a** a hypnotic state produced in a person by another's influence. **b** a doctrine concerning this. **c** an influence or process producing this. **2** fascination. [named after F. A. *Mesmer*, Austrian physician, 1734–1815] □ **mesmeric** *adj.* **mesmerist** *n.*

mesmerize *v.tr.* (also **-ise**) **1** *Psychol.* hypnotize; exercise mesmerism on. **2** fascinate, spellbind.

meso- *comb. form* middle, intermediate. [from Greek *mesos* 'middle']

mesolithic *adj. Archaeol.* of or relating to the middle phase of the Stone Age, lasting from the end of the last ice age to the start of agriculture. [based on Greek *lithos* 'stone']

mesomorph *n.* ▶ a person with a compact and muscular build of body (cf. ECTOMORPH, ENDOMORPH). [based on Greek *morphē* 'form'] □ **mesomorphic** *adj.*

meson *n. Physics* any of a class of subatomic particles believed to participate in the forces that hold nucleons together in the atomic nucleus.

mesosphere *n.* the region of the atmosphere above the stratosphere. ▷ ATMOSPHERE

Mesozoic *Geol.* ● *adj.* of or relating to an era of geological time marked by the development of dinosaurs, and with evidence of the first mammals, birds, and flowering plants. ● *n.* this era (cf. CENOZOIC, PALAEOZOIC). [based on Greek *zōion* 'animal']

mesquite /mess-**keet**/ *n.* (also **mesquit**) any N. American leguminous tree of the genus *Prosopis*, esp. *P. glandulosa*. [from Mexican Spanish *mezquite*]

mess ● *n.* **1** a dirty or untidy state of things (*the room is a mess*). **2** a state of confusion, embarrassment, or trouble. **3** something causing a mess, e.g. spilt liquid. **4** a domestic animal's excreta. **5 a** a company of persons who take meals together, esp. in the armed forces. **b** a place where such meals or recreation take place communally. **c** a meal taken there. **6** *derog.* a disagreeable concoction. **7 a** a portion of liquid or pulpy food. **b** *Brit.* a liquid or mixed food for hounds etc. ● *v.* **1** *tr.* (often foll. by *up*) **a** make a mess of; dirty. **b** muddle; make into a state of confusion. **2** *intr.* (foll. by *with*) (esp. *N. Amer.*) interfere with. **3** *intr.* take one's meals. **4** *intr.* & *tr.*

MESOMORPH

Mesomorphs are one of the three basic body shapes, or 'somatypes', identified by W. H. Sheldon in the 1950s. They have strong, muscular bodies, with wide shoulders and narrow hips. Endomorphs tend to be overweight, gaining weight in the abdominal region and with poorly developed muscle and bone. Ectomorphs, the third type, have tall, thin, lean physiques.

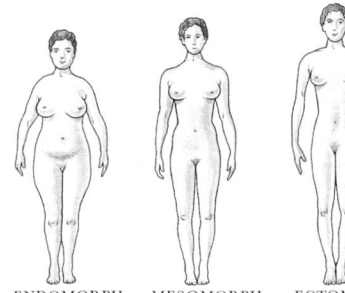

ENDOMORPH　　MESOMORPH　　ECTOMORPH

M

colloq. defecate or soil by defecating. □ **make a mess of** bungle. **mess about** (or **around**) **1** *intr.* act desultorily. **2** *tr. colloq.* make things awkward for; cause arbitrary inconvenience to. [from Late Latin *missus* 'course at dinner']

message *n.* **1** a communication sent by one person to another. **2** an inspired or significant communication from a prophet, writer, or preacher. **3** a mission or errand. □ **get the message** *colloq.* understand what is meant. [based on Latin *mittere miss-* 'to send']

Messeigneurs *pl.* of Monseigneur.

messenger *n.* **1** a person who carries a message. **2** a person employed to carry messages. [from Old French *messager*]

messenger RNA *n.* the form of RNA in which genetic information transcribed from DNA as a sequence of bases is transferred to a ribosome.

Messiah *n.* **1** a liberator or would-be liberator of an oppressed people. **2 a** the promised deliverer of the Jews. **b** (usu. prec. by *the*) Christ regarded as this. [from Hebrew *māšīaḥ* 'anointed'] □ **Messiahship** *n.*

Messianic /mess-i-**an**-ik/ *adj.* **1** of the Messiah. **2** inspired by belief in a Messiah. □ **Messianism** *n.*

Messieurs *pl.* of Monsieur.

mess kit *n.* a soldier's cooking and eating utensils.

messmate *n.* a person with whom one regularly takes meals, esp. in the armed forces.

Messrs *pl.* of Mr.

mess tin *n.* a small container as part of a mess kit.

messuage /mess-wij/ *n. Law* a dwelling house with outbuildings and land assigned to its use. [from Anglo-French]

messy *adj.* (**messier**, **messiest**) **1** untidy or dirty. **2** causing or accompanied by a mess. **3** difficult to deal with; full of awkward complications. □ **messily** *adv.* **messiness** *n.*

met[1] *past* and *past part.* of MEET[1].

met[2] *adj. colloq.* **1** meteorological. **2** metropolitan. **3** (**the Met**) **a** (in full **the Met Office**) (in the UK) the Meteorological Office. **b** the Metropolitan Police in London. **c** the Metropolitan Opera House in New York.

meta- *comb. form* (usu. **met-** before a vowel or *h*) **1** denoting change of position or condition (*metabolism*). **2** denoting position: **a** behind. **b** after or beyond (*metaphysics*; *metacarpus*). **c** of a higher or second-order kind (*metalanguage*). [from Greek *meta* 'with, after']

metabolism *n.* all the chemical processes that occur within a living organism, resulting in energy production (**destructive metabolism**) and growth (**constructive metabolism**). [based on Greek *metabolē* 'change'] □ **metabolic** *adj.* **metabolically** *adv.*

metabolite *n. Physiol.* a substance formed in or necessary for metabolism.

metabolize *v.tr. & intr.* (also **-ise**) process or be processed by metabolism.

metacarpus *n.* (*pl.* **metacarpi**) **1** the set of five bones of the hand that connects the wrist to the fingers. ▷ HAND, SKELETON. **2** this part of the hand. □ **metacarpal** *adj.*

metal ● *n.* **1 a** ▶ any of a class of substances (including many chemical elements) which are in general lustrous, malleable, fusible, ductile solids and good conductors of heat and electricity, e.g. gold, silver, iron, brass, steel. **b** material of this kind. **2** (in *pl.*) the rails of a railway line. **3** = ROAD METAL. ● *adj.* made of metal. ● *v.tr.* (**metalled**, **metalling**; *US* **metaled**, **metaling**) **1** provide or fit with metal. **2** *Brit.* make or mend (a road) with road metal. [from Greek *metallon* 'mine']

metalanguage *n.* **1** a form of language used to discuss a language. **2** a system of propositions about propositions.

metal detector *n.* an electronic device giving a signal when it locates metal.

METAL

Metals have been valued since early times for their hardness and strength, and for the ease with which they can be shaped; some are also prized for their beauty and rarity. Few occur in a pure native state: most have to be extracted by refining and smelting the ore minerals in which they occur. Some metals, such as aluminium, tin, and lead, are weaker and melt more easily than others. These are widely used in the production of alloys – metal mixtures that exploit the distinctive qualities of different metals.

EXAMPLES OF PRECIOUS METALS

PLATINUM
(native form)

GOLD
(native form)

SILVER
(native form)

EXAMPLES OF MINERAL ORES

CINNABAR
(mercury)

CASSITERITE
(tin)

BAUXITE
(aluminium)

CHALCOPYRITE
(copper)

GALENA
(lead)

NICCOLITE
(nickel)

SPHALERITE
(zinc)

RUTILE
(titanium)

HAEMATITE
(iron)

EXAMPLES OF ALLOYS

stainless steel cutlery

Chinese bronze food vessel

brass ship's bell

STAINLESS STEEL
(iron, carbon, and chromium)

BRONZE
(copper and tin)

BRASS
(copper and zinc)

M

METAMORPHIC

Metamorphic rocks are formed by the application of heat and pressure to pre-existing igneous, sedimentary, or earlier metamorphic rocks. The variations in metamorphic rock types are due to variations in the original rock type as well as the differing conditions to which the rocks were subjected. There are two main types of metamorphic rock. When rocks in a mountain-building region are transformed by both heat and pressure, regional metamorphic rock, such as slate, schist, and gneiss, is formed. Contact metamorphism occurs in the area around an igneous intrusion, where rocks may be altered by direct heat alone; marble, for example, is formed by the application of heat to limestone. A third type of metamorphism – dynamic – occurs when movements at a fault in the Earth's crust force rock masses into contact with each other, producing a very fine-grained rock called mylonite.

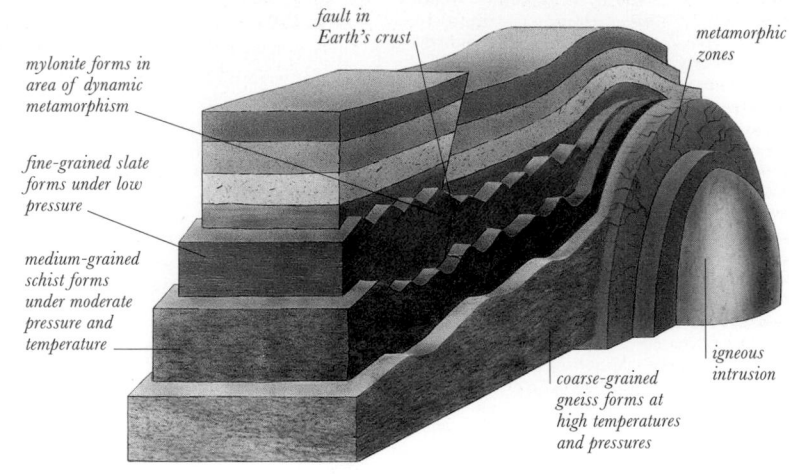

mylonite forms in area of dynamic metamorphism

fine-grained slate forms under low pressure

medium-grained schist forms under moderate pressure and temperature

fault in Earth's crust

metamorphic zones

coarse-grained gneiss forms at high temperatures and pressures

igneous intrusion

MODEL SHOWING THE FORMATION OF METAMORPHIC ROCKS

EXAMPLES OF METAMORPHIC ROCKS

REGIONAL METAMORPHIC ROCKS

SLATE   SCHIST   GNEISS

CONTACT METAMORPHIC ROCKS

METAQUARTZITE   MARBLE

DYNAMIC METAMORPHIC ROCK

MYLONITE

M

metallic *adj.* **1** of or like metal or metals. **2** sounding sharp and ringing, like struck metal. **3** having the sheen or lustre of metals. □ **metallically** *adv.*

metalliferous *adj.* bearing or producing metal.

metallize *v.tr.* (also **-ise**; *US* **metalize**) **1** render metallic. **2** coat with a thin layer of metal.

metallography *n.* the descriptive science of metals. □ **metallographic** *adj.*

metalloid ● *adj.* having the form or appearance of a metal. ● *n.* any element intermediate in properties between metals and non-metals, e.g. boron, silicon, and germanium.

metallurgy /mi-**tal**-er-ji/ *n.* the science of metals and their application. [from Greek *metallon* 'metal' + *-ourgia* 'working'] □ **metallurgical** *adj.* **metallurgist** *n.*

metalwork *n.* **1** the art of working in metal. **2** metal objects collectively. □ **metalworker** *n.*

metamorphic *adj.* **1** of or marked by metamorphosis. **2** *Geol.* ▲ (of rock) that has undergone transformation by natural agencies such as heat and pressure. ▷ ROCK CYCLE. [based on Greek *morphē* 'form'] □ **metamorphism** *n.*

metamorphose *v.tr.* **1** change in form. **2** (foll. by *to, into*) **a** turn (into a new form). **b** change the nature of.

metamorphosis *n.* (*pl.* **metamorphoses**) **1** a change of form. **2** a changed form. **3** a change of character, conditions, etc. **4** *Zool.* ▼ the transformation between an immature form and an adult form, e.g. from a pupa to an insect. [based on Greek *metamorphoun* 'to transform']

metaphor *n.* **1 a** the application of a name or descriptive term or phrase to an object or action to which it is imaginatively but not literally applicable (e.g. *a glaring error*). **b** an instance of this. **2** (often foll. by *of* or *for*) a symbol of a usu. abstract thing (*the lark was a metaphor for release*). [from Greek *metaphora*] □ **metaphoric** *adj.* **metaphorical** *adj.* **metaphorically** *adv.*

metaphysic *n.* a system of metaphysics.

metaphysical ● *adj.* **1** of or relating to metaphysics. **2** based on abstract general reasoning. **3** excessively subtle or theoretical. **4** incorporeal; supernatural. **5** (of certain 17th-c. English poets or their poetry) subtle and complex in imagery. ● *n.* (**the Metaphysicals**) the metaphysical poets. □ **metaphysically** *adv.*

metaphysics *n.pl.* (usu. treated as *sing.*) **1** the theoretical philosophy of being and knowing. **2** the philosophy of mind. **3** *colloq.* abstract talk; mere theory. [from Greek *ta meta ta phusika* 'the things after the Physics', from the sequence of Aristotle's works] □ **metaphysician** *n.*

metastable *adj.* **1** (of a state of equilibrium) stable only under small disturbances. **2** (of a substance etc.) technically unstable but so long-lived as to be stable for practical purposes. □ **metastability** *n.*

metastasis *n.* (*pl.* **metastases**) *Med.* **1** the transfer of a disease etc. from one part of the body to another. **2** a secondary tumour. [based on Greek *methistanai* ' to change'] □ **metastasize** *v.intr.* (also **-ise**). **metastatic** *adj.*

metatarsus *n.* (*pl.* **metatarsi**) **1** the part of the foot between the ankle and the toes. **2** the set of bones in this. ▷ SKELETON. □ **metatarsal** *adj.*

metathesis *n.* (*pl.* **metatheses**) **1** *Gram.* the transposition of sounds or letters in a word. **2** *Chem.* the interchange of atoms or groups of atoms between two molecules. [based on Greek *metatithenai* 'to transpose'] □ **metathetic** *adj.* **metathetical** *adj.*

mete *v.tr.* **1** (usu. foll. by *out*) *literary* apportion or allot (a punishment or reward). **2** *poet.* or *Bibl.* measure. [Old English]

meteor *n.* a small body of matter from outer space that becomes incandescent as a result of friction with the Earth's atmosphere and is visible as a streak of light. [from Greek *meteōron* 'lofty (thing)']

METAMORPHOSIS

Most invertebrates, as well as many fish and amphibians, start life as larvae. These look unlike their parents, often live in different habitats, and eat different food. They then undergo a total change of body form and appearance, called complete metamorphosis. A more gradual change in body shape, called incomplete metamorphosis, occurs in many insects. These hatch into miniature but immature versions of their parents, and progress through a series of moults to adulthood.

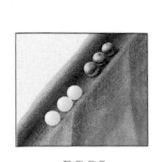

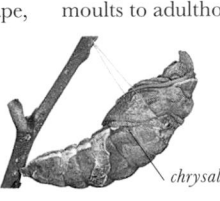

pupal case

butterfly

chrysalis

EGGS   LARVA   PUPA   MATURE BUTTERFLY

COMPLETE METAMORPHOSIS OF A BUTTERFLY

meteoric *adj.* **1** of, relating to, or derived from the atmosphere. **2** of meteors or meteorites. **3** dazzling, transient (*meteoric rise to fame*). □ **meteorically** *adv.*

meteoric stone *n.* a meteorite.

meteorite *n.* ► a rock or metal fragment formed from a meteor of sufficient size to reach the Earth's surface without burning up completely in the atmosphere. □ **meteoritic** *adj.*

meteoroid *n.* any small body moving in the solar system that becomes visible as it passes through the Earth's atmosphere as a meteor. □ **meteoroidal** *adj.*

METEORITE

meteorology *n.* **1** the study of atmospheric phenomena, esp. as a means of forecasting the weather. **2** the atmospheric character of a region. □ **meteorological** *adj.* **meteorologically** *adv.* **meteorologist** *n.*

meter[1] ● *n.* **1** ► a person or thing that measures, esp. an instrument for recording a quantity of gas, electricity, etc. **2** = PARKING METER. ● *v.tr.* measure by means of a meter. [Middle English]

meter[2] *US* var. of METRE[1].

meter[3] *US* var. of METRE[2].

-meter *comb. form* **1** forming nouns denoting measuring instruments (*barometer*). **2** *Prosody* forming nouns denoting lines of poetry with a specified number of measures (*pentameter*).

light meter

moisture gauge

METER: HOUSEPLANT LIGHT AND MOISTURE METER

methadone *n.* a potent narcotic analgesic drug. [from chemical name 6-dimethylamino-4,4-diphenyl-3-heptanone]

methamphetamine *n.* an amphetamine derivative with quicker and longer action, used as a stimulant.

methane *n. Chem.* a colourless odourless inflammable gaseous hydrocarbon, the main constituent of natural gas.

methanoic acid *n. Chem.* = FORMIC ACID. [based on METHANE]

methanol *n. Chem.* a colourless volatile inflammable liquid, used as a solvent.

methedrine *n. propr.* = METHAMPHETAMINE.

methinks /mi-**thinks**/ *v.intr.* (*past* **methought** /mi-**thort**/) *archaic* it seems to me. [Old English]

method *n.* **1** a special form of procedure esp. in any branch of mental activity. **2** orderliness. **3** a scheme of classification. **4** *Theatr.* a technique of acting based on the actor's thorough emotional identification with the character. [from Greek *methodos* 'pursuit of knowledge']

methodical *adj.* (also **methodic**) characterized by method or order. □ **methodically** *adv.*

Methodist ● *n.* **1** a member of any of several Protestant religious bodies (now united) originating in the 18th-c. Wesleyan evangelistic movement. **2** (**methodist**) a person who follows or advocates a particular method or system of procedure. ● *adj.* of or relating to Methodists or Methodism. [related to METHOD] □ **Methodism** *n.*

methodology *n.* (*pl.* **-ies**) **1** the science of method. **2** a body of methods used in a particular branch of activity. [from French *méthodologie*] □ **methodological** *adj.* **methodologically** *adv.* **methodologist** *n.*

methought *past* of METHINKS.

meths *n. Brit. colloq.* methylated spirit.

methyl *n. Chem.* the monovalent hydrocarbon radical –CH_3, present in many organic compounds. [from German] □ **methylic** *adj.*

methyl alcohol *n.* = METHANOL.

methylate *v.tr.* **1** mix or impregnate with methanol. **2** introduce a methyl group into (a molecule or compound). □ **methylation** *n.*

methylated spirit *n.* (also **methylated spirits**) alcohol saturated with methanol to make it unfit for drinking and exempt from duty.

methylbenzene *n.* = TOLUENE.

meticulous *adj.* **1** giving great or excessive attention to details. **2** very careful and precise. [from Latin *meticulosus*] □ **meticulously** *adv.* **meticulousness** *n.*

métier /**met**-yay/ *n.* **1** one's trade, profession, or department of activity. **2** one's forte. [French]

metonymy *n.* the substitution of the name of an attribute or adjunct for that of the thing meant (e.g. *Crown* for *king*). [from Greek *metōnumia* 'change of name'] □ **metonym** *n.* **metonymic** *adj.* **metonymically** *adv.*

metre[1] *n.* (*US* **meter**) a metric unit and the base SI unit of linear measure, equal to about 39.4 inches. [from Greek *metron* 'measure'] □ **metreage** *n.*

metre[2] *n.* (*US* **meter**) **1 a** any form of poetic rhythm, determined by the number and length of feet in a line. **b** a metrical group or measure. **2** the basic pulse and rhythm of a piece of music. [from Greek *metron* 'measure']

metre-kilogram-second *adj.* denoting a system of measure using the metre, kilogram, and second as the basic units of length, mass, and time.

metric *adj.* **1** of or based on the metre; esp. relating to the decimal measuring system with the metre, litre, and gram as units. See also SI 2. **2** of or relating to measurement; metrical.

metrical *adj.* **1** of, relating to, or composed in poetical or musical metre. **2** of or involving measurement. □ **metrically** *adv.*

metricate *v.intr. & tr.* change or adapt to a metric system of measurement. □ **metrication** *n.*

metric hundredweight see HUNDREDWEIGHT 2.

metric ton *n.* (also **metric tonne**) 1,000 kilograms (2,205 lb).

metro *n.* (*pl.* **-os**) an underground railway system in a city, esp. Paris. [abbreviation of French *métropolitain* 'metropolitan']

metronome *n. Mus.* a device marking time at a selected rate by giving a regular tick. [from Greek *metron* 'measure' + *nomos* 'law'] □ **metronomic** *adj.*

metropolis *n.* **1** the chief city of a country. **2** a metropolitan bishop's see. **3** a town or city as a centre of activity. [from Greek *mētropolis* 'parent state']

metropolitan ● *adj.* **1** of or relating to a metropolis, esp. as distinct from its environs (*metropolitan New York*). **2** of or forming part of a mother country as distinct from its colonies etc. (*metropolitan France*). **3** of an ecclesiastical metropolis. ● *n.* **1** (in full **metropolitan bishop**) a bishop having authority over the bishops of a province. **2** an inhabitant of a metropolis. [from Greek *mētropolitēs*] □ **metropolitanate** *n.* (in sense 1 of *n.*). **metropolitanism** *n.*

metropolitan county *n. hist.* (in England) each of six units of local government centred on a large urban area (in existence since 1974, although their councils were abolished in 1986).

metropolitan magistrate *n. Brit.* a paid professional magistrate in London.

mettle *n.* **1** the quality of a person's disposition or temperament (*a chance to show your mettle*). **2** natural ardour. **3** spirit, courage. □ **on one's mettle** incited to do one's best. [variant of METAL *n.*] □ **mettled** *adj.* (also in *comb.*). **mettlesome** *adj.*

meunière /mern-**yair**/ *adj.* (esp. of fish) cooked or served in lightly browned butter with lemon juice and parsley. [from French (*à la*) *meunière* '(in the manner of) a miller's wife']

MeV *abbr.* mega-electronvolt(s).

mew[1] ● *v.intr.* (of a cat, gull, etc.) utter its characteristic cry. ● *n.* this sound, esp. of a cat. [Middle English]

mew[2] ● *n.* a cage for hawks, esp. while moulting. ● *v.tr.* **1** put (a hawk) in a cage. **2** (often foll. by *up*) shut up; confine. [based on Old French *muer* 'to moult']

mew[3] *n.* a gull. [Old English]

mewl *v.intr.* (also **mule**) **1** cry feebly; whimper. **2** mew like a cat.

mews *n. Brit.* a set of stabling esp. round an open yard, often converted into dwellings. [pl. of MEW[2], originally referring to royal stables on the site of hawks' mews at Charing Cross, London]

Mexican ● *n.* **1 a** a native or national of Mexico. **b** a person of Mexican descent. **2** an indigenous language of Mexico. ● *adj.* **1** of or relating to Mexico or its people. **2** of Mexican descent. [from Spanish *mexicano*]

Mexican wave *n. Brit.* a rising-and-falling effect produced by successive sections of a crowd standing and sitting. [named because of its popularity at the 1986 soccer World Cup finals in Mexico City: the practice is older]

mezuzah *n.* a parchment inscribed with religious texts and attached in a case to the doorpost of a Jewish house as a sign of faith.

mezzanine /**mez**-ă-neen/ ● *n.* (also *attrib.*) **1** a low storey between two others (usu. between the ground and first floors). **2** *N. Amer. Theatr.* a dress circle. ● *adj. Commerce* designating or relating to unsecured, higher-yielding loans that are subordinate to bank and secured loans but rank above equity. [based on Latin *medianus* 'median']

mezzo /**met**-soh/ *Mus.* ● *adv.* half, moderately. ● *n.* (in full **mezzo-soprano**) (*pl.* **-os**) **1 a** a female singing voice between soprano and contralto. **b** a singer with this voice. **2** a part written for mezzo-soprano. [Italian]

mezzo forte *adj. & adv.* fairly loud.

mezzo piano *adj. & adv.* fairly soft.

mezzotint /**met**-soh-tint/ ● *n.* **1** a method of printing or engraving in which the surface of a plate is roughened by scraping to produce tones and halftones. **2** a print produced by this process. [from Italian *mezzo* 'half' + *tinto* 'tint'] □ **mezzotinter** *n.*

MF *abbr.* medium frequency.

mf *abbr.* mezzo forte.

Mg *symb. Chem.* the element magnesium.

mg *abbr.* milligram(s).

Mgr. *abbr.* **1** Manager. **2** *Monseigneur.* **3** Monsignor.

MHz *abbr.* megahertz.

MI *abbr. Brit. hist.* Military Intelligence.

mi var. of ME[2].

mi. *abbr.* mile(s).

miaow (also **meow**) ● *n.* the characteristic cry of a cat. ● *v.intr.* make this cry.

miasma *n.* (*pl.* **miasmata** or **miasmas**) *archaic* an infectious or noxious vapour. [Greek, literally 'defilement'] □ **miasmal** *adj.* **miasmic** *adj.*

miaul *v.intr.* cry like a cat; mew. [from French *miauler*]

mica /**my**-kă/ *n.* ◄ any of a group of silicate minerals with a layered structure, esp. muscovite. ▷ AGGREGATE. [Latin, literally 'crumb'] □ **micaceous** *adj.*

mice *pl.* of MOUSE.

MICA: MUSCOVITE

Michaelmas /**mik**-ĕl-măs/ *n.* the feast of St Michael, 29 September. [Old English *sancte Micheles mæsse* 'Saint Michael's Mass']

M

M

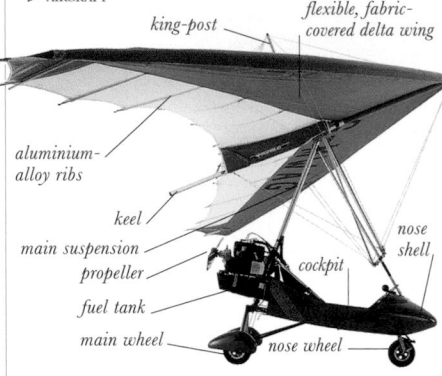

Michaelmas daisy n. ◀ an autumn-flowering aster.

mickey n. (also **micky**) □ **take the mickey** (often foll. by *out of*) *Brit. slang* tease, mock, ridicule [20th-century coinage] □ **mickey-taking** n.

MICHAELMAS DAISY
(*Aster novi-belgii*)

Mickey Finn n. *slang* **1** a drink adulterated with a narcotic or laxative. **2** the adulterant itself. [20th-century coinage]

Mickey Mouse adj. *colloq.* **1** of inferior quality. **2** ridiculous, trivial. [cartoon character created by Walt Disney, American cartoonist, 1901–66]

mickle n. (also **muckle**) *archaic* or *Sc.* a large amount. □ **many a little makes a mickle** (also *erroneous* **many a mickle makes a muckle**) many small amounts accumulate to make a large amount. [from Old Norse *mikell*]

micro n. (pl. **-os**) *colloq.* **1** = MICROCOMPUTER. **2** = MICROPROCESSOR.

micro- *comb. form* **1** small (*microchip*). **2** denoting a factor of one-millionth (10^{-6}) (*microgram*). [from Greek *mikros* 'small']

microanalysis n. the quantitative analysis of chemical compounds using a sample of a few milligrams.

microbe n. a micro-organism (esp. a bacterium causing disease or fermentation). [from Greek *mikros* 'small' + *bios* 'life'] □ **microbial** adj. **microbic** adj.

microbiology n. the scientific study of micro-organisms. □ **microbiological** adj. **microbiologically** adv. **microbiologist** n.

microchip n. a tiny wafer of semiconducting material used to make an integrated circuit.

microcircuit n. a minute electric circuit, esp. an integrated circuit. □ **microcircuitry** n.

microclimate n. ▼ the climate of a small local area or enclosed space. □ **microclimatic** adj. **microclimatically** adv.

microcomputer n. a small computer that contains a microprocessor as its central processor.

microcosm n. **1** (often foll. by *of*) a miniature representation. **2** humankind viewed as the epitome of the universe. **3** any complex unity viewed in this way. [from Greek *mikros kosmos* 'little world'] □ **microcosmic** adj.

microdot n. a microphotograph of a document etc. reduced to the size of a dot.

microeconomics n. the branch of economics dealing with individual commodities, producers, etc. □ **microeconomic** adj.

microelectronics n. the design, manufacture, and use of microchips and microcircuits. □ **microelectronic** adj.

microfiche /**my**-kroh-feesh/ n. (pl. same or **micro-**fiches) a flat rectangular piece of film bearing microphotographs of documents etc.

microfilm n. a length of film bearing microphotographs of documents etc.

microform n. microphotographic reproduction on film or paper of a manuscript etc.

micrograph n. a photograph taken by means of a microscope.

microinstruction n. a machine-code instruction that effects a basic operation in a computer system.

microlight n. ▼ a very small, light, low-speed, one- or two-seater aircraft with an open frame. ▷ AIRCRAFT

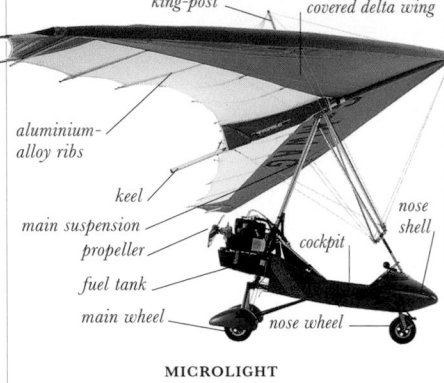

flexible, fabric-covered delta wing

king-post

aluminium-alloy ribs

keel

main suspension

propeller

fuel tank

main wheel

cockpit

nose shell

nose wheel

MICROLIGHT

micromesh n. (often *attrib.*) material, esp. nylon, consisting of a very fine mesh.

component being measured

measuring anvil

thimble scale

barrel scale

thimble

MICROMETER

micrometer /my-krom-i-ter/ n. ◀ a gauge for accurately measuring small distances, thicknesses, etc. □ **micrometry** n.

micrometre /**my**-kroh-mee-ter/ n. (*US* **micrometer**) one millionth of a metre.

micron n. one-millionth of a metre. [Greek *mikron*, literally 'small thing']

micronutrient n. a chemical element or substance required in trace amounts for the growth and development of living organisms.

micro-organism n. a microscopic organism, esp. a bacterium or virus.

microphone n. ▶ an instrument for converting sound waves into electrical energy variations that can be reconverted into sound after transmission by wire or radio or after recording.

diaphragm

wire coil

magnet

power cable

MICROPHONE:
CUTAWAY VIEW OF A MOVING
COIL MICROPHONE

microphotograph n. a photograph reduced to a very small size.

microprocessor n. an integrated circuit that contains all the functions of a computer's central processing unit. ▷ COMPUTER

microprogram n. a microinstruction program that controls the functions of a central processing unit of a computer.

microscope n. ▼ an instrument with lenses for magnifying objects and revealing details invisible to the naked eye.

microscopic adj. **1** so small as to be visible only with a microscope. **2** extremely small. **3** regarded in terms of small units. **4** of the microscope. □ **microscopical** adj. (in sense 4). **microscopically** adv.

microscopy /my-kros-kŏ-pi/ n. the use of the microscope. □ **microscopist** n.

microsecond n. one-millionth of a second.

microstructure n. (in a metal or other material) the arrangement of crystals etc. which can be made visible and examined with a microscope.

eyepiece

focusing knob

objective lens

specimen

glass slide

condenser lens

mirror to illuminate slide

base

light

MICROSCOPE: OPTICAL MICROSCOPE

microsurgery n. intricate surgery performed using microscopes, enabling the tissues to be operated on with miniaturized precision instruments. □ **microsurgical** adj.

microswitch n. a switch that can be operated rapidly by a small movement.

microwave ● n. **1** an electromagnetic wave with a wavelength in the range 0.001–0.3m. ▷ ELECTROMAGNETIC RADIATION. **2** (in full **microwave oven**) ▲ an oven that uses microwaves to cook or heat food. ● v.tr. cook in a microwave oven. □ **microwaveable** adj. (also **microwavable**).

micturition n. *formal* or *Med.* urination. [based on Latin *micturire* 'to desire to urinate']

mid prep. *poet.* = AMID.

mid- *comb. form* **1** that is the middle of (*in mid-air*). **2** that is in the middle; medium, half. [Old English, related to Greek *mesos* 'middle']

midbrain n. *Anat.* a small central part of the brainstem, developing from the middle of the primitive or embryonic brain; also called *mesencephalon*. ▷ BRAINSTEM

midday n. the middle of the day; noon.

midden n. **1** a dunghill. **2** a refuse heap. [Middle English]

middle ● *attrib.adj.* **1** at an equal distance from the extremities of a thing. **2** intermediate in rank, quality, etc. **3** average (*of middle height*). **4** (of a language) of the period between the old and modern forms. ● n. **1** (often foll. by *of*) the middle point or position or part. **2** a person's waist. ● v.tr. **1** place in the middle. **2** *Football* return (the ball) from the wing to the midfield. □ **in the middle of** (often foll. by verbal noun) in the process of; during. [Old English]

middle age n. the period between youth and old age, about 45 to 60. □ **middle-aged** adj.

Middle Ages n.pl. the period of European history esp. from *c.*1000 to 1453.

middle-age spread n. (also **middle-aged spread**) the increased bodily girth often associated with middle age.

MICROCLIMATE

Naturally occurring topographical features in an area can create a microclimate that differs greatly from the climate of the surrounding region. Features in a small area, such as a garden, can also be manipulated to create specific conditions. For example, beds can be sloped to catch the sun.

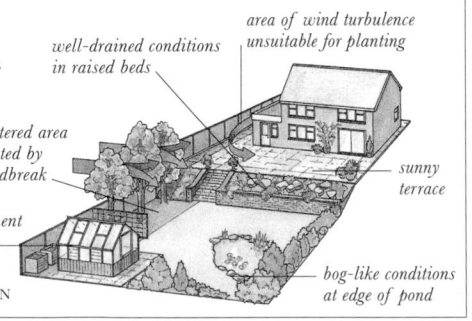

well-drained conditions in raised beds

area of wind turbulence unsuitable for planting

sheltered area created by windbreak

protected environment for tender plants

sunny terrace

bog-like conditions at edge of pond

MICROCLIMATES IN A GARDEN

MICROWAVE OVEN

In a microwave oven, high-frequency electromagnetic waves generated by a magnetron tube are bounced around the oven's metal walled interior. The waves penetrate food, causing water, fat, and sugar molecules to vibrate, thus producing heat. Heat is transferred to the centre of the food by conduction.

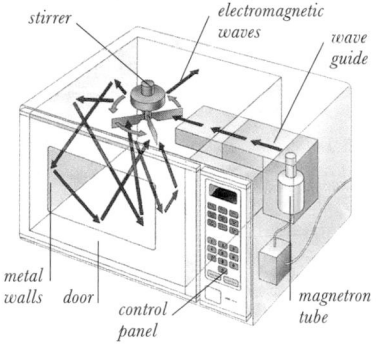

FEATURES OF A MICROWAVE OVEN

Middle America *n.* **1** Mexico and Central America. **2** the middle class in the US, esp. as a conservative political force.

middlebrow *colloq.* ● *adj.* claiming to be or regarded as only moderately intellectual. ● *n.* a middlebrow person.

middle C ● *n. Mus.* the C near the middle of the piano keyboard, the note between the treble and bass staves.

middle class ● *n.* the class of society between the upper and the lower, including professional and business workers and their families. ● *adj.* (**middle-class**) of the middle class.

middle course *n.* a compromise between two extremes.

middle distance *n.* **1** (in a painted or actual landscape) the part between the foreground and the background. **2** *Athletics* a race distance of esp. between 800 and 5,000 metres.

middle ear *n.* the cavity of the central part of the ear behind the drum. ▷ EAR

Middle East *n.* (prec. by *the*) an extensive area of SW Asia and northern Africa, stretching from the Mediterranean to Pakistan and including the Arabian peninsula. □ **Middle Eastern** *adj.*

Middle English *n.* the English language from *c.*1150 to 1500.

middle finger *n.* the finger next to the forefinger.

middle ground *n.* the thought, area, or path, tending to moderation and compromise.

middle-income *attrib.adj.* **1** of or relating to the group of people earning average salaries. **2** with an average national income (used esp. of certain Third World countries).

middleman *n.* (*pl.* **-men**) **1** a trader who handles a commodity between its producer and its consumer. **2** an intermediary.

middle management *n.* **1** the level in an organization between senior and junior management. **2** the managers at this level.

middle name *n.* **1** a person's name placed after the first name and before the surname. **2** a person's most characteristic quality (*sobriety is my middle name*).

middle-of-the-road *adj.* **1** (of a person, course of action, etc.) moderate; avoiding extremes. **2** (of music) intended to appeal to a wide audience; unadventurous.

middle school *n.* a school for children from about 9 to 13 years old.

middle-sized *adj.* of medium size.

middle way *n.* = MIDDLE COURSE.

middleweight *n.* **1** a weight in certain sports intermediate between welterweight and light heavyweight. **2** a boxer etc. of this weight.

Middle West *n.* = MIDWEST.

middling ● *adj.* **1** moderately good (esp. *fair to middling*). **2** second-rate. ● *adv.* fairly or moderately (*middling good*). □ **middlingly** *adv.*

Mideast *n. US* = MIDDLE EAST.

midfield *n. Football* the central part of the pitch, away from the goals. □ **midfielder** *n.* ▷ FOOTBALL

midge *n.* **1** any small gnatlike dipterous fly of the family Chironomidae, often seen in dancing swarms near water. **2** any similar fly, esp. a tiny biting fly of the family Ceratopogonidae, with piercing mouthparts. [Old English]

midget *n.* **1** an extremely small person or thing. **2** (*attrib.*) very small. [based on MIDGE]

MIDI /mid-i/ *n.* a system for using combinations of electronic equipment, esp. audio and computer equipment. [acronym from *musical instrument digital interface*]

midi *n.* (*pl.* **midis**) a garment of medium length, usu. reaching to mid-calf.

midi- *comb. form* medium-sized; of medium length.

midi system *n.* a set of compact stacking hi-fi equipment components.

midland ● *n.* **1** (**the Midlands**) the inland counties of central England. **2** the middle part of a country. ● *adj.* **1** (also **Midland**) of or in the Midlands. **2** of or in the midland. **3** Mediterranean. □ **Midlander** *n.*

mid-life *n.* middle age (often *attrib.*: *mid-life planning*).

mid-life crisis *n.* an emotional crisis of self-confidence that can occur in early middle age.

midline *n.* a median line, or plane of bilateral symmetry.

midmost *adj. & adv.* in the very middle.

midnight *n.* **1** the middle of the night; 12 o'clock at night. **2** intense darkness.

midnight blue ● *n.* a very dark blue. ● *adj.* (hyphenated when *attrib.*) of this colour.

midnight sun *n.* the sun visible at midnight during the summer in polar regions.

mid-off *n. Cricket* a fielder or fielding position near the bowler on the off side. ▷ CRICKET

mid-on *n. Cricket* a fielder or fielding position near the bowler on the on side. ▷ CRICKET

midrib *n.* ▼ the central rib of a leaf.

midrib

MIDRIB OF A BEECH LEAF

midriff *n.* **1 a** the region of the front of the body between the thorax and abdomen. **b** the diaphragm. **2** a garment or part of a garment covering the abdomen. [Old English, based on *hrif* 'belly']

midship *n.* the middle part of a ship or boat.

midshipman *n.* (*pl.* **-men**) **1** *Brit.* a naval officer of rank between naval cadet and sub lieutenant. **2** *US* a naval cadet.

midships *adv.* = AMIDSHIPS.

midst ● *prep. poet.* amidst. ● *n.* middle (now only in phrs. as below). □ **in the midst of** among; in the middle of. **in our** (or **your** or **their**) **midst** among us (or you or them). [Middle English]

midstream ● *n.* the middle of a stream, river, etc. ● *adv.* (also **in midstream**) in the middle of an action etc.

midsummer *n.* the period of or near the summer solstice.

Midsummer Day *n.* (also **Midsummer's Day**) 24 June.

midsummer madness *n.* extreme folly.

midway *adv.* in or towards the middle of the distance between two points.

midweek ● *n.* the middle of the week. ● *adj. & adv.* occurring at this time.

Midwest *n.* (in the US) the region of northern states from Ohio west to the Rocky mountains. □ **Midwestern** *adj.*

midwicket *n. Cricket* a fielder or fielding position on the leg side opposite the middle of the pitch. ▷ CRICKET

midwife *n.* (*pl.* **-wives**) a person trained to assist women in childbirth. [Middle English] □ **midwifery** *n.*

fertilized eggs

midwife toad *n.* ◄ a European toad, *Alytes obstetricans*, in which the male carries the developing eggs on his hind legs.

MIDWIFE TOAD (MALE)
(*Alytes obstetricans*)

midwinter *n.* the period of or near the winter solstice.

mien /meen/ *n. literary* a person's look or bearing.

miff *colloq.* ● *v.tr.* (usu. in *passive*) put out of humour; offend. ● *n.* **1** a petty quarrel. **2** a huff.

might[1] *past* of MAY, used esp.: **1** in reported speech, expressing possibility (*said he might come*) or permission (*asked if I might leave*). **2** (foll. by perfect infin.) expressing a possibility based on a condition not fulfilled (*if you'd looked you might have found it*). **3** (foll. by present infin. or perfect infin.) expressing complaint about nonfulfilment of an obligation or expectation (*they might have asked*). **4** expressing a request (*you might call in at the butcher's*). **5** *colloq.* **a** = MAY 1 (*it might be true*). **b** (in tentative questions) = MAY 2 (*might I have the pleasure of this dance?*). **c** = MAY 4 (*who might you be?*). □ **might as well** expressing that it is probably at least as desirable to do a thing as not to do it (*you might as well try*).

might[2] *n.* **1** great bodily or mental strength. **2** power to enforce one's will (usu. in contrast with *right*). [Old English]

might-have-been *n. colloq.* **1** a past possibility that no longer applies. **2** a person who could have been more eminent.

mightn't *contr.* might not.

mighty ● *adj.* (**mightier**, **mightiest**) **1** powerful or strong, in body, mind, or influence. **2** massive, bulky. **3** *colloq.* great, considerable. ● *adv. colloq.* very (*mighty difficult*). □ **mightily** *adv.* **mightiness** *n.*

mignonette /min-yŏn-et/ *n.* **1** ► any of various plants of the genus *Reseda*, with fragrant grey-green flowers. **2** a light fine narrow pillow lace. [from French *mignonnette* 'very tiny']

migraine *n.* a recurrent throbbing headache that usually affects one side of the head, often with nausea and visual disturbance. [originally referring to a headache on one side of the head; based on Greek *hēmikrania*, literally 'half skull']

migrant ● *adj.* that migrates. ● *n.* a migrant person or animal, esp. a bird.

migrate *v.intr.* **1** (of people) move from one place of abode to another, esp. in a different country.

MIGNONETTE: WILD MIGNONETTE (*Reseda lutea*)

M

M

2 (of an animal, esp. a bird or fish) change its area of habitation with the seasons. **3** move under natural forces. [based on Latin *migratus* 'moved (abode)'] □ **migration** *n.* **migrational** *adj.* **migrator** *n.* **migratory** *adj.*

mihrab /mee-**rahb**/ *n.* ▶ a niche or slab in a mosque, used to show the direction of Mecca. [from Arabic *miḥrāb* 'praying-place']

mikado /mi-**kah**-doh/ *n.* (*pl.* **-os**) *hist.* the emperor of Japan. [Japanese, from *mi* 'august' + *kado* 'gate']

mike *n. colloq.* a microphone.

mil *n. colloq.* millimetre.

milady *n.* (*pl.* **-ies**) **1** an English noblewoman or great lady. **2** a form used in speaking of or to such a person.

milage var. of MILEAGE.

Milanese ● *adj.* of or relating to Milan in N. Italy. ● *n.* (*pl.* same) a native of Milan.

milch *adj.* (of a domestic mammal) giving or kept for milk. [Middle English, from earlier *thrimilce* 'May', when cows could be milked three times a day]

milch cow *n.* a source of easy profit, esp. a person.

mild ● *adj.* **1** (esp. of a person) gentle and inoffensive. **2** (of a rule, illness, etc.) moderate; not severe. **3** (of the weather) moderately warm. **4** not sharp or strong in taste etc. **5** (of medicine) operating gently. **6** lacking energy or vivacity. ● *n. Brit.* beer not strongly flavoured with hops. [Old English] □ **mildish** *adj.* **mildness** *n.*

mildew ● *n.* **1** a destructive growth of minute fungi on plants. **2** a similar growth on paper etc. exposed to damp. ● *v.tr. & intr.* taint or be tainted with mildew. [Old English]

mildly *adv.* in a mild fashion. □ **to put it mildly** as an understatement (implying the reality is more extreme).

mild steel *n.* steel containing a small percentage of carbon, strong and tough but not readily tempered.

mile *n.* **1** (also **statute mile**) a unit of linear measure equal to 1,760 yards (approx. 1.609 kilometres). **2** *hist.* a Roman measure of 1,000 paces (approx. 1,620 yards). **3** (in *pl.*) *colloq.* a great distance or amount (*miles better*). **4** a race extending over a mile. □ **miles away** *colloq.* lost in thought. [based on Latin *mil(l)ia* 'thousands' (see sense 2)]

mileage *n.* (also **milage**) **1** a number of miles travelled, esp. by a vehicle per unit of fuel. **2** travelling expenses (per mile). **3** *colloq.* benefit, profit, advantage.

miler *n. colloq.* a person or horse qualified or trained specially to run a mile.

milestone *n.* **1** a stone set up beside a road to mark a distance in miles. **2** a significant event or stage in a life, project, etc.

milfoil *n.* **1** ▶ the common yarrow, *Achillea millefolium*, with small white to deep pink flowers and finely divided leaves. **2** (in full **water milfoil**) an aquatic plant of the genus *Myriophyllum* with whorls of fine leaves. [from Latin *mille* 'thousand' + *folium* 'leaf']

miliary *adj.* **1** like a millet seed in size or form. **2** (of a disease) having as a symptom a rash with lesions resembling millet seed.

milieu /meel-**yer**/ *n.* (*pl.* **milieux** /-yerz/ or **milieus**) one's environment or social surroundings. [French, from *mi* 'mid' + *lieu* 'place']

militant ● *adj.* **1** aggressively active esp. in support of a (usu. political) cause. **2** engaged in warfare. ● *n.* a militant person, esp. a political activist. [from Latin *militant-* 'waging war'] □ **militancy** *n.* **militantly** *adv.*

militaria *n.pl.* military articles of historical interest.

MIHRAB IN THE GREAT MOSQUE AT CORDOBA, SPAIN

militarism *n.* **1** the spirit or tendencies of a professional soldier. **2** undue prevalence of the military spirit or ideals. □ **militarist** *n.* **militaristic** *adj.*

militarize *v.tr.* (also **-ise**) **1** equip with military resources. **2** make military or warlike. **3** imbue with militarism. □ **militarization** *n.*

military ● *adj.* of, relating to, or characteristic of soldiers or armed forces. ● *n.* (treated as *sing.* or *pl.*; prec. by *the*) members of the armed forces, as distinct from civilians and the police. [from Latin *militaris*] □ **militarily** *adv.*

military honours *n.pl.* marks of respect paid by troops at the burial of a soldier, to royalty, etc.

military police *n.* (treated as *pl.*) a corps responsible for police and disciplinary duties in the army. □ **military policeman** *n.*

military tribune see TRIBUNE[1] 2b.

militate *v.intr.* (usu. foll. by *against*) (of facts or evidence) have force or effect. [based on Latin *militatus* 'served as a soldier']

■ **Usage** Care should be taken not to confuse *militate* 'have force or effect' with *mitigate* 'make less intense or severe'. Both words are illustrated by the sentence *The heavy rains militated against their attempts to mitigate the problem of flooding*.

militia /mi-**lish**-ă/ *n.* a military force, esp. one raised from the civil population and supplementing a regular army in an emergency. [Latin, literally 'military service'] □ **militiaman** *n.* (*pl.* **-men**)

milk ● *n.* **1** an opaque white fluid secreted by female mammals for the nourishment of their young. **2** the milk of cows, goats, or sheep as food. **3** a milklike juice e.g. in the coconut. ● *v.tr.* **1** draw milk from (a cow etc.). **2** exploit (a person or situation) to the utmost. **3** extract sap, venom, etc. from. □ **cry over spilt** (or *US* **spilled**) **milk** lament an irremediable loss or error. **in milk** secreting milk. [Old English] □ **milker** *n.*

milk and honey *n.* abundance, prosperity.

milk and water *n.* a feeble or insipid or mawkish discourse or sentiment.

milk bar *n.* a snack bar selling milk drinks and other refreshments.

milk chocolate *n.* chocolate made with milk.

milk fever *n.* **1** an acute illness in female cows, goats, etc. that have just produced young, caused by calcium deficiency. **2** *Med.* a fever in women caused by infection after childbirth (formerly supposed to be due to the swelling of the breasts with milk).

milk float *n. Brit.* a small usu. electric vehicle used in delivering milk.

milkmaid *n.* a girl or woman who milks cows or works in a dairy.

milkman *n.* (*pl.* **-men**) a person who sells or delivers milk.

Milk of Magnesia *n. Brit. propr.* a white suspension of hydrated magnesium carbonate usu. in water as an antacid or laxative.

milk powder *n.* milk dehydrated by evaporation.

milk pudding *n. Brit.* a pudding of rice, sago, tapioca, etc., baked with milk in a dish.

milk round *n.* **1** a fixed route on which milk is delivered regularly. **2** a regular trip or tour involving calls at several places.

MILFOIL: YARROW (*Achillea millefolium*)

milk run *n.* a routine expedition or service journey.

milk shake *n.* a drink of milk, flavouring, etc., mixed by shaking or whisking.

milksop *n.* a spiritless man or youth.

milk tooth *n.* a temporary tooth in young mammals.

milk train *n.* a train chiefly transporting milk, usu. very early in the morning.

milky *adj.* (**milkier**, **milkiest**) **1** of, like, or mixed with milk. **2** ◀ (of a gem or liquid) cloudy, not clear. **3** effeminate; weakly amiable. □ **milkiness** *n.*

Milky Way *n.* ▶ a faint band of light crossing the night sky, made up of many distant stars forming the bulk of our Galaxy. ▷ GALAXY

MILKY QUARTZ

mill ● *n.* **1 a** a building fitted with a mechanical apparatus for grinding corn. **b** ▼ such an apparatus. **2** an apparatus for grinding any solid substance to powder etc. **3 a** a building fitted with machinery for manufacturing processes etc. (*cotton mill*). **b** such machinery. ● *v.* **1** *tr.* process in a mill, esp. grind (corn), produce (flour), or hull (seeds) in a mill. **2** *tr.* produce regular ribbed markings on the edge of (a coin). **3** *tr.* cut or shape (metal) with a rotating tool. **4** *intr.* (often foll. by *about*, *around*) (of people or animals) move aimlessly, esp. in a confused mass. □ **go** (or **put**) **through the mill** undergo (or cause to undergo) intensive work, suffering, etc. [from Latin *mola* 'grindstone, mill'] □ **millable** *adj.*

grain to be milled

milled flour

water supply

millstone

horizontal water wheel drives millstone

MILL: MODEL OF A GREEK MILL, *c.*85 BC

millefeuille /meel-**fĕ**'i/ *n.* a rich confection of puff pastry split and filled with jam, cream, etc. [French, literally 'thousand-leaf']

millenary ● *n.* (*pl.* **-ies**) **1** a period of 1,000 years. **2** the festival of the 1,000th anniversary of a person or thing. **3** = MILLENARIAN *n.* ● *adj.* of or relating to a millenary. [from Late Latin *millenarius* 'consisting of a thousand']

millennium *n.* (*pl.* **millenniums** or **millennia**) **1** a period of 1,000 years. **2** *Theol.* the prophesied 1,000-year reign of Christ in person (Rev. 20:1–5). **3** a period of happiness and prosperity. [based on Latin *mille* 'thousand'] □ **millennial** *adj.* **millennialism** *n.* **millennialist** *n. & adj.*

millepede var. of MILLIPEDE.

miller *n.* **1** the proprietor or tenant of a corn mill. **2** a person who works or owns a mill. [Middle English]

millesimal ● *adj.* **1** thousandth. **2** of or belonging to a thousandth. **3** of or dealing with thousandths. ● *n.* a thousandth part. [from Latin *millesimus*]

millet *n.* **1** a cereal plant bearing a large crop of small nutritious seeds. **2** the seed of this. ▷ GRAIN. [from Latin *milium*]

milli- *comb. form* a thousand, esp. denoting a factor of one-thousandth. [from Latin *mille* 'thousand']

milliampere *n.* one-thousandth of an ampere, a measure for small electrical currents.

MILKY WAY

The Milky Way is made up of the combined light of many of the 200 billion stars and nebulae in our Galaxy. The Galaxy consists of a central bulge surrounded by a thin disc and a spheroidal halo. The central bulge contains mainly older red and yellow stars. Matter in the disc is aggregated into several spiral arms which contain young hot blue stars and nebulae. The oldest stars are situated in the sparsely populated halo. Our solar system is in one of the spiral arms (the Orion arm), about halfway out from the centre, and from this position our view of the galactic centre is completely obscured by dust clouds.

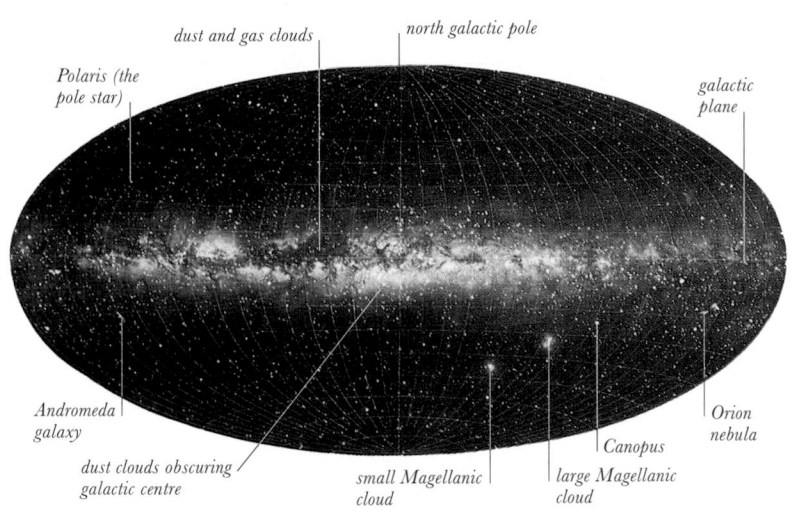

MAP OF THE GALAXY VIEWED FROM THE EARTH

north galactic pole
dust and gas clouds
Polaris (the pole star)
galactic plane
Andromeda galaxy
dust clouds obscuring galactic centre
small Magellanic cloud
large Magellanic cloud
Canopus
Orion nebula

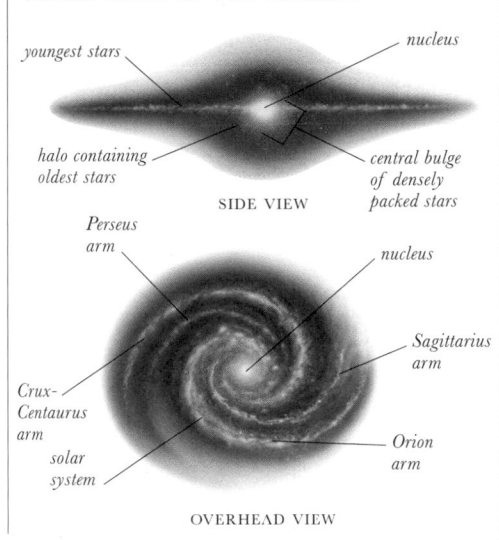

OTHER VIEWS OF THE GALAXY

youngest stars
nucleus
halo containing oldest stars
central bulge of densely packed stars
SIDE VIEW

Perseus arm
nucleus
Crux-Centaurus arm
solar system
Sagittarius arm
Orion arm
OVERHEAD VIEW

---

milliard *n. Brit.* one thousand million. [French]

■ **Usage** The term *milliard* has been largely superseded by *billion*.

millibar *n.* the cgs unit of atmospheric pressure equivalent to 100 pascals.

milligram *n.* (also **milligramme**) one-thousandth of a gram.

millilitre *n.* (*US* **milliliter**) one-thousandth of a litre (0.002 pint).

millimetre *n.* (*US* **millimeter**) one-thousandth of a metre (0.039 in.).

milliner *n.* a person who makes or sells women's hats. □ **millinery** *n.*

million ● *n.* (*pl.* same or (in sense 2) **millions**) (in *sing.* prec. by *a* or *one*) **1** a thousand thousand (1,000,000). **2** (in *pl.*) *colloq.* a very large number (*millions of times*). **3 a** *Brit.* a million pounds. **b** *N. Amer.* a million dollars. ● *adj.* that amount to a million. [from Old French] □ **millionth** *adj. & n.*

millionaire *n.* (*fem.* **millionairess**) **1** a person whose assets are worth at least one million pounds, dollars, etc. **2** a person of great wealth.

millipede *n.* (also **millepede**) ► any arthropod of the class Diplopoda, having a long segmented body with two pairs of legs on each segment. [from Latin *millepeda* 'woodlouse']

millisecond *n.* one-thousandth of a second.

MILLIPEDE

millivolt *n.* one-thousandth of a volt.

millpond *n.* a pool of water retained by a mill-dam for the operation of a mill. □ **like a millpond** (of a stretch of water) very calm.

mill-race *n.* a current of water that drives a mill-wheel.

millstone *n.* **1** each of two circular stones used for grinding corn. ▷ MILL. **2** a heavy burden or responsibility.

millstream *n.* = MILL-RACE.

mill-wheel *n.* a wheel used to drive a water mill.

milometer *n. Brit.* an instrument for measuring the number of miles travelled by a vehicle.

milord *n. hist.* an Englishman travelling in Europe in aristocratic style.

milt *n.* **1** the spleen in mammals. **2** an analogous organ in other vertebrates. **3** a sperm-filled reproductive gland or the sperm of a male fish. [Old English]

mime ● *n.* **1** theatrical expression by gesture without using words. **2** a theatrical performance using this technique. **3** (also **mime artist**) a practitioner of mime. ● *v.* **1** *tr.* (also *absol.*) convey (an idea or emotion) by gesture without words. **2** *intr.* (often foll. by *to*) (of singers etc.) mouth the words of a song etc. along with a soundtrack. [from Greek *mimos*] □ **mimer** *n.*

mimeograph ● *n.* **1** (often *attrib.*) a duplicating machine which produces copies from a stencil. **2** a copy produced in this way. ● *v.tr.* reproduce (text or diagrams) by this process. [based on Greek *mimeisthai* 'to imitate']

mimesis *n. Biol.* = MIMICRY 3. [from Greek *mimēsis*]

mimetic *adj.* relating to or habitually practising imitation or mimicry. [from Greek *mimētikos* 'imitation'] □ **mimetically** *adv.*

mimic ● *v.tr.* (**mimicked**, **mimicking**) **1** imitate (a person etc.) esp. to entertain or ridicule. **2** copy minutely or servilely. **3** (of a thing) resemble closely. ● *n.* a person skilled in imitation. [from Greek *mimikos*] □ **mimicker** *n.*

mimicry *n.* (*pl.* **-ies**) **1** the act or art of mimicking. **2** a thing that mimics another. **3** *Biol.* **a** ▼ a close external resemblance of an animal (or part of one) to another animal or to a plant or inanimate object. **b** a similar resemblance in a plant.

mimosa *n.* **1** any leguminous shrub of the genus *Mimosa*, esp. *M. pudica*, having globular usu. yellow flowers. **2** any of various acacia plants with showy yellow flowers. [modern Latin]

mimulus *n.* any flowering plant of the genus *Mimulus*, including musk and the monkey flower.

Min *n.* any of the Chinese languages or dialects spoken in the Fukien province in SE China. [Chinese]

Min. *abbr.* **1** Minister. **2** Ministry.

min. *abbr.* **1** minute(s). **2** minim (fluid measure).

mina var. of MYNAH.

M

MIMICRY

Many examples exist in nature of harmless animals and plants that have developed the appearance or behaviour of a dangerous species as a defence against predators. For example, the black and yellow banding on a hornet moth gives it a close resemblance to a hornet – a large wasp with a painful sting.

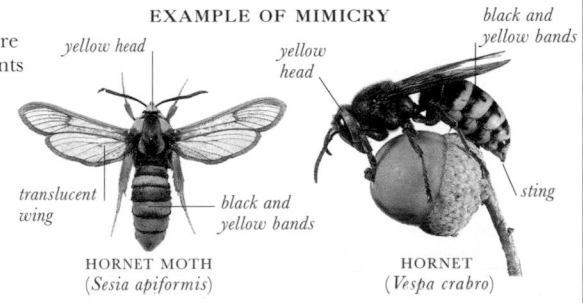

EXAMPLE OF MIMICRY

yellow head
translucent wing
black and yellow bands
HORNET MOTH (*Sesia apiformis*)

yellow head
black and yellow bands
sting
HORNET (*Vespa crabro*)

minaret *n.* ▶ a slender turret connected with a mosque, from which the muezzin calls at hours of prayer. ▷ MOSQUE. [from Arabic *manār(a)*] □ **minareted** *adj.*

minatory *adj.* threatening, menacing. [from Late Latin *minatorius*]

mince ● *v.* **1** *tr.* cut up or grind (esp. meat) into very small pieces. **2** *tr.* (usu. with *neg.*) restrain (one's words etc.) within the bounds of politeness. **3** *intr.* (usu. as **mincing** *adj.*) speak or walk with an affected delicacy. ● *n.* esp. *Brit.* minced meat. ▷ CUT. □ **mince matters** (usu. with *neg.*) use polite expressions etc. [from Old French *mincier*] □ **mincer** *n.* **mincingly** *adv.* (in sense 3 of *v.*).

mincemeat *n.* a mixture of currants, sugar, spices, suet, etc. □ **make mincemeat of** utterly defeat (a person, argument, etc.).

mince pie *n.* a usu. small round pie containing mincemeat.

mind ● *n.* **1 a** the seat of awareness, thought, volition, and feeling. **b** attention, concentration (*my mind keeps wandering*). **2** the intellect; intellectual powers. **3** memory (*I can't call it to mind*). **4** one's opinion (*we're of the same mind*). **5** a way of thinking or feeling (*to the Victorian mind*). **6** the focus of one's thoughts or desires (*put one's mind to it*). **7** the state of normal mental functioning (*lose one's mind*). **8** a person as embodying mental faculties (*a great mind*). ● *v.tr.* **1** (usu. with *neg.* or *interrog.*) object to (*I don't mind your being late*). **2 a** take care to (*mind you come on time*). **b** (often foll. by *out*) *Brit.* be careful. **3** have charge of temporarily (*mind the house while I'm away*). **4** concern oneself with (*I try to mind my own business*). **5** give heed to (*mind the step*). **6** *N. Amer. & Ir.* be obedient to (*mind what your mother says*). □ **be in** esp. *N. Amer.* **of**) **two minds** be undecided. **come** (or **spring**) **to mind** (of a thought, idea, etc.) suggest itself. **don't mind me** often *iron.* do as you please. **do you mind!** *iron.* an expression of annoyance. **give a person a piece of one's mind** scold or reproach a person. **have a good** (or **great** or **half a**) **mind to** (often as a threat, usu. unfulfilled) feel tempted to. **have** (**it**) **in mind** intend. **in one's mind's eye** in one's imagination. **mind out for** *Brit.* guard against, avoid. **mind you** an expression used to qualify a previous statement (*I won; mind you, it wasn't easy*). **never mind 1** let alone; not to mention. **2** an expression used to comfort or console. **3** (also **never you mind**) an expression used to evade a question. **open** (or **close**) **one's mind** to be receptive (or unreceptive) to (changes, new ideas, etc.). **out of one's mind** insane. **put a person in mind of** remind a person of. **put** (or **set**) **a person's mind at rest** reassure a person. **spring to mind** = *come to mind*. **to my mind** in my opinion. [Old English]

mind-bending *adj. colloq.* (esp. of a psychedelic drug) influencing or altering one's state of mind.

mind-blowing *adj. slang* **1** confusing, shattering. **2** (esp. of drugs etc.) inducing hallucinations.

mind-boggling *adj.colloq.* overwhelming, startling.

minded *adj.* **1** (in *comb.*) **a** inclined to think in some specified way (*fair-minded*). **b** having a specified kind of mind (*high-minded*). **c** interested in or enthusiastic about a specified thing (*car-minded*). **2** (usu. foll. by *to* + infin.) disposed or inclined (to an action).

minder *n.* **1 a** a person whose job it is to attend to a person or thing. **b** (in *comb.*: *childminder*). **2** esp. *Brit.slang* a bodyguard employed to protect a criminal, celebrity, etc.

mind-expanding *adj.* giving a sense of heightened or broader awareness.

mindful *adj.* (often foll. by *of*) taking heed or care; being conscious. □ **mindfully** *adv.*

mindless *adj.* **1** lacking intelligence; stupid. **2** not requiring thought or skill (*totally mindless work*). **3** (usu. foll. by *of*) heedless of (advice etc.). □ **mindlessly** *adv.* **mindlessness** *n.*

mind-numbing *adj.* (esp. of tedium) that numbs the mind. □ **mind-numbingly** *adv.*

mind-read *v.tr.* discern the thoughts of (another person). □ **mind-reader** *n.*

mindset *n.* a fixed opinion or state of mind formed by earlier events.

mine[1] ● *poss.pron.* the one or ones belonging to or associated with me (*it is mine*). ● *poss.det.* (before a vowel) *archaic* = MY (*mine host*). □ **of mine** of or belonging to me (*a friend of mine*). [Old English]

mine[2] ● *n.* **1** ▼ an excavation in the earth for extracting metal, coal, etc. **2** an abundant source (of information etc.). **3** a receptacle filled with explosive and placed in the ground or in the water for destroying enemy personnel etc. **4 a** a subterranean gallery in which explosive is placed to blow up fortifications. **b** *hist.* a subterranean passage under the wall of a besieged fortress. ● *v.tr.* **1** obtain (coal etc.) from a mine. **2** (also *absol.*, often foll. by *for*) dig in (the earth etc.) for ore etc. **3 a** dig or burrow in (usu. the earth). **b** make (a passage etc.) underground. **4** lay explosive mines under or in. [from Old French *mine* (n.), *miner* (v.)] □ **mining** *n.*

mine-detector *n.* an instrument used for detecting the presence of military mines.

minefield *n.* **1** an area planted with explosive mines. **2** a subject or situation presenting unseen hazards.

miner *n.* **1** a person who works in a mine. **2** any burrowing insect or grub.

mineral ● *n.* **1** ▶ any of the species into which inorganic substances are classified. **2** a substance obtained by mining. **3** (often in *pl.*) *Brit.* an artificial mineral water or other effervescent drink. ● *adj.* **1** of or containing a mineral or minerals. **2** obtained by mining. [from Old French]

mineralogy *n.* the scientific study of minerals. □ **mineralogical** *adj.* **mineralogist** *n.*

mineral oil *n. Brit.* petroleum or one of its distillation products.

mineral water *n.* **1** water found in nature with some dissolved salts present. **2** an artificial imitation of this. **3** *Brit.* any effervescent non-alcoholic drink.

mineral wool *n.* a wool-like substance made from inorganic material, used for packing etc.

mine shaft *n.* a shaft giving access to a mine. ▷ MINE

minestrone /min-i-**stroh**-ni/ *n.* a soup containing vegetables, pasta, and beans. [Italian]

minesweeper *n.* a ship for clearing away floating and submarine mines.

mineworker *n.* a person who works in a mine, esp. a coal mine.

Ming *n.* **1** the dynasty ruling China 1368–1644. **2** ▶ Chinese porcelain made during the rule of this dynasty. [Chinese]

mingle *v.tr. & intr.* mix, blend. □ **mingle with** go about among. [Middle English, related to AMONG]

mingy /**min**-ji/ *adj.* (**mingier**, **mingiest**) *colloq.* mean, stingy. □ **mingily** *adv.*

mini *n.* (*pl.* **minis**) **1** *colloq.* a miniskirt, minidress, etc. **2** (**Mini**) *Brit. propr.* a make of small car.

mini- *comb. form* miniature; very small or minor of its kind (*minibus*). [abbreviation of MINIATURE]

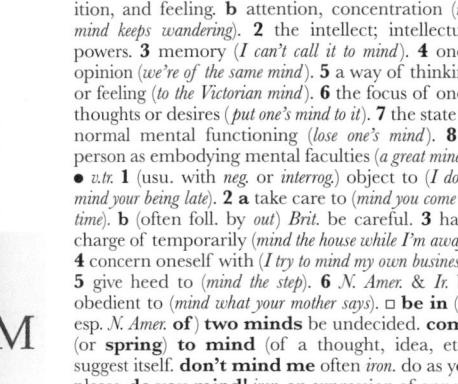
MINARET

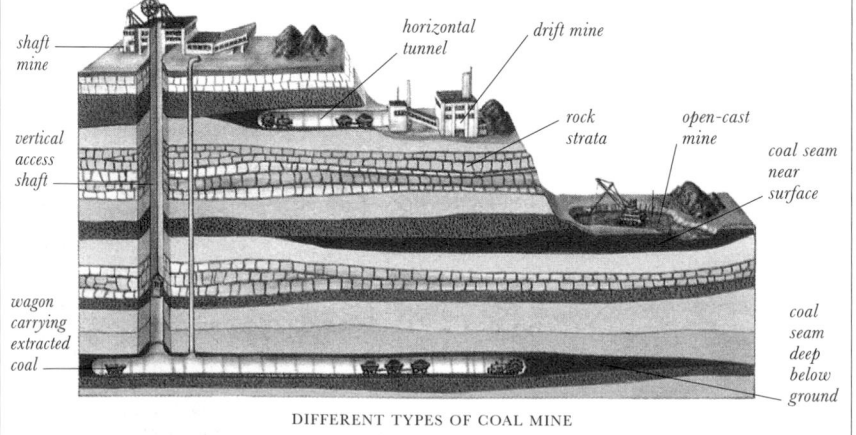

MING: 15TH-CENTURY MING FIGURINE

miniature ● *adj.* **1** much smaller than normal. **2** represented on a small scale. ● *n.* **1** any object reduced in size. **2** a small-scale minutely finished portrait. **3** this branch of painting. □ **in miniature** on a small scale. [based on Latin *miniare* 'to provide with rubrics, illuminate'] □ **miniaturist** *n.* (in senses 2, 3 of *n.*). **miniaturize** *v.tr.* (also **-ise**). **miniaturization** *n.*

minibar *n.* a selection of mainly alcoholic drinks placed in a hotel room for the use of guests and charged on the bill if used.

minibus *n.* a small bus for about twelve passengers.

minicab *n. Brit.* a car used as a taxi, but not licensed to ply for hire.

MINE

Mines are used to extract raw materials from the rocks and sediments of the Earth's interior. Ores, such as gold, silver, iron, and tin, are recovered by blasting and boring rock in underground mines. Coal mines vary with the location of the seam being worked: the deepest are reached by a vertical shaft, whereas seams nearer the surface are mined via a horizontal tunnel, known as a drift mine. In an open-cast mine, coal just below the surface is reached by stripping away the covering layers of ground.

DIFFERENT TYPES OF COAL MINE

MINERAL

Apart from the native elements – a small group of free, uncombined elements that includes gold, silver, and copper – minerals are solid, inorganic compounds. Aggregates of minerals, fused or bound together, form the rocks that make up the Earth's crust.

Minerals are classified by their chemical composition. For example, sulphides are compounds in which sulphur has combined with metallic and semimetallic elements, whereas minerals in the halide group contain one of the halogens.

EXAMPLES OF MAIN MINERAL GROUPS

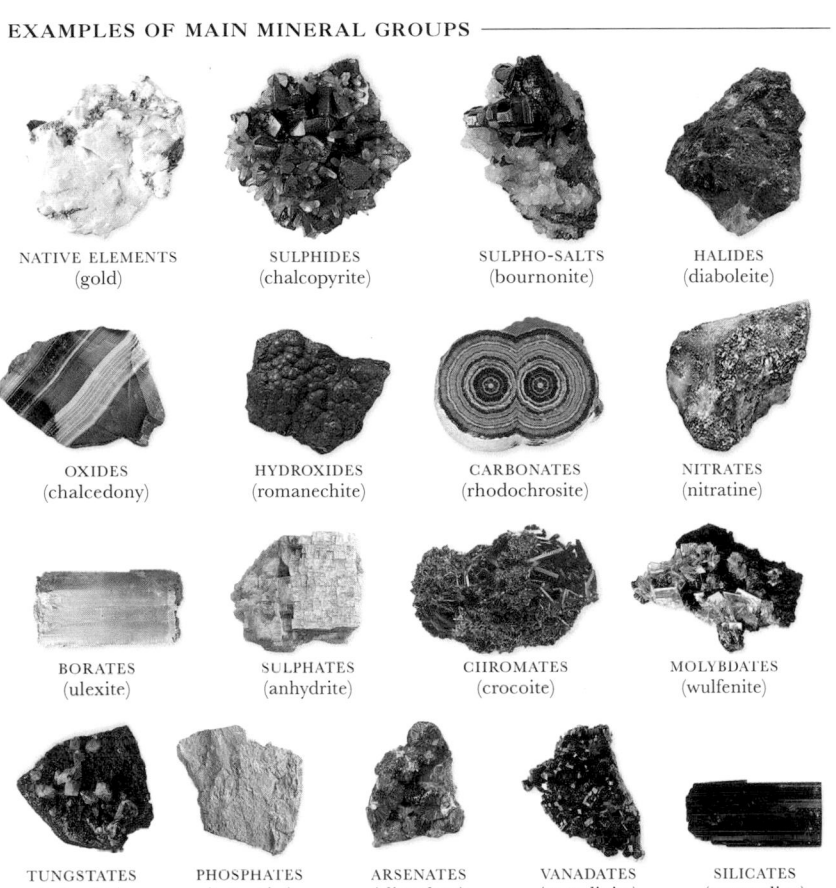

NATIVE ELEMENTS (gold)   SULPHIDES (chalcopyrite)   SULPHO-SALTS (bournonite)   HALIDES (diaboleite)

OXIDES (chalcedony)   HYDROXIDES (romanechite)   CARBONATES (rhodochrosite)   NITRATES (nitratine)

BORATES (ulexite)   SULPHATES (anhydrite)   CHROMATES (crocoite)   MOLYBDATES (wulfenite)

TUNGSTATES (scheelite)   PHOSPHATES (turquoise)   ARSENATES (clinoclase)   VANADATES (vanadinite)   SILICATES (tourmaline)

---

minicomputer *n.* a computer of medium power.

minigolf *n. Sport* a game in which a club is used to knock a small ball into a series of holes in a lawn.

minim *n.* **1** esp. *Brit. Mus.* a note having the time value of two crotchets or half a semibreve and represented by a hollow ring with a stem. ▷ NOTATION. **2** one-sixtieth of a fluid drachm; about one drop of liquid. [from Latin *minimus* 'smallest']

minima *pl.* of MINIMUM.

minimal *adj.* **1** very minute or slight. **2** being or related to a minimum. **3** the least possible in size, duration, etc. **4 a** *Art* etc. characterized by the use of simple or primary forms or structures etc. **b** *Mus.* characterized by the repetition of short phrases. [from Latin *minimus* 'smallest'] □ **minimalism** *n.* **minimalist** *n. & adj.* **minimally** *adv.* (in senses 1–3).

minimize *v.tr.* (also **-ise**) **1** reduce to, or estimate at, the smallest possible amount or degree. **2** estimate or represent at less than the true value or importance. □ **minimization** *n.*

minimum (*pl.* **minima** or **minimums**) ● *n.* the least possible or attainable amount (*reduced to a minimum*). ● *adj.* that is a minimum. [Latin]

minimum wage *n.* the lowest wage permitted by law or special agreement.

minion *n. derog.* a servile agent; a slave. [from Old French *mignot*]

minipill *n.* a contraceptive pill containing a progestogen only.

miniscule var. of MINUSCULE.

miniseries *n.* (*pl.* same) a short series of television programmes on a common theme.

miniskirt *n.* a very short skirt.

minister ● *n.* **1** (often **Minister**) *Brit.* a head of a government department. **2** (in full **minister of religion**) a member of the clergy, esp. in the Presbyterian and Nonconformist Churches. **3** a diplomatic agent, usu. ranking below an ambassador. **4** (usu. foll. by *of*) a person employed in the execution of (a purpose, will, etc.) (*a minister of justice*). ● *v. intr.* (usu. foll. by *to*) render aid or service (to a person, cause, etc.). [from Latin, literally 'servant'] □ **ministership** *n.* **ministrable** *adj.*

ministerial *adj.* **1** of a minister of religion or a minister's office. **2** instrumental or subsidiary in achieving a purpose. **3** *Brit.* of a government minister or ministry. □ **ministerially** *adv.*

Minister of State *n.* a government minister, in the UK usu. regarded as holding a rank below that of Head of Department.

Minister of the Crown *n. Brit. Parl.* a member of the Cabinet.

Minister without Portfolio *n.* a government minister not in charge of a specific department of state.

ministration *n.* **1** (usu. in *pl.*) aid or service. **2** ministering, esp. in religious matters. **3** (usu. foll. by *of*) the supplying (of help, justice, etc.). [from Latin *ministratio*] □ **ministrant** *adj. & n.* **ministrative** *adj.*

ministry *n.* (*pl.* **-ies**) **1** (often **Ministry**) **a** a government department headed by a minister. **b** the building for this. **2 a** (prec. by *the*) the vocation or profession of a religious minister. **b** the office of a priest etc. **c** the period of tenure of this. **3** (prec. by *the*) the body of ministers of a government or of a religion. **4** a period of government under one Prime Minister. **5** ministering, ministration.

mink *n.* **1** ▼ either of two small semiaquatic stoat-like animals of the genus *Mustela*. **2** the thick brown fur of these. **3** a coat made of this. [Middle English]

MINK: NORTH AMERICAN MINK (*Mustela vison*)

minke *n.* a small baleen whale, *Balaenoptera acutorostrata*, with a pointed snout. ▷ CETACEAN

minnow *n.* a small freshwater carp. [late Middle English]

Minoan *Archaeol.* ● *adj.* of or relating to the Bronze Age civilization centred on Crete (*c.*3000–1100 BC). ● *n.* **1** an inhabitant of Minoan Crete or the Minoan world. **2** the language or scripts associated with the Minoans. [from the legendary Cretan king *Minos*, to whom the palace excavated at Knossos was attributed]

minor ● *adj.* **1** lesser or comparatively small in size or importance. **2** *Mus.* **a** (of a scale) having intervals of a semitone between the second and third, fifth and sixth, and seventh and eighth degrees. **b** (of an interval) less by a semitone than a major interval. **c** (of a key) based on a minor scale. **3** *Brit.* (appended to a surname) indicating the younger of two brothers (*Smith minor*). ● *n.* **1** a person under the legal age limit or majority. **2** *Mus.* a minor key etc. **3** *US* a student's subsidiary subject or course. ● *v.intr.* (foll. by *in*) *US* (of a student) undertake study in (a subject) as a subsidiary to a main subject. [Latin, literally 'smaller, less']

Minorcan ● *adj.* of or relating to Minorca, an island in the western Mediterranean. ● *n.* a native or inhabitant of Minorca.

minor canon *n.* a cleric who is not a member of the chapter, who assists in daily cathedral services.

minority *n.* (*pl.* **-ies**) **1** (often foll. by *of*) a smaller number or part, esp. within a political party or structure. **2** the number of votes cast for this (*a minority of two*). **3** the state of being supported by less than half of the body of opinion (*in the minority*). **4** a relatively small group of people differing from others in race, religion, language, etc. **5** (*attrib.*) relating to or done by the minority (*minority interests*). **6 a** the state of being under full legal age. **b** the period of this.

minster *n.* **1** a large or important church. **2** the church of a monastery. [from Greek *monastērion* 'monastery']

minstrel *n.* **1** *hist.* a medieval singer or musician. **2** *hist.* a person who entertained patrons with singing, buffoonery, etc. **3** (usu. in *pl.*) a member of a band of public entertainers with blackened faces etc., performing songs ostensibly of black American origin. [from Provençal *menest(ai)ral* 'officer, employee, musician'] □ **minstrelsy** *n.* (*pl.* **-ies**).

MINT:
BOWLES' MINT
(*Mentha × villosa*)

mint[1] *n.* **1** ◄ any aromatic plant of the genus *Mentha* (family Labiatae). ▷ HERB. **2** a peppermint sweet or lozenge. [from Greek *minthē*] □ **minty** *adj.* (**mintier**, **mintiest**).

mint[2] ● *n.* **1** a place where money is coined, usu. under State authority. **2** *colloq.* a vast sum of money (*making a mint*). **3** a source of invention etc. (*a mint of ideas*). ● *v.tr.* **1** make (coin) by stamping metal. **2** invent, coin (a word etc.). □ **in mint condition** (or **state**) as new. [from Latin *moneta* 'money']

mint julep *n.* US a sweet iced alcoholic drink of bourbon flavoured with mint.

mint sauce *n.* chopped spearmint in vinegar and sugar, usu. eaten with lamb.

minuet /min-yoo-**et**/ ● *n.* **1** a slow stately dance for two in triple time. **2** *Mus.* the music for this, or music in the same rhythm and style. ● *v.intr.* (**minueted**, **minueting**) dance a minuet. [from French *menuet* 'fine, delicate', used as a noun]

minus ● *prep.* **1** with the subtraction of (*7 minus 4 equals 3*). **2** below zero (*minus 2°*). **3** *colloq.* lacking (*returned minus their dog*). ● *adj.* **1** *Math.* negative. **2** *Electronics* having a negative charge. ● *n.* **1** = MINUS SIGN. **2** *Math.* a negative quantity. **3** a disadvantage. [Latin neut. form of *minor* 'less']

minuscule *adj.* (also *disp.* **miniscule**) **1** lower case. **2** *colloq.* extremely small or unimportant. [from Latin *minuscula (littera)* 'lesser (letter)'] □ **minuscular** *adj.*

minus sign *n.* the symbol –, indicating subtraction or a negative value.

minute[1] /**min**-it/ ● *n.* **1** a sixtieth of an hour. **2** a distance covered in one minute (*twenty minutes from the station*). **3 a** a moment (*any minute now*). **b** (prec. by *the*) *colloq.* the present time (*what are you doing at the minute?*). **c** (foll. by *clause*) as soon as (*the minute you get back*). **4** a sixtieth of a degree of angular distance. **5** (in *pl.*) a brief summary of the proceedings at a meeting. **6** an official memorandum authorizing or recommending a course of action. ● *v.tr.* **1** record in the minutes. **2** send the minutes of a meeting to. [related to MINUTE[2]; *n.* 1, 4: from medieval Latin *pars minuta prima* 'first minute part']

minute[2] /my-**newt**/ *adj.* (**minutest**) **1** very small. **2** trifling, petty. **3** accurate, detailed. [from Latin *minutus* 'lessened'] □ **minutely** *adv.* **minuteness** *n.*

minute hand *n.* the hand on a watch or clock which indicates minutes. ▷ WATCH

minute steak *n.* a thin slice of steak to be cooked quickly.

minutia /min-yoo-**shiă**/ *n.* (*pl.* **minutiae** /-shi-ee/) (usu. in *pl.*) a precise, trivial, or minor detail. [Latin, literally 'smallness', in pl. 'trifles']

minx *n.* a pert, sly, or playful girl. [16th-century coinage]

Miocene *Geol.* ● *adj.* of or relating to the fourth epoch of the Tertiary period. ● *n.* this epoch or system. [formed irregularly from Greek *meiōn* 'less' + *kainos* 'new']

MIPS /mips/ *n.* a unit of computing speed equivalent to a million instructions per second.

mirabelle *n.* **1** a European variety of plum tree, *Prunus insititia*, bearing small round yellow fruit. **2** ► a fruit from this tree. [French]

miracle *n.* **1** an extraordinary event attributed to some supernatural agency. **2** any remarkable occurrence or development (*an economic miracle*). **3** (usu. foll. by *of*) a remarkable specimen (*a miracle of ingenuity*). [from Latin *miraculum* 'object of wonder']

miracle play *n.* a mystery play.

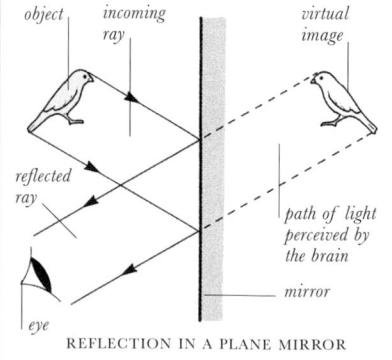

MIRABELLE
(*Prunus insititia*)

miraculous *adj.* **1** of the nature of a miracle. **2** supernatural. **3** remarkable, surprising. □ **miraculously** *adv.*

mirage /mi-**rah**zh/ *n.* **1** ► an optical illusion caused by atmospheric conditions, esp. the appearance of a sheet of water in a desert etc. from the reflection of light. **2** an illusory thing. [French]

MIRAS /**myr**-ăs/ *abbr.* (also **Miras**) (in the UK) mortgage interest relief at source.

mire ● *n.* **1** a stretch of swampy ground. **2** mud, dirt. ● *v.* **1** *tr.* plunge or sink in a mire. **2** *tr.* involve in difficulties. [from Old Norse *mýrr*]

mirk var. of MURK.

mirky var. of MURKY.

mirror ● *n.* **1** ▼ a polished surface, usu. of coated glass, reflecting an image. ▷ OBSERVATORY, PERISCOPE. **2** anything reflecting or illuminating a state of affairs etc. ● *v.tr.* reflect as in a mirror. [from Old French *mirour*]

mirror image *n.* an identical image, but with the structure reversed, as in a mirror.

mirror writing *n.* reversed writing, like ordinary writing reflected in a mirror.

mirth *n.* merriment, laughter. [Old English] □ **mirthful** *adj.* **mirthfully** *adv.* **mirthless** *adj.* **mirthlessly** *adv.* **mirthlessness** *n.*

mis- *prefix* added to verbs and verbal derivatives: meaning 'amiss', 'badly', 'wrongly', 'unfavourably' (*mislead*; *misshapen*; *mistrust*). [Old English]

misadventure *n.* **1** *Law* an accident without concomitant crime or negligence (*death by misadventure*). **2** bad luck. **3** a misfortune.

misalign *v.tr.* give the wrong alignment to. □ **misalignment** *n.*

misalliance *n.* an unsuitable alliance, esp. an unsuitable marriage.

misanthrope *n.* (also **misanthropist**) **1** a person who hates humankind. **2** a person who avoids human society. [from Greek *misanthrōpos*] □ **misanthropic** *adj.* **misanthropy** *n.*

misapply *v.tr.* (**-ies**, **-ied**) apply (esp. funds) wrongly. □ **misapplication** *n.*

misapprehend *v.tr.* misunderstand (words, a person). □ **misapprehension** *n.* **misapprehensive** *adj.*

misappropriate *v.tr.* apply (usu. another's money) to one's own use, or to a wrong use. □ **misappropriation** *n.*

misbegotten *adj.* **1** illegitimate, bastard. **2** contemptible, disreputable.

misbehave *v.intr.* & *refl.* (of a person or machine) behave badly. □ **misbehaviour** *n.*

miscalculate *v.tr.* (also *absol.*) calculate (amounts, results, etc.) wrongly. □ **miscalculation** *n.*

miscall *v.tr.* **1** call by a wrong or inappropriate name. **2** *archaic* or *dial.* call (a person) names.

miscarriage *n.* a spontaneous abortion, esp. before the 28th week of pregnancy.

miscarriage of justice *n.* any failure of the judicial system to attain the ends of justice.

miscarry *v.intr.* (**-ies**, **-ied**) **1** (of a woman) have a miscarriage. **2** (of a business, plan, etc.) fail; be unsuccessful.

miscast *v.tr.* (*past* and *past part.* **-cast**) allot an unsuitable part to (an actor).

miscegenation /mis-i-jin-**ay**-shŏn/ *n.* the interbreeding of races, esp. of whites and non-whites. [based on Latin *miscēre* 'to mix' + *genus* 'race']

miscellaneous *adj.* **1** of mixed composition or character. **2** (foll. by pl. noun) of various kinds. [from Latin *miscellus* 'mixed'] □ **miscellaneously** *adv.* **miscellaneousness** *n.*

miscellany *n.* (*pl.* **-ies**) **1** a mixture; a medley. **2** a book containing various literary compositions.

mischance *n.* **1** bad luck. **2** an instance of this.

mischief *n.* **1** conduct which is trouble-some, but not malicious, esp. in children. **2** playful malice; archness, satire (*eyes full of mischief*). **3** harm or injury caused by a person or thing. □ **get up to** (or **make**) **mischief** create discord. [from Old French *meschief*]

mischief-maker *n.* a person who encourages discord, esp. by gossip etc. □ **mischief-making** *n.*

mischievous *adj.* **1** (of a person) disposed to mischief. **2** (of conduct) playfully malicious. **3** (of a thing) harmful. [from Old French *meschever*] □ **mischievously** *adv.* **mischievousness** *n.*

miscible *adj.* (often foll. by *with*) capable of being mixed. [based on Latin *miscēre* 'to mix'] □ **miscibility** *n.*

misconceive *v.* **1** *intr.* (often foll. by *of*) have a wrong idea or conception. **2** *tr.* (as **misconceived** *adj.*) badly planned, organized, etc. □ **misconception** *n.*

misconduct ● *n.* improper or unprofessional behaviour. ● *v.refl.* misbehave.

misconstrue *v.tr.* (**-construes**, **-construed**, **-construing**) interpret (a word, action, etc.) wrongly. □ **misconstruction** *n.*

MIRAGE

A mirage occurs in hot places, such as a desert, when a layer of warm air above the ground is trapped by cooler air above. Light rays, which normally travel in straight lines, bend as they pass through the different temperatures, but eventually travel upwards. The observer perceives the light rays as if they are travelling in a straight line from the object. The mirage is an inverted, virtual image of the object.

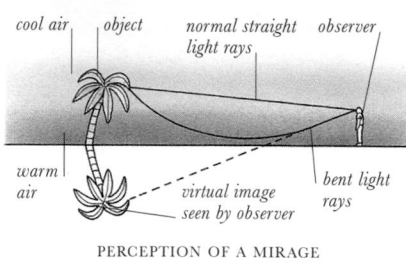

PERCEPTION OF A MIRAGE

MIRROR

Incoming light rays from an object viewed in a mirror are reflected back at exactly the same, but reversed, angle. The brain, assuming that the reflected rays have reached the eye in straight lines, works backwards along the light paths and perceives an image behind the mirror.

REFLECTION IN A PLANE MIRROR

M

miscount ● *v.tr.* (also *absol.*) count wrongly. ● *n.* a wrong count.

miscreant /mis-kri-ănt/ ● *n.* a wretch; a villain. ● *adj.* depraved. [from Old French *mescreant*]

miscue ● *n.* (in snooker etc.) the failure to strike the ball properly with the cue. ● *v.intr.* (-**cues**, -**cued**, -**cueing** or -**cuing**) make a miscue.

misdate *v.tr.* date (an event, a letter, etc.) wrongly.

misdeed *n.* an evil deed; a wrongdoing; a crime.

misdemeanour *n.* (*US* **misdemeanor**) **1** an offence, a misdeed. **2** *Law* an indictable offence, (in the UK formerly) less heinous than a felony.

misdescribe *v.tr.* describe inaccurately. □ **misdescription** *n.*

misdiagnose *v.tr.* diagnose incorrectly. □ **misdiagnosis** *n.*

misdial *v.tr.* (-**dialled**, -**dialling**; *US* -**dialed**, -**dialing**) (also *absol.*) dial (a telephone number etc.) incorrectly.

misdirect *v.tr.* **1** direct (a person, letter, blow, etc.) wrongly. **2** (of a judge) instruct (the jury) wrongly. □ **misdirection** *n.*

misdoing *n.* a misdeed.

miser *n.* **1** a person who hoards wealth and lives miserably. **2** an avaricious person. [Latin, literally 'wretched']

miserable *adj.* **1** wretchedly unhappy or uncomfortable. **2** contemptible, inadequate, mean (*a miserable attempt*). **3** causing wretchedness or discomfort (*miserable weather*). **4** *Sc.*, *Austral.*, & *NZ* (of a person) stingy, mean. **5** *colloq.* (of a person) gloomy, morose. [from Latin *miserabilis* 'pitiable'] □ **miserableness** *n.* **miserably** *adv.*

misericord /mi-ze-ri-kord/ *n.* a projection under a hinged seat in a choir stall serving (when the seat is turned up) to help support a person standing. [based on Latin *miserēri* 'to pity' + *cor cordis* 'heart']

miserly *adj.* like a miser □ **miserliness** *n.*

misery *n.* (*pl.* -**ies**) **1** a wretched state of mind, or of outward circumstances. **2** a thing causing this. **3** *Brit. colloq.* a constantly depressed or discontented person. □ **put out of its** etc. **misery 1** release (a person, animal, etc.) from suffering or suspense. **2** kill (an animal in pain).

misfield ● *v.tr.* (also *absol.*) (in cricket etc.) field (the ball) badly. ● *n. Brit.* an instance of this.

misfire ● *v.intr.* **1** (of a gun, motor engine, etc.) fail to go off or start or function regularly. **2** (of an action etc.) fail to have the intended effect. ● *n.* a failure of function or intention.

misfit *n.* a person unsuited to a particular kind of environment, occupation, etc.

misfortune *n.* **1** bad luck. **2** an instance of this.

misgiving *n.* (usu. in *pl.*) a feeling of mistrust or apprehension.

misgovern *v.tr.* govern (a state etc.) badly. □ **misgovernment** *n.*

misguide *v.tr.* **1** (as **misguided** *adj.*) mistaken in thought or action. **2** mislead, misdirect. □ **misguidedly** *adv.* **misguidedness** *n.*

mishandle *v.tr.* **1** deal with incorrectly or ineffectively. **2** handle (a person or thing) roughly or rudely; ill-treat.

mishap *n.* an unlucky accident.

mishear *v.tr.* (*past* and *past part.* -**heard**) hear incorrectly or imperfectly.

mishit ● *v.tr.* (-**hitting**; *past* and *past part.* -**hit**) hit (a ball etc.) faultily. ● *n.* a faulty or bad hit.

mishmash *n.* a confused mixture. [Middle English]

misidentify *v.tr.* (-**ies**, -**ied**) identify erroneously. □ **misidentification** *n.*

misinform *v.tr.* give wrong information to; mislead. □ **misinformation** *n.*

misinterpret *v.tr.* (-**interpreted**, -**interpreting**) **1** interpret wrongly. **2** draw a wrong inference from. □ **misinterpretation** *n.*

misjudge *v.tr.* (also *absol.*) **1** judge wrongly. **2** have a wrong opinion of. □ **misjudgement** *n.* (also **misjudgment**).

miskey *v.tr.* (-**keys**, -**keyed**) (also *absol.*) key (data) wrongly.

mislay *v.tr.* (*past* and *past part.* -**laid**) **1** unintentionally put (a thing) where it cannot readily be found. **2** *euphem.* lose.

mislead *v.tr.* (*past* and *past part.* -**led**) cause (a person) to infer what is not true. □ **misleading** *adj.* **misleadingly** *adv.*

mismanage *v.tr.* manage badly or wrongly. □ **mismanagement** *n.*

mismatch ● *v.tr.* match unsuitably or incorrectly, esp. in marriage. ● *n.* a bad match.

misname *v.tr.* call by a wrong or inappropriate name.

hatcho miso

genmai miso

MISO: SOYA-BEAN PASTE

misnomer *n.* **1** a name or term used wrongly. **2** the wrong use of a name or term. [based on Old French *mesnom(m)er*]

miso *n.* ◀ a paste made from fermented soya beans and barley or rice malt, used in Japanese cookery. [Japanese]

misogyny *n.* the hatred of women. [based on Greek *misos* 'hatred' + *gunē* 'woman'] □ **misogynist** *n.* **misogynistic** *adj.*

misplace *v.tr.* **1** put in the wrong place. **2** bestow (affections, confidence, etc.) on an inappropriate object. **3** time (words, actions, etc.) badly. □ **misplacement** *n.*

misprint ● *n.* a mistake in printing. ● *v.tr.* print wrongly.

mispronounce *v.tr.* pronounce (a word etc.) wrongly. □ **mispronunciation** *n.*

misquote *v.tr.* quote wrongly. □ **misquotation** *n.*

misread *v.tr.* (*past* and *past part.* -**read**) read or interpret (text, a situation, etc.) wrongly.

misreport ● *v.tr.* give a false or incorrect report of. ● *n.* a false or incorrect report.

misrepresent *v.tr.* represent wrongly; give a false or misleading account or idea of. □ **misrepresentation** *n.* **misrepresentative** *adj.*

misrule ● *n.* bad government; disorder. ● *v.tr.* govern badly.

miss¹ ● *v.* **1** *tr.* (also *absol.*) fail to hit, reach, find, catch, etc. (an object or goal). **2** *tr.* fail to catch (a bus, train, etc.). **3** *tr.* fail to experience, see, or attend (an occurrence or event). **4** *tr.* fail to meet (a person); fail to keep (an appointment). **5** *tr.* fail to seize (an opportunity etc.) (*I missed my chance*). **6** *tr.* fail to hear or understand (*I missed what you said*). **7** *tr.* **a** regret the loss or absence of (a person or thing) (*did you miss me?*). **b** notice the loss or absence of (an object or person) (*bound to miss the key if it isn't there*). **8** *tr.* avoid (*go early to miss the traffic*). **9** *intr.* (of an engine etc.) fail, misfire. ● *n.* a failure to hit, reach, etc. □ **be missing** not have, lack (an integral part etc.) (*the coat is missing its belt*) (see also MISSING *adj.*). **give (a thing) a miss** *Brit.* avoid; leave alone (*gave the party a miss*). **miss out 1** *Brit.* omit; leave out. **2** (usu. foll. by *on*) *colloq.* fail to get or experience (*always misses out on the good times*). **miss the boat** lose an opportunity. **not miss much** be alert. **not miss a trick** never fail to seize an opportunity, advantage, etc. [Old English] □ **missable** *adj.*

miss² *n.* **1** a girl or unmarried woman. **2** (**Miss**) **a** the title of an unmarried woman or girl. **b** the title of a beauty queen (*Miss World*). **3** usu. *derog.* or *joc.* a girl, with implications of silliness etc. **4** the title used to address a female schoolteacher, shop assistant, etc. [abbreviation of MISTRESS]

missal *n. RC Ch.* **1** a book containing the texts used in the service of the Mass throughout the year.

2 a book of prayers, esp. an illuminated one. [from ecclesiastical Latin *missale* (neut.) 'of the Mass']

missel thrush var. of MISTLE THRUSH.

misshape *v.tr.* give a bad shape or form to; distort.

misshapen *adj.* ill-shaped, deformed, distorted. □ **misshapenness** *n.*

missile *n.* **1** an object or weapon for throwing at a target or for discharge from a machine. **2** ▼ a weapon directed by remote control or automatically. [from Latin *missilis*] □ **missilery** *n.*

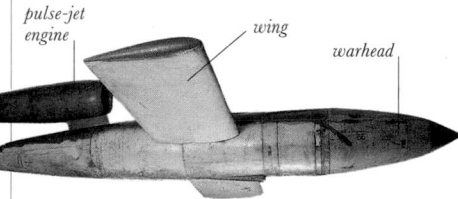

pulse-jet engine — *wing* — *warhead*

MISSILE: SECOND WORLD WAR GERMAN V1 FLYING BOMB

missing *adj.* **1** not in its place; lost. **2** (of a person) not yet traced or confirmed as alive but not known to be dead. **3** not present.

missing link *n.* **1** a thing lacking to complete a series. **2** a hypothetical intermediate type, esp. between apes and humans.

mission *n.* **1 a** a particular task or goal assigned to a person or group. **b** a journey undertaken as part of this. **c** a person's vocation (*mission in life*). **2** a body of persons sent, esp. to a foreign country, to conduct negotiations etc. **3 a** a field of missionary activity. **b** a missionary post or organization. [from Latin *missio* 'sending']

missionary ● *adj.* of, concerned with, or characteristic of, religious missions. ● *n.* (*pl.* -**ies**) a person doing missionary work. [from modern Latin *missionarius*]

missionary position *n. colloq.* a position for sexual intercourse with the woman lying on her back and the man lying on top and facing her.

missioner *n.* **1** a missionary. **2** a person in charge of a religious mission.

mission statement *n.* a declaration made by a company etc. of its general principles of operation.

missis *n.* (also **missus**) *slang* or *joc.* **1** a form of address to a woman. **2** a wife. □ **the missis** my or your wife. [corruption of MISTRESS]

missive *n.* **1** *joc.* a letter. **2** an official letter. [based on Latin *mittere miss-* 'to send']

misspell *v.tr.* (*past* and *past part.* -**spelt** or -**spelled**) spell wrongly. □ **misspelling** *n.*

misspend *v.tr.* (*past* and *past part.* -**spent**) (esp. as **misspent** *adj.*) spend amiss or wastefully.

misstate *v.tr.* state wrongly or inaccurately. □ **misstatement** *n.*

missus var. of MISSIS.

missy *n.* (*pl.* -**ies**) an affectionate or derogatory form of address to a young girl.

mist ● *n.* **1 a** water vapour near the ground in minute droplets limiting visibility. **b** condensed vapour settling on a surface and obscuring glass etc. **2** dimness or blurring of the sight caused by tears etc. **3** a cloud of particles resembling mist. ● *v.tr.* & *intr.* (usu. foll. by *up*, *over*) cover or become covered with mist or as with mist. [Old English]

mistake ● *n.* **1** an incorrect idea or opinion; a thing incorrectly done or thought. **2** an error of judgement. ● *v.tr.* (*past* **mistook**; *past part.* **mistaken**) **1** misunderstand the meaning or intention of (a person, a statement, etc.). **2** (foll. by *for*) wrongly take or identify (*mistook me for you*). □ **by mistake** accidentally; in error. □ **mistakable** *adj.*

mistaken *adj.* **1** wrong in opinion or judgement. **2** based on or resulting from this (*mistaken loyalty; mistaken identity*). □ **mistakenly** *adv.* □ **mistakenness** *n.*

M

M

misteach *v.tr.* (*past* and *past part.* **-taught**) teach wrongly or incorrectly.

mister *n.* **1** a man without a title of nobility etc. (*a mere mister*). **2** *slang* or *joc.* a form of address to a man. [weakened form of MASTER in unstressed use before a name]

mistigris *n. Cards* **1** a blank card used as a wild card in a form of draw poker. **2** this game.

mistime *v.tr.* say or do at the wrong time.

mistitle *v.tr.* give the wrong title or name to.

mistle thrush *n.* (also **missel thrush**) a large thrush, *Turdus viscivorus*, with a spotted breast, that feeds on mistletoe berries. [Old English *mistel* 'basil, mistletoe']

mistletoe *n.* ▶ a parasitic plant, *Viscum album*, growing on apple and other trees and bearing white glutinous berries in winter. [Old English *misteltān* 'mistletoe twig']

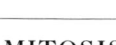

MISTLETOE
(*Viscum album*)

mistook *past* of MISTAKE.

mistral *n.* a cold northerly wind of southern France. [from Latin *magistralis* (*ventus*) 'master (wind)']

mistranslate *v.tr.* translate incorrectly □ **mistranslation** *n.*

mistreat *v.tr.* treat badly. □ **mistreatment** *n.*

mistress *n.* **1** a female head of a household. **2 a** a woman in authority over others. **b** the female owner of a pet. **3** a woman with power to control etc. (often foll. by *of: mistress of the situation*). **4** *Brit.* **a** a female teacher. **b** a female head of a college etc. **5** a woman (other than his wife) with whom a married man has a sexual relationship. [from Old French *maistresse*]

mistrial *n.* **1** a trial rendered invalid through some error. **2** *US* a trial in which the jury cannot agree on a verdict.

mistrust ● *v.tr.* **1** be suspicious of. **2** feel no confidence in (a person, oneself, one's powers, etc.). ● *n.* **1** suspicion. **2** lack of confidence.

mistrustful *adj.* **1** (foll. by *of*) suspicious. **2** lacking confidence or trust. □ **mistrustfully** *adv.*

misty *adj.* (**mistier**, **mistiest**) **1** of or covered with mist. **2** indistinct or dim in outline. **3** obscure, vague (*a misty idea*). □ **mistily** *adv.* **mistiness** *n.*

mistype *v.tr.* type wrongly.

misunderstand *v.tr.* (*past* and *past part.* **misunderstood**) **1** fail to understand correctly. **2** (usu. as **misunderstood** *adj.*) misinterpret the words or actions of (a person).

misunderstanding *n.* **1** a failure to understand correctly. **2** a slight disagreement or quarrel.

misuse ● *v.tr.* /mis-yooz/ **1** use wrongly; apply to the wrong purpose. **2** ill-treat. ● *n.* /mis-yooss/ wrong or improper use or application.

MIT *abbr.* Massachusetts Institute of Technology.

mite[1] ● *n.* a very small arachnid of the order Acarina, many of which are parasitic on plants or animals. ▷ ARACHNID. [Old English]

mite[2] ● *n.* **1** any small monetary unit. **2** a small object or person, esp. a child. **3** a modest contribution; the best one can do (*offered my mite of comfort*). ● *adv.* (usu. prec. by *a*) *colloq.* somewhat (*is a mite shy*). [from Middle Dutch *mīte*]

miter *US* var. of MITRE.

mitigate *v.tr.* make milder or less intense or severe. [based on Latin *mitigatus* 'made mild'] □ **mitigation** *n.* **mitigatory** *adj.*

■ **Usage** See Usage Note at MILITATE.

mitigating circumstance *n.* (usu. in *pl.*) *Law* a circumstance permitting greater leniency.

mitosis *n. Biol.* ▼ a type of cell division that results in two daughter cells each having the same number and kind of chromosomes as the parent nucleus. (cf. MEIOSIS 1). [based on Greek *mitos* 'thread'] □ **mitotic** *adj.*

mitre (*US* **miter**) ● *n.* **1** ▶ a tall deeply cleft headdress worn by bishops and abbots, esp. as a symbol of office. **2** (in full **mitre joint**) the joint of two pieces of wood or other material at an angle of 90°, such that the line of junction bisects this angle. ● *v.tr. & intr.* join with a mitre. [from Greek *mitra* 'girdle, turban'] □ **mitred** *adj.*

mitre box *n.* ◀ a frame with slits for guiding a saw in cutting mitre joints.

mitt *n.* **1** = MITTEN. **2** a glove leaving the fingers and thumb exposed. **3** *slang* a hand or fist. **4** a baseball glove for catching the ball.

mitten *n.* **1** a glove with two sections, one for the thumb and the other for all four fingers. **2** (in *pl.*) *slang* boxing gloves. □ **mittened** *adj.* [from Old French *mitaine*]

mix ● *v.* **1** *tr.* combine or put together (two or more substances or things) so that they are diffused into each other. **2** *tr.* prepare (a compound, cocktail, etc.) by combining the ingredients. **3** *tr.* combine (an activity etc.) with

angled slit

MITRE BOX

another simultaneously (*mix business with pleasure*). **4** *intr.* **a** join, be mixed, or combine, esp. readily (*oil and water will not mix*). **b** be compatible. **c** be sociable (*must learn to mix*). **5** *intr.* (foll. by *with*) (of a person) be harmonious or sociable with; have regular dealings with. **b** (foll. by *in*) participate in. **6** *tr.* drink different kinds of (alcoholic liquor) in close succession. **7** *tr.* combine (two or more sound signals) into one. **8** *tr. Mus.* produce (a recording) by combining a number of separate recordings or soundtracks. ● *n.* **1 a** the act or an instance of mixing; a mixture. **b** the proportion of materials etc. in a mixture. **2** *colloq.* a group of persons of different types (*social mix*). **3** the ingredients prepared commercially for making a cake etc. or for a process such as making concrete. **4** the merging of film pictures or sound. □ **be mixed up in** (or **with**) be involved in or with (esp. something undesirable). **mix and match** select from a range of alternative combinations. **mix it** (*US* **mix it up**) *colloq.* start fighting. **mix up 1** mix thoroughly. **2** confuse; mistake the identity of. [back-formation from MIXED, taken as past participle]

mixed *adj.* **1** of diverse qualities or elements. **2** containing persons from various backgrounds etc. **3** for or involving persons of both sexes (*a mixed school*). [from Latin *mixtus*]

mixed bag *n.* (also **mixed bunch**) a diverse assortment of things or persons.

mixed blessing *n.* a thing having advantages and disadvantages.

mixed crystal *n.* a crystal formed from more than one substance.

mixed doubles *n.pl. Tennis* etc. a doubles game with a man and a woman as partners on each side.

mixed economy *n.* an economic system combining private and State enterprise.

mixed farming *n.* farming of both crops and livestock.

mixed feelings *n.pl.* a mixture of pleasure and dismay about something.

mixed grill *n.* a dish of various grilled meats and vegetables etc.

mixed marriage *n.* a marriage between persons of different races or religions.

mixed media ● *n.* the use of a variety of mediums in an entertainment, work of art, etc. ● *attrib.adj.* (also **mixed-media**) = MULTIMEDIA.

mixed metaphor *n.* a combination of inconsistent metaphors (e.g. *this tower of strength will forge ahead*).

mixed-up *adj. colloq.* mentally or emotionally confused; socially ill-adjusted.

MITRE:
BISHOP'S MITRE

MITOSIS

Mitosis is a type of cell division that produces two new genetically identical cells. During prophase, the cell's genetic material (chromatin) tightens up to form chromosomes. The membrane around the nucleus begins to disintegrate, and a system of microtubules forms a structure called the spindle. This is complete by metaphase, when the chromosomes line up across the cell's centre. During anaphase, the spindle microtubules contract, pulling the chromosomes apart so that each half (or chromatid) moves to opposite poles of the cell. During telophase, the spindle disappears and a new nuclear membrane forms around each group of chromosomes. The cell's plasma membrane then begins to constrict, eventually forming two new daughter cells.

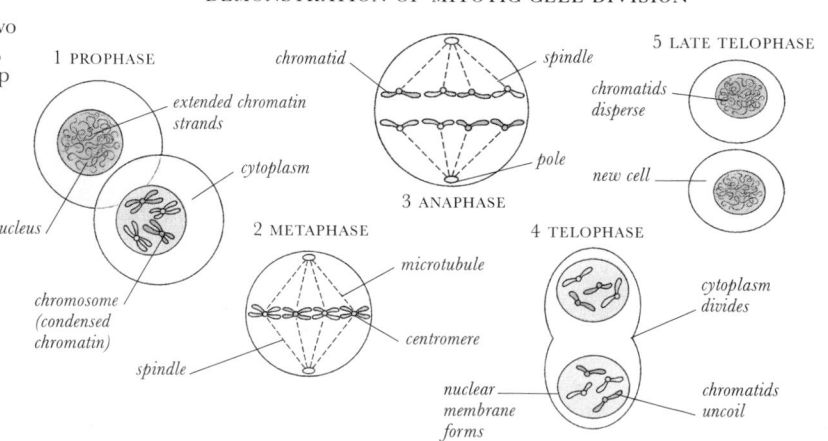

DEMONSTRATION OF MITOTIC CELL DIVISION

1 PROPHASE
extended chromatin strands
cytoplasm
nucleus
chromosome (condensed chromatin)
spindle

2 METAPHASE
microtubule
centromere
nuclear membrane forms

chromatid
spindle
pole
3 ANAPHASE

4 TELOPHASE
cytoplasm divides
chromatids uncoil

5 LATE TELOPHASE
chromatids disperse
new cell

mixer *n.* **1** ◀ a device for mixing foods etc. or for processing other materials. **2** a person who manages socially in a specified way (*a good mixer*). **3** a (usu. soft) drink to be mixed with another. **4** *Broadcasting & Cinematog.* **a** a device for merging input signals to produce a combined output in the form of sound or pictures. **b** a person who operates this.

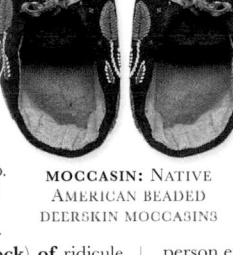

MIXER: HAND-HELD FOOD MIXER

beater

mixer tap *n. Brit.* a tap through which mixed hot and cold water is drawn by means of separate controls.

mixture *n.* **1** the process of mixing or being mixed. **2** the result of mixing; something mixed; a combination. **3** *Chem.* the product of the random distribution of one substance through another without any chemical reaction taking place between the components, as distinct from a chemical compound. **4** gas or vaporized petrol or oil mixed with air, forming an explosive charge in an internal-combustion engine. □ **the mixture as before** *Brit.* the same treatment repeated. [from Latin *mixtura*]

mix-up *n.* a confusion, misunderstanding, or mistake.

mizzen *n.* (in full **mizzen-sail**) *Naut.* the lowest fore-and-aft sail of a fully rigged ship's mizzen-mast. [from Italian *mezzana* 'mizzen-sail']

mizzen-mast *n.* the mast next aft of the mainmast. ▷ RIGGING, SHIP

ml *abbr.* **1** millilitre(s). **2** mile(s).

M.Litt. *abbr.* Master of Letters. [Latin *Magister Litterarum*]

Mlle *abbr.* (*pl.* **Mlles**) Mademoiselle.

MLR *abbr.* minimum lending rate.

m'lud see LUD.

MM *abbr.* Messieurs.

mm *abbr.* millimetre(s).

Mme *abbr.* (*pl.* **Mmes**) Madame.

Mn *symb. Chem.* the element manganese.

mnemonic /ni-mon-ik/ ● *adj.* of or designed to aid the memory. ● *n.* a mnemonic device. [from Greek *mnēmonikos*] □ **mnemonically** *adv.*

MO *abbr.* **1** Medical Officer. **2** money order.

Mo *symb. Chem.* the element molybdenum.

mo *n.* (*pl.* **mos**) *colloq.* a moment (*wait a mo*).

moa *n.* (*pl.* **moas**) ► any extinct flightless New Zealand bird of the family Dinornithidae, resembling the ostrich. [Maori]

moan ● *n.* **1** a long murmur expressing physical or mental suffering or pleasure. **2** a low plaintive sound of wind etc. **3** a complaint; a grievance. ● *v.* **1** *intr.* make a moan or moans. **2** *intr. colloq.* complain or grumble. **3** *tr.* **a** utter with moans. **b** lament. [Middle English] □ **moaner** *n.*

moat ● *n.* a deep defensive ditch round a castle, town, etc., usu. filled with water. ● *v.* surround with or as with a moat. ▷ CASTLE. [from Old French *mote*, *motte* 'mound'] □ **moated** *adj.*

mob ● *n.* **1** a disorderly crowd; a rabble. **2** (prec. by *the*) usu. *derog.* the populace. **3** *colloq.* **a** *Brit.* a gang; an associated group of persons. **b** (**the Mob**) the Mafia or a similar criminal organization. **4** *Austral.* a flock or herd. ● *v.tr.* (**mobbed**, **mobbing**) **1** crowd round in order to attack or admire. **2** *US* crowd into (a building). [short for Latin *mobile vulgus* 'excitable crowd']

MOA
(*Dinornis maximus*)

mob cap *n. hist.* ► a woman's large indoor cap covering all the hair, worn in the 18th and early 19th c. [based on obsolete (18th c.) *mob* 'slut']

mobile ● *adj.* **1** movable; not fixed; free or able to move or flow easily. **2** (of the face etc.) readily changing its expression. **3** (of a shop, library, etc.) accommodated in a vehicle so as to serve various places. **4** (of a person) able to change his or her social status. ● *n.* **1** a decorative structure hung so as to turn freely. **2** = MOBILE PHONE. [from Latin *mobilis*] □ **mobility** *n.*

mobile home *n.* a large caravan permanently parked and used as a residence.

mobile phone *n.* (also **mobile telephone**) a portable radio telephone.

mobilize *v.* (also **-ise**) **1** *tr.* organize for service or action (esp. troops in time of war). **2** *intr.* be organized in this way. □ **mobilization** *n.*

Möbius strip /**mer**-bi-ŭs/ *n. Math.* a one-sided surface formed by joining the ends of a rectangle after twisting one end through 180°. [named after A. F. *Möbius*, German mathematician, 1790–1868]

mob rule *n.* rule imposed and enforced by a mob.

mobster *n. slang* a gangster.

moccasin *n.* ► a type of soft leather shoe with combined sole and heel, as originally worn by N. American Indians. [from American Indian *mockasin*]

mocha /**mok**-ă/ *n.* **1** a coffee of fine quality. **2** a beverage or flavouring made with this. [from *Mocha*, a port on the Red Sea]

mock ● *v.* **1 a** *tr.* ridicule; scoff at. **b** *intr.* (foll. by *at*) act with scorn or contempt for. **2** *tr.* mimic contemptuously. **3** *tr.* jeer, defy, or delude contemptuously. ● *attrib.adj.* sham, imitation (esp. without intention to deceive); pretended (*a mock battle*; *mock cream*). ● *n.* (in *pl.*) *colloq.* mock examinations. □ **make mock** (or **a mock**) **of** ridicule. [from Old French *mo(c)quer* 'to deride'] □ **mockingly** *adv.*

mocker *n.* a person who mocks. □ **put the mockers on** *Brit. slang* **1** bring bad luck to. **2** put a stop to.

mockery *n.* (*pl.* **-ies**) **1** a derision, ridicule. **b** a subject or occasion of this. **2** (often foll. by *of*) a counterfeit or absurdly inadequate representation. **3** a ludicrously or insultingly futile action etc. [Middle English from Old French *moquerie* (as MOCK)]

mockingbird *n.* a long-tailed songbird of the American family Mimidae, noted as a mimic of other birds' calls, etc., esp. *Mimus polyglottos*.

MOB CAP

MOCCASIN: NATIVE AMERICAN BEADED DEERSKIN MOCCASINS

mock orange *n.* ► a white flowered heavy-scented shrub, *Philadelphus coronarius*.

mock turtle soup *n.* soup made from a calf's head etc. to resemble turtle soup.

mock-up *n.* an experimental model or replica of a proposed structure etc.

MOD *abbr.* (in the UK) Ministry of Defence.

mod *colloq.* ● *adj.* modern, esp. in style of dress. ● *n. Brit.* a young person (esp. in the 1960s) of a group aiming at sophistication and smart modern dress.

modal *adj.* **1** of or relating to mode or form as opposed to substance. **2** *Gram.* **a** of or denoting the mood of a verb. **b** (of an auxiliary verb, e.g. *would*) used to express the mood of another verb. [from medieval Latin *modalis*] □ **modality** *n.* (*pl.* **-ies**) **modally** *adv.*

mod cons *n.pl. Brit.* modern conveniences.

mode *n.* **1** a way in which a thing is done. **2** a prevailing fashion or custom. **3** *Computing* a way of operating or using a system (*print mode*). **4** *Statistics* the value that occurs most frequently in a given set of data. **5** *Mus.* any of several scale systems. **6** *N. Amer. Gram.* = MOOD[2] 1. [from Latin *modus* 'measure']

model ● *n.* **1** a representation in three dimensions of an existing person or thing or of a proposed structure, esp. on a smaller scale (often *attrib.*: *a model train*). **2** a simplified (often mathematical) description of a system etc., to assist calculations and predictions. **3** a figure in clay, wax, etc., to be reproduced in another material. **4** a particular design or style, esp. of a car. **5 a** (foll. by *of*) an exemplary person or thing (*a model of self-discipline*). **b** (*attrib.*) ideal, exemplary (*a model student*) **6 a** a person employed to pose for an artist, photographer, etc. **b** a person employed to display clothes etc. by wearing them. ● *v.* (**modelled**, **modelling**; *US* **modeled**, **modeling**) **1** *tr.* **a** fashion or shape (a figure) in clay, wax, etc. **b** (foll. by *after*, *on*, etc.) form (a thing in imitation of). **2 a** *intr.* act or pose as a model. **b** *tr.* (of a person acting as a model) display (a garment). **3** *tr.* devise (a usu. mathematical) model of (a phenomenon, system, etc.). [from Latin *modulus*] □ **modeller** *n.*

modem *n.* ▼ a combined device for modulation and demodulation, e.g. between a computer and a telephone line. [from *modulator* + *demodulator*]

moderate ● *adj.* **1** avoiding extremes; temperate in conduct or expression.

MOCK ORANGE: GOLDEN MOCK ORANGE (*Philadelphus coronarius* 'Aureus')

MODEM

A modem is a device that converts data from binary code – the string of ones and noughts that a computer reads and interprets – into an analogue signal that can be transmitted over the telephone network. It forms the basis for the transmission of e-mail and faxes and access to the Internet. An internal modem occupies an expansion slot inside a computer; an external modem plugs into a serial port on the outside of the computer.

server routes messages to addressees

service-provider's modem

monitor

telephone network

computer system

modem converts data

MODEM IN A MODERN COMMUNICATIONS SYSTEM

M

2 fairly or tolerably large or good. **3** (of the wind) of medium strength. **4** (of prices) fairly low. ● *n.* a person who holds moderate views, esp. in politics. ● *v.* **1** *tr. & intr.* make or become less violent, intense, rigorous, etc. **2** *tr.* (also *absol.*) act as a moderator of or to. [from Latin *moderatus* 'reduced, controlled'] □ **moderately** *adv.*

moderation *n.* **1** the process or an instance of moderating. **2** the quality of being moderate. □ **in moderation** in a moderate manner or degree.

moderator *n.* **1** an arbitrator or mediator. **2** a presiding officer. **3** *Eccl.* a Presbyterian minister presiding over an ecclesiastical body.

modern ● *adj.* **1** of the present and recent times. **2** in current fashion; not antiquated. ● *n.* (usu. in *pl.*) a person living in modern times. [based on Latin *modo* 'just now'] □ **modernity** *n.*

modern English *n.* English from about 1500 onwards.

modernism *n.* **1 a** modern ideas or methods. **b** the tendency of religious belief to harmonize with modern ideas. **2** a modern term or expression. □ **modernist** *n.* **modernistic** *adj.*

modernize *v.* (also **-ise**) **1** *tr.* make modern; adapt to modern needs or habits. **2** *intr.* adopt modern ways or views. □ **modernization** *n.* **modernizer** *n.*

modern Latin *n.* Latin since 1500, used esp. in scientific classification.

modest *adj.* **1** having or expressing a humble or moderate estimate of one's own merits or achievements. **2** diffident, bashful, retiring. **3** decorous. **4** moderate or restrained in amount, extent, severity, etc. (*a modest sum*). **5** (of a thing) unpretentious in appearance etc. [from Latin *modestus* 'keeping due measure'] □ **modestly** *adv.*

modesty *n.* the quality of being modest.

modicum *n.* (foll. by *of*) a small quantity. [Latin, literally 'short distance or time']

modifier *n.* **1** a person or thing that modifies. **2** *Gram.* a word, esp. an adjective or noun used attributively, that qualifies the sense of another word (e.g. *good* and *family* in *a good family house*).

modify *v.tr.* (**-ies**, **-ied**) **1** make less severe or extreme (*modify one's demands*). **2** make partial changes in; make different. **3** *Gram.* qualify or expand the sense of (a word etc.). [from Latin *modificare*] □ **modification** *n.* **modificatory** *adj.*

modish /**moh**-dish/ *adj.* fashionable. □ **modishly** *adv.* **modishness** *n.*

modiste *n.* a milliner; a dressmaker. [French]

modular *adj.* of or consisting of modules or moduli. [based on Latin *modulus* 'measure'] □ **modularity** *n.*

modulate *v.* **1** *tr.* **a** regulate or adjust. **b** moderate. **2** *tr.* adjust or vary the tone or pitch of (the speaking voice). **3** *tr.* alter the amplitude or frequency of (a wave) by a wave of a lower frequency to convey a signal. **4** *intr. & tr.* (often foll. by *from, to*) *Mus.* change or cause to change from one key to another. [based on Latin *modulatus* 'measured'] □ **modulation** *n.* **modulator** *n.*

module *n.* **1** a standardized part or independent unit used in construction, esp. of furniture, a building, or an electronic system. **2** an independent unit of a spacecraft (*lunar module*). ▷ LUNAR MODULE, SPACE-CRAFT. **3** a unit or period of training or education. [from Latin *modulus* 'small measure']

modulus *n.* (*pl.* **moduli**) *Math.* **1** the magnitude of a real number without regard to its sign. **2** a constant factor or ratio. [Latin, literally 'small measure']

modus operandi /moh-dŭs op-er-**an**-dee/ *n.* (*pl.* **modi operandi**) a way of performing a task or action. [Latin, literally 'way of operating']

modus vivendi /moh-dŭs vi-**ven**-dee/ *n.* (*pl.* **modi vivendi**) **1** a way of living or coping. **2** an arrangement between people who agree to differ. [Latin, literally 'way of living']

mog *n.* (also **moggie**) *Brit. slang* a cat. [20th-century variant of *Mag*, pet form of *Margaret*]

Mogadon *n. propr.* a benzodiazepine drug used to treat insomnia.

mogul[1] *n.* **1** *colloq.* an important or influential person. **2** (**Mogul**) *hist.* any of the emperors of Delhi in the 16th–19th c. [from Persian *mugul*]

mogul[2] *n.* a mound on a ski slope formed by skiers turning.

mohair *n.* **1** the hair of the angora goat. **2** a yarn or fabric from this. [based on Arabic *mukayyar*, literally 'choice, select']

Mohammedan var. of MUHAMMADAN.

Mohawk ● *n.* **1** (*pl.* same or **Mohawks**) a member of a N. American Indian people. **2** the Iroquoian language of this people. ● *adj.* of or relating to the Mohawks or their language. [from North American Indian *mohowawog* 'man-eaters']

Mohican ● *n.* **1** a member of a N. American Indian people of Connecticut. **2** a Mohican hairstyle. ● *adj.* **1** of or relating to this people. **2** (of a hairstyle) with the head shaved except for a strip of hair from the middle of the forehead to the back of the neck, often worn in long spikes. [native name]

moiety /**moy**-iti/ *n.* (*pl.* **-ies**) *Law* or *literary* **1** a half. **2** each of the two parts into which a thing is divided. [from Latin *medietas* 'middle']

moire /mwah/ *n.* (in full **moire antique**) watered fabric, usu. silk. [French, from MOHAIR]

moiré /**mwah**-ray/ ● *adj.* **1** ▼ (of silk) watered. **2** (of metal) having a patterned appearance like watered silk. ● *n.* **1** this patterned appearance. **2** = MOIRE. [French, literally 'made to look like moire']

MOIRÉ RIBBON

moist *adj.* slightly wet; damp. [based on Latin *mucidus* 'mouldy' and *musteus* 'fresh'] □ **moistness** *n.*

moisten *v.tr. & intr.* make or become moist.

moisture *n.* water or other liquid diffused in a small quantity as vapour, or within a solid, or condensed on a surface.

moisturize *v.tr.* (also **-ise**) make less dry (esp. the skin by use of a cosmetic). □ **moisturizer** *n.*

moke *n. slang Brit.* a donkey. [19th c.: origin unknown]

mol /mohl/ *abbr.* = MOLE[4].

molar ● *adj.* (usu. of a mammal's back teeth) serving to grind. ● *n.* ▼ a molar tooth. ▷ DENTITION, PREMOLAR, TOOTH. [based on Latin *mola* 'millstone']

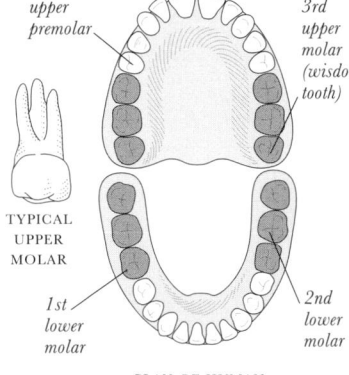

upper premolar

3rd upper molar (wisdom tooth)

TYPICAL UPPER MOLAR

1st lower molar

2nd lower molar

PLAN OF HUMAN DENTITION

MOLAR

molasses *n.pl.* (treated as *sing.*) **1** uncrystallized syrup extracted from raw sugar during refining. **2** *N. Amer.* treacle. [from Late Latin *mellaceum* 'fermenting juice']

mold *US* var. of MOULD[1], MOULD[2], MOULD[3].

molder *US* var. of MOULDER.

molding *US* var. of MOULDING.

moldy *US* var. of MOULDY.

MOLECULE

A molecule is a discrete unit made from atoms joined together by chemical bonds. All molecules of the same compound are identical. All water molecules, for example, consist of an atom of oxygen, chemically bound to two hydrogen atoms. Molecules may consist of just two atoms, or many thousands.

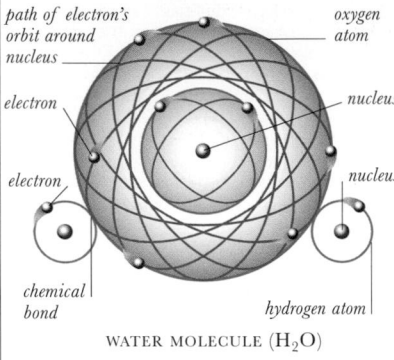

path of electron's orbit around nucleus

oxygen atom

electron

nucleus

electron

nucleus

chemical bond

hydrogen atom

WATER MOLECULE (H_2O)

mole[1] *n.* **1** any small burrowing insect-eating mammal of the family Talpidae, esp. *Talpa europaea*, with dark velvety fur and very small eyes. ▷ INSECT-IVORE, NEST. **2** *colloq.* a spy within an organization, usu. dormant for a long period while attaining a position of trust. [Middle English]

mole[2] *n.* a small often slightly raised dark blemish on the skin caused by a high concentration of melanin. [Old English]

mole[3] *n.* **1** a structure serving as a pier, breakwater, or causeway. **2** an artificial harbour. [from Latin *moles* 'mass']

mole[4] *n. Chem.* the SI unit of amount of substance equal to the quantity containing as many elementary units as there are atoms in 0.012 kg of carbon-12. [based on German *Molekül* 'molecule']

molecular *adj.* of, relating to, or consisting of molecules. □ **molecularity** *n.*

molecular biology *n.* the study of the structure and function of large molecules associated with living organisms.

molecular sieve *n.* a crystalline substance with pores of molecular dimensions which permit the passage of molecules below a certain size.

molecular weight *n.* = RELATIVE MOLECULAR MASS.

molecule *n.* **1** *Chem.* ▲ the smallest fundamental unit (usu. a group of atoms) of a chemical compound that can take part in a chemical reaction. **2** (in general use) a small particle. [from modern Latin *molecula*]

molehill *n.* a small mound pushed up by a mole in burrowing. □ **make a mountain out of a molehill** exaggerate the importance of a minor difficulty.

mole rat *n.* any of various ratlike rodents with reduced eyes which live underground, esp. of the African family Bathyergidae, often living communally. ▷ RODENT

moleskin *n.* **1** the skin of a mole used as fur. **2 a** kind of cotton fustian with its surface shaved before dyeing. **b** (in *pl.*) clothes, esp. trousers, made of this.

molest *v.tr.* **1** annoy or pester (a person) in a hostile or injurious way. **2** attack or interfere with (a person), esp. sexually. [from Latin *molestare* 'to annoy'] □ **molestation** *n.* **molester** *n.*

moll *n. slang* **1** a gangster's female companion. **2** a prostitute. [pet form of the name *Mary*]

mollify *v.tr.* (**-ies**, **-ied**) **1** appease, pacify; soften. **2** reduce the severity of; soften. [based on Latin *mollis* 'soft'] □ **mollification** *n.*

mollusc *n.* (*US* also **mollusk**) ▼ any invertebrate of the phylum Mollusca, with a soft body and usu. a hard shell, including snails, cuttlefish, mussels, etc. [from modern Latin *mollusca*] □ **molluscan** *adj.*

mollycoddle *v.tr.* coddle, pamper. [formed as MOLL + CODDLE]

Molotov cocktail *n.* a crude incendiary device usu. a bottle filled with inflammable liquid. [named after V. M. *Molotov*, Russian statesman, 1890–1986]

molt *US* var. of MOULT.

molten *adj.* melted, esp. made liquid by heat (*molten lava*; *molten lead*). [past participle of MELT]

molto *adv. Mus.* very (*molto sostenuto*; *allegro molto*). [Italian]

molybdenum *n. Chem.* a silver-white brittle metallic transition element occurring naturally in molybdenite and used in steel to give strength and resistance to corrosion. [based on Greek *molubdaina* 'plummet']

mom *n. N. Amer. colloq.* mother.

moment *n.* **1** a brief or very brief portion of time. **2** an exact or particular point of time (*at last the moment arrived*). **3** importance (*of no great moment*). **4** *Physics & Mech.* a turning effect, esp. expressed as the product of a force and the distance from its line of action to a point. □ **at the moment** at this time; now. **have one's moments** be impressive, happy, etc., on occasions. **in a moment 1** very soon. **2** instantly. **man** (or **woman** etc.) **of the moment** the one of importance at the time in question. **this moment** immediately; at once (*come here this moment*). [from Latin *momentum*]

momenta *pl.* of MOMENTUM.

Most organized religions, especially the Christian and Buddhist traditions, have monasteries where monks, who have chosen to devote their lives to their religion, live apart from society. Monastic life is dominated by prayer, so the church is a central feature, but there are also rooms for eating, washing, sleeping, and studying, as well as an infirmary. A garden, or farm, is another important feature, providing a means of sustenance and revenue for the religious community.

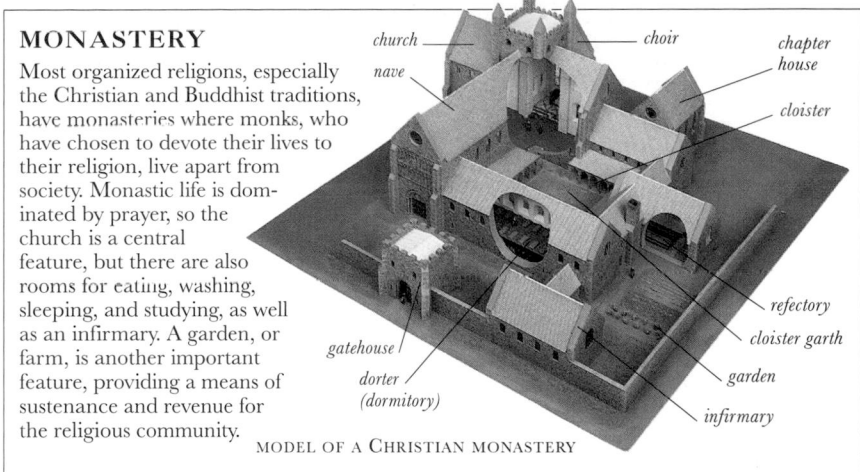

church — choir — chapter house

nave

cloister

refectory

cloister garth

gatehouse

dorter (dormitory)

garden

infirmary

MODEL OF A CHRISTIAN MONASTERY

momentarily *adv.* **1** for a moment. **2** *N. Amer.* **a** at any moment. **b** instantly.

momentary *adj.* lasting only a moment.

moment of truth *n.* a time of crisis or test (originally the final sword-thrust in a bullfight).

momentous *adj.* having great importance. □ **momentously** *adv.* **momentousness** *n.*

momentum *n.* (*pl.* **momenta**) **1** *Physics* the quantity of motion of a moving body, measured as a product of its mass and velocity. **2** the impetus gained by movement. **3** strength or continuity derived from an initial effort. [Latin]

momma *n.* var. of MAMMA.

mommy *n.* (*pl.* **-ies**) esp. *US colloq.* = MUMMY[1].

Mon. *abbr.* Monday.

monad *n.* **1** the number one; a unit. **2** *Philos.* any ultimate unit of being (e.g. a soul, an atom, a person, God). **3** *Biol.* a simple organism, e.g. one assumed as the first in the genealogy of living beings. [from Greek *monas -ados* 'unit'] □ **monadic** *adj.*

monarch *n.* a sovereign with the title of king, queen, emperor, empress, or the equivalent. [from Greek *monarkhēs*, literally 'lone ruler'] □ **monarchic** *adj.* **monarchical** *adj.*

monarchism *n.* the advocacy of or the principles of monarchy. □ **monarchist** *n.*

monarchy *n.* (*pl.* **-ies**) **1** a form of government with a monarch at the head. **2** a state with this. □ **monarchial** *adj.*

monastery *n.* (*pl.* **-ies**) ▲ the residence of a religious community, esp. of monks. [from ecclesiastical Greek *monastērion*]

monastic *adj.* of or relating to monasteries or the religious communities living in them. [based on Greek *monazein* 'to live alone'] □ **monastically** *adv.* **monasticism** *n.*

monaural *adj.* **1** = MONOPHONIC. **2** of or involving one ear. □ **monaurally** *adv.*

Monday ● *n.* the second day of the week, following Sunday. ● *adv. colloq.* **1** on Monday. **2** (**Mondays**) on Mondays; each Monday. [Old English *mōnandæg* 'day of the moon']

monetarism *n.* the theory or practice of controlling the supply of money as the chief method of stabilizing the economy. □ **monetarist** *n. & adj.*

monetary *adj.* **1** of the currency in use. **2** of or consisting of money. [from Late Latin *monetarius*]

monetize *v.tr.* (also **-ise**) **1** give a fixed value as currency. **2** put (a metal) into circulation as money. [from French *monétiser*] □ **monetization** *n.*

money *n.* **1** a current medium of exchange in the form of coins and banknotes. **2** (*pl.* **-eys** or **-ies**) (in *pl.*) sums of money. **3 a** wealth. **b** a rich person or family (*has married into money*). □ **for my money** in my opinion or judgement; for my preference (*is too aggressive for my money*). **in the money** *colloq.* having or winning a lot of money. **money for jam** (or **old rope**) *Brit. colloq.* profit for little or no trouble. **put money into** invest in. [from Latin *moneta* 'mint, money'] □ **moneyless** *adj.*

moneybags *n.pl.* (treated as *sing.*) *colloq.* usu. *derog.* a wealthy person.

money box *n. Brit.* a box for saving money dropped through a slit.

moneyed *adj.* having much money; wealthy.

MOLLUSC

With over 80,000 species, molluscs form the second largest phylum of animals on Earth, and range from tiny snails to giant squid. Most molluscs are aquatic, but some slugs and snails live on land. A typical mollusc has a soft body, protected by a shell. The shell is formed by a layer of tissue called the mantle. Most molluscs belong to one of the four main groups – gastropods, bivalves, cephalopods, and chitons. Gastropods move with the help of a single sucker-like foot, which moves in a series of muscular waves.

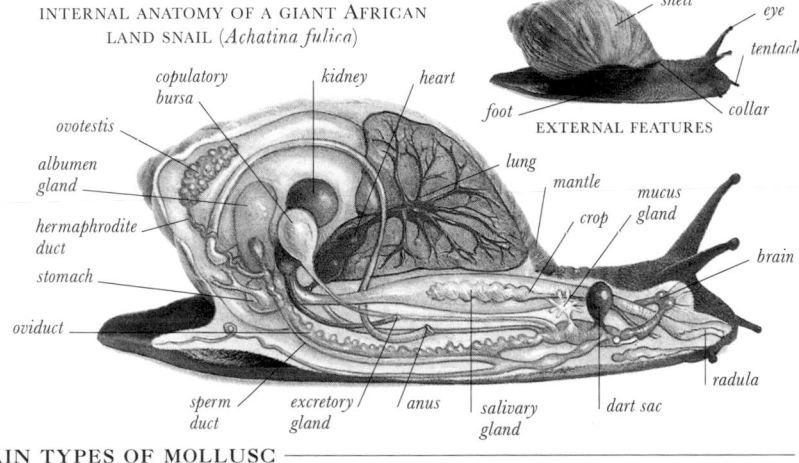

INTERNAL ANATOMY OF A GIANT AFRICAN LAND SNAIL (*Achatina fulica*)

copulatory bursa   kidney   heart
ovotestis
albumen gland
hermaphrodite duct
stomach
oviduct

sperm duct   excretory gland   anus   salivary gland   dart sac

lung
mantle
mucus gland
crop
brain
radula

shell   eye
tentacle
foot   collar

EXTERNAL FEATURES

MAIN TYPES OF MOLLUSC

GASTROPODS (slugs, snails)
▷ GASTROPOD, SNAIL

BIVALVES (clams, mussels, scallops)
▷ BIVALVE

CEPHALOPODS (octopuses, squid)
▷ CEPHALOPOD, OCTOPUS

CHITONS (chitons)

M

M

money-grubber *n. colloq.* a person greedily intent on amassing money. □ **money-grubbing** *adj. & n.*

moneylender *n.* a person who lends money, esp. as a business, at interest. □ **moneylending** *n. & adj.*

moneymaker *n.* **1** a person who earns much money. **2** a thing, idea, etc., that produces much money. □ **moneymaking** *n. & adj.*

money market *n. Stock Exch.* trade in short-term stocks, loans, etc.

money order *n.* an order for payment of a specified sum, issued by a bank or Post Office.

money spider *n.* a small household spider supposed to bring financial luck.

money-spinner *n.* esp. *Brit.* a thing that brings in a profit.

money supply *n.* the total amount of money in circulation or in being in a country.

money's-worth *n.* (prec. by *your, my, one's,* etc.) good value for one's money.

monger *n.* (usu. in *comb.*) **1** a dealer or trader (*fishmonger; ironmonger*). **2** usu. *derog.* a person who promotes or deals in something specified (*warmonger; scaremonger*). [from Latin *mango* 'dealer']

Mongol ● *adj.* **1** of or relating to the Asian people now inhabiting Mongolia in central Asia. **2** resembling this people, esp. in appearance. **3** (**mongol**) *offens.* suffering from Down's syndrome. ● *n.* **1** a Mongolian. **2** (**mongol**) *offens.* a person suffering from Down's syndrome. [Mongolian: perhaps from *mong* 'brave']

■ **Usage** In sense 3 of the adjective and sense 2 of the noun, *Down's syndrome* should be used in place of *mongol* in order to avoid offence, e.g. *a Down's syndrome baby; She suffers from Down's syndrome.*

Mongolian ● *n.* **1** a native or inhabitant of Mongolia. **2** the language of Mongolia. ● *adj.* of or relating to Mongolia or its people or language.

mongolism *n. offens.* = DOWN'S SYNDROME.

■ **Usage** The term *Down's syndrome* is now much preferred to *mongolism* which can cause offence.

Mongoloid ● *adj.* **1** characteristic of the Mongolians, esp. in having a broad flat yellowish face. **2** (**mongoloid**) *offens.* affected with Down's syndrome. ● *n.* a Mongoloid or *offens.* mongoloid person.

mongoose *n.* (*pl.* **mongooses**) ◄ any of various small flesh-eating civet-like mammals of the family Viverridae, including the genera *Herpestes* and *Mungos*. [from Marathi spoken in W. India) *mangūs*]

MONGOOSE: BANDED MONGOOSE (*Mungos mungo*)

mongrel ● *n.* **1** a dog of no definable type or breed. **2** any other animal or plant resulting from the crossing of different breeds or types. ● *adj.* of mixed origin, nature, or character.

monies see MONEY 2.

moniker *n.* (also **monicker**) *slang* a name. [19th-century coinage]

monism *n.* **1** any theory denying the duality of matter and mind. **2** *Philos. & Theol.* the doctrine that only one supreme being exists. [based on Greek *monos* 'single'] □ **monist** *n.* **monistic** *adj.*

monitor ● *n.* **1** any of various persons or devices for checking or warning about a situation, operation, etc. **2** a school pupil with disciplinary or other special duties. **3 a** a television receiver used in a studio to select or verify

adjustable jaw

MONKEY WRENCH: FRONT-RACK WRENCH

MONITOR

A computer monitor is a very precise type of television screen that displays images created by the graphics card in a computer. The display area is divided into a grid of pixels (picture elements); each pixel is made up of at least one set of three dots (one red, one blue, and one green) of phosphor – a substance that glows when stimulated by electrons. Electron beams, directed through a mask within the monitor, can vary the brightness of each dot to make any pixel produce any colour. On-screen graphics are created by manipulating the colours of pixels and the number of pixels displayed.

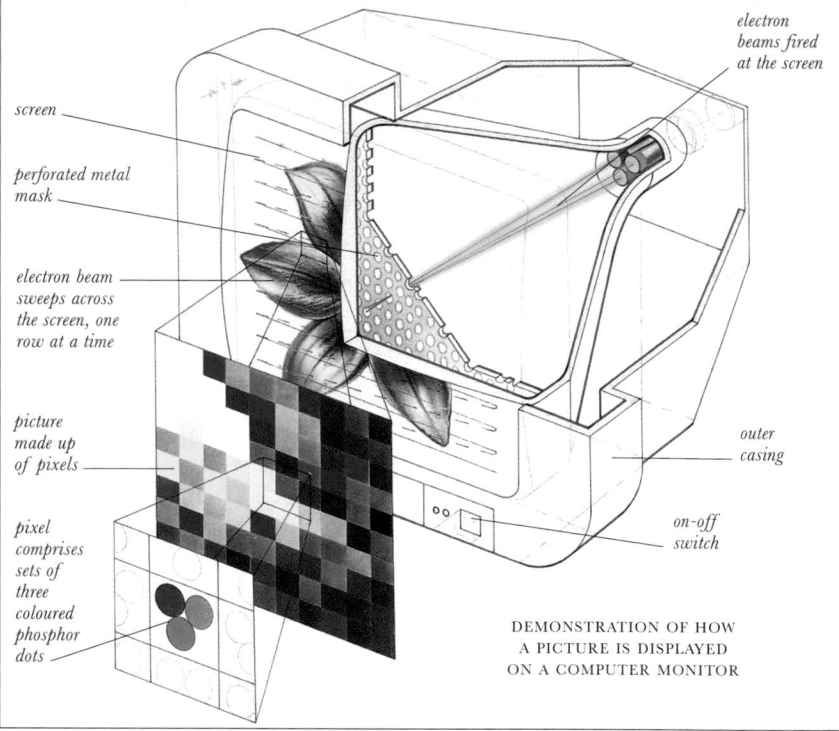

electron beams fired at the screen

screen

perforated metal mask

electron beam sweeps across the screen, one row at a time

picture made up of pixels

pixel comprises sets of three coloured phosphor dots

outer casing

on-off switch

DEMONSTRATION OF HOW A PICTURE IS DISPLAYED ON A COMPUTER MONITOR

---

the picture being broadcast. **b** esp. *Brit. Computing* ▲ a device displaying data on a screen. ▷ COMPUTER, TOUCH SCREEN. **4** a person who listens to and reports on foreign broadcasts etc. **5** *Zool.* any tropical lizard of the genus *Varanus*, supposed to give warning of the approach of crocodiles. ● *v.tr.* **1** act as a monitor of. **2** maintain regular surveillance over. [Latin] □ **monitorial** *adj.*

monitory *adj. literary* giving or serving as a warning.

monk *n.* a member of a religious community of men living under certain vows esp. of poverty, chastity, and obedience. [based on Greek *monakhos* 'solitary'] □ **monkish** *adj.*

monkey ● *n.* (*pl.* **-eys**) **1** any of various mainly long-tailed agile tree-dwelling primates of the families Cebidae, Callithricidae, and Cercopithecidae. ▷ PRIMATE. **2** a mischievous person, esp. a child (*young monkey*). **3** *Brit. slang* £500. ● *v.intr.* (**-eys, -eyed**) **1** (often foll. by *with*) tamper or play mischievous tricks. **2** (foll. by *around, about*) fool around. □ **make a monkey of** humiliate by making appear ridiculous. [16th-century coinage]

monkey bars *n.pl. N.Amer.* = CLIMBING FRAME.

monkey business *n. colloq.* mischief.

monkey-nut *n. Brit.* a peanut.

monkey-puzzle *n.* (in full **monkey-puzzle tree**) a coniferous tree, *Araucaria araucana*, native to Chile, with downward-pointing, prickly branches.

monkey tricks *n.pl. Brit. colloq.* mischief.

monkey wrench *n.* ◄ a wrench with an adjustable jaw. □ **monkeywrenching** *n.*

monkfish *n.* (*pl.* usu. same) an angler fish, esp. *Lophius piscatorius*, often used as food.

monkshood *n.* ► a poisonous garden plant *Aconitum napellus*, with hood-shaped blue or purple flowers.

mono ● *adj.* monophonic. ● *n.* (*pl.* **-os**) a monophonic record, reproduction, etc.

mono- *comb. form* (usu. **mon-** before a vowel) **1** one, alone, single. **2** *Chem.* (forming names of compounds) containing one atom or group of a specified kind. [Greek]

monochromatic *adj.* **1** *Physics* (of light or other radiation) of a single wavelength or frequency. **2** containing only one colour. □ **monochromatically** *adv.*

monochrome ● *n.* a photograph or picture done in one colour or different tones of this, or in black and white only. ● *adj.* having or using only one colour or in black and white only. [from Greek *monokhrōmatos*]

MONKSHOOD (*Aconitum napellus*)

monocle *n.* a single eyeglass. [originally French *adj.*, from Late Latin *monoculus* 'one-eyed'] □ **monocled** *adj.*

monocoque *n.* an aircraft or vehicle structure in which the chassis is integral with the body. [French]

monocot *n.* = MONOCOTYLEDON. [abbreviation]

monocotyledon /mon-oh-kot-i-**lee**-dŏn/ *n. Bot.* any flowering plant with a single cotyledon. ▷ ANGIOSPERM, FLOWER. □ **monocotyledonous** *adj.*

monocular *adj.* with or for one eye. [from Late Latin *monoculus* 'one-eyed']

monoculture *n.* the cultivation of a single crop.

monocycle *n.* = UNICYCLE.

monocyte *n. Biol.* a large leucocyte with a simple nucleus, developing into a macrophage.

monody *n.* (*pl.* **-ies**) **1** an ode sung by a single actor in a Greek tragedy. **2** a poem lamenting a person's death. [from Greek *monōidia* □ **monodic** *adj.* **monodist** *n.*

monoecious /mō-nee-shŭs/ *adj.* **1** *Bot.* with unisexual male and female organs on the same plant. **2** *Zool.* hermaphrodite. [based on Greek *monos* 'single' + *oikos* 'house']

monogamy *n.* **1** the practice or state of being married to one person at a time. **2** *Zool.* the habit of having only one mate at a time. [from Greek *monogamia*] □ **monogamist** *n.* **monogamous** *adj.* **monogamously** *adv.*

monoglot ● *adj.* using only one language. ● *n.* a monoglot person. [based on Greek *glōtta* 'tongue']

monogram *n.* two or more letters, esp. a person's initials, interwoven as a device. □ **monogrammed** *adj.*

monograph *n.* a separate treatise on a single subject. □ **monographic** *adj.*

monohull *n.* a boat with a single hull.

monokini *n.* a woman's one-piece beach garment equivalent to the lower half of a bikini.

monolingual *adj.* speaking or using only one language.

monolith *n.* **1** a single block of stone, esp. shaped into a pillar or monument. **2** a person or thing like a monolith in being massive, immovable, or solidly uniform. [based on Greek *lithos* 'stone'] □ **monolithic** *adj.*

monologue *n.* **1 a** a scene in a drama in which a person speaks alone. **b** a dramatic composition for one performer. **2** a long speech by one person in a conversation etc. □ **monologic** *adj.* **monological** *adj.* **monologist** *n.* (also **-loguist**)

monomania *n.* obsession of the mind by one idea or interest. □ **monomaniac** *n. & adj.*

monomer *n. Chem.* **1** a unit in a dimer, trimer, or polymer. **2** a molecule or compound that can be polymerized. □ **monomeric** *adj.*

monophonic *adj.* (of sound reproduction) using only one channel of transmission (cf. STEREOPHONIC). [based on Greek *phōnē* 'sound']

monoplane *n.* ▼ an aeroplane with one set of wings (cf. BIPLANE). ▷ AIRCRAFT

MONORAIL IN WUPPERTAL, GERMANY

monorail *n.* ▲ a railway in which the track consists of a single rail, usu. elevated with the trains suspended from it.

monosaccharide /mon-oh-**sak**-ă-ryd/ *n. Chem.* a sugar that cannot be hydrolysed to give a simpler sugar, e.g. glucose.

monosodium glutamate *n. Chem.* a sodium salt of glutamic acid used to flavour food (cf. GLUTAMATE).

monosyllabic *adj.* **1** (of a word) having one syllable. **2** (of a person or statement) using or expressed in monosyllables. □ **monosyllabically** *adv.*

monosyllable *n.* a word of one syllable.

monotheism *n.* the doctrine that there is only one God. [based on Greek *theos* 'god'] □ **monotheist** *n.* **monotheistic** *adj.*

monotone ● *n.* **1** a sound or utterance continuing or repeated on one note without change of pitch. **2** sameness of style in writing. ● *adj.* without change of pitch. [from late Greek *monotonos*]

monotonous *adj.* **1** lacking in variety; tedious through sameness. **2** (of a sound or utterance) without variation in tone or pitch. □ **monotonously** *adv.*

monotony *n.* **1** the state of being monotonous. **2** dull or tedious routine.

monotreme *n.* any egg-laying mammal of the order Monotremata, native to Australia and New Guinea, e.g. the platypus and echidna, having a cloaca. ▷ MAMMAL. [from Greek *monos* 'single' + *trēma* 'hole']

monotype *n.* **1** (**Monotype**) *Printing propr.* a typesetting machine that casts and sets up types in individual characters. **2** an impression on paper made from an inked design painted on glass or metal.

monounsaturated *adj. Chem.* (of a compound, esp. a fat) saturated except for one multiple bond.

monovalent *adj. Chem.* having a valency of one.

monoxide *n. Chem.* an oxide containing one oxygen atom (*carbon monoxide*).

Monseigneur /mon-sen-**yer**/ *n.* (*pl.* ***Messeigneurs*** /mes-en-**yer**/) a title given to an eminent French person, esp. a prince, cardinal, archbishop, or bishop. [French, literally 'my lord']

Monsieur /mŏ-**syer**/ *n.* (*pl.* **Messieurs** /mes-**yer**/) **1** the title or form of address used of or to a French-speaking man, corresponding to Mr or sir. **2** a Frenchman. [French, from *mon* 'my' + *sieur* 'lord']

Monsignor /mon-**seen**-yer/ *n.* (*pl.* **Monsignori** /mon-seen-**yor**-i/) the title of various Roman Catholic prelates, officers of the papal court, etc. [Italian]

monsoon *n.* **1** a wind in S. Asia, esp. in the Indian Ocean, blowing from the south-west in summer

(**wet monsoon**) and the north-east in winter (**dry monsoon**). **2** a rainy season accompanying a wet monsoon. **3** any other wind with periodic alterations. [Arabic *mawsim* 'fixed season']

monster *n.* **1** an imaginary creature, usu. large and frightening, compounded of incongruous elements. **2** an inhumanly cruel or wicked person. **3** a misshapen animal or plant. **4** a large usu. ugly animal or thing. **5** (*attrib.*) huge; extremely large of its kind. [from Latin *monstrum* 'portent, monster']

monstera *n.* any climbing plant of the genus *Monstera*, including the Swiss cheese plant.

monstrance *n. RC Ch.* a receptacle in which the consecrated Host is exposed for veneration. [Middle English in sense 'demonstration', based on Latin *monstrare* 'to show']

monstrosity *n.* (*pl.* **-ies**) **1** a huge or outrageous thing. **2** monstrousness. **3** = MONSTER 3. [from Late Latin *monstrositas*]

monstrous *adj.* **1** like a monster; abnormally formed. **2** huge. **3 a** outrageously wrong or absurd. **b** atrocious. [from Latin *monstrosus*] □ **monstrously** *adv.* **monstrousness** *n.*

montage /mon-**tah**zh/ *n.* **1 a** a process of selecting, editing, and piecing together separate sections of cinema or television film to form a continuous whole. **b** a sequence of such film. **2 a** the technique of producing a new composite whole from fragments of pictures, words, music, etc. **b** a composition produced in this way. [French]

montane *adj.* of or inhabiting mountainous country. [from Latin *montanus*]

Montessori *n.* (usu. *attrib.*) a system of education (esp. of young children) that seeks to develop natural interests and activities rather than use formal teaching methods. [named after Maria *Montessori*, Italian educationist d. 1952, who initiated it]

month *n.* **1** (in full **calendar month**) **a** each of usu. twelve periods into which a year is divided. **b** a period of time between the same dates in successive calendar months. **2** a period of 28 days or of four weeks. **3** = LUNAR MONTH. □ **month of Sundays** a very long period. [Old English, related to MOON]

monthly ● *adj.* done, produced, or occurring once a month. ● *adv.* once a month; from month to month. ● *n.* (*pl.* **ies**) a monthly periodical.

monty *n.* the full amount expected, desired, or possible (*the full monty*). [20th-century coinage]

monument *n.* **1** anything enduring that serves to commemorate or make celebrated, esp. a structure or building. **2** a stone or other structure placed over a grave or in a church etc. in memory of the dead. **3** an ancient building or site etc. that has been preserved. **4** (foll. by *of*, *to*) a typical or outstanding example (*a monument of indiscretion*). [from Latin *monumentum*]

monumental *adj.* **1 a** extremely great, stupendous (*a monumental achievement*). **b** (of a literary work) massive and permanent. **2** of or serving as a monument. □ **monumentality** *n.* **monumentally** *adv.*

monumentalize *v.tr.* (also **-ise**) commemorate by or as by a monument.

monumental mason *n.* a maker of tombstones etc.

moo ● *v.intr.* (**moos**, **mooed**) make the characteristic vocal sound of cattle. ● *n.* (*pl.* **moos**) this sound.

mooch *v. colloq.* **1** *intr. Brit.* loiter or saunter desultorily. **2** *tr.* esp. *N. Amer.* **a** steal. **b** beg. [Middle English] □ **moocher** *n.*

mood[1] *n.* **1** a state of mind or feeling. **2** a fit of melancholy or bad temper. **3** (*attrib.*) inducing a particular mood (*mood music*). □ **in the** (or **no**) **mood** (foll. by *for*, or *to* + infin.) inclined (or disinclined) (*was in no mood to agree*). [Old English *mōd* 'mind, thought']

mood[2] *n.* **1** *Gram.* a form or set of forms of a verb serving to indicate whether it is to express fact, command, wish, etc. (*subjunctive mood*). **2** the distinction of meaning, for example possibility or necessity, expressed by different moods.

---

monoplane labels: single wing · starboard elevator · nose-ring · seven-cylinder rotary engine · tailskid

MONOPLANE: 1912 BLACKBURN MONOPLANE

monopod *n.* a structure having only one foot, esp. a one-legged support for a camera. [from Greek *monopodion*]

monopole *n.* **1** *Physics* a single electric charge or magnetic pole, esp. a hypothetical isolated magnetic pole. **2** a radio aerial, pylon, etc. consisting of a single pole or rod.

monopolist *n.* a person who has or advocates a monopoly. □ **monopolistic** *adj.*

monopolize *v.tr.* (also **-ise**) **1** obtain exclusive possession or control of (a trade or commodity etc.). **2** dominate or prevent others from sharing in (a conversation etc.). □ **monopolization** *n.*

monopoly *n.* (*pl.* **-ies**) **1** the exclusive possession or control of the trade in a commodity or service. **2 a** such a commodity or service. **b** a company etc. that possesses a monopoly. **3** (foll. by *of*, *on*) exclusive possession, control, or exercise. [from Greek *monopōlion*]

M

MOON

The Moon is a natural satellite of the Earth, and takes 27.3 days to travel round its orbit. As the Moon takes the same time to rotate on its own axis, the surface seen from the Earth is always the same. The amount of the surface visible, however, varies according to how much of it is in sunlight; this produces the familiar lunar phases. The Moon is barren, with no atmosphere or liquid water, but polar craters are believed to contain small quantities of ice. Its dusty surface has been cratered by meteorites; some of the larger craters have filled with lava to form dark areas known as maria or mares ('seas').

crust of granite-like rock
partially molten outer core
thick dust layer
cratered surface
Avogadro crater
Fabry crater
Mendeleev crater
Gagarin crater
Mare Ingenii
Schrödinger crater
Leibnitz crater
Zeeman crater
Apollo crater
Mare Orientale
Galois crater
small inner core
rocky mantle
Mare Muscoviense

MOON (FAR SIDE), WITH
INTERNAL STRUCTURE REVEALED

MOONSTONE: CAMEO
BROOCH OF BLUE
MOONSTONE

moody *adj.* (**moodier, moodiest**) given to extreme changes of mood; gloomy, sullen. [Old English *mōdig* 'brave'] □ **moodily** *adv.* **moodiness** *n.*

moon ● *n.* **1 a** (also **Moon**) ▲ the natural satellite of the Earth, orbiting it monthly, illuminated by the Sun and reflecting some light to the Earth. ▷ ECLIPSE. **b** this regarded in terms of its waxing and waning in a particular month (*new moon*). ▷ LUNAR MONTH. **c** the Moon when visible (*there is no moon tonight*). **2** a satellite of any planet. **3** *poet.* a month. ● *v.* **1** *intr.* move or look listlessly. **2** *tr.* (foll. by *away*) spend (time) in a listless manner. **3** *intr.* (foll. by *over*) act aimlessly or inattentively from infatuation for (a person). **4** *intr. slang* expose one's buttocks. □ **over the moon** extremely happy. [Old English] □ **moonless** *adj.*

moonbeam *n.* a ray of moonlight.

moon boot *n.* a thickly-padded boot designed for low temperatures.

moon-faced *adj.* having a round face.

Moonie *n. colloq. offens.* a member of the Unification Church. [from the name of its founder, Sun Myung *Moon*]

moonlight ● *n.* **1** the light of the Moon. **2** (*attrib.*) lit by the Moon. ● *v.intr.* (*past* and *past part.* **-lighted**) *colloq.* have two paid occupations, esp. one by day and one by night. □ **moonlighter** *n.*

moonlight flit *n. Brit.* a hurried departure by night.

moonlit *adj.* lit by the Moon.

moonscape *n.* **1** the surface or landscape of the Moon. **2** an area resembling this; a wasteland.

moonshine *n.* **1** foolish or unrealistic talk or ideas. **2** *slang* smuggled spirit or esp. *N. Amer.* illicitly distilled liquor.

moonshiner *n. US slang* a smuggler, or esp. *N. Amer.* an illicit distiller of alcoholic liquor.

moonshot *n.* the launching of a spacecraft to the Moon.

moonstone *n.* ◄ feldspar of pearly appearance.

moonstruck *adj.* mentally deranged.

moony *adj.* (**moonier, mooniest**) **1** listless; stupidly dreamy. **2** of or like the Moon.

Moor *n.* a member of a Muslim people of mixed Berber and Arab descent, inhabiting NW Africa. [from Greek *Mauros* 'inhabitant of *Mauretania*', a region of N. Africa]

moor[1] *n.* **1** a tract of open uncultivated upland. **2** a tract of such land preserved for shooting. **3** *US* or *dial.* a fen. [Old English *mōr* 'waste land, mountain']

moor[2] *v.* **1** *tr.* make fast (a boat, buoy, etc.) by attaching a cable etc. to a fixed object. **2** *intr.* (of a boat) be moored. [Middle English]

MOORHEN
(*Gallinula chloropus*)

moorhen *n.* **1** ◄ a small aquatic bird, *Gallinula chloropus*, with mainly blackish plumage and a short red-yellow bill. **2** a female red grouse.

mooring *n.* **1 a** a fixed object to which a boat, buoy, etc., is moored. **b** (often in *pl.*) a place where a boat etc. is moored. **2** (in *pl.*) a set of permanent anchors and chains laid down for ships to be moored to.

mooring-mast see MAST[1] *n.* 4.

Moorish *adj.* ▼ of or relating to the Moors.

MOORISH PALACE
(THE ALHAMBRA, SPAIN)

moorland *n.* an extensive area of moor.

moose *n.* (*pl.* same) esp. *N. Amer.* ► the elk, *Alces alces*. [from North American Indian *moos*]

moot ● *adj.* debatable, undecided (*a moot point*). ● *v.tr.* raise (a question) for discussion. ● *n.* **1** *hist.* an assembly. *Law* a discussion of a hypothetical case as an academic exercise. [Old English]

MOOSE
(*Alces alces*)

■ **Usage** *Moot* 'debatable, undecided' is sometimes confused with *mute* 'silent, dumb', especially in the phrase *moot point*.

mop ● *n.* **1** a wad or bundle of cotton or synthetic material fastened to the end of a stick, for cleaning floors etc. **2** a similarly-shaped implement for various purposes. **3** a thick mass of hair. **4** an act of mopping or being mopped (*gave it a mop*). ● *v.tr.* (**mopped, mopping**) **1** wipe or clean with or as with a mop. **2 a** wipe tears or sweat etc. from (one's face or brow etc.). **b** wipe away (tears etc.). □ **mop up 1** wipe up with or as with a mop. **2** *colloq.* absorb (profits etc.). **3** dispatch; make an end of. **4** *Mil.* **a** complete the occupation of (a district etc.) by capturing or killing enemy troops left there. **b** capture or kill (stragglers). [Middle English]

mope ● *v.intr.* **1** be gloomily depressed or listless. **2** wander about listlessly. ● *n.* a person who mopes. [16th-century coinage]

moped *n.* a motorized bicycle with an engine capacity below 50 cc. [Swedish]

moppet *n. colloq.* a baby or small child. [from obsolete *moppe* 'baby, doll']

moquette *n.* a thick pile or looped material used for carpets and upholstery. [French]

moraine *n.* an area covered by rocks and debris carried down and deposited by a glacier. ▷ GLACIER. [based on French dialect *mor(re)* 'snout'] □ **morainic** *adj.*

moral ● *adj.* **1 a** concerned with goodness or badness of human character or behaviour, or with the distinction between right and wrong. **b** concerned with accepted rules and standards of human behaviour. **2 a** conforming to accepted standards of general conduct. **b** capable of moral action (*man is a moral agent*). **3** (of rights or duties etc.) founded on moral law. **4 a** concerned with morals or ethics (*moral philosophy*). **b** (of a literary work etc.) dealing with moral conduct. **5** concerned with or leading to a psychological effect associated with confidence in a right action (*moral courage; moral support; moral victory*). ● *n.* **1 a** a moral lesson of a fable, story, event, etc. **b** a moral maxim or principle. **2** (in *pl.*) moral behaviour. [based on Latin *mos moris* 'custom'] □ **morally** *adv.*

moral certainty *n.* probability so great as to allow no reasonable doubt.

morale /mŏ-**rahl**/ *n.* the mental attitude or bearing of a person or group, esp. as regards confidence, discipline, etc. [from French *moral*]

moralism *n.* **1** a natural system of morality. **2** religion regarded as moral practice.

moralist *n.* **1** a person who practises or teaches morality. **2** a person who follows a natural system of ethics. □ **moralistic** *adj.*

morality *n.* (*pl.* **-ies**) **1** the degree of conformity of an idea, practice, etc., to moral principles. **2** right moral conduct. **3** a lesson in morals. **4** the science of morals. **5** a particular system of morals (*commercial morality*). **6** (in *pl.*) moral principles; points of ethics. **7** (in full **morality play**) *hist.* a kind of drama with personified abstract qualities as the main characters and inculcating a moral lesson, popular in the 16th c.

moralize v. (also **-ise**) **1** intr. indulge in moral reflection or talk. **2** tr. interpret morally; point the moral of. **3** tr. make moral or more moral. □ **moralization** n. **moralizer** n.

moral law n. the conditions to be satisfied by any right course of action.

moral philosophy n. the branch of philosophy concerned with ethics.

moral pressure n. persuasion by appealing to a person's moral sense.

moral sense n. the ability to distinguish right and wrong.

morass n. **1** an entanglement; a disordered situation, esp. one impeding progress. **2** literary a bog or marsh. [from medieval Latin mariscus]

moratorium n. (pl. **moratoriums** or **moratoria**) **1** (often foll. by on) a temporary prohibition or suspension (of an activity). **2 a** a legal authorization to debtors to postpone payment. **b** the period of this postponement. [modern Latin, based on mora 'delay']

Moravian ● n. a native of Moravia, now part of the Czech Republic. ● adj. of or relating to Moravia or its people.

moray n. ▼ any voracious eel-like fish of the family Muraenidae, of warm seas, esp. Muraena helena of the Mediterranean and E. Atlantic. [from Greek muraina]

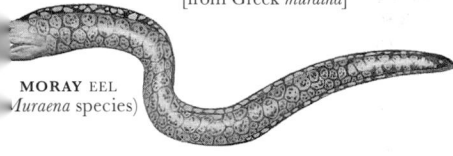

MORAY EEL
(Muraena species)

morbid adj. **1 a** (of the mind, ideas, etc.) unwholesome. **b** given to morbid feelings. **2** colloq. melancholy. **3** Med. of the nature of or indicative of disease. [based on Latin morbus 'disease'] □ **morbidity** n. **morbidly** adv.

mordant ● adj. **1** (of sarcasm etc.) caustic, biting. **2** pungent, smarting. **3** corrosive or cleansing. **4** (of a substance) serving to fix colouring matter or gold leaf on another substance. ● n. **1** a substance that enables a dye or stain to become fixed in a fabric etc. **2** an adhesive compound for fixing gold leaf. **3** a corrosive liquid used to etch the lines on a printing plate. [from French, literally 'biting'] □ **mordantly** adv.

more ● det. existing in a greater or additional quantity, amount, or degree (more problems than last time; bring some more water). ● pron. a greater quantity, number, or amount (more than three people; more to it than meets the eye). ● adv. **1** in a greater degree (do it more carefully). **2** to a greater extent (people like to walk more these days). **3** forming the comparative of adjectives and adverbs, esp. those of more than one syllable (more absurd; more easily). **4** again (once more; never more). □ **more and more** in an increasing degree. **more of** to a greater extent (more of a poet than a musician). **more or less 1** in a greater or smaller degree. **2** approximately; as an estimate. **more so** of the same kind to a greater degree. [Old English]

moreish adj. Brit. colloq. pleasant to eat, causing a desire for more.

morel n. an edible fungus, Morchella esculenta, with ridged mushroom caps. [from Dutch morilje]

morello n. (pl. **-os**) a sour kind of dark cherry. [Italian, literally 'blackish']

moreover adv. (introducing or accompanying a new statement) further, besides.

mores /mor-ayz/ n.pl. customs or conventions regarded as characteristic of a community. [Latin, literally 'customs']

morganatic adj. **1** (of a marriage) between a person of high rank and another of lower rank, the spouse and children having no claim to the possessions or title of the person of higher rank. **2** (of a wife) married in this way. [based on medieval Latin matrimonium ad morganaticam 'marriage with a morning gift', this gift being the husband's sole obligation]

morgue /morg/ n. **1** a mortuary. **2** (in a newspaper office) a room or file of miscellaneous information, esp. for future obituaries. [French, originally the name of a Paris mortuary]

moribund adj. **1** at the point of death. **2** lacking vitality. [from Latin moribundus]

Mormon n. a member of the Church of Jesus Christ of Latter-Day Saints, a religion founded in 1830 by Joseph Smith on the basis of revelations in the Book of Mormon. [name of the reputed author] □ **Mormonism** n.

morn n. poet. morning. [Old English]

mornay n. a cheese-flavoured white sauce. [20th-century coinage]

morning ● n. **1** the early part of the day, esp. from sunrise to noon (this morning; during the morning; morning coffee). **2** sunrise, daybreak. **3** a time compared with the morning, esp. the early part of one's life etc. ● int. colloq. = good morning (see GOOD adj. 14). □ **in the morning 1** during or in the course of the morning. **2** colloq. tomorrow morning. [Middle English]

morning after n. colloq. a hangover.

morning-after pill n. a contraceptive pill effective when taken some hours after intercourse.

morning coat n. a coat with tails, and with the front cut away below the waist.

morning dress n. a man's morning coat and striped trousers.

morning glory n. any of various twining plants of the genus Ipomoea, with trumpet-shaped flowers.

morning room n. a sitting room for the morning.

morning sickness n. nausea felt in the morning in pregnancy.

morning star n. a planet, esp. Venus, when visible in the east before sunrise.

Moroccan ● n. **1** a native or national of Morocco in N. Africa. **2** a person of Moroccan descent. ● adj. of or relating to Morocco.

morocco n. (pl. **-os**) a fine flexible leather made from goatskins tanned with sumac.

moron n. **1** colloq. a very stupid person. **2** an adult with a mental age of about 8–12. [Greek, literally 'foolish (thing)'] □ **moronic** adj. **moronically** adv.

morose adj. sullen and ill-tempered. [from Latin morosus 'peevish'] □ **morosely** adv. **moroseness** n.

morpheme n. Linguistics **1** a morphological element considered in respect of its functional relations in a linguistic system. **2** a meaningful morphological unit of a language that cannot be further divided (e.g. in, come, -ing, forming incoming). [based on Greek morphē 'form'] □ **morphemic** adj.

morphia n. (in general use) = MORPHINE.

morphine n. a narcotic drug obtained from opium and used to relieve pain. [based on Latin name Morpheus, god of sleep]

morphing n. a computing technique for transforming an image smoothly into a different one. [based on shortening of METAMORPHOSIS]

morphology n. the study of the forms of things, esp.: **1** Biol. the study of the forms of organisms. **2** Philol. **a** the study of the forms of words. **b** the system of forms in a language. [based on Greek morphē 'form'] □ **morphological** adj. **morphologically** adv. **morphologist** n.

morris dance n. a lively traditional English dance performed by groups often using handkerchiefs or sticks. [morris: from morys, obsolete variant of MOORISH] □ **morris dancer** n. **morris dancing** n.

morrow n. (usu. prec. by the) literary the following day. [Middle English]

Morse ● n. (in full **Morse code**) ▲ a code in which letters are represented by combinations of long and short light or sound signals. ● v.tr. & intr. signal by Morse code. [named after S. F. B. Morse, American electrician, 1791–1872]

MORSE CODE

Devised by Samuel Morse, the Morse code was an integral part of the telegraph system he developed from 1832 onwards. Operators encoded a message by tapping a key to turn the electric current in the telegraph wires on and off. Letters of the alphabet were represented by combinations of dots and dashes, which were sent as long and short pulses of power. The Morse code fell out of use in the 1940s.

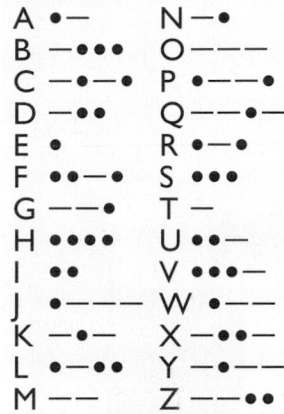

THE ALPHABET IN MORSE CODE.

morsel n. a mouthful; a small piece (esp. of food). [from Old French, literally 'little bite']

mortadella n. (pl. **mortadelle**) a large spiced pork sausage. [Italian, based on Latin murtatum 'seasoned with myrtle berries']

mortal ● adj. **1** subject to death. **2** causing death; fatal. **3** (of a battle) fought to the death. **4** associated with death (mortal agony). **5** (of an enemy) implacable. **6** (of pain, fear, an affront, etc.) intense, very serious. **7** colloq. **a** very great (in a mortal hurry). **b** long and tedious (for two mortal hours). **8** colloq. conceivable, imaginable (every mortal thing; of no mortal use). ● n. a mortal being, esp. a human. [from Latin mortalis] □ **mortally** adv.

mortality n. (pl. **-ies**) **1** the state of being subject to death. **2** loss of life on a large scale. **3 a** the number of deaths in a given period etc. **b** (in full **mortality rate**) a death rate.

mortal sin n. Theol. a sin that is regarded as depriving the soul of divine grace.

mortar ● n. **1** a mixture of lime with cement, sand, and water, used in building to bond bricks or stones. **2** a short large-bore cannon for firing bombs at high angles. **3** a contrivance for firing a lifeline or firework. **4** a usu. cup-shaped receptacle made of hard material, in which ingredients are pounded with a pestle. ▷ PESTLE. ● v.tr. **1** plaster or join with mortar. **2** attack or bombard with mortars. [from Latin mortarium]

mortarboard n. **1** an academic cap with a stiff flat square top. **2** a flat board with a handle on the undersurface, for holding mortar in bricklaying etc.

mortgage /mor-gij/ ● n. **1 a** a conveyance of property by a debtor to a creditor as security for a debt (esp. one incurred by the purchase of the property). **b** a deed effecting this. **2 a** a debt secured by a mortgage. **b** a loan resulting in such a debt. ● v.tr. **1** convey (a property) by mortgage. **2** pledge (oneself, one's powers, etc.). [from Old French, literally 'dead pledge']

mortgagee /mor-gij-ee/ n. the creditor in a mortgage.

M

mortgager /mor-gij-er/ n. (also **mortgagor** /mor-gij-**or**/) the debtor in a mortgage.

mortgage rate n. the rate of interest charged by a mortgagee.

mortice var. of MORTISE.

mortician n. N. Amer. an undertaker. [based on Latin mors mortis 'death']

mortify v. (-ies, -ied) **1** tr. **a** cause (a person) to feel shamed or humiliated. **b** wound (a person's feelings). **2** tr. bring (the body, the flesh, the passions, etc.) into subjection by self-denial or discipline. **3** intr. (of flesh) be affected by gangrene or necrosis. [from ecclesiastical Latin mortificare 'to kill, subdue'] □ **mortification** n. **mortifying** adj. **mortifyingly** adv.

mortise (also **mortice**) ● n. a hole in a framework designed to receive the end of another part, esp. a tenon. ▷ DOVETAIL. ● v.tr. **1** join securely, esp. by mortise and tenon. **2** cut a mortise in. [from Arabic murtazz 'fixed in']

mortise lock n. ▼ a lock recessed into the frame of a door or window etc.

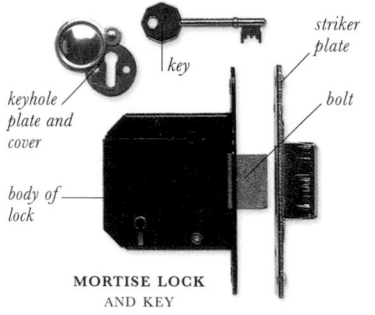

MORTISE LOCK
AND KEY

M

mortuary ● n. (pl. **-ies**) a room or building in which dead bodies are kept until burial or cremation. ● adj. of or concerning death or burial. [based on Latin mortuus 'dead']

Mosaic adj. of or associated with Moses. [from modern Latin, based on Hebrew Mōšeh 'Moses']

mosaic n. **1 a** a picture or pattern produced by an arrangement of small variously coloured pieces of glass or stone etc. **b** work of this kind as an art form. **2** a diversified thing. **3** (in full **mosaic disease**) a virus disease causing leaf-mottling in plants. **4** (attrib.) **a** of or like a mosaic. **b** diversified. [from Greek mous(e)ion 'mosaic work'] □ **mosaicist** n.

Mosaic Law n. the laws attributed to Moses.

Moselle n. (also **Mosel**) a light medium dry white wine produced in the valley of the river Moselle. [French]

mosey v.intr. (-eys, -eyed) slang walk in a leisurely manner. [19th-century coinage]

Moslem var. of MUSLIM.

mosque n. ▼ a Muslim place of worship. [based on Arabic masjid]

MOSQUE: THE BLUE MOSQUE,
ISTANBUL, TURKEY

MOTH

The order Lepidoptera comprises at least 150,000 species of moth and just 20,000 butterfly species. Although most moths are drab, some are brilliantly coloured. They vary greatly in size, ranging in wingspan from 2 mm to 30 cm (¹⁄₁₂ to 12 in.). Moths can often be distinguished by their feathered antennae, which lack the clubbed tips of butterflies' antennae. Most moths have a wing-coupling device consisting of bristles on the base of the hindwing that engage with a flap on the forewing.

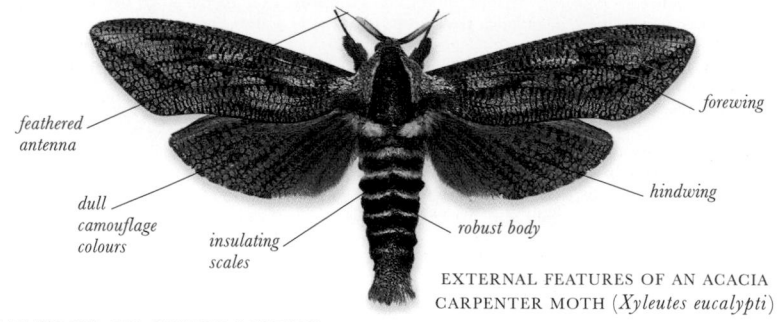

feathered antenna

forewing

dull camouflage colours

insulating scales

robust body

hindwing

EXTERNAL FEATURES OF AN ACACIA
CARPENTER MOTH (Xyleutes eucalypti)

EXAMPLES OF OTHER MOTHS

DEATH'S HEAD HAWKMOTH
(Acherontia atropos)

MAGPIE MOTH
(Abraxas grossulariata)

GARDEN TIGER
(Arctia caja)

SILKMOTH
(Bombyx mori)

ATLAS MOTH
(Attacus atlas)

SIX-SPOT BURNET
(Zygaena filipendulae)

GOLDEN CLEARWING
(Albuna oberthuri)

PINE EMPEROR
(Nudaurelia cytherea)

SILVER 'Y' MOTH
(Autographa gamma)

MADAGASCAN SUNSET MOTH
(Chrysiridia madagascariensis)

BEAUTIFUL TIGER
(Amphicallia bellatrix)

PUSS MOTH
(Cerura vinula)

mosquito n. (pl. **-oes**) ▶ any slender biting dipterous fly of the family Culicidae, esp. of the genus Culex, Anopheles, or Aedes, the female of which sucks the blood of humans and other animals. [Spanish & Portuguese, literally 'little fly']

mosquito net n. a net to keep off mosquitoes.

moss ● n. any small cryptogamous plant of the class Musci, growing in dense clusters on the surface of the ground, in bogs, on trees, stones, etc. ▷ BRYOPHYTE. ● v.tr. cover with moss. [Old English mos 'bog, moss']

piercing stylet

MOSQUITO
SUCKING BLOOD

moss agate n. agate with mosslike markings.

moss stitch n. alternate plain and purl in knitting. ▷ KNITTING

mossy adj. (**mossier, mossiest**) **1** covered in or resembling moss. **2** US slang antiquated, old-fashioned.

most ● det. **1** existing in the greatest quantity or degree (see who can make the most noise). **2** the majority of; nearly all of (most people think so). ● pron. **1** the majority (most of them are missing). **2** the greatest quantity or number (this is the most I can do). **3** (the most) slang the best of all (you are the most). ● adv. **1** in the highest degree (this is most interesting; what most annoys me). **2** forming the superlative of adjectives and adverbs, esp. those of more than one syllable (most certain; most easily). **3** N. Amer. colloq. almost (most everyone I know agrees). □ **at most** no more or better than (this is at most a makeshift). **at the most 1** as the greatest amount. **2** not more than. **for the most part 1** as regards the greater part. **2** usually. **make the most of 1** employ to the best advantage. **2** represent at its best or worst. [Old English]

mostly adv. **1** as regards the greater part. **2** usually.

Most Reverend adj. the title of an archbishop or an Irish Roman Catholic bishop.

MOT abbr. **1** hist. (in the UK) Ministry of Transport. **2** (in full **MOT test**) a compulsory annual test of motor vehicles of more than a specified age.

mot /moh/ n. (pl. **mots** pronunc. same or /mohz/) a witty saying. [French, literally 'word']

mote n. a speck of dust. [Old English]

motel *n.* a roadside hotel for motorists.

motet *n. Mus.* a short sacred choral composition. [from Old French, literally 'little word']

moth *n.* **1** ◄ an insect of the order Lepidoptera, often drably coloured, and distinguished from butterflies as having a stout body, lacking clubbed antennae, and folding the wings flat when at rest. **2** (in full **clothes-moth**) any small lepidopterous insect of the family Tineidae breeding in cloth etc., on which its larva feeds. [Old English]

mothball ● *n.* a ball of naphthalene etc. placed in stored clothes to keep away moths. ● *v.tr.* **1** place in mothballs. **2** leave unused. □ **in mothballs** stored unused for a considerable time.

moth-eaten *adj.* **1** damaged by moths. **2** timeworn.

mother ● *n.* **1 a** a woman in relation to a child to whom she has given birth. **b** (in full **adoptive mother**) a woman who has continuous care of a child, esp. by adoption. **2** any female animal in relation to its offspring. **3** a quality or condition etc. that gives rise to another (*necessity is the mother of invention*). **4** (in full **Mother Superior**) the head of a female religious community. **5** (*attrib.*) **a** designating an institution etc. regarded as having maternal authority (*Mother Church; mother earth*). **b** designating the main ship, spacecraft, etc., in a convoy or mission (*the mother craft*). ● *v.tr.* **1** give birth to; be the mother of. **2** protect as a mother. **3** give rise to; be the source of. [Old English] □ **motherhood** *n.* **motherless** *adj.*

motherboard *n. Computing* a printed circuit board containing the principal components of a microcomputer etc.

mother country *n.* a country in relation to its colonies.

mother figure *n.* an older woman who is regarded as a source of nurture, support, etc.

motherfucker *n.* esp. *N. Amer. coarse slang* an obnoxious or very unpleasant person or thing.

Mothering Sunday *n. Brit.* the fourth Sunday in Lent, traditionally a day for honouring mothers with gifts.

mother-in-law *n.* (*pl.* **mothers-in-law**) the mother of one's husband or wife.

motherland *n.* one's native country.

mother lode *n. Mining* the main vein of a system.

motherly *adj.* **1** like or characteristic of a mother in affection, care, etc. **2** of or relating to a mother. □ **motherliness** *n.*

mother-of-pearl *n.* a smooth iridescent substance forming the inner layer of the shell of some molluscs. ▷ PEARL

Mother's Day *n.* **1** *Brit.* = MOTHERING SUNDAY. **2** *N. Amer.* an equivalent day on the second Sunday in May.

Mother Superior see MOTHER *n.* 4.

mother tongue *n.* **1** one's native language. **2** a language from which others have evolved.

mothproof ● *adj.* (of clothes) treated so as to repel moths. ● *v.tr.* treat (clothes) in this way.

motif *n.* **1** a distinctive feature or dominant idea in artistic or literary composition. **2** *Mus.* = FIGURE *n.* 9. **3** a decorative design or pattern. **4** an ornament sewn separately on a garment. [French]

motile *adj. Zool.* & *Bot.* capable of motion. □ **motility** *n.*

motion ● *n.* **1** the act or process of moving or of changing position. **2** a particular manner of moving the body in walking etc. **3** a gesture. **4** a formal proposal put to a committee, legislature, etc. **5** *Law* an application for a rule or order of court. **6** *Brit.* **a** an evacuation of the bowels. **b** (in *sing.* or *pl.*) faeces. ● *v.* **1** *tr.* direct (a person) by a sign or gesture. **2** *intr.* make a gesture directing (*motioned to me to leave*). □ **go through the motions 1** do something perfunctorily or superficially. **2** simulate an action by gestures. **in motion** moving; not at rest. **put** (or **set**) **in motion** set going or working. [from Latin *motio*] □ **motionless** *adj.*

motion picture *n.* (often, with hyphen, *attrib.*) = FILM *n.* 3.

motion sickness *n.* nausea induced by motion.

motivate *v.tr.* **1** supply a motive to; be the motive of. **2** cause (a person) to act in a particular way. **3** stimulate the interest of (a person in an activity). □ **motivation** *n.* **motivational** *adj.* **motivator** *n.*

motive ● *n.* **1** a factor that induces a person to act in a particular way. **2** a motif in art, literature, or music. ● *adj.* **1** tending to initiate movement. **2** concerned with movement. [from Late Latin *motivus* 'motive, moving'] □ **motiveless** *adj.*

motive power *n.* a moving or impelling power.

mot juste /zhoost/ *n.* (*pl.* **mots justes** *pronunc.* same) the most appropriate expression. [French]

motley ● *adj.* (**motlier, motliest**) **1** diversified in colour. **2** of varied character (*a motley crew*). ● *n. hist.* the particoloured costume of a jester. [Middle English]

motocross *n.* cross-country racing on motorcycles. ▷ MOTORCYCLE

motor ● *n.* **1** a thing that imparts motion. **2** a machine supplying motive power for a vehicle etc. or for some other device with moving parts. **3** *Brit.* = MOTOR CAR. **4** (*attrib.*) **a** a giving, imparting, or producing motion. **b** driven by a motor (*motor mower*). **c** of or for motor vehicles. **d** *Anat.* relating to muscular movement or the nerves activating it. ▷ PERIPHERAL NERVOUS SYSTEM. ● *v.intr.* & *tr.* go or (*Brit.*) convey in a motor vehicle. [Latin, literally 'mover']

motorbike *n. colloq.* = MOTORCYCLE.

motor boat *n.* a motor-driven boat.

motorcade *n.* a procession of motor vehicles.

motor car see CAR 1.

motor caravan *n.* a van equipped with beds, cooking facilities, etc., like a caravan.

motor coach *n.* **1** = COACH *n.* 1. **2** a railway passenger carriage with its own motor.

motorcycle *n.* ▼ a two-wheeled motor-driven road vehicle without pedal propulsion. ▷ OFF-ROAD. □ **motorcycling** *n.* **motorcyclist** *n.*

motorhome *n.* esp. *N. Amer.* a large motor vehicle equipped as a self-contained home.

motorist *n.* the driver of a car.

motorize *v.tr.* (also **-ise**) **1** equip with motor transport. **2** provide with a motor.

motorman *n.* (*pl.* **-men**) the driver of an underground train, tram, etc.

MOTORCYCLE

One of the earliest attempts at creating a motorized bicycle, the Michaeux-Perreaux velocipede, was produced in France in 1869. A similar model was made at the same time by S. H. Roper in America. Both prototypes combined a wooden-framed bicycle and a small steam engine. Modern machines are infinitely more sophisticated, with internal-combustion engines ranging in size from 50 to over 1,000 cc. Designs are tailored to suit a wide range of uses, from competitive racing to touring and everyday use.

FEATURES OF A YAMAHA XV920 MOTORCYCLE

rear-view mirror
speedometer
fuel tank
carburettor
contoured saddle
tail-light
headlamp
920 cc engine
indicator light
front suspension
rear indicator light
front brake disc
box-section frame
five-speed gearbox
exhaust pipe
enclosed final drive chain

TYPES OF MOTORCYCLE

RACING MOTORCYCLE

FACTORY-CUSTOMIZED/TOURER

SPORTS MODEL

MOTOCROSS MOTORCYCLE

M

MOTOR RACING

Motor racing involves many different types of four and two-wheeled vehicles competing on specially prepared tracks. Motor racing on four wheels includes Formula 1, Indycar racing, rally driving, drag racing, and karting. In Formula 1 racing, drivers compete for points in a series of Grand Prix races on closed-circuit tracks around the world. Indycars are similar to Formula 1 models, but racing takes place on large oval tracks and twisting road circuits – mainly in the United States of America.

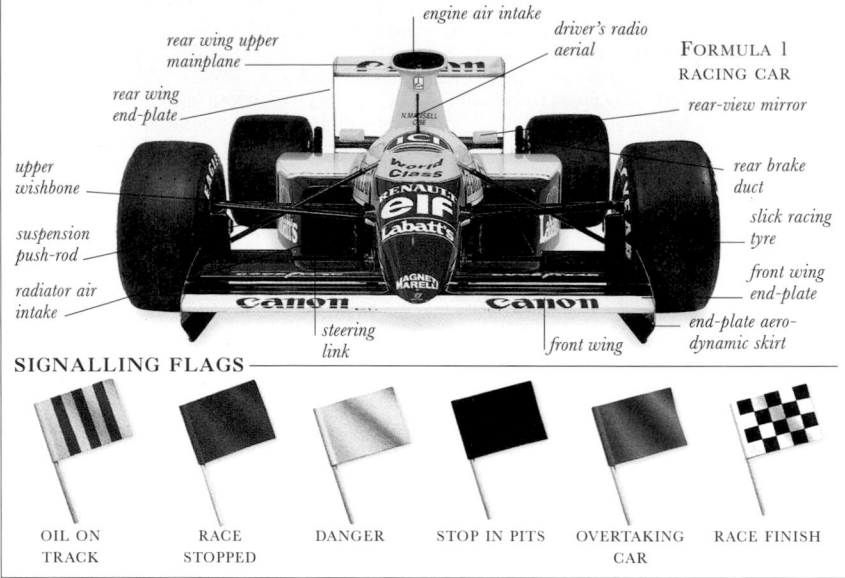

FORMULA 1 RACING CAR

rear wing upper mainplane · *engine air intake* · *driver's radio aerial* · *rear wing end-plate* · *upper wishbone* · *rear-view mirror* · *suspension push-rod* · *rear brake duct* · *radiator air intake* · *slick racing tyre* · *front wing end-plate* · *steering link* · *front wing* · *end-plate aerodynamic skirt*

SIGNALLING FLAGS

OIL ON TRACK   RACE STOPPED   DANGER   STOP IN PITS   OVERTAKING CAR   RACE FINISH

M

motor nerve *n.* a nerve carrying impulses from the brain or spinal cord to a muscle.

motor neurone disease *n. Med.* a progressive disease involving degeneration of the motor neurones and wasting of the muscles.

motor racing *n.* ▲ the racing of motorized vehicles, esp. cars, as a sport.

motor scooter see SCOOTER *n.* 2.

motor vehicle *n.* a road vehicle powered by an internal-combustion engine.

motorway *n. Brit.* a main road with separate carriageways and limited access, specially constructed and controlled for fast motor traffic.

motor yacht *n.* a motor-driven yacht. ▷ BOAT

Motown *n.* music with rhythm-and-blues and soul elements, associated with Detroit. [from *Tamla*

Motown, proprietary name of a record label (*Motown* i.e. *Motor Town* = Detroit)]

motte *n.* a mound forming the site of a castle, camp, etc. ▷ BAILEY. [from Old French *mote*, related to MOAT]

mottle ● *v.tr.* (esp. as **mottled** *adj.*) mark with spots or smears of colour. ● *n.* **1** an irregular arrangement of spots or patches of colour. **2** any of these spots or patches.

motto *n.* (*pl.* **-oes** or **-os**) **1** a maxim adopted as a rule of conduct. **2** a phrase or sentence accompanying a coat of arms. **3** a sentence inscribed on some object and expressing an appropriate sentiment. **4** verses etc. in a paper cracker. **5** a quotation prefixed to a book or chapter. **6** *Mus.* a recurrent phrase having some symbolical significance. [Italian]

mouflon /moof-lon/ *n.* (also **moufflon**) a wild mountain sheep, *Ovis orientalis*, of S. Europe. [French]

mould[1] (*US* **mold**) ● *n.* **1** a hollow container into which molten metal etc. is poured or soft material is pressed to harden into a required shape. **2 a** a hollow vessel used to give shape to puddings etc. **b** a pudding etc. made in this way. **3** a form or shape. **4** a frame or template for producing mouldings. **5** character or disposition (*in heroic mould*). ● *v.tr.* **1** make in a required shape or from certain ingredients (*was moulded out of clay*). **2** give a shape to. **3** influence the formation or development of (*consultation helps to mould policies*). **4** (esp. of clothing) fit closely to (*the gloves moulded his hands*). [Middle English] □ **moulder** *n.*

mould[2] *n.* (*US* **mold**) a furry growth of minute fungi occurring esp. in moist warm conditions. ▷ FUNGUS

mould[3] *n.* (*US* **mold**) **1** esp. *Brit.* loose earth. **2** the upper soil of cultivated land, esp. when rich in organic matter. [Old English, related to MEAL[2]]

mould-board *n.* the board in a plough that turns over the furrow-slice.

moulder *v.intr.* (*US* **molder**) **1** decay to dust. **2** (foll. by *away*) rot or crumble. **3** deteriorate. [perhaps from MOULD[3], but cf. Norwegian dialect *muldra* 'crumble']

MOUNTAIN

Mountains are formed in three main ways, although each of the processes occurs as a result of the movement of the huge tectonic plates that make up the Earth's crust. Most mountains are folds, formed where plates push together, causing the rock to buckle upwards. A few are volcanoes, which often form along plate boundaries, and are built up by successive eruptions of lava and debris. Others are block mountains, formed when a block of land is uplifted between two faults as a result of compression or tension in the Earth's crust.

MOUNTAIN RANGES OF THE WORLD

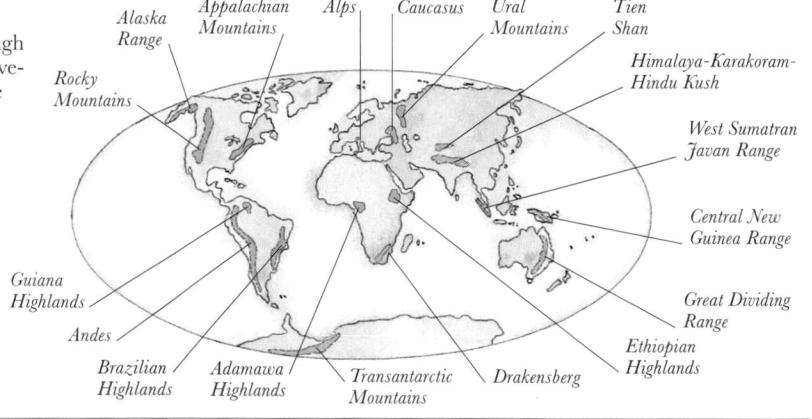

Alaska Range · *Appalachian Mountains* · *Alps* · *Caucasus* · *Ural Mountains* · *Tien Shan* · *Rocky Mountains* · *Himalaya-Karakoram-Hindu Kush* · *West Sumatran Javan Range* · *Guiana Highlands* · *Central New Guinea Range* · *Andes* · *Great Dividing Range* · *Brazilian Highlands* · *Adamawa Highlands* · *Transantarctic Mountains* · *Drakensberg* · *Ethiopian Highlands*

MAIN MOUNTAIN TYPES

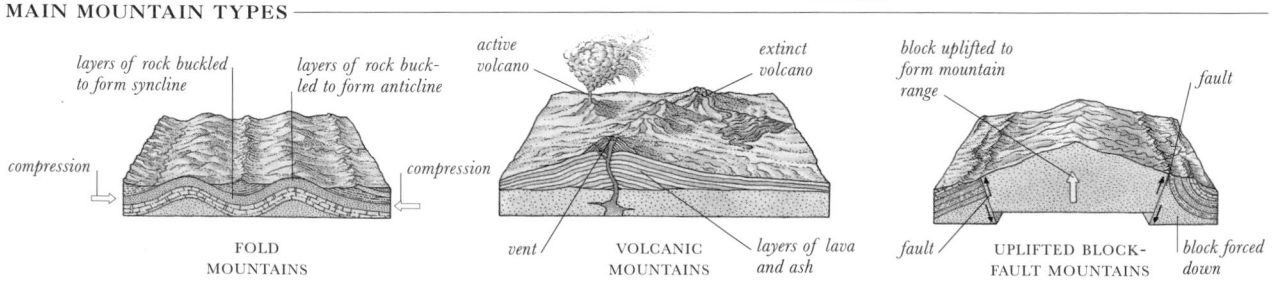

layers of rock buckled to form syncline · *layers of rock buckled to form anticline* · *active volcano* · *extinct volcano* · *block uplifted to form mountain range* · *fault* · *compression* · *compression* · *fault* · *vent* · *layers of lava and ash* · *fault* · *block forced down*

FOLD MOUNTAINS   VOLCANIC MOUNTAINS   UPLIFTED BLOCK-FAULT MOUNTAINS

moulding *n.* (*US* **molding**) **1 a** an ornamentally shaped outline as an architectural feature. **b** a strip of material in wood or stone etc. for use as moulding. **2** similar material in wood or plastic etc. used for other decorative purposes, e.g. in picture framing.

mouldy *adj.* (*US* **moldy**) (**-ier**, **-iest**) **1** covered with mould. **2** stale; out of date. **3** *colloq.* (as a general term of disparagement) dull, miserable, boring.

moult (*US* **molt**) ● *v.* **1** *intr.* shed feathers, hair, a shell, skin, etc., in the process of renewing plumage, acquiring a new growth, etc. **2** *tr.* shed (feathers, hair, etc.). ● *n.* the act or an instance of moulting (*is in moult once a year*). [from Latin *mutare* 'to change']

mound ● *n.* **1** a raised mass of earth, stones, or other compacted material. **2** a heap or pile. **3** a hillock. **4** *Baseball* a slight elevation on which the pitcher stands. ● *v.tr.* **1** heap up in a mound or mounds. **2** enclose with mounds. [16th-century coinage, originally in sense 'hedge or fence': origin unknown]

mount[1] ● *v.* **1** *tr.* ascend or climb. **2** *tr.* **a** get up on (an animal) to ride it. **b** set (a person) on horseback. **c** provide (a person) with a horse. **d** (as **mounted** *adj.*) serving on horseback (*mounted police*). **3** *tr.* go up or climb on to (a raised surface). **4** *intr.* **a** move upwards. **b** increase, accumulate. **c** (of a feeling) become stronger or more intense (*excitement was mounting*). **d** (of the blood) rise into the cheeks. **5** *tr.* (of a male animal) get on to (a female) to copulate. **6** *tr.* place (an object) on an elevated support. **7** *tr.* **a** set in or attach to a backing, setting, or other support. **b** attach (a picture etc.) to a mount or frame. **c** fix (an object for viewing) on a microscope slide. **8** *tr.* **a** arrange (a play, exhibition, etc.) or present for public view or display. **b** take action to initiate (a programme, campaign, etc.). **9** *tr.* prepare (specimens) for preservation. **10** *tr.* bring into readiness for operation. ● *n.* **1** a backing or setting on which a photograph, work of art, gem, etc. is set for display. **2** a support for a gun, camera, etc. **3** a glass microscope slide for securing a specimen etc. to be viewed. **4** a stamp hinge. **5 a** a horse available for riding. **b** an opportunity to ride a horse. □ **mount guard** perform the duty of guarding; take up sentry duty. [from Latin, related to MOUNT[2]] □ **mountable** *adj.*

mount[2] *n. archaic* (except before a name): mountain, hill (*Mount Everest; Mount of Olives*). [from Latin *mons montis* 'mountain']

mountain *n.* **1** a large natural elevation of the Earth's surface rising abruptly from the surrounding level. **2** a large heap or pile; a huge quantity (*a mountain of work*). **3** a large surplus stock (*butter mountain*). □ **make a mountain out of a molehill** see MOLEHILL. **move mountains 1** achieve spectacular results. **2** make every possible effort. [from Latin *mons montis*]

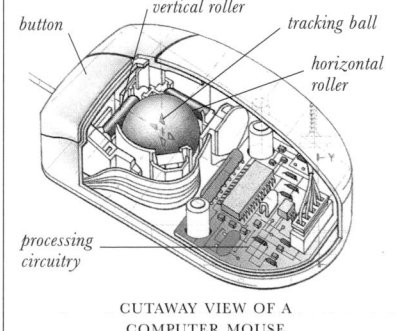

MOUNTAIN ASH
(*Sorbus aucuparia*)

mountain ash *n.* **1** ◀ a tree, *Sorbus aucuparia*, with delicate pinnate leaves and scarlet berries. **2** any of several Australian eucalypts.

mountain bike *n.* a bicycle with a light sturdy frame, broad deep-treaded tyres, and multiple gears, originally designed for riding on mountainous terrain. ▷ BICYCLE.

mountain chain *n.* a connected series of mountains.

mountaineer ● *n.* **1** a person skilled in mountain climbing. **2** a person living in an area of high mountains. ● *v.intr.* climb mountains as a sport. □ **mountaineering** *n.*

mountain goat *n.* **1** a goat which lives on mountains, proverbial for agility. **2** (in full **Rocky Mountain goat**) ► a white goatlike animal, *Oreamnos americanus*, of mountains in western N. America.

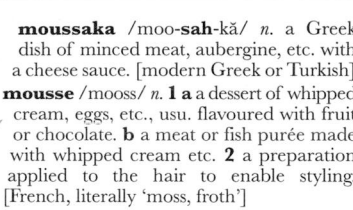

MOUNTAIN GOAT:
ROCKY MOUNTAIN GOAT
(*Oreamnos americanus*)

mountain lion *n.* a puma.

mountainous *adj.* **1** having many mountains. **2** huge.

mountain range *n.* a line of mountains connected by high ground.

mountain sickness *n.* a sickness caused by breathing the rarefied air at great heights.

mountainside *n.* the slope of a mountain below the summit.

mountebank *n.* **1** a swindler; a charlatan. **2** a clown. [from Italian *montambanco*, from *monta in banco*, literally 'climb on bench']

Mountie *n. colloq.* a member of the Royal Canadian Mounted Police.

mounting *n.* **1** = MOUNT[1] *n.* 1. **2** in senses of MOUNT[1] *v.*

mounting block *n.* a block of stone placed to help a rider mount a horse.

mourn *v.* **1** *tr.* & (foll. by *for*) *intr.* feel or show deep sorrow or regret for (a dead person, a past event, etc.). **2** *intr.* show conventional signs of grief after a person's death. [Old English]

mourner *n.* a person who mourns, esp. at a funeral.

mournful *adj.* **1** doleful, sad, sorrowing. **2** expressing or suggestive of mourning. □ **mournfully** *adv.* **mournfulness** *n.*

mourning *n.* **1** the expression of deep sorrow, esp. for a dead person, by the wearing of solemn dress. **2** the clothes worn in mourning.

mouse ● *n.* (*pl.* **mice**) **1 a** any of various small rodents esp. of the family Muridae, usu. having a pointed snout and relatively large ears and eyes. ▷ RODENT. **b** any similar small mammal, such as a shrew or vole. **2** a timid or feeble person. **3** (*pl.* also **mouses**) *Computing* ▼ a small hand-held device which controls the cursor on a VDU screen. ▷ COMPUTER. ● *v.intr.* (esp. of a cat, owl, etc.) hunt for or catch mice. [Old English] □ **mouselike** *adj.* & *adv.* **mouser** *n.*

mouse deer *n.* a chevrotain.

mousetrap *n.* **1** a sprung trap with bait for catching and usu. killing mice. **2** (often *attrib.*) *Brit.* cheese of poor quality.

mousey var. of MOUSY.

MOUSE

A mouse provides a means of pointing to items on a computer screen. The mouse is moved around on a flat surface until the cursor is in the desired position. By clicking a button, a signal is sent to the computer via the processor.

button　　*vertical roller*　　*tracking ball*

horizontal roller

processing circuitry

CUTAWAY VIEW OF A
COMPUTER MOUSE

moussaka /moo-**sah**-kă/ *n.* a Greek dish of minced meat, aubergine, etc. with a cheese sauce. [modern Greek or Turkish]

mousse /mooss/ *n.* **1 a** a dessert of whipped cream, eggs, etc., usu. flavoured with fruit or chocolate. **b** a meat or fish purée made with whipped cream etc. **2** a preparation applied to the hair to enable styling. [French, literally 'moss, froth']

mousseline /mooss-**leen**/ *n.* **1** a muslin-like fabric of silk etc. **2 a** a soft light mousse. **b** hollandaise sauce made frothy with whipped cream or egg white. [French, related to MUSLIN]

moustache /mŭs-**tahsh**/ *n.* (*US* **mustache**) **1** hair left to grow above a man's upper lip. **2** a similar growth round the mouth of some animals. [from Greek *mustax*] □ **moustached** *adj.*

mousy *adj.* (also **mousey**) (**mousier**, **mousiest**) **1** of or like a mouse. **2** (of a person) shy or timid; ineffectual. **3** of a nondescript shade of light brown, mid brown, or grey. □ **mousily** *adv.* **mousiness** *n.*

mouth ● *n.* /mowth/ (*pl.* **mouths**) **1 a** an external opening in the head, through which most animals admit food and emit communicative sounds. ▷ DIGESTION. **b** (in humans and some animals) the cavity behind it containing the means of biting and chewing and the vocal organs. **2 a** the opening of a container, cave, trumpet, etc. **b** the muzzle of a gun. **3** the place where a river enters the sea. ▷ RIVER. **4** *colloq.* **a** talkativeness. **b** impudent talk; cheek. ● *v.* /mowth/ **1** *tr.* & *intr.* utter or speak with affectations (*mouthing platitudes*). **2** *tr.* utter very distinctly. **3** *intr.* **a** move the lips silently. **b** grimace. **4** *tr.* say (words) with movement of the mouth but no sound. □ **keep one's mouth shut** *colloq.* not reveal a secret. **put words into a person's mouth** represent a person as having said something in a particular way. **take the words out of a person's mouth** say what another was about to say. [Old English] □ **mouthed** *adj.* (also in *comb.*).

mouthbrooder *n.* ▼ a fish which protects its eggs (and sometimes its young) by carrying them in its mouth.

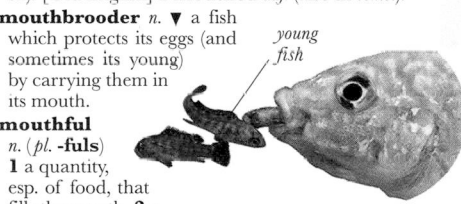

young fish

mouthful *n.* (*pl.* **-fuls**) **1** a quantity, esp. of food, that fills the mouth. **2 a** a small quantity. **3 a** long or complicated word or phrase.

MOUTHBROODER: BANDED
YELLOW MOUTHBROODER
(*Haplochromis* species)

mouth organ *n.* = HARMONICA.

mouthpart *n.* any of the (usu. paired) organs surrounding the mouth of an insect or other arthropod and adapted for feeding.

mouthpiece *n.* **1 a** the part of a musical instrument placed between or against the lips. ▷ BRASS. **b** the part of a telephone for speaking into. **c** the part of a tobacco pipe placed between the lips. **2** a person who speaks for another or others.

mouth-to-mouth *adj.* (of resuscitation) in which a person breathes into a subject's lungs through the mouth.

mouthwash *n.* a liquid antiseptic etc. for rinsing the mouth or gargling.

mouth-watering *adj.* **1** (of food etc.) having a delicious smell or appearance. **2** tempting, alluring.

movable (also **moveable**) ● *adj.* **1** that can be moved. **2** (of a feast or festival) variable in date from year to year. ● *n.* **1** an article of furniture that may be removed from a house, as distinct from a fixture. **2** (in *pl.*) personal property. □ **movability** *n.* **movably** *adv.*

movable-doh *attrib.adj.* designating a system of sight-singing in which doh is the keynote of any major scale (cf. FIXED-DOH).

M

MRI

Magnetic resonance imaging (MRI) is a medical diagnostic technique that provides high-quality cross-sectional or three-dimensional images of body structures and organs. During imaging, the patient lies inside a magnetic chamber, which causes the nuclei of hydrogen atoms in the body to line up. A pulse of radio waves is released, throwing the atoms out of alignment. As they realign, the atoms oscillate and resonate. The resonance is detected and analyzed by a computer to create an image.

back muscles
spinal cord
spine
spleen
aorta
liver

MRI SCAN (SECTION THROUGH A HUMAN TORSO)

body 'slice' being imaged

radio-frequency magnetic coil

CUTAWAY VIEW OF AN MRI SCANNER IN OPERATION

large, superconducting electromagnet

M

movable feast *n.* **1** a religious festival that occurs on a different date each year. **2** an event which takes place at no regular time.

move ● *v.* **1** *intr. & tr.* change one's position or posture, or cause to do this. **2** *tr. & intr.* put or keep in motion. **3 a** *intr.* make a move in a board game. **b** *tr.* change the position of (a piece) in a board game. **4** *intr.* (often foll. by *about, away,* etc.) go from place to place. **5** *intr.* take action (*moved to reduce unemployment*). **6** *intr.* make progress (*the project is moving fast*). **7** *tr.* (also *absol.*) change (one's place of residence or work). **8** *intr.* (foll. by *in*) be socially active in (*moves in the best circles*). **9** *tr.* affect (a person) with emotion. **10** *tr.* (foll. by *to*) provoke (a person to laughter etc.). **11** *tr.* (foll. by *to,* or *to* + infin.) prompt or incline (a person to a feeling or action). **12** *tr. & intr.* (cause to) change in opinion (*nothing can move me on this issue*). **13 a** *tr.* cause (the bowels) to be evacuated. **b** *intr.* (of the bowels) be evacuated. **14** *tr.* (often foll. by *that* + clause) propose in a meeting etc. **15** *intr.* (foll. by *for*) make a formal request or application. **16 a** *intr.* (of merchandise) be sold. **b** *tr.* sell. ● *n.* **1** the act or an instance of moving. **2** a change of house, premises, etc. **3** an initiative. **4 a** the changing of the position of a piece in a board game. **b** a player's turn to do this. □ **get a move on** *colloq.* **1** hurry up. **2** make a start. **make a move** take action. **make along** (or **on**) change to a new position, esp. to avoid crowding etc. **move away** go to live in another area. **move in 1** take possession of a new house etc. **2** get into a position of influence etc. **3** (often foll. by *on*) get into a position of readiness or proximity (for an offensive action etc.). **move in with** start to share accommodation with. **move mountains** see MOUNTAIN. **move out** change one's place of residence. **move over** (or **up**) adjust one's position to make room for another. **on the move 1** progressing. **2** moving about. [from Latin *movēre*] □ **mover** *n.*

moveable var. of MOVABLE.

movement *n.* **1** the act or an instance of moving or being moved. **2** the moving parts of a mechanism (esp. a clock or watch). **3 a** a body of persons with a common object (*the peace movement*). **b** a campaign undertaken by such a body. **4** (usu. in *pl.*) a person's activities and whereabouts. **5** *Mus.* a principal division of a longer musical work. **6** motion of the bowels. **7** a rise or fall in prices on the stock market.

movie *n.colloq.* **1** esp. *N. Amer.* a motion-picture film. **2** *US* a cinema.

movie theatre *n.* (also **movie house**) esp. *N. Amer.* a cinema.

moving *adj.* **1** that moves or causes to move. **2** affecting with emotion. □ **movingly** *adv.* (in sense 2).

moving pavement *n. Brit.* a structure like a conveyor belt for pedestrians.

mow *v.tr.* (*past part.* **mowed** or **mown**) **1** cut down (grass, hay, etc.) with a scythe or machine. **2** cut down the produce of (a field) or the grass etc. of (a lawn) by mowing. □ **mow down** kill or destroy randomly or in great numbers. [Old English] □ **mower** *n.*

mozzarella /mot-să-**rel**-ă/ *n.* an Italian curd cheese originally of buffalo milk. [Italian]

MP *abbr.* **1** Member of Parliament. **2 a** military police. **b** military policeman.

mp *abbr.* mezzo piano.

m.p.g. *abbr.* miles per gallon.

m.p.h. *abbr.* miles per hour.

M.Phil. *abbr.* Master of Philosophy.

MPV *abbr.* multi-purpose vehicle; = PEOPLE CARRIER.

MRI *abbr.* ▲ magnetic resonance imaging.

Mr /mis-ter/ *n.* (*pl.* **Messrs** /mess-erz/) **1** the title of a man without a higher or honorific or professional title (*Mr Jones*). **2** a title prefixed to a designation of office etc. (*Mr President*).

mRNA *abbr. Biol.* messenger RNA.

Mrs /miss-iz/ *n.* (*pl.* same or **Mesdames** /may-dahm/) the title of a married woman without a higher or honorific or professional title (*Mrs Jones*).

MS *abbr.* **1** manuscript. **2** multiple sclerosis.

Ms /miz, muz/ *n.* the title of a woman without a higher or honorific or professional title, used regardless of marital status. [combination of MRS and MISS²]

M.Sc. *abbr.* Master of Science.

MS-DOS /em-ess-**doss**/ *abbr. Computing propr.* Microsoft disk operating system.

MSS *abbr.* manuscripts.

Mt. *abbr.* Mount.

M.Tech. *abbr.* Master of Technology.

mu *n.* **1** the twelfth letter of the Greek alphabet (M, μ). **2** (μ, as a symbol) = MICRO- 2. [Greek]

much (**more, most**) ● *det.* existing or occurring in a great quantity (*not much rain*). ● *pron.* **1** a great quantity (*much of that is true*). **2** (usu. in *neg.*) a noteworthy or outstanding example (*not much of a party*). ● *adv.* **1 a** in a great degree (*is much the same*). **b** greatly (*they much regret the mistake*). **2** for a large part of one's time (*not here much*). □ **as much** the extent or quantity just specified (*I thought as much*). **a bit much** *colloq.* somewhat excessive. **make much of** see MAKE. **much as** even though (*much as I would like to*). **much less** see LESS. **not much in it** little difference between things being compared. **too much** *colloq.* intolerable (*that really is too much*). **too much for 1** more than a match for. **2** beyond what is endurable by. [Middle English] □ **muchly** *adv. joc.*

muchness *n.* □ **much of a muchness** very nearly the same or alike.

much obliged see OBLIGE.

mucilage *n.* a viscous solution obtained from plants. [from Late Latin *mucilago* 'musty juice'] □ **mucilaginous** *adj.*

muck ● *n.* **1** farmyard manure. **2** *colloq.* dirt or filth; anything disgusting. **3** *colloq.* a mess. ● *v.tr.* **1** (usu. foll. by *up*) *colloq.* bungle (a job), spoil, ruin. **2** (foll. by *out*) remove muck from. **3** make dirty or untidy. **4** manure with muck. □ **make a muck of** *colloq.* bungle. **muck about** (or **around**) *Brit. colloq.* **1** potter or fool about. **2** (foll. by *with*) fool or interfere with. **muck in** (often foll. by *with*) *Brit.* share tasks etc. equally. [Middle English]

mucker *n. slang Brit.* a friend or companion.

muckle var. of MICKLE.

muckrake *v.intr.* search out and reveal scandal, esp. among famous people. □ **muckraking** *n.*

muck-spreader *n.* ▼ a machine for spreading manure on fields. □ **muck-spreading** *n.*

MUCK-SPREADER

mucky *adj.* (**muckier, muckiest**) **1** covered with muck. **2** dirty.

mucosa *n.* (*pl.* **mucosae** /-see/) a mucous membrane. [modern Latin fem. of *mucosus* 'mucous']

mucous *adj.* of or covered with mucus.

mucous membrane *n.* an epithelial tissue lining many body cavities and tubular organs and secreting mucus.

mucus *n.* **1** a slimy substance secreted by a mucous membrane or gland. **2** a gummy substance found in plants. [Latin]

mud *n.* **1** wet soft earthy matter. **2** hard ground from the drying of an area of this. □ **fling** (or **sling** or **throw**) **mud** speak disparagingly or slanderously. **one's name is mud** one is unpopular or in disgrace. [Middle English]

mudbank *n.* a bank of mud on the bed of a river or the bottom of the sea.

mudbath *n.* **1** a bath in the mud of mineral springs, esp. to relieve rheumatism etc. **2** a muddy scene or occasion.

mudbrick *n.* a brick made from baked mud.

muddle ● *v.tr.* **1** (often foll. by *up, together*) bring into disorder. **2** bewilder, confuse. **3** mismanage (an affair). ● *n.* **1** disorder. **2** a muddled condition. □ **make a muddle of 1** bring into disorder. **2** bungle. **muddle along** (or **on**) progress in a haphazard way. **muddle through** succeed despite one's inefficiency. **muddle up** confuse (two or more things). □ **muddler** *n.*

muddle-headed *adj.* stupid, confused. □ **muddle-headedness** *n.*

muddy ● *adj.* (**muddier**, **muddiest**) **1** like mud. **2** covered in or full of mud. **3** (of liquid) turbid. **4** mentally confused. **5** obscure. **6** (of light) dull. **7** (of colour) impure. ● *v.tr.* (**-ies**, **-ied**) make muddy. □ **muddily** *adv.*

mudflap *n.* ▼ a flap hanging behind the wheel of a vehicle, to repel mud etc. thrown up from the road.

mudflap

MUDFLAP ON AN ALL-TERRAIN VEHICLE

mudflat *n.* a stretch of muddy land left uncovered at low tide.

mudflow *n.* **1** a fluid or hardened stream or avalanche of mud. **2** the flow or motion of such a stream.

mudguard *n.* a curved strip or cover over a wheel of a bicycle or motorcycle to reduce the amount of mud etc. thrown up from the road.

mud pack *n.* a cosmetic paste applied thickly to the face.

mud pie *n.* mud made into a pie shape by a child.

mud-slinger *n. colloq.* one given to making abusive or disparaging remarks. □ **mud-slinging** *n.*

muesli *n.* (*pl.* **mueslis**) a breakfast food of crushed cereals, dried fruits, nuts, etc., eaten with milk. [Swiss German]

muezzin /moo-ez-in/ *n.* a Muslim crier who proclaims the hours of prayer. [based on Arabic *mu'addana* 'to proclaim']

muff[1] *n.* a fur or other covering, usu. in the form of a tube in which the hands are inserted for warmth. [from medieval Latin *muff(u)la*]

muff[2] ● *v.tr.* **1** bungle. **2** fail to catch or receive (a ball etc.). ● *n.* **1** esp. *Brit.* a person who is awkward or stupid, originally in some athletic sport. **2** a failure. [19th-century coinage]

muffin *n.* **1** *Brit.* a circular spongy cake made from yeast dough and eaten toasted and buttered. **2** *N. Amer.* a small spongy cake made with eggs and baking powder. [18th-century coinage]

muffle *v.tr.* **1** (often foll. by *up*) wrap or cover for warmth. **2** cover or wrap up (a source of sound) to reduce its loudness. **3** (usu. as **muffled** *adj.*) stifle (an utterance). **4** prevent from speaking. [Middle English]

muffler *n.* **1** a wrap or scarf worn for warmth. **2** any of various devices used to deaden sound in musical instruments. **3** *N. Amer.* the silencer of a motor vehicle.

mufti *n.* plain clothes worn by a person who also wears (esp. military) uniform (*in mufti*). [19th-century coinage]

mug[1] ● *n.* **1 a** a drinking vessel, usu. cylindrical and with a handle and used without a saucer. **b** its contents. **2** *slang* the face or mouth of a person. **3** *Brit. slang* **a** a simpleton. **b** a gullible person. ● *v.tr.* (**mugged**, **mugging**) **1** rob (a person) with violence, esp. in a public place. **2** fight, thrash. □ **mugger** *n.* (in sense 1 of *v.*). **mugging** *n.* (in sense 1 of *v.*).

mug[2] *v.tr.* (**mugged**, **mugging**) (usu. foll. by *up* or *up on*) *Brit. slang* learn (a subject) by concentrated study. [19th-century coinage]

muggins *n.* (*pl.* same or **mugginses**) *Brit.* **1** *colloq.* a simpleton. **2** a person who is easily outwitted (often with allusion to oneself: *so muggins had to pay*).

muggy *adj.* (**muggier**, **muggiest**) (of the weather, a day, etc.) oppressively damp and warm; humid. [based on Old Norse *mugga* 'mist, drizzle'] □ **mugginess** *n.*

mugshot *n. slang* a photograph of a face, esp. for official purposes.

mugwort *n.* any of various plants of the genus *Artemisia*, esp. *A. vulgaris*, with silver-grey aromatic foliage. [Old English]

Muhammadan *n. & adj.* (also **Mohammedan**) *offens.* = MUSLIM. [from *Muhammad*, Arabian prophet, *c*570-632] □ **Muhammadanism** *n.*

■ **Usage** The term *Muhammadan* is not used or favoured by Muslims, and is often regarded as offensive.

mujahedin /muu-jah-hi-**deen**/ *n.pl.* (also **mujahidin**, **mujahideen**) guerrilla fighters in Islamic countries, esp. supporting Islamic fundamentalism. [from Persian & Arabic *mujāhidīn*, literally 'people who fight a jihad']

mulatto *n.* (*pl.* **-os** or **-oes**) a person of mixed white and black parentage. [from Spanish *mulato* 'young mule, mulatto']

mulberry ● *n.* (*pl.* **-ies**) **1** (also **mulberry tree** or **bush**) ▶ any deciduous tree of the genus *Morus*, grown esp. for feeding silkworms, or its fruit. **2** the dark red or white berry of such a tree. **3** a dark red or purple colour. ● *adj.* of this colour. [from Latin *morum* 'mulberry' + BERRY]

fruit

MULBERRY: BLACK MULBERRY (*Morus nigra*)

mulch ● *n.* a mixture of wet straw, leaves, etc., spread around or over a plant to enrich or insulate the soil. ● *v.tr.* treat with mulch.

mulct ● *v.tr.* **1** extract money from by fine or taxation. **2 a** (often foll. by *of*) swindle. **b** obtain by swindling. ● *n.* a fine. [from Latin *multa, mulcta* 'a fine']

mule[1] *n.* **1** ▶ the offspring of a male donkey and a female horse, or (in general use) of a female donkey and a male horse. **2** a stupid or obstinate person. [from Latin *mulus mula*]

mule[2] *n.* ▼ a light shoe or slipper without a back. [French, literally 'slipper']

mule[3] var. of MEWL.

muleteer *n.* a mule driver.

mulish *adj.* **1** like a mule. **2** stubborn. □ **mulishly** *adv.* **mulishness** *n.*

mull[1] *v.tr. & intr.* (often foll. by *over*) ponder or consider.

MULES: 19TH-CENTURY LEATHER MULES

mull[2] *v.tr.* (esp. as **mulled** *adj.*) warm (wine or beer) with added spices etc. [17th-century coinage]

mull[3] *n. Sc.* a promontory. [Middle English]

mull[4] *n.* a thin soft plain muslin. [from Hindi *malmal*]

mullah *n.* a Muslim learned in Islamic theology and sacred law. [from Arabic *mawlā*]

mullein /**mul**-in/ *n.* ▶ any herbaceous plant of the genus *Verbascum*, with woolly leaves and yellow flowers. [from Old French *moleine*]

mullet *n.* a fish of the family Mullidae or (esp. *US*) the family Mugilidae. [from Greek *mollos* 'red mullet']

mulligatawny *n.* a highly seasoned soup originally from India. [from Tamil *milagutannir* 'pepper-water']

mullion *n.* (also **munnion**) a vertical bar dividing the lights in a window. ▷ WINDOW. □ **mullioned** *adj.*

multi- *comb. form* many; more than one. [from Latin *multus* 'much, many']

multi-access *n.* (often *attrib.*) the simultaneous connection to a computer of a number of terminals.

multichannel *adj.* employing or possessing many communication or television channels.

multicolour *adj.* (also **multicoloured**) (*US* **-color**, **-colored**) of many colours.

multicultural *adj.* of, relating to or constituting several cultural groups. □ **multiculturalism** *n.* **multiculturalist** *n. & adj.* **multiculturally** *adv.*

multidimensional *adj.* of or involving more than three dimensions. □ **multidimensionality** *n.* **multidimensionally** *adv.*

multidirectional *adj.* of, involving, or operating in several directions.

multi-ethnic *adj.* composed of or involving several ethnic groups.

multifarious *adj.* **1** (foll. by pl. noun) many and various. **2** having great variety. [from Latin *multifarius*] □ **multifariousness** *n.*

multiform *adj.* **1** having many forms. **2** of many kinds. □ **multiformity** *n.*

multifunctional *adj.* (also **multifunction**) having or fulfilling several functions.

multigrade *n.* (usu. *attrib.*) an engine oil etc. meeting the requirements of several standard grades.

multihull ● *adj.* having more than one hull. ● *n.* a multihull boat.

multilateral *adj.* **1** (of an agreement etc.) in which three or more parties participate. **2** having many sides. □ **multilateralism** *n.* **multilateralist** *n. & adj.* **multilaterally** *adv.*

multilingual *adj.* in or using several languages. □ **multilingualism** *n.* **multilingually** *adv.*

multimedia ● *attrib.adj.* (of art, education, etc.) using more than one medium of expression, communication, etc. ● *n.* an extension of hypertext allowing the provision of audio and video material cross-referenced to a computer text.

MULE

M

multimillion *attrib.adj.* costing or involving several million (pounds, dollars, etc.)

multimillionaire *n.* a person with a fortune of several millions.

multinational ● *adj.* **1** (of a business organization) operating in several countries. **2** relating to or including several nationalities. ● *n.* a multinational company. □ **multinationally** *adv.*

multi-party *attrib.adj.* of or involving several esp. political parties.

multiple ● *adj.* **1** having several or many parts, elements, or individual components. **2** (foll. by pl. noun) many and various. ● *n.* a number that may be divided by another a certain number of times without a remainder (*56 is a multiple of 7*). [from Late Latin *multiplus*] □ **multiply** *adv.*

multiple-choice *adj.* (of a question in an examination) accompanied by several possible answers from which the correct one has to be chosen.

multiple sclerosis see SCLEROSIS 2.

multiple shop *n.* (also **multiple store**) *Brit.* a shop or store with branches in several places.

multiplex ● *adj.* **1** manifold; of many elements. **2** involving simultaneous transmission of several messages along a single channel of communication. **3** of or relating to a single-site complex of two or more cinemas. ● *n.* **1** a multiplex system or signal. **2** a multiplex cinema. ● *v.tr.* incorporate into a multiplex signal or system. [Latin] □ **multiplexer** *n.* (also **multiplexor**). **multiplexing** *n.*

MULLEIN: DARK MULLEIN (*Verbascum nigrum*)

multipliable *adj.* that can be multiplied.

M

multiplicand n. a quantity to be multiplied by a multiplier. [from medieval Latin *multiplicandus* 'to be multiplied']

multiplication n. **1** the arithmetical process of multiplying. **2** the act or an instance of multiplying. [from Latin *multiplicatio*] □ **multiplicative** adj.

multiplication sign n. the sign (×) to indicate that one quantity is to be multiplied by another.

multiplication table n. a list of multiples of a particular number, usu. from 1 to 12.

multiplicity n. (pl. **-ies**) **1** manifold variety. **2** (foll. by *of*) a great number. [from Late Latin *multiplicitas*]

multiplier n. a quantity by which a given number is multiplied.

multiply v. (**-ies, -ied**) **1** tr. (also *absol.*) obtain from (a number) another that is a specified number of times its value (*multiply 6 by 4 and you get 24*). **2** intr. increase in number esp. by procreation. **3** tr. produce a large number of (instances etc.). **4** tr. **a** breed (animals). **b** propagate (plants). [from Latin *multiplicare*]

multiprocessing n. *Computing* processing by a number of processors sharing a common memory and common peripherals. □ **multiprocessor** n.

multiprogramming n. *Computing* the execution of two or more independent programs concurrently.

multi-purpose adj. having several purposes.

multiracial adj. relating to or made up of many human races. □ **multiracially** adv.

multi-storey ● attrib.adj. (of a building) having several storeys. ● n. colloq. a multi-storey car park.

multitasking n. *Computing* the execution of a number of tasks at the same time. □ **multitask** v.tr. & intr.

multi-track ● attrib.adj. relating to or made by the mixing of separately recorded soundtracks. ● n. a multi-track recording. ● v.tr. & intr. record using multi-track recording. □ **multi-tracking** n.

multitude n. **1** (often foll. by *of*) a great number. **2** a large gathering of people; a crowd. **3** (**the multitude**) the common people. [from Latin *multitudo*]

multitudinous adj. **1** very numerous. **2** consisting of many individuals. □ **multitudinously** adv.

multi-user attrib.adj. (of a computer system) having a number of simultaneous users.

multivalent adj. **1** *Chem.* **a** having a valency of more than two. **b** having a variable valency. **2** having many applications, meanings, or values. □ **multivalency** n.

multivariate adj. *Statistics* involving two or more variable quantities.

multivitamin ● n. a tablet containing a combination of vitamins. ● attrib. adj. containing a combination of vitamins.

mum[1] n. *Brit. colloq.* mother.

mum[2] adj. *colloq.* silent (*keep mum*). □ **mum's the word** say nothing. [Middle English: imitative of closed lips]

mum[3] v.intr. (**mummed, mumming**) act in a traditional masked mime. [related to MUM[2] and Middle Low German *mummen* 'to mutter']

mumble ● v. **1** intr. & tr. speak or utter indistinctly. **2** tr. bite or chew with or as with toothless gums. ● n. an indistinct utterance. [Middle English] □ **mumbler** n.

mumbo-jumbo n. (pl. **-jumbos**) **1** meaningless or ignorant ritual. **2** language or action intended to mystify or confuse. **3** an object of senseless veneration. [from *Mumbo Jumbo*, a supposed African idol]

mummer n. an actor in a traditional mime.

mummery n. (pl. **-ies**) **1** ridiculous (esp. religious) ceremonial. **2** a performance by mummers.

mummy[1] n. (pl. **-ies**) *Brit. colloq.* mother.

mummy[2] n. (pl. **-ies**) **1** ▼ a body of a human being or animal embalmed for burial, esp. in ancient Egypt. **2** a dried-up body. [based on Persian *mūm* 'wax'] □ **mummify** v.tr. (**-ies, -ied**). **mummification** n.

mumps n.pl. **1** (treated as *sing.*) an infectious viral disease with swelling of the parotid salivary glands in the face. **2** *Brit.* a fit of sulks. [related to archaic *mump* 'to be sullen'] □ **mumpish** adj. (in sense 2).

mumsy adj. maternal; homely. [jocular variant of MUMMY[1]]

munch v.tr. eat steadily with a marked action of the jaws. [Middle English]

Munchausen's syndrome /muunsh-ow-zĕnz/ n. *Med.* a mental illness in which a person repeatedly feigns severe illness so as to obtain hospital treatment. [from Baron *Munchausen*, hero of a book (1785) by R.E. Raspe]

mundane adj. **1** dull, routine. **2** of this world; worldly. [based on Latin *mundus* 'world'] □ **mundanely** adv. **mundanity** n. (pl. **-ies**).

mung n. (in full **mung bean**) ▶ a leguminous plant of the genus *Vigna*, native to India and yielding a small bean used as food. [from Hindi *mūng*]

municipal adj. of or concerning a municipality or its self-government. [from Latin *municipalis*] □ **municipalize** v.tr. (also **-ise**). **municipally** adv.

municipality n. (pl. **-ies**) **1** a town or district having local government. **2** the governing body of this area.

munificent adj. (of a giver or a gift) splendidly generous, bountiful. [based on Latin *munus* 'gift'] □ **munificence** n. **munificently** adv.

muniment n. (usu. in *pl.*) a document kept as evidence of rights or privileges etc. [from Latin *munimentum* 'defence', later 'title deed']

munition n. (usu. in *pl.*) military weapons, ammunition, etc. [from Latin *munitio* 'fortification']

munnion var. of MULLION.

muntjac n. (also **muntjak**) any small deer of the genus *Muntiacus* native to SE Asia. [local name in western Java]

muon n. *Physics* an unstable subatomic particle like an electron, but with a much greater mass. [originally *mu-meson*]

mural ● n. a painting executed directly on a wall. ● adj. **1** of or like a wall. **2** on a wall. [from Latin *muralis*]

murder ● n. **1** the unlawful killing of a human being by another with malice aforethought. **2** colloq. an unpleasant state of affairs (*it was murder here on Saturday*). ● v.tr. **1** kill (a human being) unlawfully. **2** *Law* kill (a human being) unlawfully with malice aforethought. **3** colloq. **a** utterly defeat. **b** spoil by a bad performance, mispronunciation, etc. □ **cry (or scream) blue murder** slang make an extravagant outcry. **get away with murder** colloq. do whatever one wishes and escape punishment. [from Old French *murdre*] □ **murderer** n. **murderess** n.

murderous adj. **1** capable of, intending, or involving murder or great harm. **2** colloq. extremely arduous or unpleasant.

murk (also **mirk**) ● n. **1** darkness, poor visibility. **2** air obscured by fog etc. ● adj. archaic = MURKY.

murky adj. (also **mirky**) (**-ier, -iest**) **1** dark, gloomy. **2** (of darkness, liquid, etc.) thick, dirty. **3** suspiciously obscure (*murky past*). □ **murkily** adv. **murkiness** n.

murmur ● n. **1** a subdued continuous sound, as made by waves, a brook, etc. **2** a softly spoken or nearly inarticulate utterance. **3** *Med.* a recurring sound heard in the auscultation of the heart and usu. indicating abnormality. **4** a subdued expression of discontent. ● v. **1** intr. make a subdued continuous sound. **2** tr. utter (words) in a low voice. **3** intr. (usu. foll. by *at, against*) complain in low tones, grumble. [from Latin *murmurare*] □ **murmuringly** adv.

murphy n. (pl. **-ies**) slang a potato. [from an Irish surname]

Murphy's Law n. joc. the maxim that anything that can go wrong will go wrong.

murrain n. **1** an infectious disease of cattle, carried by parasites. **2** archaic a plague, esp. the potato blight during the Irish famine in the mid-19th c. [Middle English, based on Latin *mori* 'to die']

Mus.B. abbr. (also **Mus. Bac.**) Bachelor of Music. [Latin *Musicae Baccalaureus*]

muscadel var. of MUSCATEL.

muscadine n. a variety of grape with a musk flavour, used chiefly in wine-making.

muscat n. **1** a sweet fortified white wine made from muscadines. **2** a muscadine. [based on Provençal *muscat muscade* 'musky']

muscatel n. (also **muscadel**) **1** = MUSCAT. **2** a raisin from a muscadine grape. [diminutive of MUSCAT]

muscle ● n. **1** a fibrous tissue with the ability to contract, producing movement in or maintaining the position of an animal body. **2** the part of an animal body that is composed of muscles. ▷ MUSCULATURE. **3** physical power or strength. ● v.intr. (usu. foll. by *in*) colloq. force oneself on others; intrude by forceful means. □ **not move a muscle** be completely motionless. [from Latin *musculus* 'little mouse', from the fancied mouselike form of some muscles] □ **muscly** adj.

MUNG BEANS

MUMMY

The ancient Egyptians developed a way of preserving the bodies of their dead, in the belief that this would ensure their eternal survival. The liver, lungs, and brain were first removed and stored in special jars. The heart, however, was left in place, so that it could be judged in the afterlife. The body was then covered with natron (a compound of sodium carbonate and sodium bicarbonate) to stop it decaying, packed with dry material, and wrapped in bandages. Finally, the body was placed in a sarcophagus.

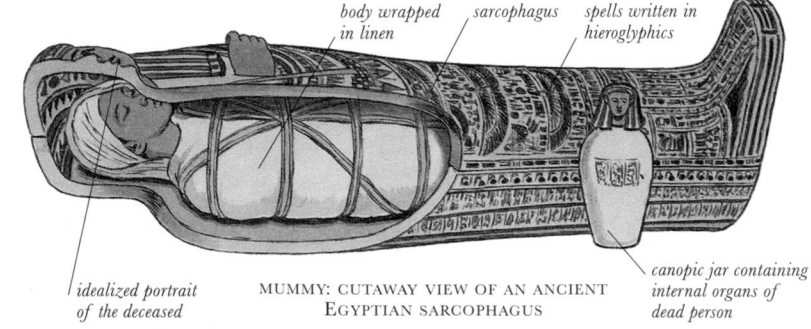

body wrapped in linen · *sarcophagus* · *spells written in hieroglyphics*

idealized portrait of the deceased

MUMMY: CUTAWAY VIEW OF AN ANCIENT EGYPTIAN SARCOPHAGUS

canopic jar containing internal organs of dead person

MUSCULATURE

All human movements depend on muscles, of which there are three types: skeletal, smooth, and cardiac. Only skeletal muscle (also known as voluntary muscle) is under our conscious control; the others work automatically and are described as involuntary. Smooth muscle is found in the digestive system, bladder, and blood vessels, whereas cardiac muscle is found only in the heart. Muscles of all three kinds have in common the ability to be stretched, to contract, to be excited by a stimulus, and to return to their original size and shape. The skeletal muscular system consists of about 620 muscles that make up over 40 per cent of body weight.

ENLARGED SECTION THROUGH A MUSCLE FASCICLE

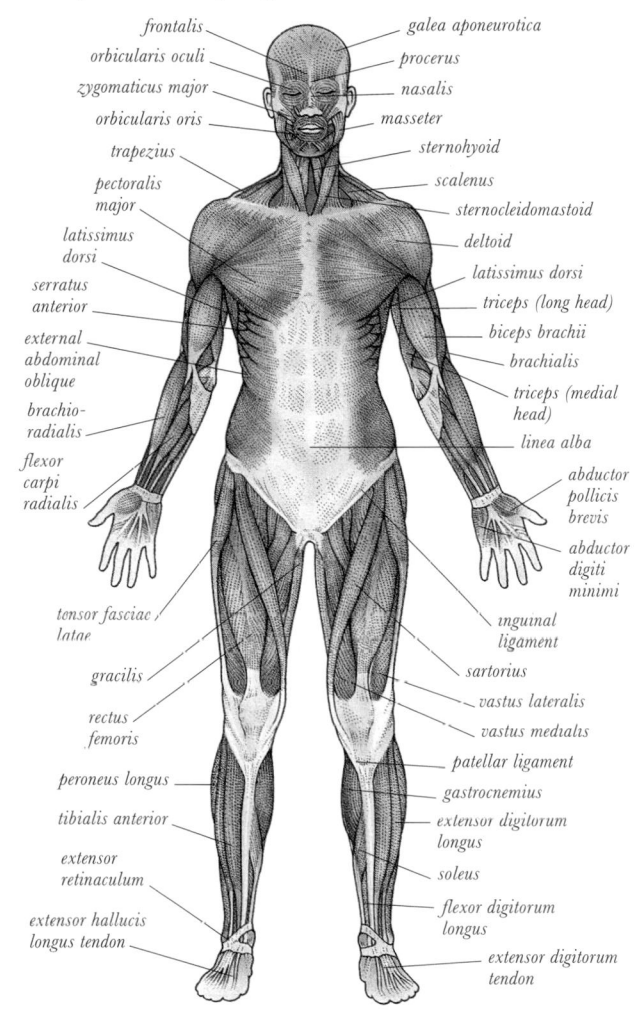

ANTERIOR VIEW OF SUPERFICIAL HUMAN MUSCLES

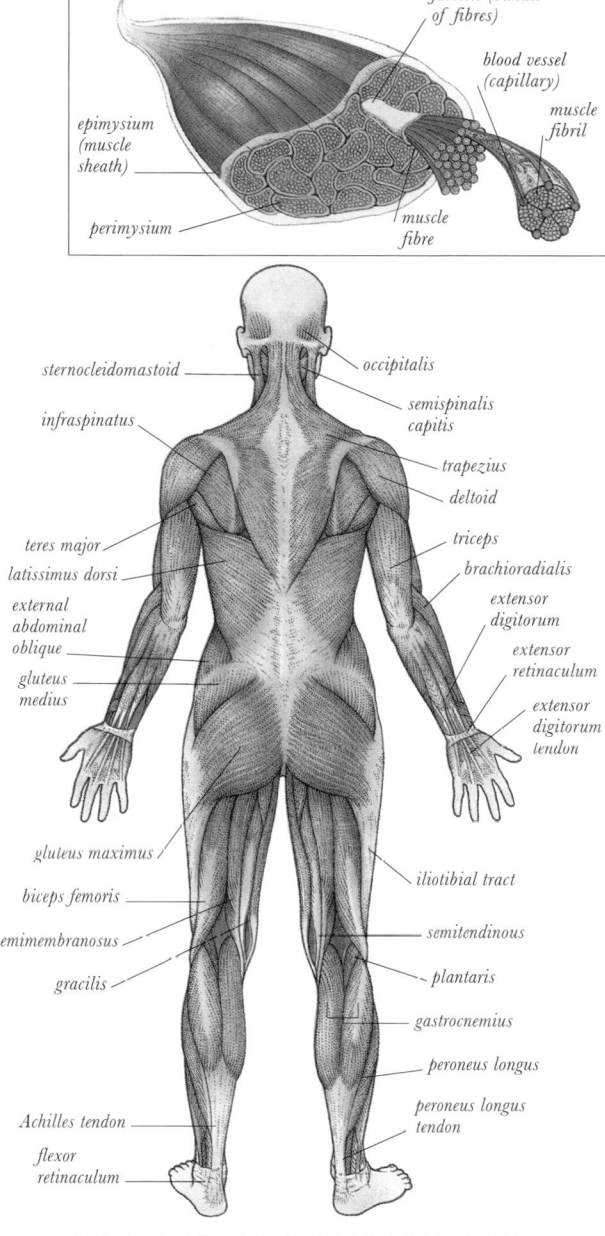

POSTERIOR VIEW OF SUPERFICIAL HUMAN MUSCLES

M

muscle-bound *adj.* with muscles stiff and inelastic through excessive exercise or training.

muscle-man *n.* a man with highly developed muscles, esp. one employed as an intimidator.

Muscovite ● *n.* **1** a native or citizen of Moscow. **2** *archaic* a Russian. ● *adj.* **1** of or relating to Moscow. **2** *archaic* of or relating to Russia. [from *Muscovia* 'Muscovy']

muscovite *n.* a silver-grey form of mica.

Muscovy *n. archaic* Russia. [from Russian *Moskva* 'Moscow']

Muscovy duck *n.* a tropical American duck, *Cairina moschata*, with red markings on its head.

muscular *adj.* **1** of or affecting the muscles. **2** having well-developed muscles. **3** robust. [related to MUSCLE] □ **muscularity** *n.* **muscularly** *adv.*

muscular dystrophy *n.* a hereditary progressive wasting of the muscles.

musculature *n.* ▲ the muscular system of a body or organ.

musculoskeletal *adj.* of or relating to the musculature and skeleton together.

Mus.D. *abbr.* (also **Mus. Doc.**) Doctor of Music. [Latin *Musicae Doctor*]

muse[1] *n.* **1 a** (**Muse**) ► (in Greek and Roman mythology) each of nine goddesses who inspire poetry, music, etc. **b** a source of inspiration for creativity. **2** (usu. prec. by *the*) **a** a poet's inspiring goddess. **b** a poet's genius. [from Greek *mousa*]

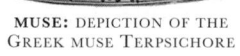

MUSE: DEPICTION OF THE GREEK MUSE TERPSICHORE

muse[2] *v. literary* **1** *intr.* **a** (usu. foll. by *on, upon*) ponder, reflect. **b** (usu. foll. by *on*) gaze meditatively. **2** *tr.* say meditatively. [from Old French *muser* 'to waste time'] □ **musingly** *adv.*

museum *n.* a building used for storing and exhibiting objects of historical, scientific, or cultural interest. [from Greek *mouseion* 'seat of the Muses']

museum piece *n.* **1** a specimen of art etc. fit for a museum. **2** *Brit. derog.* an old-fashioned or quaint person or object.

mush *n.* **1** soft pulp. **2** feeble sentimentality. **3** *N. Amer.* maize porridge. □ **mushy** *adj.* (**mushier mushiest**). **mushily** *adv.* **mushiness** *n.*

MUSHROOM

Like all fungi, mushrooms lack the green pigment chlorophyll, which plants use to make food. Instead they absorb nutrients from decaying organic matter or from living plants and animals. The part that is visible above ground is, in fact, the fruiting body of the fungus. The main body consists of hyphal threads, which form a branching web known as the mycelium; this spreads through the substrate that the fungus has colonized, absorbing nutrients. Fruiting bodies vary in shape and colour, but all are designed to spread the spores that enable a fungus to establish new colonies. Spores are produced on the underside of a mushroom and released from flaps (gills) or hollows (pores). Many types of fungi are edible, and some are considered a delicacy.

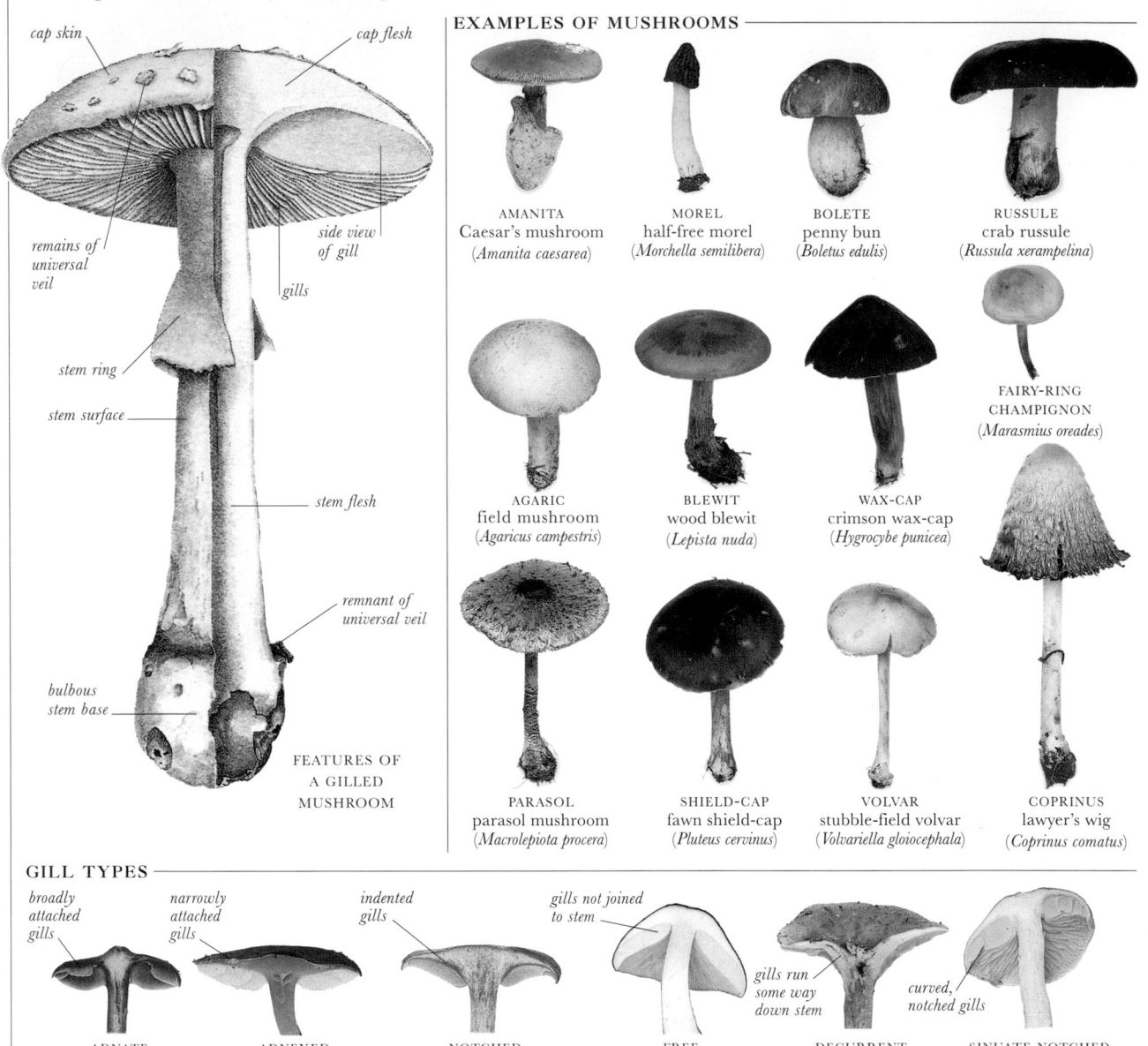

FEATURES OF A GILLED MUSHROOM

cap skin

cap flesh

remains of universal veil

side view of gill

gills

stem ring

stem surface

stem flesh

remnant of universal veil

bulbous stem base

EXAMPLES OF MUSHROOMS

AMANITA
Caesar's mushroom
(*Amanita caesarea*)

MOREL
half-free morel
(*Morchella semilibera*)

BOLETE
penny bun
(*Boletus edulis*)

RUSSULE
crab russule
(*Russula xerampelina*)

AGARIC
field mushroom
(*Agaricus campestris*)

BLEWIT
wood blewit
(*Lepista nuda*)

WAX-CAP
crimson wax-cap
(*Hygrocybe punicea*)

FAIRY-RING
CHAMPIGNON
(*Marasmius oreades*)

PARASOL
parasol mushroom
(*Macrolepiota procera*)

SHIELD-CAP
fawn shield-cap
(*Pluteus cervinus*)

VOLVAR
stubble-field volvar
(*Volvariella gloiocephala*)

COPRINUS
lawyer's wig
(*Coprinus comatus*)

GILL TYPES

broadly attached gills

narrowly attached gills

indented gills

gills not joined to stem

gills run some way down stem

curved, notched gills

ADNATE   ADNEXED   NOTCHED   FREE   DECURRENT   SINUATE NOTCHED

M

---

mushroom ● *n.* **1 ▲** the usu. edible spore-producing body of various fungi, esp. *Agaricus campestris*, with a stem and domed cap, proverbial for its rapid growth. ▷ FUNGUS. **2** the pale pinkish-brown colour of this. **3** any item resembling a mushroom in shape (*darning mushroom*). **4** (usu. *attrib.*) something that appears or develops suddenly or is ephemeral; an upstart. **●** *v.intr.* **1** appear or develop rapidly. **2** expand and flatten like a mushroom cap. **3** gather mushrooms. **●** *adj.* mushroom-coloured. [from Late Latin *mussirio -onis*]

mushroom cloud *n.* a cloud suggesting the shape of a mushroom, esp. from a nuclear explosion.

mushroom growth *n.* **1** a sudden development or expansion. **2** anything undergoing this.

music *n.* **1** the art of combining vocal or instrumental sounds (or both) to produce beauty of form, harmony, and expression of emotion. ▷ NOTATION. **2** the sounds so produced. **3** musical compositions. **4** the written or printed score of a musical composition. **5** certain pleasant natural sounds, e.g. birdsong. □ **music of the spheres** see SPHERE. **music to one's ears** something very pleasant to hear. [from Greek *mousikē (tekhnē)* '(art) of the Muses']

musical ● *adj.* **1** of or relating to music. **2** (of sounds, a voice, etc.) melodious, harmonious. **3** fond of or skilled in music (*the musical one of the family*). **4** set to or accompanied by music. **●** *n.* a film or theatrical piece (not opera or operetta) of which music is an essential element. □ **musicality** *n.* **musicalize** *v.tr.* (also **-ise**). **musically** *adv.* **musicalness** *n.*

musical box *n.* *Brit.* a mechanical musical instrument in a box, typically incorporating a toothed cylinder which plucks a row of tuned metal strips as it revolves.

musical chairs *n.pl.* **1** a party game in which the players compete in successive rounds for a decreasing number of chairs. **2** a series of changes or political manoeuvring etc.

musical comedy *n.* a light dramatic entertainment of songs, dialogue, and dancing, connected by a slender plot.

musical director *n.* the person responsible for the musical aspects of a performance or production, often the conductor or leader of a music group.

musical instrument see INSTRUMENT *n.* 2.

musical sound see SOUND[1] *n.* 6.

music centre *n. Brit.* equipment combining radio, record player, tape recorder, etc.

music drama *n.* Wagnerian-type opera without formal arias etc. and governed by dramatic considerations.

music hall *n.* (usu. hyphenated when *attrib.*) *Brit.* **1** variety entertainment, popular *c.*1850–1914, consisting of singing, dancing, and novelty acts. **2** a theatre where this took place.

musician *n.* a person who plays a musical instrument, esp. professionally, or is otherwise musically gifted. □ **musicianship** *n.*

musicology *n.* the study of music other than that directed to proficiency in performance or composition. □ **musicologist** *n.* **musicological** *adj.*

music stand *n.* a rest or frame on which sheet music or a score is supported.

music stool *n.* a stool for a pianist.

musk *n.* **1** a strong-smelling reddish-brown substance produced by a gland in the male musk deer and used in perfumes. **2** the plant, *Mimulus moschatus*, with pale green ovate leaves and yellow flowers. [from Persian *mušk*] □ **musky** *adj.* (**muskier**, **muskiest**). **muskiness** *n.*

musk deer *n.* ▼ any small Asian deer of the genus *Moschus*, having no antlers.

MUSK DEER
(*Moschus moschiferus*)

musket *n. hist.* an infantryman's (esp. smooth-bored) light gun, often supported on the shoulder. ▷ REDCOAT. [from Italian *moschetto* 'crossbow bolt']

musketeer *n. hist.* a soldier armed with a musket.

musketry *n.* **1** muskets, or soldiers armed with muskets, referred to collectively. **2** the knowledge of handling muskets.

musket shot *n. hist.* **1** a shot fired from a musket. **2** the range of this shot.

musk melon *n.* the common yellow or green melon, *Cucumis melo*, usu. with a raised network of markings on the skin. [from the aromatic flesh of some varieties]

musk ox *n.* a large goat-antelope, *Ovibos moschatus*, with a thick shaggy coat and small curved horns. [from the strong smell emitted by the male during rutting]

muskrat *n.* **1** a large aquatic rodent, *Ondatra zibethicus*, having a musky smell. **2** the fur of this.

musk-rose *n.* a rambling rose, *Rosa moschata*, with large white flowers smelling of musk.

Muslim (also **Moslem**) ● *n.* a follower of the Islamic religion. ● *adj.* of or relating to the Muslims or their religion. [Arabic, based on *aslama* 'to resign oneself']

muslin *n.* **1** a fine delicately woven cotton fabric. **2** *US* a cotton cloth in plain weave. [from *Mussolo* 'Mosul', in Iraq]

musquash *n.* = MUSKRAT. [Algonquian]

mussel *n.* **1** ▶ any bivalve mollusc of the genus *Mytilus*, living in sea water and often used for food. ▷ BIVALVE. **2** any similar freshwater mollusc of the genus *Margaritifer* or *Anodonta*, forming pearls. [Old English]

MUSTELID

Numbering about 65 species, mustelids are long-bodied mammalian carnivores. Although most mustelids are terrestrial or arboreal, some spend their time in water. They range in size from the least weasel, weighing less than 28 g (1 oz), to the sea otter, which can weigh up to 45 kg (99 lb). With their sharp teeth, acute senses, and agile bodies, they are highly effective hunters. Some species subsist on live prey, but others, such as badgers, eat carrion and a range of plant foods. Most mustelids mark their territories with a strong-smelling fluid, which is discharged from the anal glands.

dense, soft coat

anal scent glands

long tail

long body

short legs

FISHER
(*Martes pennanti*)

EXAMPLES OF MUSTELIDS

PINE MARTEN
(*Martes martes*)

WOLVERINE
(*Gulo gulo*)

SKUNK
(*Spilogale putorius*)

POLECAT
(*Mustela putorius*)

WEASEL
(*Mustela nivalis*)

COMMON OTTER
(*Lutra lutra*)

STOAT
(*Mustela erminea*)

BADGER
(*Meles meles*)

must[1] ● *v.aux.* (*3rd sing. present* **must**; *past* **had to** or in indirect speech **must**) (foll. by infin., or *absol.*) **1 a** be obliged to (*must we leave now?*). **b** in ironic questions (*must you slam the door?*). **2** be certain to (*they must have left by now*). **3** ought to (*it must be said that*). **4** expressing insistence (*I must ask you to leave*). **5** (foll. by *not* + infin.) **a** be forbidden to (*you must not smoke*). **b** ought not; need not (*you must not worry*). **c** expressing insistence that something should not be done (*they must not be told*). **6** (as past or historic present) expressing the perversity of destiny (*what must I do but break my leg*). ● *n. colloq.* a thing that cannot or should not be missed (*if you go to London St Paul's is a must*). □ **I must say** often *iron.* I cannot refrain from saying (*a fine way to behave, I must say*). **must needs** see NEEDS. [Old English]

■ **Usage** In sense 1a, the negative (i.e. lack of obligation) is expressed by *not have to* or *need not*; *must not* denotes positive forbidding, as in *you must not smoke.*

must[2] *n.* grape juice before fermentation is complete. [from Latin *mustum* 'new (thing)']

must[3] *n.* mustiness, mould.

mustache *US* var. of MOUSTACHE.

mustachio /mŭ-stah-shi-oh/ *n.* (*pl.* **-os**) (often in *pl.*) *archaic* a moustache. [from Spanish *mostacho*]

MUSSEL
(*Mytilus* species)

mustang *n.* a small wild horse native to Mexico and California. ▷ HORSE. [from Spanish *mestengo*]

mustang grape *n.* a grape from the wild vine *Vitis candicans*, of the southern US, used for making wine.

mustard ● *n.* **1 a** ▶ any of various plants of the genus *Brassica* with slender pods and yellow flowers. **b** any of various plants of the genus *Sinapis*, eaten at the seedling stage, often with cress. **2** the crushed seeds of these made into a paste and used as a spicy condiment. ▷ SPICE. **3** the brownish-yellow colour of this condiment. ● *adj.* of a brownish-yellow colour. [from Old French *mo(u)starde*: originally a condiment prepared with MUST[2]]

mustard gas *n.* a colourless oily liquid, whose vapour is a powerful irritant and vesicant.

mustelid ● *n.* ▲ a mammal of the family Mustelidae, including weasels, stoats, badgers, skunks, martens, etc. ● *adj.* of or relating to this family. [based on Latin *mustela* 'weasel']

muster ● *v.* **1** *tr.* collect (originally soldiers) for inspection, to check numbers, etc. **2** *tr. & intr.* gather together. **3** *tr.* (often foll. by *up*) summon up (courage etc.). ● *n.* **1** the assembly of persons for inspection. **2** an assembly. □ **pass muster** bear inspection; come up to a required standard. [from Latin *monstrare* 'to show'] □ **musterer** *n.*

MUSTARD:
BROWN
MUSTARD
(*Brassica juncea*)

M

MUTATION

Mutations occur as a result of the chance rearrangement of a DNA molecule or by a change in the shape or number of chromosomes. If mutation occurs in a sex cell it can be passed on from one generation to another. Most mutations are damaging, and often impair survival, but they are a source of variation in living things and allow evolution to take place. The mutant teasel shown here has curved rather than straight spines on the seed-head.

straight spines — NORMAL TEASEL

curved spines — MUTANT TEASEL

M

mustn't *contr.* must not.

musty *adj.* (**mustier, mustiest**) **1** mouldy. **2** of a mouldy or stale smell or taste. □ **mustily** *adv.* **mustiness** *n.*

mutable *adj. literary* **1** liable to change. **2** fickle. [from Latin *mutabilis*] □ **mutability** *n.*

mutagen *n.* an agent promoting mutation, e.g. radiation. □ **mutagenic** *adj.* **mutagenesis** *n.*

mutant ● *adj.* resulting from mutation. ● *n.* a mutant form. [from Latin *mutant-* 'changing']

mutate *v.intr. & tr.* undergo or cause to undergo mutation. [back-formation from MUTATION]

mutation *n.* **1** the process or an instance of change or alteration. **2** ▲ a genetic change which, when transmitted to offspring, gives rise to heritable variations. **3** a mutant. [from Latin *mutatio* 'changing'] □ **mutational** *adj.*

mutatis mutandis /moo-tah-tis moo-**tan**-dis/ *adv.* (in comparing cases) making the necessary alterations. [Latin]

mute ● *adj.* **1** silent, refraining from or temporarily bereft of speech. **2** not emitting articulate sound. **3** (of a person or animal) dumb. **4** not expressed in speech (*mute protest*). **5** (of a letter) not pronounced. ● *n.* **1** a dumb person (*a deaf mute*). **2** *Mus.* **a** a clamp for damping the resonance of the strings of a violin etc. **b** ▼ a pad or cone for damping the sound of a wind or brass instrument. **3** an unsounded consonant. **4** an actor whose part is in a dumbshow. ● *v.tr.* **1** deaden, muffle, or soften the sound of (a thing, esp. a musical instrument). **2 a** tone down, make less intense. **b** (as **muted** *adj.*) (of colours etc.) subdued (*a muted green*). [from Latin *mutus*] □ **mutely** *adv.* **muteness** *n.*

■ **Usage** See Usage Note at MOOT.

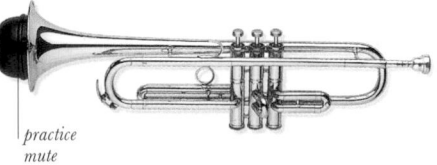

MUTE: TRUMPET WITH PRACTICE MUTE

practice mute

mute swan *n.* ► the commonest Eurasian swan, *Cygnus olor*, having white plumage and an orange-red bill with a swollen black base. ▷ WATER FOWL

MUTE SWAN (*Cygnus olor*)

mutilate *v.tr.* **1 a** deprive of a limb or organ. **b** destroy the use of (a limb or organ). **2** render (a book etc.) imperfect by excision or some act of destruction. [based on Latin *mutilatus* 'lopped off'] □ **mutilation** *n.* **mutilator** *n.*

mutineer *n.* a person who mutinies. [from French *mutinier*, based on *mutin* 'rebellious']

mutiny ● *n.* (*pl.* **-ies**) an open revolt against constituted authority, esp. by soldiers or sailors against their officers. ● *v.intr.* (**-ies, -ied**) (often foll. by *against*) revolt; engage in mutiny. [based on French *mutin* 'rebellious'] □ **mutinous** *adj.*

mutt *n.* **1** *slang* an ignorant, stupid, or blundering person. **2 a** *Brit. derog.* or *joc.* a dog. **b** *US* a mongrel. [abbreviation of *mutton-head*]

mutter ● *v.* **1** *intr.* speak low in a barely audible manner. **2** *intr.* (often foll. by *against, at*) murmur or grumble about. **3** *tr.* utter (words etc.) in a low tone. **4** *tr.* say in secret. ● *n.* **1** muttered words or sounds. **2** muttering. [Middle English, related to MUTE] □ **mutterer** *n.*

mutton *n.* **1** the flesh of sheep used for food. **2** *joc.* a sheep. □ **mutton dressed as lamb** *Brit. colloq. derog.* a usu. middle-aged or elderly woman dressed or made up to appear younger. [from medieval Latin *multo*]

mutual *adj.* **1** (of feelings, actions, etc.) experienced or done by each of two or more parties with reference to the other or others (*mutual affection*). **2** *disp.* common to two or more persons (*a mutual friend*). **3** standing in (a specified) relation to each other (*mutual beneficiaries*). [from Latin *mutuus* 'mutual, borrowed'] □ **mutuality** *n.* **mutually** *adv.*

■ **Usage** The use of *mutual* in sense 2, although often found, is considered incorrect by some people, for whom *common* is preferable.

muu-muu *n.* a woman's loose brightly coloured dress. [Hawaiian]

muzak *n.* **1** *propr.* a system of music transmission for playing in public places. **2** recorded light music. [alteration of MUSIC]

muzzle ● *n.* **1** the projecting part of an animal's face, including the nose and mouth. ▷ DOG. **2** ► a guard, usu. made of straps or wire, fitted over an animal's nose and mouth to stop it biting or feeding. **3** the open end of a firearm. ▷ GUN. ● *v.tr.* **1** put a muzzle on (an animal etc.). **2** impose silence upon. [from Old French *musel*]

MUZZLE ON A DOG

muzzle-loader *n.* ► a gun that is loaded through the muzzle. □ **muzzle-loading** *adj.*

muzzy *adj.* **1 a** mentally hazy. **b** esp. *Brit.* confused from drinking alcohol. **2** blurred. [18th-century coinage] □ **muzzily** *adv.* **muzziness** *n.*

MW *abbr.* **1** megawatt(s). **2** medium wave.

my *poss.det.* **1** of or belonging to me (*my house*). **2** as a form of address in affectionate, sympathetic, etc. contexts (*my dear boy*). **3** in various expressions of surprise (*oh my!*). □ **my Lady** (or **Lord**) the form of address to certain titled persons. [Middle English]

my- *comb. form* var. of MYO-.

myalgia *n.* a pain in a muscle or group of muscles. □ **myalgic** *adj.*

myalgic encephalomyelitis see ME.

myasthenia *n.* a condition causing abnormal weakness of certain muscles.

mycelium *n.* (*pl.* **mycelia**) the vegetative part of a fungus, consisting of microscopic threadlike hyphae. [based on Greek *mukēs* 'mushroom'] □ **mycelial** *adj.*

Mycenaean /my-si-**nee**-ăn/ ● *adj. Archaeol.* ▼ of or relating to the late Bronze Age civilization in Greece (*c.*1580–1100 BC). ● *n.* an inhabitant of Mycenae or the Mycenaean world. [from Latin *Mycenaeus*]

myco- *comb. form* fungus. [from Greek *mukēs* 'fungus, mushroom']

mycology *n.* **1** the study of fungi. **2** the fungi of a particular region. □ **mycological** *adj.* **mycologist** *n.*

MYCENAEAN CUP

mycoprotein *n.* protein derived from fungi, esp. as produced for human consumption.

myelin *n.* a white fatty substance forming an insulating sheath around certain nerve fibres. ▷ NERVOUS SYSTEM. [based on Greek *muelos* 'marrow'] □ **myelination** *n.*

myelitis *n.* inflammation of the spinal cord. [based on Greek *muelos* 'marrow']

myeloid *adj.* of or relating to bone marrow or the spinal cord.

mylodon *n.* an extinct gigantic ground sloth with cylindrical teeth. [from Greek *mulē* 'mill, molar' + *odous odontos* 'tooth']

mynah *n.* (also **myna, mina**) any of various SE Asian starlings, able to mimic the human voice. [from Hindi *mainā*]

myo- *comb. form* (also **my-** before a vowel) muscle. [from Greek *mus muos* 'muscle']

myocardium *n.* (*pl.* **myocardia**) the muscular tissue of the heart. ▷ HEART. [based on Greek *kardia* 'heart'] □ **myocardial** *adj.* **myocarditis** *n.*

MYNAH: COMMON MYNAH (*Acridotheres tristis*)

myopia *n.* **1** short-sightedness. **2** lack of imagination or intellectual insight. □ **myopic** *adj.* **myopically** *adv.*

myosin *n.* a protein which with actin forms the contractile filaments of muscle.

myosotis *n.* (also **myosote**) any plant of the genus *Myosotis* with blue, pink, or white flowers, esp. a forget-me-not. [from Greek *mus muos* 'mouse' + *ous ōtos* 'ear']

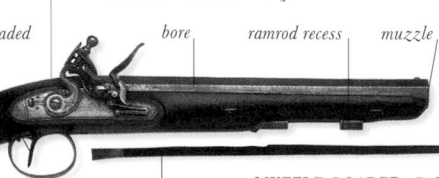

bore   ramrod recess   muzzle

spring-loaded trigger

ramrod for pushing ammunition down the bore

MUZZLE-LOADER: EARLY 19TH-CENTURY ENGLISH DUELLING PISTOL

myriad *literary* ● *n.* **1** an indefinitely great number. **2** ten thousand. ● *adj.* of an indefinitely great number. [from Greek *murias muriados* 'countless']

myriapod *n.* any land-living arthropod of the class Myriapoda, with numerous leg-bearing segments, e.g. centipedes and millipedes. [from Greek *murias* 'countless' + *pous podos* 'foot']

myrmidon *n.* **1** a hired ruffian. **2** a lowly servant. [from Greek *Murmidones*, warlike Thessalian people who went with Achilles to Troy]

myrrh /mer/ *n.* a gum resin from several trees of the genus *Commiphora* used in perfumery, incense, etc. [from Greek *murra*] □ **myrrhic** *adj.* **myrrhy** *adj.*

myrtle *n.* **1** ▶ an evergreen shrub of the genus *Myrtus* with aromatic foliage and white flowers, esp. *M. communis*, bearing purple-black ovoid berries. **2** *US* = PERIWINKLE[1]. [from medieval Latin *myrtilla*]

myself *pron.* **1** *emphat. form* of I[2] or ME[1] (*I saw it myself*). **2** *refl. form* of ME[1] (*able to dress myself*). **3** in my normal state of body and mind (*I'm not myself today*). **4** *poet.* = I[2] (*myself when young did often wander in the woods*). □ **by myself** see *by oneself.* **I myself** I for my part (*I myself am doubtful*).

MYRTLE
(*Myrtus communis*)

mysterious *adj.* **1** full of or wrapped in mystery. **2** (of a person) delighting in mystery. □ **mysteriously** *adv.* **mysteriousness** *n.*

mystery *n.* (*pl.* -**ies**) **1** a secret, hidden, or inexplicable matter. **2** secrecy or obscurity (*wrapped in mystery*). **3** (*attrib.*) secret, undisclosed (*mystery guest*). **4** the practice of making a secret of (esp. unimportant) things (*engaged in mystery and intrigue*). **5** (in full **mystery story**) a fictional work dealing with a puzzling event, esp. a crime. **6 a** a religious truth divinely revealed. **b** *RC Ch.* a decade of the rosary. **7** (in *pl.*) the secret religious rites of the ancient Greeks, Romans, etc. [from Greek *mustērion*]

　mystery play *n.* a medieval play based on the Bible or the lives of the saints.

　mystery tour *n. Brit.* a pleasure trip to an unspecified destination.

mystic ● *n.* a person who seeks by contemplation etc. to obtain unity with the Deity, or who believes in the spiritual apprehension of truths that are beyond the understanding. ● *adj.* **1** mysterious and awe-inspiring. **2** spiritually allegorical or symbolic. [based on Greek *mustēs* 'initiated person'] □ **mystical** *adj.* **mystically** *adv.* **mysticism** *n.*

mystify *v.tr.* (-**ies**, -**ied**) **1** bewilder, confuse. **2** hoax, take advantage of the credulity of. **3** wrap up in mystery. [from French *mystifier*] □ **mystification** *n.*

mystique *n.* **1** an atmosphere of mystery and veneration attending some activity or person. **2** any skill or technique, which is impressive or mystifying to the layman. [French]

myth *n.* **1** a traditional narrative usu. involving supernatural or imaginary persons and often embodying popular ideas on natural or social phenomena etc. **2** such narratives collectively. **3** a widely held but false notion. **4** a fictitious person, thing, or idea. [from Greek *muthos*] □ **mythic** *adj.* **mythical** *adj.* **mythically** *adv.*

mythology *n.* (*pl.* -**ies**) **1** a body of myths (*Greek mythology*). **2** the study of myths. □ **mythologer** *n.* **mythological** *adj.* **mythologically** *adv.* **mythologist** *n.*

mythos /my-thŭs/ *n.* (*pl.* **mythoi**) **1** *literary* a myth; a body of myths. **2** a narrative theme or pattern. [Late Latin]

myxoedema *n.* (*US* **myxedema**) a syndrome caused by hypothyroidism, resulting in thickening of the skin, weight gain, mental dullness, loss of energy, and sensitivity to cold.

myxomatosis *n.* an infectious usu. fatal viral disease in rabbits, causing swelling of the mucous membranes.

M

N

N¹ *n.* (also **n**) (*pl.* **Ns** or **N's**) the fourteenth letter of the alphabet.

N² *abbr.* (also **N.**) North; Northern.

N³ *symb. Chem.* the element nitrogen.

n¹ *abbr.* (also **n.**) neuter.

n² *symb.* **1** *Math.* an indefinite number. **2** nano-. □ **to the nth** (or **nth degree**) **1** *Math.* to any required power. **2** to any extent; to the utmost.

'n *conj.* (also **'n'**) *colloq.* and.

Na *symb. Chem.* the element sodium. [modern Latin *natrium*]

na *adv.* (in *comb.*; usu. with an auxiliary verb) *Sc.* = NOT (*I canna do it; they didna go*).

n/a *abbr.* **1** not applicable. **2** not available.

NAAFI /**naf**-i/ *abbr. Brit.* **1** Navy, Army, and Air Force Institutes. **2** a canteen, shop, etc. for service personnel run by the NAAFI.

naan var. of NAN².

nab *v.tr.* (**nabbed**, **nabbing**) *slang* **1** arrest; catch in wrongdoing. **2** seize, grab. [17th-century coinage]

nabob *n.* **1** *hist.* a Muslim official or governor under the Mogul empire. **2** a person of conspicuous wealth or high rank. [from Urdu, related to NAWAB]

nacho *n.* (*pl.* **-os**) (usu. in *pl.*) a tortilla chip, usu. topped with melted cheese and spices etc. [20th-century coinage]

nacre *n.* mother-of-pearl from any shelled mollusc. [French] □ **nacreous** *adj.*

nadir /**nay**-deer/ *n.* **1** the part of the celestial sphere directly below an observer (opp. ZENITH). **2** the lowest point in one's fortunes; a time of deep despair. [from Arabic *nazīr (as-samt)* 'opposite to the zenith')']

naevus /**nee**-vŭs/ *n.* (*US* **nevus**) (*pl.* **naevi** /**nee**-vy/) **1** a birthmark in the form of a raised red patch on the skin. **2** = MOLE². [Latin]

naff¹ *v.intr. Brit. slang* **1** (in *imper.*, foll. by *off*) go away. **2** (as **naffing** *adj.*) used as an intensive to express annoyance etc.

naff² *adj. Brit. slang* **1** unfashionable, tasteless. **2** worthless, rubbishy. [20th-century coinage]

nag¹ ● *v.* (**nagged**, **nagging**) **1 a** *tr.* annoy or irritate (a person) with persistent complaining, criticizing, or urging. **b** *intr.* (often foll. by *at*) find fault, complain, or urge, esp. persistently. **2** *intr.* (of a pain) ache dully but persistently. **3** *tr.* worry or preoccupy (a person, the mind, etc.) (*his mistake nagged him*). ● *n.* a persistently nagging person. □ **nagger** *n.* **naggingly** *adv.*

nag² *n. colloq.* a horse. [Middle English]

naiad /**ny**-ad/ *n.* (*pl.* **naiads** or **naiades** /**ny**-ă-deez/) *Mythol.* a water nymph. [from Greek *Naias -ados*]

naïf /ny-**eef**/ ● *adj.* = NAIVE. ● *n.* a naive person.

nail ● *n.* **1** a small metal spike with a broadened flat head, driven in with a hammer to join things together or to serve as a peg, protection (cf. HOBNAIL), or decoration. **2** ▸ a horny covering on the upper surface of the tip of the finger and toe. ● *v.tr.* **1** fasten with a nail or nails. **2 a** secure, catch, or get hold of (a person or thing). **b** expose or discover (a lie or a liar). □ **nail one's colours to the mast** persist; refuse to give in. **nail down 1** bind (a person) to a promise etc. **2** define precisely. **3** fasten (a thing) with nails. **nail in a person's coffin** something thought to

increase the risk of death. **on the nail** *Brit.* (esp. of payment) without delay (*cash on the nail*). [Old English] □ **nailed** *adj.* (also in *comb.*).

nail enamel *n. N. Amer.* = NAIL POLISH.

nail file *n.* a roughened metal or emery strip used for smoothing the nails.

nail polish *n.* a varnish applied to the nails to colour them or make them shiny.

nail punch *n.* (also **nail set**) a tool for sinking the head of a nail below a surface.

nail varnish *n. Brit.* = NAIL POLISH.

naive /ny-**eev**/ *adj.* (also **naïve**) **1** artless; innocent; unaffected. **2** foolishly credulous. **3** (of art etc.) produced in a sophisticated society but deliberately rejecting conventional expertise. [French, from Latin *nativus* 'native'] □ **naively** *adv.*

naivety /ny-**eev**-ti/ *n.* (also **naïvety**, **naïveté**) (*pl.* **-ies** or **naïvetés**) **1** the state or quality of being naive. **2** a naive action.

naked *adj.* **1** without clothes; nude. **2** plain; undisguised; exposed (*the naked truth; his naked soul*). **3** (of a light, flame, etc.) unprotected from the wind etc.; unshaded. **4** defenceless. **5** (of a sword etc.) unsheathed. **6** (usu. foll. by *of*) devoid; without. [Old English] □ **nakedly** *adv.* **nakedness** *n.*

naked eye *n.* (prec. by *the*) unassisted vision, e.g. without a telescope, microscope, etc.

Nama ● *n.* (*pl.* same or **Namas**) **1** a member of a people of S. Africa and Namibia. **2** the language of this people. ● *adj.* of or relating to this people or their language.

■ **Usage** The term *Hottentot* is sometimes used for this people and language, but it is often considered to be offensive.

namby-pamby ● *adj.* **1** lacking vigour or drive; weak. **2** insipidly pretty or sentimental. ● *n.* (*pl.* **-ies**) a namby-pamby person. [fanciful formation from *Ambrose* Philips, English pastoral writer, 1674–1749]

name ● *n.* **1** the word by which an individual person, animal, place, or thing is known, spoken of, etc. **2 a** a usu. abusive term used of a person etc. (*called him names*). **b** a word denoting an object or esp. a class of objects, ideas, etc. (*what is the name of that kind of vase?*). **3** a famous person. **4** a reputation, esp. a good one (*has a name for honesty*). **5** (**Name**) an underwriter of a Lloyd's syndicate. ● *v.tr.* **1** give a usu. specified name to (*named the dog Spot*). **2** call (a person or thing) by the right name (*named the man in the photograph*). **3** mention; specify; cite (*named his requirements*). **4** nominate, appoint, etc. (*was named the new chairman*). **5** specify as something desired (*named it as her dearest wish*). □ **by name** called (*Tom by name*). **have to one's name** possess. **in all but name** virtually. **in name** (or **name only**) as a mere formality; hardly at all (*is the leader in name only*). **in a**

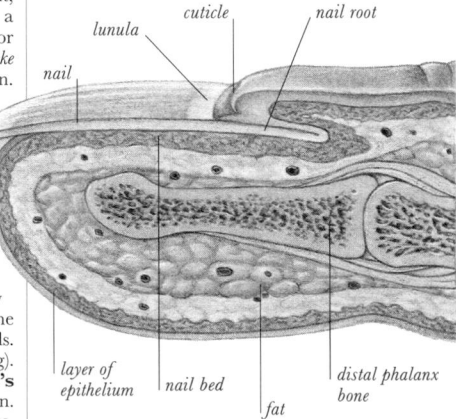

NAIL: CROSS-SECTION OF A HUMAN FINGERTIP SHOWING THE NAIL

cuticle · *nail root* · *lunula* · *nail* · *layer of epithelium* · *nail bed* · *fat* · *distal phalanx bone*

person's name = *in the name of*. **in the name of** calling to witness; invoking (*in the name of goodness*). **in one's own name** independently; without authority. **make a name for oneself** become famous. **name after** (*N. Amer.* also **for**) call (a person) by the name of (a specified person) (*named him after his uncle Roger*). **name the day** arrange a date (esp. of a woman fixing the date for her wedding). **name names** mention specific names, esp. in accusation. **name of the game** *colloq.* the purpose or essence of an action etc. **of** (or **by**) **the name of** called. **put one's name down for 1** apply for. **2** promise to subscribe (a sum). **you name it** no matter what; whatever you like. [Old English] □ **nameable** *adj.*

name-calling *n.* abusive language.

name-dropping *n.* the familiar mention of famous people as a form of boasting. □ **namedrop** *v.intr.* (**-dropped**, **-dropping**). **name-dropper** *n.*

nameless *adj.* **1** having no name or name-inscription. **2** unnamed; anonymous, esp. deliberately (*our informant, who shall be nameless*). **3** too loathsome or horrific to be named (*nameless vices*). □ **namelessly** *adv.* **namelessness** *n.*

namely *adv.* that is to say; in other words.

nameplate *n.* a plate or panel bearing the name of an occupant of a room etc.

namesake *n.* a person or thing having the same name as another (*was her aunt's namesake*). [probably from the phrase *for the name's sake*]

name-tape *n.* a tape fixed to a garment etc. and bearing the name of the owner.

nan¹ *nan n. Brit. colloq.* grandmother.

nan² /nahn/ *n.* (also **naan**) (in Indian cookery) a type of leavened bread cooked esp. in a clay oven. [from Urdu *nān*]

nana¹ /**nah**-nă/ *n. slang* a silly person; a fool.

nana² /**nan**-ă/ *n.* (also *Brit.* **nanna**) *colloq.* grandmother.

nancy *offens.* (also **nance**) *slang* ● *n.* (*pl.* **-ies**) (in full **nancy boy**) an effeminate man, esp. a homosexual. ● *adj.* effeminate. [pet form of the name *Ann*]

nanna var. of NANA².

nanny ● *n.* (*pl.* **-ies**) **1 a** a child's nurse. **b** *Brit.* an unduly protective person, institution, etc. (*the nanny state*). **2** = NAN¹. **3** (in full **nanny goat**) a female goat. ● *v.tr.* (**-ies**, **-ied**) be unduly protective towards.

nano- /**nan**-oh/ *comb. form* denoting a factor of 10^{-9}. [from Greek *nanos* 'dwarf']

nanometre *n.* (*US* **nanometer**) one thousand-millionth of a metre.

nanosecond *n.* one thousand-millionth of a second.

nanotechnology *n.* the branch of technology that deals with dimensions and tolerances of less than 100 nanometres, esp. the manipulation of individual atoms and molecules. □ **nanotechnological** *adj.* **nanotechnologist** *n.*

nap¹ ● *v.intr.* (**napped**, **napping**) sleep lightly or briefly. ● *n.* a short sleep or doze, esp. by day (*took a nap*). □ **catch a person napping 1** find a person asleep or off guard. **2** detect in negligence or error. [Old English]

nap² *n.* the raised pile on textiles, esp. velvet. [Middle English]

nap³ ● *n.* **1** a form of whist in which players declare the number of tricks they expect to take. **2** *Brit.* a racing or investment tip. ● *v.tr.* (**napped**, **napping**) *Brit.* name (a horse etc.) as a probable winner. □ **go nap** risk everything in one attempt. [abbreviation of *napoleon*, original name of the card game]

napalm /**nay**-pahm/ ● *n.* jellied petrol used in incendiary bombs. ● *v.tr.* attack with napalm bombs.

nape *n.* (in full **nape of the neck**) the back of the neck. [Middle English]

naphtha /**naf**-thă/ *n.* an inflammable oil obtained by the dry distillation of coal etc. [Latin, literally 'inflammable volatile liquid issuing from the earth']

NAPHTHALENE

naphthalene /naf-thă-leen/ n. ◀ a white crystalline aromatic substance produced by the distillation of coal tar and used in mothballs and the manufacture of dyes etc. [based on NAPHTHA] □ **naphthalic** adj.

napkin n. **1** (in full **table napkin**) a square piece of linen, paper, etc. used for wiping the lips, fingers, etc. at meals. **2** Brit. a baby's nappy. [based on Latin mappa 'sheet']

napkin ring n. a ring used to hold (and distinguish) a person's table napkin when not in use.

Napoleonic adj. of, relating to, or characteristic of Napoleon I or his time.

nappy n. (pl. **-ies**) Brit. a piece of towelling or other absorbent material wrapped round a baby to absorb and retain urine and faeces. [abbreviation of NAPKIN]

narcissism n. Psychol. excessive or erotic interest in oneself. [from Greek Narkissos, a youth who fell in love with his reflection in a pool] □ **narcissist** n. **narcissistic** adj. **narcissistically** adv.

narcissus n. (pl. **narcissi** /-sy/ or **narcissuses**) ▼ any bulbous plant of the genus Narcissus, esp. N. poeticus bearing a heavily scented single flower with an undivided corona edged with crimson and yellow. [from Greek narkissos]

— corona

— petals

NARCISSUS
(*Narcissus poeticus* var. *recurvus*)

narcolepsy n. Med. a disease with fits of sleepiness and drowsiness. [based on Greek narkoun 'to make numb'] □ **narcoleptic** adj. & n.

narcosis n. **1** Med. the working or effects of soporific narcotics. **2** a state of insensibility. [Greek, literally 'numbness']

narcotic ● adj. **1** (of a substance) inducing drowsiness, sleep, stupor, or insensibility. **2** (of a drug etc.) affecting the mind. ● n. a narcotic substance, drug, or influence. [from Greek narkōtikos] □ **narcotically** adv. **narcotize** v.tr. (also **-ise**).

nark slang ● n. **1** Brit. a police informer or decoy. **2** Austral. an annoying person or thing. ● v.tr. (usu. in passive) Brit. annoy; infuriate. [from Romany nāk 'nose']

narrate v.tr. (also absol.) **1** give a continuous story or account of. **2** provide a spoken commentary or accompaniment for (a film etc.). [based on Latin narratus 'recounted'] □ **narratable** adj. **narration** n.

narrative ● n. **1** a spoken or written account of connected events in order of happening. **2** the practice or art of narration. ● adj. in the form of, or concerned with, narration (narrative verse). □ **narratively** adv.

narrator n. **1** a person who narrates, esp. a character who recounts the events of a novel or narrative poem. **2** a person who speaks the commentary in a film etc.

narrow ● adj. (**narrower**, **narrowest**) **1 a** of small width in proportion to length; lacking breadth. **b** confined or confining; constricted (within narrow bounds). **2** of limited scope; restricted (in the narrowest sense). **3** with little margin (a narrow escape). ● n. (usu. in pl.) **1** the narrow part of a strait, river, sound, etc. **2** a narrow pass or street. ● v.tr. & intr. make or become narrow. [Old English] □ **narrowly** adv. **narrowness** n.

narrow boat n. Brit. a boat for canal navigation, esp. one less than 7 ft (2.1 metres) wide.

narrowcast esp. N. Amer. ● v.intr. & tr. (past and past part. **narrowcast** or **narrowcasted**) transmit (a television programme etc.), esp. by cable, to an audience targeted by interests or location. ● n. a transmission or programme of this kind. □ **narrowcasting** n.

narrow gauge n. a railway track of a smaller gauge than the standard one.

narrow-minded adj. rigid or restricted in one's views, intolerant, illiberal. □ **narrow-mindedness** n.

narrow squeak n. Brit. **1** a narrow escape. **2** a success barely attained.

narwhal n. ▼ a small Arctic whale, *Monodon monoceros*, the male of which has a long twisted tusk. [from Danish narhval]

NARWHAL
(*Monodon monoceros*)

nary /nair-i/ adj. colloq. or dial. not a; no (nary a one). [from ne'er a]

NASA /nas-ă/ abbr. (in the US) National Aeronautics and Space Administration.

nasal ● adj. **1** of, for, or relating to the nose. **2** Phonet. (of a speech sound) pronounced with the breath passing through the nose, e.g. m, n, ng, or French en. **3** (of the voice or speech) having an intonation caused by breathing through the nose. ● n. Phonet. a nasal sound. [based on Latin nasus 'nose'] □ **nasality** n. **nasalize** v.intr. & tr. (also **-ise**). **nasalization** n. **nasally** adv.

nascent adj. **1** in the act of being born. **2** just beginning to be; not yet mature. [from Latin nascent- 'being born'] □ **nascency** n.

nasturtium /nă-ster-shŭm/ n. a trailing plant, *Tropaeolum majus*, with rounded edible leaves and bright orange, yellow, or red flowers. [Latin]

nasty ● adj. (**nastier**, **nastiest**) **1 a** highly unpleasant. **b** annoying; objectionable (the car has a nasty habit of breaking down). **2** difficult to negotiate; dangerous, serious (a nasty fence; a nasty question; a nasty illness). **3** (of a person or animal) ill-tempered, spiteful; violent, offensive. **4** (of the weather) foul, wet, stormy. ● n. (pl. **-ies**) colloq. **1** a nasty person, object, or event. **2** a video nasty. **□ nasty bit or piece) of work** Brit. colloq. an unpleasant or contemptible person. [Middle English] □ **nastily** adv. **nastiness** n.

Nat. abbr. **1** National. **2** Nationalist. **3** Natural.

natal adj. of or from one's birth. [from Latin natalis]

natch adv. colloq. = NATURALLY.

nation n. a community of people of mainly common descent, history, language, etc., forming a state or inhabiting a territory. [from Latin natio] □ **nationhood** n.

national ● adj. **1** of or common to a nation or the nation. **2** peculiar to or characteristic of a particular nation. ● n. **1** a citizen of a specified country, usu. entitled to hold that country's passport (French nationals). **2** (**the National**) = GRAND NATIONAL. □ **nationally** adv.

national anthem n. a song adopted by a nation, intended to inspire patriotism.

national curriculum n. a common programme of study laid down for pupils in the maintained schools of England and Wales with tests at specified ages.

national debt n. the money owed by a state because of loans to it.

National Front n. a UK political party with extreme reactionary views on immigration etc.

national grid n. Brit. **1** the network of high-voltage electric power lines between major power stations. **2** the metric system of geographical coordinates used in maps of the British Isles.

National Guard n. (in the US) the primary reserve force partly maintained by the states but available for federal use.

National Health n. (also **National Health Service**) (in the UK) a system of national medical care paid for mainly by taxation.

national income n. the total money earned within a nation.

National Insurance n. (in the UK) the system of compulsory payments by employed persons (supplemented by employers) to provide state assistance in sickness, unemployment, retirement, etc.

nationalism n. **1 a** a patriotic feeling, principles, etc. **b** an extreme form of this; chauvinism. **2** a policy of national independence. □ **nationalist** n. & adj. **nationalistic** adj. **nationalistically** adv.

nationality n. (pl. **-ies**) **1** the status of belonging to a particular nation (what is your nationality?; has British nationality). **2** the condition of being national; distinctive national qualities. **3** an ethnic group forming a part of one or more political nations.

nationalize v.tr. (also **-ise**) **1** take over (industry, land, etc.) from private ownership on behalf of the State. **2** make national. □ **nationalization** n.

national park n. an area of natural beauty protected by the State for the use of the general public.

national service n. Brit. hist. service in the army etc. under conscription.

National Socialism n. hist. the doctrines of nationalism, racial purity, etc., adopted by the Nazis. □ **National Socialist** n.

National Trust n. (in the UK, Australia, etc.) an organization for maintaining and preserving historic buildings etc.

National Vocational Qualification n. (in the UK) a qualification in a vocational subject set at five levels and (at levels two and three) corresponding in standard to GCSE and GCE A levels.

nation state n. a sovereign state of which most of the citizens or subjects are united also by factors such as language, common descent, etc., which define a nation.

nationwide adj. & adv. extending over the whole nation.

native ● n. **1 a** (usu. foll. by of) a person born in a specified place (a native of Bristol). **b** a local inhabitant. **2** offens. a member of a non-white indigenous people, as regarded by the colonial settlers. **3** (usu. foll. by of) an indigenous animal or plant. ● adj. **1** (usu. foll. by to) inherent; innate (spoke with the facility native to him). **2** of one's birth or birthplace (native dress; native country). **3** (usu. foll. by to) belonging to a specified place (the anteater is native to S. America). **4 a** (esp. of a non-European) indigenous; born in a place. **b** of the natives of a place (native customs). □ **go native** (of a settler) adopt the local way of life, esp. in a non-European country. [from Latin nativus] □ **natively** adv. **nativeness** n.

Native American n. an American Indian, esp. of the US.

■ **Usage** The term *Native American* is now often preferred to *American Indian*. However, when used to include the aboriginal peoples of Canada as well as

N

N

of the US, it can cause offence. Ambiguity can be avoided by using *American Indian* or *Canadian Indian* as appropriate. See also Usage Note at INDIAN.

native speaker *n.* a person who has spoken a language from early childhood.

nativity *n.* (*pl.* **-ies**) **1** (esp. **the Nativity**) **a** the birth of Christ. **b** the festival of Christ's birth; Christmas. **2** ▼ a picture of the Nativity. **3** birth.

NATIVITY: 15TH-CENTURY NATIVITY BY FILIPPINO LIPPI

nativity play *n.* a play, usu. performed by children at Christmas, dealing with the birth of Christ.

NATO /**nay**-toh/ *abbr.* (also **Nato**) North Atlantic Treaty Organization.

natter esp. *Brit. colloq.* ● *v.intr.* chatter idly. ● *n.* aimless chatter. [originally Scots] □ **natterer** *n.*

natterjack *n.* ► a toad, *Bufo calamita*, with a bright yellow stripe down its back.

natty *adj.* (**nattier**, **nattiest**) *colloq.* **1 a** smartly or neatly dressed, dapper. **b** spruce; trim; smart (*a natty blouse*). **2** deft. □ **nattily** *adv.* **nattiness** *n.*

NATTERJACK (*Bufo calamita*)

natural ● *adj.* **1 a** existing in or caused by nature (*natural landscape*). **b** uncultivated; wild (*existing in its natural state*). **2** in the course of nature (*died of natural causes*). **3** (of human nature etc.) not surprising; to be expected (*natural for her to be upset*). **4 a** (of a person or a person's behaviour) unaffected, easy, spontaneous. **b** (foll. by *to*) spontaneous, easy (*friendliness is natural to him*). **5 a** (of qualities etc.) inherent; innate (*a natural talent for music*). **b** (of a person) having such qualities (*a natural linguist*). **6** not disguised or altered (as by make-up etc.). **7** lifelike; as if in nature (*the portrait looked very natural*). **8** likely by its or their nature to be such (*natural enemies; the natural antithesis*). **9 a** related genetically (*her natural son*). **b** illegitimate (*a natural child*). **10** *Mus.* (of a note) not sharpened or flattened (*B natural*). ● *n.* **1** (usu. foll. by *for*) *colloq.* a person or thing naturally suitable, adept, expert, etc. (*a natural for the championship*). **2** *Mus.* **a** a sign (♮) denoting a return to natural pitch after a sharp or a flat. ▷ NOTATION. **b** a natural note. [from Latin *naturalis*] □ **naturalness** *n.*

natural-born *adj.* (usu. *attrib.*) having a character or position by birth.

NATURALISM

Naturalist art and literature attempts to create an accurate representation of nature and character. This aim requires great attention to detail, but does not exclude a concern for capturing the beauty of the subject.

The Gleaners (1857), JEAN-FRANÇOIS MILLET

natural childbirth *n. Med.* childbirth with minimal medical or technological intervention.

natural death *n.* death by age or disease, not by accident, poison, violence, etc.

natural food *n.* food without preservatives etc.

natural gas *n.* an inflammable mainly methane gas found in the Earth's crust, not manufactured. ▷ GAS FIELD, OIL PLATFORM.

natural history *n.* **1** the study of animals or plants, esp. as set forth for popular use. **2** the facts concerning the flora and fauna etc. of a particular place or class (*a natural history of the Isle of Wight*). □ **natural historian** *n.*

naturalism *n.* ▲ the theory or practice in art and literature of representing nature, character, etc. realistically and in great detail. □ **naturalistic** *adj.* **naturalistically** *adv.*

naturalist *n.* **1** an expert in natural history. **2** a person who believes in or practises naturalism.

naturalize *v.tr.* (also **-ise**) **1** admit (a foreigner) to the citizenship of a country. **2** introduce (an animal, plant, etc.) into another region so that it flourishes in the wild. **3** adopt (a foreign word, custom, etc.). □ **naturalization** *n.*

natural law *n.* **1** *Philos.* unchanging moral principles common to all human beings. **2** an observable law relating to natural phenomena.

natural life *n.* the duration of one's life on Earth.

naturally *adv.* **1** in a natural manner. **2** as a natural result. **3** (qualifying a whole sentence) as might be expected; of course.

natural note *n. Mus.* a note that is neither sharp nor flat.

natural numbers *n.pl.* the integers 1, 2, 3, etc.

natural resources *n.pl.* materials or conditions occurring in nature and capable of economic exploitation.

natural science *n.* the sciences used in the study of the physical world, e.g. physics, chemistry, geology, biology, botany.

natural selection *n.* the Darwinian theory of the survival and propagation of organisms best adapted to their environment.

natural wastage *n.* = WASTAGE 3.

nature *n.* **1** a thing's or person's innate or essential qualities or character. **2** (often **Nature**) **a** the physical power causing all the phenomena of the material world. **b** these phenomena, including plants, animals, landscape, etc. **3** a kind, sort, or class (*things of this nature*). **4** the general characteristics and feelings of humankind. **5** inherent impulses determining character or action. **6** heredity as an influence on or determinant of personality. □ **by nature** innately. **from nature**

Art using natural objects as models. **in** (or **of**) **the nature of** characteristically resembling or belonging to the class of (*the answer was in the nature of an excuse*). **in the nature of things** inevitable. ● *adv.* inevitably. [from Latin *natura*, based on *natus* 'born']

natured *adj.* (in *comb.*) having a specified disposition (*good-natured; ill-natured*).

nature reserve *n.* a tract of land managed so as to preserve its flora, fauna, physical features, etc.

nature study *n.* the practical study of plant and animal life etc. as a school subject.

nature trail *n.* a signposted path through the countryside designed to draw attention to natural phenomena.

naturism *n.* nudism. □ **naturist** *n. & adj.*

naturopathy *n.* the treatment or prevention of disease etc. without drugs, usu. involving diet, exercise, massage, etc. □ **naturopath** *n.* **naturopathic** *adj.*

naught ● *n.* **1** *archaic* or *literary* nothing, nought. **2** *US* = NOUGHT 1. ● *adj.* (usu. *predic.*) *archaic* or *literary* worthless; useless. □ **come to naught** be ruined or baffled. **set at naught** disregard; despise. [Old English]

naughty *adj.* (**naughtier**, **naughtiest**) **1** (esp. of children) disobedient; badly behaved. **2** *colloq. joc.* indecent (*a naughty postcard*). [Middle English] □ **naughtily** *adv.* **naughtiness** *n.*

nausea /**naw**-ziă/ *n.* **1** an inclination to vomit. **2** loathing; revulsion. [based on Greek *naus* 'ship']

nauseate *v.tr.* affect with nausea; disgust (*was nauseated by the smell*). □ **nauseating** *adj.* **nauseatingly** *adv.*

nauseous *adj.* **1** affected with nausea, sick (*felt nauseous all day*). **2** causing nausea, offensive to the taste or smell. **3** disgusting; loathsome. □ **nauseously** *adv.*

nautical *adj.* of or concerning sailors or navigation; naval; maritime. [based on Greek *nautēs* 'sailor'] □ **nautically** *adv.*

nautical mile *n.* a unit of approx. 2,025 yards (1,852 metres).

nautilus *n.* (*pl.* **nautiluses** or **nautili** /-ly/) ► any cephalopod of the genus *Nautilus* with a light brittle spiral shell, esp. (**pearly nautilus**) one having a chambered shell with nacreous septa. ▷ SHELL. [from Greek *nautilos* 'sailor, nautilus']

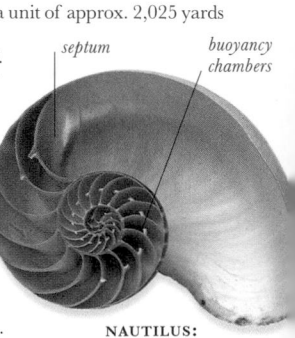

septum   buoyancy chambers

NAUTILUS: CROSS-SECTION OF A NAUTILUS SHELL

naval *adj.* **1** of, in, for, etc. the navy or a navy. **2** or concerning ships (*a naval battle*). [based on Latin *navis* 'ship']

naval academy *n.* a college for training naval officers.

naval architecture *n.* the designing of ships. □ **naval architect** *n.*

naval stores *n.pl.* all materials used in shipping.

navarin *n.* a casserole of mutton or lamb with vegetables. [French]

nave[1] *n.* ▼ the central part of a church, usu. from the west door to the chancel and excluding the side aisles. ▷ CATHEDRAL. [from Latin *navis* 'ship']

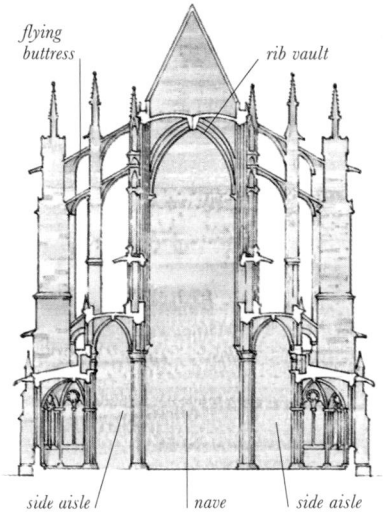

flying buttress
rib vault
side aisle | *nave* | *side aisle*

NAVE: CROSS-SECTION OF A 13TH-CENTURY FRENCH CHURCH SHOWING THE NAVE

nave[2] *n.* the hub of a wheel. [Old English]

navel *n.* a rounded knotty depression in the centre of the belly caused by the detachment of the umbilical cord. [Old English]

navel orange *n.* a large seedless orange with a navel-like formation at the top. ▷ CITRUS FRUIT

navigable *adj.* (of a river, the sea, etc.) affording a passage for ships. [from Latin *navigabilis*] □ **navigability** *n.*

navigate *v.* **1 a** *tr.* manage or direct the course of (a ship, aircraft, etc.). **b** *intr.* find one's way; steer the correct course. **2** *tr.* **a** sail on or across (a sea, river, etc.). **b** travel or fly through (the air). **3** *intr.* (of a passenger in a vehicle) assist the driver by map-reading etc. **4** *intr.* sail a ship, sail in a ship. [based on Latin *navis* 'ship' + *agere* 'to drive']

navigation *n.* **1** the act or process of navigating. **2** any of several methods of determining or planning a ship's or aircraft's position and course. □ **navigational** *adj.*

navigator *n.* **1** a person skilled or engaged in navigation. **2** an explorer by sea.

navvy /**na**-vi/ *Brit.* ● *n.* (*pl.* **-ies**) a labourer employed in building or excavating roads, canals, etc. ● *v.intr.* (**-ies, -ied**) work as a navvy.

navy /**nay**-vi/ ● *n.* (*pl.* **-ies**) **1** (often **the Navy**) **a** the whole body of a state's ships of war, including crews, maintenance systems, etc. **b** the officers and men of a navy. **2** (in full **navy blue**) a dark blue colour as used in naval uniform. ● *adj.* (in full **navy blue**; hyphenated when *attrib.*) dark blue. [based on Latin *navis* 'ship']

nawab /nă-**wahb**/ *n.* **1** the title of a distinguished Muslim in Pakistan. **2** *hist.* the title of a governor or nobleman in India. [from Arabic *nā'ib* 'deputy']

nay ● *adv.* **1** or rather; and even; and more than that (*impressive, nay, magnificent*). **2** *archaic* = NO[2] *adv.* **1**. ● *n.* **1** the word 'nay'. **2** a negative vote. [from Old Norse *nei*]

naysay *v.* (*3rd sing. present* **-says**; *past* and *past part.* **-said**) *US* **1** *intr.* utter a denial or refusal. **2** *tr.* refuse or contradict. □ **naysayer** *n.*

Nazarene ● *n.* **1 a** (prec. by *the*) Christ. **b** (esp. in Jewish or Muslim use) a Christian. **2** a native or inhabitant of Nazareth. ● *adj.* of or concerning Nazareth, Nazarenes, etc. [from Greek *Nazarēnos*]

Nazi /**naht**-si/ ● *n.* (*pl.* **Nazis**) **1** *hist.* a member of the German National Socialist party. **2** *derog.* a person holding extreme racist or authoritarian views or behaving brutally. ● *adj.* of or concerning the Nazis, Nazism, etc. [representing pronunciation of *Nati-* in German *Nationalsozialist*] □ **Nazidom** *n.* **Nazify** *v.tr.* (**-ies, -ied**) **Naziism** *n.* **Nazism** *n.*

NB *abbr.* nota bene.

Nb *symb. Chem.* the element niobium.

NCO *abbr.* non-commissioned officer.

Nd *symb. Chem.* the element neodymium.

NE *abbr.* **1** north-east. **2** north-eastern.

Ne *symb. Chem.* the element neon.

Neanderthal /ni-**an**-der-tahl/ *adj.* ▼ of or belonging to a type of fossil human widely distributed in palaeolithic Europe, with a retreating forehead and prominent brow-ridges. [from *Neanderthal*, a region in Germany where remains were found]

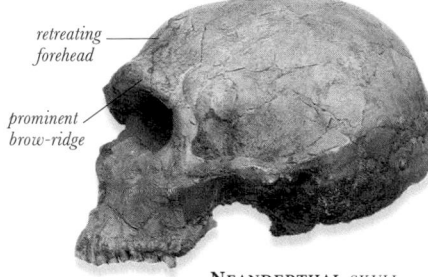

retreating forehead
prominent brow-ridge

NEANDERTHAL SKULL

neap *n.* (in full **neap tide**) a tide just after the first and third quarters of the Moon when there is least difference between high and low water. ▷ TIDE. [Old English]

Neapolitan ● *n.* a native or citizen of Naples in Italy. ● *adj.* of or relating to Naples. [based on Greek *Neapolis* 'new town, Naples']

near ● *adv.* **1** (often foll. by *to*) to or at a short distance in space or time; close by (*the time drew near; dropped near to them*). **2** closely (*as near as one can guess*). ● *prep.* (*compar.* & *superl.* also used) **1** to or at a short distance (in space, time, condition, or resemblance) from (*stood near the back; occurs nearer the end; the Sun is*

near setting). **2** (in *comb.*) that is almost (*near-hysterical; a near-Communist*). ● *adj.* **1** close at hand; close to, in place or time (*the end is near; in the near future*). **2** closely related (*a near relation*). **3** (of a part of a vehicle, animal, or road) left (*the near foreleg*). **4** close; narrow (*a near escape; a near guess*). **5** similar (to) (*is nearer the original*). **6** niggardly, mean. ● *v.* **1** *tr.* approach; draw near to (*neared the harbour*). **2** *intr.* draw near (*could distinguish them as they neared*). □ **come** (or **go**) **near** (foll. by verbal noun, or *to* + verbal noun) be on the point of; almost succeed in (*came near to falling*). **go near** (foll. by *to* + infin.) narrowly fail. **near at hand 1** within easy reach. **2** in the immediate future. **nearest and dearest** one's closest friends and relatives collectively. **near the knuckle** *Brit. colloq.* verging on the indecent. [from Old Norse *nær* 'closer'] □ **nearish** *adj.* **nearness** *n.*

nearby ● *adj.* situated in a near position (*a nearby hotel*). ● *adv.* (also **near by**) close; not far away.

Near East *n.* (prec. by *the*) = MIDDLE EAST. □ **Near Eastern** *adj.*

nearly *adv.* almost. □ **not nearly** nothing like; far from (*not nearly enough*).

near miss *n.* **1** a bomb etc. falling close to the target. **2** a situation in which a collision is narrowly avoided.

nearside *n.* (often *attrib.*) esp. *Brit.* the left side of a vehicle, animal, or road.

near sight *n.* esp. *US* = SHORT SIGHT.

near-sighted *adj.* esp. *US* = SHORT-SIGHTED. □ **near-sightedly** *adv.* **near-sightedness** *n.*

near thing *n. Brit.* a narrow escape.

neat *adj.* **1** tidy and methodical. **2** elegantly simple in form etc. **3** (of language, style, etc.) brief, clear, and pointed. **4 a** cleverly executed (*a neat piece of work*). **b** deft; dexterous. **5** (of esp. alcoholic liquor) undiluted. **6** *N. Amer. slang* (as a general term of approval) good, pleasing, excellent. [based on Latin *nitēre* 'to shine'] □ **neatly** *adv.* **neatness** *n.*

neaten *v.tr.* make neat.

neath *prep. poet.* beneath.

nebula *n.* (*pl.* **nebulae** /-lee/ or **nebulas**) *Astron.* **1** ▼ a cloud of gas and dust, sometimes glowing and sometimes appearing as a dark silhouette against other glowing matter. ▷ STAR. **2** a bright area caused by a galaxy, or a large cloud of distant stars. [Latin, literally 'mist'] □ **nebular** *adj.*

nebulizer *n.* (also **-iser**) a device for producing a fine spray of liquid. [based on Latin *nebula* 'mist'] □ **nebulize** *v.tr.* (also **-ise**).

nebulous *adj.* **1** cloudlike. **2 a** formless, clouded. **b** hazy, indistinct, vague (*put forward a few nebulous ideas*). **3** *Astron.* of or like a nebula or nebulae. [from

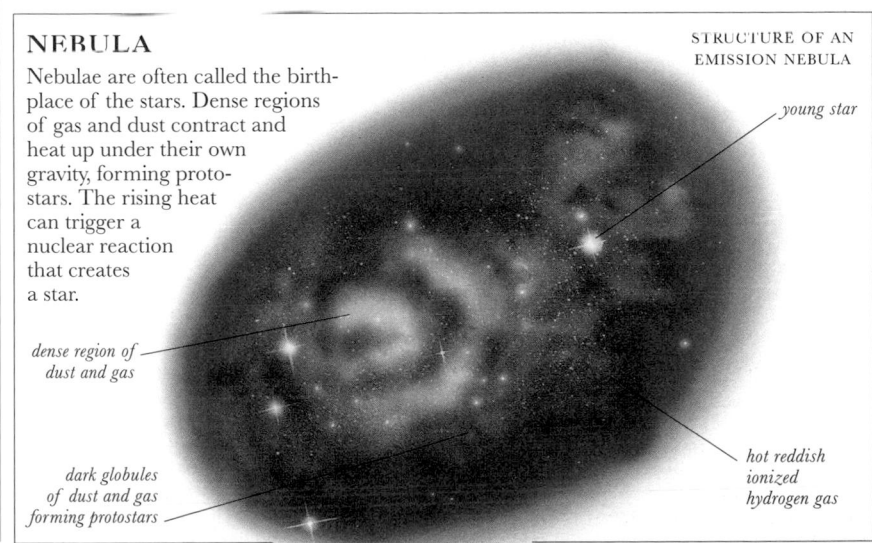

NEBULA

Nebulae are often called the birthplace of the stars. Dense regions of gas and dust contract and heat up under their own gravity, forming protostars. The rising heat can trigger a nuclear reaction that creates a star.

STRUCTURE OF AN EMISSION NEBULA

young star
dense region of dust and gas
dark globules of dust and gas forming protostars
hot reddish ionized hydrogen gas

N

N

Latin *nebulosus*] □ **nebulosity** *n*. **nebulously** *adv*. **nebulousness** *n*.

NEC *abbr*. National Executive Committee.

necessarily *adv*. as a necessary result; inevitably.

necessary ● *adj*. **1** requiring to be done, achieved, etc.; requisite, essential. **2** determined, existing, or happening by natural laws, predestination, etc., not by free will; inevitable. ● *n*. (*pl*. **-ies**) (usu. in *pl*.) any of the basic requirements of life, such as food, warmth, etc. □ **the necessary** *colloq*. **1** *Brit*. money. **2** an action, item, etc., needed for a purpose (*they will do the necessary*). [from Latin *necesse* 'needful']

necessitate *v.tr*. make necessary (esp. as a result) (*will necessitate some sacrifice*). [based on medieval Latin *necessitatus* 'compelled']

necessitous *adj*. poor; needy.

necessity *n*. (*pl*. **-ies**) **1 a** an indispensable thing; a necessary. **b** (usu. foll. by *of*) indispensability. **2** a state of things or circumstances enforcing a certain course (*there was a necessity to hurry*). **3** imperative need (*necessity is the mother of invention*). **4** want; poverty; hardship. □ **of necessity** unavoidably. [from Latin *necessitas*]

neck ● *n*. **1 a** ▽ the part of the body connecting the head to the shoulders. **b** the part of a shirt, dress, etc. round or close to the neck. **2** something resembling a neck, such as the narrow part of a cavity or vessel, an isthmus, etc. **3** the part of a violin etc. bearing the fingerboard. ▷ STRINGED. **4** the length of a horse's head and neck as a measure of its lead in a race. **5** the flesh of an animal's neck (*neck of lamb*). **6** *Brit. slang* impudence (*you've got a neck, asking that*). ● *v.intr. & tr. colloq*. kiss and caress amorously. □ **get it in the neck** *colloq*. **1** receive a severe reprimand or punishment. **2** suffer a fatal or severe blow. **neck and neck** running level in a race etc. **up to one's neck** (often foll. by *in*) *colloq*. very deeply involved; very busy. [Old English] □ **necked** *adj*. (also in *comb*.). **necker** *n*. **neckless** *adj*.

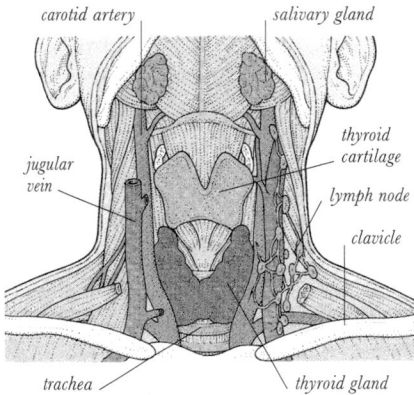

NECK: STRUCTURE OF THE
HUMAN NECK (FRONT VIEW)

carotid artery   *salivary gland*
jugular vein
thyroid cartilage
lymph node
clavicle
trachea   *thyroid gland*

neckband *n*. a strip of material round the neck of a garment.

neckerchief *n*. a square of cloth worn round the neck.

necklace ● *n*. **1** a chain or a string of beads, precious stones, etc., worn as an ornament round the neck. **2** *S.Afr*. a tyre soaked or filled with petrol, placed round a victim's neck, and set alight. ● *v.tr. S.Afr*. kill with a 'necklace'.

necklet *n*. **1** = NECKLACE *n*. 1. **2** a strip of fur worn round the neck.

neckline *n*. the edge or shape of the opening of a garment at the neck (*a square neckline*).

neck of the woods *n*. *colloq*. a locality, esp. *Brit*. a remote one.

necktie *n*. esp. *US* = TIE *n*. 2.

neckwear *n*. collars, ties, etc.

necro- *comb. form* corpse. [from Greek *nekros*]

necromancy *n*. **1** the prediction of the future by

supposed communication with the dead. **2** witchcraft. □ **necromancer** *n*. **necromantic** *adj*.

necrophilia *n*. (also **necrophily**) a morbid and esp. erotic attraction to corpses. [based on Greek *nekros* 'corpse'] □ **necrophile** *n*. **necrophiliac** *n*. **necrophilic** *adj*. **necrophilism** *n*.

necropolis *n*. an ancient cemetery or burial place. [based on Greek *polis* 'city']

necrosis *n*. *Med. & Physiol*. the death of tissue caused by injury or disease, esp. gangrene or pulmonary tuberculosis. □ **necrotic** *adj*. **necrotize** *v.intr*. (also **-ise**).

nectar *n*. **1** a sugary substance produced by plants to attract pollinating insects and made into honey by bees. **2** (in Greek and Roman mythology) the drink of the gods. **3** a drink compared to this. [from Greek *nektar*] □ **nectariferous** *adj*. **nectarous** *adj*.

nectarine *n*. ▶ a variety of peach with smooth skin. [originally as adj. in sense 'nectar-like']

neddy *n*. (*pl*. **-ies**) *Brit. colloq*. a donkey. [diminutive of *Ned*, pet form of the name *Edward*]

née /nay/ *adj*. (*US* also **nee**) (indicating a married woman's maiden name) born (*Mrs Ann Smith, née Jones*). [French]

NECTARINE
(*Prunus persica*
variety)

need ● *v.tr*. **1** stand in want of; require. **2** (foll. by *to* + infin.; *3rd sing. present neg. or interrog*. **need** without *to*) be under the necessity or obligation (*it needs to be done carefully*; *he need not come*; *need you ask?*). ● *n*. **1** a want or requirement (*my needs are few*; *the need for greater freedom*; *my greatest need is a car*). **2** circumstances requiring some course of action; necessity (*there is no need to worry*; *if need arise*). **3** destitution; poverty. □ **at need** in time of need. **have need of** require; want. **in need** requiring help. **in need of** requiring. **need not have** did not need to (but did). [Old English]

needful *adj*. **1** requisite; necessary. **2** (prec. by *the*) **a** what is necessary. **b** *colloq*. money or action needed for a purpose. □ **needfully** *adv*. **needfulness** *n*.

needle ● *n*. **1 a** a very thin small piece of smooth steel etc. pointed at one end and with a slit (eye) for thread at the other, used in sewing. ▷ SEWING MACHINE, STITCH. **b** a larger plastic, wooden, etc. slender stick without an eye, used in knitting. **2** a pointer on a dial (see MAGNETIC NEEDLE). **3** any of several small thin pointed instruments, esp.: **a** the end of a hypodermic syringe. **b** = STYLUS 1. **4 a** an obelisk (*Cleopatra's Needle*). **b** a pointed rock or crag. **5** ▼ the leaf of a fir or pine tree. ▷ LEAF. **6** (usu. prec. by *the*) *Brit. slang* a fit of bad temper or nervousness (*got the needle while waiting*). ● *v.tr. colloq*. incite or irritate; provoke (*refused to be needled by him*). [Old English]

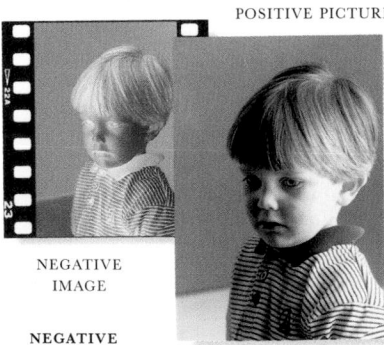

NEEDLES OF A PINE TREE

needlecord *n*. *Brit*. a fine-ribbed corduroy fabric.

needlecraft *n*. skill in needlework.

needle-lace *n*. lace made with needles not bobbins.

needlepoint *n*. **1** a very sharp point. **2** = NEEDLE-LACE. **3** = GROS POINT or PETIT POINT 1.

needless *adj*. **1** unnecessary. **2** uncalled for; gratuitous. □ **needless to say** of course; it goes without saying. □ **needlessly** *adv*. **needlessness** *n*.

needle time *n*. *Brit*. an agreed maximum allowance of time for broadcasting recorded music.

needlewoman *n*. (*pl*. **-women**) **1** a seamstress. **2** a woman or girl with specified sewing skill (*a good needlewoman*).

needlework *n*. sewing or embroidery.

needn't *contr*. need not.

needs *adv*. (usu. prec. or foll. by *must*) *archaic* of necessity (*must needs decide*).

needy *adj*. (**needier**, **neediest**) **1** (of a person) poor; destitute. **2** (of circumstances) characterized by poverty. □ **neediness** *n*.

ne'er *adv. poet*. = NEVER.

ne'er-do-well ● *n*. a good-for-nothing person. ● *adj*. good-for-nothing.

nefarious *adj*. wicked; iniquitous. [based on Latin *nefas* 'wrong'] □ **nefariously** *adv*. **nefariousness** *n*.

neg *n*. *colloq*. a photographic negative.

neg. *abbr*. negative.

negate *v.tr*. **1** nullify, make ineffective, destroy. **2** deny, deny the existence of. **3** *Gram*. make (a clause, sentence, etc.) negative in meaning. [based on Latin *negatus* 'denied']

negation *n*. **1** (often foll. by *of*) **a** the act of contradicting or denying a statement or allegation. **b** an instance of this; a contradiction or denial. **2** the absence or opposite of something actual or positive (*death is the negation of life*). **3** *Gram*. **a** the grammatical process by which the truth of a clause or sentence is denied, involving the use of a negative word, e.g. *not*, *no*, *never*. **b** an instance of this. **4** a negative or unreal thing; a nonentity. □ **negatory** *adj*.

negative ● *adj*. **1** expressing or implying denial, prohibition, or refusal (*a negative vote*; *a negative answer*). **2** (of a person or attitude) lacking positive attributes; apathetic; pessimistic. **3** marked by the absence of qualities (*a negative reaction*; *a negative result from the test*). **4** of the opposite nature to a thing regarded as positive (*debt is negative capital*). **5** *Gram*. (of a word, clause, etc.) expressing negation. **6** (of a quantity) less than zero, to be subtracted from others or from zero. **7** *Electr*. **a** of the kind of charge carried by electrons. **b** containing or producing such a charge. ● *n*. **1** a negative statement or reply. **2** *Photog*. **a** ▼ an image with black and white reversed or colours replaced by complementary ones, from which positive pictures are obtained. **b** a developed film or plate bearing such an image. **3** *Gram*. = NEGATOR 2. ● *v.tr*. **1** refuse to accept or countenance; veto; reject. **2** disprove (an inference or hypothesis). **3** contradict (a statement). **4** neutralize (an effect). □ **in the negative** with negative effect; so as to reject a proposal etc.; no (*the answer was in the negative*). [based on Latin *negare negat-* 'to deny'] □ **negatively** *adv*. **negativeness** *n*. **negativity** *n*.

POSITIVE PICTURE

NEGATIVE
IMAGE

NEGATIVE

negative equity *n*. the indebtedness arising when the market value of a property falls below the outstanding amount of a mortgage secured on it.

negative feedback *n*. **1** the return of part of an output signal to the input, tending to decrease the amplification etc. **2** esp. *Biol*. the diminution or counteraction of an effect by its own influence on the process giving rise to it. **3** a negative response to a questionnaire, an experiment, etc.

negative pole *n.* the south-seeking pole of a magnet. ▷ MAGNETIC FIELD

negative prescription *n.* the time limit within which an action or claim can be raised.

negative sign *n.* a symbol (–) indicating subtraction or a value less than zero.

negativism *n.* **1** a negative position or attitude; extreme scepticism, criticism, etc. **2** denial of accepted beliefs. □ **negativist** *n.* **negativistic** *adj.*

negator *n.* **1** a person who denies something. **2** *Gram.* a word or particle expressing negation, e.g. *not, don't.*

neglect ● *v.tr.* **1** fail to care for or to do; be remiss about (*neglected their duty; neglected his children*). **2** (foll. by verbal noun, or *to* + infin.) fail; overlook or forget the need to (*neglected to inform them; neglected telling them*). **3** not pay attention to; disregard (*neglected the obvious warning*). ● *n.* **1** lack of caring; negligence (*the house suffered from neglect*). **2 a** the act of neglecting. **b** the state of being neglected (*the house fell into neglect*). **3** (usu. foll. by *of*) disregard. [based on Latin *neglectus* 'disregarded'] □ **neglectful** *adj.* **neglectfully** *adv.*

negligee /**neg**-li-zhay/ *n.* (also **negligée, négligé**) a woman's dressing gown of thin fabric. [French, literally 'neglected']

negligence *n.* **1** a lack of proper care and attention; carelessness. **2** an act of carelessness. [from Latin *negligentia* 'disregard'] □ **negligent** *adj.* **negligently** *adv.*

negligible *adj.* not worth considering; insignificant. [obsolete French] □ **negligibility** *n.* **negligibly** *adv.*

negotiable *adj.* **1** open to discussion or modification. **2** able to be negotiated.

negotiate *v.* **1** *intr.* (usu. foll. by *with*) confer in order to reach an agreement. **2** *tr.* arrange (a matter) or bring about (a result) by negotiating (*negotiated a settlement*). **3** *tr.* find a way over, through, etc. (an obstacle, difficulty, etc.). **4** *tr.* **a** transfer (a cheque etc.) to another for a consideration. **b** convert (a cheque etc.) into money. [based on Latin *negotium* 'business'] □ **negotiation** *n.* **negotiator** *n.*

Negress *n.* a female Negro.

■ **Usage** The term *Negress* is now often considered offensive; *black* is usually preferred.

Negritude *n.* **1** the quality or state of being black. **2** the affirmation or consciousness of the value of black culture.

Negro ● *n.* (*pl.* **-oes**) a member of a dark-skinned race originally native to Africa. ● *adj.* of or concerning Negroes. [from Latin *niger nigri* 'black']

■ **Usage** The term *Negro* is now often considered offensive; *black* is usually preferred.

Negroid ● *adj.* **1** resembling or having some of the characteristic physical features of black people, e.g. dark skin, tightly curled hair, and a broad flattish nose. **2** of or concerning blacks. ● *n.* a black person.

Negro spiritual *n.* a religious song derived from the musical traditions of black people in the southern US.

neigh ● *n.* the high whinnying sound of a horse. ● *v.intr.* make such a sound. [Old English]

neighbour (*US* **neighbor**) ● *n.* **1** a person living next door to or near or nearest another. **2** a fellow human being. **3** a person or thing near or next to another. **4** (*attrib.*) neighbouring. ● *v.* **1** *tr.* border on; adjoin. **2** *intr.* (often foll. by *on, upon*) border; adjoin. [Old English, from *neah* 'nigh' + *gebūr* 'a tenant-farmer'] □ **neighbouring** *adj.* **neighbourless** *adj.* **neighbourship** *n.*

neighbourhood *n.* (*US* **neighborhood**) **1** a district, esp. one forming a community within a town or city. **2** the people of a district. □ **in the neighbourhood of** roughly; about (*paid in the neighbourhood of £100*).

neighbourhood watch *n.* systematic local

NEOCLASSICAL

In the late 18th and early 19th centuries, Europe became fascinated with the cultures of classical Greece and Rome. This interest was in part stimulated by the discovery and excavation of the remains of a number of ancient sites. Artists and architects were greatly influenced by the ancient civilizations, and imitated their style very deliberately.

The Oath of the Horatii (1784), JACQUES-LOUIS DAVID

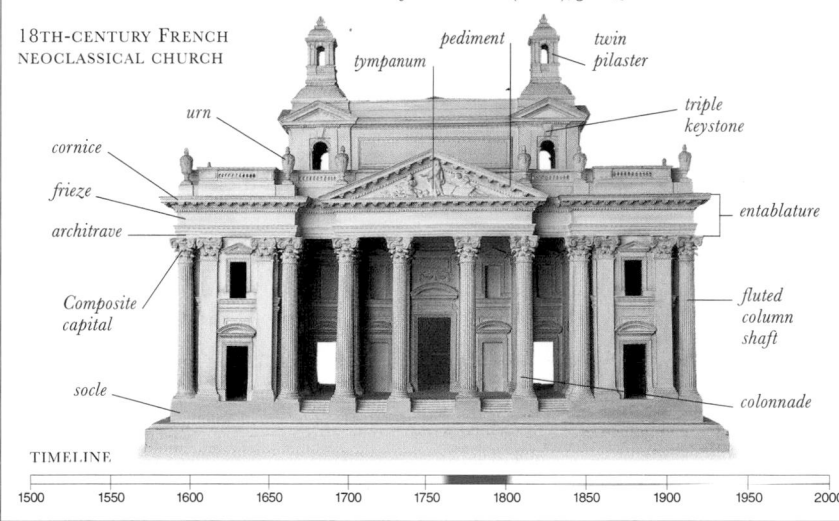

18TH-CENTURY FRENCH NEOCLASSICAL CHURCH

pediment   twin pilaster   tympanum   triple keystone   urn   entablature   cornice   frieze   architrave   fluted column shaft   Composite capital   socle   colonnade

TIMELINE

| 1500 | 1550 | 1600 | 1650 | 1700 | 1750 | 1800 | 1850 | 1900 | 1950 | 2000 |

vigilance by householders to discourage crime, esp. against property.

neighbourly *adj.* (*US* **neighborly**) characteristic of a good neighbour; friendly; kind. □ **neighbourliness** *n.*

neither ● *det. & pron.* (with a sing. verb) not the one nor the other (of two things); not either (*neither wish was granted; neither of them knows; neither went to the fair*). ● *adv.* **1** not either; not on the one hand (foll. by *nor*; introducing the first of two or more things in the negative: *neither knowing nor caring; neither the teachers nor the parents nor the children*). **2** not either; also not (*if you do not, neither shall I*). **3** (with neg.) *disp.* either (*I don't know that neither*). [Old English]

■ **Usage** It is generally considered wrong to use *neither* instead of *either* in sense 3 of the adverb to strengthen a preceding negative.

nelly *n.* □ **not on your nelly** *Brit. slang* certainly not.

nelson *n.* a wrestling hold in which one arm is passed under the opponent's arm from behind and the hand is applied to the neck (**half nelson**), or both arms and hands are applied (**full nelson**).

nematode *n.* ▼ a worm of the phylum Nematoda, with a slender unsegmented cylindrical shape. [based on Greek *nēma nēmat-* 'thread']

NEMATODE
(*Caenorhabditis elegans*)

nem. con. *abbr.* with no one dissenting. [Latin *nemine contradicente*]

nemesis /**nem**-i-sis/ *n.* (*pl.* **nemeses**) **1** retributive justice. **2** a downfall caused by this. [Greek, literally 'righteous indignation', personified as goddess of retribution]

neo- *comb. form* **1** new, modern. **2** a new or revived form of. [Greek]

neoclassical *adj.* (also **neoclassic**) ▲ of or relating to a revival of a classical style or treatment in the arts. □ **neoclassicism** *n.* **neoclassicist** *n.*

neocolonialism *n.* the use of economic, political, etc. pressures to influence other countries, esp. former dependencies. □ **neocolonialist** *n. & adj.*

neodymium *n.* *Chem.* a silver-grey naturally occurring metallic element of the lanthanide series.

neolithic *adj.* *Archaeol.* of or relating to the later Stone Age. [based on Greek *lithos* 'stone']

neologism *n.* **1** a new word or expression. **2** the coining or use of new words. □ **neologist** *n.* **neologize** *v.intr.* (also **-ise**).

neon *n.* *Chem.* an inert gaseous element giving an orange glow when electricity is passed through it (*neon sign*). [Greek, literally 'new (thing)']

neonate *n.* a newborn child (or mammal). [based on Latin *natus* 'born'] □ **neonatal** *adj.*

neophobia *n.* a fear or dislike of what is new.

neophyte *n.* **1** a new convert, esp. to a religious faith. **2** *RC Ch.* **a** a novice of a religious order. **b** a newly ordained priest. **3** a beginner; a novice. [from NT Greek *neophutos* 'newly planted']

neoplasm *n.* a new and abnormal growth of tissue in some part of the body, esp. a tumour. [based on Greek *plasma* 'formation'] □ **neoplastic** *adj.*

neoprene *n.* a synthetic rubber-like polymer. [on the pattern of *chloroprene* etc.]

Nepalese /nep-ăl-**eez**/ *adj. & n.* (*pl.* same) = NEPALI.

Nepali /ni-**paw**-li/ ● *n.* (*pl.* same or **Nepalis**) **1 a** a native or national of Nepal in central Asia. **b** a person of Nepali descent. **2** the language of Nepal. ● *adj.* of or relating to Nepal or its language or people.

nephew *n.* a son of one's brother or sister, or of one's brother-in-law or sister-in-law. [from Latin *nepos* 'grandson, nephew']

nephrite *n.* ◀ a green, yellow, or white calcium magnesium silicate form of jade. [based on Greek *nephros* 'kidney', with reference to its supposed efficacy in treating kidney disease]

NEPHRITE

nephritic *adj.* **1** of or in the kidneys; renal. **2** of or relating to nephritis.

nephritis *n.* inflammation of the kidneys. [based on Greek *nephros* 'kidney']

ne plus ultra /nay/ *n.* **1** the furthest attainable point. **2** the culmination, acme, or perfection. [Latin, literally 'not further beyond', supposed inscription on the Pillars of Hercules (at the Strait of Gibraltar) prohibiting passage]

nepotism *n.* favouritism shown to relatives or friends in conferring offices. [based on Italian *nepote* 'nephew', originally used of illegitimate sons of popes] □ **nepotist** *n.* **nepotistic** *adj.*

Neptune *n.* ▼ a distant planet of the solar system, eighth from the Sun, discovered in 1846 from mathematical computations. ▷ SOLAR SYSTEM. [Middle English from French *Neptune* or Latin *Neptunus*, the god of the sea]

neptunium *n. Chem.* a radioactive transuranic metallic element produced when uranium atoms absorb bombarding neutrons. [based on the planet *Neptune*, on the pattern of *uranium*]

nerd *n.* (also **nurd**) orig. *US slang* a foolish, feeble, or uninteresting person. [20th-century coinage] □ **nerdy** *adj.*

nereid /**neer**-i-id/ *n.* **1** *Mythol.* a sea nymph. **2** *Zool.* a carnivorous marine polychaete worm of the ragworm family Nereidae. [from Greek *Nēreïs -idos*, daughter of the sea-god Nereus]

nerve ● *n.* **1 a** a fibre or bundle of fibres that transmits impulses of sensation or motion between the brain or spinal cord and other parts of the body. ▷ NERVOUS SYSTEM, SKIN. **b** the tissue constituting these. **2 a** coolness in danger; bravery. **b** *colloq.* impudence (*they've got a nerve*). **3** (in *pl.*) a state of heightened nervousness or sensitivity; a condition

of mental or physical stress (*need to calm my nerves*). **4** a rib of a leaf, esp. the midrib. ● *v.tr.* **1** (usu. *refl.*) brace (oneself) to face danger, suffering, etc. **2** give strength, vigour, or courage to. □ **get on a person's nerves** irritate or annoy a person. [Middle English in sense 'sinew': from Latin *nervus*] □ **nerved** *adj.* (also in *comb.*).

NERVOUS SYSTEM

The nervous system is a network of fibres and neurones controlling the actions and reactions of the body. The central nervous system (CNS) comprises the brain and spinal cord, which receive and integrate signals relayed from the sense organs (such as the eyes, nose, and ears) via the peripheral nervous system. The latter includes the autonomic nervous system, which controls unconscious functions, such as heartbeat and breathing.

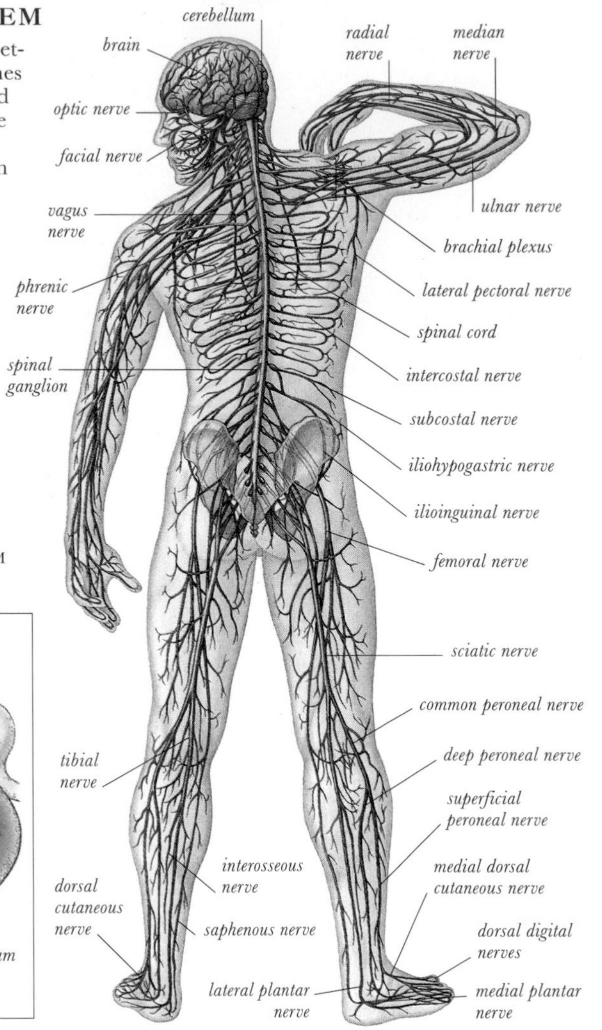

HUMAN
NERVOUS SYSTEM

cerebellum · brain · radial nerve · median nerve · optic nerve · facial nerve · vagus nerve · phrenic nerve · spinal ganglion · ulnar nerve · brachial plexus · lateral pectoral nerve · spinal cord · intercostal nerve · subcostal nerve · iliohypogastric nerve · ilioinguinal nerve · femoral nerve · sciatic nerve · common peroneal nerve · deep peroneal nerve · superficial peroneal nerve · interosseous nerve · medial dorsal cutaneous nerve · dorsal cutaneous nerve · saphenous nerve · dorsal digital nerves · lateral plantar nerve · medial plantar nerve

SECTION THROUGH
A NERVE

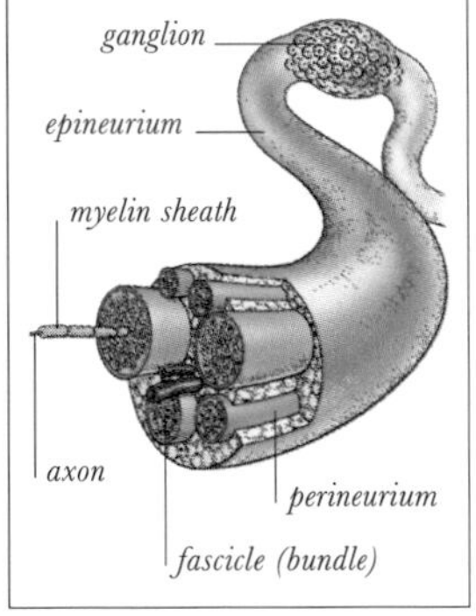

ganglion · epineurium · myelin sheath · axon · perineurium · fascicle (bundle)

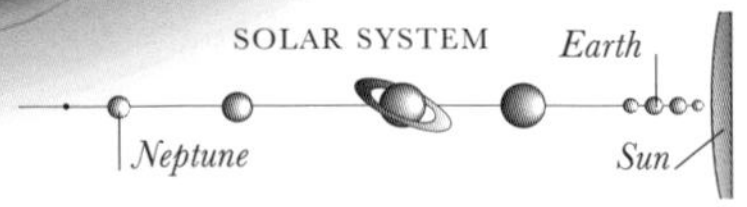

nerve cell *n.* an elongated branched cell transmitting impulses in nerve tissue. ▷ NEURONE

nerve centre *n.* **1** a group of closely connected nerve cells associated in performing some function. **2** the centre of control of an organization etc.

nerve gas *n.* a poisonous gas affecting the nervous system.

nerveless *adj.* **1** inert, lacking vigour or spirit. **2** confident; not nervous. **3** *Anat. & Zool.* without nerves. □ **nervelessly** *adv.* **nervelessness** *n.*

nerve-racking *adj.* stressful, frightening.

nervo- *comb. form* (also **nerv-** before a vowel) a nerve or the nerves.

nervous *adj.* **1** having delicate nerves. **2** timid or anxious. **3 a** excitable; easily agitated. **b** resulting from this temperament (*nervous tension*). **4** affecting or acting on the nerves. **5** (foll. by *of* + verbal noun) reluctant, afraid (*am nervous of meeting them*). □ **nervously** *adv.* **nervousness** *n.*

nervous breakdown *n.* a period of mental illness, usu. resulting from severe depression or anxiety.

nervous system *n.* ▲ the body's network of specialized cells which transmit nerve impulses. ▷ PERIPHERAL NERVOUS SYSTEM

nervous wreck *n. colloq.* a person suffering from mental stress, exhaustion, etc.

nervure *n.* **1** each of the hollow tubes that form the framework of an insect's wing; a venule. **2** the principal vein of a leaf. [from French *nerf* 'nerve']

NEPTUNE

The planet Neptune is believed to consist of a small solid core surrounded by a mixture of liquids and gases. It has four unstable rings and eight known moons.

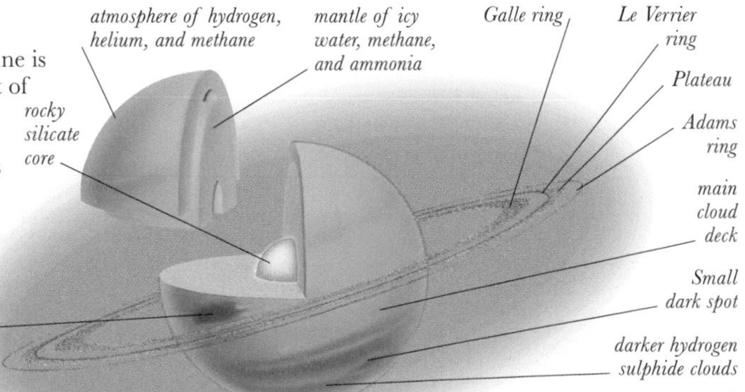

atmosphere of hydrogen, helium, and methane · mantle of icy water, methane, and ammonia · Galle ring · Le Verrier ring · Plateau · Adams ring · main cloud deck · rocky silicate core · Great dark spot · Small dark spot · darker hydrogen sulphide clouds

NEPTUNE,
WITH INTERNAL
STRUCTURE
REVEALED

SOLAR SYSTEM · Earth · Neptune · Sun

N

NEST

Many animals invest a lot of time and energy in building a nest. Construction may often involve complex techniques, such as weaving grass. It may also require a very specific building material, such as the 'paper' made by wasps, or the mixture of mud and saliva made by termites.

KESTREL NEST

TERMITE NEST (MOUND)

MOLE NEST

COMMUNAL WEAVER-BIRD NESTS

WASP NEST

nervy *adj.* (**nervier**, **nerviest**) esp. *Brit.* nervous; easily excited or disturbed. □ **nervily** *adv.* **nerviness** *n.*

nescient *adj.* (foll. by *of*) *literary* lacking knowledge; ignorant. [from Latin *nescient-* 'not knowing'] □ **nescience** *n.*

ness *n.* a headland or promontory. [Old English]

-ness *suffix* forming nouns from adjectives, and occasionally other words, expressing: **1** state or condition, or an instance of this (*bitterness*; *a kind ness*). **2** something in a certain state (*wilderness*).

nest ● *n.* **1** a structure or place where a bird lays eggs and shelters its young. **2** ▲ any creature's breeding place or lair. **3** a snug retreat or shelter. **4** (often foll. by *of*) a place fostering something undesirable (*a nest of vice*). **5** a brood or swarm. **6** a group or set of similar objects, often of different sizes and fitting together for storage (*a nest of tables*). ● *v.intr.* **1** use or build a nest. **2** take wild birds' nests or eggs. **3** (of objects) fit together or one inside another. [Old English] □ **nestful** *n.* (*pl.* **-fuls**). **nesting** *n.*

nest box *n.* (also **nesting box**) a box provided for a domestic fowl or other bird to make its nest in.

nest egg *n.* a sum of money saved for the future.

nestle *v.* **1** *intr.* (often foll. by *down*, *in*, etc.) settle oneself comfortably. **2** *intr.* press oneself against another in affection etc. **3** *tr.* (foll. by *in*, *into*, etc.) push (a head or shoulder etc.) affectionately or snugly. **4** *intr.* lie half hidden or embedded. [Old English, related to NEST]

nestling *n.* a bird that is too young to leave its nest.

net¹ ● *n.* **1** an open-meshed fabric of cord, rope, etc.; a structure resembling this. **2** a piece of net used esp. to restrain, contain, or delimit, or to catch fish etc. ▷ SEINE, TRAWL. **3 a** a structure with net used in various games. **b** (often in *pl.*) ▷ BADMINTON. **b** (often in *pl.*) a practice-ground in cricket, surrounded by nets. **4 a** a network of spies. **b** a broadcasting network. **c** *Computing* a network of interconnected computers. **d** (usu. **Net**) = INTERNET. ● *v.tr.* (**netted**, **netting**) **1 a** cover, confine, or catch with a net. **b** acquire as with a net. **2** hit (a ball) into the net, esp. of a goal. **3** (usu. as **netted** *adj.*) mark with a netlike pattern; reticulate. [Old English] □ **netful** *n.* (*pl.* **-fuls**).

net² (also *Brit.* **nett**) ● *adj.* **1** (esp. of money) remaining after all necessary deductions, or free from

deductions. **2** (of a price) to be paid in full; not reducible. **3** (of a weight) excluding that of the packaging etc. **4** (of an effect etc.) ultimate, effective. ● *v.tr.* (**netted**, **netting**) gain or yield (a sum) as net profit. [French, literally 'neat']

netball *n.* a team game in which goals are scored by throwing a ball through a high horizontal ring with a net suspended from it.

nether *adj.* *archaic* = LOWER¹. [Old English] □ **nethermost** *adj.*

nether regions *n.pl.* (also **nether world** *n.sing.*) hell; the underworld.

net profit *n.* the effective profit; the actual gain after working expenses have been paid.

netsuke /nets-ki/ *n.* (*pl* same or **netsukes**) (in Japan) ◄ a carved button-like ornament, esp. of ivory or wood. [Japanese]

nett *Brit.* var. of NET².

NETSUKE

netting *n.* **1** netted fabric. **2** a piece of this.

nettle ● *n.* **1** any plant of the genus *Urtica*, esp. *U. dioica*, with jagged leaves covered with stinging hairs. **2** a plant resembling this. ● *v.tr.* **1** irritate, annoy. **2** sting with nettles. [Old English]

nettle-rash *n.* *Med.* a rash of itching red spots on the skin caused by allergic reaction to food etc.

network ● *n.* **1** an arrangement of intersecting horizontal and vertical lines, like the structure of a net. **2** a complex system of railways, roads, etc. **3** a group of people who exchange information etc. for professional or social purposes. **4** a chain of interconnected computers, machines, or operations. **5** a system of connected electrical conductors. **6** a group of broadcasting stations connected for a simultaneous broadcast of a programme. ● *v.* **1** *tr.* *Brit.* broadcast on a network. **2** *intr.* establish a network. **3** *tr.* link (esp. computers) to operate interactively. **4** *intr.* communicate with other people to exchange information etc. (see sense 3 of *n.*). □ **networker** *n.* esp. *Computing.* **networking** *n.*

neural *adj.* of or relating to a nerve or the central nervous system. [based on Greek *neuron* 'nerve'] □ **neurally** *adv.*

neuralgia *n.* an intense intermittent pain along the course of a nerve, esp. in the head or face. □ **neuralgic** *adj.*

neural network *n.* (also **neural net**) a computer system modelled on the human brain and nervous system.

neurasthenia *n.* a general term for fatigue, anxiety, listlessness, etc. (not in medical use). [from Greek *neuron* 'nerve' + *astheneia* 'weakness'] □ **neurasthenic** *adj. & n.*

neuritis *n.* inflammation of a nerve or nerves. □ **neuritic** *adj.*

neuro- *comb. form* a nerve or the nerves. [from Greek *neuron* 'nerve']

neurology *n.* the scientific study of nerve systems. □ **neurological** *adj.* **neurologically** *adv.* **neurologist** *n.*

neuromuscular *adj.* of or relating to nerves and muscles. ▷ MUSCULATURE, NERVOUS SYSTEM

neurone *n.* (also **neuron**) ► a specialized cell transmitting nerve impulses. ▷ NERVOUS SYSTEM. [from Greek *neuron* 'nerve'] □ **neuronal** *adj.*

■ **Usage** The spelling *neuron* is often preferred to *neurone* in technical use.

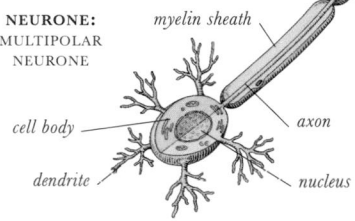

NEURONE: MULTIPOLAR NEURONE

synaptic knob

node of Ranvier

Schwann cell

myelin sheath

axon

nucleus

cell body

dendrite

neuropathology *n.* the pathology of the nervous system. □ **neuropathological** *adj.* **neuropathologist** *n.*

neuropathy *n.* a disease or dysfunction of one or more peripheral nerves. □ **neuropathic** *adj.*

neurophysiology *n.* the physiology of the nervous system. □ **neurophysiological** *adj.* **neurophysiologist** *n.*

neuropteran *n.* ▼ any insect of the order Neuroptera, including lacewings and ant-lions, having four finely veined membranous leaflike wings. ▷ INSECT. □ **neuropterous** *adj.* [NEURO- + Greek *pteron* 'wing']

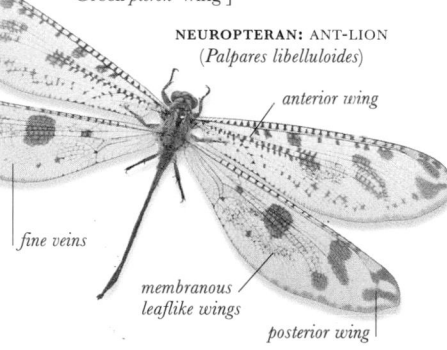

NEUROPTERAN: ANT-LION (*Palpares libelluloides*)

anterior wing

fine veins

membranous leaflike wings

posterior wing

neurosis *n.* (*pl.* **neuroses**) a relatively mild mental illness involving symptoms of stress (e.g. depression, anxiety, obsessive behaviour) without loss of contact with reality.

neurosurgery *n.* surgery performed on the nervous system, esp. the brain and spinal cord. □ **neurosurgeon** *n.* **neurosurgical** *adj.*

neurotic ● *adj.* **1** caused by or relating to neurosis. **2** (of a person) suffering from neurosis. **3** *colloq.* abnormally sensitive or obsessive. ● *n.* a neurotic person. □ **neurotically** *adv.* **neuroticism** *n.*

neurotoxin *n.* any poison which acts on the nervous system.

N

N

neurotransmitter *n.* *Biochem.* a chemical substance released from a nerve fibre that effects the transfer of an impulse to another nerve or muscle. ▷ SYNAPSE

neuter ● *adj.* **1** *Gram.* (of a noun etc.) neither masculine nor feminine. **2** (of a plant) having neither pistils nor stamen. **3** (of an animal etc.) sexually undeveloped; castrated or spayed. ● *n.* **1** *Gram.* a neuter word. **2 a** a non-fertile insect, esp. a worker bee or ant. **b** a castrated animal. ● *v.tr.* castrate or spay. [Latin *neuter* 'neither']

neutral ● *adj.* **1** not helping or supporting either of two opposing sides; impartial. **2** belonging to a neutral party, state, etc. (*neutral ships*). **3** indistinct, indeterminate. **4** (of a gear) in which the engine is disconnected from the driven parts. **5** (of colours) not strong or positive; grey or beige. **6** *Chem.* neither acid nor alkaline. **7** *Electr.* neither positive nor negative. **8** *Biol.* sexually undeveloped; asexual. ● *n.* **1 a** a neutral state or person. **b** a subject of a neutral state. **2** a neutral gear. [from Latin *neutralis* 'of neuter gender'] □ **neutrality** *n.* **neutrally** *adv.*

neutralism *n.* a policy of political neutrality. □ **neutralist** *n.*

neutralize *v.tr.* (also **-ise**) **1** make neutral. **2** counterbalance. **3** exempt or exclude (a place) from the sphere of hostilities. □ **neutralization** *n.* **neutralizer** *n.*

neutrino *n.* (*pl.* **-os**) any of a class of stable neutral subatomic particles with almost zero mass, which travel at the speed of light and rarely interact with normal matter. [Italian]

neutron *n.* a subatomic particle of about the same mass as a proton but without an electric charge. ▷ ATOM, NUCLEUS

neutron bomb *n.* a bomb producing neutrons and little blast, causing damage to life but not to property.

neutron star *n.* a very dense star composed mainly of neutrons. ▷ STAR

never *adv.* **1 a** at no time; on no occasion; not ever. **b** *colloq.* as an emphatic negative (*I never heard you come in*). **2** not at all (*never fear*). **3** *Brit. colloq.* (expressing surprise) surely not (*you never left the key in the lock!*). □ **never-never land** an imaginary utopian place. **never say die** see DIE[1]. **well I never!** *colloq.* expressing great surprise. [Old English]

nevermore *adv.* at no future time.

never-never *n.* (often prec. by *the*) *Brit. colloq.* hire purchase.

nevertheless *adv.* in spite of that; notwithstanding; all the same.

nevus *US* var. of NAEVUS.

new ● *adj.* **1 a** of recent origin or arrival. **b** made, discovered, acquired, or experienced recently or now for the first time. **2** in original condition; not worn or used. **3 a** renewed or reformed (*the new order*). **b** reinvigorated (*felt like a new person*). **4** different from a recent previous one (*has a new job*). **5** (often foll. by *to*) unfamiliar or strange (*a new sensation*). **6** (often foll. by *at*) (of a person) inexperienced (*am new at this business*). **7** (usu. prec. by *the*) often *derog.* **a** later, modern (*the new morality*). **b** newfangled. **c** recently affected by social change (*the new rich*). **8** (often prec. by *the*) advanced in method or theory (*the new formula*). **9** (in place names) discovered or founded later than and named after (*New York*). ● *adv.* (usu. in *comb.*) **1** newly, recently (*new-found; new-baked*). **2** anew, afresh. [Old English] □ **newish** *adj.* **newness** *n.*

New Age *n.* a broad movement characterized by alternative approaches to traditional Western culture, with interest in holistic ideas, environmentalism, etc. (often *attrib.*: *New Age travellers*).

new arrival *n.* *colloq.* a newborn child.

newborn *adj.* (of a child etc.) recently born.

new broom *n.* a newly appointed person eager to make changes.

newcomer *n.* **1** a person who has recently arrived. **2** a beginner in some activity.

newel *n.* **1** the supporting central post of winding stairs. **2** ► the top or bottom supporting post of a stair-rail. [from medieval Latin *nodellus* 'little knot']

newfangled *adj.* *derog.* different from what one is used to; objectionably new. [Middle English *newfangle* (now dialect) 'liking what is new']

new-laid *adj.* (of an egg) freshly laid.

newly *adv.* **1** recently (*a newly discovered country*). **2** afresh (*newly painted*). **3** in a different manner (*newly arranged*).

newly-wed *n.* a recently married person.

new man *n.* a man who rejects sexist attitudes and the traditional male role.

new mathematics *n.pl.* (also *Brit.* **new maths**) (often treated as *sing.*) a system of teaching mathematics to children, with emphasis on investigation and set theory.

new moon *n.* **1** the Moon when first seen as a crescent after conjunction with the Sun. **2** the time of its appearance.

new potatoes *n.pl.* the earliest potatoes of a new crop.

news *n.pl.* (usu. treated as *sing.*) **1** information about important or interesting recent events, esp. when published or broadcast. **2** (prec. by *the*) a broadcast report of news. **3** newly received or noteworthy information. **4** (foll. by *to*) *colloq.* information not previously known (*that's news to me*). [Middle English, translating Old French *noveles*]

news agency *n.* an organization that collects and distributes news items.

newsagent *n.* *Brit.* a seller of or shop selling newspapers etc.

newsboy *n.* a boy who sells or delivers newspapers.

news bulletin *n.* *Brit.* a collection of items of news, esp. for broadcasting.

newscast *n.* a radio or television broadcast of news reports.

newscaster *n.* = NEWSREADER.

news conference *n.* a press conference.

newsflash *n.* a single item of important news broadcast separately and often interrupting other programmes.

news-gatherer *n.* a person who researches news items, esp. for broadcast or publication. □ **news-gathering** *n.*

newsgirl *n.* a girl who sells or delivers newspapers.

news hound *n.* *colloq.* a newspaper reporter.

newsletter *n.* an informal printed report issued periodically to the members of an organization etc.

newsman *n.* (*pl.* **-men**) a newspaper reporter; a journalist.

newspaper *n.* **1** a printed publication (usu. daily or weekly) containing news, advertisements, etc. **2** the sheets of paper forming this (*wrapped in newspaper*).

newspaperman *n.* (*pl.* **-men**) a journalist.

Newspeak *n.* ambiguous euphemistic language used esp. in political propaganda. [an artificial official language in George Orwell's *Nineteen Eighty-Four* (1949)]

newsprint *n.* a type of low-quality paper on which newspapers are printed.

newsreader *n.* *Brit.* a person who reads out broadcast news bulletins.

newsreel *n.* a short cinema film of news and current affairs.

newsroom *n.* a room in a newspaper or broadcasting office where news is processed.

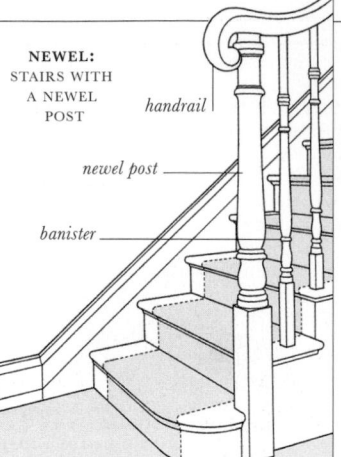

NEWEL: STAIRS WITH A NEWEL POST

handrail

newel post

banister

news-sheet *n.* a simple form of newspaper; a newsletter.

news-stand *n.* a stall for the sale of newspapers.

new star *n.* a nova.

new-style *attrib.adj.* having a new style (*new-style contracts*).

news-vendor *n.* *Brit.* a newspaper-seller.

newsworthy *adj.* topical; noteworthy as news. □ **newsworthiness** *n.*

newsy *adj.* (**newsier**, **newsiest**) *colloq.* full of news.

newt *n.* ► any of various small amphibians, esp. of the genus *Triturus*, having a well-developed tail. [Middle English, from *ewt*, with *n* from *an*]

New Testament *n.* the second part of the Christian Bible, concerned with the life and teachings of Christ and his earliest followers.

newton *n.* *Physics* the SI unit of force. [named after Sir Isaac *Newton*, English scientist, 1642–1727]

Newtonian *adj.* of or devised by Isaac Newton.

new town *n.* a town established as a completely new settlement with government sponsorship.

new wave *n.* **1** = NOUVELLE VAGUE. **2** a style of rock music popular in the 1970s.

New World *n.* North and South America regarded collectively in relation to Europe.

new year *n.* **1** the calendar year just begun or about to begin. **2** the first few days of a year.

New Year's Day *n.* 1 January.

New Year's Eve *n.* 31 December.

New Zealander *n.* **1** a native or national of New Zealand. **2** a person of New Zealand descent.

next ● *adj.* **1** (often foll. by *to*) being or positioned or living nearest. **2** the nearest in order of time; the soonest encountered (*next Friday*; *ask the next person you see*). ● *adv.* (often foll. by *to*) in the nearest place or degree (*next to last*). **2** on the first or soonest occasion (*when we next meet*). □ **next to** almost (*next to nothing left*). [Old English in sense 'nearest']

next-best *adj.* the next in order of preference.

next door *adv.* & *adj.* (as adj. often hyphenated) in or to the next house or room. □ **next door to 1** in the next house to. **2** nearly, near to.

next of kin *n.sing.* & *pl.* the closest living relative or relatives.

next world *n.* a supposed life after death.

nexus *n.* (*pl.* **nexuses**) **1** a connected group, series, or network. **2** a bond; a connection. [Latin]

NGO *abbr.* non-governmental organization.

NHS *abbr.* (in the UK) National Health Service.

NI *abbr.* **1** (in the UK) National Insurance. **2** Northern Ireland.

Ni *symb.* *Chem.* the element nickel.

niacin *n.* = NICOTINIC ACID.

nib *n.* **1** ► the point of a pen, which touches the writing surface. **2** (in *pl.*) shelled and crushed coffee or cocoa beans. **3** the point of a tool etc.

nibble ● *v.* **1** *tr.* & (foll. by *at*) *intr.* **a** take small bites at. **b** eat in small amounts. **c** bite at gently or cautiously or playfully. **2** *intr.* (foll. by *at*) show cautious interest in. ● *n.* **1** an instance of nibbling. **2** (usu. in *pl.*) a morsel or titbit of food. **3** *Computing* half a byte, i.e. 4 bits. □ **nibbler** *n.*

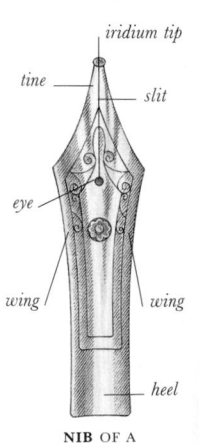

iridium tip

tine

slit

eye

wing   *wing*

heel

NIB OF A FOUNTAIN PEN

NEWT

Newts are amphibians that usually live on land for part of the year, returning to the water during the breeding season in spring. They have cylindrical bodies, four-toed feet, dry, not slippery, skin, and vertically compressed tails.

EXTERNAL FEATURES OF
A GREAT CRESTED NEWT
(*Triturus cristatus*)

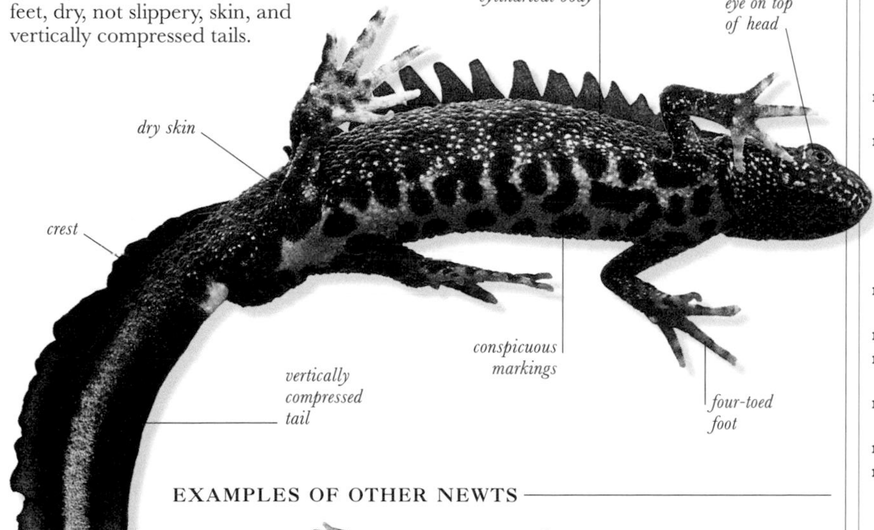

cylindrical body

*eye on top
of head*

dry skin

crest

*conspicuous
markings*

*vertically
compressed
tail*

*four-toed
foot*

EXAMPLES OF OTHER NEWTS

CALIFORNIA NEWT
(*Taricha torosa*)

MARBLED NEWT
(*Triturus marmoratus*)

FIRE-BELLIED NEWT
(*Cynops pyrrhogaster*)

MANDARIN NEWT
(*Tylototriton verrucosus*)

ITALIAN CRESTED
NEWT
('*Triturus carnifex*)

PALMATE NEWT
(*Triturus helveticus*)

ALPINE NEWT
(*Triturus alpestris*)

---

nibs *n.* □ **his nibs** *joc. colloq.* a mock title used with reference to an important or self-important person. [19th-century coinage]

nicad *n.* (often *attrib.*) a battery, often rechargeable, with a nickel anode and a cadmium cathode.

Nicam *n.* a digital system used in British television to provide video signals with high-quality stereo sound. [from *near instantaneously companded* (= compressed and expanded) *audio multiplex*]

nice *adj.* **1** pleasant, satisfactory. **2** (of a person) kind, good-natured. **3** *iron.* bad or awkward (*a nice mess you've made*). **4** fine or subtle (*a nice distinction*).

5 fastidious; delicately sensitive. **6** scrupulous (*were not too nice about their methods*). **7** (foll. by an adj., often with *and*) satisfactory or adequate in terms of the quality described (*nice and warm*). □ **nice one** *colloq.* expressing approval. **nice work** expressing approval of a task well done. [originally in sense 'stupid, wanton': from Latin *nescius* 'ignorant'] □ **nicely** *adv.* **niceness** *n.*

nicety /**ny**-si-ti/ *n.* (*pl.* **-ies**) **1** a subtle distinction or detail. **2** precision, accuracy. **3** intricate or subtle quality (*a point of great nicety*). **4** (in *pl.*) **a** minutiae. **b** refinements. □ **to a nicety** with exactness.

niche /neesh/ *n.* **1** a shallow recess, esp. in a wall to contain a statue etc. ▷ FAÇADE. **2** a comfortable or suitable position in life or employment. **3** a specialized but profitable corner of the market. [from Latin *nidus* 'nest']

nick[1] ● *n.* **1** a small cut or notch. **2** *Brit. slang* **a** a prison. **b** a police station. **3** (prec. by *in* with adj.) *Brit. colloq.* condition (*in reasonable nick*). ● *v.tr.* **1** make a nick or nicks in. **2** *Brit. slang* **a** steal. **b** arrest, catch. □ **in the nick of time** only just in time. [Middle English]

nick[2] *v.intr.* (foll. by *off*, *in*, etc.) *Austral. slang* move quickly or furtively. [19th-century coinage]

nickel ● *n.* **1** *Chem.* a malleable ductile silver-white metallic element used esp. in magnetic alloys. ▷ METAL. **2** *N. Amer. colloq.* a five-cent coin. ● *v.tr.* (**nickelled, nickelling;** *US* **nickeled, nickeling**) coat with nickel. [abbreviation of German *Kupfernickel*, the copper-coloured ore from which nickel was first obtained]

nickelodeon *n. US* **1** *colloq.* a jukebox. **2** *hist.* a cinema with an admission fee of one nickel.

nickel silver *n.* = GERMAN SILVER.

nickel steel *n.* a type of stainless steel with chromium and nickel.

nicker *n.* (*pl.* same) *Brit. slang* a pound (in money). [20th-century coinage]

nick-nack var. of KNICK-KNACK.

nickname ● *n.* a familiar or humorous name given to a person or thing instead of or as well as the real name. ● *v.tr.* **1** give a nickname to. **2** call by a nickname. [Middle English, from *eke-name*, with *n* from *an* (*eke* = addition)]

nicotine *n.* a colourless poisonous narcotic alkaloid present in tobacco. [French]

nicotinic acid *n.* a vitamin of the B complex, found in milk, liver, and yeast.

nictitate *v.intr.* esp. *Zool.* blink or wink. [from medieval Latin *nictitare* 'to blink repeatedly'] □ **nictitation** *n.*

nictitating membrane *n.* ▼ a clear membrane forming a third eyelid in amphibians, birds, and some other animals.

N

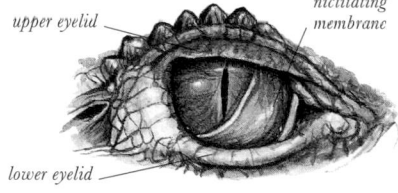

upper eyelid

*nictitating
membrane*

lower eyelid

NICTITATING MEMBRANE
ON A CROCODILE EYE

niece *n.* a daughter of one's brother or sister, or of one's brother-in-law or sister-in-law. [based on Latin *neptis* 'granddaughter']

niff *Brit. colloq.* ● *n.* a smell, esp. an unpleasant one. ● *v.intr.* smell, stink. □ **niffy** *adj.* (**niffier, niffiest**).

nifty *adj.* (**niftier, niftiest**) *colloq.* **1** clever, adroit. **2** smart, stylish. [19th-century coinage] □ **niftily** *adv.*

nigella /ny-**jel**-ă/ *n.* a plant of the genus *Nigella* (buttercup family), with showy flowers and finely cut leaves. [modern Latin]

niggard *n.* a mean or stingy person. [Middle English, alteration of earlier *nigon*]

niggardly ● *adj.* **1** stingy, parsimonious. **2** meagre, scanty. ● *adv.* in a stingy or meagre manner. □ **niggardliness** *n.*

nigger *n. offens.* **1** a black person. **2** a dark-skinned person. □ **a nigger in the woodpile** a hidden cause of trouble or inconvenience. [from Spanish *negro* 'Negro']

niggle ● *v.* **1** *intr.* be over-attentive to details. **2** *intr.* find fault in a petty way. **3** *tr.* irritate. ● *n.* a trifling complaint or criticism; a worry.

551

niggling *adj.* **1** troublesome or irritating in a petty way. **2** trifling or petty.

nigh *adv., prep., & adj. archaic* or *dial.* near. [Old English]

night ● *n.* **1** the period of darkness between one day and the next; the time from sunset to sunrise. **2** nightfall. **3** the darkness of night. **4** an evening appointed for some activity (*last night of the Proms*). ● *int. colloq.* = GOODNIGHT *int.* [Old English]

nightbird *n.* a person habitually active at night.

night-blindness *n.* = NYCTALOPIA.

nightcap *n.* **1** *hist.* a cap worn in bed. **2** a hot or alcoholic drink taken at bedtime.

nightclothes *n.* clothes worn in bed.

nightclub *n.* a club that is open at night and provides refreshment and entertainment.

nightdress *n.* a woman's or child's loose garment worn in bed.

nightfall *n.* the onset of night; the end of daylight.

night fighter *n.* an aeroplane used for interception at night.

nightgown *n.* **1** = NIGHTDRESS. **2** *hist.* a dressing gown.

nightie *n. colloq.* a nightdress.

nightingale *n.* ▶ a small brownish migratory thrush, *Luscinia megarhynchos*. ▷ SONGBIRD. [Old English]

NIGHTINGALE
(*Luscinia megarhynchos*)

nightjar *n.* any nocturnal insectivorous bird of the family Caprimulgidae, with grey-brown plumage and often a characteristic chirring call.

nightlife *n.* entertainment available at night in a town.

night light *n.* a dim light kept burning in a bedroom at night.

night-long *adj. & adv.* throughout the night.

nightly ● *adj.* **1** happening, done, or existing in the night. **2** recurring every night. ● *adv.* every night.

nightmare *n.* **1** a frightening or unpleasant dream. **2** *colloq.* a terrifying or very unpleasant experience or situation. **3** a haunting or obsessive fear. [an evil spirit (Old English *mære* 'incubus') once thought to lie on and suffocate sleepers] □ **nightmarish** *adj.* **nightmarishly** *adv.*

night nurse *n.* a nurse on duty during the night.

night owl *n. colloq.* a person habitually active or wakeful at night.

night safe *n. Brit.* a safe with access from the outer wall of a bank for the deposit of money etc. when the bank is closed.

night school *n.* an institution providing evening classes for those working by day.

nightshade *n.* ▶ any of various poisonous plants of the family Solanaceae, esp. of the genus *Solanum*, including *S. nigrum* (**black nightshade**) with black berries, and *S. dulcamara* (**woody nightshade**) with red berries. [Old English]

night shift *n.* a shift of workers employed during the night.

nightshirt *n.* a long shirt worn in bed.

nightspot *n. colloq.* a nightclub.

nightstick *n. US* a police officer's truncheon.

night terrors *n.pl.* feelings of great fear experienced on suddenly waking in the night, esp. by children.

night-time *n.* the time of darkness.

nightwatchman *n.* **1** a person whose job is to keep watch by night. **2** *Cricket* an inferior batsman sent in near the end of a day's play.

nightwear *n.* clothing suitable for wearing in bed.

nihilism /ny-il-izm/ *n.* **1** the rejection of all religious and moral principles. **2** the assertion that nothing really exists. [based on Latin *nihil* 'nothing'] □ **nihilist** *n.* **nihilistic** *adj.*

-nik *suffix* forming nouns denoting a person associated with a specified thing or quality (*refusenik*).

nil *n.* nothing; no number or amount (esp. *Brit.* as a score in games). [Latin, from *nihil*]

nimble *adj.* (**nimbler, nimblest**) **1** quick and light in movement or action. **2** (of the mind) clever, versatile. [Old English *næmel* 'quick to seize'] □ **nimbleness** *n.* **nimbly** *adv.*

nimbostratus *n. Meteorol.* cloud forming a low dense grey layer, from which rain or snow often falls. ▷ CLOUD

nimbus *n.* (*pl.* **nimbi** /-by/ or **nimbuses**) **1** a halo. **2** *Meteorol.* a rain cloud. [Latin, literally 'cloud, aureole'] □ **nimbused** *adj.*

Nimby ● *adj.* objecting to the siting of unpleasant developments in one's own locality. ● *n.* (*pl.* **-ies**) a person who so objects. [from *not in my back yard*]

nincompoop *n.* a simpleton; a fool. [17th-century coinage]

nine ● *n.* **1** one more than eight. **2** a symbol for this (9, ix, IX). **3** a size etc. denoted by nine. **4** a set or team of nine individuals. **5** nine o'clock. **6** a card with nine pips. ● *adj.* that amount to nine. □ **dressed to** (or *Brit.* **up to**) **the nines** dressed very elaborately. **nine times out of ten** nearly always. **nine to five** a designation of typical office hours. [Old English]

nine days' wonder *n.* a person or thing that is briefly famous.

ninefold *adj. & adv.* **1** nine times as much or as many. **2** consisting of nine parts.

ninepin *n.* **1** = SKITTLE *n.* 1. **2** (in *pl.*; usu. treated as *sing.*) the usual form of skittles, using nine pins. □ **go down** (or **drop** or **fall**) **like ninepins** topple or succumb in large numbers.

nineteen ● *n.* **1** one more than eighteen. **2** the symbol for this (19, xix, XIX). **3** a size etc. denoted by nineteen. ● *adj.* that amount to nineteen. □ **talk nineteen to the dozen** see DOZEN. [Old English] □ **nineteenth** *adj. & n.*

nine-to-five *attrib.adj.* of or involving standard office hours (typically 9 a.m. to 5 p.m.).

ninety ● *n.* (*pl.* **-ies**) **1** the product of nine and ten. **2** a symbol for this (90, xc, XC). **3** (in *pl.*) the numbers from 90 to 99. ● *adj.* that amount to ninety. [Old English] □ **ninetieth** *adj. & n.*

ninja *n.* a person skilled in ninjutsu. [Japanese]

ninjutsu *n.* one of the Japanese martial arts, characterized by stealthy movement and camouflage. [Japanese, from *nin* 'stealth' + *jutsu* 'art, science']

ninny *n.* (*pl.* **-ies**) *colloq.* a foolish or simple-minded person.

berries

toothed
leaves

star-shaped
flowers

NIGHTSHADE: BLACK
NIGHTSHADE (*Solanum nigrum*)

ninth ● *n.* **1** the position in a sequence corresponding to the number 9 in the sequence 1–9. **2** something occupying this position. **3** each of nine equal parts of a thing. ● *adj.* that is the ninth. □ **ninthly** *adv.*

niobium *n. Chem.* a rare grey-blue metallic element occurring naturally. [named after *Niobe*, daughter of Tantalus, because first found in tantalite, rare black mineral]

nip[1] ● *v.* (**nipped, nipping**) **1** *tr.* pinch, squeeze, or bite sharply. **2** *tr.* (often foll. by *off*) remove by pinching etc. **3** *tr.* (of the frost etc.) cause pain or harm to. **4** *intr.* (foll. by *in, out*, etc.) *Brit. colloq.* go nimbly or quickly. ● *n.* **1 a** a pinch, a sharp squeeze. **b** a bite. **2** biting cold. □ **nip in the bud** suppress or destroy (esp. an idea) at an early stage. [Middle English] □ **nipping** *adj.*

nip[2] *n.* a small quantity of spirits.

nip and tuck ● *n. colloq.* a cosmetic surgical operation. ● *adv. N. Amer.* neck and neck.

nipper *n.* **1** a person or thing that nips. **2** the claw of a crab, lobster, etc. **3** *Brit. colloq.* a young child. **4** (in *pl.*) any tool for gripping or cutting.

nipple *n.* **1 a** a small projection in which the mammary ducts of female mammals terminate and from which milk is secreted for the young. ▷ BREAST. **b** an analogous structure in the male. **2** the teat of a feeding bottle. **3** a device like a nipple which disperses liquids **4** a device on the casing of a bearing through which grease is introduced using a grease gun. **5** a nipple-like protuberance. [16th-century coinage]

nipplewort *n.* a yellow-flowered weed, *Lapsana communis*.

nippy *adj.* (**nippier, nippiest**) *colloq.* **1** quick, nimble, active. **2** chilly, cold. □ **nippily** *adv.*

nirvana *n.* (in Buddhism) perfect bliss and release from karma, attained by the extinction of individuality. [from Sanskrit *nirvāṇa*]

nisei /nee-say/ *n.* (also **Nisei**) *US* an American whose parents were immigrants from Japan. [Japanese, literally 'second generation']

Nissen hut *n.* a tunnel-shaped hut of corrugated iron with a cement floor. [named after P. N. *Nissen*, British engineer, 1871–1930, its inventor]

nit *n.* **1** the egg or young form of a louse or other parasitic insect. **2** *Brit. colloq.* a stupid person. [Old English]

niter *US* var. of NITRE.

nit-picking *n. & adj. colloq.* criticizing in a petty manner. □ **nit-pick** *v.intr.* **nit-picker** *n.*

nitrate ● *n.* **1** any salt or ester of nitric acid. **2** potassium or sodium nitrate when used as a fertilizer. ● *v.tr. Chem.* treat, combine, or impregnate with nitric acid. □ **nitration** *n.*

nitre *n.* (*US* **niter**) saltpetre, potassium nitrate. [from Greek *nitron*]

nitric *adj.* of or containing nitrogen.

nitric acid *n.* a colourless or pale yellow corrosive poisonous liquid acid. ▷ NITROGEN CYCLE

nitric oxide *n.* a colourless toxic gas, involved in physiological processes in minute quantities, and forming nitrogen dioxide in air.

nitride *n. Chem.* a compound of nitrogen with another element or radical.

nitrify *v.tr.* (**-ies, -ied**) **1** impregnate with nitrogen. **2** convert into nitrites or nitrates. ▷ NITROGEN CYCLE. [from French *nitrifier*] □ **nitrification** *n.*

nitrile *n. Chem.* an organic compound consisting of an alkyl radical bound to a cyanide radical.

nitrite *n.* any salt or ester of nitrous acid.

nitro- *comb. form* **1** of or containing nitric acid, nitre, or nitrogen. **2** made with or by use of any of these. **3** of or containing the monovalent -NO$_2$ group. [Greek]

nitrobenzene *n.* a yellow oily liquid made by the nitration of benzene and used to make aniline etc.

nitrocellulose *n.* a highly flammable material made by treating cellulose with concentrated nitric acid.

N

NITROGEN CYCLE

All living things play a part in the nitrogen cycle. Bacteria have a double role: they can fix (combine) nitrogen with oxygen to form nitrates, which most living organisms can use, and they can break the nitrates down (denitrify them) into nitrogen and oxygen.

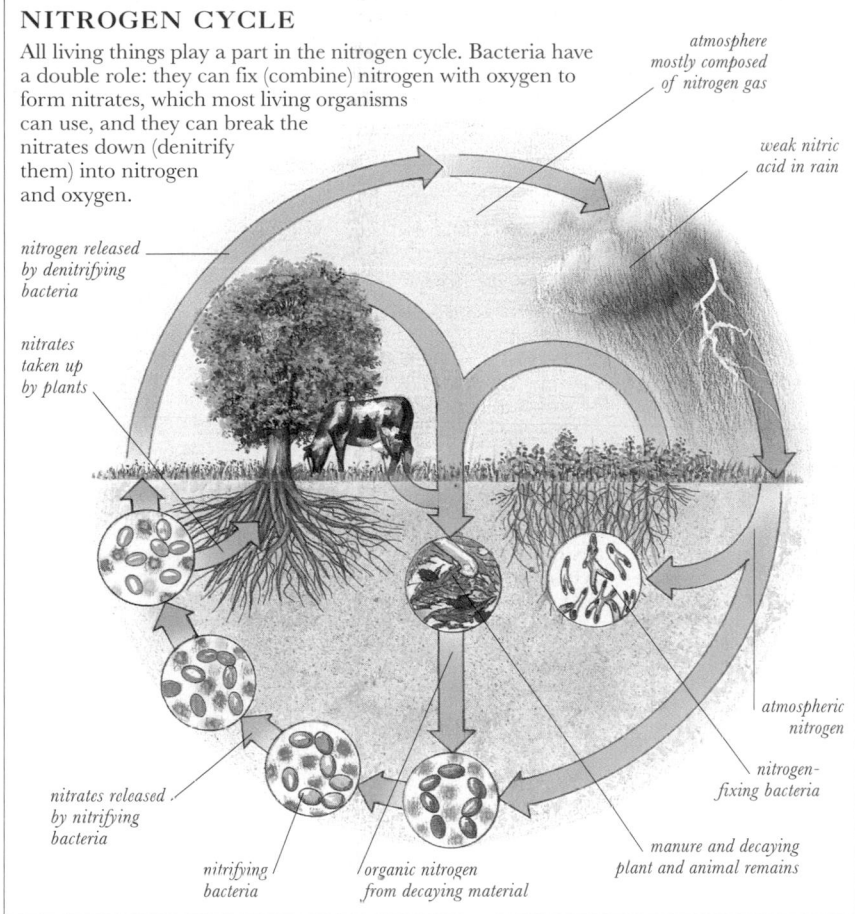

atmosphere mostly composed of nitrogen gas

weak nitric acid in rain

nitrogen released by denitrifying bacteria

nitrates taken up by plants

atmospheric nitrogen

nitrogen-fixing bacteria

nitrates released by nitrifying bacteria

nitrifying bacteria

organic nitrogen from decaying material

manure and decaying plant and animal remains

---

nitrogen *n. Chem.* a colourless odourless unreactive gaseous element that forms four-fifths of the Earth's atmosphere. ▷ NITROGEN CYCLE. [from French *nitrogène*] □ **nitrogenous** *adj.*

nitrogen cycle *n. Ecol.* ▲ the series of processes by which nitrogen is absorbed from and returned to the atmosphere by biological systems.

nitrogen dioxide *n.* a reddish-brown poisonous gas.

nitroglycerine *n.* (also **nitroglycerin**) an explosive yellow liquid made by reacting glycerol with a mixture of concentrated sulphuric and nitric acids.

nitrous *adj.* of, like, or impregnated with nitrogen.

nitrous acid *n.* a weak acid existing only in solution and in the gaseous state.

nitrous oxide *n.* a colourless gas used as an anaesthetic and as an aerosol propellant.

nitty-gritty *n. slang* the realities or practical details of a matter. [20th-century coinage]

nitwit *n. colloq.* a stupid person. □ **nitwittery** *n.*

nix *slang* ● *n.* **1** nothing. **2** a denial or refusal. ● *v.tr.* **1** cancel. **2** reject. [German, colloquial variant of *nichts* 'nothing']

NMR *abbr.* (also **nmr**) nuclear magnetic resonance.

NNE *abbr.* north-north-east.

NNW *abbr.* north-north-west.

No[1] *symb. Chem.* the element nobelium.

No[2] var. of NOH.

No. *abbr.* **1** number. **2** *US* North. [sense 1: from Latin *numero* 'by number']

no[1] *det.* **1** not any (*there is no excuse*). **2** not a, quite other than (*is no fool*). **3** hardly any (*did it in no time*). **4** used elliptically in a notice etc., to forbid, reject, or deplore the thing specified (*no parking*). □ **by no**

means see MEANS. **no dice** see DICE. **no doubt** see DOUBT. **no end** see END. **no fear** see FEAR. **no little** see LITTLE. **no man** no person, nobody. **no place** *US* nowhere. **no small** see SMALL. **no sweat** *colloq.* no bother, no trouble. **no thoroughfare** an indication that passage along a street, path, etc., is blocked or prohibited. **no through road** = *no thoroughfare*. **no time** see TIME. **no way** *colloq.* **1** it is impossible. **2** I will not agree etc. **no wonder** see WONDER. **... or no ...** regardless of the ... (*rain or no rain, I shall go out*). **there is no ...ing** it is impossible to ... (*there is no accounting for tastes*). [Middle English]

no[2] ● *int.* equivalent to a negative sentence: the answer to your question is negative, your request or command will not be complied with, the statement made or course of action intended or conclusion arrived at is not correct or satisfactory, the negative statement made is correct. ● *adv.* **1** (foll. by *compar.*) by no amount (*no better than before*). **2** *Sc.* not (*will ye no come back again?*). ● *n.* (*pl.* **noes**) **1** an utterance of the word *no*. **2** a denial or refusal. **3** a negative vote. □ **is no more** has died or ceased to exist. **no better than one should be** morally suspect. **no can do** *colloq.* I am unable to do it. **no less** (often foll. by *than*) **1** as much (*gave me £50, no less*). **2** as important (*no less a person than the President*). **3** *disp.* no fewer *no less than ten people have told me*. **no longer** not now or henceforth as formerly. **no sooner ... than** see SOON. **not take no for an answer** persist in spite of refusals. **or no** or not (*pleasant or no, it is true*). **whether or no 1** in either case. **2** (as an indirect question) which of a case and its negative (*tell me whether or no*). [Old English]

no-account *attrib.adj.* unimportant, worthless.

nob[1] *n. Brit. slang* a person of wealth or high social

position. [originally Scots *knabb*, *nab*; 17th-century coinage]

nob[2] *n. slang* the head.

no-ball *Cricket* ● *n.* an unlawfully delivered ball. ● *v.tr.* pronounce (a bowler) to have bowled a no-ball.

nobble *v.tr. Brit. slang* **1** tamper with (a racehorse) to prevent its winning. **2** try to influence, esp. unfairly. **3** steal (money). **4** seize, catch.

Nobelist *n. US* a winner of a Nobel Prize.

nobelium *n. Chem.* an artificially produced radioactive transuranic metallic element. [named after Λ. *Nobel* (see NOBEL PRIZE)]

Nobel Prize *n.* any of six international prizes awarded annually for physics, chemistry, physiology or medicine, literature, economics, and the promotion of peace. [named after Alfred *Nobel*, 1833–96, Swedish chemist and engineer, who endowed them] □ **Nobel prizewinner** *n.*

nobility *n.* (*pl.* **-ies**) **1** nobleness of character, mind, birth, or rank. **2** (prec. by *a*, *the*) a class of nobles, an aristocracy. [from Latin *nobilitas*]

noble ● *adj.* (**nobler**, **noblest**) **1** belonging by rank, title, or birth to the aristocracy. **2** having lofty ideals; free from pettiness and meanness. **3** of imposing appearance. **4** excellent, admirable (*noble horse; noble cellar*). ● *n.* a nobleman or noblewoman. □ **the noble art of self-defence** see SELF-DEFENCE. [from Latin *(g)nobilis*] □ **nobleness** *n.* **nobly** *adv.*

noble gas *n.* any gaseous element of a group that almost never combine with other elements.

nobleman *n.* (*pl.* **-men**) a man of noble rank or birth, a peer.

noble metal *n.* a metal that resists chemical action, does not corrode or tarnish in air or water, and is not easily attacked by acids.

noble rot *n.* **1** the condition of grapes affected by the mould *Botrytis cinerea* (see BOTRYTIS). **2** the mould itself. [translation of French *pourriture noble*]

noble savage *n.* primitive man idealized as in Romantic literature.

noblesse /noh-*bless*/ *n.* the class of nobles (esp. of a foreign country). □ **noblesse oblige** /o-*bleezh*/ privilege entails responsibility. [Middle English, from Old French]

noblewoman *n.* (*pl.* **-women**) a woman of noble rank or birth, a peeress.

nobody ● *pron.* no person. ● *n.* (*pl.* **-ies**) a person of no importance, authority, or position. □ **like nobody's business** see BUSINESS. **nobody's fool** see FOOL[1]. [Middle English]

nock ● *n.* **1** a notch at either end of a bow for holding the string. **2** a notch at the butt-end of an arrow for receiving the bowstring. ● *v.tr.* set (an arrow) on the string. [Middle English]

no-claims bonus *n.* (also **no-claim bonus**, **no-claim(s) discount**) *Brit.* a reduction of the insurance premium charged when the insured has not made a claim under the insurance during an agreed preceding period.

noctambulist *n.* a sleepwalker. [based on Latin *nox noctis* 'night' + *ambulare* 'to walk'] □ **noctambulism** *n.*

noctule *n.* a large W. European bat, *Nyctalus noctula*. ▷ BAT. [from Italian *nottola* 'bat']

nocturnal *adj.* of or in the night; done or active by night. [from Latin *nocturnus* 'of the night'] □ **nocturnally** *adv.*

nocturnal emission *n.* involuntary emission of semen during sleep.

nocturne *n.* **1** *Mus.* a short composition of a romantic nature, usu. for piano. **2** a picture of a night scene. [French]

nod ● *v.* (**nodded**, **nodding**) **1** *intr.* incline one's head slightly and briefly in greeting, assent, or command. **2** *intr.* let one's head fall forward in drowsiness. **3** *tr.* incline (one's head). **4** *tr.* signify (assent etc.) by a nod. **5** *intr.* (of flowers, plumes, etc.) bend downwards and sway. **6** *intr.* make a mistake due to a momentary lack of alertness or

N

attention. ● n. a nodding of the head. □ **get the nod** *N. Amer.* be chosen or approved. **nod off** *colloq.* fall asleep. **on the nod** *Brit. colloq.* **1** with merely formal assent and no discussion. **2** on credit. [Middle English]

nodding acquaintance n. (usu. foll. by *with*) a very slight acquaintance with a person or subject.

noddle n. *colloq.* the head. [Middle English]

noddy n. (*pl.* **-ies**) **1** a simpleton. **2** any usu. dark-coloured tropical tern of the genus *Anous* or *Procelsterna*.

node n. **1** *Bot.* **a** the part of a plant stem from which leaves emerge. **b** a knob on a root or branch. **2** *Anat.* **a** a small mass of differentiated tissue, esp. a lymph gland. **b** an interruption of the myelin sheath of a nerve. **3** *Astron.* either of two points at which a planet's orbit intersects the plane of the ecliptic or the celestial equator. **4** *Physics* a point of minimum disturbance in a standing wave system. **5** *Electr.* a point of zero current or voltage. **6** *Math.* a point at which a curve intersects itself. **7** a component in a computer network. [from Latin *nodus* 'knot'] □ **nodal** *adj.* **nodical** *adj.* (in sense 3).

nodule n. **1** a small rounded lump of anything. **2** a small tumour, node, or ganglion. [from Latin *nodulus* 'little knot'] □ **nodular** *adj.* **nodulated** *adj.* **nodulation** n. **nodulose** *adj.*

Noel n. (also **Noël**) Christmas (esp. as a refrain in carols). [French, based on Latin *natus* 'born']

no-fault *attrib.adj.* esp. *N. Amer.* involving no fault or blame, esp. designating a type of insurance policy.

no-fly zone n. a zone in which aircraft are forbidden to fly.

no-frills *attrib.adj.* lacking ornament or embellishment.

nog n. a small block or peg of wood. [17th-century coinage]

noggin n. **1** a small mug. **2** a small measure, usu. ¼ pint, of spirits. **3** *slang* the head. [17th-century coinage]

nogging n. ▼ brickwork or timber braces in a timber frame.

NOGGING IN A TIMBER-FRAMED GERMAN HOUSE

timber frame

brick nogging

no go *adj.* (usu. hyphenated when *attrib.*) impossible, hopeless; forbidden.

no-go area n. *Brit.* an area forbidden to unauthorized people.

no-good *colloq.* ● *attrib.adj.* useless. ● n. a useless person or thing.

Noh n. (also **No**) traditional Japanese drama with dance and song, evolved from Shinto rites. [from Japanese *nō*]

no-hitter n. *Baseball* a match in which a pitcher yields no hits.

no-hoper n. *slang* a useless person; a person or thing doomed to failure.

nohow *adv.* **1** *US* in no way; by no means. **2** *dial.* out of order; out of sorts.

noise ● n. **1** a sound, esp. a loud or unpleasant or undesired one. **2** a series or confusion of loud sounds. **3** irregular fluctuations accompanying a transmitted signal but not relevant to it. **4** (in *pl.*) conventional remarks, or speechlike sounds without actual words (*made sympathetic noises*). ● *v.tr.* (usu. in *passive*) spread abroad (a person's fame or a fact). □ **make a noise 1** (usu. foll. by *about*) talk or complain much. **2** attain notoriety. [from Latin *nausea* 'nausea']

noiseless *adj.* **1** silent. **2** characterized by the absence of extraneous noise. □ **noiselessly** *adv.* **noiselessness** n.

noise pollution n. harmful or annoying noise.

noises off *n.pl.* sounds made off stage to be heard by the audience of a play.

noisette /nwah-**zet**/ n. **1** a small round piece of meat etc. **2** a chocolate made with hazelnuts. [French, literally 'little nut']

noisome *adj.* *literary* **1** harmful, noxious. **2** evil-smelling. **3** objectionable, offensive. [Middle English, from obsolete *noy* 'annoyance'] □ **noisomeness** n.

noisy *adj.* (**noisier, noisiest**) **1** full of or attended with noise. **2** making or given to making much noise. **3** clamorous, turbulent. **4** (of a colour, garment, etc.) loud, conspicuous. □ **noisily** *adv.* **noisiness** n.

nomad n. **1** a member of a people roaming from place to place for fresh pasture. **2** a wanderer. [from Greek *nomas -ados*] □ **nomadic** *adj.* **nomadically** *adv.* **nomadism** n.

no man's land n. **1** *Mil.* the space between two opposing armies. **2** an area not assigned to any owner. **3** an area not clearly belonging to any one subject etc.

nom de guerre /nom dĕ **gair**/ n. (*pl.* **noms de guerre** *pronunc.* same) an assumed name under which a person fights, plays, writes, etc. [French, literally 'war-name']

nom de plume /nom dĕ **ploom**/ n. (*pl.* **noms de plume** *pronunc.* same) an assumed name under which a person writes. [formed in English of French words, literally 'pen-name']

nomenclature /nŏ-**meng**-klă-cher/ n. **1** a person's or community's system of names for things. **2** the terminology of a science etc. **3** systematic naming. **4** a catalogue or register. [from Latin *nomenclatura*] □ **nomenclatural** *adj.*

nominal *adj.* **1** existing in name only; not real or actual (*nominal ruler*). **2** (of a sum of money etc.) virtually nothing; much below the actual value of a thing. **3** of or in names (*nominal and essential distinctions*). **4** consisting of or giving the names (*nominal list of officers*). **5** of or as or like a noun. [from Latin *nominalis*] □ **nominally** *adv.*

nominal value n. the face value (of a coin, shares, etc.).

nominate *v.tr.* **1** propose (a candidate) for election. **2** appoint to an office (*a board of six nominated and six elected members*). **3** name or appoint (a date or place). **4** mention by name. **5** call by the name of, designate. [based on Latin *nominatus* 'named'] □ **nomination** n. **nominator** n.

nominative ● n. *Gram.* **1** the case of nouns, pronouns, and adjectives, expressing the subject of a verb. **2** a word in this case. ● *adj.* **1** *Gram.* of or in this case. **2** of, or appointed by, nomination (as distinct from election).

nominee n. **1** a person who is nominated for an office or as the recipient of a grant etc. **2** *Commerce* a person in whose name a stock etc. is registered.

no more ● n. nothing further (*have no more to say*). ● *adj.* not any more (*no more wine?*). ● *adv.* **1** no longer. **2** never again. **3** to no greater extent (*is no more a lord than I am*). **4** just as little, neither (*you did not come, and no more did he*).

non- *prefix* giving the negative sense of words with which it is combined, esp.: **1** not doing or having or involved with (*non-attendance*). **2 a** not of the kind or class described (*non-alcoholic*). **b** forming terms used adjectivally (*non-union*). **3** lack of (*non-availability*). **4** (with adverbs) not in the way described (*non-aggressively*). **5** forming adjectives from verbs, meaning 'that does not' or 'that is not meant to (or to be)' (*non-skid*). **6** used to form a neutral negative sense when a form in *in-* or *un-* has a special sense or (usu. unfavourable) connotation (*non-controversial*).

■ **Usage** The number of words that can be formed with the prefix *non-* is unlimited; consequently only a selection, considered the most current or semantically noteworthy, can be given here.

nona- *comb. form* nine. [Latin]

non-abstainer n. a person who does not abstain (esp. from alcohol).

non-acceptance n. a lack of acceptance.

non-addictive *adj.* (of a drug, habit, etc.) not causing addiction.

nonage n. **1** *hist.* the state of being under full legal age, minority. **2** a period of immaturity. [from Old French]

nonagenarian ● n. a person from 90 to 99 years old. ● *adj.* of this age. [from Latin *nonagenarius*]

non-aggression n. lack of or restraint from aggression (often *attrib.*: *non-aggression pact*).

nonagon n. ▶ a plane figure with nine sides and angles. [based on Latin *nonus* 'ninth', on the pattern of *hexagon*]

non-alcoholic *adj.* (of a drink etc.) not containing alcohol.

NONAGON

non-aligned *adj.* (of states etc.) not aligned with another (esp. major) power. □ **non-alignment** n.

non-allergic *adj.* not causing allergy; not allergic.

non-appearance n. failure to appear or be present.

non-attached *adj.* that is not attached.

■ **Usage** *Non-attached* is neutral in sense: see NON- 6, UNATTACHED.

non-attendance n. failure to attend.

non-attributable *adj.* that cannot or may not be attributed to a particular source etc. □ **non-attributably** *adv.*

non-availability n. a state of not being available.

non-believer n. a person who does not believe or has no (esp. religious) faith.

non-belligerent ● *adj.* not engaged in hostilities. ● n. a non-belligerent nation, state, etc.

non-biological *adj.* **1** not relating to biology or living organisms. **2** (of a detergent etc.) not containing enzymes.

non-black *adj.* **1** (of a person) not black. **2** of or relating to non-black people. ● n. a non-black person.

non-capital *adj.* (of an offence) not punishable by death.

non-Catholic ● *adj.* not Roman Catholic. ● n. a non-Catholic person.

nonce n. □ **for the nonce** for the time being; for the present occasion. [from wrong division in Middle English of *than anes* 'for the one (occasion)']

nonce-word n. a word coined for one occasion.

nonchalant /**non**-shă-lănt/ *adj.* calm and casual. [French, literally 'not concerned'] □ **nonchalance** n. **nonchalantly** *adv.*

non-Christian ● *adj.* not Christian. ● n. a non-Christian person.

non-citizen n. a person who is not a citizen (of a particular place).

non-clerical *adj.* not doing or involving clerical work.

N

non-com *n. colloq.* a non-commissioned officer.

non-combatant *n.* a person not fighting in a war, esp. a civilian, army chaplain, etc.

non-commissioned *adj. Mil.* (of an officer) not holding a commission.

non-committal *adj.* avoiding commitment to a definite opinion or course of action. □ **non-committally** *adv.*

non-communist (also **non-Communist** with reference to a particular party) ● *adj.* not advocating or practising communism. ● *n.* a non-communist person.

non-compliance *n.* failure to comply; a lack of compliance.

non compos mentis *adj.* (also **non compos**) not in one's right mind.

non-conductor *n.* a substance that does not conduct heat or electricity. □ **non-conducting** *adj.*

nonconformist ● *n.* **1** a person who does not conform to the doctrine or discipline of an established Church, esp. (**Nonconformist**) a member of a Protestant Church dissenting from the Anglican Church. **2** a person who does not conform to a prevailing principle. ● *adj.* of or relating to a nonconformist or to Nonconformism. □ **nonconformism** *n.* (also *Relig.* **Nonconformism**).

nonconformity *n.* **1 a** nonconformists as a body, esp. (**Nonconformity**) Protestants dissenting from the Anglican Church. **b** the principles or practice of nonconformists, esp. (**Nonconformity**) Protestant dissent. **2** (usu. foll. by *to*) failure to conform. **3** lack of correspondence between things.

non-contentious *adj.* not contentious.

non-contributory *adj.* not contributing or (esp. of a pension scheme) involving contributions.

non-controversial *adj.* not controversial.

■ **Usage** *Non-controversial* is neutral in sense: see NON-6, UNCONTROVERSIAL.

non-cooperation *n.* failure to cooperate.

non-delivery *n.* failure to deliver.

non-denominational *adj.* not restricted as regards religious denomination.

nondescript ● *adj.* lacking distinctive characteristics, not easily classified. ● *n.* a nondescript person or thing.

non-destructive *adj.* that does not involve destruction or damage.

non-drinker *n.* a person who does not drink alcoholic liquor.

non-driver *n.* a person who does not drive a motor vehicle.

none ● *pron.* **1** (foll. by *of*) **a** not any of (*none of this concerns me; none of them have found it; none of your impudence!*). **b** not any one of (*none of them has come*). **2 a** no persons (*none but fools have ever believed it*). **b** no person (*none can tell*). ● *adj.* (usu. with a preceding noun implied) **1** no; not any (*you have money and I have none*). **2** not to be counted in a specified class (*his understanding is none of the clearest; if a linguist is wanted, I am none*). ● *adv.* (foll. by *the* + *compar.*, or *so, too*) by no amount; not at all (*am none the wiser*). □ **none the less** see NONETHELESS. **none other** (usu. foll. by *than*) no other person. [Old English]

■ **Usage** In sense 1 of the pronoun, *none* can be followed by a singular or plural verb according to the sense. If the sense is 'not any one of' a singular verb is used, e.g. *None of them is any good*, while if the sense is simply 'not any of' a plural verb is used, e.g. *None of them want to come*. The use of the singular verb is more emphatic.

non-effective *adj.* that does not have an effect.

■ **Usage** *Non-effective* is neutral in sense: see NON-6, INEFFECTIVE.

nonentity *n.* (*pl.* **-ies**) **1** a person or thing of no importance. **2 a** non-existence. **b** a non-existent thing. [from medieval Latin *nonentitas* 'non-existence']

nones *n.pl.* in the ancient Roman calendar, the ninth day before the ides by inclusive reckoning, i.e. the 7th day of March, May, July, October, the 5th of other months. [from Latin *nonae* (fem. pl.) 'ninth']

non-essential ● *adj.* not essential. ● *n.* a non-essential thing.

■ **Usage** *Non-essential* is neutral in sense: see NON-6, INESSENTIAL.

nonesuch var. of NONSUCH.

nonetheless *adv.* (also **none the less**) nevertheless.

non-Euclidean *adj.* denying or going beyond Euclidean principles in geometry.

non-European ● *adj.* not European. ● *n.* a non-European person.

non-event *n.* an unimportant or anticlimactic occurrence.

non-existent *adj.* not existing. □ **non-existence** *n.*

non-explosive *adj.* (of a substance) that does not explode.

non-fattening *adj.* (of food) that does not make the consumer fat when eaten in normal amounts.

non-ferrous *adj.* (of a metal) other than iron or steel.

non-fiction *n.* literary work other than fiction. □ **non-fictional** *adj.*

non-flammable *adj.* not inflammable.

■ **Usage** See Usage Note at FLAMMABLE.

non-fulfilment *n.* failure to fulfil (an obligation).

non-functional *adj.* not having a function.

non-governmental *adj.* not belonging to or associated with a government.

non-human ● *adj.* (of a being) not human. ● *n.* a non-human being.

■ **Usage** *Non-human* is neutral in sense: see NON-6, INHUMAN, UNHUMAN.

non-infectious *adj.* (of a disease) not infectious.

non-interference *n.* a lack of interference.

non-intervention *n.* the principle or practice of not becoming involved in others' affairs, esp. by one state in regard to another. □ **non-interventionist** *adj. & n.*

non-invasive *adj.* **1** (of a medical procedure) not requiring incision into the body or the removal of tissue. **2** (of an infection etc.) not tending to spread.

non-iron *adj.* (of a fabric) that needs no ironing.

non-linear *adj.* not linear, esp. with regard to dimension.

non-literary *adj.* (of writing, a text, etc.) not literary in character.

non-magnetic *adj.* (of a substance) not magnetic.

non-member *n.* a person who is not a member (of a particular association, club, etc.). □ **non-membership** *n.*

non-metal *adj.* not made of metal. □ **non-metallic** *adj.*

non-militant *adj.* not militant.

non-military *adj.* not military; not involving armed forces, civilian.

non-natural *adj.* not involving natural means or processes.

■ **Usage** *Non-natural* is neutral in sense: see NON-6, UNNATURAL.

non-negotiable *adj.* that cannot be negotiated (esp. in financial senses).

non-nuclear *adj.* **1** not involving nuclei or nuclear energy. **2** (of a state etc.) not having nuclear weapons.

no-no *n.* (*pl.* **no-nos**) *colloq.* a thing that is not possible or acceptable.

non-objective *adj.* **1** not objective. **2** *Art* abstract.

non-observance *n.* failure to observe (esp. an agreement, requirement, etc.).

no-nonsense *attrib.adj.* serious, sensible, without flippancy.

non-operational *adj.* **1** that does not operate. **2** out of order.

non-organic *adj.* not organic.

■ **Usage** *Non-organic* is neutral in sense: see NON-6, INORGANIC.

nonpareil ● *adj.* unrivalled or unique. ● *n.* such a person or thing. [French, literally 'not equal']

non-participating *adj.* not taking part.

non-partisan *adj.* not partisan.

non-party *adj.* independent of political parties.

non-payment *n.* failure to pay.

non-penetrative *adj.* (of sexual activity) in which penetration does not take place.

non-person *n.* a person regarded as non-existent or insignificant (cf. UNPERSON).

non-personal *adj.* not personal.

■ **Usage** *Non-personal* is neutral in sense: see NON-6, IMPERSONAL.

non-physical *adj.* not physical.

non-playing *adj.* that does not play or take part (in a game etc.).

nonplus *v.tr.* (**nonplussed**, **nonplussing**) completely perplex. [from Latin *non plus* 'not more']

non-political *adj.* not political; not involved in politics.

non-porous *adj.* (of a substance) not porous.

non-productive *adj.* not productive. □ **non-productively** *adv.*

■ **Usage** *Non-productive* is neutral in sense: see NON-6, UNPRODUCTIVE.

non-professional *adj.* not professional (esp. in status).

■ **Usage** *Non-professional* is neutral in sense: see NON-6, UNPROFESSIONAL.

non-profit *adj.* not involving or making a profit.

non-profit-making *adj. Brit.* (of an enterprise) not conducted primarily to make a profit.

non-proliferation *n.* the prevention of an increase in something, esp. possession of nuclear weapons (usu. *attrib.*; *non-proliferation agreement*).

non-racial *adj.* not involving race or racial factors.

non-resident ● *adj.* **1** not residing in a particular place. **2** (of a post) not requiring the holder to reside at the place of work. ● *n. Brit.* a non-resident person, esp. a person using some of the facilities of a hotel. □ **non-residence** *n.* **non-residential** *adj.*

non-resistance *n.* failure to resist; a lack of resistance.

non-returnable *adj.* that will or need or may not be returned.

non-rigid *adj.* (esp. of materials) not rigid.

non-scientific *adj.* not involving science or scientific methods. □ **non-scientist** *n.*

■ **Usage** *Non-scientific* is neutral in sense: see NON-6, UNSCIENTIFIC.

non-sectarian *adj.* not sectarian.

nonsense *n.* **1 a** (often as *int.*) absurd or meaningless words or ideas; foolish or extravagant conduct. **b** an instance of this. **2** a scheme, arrangement, etc., that one disapproves of. **3** (often *attrib.*) a form of literature meant to amuse by absurdity (*nonsense verse*). □ **nonsensical** *adj.* **nonsensicality** *n.* (*pl.* **-ies**). **nonsensically** *adv.*

non sequitur *n.* a conclusion that does not logically follow from the premises. [Latin, literally 'it does not follow']

non-sexual *adj.* not based on or involving sex. □ **non-sexually** *adv.*

non-skid *adj.* **1** that does not skid. **2** that inhibits skidding.

N

non-slip *adj.* **1** that does not slip. **2** that inhibits slipping.

non-smoker *n.* **1** a person who does not smoke. **2** a train compartment etc. in which smoking is forbidden. □ **non-smoking** *adj. & n.*

non-specialist *n.* a person who is not a specialist (in a particular subject).

non-specific *adj.* not specific or not restricted in extent, effect, cause, etc.

non-specific urethritis *n. Med.* inflammation of the urethra due to infection other than by gonococci, esp. by chlamydiae.

non-standard *adj.* not standard.

non-starter *n.* **1** a person or animal that does not start in a race. **2** *colloq.* a person or thing that is unlikely to succeed or be effective.

non-stick *adj.* **1** that does not stick. **2** that does not allow things to stick to it.

non-stop ● *adj.* **1** (of a train etc.) not stopping at intermediate places. **2** (of a journey, performance, etc.) done without a stop or intermission. ● *adv.* without stopping or pausing.

nonsuch *n.* (also **nonesuch**) **1** a person or thing that is unrivalled, a paragon. **2** ◀ a leguminous plant, *Medicago lupulina*, with black pods.

non-swimmer *n.* a person who cannot swim.

non-technical *adj.* **1** not technical. **2** without technical knowledge.

non-toxic *adj.* not toxic.

non-transferable *adj.* that may not be transferred.

non-U *adj.* esp. *Brit. colloq.* not characteristic of the upper class.

NONSUCH
(*Medicago lupulina*)

non-uniform *adj.* not uniform.

non-union *adj.* **1** not belonging to a trade union. **2** not done or produced by members of a trade union.

non-verbal *adj.* not involving words or speech. □ **non-verbally** *adv.*

non-vintage *adj.* (of wine etc.) not vintage.

non-violence *n.* the avoidance of violence, esp. as a principle. □ **non-violent** *adj.*

non-volatile *adj.* (esp. of a substance) not volatile.

non-voting *adj.* not having or using a vote. □ **non-voter** *n.*

non-white ● *adj.* **1** (of a person) not white. **2** of or relating to non-white people. ● *n.* a non-white person.

noodle[1] *n.* a strip or ring of pasta. [from German *Nudel*]

noodle[2] *n.* **1** a simpleton. **2** *slang* the head. [18th-century coinage]

nook *n.* a corner or recess; a secluded place. [Middle English]

nooky *n.* (also **nookie**) *slang* sexual activity. [20th-century coinage]

noon *n.* **1** twelve o'clock in the day, midday. **2** the culminating point. [originally in sense '3 p.m.': from Latin *nona (hora)* 'ninth hour']

noonday *n.* midday.

no one *n.* no person; nobody.

noontide *n.* (also **noontime**) midday.

noose ● *n.* **1** a loop with a running knot, tightening as the rope or wire is pulled. **2** a snare or bond. ● *v.tr.* catch with or enclose in a noose, ensnare. □ **put one's head in a noose** bring about one's own downfall. [Middle English]

nor *conj.* **1** and not; and not either (*neither one thing nor the other; not a man nor a child was to be seen; I said I had not seen it, nor had I; all that is true, nor must we forget …; can neither read nor write*). **2** and no more; neither (*'I cannot go' – 'Nor can I'*). [Middle English]

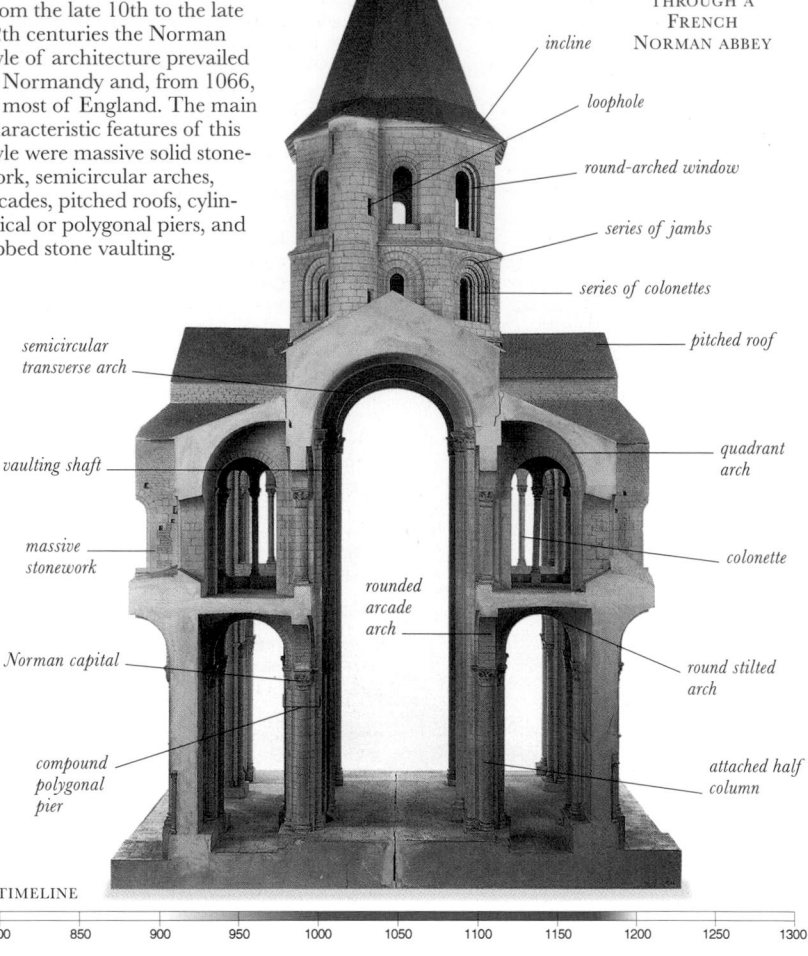

NORMAN

From the late 10th to the late 12th centuries the Norman style of architecture prevailed in Normandy and, from 1066, in most of England. The main characteristic features of this style were massive solid stonework, semicircular arches, arcades, pitched roofs, cylindrical or polygonal piers, and ribbed stone vaulting.

SECTION THROUGH A FRENCH NORMAN ABBEY

incline
loophole
round-arched window
series of jambs
series of colonettes
pitched roof
quadrant arch
colonette
round stilted arch
attached half column

semicircular transverse arch
vaulting shaft
massive stonework
Norman capital
compound polygonal pier

rounded arcade arch

TIMELINE

| 800 | 850 | 900 | 950 | 1000 | 1050 | 1100 | 1150 | 1200 | 1250 | 1300 |

nor' *n., adj., & adv.* (esp. in compounds) = NORTH (*nor'ward*).

Nordic ● *adj.* **1** of or relating to the tall blond Germanic people found in N. Europe, esp. in Scandinavia. **2** of or relating to Scandinavia or Finland. **3** (of skiing) with cross-country work and jumping. ● *n.* a Nordic person. [from French *nordique*]

Norfolk jacket *n.* a man's loose belted jacket, with box pleats. [from *Norfolk*, a county in S. England]

norm *n.* **1** a standard or pattern or type. **2** a standard quantity to be produced or amount of work to be done. **3** customary behaviour etc. [from Latin *norma* 'carpenter's square']

normal ● *adj.* **1** conforming to a standard; regular, usual, typical. **2** free from mental or emotional disorder. **3** *Geom.* (of a line) at right angles, perpendicular. ● *n.* **1 a** the normal value of a temperature etc. **b** the usual state, level, etc. **2** *Geom.* a line at right angles. [from Latin *normalis*] □ **normalcy** *n.* esp. *N. Amer.* **normality** *n.*

normal distribution *n. Statistics* a function that represents the distribution of many random variables as a symmetrical bell-shaped graph.

normalize *v.* (also **-ise**) **1** *tr.* make normal. **2** *intr.* become normal. **3** *tr.* cause to conform. □ **normalization** *n.* **normalizer** *n.*

normally *adv.* **1** in a normal manner. **2** usually.

Norman ● *n.* **1** a native or inhabitant of medieval Normandy. **2** a descendant of the people of mixed Scandinavian and Frankish origin established there in the 10th c., who conquered England in 1066.

3 Norman French. ● *adj.* **1** of or relating to the Normans. **2** ▲ of or relating to the Norman style of architecture. [from Old Norse *Northmathr* 'north man'] □ **Normanize** *v.tr. & intr.* (also **-ise**).

Norman Conquest see CONQUEST 4.

Norman French *n.* French as spoken by the Normans or (after 1066) in English law courts.

normative *adj.* of or establishing a norm. [from French *normatif -ive*] □ **normatively** *adv.* **normativeness** *n.*

Norse ● *n.* **1** the Norwegian language. **2** the Scandinavian language group. ● *adj.* **1** of or relating to Norway or the Norse language. **2** of or relating to ancient Scandinavia or its inhabitants. [from Dutch *noor(d)sch*] □ **Norseman** *n.* (*pl.* **-men**).

north ● *n.* **1 a** the point of the horizon 90° anticlockwise from east. **b** the compass point corresponding to this. ▷ COMPASS. **c** the direction in which this lies. **2** (usu. **the North**) **a** the part of the world or a country or a town lying to the north. **b** the Arctic. **c** the industrialized nations. ● *adj.* **1** towards, at, near, or facing north. **2** coming from the north (*north wind*). ● *adv.* **1** towards, at, or near the north. **2** (foll. by *of*) further north than. □ **north and south** lengthwise along a line from north to south. **to the north** (often foll. by *of*) in a northerly direction. [Old English]

North American ● *adj.* of North America. ● *n.* a native or inhabitant of North America, esp. a citizen of the US or Canada.

northbound *adj.* travelling or leading northwards.

North Country n. (also **north country**) the northern part of England (north of the Humber) (also (often hyphenated) attrib.: a north-country lad).

north-countryman n. (pl. **-men**) a native of the North Country.

North-East n. the part of a country or town lying to the north-east.

north-east ● n. **1** the point of the horizon midway between north and east. **2** the compass point corresponding to this. **3** the direction in which this lies. ● adj. of, towards, or coming from the north-east. ● adv. towards, at, or near the north-east. □ **north-eastern** adj.

northeaster n. a north-east wind.

north-easterly adj. & adv. = NORTH-EAST.

north-eastward adj. & adv. (also **north-eastwards**) towards the north-east.

northerly ● adj. & adv. **1** in a northern position or direction. **2** (of wind) blowing from the north. ● n. (pl. **-ies**) (usu. in pl.) a wind blowing from the north.

northern adj. of, in, or towards, the north. □ **northernmost** adj.

northerner n. a native or inhabitant of the north.

northern hemisphere n. the half of the Earth north of the equator.

northern lights n.pl. the aurora borealis. ▷ AURORA

Northern States n.pl. the states in the north of the US.

North Germanic n. & adj. ● n. the northern group of Germanic languages, comprising the Scandinavian languages. ● adj. of or relating to North Germanic.

north light n. good natural light without direct sun, esp. as desired by painters and in factory design.

Northman n. (pl. **-men**) a native of Scandinavia, esp. of Norway.

north-north-east n. the point or direction midway between north and north-east.

north-north-west n. the point or direction midway between north and north-west.

North Pole n. **1** the northernmost point of the Earth's axis of rotation. **2** the point in the northern sky about which the stars appear to revolve.

North Star n. the pole star.

northward ● adj. & adv. (also **northwards**) towards the north. ● n. a northward direction or region.

North-West n. the part of a country or town lying to the north-west.

north-west ● n. **1** the point of the horizon midway between north and west. **2** the compass point corresponding to this. **3** the direction in which this lies. ● adj. of, towards, or coming from the north-west. ● adv. towards, at, or near the north-west. □ **north-western** adj.

northwester n. a north-west wind.

north-westerly adj. & adv. = NORTH-WEST.

north-westward adj. & adv. (also **north-westwards**) towards the north-west.

Norway lobster n. a small European lobster, Nephrops norvegicus. [from Norway, country in N. Europe]

Norwegian ● n. **1 a** a native or national of Norway. **b** a person of Norwegian descent. **2** the language of Norway. ● adj. of or relating to Norway or its people or language. [from Old Norse Norvegr]

Nos. abbr. numbers.

no-score draw n. a draw in football in which no goals are scored.

nose ● n. **1** ▼ an organ above the mouth of a human or animal, used for smelling and breathing. ▷ RESPIRATION. **2 a** the sense of smell (dogs have a good nose). **b** the ability to detect a particular thing (a nose for scandal). **3** the odour or perfume of wine, tea, tobacco, hay, etc. **4** the open end or nozzle of a tube, pipe, pair of bellows, retort, etc. **5** the front end or projecting part of a thing, e.g. of a car or aircraft. **6** slang an informer of the police. ● v. **1** tr. (often foll. by out) **a** perceive the smell of, discover by smell. **b** detect. **2** tr. thrust or rub one's nose against or into. **3** intr. (usu. foll. by about, around, etc.) pry or search. **4 a** intr. make one's way cautiously forward. **b** tr. make (one's or its way). □ **as plain as the nose on your face** easily seen or perceived. **by a nose** by a very narrow margin (won the race by a nose). **get up a person's nose** slang annoy a person. **keep one's nose clean** slang stay out of trouble, behave properly. **keep one's nose to the grindstone** see GRINDSTONE. **on the nose 1** N. Amer. slang precisely. **2** Austral. slang annoying. **put a person's nose out of joint** colloq. embarrass, disconcert, frustrate, or supplant a person. **rub a person's nose in it** see RUB. **turn up one's nose** (usu. foll. by at) colloq. show disdain. **under a person's nose** colloq. right before a person. **with one's nose in the air** haughtily. [Old English] □ **nosed** adj. (also in comb.). **noseless** adj.

nosebag n. a bag containing fodder, hung on a horse's head.

noseband n. the lower band of a bridle, passing over the horse's nose. ▷ BRIDLE

nosebleed n. an instance of bleeding from the nose.

nose-cone n. the cone-shaped nose of a rocket etc. ▷ BALLISTIC MISSILE, ROCKET

nosedive ● n. **1** a steep downward plunge by an aeroplane. **2** a sudden plunge or drop. ● v.intr. make a nosedive.

nose flute n. ▶ a musical instrument blown with the nose in Fiji etc.

nosegay n. a bunch of flowers, esp. a sweet-scented posy. [based on (now dialect) gay 'ornament']

nosering n. a ring fixed in the nose of an animal for leading it, or of a person for ornament.

nose wheel n. a landing wheel under the nose of an aircraft.

nosey var. of NOSY.

nosh slang ● v.tr. & intr. **1** eat or drink. **2** N. Amer. eat between meals. ● n. **1** food or drink. **2** N. Amer. a snack. [Yiddish]

no-show n. a person who has reserved a seat etc. but neither uses it nor cancels the reservation.

nosh-up n. Brit. a large meal.

nostalgia n. **1** sentimental yearning for a period of the past; regretful or wistful memory of an earlier time. **2** a thing or things which evoke a former era. **3** severe homesickness. [based on Greek nostos 'return home'] □ **nostalgic** adj. **nostalgically** adv.

nostril n. either of two external openings of the nasal cavity in vertebrates. [Old English, from nosu 'nose' + thyr(e)l 'hole']

nostrum n. **1** a quack remedy, a patent medicine. **2** a pet scheme, esp. for political or social reform. [Latin, literally 'our thing', used in sense 'of our own make']

nosy adj. (also **nosey**) (**nosier**, **nosiest**) colloq. inquisitive, prying. □ **nosily** adv. **nosiness** n.

Nosy Parker n. esp. Brit. colloq. a busybody.

not adv. expressing negation, esp.: **1** (also **n't** joined to a preceding verb) following an auxiliary verb or be or (in a question) the subject of such a verb (I cannot say; she isn't there; didn't you tell me?; am I not right?; aren't we smart?). **2** used elliptically for a negative sentence or verb or phrase (Is she coming? — I hope not; Do you want it? — Certainly not!). **3** used to express the negative of other words (not a single one was left; Are they pleased? — Not they; he is not my cousin, but my nephew). **4** colloq. following and emphatically negating an affirmative statement (great party … not!). □ **not at all** (in polite reply to thanks) there is no need for thanks. **not half** see HALF. **not least** with considerable importance, notably. **not quite 1** almost (am not quite there). **2** noticeably not (not quite proper). **not in the slightest** not at all. **not a thing** nothing at all. **not that** (foll. by clause) it is not to be inferred that (if he said so — not that he ever did — he lied). **not very** see VERY. [Middle English contraction of NOUGHT]

■ **Usage** The use of not with verbs other than auxiliaries or be is now archaic (e.g. I know not; fear not), except with participles and infinitives (e.g. not realizing her mistake; We asked them not to come).

nota bene /noh-tă ben-ay/ v.tr. (as imper.) observe what follows, take notice. [Latin, literally 'note well']

notability n. (pl. **-ies**) **1** the state of being notable (names of no historical notability). **2** a prominent person.

notable ● adj. worthy of note; remarkable, eminent. ● n. an eminent person. [from Latin notabilis] □ **notably** adv.

notarize v.tr. (also **-ise**) N. Amer. certify (a document) as a notary.

notary n. (pl. **-ies**) (in full **notary public**, pl. **notaries public**) a person authorized to perform certain legal formalities, esp. to draw up or certify contracts, deeds, etc. [from Latin notarius 'secretary'] □ **notarial** adj.

notate v.tr. write in notation.

NOSE FLUTE: FIJIAN BAMBOO NOSE FLUTE

blow-hole

finger hole

N

NOSE

The nose processes the air humans breathe. Hairs and mucus filter the air, while receptors in the olfactory epithelium send messages about smell to the brain via the olfactory bulb and nerve.

olfactory epithelium
frontal sinus
olfactory bulb
olfactory nerve
nasal bone
nasal cartilage
nasal conchae
nasal cavity
nostril
hard palate
upper lip
upper tooth
soft palate

CROSS-SECTION THROUGH THE HUMAN NOSE

NOTATION

Conventional musical notation is written on a five-line staff divided into bars. Notes indicate the duration and pitch of a sound; they can be arranged in order of pitch to form scales. Clefs fix the pitch of the notes; accidentals indicate brief changes in pitch. Rests specify the duration of a silence.

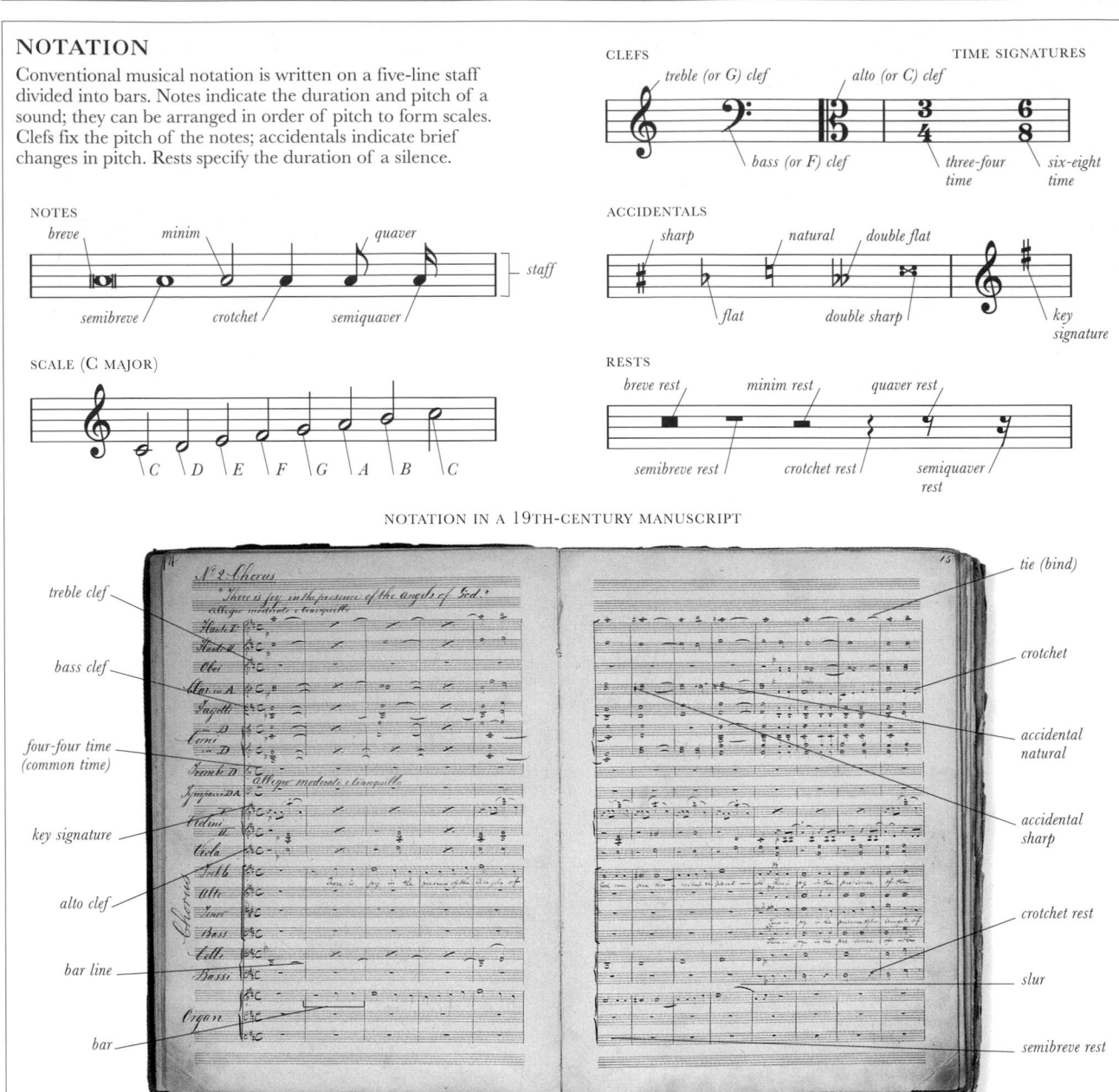

NOTATION IN A 19TH-CENTURY MANUSCRIPT

---

notation *n.* **1 a** ▲ the representation of numbers, quantities, pitch and duration etc. of musical notes, etc. by symbols. **b** any set of such symbols. **2** a set of symbols used to represent chess moves, dance steps, etc. **3** *US* **a** a note or annotation. **b** a record. [from Latin *notatio*, related to NOTE] □ **notational** *adj.*

notch ● *n.* **1** a V-shaped indentation on an edge or surface. **2** a nick made on a stick etc. in order to keep count. **3** *colloq.* a step or degree (*move up a notch*). **4** *N. Amer.* a deep narrow mountain pass. ● *v.tr.* **1** make notches in. **2** (foll. by *up*) record or score with or as with notches. **3** secure or insert by notches. [from Anglo-French *noche*] □ **notched** *adj.* **notcher** *n.* **notchy** *adj.* (**notchier, notchiest**)

note ● *n.* **1** a brief record as an aid to memory (often in *pl.*: *make notes*; *spoke without notes*). **2** an observation, usu. unwritten, of experiences etc. (*compare notes*). **3** a short or informal letter. **4** a formal diplomatic or parliamentary communication. **5** a short annotation or additional explanation in a book etc.

6 a *Brit.* = BANKNOTE (*a five-pound note*). **b** a written promise or notice of payment of various kinds. **7 a** notice, attention (*worthy of note*). **b** eminence (*a person of note*). **8 a** a written sign representing the pitch and duration of a musical sound. ▷ NOTATION. **b** a single musical tone of definite pitch. **c** a key of a piano etc. **9 a** a bird's song or call. **b** a single tone in this. **10** a quality or tone of speaking, expressing mood or attitude etc.; a hint or suggestion (*sound a note of warning*; *ended on a note of optimism*). ● *v.tr.* **1** observe, notice; give or draw attention to. **2** (often foll. by *down*) record as a thing to be remembered or observed. **3** (in *passive*; often foll. by *for*) be famous or well known (for a quality, activity, etc.) (*were noted for their generosity*). □ **hit** (or **strike**) **the right note** speak or act in exactly the right manner. **of note** important, distinguished (*a person of note*). **take note** (often foll. by *of*) observe; pay attention (to). [from Latin *nota* 'mark'] □ **noted** *adj.* (in sense 3 of *v.*). **noteless** *adj.*

notebook *n.* **1** a small book for making or taking notes. **2** a portable computer smaller than a laptop.

notecase *n. Brit.* a wallet for holding banknotes.

notelet *n.* a small folded sheet of paper for an informal letter.

notepad *n.* a pad of paper for writing notes on.

notepaper *n.* paper for writing letters.

noteworthy *adj.* worthy of attention; remarkable. □ **noteworthiness** *n.*

nothing ● *n.* **1** not anything (*nothing has been done*). **2** no thing (often foll. by compl.: *I see nothing that I want*). **3** a person or thing of no importance; a trivial event or remark. **4** non-existence; what does not exist. **5** (in calculations) no amount; nought (*a third of nothing is nothing*). ● *adv.* not at all, in no way (*helps us nothing*; *is nothing like enough*). □ **be nothing to 1** not concern. **2** not compare with. **be** (or **have**) **nothing to do with 1** have no connection with. **2** not be involved or associated with. **for nothing 1** at no cost; without payment. **2** to no purpose.

N

have nothing on 1 be naked. **2** have no engagements. **nothing doing** *colloq.* **1 a** there is no prospect of success or agreement. **b** I refuse. **2** nothing (is) happening. **nothing** (or **nothing else**) **for it** *Brit.* no alternative (*nothing for it but to pay up*). **nothing less than** at least (*nothing less than a disaster*). **nothing** (or **not much**) **to it** (or *Brit.* **in it**) **1** untrue or unimportant. **2** simple to do. **3** no (or little) advantage to be seen in one possibility over another. **think nothing of it** do not apologize or feel bound to show gratitude. [Old English]

nothingness *n.* **1** non-existence; the non-existent. **2** worthlessness, triviality.

notice ● *n.* **1** attention, observation (*it escaped my notice*). **2** a displayed sheet etc. bearing an announcement. **3 a** an intimation or warning, esp. a formal one (*give notice*). **b** a formal announcement or declaration of intention to end an agreement or leave employment at a specified time (*hand in one's notice; notice to quit*). **4** a short published review or comment about a new play, book, etc. ● *v.tr.* **1** (often foll. by *that, how,* etc. + clause) perceive, observe; take notice of. **2** remark upon; speak of. □ **at short** (or **a moment's**) **notice** with little warning. **take notice** (or **no notice**) show signs (or no signs) of interest. **take notice of 1** observe. **2** act upon. **under notice** served with a formal notice. [from Latin *notitia* 'being known']

noticeable *adj.* **1** easily seen or noticed; perceptible. **2** noteworthy. □ **noticeably** *adv.*

noticeboard *n. Brit.* a board for displaying notices.

notifiable *adj.* (of a disease, pest, etc.) that must be notified to the appropriate authorities.

notify *v.tr.* (**-ies, -ied**) **1** inform or give notice to (a person). **2** make known. [from Latin *notificare*] □ **notification** *n.*

notion *n.* **1 a** a concept or idea; a conception (*it was an absurd notion*). **b** an opinion (*has the notion that people are honest*). **c** a vague view or understanding (*have no notion what you mean*). **2** an inclination or intention (*has no notion of conforming*). [from Latin *notio* 'idea']

notional *adj.* hypothetical, imaginary. □ **notionally** *adv.*

notochord *n.* a cartilaginous skeletal rod supporting the body in all embryo and some adult chordate animals. [from Greek *nōton* 'back' + CHORD[2]]

notorious *adj.* well known, esp. unfavourably (*a notorious criminal; notorious for its climate*). [from medieval Latin *notorius*] □ **notoriety** *n.* **notoriously** *adv.*

notwithstanding ● *prep.* in spite of; without prevention by (*notwithstanding your objections; this fact notwithstanding*). ● *adv.* nevertheless. ● *conj.* (usu. foll. by *that* + clause) although. [Middle English]

nougat /noo-gah/ *n.* a sweet made from sugar or honey, nuts, and egg white. [from Provençal *nogat*]

nought *n.* **1** the digit 0; a cipher. **2** *poet.* or *archaic* (in certain phrases) nothing (cf. NAUGHT). [Old English]

noughts and crosses *n.pl.* esp. *Brit.* a game in which players seek to complete a row of three noughts or three crosses.

noun *n. Gram.* a word (other than a pronoun) or group of words used to name or identify any of a class of persons, places, or things (**common noun**), or a particular one of these (**proper noun**). [from Latin *nomen* 'name']

nourish *v.tr.* **1 a** sustain with food. **b** enrich; promote the development of (the soil etc.). **c** provide with intellectual or emotional sustenance or enrichment. **2** foster or cherish (a feeling etc.). [from Latin *nutrire*]

nourishing *adj.* (esp. of food) containing much nourishment; sustaining. □ **nourishingly** *adv.*

nourishment *n.* sustenance, food.

nous /nowss/ *n.* **1** *Brit. colloq.* common sense; gumption. **2** *Philos.* the mind or intellect. [Greek]

nouveau riche /noo-voh **reesh**/ *n.* (*pl.* **nouveaux riches** *pronunc.* same) a person who has recently acquired (usu. ostentatious) wealth. [French, literally 'new rich']

nouvelle cuisine /noo-vel/ *n.* a modern style of cookery avoiding heaviness and emphasizing presentation. [French, literally 'new cookery']

nouvelle vague /noo-vel **vagh**/ *n.* a new trend, esp. in French film-making of the early 1960s. [French, literally 'new wave']

Nov. *abbr.* November.

nova *n.* (*pl.* **novae** /-vee/ or **novas**) a star showing a sudden large increase of brightness and then subsiding. [Latin fem. of *novus* 'new', because originally thought to be a new star]

novel[1] *n.* **1** a fictitious prose story of book length. **2** (prec. by *the*) this type of literature. [from Italian *novella* (*storia*) 'new (story)']

novel[2] *adj.* of a new kind. [from Latin *novellus*] □ **novelly** *adv.*

novelette *n.* **1** a short novel. **2** esp. *Brit. derog.* a light romantic novel.

novelist *n.* a writer of novels. □ **novelistic** *adj.*

novella *n.* (*pl.* **novellas**) a short novel or narrative story. [Italian]

novelty *n.* (*pl.* **-ies**) **1 a** newness. **b** originality. **2 a** new or unusual thing or occurrence. **3** a small toy or decoration etc. of novel design. **4** (*attrib.*) having novelty (*novelty toys*). [from Old French *novelté*]

November *n.* the eleventh month of the year. [originally the ninth month of the Roman year: Latin, based on *novem* 'nine']

novena *n. RC Ch.* a devotion consisting of special prayers or services on nine successive days. [based on Latin *novem* 'nine']

novice *n.* **1 a** a probationary member of a religious order. **b** a new convert. **2** a beginner. **3** a horse, dog, etc. that has not won a major prize in a competition (also *attrib.*: *novice hurdle*). [from Latin *novicius*]

noviciate *n.* (also **novitiate**) **1** the period of being a novice. **2** a religious novice. **3** novices' quarters.

no-vote *n.* a vote in opposition to a proposal etc.

now ● *adv.* **1** at the present or mentioned time. **2** immediately (*I must go now*). **3** by this or that time (*it was now clear*). **4** under the present circumstances (*I cannot now agree*). **5** on this further occasion (*what do you want now?*). **6** in the immediate past (*just now*). **7** (esp. in a narrative or discourse) then, next (*the police now arrived; now to consider the next point*). **8** (without reference to time, giving various tones to a sentence) surely, I insist, I wonder, etc. (*now what do you mean by that?; oh come now!*). ● *conj.* (often foll. by *that* + clause) as a consequence of the fact (*now that I am older; now you mention it*). ● *n.* this time; the present (*should be there by now; has happened before now*). □ **as of now** from or at this time. **for now** until a later time (*goodbye for now*). **now and again** (or **then**) from time to time; intermittently. [Old English]

nowadays ● *adv.* at the present time or age; in these times. ● *n.* the present time.

nowhere ● *adv.* in or to no place. ● *pron.* no place. □ **come from nowhere** be suddenly evident or successful. **get nowhere** make or cause to make no progress. **in the middle of nowhere** *colloq.* remote from urban life. **nowhere near** not nearly. [Old English]

no-win *attrib.adj.* of or designating a situation in which success is impossible.

nowt *n. colloq.* or *dial.* nothing.

noxious *adj.* harmful, unwholesome. [based on Latin *noxa* 'harm'] □ **noxiousness** *n.*

nozzle *n.* a spout on a hose etc. from which a jet issues. ▷ AIRBRUSH, SPRAY-GUN. [based on NOSE]

Np *symb. Chem.* the element neptunium.

nr. *abbr.* near.

NRA *abbr.* (in the UK) National Rivers Authority.

NSPCC *abbr.* (in the UK) National Society for the Prevention of Cruelty to Children.

NSW *abbr.* New South Wales.

NT *abbr.* **1** New Testament. **2** Northern Territory (of Australia).

n't *adv.* (in *comb.*) = NOT 1 (usu. with *is, are, have, must,*

and the auxiliary verbs *can, do, should, would*: *isn't; mustn't*) (see also CAN'T, DON'T, WON'T).

nth see N[2].

nu *n.* the thirteenth letter of the Greek alphabet (N, v). [Greek]

nuance /**new**-ahnss/ ● *n.* a subtle shade of meaning, feeling, colour, etc. ● *v.tr.* give a nuance to. [French]

nub *n.* **1** the point or gist (of a matter or story). **2** a small lump, esp. of coal. **3** a stub; a small residue. □ **nubby** *adj.*

nubile *adj.* (of a woman) marriageable or sexually attractive. [from Latin *nubilis*] □ **nubility** *n.*

nuclear /**new**-kli-er/ *adj.* **1** of, relating to, or constituting a nucleus. **2** using nuclear energy (*nuclear reactor*). **3** having nuclear weapons.

nuclear bomb *n.* a bomb using the release of energy by nuclear fission or fusion or both.

nuclear disarmament *n.* the gradual or total reduction by a state of its nuclear weapons.

nuclear energy *n.* energy obtained by nuclear fission or fusion.

nuclear family *n.* a couple and their children.

nuclear fission *n.* ▼ a nuclear reaction in which a heavy nucleus splits spontaneously or on impact with another particle, with the release of energy.

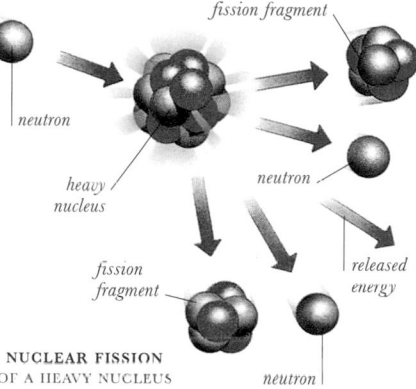

fission fragment
neutron
heavy nucleus
neutron
fission fragment
released energy

NUCLEAR FISSION
OF A HEAVY NUCLEUS

neutron

N

nuclear-free *adj.* free from nuclear weapons, power, etc.

nuclear fuel *n.* a substance that will sustain a fission chain reaction so that it can be used as a source of nuclear energy.

nuclear fusion *n.* ▼ a nuclear reaction in which atomic nuclei of low atomic number fuse to form a heavier nucleus with the release of energy.

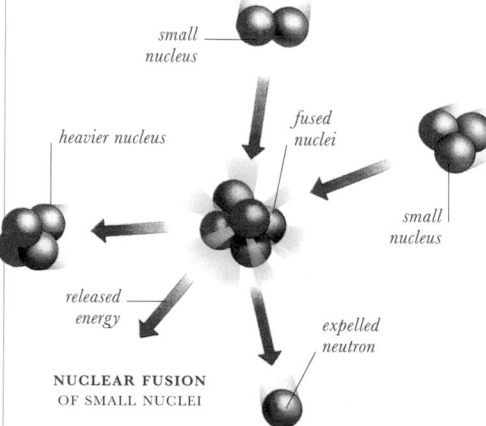

small nucleus
fused nuclei
heavier nucleus
small nucleus
released energy
expelled neutron

NUCLEAR FUSION
OF SMALL NUCLEI

nuclear magnetic resonance *n.* the absorption of electromagnetic radiation by a nucleus having a magnetic moment when in an external magnetic field, used mainly as an analytical technique and in body imaging for diagnosis.

NUCLEAR POWER

Nuclear power is produced through controlled nuclear fission inside the core of a reactor. The heat created by the fission of the fuel (usually uranium) is taken away by a coolant and used to turn water into steam. The steam powers a turbine that runs an electricity generator.

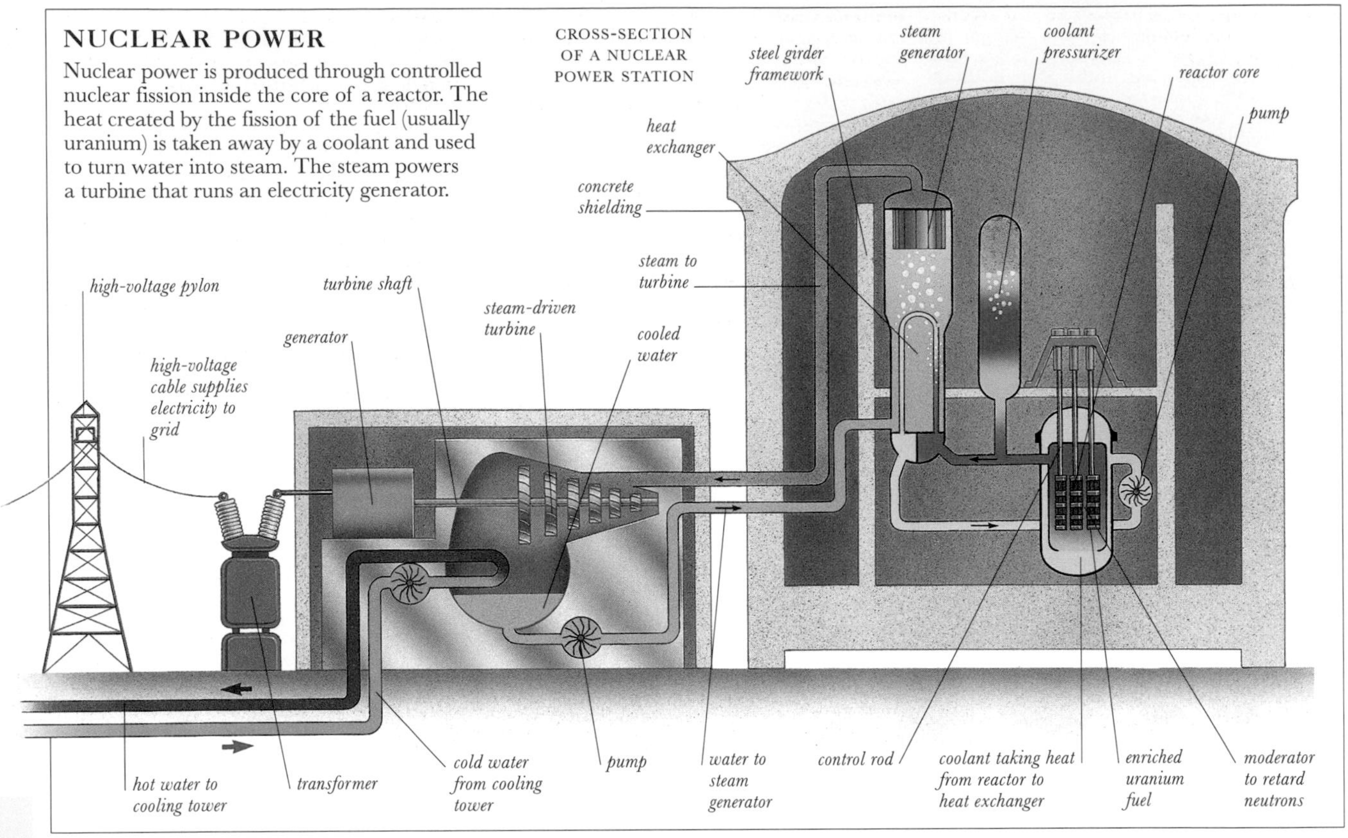

CROSS-SECTION OF A NUCLEAR POWER STATION

steam generator

coolant pressurizer

reactor core

steel girder framework

pump

heat exchanger

concrete shielding

steam to turbine

high-voltage pylon

turbine shaft

high-voltage cable supplies electricity to grid

generator

steam-driven turbine

cooled water

hot water to cooling tower

transformer

cold water from cooling tower

pump

water to steam generator

control rod

coolant taking heat from reactor to heat exchanger

enriched uranium fuel

moderator to retard neutrons

N

nuclear physics *n.* the physics of atomic nuclei and their interactions.

nuclear power *n.* **1** ▲ power generated by a nuclear reactor. **2** a country that has nuclear weapons. □ **nuclear-powered** *adj.*

nuclear reactor see REACTOR *n.* 2.

nuclear umbrella *n.* supposed protection afforded by an alliance with a country possessing nuclear weapons.

nuclear warfare *n.* warfare in which nuclear weapons are used.

nuclear waste *n.* radioactive waste material.

nuclear weapon *n.* a missile, bomb, etc., using the release of energy by nuclear fission or fusion or both.

nuclear winter *n.* a period of abnormal cold and darkness predicted to follow a nuclear war, caused by a layer of smoke and dust in the atmosphere blocking the Sun's rays.

nuclease /**new**-kli-ayz/ *n.* any enzyme that catalyses the breakdown of nucleic acids.

nucleate ● *adj.* having a nucleus. ● *v.intr. & tr.* form or form into a nucleus. □ **nucleation** *n.*

nuclei *pl.* of NUCLEUS.

nucleic acid *n.* either of two complex organic substances (DNA and RNA), whose molecules consists of many nucleotides linked in a long chain, and present in all living cells. ▷ DNA

nucleo- *comb. form* nucleus; nucleic acid.

nucleolus *n.* (*pl.* **nucleoli** /-ly/) *Biol.* a small dense spherical structure in the nucleus of a cell. [Late Latin, literally 'little kernel'] □ **nucleolar** *adj.*

nucleon *n. Physics* a proton or neutron.

nucleoside *n. Biochem.* an organic compound consisting of a purine or pyrimidine base linked to a sugar.

nucleotide *n. Biochem.* an organic compound consisting of a nucleoside linked to a phosphate group.

nucleus *n.* (*pl.* **nuclei** /**new**-kli-I/) **1 a** the central part or thing round which others are collected. ▷ ATOM. **b** the kernel of an aggregate or mass. **2** an initial part meant to receive additions. **3** *Astron.* the solid part of a comet's head. **4** *Physics* ▼ the central core of an atom that contains most of its mass. **5** *Biol.* a large dense organelle in a eukaryotic cell, containing the genetic material. ▷ CELL. [Latin, literally 'kernel, inner part']

nude ● *adj.* naked, bare, unclothed. ● *n.* **1** a painting, sculpture, photograph, etc. of a nude human figure. **2** a nude person. **3** (prec. by *the*) **a** an unclothed state. **b** the representation of an undraped human figure as a genre in art. [from Latin *nudus*]

nudge ● *v.tr.* **1** prod gently with the elbow to attract attention. **2** push gently or gradually. **3** give a gentle reminder or encouragement to (a person). ● *n.* the act or an instance of nudging; a gentle push. [17th-century coinage]

nudist *n.* a person who advocates or practises going unclothed. □ **nudism** *n.*

nudity *n.* the state of being nude; nakedness.

nugatory *adj.* **1** futile, trifling. **2** inoperative; not valid. [based on Latin *nugae* 'jests']

nugget *n.* **1 a** ▶ a lump of gold, platinum, etc., as found in the earth. **b** a lump of anything compared to this. **2** something valuable for its size (often abstract in sense: *a little nugget of information*).

nuisance *n.* **1** a person, thing, or circumstance causing trouble or annoyance. **2** anything harmful or offensive to the community or a member of it and for which a legal remedy exists. [based on Latin *nocēre* 'to hurt']

NUGGET: GOLD NUGGET

NUCLEUS

A nucleus consists of particles called protons and neutrons, which are in turn made up of quarks held together by particles called gluons.

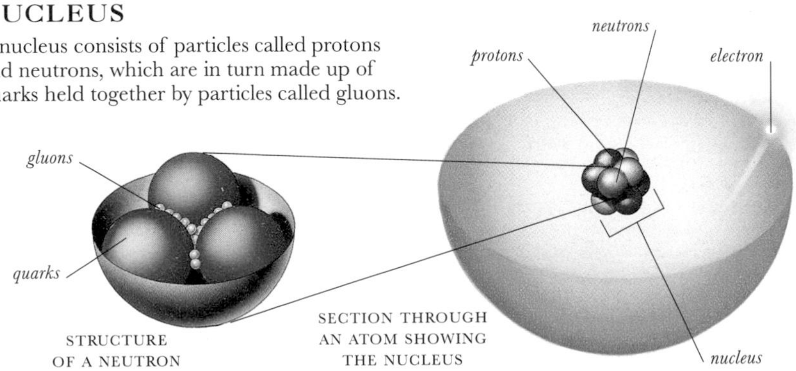

neutrons

protons

electron

gluons

quarks

STRUCTURE OF A NEUTRON

SECTION THROUGH AN ATOM SHOWING THE NUCLEUS

nucleus

nuisance value n. an advantage resulting from the capacity to harass or frustrate.

nuke colloq. ● n. a nuclear weapon. ● v.tr. bomb or destroy with nuclear weapons.

null ● adj. **1** (esp. **null and void**) invalid; not binding. **2** non-existent; amounting to nothing. **3** having or associated with the value zero. **4** Computing **a** empty; having no elements (null list). **b** all the elements of which are zeros (null matrix). **5** without character or expression. ● n. a dummy letter in a cipher. [from Latin nullus 'none'] □ **nullity** n. (pl. **-ies**).

null hypothesis n. a hypothesis suggesting that the difference between statistical samples does not imply a difference between populations.

nullify v.tr. (**-ies**, **-ied**) make null; neutralize, invalidate, cancel. □ **nullification** n. **nullifier** n.

numb ● adj. (often foll. by with) deprived of feeling (numb with cold). ● v.tr. **1** make numb. **2** stupefy, paralyse. [Middle English nome(n) 'taken'] □ **numbly** adv. **numbness** n.

number ● n. **1 a** an arithmetical value representing a particular quantity. **b** a word, symbol, or figure representing this. **c** an arithmetical value showing position in a series (registration number). **2** (often foll. by of) the total count or aggregate (the number of accidents has decreased). **3 a** numerical reckoning (the laws of number). **b** (in pl.) arithmetic (not good at numbers). **4 a** (in sing. or pl.) a quantity or amount (a large number of people). **b** (**a number of**) several (of), some (of). **c** (in pl.) numerical preponderance (force of numbers). **5 a** a person or thing having a place in a series, esp. a single issue of a magazine, an item in a programme, etc. **b** a song, dance, musical item, etc. **6** company, collection, group (among our number). **7** Gram. **a** the classification of words by their singular or plural forms. **b** a particular form so classified. **8** colloq. a person or thing regarded familiarly (usu. qualified in some way: an attractive little number). ● v.tr. **1** include (I number you among my friends). **2** assign a number or numbers to. **3** have or amount to (a specified number). **4 a** count. **b** comprise (numbering forty thousand men). □ **any number of** any particular whole quantity of. **2** colloq. a large unspecified number of. **one's days are numbered** one does not have long to live. **have a person's number** colloq. understand a person's real motives, character, etc. **one's number is up** colloq. one is finished or doomed to die. **without number** innumerable. [from Latin numerus (n.), numerare (v.)]

■ **Usage** In sense 4b of the noun, a number of is normally used with a plural verb, e.g. A number of problems remain.

number cruncher n. Computing & Math. slang a machine capable of complex calculations etc. □ **number crunching** n.

numberless adj. innumerable.

number one colloq. ● n. oneself (take care of number one). ● adj. most important (the number one priority).

number plate n. a plate on a vehicle displaying its registration number.

numbers game n. **1** usu. derog. action involving only arithmetical work. **2** a comparison, contest, etc., regarded merely in terms of numerical statistics.

number two n. a second in command.

numbskull var. of NUMSKULL.

numeral ● n. a word, figure, or group of figures denoting a number. ● adj. of or denoting a number. [from Late Latin numeralis]

numerate adj. acquainted with the basic principles of mathematics. [based on Latin numerus 'number'] □ **numeracy** n.

numeration n. **1** a method or process of numbering or computing. **2** the expression in words of a number written in figures.

numerator n. the number above the line in a vulgar fraction showing how many of the parts indicated by the denominator are taken (e.g. 2 in ⅔).

numerical adj. (also **numeric**) of or relating to a number or numbers. [from medieval Latin numericus] □ **numerically** adv.

numerology n. the study of the supposed occult significance of numbers. □ **numerological** adj. **numerologist** n.

numerous adj. **1** (with pl.) great in number. **2** consisting of many. [from Latin numerosus] □ **numerously** adv. **numerousness** n.

numinous adj. **1** indicating the presence of a divinity. **2** spiritual. **3** awe-inspiring. [based on Latin numen 'deity']

numismatic adj. of or relating to coins or medals. [based on Greek nomisma -atos 'current coin'] □ **numismatically** adv.

numismatics n. the study of coins or medals. □ **numismatist** n.

numskull n. (also **numbskull**) a stupid or foolish person.

nun n. a member of a community of women living apart under religious vows. [from ecclesiastical Latin nonna, fem. of nonnus 'monk'] □ **nunlike** adj. **nunnish** adj.

nunciature /nun-shă-tewr/ n. RC Ch. the office or tenure of a nuncio. [from Italian nunziatura]

nuncio /nun-si-oh/ n. (pl. **-os**) RC Ch. a papal ambassador. [Italian]

nunnery n. (pl. **-ies**) a religious house of nuns; a convent.

nuptial ● adj. of or relating to marriage or weddings. ● n. (usu. in pl.) a wedding. [based on Latin nuptiae 'wedding']

nurd var. of NERD.

nurse ● n. **1** a person trained to care for the sick or infirm. **2** (formerly) a person employed or trained to take charge of young children. ● v. **1 a** intr. work as a nurse. **b** tr. attend to (a sick person). **c** tr. give medical attention to (an illness or injury). **2** tr. & intr. feed or be fed at the breast. **3** tr. esp. Brit. hold or treat carefully or caressingly. **4** tr. **a** foster; promote the development of. **b** harbour (a grievance etc.). [based on Latin nutrire 'to nourish']

nursemaid n. **1** a woman in charge of a child or children. **2** a person who watches over or guides another carefully.

nursery n. (pl. **-ies**) **1 a** a room or place equipped for young children. **b** = DAY NURSERY. **2** a place where plants etc., are reared for sale or transplantation.

nurseryman n. (pl. **-men**) an owner of or worker in a plant nursery.

nursery nurse n. Brit. a person trained to take charge of babies and young children.

nursery rhyme n. a simple traditional song or story in rhyme for children.

nursery school n. a school for children between the ages of usu. three and five.

nursery slopes n.pl. Brit. Skiing gentle slopes suitable for beginners.

nursery stakes n.pl. Brit. a race for two-year-old horses.

nursing n. **1** the practice or profession of caring for the sick as a nurse. **2** (attrib.) concerned with or suitable for nursing the sick or elderly etc.

nursing officer n. Brit. a senior nurse.

nursling n. an infant that is being suckled.

nurture ● n. **1** the process of bringing up; fostering care. **2** nourishment. **3** sociological factors as a determinant of personality. ● v.tr. **1** bring up; rear. **2** nourish. [from Old French nour(e)ture] □ **nurturer** n.

nut ● n. **1 a** ▼ a fruit consisting of a hard or tough shell around an edible kernel. **b** this kernel. **2** a pod containing hard seeds. **3** a small usu. square or hexagonal flat piece of metal or other material with a threaded hole through it for screwing on the end of a bolt to secure it. **4** slang a person's head. **5** slang **a** a crazy or eccentric person. **b** an obsessive enthusiast (a health-food nut). **6** a small lump of coal, butter, etc. **7** (in pl.) coarse slang the testicles. ● v.tr. (**nutted, nutting**) slang butt with the head. □ **do one's nut** Brit. slang be extremely angry or agitated. **for nuts** Brit. colloq. even tolerably well (cannot sing for nuts). **nuts and bolts** colloq. the practical details. **off one's nut** slang crazy. [Old English] □ **nutlike** adj.

nutation n. the act or an instance of nodding.

nut brown ● n. a dark brown colour. ● adj. (hyphenated when attrib.) of this colour.

nutcase n. slang a crazy or foolish person.

nutcracker n. (usu. in pl.) a device for cracking nuts.

N

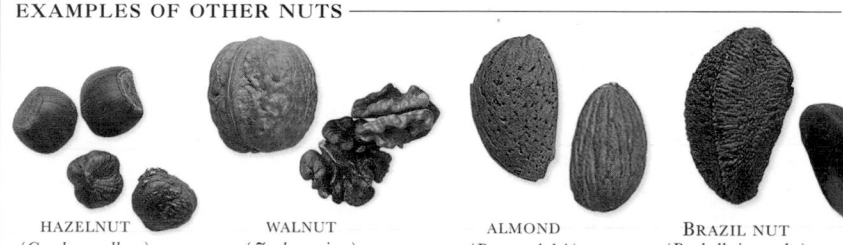

NUT

In strict botanical terms, a nut is a dry fruit with a hard non-splitting pericarp (shell) surrounding usually only one seed. In common usage, the term is widely applied to any dry fruit that has a hard shell surrounding an edible kernel.

remains of stigma

remains of style

embryo

pericarp

kernel (seed)

woody pericarp

SWEET CHESTNUT (*Castanea sativa*)

testa

EXAMPLES OF OTHER NUTS

HAZELNUT (*Corylus avellana*)

WALNUT (*Juglans nigra*)

ALMOND (*Prunus dulcis*)

BRAZIL NUT (*Bertholletia excelsa*)

nut cutlet *n. Brit.* a cutlet-shaped portion of meat-substitute, made from nuts etc.

nuthatch *n.* ◄ any small songbird of the genus *Sitta* and family Sittidae, climbing up and down tree trunks and feeding on nuts etc. [hatch: related to HACK[1], from the bird's method of pecking at nuts in a crevice]

NUTHATCH:
EURASIAN NUTHATCH
(*Sitta europaea*)

nuthouse *n. slang* a mental home or hospital.

nutmeg *n.* **1** an evergreen tree, *Myristica fragrans*, native to the Moluccas, yielding a hard aromatic spheroidal seed. **2** the seed of this grated and used as a spice. [based on Latin *nux* 'nut' + Late Latin *muscus* 'musk']

nut oil *n.* an oil obtained from hazelnuts and walnuts and used in paints and varnishes.

nutria *n.* the skin or fur of a coypu. [Spanish, literally 'otter']

nutrient ● *n.* any substance that provides essential nourishment for the maintenance of life. ● *adj.* serving as or providing nourishment. [from Latin *nutrient-* 'nourishing']

nutriment *n.* **1** nourishing food. **2** an intellectual or artistic etc. nourishment or stimulus. [from Latin *nutrimentum*] □ **nutrimental** *adj.*

nutrition *n.* **1 a** the process of providing or receiving nourishing substances. **b** food, nourishment.

2 the study of nutrients and nutrition. [from Late Latin *nutritio*] □ **nutritional** *adj.* **nutritionally** *adv.* **nutritionist** *n.*

nutritious *adj.* efficient as food; nourishing. □ **nutritiously** *adv.*

nutritive *adj.* **1** of or concerned in nutrition. **2** serving as nutritious food.

nuts *colloq.* ● *predic.adj.* crazy, mad, eccentric. ● *int.* an expression of contempt (*nuts to you*). □ **be nuts about** (or *Brit.* **on**) be enthusiastic about or very fond of.

nutshell *n.* the hard exterior covering of a nut. □ **in a nutshell** in a few words.

nutter *n. Brit. slang* a crazy or eccentric person.

nutty *adj.* (**nuttier**, **nuttiest**) **1 a** full of nuts. **b** tasting like nuts. **2** *slang* crazy, mad, eccentric. □ **nuttiness** *n.*

nux vomica *n.* **1** ▼ a southern Asian tree, *Strychnos nux-vomica*, with a poisonous fruit. **2** ▼ the seeds of this tree, containing strychnine. [medieval Latin, based on *nux* 'nut' + *vomere* 'to vomit']

oval leaves

seeds

NUX VOMICA
(*Strychnos nux-vomica*)

nuzzle *v.* **1** *tr.* prod or rub gently with the nose. **2** *intr.* (foll. by *into*, *against*, *up to*) press the nose gently. **3** *tr.* (also *refl.*) nestle; lie snug. [Middle English, based on NOSE]

NVQ *abbr.* (in the UK) National Vocation Qualification.

NW *abbr.* **1** north-west. **2** north-western.

nyctalopia *n. Med.* inability to see in dim light or at night. [from Greek *nuktalōps*]

nylon *n.* **1** any of various synthetic polyamide fibres having a protein-like structure, with tough, lightweight, elastic properties. ▷ ROPE. **2** a nylon fabric. **3** (in *pl.*) stockings made of nylon. [invented word]

nymph *n.* **1** any of various mythological semi-divine spirits regarded as maidens and associated with aspects of nature, esp. rivers and woods. **2** *poet.* a beautiful young woman. **3** ▼ an immature form of an insect that does not undergo complete metamorphosis. [from Greek *numphē*] □ **nymphal** *adj.*

NYMPH:
DAMSELFLY NYMPH

nympho *n.* (*pl.* **-os**) *colloq.* a nymphomaniac.

nymphomania *n.* excessive sexual desire in a woman. □ **nymphomaniac** *n. & adj.*

nystagmus *n.* rapid involuntary movements of the eyes. □ **nystagmic** *adj.* [Greek *nustagmos* 'nodding, drowiness' from *nustazō* 'nod, be sleepy']

NZ *abbr.* New Zealand.

N

O¹ n. (also **o**) (pl. **Os** or **O's**) **1** the fifteenth letter of the alphabet. **2** (**0**) nought, zero. **3** a human blood type.

O² symb. Chem. the element oxygen.

O³ int. **1** var. of OH¹. **2** prefixed to a name in the vocative (*O God*). [a natural exclamation]

O' prefix of Irish patronymic names (*O'Connor*). [Irish ó, ua, 'descendant']

o' prep. of, on (esp. in phrs.: *o'clock*; *will-o'-the-wisp*).

-o suffix forming usu. slang or colloq. variants or derivatives (*beano*; *wino*).

oaf n. (pl. **oafs**) **1** an awkward lout. **2** a stupid person. [originally in sense 'elf's child': from Old Norse *álfr* 'elf'] □ **oafish** adj. **oafishly** adv. **oafishness** n.

oak n. **1** (also **oak tree**) ▼ any tree of the genus *Quercus* usu. having lobed leaves and bearing acorns. ▷ DECIDUOUS. **2** the durable wood of this tree, used esp. for furniture and in building. ▷ WOOD. **3** (attrib.) made of oak (*oak table*). **4** (**the Oaks**) (treated as sing.) an annual race at Epsom for three-year-old fillies. [Old English] □ **oaken** adj.

acorn

OAK: WHITE OAK
(*Quercus alba*)

lobed leaves

oak-apple n. ◄ a spongy round gall found on oak trees, formed by the gall wasp *Biorhiza pallida*.

OAK-APPLE

oakum n. a loose fibre obtained by picking old rope to pieces and used esp. in caulking. [Old English *ǣcumbe* 'off-combings']

OAP abbr. Brit. old-age pensioner.

oar n. **1** a pole with a blade used for rowing or steering a boat by leverage against the water. ▷ ROW. **2** a rower. □ **put** (or **stick**) **one's oar in** interfere, meddle. [Old English] □ **oared** adj. (also in comb.).

oarsman n. (pl. **-men**; fem. **oarswoman**, pl. **-women**) a rower. □ **oarsmanship** n.

oasis n. (pl. **oases**) **1** a fertile spot in a desert, where water is found. **2** an area or period of calm in the midst of turbulence. [from Greek]

oast n. a kiln for drying hops. [Old English]

oast house n. a building containing an oast.

oat n. **1 a** a cereal plant, *Avena sativa*, cultivated in cool climates. **b** (in pl.) the grain yielded by this, used as food. ▷ GRAIN. **2** any related grass, esp. the wild oat, *A. fatua*. **3** (in pl.) slang sexual gratification. □ **off one's oats** colloq. lacking an appetite. [Old English] □ **oaty** adj.

oatcake n. a thin unleavened biscuit-like food made of oatmeal, common in Scotland and northern England.

oath n. (pl. **oaths**) **1** a solemn declaration or undertaking (often naming God). **2** a statement or promise contained in an oath (*oath of allegiance*). **3** a profane or blasphemous utterance; a curse. □ **under** (or *Brit.* **on**) **oath** having sworn a solemn oath. [Old English]

oatmeal ● n. **1** meal made from ground oats used esp. in porridge and oatcakes. **2** a greyish-fawn colour flecked with brown. ● adj. of this colour.

ob. abbr. he or she died. [Latin *obiit*]

obbligato n. (pl. **-os**) Mus. an accompaniment, usu. special and unusual in effect, forming an integral part of a composition. [Italian, literally 'obligatory']

obdurate adj. **1** stubborn. **2** hardened against influence. [from Latin *obduratus* 'hardened'] □ **obduracy** n. **obdurately** adv.

OBE abbr. (in the UK) Officer of the Order of the British Empire.

obedient adj. **1** obeying or ready to obey. **2** (often foll. by *to*) submissive to another's will. [from Latin *obedient-* 'obeying'] □ **obedience** n. **obediently** adv.

obeisance n. **1** a bow, curtsy, or other respectful or submissive gesture (*make an obeisance*). **2** homage. [from Old French *obeissance*]

obeli pl. of OBELUS.

obelisk n. **1** ▶ a tapering usu. four-sided stone pillar set up as a monument or landmark etc. **2** = OBELUS. [from Greek *obeliskos* 'little pointed pillar']

obelus /ob-ĕ-lŭs/ n. (pl. **obeli**) **1** a symbol (†) used as a reference mark. **2** a mark (– or ÷) used in ancient manuscripts to mark a word etc. [from Greek *obelos* 'spit, pointed pillar']

obese adj. very overweight; corpulent. [from Latin *obesus*] □ **obesity** n.

obey v. **1** tr. **a** carry out the command of. **b** carry out (a command) (*obey orders*). **2** intr. do what one is told to do. **3** tr. be actuated by (a force or impulse). [from Latin *obedire*]

obfuscate v.tr. **1** obscure or confuse (a mind, topic, etc.). **2** stupefy, bewilder. [based on Latin *obfuscatus* 'darkened'] □ **obfuscation** n. **obfuscatory** adj.

obit n. colloq. an obituary.

obituary n. (pl. **-ies**) **1** a notice of a death or deaths. **2** an account of the life of a deceased person. **3** (attrib.) of or serving as an obituary. [based on Latin *obitus* 'death'] □ **obituarial** adj.

object ● n. /ob-jekt/ **1** a material thing that can be seen or touched. **2** (foll. by *of*) a person or thing to which action or feeling is directed (*the object of attention*). **3** a thing sought or aimed at. **4** Gram. a noun or its equivalent governed by an active transitive verb or by a preposition. **5** Philos. a thing external to the thinking mind or subject. ● v. /ŏb-jekt/ **1** intr. (often foll. by *to* or *Brit.* against) express or feel opposition, disapproval, or reluctance. **2** tr. (foll. by *that* + clause) state as an objection. **3** tr. (foll. by *to*, *against*, or *that* + clause) adduce (a quality or fact) as contrary or damaging (to a case). □ **no object** not forming an important or restricting factor (*money no object*). [from medieval Latin *objectum* 'thing presented to the mind'] □ **objectless** adj. **objector** n.

objectify v.tr. (**-ies**, **-ied**) **1** make objective; express

in a concrete form. **2** present as an object of perception. □ **objectification** n.

objection n. **1** an expression or feeling of opposition or disapproval. **2** the act of objecting. **3** an adverse reason or statement.

objectionable adj. **1** open to objection. **2** unpleasant, offensive. □ **objectionableness** n. **objectionably** adv.

objective ● adj. **1** external to the mind; actually existing; real. **2** dealing with the world about us or exhibiting facts uncoloured by feelings or opinions. **3** Gram. (of a case or word) constructed as or appropriate to the object of a transitive verb or preposition. **4** aimed at (*objective point*). ● n. **1** something sought or aimed at. **2** Gram. the objective case. □ **objectively** adv. **objectivity** n. **objectivize** v.tr. (also **-ise**)

object lesson n. a striking practical example of some principle.

objet d'art /ob-zhay dar/ n. (pl. **objets d'art** pronunc. same) a small decorative object. [French, literally 'object of art']

objurgate v.tr. literary chide or scold. [based on Latin *jurgium* 'strife'] □ **objurgation** n.

oblate¹ n. a person dedicated to a monastic or religious life or work. [from medieval Latin *oblatus* 'offered']

oblate² adj. Geom. (of a spheroid) flattened at the poles. [from Latin *oblatus*, literally 'carried inversely']

oblation n. Relig. a thing offered to a divine being. □ **oblational** adj. **oblatory** adj.

obligate v.tr. **1** (usu. in passive; foll. by *to* + infin.) bind (a person) legally or morally. **2** US commit (assets) as security. [based on Latin *obligatus* 'obliged'] □ **obligator** n.

obligation n. **1** the constraining power of a law, precept, duty, contract, etc. **2** a duty; a burdensome task. **3** a binding agreement. **4 a** a kindness done or received (*repay an obligation*). **b** indebtedness for this (*be under an obligation*).

obligatory adj. **1** legally or morally binding. **2** compulsory. **3** constituting an obligation. □ **obligatorily** adv.

oblige v.tr. **1** (foll. by *to* + infin.) constrain, compel. **2** be binding on. **3 a** make indebted by conferring a favour. **b** (foll. by *with*, or *by* + verbal noun; also absol.) gratify (*oblige me by leaving*). **4** (in passive; foll. by *to*) be indebted. □ **much obliged** an expression of thanks. [from Latin *obligare*]

obliging adj. courteous, accommodating; ready to do a service or kindness. □ **obligingly** adv.

oblique ● adj. **1 a** slanting; declining from the vertical or horizontal. **b** diverging from a straight line or course. **2** not going straight to the point; indirect. **3** Geom. inclined at other than a right angle. **4** Gram. denoting any case other than the nominative or vocative. **5** Bot. (of a leaf) with unequal sides. ● n. Brit. an oblique stroke (/). [from Latin *obliquus*] □ **obliquely** adv. **obliqueness** n. **obliquity** n.

obliterate v.tr. blot out; destroy, leave no clear trace of. [based on Latin *obliteratus* 'erased'] □ **obliteration** n. **obliterative** adj. **obliterator** n.

oblivion n. **1** the state of forgetting or having forgotten. **2** the state of being forgotten (*return to oblivion*). [from Latin *oblivio*]

oblivious adj. **1** (often foll. by *of*) forgetful, unmindful. **2** (foll. by *to*, *of*) unaware or unconscious of. [from Latin *obliviosus*] □ **obliviously** adv. **obliviousness** n.

oblong ● adj. **1** rectangular with adjacent sides unequal. **2** greater in breadth than in height. ● n. an oblong figure or object. [from Latin *oblongus* 'longish']

obloquy n. **1** the state of being generally ill spoken of. **2** abuse, detraction. [from Late Latin *obloquium* 'contradiction']

obnoxious adj. offensive, objectionable, disliked. [originally in sense 'vulnerable (to harm)': from Latin *obnoxiosus*] □ **obnoxiously** adv. **obnoxiousness** n.

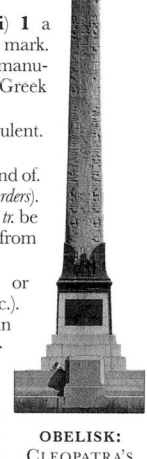

OBELISK:
CLEOPATRA'S
NEEDLE,
ENGLAND

O

OBSERVATORY

Astronomers use observatories to study the movement, position, and physical composition of celestial bodies. Observatories are built where viewing conditions are best: usually on high ground, in low-population areas with stable air and little cloud. The Keck telescopes (the largest in the world) are used in observatories on Mauna Kea, Hawaii. These telescopes have mirrors with a diameter of 10 m (33 ft).

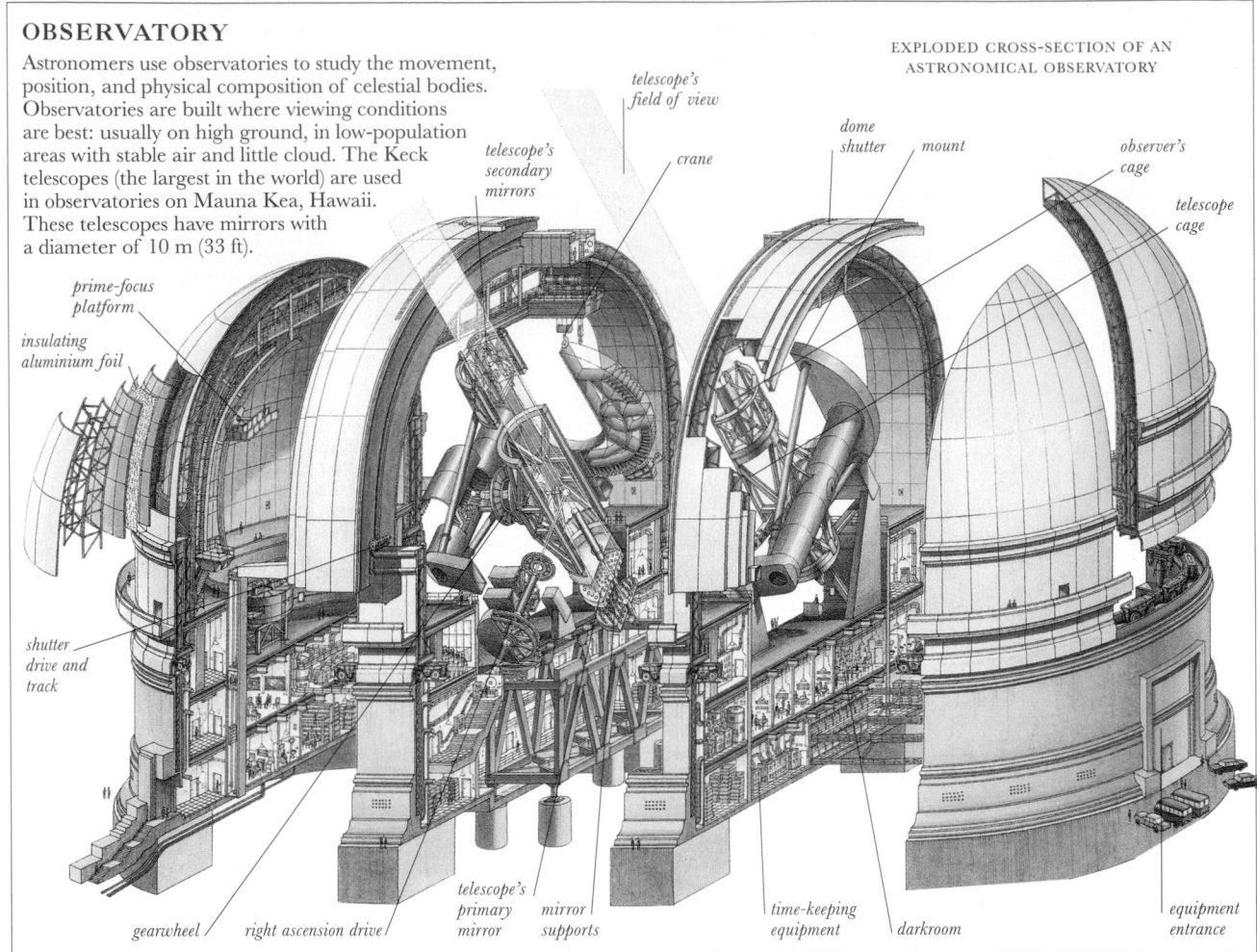

EXPLODED CROSS-SECTION OF AN ASTRONOMICAL OBSERVATORY

telescope's field of view · *telescope's secondary mirrors* · *crane* · *dome shutter* · *mount* · *observer's cage* · *telescope cage* · *prime-focus platform* · *insulating aluminium foil* · *shutter drive and track* · *gearwheel* · *right ascension drive* · *telescope's primary mirror* · *mirror supports* · *time-keeping equipment* · *darkroom* · *equipment entrance*

O

---

oboe *n.* a woodwind double-reed instrument of treble pitch and plaintive incisive tone. ▷ ORCHESTRA, WOODWIND. [from French *hautbois*, from *haut* 'high' + *bois* 'wood'] □ **oboist** *n.*

oboe d'amore *n.* an oboe wth a pear-shaped bell and mellow tone, pitched a minor third below a normal oboe, commonly used in baroque music. [Italian, literally 'oboe of love']

obscene *adj.* **1** offensively or repulsively indecent. **2** *colloq.* highly repugnant (*obscene wealth*). **3** *Brit. Law* (of a publication) tending to deprave or corrupt. [from Latin *obsc(a)enus* 'ill-omened, abominable'] □ **obscenely** *adv.*

obscenity *n.* (*pl.* **-ies**) **1** the state or quality of being obscene. **2** an obscene action, word, etc.

obscurantism *n.* opposition to knowledge and enlightenment. [based on Latin *obscurant-* 'darkening'] □ **obscurantist** *n. & adj.*

obscure ● *adj.* **1** not clearly expressed or easily understood. **2** vague, uncertain. **3** dark, dim. **4** indistinct; not clear. **5** hidden; remote from observation. **6 a** unnoticed. **b** (of a person) undistinguished, hardly known. ● *v.tr.* **1** make obscure, dark, indistinct, or unintelligible. **2** dim the glory of; outshine. **3** conceal from sight. [from Latin *obscurus* 'dark'] □ **obscuration** *n.* **obscurely** *adv.* **obscurity** *n.* (*pl.* **-ies**)

obsequies /ob-si-kwiz/ *n.pl.* **1** funeral rites. **2** a funeral. [pl. of obsolete *obsequy*, from medieval Latin *obsequiae*]

obsequious *adj.* servilely obedient or attentive. [based on Latin *obsequium* 'compliance'] □ **obsequiously** *adv.* **obsequiousness** *n.*

observance *n.* **1** the act or process of keeping or performing a law, duty, etc. **2** a customary rite.

observant *adj.* **1** acute or diligent in taking notice. **2** attentive in esp. religious observances (*an observant Jew*). [French, literally 'observing'] □ **observantly** *adv.*

observation *n.* **1** the act or an instance of noticing; the condition of being noticed. **2** perception; the faculty of taking notice. **3** a remark or statement. **4 a** the accurate watching and noting of a phenomenon etc. for the purpose of scientific investigation. **b** a result so obtained. □ **under observation** being watched or monitored. □ **observational** *adj.* **observationally** *adv.*

observation car *n.* esp. *N. Amer.* a carriage in a train built so as to afford good views.

observation post *n. Mil.* a post for watching the effect of artillery fire etc.

observatory *n.* (*pl.* **-ies**) ▲ a room or building for the observation of natural, esp. astronomical or meteorological, phenomena. [based on Latin *observare* 'to watch']

observe *v.tr.* **1** (often foll. by *that, how* + clause) perceive; become conscious of. **2** watch carefully. **3** *tr.* **a** follow or adhere to (a law, principle, etc.). **b** keep or adhere to (an appointed time). **c** maintain (silence). **d** duly perform (a rite). **e** celebrate (an anniversary). **4** examine and note (phenomena). **5** (often foll. by *that* + clause) say, esp. by way of comment. [from Latin *observare* 'to watch'] □ **observable** *adj.* **observably** *adv.*

observer *n.* **1** a person who observes. **2** an interested spectator. **3** a person who attends a conference etc. to note the proceedings but does not participate.

obsess *v.tr.* (often in *passive*) preoccupy, haunt; fill the mind of (a person) continually. [based on Latin *obsessus* 'besieged, possessed'] □ **obsessive** *adj. & n.* **obsessively** *adv.* **obsessiveness** *n.*

obsession *n.* **1** the act of obsessing or the state of being obsessed. **2** a persistent idea or thought dominating a person's mind. **3** a condition in which such ideas are present. □ **obsessional** *adj.* **obsessionally** *adv.*

obsidian *n.* ▼ a dark glassy volcanic rock formed by the rapid solidification of lava without crystallization. ▷ IGNEOUS. [from Latin *Obsius*, name (in Pliny) of the discoverer of a similar stone]

OBSIDIAN

obsolescent *adj.* becoming obsolete; going out of use or date. [from Latin *obsolescent-* 'falling into disuse'] □ **obsolescence** *n.*

obsolete *adj.* **1** disused, discarded, antiquated. **2** *Biol.* rudimentary. [from Latin *obsoletus*]

obstacle *n.* a person or thing that obstructs progress. [Middle English via Old French from Latin *obstaculum*]

obstacle race *n.* a race in which various obstacles have to be negotiated.

obstetric *adj.* (also **obstetrical**) of or relating to childbirth and associated processes. [based on Latin *obstetrix* 'midwife'] □ **obstetrically** *adv.* **obstetrician** *n.*

obstetrics *n.* the branch of medicine and surgery concerned with childbirth and midwifery.

obstinate *adj.* **1** stubborn, intractable. **2** firmly adhering to one's chosen course of action or opinion despite dissuasion. **3** not readily responding to treatment etc. [from Latin *obstinatus*] □ **obstinacy** *n.* **obstinately** *adv.*

obstreperous *adj.* **1** turbulent, unruly. **2** noisy, vociferous. [from Latin *obstreperus* 'clamorous'] □ **obstreperously** *adv.* **obstreperousness** *n.*

obstruct *v.tr.* **1** block up; make hard or impossible to pass along or through. **2** impede. [based on Latin *obstructus* 'blocked up']

obstruction *n.* **1** the act or an instance of blocking; the state of being blocked. **2** an obstacle or blockage. **3** the retarding of progress by deliberate delays, esp. of parliamentary business. **4** *Sport* the act of unlawfully obstructing another player. □ **obstructionism** *n.* (in sense 3). **obstructionist** *n.* (in sense 3).

obstructive ● *adj.* causing or intended to cause an obstruction. ● *n.* an obstructive person or thing. □ **obstructively** *adv.* **obstructiveness** *n.*

obtain *v.* **1** *tr.* acquire, secure; have granted to one. **2** *intr.* be prevalent or established or in vogue. [from Latin *obtinēre* 'to keep'] □ **obtainable** *adj.*

obtrude *v.* **1** *intr.* be or become obtrusive. **2** *tr.* (often foll. by *on*, *upon*) thrust forward (oneself, one's opinion, etc.) importunately. [from Latin *obtrudere*]

obtrusive *adj.* **1** unpleasantly or unduly noticeable. **2** obtruding oneself. [based on Latin *obtrusus* 'pushed out'] □ **obtrusively** *adv.* **obtrusiveness** *n.*

obtuse *adj.* **1** dull-witted; slow to understand. **2** blunt in form; not sharp-pointed or sharp-edged. **3** (of an angle) more than 90° and less than 180°. ▷ TRIANGLE. [from Latin *obtusus* 'blunted'] □ **obtusely** *adv.* **obtuseness** *n.*

obverse *n.* **1 a** the side of a coin or medal etc. bearing the head or principal design. **b** this design. **2** the front or proper or top side of a thing. **3** the counterpart of a fact or truth. [from Latin *obversus* 'turned towards'] □ **obversely** *adv.*

obviate *v.tr.* get round or do away with (a need, inconvenience, etc.). [based on Latin *obviatus* 'opposed'] □ **obviation** *n.*

obvious *adj.* easily seen, recognized, or understood. [from Latin *obvius* 'in the way'] □ **obviously** *adv.* **obviousness** *n.*

OC *abbr.* Officer Commanding.

ocarina *n.* ▼ a small egg-shaped ceramic (usu. terracotta) or metal wind instrument. [Italian, based on *oca* 'goose', from its shape]

OCARINA: 19TH-CENTURY
GERMAN OCARINA

occasion ● *n.* **1 a** a special or noteworthy event or happening. **b** the time or occurrence of this. **2** (often foll. by *for*, or *to* + infin.) a reason or justification (*there is no occasion to be angry*). **3** a juncture suitable for doing something. **4** an immediate but subordinate cause (*the assassination was the occasion of the war*). ● *v.tr.* **1** be the occasion or cause of. **2** (foll. by *to* + infin.) cause (a person or thing to do something). □ **on occasion** now and then; when the need arises. **rise to the occasion** produce the

necessary will, energy, etc. in unusually demanding circumstances. [from Latin *occasio* 'juncture, reason']

occasional *adj.* **1** happening irregularly and infrequently. **2** made or meant for, or associated with, a particular occasion (*occasional hymn*). □ **occasionally** *adv.*

occasional table *n.* a small table for infrequent and varied use.

Occident *n. poet.* or *literary* (prec. by *the*) **1** the West. **2** western Europe. **3** Europe, America, or both, as distinct from the Orient. **4** European or Western in contrast to oriental civilization. [from Latin *occidens occident-* 'setting, west']

occidental ● *adj.* **1** of the Occident, as distinct from oriental. **2** western. **3** of western Europe. **4** relating to European or Western (in contrast to oriental) civilization. ● *n.* (**Occidental**) a native or inhabitant of the Occident.

occiput *n.* the back of the head. ▷ SKULL. [Latin] □ **occipital** *adj.*

occlude *v.tr.* **1** stop up or close. **2** *Chem.* absorb and retain (gases or impurities). [from Latin *occludere*]

occluded front *n. Meteorol.* a front resulting from occlusion. ▷ WEATHER CHART

occlusion *n.* **1** the act or process of occluding. **2** *Meteorol.* a phenomenon in which the cold front of a depression overtakes a warm front. □ **occlusive** *adj.*

occult ● *adj.* **1** involving the supernatural; mystical. **2** esoteric. **3** beyond the range of ordinary knowledge. ● *v.tr. Astron.* (of a celestial body) conceal (an apparently smaller body) from view by passing or being in front of it. □ **the occult** occult phenomena generally. [from Latin *occultus* 'concealed'] □ **occultism** *n.* **occultist** *n.*

occupant *n.* **1** a person who occupies, resides in, or is in a place etc. **2** a person holding property, esp. land, in actual possession. [from Latin *occupant-* 'occupying'] □ **occupancy** *n.* (*pl.* **-ies**).

occupation *n.* **1** what occupies one; a means of passing one's time. **2** a person's temporary or regular employment. **3** the act of occupying or state of being occupied. **4 a** the act of taking or holding possession of (a country etc.) by military force. **b** the state or time of this. **5** tenure, occupancy.

occupational *adj.* **1** of or in the nature of an occupation or occupations. **2** (of a disease, hazard, etc.) rendered more likely by one's occupation.

occupational therapy *n.* mental or physical activity designed to assist recovery from disease or injury. □ **occupational therapist** *n.*

occupier *n. Brit.* a person residing in a property as its owner or tenant.

occupy *v.tr.* (**-ies**, **-ied**) **1** reside in; be the tenant of. **2** take up or fill (space or time or a place). **3** hold (a position or office). **4** take military possession of. **5** place oneself in (a building etc.) forcibly or without authority. **6** (usu. *refl.* or in *passive*; often foll. by *in*, *with*) keep busy or engaged. [from Latin *occupare* 'to seize']

occur *v.intr.* (**occurred**, **occurring**) **1** come into being as an event or process at or during some time. **2** exist or be encountered in some place or conditions. **3** (foll. by *to*; usu. foll. by *that* + clause) come into the mind of. [from Latin *occurrere* 'to go to meet, present itself']

occurrence *n.* **1** the act or an instance of occurring. **2** an incident or event.

ocean *n.* **1 ▲** a large expanse of sea, esp. each of the main areas called the Atlantic, Pacific, Indian, Arctic, and Southern Oceans. **2** (usu. prec. by *the*) the sea. **3** (often in *pl.*) a very large expanse or quantity of anything (*oceans of time*). [from Greek *ōkeanos* 'the great stream encircling the Earth's disc, the Atlantic'] □ **oceanic** *adj.*

oceanarium *n.* (*pl.* **oceanariums** or **oceanaria**) a large sea-water aquarium for keeping sea animals.

ocean-going *adj.* (of a ship) designed to cross oceans.

oceanography *n.* the study of the oceans. □ **oceanographer** *n.* **oceanographic** *adj.*

ocelot *n.* **1 ▼** a medium-sized cat, *Felis pardalis*, having a deep yellow or orange coat with black striped and spotted markings. **2** its fur. [from Aztec *ocelotl* 'jaguar']

OCEAN

Approximately 70 per cent of the Earth's surface is covered by oceans and seas. Owing to the action of tides, wind, and currents (flows of water that may travel thousands of kilometres), the world's oceans are constantly moving. Oceans support a huge diversity of life, with most species found in water 0–200 m (0–655 ft) deep (the sunlit zone).

OCEANS OF THE WORLD

Arctic Ocean
Pacific Ocean
Indian Ocean
Atlantic Ocean
Southern Ocean

OCELOT
(*Felis pardalis*)

och /okh/ *int. Sc. & Ir.* expressing surprise, regret, admiration, etc. [Gaelic & Irish]

oche /ok-i/ *n.* (also **hockey**) *Darts* the line behind which the players stand when throwing. [20th-century coinage]

ochre (*US* **ocher**) ● *n.* **1** a mineral of clay and ferric oxide, used as a pigment varying from light yellow to brown or red. **2** a pale brownish yellow. ● *adj.* of the colour of ochre, esp. pale brownish yellow. [from Greek *ōkhra* 'yellow ochre'] □ **ochreous** *adj.* **ochrous** *adj.*

o'clock *adv.* of the clock (used to specify the hour) (*6 o'clock*).

Oct. *abbr.* October.

oct. *abbr.* octavo.

oct- *comb. form* assim. form of OCTA-, OCTO- before a vowel.

octa- *comb. form* (also **oct-** before a vowel) eight. [Greek]

octad *n.* a group of eight. [from Greek *oktas -ados*]

octagon *n.* **1** ▶ a plane figure with eight sides and angles. **2** an object or building with this cross-section. [from Greek *octagōnos*] □ **octagonal** *adj.* **octagonally** *adv.*

octahedron *n.* (*pl.* **octahedra** or **octahedrons**) ▶ a solid figure contained by eight (esp. triangular) plane faces. [from Greek *oktaedron*] □ **octahedral** *adj.*

octal *adj.* reckoning or proceeding by eights (*octal scale*).

octane *n.* a colourless inflammable hydrocarbon of the alkane series.

octane number *n.* (also **octane rating**) a figure indicating the antiknock properties of a fuel.

octavalent *adj. Chem.* having a valency of eight.

octave *n.* **1** *Mus.* **a** a series of eight notes occupying the interval between (and including) two notes, one having twice or half the frequency of vibration of the other. **b** this interval. **c** each of the two notes at the extremes of this interval. **d** these two notes sounding together. **2** a group or stanza of eight lines. [from Latin *octava dies* 'eighth day' (reckoned inclusively)]

octavo *n.* (*pl.* **-os**) **1** a size of book or page given by folding a standard sheet three times to form eight leaves. **2** a book or sheet of this size. [from Latin *in octavo* 'in an eighth']

octet *n.* (also **octette**) **1** *Mus.* **a** a composition for eight voices or instruments. **b** the performers of such a piece. **2** a group of eight. **3** the first eight lines of a sonnet. **4** *Chem.* a stable group of eight electrons. [from Italian *ottetto*]

octo- *comb. form* (also **oct-** before a vowel) eight. [Latin & Greek]

October *n.* the tenth month of the year. [originally the eighth month of the Roman year: Latin, based on *octo* 'eight']

octogenarian *n.* a person from 80 to 89 years old. [from Latin *octogenarius* 'aged eighty']

octopod *n.* any cephalopod of the order Octopoda, with eight arms usu. having suckers, and a round saclike body, including octopuses. [from Greek *oktō* 'eight' + *pous podos* 'foot']

octopus *n.* (*pl.* **octopuses**) ▶ any cephalopod mollusc of the genus *Octopus*, *Eledone*, etc., having eight suckered arms, a soft saclike body, and strong beaklike jaws. ▷ CEPHALOPOD. [from Greek *oktō* 'eight' + *pous podos* 'foot']

octuple ● *adj.* eightfold. ● *n.* an eightfold amount. ● *v.tr. & intr.* multiply by eight. [from Latin *octuplus*]

ocular *adj.* of or connected with the eyes or sight; visual. [based on Latin *oculus* 'eye']

oculist *n.* a person who specializes in the medical treatment of eye disorders or defects. [from French *oculiste*] □ **oculistic** *adj.*

OD *slang* ● *n.* an overdose, esp. of a narcotic drug. ● *v.intr.* (**OD's**, **OD'd**, **OD'ing**) take an overdose.

odalisque *n. hist.* an Eastern female slave or concubine. [from Turkish *odalik*]

odd *adj.* **1** strange, queer, remarkable. **2** casual, occasional (*odd jobs*; *odd moments*). **3** not normally noticed or considered (*in some odd corner*). **4 a** (of numbers such as 3 and 5) not integrally divisible by two. **b** bearing such a number (*no parking on odd dates*). **5** left over when the rest have been distributed or divided into pairs (*have got an odd sock*). **6** detached from a set or series (*a few odd volumes*). **7** somewhat more than (*forty odd*). **8** by which a round number, given sum, etc., is exceeded (*we have 102 – what shall we do with the odd 2?*). [from Old Norse *odda-* in *oddamathr* 'third man, odd man'] □ **oddly** *adv.* **oddness** *n.*

oddball *n. colloq.* **1** an odd or eccentric person. **2** (*attrib.*) strange, bizarre.

odd bod *n. slang* a strange or eccentric person.

oddity *n.* (*pl.* **-ies**) **1** a strange person, thing, or occurrence. **2** a peculiar trait. **3** the state of being odd.

odd job *n.* a casual isolated piece of work.

odd man out *n.* a person or thing differing from all the others in a group in some respect.

oddment *n.* **1** an odd article; something left over. **2** (in *pl.*) miscellaneous articles.

odds *n.pl.* **1** the ratio between the amounts staked by the parties to a bet, based on the expected probability either way. **2** the balance of probability (*the odds are against it*). **3** the balance of advantage (*the odds are in your favour*). **4** an equalizing allowance to a weaker competitor. **5** a difference giving an advantage (*it makes no odds*). □ **at odds** (often foll. by *with*) in conflict or at variance. **over the odds** above a generally agreed price etc. **take odds** offer a bet with odds unfavourable to the other better. **what's the odds?** *colloq.* what does it matter?

odds and ends *n.pl.* (also *colloq.* **odds and sods**) miscellaneous articles or remnants.

odds-on ● *n.* a state when success is more likely than failure, esp. as indicated by the betting odds. ● *adj.* (of a chance) better than even; likely.

ode *n.* a lyric poem, usu. rhymed and in the form of an address, in varied or irregular metre. [from Greek *ōidē*]

odious *adj.* hateful, repulsive. □ **odiously** *adv.* **odiousness** *n.*

odium *n.* a general or widespread dislike or reprobation incurred by a person or associated with an action. [Latin, literally 'hatred']

cable-driven worm-gear

distance counter

tenths wheel

faceplate

ODOMETER: OVERHEAD VIEW OF A MOTORCYCLE ODOMETER

odometer *n.* (esp. *US*) ▲ an instrument for measuring the distance travelled by a wheeled vehicle. [based on Greek *hodos* 'way'] □ **odometry** *n.*

odontoid process *n.* a projection from the second cervical vertebra.

odor *US var.* of ODOUR.

odoriferous *adj.* diffusing a scent, esp. an agreeable one. [from Latin *odorifer* 'odour-bearing'] □ **odoriferously** *adv.*

odorous *adj.* **1** having a scent. **2** = ODORIFEROUS. □ **odorously** *adv.*

odour *n.* (*US* **odor**) **1** the property of a substance that has an effect on the nasal sense of smell. **2** a lasting quality or trace (*an odour of intolerance*). **3** regard, repute (*in bad odour*). [from Latin *odor* 'smell'] □ **odourless** *adj.* (in sense 1).

odyssey /od-i-si/ *n.* (*pl.* **-eys**) a series of wanderings; a long adventurous journey. [from Greek *Odusseia*, title of an epic poem attributed to Homer describing the adventures of Odysseus] □ **Odyssean** *adj.*

OECD *abbr.* Organization for Economic Cooperation and Development.

OED *abbr.* Oxford English Dictionary.

oedema /i-dee-mă/ *n.* (*US* **edema**) a condition characterized by an excess of watery fluid collecting in the cavities or tissues of the body. [from Greek *oidēma*] □ **oedematous** *adj.*

Oedipus complex /ee-di-pŭs/ *n. Psychol.* (according to Freud etc.) the complex of emotions aroused in a young (esp. male) child by a subconscious sexual desire for the parent of the opposite sex and wish to exclude the parent of the

---

OCTAGON

OCTAHEDRON

O

OCTOPUS

Unlike most other molluscs, the majority of octopuses have no shell (internal or external). They usually hide in rocky lairs by day and emerge to feed at night. The powerful suckers on an octopus's arms are used to hold captured prey (such as a crab). A poisonous secretion from the octopus's beak then paralyses the held creature. When threatened, octopuses can change colour to hide from, or confuse, attackers. Octopus species range in length from 5 cm (2 in.) to around 9 m (30 ft).

EXTERNAL FEATURES OF A LESSER OCTOPUS (*Eledone cirrhosa*)

single-lens eye

visceral hump

paired suckers

arm

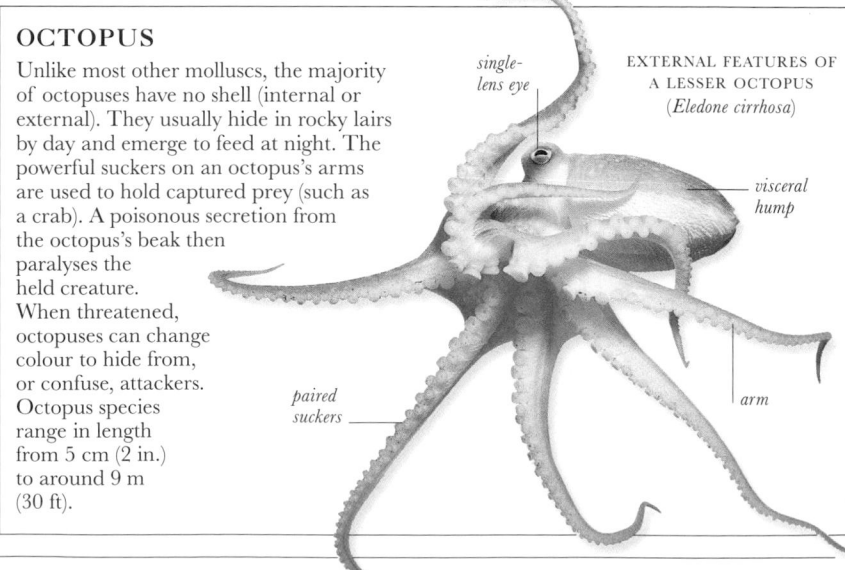

same sex. [from Greek *Oidipous*, legendary king of Thebes] □ **Oedipal** *adj.*

oenology /een-ol-ŏji/ *n.* (*US* **enology**) the study of wines. [based on Greek *oinos* 'wine'] □ **oenological** *adj.* **oenologist** *n.*

o'er /oh-er/ *adv. & prep. poet.* = OVER.

oesophagus /i-sof-ă-gŭs/ *n.* (*US* **esophagus**) (*pl.* **oesophagi** /-jy/ or **-guses**) ▼ the part of the alimentary canal from the throat to the stomach; the gullet. ▷ DIGESTION. [from Greek *oisophagos*] □ **oesophageal** /i-sof-ă-jeel/ *adj.*

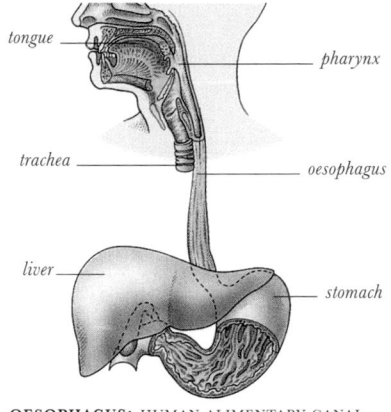

OESOPHAGUS: HUMAN ALIMENTARY CANAL
SHOWING THE OESOPHAGUS

oestradiol *n. Biochem.* a major oestrogen produced in the ovaries.

oestrogen /eess-trŏ-jĕn/ *n.* (*US* **estrogen**) **1** any of various steroid hormones developing and maintaining female characteristics of the body. **2** such a hormone produced artificially. □ **oestrogenic** *adj.* **oestrogenically** *adv.*

oestrus /eess-trŭs/ *n.* (also **oestrum**, *US* **estrus**, **estrum**) a recurring period of sexual receptivity in many female mammals. [from Greek *oistros* 'gadfly, frenzy'] □ **oestrous** *adj.*

oeuvre /ervr/ *n.* the works of an author, painter, composer, etc., esp. regarded collectively. [French, literally 'work']

of *prep.* connecting a noun (often a verbal noun) or pronoun with a preceding noun, adjective, adverb, or verb, expressing a wide range of relations broadly describable as follows: **1** origin, cause, or authorship (*paintings of Turner*; *people of Rome*). **2** the material or substance constituting or identifying a thing (*a house of cards*). **3** belonging, connection, or possession (*articles of clothing*; *tip of the iceberg*). **4** identity or close relation (*the city of Rome*; *a fool of a man*). **5** removal, separation, or privation (*north of the city*; *got rid of them*). **6** reference, direction, or respect (*beware of the dog*; *very good of you*; *the selling of goods*). **7** objective relation (*love of music*). **8** partition, classification, or inclusion (*no more of that*; *part of the story*). **9** description, quality, or condition (*the hour of prayer*; *a girl of ten*). **10** *N. Amer.* time in relation to the following hour (*a quarter of three*). □ **be of** possess intrinsically (*is of great interest*). **of all** designating the (nominally) least likely example (*you of all people!*). **of all the nerve** (or **cheek** etc.) an exclamation of indignation at a person's impudence etc. **of an evening** (or **morning** etc.) *colloq.* **1** on most evenings (or mornings etc.). **2** at some time in the evenings (or mornings etc.). **of late** recently. **of old** formerly; long ago. [Old English]

■ **Usage** *Of* should not be used instead of *have* in constructions such as *You should have asked*; *He couldn't have known*, although in rapid speech they sound the same.

Off. *abbr.* **1** Office. **2** Officer.

off ● *adv.* **1** away; at or to a distance (*drove off*; *is three miles off*). **2** out of position; not on or touching or

attached (*has come off*; *take your coat off*). **3** so as to be rid of (*sleep it off*). **4** so as to break continuity; discontinued (*take a day off*; *the game is off*). **5** not available as a choice (*chips are off*). **6** to the end; entirely (*finish off*; *pay off*). **7** situated as regards money etc. (*is badly off*). **8** off stage (*noises off*). **9** esp. *Brit.* (with preceding numeral) denoting a quantity produced or made at one time (esp. *one-off*). ● *prep.* **1 a** from; away or down or up from (*fell off the chair*). **b** not on (*was already off the pitch*). **2 a** (temporarily) relieved of or abstaining from (*off duty*). **b** not attracted by for the time being (*off their food*). **c** not achieving or doing one's best in (*off form*). **3** using as a source or means of support (*live off the land*). **4** leading from (*a street off the Strand*). **5** at a short distance to sea from (*sank off Cape Horn*). ● *adj.* **1** far, further (*the off side of the wall*). **2** *Brit.* (of a part of a vehicle, animal, or road) right (*the off front wheel*). **3** (*predic.*) *Brit. colloq.* **a** annoying or unfair. **b** unwell (*am feeling a bit off*). **c** (of food etc.) no longer fresh. ● *n.* **1** (in full **off side**) *Cricket* the half of the field (as divided lengthways through the pitch) towards which the batsman's feet are pointed. ▷ CRICKET. **2** *Brit. colloq.* the start of a race; the departure. □ **off and on** intermittently; now and then. **off form** see FORM. **off guard** see GUARD. **off one's hands** see HAND. **off one's head** see HEAD. **off of** *slang disp.* = OFF *prep.* 1a (*picked it up off of the floor*). **off the peg** see PEG. **off the point** ● *adj.* irrelevant. ● *adv.* irrelevantly. **off the record** see RECORD. [originally variant of OF, to distinguish the sense]

■ **Usage** The use of *off* for the preposition *off* (sense 1a), e.g. *lifted it up off of the table*, is non-standard and should be avoided.

off-air *adj. & adv.* involving or by the transmission of programmes by broadcasting.

offal *n.* **1** the less valuable edible parts of a carcass, esp. the entrails and internal organs. **2** refuse or waste stuff. [from Middle Dutch *afval*]

offbeat ● *adj.* **1** *Mus.* not coinciding with the beat. **2** eccentric, unconventional. ● *n. Mus.* any of the normally unaccented beats in a bar.

off-break *n. Cricket* a ball which deviates from the off side after bouncing.

off-centre *adj. & adv.* not quite coinciding with a central position.

off chance *n.* (prec. by *the*) the slight possibility.

off colour *predic.adj.* **1** *Brit.* not in good health. **2** *N. Amer.* somewhat indecent.

offcut *n.* a remnant of timber, paper, etc., after cutting.

off day *n.* a day when one is not at one's best.

offence *n.* (*US* **offense**) **1** an illegal act; a transgression or misdemeanour. **2** a wounding of the feelings (*no offence was meant*). **3** the act of attacking or taking the offensive. [originally in sense 'stumbling, stumbling block': from Latin *offensus*]

offend *v.* **1** *tr.* cause offence to or resentment in; wound the feelings of. **2** *tr.* displease or anger. **3** *intr.* commit an illegal act. **4** *intr.* (often foll. by *against*) do wrong; transgress. [from Latin *offendere*] □ **offendedly** *adv.* **offender** *n.* **offending** *adj.*

offensive ● *adj.* **1** giving or meant or likely to give offence; insulting. **2** disgusting, repulsive. **3 a** aggressive, attacking. **b** (of a weapon) meant for use in attack. ● *n.* **1** an aggressive action or attitude. **2** an attack. **3** aggressive action in pursuit of a cause. □ **offensively** *adv.* **offensiveness** *n.*

offer ● *v.* **1** *tr.* present for acceptance or refusal or consideration. **2** *intr.* (foll. by *to* + infin.) express readiness or show intention (*offered to take the children*). **3** *tr.* provide; give an opportunity for. **4** *tr.* make available for sale. **5** *tr.* (of a thing) present to one's attention (*each day offers new opportunities*). **6** *tr.* present (a sacrifice etc.) to a deity. **7** *intr.* present itself; occur (*as opportunity offers*). **8** *tr.* attempt, or try to show (violence, resistance, etc.). ● *n.* **1** an expression of readiness to do or give if desired, or to buy or sell (for a certain amount). **2** an amount offered. **3** a proposal (esp. of marriage). **4** a bid. □ **on offer** *Brit.*

for sale at a certain (esp. reduced) price. [from Latin *offerre*]

offering *n.* **1** a contribution, esp. of money, to a Church. **2** a thing offered as a sacrifice etc. **3** anything contributed or offered.

offertory *n.* (*pl.* **-ies**) **1** *Eccl.* **a** the offering of the bread and wine at the Eucharist. **b** an anthem accompanying this. **2 a** the collection of money at a religious service. **b** the money collected. [from ecclesiastical Latin *offertorium* 'offering']

offhand ● *adj.* curt or casual in manner. ● *adv.* **1** in an offhand manner. **2** without preparation or premeditation. □ **offhanded** *adj.* **offhandedly** *adv.* **offhandedness** *n.*

office *n.* **1** a room or building used as a place of business, esp. for clerical or administrative work. **2** a room, area, etc. for a particular kind of business (*post office*). **3** the local centre of a large business (*our London office*). **4** a position with duties attached to it. **5** tenure of an official esp. political position (*hold office*). **6** (**Office**) *Brit.* the quarters or staff or collective authority of a Government department etc. (*Foreign Office*). **7** a duty attaching to one's position; a task or function. **8** (usu. in *pl.*) a piece of kindness or attention (esp. *through the good offices of*). **9** *Eccl.* **a** an authorized form of worship (*Office for the Dead*). **b** (in full **divine office**) the daily service of the Roman Catholic breviary (*say the office*). [from Latin *officium* 'performance of a task', later also 'divine service']

office block *n.* a large building designed to contain business offices.

office boy *n.* (also **office girl**) a young man (or woman) employed to do minor jobs in a business office.

office hours *n.pl.* the hours during which business is normally conducted.

officer *n.* **1** a person holding a position of authority or trust, esp. one with a commission in the armed services. **2** a policeman or policewoman. **3** a holder of a post in a society (e.g. the president or secretary). **4** a holder of a public, civil, or ecclesiastical office.

office worker *n.* an employee in a business office.

official ● *adj.* **1** of or relating to an office or its tenure or duties. **2** (often *derog.*) characteristic of officials and bureaucracy. **3** properly authorized. **4** employed in a public capacity. ● *n.* a person holding office or engaged in official duties. □ **officialdom** *n.* **officially** *adv.*

official birthday *n.* (in the UK) a day in June chosen for the observance of the sovereign's birthday.

officialese *n. derog.* the formal precise language characteristic of official documents.

official receiver see RECEIVER 3.

official secrets *n.pl.* (esp. in phr. **Official Secrets Act**) *Brit.* confidential information involving national security.

officiant *n.* a person who officiates at a religious ceremony.

officiate *v.intr.* **1** act in an official capacity, esp. on a particular occasion. **2** perform a divine service or ceremony. [from medieval Latin *officiare*, related to OFFICE] □ **officiation** *n.* **officiator** *n.*

officinal /ŏ-fis-in-ăl/ *adj.* **1 a** (of a medicine) kept ready for immediate dispensing. **b** made from the pharmacopoeia recipe. **c** (of a name) adopted in the pharmacopoeia. **2** (of a herb or drug) used in medicine. [based on medieval Latin *officinalis* 'storeroom for medicines etc.'] □ **officinally** *adv.*

officious *adj.* **1** domineering. **2** intrusive in offering help etc. **3** *Diplomacy* informal, unofficial. [from Latin *officiosus* 'obliging'] □ **officiously** *adv.* **officiousness** *n.*

offing *n.* the more distant part of the sea in view. □ **in the offing** not far away; likely to appear or happen soon.

off-key *adj. & adv.* **1** out of tune. **2** not quite fitting.

off-licence *n. Brit.* **1** a shop selling alcoholic drink for consumption elsewhere. **2** a licence for this.

OFF-ROAD

Motorcycles used off-road need special modifications such as long suspensions, which make the ride smoother and help keep the rear wheel on the ground. In four-wheeled off-road vehicles, power is usually transmitted to all four wheels, which improves traction.

hand protector

plastic mudguard

telescopic fork

trials tyre

steel cradle frame

lightweight exhaust system

long suspension

alloy swing arm

two-stroke engine

OFF-ROAD COMPETITION MOTORCYCLE

off-limits *adj.* out of bounds.

off-line *Computing* ● *adj.* (of a computer terminal or process) not directly controlled by or connected to a central processor. ● *adv.* with a delay between the production of data and its processing; while not directly controlled by or connected to a central processor.

offload *v.tr.* **1** get rid of (something) by giving it to someone else. **2** unload (cargo etc.).

off-message *predic. adj. & adv.* departing from the official party line.

off-peak ● *adj.* used or for use at times other than those of greatest demand. ● *adv.* at times other than those of greatest demand.

off-piste *attrib.adj. & adv. Skiing* away from prepared ski runs.

offprint *n.* a printed copy of an article etc. originally forming part of a larger publication.

off-putting *adj.* **1** disconcerting. **2** repellent. □ **off-puttingly** *adv.*

off-road *attrib.adj.* **1** away from the road, on rough terrain. **2** ▲ (of a vehicle etc.) designed for rough terrain or for cross-country driving.

off-roading *n.* the activity of driving over rough terrain. □ **off-roader** *n.*

off-screen ● *adj.* **1** not appearing on a cinema, television, or VDU screen. **2** (*attrib.*) in one's private life or in real life as opposed to a film or television role. ● *adv.* **1** without use of a screen. **2** outside the view presented by a cinema film scene. **3** in one's private life or in real life as opposed to a film or television role.

off-season *n.* a time when business etc. is slack (often *attrib.*: *off-season prices*).

offset ● *n.* **1** a side shoot from a plant serving for propagation. **2** an offshoot or scion. **3** a compensation; a consideration or amount diminishing or neutralizing the effect of a contrary one. **4** *Archit.* a sloping ledge in a wall etc. where the thickness of the part above is diminished. **5** a bend in a pipe etc. to carry it past an obstacle. **6** (often *attrib.*) a method of printing in which ink is transferred from a plate or stone to a uniform rubber surface and from there to paper etc. (*offset litho*). ▷ PRINTING. ● *v.tr.* (**-setting**; *past* and *past part.* **-set**) **1** counterbalance, compensate. **2** place out of line. **3** print by the offset process.

offshoot *n.* **1** a side shoot or branch. **2** a derivative (*an offshoot of a right-wing group*).

offshore ● *adj.* **1** at sea some distance from the shore. **2** (of the wind) blowing seawards. **3** made or registered abroad. ● *adv.* **1** away from the shore. **2** abroad.

offside ● *adj. Sport* (of a player in a field game) in a position that is not allowed if it affects play.

● *n.* (often *attrib.*) esp. *Brit.* the right side of a vehicle, animal, etc. (cf. NEARSIDE).

off side see OFF *n.* 1.

offspring *n.* (*pl.* same) **1** a person's child or children or descendant(s). **2** an animal's young or descendant(s). **3** a result. [Old English]

off-stage *attrib.adj.* not on the stage and so not visible to the audience.

off-street *adj.* (esp. of parking) other than on a street.

off the cuff *colloq.* ● *adv.* without preparation, extempore. ● *adj.* (hyphenated when *attrib.*) made without preparation, extempore.

off-the-shelf ● *attrib.adj.* supplied ready-made; available from existing stock. ● *adv.* (**off the shelf**) ready-made; from existing stock.

off-the-shoulder *attrib.adj.* (of a dress etc.) leaving the shoulders bare.

off the wall *adj.* (hyphenated when *attrib.*) esp. *N. Amer. slang* unorthodox, unconventional.

off-white ● *n.* a white colour with a grey or yellowish tinge. ● *adj.* of this colour.

oft *adv. archaic* or *literary* often (usu. in *comb.*: *oft-recurring*; *oft-quoted*). [Old English]

often *adv.* (**oftener**, **oftenest**) **1 a** frequently; many times. **b** at short intervals. **2** in many instances. □ **as often as not** in roughly half the instances. [Middle English]

oftentimes *adv.* (also **oft-times**) *archaic* or *literary* often.

ogee /oh-jee/ *Archit.* ● *adj.* showing in section a double continuous S-shaped curve. ● *n.* an S-shaped line or moulding.

ogive /oh-jyv/ *n.* **1** a pointed arch. **2** one of the diagonal ribs of a vault. **3** an S-shaped line. [Middle English, from French] □ **ogival** *adj.*

ogle ● *v.* **1** *tr.* eye amorously or lecherously. **2** *intr.* look amorously. ● *n.* an amorous or lecherous look.

O grade *n.* = ORDINARY GRADE.

ogre *n.* (*fem.* **ogress**) **1** a man-eating giant in folklore etc. **2** a terrifying person. [first used by Perrault, French writer, in 1697] □ **ogreish** *adj.* (also **ogrish**)

oh[1] *int.* (also **O**) expressing surprise, pain, entreaty, etc. (*oh, what a mess*; *oh for a holiday*). □ **oh boy** expressing surprise, excitement, etc. **oh well** expressing resignation.

oh[2] *n.* = O[1] 2.

ohm *n. Electr.* the SI unit of resistance. [named after G. S. *Ohm*, German physicist, 1789–1854] □ **ohmic** *adj.*

OHMS *abbr.* on Her (or His) Majesty's Service.

oho *int.* expressing surprise or exultation. [Middle English]

OHP *abbr.* overhead projector.

oi *int.* calling attention or expressing alarm etc.

oik *n. colloq.* an uncouth or obnoxious person; an idiot. [20th-century coinage]

oil ● *n.* **1** any of various thick, viscous, usu. inflammable liquids insoluble in water but soluble in organic solvents (see also ESSENTIAL OIL, MINERAL OIL). ▷ OIL PLATFORM. **2** petroleum. **3** (in *comb.*) using oil as fuel (*oil-heater*). **4 a** (usu. in *pl.*) = OIL PAINT. **b** *colloq.* a picture painted in oil paints. **5** (in *pl.*) = OILSKIN 2b. ● *v.* **1** *tr.* apply oil to; lubricate. **2** *tr.* impregnate or treat with oil (*oiled silk*). **3** *tr. & intr.* supply with or take on oil as fuel. □ **oil the wheels** help make things go smoothly. [from Latin *oleum* '(olive) oil']

oilcake *n.* a mass of compressed linseed etc. left after oil has been extracted, used as fodder or manure.

oil can *n.* a can with a long nozzle for oiling machinery.

oilcloth *n.* **1** a fabric waterproofed with oil. **2** an oilskin. **3** a canvas coated with linseed or other oil and used to cover a table or floor.

oil colour *n.* = OIL PAINT.

oil drum *n.* a metal drum used for transporting oil.

oiler *n.* **1** an oil can. **2** an oil tanker. **3** *US* **a** an oil well. **b** (in *pl.*) oilskin.

oilfield *n.* an area yielding mineral oil. ▷ GAS FIELD

oil-fired *adj.* using oil as fuel.

oil lamp *n.* a lamp using oil as fuel.

oilman *n.* (*pl.* **-men**) a person who deals in oil.

oil of turpentine see TURPENTINE *n.* 2.

oil paint *n.* a mix of ground colour pigment and oil.

oil painting *n.* **1** the art of painting in oils. **2** a picture painted in oils. □ **is no oil painting** is physically unattractive.

oil platform *n.* ▶ a structure designed to stand on the seabed to provide a stable base above water for the drilling and regulation of oil wells.

oil rig *n.* a structure with equipment for drilling an oil well. ▷ OIL PLATFORM

oilseed *n.* any of various seeds from crops yielding oil.

oil-shale *n.* a fine-grained rock from which oil can be extracted. ▷ SEDIMENT

oilskin *n.* **1** cloth waterproofed with oil. **2 a** a garment made of this. **b** (in *pl.*) a suit made of this.

oil slick *n.* a smooth patch of oil, esp. on the sea.

oilstone *n.* a fine-grained flat stone used with oil for sharpening flat tools (cf. WHETSTONE).

oil tanker *n.* a ship designed to carry oil in bulk.

oil well *n.* a well from which mineral oil is drawn. ▷ OIL PLATFORM

oily *adj.* (**oilier**, **oiliest**) **1** of, like, or containing much oil. **2** covered or soaked with oil. **3** fawning, unctuous. □ **oiliness** *n.*

oink *v.intr.* (of a pig) make its characteristic grunt.

ointment *n.* a smooth greasy healing or cosmetic preparation for the skin. ▷ DRUG. [from Old French *oignement*]

OK (also **okay**) *colloq.* ● *adj.* (often as *int.*) all right; satisfactory. ● *adv.* well, satisfactorily (*that worked out OK*). ● *n.* (*pl.* **OKs**) approval. ● *v.tr.* (**OK's**, **OK'd**, **OK'ing**) approve. [originally US]

okapi *n.* (*pl.* same or **okapis**) ▼ a ruminant mammal, *Okapia johnstoni*, native to N. and NE Zaïre, with a head resembling that of a giraffe and a body resembling that of a zebra. [African native name]

OKAPI
(*Okapia johnstoni*)

OIL PLATFORM

Since most of the world's oil is trapped between layers of rock buried beneath the ocean floor, oil platforms are needed to exploit the valuable liquid. The oil rig is the part of the platform that actually drills the oil wells. The rig's motor turns the rotary table, which turns the drill string, a long shaft that may weigh hundreds of tonnes. The drill string is held by a tall support structure called the derrick. As a drill bit at the end of the drill string cuts deeper into the rock, sections of pipe are added one by one. When oil is struck, the shaft becomes a producing well. Retrieved oil is transported to shore by pipeline or tanker. Most oil platforms also recover natural gas, and if there is excess gas, it is burnt off at the flare stack.

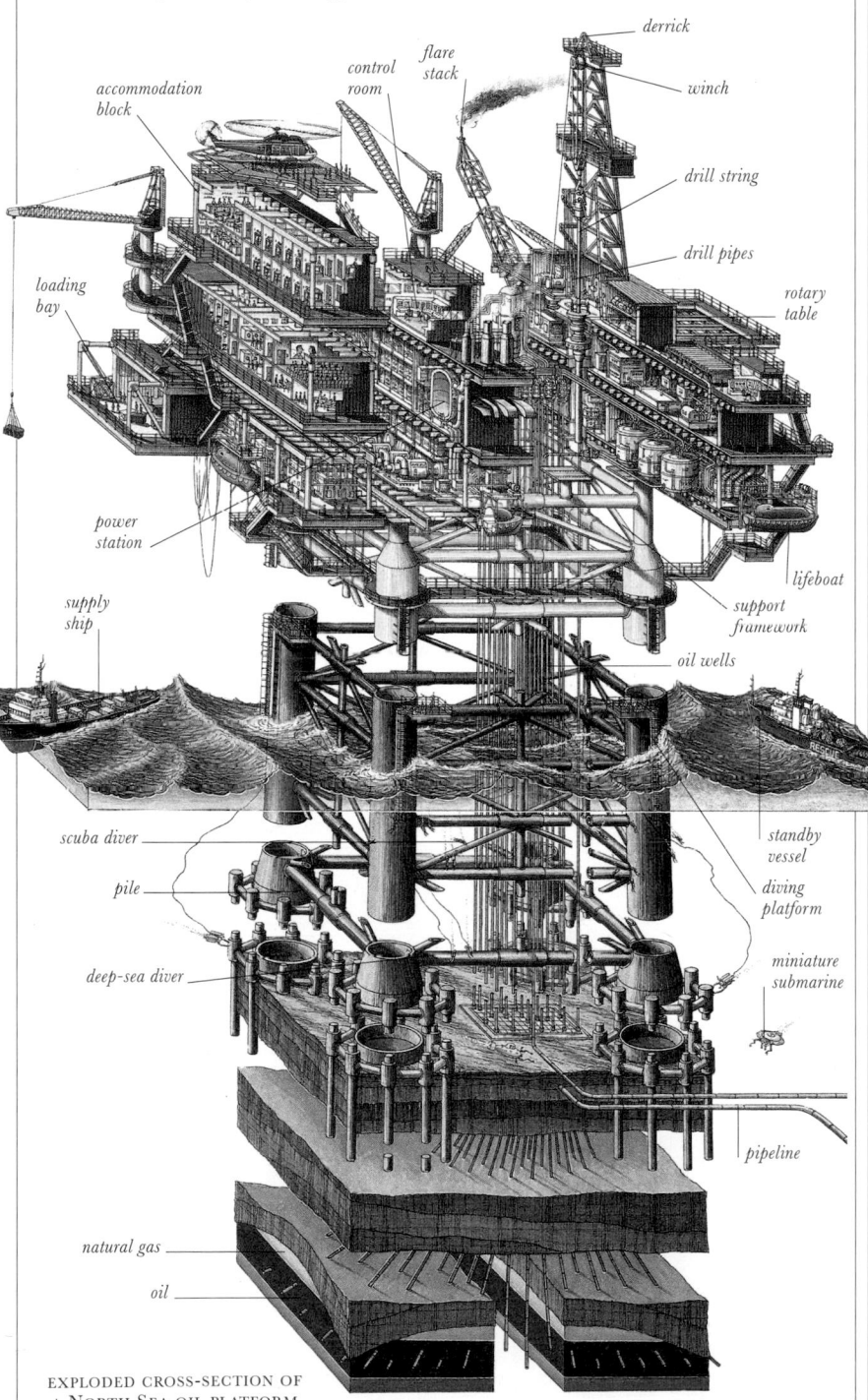

accommodation block
control room
flare stack
derrick
winch
drill string
drill pipes
rotary table
loading bay
power station
lifeboat
support framework
supply ship
oil wells
scuba diver
pile
standby vessel
diving platform
deep-sea diver
miniature submarine
pipeline
natural gas
oil

EXPLODED CROSS-SECTION OF
A NORTH SEA OIL PLATFORM

okey-dokey *adj. & adv.* (also **okey-doke**) *slang* = OK.

okra *n.* **1** an African plant, *Abelmoschus esculentus* (mallow family), yielding long ridged seed pods. **2** ▶ the seed pods eaten as a vegetable and used to thicken soups and stews. [West African native name]

old *adj.* (**older, oldest**) (cf. ELDER[1], ELDEST). **1 a** advanced in age; far on in the natural period of existence. **b** not young or near its beginning. **2** made long ago. **3** long in use. **4** worn or dilapidated or shabby from the passage of time. **5** having the characteristics of age (*the child has an old face*). **6** practised, inveterate (*an old offender; old in crime*). **7** belonging to the past; lingering on (*old times; haunted by old memories*). **8** dating from far back; long established or known; ancient, primeval (*old as the hills; old friends; an old family*). **9** (appended to a period of time) (often in *comb.*) of age (*is four years old; a four-year-old boy*). **10** (prefixed to the name of a language) as used in former or earliest times. **11** *colloq.* as a term of affection or casual reference (*good old Charlie; old shipmate*). **12** the former or first of two or more similar things (*our old house; wants his old job back*). [Old English] □ **oldish** *adj.* **oldness** *n.*

old age *n.* the later part of normal life.

old-age pension *n.* = RETIREMENT PENSION. □ **old-age pensioner** *n.*

Old Bailey *n.* the Central Criminal Court in London.

Old Bill *n. Brit. slang* the police.

old boy *n.* **1** a former male pupil of a school. **2** *colloq.* **a** an elderly man. **b** an affectionate form of address to a boy or man.

old boy network *n. Brit. colloq.* preferment in employment of those from a similar background.

old country *n.* (prec. by *the*) the native country of colonists etc.

old dear *n. colloq.* **1** an elderly woman. **2** one's mother.

olden *adj. archaic* of old; of a former age (esp. *in the olden days*).

Old English *n.* the English language up to *c.*1150.

Old English sheepdog *n.* a large sheepdog with a shaggy blue-grey and white coat. ▷ DOG

olde worlde *adj.* often *derog.* old and quaint, often in a mock old style.

old-fashioned *adj.* in or according to a fashion or tastes no longer current.

Old French *n.* the French language of the period before *c.*1400.

old fruit *n.* a familiar form of address to a man.

old girl *n.* **1** a former female pupil of a school. **2** *colloq.* **a** an elderly woman. **b** an affectionate term of address to a girl or woman.

Old Glory *n. US* the US national flag.

old gold *n.* a dull brownish-gold colour.

old guard *n.* the original or past or conservative members of a group.

old hand *n.* a person with much experience.

old hat *adj. colloq.* tediously familiar or out of date.

Old High German *n.* High German (see GERMAN) up to *c.*1200.

Old Icelandic *n.* Icelandic up to the 16th c., a form of Old Norse.

oldie *n. colloq.* an old person or thing.

old lady *n. colloq.* one's mother or wife.

old lag see LAG[3] *n.*

old maid *n.* **1** *derog.* an elderly unmarried woman. **2** a prim and fussy person. **3** a card game in which players try not to be left with an unpaired queen. □ **old-maidish** *n.*

old man *n. colloq.* **1** one's husband or father. **2** one's employer or other person in authority over one. **3** *Brit.* an affectionate form of address to a boy or man.

OKRA
(*Abelmoschus esculentus*)

old man's beard n. ▶ traveller's joy (a wild clematis), esp. in seed. [so called from the grey fluffy hairs round the seeds]

old master n. **1** a great artist of former times, esp. of the 13th–17th c. in Europe. **2** a painting by such a painter.

OLD MAN'S BEARD SEED HEAD
(*Clematis vitalba*)

Old Nick n. *colloq.* the Devil. [probably from a pet form of the name *Nicholas*]

Old Norse n. the language of Norway and its colonies until the 14th c., from which the Scandinavian languages are derived.

Old Saxon see SAXON n. 1b.

old school n. **1** traditional attitudes. **2** people having such attitudes.

old school tie n. esp. *Brit.* **1** a necktie with a characteristic pattern worn by the pupils of a particular school. **2** the group loyalty and traditionalism associated with wearing such a tie.

old soldier n. = OLD-TIMER.

old stager n. = OLD-TIMER.

oldster n. an old person.

old-style *attrib.adj.* of an old style, outmoded (*old-style communists*).

Old Testament n. the first part of the Christian Bible, containing the scriptures of the Hebrews.

old-time *attrib.adj.* belonging to former times.

old-timer n. a person with long experience.

old wives' tale n. an unscientific belief.

old woman n. *colloq.* **1** one's wife or mother. **2** a fussy or timid man. □ **old-womanish** *adj.*

Old World n. Europe, Asia, and Africa.

old-world *adj.* belonging to or associated with old times.

old year n. the year just ended or about to end.

oleaginous *adj.* **1** having the properties of or producing oil. **2** oily, greasy. **3** obsequious, ingratiating. [from Latin *oleaginus*]

oleander /oh-li-**an**-der/ n. an evergreen poisonous shrub, *Nerium oleander*, native to the Mediterranean. [medieval Latin]

olefin /**oh**-li-fin/ n. (also **olefine**) *Chem.* = ALKENE. [from French *oléfiant* 'oil-forming', with reference to oily ethylene dichloride]

oleo- *comb. form* oil. [from Latin *oleum* 'oil']

oleograph n. a print made to resemble an oil painting.

oleomargarine n. **1** a fatty substance extracted from beef fat and often used in margarine. **2** *US* margarine.

O level n. *hist.* = ORDINARY LEVEL.

olfaction n. the act or capacity of smelling; the sense of smell. [based on Latin *olfactus* 'smelling']

olfactory *adj.* of or relating to the sense of smell (*olfactory nerves*). ▷ NOSE. [based on Latin *olfacere olfact-* 'to smell']

oligarch /**ol**-i-gark/ n. a member of an oligarchy. [from Greek *oligarkhēs*]

oligarchy /**ol**-i-gar-ki/ n. (*pl.* **-ies**) **1** government by a small group of people. **2** a state governed in this way. **3** the members of such a government. □ **oligarchic** *adj.* **oligarchical** *adj.*

Oligocene *Geol.* ● *adj.* of or relating to the third epoch of the Tertiary period, with evidence of the first primates. ● *n.* this epoch or system. [based on Greek *oligos* 'small' + *kainos* 'new']

olive ● *n.* **1** (in full **olive tree**) ▶ any evergreen tree of the genus *Olea*, having dark green lance-shaped leathery leaves with silvery undersides, esp. *O. europaea* of the Mediterranean, and *O. africana* native to S. Africa. **2** the small oval fruit of this, having a hard stone and bitter flesh, green when unripe and bluish black when ripe. **3** (in full **olive green**) the greyish-green colour of an

unripe olive. **4** the wood of the olive tree. ● *adj.* **1** (in full **olive green**; hyphenated when *attrib.*) coloured like an unripe olive. **2** (of the complexion) yellowish brown, sallow. [from Greek *elaia*]

olive branch n. **1** the branch of an olive tree as a symbol of peace. **2** a gesture of reconciliation or friendship.

olive drab ● *n.* the dull olive-green colour used in certain army uniforms. ● *adj.* (hyphenated when *attrib.*) of this colour.

olive green see OLIVE n. 3, *adj.* 1.

olive oil n. an oil extracted from olives, used esp. in cookery.

olivine n. *Mineral.* a naturally occurring form of magnesium-iron silicate, usu. olive green.

Olympiad n. **1 a** a period of four years between Olympic Games, used by the ancient Greeks in dating events. **b** a four-yearly celebration of the ancient Olympic Games. **2** a celebration of the modern Olympic Games. **3** a regular international contest in chess etc. [from Greek *Olumpias Olumpiad-*]

Olympian ● *adj.* **1 a** of or associated with Mount Olympus in NE Greece, traditionally the home of the Greek gods. **b** celestial. **2** (of manners etc.) magnificent, condescending, superior. **3 a** of or relating to ancient Olympia in southern Greece. **b** = OLYMPIC. ● *n.* **1** any of the gods regarded as living on Olympus. **2** a person of great attainments or of superhuman calm and detachment. **3** a competitor in the Olympic Games. [from Greek *Olympus*]

Olympic ● *adj.* of ancient Olympia or the Olympic Games. ● *n.pl.* (**the Olympics**) the Olympic Games. [from Greek *Olumpikos* 'of Olympus or Olympia']

Olympic Games *n.pl.* **1** an ancient Greek festival held at Olympia every four years, with athletic, literary, and musical competitions. **2** a modern international revival of this as a sports festival held every four years since 1896 in different venues.

OM *abbr.* (in the UK) Order of Merit.

ombudsman n. (*pl.* **-men**) an official appointed by a government to investigate individuals' complaints against public authorities etc. [Swedish, literally 'legal representative']

omega /**oh**-mi-gă/ n. **1** the last (24th) letter of the Greek alphabet (Ω, ω). **2** the last of a series; the final development. [from Greek *ō mega*, literally 'great O']

omelette n. (also **omelet**) a dish of beaten eggs cooked in a frying pan and served plain or with a savoury or sweet filling. [French, based on earlier *lemele* 'knife blade', probably with reference to an omelette's thin flat shape]

omen n. **1** an occurrence or object regarded as portending good or evil. **2** prophetic significance (*of good omen*). [Latin]

omicron /oh-**my**-kron/ n. the fifteenth letter of the Greek alphabet (O, o). [from Greek *o mikron*, literally 'small o']

ominous *adj.* **1** threatening; indicating disaster or difficulty. **2** of evil omen; inauspicious. **3** giving or being an omen. [from Latin *ominosus*] □ **ominously** *adv.*

omission n. **1** the act or an instance of omitting or being omitted. **2** something that has been omitted. [from Late Latin *omissio*]

omit *v.tr.* (**omitted**, **omitting**) **1** leave out; not insert or

unripe fruit

OLIVE
(*Olea europaea*)

include. **2** leave undone. **3** (foll. by verbal noun or to + infin.) fail or neglect (*omitted saying anything*; *omitted to say*). [from Latin *omittere*] □ **omissible** *adj.*

omni- *comb. form* **1** all; of all things. **2** in all ways or places. [Latin]

omnibus ● *n.* **1** *formal* = BUS n. 1. **2 a** a volume containing several novels etc. previously published separately. **b** a single edition of two or more consecutive programmes previously broadcast separately. ● *adj.* **1** serving several purposes at once. **2** comprising several items. [from Latin, literally 'for all']

omnidirectional *adj.* (of an aerial etc.) receiving or transmitting in all directions.

omnipotent *adj.* **1** having great or absolute power. **2** having great influence. [from Latin *omnipotens omnipotent-*] □ **omnipotence** n.

omnipresent *adj.* **1** present everywhere at the same time. **2** widely or constantly encountered. □ **omnipresence** n.

omniscient *adj.* knowing everything. [from medieval Latin *omnisciens omniscient-*] □ **omniscience** n.

omnium gatherum n. *colloq.* a miscellany or strange mixture. [mock Latin]

omnivorous *adj.* **1** feeding on many kinds of food, esp. on both plants and flesh. **2** making use of everything available. □ **omnivore** n.

omphalos /**om**-fă-los/ n. **1** *Gk Antiq.* a conical stone (esp. that at Delphi) representing the navel of the Earth. **2** *Gk Antiq.* a boss on a shield. **3** a centre or hub. [Greek, literally 'navel, boss, hub']

on ● *prep.* **1** (so as to be) supported by or attached to or covering or enclosing (*sat on a chair*; *stuck on the wall*; *rings on her fingers*; *leaned on his elbow*). **2** carried with; about the person of (*have you a pen on you?*). **3** (of time) exactly at; during; contemporaneously with (*on 29 May*; *on the hour*; *on schedule*; *working on Tuesday*). **4** immediately after or before (*I saw them on my return*). **5** as a result of (*on further examination I found this*). **6** having, or so as to have, membership etc. of, or residence at or in (*she is on the board of directors*; *lives on the Continent*). **7** supported financially by (*lives on £50 a week*; *lives on his wits*). **8** close to; just by (*a house on the sea*; *lives on the main road*). **9** in the direction of; against. **10** so as to threaten; touching or striking (*advanced on him*; *pulled a knife on me*; *a punch on the nose*). **11** having as an axis or pivot (*turned on his heel*). **12** having as a basis or motive (*works on a ratchet*; *arrested on suspicion*). **13** having as a standard, confirmation, or guarantee (*had it on good authority*; *did it on purpose*; *I promise on my word*). **14** concerning or about (*writes on frogs*). **15** using or engaged with (*is on the pill*; *here on business*). **16** so as to affect (*walked out on her*). **17** at the expense of (*the drinks are on me*; *the joke is on him*). **18** added to (*disaster on disaster*; *ten pence on a pint of beer*). **19** in a specified manner or style (*on the cheap*; *on the run*). ● *adv.* **1** (so as to be) covering or in contact (*put your boots on*). **2** in the appropriate direction; towards something (*look on*). **3** further forward; in an advanced position or state (*time is getting on*; *it happened later on*). **4** with continued movement or action (*went plodding on*; *keeps on complaining*). **5** in operation or activity (*the light is on*; *the chase is on*). **6** due to take place as planned (*is the party still on?*). **7** *colloq.* **a** willing to participate or approve, or make a bet. **b** esp. *Brit.* practicable or acceptable (*that's just not on*). **8** being shown or performed (*a good film on tonight*). **9** on stage. **10** on duty. **11** forward (*head on*). ● *n.* (in full **on side**) *Cricket* = LEG n. 5. □ **be on about** *Brit.* refer to or discuss esp. tediously (*what are they on about?*). **be on at** *Brit. colloq.* nag or grumble at. **be on to 1** realize the significance or intentions of. **2** get in touch with. **on and off** intermittently; now and then. **on and on** continually; at tedious length. **on time** punctual, punctually. **on to** to a position or state on or in contact with (cf. ONTO). [Old English]

-on *suffix Physics* forming nouns denoting subatomic particles (*meson*; *neutron*).

onager /**on**-ă-ger/ n. a wild ass, esp. *Equus hemionus* of a race native to central Asia. [from Greek *onos* 'ass' + *agrios* 'wild']

onanism *n.* **1** masturbation. **2** coitus interruptus. [from French *onanisme*, based on the name *Onan* (Gen. 38:9)] □ **onanist** *n.* **onanistic** *adj.*

on-board *attrib.adj.* available or situated on board a ship, aircraft, etc. (*on-board facilities*). Cf. *on board* (see BOARD).

ONC *abbr. hist.* (in the UK) Ordinary National Certificate.

once ● *adv.* **1** on one occasion or for one time only (*once is not enough; have read it once*). **2** at some point or period in the past (*could once play chess*). **3** ever or at all (*if you once forget it*). **4** multiplied by one. ● *conj.* as soon as (*once they have gone we can relax*). ● *n.* one time or occasion (*just the once*). □ **all at once 1** suddenly. **2** all together. **at once 1** immediately. **2** simultaneously. **for once** on this (or that) occasion, even if at no other. **once again** (or **more**) another time. **once and for all** (or **once for all**) (done) in a final or conclusive manner. **once** (or **every once**) **in a while** from time to time. **once or twice** a few times. **once upon a time 1** at some vague time in the past. **2** formerly. [Middle English]

once-over *n. colloq.* a rapid preliminary inspection.

oncer *n.* **1** *Brit. hist. slang* a one-pound note. **2** *Brit. colloq.* a thing that occurs only once.

onco- *comb. form Med.* tumour. [from Greek *ogkos* 'swelling, mass']

oncogenic *adj. Med.* causing development of a tumour or tumours. □ **oncogenicity** *n.*

oncology *n. Med.* the study and treatment of tumours. □ **oncologist** *n.*

oncoming *adj.* approaching from the front.

OND *abbr. hist.* (in the UK) Ordinary National Diploma.

one ● *adj.* **1** single and integral in number. **2** (with a noun implied) a single person or thing of the kind expressed or implied (*one of the best; a nasty one*). **3 a** particular but undefined, esp. as contrasted with another (*that is one view; one thing after another*). **b** *esp. US colloq.* a noteworthy example of (*that is one difficult question*). **4** only such (*the one man who can do it*). **5** forming a unity (*one and undivided*). **6** identical; the same (*of one opinion*). ● *n.* **1 a** the lowest cardinal number. **b** a symbol for this (1, i, I). **2** unity; a unit (*one is half of two; came in ones and twos*). **3** a single thing or person or example (often referring to a noun previously expressed or implied: *the big dog and the small one*). **4** one o'clock. **5** *colloq.* an alcoholic drink (*have a quick one; have one on me*). **6** a story or joke (*the one about the frog*). ● *pron.* **1** a person of a specified kind (*loved ones; like one possessed*). **2** any person, as representing people in general (*one is bound to lose in the end*). **3** any person; the speaker or writer as representing people in general; I, me (*one would like to help*). □ **at one** in agreement. **for one** being one, even if the only one (*I for one do not believe it*). **for one thing** as a single consideration, ignoring others. **one and all** everyone. **one and only 1** unique. **2** superb, unequalled. **one by one** singly, successively. **one day 1** on an unspecified day. **2** at some unspecified future date. **one or two** see OR. [Old English]

■ **Usage** The use of the pronoun *one* to mean 'any person', 'I', or 'me' (see sense 3 of the pronoun) is often regarded as an affectation, but can be useful when a less personal statement is being made, e.g. *One never knows what might happen*. However, it should not be mixed with *he* (*him, his*, etc.), and repeated use in a long sentence may seem clumsy, e.g. *One never knows how one would react if one's house were to burn down*. The less formal *you* can usually replace it successfully and is safer when one is launching into a long statement.

one another *pron.* each the other or others (as a formula of reciprocity: *love one another*).

one-armed bandit *n. colloq.* a fruit machine worked by a long handle.

one-horse *attrib.adj.* **1** using a single horse. **2** *colloq.* small, poorly equipped.

one-horse race *n.* a competition etc. in which one competitor is clearly superior to all the others.

one-liner *n. colloq.* a single brief sentence, often witty or apposite.

one-man *attrib.adj.* involving, done, or operated by only one man.

oneness *n.* **1** the fact or state of being one; singleness. **2** uniqueness. **3** agreement. **4** identity, sameness.

one-night stand *n.* **1** a single performance of a play etc. in a place. **2** *colloq.* a sexual liaison lasting only one night.

one-off *esp. Brit. colloq.* ● *attrib.adj.* made or done as the only one; not repeated. ● *n.* a one-off product, event, etc.

one-piece *adj.* made in one piece, esp. as a single garment.

onerous *adj.* **1** burdensome; causing or requiring trouble. **2** *Law* involving heavy obligations. [from Latin *onerosus*]

oneself *pron.* the reflexive and emphatic form of *one* (*kill oneself; one has to do it oneself*).

one-sided *adj.* **1** favouring one side in a dispute; unfair, partial. **2** having or occurring on one side only. **3** larger or more developed on one side. □ **one-sidedly** *adv.* **one-sidedness** *n.*

one-time *attrib.adj.* former.

one-to-one *adj. & adv.* with one member of one group corresponding to one of another.

one-track mind *n.* a mind preoccupied with one subject.

one-two *n. colloq.* **1** *Boxing* the delivery of two punches in quick succession. **2** *Football* etc. a series of reciprocal passes between two advancing players.

one-up *adj. colloq.* having a particular advantage.

one-upmanship *n. colloq.* the art of gaining or maintaining a psychological advantage.

one-way *adj.* allowing movement or travel in one direction only.

ongoing *adj.* **1** continuing (*an ongoing problem*). **2** in progress (*ongoing discussions*).

■ **Usage** The vague or tautologous use of *ongoing*, as in the cliché *an ongoing situation*, should be avoided.

onion *n.* **1** an allium, *Allium cepa*, having a swollen bulb with many concentric layers and bearing greenish-white flowers. **2** the bulb of this, used for its pungent taste in cooking, pickling, etc. □ **know one's onions** be fully knowledgeable or experienced. [from Latin *unio*] □ **oniony** *adj.*

on-line *Computing* ● *adj.* (of equipment or a process) directly controlled by or connected to a central processor. ● *adv.* while thus controlled or connected.

onlooker *n.* a non-participating observer; a spectator. □ **onlooking** *adj.*

only ● *adv.* **1** solely, merely, exclusively; and no one or nothing more besides (*I only want to sit down; will only make matters worse; needed six only; is only a child*). **2** no longer ago than (*saw them only yesterday*). **3** not until (*arrives only on Tuesday*). **4** with no better result than (*hurried home only to find her gone*). ● *attrib.adj.* **1** existing alone of its or their kind (*their only son*). **2** best or alone worth knowing (*the only place to eat*). ● *conj. colloq.* **1** except that; but for the fact that (*I would go, only I feel ill*). **2** but then (as an extra consideration) (*he always makes promises, only he never keeps them*). □ **only too** extremely (*is only too willing*). [Old English]

■ **Usage** In informal English *only* is usually placed between the subject and verb regardless of what it refers to (e.g. *I only want to talk to you*); in more formal English it is often placed more exactly, especially to avoid ambiguity (e.g. *I want to talk only to you*). In speech, intonation usually serves to clarify the sense.

on-message *predic. adj. & adv.* reinforcing the official party line.

o.n.o. *abbr. Brit.* or near offer.

on-off *adj.* **1** (of a switch) having two positions, 'on' and 'off'. **2** – *on and off* (see ON).

onomastics *n.pl.* (treated as *sing.*) the study of the origin and formation of (esp. personal) proper names. □ **onomastic** *adj.*

onomatopoeia /on-ŏ-mat-ŏ-**pee**-ǎ/ *n.* **1** the formation of a word from a sound associated with what is named (e.g. *cuckoo, sizzle*). **2** the use of such words. [from Greek *onomatopoiia* 'word-making'] □ **onomatopoeic** *adj.*

onrush *n.* an onward rush.

on-screen ● *attrib.adj.* appearing on a cinema, television, or VDU screen. ● *adv.* **1** on or by means of a screen. **2** within the view presented by a cinema film scene.

onset *n.* **1** an attack. **2** a beginning, esp. an energetic or determined one.

on-set *attrib.adj.* taking place or occurring on the set of a play or film.

onshore ● *adj.* **1** on the shore. **2** (of the wind) blowing from the sea towards the land. ● *adv.* on or towards the land.

onside *adj. & adv.* (of a player in a field game) not offside.

on side see ON *n.*

on-site *attrib.adj.* taking place or available on a site or premises.

onslaught *n.* a fierce attack. [from Middle Dutch *aenslag*]

on-stage *attrib.adj.* on the stage; visible to the audience.

on-street *attrib.adj.* (with reference to parking) at the side of a street.

onto *prep. disp.* to a position or state on or in contact with (cf. *on to*).

■ **Usage** The form *onto* is still not fully accepted in the way that *into* is, although it is in wide use. It is however useful in distinguishing sense as between *We drove on to the beach* (i.e. in that direction) and *We drove onto the beach* (i.e. in contact with it).

ontogenesis *n.* the origin and development of an individual. [based on ONTOGENY + Greek *genesis* 'birth'] □ **ontogenetic** *adj.*

ontogeny *n.* = ONTOGENESIS. [based on Greek *ont-* 'being']

ontology *n.* the branch of metaphysics dealing with the nature of being. [based on Greek *ont-* 'being'] □ **ontological** *adj.* **ontologically** *adv.*

onus *n.* (*pl.* **onuses**) a burden, duty, or responsibility. [Latin]

onward ● *adv.* (also **onwards**) **1** further on. **2** towards the front. **3** with advancing motion. **4** into the future (*from 1996 onward*). ● *adj.* directed onwards.

onyx *n.* ▶ a semiprecious variety of agate with different colours in layers. ▷ GEM. [Middle English via Old French *oniche*, *onix* and Latin from Greek *onux* 'fingernail, onyx']

ONYX

oodles *n.pl. colloq.* a very great amount. [19th-century US: origin unknown]

ooh *int.* expressing surprise, delight, pain, etc.

oolite /**oh**-ŏ-lyt/ *n.* a sedimentary rock, usu. limestone, consisting of rounded grains made up of concentric layers. [from French *oölithe*] □ **oolitic** *adj.*

oompah *n. colloq.* the rhythmical sound of deeptoned brass instruments in a band.

oomph *n. slang* **1** energy, enthusiasm. **2** attractiveness, esp. sexual appeal. [20th-century coinage]

oophorectomy *n.* (*pl.* **-ies**) *Med.* the surgical removal of one or both ovaries. [based on *oophoron* 'ovary', from Greek *ōophoros* 'egg-bearing']

oops *int. colloq.* expressing surprise or apology. [a natural exclamation]

oops-a-daisy var. of UPSY-DAISY.

Oort cloud *n. Astron.* a cloud of small rocky and icy bodies thought to orbit the Sun beyond the orbit of the planet Pluto, acting as a reservoir of comets. [named after J.H. *Oort*, Dutch astronomer, 1900–92]

ooze[1] ● *v.* **1** *intr.* pass slowly through the pores of a body. **2** *intr.* trickle or leak slowly out. **3** *intr.* (of a substance) exude moisture. **4** *tr.* exude (a feeling) liberally (*oozed sympathy*). ● *n.* a sluggish flow. [originally in sense 'juice, sap': from Old English *wōs*] □ **oozy** *adj.*

ooze[2] *n.* **1** a deposit of wet mud or slime. **2** a bog or marsh; soft muddy ground. [Old English] □ **oozy** *adj.*

op *n. colloq.* operation.

op. *abbr.* **1** *Mus.* opus. **2** operator.

o.p. *abbr.* out of print.

opacity *n.* **1** the state or degree of being opaque. **2** obscurity of meaning. **3** obtuseness of understanding. [from Latin *opacitas*]

opal *n.* ▶ a quartzlike form of hydrated silica, usu. white or colourless and sometimes showing changing colours. ▷ GEM. [from Latin *opalus*]

opalescent *adj.* showing changing colours like an opal. □ **opalescence** *n.*

opaline *adj.* opal-like, opalescent, iridescent.

opaque *adj.* (**opaquer**, **opaquest**) **1** not transmitting light. **2** impenetrable to sight. **3** obscure; not lucid. **4** obtuse, dull-witted. [from Latin *opacus*] □ **opaquely** *adv.* **opaqueness** *n.*

OP ART PAINTING BY BRIDGET RILEY, *Cataract III* (1967)

op art *n.* ▼ a form of abstract art that gives the illusion of movement by the precise use of pattern and colour.

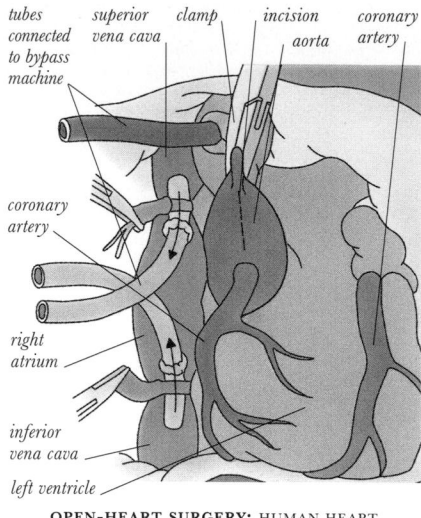

OPAL

op. cit. *abbr.* in the work already quoted. [Latin *opere citato*]

OPEC /oh-pek/ *abbr.* Organization of Petroleum Exporting Countries.

open ● *adj.* **1** not closed or locked or blocked up. **2 a** (of a room, field, or other area) having its door or gate in a position allowing access, or part of its confining boundary removed. **b** (of a container) not fastened or sealed; allowing access to the inside part. **3** unenclosed, unconfined, unobstructed (*the open road*; *open views*). **4 a** uncovered, bare, exposed (*open drain*; *open wound*). **b** *Sport* (of a goalmouth or other object of attack) unprotected, vulnerable. **5** undisguised, public, manifest (*open scandal*; *open hostilities*). **6** expanded, unfolded, or spread out (*had the map open on the table*). **7** (of a fabric) not closely woven; with gaps. **8 a** frank and communicative. **b** accessible to new ideas; unprejudiced or undecided. **9 a** accessible to visitors or customers; ready for business. **b** (of a meeting) admitting all, not restricted to members etc. **10** (also **Open**) **a** (of a race, competition, scholarship, etc.) unrestricted as to who may compete. **b** (of a champion, scholar, etc.) having won such a contest. **11** (of government) conducted in an informative manner receptive to enquiry, criticism, etc., from the public. **12** (foll. by *to*) **a** willing to receive (*is open to offers*). **b** (of a choice, offer, or opportunity) still available (*there are three courses open to us*). **c** likely to suffer from or be affected by (*open to abuse*). **13 a** (of the mouth) with lips apart. **b** (of the ears or eyes) eagerly attentive. **14** *Mus.* **a** (of a string) allowed to vibrate along its whole length. **b** (of a pipe) unstopped at each end. **c** (of a note) sounded from an open string or pipe. **15** (of an electrical circuit) having a break in the conducting path. **16** (of the bowels) not constipated. **17** (of a return ticket) not restricted as to day of travel. **18** *Brit.* (of a cheque) not crossed. **19** (of a boat) without a deck. ● *v.* **1** *tr.* & *intr.* make or become open or more open. **2 a** *tr.* change from a closed or fastened position so as to allow access (*opened the door*; *opened the box*). **b** *intr.* (of a door, lid, etc.) have its position changed to allow access (*the door opened slowly*). **3** *tr.* remove the sealing or fastening element of (a container) to get access to the contents (*opened the envelope*). **4** *intr.* (foll. by *into*, *on to*, etc.) (of a door, room, etc.) afford access as specified (*opened on to a large garden*). **5 a** *tr.* start or establish or set going (a business, activity, etc.). **b** *intr.* start (*the session opens tomorrow*; *the story opens with a murder*). **c** *tr.* (of a counsel in a law court) make a preliminary statement in (a case) before calling witnesses. **6** *tr.* **a** spread out or unfold (a map, newspaper, etc.). **b** (often *absol.*) find and refer to (the contents of a book) (*open at the first soliloquy*). **7** *intr.* begin speaking, writing, etc. (*he opened with a warning*). **8** *intr.* (of a prospect) come into view; be revealed. **9** *tr.* reveal or communicate (one's feelings, intentions, etc.). **10** *tr.* make (one's mind, heart, etc.) more sympathetic or tolerant. **11** *tr.* ceremonially declare (a building etc.) to be completed and in use. **12** *tr.* break up (ground) with a plough etc. **13** *tr.* cause evacuation of (the bowels). ● *n.* **1** (prec. by *the*) **a** open space or country or air. **b** public notice; general attention (*esp. into the open*). **2** (**Open**) an open championship, competition, or scholarship. □ **be open with** speak frankly to. **open-and-shut** straightforward and conclusive. **open out 1** unfold. **2** develop, expand. **3** esp. *Brit.* become communicative. **4** accelerate. **open up 1** unlock (premises). **2** make accessible. **3** reveal; bring to notice. **4** accelerate. **5** begin shooting or sounding. **6** talk or speak openly. [Old English] □ **openness** *n.*

open air ● *n.* (usu. prec. by *the*) a free or unenclosed space outdoors. ● *attrib.adj.* (**open-air**) out of doors.

open book *n.* a person who is easily understood.

opencast *adj. Brit.* (of a mine or mining) with removal of the surface layers and working from above, not from shafts. ▷ MINE

open college *n.* a college offering training and vocational courses mainly by correspondence.

open day *n.* a day when the public may visit a place normally closed to them.

open door *n.* free admission of international trade and immigrants.

open-ended *adj.* having no predetermined limit.

opener *n.* **1** a device for opening tins, bottles, etc. **2** *colloq.* the first item on a programme etc. **3** *Cricket* an opening batsman.

open-faced *adj.* having a frank or ingenuous expression.

open-handed *adj.* generous.

open-hearted *adj.* frank and kindly.

open-heart surgery *n.* ▼ surgery with the heart exposed and the blood made to bypass it. ▷ HEART

tubes connected to bypass machine — *superior vena cava* — *clamp* — *incision* — *coronary artery* — *aorta*

coronary artery

right atrium

inferior vena cava

left ventricle

OPEN-HEART SURGERY: HUMAN HEART REVEALED AND BYPASSED FOR SURGERY

open house *n.* **1** hospitality for all visitors. **2** *N. Amer.* = OPEN DAY.

opening ● *n.* **1** an aperture or gap. **2** an opportunity. **3** a beginning; an initial part. **4** *Chess* a recognized sequence of moves at the beginning of a game. ● *adj.* initial, first.

opening time *n. Brit.* the time at which public houses may legally open for custom.

open letter *n.* a letter addressed to an individual but published in a newspaper or journal.

openly *adv.* **1** frankly. **2** publicly.

open market *n.* an unrestricted market with free competition of buyers and sellers.

open-minded *adj.* accessible to new ideas; unprejudiced. □ **open-mindedness** *n.*

open-mouthed *adv.* & *adj.* with the mouth open, esp. in surprise.

open-plan *adj.* having large undivided rooms.

open prison *n.* a prison with the minimum of physical restraints on prisoners.

open question *n.* a matter on which differences of opinion are legitimate.

open sandwich *n.* a sandwich without a top slice of bread.

open sea *n.* an expanse of sea away from land.

open season *n.* **1** the season when restrictions on the killing of game etc. are lifted. **2** a time of no restrictions or restraint (*appears to be open season on union-bashing*).

open secret *n.* a supposed secret that is known to many people.

open sesame see SESAME.

open-top *adj.* (also **open-topped**) (of a bus, sports car, etc.) not having a fixed top.

Open University *n.* (in the UK) a university that teaches mainly by broadcasting and correspondence, and is open to those without academic qualifications.

open verdict *n. Brit.* a verdict affirming that a crime has been committed but not specifying the criminal or (in case of violent death) the cause.

O

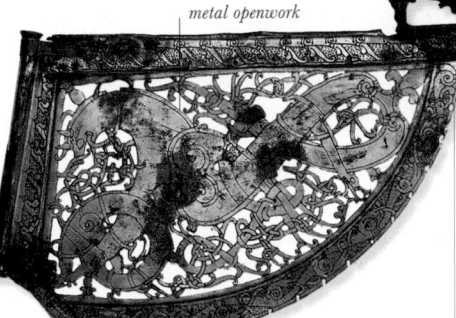

metal openwork

OPENWORK: 9TH-CENTURY
SCANDINAVIAN WEATHER VANE

openwork n. ▲ a pattern with intervening spaces in metal, leather, lace, etc.

opera[1] n. **1 a** a dramatic work set to music for singers and instrumentalists. **b** works of this kind as a genre. **2** a building for the performance of opera. [Latin, literally 'labour, work']

opera[2] pl. of OPUS.

operable adj. **1** that can be operated. **2** suitable for treatment by surgical operation. [from Late Latin operabilis] □ **operability** n.

opera glasses n.pl. small binoculars for use at the opera or theatre.

opera house n. a theatre for the performance of opera.

operand n. Math. the quantity etc. on which an operation is to be done. [from Latin operandum 'thing to be operated upon']

operate v. **1** tr. manage, work, control. **2** intr. be in action; function. **3** intr. (often foll. by on) **a** perform a surgical operation. **b** conduct a military or naval action. **c** be active in business etc., esp. dealing in stocks and shares. **4** tr. bring about; accomplish. [based on Latin operatus 'laboured']

operatic adj. **1** of or relating to opera. **2** resembling or characteristic of opera. □ **operatically** adv.

operating system n. the basic software that enables the running of a computer program.

operating table n. a table on which surgical operations are performed.

operating theatre n. (N. Amer. **operating room**) a room for surgical operations.

operation n. **1 a** the action or process or method or state of working or operating. **b** the scope or range of effectiveness of a thing's activity. **2** an active process (the operation of breathing). **3** a piece of work, esp. one in a series (often in pl.: begin operations). **4** an act of surgery performed on a patient. **5** a strategic movement of troops, ships, etc. for military action. **6** Math. the subjection of a number or quantity or function to a process affecting its value or form, e.g. multiplication, differentiation.

operational adj. **1 a** of or used for operations. **b** engaged or involved in operations. **2** able or ready to function. □ **operationally** adv.

operationalize v.tr. (also **-ise**) express in operational terms.

operative ● adj. **1** in operation; having effect. **2** having the principal relevance ('may' is the operative word). **3** of or by surgery. ● n. **1** a worker, esp. a skilled one. **2** US a private detective or secret agent. □ **operatively** adv. **operativeness** n.

operator n. **1** a person operating a machine etc., esp. making connections of lines in a telephone exchange. **2** a person operating or engaging in business. **3** colloq. a person acting in a specified way (a smooth operator). **4** Math. a symbol or function denoting an operation (e.g. ×, +).

operetta n. a light opera. [Italian, literally 'little opera']

ophidian ● n. a reptile of the suborder Serpentes (formerly Ophidia), comprising snakes. ● adj. **1** of or relating to this suborder. **2** snakelike. [based on Greek ophis 'snake']

ophthalmia n. inflammation of the eye, esp. conjunctivitis. [based on Greek ophthalmos 'eye']

ophthalmic adj. of or relating to the eye and its diseases.

ophthalmic optician n. Brit. an optician qualified to prescribe and dispense spectacles and contact lenses and to detect eye diseases.

ophthalmo- comb. form Optics denoting the eye. [from Greek ophthalmos 'eye']

ophthalmology n. the scientific study of the eye. □ **ophthalmological** adj. **ophthalmologist** n.

ophthalmoscope n. ▶ an instrument for inspecting the retina and other parts of the eye.

rotating magnifying lenses

lens adjuster

lens indicator

OPHTHALMOSCOPE

light switch

opiate ● adj. **1** containing, derived from, or resembling opium. **2** narcotic, soporific. ● n. **1** a drug containing, derived from, or resembling opium, usu. to ease pain or induce sleep. **2** a thing which soothes or stupefies. [based on Latin opium 'opium']

opine v.tr. (often foll. by that + clause) hold or express as an opinion. [from Latin opinari 'to think, believe']

opinion n. **1** a belief or assessment based on grounds short of proof. **2** a view held as probable. **3** (often foll. by on) what one thinks about a particular topic or question (my opinion on capital punishment). **4** a formal statement of professional advice (get a second opinion). **5** an estimation (had a low opinion of it). □ **a matter of opinion** a disputable point. [from Latin opinio]

opinionated adj. conceitedly assertive or dogmatic in one's opinions.

opinion poll n. = GALLUP POLL.

opioid Pharm. & Biochem. ● n. any compound resembling cocaine and morphine in its addictive properties or physiological effects. ● adj. of or relating to such a compound.

opium n. an addictive drug prepared from the juice of the opium poppy, used in medicine as an analgesic and narcotic. [from Greek opion 'poppy-juice']

opium den n. a haunt of opium-smokers.

opium poppy n. a poppy, Papaver somniferum, native to Europe and E. Asia, with white, red, pink, or purple flowers. ▷ HERB

opossum n. **1** ▼ any mainly tree-living marsupial of the family Didelphidae, native to America, having a prehensile tail. ▷ MARSUPIAL. **2** Austral. = POSSUM 2. [from Virginian Indian āpassūm]

OPOSSUM: VIRGINIA OPOSSUM
(Didelphis virginiana)

opp. abbr. opposite.

oppo n. (pl. **-os**) Brit. colloq. a colleague or friend.

opponent n. a person who opposes, or who belongs to an opposing side. [from Latin opponent- 'opposing']

opportune adj. **1** (of a time) especially favourable or appropriate (an opportune moment). **2** (of an action or event) done or occurring at a favourable or useful time. [originally of a wind blowing towards harbour: based on Latin portus 'port'] □ **opportunely** adv. **opportuneness** n.

opportunism n. the adaptation of policy or judgement to circumstances or opportunity, esp. regardless of principle. □ **opportunistic** n. **opportunistically** adv. **opportunist** n. & adj.

opportunity n. (pl. **-ies**) a good chance; a favourable occasion. □ **opportunity knocks** an opportunity occurs. [from Latin opportunitas]

opposable adj. Zool. (of the thumb in primates) capable of facing and touching the other digits on the same hand.

oppose v.tr. (often absol.) **1** set oneself against; resist, argue against. **2** take part in a game, sport, etc., against (another competitor or team). **3** (foll. by to) place in opposition or contrast. □ **as opposed to** in contrast with. [earlier also oppone: from Latin opponere]

opposite ● adj. **1** (often foll. by to) on the other or further side, facing or back to back. **2** (often foll. by to, from) **a** of a contrary kind; diametrically different. **b** being the other of a contrasted pair. **3** (of angles) between opposite sides of the intersection of two lines. ● n. an opposite thing or person or term. ● adv. in an opposite position (the tree stands opposite). ● prep. **1** in a position opposite to (opposite the house is a tree). **2** (of a leading theatrical etc. part) in a complementary role to (another performer). [from Latin oppositus 'opposed'] □ **oppositely** adv. **oppositeness** n.

opposite number n. a person holding an equivalent position in another group or organization.

opposite sex n. (prec. by the) either sex in relation to the other.

opposition n. **1** resistance, antagonism. **2** the state of being hostile or in conflict or disagreement. **3** contrast or antithesis. **4 a** a group or party of opponents or competitors. **b** (the Opposition) Brit. the principal parliamentary party opposed to that in office. **5** the act of opposing or placing opposite. □ **oppositional** adj.

oppress v.tr. **1** keep in subservience by coercion. **2** govern or treat harshly or cruelly. **3** weigh down (with cares or unhappiness). [from medieval Latin oppressare] □ **oppression** n. **oppressor** n.

oppressive adj. **1** oppressing; harsh or cruel. **2** (of weather) close and sultry. □ **oppressively** adv. **oppressiveness** n.

opprobrious adj. (of language) severely scornful; abusive. □ **opprobriously** adv.

opprobrium n. **1** disgrace. **2** a cause of this. [Latin, based on probrum 'disgraceful act']

opt v.intr. (usu. foll. by for, between) exercise an option; make a choice. □ **opt out** (often foll. by of) **1** choose not to participate (opted out of the race). **2** (in the UK) (of a school or hospital) decide to withdraw from local authority control. [from Latin optare 'to choose, wish']

optative Gram. ● adj. expressing a wish. ● n. the optative mood. [from Late Latin optativus]

optative mood n. a set of verb forms expressing a wish etc.

optic ● adj. of or relating to the eye or vision (optic nerve). ● n. **1** a lens etc. in an optical instrument. **2** Brit. propr. a device fastened to the neck of an inverted bottle for measuring out spirits etc. [based on Greek optos 'seen']

optical adj. **1** of sight; visual. **2 a** of or concerning sight and light in relation to each other. **b** belonging to optics. **3** (esp. of a lens) constructed to assist sight. □ **optically** adv.

O

optical brightener *n.* any fluorescent substance used to produce a whitening effect on laundry.

optical character recognition *n.* the identification of printed characters using photoelectric devices.

optical disc see DISC 4b.

optical fibre *n.* ▼ thin glass fibre through which light can be transmitted.

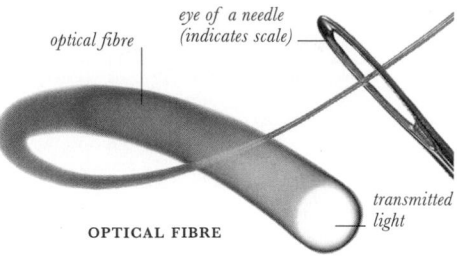

optical fibre

eye of a needle (indicates scale)

transmitted light

OPTICAL FIBRE

optical illusion *n.* 1 a thing having an appearance so resembling something else as to deceive the eye. 2 a mental misapprehension caused by this.

optical microscope *n.* a microscope using the direct perception of light (cf. ELECTRON MICROSCOPE).

optician *n.* 1 a maker or seller of optical instruments. 2 a person qualified to make and supply spectacles and contact lenses. 3 = OPHTHALMIC OPTICIAN.

optic nerve *n.* ▼ each of the second pair of cranial nerves, transmitting impulses to the brain from the retina at the back of the eye. ▷ EYE

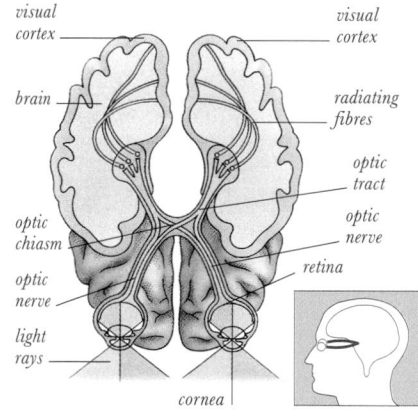

visual cortex · *visual cortex* · *brain* · *radiating fibres* · *optic tract* · *optic chiasm* · *optic nerve* · *retina* · *optic nerve* · *light rays* · *cornea*

OPTIC NERVE: PATH OF IMPULSES FROM RETINA TO BRAIN (VIEWED FROM UNDERNEATH)

optics *n.pl.* (treated as *sing.*) the scientific study of sight and the behaviour of light, or of other radiation or particles (*electron optics*).

optima *pl.* of OPTIMUM.

optimal *adj.* best or most favourable. [from Latin *optimus* 'best'] □ **optimally** *adv.*

optimism *n.* 1 an inclination to hopefulness and confidence. 2 *Philos.* a the doctrine that this world is the best of all possible worlds. b the theory that good must ultimately prevail over evil in the universe. [based on Latin *optimum*] □ **optimist** *n.* **optimistic** *adj.* **optimistically** *adv.*

optimize *v.* (also **-ise**) 1 *tr.* make the best or most effective use of (a situation, an opportunity, etc.). 2 *intr.* be an optimist. □ **optimization** *n.*

optimum ● *n.* (*pl.* **optima** or **optimums**) 1 the most favourable conditions (for growth, reproduction, etc.). 2 the best possible compromise between opposing tendencies. ● *adj.* = OPTIMAL. [Latin, literally 'best (thing)']

option *n.* 1 a the act or an instance of choosing; a choice. b a thing that is or may be chosen. 2 the liberty of choosing; freedom of choice. 3 *Stock Exch.*

etc. the right to buy or sell specified stocks etc. at a specified price within a set time. □ **have no option but to** must. **keep** (or **leave**) **one's options open** not commit oneself. [from Latin *optio*]

optional *adj.* being an option only; not obligatory. □ **optionality** *n.* **optionally** *adv.*

optional extra *n.* an accessory or other additional item which is available for purchase.

optometrist *n.* esp. *US* a person who practises optometry, an ophthalmic optician.

optometry *n.* the occupation of measuring eyesight, prescribing corrective lenses, detecting eye disease, etc. □ **optometric** *adj.*

opt-out *n.* 1 the action of opting out of something, esp. of a school or hospital opting out of local-authority control. 2 an instance of this.

opulent *adj.* 1 ostentatiously rich; wealthy. 2 luxurious. 3 abundant; profuse. [from Latin *opulentus* 'wealthy'] □ **opulence** *n.* **opulently** *adv.*

opus *n.* (*pl.* **opuses** or **opera**) 1 *Mus.* a a separate musical composition or set of compositions of any kind. b (also **op.**) used before a number given to a composer's work, usu. indicating the order of publication (*Beethoven, op. 15*). 2 any artistic work. [Latin, literally 'work']

or *conj.* 1 (often prec. by *either*) a introducing the second of two alternatives (*white or black*). b introducing all but the first, or only the last, of any number of alternatives (*white or grey or black*; *white, grey, or black*). 2 introducing a synonym or explanation of a preceding word etc. (*suffered from vertigo or giddiness*). 3 introducing a significant afterthought (*he must know — or is he bluffing?*). 4 = *or else* (*run or you'll be late*). □ **one or two** (or **two or three** etc.) *colloq.* a few. **or else** 1 otherwise (*do it now, or else you will have to do it tomorrow*). 2 *colloq.* expressing a warning or threat (*hand over the money or else*). **or rather** introducing a rephrasing or qualification of a preceding statement etc. (*he was there, or rather I heard that he was*). **or so** (after a quantity or a number) or thereabouts (*send me ten or so*). [reduced form of obsolete conjunction *other*]

oracle *n.* 1 a a place at which advice or prophecy was sought from the gods in classical antiquity. b the usu. ambiguous or obscure response given at an oracle. c a prophet or prophetess at an oracle. 2 a a person or thing regarded as an infallible guide to future action etc. b a saying etc. regarded as infallible guidance. [from Latin *oraculum*] □ **oracular** *adj.*

oracy *n.* the ability to express oneself fluently in speech. [based on Latin *os oris* 'mouth']

oral ● *adj.* 1 by word of mouth; spoken; not written (*the oral tradition*). 2 done or taken by the mouth (*oral contraceptive*). 3 of or relating to the mouth.

● *n.colloq.* a spoken examination, test, etc. [based on Latin *os oris* 'mouth'] □ **orally** *adv.*

oral sex *n.* sexual activity in which the genitals of one partner are stimulated by the mouth of the other.

oral society *n.* a society that has not reached the stage of literacy.

orange ● *n.* 1 a a large roundish juicy citrus fruit with a bright reddish-yellow tough rind. ▷ CITRUS FRUIT. b (also **orange tree**) any of various trees or shrubs of the genus *Citrus*, esp. *C. sinensis* or *C. aurantium*, bearing fragrant white flowers and yielding this fruit. 2 a fruit or plant resembling this. 3 the reddish-yellow colour of an orange. ● *adj.* orange-coloured. [from Persian *nārang*]

orangeade *n. Brit.* a usu. fizzy non-alcoholic drink flavoured with orange.

Orangeman *n.* (*pl.* **-men**) a member of a political society formed in 1795 to support Protestantism in Ireland. [named after the Protestant William of *Orange* (William III)]

orange peel *n.* 1 the skin of an orange. 2 a rough surface resembling this.

orange pekoe *n.* a type of black tea made from very small leaves.

orangery *n.* (*pl.* **-ies**) a place, esp. a special structure, where orange trees are cultivated.

orange squash *n. Brit.* a soft drink made from oranges and other ingredients, often sold in concentrated form.

orange stick *n.* a thin stick, pointed at one end, for manicuring the nails.

orang-utan /or-ang-oo-tan/ *n.* (also **orangutan**, **orang-outang**) a large red long-haired tree-living ape, *Pongo pygmaeus*, native to Borneo and Sumatra. ▷ PRIMATE. [from Malay *orang huan* 'forest person']

oration *n.* a formal speech, discourse, etc., esp. when ceremonial. [from Latin *oratio* 'discourse, prayer']

orator /o-rǎ-ter/ *n.* 1 a person making a speech. 2 an eloquent public speaker.

oratorio *n.* (*pl.* **-os**) a semi-dramatic, but not staged, work for orchestra and voices esp. on a sacred theme. [Italian, from ecclesiastical Latin *oratorium* 'oratory']

oratory *n.* (*pl.* **-ies**) 1 the art or practice of formal speaking, esp. in public. 2 a small chapel, esp. for private worship. [based on Latin *orare* 'to pray, speak'] □ **oratorical** *adj.*

orb *n.* 1 ▶ a globe surmounted by a cross, esp. carried by a sovereign at a coronation. 2 a sphere; a globe. [from Latin *orbis* 'ring']

ORB: 17TH-CENTURY ENGLISH ORB

ORBIT

In space, smaller bodies (such as a satellite) orbit larger bodies (such as the Earth) because of the gravitational pull exerted by the larger object. This is why the Earth orbits the Sun. Artificial satellites orbiting the Earth perform tasks such as recording weather patterns.

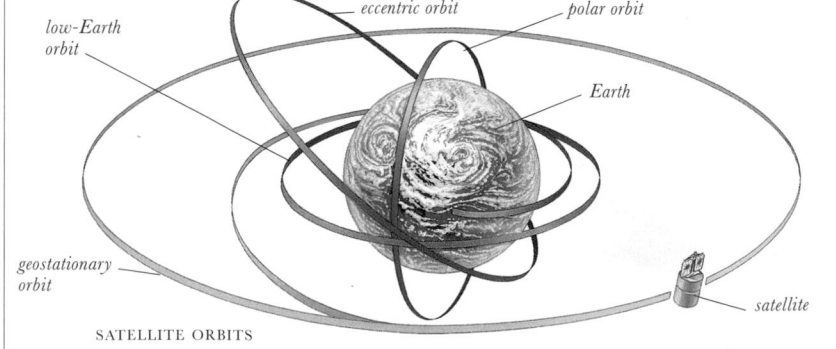

low-Earth orbit · *eccentric orbit* · *polar orbit* · *Earth* · *geostationary orbit* · *satellite*

SATELLITE ORBITS

ORCHESTRA

Orchestras as we know them today first appeared in the 17th century, but were generally fairly small. During the 19th century, instrument-making techniques improved markedly and orchestra sizes increased. Today an average orchestra may contain 40–70 players. Each of the four sections in an orchestra has a different role. The strings, almost always the largest division, usually provide the melody. The woodwinds sometimes carry the tune, but more often give colour and warmth to the overall sound. The brass instruments commonly add brightness and emphasis in dramatic passages, while the percussion section provides the orchestra's rhythmic backbone. The conductor dictates the tempo, volume, and balance of the piece.

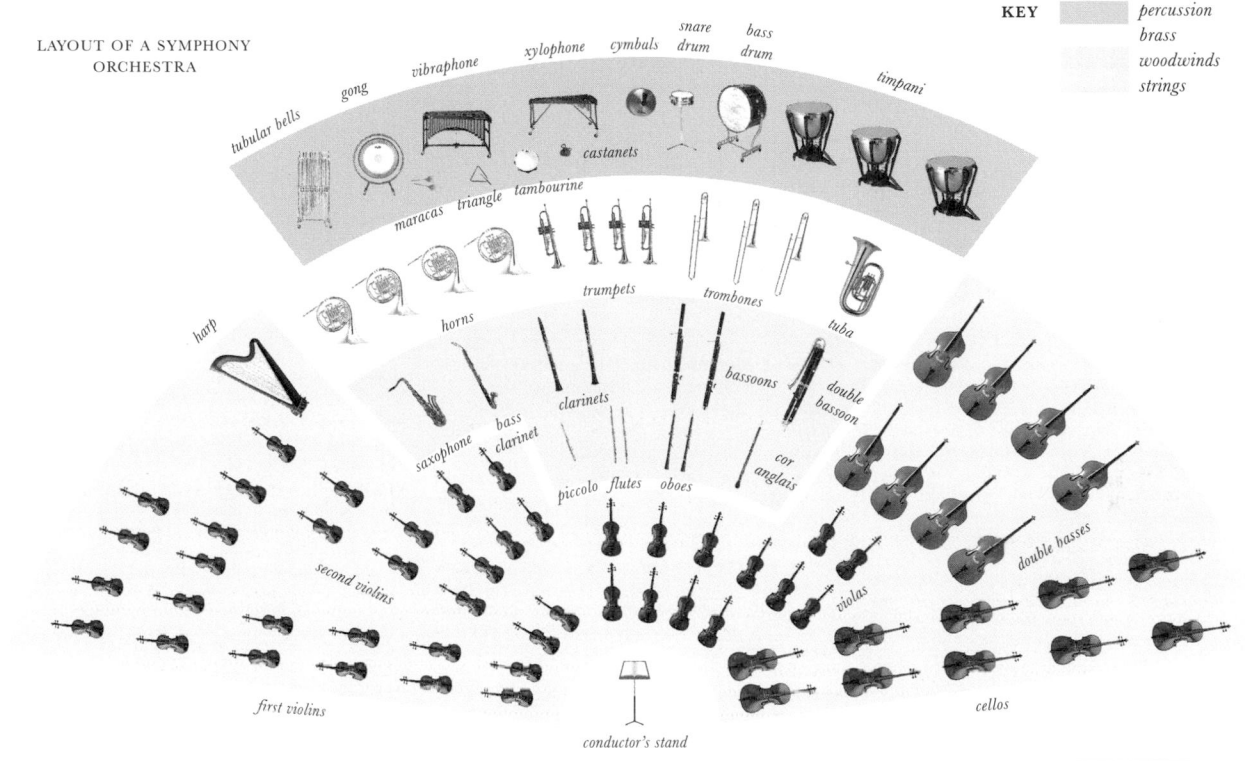

LAYOUT OF A SYMPHONY ORCHESTRA

KEY: percussion / brass / woodwinds / strings

tubular bells, gong, vibraphone, xylophone, cymbals, snare drum, bass drum, timpani, castanets, maracas, triangle, tambourine, trumpets, trombones, tuba, horns, bassoons, double bassoon, harp, clarinets, saxophone, bass clarinet, cor anglais, piccolo, flutes, oboes, violas, double basses, second violins, first violins, cellos, conductor's stand

---

orbit ● *n.* **1 a** ◄ the curved, usu. closed course of a planet, satellite, etc. ▷ SOLAR SYSTEM. **b** (prec. by *in, into, out of,* etc.) the state of motion in an orbit. **c** one complete passage in orbit around an orbited body. **2** the path of an electron round an atomic nucleus. ▷ ATOM. **3** a range or sphere of action. **4 a** the eye socket. **b** the area around the eye of a bird or insect. ● *v.* (**orbited, orbiting**) **1** *intr.* **a** (of a satellite etc.) go round in orbit. **b** fly in a circle **2** *tr.* move in orbit round. [from Latin *orbita* 'course, track', later 'eye-cavity']

orbital *adj.* **1** *Astron. & Physics* of an orbit or orbits. **2** *Brit.* (of a road) passing round the outside of a town.

orbital sander *n.* a sander having a circular and not oscillating motion.

orbiter *n.* a spacecraft designed to travel in orbit. ▷ SPACECRAFT.

orca *n.* the killer whale. [from Latin *orca*, a kind of whale]

Orcadian ● *adj.* of or relating to the Orkney Islands off the N. coast of Scotland. ● *n.* a native of the Orkney Islands. [from *Orcades*, Latin name of the Orkney Islands]

orch. *abbr.* **1** orchestrated by. **2** orchestra.

orchard *n.* a piece of enclosed land with fruit trees. [Old English *ortgeard,* literally 'garden enclosure'] □ **orchardist** *n.*

orchestra *n.* **1** ▲ a usu. large group of instrumentalists, esp. combining strings, woodwinds, brass, and percussion (*symphony orchestra*). ▷ BRASS, PERCUSSION, STRINGED, WOODWIND. **2 a** (in full **orchestra pit**) the part of a theatre, opera house, etc., where the orchestra plays, usu. in front of the stage and on a lower level. ▷ THEATRE. **b** *N. Amer.* the stalls in a theatre. **3** the semicircular space in front of an ancient Greek theatre stage where the chorus danced and sang. [from Greek *orkhēstra*] □ **orchestral** *adj.* **orchestrally** *adv.*

orchestra stalls *n.pl. Brit.* the front of the stalls.

orchestrate *v.tr.* **1** arrange, score, or compose for orchestral performance. **2** arrange, combine, or direct the elements of (a situation etc.) for maximum effect. □ **orchestration** *n.* **orchestrator** *n.*

orchid *n.* **1** a plant of the family Orchidaceae, bearing flowers in fantastic shapes and brilliant colours. ▷ EPIPHYTE. **2** ▶ a flower of such a plant. [based on Greek *orkhis,* literally 'testicle', referring to the shape of its tuber] □ **orchidaceous** *adj.*

orchitis *n. Med.* inflammation of a testicle. [modern Latin]

ordain *v.tr.* **1** confer holy orders on; appoint to the Christian ministry (*ordained him priest; was ordained in 1970*). **2 a** (often foll. by *that* + clause) decree (*ordained that he should go*). **b** (of God, fate, etc.) destine; appoint (*has ordained us to die*). [from Latin *ordinare*] □ **ordainer** *n.*

ordeal *n.* a painful or horrific experience; a severe trial. [Old English]

order ● *n.* **1 a** the condition in which every part, unit, etc. is in its right place; tidiness. **b** a usu. specified sequence, succession, etc. (*alphabetical order; the order of events*). **2** (in *sing.* or *pl.*) an authoritative command, direction, instruction, etc. **3** a state of peaceful harmony under a constituted authority (*order was restored; law and order*). **4** (esp. in *pl.*) esp. *Brit.* a social class, rank, etc., constituting a distinct group in society (*the lower orders*). **5** a kind; a sort (*talents of a high order*). **6 a** a direction to a manufacturer, tradesman, waiter, etc. to supply something. **b** the goods etc. supplied. **7** the constitution or nature of the world, society, etc. (*the moral order; the order of things*). **8** *Biol.* a taxonomic rank below a class and above a family. **9** (also **Order**) a fraternity of monks or friars, or formerly of knights, bound by a common rule of life (*the Franciscan order; the Order of Templars*). **10 a** any of the grades of the Christian ministry. **b** (in *pl.*) the status of a member of the clergy (*Anglican orders*). **11** any of the five classical styles of architecture (Doric, Ionic, Corinthian, Tuscan, and Composite). ▷ CORINTHIAN, DORIC, IONIC. **12** (esp. **Order**) **a** a company of people honoured esp. by a sovereign (*Order of the Garter; Order of Merit*). **b** the insignia worn by members of an order. **13** *Eccl.* the stated form of

ORCHID
(x *Odontocidium* cultivar)

sepal, fused style and stamen, petal, sepal, lip

ORE

A rock or mineral is considered an ore if the valuable commodity it contains (such as iron) can be profitably extracted. Some ores contain less than one per cent of the precious material. Most ores form by either sedimentary, magmatic, or hydrothermal processes.

EXAMPLES OF ORES

HAEMATITE
(iron ore)

GOLD IN QUARTZ
(gold ore)

GALENA
(lead ore)

CINNABAR
(mercury ore)

BAUXITE
(aluminium ore)

---

divine service (*the order of confirmation*). **14** the principles of procedure, decorum, etc., of a meeting, legislative assembly, etc. **15** any of the nine grades of angelic beings (seraphim, cherubim, thrones, dominations, principalities, powers, virtues, archangels, angels). ● *v.tr.* **1** (usu. foll. by *to* + infin., or *that* + clause) command; bid; prescribe (*ordered him to go*; *ordered that they should be sent*). **2** command or direct (a person) to a specified destination (*was ordered to Singapore*; *ordered them home*). **3** direct a manufacturer, waiter, tradesman, etc. to supply. **4** arrange; regulate (*ordered her affairs*). **5** (of God, fate, etc.) ordain (*fate ordered it otherwise*). **6** *US* command (a thing) done or (a person) dealt with (*ordered it settled*; *ordered him expelled*). □ **by order** according to the proper authority. **in bad** (or **good** etc.) **order** not working (or working properly etc.). **in order 1** one after another according to some principle. **2** ready or fit for use. **3** according to the rules (of procedure at a meeting etc.). **in order that** with the intention; so that. **in order to** with the purpose of doing; with a view to. **keep order** enforce orderly behaviour. **of** (or **in** or **on**) **the order of 1** approximately. **2** having the order of magnitude specified by (*of the order of one in a million*). **on order** (of goods etc.) ordered but not yet received. **order about 1** dominate; command officiously. **2** send hither and thither. **out of order 1** not working properly. **2** not in the correct sequence. **3** not according to the rules (of a meeting, organization, etc.). **4** *colloq.* **a** not behaving in an acceptable fashion. **b** (of behaviour) not acceptable. **take orders 1** accept commissions. **2** accept and carry out commands. [from Latin *ordo* 'row, degree, command']

order book *n.* **1** a book in which a tradesman enters orders. **2** the level of incoming orders.

order form *n.* a printed form in which details are entered by a customer.

Order in Council *n. Brit.* a sovereign's order on an administrative matter given by the advice of the Privy Council.

orderly ● *adj.* **1** methodically arranged; regular. **2** obedient to discipline; well-behaved; not unruly. ● *n.* (*pl.* **-ies**) **1** an esp. male cleaner in a hospital. **2** a soldier who carries orders for an officer etc. □ **orderliness** *n.*

orderly book *n. Brit. Mil.* a regimental or company book for entering orders.

orderly officer *n. Brit. Mil.* the officer of the day.

orderly room *n. Brit. Mil.* a room in a barracks used for company business.

order of magnitude *n.* a class in a system of classification determined by size, usu. by powers of 10.

Order of Merit *n.* (in the UK) an order, founded in 1902, for distinguished achievement.

Order of the Bath *n.* (in the UK) an order of knighthood. [so called from the ceremonial bath which originally preceded installation]

order of the day *n.* **1** the prevailing state of things. **2** a principal topic of action or a procedure decided upon. **3** business set down for treatment; a programme.

Order of the Garter *n.* the highest order of English knighthood. [so called from the traditional story of the order's founding, that the garter was that of the Countess of Salisbury which Edward III placed on his own leg after it fell off while she was dancing]

order paper *n.* esp. *Parl.* a written or printed order of the day; an agenda.

ordinal ● *n.* (in full **ordinal number**) a number defining a thing's position in a series, e.g. 'first', 'second', etc. ● *adj.* **1** of or relating to an ordinal number. **2** defining a thing's position in a series etc. [from Late Latin *ordinalis*]

ordinance *n.* **1** a decree. **2** an enactment by a local authority. **3** a religious rite. [from Latin *ordinantia* 'ordaining']

■ **Usage** Care should be taken not to confuse *ordinance* meaning 'a decree' or 'a religious rite' with *ordnance* meaning 'mounted guns' or 'the government service dealing with military stores and materials'. Note also *Ordnance Survey*.

ordinand *n. Eccl.* a candidate for ordination. [from Latin *ordinandus* 'to be ordained']

ordinary ● *adj.* **1** regular, normal, customary, usual (*in the ordinary course of events*). **2** boring; commonplace (*an ordinary little man*). ● *n.* (*pl.* **-ies**) (usu. **Ordinary**) *RC Ch.* **1** those parts of a service, esp. the Mass, which do not vary from day to day. **2** a rule or book laying down the order of divine service. □ **in the ordinary way** if the circumstances are or were not exceptional. **out of the ordinary** unusual. [from Latin *ordinarius* 'orderly'] □ **ordinarily** *adv.* **ordinariness** *n.*

ordinary grade *n.* (in Scotland) the lower of two main levels of examination leading to the Scottish Certificate of Education.

ordinary level *n. hist.* (in the UK except Scotland) the lower of the two main levels of the GCE examination.

ordinary seaman *n.* a sailor of the lowest rank, that below able-bodied seaman.

ordinary share *n. Brit.* a share entitling the holder to a dividend from net profits (cf. PREFERENCE SHARE).

ordinate *n. Math.* a straight line from any point drawn parallel to one coordinate axis and meeting the other, usually a coordinate measured parallel to the vertical. [from Latin *linea ordinata applicata* 'line applied parallel']

ordination *n.* the act of conferring holy orders, esp. on a priest or deacon. [from Latin *ordinatio*]

ordnance *n.* **1** mounted guns; cannon. **2** a branch of government service dealing esp. with military stores and materials. [Middle English variant of ORDINANCE]

■ **Usage** See Usage Note at ORDINANCE.

Ordnance Survey *n.* (in the UK) an official survey organization preparing large-scale detailed maps of the whole country.

Ordovician *Geol.* ● *adj.* of or relating to the second period of the Palaeozoic era. ● *n.* this period or system. [from *Ordovices*, Latin name of an ancient British tribe in N. Wales]

ordure *n.* **1** excrement; dung. **2** obscenity; filth; foul language. [based on Latin *horridus* 'horrid']

ore *n.* ◄ a naturally occurring solid material from which metal or other valuable minerals may be extracted profitably. ▷ METAL. [Old English *ōra* 'unwrought metal', *ār* 'bronze']

oregano /o-ri-gah-noh/ *n.* the dried leaves of wild marjoram used as a culinary herb (cf. MARJORAM). ▷ HERB. [Spanish, literally 'origanum']

orfe *n.* a usu. silvery freshwater fish, *Leuciscus idus*, of the carp family, fished commercially in northern Eurasia. See also GOLDEN ORFE. [German]

organ *n.* **1 a** ► a usu. large musical instrument having pipes supplied with air from bellows, sounded by keys and pedals. **b** a smaller instrument without pipes, producing similar sounds electronically. **c** a smaller keyboard wind instrument with metal reeds; a harmonium. **d** = BARREL ORGAN. **2 a** a usu. self-contained part of an organism having a special vital function (*vocal organs*; *digestive organs*). **b** esp. *joc.* the penis. **3** a medium of communication, esp. a newspaper or periodical which serves as the mouthpiece of a movement, political party, etc. [from Greek *organon* 'tool']

organdie *n.* (*US* **organdy**) (*pl.* **-ies**) a fine translucent cotton muslin, usu. stiffened. [from French *organdi*]

organelle *n. Biol.* any of various organized or specialized structures which form part of a cell. [from modern Latin *organella*]

organ-grinder *n.* the player of a barrel organ.

organic *adj.* **1 a** *Physiol.* of or relating to a bodily organ or organs. **b** *Med.* (of a disease) affecting the structure of an organ. **2** (of a plant or animal) having organs or an organized physical structure. **3** produced or involving production without chemical fertilizers, pesticides, etc. **4** *Chem.* (of a compound etc.) containing carbon (opp. INORGANIC). ▷ ALKANE, ALKENE, ALKYNE. **5 a** structural, inherent. **b** constitutional, fundamental. **6** organized, systematic, coordinated (*an organic whole*). **7** characterized by or designating continuous or natural development (*the company expanded through organic growth rather than acquisitions*). [from Greek *organikos*] □ **organically** *adv.*

organism *n.* **1** a living individual consisting of a single cell or of a group of interdependent parts. **2** an individual live plant or animal. **3** a whole with interdependent parts compared to a living being.

organist *n.* the player of an organ.

organization *n.* (also **-isation**) **1** the act or an instance of organizing; the state of being organized. **2** an organized body, esp. a business, charity, etc. **3** systematic arrangement; tidiness. □ **organizational** *adj.* **organizationally** *adv.*

organize *v.tr.* (also **-ise**) **1 a** give an orderly structure to, systematize. **b** make arrangements for (a person). **2** *Brit.* **a** arrange for or initiate (a scheme etc.). **b** provide; take responsibility for (*organized some sandwiches*). **3** (often *absol.*) **a** enrol (new

ORGAN

Depressing the keys or pedals on an organ sends air into the pipes. This causes the air in the pipes to vibrate, which creates a note. The pipes are organized in rows (called ranks or registers), and each row sounds a single pitch. When a stop is pushed in, it 'stops' air entering a particular rank. The pistons are used to select varying combinations of keyboard and stop settings, thereby creating different sound mixtures.

PIPE ORGAN CONSOLE

stops · *music stand* · *pipes* · *swell manual (keyboard)* · *stops* · *thumb piston* · *great manual (keyboard)* · *choir manual (keyboard)* · *swell pedals* · *foot pedals* · *toe pistons* · *pedal board*

---

members) in a trade union, political party, etc. **b** form (a trade union or other political group). **4** (esp. as **organized** *adj.*) make organic; make into a living being or tissue. [from medieval Latin *organizare*]

organizer *n.* (also **-iser**) **1 a** a thing used for organizing objects, such as a handbag or folder with many compartments. **b** = PERSONAL ORGANIZER. **2** in senses of ORGANIZE.

organ loft *n.* a gallery in a church or concert room for an organ.

organ pipe *n.* any of the pipes on an organ.

organ stop *n.* **1** a set of pipes of a similar tone in an organ. **2** the handle of the mechanism that brings it into action.

organza *n.* a thin stiff transparent silk or synthetic dress fabric.

orgasm ● *n.* the climax of sexual excitement. ● *v.intr.* experience an orgasm. [based on Greek *organ* 'to swell, be excited'] □ **orgasmic** *adj.* **orgasmically** *adv.*

orgiastic *adj.* of or resembling an orgy. [from Greek *orgiastikos*] □ **orgiastically** *adv.*

orgy *n.* (*pl.* **-ies**) **1** a wild drunken festivity, esp. one at which indiscriminate sexual activity takes place. **2** excessive indulgence in an activity. [from Greek *orgia* 'secret rites']

oriel *n.* (in full **oriel window**) a projecting window in an upper storey. [from Old French *oriol* 'gallery']

orient ● *n.* (**the Orient**) **1** *poet.* the east. **2** the countries east of the Mediterranean, esp. E. Asia; the East. ● *v.* **1** *tr.* **a** place or exactly determine the position of with the aid of a compass; settle or find the bearings of. **b** (often foll. by *towards*) direct. **2** *tr.* place or build (a church etc.) facing towards the east. **3** *intr.* turn eastward or in a specified direction. □ **orient oneself** determine how one stands in relation to one's surroundings. [from Latin *oriens orient-* 'rising, east']

oriental ● *adj.* **1** (often **Oriental**) of or characteristic of Eastern civilization etc. **2** of or concerning the East, esp. E. Asia. ● *n.* (esp. **Oriental**) a person of Oriental, esp. E. Asian, descent. □ **orientalism** *n.* **orientalist** *n.* **orientalize** *v.intr.* & *tr.* (also **-ise**).

■ **Usage** The term *Oriental*, when applied to people, may be considered offensive, especially in the United States where *Asian* is preferred.

orientate *v tr* & *intr.* = ORIENT *v.*

orientation *n.* **1** the act or an instance of orienting; the state of being oriented. **2 a** a relative position. **b** a person's attitude or adjustment in relation to circumstances, esp. politically or psychologically. **3** an introduction to a subject or situation; a briefing. □ **orientational** *adj.*

orienteering *n.* a competitive sport in which runners cross open country with a map, compass, etc. □ **orienteer** *n.* & *v.intr.*

orifice *n.* an opening, esp. the mouth of a cavity, a bodily aperture, etc. [based on Latin *os oris* 'mouth' + *facere* 'to make']

origami *n.* ▶ the Japanese art of folding paper into decorative shapes and figures. [Japanese, from *oru* 'fold' + *kami* 'paper']

origanum *n.* any plant of the genus *Origanum*, esp. wild marjoram (see MARJORAM). [from Greek *origanon*]

origin *n.* **1** a beginning or starting point; a derivation; a source (*a word of Latin origin*). **2** (often in *pl.*) a person's ancestry (*what are his origins?*). **3** *Math.* a fixed point from which coordinates are measured. [from Latin *origo -ginis*]

original ● *adj.* **1** existing from the beginning; innate. **2** novel; inventive; creative (*has an original*

ORIGAMI: FIGURE OF A DOG

---

mind). **3** not derivative or imitative; first-hand (*in the original Greek; has an original Rembrandt*). ● *n.* **1** an original model, pattern, picture, etc. from which another is copied or translated (*kept the copy and destroyed the original*). **2** an eccentric or unusual person. **3 a** a garment specially designed for a fashion collection. **b** a copy of such a garment made to order. □ **originally** *adv.*

original instrument *n.* a musical instrument, or a copy of one, dating from the time the music played on it was composed.

originality *n.* (*pl.* **-ies**) **1** the power of creating or thinking creatively. **2** newness or freshness (*this vase has originality*).

original sin *n.* the innate depravity of all mankind held to be a consequence of the Fall.

originate *v.* **1** *tr.* cause to begin; initiate. **2** *intr.* (usu. foll. by *from*, *in*, *with*) have as an origin; begin. □ **origination** *n.* **originator** *n.*

O-ring *n.* a gasket in the form of a ring with a circular cross-section.

oriole *n.* **1** any Old World bird of the genus *Oriolus*, many of which have brightly coloured plumage. **2** any New World bird of the genus *Icterus*, with similar coloration. ▷ SONGBIRD. [from Latin *aureolus* 'little golden (one)']

Orion *n.* ▼ a brilliant constellation on the celestial equator visible from most parts of the Earth. [from Greek *Ōrīōn*, name of a legendary hunter]

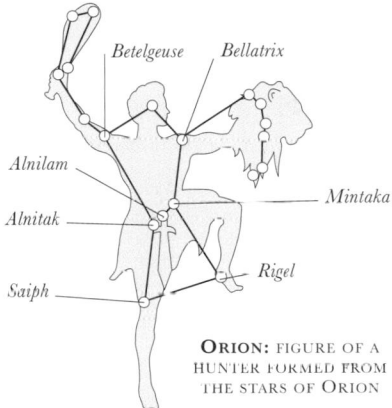

Betelgeuse · *Bellatrix* · *Alnilam* · *Mintaka* · *Alnitak* · *Rigel* · *Saiph*

ORION: FIGURE OF A HUNTER FORMED FROM THE STARS OF ORION

ormolu /or-mŏ-loo/ *n.* **1** (often *attrib.*) gilded bronze; a gold-coloured alloy of copper, zinc, and tin. **2** furniture, ornaments, etc. made of or decorated with this. [from French *or moulu* 'powdered gold', for use in gilding]

ornament ● *n.* **1** a thing used or serving to adorn, esp. a small trinket, vase, figure, etc. **2** decoration added to embellish esp. a building (*a tower rich in ornament*). **3** (in *pl.*) *Mus.* embellishments and decorations made to a melody. ● *v.tr.* adorn; beautify. [from Latin *ornamentum* 'equipment, ornament'] □ **ornamentation** *n.*

ornamental ● *adj.* serving as an ornament; decorative. ● *n.* a thing considered to be ornamental, esp. a cultivated plant. □ **ornamentalism** *n.*

ornate *adj.* **1** elaborately adorned. **2** (of literary style) convoluted; flowery. [from Latin *ornatus* 'adorned'] □ **ornately** *adv.* **ornateness** *n.*

ornery *adj.* *N. Amer. colloq.* **1** cantankerous; unpleasant. **2** of poor quality. [variant of ORDINARY] □ **orneriness** *n.*

ornithischian /or-ni-th'is-ki-ăn/ ● *adj.* of or relating to the order Ornithischia, including dinosaurs with a pelvic structure like that of birds. ● *n.* a dinosaur of this order. ▷ DINOSAUR. [based on Greek *ornis ornith-* 'bird' + *iskhion* 'hip joint']

ornitho- *comb. form* bird. [Greek]

ornithology *n.* the scientific study of birds. □ **ornithological** *adj.* **ornithologically** *adv.* **ornithologist** *n.*

ORRERY

English scientist Isaac Newton (1642–1727) proposed that the universe runs like a giant clockwork machine. An orrery is an embodiment of this view. The complex gearing in an orrery ensures the planets move around the Sun at the correct relative rates.

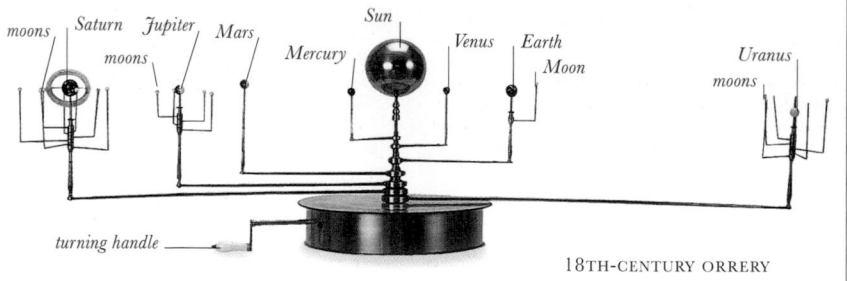

moons · Saturn · Jupiter · Mars · Sun · Mercury · Venus · Earth Moon · Uranus moons

turning handle

18TH-CENTURY ORRERY

---

ornithopod ● *n.* a bipedal herbivorous ornithischian dinosaur of the suborder Ornithopoda. ▷ DINOSAUR. ● *adj.* of or relating to this suborder.

orotund *adj.* **1** (of the voice or phrasing) full, round; imposing. **2** (of writing, style, expression, etc.) pompous; pretentious. [from Latin *ore rotundo* 'with rounded mouth']

orphan ● *n.* (often *attrib.*) a child whose parents are dead. ● *v.tr.* bereave (a child) of its parents. [from Greek *orphanos* 'bereaved'] □ **orphanhood** *n.*

orphanage *n.* a usu. residential institution for the care and education of orphans.

orrery *n.* (*pl.* **-ies**) ▲ a clockwork model of the solar system. [named after the fourth Earl of *Orrery*, for whom one was made]

orris *n.* **1** any plant of the genus *Iris*, esp. *I. florentina*. **2** = ORRIS ROOT. [16th-century coinage]

orris-powder *n.* powdered orris root.

orris root *n.* the fragrant rootstock of the orris, used in perfumery and formerly in medicine.

ortanique *n.* a citrus fruit produced by crossing an orange and a tangerine. [from *or*ange + *t*ange*r*ine + un*ique*]

ortho- *comb. form* **1** straight, rectangular, upright. **2** right, correct. [from Greek *orthos* 'straight']

orthodontics *n.pl.* (treated as *sing.*) (also **orthodontia**) the treatment of irregularities in the teeth and jaws. [based on Greek *odous odontos* 'tooth'] □ **orthodontic** *adj.* **orthodontist** *n.*

orthodox *adj.* **1** holding currently accepted opinions, esp. on religious doctrine, morals, etc. **2** (of religious doctrine, standards of morality, etc.) generally accepted as right or true; conventional. **3** (also **Orthodox**) (of Judaism) strictly keeping to traditional doctrine and ritual. **4** (**Orthodox**) of or relating to the Orthodox Church. [based on Greek *doxa* 'opinion'] □ **orthodoxly** *adv.*

Orthodox Church *n.* a Christian Church or federation of Churches acknowledging the authority of the patriarch of Constantinople, including the national Churches of Greece, Russia, Bulgaria, Romania, etc.

orthodoxy *n.* (*pl.* **-ies**) **1** the state of being orthodox. **2 a** the orthodox practice of Judaism. **b** the body of Orthodox Jews or Orthodox Christians. **3** esp. *Relig.* an authorized or generally accepted theory, doctrine, etc.

orthogonal *adj.* of or involving right angles; at right angles. [French]

orthography *n.* (*pl.* **-ies**) **1** correct or conventional spelling. **2** spelling with reference to its correctness (*dreadful orthography*). **3** the study or science of spelling. □ **orthographic** *adj.* **orthographical** *adj.* **orthographically** *adv.*

orthopaedics /or-thŏ-**pee**-diks/ *n.pl.* (*US* **-pedics**) (treated as *sing.*) the branch of medicine dealing with the treatment of disorders of the bones and joints and with the correction of deformities. [based on Greek *paideia* 'rearing of children'] □ **orthopaedic** *adj.* **orthopaedist** *n.*

orthopteran *n.* ▼ any insect of the order Orthoptera, with straight narrow forewings, and hind legs modified for jumping etc., including grasshoppers and crickets. □ **orthopterous** *adj.* [ortho- + Greek *pteros* 'wing']

orthoptics *n. Med.* the study or treatment of irregularities of the eyes, esp. with reference to the eye muscles.

orthorhombic *adj. Crystallog.* (of a crystal) characterized by three mutually perpendicular axes which are unequal in length, as in topaz and talc.

ortolan *n.* (in full **ortolan bunting**) a small European bird, *Emberiza hortulana*, formerly eaten as a delicacy. [from Latin *hortulanus*]

Orwellian *adj.* of or characteristic of the writings of George Orwell (E.A. Blair), English writer 1903–50, esp. with reference to the totalitarian development of the State as depicted in *Nineteen Eighty-Four* and *Animal Farm*.

OS *abbr.* **1** ordinary seaman. **2** (in the UK) Ordnance Survey. **3** outsize.

Os *symb. Chem.* the element osmium.

Oscar *n.* any of the statuettes awarded by the US Academy of Motion Picture Arts and Sciences for excellence in film acting, directing, etc.

oscillate *v.* **1** *intr. & tr.* swing or move to and fro. **2** *intr.* vacillate; vary between extremes of opinion, action, etc. **3** *intr. Physics* move with periodic regularity. **4** *intr. Electr.* (of a current) undergo high-frequency alternations as across a spark-gap. [based on Latin *oscillatus* 'swung'] □ **oscillation** *n.* **oscillator** *n.* **oscillatory** *adj.*

oscillogram *n.* a record obtained from an oscillograph.

oscillograph *n.* a device for recording oscillations.

oscilloscope *n.* a device for viewing oscillations by a display on the screen of a cathode ray tube.

osier *n.* **1** any of various willows, esp. *Salix viminalis*, with long flexible shoots used in basketwork. **2** a shoot of this. [from medieval Latin *auseria* 'osier bed']

osmic *adj. Chem.* containing osmium.

osmium *n. Chem.* a hard bluish-white transition element, the heaviest known metal, occurring naturally in association with platinum and used in certain alloys. [based on Greek *osmē* 'smell', from the pungent smell of its tetroxide]

osmoregulation *n. Biol.* the maintenance of constant osmotic pressure in the fluids of an organism by control of water and salt levels etc.

osmosis *n.* **1** *Biol. & Chem.* the passage of a solvent through a semi-permeable partition into a more concentrated solution. **2** any process by which something is acquired by absorption. [based on Greek *ōsmos* 'push'] □ **osmotic** *adj.* **osmotically** *adv.*

ORTHOPTERAN

There are over 20,000 species in the order Orthoptera. These insects usually travel by jumping, even though many have wings.

Orthopterans communicate by stridulation: rubbing together body parts, such as wings and legs, to produce a sound.

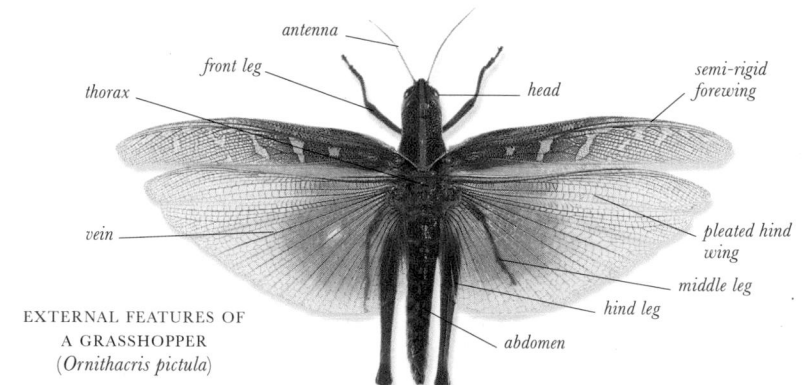

antenna · front leg · thorax · head · semi-rigid forewing · vein · pleated hind wing · middle leg · hind leg · abdomen

EXTERNAL FEATURES OF A GRASSHOPPER (*Ornithacris pictula*)

EXAMPLES OF OTHER ORTHOPTERANS

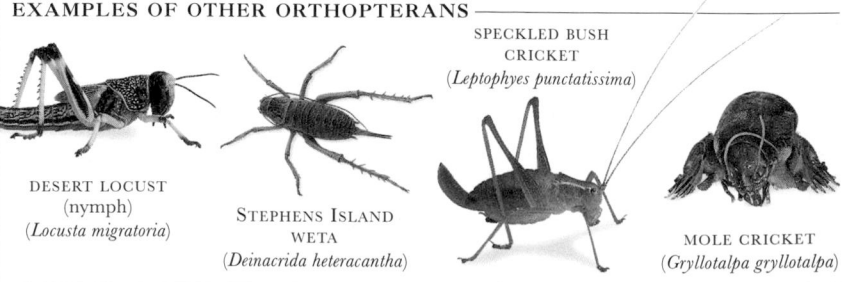

DESERT LOCUST (nymph) (*Locusta migratoria*)

STEPHENS ISLAND WETA (*Deinacrida heteracantha*)

SPECKLED BUSH CRICKET (*Leptophyes punctatissima*)

MOLE CRICKET (*Gryllotalpa gryllotalpa*)

OSPREY
(Pandion haliaetus)

osprey /**os**-pri/ *n.* (*pl.* **-eys**) ▲ a large bird of prey, *Pandion haliaetus*, with a brown back and white markings, feeding on fish. ▷ RAPTOR. [from Old French *ospres*]

osseous *adj.* **1** consisting of bone. **2** having a bony skeleton. **3** ossified. [from Latin *osseus*]

ossicle *n.* **1** *Anat.* any small bone, esp. of the middle ear. ▷ EAR. **2** a small piece of bonelike substance. [from Latin *ossiculum* 'little bone']

Ossie var. of AUSSIE.

ossify *v.tr. & intr.* (**-ies**, **-ied**) **1** turn into bone; harden. **2** make or become rigid, callous, or unprogressive. [from French *ossifier*] □ **ossification** *n.*

osso bucco /**boo**-koh/ *n.* shin of veal containing marrowbone stewed in wine with vegetables. [Italian, literally 'marrowbone']

ossuary *n.* (*pl.* **-ies**) **1** a receptacle or urn for the bones of the dead; a charnel house. **2** a cave in which ancient bones are found. [from Late Latin *ossuarium*]

ostensible *adj.* apparent but not necessarily real; professed (*his ostensible function was that of interpreter*). [based on Latin *ostensus* 'stretched out to view'] □ **ostensibly** *adv.*

ostensive *adj.* **1** directly demonstrative. **2** (of a definition) indicating by direct demonstration that which is signified by a term. [from Late Latin *ostensivus*] □ **ostensively** *adv.* **ostensiveness** *n.*

ostentation *n.* **1** a pretentious and vulgar display esp. of wealth and luxury. **2** the attempt or intention to attract notice; showing off. [from Latin *ostentatio*] □ **ostentatious** *adj.* **ostentatiously** *adv.*

osteo- *comb. form* bone. [from Greek *osteon*]

osteoarthritis *n.* degeneration of joint cartilage, causing pain and stiffness. □ **osteoarthritic** *adj.*

osteology *n.* the study of the structure and function of the skeleton and bony structures. □ **osteological** *adj.* **osteologist** *n.*

osteomyelitis *n.* inflammation of the bone or of bone marrow, usu. due to infection.

osteopathy *n.* the treatment of medical disorders through the manipulation and massage of the skeleton and musculature. □ **osteopath** *n.* **osteopathic** *adj.*

osteoporosis *n.* a condition of brittle and fragile bones caused by loss of bony tissue, esp. as a result of hormonal changes, or deficiency of calcium or vitamin D. [based on Greek *poros* 'passage, pore']

ostinato *n.* (*pl.* **-os** or **ostinati**) (often *attrib.*) *Mus.* a persistent phrase or rhythm repeated through all or part of a piece. [Italian, literally 'obstinate']

ostler /**os**-ler/ *n. Brit. hist.* a person who works in the stable of an inn. [from Old French *(h)ostelier* 'keeper of a hostelry']

ostracize *v.tr.* (also **-ise**) exclude (a person) from a society, favour, common privileges, etc.; refuse to associate with. [from Greek *ostrakizein*] □ **ostracism** *n.*

ostrich *n.* **1** a large African swift-running flightless bird, *Struthio camelus*, with long legs and two toes on each foot. ▷ FLIGHTLESS. **2** a person who refuses to accept facts. [based on Latin *avis* 'bird' + Greek *strouthiōn* 'ostrich']

OT *abbr.* Old Testament.

other ● *adj.* **1** not the same as one or some already mentioned or implied (*other people; use other means; my reason is quite other*). **2 a** further; additional (*a few other examples*). **b** alternative of two (*open your other eye*) (cf. *every other*). **3** (prec. by *the*) remaining (*must be in the other pocket; where are the other two?*). **4** (foll. by *than*) apart from; excepting (*any person other than you*). ● *n. & pron.* **1** an additional, different, or extra person, thing, example, etc. (*one or other of us will be there; some others have come*) (see also ANOTHER, EACH OTHER). **2** (in *pl.*; prec. by *the*) the ones remaining (*where are the others?*). ● *adv.* (usu. foll. by *than*) disp. otherwise (*cannot react other than angrily*). □ **on the other hand** see HAND. **the other day** (or **night** or **week** etc.) a few days etc. ago (*heard from him the other day*). **someone** (or **something** or **somehow** etc.) **or other** some unspecified person, thing, manner, etc. [Old English]

■ **Usage** The use of *other* as an adverb (see example above) is non-standard. *Otherwise* should be used instead, e.g. *It is impossible to do the job otherwise than very superficially in the time allotted.*

other half *n. colloq.* one's wife or husband.

otherness *n.* **1** the state of being different; diversity. **2** a thing or existence other than the thing mentioned and the thinking subject.

other ranks *n.pl. Brit.* soldiers other than commissioned officers.

otherwise ● *adv.* **1** else; or else; in the circumstances other than those considered etc. (*bring your umbrella, otherwise you will get wet*). **2** in other respects (*he is untidy, but otherwise very suitable*). **3** (often foll. by *than*) in a different way (*could not have acted otherwise; cannot react otherwise than angrily*). **4** as an alternative (*otherwise known as Jack*). ● *predic.adj.* in a different state (*the matter is quite otherwise*). □ **and** (or **or**) **otherwise** the negation or opposite (of a specified thing) (*the merits or otherwise of the Bill; experiences pleasant and otherwise*). [Old English]

■ **Usage** See Usage Note at OTHER.

other woman *n.* (*masc.* **other man**) (prec. by *the*) the lover of a married or similarly attached woman or man.

other-worldly *adj.* **1** not of this world; of an imaginary other world. **2** relating to life after death etc. □ **other-worldliness** *n.*

otiose *adj.* serving no practical purpose; not required; functionless. [based on Latin *otium* 'leisure'] □ **otiosely** *adv.* **otioseness** *n.*

otitis *n.* inflammation of the ear, esp. (in full **otitis media**) of the middle ear.

oto- *comb. form* ear. [Greek]

otology *n.* the study of the anatomy and diseases of the ear. □ **otological** *adj.* **otologist** *n.*

OTT *abbr. colloq.* over-the-top.

otter *n.* **1** ▶ any of several semiaquatic fish-eating mammals of the genus *Lutra* or a related genus of the weasel family, with dense fur and webbed feet. ▷ MUSTELID. **2** its fur or pelt. [Old English]

otter-board *n.* a device for keeping the mouth of a trawl net open.

otto var. of ATTAR.

Ottoman *hist.* ● *adj.* **1** of or relating to: **a** the dynasty of Osman I (Othman I). **b** the branch of the Turks to which he belonged. **c** the empire ruled by his descendants. **2** Turkish. ● *n.* (*pl.* **Ottomans**) an Ottoman person; a Turk. [based on Arabic *'utmān* 'Othman']

ottoman *n.* (*pl.* **ottomans**) an upholstered seat, usu. square and without a back or arms, sometimes a box with a padded top. [French, related to OTTOMAN]

OU *abbr. Brit.* **1** Open University. **2** Oxford University.

oubliette /oo-bli-**et**/ *n.* a secret dungeon with access only through a trapdoor. [French, based on *oublier* 'to forget']

ouch *int.* expressing pain. [a natural exclamation]

ought *v.aux.* (usu. foll. by *to* + infin.; present and past indicated by the following infin.) **1** expressing duty or rightness (*we ought to love our neighbours*). **2** expressing shortcoming (*it ought to have been done long ago*). **3** expressing advisability or prudence (*you ought to go for your own good*). **4** expressing esp. strong probability (*he ought to be there by now*). □ **ought not** the negative form of *ought* (*he ought not to have stolen it*). [Old English *āhte* 'owed']

oughtn't *contr.* ought not.

Ouija /**wee**-jă/ *n.* (in full **Ouija board**) *propr.* a board having letters or signs at its rim to which a planchette, movable pointer, or upturned glass supposedly points in answer to questions from attenders at a seance etc. [from French *oui* 'yes' + German *ja* 'yes']

ounce *n.* **1** a unit of weight of one-sixteenth of a pound avoirdupois (approx. 28 grams). **2** a small quantity. [from Latin *uncia* 'twelfth part']

our *poss.det.* **1** of or belonging to us or ourselves (*our house*). **2** of or belonging to all people (*our children's future*). **3** (esp. as **Our**) of Us the royal, imperial, etc., personage (*given under Our seal*). **4** of us, the editorial staff of a newspaper etc. (*a foolish adventure in our view*). [Old English]

Our Father *n.* **1** the Lord's Prayer. **2** God.

Our Lady *n.* the Virgin Mary.

Our Lord *n.* **1** Jesus Christ. **2** God.

ours *poss.pron.* the one or ones belonging to or associated with us (*it is ours*). □ **of ours** of or belonging to us (*a friend of ours*).

ourself *pron.* **1** *archaic* a word formerly used instead of *myself* by a sovereign, newspaper editorial staff, etc. **2** *disp.* = OURSELVES.

■ **Usage** The use of *ourself* rather than *ourselves*, in contexts such as *We see ourself as the biggest club in Britain*, is considered incorrect by some people.

ourselves *pron.* **1 a** *emphat. form* of WE or US (*we ourselves did it*). **b** *refl. form* of US (*are pleased with ourselves*). **2** in our normal state of body or mind (*not quite ourselves today*). □ **be ourselves** act in our normal unconstrained manner. **by ourselves** see by *oneself.*

ousel var. of OUZEL.

oust *v.tr.* (usu. foll. by *from*) drive out or expel, esp. by forcing oneself into the place of. [from Latin *obstare* 'to oppose, hinder']

out ● *adv.* **1** away from or not in or at a place etc. (*keep him out*). **2** (forming part of phrasal verbs) **a** indicating dispersal away from a centre etc. (*hire out*). **b** indicating a progression to a conclusion or resolution (*die out*). **c** indicating coming or bringing into the open (*send out; shine out*). **d** indicating a need for attentiveness (*watch out; listen out*). **3 a** not in one's house, office, etc. (*went out for a walk*). **b** occupied elsewhere, esp. socially (*out with friends*). **c** no longer detained in prison. **4 a** completely; thoroughly (*tired out*). **b** in its entirety (*typed it out*). **5** (of a fire, light, etc.) not burning; no longer lit. **6** in error (*was 3% out in my calculations*). **7** *colloq.* unconscious (*she was out for five minutes*). **8 a** (of a tooth) extracted. **b** (of a joint, bone, etc.) dislocated. **9** (of a party, politician, etc.) not in office. **10** (of a jury) considering its verdict in secrecy. **11** (of workers) on strike. **12** (of a secret) revealed. **13** (of a flower) blooming, open.

OTTER: EUROPEAN OTTER
(Lutra lutra)

waterproof fur

strong tail

webbed feet

sharp claws

forward-facing eyes

14 (of a book) published. **15** (of a star) visible after dark. **16** unfashionable (*turn-ups are out*). **17 a** (of a batsman etc.) no longer taking part, having been caught, stumped, etc. **b** (of a shot, serve, etc.) outside the boundary of the playing area. **18** not worth considering (*that idea is out*). **19** (prec. by *superl.*) *colloq.* known to exist (*the best game out*). **20** (of a stain etc.) removed (*painted out the sign*). **21** (of time) not spent working (*took five minutes out*). **22** (of a rash, bruise, etc.) visible. **23** (of the tide) at the lowest point. **24** *Boxing* unable to rise from the floor. **25 a** at an end (*before the week is out*). **b** (in a radio conversation etc.) transmission ends (*over and out*). • *prep. disp.* out of (*looked out of the window*). • *n. colloq.* an excuse. • *adj.* **1** *Brit.* (of a match) played away. **2** (of an island) away from the mainland. • *int.* a peremptory dismissal, reproach, etc. (*out, you scoundrel!*) • *v.* **1** *tr.* **a** put out. **b** *colloq.* eject forcibly. **2** *intr.* come or go out; emerge (*murder will out*). **3** *tr. Boxing* knock out. **4** *tr. colloq.* reveal the homosexuality of (a prominent person). □ **out and about** (of a person, esp. after an illness) engaging in normal activity. **out and away** by far. **out for** having one's interest or effort directed to; intent on. **out of 1** from within (*came out of the house*). **2** not within (*never out of England*). **3** from among (*nine people out of ten*). **4** beyond the range of (*is out of reach*). **5** without or so as to be without (*out of breath*). **6** from (*get money out of him*). **7** owing to (*out of curiosity*). **8** by the use of (material) (*what did you make it out of?*). **9** at a specified distance from (*seven miles out of Liverpool*). **10** beyond (*something out of the ordinary*). **11** *Racing* (of an animal, esp. a horse) born of. **out of bounds** see BOUND². **out of hand** see HAND. **out of it 1** not included; forlorn. **2** *colloq.* unaware of what is happening. **out of order** see ORDER. **out of pocket** see POCKET. **out of the question** see QUESTION. **out of sorts** see SORT. **out of temper** see TEMPER. **out of this world** see WORLD. **out of the way** see WAY. **out to** keenly striving to do. **out with it** say what you are thinking. [Old English]

■ **Usage** The use of *out* as a preposition, as in *He threw it out the window* or *I jumped out the boat*, is considered incorrect by some people. *Out of* is preferable in formal contexts.

outact *v.tr.* surpass in acting or performing.

outage *n.* a period of time during which a power supply etc. is not operating.

out and out • *adj.* thorough; surpassing. • *adv.* thoroughly; surpassingly.

outback *n.* esp. *Austral.* the remote and usu. uninhabited inland districts. □ **outbacker** *n.*

outbalance *v.tr.* **1** count as more important than. **2** outweigh.

outbid *v.tr.* (**-bidding**; *past* and *past part.* **-bid**) **1** bid higher than (another person) at an auction. **2** surpass in exaggeration etc.

outboard • *adj.* **1** ▶ (of a motor) portable and attachable to the outside of the stern of a boat. **2** (of a boat) having an outboard motor. • *adj. & adv.* on, towards, or near the outside of esp. a ship, an aircraft, etc. • *n.* **1** an outboard engine. **2** a boat with an outboard engine.

throttle / tiller

MERCURY

engine cowling

clamp

cavitation plate

propeller

skeg

OUTBOARD MOTOR

outbreak *n.* **1** a usu. sudden eruption of war, disease, rebellion, etc. **2** an outcrop.

outbreeding *n.* the theory or practice of breeding from animals not closely related. □ **outbreed** *v.intr. & tr.* (*past* and *past part.* **-bred**).

outbuilding *n.* a detached shed, barn, etc. within the grounds of a main building.

outburst *n.* **1** an explosion of anger etc., expressed in words. **2** an act or instance of bursting out. **3** an outcrop.

outcast • *n.* **1** a person cast out from or rejected by his or her home, country, etc. **2** a tramp or vagabond. • *adj.* rejected; homeless.

outclass *v.tr.* **1** belong to a higher class than. **2** defeat easily.

outcome *n.* a result; a visible effect.

outcrop • *n.* **1 a** ▶ the emergence of a stratum, vein, or rock, at the surface. **b** a stratum etc. emerging. **2** a noticeable manifestation or occurrence. • *v.intr.* (**-cropped**, **-cropping**) appear as an outcrop; crop out.

outcrop of harder, unweathered rocks

OUTCROP

softer, weathered rocks

outcry *n.* (*pl.* **-ies**) **1** the act or an instance of crying out. **2** an uproar. **3** a public protest.

outdance *v.tr.* surpass in dancing.

outdated *adj.* out of date; obsolete.

outdistance *v.tr.* leave (a competitor) behind completely.

outdo *v.tr.* (*3rd sing. present* **-does**; *past* **-did**; *pres. part.* **-doing**; *past part.* **-done**) exceed or excel in doing or performance.

outdoor *attrib.adj.* **1** done, existing, or used out of doors. **2** fond of the open air (*an outdoor type*).

outdoor pursuits *n.pl.* usu. organized sporting or leisure activities undertaken out of doors.

outdoors • *adv.* in or into the open air; out of doors. • *n.* the open air.

outer • *adj.* **1** outside; external (*pierced the outer layer*). **2** farther from the centre or inside. **3** objective or physical, not subjective or psychical. • *n. Brit.* the division of a target furthest from the bull's-eye. [Middle English]

outermost *adj.* furthest from the inside; the most far out.

outer space see SPACE *n.* 3a.

outface *v.tr.* disconcert or defeat by staring or by a display of confidence.

outfall *n.* the mouth of a river, drain, etc., where it empties into the sea etc.

outfield *n.* **1** the outer part of a cricket or baseball field. ▷ BASEBALL. **2** outlying land. □ **outfielder** *n.*

outfight *v.tr.* fight better than; beat in a fight.

outfit • *n.* **1** a set of clothes worn or esp. designed to be worn together. **2** a complete set of equipment etc. for a specific purpose. **3** *colloq.* a group of people regarded as a unit etc. • *v.tr.* (**-fitted**, **-fitting**) (also *refl.*) provide with an outfit, esp. of clothes.

outfitter *n.* a supplier of equipment, esp. (*Brit.*) of conventional styles of clothing or (*N. Amer.*) of equipment for outdoor expeditions.

outflank *v.tr.* **1 a** extend one's flank beyond that of (an enemy). **b** outmanoeuvre (an enemy) in this way. **2** get the better of; confound (an opponent).

outflow *n.* **1** an outward flow. **2** the amount that flows out.

outflung *adj.* (esp. of an arm) flung out to one side.

outfly *v.tr.* (**-flies**; *past* **-flew**; *past part.* **-flown**) **1** surpass in flying. **2** fly faster or farther than.

outfox *v.tr. colloq.* outwit.

outgas *v.* (**outgases**, **outgassed**, **outgassing**) **1** *intr.* release or give off a dissolved or adsorbed gas or vapour. **2** *tr.* **a** release or give off (a substance) as a gas or vapour. **b** drive off a gas or vapour from.

outgeneral *v.tr.* (**-generalled**, **-generalling**; *US* **-generaled**, **-generaling**) **1** outdo in generalship. **2** get the better of by superior strategy or tactics.

outgoing • *adj.* **1** friendly; sociable; extrovert. **2** retiring from office. **3** going out or away. • *n. Brit.* (in *pl.*) expenditure.

outgrow *v.tr.* (*past* **-grew**; *past part.* **-grown**) **1** grow too big for (one's clothes). **2** leave behind (a childish habit, ailment, etc.) as one matures. **3** grow faster or taller than. □ **outgrow one's strength** *Brit.* (esp. of a plant) become lanky and weak through rapid growth.

outgrowth *n.* **1** something that grows out. **2** an offshoot. **3** the process of growing out.

outguess *v.tr.* guess correctly what is intended by (another person).

outgun *v.tr.* (**-gunned**, **-gunning**) **1** surpass in military or other power or strength. **2** shoot better than.

outhouse *n.* **1** esp. *Brit.* a building, esp. a shed, barn, etc. built next to or in the grounds of a house. **2** *N. Amer.* an outdoor lavatory.

outing *n.* **1** a short holiday away from home, esp. of one day or part of a day. **2** any brief journey from home. **3** an appearance in an outdoor match, race, etc. **4** *colloq.* the practice or policy of revealing the homosexuality of a prominent person.

outjump *v.tr.* surpass in jumping.

outlandish *adj.* **1** looking or sounding foreign. **2** bizarre, strange, unfamiliar. [Old English, from *ūtland* 'foreign country'] □ **outlandishly** *adv.* **outlandishness** *n.*

outlast *v.tr.* last longer than.

outlaw • *n.* **1** a fugitive from the law. **2** *hist.* a person deprived of the protection of the law. • *v.tr.* **1** declare an outlaw. **2** make illegal. [from Old Norse *útlagi*] □ **outlawry** *n.*

outlay *n.* the money spent on something.

outlet *n.* **1** a means of exit or escape. **2** (usu. foll. by *for*) a means of expression (*find an outlet for tension*). **3** an agency, distributor, or market for goods (*a new retail outlet*). **4** *N. Amer.* a power point.

outline • *n.* **1** a rough draft of a diagram, plan, etc. **2 a** a précis of a proposed novel, article, etc. **b** a verbal description of essential parts only; a summary. **3** a sketch containing only contour lines. **4** (in *sing.* or *pl.*) **a** lines enclosing or indicating an object (*the outline of a shape under the blankets*). **b** a contour. **c** an external boundary. **5** (in *pl.*) the main features or general principles (*the outlines of a plan*). • *v.tr.* **1** draw or describe in outline. **2** mark the outline of. □ **in outline** sketched or represented as an outline.

outlive *v.tr.* **1** live longer than (another person). **2** live beyond (a specified date or time). **3** live through (an experience).

outlook *n.* **1** the prospect for the future (*the outlook is bleak*). **2** one's mental attitude or point of view (*narrow in their outlook*). **3** what is seen on looking out.

outlying *attrib.adj.* situated far from a centre; remote.

outmanoeuvre *v.tr.* (*US* **-maneuver**) **1** use skill and cunning to secure an advantage over (a person). **2** outdo in manoeuvring.

outmatch *v.tr.* be more than a match for (an opponent etc.); surpass.

outmoded *adj.* **1** no longer in fashion. **2** obsolete.

outnumber *v.tr.* exceed in number.

out-of-body experience *n.* a sensation of being outside one's body, esp. of floating and being able to observe oneself from a distance.

out-of-court *attrib.adj.* (esp. of a settlement) made or done outside or without the intervention of a court.

out of date *adj.* (hyphenated when *attrib.*) old-fashioned, obsolete.

out of doors *adj. & adv.* in or into the open air.

out-of-pocket expenses *n.pl.* the actual outlay of cash incurred.

out-of-town *attrib.adj.* situated or taking place outside a town.

outpace *v.tr.* **1** go faster than. **2** outdo in a contest.

outpatient *n.* a patient who attends a hospital without staying there overnight.

outperform *v.tr.* **1** perform better than. **2** surpass in a specified field or activity. □ **outperformance** *n.*

outplacement *n.* the act or process of finding new employment for esp. executive workers after redundancy.

outplay *v.tr.* surpass in playing; play better than.

outpost *n.* **1** a detachment set at a distance from the main body of an army, esp. to prevent surprise. **2** a distant branch or settlement.

outpouring *n.* **1** (usu. in *pl.*) a copious spoken or written expression of emotion. **2** what is poured out.

output ● *n.* **1** the product of a process, esp. of manufacture, or of mental or artistic work. **2** the quantity or amount of this. **3** the printout etc. supplied by a computer. **4** the power etc. delivered by an apparatus. **5** a place where energy etc. leaves a system. ● *v.tr.* (**-putting**; *past* and *past part.* **-put** or **-putted**) **1** put or send out. **2** (of a computer) supply (results etc.).

outrage ● *n.* **1** an extreme violation of others' rights, sentiments, etc. **2** a gross offence or indignity. **3** fierce anger or resentment (*a feeling of outrage*). ● *v.tr.* **1** subject to outrage. **2** insult, etc. flagrantly. **3** shock and anger [based on Old French *outrer* 'to exceed']

outrageous *adj.* **1** immoderate. **2** shocking. **3** grossly cruel. **4** immoral, offensive □ **outrageously** *adv.* **outrageousness** *n.*

outran *past* of OUTRUN.

outrank *v.tr.* **1** be superior in rank to. **2** take priority over.

outré /oo-tray/ *adj.* **1** outside the bounds of what is usual or proper. **2** eccentric or indecorous. [French, literally 'exceeded']

outreach *n.* any organization's involvement with or influence in the community, esp. in the context of social welfare.

outride *v.tr.* (*past* **-rode**; *past part.* **-ridden**) **1** ride better, faster, or further than. **2** (of a ship) come safely through (a storm etc.).

outrider *n.* **1** a mounted attendant riding ahead of, or with, a carriage etc. **2** a motorcyclist acting as a guard in a similar manner. □ **outriding** *n.*

outrigger *n.* **1** a beam, spar, or framework, rigged out and projecting from or over a ship's side. **2** a similar projecting beam etc. in a building. **3** ► a log etc. fixed parallel to a canoe to stabilize it. **4 a** an iron bracket bearing a rowlock attached horizontally to a boat's side to increase the leverage of the oar. ▷ SCULL. **b** a boat fitted with these.

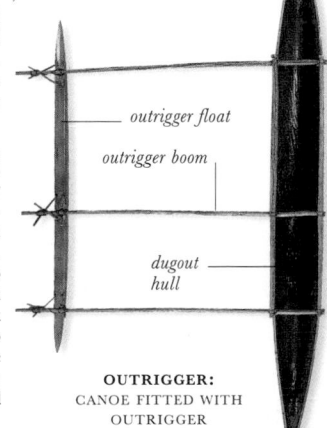

OUTRIGGER:
CANOE FITTED WITH
OUTRIGGER

outrigger float
outrigger boom
dugout hull

outright ● *adv.* **1** altogether, entirely (*proved outright*). **2** not gradually, nor by degrees, nor by instalments (*bought it outright*). **3** without reservation (*denied the charge outright*). ● *attrib.adj.* **1** downright, direct, complete (*resentment turned to outright anger*). **2** undisputed, clear (*the outright winner*).

outro *n.* (*pl.* **-os**) *colloq.* a concluding section, esp. of a broadcast programme or a piece of music. [on the pattern of *intro*]

outrode *past* of OUTRIDE.

outrun *v.tr.* (**-running**; *past* **-ran**; *past part.* **-run**) **1 a** run faster or farther than. **b** escape from. **2** go beyond (a specified point or limit).

outrush *n.* **1** a rushing out. **2** a violent overflow.

outsail *v.tr.* sail better or faster than.

outsell *v.tr.* (*past* and *past part.* **-sold**) **1** sell more than. **2** be sold in greater quantities than.

outset *n.* the start, beginning. □ **at** (or **from**) **the outset** at or from the beginning.

outshine *v.tr.* (*past* and *past part.* **-shone**) **1** shine brighter than. **2** surpass in ability etc.

outshoot *v.tr.* (*past* and *past part.* **-shot**) **1** shoot better or further than (another person). **2** esp. *N. Amer.* attempt or score more goals etc. than.

outside ● *n.* **1** the external side or surface (*painted blue on the outside*). **2** the outward aspect of a building etc. **3** (also *attrib.*) all that is without; (*learn about the outside world*). **4** a position on the outer side (*the gate opens from the outside*). **5** *colloq.* the highest computation (*it is a mile at the outside*). **6** *Brit.* an outside player in football etc. ● *adj.* **1** of or on or nearer the outside; outer. **2** not of or belonging to some circle or institution (*outside help*). **3** (of a chance etc.) remote; very unlikely. **4** (of an estimate etc.) the greatest or highest possible (*the outside price*). **5** (of a player in football etc.) positioned nearest to the edge of the field. ● *adv.* **1** on or to the outside. **2** in or to the open air. **3** not within or enclosed or included. **4** *slang* not in prison. ● *prep.* (also *disp.* foll. by *of*) **1** to or at the exterior of (*meet me outside the post office*). **2** beyond the limits of (*outside the law*). □ **at the outside** (of an estimate etc.) at the most. **outside in** = INSIDE OUT. **outside of** esp. *N. Amer. colloq.* apart from.

■ **Usage** The use of *outside of* as a preposition, e.g. *There is nothing like it outside of Japan* is considered incorrect by some people. *Outside* on its own is preferable.

outside broadcast *n. Brit.* a broadcast made on location and not in a studio.

outside interest *n.* an interest not connected with one's work or normal way of life.

outsider *n.* **1 a** a non-member of some circle, party, etc. **b** an uninitiated person, a layman. **2** a competitor, applicant, etc. thought to have little chance of success.

outsize *adj.* **1** unusually large. **2** (of garments etc.) of an exceptionally large size. □ **outsizeness** *n.*

outskirts *n.pl.* the outer border or fringe of a town etc.

outsmart *v.tr. colloq.* outwit, be cleverer than.

outsold *past* and *past part.* of OUTSELL.

outsource *v.tr.* esp. *N. Amer. Commerce* **1** obtain (goods etc.) by contract from an outside source. **2** contract (work) out. □ **outsourcing** *n.*

outspend *v.tr.* (*past* and *past part.* **-spent**) spend more than (one's resources or another person).

outspoken *adj.* given to or involving plain speaking; frank in stating one's opinions. □ **outspokenly** *adv.* **outspokenness** *n.*

outspread ● *adj.* spread out; fully extended or expanded. ● *v.tr. & intr.* (*past* and *past part.* **-spread**) spread out; expand.

outstanding *adj.* **1 a** conspicuous, eminent, esp. because of excellence. **b** (usu. foll. by *at, in*) remarkable (in a specified field). **2** (esp. of a debt) not yet settled (*£200 still outstanding*). □ **outstandingly** *adv.*

outstare *v.tr.* **1** outdo in staring. **2** abash by staring.

outstation *n.* a remote branch or outpost.

outstay *v.tr.* **1** stay beyond the limit of (one's welcome etc.). **2** stay or endure longer than (another person etc.).

outstep *v.tr.* (**-stepped**, **-stepping**) step outside or beyond.

outstretch *v.tr.* **1** (usu. as **outstretched** *adj.*) reach out or stretch out (esp. one's hands or arms). **2** reach or stretch further than.

outstrip *v.tr.* (**-stripped**, **-stripping**) **1** pass in running etc. **2** surpass in competition or relative progress or ability.

out-take *n.* a length of film or tape rejected in editing.

out-talk *v.tr.* outdo or overcome in talking.

out-think *v.tr.* (*past* and *past part.* **-thought**) outwit; outdo in thinking.

out-thrust *adj.* extended; projected (*with out-thrust arms*).

out to lunch *adj. colloq.* crazy, mad.

out-tray *n.* a tray for outgoing documents, letters, etc.

out-turn *n.* **1** the quantity produced. **2** the result of a process or sequence of events.

outvote *v.tr.* defeat by a majority of votes.

outward ● *adj.* **1** situated on or directed towards the outside. **2** going out (*on the outward voyage*). **3** external, apparent, superficial (*in all outward respects*). ● *adv.* (also **outwards**) in an outward direction; towards the outside. ● *n.* the outward appearance of something; the exterior. [Old English] □ **outwardly** *adv.*

outward bound ● *adj.* (of a ship, passenger, etc.) going away from home. ● *n.* (**Outward Bound**) *propr.* a movement to provide adventure training etc. for young people.

outward form *n.* appearance.

outwardness *n.* external existence; objectivity.

outwards var. of OUTWARD *adv.*

outwash *n.* ▼ the material carried from a glacier by melt water and deposited beyond the moraine. ▷ GLACIER

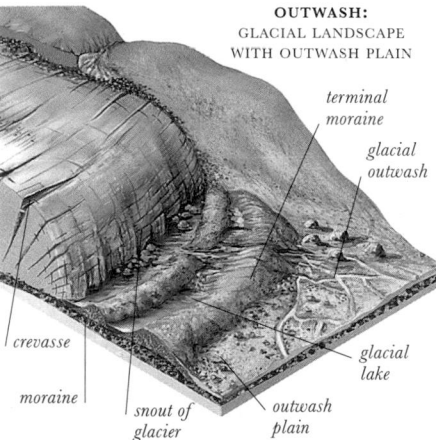

OUTWASH:
GLACIAL LANDSCAPE
WITH OUTWASH PLAIN

terminal moraine
glacial outwash
crevasse
moraine
snout of glacier
outwash plain
glacial lake

outweigh *v.tr.* exceed in weight, value, importance, or influence.

outwent *past* of OUTGO.

outwit *v.tr.* (**-witted**, **-witting**) be too clever or crafty for; deceive by greater ingenuity.

outwith *prep. Sc.* outside, beyond.

outwork *n.* **1** an advanced or detached part of a fortification. **2** *Brit.* work done outside the shop or factory which supplies it. □ **outworker** *n.* (in sense 2).

outworking *n.* (usu. foll. by *of*) the action or process of working out; practical operation.

outworn *adj.* out of date, obsolete.

ouzel /oo-zĕl/ *n.* (also **ousel**) **1** = RING OUZEL. **2** = DIPPER 1. **3** *archaic* a blackbird. [Old English *ōsle* 'blackbird']

ouzo /oo-zoh/ *n.* (*pl.* **-os**) a Greek aniseed-flavoured spirit. [modern Greek]

ova *pl.* of OVUM.

oval ● *adj.* **1** egg-shaped, ellipsoidal. **2** having the outline of an egg. ● *n.* **1** an egg-shaped or elliptical closed curve. **2** any object with an oval outline. **3** a sports ground with an oval field. [from medieval Latin *ovalis*]

Oval Office *n.* the office of the US President in the White House.

ovary *n.* (*pl.* **-ies**) **1** ▼ each of a pair of female reproductive organs in which ova are produced. ▷ ENDOCRINE, REPRODUCTIVE ORGANS. **2** the hollow base of the carpel of a flower, containing one or more ovules. ▷ FLOWER. [related to OVUM] □ **ovarian** *adj.* **ovariectomy** *n.* (*pl.* **-ies**) (in sense 1). **ovariotomy** *n.* (*pl.* **-ies**) (in sense 1). **ovaritis** *n.* (in sense 1).

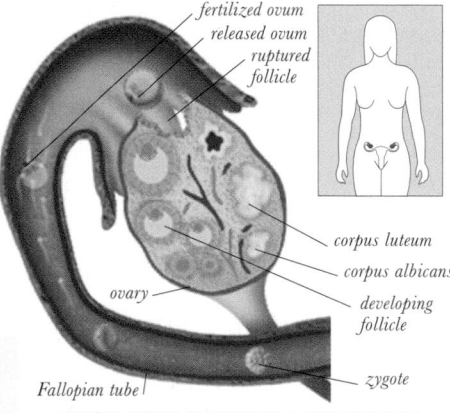

OVARY: CROSS-SECTION OF A HUMAN OVARY AND FALLOPIAN TUBE

Labels: fertilized ovum · released ovum · ruptured follicle · corpus luteum · corpus albicans · ovary · developing follicle · zygote · Fallopian tube

ovate *adj.* esp. *Biol.* egg-shaped as a solid or in outline; oval. [from Latin *ovatus*]

ovation *n.* an enthusiastic reception, esp. spontaneous and sustained applause. [based on Latin *ovare* 'to exult'] □ **ovational** *adj.*

oven *n.* **1** an enclosed compartment of brick, stone, or metal for cooking food. **2** a chamber for heating or drying. [Old English]

ovenbird *n.* any Central or S. American bird of the family Furnariidae, many of which make domed nests.

ovenproof *adj.* suitable for use in an oven; heat-resistant.

oven-ready *adj.* (of food) prepared before sale so as to be ready for immediate cooking in the oven.

ovenware *n.* dishes that can be used for cooking food in the oven.

over ● *adv.* expressing movement or position or state above or beyond something stated or implied: **1** outward and downward from a brink or from any erect position (*knocked the man over*). **2** so as to cover or touch a whole surface (*paint it over*). **3** so as to produce a fold, or reverse a position; with the effect of being upside down. **4 a** across a street or other space (*decided to cross over*). **b** for a visit etc. (*invited them over last night*). **5** with transference from one hand or part to another (*swapped them over*). **6** with motion above something (*climb over*). **7** from beginning to end with repetition or detailed concentration (*think it over*). **8** in excess (*left over*). **9** for or until a later time (*hold it over*). **10** at an end (*the crisis is over*). **11** (in full **over to you**) (as *int.*) (in radio conversations etc.) said to indicate that it is the other person's turn to speak. ● *prep.* **1** above, in, or to a

position higher than; upon. **2** out and down from; down from the edge of (*fell over the cliff*). **3** so as to cover (*a hat over his eyes*). **4** above and across (*a bridge over the Thames*). **5** concerning; as a result of; while occupied with (*laughed over a good joke*). **6 a** in superiority of; in charge of (*a victory over the enemy*). **b** in preference to. **7** *Math.* divided by. **8 a** throughout; covering (*a blush spread over his face*). **b** so as to deal with completely (*went over the plans*). **9 a** for the duration of (*stay over Saturday night*). **b** at any point during the course of (*I'll do it over the weekend*). **10** more than (*bids of over £50*). **11** transmitted by (*heard it over the radio*). **12** in comparison with (*gained 20% over last year*). **13** having recovered from (*am now over my cold*). ● *n. Cricket* **1** a sequence of balls (now usu. six), bowled from one end of the pitch. **2** the period of play during which such a sequence is bowled. ● *adj.* **1** upper, outer. **2** superior. **3** extra. □ **begin** (or **start** etc.) **over** *N. Amer.* begin again. **get it over with** do or undergo something unpleasant etc. so as to be rid of it. **give over** (usu. as *int.*) *colloq.* desist. **not over** not very; not at all (*not over friendly*). **over again** once again. **over against** in an opposite situation to; adjacent to, in contrast with. **over all** taken as a whole. **over and above** in addition to (*asking price £100 over and above the basic fee of £500*). **over and over** so that the same thing or the same point comes up again and again. **over one's head** see HEAD. **over the hill** see HILL. **over the moon** see MOON. **over to you** see OVER *adv.* 11. **over the way** *Brit.* (in a street etc.) facing or opposite. [Old English]

over-abundant *adj.* in excessive quantity. □ **over-abundance** *n.* **over-abundantly** *adv.*

overachieve *v.* **1** *intr.* do more than might be expected (esp. scholastically). **2** *tr.* achieve more than (an expected goal or objective etc.). □ **over-achievement** *n.* **overachiever** *n.*

overact *v.tr.* & *intr.* act (a role) in an exaggerated manner.

overactive *adj.* excessively active. □ **overactivity** *n.*

over age *adj.* (usu. hyphenated when *attrib.*) over a certain age limit; too old.

overall ● *adj.* **1** total, inclusive of all (*overall cost*). **2** taking everything into account (*overall improvement*). **3** from end to end (*overall length*). ● *adv.* taken as a whole (*overall, it was excellent*). ● *n.* **1** *Brit.* an outer garment worn to keep out dirt, wet, etc. **2** (in *pl.*) protective trousers, dungarees, or a combination suit, worn by workmen etc. □ **overalled** *adj.*

overambitious *adj.* excessively ambitious. □ **over-ambition** *n.* **overambitiously** *adv.*

over-anxious *adj.* excessively anxious. □ **over-anxiety** *n.* **over-anxiously** *adv.*

overarch *v.tr.* form an arch over. □ **overarching** *adj.*

overarm *adj.* & *adv.* **1** ▶ *Cricket* & *Tennis* etc. with the hand above the shoulder (*an overarm service*). **2** *Swimming* with one or both arms lifted out of the water during a stroke.

overate *past* of OVEREAT.

overawe *v.tr.* **1** restrain by awe. **2** keep in awe.

overbalance *v.* **1** *tr.* esp. *Brit.* cause to lose its balance and fall. **2** *intr.* fall over, capsize. **3** *tr.* outweigh.

overbear *v.tr.* (*past* **-bore**; *past part.* **-borne**) **1** (as **overbearing** *adj.*) **a** domineering, masterful. **b** overpowering. **2** bear down; upset by weight, force, or emotional pressure. **3** put down or repress by power or authority. □ **overbearingly** *adv.* **overbearingness** *n.*

overbid ● *v.tr.* (**-bidding**; *past* and *past part.* **-bid**) **1** make a higher bid than. **2** (also *absol.*) *Bridge* **a** bid more on (one's hand) than warranted. **b** = OVERCALL 1. ● *n.* **1 a** a bid that is higher than another, or a higher than is justified. □ **overbidder** *n.*

OVERARM
TENNIS STROKE

overbite *n. Dentistry* the overlapping of the lower teeth by the upper.

overblouse *n.* a garment like a blouse, but worn without tucking it into a skirt or trousers.

overblown *adj.* **1** excessively inflated or pretentious. **2** (of a flower, or a woman's beauty etc.) past its prime.

overboard *adv.* from on a ship into the water (*fall overboard*). □ **go overboard 1** be highly enthusiastic. **2** behave immoderately; go too far. **throw overboard** abandon, discard.

overbook *v.tr.* (also *absol.*) make too many bookings for (an aircraft, hotel, etc.) in respect of the space available.

overbore *past* of OVERBEAR.

overborne *past part.* of OVERBEAR.

overburden *v.tr.* burden (a person, thing, etc.) to excess. □ **overburdensome** *adj.*

overcall ● *v.tr.* (also *absol.*) *Bridge* **1** make a higher bid than (a previous bid or opponent). **2** *Brit.* = OVERBID *v.* 2a. ● *n.* an act or instance of overcalling.

overcame *past* of OVERCOME.

overcapacity *n.* a state of saturation or an excess of productive capacity.

overcapitalize *v.tr.* (also **-ise**) fix or estimate the capital of (a company etc.) too high.

overcareful *adj.* excessively careful. □ **overcarefully** *adv.*

overcast ● *adj.* **1** covered with cloud; dull and gloomy. **2** (in sewing) edged with stitching to prevent fraying. ▷ STITCH. ● *v.tr.* (*past* and *past part.* **-cast**) **1** cover with clouds or darkness. **2** stitch over to prevent fraying.

overcautious *adj.* excessively cautious. □ **overcaution** *n.* **overcautiously** *adv.* **overcautiousness** *n.*

overcharge *v.tr.* **1 a** charge too high a price to (a person) for a thing. **b** charge (a specified sum) beyond the right price. **2** put too much charge into (a battery, gun, etc.).

overcoat *n.* a heavy coat, esp. one worn over indoor clothes for warmth outdoors in cold weather.

overcome *v.* (*past* **-came**; *past part.* **-come**) **1** *tr.* prevail over, master, conquer. **2** *tr.* (as **overcome** *adj.*) **a** exhausted, made helpless. **b** (usu. foll. by *with, by*) affected by (emotion etc.). **3** *intr.* be victorious.

overcommit *v.tr.* (**overcommitted, overcommitting**) (usu. *refl.*) commit (esp. oneself) to an excessive degree. □ **overcommitment** *n.*

overcompensate *v.* **1** *tr.* (usu. foll. by *for*) compensate excessively for (something). **2** *intr. Psychol.* strive for power etc. in an exaggerated way, esp. to make up for a grievance, handicap, etc. □ **overcompensation** *n.* **overcompensatory** *adj.*

overconfident *adj.* excessively confident. □ **overconfidence** *n.* **overconfidently** *adv.*

overcook *v.tr.* cook too much or for too long. □ **overcooked** *adj.*

overcritical *adj.* excessively critical; quick to find fault.

overcrowd *v.tr.* fill (a space, object, etc.) beyond what is usual or comfortable. □ **overcrowding** *n.*

overdetermine *v.tr.* **1** determine, account for, or cause in more than one way, or with more conditions than are necessary. **2** (as **overdetermined** *adj.*) have more determining factors than the minimum necessary. □ **overdetermination** *n.*

overdevelop *v.tr.* (**-developed, -developing**) **1** develop too much. **2** *Photog.* treat with developer for too long.

overdo *v.tr.* (*3rd sing. present* **-does**; *past* **-did**; *past part.* **-done**) **1** carry to excess (*I think you overdid the sarcasm*). **2** (esp. as **overdone** *adj.*) overcook. □ **overdo it** (or **things**) exhaust oneself. [Old English]

overdose ● *n.* an excessive dose (of a drug etc.). ● *v.* **1** *tr.* give an overdose of a drug etc. to (a person). **2** *intr.* (often foll. by *on*) take an overdose of a drug. □ **overdosage** *n.*

overdraft *n.* **1** a deficit in a bank account caused by drawing more money than is credited to it. **2** the amount of this.

overdramatize *v.tr.* (also **-ise**) (also *absol.*) express or react to in an excessively dramatic way. □ **overdramatic** *adj.*

overdraw *v.* (*past* **-drew**; *past part.* **-drawn**) **1** *tr.* **a** draw a sum of money in excess of the amount credited to (one's bank account). **b** (as **overdrawn** *adj.*) having overdrawn one's account. **2** *intr.* overdraw one's account.

overdress ● *v.* **1** *tr.* dress with too much display or formality. **2** *intr.* overdress oneself. ● *n.* esp. *Brit.* a dress worn over another dress or a blouse etc.

overdrive *n.* **1** an additional speed-increasing gear in a motor vehicle providing a gear ratio higher than that of top gear. **2** (usu. prec. by *in, into*) a state of high or excessive activity.

overdue *adj.* **1** past the time when due or ready. **2** not yet paid, arrived, born, etc., though after the expected time.

overeager *adj.* excessively eager. □ **overeagerly** *adv.* **overeagerness** *n.*

overeat *v.intr. & refl.* (*past* **-ate**; *past part.* **-eaten**) eat too much.

over-elaborate ● *adj.* excessively elaborate. ● *v.tr.* (also *absol.*) explain in excessive detail. □ **over-elaborately** *adv.* **over-elaborateness** *n.* **over-elaboration** *n.*

over-emotional *adj.* excessively emotional. □ **over-emotionally** *adv.*

overemphasis *n.* excessive emphasis. □ **over-emphasize** *v.tr. & intr.* (also **-ise**).

overenthusiasm *n.* excessive enthusiasm. □ **over-enthusiastic** *adj.* **overenthusiastically** *adv.*

overestimate ● *v.tr.* (also *absol.*) form too high an estimate of (a person, cost, etc.). ● *n.* too high an estimate. □ **overestimation** *n*

overexcite *v.tr.* excite excessively. □ **overexcitement** *n.*

over-exercise ● *v.* **1** *tr.* use or exert (a part of the body, one's authority, etc.) too much. **2** *intr.* take too much exercise; overexert oneself. ● *n.* excessive exercise.

overexert *v.tr. & refl.* exert too much. □ **overexertion** *n.*

overexpose *v.tr.* (also *absol.*) **1** expose too much, esp. to the public eye. **2** *Photog.* expose (film) for too long a time. □ **overexposure** *n.*

overextend *v.tr.* **1** extend (a thing) too far. **2** (also *refl.*) take on (oneself) or impose on (another person) an excessive burden of work.

overfamiliar *adj.* excessively familiar. □ **over-familiarity** *n.*

overfeed *v.tr.* (*past* and *past part.* **-fed**) feed excessively.

overfill *v.tr. & intr.* fill to excess or to overflowing.

overfish *v.tr.* deplete (a stream, stock of fish, etc.) by too much fishing.

overflow ● *v.* **1** *tr.* **a** flow over (the brim etc.). **b** flow over the brim or limits of. **2** *intr.* **a** (of a receptacle etc.) be so full that the contents overflow it. **b** (of contents) overflow a container. **3** *tr.* (of a crowd etc.) extend beyond the limits of (a room etc.). **4** *tr.* flood (a surface or area). **5** *intr.* (foll. by *with*) be full of. **6** *intr.* (of kindness, a harvest, etc.) be very abundant. ● *n.* (also *attrib.*) **1** what overflows or is superfluous (*mop up the overflow*). **2** an instance of overflowing. **3** (esp. in a bath or sink) an outlet for excess water etc. **4** *Computing* the generation of a number having more digits than the assigned location. [Old English]

overflow meeting *n.* a meeting for those who cannot be accommodated at the main gathering.

overfly *v.tr.* (**-flies**; *past* **-flew**; *past part.* **-flown**) fly over or beyond (a place or territory). □ **overflight** *n.*

overfond *adj.* (often foll. by *of*) having too great an affection or liking (for a person or thing). □ **overfondly** *adv.* **overfondness** *n.*

overfull *adj.* filled excessively or to overflowing.

overgarment *n.* a garment worn over others; an outer garment.

overgeneralize *v.* (also **-ise**) **1** *intr.* draw general conclusions from inadequate data etc. **2** *intr.* argue more widely than is justified by the available evidence etc. **3** *tr.* draw an excessively general conclusion from (data etc.). □ **overgeneralization** *n.*

overgenerous *adj.* excessively generous. □ **overgenerously** *adv.*

overgraze *v.tr.* allow excessive grazing of (grassland), so that vegetation is damaged. □ **overgrazing** *n.*

overground *adv. & adj.* **1** above the ground. **2** in or into the open; unconcealed.

overgrow *v.* (*past* **-grew**; *past part.* **-grown**) **1** (as **overgrown** *adj.*) **a** abnormally large in stature (*a great overgrown child*). **b** grown over with vegetation (*an overgrown pond*). **2** grow over, esp. so as to choke (*nettles have overgrown the pathway*). □ **overgrowth** *n.*

overhang ● *v.* (*past* and *past part.* **-hung**) **1** *tr. & intr.* project or hang over. **2** *tr.* menace, preoccupy, threaten. ● *n.* **1** an instance of overhanging. **2** the overhanging part of a structure or rock formation. **3** the amount by which a thing overhangs.

overhaul ● *v.tr.* **1 a** take to pieces in order to examine. **b** examine the condition of (and repair if necessary). **2** overtake. ● *n.* a thorough examination, with repairs if necessary. [originally nautical, literally 'to release (rope-tackle) by slackening']

overhead ● *adv.* **1** above one's head. **2** in the sky or in the storey above. ● *adj.* **1** placed overhead. **2** (of a driving mechanism etc.) above the object driven. **3** (of expenses) arising from general running costs, as distinct from particular business transactions. ● *n.* (in *pl.* or *N. Amer.* in *sing.*) overhead expenses.

overhead projector *n.* a device that projects an enlarged image of a transparency on to a surface above and behind the user.

overhear *v.tr.* (*past* and *past part.* **-heard**) (also *absol.*) hear as an eavesdropper or as an unintentional listener.

overheat *v.* **1** *tr. & intr.* make or become too hot; heat to excess. **2** *tr.* (as **overheated** *adj.*) too passionate about a matter. **3** *intr. & tr. Econ* suffer, or cause to suffer, from marked inflation, as a result of placing excessive pressure on resources at a time of expanding demand.

over-indulge *v.tr. & intr.* indulge to excess. □ **over-indulgence** *n.* **over-indulgent** *adj.*

over-inflated *adj.* excessively large or aggrandized; exaggerated.

over-insure *v.tr.* insure (property etc.) for more than its real value; insure excessively. □ **over-insurance** *n.*

overjoyed *adj.* (often foll. by *at, to hear*, etc.) filled with great joy.

overkill *n.* **1** the excess of capacity to kill or destroy. **2** unwarranted thoroughness of treatment.

overladen *adj.* bearing or carrying too large a load.

overlaid *past* and *past part.* of OVERLAY¹.

overlain *past part.* of OVERLIE.

overland *adj. & adv.* by land; not by sea.

overlap ● *v.* (**-lapped**, **-lapping**) **1** *tr.* (of part of an object) partly cover (another object). **2** *tr.* cover and extend beyond. **3** *intr.* (of two things) partly coincide; not be completely separate. ● *n.* **1** an instance of overlapping. **2** the amount of this.

over-large *adj.* too large.

overlay¹ ● *v.tr.* (*past* and *past part.* **-laid**) **1** lay over. **2** (foll. by *with*) cover the surface of (a thing) with (a coating etc.). **3** overlie. ● *n.* a thing laid over another.

overlay² *past* of OVERLIE.

overleaf *adv.* on the other side of the leaf (of a book) (*the diagram overleaf*).

overlie *v.tr.* (**-lying**; *past* **-lay**; *past part.* **-lain**) **1** lie on top of. **2** smother (a child etc.) by lying on top.

overload ● *v.tr.* load excessively; force (a person, thing, etc.) beyond normal or reasonable capacity. ● *n.* an excessive quantity or demand.

overlong *adj. & adv.* too excessively long.

overlook *v.tr.* **1** fail to notice; ignore, condone (an offence etc.). **2** have a view from above, be higher than. **3** supervise, oversee. **4** bewitch with the evil eye. □ **overlooker** *n.*

overlord *n.* a supreme lord. □ **overlordship** *n.*

overly *adv.* excessively; too.

overlying *pres. part.* of OVERLIE.

overman *v.tr.* (**-manned**, **-manning**) provide with too large a crew, staff, etc.

overmantel *n.* ornamental shelves etc. over a mantelpiece.

over-many *adj.* too many; an excessive number.

overmaster *v.tr.* master completely, conquer. □ **overmastering** *adj.* **overmastery** *n.*

overmuch ● *adv.* to too great an extent; excessively. ● *adj.* excessive; superabundant.

overnice *adj.* excessively fussy etc. □ **overniceness** *n.*

overnight ● *adv.* **1** for the duration of a night (*stay overnight*). **2** during the course of a night. **3** suddenly, immediately (*the situation changed overnight*). ● *adj.* **1** for use overnight (*an overnight bag*). **2** done etc. overnight (*an overnight stop*).

overnighter *n.* **1** a person who stops at a place overnight. **2** an overnight bag.

over-optimistic *adj.* excessively or unjustifiably optimistic. □ **over-optimism** *n.*

overpaid *past* and *past part.* of OVERPAY.

over-particular *adj.* excessively particular or fussy.

overpass *n.* a road or railway line that passes over another by means of a bridge.

overpay *v.tr.* (*past* and *past part.* **-paid**) recompense (a person, service, etc.) too highly. □ **overpayment** *n.*

overplay *v.tr.* play (a part) to excess; give undue importance to. □ **overplay one's hand 1** be unduly optimistic about one's capabilities. **2** spoil a good case by exaggerating its value.

overpopulated *adj.* having too large a population. □ **overpopulation** *n.*

overpower *v.tr.* **1** reduce to submission, subdue. **2** make (a thing) ineffective or imperceptible by greater intensity. **3** (of heat, emotion, etc.) overwhelm. □ **overpowering** *adj.* **overpoweringly** *adv.*

over-prescribe *v.tr.* (also *absol.*) prescribe an excessive amount of (a drug) or too many (drugs). □ **over-prescription** *n.*

overprice *v.tr.* price (a thing) too highly.

overprint ● *v.tr.* **1** print further matter on (a surface already printed, esp. a postage stamp). **2** print (further matter) in this way. ● *n.* the words etc. over-printed.

overproduce *v.tr.* (usu. *absol.*) **1** produce more of (a commodity) than is wanted. **2** produce to an excessive degree. □ **overproduction** *n.*

overprotective *adj.* excessively protective, esp. of a person in one's charge.

overqualified *adj.* too highly qualified (esp. for a particular job etc.).

overran *past* of OVERRUN.

overrate *v.tr.* (often as **overrated** *adj.*) assess or value too highly.

overreach *v.tr.* circumvent, outwit. □ **overreach oneself 1** strain oneself by reaching too far. **2** defeat one's object by going too far.

overreact *v.intr.* respond more forcibly etc. than is justified. □ **overreaction** *n.*

over-refine *v.tr.* (also *absol.*) **1** refine too much. **2** make too subtle distinctions in (an argument etc.). □ **over-refinement** *n.*

override ● *v.tr.* (*past* **-rode**; *past part.* **-ridden**) **1** have or claim precedence over (*an overriding consideration*). **2 a** intervene and make ineffective. **b** interrupt the action of (an automatic device) esp. to take manual control. **3 a** trample down or underfoot. **b** supersede arrogantly. ● *n*. **1** the action or process of suspending an automatic function. **2** a device for this.

overripe *adj*. (esp. of fruit etc.) past its best; excessively ripe; full-blown.

overrode *past* of OVERRIDE.

overrule *v.tr*. **1** set aside (a decision etc.) by exercising a superior authority. **2** annul a decision by or reject a proposal of (a person) in this way.

overrun ● *v.tr*. (**-running**; *past* **-ran**; *past part*. **-run**) **1** (of vermin, weeds, etc.) swarm or spread over. **2** conquer or ravage (territory) by force. **3** (of time, expenditure, etc.) exceed (a fixed limit). **4** *Printing* carry over (a word etc.) to the next line or page. ● *n*. **1** an instance of overrunning. **2** the amount of this. [Old English]

oversaw *past* of OVERSEE.

overscrupulous *adj*. excessively scrupulous or particular.

overseas ● *adv*. (also **oversea**) abroad. ● *attrib.adj*. (also **oversea**) foreign; across or beyond the sea.

oversee *v.tr*. (**-sees**; *past* **-saw**; *past part*. **-seen**) officially supervise (workers etc.). □ **overseer** *n*.

oversell *v.tr*. (*past* and *past part*. **-sold**) (also *absol*.) **1** sell more of (a commodity etc.) than one can deliver. **2** exaggerate the merits of.

oversensitive *adj*. excessively sensitive; easily hurt or too quick to react. □ **oversensitiveness** *n*. **oversensitivity** *n*.

oversew *v.tr*. (*past part*. **-sewn** or **-sewed**) sew (two edges) with every stitch passing over the join.

oversexed *adj*. having unusually strong sexual desires.

overshadow *v.tr*. **1** appear much more prominent or important than. **2** cast into the shade. [Old English]

overshoe *n*. a shoe of rubber, felt, etc., worn over another as protection from wet, cold, etc.

overshoot ● *v.tr*. (*past* and *past part*. **-shot**) **1** pass or send beyond (a target or limit). **2** (of an aircraft) proceed beyond (the runway) when landing or taking off. ● *n*. **1** the act of overshooting. **2** the amount of this. □ **overshoot the mark** go beyond what is intended or proper; go too far.

oversight *n*. **1** a failure to notice something. **2** an inadvertent mistake. **3** supervision.

oversimplify *v.tr*. (**-ies**, **-ied**) (also *absol*.) distort (a problem etc.) by stating it in too simple terms. □ **oversimplification** *n*.

oversize *adj*. (also **-sized**) of more than the usual size.

overskirt *n*. an outer or second skirt.

oversleep *v.intr. & refl*. (*past* and *past part*. **-slept**) continue sleeping beyond the intended time of waking; sleep too long.

oversold *past* and *past part*. of OVERSELL.

oversolicitous *adj*. excessively worried, anxious, eager, etc. □ **oversolicitude** *n*.

overspecialize *v.intr*. (also **-ise**) concentrate too much on one aspect or area. □ **overspecialization** *n*.

overspend *v*. (*past* and *past part*. **-spent**) **1** *intr. & refl*. spend too much. **2** *tr*. spend more than (a specified amount).

overspill *n*. **1** what is spilt over or overflows. **2** *Brit*. the surplus population moving to a new area.

overspread *v.tr*. (*past* and *past part*. **-spread**) **1** become spread or diffused over. **2** cover or occupy the surface of. [Old English]

overstaff *v.tr*. provide with too large a staff.

overstate *v.tr*. **1** state (a case etc.) too strongly. **2** exaggerate. □ **overstatement** *n*.

overstay *v.tr*. stay longer than (one's welcome etc.).

oversteer ● *v.intr*. (of a motor vehicle) have a tendency to turn more sharply than was intended. ● *n*. this tendency.

overstep *v.tr*. (**-stepped**, **-stepping**) **1** pass

OWL

There are about 130 owl species, most of which are nocturnal hunters. They have large, forward-facing eyes for long-range binocular vision, and hearing so acute they can locate prey in total darkness. Owls have no external ears, although some do have tufts of feathers that look like ears. Instead the broad facial disc gathers sound waves (like an external ear does) and directs them to the internal ear drum. Owls typically have fringed feathers that reduce air turbulence; this means quarry can be approached almost silently. Most owls have feathers covering their legs and feet, which helps further quieten their flight. An owl's diet consists mainly of small birds, insects, frogs, and rodents.

EXTERNAL FEATURES OF A BARN OWL (*Tyto alba*)

EXAMPLES OF OTHER OWLS

TAWNY OWL (*Strix aluco*)

SNOWY OWL (*Nyctea scandiaca*)

SOUTHERN BOOBOOK (*Ninox novaeseelandiae*)

EURASIAN EAGLE OWL (*Bubo bubo*)

beyond (a boundary or mark). **2** violate (certain standards of behaviour etc.). □ **overstep the mark** violate conventions of behaviour.

overstock ● *v.tr*. stock excessively. ● *n*. esp. *US* a supply in excess of demand or requirement.

overstrain *v.tr*. strain too much.

overstress *v.tr*. stress too much.

overstretch *v.tr*. **1** stretch too much. **2** (esp. as **overstretched** *adj*.) make excessive demands on (resources, a person, etc.).

overstrung *adj*. (of a person, disposition, etc.) intensely strained, highly strung.

overstuff *v.tr*. **1** stuff more than is necessary. **2** (as **overstuffed** *adj*.) (of furniture) made soft and comfortable by thick upholstery.

oversubscribe *v.tr*. (usu. as **oversubscribed** *adj*.) subscribe for more than the amount available of (*the offer was oversubscribed*).

oversubtle *adj*. excessively subtle; not plain or clear.

oversupply ● *v.tr*. (**-ies**, **-ied**) supply with too much. ● *n*. an excessive supply.

oversusceptible *adj*. too susceptible or vulnerable.

overt *adj*. unconcealed; done openly. [from Old French, literally 'opened'] □ **overtly** *adv*. **overtness** *n*.

overtake *v.tr*. (*past* **-took**; *past part*. **-taken**) **1** (also (*Brit*.) *absol*.) catch up with and pass while travelling in the same direction. **2** (of a misfortune etc.) come suddenly upon.

overtax *v.tr*. **1** make excessive demands on (a person's strength etc.). **2** tax too heavily.

over-the-counter *attrib.adj*. obtainable from a

shop, esp. (of drugs) without a prescription (see also *over the counter* (COUNTER¹)).

over-the-top see *over the top* 2 (TOP¹).

overthrow ● *v.tr*. (*past* **-threw**; *past part*. **-thrown**) **1** remove forcibly from power. **2** put an end to (an institution etc.). **3** conquer, overcome. **4** knock down, upset. ● *n*. a defeat or downfall.

overtime ● *n*. **1** the time during which a person works at a job in addition to the regular hours. **2** payment for this. ● *adv*. in addition to regular hours.

overtire *v.tr. & refl*. exhaust or wear out (esp. an invalid etc.).

overtone *n*. **1** *Mus*. any of the tones above the lowest in a harmonic series. **2** a subtle or elusive quality or implication (*sinister overtones*).

overtrain *v.tr. & intr*. subject to or undergo too much (esp. athletic) training with a consequent loss of proficiency.

overture *n*. **1** an orchestral piece opening an opera etc. **2** a one-movement composition in this style. **3** (usu. in *pl*.) **a** an opening of negotiations. **b** a formal proposal or offer initiating negotiation etc. (esp. *make overtures to*). [from Latin *apertura* 'aperture']

overturn ● *v*. **1** *tr*. cause to fall down or turn over; upset. **2** *tr*. reverse; invalidate. **3** *intr*. turn over. ● *n*. a subversion, an act of upsetting.

overuse ● *v.tr*. /oh-ver-yooz/ use too much. ● *n*. /oh-ver-**yooss**/ excessive use.

overvalue *v.tr*. (**-values**, **-valued**, **-valuing**) value too highly; have too high an opinion of.

overview *n*. a general survey.

overwater ● *v.tr*. (also *absol*.) water (a plant etc.) too much. ● *attrib.adj*. situated above the water.

overweening adj. arrogant, presumptuous. [based on archaic ween 'to have an opinion'] □ **overweeningly** adv.

overweight ● adj. **1** in excess of a weight considered normal or desirable. **2** beyond an allowed or suitable weight. **●** n. excessive or extra weight; preponderance. **●** v.tr. (usu. foll. by with) load unduly.

overwhelm v.tr. **1** overpower with emotion. **2** (usu. foll. by with) overpower with an excess of business etc. **3** bring to sudden ruin or destruction. **4** submerge utterly.

overwhelming adj. irresistible by force of numbers, influence, amount, etc. □ **overwhelmingly** adv.

overwind v.tr. (past and past part. **-wound**) wind (a mechanism, esp. a watch) beyond the proper stopping point.

overwinter v. **1** intr. (usu. foll. by at, in) spend the winter. **2** intr. (of insects, fungi, etc.) live through the winter. **3** tr. keep (animals, plants, etc.) alive through the winter.

overwork ● v. **1** intr. work too hard. **2** tr. cause (another person) to work too hard. **3** tr. weary or exhaust with too much work. **4** tr. (esp. as **overworked** adj.) make excessive use of. **●** n. excessive work.

overwound past and past part. of OVERWIND.

overwrite v. (past **-wrote**; past part. **-written**) **1** tr. write on top of (other writing). **2** tr. Computing destroy (data) in (a file etc.) by entering new data. **3** intr. (esp. as **overwritten** adj.) write too elaborately or too ornately.

overwrought adj. **1** overexcited, nervous, distraught. **2** overdone; too elaborate.

overzealous adj. too zealous in one's attitude, behaviour, etc.; excessively enthusiastic.

ovi- comb. form egg, ovum. [from Latin ovum 'egg']

oviduct n. the tube through which an ovum passes from the ovary. □ **oviductal** adj.

oviform adj. egg-shaped.

ovine adj. of or like sheep. [based on Latin ovis 'sheep']

oviparous adj. Zool. producing young by means of eggs expelled from the body before they are hatched. □ **oviparity** n. **oviparously** adv.

ovipositor n. ▶ a pointed tubular organ with which a female insect deposits her eggs. [modern Latin]

ovoid ● adj. **1** (of a solid or of a surface) egg-shaped. **2** oval, with one end more pointed than the other. **●** n. an ovoid body or surface. [from French ovoïde, related to OVUM]

ovulate v.intr. produce ova or ovules, or discharge them from the ovary. □ **ovulation** n. **ovulatory** adj.

ovule n. the part of the ovary of seed plants that contains the germ cell; an unfertilized seed. ▷ FLOWER. [from medieval Latin ovulum 'little egg'] □ **ovular** adj.

ovum n. (pl. **ova**) **1** a mature reproductive cell of female animals, produced by the ovary. ▷ OVARY. **2** the egg cell of plants. [Latin, literally 'egg']

ow int. expressing sudden pain. [a natural exclamation]

owe v.tr. **1 a** be under obligation (to a person etc.) to pay or repay (money etc.). **b** (absol.; usu. foll. by for) be in debt (still owe for my car). **2** (often foll. by to) be under obligation to render (owe grateful thanks to). **3** (usu. foll. by to) be indebted to a person or thing for (we owe the principle to Newton). □ **owe it to oneself** (often foll. by to + infin.) need (to do) something to protect one's own interests. [Old English]

owing predic.adj. **1** owed; yet to be paid (the balance owing). **2** (foll. by to) **a** caused by; attributable to. **b** (as prep.) because of (owing to bad weather).

■ **Usage** The use of owing to as a preposition meaning 'because of' is entirely acceptable (see example above), unlike this use of due to.

owl n. **1** ◀ any nocturnal bird of prey of the order Strigiformes, with large eyes and a hooked beak. **2** colloq. a person compared to an owl, esp. in looking wise. [Old English] □ **owlery** n. (pl. **-ies**). **owlish** adj. **owlishly** adv. **owl-like** adj.

owlet n. a young or small owl.

own ● adj. (prec. by possessive) **1 a** belonging to oneself or itself (saw it with my own eyes). **b** individual, particular (has its own charm). **2** used to emphasize identity rather than possession (cooks his own meals). **3** (absol.) **a** private property (is it your own?). **b** kindred (among my own). **●** v. **1** tr. have as property; possess. **2 a** tr. confess (own their faults). **b** intr. (foll. by to) confess to (owned to a prejudice). **3** tr. acknowledge paternity, authorship, or possession of. □ **come into one's own 1** receive one's due. **2** achieve recognition. **get one's own back** (often foll. by on) colloq. get revenge. **hold one's own** maintain one's position. **of one's own** belonging to oneself alone. **on one's own 1** alone. **2** independently, without help. **own up** (often foll. by to) confess frankly. [Old English āgen 'owed'] □ **-owned** adj. (in comb.).

own brand n. Brit. **1** a make of goods manufactured specially for a retailer and bearing the retailer's name. **2** (foll. by of) a kind particular to a person or group (own brand of gay activism).

owner n. **1** a person who owns something. **2** slang the captain of a ship. □ **ownership** n.

owner-occupier n. Brit. a person who owns the house etc. he or she lives in. □ **owner-occupied** adj.

own goal n. Brit. **1** a goal scored (usu. by mistake) against the scorer's own side. **2** colloq. an act that unintentionally harms one's own interests.

owt n. Brit. colloq. or dial. anything. [variant of AUGHT]

ox n. (pl. **oxen**) **1** any bovine animal, esp. a large usu. horned domesticated ruminant used for draught, milk, and meat. ▷ RUMINANT. **2** a castrated male of a domesticated species of cattle, Bos taurus. [Old English]

ox- var. of OXY-.

oxalic acid n. Chem. a very poisonous and sour acid found in sorrel and rhubarb leaves. [based on Greek oxalis 'wood sorrel'] □ **oxalate** n.

oxalis n. any plant of the genus Oxalis, with trifoliate leaves and white, yellow, or pink flowers, e.g. wood sorrel. [based on Greek oxus 'sour']

oxbow n. **1** a U-shaped collar of an ox-yoke. **2 a** a loop formed by a horseshoe bend in a river. **b** a lake formed when the river cuts across the narrow end of the loop. ▷ LAKE, RIVER

OVIPOSITOR: ICHNEUMON WASP DEPOSITING EGGS

Oxbridge n. Brit. **1** (also attrib.) Oxford and Cambridge universities regarded together, esp. in contrast to newer institutions. **2** (often attrib.) the characteristics of these universities. [blend of Ox(ford) and (Cam)bridge]

oxen pl. of OX.

ox-eye n. any of various plants of the daisy family with conspicuously rayed flowers.

Oxfam /**oks**-fam/ abbr. Oxford Committee for Famine Relief.

Oxford blue ● n. **1** a dark blue, sometimes with a purple tinge. **2** = BLUE[1] n. 3a. **●** adj. (hyphenated when attrib.) of this colour. [adopted by Oxford University in S. England]

oxherd n. a cowherd.

oxhide n. **1** the hide of an ox. **2** leather made from this.

oxidant n. an oxidizing agent. [French]

oxidation n. the process or result of oxidizing or being oxidized.

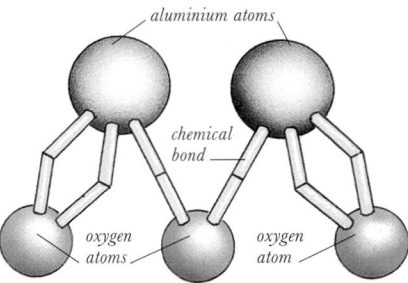

OXIDE: ALUMINIUM OXIDE MOLECULE

oxide n. ▲ a binary compound of oxygen. [French, from oxygène 'oxygen' + -ide as in acide 'acid']

oxidize v. (also **-ise**) **1** intr. & tr. combine or cause to combine with oxygen. **2** tr. & intr. cover or become covered with a coating of oxide etc.; make or become rusty. □ **oxidization** n. **oxidizer** n.

Oxon abbr. **1** Oxfordshire. **2** of Oxford University (esp. in degree titles). [abbreviation of medieval Latin Oxoniensis from Oxonia (see OXONIAN)]

Oxonian ● adj. of or relating to Oxford or Oxford University. **●** n. **1** a member of Oxford University. **2** a native or inhabitant of Oxford. [from Oxonia, Latinized name of Ox(en)ford]

oxtail n. the tail of an ox, esp. as an ingredient in soup.

oxy- comb. form (also **ox-**) Chem. oxygen (oxyacetylene). [abbreviation]

oxyacetylene adj. of or using oxygen and acetylene, esp. in cutting or welding metals (oxyacetylene burner).

oxygen n. Chem. a colourless tasteless odourless gaseous element essential to plant and animal life. [from French oxygène in sense 'acidifying principle', first held to be the essential principle in acid formation] □ **oxygenous** adj.

oxygenate v.tr. supply or treat with oxygen. □ **oxygenation** n.

oxygen mask n. a mask placed over the nose and mouth to supply oxygen from an attached cylinder for breathing.

oxygen tent n. a tentlike enclosure supplying a patient with air rich in oxygen.

oxyhaemoglobin /ok-si-hee-mŏ-**gloh**-bin/ n. Biochem. a bright red complex formed when haemoglobin combines with oxygen.

oxymoron n. Rhet. a figure of speech in which apparently contradictory terms appear in conjunction (e.g. faith unfaithful kept him falsely true). [based on Greek oxus 'sharp' + mōros 'foolish']

oxytocin n. **1** a hormone released by the pituitary gland that causes increased contraction of the womb during labour and stimulates the ejection of milk into the ducts of the breasts. **2** a synthetic form of this used to induce labour etc. [based on Greek oxutokia 'sudden delivery']

oyez /oh-**yes**/ int. (also **oyes**) uttered, usu. three times, by a public crier or a court officer to command silence and attention. [from Old French, literally 'hear ye']

oyster n. **1** any of various bivalve molluscs of the families Ostreidae and Aviculidae. ▷ BIVALVE. **2** an oyster-shaped morsel of meat in a fowl's back. **3** something regarded as containing all that one desires (the world is my oyster). [from Greek ostreon]

oystercatcher n. any usu. coastal wading bird of the genus Haematopus, with a strong orange-coloured bill, feeding on shellfish. ▷ WADING BIRD

oz abbr. ounce(s). [Italian, from onza 'ounce']

ozone n. **1** Chem. a colourless unstable toxic gas with a pungent odour and powerful oxidizing properties. **2** colloq. invigorating air at the seaside etc. [based on Greek ozein 'to smell'] □ **ozonic** adj. **ozonize** v.tr. (also **-ise**). **ozonization** n. **ozonizer** n.

ozone-friendly adj. not containing chemicals destructive to the ozone layer.

ozone layer n. a layer in the stratosphere containing a high concentration of ozone that absorbs most of the Sun's ultraviolet radiation. ▷ ATMOSPHERE

P

P[1] *n.* (also **p**) (*pl.* **Ps** or **P's**) the sixteenth letter of the alphabet.

P[2] *abbr.* (also **P.**) **1** (on road signs) parking. **2** *Chess* pawn.

P[3] *symb.* **1** *Chem.* the element phosphorus. **2** *Physics* poise (unit).

p *abbr.* (also **p.**) **1** *Brit.* penny, pence. **2** page. **3** pico-. **4** *Mus.* piano (softly).

PA *abbr.* **1** *Brit.* personal assistant. **2** public address (esp. *PA system*).

Pa *symb. Chem.* the element protactinium.

pa *n. colloq.* father. [abbreviation of PAPA]

p.a. *abbr.* per annum.

pabulum *n.* **1** food, esp. for the mind. **2** bland or insipid intellectual fare. [Latin]

PABX *abbr. Brit.* private automatic branch exchange.

pace[1] ● *n.* **1 a** a single step in walking or running. **b** the distance covered in this. **2** speed in walking or running. **3** *Theatr. & Mus.* speed or tempo in performance (*played with great pace*). **4 a** the rate at which something progresses (*the pace of technological change*). **b** the speed at which life is led (*the pace of city life*). **5 a** a manner of walking or running. **b** any of various gaits, esp. of a trained horse etc. ● *v.* **1** *intr.* a walk (esp. repeatedly or methodically) with a slow or regular pace (*pacing up and down*). **b** (of a horse) = AMBLE 2. **2** *tr.* traverse by pacing. **3** *tr.* set the pace for (a rider, runner, etc.). **4** *tr.* (often foll. by *out*) measure (a distance) by pacing. □ **keep pace** (often foll. by *with*) advance at an equal rate (to that of). □ **put a person through his** (or **her**) **paces** test a person's qualities in action etc. **set the pace** determine the speed, esp. by leading. **stand the pace** be able to keep up with others. [from Latin *passus*, literally 'stretch (of the legs)'] □ **-paced** *adj.* (in *comb.*) **pacer** *n.*

pace[2] /**pah**-chay/ *prep.* with due deference to; despite the opinion of (*I was not* (pace *Mr Smith*) *defending the legalization of drugs*). [Latin, literally 'in peace']

■ **Usage** *Pace* does not mean 'according to (someone)' or 'notwithstanding (something)'.

pacemaker *n.* **1** a competitor who sets the pace in a race. **2** ▲ a natural or artificial device for stimulating the heart muscle and regulating its contractions. □ **pacemaking** *n. & adj.*

pace-setter *n.* **1** a leader. **2** = PACEMAKER 1. □ **pace-setting** *adj. & n.*

pacey var. of PACY.

pacha var. of PASHA.

pachinko *n.* a Japanese form of pinball. [Japanese]

pachyderm /**pak**-i-derm/ *n.* any thick-skinned mammal, esp. an elephant or rhinoceros. ▷ ELEPHANT, RHINOCEROS. [from Greek *pakhus* 'thick' + *derma* 'skin']

pacific ● *adj.* **1** characterized by or tending to peace; tranquil. **2** (**Pacific**) of or adjoining the Pacific. ● *n.* (**the Pacific**) = PACIFIC OCEAN. □ **pacifically** *adv.*

pacification *n.* the act of pacifying or the process of being pacified.

Pacific Ocean *n.* the largest of the world's oceans, lying between America to the east and Asia and Australasia to the west. ▷ OCEAN

PACEMAKER

An artificial pacemaker is implanted in the human body when the natural pacemaker – a knot of tissue in the heart muscle that initiates the rhythmic heartbeat – does not function properly. It consists of a battery-powered generator that delivers short pulses of electricity to the heart to stimulate or regulate the heartbeat. The illustration below shows the position of a common pacemaker.

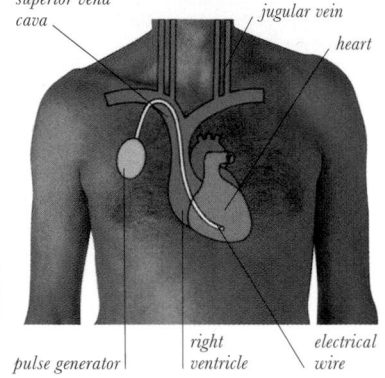

PACEMAKER IN POSITION

superior vena cava — jugular vein — heart — pulse generator — right ventricle — electrical wire

Pacific Rim *n.* (usu. prec. by *the*) the countries and regions bordering the Pacific Ocean, esp. the small nations of eastern Asia.

pacifier *n.* **1** a person or thing that pacifies. **2** *N. Amer.* a baby's dummy.

pacifism *n.* the belief that war and violence are morally unjustified and that all disputes should be settled by peaceful means. □ **pacifist** *n. & adj.*

pacify *v.tr.* (**-ies, -ied**) **1** appease (a person, anger, etc.). **2** bring (a country etc.) to a state of peace. [from Latin *pacificare*]

pack[1] ● *n.* **1 a** a collection of things wrapped up or tied together for carrying. **b** = BACKPACK. **2** a set of items packaged for use or disposal together. **3** usu. *derog.* a lot or set (of similar things or persons) (*a pack of lies; a pack of thieves*). **4** *Brit.* a set of playing cards. **5** a group of hounds or wild animals, esp. wolves, hunting together. **6** an organized group of Cub Scouts or Brownies. **7 a** *Rugby* a team's forwards. **b** *Sport* the main body of competitors following the leader or leaders esp. in a race. **8** a medicinal or cosmetic substance applied to the skin; = FACE PACK. ● *v.* **1** *tr.* (often foll. by *up*) **a** fill (a suitcase, bag, etc.) with clothes and other items. **b** put (things) together in a bag or suitcase, esp. for travelling. **2** *intr. & tr.* come or put closely together; crowd or cram. **3** *tr.* (in *passive*; often foll. by *with*) be filled (with); (*the restaurant was packed; the book is packed with information*). **4** *tr.* fill (a hall, theatre, etc.) with an audience etc. **5** *tr.* cover (a thing) with something pressed tightly round. **6** *intr.* be suitable for packing. **7** *tr. colloq.* **a** carry (a gun etc.). **b** be capable of delivering (a punch) with skill or force. □ **pack in** *colloq.* stop, give up (*packed in his job*). **pack off** *colloq.* send (a person) away, esp. abruptly or promptly. **pack up** *Brit. colloq.* **1** (esp. of a machine) stop functioning; break down. **2** retire from an activity, contest, etc. **send packing** *colloq.* dismiss (a person) summarily. [from Middle Dutch *pak*] □ **packable** *adj.*

pack[2] *v.tr.* select (a jury etc.) or fill (a meeting) so as to secure a decision in one's favour.

package ● *n.* **1 a** a bundle of things packed. **b** a parcel, box, etc., in which things are packed. **2** (in full **package deal**) a set of proposals or items offered or agreed to as a whole. **3** *Computing* a piece of software suitable for various applications rather than one which is custom-built. **4** *colloq.* = PACKAGE HOLIDAY. ● *v.tr.* **1** make up into or enclose in a package. **2** present (a product, person, or message) so as to appeal to the public. [based on PACK[1]] □ **packager** *n.*

package holiday *n.* (also **package tour** etc.) a holiday or tour etc. with all arrangements made at an inclusive price.

packaging *n.* **1** a wrapping or container for goods. **2** the process of packing goods.

pack animal *n.* an animal for carrying packs.

pack drill *n.* a military punishment of marching up and down carrying full equipment.

packed lunch *n.* a lunch carried in a bag, box, etc., esp. to work, school, etc.

packed out *adj. Brit. colloq.* full, crowded.

packer *n.* a person or thing that packs, esp. a dealer who prepares and packs food.

packet ● *n.* **1** a small package. **2** esp. *Brit. colloq.* a large sum of money won, lost, or spent. **3** (in full **packet-boat**) *hist.* a mailboat or passenger ship. ● *v.tr.* make up into or wrap up in a packet. [based on PACK[1]]

packet switching *n.* a method of data transmission in which parts of a message are sent independently by the optimum route for each part and then reassembled.

packhorse *n.* a horse for carrying loads.

pack ice *n.* an area of large crowded pieces of floating ice in the sea.

packing *n.* **1** the act or process of packing. **2** material used to fill up a space around or in something.

packing case *n.* a case (usu. wooden) or framework for packing goods in.

packsaddle *n.* a horse's saddle adapted for supporting packs.

pact *n.* an agreement or a treaty. [from Latin *pactum* '(thing) agreed']

pacy *adj.* (also **pacey**) (**pacier, paciest**) fast-moving.

pad[1] ● *n.* **1** a piece of soft material used to reduce friction or jarring, fill out hollows, hold or absorb liquid, etc. **2** a number of sheets of blank paper fastened together at one edge, for writing or drawing on. **3** ◀ the fleshy underpart of an animal's foot or of a human finger. **4** a guard for the leg and ankle in sports. ▷ CRICKET. **5** a flat surface for helicopter take-off or rocket-launching. **6** *colloq.* a lodging, esp. a bedsitter or flat. ● *v.tr.* (**padded, padding**) **1** provide with a pad or padding; stuff. **2** (foll. by *out*) lengthen or fill out (a book etc.) with unnecessary material.

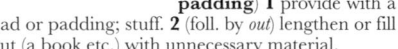

claw — dewclaw — toe pad — metacarpal pad

PAD OF A DOMESTIC CAT

pad[2] ● *v.* (**padded, padding**) **1** *intr.* walk with a soft dull steady step. **2 a** *tr.* tramp along (a road etc.) on foot. **b** *intr.* travel on foot. ● *n.* the sound of soft steady steps. [from Low German *padden* 'to tread', *pad* 'path']

padded cell *n.* a room with padded walls in a psychiatric hospital.

padding *n.* soft material used to pad or stuff with.

paddle[1] ● *n.* **1** a short broad-bladed oar used without a rowlock. ▷ CANOE. **2** a paddle-shaped instrument. **3** *Zool.* a fin or flipper. **4** each of the boards fitted round the circumference of a paddle wheel or mill-wheel. **5** the action or a spell of paddling. ● *v.intr. & tr.* **1** move on water or propel (a boat) by means of paddles. **2** row gently. [Middle English] □ **paddler** *n.*

paddle² ● *v.intr.* **1** *Brit.* walk, esp. barefoot, in shallow water. **2** dabble the feet or hands in shallow water. ● *n.* the action or a spell of paddling. □ **paddler** *n.*

paddle boat *n.* (also **paddle steamer** etc.) ► a boat, steamer, etc., propelled by a paddle wheel.

paddle wheel *n.* a wheel for propelling a ship, with boards round the circumference so as to press backwards against the water. ▷ PADDLE BOAT

paddock *n.* **1** a small field, esp. for keeping horses in. **2** an enclosure adjoining a racecourse or race-track where horses or cars are assembled before a race. ▷ RACECOURSE. **3** *Austral.* & *NZ* a field; a plot of land.

Paddy *n.* (*pl.* **-ies**) *colloq.* often *offens.* an Irishman. [pet form of the Irish name *Padraig* 'Patrick']

paddy¹ *n.* (*pl.* **-ies**) **1** (in full **paddy field**) a field where rice is grown. **2** rice before threshing or in the husk. [from Malay *pādī*]

paddy² *n.* (*pl.* **-ies**) *Brit. colloq.* a rage; a fit of temper. [based on PADDY]

padlock ● *n.* a detachable lock hanging by a pivoted or sliding hook on the object fastened. ● *v.tr.* secure with a padlock. [Middle English]

padre /**pah**-dray/ *n.* a chaplain in any of the armed services. [Italian, Spanish, & Portuguese]

padsaw *n.* a saw with a narrow blade, for cutting curves.

paean /**pee**-ăn/ *n.* a song of praise or triumph. [from Greek *paian* 'hymn of thanksgiving to Apollo' invoked as *Paian*, the name used by Homer for the physician of the gods]

paediatrics /pee-di-**at**-riks/ *n.pl.* (*US* **pediatrics**) (treated as *sing.*) the branch of medicine dealing with children and their diseases. □ **paediatric** *adj.* **paediatrician** *n.*

paedo- /**pee**-doh/ *comb. form* (*US* **pedo-**) child. [from Greek *pais paid-*]

paedophile /**pee**-dŏ-fyl/ *n.* (*US* **pedophile**) a person who displays paedophilia.

paedophilia /pee-dŏ-**fil**-iă/ *n.* (*US* **pedophilia**) sexual desire directed towards children.

paella /py-**el**-ă/ *n.* a Spanish dish of rice, saffron, chicken, seafood, etc. [Catalan, based on Latin *patella* 'pan']

paeony var. of PEONY.

pagan ● *n.* a person not subscribing to any of the main religions of the world. ● *adj.* **1 a** of or relating to or associated with pagans. **b** irreligious. **2** pantheistic. [from Latin *paganus* 'villager, rustic'] □ **paganism** *n.* **paganize** *v.tr. & intr.* (also **-ise**)

page¹ ● *n.* **1 a** a leaf of a book, periodical, etc. **b** each side of this. **c** what is written or printed on this. **2** *Computing* a section of stored data, esp. that can be displayed on a screen at one time. **3** an episode of history etc.; a record. ● *v.* **1** *tr.* paginate. **2** *intr.* **a** (foll. by *through*) leaf through (a book etc.). **b** (foll. by *through, up, down*) *Computing* display (text etc.) one page at a time. [from Latin *pagina*]

page² ● *n.* **1** a boy or man, usu. in livery, employed to run errands, attend to a door, etc. **2** a boy employed as a personal attendant of a person of rank, a bride, etc. **3** *hist.* a boy in training for knighthood and attached to a knight's service. ● *v.tr.* **1** (in hotels, airports, etc.) summon by making an announcement or by sending a messenger. **2** summon by means of a pager. [from Old French]

pageant /**paj**-ĕnt/ *n.* **1** a spectacular procession, or play performed in the open, illustrating historical events. **2** a brilliant spectacle, esp. an elaborate parade. **3** a tableau etc. on a fixed stage or moving vehicle. [Middle English]

PADDLE BOAT

The invention of the steam engine in the 18th century made paddle boats a viable alternative to ships propelled by sails. As the wheels of a paddle boat turn, their floats (boards) dip in the water and drive the boat. Paddle wheels are suited to rivers and lakes, but were superseded by the propeller on ocean-going vessels in the mid-19th century.

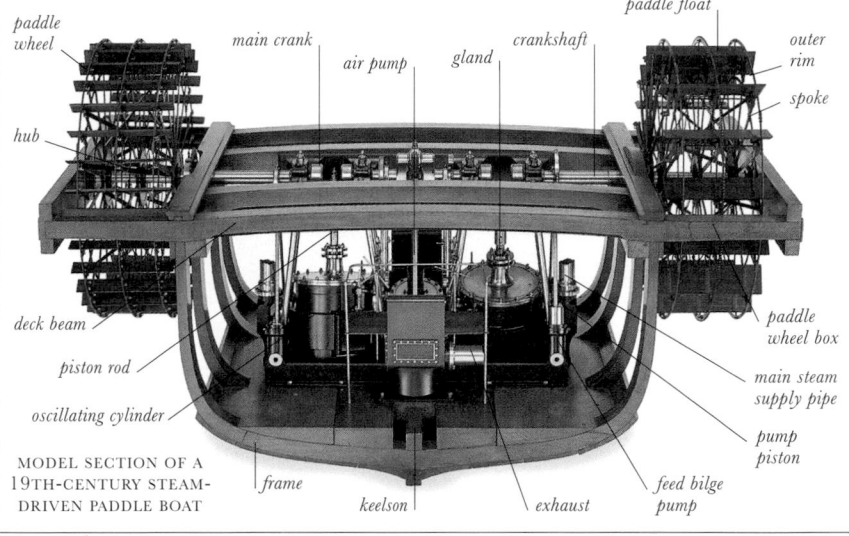

MODEL SECTION OF A 19TH-CENTURY STEAM-DRIVEN PADDLE BOAT

---

pageantry /**paj**-ĕn-tri/ *n.* (*pl.* **-ies**) **1** elaborate or sumptuous show or display. **2** an instance of this.

page-boy *n.* **1** = PAGE² *n.* 2. **2** a woman's hairstyle with the hair reaching to the shoulder and rolled under at the ends.

pager *n.* a radio device with a bleeper, activated from a central point to alert the person wearing it.

paginate *v.tr.* assign numbers to the pages of a book etc. [based on Latin *pagina* 'page'] □ **pagination** *n.*

pagoda *n.* **1** ◄ a Hindu or Buddhist temple or sacred building, esp. a many-tiered tower, in India and the Far East. **2** an ornamental imitation of this. [from Portuguese *pagode*]

pah *int.* expressing disgust or contempt. [a natural utterance]

paid *past* and *past part.* of PAY¹.

paid-up member *n.* **1** a person (esp. a trade-union member) who has paid his or her subscription in full. **2** *colloq.* a fully committed supporter of a cause, organization, etc.

pail *n.* **1** a bucket. **2** an amount contained in this. [Old English *pægel* 'gill'] □ **pailful** *n.* (*pl.* **-fuls**).

paillette *n.* **1** a piece of bright metal used in enamel painting. **2** a spangle.

pain ● *n.* **1** a strongly unpleasant bodily sensation produced by illness, injury, or other harmful physical contact etc. **2** mental suffering or distress. **3** (in *pl.*) careful effort; trouble taken (*take pains; got nothing for my pains*). **4** (also **pain in the neck** etc.) *colloq.* a troublesome person or thing; a nuisance. ● *v.tr.* **1** cause pain to. **2** (as **pained** *adj.*) expressing pain (*a pained expression*). □ **in pain** suffering pain. **on** (or **under**) **pain of** with (death etc.) as the penalty. [from Latin *poena* 'penalty']

PAGODA: MODEL OF A 9TH–10TH-CENTURY BURMESE PAGODA

---

painful *adj.* **1** causing bodily or mental pain or distress. **2** (esp. of part of the body) suffering pain. **3** causing trouble or difficulty; laborious (*a painful climb*). □ **painfully** *adv.* **painfulness** *n.*

painkiller *n.* a medicine or drug for alleviating pain. □ **painkilling** *adj.*

painless *adj.* not causing or suffering pain. □ **painlessly** *adv.* **painlessness** *n.*

painstaking *adj.* careful, industrious, thorough. □ **painstakingly** *adv.*

paint ● *n.* **1** colouring matter, esp. in liquid form for imparting colour to a surface. **2** this as a dried film or coating. ● *v.tr.* **1 a** cover the surface of (a wall, object, etc.) with paint. **b** apply paint of a specified colour to (*paint the door green*). **2** depict (an object, scene, etc.) with paint; produce (a picture) by painting. **3** describe vividly as if by painting (*painted the scene in vivid terms*). **4** apply a liquid or (*joc.* or *archaic*) cosmetics to (the face, skin, etc.). **5** apply (a liquid) to a surface with a brush etc. □ **paint out** efface with paint. **paint the town red** *colloq.* enjoy oneself flamboyantly. [from Latin *pingere* 'to paint'] □ **paintable** *adj.*

paintball *n.* a game in which participants simulate military combat using airguns to shoot capsules of paint at each other. □ **paintballer** *n.*

paintbox *n.* a box holding dry paints for painting pictures.

paintbrush *n.* a brush for applying paint.

painted lady *n.* ▼ an orange-red butterfly, esp. *Cynthia cardui*, with black and white spots.

PAINTED LADY (*Cynthia cardui*)

P

painter[1] *n.* a person who paints, esp. an artist or decorator.

painter[2] *n.* a rope attached to the bow of a boat for tying it to a quay etc. [Middle English]

painterly *adj.* **1** using paint well; artistic. **2** characteristic of a painter or paintings. □ **painterliness** *n.*

painting *n.* **1** the process or art of using paint. **2** a painted picture.

paint shop *n.* the part of a factory where goods are painted, esp. by spraying.

paintwork *n.* esp. *Brit.* a painted surface or area in a building etc.

pair ● *n.* **1** a set of two persons or things used together or regarded as a unit (*a pair of gloves; a pair of eyes*). **2** an article (e.g. scissors, trousers, or tights) consisting of two joined or corresponding parts not used separately. **3 a** an engaged or married couple. **b** a mated couple of animals. **4** two horses harnessed side by side (*a coach and pair*). **5** the second member of a pair in relation to the first (*cannot find its pair*). **6** two playing cards of the same denomination. **7** *Parl.* either or both of two members of a legislative assembly on opposite sides absenting themselves from voting by mutual arrangement. ● *v.tr. & intr.* **1** (often foll. by *off*) arrange or be arranged in couples. **2 a** join or be joined in marriage. **b** (of animals) mate. **3** *Parl.* form a pair (see sense 7 of *n.*). □ **in pairs** in twos. [from Latin *paria* 'equal things'] □ **paired** *adj.* **pairing** *n.*

Paisley *n.* (often *attrib.*) ▼ a distinctive intricate pattern of curved feather-shaped figures. [from *Paisley*, a town in Scotland]

PAISLEY PATTERN ON SILK

pajamas *US* var. of PYJAMAS.

pakeha /pah-ki-hah/ *NZ* ● *n.* a white person as opposed to a Maori. ● *adj.* of or relating to white people. [Maori]

Pakistani ● *n.* (*pl.* **Pakistanis**) **1** a native or national of Pakistan. **2** a person of Pakistani descent. ● *adj.* of or relating to Pakistan.

pakora /pă-kor-ă/ *n.* a piece of cauliflower, carrot, or other vegetable, coated in seasoned batter and deep-fried. [Hindi]

pal ● *n. colloq.* a friend, mate, or comrade. ● *v.intr.* (**palled**, **palling**) (usu. foll. by *up*) associate; form a friendship. [Romany, literally 'brother, mate']

palace *n.* **1** the official residence of a sovereign, president, archbishop, or bishop. **2** a splendid mansion; a spacious building. [from Latin *Palatium*, the Palatine hill in Rome, site of the emperor's house]

paladin *n. hist.* **1** any of the twelve peers of Charlemagne's court, of whom the Count Palatine was the chief. **2** a knight errant; a champion. [French]

palaeo- /**pal**-i-oh/ *comb. form* (*US* **paleo-**) ancient, old; of ancient (esp. prehistoric) times. [from Greek *palaios* 'ancient']

Palaeocene /**pal**-i-ŏ-seen/ (*US* **Paleocene**) *Geol.* ● *adj.* of or relating to the earliest epoch of the Tertiary period. ● *n.* this epoch or system. [based on Greek *kainos* 'new']

palaeography /pal-i-**og**-ră-fi/ *n.* (*US* **paleography**) the study of writing and documents from the past. □ **palaeographer** *n.* **palaeographic** *adj.*

palaeolithic /pal-i-ŏ-**lith**-ik/ (*US* **paleolithic**) *Archaeol.* ● *adj.* of or relating to the early phase of the Stone Age. ● *n.* the palaeolithic period. [based on Greek *lithos* 'stone']

palaeontology /pal-i-ŏn-**tol**-ŏji/ *n.* (*US* **paleontology**) the branch of science that deals with extinct and fossil animals and plants. [based on Greek *onta* 'existing things'] □ **palaeontological** *adj.* **palaeontologist** *n.*

Palaeozoic /pal-i-ŏ-**zoh**-ik/ (*US* **Paleozoic**) *Geol.* ● *adj.* of or relating to an era of geological time marked by the appearance of marine and terrestrial plants and animals, esp. invertebrates. ● *n.* this era (cf. CENOZOIC, MESOZOIC). [based on Greek *zōē* 'life']

palais /**pal**-ay/ *n. Brit. colloq.* a public hall for dancing. [French *palais* (*de danse*) '(dancing) hall']

palanquin /pal-ăn-**keen**/ *n.* (in India and the East) a covered litter for one passenger. [from Sanskrit *palyanka* 'bed, couch']

palatable *adj.* **1** pleasant to taste. **2** (of an idea, suggestion, etc.) acceptable, satisfactory. □ **palatability** *n.* **palatably** *adv.*

palatal ● *adj.* **1** of the palate. **2** (of a speech sound) made by placing the surface of the tongue against the hard palate (e.g. *y* in *yes*). ● *n.* a palatal sound. □ **palatalize** *v.tr.* (also **-ise**). **palatalization** *n.*

palate /**pal**-ăt/ *n.* **1** the roof of the mouth in vertebrates. **2** the sense of taste. **3** a mental taste or inclination; liking. [from Latin *palatum*]

palatial *adj.* (of a building) like a palace, esp. spacious and splendid. [from Latin, related to PALACE] □ **palatially** *adv.*

palatinate *n.* a territory under the jurisdiction of a Count Palatine.

palatine *adj.* (also **Palatine**) *hist.* **1** (of an official or feudal lord) having local authority that elsewhere belongs only to a sovereign (*Count Palatine*). **2** (of a territory) subject to this authority. [from Latin *palatinus* 'of the palace']

palaver /pă-**lah**-ver/ *n.* **1** fuss and bother, esp. prolonged. **2** profuse or idle talk. **3** cajolery. **4** *colloq.* a prolonged or tiresome affair or business. [from Portuguese *palavra* 'word']

PALLADIAN

Palladian is a neoclassical architectural style derived from the Renaissance buildings and writings of Andrea Palladio (1508–80). Palladio's Villa Rotonda (shown below) bears many of his hallmarks. The villa's design, both plan and elevation, is symmetrical, and centres on a domed room. Each of the four façades is identical, and is dominated by huge columns and a pedimented temple porch, a favourite motif of Palladio.

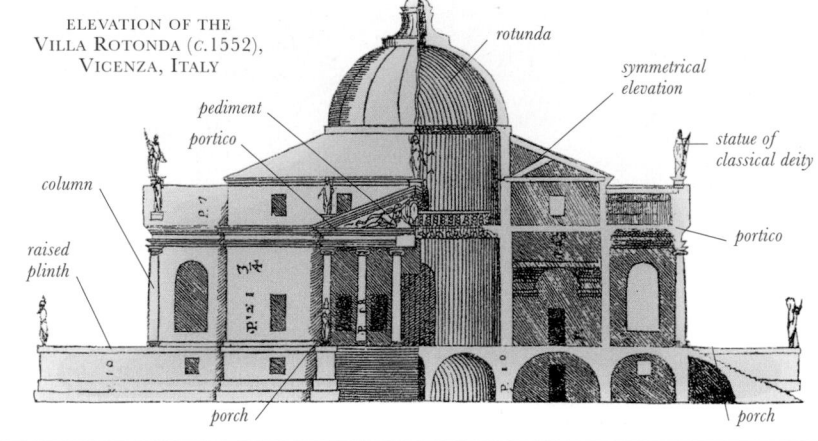

ELEVATION OF THE
VILLA ROTONDA (*c.*1552),
VICENZA, ITALY

rotunda

symmetrical elevation

pediment

portico

statue of classical deity

column

portico

raised plinth

porch

porch

pale[1] ● *adj.* **1** (of a person or complexion) of a whitish or ashen appearance. **2 a** (of a colour) faint; not dark or deep. **b** faintly coloured. **3** of faint lustre; dim. ● *v.* **1** *intr. & tr.* grow or make pale. **2** *intr.* (often foll. by *before, beside*) seem feeble in comparison (with). [from Latin *pallidus*] □ **palely** *adv.* **paleness** *n.* **palish** *adj.*

pale[2] *n.* **1** a pointed piece of wood for fencing etc.; a stake. **2** a boundary. **3** an enclosed or delimited area. □ **beyond the pale** outside the bounds of acceptable behaviour. **in pale** *Heraldry* arranged vertically. [from Latin *palus* 'stake']

paleface *n.* a name supposedly used by the N. American Indians for a white person.

paleo- *US* var. of PALAEO-.

Paleocene *US* var. of PALAEOCENE.

Paleozoic *US* var. of PALAEOZOIC.

Palestinian ● *adj.* of or relating to Palestine, a region (in ancient and modern times) and former mandated territory on the E. Mediterranean coast. ● *n.* **1** a native of Palestine in ancient or modern times. **2** an Arab, or a descendant of one, born or living in the area formerly called Palestine.

palette /**pal**-it/ *n.* **1** ▼ a thin board or slab or other surface, usu. with a hole for the thumb, on which an artist lays and mixes colours. **2** the range of colours used by an artist. [French, literally 'little shovel']

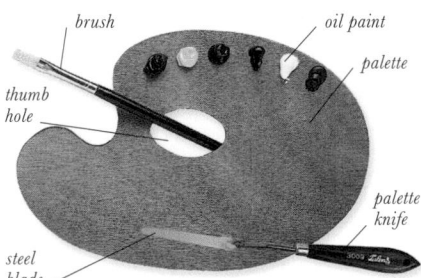

brush

oil paint

thumb hole

palette

palette knife

steel blade

PALETTE AND PALETTE KNIFE

palette knife *n.* **1** a thin steel blade with a handle for mixing colours or applying or removing paint. ▷ PALETTE. **2** *Brit.* a kitchen knife with a long blunt round-ended flexible blade.

P

palfrey *n.* (*pl.* **-eys**) *archaic* a horse for ordinary riding, esp. for women. [based on Greek *para* 'beside, extra' + Latin *veredus* 'light horse']

palimony *n.* esp. *US colloq.* an allowance made by one member of an unmarried couple to the other after separation. [blend of PAL and ALIMONY]

palimpsest *n.* a piece of writing material or manuscript on which later writing has been written over the effaced original writing. [from Greek *palin* 'again' + *psēstos* 'rubbed smooth']

palindrome *n.* a word or phrase that reads the same backwards as forwards (e.g. *rotator*, *nurses run*). [from Greek *palindromos* 'running back again'] □ **palindromic** *adj.*

paling *n.* **1** a fence of pales. **2** a pale.

palisade ● *n.* **1 a** a fence of pales or iron railings. **b** a strong pointed wooden stake used in a close row for defence. **2** (in *pl.*) *US* a line of high cliffs. ● *v.tr.* enclose or provide with a palisade. [from Provençal *palissada*]

pall[1] /pawl/ *n.* **1** a cloth spread over a coffin, hearse, or tomb. **2** a dark covering (*a pall of smoke*). [from Latin *pallium* 'cloak']

pall[2] /pawl/ *v.* **1** *intr.* (often foll. by *on*) become uninteresting (to). **2** *tr.* satiate, cloy. [Middle English]

Palladian *adj. Archit.* ◄ in the neoclassical style of Palladio. [from A. *Palladio*, Italian architect, 1508–80] □ **Palladianism** *n.*

palladium *n. Chem.* a white ductile metallic element used in chemistry as a catalyst and for making jewellery. [based on *Pallas*, name given to an asteroid discovered (1803) just before the element]

pall-bearer *n.* a person helping to carry or officially escorting a coffin at a funeral.

pallet[1] *n.* **1** a straw mattress. **2** a crude or makeshift bed. [based on Latin *palea* 'straw']

pallet[2] *n.* **1** a portable platform for transporting and storing loads. **2** a flat wooden blade with a handle, used to shape clay in ceramics. [from French *palette*] □ **palletize** *v.tr.* (also **-ise**)

palliasse *n.* a straw mattress. [based on Latin *palea* 'straw']

palliate *v.tr.* **1** alleviate (disease) without curing it. **2** excuse, extenuate. [based on Latin *palliatus* 'cloaked'] □ **palliation** *n.*

palliative ● *n.* something used to alleviate pain, anxiety, etc. ● *adj.* serving to alleviate. □ **palliatively** *adv.*

pallid *adj.* pale, esp. from illness. [from Latin *pallidus*] □ **pallidly** *adv.* **pallidness** *n.*

pallor *n.* the state or quality of being pallid; paleness. [Latin]

pally *adj.* (**pallier**, **palliest**) *colloq.* like a pal; friendly.

PALM TREE
(*Borassus flabellifer*)

palm[1] *n.* **1** (in full **palm tree**) ◄ a tree of the mainly tropical family Palmae, with no branches and a mass of large pinnate or fan-shaped leaves at the top. **2** the leaf of this tree as a symbol of victory. **3** a branch of various trees used instead of a palm in non-tropical countries. [from Latin *palma* 'palm', its leaf being likened to a spread hand]

palm[2] ● *n.* **1** the inner surface of the hand between the wrist and fingers. **2** the part of a glove that covers this. ● *v.tr.* conceal in the hand, esp. to steal. □ **in the palm of one's hand** under one's control or influence. **palm off 1** (often foll. by *on*) **a** impose or thrust fraudulently (on a person). **b** cause a person to accept unwillingly or unknowingly (*palmed my old typewriter off on him*). **2** (often foll. by *with*) cause (a person) to accept unwillingly or unknowingly (*palmed him off with my old typewriter*). [from Latin *palma*] □ **palmar** *adj.* **palmful** *n.* (*pl.* **-fuls**).

palmate /pal-mayt/ *adj. Bot. & Zool.* **1** shaped like an open hand. **2** having lobes etc. like spread fingers. ▷ LEAF

palmetto /pal-met-oh/ *n.* (*pl.* **-os**) a small palm tree, e.g. any of various fan palms of the genus *Sabal* or *Chamaerops*. [from Spanish *palmito* 'little palm']

palmistry *n.* ▲ supposed divination from lines and other features on the palm of the hand. □ **palmist** *n.*

palm oil *n.* oil from the fruit of any of various palms, esp. *Elaeis guineensis* of W. Africa.

Palm Sunday *n.* the Sunday before Easter, celebrating Christ's entry into Jerusalem.

palmtop *n.* a computer small and light enough to be held in one hand.

palm wine *n.* an alcoholic drink made from fermented palm sap.

palmy *adj.* (**palmier**, **palmiest**) triumphant, flourishing (*palmy days*).

PALMISTRY

Palmistry is the practice of interpreting character and telling fortunes by examining the lines, and other features such as mounts, on a person's palm. The four main lines are claimed to relate to vitality of life (life line), emotional security (heart line), intelligence (head line), and to external influences that might affect your life (fate line).

HAND FEATURES USED IN PALMISTRY

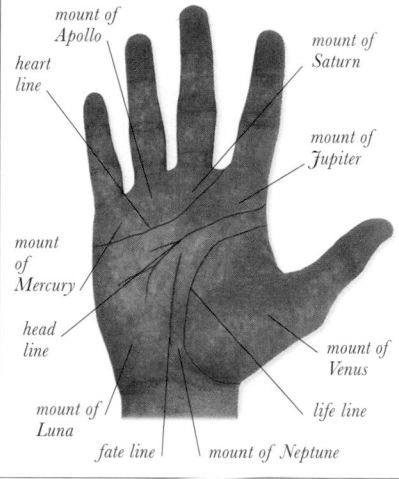

mount of Apollo

heart line

mount of Saturn

mount of Jupiter

mount of Mercury

mount of Venus

head line

mount of Luna

life line

fate line

mount of Neptune

palomino *n.* (*pl.* **-os**) ▼ a golden or tan-coloured horse with a light-coloured mane and tail. [Latin American Spanish]

PALOMINO

palp *n.* (also **palpus**) (*pl.* **palps** or **palpi**) a segmented sense organ at the mouth of an arthropod; a feeler. ▷ SPIDER. [from Latin *palpus*]

palpable *adj.* **1** that can be touched or felt. **2** readily perceived by the senses or mind. [from Late Latin *palpabilis*] □ **palpability** *n.* **palpably** *adv.*

palpate *v.tr.* examine (esp. medically) by touch. [based on Latin *palpatus* 'touched gently'] □ **palpation** *n.*

palpitate *v.intr.* **1** (of the heart) beat strongly and rapidly; undergo palpitations. **2** throb, tremble. [based on Latin *palpitatus* 'throbbed']

palpitation *n.* **1** throbbing, trembling. **2** (often in *pl.*) a noticeably rapid, strong, or irregular heartbeat due to exertion, agitation, or disease.

palpus var. of PALP.

palsy ● *n.* (*pl.* **-ies**) paralysis, esp. with involuntary tremors. ● *v.tr.* (**-ies**, **-ied**) affect with palsy. [from Latin *paralysis*]

paltry *adj.* (**paltrier**, **paltriest**) worthless, contemptible, trifling. [16th-century coinage] □ **paltriness** *n.*

pampas *n.pl.* large treeless plains in S. America. [from Quechua *pampa* 'plain']

pampas grass *n.* ▼ a tall grass, *Cortaderia selloana*, from S. America, with silky flowering plumes.

PAMPAS GRASS (*Cortaderia selloana*)

pamper *v.tr.* **1** over-indulge (a person, taste, etc.), cosset. **2** spoil (a person) with luxury. [Middle English]

pamphlet ● *n.* a small usu. unbound booklet or leaflet containing information or a short treatise. ● *v.tr.* (**pamphleted**, **pamphleting**) distribute pamphlets to. [from *Pamphilet*, familiar name of the 12th-century Latin love poem *Pamphilus seu de Amore*]

pamphleteer ● *n.* a writer of (esp. political) pamphlets. ● *v.intr.* (usu. as **pamphleteering** *n.*) write pamphlets.

pan[1] ● *n.* **1 a** a vessel of metal, earthenware, or plastic, usu. broad and shallow, used for cooking and other domestic purposes. **b** the contents of this. **2** any similar shallow container such as the bowl of a balance scale or that used for washing gravel etc. to separate gold. **3** *Brit.* the bowl of a lavatory. **4** part of the lock that held the gunpowder in old guns. **5** a hollow in the ground (*salt pan*). ● *v.* (**panned**, **panning**) **1** *tr. colloq.* criticize severely. **2 a** *tr.* (often foll. by *off*, *out*) wash (gold-bearing gravel) in a pan. **b** *intr.* search for gold by panning gravel. □ **pan out** (of an action etc.) turn out well or in a specified way. [Old English] □ **panful** *n.* (*pl.* **-fuls**). **panlike** *adj.*

pan[2] ● *v.* (**panned**, **panning**) **1** *tr.* swing (a camera) horizontally to give a panoramic effect or to follow a moving object. **2** *intr.* (of a camera) be moved in this way. ● *n.* a panning movement. [abbreviation of PANORAMA]

pan- *comb. form* **1** all; the whole of. **2** relating to the whole or all the parts of a continent, racial group, religion, etc. (*pan-American*; *pan-African*; *pan-Hellenic*; *pan-Anglican*). [Greek]

P

PANCREAS

In vertebrates, the pancreas gland is located behind the stomach and close to the duodenum. Part of the pancreas produces enzymes, which flow through the pancreatic duct into the duodenum to help digest foods. The pancreas also has groups of cells called islets, which produce two hormones: glucagon and insulin. These hormones, which play an important role in regulating blood sugar levels, pass directly into the bloodstream.

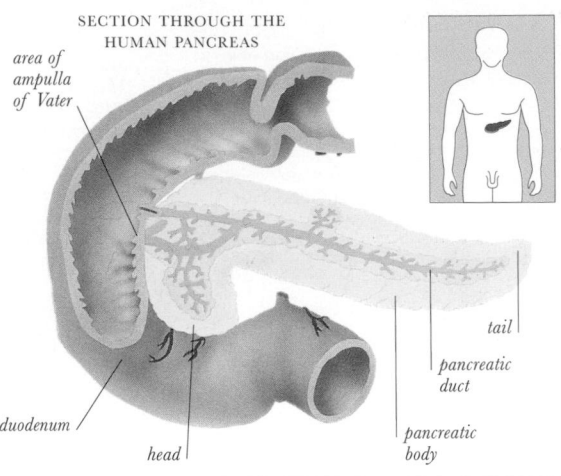

SECTION THROUGH THE HUMAN PANCREAS

area of ampulla of Vater

duodenum

head

tail

pancreatic duct

pancreatic body

panacea /pan-ă-see-ă/ n. a universal remedy. [from Greek *panakeia*]

■ **Usage** The phrase *universal panacea* should be avoided since it is tautologous.

panache /pă-nash/ n. flamboyant confidence of style or manner. [based on Late Latin *pinnaculum* 'little feather']

panama n. a hat of strawlike material made from the leaves of a pine tree. [from *Panama* in Central America]

panatella n. a long thin cigar. [from Latin American Spanish *panatela* 'long thin biscuit']

pancake ● n. 1 a thin flat cake of batter usu. fried and turned in a pan and often rolled up with a filling. 2 (also **Pan-Cake** *propr.*) a flat cake of make-up etc. ● v. 1 *intr.* make a pancake landing. 2 *tr.* cause (an aircraft) to pancake. □ **flat as a pancake** completely flat.

Pancake Day n. Shrove Tuesday (on which pancakes are traditionally eaten).

pancake landing n. an emergency landing in which an aircraft lands with its undercarriage still retracted.

panchromatic adj. *Photog.* (of a film etc.) sensitive to all visible colours of the spectrum.

pancreas /pank-ri-ăs/ n. ▲ a gland near the stomach supplying the duodenum with digestive enzymes and secreting insulin into the blood. ▷ DIGESTION, ENDOCRINE. [from Greek *pagkreas*] □ **pancreatic** adj. **pancreatitis** n.

panda n. 1 (also **giant panda**) a large rare black and white bearlike mammal, *Ailuropoda melanoleuca*, native to certain mountain forests in China and Tibet. 2 (also **red panda**) ▼ a Himalayan raccoon-like

mammal, *Ailurus fulgens*, with reddish-brown fur and a long bushy tail. [Nepali]

panda car n. *Brit.* a police patrol car.

pandemic ● adj. (of a disease) prevalent over a whole country or the world. ● n. an outbreak of such a disease. [from Greek *pandēmos* 'public']

pandemonium n. 1 uproar; utter confusion. 2 a scene of this. [modern Latin (place of all demons in Milton's *Paradise Lost*)]

pander v.*intr.* (foll. by *to*) gratify or indulge a person, a desire or weakness, etc. [from *Pandare*, a character in Boccaccio and in Chaucer's *Troilus and Criseyde*]

pandit var. of PUNDIT 1.

Pandora's box n. a process that once activated will generate many unmanageable problems. [in Greek mythology, the box from which the ills of humankind were released by *Pandora*]

p. & p. abbr. *Brit.* postage and packing.

pane n. a single sheet of glass in a window or door. [Middle English in sense 'piece of cloth': from Latin *pannus*]

panegyric /pan-i-ji-rik/ n. a laudatory discourse; a eulogy. [from Greek *panēgurikos* 'of public assembly'] □ **panegyrical** adj.

panel ● n. 1 a a distinct, usu. rectangular, section of a surface (e.g. of a wall, door, or vehicle). b a board on which controls, dials, etc., are mounted. 2 a strip of material as part of a garment. 3 a group of people forming a team in a broadcast game, discussion, etc. 4 a list of available jurors; a jury. ● v.*tr.* (**panelled, panelling;** *US* **paneled, paneling**) 1 fit or provide with panels. 2 cover or decorate with panels. [from Old French, literally 'piece of cloth']

panel beater n. *Brit.* a person whose job is to beat out the metal panels of motor vehicles.

panel game n. a broadcast quiz etc. played by a panel.

panelling n. (*US* **paneling**) 1 panelled work. 2 wood for making panels.

panellist n. (*US* **panelist**) a member of a panel (esp. in broadcasting).

panel pin n. *Brit.* a thin nail with a very small head.

pan-fry v.*tr.* fry in a pan in shallow fat.

pang n. (often in *pl.*) a sudden sharp pain or painful emotion. [variant of PRONG]

pangolin n. ▶ a mammal of the genus *Manis* (native to Asia) or *Phataginus* (native to Africa), having a small head with elongated snout and tongue. [from Malay *peng-gōling* 'roller', from its habit of rolling itself up]

panhandle *N. Amer.* ● n. a narrow strip of territory projecting from the main territory of one state into another. ● v.*tr. & intr. colloq.* beg for money in the street. □ **panhandler** n.

panic ● n. 1 sudden uncontrollable fear or alarm. 2 infectious apprehension or fright esp. in commercial dealings. 3 (*attrib.*) characterized or caused by panic (*panic measure; panic buying*). ● v.*tr. & intr.* (**panicked, panicking**) (often foll. by *into*) affect or be affected with panic (*was panicked into buying*). [from Greek *panikos* based on *Pan*, name of a rural god causing terror] □ **panicky** adj.

panic button n. a button for summoning help in an emergency.

panicle n. *Bot.* a loose branching cluster of flowers, as in oats. ▷ INFLORESCENCE. [from Latin *paniculum* 'little thread'] □ **panicled** adj.

panic stations n.pl. *Brit.* a state of emergency.

panic-stricken adj. (also **panic-struck**) affected with panic; very apprehensive.

panjandrum n. 1 a mock title for an important person. 2 a pompous or pretentious official etc.

pannier n. 1 a basket, esp. one of a pair carried by a beast of burden. 2 each of a pair of bags or boxes on either side of the rear wheel of a bicycle or motorcycle. [from Latin *panarium* 'bread basket']

panoply n. (*pl.* **-ies**) 1 a complete or splendid array. 2 a complete suit of armour. [based on Greek *pan-* 'all' + *hopla* 'arms'] □ **panoplied** adj.

panorama n. 1 an unbroken view of a surrounding region. 2 a complete survey or presentation of a subject, sequence of events, etc. 3 a picture or photograph containing a wide view. 4 a continuous passing scene. [based on Greek *horama* 'view'] □ **panoramic** adj. **panoramically** adv.

pan pipes n.pl. ▼ a musical instrument made of a series of short pipes graduated in length and fixed together with the mouthpieces in line.

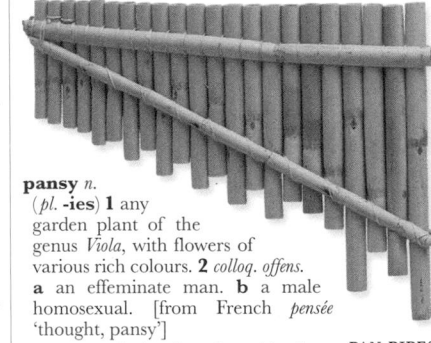

pansy n. (*pl.* **-ies**) 1 any garden plant of the genus *Viola*, with flowers of various rich colours. 2 *colloq. offens.* a an effeminate man. b a male homosexual. [from French *pensée* 'thought, pansy']

pant ● v. 1 *intr.* breathe with short quick breaths. 2 *tr.* (often foll. by *out*) utter breathlessly. 3 *intr.* (often foll. by *for*) yearn or crave. ● n. a panting breath. [from Old French *pantaisier* 'to be agitated, gasp'] □ **pantingly** adv.

PAN PIPES

pantaloon n. (in *pl.*) 1 *hist.* men's close-fitting breeches fastened below the calf or at the foot. 2 baggy trousers (esp. for women) gathered at the ankles. [from Italian *Pantalone*, a character in Italian comedy]

pantechnicon n. *Brit.* a large van for transporting furniture. [invented as the name of a bazaar for artistic work, later in sense 'furniture warehouse']

pantheism n. 1 the belief that God is identifiable with the forces of nature and with natural substances. 2 worship that admits or tolerates all

PANGOLIN (*Manis tricuspis*)

overlapping scales

PANDA: RED PANDA (*Ailurus fulgens*)

P

gods. [based on Greek *theos* 'god'] □ **pantheist** *n.* **pantheistic** *adj.*

pantheon *n.* **1** a building in which illustrious dead are buried or have memorials. **2** the deities of a people collectively. **3** ▶ a temple dedicated to all the gods, esp. the circular one at Rome. **4** a group of individuals who are admired, respected, or distinguished. [from Greek, literally 'all holy']

panther *n.* **1** a leopard, esp. with black fur. **2** *US* a puma. [from Greek]

panties *n.pl. colloq.* short-legged or legless underpants worn by women and girls.

pantihose var. of PANTYHOSE.

pantile *n.* a roof tile curved to form an S-shaped section, fitted to overlap. □ **pantiled** *adj.*

panto *n.* (*pl.* **-os**) *Brit. colloq.* = PANTOMIME 1.

pantograph *n.* **1** an instrument for copying a plan or drawing etc. on a different scale by a system of jointed rods. **2** ▶ a jointed framework conveying a current to an electric vehicle from overhead wires.

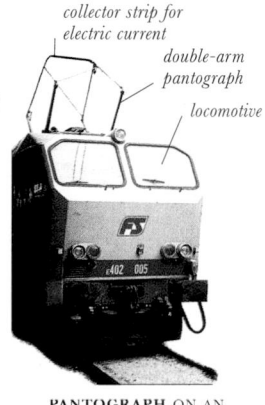

collector strip for electric current
double-arm pantograph
locomotive

PANTOGRAPH ON AN ELECTRIC LOCOMOTIVE

pantomime *n.* **1** *Brit.* a theatrical entertainment based on a fairy tale, with music, topical jokes, etc., usu. produced around Christmas. **2** the use of gestures and facial expression to convey meaning, esp. in drama and dance. **3** *colloq.* an absurd or outrageous piece of behaviour. [from Greek *pantomimos*] □ **pantomimic** *adj.*

pantothenic acid *n.* a vitamin of the B complex, found in rice, bran, and many other foods, and essential for the oxidation of fats and carbohydrates. [based on Greek *pantothen* 'from every side' with allusion to its widespread occurrence]

pantry *n.* (*pl.* **-ies**) **1** a small room or cupboard in which crockery, cutlery, table linen, etc., are kept. **2** a larder. [from Old French *paneterie* 'bread closet']

pants *n.pl.* **1** *Brit.* underpants or knickers. **2** *N. Amer.* trousers or slacks. □ **bore** (or **scare** etc.) **the pants off** *colloq.* bore, scare, etc., to an intolerable degree. **with one's pants down** *colloq.* in an embarrassingly unprepared state. [abbreviation of *pantaloons*]

pants suit *n.* (also **pant suit**) esp. *N. Amer.* a trouser suit.

panty girdle *n.* a woman's girdle with a crotch shaped like pants.

pantyhose *n.* (also **pantihose**) (usu. treated as *pl.*) esp. *N. Amer.* women's usu. sheer tights.

panzer *n.* **1 a** (in *pl.*) (esp. German) armoured troops. **b** a German tank. **2** (*attrib.*) heavily armoured (*panzer division*). [German, literally 'coat of mail']

pap[1] *n.* **1 a** soft or semi-liquid food for infants or invalids. **b** a mash or pulp. **2** light or trivial reading matter; nonsense. [Middle English] □ **pappy** *adj.*

pap[2] *n. archaic* or *dial.* the nipple of a breast. [Middle English, of Scandinavian origin]

papa *n. US* or *archaic* father (esp. as a child's word). [from Greek *papas*]

papacy *n.* (*pl.* **-ies**) **1** a pope's office or tenure. **2** the papal system. [based on Latin *papa* 'pope']

papal *adj.* of or relating to a pope or to the papacy. [from medieval Latin *papalis*] □ **papally** *adv.*

paparazzo /pap-ă-**rat**-soh/ *n.* (*pl.* **paparazzi**) a freelance photographer who pursues celebrities to photograph them. [Italian, from the name of a character in Fellini's film *La Dolce Vita* (1960)]

papaya see PAWPAW.

paper ● *n.* **1** ▼ a material manufactured in thin sheets from the pulp of wood or other fibrous substances, used for writing or drawing or printing on, or as wrapping material etc. **2** (*attrib.*) **a** made of or using paper. **b** flimsy like paper. **3** = NEWSPAPER. **4 a** a document printed on paper. **b** (in *pl.*) documents attesting identity or credentials. **c** (in *pl.*) documents belonging to a person or relating to a matter. **5** *Commerce* **a** negotiable documents, e.g. bills of exchange. **b** (*attrib.*) recorded on paper though not existing (*paper profits*). **6 a** a set of questions to be answered at one session in an examination. **b** the written answers to these. **7** = WALLPAPER 1. **8** an essay or dissertation, esp. one read to a learned society or published in a learned journal. **9** a piece of paper, esp. as a wrapper etc. ● *v.tr.* **1** decorate (a wall etc.) with wallpaper. **2** (foll. by *over*) **a** cover (a hole or blemish) with paper. **b** disguise or try to hide (a fault etc.). □ **on paper 1** in writing. **2** in theory; to judge from written or printed evidence. [from Latin *papyrus*] □ **paperer** *n.* **paperless** *adj.*

paperback ● *adj.* (of a book) bound in stiff paper not boards. ● *n.* a paperback book.

paper boy *n.* (*fem.* **paper girl**) a boy or girl who delivers or sells newspapers.

paperchase *n.* a cross-country run in which the runners follow a trail marked by torn-up paper.

paper clip *n.* a clip of bent wire or of plastic for holding several sheets of paper together.

PANTHEON

The term pantheon is often used to refer specifically to the Pantheon at Rome, which was built by the Roman emperor Hadrian (AD 76–138). Its huge hemispherical dome is a symbolic reference to the temple's dedication to all the gods in the universe.

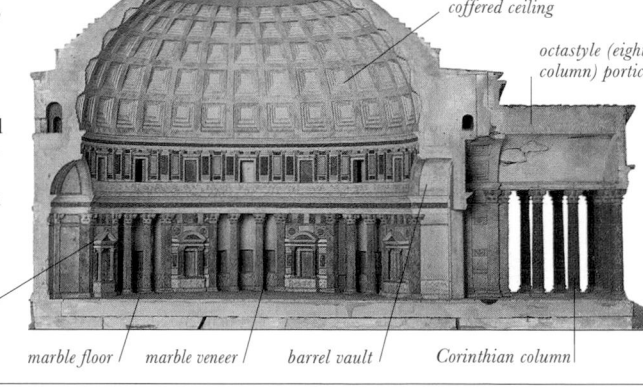

MODEL OF THE PANTHEON (AD 118–128), ROME, ITALY

unglazed oculus (circular opening)
hemispherical dome
coffered ceiling
octastyle (eight-column) portico
pediment
marble floor
marble veneer
barrel vault
Corinthian column

PAPER

Most paper is made from the pulped wood of trees. Softwood logs are broken into pieces and treated with chemicals in a pulping machine, which converts the wood to a mass of fibres known as pulp. Wet wood pulp flows on to a paper-making machine. Water is sucked out, and the damp paper passes through rollers and cylinders that press and dry it. Recycled paper is made in the same way, using waste paper.

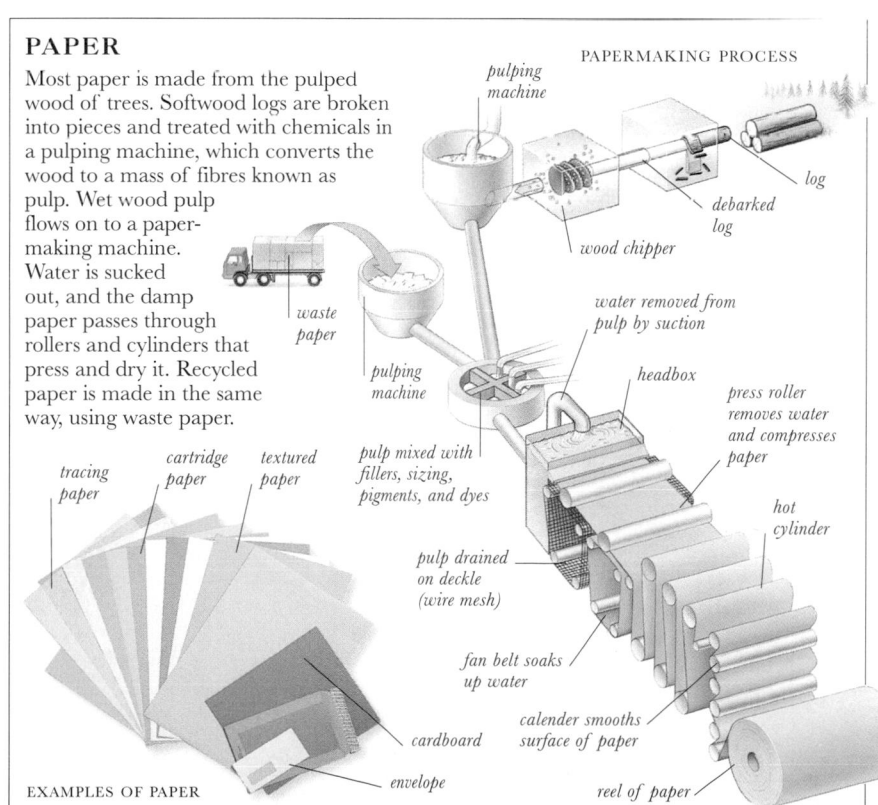

PAPERMAKING PROCESS

pulping machine
log
debarked log
wood chipper
waste paper
pulping machine
water removed from pulp by suction
headbox
press roller removes water and compresses paper
pulp mixed with fillers, sizing, pigments, and dyes
hot cylinder
pulp drained on deckle (wire mesh)
fan belt soaks up water
calender smooths surface of paper
reel of paper

tracing paper
cartridge paper
textured paper
cardboard
envelope

EXAMPLES OF PAPER

paperhanger *n.* a person who decorates with wall-paper, esp. professionally.

paperknife *n.* (*pl.* **paperknives**) *Brit.* a blunt knife for opening letters etc.

papermaker *n.* a person who makes paper for a living. □ **papermaking** *n. & adj.* ▷ PAPER

paper mill *n.* a mill in which paper is made.

paper money *n.* money in the form of banknotes.

paper round *n.* (*N. Amer.* **paper route**) **1** a job of regularly delivering newspapers. **2** a route taken doing this.

paper-thin ● *adj.* very thin; of no substance (*paper-thin slices*). ● *adv.* very thinly.

paper tiger *n.* an apparently threatening, but ineffectual, person or thing.

paperweight *n.* a small heavy object for keeping loose papers in place.

paperwork *n.* routine clerical or administrative work.

papery *adj.* like paper in thinness or texture.

papier mâché /pap-yay **mash**-ay/ *n.* paper pulp used for moulding into boxes, trays, etc. [French, literally 'chewed paper']

papilla *n.* (*pl.* **papillae** /-lee/) **1** a small nipple-like protuberance in a part or organ of the body. **2** a small fleshy projection on a plant. [Latin, literally 'nipple'] □ **papillary** *adj.* **papillate** *adj.* **papillose** *adj.*

papilloma *n.* (*pl.* **papillomas** or **papillomata**) a wartlike usu. benign tumour.

papist often *derog.* ● *n.* a Roman Catholic. ● *adj.* of or relating to Roman Catholics. [from French *papiste*] □ **papism** *n.* **papistical** *adj.* **papistry** *n.*

papoose *n.* a young N. American Indian child. [from Algonquian]

paprika *n.* **1** *Bot.* a red pepper. **2** a condiment made from it. ▷ SPICE. [Hungarian]

Pap test *n.* (also **pap test**) a test carried out on a cervical smear to detect cancer of the cervix or womb. [named after G. N. *Papanicolaou*, US scientist, 1883–1962]

papyrus /pă-**py**-rŭs/ *n.* (*pl.* **papyri**) **1** ▼ an aquatic plant, *Cyperus papyrus*, with dark green stems topped with fluffy inflorescences. **2 a** a writing material prepared in ancient Egypt from the pithy stem of this. **b** a document written on this. [from Greek *papuros*]

PAPYRUS (*Cyperus papyrus*)

par *n.* **1** the average or normal amount, degree, condition, etc. (*feel below par*; *be up to par*). **2** equality; an equal status or footing (*on a par with*). **3** *Golf* the number of strokes a first-class player should normally require for a hole or course. **4** *Stock Exch.* the face value of stocks and shares etc. (*at par*; *below par*). □ **par for the course** *colloq.* what is normal or expected in any given circumstances. [Latin (adj. & n.), literally 'equal, equality']

para *n. colloq.* a paratrooper.

parable *n.* **1** a narrative of imagined events used to illustrate a moral or spiritual lesson. **2** an allegory. [from Latin *parabola* 'comparison']

parabola /pă-**rab**-ŏ-lă/ *n.* (*pl.* **parabolas** or **parabolae** /-lee/) ▼ a symmetrical open plane curve formed by the intersection of a cone with a plane parallel to its side. [from Greek *parabolē* 'placing side by side, comparison'] □ **parabolic** *adj.*

paraboloid *n.* **1** (in full **paraboloid of revolution**) ▼ a solid generated by the rotation of a parabola about its axis of symmetry. **2** a solid having two or more non-parallel parabolic cross-sections. □ **paraboloidal** *adj.*

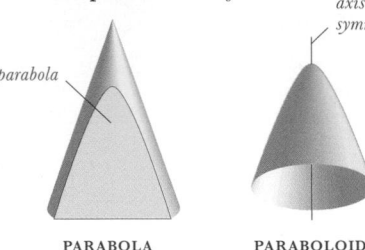

PARABOLA　　　　　PARABOLOID

paracetamol *n. Brit.* **1** a drug used to relieve pain and reduce fever. **2** a tablet of this. [from *para-acetylaminophenol*]

parachute ● *n.* **1** a rectangular or umbrella-shaped apparatus allowing a person or heavy object attached to it to descend slowly from a height, esp. from an aircraft, or to retard motion in other ways. **2** (*attrib.*) dropped by parachute (*parachute troops*; *parachute flare*). ● *v.tr. & intr.* convey or descend by parachute. [French] □ **parachutist** *n.*

parade ● *n.* **1** a formal or ceremonial muster of troops for inspection. **2** a public procession. **3** *Brit.* a public square, promenade, or row of shops. ● *v.* **1** *intr.* assemble for parade. **2 a** *tr.* march through (streets etc.) in procession. **b** *intr.* march ceremonially. **3** *tr.* display ostentatiously. □ **on parade** **1** taking part in a parade. **2** on display. [French, literally 'show']

parade ground *n.* a place for the muster of troops.

paradigm /**pa**-ră-dym/ *n.* **1** an example or pattern, esp. one underlying a theory or methodology. **2** a representative set of the inflections of a noun, verb, etc. [from Greek *paradeigma*] □ **paradigmatic** /pa-ră-dig-**mat**-ik/ *adj.* **paradigmatically** *adv.*

paradigm shift *n.* a fundamental change (in approach, philosophy, etc.).

paradise *n.* **1** (in some religions) heaven as the ultimate abode of the just. **2** a place or state of complete happiness. **3** (in full **earthly paradise**) the garden of Eden. [from Avestan (Iranian)

pairidaēza 'park'] □ **paradisaical** *adj.* **paradisal** *adj.* **paradisiacal** *adj.* **paradisical** *adj.*

parador *n.* (*pl.* **paradors** or **paradores** /pa-ră-**dor**-ez/) a hotel owned and administered by the Spanish government. [Spanish]

paradox *n.* **1 a** a seemingly absurd or contradictory statement, even if actually well-founded. **b** a self-contradictory or absurd statement. **2** a person or thing conflicting with a preconceived notion of what is reasonable or possible. **3** a paradoxical quality or character. [originally in sense 'a statement contrary to accepted opinion': from Greek *paradoxon*] □ **paradoxical** *adj.* **paradoxically** *adv.*

paraffin *n.* **1** *Brit.* an inflammable waxy or oily substance obtained by distillation from petroleum or shale, used in liquid form (also **paraffin oil**) esp. as a fuel. **2** *Chem.* = ALKANE. [based on Latin *parum* 'little' + *affinis* 'related', from its low reactivity]

paraffin wax *n.* paraffin in its solid form.

paragliding *n.* a sport resembling hang-gliding, using a wide parachute-like canopy attached to the body by a harness. □ **paraglide** *v.intr.* **paraglider** *n.*

paragon *n.* **1 a** a model of excellence. **b** a supremely excellent person or thing. **2** (foll. by *of*) a model (of virtue etc.). [from Italian *paragone* 'touchstone']

paragraph *n.* **1** a distinct section of a piece of writing, beginning on a new usu. indented line. **2** a symbol (usu. ¶) used to mark a new paragraph, and also as a reference mark. [from Greek *paragraphos* 'short stroke marking a break in sense'] □ **paragraphic** *adj.*

parakeet *n.* any of various small usu. long-tailed parrots. [from Spanish *periquito*]

paralegal esp. *N. Amer.* ● *adj.* of or relating to auxiliary aspects of the law. ● *n.* a person trained in subsidiary legal matters.

parallax *n.* **1** ▼ the apparent difference in the position or direction of an object when viewed from different positions. **2** the angular amount of this. [from Greek *parallaxis* 'change'] □ **parallactic** *adj.*

parallel ● *adj.* **1 a** (of lines or planes) side by side and having a constant distance between them. **b** (foll. by *to*, *with*) (of a line or plane) having this relation (to another). **2** (of circumstances etc.) precisely similar, analogous, or corresponding. **3 a** (of processes etc.) occurring or performed simultaneously. **b** *Computing* involving the simultaneous performance of operations. ● *n.* **1** a person or thing precisely analogous or equal to another. **2** a comparison (*drew a parallel between the two situations*). **3** (in full **parallel of latitude**) *Geog.* **a** each

PARALLAX

In astronomy, the term parallax refers to the apparent displacement of nearby stars against the background of more distant stars when viewed from opposite sides of the Earth's orbit. The greater the parallax, the nearer the star is to Earth. In the illustration shown here, star B has the greater shift and is closer to Earth than star A.

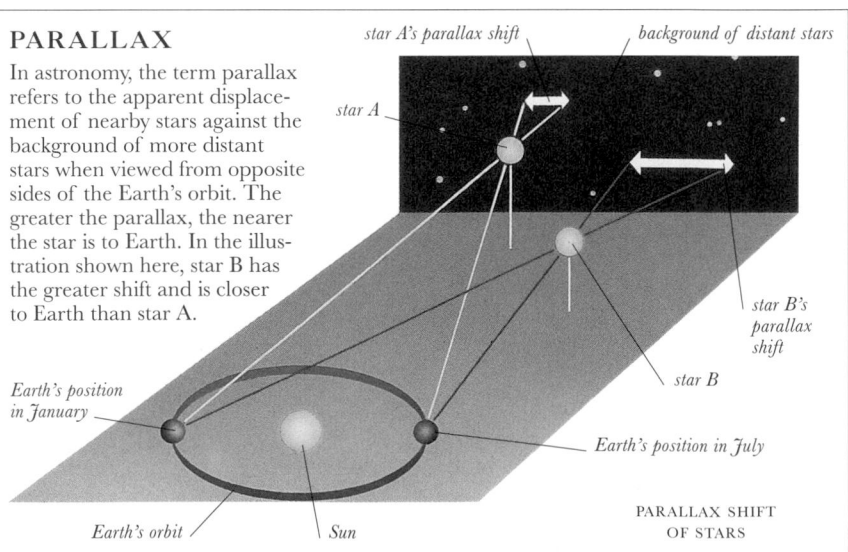

star A's parallax shift　　background of distant stars

star A

star B's parallax shift

star B

Earth's position in January

Earth's position in July

Earth's orbit　　Sun

PARALLAX SHIFT OF STARS

of the imaginary parallel circles of constant latitude on the Earth's surface. **b** a corresponding line on a map (*the 49th parallel*). **4** *Printing* two parallel lines (‖) as a reference mark. ● *v.tr.* (**paralleled**, **paralleling**) **1** be parallel to; correspond to. **2** represent as similar; compare. □ **in parallel** (of electric circuits) arranged so as to join at common points at each end. [from Greek *parallēlos*] □ **parallelism** *n.*

parallel bars *n.pl.* a pair of parallel rails on posts for gymnastics.

parallelepiped *n. Geom.* a solid body of which each face is a parallelogram. [based on Greek *epipedon* 'plane surface']

parallelogram *n.* ◄ a four-sided plane rectilinear figure with opposite sides parallel. [based on Greek *grammē* 'line']

parallel parking *n.* the parking of a vehicle or vehicles parallel to the roadside.

Paralympics *n.pl.* an international athletic competition for disabled athletes. □ **Paralympic** *attrib.adj.*

PARALLELOGRAM

paralyse *v.tr.* (*US* **paralyze**) **1** affect with paralysis. **2** render powerless; cripple. **3** bring to a standstill. [from French *paralyser*] □ **paralysingly** *adv.*

paralysis *n.* (*pl.* **paralyses**) **1** a nervous condition with impairment or loss of esp. the motor function of the nerves. **2** a state of utter powerlessness. [from Greek *paralusis* 'disabling']

paralytic ● *adj.* **1** affected by paralysis. **2** esp. *Brit. slang* very drunk. ● *n.* a person affected by paralysis. [from Greek *paralutikos*] □ **paralytically** *adv.*

paramedic *n.* a paramedical worker.

paramedical *adj.* (of services etc.) supplementing and supporting medical work.

parameter /pă-**ram**-i-ter/ *n.* **1** *Math.* a quantity constant in the case considered but varying in different cases. **2 a** an (esp. measurable or quantifiable) characteristic or feature. **b** *disp.* (loosely) a constant element or factor, esp. serving as a limit or boundary (*within the parameters of the inquiry*). [from Greek *para* 'beside' + *metron* 'measure'] □ **parametric** *adj.* **parametrize** *v.tr.* (also **-ise**).

■ **Usage** The very common use of *parameter* in sense 2b, probably influenced by *perimeter* is frowned upon by some people.

paramilitary ● *adj.* (of forces) organized similarly to military forces. ● *n.* (*pl.* **-ies**) a member of an unofficial paramilitary organization, esp. in Northern Ireland.

paramount *adj.* **1** supreme; pre-eminent (*of paramount importance*). **2** in supreme authority. [from Old French *par* 'by' + *amont* 'above'] □ **paramountcy** *n.*

paramour /pa-ră-**moor**/ *n. archaic* or *derog.* an illicit lover of a married person. [from Old French *par amour* 'by love']

paranoia *n.* **1** a mental disorder esp. characterized by delusions of persecution and self-importance. **2** an abnormal tendency to suspect and mistrust others. [based on Greek *paranoos* 'distracted'] □ **paranoiac** *adj. & n.* **paranoiacally** *adv.* **paranoic** *adj.* **paranoically** *adv.* **paranoid** *adj. & n.*

paranormal *adj.* beyond the scope of normal objective investigation or explanation. □ **paranormally** *adv.*

parapet *n.* **1** a low wall at the edge of a roof, balcony, etc., or the side of a bridge. **2** a defence of earth or stone to conceal and protect troops. [French, literally 'breast-high wall'] □ **parapeted** *adj.*

paraphernalia *n.pl.* (also treated as *sing.*) miscellaneous belongings, items of equipment, accessories, etc. [originally in sense 'property owned by a married woman': from Greek *parapherna*]

paraphrase ● *n.* a free rendering or rewording of a passage. ● *v.tr.* express the meaning of (a passage) in other words. [from Greek *paraphrasis*]

PARASITE

Parasitic lifestyles are common in invertebrates, flowering plants, fungi, and single-celled organisms. Endoparasites live inside their host. Tapeworms, for example, use hooks and suckers on their head to grip their host's intestine. Ectoparasites, such as lice, live on the surface of their host's body and often attach themselves by their claws or sharp mouthparts. Some parasitic plants live entirely within their hosts, but most – such as the dodder – invade their host's tissue through specially adapted roots or stems.

TYPES OF PARASITE

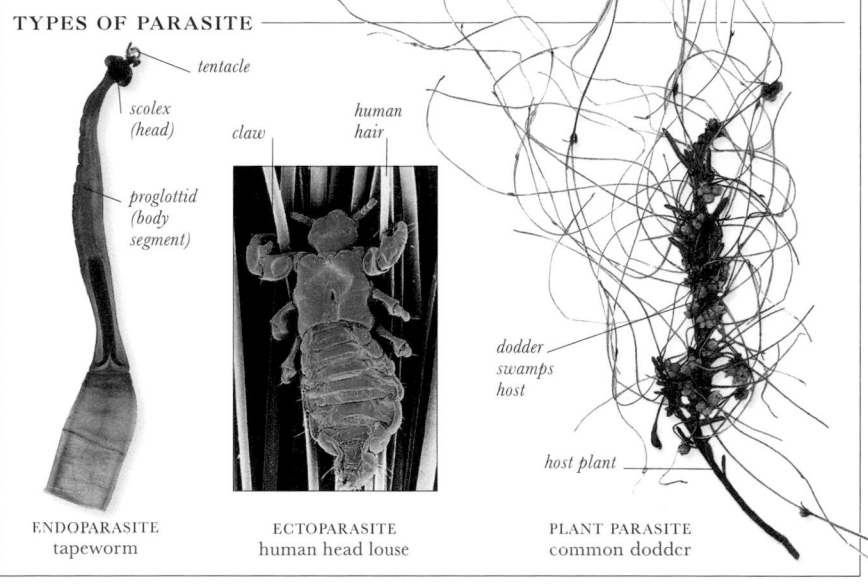

- tentacle
- scolex (head)
- claw
- human hair
- proglottid (body segment)
- dodder swamps host
- host plant

ENDOPARASITE
tapeworm

ECTOPARASITE
human head louse

PLANT PARASITE
common dodder

paraplegia *n.* paralysis of the legs and part or the whole of the trunk. [based on Greek *paraplēssein* 'to strike at the side'] □ **paraplegic** *adj. & n.*

parapsychology *n.* the study of mental phenomena outside the sphere of ordinary psychology (hypnosis, telepathy, etc.). □ **parapsychological** *adj.* **parapsychologist** *n.*

paraquat *n.* a toxic fast-acting herbicide. [from the position of the bond between the two parts of the molecule relative to *quat*ernary nitrogen atoms]

parasailing *n.* a sport in which a person wearing an open parachute glides through the air attached to the back of a motor boat. □ **parasail** *v.intr. & n.*

parascending *n. Brit.* = PARAGLIDING, PARASAILING. □ **parascend** *v.intr.* **parascender** *n.*

parasite *n.* **1** ▲ an organism living in or on another and benefiting at the expense of the other. **2** a person who lives off or exploits others. [from Greek *parasitos* 'a person who eats at another's table'] □ **parasitic** *adj.* **parasitical** *adj.* **parasitically** *adv.* **parasitism** *n.* **parasitology** *n.* **parasitologist** *n.*

parasitize *v.tr.* (also **-ise**) infest as a parasite. □ **parasitization** *n.*

parasitoid *Zool.* ● *n.* an insect whose larvae live as parasites which eventually kill their hosts, e.g. an ichneumon wasp. ● *adj.* of, relating to, or designating such an insect.

parasol *n.* **1** a light umbrella used to give shade from the Sun. **2** (in full **parasol mushroom**) ► a tall fungus of the genus *Lepiota* with a broad shaggy domed cap, esp. the edible *L. procera*. [French]

parastatal ● *adj.* (of an industrial organization etc.) having some political authority and serving the State indirectly, esp. in some African countries. ● *n.* a parastatal organization.

paratha /pă-**rah**-tă/ *n.* (in Indian cookery) a piece of flat unleavened bread fried on a griddle. [from Hindi *parāṭhā*]

parathion *n.* a highly toxic organic compound of phosphorus and sulphur used as an agricultural insecticide.

parathyroid *Anat.* ● *n.* a gland next to the thyroid, secreting a hormone that regulates calcium levels in the body. ▷ ENDOCRINE. ● *adj.* of or associated with this gland.

paratrooper *n.* a member of a body of paratroops.

paratroops *n.pl.* troops equipped to be dropped by parachute from aircraft. □ **paratroop** *attrib.adj.*

paratyphoid ● *n.* a fever resembling typhoid but caused by various different bacteria. ● *adj.* of, relating to, or caused by this fever.

par avion *adv.* by airmail. [French, literally 'by aeroplane']

parboil *v.tr.* partly cook by boiling. [from Late Latin *perbullire* 'to boil thoroughly', confused with *part*]

parcel ● *n.* **1 a** goods etc. wrapped up in a single package. **b** a bundle of things wrapped up, usu. in paper. **2** a piece of land. **3** a quantity dealt with in one commercial transaction. ● *v.tr.* (**parcelled**, **parcelling**; *US* **parceled**, **parceling**) **1** (foll. by *up*) wrap as a parcel. **2** (foll. by *out*) divide into portions. □ **part and parcel** see PART. [from Latin *particula*]

parch *v.* **1** *tr. & intr.* make or become hot and dry. **2** *tr.* roast (peas, corn, etc.) slightly. [Middle English]

parched *adj.* **1** hot and dry; dried out with heat. **2** *colloq.* thirsty.

parchment *n.* **1 a** a skin, esp. that of a sheep or goat, prepared as a writing or painting surface. ▷ SCROLL. **b** a manuscript written on this. **2** high-grade paper made to resemble parchment. [from a blend of Late Latin *pergamina* 'writing material from Pergamum' (in Asia Minor) with *Parthica pellis* 'Parthian skin' (leather)]

PARASOL MUSHROOM (*Lepiota aspera*)

P

pardner *n. US dial.* or *joc.* a partner or comrade.

pardon ● *n.* **1** the act of forgiving an offence, error, etc. **2** (in full **free pardon**) *Brit.* a remission of the legal consequences of a crime or conviction. ● *v.tr.* **1** release from the consequences of an offence, error, etc. **2** forgive a person for (an offence etc.). **3** make allowances for; excuse. ● *int.* (also **pardon me** or **I beg your pardon**) **1** a formula of apology or disagreement. **2** a request to a speaker to repeat something said. [from medieval Latin *perdonare* 'to concede, remit'] □ **pardonable** *adj.* **pardonably** *adv.*

pardoner *n. hist.* a person licensed to sell papal pardons or indulgences.

pare *v.tr.* **1 a** trim or shave by cutting away the surface or edge. **b** cut off (the surface or edge). **2** diminish little by little. [from Latin *parare* 'to prepare']

parent ● *n.* **1** a person who has begotten or borne offspring; a father or mother. **2** a person who has adopted a child or who holds the position or exercises the function of a parent. **3** *archaic* a forefather. **4** an animal or plant from which others are derived. **5** a source or origin. **6** an initiating organization or enterprise. ● *v.tr.* (also *absol.*) be a parent of. □ **parent–teacher association** a local organization of parents and teachers for promoting closer relations and improving educational facilities at a school. [from Latin *parent-* 'bringing forth'] □ **parental** *adj.* **parenthood** *n.*

parentage *n.* lineage; descent from or through parents (*their parentage is unknown*).

parent company *n.* a company of which others are subsidiaries.

parenthesis *n.* (*pl.* **parentheses**) **1 a** a word, clause, or sentence inserted as an explanation or afterthought into a passage which is grammatically complete without it, and usu. marked off by brackets or dashes or commas. **b** (in *pl.*) a pair of round brackets ( ) used for this. **2** an interlude or interval. □ **in parenthesis** as a parenthesis or afterthought. [based on Greek *parentithenai* 'to put in beside']

parenthetic *adj.* **1** of or by way of a parenthesis. **2** interposed. □ **parenthetical** *adj.* **parenthetically** *adv.*

parenting *n.* the occupation or concerns of parents.

par excellence *adv.* being the supreme example of its kind (*the short story par excellence*). [French, literally 'by excellence']

parfait /par-**fay**/ *n.* **1** a rich iced pudding of whipped cream, eggs, etc. **2** layers of ice cream, meringue, etc., served in a tall glass. [French, literally 'perfect']

pargeting /par-jit-ing/ *n. Building* ▼ plaster, esp. with an ornamental pattern. [based on Old French *parjeter* 'to cast over a surface']

PARGETING: ROYAL COAT OF ARMS ON
A 17TH-CENTURY HOUSE

pariah /pă-**ry**-ă/ *n.* **1** a social outcast. **2** *hist.* a member of a low caste or of no caste in southern India. [from Tamil pl. of *paṛaiyan* 'hereditary drummer']

pariah dog *n.* = PYE-DOG.

parietal /pă-**ry**-i-tăl/ *adj. Anat.* of the wall of the body or any of its cavities. [based on Latin *paries -etis* 'wall']

parietal bone *n.* either of a pair of bones forming the central part of the sides and top of the skull. ▷ SKULL

parietal lobe *n.* either of the paired lobes of the brain at the top of the head.

paring *n.* a strip or piece cut off.

pari passu /pah-ri **pass**-oo/ *adv.* **1** with equal speed. **2** simultaneously and equally. [Latin]

parish *n.* **1** an area having its own church and clergy. **2** (in full **civil parish**) *Brit.* a district constituted for purposes of local government. **3** the inhabitants of a parish. [based on Greek *paroikia* 'sojourning']

parish clerk *n.* an official in charge of the public records of a parish.

parish council *n. Brit.* the administrative body in a civil parish.

parishioner *n.* an inhabitant of a parish.

parish pump *n.* (often *attrib.*) *Brit.* a symbol of a parochial or restricted outlook.

parish register *n.* a book recording christenings, marriages, and burials, at a parish church.

Parisian ● *adj.* of or relating to Paris in France. ● *n.* a native or inhabitant of Paris. [from French *parisien*]

parity *n.* **1** equality, esp. as regards status or pay. **2** parallelism or analogy (*parity of reasoning*). **3** equivalence of one currency with another; being at par. **4** (of a number) the fact of being even or odd. [from Late Latin *paritas*]

park ● *n.* **1** a large public garden in a town, for recreation. **2** a large enclosed piece of ground attached to a country house etc. **3 a** a large area of land kept in its natural state for public recreational use. **b** a large enclosed area of land used to accommodate wild animals in captivity (*wildlife park*). **4** esp. *Brit.* an area for motor vehicles etc. to be left in (*car park*). **5** an area devoted to a specified purpose (*business park*). **6 a** *N. Amer.* an enclosed sports ground. **b** (usu. prec. by the) *Brit. colloq.* a football pitch. ● *v.tr.* **1** (also *absol.*) leave (a vehicle) temporarily. **2** *colloq.* deposit and leave, usu. temporarily. □ **park oneself** *colloq.* sit down. [from medieval Latin *parricus*]

parka *n.* **1** ▶ a skin jacket with a hood, worn by Eskimos. **2** a windproof fabric garment of similar design worn in cold weather. [from Russian]

hood

reindeer skin

mittens sewn into sleeves

fur trim

PARKA

parkin *n. Brit.* a cake made with oatmeal, ginger, and treacle or molasses.

parking light *n.* a small light on the side of a vehicle, for use when the vehicle is parked at night.

parking lot *n. US* an outdoor area for parking vehicles.

parking meter *n.* a coin-operated meter which

receives fees for vehicles parked in the street and indicates the time available.

parking ticket *n.* a notice of a penalty imposed for parking illegally.

Parkinsonism *n.* = PARKINSON'S DISEASE.

Parkinson's disease *n.* a progressive disease of the nervous system with tremor, muscular rigidity, and emaciation. [named after J. *Parkinson*, English surgeon, 1755 –1824]

Parkinson's law *n.* the notion that work expands so as to fill the time available for its completion. [named after C.N. *Parkinson*, English writer, 1909–93]

parkland *n.* open grassland with clumps of trees etc.

parkway *n.* **1** *US* an open landscaped highway. **2** *Brit.* a railway station with extensive parking facilities, used esp. in names (*Bristol Parkway*).

parky *adj.* (**parkier**, **parkiest**) *Brit. colloq.* chilly. [19th-century coinage]

parlance *n.* a particular way of speaking, esp. as regards choice of words, idiom, etc. [from Old French]

parley ● *n.* (*pl.* **-eys**) a conference for debating points in a dispute, esp. a discussion of terms for an armistice etc. ● *v.intr.* (**-leys**, **-leyed**) (often foll. by *with*) hold a parley.

parliament *n.* **1** (**Parliament**) (in the UK) **a** the highest legislature, consisting of the Sovereign, the House of Lords, and the House of Commons. **b** the members of this legislature for a particular period, esp. between one dissolution and the next. **2** a similar legislature in other states. [from Old French *parlement* 'speaking']

parliamentarian *n.* a member of a parliament, esp. one well-versed in its procedures.

parliamentary *adj.* **1** of or relating to a parliament. **2** enacted or established by a parliament. **3** (of language) admissible in a parliament; polite.

Parliamentary Commissioner for Administration *n.* the official title of the ombudsman in the UK.

parliamentary private secretary *n.* a Member of Parliament assisting a government minister.

parlour *n.* (*US* **parlor**) **1** a sitting room in a private house. **2** a room in a hotel, convent, etc., for the private use of residents. **3** esp. *US* a shop providing specified goods or services (*beauty parlour, ice-cream parlour*). **4** a room or building equipped for milking cows. [from Old French *parleur*]

parlour game *n.* an indoor game, esp. a word game.

parlourmaid *n. hist.* a maid who waits at table.

parlous *adj. archaic* or *joc.* **1** dangerous or difficult. **2** hard to deal with. [Middle English, literally 'perilous']

Parma ham *n.* a type of ham which is eaten uncooked. [from *Parma*, a city and province in Italy]

Parmesan /par-mi-**zan**/ *n.* a kind of hard dry cheese made originally at Parma and used esp. in grated form. ▷ CHEESE. [from Italian *parmegiano* 'of *Parma*' a city and province in Italy]

parochial *adj.* **1** of or concerning a parish. **2** (of affairs, views, etc.) merely local, narrow or restricted in scope. [from ecclesiastical Latin *parochialis*] □ **parochialism** *n.* **parochiality** *n.* **parochially** *adv.*

parody ● *n.* (*pl.* **-ies**) **1 a** a humorous exaggerated imitation of an author, literary work, style, etc. **b** a work of this kind. **2** a feeble imitation; a travesty. ● *v.tr.* (**-ies**, **-ied**) **1** compose a parody of. **2** mimic humorously. [from Greek *parōidia* 'burlesque poem'] □ **parodic** *adj.* **parodist** *n.*

parole ● *n.* **1 a** the temporary or permanent release of a prisoner before the expiry of a sentence, on the promise of good behaviour. **b** such a promise. **2** a word of honour. ● *v.tr.* put (a prisoner) on parole. □ **on parole** released on the terms of parole. [French, literally 'word'] □ **parolee** *n.*

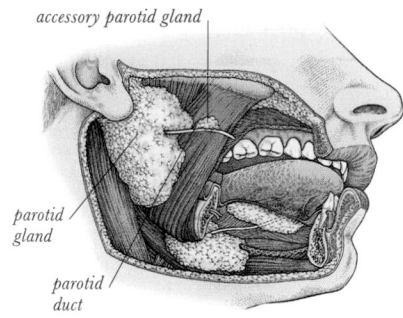

PAROTID GLAND: HUMAN HEAD SHOWING
THE PAROTID GLAND

accessory parotid gland

parotid gland

parotid duct

parotid *Anat.* ● *adj.* situated near the ear. ● *n.* (in full **parotid gland**) ▲ a salivary gland in front of the ear. [based on Greek *ous ōtos* 'ear']

parotitis *n. Med.* **1** inflammation of the parotid gland. **2** mumps.

paroxysm *n.* **1** a sudden attack or outburst (of rage, laughter, etc.). **2** a fit of disease. [from Greek *paroxusmos* 'exasperation'] □ **paroxysmal** *adj.*

parquet /**par**-kay/ ● *n.* **1** (often *attrib.*) a flooring of wooden blocks arranged in a pattern. **2** *US* **a** the ground floor of a theatre auditorium. **b** the front part of this. ● *v.tr.* (**parqueted, parqueting**) furnish (a room) with a parquet floor. [French, literally 'small compartment, floor']

parquetry /**par**-kit-ri/ *n.* the use of wooden blocks to make floors or inlay for furniture.

parr *n.* a young salmon. [18th-century coinage]

parricide *n.* **1** the killing of a near relative, esp. of a parent. **2** a person who commits parricide. [from Latin *parricidium* (sense 1), *parricida* (sense 2)] □ **parricidal** *adj.*

■ **Usage** *Parricide*, the killing of a near relative, especially of a parent, is sometimes confused with *patricide*, the killing of one's father.

parrot ● *n.* **1** ▶ any of various mainly tropical birds of the order Psittaciformes, with a short hooked bill, often having vivid plumage and sometimes able to mimic the human voice. **2** a person who mechanically repeats the words or actions of another. ● *v.tr.* (**parroted, parroting**) repeat mechanically.

parrot-fashion *adv.* (learning or repeating) mechanically without understanding.

parrotfish *n.* (*pl.* usu. same) ◀ any fish of the family Scaridae, with a mouth like a parrot's bill and forming a protective mucous cocoon against predators.

parry ● *v.tr.* (**-ies, -ied**) **1** avert or ward off (a weapon or attack). **2** deal skilfully with (an awkward question etc.). ● *n.* (*pl.* **-ies**) an act of parrying.

parse *v.tr.* **1** describe (a word in context) grammatically, stating its inflection, relation to the sentence, etc. **2** resolve (a sentence) into its component parts and describe them grammatically. **3** *Computing* analyse (a string) into syntactic components. □ **parser** *n.* (esp. in sense 3).

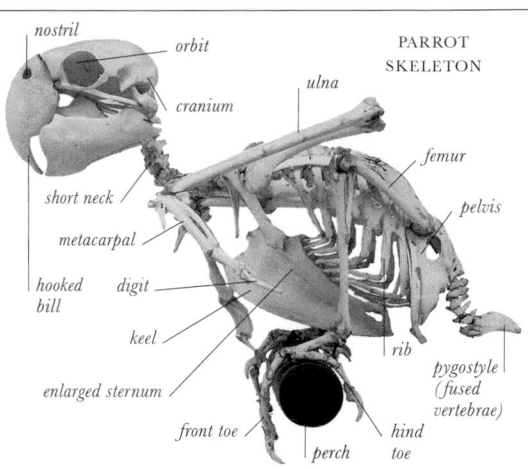

PARROT SKELETON

nostril
orbit
cranium
ulna
femur
pelvis
short neck
metacarpal
digit
rib
hooked bill
keel
pygostyle (fused vertebrae)
enlarged sternum
front toe
perch
hind toe

PARROT

The more than 300 species of parrot share common features including: a large head; hooked bill; and strong grasping feet with two toes in front and two toes behind, which aid in grasping food and climbing. Parrots often gather in flocks, within which they are commonly in pairs. Most species are diurnal birds that live in trees, while a few aberrant species are nocturnal and remain on the ground. Nearly all parrot species are monogamous, commonly mating for years and sometimes for life.

EXAMPLES OF PARROTS

CELESTIAL PARROTLET
(*Forpus coelestis*)

ECLECTUS PARROT
(*Eclectus roratus*)

AFRICAN GREY PARROT
(*Psittacus erithacus*)

GREEN-WINGED MACAW
(*Ara chloroptera*)

BLUE-CROWNED HANGING PARROT
(*Loriculus galgulus*)

GALAH
(*Eolophus roseicapillus*)

UMBRELLA COCKATOO
(*Cacatua alba*)

CHATTERING LORY
(*Lorius garrulus*)

RAINBOW LORIKEET
(*Trichoglossus haematodus*)

PARROTFISH
(*Bolbometaon bicolor*)

parsec *n.* a unit of astronomical distance, equal to about 3.25 light years, the distance at which the mean radius of the Earth's orbit subtends an angle of one second of arc. [blend of PARALLAX and SECOND²]

Parsee *n.* an adherent of Zoroastrianism, esp. a descendant of those Zoroastrians who fled to India during the 7th–8th c. [from Persian *pārsī* 'Persian']

parsimony *n.* **1** carefulness in the use of money or other resources. **2** meanness, stinginess. [from Latin *parsimonia* 'saving'] □ **parsimonious** *adj.* **parsimoniously** *adv.*

parsley *n.* a biennial herb, *Petroselinum crispum*, with crinkly aromatic leaves, used for seasoning and garnishing food. ▷ HERB. [from Greek *petroselinon*]

parsnip *n.* **1** a biennial umbelliferous plant, *Pastinaca sativa*, with a large pale yellow tapering root. **2** this root eaten as a vegetable. [from Latin *pastinaca*]

parson *n.* **1** a rector. **2** a vicar or any beneficed member of the clergy. **3** *colloq.* any member of the clergy. [from Latin *persona* 'person', later 'rector']

parsonage *n.* a church house provided for a parson.

parson's nose *n.* the piece of fatty flesh at the rump of a fowl.

part ● *n.* **1** some but not all of a thing or number of things. **2** an essential member or constituent of anything (*part of the family; a large part of the job*). **3** a component of a machine etc. (*spare parts; needs a new part*). **4** a portion of a human or animal body. **5** a division of a book, broadcast serial, etc., esp. as much as is issued or broadcast at one time. **6 a** each of several equal portions of a whole (*the recipe has 3 parts sugar to 2 parts flour*). **b** (prec. by ordinal number) a specified fraction of a whole (*each received a fifth part*). **7 a** a portion allotted; a share. **b** a person's share in an action or enterprise (*will have no part in it*). **c** one's duty (*was not my part to interfere*). **8 a** a character assigned to an actor. **b** the words spoken by an actor. **c** a copy of these. **9** *Mus.* **a** a melody or other constituent of harmony assigned to a particular voice or instrument (often in *comb.*: *four-part harmony*). **b** a copy of the music for a particular musician. **10** each of the sides in an agreement or dispute. **11** (in *pl.*) a region or district (*am not from these parts*). **12** (in *pl.*) abilities (*a man of many parts*). ● *v.* **1** *tr. & intr.* divide or separate into parts (*the crowd parted to let them through*). **2** *intr.* **a** leave one another's company (*they parted the best of friends*). **b** (foll. by *from*) say goodbye to. **3** *tr.* cause to separate (*they fought hard and had to be parted*). **4** *intr.* (foll. by *with*) give up

P

possession of; hand over. **5** *tr.* separate (the hair of the head on either side of the parting). ● *adv.* to some extent; partly (*is part iron and part wood*; *a lie that is part truth*). □ **for the most part** see MOST. **for one's part** as far as one is concerned. **in part** (or **parts**) to some extent; partly. **look the part** appear suitable for a role. **on the part of** proceeding from, on the initiative of (*a long struggle on the part of the scholars*; *no objection on my part*). **part and parcel** (usu. foll. by *of*) an essential part. **part company** see COMPANY. **play a part 1** be significant or contributory. **2** act deceitfully. **3** perform a dramatic role. **take part** assist or have a share. **take the part of** support; back up. [from Latin *pars partis* (n.), *partire* (v.)]

■ **Usage** See Usage Note at BEHALF.

partake *v.intr.* (*past* **partook**; *past part.* **partaken**) **1** (foll. by *of*, *in*) take a share or part. **2** (foll. by *of*) eat or drink some or *colloq.* all (of a thing). **3** (foll. by *of*) have some (of a quality etc.) (*their manner partook of insolence*). [16th-century coinage] □ **partaker** *n.*

parterre /par-**tair**/ *n.* **1** a level space in a garden occupied by flower beds arranged formally. **2** *US* the ground floor of a theatre auditorium, esp. the pit. [French, literally *par terre* 'on the ground']

part exchange ● *n. Brit.* a transaction in which goods are given as part of the payment for other goods, with the balance in money. ● *v.tr.* (**part-exchange**) give (goods) in such a transaction.

parthenogenesis *n. Biol.* reproduction from an ovum without fertilization, esp. as a normal process in invertebrates and lower plants. [from Greek *parthenos* 'virgin' + *genesis* 'genesis'] □ **parthenogenetic** *adj.*

Parthian shot *n.* a remark or glance etc. reserved for the moment of departure. [from the custom among horsemen of *Parthia* (ancient Asian kingdom) of firing, in retreat, at the enemy]

partial *adj.* **1** not complete; forming only part (*a partial success*). **2** biased. **3** (foll. by *to*) having a liking for. [from Late Latin *partialis*] □ **partially** *adv.*

partiality *n.* **1** bias, favouritism. **2** (foll. by *for*) fondness.

participant *n.* a participator.

participate *v.intr.* share or take part. [based on Latin *participatus* 'made to share'] □ **participation** *n.* **participative** *adj.* **participator** *n.* **participatory** *adj.*

P

participle *n. Gram.* a word formed from a verb (e.g. *going*, *gone*, *being*, *been*) and used in compound verb forms (e.g. *is going*, *has been*), or as an adjective (e.g. *working woman*, *burnt toast*), or to form verbal nouns (e.g. *workings*, *leavings*). [from Latin *participium*] □ **participial** *adj.*

particle *n.* **1** a minute portion of matter. **2** the least possible amount (*not a particle of sense*). **3** *Gram.* **a** a minor part of speech. **b** a common prefix or suffix such as *in-*, *-ness*. [from Latin *particula* 'little part']

particle physics *n.* the branch of physics concerned with the properties and interactions of subatomic particles.

particoloured *adj.* (*US* **particolored**) partly of one colour, partly of another or others.

particular ● *adj.* **1** relating to or considered as one thing or person as distinct from others; individual (*in this particular instance*). **2** more than is usual; special (*took particular trouble*). **3** scrupulously exact; fastidious. **4** detailed (*a full and particular account*). ● *n.* **1** a detail; an item. **2** (in *pl.*) points of information; a detailed account. □ **in particular** especially, specifically. [from Latin *particularis*, related to PARTICLE]

particularity *n.* (*pl.* **-ies**) **1** the quality of being individual or particular. **2** fullness or minuteness of detail. **3** (usu. in *pl.*) detail, particular.

particularize *v.tr.* (also **-ise**) (also *absol.*) **1** name specially or one by one. **2** specify (items). □ **particularization** *n.*

particularly *adv.* **1** especially, very. **2** specifically (*they particularly asked for you*). **3** in a particular or fastidious manner.

particulate ● *adj.* in the form of separate particles. ● *n.* (usu. in *pl.*) matter in this form. [based on Latin *particula* 'particle']

parting *n.* **1** a leave-taking or departure (often *attrib.*: *parting words*). **2** *Brit.* the dividing line of combed hair. **3** a division; an act of separating.

parting shot *n.* = PARTHIAN SHOT.

partisan (also **partizan**) ● *n.* **1** a strong supporter of a party, cause, etc. **2** *Mil.* a guerrilla. ● *adj.* **1** of or characteristic of partisans. **2** biased. [from Italian dialect *partigiano*] □ **partisanship** *n.*

partita *n.* (*pl.* **partitas** or **partite**) *Mus.* **1** a suite. **2** an air with variations. [Italian, literally 'divided' (fem.)]

partition ● *n.* **1** division into parts, esp. of a country with separate areas of government. **2** a structure dividing a space esp. a light interior wall. ● *v.tr.* **1** divide into parts. **2** (foll. by *off*) separate (part of a room etc.) with a partition. [from Latin *partitio*] □ **partitioned** *adj.*

partitive *Gram.* ● *adj.* (of a word, form, etc.) denoting part of a collective group or quantity. ● *n.* a partitive word (e.g. *some*, *any*) or form. [from medieval Latin *partitivus*]

partizan var. of PARTISAN.

partly *adv.* **1** with respect to a part or parts. **2** to some extent.

partner ● *n.* **1** a person who shares or takes part with another or others, esp. in a business. **2** a companion in dancing. **3** a player (esp. one of two) on the same side in a game. **4** either member of a married couple, or of an established unmarried couple. ● *v.tr.* **1** be the partner of. **2** associate as partners. [Middle English, alteration of *parcener* 'joint heir']

partnership *n.* **1** the state of being a partner or partners. **2** a joint business. **3** a pair or group of partners.

part of speech *n.* each of the categories to which words are assigned in accordance with their grammatical and semantic functions.

partook *past* of PARTAKE.

partridge *n.* (*pl.* same or **partridges**) **1** any game bird of the genus *Perdix*, esp. *P. perdix* of Europe and Asia. **2** any similar bird of the family Phasianidae. [from Latin *perdix*]

part-song *n.* a song with three or more voice parts.

part-time *adj.* & *adv.* occupying or using only part of the usual working week (*a part-time gardener*; *he only works part-time*). □ **part-timer** *n.*

parturient *adj.* about to give birth. [from Latin *parturient-* 'being in labour']

parturition *n. formal* childbirth. [from Late Latin *parturitio*]

part-way *adv.* **1** part of the way. **2** partly.

part-work *n. Brit.* a publication appearing in several parts over a period of time.

party ● *n.* (*pl.* **-ies**) **1** a social gathering, usu. of invited guests. **2** a body of persons engaged in an activity or travelling together (*fishing party*; *search party*). **3** a group of people united in a cause, opinion, etc., esp. a political group organized on a national basis. **4** a person or persons forming one side in an agreement or dispute. **5** (foll. by *to*) *Law* an accessory (to an action). **6** *colloq.* a person. ● *v.tr.* & *intr.* (**-ies, -ied**) entertain at or attend a party. [based on Latin *partire* 'to separate']

party-goer *n.* a person who attends a party or who frequents parties.

party line *n.* **1** the policy adopted by a political party. **2** a telephone line shared by two or more subscribers.

party political ● *adj.* of or relating to party politics. ● *n.* (in full **party political broadcast**) a television or radio programme on which a representative of a political party presents material intended to foster support for it.

party politics *n.pl.* (also treated as *sing.*) politics as it relates to political parties.

party-poop *n.* (also **party-pooper**) esp. *N. Amer. slang* a person who throws gloom over social enjoyment. □ **party-pooping** *n.*

party popper *n.* a device which rapidly ejects a paper streamer, used as an amusement at parties.

party wall *n.* a wall common to two adjoining buildings or rooms.

parvenu /**par**-vĕ-noo/ ● *n.* (*fem.* **parvenue**) **1** a person of obscure origin who has gained wealth or position. **2** an upstart. ● *adj.* **1** associated with or characteristic of such a person. **2** upstart. [French, literally 'arrived']

parvovirus *n.* any of a class of small viruses affecting vertebrate animals. [based on Latin *parvus* 'small']

pas *n.* (*pl.* same) a step, esp. in ballet. [French, literally 'step']

pascal *n.* **1** the SI unit of pressure, equal to one newton per square metre. **2** (**Pascal**) *Computing* a programming language esp. used in education. [named after B. *Pascal*, French scientist, 1623–62]

paschal /**pas**-kăl/ *adj.* **1** of or relating to the Passover. **2** of or relating to Easter. [based on Aramaic *pasḥa* 'Passover']

pas de deux /pah dĕ **der**/ *n.* (*pl.* same) a dance for two. [French]

pash *n. slang* a brief infatuation. [abbreviation of PASSION]

pasha *n.* (also **pacha**) *hist.* the title (placed after the name) of a Turkish officer of high rank. [from Turkish *paşa*]

paso doble /pas-oh **doh**-blay/ *n.* a ballroom dance based on a Latin American style of marching. [Spanish, literally 'double step']

PASQUE FLOWER (*Pulsatilla vulgaris*)

pasque flower *n.* ◄ a plant of the buttercup family, *Pulsatilla vulgaris*, with bell-shaped purple flowers. [from French *passefleur*, assimilated to *pasque* 'Easter']

pass[1] ● *v.* (*past part.* **passed**) (see also PAST). **1** *intr.* move onward, esp. past some point of reference (*saw the procession passing*). **2** *tr.* **a** go past; leave (a thing etc.) on one side or behind. **b** overtake. **c** go across (a frontier, mountain range, etc.). **3** *intr.* & *tr.* be transferred or cause to be transferred from one person or place to another (*pass the butter*; *the title passes to his son*). **4** *tr.* surpass; be too great for (*it passes my comprehension*). **5** *intr.* get through. **6** *intr.* **a** be accepted as adequate; go uncensured (*let the matter pass*). **b** (foll. by *as*, *for*) be accepted or known as. **7** *tr.* move; cause to go (*passed her hand over her face*; *passed a rope round it*). **8 a** *intr.* (of a candidate in an examination) be successful. **b** *tr.* be successful in (an examination or course). **c** *tr.* (of an examiner) judge the performance of (a candidate) to be satisfactory. **9 a** *tr.* (of a bill) be examined and approved by (a parliamentary body or process). **b** *tr.* cause or allow (a bill) to proceed. **c** *intr.* (of a bill or proposal) be approved. **10** *intr.* **a** occur, elapse (*time passes slowly*). **b** happen; be done or said (*heard what passed between them*). **11 a** *intr.* circulate; be current. **b** *tr.* put into circulation (*was passing forged cheques*). **12** *tr.* spend or use up (a certain time or period) (*passed the afternoon reading*). **13** *tr.* (also *absol.*) (in field games) send (the ball) to a team-mate. **14** *intr.* forgo one's turn or chance in a game etc. **15** *intr.* (foll. by *to*, *into*) change from one form (to another). **16** *intr.* come to an end. **17** *tr.* discharge from the body as or with excreta. **18** *tr.* (foll. by *on*, *upon*) **a** utter (criticism) about. **b** pronounce (a judicial sentence) on. ● *n.* **1** an act or instance of passing. **2** *Brit.* **a** success in an examination. **b** a university degree without honours. **3** written permission to pass into or out of a place, or to be absent from quarters. **4** a ticket or permit giving free entry or access etc. **5** (in field games) a transference of the ball to a team-mate. **6** a thrust in fencing. **7** a juggling trick. **8** an act of passing the hands over anything, as in conjuring or hypnotism. **9** a critical position (*has come to a fine pass*). □ **in passing 1** by the way. **2** in the course of speech, conversation, etc. **make a pass at** *colloq.* make sexual advances to. **pass away 1** *euphem.* die. **2** cease to exist; come to an end. **pass the buck** see BUCK³. **pass by 1** go past. **2** disregard, omit. **pass the hat round** see HAT. **pass muster** see MUSTER. **pass off 1** (of feelings etc.) disappear gradually. **2** (of proceedings) be carried through (in a specified way). **3** (foll. by *as*) misrepresent (a person or thing) as something else. **4** evade or lightly dismiss (an awkward remark etc.). **pass on 1** proceed on one's way. **2** *euphem.* die. **3** transmit to the next person in a series. **pass out 1** become unconscious. **2** *Brit. Mil.* complete one's training. **3** distribute. **pass over 1** omit, ignore, or disregard. **2** ignore the claims of (a person) to promotion. **3** *euphem.* die. **pass round** (*US* **around**) **1** distribute. **2** send or give to each of a number in turn. **pass through** experience. **pass the time of day** see TIME. **pass up** *colloq.* refuse or neglect (an opportunity etc.). **pass water** urinate. [based on Latin *passus* 'pace'] □ **passer** *n.*

pass² *n.* a narrow passage through mountains. □ **sell the pass** *Brit.* betray a cause. [Middle English]

passable *adj.* **1** barely satisfactory; just adequate. **2** (of a road, pass, etc.) that can be passed. □ **passably** *adv.*

passage *n.* **1** the process or means of passing; transit. **2** = PASSAGEWAY. **3** the liberty or right to pass through. **4 a** the right of conveyance as a passenger by sea or air. **b** a journey by sea or air. **5** a transition from one state to another. **6 a** a short extract from a book etc. **b** a section of a piece of music. **7** the passing of a bill etc. into law. **8** (in *pl.*) an interchange of words etc. **9** *Anat.* a duct etc. in the body. □ **work one's passage** earn a right by working for it. [from Old French]

passageway *n.* a narrow way for passing along; a corridor.

passbook *n.* a book issued by a bank or building society etc. to an account-holder recording sums deposited and withdrawn.

passé /**pas**-ay/ *adj.* **1** no longer fashionable; out of date. **2** *archaic* past one's prime. [French, literally 'passed']

passenger *n.* **1** a traveller in or on a conveyance (other than the driver, pilot, crew, etc.). **2** *colloq.* a member of a team, crew, etc., who does no effective work. **3** (*attrib.*) for the use of passengers (*passenger seat*). [from Old French *passager* '(person) passing']

passenger pigeon *n.* an extinct wild pigeon of N. America, noted for migrating in huge flocks and hunted to extinction by 1914.

passer-by *n.* (*pl.* **passers-by**) a person who goes past, esp. by chance.

passerine ● *n.* ▶ any bird of the order Passeriformes, comprising the perching birds. ▷ SONGBIRD. ● *adj.* **1** of or relating to this order. **2** of the size of a sparrow. [based on Latin *passer* 'sparrow']

passim *adv.* (of references in a published work) to be found at various places throughout the text. [Latin]

passing ● *adj.* **1** in senses of PASS¹ *v.* **2** transient, fleeting (*a passing glance*). **3** cursory, incidental (*a passing reference*). ● *n.* **1** in senses of PASS¹ *v.* **2** *euphem.* the death of a person (*mourned his passing*). □ **passingly** *adv.*

passing shot *n.* *Tennis* etc. a shot aiming the ball beyond and out of reach of the other player.

passion *n.* **1** strong emotion. **2** an outburst of anger (*flew into a passion*). **3** intense sexual love. **4 a** strong enthusiasm (*has a passion for football*). **b** a thing arousing this. **5** (**the Passion**) **a** the suffering of Christ during his last days. **b** a narrative of this from the Gospels. **c** a musical setting of any of these narratives. [from Late Latin *passio* 'suffering'] □ **passionless** *adj.*

passionate *adj.* **1** dominated by or easily moved to strong feeling. **2** showing or caused by passion. □ **passionately** *adv.* **passionateness** *n.*

PASSERINE

The passerines, also known as the perching birds, are the largest bird order, containing approximately half of the world's birds. All passerines have four unwebbed toes – three facing forwards, and a hind toe facing backwards. When a passerine lands on a perch, its weight makes its leg tendons tighten and its toes clamp tightly shut. The passerines comprise two sub-orders. The oscines, also known as songbirds, can produce complex vocalizations, but the sub-oscine families have fairly limited vocal powers.

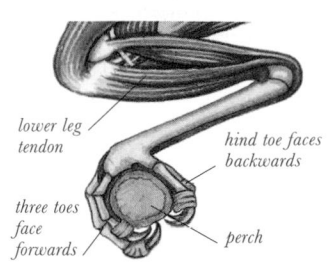

LOWER LEG OF A PASSERINE

lower leg tendon

hind toe faces backwards

three toes face forwards

perch

EXAMPLES OF PASSERINES

OSCINES

CACTUS WREN
(*Campylorhynchus brunneicapillus*)

WOOD WARBLER
(*Phylloscopus sibilatrix*)

SWALLOW
(*Hirundo rustica*)

KING BIRD OF PARADISE
(*Cicinnurus regius*)

JAY
(*Garrulus glandarius*)

SCARLET-TUFTED
MALACHITE
SUNBIRD
(*Nectarinia johnstoni*)

AMERICAN ROBIN
(*Turdus migratorius*)

BLUE TIT
(*Parus caeruleus*)

SUB-OSCINES

RUFOUS HORNERO
(*Furnarius rufus*)

SUPERB LYREBIRD
(*Menura novaehollandiae*)

P

PASSION FLOWER (*Passiflora caerulea*)

passion flower *n.* ▲ any climbing plant of the genus *Passiflora*, with a flower that was supposed to suggest the instruments of the Crucifixion.

passion fruit *n.* the edible fruit of some species of passion flower, esp. *Passiflora edulis*.

passion play *n.* a miracle play representing Christ's Passion.

Passion Sunday *n.* the fifth Sunday in Lent.

passive *adj.* **1** suffering action; acted upon. **2** offering no opposition; submissive. **3** not active; inert. **4** *Gram.* designating the voice in which the subject undergoes the action of the verb (e.g. in *they were killed*). [from Latin *passivus*, based on *pati pass-* 'to suffer'] □ **passively** *adv.* **passiveness** *n.* **passivity** *n.*

passive resistance *n.* non-violent refusal to co-operate.

passive smoking *n.* the involuntary inhaling of smoke from others' cigarettes etc.

pass-key *n.* **1** a private key to a gate etc. **2** a master key.

pass-mark *n. Brit.* the minimum mark needed to pass an examination.

Passover *n.* the Jewish spring festival commemorating the liberation of the Israelites from Egyptian bondage. [from *pass over*, 'pass without touching (the first-born)' (see Exod. 12)]

passport *n.* **1** an official document certifying the holder's identity and citizenship, and entitling the holder to travel to and from foreign countries. **2** (foll. by *to*) a thing that ensures admission or attainment (*a passport to success*).

password *n.* a selected word, phrase, or string of characters, securing recognition, admission, access to a computing system, etc.

past ● *adj.* **1** gone by in time (*in past years*; *the time is past*). **2** recently gone by (*the past month*). **3** relating to a former time (*past president*). **4** *Gram.* expressing a past action or state. ● *n.* **1** (prec. by *the*) **a** past time. **b** what has happened in past time (*cannot undo the past*). **2** a person's past life or career, esp. if discreditable (*a man with a past*). **3** a past tense or form. ● *prep.* **1** beyond in time or place (*is past two o'clock*; *ran past the house*). **2** beyond the range, duration, or compass of (*past belief*; *past endurance*). ● *adv.* so as to pass by (*hurried past*). □ **not put it past** believe it possible of. **past it** *colloq.* old and useless. [past participle of PASS[1]]

pasta *n.* **1** ► a type of dough extruded or stamped into various shapes for cooking (e.g. lasagne, spaghetti). **2** a dish made from this. [Italian, literally 'paste']

paste ● *n.* **1** a moist fairly stiff mixture, esp. of powder and liquid. **2** a dough of flour with fat, water, etc. **3** an adhesive of flour, water, etc., esp. for sticking paper. **4** an easily spread preparation of ground meat, fish, etc. (*anchovy paste*). **5 a** a hard vitreous composition used in making imitation gems. **b** imitation jewellery made of this. ● *v.tr.* **1** fasten or coat with paste. **2** *slang* **a** beat or thrash. **b** bomb or bombard heavily. [from Greek *pastē*] □ **pasting** *n.* (esp. in sense 2 of *v.*).

pasteboard *n.* **1** a sheet of stiff material made by pasting together sheets of paper. **2** (*attrib.*) **a** flimsy, unsubstantial. **b** fake.

pastel ● *n.* **1** a crayon consisting of powdered pigments bound with a gum solution. **2** a work of art in pastel. **3** a light shade of a colour. ● *adj.* of a light shade or colour. [from Italian *pastello*, diminutive of *pasta* 'paste'] □ **pastellist** *n.*

pastern *n.* the part of a horse's foot between the fetlock and the hoof. ▷ HORSE. [from Old French *pasturon*, from *pasture* 'hobble']

paste-up *n.* a document prepared for copying etc. by pasting various sections on a backing.

pasteurize /**pahss**-chĕ-ryz/ *v.tr.* (also **-ise**) subject (milk etc.) to the process of partial sterilization by heating. [named after L. *Pasteur*, French chemist, 1822–95] □ **pasteurization** *n.*

pastiche /pas-**teesh**/ *n.* **1** a picture or musical composition made up from or imitating various sources. **2** a literary or other work of art composed in the style of a well-known writer, artist, etc. [from Late Latin *pasta* 'paste']

pastille *n.* **1** a small sweet or lozenge. **2** a small roll of aromatic paste burnt as a fumigator etc. [from Latin *pastillus* 'little loaf, lozenge']

pastime *n.* **1** a recreation or hobby. **2** a sport or game.

pastis *n.* (*pl.* same) an aniseed-flavoured aperitif. [French]

past master *n.* **1** a person who is especially adept or expert in an activity, subject, etc. **2** a person who has been a master in a guild, Freemason's lodge, etc.

PASTA

Most pasta is made from durum wheat flour, which, because of its high gluten content, makes a strong elastic dough. The flour is mixed with water, kneaded to form a thick paste, and then forced through perforated plates or dies that shape it into one of more than a hundred different forms. Pasta can be coloured with spinach or beet juice.

EXAMPLES OF PASTA

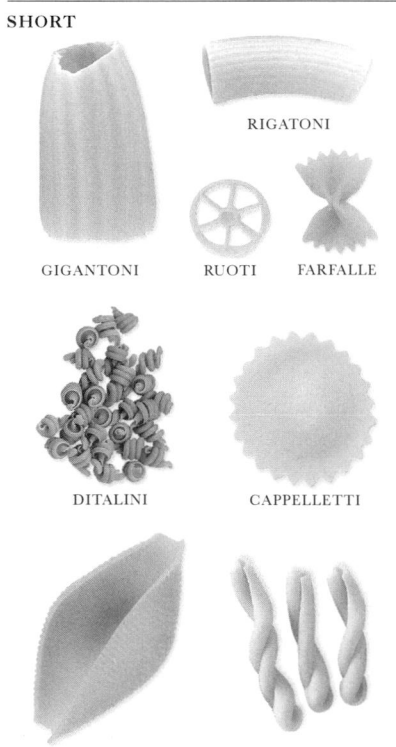

LONG

CAPELLINI

TAGLIATELLE VERDE

FEDELI

SPAGHETTI

SHORT

RIGATONI

GIGANTONI

RUOTI

FARFALLE

DITALINI

CAPPELLETTI

CONCHIGLIE

STROZZAPRETI

STUFFED AND LAYERED

CANNELLONI

TORTELLINI VERDE

RAVIOLI

LASAGNE VERDE

P

pastor ● *n.* **1** a minister in charge of a church or a congregation. **2** a person exercising spiritual guidance. ● *v.* **1** *tr.* **a** be minister of (a church). **b** have the spiritual care of (a congregation). **2** *intr.* be a pastor. [from Latin, literally 'feeder, shepherd']

pastoral ● *adj.* **1** of, relating to, or associated with shepherds or flocks and herds. **2** (of land) used for pasture. **3** (of a poem, picture, etc.) portraying country life, usu. in a romantic or idealized form. **4** of or appropriate to a pastor. **5** of or relating to a teacher's responsibility for the general well-being of pupils or students. ● *n.* **1** a pastoral poem, play, picture, etc. **2** a letter from a pastor (esp. a bishop) to the clergy or people. □ **pastoralism** *n.* **pastorally** *adv.*

pastoralist *n. Austral.* a farmer of sheep or cattle.

pastorate *n.* **1** the office or tenure of a pastor. **2** a body of pastors.

pastrami *n.* seasoned smoked beef. [Yiddish]

pastry *n.* (*pl.* **-ies**) **1** a dough of flour, fat, and water, used as a base and covering for pies etc. **2 a** food, esp. cake, made wholly or partly of this. **b** a piece or item of this food. [based on PASTE]

pastry-cook *n.* a cook who specializes in pastry.

pasturage *n.* **1** land for pasture. **2** the process of pasturing cattle etc.

pasture ● *n.* **1** land covered with grass etc. suitable for grazing. **2** herbage for animals. ● *v.* **1** *tr.* put (animals) to graze in a pasture. **2** *intr. & tr.* (of animals) graze. [from Late Latin *pastura*]

pastureland *n.* = PASTURE *n.* 1.

pasty[1] /**pas**-ti/ *n.* (*pl.* **-ies**) esp. *Brit.* a pastry case with a usu. savoury filling, baked without a dish to shape it. [based on Late Latin *pasta* 'paste']

pasty[2] /**payss**-ti/ *adj.* (**pastier**, **pastiest**) **1** of or like or covered with paste. **2** unhealthily pale (esp. in complexion). □ **pastiness** *n.*

Pat. *abbr.* Patent.

pat[1] ● *v.* (**patted**, **patting**) **1** *tr.* strike gently with the hand or a flat surface. **2** *tr.* flatten or mould by patting. **3** *tr.* strike gently with the inner surface of the hand, esp. as a sign of affection, sympathy, or congratulation. **4** *intr.* (foll. by *on*, *upon*) beat lightly. ● *n.* **1** a light stroke or tap, esp. with the hand in affection etc. **2** the sound made by this. **3** a small mass (esp. of butter) formed by patting. □ **pat on the back** a gesture of congratulation. [Middle English]

pat[2] ● *adj.* **1** known thoroughly and ready for any occasion. **2** apposite or opportune, esp. unconvincingly so (*gave a pat answer*). ● *adv.* **1** in a pat manner. **2** appositely. □ **have off** (or **down**) **pat** know or have memorized perfectly. **stand pat** esp. *N. Amer.* **1** stick stubbornly to one's opinion or decision. **2** *Poker* retain one's hand as dealt; not draw other cards. [16th-century coinage] □ **patly** *adv.* **patness** *n.*

patch ● *n.* **1** a piece of material used to mend a hole or as reinforcement. **2** a shield worn over an eye or eye socket. **3** a dressing etc. put over a wound. **4** a large or irregular distinguishable area. **5** *Brit. colloq.* a period of time in terms of its characteristic quality (*went through a bad patch*). **6** a piece of ground. **7** *Brit. colloq.* an area assigned to or patrolled by an authorized person, esp. a police officer. **8** a number of plants growing in one place (*brier patch*). **9** a scrap or remnant. **10 a** a temporary electrical connection. **b** *Computing* a small piece of code inserted to correct or enhance a program. ● *v.tr.* **1** repair with a patch or patches; put a patch or patches on. **2** (of material) serve as a patch to. **3** put together, esp. hastily. **4** (foll. by *up*) settle (a quarrel etc.) esp. hastily or temporarily. □ **not a patch on** *Brit. colloq.* greatly inferior to. [Middle English] □ **patcher** *n.*

patchouli *n.* **1** ▶ a strongly scented S. Asian shrub of the genus *Pogostemon*. **2** the perfume obtained from this. [from Tamil *paccuḷi*]

PATCHOULI
(*Pogostemon cablin*)

patch pocket *n.* one made of a piece of cloth sewn on a garment.

patch test *n.* a test for allergy by applying to the skin patches containing allergenic substances.

patchwork ● *n.* **1** ▼ needlework in which small pieces of cloth in different designs are sewn together to form one article such as a quilt. **2** a thing composed of various small pieces or fragments. ● *attrib.adj.* **1** composed of patchwork pieces. **2 a** resembling patchwork (*patchwork fields*). **b** pieced together with lack of uniformity (*patchwork political philosophy*).

PATCHWORK OF BROCADES AND VELVETS

patchy *adj.* (**patchier**, **patchiest**) **1** uneven in quality. **2** having or existing in patches. □ **patchily** *adv.* **patchiness** *n.*

pate *n. archaic* or *joc.* the head. [Middle English]

pâté /**pat**-ay/ *n.* a paste of mashed and spiced meat or fish etc. [from Old French *pasté* 'pasty']

pâté de foie gras /pat-ay dĕ fwah **grah**/ *n.* a paste of fatted goose liver. [French]

patella *n.* (*pl.* **patellae** /-lee/) the kneecap. ▷ KNEE, SKELETON. [Latin, literally 'little dish'] □ **patellar** *adj.*

paten /**pat**-ĕn/ *n.* a shallow dish used for the bread at the Eucharist. [from Greek *patanē* 'a plate']

patent ● *n.* **1** a government authority to an individual or organization conferring a right or title, esp. the sole right to make or use or sell some invention. **2** a document granting this authority. **3** an invention or process protected by it. ● *adj.* **1** obvious, plain. **2** conferred or protected by patent. **3 a** made and marketed under a patent; proprietary. **b** to which one has a proprietary claim. **4** ingenious, well-contrived. ● *v.tr.* obtain a patent for (an invention). [from Latin *patent-* 'lying open'; *n.* sense 2: shortening of *letters patent*]. □ **patency** *n.* **patentable** *adj.* **patently** *adv.* (in sense 1 of *adj.*).

patentee *n.* **1** a person who takes out or holds a patent. **2** a person for the time being entitled to the benefit of a patent.

patent leather *n.* leather with a glossy varnished surface.

patent **medicine** *n.* medicine made and marketed under a patent and available without prescription.

patent office *n.* an office from which patents are issued.

pater *n. Brit. slang* father. [Latin]

■ **Usage** *Pater* is now only found in jocular or affected use.

paterfamilias *n.* the male head of a family or household. [Latin, literally 'father of the family']

paternal *adj.* **1** of or like or appropriate to a father. **2** fatherly. **3** related through the father. **4** (of a government etc.) limiting freedom and responsibility by well-meant regulations. [from Latin *paternus*] □ **paternally** *adv.*

paternalism *n.* the policy or practice of governing or behaving in a paternal way. □ **paternalist** *n.* **paternalistic** *adj.* **paternalistically** *adv.*

paternity *n.* **1** fatherhood. **2** one's paternal origin. [from Late Latin *paternitas*]

paternity suit *n.* a lawsuit held to determine whether a certain man is the father of a certain child.

paternoster *n.* **1 a** the Lord's Prayer, esp. in Latin. **b** a rosary bead indicating that this is to be said. **2** a lift consisting of a series of linked doorless compartments circulating continuously. [from Latin *pater noster* 'our father', first words of the prayer]

path *n.* (*pl.* **paths**) **1** a way or track laid down for walking or made by continual treading. **2** the line along which a person or thing moves (*flight path*). **3** a course of action or conduct. **4** a sequence of operations taken by a system. [Old English] □ **pathless** *adj.*

pathetic *adj.* **1** arousing pity, sadness, or contempt. **2** *colloq.* miserably inadequate. [from Greek *pathētikos*, related to PATHOS] □ **pathetically** *adv.*

pathetic fallacy *n.* the attribution of human feelings and responses to inanimate things, esp. in art and literature.

pathfinder *n.* **1** a person who explores new territory etc. **2** an aircraft or its pilot sent ahead to locate and mark the target area for bombing.

patho- *comb. form* disease.

pathogen *n.* an agent causing disease. □ **pathogenic** *adj.* **pathogenous** *adj.*

pathological *adj.* **1** of pathology. **2** of or caused by a physical or mental disorder. □ **pathologically** *adv.*

pathology *n.* **1** the science of bodily diseases. **2** the symptoms of a disease. □ **pathologist** *n.*

pathos *n.* a quality in speech, writing, etc., that excites pity or sadness. [Greek, literally 'suffering']

pathway *n.* a path or its course.

patience *n.* **1** calm endurance of hardship, provocation, delay, etc. **2** tolerant perseverance or forbearance. **3** the capacity for calm self-possessed waiting. **4** esp. *Brit.* a solo card game.

patient ● *adj.* having or showing patience. ● *n.* a person receiving or registered to receive medical treatment. [from Latin *patient-* 'suffering'] □ **patiently** *adv.*

patina *n.* (*pl.* **patinas**) **1** a film, usu. green, formed on the surface of old bronze. **2** a similar film on other surfaces. **3** a gloss produced by age on woodwork. [Italian, from Latin *patina* 'dish'] □ **patinated** *adj.* **patination** *n.*

patio *n.* (*pl.* **-os**) **1** a paved usu. roofless area adjoining a house. **2** an inner court open to the sky in a Spanish or Spanish-American house. [Spanish]

patisserie /pă-**teess**-ĕ-ri/ *n.* **1** a shop where pastries are made and sold. **2** pastries collectively. [based on medieval Latin *pasticium* 'pastry']

Patna rice *n.* a variety of rice with long firm grains. [from *Patna*, a district in India]

patois /**pat**-wah/ *n.* (*pl.* same) the dialect in a region, differing fundamentally from the literary language. [French, literally 'rough speech']

patriarch *n.* **1** a man who is the head of a family or tribe. **2** (often in *pl.*) *Bibl.* any of those regarded as fathers of the human race. **3** *Eccl.* the title of a chief bishop in the Orthodox Church. **4 a** the founder of an order, science, etc. **b** a venerable old man. [from Greek *patēr* 'father' + *arkhēs* 'ruler'] □ **patriarchal** *adj.*

patriarchate *n.* **1** the office, see, or residence of an ecclesiastical patriarch. **2** the rank of a tribal patriarch.

patriarchy *n.* (*pl.* **-ies**) a form of social organization etc. in which a man or men rule and descent is reckoned through the male line.

P

patrician ● *n.* **1** *hist.* a member of the ancient Roman nobility. **2** an aristocrat. ● *adj.* **1** noble, aristocratic. **2** *hist.* of the ancient Roman nobility. [from Latin *patricius* 'having a noble father']

patricide *n.* **1** the killing of one's father. **2** a person who commits patricide. [based on Latin *parricida*, *parricidium* 'parricide'] □ **patricidal** *adj.*

■ **Usage** See Usage Note at PARRICIDE.

patrimony *n.* (*pl.* **-ies**) **1** property inherited from one's father or ancestor. **2** a heritage. [from Latin *patrimonium*] □ **patrimonial** *adj.*

patriot *n.* a person who is devoted to and ready to defend his or her country. [based on Greek *patrios* 'of one's fathers'] □ **patriotic** *adj.* **patriotically** *adv.* **patriotism** *n.*

patrol ● *n.* **1** the act of walking or travelling around an area, esp. at regular intervals, in order to protect or supervise it. **2** one or more persons or vehicles assigned or sent out on patrol. **3 a** a detachment of troops sent out to reconnoitre. **b** such reconnaissance. **4** a routine operational voyage of a ship or aircraft. **5** *Brit.* an official controlling traffic where children cross the road. **6** a unit of six to eight Scouts or Guides. ● *v.* (**patrolled**, **patrolling**) **1** *tr.* carry out a patrol of. **2** *intr.* act as a patrol. [from French *patrouiller* 'to paddle in mud'] □ **patroller** *n.*

patrol car *n.* a police car used in patrolling roads and streets.

patrolman *n.* (*pl.* **-men**) *US* a police officer of the lowest rank.

patron *n.* (*fem.* **patroness**) **1** a person who gives financial etc. support to a person, cause, etc. **2** a usu. regular customer of a shop etc. [from Latin *patronus* 'protector of clients, defender']

patronage *n.* **1** the support, promotion, or encouragement given by a patron. **2** the control of appointments to office, privileges, etc. **3** a patronizing or condescending manner. **4** a customer's support for a shop etc.

patronal *adj.* of or relating to a patron saint (*the patronal festival*). [from French]

patronize *v.tr.* (also **-ise**) **1** treat condescendingly. **2** act as a patron towards. **3** frequent (a shop etc.) as a customer. □ **patronizing** *adj.* **patronizingly** *adv.*

patron saint *n.* the protecting or guiding saint of a person, place, etc.

patronymic ● *n.* a name derived from the name of a father or ancestor, e.g. *Johnson*, *Ivanovich*. ● *adj.* (of a name) so derived. [from Greek *patrōnumikos*]

patsy *n.* (*pl.* **-ies**) esp. *N. Amer. slang* a person who is deceived, ridiculed, etc. [19th-century coinage]

patten *n. hist.* ▼ a shoe or clog with a raised sole or set on an iron ring, for walking in mud etc. [from Old French *patin*]

leather strap

wooden base

iron ring

PATTEN

patter[1] ● *v.intr.* make a rapid succession of taps, as of rain on a window pane. ● *n.* a rapid succession of taps etc. [based on PAT[1]]

patter[2] ● *n.* **1** the rapid speech used by a comedian or introduced into a song. **2** a sales pitch. **3** the special language or jargon of a profession etc. ● *v.* **1** *tr.* repeat (prayers etc.) in a rapid mechanical way. **2** *intr.* talk glibly or mechanically. [Middle English, from *pater*, shortening of PATERNOSTER]

pattern ● *n.* **1** a repeated decorative design on cloth etc. **2** a regular or logical form, order, or arrangement of parts (*behaviour pattern*). **3** a model or design from which copies can be made. **4** an example of

excellence (*a pattern of elegance*). **5** a wooden or metal figure from which a mould is made for a casting. **6** a sample (of cloth etc.). **7** the marks made by bombs etc. on a target or target area. **8** a random combination of shapes or colours. ● *v.tr.* **1** (usu. foll. by *after*, *on*) model (a thing) on a design etc. **2** decorate with a pattern. [Middle English *patron* (see PATRON); differentiated in sense and spelling since the 16th–17th century]

pattern bombing *n.* bombing over a large area, not on a single target.

patty *n.* (*pl.* **-ies**) **1** a little pie or pastry. **2** a small flat cake of minced meat etc. [from French *pâté* 'pasty']

pattypan *n.* a pan for baking a patty.

paucity *n.* smallness of number or quantity. [based on Latin *paucus* 'few']

Pauline /ˈpawˈlyn/ *adj.* of or relating to St Paul (*the Pauline Epistles*). [based on Latin *Paulus* 'Paul']

Paul Jones *n.* a ballroom dance in which partners are exchanged according to a pattern. [name of an American naval officer, 1747–92]

paunch *n.* the belly or stomach, esp. when protruding. [from Latin *pantex panticis* 'bowels'] □ **paunchy** *adj.* (**paunchier**, **paunchiest**). **paunchiness** *n.*

pauper *n.* **1** a person without means; a beggar. **2** *hist.* a recipient of poor-law relief. [Latin, literally 'poor'] □ **pauperism** *n.* **pauperize** *v.tr.* (also **-ise**). **pauperization** *n.*

pause ● *n.* **1** an interval of inaction, esp. when due to hesitation. **2** a break in speaking or reading; a silence. **3** *Mus.* a mark (⌒) over a note or rest that is to be lengthened. **4** a control allowing the interruption of the operation of a tape recorder etc. ● *v.intr.* **1** make a pause; wait. **2** (usu. foll. by *upon*) linger over (a word etc.). [from Greek *pausein* 'to stop']

pavane *n.* (also **pavan**) **1** *hist.* a stately dance in slow duple time, performed in elaborate clothing. **2** the music for this. [French, from Spanish]

pave *v.tr.* **1 a** cover (a street, floor, etc.) with asphalt, stone, etc. **b** cover or strew (a floor etc.) with anything (*paved with flowers*). **2** prepare (*paved the way for her arrival*). [from Old French *paver*] □ **paver** *n.* **paving** *n.* **pavior** *n.* (also **paviour**).

pavement *n.* **1** *Brit.* a paved path for pedestrians at the side of and a little higher than a road. **2** the covering of a street, floor, etc., made of usu. rectangular stones. **3** *N. Amer.* a roadway. [from Latin *pavimentum*]

pavilion *n.* **1** *Brit.* a building at a cricket or other sports ground used for changing, refreshments, etc. **2** a summer house or other decorative building in a garden. **3** a large tent at a show, fair, etc. **4** a building used for entertainments. **5** a temporary stand at an exhibition. [from Latin *papilio* 'butterfly, tent']

paving stone *n.* a large flat usu. rectangular piece of stone etc. for paving.

pavior, paviour see PAVE.

pavlova *n.* a meringue cake with cream and fruit. [named after A. *Pavlova*, Russian ballerina, 1881–1931]

paw ● *n.* **1** a foot of an animal having claws or nails. **2** *colloq.* a person's hand. ● *v.tr.* **1** strike or scrape with a paw or foot. **2** *colloq.* fondle awkwardly or indecently. [from Old French *poue*]

pawky *adj.* (**pawkier**, **pawkiest**) *Sc.* & *dial.* **1** drily humorous. **2** shrewd. [from Scots & northern English dialect *pawk* 'trick'] □ **pawkily** *adv.* **pawkiness** *n.*

pawl *n.* **1** a lever with a catch for the teeth of a wheel or bar. **2** *Naut.* a short bar used to lock a capstan, windlass, etc.

pawn[1] *n.* **1** *Chess* a piece of the smallest size and value. ▷ CHESS. **2** a person used by others for their own purposes. [from medieval Latin *pedo -onis* 'foot soldier']

pawn[2] ● *v.tr.* **1** deposit an object, esp. with a pawnbroker, as security for money lent. **2** pledge or wager (one's life, honour, etc.). ● *n.* an object left as

security for money etc. lent. □ **in** (or **at**) **pawn** (of an object etc.) held as security. [from Old French *pan*, *pand*, *pant* 'pledge, security']

pawnbroker *n.* a person who lends money at interest on the security of personal property pawned. □ **pawnbroking** *n.*

pawnshop *n.* a shop where pawnbroking is conducted.

pawpaw /ˈpăˈpaw/ *n.* (also **papaw**, **papaya** /păˈpyr/) **1** ▼ an elongated melon-shaped fruit with edible orange flesh and small black seeds. **2** a tropical tree, *Carica papaya*, bearing this. [from Spanish & Portuguese *papaya*]

edible flesh

seeds

PAWPAW (*Carica papaya*)

pax *n.* **1** the kiss of peace. **2** (as *int.*) *Brit. slang* a call for a truce (used esp. by schoolchildren). [Latin, literally 'peace']

pay ● *v.tr.* (*past* and *past part.* **paid**) **1** (also *absol.*) give (a person etc.) what is due for goods received, debts incurred, etc. **2 a** give a (usu. specified amount) for work done, a ransom, etc. **b** (foll. by *to*) hand over the amount of (wages etc.) to. **3 a** give, bestow, or express (attention, respect, etc.) (*paid them no heed*). **b** make (a visit, a call, etc.). **4** (also *absol.*) (of a business etc.) be profitable or advantageous to (a person etc.). **5** reward or punish. **6** (usu. as **paid** *adj.*) recompense (work, time, etc.) (*paid holiday*). **7** (usu. foll. by *out*, *away*) let out (a rope) by slackening it. ● *n.* wages; payment. □ **in the pay of** employed by. **pay back 1** return (money). **2** take revenge on (a person). **pay dearly** (usu. foll. by *for*) suffer for a wrongdoing etc. **pay for 1** hand over the price of. **2** bear the cost of. **3** suffer or be punished for (a fault etc.). **pay in** pay (money) into a bank account. **pay its** (or **one's**) **way** cover costs. **pay one's last respects** show respect towards a dead person by attending the funeral. **pay off 1** dismiss (workers) with a final payment. **2** *colloq.* yield good results; succeed. **3** pay (a debt) in full. **pay out 1** pay (money) from funds under one's control; spend. **2** punish, take revenge on (a person). **pay one's respects** make a polite visit. **pay through the nose** *colloq.* pay much more than a fair price. **pay up** pay the full amount, or the full amount of. **put paid to** *Brit. colloq.* **1** deal effectively with (a person). **2** terminate (hopes etc.). [from Latin *pacare* 'to appease'] □ **payee** *n.* **payer** *n.*

payable ● *adj.* **1** that must be paid; due (*payable in April*). **2** that may be paid. **3** (of a mine etc.) profitable. ● *n.* (in *pl.*) debts owed by a business; liabilities.

pay-as-you-earn *n.* (often *attrib.*) *Brit.* the deduction of income tax from wages at source.

payback *n.* **1** a financial return; a reward. **2** the profit from an investment etc.

payback period *n.* the length of time required for an investment to pay for itself in terms of profits or savings.

pay bed *n. Brit.* a hospital bed for private patients.

pay claim *n. Brit.* a demand for an increase in pay, esp. by a trade union.

PAYE *abbr. Brit.* pay-as-you-earn.

paying guest *n.* a boarder.

payload *n.* **1** the part of an aircraft's load yielding revenue. **2 a** the explosive warhead carried by an

P

aircraft or rocket. **b** the instruments etc. carried by a spaceship. ▷ ROCKET. **3** the goods carried by a road vehicle.

paymaster *n.* **1** an official who pays troops, workers, etc. **2** a person, organization, etc., to whom another owes loyalty because of payment given. **3** (in full **Paymaster General**) *Brit.* the Treasury minister responsible for payments.

payment *n.* **1** the act or an instance of paying. **2** an amount paid. **3** reward, recompense.

pay-off *n. colloq.* **1** an act of payment, esp. a bribe. **2** return on investment or on a bet. **3** a final outcome.

payola *n.* esp. *US* **1** a bribe offered in return for unofficial promotion of a product etc. in the media. **2** the practice of such bribery.

pay-out *n.* an instance of money being paid out, esp. compensation or dividends.

pay packet *n. Brit.* a packet or envelope containing an employee's wages.

pay-per-view *attrib.adj.* designating a system of charging for watching television based on the actual time spent viewing.

payphone *n.* a coin box telephone.

payroll *n.* a list of employees receiving regular pay.

payslip *n.* a note given to an employee when paid detailing the amount of pay, and of tax and insurance deducted.

Pb *symb. Chem.* the element lead. [Latin *plumbum*]

PBX *abbr.* private branch exchange (private telephone switchboard).

PC *abbr.* **1** police constable. **2** Privy Counsellor. **3** personal computer. **4** politically correct; political correctness.

p.c. *abbr.* **1** per cent. **2** postcard.

PCB *abbr.* **1** *Computing* ▼ printed circuit board. **2** *Chem.* polychlorinated biphenyl, any of several toxic aromatic compounds formed as waste in industrial processes.

pct. *abbr. US* per cent.

Pd *symb. Chem.* the element palladium.

pd. *abbr.* paid.

PE *abbr.* physical education.

pea *n.* **1 a** a hardy climbing plant, *Pisum sativum*

(family Leguminosae), with seeds growing in pods and used for food. ▷ VEGETABLE. **b** its seed. ▷ SEED. **2** any of several similar leguminous plants (*sweet pea*). [back-formation from PEASE, taken as pl.]

pea-brain *n. colloq.* a stupid or dim-witted person. □ **pea-brained** *adj.*

peace *n.* **1 a** quiet; tranquillity. **b** mental calm. **2 a** (often *attrib.*) freedom from or the cessation of war. **b** (esp. **Peace**) a treaty of peace between states etc. at war. **3** freedom from civil disorder. **4** *Eccl.* a ritual liturgical greeting. **5** (**the peace**) civil order. □ **at peace** in a state of friendliness. **2** serene. **3** *euphem.* dead. **hold one's peace** keep silent. **keep the peace** prevent, or refrain from, strife. **make one's peace** (often foll. by *with*) re-establish friendly relations. **make peace** bring about peace. [from Latin *pax pacis*]

peaceable *adj.* **1** disposed to peace; unwarlike. **2** free from disturbance; peaceful. □ **peaceableness** *n.* **peaceably** *adv.*

Peace Corps *n. US* an organization sending young people to work as volunteers in developing countries.

peace dividend *n.* public money which becomes available when spending on defence is reduced.

peaceful *adj.* **1** characterized by peace. **2** not violating peace (*peaceful coexistence*). □ **peacefully** *adv.* **peacefulness** *n.*

peacekeeper *n.* a person or organization that keeps or maintains peace. □ **peacekeeping** *n.* & *attrib.adj.*

peacemaker *n.* a person who brings about peace. □ **peacemaking** *n.* & *adj.*

peace-offering *n.* a propitiatory or conciliatory gift.

peace pipe *n.* a tobacco pipe as a token of peace among N. American Indians.

peacetime *n.* a period when a country is not at war.

peach[1] ● *n.* **1 a** a round juicy stone fruit with downy cream or yellow skin flushed with red. ▷ FRUIT. **b** (in full **peach tree**) the tree, *Prunus persica*, bearing it. **2** the yellowish-pink colour of a peach. **3** *colloq.* **a** a

---

person or thing of superlative quality. **b** an attractive young woman. ● *adj.* of a yellowish-pink colour. [from Latin *persicum* (malum) 'Persian (apple)'] □ **peachy** *adj.* (**peachier**, **peachiest**).

peach[2] *v.intr.* (usu. foll. by *against*, *on*) esp. *Brit. colloq.* turn informer; inform. [from Old French *empechier* 'to impeach']

peach Melba *n.* a dish of ice cream and peaches with liqueur or sauce. [named after Nellie *Melba* (see MELBA SAUCE)]

peacock *n.* a male peafowl, having brilliant plumage and a tail (with eyelike markings) that can be expanded erect in display like a fan. [Middle English]

peacock blue ● *n.* the lustrous greenish blue of a peacock's neck. ● *adj.* (hyphenated when *attrib.*) of this colour.

peacock butterfly *n.* ◀ a butterfly, *Inachis io*, with eyelike markings on its wings.

peafowl *n.* a pheasant of the genus *Pavo*, a peacock or peahen.

pea green ● *n.* a bright green colour. ● *adj.* (hyphenated when *attrib.*) of this colour.

peahen *n.* a female peafowl.

peak[1] ● *n.* **1** a projecting usu. pointed part, esp.: **a** the pointed top of a mountain. **b** a mountain with a peak. **c** a stiff brim at the front of a cap. **2 a** the highest point in a curve (*on the peak of the wave*). **b** the time of greatest success (in a career etc.). **c** the highest point on a graph etc. ● *v.intr.* reach the highest value, quality, etc. (*output peaked in September*). ● *attrib.adj.* of or at the highest frequency, rate, level, etc. (*peak shopping times*). □ **peaked** *adj.* **peaky** *adj.* **peakiness** *n.*

peak[2] *v.intr.* **1** waste away. **2** (as **peaked** *adj.*) pinched; sickly-looking. [Middle English]

peak hour *n.* esp. *Brit.* the time of the most intense traffic etc.

peaky *adj.* (**peakier**, **peakiest**) **1** sickly; puny. **2** white-faced.

peal ● *n.* **1 a** the loud ringing of a bell or bells, esp. a series of changes. **b** a set of bells. **2** a loud repeated sound, esp. of thunder, laughter, etc. ● *v.* **1** *intr.* sound forth in a peal. **2** *tr.* utter sonorously. **3** *tr.* ring (bells) in peals. [Middle English, related to APPEAL]

peanut *n.* **1** a leguminous plant, *Arachis hypogaea*, bearing pods that ripen underground and contain seeds used as food and yielding oil. **2** the seed of this plant. **3** (in *pl.*) *colloq.* a paltry or trivial thing or amount, esp. of money.

peanut butter *n.* a paste of ground roasted peanuts.

pear *n.* **1** a yellowish or brownish-green fleshy fruit, tapering towards the stalk. **2** (in full **pear tree**) any of various trees of the genus *Pyrus* bearing it. [from Latin *pirum*]

pear drop *n.* a small sweet with the shape of a pear.

pearl[1] ● *n.* **1 a** (often *attrib.*) ▼ a usu. white or bluish-grey hard mass formed within the shell of a pearl-oyster or other bivalve mollusc, highly prized as a gem. ▷ GEM. **b** an imitation of this. **c** (in *pl.*) a necklace of pearls. **d** (usu. *attrib.*) = MOTHER-OF-PEARL. **2** a precious thing; the finest example. **3** anything resembling a pearl, e.g. a dewdrop, tear, etc. ● *adj.* of the colour of pearl; bluish grey. ● *v.* **1** *tr. poet.* sprinkle with pearly drops. **2** *tr.* reduce (barley etc.) to small rounded grains. **3** *intr.* fish for pearl-oysters. **4** *intr. poet.* form pearl-like drops. [from Old French *perle*] □ **pearler** *n.*

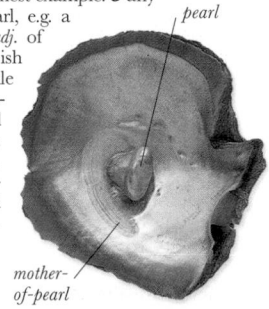

pearl

PEARL IN AN OYSTER SHELL   *mother-of-pearl*

PEACOCK BUTTERFLY (*Inachis io*)

P

PCB

A PCB, or printed circuit board, is an electrical circuit used in most digital equipment, including computers. It is made by laying tracks of a conductor such as copper on to one or both sides of an insulating board.

Components such as integrated circuits, resistors, and capacitors can be soldered to the surface of the board, or attached by inserting their connecting pins or wires into holes drilled in the board.

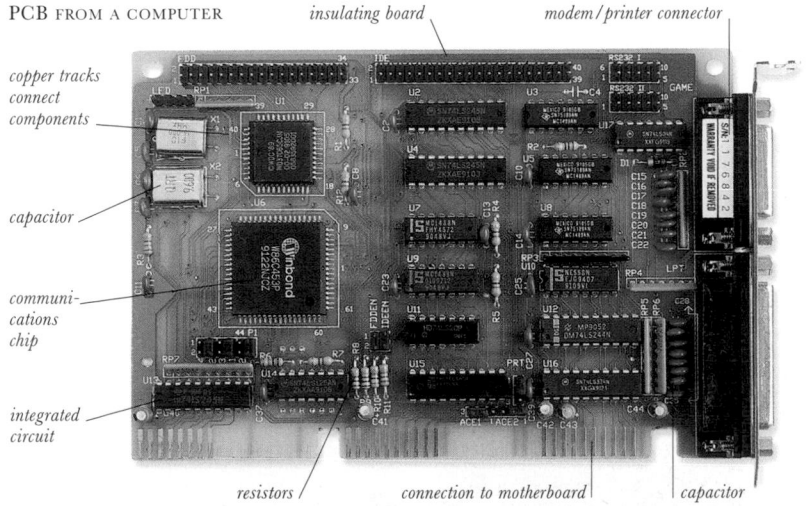

PCB FROM A COMPUTER   *insulating board*   *modem / printer connector*

copper tracks connect components

capacitor

communications chip

integrated circuit

resistors   *connection to motherboard*   *capacitor*

pearl[2] *n. Brit.* = PICOT. [variant of PURL[1]]

pearl barley *n.* barley reduced to small round grains by grinding.

pearl bulb *n. Brit.* a translucent electric light bulb.

pearl-diver *n.* a person who dives for pearl-oysters.

pearl onion *n.* a very small onion used in pickles.

pearl-oyster *n.* any of various marine bivalve molluscs of the genus *Pinctada*, bearing pearls.

pearly ● *adj.* (**pearlier**, **pearliest**) **1** resembling a pearl; lustrous. **2** containing pearls or mother-of-pearl. **3** adorned with pearls. ● *n.* (*pl.* **-ies**) (in *pl.*) *Brit.* **1** pearly kings and queens. **2** a pearly king's or queen's clothes or pearl buttons. **3** *slang* teeth. □ **pearliness** *n.*

Pearly Gates *n.pl. colloq.* the gates of Heaven.

pearly king *n.* (also **pearly queen**) *Brit.* a London costermonger (or his wife) wearing clothes covered with pearl buttons.

pearly nautilus see NAUTILUS.

pearmain *n.* a variety of apple with firm white flesh. [Middle English in sense 'pear': from Old French *parmain*]

peasant *n.* **1** a worker on the land, a farm labourer or small farmer. **2** *derog.* a boor, a lout. [from Old French *païsent*] □ **peasantry** *n.* (*pl.* **-ies**). **peasanty** *adj.*

pease *n.pl. archaic* peas. [from Greek *pison* (see PEA)]

pease pudding *n.* esp. *Brit.* a dish of split peas (served esp. with boiled ham).

pea-shooter *n.* a small tube for blowing dried peas through as a toy.

pea-souper *n. Brit. colloq.* a thick yellowish fog.

peat *n.* **1** vegetable matter partly decomposed in wet acid conditions to form a brown deposit like soil, used for fuel etc. ▷ BOG, COAL. **2** a cut piece of this. [from Anglo-Latin *peta*] □ **peaty** *adj.*

peatbog *n.* a bog composed of peat.

peatmoss *n.* **1** a peatbog. **2** = SPHAGNUM.

pebble *n.* a small smooth stone worn by the action of water. [Old English *papel-stān* 'pebble-stone', *pyppelrīpig* 'pebble-stream'] □ **pebbled** *adj.* **pebbly** *adj.*

pebble-dash *n.* esp. *Brit.* mortar with pebbles in it used as a coating for external walls. □ **pebble-dashed** *adj.*

P

pecan *n.* **1** ► a pinkish-brown smooth nut with an edible kernel. **2** a hickory, *Carya illinoensis*, producing this. [earlier *paccan*, of Algonquian origin]

kernel   *nut*

PECAN (*Carya illinoensis*)

peccadillo *n.* (*pl.* **-oes** or **-os**) a trifling offence; a venial sin. [from Spanish *pecadillo* 'little sin']

peccary *n.* (*pl.* **-ies**) any American wild piglike mammal of the family Tayassuidae. [from Carib *pakira*]

peck[1] ● *v.tr.* **1** strike or bite (something) with a beak. **2** kiss hastily or perfunctorily. **3 a** make (a hole) by pecking. **b** (foll. by *out*, *off*) remove by pecking. **4** (also *absol.*) *colloq.* nibble at. ● *n.* **1 a** a stroke or bite with a beak. **b** a mark made by this. **2** a hasty or perfunctory kiss. □ **peck at 1** eat (food) listlessly. **2** carp at. **3** strike repeatedly with a beak. [Middle English]

peck[2] *n.* **1** a measure of capacity for dry goods, equal to a quarter of a bushel. **2** a vessel used to contain this amount. □ **a peck of** a large number or amount of. [from Anglo-French *pek*]

pecker *n.* **1** a bird that pecks (*woodpecker*). **2** *N. Amer. coarse slang* the penis. □ **keep your pecker up** *Brit. colloq.* remain cheerful.

pecking order *n.* (also **peck order**) a social hierarchy.

peckish *adj. colloq.* **1** esp. *Brit.* hungry. **2** *US* irritable.

pectin *n. Biochem.* any of various soluble gelatinous polysaccharides found in ripe fruits etc. and used as a setting agent in jams etc. [based on Greek *pēktos* 'congealed'] □ **pectic** *adj.*

pectoral ● *adj.* **1** of or relating to the breast or chest (*pectoral fin*). **2** worn on the chest (*pectoral cross*). ● *n.* **1** (esp. in *pl.*) a pectoral muscle. **2** a pectoral fin. ▷ FISH. [based on Latin *pectus pectoris* 'breast, chest']

peculate *v.tr.* & *intr.* embezzle (money). [based on Latin *peculatus* 'embezzled'] □ **peculation** *n.*

peculiar *adj.* **1** strange; odd; unusual. **2 a** (usu. foll. by *to*) belonging exclusively (*a fashion peculiar to the time*). **b** belonging to the individual (*in their own peculiar way*). **3** special (*a point of peculiar interest*). [from Latin *peculiaris* 'of private property']

peculiarity *n.* (*pl.* **-ies**) **1 a** idiosyncrasy; unusualness; oddity. **b** an instance of this. **2** a characteristic (*meanness is his peculiarity*). **3** the state of being peculiar.

peculiarly *adv.* **1** more than usually; especially (*peculiarly annoying*). **2** oddly. **3** as regards oneself alone (*does not affect him peculiarly*).

pecuniary *adj.* **1** of, concerning, or consisting of money (*pecuniary aid*). **2** (of an offence) entailing a money penalty. [based on Latin *pecunia* 'money'] □ **pecuniarily** *adv.*

pedagogue *n.* **1** *archaic* a schoolmaster. **2** a usu. strict or pedantic teacher. [from Greek *pais paidos* 'boy' + *agōgos* 'guide'] □ **pedagogic** *adj.* **pedagogical** *adj.* **pedagogically** *adv.*

pedagogy *n.* the science of teaching. [from Greek *paidagōgia*] □ **pedagogics** *n.*

pedal[1] ● *n.* any of several types of foot-operated levers or controls for mechanisms, esp.: **1** either of a pair of levers for transmitting power to a bicycle wheel etc. ▷ BICYCLE. **2** any of the foot-operated controls in a motor vehicle. **3** any of the foot-operated keys of an organ. ▷ ORGAN. **4** each of the foot-levers on a piano, harp, etc. ▷ PIANO, UPRIGHT. ● *v.* (**pedalled**, **pedalling**; *US* **pedaled**, **pedaling**) **1** *intr.* operate a bicycle, organ, etc. by using the pedals. **2** *tr.* work (a bicycle etc.) with the pedals. [from Latin, related to PEDAL[2]] □ **pedaller** *n.* (*US* **pedaler**).

pedal[2] *adj. Zool.* of the foot or feet (esp. of a mollusc). [based on Latin *pes pedis* 'foot']

pedal bin *n.* a rubbish bin with a lid opened by a pedal.

pedal cycle *n.* a bicycle.

pedalo *n. Brit.* (*pl.* **-os** or **-oes**) a pedal-operated pleasure boat.

pedant *n.* **1** a person who insists on strict adherence to formal rules or literal meaning at the expense of a wider view. **2** a person who rates academic learning or technical knowledge above everything. [from French *pédant*] □ **pedantic** *adj.* **pedantically** *adv.* **pedantry** *n.* (*pl.* **-ies**).

peddle *v.* **1** *tr.* **a** sell (goods), esp. in small quantities, as a pedlar. **b** advocate or promote (ideas etc.). **2** *tr.* sell (drugs) illegally. **3** *intr.* engage in selling, esp. as a pedlar. [back-formation from PEDLAR]

peddler *n.* **1** a person who sells drugs illegally. **2** *US* var. of PEDLAR.

pederast *n.* a man who performs pederasty.

pederasty *n.* anal intercourse between a man and a boy. [based on Greek *pais paidos* 'boy' + *erastēs* 'lover']

pedestal *n.* **1** ► the part of a column below the base, comprising the plinth and the dado if present. **2** the stone etc.

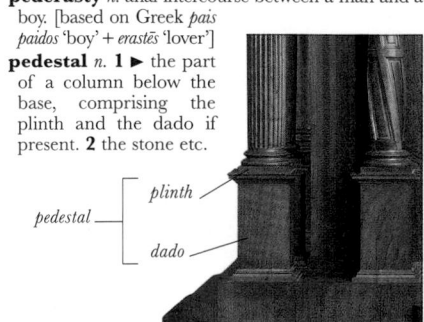

plinth

pedestal —

dado

PEDESTAL

base of a statue etc. **3** either of the two supports of a kneehole desk or table, usu. containing drawers. **4** an upright support of a machine, apparatus, etc. □ **put** (or **set**) **on a pedestal** admire disproportionately, idolize. [from Italian *piedestallo*]

pedestal table *n.* a table with a single central support.

pedestrian ● *n.* **1** (often *attrib.*) a person who is walking, esp. in a town. **2** a person who walks competitively. ● *adj.* prosaic; dull. [from Latin *pedester*] □ **pedestrianism** *n.* **pedestrianize** *v.tr.* & *intr.* (also **-ise**). **pedestrianization** *n.*

pedestrian crossing *n.* a specified part of a road where pedestrians have right of way to cross.

pedestrian precinct *n.* an area of a town restricted to pedestrians.

pediatrics *US* var. of PAEDIATRICS.

pedicure *n.* **1** the care or treatment of the feet, esp. of the toenails. **2** a person practising this. [based on Latin *pes pedis* 'foot' + *curare* 'take care of']

pedigree *n.* **1** (often *attrib.*) a recorded line of descent of a person or esp. a pure-bred domestic animal. **2** a genealogical table. [from Anglo-French *pé de grue* 'crane's foot', a mark denoting succession in pedigrees] □ **pedigreed** *adj.*

pediment *n.* **1** ▼ the triangular front part of a building in classical style, surmounting esp. a portico of columns. ▷ FACADE. **2** a similar part of a building in baroque or mannerist style. □ **pedimental** *adj.* **pedimented** *adj.*

PEDIMENT

pedlar *n.* (*US* **peddler**) **1** a travelling seller of small items. **2** (usu. foll. by *of*) a retailer of gossip etc. [Middle English] □ **pedlary** *n.*

pedo- *US* var. of PAEDO-.

pedometer *n.* an instrument for estimating the distance travelled on foot by recording the number of steps taken. [from French *pédomètre*]

peduncle *n. Bot.* the stalk of a flower, fruit, or cluster, esp. a main stalk bearing a solitary flower or subordinate stalks. ▷ INFLORESCENCE. [based on Latin *pes pedis* 'foot'] □ **peduncular** *adj.* **pedunculate** *adj.*

pedunculate oak *n.* a common oak, *Quercus robur*, in which clusters of acorns are borne on long stalks.

pee *colloq.* ● *v.* (**pees**, **peed**) **1** *intr.* urinate. **2** *tr.* discharge (blood etc.) when urinating. ● *n.* **1** an act of urinating. **2** urine. [initial letter of PISS]

peek ● *v.intr.* (usu. foll. by *in*, *out*, *at*) look quickly or slyly; peep. ● *n.* a quick or sly look. [Middle English]

peekaboo ● *adj.* **1** (of a garment etc.) transparent or having a pattern of holes which reveal the skin below. **2** (of a hairstyle) concealing one eye with a fringe or wave. ● *n.* a game of hiding and suddenly reappearing, played with a young child (also as *int.*).

peel ● *v.* **1** *tr.* **a** strip the skin, rind, bark, wrapping, etc. from. **b** (usu. foll. by *off*) strip (skin, peel, etc.) from. **2** *intr.* **a** (of a tree, a body, etc.) become bare of bark, skin, etc. **b** (often foll. by *off*) (of bark, skin, etc.) flake off. **3** *intr.* (often foll. by *off*) *colloq.* (of a person) strip for exercise etc. ● *n.* the outer covering of a fruit, vegetable, etc. □ **peel off 1** veer away and detach oneself from a group, formation, etc. **2** *colloq.* strip off one's clothes. [from Latin *pilare* 'to strip hair from'] □ **peeler** *n.* (in sense 1 of *v.*).

peeling *n.* a strip of the outer skin of a vegetable, fruit, etc. (*potato peelings*).

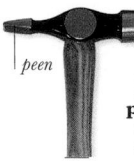

**PEEN:
HAMMER
WITH A
PEEN**

peen ● *n.* ◄ the wedge-shaped or thin or curved end of a hammer head. ● *v.tr.* hammer with a peen. [16th-century coinage]

peep[1] ● *v.intr.* **1** (usu. foll. by *at, in, out, into*) look through a narrow opening; look furtively. **2** (usu. foll. by *out*) **a** (of daylight, a flower etc.) emerge. **b** (of a quality etc.) show itself unconsciously. ● *n.* **1** a furtive or peering glance. **2** the first appearance (*at peep of day*). [Middle English]

peep[2] ● *v.intr.* make a shrill feeble sound as of young birds etc. ● *n.* **1** such a sound. **2** a slight sound or utterance (*not a peep out of them*).

peeper *n.* **1** a person who peeps. **2** *colloq.* an eye. **3** *US slang* a private detective.

peephole *n.* a small hole that may be looked through.

peeping Tom *n.* a furtive voyeur.

peep-show *n.* a small exhibition of pictures etc. viewed through a lens or hole set into a box etc.

peep-toe *attrib.adj.* (also **peep-toed**) *Brit.* (of a shoe) leaving the toes partly exposed.

peer[1] *v.intr.* **1** (usu. foll. by *into, at,* etc.) look keenly or with difficulty (*peered into the fog*). **2** peep out. [variant of obsolete (except dialect) *pire*]

peer[2] ● *n.* **1 a** (*fem.* **peeress**) a member of one of the degrees of the nobility in Britain or Ireland. **b** a noble of any country. **2** a person who, or thing which, is equal in ability, standing, age, etc. ● *v.intr. & tr.* (usu. foll. by *with*) rank or cause to rank equally. [from Latin *par* 'equal'] □ **peerless** *adj.* (in sense 2 of *n.*)

peerage *n.* **1** peers as a class. **2** the rank of peer or peeress (*a life peerage*).

peer group *n.* a group of people of the same age, status, etc.

peer of the realm *n.* (also **peer of the United Kingdom**) any of the class of peers whose adult members may all sit in the House of Lords.

peer pressure *n.* influence from members of one's peer group.

peeve *colloq.* ● *v.tr.* (usu. as **peeved** *adj.*) annoy; vex. ● *n.* **1** a cause of annoyance. **2** vexation. [back-formation from PEEVISH]

peevish *adj.* querulous; irritable. [Middle English in sense 'foolish, mad, spiteful'] □ **peevishly** *adv.* **peevishness** *n.*

peewit *n.* (also **pewit**) **1** a lapwing. **2** its cry.

peg ● *n.* **1 a** a usu. cylindrical pin or bolt of wood, metal, etc., often tapered at one end, and used for holding things together, hanging garments on, securing a tent, etc. **b** a bung for stoppering a cask etc. **c** each of several pegs used to tighten or loosen the strings of a violin etc. ▷ STRINGED. **d** a small matchstick etc. stuck into holes in a board for calculating the scores at cribbage. **2** *Brit.* = CLOTHES-PEG. **3** *Brit.* a measure of spirits or wine. ● *v.tr.* (**pegged**, **pegging**) **1** (usu. foll. by *down, in, out,* etc.) fix (a thing) with a peg. **2** *Econ.* stabilize (prices, wages, etc.). **3** mark (the score) with pegs on a cribbage board. □ **off the peg** esp. *Brit.* (of clothes) ready-made. **peg away** (often foll. by *at*) *Brit.* work consistently and esp. for a long period. **peg down** restrict (a person etc.) to rules, a commitment, etc. **peg on** = peg away. **peg out 1** *Brit. slang* die. **2** mark the boundaries of (land etc.). **a square peg in a round hole** a misfit. **take a person down a peg or two** humble a person. [Middle English] □ **pegged** *adj.*

pegboard *n.* a board having a regular pattern of small holes for pegs, used for commercial displays, games, etc.

peg-leg *n. colloq.* **1** an artificial leg. **2** a person with an artificial leg.

pejorative ● *adj.* (of a word etc.) depreciatory. ● *n.* a depreciatory word. [based on Latin *pejor* 'worse'] □ **pejoratively** *adv.*

peke *n. colloq.* a Pekinese dog.

Pekingese (also **Pekinese**) ● *n.* (*pl.* same) **1** (usu. **Pekinese**) a lapdog of a short-legged breed with long hair and a snub nose. ▷ DOG. **2** a citizen of

Beijing (Peking) in China. **3** the form of the Chinese language used in Beijing. ● *adj.* of or concerning Beijing or its language or citizens.

pekoe *n.* a superior kind of black tea. [from Chinese dialect *pek-ho*]

pelagian ● *adj.* inhabiting the open sea. ● *n.* an inhabitant of the open sea. [from Greek *pelagios* 'of the sea']

pelagic *adj.* **1** of or performed on the open sea. **2** (of marine life) belonging to the upper layers of the open sea. [from Greek *pelagikos*]

pelargonium *n.* a plant of the genus *Pelargonium*, with red, pink, or white flowers and often fragrant leaves. [modern Latin]

pelf *n. derog.* or *joc.* money; wealth. [from Old French *pelfre, peufre* 'spoils', related to PILFER]

pelican *n.* ▼ any large waterbird of the family Pelecanidae, with a long bill and a pouch for storing fish. [from Greek *pelekan*]

pouch

**PELICAN:
DALMATIAN PELICAN
(*Pelecanus crispus*)**

pelican crossing *n.* (in the UK) a pedestrian crossing with traffic lights operated by pedestrians. [from *pe*destrian *li*ght *con*trolled, respelt after the bird name]

pelisse *n. hist.* **1** a woman's long cloak with armholes or sleeves. **2** a fur-lined cloak, esp. as part of a hussar's uniform. [from medieval Latin *pellicia* (*vestis*) '(garment) of fur']

pellagra *n.* a disease caused by deficiency of nicotinic acid, characterized by cracking of the skin. [Italian, based on *pelle* 'skin'] □ **pellagrous** *adj.*

pellet ● *n.* **1** a small compressed ball of paper, bread, etc. **2** a pill. **3 a** a small mass of bones etc. regurgitated by a bird of prey. **b** a small hard piece of usu. rodent excreta. **4** a piece of small shot. ● *v.tr.* (**pelleted**, **pelleting**) make into a pellet or pellets. [from Latin *pila* 'ball'] □ **pelletize** *v.tr.* (also **-ise**)

pellicle *n.* a thin skin, membrane, or film. [from Latin *pellicula* 'little skin'] □ **pellicular** *adj.*

pell-mell ● *adv.* **1** headlong, recklessly. **2** in disorder or confusion. ● *adj.* confused, tumultuous. ● *n.* confusion; a mixture. [from Old French *pesle mesle, mesle pesle*, etc., reduplication based on *mesler* 'to mix']

pellucid *adj.* **1** (of water, light, etc.) transparent, clear. **2** (of style, speech, etc.) not confused. **3** mentally clear. [based on Latin *perlucere* 'to shine through'] □ **pellucidity** *n.* **pellucidly** *adv.*

pelmet *n.* a narrow border of cloth, wood, etc. above esp. a window, concealing the curtain rail.

pelota *n.* **1** a Basque or Spanish game played in a walled court with a ball and basket-like rackets attached to the hand. **2** the ball used in this. [Spanish, literally 'ball']

pelt[1] ● *v.* **1** *tr.* (usu. foll. by *with*) **a** hurl many small missiles at. **b** strike repeatedly with missiles. **c** assail with insults etc. **2** *intr.* (usu. foll. by *down*) (of rain etc.) fall quickly and torrentially. **3** *intr.* run fast. ● *n.* the act or an instance of pelting. □ **at full pelt** as fast as possible. [Middle English]

pelt[2] *n.* the undressed skin of a fur-bearing mammal. [Middle English, from Latin *pellis* 'skin'] □ **peltry** *n.*

pelvic *adj.* of or relating to the pelvis or the organs it encloses (e.g. the uterus).

pelvic girdle *n.* the bony or cartilaginous structure in vertebrates to which the posterior limbs are attached.

pelvis *n.* (*pl.* **pelvises** or **pelves** /-veez/) a basin-shaped cavity in most vertebrates, formed from the bones of the haunch with the sacrum and other vertebrae. ▷ HIP JOINT, SKELETON. [Latin, literally 'basin']

pemmican *n.* **1** a cake of dried pounded meat mixed with melted fat, originally made by N. American Indians. **2** beef so treated and flavoured with currants etc. for use by Arctic travellers etc. [from Algonquian *pimecan*]

PEN *abbr.* International Association of Poets, Playwrights, Editors, Essayists, and Novelists.

pen[1] ● *n.* **1** ▼ an instrument for writing or drawing with ink. ▷ CALLIGRAPHY. **2 a** (usu. prec. by *the*) the occupation of writing. **b** a style of writing. **3** *Zool.*

PEN

The basic components of a pen are a writing point, ink reservoir, and external housing. Types of writing points used include nibs (fountain pen), rotating ball (ballpoint pen), or felt or nylon point (felt-tip pen). Ink reservoirs are usually replaced when depleted, but some, such as the one shown here, can be refilled.

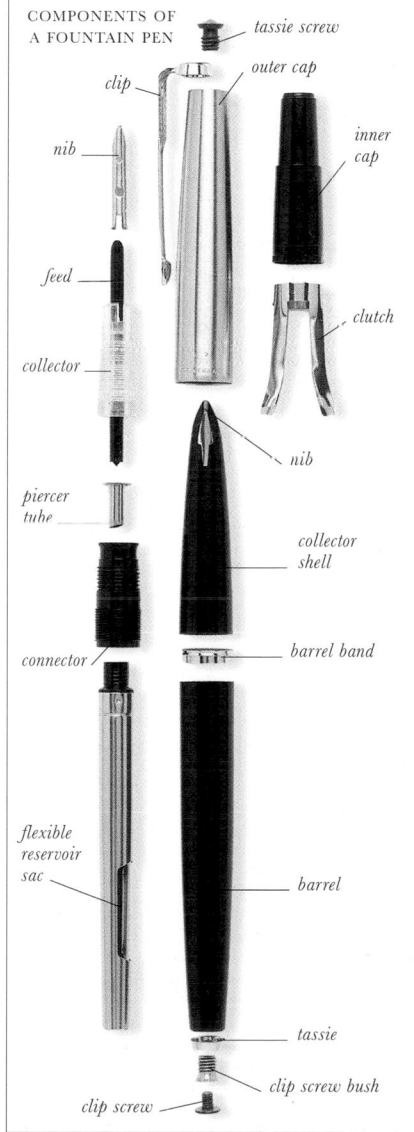

**COMPONENTS OF
A FOUNTAIN PEN**

tassie screw

clip

outer cap

nib

inner cap

feed

clutch

collector

nib

piercer tube

collector shell

connector

barrel band

flexible reservoir sac

barrel

tassie

clip screw bush

clip screw

P

the tapering internal cartilaginous shell of a squid. ● *v.tr.* (**penned, penning**) **1** write. **2** compose and write. □ **put pen to paper** begin writing. [from Latin *penna* 'feather']

pen² ● *n.* **1** a small enclosure for cows, sheep, etc. **2** a place of confinement. ● *v.tr.* (**penned, penning**) (often foll. by *in, up*) enclose or shut up, esp. in a pen. [Old English]

pen³ *n.* a female swan. [16th-century coinage]

pen⁴ *n. US slang* = PENITENTIARY *n.*

penal *adj.* **1 a** of or concerning punishment or its infliction. **b** (of an offence) punishable, esp. by law. **2** extremely severe (*penal taxation*). [based on Latin *poena* 'pain'] □ **penally** *adv.*

penalize *v.tr.* (also **-ise**) **1** subject (a person) to a penalty or comparative disadvantage. **2** make or declare (an action) penal. □ **penalization** *n.*

penal servitude *n. hist.* imprisonment with compulsory labour.

penalty *n.* (*pl.* **-ies**) **1 a** a punishment, esp. a fine, for a breach of contract etc. **b** a fine paid. **2** a disadvantage, loss, etc., esp. as a result of one's own actions. **3** a disadvantage imposed in a game etc. for a breach of the rules etc. □ **under** (or **on**) **penalty of** under the threat of (dismissal etc.). [from medieval Latin *penalitas*, related to PENAL]

penalty area *n. Football* the ground in front of the goal in which a foul by defenders involves the award of a penalty kick. ▷ FOOTBALL

penalty kick *n. Football* a free-kick at the goal, given after a foul in the penalty area.

penalty shoot-out see SHOOT-OUT 2.

penalty spot see SPOT *n.* 2c.

penance ● *n.* **1** an act of self-punishment as reparation for guilt. **2 a** (in the RC and Orthodox Church) a sacrament including confession of and absolution for a sin. **b** a penalty imposed, esp. by a priest, for a sin. ● *v.tr.* impose a penance on. □ **do penance** perform a penance. [from Latin *paenitentia*]

pen and ink ● *n.* **1** the instruments of writing. **2** writing. ● *adj.* (**pen-and-ink**) drawn or written with ink.

pence *n.* **1** *pl.* of PENNY. **2** *colloq.* = PENNY 1.

penchant /*pahn*-shahn/ *n.* an inclination or liking. [French, literally 'inclining']

pencil ● *n.* **1** (often *attrib.*) **a** an instrument for writing or drawing, usu. consisting of a thin rod of graphite etc. enclosed in a wooden cylinder. **b** a similar instrument with a metal or plastic cover and retractable lead. **c** a cosmetic in pencil form. **2** (*attrib.*) resembling a pencil in shape (*pencil skirt*). ● *v.tr.* (**pencilled, pencilling**; *US* **penciled, penciling**) **1** tint or mark with or as if with a pencil. **2** (usu. foll. by *in*) **a** write, esp. tentatively or provisionally. **b** (esp. as **pencilled** *adj.*) fill (an area) with soft pencil strokes. [from Latin *penicillum* 'paintbrush'] □ **penciller** *n.*

pencil case *n.* a container for pencils etc.

pencil sharpener *n.* a device for sharpening a pencil by rotating it against a cutting edge.

pendant *n.* **1** ◀ a hanging jewel etc., esp. one attached to a necklace etc. **2** a light fitting etc., hanging from a ceiling. [from Old French]

pendent *adj.* (also **pendant**) **1 a** hanging. **b** overhanging. **2** undecided; pending. [based on Latin *pendere* 'to hang'] □ **pendency** *n.*

pending ● *predic.adj.* **1** awaiting decision or settlement (*a settlement was pending*). **2** about to come into existence (*patent pending*). ● *prep.* **1** during (*pending these negotiations*). **2** until (*pending his return*). [suggested by French *pendant* 'hanging']

pending tray *n. Brit.* a tray for documents etc. awaiting attention.

necklace

link

crystal pendant

PENDANT

---

pendulous *adj.* **1** (of ears, breasts, flowers, branches, etc.) hanging down; drooping. **2** swinging; oscillating. [from Latin *pendulus*] □ **pendulously** *adv.*

pendulum *n.* ▶ a weight suspended so as to swing freely, esp. a rod with a weighted end regulating the movement of a clock's works. [Latin, literally 'free-hanging thing']

penetrate *v.* **1** *tr.* **a** find access into or through, esp. forcibly. **b** (usu. foll. by *with*) imbue (a person or thing) with; permeate. **2** *tr.* see into, find out, or discern (a person's mind, the truth, a meaning, etc.). **3** *tr.* see through (darkness, fog, etc.) (*could not penetrate the gloom*). **4** *intr.* be absorbed by the mind (*my hint did not penetrate*). **5** *tr.* (as **penetrating** *adj.*) **a** having or suggesting sensitivity or insight (*a penetrating remark*). **b** (of a voice etc.) easily heard through or above other sounds. **6** *tr.* (of a man) put the penis into the vagina of (a woman). **7** *intr.* (usu. foll. by *into, through, to*) make a way. [based on Latin *penetratus* 'placed or entered within'] □ **penetrable** *adj.* **penetrability** *n.* **penetrant** *adj. & n.* **penetratingly** *adv.* **penetration** *n.* **penetrative** *adj.* **penetrator** *n.*

pen-feather *n.* a quill-feather of a bird's wing.

penfriend *n. Brit.* a friend communicated with by letter only.

penguin *n.* ▼ any flightless seabird of the family Spheniscidae of the southern hemisphere, with black upper parts and white underparts, and wings developed into scaly flippers for swimming underwater. [16th-century coinage, originally in sense 'great auk']

penicillate *adj. Biol.* **1** having or forming a small

clock's mechanism

rod

pendulum controls clock's movement

falling weight drives clock's mechanism

PENDULUM
OF A CLOCK

---

tuft or tufts. **2** marked with streaks as of a pencil or brush.

penicillin *n.* any of various antibiotics produced naturally by moulds of the genus Penicillum, or synthetically, and able to prevent the growth of certain disease-causing bacteria. [from Latin *penicillum* 'paintbrush']

penile *adj.* of or concerning the penis.

peninsula *n.* a piece of land almost surrounded by water or projecting far into a sea or lake etc. [from Latin *paene* 'almost' + *insula* 'island'] □ **peninsular** *adj.*

penis *n.* (*pl.* **penises** or **penes** /-neez/) **1** the male organ of copulation and (in mammals) urination. ▷ REPRODUCTIVE ORGANS. **2** the male copulatory organ in lower vertebrates. [Latin, literally 'tail']

penitent ● *adj.* regretting and wishing to atone for sins etc. ● *n.* **1** a repentant sinner. **2** a person doing penance under the direction of a confessor. **3** (in *pl.*) various RC orders associated for mutual discipline and the giving of aid to criminals, prostitutes, etc. [from Latin *paenitent-* 'repenting'] □ **penitence** *n.* **penitently** *adv.*

penitential *adj.* of or concerning penitence or penance. □ **penitentially** *adv.*

penitentiary ● *n.* (*pl.* **-ies**) *N. Amer.* a reformatory prison. ● *adj.* **1** of or concerning penance. **2** of or concerning reformatory treatment. [from medieval Latin *paenitentiarius*]

penknife *n.* (*pl.* **penknives**) a small folding knife.

penlight *n.* a small electric torch shaped like a fountain pen.

penman *n.* (*pl.* **-men**) **1** a person who writes by hand with a specified skill. **2** an author. □ **penmanship** *n.*

pen-name *n.* a literary pseudonym.

pennant *n.* **1** *Naut.* a tapering flag, esp. that flown at the masthead of a vessel in commission. **2** = PENNON. **3** *N. Amer.* a flag denoting a sports championship etc. [blend of PENDANT and PENNON]

penne /*pen*-ay/ *n.* pasta in the form of short wide tubes. [Italian, literally 'quills']

penniless *adj.* having no money; destitute. □ **pennilessly** *adv.* **pennilessness** *n.*

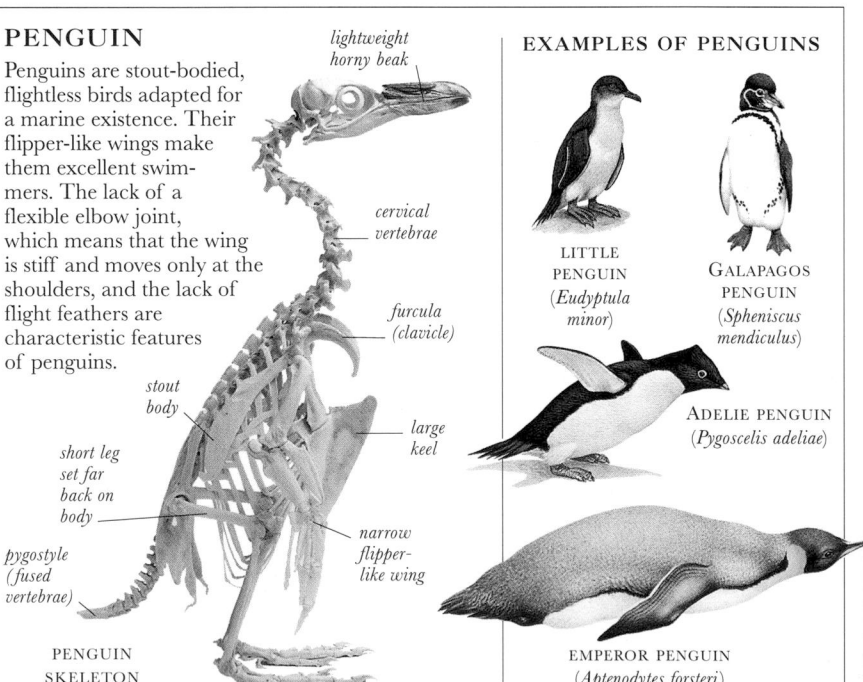

PENGUIN

Penguins are stout-bodied, flightless birds adapted for a marine existence. Their flipper-like wings make them excellent swimmers. The lack of a flexible elbow joint, which means that the wing is stiff and moves only at the shoulders, and the lack of flight feathers are characteristic features of penguins.

lightweight horny beak

cervical vertebrae

furcula (clavicle)

stout body

large keel

short leg set far back on body

pygostyle (fused vertebrae)

narrow flipper-like wing

PENGUIN SKELETON

EXAMPLES OF PENGUINS

LITTLE PENGUIN (*Eudyptula minor*)

GALAPAGOS PENGUIN (*Spheniscus mendiculus*)

ADELIE PENGUIN (*Pygoscelis adeliae*)

EMPEROR PENGUIN (*Aptenodytes forsteri*)

P

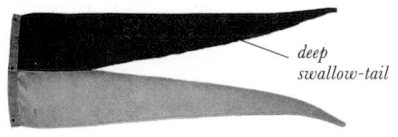

*deep
swallow-tail*

PENNON

pennon *n.* **1** ▲ a long narrow flag, triangular or swallow-tailed, esp. as the military ensign of lancer regiments. **2** *Naut.* a long pointed streamer on a ship. [from Latin *penna* 'feather'] □ **pennoned** *adj.*

penn'orth var. of PENNYWORTH.

penny *n.* (*pl.* for separate coins **-ies**, for a sum of money **pence**) **1** a British bronze coin and monetary unit equal to one-hundredth of a pound. **2** *hist.* a former British coin and monetary unit equal to one two-hundred-and-fortieth of a pound. **3** *N. Amer.* a one-cent coin. □ **like a bad penny** continually returning when unwanted. **pennies from heaven** unexpected benefits. **the penny drops** *Brit. colloq.* one begins to understand at last. **a pretty penny** a large sum of money. **two a penny** almost worthless though easily obtained. [Old English]

penny black *n. hist.* the first adhesive postage stamp (1840, value one penny).

penny dreadful *n. Brit.* a cheap sensational comic or story book.

penny-farthing *n. Brit. hist.* ▼ an early type of bicycle with one large and one small wheel.

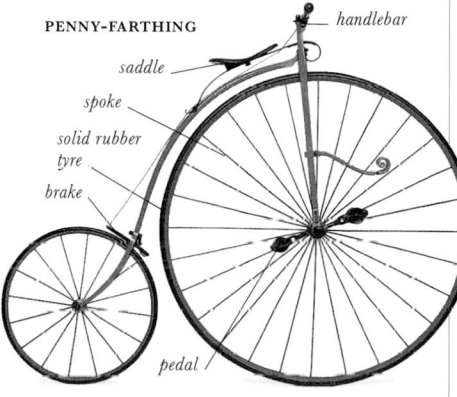

PENNY-FARTHING

handlebar

saddle

spoke

*solid rubber
tyre*

brake

pedal

penny-pinching ● *n.* meanness. ● *adj.* mean. □ **penny-pincher** *n.*

pennyweight *n.* a unit of weight, 24 grains or one-twentieth of an ounce troy.

penny whistle *n.* a tin pipe with six holes giving different notes.

pennywort *n.* any of several wild plants with rounded leaves. [Middle English]

pennyworth *n.* (also **penn'orth** /pen-ŏth/) esp. *Brit.* **1** as much as can be bought for a penny. **2** a bargain of a specified kind (*a bad pennyworth*).

penology *n.* the study of the punishment of crime and of prison management. [based on Latin *poena* 'penalty'] □ **penological** *adj.* **penologist** *n.*

pen pal *n. colloq.* = PENFRIEND.

pen-pushing *n. colloq. derog.* clerical work. □ **pen-pusher** *n.*

pensile *adj.* **1** hanging down; pendulous. **2** (of a bird etc.) building a pensile nest. [from Latin *pensilis*]

pension¹ ● *n.* **1 a** (in full *Brit.* **state pension** or *US* **government pension**) a regular payment made by a government to people above a specified age, to widows, or to the disabled. **b** similar payments made by an employer etc. on the retirement of an employee. **2** a regular payment paid to a scientist, artist, etc. for services to the state, or to fund work. ● *v.tr.* grant a pension to. □ **pension off 1** dismiss with a pension. **2** cease to employ or use. [from

Latin *pensio* 'payment'] □ **pensionary** *n. & adj.* **pensionless** *adj.*

pension² /pahn-si-ahn/ *n.* a boarding house in France or continental Europe etc., providing full or half board at a fixed rate. □ **en pension** as a boarder. [French]

pensionable *adj.* **1** entitled to a pension. **2** (of a job etc.) entitling an employee to a pension. □ **pensionability** *n.*

pensioner *n.* a recipient of a pension, esp. the retirement pension.

pensive *adj.* **1** deep in thought. **2** sorrowfully thoughtful. [from Old French *pensif -ive*] □ **pensively** *adv.* **pensiveness** *n.*

pent *adj.* (often foll. by *in, up*) closely confined; shut in (*pent-up feelings*). [past participle of obsolete *pend* 'to shut in']

penta- *comb. form* **1** five. **2** *Chem.* (forming the names of compounds) containing five atoms or groups of a specified kind. [Greek]

pentacle *n.* a pentagram or similar figure used as a mystic symbol. [from medieval Latin *pentaculum*]

pentad *n.* **1** the number five. **2** a group of five. [from Greek *pentas -ados*]

pentagon *n.* **1** ► a plane figure with five sides and angles. **2** (**the Pentagon**) **a** the pentagonal Washington headquarters of the US defence forces. **b** the leaders of the US defence forces. [from Greek *penta-gōnon*] □ **pentagonal** *adj.*

PENTAGON

pentagram *n.* ► a five-pointed star formed by extending the sides of a pentagon both ways until they intersect. [from Greek *pentagrammon*|

pentahedron *n.* (*pl.* **pentahedra** or **pentahedrons**) ▼ a solid figure with five faces. □ **pentahedral** *adj.*

PENTAGRAM

pentameter /pen-tam-i-ter/ *n.* a verse of five feet. [from Greek *pentametros*]

pentane *n. Chem.* a hydrocarbon of the alkane series.

pentangle *n.* = PENTAGRAM. [Middle English]

pentaprism *n.* a five-sided prism with two silvered surfaces used in a viewfinder to obtain a constant deviation of all rays of light through 90°. ▷ CAMERA

PENTAHEDRON

Pentateuch *n.* the first five books of the Old Testament. [from ecclesiastical Greek *pentateukhos*] □ **Pentateuchal** *adj.*

pentathlon *n.* an athletic event comprising five different events for each competitor. [from Greek *pente* 'five' + *athlon* 'contest'] □ **pentathlete** *n.*

pentatonic *adj. Mus.* **1** consisting of five notes. **2** relating to such a scale.

pentavalent *adj. Chem.* having a valency of five.

Pentecost *n.* **1 a** Whit Sunday. **b** a festival celebrating the descent of the Holy Spirit on Whit Sunday. **2** the Jewish harvest festival, on the fiftieth day after the second day of Passover. [from Greek *pentēkostē (hēmera)* 'fiftieth (day)']

Pentecostal ● *adj.* (also **pentecostal**) **1** of or relating to Pentecost. **2** of or designating Christian sects, often fundamentalist, who emphasize baptism in the Holy Spirit evidenced by 'speaking in tongues'. ● *n.* a Pentecostalist. □ **Pentecostalism** *n.* **Pentecostalist** *adj. & n.*

penthouse *n.* **1** a house or flat on the roof or the top floor of a tall building. **2** a sloping roof, esp. of an outhouse built on to another building. [Middle

English *pentis*, from Late Latin *appendicium* 'appendage']

Pentothal *n. propr.* = THIOPENTONE.

penult ● *n.* the last but one (esp. syllable). ● *adj.* last but one.

penultimate ● *adj.* last but one. ● *n.* the last but one. [based on Latin *paene* 'almost' + *ultimus* 'last']

penumbra *n.* (*pl.* **penumbrae** /-bree/ or **penumbras**) **1** the partly shaded outer region of the shadow cast by an opaque object, esp. (*Astron.*) that of the shadow cast by the Earth or Moon over an area experiencing a partial eclipse. ▷ ECLIPSE. **2 a** a partial shadow. **b** an area of obscurity or uncertainty. [from Latin *paene* 'almost' + *umbra* 'shadow'] □ **penumbral** *adj.*

penurious *adj.* **1** poor; destitute. **2** stingy; grudging. **3** scanty. □ **penuriously** *adv.*

penury *n.* (*pl.* **-ies**) **1** destitution; poverty. **2** a lack; scarcity. [from Latin *penuria*]

peon *n.* **1** a Spanish-American day labourer or farmworker. **2** *N. Amer.* a menial or drudge. [Spanish, from medieval Latin *pedo pedonis* 'foot soldier'] □ **peonage** *n.*

peony *n.* (also **paeony**) (*pl.* **-ies**) ► any herbaceous plant of the genus *Paeonia*, with large globular red, pink, or white flowers, often double in cultivated varieties. [from Greek, based on *Paiōn*, name of the physician of the gods]

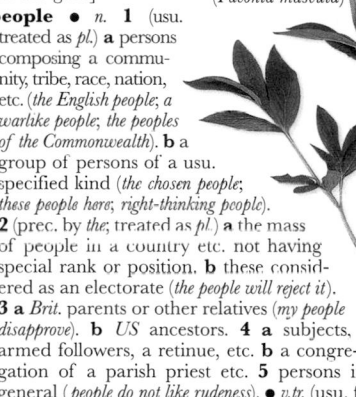

PEONY
(*Paeonia mascula*)

people ● *n.* **1** (usu. treated as *pl.*) **a** persons composing a community, tribe, race, nation, etc. (*the English people; a warlike people; the peoples of the Commonwealth*). **b** a group of persons of a usu. specified kind (*the chosen people; these people here; right-thinking people*). **2** (prec. by *the;* treated as *pl.*) **a** the mass of people in a country etc. not having special rank or position. **b** these considered as an electorate (*the people will reject it*). **3 a** *Brit.* parents or other relatives (*my people disapprove*). **b** *US* ancestors. **4 a** subjects, armed followers, a retinue, etc. **b** a congregation of a parish priest etc. **5** persons in general (*people do not like rudeness*). ● *v.tr.* (usu. foll. by *with*) **1** fill with people, animals, etc.; populate. **2** inhabit; occupy; fill (*thickly peopled*). [from Latin *populus*]

people carrier *n.* a motor vehicle of the size and shape of a small minibus but with approximately eight seats which may swivel, be removable, or convert into a table. ▷ CAR

people's democracy *n.* a political system, formerly esp. in E. Europe, with power regarded as invested in the people.

PEP /pep/ *abbr. Brit.* **1** Political and Economic Planning. **2** Personal Equity Plan.

pep *colloq.* ● *n.* vigour; go; spirit. ● *v.tr.* (**pepped, pepping**) (usu. foll. by *up*) fill with vigour.

peperino *n.* a light porous (esp. brown) volcanic rock formed of small grains of sand, cinders, etc.

peperoni var. of PEPPERONI.

peplum *n.* **1** a short flounce etc. at waist level, esp. of a blouse or jacket over a skirt. **2** *Gk Antiq.* a woman's outer garment. [from Greek *peplos*]

pepo *n.* (*pl.* **-os**) any fleshy fruit of the melon or cucumber type, with numerous seeds and surrounded by a hard skin.

pepper ● *n.* **1 a** a hot aromatic condiment from the dried berries of certain plants used whole or ground. ▷ SPICE. **b** any climbing vine of the genus *Piper*, esp. *P. nigrum*, yielding these berries. **2** anything hot or pungent. **3 a** = CAPSICUM. **b** = CAYENNE. ● *v.tr.* **1**

P

P

sprinkle or treat with or as if with pepper. **2** pelt with missiles. **3** punish severely. [from Sanskrit *pippalī-* 'berry, peppercorn']

peppercorn *n.* **1** the dried berry of *Piper nigrum* as a condiment. ▷ BLACK PEPPER. **2** (in full **peppercorn rent**) *Brit.* a nominal rent.

pepper mill *n.* a device for grinding pepper by hand.

peppermint *n.* **1** a mint plant, *Mentha piperita*, grown for the strong-flavoured oil obtained from its leaves. **2** a sweet flavoured with peppermint. □ **pepperminty** *adj.*

pepperoni *n.* (also **peperoni**) beef and pork sausage seasoned with pepper. [from Italian *peperone* 'chilli']

pepper pot *n. Brit.* a small container with a perforated lid for sprinkling pepper.

pepper shaker *n. N. Amer.* = PEPPER POT.

peppery *adj.* **1** of, like, or containing much pepper. **2** hot-tempered. **3** pungent; stinging. □ **pepperiness** *n.*

pep pill *n.* a pill containing a stimulant drug.

peppy *adj.* (**peppier**, **peppiest**) *colloq.* vigorous, energetic, bouncy.

pepsin *n.* a digestive enzyme contained in the gastric juice. [German, based on Greek *pepsis* 'digestion']

pep talk *n.* a usu. short talk intended to enthuse, encourage, etc.

peptic *adj.* concerning or promoting digestion. [from Greek *peptikos* 'able to digest']

peptic ulcer *n.* an ulcer in the stomach or duodenum caused by the action of pepsin and stomach acid.

peptide *n. Biochem.* a compound consisting of two or more amino acids linked in sequence. [from German *Peptid*]

per *prep.* **1** for each; for every (*two sweets per child; five miles per hour*). **2** by means of; by; through (*per post; per rail*). **3** (in full **as per**) in accordance with (*as per instructions*). □ **as per usual** *colloq.* as usual. [Latin]

peradventure *archaic* or *joc.* ● *adv.* perhaps. ● *n.* uncertainty; chance; conjecture; doubt (esp. *beyond* or *without peradventure* 'by chance']

perambulate *v.* **1** *tr.* walk through, over, or about (streets, the country, etc.). **2** *intr.* walk from place to place. [based on Latin *perambulatus* 'walked through'] □ **perambulation** *n.* **perambulatory** *adj.*

perambulator *n. Brit. formal* = PRAM.

per annum *adv.* for each year. [Latin]

percale *n.* a closely woven cotton fabric like calico. [French]

per capita *adv. & adj.* (also **per caput**) for each person. [Latin, literally 'by heads']

perceive *v.tr.* **1** apprehend, esp. through the sight; observe. **2** (usu. foll. by *that*, *how*, etc. + clause) apprehend with the mind; understand. **3** regard mentally in a specified manner (*perceives the universe as infinite*). [from Latin *percipere*] □ **perceivable** *adj.* **perceiver** *n.*

per cent (*US* **percent**) ● *adv.* in every hundred. ● *n.* **1** percentage. **2** one part in every hundred (*half a per cent*). [from Latin *per centum* 'by the hundred']

percentage *n.* **1** a rate or proportion per cent. **2** a proportion.

percentile *n. Statistics* **1** one of 99 values of a variable dividing a population into 100 equal groups as regards the value of that variable. **2** each of these groups.

percept *n. Philos.* **1** an object of perception. **2** a mental concept resulting from perceiving, esp. by sight. [from Latin *perceptum* 'thing) perceived']

perceptible *adj.* capable of being perceived by the senses or intellect. [from Old French] □ **perceptibility** *n.* **perceptibly** *adv.*

perception *n.* **1** the faculty or an instance of perceiving. **2** (often foll. by *of*) **a** the intuitive recognition of a truth, aesthetic quality, etc. **b** an

instance of this (*a sudden perception of the true position*). **3** an interpretation or impression based on one's understanding of something. [from Latin *perceptio*] □ **perceptual** *adj.* **perceptually** *adv.*

perceptive *adj.* **1** capable of perceiving. **2** sensitive; discerning; observant (*a perceptive remark*). [from medieval Latin *perceptivus*] □ **perceptively** *adv.* **perceptiveness** *n.*

perch¹ ● *n.* **1** a usu. horizontal bar, branch, etc. used by a bird to rest on. **2** a usu. high or precarious place for a person or thing to rest on. **3** esp. *Brit. hist.* a measure of length, esp. for land, of 5½ yards. ● *v.intr. & tr.* (usu. foll. by *on*) settle or rest, or cause to settle or rest on or as if on a perch etc. (*the bird perched on a branch; a town perched on a hill*). □ **knock a person off his** (or **her**) **perch 1** vanquish, destroy. **2** make less confident or secure. [from Latin *pertica* 'pole']

perch² *n.* (*pl.* same or **perches**) ▼ any spiny-finned freshwater edible fish of the genus *Perca*, esp. *P. fluviatilis* of Europe. ▷ FISH. [from Greek *perkē*]

PERCH (*Perca fluviatilis*)

perchance *adv. archaic* or *poet.* **1** by chance. **2** possibly; maybe. [from Anglo-French *par chance* 'by chance']

percipient *adj.* discerning; observant. [from Latin *percipient-* 'perceiving'] □ **percipience** *n.* **percipiently** *adv.*

percolate *v.* **1** *intr.* (often foll. by *through*) **a** (of liquid etc.) filter or ooze gradually (esp. through a porous surface). **b** (of an idea etc.) permeate gradually. **2** *tr.* prepare (coffee) by repeatedly passing boiling water through ground beans. [based on Latin *percolatus* 'strained through'] □ **percolation** *n.*

percolator *n.* a machine for percolating coffee.

percussion *n.* **1** *Mus.* **a** (often *attrib.*) ▶ the playing of music by striking instruments with sticks etc. (*a percussion instrument*). **b** the section of such instruments in an orchestra. ▷ ORCHESTRA. **2** the forcible striking of one esp. solid body against another. □ **percussionist** *n.* **percussive** *adj.* **percussively** *adv.* **percussiveness** *n.*

percussion cap *n.* a small amount of explosive powder contained in metal or paper and exploded by striking, used esp. in toy guns and formerly in some firearms.

per diem /per **dee**-em/ *adv. & adj.* for each day. [Latin]

perdition *n.* eternal death; damnation. [from ecclesiastical Latin *perditio* 'destruction']

Père David's deer *n.* a large slender-antlered deer, *Elaphurus davidianus*. [named after Father A. *David*, French missionary, 1826–1900]

peregrine *n.* (in full **peregrine falcon**) ▶ a powerful falcon, *Falco peregrinus*, breeding esp. on coastal cliffs and much used for falconry. [from Latin *peregrinus*]

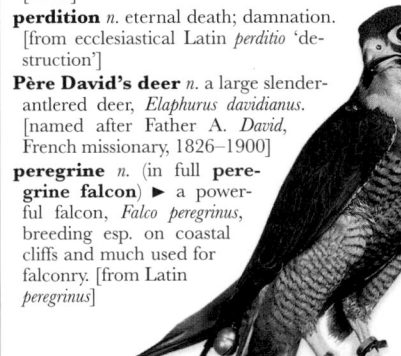

PEREGRINE FALCON (*Falco peregrinus*)

peremptory *adj.* **1** (of a statement or command) admitting no denial or refusal. **2** (of a person, a person's manner, etc.) dogmatic; imperious; dictatorial. [from Latin *peremptorius* 'deadly, decisive'] □ **peremptorily** *adv.* **peremptoriness** *n.*

perennial ● *adj.* **1** lasting through a year or several years. **2** (of a plant) lasting several years (cf. ANNUAL *adj.* 3). **3** lasting a long time or for ever. ● *n.* a perennial plant. [from Latin *perennis*] □ **perenniality** *n.* **perennially** *adv.*

perestroika /pe-ri-**stroy**-kǎ/ *n.* (in the former Soviet Union) the policy or practice of restructuring or reforming the economic and political system. [Russian, literally 'restructuring']

perfect ● *adj.* /**per**-fikt/ **1** complete; not deficient. **2** faultless (*a perfect diamond*). **3** very satisfactory (*a perfect evening*). **4** exact; precise (*a perfect circle*). **5** entire; unqualified (*a perfect stranger*). **6** *Gram.* (of a tense) denoting a completed action or event in the past, formed in English with *have* and the past participle, as in *he has gone*. ● *v.tr.* /per-**fekt**/ **1** make perfect. **2** carry through; complete. ● *n.* /**per**-fikt/ *Gram.* the perfect tense. [from Latin *perfectus* 'completed'] □ **perfecter** *n.* **perfectible** *adj.* **perfectibility** *n.*

perfect interval *n. Mus.* a fourth or fifth as it would occur in a major or minor scale starting on the lower note of the interval, or octave.

perfection *n.* **1** the act or process of making perfect. **2** the state of being perfect. **3** a perfect person, thing, or example. □ **to perfection** exactly; completely.

perfectionism *n.* the uncompromising pursuit of excellence. □ **perfectionist** *n. & adj.*

perfectly *adv.* **1** quite, completely (*is perfectly capable of doing it*). **2** in a perfect way.

perfect pitch *n.* = ABSOLUTE PITCH 1.

perfidy *n.* breach of faith; treachery. [from Latin *perfidia*] □ **perfidious** *adj.* **perfidiously** *adv.*

perforate ● *v.tr.* **1** make a hole or holes through; pierce. **2** make a row of small holes in (paper etc.) so that a part may be torn off easily. ● *adj.* perforated. [based on Latin *perforatus* 'perforated'] □ **perforation** *n.* **perforator** *n.*

perforce *adv. archaic* unavoidably; necessarily. [from Old French *par force* 'by force']

perform *v.* **1** *tr.* (also *absol.*) carry into effect; do (a command, promise, task, etc.). **2** *tr.* go through, execute (a public function, play, piece of music, etc.). **3** *intr.* act in a play; play music, sing, etc. (*is performing*). **4** *intr.* (of a trained animal) execute tricks etc. at a public show. **5** *intr.* function, esp. satisfactorily (*the car performs well at speed*). **6** *intr.* (of an investment) yield a return, esp. a profit. [from Old French *parfournir*] □ **performable** *adj.* **performer** *n.* **performing** *adj.*

performance *n.* **1** (usu. foll. by *of*) **a** the act or process of performing or carrying out. **b** the execution or fulfilment (of a duty etc.). **2** a staging or production (of a drama, piece of music, etc.) (*the afternoon performance*). **3** a person's achievement under test conditions etc. (*put up a good performance*). **4** *colloq.* a fuss; a scene (*made such a performance about leaving*). **5** **a** the capabilities of a machine, esp. a car or aircraft. **b** (*attrib.*) of high capability (*a performance car*).

performance art *n.* a kind of visual art in which the activity of the artist forms a central feature. □ **performance artist** *n.*

performing arts *n.pl.* the arts, such as drama, music, and dance, that require performance for their realization.

perfume ● *n.* **1** a sweet smell. **2** fluid containing the essence of flowers etc.; scent. ● *v.tr.* (usu. as **perfumed** *adj.*) impart a sweet scent to. [originally in sense 'odorous fumes': from obsolete Italian *parfumare* 'to smoke through'] □ **perfumy** *adj.*

perfumer *n.* a maker or seller of perfumes. □ **perfumery** *n.* (*pl.* **-ies**)

perfunctory *adj.* **1** done merely for the sake of getting through a duty. **2** superficial; mechanical.

PERCUSSION

Percussion instruments, played by being struck, shaken, or scraped or clashed together, are the oldest of the instrumental groups. Most percussion instruments, such as a side drum, do not have a definite pitch and are used for rhythm and impact, and the distinctive timbre of their sound. Other percussion instruments, such as tubular bells, are tuned to a definite pitch and can play melody, harmony, and rhythms.

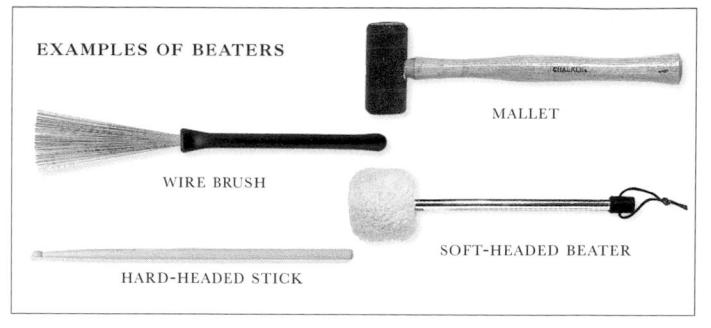

EXAMPLES OF BEATERS

MALLET

WIRE BRUSH

SOFT-HEADED BEATER

HARD-HEADED STICK

UNTUNED INSTRUMENTS

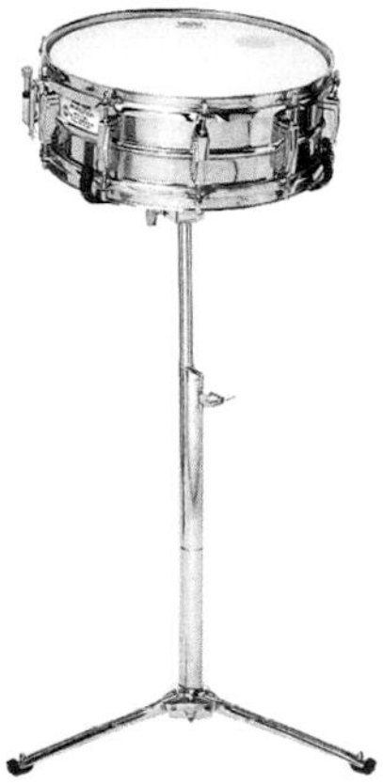

SIDE DRUM

CONGAS

BASS DRUM

TABLA

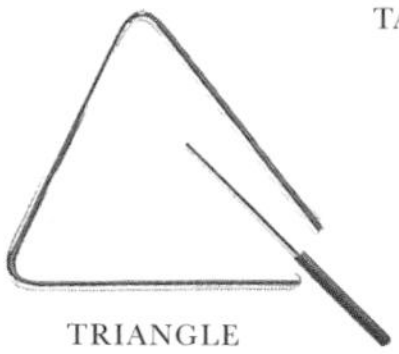

CLAVES

TRIANGLE

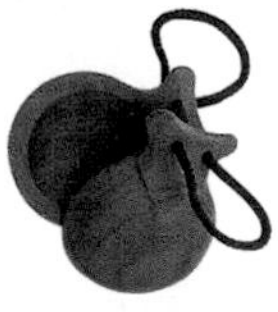

CASTANETS

TAMBOURINE

MARACAS

CYMBALS

TUNED INSTRUMENTS

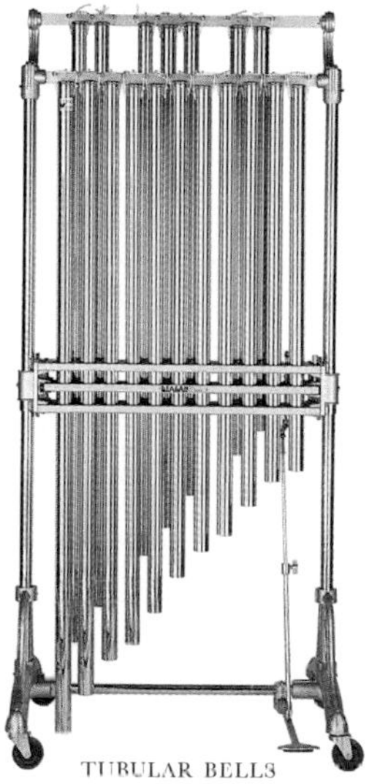

TUBULAR BELLS

TIMPANUM
(KETTLEDRUM)

P

XYLOPHONE

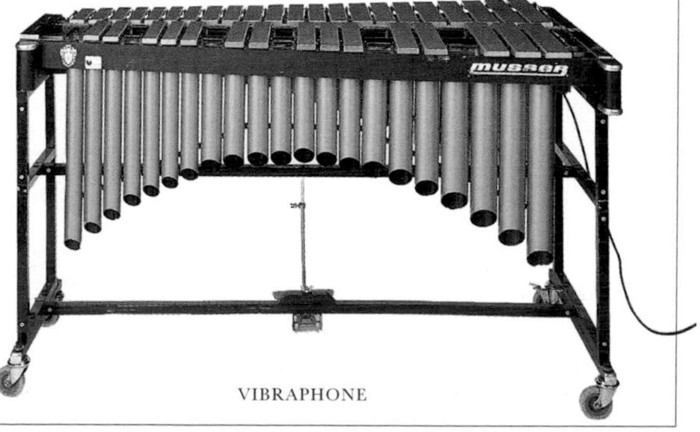

VIBRAPHONE

[from Late Latin *perfunctorius* 'careless'] □ **perfunctorily** *adv.* **perfunctoriness** *n.*

pergola *n.* an arbour or covered walk, formed of growing plants trained over trellis-work. [from Latin *pergula* 'projecting roof']

perhaps *adv.* **1** it may be; possibly (*perhaps it is lost*). **2** introducing a polite request (*perhaps you would open the window?*). [based on HAP]

peri- *prefix* **1** round, about. **2** *Astron.* the point nearest to. [from Greek *peri* 'around']

perianth *n.* the outer part of a flower. ▷ CORONA. [from French *périanthe*]

pericardium *n.* (*pl.* **pericardia**) the membranous sac enclosing the heart. ▷ HEART. [based on Greek *kardia* 'heart'] □ **pericardial** *adj.* **pericarditis** *n.*

pericarp *n.* ▶ the part of a fruit formed from the wall of the ripened ovary. ▷ NUT. [from Greek *perikarpion* 'pod, shell']

perigee *n.* the point in a body's orbit at which it is nearest the Earth (opp. APOGEE 1). [from Greek *perigeion* 'round the Earth'] □ **perigean** *adj.*

perihelion *n.* (*pl.* **perihelia**) the point in the orbit of a planet, comet, etc. at which it is closest to the Sun (opp. APHELION). [based on Greek *hēlios* 'Sun']

peril *n.* serious and immediate danger. □ **at one's peril** at one's own risk. **in peril of** with great risk to (*in peril of your life*). [from Latin *peric(u)lum*] □ **perilous** *adj.* **perilously** *adv.* **perilousness** *n.*

perilune *n.* the point at which a body orbiting the Moon is closest to it (opp. APOLUNE). [based on Latin *luna* 'Moon']

perimeter /pĕ-**rim**-i-ter/ *n.* **1 a** the circumference or outline of a closed figure. **b** the length of this. **2 a** the outer boundary of an enclosed area. **b** a defended boundary. [from Greek *perimetros*] □ **perimetric** *adj.*

perinatal *adj.* of or relating to the time immediately before and after birth.

---

perineum *n.* the region of the body between the anus and the scrotum or vulva. [from Greek *perinaion*] □ **perineal** *adj.*

period ● *n.* **1** a length or portion of time. **2** a distinct portion of history, a person's life, etc. **3** *Geol.* a time forming part of a geological era (*the Quaternary period*). **4** an interval between recurrences of an astronomical or other phenomenon. **5** the time allowed for a lesson in school. **6** an occurrence of menstruation. **7** esp. *N. Amer.* **a** = FULL STOP 1. **b** used at the end of a sentence etc. to indicate finality, absoluteness, etc. (*we want the best, period*). ● *adj.* belonging to or characteristic of some past period (*period furniture*). [from Greek *periodos* 'orbit, recurrence, course']

periodic *adj.* appearing or occurring at esp. regular intervals. □ **periodicity** *n.*

periodical ● *n.* a newspaper, magazine, etc. issued at regular intervals, usu. monthly or weekly. ● *adj.* **1** published at regular intervals. **2** periodic, occasional. □ **periodically** *adv.*

periodic table *n.* a table of the chemical elements arranged in order of atomic number, usu. in rows, so that elements with similar atomic structure appear in columns.

period piece *n.* an object or work whose main interest lies in its historical etc. associations.

peripatetic ● *adj.* **1** (of a teacher) working in more than one school or college etc. **2** going from place to place; itinerant. ● *n.* a peripatetic person, esp. a teacher. [from Greek *peripatētikos*] □ **peripatetically** *adv.*

peripheral ● *adj.* **1** of minor importance; marginal. **2** of the periphery; on the fringe. **3** (of equipment) used with a computer etc. but not an integral part of it. ● *n.* *Computing* a peripheral device or piece of equipment. □ **peripherality** *n.* **peripherally** *adv.*

peripheral nervous system *n.* *Anat.* ▼ the nervous system outside the brain and spinal cord. ▷ AUTONOMIC NERVOUS SYSTEM, NERVOUS SYSTEM

periphery *n.* (*pl.* **-ies**) **1** the boundary of an area or surface. **2** an outer or surrounding region (*built on the periphery of the old town*). [from Greek *periphereia* 'circumference']

periphrasis /pĕ-**rif**-ră-sis/ *n.* (*pl.* **periphrases**) **1** a roundabout way of speaking; circumlocution. **2** a roundabout phrase. [Latin, from Greek] □ **periphrastic** *adj.* **periphrastically** *adv*

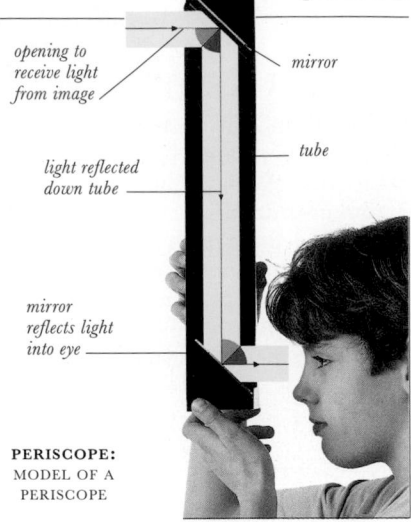

opening to receive light from image

light reflected down tube

mirror

tube

mirror reflects light into eye

PERISCOPE: MODEL OF A PERISCOPE

periscope *n.* ▲ an apparatus with a tube and mirrors or prisms, by which an observer in a trench, submerged submarine, or at the rear of a crowd etc., can see things otherwise out of sight. ▷ SUBMARINE

perish *v.* **1** *intr.* be destroyed; suffer death or ruin. **2 a** *intr.* (esp. of rubber, a rubber object, etc.) deteriorate, rot. **b** *tr. Brit.* cause to deteriorate or rot. **3** *tr.* (in *passive*) *Brit.* suffer from cold or exposure (*were perished standing outside*). □ **perish the thought** an exclamation of horror against an unwelcome idea. [from Latin *perire* 'to pass away']

perishable ● *adj.* liable to perish; subject to decay. ● *n.* a thing, esp. a foodstuff, subject to speedy decay. □ **perishability** *n.*

perisher *n. Brit. slang* an annoying person.

perishing *Brit. colloq.* ● *adj.* **1** confounded. **2** freezing cold, extremely chilly. ● *adv.* confoundedly. □ **perishingly** *adv.*

perissodactyl *Zool.* ● *adj.* ▶ of or relating to the order Perissodactyla of ungulate mammals with one main central toe, or a single toe, on each foot, including horses, rhinoceroses, and tapirs. ● *n.* an animal of this order. ▷ UNGULATE. [from modern Latin *Perissodactyla*, from Greek *perissos* 'uneven' + *daktulos* 'finger, toe']

single toe

PERISSODACTYL: HORSE'S HOOF

peristalsis *n.* ▼ an involuntary muscular wavelike movement by which the contents of the alimentary canal etc. are propelled along. [based on Greek *peristellein* 'to wrap around'] □ **peristaltic** *adj.* **peristaltically** *adv.*

P

PERIPHERAL NERVOUS SYSTEM

The peripheral nervous system is a network of nerves that links the central nervous system (brain and spinal cord) and the rest of the body. It has three divisions: autonomic, sensory, and motor. Autonomic nerve fibres, which may join the autonomic nerve ganglia, regulate involuntary actions, such as heartbeat. Sensory nerve fibres receive external stimuli via sense receptors. Motor nerve fibres initiate the relaxation and contraction of the muscles.

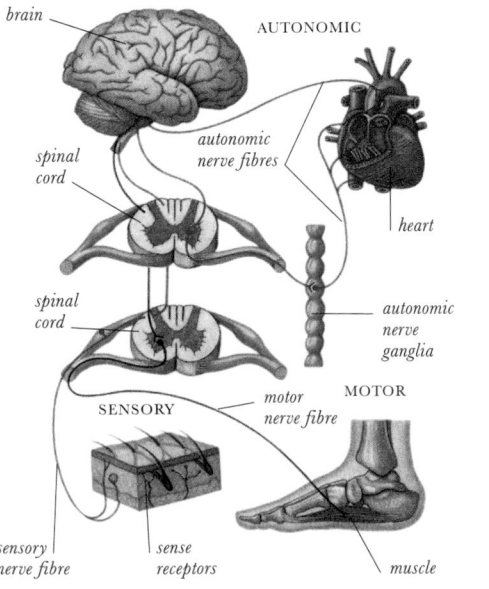

brain

AUTONOMIC

autonomic nerve fibres

spinal cord

heart

spinal cord

autonomic nerve ganglia

MOTOR

motor nerve fibre

SENSORY

STRUCTURE OF THE PERIPHERAL NERVOUS SYSTEM IN THE HUMAN BODY

sensory nerve fibre

sense receptors

muscle

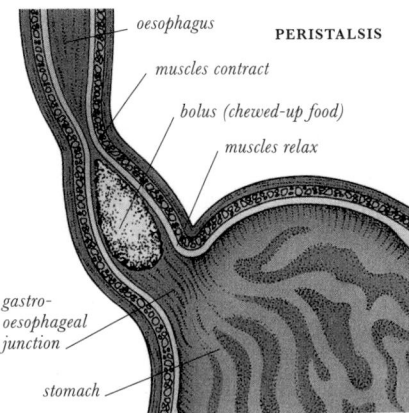

oesophagus

PERISTALSIS

muscles contract

bolus (chewed-up food)

muscles relax

gastro-oesophageal junction

stomach

---

aril   pericarp

seed

PERICARP: CROSS-SECTION OF A LYCHEE SHOWING THE PERICARP

peristyle *n.* a row of columns surrounding a temple, court, cloister, etc.; a space surrounded by columns. [from Greek *peristulon*]

peritoneum *n.* (*pl.* **peritoneums** or **peritonea**) the serous membrane lining the cavity of the abdomen. [Late Latin, from Greek] □ **peritoneal** *adj.*

peritonitis *n.* an inflammatory disease of the peritoneum.

periwig *n.* esp. *hist.* ▼ a wig. [alteration of *peruke*, in same sense] □ **periwigged** *adj.*

PERIWIG:
TWO-HORNED
PERIWIG

periwinkle[1] *n.* ► any plant of the genus *Vinca*, esp. an evergreen trailing plant with blue or white flowers. [from Late Latin *pervinca*]

periwinkle[2] *n.* = WINKLE. [16th-century coinage]

perjure *v.refl. Law* **1** wilfully tell an untruth when on oath. **2** (as **perjured** *adj.*) guilty of or involving perjury. [from Latin *perjurare*] □ **perjurer** *n.*

perjury *n.* (*pl.* **-ies**) *Law* **1** a breach of an oath, esp. the act of wilfully telling an untruth when on oath. **2** the practice of this. [from Latin *perjurium*] □ **perjurious** *adj.*

PERIWINKLE
(*Vinca
difformis*)

perk[1] ● *v.tr.* (often foll. by *up*) raise (one's head etc.) briskly. ● *adj.* perky; pert. □ **perk up 1** recover confidence, courage, life, or zest. **2** restore confidence or courage or liveliness in (esp. another person). **3** smarten up. [Middle English]

perk[2] *n. colloq.* a perquisite. [abbreviation]

perk[3] *v. colloq.* **1** *intr.* (of coffee) percolate, make a bubbling sound in the percolator. **2** *tr.* percolate (coffee).

perky *adj.* (**perkier, perkiest**) **1** self-assertive; saucy; pert. **2** lively; cheerful. □ **perkily** *adv.* **perkiness** *n.*

perlite *n.* a glassy type of vermiculite, expandable to a solid form by heating, used for insulation etc. [French, based on *perle* 'pearl']

perm[1] ● *n.* a permanent wave. ● *v.tr.* give a permanent wave to (a person or a person's hair). [abbreviation]

perm[2] *Brit. colloq.* ● *n.* a permutation. ● *v.tr.* make a permutation of. [abbreviation]

permaculture *n.* the development of agricultural ecosystems intended to be complete and self-sustaining.

permafrost *n.* subsoil which remains below freezing point throughout the year. ▷ TUNDRA

permanent *adj.* lasting, or intended to last or function, indefinitely (opp. TEMPORARY). [from Latin *permanent-* 'remaining to the end'] □ **permanence** *n.* **permanency** *n.* **permanently** *adv.*

permanent magnet *n.* a magnet retaining its magnetic properties in the absence of an inducing field or current.

permanent wave *n.* an artificial wave in the hair, intended to last for some time.

permanent way *n. Brit.* the finished foundation structure of a railway.

permanganate *n. Chem.* any salt of permanganic acid, esp. potassium permanganate.

permanganic acid *n. Chem.* an acid containing heptavalent manganese.

permeable *adj.* capable of being permeated. [from Latin *permeabilis*] □ **permeability** *n.*

permeate *v.* **1** *tr.* penetrate throughout; pervade; saturate. **2** *intr.* (usu. foll. by *through, among,* etc.) diffuse itself. [based on Latin *permeatus* 'permeated'] □ **permeation** *n.*

permethrin *n.* a synthetic pyrethroid used as an insecticide, esp. against disease-carrying insects. [based on *pyrethrin*, found in pyrethrum flowers]

Permian *Geol.* ● *adj.* of or relating to the last period of the Palaeozoic era. ● *n.* this period or system. [based on *Perm*, a province in Russia]

permissible *adj.* allowable. [from medieval Latin *permissibilis*] □ **permissibility** *n.*

permission *n.* (often foll. by *to* + infin.) consent; authorization. [from Latin *permissio*]

permissive *adj.* **1** tolerant; liberal, esp. in sexual matters (*the permissive society*). **2** giving permission. [from medieval Latin *permissivus*] □ **permissively** *adv.* **permissiveness** *n.*

permit ● *v.* /per-**mit**/ (**permitted, permitting**) **1** *tr.* give permission or consent to; authorize (*permit me to say*). **2 a** *tr.* allow; give an opportunity to (*permit the traffic to flow again*). **b** *intr.* give an opportunity (*circumstances permitting*). **3** *intr.* (foll. by *of*) admit; allow for. ● *n.* /per-mit/ a document giving permission. [from Latin *permittere*] □ **permittee** *n.*

permittivity *n. Electr.* a quantity measuring the ability of a substance to store electrical energy in an electric field.

permutate *v.tr.* = PERMUTE.

permutation *n.* **1** an ordered arrangement or grouping of a set of numbers, items, etc. **2** any combination or selection of a specified number of things from a larger group, esp. *Brit.* matches in a football pool. [from Latin *permutatio*] □ **permutational** *adj.*

permute *v.tr.* alter the sequence or arrangement of. [from Latin *permutare* 'to change thoroughly']

pernicious *adj.* destructive; ruinous; fatal. [based on Latin *pernicies* 'ruin'] □ **perniciously** *adv.* **perniciousness** *n.*

pernicious anaemia *n.* a defective formation of red blood cells through a lack of vitamin B_{12} or folic acid.

pernickety *adj. colloq.* **1** fastidious. **2** precise or over-precise. [19th-century Scots]

peroration *n.* the concluding part of a speech, forcefully summing up what has been said.

peroxide ● *n. Chem.* **1 a** = HYDROGEN PEROXIDE. **b** (often *attrib.*) a solution of hydrogen peroxide used to bleach the hair or as an antiseptic. **2** a compound of oxygen with another element containing the greatest possible proportion of oxygen. ● *v.tr.* bleach (the hair) with peroxide.

perpendicular ● *adj.* **1 a** at right angles to the plane of the horizon. **b** (usu. foll. by *to*) Geom. at right angles (to a given line, plane, or surface). **2** upright, vertical. **3** (of a slope etc.) very steep. **4** (**Perpendicular**) *Archit.* ► of the third stage of English Gothic (15th–16th c.) with vertical tracery in large windows. ● *n.* **1** a perpendicular line. **2** (prec. by *the*) a perpendicular line or

orientation (*is out of the perpendicular*). [based on Latin *perpendiculum* 'plumb line'] □ **perpendicularity** *n.* **perpendicularly** *adv.*

perpetrate *v.tr.* commit (a crime, blunder, or anything outrageous). [based on Latin *perpetratus* 'perpetrated'] □ **perpetration** *n.* **perpetrator** *n.*

perpetual *adj.* **1** eternal; lasting for ever or indefinitely. **2** continuous, uninterrupted. **3** frequent, much repeated (*perpetual interruptions*). [from Latin *perpetualis*] □ **perpetually** *adv.*

perpetual motion *n.* the motion of a hypothetical machine which once set in motion would run for ever unless subject to an external force or to wear.

perpetuate *v.tr.* make perpetual. **2** preserve from oblivion. [based on Latin *perpetuatus* 'made continuous'] □ **perpetuation** *n.* **perpetuator** *n.*

perpetuity *n.* (*pl.* **-ies**) **1** the state or quality of being perpetual. **2** a perpetual annuity. **3** a perpetual possession or position. □ **in perpetuity** for ever. [from Latin *perpetuitas*]

perplex *v.tr.* **1** puzzle, bewilder, or disconcert (a person, a person's mind, etc.). **2** complicate or confuse (a matter). [from Latin *perplexus* 'plaited through, intricate'] □ **perplexedly** *adv.* **perplexing** *adj.* **perplexingly** *adv.*

perplexity *n.* (*pl.* **-ies**) **1** the state of being perplexed. **2** a thing which perplexes.

per pro. *abbr.* through the agency of (used in signatures). [Latin *per procurationem*]

■ **Usage** The correct sequence of signatures is A *per pro.* B, where B is signing on behalf of A. The abbreviation *p.p.* is commonly used instead.

perquisite *n.* **1** an extra profit or allowance additional to a main income etc. **2** a customary extra right or privilege. **3** an incidental benefit attached to employment etc. **4** a thing which has served its primary use and to which a subordinate or employee has a customary right. [from Latin *perquisitum* '(thing) diligently sought']

■ **Usage** *Perquisite* is sometimes confused with *prerequisite*, which means 'a thing required as a precondition'.

perry *n.* (*pl.* **-ies**) *Brit.* a drink like cider, made from the fermented juice of pears. [from Latin *pirum* 'pear']

per se /per **say**/ *adv.* by or in itself; intrinsically. [Latin]

persecute *v.tr.* **1** subject (a person etc.) to hostility or ill-treatment, esp. on the grounds of political or religious belief. **2** harass; worry. [based on Latin *persecutus* 'pursued'] □ **persecution** *n.* **persecutor** *n.* **persecutory** *adj.*

persecution complex *n.* (also **persecution mania**) an irrational obsessive fear that others are scheming against one.

perseverance *n.* **1** the steadfast pursuit of an objective. **2** (often foll. by *in*) constant persistence (in a belief etc.). [from Latin *perseverantia*]

persevere *v.intr.* (often foll. by *in, at, with*) continue steadfastly or determinedly; persist. [from Latin *perseverare* 'to persist']

Persian ● *n.* **1 a** a native or inhabitant of ancient or modern Persia (now Iran). **b** a person of Persian descent. **2** the language of ancient Persia or modern Iran. **3** (in full **Persian cat**) a cat of a breed with long silky hair and a thick tail. ▷ CAT. ● *adj.* of or relating to Persia or its people or language. [from medieval Latin]

■ **Usage** The preferred terms for the language (see sense 2 of the noun) are *Iranian* and *Farsi* respectively.

tracery

PERPENDICULAR WINDOW

P

Persian lamb *n.* the silky tightly curled fur of a young karakul, used in clothing.

persiflage /per-si-flah*zh*/ *n.* light raillery, banter. [French]

persimmon *n.* **1** any evergreen tree of the genus *Diospyros* bearing edible orange pulpy fruits. **2** ▶ the fruit of this. [corruption of Algonquian *pessemmins*]

persist *v.intr.* **1** (often foll. by *in*) continue firmly or obstinately (in an opinion or a course of action) esp. despite obstacles, remonstrance, etc. **2** (of a custom, phenomenon, etc.) continue in existence; survive. [from Latin *persistere*]

persistent *adj.* **1** continuing obstinately; persisting. **2** enduring. **3** constantly repeated (*persistent nagging*). **4** *Biol.* (of horns, leaves, etc.) remaining instead of falling off in the normal manner. □ **persistence** *n.* **persistently** *adv.*

PERSIMMON
(*Diospyros virginiana*)

persistent vegetative state *n. Med.* the state of a person whose body is kept functioning by medical means but who manifests no sign of higher brain functions.

person *n.* **1** an individual human being (*a cheerful and forthright person*). **2** the living body of a human being (*hidden about your person*). **3** *Gram.* a category used in the classification of pronouns, verb forms, etc., according to whether they indicate the speaker (**first person**); the addressee (**second person**); a third party (**third person**). **4** (in *comb.*) used to replace *-man* in offices open to either sex (*salesperson*). **5** (in Christianity) God as Father, Son, or Holy Ghost (*three persons in one God*). **6** a type of person who enjoys something specified (*not a party person*). □ **in person** physically present. [from Latin *persona* 'actor's mask, human being']

persona /per-**soh**-nă/ *n.* (*pl.* **personas** or **personae** /-nee/) **1** an aspect of the personality as shown to or perceived by others (opp. ANIMA 1). **2** *Literary Criticism* an author's assumed character in his or her writing. [Latin]

personable *adj.* pleasing in appearance and behaviour. □ **personableness** *n.* **personably** *adv.*

personage *n.* a person, esp. of rank or importance.

persona grata /**grah**-tă/ *n.* (*pl.* **personae gratae** /-tee/) a person, esp. a diplomat, acceptable to certain others. [Latin, literally 'pleasing character']

personal ● *adj.* **1** one's own; individual; private. **2** done or made in person (*made a personal appearance*; *my personal attention*). **3** directed to or concerning an individual (*a personal letter*). **4** referring (esp. in a hostile way) to an individual's private life or concerns (*making personal remarks*; *no need to be personal*). **5** of the body and clothing (*personal hygiene*; *personal appearance*). **6** existing as a person, not as an abstraction or thing (*a personal God*). **7** *Gram.* of or denoting one of the three persons (*personal pronoun*). ● *n.* esp. *N. Amer.* an advertisement or notice in the personal column of a newspaper.

personal ad *n.* esp. *US colloq.* = PERSONAL *n.*

personal column *n.* the part of a newspaper devoted to private advertisements or messages.

personal computer *n.* a computer designed for use by a single individual, esp. in an office or business environment. ▷ COMPUTER

personal equity plan *n. Brit.* a scheme for limited personal investment in shares, unit trusts, etc.

personal identification number *n.* a number allocated to an individual, serving as a password esp. for a cash dispenser, computer, etc.

personality *n.* (*pl.* **-ies**) **1 a** the distinctive character or qualities of a person, often as distinct from others (*an attractive personality*). **b** socially attractive qualities (*was clever but had no personality*). **2** a famous person; a celebrity (*a TV personality*). **3** a person who stands out from others by virtue of his or her character (*is a real personality*). [from Late Latin *personalitas*]

personality cult *n.* the extreme adulation of an individual.

personalize *v.tr.* (also **-ise**) **1** make personal, esp. by marking with one's name etc. **2** personify. □ **personalization** *n.*

personally *adv.* **1** in person (*see to it personally*). **2** for one's own part (*speaking personally*). **3** in a personal manner (*took the criticism personally*).

personal organizer *n.* **1** a loose-leaf notebook with sections for various kinds of information, including a diary etc. **2** a hand-held microcomputer serving the same purpose.

PERSPECTIVE

In the early 15th century, Battista Alberti, a writer and architect, formulated a method of perspective construction that artists, such as Paolo Uccello, could follow. In Alberti's system, the picture surface is imagined as an 'open window' through which a painted world is seen. He showed how a perspectival construction can be created by using parallel lines, known as orthogonals, to represent visual rays that connect the viewer's eye to a spot in the distance. The spot on which all the rays converge is known as the vanishing point, and is positioned opposite the spectator's viewpoint. The single viewpoint meant that the artist could now control and focus the way that the spectator looked at the picture.

P

PERSPECTIVE ANALYSIS OF UCCELLO'S
The Hunt in the Forest

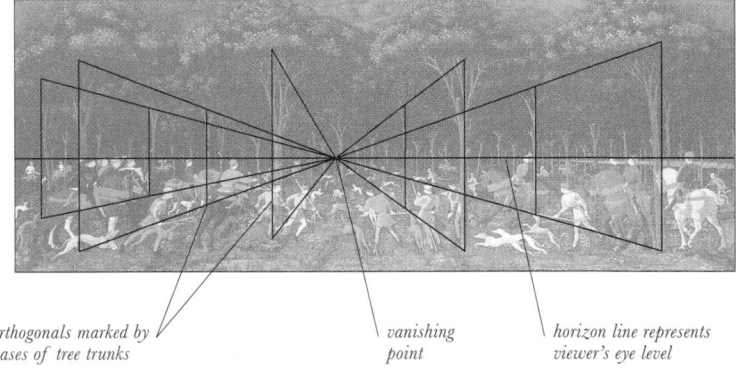

orthogonals marked by
bases of tree trunks

*vanishing
point*

*horizon line represents
viewer's eye level*

The Hunt in the Forest (*c.*1460),
PAOLO UCCELLO

personal pronoun *n.* each of the pronouns (*I, you, he, she, it, we, they, me, him, her, us, them*) comprising a set that shows contrast of person, gender, number, and case.

■ **Usage** Reflexive pronouns (*myself, ourselves,* etc.) and possessive pronouns (*my, your,* etc.) are sometimes included in the category of personal pronouns.

personal property *n. Law* all one's property except land and those interests in land that pass to one's heirs (cf. REAL[1] *adj.* 3).

personal stereo *n.* a small portable audio cassette player, often with radio, or compact disc player, used with lightweight headphones.

persona non grata /grah-tă/ *n.* (*pl. **personae non gratae*** /-tee/) an unacceptable or unwelcome person. [Latin, literally 'non-pleasing character']

personate *v.tr.* = IMPERSONATE. □ **personation** *n.* **personator** *n.*

personification *n.* **1** the act of personifying. **2** (foll. by *of*) a person or thing viewed as a striking example of (a quality etc.) (*the personification of ugliness*).

personify *v.tr.* (**-ies, -ied**) **1** attribute a personal nature to (an abstraction or thing). **2** symbolize (a quality etc.) by a figure in human form. **3** (usu. as **personified** *adj.*) embody (a quality) in one's own person (*has always been kindness personified*). □ **personifier** *n.*

personnel *n.* a body of employees, persons involved in a public undertaking, armed forces, etc. [French, originally as adj. in sense 'personal']

personnel carrier *n.* an armoured vehicle for transporting troops etc.

personnel department *n.* the part of an organization concerned with the appointment, training, and welfare of employees.

person-to-person *attrib.adj.* (of a phone call) booked through the operator to a specified person.

perspective ● *n.* **1 a** ◄ the art of drawing solid objects on a two-dimensional surface so as to give the right impression of relative positions, size, etc. **b** a picture drawn in this way. **2** the apparent relation between visible objects as to position, distance, etc. **3** a mental view of the relative importance of things (*keep the right perspective*). **4** a geographical or imaginary prospect. ● *adj.* of or in perspective. □ **in** (or **out of**) **perspective 1** drawn or viewed according (or not according) to the rules of perspective. **2** correctly (or incorrectly) regarded in terms of relative importance. [Middle English in sense 'science of sight': from medieval Latin *perspectiva ars*] □ **perspectival** *adj.*

perspex *n. Brit. propr.* a tough light transparent acrylic thermoplastic used instead of glass. [based on Latin *perspicere* 'to look through']

perspicacious *adj.* having mental penetration or discernment. [from Latin *perspicax -acis*] □ **perspicaciously** *adv.* **perspicacity** *n.*

■ **Usage** *Perspicacious*, meaning 'having or showing insight', is sometimes confused with *perspicuous*, meaning 'expressing things clearly' or 'clearly expressed'.

perspicuous *adj.* **1** easily understood; clearly expressed. **2** (of a person) expressing things clearly. [Middle English in sense 'transparent': from Latin *perspicuus*] □ **perspicuity** *n.* **perspicuously** *adv.*

■ **Usage** See Usage Note at PERSPICACIOUS.

perspiration *n.* **1** = SWEAT *n.* 1. **2** sweating. [French] □ **perspiratory** *adj.*

perspire *v.* **1** *intr.* sweat or exude perspiration, esp. as the result of heat, exercise, anxiety, etc. **2** *tr.* sweat or exude (fluid etc.). [from Latin *perspirare*]

persuade *v.tr. & refl.* **1** (often foll. by *of*, or *that* + clause) cause (another person or oneself) to believe; convince. **2 a** (often foll. by *to* + infin.) induce (another person or oneself) (*persuaded us to join them*).

b (foll. by *away from*, *down to*, etc.) lure, attract, entice, etc. [from Latin *persuadēre*] □ **persuadable** *adj.* **persuadability** *n.* **persuader** *n.*

persuasion *n.* **1** persuading. **2** persuasiveness. **3** a belief or conviction. **4** a religious belief, or the group or sect holding it. [from Latin *persuasio*]

persuasive *adj.* able to persuade. □ **persuasively** *adv.* **persuasiveness** *n.*

pert *adj.* **1** saucy or impudent, esp. in speech or conduct. **2** (of clothes etc.) neat and suggestive of jauntiness. [from Latin *apertus* 'open'] □ **pertly** *adv.* **pertness** *n.*

pertain *v.intr.* **1** (foll. by *to*) **a** relate or have reference to. **b** belong to as a part or appendage or accessory. **2** (usu. foll. by *to*) be appropriate to. [from Latin *pertinēre*]

pertinacious *adj.* stubborn; persistent; obstinate (in a course of action etc.). [from Latin *pertinax -acis*] □ **pertinaciously** *adv.* **pertinacity** *n.*

pertinent *adj.* **1** (often foll. by *to*) relevant to the matter in hand; apposite. **2** to the point. [from Latin *pertinent-* 'extending, belonging (to)'] □ **pertinence** *n.* **pertinently** *adv.*

perturb *v.tr.* **1** throw into confusion or disorder. **2** disturb mentally; agitate. [from Latin *perturbare*] □ **perturbation** *n.* **perturbingly** *adv.*

peruse *v.tr.* **1** (also *absol.*) read or study, esp. thoroughly or carefully. **2** examine (a person's face etc.) carefully. [Middle English in sense 'to use up'] □ **perusal** *n.* **peruser** *n.*

pervade *v.tr.* **1** spread throughout, permeate. **2** be rife among or through. [from Latin *pervadere*] □ **pervasion** *n.*

pervasive *adj.* **1** pervading. **2** able to pervade. □ **pervasively** *adv.* **pervasiveness** *n.*

perve *slang* ● *n.* (also **perv**) **1** *Brit.* a sexual pervert. **2** *Austral.* an erotic gaze. ● *v.intr.* **1** act like a sexual pervert. **2** (foll. by *at, on*) *Austral.* gaze with erotic interest.

perverse *adj.* **1** (of a person or action) deliberately or stubbornly departing from what is reasonable or required. **2** persistent in error. **3** (of a verdict etc.) against the weight of evidence or the judge's direction. [from Latin *perversus*] □ **perversely** *adv.* **perverseness** *n.* **perversity** *n.* (*pl.* -**ies**).

perversion *n.* **1** an act of perverting; the state of being perverted. **2** a perverted form of an act or thing. **3 a** preference for an abnormal form of sexual activity. **b** such an activity.

pervert ● *v.tr.* /per-**vert**/ **1** turn (a person or thing) aside from its proper use or nature. **2** misapply or misconstrue (words etc.). **3** lead astray (a person, a person's mind, etc.) from right opinion or conduct, or esp. religious belief. **4** (as **perverted** *adj.*) showing perversion. ● *n.* /**per**-vert/ **1** a perverted person. **2** a person showing sexual perversion. [from Latin *pervertere*] □ **pervertedly** *adv.* **perverter** *n.*

pervious *adj.* **1** permeable. **2** (usu. foll. by *to*) **a** affording passage. **b** accessible (to reason etc.). [from Latin *pervius*] □ **perviousness** *n.*

peseta /pě-say-tă/ *n.* the chief monetary unit of Spain. [Spanish, literally 'little weight']

pesky *adj.* (**peskier, peskiest**) esp. *US colloq.* troublesome; confounded; annoying. [18th-century coinage] □ **peskily** *adv.* **peskiness** *n.*

peso /pay-soh/ *n.* (*pl.* -**os**) the chief monetary unit of several Latin American countries and of the Philippines. [Spanish, literally 'weight', from Latin *pensum*]

pessary *n.* (*pl.* -**ies**) *Med.* **1** a device worn in the vagina to support the uterus or as a contraceptive. **2** a vaginal suppository. [based on Greek *pessos* 'oval stone']

pessimism *n.* **1** a tendency to take the worst view or expect the worst outcome. **2** *Philos.* a belief that this world is as bad as it could be or that all things tend to evil. [based on Latin *pessimus* 'worst'] □ **pessimist** *n.* **pessimistic** *adj.* **pessimistically** *adv.*

PEST: SOLOMON'S SEAL SAWFLY LARVAE ATTACKING A PLANT

pest *n.* **1** a troublesome or annoying person or thing. **2** ▲ a destructive animal, esp. an insect which attacks crops, livestock, etc. [from Latin *pestis* 'plague']

pester *v.tr.* trouble or annoy, esp. with persistent requests. [from French *empestrer* 'to encumber'] □ **pesterer** *n.*

pesticide *n.* a substance used for destroying insects or other organisms harmful to cultivated plants or to animals. □ **pesticidal** *adj.*

pestiferous *adj.* noxious; pestilent. [from Latin *pestifer*]

pestilence *n.* a fatal epidemic disease, esp. bubonic plague. [from Latin *pestilentia*]

pestilent *adj.* **1** destructive to life, deadly. **2** *colloq.* troublesome; annoying. [based on Latin *pestis* 'plague']

pestilential *adj.* **1** of or relating to pestilence. **2** dangerous; troublesome; pestilent. □ **pestilentially** *adv.*

pestle *n.* ▼ a club-shaped instrument for pounding substances in a mortar. [from Latin *pistillum*]

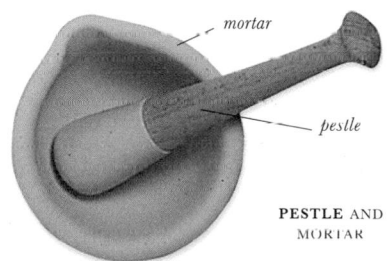

PESTLE AND MORTAR

pesto *n.* an Italian sauce of crushed basil leaves, pine nuts, garlic, Parmesan cheese, and olive oil, usu. served with pasta. [Italian, literally 'pounded']

pet[1] ● *n.* **1** a domestic or tamed animal kept for pleasure or companionship. **2** a darling, a favourite (often as a term of endearment). ● *attrib.adj.* **1** kept as a pet (*pet lamb*). **2** of or for pet animals (*pet food*). **3** often *joc.* favourite or particular (*my pet hate is filling in forms*). **4** expressing fondness or familiarity (*pet form*). ● *v.tr.* (**petted, petting**) **1** treat as a pet. **2** (also *absol.*) fondle, esp. erotically. [16th-century Scots & northern English dialect]

pet[2] *n.* a feeling of petty resentment or ill humour (esp. *be in a pet*). [16th-century coinage]

petal *n.* each of the parts of the corolla of a flower. ▷ FLOWER. [from Greek *petalon* 'leaf'] □ **petaline** *adj.* **petalled** *adj.* (also in *comb.*). **petal-like** *adj.* **petaloid** *adj.*

petard *n. hist.* a small bomb used to blast down a door etc. □ **hoist with** (or **by**) **one's own petard** affected adversely by one's schemes against others. [from French *pétard*]

peter *v.intr.* (foll. by *out*) (originally of a vein of ore etc.) diminish, come to an end. [19th-century coinage]

P

P

Peter Pan *n.* a person who retains youthful features, or who is immature. [hero of J. M. Barrie's play of the same name (1904)]

petersham *n.* thick corded silk ribbon used for stiffening in dressmaking etc. [named after Lord *Petersham*, English army officer, 1790–1851]

pethidine *n.* esp. *Brit.* a synthetic analgesic drug used esp. in childbirth.

petiole *n.* ◀ the slender stalk joining a leaf to a stem. [from Latin *petiolus* 'little foot, stalk'] □ **petiolar** *adj.* **petiolate** *adj.*

petit bourgeois /pet-i/ *n.* (*pl.* **petits bourgeois** *pronunc.* same) a member of the lower middle classes. [French, literally 'little citizen']

petite /pĕ-**teet**/ *adj.* (of a woman) of small and dainty build. [French]

petite bourgeoisie *n.* the lower middle classes. [French]

PETIOLE OF A COMMON MULBERRY LEAF

petiole

petit four /pet-i **for**/ *n.* (*pl.* **petits fours**) a very small fancy cake, biscuit, or sweet. [French, literally 'little oven']

petition ● *n.* **1** a supplication or request. **2** a formal written request, esp. one signed by many people, appealing to authority in some cause. **3** *Law* an application to a court for a writ etc. ● *v.* **1** *tr.* make or address a petition to (*petition your MP*). **2** *intr.* (often foll. by *for, to*) appeal earnestly or humbly. [from Latin *petitio*] □ **petitionary** *adj.* **petitioner** *n.*

petit mal /pĕ-ti **mal**/ *n.* a mild form of epilepsy with only momentary loss of consciousness (often *attrib.: petit mal epilepsy*). [French, literally 'little sickness']

petit point /pĕ-ti **pwahng**/ *n.* **1** embroidery on canvas using small stitches. **2** tent stitch. [French, literally 'little point']

petits pois /pet-i **pwah**/ *n.pl.* small green peas. [French]

petrel *n.* any of various seabirds of the family Procellariidae or Hydrobatidae, usu. flying far from land. ▷ SEABIRD. [17th-century coinage]

Petri dish *n.* a shallow covered dish used for the culture of bacteria etc. [named after J. R. *Petri*, German bacteriologist, 1852–1921]

petrify *v.* (**-ies**, **-ied**) **1** *tr.* paralyse with fear, astonishment, etc. **2** *tr.* ▼ change (organic matter) into a stony substance. **3** *intr.* become like stone. [based on Latin *petra* 'rock'] □ **petrifaction** *n.*

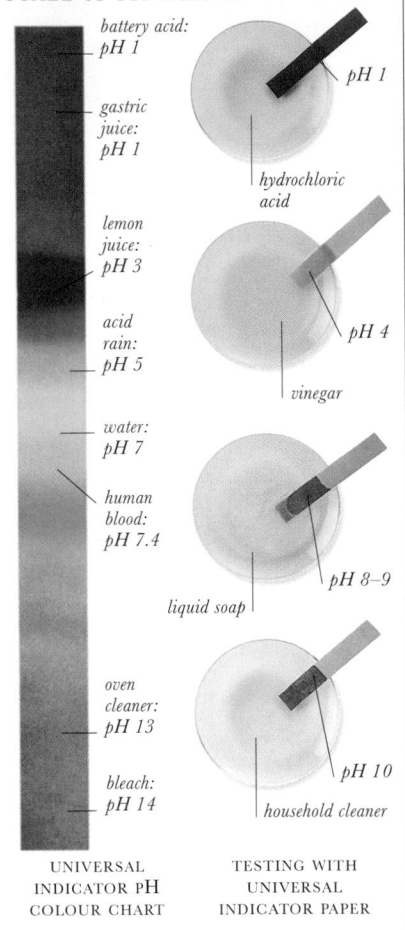

petrified egg

petrified nest

PETRIFY: PETRIFIED BIRD'S NEST

petro- *comb. form* **1** rock. **2** petroleum. [from Greek *petros* 'stone' or *petra* 'rock']

petrochemical ● *n.* a substance obtained from petroleum or natural gas. ● *adj.* of or relating to petrochemicals.

petrodollar *n.* a notional unit of currency earned by a country exporting petroleum.

petrol *n. Brit.* **1** refined petroleum used as a fuel in motor vehicles, aircraft, etc. **2** (*attrib.*) concerned

with the supply of petrol (*petrol pump; petrol station*). [from medieval Latin *petroleum*]

petrol bomb *n. Brit.* a simple bomb made of a petrol-filled bottle and a wick.

petroleum *n.* a hydrocarbon oil found in the upper strata of the Earth, refined for use as a fuel for heating, lighting, and internal-combustion engines, for dry-cleaning etc. [medieval Latin]

petroleum jelly *n.* a translucent solid mixture of hydrocarbons used as a lubricant, ointment, etc.

petrology *n.* the study of the origin, structure, composition, etc., of rocks. □ **petrological** *adj.* **petrologist** *n.*

petticoat *n.* a woman's or girl's undergarment in the form of a skirt or a skirt and bodice. [Middle English, from *petty coat*] □ **petticoated** *adj.*

pettifog *v.intr.* (**pettifogged, pettifogging**) **1** practise legal deception or trickery. **2** quibble or wrangle about petty points.

pettifogging *adj.* **1** mean, shifty. **2** petty, quibbling. [based on archaic *fogger* 'underhand dealer']

pettish *adj.* peevish, petulant; easily put out. □ **pettishly** *adv.* **pettishness** *n.*

petty *adj.* (**pettier, pettiest**) **1** unimportant; trivial. **2** mean, small-minded; contemptible. **3** minor; inferior; on a small scale (*petty princes*). **4** *Law* (of a crime) of lesser importance (*petty larceny*). [Middle English] □ **pettily** *adv.* **pettiness** *n.*

petty bourgeois *n.* = PETIT BOURGEOIS.

petty bourgeoisie *n.* = PETITE BOURGEOISIE.

petty cash *n.* money from or for small items of receipt or expenditure.

petty officer *n.* a naval NCO.

petty treason see TREASON 2.

petulant *adj.* peevishly impatient or irritable. [from Latin *petulans petulant-* 'insolent, wanton'] □ **petulance** *n.* **petulantly** *adv.*

petunia *n.* ◀ any plant of the genus *Petunia* with white, purple, red, etc., funnel-shaped flowers. [based on South American Indian *pety* 'tobacco', to which these plants are related]

PETUNIA CULTIVAR

pew *n.* **1** (in a church) a long bench with a back; an enclosed compartment. **2** *Brit. colloq.* a seat (esp. *take a pew*). [originally usu. raised and enclosed for particular worshippers: based on Latin *podia* 'podia']

pewit var. of PEEWIT.

pewter *n.* **1** a grey alloy of tin with copper and antimony (formerly, tin and lead). **2** utensils made of this. [from Old French *peutre*] □ **pewterer** *n.*

peyote /pay-**oh**-ti/ *n.* **1** a Mexican cactus, *Lophophora williamsii*, having no spines and button-like tops when dried. **2** a hallucinogenic drug containing mescaline prepared from this. [from Aztec *peyotl*]

pfennig *n.* **1** a German monetary unit, equal to one-hundredth of a mark. **2** a coin of this value. [German]

PG *abbr.* **1** (of films) classified as suitable for children subject to parental guidance. **2** paying guest.

PGCE *abbr.* Postgraduate Certificate in Education.

pH *n. Chem.* ▲ a logarithm of the reciprocal of the hydrogen ion concentration in moles per litre of a solution, giving a measure of its acidity or alkalinity. [German, from *Potenz* 'power' + *H*, symbol for hydrogen]

phaeton *n.* **1** a light open four-wheeled carriage, usu. drawn by a pair of horses. **2** *US* a vintage touring car. [from Greek *Phaethōn*, allowed to drive his father's sun-chariot, with disastrous results]

phagocyte *n.* ▶ a type of cell capable of engulfing

pH

The concentration of hydrogen ions in a solution is known as its pH. This value gives an indication of the acidity or alkalinity of a substance. The pH value can be determined by the use of indicators, such as universal indicator paper, which contain compounds that change colour over a certain pH range. A pH value may fall anywhere on a scale from 0 (strongly acidic) to 14 (strongly alkaline), with a value of 7 representing neutrality.

SCALE OF pH VALUES

battery acid: pH 1
gastric juice: pH 1
lemon juice: pH 3
acid rain: pH 5
water: pH 7
human blood: pH 7.4
oven cleaner: pH 13
bleach: pH 14

pH 1
hydrochloric acid

pH 4
vinegar

pH 8–9
liquid soap

pH 10
household cleaner

UNIVERSAL INDICATOR pH COLOUR CHART

TESTING WITH UNIVERSAL INDICATOR PAPER

and absorbing foreign matter, esp. a leucocyte ingesting bacteria in the body. [based on Greek *phagein* 'to eat'] □ **phagocytic** *adj.*

phalanger *n.* any of various arboreal marsupials of the family Phalangeridae, including brush-tailed possums. [from Greek *phalaggion* 'spider's web', from the webbed toes of their hind feet]

phalanx *n.* (*pl.* **phalanxes** or **phalanges** /fă-**lan**-jeez/) **1** a set of people etc. forming a compact mass, or banded together for a common purpose. **2** *Gk Antiq.* a line of battle, esp. a body of infantry drawn up in close order. [from Greek *phalanx*]

phalli *pl.* of PHALLUS.

phallic *adj.* of, relating to, or resembling a phallus. [from Greek *phallikos*] □ **phallically** *adv.*

phallocentric *adj.* centred on the phallus or on male attitudes. □ **phallocentrism** *n.*

phallus *n.* (*pl.* **phalli** or **phalluses**) **1** the (esp. erect) penis. **2** an image of this as a symbol of generative power in nature. [from Greek *phallos*] □ **phallicism** *n.* **phallism** *n.*

phantasize var. of FANTASIZE.

phantasm *n.* an illusion; a phantom. [based on Greek *phantazein* 'to make visible'] □ **phantasmal** *adj.* **phantasmic** *adj.*

phantasmagoria *n.* a shifting series of real or imaginary figures as seen in a dream. □ **phantasmagoric** *adj.* **phantasmagorical** *adj.*

phantasy var. of FANTASY.

phantom ● *n.* **1** a ghost; an apparition; a spectre. **2** a form without substance or reality; a mental illusion. ● *adj.* merely apparent; illusory. [related to PHANTASM]

phantom circuit *n.* an arrangement of telegraph or other electrical wires equivalent to an extra circuit.

phantom limb *n.* a continuing sensation of the presence of a limb which has been amputated.

phantom pregnancy *n.* Med. the symptoms of pregnancy in a person not actually pregnant.

Pharaoh /fair-oh/ *n.* **1** the ruler of ancient Egypt. **2** the title of this ruler. [based on Egyptian *pr-ʿo* 'great house'] □ **Pharaonic** *adj.*

Pharaoh's serpent *n.* an indoor firework burning and uncoiling in serpentine form.

Pharisee *n.* **1** a member of an ancient Jewish sect, distinguished by strict observance of the traditional and written law. **2** a self-righteous person. [based on Hebrew *pārûš* 'separated'] □ **Pharisaic** *adj.* **Pharisaical** *adj.* **Pharisaism** *n.*

pharmaceutical *adj.* **1** of or engaged in pharmacy. **2** of the use or sale of medicinal drugs. [from Greek *pharmakeutikos*] □ **pharmaceutically** *adv.* **pharmaceutics** *n.*

pharmacist *n.* a person qualified to prepare and dispense drugs.

pharmacology *n.* the branch of medicine that deals with the uses, effects, and modes of action of drugs. [based on Greek *pharmakon* 'drug'] □ **pharmacological** *adj.* **pharmacologically** *adv.* **pharmacologist** *n.*

pharmacopoeia /far-mă-kŏ-pee-ă/ *n.* **1** a book containing a list of drugs with directions for use. **2** a stock of drugs. [from Greek *pharmakopoiia* 'art of preparing drugs'] □ **pharmacopoeial** *adj.*

pharmacy *n.* (*pl.* **-ies**) **1** the preparation and the (esp. medicinal) dispensing of drugs. **2** a pharmacist's shop. [from Greek *pharmakeia* 'practice of the druggist']

pharynx *n.* (*pl.* **pharynges** /fă-rin-jeez/) *Anat.* & *Zool.* ▶ a membrane-lined cavity behind the nose and mouth, connecting them to the oesophagus. [from Greek *pharugx*] □ **pharyngeal** *adj.* **pharyngitis** *n.*

PHARYNX

The pharynx is a muscular passage lined with mucous membrane that extends from the nasal cavity to the oesophagus. The upper part, the nasopharynx, connects to the ear via the Eustachian tube and acts as an air passage. The oropharynx, a passage for air and food, lies between the soft palate and the upper edge of the epiglottis. The laryngopharynx lies below the epiglottis and opens into both the larynx for breathing and the oesophagus for swallowing.

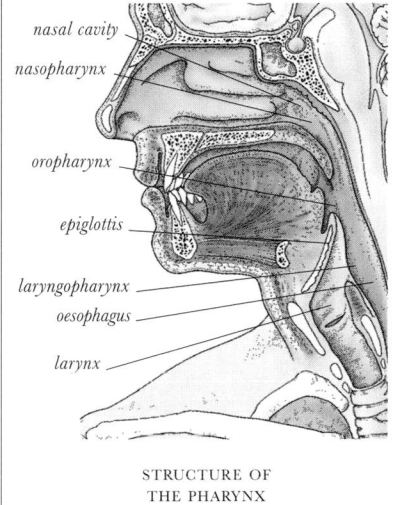

nasal cavity
nasopharynx
oropharynx
epiglottis
laryngopharynx
oesophagus
larynx

STRUCTURE OF
THE PHARYNX

phase ● *n.* **1** a distinct period or stage in a process of change or development. **2** each of the aspects of the Moon or a planet, according to the amount of its illumination, esp. the new Moon, the first quarter, the full Moon, and the last quarter. **3** *Physics* a stage in a periodically recurring sequence, esp. of alternating electric currents or light vibrations. ● *v.tr.* carry out (a programme etc.) in phases or stages. □ **in phase** having the same phase at the same time. **out of phase** not in phase. **phase in** (or **out**) bring gradually into (or out of) use. [from Greek *phasis* 'appearance'] □ **phasic** *adj.*

phatic *adj.* (of speech etc.) used to convey general sociability rather than to communicate a specific meaning, e.g. 'nice morning, isn't it?'. [based on Greek *phatos* 'spoken']

Ph.D. *abbr.* Doctor of Philosophy. [Latin *philosophiae doctor*]

pheasant *n.* ◀ any of several long-tailed game birds of the family Phasianidae. [from Greek *phasianos* '(bird) of *Phasis*', a river in Asia Minor]

PHEASANT: GOLDEN PHEASANT
(*Chrysolophus pictus*)

pheasantry *n.* (*pl.* **-ies**) a place where pheasants are reared or kept.

phenacetin *n.* an acetyl derivative of phenol used to treat fever etc.

phencyclidine *n.* a drug used as a veterinary anaesthetic and as a hallucinogen.

pheno- *comb. form* **1** *Chem.* derived from benzene (*phenol*). **2** showing (*phenotype*). [based on Greek *phainein* 'to show', with reference to substance used for illumination]

phenobarbitone *n.* (*US* **phenobarbital**) a narcotic and sedative barbiturate drug used esp. to treat epilepsy.

phenol *n.* *Chem.* **1** a white crystalline solid, used in dilute form as an antiseptic and disinfectant. **2** any hydroxyl derivative of an aromatic hydrocarbon. [from French *phénole*] □ **phenolic** *adj.*

phenolphthalein /fee-nolf-thal-een/ *n.* *Chem.* a white crystalline solid used in solution as an acid–base indicator and medicinally as a laxative. [based on PHENOL and NAPHTHALENE]

phenom *n.* US *colloq.* an unusually gifted person.

phenomena *pl.* of PHENOMENON.

phenomenal *adj.* **1** of the nature of a phenomenon. **2** extraordinary, remarkable. □ **phenomenally** *adv.*

phenomenology *n.* *Philos.* **1** the science of phenomena as distinct from that of being (ontology). **2** a philosophical approach concentrating on the study of consciousness and the objects of direct experience. □ **phenomenological** *adj.* **phenomenologically** *adv.* **phenomenologist** *n.*

phenomenon *n.* (*pl.* **phenomena**) **1** a fact or occurrence that appears or is perceived, esp. one of which the cause is in question. **2** a remarkable person or thing. [from Greek *phainomenon*, literally '(thing) appearing']

■ **Usage** The plural form of *phenomenon*, *phenomena*, is often used mistakenly for the singular. This should be avoided.

phenotype *n.* *Biol.* a set of observable characteristics of an individual or group resulting from the interaction of its genotype with its environment. [from German *Phaenotypus*] □ **phenotypic** *adj.* **phenotypically** *adv.*

pheromone *n.* a substance secreted and released by an animal for detection and response by another usu. of the same species. [based on Greek *pherein* 'to convey' + HORMONE] □ **pheromonal** *adj.*

phew *int.* an expression of impatience, discomfort, relief, astonishment, or disgust.

phi *n.* the twenty-first letter of the Greek alphabet (Φ, φ). [Greek]

phial *n.* a small glass bottle. [from Greek *phialē*, a broad flat vessel]

phil- var. of PHILO-.

philadelphus *n.* a highly-scented deciduous flowering shrub of the genus *Philadelphus*, esp. the mock orange. [from Greek *philadelphon*]

P

PHAGOCYTE

A phagocyte is a cell that can surround, engulf, and digest micro-organisms (such as viruses), foreign particles that have entered the body (such as dust inhaled into the lungs), and cellular debris. Phagocytes form part of the body's immune system and are found in the blood, spleen, lymph nodes, alveoli, and elsewhere. Some types of white blood cell are 'free' phagocytes, able to wander through tissue and absorb micro-organisms.

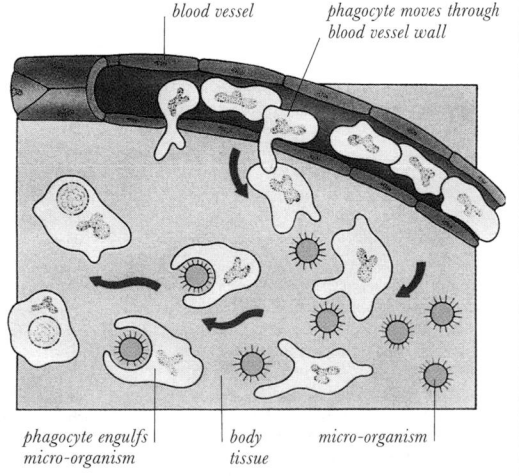

blood vessel
phagocyte moves through
blood vessel wall

CROSS-SECTION OF A HUMAN
BLOOD VESSEL AND TISSUE

phagocyte engulfs
micro-organism

body
tissue

micro-organism

philander v.intr. flirt or have casual affairs with women. [earlier in noun sense 'lover': from Greek *philandros* 'fond of men'] □ **philanderer** n.

philanthropic adj. loving one's fellow men; benevolent. □ **philanthropically** adv.

philanthropy n. **1** a love of humankind. **2** practical benevolence. □ **philanthropist** n.

philately n. the collection and study of postage stamps. [from French *philatélie*] □ **philatelic** adj. **philatelically** adv. **philatelist** n.

-phile comb. form forming nouns and adjectives denoting fondness for what is specified (*bibliophile*; *Francophile*). [from Greek *philos* 'dear, loving']

philharmonic adj. **1** fond of music. **2** used characteristically in the names of orchestras, choirs, etc. (*Royal Philharmonic Orchestra*). [from Italian *filarmonico*]

-philia comb. form **1** denoting fondness or love for what is specified (*necrophilia*). **2** denoting undue inclination (*haemophilia*). [Greek] □ **-philiac** comb. form forming nouns and adjectives. **-philic** comb. form forming adjectives. **-philous** comb. form forming adjectives.

philippic n. a bitter verbal attack. [from Greek *philippikos*, name of Demosthenes' speeches against Philip II of Macedon]

Philistine ● n. **1** a member of a people in ancient Palestine. **2** (usu. **philistine**) a person who is hostile or indifferent to culture. ● adj. (usu. **philistine**) hostile or indifferent to culture. [from Hebrew *p'lištī*] □ **philistinism** n.

Phillips n. (usu. attrib.) propr. denoting a screw with a cross-shaped slot, or a corresponding screwdriver. [name of the original US manufacturer]

philo- comb. form (also **phil-** before a vowel or h) denoting a liking for what is specified.

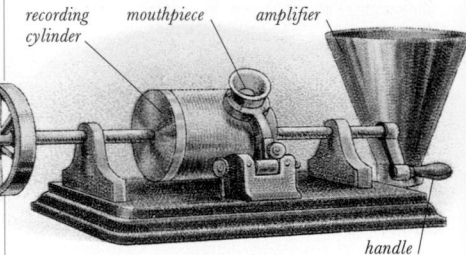

PHILODENDRON
(*Philodendron erubescens* 'Red Emerald')

philodendron n. (pl. **philodendrons** or **philodendra**) ◄ a tropical American climbing plant of the genus *Philodendron* (arum family). [based on Greek *dendron* 'tree']

philology n. **1** the science of language, esp. in its historical and comparative aspects. **2** the love of learning and literature. □ **philological** adj. **philologically** adv. **philologist** n.

philosopher n. **1** a person engaged or learned in philosophy or a branch of it. **2** a person who shows philosophic calmness in trying circumstances. [from Greek *philosophos*]

philosophers' stone n. (also **philosopher's stone**) the supreme object of alchemy, a substance supposed to change other metals into gold or silver.

philosophical adj. (also **philosophic**) **1** of or according to philosophy. **2** skilled in or devoted to philosophy (*philosophical society*). **3** wise; serene; temperate. **4** calm in adverse circumstances. □ **philosophically** adv.

philosophize v. (also **-ise**) **1** intr. reason like a philosopher. **2** intr. moralize. **3** intr. speculate; theorize. **4** tr. render philosophic. □ **philosophizer** n.

philosophy n. (pl. **-ies**) **1** the use of reason and argument in seeking truth and knowledge of reality, esp. of the causes and nature of things and of the principles governing existence. **2 a** a particular system or set of beliefs reached by this. **b** a personal rule of life. **3** advanced learning in general (*doctor of philosophy*). **4** serenity; calmness. [based on Greek *sophos* 'wise']

philtre n. (US **philter**) a drink supposed to excite sexual love in the drinker. [from Greek *philtron*]

phlebitis n. inflammation of a vein. [based on Greek *phleps phlebos* 'vein'] □ **phlebitic** adj.

phlegm flem n. **1** the thick viscous substance secreted by the mucous membranes of the respiratory passages, discharged by coughing. **2** phlegmatic character or behaviour. **3** hist. one of the four bodily humours, characterized as cold and moist, and associated with a calm, stolid or apathetic temperament (see HUMOUR n. 4). [from Greek *phlegma* 'inflammation'] □ **phlegmy** adj.

phlegmatic adj. stolidly calm; unexcitable. □ **phlegmatically** adv.

phloem n. Bot. the tissue conducting food material in plants. ▷ STEM. [from Greek *phloos* 'bark']

phlogiston n. hist. a substance formerly supposed to exist in all combustible bodies, and to be released in combustion. [based on Greek *phlogizein* 'to set on fire']

phlox n. any cultivated plant of the genus *Phlox*, with clusters of esp. white, purple, or red flowers. [Latin, from Greek]

-phobe comb. form forming nouns and adjectives denoting a person having a fear or dislike of what is specified (*xenophobe*). [from Greek *phobos* 'fear']

phobia n. an abnormal or morbid fear or aversion. [-PHOBIA used as a separate word] □ **phobic** adj. & n.

-phobia comb. form forming nouns denoting a fear or dislike of what is specified (*agoraphobia*; *xenophobia*). [Latin, from Greek] □ **-phobic** comb. form forming adjectives.

Phoenician /fĕ-neesh-ăn/ ● n. a member of a Semitic people of ancient Phoenicia in S. Syria or of its colonies. ● adj. of or relating to Phoenicia. [from Greek *Phoinikē* 'Phoenicia']

phoenix /fee-niks/ n. **1** a mythical bird, the only one of its kind, that burnt itself on a funeral pyre and rose from the ashes with renewed youth. **2** a unique person or thing. [from Greek *phoinix* 'Phoenician, purple, phoenix']

phone n. & v. = TELEPHONE.

-phone comb. form forming nouns and adjectives meaning: **1** an instrument using or connected with sound (*telephone*; *xylophone*). **2** a person who uses a specified language (*anglophone*). [from Greek *phōnē* 'voice, sound']

phone book n. = TELEPHONE DIRECTORY.

phonecard n. esp. Brit. a card containing prepaid units for use with a cardphone.

phone-in n. a broadcast programme during which the listeners or viewers telephone the studio and participate.

phoneme n. any of the units of sound in a specified language that distinguish one word from another (e.g. *p*, *b*, *d*, *t* in the English words pad, pat, bad, bat). [from Greek *phōnēma* 'sound, speech'] □ **phonemic** adj. **phonemics** n.

phonetic adj. **1** representing vocal sounds. **2** (of spelling etc.) having a direct correspondence between symbols and sounds. **3** of or relating to phonetics. [from Greek *phōnētikos*] □ **phonetically** adv.

phonetics n.pl. (usu. treated as sing.) **1** vocal sounds. **2** the study of these. □ **phonetician** n.

phoney (also **phony**) colloq. ● adj. (**phonier**, **phoniest**) **1** sham; counterfeit. **2** fictitious. ● n. (pl. **-eys** or **-ies**) a phoney person or thing. [19th-century coinage] □ **phonily** adv. **phoniness** n.

phonic ● adj. of sound; of vocal sounds. ● n. (in pl.) a method of teaching reading based on sounds. [based on Greek *phōnē* 'voice'] □ **phonically** adv.

phono attrib.adj. designating a type of plug (and the corresponding socket) used with audio and video equipment, in which one conductor is cylindrical and the other is a central part that extends beyond it.

phono- comb. form denoting sound. [from Greek *phōnē* 'voice, sound']

phonograph n. **1** Brit. ▼ an early form of gramophone using cylinders and able to record as well as reproduce sound. **2** N. Amer. a gramophone.

PHONOGRAPH DESIGNED BY
THOMAS EDISON (1877)

phonology n. the study of sounds in a language. □ **phonological** adj. **phonologically** adv. **phonologist** n.

phonon n. Physics a quantum of sound or elastic vibrations.

phony var. of PHONEY.

phooey int. colloq. an expression of disgust or disbelief.

phoresy n. Zool. an association in which one organism is carried by another, without being a parasite. □ **phoretic** adj. [based on Greek *phorēsis* being carried]

phormium n. a fibre-yielding New Zealand plant of the genus *Phormium* (agave family). [from Greek *phormion*, a species of plant]

phosgene n. a colourless poisonous gas (carbonyl chloride), formerly used in warfare. [based on Greek *phōs* 'light', sunlight being used in the original production process]

phosphate n. any salt or ester of phosphoric acid, esp. used as a fertilizer. [French, based on *phosphore* 'phosphorus'] □ **phosphatic** adj.

phosphine n. Chem. a colourless foul-smelling gas, phosphorus trihydride. □ **phosphinic** adj.

phosphite n. Chem. any salt or ester of phosphorous acid.

phospho- comb. form denoting phosphorus.

phospholipid n. Biochem. any lipid consisting of a phosphate group and one or more fatty acids, including those forming cell membranes.

phosphor n. **1** = PHOSPHORUS. **2** a synthetic fluorescent or phosphorescent substance. [from Latin *phosphorus* 'phosphorus']

phosphor bronze n. a tough hard bronze alloy containing a small amount of phosphorus, used esp. for bearings.

phosphorescence n. **1** radiation similar to fluorescence but detectable after excitation ceases. **2** the emission of light without combustion or perceptible heat. □ **phosphoresce** v.intr. **phosphorescent** adj.

phosphoric adj. **1** Chem. containing phosphorus, esp. in its higher valency of five. **2** phosphorescent.

phosphoric acid n. a crystalline solid which has many commercial uses.

phosphorite n. a non-crystalline form of apatite.

phosphorous adj. **1** Chem. containing phosphorus, esp. in its lower valency of three (*phosphorous acid*). **2** phosphorescent.

phosphorus n. Chem. a non-metallic element existing in allotropic forms, esp. as a whitish waxy substance burning slowly at ordinary temperatures and so luminous in the dark, and a reddish form used in matches, fertilizers, etc. [from Greek *phōsphoros* 'the morning star']

phossy jaw n. colloq. hist. gangrene of the jawbone caused by phosphorous poisoning.

P

photic *adj.* **1** of or relating to light. **2** (of ocean layers) reached by sunlight.

photism *n.* a hallucinatory sensation or vision of light.

photo ● *n.* (*pl.* **-os**) = PHOTOGRAPH *n.* ● *v.tr.* (**-oes, -oed**) = PHOTOGRAPH *v.*

photo- *comb. form* denoting: **1** light (*photosensitive*). **2** photography (*photocomposition*). [from Greek *phōs, phōtos* 'light', or abbreviation of PHOTOGRAPH]

photobiology *n.* the study of the effects of light on living organisms.

photocall *n. Brit.* an occasion on which theatrical performers, famous personalities, etc., pose for photographers by arrangement.

photocell *n.* = PHOTOELECTRIC CELL.

photochemical *adj.* of or relating to the chemical action of light.

photochemical smog *n.* a condition of the atmosphere caused by the action of sunlight on pollutants, resulting in haze and high levels of ozone and nitrogen oxide.

photochemistry *n.* the study of the chemical effects of light.

photocomposition *n.* = FILMSETTING.

photoconductivity *n.* conductivity caused by the action of light. □ **photoconductive** *adj.*

photocopier *n.* ▼ a machine for producing photocopies.

photocopy ● *n.* (*pl.* **-ies**) a photographic copy of printed or written material. ● *v.tr.* (**-ies, -ied**) make a photocopy of. □ **photocopiable** *adj.*

photodegradable *adj.* capable of being decomposed by the action of light, esp. sunlight.

photodiode *n.* a semiconductor diode responding electrically to illumination.

photoelectric *adj.* marked by or using emissions of electrons from substances exposed to light. □ **photoelectricity** *n.*

photoelectric cell *n.* a device using a photoelectric effect to generate current.

photoelectron *n.* an electron emitted from an atom by interaction with a photon, esp. one emitted from a solid surface by the action of light.

photo finish *n.* a close finish of a race or contest, esp. one where the winner is distinguishable only from a photograph.

photofit *n. Brit.* a reconstructed picture of a person (esp. one sought by the police) made from composite photographs of facial features.

photogenic *adj.* having an appearance that looks pleasing in photographs.

PHOTOSYNTHESIS

Photosynthesis takes place in chloroplasts, the microscopic green organelles inside the cells of green plant tissue, especially leaves. During photosynthesis, a plant uses the energy in sunlight to carry out a chain of chemical reactions. It makes the food substance glucose, which is the energy source for the whole plant, from molecules of carbon dioxide and water. Oxygen is formed as a by-product. Photosynthesis is vital to life on Earth, since all animals are directly or indirectly dependent on plants for food.

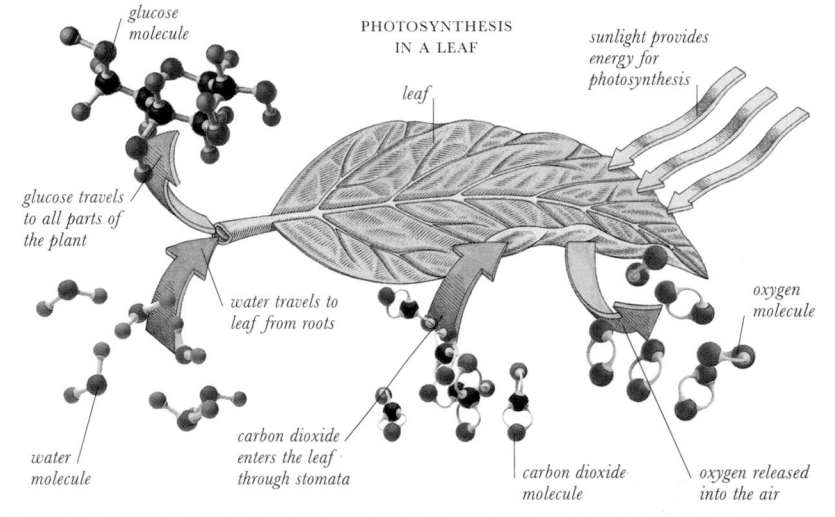

PHOTOSYNTHESIS IN A LEAF

glucose molecule

leaf

sunlight provides energy for photosynthesis

glucose travels to all parts of the plant

water travels to leaf from roots

water molecule

carbon dioxide enters the leaf through stomata

carbon dioxide molecule

oxygen molecule

oxygen released into the air

photograph ● *n.* a picture formed by means of the chemical action of light or other radiation on sensitive film. ● *v.tr.* (also *absol.*) take a photograph of. □ **photographable** *adj.* **photographer** *n.* **photographic** *adj.* **photographically** *adv.*

photographic memory *n.* a memory allowing the recall of visual images with great accuracy.

photography *n.* the taking and processing of photographs.

photogravure *n.* **1** an image produced from a photographic negative transferred to a metal plate and etched in. **2** this process. [French, based on *gravure* 'engraving']

photojournalism *n.* the art or practice of relating news by photographs. □ **photojournalist** *n.*

photolithography *n.* (also **photolitho**) lithography using plates made photographically.

□ **photolithographic** *adj.* **photolithographically** *adv.*

photometer /foh-tom-i-ter/ *n.* an instrument for measuring light. □ **photometric** *adj.* **photometry** *n.*

photomicrograph *n.* a photograph of an image produced by a microscope. □ **photomicrography** *n.*

photomontage *n.* **1** the technique of constructing a montage from photographic images. **2** a composite picture so produced.

photomultiplier *n.* an instrument containing a photocell and a series of electrodes, used to detect and amplify the light from very faint sources.

photon *n.* a quantum of electromagnetic radiation energy, proportional to the frequency of radiation. [from Greek *phōs phōtos* 'light']

photonovel *n.* a novel told in a series of photographs with superimposed speech bubbles.

photo-offset *n.* offset printing with plates made photographically.

photo op *n. N. Amer. colloq.* = PHOTO OPPORTUNITY.

photo opportunity *n.* = PHOTOCALL.

photophobia *n.* an abnormal fear of or aversion to light. □ **photophobic** *adj.*

photoreceptor *n.* a structure in a living organism, esp. a sensory cell or sense organ, that responds to incident light.

photosensitive *adj.* reacting to light. □ **photosensitivity** *n.*

photo session *n.* a pre-arranged session in which a photographer takes photographs of a person for use in advertising etc.

photosetting *n.* = FILMSETTING. □ **photoset** *v.tr.* (*past* and *past part.* **-set**). **photosetter** *n.*

photo shoot *n.* = PHOTO SESSION.

photostat ● *n. propr.* **1** a type of photocopier. **2** a copy made by this means. ● *v.tr.* (**-statted, -statting**) make a photostat of. □ **photostatic** *adj.*

photosynthesis *n.* ▲ the process by which the energy of sunlight is used by organisms, esp. green plants, to synthesize carbohydrates from carbon dioxide and water. □ **photosynthesize** *v.tr. & intr.* (also **-ise**). **photosynthetic** *adj.* **photosynthetically** *adv.*

P

PHOTOCOPIER

At the heart of a photocopier is a charged photoconductive drum. The image to be copied is projected via a lens and mirrors on to the drum. Light from white areas of the image disperses the charge where it hits the drum. The drum is left with charged areas that correspond to the black parts of the document. These attract toner from a roller to form a copy of the document on the drum, which is then transferred to a sheet of paper.

INSIDE A BLACK AND WHITE PHOTOCOPIER

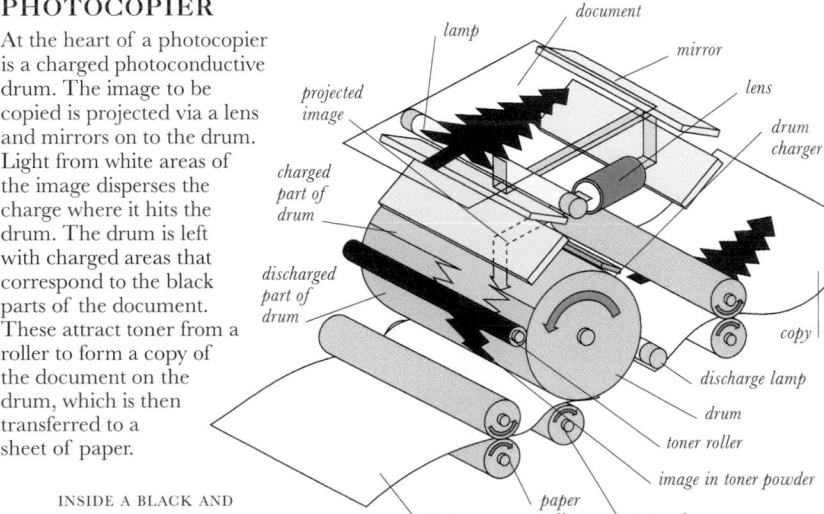

lamp

document

mirror

projected image

lens

drum charger

charged part of drum

discharged part of drum

copy

discharge lamp

drum

toner roller

image in toner powder

paper

paper roller

paper charger

PHOTOTROPISM

Phototropism in a plant is manifested by the growth of the roots or shoots towards or away from a source of light. Shoots show positive phototropism, detecting the source of light and orientating themselves to receive the maximum amount (as demonstrated here). Roots show negative phototropism by growing away from light.

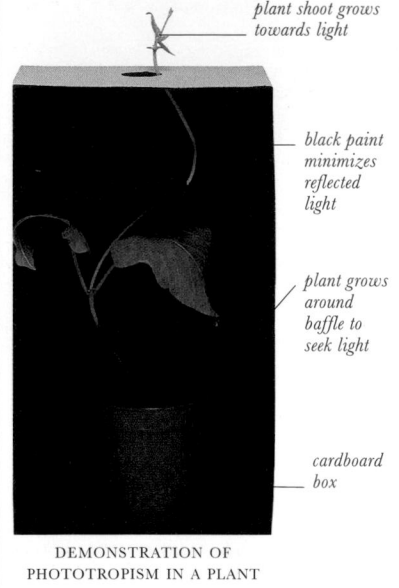

plant shoot grows towards light

black paint minimizes reflected light

plant grows around baffle to seek light

cardboard box

DEMONSTRATION OF
PHOTOTROPISM IN A PLANT

phototropism *n.* ▲ the tendency of a plant etc. to turn towards or away from a source of light. □ **phototropic** *adj.*

phototypesetter *n.* a machine for filmsetting. □ **phototypeset** *adj.* **phototypesetting** *n.*

photovoltaic *adj.* relating to the production of electric current at the junction of two substances exposed to light.

phrasal *adj. Gram.* consisting of a phrase.

phrasal verb *n.* an idiomatic phrase consisting of a verb and an adverb (e.g. *break down*) or a verb and a preposition (e.g. *see to*), or a combination of both (e.g. *look down on*).

phrase ● *n.* **1** a group of words forming a conceptual unit, but not a sentence. **2** an idiomatic or short pithy expression. **3** a mode of expression (*a nice turn of phrase*). **4** *Mus.* a group of notes forming a distinct unit within a larger piece. ● *v.tr.* **1** express in words (*phrased the reply badly*). **2** (esp. when reading aloud or speaking) divide (sentences etc.) into units so as to convey the meaning of the whole. **3** *Mus.* divide (music) into phrases, esp. in performance. [based on Greek *phrazein* 'to declare, tell'] □ **phrasing** *n.*

phrase book *n.* a book for tourists etc. listing useful expressions with their equivalent in a foreign language.

phraseology *n.* (*pl.* **-ies**) **1** a choice or arrangement of words. **2** a mode of expression.

phrenology *n. hist.* the study of the shape and size of the cranium as a supposed indication of character and mental faculties. [based on Greek *phren* 'mind'] □ **phrenological** *adj.* **phrenologist** *n.*

phthisis /fthy-sis/ *n.* any progressive wasting disease. [Latin, based on Greek *phthinein* 'to decay']

phut *n.* a dull abrupt sound as of an impact or explosion. □ **go phut** *colloq.* collapse, break down.

phyla *pl.* of PHYLUM.

phylactery *n.* (*pl.* **-ies**) a small leather box containing Hebrew texts worn by Jewish men at morning prayer. [from Greek *phulaktērion* 'amulet']

phyllo var. of FILO.

phyllo- *comb. form* leaf. [from Greek]

phylloquinone *n.* one of the K vitamins, found in leafy green vegetables, and essential for the blood-clotting process.

phylloxera /fil-oks-eer-a/ *n.* any plant-louse of (or formerly of) the genus *Phylloxera*, esp. *Daktulosphaira vitifoliae*, a pest of vines. [from Greek *phullon* 'leaf' + *xēros* 'dry']

phylogeny *n.* the evolutionary development and diversification of groups of organisms, or particular features of organisms. [based on Greek *phulon* 'race'] □ **phylogenetic** *adj.*

phylum *n.* (*pl.* **phyla**) *Biol.* a taxonomic rank below a kingdom and above a class. [from Greek *phulon* 'race']

physalis /fy-să-lis/ *n.* any plant of the genus *Physalis*, bearing fruit surrounded by lantern-like calyxes. [from Greek *physallis* 'bladder', with reference to the inflated calyx]

physic *n. archaic* **1** a medicine (*a dose of physic*). **2** the art of healing. **3** the medical profession. [from Greek *phusikē (epistēmē)* '(knowledge) of nature']

physical ● *adj.* **1** of or concerning the body (*physical exercise*; *physical education*). **2** of matter; material (*both mental and physical force*). **3 a** of, or according to, the laws of nature (*a physical impossibility*). **b** belonging to physics (*physical science*). ● *n.* (in full **physical examination**) a medical examination. □ **physicality** *n.* **physically** *adv.* **physicalness** *n.*

physical chemistry *n.* the application of physics to the study of chemical behaviour.

physical education *n.* instruction in physical exercise and games, esp. in schools.

physical geography *n.* geography dealing with natural features.

physical jerks *n.pl. Brit. colloq.* physical exercises.

physical science *n.* the sciences used in the study of inanimate natural objects.

physical training *n.* exercises promoting bodily fitness and strength.

physic garden *n.* a garden for cultivating medicinal herbs etc.

physician *n.* **1 a** a person legally qualified to practise medicine and surgery. **b** a specialist in medical diagnosis and treatment. **c** any medical practitioner. **2** a healer (*work is the best physician*).

physicist *n.* a person skilled in physics.

physico- *comb. form* **1** physical (and). **2** of physics (and).

physics *n.* the science dealing with the properties and interactions of matter and energy. [pl. of archaic *physic* 'physical (thing)', suggested by Greek *phusika* 'natural things']

physio *n.* (*pl.* **-os**) *colloq.* a physiotherapist.

physio- *comb. form* nature; what is natural. [from Greek *phusis* 'nature']

physiognomy /fiz-i-on-ŏmi/ *n.* (*pl.* **-ies**) **1 a** the cast or form of a person's features, expression, etc. **b** the art of supposedly judging character from facial characteristics etc. **2** the external features of a landscape etc. [from Greek *phusiognōmonia* 'judging of a man's nature (by his features)'] □ **physiognomic** *adj.* **physiognomical** *adj.* **physiognomist** *n.*

physiography *n.* the description of nature, of natural phenomena, or of a class of objects. □ **physiographic** *adj.* **physiographical** *adj.*

physiological *adj.* (also **physiologic**) of or concerning physiology. □ **physiologically** *adv.*

physiology *n.* **1** the science of the functions of living organisms and their parts. **2** these functions. □ **physiologist** *n.*

physiotherapy *n.* the treatment of disease, injury, deformity, etc., by physical methods including manipulation, massage, infra-red heat treatment, remedial exercise, etc. □ **physiotherapist** *n.*

physique *n.* the bodily structure, development, and organization of an individual (*an undernourished physique*). [French]

phyto- *comb. form* denoting a plant.

PIANO

A piano frame is either vertical – as in the upright piano – or horizontal – as in the grand piano (shown here). Metal strings are stretched on the frame with great force. Pressing a key makes a felt-tipped hammer strike a string, which vibrates. This causes the soundboard underneath the strings to resonate, making the piano's distinctive sound.

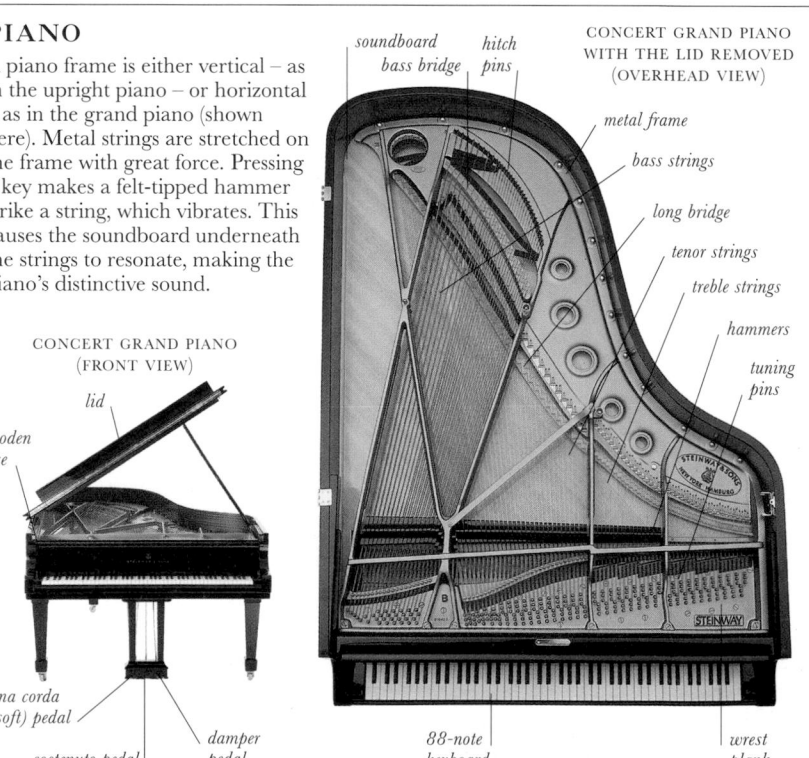

CONCERT GRAND PIANO
(FRONT VIEW)

lid

wooden case

una corda (soft) pedal

sostenuto pedal

damper pedal

soundboard

bass bridge

hitch pins

CONCERT GRAND PIANO
WITH THE LID REMOVED
(OVERHEAD VIEW)

metal frame

bass strings

long bridge

tenor strings

treble strings

hammers

tuning pins

88-note keyboard

wrest plank

P

phytochemistry *n.* the chemistry of plant products. □ **phytochemical** *adj.*

phytoplankton *n.* the component of plankton consisting of microscopic plants.

pi[1] *n.* **1** the sixteenth letter of the Greek alphabet (Π, π). **2** (as π) the symbol of the ratio of the circumference of a circle to its diameter (approx. 3.14159). [Greek; sense 2: from Greek *periphereia* 'circumference']

pi[2] *adj. Brit. slang* pious.

pi[3] *US* var. of PIE[3].

piani *pl.* of PIANO[2].

pianism *n.* **1** the art or technique of piano playing. **2** the skill or style of a composer of piano music. □ **pianistic** *adj.* **pianistically** *adv.*

pianissimo *Mus.* ● *adj.* performed very softly. ● *adv.* very softly. ● *n.* (*pl.* **-os** or **pianissimi**) a passage to be performed very softly. [Italian]

pianist *n.* the player of a piano. [from French *pianiste*]

piano[1] *n.* (*pl.* **-os**) ◀ a large musical instrument played by pressing down keys on a keyboard and causing hammers to strike metal strings. ▷ UPRIGHT. [Italian, abbreviation of PIANOFORTE]

piano[2] ● *adj.* **1** *Mus.* performed softly. **2** subdued. ● *adv.* **1** *Mus.* softly. **2** in a subdued manner. ● *n.* (*pl.* **-os** or **piani**) *Mus.* a passage to be performed softly. [from Latin *planus* 'flat', (of sound) 'soft']

piano accordion *n.* an accordion with a small vertical keyboard like that of a piano.

pianoforte *n. Mus. formal* or *archaic* a piano. [Italian, earlier *piano e forte* 'soft and loud', expressing its gradation of tone]

pianola *n. propr.* a kind of automatic piano.

piano nobile /pi-**ah**-noh **noh**-bi-lay/ *n. Archit.* the main storey of a large house. [Italian, literally 'noble floor']

piano trio *n.* a trio for piano and two stringed instruments.

piano-tuner *n.* a person who tunes pianos for a living.

piassava *n.* a stout fibre obtained from the leafstalks of various American and African palm trees.

piastre *n.* (*US* also **piaster**) a small coin and monetary unit of several Middle Eastern countries. [from Italian *piastra (d'argento)* 'plate (of silver)']

piazza /pee-**at**-să/ *n.* **1** a public square or market place. **2** *US* the veranda of a house. [Italian]

pibroch /**pee**-brok/ *n.* a series of esp. martial or funerary variations on a theme for the bagpipes. [from Gaelic *piobaireachd* 'art of piping']

pic *n. colloq.* a picture, esp. a cinema film.

pica /**py**-kă/ *n. Printing* **1** a unit of type size (⅙ inch). **2** a size of letters in typewriting (10 per inch). [from Anglo-Latin *pica*, a 15th-century book of rules about Church feasts]

picador *n.* (in bullfighting) a person on horseback who goads the bull with a lance. [Spanish, literally 'pricker']

picaresque *adj.* (of a style of fiction) dealing with the episodic adventures of rogues etc. [from Spanish *picaresco*]

■ **Usage** *Picaresque* is sometimes used to mean 'transitory' or 'roaming', but this is considered incorrect in standard English.

picaroon *n. archaic* **1 a** a rogue. **b** a thief. **2 a** a pirate. **b** a pirate ship.

picayune /pik-ă-**yoon**/ *N. Amer.* ● *n.* **1** a small coin of little value, esp. a 5-cent piece. **2** *colloq.* an insignificant person or thing. ● *adj. colloq.* mean; contemptible; petty. [from French *picaillon*, a Piedmontese coin]

piccalilli *n.* (*pl.* **piccalillis**) a pickle of chopped vegetables, mustard, and hot spices. [18th-century coinage]

piccaninny *n.* (*US* **pickaninny**) (*pl.* **-ies**) often *offens.* a small black or Australian Aboriginal child. [W. Indian Creole, from Spanish *pequeño* 'little']

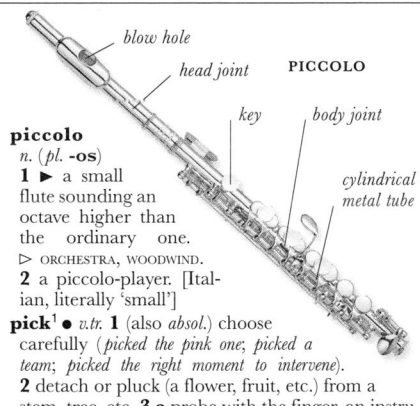

blow hole / head joint / PICCOLO / key / body joint / cylindrical metal tube

piccolo *n.* (*pl.* **-os**) **1** ▶ a small flute sounding an octave higher than the ordinary one. ▷ ORCHESTRA, WOODWIND. **2** a piccolo-player. [Italian, literally 'small']

pick[1] ● *v.tr.* **1** (also *absol.*) choose carefully (*picked the pink one; picked a team; picked the right moment to intervene*). **2** detach or pluck (a flower, fruit, etc.) from a stem, tree, etc. **3 a** probe with the finger, an instrument, etc. to remove unwanted matter. **b** clear (a bone, carcass, etc.) of scraps of meat etc. **4** (also *absol.*) (of a person) eat (food, a meal, etc.) in small bits. **5** (also *absol.*) esp. *N. Amer.* pluck the strings of (a banjo etc.). **6 a** select (a route or path) carefully over difficult terrain on foot. **b** place (one's steps etc.) carefully. **7** pull apart (*pick oakum*). ● *n.* **1** the act or an instance of picking. **2 a** a selection or choice. **b** the right to select (*had first pick of the prizes*). **3** (usu. foll. by *of*) the best (*the pick of the bunch*). □ **pick and choose** select carefully or fastidiously. **pick at 1** eat (food) without interest. **2** = *pick on* 1. **pick a person's brains** extract ideas, information, etc., from a person for one's own use. **pick a fight** = *pick a quarrel*. **pick holes** (or *a hole*) **in 1** make holes in (material etc.) by plucking, poking, etc. **2** find fault with (an idea etc.). **pick a lock** open a lock with an instrument other than the proper key. **pick off 1** pluck (leaves etc.) off. **2** shoot (people etc.) one by one without haste. **3** eliminate (opposition etc.) singly. **pick on 1** find fault with; nag at. **2** select. **pick out 1** take from a larger number (*picked him out from the others*). **2** distinguish from surrounding objects or at a distance (*can just pick out the church spire*). **3** play (a tune) by ear on the piano etc. **4** esp. *Brit.* **a** highlight (a painting etc.) with touches of another colour. **b** accentuate (decoration, a painting, etc.) with a contrasting colour (*picked out the handles in red*). **5** make out (the meaning of a passage etc.). **pick over** select the best from. **pick a person's pockets** steal the contents of a person's pockets. **pick a quarrel** start an argument or a fight deliberately. **pick to pieces** = *take to pieces* (see PIECE). **pick up 1** grasp and raise. **2** acquire by chance or without effort (*picked up a cold; picked up French easily*). **3 a** fetch (a person, animal, or thing) left in another person's charge. **b** stop for and take along with one, esp. in a vehicle (*pick me up on the corner*). **4** make the acquaintance of (a person) casually, esp. as a sexual overture. **5** (of one's health, the weather, share prices, etc.) recover, improve. **6** (of an engine etc.) recover speed; accelerate. **7** (of the police etc.) arrest. **8** detect by scrutiny or with a telescope, searchlight, radio, etc. (*picked up most of the mistakes; picked up a distress signal*). **9 a** form or renew (a friendship). **b** resume, take up anew (*pick up where we left off*). **10** (esp. in phr. **pick up the tab**) accept the responsibility of paying (a bill etc.). **11** (*refl.*) raise (oneself etc.) after a fall etc. **12** raise (the feet etc.) clear of the ground. **take one's pick** make a choice from a range of things. [Middle English]

pick[2] ● *n.* **1** a long-handled tool having a usu. curved iron bar pointed at one or both ends, used for breaking up hard ground, masonry, etc. **2** *colloq.* a plectrum. **3** any instrument for picking. ● *v.tr.* **1** break the surface of (the ground etc.) with or as if with a pick. **2** make (holes etc.) in this way. [Middle English]

pickaback var. of PIGGYBACK.

pickaninny *US* var. of PICCANINNY.

pickaxe *n.* (*US* **pickax**) = PICK[2] *n.* 1. [from Old French *picois*, assimilated to AXE]

picker *n.* **1** a person or thing that picks something. **2** (often in *comb.*) a person who gathers something (*hop-picker*).

picket ● *n.* **1** a person or group of people outside a place of work, intending to persuade esp. workers not to enter during a strike etc. **2** a pointed stake driven into the ground. **3** (also **picquet**, **piquet**) *Mil.* **a** a small body of troops or a single soldier sent out to watch for the enemy, held in readiness, etc. **b** a party of sentries. **c** an outpost. **d** a camp guard on police duty. ● *v.* (**picketed**, **picketing**) **1 a** *tr. & intr.* station or act as a picket. **b** *tr.* beset or guard with a picket or pickets. **2** *tr.* secure with stakes. **3** *tr.* tether (an animal). [from French *piquet* 'pointed stake'] □ **picketer** *n.*

picket line *n.* a boundary established by workers on strike, esp. at the entrance to the place of work, which others are asked not to cross.

pickings *n.pl.* **1** perquisites; pilferings (*rich pickings*). **2** remaining scraps; gleanings.

pickle ● *n.* **1 a** (often in *pl.*) food, esp. vegetables, preserved in brine, vinegar, mustard, etc. **b** the brine, vinegar, etc. in which food is preserved. **c** *US* a cucumber preserved thus. **2** *colloq.* a plight (*a fine pickle we are in!*). **3** *Brit. colloq.* a mischievous child. ● *v.tr.* **1** preserve in pickle. **2** treat with pickle. **3** (as **pickled** *adj.*) *slang* drunk. [from Middle Dutch *pekel*]

pickler *n.* **1** a person who pickles vegetables etc. **2** a vegetable suitable for pickling.

picklock *n.* **1** a person who picks locks. **2** an instrument for this.

pick-me-up *n.* **1** a tonic for the nerves etc. **2** an experience that cheers.

pickpocket *n.* a person who steals from the pockets of others. □ **pickpocketing** *n.*

pick-up *n.* **1** (in full **pick-up truck**) a small open motor truck. **2** a device that produces an electrical signal in response to some other kind of signal or change, esp. **a** the part of a record player carrying the stylus. **b** ▼ a device on a musical instrument which converts sound vibrations into electrical signals for amplification. **3** *slang* a person met casually, esp. for sexual purposes. **4** the act of picking up, esp. of giving a person a lift. **5** an increase in, or recovery of, speed or prosperity. **6** *Mus.* a series of introductory notes leading into the opening part of a tune.

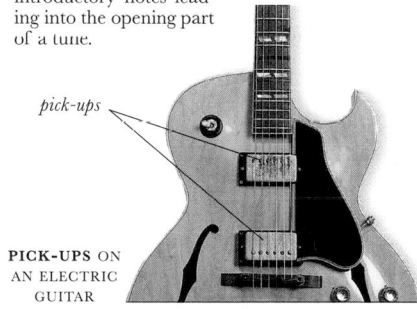

pick-ups

PICK-UPS ON AN ELECTRIC GUITAR

Pickwickian *adj.* **1** of or like Mr Pickwick in Dickens's *Pickwick Papers*, esp. in being jovial, plump, etc. **2** (of words or their sense) misunderstood or misused, esp. to avoid offence.

picky *adj.* (**pickier**, **pickiest**) *colloq.* excessively fastidious.

pick-your-own *adj.* (usu. *attrib.*) (of commercially grown fruit and vegetables) dug or picked by the customer at the place of production.

picnic ● *n.* **1** an outing taking a packed meal to be eaten out of doors. **2** any meal eaten out of doors or without preparation, tables, chairs, etc. **3** (usu. with *neg.*) *colloq.* something agreeable or easily accomplished etc. (*it was no picnic organizing the meeting*). ● *v.intr.* (**picnicked**, **picnicking**) take part in a picnic. [from French *pique-nique*] □ **picnicker** *n.* **picnicky** *adj.*

pico- *comb. form* denoting a factor of 10^{-12} (*picometre; picosecond*). [from Spanish *pico* 'beak, peak, little bit']

P

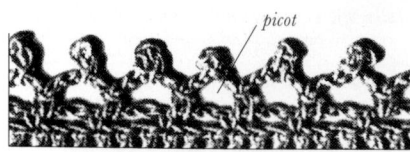

picot

PICOT

picot /pee-koh/ n. ▲ a small loop of twisted thread in a lace edging etc. [French, literally 'little peak']

picquet var. of PICKET n. 3.

picric acid n. a very bitter yellow compound used in dyeing and surgery and in explosives. [based on Greek *pikros* 'bitter'] □ **picrate** n.

Pict n. a member of an ancient people of N. Britain. [from Late Latin *Picti*] □ **Pictish** adj.

pictograph n. (also **pictogram**) **1 a** ▼ a pictorial symbol for a word or phrase. **b** an ancient record consisting of these. **2** a pictorial representation of statistics etc. on a chart, graph, etc. [based on Latin *pingere pict-* 'to paint'] □ **pictographic** adj. **pictography** n.

HOUSE   PLATE   CHILD

NO   TO GIVE   TO GO

PICTOGRAPHS FROM CAMEROON *c.*1900

pictorial ● adj. **1** of or expressed in a picture or pictures. **2** illustrated. **3** picturesque. ● n. a journal, postage stamp, etc., with a picture or pictures as the main feature. [based on Latin *pictor* 'painter'] □ **pictorially** adv.

picture ● n. **1 a** (often attrib.) a painting, drawing, photograph, etc., esp. as a work of art. **b** a portrait, esp. a photograph, of a person (*does not like to have her picture taken*). **c** a beautiful object (*her hat is a picture*). **2 a** a total visual or mental impression produced; a scene (*the picture looks bleak*). **b** a written or spoken description (*drew a vivid picture of moral decay*). **3 a** a film. **b** (in pl.; prec. by the) a showing of films at a cinema (*went to the pictures*). **c** (in pl.) films in general. **4** an image on a television screen. **5** colloq. **a** esp. iron. a person or thing exemplifying something (*he was the picture of innocence*). **b** a person or thing resembling another closely (*the picture of her aunt*). **c** iron. a striking expression, pose, etc.; a comic or striking sight (*her face was a picture*). ● v.tr. **1** represent in a picture. **2** (also refl.) imagine (*pictured it to herself*). **3** describe graphically. □ **get the picture** colloq. grasp the tendency or drift of circumstances, information, etc. **in the picture** fully informed. **out of the picture** uninvolved, inactive; irrelevant. [from Latin *pictura*]

picture book n. a book containing many illustrations.

picture frame n. a frame made to hold a picture.

picture gallery n. a place containing an exhibition or collection of pictures.

picturegoer n. a person who frequents the cinema.

picture hat n. a woman's wide-brimmed highly decorated hat as in pictures in the 18th-c. English painters such as Reynolds and Gainsborough.

picture palace n. Brit. archaic a cinema.

picture postcard n. a postcard with a picture on one side.

picture rail n. a horizontal rail on a wall for hanging pictures from. ▷ COVE

picturesque adj. **1** beautiful or striking. **2** (of language etc.) strikingly graphic. [from Italian *pittoresco*] □ **picturesquely** adv. **picturesqueness** n.

picture window n. a very large window consisting of one pane of glass.

picture-writing n. a mode of recording events etc. by pictorial symbols as in early hieroglyphics etc.

piddle ● v.intr. **1** colloq. urinate. **2** work or act in a trifling way. **3** (as **piddling** adj.) colloq. trivial; trifling. ● n. colloq. **1** an act of urinating. **2** urine.

piddock n. any rock-boring bivalve mollusc of the family Pholadidae, used for bait.

pidgin n. a simplified language containing vocabulary from two or more languages, used for communication between people not having a common language. [Chinese corruption of *business*]

pidgin English n. a pidgin in which the chief language is English, used originally between Chinese and Europeans.

pi-dog var. of PYE-DOG.

pie[1] n. **1 a** a baked dish of meat, fish, fruit, etc., usu. with a top and base of pastry. **2** anything resembling a pie in form (*a mud pie*). □ **easy as pie** colloq. very easy. **pie in the sky** colloq. an unrealistic prospect of future happiness. [Middle English]

pie[2] n. archaic **1** a magpie. **2** a pied animal. [from Latin *pica* 'magpie']

pie[3] n. (US **pi**) **1** a confused mass of printers' type. **2** chaos.

piebald ● adj. **1** (usu. of an animal, esp. a horse) having irregular patches of two colours, esp. black and white. **2** motley; mongrel. ● n. a piebald animal, esp. a horse.

piece ● n. **1 a** one of the distinct portions forming part of or broken off from a larger object (*a piece of string*). **b** each of the parts of which a set or category is composed (*a five-piece band*; *a piece of furniture*). **2** a coin of specified value (*50p piece*). **3 a** a usu. short literary or musical composition or a picture. **b** a theatrical play. **4** an item, instance, or example (*a piece of impudence*; *a piece of news*). **5 a** any of the objects used to make moves in board games. **b** a chessman (strictly, other than a pawn). **6** a definite quantity in which a thing is sold. **7** an enclosed portion (of land etc.). **8** slang offens. a woman. **9** (foll. by of) colloq. a share in, involvement in; a financial share or investment in (*has a piece of the new production*). **10** esp. N. Amer. slang a portable firearm; a handgun. ● v.tr. **1** (usu. foll. by together) form into a whole; put together; join (*finally pieced his story together*). **2** (usu. foll. by out) **a** eke out. **b** form (a theory etc.) by combining parts etc. **3** (usu. foll. by up) patch. **4** join (threads) in spinning. □ **by the piece** (paid) according to the quantity of work done. **go to pieces** collapse emotionally. **in one piece 1** unbroken. **2** unharmed. **in pieces** broken. **of a piece** uniform, consistent, in keeping. **a piece of the action** slang **1** a share in the profits accruing from something. **2** a share in the excitement. **a piece of cake** see CAKE. **a piece of one's mind** a sharp rebuke or lecture. **say one's piece** give one's opinion or make a prepared statement. **take to pieces 1** break up or dismantle. **2** criticize harshly. [from Old French] □ **piecer** n. (in sense 4 of v.).

pièce de résistance /pee-ess dĕ ray-**zeess**-tahnss/ n. (pl. **pièces de résistance** pronunc. same) **1** the most important or remarkable item. **2** the most substantial dish at a meal. [French]

piece-goods n.pl. fabrics woven in standard lengths.

piecemeal ● adv. piece by piece; gradually. ● adj. gradual; unsystematic. [Middle English]

piece of eight n. hist. a Spanish dollar, equivalent to 8 reals.

piece-rate n. a rate of payment for piecework.

piecework n. work paid for by the amount produced.

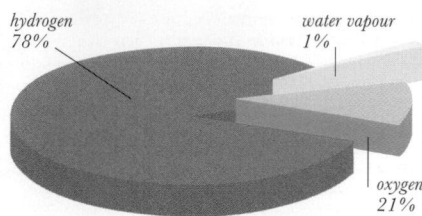

hydrogen 78%

water vapour 1%

oxygen 21%

PIE CHART SHOWING THE RELATIVE CONSTITUENTS OF THE EARTH'S ATMOSPHERE

pie chart n. ▲ a circle divided into sectors to represent relative quantities.

piecrust n. the baked pastry crust of a pie.

pied adj. particoloured. [Middle English]

pied-à-terre /p'yayd ah **tair**/ n. (pl. **pieds-à-terre** pronunc. same) a flat, house, etc. kept for occasional use. [French, literally 'foot to earth']

pie-dog var. of PYE-DOG.

Pied Piper n. a person enticing followers, esp. to their doom.

pie-eyed adj. slang drunk.

pier n. **1 a** a structure raised on piles and leading out to sea, a lake, etc., used as a promenade and landing stage, and Brit. often with entertainment arcades etc. **b** a breakwater. **2 a** a support of an arch or of the span of a bridge; a pillar. **b** solid masonry between windows etc. **3** a long narrow structure projecting from the main body of an airport terminal, along which passengers walk to and from their aircraft. [Middle English *per*, from Anglo-Latin *pera*]

pierce v. **1** tr. **a** (of a sharp instrument etc.) penetrate. **b** prick with a sharp instrument, esp. to make a hole. **c** make a hole, opening, or tunnel into or through (something), bore through. **d** make (a hole etc.) (*pierced a hole in the belt*). **e** (of cold, grief, etc.) affect keenly or sharply. **f** (of a light, glance, sound, etc.) penetrate keenly or sharply. **2** intr. (as **piercing** adj.) (of a glance, intuition, high noise, etc.) keen, sharp, or unpleasantly penetrating. **3** tr. force a way through or into (*pierced the German line*). **4** intr. (usu. foll. by through, into) penetrate. [from Latin *pertundere* 'to bore through'] □ **piercer** n. **piercingly** adv.

pier glass n. a large mirror, used originally to fill wall-space between windows.

pierrot /**peer**-oh/ n. (fem. **pierrette** /peer-**et**/) Theatr. a white-faced entertainer in pier shows etc. with a loose white clown's costume. [French, literally 'little Peter']

pietà /pee-ay-**tah**/ n. a picture or sculpture of the Virgin Mary holding the dead body of Christ on her lap or in her arms. [Italian, from Latin]

pietism n. **1** pious sentiment. **2** an exaggerated or affected piety. □ **pietist** n. **pietistic** adj. **pietistical** adj.

piety n. (pl. **-ies**) **1** the quality of being pious. **2** a pious act. [from Latin *pietas* 'dutifulness']

piezoelectricity /peet-soh-i-lek-**tris**-iti/ n. electric polarization in a substance resulting from the application of mechanical stress, esp. in certain crystals. [based on Greek *piezein* 'to press'] □ **piezoelectric** adj. **piezoelectrically** adv.

piffle colloq. ● n. nonsense; empty speech. ● v.intr. talk or act feebly; trifle. □ **piffler** n.

piffling adj. colloq. trivial; worthless.

pig ● n. **1 a** any omnivorous hoofed broad-snouted bristly mammal of the family Suidae. ▷ UNGULATE. **b** US a young pig; a piglet. **c** (often in comb.) any similar animal (*guinea pig*). **2** the flesh of esp. a young or sucking pig as food. **3** colloq. **a** a greedy, dirty, obstinate, or annoying person. **b** an unpleasant, awkward, or difficult thing, task, etc. **4** an oblong mass of metal from a smelting furnace. **5** slang offens. a police officer. **6** Sc. dial. an earthenware hot-water bottle. ● v.tr. (**pigged**, **pigging**) **1** (also absol.) (of a sow) bring forth (piglets). **2** colloq. eat (food) greedily. □ **buy a pig in a poke** buy, accept, etc. something without knowing its value or esp. seeing it. **make a pig of oneself** overeat. **make a pig's ear of** *colloq.* make a mess of; bungle. **pig it** live in a disorderly, untidy, or filthy fashion. **pig out** (often foll. by *on*) esp. *N. Amer. slang* make a pig of oneself; overeat. [Middle English] ▷ **piglet** *n.* **pigling** *adj.* **pigling** *n.*

pigeon[1] *n.* **1** any of several large usu. grey and white birds of the family Columbidae; a dove. **2** *slang* a person easily swindled. [from Old French *pijon*] ▷ **pigeonry** *n.* (*pl.* **-ies**).

pigeon[2] *n.* **1** = PIDGIN. **2** *colloq.* a particular concern, job, or business (*that's not my pigeon*).

pigeon-breast *n.* (also **pigeon-chest**) a deformed human chest with a projecting breastbone. ▷ **pigeon-breasted** *adj.* also **pigeon-chested**).

pigeon fancier *n.* a person who keeps and breeds fancy pigeons. ▷ **pigeon-fancying** *n.*

pigeon-hole ● *n.* **1** each of a set of compartments in a cabinet or on a wall for letters etc. **2** a small recess for a pigeon to nest in. ● *v.tr.* **1** assign (a person or thing) to a preconceived category. **2** put (a matter) aside for the time being. **3** deposit (a document) in a pigeon-hole.

pigeon-toed *adj.* (of a person) having the toes turned inwards.

piggery *n.* (*pl.* **-ies**) **1** a pig-breeding farm etc. **2** = PIGSTY 1. **3** piggishness.

piggish *adj.* **1** of or relating to pigs. **2** having a quality associated with pigs. ▷ **piggishness** *n.*

piggy ● *n.* (also **piggie**) (*pl.* **piggies**) *colloq.* **1** a little pig. **2 a** a child's word for a pig. **b** a child's word for a toe. ● *adj.* (**piggier**, **piggiest**) **1** like a pig. **2** (of features etc.) like those of a pig (*little piggy eyes*). ▷ **piggy in the middle** = PIG IN THE MIDDLE.

piggyback (also **pickaback**) ● *n.* a ride on the back and shoulders of another person. ● *v.* **1** *intr.* ride (as if) on a person's back and shoulders. **2** *tr.* **a** give a piggyback to. **b** carry or mount on top of another thing. ● *adv.* **1** on the back and shoulders of another person. **2** on the back or top of a larger object. [16th-century coinage]

piggy bank *n.* a pig-shaped money box.

pig-headed *adj.* obstinate. ▷ **pig-headedly** *adv.* **pig-headedness** *n.*

pig-ignorant *adj. colloq.* extremely ignorant.

pig in the middle *n.* esp. *Brit.* a person who is placed in an awkward situation between two others (after a ball game for three with one in the middle).

pig-iron *n.* crude iron from a smelting furnace.

pigment ● *n.* **1** colouring matter used as paint or dye. ▷ FRESCO. **2** the natural colouring matter of animal or plant tissue. ● *v.tr.* colour with or as if with pigment. [from Latin *pigmentum*] ▷ **pigmentary** *adj.*

pigmentation *n.* **1** the natural colouring of plants, animals, etc. **2** the excessive colouring of tissue by the deposition of pigment.

pigmy var. of PYGMY.

pigskin *n.* **1** the hide of a pig. **2** leather made from this. **3** *N. Amer.* a football.

pigsticking *n.* **1** the hunting of wild boar with a spear on horseback. **2** the butchering of pigs.

pigsty *n.* (*pl.* **-ies**) **1** a pen or enclosure for a pig or pigs. **2** a filthy house, room, etc.

pigswill *n.* kitchen refuse and scraps fed to pigs.

pigtail *n.* a plait of hair hanging from the back of the head, or either of a pair at the sides. ▷ **pigtailed** *adj.*

pika /pee-ay-**tah**/ *n.* any small rabbit-like mammal of the genus *Ochotona* with small ears, short legs, and a very short tail. Also called a *mouse hare*. ▷ LAGOMORPH. [from Tungus *piika*]

pike[1] *n.* (*pl.* same) **1** ▶ a large voracious freshwater fish of the family Esocidae, with a long narrow snout and sharp teeth. ▷ FISH. **2** a similar fish. [Middle English, related to PIKE[2], because of its pointed jaw]

pike[2] *n.* **1** *hist.* an infantry weapon with a pointed steel or iron head on a long wooden shaft. **2** *N.Engl.* the peaked top of a hill. ▷ **pike on** esp. *Austral. colloq.* withdraw timidly from. [Old English *pīc* 'point, prick']

pike[3] *n.* **1** a toll gate; a toll. **2** a turnpike road. [abbreviation of TURNPIKE]

pike[4] *n.* a jackknife position in diving or gymnastics. [20th-century coinage]

pikelet *n.* *N.Engl.* a thin kind of crumpet. [Welsh *(bara) pyglyd* 'pitchy (bread)']

pikestaff *n.* **1** *hist.* the wooden shaft of a pike. **2** a walking stick with a metal point. ▷ **as plain as a pikestaff** quite plain or obvious.

pilaf *n.* (also **pilaff**, **pilau** /*rhymes with* allow/, **pilaw** /pi-**lor**/) a Middle Eastern or Indian dish of spiced rice or wheat with meat, fish, vegetables, etc. [from Turkish *pilâv*]

pilaster *n.* a rectangular column, esp. one projecting from a wall. ▷ FACADE. [based on Latin *pila* 'pillar'] ▷ **pilastered** *adj.*

pilchard *n.* a small marine fish, *Sardinia pilchardus* of the herring family. [16th-century coinage]

pile[1] ● *n.* **1** a heap of things laid or gathered upon one another (*a pile of leaves*). **2 a** a large imposing building (*a stately pile*). **b** a large group of tall buildings. **3** *colloq.* **a** a large quantity. **b** a fortune (*made his pile*). **4 a** a series of plates of dissimilar metals laid one on another alternately to produce an electric current. **b** = ATOMIC PILE. **5** a funeral pyre. ● *v.* **1** *tr.* **a** (often foll. by *up*, *on*) heap up. **b** (foll. by *with*) load. **2** *intr.* (usu. foll. by *in*, *into*, *on*, *out of*, etc.) crowd hurriedly or tightly. ▷ **pile it on** *colloq.* exaggerate. **pile on the agony** *colloq.* exaggerate for effect. **pile up 1** accumulate; heap up. **2** *colloq.* run (a ship) aground or cause (a vehicle etc.) to crash. [from Latin *pila* 'pillar, pier, mole']

pile[2] ● *n.* **1** a heavy beam driven vertically into soft ground, etc., to support the foundations of a superstructure. ▷ OIL PLATFORM. **2** a pointed stake or post. ● *v.tr.* **1** provide with piles. **2** drive (piles) into the ground etc. [from Latin *pilum* 'javelin']

pile[3] *n.* the soft projecting surface on velvet, a carpet, etc. [Middle English] ▷ **pileless** *adj.*

piledriver *n.* a machine for driving piles into the ground. ▷ **piledriving** *n. & attrib.adj.*

piles *n.pl. colloq.* haemorrhoids. [Middle English]

pile-up *n. colloq.* a multiple crash of road vehicles.

pilfer *v.tr.* (also *absol.*) steal (objects) esp. in small quantities. [from Old French *pelfrer* 'to pillage'] ▷ **pilferage** *n.* **pilferer** *n.*

pilgrim *n.* **1** a person who journeys to a sacred place for religious reasons. **2** a traveller. [from Latin *peregrinus* 'stranger']

pilgrimage ● *n.* **1** a pilgrim's journey (*go on a pilgrimage*). **2** any journey taken for nostalgic or sentimental reasons. ● *v.intr.* go on a pilgrimage.

Pilgrim Fathers *n.pl.* English Puritans who founded the colony of Plymouth, Massachusetts, in 1620.

pill *n.* **1 a** a ball or disc etc. of solid medicine for swallowing whole. **b** (usu. prec. by *the*) a contraceptive pill. **2** an unpleasant or painful necessity (*a bitter pill*). ▷ **sugar** (or **sweeten**) **the pill** make an unpleasant necessity acceptable. [from Middle Dutch *pille*]

pillage ● *v.tr.* (also *absol.*) plunder; sack (a place or a person). ● *n.* the act or an instance of pillaging. [from Old French] ▷ **pillager** *n.*

pillar *n.* **1 a** a usu. slender vertical structure of esp. stone used as a support for a roof etc. **b** a similar structure used for ornament. **c** a post supporting a structure. **2** a person regarded

as a mainstay or support. **3** an upright mass of ice, rock, etc. ▷ **from pillar to post** (driven etc.) from one place to another; to and fro. [from Latin *pila* 'pillar'] ▷ **pillared** *adj.*

pillar box *n. Brit.* a public postbox shaped like a pillar.

pillar-box red *Brit.* ● *n.* a bright red colour, as of pillar boxes. ● *adj.* of this colour.

pillbox *n.* **1** a small shallow cylindrical box for holding pills. **2** a hat of a similar shape. **3** *Mil.* a small partly underground enclosed concrete fort used as an outpost.

pillion *n.* seating for a passenger behind a motorcyclist. ▷ **ride pillion** travel seated behind a motorcyclist etc. [from Gaelic *pillean* 'little cushion']

pillock *n. Brit. slang* a stupid person; a fool. [variant of obsolete *pillicock* 'penis']

pillory ● *n.* (*pl.* **-ies**) *hist.* a wooden framework with holes for the head and hands, enabling the public to assault or ridicule a person so imprisoned. ● *v.tr.* (**-ies**, **-ied**) expose (a person) to ridicule or public contempt. [from Old French *pilori*]

pillow ● *n.* **1 a** a usu. oblong support for the head, esp. in bed, with a cloth cover stuffed with feathers, flock, etc. **b** any pillow-shaped block or support. **2** = LACE-PILLOW. ● *v.tr.* **1** rest (the head etc.) on or as if on a pillow. **2** serve as a pillow for. [from Latin *pulvinus* 'cushion'] ▷ **pillowy** *adj.*

pillowcase *n.* a washable cotton etc. cover for a pillow.

pillow-fight *n.* a mock fight with pillows, esp. by children.

pillow lace *n.* lace made on a lace-pillow.

pillowslip *n.* = PILLOWCASE.

pillow talk *n.* romantic or intimate conversation in bed.

pill-popper *n. colloq.* **1** a person who takes pills freely. **2** a drug addict. ▷ **pill-popping** *n. & attrib.adj.*

pillule var. of PILULE.

pilot ● *n.* **1** a person who operates the flying controls of an aircraft. **2** a person qualified to take charge of a ship entering or leaving harbour. **3** (usu. *attrib.*) an initial experimental undertaking (*a pilot project*). **4** a guide. **5** *archaic* a steersman. ● *v.tr.* (**piloted**, **piloting**) **1** act as a pilot on (a ship) or of (an aircraft). **2** conduct or initiate as a pilot (*piloted the new scheme*). [based on Greek *pēdon* 'oar', in pl. 'rudder'] ▷ **pilotage** *n.* **pilotless** *adj.*

pilot-bird *n.* a rare dark-brown Australian warbler, *Pycnoptilus floccosus*, with a distinctive loud cry.

pilot chute *n.* a small parachute used to bring the main one into operation.

pilot-cloth *n.* thick blue woollen cloth for seamen's coats etc.

pilot fish *n.* a small fish, *Naucrates ductor*, said to act as a pilot leading a shark to food.

pilot house *n.* = WHEELHOUSE.

pilot light *n.* **1** a small gas burner kept alight to light another. **2** an electric indicator light or control light.

pilot officer *n.* a rank in the RAF above acting pilot officer.

pilot whale *n.* a small whale of the genus *Globicephalus*, of temperate or subtropical waters.

Pilsner *n.* (also **Pilsener**) a lager beer brewed or like that brewed at *Pilsen* (Plzeň) in the Czech Republic.

pilule *n.* (also **pillule**) a small pill. [from Latin *pilula*]

pimento *n.* (*pl.* **-os**) **1** = PIMIENTO. **2** esp. *W. Indies* = ALLSPICE 1. [from Spanish *pimiento*]

pimiento *n.* (*pl.* **-os**) a red pepper (capsicum). [from Latin *pigmentum* 'pigment', later 'spice']

pimp ● *n.* a man who lives off the earnings of a prostitute or a brothel. ● *v.intr.* act as a pimp. [16th-century coinage]

P

PIKE
(*Esox lucius*)

pimpernel *n.* ◄ any plant of the genus *Anagallis*. [based on Latin *piper* 'pepper']

pimple *n.* **1** a small hard inflamed spot on the skin. **2** anything resembling a pimple, esp. in relative size. [Middle English, from earlier *piplian* 'to break out in pustules'] □ **pimpled** *adj.* **pimply** *adj.*

PIN pin *n.* (also **PIN number**) personal identification number.

■ **Usage** The variant *PIN number* is common, even though the element *number* is redundant. The reason is probably that it is more readily understood than *PIN* in examples such as *He'd forgotten his PIN.*

PIMPERNEL:
BLUE PIMPERNEL
(*Anagallis foemina*)

pin ● *n.* **1 a** a small thin pointed piece of esp. steel wire with a round or flattened head, used esp. in sewing for holding things in place. **b** any of several types of pin (*drawing pin*). **c** a small brooch (*diamond pin*). **d** a badge fastened with a pin. **2** a peg of wood or metal for various purposes, e.g. a wooden skittle in bowling. **3** something of small value (*don't care a pin*). **4** (in *pl.*) *colloq.* legs (*quick on his pins*). **5** *Med.* a steel rod used to join the ends of fractured bones while they heal. **6** *Golf* a stick with a flag placed in a hole to mark its position. **7** *Brit.* a half-firkin cask for beer. ● *v.tr.* (**pinned**, **pinning**) **1 a** (often foll. by *to*, *up*, *together*) fasten with a pin or pins. **b** transfix with a pin, lance, etc. **2** (usu. foll. by *on*) fix (blame, responsibility, etc.) on a person etc. **3** (often foll. by *against*, *on*, etc.) seize and hold fast. □ **on pins and needles** in an agitated state of suspense. **pin down 1** (often foll. by *to*) bind (a person etc.) to a promise etc. **2** force (a person) to declare his or her intentions. **3** restrict the actions or movement of (an enemy etc.). **4** specify (a thing) precisely (*could not pin it down to a particular cause*). **5** hold (a person etc.) down by force. **pin one's faith** (or **hopes** etc.) **on** rely implicitly on. [from Latin *pinna* 'point' etc.]

pina colada /pee-nǎ kǒ-lah-dǎ/ *n.* a drink made from pineapple juice, rum, and coconut. [Spanish, literally 'strained pineapple']

pinafore *n.* **1** *Brit.* an apron, esp. with a bib. **2** (in full **pinafore dress**) a collarless sleeveless dress usu. worn over a blouse or jumper. [PIN + AFORE, because originally pinned on the front of a dress]

pinball *n.* a game in which small metal balls are shot across a board and score points by striking pins with lights etc.

pince-nez /panss-nay/ *n.* (*pl.* same) a pair of eyeglasses with a nose clip instead of side pieces. [French, literally 'pinch-nose']

pincer movement *n. Mil.* a movement by two wings of an army converging on the enemy.

pincers *n.pl.* **1** (also **pair of pincers** *sing.*) a gripping-tool resembling scissors but with blunt usu. concave jaws to hold a nail etc. for extraction. **2** the front claws of lobsters and some other crustaceans. [based on Old French *pincier* 'to pinch']

pinch ● *v.* **1** *tr.* **a** grip tightly, esp. between finger and thumb. **b** (often *absol.*) (of a shoe etc.) constrict (the flesh) painfully. **2** *tr.* (of cold, hunger, etc.) grip (a person) painfully. **3** *tr.* **a** esp. *Brit. colloq.* steal; take without permission. **b** *slang* arrest (a person). **4** *tr.* (as **pinched** *adj.*) (of the features) drawn, as with cold, hunger, etc. **5 a** *tr.* (usu. foll. by *in*, *of*, *for*, etc.) stint (a person). **b** *intr.* be niggardly with money, food, etc. **6** *tr.* (usu. foll. by *out*, *back*, *down*) remove (leaves etc.) to encourage bushy growth. ● *n.* **1** the act or an instance of pinching etc. the flesh. **2** an amount that can be taken up with fingers and thumb. **3** the

PINE MARTEN
(*Martes martes*)

stress or pain caused by poverty, cold, hunger, etc. **4** *slang* **a** an arrest. **b** a theft. □ **at** (or **in**) **a pinch** in an emergency. **feel the pinch** experience the effects of poverty. [from Latin *pungere* 'to prick']

pinchbeck ● *n.* an alloy of copper and zinc resembling gold and used in cheap jewellery etc. ● *adj.* **1** counterfeit; sham. **2** cheap; tawdry. [named after C. *Pinchbeck*, English watchmaker, *c.*1670–1732]

pinchpenny *n.* (*pl.* **-ies**) (also *attrib.*) a miserly person.

pinch-run *v.intr. Baseball* substitute as a runner between bases, esp. at a critical point in the game. □ **pinch-runner** *n.*

pincushion *n.* a small cushion for holding pins.

pin-down *n.* the action or policy of putting children in care into solitary confinement for long periods of time.

pine[1] *n.* **1** (in full **pine tree**) ► any evergreen tree of the genus *Pinus* with needle-shaped leaves growing in clusters. **2** the soft timber of this. **3** (*attrib.*) made of pine. [from Latin *pinus*] □ **pinery** *n.* (*pl.* **-ies**)

pine[2] *v.intr.* **1** (often foll. by *away*) decline or waste away, esp. from grief etc. **2** (usu. foll. by *for*, *after*, or *to* + infin.) long eagerly. [earlier in sense 'to (cause to) suffer': based on Latin *poena* 'pain']

pineal *adj.* shaped like a pine cone. [based on Latin *pinea* 'pine cone']

pineal body *n.* (also **pineal gland**) a pea-sized conical mass of tissue in the brain, secreting a hormone-like substance. ▷ ENDOCRINE

pineapple *n.* **1** a tropical plant, *Ananas comosus*, with a spiral of sword-shaped leaves and a thick stem bearing a large fruit. **2** the fruit of this, consisting of yellow flesh surrounded by a tough segmented skin and topped with a tuft of leaves. [based on PINE[1], from the fruit's resemblance to a pine cone]

pine cone *n.* the cone-shaped fruit of the pine tree.

pine marten *n.* ◄ a weasel-like mammal, *Martes martes*, having a dark brown coat with a yellowish throat.

pine nut *n.* the edible seed of various pine trees.

piney var. of PINY.

ping ● *n.* a single short high ringing sound. ● *v.* **1** *intr. & tr.* make or cause to make a ping. **2** *intr. US* = PINK[3].

pinger *n.* **1** a device that transmits pings at short intervals for purposes of detection, measurement, etc. **2** *Brit.* a timer that pings after a pre-set time.

ping-pong *n.* = TABLE TENNIS.

pinhead *n.* **1** the flattened head of a pin. **2** a very small thing. **3** *colloq.* a stupid or foolish person.

pinheaded *adj. colloq.* stupid, foolish. □ **pinheadedness** *n.*

pinhole *n.* **1** a hole made by a pin. **2** a hole into which a peg fits.

pinhole camera *n.* a camera with a pinhole aperture and no lens.

pinion[1] ● *n.* **1** the outer part of a bird's wing. **2** *poet.* a wing; a flight feather. ● *v.tr.* **1** cut off the pinion of (a wing or bird) to prevent flight. **2 a** bind the arms of (a person). **b** (often foll. by *to*) bind (the arms, a person, etc.) esp. to a thing. [from Latin *pinna*]

pinion[2] *n.* **1** a small cogwheel engaging with a larger one. ▷ RACK-AND-PINION, RACK RAILWAY. **2** a cogged spindle engaging with a wheel. [from Latin *pinea* 'pine cone']

pink[1] ● *n.* **1** a pale red colour. **2** ► any cultivated plant of the genus *Dianthus*, with sweet-smelling white, pink, crimson, etc. flowers. **3** (prec. by *the*) the most perfect condition etc. (*the pink of elegance*). **4** (also **hunting pink**) a fox-hunter's red coat. ● *adj.* **1** (often in *comb.*) of a pale red colour of any of various shades (*rose pink*). **2** *colloq.* often *derog.* tending to socialism. **3** of or associated with homosexuals. □ **in the pink** *colloq.* in very good health. [earliest in sense 2 of noun] □ **pinkish** *adj.*

PINK
(*Dianthus* 'Dad's Favourite')

pinkness *n.* **pinky** *adj.*

pink[2] *v.tr.* **1** pierce slightly with a sword etc. **2** cut a scalloped or zigzag edge on. [Middle English]

pink[3] *v.intr. Brit.* (of a vehicle engine) emit a series of high-pitched explosive sounds caused by faulty combustion.

pink-collar *adj.* (usu. *attrib.*) (of a profession etc.) traditionally associated with women.

pink-eye *n.* **1** a contagious fever in horses. **2** conjunctivitis in humans and some livestock.

pink gin *n. Brit.* gin flavoured with Angostura Bitters.

pinkie *n.* esp. *US & Sc. colloq.* the little finger. [partly from PINK[1], partly from Dutch *pink* 'the little finger']

pinking shears *n.pl.* (also **pinking scissors**) ▼ a dressmaker's serrated shears for cutting a zigzag edge.

pinked edge

pink slip *n.* esp. *N. Amer.* a notice of dismissal from employment.

pin money *n.* **1** *hist.* an allowance to a woman from her husband. **2** a small sum of money.

pinna *n.* (*pl.* **pinnae** /pin-ee/ or **pinnas**) the external part of the ear. ▷ EAR, ELEPHANT. [Latin variant of *penna* 'feather, wing, fin']

pinnace *n. Naut.* a ship's small boat. [based on Latin *pinus* 'pine']

PINKING SHEARS

pinnacle ● *n.* **1** the culmination or climax. **2** a natural peak. **3** a small ornamental turret crowning a buttress, roof, etc. ▷ CATHEDRAL. ● *v.tr.* **1** set on or as if on a pinnacle. **2** form the pinnacle of. **3** provide with pinnacles. [from Late Latin *pinnaculum*]

pinnae *pl.* of PINNA.

pinnate *adj.* **1** (of a compound leaf) having leaflets arranged on either side of the stem, usu. in pairs opposite each other. ▷ LEAF. **2** having branches, tentacles, etc., on each side of an axis. [from Latin *pinnatus* 'feathered'] □ **pinnated** *adj.* **pinnately** *adv.* **pinnation** *n.*

pinniped ● *adj.* denoting any aquatic mammal with limbs ending in flippers, e.g. a seal. ▷ SEAL. ● *n.* ▲ a pinniped mammal. [based on Latin *pinna* 'wing']

PINNIPED

Pinniped mammals belong to the order Pinnipedia, which contains the two main groups of seals – true seals and eared seals – and the walrus, which is the sole member of its family. Highly adapted to an aquatic life, pinnipeds have limbs modified into flippers and streamlined bodies. All pinnipeds must emerge on to shores or ice to breed, typically gathering in large groups at traditional breeding sites, known as rookeries.

TYPES OF PINNIPED

EARED SEALS
Californian sea lion
(*Zalophus californianus*)

WALRUS
walrus
(*Odobenus rosmarus*)

TRUE SEALS
grey seal
(*Halichoerus grypus*)

PIN number var. of PIN.

pinny *n.* (*pl.* **-ies**) *colloq.* a pinafore.

piñon /pin-yon/ *n.* (also **pinyon**) **1** any of several small N. American pines. **2** the seed of such a tree, a type of pine nut. [Spanish]

pinpoint ● *n.* **1** the point of a pin. **2** something very small or sharp. **3** (*attrib.*) **a** very small. **b** precise, accurate. ● *v.tr.* locate with precision (*pinpointed the target*).

pinprick *n.* **1** a prick caused by a pin. **2** a trifling irritation.

pins and needles *n pl.* a tingling sensation in a limb recovering from numbness.

pinstripe *n.* **1** (often *attrib.*) a very narrow stripe in (esp. worsted or serge) cloth. **2** (in *sing* or *pl.*) a pinstripe suit (*came wearing his pinstripes*). □ **pinstriped** *adj.*

pint *n.* **1** a unit of liquid or dry capacity equal to one-eighth of a gallon: **a** (in full **imperial pint**) (in Britain) 20 fluid oz, 34.66 cu. in., or 0.565 litre. **b** (in full **US pint**) (in the US) 28.87 cu. in. or 0.473 litre (for liquid measure), or 33.60 cu. in. or 0.551 litre (for dry measure). **2** *Brit.* **a** *colloq.* a pint of beer. **b** a pint of a liquid, esp. milk. **3** *Brit.* a measure of shellfish, being the amount containable in a pint mug. [from Old French *pinte*]

pinta *n. Brit. colloq.* a pint of milk.

pin-table *n. Brit.* a table used in playing pinball.

pintail *n.* a duck, esp. *Anas acuta*, or grouse, with a pointed tail.

pintle *n.* a pin or bolt, esp. one on which some other part turns. [Old English *pintel* 'penis']

pinto *N. Amer.* ● *adj.* piebald. ● *n.* (*pl.* **-os**) ▼ a piebald horse. [Spanish, literally 'mottled', from Latin *pictus* 'painted']

ovaro (brown and white) markings

PINTO

pint pot *n.* a pot, esp. of pewter, holding one pint, esp. of beer.

pint-sized *adj. colloq.* very small, esp. of a person.

pin-tuck *n.* a very narrow ornamental tuck.

pin-up *n.* **1** a photograph of a popular or sexually attractive person, designed to be hung on the wall. **2** a person shown in such a photograph.

pinwheel *n.* **1** a small Catherine wheel (firework). **2** a flat rotating spiral.

pinworm *n.* any of various small thread-like parasitic nematode worms, esp. *Enterobus vermicularis* found in the human intestine.

piny *adj.* (also **piney**) of, like, or full of pines (*a piny smell*).

Pinyin *n.* a system of romanized spelling for transliterating Chinese. [Chinese *pīn-yīn*, literally 'spell sound']

pinyon var. of PIÑON.

piolet *n.* a two-headed ice-axe for mountaineering.

pion *n. Physics* a meson having a mass approximately 270 times that of an electron. □ **pionic** *adj.*

pioneer ● *n.* **1** an initiator of a new enterprise, an inventor etc. **2** an explorer or settler. **3** *Mil.* a member of an infantry group preparing terrain etc. for the main body of troops. ● *v.* **1** *tr.* originate (an enterprise etc.). **2** *intr.* act or prepare the way as a pioneer. [from French *pionnier* 'foot soldier, pioneer']

pious *adj.* **1** devout; religious. **2** hypocritically virtuous. **3** dutiful. [from Latin *pius* 'dutiful, pious'] □ **piously** *adv.* **piousness** *n.*

pious fraud *n.* a deception intended to benefit those deceived, esp. religiously.

pip[1] ● *n.* the seed of an apple, pear, etc. ▷ SEED. ● *v.tr.* (**pipped**, **pipping**) remove the pips from (fruit etc.). □ **pipless** *adj.*

pip[2] *n. Brit.* a short high-pitched sound, usu. mechanically produced, esp. as a radio time signal.

pip[3] *n.* **1** any of the spots on a playing card, dice, or domino. **2** *Brit.* a star on the shoulder of an army officer's uniform. **3** an image of an object on a radar screen. [shortening of earlier *peep*]

pip[4] *n.* **1** a disease of poultry etc. causing thick mucus in the throat and white scale on the tongue. **2** *colloq.* a fit of disgust (esp. *give one the pip*). [from Middle Dutch *pippe*]

pip[5] *v.tr.* (**pipped**, **pipping**) *Brit. colloq.* **1** hit with a shot. **2** defeat. **3** blackball. □ **pip at** (or **to**) **the post** defeat at the last moment. **pip out** die.

pipe ● *n.* **1** a tube used to convey water, gas, etc. **2** (also **tobacco pipe**) a narrow wooden or clay etc. tube with a bowl at one end containing burning tobacco, the smoke from which is drawn into the mouth. **3** *Mus.* **a** a wind instrument consisting of a single tube. **b** any of the tubes of an organ. ▷ ORGAN. **c** (in *pl.*) bagpipes. **d** (in *pl.*) a set of pipes joined together, e.g. pan pipes. **4** a tubal organ, vessel, etc. in an animal's body. **5** a high note or song, esp. of a bird. **6 a** a boatswain's whistle. **b** the sounding of this. **7** a cask for wine, esp. as a measure of two hogsheads. ● *v.tr.* **1** (also *absol.*) play (a tune etc.) on a pipe or pipes. **2 a** convey (oil etc.) by pipes. **b** provide with pipes. **3** transmit (music etc.) by wire or cable. **4** (usu. foll. by *up, on, to,* etc.) *Naut.* **a** summon (a crew). **b** signal the arrival of (an officer etc.) on board. **5** utter in a shrill voice. **6 a** arrange (icing, cream, etc.) decoratively on a cake etc. **b** ornament (a cake etc.) with piping. **7** trim (a dress etc.) with piping. **8** lead or bring (a person etc.) by the sound of a pipe. □ **pipe down** *colloq.* be quiet or less insistent. **pipe up** begin to play, speak, etc. **put that in your pipe and smoke it** *colloq.* a challenge to another to accept something frank or unwelcome. [from Latin *pipare* 'to peep, chirp'] □ **pipeful** *n.* (*pl.* **-fuls**).

pipe band *n.* a (esp. military) band consisting of bagpipe players, drummers, and a drum major.

pipeclay ● *n.* a fine white clay used for tobacco pipes, whitening leather, etc. ● *v.tr.* **1** whiten (leather etc.) with this. **2** put in order.

pipe-cleaner *n.* a piece of flexible covered wire for cleaning a tobacco pipe.

piped music *n.* pre-recorded music played through loudspeakers in a public place.

pipe dream *n.* an unattainable or fanciful hope or scheme. [originally as experienced when smoking an opium pipe]

pipefish *n.* (*pl.* usu. same) ▼ any of various long slender fish of the family Syngnathidae, with an elongated snout.

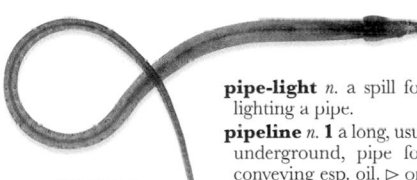

PIPEFISH
(*Syngnathus* species)

pipe-light *n.* a spill for lighting a pipe.

pipeline *n.* **1** a long, usu. underground, pipe for conveying esp. oil. ▷ OIL PLATFORM. **2** a channel supplying goods, information, etc. □ **in the pipeline** awaiting completion or processing.

pipe major *n.* an NCO commanding regimental pipers.

pip emma *adv.* & *n. Brit. colloq.* = P.M. [formerly signallers' names for letters *PM*]

pipe organ *n. Mus.* an organ using pipes instead of or as well as reeds. ▷ ORGAN

piper *n.* a person who plays a pipe, esp. the bagpipes.

pipe-rack *n.* a rack for holding tobacco pipes.

piperidine *n Chem.* a peppery-smelling liquid formed by the reduction of pyridine.

pipe-stem *n.* the shaft of a tobacco pipe.

pipe-stone *n.* a hard red clay used by N. American Indians for tobacco pipes.

pipette ● *n* ▼ a slender tube for transferring or measuring small quantities of liquids esp. in chemistry. ● *v.tr.* transfer or measure (a liquid) using a pipette. [French, literally 'little pipe']

PIPETTE

P

pipework *n.* pipes collectively.

piping ● *n.* **1** the act or an instance of piping, esp. whistling or singing. **2** a thin pipelike fold used for edging hems, seams, etc. **3** ▼ ornamental lines of icing, cream, potato, etc. **4** lengths of pipe, or a system of pipes, esp. in domestic use. ● *adj.* (of a noise) high; whistling.

PIPING: WHORLS OF MERINGUE PIPING

piping hot *adj. & adv.* very or suitably hot (esp. as required of food, water, etc.).

pipistrelle *n.* any bat of the genus *Pipistrellus*, native to temperate regions and feeding on insects. [from Latin *vespertilio* 'bat']

pipit *n.* any of various mainly ground-dwelling songbirds of the genus *Anthus*, having brown-streaked plumage.

pippin *n.* **1** an apple grown from seed. **2** a red and yellow dessert apple. [from Old French *pepin*]

pipsqueak *n. colloq.* an insignificant or contemptible person or thing.

piquant *adj.* **1** agreeably pungent, sharp, or appetizing. **2** pleasantly stimulating to the mind. [French, literally 'stinging'] □ **piquancy** *n.* **piquantly** *adv.*

pique peek ● *v.tr.* (**piques, piqued, piquing**) **1** wound the pride of, irritate. **2** arouse (curiosity, interest, etc.). ● *n.* ill feeling; enmity; resentment (*in a fit of pique*). [from French *piquer* 'to prick, irritate']

piqué /**pee**-kay/ *n.* a stiff ribbed cotton or other fabric. [French, literally 'pricked']

piquet[1] /**pee**-kay/ *n.* a game for two players with a pack of 32 cards. [French]

piquet[2] var. of PICKET *n.* 3.

piracy *n.* (*pl.* **-ies**) **1** robbery of ships at sea. **2** a similar practice, esp. hijacking. **3** the infringement of copyright by unauthorized reproduction or use of something. [from Greek *pirateia*]

piranha /pi-**rah**-nă/ *n.* (also **piraya** /pi-**rah**-yă/) ▼ a predatory S. American freshwater fish, noted for its voracity. [Portuguese]

PIRANHA (*Serrasalmus niger*)

pirate ● *n.* **1 a** a person who commits piracy. **b** a ship used by pirates. **2** a person who infringes another's copyright or business rights or who broadcasts without official authorization. ● *v.tr.* **1** appropriate or reproduce (another's works or ideas etc.) without permission, for one's own benefit. **2** plunder. [based on Greek *peiran* 'to attack, assault'] □ **piratic** *adj.* **piratical** *adj.*

piraya var. of PIRANHA.

pirouette /pi-roo-**et**/ ● *n.* a dancer's spin on one

foot or the point of the toe. ● *v.intr.* perform a pirouette. [French, literally 'spinning top']

piscatorial *adj.* = PISCATORY 1. □ **piscatorially** *adv.*

piscatory *adj.* of or concerning fishermen or fishing. [from Latin *piscatorius*]

Pisces /**py**-seez/ *n.* (*pl.* same) **1** *Astron.* ▼ a large constellation (the Fish or Fishes). **2** *Astrol.* **a** the twelfth sign of the zodiac, which the Sun enters about 20 Feb. **b** a person born when the Sun is in this sign. ▷ ZODIAC. [Latin, literally 'fishes'] □ **Piscean** *n. & adj.*

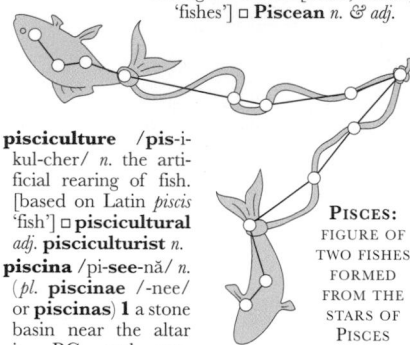

PISCES: FIGURE OF TWO FISHES FORMED FROM THE STARS OF PISCES

pisciculture /**pis**-i-kul-cher/ *n.* the artificial rearing of fish. [based on Latin *piscis* 'fish'] □ **piscicultural** *adj.* **pisciculturist** *n.*

piscina /pi-**see**-nă/ *n.* (*pl.* **piscinae** /-nee/ or **piscinas**) **1** a stone basin near the altar in RC and pre-Reformation churches for draining water used in the Mass. **2** a fish pond. [Latin, based on *piscis* 'fish']

piscine /**pi**-syn/ *adj.* of or concerning fish. [based on Latin *piscis* 'fish']

piss *coarse slang* ● *v.* **1** *intr.* urinate. **2** *tr.* discharge (blood etc.) when urinating. **3** *tr.* (as **pissed** *adj.*) *Brit.* drunk. **4** *refl.* **a** wet one's clothing with urine. **b** be very frightened, amused, or excited. ● *n.* **1** urine. **2** an act of urinating. □ **piss about** *Brit.* fool or mess about. **piss down** rain heavily. **piss off** *Brit.* **1** go away. **2** (often as **pissed off** *adj.*) annoy; depress. **take the piss** (often foll. by *out of*) *Brit.* mock. [from Old French *pisser*]

piss artist *n. Brit. coarse slang* **1** a drunkard. **2** a person who fools about. **3** a glib person.

pissoir /peess-**wah**/ *n.* a public urinal. [French]

piss-take *n. Brit. coarse slang* a parody.

piss-taker *n. Brit. coarse slang* a person who mocks. □ **piss-taking** *n.*

piss-up *n. Brit. coarse slang* a drinking spree.

pistachio /pis-**tash**-i-oh/ ● *n.* (*pl.* **-os**) **1** an evergreen tree, *Pistacia vera*, bearing small brownish-green flowers and ovoid reddish fruit. **2** (in full **pistachio nut**) the edible pale green seed of this. **3** (in full **pistachio green**) a pale green colour. ● *adj.* (in full **pistachio green**; hyphenated when *attrib.*) pale green. [based on Persian *pistah*]

piste /peest/ *n.* a ski run of compacted snow. [French, literally 'racetrack']

pisteur /peess-**ter**/ *n.* a person employed to prepare the snow on a skiing piste. [French]

pistil *n.* the female organs of a flower, comprising the stigma, style, and ovary. ▷ HERMAPHRODITE. [from Latin *pistillum* 'pestle']

pistol *n.* **1** ▼ a small hand-held firearm. **2** anything of a similar shape. ▷ GUN. [from Czech *píšťal*]

PISTOL: SECOND WORLD WAR JAPANESE AUTOMATIC PISTOL

safety switch
cocking boss
barrel
foresight
lanyard loop
trigger guard
rear sight
trigger
magazine release catch
base of magazine

pistol grip *n.* a handle shaped like a pistol-butt.

pistol shot *n.* **1** the range of a pistol. **2** a shot fired from a pistol.

pistol-whip *v.tr.* (**-whipped, -whipping**) beat with a pistol.

piston *n.* **1** a disc or short cylinder fitting closely within a tube in which it moves up and down against a liquid or gas deriving or imparting motion. ▷ PNEUMATIC, SHOCK ABSORBER. **2** a sliding valve in a trumpet etc. [from Italian *pistone*]

piston engine *n.* an engine, esp. in an aircraft, in which motion is derived from a piston. □ **piston-engined** *adj.*

piston ring *n.* a ring on a piston sealing the gap between the piston and the cylinder wall.

piston rod *n.* a rod or crankshaft attached to a piston to drive a wheel or to impart motion.

pit[1] ● *n.* **1 a** a usu. large deep hole in the ground. **b** a hole made in digging for industrial purposes (*chalk pit*). **c** a covered hole as a trap for esp. wild animals. **2 a** an indentation left after smallpox, acne, etc. **b** a hollow in a plant or animal body or on any surface. **3 a** = ORCHESTRA 2a. **b** *Brit. Theatr.* (usu. *hist.*) seating at the back of the stalls, or the people seated there. **4 a** (**the pit** or **bottomless pit**) hell. **b** (**the pits**) *slang* the worst imaginable place, person, etc. **5 a** an area at the side of a track where racing cars are serviced and refuelled. **b** a sunken area in a workshop floor for access to a car's underside. **6** *Brit. slang* a bed. ● *v.tr.* (**pitted, pitting**) **1** (usu. foll. by *against*) **a** set (one's wits etc.) in opposition. **b** set (a cock etc.) to fight, originally in a pit, against another. **2** (usu. as **pitted** *adj.*) make pits, esp. scars, in. □ **dig a pit for** try to ensnare. [from Latin *puteus* 'well']

pit[2] esp. *US* ● *n.* the stone of a fruit. ● *v.tr.* (**pitted, pitting**) remove pits from (fruit).

pita var. of PITTA.

pit-a-pat (also **pitter-patter**) ● *adv.* **1** with a sound like quick light steps. **2** with a faltering sound. ● *n.* such a sound.

pit bull *n.* (in full **pit bull terrier**) ▶ a dog of an American variety of bull terrier, noted for its ferocity.

pitch[1] ● *v.* **1** *tr.* (also *absol.*) erect and fix (a tent etc.). **2** *tr.* **a** throw; fling. **b** (in games) throw (a flat object) towards a mark. **3** *tr.* fix or plant (a thing) in a definite position. **4** *tr.* express in a particular style or at a particular level. **5** *intr.* (often foll. by *against, into*, etc.) fall heavily, esp. headlong. **6** *intr.* (of a moving ship etc.) rock so that the front moves up and down. **7** *tr. Mus.* set at a particular pitch. **8** *intr.* (of a roof etc.) slope downwards. **9** *intr.* (often foll. by *about*) move with a vigorous jogging motion, as in a train etc. **10** *Cricket* **a** *tr.* cause (a bowled ball) to strike the ground at a specified point etc. **b** *intr.* (of a bowled ball) strike the ground. ● *n.* **1 a** *Brit.* the area of play in a field game. **b** *Cricket* the area between the creases. **2** degree, intensity, etc. (*the pitch of despair*). **3** the steepness of a slope, esp. of a roof etc. **4** *Mus.* **a** that quality of a sound which is governed by the rate of vibrations producing it; the highness or lowness of a tone. **b** a standard scale of this used in performance etc. **5** the pitching motion of a ship etc. **6** *Cricket* the act or mode of delivery in bowling, or the spot where the ball bounces. **7** *colloq.* a salesman's advertising or selling approach. **8** *Brit.* a place where a street vendor sells wares etc. **9** the delivery of a baseball by a pitcher. □ **pitch in** *colloq.* set to work vigorously. **pitch into** *colloq.* **1** attack forcibly. **2** assail (food, work, etc.) vigorously. **pitch on** (or **upon**) *Brit.* happen to select. [earlier in sense 'to thrust a stake etc. into the ground': Middle English]

PIT BULL TERRIER

pitch[2] ● *n.* **1** a sticky resinous black or dark brown substance obtained by distilling tar or turpentine, used for caulking the seams of ships etc. **2** any of various bituminous substances including asphalt. ● *v.tr.* cover, coat, or smear with pitch. [from Latin *pix picis*] □ **pitchy** *adj.* (**pitchier**, **pitchiest**).

pitch-and-toss *n.* a gambling game in which coins are pitched at a mark and then tossed.

pitch-black *adj.* (also **pitch-dark**) very or completely dark.

pitchblende *n.* a mineral form of uranium oxide occurring in pitchlike masses and also containing radium.

pitched battle *n.* **1** a vigorous argument etc. **2** *Mil.* a battle planned beforehand and fought on chosen ground.

pitched roof *n.* a sloping roof. ▷ ROOF

pitcher[1] *n.* **1** *Brit.* a large usu. earthenware jug with a lip and a handle, for holding liquids. **2** *US* = JUG *n.* 1. [from Old French *pichier*] □ **pitcherful** *n.* (*pl.* **-fuls**).

pitcher[2] *n.* **1** a person or thing that pitches. **2** *Baseball* a player who delivers the ball to the batter.

pitcher plant *n.* ◀ any of various plants of the families Nepenthaceae and Sarraceniaceae with leaves modified into deep pouches.

pitchfork ● *n.* a long-handled two-pronged fork for pitching hay etc. ● *v.tr.* **1** throw with or as if with a pitchfork. **2** (usu. foll. by *into*) thrust (a person) forcibly into a position etc. [Middle English alteration of *pickfork*]

pitch pine *n.* any of various pine trees with very resinous wood.

pitch-pipe *n. Mus.* a small pipe blown to set the pitch for singing or tuning.

piteous *adj.* deserving or causing pity; wretched. □ **piteously** *adv.* **piteousness** *n.*

pitfall *n.* **1** an unsuspected snare, danger, or drawback. **2** a covered pit for trapping animals etc.

pith *n.* **1** spongy white tissue lining the rind of an orange etc. **2** the essential part (*the pith of his argument*). **3** *Bot.* the spongy cellular tissue in the stems and branches of dicotyledonous plants. **4** vigour; energy. [Old English]

pithead *n.* **1** the top of a mine shaft. **2** the area surrounding this.

pith helmet *n.* ▶ a lightweight sun-helmet made from the dried pith of the sola etc.

pithy *adj.* (**pithier**, **pithiest**) **1** (of style, speech, etc.) condensed, terse, and forcible. **2** of, like, or containing much pith. □ **pithily** *adv.* **pithiness** *n.*

pitiable *adj.* **1** deserving or causing pity. **2** contemptible. □ **pitiableness** *n.* **pitiably** *adv.*

pitiful *adj.* **1** causing pity. **2** contemptible. **3** *archaic* compassionate. □ **pitifully** *adv.* **pitifulness** *n.*

pitiless *adj.* showing no pity. □ **pitilessly** *adv.* **pitilessness** *n.*

pitman *n.* **1** (*pl.* **-men**) a collier. **2** *US* (*pl.* **-mans**) a connecting rod in machinery.

nectar on rim attracts insects

partially digested insects

PITCHER PLANT:
CROSS-SECTION OF
THE LEAF POUCH

PITH HELMET

---

pit of the stomach *n.* **1** the floor of the stomach. **2** the depression below the bottom of the breastbone.

piton /pee-ton/ *n.* a peg or spike driven into a rock or crack to support a climber or a rope. [French, literally 'eye bolt']

pit pony *n. Brit. hist.* a pony kept underground for haulage in coal mines.

pit prop *n.* a baulk of wood used to support the roof of a coal mine.

pit stop *n. Motor Racing* a stop at a pit for servicing and refuelling.

pitta *n.* (also **pita**) a flat hollow unleavened bread which can be split and filled with salad etc. [modern Greek, literally 'a cake']

pittance *n.* a scanty or meagre allowance, remuneration, etc. [based on Latin *pietas* 'pity']

pitter-patter var. of PIT-A-PAT.

pittosporum *n.* ▶ any evergreen shrub of the genus *Pittosporum*, with small often fragrant flowers. [modern Latin, based on Greek *pitta* 'pitch' + *sporos* 'seed']

pituitary ● *n.* (*pl.* **-ies**) (also **pituitary gland** or **pituitary body**) a small ductless gland at the base of the brain secreting various hormones essential for growth etc. ▷ BRAIN, ENDOCRINE. ● *adj.* of or relating to this gland. [from Latin *pituitarius* 'secreting phlegm']

pity ● *n.* (*pl.* **-ies**) **1** sorrow and compassion aroused by another's condition. **2** something to be regretted; grounds for regret. ● *v.tr.* (**-ies**, **-ied**) feel (often contemptuous) pity for. □ **for pity's sake** an exclamation of urgent supplication, anger, etc. **more's the pity** so much the worse. **take pity on** feel or act compassionately towards. [from Latin *pietas* 'piety'] □ **pitying** *adj.* **pityingly** *adv.*

pivot ● *n.* **1** a short shaft or pin on which something turns or oscillates. **2** a crucial or essential person, point, etc., in a scheme or enterprise. **3** *Mil.* the man or men about whom a body of troops wheels. ● *v.* (**pivoted, pivoting**) **1** *intr.* turn on or as if on a pivot. **2** *intr.* (foll. by *on, upon*) hinge on. **3** *tr.* provide with or attach by a pivot. [French] □ **pivotability** *n.* **pivotable** *adj.* **pivotal** *adj.*

pix[1] *n.pl. colloq.* pictures, esp. photographs.

pix[2] var. of PYX.

pixel *n. Electronics* any of the minute areas of uniform illumination of which an image on a display screen is composed. ▷ MONITOR. [from abbreviation of *pictures* + ELEMENT]

pixelate *v.tr. Electronics* display as or divide into pixels. □ **pixelation** *n.*

pixie *n.* (also **pixy**) (*pl.* **-ies**) a being like a fairy; an elf. [17th-century coinage]

pixie hat *n.* (also **pixie hood**) a child's hat with a pointed crown.

pixilated *adj.* (also **pixillated**) **1** bewildered; crazy. **2** drunk. [variant of *pixie-led* 'led astray by pixies']

pizazz *n.* (also **pizzazz**, **pzazz**, etc.) *slang* verve, energy, liveliness, sparkle.

pizza /peet-sǎ/ *n.* a flat round base of dough baked with a topping of tomatoes, cheese, onions, etc. [Italian, literally 'pie']

pizzeria /peet-sě-ree-ǎ/ *n.* a place where pizzas are made or sold.

pizzicato /pit-si-kah-toh/ *Mus.* ● *adv.* plucking the strings of a violin etc. with the finger. ● *adj.* performed pizzicato. ● *n.* (*pl.* **pizzicatos** or **pizzicati**) a note, passage, etc. played pizzicato. [Italian, literally 'twitched']

PITTOSPORUM: JAPANESE
PITTOSPORUM
(*Pittosporum tobira*)

---

pl. *abbr.* **1** place. **2** plate. **3** esp. *Mil.* platoon. **4** plural.

placable *adj.* easily placated; mild; forgiving. [from Latin *placabilis*]

placard ● *n.* a printed or handwritten poster esp. for advertising. ● *v.tr.* **1** set up placards on (a wall etc.). **2** advertise by placards. **3** display (a poster etc.) as a placard. [from Old French *placquart*]

placate *v.tr.* pacify; conciliate. [based on Latin *placatus* 'appeased'] □ **placatingly** *adv.* **placation** *n.* **placatory** *adj.*

place ● *n.* **1 a** a particular portion of space. **b** a portion of space occupied by a person or thing. **c** a proper or natural position (*out of his place*). **2** a city, village, etc. (*was born in this place*). **3** a residence (*come round to my place*). **4 a** a group of houses in a town etc., esp. a square. **b** a country house with its surroundings. **5** a person's rank or status (*know their place*). **6** a space, esp. a seat, for a person. **7** a building or area for a specific purpose (*place of worship*). **8 a** a point reached in a book etc. **b** a passage in a book. **9** a particular spot on a surface, esp. of the skin. **10 a** employment or office, esp. government employment. **b** the duties or entitlements of office etc. (*is his place to hire staff*). **11** a position as a member of a team, a student in a college, etc. **12** *Brit.* any of the first three or sometimes four final positions in a race, esp. other than the winner (*backed it for a place*). **13** the position of a figure in a series indicated in decimal or similar notation. ● *v.tr.* **1** put (a thing etc.) in a particular place or state. **2** identify, classify, or remember correctly (*cannot place him*). **3** locate. **4 a** appoint (a person, esp. a member of the clergy) to a post. **b** find a situation, living, etc. for. **c** (usu. foll. by *with*) consign to a person's care etc. **5** assign rank, importance, or worth to. **6 a** dispose of (goods) to a customer. **b** make (an order for goods etc.). **7** (often foll. by *in, on,* etc.) have (confidence etc.). **8** invest (money). **9** *Brit.* state the position of (any of esp. the first three runners) in a race. **10** *tr.* (as **placed** *adj.*) **a** esp. *Brit.* among the first three or sometimes four in a race. **b** *US* second in a race. **11** *Football* get (a goal) by a place-kick. □ **all over the place** in disorder; chaotic. **give place to 1** make room for. **2** yield precedence to. **3** be succeeded by. **go places** *colloq.* be successful. **in place 1** in the right position; suitable. **2** *US* on the spot (*running in place*). **in place of** instead of. **in places** at some places or in some parts, but not others. **keep a person in his** or **her place** suppress a person's aspirations or pretensions. **out of place 1** in the wrong position. **2** unsuitable. **put oneself in another's place** imagine oneself in another's position. **put a person in his** or **her place** deflate or humiliate a person. **take place** occur. **take one's place** go to one's correct position etc. **take the place of** be substituted for. [from Greek *plateia (hodos)* 'broad (way)'] □ **placeless** *adj.* **placement** *n.* **placing** *n.*

place-bet *n.* **1** *Brit.* a bet on a horse to come first, second, third, or sometimes fourth in a race. **2** *US* a bet on a horse to come second.

placebo /plǎ-see-boh/ *n.* (*pl.* **-os**) **1 a** a pill, medicine, etc. prescribed for psychological reasons but having no physiological effect. **b** a blank sample used as a control in testing new drugs etc. **2** something that is said or done to calm or humour a person. [Latin, literally 'I shall be pleasing']

placebo effect *n.* a beneficial (or adverse) effect produced by a placebo and not due to any property of the placebo itself.

place card *n.* a card marking a person's place at a table etc.

place in the sun *n.* a favourable situation, position, etc.

P

place-kick *n.* *Football* a kick made when the ball is previously placed on the ground. □ **place-kicker** *n.*

placeman *n.* (*pl.* **-men**) a person appointed to a position chiefly to implement the political policies of a higher authority.

place mat *n.* a small mat on a table underneath a person's plate.

place name *n.* the name of a town, hill, lake, etc.

placenta *n.* (*pl.* **placentae** /-tee/ or **placentas**) a flattened circular organ in the uterus of certain mammals when pregnant, nourishing and maintaining the foetus through the umbilical cord and expelled after birth. ▷ FOETUS. [from Greek *plakous -ountos* 'flat cake'] □ **placental** *adj.*

placer *n.* a deposit of sand, gravel, etc., in the bed of a stream etc., containing valuable minerals in particles. [Latin American Spanish]

place setting *n.* a set of plates, cutlery, etc. for one person at a meal.

placid *adj.* **1** (of a person) not easily aroused or disturbed. **2** mild; calm; serene. [from Latin *placidus*] □ **placidity** *n.* **placidly** *adv.* **placidness** *n.*

placket *n.* **1** an opening or slit in a garment, for fastenings or access to a pocket. **2** the flap of fabric under this. [variant of obsolete *placard* 'garment worn under an open coat']

plagiarize /play-jă-ryz/ *v.tr.* (also **-ise**) (also *absol.*) **1** take and use (the thoughts, inventions, etc. of another person) as one's own. **2** pass off the thoughts etc. of (another person) as one's own. [based on Greek *plagion* 'a kidnapping'] □ **plagiarism** *n.*

plague *n.* **1 a** (prec. by *the*) a contagious bacterial disease characterized by fever and delirium, with the formation of buboes (**bubonic plague**) and sometimes infection of the lungs (**pneumonic plague**). **b** any severe or fatal contagious disease spreading rapidly over a wide area. **2** (foll. by *of*) an unusual infestation (*a plague of frogs*). **3 a** great trouble. **b** an affliction, esp. as regarded as divine punishment. **4** *colloq.* a nuisance. ● *v.tr.* (**plagues**, **plagued**, **plaguing**) **1** afflict, torment (*plagued by war*). **2** *colloq.* pester or harass continually. [from Latin *plaga* 'stroke, wound']

plaice *n.* (*pl.* same) **1** ▼ a European flatfish, *Pleuronectes platessa*, having a brown back with orange spots and a white underside, much used for food. **2** (in full **American plaice**) a N. Atlantic fish, *Hippoglossoides platessoides*. [from Late Latin *platessa*]

white underside

upper side

PLAICE (*Pleuronectes platessa*)

plaid /plad/ *n.* **1** (often *attrib.*) chequered or tartan, esp. woollen, twilled cloth (*a plaid skirt*). **2** a long piece of plaid worn over the shoulder as part of Scottish Highland dress. [from Gaelic]

plain ● *adj.* **1** clear; evident. **2** readily understood. **3 a** (of food, decoration, etc.) uncomplicated; not elaborate. **b** without a decorative pattern. **4** (esp. of a woman or girl) not beautiful or pretty. **5** outspoken. **6** (of manners, dress, etc.) unsophisticated; homely. **7** (of a knitting stitch) made by putting the needle through the front of the stitch from left to right. ▷ KNITTING. ● *adv.* **1** unequivocally (*to speak plain, I don't approve*). **2** simply (*that is plain stupid*). ● *n.* a level tract of esp. treeless country. [from Latin *planus* (adj.), *planum* (n.)] □ **plainly** *adv.* **plainness** *n.*

plainchant *n.* = PLAINSONG.

plain chocolate *n.* *Brit.* chocolate without added milk and therefore dark.

plain clothes *n.pl.* ordinary clothes worn esp. as a disguise by police officers etc. (hyphenated when *attrib.*: *plain-clothes policeman*).

plain dealing *n.* candour; straightforwardness.

plain flour *n.* flour not containing a raising agent.

plain sailing *n.* **1** sailing a straightforward course. **2** an uncomplicated situation or course of action.

plainsman *n.* (*pl.* **-men**) a person who lives on a plain, esp. in N. America.

plainsong *n.* unaccompanied church music sung in unison in medieval modes and in free rhythm corresponding to the accentuation of the words.

plain-spoken *adj.* outspoken; blunt.

plaint *n.* **1** *Brit. Law* an accusation; a charge. **2** *literary* or *archaic* a lamentation. [from Latin *planctus*]

plaintiff *n.* *Law* a person who brings a case against another into court. [from Old French *plaintif* 'plaintive (person)']

plaintive *adj.* **1** expressing sorrow; mournful. **2** mournful-sounding. [from Old French *plaintif -ive*] □ **plaintively** *adv.* **plaintiveness** *n.*

plait plat ● *n.* **1** a length of hair, straw, etc., in three or more interlaced strands. **2** = PLEAT *n.* ● *v.tr.* **1** form (hair etc.) into a plait. **2** make (a belt, mat, etc.) by plaiting. [from Old French *pleit* 'a fold']

plan ● *n.* **1 a** a formulated and esp. detailed method by which a thing is to be done. **b** an intention or proposed proceeding (*plan of campaign*). **2** a drawing or diagram made by projection on a horizontal plane, esp. showing a building (cf. ELEVATION 2a). **3** a fairly large-scale map of a town or district. **4 a** a table etc. indicating times, places, etc. of intended proceedings. **b** a diagram of an arrangement (*seating plan*). **5** an imaginary plane perpendicular to the line of vision and containing the objects shown in a picture. ● *v.* (**planned**, **planning**) **1** *tr.* (often foll. by *that* + clause or *to* + infin.) arrange (a procedure etc.) beforehand; form a plan. **2** *tr.* **a** design (a building, new town, etc.). **b** make a plan of (an existing building, an area, etc.). **3** *tr.* (as **planned** *adj.*) in accordance with a plan (*planned parenthood*). **4** *intr.* make plans. □ **plan on** *colloq.* aim at doing or having; intend. [from Italian *pianta* 'plan of building'] □ **planning** *n.*

planarian *n.* any flatworm of the division Tricladida, usu. living in fresh water.

planchet *n.* a plain metal disc from which a coin is made.

planchette /plahn-**shet**/ *n.* a small usu. heart-shaped board on castors with a pencil that is supposedly caused to write spirit messages when a person's fingers rest lightly on it. [French, literally 'little plank']

plane[1] ● *n.* **1 a** a flat surface on which a straight line joining any two points on it would wholly lie. **b** an imaginary flat surface through or joining etc. material objects. **2** a level surface. **3** = AEROPLANE. **4** a flat surface producing lift by the action of air or water over and under it (usu. in *comb.*: *hydroplane*). **5** (often foll. by *of*) a level of attainment, thought, etc. **6** a flat thin object such as a table top. ● *adj.* **1** (of a surface etc.) perfectly level. **2** (of an angle, figure, etc.) lying in a plane. ● *v.intr.* **1** (often foll. by *down*) travel or glide in an aeroplane. **2** (of a speedboat etc.) skim over water. **3** soar. [from Latin *planum* 'flat surface'] □ **planar** *adj. Math.*

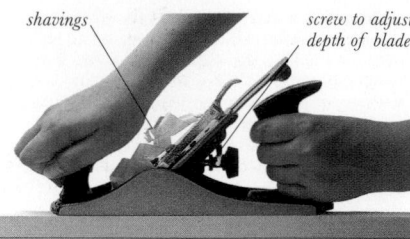

shavings   screw to adjust depth of blade

PLANE

plane[2] ● *n.* **1** ▲ a tool consisting of a wooden or metal block with a projecting steel blade, used to smooth a wooden surface by paring shavings from it. **2** a similar tool for smoothing metal. ● *v.tr.* **1** smooth (wood, metal, etc.) with a plane. **2** (often foll. by *away*, *down*) pare with a plane. [from Latin *planus* 'plain']

plane[3] *n.* (in full **plane tree**) ◀ any tree of the genus *Platanus* often growing to great heights, with maple-like leaves and bark. [from Greek *platanos*]

bristly fruit

PLANE: ORIENTAL PLANE
(*Platanus orientalis*)

plane polarization *n.* (also **-isation**) a process restricting the vibrations of electromagnetic radiation, esp. light, to one direction.

planer *n.* a machine for planing esp. wood.

plane sailing *n.* **1** the practice of determining a ship's position on the theory that it is moving on a plane. **2** = PLAIN SAILING.

planet *n.* **1** a celestial body moving in an elliptical orbit round a star. **2** (prec. by *the*) the Earth. ▷ SOLAR SYSTEM. [from Greek *planētēs* 'wanderer, planet']

planetarium *n.* (*pl.* **planetariums** or **planetaria**) **1** a domed building in which images of stars, planets, etc. are projected for entertainment or education. **2** the device used for such projection. **3** = ORRERY. [modern Latin]

planetary *adj.* **1** of or like planets. **2** terrestrial; mundane. **3** wandering; erratic.

planetary nebula *n.* ▼ a ring-shaped nebula formed by an expanding shell of gas round a star. ▷ NEBULA, STAR

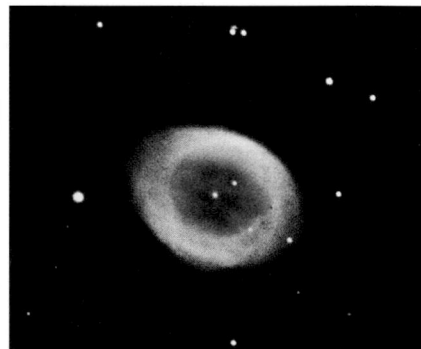

PLANETARY NEBULA IN THE CONSTELLATION LYRA

planetoid *n.* = ASTEROID 1.

plangent *adj.* **1** loud and reverberating. **2** plaintive; sad. [from Latin *plangent-* 'lamenting'] □ **plangency** *n.* **plangently** *adv.*

planimeter /plă-**nim**-i-ter/ *n.* an instrument for mechanically measuring the area of a plane figure. [based on Latin *planus* 'level'] □ **planimetric** *adj.* **planimetry** *n.*

planisphere *n.* a map formed by the projection of a sphere or part of a sphere on a plane, esp. an

P

adjustable circular star map. [from medieval Latin *planisphaerium*]

plank ● *n.* **1** a long flat piece of timber used esp. in flooring etc. **2** an item of a political or other programme. ● *v.tr.* **1** provide, cover, or floor with planks. **2** (usu. foll. by *down*; also *absol.*) esp. *US colloq.* **a** put down roughly or violently. **b** pay (money) on the spot or abruptly. □ **walk the plank** *hist.* (of a pirate's captive etc.) be made to walk blindfold along a plank over the side of a ship to one's death. [from Late Latin *planca* 'board']

planking *n.* planks as flooring etc.

plankton *n.* the small and microscopic organisms drifting or floating in the sea or fresh water. [from Greek *plagktos* 'wandering'] □ **planktonic** *adj.*

planned economy *n.* an economy in which production, prices, incomes, etc. are determined centrally by government.

planner *n.* **1** a person who controls or plans the development of new towns etc. **2** a person who makes plans. **3** a list, table, etc., with information helpful in planning.

planning permission *n. Brit.* formal permission for building development etc., esp. from a local authority.

plano- *comb. form* level, flat. [from Latin *planus*]

planoconcave *adj.* (of a lens etc.) with one surface plane and the other concave.

planoconvex *adj.* (of a lens etc.) with one surface plane and the other convex.

plant ● *n.* **1 a** any living organism of the kingdom Plantae, usu. containing chlorophyll enabling it to live wholly on inorganic substances and lacking specialized sense organs and the power of voluntary movement. **b** a small organism of this kind, as distinguished from a shrub or tree. **2 a** machinery, fixtures, etc., used in industrial processes. **b** a factory. **3** *colloq.* **a** something positioned or concealed to incriminate another. **b** a person stationed as a spy or source of information. ● *v.tr.* **1** place (a seed, bulb, etc.) in the ground so that it may take root and flourish. **2** (often foll. by *in*, *on*, etc.) **a** put or fix in position. **b** *refl.* take up a position (*planted myself by the door*). **c** place (a bomb) in a building etc. **3** station (a person etc.), esp. as a spy or source of information. **4** cause (an idea etc.) to be established, esp. in another person's mind. **5** deliver (a blow, kiss, etc.) with a deliberate aim. **6** *colloq.* position or conceal (something incriminating or compromising) for later discovery. **7** bury. □ **plant out** transfer (a plant) from a pot or frame to the open ground; set out (seedlings) at intervals. [from Latin *planta* 'sprout, slip, cutting'] □ **plantlet** *n.* **plantlike** *adj.*

Plantagenet ● *adj.* of or relating to the kings of England from Henry II to Richard III. ● *n.* any of these kings. [from Latin *planta genista* 'sprig of broom', worn as a crest and origin of the surname]

plantain[1] *n.* ► any low-growing plant of the genus *Plantago*, with usu. broad flat leaves forming a rosette on the ground. [from Latin *plantago*]

plantain[2] *n.* **1** a plant, *Musa paradisiaca*, related to the banana and widely grown in warm countries for its fruit. **2** the starchy fruit of this. [from Spanish *plá(n)tano* 'plane tree']

plantar *adj.* of or relating to the sole of the foot. [from Latin *plantaris*]

plantation *n.* **1** an estate on which cotton, tobacco, etc.,

PLANTAIN:
COMMON PLANTAIN
(*Plantago major*)

is cultivated. **2** an area planted with trees etc. **3** *hist.* a colony. [from Latin *plantatio*]

plantation song *n.* a song of the kind formerly sung by blacks on American plantations.

planter *n.* **1** a person who cultivates the soil. **2** the manager or occupier of a plantation. **3** a large container for decorative plants. **4** a machine for planting seeds etc.

plant-louse *n.* a small insect that infests plants, esp. an aphis. ▷ HEMIPTERA

plantsman *n.* (*pl.* **-men**; *fem.* **plantswoman**, *pl.* **-women**) an expert in garden plants and gardening.

plaque *n.* **1** an ornamental tablet of metal, porcelain, etc., esp. affixed to a building in commemoration. **2** a deposit on teeth where bacteria proliferate. [from Dutch *plak* 'tablet'] □ **plaquette** *n.*

plash[1] ● *n.* **1** a splash; a plunge. **2 a** a marshy pool. **b** a puddle. ● *v.* **1** *tr. & intr.* splash. **2** *tr.* strike the surface of (water). [Old English]

plash[2] *v.tr.* esp. *Brit.* bend down and interweave (branches, twigs, etc.) to form a hedge. [from Latin *plectere* 'to plait']

plasma *n.* (also **plasm**) **1** the colourless fluid part of blood, lymph, or milk, in which corpuscles or fat-globules are suspended. ▷ BLOOD. **2** = PROTOPLASM. **3** a gas of positive ions and free electrons with approximately equal positive and negative charges. [Greek, literally 'mould, image'] □ **plasmic** *adj.*

plaster ● *n.* **1** a soft mixture esp. of lime putty with sand or Portland cement etc. for spreading on walls, ceilings, etc., to form a smooth hard surface when dried. **2** *Brit.* = STICKING PLASTER. **3** = PLASTER OF PARIS. ● *v.tr.* **1** cover (a wall etc.) with plaster or a similar substance. **2** (often foll. by *with*) coat thickly or to excess; daub (*plastered the bread with jam; the wall was plastered with slogans*). **3** stick or apply (a thing) thickly like plaster (*plastered glue all over it*). **4** (often foll. by *down*) make (esp. hair) smooth with water, cream, etc. **5** (as **plastered** *adj.*) *slang* drunk. **6** apply a plaster cast to. **7** *slang* bomb or shell heavily. [from Greek *emplastron*] □ **plasterer** *n.* **plastery** *adj.*

plasterboard *n.* two boards with a filling of plaster used to form or line the inner walls of houses etc.

plaster cast *n.* **1** a rigid casing for a broken limb etc., made from a bandage stiffened with plaster of Paris. **2** ► a statue or mould made of plaster.

plaster of Paris *n.* fine white plaster made of gypsum and used for making plaster casts etc. ▷ CORNICE

PLASTER CAST
OF A FOSSIL

plaster saint *n. iron.* a person regarded as being without moral faults or human frailty.

plasterwork *n.* work done in plaster, esp. the plaster-covered surface of a wall or decorative plaster surfaces.

plastic ● *n.* **1** ▲ any of a number of synthetic polymeric substances that can be given any required shape. **2** (*attrib.*) **a** made of plastic (*plastic bag*). **b** artificial, insincere. **3** *colloq.* = PLASTIC MONEY. ● *adj.* **1** capable of being moulded. **2** moulding or giving form to clay, wax, etc. [from Greek *plastikos*] □ **plastically** *adv.* **plasticity** *n.* **plasticization** *n.* **plasticize** *v.tr.* (also **-ise**). **plasticizer** *n.* **plasticky** *adj.*

plastic arts *n.pl.* art forms involving modelling or moulding, e.g. sculpture and ceramics.

plastic bomb *n.* a bomb containing plastic explosive.

plastic bullet *n.* a bullet made of PVC or another plastic material.

plastic explosive *n.* a putty-like explosive capable of being moulded by hand.

PLASTIC

Plastics fall into two main classes according to the way they react to heat. Thermoplastics, such as polythene and perspex, can be repeatedly softened and hardened by heating and cooling. Thermosetting plastics, such as epoxy resins and polyurethane, are initially soft but set hard after heating, and cannot be softened again by further heating. Some plastics are given added strength by reinforcing them with fibres; these are known as composites.

EXAMPLES OF PLASTICS

THERMOPLASTIC
(POLYTHENE BAG)

THERMOSETTING
PLASTIC (EPOXY
CYCLE HELMET)

COMPOSITE
PLASTIC
(TENNIS RACKET)

plasticine *n. propr.* a soft plastic material used, esp. by children, for modelling.

plastic money *n. colloq.* credit cards or other types of plastic card that can be used instead of money.

plastic surgery *n.* the process of reconstructing or repairing injured or unsightly parts of the body by the transfer of tissue. □ **plastic surgeon** *n.*

plastic wood *n.* a mouldable material which hardens to resemble wood, used for filling crevices etc.

plastid *n.* any small organelle in the cytoplasm of a plant cell, containing pigment or food. ▷ DIATOM. [German]

plate ● *n.* **1 a** a shallow vessel, usu. circular and of earthenware or china, from which food is eaten or served. **b** the contents of this (*a plate of sandwiches*). **2** a similar vessel usu. of metal or wood, used esp. for making a collection in a church etc. **3** *US* a main course of a meal, served on one plate. **4** (*collect.*) **a** utensils of silver, gold, or other metal. **b** objects of plated metal. **5 a** a piece of metal with a name or inscription for affixing to a door, container, etc. **b** = NUMBER PLATE. **6** an illustration on special paper in a book. **7** a thin sheet of metal, glass, etc. with a light-sensitive coating, used for photography. **8** a flat thin usu. rigid sheet of metal etc. with an even surface and uniform thickness, often as part of a mechanism. **9 a** a smooth piece of metal etc. for engraving. **b** an impression made from this. **10 a** a silver or gold cup as a prize for a horse race etc. **b** a race with this as a prize. **11 a** a thin piece of plastic material, moulded to the shape of the mouth, to which artificial teeth or another orthodontic appliance are attached. **b** *colloq.* a complete denture or orthodontic appliance. **12** *Geol.* each of several sheets of rock thought to form the Earth's outer crust. ▷ PLATE TECTONICS. **13** a stereotype, electrotype, or plastic cast of a page of composed movable types, or a metal or plastic copy of filmset matter,

P

from which sheets are printed. **14** *Baseball* a flat piece of whitened rubber marking the station of a batter or pitcher. **15** *US* the anode of a thermionic valve. **16** a horizontal timber laid along the top of a wall to support the ends of joists or rafters. ● *v.tr.* **1** apply a thin coat esp. of silver, gold, or tin to (another metal). **2** cover (esp. a ship) with plates of metal, esp. for protection. **3** make a plate of (type etc.) for printing. □ **on a plate** *colloq.* available with little trouble to the recipient. **on one's plate** esp.

Brit. for one to deal with or consider. [based on Greek *platus* 'flat'] □ **plateful** *n.* (*pl.* **-fuls**). **plater** *n.*

plate armour *n.* armour of metal plates, for a man, ship, etc. ▷ ARMOUR

plateau /plat-oh/ ● *n.* (*pl.* **plateaux** /-tohz/ or **plateaus**) **1** an area of fairly level high ground. **2** a state of little variation after an increase. ● *v.intr.* (**plateaus, plateaued**) (often foll. by *out*) reach a level or stable state after an increase. [from Old French *platel* 'small flat surface']

plate glass *n.* thick fine-quality glass for shop windows etc., originally cast in plates.

platelayer *n. Brit.* a person employed in fixing and repairing railway rails.

platelet *n.* a small colourless disc-shaped cell fragment without a nucleus, found in blood and involved in clotting. ▷ BLOOD

platen *n.* **1** a plate in a printing press which presses the paper against the type. **2** a cylindrical roller in a typewriter against which the paper is held. [from Old French *platine* 'flat piece']

plate rack *n. Brit.* a rack in which plates are stored or placed to drain.

plateresque *adj.* richly ornamented in a style suggesting silverware.

plate tectonics *n.pl.* (usu. treated as *sing.*) ◄ a theory about the nature of the Earth's surface involving rigid lithospheric plates moving slowly on the underlying mantle. ▷ SEABED

plate tracery *n. Archit.* tracery with perforations in otherwise continuous stone.

platform *n.* **1** a raised level surface, esp. one from which a speaker addresses an audience. **2** a raised structure along the side of a track in a railway station. **3** the floor area at the entrance to a bus. **4** a thick sole of a shoe. **5** the declared policy of a political party. [from French *plateforme* 'ground plan']

plating *n.* a coating of gold, silver, etc.

platinize *v.tr.* (also **-ise**) coat with platinum. □ **platinization** *n.*

platinum *n. Chem.* ► a ductile malleable silvery-white metallic element, unaffected by simple acids and fusible only at a very high temperature, used in making jewellery and laboratory apparatus. [earlier *platina* from Spanish, literally 'little silver']

platinum blonde (also **platinum blond**) ● *adj.* (hyphenated when *attrib.*) silvery-blond. ● *n.* a person with silvery-blond hair.

PLATINUM NUGGET

platinum disc *n.* the highest of a series of awards given to a recording artist or group for sales of a record etc. exceeding a specified high figure (cf. GOLD DISC).

platinum metal *n.* any metallic element found with and resembling platinum, e.g. osmium, iridium, and palladium.

platitude *n.* a trite or commonplace remark, esp. one solemnly delivered. [French, based on *plat* 'flat'] □ **platitudinize** *v.intr.* (also **-ise**). **platitudinous** *adj.*

Platonic *adj.* **1** of or associated with the Greek philosopher Plato (d. 347 BC) or his ideas. **2** (**platonic**) (of love or friendship) purely spiritual, not sexual. **3** (**platonic**) confined to words or theory; not leading to action; harmless. [from Greek *Platōn* 'Plato'] □ **Platonically** *adv.*

Platonic solid *n.* (also **Platonic body**) any of the five regular solids (tetrahedron, cube, octahedron, dodecahedron, icosahedron).

Platonism *n.* the philosophy of Plato or his followers. □ **Platonist** *n.*

platoon *n.* **1** *Mil.* a subdivision of a company, commanded by a lieutenant and usu. divided into three sections. **2** a group of persons acting together. [from French *peloton* 'small ball']

platteland *n. S.Afr.* remote country districts. [Afrikaans, literally 'flat land'] □ **plattelander** *n.*

platter *n.* **1** a large flat dish or plate, esp. for food. **2** *slang* a gramophone record. **3** the rotating metal disc of a record player turntable. **4** *Computing* a rigid disc used to store data magnetically. □ **on a platter** = *on a plate* (see PLATE). [based on Anglo-French *plat* 'plate']

PLATE TECTONICS

The Earth's lithosphere is thought to consist of semi-rigid plates that move relative to each other on the underlying asthenosphere (a partly molten layer of the mantle). The movement of these tectonic plates may be caused by convection currents in the Earth's mantle. Mountain-building, earth-quakes, and volcanoes occur mostly near plate boundaries, where the plates may be moving apart or together, or sliding past each other. The effect this movement has depends on whether the boundary is between two continental plates, two oceanic plates, or an oceanic and a continental plate.

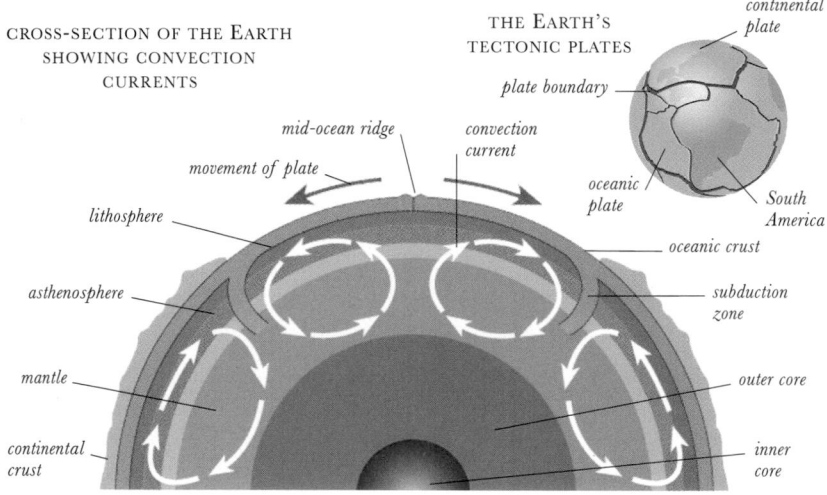

CROSS-SECTION OF THE EARTH SHOWING CONVECTION CURRENTS

mid-ocean ridge · movement of plate · convection current · lithosphere · asthenosphere · mantle · continental crust

THE EARTH'S TECTONIC PLATES

continental plate · plate boundary · oceanic plate · South America · oceanic crust · subduction zone · outer core · inner core

EXAMPLES OF PLATE MOVEMENT

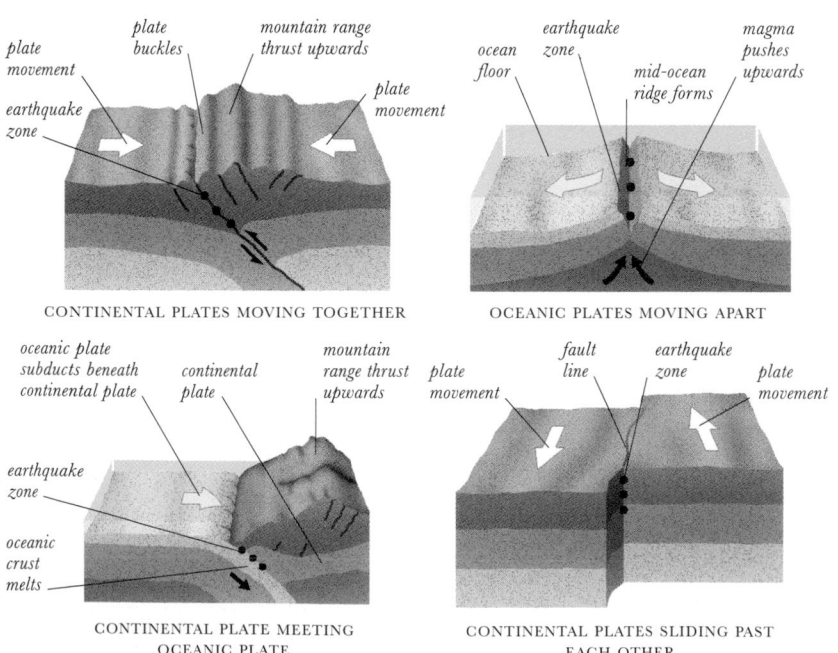

plate movement · earthquake zone · plate buckles · mountain range thrust upwards · plate movement
CONTINENTAL PLATES MOVING TOGETHER

earthquake zone · ocean floor · mid-ocean ridge forms · magma pushes upwards
OCEANIC PLATES MOVING APART

oceanic plate subducts beneath continental plate · continental plate · mountain range thrust upwards · earthquake zone · oceanic crust melts
CONTINENTAL PLATE MEETING OCEANIC PLATE

plate movement · fault line · earthquake zone · plate movement
CONTINENTAL PLATES SLIDING PAST EACH OTHER

P

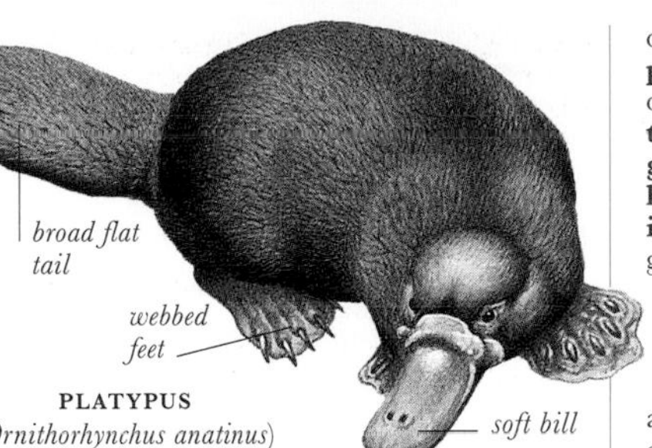

PLATYPUS
(*Ornithorhynchus anatinus*)

platypus *n.* (in full **duck-billed platypus**) (*pl.* **platypuses**) ▲ an Australian aquatic egg-laying mammal, *Ornithorhynchus anatinus*, having a soft pliable bill shaped like a duck's, webbed feet, and sleek grey fur. [from Greek *platupous* 'flat-footed']

plaudit *n.* (usu. in *pl.*) **1** a round of applause. **2** an emphatic expression of approval. [shortened from Latin *plaudite*, literally 'applaud!', said by Roman actors at the end of a play]

plausible *adj.* **1** (of an argument, statement, etc.) seeming reasonable or probable. **2** (of a person) persuasive but deceptive. [from Latin *plausibilis*] □ **plausibility** *n.* **plausibly** *adv.*

play ● *v.* **1** *intr.* (often foll. by *with*) occupy or amuse oneself pleasantly with some recreation, game, exercise, etc. **2** *intr.* (foll. by *with*) act light-heartedly or flippantly (with feelings etc.). **3 a** *tr.* perform on or be able to perform on (a musical instrument). **b** *tr.* perform (a piece of music etc.). **c** *tr.* cause (a record, record player, etc.) to produce sounds. **d** *intr.* (of a record, record player, etc.) produce sounds. **4 a** *intr.* (foll. by *in*) perform a role in (a drama etc.). **b** *tr.* perform (a drama or role) on stage, or in a film or broadcast. **c** *tr.* give a dramatic performance at (a particular theatre or place). **5** *tr.* act in real life the part of (*play truant*; *play the fool*). **6** *tr.* (foll. by *on*) perform (a trick or joke etc.) on (a person). **7** *intr. colloq.* participate, cooperate (*they won't play*). **8** *intr.* gamble. **9** *tr.* gamble on. **10** *tr.* **a** (also *absol.*) take part in (a game or recreation). **b** compete with (another player or team) in a game. **c** occupy (a specified position) in a team for a game. **d** (foll. by *in*, *on*, *at*, etc.) assign (a player) to a position. **11** *tr.* move (a piece) or display (a playing card) in one's turn in a game. **12** *tr.* (also *absol.*) strike (a ball etc.) or execute (a stroke) in a game. **13** *intr.* move about in a lively or unrestrained manner. **14** *intr.* (often foll. by *on*) **a** touch gently. **b** emit light, water, etc. (*fountains gently playing*). **15** *tr.* allow (a fish) to exhaust itself pulling against a line. **16** *intr.* (often foll. by *at*) **a** engage in a half-hearted way (in an activity). **b** pretend to be. ● *n.* **1** recreation, amusement, esp. as the spontaneous activity of children and young animals. **2 a** the playing of a game. **b** the action or manner of this. **c** the status of the ball etc. in a game as being available to be played according to the rules (*in play*; *out of play*). **3** a dramatic piece for the stage etc. **4** activity or operation (*are in full play*; *brought into play*). **5 a** freedom of movement. **b** space or scope for this. **6** brisk, light, or fitful movement. **7** gambling. **8** an action or manoeuvre, esp. in or as in a game. □ **at play** engaged in recreation. **in play** for amusement; not seriously. **make play** act effectively. **make a play for** *colloq.* make a conspicuous attempt to acquire. **make play with** use ostentatiously. **play about** (or **around**) behave irresponsibly. **play along** pretend to cooperate. **play back** play (sounds recently recorded), esp. to monitor recording quality etc. **play ball** see BALL[1]. **play by ear 1** perform (music) without having seen a score of it. **2** (also **play it by ear**) proceed instinctively or step by step according to results and circumstances. **play one's cards close to one's chest** see CHEST. **play one's cards right** (or **well**) make good use of opportunities; act shrewdly. **play down** minimize the importance of. **played out** exhausted of energy or usefulness. **play false** act, or treat (a person), deceitfully or treacherously. **play fast and loose** act unreliably; ignore one's obligations. **play the field** see FIELD. **play for time** seek to gain time by delaying. **play the game** see GAME[1]. **play havoc with** see HAVOC. **play hell with** see HELL. **play hookey** see HOOKEY. **play into a person's hands** act so as unwittingly to give a person an advantage. **play it cool** *colloq.* **1** affect indifference. **2** be relaxed or unemotional. **play the man** = *be a man* (see MAN). **play the market** speculate in stocks etc. **play off** (usu. foll. by *against*) **1** oppose (one person against another), esp. for one's own advantage. **2** play an extra match to decide a draw or tie. **play on 1** continue to play. **2** take advantage of (a person's feelings etc.). **play oneself in** *Brit.* become accustomed to the prevailing conditions in a game etc. **play on words** a pun. **play safe** (or **for safety**) avoid risks. **play to the gallery** see GALLERY. **play up 1** *Brit.* **a** behave mischievously. **b** obstruct or annoy in this way (*played the teacher up*). **c** cause trouble; be irritating (*my rheumatism is playing up again*). **2** emphasize, make the most of. **3** *Brit.* put all one's energy into a game. **play up to** flatter, esp. to win favour. **play with fire** take foolish risks. [Old English, originally in sense 'exercise'] □ **playable** *adj.* **playability** *n.*

play-act *v.intr.* **1** act in a play. **2** behave affectedly or insincerely. □ **play-acting** *n.* **play-actor** *n.*

playback *n.* the playing back of a sound or sounds; an instance of this.

playbill *n.* **1** a poster announcing a theatrical performance. **2** *US* a theatre programme.

playboy *n.* an irresponsible pleasure-seeking man, esp. a wealthy one.

player *n.* **1** a person taking part in a sport or game. **2** a person playing a musical instrument (often in *comb.*: *flute-player*). **3** an actor. **4** any device for playing records, compact discs, cassettes, etc.

player-manager *n.* a person who both plays in a team and manages it.

player-piano *n.* a piano fitted with an apparatus enabling it to be played automatically.

playfellow *n.* a playmate.

playful *adj.* **1** fond of or inclined to play. **2** done in fun; jocular. □ **playfully** *adv.* **playfulness** *n.*

playgoer *n.* a person who goes often to the theatre.

playground *n.* an outdoor area for children to play on.

playgroup *n. Brit.* a group of pre-school children who play regularly together at a particular place under supervision.

playhouse *n.* **1** a theatre. ▷ THEATRE. **2** a toy house for children to play in.

playing card *n.* each of a set of usu. 52 oblong pieces of card with an identical pattern on one side and different values represented by numbers and symbols on the other, used to play various games.

playing field *n.* a field used for outdoor team games.

playlet *n.* a short play or dramatic piece.

playlist ● *n.* a list of pieces to be played, esp. of musical recordings to be broadcast on radio. ● *v.tr.* place on a playlist.

playmaker *n.* a player in a team game who leads attacks or enables fellow team members to score.

playmate *n.* a child's companion in play.

play-off *n.* a match played to decide a draw or tie.

playpen *n.* a portable enclosure for young children to play in.

play-reading *n.* **1** the activity of reading through a play. **2** an instance of this.

playroom *n.* a room set aside for children to play in.

play school *n.* a nursery school or kindergarten.

plaything *n.* **1** a toy or other thing to play with. **2** a person treated as a toy.

playtime *n.* time for play or recreation.

playwright *n.* a person who writes plays.

plaza *n.* a market place or open square (esp. in a Spanish town). [Spanish, literally 'place']

plc *abbr.* (also **PLC**) *Brit.* Public Limited Company.

plea *n.* **1** an earnest appeal or entreaty. **2** *Law* a formal statement by or on behalf of a defendant. [from Latin *placitum* 'a decree']

plea bargaining *n.* orig. *US* an arrangement between prosecutor and defendant whereby the defendant pleads guilty to a lesser charge in the expectation of leniency. □ **plea bargain** *n.* & *v.intr.*

plead *v.* (*past* and *past part.* **pleaded** or esp. *N. Amer.*, *Sc.*, & *dial.* **pled**) **1** *intr.* (foll. by *with*) make an earnest appeal to. **2** *intr. Law* address a law court as an advocate on behalf of a party. **3** *tr.* maintain (a cause) esp. in a law court. **4** *tr. Law* declare to be one's state as regards guilt in or responsibility for a crime (*plead guilty*; *plead insanity*). **5** *tr.* offer or allege as an excuse (*pleaded forgetfulness*). **6** *intr.* make an appeal or entreaty. [from Old French *plaidier*] □ **pleader** *n.* **pleadingly** *adv.*

pleading *n.* (usu. in *pl.*) a formal statement of the cause of an action or defence.

pleasant *adj.* (**pleasanter**, **pleasantest**) pleasing to the mind, feelings, or senses. [from Old French *plaisant*] □ **pleasantly** *adv.* **pleasantness** *n.*

pleasantry *n.* (*pl.* **-ies**) **1** (usu. in *pl.*) a courteous or polite remark, esp. made in casual conversation. **2** (esp. in *pl.*) an amusing remark. **3** jocularity.

please *v.* **1** *tr.* (also *absol.*) be agreeable to; make glad; give pleasure to (*the gift will please them*; *anxious to please*). **2** *tr.* (in *passive*) **a** (foll. by *to* + infin.) be glad or willing to (*am pleased to help*). **b** (often foll. by *about*, *at*, *with*) derive pleasure or satisfaction (from). **3** *tr.* (prec. by *it* as subject; usu. foll. by *to* + infin.) be the inclination or wish of (*it did not please them to attend*). **4** *intr.* think fit; have the will or desire (*take as many as you please*). **5** *tr.* used in polite requests (*come in, please*). □ **(as) pleased as Punch** see PUNCH[4]. **if you please** if you are willing, esp. *iron.* to indicate unreasonableness (*then, if you please, we had to pay*). **please oneself** do as one likes. [from Latin *placēre*] □ **pleased** *adj.* **pleasing** *adj.* **pleasingly** *adv.*

pleasurable *adj.* causing pleasure; agreeable. □ **pleasurableness** *n.* **pleasurably** *adv.*

pleasure ● *n.* **1** a feeling of satisfaction or joy. **2** enjoyment. **3** a source of pleasure or gratification. **4** *formal* a person's will or desire (*what is your pleasure?*). **5** sensual gratification (*a life of pleasure*). **6** (*attrib.*) done or used for pleasure (*pleasure boat*; *pleasure trip*). ● *v.* **1** *tr.* give (esp. sexual) pleasure to. **2** *intr.* (often foll. by *in*) take pleasure. □ **take pleasure in** like doing. **with pleasure** gladly. [from Old French *plaisir* 'to please']

pleat ● *n.* a fold or crease, esp. a flattened fold in cloth doubled upon itself. ● *v.tr.* make a pleat or pleats in. [Middle English variant of PLAIT]

pleb *n. colloq.* usu. *derog.* = PLEBEIAN *n.* 2. □ **plebby** *adj.*

plebeian /pli-**bee**-ăn/ ● *n.* **1** a commoner, esp. in ancient Rome. **2** a working-class person, esp. an uncultured one. ● *adj.* **1** of low birth; of the common people. **2** uncultured. [based on Latin *plebs plebis* 'the common people'] □ **plebeianism** *n.*

plebiscite /**pleb**-i-syt/ *n.* the direct vote of all the electors of a state etc. on an important question, e.g. a change in the constitution. [from Latin *plebiscitum*] □ **plebiscitary** *adj.*

plectrum *n.* (*pl.* **plectrums** or **plectra**) a thin flat piece of plastic or horn etc. used to pluck a string, esp. of a guitar. [from Greek *plēktron*]

pled see PLEAD.

pledge ● *n.* **1** a solemn promise or undertaking. **2** a thing given as security for the fulfilment of a contract, the payment of a debt, etc. **3** a thing put in pawn. **4 a** the promise of a donation to charity. **b** such a donation. **5** a thing given as a token of love, favour, or something to come. **6** a solemn undertaking to abstain from alcohol (*sign the pledge*). ● *v.tr.* **1 a** deposit as security. **b** pawn. **2** promise solemnly by the pledge of (one's honour, word, etc.). **3** (often *refl.*) bind by a solemn promise.

P

□ **pledge one's troth** see TROTH. [from Late Latin *plebium*] □ **pledger** *n.* **pledgor** *n. Law.*

Pleiades /ply-ă-deez/ *n.pl.* a cluster of stars in the constellation Taurus. [Greek, the seven mythical daughters of Atlas and Pleione]

Pleistocene /ply-stŏ-seen/ *Geol.* ● *adj.* of or relating to the first epoch of the Quaternary period. ● *n.* this epoch or system. [from Greek *pleistos* 'most' + *kainos* 'new']

plenary *adj.* **1** entire, unqualified, absolute (*plenary indulgence*). **2** (of an assembly) to be attended by all members. [from Late Latin *plenarius*]

plenipotentiary ● *n.* (*pl.* **-ies**) a person (esp. a diplomat) invested with the full power of independent action. ● *adj.* having this power. [based on Latin *plenus* 'full' + *potentia* 'power']

plenitude *n. literary* **1** fullness, completeness. **2** abundance. [from Late Latin *plenitudo*]

plenteous *adj. poet.* plentiful. □ **plenteously** *adv.* **plenteousness** *n.*

plentiful *adj.* abundant, copious. □ **plentifully** *adv.*

plenty ● *n.* (often foll. by *of*) a great or ample quantity or number. ● *adj. colloq.* existing in an ample quantity. ● *adv. colloq.* fully, entirely (*it is plenty large enough*). [from Latin *plenitas*]

plenum *n.* a full assembly of people or a committee etc. [Latin, literally 'full thing']

pleonasm *n.* the use of more words than are needed to give the sense (e.g. *see with one's eyes*). [based on Greek *pleonazein* 'to be superfluous'] □ **pleonastic** *adj.* **pleonastically** *adv.*

plesiosaurus *n.* (also **plesiosaur**) any of a group of large extinct marine reptiles with large paddle-like limbs and often a long flexible neck. ▷ ELASMOSAURUS. [from Greek *plēsios* 'near' + *sauros* 'lizard']

plethora /pleth-ŏ-ra/ *n.* an oversupply, glut, or excess. [from Greek *plēthōrē*] □ **plethoric** *adj.*

pleura *n.* (*pl.* **pleurae** /-ree/) each of a pair of serous membranes enveloping the lungs in mammals. [Greek, literally 'side of the body, rib'] □ **pleural** *adj.*

pleurisy *n.* inflammation of the pleurae, marked by pain, fever, etc. [from Late Latin *pleurisis*] □ **pleuritic** *adj.*

plexiglas *n. propr.* = PERSPEX. [based on *plexor* 'hammer for testing percussion']

P

plexus *n.* (*pl.* same or **plexuses**) **1** *Anat.* a network of nerves or vessels in an animal body (*gastric plexus*). **2** any network or weblike formation. [Latin] □ **plexiform** *adj.*

pliable *adj.* **1** bending easily; supple. **2** yielding, compliant. [French, literally 'bendable'] □ **pliability** *n.*

pliant *adj.* = PLIABLE 1. [from Old French] □ **pliancy** *n.* **pliantly** *adv.*

plié /plee-ay/ *n.* (*pl.* **pliés**) *Ballet* a bending of the knees with the feet on the ground. [French, literally 'bent']

pliers *n.pl.* ◄ pincers with flat usu. serrated surfaces for holding small objects, bending wire, etc. [based on French *plier* 'to bend']

plight[1] *n.* a condition or state, esp. an unfortunate one. [Middle English & Anglo-French *plit* 'fold']

plight[2] *v.tr. archaic* **1** pledge or promise solemnly (one's faith, loyalty, etc.). **2** (foll. by *to*) engage, esp. in marriage. □ **plight one's troth** see TROTH. [Old English *pliht* 'danger']

plimsoll *n.* (also **plimsole**) *Brit.* a rubber-soled canvas sports shoe. [probably from the resemblance of the side of the sole to a PLIMSOLL LINE]

Plimsoll line *n.* (also **Plimsoll mark**) a marking on a ship's side showing the limit of legal submersion under various conditions. [named after S. *Plimsoll*, English politician, 1824–98, promoter of the 1876 Merchant Shipping Act]

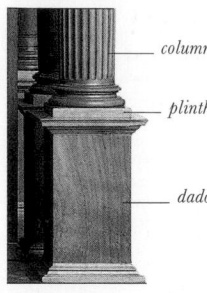

PLINTH

column

plinth

dado

plinth *n.* **1** *Archit.* ◄ the lower square slab at the base of a column. **2** a base supporting a vase or statue etc. [from Greek *plinthos* 'tile, brick, squared stone']

Pliocene *Geol.* ● *adj.* of or relating to the last epoch of the Tertiary period. ● *n.* this epoch or system. [from Greek *pleiōn* 'more' + *kainos* 'new']

PLO *abbr.* Palestine Liberation Organization.

plod ● *v.* (**plodded**, **plodding**) **1** *intr.* (often foll. by *along*, *on*, etc.) walk doggedly or laboriously; trudge. **2** *intr.* (often foll. by *at*) work slowly and steadily. **3** *tr.* tread or make (one's way) laboriously. ● *n.* the act or a spell of plodding. [16th-century coinage] □ **plodder** *n.* **ploddingly** *adv.*

ploidy *n.* the number of sets of chromosomes in a cell.

plonk[1] ● *v.tr.* **1** set down hurriedly or clumsily. **2** (usu. foll. by *down*) set down firmly. ● *n.* **1** an act of plonking. **2** a heavy thud.

plonk[2] *n. Brit. colloq.* cheap or inferior wine. [originally Australian]

plonker *n. coarse slang* a foolish or inept person.

plop ● *n.* **1** a sound as of a smooth object dropping into water without a splash. **2** an act of falling with this sound. ● *v.intr. & tr.* (**plopped**, **plopping**) fall or drop with a plop. ● *adv.* with a plop. [19th-century coinage]

plosive *Phonet.* ● *adj.* denoting a consonant that is produced by stopping the airflow using the lips, teeth, or palate, followed by a sudden release of air. ● *n.* a plosive speech sound.

plot ● *n.* **1** a defined and usu. small piece of ground. **2** the interrelationship of the main events in a play, novel, film, etc. **3** a conspiracy or secret plan, esp. to achieve an unlawful end. **4** a graph showing the relation between two variables. ● *v.tr.* (**plotted**, **plotting**) **1** make a plan or map of. **2** (also *absol.*) plan or contrive secretly (a crime, conspiracy, etc.). **3 a** mark (a point or course etc.) on a chart, diagram, or graph. **b** make (a curve etc.) by marking out points. [from Old French *complot* 'secret plan'] □ **plotless** *adj.* **plotlessness** *n.* **plotter** *n.*

plough /plow/ (esp. *N. Amer.* **plow**) ● *n.* **1** ▼ an implement drawn by a tractor or by horses, for cutting furrows in the soil and turning it up. **2** an implement resembling this (*snowplough*). **3** (**the Plough**) the constellation Ursa Major or its seven bright stars. ● *v.* **1** *tr.* (also *absol.*) turn up (the earth) with a plough. **2** *tr.* (foll. by *out*, *up*, *down*, etc.) turn or extract (roots, weeds, etc.) with a plough. **3** *tr.* furrow or scratch (a surface) as if with a plough. **4** *tr.* produce (a furrow or line) in this way. **5** *intr.* (foll. by *through*) advance laboriously, esp. through work, a book, etc. **6** *intr.* (foll. by *through*, *into*) travel or be propelled clumsily or violently. □ **plough back** reinvest (profits) in the business producing them. **put one's hand to the plough** undertake

a task (Luke 9:62). [from Old Norse *plógr*] □ **ploughable** *adj.*

ploughman *n.* (*N. Amer.* **plowman**) (*pl.* **-men**) a person who uses a plough.

ploughman's lunch *n. Brit.* a meal of bread and usu. cheese with pickle or salad.

ploughshare *n.* (*N. Amer.* **plowshare**) the cutting blade of a plough. [Middle English, based on earlier *scaer* 'ploughshare']

plover *n.* any short-billed gregarious bird of the family Charadriidae, esp. of the genus *Charadrius*, often found by water. [based on Latin *pluvia* 'rain']

plow *N. Amer.* var. of PLOUGH.

ploy *n.* a stratagem; a cunning manoeuvre to gain an advantage. [17th century coinage, originally Scots]

PLR *abbr.* (in the UK) Public Lending Right.

pluck ● *v.* **1** *tr.* (often foll. by *out*, *off*, etc.) pick or pull out or away. **2** *tr.* strip (a bird) of feathers. **3** *tr.* pull at; twitch. **4** *intr.* (foll. by *at*) tug or snatch at. **5** *tr.* sound (the string of a musical instrument) with the finger or a plectrum etc. ● *n.* **1** courage, spirit. **2** an act of plucking; a twitch. □ **pluck up** summon up (one's courage, spirits, etc.). [Old English] □ **plucker** *n.*

plucky *adj.* (**pluckier**, **pluckiest**) brave, spirited. □ **pluckily** *adv.*

plug ● *n.* **1** a piece of solid material fitting tightly into a hole, used to fill a gap or cavity or act as a wedge or stopper. **2 a** a device of metal pins in an insulated casing fitting into holes in a socket for making an electrical connection. **b** *colloq.* an electric socket. **3** = SPARK PLUG. **4** *colloq.* a piece of (often free) publicity for an idea, product, etc. **5** ▼ a mass of solidified lava filling the neck of a volcano. ● *v.* (**plugged**, **plugging**) **1** *tr.* (often foll. by *up*) stop (a hole etc.) with a plug. **2** *tr. slang* shoot or hit (a person etc.). **3** *tr. colloq.* seek to popularize (an idea, product, etc.) by constant recommendation. **4** *intr.* (often foll. by *at*) *colloq.* work steadily away (at). □ **plug in** connect electrically by inserting a plug in a socket. [from Middle Dutch *plugge*] □ **plugger** *n.*

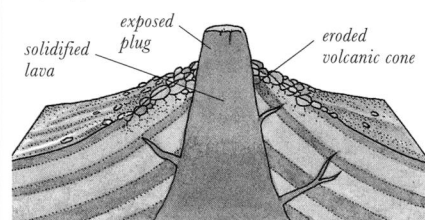

exposed plug

solidified lava

eroded volcanic cone

PLUG: EXPOSED VOLCANIC PLUG

plughole *n.* a hole in a bath, basin, sink, etc., which can be stopped with a plug.

plug-in *attrib.adj.* able to be connected by means of a plug.

plug-ugly *US slang* ● *n.* (*pl.* **-ies**) a thug or ruffian. ● *adj.* villainous-looking.

plum ● *n.* **1 a** a sweet oval fleshy fruit, usu. purple or reddish when ripe, with a flattish pointed stone. **b** (also **plum tree**) any deciduous tree of the genus *Prunus* (rose family), esp. *P. domestica*, which bears this fruit. **2** a reddish-purple colour. **3** a dried grape or raisin used in cooking (*plum pudding*). **4** the best of a collection; something especially prized (often *attrib.*: *a plum job*). ● *adj.* of a reddish-purple colour. □ **a plum in one's mouth** a rich-sounding voice or affected accent. [from Latin *prunum*]

plumage *n.* a bird's feathers. [from Old French] □ **plumaged** *adj.* (usu. in *comb.*).

PLIERS

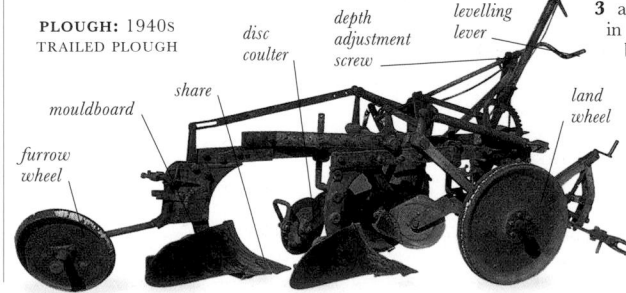

PLOUGH: 1940s TRAILED PLOUGH

mouldboard

furrow wheel

share

disc coulter

depth adjustment screw

levelling lever

land wheel

plumb

PLUMB AND LINE

plumb[1] ● *n.* ◀ a ball of lead or other heavy material, esp. one attached to the end of a line for finding the depth of water or determining the vertical on an upright surface. ● *adv.* **1** exactly (*plumb in the centre*). **2** vertically. **3** *N. Amer. slang* quite, utterly (*plumb crazy*). ● *adj.* **1** vertical. **2** downright, sheer (*plumb nonsense*). ● *v.tr.* **1 a** measure the depth of (water) with a plumb. **b** determine (a depth). **2** test (an upright surface) to determine the vertical. **3** reach or experience in extremes (*plumb the depths of fear*). **4** learn in detail the facts about (a matter). □ **out of plumb** not vertical. [Middle English]

plumb[2] *v.tr.* **1** provide (a building or room etc.) with plumbing. **2** (often foll. by *in*) fit as part of a plumbing system. [back-formation from PLUMBER]

plumbago *n.* (*pl.* **-os**) **1** = GRAPHITE. **2** ▼ any plant of the genus *Plumbago*, with grey or blue flowers. [Latin]

PLUMBAGO
(*Plumbago auriculata*)

plumber *n.* a person who fits and repairs plumbing. [based on Latin *plumbum* 'lead']

plumbing *n.* **1** the system or apparatus of water supply, heating, etc., in a building. **2** the work of a plumber.

plumb line *n.* ▲ a line with a plumb attached.

plum duff *n. Brit.* a plain flour pudding with raisins or currants.

plume ● *n.* **1** a feather, esp. a large one used for ornament. **2** an ornament of feathers etc. attached to a helmet or hat or worn in the hair. ▷ SHAKO. **3** something resembling this (*a plume of smoke*). ● *v.* **1** *tr.* decorate or provide with a plume or plumes. **2** *refl.* (foll. by *on, upon*) pride (oneself on esp. something trivial). **3** *tr.* (of a bird) preen (itself or its feathers). [from Latin *pluma* 'down'] □ **plumelike** *adj.*

plummet ● *n.* **1** a plumb or plumb line. **2** a plumb line. **3** a weight attached to a fishing line to keep the float upright. ● *v.intr.* (**plummeted, plummeting**) fall or plunge rapidly. [from Old French *plommet* 'little plumb']

plummy *adj.* (**plummier, plummiest**) **1** abounding or rich in plums. **2** *colloq.* (of a voice) sounding affectedly rich or deep in tone. **3** *colloq.* good, desirable.

plump[1] ● *adj.* (esp. of a person or animal or part of the body) having a full rounded shape; fleshy. ● *v.tr. & intr.* (often foll. by *up, out*) make or become plump. [from Middle Dutch *plomp* 'blunt'] □ **plumpish** *adj.* **plumply** *adv.* **plumpness** *n.* **plumpy** *adj.*

plump[2] ● *v.* **1** *intr. & tr.* (often foll. by *down*) drop or fall abruptly. **2** *intr.* (foll. by *for*) decide definitely in favour of (one of two or more possibilities). ● *n.* an abrupt plunge; a heavy fall. ● *adv. colloq.* with a sudden or heavy fall. [from Middle Dutch *plompen*]

plum pudding *n.* a rich boiled suet pudding with raisins, currants, spices, etc.

plumy *adj.* (**plumier, plumiest**) **1** plumelike, feathery. **2** adorned with plumes.

plunder ● *v.tr.* **1** rob (a place or person) or steal (goods), esp. systematically or as in war. **2** steal from (another's writings etc.). ● *n.* **1** the violent or dishonest acquisition of property. **2** property acquired by plundering. [from Low German *plündern*, literally 'to rob of household goods'] □ **plunderer** *n.*

plunge ● *v.* **1** (usu. foll. by *in, into*) **a** *tr.* thrust forcefully or abruptly. **b** *intr.* dive; propel oneself forcibly. **c** *intr. & tr.* enter or cause to enter a certain condition or embark on a certain course abruptly or impetuously (*they plunged into a lively discussion; the room was plunged into darkness*). **2** *tr.* immerse completely. **3** *intr.* **a** move suddenly and dramatically downward. **b** (foll. by *down, into*, etc.) move with a rush (*plunged down the stairs*). ● *n.* a plunging action or movement; a dive. □ **take the plunge** *colloq.* commit oneself to a (usu. risky) course of action. [based on Latin *plumbum* 'plumbline, lead']

plunger *n.* **1** a part of a mechanism that works with a plunging or thrusting movement. **2** a rubber cup on a handle for clearing blocked pipes by a plunging and sucking action.

plunging neckline *n.* (also **plunge neckline**) a low-cut neckline.

plunk ● *n.* the sound made by the sharply plucked string of a stringed instrument. ● *v.intr. & tr.* sound or cause to sound with a plunk.

pluperfect *Gram.* ● *adj.* (of a tense) denoting an action completed prior to some past point of time specified or implied, formed in English by *had* and the past participle, as: *he had gone by then*. ● *n.* the pluperfect tense. [based on Latin *plus quam perfectum* 'more than perfect']

plural ● *adj.* **1** more than one in number. **2** *Gram.* (of a word or form) denoting more than one. ● *n. Gram.* **1** a plural word or form. **2** the plural number. [from Latin *pluralis*] □ **plurally** *adv.*

pluralism *n.* **1** holding more than one office, esp. an ecclesiastical office or benefice, at a time. **2** a

form of society in which the members of minority groups maintain their independent cultural traditions. □ **pluralist** *n.* **pluralistic** *adj.* **pluralistically** *adv.*

plurality *n.* (*pl.* **-ies**) **1** the state of being plural. **2** = PLURALISM 1. **3** a large or the greater number. **4** *US* a majority of votes that is not absolute.

pluralize *v.* (also **-ise**) **1** *tr. & intr.* make or become plural. **2** *tr.* express in the plural. □ **pluralization** *n.*

plus ● *prep.* **1** *Math.* with the addition of (*3 plus 4 equals 7*) (symbol +). **2** (of temperature) above zero (*plus 2 °C*). **3** *colloq.* with; having gained (*returned plus a new car*). ● *adj.* **1** (after a number) at least (*fifteen plus*). **2** (after a grade etc.) rather better than (*beta plus*). **3** *Math.* positive. **4** having a positive electrical charge. ● *n.* **1** = PLUS SIGN. **2** *Math.* an additional or positive quantity. **3** an advantage (*experience is a definite plus*). ● *conj. colloq. disp.* also; and furthermore (*they arrived late, plus they were hungry*). [Latin, literally 'more']

■ **Usage** The use of *plus* as a conjunction, as in *They arrived late, plus they wanted a meal*, is considered incorrect by some people.

plus fours *n.* ◀ men's long wide knickerbockers usu. worn for golf etc.

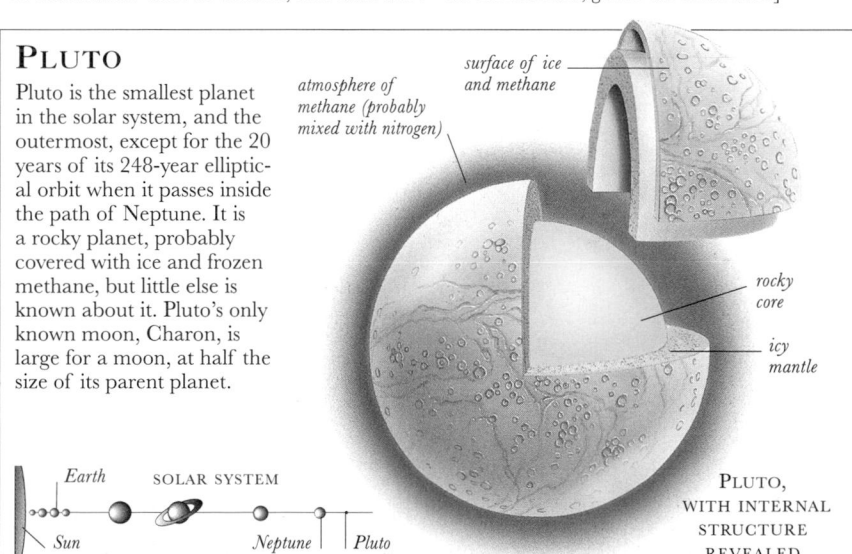

plus fours

plush ● *n.* cloth of silk or cotton etc., with a long soft nap. ● *adj.* **1** made of plush. **2** *colloq.* plushy. [based on Latin *pilus* 'hair'] □ **plushly** *adv.* **plushness** *n.*

plushy *adj.* (**plushier, plushiest**) *colloq.* stylish, luxurious. □ **plushiness** *n.*

plus sign *n.* the symbol +, indicating addition or a positive value.

Pluto *n.* ▼ a small planet, for most of its orbit the outermost planet of the solar system. ▷ SOLAR SYSTEM. [Latin from Greek *Ploutōn*, the god of the underworld]

plutocracy *n.* (*pl.* **-ies**) **1 a** government by the wealthy. **b** a state governed in this way. **2** a wealthy elite or ruling class. [based on Greek *ploutos* 'wealth'] □ **plutocratic** *adj.* **plutocratically** *adv.*

plutocrat *n.* esp. *derog. or joc.* **1** a member of a plutocracy or wealthy elite. **2** a wealthy and influential person.

PLUS FOURS

pluton *n. Geol.* a body of plutonic rock.

plutonic *adj.* **1** *Geol.* (of rock) formed as igneous rock by solidification below the surface of the Earth. **2** (**Plutonic**) of the infernal regions. [based on Greek *Ploutōn*, god of the underworld]

P

PLUTO

Pluto is the smallest planet in the solar system, and the outermost, except for the 20 years of its 248-year elliptical orbit when it passes inside the path of Neptune. It is a rocky planet, probably covered with ice and frozen methane, but little else is known about it. Pluto's only known moon, Charon, is large for a moon, at half the size of its parent planet.

atmosphere of methane (probably mixed with nitrogen)

surface of ice and methane

rocky core

icy mantle

SOLAR SYSTEM

Earth

Sun

Neptune | *Pluto*

PLUTO, WITH INTERNAL STRUCTURE REVEALED

plutonium *n. Chem.* a dense silvery radioactive metallic transuranic element of the actinide series, used in some nuclear reactors and weapons. [based on *Pluto*, on the pattern of *neptunium* (Pluto being the next planet beyond Neptune)]

pluvial *adj.* **1** of rain; rainy. **2** *Geol.* caused by rain. [based on Latin *pluvia* 'rain'] □ **pluvious** *adj.* (in sense 1).

ply[1] *n.* (*pl.* **-ies**) **1** a thickness or layer of material, esp. wood or cloth (*three-ply*). **2** a strand of yarn or rope etc. [based on Latin *plicare* 'to fold']

ply[2] *v.* (**-ies**, **-ied**) **1** *tr.* use or wield vigorously (a tool, weapon, etc.). **2** *tr.* work steadily at (one's business or trade). **3** *tr.* (foll. by *with*) **a** supply (a person) continuously (with food, drink, etc.). **b** approach repeatedly (with questions, demands, etc.). **4 a** *intr.* (often foll. by *between*) (of a vehicle etc.) travel regularly to and fro. **b** *tr.* work (a route) in this way. **5** *intr.* (of a taxi driver, boatman, etc.) attend regularly for custom (*ply for trade*). [Middle English, related to APPLY]

Plymouth Brethren *n.pl.* a strict Calvinistic religious body having no formal creed and no official order of ministers.

plywood *n.* a strong board consisting of two or more layers glued together with the direction of the grain alternating.

PM *abbr.* **1** Prime Minister. **2** post-mortem.

Pm *symb. Chem.* the element promethium.

p.m. *abbr.* after noon. [Latin *post meridiem*]

PNEUMATIC DRILL

A pneumatic drill is used to break up concrete and tarmac, often on roads. Compressed air forces the tool of the drill up and down in a four-stage cycle. In the stage shown here, compressed air enters a cylinder above a piston, forcing it down. The piston strikes the anvil, driving the tool into the road surface.

P

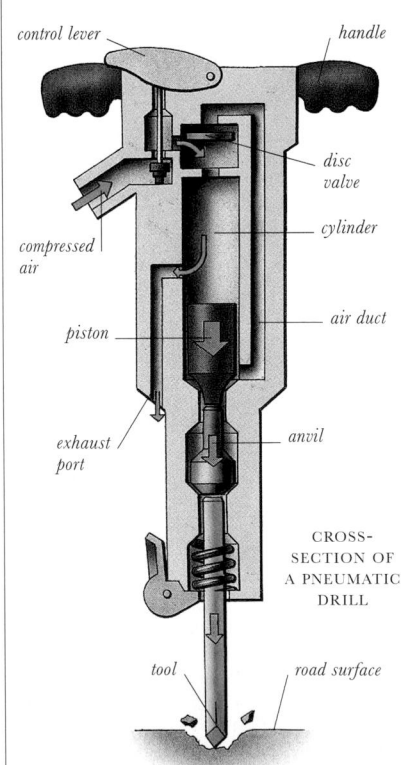

control lever
handle
disc valve
compressed air
cylinder
piston
air duct
exhaust port
anvil
CROSS-SECTION OF A PNEUMATIC DRILL
tool
road surface

PMS *abbr. Med.* premenstrual syndrome.

PMT *abbr.* esp. *Brit.* premenstrual tension.

pneumatic /new-**mat**-ik/ *adj.* **1** of or relating to air or wind. **2** containing or operated by compressed air. [from Greek *pneumatikos*] □ **pneumatically** *adv.*

pneumatic drill *n.* ▼ a drill driven by compressed air, for breaking up a hard surface.

pneumatics *n.* the science of the mechanical properties of gases.

pneumo- /**new**-moh/ *comb. form* denoting the lungs. [from Greek *pneumōn* 'lung']

pneumococcus /new-mŏ-**kok**-ŭs/ *n.* (*pl.* **pneumococci**) *Med.* a paired bacterium, *Streptococcus pneumoniae*, associated with pneumonia and sometimes meningitis.

pneumoconiosis /new-mŏ-koh-ni-**oh**-sis/ *n.* a lung disease caused by inhalation of dust or small particles. [based on Greek *konis* 'dust']

pneumonia /new-**moh**-niă/ *n.* a bacterial or other inflammation of one lung (**single pneumonia**) or both lungs (**double pneumonia**) causing the air sacs to fill with pus and become solid. [based on Greek *pneumōn* 'lung'] □ **pneumonic** *adj.*

PO *abbr.* **1** Post Office. **2** postal order. **3** Petty Officer. **4** Pilot Officer.

Po *symb. Chem.* the element polonium.

po *n.* (*pl.* **pos**) *Brit. colloq.* a chamber pot.

poach[1] *v.tr.* **1** cook (an egg) without its shell in or over boiling water. **2** cook (fish etc.) by simmering in a small amount of liquid. [from Old French *pochier*, originally in sense 'to enclose in a bag'] □ **poacher** *n.*

poach[2] *v.* **1** *tr.* (also *absol.*) catch (game or fish) illegally. **2** *intr.* (often foll. by *on*) trespass or encroach (on another's property, ideas, etc.). **3** *tr.* appropriate illicitly or unfairly (a person, thing, idea, etc.). □ **poacher** *n.*

pochard *n.* (*pl.* same or **pochards**) any duck of the genus *Aythya*, esp. *A. ferina*, the male of which has a bright reddish-brown head and neck. [16th-century coinage]

pock *n.* = POCKMARK. [Old English] □ **pocked** *adj.*

pocket ● *n.* **1** a small bag sewn into or on clothing, for carrying small articles. **2** a pouchlike compartment in a suitcase, car door, etc. **3** one's financial resources (*it is beyond my pocket*). **4** an isolated group or area (*a few pockets of resistance remain*). **5** a cavity in a rock or stratum, usu. filled with ore (esp. gold) or water. **6** a pouch at the corner or on the side of a billiard or snooker table into which balls are driven. ▷ POOL. **7** = AIR POCKET 2. **8** (*attrib.*) **a** of a suitable size and shape for carrying in a pocket. **b** smaller than the usual size. ● *v.tr.* (**pocketed**, **pocketing**) **1** put into one's pocket. **2** appropriate, esp. dishonestly. **3** *Billiards* etc. drive (a ball) into a pocket. □ **in pocket** having gained in a transaction. **in a person's pocket 1** under a person's control. **2** close to or intimate with a person. **out of pocket** having lost in a transaction. **put one's hand in one's pocket** spend or provide money. [from Anglo-French *poket(e)* 'little bag'] □ **pocketable** *adj.* **pocketless** *adj.*

pocket battleship *n. hist.* a warship armoured and equipped like, but smaller than, a battleship.

pocketbook *n.* **1** a notebook. **2** a booklike case for papers or money carried in a pocket. **3** *US* a purse or handbag. **4** *N. Amer.* a paperback or other small book.

pocketful *n.* (*pl.* **-fuls**) as much as a pocket will hold:

pocket knife *n.* a knife with a folding blade or blades, for carrying in the pocket.

pocket money *n.* **1** money for minor expenses. **2** *Brit.* an allowance of money made to a child.

pockmark *n.* **1** a small pus-filled spot on the skin, esp. caused by chickenpox or smallpox. **2** a mark resembling this. □ **pock-marked** *adj.*

pod[1] ● *n.* **1** a long seed vessel esp. of a leguminous plant, e.g. a pea. ▷ LEGUME. **2** a compartment suspended under an aircraft for equipment etc. ● *v.* (**podded**, **podding**) **1** *intr.* bear or form pods. **2** *tr.* remove (peas etc.) from pods. [back-formation from dialect *podware, podder* 'field crops']

pod[2] *n.* a small herd or school of marine animals, esp. whales. [19th-century coinage, originally *US*]

podagra *n. Med.* gout of the foot, esp. the big toe. [from Greek *pous podos* 'foot' + *agra* 'seizure']

podgy *adj.* (**podgier**, **podgiest**) *Brit.* **1** (of a person) short and fat. **2** (of a face etc.) plump, fleshy. [19th-century coinage: from *podge* 'a short fat person'] □ **podginess** *n.*

podiatry /pŏ-**dy**-ătri/ *n.* = CHIROPODY. [based on Greek *pous podos* 'foot' + *iatros* 'physician'] □ **podiatrist** *n.*

podium *n.* (*pl.* **podiums** or **podia**) a platform or rostrum. [from Greek *podion* 'little foot']

poem *n.* **1** a metrical composition, usu. concerned with feeling or imaginative description. **2** an elevated composition in verse or prose. [from Greek *poēma*]

poesy *n. archaic* poetry. [from Greek *poiēsis* 'making, poetry']

poet *n.* (*fem.* **poetess**) **1** a writer of poems. **2** a person possessing high powers of imagination or expression etc. [from Greek *poētēs* 'maker, poet']

poetaster *n.* an inferior poet. [modern Latin]

poetic *adj.* (also **poetical**) **1 a** of or like poetry or poets. **b** written in verse. **2** elevated or sublime in expression. □ **poetically** *adv.*

poeticize *v.tr.* (also **-ise**) make (a theme) poetic.

poetic justice *n.* well-deserved unforeseen retribution or reward.

poetic licence *n.* a writer's or artist's transgression of established rules for effect.

Poet Laureate *n.* (*pl.* **Poets Laureate**) (in the UK) a poet appointed to write poems for state occasions.

poetry *n.* **1** the art or work of a poet. **2** poems collectively. **3** a poetic or tenderly pleasing quality.

Poets' Corner *n.* part of Westminster Abbey where several poets are buried or commemorated.

po-faced *adj. Brit.* solemn-faced, humourless. [20th-century coinage]

pogo *n.* (*pl.* **-os**) (also **pogo stick**) a toy consisting of a spring-loaded stick with rests for the feet, for springing about on. [20th-century coinage]

pogrom *n.* an organized massacre. [Russian, literally 'devastation']

poignant /**poyn**-yănt/ *adj.* **1** painfully sharp to the emotions or senses; deeply moving. **2** arousing sympathy. **3** sharp or pungent in taste or smell. **4** pleasantly piquant. [from Old French, literally 'pricking'] □ **poignance** *n.* **poignancy** *n.* **poignantly** *adv.*

poinsettia *n.* ▶ a shrub, *Euphorbia pulcherrima*, with large scarlet or pink bracts surrounding small yellow flowers. [named after J. R. Poinsett, American diplomat, 1779–1851]

bright red bract

POINSETTIA
(*Euphorbia pulcherrima*)

point ● *n.* **1** the sharp or tapered end of a tool, weapon, pencil, etc. **2** a tip or extreme end. **3** that which in geometry has position but not magnitude, e.g. the intersection of two lines. **4** a particular place or position (*Bombay and points east*). **5 a** a precise or particular moment (*at the point of death*). **b** the critical or decisive moment (*when it came to the* *point, he refused*). **6** a very small mark on a surface. **7** a dot or other punctuation mark, esp. = FULL STOP 1. **8** = DECIMAL POINT. **9** a stage or degree in progress or increase (*abrupt to the point of rudeness; at that point we gave up*). **10** a temperature at which a change of state occurs (*freezing point*). **11** a single item; a detail or particular (*we differ on these points; it is a point of principle*). **12 a** a unit of scoring in games or of measuring value etc. **b** an advantage or success in an argument, discussion etc. **13 a** (usu. prec. by *the*) the significant or essential thing; what is actually intended or under discussion (*that was the point of the question*). **b** (usu. with *neg.* or *interrog.*) often foll. by *in*) sense or purpose; advantage or value (*saw no point in staying*). **14** a distinctive feature or characteristic (*it has its points; tact is not his good point*). **15 a** each of 32 directions marked at equal distances round a compass. **b** the corresponding direction towards the horizon. **16** (usu. in *pl.*) *Brit.* a junction of two sets of railway lines, with a pair of linked tapering rails that can be moved laterally to allow a train to pass from one line to the other. **17** (in *pl.*) the pair of electrical contacts in the distributor of an internal-combustion engine. **18** *Cricket* **a** a fielder on the off side near the batsman. **b** this position. ▷ CRICKET. **19** the tip of the toe in ballet. **20** a promontory. **21** *Printing* a unit of measurement for type bodies (in the UK and US 0.351 mm, in Europe 0.376 mm). ● *v.* **1** (usu. foll. by *to, at*) **a** *tr.* direct or aim (a finger, weapon, etc.). **b** *intr.* direct attention in a certain direction (*pointed to the house across the road*). **2** *intr.* (foll. by *at, towards*) **a** aim or be directed to. **b** tend towards. **3** *intr.* (foll. by *to*) indicate; be evidence of (*it all points to murder*). **4** *tr.* give point or force to (words or actions). **5** *tr.* fill in or repair the joints of (brickwork) with smoothly finished mortar or cement. **6** *tr.* (also *absol.*) (of a dog) indicate the presence of (game) by acting as pointer. □ **at all points** in every part or respect. **beside the point** irrelevant or irrelevantly. **have a point** be correct or effective in one's contention. **in point** apposite, relevant. **in point of fact** see FACT. **make** (or **prove**) **a** (or **one's**) **point** establish a proposition; prove one's contention. **make a point of** (often foll. by verbal noun) insist on; treat or regard as essential. **on** (or **upon**) **the point of** (foll. by verbal noun) about to do (the action specified). **point out** (often foll. by *that* + clause) indicate, show; draw attention to. **point up** emphasize; show as important. **score points off** get the better of in an argument etc. **take a person's point** esp. *Brit.* concede that a person has made a valid contention. **to the point** relevant or relevantly. **up to a point** to some extent but not completely. **win on points** *Boxing* win by scoring more points, not by a knockout. [from Latin *punctum*]

point-blank ● *adj.* **1 a** (of a shot) aimed or fired horizontally at a range very close to the target. **b** (of a range) very close. **2** (of a remark, question, etc.) blunt, direct. ● *adv.* **1** at very close range. **2** bluntly, directly.

point duty *n. Brit.* the duty of a police officer or traffic warden stationed at a crossroad or other point to control traffic.

pointed *adj.* **1** sharpened or tapering to a point. **2** (of a remark etc.) having point; penetrating, cutting. **3** emphasized; made evident. □ **pointedly** *adv.* **pointedness** *n.*

pointer *n.* **1** a thing that points, e.g. the index hand of a gauge etc. **2** a rod for pointing to features on a map, chart, etc. **3** *colloq.* a hint, clue, or indication. **4** a dog of a breed that on scenting game stands rigid looking towards it. ▷ DOG

pointillism *n. Art* ▶ a technique of Impressionist painting using tiny dots of various pure colours, which become blended in the viewer's eye. [from French *pointillisme*] □ **pointillist** *n. & adj.* **pointillistic** *adj.*

pointing *n.* **1** cement or mortar filling the joints of brickwork. **2** the process of applying this.

pointless *adj.* lacking force, purpose, or meaning. □ **pointlessly** *adv.* **pointlessness** *n.*

point of honour *n.* an action or circumstance that affects one's reputation or conscience.

point of no return *n.* a point in a journey or enterprise at which it becomes essential or more practical to continue to the end.

point of order *n.* a query in a debate etc. as to whether correct procedure is being followed.

point of sale *n.* (hyphenated when *attrib.*) the place at which goods are retailed.

point of view *n.* **1** a position from which a thing is viewed. **2** a particular way of considering a matter.

point-to-point *n.* a steeplechase for horses used regularly in hunting.

pointy *adj.* (**pointier**, **pointiest**) having a sharp end; pointed.

poise ● *n.* **1** composure or self-possession of manner. **2** equilibrium; a stable state. **3** carriage (of the head etc.). ● *v.* **1** *tr.* balance; hold suspended or supported. **2** *intr.* be balanced; hover in the air etc. [from Latin *pensum* 'weight']

poised *adj.* **1** composed, self-assured. **2** (often foll. by *for*, or *to* + infin.) ready for action.

poison ● *n.* **1** a substance that when introduced into or absorbed by a living organism causes death or injury. **2** a harmful influence or principle etc. ● *v.tr.* **1** administer poison to (a person or animal). **2** kill or injure or infect with poison. **3** infect (air, water, etc.) with poison. **4** (esp. as **poisoned** *adj.*) treat (a weapon) with poison. **5** corrupt or pervert (a person or mind). **6** render (land etc.) foul and unfit for its purpose by a noxious application etc. [from Old French, related to POTION] □ **poisoner** *n.* **poisonous** *adj.* **poisonously** *adv.*

poisoned chalice *n.* an assignment, award, honour, etc. which is likely to prove a disadvantage or source of problems to the recipient.

poison gas *n.* = GAS *n.* 4.

poison ivy *n.* ▶ a N. American climbing plant, *Rhus radicans*, secreting an irritant oil from its leaves.

poison pen letter *n.* an anonymous libellous or abusive letter.

poison pill *n.* **1** a pill containing esp. fast-acting poison. **2** *Finance* any of various ploys used by a company threatened with an unwelcome takeover bid to make itself unattractive to the bidder.

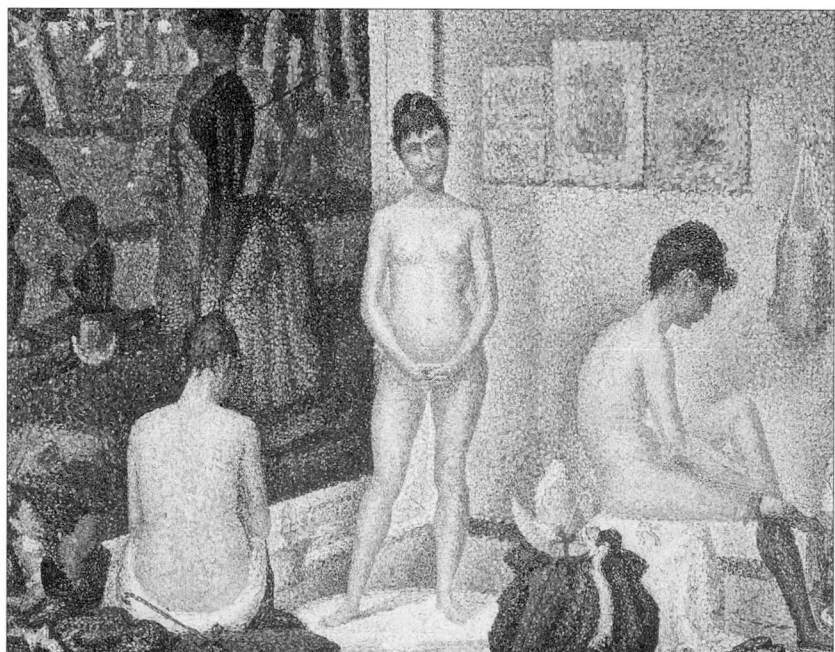

POISON IVY
(*Rhus radicans*)

poke[1] ● *v.* **1 a** *tr.* thrust or push with the hand, point of a stick, etc. **b** *intr.* be thrust forward. **2** *intr.* (foll. by *at* etc.) make thrusts with a stick etc. **3** *tr.* thrust the end of a finger etc. against. **4** (foll. by *in*) produce (a hole etc. in a thing) by poking. **5** *tr.* stir (a fire) with a poker. **6** *intr.* **a** (often foll. by *about, around*) move or act desultorily; potter. **b** (foll. by

POINTILLISM

Pointillism was a technique used by certain Impressionists, and developed by Georges Seurat and Paul Signac into a systematic approach to the use of colour based on 19th-century scientific colour theories. Dots or small dabs of pure, unmixed colour are methodically applied to the canvas so that when viewed from an appropriate distance they seem to react together optically, creating more vibrant effects than if the same colours were physically mixed together. Pointillism was adopted by the neo-Impressionists, and was extensively used in early 20th-century art.

DETAIL FROM
Les Poseuses

image composed of tiny dots

Les Poseuses (*c.*1888),
GEORGES SEURAT

about, into) pry; search casually. ● *n.* **1** the act or an instance of poking. **2** a thrust or nudge. □ **poke fun at** ridicule, tease. **poke one's nose into** *colloq.* pry or intrude into (esp. a person's affairs). [from Middle Dutch *poken*]

poke[2] *n. dial.* a bag or sack. □ **buy a pig in a poke** see PIG. [from Old Northern French, related to POUCH]

poker[1] *n.* a metal rod with a handle, for stirring an open fire.

poker[2] *n.* a card game in which bluff is used as players bet on the value of their hands. [19th-century coinage]

poker-face *n.* the impassive countenance appropriate to a poker player. □ **poker-faced** *adj.*

pokerwork *n. Brit.* the technique of burning designs on white wood etc. with a heated metal rod.

poky *adj.* (**pokier**, **pokiest**) **1** (of a room etc.) small and cramped. **2** *US* annoyingly slow. [based on POKE[1], in colloquial sense 'to confine'] □ **pokily** *adv.* **pokiness** *n.*

polar *adj.* **1 a** of or near a pole of the Earth or a celestial body, or of the celestial sphere. **b** (of a species or variety) living in the north polar region. **2** having magnetic polarity. **3 a** (of a molecule) having a positive charge at one end and a negative charge at the other. **b** (of a compound) having electric charges. **4** directly opposite in character or tendency. [from French *polaire*] □ **polarly** *adv.*

polar bear *n.* ▼ a white bear, *Thalarctos maritimus*, of the Arctic regions. ▷ BEAR

POLAR BEAR
(*Thalarctos maritimus*)

P

polarity *n.* (*pl.* **-ies**) **1** the tendency of a lodestone, magnetized bar, etc., to point with its extremities to the magnetic poles of the Earth. **2** the condition of having two poles with contrary qualities. **3** the state of having two opposite tendencies, opinions, etc. **4** the electrical condition of a body (positive or negative).

polarize *v.* (also **-ise**) **1** *tr.* ▲ restrict the vibrations of (a transverse wave, esp. light) to one direction. **2** *tr.* give magnetic or electric polarity to (a substance or body). **3** *tr. & intr.* divide into two groups of opposing opinion etc. □ **polarizable** *adj.* **polarization** *n.* **polarizer** *n.*

Polaroid *n. propr.* **1** material in thin plastic sheets that produces a high degree of plane polarization in light passing through it. **2 a** a type of camera that produces a finished print rapidly after each exposure. **b** a photograph taken with such a camera. **3** (in *pl.*) sunglasses with lenses made from Polaroid.

polder *n.* a piece of land reclaimed from the sea or a river, esp. in the Netherlands. [Dutch]

Pole *n.* **1** a native or national of Poland. **2** a person of Polish descent. [based on Polish *Polanie*, literally 'field-dwellers']

pole[1] ● *n.* **1** a long slender rounded piece of wood or metal, esp. with one end fixed in the ground. **2** *Athletics* a long slender flexible rod of wood, fibreglass, etc. used by a competitor in pole-vaulting. **3** esp. *US* a simple fishing rod. **4** *hist.* = PERCH[1] 3. ● *v.tr. & intr.* push (a punt etc.) with a pole. □ **up the**

---

pole *Brit. slang* **1** crazy, eccentric. **2** in difficulty. [from Latin *palus* 'stake']

pole[2] *n.* **1** (in full **north pole, south pole**) **a** each of the two points in the celestial sphere about which the stars appear to revolve. ▷ EQUATOR. **b** each of the extremities of the axis of rotation of the Earth or another body. **c** see MAGNETIC POLE. **2** each of the two opposite points on the surface of a magnet at which magnetic forces are strongest. **3** each of two terminals (positive and negative) of an electric cell or battery etc. **4** each of two opposed principles or ideas. □ **be poles apart** differ greatly, esp. in nature or opinion. [from Greek *polos* 'pivot, axis, sky'] □ **poleward** *adj.* **polewards** *adj. & adv.*

■ **Usage** In sense 1, the spelling is *North Pole* and *South Pole* (capitals) when used as geographical designations.

pole-axe (*US* **poleax**) ● *n.* **1** *hist.* = BATTLEAXE 1. **2** a butcher's axe. ● *v.tr.* hit or kill with or as if with a pole-axe. [from Middle Dutch *pol(l)aex*, based on POLL]

polecat *n.* **1** *Brit.* ▶ a small European brownish-black fetid flesh-eating mammal, *Mustela putorius*, of the weasel family. **2** *US* a skunk.

polemic ● *n.* **1** (also in *pl.*) a controversial discussion. **2** *Polit.* a verbal or written attack, esp. on a political opponent. **3** (in *pl.*; also treated as *sing.*) the art of controversial discussion, esp. in theology. ● *adj.* (also **polemical**) involving dispute; controversial. [from Greek *polemikos*] □ **polemically** *adv.* **polemicist** *n.* **polemicize** *v.intr.* (also **-ise**).

POLECAT
(*Mustela putorius*)

polenta *n.* porridge made of maize meal etc. [Latin, literally 'pearl barley']

pole position *n.* the most favourable position at the start of a motor race.

pole star *n. Astron.* a star in Ursa Minor now about 1° distant from the celestial North Pole. ▷ LODESTAR

pole vault ● *n.* the athletic sport of vaulting over a high bar with the aid of a long flexible pole held in the hands and giving extra spring. ● *v.intr.* (**pole-vault**) take part in this sport. □ **pole-vaulter** *n.*

police ● *n.* **1** (usu. prec. by *the*; usu. treated as *pl.*) the civil force of a state, responsible for maintaining public order. **2** (treated as *pl.*) the members of a police force. **3** (usu. treated as *pl.*) a force with similar functions (*military police*; *railway police*). ● *v.tr.* **1** control (a country or area) by means of police. **2** provide with police. **3** keep order in; control; monitor. [based on medieval Latin *politia* 'policy']

police constable see CONSTABLE 1b.

police dog *n.* a dog, esp. an Alsatian, used in police work.

police force *n.* the body of police of a country, district, or town.

police informer *n.* a person who gives police information about crimes and offenders.

policeman *n.* (*pl.* **-men**) a male member of a police force.

police officer *n.* a policeman or policewoman.

police procedural *n.* a crime novel that focuses on the procedures used by the police in solving a crime.

police state *n.* a totalitarian state controlled by political police supervising the citizens' activities.

police station *n.* the office of a local police force.

policewoman *n.* (*pl.* **-women**) a female member of a police force.

policy[1] *n.* (*pl.* **-ies**) **1** a course or principle of action adopted or proposed by a government, party, business, etc. **2** prudent conduct; sagacity. [from Greek *politeia* 'citizenship']

■ **Usage** See Usage Note at POLITY.

policy[2] *n.* (*pl.* **-ies**) **1** a contract of insurance. **2** a document containing this. [from French *police* 'bill of lading, contract of insurance']

policyholder *n.* a person or body holding an insurance policy.

polio *n.* = POLIOMYELITIS.

poliomyelitis *n. Med.* an infectious viral disease that affects the central nervous system and which can cause temporary or permanent paralysis. [based on Greek *polios* 'grey' + *muelos* 'marrow']

Polish /poh-lish/ ● *adj.* **1** of or relating to Poland. **2** of the Poles or their language. ● *n.* the language of Poland.

polish /pol-ish/ ● *v.* **1** *tr. & intr.* make or become smooth or glossy by rubbing. **2** *tr.* (esp. as **polished** *adj.*) refine or improve. ● *n.* **1** a substance used for polishing. **2** smoothness or glossiness produced by friction. **3** the act or an instance of polishing. **4** refinement or elegance of manner, conduct, etc. □ **polish off** finish (esp. food) quickly. **polish up** revise or improve (a skill etc.). [from Latin *polire*] □ **polishable** *adj.* **polisher** *n.*

politburo *n.* (*pl.* **-os**) the principal policy-making committee of a Communist party, esp. in the former USSR. [from Russian *politícheskoe byuró* 'political bureau']

polite *adj.* (**politer**, **politest**) **1** having good manners; courteous. **2** cultivated, cultured. [from

Latin *politus* 'polished'] □ **politely** *adv.* **politeness** *n.*

politic ● *adj.* **1** (of an action) judicious, expedient. **2** (of a person) prudent, sagacious. **3** political (now only in *body politic*). ● *v.intr.* (**politicked, politicking**) engage in politics. [from Greek *politikos* 'civic, civil'] □ **politicly** *adv.*

political *adj.* **1 a** of or concerning the state or its government, or public affairs generally. **b** of, relating to, or engaged in politics. **c** belonging to or forming part of a civil administration. **2** taking or belonging to a side in politics or in controversial matters. **3** relating to interests of status or authority in an organization (*a political decision*). □ **politically** *adv.*

political asylum *n.* protection given by a state to a political refugee from another country.

political correctness *n.* the avoidance of forms of expression or action that exclude, marginalize, or insult certain racial, cultural, or other groups.

political economy *n.* the study of the economic aspects of government. □ **political economist** *n.*

politically correct *adj.* (also **politically incorrect**) exhibiting (or failing to exhibit) political correctness.

political prisoner *n.* a person imprisoned for political beliefs or actions.

political science *n.* the study of the state and systems of government. □ **political scientist** *n.*

politician *n.* **1** a person engaged in or concerned with politics, esp. as a practitioner. **2** esp. *Brit.* a person skilled in politics.

politicize *v.tr.* (also **-ise**) **1** give a political character to. **2** make politically aware. □ **politicization** *n.*

politico *n.* (*pl.* **-os**) *colloq.* a politician or political enthusiast. [Spanish]

politico- *comb. form* **1** politically. **2** political and (*politico-social*).

politics *n.pl.* **1** (treated as *sing.* or *pl.*) **a** the art and science of government. **b** public life and affairs as involving authority and government. **2** (usu. treated as *pl.*) **a** a set of ideas or principles in politics (*what are her politics?*). **b** activities concerned with the acquisition or exercise of authority or government. **c** an organizational process or principle affecting authority, status, etc. (*the politics of the decision*).

polity *n.* (*pl.* **-ies**) **1** a form or process of civil government or constitution. **2** an organized society; a state. [from Greek *politeia*]

■ **Usage** This word is sometimes confused with *policy*. It means neither 'policy' nor 'politics'.

polka ● *n.* **1** a lively dance of Bohemian origin in duple time. **2** the music for this. ● *v.intr.* (**polkas, polkaed** or **polka'd, polkaing**) dance the polka. [from Czech *půlka* 'half-step']

polka dot *n.* any of many uniform round dots forming a regular pattern on a textile fabric etc.

poll ● *n.* **1 a** the process of voting at an election. **b** the counting of votes at an election. **c** the result of voting. **d** the number of votes recorded (*a heavy poll*). **e** (usu. in *pl.*) a place where votes are cast. **2** = GALLUP POLL. **3 a** *Sc.* & *dial.* a human head. **b** the part of this on which hair grows (*flaxen poll*). **4** a hornless animal. ● *v.* **1** *tr.* **a** take the vote or votes of. **b** (in *passive*) have one's vote taken. **c** (of a candidate) receive (so many votes). **d** give (a vote). **2** *tr.* record the opinion of (a person or group) in an opinion poll. **3** *intr.* give one's vote. **4** *tr.* cut off the top of (a tree or plant), esp. make a pollard of. **5** *tr.* (esp. as **polled** *adj.*) cut the horns off (cattle). [Middle English]

pollard ● *n.* **1** an animal that has lost or cast its horns; an ox, sheep, or goat of a hornless breed. **2** a tree whose branches have been cut off to encourage the growth of new branches, esp. a riverside willow **3a** the bran sifted from flour. **b** a fine bran containing some flour. ● *v.tr.* make (a tree) a pollard. [based on POLL]

pollen *n.* ► the fine dust-like grains discharged from the male part of a flower, each containing a gamete that can fertilize the female ovule. ▷ POLLINATE. [Latin, literally 'fine flour, dust']

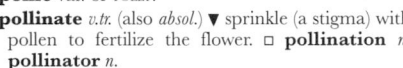

POLLEN: GRAIN OF PINE POLLEN (MAGNIFIED)

pollen count *n.* an index of the amount of pollen in the air.

pollie var. of POLLY.

pollinate *v.tr.* (also *absol.*) ▼ sprinkle (a stigma) with pollen to fertilize the flower. □ **pollination** *n.* **pollinator** *n.*

polling *n.* the registering or casting of votes.

polling booth *n.* a compartment in which a voter stands to mark a ballot paper.

polling day *n.* the day of an election.

polling station *n.* a building where voting takes place during an election.

pollinic *adj.* of or relating to pollen.

pollster *n.* a person who conducts or analyses opinion polls.

poll tax *n. hist.* **1** a tax levied on every adult. **2** = COMMUNITY CHARGE.

pollute *v.tr.* **1** contaminate or defile (the environment). **2** make foul or filthy. **3** destroy the purity or sanctity of. [based on Latin *pollutus* 'defiled'] □ **pollutant** *adj.* & *n.* **polluter** *n.* **pollution** *n.*

polly *n.* (also **pollie**) (*pl.* **-ies**) *Austral.* a politician.

polo *n.* a game of Eastern origin resembling hockey, played on horseback with a long-handled mallet. [from Tibetan *pholo*, literally 'ball game']

polonaise /pol-ŏn-ayz/ *n.* **1** a dance of Polish origin in triple time. **2** the music for this. [French fem. of *polonais* 'Polish']

polo neck *n.* (hyphenated when *attrib.*) *Brit.* **1** a high round turned-over collar. **2** a pullover with this.

polonium *n. Chem.* a rare radioactive metallic element, occurring naturally in uranium ores. [based on medieval Latin *Polonia* 'Poland', native country of Marie Curie, its co-discoverer]

polo shirt *n.* a short-sleeved casual shirt with a collar and only partly buttoned down the front.

polo stick *n.* a mallet for playing polo.

POLLINATE

For a flower to be pollinated, pollen must be transferred from the male to the female part. The main pollen-carrying agents are the wind and animals (mostly insects, but also birds and bats). Animal pollinators carry the pollen on their bodies, and are attracted to the flower by scent or by the sight of the petals.

sticky pollen attaches to bee

bee feeds on nectar

scented petal attracts insects

INSECT POLLINATION

poltergeist /pol-ter-gyst/ *n.* a noisy mischievous ghost. [German]

poltroon *n.* a spiritless coward. [from Italian *poltrone*] □ **poltroonery** *n.*

poly *n.* (*pl.* **polys**) *Brit. colloq.* polytechnic.

poly- *comb. form* **1** denoting many or much. **2** *Chem.* denoting the presence of many radicals etc. of a particular kind in a molecule (*polysaccharide*; *polystyrene*). [from Greek *polus* 'much', *polloi* 'many']

polyamide *n. Chem.* any of a class of condensation polymers which includes many synthetic fibres such as nylon.

polyandry *n.* polygamy in which a woman has more than one husband. [based on Greek *anēr andros* 'male'] □ **polyandrous** *adj.*

polyanthus *n.* (*pl.* **polyanthuses**) a flower cultivated from hybridized primulas. [based on Greek *anthos* 'flower']

polycarbonate *n.* any of a class of polymers in which the units are linked through a carbonate group, mainly used as moulding materials.

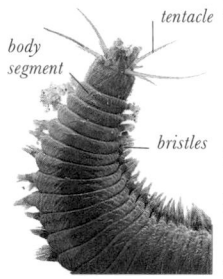

tentacle

body segment

bristles

polychaete /pol-i-keet/ *n.* ◄ any aquatic annelid worm of the class Polychaeta, having numerous bristles on the fleshy lobes of each body segment.

POLYCHAETE: KING RAGWORM (*Nereis pelagica*)

polychlorinated biphenyl see PCB 2.

polychromatic *adj.* many-coloured. □ **polychromatism** *n.*

polychrome ● *adj.* painted, printed, or decorated in many colours. ● *n.* **1** a work of art in several colours. **2** varied colouring. [based on Greek *khrōma* 'colour']

polycotton *n.* fabric made from a mixture of cotton and polyester fibre.

polyester *n.* **1** any of a group of condensation polymers used to form synthetic fibres such as Terylene or to make resins. **2** a fabric made from such a polymer. ▷ ROPE

polyethene *n. Chem.* = POLYTHENE.

polyethylene *n. Chem.* = POLYTHENE.

polygamous *adj.* **1** having more than one wife or husband at the same time. **2** having more than one mate. [from Greek *polugamos*] □ **polygamist** *n.* **polygamy** *n.*

polyglot ● *adj.* **1** of many languages. **2** speaking or writing several languages. ● *n.* a polyglot person. [based on Greek *glōtta* 'tongue']

polygon *n.* a plane figure with many sides and angles. [from Greek *polugōnon* 'many-angled (thing)'] □ **polygonal** *adj.*

polygraph *n.* a machine designed to detect and record changes in physiological characteristics, used esp. as a lie detector.

polygyny *n.* polygamy in which a man has more than one wife. [based on Greek *gunē* 'woman'] □ **polygynous** *adj.*

polyhedron *n.* (*pl.* **polyhedra** or **polyhedrons**) a solid figure with many faces. [based on Greek *hedra* 'base'] □ **polyhedral** *adj.*

polymath *n.* a person of much or varied learning. [based on Greek *manthanein* 'to learn'] □ **polymathic** *adj.* **polymathy** *n.*

polymer *n.* a compound composed of one or more large molecules that are formed from repeated units of smaller molecules. [from Greek *polumeros* 'having many parts'] □ **polymeric** *adj.* **polymerize** *v.intr.* & *tr.* (also **-ise**). **polymerization** *n.*

polymerase *n. Biochem.* any enzyme which catalyses the formation of a polymer, esp. of DNA or RNA.

P

Polynesian ● *adj.* of or relating to Polynesia, a group of Pacific islands including New Zealand, Hawaii, Samoa, etc. ● *n.* **1 a** a native of Polynesia. **b** a person of Polynesian descent. **2** the Polynesian languages as a group. [based on Greek *nēsos* 'island']

polynomial *Math.* ● *n.* an expression of more than two algebraic terms. ● *adj.* of or being a polynomial.

polyp *n.* **1** *Zool.* an individual cnidarian. **2** *Med.* a small usu. benign growth protruding from a mucous membrane. [from French *polype*]

polypeptide *n.* *Biochem.* a peptide formed by the combination of about ten or more amino acids. [from German *Polypeptid*]

polyphonic *adj.* *Mus.* (of vocal music etc.) in two or more relatively independent parts; contrapuntal. [based on Greek *phōnē* 'voice, sound']

polyphony *n.* (*pl.* **-ies**) *Mus.* polyphonic style in musical composition; counterpoint.

polyphosphate *n.* any of various complex phosphates, used esp. in detergents or as food additives.

polyploid *Biol.* ● *n.* a nucleus or organism that contains more than two sets of chromosomes. ● *adj.* of or being a polyploid. □ **polyploidy** *n.*

polypropene *n.* = POLYPROPYLENE.

polypropylene *n.* *Chem.* any of various polymers of propylene including thermoplastic materials used for films, fibres, or moulding materials. ▷ ROPE

polysaccharide /pol-i-sak-ă-ryd/ *n.* any carbohydrate whose molecules consist of long chains of monosaccharides.

polysemy *n.* *Philol.* the existence of many meanings (of a word etc.). [based on Greek *sēma* 'sign'] □ **polysemic** *adj.* **polysemous** *adj.*

polystyrene *n.* a polymer of styrene, esp. a thermoplastic polymer often expanded with a gas to produce a lightweight rigid white substance used for insulation and in packaging.

polysyllabic *adj.* **1** having many syllables. **2** characterized by the use of words of many syllables.

polysyllable *n.* a polysyllabic word.

polytechnic ● *n.* an institution of higher education offering courses in many (esp. vocational) subjects at degree level or below. ● *adj.* dealing with or devoted to various vocational or technical subjects. [based on Greek *tekhnē* 'art']

■ **Usage** In 1989 British polytechnics gained autonomy from their local education authorities and in 1992 were able to call themselves universities.

polytetrafluoroethylene *n.* *Chem.* a tough translucent polymer resistant to chemical action and with a low coefficient of friction, used for seals and bearings, to coat non-stick cooking utensils, etc. Cf. TEFLON.

polytheism *n.* the belief in or worship of more than one god. [based on Greek *polutheos* 'of many gods'] □ **polytheist** *n.* **polytheistic** *adj.*

polythene *n.* esp. *Brit.* a tough light plastic, a thermoplastic polymer of ethylene, used for packaging and insulating materials.

polyunsaturate *n.* a polyunsaturated fat or fatty acid.

polyunsaturated *adj.* *Chem.* (of a compound, esp. a fat or oil molecule) containing several double or triple bonds and therefore capable of further reaction.

polyurethane *n.* any polymer containing the urethane group, used in adhesives, paints, plastics, rubbers, foams, etc.

polyvalent *adj.* *Chem.* having a valency of more than two, or several valencies

polyvinyl acetate *n.* *Chem.* a soft plastic polymer used in paints and adhesives.

polyvinyl chloride *n.* a tough transparent solid polymer of vinyl chloride, used for a wide variety of products including pipes, flooring, etc.

Pom *n.* *Austral.* & *NZ slang offens.* = POMMY.

pomace *n.* the mass of crushed apples in cider-making. [based on Latin *pomum* 'apple']

pomade ● *n.* scented dressing for the hair and the skin of the head. ● *v.tr.* dress with pomade. [based on Latin *pomum* 'apple', from which it was originally made]

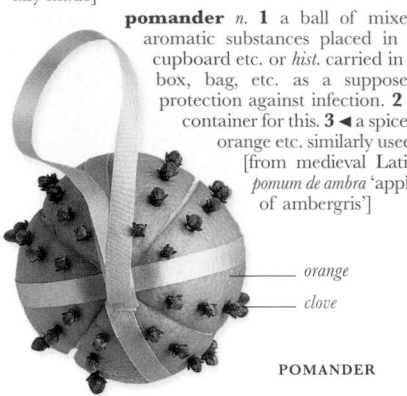

pomander *n.* **1** a ball of mixed aromatic substances placed in a cupboard etc. or *hist.* carried in a box, bag, etc. as a supposed protection against infection. **2** a container for this. **3** ◀ a spiced orange etc. similarly used. [from medieval Latin *pomum de ambra* 'apple of ambergris']

orange

clove

POMANDER

pome *n.* a firm-fleshed fruit in which the carpels from the central core enclose the seeds, e.g. the apple, pear, and quince. ▷ FRUIT. [from Latin *poma* 'fruit, apples']

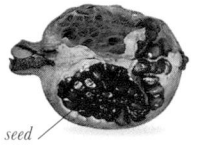

pomegranate *n.* **1** ▶ an orange-sized fruit with a tough skin containing many seeds in a red pulp. **2** the tree bearing this fruit, *Punica granatum*, native to N. Africa and W. Asia. [from Old French *pome grenate*, literally 'many-seeded apple']

seed

POMEGRANATE
(*Punica granatum*)

pomelo *n.* (*pl.* **-os**) **1** = SHADDOCK. **2** = GRAPEFRUIT. [19th-century coinage]

Pomeranian *n.* a small dog of a breed with long silky hair, a pointed muzzle, and pricked ears. [from *Pomerania* in Germany and Poland]

pomfret-cake *n.* (also **Pontefract-cake**) *Brit.* a small round flat liquorice sweet originally made at Pontefract (earlier *Pomfret*) in Yorkshire.

pommel /pum-ĕl/ *n.* **1** a knob, esp. at the end of a sword-hilt. **2** the upward projecting front part of a saddle. ▷ SADDLE, SIDE-SADDLE. ● *v.tr.* (**pommelled**, **pommelling**; *US* **pommeled**, **pommeling**) = PUMMEL. [from Old French *pomel*]

Pommy *n.* (also **Pommie**) (*pl.* **-ies**) *Austral.* & *NZ slang offens.* a British person, esp. a recent immigrant. [20th-century coinage]

pomp *n.* a splendid display; splendour. [from Greek *pompē* 'procession, pomp']

pompadour /pom-pă-door/ *n.* a woman's hairstyle with the hair in a high turned-back roll round the face. [named after the Marquise de *Pompadour*, mistress of Louis XV of France, 1721–64]

pom-pom *n.* an automatic quick-firing gun, esp. on a ship.

pompon *n.* (also **pompom**) **1** an ornamental ball or bobble made of wool, silk, or ribbons, usu. worn on women's or children's hats or clothing. **2** ◀ the round tuft on a soldier's cap, the front of a shako, etc. **3** (often *attrib.*)

pompon

POMPON ON A
FRENCH FUSILIER'S
SHAKO

a dahlia or chrysanthemum with small tightly-clustered petals. [French]

pompous *adj.* **1** self-important, affectedly grand or solemn. **2** (of language) pretentious; unduly grand in style. [from Late Latin *pomposus*, related to POMP] □ **pomposity** *n.* (*pl.* **-ies**). **pompously** *adv.* **pompousness** *n.*

ponce *Brit. slang* ● *n.* **1** a man who lives off a prostitute's earnings; a pimp. **2** *offens.* a homosexual; an effeminate man. ● *v.intr.* act as a ponce. □ **ponce about** move about effeminately or ineffectually. □ **poncey** *adj.* (also **poncy**) (in sense 2 of *n.*).

poncho *n.* (*pl.* **-os**) a cloak made of a blanket-like piece of cloth with a slit in the middle for the head. ▷ GAUCHO. [Latin American Spanish]

pond *n.* a fairly small body of still water. [Middle English variant of POUND[3]]

ponder *v.* **1** *tr.* think over; consider. **2** *intr.* think; muse. [from Latin *ponderare*]

ponderable *adj.* *literary* having appreciable weight or significance.

ponderosa *n.* *US* **1** a N. American pine tree, *Pinus ponderosa*. **2** the timber of this tree. [modern Latin fem. of *ponderosus* 'heavy']

ponderous *adj.* **1** heavy; unwieldy. **2** laborious. **3** (of style etc.) dull; tedious. [from Latin *ponderosus*] □ **ponderously** *adv.* **ponderousness** *n.*

pond life *n.* animals that live in ponds.

pondweed *n.* ▶ any of various aquatic plants, esp. of the genus *Potamogeton*.

pong *Brit. colloq.* ● *n.* an unpleasant smell. ● *v.intr.* stink. [20th-century coinage] □ **pongy** *adj.* (**pongier**, **pongiest**).

pongee /pun-jee/ *n.* **1** a soft type of Chinese silk fabric. **2** an imitation of this in cotton etc. [from Chinese *běnjī*, literally 'own loom']

pont *n.* *S.Afr.* a flat-bottomed ferry boat. [Dutch]

Pontefract-cake var. of POMFRET-CAKE.

PONDWEED:
CURLED
PONDWEED
(*Potamogeton crispus*)

pontiff *n.* (in full **sovereign** or **supreme pontiff**) *RC Ch.* the Pope. [from French *pontife*]

pontifical *adj.* **1** *RC Ch.* papal. **2** pompously dogmatic.

pontificate ● *v.intr.* **1** play the pontiff. **2** be pompously dogmatic. ● *n.* **1** the office of bishop or pope. **2** the period of this. [based on medieval Latin *pontificatus* 'pontificated upon']

pontoon[1] *n.* *Brit.* a card game in which players try to acquire cards with a face value totalling 21.

pontoon[2] *n.* **1** a flat-bottomed boat. **2 a** each of several boats, hollow metal cylinders, etc., used to support a temporary bridge. **b** (also **pontoon bridge**) such a bridge. **3** = CAISSON 1, 2. [from Latin *ponto -onis*]

pony *n.* (*pl.* **-ies**) **1** a horse of any small breed. ▷ HORSE. **2** a small drinking glass.

ponytail *n.* a hairstyle in which the hair is drawn back and tied, causing it to hang down like a pony's tail.

pony-trekking *n.* *Brit.* travelling across country on a pony for pleasure. □ **pony-trekker** *n.*

poo var. of POOH.

pooch *n.* *colloq.* a dog. [20th-century coinage]

poodle *n.* **1** a dog of a breed with a curly coat that is usually clipped. ▷ DOG. **2** *Brit.* a servile follower. [from German *Pudel(hund)*]

poof[1] *n.* (also **pouf**, **poove**) *Brit. slang offens.* **1** an effeminate man. **2** a male homosexual. [19th-century coinage] □ **poofy** *adj.*

poof[2] *int.* expressing contemptuous rejection or announcing a sudden disappearance.

POOL

Pool is played using a cue to hit a cue ball against a coloured or striped ball, causing it to fall into a pocket. The most popular form of pool is eight-ball, in which one player shoots only at coloured balls, the other player only at striped balls. After a player pockets an entire group, the 8-ball must be pocketed to end the game. Other forms include sinking balls in numerical order (rotation), or sinking a designated ball into a designated pocket (straight pool).

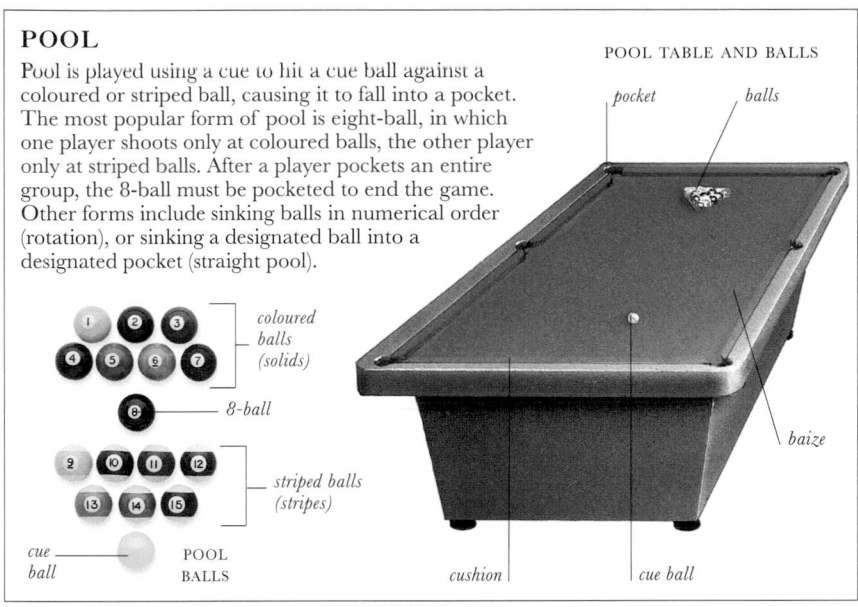

POOL TABLE AND BALLS

pocket · *balls* · *baize* · *coloured balls (solids)* · *8-ball* · *striped balls (stripes)* · *cue ball* · POOL BALLS · *cushion* · *cue ball*

---

poofter *n. Brit. slang offens.* = POOF¹.

pooh (also **poo**) ● *int.* expressing impatience or contempt. ● *n. slang* (a child's word for) excrement.

pooh-pooh *v.tr.* express contempt for; ridicule.

pooja var. of PUJA.

pool¹ ● *n.* **1** a small body of still water. **2** a small shallow body of any liquid. **3** = SWIMMING POOL. **4** a deep place in a river. ● *v. intr.* (of water etc.) form a pool. [Old English]

pool² ● *n.* **1 a** (often *attrib.*) a common supply of persons, vehicles, commodities, etc. for sharing by a group of people (*a typing pool; a pool car*). **b** a group of persons sharing duties etc. **2 a** the collective amount of players' stakes in gambling etc. **b** a receptacle for this. **3 a** a joint commercial venture, esp. an arrangement between competing parties to fix prices and share business to eliminate competition. **b** the common funding for this. **4** *N. Amer.* ▲ a game on a billiard table with usu. 16 balls. ● *v.tr.* **1** put into a common fund. **2** share (things) in common. **3** (of transport or organizations etc.) share (traffic, receipts). **4** *Austral. slang* **a** involve (a person) in a scheme etc., often by deception. **b** implicate, inform on. □ **the pools** *Brit.* = FOOTBALL POOL. [originally in Cards sense: from French *poule* 'stake, kitty']

pool room *n. US* **1** a betting shop. **2** a place for playing pool.

poolside *n.* the side of a swimming pool (often *attrib.*: *poolside bar*).

poop¹ *n.* **1** the stern of a ship. **2** (also **poop deck**) the aftermost and highest deck of a ship. ▷ MAN-OF-WAR. [from Latin *puppis*]

poop² *v.tr.* (esp. as **pooped** *adj.*) *US colloq.* exhaust; tire out. [20th-century coinage]

poop³ ● *n.* **1** a short blast made in a hollow tube; a toot. **2** *slang* an act of breaking wind or defecating. ● *v.intr. slang* break wind; defecate.

pooper scooper *n.* (also **poop scoop**) *colloq.* an implement for clearing up (esp. dog) excrement. [based on POOP³]

poor *adj.* **1** lacking adequate money or means to live comfortably. **2** (foll. by *in*) deficient in (a possession or quality) (*the poor in spirit*). **3 a** scanty, inadequate (*a poor crop*). **b** less good than is usual or expected (*poor visibility; is a poor driver; in poor health*). **c** paltry; inferior (*poor condition; came a poor third*). **4 a** deserving pity or sympathy; unfortunate (*you poor thing*). **b** with reference to a dead person (*as my poor father used to say*). **5** spiritless; despicable (*is a poor creature*). □ **poor man's** an inferior or cheaper substitute for.

take a poor view of regard with disfavour or pessimism. [from Latin *pauper*]

poor box *n.* a collection box for the relief of the poor.

poorhouse *n. hist.* = WORKHOUSE 1.

poor law *n. hist.* a law relating to the support of paupers.

poorly ● *adv.* **1** scantily; defectively. **2** with no great success. **3** meanly; contemptibly. ● *predic.adj.* esp. *Brit.* unwell.

poorness *n.* **1** defectiveness. **2** the lack of some good quality or constituent.

poor relation *n.* an inferior or subordinate member of a family or any other group.

poor white *n.* esp. *US offens.* a member of a group of white people regarded as socially inferior.

pootle *v.intr. colloq.* move or travel in a leisurely manner. [blend of TOOTLE and *poodle*, in same sense]

poove var. of POOF¹.

pop¹ ● *n.* **1** a sudden sharp explosive sound as of a cork when drawn. **2** *colloq.* an effervescent sweet drink. ● *v.* (**popped**, **popping**) **1** *intr. & tr.* make or cause to make a pop. **2** *intr. & tr.* (foll. by *in, out, up, down,* etc.) go, move, come, or put unexpectedly or in a quick or hasty manner (*pop out to the shops; pop in for a visit; pop it on your head*). **3 a** *intr. & tr.* burst, making a popping sound. **b** *tr.* heat (popcorn etc.) until it pops. **4** *intr. colloq.* fire a gun. **5** *tr. Brit. slang* pawn. **6** *tr. slang* take or inject (a drug etc.). **7** *intr.* (often foll. by *up*) (of a cricket ball) rise sharply off the pitch. ● *adv.* with the sound of a pop (*heard it go pop*). □ **pop off** *colloq.* **1** die. **2** quietly slip away (cf. sense 2 of *v.*). **pop the question** *colloq.* propose marriage. [Middle English]

pop² *colloq.* ● *adj.* (usu. *attrib.*) **1** in a popular or modern style. **2** of, performing, or relating to pop music (*pop concert; pop group*). ● *n.* **1** (in full **pop music**) commercial popular music, esp. that since the 1950s. **2** a pop record or song (*top of the pops*).

pop³ *n.* esp. *US colloq.* father.

pop. *abbr.* population.

popadom (also **popadam**) var. of POPPADOM.

pop art *n.* ▼ art based on modern popular culture and the mass media.

popcorn *n.* **1** maize which bursts open when heated. **2** these kernels when popped.

pop culture *n.* commercial culture based on popular taste.

pope *n.* (as title usu. **Pope**) the Bishop of Rome as head of the Roman Catholic Church. [from Greek *pappas* 'father']

Popemobile *n.* a bulletproof vehicle with a raised viewing area, used by the Pope on official visits.

popery *n. derog.* **1** the papal system. **2 a** the Roman Catholic Church. **b** the doctrines and ceremonies associated with Roman Catholicism.

pop-eyed *adj. colloq.* **1** having bulging eyes. **2** wide-eyed.

pop festival *n.* a festival at which popular music etc. is performed.

popgun *n.* a child's toy gun which shoots a pellet etc. by the compression of air.

popinjay *n.* **1** a fop, a conceited person, a coxcomb. **2** *archaic* a parrot. [from Arabic *babaġā*, assimilated to JAY]

popish *adj. derog.* Roman Catholic.

poplar *n.* **1** any tree of the genus *Populus*, typically tall and fast growing. *N. Amer.* = TULIP TREE. [from Latin *populus*]

P

POP ART

The term pop art was coined in the 1950s by the critic Lawrence Alloway. He used it to describe works by artists who employed popular imagery drawn from advertising, comic strips, film, and television. The materials and techniques long used by abstract and action painters – acrylic paints, stencils, silk screens, spray guns – were applied to figurative uses by pop artists. The leading pop artists include Roy Lichtenstein, Peter Blake, Richard Hamilton, and Andy Warhol.

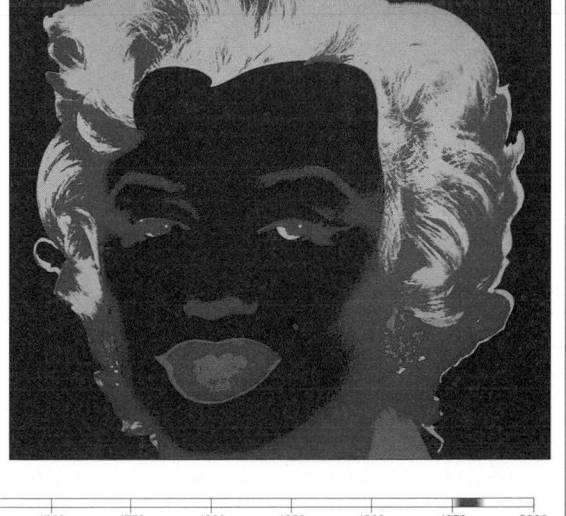

Marilyn, ANDY WARHOL

TIMELINE

1500	1550	1600	1650	1700	1750	1800	1850	1900	1950	2000

poplin *n.* a plain-woven fabric usu. of cotton, with a corded surface. [from obsolete French *papeline*]

pop music see POP² *n.* 1.

poppa *n. US colloq.* father.

poppadom *n.* (also **poppadam**, **popadom**, **popadam**) (in Indian cookery) a thin, crisp, spiced bread eaten with curry etc. [from Tamil *pappadam*]

popper *n.* **1** *Brit. colloq.* a press stud. **2** a person or thing that pops.

poppet *n.* **1** *Brit. colloq.* a small or dainty person. **2** the head of a lathe. [from Latin *pup(p)a*, related to PUPPET]

poppet-valve *n. Engin.* a mushroom-shaped valve, lifted bodily from its seat rather than hinged.

popping crease *n. Cricket* a line in front of and parallel to the wicket, inside which the batsman must keep the bat or one foot grounded to avoid the risk of being stumped.

poppy¹ *n.* (*pl.* **-ies**) ▼ any plant of the genus *Papaver*, with showy flowers, milky sap and rounded seed-capsules, esp. the red-flowered corn poppy, *P. rhoeas*, and the opium poppy. [from Latin *papaver*]

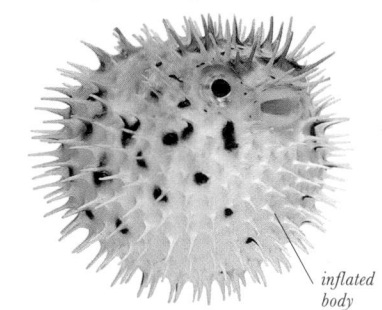

seeds

poppy-head

POPPY: OPIUM POPPY
(*Papaver somniferum*)

poppy² *adj.* having a sound characteristic of pop music.

poppycock *n. slang* nonsense. [from Dutch dialect *pappekak*, from *pap* 'soft' + *kak* 'dung']

Poppy Day *n. Brit.* = REMEMBRANCE SUNDAY.

poppy-head *n.* **1** the seed capsule of the poppy. **2** an ornamental top on the end of a church pew.

Popsicle *n.* esp. *N. Amer. propr.* an ice lolly.

popsy *n.* (also **popsie**) (*pl.* **-ies**) esp. *Brit. colloq.* a young woman. [shortening of POPPET]

populace *n.* the common people. [from Italian *popolaccio*]

popular *adj.* **1** liked or admired by many people or by a specified group (*popular teachers; a popular hero*). **2 a** of or carried on by the general public (*popular meetings*). **b** prevalent among the general public (*popular discontent*). **3** adapted to the understanding, taste, or means of the people (*popular science; popular medicine*). [from Latin *popularis*] □ **popularism** *n.* **popularity** *n.* **popularly** *adv.*

popular front *n.* a party or coalition representing left-wing elements.

popularize *v.tr.* (also **-ise**) **1** make popular. **2** cause (a person, principle, etc.) to be generally known or liked. **3** present (a technical subject etc.) in a popular or readily understandable form. □ **popularization** *n.* **popularizer** *n.*

popular music *n.* music appealing to a wide public.

populate *v.tr.* **1** inhabit; form the population of. **2** supply with inhabitants (*a densely populated district*). [based on medieval Latin *populatus* 'peopled']

population *n.* **1 a** the inhabitants of a place, country, etc. **b** any specified group within this (*the Irish population of Liverpool*). **2** the total number of any of these (*a population of eight million; the seal population*). **3** the act or process of supplying with inhabitants (*the population of forest areas*). **4** *Statistics* any finite or infinite collection of items under consideration.

population explosion *n.* a sudden large increase of population.

populist ● *n.* a member or adherent of a political party seeking support mainly from the ordinary people. ● *adj.* of or relating to a populist or populist ideology. [based on Latin *populus* 'people'] □ **populism** *n.*

populous *adj.* densely populated. [from Late Latin *populosus*]

pop-up *attrib.adj.* **1** (of a toaster etc.) operating so as to move the object (toast when ready etc.) quickly upwards. **2** (of a book, greetings card, etc.) containing three-dimensional figures, illustrations, etc., that rise up when the page is turned. **3** *Computing* (of a menu) able to be superimposed on the screen being worked on and suppressed rapidly.

porbeagle *n.* a large shark, *Lamna nasus*, having a pointed snout. [18th-century Cornish dialect]

porcelain *n.* **1** a hard vitrified translucent ceramic. **2** objects made of this. [from Italian *porcellana* 'cowrie shell']

porch *n.* **1** a covered shelter for the entrance of a building. ▷ HOUSE. **2** *N. Amer.* a veranda. [from Latin *porticus*, translation of Greek *stoa*] □ **porched** *adj.*

porcine /por-syn/ *adj.* of or like pigs. [from Latin *porcinus*]

porcupine *n.* any rodent of the family Hystricidae native to Africa, Asia, and SE Europe, or the family Erethizontidae native to America, having defensive spines or quills. ▷ RODENT. [from Latin *porcus* 'pig' + *spina* 'thorn']

porcupine fish *n.* ▼ a marine fish, *Diodon hystrix*, covered with sharp spines and often distending itself into a spherical shape.

inflated body

PORCUPINE FISH
(*Diodon hystrix*)

pore¹ *n.* esp. *Biol.* a minute opening in a surface through which gases, liquids, or fine solids may pass. ▷ SKIN. [from Greek *poros* 'passage, pore']

pore² *v.intr.* (foll. by *over*) **1** be absorbed in studying (a book etc.). **2** meditate on. [Middle English]

pork *n.* the flesh of a pig, used as food. ▷ CUT. [from Latin *porcus* 'pig']

pork barrel *n.* (hyphenated when *attrib.*) *N. Amer. colloq.* **1** a source of government funds for projects designed to win votes (*disapproved of pork-barrel funding*). **2** the funds themselves. □ **pork-barrelling** *n.*

pork butcher *n.* a person who slaughters pigs for sale, or who sells pork rather than other meats.

porker *n.* **1** a pig raised for food. **2** a young fattened pig.

pork pie *n.* a pie of minced pork etc. eaten cold.

pork-pie hat *n.* a hat with a flat crown and a brim turned up all round.

porky ● *adj.* (**porkier**, **porkiest**) **1** *colloq.* fat. **2** of or like pork. ● *n.* (*pl.* **porkies**) (also **porky-pie**) *Brit. rhyming slang* a lie.

porn (also **porno**) *colloq.* ● *n.* pornography. ● *attrib. adj.* pornographic.

pornography *n.* **1** the explicit description or exhibition of sexual activity in literature, films, etc., intended to stimulate erotic rather than aesthetic or emotional feelings. **2** literature etc. characterized by this. [from Greek *pornographos* 'writing of harlots'] □ **pornographer** *n.* **pornographic** *adj.*

porous *adj.* **1** full of pores. **2** letting through air, water, etc. **3** (of an argument, security system, etc.) leaky, admitting infiltration. [based on Latin *porus* 'pore'] □ **porosity** *n.*

porphyria *n.* any of a group of genetic disorders involving abnormal metabolism of certain pigments and their excretion in the urine. [based on *porphyrin*, deep red or purple pigment]

porphyry *n.* (*pl.* **-ies**) **1** a hard rock composed of crystals of white or red feldspar in a red matrix. **2** *Geol.* an igneous rock with large crystals scattered in a matrix of much smaller crystals. [based on Greek *porphura* 'purple'] □ **porphyritic** *adj.*

porpoise *n.* ▼ any of various small toothed whales of the family Phocoenidae, with a blunt rounded snout. ▷ CETACEAN. [from Latin *porcus* 'pig' + *piscis* 'fish']

porridge *n.* **1** a dish consisting of oatmeal or another meal or cereal boiled in water or milk. **2** *Brit. slang* imprisonment. [16th-century coinage, alteration of POTTAGE] □ **porridgy** *adj.*

PORPOISE

The six species of porpoise are typically smaller than other cetaceans (whales and dolphins), and have blunt snouts without beaks. Porpoise teeth are spade-shaped, whereas those of the dolphin are conical.

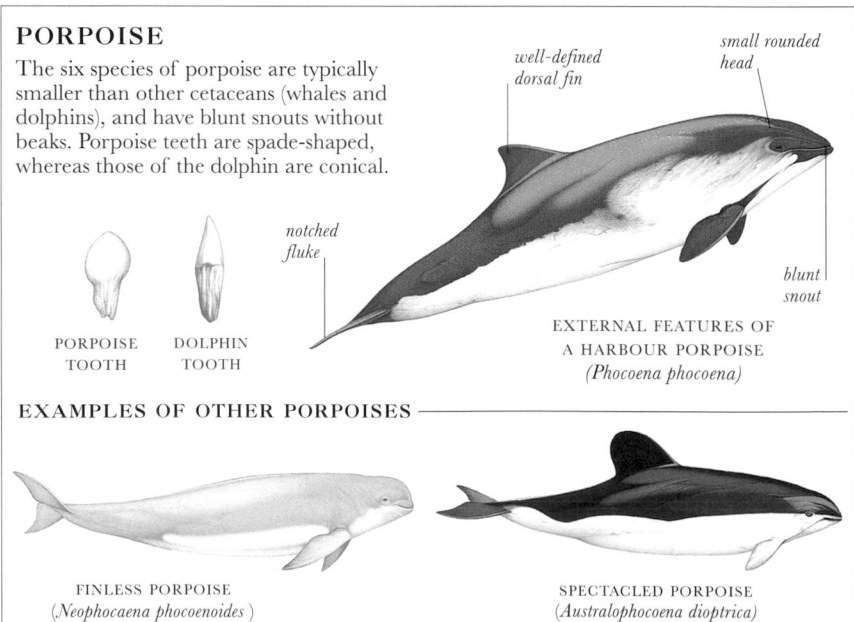

well-defined dorsal fin

small rounded head

notched fluke

blunt snout

PORPOISE TOOTH

DOLPHIN TOOTH

EXTERNAL FEATURES OF A HARBOUR PORPOISE
(*Phocoena phocoena*)

EXAMPLES OF OTHER PORPOISES

FINLESS PORPOISE
(*Neophocaena phocoenoides*)

SPECTACLED PORPOISE
(*Australophocaena dioptrica*)

PORT

A port is a protected body of water that provides facilities for boats to berth and manage passengers and goods. Large ports can deal with many types of vessel, and have warehouses for goods and dry docks for repairing ships. Most ports are designed to handle containers, which can be loaded straight off ships on to trains and lorries.

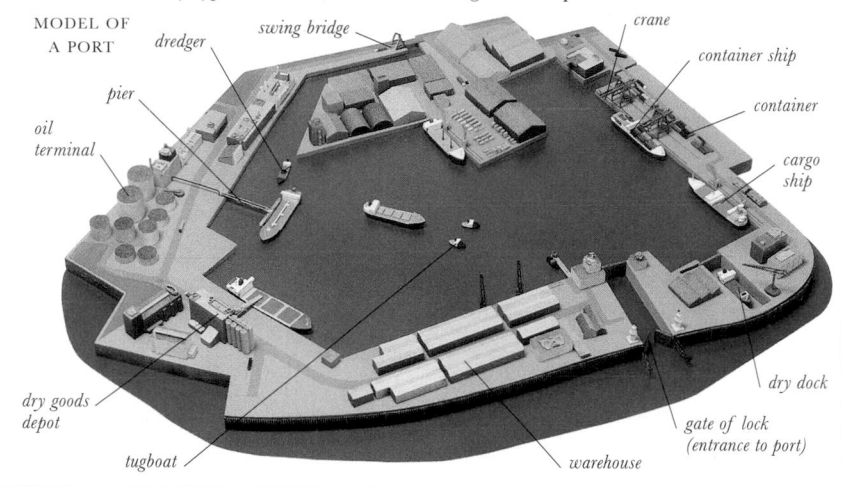

MODEL OF A PORT

swing bridge · crane · dredger · pier · container ship · container · oil terminal · cargo ship · dry goods depot · dry dock · tugboat · gate of lock (entrance to port) · warehouse

---

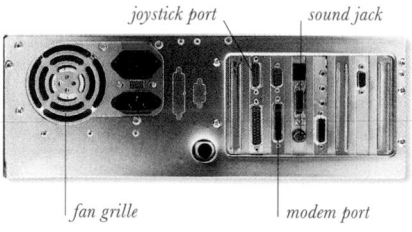

PORT: INPUT/OUTPUT PORTS ON THE BACK OF A COMPUTER

joystick port · sound jack · fan grille · modem port

---

porringer *n.* a small bowl, often with a handle, for soup, stew, etc. [earlier *pottinger*, from Old French *potager*]

port[1] *n.* **1** ▲ a harbour. **2** a place of refuge. **3** a town possessing a harbour. [from Latin *portus*]

port[2] *n.* (in full **port wine**) a strong sweet fortified wine of Portugal. [shortened form of *Oporto*, Portuguese *port*]

port[3] ● *n.* the left-hand side (looking forward) of a ship, boat, or aircraft (cf. STARBOARD). ● *v.tr.* (also *absol.*) turn (the helm) to port.

port[4] *n.* **1 a** an opening in the side of a ship for entrance, loading, etc. **b** a porthole. **2** an aperture for the passage of steam, water, etc. **3** *Electr.* ▼ a socket or aperture in an electronic circuit, esp. in a computer network, where connections can be made with peripheral equipment or disks etc. inserted. [from Latin *porta*]

port[5] *Mil.* ● *v.tr.* carry (a rifle, or other weapon) diagonally across and close to the body with the barrel etc. near the left shoulder (esp. *port arms!*). ● *n.* this position. [from Latin *portare* 'to carry']

port[6] *n. Austral. colloq.* **1** a suitcase or travelling bag. **2** a bag of a specified kind. [abbreviation of PORTMANTEAU]

portable ● *adj.* **1** easily movable, convenient for carrying (*portable TV*; *portable computer*). **2** (of a right, privilege, etc.) capable of being transferred or adapted in altered circumstances (*portable pension*). ● *n.* a portable object, e.g. a radio, typewriter, etc. [from Late Latin *portabilis*] □ **portability** *n.*

portage ● *n.* **1** the carrying of boats or goods between two navigable waters. **2** a place at which this is necessary. ● *v.tr.* convey (a boat or goods) between navigable waters. [from Old French]

Portakabin *n. Brit. propr.* a portable room or building designed for quick assembly.

portal[1] *n.* a doorway or gate etc., esp. an elaborate one. [from medieval Latin *portale* 'city gate, porch']

portal[2] *adj.* of or relating to the transverse fissure of the liver, through which pass blood vessels etc. [based on Latin *porta* 'gate']

portal vein *n.* a vein conveying blood to the liver from the spleen, stomach, pancreas, and intestines.

portamento *n.* (*pl.* **-os** or **portamenti**) *Mus.* the act or an instance of gliding from one note to another in singing, playing the violin, etc. [Italian, literally 'carrying']

portcullis *n.* ► a strong heavy grating lowered to block a gateway in a fortress etc. [from Old French *porte coleïce* 'sliding door']

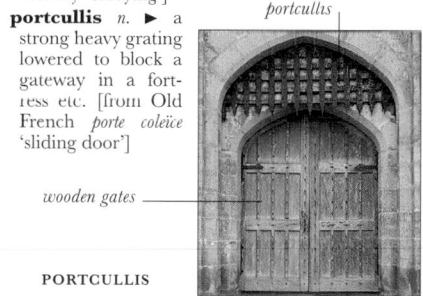

portcullis · wooden gates

PORTCULLIS

portend *v.tr.* **1** foreshadow as an omen. **2** give warning of. [from Latin *portendere*]

portent *n.* **1** an omen, a sign of something to come. **2** a prodigy; a marvellous thing. [from Latin *portentum*, related to PORTEND]

portentous *adj.* **1** like or serving as a portent. **2** pompously solemn. □ **portentously** *adv.* **portentousness** *n.*

■ **Usage** The spelling *portentious* (due to the influence of *pretentious*) is wrong.

porter[1] *n.* **1 a** a person employed to carry luggage etc. **b** a hospital employee who moves equipment, trolleys, etc. **2** a dark brown bitter beer brewed from charred or browned malt (apparently originally made esp. for porters). **3** *US* a sleeping car attendant. [from medieval Latin *portator*]

porter[2] *n. Brit.* a gatekeeper or doorkeeper. [based on Latin *porta* 'door']

porterage *n.* **1** the work of carrying luggage etc. **2** a charge for this.

---

porterhouse *n.* esp. *N. Amer. hist.* **1** a house at which porter and other drinks were retailed. **2** a house where steaks, chops, etc. were served.

porterhouse steak *n.* a thick steak cut from the thick end of a sirloin.

portfolio *n.* (*pl.* **-os**) **1** a case for keeping loose sheets of paper, drawings, etc. **2** a range of investments held by a person, a company, etc. **3** the office of a Minister of State (cf. MINISTER WITHOUT PORTFOLIO). **4** samples of an artist's work. [from Italian *portafogli*]

porthole *n.* **1** an aperture in a ship's or aircraft's side for the admission of light. **2** *hist.* an aperture for pointing a cannon through.

portico *n.* (*pl.* **-oes** or **-os**) ▼ a colonnade; a roof supported by columns at regular intervals usu. attached as a porch to a building. ▷ FAÇADE. [Italian]

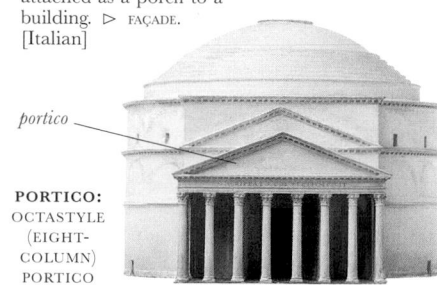

portico

PORTICO: OCTASTYLE (EIGHT-COLUMN) PORTICO

portière *n.* a curtain hung over a door or doorway. [French]

portion ● *n.* **1** a part or share. **2** the amount of food allotted to one person. **3** a specified or limited quantity. **4** one's destiny or lot. **5** a dowry. ● *v.tr.* **1** divide (a thing) into portions. **2** (foll. by *out*) distribute. **3** give a dowry to. **4** (foll. by *to*) assign (a thing) to (a person). [from Latin *portio*]

Portland cement *n.* a cement manufactured from chalk and clay which when hard resembles Portland stone in colour.

Portland stone *n.* a limestone from the Isle of Portland in Dorset, used in building.

portly *adj.* (**portlier**, **portliest**) corpulent; stout. [based on PORT[5], in literary sense 'bearing'] □ **portliness** *n.*

portmanteau /port-man-toh/ *n.* (*pl.* **portmanteaus** or **portmanteaux** /-tohz/) a travelling bag for clothes etc., opening into two equal parts. [from French, based on *porter* 'to carry' | *manteau* 'mantle']

portmanteau word *n.* a word blending the sounds and combining the meanings of two others, e.g. *motel*, *Oxbridge*.

port of call *n.* a place where a ship, person, etc. stops on a journey.

portrait *n.* **1** a representation of a person or animal, esp. of the face, made by drawing, painting, photography, etc. **2** a verbal picture; a graphic description. **3** a person etc. resembling or typifying another (*is the portrait of his father*). **4** (in graphic design etc.) a format in which the height of an illustration etc. is greater than the width. [French, literally 'portrayed']

portraitist *n.* a person who takes or paints portraits.

portraiture *n.* **1** the art of painting or taking portraits. **2** graphic description. **3** a portrait.

portray *v.tr.* **1** make a likeness of. **2** describe graphically; depict in words. [from Old French *portraire*] □ **portrayal** *n.*

Port Salut *n.* a pale mild type of cheese.

port tack see TACK[1] 4.

Portuguese /port-yuu-**g'eez**/ ● *n.* (*pl.* same) **1 a** a native or national of Portugal. **b** a person of Portuguese descent. **2** the language of Portugal. ● *adj.* of or relating to Portugal or its people or language. [from medieval Latin *portugalensis*]

P

PORTUGUESE MAN-OF-WAR (*Physalia* species)

crest

tentacles

Portuguese man-of-war *n.* ◄ a jellyfish of the genus *Physalia* with a large crest and a poisonous sting.

port watch see WATCH *n.* 3b.

port wine see PORT².

pose ● *v.* **1** *intr.* assume a certain attitude of body, esp. when being photographed or painted. **2** *intr.* (foll. by *as*) set oneself up as or pretend to be (another person etc.) (*posing as a celebrity*). **3** *intr.* behave affectedly in order to impress others. **4** *tr.* put forward or present (a question etc.). **5** *tr.* place (an artist's model etc.) in a certain attitude. ● *n.* **1** an attitude of body or mind. **2** an attitude or pretence, esp. one assumed for effect (*his generosity is a mere pose*). [from Late Latin *pausare* 'to pause']

poser *n.* **1** a person who poses (see POSE *v.* 3). **2** a puzzling question or problem.

poseur /poh-zer/ *n.* (*fem.* **poseuse**) = POSER 1. [French]

posh *colloq.* ● *adj.* **1** smart; stylish. **2** esp. *Brit.* of or associated with the upper classes (*spoke with a posh accent*). ● *adv.* esp. *Brit.* in a stylish or upper-class way (*talk posh; act posh*). □ **posh up** esp. *Brit.* smarten up. [20th-century coinage] □ **poshly** *adv.* **poshness** *n.*

posit *v.tr.* (**posited**, **positing**) assume as a fact, postulate. [based on Latin *positus* 'placed']

position ● *n.* **1** a place occupied by a person or thing. **2** the way in which a thing or its parts are placed or arranged (*sitting in an uncomfortable position*). **3** the proper place (*in position*). **4** the state of being advantageously placed (*jockeying for position*). **5** a person's mental attitude; a way of looking at a question (*changed their position on nuclear disarmament*). **6** a person's situation in relation to others (*puts one in an awkward position*). **7** rank or status; high social standing. **8** paid employment; a job. **9** a place where troops etc. are posted for strategic purposes (*the position was stormed*). ● *v.tr.* place in position. □ **in a position to** enabled by circumstances, resources, information, etc. to. [from Latin *positio*] □ **positional** *adj.* **positionally** *adv.* **positioner** *n.*

positive ● *adj.* **1** formally or explicitly stated; definite, unquestionable (*positive proof*). **2** (of a person) convinced or confident in his or her opinion (*positive that I was not there*). **3 a** absolute; not relative. **b** *Gram.* (of an adjective or adverb) expressing a simple quality without comparison (cf. COMPARATIVE *adj.* 4, SUPERLATIVE *adj.* 2). **4** *colloq.* downright (*it would be a positive miracle*). **5** constructive (*positive criticism; positive thinking*). **6** marked by the presence rather than absence of qualities or *Med.* symptoms (*a positive reaction to the plan; the test was positive*). **7** greater than zero (*positive and negative integers*). **8** *Electr.* of, containing, or producing the kind of electrical charge produced by rubbing glass with silk; lacking electrons. **9** (of a photographic image) showing lights and shades or colours true to the original. ● *n.* a positive adjective, photograph, quantity, etc. [from Latin *positivus*] □ **positively** *adv.* **positiveness** *n.* **positivity** *n.*

positive discrimination *n. Brit.* the practice of making distinctions in favour of groups considered to be underprivileged.

positive feedback *n.* **1** *Electronics* the return of part of an output signal to the input, tending to increase the amplification etc. **2** esp. *Biol.* the enhancing or amplification of an effect by its own influence on the process which gives rise to it.

positive pole *n.* the north-seeking pole. ▷ MAGNETIC FIELD

positive sign *n.* = PLUS SIGN.

positive vetting *n. Brit.* an inquiry into the background and character of a candidate for a post in the Civil Service that involves access to secret material.

positivism *n. Philos.* **1 a** the philosophical system of Auguste Comte (d. 1857), recognizing only non-metaphysical facts and observable phenomena. **b** a religious system founded on this. **2** = LOGICAL POSITIVISM. □ **positivist** *n.* & *adj.*

positron *n. Physics* ▼ a subatomic particle with a positive charge equal to the negative charge of an electron and having the same mass as an electron.

posse /poss-i/ *n.* **1** a strong force or company or assemblage. **2** (in full **posse comitatus** /kom-i-tay-tŭs/) **a** a body of constables, law-enforcers, etc. **b** esp. *US* a body of men summoned by a sheriff etc. to enforce the law. [Latin, literally 'to be able'; sense 2: *comitatus* 'of the county']

possess *v.tr.* **1** hold as property; own. **2** have as a faculty, quality, etc. (*they possess a special value for us*). **3** (also *refl.*; foll. by *in*) maintain (oneself, one's soul, etc.) in a specified state (*possess oneself in patience*). **4 a** (of a demon etc.) occupy; have power over (a person etc.) (*possessed by the Devil*). **b** (of an emotion, infatuation, etc.) dominate, be an obsession of (*possessed by fear*). **5** have sexual intercourse with (esp. a woman). □ **be possessed of** own, have. **possess oneself of** take or get for one's own. **what possessed you?** an expression of incredulity. [based on Latin *possessus* 'possessed'] □ **possessor** *n.* **possessory** *adj.*

possession *n.* **1** the act or state of possessing or being possessed. **2** the thing possessed. **3** the act or state of holding or occupancy. **4** *Law* power or control similar to lawful ownership but which may exist separately from it (*prosecuted for possession of drugs*). **5** (in *pl.*) property, wealth, subject territory, etc. **6** *Football* etc. control of the ball by a particular player. □ **in possession 1** (of a person) possessing. **2** (of a thing) possessed. **in possession of 1** having in one's possession. **2** maintaining control over (*in possession of one's wits*). **in the possession of** held or owned by. **take possession** (often foll. by *of*) become the owner or possessor (of a thing). [from Latin *possessio*] □ **possessionless** *adj.*

possession order *n. Brit.* an order made by a court directing that possession of a property be given to the owner.

possessive ● *adj.* **1** showing a desire to possess or retain what one already owns. **2** showing jealous and domineering tendencies towards another person. **3** *Gram.* indicating possession. ● *n.* (in full **possessive case**) *Gram.* the case of nouns and pronouns expressing possession. □ **possessively** *adv.* **possessiveness** *n.*

possessive pronoun *n.* each of the pronouns indicating possession (*my, your, his, their*, etc.) or the corresponding absolute forms (*mine, yours, his, theirs*, etc.).

possibility *n.* (*pl.* **-ies**) **1** the state or fact or an occurrence of being possible. **2** a thing that may exist or happen. **3** (usu. in *pl.*) the capability of being used, improved, etc.; the potential of an object or situation (esp. *have possibilities*). [from Late Latin *possibilitas*]

possible ● *adj.* **1** capable of existing or happening; that may be managed, achieved, etc. (*came as early as possible; few thought their victory possible*). **2** acceptable; potential (*a possible way of doing it*). ● *n.* **1** a possible candidate, member of a team, etc. **2** (prec. by *the*) whatever is likely, manageable, etc. [from Latin *possibilis*]

possibly *adv.* **1** perhaps. **2** in accordance with possibility (*cannot possibly refuse*).

possum *n.* **1** *colloq.* = OPOSSUM 1. **2** *Austral.* ► a phalanger resembling an American opossum. □ **play possum** pretend to be asleep or unconscious. [abbreviation]

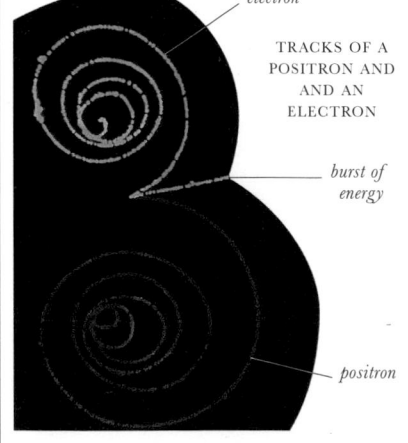

POSSUM: HONEY POSSUM (*Tarsipes spenserae*)

post¹ ● *n.* **1** a long stout piece of timber or metal set upright in the ground etc. to support something, mark a boundary, etc. **2** a pole etc. marking the start or finish of a race. ● *v.tr.* **1** (often foll. by *up*) **a** attach (a paper etc.) in a prominent place; stick up (*post no bills*). **b** announce or advertise by placard or in a published text. **2** *N. Amer.* achieve (a score in a game etc.). [from Latin *postis*]

post² ● *n.* **1** *Brit.* **a** the official conveyance of parcels, letters, etc. (*send it by post*). **b** these parcels, letters, etc. **2** *Brit.* a single collection, dispatch, or delivery of these; the letters etc. dispatched (*has the post arrived yet?*). **3** *Brit.* a place where letters etc. are dealt with; a post office or postbox (*take it to the post*). ● *v.tr.* **1** put (a letter etc.) in the post. **2** (esp. as **posted** *adj.*) (*US* often foll. by *up*) supply a person with information (*keep me posted*). **3 a** enter (an item) in a ledger. **b** (often foll. by *up*) complete (a ledger) in this way. [from Italian *posta*, based on Latin *positus* 'placed']

post³ ● *n.* **1** a place where a soldier is stationed or which he or she patrols. **2** a place of duty. **3 a** a position taken up by a body of soldiers. **b** a force occupying this. **c** a fort. **4** a situation, paid employment. **5** = TRADING POST. ● *v.tr.* **1** place or station (soldiers, an employee, etc.). **2** appoint to a post or command. [from Italian *posto*, based on Latin *positus* 'placed']

post- *prefix* after in time or order.

postage *n.* the amount charged for sending a letter etc. by post.

postage meter *n. N. Amer.* a franking machine.

postage stamp *n.* an official stamp affixed to a letter etc. indicating the amount of postage paid.

postal ● *adj.* **1** of the post. **2** esp. *Brit.* by post (*postal vote*). ● *n. US* a postcard.

postal card *n. US* = POSTCARD.

postal code *n.* = POSTCODE.

POSITRON

A positron is the antiparticle of an electron and has a positive charge. Pairs of particles and their antiparticles can be created in particle accelerators. Shown here, a burst of energy produces a positron and an electron, which spiral in opposite directions due to their opposing charges.

electron

TRACKS OF A POSITRON AND AND AN ELECTRON

burst of energy

positron

P

postal note *n. Austral.* & *NZ* = POSTAL ORDER.

postal order *n. Brit.* a money order issued by the Post Office.

postbag *n. Brit.* = MAILBAG.

postbox *n. Brit.* a public box in which mail is posted.

postcard *n.* a card, often with a photograph etc. on one side, for sending a short message by post without an envelope.

postcode *n. Brit.* a group of figures or letters and figures which are added to a postal address to assist sorting.

post-coital *adj.* occurring or existing after sexual intercourse. □ **post-coitally** *adv.*

post-date ● *v.tr.* affix or assign a date later than the actual one to (a document, event, etc.). ● *n.* such a date.

postdoctoral *adj.* of or relating to research undertaken after the completion of doctoral research.

poster *n.* **1** a placard in a public place. **2** a large printed picture. **3** a billposter.

poste restante /pohst rest-**ahnt**/ *n. Brit.* the department in a post office keeping letters until collected by the addressees. [French, literally 'letter(s) remaining']

posterior ● *adj.* **1** later; coming after in series, order, or time. **2** situated at the back. ● *n.* the buttocks. [Latin, literally 'further behind'] □ **posteriorly** *adv.*

posterity *n.* **1** all succeeding generations. **2** the descendants of a person. [from Latin *posteritas*]

postern *n.* **1** a back door. **2** a side way or entrance. [from Late Latin *posterula* 'a back way']

poster paint *n.* a gummy opaque paint.

postgrad *adj.* & *n. colloq.* = POSTGRADUATE.

postgraduate ● *adj.* of, relating to, or designating a course of study carried on after taking a first degree. ● *n.* a postgraduate student.

post-haste *adv.* with great speed.

post-horn *n. hist.* ▼ a valveless horn formerly used to announce the arrival of the post.

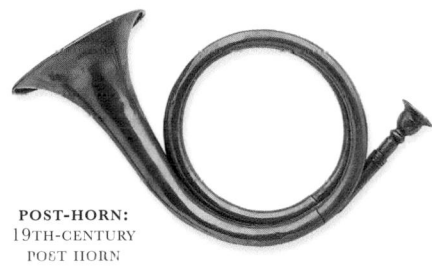

POST-HORN:
19TH-CENTURY
POST HORN

posthumous *adj.* **1** occurring after death. **2** (of a child) born after the death of its father. **3** (of a book etc.) published after the author's death. [from Latin *postumus* 'last'] □ **posthumously** *adv.*

postilion *n.* (also **postillion**) the rider on the near (left-hand side) horse drawing a coach etc. when there is no coachman. [from Italian *postiglione* 'post-boy']

post-Impressionism *n.* ▲ a style or movement in art seeking to express the individual artist's conception of the objects represented rather than the general observer's view. □ **post-Impressionist** *n.* & *adj.*

post-industrial *adj.* relating to or characteristic of a society or economy which no longer relies on heavy industry.

Post-it note *n. propr.* a piece of paper for writing notes on, with an adhesive strip on one side, designed to be stuck prominently to a surface and easily removed when necessary.

postlude *n. Mus.* a concluding voluntary.

postman *n.* (*pl.* **-men**) a man who is employed to deliver and collect letters etc.

postmark ● *n.* an official mark stamped on a letter,

POST-IMPRESSIONISM

Post-Impressionism is a term first used by British art critic Roger Fry in 1910 to describe the various styles of painting that flourished in France from 1880 to 1910. Generally, the term is used to cover the generation of artists who sought new forms of expression following the pictorial revolution brought about by Impressionism. Among the principal figures in this group were Paul Cezanne, Paul Gauguin, Georges Seurat, and Vincent Van Gogh. Although their individual styles differed markedly, all of these artists developed the Impressionist style far beyond the representational.

The Italian Woman (1888),
VINCENT VAN GOGH

TIMELINE
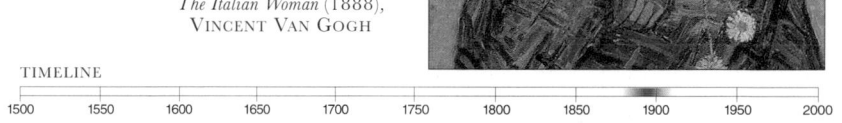
1500   1550   1600   1650   1700   1750   1800   1850   1900   1950   2000

esp. one giving the place, date, etc. and cancelling the stamp. ● *v.tr.* mark (an envelope etc.) with this.

postmaster *n.* a man in charge of a post office.

post-mill *n.* a windmill pivoted on a post and turning to catch the wind.

postmistress *n.* a woman in charge of a post office.

postmodern *adj.* ▼ (in literature, architecture, the arts, etc.) denoting a movement reacting against modern tendencies, esp. by drawing attention to former conventions. □ **postmodernism** *n.* **postmodernist** *n.* & *adj.* **postmodernity** *n.*

post-mortem ● *n.* **1** (in full **post-mortem examination**) an examination made after death, esp. to determine its cause. **2** a discussion analysing the course and result of a game, election, etc. ● *adv.* & *adj.* after death. [Latin]

post-natal *adj.* characteristic of or relating to the period after childbirth. □ **post-natally** *adv.*

post-natal depression *n.* depression suffered by a mother following childbirth.

Post Office *n.* **1** the public department or corporation responsible for postal services and (in some countries) telecommunications. **2** (**post office**) a room or building where postal business is carried on.

post office box *n.* a numbered place in a post office where letters are kept until called for.

post-operative *adj.* of the period following a surgical operation.

post-paid *adj.* & *adv.* on which postage has been paid.

postpone *v.tr.* cause or arrange (an event etc.) to take place at a later time. [from Latin *postponere*] □ **postponable** *adj.* **postponement** *n.*

postprandial *adj. formal* or *joc.* after dinner or lunch. [based on Latin *prandium* 'a meal']

post-production *n.* work done on a film, broadcast, etc. after filming or recording has taken place (usu. *attrib.: post-production costs*).

P

POSTMODERN

Postmodernism is a late 20th-century term used in various disciplines to refer to a rejection of modernism's preoccupation with pure form and technique. Postmodern designers use an amalgam of style elements from the past, such as the classical and baroque, introducing ornament, colour, and sculpture, often with ironic intent.

pediment

ornamental motif

classical column

columned gateway

TIMELINE
PUMPING STATION (1989), LONDON, ENGLAND
1500   1550   1600   1650   1700   1750   1800   1850   1900   1950   2000

P

post room *n. Brit.* the department of a company that deals with incoming and outgoing mail.

postscript *n.* an additional paragraph or remark, usu. at the end of a letter after the signature and introduced by 'PS'. [from Latin *postscriptum* 'that written afterwards']

post-structuralism *n.* an extension and critique of structuralism, esp. as used in critical textual analysis. □ **post-structuralist** *n. & adj.*

post town *n. Brit.* a town with a post office, esp. one that is not a sub-office of another.

post-traumatic stress disorder *n. Med.* a condition of persistent mental and emotional stress occurring after injury or severe psychological shock.

postulant *n.* a candidate, esp. for admission into a religious order. [from Latin *postulant-* 'demanding']

postulate ● *v.tr.* **1** (often foll. by *that* + clause) assume as a necessary condition, esp. as a basis for reasoning; take for granted. **2** claim. ● *n.* **1** a thing postulated. **2** a fundamental prerequisite or condition. [based on Latin *postulatus* 'demanded'] □ **postulation** *n.*

posture ● *n.* **1** the relative position of parts, esp. of the body (*in a reclining posture*). **2** carriage or bearing (*improved by good posture and balance*). **3** a mental or spiritual attitude or condition. **4** the condition or state (of affairs etc.) (*in more diplomatic postures*). ● *v.* **1** *intr.* assume a mental or physical attitude, esp. for effect (*inclined to strut and posture*). **2** *tr.* pose (a person). [from Latin *positura*] □ **postural** *adj.*

post-war *adj.* occurring or existing after a war (esp. the most recent major war).

postwoman *n.* (*pl.* **-women**) a woman who is employed to deliver and collect letters etc.

posy *n.* (*pl.* **-ies**) a small bunch of flowers. [alteration of POESY]

pot[1] ● *n.* **1 a** a vessel, usu. rounded, of ceramic ware or metal or glass for holding liquids or solids or for cooking in. **b** such a vessel designed to hold a particular substance (*coffee pot; teapot*). **2 a** = FLOWERPOT. **b** = CHIMNEY POT. **c** = LOBSTER POT. **d** = CHAMBER POT, POTTY[2]. **3** a drinking vessel of pewter etc. **4** the contents of a pot. **5** the total amount of the bet in a game etc. **6** *colloq.* a large sum (*pots of money*). **7** *slang* a vessel given as a prize in an athletic contest, esp. a silver cup. **8** = POT BELLY 1. ● *v.tr.* (**potted**, **potting**) **1** place in a pot. **2** (usu. as **potted** *adj.*) preserve in a sealed pot (*potted shrimps*). **3** *Brit.* pocket (a ball) in billiards etc. **4** shoot at, hit, or kill (an animal) with a pot-shot. **5** seize or secure. **6** (esp. as **potted** *adj.*) *Brit.* abridge or epitomize (*in a potted version; potted wisdom*). □ **go to pot** *colloq.* deteriorate; be ruined. **pot of gold** an imaginary reward; an ideal; a jackpot. [Old English] □ **potful** *n.* (*pl.* **-fuls**).

pot[2] *n. slang* marijuana.

potable /**poht**-ăbŭl/ *adj.* drinkable. [French] □ **potability** *n.*

potage *n.* thick soup. [French]

potash *n.* an alkaline potassium compound, usu. potassium carbonate or hydroxide. [from Dutch *pot-asschen* 'pot-ashes', originally obtained by evaporating solution from leached vegetable ashes in iron pots]

potassium *n. Chem.* ▼ a soft silver-white metallic element occurring naturally in sea water and various minerals, an essential element for living organisms, and forming many useful compounds. [based on POTASH] □ **potassic** *adj.*

POTASSIUM:
PURE FORM

potassium–argon dating *n. Geol.* a method of dating rocks from the relative proportions of radioactive potassium-40 and its decay product, argon-40.

potassium carbonate *n.* a hygroscopic white crystalline solid, alkaline in solution, with many industrial applications.

potassium chloride *n.* a white crystalline solid used as a fertilizer and in photographic processing.

potassium cyanide *n.* a highly toxic solid that releases poisonous hydrogen cyanide gas when hydrolysed.

potassium iodide *n.* a white crystalline solid used as an additive in table salt to prevent iodine deficiency.

potassium permanganate *n.* a purple crystalline solid that is used in solution as an oxidizing agent and disinfectant.

potation *n. formal* or *joc.* **1** a drink. **2** the act or an instance of drinking. [from Latin *potatio*]

potato *n.* (*pl.* **-oes**) **1** a starchy plant tuber that is cooked for food. **2** ▼ the plant, *Solanum tuberosum*, bearing this. [from Spanish *patata* 'sweet potato']

flower

POTATO
(*Solanum tuberosum*)

tuber (potato)

root

potato chip *n.* = CHIP *n.* 3b.

potato crisp see CRISP *n.*

pot-au-feu /pot-oh-**fer**/ *n.* (*pl.* same) **1** French soup of usu. boiled beef and vegetables cooked in a large pot. **2** the broth from this. [French, literally 'pot on the fire']

pot belly *n.* (*pl.* **-ies**) a protruding stomach. □ **pot-bellied** *adj.*

potboiler *n.* a work of literature or art executed merely to make the writer or artist a living.

pot-bound *adj.* (of a plant) having roots which fill the flowerpot, leaving no room to expand.

pot cheese *n. US* cottage cheese.

poteen /pot-**een**/ *n.* (also **potheen** /poth-**een**/) *Ir.* alcohol made illicitly, usu. from potatoes. [from Irish *poitín* 'little pot']

potent *adj.* **1** powerful; strong. **2** (of a reason) cogent; forceful. **3** (of a male) capable of sexual erection or orgasm. [from Latin *potent-* 'being able'] □ **potency** *n.* **potently** *adv.*

potentate *n.* a monarch or ruler. [from Late Latin *potentatus* 'dominion', later 'potentate']

potential ● *adj.* capable of coming into being or action; latent. ● *n.* **1** the capacity for use or development. **2** usable resources. **3** *Physics* the quantity determining the energy of mass in a gravitational field or of charge in an electric field. [from Late Latin *potentialis*] □ **potentiality** *n.* **potentially** *adv.*

potential difference *n.* ▶ the difference of electric potential between two points.

potential energy *n.* a body's ability to do work by

virtue of its position relative to others, stresses within itself, electric charge, etc.

potentiate *v.tr.* **1** make more powerful. **2** make possible.

potentilla *n.* any plant or shrub of the genus *Potentilla*. [medieval Latin]

potentiometer *n.* ▼ an instrument for measuring or adjusting small electrical potentials. ▷ RESISTOR. □ **potentiometric** *adj.* **potentiometry** *n.*

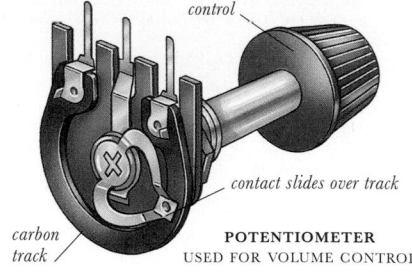

control

contact slides over track

carbon track

POTENTIOMETER
USED FOR VOLUME CONTROL

potheen var. of POTEEN.

pother *n. literary* a noise; commotion. [16th-century coinage]

pot-herb *n.* any herb grown for culinary use.

pothole ● *n.* **1** a deep hole or system of caves and underground river beds formed by the erosion of rock. **2** a hole in a road surface. ● *v.intr. Brit.* explore potholes. [based on northern dialect *pot* 'pit'] □ **potholer** *n.* **potholing** *n.*

potion *n.* a liquid medicine, poison, etc. [from Latin *potio*]

potluck *n.* (also **pot luck**) whatever is available.

pot plant *n. Brit.* a plant grown in a flowerpot.

pot-pourri /poh poor-i/ *n.* (*pl.* **pot-pourris**) **1** a mixture of dried petals and spices used to perfume a room etc. **2** a musical or literary medley. [earlier in sense 'a stew made of different kinds of meat': French, literally 'rotten pot']

POTENTIAL DIFFERENCE

Electric potential is a measure of the energy of electrons or other charged particles. Current is the movement of electric charge between positions with different electric potentials. The potential difference (p.d.) between two points is measured in volts.

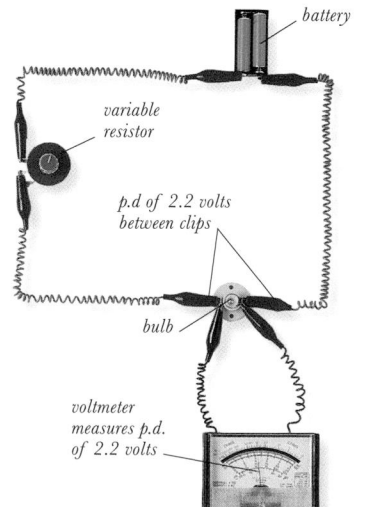

battery

variable resistor

p.d of 2.2 volts between clips

bulb

voltmeter measures p.d. of 2.2 volts

DEMONSTRATION OF POTENTIAL DIFFERENCE
IN AN ELECTRICAL CIRCUIT

pot roast ● *n.* a piece of meat cooked slowly in a covered dish. ● *v.tr.* (**pot-roast**) cook in this way.

potsherd *n.* a broken piece of ceramic material.

pot-shot *n.* **1** a random shot. **2** a shot aimed at an animal etc. within easy reach.

pottage *n. archaic* soup, stew. [from Old French *potage*]

potter[1] *v.intr.* (*US* **putter**) **1 a** (often foll. by *about*, *around*) work or occupy oneself in a desultory but pleasant manner. **b** (often foll. by *at*, *in*) dabble in a subject or occupation. **2** *Brit.* go slowly, dawdle. [from dialect *pote* (Old English *potian*) 'to push'] □ **potterer** *n.*

potter[2] *n.* a maker of ceramic vessels. [Old English]

potter's wheel *n.* ◀ a horizontal revolving disc to carry clay for making pots.

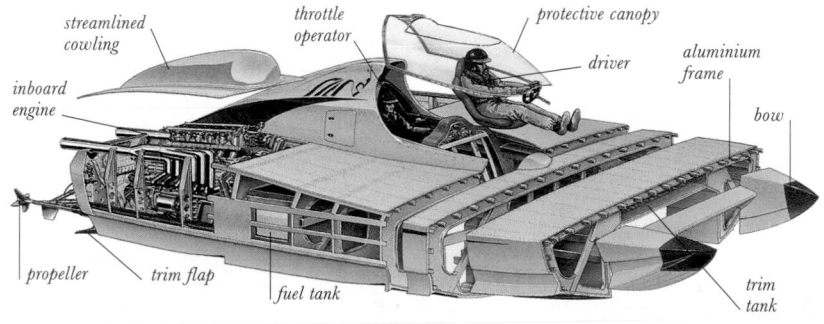

POTTER'S WHEEL

wheel

pedal turns wheel

pottery *n.* (*pl.* -**ies**) **1** vessels etc. made of fired clay. **2** a potter's work. **3** a potter's workshop. [from Old French *poterie*]

potting shed *n.* a building in which plants are potted and tools etc. are stored.

potty[1] *adj.* (**pottier**, **pottiest**) *Brit. colloq.* **1** foolish or crazy. **2** (usu. foll. by *little*) insignificant. [19th-century coinage] □ **pottiness** *n.*

potty[2] *n.* (*pl.* -**ies**) *colloq.* a chamber pot, esp. for a child.

potty-train *v.tr.* train (a small child) to use a potty.

pouch ● *n.* **1** a small bag or detachable outside pocket. **2** a baggy area of skin underneath the eyes etc. **3 a** a pocket-like receptacle of marsupials. **b** any similar structure in various animals, e.g. in the cheeks of rodents. ● *v.tr.* put or make into a pouch. [from Old Northern French *pouche*] □ **pouched** *adj.* **pouchy** *adj.*

pouf var. of POOF[1], POUFFE.

pouffe /poof/ *n.* (also **pouf**) a large firm cushion used as a low seat or footstool. [from French *pouf*]

poult /pohlt/ *n.* a young domestic fowl, pheasant, etc. [Middle English contraction of PULLET]

poulterer *n. Brit.* a dealer in poultry and usu. game. [from Old French *pouletier*]

poultice ● *n.* a soft medicated and usu. heated mass applied to the body and kept in place with muslin etc., for relieving soreness. ● *v.tr.* apply a poultice to. [from Latin *puls pultis* 'pottage, pap']

poultry *n.* domestic fowls, esp. as a source of food. [from Old French *pouletrie*]

pounce ● *v.intr.* **1** spring or swoop, esp. as in capturing prey. **2** (often foll. by *on*, *upon*) **a** make a sudden attack. **b** seize eagerly upon an object, remark, etc. ● *n.* the act or an instance of pouncing.

pound[1] *n.* **1** a unit of weight equal to 16 oz avoirdupois (0.4536 kg), or 12 oz troy (0.3732 kg). **2** (in full **pound sterling**) (*pl.* same or **pounds**) the chief monetary unit of the UK and several other countries. [from Latin *pondo*, a Roman pound weight of 12 ounces]

pound[2] *v.* **1** *tr.* crush or beat with repeated heavy blows. **2** *intr.* (foll. by *at*, *on*) deliver heavy blows or gunfire. **3** *intr.* (foll. by *along* etc.) make one's way heavily or clumsily. **4** *intr.* (of the heart) beat heavily. □ **pound out** produce with or as if with heavy blows. [Old English] □ **pounder** *n.*

pound[3] *n.* **1** an enclosure where stray animals or officially removed vehicles are kept until redeemed. **2** a place of confinement. [Old English]

poundage *n.* **1** *Brit.* a commission or fee of so much per pound sterling or weight. **2** *Brit.* a percentage of the total earnings of a business, paid as wages. **3** a person's weight, esp. that which is regarded as excess.

pound coin *n.* a coin worth one pound sterling.

pounder *n.* (usu. in *comb.*) **1** a thing or person weighing a specified number of pounds (*a five-pounder*). **2** a gun carrying a shell of a specified number of pounds. **3** a thing worth, or a person possessing, so many pounds sterling.

pound of flesh *n.* any legitimate but crippling demand. [with allusion to Shakespeare's *Merchant of Venice*]

pound sign *n.* the sign £, representing a pound.

pound sterling see POUND[1] 2.

pour *v.* **1** *intr.* & *tr.* (usu. foll. by *down*, *out*, *over*, etc.) flow or cause to flow esp. downwards in a stream or shower. **2** *tr.* dispense (a drink, e.g. tea) by pouring. **3** *intr.* (of rain, or prec. by *it* as subject) fall heavily. **4** *intr.* (usu. foll. by *in*, *out*, etc.) come or go in profusion. **5** *tr.* discharge or send freely (*poured forth arrows*). **6** *tr.* (often foll. by *out*) utter at length or in a rush. □ **pour cold water on** see COLD. **pour oil on the waters** (or **on troubled waters**) calm a disagreement or disturbance, esp. with conciliatory words. **pour scorn on** see SCORN. [Middle English] □ **pourable** *adj.* **pourer** *n.*

poussin /ˈpooss-ang/ *n.* a young chicken bred for eating. [French]

pout ● *v.* **1** *intr.* **a** push the lips forward as an expression of displeasure or sulking. **b** (of the lips) be pushed forward. **2** *tr.* push (the lips) forward in pouting. ● *n.* such an action or expression. [Middle English] □ **pouty** *adj.*

pouter *n.* **1** a person who pouts. **2** a kind of pigeon able to inflate its crop considerably.

poverty *n.* **1** the state of being poor; want of the necessities of life. **2** (often foll. by *of*, *in*) scarcity or lack. **3** inferiority, poorness. [from Latin *paupertas*]

poverty line *n.* the minimum income level needed to secure the necessities of life.

poverty-stricken *adj.* extremely poor.

poverty trap *n. Brit.* a situation in which an increase of income incurs a corresponding or greater loss of state benefits, making real improvement impossible.

POW *abbr.* prisoner of war.

pow *int.* expressing the sound of a blow or explosion.

powder ● *n.* **1** a substance in the form of fine dry particles. **2** a medicine or cosmetic in this form. **3** = GUNPOWDER 1. ● *v.tr.* **1** apply powder to. **b** sprinkle or decorate with or as with powder. **2** (esp. as **powdered** *adj.*) reduce to a fine powder. □ **keep one's powder dry** be cautious and alert. **take a powder** *slang* depart quickly. [from Latin *pulvis pulveris* 'dust'] □ **powdery** *adj.*

powder blue ● *n.* pale blue. ● *adj.* (hyphenated when *attrib.*) of this colour.

powder keg *n.* **1** a barrel of gunpowder. **2** a dangerous or volatile situation.

powder puff *n.* a soft pad for applying powder to the skin, esp. the face.

powder room *n.* a women's cloakroom or lavatory in a public building.

powder snow *n.* loose dry snow on a ski run etc.

power ● *n.* **1** the ability to do or act (*the power to change colour*). **2** a particular faculty of body or mind (*power of speech*). **3 a** a government, influence, or authority. **b** political or social ascendancy (*the party in power*). **4** delegated authority (*power of attorney*). **5** (often foll. by *over*) personal ascendancy. **6** an influential person, group, or organization (*a power in the land*). **7 a** a military strength. **b** a state having international influence (*the leading powers*). **8** vigour, energy. **9** an active property or function (*has a high heating power*). **10** *colloq.* a large number or amount (*a power of good*). **11** the capacity for exerting mechanical force or doing work (*horsepower*). **12** mechanical or electrical energy (often *attrib.: power tools*). **13 a** a public supply of (esp. electrical) energy. **b** a particular source or form of energy (*hydroelectric power*). **14** a mechanical force applied e.g. by means of a lever. **15** *Math.* the product obtained when a number is multiplied by itself (*2 to the power of 3 = 8*). **16** the magnifying capacity of a lens. ● *v.tr.* **1** supply with mechanical or electrical energy. **2** (foll. by *up*, *down*) increase or decrease the power supplied to (a device); switch on or off. □ **in the power of** under the control of. **power behind the throne** a person who asserts authority or influence without having formal status. **the powers that be** those in authority (after Rom. 13:1). [based on Latin *posse* 'to be able'] □ **powered** *adj.* (also in *comb.*).

power-assisted *adj.* (esp. of steering and brakes in a motor vehicle) employing an inanimate source of power to assist manual etc. operation.

power base *n.* a source of authority or support.

power block *n.* a group of nations constituting an international political force.

powerboat *n.* ▼ a powerful motor boat. ▷ BOAT

POWERBOAT

Powerboats are fitted with high-powered inboard or outboard engines and are used to race over courses. Offshore powerboats race on ocean courses up to 160 miles (257 km) long, and reach speeds of over 100 m.p.h. (160 k.p.h). The driver steers using satellite navigation systems, while the throttle operator controls the trim and engine speed.

streamlined cowling
throttle operator
protective canopy
driver
aluminium frame
inboard engine
bow
propeller
trim flap
fuel tank
trim tank

EXPLODED VIEW OF AN OFFSHORE CATAMARAN POWERBOAT

P

power-broker *n.* esp. *N. Amer.* a person who exerts influence or affects the equilibrium of political power by intrigue. □ **power-broking** *n. & adj.*

power cut *n.* a temporary withdrawal or failure of an electric power supply.

power-dive ● *n.* a steep dive of an aircraft with the engines providing thrust. ● *v.intr.* perform a power-dive.

powerful *adj.* **1** having much power or strength. **2** politically or socially influential. **3** having a strong emotional effect (*powerful drama*). □ **powerfully** *adv.*

powerhouse *n.* **1** = POWER STATION. **2** a person or thing of great energy.

powerless *adj.* **1** without power or strength. **2** (often foll. by *to* + infin.) wholly unable. □ **powerlessness** *n.*

power line *n.* a conductor supplying electrical power, esp. one supported by pylons or poles.

power of attorney *n.* the authority to act for another person in legal or financial matters.

power pack *n.* **1** a unit for supplying power. **2** the equipment for converting an alternating current (from the mains) to a direct current.

power plant *n.* an apparatus or an installation which provides power for industry, a machine, etc.

power play *n.* **1** tactics involving the concentration of players at a particular point. **2** similar tactics in business etc., involving a concentration of resources, effort, etc.

power point *n. Brit.* a socket in a wall etc. for connecting an electrical device to the mains.

power politics *n.pl.* (treated as *sing.* or *pl.*) political action based on power or influence.

power-sharing *n.* a policy agreed between parties to share responsibility for decision-making and political action.

power station *n.* ▼ a building where electrical power is generated for distribution. ▷ HYDROELECTRIC, NUCLEAR POWER

power stroke *n.* the stroke of an internal-combustion engine, in which the piston is moved downward by the expansion of gases.

power tool *n.* an electrically powered tool.

power train *n. Mech.* **1** the mechanism that transmits the drive from the engine of a vehicle to its axle. **2** this together with the engine and axle.

powwow ● *n.* a conference or meeting for discussion (originally among N. American Indians). ● *v.intr.* hold a powwow. [from Algonquian *powwaw* 'magician' (literally 'he dreams')]

pox *n.* **1** any virus disease producing a rash of pimples that become pus-filled and leave pockmarks on healing. **2** *colloq.* = SYPHILIS. [alteration of *pocks*, pl. of POCK]

poxy *adj.* (**poxier**, **poxiest**) esp. *Brit.* **1** infected by pox. **2** *slang* of poor quality; worthless.

pp *abbr.* pianissimo.

pp. *abbr.* pages.

p.p. *abbr.* (also **pp**) *per pro.*

■ **Usage** See Usage Note at PER PRO.

p.p.m. *abbr.* parts per million.

PPS *abbr.* **1** *Brit.* Parliamentary Private Secretary. **2** additional postscript.

PR *abbr.* **1** public relations. **2** proportional representation.

Pr *symb. Chem.* the element praseodymium.

pr. *abbr.* pair.

practicable *adj.* **1** that can be done or used. **2** possible in practice. [from French *praticable*] □ **practicability** *n.* **practicably** *adv.*

practical ● *adj.* **1** of or concerned with practice or use rather than theory. **2** suited to use or action (*practical shoes*). **3** (of a person) **a** inclined to action rather than speculation. **b** skilled at manual tasks. **4 a** that is such in effect, though not nominally (*for all practical purposes*). **b** virtual (*in practical control*). **5** concerned with what is actually possible (*practical solutions*). ● *n. Brit.* a practical examination or lesson. [earlier *practic*, from Greek *praktikos*] □ **practicality** *n.* (*pl.* **-ies**). **practicalness** *n.*

practical joke *n.* a humorous trick played on a person. □ **practical joker** *n.*

practically *adv.* **1** virtually, almost (*practically nothing*). **2** in a practical way.

practice ● *n.* **1** habitual action or performance. **2** a habit or custom. **3 a** repeated exercise in an activity requiring the development of skill. **b** a session of this. **4** action or execution as opposed to theory. **5** the professional work or business of a doctor, lawyer, etc. **6** procedure generally (*bad practice*). ● *v.tr. & intr. US* var. of PRACTISE. □ **in practice 1** in reality. **2** skilful because of recent exercise in a particular pursuit. **out of practice** lacking a former skill from lack of recent

practice. **put into practice** actually apply (an idea, method, etc.). [Middle English]

practise *v.* (*US* **practice**) **1** *tr.* perform habitually; carry out in action. **2** *tr. &* (foll. by *in, on*) *intr.* do repeatedly as an exercise to improve a skill; exercise oneself in or on (an activity requiring skill). **3** *tr.* (as **practised** *adj.*) experienced, expert. **4** *tr.* **a** pursue or be engaged in (a profession, religion, etc.). **b** (as **practising** *adj.*) currently active or engaged in (a profession or activity). **5** *intr.* (foll. by *on, upon*) take advantage of; impose upon. [from Old French *pra(c)tiser*]

practitioner *n.* a person practising a profession, esp. medicine. [from obsolete *practitian*]

praenomen /pree-**noh**-men/ *n.* an ancient Roman's first or personal name (e.g. *Marcus* Tullius Cicero). [Latin, from *prae* 'before' + *nomen* 'name']

praesidium var. of PRESIDIUM.

praetor /**pree**-ter/ *n.* (*US* also **pretor**) *Rom.Hist.* each of two ancient Roman magistrates ranking below consul. [Latin] □ **praetorial** *adj.* **praetorian** *adj. & n.* (*US* also **pretorian**). **praetorship** *n.*

praetorian guard *n.* the bodyguard of the Roman emperor.

pragmatic *adj.* **1** dealing with matters with regard to their practical requirements or consequences. **2** treating the facts of history with reference to their practical lessons. [from Greek *pragmatikos*] □ **pragmaticality** *n.* **pragmatically** *adv.*

pragmatism *n.* **1** a pragmatic attitude or procedure. **2** a philosophy that evaluates assertions solely by their practical consequences and bearing on human interests. [based on Greek *pragma* 'deed'] □ **pragmatist** *n.*

prairie *n.* a large area of usu. treeless grassland esp. in N. America. [from Latin *pratum* 'meadow']

prairie chicken *n.* (also **prairie hen**) a N. American grouse, *Tympanuchus cupido*.

prairie dog *n.* ◀ any N. American rodent of the genus *Cynomys*, living in burrows and making a barking sound.

prairie oyster *n.* a seasoned raw egg, often served in spirits and swallowed in one gulp as a cure for a hangover.

prairie wolf *n.* = COYOTE.

praise ● *v.tr.* **1** express warm approval or admiration of. **2** glorify (God) in words. ● *n.* the act or an instance of praising; commendation. □ **praise be!** an exclamation of pious gratitude. **sing the praises of** commend (a person)

PRAIRIE DOG
(*Cynomys ludovicianus*)

highly. [from Old French *preisier* 'to price, prize, praise']

praiseworthy *adj.* worthy of praise; commendable.

praline /**prah**-leen/ *n.* a smooth sweet substance made by boiling nuts in sugar. [French, named after Marshal de Plessis-*Praslin*, French soldier, 1598–1675, whose cook invented it]

pram *n. Brit.* a four-wheeled carriage for a baby, pushed by a person on foot.

prana *n.* **1** (in Hinduism) breath as a life-giving force. **2** the breath; breathing. [Sanskrit]

prance ● *v.intr.* **1** (of a horse) raise the forelegs and spring from the hind legs. **2** (often foll. by *about*) walk or behave in an elated or arrogant manner. ● *n.* **1** the act of prancing. **2** a prancing movement. [Middle English] □ **prancer** *n.*

prandial *adj. formal* or *joc.* of or relating to dinner or lunch. [based on Latin *prandium* 'luncheon']

prang *Brit. slang* ● *v.tr.* **1** crash or damage (an aircraft or vehicle). **2** bomb (a target) successfully. ● *n.* the act or an instance of pranging.

prank *n.* a practical joke; a piece of mischief. [16th-century coinage] □ **prankish** *adj.*

prankster *n.* a person fond of playing pranks.

POWER STATION

Virtually all commercial electric energy is produced by power stations driven by steam from the burning of fossil fuels, or from nuclear sources or by hydropower. Inside a coal- or oil-fired power station, energy stored within fuel is released in a furnace. The heat is used to boil water into steam, which drives turbines linked to electricity generators. The electricity reaches consumers via a network of cables called a grid.

concrete tower for cooling water

boiler house

chimney

coal store

turbine house

connections to electricity grid

MODEL OF A
COAL-FIRED
POWER STATION

P

prase *n.* a translucent leek-green type of quartz. [from Greek *prasios* 'leek-green']

praseodymium *n. Chem.* a soft silvery metallic element of the lanthanide series, occurring naturally in various minerals and used in catalyst mixtures. [from German *Praseodym*].

prat *n. slang* **1** *Brit.* a silly or foolish person. **2** the buttocks. [sense 2: 16th-century slang]

prate ● *v.* **1** *intr.* chatter; talk too much. **2** *intr.* talk foolishly or irrelevantly. **3** *tr.* tell or say in a prating manner. ● *n.* prating; idle talk. [from Middle Dutch *praten*] □ **prater** *n.* **prating** *adj.*

pratfall *n. slang* **1** a fall on the buttocks. **2** a humiliating failure.

pratincole *n.* a fork-tailed insectivorous plover-like bird of the genus *Glareola*, living near water.

pratique *n.* a licence to have dealings with a port, granted to a ship after quarantine or on showing a clean bill of health. [French, literally 'practice', 'intercourse', via Italian *practica* from medieval Latin *practica*]

prattle ● *v.intr. & tr.* chatter or say in a childish or inconsequential way. ● *n.* **1** childish chatter. **2** inconsequential talk. [from Middle Low German *pratelen*] □ **prattler** *n.* **prattling** *adj.*

prawn *n.* ▼ any of various marine crustaceans, resembling a shrimp but usu. larger. [Middle English]

PRAWN

carapace

antenna

segmented abdomen

telson (tail fan)

praxis *n.* **1** accepted practice or custom. **2** the practising of an art or skill. [Greek, literally 'doing']

pray *v.* (often foll. by *for*, or *to* + infin., or *that* + clause) **1** *intr.* (often foll. by *to*) say prayers (to God etc.). **2 a** *tr.* entreat. **b** *tr. & intr.* ask earnestly (*pray to be released*). **3** *tr.* (as *imper.*) *formal* or *joc.* please (*pray tell me*). [from Latin *precari* 'to entreat']

prayer[1] *n.* **1 a** a solemn request or thanksgiving to God or an object of worship. **b** a formula or form of words used in praying (*the Lord's prayer*). **c** the act of praying (*be at prayer*). **d** a religious service consisting largely of prayers (*morning prayers*). **2 a** an entreaty to a person. **b** a thing entreated or prayed for. □ **not have a prayer** *N. Amer. colloq.* have no chance (of success etc.). □ **prayerless** *adj.* [from Latin *prex precis* 'prayer']

prayer[2] *n.* a person who prays.

prayer book *n.* a book containing the forms of prayer in regular use, esp. the Book of Common Prayer.

prayerful *adj.* **1** (of a person) given to praying; devout. **2** (of speech, actions, etc.) characterized by or expressive of prayer. □ **prayerfully** *adv.* **prayerfulness** *n.*

prayer mat *n.* ◄ a small carpet used by Muslims when praying.

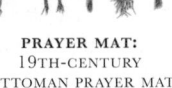

PRAYER MAT:
19TH-CENTURY
OTTOMAN PRAYER MAT

prayer wheel *n.* ► a revolving cylindrical box inscribed with or containing prayers, used esp. by Tibetan Buddhists.

praying mantis see MANTIS.

pre- *prefix* before (in time, place, order, degree, or importance).

preach *v.* **1 a** *intr.* deliver a sermon or religious address. **b** *tr.* deliver (a sermon); proclaim or expound (the Gospel etc.). **2** *intr.* give moral advice in an obtrusive way. **3** *tr.* advocate or inculcate (a quality or practice etc.). □ **preach to the converted** commend an opinion to a person or persons already in agreement. [from Latin *praedicare* 'to proclaim']

preacher *n.* a person who preaches, esp. a minister of religion.

preachify *v.intr.* (**-ies**, **-ied**) *colloq.* preach or moralize tediously.

pre-adolescent ● *adj.* **1** (of a child) having nearly reached adolescence. **2** of or relating to the two or three years preceding adolescence. ● *n.* a pre-adolescent child. □ **pre-adolescence** *n.*

preamble *n.* **1** a preliminary statement or introduction. **2** the introductory part of a statute or deed etc. [from medieval Latin *praeambulum* '(thing) going before'] □ **preambular** *adj.*

preamp *n.* = PREAMPLIFIER.

preamplifier *n.* an electronic device that amplifies a very weak signal (e.g. from a microphone or pick-up) and transmits it to a main amplifier. □ **preamplified** *adj.*

pre-arrange *v.tr.* arrange beforehand. □ **pre-arrangement** *n.*

preatomic *adj.* existing or occurring before the use of atomic energy.

prebend /preb-ĕnd/ *n.* **1** = PREBENDARY 1. **2** *hist.* the stipend of a canon or member of chapter. **3** *hist.* a portion of land or tithe from which this is drawn. [from Late Latin *praebenda* 'pension', literally 'things that should be provided']

prebendal /pri-bend-ăl/ *adj.* of or relating to a prebend or a prebendary.

prebendary /preb-ĕn-dri/ *n.* (*pl.* **-ies**) **1** an honorary canon. **2** *hist.* the holder of a prebend.

pre-book *v.tr.* book in advance. □ **pre-bookable** *adj.*

Precambrian *Geol.* ● *adj.* of or relating to the earliest era of geological time from the formation of the Earth to the first forms of life. ● *n.* this era.

precancerous *adj.* tending to develop into cancer.

precarious *adj.* **1** uncertain; dependent on chance. **2** insecure, perilous. [from Latin *precarius*, related to PRAYER[1]] □ **precariously** *adv.* **precariousness** *n.*

pre-cast *adj.* (of concrete) cast in its final shape before positioning.

precaution *n.* **1** an action taken beforehand to avoid risk or ensure a good result. **2** (in *pl.*) *colloq.* the use of contraceptives. [based on Latin *praecavēre* 'to beware of in advance'] □ **precautionary** *adj.*

precede *v.tr.* **1 a** come or go before in time, order, importance, etc. **b** walk etc. in front of (*preceded by our guide*). **2** (foll. by *by*) cause to be preceded. [from Latin *praecedere*]

precedence *n.* (also **precedency**) **1** priority in time, order, or importance, etc. **2** the right of preceding others on formal occasions. □ **take precedence** (often foll. by *over, of*) have priority (over).

precedent /press-i-dĕnt/ ● *n.* a previous case or legal decision etc. taken as a guide for subsequent cases or as a justification. ● *adj.* preceding in time, order, importance, etc. [from Old French *précédent*]

precedented *adj.* having or supported by a precedent.

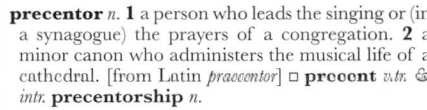

mantra

PRAYER WHEEL
WITH MANTRA
REVEALED

precentor *n.* **1** a person who leads the singing or (in a synagogue) the prayers of a congregation. **2** a minor canon who administers the musical life of a cathedral. [from Latin *praecentor*] □ **precent** *v.tr. & intr.* **precentorship** *n.*

precept *n.* **1** a rule of conduct. **2** moral instruction (*example is better than precept*). **3 a** a writ. **b** *Brit.* an order for payment of money under a local rate. [from Latin *praeceptum* '(thing) advised'] □ **preceptive** *adj.*

preceptor *n.* (*fem.* **preceptress**) a teacher or instructor. □ **preceptorial** *adj.* **preceptorship** *n.*

precession *n.* ▼ the slow movement of the axis of a spinning body around another axis. [from Late Latin *praecessio*] □ **precessional** *adj.*

precession of the equinoxes *n.* **1** the slow retrograde motion of equinoctial points along the ecliptic. **2** the resulting earlier occurrence of equinoxes in each successive sidereal year.

pre-Christian *adj.* before Christ or the advent of Christianity.

precinct *n.* **1** an enclosed or clearly defined area, e.g. around a cathedral, college, etc. **2** a specially designated area in a town, esp. with the exclusion of traffic. **3** (in *pl.*) **a** the surrounding area or environs. **b** the boundaries. **4** *US* **a** a subdivision of a county, city, etc. **b** *colloq.* the police station of such a subdivision. **c** (in *pl.*) a neighbourhood. [from medieval Latin *praecinctum* 'encircled (thing)']

preciosity *n.* over-refinement in art or language, esp. in the choice of words. [from Latin *pretiositas*]

precious ● *adj.* **1** of great value or worth. **2** much prized (*precious memories*). **3** affectedly refined, esp. in language or manner. **4** *colloq.* expressing disdain (*you can keep your precious flowers*). ● *adv. colloq.* extremely, very (*had precious little left*). [based on Latin *pretium* 'price'] □ **preciously** *adv.* **preciousness** *n.*

precious metals *n.pl.* gold, silver, and platinum.

precious stone *n.* a piece of mineral having great value, esp. as used in jewellery. ▷ GEM

precipice *n.* **1** a vertical or steep face of a rock etc. **2** a dangerous situation. [from Latin *praecipitium* 'falling headlong']

PRECESSION

Although the Earth's axis is always tilted at an angle of 23.5°, the direction in space to which it points changes continuously, tracing out a circle every 25,800 years. This phenomenon is called precession.

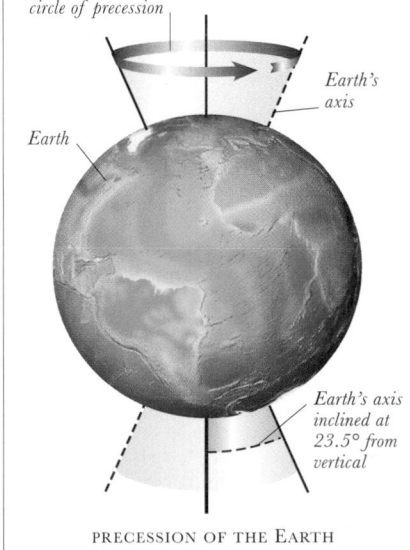

circle of precession

Earth's axis

Earth

Earth's axis inclined at 23.5° from vertical

PRECESSION OF THE EARTH

P

precipitate ● *v.tr.* **1** hasten the occurrence of. **2** (foll. by *into*) send rapidly into a certain state or condition. **3** throw down headlong. **4** *Chem.* cause (a substance) to be deposited in solid form from a solution. **5** *Physics* **a** cause (dust etc.) to be deposited from the air on a surface. **b** condense (vapour) into drops and so deposit it. ● *adj.* **1** violently hurried. **2** (of a person or act) rash, inconsiderate. ● *n.* **1** *Chem.* a substance precipitated from a solution. **2** *Physics* moisture condensed from vapour, e.g. rain or dew. [based on Latin *praecipitatus* 'thrown headlong'] □ **precipitable** *adj.* **precipitately** *adv.* **precipitateness** *n.* **precipitator** *n.*

precipitation *n.* **1** the act of precipitating or the process of being precipitated. **2** rash haste. **3 a** rain or snow etc. falling to the ground. **b** a quantity of this.

precipitous *adj.* **1 a** of or like a precipice. **b** dangerously steep. **2** = PRECIPITATE *adj.* □ **precipitously** *adv.* **precipitousness** *n.*

précis /pray-see/ ● *n.* (*pl.* same) a summary or abstract, esp. of a text or speech. ● *v.tr.* (**précises** /-seez/, **précised** /-seed/, **précising** /-see-ing/) make a précis of. [French, literally 'precise', used as a noun]

precise *adj.* **1 a** accurately expressed; exact in statement. **b** exact in measurement, value, etc. **2** punctilious; scrupulous in being exact, observing rules, etc. **3** same (*at that precise moment*). [from Latin *praecisus* 'shortened'] □ **preciseness** *n.*

precisely *adv.* **1** in a precise manner; exactly. **2** (as a reply) quite so; as you say.

precision *n.* **1** the condition of being precise; accuracy. **2** the degree of refinement in measurement etc. **3** (*attrib.*) marked by or adapted for precision (*precision instruments*). □ **precisionism** *n.* **precisionist** *n.* & *adj.*

preclinical *adj.* **1** of or relating to the first, chiefly theoretical, stage of a medical education. **2** (of a stage in a disease) before symptoms can be identified.

preclude *v.tr.* **1** (foll. by *from*) prevent, exclude. **2** make impossible (*so as to preclude all doubt*). [from Latin *praecludere*] □ **preclusion** *n.* **preclusive** *adj.*

precocious *adj.* **1** often *derog.* (esp. of a child) prematurely developed in some faculty or characteristic. **2** (of an action etc.) indicating such development. [from Latin *praecox -cocis*] □ **precociously** *adv.* **precociousness** *n.* **precocity** *n.*

precognition *n.* (supposed) foreknowledge, esp. of a supernatural kind. [from Late Latin *praecognitio*] □ **precognitive** *adj.*

preconceive *v.tr.* form (an idea or opinion etc.) beforehand.

preconception *n.* **1** a preconceived idea. **2** a prejudice.

precondition ● *n.* a prior condition, that must be fulfilled before other things can be done. ● *v.tr.* bring into a required condition beforehand.

pre-cook *v.tr.* cook in advance.

pre-cool *v.tr.* cool in advance.

precursor *n.* **1 a** a forerunner. **b** a person who precedes in office etc. **2** a harbinger. [from Latin *praecursor*]

precursory *adj.* (also **precursive**) **1** preliminary, introductory. **2** (foll. by *of*) serving as a harbinger of.

pre-cut *v.tr.* (**-cutting**; *past* and *past part.* **-cut**) cut in advance.

predacious *adj.* (also **predaceous**) **1** (of an animal) predatory. **2** relating to such animals (*predacious instincts*). [based on Latin *praeda* 'booty']

pre-date *v.tr.* exist or occur at a date earlier than.

predation *n.* **1** (usu. in *pl.*) = DEPREDATION. **2** *Zool.* the natural preying of one animal on others. ▷ FOOD CHAIN. [from Latin *praedatio* 'taking of booty']

predator /pred-ă-ter/ *n.* **1** an animal naturally preying on others. **2** a rapacious, exploitative person, state, etc. [from Latin *praedator* 'plunderer'] □ **predatory** *adj.*

predecease ● *v.tr.* die earlier than (another person). ● *n.* a death preceding that of another.

predecessor *n.* **1** a former holder of an office or position with respect to a later holder. **2** an ancestor. **3** a thing to which another has succeeded. [from Late Latin *praedecessor*]

pre-decimal *adj.* of or relating to a time before the introduction of a decimal system, esp. of coinage.

predestine *v.tr.* **1** determine beforehand. **2** ordain in advance by divine will or as if by fate. [from ecclesiastical Latin *praedestinare*] □ **predestination** *n.*

predetermine *v.tr.* **1** determine or decree beforehand. **2** predestine. [from Late Latin *praedeterminare*] □ **predeterminate** *adj.* **predetermination** *n.*

predeterminer *n. Gram.* a word or phrase that occurs before a determiner, generally quantifying the noun group, e.g. *both*, *all*, *a lot of*.

predicable *adj.* that may be predicated or affirmed. [from medieval Latin *praedicabilis* 'that may be affirmed'] □ **predicability** *n.*

predicament *n.* **1** a difficult, unpleasant, or embarrassing situation. **2** *Philos.* a category in (esp. Aristotelian) logic. [from Late Latin *praedicamentum* 'thing predicated']

predicate ● *v.tr.* **1** assert (something) about the subject of a proposition. **2** (foll. by *on*) found or base (a statement etc.) on. ● *n.* **1** *Gram.* what is said about the subject of a sentence etc. (e.g. *went home* in *John went home*). **2** *Logic* **a** what is predicated. **b** what is affirmed or denied of the subject by means of the copula (e.g. *mortal* in *all men are mortal*). [based on Latin *praedicatus* 'proclaimed'] □ **predication** *n.*

predicative *adj.* **1** *Gram.* (of an adjective or noun) forming or contained in the predicate, as *old* in *the dog is old* (but not in *the old dog*) and *house* in *there is a large house*. **2** that predicates. □ **predicatively** *adv.*

predict *v.tr.* (often foll. by *that* + clause) make a statement about the future; foretell, prophesy. [based on Latin *praedictus* 'predicted'] □ **predictive** *adj.* **predictor** *n.*

predictable *adj.* **1** that can be predicted or is to be expected. **2** (of a person) likely to behave in a way that is easy to predict. □ **predictability** *n.* **predictably** *adv.*

prediction *n.* **1** the art of predicting or the process of being predicted. **2** a thing predicted; a forecast.

predigest *v.tr.* **1** render (food) easily digestible before being eaten. **2** make (reading matter) easier to read or understand. □ **predigestion** *n.*

predilection *n.* (often foll. by *for*) a preference or special liking. [from French *prédilection*]

predispose *v.tr.* **1** influence favourably in advance. **2** (foll. by *to*, or *to* + infin.) render liable or inclined beforehand. □ **predisposition** *n.*

predominant *adj.* **1** predominating. **2** being the strongest or main element. □ **predominance** *n.* **predominantly** *adv.*

predominate *v.intr.* **1** (foll. by *over*) have or exert control. **2** be superior. **3** be the strongest or main element; preponderate. [from medieval Latin *praedominari praedominat-*]

predominately *adv.* = PREDOMINANTLY (see PREDOMINANT).

pre-echo *n.* (*pl.* **-oes**) **1** a faint copy heard just before an actual sound in a recording, caused by the accidental transfer of signals. **2** a foreshadowing.

pre-eclampsia *n.* a condition of pregnancy characterized esp. by high blood pressure. □ **pre-eclamptic** *adj.* & *n.*

pre-elect *v.tr.* elect beforehand. □ **pre-election** *n.* & *attrib.adj.*

pre-embryo *n. Med.* a human embryo in the first fourteen days after fertilization. □ **pre-embryonic** *adj.*

pre-eminent *adj.* **1** excelling others. **2** outstanding; distinguished in some quality. [from Latin *praeeminent-* 'excelling'] □ **pre-eminence** *n.* **pre-eminently** *adv.*

pre-empt *v.tr.* **1 a** forestall. **b** acquire or appropriate in advance. **2** obtain by pre-emption. □ **pre-emptor** *n.*

■ **Usage** *Pre-empt* is sometimes used to mean 'prevent', but this is considered incorrect in standard English.

pre-emption *n.* **1 a** the purchase or appropriation by one person or party before the opportunity is offered to others. **b** the right to purchase in this way. **2** prior appropriation or acquisition. [from medieval Latin *praeemptio*]

pre-emptive *adj.* **1** pre-empting. **2** (of military action) intended to prevent attack by disabling the enemy.

preen *v.tr.* & *refl.* **1** ▼ (of a bird) tidy (the feathers or itself) with its beak. **2** (of a person) smarten or admire (oneself, one's hair, etc.). **3** (often foll. by *on*) congratulate or pride (oneself). [Middle English] □ **preener** *n.*

PREEN: QUAKER PARROT PREENING ITS FEATHERS

pre-establish *v.tr.* establish beforehand.

pre-exist *v.* **1** *intr.* exist at an earlier time. **2** *tr.* exist earlier than. □ **pre-existence** *n.* **pre-existent** *adj.*

prefab *n. colloq.* a prefabricated building (often *attrib.*: *prefab houses*).

prefabricate *v.tr.* **1** manufacture sections of (a building etc.) prior to their assembly on a site. **2** produce in an artificially standardized way. □ **prefabrication** *n.*

preface /pref-ăs/ ● *n.* **1** an introduction to a book stating its subject, scope, etc. **2** the preliminary part of a speech. ● *v.tr.* **1** (foll. by *with*) introduce or begin (a speech or event). **2** provide (a book etc.) with a preface. **3** (of an event etc.) lead up to (another). [based on Latin *praefari* 'to say beforehand'] □ **prefatory** *adj.*

prefect *n.* **1 a** a chief officer, magistrate, or governor. **b** the chief administrative officer of a department in France. **2** esp. *Brit.* a senior pupil in a school etc. authorized to enforce discipline. [from Latin *praefectus* '(one) set in authority over'] □ **prefectoral** *adj.* **prefectorial** *adj.*

prefecture *n.* **1** a district under the government of a prefect. **2 a** a prefect's office or tenure. **b** the official residence of a prefect. □ **prefectural** *adj.*

prefer *v.tr.* (**preferred**, **preferring**) **1** (often foll. by *to*, or *to* + infin.) choose rather; like better. **2** submit (information, an accusation, etc.) for consideration. **3** promote or advance (a person). [from Latin *praeferre* 'to bear or put before']

preferable *adj.* **1** to be preferred. **2** (often foll. by *to*) more desirable. □ **preferability** *n.* **preferably** *adv.*

■ **Usage** *Preferable to* means 'more desirable than', and should, therefore, be intensified by *far*, *greatly*, or *much*, rather than *more*, e.g. *Travelling by train is far/greatly/much preferable to driving.*

preference *n.* **1** the act or an instance of preferring or being preferred. **2** a preferred thing. **3** the favouring of one person etc. before others. □ **in preference to** as a thing preferred over (another). [from medieval Latin *praeferentia*]

preference share *n.* (*US* **preferred share**) a share whose entitlement to dividend takes priority over that of an ordinary share.

preference stock *n. Brit.* (*US* also **preferred**

P

stock) stock whose entitlement to dividend takes priority over that of ordinary stock.

preferential *adj.* **1** of or involving preference. **2** giving or receiving a favour. **3** *Commerce* (of a tariff etc.) favouring particular countries. **4** (of voting) in which the voter puts candidates in order of preference. □ **preferentially** *adv.*

preferment *n.* promotion to office.

prefigure *v.tr.* **1** represent beforehand by a figure or type. **2** imagine beforehand. [from ecclesiastical Latin *praefigurare*] □ **prefiguration** *n.* **prefigurative** *adj.* **prefigurement** *n.*

prefix ● *n.* **1** a verbal element placed at the beginning of a word to adjust or qualify its meaning (e.g. *ex-*, *non-*, *re-*) or (in some languages) as an inflectional formative. **2** a title placed before a name (e.g. *Mr*). ● *v.tr.* (often foll. by *to*) **1** add as an introduction. **2** join (a word or element) as a prefix. [*v.*: from Old French *prefixer* 'to fix before'; *n.*: from Latin *praefixum*] □ **prefixation** *n.* **prefixion** *n.*

pre-flight *attrib.adj.* occurring or provided before an aircraft flight.

preform *v.tr.* form beforehand. □ **preformation** *n.*

pregnable *adj.* able to be captured etc.; not impregnable. [from Old French *prenable* 'takable']

pregnancy *n.* (*pl.* **-ies**) the condition or an instance of being pregnant.

pregnant *adj.* **1** (of a woman or female animal) having a child or young developing in the uterus. **2** full of meaning; significant or suggestive. **3** (esp. of a person's mind) imaginative, inventive. **4** (foll. by *with*) plentifully provided. [from Latin *praegnans praegnant-*] □ **pregnantly** *adv.* (in sense 2).

preheat *v.tr.* heat beforehand.

tail gripping branch

prehensile *adj. Zool.* ► (of a tail or limb) capable of grasping. ▷ DUGONG, SEA HORSE. [based on Latin *prehens-* 'grasping']

PREHENSILE: BLACK SPIDER MONKEY WITH PREHENSILE TAIL

prehistoric *adj.* **1** of or relating to the period before written records. **2** *colloq.* utterly out of date. □ **prehistorian** *n.* **prehistorically** *adv.* **prehistory** *n.*

pre-human *adj.* existing before the time of man.

pre-ignition *n.* the premature firing of the explosive mixture in an internal-combustion engine.

pre-industrial *adj.* of or relating to the time before industrialization.

prejudge *v.tr.* **1** form a premature judgement on (a person, issue, etc.). **2** pass judgement on (a person) before a trial or proper inquiry. □ **prejudgement** *n.*

prejudice ● *n.* **1 a** a preconceived opinion. **b** (foll. by *against*, *in favour of*) bias or partiality. **2** harm or injury that results or may result from some action or judgement (*to the prejudice of*). ● *v.tr.* **1** impair the validity or force of (a right, statement, etc.). **2 a** (often as **prejudiced** *adj.*) cause (a person) to have a prejudice. **b** (as **prejudiced** *adj.*) not impartial; bigoted. □ **without prejudice** (often foll. by *to*) without detriment (to any existing right or claim). [from Latin *praejudicium*]

prejudicial *adj.* causing prejudice; detrimental. □ **prejudicially** *adv.*

prelacy *n.* (*pl.* **-ies**) **1** Church government by

prelates. **2** (prec. by *the*) prelates collectively. **3** the office or rank of prelate. [from medieval Latin *prelatia*]

prelate *n.* a high ecclesiastical dignitary, e.g. a bishop. [from medieval Latin *praelatus* '(one) placed before'] □ **prelatical** *adj.*

prelim *n. colloq.* **1** a preliminary examination, esp. at a university. **2** (in *pl.*) the pages preceding the text of a book.

preliminary ● *adj.* introductory, preparatory. ● *n.* (*pl.* **-ies**) (usu. in *pl.*) **1** a preliminary action or arrangement. **2** a preliminary trial or contest. ● *adv.* (foll. by *to*) preparatory to; in advance of. [based on Latin *limen liminis* 'threshold'] □ **preliminarily** *adv.*

pre-linguistic *adj.* existing or occurring before the development of language or the acquisition of speech.

preliterate *adj.* of or relating to a society or culture that has not developed the use of writing.

prelude ● *n.* (often foll. by *to*) **1** an action, event, or situation serving as an introduction. **2** the introductory part of a poem etc. **3 a** an introductory piece to a fugue, suite, etc. **b** a short piece of music of a similar type, esp. for the piano. ● *v.tr.* **1** serve as a prelude to. **2** introduce with a prelude. [from medieval Latin *praeludium*] □ **preludial** *adj.*

premarital *adj.* existing or (esp. of sexual relations) occurring before marriage. □ **premaritally** *adv.*

premature *adj.* **1 a** occurring or done before the usual or proper time. **b** too hasty. **2** (of a baby) born (esp. three or more weeks) before the end of the full term of gestation. [from Latin *praematurus* 'very early'] □ **prematurely** *adv.* **prematurity** *n.*

pre-med *n. colloq.* **1** = PRE-MEDICATION. **2** (**premed**) a premedical course or student.

premedical *adj.* of or relating to study in preparation for a course in medicine.

pre-medication *n.* medication to prepare for an operation or other treatment.

premeditate *v.tr.* think out or plan (an action) beforehand. [based on Latin *praemeditatus* 'premeditated'] □ **premeditation** *n.*

premenstrual *adj.* of, occurring, or experienced before menstruation. □ **premenstrually** *adv.*

premenstrual syndrome *n.* any of a complex of symptoms (including tension, fluid retention, etc.) experienced by some women in the days immediately before menstruation.

premier ● *n.* (usu. **Premier**) a prime minister or other head of government. ● *adj.* **1** first in importance, order, or time. **2** of earliest creation (*premier earl*). [from Old French, literally 'first'] □ **premiership** *n.*

premiere /prem-i-air/ (also **première**) ● *n.* the first performance or showing of a play or film. ● *v.tr.* give a premiere of. [French fem. of *premier* 'first']

premillenial *adj.* existing or occurring before the millenium, esp. with reference to the prophesied second coming of Christ.

premise ● *n.* /prem-iss/ **1** *Logic* = PREMISS. **2** (in *pl.*) a house or building with its grounds and appurtenances. ● *v.tr.* /pri-**myz**/ say or write by way of introduction. □ **on the premises** in the building etc. concerned. [from medieval Latin *praemissa (propositio)* '(proposition) set in front']

premiss *n. Brit. Logic* a previous statement from which another is inferred. [variant of PREMISE]

premium *n.* (*pl.* **premiums**) **1** an amount to be paid for a contract of insurance. **2** a sum added to interest, wages, charges, etc. **3** a reward or prize. **4** (*attrib.*) (of a commodity) of best quality and therefore more expensive. □ **at a premium 1** above the usual or nominal price. **2** scarce and in demand. **put a premium on 1** provide or act as an incentive to. **2** attach special value to. [from Latin *praemium* 'booty, reward']

Premium Bond *n.* (also **Premium Savings Bond**) *Brit.* a government security without interest but with a draw for cash prizes.

upper premolars

premolar *n.* ◄ (in an adult human) a tooth situated between the canines and molars. ▷ DENTITION, TOOTH.

premonition *n.* a forewarning; a presentiment. [based on Latin *praemonitus* 'forewarned'] □ **premonitory** *adj.*

prenatal *adj.* of or concerning the period before birth. □ **prenatally** *adv.*

prenuptial *adj.* existing or occurring before marriage.

preoccupation *n.* **1** the state of being preoccupied. **2** a thing that engrosses the mind. [from Latin *praeoccupatio*]

preoccupy *v.tr.* (**-ies**, **-ied**) **1** dominate the mind of (a person) to the exclusion of other thoughts. **2** (as **preoccupied** *adj.*) otherwise engrossed; mentally distracted. **3** occupy beforehand.

upper premolars

lower premolars   *lower premolars*   INDIVIDUAL PREMOLAR

PLAN OF HUMAN DENTITION   **PREMOLAR**

preordain *v.tr.* ordain or determine beforehand.

pre-owned *adj.* esp. *US* second-hand.

prep[1] ● *n. colloq.* **1** *Brit.* **a** school work done outside lessons, esp. in an independent school. **b** a period when this is done. **2** *US* a student in a preparatory school. ● *attrib.adj. Brit.* **1** relating to work set as prep or the time allocated for this. **2** relating to education in a preparatory school (*prep department*).

prep[2] *v.* (**prepped**, **prepping**) *colloq.* **1** *tr. N. Amer.* prepare, make ready or suitable. **2** *intr. US* prepare oneself for an event.

prep. *abbr.* preposition.

pre-pack *v.tr.* (also **pre-package**) pack (goods) on the site of production or before retail.

prepaid *past* and *past part.* of PREPAY.

preparation *n.* **1** the act or an instance of preparing; the process of being prepared. **2** (often in *pl.*) something done to make ready. **3** a specially prepared substance. **4** = PREP[1] *n.* 1. [from Latin *praeparatio*]

preparatory ● *adj.* **1** (often foll. by *to*) serving to prepare; introductory. **2** *Brit.* = PREP[1] *adj.* 2. ● *adv.* (often foll. by *to*) in a preparatory manner. [related to PREPARE] □ **preparatorily** *adv.*

preparatory school *n.* a usu. private school preparing pupils *Brit.* for esp. a public school or *US* for college or university.

prepare *v.* **1** *tr.* make or get ready for use, consideration, etc. **2** *tr.* make ready or assemble (food etc.) for eating. **3 a** *tr.* make (a person or oneself) ready or disposed in some way. **b** *intr.* get ready. □ **be prepared 1** (usu. foll. by *for*) be ready or disposed. **2** (foll. by *to*) be willing to. [from Latin *praeparare* 'to make ready before'] □ **preparer** *n.*

■ **Usage** The use of *be prepared* in the sense 'be willing' was criticized in the past by some authorities, but it is now established usage.

preparedness *n.* a state of readiness, esp. for war.

prepay *v.tr.* (*past* and *past part.* **prepaid**) **1** pay (a charge) in advance. **2** pay postage on (a letter etc.) before posting. □ **prepayable** *adj.* **prepayment** *n.*

prepense *adj.* (usu. placed after noun) esp. *Law* deliberate, intentional. [earlier *prepensed*: from Old French *purpenser* 'to think before'] □ **prepensely** *adv.*

pre-plan *v.tr.* (**pre-planned**, **pre-planning**) plan in advance.

preponderant *adj.* surpassing in influence, power, number, or importance. □ **preponderance** *n.* **preponderantly** *adv.*

preponderate *v.intr.* (often foll. by *over*) **1 a** be

P

greater in influence, quantity, or number. **b** predominate. **2 a** be of greater importance. **b** weigh more. [based on Latin *praeponderatus* 'outweighed']

preposition *n. Gram.* a word governing (and usu. preceding) a noun or pronoun and expressing a relation to another word or element, e.g. 'came *after* dinner', 'what did you do it *for*?'. [from Latin *praepositio*] □ **prepositional** *adj.* **prepositionally** *adv.*

prepossess *v.tr.* **1** (usu. in *passive*) (of an idea, feeling, etc.) take possession of (a person); imbue. **2 a** prejudice (usu. favourably and spontaneously). **b** (as **prepossessing** *adj.*) attractive, appealing. □ **prepossession** *n.*

preposterous *adj.* **1** utterly absurd; outrageous. **2** contrary to nature, reason, or common sense. [from Latin *praeposterus* 'reversed, absurd'] □ **preposterously** *adv.* **preposterousness** *n.*

preppy (also **preppie**) *N. Amer. colloq.* ● *n.* (*pl.* **-ies**) a person attending an expensive private school or who looks like such a person (with short hair, blazer, etc.). ● *adj.* (**preppier, preppiest**) **1** like a preppy. **2** neat and fashionable.

pre-prandial *adj. formal* or *joc.* before dinner or lunch.

pre-print *n.* a printed document issued in advance of general publication.

pre-process *v.tr.* subject to a preliminary processing.

pre-processor *n.* a computer program that modifies data to conform with the input requirements of another program.

pre-production *n.* work done on a film, broadcast, etc. before production begins (usu. *attrib.*: *pre-production discussions*).

pre-program *v.tr.* (**-programmed, -programming**) program (a computer etc.) beforehand.

prep school *n.* = PREPARATORY SCHOOL.

pre-pubescent *adj.* (also **pre-pubertal**) **1** occurring prior to puberty. **2** that has not yet reached puberty. ● *n.* a pre-pubescent boy or girl.

pre-publication ● *attrib.adj.* produced or occurring before publication. ● *n.* publication in advance or beforehand.

prepuce *n.* **1** = FORESKIN. **2** the fold of skin surrounding the clitoris. [from Latin *praeputium*] □ **preputial** *adj.*

P

---

pre-qualify *v.intr.* qualify in advance, esp. in advance of a sporting event.

prequel *n.* a story, film, etc., whose events or concerns precede those of an existing work.

Pre-Raphaelite ● *n.* ▼ a member of a group of English 19th-c. artists emulating the work of Italian artists from before the time of Raphael. ● *adj.* **1** of or relating to the Pre-Raphaelites. **2** (**pre-Raphaelite**) (esp. of a woman) like a type painted by a Pre-Raphaelite (e.g. with long thick curly auburn hair). □ **Pre-Raphaelitism** *n.*

pre-record *v.tr.* (esp. as **pre-recorded** *adj.*) record (esp. material for broadcasting) in advance.

prerequisite ● *adj.* required as a precondition. ● *n.* a prerequisite thing.

■ **Usage** See Usage Note at PERQUISITE.

prerogative *n.* **1** a right or privilege exclusive to an individual or class. **2** (in full **royal prerogative**) *Brit.* the right of the sovereign, theoretically subject to no restriction. [from Latin *praerogativa* 'privilege']

Pres. *abbr.* President.

presage /press-ij/ ● *n.* **1** an omen or portent. **2** a presentiment or foreboding. ● *v.tr.* **1** portend, foreshadow. **2** give warning of (an event etc.) by natural means. **3** (of a person) predict or have a presentiment of. [from Latin *praesagium*]

presbyopia *n.* long-sightedness caused by loss of elasticity of the eye lens, occurring esp. in middle and old age. [based on Greek *presbus* 'old man' + *ōps ōpos* 'eye'] □ **presbyopic** *adj.*

presbyter *n.* **1** (in the Episcopal Church) a minister of the second order; a priest. **2** (in the Presbyterian Church) an elder. [from Greek *presbuteros* 'elder'] □ **presbyteral** *adj.* **presbyterate** *n.* **presbyterial** *adj.*

Presbyterian ● *adj.* (of a Church) governed by elders all of equal rank, esp. with reference to the national Church of Scotland. ● *n.* a member of a Presbyterian Church. [based on ecclesiastical Latin *presbyterium* 'presbytery'] □ **Presbyterianism** *n.*

presbytery *n.* (*pl.* **-ies**) **1** the eastern part of a chancel beyond the choir. **2 a** a body of presbyters. **b** a district represented by this. **3** the house of a Roman Catholic priest. [from Greek *presbuterion*]

pre-school *adj.* of or relating to the time before a child is old enough to go to school. □ **pre-schooler** *n.*

---

prescient /press-i-ənt/ *adj.* having foreknowledge or foresight. [from Latin *praescient-* 'knowing beforehand'] □ **prescience** *n.* **presciently** *adv.*

prescribe *v.* **1** *tr.* **a** advise the use of (a medicine etc.), esp. by an authorized prescription. **b** recommend, esp. as a benefit. **2** *tr.* lay down or impose authoritatively. **3** *intr.* (foll. by *to, for*) assert a prescriptive right or claim. [from Latin *praescribere* 'to direct in writing'] □ **prescriber** *n.*

■ **Usage** *Prescribe*, meaning 'advise, recommend, impose authoritatively', is sometimes confused with *proscribe*, meaning 'to forbid'. Note the difference in sense between *prescribed drugs* and *proscribed drugs*.

prescript *n.* an ordinance, law, or command. [from Latin *praescriptum*]

prescription *n.* **1** the act or an instance of prescribing. **2 a** a doctor's (usu. written) instruction for the composition and use of a medicine. **b** a medicine prescribed. [from Latin *praescriptio*]

prescriptive *adj.* **1** prescribing. **2** *Linguistics* concerned with or laying down rules of usage. □ **prescriptively** *adv.* **prescriptiveness** *n.* **prescriptivism** *n.* **prescriptivist** *n. & adj.*

pre-select *v.tr.* select in advance. □ **pre-selection** *n.* **pre-selective** *adj.*

pre-selector *n.* any of various devices for selecting a mechanical or electrical operation in advance of its execution, e.g. of a gear change in a motor vehicle.

presence *n.* **1** the state or condition of being present. **2** a place where a person is. **3 a** a person's appearance or bearing, esp. when imposing. **b** a person's force of personality (esp. *have presence*). **4** a person or thing that is present. **5** representation for reasons of political influence (*maintained a presence*). □ **in the presence of** in front of; observed by. [from Latin *praesentia*]

presence of mind *n.* calmness and self-command in sudden difficulty etc.

present[1] /prez-ent/ ● *adj.* **1** (usu. *predic.*) being in the place in question. **2 a** now existing, occurring, or being such (*the present Duke*). **b** now being considered etc. (*in the present case*). **3** *Gram.* expressing an action etc. now going on or habitually performed (*present tense*). ● *n.* (prec. by *the*) **1** the time now passing (*no time like the present*). **2** *Gram.* the present tense. □ **at present** now. **for the present 1** just now. **2** as far as the present is concerned. [from Latin *praesent-* 'being at hand']

present[2] /pri-zent/ ● *v.tr.* **1** introduce, offer, or exhibit, esp. for public attention or consideration. **2 a** (with a thing as object, foll. by *to*) offer, award, or give as a gift (to a person), esp. formally or ceremonially. **b** (with a person as object, foll. by *with*) make available to; cause to have (*presents us with a problem*). **3 a** (of a company, producer, etc.) put (a form of entertainment) before the public. **b** (of a performer, compère, etc.) introduce or put before an audience. **4** introduce (a person) formally (*may I present my fiancé?*). **5** offer, give (compliments etc.). **6 a** (of a circumstance) reveal (some quality etc.) (*this presents some difficulty*). **b** exhibit (*presented a rough exterior*). **7** (of an idea etc.) offer or suggest itself. **8** deliver (a cheque, bill, etc.) for acceptance or payment. **9 a** (usu. foll. by *at*) aim (a weapon). **b** hold out (a weapon) in a position for aiming. ● *n.* the position of presenting arms in salute. □ **present arms** hold a rifle etc. vertically in front of the body as a salute. **present oneself 1** appear. **2** come forward for examination etc. [from Latin *praesentare*] □ **presenter** *n.* (esp. in sense 3b of *v.*).

present[3] /prez-ent/ ● *n.* a gift; a thing given or presented. □ **make a present of** give as a gift. [from Old French, originally in phrase *mettre une chose en present à quelqu'un* 'to put a thing into the presence of a person']

presentable *adj.* **1** of good appearance; fit to be presented to other people. **2** fit for presentation. □ **presentability** *n.* **presentably** *adv.*

presentation *n.* **1 a** the act or an instance of

PRE-RAPHAELITE

The Pre-Raphaelites, formed in 1848, were a coalition of British artists united in their distaste for formal academic art and the neoclassical style dominating the art of the early 19th century. The principal members of the movement were Holman Hunt, John Everett Millais, and Dante Gabriel Rosetti. Despite individual differences, the group shared certain characteristics of style, looking to the past for inspiration and dealing primarily with religious, historical, and literary subjects. They painted directly from nature and tried to represent historical events exactly as they might have occurred.

Horatio Discovering the Madness of Ophelia (1864), DANTE GABRIEL ROSSETTI

TIMELINE

| 1500 | 1550 | 1600 | 1650 | 1700 | 1750 | 1800 | 1850 | 1900 | 1950 | 2000 |

presenting; the process of being presented. **b** a thing presented. **2** the manner or quality of presenting. **3** a demonstration or display of materials, information, etc., a lecture. [from Late Latin *praesentatio*] □ **presentational** *adj.* **presentationally** *adv.*

present-day *attrib.adj.* of this time; modern.

presentient *adj.* (often foll. by *of*) having a presentiment.

presentiment *n.* a vague expectation; a foreboding (esp. of misfortune).

presently *adv.* **1** soon; after a short time. **2** esp. *N. Amer.* & *Sc.* at the present time; now.

presentment *n.* the act of presenting information, esp. a statement on oath by a jury of a fact known to them.

preservation *n.* **1** the act of preserving or process of being preserved. **2** a state of being well or badly preserved.

preservationist *n.* a supporter or advocate of preservation, esp. of antiquities and historic buildings.

PRESERVATIVE:
PICKLING SPICE

preservative ● *n.* ◄ a substance for preserving perishable foodstuffs, wood, etc. ● *adj.* tending to preserve.

preserve ● *v.tr.* **1 a** keep safe or free from harm, decay, etc. **b** keep alive (a name, memory, etc.). **2** maintain (a thing) in its existing state. **3** retain (a quality or condition). **4 a** treat or refrigerate (food) to prevent decomposition or fermentation. **b** prepare (fruit) by boiling it with sugar, for long-term storage. **5** keep (game, a river, etc.) undisturbed for private use. ● *n.* (in *sing.* or *pl.*) **1** preserved fruit; jam. **2** a place where game or fish etc. are preserved. **3** a sphere or area of activity regarded as a person's own. [from Late Latin *praeservare*] □ **preservable** *adj.* **preserver** *n.*

pre-set *v.tr.* (**-setting**, *past* and *past part.* **-set**) **1** set or fix (a device) in advance of its operation. **2** settle or decide beforehand.

pre-shrunk *adj.* (of a fabric or garment) treated so that it shrinks during manufacture and not in use.

preside *v.intr.* **1** (often foll. by *at, over*) be in a position of authority, esp. as the chairperson or president of a meeting. **2** exercise control or authority. [from Latin *praesidēre* 'to sit before']

presidency *n.* (*pl.* **-ies**) **1** the office of president. **2** the period of this. [from medieval Latin *praesidentia*]

president *n.* **1** the head of a republican state. **2** the head of a society or council etc. **3** the head of certain colleges. **4** *N. Amer.* **a** the head of a university. **b** the head of a company etc. **5** a person in charge of a meeting, council, etc. [related to PRESIDE] □ **presidential** *adj.* **presidentially** *adv.*

president-elect *n.* (*pl.* **presidents-elect**) a president who has been elected but has not yet taken up office.

presidium *n.* (also **praesidium**) a standing executive committee in a Communist country. [from Latin *praesidium* 'protection']

press[1] ● *v.* **1** *tr.* apply steady force to (a thing in contact) (*press a switch*; *pressed the two surfaces together*). **2** *tr.* **a** compress or apply pressure to (a thing) to flatten, shape, or smooth it, as by ironing (*got the curtains pressed*). **b** squeeze (a fruit etc.) to extract its juice. **c** manufacture (a gramophone record etc.) by moulding under pressure. **3** *tr.* (foll. by *out of, from*, etc.) squeeze (juice etc.). **4** *tr.* embrace or caress by squeezing (*pressed my hand*). **5** *intr.* (foll. by *on, against*, etc.) exert pressure. **6** *intr.* be urgent; demand immediate action (*time was pressing*). **7** *intr.* (foll. by *for*) make an insistent demand. **8** *intr.* (foll. by *up*,

PRESS FOR EXTRACTING JUICE FROM FRUIT

juice

round, etc.) form a crowd. **9** *intr.* (foll. by *on, forward*, etc.) hasten insistently. **10** *tr.* (often in *passive*) (of an enemy etc.) bear heavily on. **11** *tr.* (often foll. by *for*, or *to* + *infin.*) urge or entreat (*pressed me to stay*; *pressed me for an answer*). **12** *tr.* (foll. by *on, upon*) **a** put forward or urge (an opinion, claim, or course of action). **b** insist on the acceptance of (an offer, a gift, etc.). **13** *tr.* insist on (*did not press the point*). **14** *intr.* (foll. by *on*) produce a strong mental or moral impression; oppress; weigh heavily. **15** *intr* *Golf* try too hard for a long shot etc. and so strike the ball imperfectly. ● *n.* **1** the act or an instance of pressing (*give it a slight press*). **2 a** ▲ a device for compressing, flattening, shaping, extracting juice, etc. (*trouser press; flower press; wine press*). **b** a frame for preserving the shape of a racket when not in use. **c** a machine that applies pressure to a workpiece by means of a tool, in order to punch shapes, bend it, etc. **3** = PRINTING PRESS. **4** (*prec. by the*) **a** the art or practice of printing. **b** newspapers, journalists, etc., generally or collectively (*read it in the press*; *pursued by the press*). **5** a notice or piece of publicity in newspapers etc. (*got a good press*). **6** (**Press**) **a** a printing house or establishment. **b** a publishing company. **7 a** a crowding. **b** a crowd (of people etc.). **8** the pressure of affairs. **9** esp. *Ir.* & *Sc.* a large usu. shelved cupboard. □ **at** (or **in**) **press** (or **the press**) being printed. **be pressed for** have barely enough (time etc.). **go** (or **send**) **to press** go or send to be printed. **press the button 1** set machinery in motion. **2** *colloq.* initiate an action or train of events. [from Latin *pressare* 'to keep pressing']

press[2] ● *v.tr.* **1** *hist.* force to serve in the army or navy. **2** bring into use as a makeshift (*was pressed into service*). ● *n.* *hist.* compulsory enlistment, esp. in the navy. [alteration of obsolete *prest* 'to pay on enlistment': from Latin *praestare* 'to furnish']

press agent *n.* a person employed to attend to advertising and press publicity.

press box *n.* a reporters' enclosure, esp. at a sports event.

press-button *n.* & *attrib.adj. Brit.* = PUSH-BUTTON.

press conference *n.* an interview given to a number of journalists.

press cutting *n.* a cutting taken from a newspaper etc.

pressed steel *n.* steel moulded under pressure.

press gallery *n.* a gallery for reporters, esp. in a legislative assembly.

press-gang ● *n.* **1** *hist.* a body of men employed to press men into service in the army or navy. **2** any group using similar coercive methods. ● *v.tr.* force into service.

pressie var. of PREZZIE.

pressing ● *adj.* **1** urgent (*pressing business*). **2 a** urging strongly (*a pressing invitation*). **b** persistent, importunate (*since you are so pressing*). ● *n.* **1** a thing made by pressing, esp. a gramophone record. **2** a series of these made at one time. **3** the act or an instance of pressing a thing, esp. a gramophone record, grapes, etc. (*all at one pressing*). □ **pressingly** *adv.*

pressman *n.* (*pl.* **-men**) **1** a journalist. **2** an operator of a printing press.

pressmark *n. Brit.* a library shelf mark showing the location of a book etc.

press-on *adj.* that can be pressed or ironed on to something.

press release *n.* an official statement issued to newspapers for information.

press stud *n. Brit.* a small fastening device engaged by pressing its two halves together.

press-up *n. Brit.* an exercise in which the prone body is raised from the legs or trunk upwards by pressing down on the hands to straighten the arms.

pressure ● *n.* **1 a** ▼ the exertion of continuous force on or against a body by another in contact with it. **b** the force exerted. **c** the amount of this (expressed by the force on a unit area) (*atmospheric pressure*). **2** urgency; the need to meet a deadline etc. (*work under pressure*). **3** affliction or difficulty (*under financial pressure*). **4** constraining influence (*if pressure is brought to bear*). ● *v.tr.* **1** apply (esp. psychological or moral) pressure to. **2** (often foll. by *into*) persuade; coerce (*was pressured into attending*).

PRESSURE

Pressure may be exerted by solids, liquids, and gases, and is normally measured in newtons per square metre. In the experiment shown here, a liquid (water) in a tall tank exerts pressure on the sides of the tank. The water escapes more quickly from holes at the bottom of the tank compared to holes at the top. This is because pressure exerted by the water is greatest at the bottom of the tank, due to the weight of the water above it.

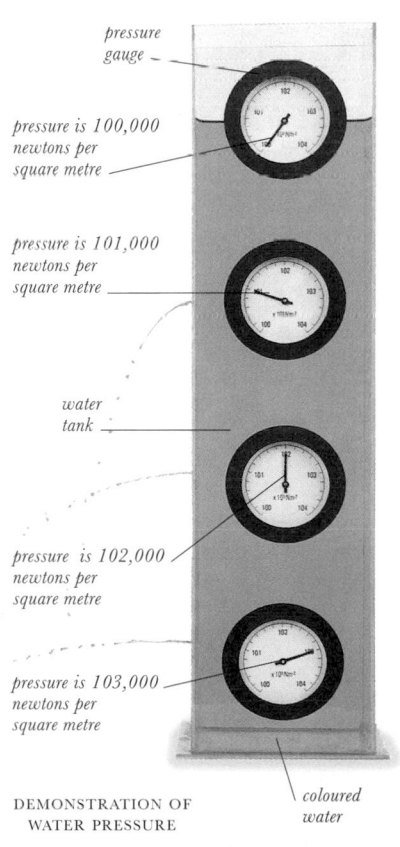

pressure gauge

pressure is 100,000 newtons per square metre

pressure is 101,000 newtons per square metre

water tank

pressure is 102,000 newtons per square metre

pressure is 103,000 newtons per square metre

coloured water

DEMONSTRATION OF WATER PRESSURE

P

PRESSURE COOKER

Inside a sealed pressure cooker, air pressure is increased by heating water to produce steam. The higher pressure raises both the boiling point of the water and the temperature of the steam, so that food suspended inside cooks more quickly.

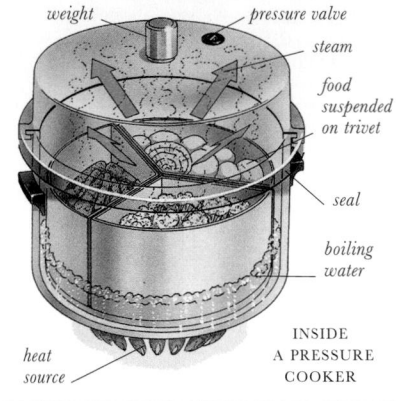

weight

pressure valve

steam

food suspended on trivet

seal

boiling water

heat source

INSIDE A PRESSURE COOKER

pressure cooker *n.* ▲ an airtight pan for cooking quickly under steam pressure. □ **pressure-cook** *v.tr.*

pressure gauge *n.* a gauge showing the pressure of steam etc.

pressure group *n.* a group or association formed to promote a particular interest or cause by influencing public policy.

pressure point *n.* **1** ▼ a point where an artery can be pressed against a bone to inhibit bleeding. **2** a point on the skin sensitive to pressure. **3** a target for political pressure or influence.

pressure suit *n.* an inflatable suit for flying at a high altitude.

---

pressurize *v.tr.* (also **-ise**) **1** (esp. as **pressurized** *adj.*) maintain normal atmospheric pressure in (an aircraft cabin etc.) at a high altitude. **2** raise to a high pressure. **3** pressure (a person). □ **pressurization** *n.*

pressurized-water reactor *n.* a nuclear reactor in which the coolant is water at high pressure.

Prestel *n. propr.* (in the UK) the computerized visual information system operated by British Telecom.

prestidigitator *n. formal* a conjuror. [from French *prestidigitateur*] □ **prestidigitation** *n.*

prestige /press-**teezh**/ *n.* **1** respect, reputation, or influence derived from achievements, power, associations, etc. **2** (*attrib.*) having or conferring prestige. [French, literally 'illusion, glamour']

prestigious /press-**tij**-ŭs/ *adj.* having or showing prestige. [originally in sense 'deceptive': based on Latin *praestigiae* 'juggler's tricks'] □ **prestigiously** *adv.*

presto ● *adv. & adj. Mus.* in quick tempo. ● *n.* (*pl.* **-os**) *Mus.* a presto passage or movement. ● *int.* = HEY PRESTO! [from Latin *praesto* 'ready']

prestressed *adj.* strengthened by stressing in advance, esp. of concrete by means of stretched rods or wires put in during manufacture.

presumably *adv.* as may reasonably be presumed.

presume *v.* **1** *tr.* suppose to be true; take for granted. **2** *tr.* **a** take the liberty; be impudent enough (*presumed to question their authority*). **b** dare, venture (*may I presume to ask?*). **3** *intr.* be presumptuous. **4** *intr.* (foll. by *on*, *upon*) take advantage of or make unscrupulous use of (a person's good nature etc.). [from Latin *praesumere* 'to anticipate, venture'] □ **presumable** *adj.*

presumption *n.* **1** arrogance; presumptuous behaviour. **2 a** the act of presuming a thing to be true. **b** a thing that is or may be presumed to be true. **3** a ground for presuming (*a strong presumption against their being guilty*). [from Latin *praesumptio*]

presumptive *adj.* giving grounds for presumption (*presumptive evidence*). □ **presumptively** *adv.*

presumptuous *adj.* unduly or overbearingly confident. [related to PRESUME] □ **presumptuously** *adv.* **presumptuousness** *n.*

---

presuppose *v.tr.* **1** assume beforehand. **2** imply.

presupposition *n.* **1** the act or an instance of presupposing. **2** a thing assumed beforehand as the basis of argument etc.

pre-tax *attrib.adj.* (of income or profits) before the deduction of taxes.

pre-teen *adj.* of or relating to a child just under the age of thirteen.

pretence *n.* (*US* **pretense**) **1** pretending, make-believe. **2 a** a pretext or excuse (*on the slightest pretence*). **b** a false show of intentions or motives (*under the pretence of friendship*). **3** (foll. by *to*) a claim (*has no pretence to any great talent*). **4 a** affectation, display. **b** ostentation (*stripped of all pretence*). [from Anglo-French *pretense*]

pretend ● *v.* **1** *tr.* claim or assert falsely so as to deceive (*pretend knowledge*; *pretended that they were foreigners*). **2** *tr.* imagine to oneself in play (*pretended to be monsters*; *pretended it was night*). **3** *tr.* **a** profess (*does not pretend to be a scholar*). **b** (as **pretended** *adj.*) falsely claim to be such (*a pretended friend*). **4** *intr.* (foll. by *to*) **a** lay claim to (a right or title etc.). **b** profess to have (a quality etc.). ● *adj. colloq.* pretended; in pretence (*pretend money*). [from French *prétendre*]

pretender *n.* **1** a person who claims a throne or title etc. **2** a person who pretends.

pretense *US* var. of PRETENCE.

pretension *n.* **1 a** an assertion of a claim. **b** a justifiable claim (*has no pretensions to the name*; *has some pretensions to be included*). **2** pretentiousness. [from medieval Latin *praetensio*, related to PRETEND]

pretentious *adj.* **1** making an excessive claim to great merit or importance. **2** ostentatious. □ **pretentiously** *adv.* **pretentiousness** *n.*

preter- *comb. form* more than. [from Latin *praeter* 'past, beyond']

preterite (*US* also **preterit**) *Gram.* ● *adj.* expressing a past action or state. ● *n.* a preterite tense or form. [from Latin *praeteritus*]

pre-term *adj. & adv.* born or occurring prematurely.

preternatural *adj.* outside the ordinary course of nature; supernatural. □ **preternaturally** *adv.*

pretext *n.* **1** an ostensible reason or intention. **2** an excuse offered. □ **on** (or **under**) **the pretext** (foll. by *of*, or *that* + clause) professing as one's object or intention. [from Latin *praetextus* 'outward display']

pretor *US* var. of PRAETOR.

pretreat *v.tr.* treat beforehand. □ **pretreatment** *n.*

prettify *v.tr.* (**-ies**, **-ied**) make pretty esp. in an affected way. □ **prettification** *n.*

pretty ● *adj.* (**prettier**, **prettiest**) **1** attractive in a delicate way without being truly beautiful or handsome (*a pretty child*; *a pretty dress*). **2** fine or good of its kind (*a pretty wit*). **3** *colloq. iron.* considerable, fine (*a pretty penny*; *a pretty mess you have made*). ● *adv. colloq.* fairly, moderately; considerably (*am pretty well*; *find it pretty difficult*). ● *n.* (*pl.* **-ies**) a pretty person. ● *v.tr.* (**-ies**, **-ied**) make pretty or attractive. □ **pretty much** (or **nearly** or **well**) *colloq.* almost; very nearly. [Old English] □ **prettily** *adv.* **prettiness** *n.*

pretty-pretty *adj. Brit.* too pretty.

pretzel *n.* ▼ a crisp knot-shaped or stick-shaped salted biscuit. [German]

prevail *v.intr.* **1** be victorious or gain mastery. **2** be the more usual or predominant. **3** exist or occur in general use or experience. **4** (foll. by *on*, *upon*) persuade. [from Latin *praevalēre* 'to have power over']

P

PRESSURE POINT

Bleeding from a wound can be controlled by applying pressure directly to it, or by applying pressure to certain points on the body (pressure points) where it is possible to press an artery against underlying bone. By pressing the appropriate artery, the flow of blood from the heart to the injured part of the body will be reduced.

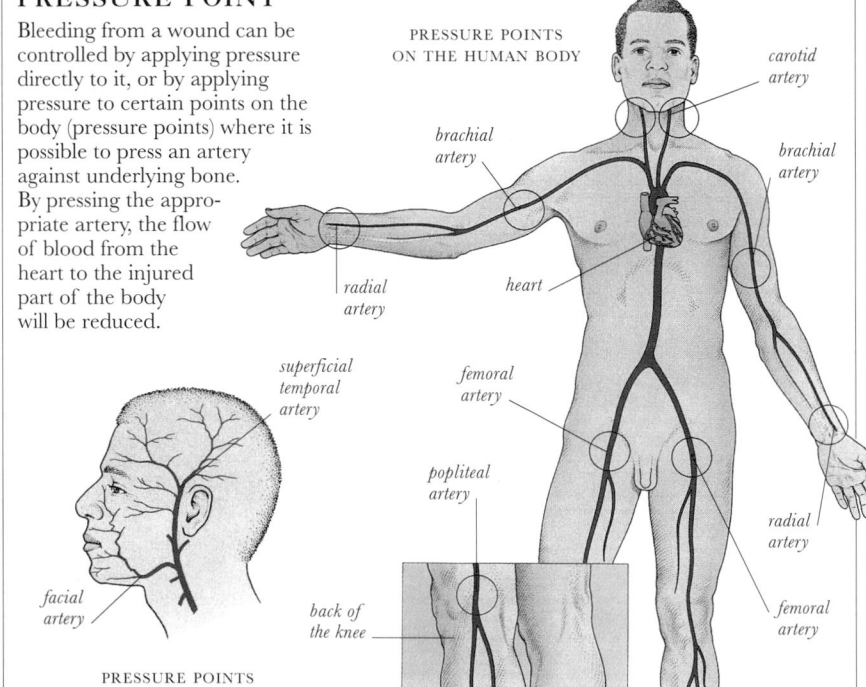

PRESSURE POINTS ON THE HUMAN BODY

carotid artery

brachial artery

brachial artery

radial artery

heart

femoral artery

superficial temporal artery

radial artery

femoral artery

popliteal artery

facial artery

back of the knee

PRESSURE POINTS ON THE HEAD

PRETZELS

prevailing wind *n.* the wind that most frequently occurs at a place.

prevalent /prev-ă-lĕnt/ *adj.* **1** generally existing or occurring. **2** predominant. [from Latin *praevalent-* 'powerful'] □ **prevalence** *n.*

prevaricate *v.intr.* **1** speak or act evasively or misleadingly. **2** quibble, equivocate. [from Latin *praevaricari praevaricat-* 'to walk crookedly, practise collusion'] □ **prevarication** *n.* **prevaricator** *n.*

■ **Usage** *Prevaricate* is often confused with *procrastinate*, which means 'to defer or put off an action'.

prevent *v.tr.* stop from happening or doing something; hinder; make impossible (*the weather prevented me from going*). [based on Latin *praeventus* 'hindered'] □ **preventable** *adj.* (also **preventible**). **preventer** *n.* **prevention** *n.*

■ **Usage** The use of *prevent* in sense 1 without *from*, as in *prevented me going*, is informal. An acceptable alternative is *prevented my going*.

preventative *adj. & n.* = PREVENTIVE.

preventive ● *adj.* serving to prevent, esp. preventing disease, breakdown, etc. (*preventive medicine*; *preventive maintenance*). ● *n.* a preventive agent, measure, drug, etc. □ **preventively** *adv.*

preview ● *n.* **1** the act of seeing in advance. **2 a** the showing of a film, play, exhibition, etc., before the official opening. **b** (*N. Amer.* also **prevue**) a film trailer. ● *v.tr.* see or show in advance.

previous ● *adj.* **1** coming before in time or order (*previous afternoon*; *previous attempts*). **2** *colloq.* done or acting hastily. ● *adv.* (foll. by *to*) before (*had called previous to writing*). [from Latin *praevius*] □ **previously** *adv.*

pre-war *adj.* existing, occurring, or built before a war, esp. the First or Second World War.

■ **Usage** *Pre-war* should not be used as an adverb, e.g. *Pre-war, my father used to smoke. Before the war* is preferable.

pre-wash ● *n.* a preliminary wash, esp. as performed in an automatic washing machine. ● *v.tr.* give a preliminary wash to, esp. before putting on sale.

prey ● *n.* **1** an animal that is hunted or killed by another for food. **2** (foll. by *to*) a person or thing that is influenced by or vulnerable to (something undesirable) (*became a prey to morbid fears*). ● *v.intr.* (foll. by *on, upon*) **1** seek or take as prey. **2** make a victim of. **3** (of a disease, emotion, etc.) exert a harmful influence (*fear preyed on his mind*). [from Latin *praeda* 'booty']

prezzie *n.* (also **pressie**) *Brit. colloq.* a present or gift.

priapic *adj.* phallic.

priapism *n.* **1** lewdness, licentiousness. **2** *Med.* persistent erection of the penis. [based on *Priapos*, god of procreation]

price ● *n.* **1 a** the amount of money or goods for which a thing is bought or sold. **b** value or worth (*a pearl of great price*; *beyond price*). **2** what is or must be given, done, sacrificed, etc., to obtain or achieve something. **3** the odds in betting (*starting price*). ● *v.tr.* **1** fix or find the price of (a thing for sale). **2** estimate the value of. □ **above** (or **beyond** or **without**) **price** so valuable that no price can be stated. **at any price** no matter what the cost, sacrifice, etc. (*peace at any price*). **at a price** at a high cost. **price on a person's head** a reward for a person's capture or death. **price oneself out of the market** lose to one's competitors by charging more than customers are willing to pay. **set a price on** declare the price of. **what price ...?** *colloq.* **1** what is the chance of ...? (*what price your finishing the course?*). **2** *iron.* the expected or much boasted ... proves disappointing (*what price your friendship now?*). [*n.*: from Latin *pretium*; *v.*: a variant of archaic *prise*] □ **priced** *adj.* (also in *comb.*). **pricer** *n.*

price-fixing *n.* the maintaining of prices at a certain level by agreement between competing sellers.

priceless *adj.* **1** invaluable. **2** *colloq.* very amusing or absurd. □ **pricelessly** *adv.*

price ring *n.* a group of traders acting illegally to control certain prices.

price-sensitive *adj.* **1** (of a product) whose sales are greatly influenced by its price. **2** (of information) that would affect prices if it were made public.

price tag *n.* **1** the label on an item showing its price. **2** the cost of an undertaking.

price war *n.* fierce competition among traders cutting prices.

pricey *adj.* (also **pricy**) (**pricier, priciest**) *colloq.* expensive.

prick ● *v.* **1** *tr.* pierce slightly; make a small hole in. **2** *tr.* (foll. by *off, out*) mark with small holes or dots. **3** *tr.* trouble mentally (*my conscience is pricking me*). **4** *intr.* feel a pricking sensation. **5** *intr.* (foll. by *at, into,* etc.) make a thrust as if to prick. **6** *tr.* (foll. by *in, off, out*) plant (seedlings etc.) in small holes pricked in the earth. **7** *tr. Brit. archaic* mark off (a name in a list) by pricking. **8** *tr. archaic* spur or urge on (a horse etc.). ● *n.* **1** the act or an instance of pricking. **2** a small hole or mark made by pricking. **3** a pain caused as by pricking. **4** a mental pain (*felt the pricks of conscience*). **5** *coarse slang* the penis. **b** *derog.* (as a term of contempt) a man. **6** *archaic* a goad for oxen. □ **kick against the pricks** persist in futile resistance. **prick up one's ears 1** (of a dog etc.) make the ears erect when on the alert. **2** (of a person) become suddenly attentive. [Old English] □ **pricker** *n.*

pricket *n.* a male fallow deer in its second year, having straight unbranched horns.

prickle ● *n.* **1 a** a small thorn. **b** *Bot.* a thornlike process developed from the epidermis of a plant. **2** a hard-pointed spine of a hedgehog etc. **3** a prickling sensation. ● *v.tr. & intr.* be affected with a sensation as of pricking. [Old English]

prickly *adj.* (**pricklier, prickliest**) **1** having prickles. **2** ready to take offence. **3** tingling. □ **prickliness** *n.*

prickly heat *n.* an itchy inflammation of the skin, causing a tingling sensation and common in hot countries.

prickly pear *n.* **1** any cactus of the genus *Opuntia*, native to arid regions of America, bearing large pear-shaped prickly fruits. **2** ▼ its fruit.

PRICKLY PEAR
(*Opuntia ficus indica*)

prickly poppy *n.* a tropical poppy, *Argemone mexicana*, with prickly leaves and yellow flowers.

pricy var. of PRICEY.

pride ● *n.* **1 a** a feeling of elation or satisfaction at achievements or qualities or possessions etc. that do one credit. **b** (prec. by *the*; foll. by *of*) the object of this feeling (*the pride of the museum's collection*). **2** a high or overbearing opinion of one's worth or importance. **3** (in full **proper pride**) a proper sense of what befits one's position; self-respect. **4** a group of animals, esp. lions. **5** esp. *literary* the best condition; the prime. ● *v.refl.* (foll. by *on, upon*) be proud of. □ **my, his,** etc. **pride and joy** a thing of which one is very proud. **take pride** (or **a pride**) **in 1** be proud of. **2** maintain in good condition or appearance. [Old English] □ **prideful** *adj.* **pridefully** *adv.*

pride of place *n.* the most important or prominent position.

pride of the morning *n.* a mist or shower at sunrise supposedly indicating a fine day to come.

prie-dieu /pree-d'yer/ *n.* (*pl.* **prie-dieux** *pronunc.* same) a kneeling-desk for prayer. [French, literally 'pray God']

priest *n.* **1** an ordained minister of the Roman Catholic or Orthodox Church, or of the Anglican Church (above a deacon and below a bishop). **2** an official minister of a non-Christian religion. [from ecclesiastical Latin *presbyter*] □ **priestlike** *adj.*

priestess *n.* a female priest of a non-Christian religion.

priesthood *n.* (usu. prec. by *the*) **1** the office or position of priest. **2** priests in general.

priest-in-charge *n.* (*pl.* **priests-in-charge**) a minister in charge of a parish which for the time being lacks an incumbent priest.

priestly *adj.* of or associated with priests.

priest's hole *n. hist.* a hiding place for a Roman Catholic priest during times of religious persecution.

prig *n.* a self-righteous or moralistic person. [16th-century slang in sense 'tinker', hence 'an unpleasant person'] □ **priggery** *n.* **priggish** *adj.* **priggishly** *adv.* **priggishness** *n.*

prim *adj.* (**primmer, primmest**) **1** stiffly formal and precise. **2** (of a woman or girl) demure. **3** prudish. [18th-century coinage] □ **primly** *adv.* **primness** *n.*

prima ballerina /pree-mă/ *n.* (*pl.* **prima ballerinas**) the chief female dancer in a ballet or ballet company. [Italian]

primacy *n.* (*pl.* **-ies**) **1** pre-eminence. **2** the office of a primate. [from medieval Latin *primatia*]

prima donna /pree-mă/ *n.* (*pl.* **prima donnas**) **1** the chief female singer in an opera or opera company. **2** a temperamentally self-important person. [Italian]

primaeval var. of PRIMEVAL.

prima facie /pry-mă fay-shee/ ● *adv.* at first sight (*seems prima facie to be guilty*). ● *adj.* (of evidence) based on the first impression (*can see a prima facie reason for it*). [Latin]

primal *adj.* **1** primitive, primeval. **2** chief, fundamental. [from medieval Latin *primalis*]

primary ● *adj.* **1 a** of the first importance; chief (*that is our primary concern*). **b** fundamental, basic. **2** earliest, original; first in a series. **3** of the first rank in a series; not derived (*the primary meaning of a word*). **4** (of a battery or cell) generating electricity by irreversible chemical reaction. **5** (of education) for children below the age of 11. **6** (**Primary**) *Geol.* of the lowest series of strata. **7** *Biol.* belonging to the first stage of development. **8** (of an industry or source of production) concerned with obtaining or using raw materials. ● *n.* (*pl.* **-ies**) **1** a thing that is primary. **2** (in full **primary election**) (in the US) a preliminary election to appoint delegates to a party conference or to select the candidates for a principal (esp. presidential) election. **3** (**Primary**) *Geol.* the Primary period. **4** = PRIMARY FEATHER. [based on Latin *primus* 'first'] □ **primarily** *adv.*

primary coil *n.* a coil to which current is supplied in a transformer.

primary colour *n.* any of the colours red, green, and blue, or (for pigments) red, blue, and yellow, from which all other colours can be obtained by mixing. ▷ COLOUR

primary feather *n.* a large flight feather of a bird's wing. ▷ FEATHER

primary planet *n.* a planet that directly orbits the Sun.

primary school *n.* a school where children below the age of 11 are taught.

P

PRIMATE

Primates are mostly tree-dwelling animals with forward-pointing eyes, long arms, and gripping fingers. The majority have large brains and a high level of intelligence, and live in social groups. There are two sub-orders: anthropoids, the advanced primates, which include monkeys, apes, and humans; and prosimians, the primitive primates, which include lemurs, tarsiers, and lorises.

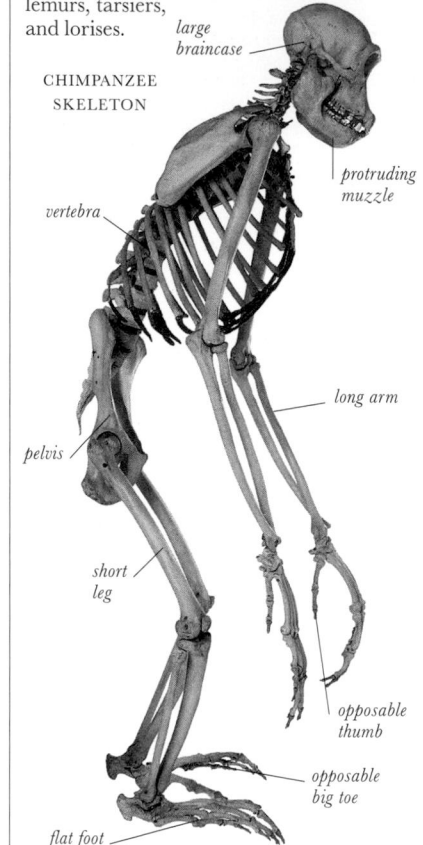

CHIMPANZEE SKELETON

large braincase

protruding muzzle

vertebra

long arm

pelvis

short leg

opposable thumb

opposable big toe

flat foot

TYPES OF PRIMATE

ANTHROPOIDS

PROBOSCIS MONKEY
(*Nasalis larvatus*)

RED HOWLER MONKEY
(*Alouatta seniculus*)

SPIDER MONKEY
(*Ateles geoffroyi*)

ORANG-UTAN
(*Pongo pygmaeus*)

GORILLA
(*Gorilla gorilla*)

PROSIMIANS

AYE-AYE
(*Daubentonia madagascariensis*)

INDRI
(*Indri indri*)

P

primate *n.* **1** ▲ any animal of the order Primates, the highest order of mammals, including tarsiers, lemurs, apes, monkeys, and humans. **2** an archbishop. [from Latin *primas -atis* 'of the first rank'] □ **primatial** *adj.*

primatology *n.* the branch of zoology that deals with primates. □ **primatological** *adj.* **primatologist** *n.*

prime¹ ● *adj.* **1** chief, most important (*the prime agent*; *the prime motive*). **2** first-rate, excellent. **3** primary, fundamental. **4** *Math.* (of a number) divisible only by itself and unity (e.g. 2, 3, 5, 7, 11). ● *n.* **1** the state of the highest perfection of something (*in the prime of life*). **2** (prec. by *the*; foll. by *of*) the best part. **3** the beginning or first age of anything. **4** *Eccl.* the office of the second canonical hour of prayer, originally said at the first hour of the day (i.e. 6 a.m.). **5** a prime number. [*n.*: from Latin *prima (hora)* 'first (hour)'; *adj.*: from Latin *primus* 'first']

prime² *v.tr.* **1** prepare (a thing) for use or action. **2** prepare (a gun) for firing or (an explosive) for detonation. **3 a** pour a liquid into (a pump) to prepare it for working. **b** inject petrol into (the cylinder or carburettor of an internal-combustion engine). **4** prepare (wood etc.) for painting by applying a substance that prevents paint from being absorbed. **5** equip (a person) with information etc. **6** ply (a person) with food or drink in preparation for something. [16th-century coinage]

prime minister *n.* the head of an elected government; the principal minister of a sovereign or state.

prime mover *n.* **1** an initial source of motive power. **2** the author of a fruitful idea.

primer¹ *n.* **1** a substance used to prime wood etc. ▷ UNDERCOAT. **2** a cap, cylinder, etc., used to ignite the powder of a cartridge etc.

primer² *n.* **1** an elementary textbook for teaching children to read. **2** an introductory book. [based on Latin *primus* 'first']

prime time *n.* the time at which a radio or television audience is expected to be at its highest (hyphenated when *attrib.*: *prime-time viewing*).

primeval *adj.* (also **primaeval**) **1** of or relating to the first age of the world. **2** ancient, primitive. [based on Latin *primus* 'first' + *aevum* 'age'] □ **primevally** *adv.*

primitive ● *adj.* **1** early, ancient; at an early stage of civilization (*primitive man*). **2** undeveloped, crude, simple (*primitive methods*). **3** original, primary. ● *n.* **1** a painter of the period before the Renaissance. **2** a modern imitator of such. **3** an untutored painter with a direct naive style. [from Latin *primitivus* 'first of its kind'] □ **primitively** *adv.* **primitiveness** *n.*

primitivism *n.* **1** primitive behaviour. **2** belief in the superiority of what is primitive. **3** the practice of primitive art. □ **primitivist** *n. & adj.*

primogeniture *n.* **1** the fact of being the first-born child. **2** (in full **right of primogeniture**) the right of succession belonging to the first-born. [from medieval Latin *primogenitura*] □ **primogenital** *adj.* **primogenitary** *adj.*

primordial *adj.* **1** existing at or from the beginning, primeval. **2** original, fundamental. [from Late Latin *primordialis*] □ **primordially** *adv.*

primp *v.tr.* **1** make (the hair, one's clothes, etc.) tidy. **2** *refl.* make (oneself) smart. [dialect variant of PRIM]

primrose ● *n.* **1** ▶ any plant of the genus *Primula*, esp. *P. vulgaris*, bearing pale yellow flowers. **2** (in full **primrose yellow**) a pale yellow colour. ● *adj.* (in full **primrose**

PRIMROSE
(*Primula vulgaris*)

yellow; hyphenated when *attrib.*) pale yellow. [based on medieval Latin *prima rosa* 'first rose']

primrose path *n.* the pursuit of pleasure, esp. with disastrous consequences. [with reference to Shakespeare's *Hamlet* I. iii. 50]

primula *n.* any plant of the genus *Primula*, bearing primrose-like flowers in a wide variety of colours during the spring, including primroses, cowslips, and polyanthuses. [medieval Latin, literally 'little first (flower)']

Primus *n. Brit. propr.* a brand of portable stove burning vaporized oil for cooking etc. [Latin literally 'first']

prince *n.* (as a title usu. **Prince**) **1** a male member of a royal family other than a reigning king. **2** (in full **prince of the blood**) a son or grandson of a British monarch. **3** a ruler of a small state. **4** (as an English rendering of foreign titles) a noble usu. ranking next below a duke. **5** the chief or greatest (*the prince of novelists*). [from Latin *princeps* 'first, chief, sovereign'] □ **princedom** *n.*

Prince Charming *n.* an idealized young hero or lover.

prince consort *n.* **1** the husband of a reigning female sovereign who is himself a prince. **2** the title conferred on him.

princeling *n.* **1** a young prince. **2** often *derog.* the ruler of a small principality or domain.

princely *adj.* (**princelier**, **princeliest**) **1 a** of or worthy of a prince. **b** held by a prince. **2** sumptuous, generous, splendid.

Prince of Darkness *n.* Satan.

Prince of Peace *n.* Christ.

prince of the blood see PRINCE 2.

Prince of Wales *n.* the heir apparent to the British throne, the eldest son of the sovereign.

Prince Regent *n.* a prince who acts as regent, esp. George (afterwards IV) as regent 1811–20.

princess *n.* (as a title usu. **Princess**) **1** the wife of a prince. **2** a female member of a royal family other than a reigning queen. **3** (in full **princess of the blood**) a daughter or granddaughter of a British monarch. **4** a pre-eminent woman or thing personified as a woman. [related to PRINCE]

Princess Royal *n.* the eldest daughter of a reigning monarch, esp. as a title conferred by the British monarch.

principal ● *adj.* **1** (usu. *attrib.*) first in rank or importance; chief (*the principal town of the district*). **2** main, leading (*a principal cause of my success*). **3** (of money) constituting the original sum invested or lent. ● *n.* **1** a head, ruler, or superior. **2** the head of some schools, colleges, and universities. **3** the leading performer in a concert, play, etc. **4** a capital sum as distinguished from interest or income. **5** a person for whom another acts as agent etc. **6** (in the UK) a civil servant of the grade below Secretary. **7** the person actually responsible for a crime. [from Latin *principalis* 'first, original'] □ **principalship** *n.*

principal boy *n.* (also **principal girl**) *Brit.* an actress who takes the leading male (or female) part in a pantomime.

principality *n.* (*pl.* **-ies**) **1** a state ruled by a prince. **2** the government of a prince. **3** (**the Principality**) *Brit.* Wales.

principally *adv.* for the most part; chiefly.

principal parts *n.pl. Gram.* the parts of a verb from which all other parts can be deduced.

principle *n.* **1** a fundamental truth or law as the basis of reasoning or action (*arguing from first principles*; *moral principles*). **2 a** a personal code of conduct (*a person of high principle*). **b** (in *pl.*) such rules of conduct (*has no principles*). **3** a general law in physics etc. (*the uncertainty principle*). **4** a natural law forming the basis for the construction or working of a machine etc. **5** a fundamental source; a primary element (*held water to be the first principle of all things*). **6** *Chem.* a constituent of a substance. □ **in principle** as regards fundamentals but not necessarily in detail. **on principle** on the basis of a moral

attitude (*I refuse on principle*). [from Latin *principium* 'source']

principled *adj.* based on or having (esp. praiseworthy) principles of behaviour.

prink *v.* **1** *tr.* (usu. *refl.*) **a** make (oneself etc.) smart. **b** (foll. by *up*) smarten (oneself) up. **c** (of a bird) preen. **2** *intr.* dress oneself up. [16th-century coinage]

print ● *n.* **1** an indentation or mark on a surface left by the pressure of a thing in contact with it. **2 a** printed lettering or writing (*large print*). **b** words in printed form. **c** a printed publication, esp. a newspaper. **d** the state of being printed. **3** a picture or design printed from a block or plate. **4** *Photog.* a picture produced on paper from a negative. **5** a printed cotton fabric. ● *v.tr.* **1 a** produce or reproduce (a book, picture, etc.) by applying inked types, blocks, or plates, to paper, vellum, etc. **b** (of an author, publisher, or editor) cause (a book or manuscript etc.) to be produced or reproduced in this way. **2** express or publish in print. **3 a** impress or stamp (a mark or figure on a surface). **b** impress or stamp (a soft surface with a seal, die, etc.). **4** (often *absol.*) write (words or letters) without joining. **5** *Photog.* produce (a picture) by the transmission of light through a negative. **6** (usu. foll. by *out*) (of a computer etc.) produce output in printed form. **7** mark (a textile fabric) with a decorative design in colours. **8** (foll. by *on*) impress (an idea, scene, etc. on the mind or memory). □ **appear in print** have one's work published. **in print 1** (of a book etc.) available from the publisher. **2** in printed form. **out of print** no longer available from the publisher.

[from Old French *preinte* (fem.) 'pressed'] □ **printable** *adj.* **printability** *n.*

printed circuit *n.* an electric circuit with thin strips of conductor on a flat insulating sheet.

printer *n.* **1** a person who prints books, magazines, advertising matter, etc. **2** the owner of a printing business. **3** a device that prints, esp. as part of a computer system.

printhead *n.* the component in a printer (see PRINTER 3) that assembles and prints the characters on the paper.

printing *n.* **1** ▼ the production of printed books etc. **2** a single impression of a book. **3** printed letters or writing imitating them.

printing press *n.* a machine for printing from types or plates etc. ▷ PRINTING

printmaker *n.* a person who makes prints. □ **printmaking** *n.*

printout *n.* **1** output in printed form. **2** an instance of this.

prior ● *adj.* **1** earlier. **2** coming before in time, order, or importance. ● *adv.* (foll. by *to*) before (*decided prior to their arrival*). ● *n.* (*fem.* **prioress**) **1** the superior of a religious house or order. **2** (in an abbey) the officer next under the abbot (or abbess). [Latin, literally 'former, elder']

priority *n.* (*pl.* **-ies**) **1** the fact or condition of being earlier or antecedent. **2** precedence in rank etc. **3** an interest having prior claim to consideration. □ **prioritize** *v.tr.* (also **-ise**). **prioritization** *n.*

priory *n.* (*pl.* **-ies**) a monastery governed by a prior or a nunnery governed by a prioress. [from medieval Latin *prioria*, related to PRIOR]

P

PRINTING

There are four basic printing processes – intaglio, lithographic, relief, and screen – each of which can be used by a printing press to make multiple copies. In intaglio printing a design is etched or engraved into a metal plate. In lithography, the printing image on the plate is greasy and attracts ink. A relief printing plate has raised images. In screen printing, the printing surface is a mesh. Colour printing uses four plates that print a picture in black, cyan, magenta, and yellow inks to create a complete colour image.

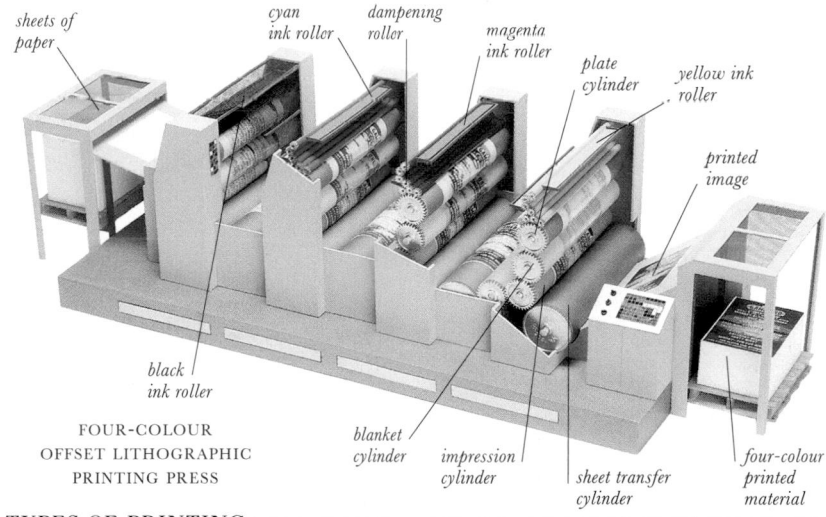

FOUR-COLOUR OFFSET LITHOGRAPHIC PRINTING PRESS

TYPES OF PRINTING

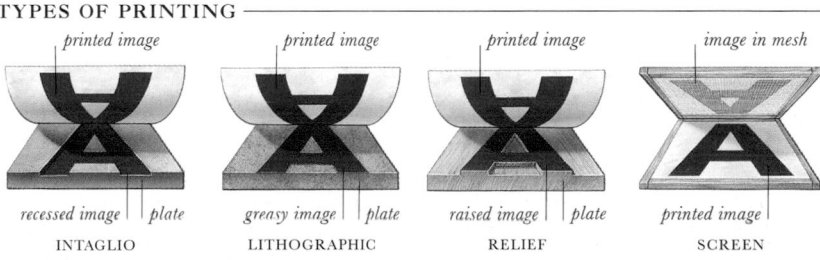

INTAGLIO   LITHOGRAPHIC   RELIEF   SCREEN

prise v.tr. (US **prize**) **1** force open or out by leverage (*prised up the lid*; *prised the box open*). **2** move or remove with difficulty (*could not be prised from his vantage point*). [based on Old French *prise* 'levering instrument']

prism n. **1** ▶ a solid figure whose two ends are equal parallel rectilinear figures, and whose sides are parallelograms. **2** a transparent body in this form, usu. triangular with refracting surfaces at an acute angle with each other, which separates white light into a spectrum of colours. [from Greek *prisma* 'thing sawn']

PRISM

prismatic adj. **1** of, like, or using a prism. **2 a** (of colours) distributed by or as if by a transparent prism. **b** (of light) displayed in the form of a spectrum. □ **prismatically** adv.

prison n. **1** a place in which a person is kept in captivity, esp. a building to which persons are legally committed while awaiting trial or for punishment; a jail. **2** custody, confinement (*in prison*). [from Latin *prehensio* 'seizure']

prison camp n. a camp for prisoners of war or of state.

prisoner n. **1** a person kept in prison. **2** (in full **prisoner at the bar**) a person in custody on a criminal charge and on trial. **3** a person or thing confined by illness, another's grasp, etc. **4** = PRISONER OF WAR. □ **take prisoner** seize and hold as a prisoner.

prisoner of conscience n. a person imprisoned by a state for holding political or religious views it does not tolerate.

prisoner of state n. (also **state prisoner**) a person confined for political reasons.

prisoner of war n. a person who is captured in war (hyphenated when *attrib.*: *prisoner-of-war camp*).

prissy adj. (**prissier**, **prissiest**) prim, prudish. □ **prissily** adv. **prissiness** n.

pristine adj. **1** in its original condition; unspoilt. **2** *disp.* spotless; fresh as if new. **3** ancient, primitive. [from Latin *pristinus* 'former']

■ **Usage** The use of *pristine* in sense 2 is considered incorrect by some people.

privacy n. **1 a** the state of being private and undisturbed. **b** a person's right to this. **2** freedom from intrusion or public attention. **3** avoidance of publicity.

private ● adj. **1** belonging to an individual; one's own; personal (*private property*). **2** confidential; not to be disclosed to others (*private talks*). **3** kept or removed from public knowledge or observation. **4 a** not open to the public. **b** for an individual's exclusive use (*private room*). **5** (of a place) secluded. **6** (of a person) not holding public office or an official position. **7** (of education or *Brit.* medical treatment) conducted outside the state system, at the individual's expense. ● n. **1** a private soldier. **2** (in *pl.*) *colloq.* the genitals. □ **in private** privately. [from Latin *privatus* 'bereaved', later 'withdrawn from public life'] □ **privately** adv.

private bill n. a legislative bill affecting an individual or corporation only.

private company n. *Brit.* a company with restricted membership and no issue of shares.

private detective n. a usu. freelance detective carrying out investigations for a private employer.

private enterprise n. **1** a business or businesses not under state control. **2** individual initiative.

privateer n. *hist.* **1** an armed vessel owned and officered by private individuals holding a government commission and authorized for war service. **2 a** a commander of such a vessel. **b** (in *pl.*) its crew. □ **privateering** n.

private eye n. *colloq.* a private detective.

private hotel n. a hotel not obliged to take all comers.

private house n. the dwelling house of a private person.

private life n. life as a private person.

private means n.pl. income from investments etc.

private member n. a member of a legislative body not holding a government office.

private member's bill n. *Brit.* a bill introduced by a private member, not part of government legislation.

private parts n.pl. the genitals.

private patient n. *Brit.* a patient treated by a doctor other than under the National Health Service.

private practice n. **1** *Brit.* medical practice that is not part of the National Health Service. **2** *US* the work of a doctor, lawyer, etc. who is self-employed.

private school n. **1** *Brit.* a school supported wholly by the payment of fees. **2** *US* a school not supported mainly by the State.

private secretary n. a secretary dealing with the personal and confidential concerns of a businessman or businesswoman.

private sector n. the part of the economy not under direct state control.

private soldier n. an ordinary soldier other than the officers (and *US* other than recruits).

private view n. the viewing of an exhibition (esp. of paintings) before it is open to the public.

privation n. lack of the comforts or necessities of life (*suffered many privations*). [from Latin *privatio*, related to PRIVATE]

privative adj. **1** consisting in or marked by the loss or removal or absence of some quality or attribute. **2** (of a term) denoting the absence of a quality etc. [from Latin *privativus*]

privatize v.tr. (also **-ise**) assign (a business etc.) to private as distinct from state control or ownership. □ **privatization** n. **privatizer** n.

privet n. ▼ any partly evergreen shrub of the genus *Ligustrum*, much used for hedges. [16th-century coinage]

PRIVET: CHINESE PRIVET
(*Ligustrum sinense*)

privilege ● n. **1 a** a right, advantage, or immunity, belonging to a person, class, or office. **b** the freedom of members of a legislative assembly when speaking at its meetings. **2** a special benefit or honour (*it is a privilege to meet you*). ● v.tr. **1** invest with a privilege. **2** (foll. by *to* + infin.) allow (a person) as a privilege (to do something). [from Latin *privilegium* 'bill or law affecting an individual'] □ **privileged** adj.

privy ● adj. **1** (foll. by *to*) sharing in the secret of (a person's plans etc.). **2** *archaic* hidden, secret. ● n. (*pl.* **-ies**) *US* or *archaic* a lavatory, esp. an outside one. [from Latin *privatus* 'withdrawn from public life'] □ **privily** adv.

Privy Council n. a body of advisers appointed by a sovereign or a Governor-General (now chiefly on

an honorary basis and including present and former government ministers etc.).

privy counsellor n. (also **privy councillor**) a private adviser, esp. a member of a Privy Council.

privy purse n. *Brit.* **1** an allowance from the public revenue for the monarch's private expenses. **2** the keeper of this.

prize[1] ● n. **1** something that can be won in a competition or lottery etc. **2** a reward given as a symbol of victory or superiority. **3** something striven for or worth striving for (*missed all the great prizes of life*). **4** (*attrib.*) **a** to which a prize is awarded (*a prize bull*; *a prize poem*). **b** excellent of its kind. ● v.tr. value highly (*a much prized possession*). [n.: Middle English variant of PRICE; v.: from Old French *preisier* 'to praise']

prize[2] n. a ship or property captured in naval warfare. [based on Latin *prehensus* 'seized']

prize[3] *US* var. of PRISE.

prizefight n. a boxing match fought for prize money. □ **prizefighter** n.

prize-giving n. *Brit.* an award of prizes, esp. formally at a school etc.

prize money n. money offered as a prize.

prizewinner n. a winner of a prize. □ **prizewinning** adj.

PRO abbr. **1** Public Record Office. **2** public relations officer.

pro[1] *colloq.* ● n. (*pl.* **-os**) a professional. ● adj. professional.

pro[2] ● adj. (of an argument or reason) for; in favour. ● n. (*pl.* **-os**) a reason or argument for or in favour. ● prep. & adv. in favour of (cf. CON[2]). [Latin, literally 'for, on behalf of']

pro- prefix **1** favouring or supporting (*pro-government*). **2** acting as a substitute or deputy for (*proconsul*). **3** forwards (*produce*). **4** forwards and downwards (*prostrate*). **5** onwards (*progress*). **6** in front of (*protect*).

proactive adj. creating or controlling a situation by taking the initiative. □ **proactively** adv. **proactivity** n.

pro-am ● adj. involving professionals and amateurs. ● n. a pro-am event.

probabilistic adj. relating to probability; involving chance variation.

probability n. (*pl.* **-ies**) **1** the state or condition of being probable. **2** the likelihood of something happening. **3** a probable or most probable event (*the probability is that they will come*). **4** *Math.* the extent to which an event is likely to occur, measured by the ratio of the cases of or conducive to such an occurrence to the whole number of cases possible. □ **in all probability** most probably. [from Latin *probabilitas*]

probable ● adj. that may be expected to happen or prove true; likely (*the probable explanation*; *it is probable that they forgot*). ● n. a probable candidate, member of a team, etc. [from Latin *probabilis*] □ **probably** adv.

probate n. **1** the official proving of a will. **2** a verified copy of a will with a certificate as handed to the executors. [from Latin *probatum* '(thing) proved']

probation n. **1** *Law* a system of supervising and monitoring the behaviour of offenders. **2** a process or period of testing the character or abilities of a person in a certain role, esp. of a new employee. □ **on probation** undergoing probation. [from Latin *probatio*] □ **probationary** adj.

probationer n. **1** a person on probation, e.g. a newly appointed nurse, teacher, etc. **2** an offender on probation.

probation officer n. an official supervising offenders on probation.

probative adj. affording proof.

probe ● n. **1** a penetrating investigation. **2** any small device, esp. an electrode, for measuring, testing, etc. **3** a blunt-ended surgical instrument for exploring a wound etc. **4** (in full **space probe**) an unmanned exploratory spacecraft transmitting information about its environment. ▷ SPACECRAFT.

P

● *v.tr.* **1** examine or enquire into closely. **2** explore (a wound or part of the body) with a probe. **3** penetrate with a sharp instrument. [from Latin *probare* 'to test'] □ **prober** *n.*

probity *n.* uprightness, honesty. [based on Latin *probus* 'good']

problem *n.* **1** a doubtful or difficult matter requiring a solution (*how to prevent it is a problem; the problem of ventilation*). **2** something hard to understand or accomplish. **3** (*attrib.*) causing problems (*problem child*). **4** *Physics & Math.* an inquiry starting from given conditions to investigate or demonstrate a fact, result, or law. **5 a** (in various games, esp. chess) an arrangement of men, cards, etc., in which the solver has to achieve a specified result. **b** a puzzle or question for solution. [from Greek *problēma*]

problematic *adj.* (also **problematical**) **1** attended by difficulty. **2** doubtful or questionable. □ **problematically** *adv.*

problematize *v.tr.* (also **-ise**) make into or regard as a problem requiring a solution. □ **problematization** *n.*

proboscidean (also **proboscidian**) ● *adj.* **1** having a proboscis. **2** of or like a proboscis. **3** of the mammalian order Proboscidea, including elephants and their extinct relatives. ▷ ELEPHANT, MAMMOTH. ● *n.* a mammal of this order. [modern Latin *Proboscidea* (as PROBOSCIS)]

proboscis /prŏ-**boss**-iss/ *n.* (*pl.* **probosces** /-seez/ or **-scides** /-si-deez/ or **-scises**) **1** the long flexible trunk or snout of some mammals, e.g. an elephant or tapir. ▷ ELEPHANT. **2** ▼ the elongated mouthparts of some insects. ▷ BUTTERFLY, HOUSEFLY. **3** the sucking organ in some worms. **4** *joc.* the human nose. [from Greek *proboskis*]

moth

flower

proboscis

PROBOSCIS:
DARWIN'S HAWK-MOTH
USING ITS PROBOSCIS
TO DRINK NECTAR

proboscis monkey *n.* a monkey, *Nasalis larvatus*, native to Borneo, the male of which has a large pendulous nose. ▷ PRIMATE

procedure *n.* **1** a way of proceeding, esp. a mode of conducting business or a legal action. **2** a mode of performing a task. **3** a series of actions conducted in a certain order or manner. **4** a proceeding. **5** *Computing* = SUBROUTINE. [from French *procédure*] □ **procedural** *adj.* **procedurally** *adv.*

proceed *v.intr.* **1** go forward or on further; make one's way. **2** continue; go on with an activity (*proceeded with their work; proceeded to tell the whole story*). **3** (of an action) be carried on or continued (*the case will now proceed*). **4** adopt a course of action (*how shall we proceed?*). **5** go on to say. **6** (foll. by *against*) start a lawsuit (against a person). **7** come forth or originate (*shouts proceeded from the bedroom*). [from Latin *procedere*]

proceeding *n.* **1** an action or piece of conduct (*a high-handed proceeding*). **2** (in *pl.*) (in full **legal proceedings**) a lawsuit. **3** (in *pl.*) a published report of discussions or a conference.

proceeds *n.pl.* money produced by a transaction or other undertaking. [pl. of obsolete noun *proceed*]

process¹ ● *n.* **1** a course of action or a procedure, esp. a series of stages in manufacture or some other operation. **2 a** the progress or course of something (*in process of construction*). **b** the course of becoming, happening, etc. (*regeneration is in process*). **3** a natural

or involuntary operation or series of changes (*the process of growing old*). **4** an action at law; a summons or writ. **5** *Anat., Zool., & Bot.* a natural appendage or outgrowth on an organism. ● *v.tr.* **1** deal with by a particular process. **2** treat (food, esp. to prevent decay) (*processed cheese*). **3** *Computing* operate on (data) by means of a program. □ **in process of time** as time goes on. [from Latin *processus* 'progress, process']

process² *v.intr.* walk in procession. [back-formation from PROCESSION]

procession *n.* **1** a number of people or vehicles etc. moving forward in orderly succession, esp. at a ceremony, demonstration, or festivity. **2** the movement of such a group (*go in procession*). [from Latin *processio*, related to PROCEED]

processional ● *adj.* **1** of or relating to processions. **2** used, carried, or sung in processions. ● *n. Eccl.* a processional hymn.

processor *n.* a machine that processes things, esp.: **1** = CENTRAL PROCESSOR (see CENTRAL PROCESSING UNIT). **2** = FOOD PROCESSOR.

pro-choice *adj.* favouring the right of a woman to choose to have an abortion.

proclaim *v.tr.* **1** (often foll. by *that* + clause) announce or declare publicly or officially. **2** declare (a person) to be (a king, traitor, etc.). [from Latin *proclamare* 'to cry out'] □ **proclaimer** *n.* **proclamation** *n.* **proclamatory** *adj.*

proclivity *n.* (*pl.* **-ies**) a tendency or inclination. [from Latin *proclivitas*]

procrastinate *v.intr.* defer action; be dilatory. [based on Latin *procrastinatus* 'deferred'] □ **procrastination** *n.* **procrastinator** *n.* **procrastinatory** *adj.*

■ **Usage** See Usage Note at PREVARICATE.

procreate *v.tr.* (often *absol.*) bring (offspring) into existence by the natural process of reproduction. [based on Latin *procreatus* 'begotten'] □ **procreation** *n.* **procreative** *adj.* **procreator** *n.*

Procrustean *adj.* seeking to enforce uniformity by forceful or ruthless methods. [from *Prokroustēs*, legendary Greek robber who fitted victims to a bed by stretching or mutilation]

proctor *n.* **1** *Brit.* an officer (usu. one of two) at certain universities, having mainly disciplinary functions. **2** *US* a supervisor of students in an examination etc. [Middle English syncopation of PROCURATOR] □ **proctorial** *adj.* **proctorship** *n.*

procurator *n.* an agent or proxy, esp. one who has power of attorney. □ **procuratorial** *adj.*

procurator fiscal *n.* (in Scotland) a local coroner and public prosecutor.

procure *v.tr.* **1** obtain, esp. by care or effort; acquire. **2** bring about. **3** (also *absol.*) obtain (women) for prostitution. [from Latin *procurare* 'to take care of, manage'] □ **procurable** *adj.* **procurement** *n.*

procurer *n.* (*fem.* **procuress**) a person who obtains women for prostitution.

prod ● *v.* (**prodded**, **prodding**) **1** *tr.* poke with the finger or a pointed object. **2** *tr.* stimulate or goad to action. **3** *intr.* (foll. by *at*) make a prodding motion. ● *n.* **1** a poke or thrust. **2** a stimulus to action. **3** a pointed instrument. [16th-century coinage] □ **prodder** *n.*

prodigal ● *adj.* **1** recklessly wasteful. **2** (foll. by *of*) lavish. ● *n.* **1** a prodigal person. **2** (in full **prodigal son**) a repentant wastrel, returned wanderer, etc. [from Latin *prodigus* 'lavish'] □ **prodigality** *n.* **prodigally** *adv.*

prodigious *adj.* **1** marvellous or amazing. **2** enormous. **3** abnormal. [from Latin *prodigiosus*, related to PRODIGY] □ **prodigiously** *adv.* **prodigiousness** *n.*

prodigy *n.* (*pl.* **-ies**) **1** a person endowed with exceptional qualities or abilities, esp. a precocious child. **2** a marvellous, esp. extraordinary, thing. [from Latin *prodigium* 'portent']

produce ● *v.tr.* /prŏ-**dewss**/ **1** bring forward for consideration, inspection, or use (*will produce evidence*). **2** manufacture (goods) from raw materials etc. **3** bear or yield (offspring, fruit, etc.). **4** cause or bring about (a reaction, sensation, etc.). **5** *Geom.* extend or continue (a line). **6** supervise the making of (a film, broadcast, record, etc.). ● *n.* /**prod**-yooss/ **1** what is produced, esp. agricultural and natural products collectively (*dairy produce*). **2** (often foll. by *of*) a result (of labour, efforts, etc.). [from Latin *producere*] □ **producible** *adj.* **producibility** *n.*

producer *n.* **1 a** *Econ.* a person who produces goods or commodities. **b** a person or thing which produces something or someone. **2** a person generally responsible for the production of a film or play (apart from the direction of the acting) or of a broadcast programme, record, etc.

product *n.* **1** a thing or substance produced by natural process or manufacture. **2** a result (*the product of their labours*). **3** *Math.* a quantity obtained by multiplying quantities together. [from Latin *productum* 'thing) produced']

production *n.* **1** the act or an instance of producing; the process of being produced. **2** a total yield. **3 a** the process or administrative management of making a film, play, record, etc. **b** a film, play, record, etc., produced. □ **productional** *adj.*

production line *n.* a systematized sequence of operations involved in producing a commodity.

productive *adj.* **1** of or engaged in the production of goods. **2** producing much. **3** *Econ.* producing commodities of exchangeable value (*productive labour*). **4** (foll. by *of*) producing or giving rise to (*productive of great annoyance*). □ **productively** *adv.* **productiveness** *n.*

productivity *n.* **1** the capacity to produce; the state of being productive. **2** the effectiveness of productive effort, esp. in industry.

Prof. *abbr.* Professor.

prof *n. colloq.* a professor.

profane ● *adj.* **1** not sacred or biblical; secular. **2 a** irreverent, blasphemous. **b** (of language) blasphemous or obscene. **3** (of a rite etc.) heathen. ● *v.tr.* **1** treat (a sacred thing) with irreverence or disregard. **2** violate or sully (what is entitled to respect). [from Latin *profanus* 'before (i.e. outside) the temple'] □ **profanation** *n.* **profanely** *adv.* **profaneness** *n.* **profaner** *n.*

profanity *n.* (*pl.* **-ies**) **1** a profane act. **2 a** profane language. **b** an oath, a swear word.

profess *v.tr.* **1** claim openly to have (a quality or feeling). **2** (foll. by *to* + infin.) pretend. **3** (often foll. by *that* + clause; also *refl.*) declare (*profess ignorance; professed herself satisfied*). **4** affirm one's faith in or allegiance to. [based on Latin *professus* 'declared publicly']

professed *adj.* **1** self-acknowledged (*a professed Christian*). **2** alleged, ostensible. **3** (of a monk or nun) having taken the vows of a religious order. □ **professedly** *adv.* (in senses 1, 2).

profession *n.* **1** a vocation or calling, esp. one that involves some branch of advanced learning or science (*the medical profession*). **2** a body of people engaged in a profession. **3** a declaration or avowal. **4** a declaration of belief in a religion. □ **professionless** *adj.*

professional ● *adj.* **1** of or belonging to or connected with a profession. **2 a** having or showing the skill of a professional; competent. **b** worthy of a professional (*professional conduct*). **3** engaged in a specified activity as one's main paid occupation (*a professional boxer*). **4** *derog.* engaged in a specified habitual activity regarded with disfavour (*a professional agitator*). ● *n.* a professional person. □ **professionally** *adv.*

professional foul *n. Brit.* a deliberate foul in football etc., esp. to prevent an opponent from scoring.

professionalism *n.* the qualities or typical features of a profession or of professionals, esp. competence, skill, etc.

P

professionalize *v.tr.* (also **-ise**) make (an occupation, activity, etc.) professional. □ **professionalization** *n.*

professor *n.* **1 a** (often as a title) a university academic of the highest rank; the holder of a university chair. **b** *US* a university teacher. **2** a person who professes a religion. [from Latin] □ **professorial** *adj.* **professorially** *adv.* **professoriate** *n.* **professorship** *n.*

proffer *v.tr.* offer (a gift, services, a hand, etc.). [from Old French *proffrir*]

proficient ● *adj.* (often foll. by *in*, *at*) adept, expert. ● *n.* a person who is proficient. [from Latin *proficient-* 'profiting'] □ **proficiency** *n.* **proficiently** *adv.*

profile ● *n.* **1 a** an outline (esp. of a human face) as seen from one side. **b** a representation of this. **2** a short biographical or character sketch. ● *v.tr.* **1** represent in profile. **2** give a profile to. □ **in profile** as seen from one side. **keep a low profile** remain inconspicuous. [from obsolete Italian *profilo* (n.), *profilare* (v.)] □ **profiler** *n.*

profit ● *n.* **1** an advantage or benefit. **2** financial gain; excess of returns over outlay. ● *v.* (**profited**, **profiting**) **1** *tr.* (also *absol.*) be beneficial to. **2** *intr.* obtain an advantage or benefit (*profited by the experience*). □ **at a profit** with financial gain. [from Latin *profectus* 'progress, profit'] □ **profitless** *adj.*

profitable *adj.* **1** yielding profit. **2** beneficial; useful. □ **profitability** *n.* **profitableness** *n.* **profitably** *adv.*

profit and loss account *n.* an account to which incomes and gains are credited and expenses and losses debited, so as to show the net profit or loss over a given period.

profiteer ● *v.intr.* make or seek to make excessive profits, esp. illegally or in black market conditions. ● *n.* a person who profiteers.

profiterole *n.* a small hollow case of choux pastry usu. filled with cream and covered with chocolate sauce. [French, literally 'little profit']

profit margin *n.* the profit remaining in a business after costs have been deducted.

profit-sharing *n.* the sharing of profits esp. between employer and employees.

profit-taking *n.* the sale of shares etc. at a time when profit will accrue.

profligate ● *adj.* **1** licentious; dissolute. **2** recklessly extravagant. ● *n.* a profligate person. [from Latin *profligatus* 'dissolute'] □ **profligacy** *n.* **profligately** *adv.*

pro forma ● *adv. & adj.* as or being a matter of form. ● *n.* (in full **pro forma invoice**) an invoice sent in advance of goods supplied. [Latin]

profound *adj.* (**profounder**, **profoundest**) **1 a** having or showing great knowledge or insight (*a profound treatise*). **b** demanding deep study or thought (*profound doctrines*). **2** (of a state or quality) deep, intense, unqualified (*a profound sleep*; *profound indifference*). **3** at or extending to a great depth (*profound crevasses*). **4** (of a sigh) deep-drawn. [from Latin *profundus* 'deep'] □ **profoundly** *adv.* **profoundness** *n.* **profundity** *n.* (*pl.* **-ies**)

profuse *adj.* **1** (often foll. by *in*) lavish; extravagant. **2** (of a thing) plentiful; abundant (*profuse bleeding*; *a profuse variety*). [from Latin *profusus* 'poured forth'] □ **profusely** *adv.* **profuseness** *n.* **profusion** *n.*

prog *n. slang* a television or radio programme.

progenitor *n.* **1** the ancestor of a person, animal, or plant. **2** a political or intellectual predecessor. [Latin] □ **progenitorial** *adj.*

progeny *n.* **1** the offspring of a person or other organism. **2** a descendant or descendants. [from Latin *progenies*]

progesterone *n.* a steroid hormone released by the corpus luteum which stimulates the preparation of the uterus for pregnancy (see also PROGESTOGEN). [from *progest*in + lute*osterone*]

progestogen *n.* **1** any of a group of steroid hormones (including progesterone) that maintain pregnancy and prevent further ovulation during it. **2** a similar hormone produced synthetically.

prognosis *n.* (*pl.* **prognoses**) **1** a forecast; a prognostication. **2** a forecast of the course of a disease. [Late Latin, from Greek]

prognostic *adj.* foretelling; predictive (*prognostic of a good result*). [from Greek *prognōstikon*] □ **prognostically** *adv.*

prognosticate *v.tr.* **1** (often foll. by *that* + clause) foretell; foresee; prophesy. **2** (of a thing) betoken; indicate (future events etc.). [based on medieval Latin *prognosticatus* 'known beforehand'] □ **prognostication** *n.* **prognosticator** *n.*

programme (*US & Austral.* **program**) ● *n.* **1** a usu. printed list of a series of events, performers, etc. at a public function etc. **2** a radio or television broadcast. **3** a plan of future events (*the programme is dinner and then a show*). **4** a course or series of studies, lectures, etc.; a syllabus. **5** (usu. **program**) a series of coded instructions to control the operation of a computer or other machine. ● *v.tr.* (**programmed**, **programming**) **1** make a programme or definite plan of. **2** (usu. **program**) **a** provide (a computer etc.) with coded instructions for the automatic performance of a particular task. **b** train to behave in a predetermined way. [from Greek *programma*] □ **programmable** *adj.* **programmability** *n.* **programmatic** *adj.* **programmatically** *adv.* **programmer** *n.*

programme music *n.* a piece of music intended to tell a story, evoke images, etc.

progress ● *n.* /**proh**-gress/ **1** forward or onward movement towards a destination. **2** advance or development; improvement (*has made little progress*; *the progress of civilization*). **3** *Brit. archaic* a state journey or official tour, esp. by royalty. ● *v.* /pro̅-**gress**/ **1** *intr.* move or be moved forward or onward; continue (*the argument is progressing*). **2** *intr.* advance or develop; improve (*science progresses*). **3** *tr.* cause (work etc.) to make regular progress. □ **in progress** in the course of developing; going on. [from Latin *progressus* 'progressed'; *v.*: readopted from US after becoming obsolete (17th c.) in British use]

progress-chaser *n. Brit.* a person employed to check the regular progress of manufacturing work.

progression *n.* **1** the act or an instance of progressing (*a mode of progression*). **2** a succession; a series. **3** *Math.* **a** = ARITHMETIC PROGRESSION. **b** = GEOMETRIC PROGRESSION. □ **progressional** *adj.*

progressive ● *adj.* **1** moving forward (*progressive motion*). **2** proceeding step by step; cumulative (*progressive drug use*). **3 a** (of a political party, government, etc.) favouring or implementing rapid progress or social reform. **b** modern; efficient (*this is a progressive company*). **4** (of disease, violence, etc.) increasing in severity or extent. **5** (of taxation) at rates increasing with the sum taxed. **6** (of a card game, dance, etc.) with periodic changes of partners. **7** *Gram.* (of an aspect) expressing an action in progress, e.g. *am writing*, *was writing*. **8** (of education) informal and without strict discipline, stressing individual needs. ● *n.* (also **Progressive**) an advocate of progressive political policies or social reform. □ **progressively** *adv.* **progressiveness** *n.* **progressivism** *n.* **progressivist** *n. & adj.*

progress report *n.* an account of progress made.

prohibit *v.tr.* (**prohibited**, **prohibiting**) (often foll. by *from* + verbal noun) **1** forbid, esp. by authority. **2** prevent. [based on Latin *prohibitus* 'held back'] □ **prohibitory** *adj.*

prohibition *n.* **1** the act or an instance of forbidding; a state of being forbidden. **2** *Law* an edict or order that forbids. **3** (usu. **Prohibition**) the prevention by law of the manufacture and sale of alcohol, esp. in the US (1920–33). □ **prohibitionist** *n.*

prohibitive *adj.* **1** prohibiting. **2** (of prices, taxes, etc.) so high as to prevent purchase, use, abuse, etc. □ **prohibitively** *adv.*

project ● *n.* /**proj**-ekt/ **1** a plan; a scheme. **2** a planned undertaking. **3** a usu. long-term task undertaken by a student to be submitted for assessment. ● *v.* /pro̅-**jekt**/ **1** *tr.* plan or contrive (a course of action, scheme, etc.). **2** *intr.* protrude; jut out. **3** *tr.* throw; cast; impel (*projected the stone into the water*). **4** *tr.* extrapolate (results etc.) to a future time; forecast (*I project that we shall produce two million next year*). **5** *tr.* cause (light, shadow, images, etc.) to fall on a surface, screen, etc. **6** *tr.* cause (a sound, esp. the voice) to be heard at a distance. **7** *tr.* (often *refl.* or *absol.*) express or promote (oneself or a positive image) forcefully or effectively. **8** *tr.* make a projection of (the Earth, sky, etc.). **9** *tr. Psychol.* **a** (also *absol.*) attribute (an emotion etc.) to an external object or person, esp. unconsciously. **b** (*refl.*) project (oneself) into another's feelings, the future, etc. [from Latin *projectum* '(thing) thrown forth']

PROJECTOR

Inside a film projector, light from a lamp is condensed into a strong beam. The beam shines through a rotating shutter on to a moving strip of film. The shutter lets light through only when each picture on the film is in the right position. The images are flashed on to a screen in such rapid succession that the picture appears to be moving continuously.

feed spool

image on screen

film

lamp

mirror reflects light

shutter

lens

fan cooler

condenser lens

claw moves film

take-up spool

reel

FILM PROJECTOR IN OPERATION

P

projectile ● *n.* **1** a missile, esp. fired by a rocket. **2** a bullet, shell, etc. fired from a gun. **3** any object thrown as a weapon. ● *adj.* **1** capable of being projected by force, esp. from a gun. **2** projecting or impelling.

projection *n.* **1** the act or an instance of projecting; the process of being projected. **2** a thing that projects or obtrudes. **3** the presentation of an image etc. on a surface or screen. **4** a forecast or estimate based on present trends. **5 a** a mental image or preoccupation viewed as an objective reality. **b** the unconscious transfer of one's own impressions or feelings to external objects or persons. **6** the representation on a plane surface of any part of the surface of the Earth or a celestial sphere. ▷ AZIMUTHAL PROJECTION, MERCATOR PROJECTION. □ **projectionist** *n.* (in sense 3).

projector *n.* ▼ an apparatus for projecting slides or film on to a screen.

prokaryote *n.* (also **procaryote**) a single-celled organism which has neither a distinct nucleus with a membrane nor other specialized organelles, e.g. a bacterium, a blue-green alga (cf. EUKARYOTE). □ **prokaryotic** *adj.*

prolactin *n.* a hormone released from the anterior pituitary gland that stimulates milk production after childbirth. [based on *lactation* (LACTATE[1])]

prolapse ● *n.* (also **prolapsus**) **1** the forward or downward displacement of a part or organ. **2** the prolapsed part or organ, esp. the womb or rectum. ● *v.intr.* undergo prolapse. [from Latin *prolapsus* 'slipped forwards']

prolate *adj. Geom.* (of a spheroid) lengthened in the direction of a polar diameter (cf. OBLATE[2]). [from Latin *prolatus* 'prolonged'] □ **prolately** *adv.*

prole *derog. colloq.* ● *adj.* proletarian. ● *n.* a proletarian.

prolegomenon /proh-li-**gom**-i-nŏn/ *n.* (*pl.* **prolegomena**) (usu. in *pl.*) an esp. critical or discursive introduction or preface to a book etc. [Greek, literally 'being said beforehand']

proletarian ● *adj.* of or concerning the proletariat. ● *n.* a member of the proletariat. [from Latin *proletarius*, a person who served the State with offspring (*proles*), not property] □ **proletarianism** *n.* **proletarianize** *v.tr.* (also **-ise**).

proletariat *n.* **1 a** *Econ.* wage earners collectively. **b** esp. *derog.* the lowest class of the community, esp. considered uncultured. **2** *Rom.Hist.* the lowest class of citizens. [from French, related to PROLETARIAN]

pro-life *adj.* in favour of preserving life, esp. in opposing abortion.

proliferate *v.* **1** *intr.* reproduce; increase rapidly in numbers. **2** *tr.* produce (cells etc.) rapidly. [based on Latin *proles* 'offspring'] □ **proliferation** *n.* **proliferative** *adj.* **proliferator** *n.*

prolific *adj.* **1** producing many offspring or much output. **2** (often foll. by *in*) abounding, copious. [from medieval Latin *prolificus*] □ **prolificacy** *n.* **prolifically** *adv.*

prolix *adj.* (of speech, writing, etc.) lengthy; tedious. [from Latin *prolixus* 'poured forth, extended'] □ **prolixity** *n.* **prolixly** *adv.*

prologue ● *n.* **1 a** a preliminary speech, poem, etc., esp. introducing a play (cf. EPILOGUE 2). **b** the actor speaking the prologue. **2** (usu. foll. by *to*) any introductory act or event. ● *v.tr.* (**prologues**, **prologued**, **prologuing**) introduce with or provide with a prologue. [from Greek *prologos*]

prolong *v.tr.* **1** extend (an action, condition, etc.) in time or space. **2** (as **prolonged** *adj.*) lengthy, esp. tediously so. [from Late Latin *prolongare*] □ **prolongation** *n.*

prom *n. colloq.* **1** *Brit.* = PROMENADE *n.* 1. **2** *Brit.* = PROMENADE CONCERT. **3** *US* = PROMENADE *n.* 3.

promenade /prom-ĕ-**nahd**/ ● *n.* **1** a paved public walk, esp. *Brit.* along the seafront at a resort. **2** a walk, ride, or drive, taken esp. for display, leisure, etc. **3** *US* a school or university dance, esp. for one class. ● *v.* **1** *intr.* make a promenade. **2** *tr.* lead (a person etc.) about a place esp. for display. **3** *tr.* make a promenade through (a place). [French]

promenade concert *n.* esp. *Brit.* a concert of usu. classical music at which many of the audience stand.

promenade deck *n.* an upper deck on a passenger ship where passengers may promenade.

promenader *n.* **1** a person who promenades. **2** *Brit.* a person who attends a promenade concert.

Promethean *adj.* daring or inventive. [based on *Prometheus*, who in Greek myth stole fire from the gods for human use]

promethium *n. Chem.* a radioactive metallic element of the lanthanide series occurring in nuclear-waste material. [based on *Prometheus* (see PROMETHEAN)]

prominence *n.* **1** the state of being prominent. **2** a prominent thing, esp. a jutting outcrop, mountain, etc.

prominent *adj.* **1** jutting out; projecting. **2** conspicuous. **3** distinguished; important. [from Latin *prominent-* 'jutting out'] □ **prominently** *adv.*

promiscuous *adj.* **1** having frequent and diverse sexual relationships. **2** mixed and indiscriminate (*promiscuous hospitality*). **3** *colloq.* carelessly irregular; casual. [from Latin *promiscuus*] □ **promiscuity** *n.* **promiscuously** *adv.*

promise ● *n.* **1** an assurance that one will or will not undertake a certain action, behaviour, etc. (*a promise of help; gave a promise to be generous*). **2** a sign or signs of future achievements, good results, etc. (*a writer of great promise*). ● *v.tr.* **1** (usu. foll. by *to* + infin., or *that* + clause; also *absol.*) make (a person) a promise, esp. to do, give, or procure (a thing) (*I promise you a fair hearing*). **2 a** afford expectations of (*such a leaden sky promises rain*). **b** (foll. by *to* + infin.) seem likely to (*is promising to rain*). **3** *colloq.* assure, confirm (*I promise you, it will not be easy*). □ **promise oneself** look forward to (a pleasant time etc.). **promise well** (or **ill** etc.) hold out good (or bad etc.) prospects. [from Latin *promissum* '(thing) promised'] □ **promisee** *n.* esp. *Law.* **promisor** *n.* esp. *Law.*

promised land *n.* (prec. by *the*) **1** *Bibl.* Canaan (originally west of the River Jordan; Gen. 12:7 etc.). **2 a** any place where happiness is expected, esp. heaven. **b** any coveted situation (*a promised land of economic freedom*).

promising *adj.* likely to turn out well (*a promising start*). □ **promisingly** *adv.*

promissory *adj.* conveying or implying a promise. [from medieval Latin *promissorius*]

promissory note *n.* a signed document containing a written promise to pay a stated sum.

promo *colloq.* ● *n.* (*pl.* **-os**) **1** publicity, advertising. **2** a trailer for a television programme. ● *adj.* promotional.

promontory *n.* (*pl.* **-ies**) a point of high land jutting out into the sea etc.; a headland. [from medieval Latin *promontorium*]

promote *v.tr.* **1** (often foll. by *to*) **a** advance or raise (a person) to a higher office, rank, etc. (*was promoted to captain*). **b** transfer (a sports team) to a higher division of a league etc. **2** help forward; support actively (a cause, process, desired result, etc.). **3** publicize and sell (a product). [based on Latin *promotus* 'moved forward'] □ **promotable** *adj.* **promotability** *n.* **promotion** *n.* **promotional** *adj.* **promotive** *adj.*

promoter *n.* **1** a person who promotes. **2** a person who finances, organizes, etc. a sporting event, theatrical production, etc.

prompt ● *adj.* acting, made, or done with alacrity. ● *adv. Brit.* punctually (*at six o'clock prompt*). ● *v.tr.* **1** (usu. foll. by *to*, or *to* + infin.) incite; urge (*prompted them to action*). **2 a** (also *absol.*) supply a forgotten word, sentence, etc., to (an actor, reciter, etc.). **b** assist (a hesitating speaker) with a suggestion. **3** give rise to; inspire (a thought, action, etc.). ● *n.* **1** an act of prompting. **2** something spoken to help the memory of an actor etc. **3** = PROMPTER. **4** *Computing* an indication or sign on a VDU screen to show that the system is waiting for input. [from Latin *promptus* 'produced'] □ **prompting** *n.* **promptitude** *n.* **promptly** *adv.* **promptness** *n.*

prompt book *n.* a copy of a play for a prompter's use.

prompter *n. Theatr.* a person who prompts actors.

promulgate *v.tr.* **1** make known to the public; disseminate. **2** proclaim (a decree, news, etc.). [based on Latin *promulgatus* 'published'] □ **promulgation** *n.* **promulgator** *n.*

prone *adj.* **1 a** lying face downwards (cf. SUPINE 1). **b** lying flat; prostrate. **c** having the front part downwards, esp. the palm of the hand. **2** (usu. foll. by *to*, or *to* + infin.) disposed or liable (*is prone to bite his nails*). **3** (usu. in *comb.*) more than usually likely to suffer (*accident-prone*). [from Latin *pronus*] □ **proneness** *n.*

■ **Usage** *Prone* in sense 2 means the same as *liable*, but is usually used with a person as its subject.

prong ● *n.* each of two or more projecting pointed parts at the end of a fork etc. ▷ TUNING FORK. ● *v.tr.* **1** pierce or stab with a fork. **2** turn up (soil) with a fork. [Middle English] □ **pronged** *adj.* (also in *comb.*).

pronghorn *n.* ► a N. American deerlike ruminant, *Antilocapra americana*, the male of which has horns with forward-pointing prongs

PRONGHORN
(*Antilocapra americana*)

pronominal *adj.* of, relating to, or serving as, a pronoun. [based on Latin *pronomen* 'pronoun'] □ **pronominalize** *v.tr.* (also **-ise**). **pronominally** *adv.*

pronoun *n.* a word used instead of a noun already mentioned or known, esp. to avoid repetition (e.g. *we, their, this, ourselves*)

pronounce *v.tr.* **1** (also *absol.*) utter or speak (words, sounds, etc.) in a certain way. **2 a** utter or deliver (a judgement, curse, etc.) formally or solemnly. **b** proclaim or announce officially (*I pronounce you man and wife*). **3** state or declare, as being one's opinion (*the apples were pronounced excellent*). [from Latin *pronuntiare*] □ **pronounceable** *adj.* **pronounceability** *n.* **pronouncement** *n.* **pronouncer** *n.*

P

pronounced *adj.* **1** (of a word, sound, etc.) uttered. **2** strongly marked; decided (*a pronounced limp*). □ **pronouncedly** *adv.*

pronto *adv. colloq.* promptly, quickly. [Spanish]

pronunciation *n.* **1** the way in which a word is pronounced, esp. with reference to a standard. **2** the act or an instance of pronouncing. **3** a person's way of pronouncing words etc. [from Latin *pronuntiatio*]

■ **Usage** *Pronunciation* is often pronounced with the second syllable rhyming with *bounce* instead of with *dunce*. This should be avoided.

proof ● *n.* **1** facts, evidence, argument, etc. establishing or helping to establish a fact. **2** a demonstration or act of proving (*not capable of proof; in proof of my assertion*). **3** a test or trial (*the proof of the pudding is in the eating*). **4** the standard of strength of distilled alcoholic liquors. **5** *Printing* a trial impression taken from type or film, used for making corrections before final printing. **6** a photographic print made for selection etc. **7** any of various preliminary impressions of coins struck as specimens. ● *adj.* **1** impervious to penetration, ill effects, etc. (*proof against the severest weather*). **2** (in *comb.*) able to withstand damage or destruction by a specified agent (*soundproof; childproof*). **3** being of proof alcoholic strength. ● *v.tr.* **1** make (something) proof, esp. make (fabric) waterproof. **2** make a proof of (a printed work etc.). [from Late Latin *proba*]

proof positive *n.* absolutely certain proof.

proof-read *v.tr.* (*past* and *past part.* **-read**) read (printer's proofs) and mark any errors. □ **proof-reader** *n.* **proof-reading** *n.*

proof-sheet *n.* a sheet of printer's proof.

proof spirit *n.* a mixture of alcohol and water having proof strength.

prop[1] *n.* **1** a rigid support, esp. one not an integral part of the thing supported. **2** a person who supplies assistance, comfort, etc. **3** (in full **prop forward**) *Rugby* a forward at either end of the front row of a scrum. ▷ RUGBY. ● *v.tr.* (**propped, propping**) (often foll. by *against, up,* etc.) support with or as if with a prop (*propped him against the wall; propped it up with a brick*). [Middle English]

prop[2] *n. Theatr. colloq.* = PROPERTY 3.

prop[3] *n. colloq.* a propeller.

propaganda *n.* **1** an organized programme of publicity, selected information, etc., used to propagate a doctrine, practice, etc. **2** usu. *derog.* the information, doctrines, etc., propagated in this way. [from modern Latin *congregatio de propaganda fide* 'congregation for propagation of the faith']

propagandist ● *n.* a person who spreads propaganda. ● *adj.* consisting of or spreading propaganda. □ **propagandism** *n.* **propagandistic** *adj.* **propagandistically** *adv.* **propagandize** *v.intr. & tr.* (also **-ise**).

propagate *v.tr.* **1 a** breed specimens of (a plant, animal, etc.) by natural processes from the parent stock. **b** (*refl.* or *absol.*) (of a plant, animal, etc.) reproduce itself. **2** disseminate; spread (a statement, belief, theory, etc.). **3** extend the operation of; transmit (a vibration, earthquake, etc.). [based on Latin *propagatus* '(of plants) multiplied from layers'] □ **propagation** *n.* **propagative** *adj.*

propagator *n.* **1** a person or thing that propagates. **2** ▼ a small box that can be heated, used for germinating seeds or raising seedlings.

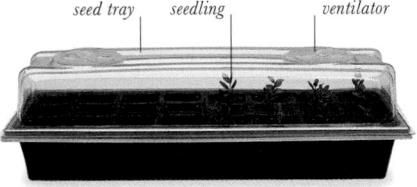

seed tray   seedling   ventilator

PROPAGATOR

propane *n.* a gaseous hydrocarbon of the alkane series used as bottled fuel. ▷ ALKANE

propanoic acid *n. Chem.* a colourless sharp-smelling liquid acid used for inhibiting the growth of mould in bread. [based on PROPANE]

propel *v.tr.* (**propelled, propelling**) **1** drive or push forward. **2** urge on; encourage. [Middle English in sense 'to expel': from Latin *propellere* 'to drive forth']

propellant *n.* **1** a thing that propels. **2** an inert compressed fluid in which the active contents of an aerosol are dispersed. **3** a substance used as rocket fuel.

propeller *n.* **1** a person or thing that propels. **2** a revolving shaft with blades, esp. for propelling a ship or aircraft (cf. *screw propeller*). ▷ AIRCRAFT, OUTBOARD, SCREW PROPELLER

propeller shaft *n. Brit.* a shaft transmitting power from an engine to a propeller or to the wheels of a vehicle.

propelling pencil *n. Brit.* a pencil with the lead advanced or retracted by twisting the outer case.

propensity *n.* (*pl.* **-ies**) an inclination or tendency (*has a propensity for wandering*). [based on Latin *propensus* 'inclined']

proper ● *adj.* **1 a** accurate, correct (*the proper sense of the word; the proper amount*). **b** fit, suitable, right (*at the proper time; do it the proper way*). **2** decent; respectable, esp. excessively so. **3** (usu. foll. by *to*) belonging or

relating exclusively or distinctively (*with the respect proper to them*). **4** (usu. placed after noun) strictly so called; real; genuine (*this is the crypt, not the cathedral proper*). **5** esp. *Brit. colloq.* thorough; complete (*had a proper row about it*). ● *adv. Brit. dial.* or *colloq.* **1** completely; very (*felt proper daft*). **2** (with reference to speech) in a genteel manner (*learn to talk proper*). [from Latin *proprius* 'one's own, special'] □ **properness** *n.*

proper fraction *n.* a fraction that is less than unity, with the numerator less than the denominator.

properly *adv.* **1** fittingly; suitably (*do it properly*). **2** accurately; correctly (*properly speaking*). **3** rightly (*he very properly refused*). **4** with decency; respectably (*behave properly*). **5** esp. *Brit. colloq.* thoroughly (*they were properly ashamed*).

proper name *n.* (also **proper noun**) *Gram.* a name used for an individual person, place, animal, country, title, etc., and spelt with a capital letter, e.g. *Jane, London, Everest.*

proper pride see PRIDE *n.* 3.

propertied *adj.* having property, esp. land.

property *n.* (*pl.* **-ies**) **1 a** something owned; a possession, esp. a house, land, etc. **b** possessions collectively, esp. real estate (*has money in property*). **2** an attribute, quality, or characteristic (*has the property of dissolving grease*). **3** a movable object used on a theatre stage, in a film, etc. [from Latin *proprietas*, related to PROPER]

property man *n.* (*fem.* **property mistress**) a man (or woman) in charge of theatrical properties.

prop forward see PROP[1] *n.* 3.

prophecy *n.* (*pl.* **-ies**) **1 a** a prophetic utterance, esp. biblical. **b** a prediction of future events (*a prophecy of massive inflation*). **2** the faculty, function, or practice of prophesying (*the gift of prophecy*). [from Greek *prophēteia*, related to PROPHET]

prophesy *v.* (**-ies, -ied**) **1** *tr.* (usu. foll. by *that, who,* etc.) foretell (an event etc.). **2** *intr.* speak as a prophet; foretell future events. [from Old French *profecier*]

prophet *n.* (*fem.* **prophetess**) **1** a teacher or interpreter of the supposed will of God. **2 a** a person who foretells events. **b** a person who advocates and speaks innovatively for a cause (*a prophet of the new order*). **3** (**the Prophet**) **a** Muhammad. **b** Joseph Smith, founder of the Mormons, or one of his successors. [from Greek *prophētēs* 'spokesman'] □ **prophethood** *n.* **prophetism** *n.*

prophetic *adj.* **1** (often foll. by *of*) containing a prediction; predicting. **2** of or concerning a prophet. □ **prophetical** *adj.* **prophetically** *adv.*

prophylactic ● *adj.* tending to prevent disease. ● *n.* **1** a preventive medicine or course of action. **2** esp. *N. Amer.* a condom. [from Greek *prophulaktikos*]

prophylaxis *n.* preventive treatment against disease. [based on Greek *phulaxis* 'act of guarding']

propinquity *n.* **1** nearness in space; proximity. **2** close kinship. **3** similarity. [from Latin *propinquitas*]

propitiate /prŏ-pish-i-ayt/ *v.tr.* appease (an offended person etc.). [based on Latin *propitiatus* 'appeased'] □ **propitiator** *n.* **propitiatory** *adj.*

propitiation /prŏ-pish-i-ay-shŏn/ *n.* **1** appeasement. **2** *Bibl.* atonement, esp. Christ's.

propitious /prŏ-pish-ŭs/ *adj.* **1** (of an omen etc.) favourable. **2** (often foll. by *for, to*) (of the weather, an occasion, etc.) suitable. **3** well disposed (*the fates were propitious*). [from Latin *propitius*] □ **propitiously** *adv.* **propitiousness** *n.*

propolis *n.* a red or brown resinous substance collected by bees from buds for use in constructing hives. [from Greek *propolis* 'suburb, bee-glue']

proponent *n.* a person advocating a motion, theory, or proposal. [from Latin *proponent-* 'placing before']

proportion ● *n.* **1 a** a comparative part or share (*a large proportion of the profits*). **b** a comparative ratio (*the proportion of births to deaths*). **2** the correct or pleasing relation of things or parts of a thing (*the*

house has fine proportions; exaggerated out of all proportion). **3** (in *pl.*) dimensions; size (*large proportions*). **4** *Math.* an equality of ratios between two pairs of quantities, e.g. 3:5 and 9:15. See also DIRECT PROPORTION, INVERSE PROPORTION. ● *v.tr.* (usu. foll. by *to*) make (a thing etc.) proportionate (*must proportion the punishment to the crime*). □ **in proportion 1** by the same factor. **2** without exaggerating (importance etc.) (*must get the facts in proportion*). [from Latin *proportio*] □ **proportioned** *adj.* (also in *comb.*).

■ **Usage** *Proportion* as a noun means 'comparative part or share' (see sense 1); it should not be used as a mere synonym for *part*.

proportional *adj.* in due proportion; comparable (*a proportional increase in the expense*). □ **proportionality** *n.* **proportionally** *adv.*

proportional representation *n.* an electoral system in which all parties gain seats in proportion to the number of votes cast for them.

proportionate *adj.* = PROPORTIONAL. □ **proportionately** *adv.*

proposal *n.* **1 a** the act or an instance of proposing something. **b** a course of action etc. so proposed (*the proposal was never carried out*). **2** an offer of marriage.

propose *v.* **1** *tr.* (also *absol.*) put forward for consideration or as a plan. **2** *tr.* (usu. foll. by *to* + infin., or verbal noun) intend; purpose (*propose to open a restaurant*). **3** *intr.* (usu. foll. by *to*) offer oneself in marriage. **4** *tr.* nominate (a person) as a member of a society, for an office, etc. **5** *tr.* offer (a person's health, a person, etc.) as a subject for a toast. [from Old French *proposer*] □ **proposer** *n.*

proposition ● *n.* **1** a statement or assertion. **2** a scheme proposed; a proposal. **3** *colloq.* a problem, opponent, prospect, etc. that is to be dealt with (*a difficult proposition*). **4** *Math.* a formal statement of a theorem or problem, often including the demonstration. **5 a** an enterprise etc. with regard to its likelihood of commercial etc. success. **b** a person regarded similarly. **6** *colloq.* a sexual proposal. ● *v.tr. colloq.* make a proposal (esp. of sexual intercourse) to. □ **propositional** *adj.*

propound *v.tr.* offer for consideration; propose. [earlier *propone*: from Latin *proponere*] □ **propounder** *n.*

proprietary *adj.* **1** of or relating to a proprietor (*proprietary rights*). **2** held in private ownership. **3** (of a product, esp. a drug or medicine) marketed under and protected by a registered trade name. [from Late Latin *proprietarius*]

proprietary name *n.* (also **proprietary term**) a name of a product etc. registered as a trade mark.

proprietor *n.* (*fem.* **proprietress**) **1** a holder of property. **2** the owner of a business etc. □ **proprietorial** *adj.* **proprietorially** *adv.* **proprietorship** *n.*

propriety *n.* (*pl.* **-ies**) **1** fitness; rightness (*doubt the propriety of refusing him*). **2** correctness of behaviour or morals (*highest standards of propriety*). **3** (in *pl.*) the details or rules of correct conduct (*must observe the proprieties*). [Middle English in sense 'ownership, peculiarity': from Old French *propriété* 'property']

propulsion *n.* the act or an instance of driving or pushing forward. [from medieval Latin *propulsio*] □ **propulsive** *adj.*

propylene *n. Chem.* a gaseous hydrocarbon of the alkene series used in the manufacture of chemicals.

pro rata ● *adj.* proportional. ● *adv.* proportionally. [Latin, literally 'according to the rate']

prorate *v.tr.* allocate or distribute pro rata. □ **proration** *n.*

prorogue /proh-rohg/ *v.* (**prorogues, prorogued, proroguing**) **1** *tr.* discontinue the meetings of (a parliament etc.) without dissolving it. **2** *intr.* (of a parliament etc.) be prorogued. [from Latin *prorogare* 'to prolong'] □ **prorogation** *n.*

prosaic *adj.* **1** like prose, lacking poetic beauty. **2** unromantic; dull; commonplace (*took a prosaic view of life*). [from Late Latin *prosaicus*] □ **prosaically** *adv.*

P

pros and cons *n.pl.* reasons or considerations for and against a proposition etc.

proscenium /prŏ-see-ni-ŭm/ *n.* (*pl.* **prosceniums** or **proscenia**) the part of a stage in front of the curtain. ▷ THEATRE. [based on Greek *skēnē* 'stage']

prosciutto /prŏ-shoo-toh/ *n.* Italian ham, esp. raw and eaten as an hors d'oeuvre. [Italian]

proscribe *v.tr.* **1** forbid, esp. by law (*proscribed drugs*). **2** reject or denounce (a practice etc.) as unwanted or dangerous. **3** esp. *hist.* outlaw (a person). [from Latin *proscribere*] □ **proscription** *n.* **proscriptive** *adj.*

■ **Usage** See Usage Note at PRESCRIBE.

prose *n.* **1** the ordinary form of the written or spoken language (opp. POETRY 2, VERSE *n.* 1a) (also *attrib.: Milton's prose works*). **2** a passage of prose, esp. for translation into a foreign language. **3 a** dull or commonplace speech, writing, etc. **b** an instance of this. [from Latin *prosa (oratio)* 'straightforward (discourse)']

prosecute *v.tr.* **1** (also *absol.*) institute legal proceedings against (a person) or with reference to (a crime, action, etc.). **2** carry on (a trade, pursuit, etc.). [based on Latin *prosecutus* 'pursued'] □ **prosecutable** *adj.*

prosecution *n.* **1 a** the institution and carrying on of (esp. criminal) legal proceedings. **b** the prosecuting party in a court case (*the prosecution denied this*). **2** the act or an instance of prosecuting (*met her in the prosecution of his hobby*).

prosecutor *n.* (*fem.* **prosecutrix**) a person who prosecutes, esp. in a criminal court. □ **prosecutorial** *adj.*

proselyte *n.* **1** a person converted, esp. recently, from one opinion, creed, party, etc., to another. **2** a convert to Judaism. [from Greek *prosēluthos* 'stranger, convert'] □ **proselytism** *n.*

proselytize *v.tr.* (also **-ise**) (also *absol.*) convert (a person) from one belief etc. to another. □ **proselytizer** *n.*

prose poem *n.* (also **prose poetry**) a piece of imaginative poetic writing in prose.

prosimian *Zool.* ● *n.* ▼ a primitive primate of the suborder Prosimii, which includes lemurs, lorises, galagos, and tarsiers. ● *adj.* of or relating to this suborder. ▷ PRIMATE

prosody *n.* **1** the theory and practice of versification. **2** the study of speech rhythms. [from Greek *prosōidia*] □ **prosodic** *adj.* **prosodist** *n.*

prospect ● *n.* /pros-pekt/ **1 a** (often in *pl.*) an expectation, esp. of success in a career etc. (*his prospects were brilliant; no prospect of success*). **b** something one has to look forward to (*don't relish the prospect of meeting him*). **2** an extensive view of landscape etc. (*a striking prospect*). **3** a possible or probable customer, subscriber, etc. ● *v.* /prŏ-spekt/ **1** intr. (usu. foll. by *for*) **a** explore a region for gold etc. **b** look out for or search for something. **2** *tr.* explore (a region) for gold etc. [from Latin *prospectus*] □ **prospector** *n.*

prospective *adj.* **1** concerned with or applying to the future (*implies a prospective obligation*) (cf. RETROSPECTIVE *adj.* 1). **2** some day to be; expected; future

(*prospective bridegroom*). [from Late Latin *prospectivus*] □ **prospectively** *adv.*

prospectus *n.* (*pl.* **prospectuses**) a printed document advertising or describing a school, commercial enterprise, forthcoming book, etc. [Latin, literally 'prospect']

prosper *v.* **1** *intr.* succeed; thrive. **2** *tr.* make successful (*Heaven prosper him*). [from Latin *prosperare*]

prosperous *adj.* **1** successful; rich (*a prosperous merchant*). **2** flourishing; thriving (*a prosperous enterprise*). □ **prosperity** *n.* **prosperously** *adv.*

prostaglandin *n. Biochem.* any of a group of cyclic fatty acids with varying hormone-like effects in mammals, including the promotion of uterine contractions. [German]

prostate *n.* (in full **prostate gland**) a gland surrounding the neck of the bladder in male mammals and releasing a fluid forming part of the semen. ▷ URINARY SYSTEM. [from Greek *prostatēs* 'one that stands before'] □ **prostatic** *adj.*

prosthesis *n.* (*pl.* **prostheses**) **1** ▼ an artificial arm, leg, etc., a false breast, tooth, etc. **2** the branch of surgery supplying and fitting prostheses. [Late Latin, from Greek] □ **prosthetic** *adj.*

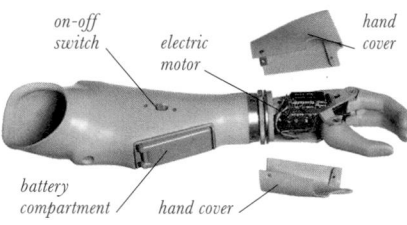

on-off switch   electric motor   hand cover

battery compartment   hand cover

PROSTHESIS: PROSTHETIC ARM

prosthetics *n.pl.* (usu. treated as *sing.*) = PROSTHESIS 2.

prostitute ● *n.* **1 a** a woman or girl who engages in sexual activity for payment. **b** (usu. **male prostitute**) a man or boy who engages in sexual activity, esp. with homosexual men, for payment. **2** a person who debases himself or herself for personal gain. ● *v.tr.* **1** (esp. *refl.*) make a prostitute of (esp. oneself). **2 a** misuse (one's talents, skills, etc.) for money. **b** offer (oneself, one's honour, etc.) for unworthy ends, esp. for money. [based on Latin *prostitutus* 'offered for sale'] □ **prostitution** *n.*

prostrate ● *adj.* **1 a** lying face downwards, esp. in submission. **b** lying horizontally. **2** overcome, esp. by grief, exhaustion, etc. (*prostrate with self-pity*). **3** *Bot.* growing along the ground. ● *v.tr.* **1** lay (a person etc.) flat on the ground. **2** (*refl.*) throw (oneself) down in submission etc. **3** (of fatigue, illness, etc.) overcome; reduce to extreme physical weakness. [from Latin *prostratus*] □ **prostration** *n.*

prosy *adj.* (**prosier**, **prosiest**) tedious; commonplace; dull (*prosy talk*). □ **prosily** *adv.*

protactinium *n. Chem.* a radioactive metallic element whose chief isotope yields actinium by decay. [German]

protagonist *n.* **1** the chief person in a drama, story, etc. **2** the leading person in a contest etc.; a principal performer. **3** (usu. foll. by *of*, *for*) *disp.* an advocate or champion of a cause etc. (*a protagonist of women's rights*). [from Greek *prōtagōnistēs*]

■ **Usage** The use of *protagonist* in sense 3 is considered incorrect in standard English. The word contains the Greek prefix *prōto-* meaning 'first', not the prefix *pro-* meaning 'in favour of'.

protean *adj.* variable, taking many forms. [from *Proteus*, Greek sea-god who could change form at will]

protect *v.tr.* **1** (often foll. by *from*, *against*) keep (a person, thing, etc.) safe; defend; guard. **2** *Econ.* shield (home industry) from competition by imposing import duties on foreign goods. [based on Latin *protectus* 'protected']

protection *n.* **1 a** the act or an instance of protecting. **b** the state of being protected; defence. **c** a

thing, person, or animal that provides protection. **2** (also **protectionism**) *Econ.* the theory or practice of protecting home industry. **3** *colloq.* **a** immunity from molestation, obtained by payment to gangsters etc. under threat of violence. **b** (in full **protection money**) the money so paid, esp. on a regular basis. **4** = SAFE CONDUCT. □ **protectionist** *n.*

protective ● *adj.* intended or intending to protect. ● *n. Brit.* something that protects, esp. a condom. □ **protectively** *adv.* **protectiveness** *n.*

protective clothing *n.* clothing worn to shield the body from dangerous substances or a hostile environment.

protective colouring *n.* colouring disguising or camouflaging a plant or animal.

protective custody *n.* the detention of a person for his or her own protection.

protector *n.* (*fem.* **protectress**) **1 a** a person who protects. **b** a guardian or patron. **2** (usu. **Protector**) *hist.* a regent in charge of a kingdom during the minority, absence, etc. of the sovereign. **3** (often in *comb.*) a thing or device that protects. [from Late Latin] □ **protectorship** *n.*

protectorate *n.* **1** a state that is controlled and protected by another. **2** (usu. **Protectorate**) *hist.* **a** the office of the protector of a kingdom or state. **b** the period of this.

protégé /prot-ĕ-zhay/ *n.* (*fem.* **protégée** *pronunc.* same) a person under the protection, patronage, tutelage, etc. of another. [French, literally 'protected']

protein *n.* **1** any of a class of nitrogenous organic compounds composed of one or more chains of amino acids and forming an essential part of all living organisms. ▷ ALGA. **2** such substances collectively, esp. as a dietary component. [based on Greek *prōteios* 'primary'] □ **proteinaceous** *adj.*

pro tem *adj.* & *adv. colloq.* = PRO TEMPORE.

pro tempore /proh tem-pŏ-ri/ *adj.* & *adv.* for the time being. [Latin]

Proterozoic *Geol.* ● *adj.* of or relating to the later part of the Precambrian era, characterized by the oldest forms of life (cf. ARCHAEAN). ● *n.* this era. [based on Greek *proteros* 'former' + *zōē* 'life']

protest ● *n.* /proh-test/ **1** a statement of dissent or disapproval. **2** (often *attrib.*) a usu. public demonstration of objection to government etc. policy (*marched in protest; protest demonstration*). ● *v.* /prŏ-test/ **1** *intr.* (usu. foll. by *against*, *at*, *about*, etc.) make a protest against an action, proposal, etc. **2** *tr.* (often foll. by *that* + clause; also *absol.*) affirm (one's innocence etc.) solemnly, esp. in reply to an accusation etc. **3** *tr. N. Amer.* object to (a decision etc.). □ **under protest** unwillingly. [from Latin *protestari*] □ **protester** *n.* **protestingly** *adv.* **protestor** *n.*

Protestant ● *n.* a member or follower of any of the western Christian Churches that are separate from the Roman Catholic Church in accordance with the principles of the Reformation. ● *adj.* of or relating to any of the Protestant Churches or their members etc. □ **Protestantism** *n.* **Protestantize** *v.tr.* & *intr.* (also **-ise**).

protestation *n.* **1** a strong affirmation. **2** a protest.

protist *n.* any primitive organism of the kingdom Protista, with both plant and animal characteristics, including protozoans and simple algae and fungi. ▷ PROTOZOAN. [from Greek *prōtista* 'very first (things)']

protium *n.* the ordinary isotope of hydrogen (cf. DEUTERIUM, TRITIUM).

proto- *comb. form* **1** original, primitive (*proto-Germanic*). **2** first, original (*prototype*). [Greek]

protocol ● *n.* **1 a** official, esp. diplomatic, formality and etiquette observed on state occasions etc. **b** the rules, formalities, etc. of any procedure, group, etc. **2** the original draft of a diplomatic document, esp. a treaty. **3** a formal statement of a transaction. ● *v.* (**protocolled**, **protocolling**) **1** *intr.* draw up a protocol or protocols. **2** *tr.* record in a protocol. [originally Scots *prothocoll*: from Greek *protokollon* 'first page, flyleaf']

P

PROTOZOAN

Most protozoans live in damp environments. They can be found in water, in the films of moisture around soil grains, and sometimes within other organisms. The majority of protozoans are solitary, but some – such as *Vorticella* – form aggregations composed of many individuals.

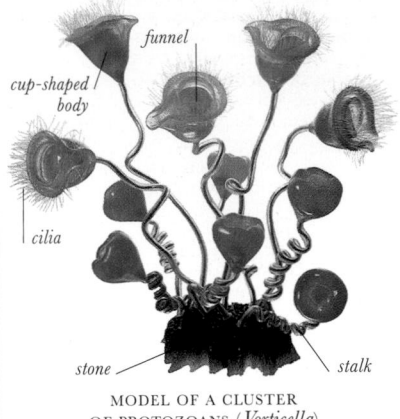

funnel

cup-shaped
body

cilia

stone   stalk

MODEL OF A CLUSTER
OF PROTOZOANS (*Vorticella*)

proton *n. Physics* a stable subatomic particle occurring in all atomic nuclei, with a positive electric charge equal in magnitude to that of an electron. ▷ ATOM. [Greek, literally 'first (thing)'] □ **protonic** *adj.*

protoplasm *n. Biol.* the material comprising the living part of a cell, consisting of a nucleus embedded in membrane-enclosed cytoplasm. [from Greek *protoplasma*] □ **protoplasmic** *adj.*

prototype *n.* **1** an original thing or person of which or whom copies, improved forms, etc. are made. **2** a trial model or preliminary version of a vehicle, machine, etc. [from Greek *prototupos*] □ **prototypal** *adj.* **prototypic** *adj.* **prototypical** *adj.* **prototypically** *adv.*

P

protozoan /proh-tŏ-zoh-ăn/ ● *n.* (also **protozoon**) (*pl.* **protozoa** or **protozoans**) ▲ a usu. unicellular and microscopic organism of the phylum or subkingdom Protozoa, e.g. an amoeba. ● *adj.* (also **protozoic**) of or relating to this group of organisms. [based on Greek *zōion* 'animal'] □ **protozoal** *adj.*

protract *v.tr.* prolong or lengthen in space or esp. time. [based on Latin *protractus* 'drawn forth'] □ **protraction** *n.*

protractor *n.* ▶ an instrument for measuring angles, usu. in the form of a graduated semicircle.

PROTRACTOR

protrude *v.* **1** *intr.* extend beyond or above a surface; project. **2** *tr.* thrust or cause to thrust out. [from Latin *protrudere*] □ **protrusible** *adj.* **protrusion** *n.* **protrusive** *adj.*

protuberant *adj.* bulging out; prominent. [from Late Latin *protuberant-* 'swelling out'] □ **protuberance** *n.*

proud *adj.* **1** feeling greatly honoured or pleased (*am proud to know him*). **2 a** (often foll. by *of*) haughty; arrogant (*proud of his ancient name*). **b** (often in *comb.*) having a proper pride; satisfied (*house-proud; proud of a job well done*). **3 a** (of an occasion etc.) justly arousing pride (*a proud day for us*). **b** (of an action etc.) showing justified pride (*a proud wave of the hand*). **4** (of a thing) imposing; splendid. **5** *Brit.* slightly projecting from a surface etc. (*the nail stood proud of*

the *plank*). □ **do proud** *colloq.* **1** treat with lavish generosity or honour (*they did us proud on our anniversary*). **2** (*refl.*) act honourably or worthily. [based on Latin *prodesse* 'to be of value'] □ **proudly** *adv.*

prove *v.* (*past part.* **proved** or **proven**) **1** *tr.* (often foll. by *that* + clause) demonstrate the truth of by evidence or argument. **2** *intr.* **a** (usu. foll. by *to* + infin.) be found (*it proved to be untrue*). **b** emerge incontrovertibly as (*will prove the winner*). **3** *tr.* establish the genuineness and validity of (a will). **4** *intr.* (of dough) rise in breadmaking. **5** *tr. archaic* test the qualities of; try. □ **not proven** (in Scottish Law) a verdict that there is insufficient evidence to establish guilt or innocence. **prove oneself** show one's abilities, courage, etc. [from Latin *probare* 'to test, approve, demonstrate'] □ **provable** *adj.* **provability** *n.* **provably** *adv.*

■ **Usage** The use of *proven* as the past participle is uncommon except in certain expressions, such as *of proven ability*. It is, however, standard in Scots and American English.

provenance *n.* **1** the place of origin or earliest known history, esp. of a work of art, manuscript, etc. **2** origin. [French]

Provençal /prov-on-sahl/ ● *adj.* of or concerning the language, inhabitants, landscape, etc. of Provence, a former province of SE France. ● *n.* **1** a native of Provence. **2** the language of Provence. [French, based on Latin *provincia* 'province', colloquial name for southern Gaul under Roman rule]

provender *n.* **1** animal fodder. **2** *joc.* food for humans. [from Latin *praebenda* 'prebend']

proverb *n.* a short pithy saying in general use, held to embody a general truth. [from Latin *proverbium*]

proverbial *adj.* **1** (esp. of a specific characteristic etc.) famous, notorious (*his proverbial honesty*). **2** of or referred to in a proverb; familiar as a proverb or catchphrase or as a stock character (*the proverbial ill wind*). □ **proverbially** *adv.*

provide *v.* **1** *tr.* supply; furnish (*provided them with food; provided food for them*). **2** *intr.* **a** (usu. foll. by *for, against*) make due preparation. **b** (usu. foll. by *for*) see to the maintenance of a person etc. **3** *tr.* (usu. foll. by *that*) stipulate in a will, statute, etc. [from Latin *providēre*]

provided ● *adj.* supplied, furnished. ● *conj.* (often foll. by *that*) on the condition or understanding (that).

providence *n.* **1** the protective care of God or nature. **2** (**Providence**) God in this aspect. **3** timely care or preparation; foresight; thrift.

provident *adj.* having or showing foresight; thrifty. [from Latin *provident-* 'foreseeing'] □ **providently** *adv.*

providential *adj.* **1** of or by divine foresight or interposition. **2** opportune, lucky. □ **providentially** *adv.*

provider *n.* **1** a person or thing that provides. **2** the breadwinner of a family etc.

providing *conj.* = PROVIDED *conj.*

province *n.* **1** a principal administrative division of a country etc. **2** (**the Province**) *Brit.* Northern Ireland. **3** (**the provinces**) the whole of a country outside the capital or *US* other major cities, esp. regarded as uncultured, unsophisticated, etc. **4** a sphere of action; business (*outside my province as a teacher*). [from Latin *provincia* 'charge, province']

provincial ● *adj.* **1 a** of or concerning a province. **b** of or concerning the provinces. **2** unsophisticated or uncultured. ● *n.* **provincialism** *n.* **provinciality** *n.* **provincially** *adv.*

provision ● *n.* **1 a** the act or an instance of providing. **b** something provided. **2** (in *pl.*) food, drink, etc., esp. for an expedition. **3 a** a legal or formal statement providing for something. **b** a clause of this. ● *v.tr.* supply (an expedition etc.) with provisions. [from Latin *provisio*] □ **provisioner** *n.*

provisional *adj.* providing for immediate needs only; temporary. □ **provisionality** *n.* **provisionally** *adv.*

proviso /prŏ-vy-zoh/ *n.* (*pl.* **-os**) **1** a stipulation.

2 a clause of stipulation or limitation in a document. [Latin, from medieval phrase *proviso quod* 'it being provided that']

provisory *adj.* **1** conditional; having a proviso. **2** making provision (*provisory care*). [from medieval Latin *provisorius*]

Provo *n.* (*pl.* **-os**) *colloq.* a member of the Provisional IRA.

provocation *n.* **1** the act or an instance of provoking; a state of being provoked. **2** a cause of annoyance. [from Latin *provocatio*]

provocative *adj.* **1** (usu. foll. by *of*) tending to provoke, esp. anger or sexual desire. **2** intentionally annoying. [from Late Latin *provocativus*] □ **provocatively** *adv.* **provocativeness** *n.*

provoke *v.tr.* **1 a** incite to anger. **b** (often foll. by *to, to* + infin., or *into*) rouse or incite (*provoked him to fury*). **c** (as **provoking** *adj.*) exasperating; irritating. **2** call forth; instigate (indignation, an inquiry, etc.). **3** tempt; allure. **4** cause (*will provoke fermentation*). [from Latin *provocare*] □ **provokable** *adj.* **provoker** *n.* **provokingly** *adv.*

provost *n.* **1** *Brit.* the head of some colleges esp. at Oxford or Cambridge. **2** *Sc.* the head of a municipal corporation or burgh. **3** *US* a high administrative officer in a university. **4** = PROVOST MARSHAL. [from medieval Latin *propositus*, for *praepositus* '(person) placed at the head'] □ **provostship** *n.*

provost marshal *n.* **1** the head of military police in camp or on active service. **2** the master-at-arms of a ship in which a court martial is held.

prow *n.* **1** the forepart or bow of a ship adjoining the stern. **2** a pointed or projecting front part. ▷ TRIREME. [from Greek *prōira*]

prowess *n.* **1** skill; expertise. **2** valour. [from Old French *proesce*]

prowl ● *v.* **1** *tr.* roam (a place) in search or as if in search of prey, plunder, etc. **2** *intr.* (often foll. by *about, around*) move about like a hunter. ● *n.* the act or an instance of prowling. □ **on the prowl** moving about secretively or rapaciously. [Middle English] □ **prowler** *n.*

prox. *abbr.* proximo.

proximate *adj.* **1** nearest or next before or after (in place, order, time, causation, etc.). **2** approximate. [from Latin *proximatus* 'approached'] □ **proximately** *adv.*

proximity *n.* nearness in space, time, etc. [from Latin *proximitas*]

proximo *adj. Commerce* of next month. [from Latin *proximo mense* 'in the next month']

proxy *n.* (*pl.* **-ies**) (also *attrib.*) **1** the authorization given to a substitute or deputy. **2** a person authorized to act as a substitute etc. **3 a** a document giving the power to act as a proxy, esp. in voting. **b** a vote given by this. [from obsolete *procuracy*: from medieval Latin *procuratia* 'procurement']

Prozac *n. propr.* an antidepressant drug, fluoxetine hydrochloride.

prude *n.* a person having or affecting an attitude of extreme propriety or modesty esp. in sexual matters. [French, back-formation from *prudefemme* 'good woman and true'] □ **prudery** *n.* (*pl.* **-ies**). **prudish** *adj.* **prudishly** *adv.* **prudishness** *n.*

prudent *adj.* **1** (of a person or conduct) careful to avoid undesired consequences; circumspect. **2** discreet. [from contraction of Latin *providens provident-* 'provident'] □ **prudence** *n.* **prudently** *adv.*

prudential *adj.* of, involving, or marked by prudence. □ **prudentially** *adv.*

prune[1] *n.* **1** a plum preserved by drying. **2** *colloq.* a silly or disliked person. [from Greek *prou(m)non* 'plum']

prune[2] *v.tr.* **1 a** (often foll. by *down*) trim (a tree etc.) by cutting away dead or overgrown branches etc. **b** (usu. foll. by *off, away*) lop (branches etc.) from a tree. **2** reduce (costs etc.). **3 a** (often foll. by *of*) clear (a book etc.) of superfluities. **b** remove (superfluities). [from Old French *pro(o)ignier*] □ **pruner** *n.*

prurient *adj.* **1** having an unhealthy obsession with sexual matters. **2** encouraging such an obsession. [from Latin *prurient-* 'itching, being wanton'] □ **prurience** *n.* **pruriency** *n.* **pruriently** *adv.*

Prussian ● *adj.* of or relating to Prussia or the militaristic tradition associated with it. ● *n.* a native of Prussia.

Prussian blue ● *n.* a deep blue pigment. ● *adj.* (hyphenated when *attrib.*) of this colour.

prussic acid *n.* hydrocyanic acid. [from French *prussique*, based on *Prusse* 'Prussia']

pry[1] *v.intr.* (**pries**, **pried**) **1** (usu. foll. by *into*) enquire impertinently. **2** (usu. foll. by *into*, *about*, etc.) look or peer inquisitively. [Middle English] □ **prying** *adj.* **pryingly** *adv.*

pry[2] *v.tr.* (**pries**, **pried**) (often foll. by *out of*, *open*, etc.) *N. Amer.* = PRISE.

PS *abbr.* **1** Police Sergeant. **2** postscript.

psalm /sahm/ *n.* **1** *Bibl.* **a** (also **Psalm**) any of the sacred songs contained in the Book of Psalms. **b** (**the Psalms** or **the Book of Psalms**) the book of the Old Testament containing the Psalms. **2** a sacred song or hymn. [from Greek *psalmos* 'song sung to a harp'] □ **psalmic** *adj.*

psalmist /sahm-ist/ *n.* **1** the author or composer of a psalm. **2** (**the Psalmist**) David or the author of any of the Psalms.

psalmody /sahm-ŏdi/ *n.* the practice or art of singing psalms, hymns, etc., esp. in public worship. [from Greek *psalmōidia* 'singing to a harp'] □ **psalmodic** *adj.* **psalmodist** *n.*

psalter /sawl-ter/ *n.* (also **Psalter**) **1 a** the Book of Psalms. **b** a version of this (*the English Psalter*). **2** a copy of the Psalms, esp. for liturgical use. [from Greek *psaltērion*, a stringed instrument (in ecclesiastical Latin and Greek sense 'Book of Psalms')]

psaltery /sawl-tĕ-ri/ *n.* (*pl.* **-ies**) an ancient and medieval instrument like a dulcimer but played by plucking the strings. [related to PSALTER]

PSBR *abbr. Brit.* public sector borrowing requirement.

psephology /sef-ol-ŏji/ *n.* the statistical study of voting etc. [based on Greek *psephos* 'pebble, vote'] □ **psephological** *adj.* **psephologically** *adv.* **psephologist** *n.*

pseud /s'yood/ *colloq.* ● *adj.* intellectually or socially pretentious, not genuine. ● *n.* such a person, a poseur.

pseudo /s'yoo-doh/ ● *adj.* **1** sham; spurious. **2** insincere. ● *n.* (*pl.* **-os**) a pretentious or insincere person. [Greek, from *pseudēs* 'false']

pseudo- /s'yoo-doh/ *comb. form* (also **pseud-** before a vowel) **1** supposed or purporting to be but not really so; false; not genuine (*pseudo-intellectual*). **2** resembling (often in technical applications) (*pseudo-acid*). [Greek]

pseudonym /s'yoo-dŏ-nim/ *n.* a fictitious name, esp. one assumed by an author. [from Greek *pseud-ōnymon*]

pseudonymous /s'yoo-don-i-mŭs/ *adj.* writing or written under a false name. □ **pseudonymity** *n.* **pseudonymously** *adv.*

pseudopodium *n.* (*pl.* **pseudopodia**) ▼ (in amoeboid cells) a temporary protrusion of the cell surface for movement, feeding, etc. [modern Latin (as PSEUDO-, PODIUM)]

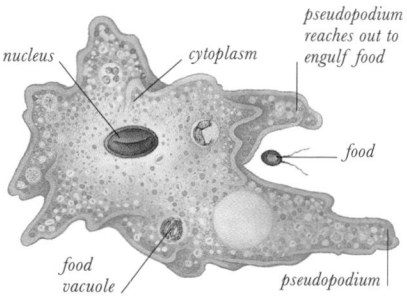

pseudopodium reaches out to engulf food

nucleus   *cytoplasm*

food

food vacuole   *pseudopodium*

PSEUDOPODIA OF AN AMOEBA

pseudo-science *n.* a pretended or spurious science. □ **pseudo-scientific** *adj.*

psi *n.* **1** the twenty-third letter of the Greek alphabet (Ψ, ψ). **2** supposed parapsychological faculties, phenomena, etc. regarded collectively. [Greek]

p.s.i. *abbr.* pounds per square inch.

psilocybin /sy-lō-sy-bin/ *n.* a hallucinogenic alkaloid found in toadstools of the genus *Psilocybe*. [based on Greek *psilos* 'bald' + *kubē* 'head']

psittacosis *n.* a contagious disease of birds, caused by chlamydiae and transmissible to human beings as a form of pneumonia. [based on Latin *psittacus* 'parrot']

psoriasis /sŏ-ry-ă-sis/ *n.* a skin disease marked by red scaly patches. [modern Latin, from Greek] □ **psoriatic** *adj.*

psst *int.* (also **pst**) a whispered exclamation seeking to attract a person's attention surreptitiously.

PSV *abbr. Brit.* public service vehicle.

psych syk *v.tr.* (also **psyche**) *colloq.* **1** (usu. foll. by *up*; often *refl.*) prepare (oneself or another person) mentally for an ordeal etc. **2 a** (usu. foll. by *out*) analyse for one's own advantage (*can't psych him out*). **b** subject to psychoanalysis. **3** (often foll. by *out*) intimidate, frighten. □ **psych out** break down mentally; become confused or deranged.

psyche /sy-ki/ *n.* **1** the soul; the spirit. **2** the mind. [from Greek *psukhē* 'breath, life, soul']

psychedelia /sy-kĕ-dee-liă/ *n.pl.* **1 a** ▼ psychedelic articles, esp. posters, paintings, etc. **b** subculture associated with these. **2** psychedelic drugs.

PSYCHEDELIA: 1960S PSYCHEDELIC POSTER

psychedelic /sy-kĕ-del-ik/ *adj.* **1 a** expanding the mind's awareness etc., esp. through the use of hallucinogenic drugs. **b** hallucinatory. **2** *colloq.* **a** producing an effect resembling that of a psychedelic drug. **b** (of colours etc.) bright, bold, and often abstract. [based on Greek *psukhē* 'soul' + *dēlos* 'clear, manifest'] □ **psychedelically** *adv.*

psychiatric nurse *n.* a nurse dealing with mentally ill patients.

psychiatric patient *n.* a patient suffering from mental illness.

psychiatry /sy-ky-ătri/ *n.* the study and treatment of mental disease. [from Greek *psukhē* 'soul' + *iatreia* 'healing'] □ **psychiatric** *adj.* **psychiatrically** *adv.* **psychiatrist** *n.*

psychic /sy-kik/ ● *adj.* **1 a** (of a person) considered to have occult powers, such as clairvoyance etc. **b** (of a phenomenon etc.) inexplicable by natural laws. **2** of the soul or mind. ● *n.* **1** a person considered to have psychic powers; a medium. **2** (in *pl.*) the study of psychic phenomena. [from Greek *psukhikos*] □ **psychicist** *n.* **psychism** *n.*

psychical /sy-ki-kăl/ *adj.* **1** concerning psychic phenomena or faculties (*psychical research*). **2** of the soul or mind. □ **psychically** *adv.*

psycho /sy-koh/ *colloq.* ● *n.* (*pl.* **-os**) a psychopath. ● *adj.* psychopathic.

psycho- /sy-koh/ *comb. form* relating to the mind or psychology. [from Greek *psukhē* 'life, soul']

psychoactive *adj.* affecting the mind.

psychoanalysis *n.* a therapeutic method of treating mental disorders by investigating and bringing repressed fears and conflicts into the conscious mind. □ **psychoanalyse** *v.tr.* (*US* **-analyze**). **psychoanalyst** *n.* **psychoanalytic** *adj.* **psychoanalytical** *adj.* **psychoanalytically** *adv.*

psychobabble *n. US colloq. derog.* jargon used in popular psychology.

psychodrama *n.* **1** a form of psychotherapy in which patients act out events from their past. **2** a play or film etc. in which psychological elements are the main interest.

psychokinesis *n.* the movement of objects supposedly by mental effort without the action of physical forces.

psycholinguistics *n.pl.* (treated as *sing.*) the study of the psychological aspects of language and language-learning. □ **psycholinguist** *n.* **psycholinguistic** *adj.*

psychological *adj.* **1** of, relating to, or arising in the mind. **2** of or relating to psychology. **3** *colloq.* (of an ailment etc.) imaginary. □ **psychologically** *adv.*

psychological block *n.* = MENTAL BLOCK.

psychological moment *n.* the most appropriate time for achieving a particular effect or purpose.

psychological warfare *n.* a campaign directed at reducing an opponent's morale.

psychology *n.* (*pl.* **-ies**) **1** the scientific study of the human mind. **2** a treatise on or theory of this. **3 a** the mental characteristics or attitude of a person or group. **b** the mental factors in a situation, activity, etc. (*psychology of crime*). [from modern Latin *psychologia*] □ **psychologist** *n.* **psychologize** *v.tr. & intr.* (also **-ise**).

psychometrics *n.pl.* (treated as *sing.*) the science of measuring mental capacities and processes.

psychometry /sy-kom-i-tri/ *n.* **1** the supposed divination of facts about events, people, etc. from inanimate objects associated with them. **2** the measurement of mental abilities. □ **psychometric** *adj.*

psychopath *n.* **1** a person suffering from chronic mental disorder esp. with abnormal or violent social behaviour. **2** a mentally or emotionally unstable person. □ **psychopathic** *adj.* **psychopathically** *adv.*

psychopathology *n.* **1** the scientific study of mental disorders. **2** a mentally or behaviourally disordered state. □ **psychopathological** *adj.*

psychopathy /sy-kop-ă-thi/ *n.* psychopathic or psychologically abnormal behaviour.

psychosexual *adj.* of or involving the psychological aspects of the sexual impulse. □ **psychosexually** *adv.*

psychosis /sy-koh-sis/ *n.* (*pl.* **psychoses**) a severe mental derangement, esp. when resulting in delusions and loss of contact with external reality. [based on Greek *psukhein* 'to give life to']

psychosocial *adj.* of or involving the influence of social factors or human interactive behaviour. □ **psychosocially** *adv.*

psychosomatic *adj.* **1** (of an illness etc.) caused or aggravated by mental conflict, stress, etc. **2** of the mind and body together. □ **psychosomatically** *adv.*

psychosurgery *n.* brain surgery as a means of treating mental disorder. □ **psychosurgical** *adj.*

psychotherapy *n.* the treatment of mental disorder by psychological means. □ **psychotherapeutic** *adj.* **psychotherapist** *n.*

psychotic /sy-kot-ik/ ● *adj.* of or characterized by a psychosis. ● *n.* a person suffering from a psychosis. □ **psychotically** *adv.*

psychotropic *n.* (of a drug) acting on the mind.

P

PT *abbr.* physical training.

Pt *symb. Chem.* the element platinum.

pt. *abbr.* **1** part. **2** pint. **3** point. **4** port.

PTA *abbr.* **1** parent–teacher association. **2** Passenger Transport Authority.

ptarmigan /tar-mi-găn/ *n.* any of various grouse-like northern game birds of the genus *Lagopus*, with feathered legs and feet. [from Gaelic *tàrmachan*]

Pte. *abbr.* Private (soldier).

ptero- /te-roh/ *comb. form* wing. [from Greek *pteron*]

pterodactyl /te-ro-**dak**-til/ *n.* a pterosaur with teeth and a long slender head, neck, and tail.

pterosaur /**te**-rŏ-sor/ *n.* any of a group of extinct flying reptiles with large bat-like wings, including pterodactyls. [based on Greek *saura* 'lizard']

PTFE *abbr.* polytetrafluoroethylene.

PTO *abbr.* please turn over.

Ptolemaic /tol-ĕ-**may**-ik/ *adj. hist.* of or relating to Ptolemy, a 2nd-c. Alexandrian astronomer, or his theories. [from Greek *Ptolemaios* 'Ptolemy']

Ptolemaic system *n. hist.* ▼ the theory that the Earth is the stationary centre of the Universe.

ptomaine /**toh**-mayn/ *n.* any of various amine compounds of unpleasant taste and odour found in putrefying animal and vegetable matter. [based on Greek *ptōma* 'corpse']

Pu *symb. Chem.* the element plutonium.

pub *n.* **1** *Brit.* a public house. **2** *Austral.* a hotel.

pub crawl *n. esp. Brit. colloq.* a drinking tour of several pubs.

puberty *n.* the period during which an adolescent reaches sexual maturity and becomes capable of reproduction. [from Latin *pubertas*] □ **pubertal** *adj.*

pubes[1] *n.* (*pl.* same) **1** the lower part of the abdomen at the front of the pelvis, covered with hair from puberty. **2** *colloq.* the pubic hair. [Latin]

pubes[2] *pl.* of PUBIS.

pubescence *n.* **1** the time when puberty begins. **2** soft down on plants or on animals, esp. insects. [from medieval Latin *pubescentia*] □ **pubescent** *adj.*

pubic *adj.* of or relating to the pubes or pubis.

pubis *n.* (*pl.* **pubes**) either of a pair of bones forming the two sides of the pelvis. ▷ SKELETON. [from Latin *os pubis* 'bone of the pubes']

public ● *adj.* **1** of or concerning the people as a whole (*a public holiday*). **2** open to or shared by all the people (*public baths*). **3** done or existing openly (*a public protest*). **4** provided by or concerning local or central government (*public money*). **5 a** of or involved in the affairs of the community (*public figures*). **b** of or relating to a person in his or her capacity as a public figure (*a likeable public face*). **6** *Brit.* of, for, or acting for, a university (*public examination*). ● *n.* **1** (treated as *sing.* or *pl.*) the community in general, or members of the community. **2** a section of the community having a particular interest or in some special connection (*the reading public*). **3** *Brit. colloq.* **a** = PUBLIC BAR. **b** = PUBLIC HOUSE. □ **go**

public 1 become a public company. **2** make one's intentions plain. **in public** openly, publicly. **in the public domain** belonging to the public as a whole, esp. not subject to copyright. **in the public eye** famous or notorious. [from Latin *publicus*] □ **publicly** *adv.*

public address system *n.* loudspeakers, amplifiers, etc., used in addressing large audiences.

publican *n.* **1 a** *Brit.* the keeper of a public house. **b** *Austral.* the keeper of a hotel. **2** *Rom.Hist.* & *Bibl.* a tax collector or tax farmer. [from Latin *publicanus*]

public analyst *n.* a member of a body that analyses foodstuffs for toxic substances etc.

publication *n.* **1 a** the preparation and issuing of a book, music, etc. to the public. **b** a book etc. so issued. **2** the act or an instance of making something publicly known. [from Latin *publicatio*]

public bar *n. Brit.* the least expensive bar in a public house.

public company *n. Brit.* a company that sells shares to all buyers on the open market.

public domain *n.* (prec. by *the*) the state of belonging or being available to the public as a whole, esp. by not being subject to legal restrictions such as copyright.

public enemy *n.* a notorious wanted criminal.

public figure *n.* a famous person.

public health *n.* the provision of adequate sanitation, drainage, etc. by government.

public house *n.* **1** *Brit.* an inn providing alcoholic drinks for consumption on the premises. **2** an inn.

publicist *n.* a publicity agent or public relations officer. [based on Latin *(jus) publicum* 'public law'] □ **publicistic** *adj.*

publicity *n.* **1 a** the professional exploitation of a product, person, etc., by advertising or popularizing. **b** material or information used for this. **2** public exposure.

publicity agent *n.* a person employed to produce or heighten public exposure.

publicize *v.tr.* (also **-ise**) advertise; make publicly known.

public lending right *n.* (in the UK) the right of authors to payment when their books etc. are lent by public libraries.

public opinion *n.* views, esp. moral, prevalent among the general public.

public orator see ORATOR 2.

public ownership *n.* state ownership of the means of production, distribution, and exchange.

public prosecutor *n.* a law officer conducting criminal proceedings on behalf of the state or in the public interest.

public purse *n.* the national treasury.

Public Record Office *n.* (in the UK) an institution keeping official archives for public inspection.

public relations *n.pl.* the professional maintenance of a favourable public image by a company etc.

public relations officer *n.* a person employed by a company etc. to promote a favourable public image.

public school *n.* **1** (in England and Wales) a private fee-paying secondary school, esp. for boarders. **2** (in Scotland, N. America, etc.) a non-fee-paying school.

public sector *n.* that part of an economy, industry, etc. that is controlled by the State.

public servant *n.* a State official.

public spirit *n.* a willingness to engage in community action. □ **public-spirited** *adj.* **public-spiritedly** *adv.* **public-spiritedness** *adj.*

public transport *n.* buses, trains, etc., charging set fares and running on fixed routes.

public utility *n.* an organization supplying water, gas, etc. to the community.

public works *n.pl.* building operations etc. done by or for the State on behalf of the community.

publish *v.tr.* **1** (also *absol.*) prepare and issue (a book, newspaper, etc.) for public sale. **2** make generally known. **3** announce formally; read (marriage banns). **4** (esp. as **published** *adj.*) publish the works of (*a published poet*). [from Latin *publicare* 'to make public'] □ **publishable** *adj.*

publisher *n.* a person or esp. a company that produces and distributes copies of a book, newspaper, etc. for sale.

puce ● *n.* a dark red or purple-brown colour. ● *adj.* of this colour. [French, literally 'flea(-colour)']

puck[1] *n.* a rubber disc used as a ball in ice hockey. ▷ HOCKEY. [19th-century coinage]

puck[2] *n.* **1** a mischievous or evil sprite. **2** a mischievous child. [Old English] □ **puckish** *adj.* **puckishly** *adv.* **puckishness** *n.*

pucka var. of PUKKA.

pucker ● *v.tr. & intr.* (often foll. by *up*) gather or cause to gather into wrinkles, folds, or bulges. ● *n.* such a wrinkle etc. □ **puckery** *adj.*

pud *n. Brit. colloq.* = PUDDING.

pudding *n.* **1 a** any of various sweet cooked dishes. **b** a savoury dish containing flour, suet, etc. (*Yorkshire pudding*). **c** *Brit.* the sweet course of a meal. **d** the intestines of a pig etc. stuffed with oatmeal, spices, blood, etc. (*black pudding*). **e** *US* a cold dessert with a soft or creamy consistency. **2** *colloq.* a fat, dumpy, or stupid person. [from Old French *boudin* 'black pudding'] □ **puddingy** *adj.*

pudding basin *n.* a basin in which puddings are made and often steamed.

puddle ● *n.* **1** a small pool, esp. of rainwater on a road etc. **2** clay and sand mixed with water and used as a watertight covering for embankments etc. ● *v.* **1** *tr.* **a** knead (clay and sand) into puddle. **b** line (a canal etc.) with puddle. **2** *tr.* make puddle from clay etc. **3** *tr.* stir (molten iron) to produce wrought iron by expelling carbon. [Middle English] □ **puddler** *n.* **puddly** *adj.*

pudendum *n.* (*pl.* **pudenda**) (usu. in *pl.*) the genitals, esp. of a woman. [sing. of Latin *pudenda (membra)* '(parts) to be ashamed of'] □ **pudendal** *adj.*

pudgy *adj.* (**pudgier**, **pudgiest**) *colloq.* (esp. of a person) plump, thickset.

pueblo /**pweb**-loh/ *n.* (*pl.* **-os**) ▲ a town or village in Spain or Spanish America, esp. a N. American Indian settlement. [Spanish, literally 'people']

puerile /**pewr**-ryl/ *adj.* **1** trivial, childish, immature. **2** of or like a child. [based on Latin *puer* 'boy'] □ **puerilely** *adv.* **puerility** *n.* (*pl.* **-ies**).

puerperal /pew-**er**-per-ăl/ *adj.* of or caused by childbirth. [from Latin *puer* 'boy' + *-parus* 'bearing']

Puerto Rican /pwer-toh **ree**-kăn/ ● *n.* **1** a native of Puerto Rico, an island of the Greater Antilles. **2** a person of Puerto Rican descent. ● *adj.* of or relating to Puerto Rico or its inhabitants.

puff ● *n.* **1 a** a short quick light blast of breath or wind. **b** the sound of this. **c** a small quantity of vapour etc., emitted in one blast. **2** a light pastry cake containing jam, cream, etc. **3** a gathered mass

PTOLEMAIC SYSTEM

Ptolemy, a 2nd-century Egyptian astronomer, saw the Earth as the centre of the universe, with the Sun, Moon, and the five known planets moving around it. This theory, known as the Ptolemaic or geocentric system, was universally accepted until the 16th century, when Nicolaus Copernicus, a Polish astronomer, proposed that the Sun was the centre of the universe, a theory known as the heliocentric system.

ILLUSTRATION OF THE
PTOLEMAIC SYSTEM (1708)

PUEBLO

The Pueblo Indians of North America built settlements, known as pueblos, composed of rows of adjoining rooms, often several storeys high. The largest, Pueblo Bonito (completed in about AD 1115), contained over 800 rooms. Each pueblo had a number of underground circular chambers – known as kivas – where ceremonies were held.

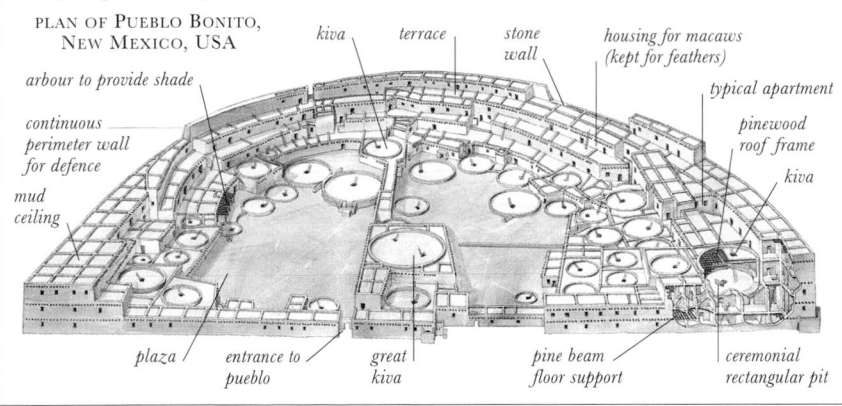

PLAN OF PUEBLO BONITO, NEW MEXICO, USA

kiva · *terrace* · *stone wall* · *housing for macaws (kept for feathers)*
arbour to provide shade · *typical apartment*
continuous perimeter wall for defence · *pinewood roof frame*
mud ceiling · *kiva*
plaza · *entrance to pueblo* · *great kiva* · *pine beam floor support* · *ceremonial rectangular pit*

---

of material in a dress etc. (*puff sleeve*). **4 a** an extravagantly enthusiastic review, esp. in a newspaper. **b** *Brit.* an advertisement for goods etc., esp. in a newspaper. **5** = POWDER PUFF. ● *v.* **1** *intr.* emit a puff of air or breath; blow with short blasts. **2** *intr.* (usu. foll. by *away*, *out*, etc.) emit or move with puffs. **3** *tr.* put out of breath (*arrived puffed out*). **4** *intr.* breathe hard; pant. **5** *intr. & tr.* (usu. foll. by *up*, *out*) swell (*inflamed and puffed up*). **6** *tr.* (usu. foll. by *out*, *up*, *away*) blow or emit (smoke etc.) with a puff. **7** *tr.* smoke (a pipe etc.) in puffs. **8** *tr.* (usu. as **puffed up** *adj.*) elate; make proud or boastful. **9** *tr.* advertise or promote (goods, a book, etc.) with exaggerated or false praise. [Middle English] □ **puffer** *n.*

puff-adder *n.* a large venomous African viper, *Bitis arietans*, which inflates the upper part of its body and hisses when excited. ▷ SNAKE

puffball *n.* **1** any of various fungi having a ball-shaped spore case. ▷ FUNGUS. **2** a short full skirt gathered around the hemline to produce a soft puffy shape.

puffery *n.* exaggerated praise or commendation.

puffin *n.* any of various seabirds of the family Alcidae, having a large head with a brightly coloured triangular bill. ▷ SEABIRD. [Middle English, originally in sense 'shearwater']

puffin crossing *n.* (in the UK) a pedestrian crossing with traffic lights operated as long as pedestrians are detected on the crossing by infra-red detectors and mats. [from *p*edestrian *us*er *f*riendly *in*telligent, respelt after the bird name]

puff pastry *n.* light flaky pastry.

puffy *adj.* (**puffier**, **puffiest**) **1** swollen, esp. of the face etc. **2** fat. **3** gusty. **4** short-winded. □ **puffily** *adv.* **puffiness** *n.*

pug *n.* **1** (in full **pug-dog**) a dwarf breed of dog like a bulldog with a broad flat nose and deeply wrinkled face. [16th-century coinage] □ **puggish** *adj.* **puggy** *adj.*

pugilist /pew-ji-list/ *n.* a boxer, esp. a professional. [based on Latin *pugil* 'boxer'] □ **pugilism** *n.* **pugilistic** *adj.*

pugnacious *adj.* quarrelsome; disposed to fight. [from Latin *pugnax -acis*] □ **pugnaciously** *adv.* **pugnaciousness** *n.* **pugnacity** *n.*

pug-nose *n.* a short squat or snub nose. □ **pug-nosed** *adj.*

puisne /pew-ni/ *adj. Brit. Law* denoting a judge of a superior court inferior in rank to chief justices. [earlier in sense 'junior': from Old French *puis* 'afterwards' + *né* 'born']

puissance /pwee-sahnss/ *n.* a test of a horse's ability to jump large obstacles in showjumping. [from Old French]

puissant /pew-i-sănt/ *adj. literary* or *archaic* having great power or influence. [based on Latin *posse* 'to be able'] □ **puissantly** *adv.*

puja *n.* (also **pooja**) a Hindu rite of worship; an offering. [Sanskrit]

puke *slang* ● *v.tr. & intr.* vomit. ● *n.* vomit. [16th-century coinage] □ **pukey** *adj.*

pukka *adj.* (also **pukkah**, **pucka**) *Anglo-Ind.* **1** genuine. **2** of good quality (*did a pukka job*). [from Hindi *pakkā* 'cooked, ripe, substantial']

pulchritude *n. literary* beauty. [from Latin *pulchritudo*] □ **pulchritudinous** *adj.*

pull ● *v.* **1** *tr.* exert force on (a thing) tending to move it towards the origin of the force. **2** *tr.* cause to move in this way (*pulled it nearer*). **3** *intr.* exert a pulling force (*the horse pulls well*). **4** *tr.* extract (a cork or tooth) by pulling. **5** *tr.* damage (a muscle etc.) by abnormal strain. **6 a** *tr.* move (a boat) by pulling on the oars. **b** *intr.* (of a boat etc.) be caused to move, esp. in a specified direction. **7** *intr.* (often foll. by *up*) proceed with effort (up a hill etc.). **8** *tr.* (foll. by *on*) bring out (a weapon) for use. **9 a** *tr.* check the speed of (a horse), esp. to lose a race. **b** *intr.* (of a horse) strain against the bit. **10** *tr.* attract or secure (custom or support). **11** *tr. Brit.* draw (liquor) from a barrel etc. **12** *intr.* (foll.

by *at*) tear or pluck at. **13** *intr.* (often foll. by *on*, *at*) draw or suck (on a pipe etc.). **14** *tr.* (often foll. by *up*) remove (a plant) by the root. **15** *tr.* **a** *Cricket* play (the ball) round to the leg side from the off. **b** *Golf & Baseball* strike (the ball) widely to the left or right. **16** *tr.* print (a proof etc.). **17** *tr. colloq.* achieve or accomplish (esp. something illicit). **18** *tr.* (also *absol.*) *slang* succeed in attracting sexually; pick up (a sexual partner). ● *n.* **1** the act of pulling. **2** the force exerted by this. **3** influence; an advantage. **4** something that attracts or draws attention. **5** a deep draught of liquor. **6** a prolonged effort, e.g. in going up a hill. **7** a handle etc. for applying a pull. **8** a printer's rough proof. **9** *Cricket & Golf* a pulling stroke. **10** a suck at a cigarette. □ **pull about 1** treat roughly. **2** pull from side to side. **pull all the stops out** exert extreme effort. **pull apart** (or **to pieces**) = *take to pieces* (see PIECE). **pull back** retreat or cause to retreat. **pull down 1** demolish (esp. a building). **2** humiliate. **pull a face** esp. *Brit.* assume a distinctive or specified expression. **pull a fast one** see FAST[1]. **pull in 1** (of a bus, train, etc.) arrive to take passengers. **2** (of a vehicle) move to the side of or off the road. **3** earn or acquire. **4** *colloq.* arrest. **5** rein in. **pull a person's leg** deceive a person playfully. **pull off 1** remove by pulling. **2** succeed in achieving. **pull oneself together** recover control of oneself. **pull the other one** *Brit. colloq.* expressing disbelief. **pull out 1** take out by pulling. **2** depart. **3** withdraw from an undertaking. **4** (of a bus, train, etc.) leave with its passengers. **5** (of a vehicle) move off, or out to overtake. **pull over** (of a vehicle) pull in. **pull the plug** (often foll. by *on*) *colloq.* put an end to an enterprise etc. **pull one's punches** avoid using one's full force. **pull rank** take advantage of one's seniority. **pull round** esp. *Brit.* recover or cause to recover from an illness. **pull strings** exert (esp. clandestine) influence. **pull the strings** be the real actuator of what another does. **pull through 1** get through an illness etc. **2** enable (a person) to do this. **pull together** work in harmony. **pull up 1** stop or cause to stop moving. **2** pull out of the ground. **3** reprimand. **4** check oneself. [Old English] □ **puller** *n.*

pull-down *attrib.adj.* that may be, or is designed to be, pulled down.

pullet *n.* a young hen, esp. one less than one year old. [from Old French *poulet*]

pulley *n.* (*pl.* **-eys**) **1** ▼ a grooved wheel or set of wheels for a cord etc. to pass over, set in a block and used for changing the direction of a force. **2** a wheel or drum fixed on a shaft and turned by a belt, used esp. to increase speed or power. ▷ HOIST, SEIZE. [from Old French *polie*]

P

PULLEY

A simple pulley, with one pulley wheel, changes the direction of a force but not its size: a 1 kg mass weighing 10 newtons is lifted by a 10 newton force. Adding more pulley wheels increases the mechanical advantage – the ratio of the load overcome to the effort expended. A double pulley will lift a 1 kg mass with a 5 newton effort, because the load is shared between two ropes. A quadruple pulley will lift a 1 kg mass with a 2.5 newton effort because the load is shared between four ropes.

EXAMPLES OF PULLEYS

SIMPLE PULLEY
meter reads 10 newtons
wheel
1 kg mass
10 newton weight (load)
10 newton force (effort)

DOUBLE PULLEY
upper wheel
meter reads 5 newtons
lower wheel
1 kg mass
10 newton weight (load)
5 newton force (effort)

QUADRUPLE PULLEY
upper wheel
meter reads 2.5 newtons
lower wheel
10 newton weight (load)
1 kg mass
2.5 newton force (effort)

P

PULSAR

As neutron stars rotate, they emit beams of light and radio waves which, if they sweep past the Earth, are detected as pulses. This has led astronomers to call them pulsars (from pulsating stars). The fastest pulsars rotate at almost one thousand times per second. Over 400 are known to exist in our galaxy.

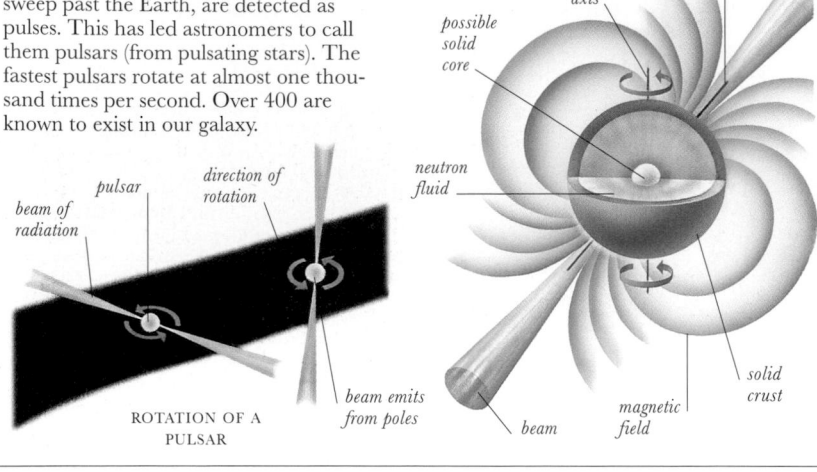

INTERNAL STRUCTURE OF A PULSAR

magnetic axis

rotational axis

possible solid core

neutron fluid

solid crust

magnetic field

beam

beam of radiation

pulsar

direction of rotation

beam emits from poles

ROTATION OF A PULSAR

---

pull-in *n. Brit.* a roadside café or other stopping place.

Pullman *n.* (*pl.* **Pullmans**) **1** a railway carriage or motor coach affording special comfort. **2** a sleeping car. **3** a train consisting of Pullman carriages. [named after G. M. *Pullman*, American designer, 1831–97]

pull-off ● *attrib.adj.* that may be, or is designed to be, pulled off. ● *n.* a lay-by.

pull-on ● *attrib.adj.* designating a garment without fasteners that is pulled on. ● *n.* such a garment.

pull-out *n.* **1** something that can be pulled out, esp. a section of a magazine. **2** the act of pulling out; a withdrawal, esp. from military involvement.

pullover *n.* a knitted garment put on over the head and covering the top half of the body.

pullulate *v.intr.* **1** (of a seed etc.) bud, sprout. **2** (esp. of an animal) swarm; breed prolifically. **3** develop; spring up. **4** (foll. by *with*) abound. [based on Latin *pullulatus* 'sprouted'] □ **pullulant** *adj.* **pullulation** *n.*

pull-up *n.* an exercise involving raising oneself with one's arms by pulling up against a horizontal bar etc. fixed above one's head.

pulmonary *adj.* **1** of or relating to the lungs. ▷ CARDIOVASCULAR, HEART, RESPIRATION. **2** having lungs or lunglike organs. **3** affected with or susceptible to

lung disease. [based on Latin *pulmo -onis* 'lung'] □ **pulmonate** *adj.*

pulmonary tuberculosis *n.* a form of tuberculosis caused by inhaling the tubercle bacillus into the lungs.

pulp ● *n.* **1** the soft fleshy part of fruit etc. **2** any soft thick wet mass. **3** a soft shapeless mass derived from rags, wood, etc., used in papermaking. **4** (often *attrib.*) cheap fiction etc. (originally printed on rough paper). ● *v.* **1** *tr.* reduce to pulp. **2** *tr.* withdraw (a publication) from the market, usu. recycling the paper. **3** *tr.* remove pulp from. **4** *intr.* become pulp. [from Latin *pulpa*] □ **pulper** *n.* **pulpy** *adj.* **pulpiness** *n.*

pulpit *n.* **1** a raised enclosed platform in a church etc. from which the preacher delivers a sermon. ▷ CHURCH. **2** (prec. by *the*) preachers or preaching collectively. [from Latin *pulpitum* 'scaffold, platform']

pulpwood *n.* timber suitable for making pulp.

pulsar *n. Astron.* ◄ a celestial object, thought to be a rapidly rotating neutron star, emitting regular pulses of radiation. [from *pulsating sta*r]

pulsate *v.intr.* **1** expand and contract rhythmically. **2** quiver, thrill. [based on Latin *pulsatus* 'beaten'] □ **pulsation** *n.* **pulsator** *n.* **pulsatory** *adj.*

pulse[1] ● *n.* **1 a** a rhythmical throbbing of the arteries as blood is propelled through them, esp. as felt in the wrists, temples, etc. **b** each successive beat of the arteries or heart. **2** a throb or thrill of life or emotion. **3** a general feeling or opinion. **4** a single vibration of sound, light, etc., esp. as a signal. **5** a musical beat. **6** any regular or recurrent rhythm. ● *v.intr.* **1** pulsate. **2** (foll. by *out, in,* etc.) transmit etc. by rhythmical beats. [from Latin *pulsus* 'beating']

pulse[2] *n.* (treated as *sing.* or *pl.*) **1** ◄ the edible seeds of various leguminous plants, e.g. chickpeas, lentils, etc. **2** the plant or plants producing this. [from Latin *puls* 'porridge of meal or pulse']

pulverize *v.* (also **-ise**) **1** *tr.* reduce to fine particles. **2** *tr. & intr.* crumble to dust. **3** *colloq. tr.* **a** demolish. **b** defeat utterly. [from Late Latin *pulverizare*] □ **pulverizable** *adj.* **pulverization** *n.* **pulverizer** *n.*

puma *n.* ▼ a wild American cat, *Felis concolor*, usu. with a tawny or greyish coat. [from Quechua]

PUMA
(*Felis concolor*)

PULSE

Pulse crops are leguminous plants that are primarily grown for their seeds. They are derived from wild members of the pea family, such as *Phaseolus vulgaris* – an annual plant that originated in South America. Their seeds (pulses) are a major source of protein, and make a vital contribution to human diets in areas where meat is scarce.

EXAMPLES OF PULSES

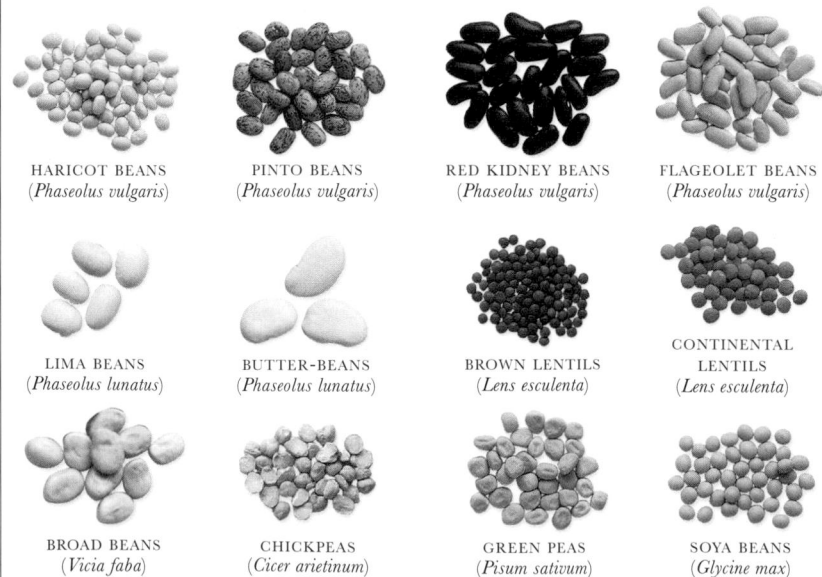

HARICOT BEANS
(*Phaseolus vulgaris*)

PINTO BEANS
(*Phaseolus vulgaris*)

RED KIDNEY BEANS
(*Phaseolus vulgaris*)

FLAGEOLET BEANS
(*Phaseolus vulgaris*)

LIMA BEANS
(*Phaseolus lunatus*)

BUTTER-BEANS
(*Phaseolus lunatus*)

BROWN LENTILS
(*Lens esculenta*)

CONTINENTAL LENTILS
(*Lens esculenta*)

BROAD BEANS
(*Vicia faba*)

CHICKPEAS
(*Cicer arietinum*)

GREEN PEAS
(*Pisum sativum*)

SOYA BEANS
(*Glycine max*)

pumice /pum-iss/ *n.* (in full **pumice stone**) **1** ▼ a light porous volcanic rock often used as an abrasive in cleaning or polishing. **2** a piece of this used for removing hard skin etc. ● *v.tr.* rub or clean with a pumice. [from Latin *pumex pumicis*] □ **pumiceous** *adj.*

pummel *v.tr.* (**pummelled**, **pummelling**; *US* **pummeled**, **pummeling**) strike repeatedly esp. with the fist. [alteration of POMMEL]

PUMICE STONE

pump[1] ● *n.* **1** ▲ a machine for raising or moving liquids, compressing gases, inflating tyres, etc. **2** an instance of pumping; a stroke of a pump. ● *v.* **1** *tr.* (often foll. by *in, out, into, up,* etc.) raise or remove (liquid, gas, etc.) with a pump. **2** *tr.* (often foll. by *up*) fill (a tyre etc.) with air. **3** *tr.* remove (water etc.) with a pump. **4** *intr.* work a pump. **5** *tr.*

PUMP

The simplest pump is the lift pump, which is used for drawing up water from underground. During the intake stroke, an inlet valve opens, the cylinder volume is increased, and water is drawn in. Water above the plunger is lifted up and pours out of the spout.

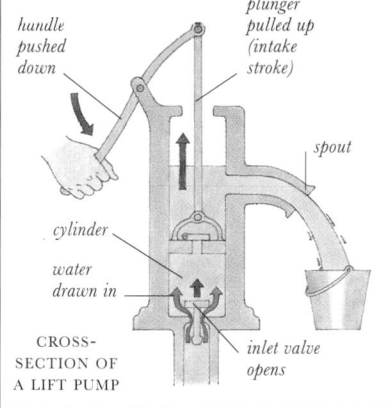

handle pushed down

plunger pulled up (intake stroke)

spout

cylinder

water drawn in

inlet valve opens

CROSS-SECTION OF A LIFT PUMP

(often foll. by *out*) cause to move, pour forth, etc., as if by pumping. **6** *tr.* try to elicit information from (a person) by persistent questioning. **7** *tr.* move vigorously up and down. □ **pump iron** *colloq.* exercise with weights. [Middle English]

pump² *n.* **1** a plimsoll. **2** a light shoe for dancing etc. **3** *N. Amer.* a court shoe. [16th-century coinage]

pump-action *attrib.adj.* designating a repeating firearm activated by a horizontally operating slide action.

pumpernickel *n.* German wholemeal rye bread. [German, earlier in sense 'lout, bumpkin']

pumpkin *n.* **1** any of various plants of the genus *Cucurbita*, esp. *C. maxima*, with large lobed leaves and tendrils. **2** ▶ the large rounded edible yellow fruit of this. [based on Greek *pepōn* 'large melon']

PUMPKIN
(*Cucurbita maxima*)

seeds

pump-priming *n.* **1** the introduction of fluid etc. into a pump to prepare it for working. **2** esp. *US* the stimulation of commerce etc. by investment.

pump room *n.* a room at a spa etc. where medicinal water is dispensed.

pun ● *n.* the humorous use of a word to suggest different meanings, or of words of the same sound and different meanings. ● *v.intr.* (**punned, punning**) (foll. by *on*) make a pun or puns with (words). [17th-century coinage] □ **punningly** *adv.*

punch¹ ● *v.tr.* **1** strike bluntly, esp. with a closed fist. **2** prod or poke with a blunt object. **3 a** pierce a hole in (paper etc.) as or with a punch. **b** pierce (a hole) by punching. **4** *N. Amer.* drive (cattle) by prodding with a stick etc. ● *n.* **1** a blow with a fist. **2** the ability to deliver this. **3** *colloq.* vigour, momentum. [Middle English variant of POUNCE] □ **puncher** *n.*

punch² *n.* **1** a device or machine for punching holes in materials. **2** a tool or machine for impressing a design or stamping a die on a material.

punch³ *n.* a drink of wine or spirits mixed with water, fruit juices, spices, etc., and usu. served hot.

punch⁴ *n.* **1** (**Punch**) a grotesque humpbacked figure in a puppet show called *Punch and Judy*. **2** (in

full **Suffolk punch**) a short-legged thickset draught horse. □ (**as**) **pleased as Punch** showing great pleasure. [abbreviation of *Punchinello*, character in a traditional Italian puppet show]

punchbag *n. Brit.* a stuffed bag suspended at a height for boxers etc. to practise punching.

punchball *n. Brit.* a stuffed or inflated ball suspended or mounted on a stand, used for punching practice by boxers etc.

punchbowl *n.* **1** a bowl in which punch is mixed. **2** a deep round hollow in a hill.

punch-drunk *adj.* stupefied from or as though from a series of heavy blows.

punchline *n.* words giving the point of a joke or story.

punch-up *n. Brit. colloq.* a fight with bare fists; a brawl.

punchy *adj.* (**punchier, punchiest**) having punch or vigour. □ **punchily** *adv.* **punchiness** *n.*

punctilio *n.* (*pl.* **-os**) **1** a delicate point of ceremony or honour. **2** the etiquette of such points. **3** petty formality. [from Italian *puntiglio* 'little point']

punctilious *adj.* **1** attentive to formality or etiquette. **2** precise in behaviour. [related to PUNCTILIO] □ **punctiliously** *adv.* **punctiliousness** *n.*

punctual *adj.* observing the appointed time; neither early nor late. [based on Latin *punctum* 'point'] □ **punctuality** *n.* **punctually** *adv.*

punctuate *v.tr.* **1** insert punctuation marks in. **2** interrupt at intervals. [based on medieval Latin *punctuatus* 'punctuated'] □ **punctuation** *n.*

punctuation mark *n.* a mark (e.g. a full stop, comma, etc.) used in writing to separate sentences and phrases etc. and to clarify meaning.

puncture ● *n.* **1** a prick or pricking, esp. the accidental piercing of a pneumatic tyre. **2** a hole made in this way. ● *v.* **1** *tr.* make a puncture in. **2** *intr.* undergo puncture. **3** *tr.* prick or pierce. [from Latin *punctura*]

pundit *n.* **1** (also **pandit**) a learned Hindu. **2** often *iron.* a learned expert or teacher. [based on Sanskrit *paṇḍita* 'learned'] □ **punditry** *n.*

pungent *adj.* **1** having a sharp or strong taste or smell, esp. so as to produce a pricking sensation. **2** (of remarks) penetrating, caustic. **3** mentally stimulating. [from Latin *pungent-* 'pricking'] □ **pungency** *n.* **pungently** *adv.*

Punic *adj.* of or relating to ancient Carthage in N. Africa or its language. [from Greek *Phoinix* 'Phoenician']

punish *v.tr.* **1** cause (an offender) to suffer for an offence. **2** inflict a penalty for (an offence). **3** *colloq.* inflict severe blows on (an opponent). **4 a** subject to severe treatment. **b** treat improperly. [from Latin *punire*] □ **punishable** *adj.* **punisher** *n.* **punishing** *adj.* (in sense 4a). **punishingly** *adv.*

punishment *n.* **1** the act or an instance of punishing; the condition of being punished. **2** the loss or suffering inflicted in this. **3** *colloq.* severe treatment or suffering.

punitive *adj.* **1** inflicting or intended to inflict punishment. **2** (of taxation etc.) extremely severe. [from medieval Latin *punitivus*] □ **punitively** *adv.*

Punjabi ● *n.* (*pl.* **Punjabis**) **1 a** *hist.* a native of the Punjab in India, now divided between India and Pakistan. **b** a native of the state of Punjab in India or the province Punjab in Pakistan. **2** the language spoken in these areas. ● *adj.* of or relating to these areas, their inhabitants, or their language. [from Hindi *pañjābī*]

punk ● *n.* **1 a** a worthless person or thing. **b** nonsense. **2 a** (in full **punk rock**) a loud fast-moving form of rock music with crude and aggressive effects. **b** (in full **punk rocker**) a devotee of this. **3** *N. Amer.* a hoodlum or ruffian. ● *adj.* **1** worthless, rotten. **2** denoting punk rock and its associations. [17th-century coinage] □ **punkish** *adj.* **punky** *adj.*

punkah *n.* a large swinging cloth fan on a frame worked by a cord or electrically. [based on Sanskrit *pakṣa* 'wing']

punnet *n. Brit.* a small light basket or container for fruit or vegetables. [19th-century coinage]

punster *n.* a person who makes puns, esp. habitually.

punt¹ ● *n.* ▼ a narrow flat-bottomed pleasure boat, square at both ends, used mainly for pleasure on rivers and propelled using a long pole. ● *v.* **1** *tr.* propel (a punt) with a pole. **2** *intr. & tr.* travel or convey in a punt. [from Latin *ponto*, a Gaulish transport vessel] □ **punter** *n.*

PUNT ON A RIVER

punt² ● *v.tr.* kick (a ball, esp. in rugby and American football) after it has dropped from the hands and before it reaches the ground. ● *n.* such a kick. □ **punter** *n.*

punt³ ● *v.intr.* **1** (in some card games) lay a stake against the bank. **2** *Brit. colloq.* **a** bet on a horse etc. **b** speculate in shares etc. ● *n.* **1** esp. *Brit.* a bet. **2** a point in faro. [from French *ponte* 'player against the bank']

punt⁴ *n.* the chief monetary unit of the Republic of Ireland. [Irish, literally 'pound']

punter *n.* **1** *Brit.* a person who gambles or lays a bet. **2** *Brit. colloq.* a customer or client, a member of an audience; a member of the general public. **b** *slang* a prostitute's client.

puny *adj.* (**punier, puniest**) **1** undersized. **2** weak, feeble. **3** petty. [phonetic spelling of PUISNE] □ **punily** *adv.* **puniness** *n.*

pup ● *n.* **1** a young dog. **2** a young wolf, rat, seal, etc. **3** esp. *Brit.* an unpleasant or arrogant young man. ● *v.tr.* (**pupped, pupping**) (also *absol.*) (of a bitch etc.) bring forth (young). □ **in pup** (of a bitch) pregnant. **sell a person a pup** *Brit.* swindle a person, esp. by selling something worthless. [back-formation from PUPPY]

pupa /pew-pă/ *n.* (*pl.* **pupae** /-pee/) ▶ an inactive transitional stage in an insect's life cycle, between larva and adult. ▷ METAMORPHOSIS. [Latin, literally 'girl, doll'] □ **pupal** *adj.*

pupate *v.intr.* become a pupa. □ **pupation** *n.*

pupil¹ *n.* a person who is taught by another, esp. a schoolchild or student in relation to a teacher. [from Latin *pupillus* 'little boy', *pupilla* 'little girl'] □ **pupillage** *n.* (also **pupilage**). **pupillary** *adj.* (also **pupilary**).

pupil² *n.* the dark circular opening in the centre of the iris of the eye, varying in size to regulate the passage of light to the retina. ▷ EYE. [from Latin *pupilla* 'little doll', so called from the tiny reflected images visible in the eye] □ **pupillar** *adj.* (also **pupilar**). **pupillary** *adj.* (also **pupilary**).

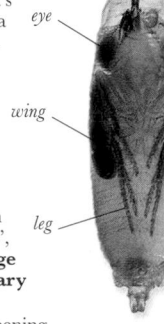

eye

wing

leg

PUPA OF A FRUITFLY MAGGOT

P

puppet n. **1** ◄ a small figure moved by various means as entertainment. ▷ MARIONETTE. **2** a person controlled by another. [later form of POPPET] □ **puppetry** n.

puppeteer n. **1** a person who works puppets. **2** a person who manipulates others. □ **puppeteering** n.

thin rod moves puppet

PUPPET: JAVANESE SHADOW PUPPET

puppet state n. a country that is nominally independent but actually under the control of another power.

puppy n. (pl. **-ies**) **1** a young dog. **2** colloq. a conceited or arrogant young man. [Middle English] □ **puppyhood** n. **puppyish** adj.

puppy fat n. temporary fatness of a child or adolescent.

puppy love n. = CALF LOVE.

purblind adj. **1** partly blind; dim-sighted. **2** obtuse, dim-witted. [originally in sense 'completely blind': Middle English pur(e) (= 'utterly') blind] □ **purblindness** n.

purchase ● v.tr. **1** acquire by payment; buy. **2** obtain or achieve at some cost. ● n. **1** the act or an instance of buying. **2** something bought. **3** a firm hold to prevent slipping; leverage. [from Old French pourchacier 'to seek to obtain'] □ **purchasable** adj. **purchaser** n.

purchase tax n. Brit. hist. a tax on goods bought, levied at higher rates for non-essential or luxury goods.

purchasing power n. **1** a person's financial ability to make purchases. **2** the amount that a sum of money etc. can purchase.

purdah n. **1** a system in certain Muslim and Hindu societies of screening women from strangers by means of a curtain. **2** a curtain for this purpose. [from Urdu & Persian pardah 'veil, curtain']

pure adj. **1** unmixed, unadulterated. **2** of unmixed origin or descent. **3** chaste. **4** morally or sexually undefiled. **5** guiltless. **6** sincere. **7** mere, nothing but (it was pure malice). **8** (of a sound) not discordant. **9** (of a subject of study) dealing with abstract concepts and not practical application. [from Latin purus] □ **pureness** n.

pure-bred ● adj. (of an animal) bred from parents of the same breed or variety; of unmixed ancestry. ● n. such an animal.

purée /pewr-ay/ ● n. a pulp of vegetables or fruit etc. reduced to a smooth cream. ● v.tr. (**purées**, **puréed**) make a purée of. [French, literally 'purified']

purely adv. **1** in a pure manner. **2** merely, solely, exclusively.

pure mathematics see MATHEMATICS 1.

purgation n. **1** purification. **2** purging of the bowels. [from Latin purgatio]

purgative ● adj. **1** serving to purify. **2** strongly laxative. ● n. **1** a purgative thing. **2** a laxative.

purgatory ● n. (pl. **-ies**) **1** the condition or supposed place of spiritual cleansing after death before entering heaven. **2** a place or state of temporary suffering or expiation. ● adj. purifying. [from medieval Latin purgatorium, related to PURGE] □ **purgatorial** adj.

purge ● v.tr. **1** (often foll. by of, from) make physically or spiritually clean. **2** remove by a cleansing process. **3** rid of persons regarded as undesirable.

4 a empty (the bowels). **b** administer a laxative to empty the bowels of. **5** Law atone for or wipe out (an offence). ● n. **1** the act or an instance of purging. **2** a purgative. [from Latin purgare 'to purify'] □ **purger** n.

purify v.tr. (**-ies**, **-ied**) **1** (often foll. by of, from) cleanse or make pure. **2** make ceremonially clean. **3** clear of extraneous elements. [from Latin purificare] □ **purification** n. **purificatory** adj. **purifier** n.

purine n. **1** Chem. a cyclic organic nitrogenous base forming uric acid on oxidation. **2** any of a group of compounds with a similar structure.

purist ● n. a stickler for or advocate of scrupulous purity, esp. in language or art. ● adj. of or relating to purism or purists. [from French puriste] □ **purism** n.

puritan ● n. **1** (**Puritan**) hist. a member of a group of English Protestants who sought to simplify and regulate forms of worship after the Reformation. **2** a purist member of any party. **3** a person practising or affecting extreme strictness in religion or morals. ● adj. **1** (usu. **Puritan**) hist. of the Puritans. **2** scrupulous and austere in religion or morals. [based on Late Latin puritas 'purity'] □ **puritanism** n. (also **Puritanism**).

puritanical adj. often derog. practising or affecting strict religious or moral behaviour. □ **puritanically** adv.

purity n. pureness, cleanness. [from Old French pureté]

purl[1] ● adj. (of a knitting stitch) made by putting the needle through the front of the stitch from right to left. ● n. **1** a cord of twisted gold or silver wire for bordering. **2** a chain of minute loops. ● v.tr. (also absol.) knit with a purl stitch. [from Scots pirl 'twist']

purl[2] ● v.intr. (of a brook etc.) flow with a swirling motion and babbling sound. ● n. this motion or sound. [16th-century coinage]

purler n. Brit. colloq. a headlong fall. [from dialect purl 'to upset', related to PURL[1]]

purlieu /perl-yoo/ n. (pl. **purlieus**) **1** a person's bounds or limits. **2** a person's usual haunts. **3** Brit. hist. a tract on the border of a forest. **4** (in pl.) the outskirts. [earlier purlew: Middle English]

purlin n. a horizontal beam along the length of a roof. ▷ ROOF. [Middle English]

purloin v.tr. literary or joc. steal, pilfer. [from Anglo-French purloigner 'to put away, do away with'] □ **purloiner** n.

purple ● n. **1** a colour intermediate between red and blue. **2** (in full **Tyrian purple** /ti-ri-ăn/) a crimson dye obtained from some molluscs. **3** a purple robe, esp. of an emperor or senior magistrate. **4** the scarlet official dress of a cardinal. ● adj. of a purple colour. ● v.tr. & intr. make or become purple. [from Latin purpura] □ **purpleness** n.

purplish adj. **purply** adj.

ribbon

PURPLE HEART

purple heart n. **1** Brit. colloq. a heart-shaped stimulant tablet, esp. of amphetamine. **2** (**Purple Heart**) ◄ (in the US) a decoration for those wounded in action.

purple passage n. an ornate or elaborate passage in a literary composition.

purple patch n. **1** = PURPLE PASSAGE. **2** colloq. a period of success or good fortune.

purple prose n. prose that is too elaborate or ornate.

purport ● v.tr. /per-port/ **1** profess; be intended to. **2** (often foll. by that + clause) (of a document or speech) have as its meaning. ● n. /per-port/ **1** the ostensible meaning of something. **2** the sense or tenor (of a document or statement). [from medieval Latin proportare] □ **purportedly** adv.

purpose ● n. **1** an object to be attained; a thing intended. **2** the intention to act. **3** resolution, determination. ● v.tr. have as one's purpose. □ **on purpose** intentionally. **to no purpose** with no result or effect. **to the purpose** **1** relevant. **2** useful. [Middle English, related to PROPOUND]

purpose-built adj. Brit. built or made for a specific purpose.

purposeful adj. **1** having or indicating purpose. **2** intentional. **3** resolute. □ **purposefully** adv. **purposefulness** n.

purposeless adj. having no aim or plan. □ **purposelessly** adv. **purposelessness** n.

purposely adv. on purpose; intentionally.

purposive adj. **1** having or serving a purpose. **2** done with a purpose. **3** (of a person or conduct) having purpose or resolution; purposeful. □ **purposively** adv. **purposiveness** n.

purr ● v. **1** intr. (of a cat) make a low vibratory sound expressing contentment. **2** intr. (of machinery etc.) make a similar sound. **3** intr. (of a person) express pleasure by making low contented sounds. **4** tr. utter or express (words or pleasure) in a contented or seductive way. ● n. a purring sound.

purse ● n. **1** a small pouch of leather etc. for carrying money. **2** N. Amer. a handbag. **3** money, funds. **4** a sum collected as a present or given as a prize. ● v. **1** tr. (often foll. by up) pucker or contract (the lips). **2** intr. become contracted and wrinkled. □ **hold the purse strings** have control of expenditure. [from Greek bursa 'hide, leather']

purser n. an officer on a ship who keeps the accounts, esp. the head steward in a passenger vessel.

purse seine /sayn/ n. a fishing net or seine which may be drawn into the shape of a bag, used for catching shoal fish (hyphenated when attrib.: purse-seine vessels). ▷ SEINE. □ **purse-seiner** n.

purslane n. ► any of various plants of the genus *Portulaca*, esp. *P. oleracea*, with green or golden leaves, used as a herb and salad vegetable. [from Old French porcelaine]

pursuance n. (foll. by of) the carrying out or observance (of a plan, idea, etc.).

pursuant ● adj. pursuing. ● adv. (foll. by to) conforming to or in accordance with. [Middle English in sense 'prosecuting': from Old French po(u)rsuiant]

PURSLANE
(*Portulaca oleracea*)

pursue v. (**pursues**, **pursued**, **pursuing**) **1** tr. follow with intent to overtake or capture or do harm to. **2** tr. continue or proceed along (a route or course of action). **3** tr. follow or engage in (study etc.). **4** tr. proceed in compliance with (a plan etc.). **5** tr. seek after, aim at. **6** tr. continue to investigate or discuss (a topic). **7** tr. importune (a person) persistently. **8** tr. (of misfortune etc.) persistently assail. **9** tr. persistently attend, stick to. **10** intr. go in pursuit. [from Latin prosequi 'to follow after'] □ **pursuable** adj. **pursuer** n.

pursuit n. **1** the act or an instance of pursuing. **2** an occupation or activity pursued. □ **in pursuit of** pursuing. [from Old French poursuite]

purulent /pewr-uul-ĕnt/ adj. **1** consisting of or containing pus. **2** discharging pus. [from French] □ **purulence** n.

purvey v. **1** tr. provide or supply (food) as one's business. **2** intr. (often foll. by for) **a** make provision. **b** act as supplier. [from Latin providēre 'to provide'] □ **purveyor** n.

purview n. **1** the scope or range of a document, scheme, etc. **2** the range of physical or mental vision. [from Old French porveü 'purveyed']

P

pus *n.* a thick yellowish or greenish liquid produced from infected tissue. [Latin]

push ● *v.* **1** *tr.* exert a force on (a thing) to move it away from the origin of the force. **2** *tr.* cause to move in this direction. **3** *intr.* exert such a force. **4** *intr.* & *tr.* **a** thrust forward or upward. **b** project or cause to project (*pushes out new roots*). **5** *intr.* move forward by force or persistence. **6** *tr.* make (one's way) by pushing. **7** *intr.* exert oneself, esp. to surpass others. **8** *tr.* (often foll. by *to*, *into*, or *to* + infin.) urge or impel. **9** *tr.* tax the abilities or tolerance of. **10** *tr.* pursue (a claim etc.). **11** *tr.* promote the use or sale or adoption of, e.g. by advertising. **12** *intr.* (foll. by *for*) demand persistently. **13** *tr. colloq.* sell (a drug) illegally. ● *n.* **1** the act or an instance of pushing; a shove or thrust. **2** the force exerted in this. **3** a vigorous effort. **4** a military attack in force. **5** enterprise; determination to succeed. **6** the use of influence to advance a person. **7** the pressure of affairs. **8** a crisis. □ **be pushed for** *colloq.* have very little of (esp. time). **get the push** *Brit. colloq.* be dismissed or sent away. **give a person the push** *Brit. colloq.* dismiss or send away a person. **push about** *colloq.* = *push around*. **push around** *colloq.* **1** move (a person) roughly from place to place. **2** bully. **push one's luck 1** take undue risks. **2** act presumptuously. **push off 1** push with an oar etc. to get a boat out into a river etc. **2** (often in *imper.*) *colloq.* go away. **push through** get (a scheme etc.) completed or accepted quickly. **when push comes to shove** *colloq.* when action must be taken. [from Latin *pulsare*]

push-bike *n. Brit. colloq.* a bicycle worked by pedals.

push-button *n.* **1** a button to be pushed esp. to operate an electrical device. **2** (*attrib.*) operated in this way.

pushcart *n.* a handcart or barrow.

pushchair *n. Brit.* a folding chair on wheels, in which a child can be pushed along.

pusher *n.* **1** *colloq.* an illegal seller of drugs. **2** a child's utensil for pushing food on to a spoon etc.

pushing *adj.* **1** pushy; aggressively ambitious. **2** *colloq.* having nearly reached (a specified age).

pushover *n. colloq.* **1** something that is easily done. **2** a person who can easily be persuaded etc.

push-pull *adj.* **1** operated by pushing and pulling. **2** *Electronics* consisting of two valves etc. operated alternately.

push-start ● *n.* the starting of a motor vehicle by pushing it to turn the engine. ● *v.tr.* start (a vehicle) in this way.

push-up *n.* = PRESS-UP.

pushy *adj.* (**pushier**, **pushiest**) *colloq.* **1** excessively or unpleasantly self-assertive. **2** selfishly determined to succeed. □ **pushily** *adv.* **pushiness** *n.*

pusillanimous *adj.* lacking courage; timid. [from ecclesiastical Latin *pusillanimis*] □ **pusillanimity** *n.* **pusillanimously** *adv.*

puss *n. colloq.* **1** a cat (esp. as a form of address). **2** a playful or coquettish girl.

pussy *n.* (*pl.* **-ies**) **1** (also **pussy cat**) *colloq.* a cat. **2** *coarse slang* **a** the vulva. **b** *offens.* women considered sexually.

pussyfoot *v.intr.* **1** move stealthily or warily. **2** act cautiously or non-committally. □ **pussyfooter** *n.*

pussy willow *n.* any of various willows with soft fluffy catkins appearing before the leaves.

pustulate ● *v.tr.* & *intr.* form into pustules. ● *adj.* of or relating to a pustule or pustules. [from Late Latin *pustulatus* 'formed into pustules'] □ **pustulation** *n.*

pustule *n.* a pimple containing pus. [from Latin *pustula*] □ **pustular** *adj.*

put[1] ● *v.* (**putting**; *past* and *past part.* **put**) **1** *tr.* move to or cause to be in a specified place or position. **2** *tr.* bring into a specified condition, relation, or state (*puts me in great difficulty*). **3** *tr.* **a** (often foll. by *on*) impose or assign (*put a tax on beer*). **b** (foll. by *on*, *to*) impose or enforce the existence of (*put a veto on it*). **4** *tr.* **a** cause (a person) to go or be, habitually or temporarily (*put them at their ease*). **b** *refl.* imagine (oneself) in a specified situation (*put yourself in my shoes*). **5** *tr.* (foll. by *for*) substitute (one thing for another). **6** *tr.* express (a thought or idea) in a specified way (*to put it mildly*). **7** *tr.* (foll. by *at*) estimate (an amount etc. at a specified amount) (*put the cost at £50*). **8** *tr.* (foll. by *into*) express or translate in (words, or another language). **9** *tr.* (foll. by *into*) invest (money in an asset, e.g. land). **10** *tr.* (foll. by *on*) stake (money) on (a horse etc.). **11** *tr.* (foll. by *to*) apply or devote to a use or purpose (*put it to good use*). **12** *tr.* (foll. by *to*) submit for consideration or attention (*let me put it to you another way*; *shall now put it to a vote*). **13** *tr.* (foll. by *to*) subject (a person) to (death, suffering, etc.). **14** *tr.* throw (esp. a shot or weight) as an athletic sport or exercise. ▷ SHOT-PUT. **15** *intr.* (foll. by *back*, *off*, *out*, etc.) (of a ship etc.) proceed or follow a course in a specified direction. ● *n.* a throw of the shot or weight. □ **put about 1** spread (information, rumour, etc.). **2** *Naut.* turn round; put (a ship) on the opposite tack. **3** esp. *Sc.* & *N.Engl.* trouble, distress. **put across 1** make acceptable or effective. **2** express in an understandable way. **put away 1** put (a thing) back in the place where it is normally kept. **2** lay (money etc.) aside for future use. **3 a** confine or imprison. **b** commit to a home or mental institution. **4** *colloq.* consume (food and drink), esp. in large quantities. **put back 1** restore to its proper or former place. **2** change (a planned event) to a later date or time. **3** move back the hands of (a clock or watch). **4** check the advance of. **put a bold** etc. **face on it** see FACE. **put the boot in** see BOOT[1]. **put by** lay (money etc.) aside for future use. **put down 1** suppress by force or authority. **2** *colloq.* snub or humiliate. **3** record or enter in writing. **4** enter the name of (a person) on a list, esp. as a member or subscriber. **5** (foll. by *as*, *for*) account or reckon. **6** (foll. by *to*) attribute (*put it down to bad planning*). **7** put (an old or sick animal) to death. **8** pay (a specified sum) as a deposit. **9** land (an aircraft). **10** stop to let (passengers) get off. **put an end to** see END. **put one's finger on** see FINGER. **put the finger on** see FINGER. **put one's foot down** see FOOT. **put one's foot in it** see FOOT. **put forward 1** suggest or propose. **2** advance the hands of (a clock or watch). **3** (often *refl.*) put into a prominent position, draw attention to. **put one's hands on** = *lay one's hands on* (see LAY[1]). **put in 1 a** enter or submit (a claim etc.). **b** (foll. by *for*) submit a claim for (a specified thing). **2** (foll. by *for*) be a candidate for (an appointment, election, etc.). **3** spend (time). **put a person in mind of** see MIND. **put off 1 a** postpone. **b** postpone an engagement with (a person). **2** (often foll. by *with*) evade (a person) with an excuse etc. **3** hinder or dissuade. **4** *Brit.* offend, disconcert; cause (a person) to lose interest in something. **put on 1** clothe oneself with. **2** cause (an electrical device, light, etc.) to function. **3** cause (transport) to be available. **4** stage (a play, show, etc.). **5** advance the hands of (a clock or watch). **6 a** pretend to be affected by (an emotion). **b** assume, take on (a character or appearance). **c** (**put it on**) exaggerate one's feelings etc. **7** increase one's weight by (a specified amount). **8** (foll. by *to*) make aware of or put in touch with (*put us on to their new accountant*). **put one across** (or **over**) (foll. by *on*) *colloq.* get the better of; trick. **put out 1 a** (often as **put out** *adj.*) disconcert or annoy. **b** (often *refl.*) inconvenience (*don't put yourself out*). **2** extinguish (a fire or light). **3** dislocate (a joint). **put over 1** make acceptable or effective. **2** express in an understandable way. **3** *US* postpone. **4** (often foll. by *on*) *US* achieve by deceit. **put the screws on** see SCREW. **put a sock in it** see SOCK[1]. **put store by** see STORE. **put through 1** carry out or complete (a task or transaction). **2** (often foll. by *to*) connect (a person) by telephone to another. **put to bed** see BED. **put to flight** see FLIGHT[2]. **put together 1** assemble (a whole) from parts. **2** combine (parts) to form a whole. **put two and two together** see TWO. **put under** render unconscious by anaesthetic etc. **put up 1** build or erect. **2 a** raise (a hand) to answer or ask a question. **b** raise (one's hands) to indicate surrender. **3** esp. *Brit.* increase (a price etc.). **4** take or provide with accommodation (*friends put me up for the night*). **5** engage in (a fight, struggle, etc.) as a form of resistance. **6** present (a proposal). **7 a** present oneself for election. **b** propose for election. **8** provide (money) as a backer in an enterprise. **9** display (a notice). **10** offer for sale or competition. **put upon** (usu. in *passive*; hyphenated when *attrib.*) *colloq.* make unfair or excessive demands on; take advantage of (a person). **put a person up to 1** inform or instruct a person about. **2** (usu. foll. by verbal noun) instigate a person in (*put them up to stealing the money*). **put up with** endure, tolerate; submit to. **put the wind up** see WIND[1]. **put words into a person's mouth** see MOUTH. [Middle English] □ **putter** *n.*

put[2] var. of PUTT.

putative *adj.* reputed, supposed (*his putative father*). [from Late Latin *putativus*] □ **putatively** *adv.*

put-down *n. colloq.* a snub or humiliating criticism.

put-in *n.* the act of putting the ball into a scrum in rugby.

put-on *n. colloq.* a deception or hoax.

putrefy *v.* (**-ies, -ied**) **1** *intr.* & *tr.* become or make putrid; go bad. **2** *intr.* fester, suppurate. **3** *intr.* become morally corrupt. [based on Latin *puter putris* 'rotten'] □ **putrefacient** *adj.* **putrefaction** *n.* **putrefactive** *adj.*

putrescent *adj.* in the process of rotting. [from Latin *putrescent-* 'turning rotten'] □ **putrescence** *n.*

putrid *adj.* **1** decomposed, rotten. **2** foul, noxious. **3** corrupt. **4** *slang* of poor quality; contemptible; very unpleasant. [from Latin *putridus*] □ **putridity** *n.* **putridly** *adv.*

putsch /puuch/ *n.* an attempt at political revolution; a violent uprising. [Swiss German, literally 'thrust, blow']

putt (also **put**) ● *v.tr.* (**putted**, **putting**) strike (a golf ball) gently on a putting green. ● *n.* a putting stroke. [differentiated from PUT[1]]

PUTTEE

puttee *n.* **1** ◀ a long strip of cloth wound spirally round the leg from ankle to knee for protection and support. **2** *US* a leather legging. [from Hindi *paṭṭī* 'band, bandage']

putter[1] *n.* a golf club used in putting. ▷ GOLF

putter[2] *US* var. of POTTER[1].

putting green *n.* (in golf) the smooth area of grass round a hole. ▷ GOLF

putty ● *n.* (*pl.* **-ies**) a cement made from ground chalk and raw linseed oil, used for fixing panes of glass, filling holes in woodwork, etc. ● *v.tr.* (**-ies, -ied**) cover, fix, join, or fill up with putty. [from French *potée*, literally 'potful']

put-up *adj.* (usu. in phr. **put-up job**) fraudulently presented or devised.

put-you-up *n. Brit.* a makeshift or temporary bed; a camp bed.

puzzle ● *n.* **1** a difficult or confusing problem; an enigma. **2** a problem or toy designed to test knowledge or ingenuity. ● *v.* **1** *tr.* (often as **puzzling** *adj.*) confound or disconcert mentally. **2** *intr.* (usu. foll. by *over* etc.) be perplexed (about). **3** *tr.* (foll. by *out*) solve or understand by hard thought. [16th-century coinage] □ **puzzlement** *n.* **puzzlingly** *adv.*

puzzler *n.* a difficult question or problem.

PVA *abbr.* polyvinyl acetate.

PVC *abbr.* polyvinyl chloride.

Pvt. *abbr.* **1** private. **2** *US* private soldier.

p.w. *abbr.* per week.

PWA *n.* (*pl.* **PWAs**) esp. *US* person with Aids.

P

PWR *abbr.* pressurized-water reactor.

pyaemia /py-**eem**-iă/ *n.* (*US* **pyemia**) blood poisoning caused by the spread of pus-forming bacteria in the bloodstream from a source of infection. [based on Greek *puon* 'pus' + *haima* 'blood'] □ **pyaemic** *adj.*

pye-dog *n.* (also **pie-dog**, **pi-dog**) a vagrant mongrel, esp. in Asia. [based on Hindi *pāhī* 'outsider']

pygmy *n.* (also **pigmy**) (*pl.* **-ies**) **1** a member of a dwarf people of equatorial Africa and parts of SE Asia. **2** a very small person, animal, or thing. **3** (*attrib.*) **a** of or relating to pygmies. **b** (of a person, animal, etc.) dwarf. [from Greek *pugmaios* 'dwarf'] □ **pygmaean** *adj.* **pygmean** *adj.*

pygmy chimpanzee see CHIMPANZEE.

pyjamas *n.pl.* (*US* **pajamas**) **1** a suit of loose trousers and jacket for sleeping in. **2** loose trousers worn by both sexes in some Asian countries. **3** (**pyjama**) (*attrib.*) designating parts of a suit of pyjamas (*pyjama trousers*). [Urdu & Persian, from *pay* 'leg' + *jāma* 'clothing']

pylon *n.* a tall structure erected esp. as a support for electric power cables. [from Greek *pulōn*]

pyorrhoea /py-ŏ-**ree**-ă/ *n.* (*US* **pyorrhea**) **1** a disease of periodontal tissue causing shrinkage of the gums and loosening of the teeth. **2** any discharge of pus. [Greek *puo-* (from *puon* 'pus') + *rhoia* 'flux' from *rheō* 'flow']

pyracantha *n.* ◀ any evergreen thorny shrub of the genus *Pyracantha*, having white flowers and bright red or yellow berries. [from Greek *pur* 'fire' + *akantha* 'thorn']

pyramid *n.* **1** ▲ a monumental structure, usu. of stone, with a square base and sloping sides meeting centrally at an apex, esp. an ancient Egyptian royal tomb. **2** a polyhedron or solid figure of this type with a base of three or more sides. **3** a pyramid-shaped thing or pile of things. [from Greek *puramis -idos*] □ **pyramidal** *adj.* **pyramidally** *adv.* **pyramidically** *adv.*

pyramid selling *n.* a system of selling goods in which agency rights are sold to an increasing number of distributors at successively lower levels.

pyre *n.* a heap of combustible material, esp. for burning a corpse. [based on Greek *pur* 'fire']

pyrethroid *n. Chem.* any of a group of substances used in the manufacture of insecticides.

pyrethrum *n.* **1** any of several aromatic plants of the genus *Tanacetum* (daisy family), esp. *T. coccineum*. **2** an insecticide made from the dried flowers of these plants, esp. *Tanacetum cinerariifolium*. [from Greek *purethron* 'feverfew']

PYRACANTHA
(*Pyracantha rogersiana*)

P

pyretic *adj.* of, for, or producing fever. [based on Greek *puretos* 'fever']

Pyrex *n. propr.* a heat-resistant type of glass, often used for ovenware. [invented word]

pyridoxine *n.* a vitamin of the B complex found in yeast, and important in the body's use of unsaturated fatty acids.

pyrimidine *n.* **1** *Chem.* a cyclic organic nitrogenous base. **2** any of a group of compounds with similar structure.

pyrites /py-ry-teez/ *n.* (in full **iron pyrites**) a yellow lustrous form of iron disulphide. [from Greek *puritēs* 'of fire'] □ **pyritic** *adj.* **pyritize** *v.tr.* (also **-ise**). **pyritous** *adj.*

pyro- *comb. form* **1** denoting fire. **2** *Chem.* denoting a new substance formed from another by elimination of water (*pyrophosphate*). [from Greek *pur* 'fire']

pyromania *n.* an obsessive desire to set fire to things. □ **pyromaniac** *n.*

pyrotechnics *n.pl.* **1** (treated as *sing.*) the art of making fireworks. **2** a display of fireworks. **3** any brilliant display. □ **pyrotechnic** *adj.* **pyrotechnical** *adj.* **pyrotechnist** *n.*

pyrrhic /pi-rik/ *adj.* (of a victory) won at too great a cost to be of use to the victor. [from *Pyrrhus* of Epirus, who defeated the Romans at Asculum (279 BC) but sustained heavy losses]

Pythagoras' theorem *n.* the theorem that the square on the hypotenuse of a right-angled triangle is equal to the sum of the squares on the other two sides.

Pythagorean ● *adj.* of or relating to the Greek philosopher Pythagoras (6th c. BC) or his philosophy. ● *n.* a follower of Pythagoras.

python *n.* ▼ any non-venomous snake of the family Pythonidae, esp. of the genus *Python*, found throughout the tropics in the Old World, and killing prey by compressing and asphyxiating it. ▷ EGG, SNAKE. [from Greek *Puthōn*, a huge monster killed by Apollo] □ **pythonic** *adj.*

PYTHON: RETICULATED PYTHON
(*Python reticulatus*)

pyx *n.* (also **pix**) *Eccl.* the vessel in which the consecrated bread of the Eucharist is kept. [from Latin *pyxis*]

pzazz var. of PIZAZZ.

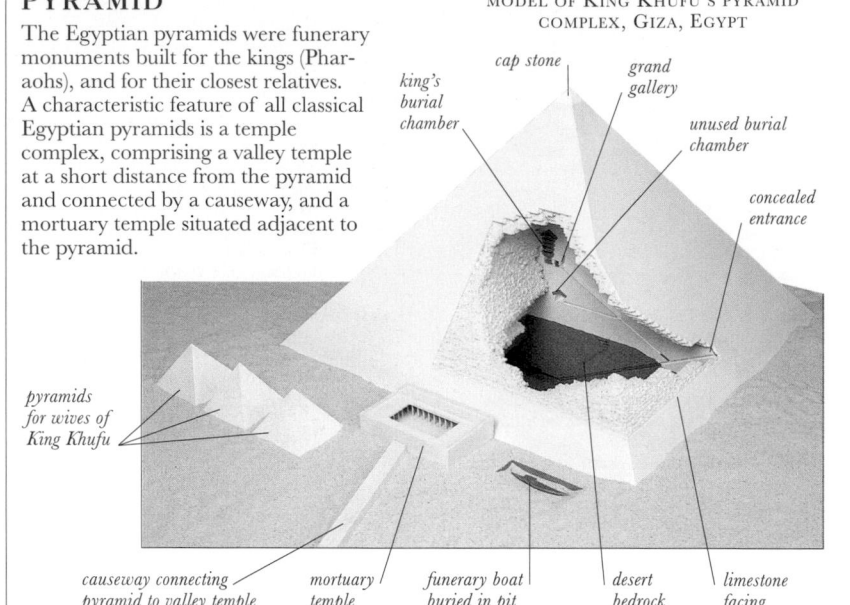

PYRAMID

The Egyptian pyramids were funerary monuments built for the kings (Pharaohs), and for their closest relatives. A characteristic feature of all classical Egyptian pyramids is a temple complex, comprising a valley temple at a short distance from the pyramid and connected by a causeway, and a mortuary temple situated adjacent to the pyramid.

MODEL OF KING KHUFU'S PYRAMID COMPLEX, GIZA, EGYPT

king's burial chamber

cap stone

grand gallery

unused burial chamber

concealed entrance

pyramids for wives of King Khufu

causeway connecting pyramid to valley temple

mortuary temple

funerary boat buried in pit

desert bedrock

limestone facing

Q[1] *n.* (also **q**) (*pl.* **Qs** or **Q's**) the seventeenth letter of the alphabet.

Q[2] *abbr.* (also **Q.**) **1** Queen, Queen's. **2** question.

QC *abbr. Law* Queen's Counsel.

QED *abbr. quod erat demonstrandum.*

qigong /chee **gong**/ *n.* a Chinese system of physical exercises and breathing control related to t'ai chi. [Chinese]

qr. *abbr.* quarter(s).

QSO *abbr.* quasi-stellar object, quasar.

qt. *abbr.* quart(s).

q.t. *n. colloq.* quiet (esp. in phr. **on the q.t.**). [abbreviation]

qu. *abbr.* **1** query. **2** question.

qua /kway, kwah/ *conj.* in the capacity of (*Napoleon qua general*). [Latin]

quack[1] ● *n.* the harsh sound made by ducks. ● *v.intr.* **1** utter this sound. **2** *colloq.* talk loudly and foolishly.

quack[2] *n.* **1 a** an unqualified practiser of medicine. **b** (*attrib.*) of or characteristic of unskilled medical practice (*quack cure*). **2** *slang* any doctor. **3** a charlatan. [abbreviation of *quacksalver*, from Dutch] □ **quackery** *n.*

quad[1] *n. colloq.* a quadrangle.

quad[2] *n. colloq.* = QUADRUPLET.

quad[3] ● *n.* quadraphony. ● *adj.* quadraphonic.

Quadragesima *n.* the first Sunday in Lent. [Latin fem. of *quadragesimus* 'fortieth', Lent having 40 days]

quadrangle *n.* **1** a four-sided plane figure, esp. a square or rectangle. **2 a** ▼ a four-sided court, esp. in colleges. **b** such a court with the buildings round it. [from Late Latin *quadrangulum* 'square'] □ **quadrangular** *adj.*

quadrangle

QUADRANGLE AT BUCKINGHAM PALACE, LONDON, ENGLAND

quadrant *n.* **1** a quarter of a circle's circumference. **2** a quarter of a circle enclosed by two radii at right angles. ▷ CIRCLE. **3** a quarter of a sphere etc. **4** any of four parts of a plane divided by two lines at right angles. **5 a** a graduated strip of metal shaped like a quarter-circle. **b** ▶ an instrument graduated for taking angular measurements. [from Latin *quadrans -antis* 'quarter']

quadraphonic *adj.* (also **quadrophonic**) (of sound reproduction) using four transmission channels. □ **quadraphonically** *adv.* **quadraphonics** *n.pl.*

quadrat *n. Ecol.* a small square area marked out for study. [variant of QUADRATE]

quadrate ● *adj.* esp. *Anat. & Zool.* square or rectangular (*quadrate bone; quadrate muscle*). ● *n.* **1** a quadrate bone or muscle. **2** a rectangular object. ● *v.tr.* make square. [from Latin *quadratus* 'made square']

quadratic *Math.* ● *adj.* **1** involving the second and no higher power of an unknown quantity or variable (*quadratic equation*). **2** square. ● *n.* **1** a quadratic equation. **2** (in *pl.*) the branch of algebra dealing with these.

quadrennial *adj.* **1** lasting four years. **2** recurring every four years.

quadri- *comb. form* denoting four. [from Latin *quattuor* 'four']

quadrilateral ● *adj.* having four sides. ● *n.* a four-sided figure. [from Late Latin *quadrilaterus*]

quadrille *n.* **1** a square dance containing usu. five figures. **2** the music for this. [from Spanish *cuadrilla* 'troop, company']

quadripartite *adj.* **1** consisting of four parts. **2** shared by or involving four parties.

quadriplegia *n. Med.* paralysis of all four limbs. [based on Greek *plēgē* 'blow, stroke'] □ **quadriplegic** *adj. & n.*

quadrivalent *adj. Chem.* = TETRAVALENT.

quadrophonic var. of QUADRAPHONIC.

quadruped ● *n.* a four-footed animal, esp. a mammal. ● *adj.* four-footed. [from Latin *quadrupes -pedis*] □ **quadrupedal** *adj.*

quadruple ● *adj.* **1** fourfold. **2 a** having four parts. **b** involving four participants (*quadruple alliance*). **3** being four times as many or as much. **4** (of time in music) having four beats in a bar. ● *n.* a fourfold number or amount. ● *v.tr. & intr.* multiply by four; increase fourfold. [from Latin *quadruplus*] □ **quadruply** *adv.*

quadruplet *n.* each of four children born at one birth.

quadruplicate ● *adj.* **1** fourfold. **2** of which four copies are made. ● *v.tr.* **1** multiply by four. **2** make four identical copies of. □ **in quadruplicate** in four identical copies. [from Latin *quadruplicatus* 'quadrupled']

quaff *v. literary* **1** *tr. & intr.* drink deeply. **2** *tr.* drain (a cup etc.) in long draughts. [16th-century coinage] □ **quaffable** *adj.* **quaffer** *n.*

quag *n.* a marshy or boggy place. [related to dialect verb *quag* 'to shake'] □ **quaggy** *adj.*

quagga *n.* ▶ an extinct zebra formerly native to S. Africa, which was yellowish-brown with stripes on the head, neck, and forebody. [from Nama *qua-ha'*]

peep-hole *sight line* *peep-hole*

apex

degree scale

angle read where string crosses scale

plumb bob

QUADRANT:
MEASURING ALTITUDE
USING A QUADRANT

quagmire *n.* **1** a soft boggy or marshy area. **2** a hazardous situation.

quail[1] *n.* (*pl.* same or **quails**) ▶ any small short-tailed game bird of the genus *Coturnix*, related to the partridge, esp. the migratory *C. coturnix*. [from medieval Latin *coacula*]

QUAIL: JAPANESE QUAIL
(*Coturnix japonica*)

quail[2] *v.intr.* flinch; be apprehensive. [Middle English]

quaint *adj.* **1** attractively unfamiliar or old-fashioned. **2** daintily odd. [earlier in senses 'wise, cunning': from Latin *cognitus* 'ascertained'] □ **quaintly** *adv.* **quaintness** *n.*

quake ● *v.intr.* **1** shake, tremble. **2** rock to and fro. **3** (of a person) shake or shudder (*was quaking with fear*). ● *n. colloq.* an earthquake. [Old English]

Quaker *n.* (also *attrib.*) a member of the Society of Friends, a Christian movement devoted to peaceful principles and eschewing formal doctrine, sacraments, and ordained ministers. [originally derogatory] □ **Quakerish** *adj.* **Quakerism** *n.*

qualification *n.* **1** the act or an instance of qualifying. **2** an accomplishment fitting a person for a position or purpose. **3 a** a circumstance, condition, etc., that modifies or limits (*the statement had many qualifications*). **b** a thing that detracts from completeness or absoluteness (*their relief had one qualification*). **4** a condition that must be fulfilled before a right can be acquired etc. **5** an attribution of a quality (*the qualification of our policy as opportunist is unfair*). □ **qualificatory** *adj.*

qualify *v.* (**-ies, -ied**) **1** *tr.* make competent or fit for a position or purpose. **2** *tr.* make legally entitled. **3** *intr.* (usu. foll. by *for*) satisfy conditions or requirements. **4** *tr.* add reservations to; modify or make less absolute (a statement or assertion). **5** *tr. Gram.* (of a word) attribute a quality to another word. **6** *tr.* moderate, mitigate; make less severe or extreme. **7** *tr.* alter the strength or flavour of. **8** *tr.* (foll. by *as*) attribute a specified quality to; describe as (*the idea was qualified as absurd*). **9** *tr.* (as **qualifying** *adj.*) serving to determine those that qualify (*qualifying examination*). [from medieval Latin *qualificare*] □ **qualifier** *n.*

QUAGGA
(*Equus quagga*)

qualitative *adj.* concerned with or depending on quality (*led to a qualitative change in society*). □ **qualitatively** *adv.*

quality *n.* (*pl.* **-ies**) **1** the degree of excellence of a thing (*of good quality; poor in quality*). **2 a** general excellence (*their work has quality*). **b** (*attrib.*) of high quality (*a quality product*). **3** a distinctive attribute or faculty. **4** the relative nature or character of a thing (*is made in three qualities*). **5** the distinctive timbre of a voice or sound. **6** *archaic* high social standing (*people of quality*). [from Latin *qualitas*]

quality control *n.* a system of maintaining standards in products by testing a sample of the output.

quality paper *n.* (also **quality newspaper**) a newspaper considered to be of a high cultural standard.

quality time *n.* time spent productively or profitably, esp. with reference to the limited time working parents can spend with their children.

Q

qualm *n.* **1** a misgiving; an uneasy doubt. **2** a scruple of conscience. **3** a momentary faint or sick feeling. [16th-century coinage] □ **qualmish** *adj.*

quandary *n.* (*pl.* **-ies**) **1** a state of perplexity. **2** a practical dilemma. [16th-century coinage]

quango *n.* (*pl.* **-os**) *Brit.* a semi-public body with financial support from and senior appointments made by the government. [abbreviation of *qua*si (or *qua*si-*au*tonomous *n*on-government(al) *o*rganization]

quanta *pl.* of QUANTUM.

quantal *adj.* **1** composed of discrete units; varying in steps, not continuously. **2** of or relating to a quantum or quantum theory. [from Latin *quantus* 'how much']

quantify *v.tr.* (**-ies**, **-ied**) **1** determine the quantity of. **2** express as a quantity. [from medieval Latin *quantificare*] □ **quantifiable** *adj.* **quantification** *n.* **quantifier** *n.*

quantitative *adj.* **1 a** concerned with quantity. **b** measured or measurable by quantity. **2** of or based on the quantity of syllables. [from medieval Latin *quantitativus*] □ **quantitatively** *adv.*

quantitative analysis *n. Chem.* measurement of the amounts of the constituents of a substance.

quantitive *adj.* = QUANTITATIVE. □ **quantitively** *adv.*

quantity *n.* (*pl.* **-ies**) **1** that property of things that is measurable. **2** the size or extent or weight or amount or number. **3** a specified or considerable portion or number or amount (*buys in quantity; the quantity of heat in a body*). **4** (in *pl.*) large amounts or numbers; an abundance (*quantities of food; is found in quantities on the shore*). **5** the length or shortness of vowel sounds or syllables. **6** *Math.* **a** a value, component, etc. that may be expressed in numbers. **b** the figure or symbol representing this. [from Latin *quantitas*]

quantity surveyor *n. Brit.* a person who measures and prices building work.

quantum *n.* (*pl.* **quanta**) **1** *Physics* **a** a discrete quantity of energy proportional in magnitude to the frequency of the radiation it represents. **b** an analogous discrete amount of any other physical quantity. **2 a** a required or allowed amount. **b** a share or portion. [Latin neut. of *quantus* 'how great']

quantum jump *n.* (also **quantum leap**) **1** a sudden large increase or advance. **2** *Physics* an abrupt transition in an atom or molecule from one quantum state to another.

quantum mechanics *n. Physics* a mathematical form of quantum theory dealing with the motion and interaction of particles and incorporating the concept that these particles can also be regarded as waves.

quantum theory *n. Physics* the body of theory based on the concept of quanta of energy.

quarantine ● *n.* **1** isolation imposed on persons or animals that have arrived from elsewhere or been exposed to infectious or contagious disease. **2** the period of this isolation. ● *v.tr.* put in quarantine. [from Italian *quarantina* 'forty days']

quark[1] *n. Physics* any of a class of unobserved subatomic particles with a fractional electric charge, of which hadrons are thought to be composed. ▷ NUCLEUS. [invented word, associated with 'Three quarks for Muster Mark' in Joyce's *Finnegans Wake* (1939)]

quark[2] *n.* a type of low-fat curd cheese. [German]

quarrel ● *n.* **1** a violent contention or altercation. **2** a rupture of friendly relations. **3** an occasion of complaint. ● *v.intr.* (**quarrelled, quarrelling**; *US* **quarreled, quarreling**) **1** have a dispute; break off friendly relations. **2** find fault. [from Latin *querel(l)a* 'complaint'] □ **quarreller** *n.*

quarrelsome *adj.* given to quarrelling. □ **quarrelsomeness** *n.*

quarry[1] ● *n.* (*pl.* **-ies**) **1** an excavation made by taking stone etc. for building etc. from its bed. **2** a place from which stone etc. may be extracted. ● *v.tr.* (**-ies, -ied**) extract (stone) from a quarry. [from Latin *quadrum* 'square']

QUARTZ

Quartz is one of the most common types of mineral, and can be found in sedimentary, igneous, and metamorphic rocks, and in mineral veins with metal ores. Quartz faces are often striated, with twinned and distorted crystals. Its varied colours include white, grey, red, purple, pink, yellow, green, brown, and black, or it may be colourless. Semi-precious varieties of quartz include citrine and amethyst.

EXAMPLES OF QUARTZ — ROCK CRYSTAL / AMETHYST / CITRINE / ROSE QUARTZ / SMOKY QUARTZ

---

quarry[2] *n.* (*pl.* **-ies**) **1** the object of pursuit by a bird of prey, hounds, hunters, etc. **2** an intended victim or prey. [originally in sense 'parts of deer placed on the hide and given to hounds': from Old French *cuiree*]

quarry[3] *n.* (*pl.* **-ies**) **1** a diamond-shaped pane of glass. **2** (in full **quarry tile**) an unglazed floor-tile. [a form of earlier *quarrel*, in same sense]

quarryman *n.* (*pl.* **-men**) a worker in a quarry.

quart *n.* **1** a liquid measure equal to a quarter of a gallon; two pints. **2** a vessel containing this amount. **3** *US* a dry measure, equivalent to one-thirty-second of a bushel (1.1 litre). □ **a quart into a pint pot** *Brit.* **1** a large amount etc. fitted into a small space. **2** something impossible to achieve. [from Latin *quarta* (fem.) 'fourth']

quarter ● *n.* **1** each of four equal parts into which a thing is or might be divided. **2** a period of three months. **3** a point of time 15 minutes before or after any hour. **4** a school or *US* university term. **5 a** 25 *US* or Canadian cents. **b** a coin of this denomination. **6** a part of a town (*residential quarter*). **7 a** a point of the compass. **b** a region at such a point. **8** the direction, district, or source of supply etc. (*help from any quarter; came from all quarters*). **9** (in *pl.*) **a** lodgings. **b** *Mil.* the accommodation of troops etc. **10 a** one-fourth of a lunar month. ▷ LUNAR MONTH. **b** the Moon's position between the first and second (**first quarter**) or third and fourth (**last quarter**) of these. **11 a** each of the four parts into which a carcass is divided. **b** (in *pl.*) = HINDQUARTERS. **12** mercy offered or granted to an enemy on condition of surrender. **13 a** one-fourth of a pound weight. **b** *Brit.* a grain measure equivalent to 8 bushels. **c** one-fourth of a hundredweight (28 lb or *US* 25 lb). **14** each of four divisions on a shield. **15** (in American and Australian football) each of four equal periods into which a match is divided. ● *v.tr.* **1** divide into quarters. **2** *hist.* divide (the body of an executed person) in this way. **3 a** put (troops etc.) into quarters. **b** station or lodge in a specified place. **4** (foll. by *on*) impose (a person) on another as a lodger. **5** (esp. of a hunting dog or bird of prey) range or traverse (the ground) in every direction. **6** *Heraldry* place or bear (charges or coats of arms) on the four quarters of a shield's surface. ▷ QUARTERING. [from Latin *quartarius* 'fourth part (of a measure)']

quarterback *n.* a player in American football who directs attacking play.

quarter day *n. Brit.* one of four days on which quarterly payments are due, tenancies begin and end, etc.

quarterdeck *n.* part of a ship's upper deck near the stern, usu. reserved for officers. ▷ MAN-OF-WAR

quarter-final *n.* a match or round preceding the semi-final.

---

quarter-hour *n.* (also **quarter of an hour**) **1** a period of 15 minutes. **2** = QUARTER *n.* 3.

quartering *n.* **1** (in *pl.*) ▼ the coats of arms marshalled on a shield to denote the alliances of a family with the heiresses of others. **2** the provision of quarters for soldiers. **3** the act or an instance of dividing, esp. into four equal parts.

quartered shield

QUARTERING: 15TH-CENTURY SPANISH DISH SHOWING QUARTERED COAT OF ARMS

quarter-light *n. Brit.* a window in the side of a motor vehicle, closed carriage, etc. other than the main door window.

quarterly ● *adj.* **1** produced or occurring once every quarter of a year. **2** (of a shield) quartered. ▷ QUARTERING. ● *adv.* **1** once every quarter of a year. **2** in the four, or in two diagonally opposite, quarters of a shield. ● *n.* (*pl.* **-ies**) a quarterly review or magazine.

quartermaster *n.* **1** a regimental officer in charge of quartering, rations, etc. **2** a naval petty officer in charge of steering, signals, etc.

Quartermaster General *n.* (*pl.* **Quartermaster Generals**) the head of the army department in charge of quartering etc.

quarter note *n.* esp. *N. Amer. Mus.* a crotchet.

quarter sessions *n.pl. hist.* (in the UK) a court of limited criminal and civil jurisdiction usu. held quarterly.

quarter-tone *n. Mus.* half a semitone.

quartet *n.* (also **quartette**) **1** *Mus.* **a** a composition for four voices or instruments. **b** the performers of such a piece. **2** any group of four. [French *quartette* from Italian *quartetto*]

quarto *n.* (*pl.* **-os**) *Printing* **1** the size of book or paper given by folding a (usu. specified) sheet of paper

Q

twice to form four leaves. **2** a book consisting of sheets folded in this way. [Latin *(in) quarto* '(in) the fourth']

quartz *n.* ◀ a mineral form of silica that crystallizes as hexagonal prisms. ▷ AGGREGATE, ORE. [from West Slavonic *kwardy*]

quartz clock *n.* (also **quartz watch**) ▼ a clock or watch operated by vibrations of an electrically driven quartz crystal.

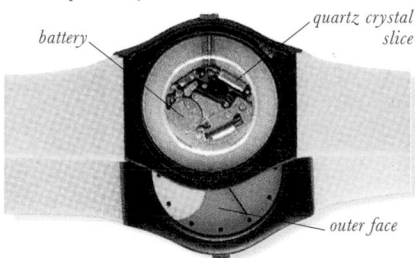

battery   *quartz crystal slice*

outer face

QUARTZ WATCH: INTERNAL MECHANISM
AND OUTER FACE

quartzite *n.* a metamorphic rock consisting mainly of quartz.

quartz lamp *n.* a quartz tube containing mercury vapour and used as a light source.

quasar *n. Astron.* ▼ any of a class of starlike celestial objects often associated with intense radio emission. [from *quasi*-stell*ar*]

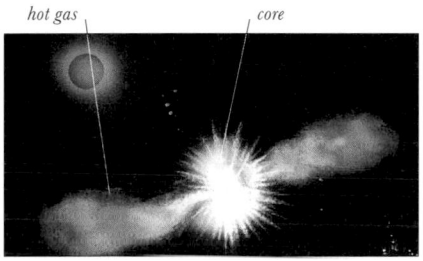

hot gas   *core*

QUASAR: ARTIST'S IMPRESSION OF A QUASAR

quash *v.tr.* **1** annul; reject as not valid, esp. by a legal procedure. **2** suppress, crush. [from Late Latin *cassare* 'to annul']

quasi- *comb. form* **1** seemingly; apparently but not really (*quasi-scientific*). **2** almost (*quasi-independent*).

quassia /kwass-iă/ *n.* **1** an evergreen tree, *Quassia amara*, native to S. America. **2** the wood, bark, or root of this tree, yielding a bitter medicinal tonic and insecticide. [named after G. *Quassi*, 18th-century Suriname slave, who discovered its medicinal properties]

quatercentenary ● *n.* (*pl.* **-ies**) a four-hundredth anniversary. ● *adj.* of this anniversary. [based on Latin *quater* 'four times']

quaternary ● *adj.* **1** fourth in order or rank etc. **2** (**Quaternary**) *Geol.* of or relating to the most recent period in the Cenozoic era. ● *n.* (*pl.* **-ies**) **1** a quaternary thing, compound, etc. **2** (**Quaternary**) *Geol.* the Quaternary period or system. [from Latin *quaternarius*]

quatrain *n.* a stanza of four lines. [French]

quatrefoil /kat-rĕ-foil/ *n.* ▶ a four-pointed or four-leafed figure, esp. as an ornament in architectural tracery. [from Anglo-French *quatre* 'four' + *foil* 'leaf']

quatrefoil

QUATREFOIL
DECORATION ON A MODEL
OF A 12TH-CENTURY
CATHEDRAL SPIRE

QUATTROCENTO

The term quattrocento is often used to describe the Italian Renaissance of the 15th century. New ideas flourished during this period. These included rules governing perspective, more naturalistic and expressive painting and sculpture, and a revival of themes from classical Italy. Key artists included Botticelli, Donatello, and Masaccio.

use of perspective gives three-dimensional effect

ancient Roman architectural styles

Crucifixion of Jesus Christ, a common 15th-century subject

realistic, not idealized, figures of the Virgin and St John

Masaccio's patron, Lorenzo Lenzi

The Trinity (*c.*1427), MASACCIO

TIMELINE

1000   1050   1100   1150   1200   1250   1300   1350   1400   1450   1500

---

quattrocento /kwat-roh-**chen**-toh/ *n.* ▲ the style of Italian art of the 15th c. ▷ RENAISSANCE. [Italian, short for *milquattrocento* '1400', referring to the years 1400–99] □ **quattrocentist** *n. & adj.*

quaver ● *v.* **1** *intr.* **a** (esp. of a voice or musical sound) vibrate, shake, tremble. **b** use trills or shakes in singing. **2** *tr.* **a** sing (a note or song) with quavering. **b** say in a trembling voice. ● *n.* **1** *Mus.* a note having the time value of half a crotchet and represented by a large dot with a hooked stem. ▷ NOTATION. **2** a trill in singing. **3** a tremble in speech. [Middle English] □ **quaveringly** *adv.* **quavery** *adj.*

quay /kee/ *n.* a stationary artificial landing place for loading and unloading ships. [from Old French *kay*]

quayside *n.* the land forming or near a quay.

queasy *adj.* (**-ier**, **-iest**) **1 a** (of a person) nauseous. **b** (of a person's stomach) easily upset; weak of digestion. **2** (of the conscience etc.) overscrupulous. [Middle English] □ **queasily** *adv.* **queasiness** *n.*

Quechua /kech-wă/ (also **Quichua** /kich-wă/) ● *n.* (*pl.* same or **Quechuas**) **1** a member of a S. American Indian people of Peru and neighbouring countries. **2** the language of this people. ● *adj.* of or relating to this people or their language. [from Quechua] □ **Quechuan** *adj.*

queen ● *n.* **1** (as a title usu. **Queen**) a female sovereign etc., esp. the hereditary ruler of an independent state. **2** (in full **queen consort**) a king's wife. **3** a woman, country, or thing pre-eminent of its kind (*tennis queen*; *the queen of roses*). **4** the fertile female among ants, bees, etc. **5** the most powerful piece in chess. ▷ CHESS. **6** a playing card with a picture of a queen. ▷ COURT CARD. **7** *slang offens.* a male homosexual, esp. an effeminate one. **8** (as a title usu. **Queen**) **a** an honoured female, e.g. the Virgin Mary (*Queen of Heaven*). **b** an ancient goddess (*Venus, Queen of love*). **9** a belle or mock sovereign on some occasion (*beauty queen*; *queen of the May*). **10** (**the Queen**) the national anthem when there is a female sovereign. ● *v.tr.* **1** make (a woman) queen. **2** *Chess* convert (a pawn) into a queen when it reaches the opponent's side of the board. □ **queen it** play the queen. [Old English] □ **queendom** *n.* **queenship** *n.*

Queen-Anne *adj.* (usu. *attrib.*) in the style of English architecture, furniture, etc., in or about Queen Anne's time, the early 18th century.

Queen Anne's lace *n. Bot.* = COW-PARSLEY.

queen bee *n.* **1** the fertile female in a hive. **2** the chief or controlling woman in a group.

queen consort see QUEEN *n.* 2.

queen dowager *n.* the widow of a king.

queenly *adj.* (**queenlier**, **queenliest**) **1** fit for or appropriate to a queen. **2** majestic. □ **queenliness** *n.*

queen mother *n.* the dowager who is mother of the sovereign.

queen of puddings *n.* a pudding made with bread, jam, and meringue.

Queen of the May *n.* = MAY QUEEN.

queen post *n.* ▼ either of two upright timbers between the tie-beam and principal rafters of a roof-truss.

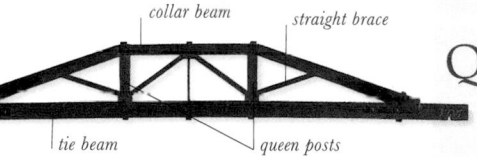

collar beam   *straight brace*

tie beam   *queen posts*

QUEEN POSTS IN A ROOF TRUSS

Q

Queen's Bench *n.* (in the UK) a division of the High Court of Justice.

Queensberry Rules *n.pl.* the standard rules, esp. of boxing. [named after the 8th Marquess of *Queensberry*, English nobleman, 1844–1900, who supervised the drafting of boxing laws (1867)]

Queen's Counsel *n.* (in the UK) counsel to the Crown, taking precedence over other barristers.

Queen's English *n.* the English language as correctly written or spoken in Britain.

Queen's evidence *n. Brit. Law* evidence for the prosecution given by a participant in the crime at issue.

Queen's Guide *n.* (in the UK) a Guide (see GUIDE *n.* 9) who has reached the highest rank of proficiency.

Queen's highway *n. Brit.* a public road, regarded as being under the sovereign's protection.

queen-size *adj.* (also **queen-sized**) of a larger than normal size, usu. smaller than king-size.

Queen's Scout *n.* (in the UK) a Scout (see SCOUT *n.* 4) who has reached the highest standard of proficiency.

Queen's Speech n. (in the UK) a statement including the Government's proposed measures read by the sovereign at the opening of Parliament.

queer ● adj. **1** strange; odd; eccentric. **2** shady; suspect; of questionable character. **3** Brit. **a** slightly ill; faint. **b** slang drunk. **4** slang offens. (esp. of a man) homosexual. ● n. slang offens. a homosexual. ● v.tr. slang spoil; put out of order. □ **in Queer Street** Brit. slang in a difficulty, in debt or trouble or disrepute. **queer a person's pitch** Brit. spoil a person's chances. □ **queerly** adv. **queerness** n.

quell v.tr. **1 a** crush or put down (a rebellion etc.). **b** reduce (rebels etc.) to submission. **2** suppress or alleviate (fear, anger, etc.). [Old English cwellan 'to kill']

quench v.tr. **1** satisfy (thirst) by drinking. **2** extinguish (a fire or light etc.). **3** cool, esp. with water. **4** Metallurgy cool (esp. hot metal) rapidly in cold water, air, oil, etc. **5 a** stifle or suppress (desire etc.). **b** Physics & Electronics inhibit or prevent (oscillation, luminescence, etc.) by counteractive means. **6** Brit. slang reduce (an opponent) to silence. [Old English] □ **quencher** n. **quenchless** adj.

quenelle /kĕ-**nel**/ n. a small seasoned ball or roll of pounded fish or meat. [French]

quern n. **1** ▶ a mill for grinding corn, typically consisting of two stones. **2** a small hand mill for pepper etc. [Old English]

querulous adj. complaining, peevish. [from Latin querulus] □ **querulously** adv. **querulousness** n.

query ● n. (pl. **-ies**) **1** a question. **2** a question mark, or the word query spoken or written to question accuracy or as a mark of interrogation. ● v. (**-ies, -ied**) **1** tr. ask or enquire. **2** tr. call in question. **3** tr. dispute the accuracy of. **4** intr. put a question. [from Latin quaerere 'to ask']

QUERN:
STONE QUERN
c.4000–2000 BC

quest ● n. **1** a search or the act of seeking. **2** the thing sought, esp. the object of a medieval knight's pursuit. ● v. **1** intr. **a** go about in search of something. **b** (of a dog etc.) search about for game. **2** tr. poet. search for; seek out. □ **in quest of** seeking. [based on Latin quaerere quaest- 'to seek'] □ **quester** n. (also **questor**). **questingly** adv.

question ● n. **1** a sentence worded or expressed so as to seek information. **2 a** doubt about or objection to a thing's truth, credibility, advisability, etc. (is there any question as to its validity?). **b** the raising of such doubt etc. **3** a matter to be discussed or decided or voted on. **4** a problem requiring an answer or solution. **5** (foll. by of) a matter or concern depending on conditions (it's a question of money). ● v.tr. **1** ask questions of; interrogate. **2** subject (a person) to examination. **3** throw doubt upon; raise objections to. **4** seek information from the study of (phenomena, facts). □ **be a question of time** be certain to happen sooner or later. **beyond all question** undoubtedly. **come into question** be discussed; become of practical importance. **in question** that is being discussed or referred to (the person in question). **is not the question** is irrelevant. **no question of** no possibility of (there's no question of my giving in). **out of the question** too impracticable etc. to be worth discussing; impossible. **put the question** require supporters and opponents of a proposal to record their votes. [from Latin quaestio 'seeking'] □ **questioner** n. **questioningly** adv. **questionless** adj.

questionable adj. **1** doubtful as regards truth or quality. **2** not clearly in accordance with honesty, honour, wisdom, etc. □ **questionability** n. **questionableness** n. **questionably** adv.

question mark n. **1** a punctuation mark (?) indicating a question. **2** a cause for doubt or uncertainty (there's still a question mark over the plans).

question master n. Brit. a person who presides over a quiz game etc.

questionnaire n. **1** a formulated series of questions, esp. for statistical study. **2** a document containing these.

question time n. a period during parliamentary proceedings when MPs may question ministers.

quetzal /**ket**-săl/ n. ▶ any of various brilliantly coloured birds of the family Trogonidae, esp. the Central and S. American Pharomachrus mocinno. [Spanish]

female

male

queue /kew/ ● n. a line or sequence of persons, vehicles, etc., awaiting their turn to be attended to or to proceed. ● v.intr. (**queues, queued, queuing** or **queueing**) (of persons etc.) form a queue; take one's place in a queue. [from Latin cauda 'tail']

QUETZAL
(Pharomachrus
mocinno)

queue-jump v.intr. Brit. push forward out of turn in a queue.

quibble ● n. **1** a petty objection; a trivial point of criticism. **2** a pun. **3** an evasion; an insubstantial argument which relies on an ambiguity etc. ● v.intr. use quibbles. [from obsolete quib, in same sense] □ **quibbling** adj.

quiche /keesh/ n. an open flan or tart with a savoury filling. [French]

Quichua var. of QUECHUA.

quick ● adj. **1** taking only a short time (a quick worker). **2** arriving after a short time, prompt (quick action; quick results). **3** with only a short interval (in quick succession). **4** lively, intelligent. **5** acute, alert (has a quick ear). **6** (of a temper) easily roused. **7** archaic living, alive (the quick and the dead). ● adv. quickly; at a rapid rate. ● n. **1** the soft flesh below the nails, or the skin, or a sore. **2** the seat of feeling or emotion (cut to the quick). □ **be quick** act quickly. [Old English cwic(u) 'alive'] □ **quickly** adv. **quickness** n.

sandstone grinder

quicken v. **1** tr. & intr. make or become quicker; accelerate. **2** tr. give life or vigour to; rouse. **3** intr. **a** (of a woman) reach a stage in pregnancy when movements of the foetus can be felt. **b** (of a foetus) begin to show signs of life. **4** intr. come to life.

quick-fire attrib.adj. **1** (of repartee etc.) rapid. **2** firing shots in quick succession.

quick fix n. a rapid (esp. inadequate) solution to a problem.

quick-freeze v.tr. freeze (food) rapidly so as to preserve its natural qualities.

quickie colloq. ● n. **1** a thing done or made quickly or hastily. **2** an alcoholic drink taken quickly. ● adj. made or executed quickly (quickie divorce; quickie production).

quicklime n. = LIME¹ n. 1.

quick march Mil. ● n. a march at about 120 paces per minute. ● int. the command to begin this.

quick one n. colloq. an alcoholic drink taken quickly.

quicksand n. **1 a** loose wet sand that sucks in anything placed or falling into it. **b** a bed of this. **2** a treacherous thing or situation.

quickset Brit. ● adj. (of a hedge) formed of slips of plants, esp. hawthorn, set in the ground to grow. ● n. **1** such slips. **2** a hedge formed in this way.

quicksilver n. **1** mercury. **2** mobility of temperament or mood.

quickstep ● n. **1** a fast foxtrot. **2** (**quick step**) Mil. a step used in quick time. ● v.intr. (**-stepped, -stepping**) dance the quickstep.

quick-tempered adj. easily angered.

quick-witted adj. quick to grasp a situation, make repartee, etc. □ **quick-wittedness** n.

quid¹ n. (pl. same) Brit. slang one pound sterling. □ **not the full quid** Austral. slang mentally deficient. **quids in** slang in a position of profit.

quid² n. a lump of tobacco for chewing. [dialect variant of CUD]

quiddity n. (pl. **-ies**) **1** Philos. the essence of a thing. **2** a quibble; a trivial objection. [from medieval Latin quidditas]

quid pro quo n. (pl. **quid pro quos**) **1** a thing given as compensation. **2** return made (for a gift, favour, etc.). [Latin, literally 'something for something']

quiescent /kwi-**ess**-ĕnt/ adj. **1** motionless, inert. **2** silent, dormant. [from Latin quiescent- 'being quiet'] □ **quiescence** n.

quiet ● adj. (**quieter, quietest**) **1** with little or no sound or motion. **2** of gentle or peaceful disposition. **3** unobtrusive; not showy. **4** not overt; disguised (quiet resentment). **5** undisturbed; uninterrupted; free or far from vigorous action (a quiet time for prayer). **6** informal (just a quiet wedding). **7** enjoyed in quiet (a quiet smoke). **8** not anxious or remorseful. ● n. **1** silence; stillness. **2** an undisturbed state; tranquillity. **3** a state of being free from urgent tasks or agitation (a time of quiet at work). **4** a peaceful state of affairs (there was quiet along the frontier). ● v. **1** tr. soothe; make quiet. **2** intr. become quiet or calm. □ **be quiet** (esp. in imper.) cease talking etc. **keep quiet 1** refrain from making a noise. **2** suppress or refrain from disclosing information etc. **on the quiet** colloq. secretly. [from Latin quietus] □ **quietly** adv. **quietness** n.

quieten v.tr. & intr. Brit. = QUIET v.

quietism n. **1** a passive attitude towards life, as a form of religious mysticism. **2** the principle of non-resistance. □ **quietist** n. & adj.

quietude n. a state of quiet.

quietus n. (pl. **quietuses**) **1** release from life; death; that which brings death. **2** something which quiets or represses; a sedative. [from medieval Latin quietus est 'he is quit', used in discharge of a debt]

quiff n. esp. Brit. **1** a man's tuft of hair, brushed upward over the forehead. **2** a curl plastered down on the forehead. [19th-century coinage]

quill n. **1** (in full **quill-feather**) a large feather in a wing or tail. ▷ FEATHER. **2** the hollow stem of this. **3** (in full **quill pen**) ▼ a pen made of a quill. **4** (usu. in pl.) the spines of a porcupine. [Middle English]

QUILL PEN MADE FROM
A GOOSE FEATHER

quilling n. US the art of making ornamental filigree from tightly rolled columns of paper.

quilt ● n. **1** ◀ a bed-covering made of padding enclosed between layers of cloth etc. and kept in place by cross lines of stitching. **2** a bedspread of similar design (patchwork quilt). ● v.tr.

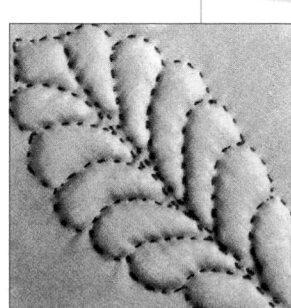

QUILT: DETAIL OF PADDED
(TRAPUNTO) QUILTING

Q

1 cover or line with padded material. **2** make or join together (pieces of cloth with padding between) after the manner of a quilt. [from Latin *culcita* 'mattress, cushion'] □ **quilter** *n.* **quilting** *n.*

quim *n.* *coarse slang* the female genitals. [18th-century coinage]

quin *n.* *esp. Brit. colloq.* a quintuplet.

quince *n.* **1** ▶ a hard acid pear-shaped fruit used as a preserve or flavouring. **2** any shrub or small tree of the genus *Cydonia* (rose family), esp. *C. oblonga*, bearing this fruit. See also JAPANESE QUINCE. [based on Latin *cydoneum (malum)* '(apple) of *Cydonia*', now Canea in Crete]

QUINCE
(*Cydonia oblonga*)

quincentenary ● *n.* (*pl.* **-ies**) **1** a five-hundredth anniversary. **2** a festival marking this. ● *adj.* of this anniversary. [based on Latin *quinque* 'five' + CENTENARY]

quincentennial ● *n.* a quincentenary. ● *adj.* **1** lasting five hundred years or occurring every five hundred years. **2** of or concerning a quincentenary.

quincunx *n.* **1** five objects set so that four are at the corners of a square or rectangle and the fifth is at its centre. **2** this arrangement. [Latin, literally 'five-twelfths'] □ **quincuncial** *adj.*

quinine *n.* **1** ◀ an alkaloid found esp. in the bark of the S. American evergreen cinchona tree. **2** a bitter toxic drug containing this, formerly used as a tonic and esp. as a remedy for malaria. [based on Quechua *kina* 'bark']

Quinquagesima *n.* (in full **Quinquagesima Sunday**) the Sunday before the beginning of Lent. [medieval Latin]

quinque- *comb. form* five.

quinquennial *adj.* **1** lasting five years. **2** recurring every five years. □ **quinquennially** *adv.*

quinquennium *n.* (*pl.* **quinquenniums** or **quinquennia**) a period of five years. [Latin, from *quinque* 'five' + *annus* 'year']

quinsy *n.* an inflammation of the throat, esp. an abscess in the region of the tonsils. [from Greek *kunagkhē* 'canine quinsy'] □ **quinsied** *adj.*

quint *n.* *N. Amer.* a quintuplet. [based on Latin *quintus* 'fifth']

quintessence *n.* **1** (usu. foll. by *of*) the purest and most perfect, or most typical, form, manifestation, or embodiment of some quality or class. **2** a refined extract. [from medieval Latin *quinta essentia* 'fifth essence (pervading all things)'] □ **quintessential** *adj.* **quintessentially** *adv.*

QUININE: BARK OF THE CINCHONA TREE, SOURCE OF QUININE

quintet *n.* (also **quintette**) **1** *Mus.* **a** a composition for five voices or instruments. **b** the performers of such a piece. **2** any group of five. [from French *quintette*]

quintuple ● *adj.* **1** fivefold; consisting of five parts. **2** involving five parties. **3** (of time in music) having five beats in a bar. ● *n.* a fivefold number or amount. ● *v.tr. & intr.* multiply by five; increase fivefold. [French]

quintuplet *n.* each of five children born at one birth.

quintuplicate ● *adj.* **1** fivefold. **2** of which five copies are made. ● *v.tr. & intr.* multiply by five. □ **in quintuplicate 1** in five identical copies. **2** in groups of five.

quip ● *n.* a clever saying; an epigram. ● *v.intr.* (**quipped, quipping**) make quips. □ **quipster** *n.*

quire *n.* **1** four sheets of paper etc. folded to form eight leaves. **2** any collection of leaves one within another in a manuscript or book. **3** 25 (formerly 24) sheets of paper. □ **in quires** unbound; in sheets. [based on Latin *quaterni* 'set of four']

quirk *n.* **1** a peculiarity of behaviour. **2** a trick of fate; a freak. **3** a flourish in writing. [16th-century coinage] □ **quirkish** *adj.* **quirky** *adj.* (**quirkier, quirkiest**). **quirkily** *adv.* **quirkiness** *n.*

quirt *n.* a short-handled riding whip with a braided leather lash. [from Spanish *cuerda* 'cord']

quisling *n.* **1** a person cooperating with an occupying enemy; a collaborator or fifth columnist. **2** a traitor. [from V. *Quisling*, renegade Norwegian Army officer, 1887–1945]

quit ● *v.tr.* (**quitting**; *past* and *past part.* **quitted** or **quit**) **1** (also *absol.*) give up; let go; abandon (a task etc.). **2** *N. Amer.* cease; stop (*quit grumbling*). **3 a** leave or depart from. **b** (*absol.*) (of a tenant) leave occupied premises (esp. *notice to quit*). **4** (*refl.*) acquit; behave (*quit oneself well*). ● *predic.adj.* (foll. by *of*) rid (*glad to be quit of the problem*). □ **quit hold of** loose. [based on Latin *quietus* 'quiet']

quitch *n.* (in full **quitch-grass**) = COUCH[2]. [Old English]

quite *adv.* **1** completely; entirely; wholly (*I quite agree*). **2** rather; to some extent (*she's quite nice*). **3** (often foll. by *so*) said to indicate agreement. □ **quite a** a remarkable or outstanding (person or thing) (*it was quite an event*). **quite another** (or **other**) very different (*that's quite another matter*). **quite a few** *colloq.* a fairly large number of. **quite some** a large amount of (*quite some time*). **quite something** a remarkable thing. [Middle English]

quits *predic.adj.* on even terms by retaliation or repayment (*then we'll be quits*). □ **call it** (or **cry**) **quits** acknowledge that things are now even; agree not to proceed further in a quarrel etc.

quittance *n.* *archaic* or *poet.* **1** (foll. by *from*) a release. **2** an acknowledgement of payment; a receipt. [from Old French *quitance*]

quitter *n.* *colloq.* **1** a person who gives up easily. **2** a shirker.

quiver[1] ● *v.* **1** *intr.* tremble or vibrate with a slight rapid motion, esp.: **a** (usu. foll. by *with*) as the result of emotion (*quiver with anger*). **b** (usu. foll. by *in*) as the result of air currents etc. (*quiver in the breeze*). **2** *tr.* (of a bird, esp. a skylark) make (its wings) quiver. ● *n.* a quivering motion or sound. [Middle English, from obsolete adj. *quiver* 'rapid'] □ **quiveringly** *adv.* **quivery** *adj.*

quiver[2] *n.* ▶ an archer's portable case for holding arrows. ▷ ARCHERY. [from Old French *quivre*]

quiverful *n.* (*pl.* **-fuls**) **1** as much as a quiver can hold. **2** many children of one parent (Ps. 127:5).

qui vive /kee veev/ *n.* □ **on the qui vive** on the alert; watching for something to happen. [French, literally '(long) live who?', i.e. 'on whose side are you?', a sentry's challenge]

quixotic *adj.* extravagantly and romantically chivalrous; naively idealistic; impractical. [from the name of Don *Quixote*, hero of Cervantes' romance (1605–15)] □ **quixotically** *adv.* **quixotism** *n.* **quixotry** *n.*

quiz ● *n.* (*pl.* **quizzes**) **1** a test of knowledge, esp. as a form of entertainment. **2** an interrogation, examination, or questionnaire. ● *v.tr.* (**quizzed, quizzing**) examine by questioning. [19th-century coinage, originally US]

quizmaster *n.* a person who presides over a quiz.

quiz show *n.* a light-entertainment programme on

arrow

QUIVER

television or radio in which people compete in a quiz, often for prizes.

quizzical *adj.* **1** expressing or done with mild or amused perplexity. **2** strange; comical. □ **quizzically** *adv.* **quizzicalness** *n.*

quod *n.* *Brit. slang* prison. [17th-century coinage]

quod erat demonstrandum which was the thing to be proved. [Latin]

quod vide /kwod *vee*-day/ which see (in cross-references etc.). [Latin]

quoin *n.* **1** an external angle of a building. **2** a cornerstone. [variant of COIN]

quoit /koyt/ *n.* **1** a heavy flattish sharp-edged iron ring thrown to encircle an iron peg or to land as near as possible to the peg. **2** (in *pl.*) a game consisting of aiming and throwing these. **3** a ring of rope, rubber, etc. for use in a similar game. **4 a** ▼ the flat stone of a dolmen. **b** the dolmen itself. [Middle English]

quoit

support stone

QUOIT ON A PREHISTORIC DOLMEN, ENGLAND

quondam *attrib.adj.* that once was; sometime; former. [Latin, literally 'formerly']

Quonset *n.* *US propr.* a prefabricated metal building with a semicylindrical corrugated roof. [named after *Quonset* Point, Rhode Island]

quorate *adj.* *Brit.* attended by a quorum. [related to QUORUM]

Quorn *n.* *propr.* a type of textured vegetable protein made from an edible fungus and used as a meat substitute. [former name of a Leicestershire village, incorporated into original maker's name]

quorum *n.* the minimum number of members that must be present to constitute a valid meeting. [Latin, literally 'of whom (we wish that you be two, three, etc.)', in the wording of commissions]

quota *n.* (*pl.* **quotas**) **1** the share that an individual person or company is bound to contribute to or entitled to receive from a total. **2** a quantity of goods etc. which under official controls must be manufactured, exported, imported, etc. **3** the number of yearly immigrants allowed to enter a country, students allowed to enrol for a course, etc. [from medieval Latin *quota (pars)* 'how great (a part)']

quotable *adj.* worth quoting. □ **quotability** *n.*

quotation *n.* **1** the act or an instance of quoting or being quoted. **2** a passage or remark quoted. **3** a contractor's estimate. **4** *Stock Exch.* an amount stated as the current price of stocks or commodities. **5** *Mus.* a short passage or tune taken from one piece of music to another. [from medieval Latin *quotatio*]

quotation mark *n.* each of a set of punctuation marks, single (' ') or double (" "), used to mark the

Q

beginning and end of a quoted passage, a book title, etc., or words regarded as slang or jargon.

quote ● *v.tr.* **1** cite or appeal to (an author, book, etc.) in confirmation of some view. **2** repeat a statement by (another person) or copy out a passage from (*don't quote me*). **3** (often *absol.*) **a** repeat or copy out (a passage) usu. with an indication that it is borrowed. **b** (foll. by *from*) cite (an author, book, etc.). **4** (foll. by *as*) cite (an author etc.) as proof, evidence, etc. **5 a** enclose (words) in quotation marks. **b** (as *int.*) (in dictation, reading aloud, etc.) indicate the presence of opening quotation marks (*he said, quote, 'I shall stay'*). **6** state (the price of a job) to a person (*they quoted £600 for the work*). **7** *Stock* *Exch.* regularly list the price of. ● *n. colloq.* **1** a passage quoted. **2** a price quoted. **3** (usu. in *pl.*) quotation marks. [earlier in sense 'to mark with numbers': from medieval Latin *quotare*]

quoth *v.tr.* (only in 1st and 3rd person) *archaic* said. [Old English]

quotidian ● *adj.* **1** daily; of every day. **2** commonplace, trivial. ● *n.* (in full **quotidian fever**) a fever recurring every day. [based on Latin *cotidiē* 'daily']

quotient /**kwoh**-shĕnt/ *n.* a result obtained by dividing one quantity by another. [from Latin *quotiens* 'how many times']

Quran (also **Qur'an**) var. of KORAN.

q.v. *abbr. quod vide.*

qwerty *attrib.adj.* (also **QWERTY**) ▼ denoting the standard keyboard on English-language typewriters, word processors, etc., with *q, w, e, r, t,* and *y* as the first keys on the top row of letters.

QWERTY KEYBOARD OF A
WORD PROCESSOR

Q

R

R¹ *n.* (also **r**) (*pl.* **Rs** or **R's**) the eighteenth letter of the alphabet.

R² *abbr.* (also **R.**) **1** *Regina* (*Elizabeth R*). **2** *Rex*. **3** River. **4** (also ®) registered as a trade mark. **5** *Chess* rook. **6** right. **7** rand. **8** radius. **9** reverse (gear).

R³ *symb.* **1** roentgen. **2** electrical resistance. **3** (in chemical formulae) an organic radical or group.

r *abbr.* (also **r.**) **1** right. **2** recto. **3** run(s). **4** radius.

RA *abbr.* **1 a** (in the UK) Royal Academy. **b** (in the UK) Royal Academician. **2** (in the UK) Royal Artillery.

Ra *symb. Chem.* the element radium.

RAAF *abbr.* Royal Australian Air Force.

rabbet ● *n.* a step-shaped channel etc. cut along the edge or face or projecting angle of a length of wood etc. ▷ WINDOW. ● *v.tr.* (**rabbeted**, **rabbeting**) **1** join or fix with a rabbet. **2** make a rabbet in. [from Old French *rab(b)at* 'abatement, recess']

rabbi *n.* (*pl.* **rabbis**) **1** a Jewish scholar or teacher, esp. of the law. **2** a person appointed as a Jewish religious leader. [from Hebrew *rabbi* 'my master'] □ **rabbinate** *n.*

rabbinical *adj.* (also **rabbinic**) of or relating to rabbis, or to Jewish law or teaching. □ **rabbinically** *adv.*

rabbit ● *n.* **1** any of various burrowing gregarious plant-eating mammals of the family Leporidae, with long ears and a short tail. ▷ LAGOMORPH. **2** *US* a hare. **3** the fur of the rabbit. ● *v.intr.* (**rabbited**, **rabbiting**) **1** hunt rabbits. **2** (often foll. by *on*, *away*) *Brit. colloq.* talk excessively or pointlessly; chatter. [Middle English] □ **rabbity** *adj.*

rabbit punch *n.* a short chop with the edge of the hand to the nape of the neck.

rabble *n.* **1** a disorderly crowd; a mob. **2** a contemptible or inferior set of people. **3** (prec. by *the*) the lower classes or disorderly section of the populace. [Middle English]

rabble-rouser *n.* a person who stirs up a crowd of people to agitate for change. □ **rabble-rousing** *adj.* & *n.*

Rabelaisian *adj.* **1** of or like Rabelais or his writings. **2** marked by coarse humour and exuberant imagination and language. [from F. *Rabelais*, French satirist, *c*.1494–1553]

rabid *adj.* **1** furious, violent (*rabid hate*). **2** unreasoning; headstrong; fanatical (*a rabid anarchist*). **3** (esp. of a dog) affected with rabies; mad. **4** of or connected with rabies. [from Latin *rabidus*] □ **rabidly** *adv.* **rabidness** *n.*

rabies *n.* a contagious and fatal viral disease of dogs and other mammals, transmissible to humans etc. and causing madness and convulsions. [based on Latin *rabere* 'to rave']

RAC *abbr.* **1** (in the UK) Royal Automobile Club. **2** (in the UK) Royal Armoured Corps.

raccoon *n.* (also **racoon**) **1** a furry N. American nocturnal mammal of the genus *Procyon*, with a bushy tail and sharp snout. **2** the fur of the raccoon. [Algonquian dialect]

race¹ ● *n.* **1** a contest of speed between runners, vehicles, etc. **2** (in *pl.*) a series of these for horses, dogs, etc. at a fixed time on a regular course. **3** a contest between persons to be first to achieve something. **4 a** a strong or rapid current flowing through

RACECOURSE

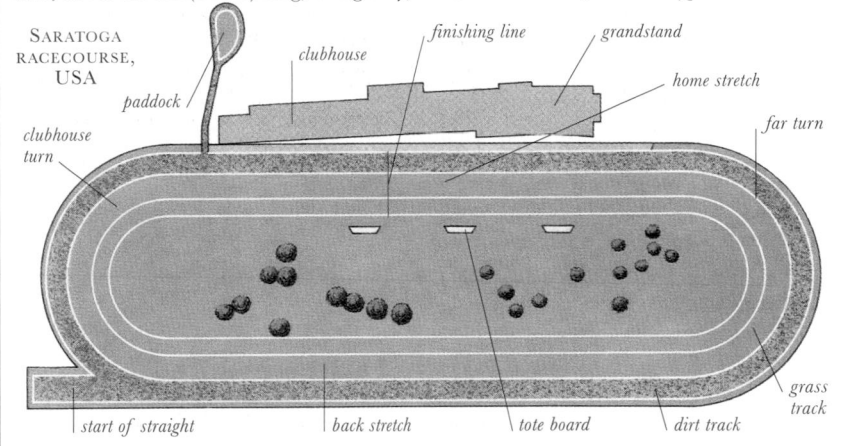

While many early racecourses were adapted to the landscape, most modern tracks are oval, about 1.6 km (1 mile) long, and grassy; some have a dirt surface. They vary mainly in the distance to the first turn, the sharpness of the turns, and the type of soil.

SARATOGA RACECOURSE, USA

paddock
clubhouse
finishing line
grandstand
home stretch
far turn
clubhouse turn
start of straight
back stretch
tote board
dirt track
grass track

a narrow sea or river channel. **b** the channel of a stream etc. (*a mill-race*). ● *v.* **1** *intr.* take part in a race. **2** *tr.* have a race with. **3** *tr.* try to surpass in speed. **4** *intr.* (foll. by *with*) compete in speed with. **5** *tr.* cause (a horse, car, etc.) to race. **6 a** *intr.* go at full or (of an engine etc.) excessive speed. **b** *tr.* cause (a person or thing) to do this (*raced the bill through*). **7** *intr.* (usu. as **racing** *adj.*) follow horse racing (*a racing man*). [from Old Norse *rás*]

race² *n.* **1** each of the major divisions of humankind, having distinct physical characteristics. **2** a nation etc., regarded as of a distinct ethnic stock. **3** the fact or concept of division into races (*based on race*). **4** a genus, species, breed, or variety of animals, plants, or micro-organisms. **5** a group of persons, animals, or plants connected by common descent. **6** descent; kindred (*of noble race*). [from Italian *razza*]

racecourse *n.* ▲ a ground or track for horse racing.

racegoer *n.* a person who frequents horse races.

racehorse *n.* a horse bred or kept for racing.

raceme /rass-eem/ *n. Bot.* a flower cluster with the separate flowers attached by short equal stalks at equal distances along a central stem. ▷ INFLORESCENCE. [from Latin *racemus* 'grape-bunch']

race meeting *n. Brit.* a sporting event consisting of a sequence of horse races at one place.

racer *n.* **1** a horse, yacht, bicycle, etc., of a kind used for racing. **2** a person or thing that races.

race relations *n.pl.* relations between members of different races usu. in the same country.

race riot *n.* an outbreak of violence due to racial antagonism.

racetrack *n.* **1** = RACECOURSE. **2** a track for motor racing.

rachitis /ră-ky-tis/ *n.* rickets. [based on Greek *rhakhis* 'spine'] □ **rachitic** *adj.*

Rachmanism *n. Brit.* the exploitation and intimidation of tenants by unscrupulous landlords. [named after P. *Rachman*, London landlord in the 1960s]

racial *adj.* **1** of or concerning race. **2** on the grounds of or connected with difference in race. □ **racially** *adv.*

racialism *n.* = RACISM 1. □ **racialist** *n.* & *adj.*

racing car *n.* a motor car built for racing on a prepared track. ▷ MOTOR RACING

racing driver *n.* a driver of racing cars.

racism *n.* **1 a** a belief in the superiority of a particular race; prejudice based on this. **b** antagonism towards, or discrimination against, other races. **2** the theory that human abilities etc. are determined by race. □ **racist** *n.* & *adj.*

rack¹ ● *n.* **1 a** a framework usu. with rails, hooks, etc., for holding or storing things. **b** a frame for holding animal fodder. **2** a cogged or toothed bar or rail engaging with a wheel or pinion etc. ▷ RACK-AND-PINION, RACK RAILWAY. **3** *hist.* an instrument of torture stretching the victim's joints by the turning of rollers to which the wrists and ankles were tied. ● *v.tr.* **1** (of disease or pain) inflict suffering on. **2** *hist.* torture (a person) on the rack. **3** place in or on a rack. **4** shake violently. **5** injure by straining. □ **on the rack** suffering intense distress or strain. **rack one's brains** make a great mental effort. [from Middle Dutch *rak*]

rack² *n.* destruction (esp. *rack and ruin*). [variant of WRACK, WRECK]

rack³ *n.* a joint of lamb etc. including the front ribs.

rack⁴ *v.tr.* (often foll. by *off*) draw off (wine etc.) from the lees. [based on Provençal *raca* 'stems and husks of grapes']

rack-and-pinion *attrib.adj.* ▼ (esp. of a steering system) using a rack and pinion.

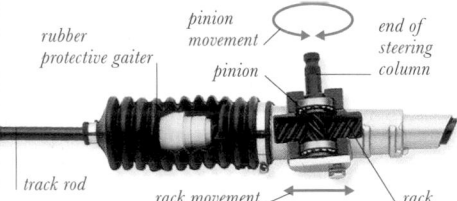

rubber protective gaiter
pinion movement
pinion
end of steering column
link to wheel
track rod
rack movement
swivelling ball joint
rack

RACK-AND-PINION CAR STEERING SYSTEM (CUTAWAY VIEW)

racket¹ *n.* (also **racquet**) **1** a bat with a round or oval frame strung with catgut, nylon, etc., used in tennis, squash, etc. **2** (in *pl.*) a ball game for two or four persons played with rackets in a plain four-walled court. [based on Arabic *rāḥa* 'palm of the hand']

racket² *n.* **1 a** a disturbance; a din. **b** social excitement; gaiety. **2** *slang* **a** a scheme for obtaining money etc. by fraudulent and often violent means. **b** a dodge; a sly game. **3** *colloq.* an activity; a way of life; a line of business. [16th-century coinage] □ **rackety** *adj.*

R

RACK RAILWAY

Early trains needed a rack rail in order to climb steep slopes. As the pinion wheel turns, its teeth lock into slots in the rack, pulling the train up and preventing it from sliding back. Some mountain tracks still use rack rails.

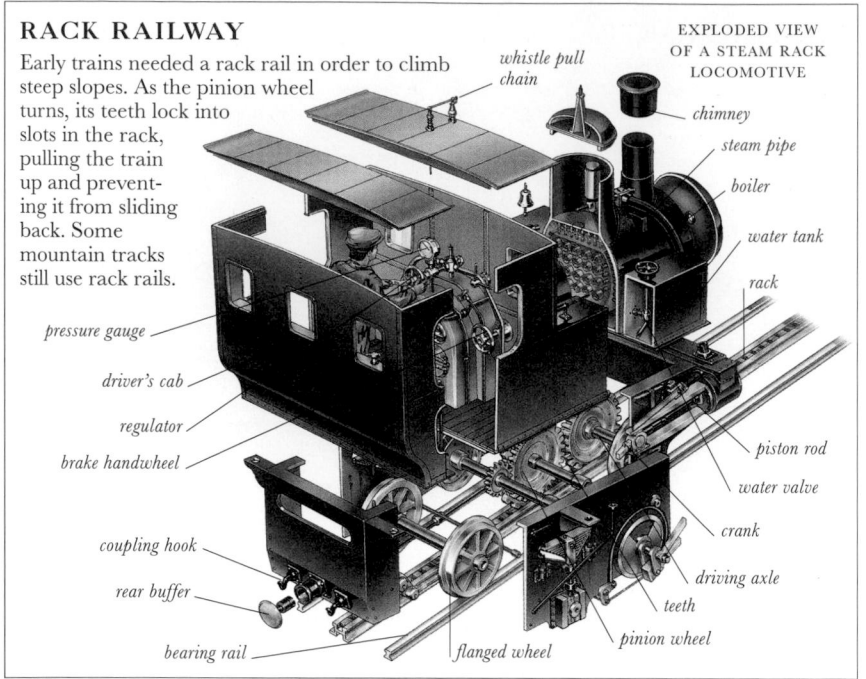

EXPLODED VIEW OF A STEAM RACK LOCOMOTIVE

whistle pull chain · *chimney* · *steam pipe* · *boiler* · *water tank* · *rack* · *piston rod* · *water valve* · *crank* · *driving axle* · *teeth* · *pinion wheel* · *flanged wheel* · *bearing rail* · *rear buffer* · *coupling hook* · *brake handwheel* · *regulator* · *driver's cab* · *pressure gauge*

racketeer *n.* a person who operates a dishonest business. □ **racketeering** *n.*

rack railway *n.* ▲ a railway with a cogged rail between the bearing rails.

rack-rent ● *n.* **1** a high rent, annually equalling the full value of the property to which it relates. **2** an extortionate rent. ● *v.tr.* exact this from (a tenant) or for (property).

raclette *n.* a Swiss dish of melted cheese, usu. eaten with potatoes. [French, literally 'small scraper', from the practice of scraping melted cheese on to a plate]

raconteur /rak-on-**ter**/ *n.* (*fem.* **raconteuse**) a teller of anecdotes. [French]

racoon var. of RACCOON.

racquet var. of RACKET[1].

racy *adj.* (**racier**, **raciest**) **1** lively and vigorous in style. **2** risqué, suggestive. [based on RACE[2]] □ **racily** *adv.* **raciness** *n.*

rad[1] *n. Physics* a unit of absorbed dose of ionizing radiation. [from *r*adiation *a*bsorbed *d*ose]

rad[2] *adj. slang* excellent, fantastic, cool. [probably abbreviation of RADICAL]

rad[3] *n. colloq.* radiator.

RADA /**rah**-dǎ/ *abbr.* (in the UK) Royal Academy of Dramatic Art.

radar *n.* **1** ▼ a system for detecting the presence etc. of aircraft, ships, etc. by sending out pulses of high-frequency electromagnetic waves. **2** the apparatus used for this. [from *ra*dio *d*etection *a*nd *r*anging]

radar trap *n.* the use of radar to detect vehicles exceeding a speed limit.

RADC *abbr.* (in the UK) Royal Army Dental Corps.

raddle ● *n.* red ochre (often used to mark sheep). ● *v.tr.* **1** colour with raddle or too much rouge. **2** (as **raddled** *adj.*) worn out; untidy, unkempt. [variant of RUDDLE]

RADAR

Primary radar locates a target by measuring the time it takes for the echo of a pulse to return to the antenna, and by recording the direction it travels back from. In secondary radar, a transponder sends more detailed information in response to a pulse from a radar scanner.

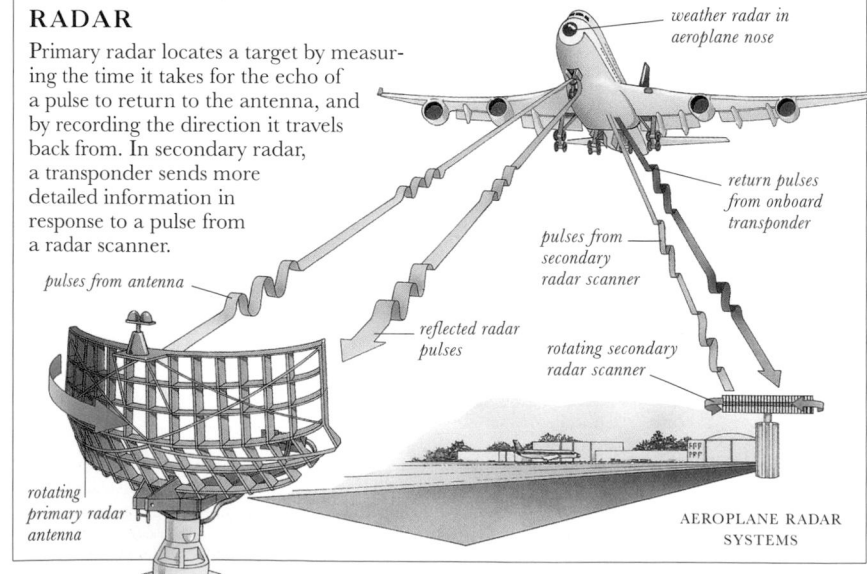

weather radar in aeroplane nose · *return pulses from onboard transponder* · *pulses from secondary radar scanner* · *reflected radar pulses* · *rotating secondary radar scanner* · *pulses from antenna* · *rotating primary radar antenna* · AEROPLANE RADAR SYSTEMS

radial ● *adj.* **1** of, concerning, or in rays. **2 a** arranged like rays or radii; having the position or direction of a radius. **b** having spokes or radiating lines. **c** acting or moving along lines diverging from a centre. **3** (in full **radial-ply**) (of a vehicle tyre) having the core fabric layers arranged radially and the tread strengthened. ● *n.* a radial-ply tyre (see sense 3 of *adj.*). ▷ TYRE. [from medieval Latin *radialis*] □ **radially** *adv.*

radial engine *n.* ▼ an engine having cylinders arranged along radii.

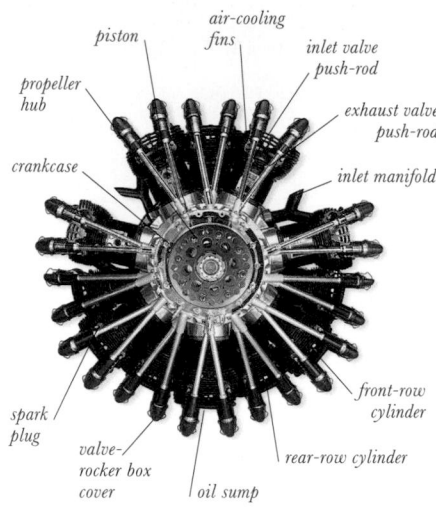

air-cooling fins · *inlet valve push-rod* · *exhaust valve push-rod* · *inlet manifold* · *front-row cylinder* · *rear-row cylinder* · *oil sump* · *valve-rocker box cover* · *spark plug* · *crankcase* · *propeller hub* · *piston*

RADIAL ENGINE: EARLY 20TH-CENTURY 14-CYLINDER RADIAL ENGINE

radial keratotomy see KERATOTOMY.

radial symmetry *n.* symmetry occurring about any number of lines or planes passing through the centre of an organism etc.

radian *n. Geom.* ▶ a unit of angle, equal to an angle at the centre of a circle the arc of which is equal in length to the radius.

radian · *radius* · *arc* · RADIAN

radiant ● *adj.* **1** emitting rays of light. **2** (of eyes or looks) beaming with joy etc. **3** (of beauty) splendid or dazzling. **4** (of light) issuing in rays. **5** operating radially. **6** extending radially; radiating. ● *n.* the point or object from which light or heat radiates. [from Latin *radiant-* 'shining'] □ **radiance** *n.* **radiantly** *adv.*

radiant heat *n.* heat transmitted by radiation. □ **radiant heater** *n.*

radiate ● *v.* **1** *intr.* **a** emit rays of light, heat, etc. **b** (of light or heat) be emitted in rays. **2** *tr.* emit (light, or sound) from a centre. **3** *tr.* transmit or demonstrate (joy etc.). **4** *intr.* & *tr.* diverge or cause to diverge or spread from a centre. **5** *tr.* (as **radiated** *adj.*) with parts arranged in rays. ● *adj.* having divergent rays or parts radially arranged. [based on Latin *radiatus* 'furnished with rays'] □ **radiative** *adj.*

radiation *n.* **1** the act or an instance of radiating; the process of being radiated. **2** *Physics* **a** the emission of energy as electromagnetic waves or as moving particles. ▷ ELECTROMAGNETIC RADIATION. **b** the energy transmitted in this way, esp. invisibly.

radiation sickness *n.* sickness caused by exposure to radiation, such as X-rays or gamma rays.

radiator *n.* **1** a person or thing that radiates. **2 a** a device for heating a room etc., consisting of a metal case through which hot water or steam circulates. **b** a usu. portable oil or electric heater resembling

R

this. **3** an engine-cooling device in a motor vehicle or aircraft. ▷ AIRCRAFT, CAR

radiator grille *n.* a grille at the front of a motor vehicle allowing air to circulate to the radiator.

radical ● *adj.* **1** of the root or roots; fundamental. **2** far-reaching; thorough (*radical change*). **3 a** advocating thorough reform; holding extreme political views. **b** (of a measure etc.) advanced by or according to principles of this kind. **4** forming the basis; primary (*the radical idea*). **5** *Math.* of the root of a number or quantity. **6** (of surgery etc.) seeking to ensure the removal of all diseased tissue. **7** of the roots of words. **8** *slang* excellent, outstanding, cool. ● *n.* **1** a person holding radical views or belonging to a radical party. **2** *Chem.* **a** a free radical. **b** an element or atom or a group of these normally forming part of a compound and remaining unaltered during the compound's ordinary chemical changes. **3 a** the root of a word. **b** any of the basic set of approximately 214 Chinese characters from which more complex ones are mainly derived. **4** a fundamental principle; a basis. **5** *Math.* a quantity forming or expressed as the root of another. [from Late Latin *radicalis*] □ **radicalism** *n.* **radicalize** *v.tr. & intr.* (also **-ise**). **radically** *adv.* **radicalness** *n.*

radicchio /rǎ-dee-ki-oh/ *n.* (*pl.* **-os**) a variety of chicory with dark red leaves. [Italian, literally 'chicory']

radices *pl.* of RADIX.

radicle *n.* ▶ the part of a plant embryo that develops into the primary root. [from Latin *radicula*, related to RADIX]

radii *pl.* of RADIUS.

radio ● *n.* (*pl.* **-os**) **1** (often *attrib.*) **a** the transmission and reception of sound messages etc. by electromagnetic waves of radio frequency. ▷ ELECTROMAGNETIC RADIATION. **b** ▼ an apparatus for receiving, broadcasting, or transmitting radio signals. **c** a message sent or received by radio. **2 a** a sound broadcasting in general (*prefers the radio*). **b** a broadcasting station or channel (*Radio One*). ● *v.* (**-oes**, **-oed**) **1** *tr* **a** send (a message) by radio. **b** send a message to (a person) by radio. **2** *intr.* communicate or broadcast by radio. [short for *radio-telegraphy* etc.]

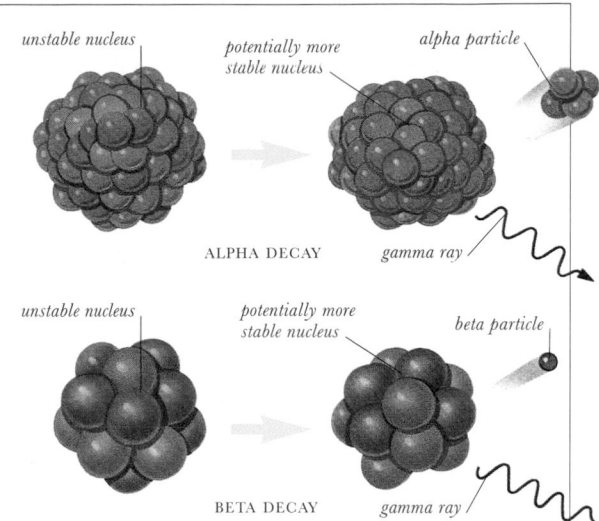

RADIOACTIVITY

A nucleus is composed of protons and neutrons. All the protons are positively charged and so repel each other. An equivalent nuclear force holds the nucleus together. If there is an imbalance between the two forces, the nucleus becomes unstable and breaks up (decays). In alpha decay, an alpha particle (two neutrons and two protons) is released. In beta decay, a beta particle (a fast electron) is released. In both cases, gamma radiation may also be emitted.

unstable nucleus　*potentially more stable nucleus*　*alpha particle*

ALPHA DECAY　*gamma ray*

unstable nucleus　*potentially more stable nucleus*　*beta particle*

BETA DECAY　*gamma ray*

RADICLE EMERGING FROM A BROAD BEAN SEED

radicle

radio- *comb. form* **1** denoting radio or broadcasting. **2** connected with radioactivity. **3** connected with rays or radiation.

radioactive *adj.* of or exhibiting radioactivity. □ **radioactively** *adv.*

radioactivity *n.* **1** ▲ the spontaneous disintegration of atomic nuclei, with the emission of usu. penetrating radiation or particles. **2** radioactive substances, or the radiation they emit.

radio astronomy *n.* the branch of astronomy concerned with the radio-frequency range of the electromagnetic spectrum.

radio cab *n.* (also **radio car**) a cab or car equipped with a two-way radio.

radiocarbon *n.* a radioactive isotope of carbon.

radiocarbon dating *n.* = CARBON DATING.

radio cassette player *n.* a cassette player and radio in one unit.

radio-controlled *adj.* (of a model aircraft etc.) controlled from a distance by radio.

radio-element *n.* a natural or artificial radioactive element or isotope.

radio frequency *n.* (*pl.* **-ies**) the frequency band of telecommunication, ranging from 10^4–10^{11} or 10^{12} Hz (hyphenated when *attrib.*: *radio-frequency spectrum*).

radio galaxy *n.* a galaxy emitting radiation in the radio-frequency range of the electromagnetic spectrum.

radiogenic *adj.* **1** produced by radioactivity. **2** suitable for broadcasting by radio. □ **radiogenically** *adv.*

radiogram *n.* **1** *Brit.* a combined radio and record player. **2** a picture obtained by X-rays, gamma rays, etc. **3** a radio-telegram.

radiograph ● *n.* **1** an instrument recording the intensity of radiation. **2** = RADIOGRAM 2. ● *v.tr.* obtain a picture of by X-ray, gamma ray, etc. □ **radiographer** *n.* **radiographic** *adj.* **radiographically** *adv.* **radiography** *n.*

radioisotope *n.* a radioactive isotope. □ **radioisotopic** *adj.*

radiolarian *n.* any marine protozoan of the superclass Actinopoda, having a siliceous skeleton and radiating surface protrusions for movement, feeding, etc. [based on Latin *radiolus* 'little radius']

radiology *n.* the scientific study of X-rays and other high-energy radiation, esp. as used in medicine. □ **radiologic** *adj.* **radiological** *adj.* **radiologically** *adv.* **radiologist** *n.*

radiometer *n.* an instrument for measuring the intensity or force of radiation. □ **radiometric** *adj.* **radiometry** *n.*

radiophonic *adj.* of or relating to synthetic sound, esp. music, produced electronically.

radioscopy *n.* the examination by X-rays etc. of objects opaque to light. □ **radioscopic** *adj.*

radiosonde *n.* a miniature radio transmitter of information about pressure, temperature, etc., from various levels of the atmosphere. [based on German *Sonde* 'probe']

radio-telegram *n.* a telegram sent by radio, usu. from a ship to land.

radio-telegraphy *n.* telegraphy using radio transmission. □ **radio-telegraph** *n.*

radio-telephony *n.* telephony using radio transmission. □ **radio-telephone** *n.*

radio telescope *n.* a directional aerial system for collecting and analysing radiation in the radio-frequency range from stars etc.

radiotelex *n.* a telex sent usu. from a ship to land.

radiotherapy *n.* the treatment of cancer and other diseases by X-rays or other forms of radiation. □ **radiotherapeutic** *adj.* **radiotherapist** *n.*

radish *n.* **1** a cruciferous plant, *Raphanus sativus*, with a fleshy pungent root. ▷ VEGETABLE. **2** this root, eaten esp. raw. [from Latin *radix radicis* 'root']

R

RADIO

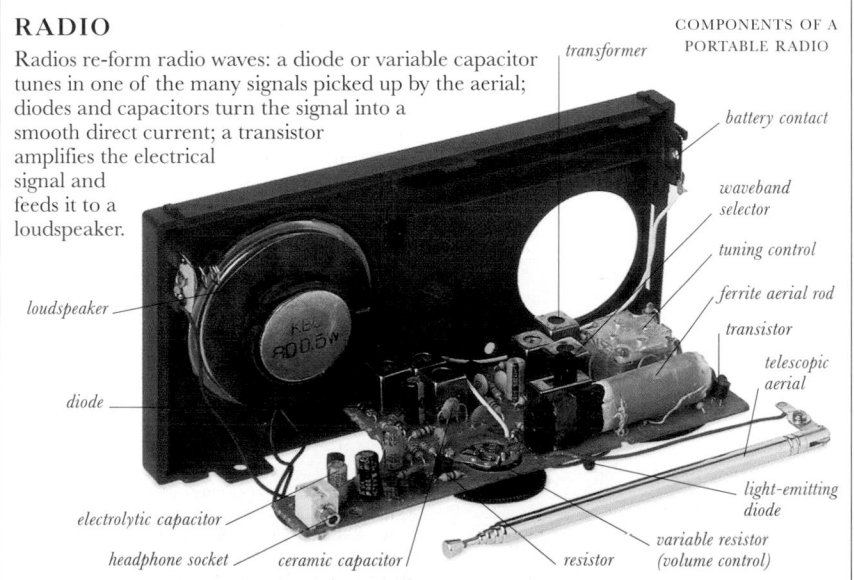

Radios re-form radio waves: a diode or variable capacitor tunes in one of the many signals picked up by the aerial; diodes and capacitors turn the signal into a smooth direct current; a transistor amplifies the electrical signal and feeds it to a loudspeaker.

COMPONENTS OF A PORTABLE RADIO

transformer
battery contact
waveband selector
tuning control
ferrite aerial rod
transistor
telescopic aerial
light-emitting diode
variable resistor (volume control)
resistor
ceramic capacitor
headphone socket
electrolytic capacitor
diode
loudspeaker

radium *n. Chem.* a radioactive metallic element present in pitchblende etc. used esp. in radiotherapy. [based on Latin *radius* 'ray']

radius *n.* (*pl.* **radii** /-di-I/ or **radiuses**) **1** *Math.* **a** ◄ a straight line from the centre to the circumference of a circle or sphere. **b** a radial line from the focus to any point of a curve. **c** the length of the radius of a circle etc. **2** usu. specified distance from a centre in all directions.

RADIUS (1a)

3 a ► the thicker and shorter of the two bones in the human forearm. ▷ SKELETON. **b** the corresponding bone in a vertebrate's foreleg or a bird's wing. **4** any of the five arm-like structures of a starfish. [Latin, literally 'ray']

radix *n.* (*pl.* **radices** /rad-i-seez/) **1** *Math.* a number or symbol used as the basis of a numeration scale (e.g. ten in the decimal system). **2** (usu. foll. by *of*) a source or origin. [Latin, literally 'root']

radius

RADIUS (3a): HUMAN FOREARM SHOWING THE RADIUS

radon *n. Chem.* a naturally occurring gaseous radioactive inert element arising from the disintegration of radium, and used in radiotherapy. [based on RADIUM]

RAF *colloq.* raf *abbr.* (in the UK) Royal Air Force.

raffia *n.* **1** a palm tree, *Raphia ruffia*, native to Madagascar, having very long leaves. **2 ▼** the fibre from its leaves used for weaving and for tying plants etc. [Malagasy (language of Madagascar)]

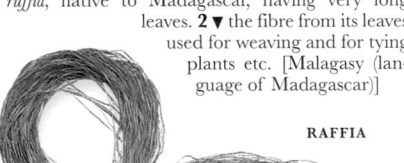

RAFFIA

R

raffish *adj.* **1** disreputable; rakish. **2** tawdry. [based on RAFT²] □ **raffishly** *adv.* **raffishness** *n.*

raffle ● *n.* a fund-raising lottery with goods as prizes. ● *v.tr.* (often foll. by *off*) dispose of by means of a raffle. [Middle English, a kind of dice game: from Old French *raf(f)le*]

raft¹ *n.* **1** a flat floating structure of timber or other materials for conveying persons or things. **2** a lifeboat or small (often inflatable) boat, esp. for use in emergencies. **3** a floating accumulation of trees, ice, etc. [originally in sense 'rafter': from Old Norse *raptr*]

raft² *n. colloq.* **1** a large collection. **2** (foll. by *of*) a crowd. [alteration of Middle English *raff* 'rubbish']

rafter¹ *n.* each of the sloping beams forming the framework of a roof. ▷ ROOF. □ **raftered** *adj.*

rafter² *n.* a person who travels by raft.

rag¹ *n.* **1** a torn, frayed, or worn piece of woven material. **2** (in *pl.*) old or worn clothes. **3** (*collect.*) scraps of cloth used as material for paper, stuffing, etc. **4** *derog.* **a** a newspaper. **b** a flag, handkerchief, curtain, etc. □ **in rags 1** much torn. **2** in old torn clothes. [Middle English]

rag² ● *n. Brit.* **1** a fund-raising programme of stunts, parades, and entertainment organized by students. **2** *colloq.* a prank. **3 a** a rowdy celebration. **b** a noisy disorderly scene. ● *v.* (**ragged**, **ragging**) **1** *tr.* tease; torment. **2** *tr.* scold. **3** *intr. Brit.* engage in rough play; be noisy and riotous. [18th-century coinage]

rag³ *n.* **1** a large coarse roofing slate. **2** *Brit.* any of various kinds of hard coarse sedimentary stone that break into thick slabs. [Middle English]

rag⁴ *n. Mus.* a ragtime composition or tune.

raga *n.* (also **rag**) (in Indian music) **1** a pattern of notes used as a basis for improvisation. **2** a piece using a particular raga. [Sanskrit, literally 'colour, musical tone']

ragamuffin *n.* **1** a person in ragged dirty clothes, esp. a child. **2** (also **raggamuffin**) **a** an exponent or follower of ragga, typically dressing in ragged clothes. **b** = RAGGA.

rag-and-bone man *n. Brit.* an itinerant dealer in old clothes, furniture, etc.

ragbag *n.* **1** a bag in which scraps of fabric etc. are kept for use. **2** (often foll. by *of*) a miscellaneous collection. **3** *slang* a sloppily-dressed woman.

rag doll *n.* a stuffed doll made of cloth.

rage ● *n.* **1** fierce or violent anger. **2** a fit of this. **3** the violent action of a natural force. **4** (foll. by *for*) **a** a vehement desire or passion. **b** a widespread temporary enthusiasm or fashion. ● *v.intr.* **1** be full of anger. **2** (often foll. by *at, against*) speak furiously or madly; rave. **3 a** (of wind, fever, etc.) be violent; be at its height. **b** (as **raging** *adj.*) extreme (*raging thirst*). □ **all the rage** very popular, fashionable. [from Old French *rager*]

ragga *n.* a style of popular music combining elements of reggae and hip hop. [from RAGAMUFFIN, from the style of clothing worn by its followers]

raggamuffin var. of RAGAMUFFIN 2.

ragged *adj.* **1** (of clothes etc.) torn; frayed. **2** rough; shaggy. **3** (of a person) in ragged clothes. **4** with a broken or jagged outline or surface. **5** *Printing* (esp. of a right margin) unjustified and so uneven. **6** faulty; imperfect. **7** lacking finish, smoothness, or uniformity (*ragged rhymes*). **8** exhausted (esp. *be run ragged*). [from Old Norse *roggvathr* 'tufted'] □ **raggedly** *adv.* **raggedness** *n.* **raggedy** *adj.*

ragged robin *n.* a pink-flowered campion, *Lychnis flos-cuculi*, with tattered petals.

raggle-taggle *adj.* (also **wraggle-taggle**) rambling, straggling.

raglan *n.* (often *attrib.*) an overcoat without shoulder seams, the sleeves running up to the neck. [named after Lord *Raglan*, British commander, 1788–1855]

raglan sleeve *n.* a sleeve which runs up to the neck of a garment.

ragout /ra-goo/ ● *n.* a highly-seasoned dish of meat cut into small pieces and stewed with vegetables. ● *v.tr.* make a ragout of. [from French *ragoûter* 'to revive the taste of']

ragstone *n.* = RAG³ 2.

rags-to-riches *attrib.adj.* denoting a person who starts out poor and ends up rich, or a story describing such a development.

ragtag *n.* (in full **ragtag and bobtail**) *derog.* the rabble or common people.

ragtime *n.* music characterized by a syncopated melodic line and regularly accented accompaniment played esp. on the piano.

rag trade *n. colloq.* the business of designing, making, and selling clothes.

ragweed *n.* **1** = RAGWORT. **2** *N. Amer.* any plant of the genus *Ambrosia*, with allergenic pollen.

ragworm *n.* ► a carnivorous marine polychaete worm of the family Nereidae, esp. *Nereis diversicolor*, often used for bait.

RAGWORM
(*Nereis diversicolor*)

ragwort *n.* ► any yellow-flowered ragged-leaved plant of the genus *Senecio*.

rah-rah *adj. US slang* marked by great enthusiasm or excitement.

rai *n.* a style of music fusing Arabic and Algerian folk elements with Western rock. [Arabic]

raid ● *n.* **1** a rapid surprise attack, esp.: **a** in warfare. **b** to commit a crime or do harm. **2** a surprise attack by police etc. to arrest suspected persons or seize illicit goods. ● *v.tr.* **1** make a

RAGWORT
(*Senecio jacobaea*)

raid on (a person, place, or thing). **2** plunder, deplete. [Scottish form of Old English *rād* 'road'] □ **raider** *n.*

rail¹ ● *n.* **1** a level or sloping bar or series of bars: **a** used to hang things on. **b** running along the top of a set of banisters. **c** forming part of a fence or barrier as protection against contact, falling over, etc. **2 ▼** a steel bar or continuous line of bars laid on the ground, usu. as one of a pair forming a railway track. **3** (often *attrib.*) a railway (*by rail*). **4** (in *pl.*) the inside boundary fence of a racecourse. ● *v.tr.* **1** furnish with a rail or rails. **2** (usu. foll. by *in, off*) enclose with rails. **3** convey (goods) by rail. □ **off the rails** deranged; astray. [from Old French *reille* 'iron rod'] □ **railless** *adj.*

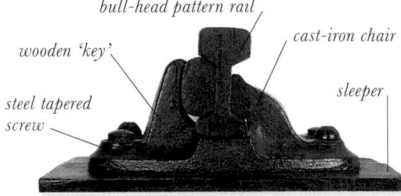

bull-head pattern rail

wooden 'key'   *cast-iron chair*

steel tapered screw   *sleeper*

RAIL: CROSS-SECTION OF A BULL-HEAD RAIL

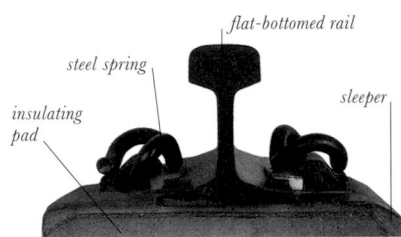

flat-bottomed rail

steel spring   *sleeper*

insulating pad

RAIL: CROSS-SECTION OF A FLAT-BOTTOMED RAIL

rail² *v.intr.* (often foll. by *at, against*) complain using abusive language. [from Provençal *ralhar* 'to jest'] □ **railer** *n.* **railing** *n.*

rail³ *n.* any bird of the family Rallidae, often inhabiting marshes. [from Old Northern French *raille*]

railcar *n.* a railway vehicle consisting of a single powered coach.

railcard *n. Brit.* a pass entitling the holder to reduced rail fares.

rail gun *n.* an electromagnetic projectile launcher used esp. as an anti-missile weapon.

railhead *n.* **1** the furthest point reached by a railway under construction. **2** the point on a railway at which road transport of goods begins.

railing *n.* **1** (usu. in *pl.*) a fence or barrier made of rails. **2** the material for these.

raillery *n.* (*pl.* **-ies**) **1** good-humoured ridicule; rallying. **2** an instance of this. [from French *raillerie*]

RAIN

Rain forms when warm air rises and cools, the water vapour in it condensing into small droplets. These droplets collide with each other, forming larger drops that fall as rain.

At very low temperatures, the droplets are supercooled, often forming crystals. These grow into snowflakes, which melt into rain as they fall into warmer air.

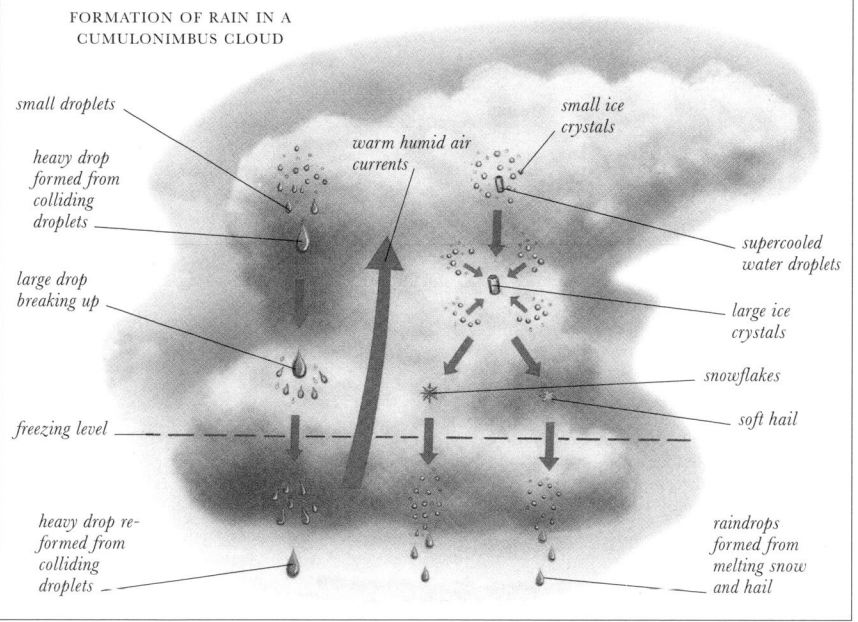

FORMATION OF RAIN IN A
CUMULONIMBUS CLOUD

small droplets

heavy drop formed from colliding droplets

warm humid air currents

small ice crystals

large drop breaking up

supercooled water droplets

large ice crystals

snowflakes

freezing level

soft hail

heavy drop re-formed from colliding droplets

raindrops formed from melting snow and hail

---

railman *n.* (*pl.* **-men**) = RAILWAYMAN.

railroad ● *n.* esp. *US* = RAILWAY. ● *v.tr.* (often foll. by *to*, *into*, *through*, etc.) rush or coerce (a person or thing) (*railroaded me into going too*).

railway *n.* **1** a track or set of tracks made of steel rails along which trains run. **2** such a system worked by a single company (*Great Western Railway*). **3** the organization and personnel required for its working.

railwayman *n.* (*pl.* **-men**) esp. *Brit.* a railway employee.

raiment *n. archaic* clothing. [Middle English, from obsolete *arrayment*]

rain ● *n.* **1 a** ▲ the condensed moisture of the atmosphere falling visibly in separate drops. **b** the fall of such drops. **2** (in *pl.*) **a** (prec. by *the*) the rainy season in tropical countries. **b** rainfalls. **3 a** falling liquid or solid particles or objects. **b** the rainlike descent of these. ● *v.* **1** *intr.* (prec. by *it* as subject) rain falls (*if it rains*). **2 a** *intr.* fall in showers or like rain (*blows rain upon him*). **b** *tr.* (prec. by *it* as subject) send in large quantities (*it rained blood*). **3** *tr.* lavishly

bestow (*rained benefits on us*). **4** *intr.* (of the sky etc.) send down rain. □ **rain cats and dogs** see CAT.

rain off (or *N. Amer.* **out**) (esp. in *passive*) cause (an event etc.) to be stopped or cancelled because of rain. [Old English] □ **rainless** *adj.*

rainbow ● *n.* **1** ▼ an arch of colours formed in the sky by reflection, twofold refraction, and dispersion of the Sun's rays in falling rain or in spray or mist. ▷ LIGHT, REFLECTION, REFRACTION. **2** a similar effect formed by the Moon's rays. **3** a wide variety of related things. ● *adj.* many-coloured. [Old English]

rainbow coalition *n.* a political alliance of minority peoples and other disadvantaged groups.

rainbow trout *n.* a large trout, *Oncorhynchus mykiss*.

rain check *n.* esp. *N. Amer.* **1** a ticket given for later use when an outdoor event is interrupted or postponed by rain. **2** a promise that an offer will be maintained though deferred.

raincoat *n.* a waterproof or water-resistant coat.

raindrop *n.* a single drop of rain. [Old English]

rainfall *n.* **1** a fall of rain. **2** the quantity of rain falling within a given area in a given time.

rainforest *n.* ▼ luxuriant forest in esp. tropical areas with consistently heavy rainfall.

emergent layer

canopy layer

understorey

liana

RAINFOREST LAYERS

forest floor

rain gauge *n.* an instrument measuring rainfall.

rainmaker *n.* **1** a person who seeks to cause rain to fall, either by magic or by a technique such as seeding. **2** *N. Amer. slang* a person who is highly successful esp. in business. □ **rainmaking** *n.*

rainproof *adj.* (esp. of a building, garment, etc.) resistant to rainwater.

rain shadow *n.* a region shielded from rain by mountains etc.

rainstorm *n.* a storm with heavy rain.

rainswept *adj.* exposed to the rain.

rainwater *n.* water obtained from collected rain, as distinct from a well etc.

rainy *adj.* (**rainier**, **rainiest**) **1** (of weather, a climate, day, region, etc.) in or on which rain is falling or much rain usually falls. **2** (of cloud, wind, etc.) laden with or bringing rain. □ **rainily** *adv.* **raininess** *n.*

rainy day *n.* a time of special usu. financial need in the future.

raise ● *v.tr.* **1** put or take into a higher position. **2** (often foll. by *up*) cause to rise or be vertical. **3** increase the amount or value or strength of. **4** (often foll. by *up*) construct or build up. **5** levy or collect or bring together. **6** cause to be heard or considered (*raise an objection*). **7** bring into being; arouse (*raise hopes*). **8** rouse from sleep or death, or

RAINBOW

Sunlight is a mixture of colours, each with its own wavelength. As light enters a drop of water, each wavelength is refracted at a different angle. It is then reflected at the back of the droplet and refracts again as it exits. This splits the light into a spectrum that is visible as bands of colour: a rainbow.

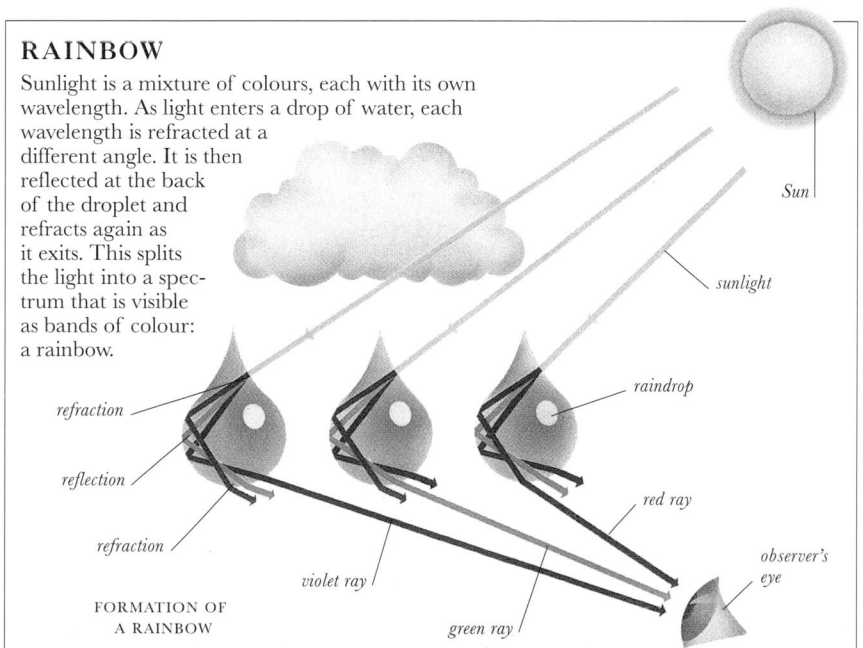

Sun

sunlight

refraction

reflection

refraction

raindrop

violet ray

green ray

red ray

observer's eye

FORMATION OF
A RAINBOW

R

R

RAKE

Rakes can be used to level, clear, or break up ground. Garden rakes are general-purpose tools, spring-tined lawn rakes are suited to clearing light debris, and scarifying rakes aerate a lawn.

GARDEN RAKE

tine

SPRING-TINED LAWN RAKE

SCARIFYING RAKE

from a lair. **9** bring up; educate. **10** breed or grow (*raise vegetables*). **11** promote to a higher rank. **12** (foll. by *to*) *Math.* multiply a quantity to a specified power. **13** cause (bread) to rise, esp. with yeast. **14** *Cards* **a** bet more than (another player). **b** increase (a stake). **c** *Bridge* make a bid contracting for more tricks in the same suit as (one's partner); increase (a bid) in this way. **15** abandon or force an enemy to abandon (a siege or blockade). **16** remove (a barrier or blockade). **17** cause (a ghost etc.) to appear. **18** *colloq.* find (a person etc. wanted). **19** establish contact with (a person etc.) by radio or telephone. **20** (usu. as **raised** *adj.*) cause (pastry etc.) to stand without support (*a raised pie*). ● *n.* **1** *Cards* an increase in a stake or bid. **2** esp. *N. Amer.* an increase in salary. □ **raise Cain** see CAIN. **raise one's eyebrows** see EYEBROW. **raise from the dead** restore to life. **raise one's hand to** make as if to strike (a person). **raise hell** *colloq.* make a disturbance. **raise a laugh** cause others to laugh. **raise a person's spirits** give him or her new courage or cheerfulness. **raise one's voice** speak, esp. louder. [from Old Norse *reisa*, related to REAR[2]] □ **raisable** *adj.*

raisin *n.* a partially dried grape. [based on Latin *racemus* 'grape-bunch'] □ **raisiny** *adj.*

raison d'être /ray-zawn detr/ *n.* (*pl.* **raisons d'être** *pronunc.* same) a purpose or reason that accounts for or justifies or originally caused a

thing's existence. [French, literally 'reason for being']

raita *n.* an Indian side dish of chopped cucumber (or other vegetables) and spices in yogurt. [from Hindi *rāytā*]

Raj *n.* (prec. by *the*) *hist.* British sovereignty in India. [from Hindi *rāj* 'reign']

raja *n.* (also **rajah**) *hist.* **1** an Indian king or prince. **2** a petty dignitary or noble in India. [from Sanskrit *rājan* 'king']

rake[1] ● *n.* **1** ◄ an implement consisting of a pole with a crossbar toothed like a comb at the end, or with several tines held together by a crosspiece, for drawing together hay etc. or smoothing loose soil or gravel. **2** a similar implement used for other purposes, e.g. by a croupier. ● *v.* **1** *tr.* collect or gather or remove with or as with a rake. **2** *tr.* make tidy or smooth with a rake. **3** *intr.* use a rake. **4** *tr.* & *intr.* search thoroughly, ransack. **5** *tr.* **a** direct gunfire along (a line) from end to end. **b** sweep with the eyes. **6** *tr.* scratch or scrape. □ **rake in** *colloq.* amass (profits etc.). **rake up** (or **over**) revive the memory of (past quarrels etc.). [Old English] □ **raker** *n.*

rake[2] *n.* a dissolute man of fashion. [short for archaic *rakehell*, in same sense]

rake[3] ● *v.* **1** *tr.* & *intr.* set or be set at a sloping angle. **2** *intr.* (of a mast or funnel) incline from the perpendicular towards the stern. ● *n.* **1** a raking position or build. **2** the amount by which a thing rakes. [17th-century coinage]

rake-off *n.* *colloq.* a commission or share, esp. in a disreputable deal.

rakish[1] *adj.* of or like a rake (see RAKE[2]); dashing, jaunty. □ **rakishly** *adv.* **rakishness** *n.*

rakish[2] *adj.* (of a ship) smart and fast-looking, open to suspicion of piracy. [based on RAKE[3], associated with RAKE[2]]

rallentando *Mus.* ● *adv.* & *adj.* with a gradual decrease of speed. ● *n.* (*pl.* **-os** or **rallentandi**) a passage to be performed in this way. [Italian]

rally[1] ● *v.* (**-ies**, **-ied**) **1** *tr.* & *intr.* (often foll. by *round*, *behind*, *to*) bring or come together as support or for concerted action. **2** *tr.* & *intr.* bring or come together again after a rout or dispersion. **3 a** *tr.* revive (courage etc.) by an effort of will. **b** *tr.* rouse (a person or animal) to fresh energy. **c** *intr.* pull oneself together. **4** *intr.* recover after illness or prostration or fear. **5** *intr.* (of share prices etc.) increase after a fall. ● *n.* (*pl.* **-ies**) **1** an act of reassembling forces or renewing conflict. **2** a recovery of energy after or in the middle of exhaustion or illness. **3** a mass meeting of supporters or persons having a common interest. **4** a competition for motor vehicles over rough terrain etc. **5** *Tennis* etc. an extended exchange of strokes between players. [from French *rallier*] □ **rallier** *n.*

rally[2] *v.tr.* (**-ies**, **-ied**) subject to good-humoured ridicule. [from French *railler*]

rallycross *n.* *Brit.* a form of motor racing over roads and cross-country.

RAM *abbr.* **1** *Computing* random-access memory. ▷ COMPUTER. **2** (in the UK) Royal Academy of Music.

ram ● *n.* **1** an uncastrated male sheep. **2** (**the Ram**) the zodiacal sign or constellation Aries. ▷ ARIES. **3** *hist.* = BATTERING RAM. **4** the falling weight of a piledriving machine. **5** a hydraulic machine for raising water or for lifting. ● *v.tr.* (**rammed**, **ramming**) **1** force or squeeze into place by pressure. **2** (usu. foll. by *down*, *in*, *into*) beat down or in by heavy blows. **3** (of a ship etc.) strike violently, crash against. **4** (foll. by *against*, *at*, *on*, *into*) violently impel. □ **ram home** stress forcefully (a lesson etc.). [Old English] □ **rammer** *n.* (in senses 1 and 2 of *v.*).

Ramadan *n.* the ninth month of the Muslim year, during which strict fasting is observed from sunrise to sunset. [from Arabic *ramaḍān*]

ramble ● *v.intr.* **1** walk for pleasure, with or without a definite route. **2** wander in discourse, write disconnectedly. ● *n.* a walk taken for pleasure.

rambler *n.* **1** a person who rambles. **2** a straggling or climbing rose.

rambling *adj.* **1** peripatetic, wandering. **2** desultory, incoherent. **3** (of a house etc.) irregularly arranged. **4** (of a plant) straggling. □ **ramblingly** *adv.*

rambutan *n.* **1** ▼ a red plum-sized prickly fruit. **2** a Malaysian tree, *Nephelium lappaceum*, that bears this. [Malay, based on *rambut* 'hair', in allusion to its spines]

edible flesh

RAMBUTAN (*Nephelium lappaceum*)

RAMC *abbr.* (in the UK) Royal Army Medical Corps.

ramekin /ram-i-kin/ *n.* **1** (in full **ramekin case** or **dish**) a small dish for baking and serving an individual portion of food. **2** food served in such a dish. [from French *ramequin*]

ramification *n.* **1** the act or an instance of ramifying; the state of being ramified. **2** a subdivision of a complex structure or process comparable to a tree's branches. **3** a consequence, esp. when complex or unwelcome.

ramify *v.* (**-ies**, **-ied**) **1** *intr.* form branches or subdivisions or offshoots. **2** *tr.* (usu. in *passive*) cause to branch out; arrange in a branching manner. [based on Latin *ramus* 'branch']

ramjet *n.* a type of jet engine in which the air drawn in for combustion is compressed solely by the forward motion of the aircraft.

rammer see RAM.

ramp[1] ● *n.* **1** a slope or inclined plane, esp. for joining two levels of ground etc. **2** movable stairs for entering or leaving an aircraft. **3** *Brit.* a transverse ridge in a road to control the speed of vehicles. ● *v.* **1** *tr.* furnish or build with a ramp. **2** *intr.* **a** assume or be in a threatening posture. **b** (often foll. by *about*) storm, rage, rush. **c** *Heraldry* be rampant. [from Old French *ramper* 'to creep, crawl']

ramp[2] *Brit.* *slang* ● *n.* a swindle or racket, esp. one conducted by the levying of exorbitant prices. ● *v.* **1** *intr.* engage in a ramp. **2** *tr.* subject (a person etc.) to a ramp. [16th-century coinage]

rampage ● *v.intr.* /ram-**payj**/ **1** (often foll. by *about*) rush wildly or violently about. **2** rage, storm. ● *n.* /**ram**-payj/ wild or violent behaviour. □ **on the rampage** rampaging. [17th-century coinage] □ **rampageous** *adj.* **rampager** *n.*

rampant *adj.* **1** (placed after noun) *Heraldry* ▼ (of an animal) standing on its left hind foot with its forepaws in the air (*bear rampant*). **2** unchecked, flourishing excessively (*rampant violence*). **3** violent or extravagant in action or opinion (*rampant theorists*). **4** rank, luxuriant. [from Old French, literally 'crawling'] □ **rampancy** *n.* **rampantly** *adv.*

rampart *n.* **1 a** a defensive wall with a broad top and usu. a stone parapet. **b** a walkway on top of such a wall. **2** a defence or protection. [from French *rempart*]

RAMPANT: SHIELD WITH BEAR RAMPANT

ram-raid *n.* a robbery in which a shop window is rammed with a vehicle and looted. □ **ram-raider** *n.* **ram-raiding** *n*

ramrod *n.* **1** ► a rod for ramming down the charge of a muzzle-loading firearm. **2** a thing that is very straight or rigid.

ramshackle *adj.* (usu. of a house or vehicle) tumbledown, rickety. [from obsolete *ransackled* 'ransacked']

RAN *abbr.* Royal Australian Navy.

ran *past of* RUN.

ranch ● *n.* **1 a** a cattle-breeding establishment, esp. in the western US and Canada. **b** a farm where other animals are bred (*mink ranch*). **2** (in full **ranch house**) *N. Amer.* a single-storey or split-level house. ● *v.intr.* farm on a ranch. [from Spanish *rancho* 'group of persons eating together']

rancher *n.* **1** a person who farms on a ranch. **2** *N. Amer.* a modern single-storey house.

ramming end

cleaning brush

RAMROD

rancid *adj.* smelling or tasting like rank stale fat. [from Latin *rancidus* 'stinking'] □ **rancidity** *n.*

rancour *n.* (*US* **rancor**) inveterate bitterness, malignant hate. [from Late Latin *rancor*, related to RANCID] □ **rancorous** *adj.* **rancorously** *adv.*

rand *n.* the chief monetary unit of South Africa and Namibia. [from *the Rand*, goldfield district near Johannesburg]

R & B *abbr.* (also **R. & B.**) rhythm and blues.

R & D *abbr.* (also **R. & D.**) research and development.

random *adj.* **1** made, done, etc., without method or conscious choice. **2** *Statistics* **a** with equal chances for each item. **b** given by a random process. □ **at random** without aim or purpose or principle [from Old French *random* 'great speed'] □ **randomize** *v.tr.* (also **-ise**). **randomization** *n.* **randomly** *adv.* **randomness** *n.*

random-access *adj. Computing* (of a memory or file) having all parts directly accessible, so that it need not be read sequentially.

random error *n. Statistics* an error in measurement caused by factors which vary from one measurement to another.

R and R *abbr.* (also **R. and R.**) **1** rescue and resuscitation. **2** rest and recreation.

randy *adj.* (**randier**, **randiest**) **1** lustful; eager for sexual gratification. **2** *Sc.* loud-tongued, boisterous. □ **randily** *adv.* **randiness** *n.*

ranee /rah-nee/ *n.* (also **rani**) *hist.* a raja's wife or widow; a Hindu queen. [from Sanskrit *rājñī*]

rang *past of* RING[2].

range ● *n.* **1 a** the region between limits of variation, esp. as representing a scope of effective operation (*whole range of politics*). **b** such limits. **c** a limited scale or series (*the range is about 10 degrees*). **2** the area included in or concerned with something. **3 a** the distance attainable by a gun or projectile. **b** the distance between a gun or projectile and its objective. **4** a row, series, line, or tier, esp. of mountains or buildings. **5 a** an open or enclosed area with targets for shooting. **b** a testing ground for military equipment. **6** a large cooking stove of which the burners and oven(s) are kept continually hot. **7** the area over which a thing, esp. a plant or animal, is distributed. **8** the distance that can be covered by a vehicle or aircraft without refuelling. **9** the distance between a camera and the subject to be photographed. **10** the extent of time covered by a forecast etc. **11 a** a large area of open land for grazing or hunting. **b** a tract over which one wanders. ● *v.* **1** *intr.* **a** reach; lie spread out; extend; vary between limits. **b** run in a line (*ranges north and south*). **2** *tr.* (usu. in *passive* or *refl.*) place or arrange in ranks or in a specified situation or order or company. **3** *intr.* rove, wander (*ranged through the woods*). **5** *intr.* **a** (often foll. by *with*) be level. **b** (foll. by *with*, *among*) rank (*ranges with the great writers*). **6** *intr.* **a** (of a gun) send a projectile over a specified distance (*ranges over a mile*). **b** obtain the range of a target by adjustment after firing past it or short of it. [from Old French, literally 'row, rank']

rangefinder *n.* an instrument for estimating the distance of an object, esp. one to be shot at or photographed.

ranger *n.* **1** a keeper of a royal or national park, or of a forest. **2** a member of a body of armed men, esp.: **a** a mounted soldier. **b** *US* a commando. **3** (**Ranger**) *Brit.* a senior Guide. □ **rangership** *n.*

rangy /rayn-ji/ *adj.* (**rangier**, **rangiest**) (of a person) tall and slim.

rani *var. of* RANEE.

rank[1] ● *n.* **1 a** a position in a hierarchy, a grade of advancement. **b** a grade of dignity or achievement (*in the top rank of performers*). **c** high social position (*persons of rank*). **d** a place in a scale. **2** a row or line. **3** a single line of soldiers drawn up abreast. **4** *Brit.* a place where taxis stand to await customers. ● *v.* **1** *intr.* have rank or place (*ranks next to the king*). **2** *tr.* classify. **3** *tr.* arrange (esp. soldiers) in a rank or ranks. **4** *US* **a** *tr.* take precedence over (a person) in respect to rank. **b** *intr.* have the senior position among the members of a hierarchy etc. □ **break rank** (or **ranks**) fail to remain in line; fail to maintain solidarity. **close ranks** maintain solidarity. **keep rank** remain in line. **the ranks** the common soldiers, i.e. privates and corporals. [from Old French *ranc*, *renc*]

rank[2] *adj.* **1** too luxuriant; choked with or apt to produce weeds or excessive foliage. **2 a** foul-smelling, offensive. **b** loathsome, indecent, corrupt. **3** flagrant, virulent, gross, complete (*rank outsider*). [Old English] □ **rankly** *adv.* **rankness** *n.*

rank and file *n.* (usu. treated as *pl.*) ordinary undistinguished people (hyphenated when *attrib.*: *rank-and-file members*).

ranker *n. Brit.* **1** a soldier in the ranks. **2** a commissioned officer who has been in the ranks.

ranking ● *n.* ordering by rank; classification. ● *adj. US* having a high rank or position.

rankle *v.intr.* (of envy, disappointment, etc.) cause persistent annoyance or resentment. [based on Old French *rancle*, *draoncle* 'festering sore']

ransack *v.tr.* **1** pillage or plunder. **2** thoroughly search (a receptacle, a person's pockets, etc.). [from Old Norse *rannsaka*] □ **ransacker** *n.*

ransom ● *n.* **1** a sum of money or other payment demanded or paid for the release of a prisoner. **2** the liberation of a prisoner in return for this. ● *v.tr.* **1** buy the freedom or restoration of; redeem. **2** hold to ransom. **3** release for a ransom. [from Latin *redemptio* 'redemption']

rant ● *v.* **1** *intr.* use bombastic language. **2** *tr. & intr.* declaim, recite theatrically. **3** *intr.* speak vehemently or wildly. **4** *tr. & intr.* preach noisily. ● *n.* **1** a piece of ranting, a tirade. **2** empty turgid talk. □ **rant and rave** express anger noisily and forcefully. [from Dutch *ranten* 'to rave'] □ **ranter** *n.* **rantingly** *adv.*

ranunculus *n.* (*pl.* **ranunculuses** or **ranunculi**) any plant of the genus *Ranunculus*, usu. having bowl-shaped flowers with many stamens and carpels. [Latin, originally in sense 'little frog']

RAOC *abbr.* (in the UK) Royal Army Ordnance Corps.

rap[1] ● *n.* **1** a smart slight blow. **2** a knock, a sharp tapping sound. **3** *slang* blame, censure, or punishment. **4** *slang* a conversation. **5 a** a rhyming monologue recited rhythmically to pre-recorded music.

b (in full **rap music**) a style of black popular music with a pronounced beat to which words are recited rather than sung. ● *v.* (**rapped**, **rapping**) **1** *tr.* strike smartly. **2** *intr.* make a sharp tapping sound. **3** *tr.* criticize adversely. **4** *intr. slang* talk. **5** *intr.* perform rap music, talk in the style of rap. □ **beat the rap** *N. Amer.* escape punishment. **rap on** (or **over**) **the knuckles** a reprimand or reproof. **rap out 1** utter abruptly or on the spur of the moment. **2** express or reproduce (a rhythm etc.) by raps. **take the rap** suffer the consequences. [Middle English] □ **rapper** *n.*

rap[2] *n.* a small amount, the least bit. [from Irish *ropaire* 'robber', used as the name of an Irish counterfeit coin]

rapacious *adj.* grasping, extortionate, predatory. [from Latin *rapax -acis*] □ **rapaciously** *adv.* **rapaciousness** *n.* **rapacity** *n.*

RAPC *abbr.* (in the UK) Royal Army Pay Corps.

rape[1] ● *n.* **1 a** the act of forcing a woman or girl to have sexual intercourse against her will. **b** forcible sodomy. **2** (often foll. by *of*) violent assault, forcible interference, violation. **3** an instance of rape. ● *v.tr.* **1** commit rape on (a person, usu. a woman or girl). **2** violate, assault, pillage. [from Latin *rapere* 'to seize']

rape[2] *n.* ► a plant, *Brassica napus*, grown as fodder and for its seed, from which oil is made. [from Latin *rapum*, *rapa* 'turnip']

rapeseed *n.* the seed of the rape plant.

raphide *n.* a needle-shaped crystal of calcium oxalate formed within the tissues of a plant. [from Greek *rhaphis -idos* 'needle']

RAPE
(*Brassica napus*)

rapid ● *adj.* (**rapider**, **rapidest**) **1** quick, swift. **2** taking or completed in a short time. **3** (of a slope) descending steeply. ● *n.* (usu. in *pl.*) a steep descent in a river bed, with a swift current. [from Latin *rapidus*] □ **rapidity** *n.* **rapidly** *adv.*

rapid eye-movement *n.* a type of jerky movement of the eyes during periods of dreaming.

rapid-fire *attrib.adj.* fired, asked, etc., in quick succession.

rapier *n.* **1** ◄ a light slender sword used for thrusting. ▷ SWORD. **2** (*attrib.*) sharp (*rapier wit*).

rapine *n. literary* plundering, robbery. [from Latin *rapina* 'seizing']

rapist *n.* a person who commits rape.

rapport /ra-por/ *n.* relationship or communication, esp. when useful and harmonious (*in rapport with*; *establish a rapport*). [French]

rapprochement /ra-prosh-mahn/ *n.* the resumption of harmonious relations, esp. between states. [French]

rapscallion *n. archaic* or *joc.* a rascal, scamp, or rogue.

rapt *adj.* **1** fully absorbed or intent, enraptured (*listen with rapt attention*). **2** carried away with joyous feeling or lofty thought. **3** *poet.* carried away bodily. **4** *Austral. colloq.* overjoyed, delighted. [from Latin *raptus* 'seized'] □ **raptly** *adv.* **raptness** *n.*

RAPIER: 17TH-CENTURY PAPPENHEIMER RAPIER

R

RAPTOR

The majority of raptors belong to the order Falconiformes; owls constitute a separate order, Strigiformes. Although some raptors, e.g. vultures, are carrion eaters, most are highly adapted to hunting live prey. Forward-facing eyes provide excellent binocular vision, powerful talons kill and grasp the quarry, and a sharp, hooked beak tears flesh.

large primary feathers

broad wingspan

forward-facing eyes

broad secondary feathers

powerful breast muscles

strong, hooked beak

tail feathers for steering, soaring, and braking

soft leg feathers

EXTERNAL FEATURES OF A RED-TAILED HAWK (*Buteo jamaicensis*)

powerful talons

TYPES OF RAPTOR

PANDIONIDAE (osprey) ▷ OSPREY

CATHARTIDAE (New World vultures) ▷ VULTURE

STRIGIFORMES (owls) ▷ OWL

ACCIPITRIDAE (eagles, buzzards, hawks, kites, Old World vultures) ▷ EAGLE, HAWK, VULTURE

FALCONIDAE (caracaras, falcons) ▷ FALCON

R

raptor *n.* ▲ any bird of prey. [Latin, literally 'ravisher, plunderer'] □ **raptorial** *adj.*

rapture *n.* **1** ecstatic delight, mental transport. **2** (in *pl.*) great pleasure or enthusiasm or the expression of it. □ **go into** (or **be in**) **raptures** be enthusiastic; talk enthusiastically. [from medieval Latin *raptura*, related to RAPT] □ **rapturous** *adj.* **rapturously** *adv.* **rapturousness** *n.*

rare[1] *adj.* (**rarer**, **rarest**) **1** seldom done, found, or occurring; uncommon. **2** esp. *Brit.* exceptionally good (*had a rare time*). **3** of less than the usual density (*rare atmosphere*). [from Latin *rarus*] □ **rareness** *n.*

rare[2] *adj.* (**rarer**, **rarest**) (of meat) underdone. [Old English]

rarebit *n.* = WELSH RABBIT.

rare earth *n.* **1** a lanthanide element. **2** an oxide of such an element.

rarefy *v.* (also **rarify**) (**-ies**, **-ied**) **1** *tr.* & *intr.* make or become less dense (*rarefied air*). **2** *tr.* refine (a person's nature etc.). **3** *tr.* make (an idea etc.) subtle. [from Latin *rarefacere* 'to make rare'] □ **rarefaction** *n.* **rarefactive** *adj.* **rarefication** *n.*

rare gas *n.* = NOBLE GAS.

rarely *adv.* **1** seldom; not often. **2** in an unusual degree; exceptionally. **3** exceptionally well.

raring *adj.* (foll. by *to* + infin.) *colloq.* enthusiastic, eager (*raring to go*). [from *rare*, dialect variant of ROAR or REAR[2]]

rarity *n.* (*pl.* **-ies**) **1** rareness. **2** an uncommon thing, esp. one valued for being rare. [from Latin *raritas*]

rascal *n.* often *joc.* a dishonest or mischievous person, esp. a child. [from Old French *rascaille* 'rabble'] □ **rascality** *n.* (*pl.* **-ies**). **rascally** *adj.*

rase var. of RAZE.

rash[1] *adj.* reckless, impetuous, hasty. [Middle English] □ **rashly** *adv.* **rashness** *n.*

rash[2] *n.* **1** an eruption of the skin in spots or patches. **2** (usu. foll. by *of*) a sudden widespread phenomenon (*a rash of strikes*). [18th-century coinage]

rasher *n.* a thin slice of bacon or ham. [16th-century coinage]

rasp ● *n.* **1** a coarse kind of file having separate teeth. **2** a grating noise or utterance. ● *v.* **1** *tr.* **a** scrape with a rasp. **b** scrape roughly. **c** (foll. by *off*, *away*) remove by scraping. **2 a** *intr.* make a grating sound. **b** *tr.* say gratingly or hoarsely. **3** *tr.* grate upon (a person or a person's feelings). [from Old French *raspe(r)*] □ **raspingly** *adv.* **raspy** *adj.*

raspberry ● *n.* (*pl.* **-ies**) **1 a** a bramble, *Rubus idaeus*, having usu. red berries. ▷ FRUIT. **b** its berry. **2** the red colour of a raspberry. **3** *colloq.* **a** a sound made with the lips expressing derision or disapproval. **b** a show of strong disapproval (*got a raspberry from the audience*). ● *adj.* of the colour of a raspberry. [from obsolete *raspis(-berry)*]

raspberry cane *n.* a raspberry plant.

Rasta *n.* & *adj. colloq.* = RASTAFARIAN.

Rastafarian ● *n.* a member of a sect of Jamaican origin regarding the former Emperor Haile Selassie of Ethiopia as the Messiah. ● *adj.* of or relating to this sect. [from *Ras Tafari*, name by which Haile Selassie was known 1916–30] □ **Rastafarianism** *n.*

raster *n.* a pattern of scanning lines for a cathode ray tube picture. [German, literally 'screen']

rasterize *v.tr.* (also **-ise**) *Computing* convert (a digitized image) into a form that can be displayed on a cathode ray tube or printed. □ **rasterization** *n.* **rasterizer** *n.*

rat ● *n.* **1 a** any of several rodents of the genus *Rattus*. ▷ RODENT. **b** any similar rodent (*muskrat*). **2 a** deserter from a party, cause, etc. **3** *colloq.* an

unpleasant person. **4** (in *pl.*) *slang* an exclamation of contempt, annoyance, etc. ● *v.intr.* (**ratted**, **ratting**) **1** (of a person or dog) hunt or kill rats. **2** *colloq.* desert a cause, party, etc. **3** (foll. by *on*) *colloq.* **a** betray; let down. **b** inform on. [Old English]

ratable var. of RATEABLE.

ratafia /rat-ă-feer/ *n.* **1** a liqueur flavoured with almonds or kernels of peach, apricot, or cherry. **2** a kind of biscuit similarly flavoured. [French]

ratan var. of RATTAN.

ratatat (also **rat-a-tat**) var. of RAT-TAT.

ratatouille /rat-ă-too-i/ *n.* a vegetable dish of onions, courgettes, tomatoes, aubergines, and peppers, fried and stewed in oil. [French dialect]

ratbag *n. Brit. slang* an unpleasant or disgusting person.

rat-catcher *n.* a person who rids buildings of rats etc.

ratchet ● *n.* **1** a set of teeth on the edge of a bar or wheel in which a device engages to ensure motion in one direction only. **2** (in full **ratchet-wheel**) a wheel with a rim so toothed. ● *v.* (**ratcheted**, **ratcheting**) **1** *tr.* **a** provide with a ratchet. **b** make into a ratchet. **2** *tr.* & *intr.* (often foll. by *up*) move as under the control of a ratchet. [from French *rochet* 'blunt lance-head, ratchet']

rate[1] ● *n.* **1** a stated numerical proportion between two sets of things (*at a rate of 50 miles per hour*) or as the basis of calculating an amount or value (*rate of taxation*). **2** a fixed or appropriate charge or cost or value; a measure of this (*postal rates*). **3** rapidity of movement or change (*a great rate*). **4** class or rank (*first-rate*). **5** *Brit.* **a** a tax levied by local authorities on commercial properties at so much per pound of the assessed value of buildings and land owned or leased (now replaced by the council tax for dwellings). **b** (in *pl.*) the amount payable by this.

● *v.* **1** *tr.* **a** estimate the worth or value of (*I rate him very highly*). **b** assign a fixed value to (a coin or metal) in relation to a monetary standard. **2** *tr.* consider; regard as. **3** *intr.* (foll. by *as*) rank or be rated. **4** *tr. Brit.* **a** subject to the payment of a local rate. **b** value for the purpose of assessing rates. **5** *tr.* be worthy of, deserve. **6** *tr.* place (a film etc.) in a category relative to its suitability for viewing. □ **at any rate** in any case, whatever happens. **at this** (or **that**) **rate** if this example is typical or this assumption is true. [based on Latin *ratus* 'reckoned']

rate[2] *v.tr.* scold angrily. [Middle English]

rateable *adj.* (also **ratable**) **1** *Brit. esp. hist.* liable to the levy of rates (see RATE[1] *n.* 5). **2** able to be rated or estimated.

rateable value *n. Brit.* the value at which a house etc. is assessed for payment of rates.

ratepayer *n.* **1** *Brit. esp. hist.* a person liable to pay rates (see RATE[1] *n.* 5). **2** *N. Amer.* a customer of a public utility.

rather *adv.* **1** (often foll. by *than*) by preference (*would rather not go*). **2** (usu. foll. by *than*) as a more likely alternative (*is stupid rather than honest*). **3** more precisely (*a book, or rather, a pamphlet*). **4** slightly; somewhat (*rather drunk*). **5** *Brit.* (as an emphatic response) indeed, assuredly (*Did you like it? – Rather!*). □ **had rather** *archaic* or *literary* would rather. [Old English *hrathor* 'sooner, earlier']

ratify *v.tr.* (**-ies**, **-ied**) confirm or accept (an agreement made in one's name) by formal consent, signature, etc. [from medieval Latin *ratificare*] □ **ratifiable** *adj.* **ratification** *n.* **ratifier** *n.*

rating[1] *n.* **1** the act or an instance of placing in a rank or class or assigning a value to. **2** the estimated standing of a person as regards credit etc. **3** *Naut. Brit.* a non-commissioned sailor. **4** *Brit. esp. hist.* an amount fixed as a local rate (cf. RATE[1] *n.* 5). **5** the relative popularity of a broadcast programme as determined by the estimated size of the audience.

rating[2] *n.* an angry reprimand.

ratio *n.* (*pl.* **-os**) the quantitative relation between two similar magnitudes determined by the number of times one contains the other integrally or fractionally. [Latin]

ratiocinate /rat-i-os-i-nayt/ *v.intr. literary* go through logical processes, reason, esp. using syllogisms. [based on Latin *ratiocinatus* 'calculated'] □ **ratiocination** *n.* **ratiocinative** *adj.*

ration ● *n.* **1** a fixed official allowance of food, clothing, etc., in a time of shortage. **2** (foll. by *of*) a single portion of provisions etc. **3** (usu. in *pl.*) a fixed daily allowance of food, esp. in the armed forces. **4** (in *pl.*) provisions. ● *v.tr.* **1** limit (persons or provisions) to a fixed ration. **2** (usu. foll. by *out*) share out (food etc.) in fixed quantities. [from Latin *ratio* 'reckoning']

rational *adj.* **1** of or based on reasoning or reason. **2** sensible, sane, moderate. **3** endowed with reason, reasoning. **4** rejecting what is unreasonable or cannot be tested by reason in religion or custom. **5** *Math.* (of a quantity or ratio) expressible as a ratio of whole numbers. □ **rationality** *n.* **rationally** *adv.*

rationale /rash-ŏ-**nahl**/ *n.* **1** (often foll. by *for*) the fundamental reason or logical basis of anything. **2** a reasoned exposition. [modern Latin]

rationalism *n.* the practice of treating reason as the basis of belief and knowledge. □ **rationalist** *n.* **rationalistic** *adj.* **rationalistically** *adv.*

rationalize *v.* (also **-ise**) **1 a** *tr.* offer a rational but specious explanation of (one's behaviour or attitude). **b** *intr.* explain one's behaviour or attitude in this way. **2** *tr.* make logical and consistent. **3** *tr.* make (a business etc.) more efficient by reorganizing it to reduce or eliminate waste. **4** *tr.* (often foll. by *away*) explain or explain away rationally. □ **rationalization** *n.* **rationalizer** *n.*

ration book *n.* (also **ration card**) a document entitling the holder to a ration.

ratline *n.* (also **ratlin**) (usu. in *pl.*) ► any of the small lines fastened across a sailing ship's shrouds like ladder rungs.

rat race *n.* a fiercely competitive struggle for position, power, etc.

rat-run *n. colloq.* a route on minor roads used by traffic to avoid congestion at peak periods.

rat's tail *n.* a thing shaped like a rat's tail, e.g. a tapering cylindrical file.

rattan *n.* (also **ratan**) **1** any Malaysian climbing palm of the genus *Calamus* etc. with long thin jointed pliable stems. **2** a piece of rattan stem used as a walking stick etc. [earlier *rot(t)ang*, from Malay *rōtan*]

rat-tat *n.* (also **rat-tat-tat**, **ratatat**, **rat-a-tat**) a rapping sound, esp. of a knocker.

ratter *n.* **1** a dog or other animal that hunts rats. **2** *slang* a person who betrays a cause, friend, etc.

rattle ● *v.* **1 a** *intr.* give out a rapid succession of short sharp hard sounds. **b** *tr.* make (a window, crockery, etc.) do this. **c** *intr.* cause such sounds by shaking something. **2 a** *intr.* move with a rattling noise. **b** *intr.* ride or run briskly. **3 a** *tr.* (usu. foll. by *off*) say or recite rapidly. **b** *intr.* (usu. foll. by *on*) talk in a lively thoughtless way. **4** *tr. colloq.* disconcert, alarm. ● *n.* **1** a rattling sound. **2** an instrument or plaything made to rattle. **3** the set of horny rings in a rattlesnake's tail. **4 a** a noisy flow of words. **b** empty chatter, trivial talk. □ **rattle the sabre** threaten war. [Middle English] □ **rattly** *adj.*

rattler *n.* **1** a thing that rattles, esp. an old or rickety vehicle. **2** *colloq.* a rattlesnake.

rattlesnake *n.* ▼ any of various poisonous American snakes of the family Viperidae, esp. of the genus *Crotalus* or *Sistrurus*, with a rattling structure of horny rings in its tail. ▷ SNAKE

horny rings

RATTLESNAKE: EASTERN DIAMONDBACK RATTLESNAKE (*Crotalus adamanteus*)

rattletrap *colloq.* ● *n.* a rickety old vehicle etc. ● *adj.* rickety.

rattling ● *adj.* **1** that rattles. **2** brisk, vigorous (*a rattling pace*). ● *adv.* remarkably (*a rattling good story*).

ratty *adj.* (**rattier**, **rattiest**) **1** relating to or infested with rats. **2** *Brit. colloq.* irritable or angry. **3** *colloq.* wretched, shabby, nasty. □ **rattily** *adv.* **rattiness** *n.*

raucous *adj.* harsh-sounding, loud and hoarse. [from Latin *raucus*] □ **raucously** *adv.* **raucousness** *n.*

raunchy *adj.* (**raunchier**, **raunchiest**) *colloq.* coarse, boisterous; sexually provocative. [20th-century coinage] □ **raunchily** *adv.* **raunchiness** *n.*

ravage ● *v.tr. & intr.* devastate, plunder. ● *n.* **1** the act or an instance of ravaging; devastation, damage. **2** (usu. in *pl.*; foll. by *of*) destructive effect (*survived*

RATLINES *ON A 16TH-CENTURY WARSHIP*

ratline

ratline

shroud

the ravages of winter). [French, alteration of *ravine* 'rush of water'] □ **ravager** *n.*

rave ● *v.* **1** *intr.* talk wildly or furiously in or as in delirium. **2** *intr.* speak with rapturous admiration; go into raptures. **3** *tr. & intr. colloq.* enjoy oneself freely (esp. *rave it up*). ● *n.* **1** (usu. *attrib.*) *colloq.* a highly enthusiastic review (*a rave review*). **2** *Brit. slang* an infatuation. **3** *Brit. colloq.* **a** (also **rave-up**) a lively party. **b** a large often illicit party or event with dancing to loud fast pop music. [Middle English]

ravel ● *v.* (**ravelled**, **ravelling**; *US* **raveled**, **raveling**) **1** *tr. & intr.* entangle or become entangled. **2** *tr.* confuse or complicate (a question or problem). **3** *intr.* fray out. **4** *tr.* disentangle, unravel, separate into threads. ● *n.* **1** a tangle or knot. **2** a complication. **3** a frayed or loose end.

raven[1] ● *n.* a large glossy blue-black crow, *Corvus corax*, having a hoarse cry. ● *adj.* glossy black (*raven tresses*). [Old English]

raven[2] *v.* **1** *intr.* **a** plunder. **b** (foll. by *after*) seek prey or booty. **c** (foll. by *about*) go plundering. **d** prowl for prey (*ravening beast*). **2 a** *tr.* devour voraciously. **b** *intr.* (esp. as **ravening** *adj.*) have a ravenous appetite. **c** *intr.* feed voraciously. [from Old French *raviner* 'to ravage']

ravenous *adj.* **1** very hungry. **2** voracious. **3** rapacious. [from Old French *ravineus*] □ **ravenously** *adv.*

raver *n.* **1** *colloq.* **a** an uninhibited pleasure-loving person. **b** a person who goes to raves. **2** a person who raves.

rave-up var. of RAVE *n.* 3a.

ravine *n.* a deep narrow gorge. [French] □ **ravined** *adj.*

raving ● *n.* (usu. in *pl.*) wild or delirious talk. ● *adj.* delirious, frenzied. ● *adj. & adv. colloq.* as an intensive (*a raving beauty; raving mad*).

ravioli /rav-i-oh-li/ *n.* small pasta envelopes containing minced meat etc. ▷ PASTA. [Italian]

ravish *v.tr.* **1** rape. **2** enrapture. [from Latin *rapere* 'to seize'] □ **ravisher** *n.* **ravishment** *n.*

ravishing *adj.* entrancing, delightful. □ **ravishingly** *adv.*

raw ● *adj.* **1** uncooked. **2** in the natural state; not processed or manufactured (*raw sewage*). **3** (of alcoholic spirit) undiluted. **4** (of statistics etc.) not analysed or processed. **5** inexperienced, untrained (*raw recruits*). **6 a** stripped of skin; having the flesh exposed. **b** sensitive to the touch from having the flesh exposed. **c** abnormally sensitive (*touched a raw nerve*). **7** (of the atmosphere, day, etc.) chilly and damp. **8** crude in artistic quality; lacking finish. **9** (of the edge of cloth) without hem or selvedge. ● *n.* a raw place on a person's or horse's body. □ **in the raw 1** in its natural state without mitigation (*life in the raw*). **2** naked. **touch on the raw** upset (a person) on a sensitive matter. [Old English] □ **rawly** *adv.* **rawness** *n.*

raw-boned *adj.* gaunt.

raw deal *n.* harsh or unfair treatment.

rawhide *n.* **1** untanned hide. **2** a rope or whip of this.

Rawlplug *n. Brit. propr.* a thin cylinder of fibre or plastic for holding a screw or nail in masonry. [from *Rawl*ings, name of the engineers who introduced it]

RAW SIENNA

raw material *n.* that from which the process of manufacture makes products.

raw sienna *n.* ► a brownish-yellow earth used as a pigment.

raw umber *n.* ► umber in its natural state, yellowish-brown in colour.

RAW UMBER

R

RAY

Rays are adapted to life on or near the sea-bed. Their flattened bodies allow them to lie on the bottom, often camouflaged and un-detected. Their gills are on the underside of their bodies, but clean water is admitted to the gill chambers through a spiracle on the upper side, just behind the eye. Rays feed primarily on shellfish, crustaceans, and fish, which they hunt largely by scent. Mantas can have a wingspan of over 6 m (20 ft).

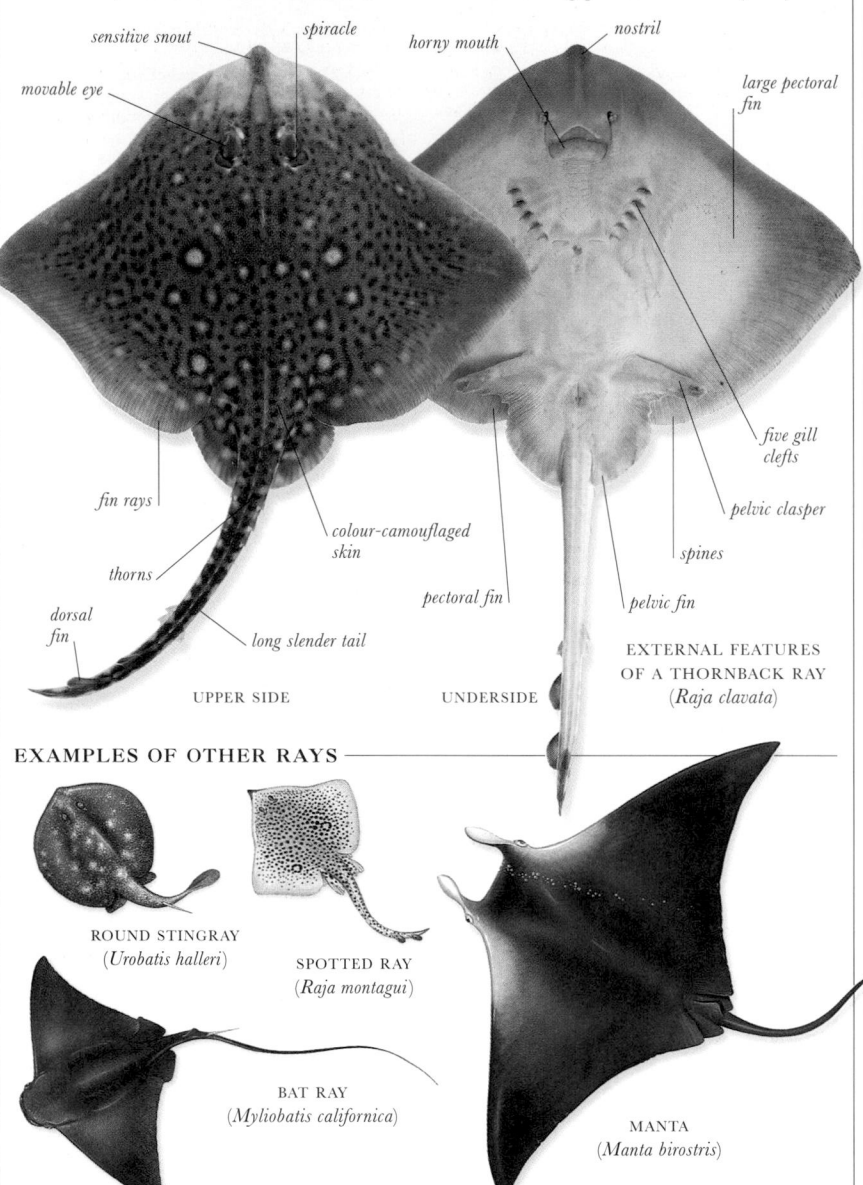

sensitive snout

spiracle

movable eye

horny mouth   *nostril*

large pectoral fin

fin rays

colour-camouflaged skin

thorns

five gill clefts

pelvic clasper

spines

dorsal fin

long slender tail

pectoral fin

pelvic fin

UPPER SIDE   UNDERSIDE

EXTERNAL FEATURES OF A THORNBACK RAY (*Raja clavata*)

EXAMPLES OF OTHER RAYS

ROUND STINGRAY (*Urobatis halleri*)

SPOTTED RAY (*Raja montagui*)

BAT RAY (*Myliobatis californica*)

MANTA (*Manta birostris*)

R

ray¹ *n.* **1** a single line or narrow beam of light from a small or distant source. **2** a straight line in which radiation travels to a given point. **3** (in *pl.*) radiation of a specified type (*gamma rays*; *X-rays*). **4** a trace or beginning of an enlightening or cheering influence (*a ray of hope*). **5 a** any of a set of radiating lines or parts or things. **b** any of a set of straight lines passing through one point. **6** the marginal portion of a composite flower, e.g. a daisy. [from Latin *radius*] □ **rayed** *adj.* **rayless** *adj.*

ray² *n.* ▲ a cartilaginous fish of the order Batiformes, with a broad flat body, winglike pectoral fins and a long slender tail. ▷ FISH. [from Latin *raia*]

ray³ *n.* (also **re**) *Mus.* **1** (in tonic sol-fa) the second note of a major scale. **2** the note D in the fixed-doh system. [Middle English *re*, from Latin *resonare* 'to resound']

ray gun *n.* (esp. in science fiction) a gun causing injury or damage by the emission of rays.

rayon *n.* any of various textile fibres or fabrics made from viscose. [arbitrary formation from RAY¹]

raze *v.tr.* (also **rase**) completely destroy; tear down (esp. *raze to the ground*). [Middle English *rase* 'to wound slightly': based on Latin *rasus* 'scraped']

razor ● *n.* an instrument with a sharp blade used in cutting hair esp. from the skin. ● *v.tr.* **1** use a razor on. **2** shave; cut down close. [related to RAZE]

razorbill *n.* a black and white auk, *Alca torda*, with a deep bill likened to a cut-throat razor.

razor blade *n.* a flat piece of metal with a sharp edge or edges used in a safety razor.

razor cut *n.* a haircut made with a razor.

razor edge *n.* (also **razor's edge**) **1** a keen edge. **2** a sharp mountain ridge. **3** a critical situation (*found themselves on a razor edge*). **4** a sharp line of division. □ **razor-edged** *adj.*

razor-fish *n.* (*pl.* usu. same) = RAZOR-SHELL.

razor-sharp *adj.* extremely sharp.

razor-shell *n.* ▶ any of various bivalve molluscs of the superfamily Solenacea, with a shell like the handle of a cut-throat razor. ▷ SHELL.

razor wire *n.* a type of sharp wire used as a barrier or run along the top of walls etc. to discourage intruders.

razzle-dazzle *n.* (also **razzle**) *slang* **1 a** excitement; bustle. **b** a spree. **2** extravagant publicity. [reduplication of DAZZLE]

razzmatazz *n.* (also **razzamatazz**) *colloq.* **1** = RAZZLE-DAZZLE. **2** insincere actions.

Rb *symb. Chem.* the element rubidium.

RC *abbr.* **1** Roman Catholic. **2** Red Cross.

RCA *abbr.* (in the UK) Royal College of Art.

RCM *abbr.* (in the UK) Royal College of Music.

RCMP *abbr.* Royal Canadian Mounted Police.

RCN *abbr.* (in the UK) Royal College of Nursing.

foot

RAZOR-SHELL (*Ensis siliqua*)

RCP *abbr.* (in the UK) Royal College of Physicians.

RCS *abbr.* (in the UK): **1** Royal College of Scientists. **2** Royal College of Surgeons. **3** Royal Corps of Signals.

RCVS *abbr.* (in the UK) Royal College of Veterinary Surgeons.

Rd. *abbr.* Road (in names).

RE *abbr.* **1** (in the UK) Royal Engineers. **2** religious education.

Re *symb. Chem.* the element rhenium.

re¹ *prep.* **1** in the matter of (as the first word in a heading). **2** *colloq.* about, concerning. [Latin]

■ **Usage** The use of *re* in sense 2 to mean simply 'about' or 'concerning' is best avoided.

re² var. of RAY³.

re- *prefix* **1** attachable to almost any verb or its derivative, meaning: **a** once more; afresh, anew (*readjust*; *renumber*). **b** back; with return to a previous state (*reassemble*; *reverse*). **2** (also **red-** before a vowel, as in *redolent*) in verbs and verbal derivatives denoting: **a** in return; mutually (*react*; *resemble*). **b** opposition (*repel*; *resist*). **c** behind or after (*relic*; *remain*). **d** retirement or secrecy (*recluse*; *reticence*). **e** off, away, down (*recede*; *relegate*; *repress*). **f** frequentative or intensive force (*redouble*; *refine*; *resplendent*). **g** negative force (*recant*; *reveal*).

■ **Usage** In sense 1, a hyphen is normally used when the word begins with e (*re-enact*), or to distinguish the compound from a more familiar one-word form (*re-form* = form again).

're *abbr. colloq.* (usu. after pronouns) are (*we're*; *you're*).

reabsorb *v.tr.* absorb again. □ **reabsorption** *n.*

reach ● *v.* **1** *intr. & tr.* stretch out; extend. **2** *intr.* stretch out a limb, the hand, etc.; make a reaching motion or effort. **3** *intr.* make a motion or effort to touch or get hold of, or to attain (*reached for his pipe*). **4** *tr.* get as far as (*reached Lincoln at lunchtime*; *your letter reached me today*). **5** *tr.* get to or attain (a specified point) on a scale (*the temperature reached 90°*; *the number of applications reached 100*). **6** *intr.* (foll. by *to*) attain to; be adequate for (*my income will not reach to it*). **7** *tr.*

succeed in achieving; attain (*have reached agreement*). **8** *tr.* make contact with the hand etc., or by telephone etc. (*was out all day and could not be reached*). **9** *tr.* (of a broadcast, broadcasting station, etc.) be received by. **10** *tr.* succeed in influencing or having the required effect on (*could not manage to reach their audience*). **11** *tr.* hand, pass (*reach me that book*). **12** *tr.* take with an outstretched hand. **13** *intr. Naut.* sail with the wind abeam or abaft the beam. • *n.* **1** the extent to which a hand etc. can be reached out, influence exerted, motion carried out, or mental powers used. **2** an act of reaching out. **3** a continuous extent, esp. a stretch of river between two bends, or the part of a canal between locks. **4** *Naut.* a distance traversed in reaching. □ **out of reach** not able to be reached or attained. [Old English] □ **reachable** *adj.*

reach-me-down *adj. Brit.* ready-made.

reacquaint *v.tr. & refl.* (usu. foll. by *with*) make acquainted again. □ **reacquaintance** *n.*

react *v.* **1** *intr.* (foll. by *to*) respond to a stimulus; undergo a change or show behaviour due to some influence (*how did they react to the news?*). **2** *intr.* (often foll. by *against*) be actuated by repulsion to; tend in a reverse or contrary direction. **3** *intr.* (often foll. by *upon*) produce a reciprocal or responsive effect; act upon the agent (*they react upon each other*). **4** *intr.* (foll. by *with*) *Chem.* & *Physics* (of a substance or particle) be the cause of activity or interaction with another (*nitrous oxide reacts with the metal*). **5** *tr.* (foll. by *with*) *Chem.* cause (a substance) to react with another. [from medieval Latin *reagere react-*]

reaction *n.* **1** the act or an instance of reacting; a responsive or reciprocal action. **2 a** a responsive feeling (*what was your reaction to the news?*). **b** an immediate or first impression. **3** the occurrence of a condition after a period of its opposite. **4 a** a bodily response to an external stimulus. **b** an adverse response to a drug. **5** a tendency to oppose change or to advocate return to a former system. **6** the interaction of substances undergoing chemical change. □ **reactionist** *n. & adj.*

reactionary • *adj.* tending to oppose change and advocate return to a former system. • *n.* (*pl.* **-ies**) a reactionary person.

reactivate *v.tr.* restore to a state of activity. □ **reactivation** *n.*

reactive *adj.* **1** showing reaction. **2** reacting rather than taking the initiative. **3** having a tendency to react chemically. □ **reactivity** *n.*

reactor *n.* **1** a person or thing that reacts. **2** (in full **nuclear reactor**) an apparatus or structure in which a controlled nuclear chain reaction releases energy. ▷ NUCLEAR POWER

read /reed/ • *v.* (*past* and *past part.* **read** red) **1** *tr.* (also *absol.*) reproduce mentally or vocally the written or printed words of (a book, author, etc.). **2** *tr.* convert or be able to convert into the intended words or meaning (written or other symbols or the things expressed in this way). **3** *tr.* interpret mentally. **4** *tr.* deduce or declare an interpretation of (*read the expression on my face*). **5** *tr.* find (a thing) recorded or stated in print etc. (*I read somewhere that you are leaving*). **6** *tr.* interpret (a statement or action) in a certain sense (*my silence is not to be read as consent*). **7** *tr.* assume as intended or deducible (*you read too much into my letter*). **8** *tr.* bring into a specified state by reading (*read myself to sleep*). **9 a** *tr.* (of a recording instrument) show (a specified figure etc.) (*the thermometer reads 20°*). **b** inspect and record the figure shown on such an instrument (*read the meter*). **10** *intr.* convey meaning in a specified manner when read (*it reads persuasively*). **11** *intr.* sound or affect a hearer or reader as specified when read (*the book reads like a parody*). **12 a** *tr.* esp. *Brit.* study by reading (esp. a subject at university). **b** *intr.* carry out a course of study by reading (*is reading for the Bar*). **13** *tr.* (as **read** *adj.*) versed in a subject by reading (*a well-read person; was widely read in law*). **14** *tr.* **a** (of a computer) copy or transfer (data). **b** (foll. by *in, out*) enter or extract (data) in an electronic storage device. **15** *tr.* receive and understand the words of (a person) by radio or telephone (*do you read me?*). **16** *tr.* **a** understand (a person) by interpretation of outward signs etc. **b** interpret (cards, a person's hand, etc.) as a fortune-teller. **17** *tr. Printing* check the correctness of and emend (a proof). **18** *tr.* **a** (of a text) have at a particular place (*reads 'battery' not 'buttery'*). **b** substitute (a word etc.) for an incorrect one (*for 'illitterate' read 'illiterate'*). • *n.* **1** esp. *Brit.* a spell of reading. **2** *colloq.* a book etc. as regards its readability (*is a really good read*). □ **read between the lines** look for or find hidden meaning. **read up** (often foll. by *on*) make a special study of (a subject). [Old English *rǣdan* 'to advise, consider, discern']

readable *adj.* **1** able to be read; legible. **2** interesting or pleasant to read. □ **readability** *n.* **readably** *adv.*

readdress *v.tr.* **1** change the address of (a letter or parcel). **2** address (a problem etc.) anew. **3** speak or write to anew.

reader *n.* **1** a person who reads or is reading. **2** a book of extracts for learning. **3** a device for producing an image that can be read from microfilm etc. **4** (also **Reader**) *Brit.* a university lecturer of the highest grade below professor. **5** a publisher's employee who reports on submitted manuscripts. **6** a printer's proof-corrector. □ **readerly** *adj.*

readership *n.* **1** the readers of a newspaper etc. **2** the number or extent of these. **3** (also **Readership**) *Brit.* the position of reader at a university.

readily *adv.* **1** without showing reluctance; willingly. **2** without difficulty.

reading *n.* **1 a** the act or an instance of reading (*the reading of the will*). **b** matter to be read (*have plenty of reading with me*). **c** the specified quality of this (*it made exciting reading*). **2** (in *comb.*) used for reading (*reading-lamp; reading-room*). **3** literary knowledge (*a person of wide reading*). **4** an entertainment at which a play, poems, etc., are read (*poetry reading*). **5** a figure etc. shown by a recording instrument. **6** an interpretation or view taken (*what is your reading of the facts?*) **7** an interpretation made (of drama, music, etc.). **8** each of the successive occasions on which a bill must be presented to a legislature for acceptance.

reading age *n.* reading ability expressed as the age for which the same ability is calculated as average (*has a reading age of eight*).

readjust *v.tr.* adjust again or to a former state. □ **readjustment** *n.*

readmit *v.tr.* (**readmitted**, **readmitting**) admit again. □ **readmission** *n.*

read-only memory *n. Computing* a memory read at high speed but not capable of being changed by program instructions. ▷ COMPUTER

readopt *v.tr.* adopt again. □ **readoption** *n.*

read-out *n.* a record or display of the output from a computer or scientific instrument.

re-advertise *v.tr. & intr.* advertise again. □ **re-advertisement** *n.*

read-write *adj. Computing* capable of reading existing data and accepting alterations or further input. ▷ HARD DISK

ready • *adj.* (**readier**, **readiest**) (usu. *predic.*) **1** with preparations complete (*dinner is ready*). **2** in an appropriate state (*are you ready to go?*). **3** willing, inclined, or resolved (*he is always ready to complain; I am ready for anything*). **4** within reach; easily secured (*a ready source of income*). **5** fit for immediate use (*was ready to hand*). **6** immediate, unqualified (*found ready acceptance*). **7** prompt (*is always ready with excuses; has a ready wit*). **8** (foll. by *to* + infin.) about to do something (*a bud just ready to burst*). **9** provided beforehand. • *adv.* esp. *Brit.* **1** beforehand. **2** so as not to require doing when the time comes for use (*the cases are ready packed*). • *n.* (*pl.* **-ies**) esp. *Brit. slang* **1** (prec. by *the*) = READY MONEY. **2** (in *pl.*) bank notes. • *v.tr.* (**-ies**, **-ied**) make ready; prepare. □ **at the ready** ready for action. **make ready** prepare. **ready, steady** (or **get set**), **go** the usual formula for starting a race. [Middle English] □ **readiness** *n.*

ready-made *adj.* made in a standard size, not to measure.

ready-mixed *adj.* (also **ready-mix**) having some or all of the constituents already mixed together.

ready money *n.* **1** actual coin or notes. **2** payment on the spot.

ready reckoner *n.* a book or table listing standard numerical calculations as used esp. in commerce.

ready-to-wear *adj.* made in a standard size, not to measure.

reaffirm *v.tr.* affirm again. □ **reaffirmation** *n.*

reafforest *v.tr.* esp. *Brit.* replant (former forest land) with trees. □ **reafforestation** *n.*

reagent *n. Chem.* **1** a substance used to cause a reaction, esp. to detect another substance. **2** a reactive substance or force.

real[1] • *adj.* **1** actually existing or occurring. **2** genuine; rightly so called; not artificial. **3** *Law* consisting of or relating to immovable property such as land or houses (*real estate*) (cf. PERSONAL PROPERTY). **4** appraised by purchasing power; adjusted for changes in the value of money (*real value; income in real terms*). • *adv. Sc.* & *N. Amer. colloq.* really, very. □ **for real** *colloq.* as a serious concern; in earnest. **the real McCoy** see MCCOY. **the real thing 1** not illusory, simulated, or inferior. **2** true love, not infatuation. [based on Latin *res* 'thing'] □ **realness** *n.*

real[2] *n.* **1** the chief monetary unit of Brazil since 1994. **2** *hist.* a former coin and monetary unit of various Spanish-speaking countries. [Spanish, literally 'royal', used as a noun]

real ale *n.* esp. *Brit.* beer regarded as brewed in a traditional way, with secondary fermentation in the cask.

realign *v.tr.* **1** align again. **2** regroup in politics etc. □ **realignment** *n.*

realism *n.* **1** the practice of regarding things in their true nature and dealing with them as they are. **2** fidelity to nature in representation; the showing of life etc. as it is. □ **realist** *n.*

realistic *adj.* **1** regarding things as they are; following a policy of realism. **2** based on facts rather than ideals. □ **realistically** *adv.*

reality *n.* (*pl.* **-ies**) **1** what is real or existent or underlies appearances. **2** (foll. by *of*) the real nature of. **3** real existence; the state of being real. **4** resemblance to an original (*the model was impressive in its reality*). □ **in reality** in fact. [from medieval Latin *realitas*]

realize *v.tr.* (also **-ise**) **1** (often foll. by *that* + clause; also *absol.*) be fully aware of; conceive as real. **2** (also *absol.*) understand clearly. **3** present as real (*the story was powerfully realized on stage*). **4 a** convert into actuality; achieve (*realized a childhood dream*). **b** *refl.* develop one's own faculties, abilities, etc. **5 a** convert into money. **b** acquire (profit). **c** be sold for (a specified price). □ **realizable** *adj.* **realization** *n.* **realizer** *n.*

real life *n.* **1** that lived by actual people, as distinct from fiction, drama, etc. **2** (**real-life**) (*attrib.*) actual, not fictional (*real-life husband*).

real live *attrib.adj.* often *joc.* actual; not pretended or simulated (*a real live burglar*).

reallocate *v.tr.* allocate again or differently. □ **reallocation** *n.*

really *adv.* **1** in reality. **2** positively, assuredly (*really useful*). **3** indeed, I assure you. **4** an expression of mild protest or surprise. **5** (in *interrog.*) is that so? (*They're musicians. — Really?*).

realm *n.* **1** *formal* esp. *Law* a kingdom. **2** a sphere or domain (*the realm of imagination*). [from Old French *realme*, influenced by *reiel* 'royal']

real money *n.* **1** current coin or notes; cash. **2** *colloq.* a large sum of money.

R

R

realpolitik /ray-**ahl**-pol-i-teek/ n. politics based on realities and material needs, rather than on morals or ideals. [German]

real tennis n. Brit. the original form of tennis played on an indoor court.

real time n. **1** the actual time during which a process or event occurs. **2** (**real-time**) (attrib.) Computing **a** (of a system) in which input data is processed within milliseconds so that it is available virtually immediately as feedback to the process from which it is coming. **b** (of information, an image, etc.) responding virtually immediately to changes in the state of affairs it reflects (real-time stock-exchange prices).

realtor n. N. Amer. a real-estate agent, esp. (**Realtor** propr.) a member of the National Association of Realtors.

ream[1] n. **1** twenty quires of paper. **2** (in pl.) a large quantity of paper or writing (wrote reams about it). [from Arabic rīzma 'bundle']

ream[2] v.tr. widen (a hole in metal etc.) with a cutting tool. [18th-century coinage] □ **reamer** n.

reanimate v.tr. **1** restore to life. **2** restore to activity or liveliness. □ **reanimation** n.

reap v.tr. **1** cut or gather (a crop, esp. grain) as a harvest. **2** harvest the crop of (a field etc.). **3** receive as the consequence of one's own or others' actions. [Old English]

reaper n. **1** a person who reaps. **2** a machine for reaping. □ **the Reaper** (or **Grim Reaper**) death personified.

reappear v.intr. appear again or as previously. □ **reappearance** n.

reapply v.tr. & intr. (-ies, -ied) apply again, esp. submit a further application (for a position etc.). □ **reapplication** n.

reappoint v.tr. appoint again to a position previously held. □ **reappointment** n.

reapportion v.tr. apportion again or differently. □ **reapportionment** n.

reappraise v.tr. appraise or assess again. □ **reappraisal** n.

rear[1] • n. **1** the back part of anything. **2** the space behind, or position at the back of, anything (a large house with a terrace at the rear). **3** the hindmost part of an army or fleet. **4** colloq. the buttocks. • adj. at the back. □ **bring up the rear** come last. **in the rear** behind; at the back. [from Old French retro 'back']

rear[2] v. **1** tr. **a** bring up and educate (children). **b** breed and care for (animals). **c** cultivate (crops). **2** intr. (of a horse etc.) raise itself on its hind legs. **3** tr. **a** set upright. **b** build. **c** hold upwards (rear one's head). **4** intr. extend to a great height. [Old English] □ **rearer** n.

rear admiral n. a naval officer ranking below vice admiral.

rearguard n. **1** a body of troops detached to protect the rear, esp. in retreats. **2** a defensive or conservative element in an organization etc. [from Old French rereguarde]

rearguard action n. **1** Mil. an engagement undertaken by a rearguard. **2** a defensive stand in argument etc., esp. when losing.

rear lamp n. (also **rear light**) esp. Brit. a usu. red light at the rear of a vehicle.

rearm v.tr. (also absol.) arm again, esp. with improved weapons. □ **rearmament** n.

rearmost adj. furthest back.

rearrange v.tr. arrange again in a different way. □ **rearrangement** n.

rearrest • v.tr. arrest again. • n. an instance of re-arresting or being rearrested.

rear sight n. the sight nearest to the stock on a firearm. ▷ GUN

rear-view mirror n. a mirror fixed inside the windscreen of a motor vehicle enabling the driver to see traffic etc. behind.

rearward • n. (esp. in prepositional phrases) rear (to the rearward of; in the rearward). • adj. to the rear. • adv. (also **rearwards**) towards the rear. [from Anglo-French rerewarde]

rear-wheel drive n. drive acting on the rear wheels of a motor vehicle (see DRIVE n. 6a).

reason • n. **1** a motive, cause, or justification (has good reasons for doing this; there is no reason to be angry). **2** a fact adduced or serving as this (I can give you my reasons). **3** the intellectual faculty by which conclusions are drawn from premisses. **4** sanity (has lost his reason). **5** a faculty transcending the understanding and providing a priori principles; intuition. **6** sense; sensible conduct; what is right or practical or practicable; moderation. • v. **1** intr. form or try to reach conclusions by connected thought. **2** intr. (foll. by with) use an argument (with a person) by way of persuasion. **3** tr. (foll. by that + clause) conclude or assert in argument. **4** tr. (foll. by why, whether, what + clause) discuss; ask oneself. **5** tr. (foll. by into, out of) persuade or move by argument (I reasoned them out of their fears). **6** tr. (foll. by out) think or work out (consequences etc.). **7** tr. (often as **reasoned** adj.) express in logical and methodical form. **8** tr. embody reason in (an amendment etc.). □ **by reason of** owing to. **in** (or **within**) **reason** within the bounds of moderation. **it stands to reason** it is evident or logical. **listen to reason** be persuaded to act sensibly. **see reason** acknowledge the force of an argument. **with reason** justifiably. [from Old French reisun (n.), raisoner (v.)] □ **reasoner** n. **reasoning** n.

■ **Usage** *The reason (why) … is …* should be followed by *that*, not *because*, e.g. *The reason why I can't stay any longer is that I have an urgent appointment.*

reasonable adj. **1** having sound judgement; moderate; ready to listen to reason. **2** not absurd. **3 a** not greatly less or more than might be expected. **b** inexpensive. **c** tolerable, fair. □ **reasonableness** n. **reasonably** adv.

reassemble v.intr. & tr. assemble again or into a former state. □ **reassembly** n.

reassert v.tr. assert again. □ **reassertion** n.

reassess v.tr. assess again, esp. differently. □ **reassessment** n.

reassign v.tr. assign again or differently. □ **reassignment** n.

reassure v.tr. **1** restore confidence to; dispel the apprehensions of. **2** confirm in an opinion or impression. □ **reassurance** n. **reassuring** adj. **reassuringly** adv.

reattach v.tr. attach again or in a former position. □ **reattachment** n.

reattempt v.tr. attempt again, esp. after failure.

reawaken v.tr. & intr. awaken again.

rebadge v.tr. relaunch (a product etc.) under a different name, logo, etc.

rebase v.tr. establish a new base level for (a price index etc.).

rebate[1] • n. **1** a partial refund. **2** a deduction from a sum to be paid; a discount. • v.tr. pay back as a rebate. [earlier in sense 'to diminish': from Old French rabattre]

rebate[2] n. & v.tr. = RABBET. [respelling of RABBET, after REBATE[1]]

rebel • n. /**reb**-ĕl/ **1** a person who fights against, resists, or refuses allegiance to, the established government. **2** a person or thing that resists authority or control. • adj. /**reb**-ĕl/ (attrib.) **1** rebellious. **2** of or concerning rebels. **3** in rebellion. • v.intr. /ri-**bel**/ (**rebelled**, **rebelling**) (usu. foll. by against) **1** act as a rebel; revolt. **2** feel or display repugnance. [from Latin rebellis]

rebellion n. **1** open resistance to authority, esp. organized armed resistance to an established government. **2** an instance of this. [from Latin rebellio]

rebellious adj. **1** tending to rebel. **2** in rebellion. **3** defying lawful authority. **4** (of a thing) unmanageable, refractory. □ **rebelliously** adv. **rebelliousness** n.

rebind v.tr. (past and past part. **rebound**) bind (esp. a book) again or differently.

rebirth n. **1** a new incarnation. **2** spiritual enlightenment. **3** a revival (the rebirth of learning). □ **reborn** adj.

rebirthing n. a therapeutic technique involving controlled breathing and intended to penetrate psychological defences so that the subject re-experiences and releases the birth trauma. □ **rebirther** n.

reboot v.tr. (often absol.) Computing boot up (a system) again.

rebore • v.tr. make a new boring in, esp. widen the bore of (the cylinder in an internal-combustion engine). • n. **1** the process of doing this. **2** a rebored engine.

rebound[1] • v.intr. **1** spring back after action or impact. **2** (foll. by on, upon) (of an action) have an adverse effect upon (the doer). • n. **1** the act or an instance of rebounding; recoil. **2** a reaction after a strong emotion. □ **on the rebound** while still recovering from an emotional shock, esp. rejection by a lover.

rebound[2] past and past part. of REBIND.

rebroadcast • v.tr. (past **rebroadcast** or **rebroadcasted**; past part. **rebroadcast**) broadcast again. • n. a repeat broadcast.

rebuff • n. **1** a rejection of a person who makes advances, proffers help, shows interest, makes a request, etc. **2** a snub. • v.tr. give a rebuff to. [from Italian ribuffo]

rebuild v.tr. (past and past part. **rebuilt**) build again or differently. □ **rebuilder** n.

rebuke • v.tr. reprove sharply; subject to protest or censure. • n. **1** the act of rebuking. **2** the process of being rebuked. **3** a reproof. [from Old Northern French rebuker] □ **rebuker** n. **rebukingly** adv.

rebus /**ree**-bŭs/ n. (pl. **rebuses**) a representation of a word (esp. a name), by pictures etc. suggesting its parts. [Latin, literally 'by things']

rebut v.tr. (**rebutted**, **rebutting**) **1** refute or disprove (evidence or a charge). **2** force or turn back; check. [from Old French rebo(u)ter] □ **rebuttable** adj. **rebuttal** n.

recalcitrant • adj. **1** obstinately disobedient. **2** objecting to restraint. • n. a recalcitrant person. [from Latin recalcitrant- 'kicking out with the heels'] □ **recalcitrance** n.

recalculate v.tr. calculate again. □ **recalculation** n.

recall • v.tr. **1** summon to return. **2** recollect, remember. **3** bring back to memory; serve as a reminder of. **4** revoke or annul. • n. **1** a summons to come back. **2** the act of remembering. **3** the ability to remember. **4** the possibility of recalling, esp. in the sense of revoking (beyond recall). □ **recallable** adj.

recant v. **1** tr. withdraw and renounce (a former belief or statement) as erroneous or heretical. **2** intr. disavow a former opinion. [from Latin recantare 'revoke'] □ **recantation** n. **recanter** n.

recap colloq. • v.tr. & intr. (**recapped**, **recapping**) recapitulate. • n. recapitulation.

recapitulate v.tr. **1** go briefly through again; summarize. **2** go over the main points or headings of. [based on Latin recapitulatus 'redrawn under headings'] □ **recapitulatory** adj.

recapitulation n. **1** the act or an instance of recapitulating. **2** Mus. part of a movement in which themes are restated.

recapture • v.tr. **1** capture again; recover by capture. **2** re-experience (a past emotion etc.). • n. the act or an instance of recapturing.

recast • v.tr. (past and past part. **recast**) **1** put into a new form. **2** improve the arrangement of. **3** change the cast of (a play etc.). • n. **1** the act or an instance of recasting. **2** a recast form.

recce /rek-i / esp. *Brit. colloq.* ● *n.* a reconnaissance. ● *v.tr. & intr.* (**recced, recceing**) reconnoitre.

recede *v.intr.* **1** go or shrink back or further off. **2** be left at an increasing distance by an observer's motion. **3** slope backwards (*a receding chin*). **4** decline in force or value. **5** (of a man's hair) cease to grow at the front, sides, etc. [from Latin *recedere*]

receipt /ri-seet/ ● *n.* **1** the act or an instance of receiving or being received into one's possession (*will pay on receipt of the goods*). **2** a written acknowledgement of this, esp. of the payment of money. **3** (usu. in *pl.*) an amount of money etc. received. **4** *archaic* a recipe. ● *v.tr.* place a written or printed receipt on (a bill). □ **in receipt of** having received. [from medieval Latin *recepta* (fem.) 'received']

receive *v.tr.* **1** take or accept (something offered or given). **2** acquire; be provided with (*have received no news; will receive a small fee*). **3** accept delivery of (something sent). **4** have conferred or inflicted on one (*received many honours; received a heavy blow on the head*). **5 a** stand the force or weight of. **b** bear up against; encounter with opposition. **6** consent to hear (a confession or oath) or consider (a petition). **7** (also *absol.*) accept (stolen property), knowing of the theft. **8** admit; consent or prove able to hold; provide accommodation for (*received many visitors*). **9** (of a receptacle) be able to hold. **10** greet or welcome, esp. in a specified manner (*how did they receive your offer?*). **11** react to (news, a play, etc.) in a specified way (*the novel was warmly received*). **12** entertain as a guest etc. **13** admit to membership. **14** be marked with (an impression etc.). **15** convert (broadcast signals) into sound or pictures. **16** *Tennis* etc. be the player to whom the server serves (the ball etc.). **17** (often as **received** *adj.*) give credit to; accept as authoritative or true (*received opinion*). □ **be at** (or **on**) **the receiving end** *colloq.* bear the brunt of something unpleasant. [from Latin *recipere*] □ **receivable** *adj.*

received pronunciation *n.* (also **Received Standard**) the form of spoken English based on educated speech in southern England.

receiver *n.* **1** a person or thing that receives. **2** ▼ the part of a machine or instrument that receives sound, signals, etc. (esp. the part of a telephone that contains the earpiece). ▷ TELEPHONE. **3** (in full *Brit.* **official receiver**) a person appointed by a court to administer the property of a bankrupt or insane person, or property under litigation. **4** a radio or television receiving apparatus. **5** a person who receives stolen goods.

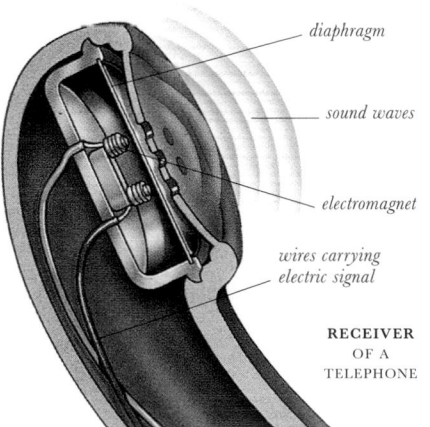

diaphragm

sound waves

electromagnet

wires carrying electric signal

RECEIVER OF A TELEPHONE

receivership *n.* **1** the office of official receiver. **2** (esp. in phr. **in receivership**) the state of being dealt with by a receiver.

receiving order *n. Brit.* an order of a court authorizing a receiver (see RECEIVER 3) to act.

recent ● *adj.* **1** not long past; that happened, appeared, began to exist, or existed lately. **2** not long established; lately begun; modern. **3** (**Recent**) *Geol.* = HOLOCENE. ● *n.* (**Recent**) *Geol.* = HOLOCENE. [from Latin *recens recentis*] □ **recency** *n.* **recently** *adv.* **recentness** *n.*

receptacle *n.* **1** a containing vessel, place, or space. **2** *Bot.* ▼ the common base of floral organs. [from Latin *receptaculum*]

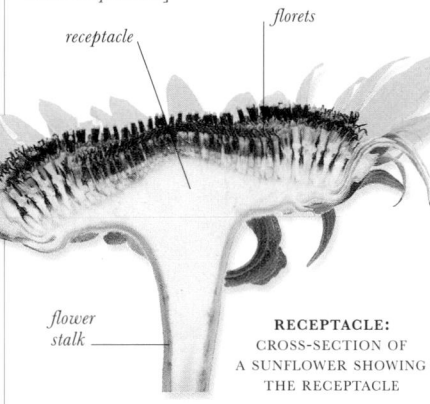

receptacle

florets

flower stalk

RECEPTACLE: CROSS-SECTION OF A SUNFLOWER SHOWING THE RECEPTACLE

reception *n.* **1** the act or an instance of receiving or the process of being received. **2** the manner in which a person or thing is received (*got a cool reception*). **3** a social occasion for receiving guests, esp. after a wedding. **4** a formal or ceremonious welcome. **5** a place where guests or clients etc. report on arrival at a hotel, office, etc. **6 a** the receiving of broadcast signals. **b** the quality of this (*we have excellent reception*). [from Latin *receptio*]

receptionist *n.* a person employed in an office or *Brit.* a hotel to receive clients, guests, etc.

reception room *n.* esp. *Brit.* a room for receiving visitors.

receptive *adj.* **1** able or quick to receive impressions or ideas. **2** concerned with receiving stimuli etc. □ **receptively** *adv.* **receptiveness** *n.* **receptivity** *n.*

receptor *n.* (often *attrib.*) *Biol.* an organ or cell able to respond to an external stimulus such as light, heat, or a drug, and transmit a signal to a sensory nerve. [Latin]

recess ● *n.* **1** a space set back in a wall. **2** (often in *pl.*) a remote or secret place (*the innermost recesses*). **3** a temporary cessation from work, esp. of Parliament, or *N. Amer.* of a law court or during a school day. ● *v.* **1** *tr.* make a recess in. **2** *tr.* place in a recess. **3** *N. Amer.* **a** *intr.* take a recess; adjourn. **b** *tr.* order a temporary cessation from the work of (a court etc.). [from Latin *recessus*]

recession *n.* **1** a temporary decline in economic activity or prosperity. **2** a receding or withdrawal from a place or point. [from Latin *recessio*] □ **recessionary** *adj.*

recessional *adj.* sung while the clergy and choir withdraw after a service.

recessive *adj.* **1** tending to recede. **2** *Genetics* (of an inherited characteristic) appearing in offspring only when not masked by a dominant characteristic. ▷ MENDELISM. □ **recessively** *adv.* **recessiveness** *n.*

recharge *v.tr.* **1** charge again. **2** reload. □ **rechargeable** *adj.*

recheck ● *v.tr. & intr.* check again. ● *n.* a further check or inspection.

recherché /rĕ-shair-shay/ *adj.* **1** carefully sought out; rare or exotic. **2** far-fetched. [French, literally 'sought out']

rechristen *v.tr.* **1** christen again. **2** give a new name to.

recidivist /ri-sid-i-vist/ *n.* a person who relapses into crime. [from Latin *recidivus*] □ **recidivism** *n.*

recipe *n.* **1** a statement of the ingredients and procedure required for preparing a culinary dish.

2 an expedient; a device for achieving something. **3** a medical prescription. [Latin imperative, literally 'take, receive!']

recipient ● *n.* a person who receives something. ● *adj.* **1** receiving. **2** receptive. [from Latin *recipient-* 'receiving']

reciprocal ● *adj.* **1** in return (*offered a reciprocal greeting*). **2** mutual (*their feelings are reciprocal*). **3** *Gram.* (of a pronoun) expressing mutual action or relation (as in *each other*). ● *n. Math.* an expression or function so related to another that their product is unity (*½ is the reciprocal of* 2). [from Latin *reciprocus*] □ **reciprocally** *adv.*

reciprocate *v.* **1** *tr.* return or requite (affection etc.). **2** *intr.* (foll. by *with*) offer or give something in return (*reciprocated with an invitation to lunch*). **3** *tr.* give and receive mutually; interchange. **4 a** *intr.* (of a part of a machine) move backwards and forwards. **b** *tr.* cause to do this. [based on Latin *reciprocatus* 'reciprocated'] □ **reciprocation** *n.* **reciprocator** *n.*

reciprocating engine *n.* an engine using a piston or pistons moving up and down in cylinders.

reciprocity *n.* **1** the condition of being reciprocal. **2** mutual action. **3** give and take, esp. the interchange of privileges. [from French *réciprocité*]

recirculate *v.tr. & intr.* circulate again, esp. make available for reuse. □ **recirculation** *n.*

recital *n.* **1** the act or an instance of reciting or being recited. **2** the performance of a programme of music by a solo instrumentalist or singer or by a small group. **3** (foll. by *of*) a detailed account of (connected things or facts); a narrative. □ **recitalist** *n.*

recitation *n.* **1** the act or an instance of reciting. **2** a thing recited.

recitative /ress-i-ta-teev/ *n.* **1** musical declamation of the kind usual in the narrative and dialogue parts of opera and oratorio. **2** the words or part given in this form.

recite *v.* **1** *tr.* repeat aloud or declaim (a poem or passage) from memory. **2** *intr.* give a recitation. **3** *tr.* enumerate. [from Latin *recitare*] □ **reciter** *n.*

reckless *adj.* disregarding the consequences or danger etc.; rash. [Old English] □ **recklessly** *adv.* **recklessness** *n.*

reckon *v.* **1** *tr.* count or compute by calculation. **2** *tr.* (foll. by *in*) count in or include in computation. **3** *tr.* consider or regard (*reckon him wise, reckon them to be beyond hope*). **4** *tr.* **a** (foll. by *that* + clause) be of the considered opinion. **b** (foll. by *to* + infin.) *colloq.* expect (*reckons to finish by Friday*). **c** *colloq.* think, suppose. **5** *intr.* **a** make calculations; add up an account or sum. **b** (foll. by *with*) settle accounts with. **6** *intr.* (foll. by *on, upon*) rely on, count on, or base plans on. **7** *intr.* (foll. by *with* or *without*) take (or fail to take) into account. □ **reckon up 1** count up; find the total of. **2** settle accounts. **to be reckoned with** of considerable importance; not to be ignored. [Old English]

reckoner *n.* = READY RECKONER.

reckoning *n.* **1** the act or an instance of counting or calculating. **2** a consideration or opinion. **3 a** the settlement of an account. **b** an account.

reclaim ● *v.tr.* **1** seek the return of (one's property). **2** claim in return or as a rebate etc. **3** bring under cultivation, esp. from a state of being under water. **4** win back or away from vice or error or a waste condition. ● *n.* the act or an instance of reclaiming; the process of being reclaimed. [from Latin *reclamare* 'to cry out against'] □ **reclaimable** *adj.* **reclaimer** *n.* **reclamation** *n.*

reclassify *v.tr.* (**-ies, -ied**) classify again or differently. □ **reclassification** *n.*

recline *v.* **1** *intr.* assume or be in a horizontal or leaning position, esp. in resting. **2** *tr.* cause to recline or move from the vertical. [from Latin *reclinare* 'to bend back']

recliner *n.* **1** a comfortable chair for reclining in. **2** a person who reclines.

reclothe *v.tr.* clothe again or differently.

RECORD

Sound recording converts sound waves into electrical signals and stores them in a retrievable format. There are two main types of recording: analogue (records and tapes) and digital (such as CDs). On records, the signals are stored as a spiral groove; on tapes, they are recorded as varying levels of magnetism on two tracks. On CDs, the signals are transformed into binary numbers, represented by pits and spaces.

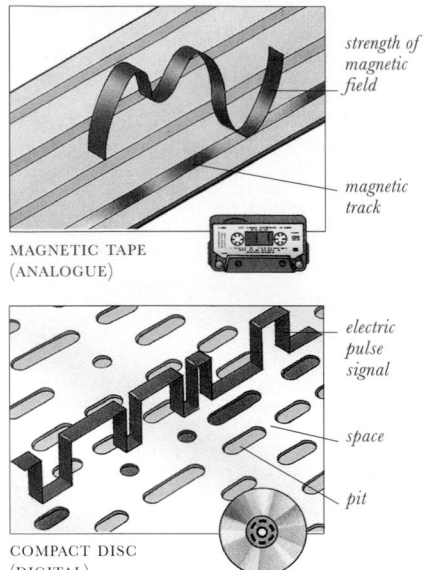

strength of magnetic field

magnetic track

MAGNETIC TAPE
(ANALOGUE)

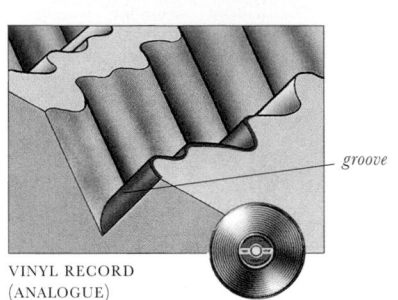

groove

VINYL RECORD
(ANALOGUE)

electric pulse signal

space

pit

COMPACT DISC
(DIGITAL)

R

recluse n. a person given to or living in seclusion or isolation, esp. as a religious discipline. [from Old French *reclus(e)* 'shut away'] □ **reclusive** adj. **reclusiveness** n.

recode v.tr. code again or differently.

recognition n. the act or an instance of recognizing or being recognized. [from Latin *recognitio*]

recognizance /ri-**kog**-ni-zănss/ n. (also **recognisance**) **1** a bond by which a person undertakes before a court or magistrate to observe some condition, e.g. to appear when summoned. **2** a sum pledged as surety for this. [from Old French *recon(n)issance*]

recognize v.tr. (also **-ise**) **1** identify as already known. **2** realize or discover the nature of. **3** (foll. by *that*) realize or admit. **4** acknowledge the existence, validity, character, or claims of. **5** show appreciation of; reward. **6** (foll. by *as, for*) treat or acknowledge. [from Latin *recognoscere*] □ **recognizable** adj. **recognizability** n. **recognizably** adv. **recognizer** n.

recoil ● v.intr. **1** suddenly move or spring back in fear, horror, or disgust. **2** shrink mentally in this way. **3** rebound after an impact. **4** (foll. by *on, upon*) have an adverse reactive effect on (the originator). **5** (of a gun) be driven backwards by its discharge. **6** retreat under an enemy's attack. ● n. **1** the act or an instance of recoiling. **2** the sensation of recoiling. [from Old French *reculer*]

recollect v.tr. **1** remember. **2** succeed in remembering; call to mind.

recollection n. **1** the act or power of recollecting. **2** a thing recollected. **3 a** a person's memory (*to the best of my recollection*). **b** the time over which memory extends (*happened within my recollection*). □ **recollective** adj.

recolonize v.tr. (also **-ise**) colonize again. □ **recolonization** n.

recombination n. *Biol.* the rearrangement of genes, esp. by exchange between homologous chromosomes, to form a combination different from that of the parents.

recombine v.tr. & intr. combine again or differently.

recommence v.tr. & intr. begin again. □ **recommencement** n.

recommend v.tr. **1** suggest as fit for some purpose or use. **2** advise as a course of action etc. (*I recommend that you stay where you are*). **3** (of qualities, conduct, etc.) make acceptable or desirable. **4** (foll.

by *to*) *Brit.* commend or entrust (to a person or a person's care). □ **recommendable** adj. **recommendation** n. **recommendatory** adj.

recompense ● v.tr. **1** make amends to (a person) or for (a loss etc.). **2** requite; reward or punish (a person or action). ● n. **1** a reward; requital. **2** retribution. [based on Late Latin *recompensatus* 'compensated in return']

recon n. (often *attrib.*) *US slang* military reconnaissance.

reconcile v.tr. **1** make friendly again after an estrangement. **2** (usu. in *refl.* or *passive*; foll. by *to*) make acquiescent or contentedly submissive to (something disagreeable) (*was reconciled to failure*). **3** settle (a quarrel etc.). **4** harmonize; make compatible. [from Latin *reconciliare*] □ **reconcilable** adj. **reconciler** n. **reconciliation** n.

recondite adj. **1** (of a subject or knowledge) abstruse; out of the way; little known. **2** (of an author or style) dealing in abstruse knowledge or allusions; obscure. [from Latin *reconditus* 'hidden']

recondition v.tr. **1** overhaul, refit, renovate. **2** make usable again.

reconfigure v.tr. configure again or differently. □ **reconfiguration** n.

reconfirm v.tr. confirm, establish, or ratify anew. □ **reconfirmation** n.

reconnaissance /ri-**kon**-i-sănss/ n. **1** a survey of a region, esp. to locate an enemy or ascertain strategic features. **2** a preliminary survey. [French]

reconnect v.tr. connect again. □ **reconnection** n.

reconnoitre /rek-ŏn-**oi**-ter/ (*US* **reconnoiter**) ● v. **1** tr. make a reconnaissance of. **2** intr. make a reconnaissance. ● n. a reconnaissance. [from Old French *recognoscere* 'to recognize']

reconquer v.tr. conquer again. □ **reconquest** n.

reconsider v.tr. & intr. consider again, esp. for a possible change of decision. □ **reconsideration** n.

reconstitute v.tr. **1** reconstruct. **2** reorganize. **3** restore the previous constitution of (dried food etc.) by adding water. □ **reconstitution** n.

reconstruct v.tr. **1** build or form again. **2 a** form a mental or visual impression of (past events) by assembling the evidence for them. **b** re-enact (a crime). **3** reorganize. □ **reconstructable** adj. (also **reconstructible**). **reconstruction** n. **reconstructive** adj. **reconstructor** n.

reconvene v.tr. & intr. convene again, esp. after a pause in proceedings.

reconvert v.tr. convert back to a former state. □ **reconversion** n.

record ● n. /**rek**-ord/ **1 a** a piece of evidence or information constituting an account of something that has occurred, been said, etc. **b** a document preserving this. **2** the state of being set down or preserved in writing or some other permanent form (*is a matter of record*). **3** (in full **gramophone record** or *N. Amer.* **phonograph record**) a disc carrying recorded sound in grooves on each surface, for reproduction by a record player. ▷ RECORD. **4** an official report of the proceedings and judgement in a court of justice. **5** the facts known about a person's past (*has an honourable record of service*). **6** (in full **criminal record**) **a** a list of a person's previous criminal convictions. **b** a history of being convicted for crime (*has a record*). **7** the best performance (esp. in sport) or most remarkable event of its kind on record (often *attrib.*: *a record attempt*). **8** an object serving as a memorial; a portrait. **9** *Computing* a number of related items of information which are handled as a unit. ● v.tr. /ri-**kord**/ **1** set down in writing or some other permanent form for later reference. **2** ◄ convert (sound, a broadcast, etc.) into permanent form for later reproduction. **3** establish or constitute a historical or other record of. □ **break** (or **beat**) **the record** outdo all previous performances etc. **for the record** as an official statement etc. **go on record** state one's opinion openly, so that it is recorded. **a matter of record** a thing established as a fact by being recorded. **off the record** as an unofficial or confidential statement etc. **on record** officially recorded; publicly known. **put** (or **set**) **the record straight** correct a misapprehension. [from Latin *recordari* 'to remember'] □ **recordable** adj.

record-breaking *attrib.adj.* that breaks a record (see RECORD n. 7).

recorded delivery n. *Brit.* a Post Office service in which the dispatch and receipt of a letter or parcel are recorded.

recorder n. **1** an apparatus for recording, esp. a tape recorder. **2 a** a keeper of records. **b** a person who makes an official record. **3** (usu. **Recorder**) (in England and Wales) a barrister or solicitor of at least ten years' standing, appointed to serve as a part-time judge. **4** *Mus.* ◄ a woodwind instrument like a flute but blown through the end and having a more hollow tone. ▷ WOODWIND. □ **recordership** n. (in sense 3).

record holder n. a person who holds a record (see RECORD n. 7).

recording n. **1** the process by which audio or video signals are recorded for later reproduction. **2** material or a programme recorded.

recordist n. esp. *Brit.* a person who records sound.

record player n. an apparatus for reproducing sound from gramophone records by means of a turntable and stylus etc.

recount v.tr. **1** narrate. **2** tell in detail.

re-count ● v.tr. count again. ● n. a re-counting, esp. of votes in an election.

mouthpiece

finger holes

hollow shaft

RECORDER:
EARLY 18TH-CENTURY
TREBLE RECORDER

recoup v.tr. **1** recover or regain (a loss). **2** compensate or reimburse for a loss. □ **recoup oneself** recover a loss. [from Old French *recouper* 'to retrench'] □ **recoupable** adj. **recoupment** n.

recourse n. **1** resorting to a possible source of help. **2** a person or thing resorted to. □ **have recourse to** turn to (a person or thing) for help.

recover *v.* **1** *tr.* regain possession or use or control of; reclaim. **2** *intr.* return to health or consciousness or to a normal state or position. **3** *tr.* obtain or secure (compensation etc.) by legal process. **4** *tr.* retrieve or make up for (a loss, setback, etc.). **5** *refl.* regain composure or consciousness or control of one's limbs. **6** *tr.* retrieve (reusable substances) from industrial waste. [from Latin *recuperare* 'to recuperate'] □ **recoverable** *adj.* **recoverability** *n.* **recoverer** *n.*

re-cover *v.tr.* **1** cover again. **2** provide (a chair etc.) with a new cover.

recovery *n.* (*pl.* **-ies**) the act or an instance of recovering; the process of being recovered.

recreate *v.tr.* create over again; reconstruct. □ **re-creation** *n.*

recreation *n.* **1** the process or means of refreshing or entertaining oneself. **2** a pleasurable activity. [from Latin *recreatio*] □ **recreational** *adj.* **recreationally** *adv.* **recreative** *adj.*

recreation ground *n.* *Brit.* public land for games etc.

recriminate *v.intr.* make mutual or counter accusations. [based on medieval Latin *recriminatus* 'accused in return'] □ **recrimination** *n.* **recriminatory** *adj.*

recross *v.tr. & intr.* cross or pass over again.

recrudesce *v.intr.* (of a disease or difficulty etc.) break out again. [from Latin *recrudescere* 'to become raw again'] □ **recrudescence** *n.* **recrudescent** *adj.*

recruit ● *n.* **1** a serviceman or servicewoman newly enlisted and not yet fully trained. **2** a new member of a society etc. **3** a beginner. ● *v.* **1** *tr.* enlist (a person) as a recruit. **2** *tr.* form (an army etc.) by enlisting recruits. **3** *intr.* get or seek recruits. **4** *tr.* replenish or reinvigorate (numbers, strength, etc.). [earlier in sense 'reinforcement': based on Latin *recrescere* 'to increase again'] □ **recruiter** *n.* **recruitment** *n.*

recta *pl.* of RECTUM.

rectal *adj.* of or by means of the rectum. □ **rectally** *adv.*

rectangle *n.* a plane figure with four straight sides and four right angles, esp. one with adjacent sides unequal. [from Latin *rectus* 'straight' + *angulus* 'angle'] □ **rectangular** *adj.* **rectangularity** *n.* **rectangularly** *adv.*

rectify *v.tr.* (**-ies, -ied**) **1** adjust or make right; correct, amend. **2** purify or refine, esp. by repeated distillation. **3** convert (alternating current) to direct current. [from medieval Latin *rectificare*] □ **rectifiable** *adj.* **rectification** *n.* **rectifier** *n.*

rectilinear *adj.* (also **rectilineal**) **1** bounded or characterized by straight lines. **2** in or forming a straight line. [from Late Latin *rectilineus*] □ **rectilinearity** *n.* **rectilinearly** *adv.*

rectitude *n.* **1** moral uprightness. **2** righteousness. **3** correctness. [based on Latin *rectus* 'right']

recto *n.* (*pl.* **-os**) **1** the right-hand page of an open book. **2** the front of a printed leaf of paper or manuscript. [Latin *recto (folio)* 'on the right (leaf)']

rector *n.* **1 a** (in the Church of England) the incumbent of a parish where all tithes formerly passed to the incumbent (cf. VICAR 1a). **b** (in other Anglican churches) a member of the clergy who has charge of a parish. **2** *RC Ch.* a priest in charge of a church or of a religious institution. **3 a** the head of some schools, universities, and colleges. **b** (in Scotland) an elected representative of students on a university's governing body. [Latin, literally 'ruler'] □ **rectorial** *adj.* **rectorship** *n.*

rectory *n.* (*pl.* **-ies**) **1** a rector's house. **2** (in the Church of England) a rector's benefice. [from medieval Latin *rectoria*]

rectum *n.* (*pl.* **rectums** or **recta**) the final section of the large intestine, terminating at the anus. ▷ DIGESTION. [from Latin *rectum (intestinum)* 'straight (intestine)']

recumbent *adj.* lying down; reclining. [from Latin *recumbent-* 'lying back'] □ **recumbency** *n.* **recumbently** *adv.*

recuperate *v.* **1** *intr.* recover from illness, exhaustion, loss, etc. **2** *tr.* regain (health, something lost, etc.). [based on Latin *recuperatus* 'recovered'] □ **recuperable** *adj.* **recuperation** *n.* **recuperative** *adj.* **recuperator** *n.*

■ **Usage** In sense 2, *recover* is preferable to *recuperate*.

recur *v.intr.* (**recurred, recurring**) **1** occur again; be repeated. **2** (of a thought etc.) come back to one's mind. **3** (foll. by *to*) go back in thought or speech. [from Latin *recurrere*]

recurrent *adj.* recurring; happening repeatedly. □ **recurrence** *n.* **recurrently** *adv.*

recurring decimal *n.* a decimal fraction in which the same figures are repeated indefinitely.

recursive *adj.* characterized by recurrence or repetition. [based on Late Latin *recursus* 'recurred'] □ **recursively** *adv.*

recusant /**rek**-yuu-zănt/ *n.* a person who refuses submission to an authority or compliance with a regulation, esp. *hist.* one who refused to attend services of the Church of England. [from Latin *recusant-* 'refusing'] □ **recusance** *n.* **recusancy** *n.*

recycle *v.tr.* return (material) to a previous stage of a cyclic process, esp. convert (waste) to reusable material. □ **recyclable** *adj.* **recycler** *n.*

red ● *adj.* (**redder, reddest**) **1** of or near the colour seen at the least-refracted end of the visible spectrum, of shades ranging from that of blood to pink or deep orange. **2** flushed in the face with shame, anger, etc. **3** (of the eyes) bloodshot or red-rimmed with weeping. **4** (of the hair) reddish brown, orange, tawny. **5** having to do with bloodshed, burning, violence, or revolution. **6** *colloq.* communist or socialist. **7** (**Red**) *hist.* Russian, Soviet (*the Red Army*). ● *n.* **1** a red colour or pigment. **2** red clothes or material. **3** *colloq.* a communist or socialist. **4** the debit side of an account. **5** a red light. [Old English] □ **reddish** *adj.* **reddy** *adj.* **redly** *adv.* **redness** *n.*

red admiral *n.* ▼ a butterfly, *Vanessa atalanta*, with red bands on each pair of wings.

UNDERSIDE

UPPER SIDE

RED ADMIRAL (*Vanessa atalanta*)

red blood cell var. of RED CELL.

red-blooded *adj.* virile, vigorous.

redbreast *n.* esp. *Brit. colloq.* a robin.

red-brick *attrib.adj.* (of a British university) founded in the late 19th or early 20th century.

redcap *n.* **1** *Brit. slang* a member of the military police. **2** *N Amer.* a railway porter.

red card *n.* *Football* a card shown by the referee to a player being sent off the field.

red carpet *n.* privileged treatment of an eminent visitor.

red cell *n.* (also **red blood cell**) = ERYTHROCYTE.

redcoat *n.* *hist.* ▼ a British soldier (so called from the scarlet uniform of most regiments).

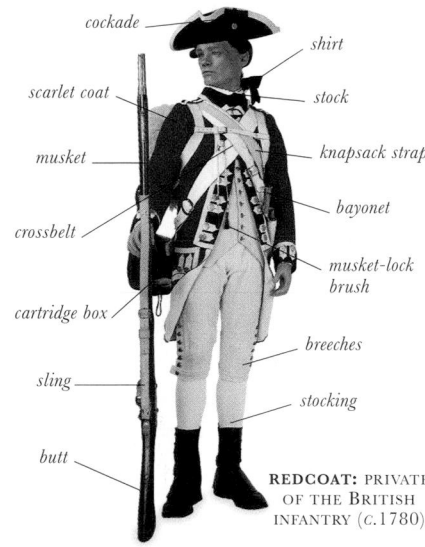

cockade
shirt
scarlet coat
stock
musket
knapsack strap
bayonet
crossbelt
musket-lock brush
cartridge box
breeches
sling
stocking
butt

REDCOAT: PRIVATE OF THE BRITISH INFANTRY (*c.*1780)

red coral see CORAL *n.* 1b.

Red Crescent *n.* an organization like the Red Cross in Muslim countries.

Red Cross *n.* **1** an international organization (originally medical) bringing relief to victims of war or natural disaster. **2** the emblem of this organization.

redcurrant *n.* **1** a widely cultivated shrub, *Ribes rubrum*. **2** a small red edible berry of this plant.

red deer *n.* a deer, *Cervus elaphus*, with a rich red-brown summer coat turning dull brown in winter. ▷ DEER

redden *v.* **1** *tr. & intr.* make or become red. **2** *intr.* blush.

reddle *n.* red ochre; ruddle. [variant of RUDDLE]

red dwarf *n.* an old relatively cool star.

redecorate *v.tr.* decorate again or differently. □ **redecoration** *n.*

rededicate *v.tr.* dedicate anew. □ **rededication** *n.*

redeem *v.tr.* **1** recover by expenditure of effort or by a stipulated payment. **2** make a single payment to discharge (a regular charge or obligation). **3** convert (tokens or bonds etc.) into goods or cash. **4** deliver from sin and damnation. **5** be a compensating factor in. **6** (foll. by *from*) save from (a defect). **7** *refl.* save (oneself) from blame. **8** purchase the freedom of (a person). **9** save (a person's life) by ransom. **10** save or rescue or reclaim. **11** fulfil (a promise). [from Latin *redimere*] □ **redeemable** *adj.*

redeemer *n.* **1** a person who redeems. **2** (**the Redeemer**) Christ.

redefine *v.tr.* define again or differently. □ **redefinition** *n.*

redemption *n.* **1** the act or an instance of redeeming; the process of being redeemed. **2** a thing that redeems. [from Latin *redemptio*] □ **redemptive** *adj.*

redeploy *v.tr.* send (troops, workers, etc.) to a new place or task. □ **redeployment** *n.*

redesign *v.tr.* design again or differently.

redevelop *v.tr.* develop anew (esp. an urban area). □ **redeveloper** *n.* **redevelopment** *n.*

red-eye *n.* **1** *US slang* cheap whisky. **2** a red reflection from a person's retina, seen in a flash photograph taken with the flashgun too near the camera lens. **3** (in full **red-eye flight**) *colloq.* an airline flight on which a traveller is unable to get adequate sleep.

red-faced *adj.* embarrassed, ashamed.

R

red flag *n.* **1** the symbol of socialist revolution. **2** a warning of danger.

red giant *n.* a relatively cool giant star. ▷ STAR

red-handed *adv.* in or just after the act of committing a crime, doing wrong, etc.

red hat *n.* **1** a cardinal's hat. **2** the symbol of a cardinal's office.

redhead *n.* a person with red hair.

red heat *n.* **1** the temperature or state of something so hot as to emit red light. **2** great excitement.

red herring *n.* **1** dried smoked herring. **2** a misleading clue or distraction.

red-hot *adj.* **1** heated until red. **2** highly exciting. **3** (of news) fresh. **4** intensely excited. **5** enraged.

red-hot poker *n.* ▶ a cultivated kniphofia, with the upper flowers in the spike red and the lower ones yellow.

redial *v.tr. & intr.* (**redialled**, **redialling**; *US* **redialed**, **redialing**) dial again.

redid *past* of REDO.

rediffusion *n. Brit.* the relaying of broadcast programmes esp. by cable from a central receiver.

Red Indian *n. esp. Brit. offens.* an American Indian.

redirect *v.tr.* direct again, esp. change the address of (a letter). □ **redirection** *n.*

rediscover *v.tr.* discover again. □ **rediscovery** *n.* (*pl.* **-ies**).

redistribute *v.tr.* distribute again or differently. □ **redistribution** *n.* **redistributive** *adj.*

redivide *v.tr.* divide again or differently. □ **redivision** *n.*

red lead *n.* a red form of lead oxide used as a pigment.

Red Leicester see LEICESTER.

red-letter day *n.* a day that is pleasantly noteworthy or memorable.

red light *n.* **1** a red light used as a signal to stop on a road, railway, etc. **2** a warning or refusal.

red-light district *n.* a district containing many brothels, strip clubs, etc.

red-lining *n.* the practice of discriminating against certain neighbourhoods with regard to giving loans, mortgages, etc. [from the act of drawing a red line round such areas]

red meat *n.* meat that is red when raw (e.g. beef or lamb).

red mullet *n.* ▼ a mullet of the family Mullidae, esp. *Muletus surmuletus* of Europe, valued as food.

RED MULLET
(*Muletus surmuletus*)

redneck *n. N. Amer. offens.* a politically conservative working-class white in the southern US.

redo *v.tr.* (*3rd sing. present* **redoes**; *past* **redid**; *past part.* **redone**) **1** do again or differently. **2** redecorate.

redolent /red-ŏ-lěnt/ *adj.* **1** (foll. by *of*, *with*) strongly reminiscent or suggestive or mentally associated. **2** fragrant. [from Latin *redolent-* 'rediffusing a smell'] □ **redolence** *n.* **redolently** *adv.*

redouble *tr. & intr.* make or grow greater or more intense; intensify.

redoubt *n. Mil.* an outwork or fieldwork usu. square or polygonal and without flanking defences. [from medieval Latin *reductus* 'refuge']

redoubtable *adj.* formidable, esp. as an opponent. [from Old French *redoutable*] □ **redoubtably** *adv.*

redound *v.intr.* **1** (foll. by *to*) (of an action etc.) make a great contribution to (one's credit or advantage etc.). **2** (foll. by *upon*, *on*) come as the final result to; come back or recoil upon. [originally in sense 'to overflow': from Latin *redundare* 'to surge']

red pepper *n.* the ripe fruit of *Capsicum annuum*.

redraft *v.tr.* draft (a document etc.) again.

red rag *n.* something that excites a person's rage.

redraw *v.tr.* (*past* **redrew**; *past part.* **redrawn**) draw again or differently.

redress ● *v.tr.* **1** remedy or rectify (a wrong etc.). **2** readjust; set straight again. ● *n.* **1** reparation for a wrong. **2** (foll. by *of*) the act or process of redressing (a grievance etc.). □ **redress the balance** restore equality. [from Old French *redresse* (n.), *redresser* (v.)] □ **redressable** *adj.* **redressal** *n.* **redresser** *n.* (also **redressor**).

red rose *n.* the emblem of Lancashire or the Lancastrians.

redshank *n.* either of two sandpipers, *Tringa totanus* and *T. erythropus*, with bright red legs.

red shift *n.* the displacement of the spectrum to longer wavelengths in the light coming from distant galaxies, quasars, etc. in recession.

redskin *n. colloq. offens.* an American Indian.

red snapper *n.* an edible marine fish of the family Lutjanidae.

red spider *n.* (also **red spider mite**) = SPIDER MITE.

red squirrel *n.* ▼ the common Eurasian squirrel, *Sciurus vulgaris*, with reddish fur.

RED SQUIRREL
(*Sciurus vulgaris*)

redstart *n.* **1** any red-tailed European songbird of the genus *Phoenicurus*. **2** any of various American warblers of the family Parulidae with orange-red markings. [based on obsolete *start* (Old English *steort*) 'tail']

red tape *n.* excessive bureaucracy or adherence to formalities. [from the red or pink tape used to secure official documents]

reduce *v.* **1** *tr. & intr.* make or become smaller or less. **2** *tr.* (foll. by *to*) bring by force or necessity (to some undesirable state or action). **3** *tr.* convert to another (esp. simpler) form (*reduced to a powder*). **4** *tr.* convert (a fraction) to the form with the lowest terms. **5** *tr.* (foll. by *to*) simplify or adapt by classification or analysis (*reduced to three issues*). **6** *tr.* make lower in status or rank. **7** *tr.* lower the price of. **8** *intr.* lessen one's weight or size. **9** *tr.* weaken (*in a reduced state*). **10** *tr.* impoverish. **11** *tr.* subdue; bring back to obedience. **12** *intr. & tr. Chem.* **a** ▲ combine or cause to combine with hydrogen. **b** undergo or cause to undergo addition of electrons. **13** *tr. Chem.* convert

REDUCE

In chemistry, a substance is reduced when it gains hydrogen during a chemical reaction. The substance providing the hydrogen is referred to as the reducing agent. Oxidation, the gaining of oxygen, occurs simultaneously with reduction.

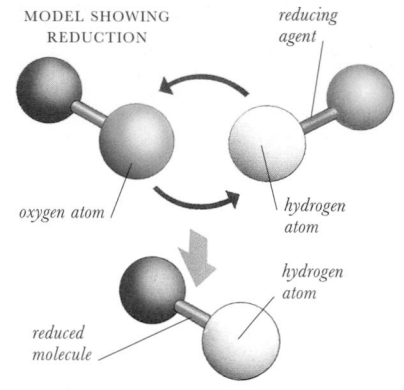

MODEL SHOWING REDUCTION

reducing agent

oxygen atom

hydrogen atom

hydrogen atom

reduced molecule

(oxide etc.) to metal. **14** *tr.* **a** (in surgery) restore (a dislocated etc. part) to its proper position. **b** remedy (a dislocation etc.) in this way. **15** *tr. Cookery* boil so as to concentrate (a sauce etc.). □ **reduce to the ranks** demote (an NCO) to the rank of private. [Middle English in sense 'to restore to original position': from Latin *reducere*] □ **reducer** *n.* **reducible** *adj.* **reducibility** *n.*

reduced circumstances *n.pl.* poverty after relative prosperity.

reductio ad absurdum /ri-duk-ti-oh ad ăb-ser-dŭm/ *n.* a method of proving the falsity of a premiss by showing that the logical consequence is absurd; an instance of this. [Latin, literally 'reduction to the absurd']

reduction *n.* **1** the act or an instance of reducing; the process of being reduced. **2** an amount by which prices etc. are reduced. **3** a reduced copy of a picture etc. [from Latin *reductio*] □ **reductive** *adj.*

reductionism *n.* **1** the tendency to or principle of analysing complex things into simple constituents. **2** often *derog.* the doctrine that a system can be fully understood in terms of its isolated parts. □ **reductionist** *n. & adj.* **reductionistic** *adj.*

redundant *adj.* **1** superfluous; not needed. **2** that can be omitted without any loss of significance. **3** *Brit.* (of a person) no longer needed at work and therefore unemployed. [from Latin *redundant-* 'surging, overflowing'] □ **redundancy** *n.* (*pl.* **-ies**). **redundantly** *adv.*

reduplicate *v.tr.* **1** make double. **2** repeat. **3** repeat (a letter or syllable or word) exactly or with a slight change (e.g. hurly-burly, see-saw). □ **reduplication** *n.* **reduplicative** *adj.*

redwing *n.* a migratory thrush, *Turdus iliacus*, with red underwings showing in flight.

redwood *n.* **1** a sequoia, esp. the very tall *Sequoia sempervirens* of the western US. **2** any tree with reddish wood.

reebok var. of RHEBOK.

re-echo *v.intr. & tr.* (**-oes**, **-oed**) **1** echo. **2** echo repeatedly; resound.

reed ● *n.* **1** **a** any of various water or marsh plants with a firm stem. **b** a tall straight stalk of this. **2** (*collect.*) reeds growing in a mass or used as material esp. for thatching. **3** **a** the vibrating part of the mouthpiece of some wind instruments, made of reed etc. and producing the sound. ▷ WOODWIND. **b** a

RED-HOT POKER
(*Kniphofia* 'Atlanta')

reed instrument. **c** (in *pl.*) the section of the orchestra playing such instruments. ● *v.tr.* **1** thatch with reed. **2** fit (a musical instrument) with a reed. [Old English]

reed-bed *n.* a bed or growth of reeds.

reed bunting *n.* a small brown bird, *Emberiza schoeniclus*, of reed-beds and similar habitats.

reeded *adj. Mus.* (of an instrument) having a vibrating reed.

re-edit *v.tr.* (**-edited**, **-editing**) edit again or differently.

reed mace *n.* ► a tall reedlike water plant, *Typha latifolia*, with straplike leaves and a head of tiny red-brown flowers.

re-educate *v.tr.* educate again, esp. to change a person's views. □ **re-education** *n.*

reed warbler *n.* any bird of the genus *Acrocephalus*, esp. *A. scirpaceus*, frequenting reed-beds.

reedy *adj.* (**reedier**, **reediest**) **1** full of reeds. **2** like a reed, esp. in weakness or slenderness. **3** (of a voice) not full. □ **reediness** *n.*

reef[1] *n.* a ridge of rock or coral etc. at or near the surface of the sea. [from Old Norse *rif* 'rib']

reef[2] *Naut.* ● *n.* each of several strips across a sail, for taking it in or rolling it up to reduce the surface area in a high wind. ● *v.tr.* take in a reef or reefs of (a sail). [from Old Norse *rif* 'rib']

reefer *n.* **1** *slang* a marijuana cigarette. **2** = REEFER JACKET. [based on REEF[2]]

reefer jacket *n.* a thick close-fitting double-breasted jacket.

reef knot *n.* ► a double knot made symmetrically to hold securely and cast off easily. ▷ KNOT

reek ● *v.intr.* (often foll. by *of*) **1** smell strongly and unpleasantly. **2** have unpleasant or suspicious associations. **3** give off smoke or fumes. ● *n.* **1** a foul or stale smell. **2** esp. *Sc.* smoke. **3** vapour; a visible exhalation (esp. from a chimney). [Old English]

reel ● *n.* **1** a cylindrical device on which film, tape, etc., or *Brit.* thread etc., is wound. **2** a quantity of thread etc. wound on a reel. **3** ▼ a device for winding and unwinding a line as required, esp. in fishing. **4** a revolving part in various machines. **5 a** a lively folk or Scottish dance, of two or more couples facing each other. **b** a piece of music for this. ● *v.* **1** *tr.* wind on a reel. **2** *tr.* (foll. by *in*, *up*) draw (fish etc.) in or up by the use of a reel. **3** *intr.* stand or walk or run unsteadily. **4** *intr.* be shaken mentally or physically. **5** *intr.* rock from side to side, or swing violently. **6** *intr.* dance a reel. □ **reel off** say or recite very rapidly and without apparent effort. [Old English] □ **reeler** *n.*

REED MACE
(*Typha latifolia*)

REEF KNOT

drag adjuster

spool spindle   reel cage

handle

reel foot

spool 'endfloat' adjuster

REEL: MULTIPLIER REEL USED ON A FISHING ROD

re-elect *v.tr.* elect again, esp. to a further term of office. □ **re-election** *n.*

re-eligible *adj.* eligible for re-election to a further term of office.

re-embark *v.intr. & tr.* go or put on board ship again. □ **re-embarkation** *n.*

re-emerge *v.intr.* emerge again. □ **re-emergence** *n.* **re-emergent** *adj.*

re-emphasize *v.tr.* (also **-ise**) place renewed emphasis on. □ **re-emphasis** *n.*

re-employ *v.tr.* employ again. □ **re-employment** *n.*

re-enact *v.tr.* act out (a past event). □ **re-enactment** *n.*

re-enlist *v.intr.* enlist again, esp. in the armed services.

re-enter *v.tr. & intr.* go back in. □ **re-entrance** *n.*

re-entrant *adj.* **1** (of an angle, esp. in fortification) pointing inwards. **2** *Geom.* reflex.

re-entry *n.* (*pl.* **-ies**) **1** the act of entering again, esp. (of a spacecraft etc.) re-entering the Earth's atmosphere. **2** *Law* an act of retaking or repossession.

re-equip *v.tr. & intr.* (**-equipped**, **-equipping**) provide or be provided with new equipment.

re-erect *v.tr.* erect again. □ **re-erection** *n.*

re-establish *v.tr.* establish again or anew. □ **re-establishment** *n.*

re-evaluate *v.tr.* evaluate again or differently. □ **re-evaluation** *n.*

reeve[1] *n. hist.* **1** the chief magistrate of a town or district. **2** an official supervising a landowner's estate. **3** any of various minor local officials. [Old English]

reeve[2] *v.tr.* (*past* **rove** or **reeved**) *Naut.* **1** (usu. foll. by *through*) thread (a rope or rod etc.) through a ring or other aperture. **2** pass a rope through (a block etc.). **3** fasten (a rope or block) in this way.

reeve[3] *n.* a female ruff (see RUFF[1] 3). [17th-century coinage]

re-examine *v.tr.* examine again or further (esp. a witness after cross-examination). □ **re-examination** *n.*

re-export ● *v.tr.* export again (esp. imported goods after further processing or manufacture). ● *n.* **1** the process of re-exporting. **2** something re-exported. □ **re-exportation** *n.* **re-exporter** *n.*

ref *n. colloq.* a referee in sports.

reface *v.tr.* put a new facing on (a building).

refashion *v.tr.* fashion again or differently.

refectory *n.* (*pl.* **-ies**) a room used for communal meals, esp. in a monastery or college. ▷ MONASTERY. [based on Latin *reficere* 'to refresh']

refectory table *n.* a long narrow table.

refer *v.* (**referred**, **referring**) (usu. foll. by *to*) **1** *tr.* trace or ascribe (*referred their success to their popularity*). **2** *tr.* consider as belonging (to a certain date or place or class). **3** *tr.* send on or direct (a person, or a question for decision). **4** *intr.* make an appeal or have recourse to (*referred to his notes*). **5** *tr.* send or direct (a person) to a medical specialist etc. **6** *tr.* (foll. by *back*) send (a proposal etc.) back to (a lower body, court, etc.). **7** *intr.* (foll. by *to*) (of a person speaking) make an allusion or direct the hearer's attention (*decided not to refer to our other problems*). **8** *intr.* (foll. by *to*) (of a statement etc.) have a particular relation or be directed to (*this paragraph refers to the events of last year*). **9** (foll. by *to*) interpret (a statement) as being directed to (a particular context etc.). **10** *tr.* fail (a candidate in an examination). [from Latin *referre* 'to carry back'] □ **referable** *adj.*

referee ● *n.* **1** an umpire esp. in football or boxing.

2 a person whose opinion or judgement is sought in a dispute etc. **3** a person willing to testify to the character of an applicant for employment etc. ● *v.* (**referees**, **refereed**) **1** *intr.* act as referee. **2** *tr.* be the referee of (a game etc.).

reference ● *n.* **1** the referring of a matter for decision or settlement or consideration to some authority. **2** the scope given to this authority. **3** (foll. by *to*) **a** a relation or respect or correspondence (*success has little reference to merit*). **b** an allusion (*made no reference to it*). **c** a direction to a book etc. (or a passage in it) where information may be found. **d** a book or passage so cited. **4 a** the act of looking up a passage etc. or looking in a book for information. **b** the act of referring to a person etc. for information. **5 a** a written testimonial supporting an applicant for employment etc. **b** a person giving this. ● *v.tr.* provide (a book etc.) with references to authorities. □ **with** (or **in**) **reference to** regarding; as regards. **without reference to** not taking account of. □ **referential** *adj.* **referentiality** *n.*

reference book *n.* a book intended to be consulted for information on individual matters rather than read continuously.

reference library *n.* a library in which the books are for consultation not loan.

referendum *n.* (*pl.* **referendums** or **referenda**) **1** the process of referring a political question to the electorate for a direct decision by general vote. **2** a vote taken by referendum. [Latin, literally 'thing to be referred']

referent *n.* the idea or thing that a word etc. symbolizes. [from Latin *referent-* 'referring']

referral *n.* the referring of an individual, esp. a patient, to an expert or specialist for advice or treatment.

referred pain *n.* pain felt in a part of the body other than its actual source.

refill ● *v.tr.* **1** fill again. **2** provide a new filling for. ● *n.* **1** a new filling. **2** the material for this. □ **refillable** *adj.*

refinance *v.tr.* provide with further capital.

refine *v.* **1** *tr.* free from impurities or defects. **2** *tr. & intr.* make or become more polished or elegant or cultured. **3** *tr. & intr.* make or become more subtle or delicate in feelings etc. [influenced by French *raffiner*] □ **refinable** *adj.*

refined *adj.* characterized by polish or elegance or subtlety.

refinement *n.* **1** the act of refining or the process of being refined. **2** fineness of feeling or taste. **3** polish or elegance in manner. **4** an added development or improvement (*a car with several refinements*). **5** a piece of subtle reasoning. **6** a fine distinction. **7** a subtle or ingenious example or display (*all the refinements of reasoning*).

refiner *n.* a person or company whose business is to refine crude oil, metal, sugar, etc.

refinery *n.* (*pl.* **-ies**) a place where oil etc. is refined.

refit ● *v.tr. & intr.* (**refitted**, **refitting**) make or become fit or serviceable again (esp. of a ship undergoing renewal and repairs). ● *n.* the act or an instance of refitting; the process of being refitted. □ **refitment** *n.*

reflag *v.tr.* (**reflagged**, **reflagging**) change the national registration of (a ship).

reflate *v.tr.* cause reflation of (a currency or economy etc.). [on the pattern of *inflate*, *deflate*] □ **reflation** *n.* **reflationary** *adj.*

reflect *v.* **1** *tr.* (of a surface or body) throw back (heat, light, etc.). **2** *tr.* (of a mirror) show an image of; reproduce to the eye or mind. **3** *tr.* correspond in appearance or effect to (*their behaviour reflects a wish to succeed*). **4** *tr.* **a** (of an action, result, etc.) show or bring (credit, discredit, etc.). **b** (*absol.*; usu. foll. by *on*, *upon*) bring discredit on. **5 a** *intr.* (often foll. by *on*, *upon*) meditate on. **b** *tr.* (foll. by *that*, *how*, etc. + clause) consider; remind oneself. [from Latin *reflectere*]

reflectance *n. Physics* a measure of the proportion of light or other radiation falling on a surface and then being reflected or scattered.

reflection *n.* (also *Brit.* **reflexion**) **1 ▼** the act or an instance of reflecting; the process of being reflected. **2 a** reflected light, heat, or colour. **b** a reflected image. **3** meditation; reconsideration (*on reflection*). **4** (often foll. by *on*) discredit or a thing bringing discredit. **5** (often foll. by *on, upon*) an idea arising in the mind; a comment or apophthegm.

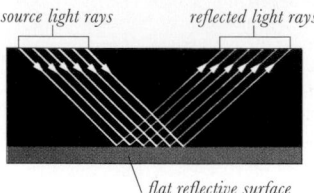

REFLECTION: LIGHT RAYS REFLECTED FROM A SMOOTH SURFACE

reflective *adj.* **1** (of a surface etc.) giving a reflection or image. **2** (of mental faculties) concerned with reflection or thought. **3** (of a person or mood etc.) thoughtful; given to meditation. □ **reflectively** *adv.* **reflectiveness** *n.*

reflectivity *n. Physics* the property of reflecting light or radiation, esp. reflectance as measured independently of the thickness of a material.

reflector *n.* **1** a piece of glass, metal, etc. for reflecting light in a required direction, e.g. on the back of a bicycle. ▷ BICYCLE. **2 a** a telescope etc. using a mirror to produce images. ▷ TELESCOPE. **b** the mirror itself.

reflex ● *adj.* **1** (of an action) independent of the will, as an automatic response to the stimulation of a nerve (e.g. a sneeze). **2** (of an angle) exceeding 180°. **3** bent backwards. ● *n.* **1** a reflex action. **2** a sign or secondary manifestation (*law is a reflex of public opinion*). **3** reflected light or a reflected image. [from Latin *reflexus*] □ **reflexly** *adv.*

reflex camera *n.* a camera with a ground-glass focusing screen on which the image is formed by a combination of lens and mirror.

reflexible *adj.* capable of being reflected. □ **reflexibility** *n.*

reflexion *Brit.* var. of REFLECTION.

reflexive *Gram.* ● *adj.* **1** (of a word or form) referring back to the subject of a clause (e.g. *myself*). **2** (of a verb) having a reflexive pronoun as its object (as in *to wash oneself*). ● *n.* a reflexive word or form, esp. a pronoun. □ **reflexively** *adv.* **reflexiveness** *n.* **reflexivity** *n.*

reflexology *n.* **▼** a system of massage through reflex points on the feet, hands, and head, used to relieve tension and treat illness. □ **reflexologist** *n.*

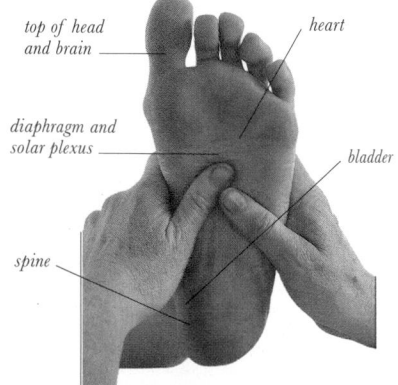

REFLEXOLOGY: REFLEX POINTS AND THE PARTS OF THE BODY THEY RELATE TO

refloat *v.tr.* set (a stranded ship) afloat again.

refocus *v.tr.* (**refocused**, **refocusing** or **refocussed**, **refocussing**) focus again or adjust the focus of.

reforest *v.tr.* = REAFFOREST. □ **reforestation** *n.*

reform ● *v.* **1** *tr. & intr.* make or become better by the removal of faults and errors. **2** *tr.* abolish or cure (an abuse or malpractice). ● *n.* **1** the removal of faults or abuses, esp. of a moral or political or social kind. **2** an improvement made or suggested. [from Latin *reformare*] □ **reformable** *adj.* **reformative** *adj.*

re-form *v.tr. & intr.* form again. □ **re-formation** *n.*

reformat *v.tr.* (**reformatted**, **reformatting**) revise or represent in another format.

reformation *n.* **1** the act of reforming or process of being reformed, esp. a radical change for the better in political or religious or social affairs. **2** (**the Reformation**) *hist.* a 16th-c. movement for the reform of abuses in the Roman Church ending in the establishment of the Reformed and Protestant Churches. [Middle English] □ **Reformational** *adj.*

reformatory ● *n.* (*pl.* **-ies**) *N. Amer. & hist.* = REFORM SCHOOL. ● *adj.* reformative.

Reformed Church *n.* a Church that has accepted the principles of the Reformation, esp. a Calvinist Church.

reformer *n.* a person who advocates or brings about (esp. political or social) reform.

reformism *n.* a policy of reform rather than abolition or revolution. □ **reformist** *n.*

Reform Judaism *n.* a simplified and rationalized form of Judaism.

reform school *n.* an institution to which young offenders are sent to be reformed.

reformulate *v.tr.* formulate again or differently. □ **reformulation** *n.*

refract *v.tr.* **▼** (of water, air, glass, etc.) deflect (a ray of light etc.) at a certain angle when it enters obliquely from another medium. ▷ LIGHT. [based on Latin *refractus* 'broken again'] □ **refraction** *n.* **refractive** *adj.*

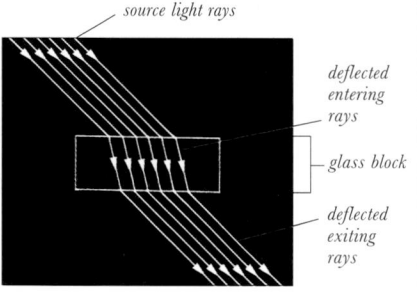

REFRACT: LIGHT RAYS REFRACTED BY A GLASS BLOCK

refractive index *n.* the ratio of the velocity of light in a vacuum to its velocity in a specified medium.

refractor *n.* **1** a refracting medium or lens. **2** a telescope using a lens to produce an image. ▷ TELESCOPE

refractory *adj.* **1** stubborn, unmanageable, rebellious. **2 a** (of a wound, disease, etc.) not yielding to treatment. **b** (of a person etc.) resistant to infection. **3** (of a substance) hard to fuse or work. □ **refractorily** *adv.* **refractoriness** *n.*

refrain[1] *v.intr.* (foll. by *from*) avoid doing (an action); forbear, desist. [from Latin *refrenare* 'to bridle']

refrain[2] *n.* **1** a recurring phrase or number of lines, esp. at the ends of stanzas. **2** the music accompanying this. [based on Latin *refringere* 'to break again', because the refrain 'broke' the sequence]

refrangible *adj.* that can be refracted. [based on Latin *refringere* 'to break again'] □ **refrangibility** *n.*

refreeze *v.tr. & intr.* (*past* **refroze**; *past part.* **refrozen**) freeze again.

refresh *v.tr.* **1** give fresh spirit or vigour to. **2** revive or stimulate (the memory), esp. by consulting the source of one's information. **3** make cool. [from Old French *refreschi(e)r*]

refresher *n.* **1** something that refreshes, esp. a drink. **2** *Brit. Law* an extra fee payable to counsel in a prolonged case.

refresher course *n.* a course reviewing or updating previous studies.

refreshing *adj.* **1** serving to refresh. **2** welcome or stimulating. □ **refreshingly** *adv.*

refreshment *n.* **1** the act of refreshing or the process of being refreshed in mind or body. **2** (usu. in *pl.*) food or drink that refreshes. **3** something that refreshes or stimulates the mind.

refrigerant ● *n.* **1** a substance used for refrigeration. ▷ REFRIGERATOR. **2** *Med.* a substance that cools or allays fever. ● *adj.* cooling. [from Latin *refrigerant-* 'cooling down']

refrigerate *v.* **1** *tr. & intr.* make or become cool or cold. **2** *tr.* subject (food etc.) to cold in order to freeze or preserve it. [based on Latin *refrigeratus* 'cooled down'] □ **refrigeration** *n.*

refrigerator *n.* **▶** a cabinet or room in which food etc. is kept cold.

refroze *past* of REFREEZE.

refrozen *past part.* of REFREEZE.

refuel *v.* (**refuelled**, **refuelling**; *US* **refueled**, **refueling**) **1** *intr.* replenish a fuel supply. **2** *tr.* supply with more fuel.

refuge *n.* **1** a shelter from pursuit or danger or trouble. **2** a person or place etc. offering this. **3** a traffic island. [from Latin *refugium*]

refugee *n.* a person taking refuge, esp. in a foreign country.

refulgent *adj. literary* shining; gloriously bright. [from Latin *refulgent-* 'shining anew'] □ **refulgence** *n.* **refulgently** *adv.*

refund ● *v.tr.* **1** pay back (money or expenses). **2** reimburse (a person). ● *n.* **1** an act of refunding. **2** a sum refunded; a repayment. [originally in sense 'to pour back': from Latin *refundere*] □ **refundable** *adj.*

refurbish *v.tr.* **1** brighten up. **2** restore and redecorate. □ **refurbishment** *n.*

refurnish *v.tr.* furnish again or differently.

refusal *n.* **1** the act or an instance of refusing; the state of being refused. **2** (in full **first refusal**) the right or privilege of deciding to take or leave a thing before it is offered to others.

refuse[1] /ri-fewz/ *v.tr.* **1** withhold acceptance of or consent to. **2** (often foll. by *to* + infin.; also *absol.*) indicate unwillingness (*I refuse to go*). **3** (often with double object) not grant (a request) made by (a person) (*refused me a day off*). **4** (also *absol.*) (of a horse) be unwilling to jump (a fence etc.). [from Old French] □ **refuser** *n.*

refuse[2] /ref-yooss/ *n.* items rejected as worthless; waste. [Middle English]

refusenik *n.* **1** *hist.* a Jew in the former Soviet Union who was refused permission to emigrate to Israel. **2** a person who refuses to follow orders or obey the law, esp. as a protest.

refute *v.tr.* **1** prove the falsity or error of (a statement etc. or the person advancing it). **2** rebut or repel by argument. **3** *disp.* deny or contradict (without argument). [from Latin *refutare*] □ **refutable** *adj.* **refutal** *n.* **refutation** *n.* **refuter** *n.*

■ **Usage** The use of *refute* in sense 3 is considered incorrect by some people. It is often confused in this sense with *repudiate*.

reg *n. Brit. colloq.* = REGISTRATION MARK.

regain *v.tr.* obtain possession or use of after loss.

regal *adj.* **1** royal; of or by a monarch or monarchs. **2** fit for a monarch; magnificent. [from Latin *regalis*] □ **regality** *n.* **regally** *adv.*

regale *v.tr.* **1** entertain lavishly with feasting. **2** (foll.

REFRIGERATOR

In a refrigerator, a gas (refrigerant) is compressed (becoming warm) and then cools into a liquid in the condenser. When it reaches the evaporator, the pressure is released and the liquid expands into a cold gas that cools the air in the cabinet. The gas then returns to the compressor.

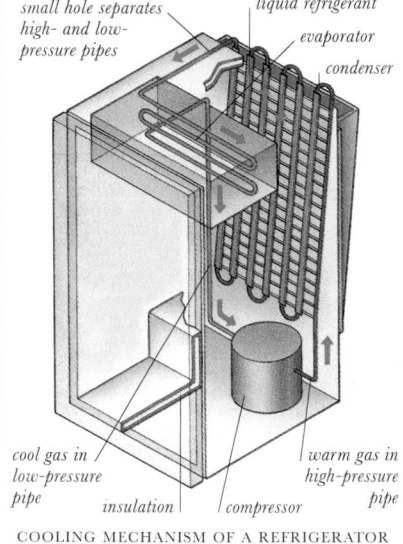

small hole separates high- and low-pressure pipes

liquid refrigerant

evaporator

condenser

cool gas in low-pressure pipe

insulation   compressor

warm gas in high-pressure pipe

COOLING MECHANISM OF A REFRIGERATOR

by *with*) entertain with (talk etc.). **3** (of beauty etc.) give delight to. [from French *régaler*]

regalia *n.pl.* **1** the insignia of royalty used at coronations. **2** the insignia of an order or of civic dignity. [medieval Latin, literally 'royal privileges']

■ **Usage** Note that *regalia* is a plural noun with no singular form in English.

regard ● *v.tr.* **1** give heed to; take into account. **2** look upon or contemplate mentally in a specified way (*I regard it as an insult*). **3** gaze on steadily (*regarded them suspiciously*). **4** (of a thing) have relation to; have some connection with. ● *n.* **1** (foll. by *to, for*) attention or care. **2** (foll. by *for*) esteem; kindly feeling. **3** a gaze; a steady or significant look. **4** a point attended to (*in this regard*). **5** (in *pl.*) an expression of friendliness in a letter etc. (*sent my best regards*). □ **as regards** concerning; in respect of. **in** (or **with**) **regard to** as concerns; in respect of. [from Old French]

regardful *adj.* (foll. by *of*) mindful of; paying attention to.

regarding *prep.* concerning; in respect of.

regardless ● *adj.* (foll. by *of*) without regard or consideration for. ● *adv.* without paying attention (*carried on regardless*). □ **regardlessly** *adv.* **regardlessness** *n.*

regatta *n.* a sporting event consisting of a series of boat or yacht races. [Italian (Venetian), literally 'a fight, a contest']

regency *n.* (*pl.* **-ies**) **1** the office of regent. **2** a commission acting as regent. **3 a** the period of office of a regent or regency commission. **b** (**Regency**) a particular period of a regency, esp. (in Britain) from 1811 to 1820. [from medieval Latin *regentia*]

regenerate ● *v.* **1** *tr. & intr.* bring or come into renewed existence; generate again. **2** *tr.* improve the moral condition of. **3** *tr.* impart new and more vigorous life to (a person or institution etc.). **4** *intr.* reform oneself. **5** *tr.* invest with a new and higher spiritual nature. **6** *intr. & tr. Biol.* regrow or cause

(new tissue) to regrow. ● *adj.* **1** spiritually born again. **2** reformed. □ **regeneration** *n.* **regenerative** *adj.* **regeneratively** *adv.* **regenerator** *n.*

regent ● *n.* a person appointed to administer a state because the monarch is a minor or is absent or incapacitated. ● *adj.* (placed after noun) acting as regent (*Prince Regent*). [from Latin *regent-* 'ruling']

reggae *n.* a W. Indian style of music with a strongly accented subsidiary beat. [W. Indian]

regicide *n.* **1** a person who kills or takes part in killing a king. **2** the act of killing a king. [based on Latin *rex regis* 'king'] □ **regicidal** *adj.*

regime /ray-*zheem*/ *n.* (also **régime**) **1** a method or system of government. **2** a prevailing order or system of things. **3** the conditions under which a scientific or industrial process occurs. **4** a (medical) regimen. [from French, related to REGIMEN]

regimen *n.* esp. *Med.* a prescribed course of exercise, way of life, and diet. [Latin]

regiment ● *n.* **1 a** a permanent unit of an army usu. commanded by a colonel and divided into several companies or troops or batteries. **b** an operational unit of artillery etc. **2** (usu. foll. by *of*) a large array or number. **3** *archaic* rule, government. ● *v.tr.* **1** organize (esp. oppressively) in groups or according to a system. **2** form into a regiment or regiments. [from Late Latin *regimentum*] □ **regimentation** *n.*

regimental ● *adj.* of or relating to a regiment. ● *n.* (in *pl.*) military uniform, esp. of a particular regiment. □ **regimentally** *adv.*

regimental sergeant major see SERGEANT MAJOR 1.

Regina /ri-*jy*-nā/ *n.* the reigning queen (following a name or in the titles of lawsuits, e.g. *Regina v. Jones* the Crown versus Jones). [Latin, literally 'queen']

region *n.* **1** an area of land, or division of the Earth's surface, having definable boundaries or characteristics (*a mountainous region*). **2** an administrative district esp. in Scotland. **3** a part of the body round or near some organ etc. (*the lumbar region*). **4** a sphere or realm (*the region of metaphysics*). □ **in the region of** approximately. [from Latin *regio* 'direction, district'] □ **regional** *adj.* **regionalism** *n.* **regionalist** *n. & adj.* **regionalize** *v.tr.* (also **-ise**). **regionally** *adv.*

register ● *n.* **1** an official list e.g. of births, marriages, and deaths, of shipping, of professionally qualified persons, or of qualified voters in a constituency. **2** a book in which items are recorded for reference. **3** a device recording speed, force, etc. **4** (in electronic devices) a location in a store of data. **5 a** the compass of a voice or instrument. **b** a part of this compass (*lower register*). **6** an adjustable plate for widening or narrowing an opening and regulating a draught, esp. in a fire-grate. **7 a** a set of organ pipes. ▷ ORGAN. **b** a sliding device controlling this. **8** = CASH REGISTER. ● *v.* **1** *tr.* set down (a name, fact, etc.) formally; record in writing. **2** *tr.* make a mental note of; notice. **3** *tr.* enter or cause to be entered in a particular register. **4** *tr.* entrust (a letter etc.) to registered post. **5** *intr. & refl.* put one's name on a register, esp. as an eligible voter, hotel guest, etc. **6** *tr.* (of an instrument) record automatically; indicate. **7 a** *tr.* express (an emotion) facially or by gesture (*registered surprise*). **b** *intr.* (of an emotion) show in a person's face or gestures. **8** *intr.* make an impression on a person's mind (*did not register*). [from Late Latin *regesta* 'things recorded'] □ **registrable** *adj.*

registered nurse *n.* a nurse with a State certificate of competence.

registered post *n. Brit.* a postal procedure with special precautions for safety and for compensation in case of loss.

register office *n. Brit.* a State office where civil marriages are conducted and births, marriages, and deaths are certified.

■ **Usage** *Register office* is the official name, although *registry office* is often heard in colloquial usage.

registrar *n.* **1** an official responsible for keeping a register or official records. **2** *Brit.* the chief administrative officer in a university. **3** a middle-ranking hospital doctor undergoing training as a specialist. [from medieval Latin *registrarius*] □ **registrarship** *n.*

registration *n.* the act or an instance of registering; the process of being registered. [from medieval Latin *registratio*]

registration document *n. Brit.* a document stating the registered keeper of a motor vehicle.

■ **Usage** The official name is *vehicle registration document*.

registration mark *n.* (also **registration number**) a combination of letters and figures identifying a motor vehicle etc.

registry *n.* (*pl.* **-ies**) **1** a place or office where registers or records are kept. **2** registration. [from medieval Latin *registerium*]

registry office *n.* = REGISTER OFFICE.

■ **Usage** See Usage Note at REGISTER OFFICE.

Regius professor /*ree*-ji-ŭs/ *n.* (in the UK) the holder of a chair founded by a sovereign or filled by Crown appointment. [Latin *regius* 'royal']

regrade *v.tr.* grade again or differently.

regress ● *v.* **1** *intr.* move backwards, esp. (in abstract senses) return to a former state. **2** *intr. & tr. Psychol.* return or cause to return mentally to a former stage of life. ● *n.* the act or an instance of going back. [based on Latin *regressus* 'stepped back']

regression *n.* **1** a backward movement, esp. a return to a former state. **2** a relapse or reversion. **3** *Psychol.* a return to an earlier stage of development.

regressive *adj.* **1** regressing; characterized by regression. **2** (of a tax) proportionally greater on lower incomes. □ **regressively** *adv.* **regressiveness** *n.*

regret ● *v.tr.* (**regretted**, **regretting**) (often foll. by *that* + clause) **1** feel or express sorrow or repentance or distress over (an action or loss etc.). **2** acknowledge with sorrow or remorse (*I regret to say*). ● *n.* **1** a feeling of sorrow, repentance, etc., over an action or loss etc. **2** (often in *pl.*) an (esp. polite or formal) expression of disappointment or sorrow at an occurrence, inability to comply, etc. □ **give** (or **send**) **one's regrets** formally decline an invitation. [from Old French *regreter* 'to bewail']

regretful *adj.* feeling or showing regret. □ **regretfully** *adv.* **regretfulness** *n.*

■ **Usage** *Regretfully* should be used only when 'in a regretful manner' is meant, e.g. *She shook her head regretfully*, and not where *regrettably* is meant, e.g. *Regrettably, he cannot be here tonight.*

regrettable *adj.* (of events or conduct) undesirable, unwelcome; deserving censure. □ **regrettably** *adv.*

■ **Usage** See Usage Note at REGRETFUL.

regroup *v.tr. & intr.* group or arrange again or differently. □ **regroupment** *n.*

regrow *v.intr. & tr.* (*past* **-grew**, *past part.* **-grown**) grow again, esp. after an interval. □ **regrowth** *n.*

regulable *adj.* able to be regulated.

regular ● *adj.* **1** conforming to a rule or principle; systematic. **2** harmonious, symmetrical (*regular features*). **3** acting or done or recurring uniformly or calculably in time or manner. **4** conforming to a standard of etiquette or procedure. **5** properly constituted or qualified; pursuing an occupation as one's main pursuit (*has no regular profession*). **6** *Gram.* (of a noun, verb, etc.) following the normal type of inflection. **7** *colloq.* complete, thorough, absolute (*a regular hero*). **8** *Eccl.* (placed before or after noun) **a** bound by religious rule. **b** belonging to a religious or monastic order (*canon regular*). **9** relating to or constituting a permanent professional body (*regular soldiers*). ● *n.* **1** a regular soldier. **2** *colloq.* a regular customer, visitor, etc. **3** *Eccl.* one of the regular

R

clergy. [from Latin *regularis*] □ **regularity** *n*. **regularize** *v.tr.* (also **-ise**). **regularization** *n*. **regularly** *adv.*

regulate *v.tr.* **1** control by rule. **2** subject to restrictions. **3** adapt to requirements. **4** alter the speed of (a machine or clock) so that it may work accurately. [based on Latin *regula* 'rule'] □ **regulative** *adj.* **regulator** *n*. **regulatory** *adj.*

regulation *n.* **1** the act or an instance of regulating; the process of being regulated. **2** a prescribed rule. **3** (*attrib.*) in accordance with regulations; of the correct type etc.

regulo *n.* (usu. foll. by a numeral) *Brit.* each of the numbers of a scale denoting temperature in a gas oven. [from *Regulo*, proprietary term for a thermostatic gas oven control]

regurgitate *v.tr.* **1** bring (swallowed food) up again to the mouth. **2** cast or pour out again (*regurgitate facts*). [based on medieval Latin *regurgitatus* 'gushed back'] □ **regurgitation** *n*.

rehabilitate *v.tr.* **1** restore to effectiveness or normal life by training etc., esp. after imprisonment or illness. **2** restore to former privileges or reputation or a proper condition. □ **rehabilitation** *n*. **rehabilitative** *adj.*

rehang *v.tr.* (*past* and *past part.* **rehung**) hang (esp. a picture or a curtain) again or differently.

rehash ● *v.tr.* put (old material) into a new form without significant change or improvement. ● *n.* **1** material rehashed. **2** the act or an instance of rehashing.

rehear *v.tr.* (*past* and *past part.* **reheard**) hear again.

rehearsal *n.* **1** the act or an instance of rehearsing. **2** a trial performance or practice of a play, recital, etc.

rehearse *v.* **1** *tr.* practise (a play etc.) for later public performance. **2** *intr.* hold a rehearsal. **3** *tr.* train (a person) by rehearsal. **4** *tr.* recite or say over. **5** *tr.* give a list of; enumerate. [from Old French *reherc(i)er*] □ **rehearser** *n*.

reheat *v.tr.* heat again. □ **reheater** *n*.

reheel *v.tr.* fit (a shoe etc.) with a new heel.

rehome *v.tr.* find a new home for (a pet).

rehouse *v.tr.* provide with new housing.

rehung *past* and *past part.* of REHANG.

rehydrate *v.* **1** *intr.* absorb water again after dehydration. **2** *tr.* add water to (esp. food) again to restore to a palatable state. □ **rehydratable** *adj.* **rehydration** *n*.

Reich /rykh/ *n.* the former German State, esp. the Third Reich. [German, literally 'empire']

■ **Usage** Only *Third Reich* is normal historical terminology.

reign ● *v.intr.* **1** hold royal office; be king or queen. **2** have power or predominance; prevail (*confusion reigns*). **3** (as **reigning** *adj.*) (of a champion etc.) currently holding the title etc. ● *n.* **1** sovereignty, rule. **2** the period during which a sovereign rules. [from Old French *reigne* 'kingdom', *reignier* 'to reign']

reignite *v.tr.* & *intr.* ignite again.

Reilly var. of RILEY.

reimburse *v.tr.* **1** repay (a person who has expended money). **2** repay (a person's expenses). [based on medieval Latin *imbursare* 'to put in a purse'] □ **reimbursable** *adj.* **reimbursement** *n*.

reimport ● *v.tr.* import (goods processed from exported materials). ● *n.* **1** the act or an instance of reimporting. **2** a reimported item. □ **reimportation** *n*.

reimpose *v.tr.* impose again, esp. after a lapse. □ **reimposition** *n*.

rein ● *n.* (in *sing.* or *pl.*) **1** a long narrow strap with each end attached to the bit, used to guide or check a horse etc. ▷ HARNESS, SHOWJUMPING. **2** a similar device used to restrain a young child. **3** a means of control. ● *v.tr.* **1** check or manage with reins. **2** (foll. by *up, back*) pull up or back with reins. **3** (foll. by *in*)

hold in as with reins; restrain. **4** govern, restrain, control. □ **give free rein to** remove constraints from; allow full scope to. **keep a tight rein on** allow little freedom to. [based on Latin *retinēre* 'to retain']

reincarnation *n.* (in some beliefs) the rebirth of a soul in a new body. □ **reincarnate** *v.tr.* **reincarnate** *adj.*

reincorporate *v.tr.* incorporate afresh. □ **reincorporation** *n*.

reindeer *n.* (*pl.* same or **reindeers**) ◄ a subarctic deer, *Rangifer tarandus*, both sexes of which have large antlers. ▷ DEER. [from Old Norse *hreindýri*]

REINDEER
(*Rangifer tarandus*)

reinfect *v.tr.* infect again. □ **reinfection** *n*.

reinforce *v.tr.* strengthen or support, esp. with additional personnel or material or by an increase of quantity, size, etc. [from French *renforcer*] □ **reinforcer** *n*.

reinforced concrete *n.* ▼ concrete with metal bars or wire etc. embedded to increase its tensile strength.

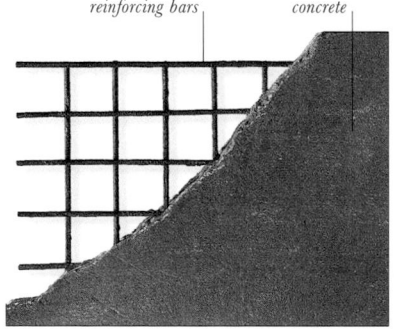

reinforcing bars   *concrete*

REINFORCED CONCRETE

reinforcement *n.* **1** the act or an instance of reinforcing; the process of being reinforced. **2** a thing that reinforces. **3** (in *pl.*) reinforcing personnel or equipment etc.

reinsert *v.tr.* insert again. □ **reinsertion** *n*.

reinstate *v.tr.* **1** replace in a former position. **2** restore (a person etc.) to former privileges. □ **reinstatement** *n*.

reinsure *v.tr.* & *intr.* insure again (esp. of an insurer securing himself by transferring some or all of the risk to another insurer). □ **reinsurance** *n*. **reinsurer** *n*.

reintegrate *v.tr.* integrate back into society. □ **reintegration** *n*.

reinter *v.tr.* inter (a corpse) again. □ **reinterment** *n*.

reinterpret *v.tr.* (**reinterpreted, reinterpreting**) interpret again or differently. □ **reinterpretation** *n*.

reintroduce *v.tr.* introduce again. □ **reintroduction** *n*.

reinvent *v.tr.* invent again. □ **reinvention** *n*.

reinvest *v.tr.* invest again (esp. money in other property etc.). □ **reinvestment** *n*.

reinvigorate *v.tr.* impart fresh vigour to. □ **reinvigoration** *n*.

reissue ● *v.tr.* (**reissues, reissued, reissuing**) issue again or in a different form. ● *n.* a new issue, esp. of a record or previously published book.

reiterate *v.tr.* say or do again or repeatedly. [based on Latin *reiteratus* 'repeated again'] □ **reiteration** *n*. **reiterative** *adj.*

reject ● *v.tr.* **1** put aside or send back as not to be used or done or complied with etc. **2** refuse to accept or believe in. **3** rebuff or snub (a person). **4** (of a body or digestive system) cast up again; vomit, evacuate. **5** *Med.* show an immune response to (a transplanted organ or tissue) so that it fails to survive. ● *n.* a thing or person rejected as unfit or below standard. [based on Latin *rejectus* 'thrown back'] □ **rejectable** *adj.* **rejection** *n*. **rejective** *adj.* **rejector** *n*.

rejectionist *n.* a person who rejects a proposed policy etc., esp. an Arab who refuses to accept a negotiated peace with Israel (often *attrib.: rejectionist groups*).

rejig *v.tr.* (**rejigged, rejigging**) esp. *Brit.* **1** re-equip (a factory etc.) for a new kind of work. **2** rearrange.

rejoice *v.intr.* **1** feel great joy. **2** (foll. by *that* + clause or *to* + infin.) be glad. **3** (foll. by *in, at*) take delight. **4** celebrate some event. [from Old French *rejoir*, *rejoiss-*] □ **rejoicer** *n*. **rejoicingly** *adv.*

rejoin[1] *v.* **1** *tr.* & *intr.* join together again; reunite. **2** *tr.* join (a companion etc.) again.

rejoin[2] *v.* **1** *tr.* say in answer; retort. **2** *intr.* *Law* reply to a charge or pleading in a lawsuit.

rejoinder *n.* **1** what is said in reply. **2** a retort. **3** *Law* a reply by rejoining.

rejuvenate *v.tr.* make young or as if young again. [based on Latin *juvenis* 'young'] □ **rejuvenation** *n*. **rejuvenator** *n*.

rejuvenesce *v.* **1** *intr.* become young again; regain vitality. **2** *Biol.* **a** *intr.* (of cells) change to a more active form. **b** *tr.* change (cells) into a more active form. [Late Latin *rejuvenescere* (as RE-, Latin *juvenis* 'young')] □ **rejuvenescent** *adj.* **rejuvenescence** *n*.

rekey *v.tr.* esp. *Computing* re-enter (text or other data) using a keyboard.

rekindle *v.tr.* & *intr.* kindle again.

relabel *v.tr.* (**relabelled, relabelling**; *US* **relabeled, relabeling**) label (esp. a commodity) again or differently.

relaid *past* and *past part.* of RELAY[2].

relapse ● *v.intr.* (usu. foll. by *into*) fall back or sink again (into a worse state after an improvement). ● *n.* the act or an instance of relapsing, esp. a deterioration in a patient's condition after a partial recovery. [from Latin *relapsus* 'slipped back'] □ **relapser** *n*.

relapsing fever *n.* an infectious disease marked by recurrent fever, caused by spirochaetes of the genus *Borrelia*.

relate *v.* **1** *tr.* narrate or recount. **2** *tr.* (in *passive*; often foll. by *to*) be connected by blood or marriage. **3** *tr.* (usu. foll. by *to, with*) bring into relation (with one another); establish a connection between. **4** *intr.* (foll. by *to*) have reference to. **5** *intr.* (foll. by *to*) bring oneself into relation to. [based on Latin *relatus* 'brought back'] □ **relatable** *adj.*

related *adj.* connected, esp. by blood or marriage. □ **relatedness** *n*.

relation *n.* **1 a** the way in which one person or thing is related to another. **b** the existence or effect of a connection, correspondence, contrast, or feeling prevailing between persons or things, esp. when qualified in some way (*bears no relation to the facts*; *enjoyed good relations for many years*). **2** a relative. **3** (in *pl.*) **a** (foll. by *with*) dealings (with others). **b** sexual

R

RELATIVITY

According to Albert Einstein's general theory of relativity, astronomical bodies distort space-time, making it curve. This distortion creates gravitational fields: the larger the body and subsequent distortion, the greater the field produced. As other astronomical objects travel into the distortion, their path is curved as the gravitational fields pull them in. Light is also curved in this way.

DEMONSTRATION OF THE DISTORTION OF SPACE-TIME

path of passing comet

Sun

space-time distortion

curved path of comet

comet

---

intercourse. **4** = RELATIONSHIP 1, 3. **5 a** narration (*his relation of the events*). **b** a narrative. □ **in relation to** as regards.

relational *adj.* **1** of, belonging to, or characterized by relation. **2** having relation.

relational database *n. Computing* a database structured to recognize the relation of stored items of information.

relationship *n.* **1** the fact or state of being related. **2 a** a connection or association (*a working relationship*). **b** an emotional (esp. sexual) association between two people. **3** a condition or character due to being related. **4** kinship.

relative ● *adj.* **1** considered or having significance in relation to something else (*in relative comfort*). **2** (foll. by *to*) proportionate to (something else) (*growth is relative to input*). **3** (foll. by *to*) in comparison with; compared with (*low levels relative to the rest of the South-East*). **4 a** compared one with another (*their relative advantages*). **b** (foll. by *to*) in relation to (*move slowly relative to each other*). **5** (usu. foll. by *to*) having reference (*the facts relative to the issue*). **6** having mutual relations; corresponding in some way; related to each other. **7** *Gram.* **a** (of a word, esp. a pronoun) referring to an expressed or implied antecedent and attaching a subordinate clause to it, e.g. *which, who*. **b** (of a clause) attached to an antecedent by a relative word. ● *n.* **1** a person connected by blood or marriage. **2** a species related to another by common origin. **3** *Gram.* a relative word, esp. a pronoun. [from Late Latin *relativus* 'having reference'] □ **relatival** *adj.* (in sense 3 of *n.*). **relatively** *adv.*

relative atomic mass *n.* the ratio of the average mass of one atom of an element to one-twelfth of the mass of an atom of carbon-12.

relative density *n. Chem.* the ratio of the density of a substance to the density of a standard, usu. water or air.

relative humidity *n.* the proportion of moisture to the value for saturation at the same temperature.

relative molecular mass *n.* the ratio of the average mass of one molecule of an element or compound to one-twelfth of the mass of an atom of carbon-12.

relativism *n.* the doctrine that knowledge, truth, morality, etc., are relative and not absolute. □ **relativist** *n.*

relativistic *adj. Physics* (of phenomena etc.) accurately described only by the theory of relativity. □ **relativistically** *adv.*

relativity *n.* **1** the fact or state of being relative. **2** *Physics* **a** (**special theory of relativity**) a theory based on the principle that all motion is relative and that light has constant velocity. **b** (**general theory of relativity**) ▲ a theory extending this to gravitation and accelerated motion.

---

relaunch ● *v.tr.* launch again. ● *n.* an instance of relaunching something, esp. a business or product.

relax *v.* **1** *tr. & intr.* make or become less stiff or rigid or tense. **2** *tr. & intr.* make or become less formal or strict (*rules were relaxed*). **3** *tr.* reduce or abate (one's attention, efforts, etc.). **4** *intr.* cease work or effort. **5** *tr.* (as **relaxed** *adj.*) at ease; unperturbed. [from Latin *relaxare*]

relaxant ● *n.* a drug etc. that relaxes and reduces tension. ● *adj.* causing relaxation.

relaxation *n.* **1** the act of relaxing or state of being relaxed. **2** recreation. **3** a partial remission or relaxing of a penalty, duty, etc. **4** a lessening of severity, precision, etc.

relaxing *adj.* conducive to relaxation.

relay[1] ● *n.* **1** a fresh set of people or horses substituted for tired ones. **2** a gang of workers, supply of material, etc., deployed on the same basis (*operated in relays*). **3** = RELAY RACE. **4** a device activating changes in an electric circuit etc. in response to other changes affecting itself. **5 a** a device to receive, reinforce, and transmit a message, broadcast, etc. **b** a relayed message or transmission. ● *v.tr.* **1** receive (a message, broadcast, etc.) and transmit it to others. **2 a** arrange in relays. **b** provide with or replace by relays. [from Old French *relai* (n.), *relayer* (v.)]

relay[2] *v.tr.* (*past* and *past part.* **relaid**) lay again or differently.

relay race *n.* a race between teams whose members each in turn cover part of the distance.

relearn *v.tr.* (*past* and *past part.* **relearned** or **relearnt**) learn again.

release ● *v.tr.* **1** (often foll. by *from*) set free; liberate, unfasten. **2** allow to move from a fixed position. **3 a** make (information, a recording, etc.) publicly or generally available. **b** issue (a film etc.) for general exhibition. **4** *Law* make over (property or money) to another. ● *n.* **1** deliverance or liberation from a restriction, duty, or difficulty. **2** a handle or catch that releases part of a mechanism. **3** a document or item of information made available for publication (*press release*). **4 a** a film or record etc. that is released. **b** the act or an instance of releasing or the process of being released in this way. [from Old French *reles* (n.), *relesser* (v.), related to RELAX] □ **releasable** *adj.* **releaser** *n.*

relegate *v.tr.* **1** consign or dismiss to an inferior position; demote. **2** transfer (a sports team) to a lower division of a league etc. **3** banish. **4** (foll. by *to*) **a** transfer (a matter) for decision or implementation. **b** refer (a person) for information. [based on Latin *relegatus* 'sent back'] □ **relegation** *n.*

relent *v.intr.* **1** abandon a harsh intention. **2** yield to compassion. **3** relax one's severity; become less stern. [based on Latin *lentāre* 'to bend']

---

relentless *adj.* **1** unrelenting; insistent and uncompromising. **2** continuous; oppressively constant (*the pressure was relentless*). □ **relentlessly** *adv.* **relentlessness** *n.*

relet esp. *Brit.* ● *v.tr.* (**-letting**; *past* and *past part.* **-let**) let (a property) for a further period or to a new tenant. ● *n.* a relet property.

relevant *adj.* (often foll. by *to*) bearing on or having reference to the matter in hand. [from medieval Latin *relevant-* 'raising up'] □ **relevance** *n.* **relevancy** *n.* **relevantly** *adv.*

reliable *adj.* **1** that may be relied on. **2** of sound and consistent character or quality. □ **reliability** *n.* **reliably** *adv.*

reliance *n.* (foll. by *in, on*) trust, confidence (*put full reliance in you*). □ **reliant** *adj.*

relic *n.* **1** an object interesting because of its age or association. **2** a part of a deceased holy person's body or belongings kept as an object of reverence. **3** a surviving custom or belief etc. from a past age. **4** a memento or souvenir. [from Latin *reliquiae* 'relics']

relict *n.* an object surviving in its primitive form. [from Latin *relictus* '(thing or person) left behind']

relief *n.* **1 a** the alleviation of or deliverance from pain, distress, anxiety, etc. **b** the feeling accompanying such deliverance. **2** a feature etc. that diversifies monotony or relaxes tension. **3** assistance given to those in special need or difficulty (*rent relief*). **4 a** the replacing of a person or persons on duty by another or others. **b** a person or persons replacing others in this way. **5** (usu. *attrib.*) *Brit.* a thing supplementing another in some service, esp. an extra vehicle providing public transport at peak times. **6** ▲ a method of moulding or carving or stamping in which the design stands out from the surface, with projections proportioned and more (**high relief**) or less (**low relief**) closely approximating to those of the objects depicted (cf. ROUND *n.* 8). ▷ PRINTING. **7** vividness, distinctness (*brings the facts out in sharp relief*). **8** (foll. by *of*) the reinforcement (esp. the raising of a siege) of a place. **9** esp. *Law* the redress of a hardship or grievance. □ **on relief** esp. *N. Amer.* receiving State assistance because of need. [from Italian *rilievo*]

RELIEF: ANCIENT GREEK LOW-RELIEF CARVING

relief map *n.* ▶ a map indicating hills and valleys by shading etc. rather than by contour lines alone.

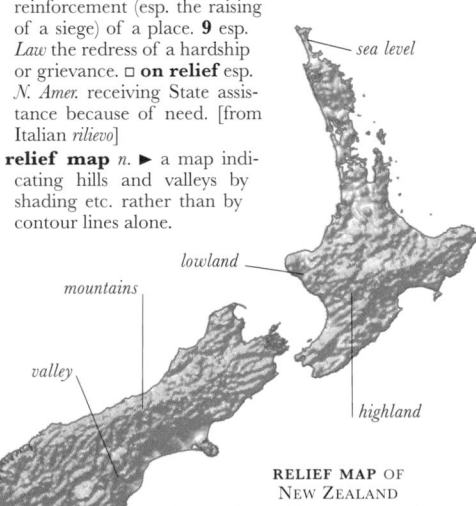

sea level

lowland

mountains

valley

highland

RELIEF MAP OF NEW ZEALAND

R

relief road *n. Brit.* a road taking traffic around a congested area.

relieve *v.tr.* **1** bring or provide aid or assistance to. **2** alleviate or reduce (pain, suffering, etc.). **3** mitigate the tedium or monotony of. **4** bring military support for (a besieged place). **5** release (a person) from a duty by acting as or providing a substitute. **6** (foll. by *of*) take (a burden or responsibility) away from (a person). **7** bring into relief; cause to appear solid or detached. □ **relieve one's feelings** use strong language or vigorous behaviour when annoyed. **relieve oneself** urinate or defecate. [from Latin *relevare* 'to raise again'] □ **relievable** *adj.* **reliever** *n.*

relieved *predic.adj.* freed from anxiety or distress (*am very relieved to hear it*). □ **relievedly** *adv.*

relievo /ril-ee-voh/ *n.* (also **rilievo** /ril-yay-voh/) (*pl.* **-os**) = RELIEF 6. [from Italian *rilievo*]

relight *v.tr.* (*past* and *past part.* **relighted** or **relit**) light (a fire etc.) again.

religio- *comb. form* **1** religion. **2** religious.

religion *n.* **1** the belief in a superhuman controlling power, esp. in a personal God or gods entitled to obedience and worship. **2** the expression of this in worship. **3** a particular system of faith and worship. **4** life under monastic vows (*the way of religion*). [from Latin *religio* 'obligation, bond, reverence']

religiose *adj.* excessively religious.

religiosity *n.* the condition of being religious or religiose.

religious ● *adj.* **1** devoted to religion; pious, devout. **2** of or concerned with religion. **3** of or belonging to a monastic order. **4** scrupulous, conscientious (*a religious attention to detail*). ● *n.* (*pl.* same) a person bound by monastic vows. [from Latin *religiosus*] □ **religiously** *adv.* **religiousness** *n.*

reline *v.tr.* renew the lining of (a garment, boiler, etc.).

relinquish *v.tr.* **1** surrender or resign (a right or possession). **2** give up or cease from (a habit, plan, belief, etc.). **3** relax hold of. [from Latin *relinquere*] □ **relinquishment** *n.*

reliquary *n.* (*pl.* **-ies**) ▼ a receptacle for relics. [from French *reliquaire*]

RELIQUARY: 12TH-CENTURY
RELIQUARY CASKET

relish ● *n.* **1 a** great liking or enjoyment. **b** keen or pleasurable longing (*had no relish for travelling*). **2 a** an appetizing flavour. **b** an attractive quality (*fishing loses its relish in winter*). **3** a condiment eaten with plainer food to add flavour. ● *v.tr.* **1 a** get pleasure out of; enjoy greatly. **b** anticipate with pleasure (*did not relish what lay before her*). **2** add relish to. [based on Old French *reles, relais* 'remainder']

relive *v.tr.* live (an experience etc.) over again, esp. in the imagination.

reload *v.tr.* (also *absol.*) load again.

relocate *v.* **1** *tr.* locate in a new place. **2** *tr. & intr.* move to a new place. □ **relocation** *n.*

reluctant *adj.* unwilling or disinclined (*most reluctant*

R

to agree). [from Latin *reluctant-* 'struggling against'] □ **reluctance** *n.* **reluctantly** *adv.*

rely *v.intr.* (**-ies, -ied**) (foll. by *on, upon*) **1** depend on with confidence or assurance (*am relying on your judgement*). **2** be dependent on (*relies on her for everything*). [earlier in senses 'to rally, be a vassal of': from Latin *religare* 'to bind together']

REM /rem/ *abbr.* rapid eye-movement.

rem *n.* (*pl.* same or **rems**) a unit of effective absorbed dose of ionizing radiation in human tissue. [from *roentgen* equivalent *man*]

remade *past* and *past part.* OF REMAKE.

remain *v.intr.* **1** be left over after others or other parts have been removed or used or dealt with. **2** be in the same place or condition during further time (*remained at home*). **3** (foll. by *compl.*) continue to be (*remained calm; remains President*). [from Latin *remanēre*]

remainder ● *n.* **1** a part remaining or left over. **2** remaining persons or things. **3** a number left after division or subtraction. **4** the copies of a book left unsold when demand has fallen. ● *v.tr.* dispose of (a remainder of books) at a reduced price.

remains *n.pl.* **1** what remains after other parts have been removed or used etc. **2** relics of antiquity (*Roman remains*). **3** a person's body after death.

remake ● *v.tr.* (*past* and *past part.* **remade**) make again or differently. ● *n.* a thing that has been remade, esp. a cinema film.

remand ● *v.tr.* return (a prisoner) to custody, esp. to allow further inquiries. ● *n.* a return to custody. □ **on remand** in custody pending trial. [from Late Latin *remandare* 'to commit afresh']

remark ● *v.* **1** *tr.* **a** say by way of comment. **b** take notice of; regard with attention. **2** *intr.* (usu. foll. by *on, upon*) make a comment. ● *n.* **1** a written or spoken comment; anything said. **2 a** the act of noticing or observing (*worthy of remark*). **b** the act of commenting (*let it pass without remark*). [from French *remarque* (n.), *remarquer* (v.)]

remarkable *adj.* **1** worthy of notice; exceptional. **2** striking, conspicuous. □ **remarkably** *adv.*

remarry *v.intr. & tr.* (**-ies, -ied**) marry again. □ **remarriage** *n.*

remaster *v.tr.* make a new master of (a recording).

rematch *n.* a return match or game.

REME /ree-mi/ *abbr.* (in the UK) Royal Electrical and Mechanical Engineers.

remedial *adj.* **1** affording or intended as a remedy (*remedial therapy*). **2** (of teaching) for slow or backward children. [based on Latin *remedium* 'remedy']

remedy ● *n.* (*pl.* **-ies**) (often foll. by *for, against*) **1** a medicine or treatment (for a disease etc.). **2 a** means of counteracting or removing anything undesirable. **3** redress; legal or other reparation. ● *v.tr.* (**-ies, -ied**) rectify; make good. [from Latin *remedium*] □ **remediable** *adj.*

remember *v.tr.* **1** keep in the memory; not forget. **2** (also *absol.*) **a** bring back into one's thoughts. **b** (foll. by *to* + infin. or *that* + clause) have in mind (a duty, commitment, etc.) (*will you remember to lock the door?*). **3** think of or acknowledge (a person), esp. in making a gift etc. **4** (foll. by *to*) convey greetings from (one person) to (another) (*remember me to your mother*). **5** mention (in prayer). [from Late Latin *rememorari*]

remembrance *n.* **1** the act of remembering or process of being remembered. **2** a memory or recollection. **3** a keepsake or souvenir. **4** (in *pl.*) greetings conveyed through a third person.

Remembrance Day *n.* **1** = REMEMBRANCE SUNDAY. **2** *hist.* Armistice Day.

Remembrance Sunday *n.* (in the UK) the Sunday nearest 11 Nov., when those who were killed in the First and Second World Wars and later conflicts are commemorated.

remind *v.tr.* **1** (foll. by *of*) cause (a person) to think of. **2** (usu. foll. by *to* + infin. or *that* + clause) cause (a person) to remember a commitment etc.

reminder *n.* **1 a** a thing that reminds, esp. a letter or bill. **b** a means of reminding (*leave it here as a reminder*). **2** a memento or souvenir.

reminisce *v.intr.* indulge in reminiscence. □ **reminiscer** *n.*

reminiscence *n.* **1** the act of remembering things past. **2 a** a past fact or experience that is remembered. **b** the process of narrating this. **3** (in *pl.*) a collection in literary form of incidents and experiences that a person remembers. [based on Latin *reminisci* 'to remember']

reminiscent *adj.* **1** (foll. by *of*) tending to remind one of or suggest. **2** concerned with reminiscence. **3** (of a person) given to reminiscing. □ **reminiscently** *adv.*

remiss *adj.* careless of duty; lax, negligent. [from Latin *remissus* 'slackened'] □ **remissness** *n.*

remission *n.* **1** *Brit.* the reduction of a prison sentence on account of good behaviour. **2** the remitting of a debt or penalty etc. **3** a diminution of force, effect, or degree (esp. of disease or pain). **4** (often foll. by *of*) forgiveness (of sins etc.). [from Latin *remissio*]

remit ● *v.* (**remitted, remitting**) **1** *tr.* cancel or refrain from exacting or inflicting (a debt or punishment etc.). **2** *intr. & tr.* abate or slacken; cease or cease from partly or entirely. **3** *tr.* send (money etc.) in payment. **4** *tr.* **a** (foll. by *to*) refer (a matter for decision etc.) to some authority. **b** *Law* send back (a case) to a lower court. **5** *tr.* **a** postpone or defer. **b** (foll. by *in, into*) send or put back into a previous state. **6** *tr. Theol.* pardon (sins etc.). ● *n.* **1** the terms of reference of a committee etc. **2** an item remitted for consideration. [from Latin *remittere*] □ **remittable** *adj.*

remittance *n.* **1** money sent, esp. by post. **2** the act of sending money.

remix ● *v.tr.* mix again. ● *n.* a sound recording that has been remixed to produce a new version (see MIX *v.* 8). □ **remixer** *n.*

remnant *n.* **1** a small remaining quantity. **2** a piece of cloth etc. left when the greater part has been used or sold. **3** (foll. by *of*) a surviving trace (*a remnant of empire*). [from Old French *remenant*]

remodel *v.tr.* (**remodelled, remodelling**; *US* **remodeled, remodeling**) **1** model again or differently. **2** reconstruct.

remold *US* var. of REMOULD.

remonstrance *n.* **1** the act or an instance of remonstrating. **2** an expostulation or protest. [from medieval Latin *remonstrantia*]

remonstrate *v.* **1** *intr.* (foll. by *with*) make a protest; argue forcibly (*remonstrated with them over the delays*). **2** *tr.* (often foll. by *that* + clause) urge protestingly. [based on medieval Latin *remonstratus* 'demonstrated'] □ **remonstration** *n.*

remorse *n.* **1** deep regret for a wrong committed. **2** compunction; a compassionate reluctance to inflict pain (esp. *without remorse*). [based on Latin *remorsus* 'vexed']

remorseful *adj.* filled with repentance. □ **remorsefully** *adv.*

remorseless *adj.* without compassion or compunction. □ **remorselessly** *adv.* **remorselessness** *n.*

remortgage ● *v.tr.* (also *absol.*) mortgage again; revise the terms of an existing mortgage on (a property). ● *n.* a different or altered mortgage.

remote *adj.* (**remoter, remotest**) **1** far away in place or time. **2** situated away from the main centres of population, society, etc. **3** distantly related (*a remote ancestor*). **4** slight, faint (esp. *not the remotest chance, idea, etc.*). **5** aloof; not friendly. **6** (foll. by *from*) widely different; separate by nature (*ideas remote from the subject*). [from Latin *remotus* 'removed'] □ **remotely** *adv.* **remoteness** *n.*

remote control *n.* **1** control of a machine or apparatus from a distance by means of signals transmitted from a radio or electronic device. **2** such a device. □ **remote-controlled** *adj.*

remote sensing *n.* the scanning of the Earth by satellite or high-flying aircraft.

remould (*US* **remold**) ● *v.tr.* **1** mould again; refashion. **2** *Brit.* re-form the tread of (a tyre). ● *n.* a remoulded tyre.

remount ● *v.* **1 a** *tr.* mount (a horse etc.) again. **b** *intr.* get on horseback again. **2** *tr.* get on to or ascend (a ladder, hill, etc.) again. **3** *tr.* provide (a person) with a fresh horse etc. **4** *tr.* put (a picture etc.) on a fresh mount. ● *n.* **1** a fresh horse for a rider. **2** a supply of fresh horses for a regiment.

removal *n.* **1** the act or an instance of removing; the process of being removed. **2** esp. *Brit.* the transfer of furniture and other contents on moving house.

remove ● *v.tr.* **1** take off or away from the place or position occupied; detach (*remove the top carefully*). **2 a** move or take to another place; change the situation of (*will you remove the tea things?*). **b** get rid of; eliminate (*will remove all doubts*). **3** cause to be no longer present or available; take away (*all privileges were removed*). **4** dismiss (from office). **5** (in *passive*; foll. by *from*) distant or remote in condition (*the country is not far removed from anarchy*). **6** (as **removed** *adj.*) (esp. of cousins) separated by a specified number of steps of descent (*a first cousin twice removed* = a grandchild of a first cousin). ● *n.* **1** a degree of remoteness; a distance. **2** a stage in a gradation; a degree (*is several removes from what I expected*). **3** a form or division in some British schools. [from Latin *removēre*] □ **removable** *adj.* **removability** *n.* **remover** *n.*

remunerate *v.tr.* **1** reward; pay for services rendered. **2** serve as or provide recompense for (toil etc.) or to (a person). [based on Latin *remuneratus* 'rewarded'] □ **remuneration** *n.* **remunerative** *adj.*

Renaissance /ri-**nay**-sănss/ *n.* **1** the revival of art and literature in the 14th–16th c. **2** the period of this. **3** ► the culture and style of art, architecture, etc. developed during this era. **4** (**renaissance**) any similar revival. [French, literally 'rebirth']

Renaissance man *n.* a person with many talents or pursuits.

renal *adj.* of or concerning the kidneys. ▷ KIDNEY [based on Latin *renes* 'kidneys']

rename *v.tr.* name again; give a new name to.

renascence *n.* **1** rebirth; renewal. **2** = RENAISSANCE.

renascent *adj.* springing up anew; being reborn or renewed. [from Latin *renascent-* 'being reborn']

renationalize *v.tr.* (also **-ise**) take (a privatized industry) back into state control. □ **renationalization** *n.*

rend *v.* (*past* and *past part.* **rent**) *archaic* or *literary* **1** *tr.* tear or wrench forcibly. **2** *tr. & intr.* split or divide in pieces or into factions (*a country rent by civil war*). **3** *tr.* cause emotional pain to (the heart etc.). [Old English]

render *v.tr.* **1** cause to be or become (*rendered us helpless*). **2** give or pay (money, service, etc.), esp. in return or as a thing due (*render thanks; rendered good for evil*). **3 a** give (assistance) (*rendered aid to the injured man*). **b** show (obedience etc.). **c** do (a service etc.). **4** submit; send in; present (an account, reason, etc.). **5 a** represent or portray artistically, musically, etc. **b** act (a role); represent (a character, idea, etc.) (*the dramatist's conception was well rendered*). **c** *Mus.* perform; execute. **6** translate (*rendered the poem into French*). **7** (often foll. by *down*) melt down (fat etc.), esp. to clarify; extract by melting. **8** cover (stone or brick) with a coat of plaster. **9** *literary* give back; hand over; deliver, give up; surrender (*render unto Caesar the things that are Caesar's*). [from Latin *reddere* 'to give back'] □ **renderer** *n.*

rendering *n.* **1 a** the act or an instance of performing music, drama, etc.; an interpretation or performance (*an excellent rendering of the part*). **b** a translation. **2 a** the act or an instance of plastering stone, brick, etc. **b** a first coating of this kind.

rendezvous /**ron**-day-voo/ ● *n.* (*pl.* same) **1** an agreed or regular meeting place. **2** a meeting by arrangement. ● *v.intr.* (**rendezvouses, rendezvoused, rendezvousing**) meet at a rendezvous. [French, literally 'present yourselves']

rendition *n.* an interpretation or rendering of a dramatic role, piece of music, etc. [obsolete French, from *rendre* 'to render']

renegade ● *n.* a person who deserts a party or principles. ● *adj.* **1** traitorous, rebellious. **2** of changed allegiance. [from medieval Latin *renegatus*]

renege /ri-**nayg**/ *v.* (also **renegue**) **1** *intr.* **a** go back on one's word; change one's mind; recant. **b** (foll. by *on*) go back on (a promise or undertaking or contract). **2** *tr.* deny, renounce, abandon (a person, faith, etc.). [from medieval Latin *renegare* 'to deny again']

renegotiate *v.tr.* (also *absol.*) negotiate again or on different terms. □ **renegotiable** *adj.* **renegotiation** *n.*

renew *v.tr.* **1** revive; make new again; restore to the original state. **2** reinforce; resupply; replace. **3** repeat or re-establish; resume after an interruption (*renewed our acquaintance; a renewed attack*). **4** get, begin, make, say, give, etc. anew. **5** (also *absol.*) grant or be granted a continuation of (a licence, subscription, lease, etc.). **6** recover (one's youth, strength, etc.). □ **renewable** *adj. & n.* **renewal** *n.*

rennet *n.* **1** curdled milk found in the stomach of an unweaned calf, used in curdling milk for cheese, junket, etc. **2** a preparation made from the stomach membrane of a calf or from certain fungi, used for the same purpose. [Middle English]

renominate *v.tr.* nominate for a further term of office. □ **renomination** *n.*

renounce *v.tr.* **1** consent formally to abandon (a claim, right, possession, etc.). **2** repudiate; refuse to recognize any longer (*renouncing their father's authority*). **3 a** decline further association or disclaim relationship with (*renounced my former friends*). **b** withdraw from; discontinue; forsake. [from Latin *renuntiare*] □ **renouncement** *n.* **renouncer** *n.*

renovate *v.tr.* **1** restore to good condition; repair. **2** make new again. [based on Latin *renovatus* 'renewed'] □ **renovation** *n.* **renovator** *n.*

renown *n.* fame; high distinction (*a city of great renown*). [from Old French *renon*]

renowned *adj.* famous; celebrated.

rent[1] ● *n.* **1** a tenant's periodical payment to an owner for the use of land or premises. **2** payment for the use of a service, equipment, etc. ● *v.* **1** *tr.* (often foll. by *from*) take, occupy, or use at a rent (*rented a cottage from the local farmer*). **2** *tr.* (often foll. by *out*) let or hire (a thing) for rent. **3** *intr.* (foll. by *at, for*) esp. *N. Amer.* be let or hired out at a specified rate (*the land rents at £100 per month*). [from Old French *rente*]

rent[2] *n.* **1** a large tear in a garment etc. **2** an opening in clouds etc. [from an obsolete variant of REND]

rent[3] *past* and *past part.* of REND.

rent-a- *comb.form* often *joc.* denoting availability for hire (*rent-a-van; rent-a-crowd*).

rental *n.* **1** the amount paid or received as rent. **2** the act of renting. **3** *N. Amer.* a rented house etc.

rent boy *n.* *Brit.* a young male prostitute.

renumber *v.tr.* change the number or numbers given to.

renunciation *n.* **1** the act or an instance of renouncing or giving up. **2** self-denial. **3** a document expressing renunciation. [from Late Latin *renuntiatio*] □ **renunciant** *n. & adj.* **renunciatory** *adj.*

reoccupy *v.tr.* (**-ies, -ied**) occupy again. □ **reoccupation** *n.*

reoccur *v.intr.* (**reoccurred, reoccurring**) occur again or habitually. □ **reoccurrence** *n.*

reoffend *v.intr.* offend again; commit a further offence. □ **reoffender** *n.*

reopen *v.tr. & intr.* open again.

reorder ● *v.tr.* order again. ● *n.* a renewed or repeated order for goods.

RENAISSANCE

The Birth of Venus (*c.*1486), SANDRO BOTTICELLI

The Renaissance saw an intellectual and artistic 'rebirth' in Europe, built around an interest in naturalism and the revival of the art and literature of classical Rome. Architects studied proportions and features of Roman buildings, while painters developed an interest in allegory, myth, history, and the technique of perspective.

PALAZZO STROZZI (1489), ITALY

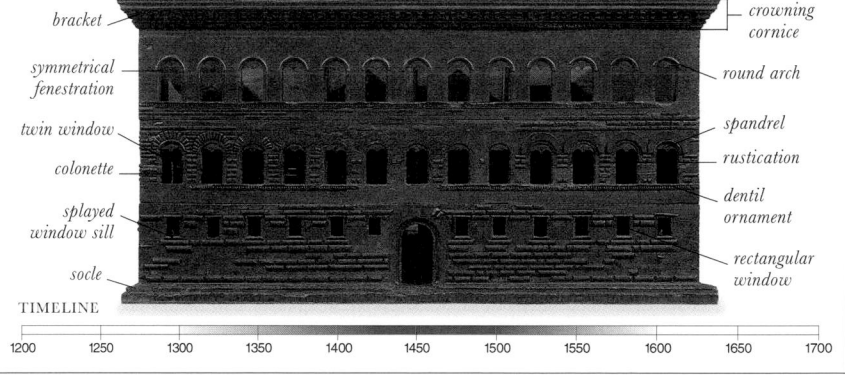

bracket — symmetrical fenestration — twin window — colonette — splayed window sill — socle — crowning cornice — round arch — spandrel — rustication — dentil ornament — rectangular window

TIMELINE
1200   1250   1300   1350   1400   1450   1500   1550   1600   1650   1700

R

reorganize *v.tr.* (also **-ise**) organize differently. □ **reorganization** *n.*

reorient *v.tr.* **1** give a new direction to (ideas etc.); redirect (a thing). **2** help (a person) find his or her bearings again. **3** change the outlook of (a person). **4** (refl., often foll. by *to*) adjust oneself to or come to terms with something.

reorientate *v.tr.* = REORIENT. □ **reorientation** *n.*

rep[1] *colloq.* ● *n.* a representative, esp. a commercial traveller. ● *v.intr.* (**repped, repping**) act as a representative for a company, product, etc.

rep[2] *n. colloq.* **1** repertory. **2** a repertory theatre or company.

rep[3] *n.* (also **repp**) a textile fabric with a corded surface, used in curtains and upholstery. [from French *reps*]

repack *v.tr.* pack again.

repackage *v.tr.* **1** package again or differently. **2** present in a new form. □ **repackaging** *n.*

repaginate *v.tr.* paginate again; renumber the pages of.

repaid *past* and *past part.* of REPAY.

repaint ● *v.tr.* **1** paint again or differently. **2** restore the paint or colouring of. ● *n.* an act of repainting.

repair[1] ● *v.tr.* **1** restore to good condition after damage or wear. **2** renovate or mend by replacing or fixing parts or by compensating for loss or exhaustion. **3** set right or make amends for (loss, wrong, error, etc.). ● *n.* **1** the act or an instance of restoring to sound condition (*in need of repair; closed during repair*). **2** the result of this (*the repair is hardly visible*). **3** good or relative condition for working or using (*must be kept in repair; in good repair*). [from Latin *reparare*] □ **repairable** *adj.* **repairer** *n.*

repair[2] *v.intr.* (foll. by *to*) resort; have recourse; go often or in great numbers or for a specific purpose (*repaired to Spain*). [from Late Latin *repatriare* 'to repatriate']

repairman *n.* (*pl.* **-men**) a man who repairs machinery etc.

repaper *v.tr.* paper (a wall etc.) again.

reparable /rep-ă-ră-bŭl/ *adj.* (of a loss etc.) that can be made good. [from Latin *reparabilis*]

reparation *n.* **1** the act or an instance of making amends. **2 a** compensation. **b** (esp. in *pl.*) compensation for war damage paid by a defeated state. [from Late Latin *reparatio*]

repartee /rep-ar-tee/ *n.* **1** the practice or faculty of making witty retorts. **2 a** a witty retort. **b** witty retorts collectively. [from French *repartie* (fem.) 'retorted', used as a noun]

repast *n.* esp. *formal* **1** a meal, esp. of a specified kind (*a light repast*). **2** food and drink supplied for or eaten at a meal. [based on Late Latin *repastus* 'fed']

repatriate ● *v.tr.* restore (a person) to his or her native land. ● *n.* a person who has been repatriated. [based on Late Latin *repatriatus* 'repatriated'] □ **repatriation** *n.*

repay *v.* (*past* and *past part.* **repaid**) **1** *tr.* pay back (money). **2** *tr.* return (a blow, visit, etc.). **3** *tr.* make repayment to (a person). **4** *tr.* requite (a service, action, etc.) (*must repay their kindness; the book repays close study*). **5** *tr.* give in recompense. **6** *intr.* make repayment. □ **repayable** *adj.* **repayment** *n.*

repeal ● *v.tr.* revoke or annul (a law, an Act of Parliament, etc.). ● *n.* the act or an instance of repealing. [from Old French *rapeler*]

repeat ● *v.* **1** *tr.* say or do over again. **2** *tr.* recite, rehearse, or reproduce (something from memory) (*repeated a poem*). **3** *tr.* say or report (something heard). **4** *tr.* imitate (an action etc.). **5** *intr.* recur; appear again (*a repeating pattern*). **6** *tr.* used for emphasis (*am not, repeat not, going*). **7** *intr.* (of food) be tasted intermittently for some time after being swallowed as a result of belching or indigestion. ● *n.* **1 a** the act or an instance of repeating. **b** a thing repeated (often *attrib.*: *repeat prescription*). **2** a repeated broadcast. **3** *Mus.* **a** a passage intended to be repeated. **b** a

mark indicating this. **4** a pattern repeated in wallpaper etc. □ **repeat itself** recur in the same form. **repeat oneself** say or do the same thing over again. [from Latin *repetere* 'to seek again'] □ **repeatable** *adj.* **repeatability** *n.* **repeatedly** *adv.*

repeater *n.* **1** a person or thing that repeats. **2** a firearm which fires several shots without reloading. **3** a watch or clock which repeats its last strike when required. **4** a device for the automatic retransmission or amplification of an electrically transmitted message.

repel *v.tr.* (**repelled, repelling**) **1** drive back; ward off (*repel an assailant*). **2** refuse to accept. **3** be repulsive to. **4** resist mixing with or admitting (*oil repels water*). **5** (often *absol.*) ▼ (of a magnetic pole) push away from itself (*like poles repel*). [from Latin *repellere*] □ **repeller** *n.*

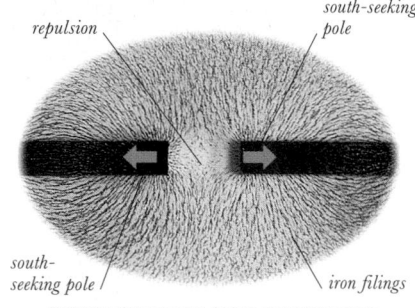

repulsion · south-seeking pole · south-seeking pole · iron filings

REPEL: DEMONSTRATION OF REPULSION BETWEEN MAGNETIC POLES

repellent ● *adj.* **1** that repels. **2** disgusting, repulsive. ● *n.* a substance that repels esp. insects etc. □ **repellence** *n.* **repellency** *n.* **repellently** *adv.*

repent *v.* **1** *intr.* (often foll. by *of*) feel deep sorrow about one's actions etc. **2** *tr.* (also *absol.*) wish one had not done, regret (one's wrong, omission, etc.); resolve not to continue (a wrongdoing etc.). [from Old French *repentir*] □ **repentance** *n.* **repentant** *adj.* **repenter** *n.*

repercussion *n.* **1** an indirect effect or reaction following an event or action (*consider the repercussions of moving*). **2** the recoil after impact. **3** an echo. [from Latin *repercussio*]

repertoire /rep-er-twah/ *n.* **1** a stock of pieces etc. that a company or a performer knows or is prepared to give. **2** a stock of regularly performed pieces, regularly used techniques, etc. (*went through his repertoire of excuses*). [from French *répertoire*]

repertory *n.* (*pl.* **-ies**) = REPERTOIRE. **2** the theatrical performance of various plays for short periods by one company. **3 a** a repertory company. **b** repertory theatres regarded collectively. **4** a store or collection, esp. of information, instances, etc. [from Late Latin *repertorium*]

repertory company *n.* a theatrical company that performs plays from a repertoire.

répétiteur *n.* **1** a tutor or coach of musicians, esp. opera singers. **2** a person who supervises ballet rehearsals etc. [French]

repetition *n.* **1 a** the act or an instance of repeating or being repeated. **b** the thing repeated. **2** a copy. [from French *répétition*]

repetitious *adj.* characterized by repetition, esp. when unnecessary or tiresome. □ **repetitiously** *adv.* **repetitiousness** *n.*

repetitive *adj.* = REPETITIOUS. □ **repetitively** *adv.* **repetitiveness** *n.*

repetitive strain injury *n.* injury arising from the prolonged use of particular muscles.

rephrase *v.tr.* express in an alternative way.

repine *v.intr. literary* fret; be discontented.

replace *v.tr.* **1** put back in place. **2** take the place of; be substituted for. **3** find or provide a substitute for. **4** (often foll. by *with*, *by*) fill up the place of. **5** (in

passive, often foll. by *by*) be succeeded or have one's place filled by another; be superseded. □ **replaceable** *adj.* **replacer** *n.*

replacement *n.* **1** the act or an instance of replacing or being replaced. **2** a person or thing that takes the place of another.

replan *v.tr.* (**replanned, replanning**) plan again or differently.

replant *v.tr.* **1** transfer (a plant etc.) to a larger pot, a new site, etc. **2** plant (ground) again.

replay ● *v.tr.* play (a match, recording, etc.) again. ● *n.* the act or an instance of replaying a match, a recording, or a recorded incident in a game etc.

replenish *v.tr.* **1** fill up again. **2** renew (a supply etc.). **3** (as **replenished** *adj.*) filled; fully stored or stocked; full. [from Old French *replenir*] □ **replenishment** *n.*

replete *adj.* **1** filled or well-supplied. **2** stuffed; gorged; sated. [from Latin *repletus* 'refilled'] □ **repletion** *n.*

replica *n.* **1** a duplicate of a work made by the original artist. **2** ► a facsimile, an exact copy. **3** a copy or model, esp. on a smaller scale. [Italian]

replicate *v.tr.* **1** repeat (an experiment etc.). **2** make a replica of. **3** fold back. [from Latin *replicatus* 'refolded'] □ **replicable** *adj.* (in sense 1). **replicability** *n.* (in sense 1). **replicative** *adj.* **replicator** *n.* (esp. in sense 2).

REPLICA OF AN ANCIENT ROMAN HELMET

replication *n.* **1** the act or an instance of copying. **2** a copy. **3** the process by which genetic material or a living organism gives rise to a copy of itself.

reply ● *v.* (**-ies, -ied**) **1** *intr.* make an answer, respond in word or action. **2** *tr.* say in answer (*he replied, 'Please yourself'*). ● *n.* (*pl.* **-ies**) **1** the act of replying (*what did they say in reply?*). **2** what is replied; a response. [from Latin *replicare* 'to unfold', later 'to reply']

reply-paid *adj.* **1** (of an envelope etc.) for which the addressee undertakes to pay postage. **2** *hist.* (of a telegram) with the cost of a reply prepaid by the sender.

repoint *v.tr.* point (esp. brickwork) again.

repopulate *v.tr.* populate again or increase the population of. □ **repopulation** *n.*

report ● *v.* **1** *tr.* **a** bring back or give an account of. **b** state as fact or news, narrate or describe or repeat, esp. as an eyewitness or hearer etc. **c** relate as spoken by another. **2** *tr.* make an official or formal statement about. **3** *tr.* name or specify (an offender or offence) (*shall report you for insubordination; reported them to the police*). **4** *intr.* present oneself as having returned or arrived (*report to the manager on arrival*). **5** *tr.* (also *absol.*) take down word for word or summarize or write a description of for publication. **6** *intr.* **a** make, draw up, or send in a report. **b** (usu. foll. by *on*) investigate as a journalist; act as a reporter. **7** *intr.* (foll. by *to*) be responsible to (a superior, supervisor, etc.) (*reports directly to the managing director*). ● *n.* **1** an account given or opinion formally expressed after investigation or consideration. **2** a description, summary, or reproduction of an event, speech, or law case, esp. for the media. **3** common talk; rumour. **4** the way a person or thing is spoken of (*I hear a good report of you*). **5** a periodical statement on (esp. a school pupil's) work, conduct, etc. **6** the sound of an explosion. □ **report back** deliver a report to the person, organization,

R

etc. for whom one acts etc. **report progress** state what has been done so far. [from Latin *reportare*] □ **reportable** *adj.* **reportedly** *adv.*

reportage /re-por-**tah**zh/ *n.* **1** the reporting of news etc. for the media. **2** the typical style of this. **3** factual presentation in a book etc.

reported speech *n.* the speaker's words with the changes of person, tense, etc. usual in reports, e.g. *he said that he would go.*

reporter *n.* **1** a person employed to report news etc. for the media. **2** a person who reports.

report stage *n.* (in the UK) the debate on a bill in the House of Commons or House of Lords after it is reported.

repose[1] ● *n.* **1** the cessation of activity or excitement or toil. **2** sleep. **3** a peaceful or quiescent state; stillness; tranquillity. **4** *Art* a restful effect; harmonious combination. ● *v.* **1** *intr. & refl.* lie down in rest (*reposed on a sofa*). **2** *tr.* (often foll. by *on*) lay (one's head etc.) to rest (on a pillow etc.). **3** *intr.* lie, be lying or laid, esp. in sleep or death. **4** *tr.* give rest to; refresh with rest. **5** *intr.* (foll. by *on*, *upon*) be supported or based on. [from Late Latin *repausare* 'to pause again'] □ **reposeful** *adj.* **reposefully** *adv.*

repose[2] *v.tr.* (foll. by *in*) place (trust etc.) in. [earlier in sense 'to replace, restore': suggested by Latin *repositus* 'replaced']

reposition *v.* **1** *tr.* move or place in a different position. **2** *intr.* alter one's position.

repository *n.* (*pl.* **-ies**) **1** a place where things are stored or may be found, esp. a warehouse or museum. **2** a receptacle. **3 a** a book, person, etc. regarded as a store of information etc. **b** the recipient of confidences or secrets. [from Latin *repositorium*]

repossess *v.tr.* regain possession of (esp. property or goods on which repayment of a debt is in arrears). □ **repossession** *n.*

repot *v.tr.* (**repotted**, **repotting**) put (a plant) in another pot.

repp var. of REP[3].

reprehend *v.tr.* rebuke; find fault with. [from Latin *reprehendere*] □ **reprehension** *n.*

reprehensible *adj.* deserving censure or rebuke; blameworthy. [from Late Latin *reprehensibilis*] □ **reprehensibility** *n.* **reprehensibly** *adv.*

represent *v.tr.* **1** stand for or correspond to (*the comment does not represent all our views*). **2** be a specimen or example of (*all types of people were represented in the audience*). **3** act as an embodiment of; symbolize (*the sovereign represents the majesty of the state*; *numbers are represented by letters*). **4** call up in the mind by description or portrayal or imagination; place a likeness of before the mind or senses. **5** serve or be meant as a likeness of. **6 a** state by way of expostulation or persuasion (*represented the rashness of it*). **b** (foll. by *to*) try to bring (the facts influencing conduct) home to (*represented the risks to his client*). **7** (often foll. by *as*, *to be*) describe or depict as; declare or make out (*represented them as martyrs*; *not what you represent it to be*). **8** (foll. by *that* + clause) allege. **9** show, or play the part of, on stage. **10** be a substitute or deputy for; be entitled to act or speak for (*the Queen was represented by the Duke of Edinburgh*). **11** be elected as a member of a legislature etc. by (*represents a rural constituency*). [from Latin *repraesentare*] □ **representable** *adj.*

re-present *v.tr.* present (esp. a cheque) again. □ **re-presentation** *n.*

representation *n.* **1** the act or an instance of representing or being represented. **2** an image, likeness, or reproduction of a thing. **3** (esp. in *pl.*) a statement made by way of allegation or to convey opinion. □ **representational** *adj.*

representative ● *adj.* **1** typical of a class. **2** containing typical specimens of all or many classes (*a representative sample*). **3 a** consisting of elected deputies etc. **b** based on representation by such deputies (*representative government*). **4** (foll. by *of*) serving as a portrayal or symbol of (*representative of their attitude to work*). ● *n.* **1** (foll. by *of*) a sample, specimen, or typical embodiment of. **2 a** the agent of a person or society. **b** a commercial traveller. **3** a delegate; a substitute. **4** a deputy in a representative assembly. □ **representatively** *adv.* **representativeness** *n.*

repress *v.tr.* **1 a** keep under; quell. **b** suppress; prevent from sounding, rioting, or bursting out. **2 a** suppress or control (thoughts, desires, etc.) in oneself or another. **b** *Psychol.* actively exclude (an unwelcome thought) from conscious awareness. **3** (usu. as **repressed** *adj.*) subject (a person) to the suppression of his or her thoughts or impulses. [based on Latin *repressus* 'pressed back'] □ **repressible** *adj.* **repression** *n.* **repressive** *adj.* **repressively** *adv.* **repressiveness** *n.* **repressor** *n. Biochem.*

reprieve ● *v.tr.* **1 a** relieve or rescue from impending punishment. **b** remit, commute, or postpone the execution of (a condemned person). **2** give respite to. ● *n.* **1 a** the act or an instance of reprieving or being reprieved. **b** a warrant for this. **2** respite; a respite or temporary escape. [based on Old French *repris* 'taken back']

reprimand ● *n.* an official or sharp rebuke. ● *v.tr.* administer this to. [based on Latin *reprimenda* '(things) to be repressed']

reprint ● *v.tr.* print again. ● *n.* **1** the act or an instance of reprinting a book etc. **2 a** a book etc. reprinted. **b** an offprint. **3** the quantity reprinted.

reprisal *n.* an act of retaliation. [from medieval Latin *reprisalia*]

reprise ● *n.* **1** a repeated passage in music. **2** a repeated item in a musical programme. ● *v.tr.* repeat (a performance, song, etc.); restage, rewrite. [French fem. of *repris* 'taken again']

repro *n.* (*pl.* **-os**) (often *attrib.*) *colloq.* a reproduction or copy.

reproach ● *v.tr.* **1** express disapproval to (a person) for a fault etc. **2** scold; rebuke; censure. ● *n.* **1** a rebuke or censure (*heaped reproaches on them*). **2** a thing that brings disgrace or discredit (*their behaviour is a reproach to us all*). **3** a disgraced or discredited state (*live in reproach and ignominy*). □ **above** (or **beyond**) **reproach** perfect. [from Old French *reproche* (n.), *reprocher* (v.)]

reproachful *adj.* full of or expressing reproach. □ **reproachfully** *adv.*

reprobate ● *n.* an unprincipled person; a person of highly immoral character. ● *adj.* **1** immoral. **2** hardened in sin. ● *v.tr.* express or feel disapproval of; censure. [from Latin *reprobatus* 'disapproved'] □ **reprobation** *n.*

reprocess *v.tr.* process again or differently.

reproduce *v.* **1** *tr.* produce a copy or representation of. **2** *tr.* replicate or cause to be seen or heard etc. again (*tried to reproduce the sound exactly*). **3** *intr.* produce further members of the same species by natural means. **4** *refl.* produce offspring (*reproduced itself several times*). □ **reproducer** *n.* **reproducible** *adj.* **reproducibility** *n.* **reproducibly** *adv.*

reproduction *n.* **1** the act or an instance of reproducing. **2** a copy of a work of art. **3** (*attrib.*) (of furniture etc.) made in imitation of a certain style or of an earlier period. **4** the quality of reproduced sound. □ **reproductive** *adj.* **reproductively** *adv.*

reproductive organs *n.* ▼ the internal and external structures of a person, animal, or plant which are concerned with reproduction, especially sexual reproduction.

reprogram *v.tr.* (also **reprogramme**) (**reprogrammed**, **reprogramming**) program (esp. a computer) again or differently. □ **reprogrammable** *adj.*

reprographics *n.pl.* (usu. treated as *sing.*) = REPROGRAPHY.

reprography *n.* the science and practice of copying documents by photography, xerography, etc. □ **reprographic** *adj.*

reproof *n.* **1** blame (*a glance of reproof*). **2** a rebuke. [from Old French *reprove*]

R

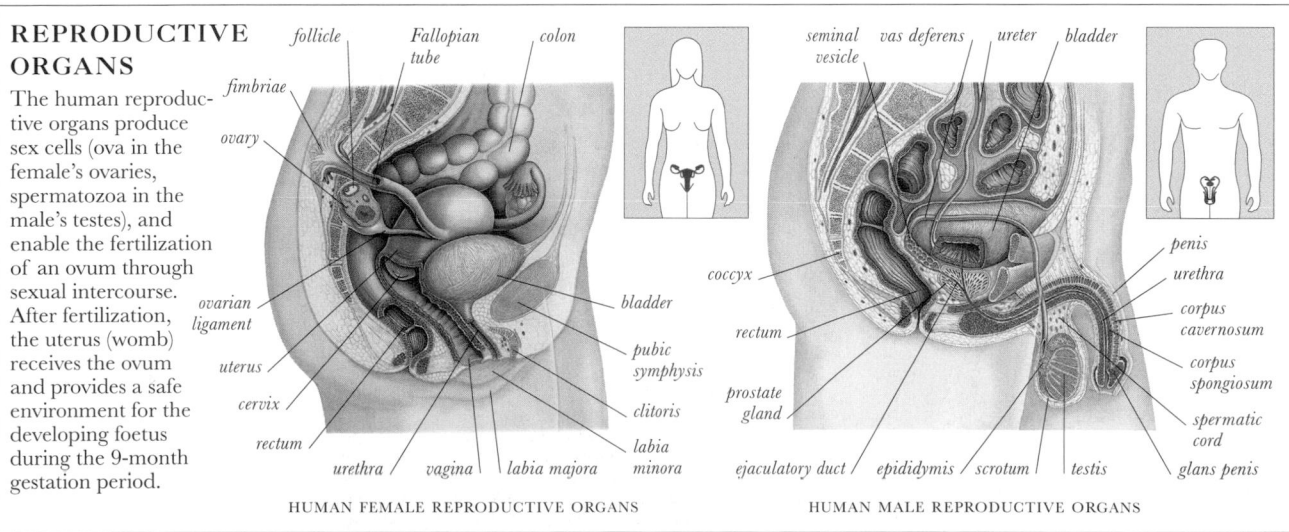

REPRODUCTIVE ORGANS

The human reproductive organs produce sex cells (ova in the female's ovaries, spermatozoa in the male's testes), and enable the fertilization of an ovum through sexual intercourse. After fertilization, the uterus (womb) receives the ovum and provides a safe environment for the developing foetus during the 9-month gestation period.

follicle *Fallopian tube* *colon* *fimbriae* *ovary* *ovarian ligament* *uterus* *cervix* *rectum* *urethra* *vagina* *labia majora* *labia minora* *clitoris* *pubic symphysis* *bladder*

HUMAN FEMALE REPRODUCTIVE ORGANS

seminal vesicle *vas deferens* *ureter* *bladder* *coccyx* *rectum* *prostate gland* *ejaculatory duct* *epididymis* *scrotum* *testis* *penis* *urethra* *corpus cavernosum* *corpus spongiosum* *spermatic cord* *glans penis*

HUMAN MALE REPRODUCTIVE ORGANS

reprove *v.tr.* rebuke. [from Late Latin *reprobare* 'to disapprove'] □ **reprovingly** *adv.*

reptile *n.* **1** ▼ any cold-blooded scaly animal of the class Reptilia, including snakes, lizards, crocodiles, turtles, tortoises, etc. **2** a mean, grovelling, or repulsive person. [from Latin *reptilis* 'crawling'] □ **reptilian** *adj. & n.*

republic *n.* a state in which supreme power is held by the people or their elected representatives or by an elected or nominated president, not by a monarch etc. [from Latin *res* 'concern' + *publicus* 'public']

republican ● *adj.* **1** of or constituted as a republic. **2** characteristic of a republic. **3** advocating or supporting republican government. ● *n.* **1** a person advocating or supporting republican government. **2** (**Republican**) (in the US) a member or supporter of the Republi-

can Party. **3** (also **Republican**) an advocate of a united Ireland. □ **republicanism** *n.*

republish *v.tr.* (also *absol.*) publish again or in a new edition etc. □ **republication** *n.*

repudiate *v.tr.* **1** a disown; disavow; reject. **b** refuse dealings with. **c** deny. **2** refuse to recognize or obey (authority or a treaty). **3** refuse to discharge (an obligation or debt). [based on Latin *repudiatus* 'divorced'] □ **repudiation** *n.*

■ **Usage** See Usage Note at REFUTE.

repugnance *n.* (also **repugnancy**) **1** antipathy; aversion. **2** inconsistency or incompatibility of ideas, statements, etc. [from Latin *repugnantia*]

repugnant *adj.* **1** extremely distasteful. **2** contradictory. **3** incompatible. [from French *répugnant*]

repulse ● *v.tr.* **1** drive back by force of arms. **2** a rebuff. **b** refuse. **3** be repulsive to, repel. ● *n.* **1** the act or an instance of repulsing or being repulsed. **2** a rebuff. [based on Latin *repulsus* 'driven back']

repulsion *n.* **1** aversion; disgust. **2** esp. *Physics* the force by which bodies tend to repel each other or increase their mutual distance.

repulsive *adj.* causing aversion or loathing; disgusting. □ **repulsively** *adv.* **repulsiveness** *n.*

repurchase ● *v.tr.* purchase again. ● *n.* the act or an instance of purchasing again.

reputable /rep-yuu-tă-bŭl/ *adj.* of good repute; respectable. □ **reputably** *adv.*

reputation *n.* **1** what is generally said or believed about a person's or thing's character (*has a reputation for dishonesty*). **2** the state of being well thought of; distinction; respectability (*an international reputation in her field*). **3** (foll. by *of, for* + verbal noun) credit, fame, or notoriety (*has the reputation of driving hard bargains*). [from Latin *reputatio*]

repute ● *n.* reputation (*known by repute*). ● *v.tr.* **1** (as **reputed** *adj.*) be generally considered or reckoned (*is reputed to be the best*). **2** (as **reputed** *adj.*) passing as, but probably not (*his reputed father*). [from Latin *reputare*] □ **reputedly** *adv.*

request ● *n.* **1** the act or an instance of asking for something (*came at his request*). **2** a thing asked for. **3** the state of being sought after; demand (*in great request*). **4** a a letter etc. asking for a particular record etc. to be played on a radio programme, often with a personal message. **b** the record etc. played in response to such a letter etc. ● *v.tr.* **1** ask to be given or allowed or favoured with (*request a hearing*; *requests your presence*). **2** (foll. by *to* + infin.) ask a person to do something (*requested her to answer*). **3** (foll. by *that* + clause) ask that. □ **by** (or **on**) **request** in response to an expressed wish. [based on Latin *requaestus* 'sought again'] □ **requester** *n.*

request programme *n.* a radio etc. programme composed of items requested by the audience.

request stop *n. Brit.* a stop at which a bus halts only on a passenger's request.

requiem /rek-wi-em/ *n.* **1** (**Requiem**) (also *attrib.*) esp. *RC Ch.* a Mass for the repose of the souls of the dead. **2** *Mus.* a musical setting for this. **3** (often foll. by *for*) a memorial (*his book was a fitting requiem*). [Latin accusative of *requies* 'rest', initial word of the Mass]

require *v.tr.* **1** need; depend on for success or fulfilment (*the work requires patience*). **2** lay down as an imperative (*required by law*). **3** command; instruct (a person etc.). **4** order; insist on (an action or measure). **5** demand (of or from a person) as a right. **6** wish to have (*is there anything else you require?*). [from Latin *requirere* 'to search for'] □ **requirement** *n.*

requisite ● *adj.* required by circumstances; necessary to success etc. ● *n.* a thing needed. [from Latin *requisitus* 'necessary']

requisition ● *n.* **1** an official order laying claim to the use of property or materials. **2** a formal written demand that some duty should be performed. **3** being called or put into service. ● *v.tr.* demand the

REPTILE

Reptiles have waterproof skin covered in keratinous scales or shields, which enables them to survive in dry habitats. Most reptiles lay eggs. Unlike amphibians, they do not have a larval stage, and the young hatch as miniature forms of their parent. There are more than 6,000 species of reptile, over 95 per cent of which belong to the order Squamata.

EXTERNAL FEATURES OF AN ASIATIC WATER MONITOR (*Varanus salvator*)

well-developed muscular tail

forked tongue

ear opening

overlapping, granular scales

clawed limbs

banded markings

legs splayed laterally

spots on juvenile

five digits

SKELETON OF A MONITOR LIZARD

maxilla   *orbit*   *rib*   *thoracolumbar vertebrae*   *sacrum*   *caudal vertebrae*

mandible   *scapula*   *ulna*   *radius*   *tibia*   *fibula*

REPTILE ORDERS

SQUAMATA (lizards, snakes)
▷ LIZARD, SNAKE

RHYNCHOCEPHALIA (tuatara)

CROCODILIA (alligators, crocodiles, gharial)
▷ ALLIGATOR, CROCODILE

CHELONIA (terrapins, tortoises, turtles)
▷ CHELONIAN

R

use or supply of, esp. by requisition order. □ **under** (or **in**) **requisition** being used or applied. □ **requisitioner** *n.*

requite *v.tr.* **1** make return for (a service). **2** reward or avenge (a favour or injury). **3** make return to (a person). **4** repay with good or evil (*requite like for like*; *requite hate with love*). [based on obsolete *quite*, variant of QUIT] □ **requital** *n.*

reran *past* of RERUN.

reread *v.tr.* (*past* and *past part.* **reread**) read again. □ **re-readable** *adj.*

re-record *v.tr.* record again.

reredos *n.* *Eccl.* ▼ an ornamental screen covering the wall at the back of an altar. ▷ CATHEDRAL. [from Old French *arere* 'behind' + *dos* 'back']

REREDOS: INTERIOR OF A CHURCH SHOWING THE ALTAR AND REREDOS

re-release ● *v.tr.* release (a record, film, etc.) again. ● *n.* a re-released record, film, etc.

re-roof *v.tr.* provide (a building etc.) with a new roof.

re-route *v.tr.* (**-routeing** or **-routing**) send or carry by a different route.

rerun ● *v.tr.* (**rerunning**; *past* **reran**; *past part.* **rerun**) run (a race, film, etc.) again. ● *n.* **1** the act or an instance of rerunning. **2** a film, television programme, etc. shown again.

resale *n.* the sale of a thing previously bought. □ **resaleable** *adj.* (also **resalable**).

resat *past* and *past part.* of RESIT.

reschedule *v.tr.* alter the schedule of; replan.

rescind *v.tr.* abrogate, revoke, cancel. [from Latin *rescindere* 'to divide off'] □ **rescission** *n.*

rescue ● *v.tr.* (**rescues**, **rescued**, **rescuing**) save or set free from danger or harm. ● *n.* the act or an instance of rescuing or being rescued; deliverance. [from Old French *rescoure*] □ **rescuable** *adj.* **rescuer** *n.*

reseal *v.tr.* seal again. □ **resealable** *adj.*

research ● *n.* **1 a** the systematic investigation into and study of materials, sources, etc., in order to establish facts and reach new conclusions. **b** (usu. in *pl.*) an endeavour to discover new or collate old facts etc. by the scientific study of a subject or by a course of critical investigation. **2** (*attrib.*) engaged in or intended for research. ● *v.* **1** *tr.* do research into (a subject) or for (a book etc.). **2** *intr.* make researches. [from obsolete French *recerche*] □ **researchable** *adj.* **researcher** *n.*

research and development *n.* (in industry etc.) work directed towards the innovation, introduction, and improvement of products and processes.

reseat *v.tr.* **1** (also *refl.*) seat (oneself, a person, etc.) again. **2** provide with a fresh seat or seats. **3** realign or repair in order to fit (a tap, nail, etc.) into its former correct position.

reseed *v.tr.* sow (an area of land) with seed again, esp. grass seed.

reselect *v.tr.* select again or differently. □ **reselection** *n.*

resell *v.tr.* (*past* and *past part.* **resold**) sell (an object etc.) after buying it. □ **reseller** *n.*

resemblance *n.* (often foll. by *to*, *between*, *of*) a likeness or similarity. [from Anglo-French] □ **resemblant** *adj.*

resemble *v.tr.* be like; have a similarity to, or the same appearance as. [from Old French *resembler*]

resent /ri-**zent**/ *v.tr.* show or feel indignation at; be aggrieved by. [from obsolete French *resentir*]

resentful *adj.* feeling resentment. □ **resentfully** *adv.* **resentfulness** *n.*

resentment *n.* (often foll. by *at*, *of*) indignant or bitter feelings; anger.

reservation *n.* **1** the act or an instance of reserving or being reserved. **2** a booking (of a room etc.). **3** the thing booked, e.g. a hotel room. **4** an express or tacit limitation or exception to an agreement etc. **5** (in full **central reservation**) *Brit.* a strip of land between road carriageways. **6** an area of land reserved for occupation by N. American Indians etc.

reserve ● *v.tr.* **1** postpone, put aside, keep back for a later occasion or special use. **2** order to be specially retained or allocated for a particular person or at a particular time. **3** retain or secure (*reserve the right to*). **4** postpone delivery of (judgement etc.). ● *n.* **1** a thing reserved for future use; an extra amount (*energy reserves*). **2** a limitation, qualification, or exception attached to something (*without reserve*). **3** self-restraint; reticence. **4** *Brit.* a company's profit added to capital. **5** (in *sing.* or *pl.*) assets kept readily available as cash or at a central bank, or as gold or foreign exchange (*reserve currency*). **6** (in *sing.* or *pl.*) **a** troops withheld from action to reinforce or protect others. **b** additional military forces, available in an emergency. **7** a member of the military reserve. **8 a** an extra player chosen to be a possible substitute in a team. **b** (in *pl.*: prec. by *the*) the second-choice team. **9** a place reserved for special use, esp.: **a** as a habitat for a native people. **b** for wildlife. □ **in reserve** unused and available if required. [from Latin *reservare*] □ **reservable** *adj.* **reserver** *n.*

reserved *adj.* **1** reticent; slow to reveal emotion or opinions. **2 a** set apart, destined for some use or fate. **b** (often foll. by *for*, *to*) left by fate for; falling first or only to. □ **reservedly** *adv.* **reservedness** *n.*

reserve price *n.* the lowest acceptable price stipulated for an item sold at an auction.

reservist *n.* a member of the reserve forces.

reservoir   *dam*   **reservoir** /**rez**-er-vwah/ *n.* **1** ◀ a large natural or artificial lake used as a source of water supply. **2 a** any natural or artificial receptacle for or of fluid. **b** a place where fluid etc. collects. **3** a part of a machine etc. holding fluid. **4** (usu. foll. by *of*) a reserve or supply, esp. of information etc. [from French *réservoir*]

reset *v.tr.* (**resetting**; *past* and *past part.* **reset**) set again or differently. □ **resettable** *adj.*

resettle *v.tr.* & *intr.* settle again in a new or former place. □ **resettlement** *n.*

RESERVOIR

reshape *v.tr.* shape or form again or differently.

reshuffle ● *v.tr.* **1** shuffle (cards) again. **2** interchange the posts of (government ministers etc.). ● *n.* the act or an instance of reshuffling.

reside *v.intr.* **1** (of a person) have one's home, dwell permanently. **2** (of power, a right, etc.) rest or be vested in. **3** (of an incumbent official) be in residence. **4** (foll. by *in*) (of a quality) be present or inherent in. [Middle English]

residence *n.* **1** the act or an instance of residing. **2 a** the place where a person resides. **b** the official house of a government minister etc. **c** a mansion. □ **in residence** living in or occupying a specified place, esp. for the performance of duties or work. [based on Latin *residēre* 'to reside']

residency *n.* (*pl.* **-ies**) **1** = RESIDENCE 1, 2b. **2** *N. Amer.* a period of specialized medical training; the position of a resident.

resident ● *n.* **1** (often foll. by *of*) **a** a permanent inhabitant. **b** a bird of a non-migratory species. **2 a** *Brit.* a guest in a hotel etc. staying overnight. **b** *US* a person who boards at a boarding school. ● *adj.* **1** residing; in residence. **2 a** having quarters on the premises of one's work etc. **b** working regularly in a particular place. **3** located; inherent (*resident in the nerves*). **4** (of birds etc.) non-migratory. [from Latin *resident-* 'residing'] □ **residentship** *n.* (in sense 3 of *n.*).

residential *adj.* **1** suitable for or occupied by private houses (*residential area*). **2** used as a residence (*residential hotel*). **3** based on or connected with residence (*residential qualification for voters*). □ **residentially** *adv.*

residua *pl.* of RESIDUUM.

residual *adj.* remaining; left as a residue or residuum. □ **residually** *adv.*

residuary *adj.* **1** of the residue of an estate (*residuary bequest*). **2** of or being a residuum; residual; still remaining.

residue *n.* **1** what is left over or remains; a remainder; the rest. **2** *Law* what remains of an estate after the payment of charges, debts, and bequests. **3** esp. *Chem.* a residuum. [from Latin *residuum*]

residuum *n.* (*pl.* **residua**) **1** *Chem.* ▶ a substance left after combustion or evaporation. **2** a remainder or residue. [Latin, literally 'that remaining']

evaporating dish   *crystalline residuum*

tripod

bunsen burner

R

RESIDUUM: EXPERIMENT TO PRODUCE A RESIDUUM FROM A SOLUTION

resign *v.* **1** *intr.* (often foll. by *from*) give up office, one's employment, etc. **2** *tr.* (often foll. by *to*, *into*) give up (office, one's employment, etc.); surrender; hand over (a right, charge, task, etc.). **3** *tr.* give up (hope etc.). **4** *refl.* (usu. foll. by *to*) reconcile (oneself, one's mind, etc.) to the inevitable. [from Latin *resignare* 'to unseal, cancel'] □ **resigner** *n.*

resignation *n.* **1** the act or an instance of resigning, esp. from one's job or office. **2** the state of being resigned; the uncomplaining endurance of a sorrow or difficulty.

resigned *adj.* (often foll. by *to*) having resigned oneself; submissive, acquiescent. □ **resignedly** *adv.* **resignedness** *n.*

resilient *adj.* **1** (of a substance etc.) springing back; resuming its original shape after bending, compression, etc. **2** (of a person) readily recovering from shock, grief, etc. [from Latin *resilient-* 'springing back'] □ **resilience** *n.* **resiliency** *n.* **resiliently** *adv.*

resin ● *n.* **1** ► an adhesive inflammable substance insoluble in water, secreted by some plants, and often extracted by incision, esp. from fir and pine. **2** (in full **synthetic resin**) a solid or liquid organic compound made by polymerization etc. and used in plastics etc. ● *v.tr.* (**resined**, **resining**) rub or treat with resin. [from Latin *resina*] □ **resinate** *v.tr.* **resinoid** *adj. & n.* **resinous** *adj.*

resist ● *v.* **1** *tr.* withstand the action or effect of; repel. **2** *tr.* stop the course or progress of; prevent from reaching, penetrating, etc. **3** *tr.* abstain from (pleasure, temptation, etc.). **4** *tr.* strive against; try to impede; refuse to comply with (*resist arrest*). **5** *intr.* offer opposition; refuse to comply. ● *n.* a protective coating of a resistant substance, applied esp. to parts of calico that are not to take dye or to parts of pottery that are not to take glaze or lustre. □ **cannot** (or **could not** etc.) **resist 1** (foll. by verbal noun) feel very strongly inclined to (*cannot resist teasing me*). **2** is certain to be attracted etc. by (*can't resist chocolate*). [from Latin *resistere*] □ **resistant** *adj.* **resister** *n.* **resistible** *adj.*

resistance *n.* **1** the act or an instance of resisting; refusal to comply. **2** the power of resisting. **3 a** *Biol.* the ability to withstand adverse conditions. **b** *Med. & Biol.* lack of sensitivity to a drug, insecticide, etc., esp. owing to continued exposure or genetic change. **4** the impeding or stopping effect exerted by one material thing on another. **5** *Physics* **a** the property of hindering the conduction of electricity, heat, etc. **b** the measure of this in a body. **6** a resistor. **7** (in full **resistance movement**) a secret organization resisting authority, esp. in an occupied country.

resistive *adj.* **1** able to resist. **2** *Electr.* of or concerning resistance.

resistivity *n. Electr.* a measure of the resisting power of a specified material to the flow of an electric current.

resistor *n. Electr.* ▼ a device having resistance to the passage of an electrical current. ▷ RADIO

resit *Brit.* ● *v.tr.* (**resitting**; *past* and *past part.* **resat**) sit (an examination) again after failing. ● *n.* the act or an instance of resitting an examination.

resite *v.tr.* place on another site; relocate.

resize *v.tr.* alter the size of.

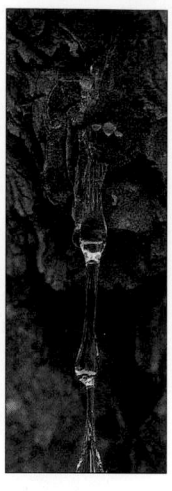
RESIN SECRETED FROM THE TRUNK OF A SCOTS PINE

reskill *v.tr.* teach, or equip with, new skills.

resold *past* and *past part.* of RESELL.

resoluble *adj.* **1** that can be resolved. **2** (foll. by *into*) analysable. [from Latin *resolubilis*]

resolute *adj.* (of a person or a person's mind or action) determined; firm of purpose. [from Latin *resolutus* 'resolved'] □ **resolutely** *adv.* **resoluteness** *n.*

resolution *n.* **1** a resolute temper or character; boldness and firmness of purpose. **2** a thing resolved on; an intention. **3 a** a formal expression of opinion or intention by a legislative body or public meeting. **b** the formulation of this (*passed a resolution*). **4** (usu. foll. by *of*) the act or an instance of solving doubt or a problem or question (*towards a resolution of the difficulty*). **5** esp. *Chem.* separation into components; decomposition. **6** (foll. by *into*) analysis; conversion into another form. **7** *Mus.* causing discord to pass into concord. **8** *Physics* etc. **a** the smallest interval measurable by a scientific (esp. optical) instrument; its ability to distinguish very small or very close objects. **b** the degree of detail visible in a photographic or television image.

resolve ● *v.* **1** *intr.* make up one's mind; decide firmly. **2** *tr.* (of circumstances etc.) cause (a person) to do this (*events resolved him to leave*). **3** *tr.* (foll. by *that* + clause) (of an assembly or meeting) pass a resolution by vote. **4** *intr. & tr.* (often foll. by *into*) separate or cause to separate into constituent parts; analyse. **5** *tr.* solve; clear up; settle (doubt, argument, etc.). **6** *tr. & intr. Mus.* convert or be converted into concord. ● *n.* **1 a** a firm mental decision or intention; a resolution. **b** *US* a formal resolution by a legislative body or public meeting. **2** resoluteness; steadfastness. [from Latin *resolvere*] □ **resolvable** *adj.* **resolvability** *n.* **resolver** *n.*

resolved *adj.* resolute, determined. □ **resolvedly** *adv.* **resolvedness** *n.*

resolving power *n. Physics* an instrument's ability to distinguish very small or very close objects.

resonance *n.* **1** the reinforcement or prolongation of sound by reflection or synchronous vibration. **2** *Mech.* a condition in which an object or system is subjected to an oscillating force having a frequency close to its own natural frequency. **3** *Chem.* the property of a molecule having a structure best represented by two or more forms rather than a single structural formula. **4** *Physics* a short-lived subatomic particle that is an excited state of a more

stable particle. [Old French, from Latin *resonantia* 'echo']

resonant *adj.* **1** (of sound) echoing, resounding; continuing to sound; reinforced or prolonged by reflection or synchronous vibration. **2** (of a body, room, etc.) tending to reinforce or prolong sounds esp. by synchronous vibration. **3** (often foll. by *with*) (of a place) resounding. **4** of or relating to resonance. [from Latin *resonant-* 'echoing'] □ **resonantly** *adv.*

resonate *v.intr.* produce or show resonance; resound. [based on Latin *resonatus* 'echoed'] □ **resonator** *n.*

resort ● *n.* **1** a place frequented esp. for holidays or for a specified purpose or quality. **2 a** a thing to which one has recourse; an expedient or measure (*a taxi was our best resort*). **b** (foll. by *to*) recourse; use of (*without resort to violence*). ● *v.intr.* **1** (foll. by *to*) turn to as an expedient. **2** (foll. by *to*) go or in large numbers to. □ **in the** (or **as a**) **last resort** when all else has failed. [from Old French *resortir* 'to come or go out again']

re-sort *v.tr.* sort again or differently.

resound *v.intr.* **1** (often foll. by *with*) (of a place) ring or echo. **2** (of a voice, sound, etc.) produce echoes; go on sounding. **3 a** (of fame etc.) be much talked of. **b** (foll. by *through*) produce a sensation (*resounded through Europe*). [Middle English, suggested by Old French *resoner*]

resounding *adj.* **1** in senses of RESOUND. **2** unmistakable; emphatic (*was a resounding success*). □ **resoundingly** *adv.*

resource ● *n.* **1** an expedient or device. **2** (usu. in *pl.*) **a** the means available to achieve an end, fulfil a function, etc. **b** a stock or supply that can be drawn on. **c** *N. Amer.* available assets. **3** (in *pl.*) a country's collective wealth or means of defence. **4** (often in *pl.*) skill in devising expedients (*a person of great resource*). ● *v.tr.* provide with resources. □ **one's own resources** one's own abilities, ingenuity, etc. [from French *ressource*] □ **resourceful** *adj.* **resourcefully** *adv.* **resourcefulness** *n.* **resourceless** *adj.* **resourcelessness** *n.*

respect ● *n.* **1** deferential esteem felt or shown towards a person or quality. **2 a** (foll. by *of, for*) heed or regard. **b** (foll. by *to*) attention to or consideration of (*without respect to the results*). **3** an aspect, detail, etc. (*except in this one respect*). **4** relation (*a morality that has no respect to religion*). **5** (in *pl.*) a person's polite messages or attentions (*give my respects to your mother*). ● *v.tr.* **1** regard with deference, esteem, or honour. **2 a** avoid interfering with, harming, degrading, insulting, injuring, or interrupting. **b** treat with consideration. **c** refrain from offending (a person, a person's feelings, etc.). □ **in respect of** (or **with respect to**) as concerns; with reference to. **with** (or **with all due**) **respect** a mollifying formula preceding an expression of disagreement with another's views. [from Old French] □ **respecter** *n.*

respectability *n.* **1** the state of being respectable. **2** those who are respectable.

respectable *adj.* **1** deserving respect. **2 a** of fair social standing. **b** having the qualities necessary for such standing. **3** honest and decent in conduct etc. **4** of some merit or importance. **5** fairly good or competent (*a respectable try*). **6** (of activities, clothes, etc.) befitting a respectable person. **7** reasonably good in condition or appearance. **8** appreciable in number, size, etc. □ **respectably** *adv.*

respectful *adj.* showing deference. □ **respectfully** *adv.* **respectfulness** *n.*

respecting *prep.* with reference or regard to; concerning.

respective *adj.* concerning or appropriate to each of several individuals.

respectively *adv.* for each separately or in turn, and in the order mentioned (*she and I gave £10 and £1 respectively*).

R

RESISTOR

Resistors provide the electrical equivalent of friction. When current flows through a resistor, an opposing voltage is set up. This limits the current or produces a voltage proportional to it. Most resistors have a set resistance but some, such as potentiometers used as volume controls, are variable.

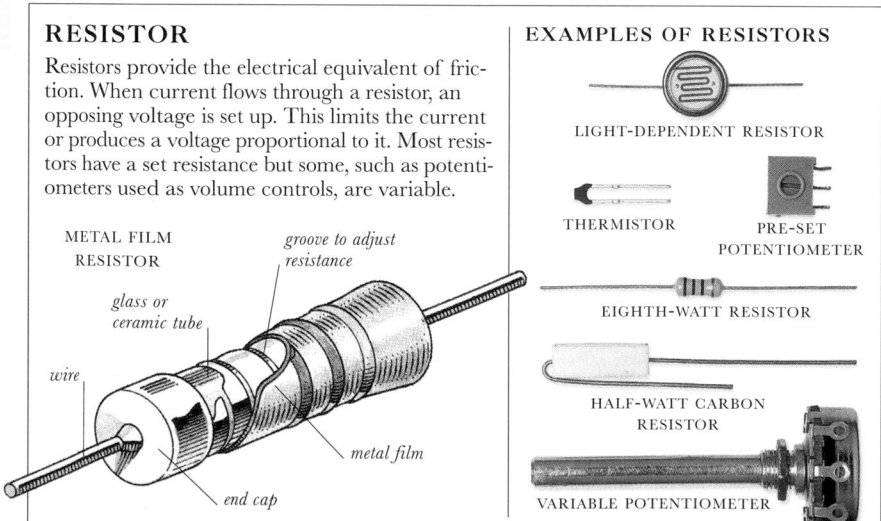

EXAMPLES OF RESISTORS

METAL FILM RESISTOR

groove to adjust resistance

glass or ceramic tube

wire

metal film

end cap

LIGHT-DEPENDENT RESISTOR

THERMISTOR

PRE-SET POTENTIOMETER

EIGHTH-WATT RESISTOR

HALF-WATT CARBON RESISTOR

VARIABLE POTENTIOMETER

RESPIRATION

Human respiration relies on an involuntary muscle reflex that makes the diaphragm and external intercostal muscles contract. This increases the volume of the chest cavity, and the pressure inside it drops. Air rushes in through the nose, down the trachea, and into the lungs, where an exchange of oxygen and carbon dioxide takes place. As the muscles relax, the air (partly waste carbon dioxide) is forced back out of the lungs.

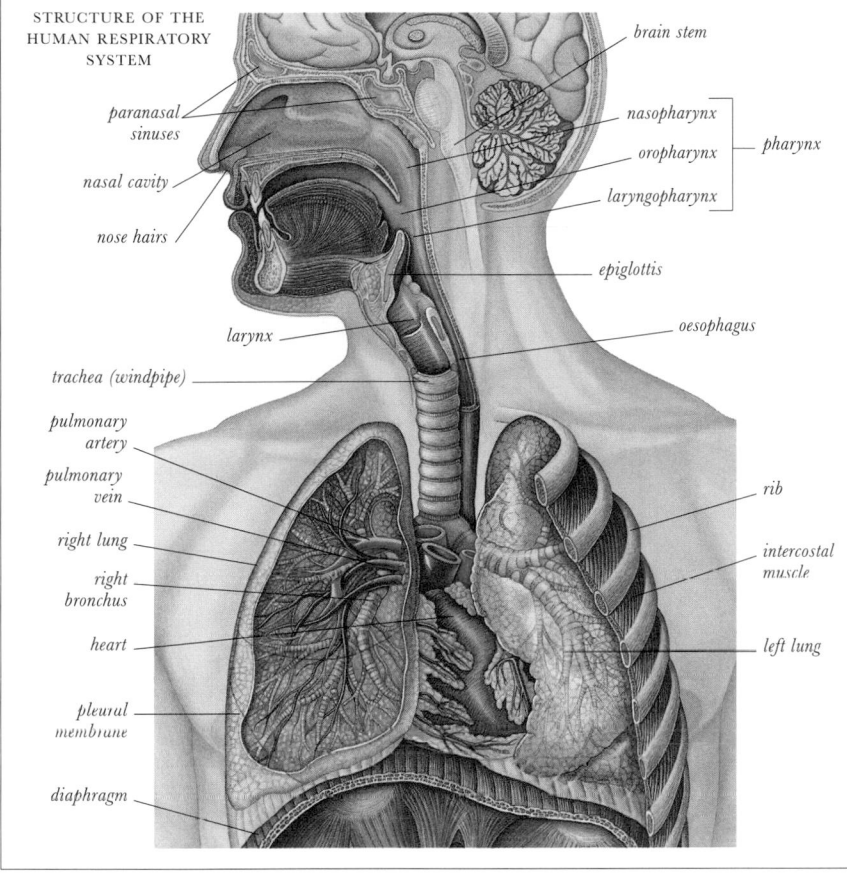

STRUCTURE OF THE HUMAN RESPIRATORY SYSTEM

- paranasal sinuses
- nasal cavity
- nose hairs
- larynx
- trachea (windpipe)
- pulmonary artery
- pulmonary vein
- right lung
- right bronchus
- heart
- pleural membrane
- diaphragm
- brain stem
- nasopharynx
- oropharynx
- laryngopharynx
- pharynx
- epiglottis
- oesophagus
- rib
- intercostal muscle
- left lung

respell *v.tr.* (*past* and *past part.* **respelt** or **respelled**) spell again or differently, esp. phonetically.

respiration *n.* **1 a** ▲ the act or an instance of breathing. **b** a single inspiration or expiration; a breath. **2** *Biol.* in living organisms, the process involving the production of energy and release of carbon dioxide from the oxidation of complex organic substances. [from Latin *respiratio*]

respirator *n.* **1** an apparatus worn over the face to prevent poison gas, cold air, dust particles, etc., from being inhaled. **2** *Med.* an apparatus for maintaining artificial respiration.

respire *v.* **1** *intr.* breathe air. **2** *intr.* inhale and exhale air. **3** *intr.* (of a plant) carry out respiration. **4** *tr.* breathe (air etc.). [from Latin *respirare*] □ **respiratory** *adj.*

respite ● *n.* **1** an interval of rest or relief. **2** a delay permitted before the discharge of an obligation or the suffering of a penalty. ● *v.tr.* grant respite to; reprieve. [from Old French *respit*]

resplendent *adj.* brilliant; dazzlingly or gloriously bright. [from Latin *resplendent-* 'glittering anew'] □ **resplendence** *n.* **resplendency** *n.* **resplendently** *adv.*

respond *v.intr.* **1** answer, give a reply. **2** act or behave in an answering or corresponding manner. **3** (usu. foll. by *to*) show sensitiveness to by behaviour or change (*does not respond to kindness*). **4** (of a congre-

gation) make answers to a priest etc. [from Latin *respondēre*] □ **respondence** *n.* **responder** *n.*

respondent ● *n.* **1** a defendant, esp. in an appeal or divorce case. **2** a person who makes an answer or defends an argument etc. ● *adj.* **1** making answer. **2** (foll. by *to*) responsive. **3** in the position of defendant.

response *n.* **1** an answer given in word or act; a reply. **2** a feeling, movement, change, etc., caused by a stimulus or influence. **3** (often in *pl.*) *Eccl.* any part of the liturgy said or sung in answer to the priest. [from Latin *responsum*]

responsibility *n.* (*pl.* **-ies**) **1 a** (often foll. by *for, of*) the state or fact of being responsible. **b** the ability to act independently and make decisions (*a job with more responsibility*). **2** the person or thing for which one is responsible (*she's my responsibility*).

responsible *adj.* **1** (often foll. by *to, for*) liable to be called to account (to a person or for a thing). **2** morally accountable for one's actions; capable of rational conduct. **3** of good credit, position, or repute; respectable; evidently trustworthy. **4** (often foll. by *for*) being the primary cause (*a short circuit was responsible*). **5** involving responsibility (*a responsible job*). [based on Latin *respondēre respons-* 'to respond'] □ **responsibleness** *n.* **responsibly** *adv.*

responsive *adj.* **1** (often foll. by *to*) responding readily (to some influence). **2** sympathetic; impressionable. □ **responsively** *adv.* **responsiveness** *n.*

respray ● *v.tr.* spray again (esp. to change the colour of the paint on a vehicle). ● *n.* the act or an instance of respraying.

rest[1] ● *v.* **1** *intr.* cease, abstain, or be relieved from exertion, action, etc. **2** *intr.* be still or asleep, esp. to refresh oneself. **3** *tr.* give relief or repose to (*a stool to rest my legs*). **4** *intr.* (foll. by *on, upon, against*) lie on; be supported by; be spread out on; be propped against. **5** *intr.* (foll. by *on, upon*) depend, be based, or rely on. **6** *intr.* (foll. by *on, upon*) (of a look) alight or be steadily directed on. **7** *tr.* (foll. by *on, upon*) place for support or foundation. **8** *intr.* (of a problem or subject) be left without further investigation or discussion (*let the matter rest*). **9** *intr.* **a** lie in death. **b** (foll. by *in*) lie buried in (a churchyard etc.). **10** *tr.* (as **rested** *adj.*) refreshed or reinvigorated by resting. ● *n.* **1** repose or sleep, esp. in bed at night. **2** the cessation of exertion, worry, etc. **3** a period of resting. **4** a support or prop for holding or steadying something. **5** *Mus.* **a** an interval of silence of a specified duration. ▷ NOTATION. **b** the sign denoting this. □ **at rest** not moving; not agitated or troubled; dead. **be resting** *Brit. euphem.* (of an actor) be out of work. **rest one's case** conclude one's argument etc. **rest on one's laurels** see LAUREL. **rest up** *US* rest oneself thoroughly. **set at rest** settle or relieve (a question, a person's mind, etc.). [Old English]

rest[2] ● *n.* (prec. by *the*) the remaining part or parts; the others; the remainder of some quantity or number. ● *v.intr.* **1** remain in a specified state (*rest assured*). **2** (foll. by *with*) be left in the hands or charge of. □ **for the rest** as regards anything else. [from Latin *restare*]

restage *v.tr.* stage (a play etc.) again or differently.

restart ● *v.tr. & intr.* begin again. ● *n.* a new beginning.

restate *v.tr.* express again or differently, esp. more clearly or convincingly. □ **restatement** *n.*

restaurant *n.* public premises where meals or refreshments may be had. [French]

restaurant car *n. Brit.* a dining car on a train.

restaurateur *n.* a restaurant-keeper. [French]

■ **Usage** The word *restaurateur* is frequently misspelt *restauranteur* under the influence of the word *restaurant*.

rest-cure *n.* a rest usu. of some weeks as a medical treatment.

restful *adj.* **1** favourable to quiet or repose. **2** free from disturbing influences. **3** soothing. □ **restfully** *adv.* **restfulness** *n.*

rest home *n.* a place where old or frail people can be cared for.

restitution *n.* **1** (often foll. by *of*) the act or an instance of restoring a thing to its proper owner. **2** reparation for an injury (esp. *make restitution*). [from Latin *restitutio*] □ **restitutive** *adj.*

restive *adj.* **1** fidgety; restless. **2** (of a horse) refusing to advance. [from Old French *restif -ive*] □ **restively** *adv.* **restiveness** *n.*

restless *adj.* **1** finding or affording no rest. **2** uneasy; agitated. **3** constantly in motion, fidgeting, etc. □ **restlessly** *adv.* **restlessness** *n.*

restock *v.tr.* (also *absol.*) stock again or differently.

restoration *n.* **1** the act or an instance of restoring or being restored. **2** a model or drawing representing the supposed original form of a thing. **3** (**Restoration**) *hist.* (prec. by *the*) the re-establishment of Charles II as King of England in 1660.

restorative ● *adj.* tending to restore health or strength. ● *n.* a restorative medicine, food, etc.

restore *v.tr.* **1** bring back or attempt to bring back to the original state by rebuilding, repairing, repainting, emending, etc. **2** bring back to health etc.; cure. **3** give back to the original owner etc. **4** reinstate; bring back to dignity or right. **5** replace; put back; bring back to a former condition. [from Latin *restaurare*] □ **restorable** *adj.* **restorer** *n.*

R

restrain *v.tr.* **1** (often *refl.*; usu. foll. by *from*) check or hold in; keep in check or under control or within bounds. **2** repress; keep down. **3** confine; imprison. [from Latin *restringere* 'to bind fast'] □ **restrainable** *adj.* **restrainer** *n.*

restrainedly *adv.* with self-restraint.

restraint *n.* **1** the act or an instance of restraining or being restrained. **2** a stoppage; a check; a controlling agency or influence. **3 a** self-control; avoidance of excess or exaggeration. **b** austerity of literary expression. **4** reserve of manner. **5** confinement, esp. because of insanity. **6** something which restrains or holds in check. [from Old French *restreinte*]

restrict *v.tr.* (often foll. by *to*, *within*) **1** confine, bound, limit. **2** subject to limitation. [based on Latin *restrictus* 'restrained'] □ **restrictedly** *adv.* **restrictedness** *n.*

restricted area *n.* **1** *Brit.* an area in which there is a special speed limit for vehicles. **2** *US* an area which military personnel, unauthorized people, etc., are not allowed to enter.

restriction *n.* **1** the act or an instance of restricting; the state of being restricted. **2** a thing that restricts. **3** a limitation placed on action. □ **restrictionist** *adj. & n.*

restrictive *adj.* imposing restrictions. □ **restrictively** *adv.* **restrictiveness** *n.*

restrictive practice *n. Brit.* an agreement to limit competition or output in industry.

restring *v.tr.* (*past* and *past part.* **restrung**) **1** fit (a musical instrument) with new strings. **2** thread (beads etc.) on a new string.

restroom *n.* esp. *US* a public lavatory in a factory, shop, etc.

restructure *v.tr.* give a new structure to; rebuild; rearrange.

restyle ● *v.tr.* **1** reshape; remake in a new style. **2** give a new designation to (a person or thing). ● *n.* an instance of restyling; a new style.

resubmit *v.tr.* submit (a plan, application, etc.) again.

result ● *n.* **1** a consequence, issue, or outcome of something. **2** a satisfactory outcome (*gets results*). **3** an end product of calculation. **4** (in *pl.*) a list of scores or winners etc. ● *v.intr.* **1** (often foll. by *from*) arise as the actual consequence or follow as a logical consequence. **2** (often foll. by *in*) have a specified end or outcome (*resulted in a large profit*). □ **without result** in vain; fruitless. [from medieval Latin *resultare* 'to spring back'] □ **resultless** *adj.*

resultant *adj.* resulting, esp. as the total outcome of more or less opposed forces.

resume *v.* **1** *tr. & intr.* begin again or continue after an interruption. **2** *tr. & intr.* begin to speak, work, or use again; recommence. **3** *tr.* recover; reoccupy (*resume one's seat*). [from Latin *resumere*] □ **resumable** *adj.*

résumé /rez-yoo-may/ *n.* (also **resumé**) **1** a summary. **2** *N. Amer.* a curriculum vitae. [French, literally 'resumed']

resumption *n.* the act or an instance of resuming. [from Late Latin *resumptio*] □ **resumptive** *adj.*

resupply ● *v.* (**-ies, -ied**) **1** *tr.* supply again; provide with a fresh supply. **2** *intr.* take on or acquire a fresh supply. ● *n.* the act of resupplying something or being resupplied.

resurface *v.* **1** *tr.* lay a new surface on (a road etc.). **2** *intr.* rise or arise again; turn up again.

resurgent *adj.* **1** rising or arising again. **2** tending to rise again. [from Latin *resurgent-* 'rising again'] □ **resurgence** *n.*

resurrect *v.* **1** *tr. colloq.* revive the practice, use, or memory of. **2** *tr.* take from the grave; exhume. **3** *tr.* dig up. **4** *tr. & intr.* raise or rise from the dead.

resurrection *n.* **1** the act or an instance of rising from the dead. **2** (**Resurrection**) Christ's rising from the dead. **3** a revival after disuse, inactivity, or

decay. **4** exhumation. **5** restoration to vogue or memory. [from Late Latin *resurrectio*] □ **resurrectional** *adj.*

resurvey ● *v.tr.* survey again; reconsider. ● *n.* the act or an instance of resurveying.

resuscitate *v.tr. & intr.* **1** revive from unconsciousness or apparent death. **2** return or restore to vogue, vigour, or vividness. [based on Latin *resuscitatus* 'raised again'] □ **resuscitation** *n.* **resuscitative** *adj.* **resuscitator** *n.*

retail ● *n.* the sale of goods in relatively small quantities to the public, and usu. not for resale (cf. WHOLESALE). ● *adj. & adv.* by retail; at a retail price. ● *v.* **1** *tr.* sell (goods) in retail trade. **2** *intr.* (often foll. by *at, for*) (of goods) be sold in this way (esp. for a specified price). **3** *tr.* recount; relate details of. [from Old French *retaille* 'a piece cut off'] □ **retailer** *n.*

retail price index *n.* an index of the variation in the prices of retail goods.

retain *v.tr.* **1 a** keep possession of; not lose; continue to have. **b** not abolish, discard, or alter. **2** keep in one's memory. **3** keep in place; hold fixed. **4** secure the services of (a person) with a preliminary payment. [from Latin *retinēre*] □ **retainable** *adj.* **retainability** *n.* **retainment** *n.*

retainer *n.* **1** a person or thing that retains. **2** esp. *Law* a fee for retaining a barrister etc. **3 a** *hist.* a dependant of a person of rank. **b** *joc.* a faithful friend or servant (esp. *old retainer*). **4** *Brit.* a reduced rent paid to retain accommodation during a period of non-occupancy. **5** *Dentistry* a structure cemented to a tooth to keep a bridge in place.

retaining wall *n.* a wall supporting and confining a mass of earth or water.

retake ● *v.tr.* (*past* **retook**; *past part.* **retaken**) **1** take again. **2** recapture. ● *n.* **1 a** the act or an instance of retaking. **b** a thing retaken, e.g. an examination. **2 a** the act or an instance of filming a scene or recording music etc. again. **b** the scene or recording obtained in this way.

retaliate *v.* **1** *intr.* repay an injury, insult, etc., in kind; attack in return; make reprisals. **2** *tr. a* (usu. foll. by *upon*) cast (an accusation) back upon a person. **b** repay (an injury or insult) in kind. [based on Latin *retaliatus* 'requited'] □ **retaliation** *n.* **retaliator** *n.* **retaliatory** *adj.*

retard *v.tr.* make slow or late. **2** delay the progress or accomplishment of. [from Latin *retardare*] □ **retardant** *adj. & n.* **retardation** *n.* **retardatory** *adj.* **retarder** *n.* **retardment** *n.*

retarded *adj.* backward in mental or physical development.

retch ● *v.intr.* make a motion of vomiting, esp. involuntarily and without effect. ● *n.* such a motion or the sound of it. [variant of (now dialect) *reach*, from Old Norse *hrækja*]

retell *v.tr.* (*past* and *past part.* **retold**) tell again or in a different version.

retention *n.* **1** the act or an instance of retaining; the state of being retained. **2** the ability to retain things experienced or learnt; memory. [from Latin *retentio*]

retentive *adj.* **1** (often foll. by *of*) tending to retain (moisture etc.). **2** (of memory or a person) not forgetful. [from medieval Latin *retentivus*] □ **retentively** *adv.* **retentiveness** *n.*

retexture *v.tr.* treat (material etc.) so as to restore its original texture.

rethink ● *v.tr.* (*past* and *past part.* **rethought**) think about (something) again, esp. with a view to making changes. ● *n.* a reassessment.

reticence *n.* **1** the avoidance of saying all one knows or feels, or more than is necessary. **2** a disposition to silence. **3** the act or an instance of holding back some fact. [from Latin *reticentia*] □ **reticent** *adj.* **reticently** *adv.*

reticulate ● *v.tr. & intr.* **1** ▶ divide or be divided in fact or appearance into a network. **2** arrange or be arranged in small squares or with intersecting lines. ● *adj.* reticulated. [from Latin *reticulatus* 'reticulated'] □ **reticulation** *n.*

reticule *n.* esp. *hist.* ▼ a woman's netted or other bag, esp. with a drawstring, carried or worn to serve the purpose of a pocket. [from French *réticule*]

reticulum *n.* (*pl.* **reticula**) a netlike structure; a fine network, esp. of membranes etc. in living organisms.

retie *v.tr.* (**retying**) tie again.

retiform *adj.* netlike, reticulated. [Latin *rete* 'net' + -FORM]

re-time *v.tr.* esp. *Railways* set a new or different time for; reschedule.

retina *n.* (*pl.* **retinas**, **retinae** /-nee/) a layer at the back of the eyeball sensitive to light, and triggering nerve impulses via the optic nerve to the brain where the visual image is formed. ▷ EYE, OPTIC NERVE. [based on Latin *rete* 'net'] □ **retinal** *adj.*

drawstring

RETICULE: 19TH-CENTURY EMBROIDERED RETICULE

retinol *n.* a vitamin found in green and yellow vegetables, egg yolk, and fish-liver oil, essential for growth and vision in dim light. Also called *vitamin A*. [based on RETINA]

retinue *n.* a body of attendants accompanying an important person. [from Old French *retenue* (fem.) 'retained']

retire *v.* **1 a** *intr.* leave office or employment, esp. because of age. **b** *tr.* cause (a person) to retire from work. **2** *intr.* withdraw; go away; retreat. **3** *intr.* seek seclusion or shelter. **4** *intr.* go to bed. **5** *tr.* withdraw (troops). **6 a** *intr. & tr. Cricket* (of a batsman) voluntarily end or be compelled to suspend one's innings. **b** *tr. Baseball* put out (a batter); cause (a side) to end a turn at bat. [from French *retirer*] □ **retirer** *n.*

retired *adj.* **1 a** having retired from employment. **b** relating to a retired person (*retired pay*). **2** withdrawn from society or observation. □ **retiredness** *n. archaic.*

retirement *n.* **1 a** the act or an instance of retiring. **b** the condition of having retired. **2 a** seclusion or privacy. **b** a secluded place.

retirement age *n.* the age at which most people normally retire from work.

retirement home *n.* **1** a house, flat, etc. to which a person moves in old age. **2** an institution for elderly people needing care.

retirement pension *n. Brit.* a pension paid by the state to retired people above a certain age.

retiring *adj.* shy; fond of seclusion. □ **retiringly** *adv.*

retold *past* and *past part.* of RETELL.

retook *past* of RETAKE.

retort[1] ● *n.* **1** an incisive or witty or angry reply. **2** the turning of a charge or argument against its originator. **3** a retaliation. ● *v.* **1 a** *tr.* say by way of a retort. **b** *intr.* make a retort. **2** *tr.* repay (an insult or attack) in kind. **3** *tr.* (often followed by *on*, *upon*)

R

return (mischief, a charge, sarcasm, etc.) to its originator. [based on Latin *retortus* 'twisted back']

retort[2] ● *n.* **1** ▼ a container, usu. of glass, with a long bent-back neck, used in distilling liquids. **2** a large receptacle or furnace for heating mercury for purification, coal to generate gas, or iron and carbon to make steel. ● *v.tr.* purify (mercury) by heating in a retort. [medieval Latin *retorta* (fem.) 'twisted back']

RETORT: EARLY GLASS RETORT ON A FURNACE

neck

furnace

retouch ● *v.tr.* improve (a composition, picture, etc.) by fresh touches or alterations. ● *n.* the act or an instance of retouching. □ **retoucher** *n.*

retrace *v.tr.* **1** go back over (one's steps etc.). **2** trace back to a source or beginning. **3** recall the course of in one's memory. [from French *retracer*]

retract *v.* **1** *tr.* (also *absol.*) withdraw or revoke (a statement or undertaking). **2 a** *tr.* & *intr.* (esp. with reference to part of the body) draw or be drawn back or in. **b** *tr.* draw (an undercarriage etc.) into the body of an aircraft. [based on Latin *retractus* 'drawn back'; sense 1 from *retractare*] □ **retractable** *adj.* **retraction** *n.* **retractive** *adj.*

retractile *adj.* capable of being retracted. □ **retractility** *n.*

retractor *n.* **1** a muscle used for retracting. **2** a device for retracting.

retrain *v.tr.* & *intr.* train again or further, esp. for new work.

retranslate *v.tr.* translate again, esp. translate (a translation) back into the original language. □ **retranslation** *n.*

retransmit *v.tr.* (**retransmitted, retransmitting**) transmit (esp. radio signals or broadcast programmes) back again or to a greater distance. □ **retransmission** *n.*

retread ● *v.tr.* **1** (*past* **retrod**; *past part.* **retrodden**) tread (a path etc.) again. **2** (*past* and *past part.* **retreaded**) put a fresh tread on (a tyre). ● *n.* **1** a retreaded tyre. **2** a person recalled to service or retrained for new work. **3** a thing or person superficially altered but essentially the same as a predecessor.

retreat ● *v.* **1 a** *intr.* (esp. of military forces) go back, retire; relinquish a position. **b** *tr.* cause to retreat; move back. **2** *intr.* (esp. of features) recede; slope back. ● *n.* **1 a** the act or an instance of retreating. **b** *Mil.* a signal for this. **2** withdrawal into privacy or security. **3** a place of shelter or seclusion. **4** a period of seclusion for prayer and meditation. **5** *Mil.* a bugle call at sunset. [from Latin *retrahere* 'to draw back']

retrench *v.* **1** *tr.* reduce the amount of (costs). **2** *intr.* cut down expenses; introduce economies. **3** *tr.* esp. *Austral.* make (an employee) redundant; sack. □ **retrenchment** *n.*

retrial *n.* a second or further (judicial) trial.

retribution *n.* requital usu. for evil done; vengeance. [from Late Latin *retributio*] □ **retributive** *adj.* **retributory** *adj.*

retrieve *v.tr.* **1 a** regain possession of. **b** recover by investigation or effort of memory. **2 a** restore to knowledge or recall to mind. **b** obtain (information stored in a computer etc.). **3** (of a dog) find and bring in (killed or wounded game etc.). **4** (foll. by *from*) recover or rescue (esp. from a bad state). **5** restore to a flourishing state; revive. **6** repair or set right (a loss or error etc.) (*managed to retrieve the situation*). [based on stressed stem of Old French *retrover*] □ **retrievability** *n.* **retrievable** *adj.* **retrieval** *n.*

retriever *n.* **1** ▶ a dog of a breed used for retrieving game. ▷ DOG. **2** a person who retrieves something.

retro ● *n.* (*pl.* **-os**) **1** a thing imitating something from the past. **2** a nostalgic style or fashion in dress, music, etc. ● *adj.* imitative of a style or fashion from the past. [from French *rétro*, abbreviation of *rétrograde*]

retro- *comb. form* **1** denoting action back or in return (*retroactive*). **2** *Anat.* & *Med.* denoting location behind. [from Latin *retro* 'backwards']

retroactive *adj.* (esp. of legislation) having retrospective effect. □ **retroactively** *adv.* **retroactivity** *n.*

retrod *past* of RETREAD 1.

retrodden *past part.* of RETREAD 1.

retrofit *v.tr.* (**-fitted, -fitting**) modify (machinery, vehicles, etc.) to incorporate changes and developments introduced after manufacture.

retrograde ● *adj.* **1** directed backwards; retreating. **2** reverting esp. to an inferior state; declining. **3** inverse, reversed (*in retrograde order*). ● *n.* a degenerate person. ● *v.intr.* **1** move backwards; recede, retire. **2** decline, revert. [from Latin *retrogradus*] □ **retrogradely** *adv.*

retrogress *v.intr.* **1** go back; move backwards. **2** deteriorate. [on the pattern of *progress*] □ **retrogression** *n.* **retrogressive** *adj.*

retro-rocket *n.* an auxiliary rocket for slowing down a spacecraft etc.

retrospect *n.* **1** (foll. by *to*) regard or reference to precedent or authority, or to previous conditions. **2** a survey of past time or events. □ **in retrospect** **1** when looked back on. **2** when looking back; with hindsight.

retrospection *n.* the action of looking back, esp. into the past.

retrospective ● *adj.* **1** looking back on or dealing with the past. **2** (of an exhibition, recital, etc.) showing an artist's development over his or her lifetime. **3** esp. *Brit.* (of a statute etc.) applying to the past as well as the future; retroactive. ● *n.* a retrospective exhibition, recital, etc. □ **retrospectively** *adv.*

retroussé *adj.* (of the nose) turned up at the tip. [French, literally 'tucked up']

retrovert *v.tr.* **1** turn backwards. **2** (as **retroverted** *adj.*) *Med.* (of the womb) having a backward inclination. [from Late Latin *retrovertere*] □ **retroversion** *n.*

retrovirus *n. Biol.* any of a group of RNA viruses which insert a DNA copy of their genome into the host cell in order to replicate, e.g. HIV. [modern Latin]

retry *v.tr.* (**-ies, -ied**) try (a defendant or lawsuit) a second or further time.

retsina *n.* a Greek usu. white wine flavoured with resin. [modern Greek]

retune *v.tr.* **1** tune (a musical instrument) again or differently. **2** tune (a radio etc.) to a different frequency.

returf *v.tr. Brit.* provide with new turf.

return ● *v.* **1** *intr.* come or go back. **2** *tr.* bring, put, or send back. **3** *tr.* pay back or reciprocate; give in response. **4** *tr.* yield (a profit). **5** *tr.* say in reply; retort. **6** *tr.* (in cricket, tennis, etc.) hit or send (the ball) back after receiving it. **7** *tr.* state or mention or describe officially, esp. in answer to a writ or formal demand. **8** *tr. Brit.* (of an electorate) elect as an MP, government, etc. ● *n.* **1** the act or an instance of coming or going back. **2 a** the act or an instance of giving or sending or putting or paying back. **b** a thing given or sent back. **3** (in full **return ticket**) esp. *Brit.* a ticket for a journey to a place and back to the starting point. **4** (in *sing.* or *pl.*) **a** the proceeds or profit of an undertaking. **b** the acquisition of

RETRIEVER: FLAT-COATED RETRIEVER

these. **5** a formal report or statement compiled or submitted by order (*an income tax return*). **6** (in full **return match** or **game**) a second match etc between the same opponents. □ **by return** (**of post**) *Brit.* by the next available post in the return direction. **in return** as an exchange or reciprocal action. **many happy returns** (**of the day**) a greeting on a birthday. [from Old French *returner*] □ **returnable** *adj.* **returner** *n.*

returnee *n.* **1** a person who returns home from abroad, esp. after war service. **2** a person who returns to work, esp. after bringing up a family.

returning officer *n. Brit.* an official conducting an election in a constituency and announcing the results.

retying *pres. part.* of RETIE.

retype *v.tr.* type again, esp. to correct errors.

reunify *v.tr.* (**-ies, -ied**) restore (esp. separated territories) to a political unity. □ **reunification** *n.*

reunion *n.* **1 a** the act or an instance of reuniting. **b** the condition of being reunited. **2** a social gathering esp. of people formerly associated. [based on Latin *reunire* 'to reunite']

reunite *v.tr.* & *intr.* bring or come back together.

reupholster *v.tr.* upholster anew. □ **reupholstery** *n.*

reuse ● *v.tr.* /ree-**yooz**/ use again or more than once. ● *n.* /ree-**yooss**/ a second or further use. □ **reusable** *adj.*

reutilize *v.tr.* (also **-ise**) utilize again or for a different purpose. □ **reutilization** *n.*

Rev. *abbr.* **1** Reverend. **2** Revelation (New Testament).

rev *colloq.* ● *n.* (in *pl.*) the number of revolutions of an engine per minute. ● *v.* (**revved, revving**) **1** *intr.* (of an engine) revolve; turn over. **2** *tr.* (also *absol.*; often foll. by *up*) cause (an engine) to run quickly.

revalue *v.tr.* (**revalues, revalued, revaluing**) *Econ.* give a different value to, esp. give a higher value to (a currency) in relation to other currencies or gold. □ **revaluation** *n.*

revamp *v.tr.* **1** renovate, revise, improve. **2** patch up.

Revd *abbr.* Reverend.

reveal[1] *v.tr.* **1** display or show; allow to appear. **2** (often as **revealing** *adj.*) disclose, divulge, betray. **3** (in *refl.* or *passive*) come to sight or knowledge. [from Latin *revelare*] □ **revealable** *adj.* **revealer** *n.* **revealingly** *adv.*

reveal[2] *n.* an internal side surface of an opening or recess, esp. of a doorway or window aperture. [from obsolete *revail* 'to lower, provide with a reveal']

reveille /ri-**val**-i/ *n.* a military waking-signal. [from French imperative *réveillez* 'wake up!']

revel ● *v.intr.* (**revelled, revelling**; *US* **reveled, reveling**) **1** have a good time; be extravagantly festive. **2** (foll. by *in*) take keen delight in. ● *n.* (in *sing.* or *pl.*) the act or an instance of revelling. [from Old French *reveler* 'to riot'] □ **reveller** *n.* **revelry** *n.* (*pl.* **-ies**)

revelation *n.* **1 a** the act or an instance of revealing, esp. the supposed disclosure of knowledge to

R

humankind by a divine or supernatural agency. **b** knowledge disclosed in this way. **2** a striking disclosure. **3** (**Revelation** or *colloq.* **Revelations**) (in full **the Revelation of St John the Divine**) the last book of the New Testament. [from Late Latin *revelatio*] □ **revelational** *adj.*

revelatory *adj.* serving to reveal, esp. something significant.

revenant *n.* a person who has returned, esp. supposedly from the dead. [French, literally '(one) coming back']

revenge ● *n.* **1** retaliation for an offence or injury. **2** an act of retaliation. **3** the desire for this; a vindictive feeling. **4** (in games) a chance to win after an earlier defeat. ● *v.tr.* **1** (*refl.* or in *passive*; often foll. by *on*, *upon*) inflict retaliation for an offence. **2** inflict retaliation for (an offence). **3** inflict retaliation on behalf of (a person). [from Late Latin *revindicare*] □ **revenger** *n.*

■ **Usage** The verb *revenge* is usually used in the passive or as a reflexive verb, often followed by *on* or *upon* (see sense 1 above). *Avenge* is also, but less commonly, used in these constructions. Like *avenge*, *revenge* can mean 'inflict retaliation for (an offence)' or on behalf of (a person)', but it is less common than *avenge* in these senses (see senses 2 and 3 above). See also Usage Note at AVENGE.

revengeful *adj.* eager for revenge. □ **revengefully** *adv.*

revenue *n.* **1 a** income, esp. of a large amount, from any source. **b** (in *pl.*) items constituting this. **2** a state's annual income from which public expenses are met. **3** the civil service department collecting this. [from Old French *revenu(e)* 'returned']

reverberate *v.* **1 a** *intr.* (of sound, light, or heat) be returned or echoed repeatedly. **b** *tr.* return (a sound etc.) in this way. **2** *intr.* **a** (of a rumour etc.) be heard much or repeatedly. **b** (of an event) have continuing effects. [based on Latin *reverberatus* 'lashed again'] □ **reverberant** *adj.* **reverberantly** *adv.* **reverberation** *n.* **reverberative** *adj.* **reverberator** *n.* **reverberatory** *adj.*

revere *v.tr.* hold in deep and usu. affectionate or religious respect; venerate. [from Latin *reverēri*]

reverence ● *n.* **1** the act of revering or the state of being revered. **2** the capacity for revering. ● *v.tr.* regard or treat with reverence.

reverend ● *adj.* (esp. as the title of a clergyman) deserving reverence. ● *n. colloq.* a clergyman. [from Latin *reverendus* 'to be revered']

■ **Usage** Note the difference between *reverend* 'deserving reverence' and *reverent* 'showing reverence'.

Reverend Mother *n.* the title of the Mother Superior of a convent.

reverent *adj.* feeling or showing reverence. □ **reverently** *adv.*

■ **Usage** See Usage Note at REVEREND.

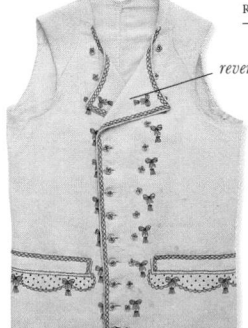

REVERS ON A DRESS WAISTCOAT

reverential *n.* of the nature of, due to, or characterized by reverence. □ **reverentially** *adv.*

reverie /rev-ĕ-ri/ *n.* a fit of abstracted musing. [from Old French, literally 'rejoicing, revelry']

revers **revers** /ri-veer/ *n.* (*pl.* same) **1** ◄ the turned-back edge of a garment revealing the undersurface. **2** the material on this surface. [French, literally 'reverse']

reverse ● *v.* **1** *tr.* turn the other way round or up or inside out. **2** *tr.* change to the opposite character or effect. **3** *intr. & tr.* travel or cause to travel backwards. **4** *tr.* make (an engine etc.) work in a contrary direction. **5** *tr.* revoke or annul (a decree, act, etc.). ● *adj.* **1** placed or turned in an opposite direction or position. **2** opposite or contrary in character or order; inverted. ● *n.* **1** the opposite or contrary. **2** the contrary of the usual manner. **3** an occurrence of misfortune; a disaster, esp. a defeat. **4** reverse gear or motion. **5** the reverse side of something. **6** the side of a coin or medal etc. bearing the secondary design. □ **reverse arms** hold a rifle with the butt upwards. **reverse the charges** make the recipient of a telephone call responsible for payment. [from Latin *reversus* 'reversed'] □ **reversal** *n.* **reversely** *adv.* **reverser** *n.* **reversible** *adj.* **reversibility** *n.* **reversibly** *adv.*

■ **Usage** *Reversal* is the noun corresponding to the verb *reverse*, e.g. *The reversal of the decision*, while *reversion* is the noun corresponding to the verb *revert*, e.g. *The reversion of the building to its original use.*

reverse-charge *adj. Brit.* (of a telephone call) for which the recipient pays.

reverse gear *n.* a gear used to make a vehicle etc. travel backwards.

reverse take-over *n.* the take-over of a public company by a smaller esp. private one.

reversing light *n. Brit.* a white light at the rear of a vehicle which comes on automatically when reverse gear is engaged.

reversion *n.* **1** a return to a previous state, habit, etc. **2** the legal right (esp. of the original owner, or his or her heirs) to possess or succeed to property on the death of the present possessor. **3** *Biol.* a return to ancestral type. **4** a sum payable on a person's death, esp. by way of life insurance. □ **reversional** *adj.* **reversionary** *adj.*

■ **Usage** See Usage Note at REVERSE.

revert *v.* **1** *intr.* (foll. by *to*) return to a former state, practice, opinion, etc. **2** *intr.* (of property, an office, etc.) return by reversion. **3** *intr.* fall back into a wild state. **4** *tr.* turn (one's eyes or steps) back. [from Latin *revertere*] □ **reverter** *n.* (in sense 2).

revertible *adj.* (of property) subject to reversion.

revetment *n.* (esp. in fortification) a retaining wall or facing of masonry etc. [from French *revêtement*]

review ● *n.* **1** a general survey or assessment of a subject or thing. **2** a retrospect or survey of the past. **3** revision or reconsideration (*is under review*). **4** a display and formal inspection of troops etc. **5** a published account or criticism of a book, play, etc. **6** a periodical publication with critical articles on the arts etc. ● *v.tr.* **1** survey or look back on. **2** reconsider or revise. **3** hold a review of (troops etc.). **4** write a review of (a book, play, etc.). [from obsolete French *reveue*] □ **reviewable** *adj.* **reviewer** *n.*

revile *v.* **1** *tr.* abuse; criticize abusively. **2** *intr.* talk abusively; rail. [from Old French *reviler*] □ **revilement** *n.* **reviler** *n.* **reviling** *n.*

revise ● *v.tr.* **1** examine or re-examine and improve or amend (esp. written or printed matter). **2** consider and alter (an opinion etc.). **3** (also *absol.*) *Brit.* read again (work learnt or done), esp. for an examination. ● *n. Printing* a proof-sheet including corrections made in an earlier proof. [from French *réviser* 'to look at'] □ **revisable** *adj.* **revisal** *n.* **reviser** *n.*

Revised Standard Version *n.* a revision of the American Standard Version of the Bible (which was based on the Revised Version), published in 1946–57.

Revised Version *n.* a revision of the Authorized Version of the Bible, published in 1881–95.

revision *n.* **1** the act or an instance of revising; the process of being revised. **2** a revised edition or form. □ **revisionary** *adj.*

revisionism *n.* often *derog.* a policy of revision or modification, esp. of Marxism. □ **revisionist** *n. & adj.*

revisit *v.tr.* (**revisited**, **revisiting**) visit again.

revitalize *v.tr.* (also **-ise**) imbue with new life and vitality. □ **revitalization** *n.*

revival *n.* **1** the act or an instance of reviving; the process of being revived. **2** a new production of an old play etc. **3** a revived use of an old practice, custom, etc. **4 a** a reawakening of religious fervour. **b** a series of evangelistic meetings to promote this.

revivalism *n.* belief in or the promotion of a revival of religious fervour. □ **revivalist** *n. & adj.* **revivalistic** *adj.*

revive *v.intr. & tr.* **1** come or bring back to consciousness or life or strength. **2** come or bring back to existence, use, notice, etc. [from Late Latin *revivere*] □ **revivable** *adj.* **reviver** *n.*

revivify *v.tr.* (**-ies**, **-ied**) restore to animation, activity, vigour, or life. [from Late Latin *revivificare*] □ **revivification** *n.*

revoke ● *v.* **1** *tr.* rescind, withdraw, or cancel. **2** *intr. Cards* fail to follow suit when able to do so. ● *n. Cards* the act of revoking. [from Latin *revocare*] □ **revocable** *adj.* **revocation** *n.* **revocatory** *adj.* **revoker** *n.*

revolt ● *v.* **1** *intr.* **a** rise in rebellion. **b** (as **revolted** *adj.*) having revolted. **2 a** *tr.* (often in *passive*) affect with loathing; nauseate. **b** *intr.* (often foll. by *at*, *against*) feel strong disgust. ● *n.* **1** an act of rebelling. **2** a state of insurrection. **3** a sense of loathing. **4** a mood of protest or defiance. [from Italian *rivoltare*, related to REVOLVE]

revolting *adj.* disgusting, horrible. □ **revoltingly** *adv.*

revolution *n.* **1** the forcible overthrow of a government or social order. **2** any fundamental change or reversal of conditions. **3** the act or an instance of revolving. **4 a** the single completion of an orbit or rotation. **b** the time taken for this. **5** a cyclic recurrence. [from Late Latin *revolutio*, related to REVOLVE] □ **revolutionism** *n.* **revolutionist** *n.*

revolutionary ● *adj.* **1** involving great and often violent change or innovation. **2** of or causing political revolution. ● *n.* (*pl.* **-ies**) an instigator or supporter of political revolution.

revolutionize *v.tr.* (also **-ise**) introduce fundamental change to.

revolve *v.* **1** *intr. & tr.* turn or cause to turn round, esp. on an axis; rotate. **2** *intr.* move in a circular orbit. **3** *tr.* ponder (a problem etc.) in the mind. **4** *intr.* (foll. by *around*) have as its chief concern; be centred upon. [from Latin *revolvere*]

revolver *n.* ▼ a pistol with revolving chambers enabling several shots to be fired without reloading. ▷ GUN

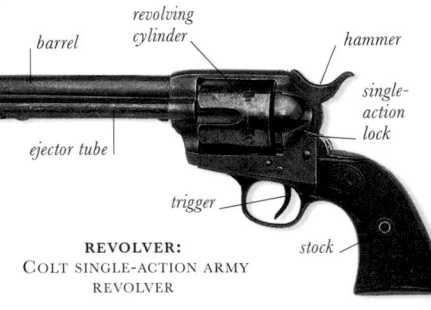

revolving cylinder · *barrel* · *hammer* · *single-action lock* · *sight* · *ejector tube* · *trigger* · *stock*

REVOLVER: COLT SINGLE-ACTION ARMY REVOLVER

revolving door *n.* a door with usu. four partitions turning round a central axis.

revue *n.* a theatrical entertainment of a series of short usu. satirical sketches and songs. [French, literally 'review']

revulsion *n.* **1** abhorrence. **2** a sudden violent change of feeling. [French]

reward ● *n.* **1 a** a return or recompense for service

R

or merit. **b** requital for good or evil; retribution. **2** a sum offered for the detection of a criminal, the restoration of lost property, etc. ● *v.tr.* give a reward to (a person) or for (a service etc.). [from Old Northern French, literally 'regard']

rewarding *adj.* (of an activity etc.) well worth doing; providing satisfaction. □ **rewardingly** *adv.*

rewind *v.tr.* (*past* and *past part.* **rewound**) wind (a film or tape etc.) back. ● *n.* **1** a mechanism for rewinding film etc. **2** the action or process of rewinding film etc. □ **rewinder** *n.*

rewire *v.tr.* provide (a building etc.) with new wiring. □ **rewirable** *adj.*

reword *v.tr.* change the wording of.

rework *v.tr.* revise; refashion, remake. □ **reworking** *n.*

rewound *past* and *past part.* of REWIND.

rewrite ● *v.tr.* (*past* **rewrote**; *past part.* **rewritten**) write again or differently. ● *n.* **1** the act or an instance of rewriting. **2** a thing rewritten.

Rex *n.* the reigning king (following a name or in the titles of lawsuits, e.g. *Rex v. Jones* the Crown versus Jones). [Latin]

Rf *symb. Chem.* the element rutherfordium.

r.f. *abbr.* radio frequency.

Rh *symb.* **1** *Chem.* the element rhodium. **2** *Med.* rhesus (factor).

r.h. *abbr.* right hand.

rhapsodize *v.intr.* (also **-ise**) write rhapsodies or talk in a rhapsodic manner.

rhapsody *n.* (*pl.* **-ies**) **1** an enthusiastic, ecstatic, or extravagant utterance or composition. **2** *Mus.* a piece of music in one extended movement, usu. emotional in character. [from Greek *rhapsōidia*] □ **rhapsodic** *adj.* **rhapsodical** *adj.* (in senses 1, 2). **rhapsodist** *n.*

rhea /ree-ă/ *n.* ◀ a S. American flightless bird of the family Rheidae, like but smaller than an ostrich. [from Greek *Rhea*, mother of Zeus]

RHEA:
GREATER RHEA
(*Rhea americana*)

rhebok *n.* (also **reebok**) a small southern African antelope, *Pelea capreolus*, with a long slender neck and short straight horns. [from Dutch *reebok* 'roebuck']

rhenium *n. Chem.* a rare metallic element of the manganese group, occurring naturally in molybdenum ores. [modern Latin, based on *Rhenus* 'Rhine']

rheostat *n. Electr.* ▲ an instrument used to control a current by varying the resistance. [based on Greek *rheos* 'stream'] □ **rheostatic** *adj.*

rhesus *n.* (in full **rhesus monkey**) a small monkey, *Macaca mulatta*, common in N. India. [arbitrary use from Greek *Rhēsos*, a mythical king of Thrace]

rhesus baby *n.* an infant with a blood disorder caused by the incompatibility of its own rhesus-positive blood with its mother's rhesus-negative blood.

rhesus factor *n.* an antigen occurring on the red blood cells of most humans and some other primates.

rhesus-negative *adj.* lacking the rhesus factor.

RHEOSTAT

In a rheostat, a current enters one terminal and flows through the resistance wire. On reaching the sliding contact it is diverted along the bar. The more wire it travels through, the higher the resistance.

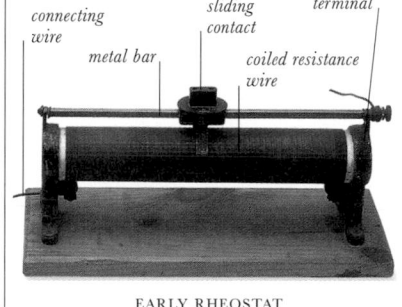

connecting wire *sliding contact* *terminal*
metal bar *coiled resistance wire*

EARLY RHEOSTAT

rhesus-positive *adj.* having the rhesus factor.

rhetoric *n.* **1** the art of effective or persuasive speaking or writing. **2** language designed to persuade or impress (often with an implication of exaggeration etc.). [from Greek *rhētorikē (tekhnē)* '(art) of rhetoric']

rhetorical *adj.* **1** expressed with a view to persuasive or impressive effect. **2** of the nature of rhetoric. □ **rhetorically** *adv.*

rhetorical question *n.* a question asked not for information but to produce an effect, e.g. *who cares?* for *nobody cares.*

rheum *n.* a watery discharge from a mucous membrane, esp. of the eyes or nose. [from Greek *rheuma* 'stream'] □ **rheumy** *adj.*

rheumatic ● *adj.* **1** of, relating to, or suffering from rheumatism. **2** producing or produced by rheumatism. ● *n.* a person suffering from rheumatism. [from Greek *rheumatikos*] □ **rheumatically** *adv.* **rheumaticky** *adj. colloq.*

rheumatic fever *n.* a non-infectious fever with inflammation and pain in the joints.

rheumatics *n.pl.* (usu. treated as *sing.*; often prec. by *the*) *colloq.* rheumatism.

rheumatism *n.* any disease marked by inflammation and pain in the joints, muscles, or fibrous tissue, esp. rheumatoid arthritis. [from Greek *rheumatismos*]

rheumatoid *adj.* having the character of rheumatism.

rheumatoid arthritis *n.* a chronic progressive disease causing inflammation and stiffening of the joints.

rheumatology *n.* the study of rheumatic diseases. □ **rheumatological** *adj.* **rheumatologist** *n.*

rhinal *adj. Anat.* of a nostril or the nose. [from Greek *rhis rhinos* 'nose']

rhinestone *n.* an imitation diamond. [based on *Rhine*, a river and region in Germany]

rhinitis *n.* inflammation of the mucous membrane of the nose. [based on Greek *rhis rhinos* 'nose']

rhino *n.* (*pl.* **-os** or same) *colloq.* a rhinoceros.

rhino- *comb. form Anat.* the nose. [from Greek *rhis rhinos* 'nose']

rhinoceros *n.* (*pl.* same or **rhinoceroses**) ▼ any of various large thick-skinned plant-eating ungulates of the family Rhinocerotidae, with usu. one horn. ▷ UNGULATE. [from Greek *rhinokerōs*]

rhinoceros horn *n.* a mass of keratinized fibres, reputed to have medicinal or aphrodisiac powers.

rhinoplasty *n.* plastic surgery performed on the nose. □ **rhinoplastic** *adj.*

rhizobium *n.* a nitrogen-fixing soil bacterium of the genus *Rhizobium*, found esp. in the root nodules of leguminous plants. [based on Greek *rhiza* 'root' + *bios* 'life']

rhizome *n.* ▶ an underground rootlike stem bearing both roots and shoots. [from Greek *rhizōma*]

rho *n.* the seventeenth letter of the Greek alphabet (Ρ, ρ). [Greek]

rhodium *n. Chem.* a hard white metallic element of the platinum group, occurring naturally in platinum ores and used in making alloys and plating jewellery. [based on Greek *rhodon* 'rose', from the colour of its salts in solution]

shoot
rhizome
roots

RHIZOME
OF AN IRIS

RHINOCEROS

There are five species of rhinoceros, two from Africa and three from Asia. They have poor eyesight, but compensate with a highly developed sense of smell and acute hearing. Rhinoceroses are solitary and fiercely territorial animals, with a lifespan of up to 40 years.

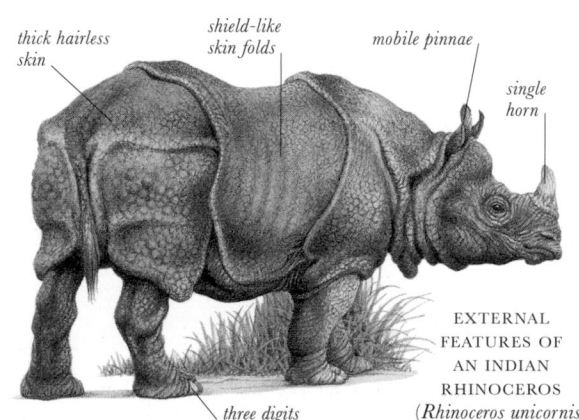

thick hairless skin *shield-like skin folds* *mobile pinnae* *single horn*

EXTERNAL FEATURES OF AN INDIAN RHINOCEROS
(*Rhinoceros unicornis*)

three digits

OTHER SPECIES OF RHINOCEROS

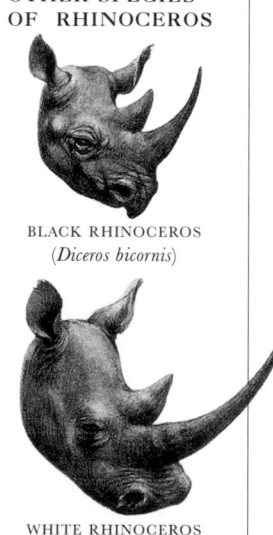

BLACK RHINOCEROS
(*Diceros bicornis*)

WHITE RHINOCEROS
(*Ceratotherium simum*)

R

rhododendron *n.* ▶ a shrub of the genus *Rhododendron*, esp. an evergreen one, with large clusters of bell-shaped flowers. [from Greek *rhodon* 'rose' + *dendron* 'tree']

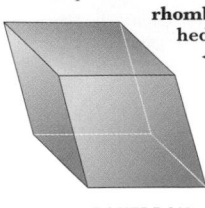

RHODODENDRON
(*Rhododendron yakushimanum*)

rhomb *n.* = RHOMBUS. [from Latin *rhombus*] □ **rhombic** *adj.*

rhombi *pl.* of RHOMBUS.

rhombohedron *n.* (*pl.* **rhombohedra** or **rhombohedrons**) ◀ a solid bounded by six equal rhombuses. □ **rhombohedral** *adj.*

RHOMBOHEDRON

rhomboid ● *adj.* (also **rhomboidal**) having or nearly having the shape of a rhombus. ● *n.* a quadrilateral of which only the opposite sides and angles are equal. [from Greek *rhomboeidēs*]

rhombus *n.* (*pl.* **rhombuses** or **rhombi** /-by/) *Geom.* a parallelogram with oblique angles and equal sides. [from Greek *rhombos*]

rhubarb *n.* **1 a** any of various plants of the genus *Rheum*, producing long fleshy dark red leaf-stalks used cooked as food. **b** the leaf-stalks of this. **2 a** a root of a Chinese and Tibetan plant of the genus *Rheum*. **b** a purgative made from this. **3** *Brit.* **a** *colloq.* a murmurous conversation or noise; the repetition of the word 'rhubarb' by crowd actors. **b** *slang* nonsense. [based on medieval Latin *rhabarbarum* 'foreign rhubarb']

rhumba var. of RUMBA.

rhyme (also *archaic* **rime**) ● *n.* **1** identity of sound between words or the endings of words, esp. in verse. **2** (in *sing.* or *pl.*) verse having rhymes. **3 a** the use of rhyme. **b** a poem having rhymes. **4** a word providing a rhyme. ● *v.* **1** *intr.* **a** (of words or lines) produce a rhyme. **b** (foll. by *with*) act as a rhyme (with another). **2** *intr.* make or write rhymes. **3** *tr.* put or make (a story etc.) into rhyme. **4** *tr.* (foll. by *with*) treat (a word) as rhyming with another. □ **rhyme or reason** sense, logic. [from Greek *rhuthmos* 'rhythm'] □ **rhymeless** *adj.* **rhymer** *n.*

rhymester *n.* a writer of (esp. simple) rhymes.

rhyming slang *n.* (esp. Cockney) slang that replaces words by rhyming words or phrases, e.g. *stairs* by *apples and pears*.

rhythm *n.* **1** a measured flow of words and phrases in verse or prose determined by the length of and stress on syllables. **2 a** the aspect of musical composition concerned with periodical accent and the duration of notes. **b** a particular type of pattern formed by this (*samba rhythm*). **3** *Physiol.* movement with a regular succession of strong and weak elements. **4** a regularly recurring pattern of events or actions. [from Greek *rhuthmos*] □ **rhythmless** *adj.*

rhythm and blues *n.* popular music with a blues theme and a strong rhythm.

rhythmic *adj.* (also **rhythmical**) **1** relating to or characterized by rhythm. **2** regularly occurring. □ **rhythmically** *adv.* **rhythmicity** *n.*

rhythm method *n.* birth control by avoiding sexual intercourse when ovulation is likely to occur.

rhythm section *n.* the part of a dance band or jazz band mainly supplying rhythm, usu. consisting of piano or guitar etc., bass, and drums.

rib ● *n.* **1** each of the curved bones articulated in pairs to the spine and protecting the thoracic cavity and its organs. ▷ SKELETON. **2** a joint of meat from this part of an animal. ▷ CUT. **3** a supporting ridge, timber, rod, etc. across a surface or through a structure. **4** ▶ any of a ship's transverse curved timbers forming the framework of the hull. **5** *Knitting* a

combination of plain and purl stitches producing a ribbed somewhat elastic fabric. **6** each of the hinged rods supporting the fabric of an umbrella. **7** a vein of a leaf or an insect's wing. ● *v.tr.* (**ribbed**, **ribbing**) **1** provide with ribs; act as the ribs of. **2** *colloq.* make fun of; tease. **3** mark with ridges. **4** plough with spaces between the furrows. [Old English] □ **ribless** *adj.*

ribald /rib-ăld/ *adj.* (of language or its user) coarsely or disrespectfully humorous. [from Old French *ribau(l)d*]

ribaldry /rib-ăld-ri/ *n.* ribald talk or behaviour.

riband /rib-ănd/ *n.* a ribbon. [from Old French *riban*]

ribbed *adj.* having ribs or riblike markings.

ribbing *n.* **1** ribs or a riblike structure, esp. a band of knitting in rib. **2** *colloq.* the act or an instance of teasing.

ribbon *n.* **1 a** a narrow strip or band of fabric, used esp. for trimming or decoration. **b** material in this form. **2** a ribbon of a special colour etc. worn to indicate some honour or membership of a sports team etc. **3** a long narrow strip of anything (*typewriter ribbon*). **4** (in *pl.*) ragged strips (*torn to ribbons*). [variant of RIBAND] □ **ribboned** *adj.*

ribbon development *n. Brit.* the building of houses along a main road, usu. one leading out of a town or village.

ribcage *n.* the wall of bones formed by the ribs round the chest. ▷ STERNUM

riboflavin *n.* (also **riboflavine**) a vitamin of the B complex, found in liver, milk, and eggs, essential for energy production. [based on RIBOSE + Latin *flavus* 'yellow']

ribonucleic acid *n.* a nucleic acid yielding ribose on hydrolysis, present in living cells, esp. in ribosomes where it is involved in protein synthesis. [RIBOSE + NUCLEIC ACID]

ribose *n.* a sugar found in many nucleosides and in several vitamins and enzymes. [German, alteration of *Arabinose*, a related sugar]

ribosome *n. Biochem.* each of the minute particles consisting of RNA and associated proteins found in the cytoplasm of living cells, concerned with the synthesis of proteins. ▷ BACTERIUM, CELL. □ **ribosomal** *adj.*

rice ● *n.* **1** a swamp grass, *Oryza sativa*, cultivated in marshes, esp. in Asia. **2** the grains of this, used as cereal food. ● *v.tr.* US sieve (cooked potatoes etc.) into thin strings. [from Greek *oruza*] □ **ricer** *n.*

rice-paper *n.* edible paper made from the pith of an oriental tree and used for painting and in cookery.

rich *adj.* **1** having much wealth. **2** (often foll. by *in*, *with*) splendid, costly, elaborate. **3** valuable (*rich offerings*). **4** copious, abundant, ample (*a rich supply of ideas*). **5** (often foll. by *in*, *with*) (of soil or a region etc.) abounding in natural resources etc. (*rich in nutrients*). **6** (of food or diet) containing much fat or spice etc. **7** (of the mixture in an internal-combustion engine) containing a high proportion of fuel. **8** (of colour, sound, or smell) mellow and deep, strong and full. **9 a** (of an incident or assertion etc.) ludicrous. **b** (of humour) earthy. [Old English] □ **richen** *v.intr. & tr.* **richness** *n.*

riches *n.pl.* abundant means; valuable possessions. [from Old French *richeise*]

richly *adv.* **1** in a rich way. **2** fully, thoroughly.

Richter scale *n.* a logarithmic scale of 0 to 10 for representing the strength of an earthquake. [named after C. F. *Richter*, American seismologist, 1900–85]

rick[1] ● *n.* ▼ a stack of hay, corn, etc., built into a regular shape and usu. thatched. ● *v.tr.* form into a rick or ricks. [Old English]

RICK OF HAY

thatched top

rick[2] *Brit.* (also **wrick**) ● *n.* a slight sprain or strain. ● *v.tr.* sprain or strain slightly. [from Middle Low German *wricken* 'to move about, sprain']

rickets *n.* (treated as *sing.* or *pl.*) a disease of children with softening of the bones, caused by a deficiency of vitamin D. [17th-century coinage]

rickety *adj.* **1 a** insecure or shaky in construction. **b** feeble. **2** suffering from rickets. □ **ricketiness** *n.*

rickrack var. of RICRAC.

rickshaw *n.* (also **ricksha**) a light two-wheeled hooded vehicle drawn by one or more persons. [from Japanese *jinrikisha*, from *jin* 'person' + *riki* 'power' + *sha* 'vehicle']

ricochet /rik-ŏ-shay/ ● *n.* **1** the action of esp. a shell or bullet, in rebounding off a surface. **2** a hit made after this. ● *v.intr.* (**ricocheted**, **ricocheting** or **ricochetted**, **ricochetting**) (of a projectile) rebound one or more times from a surface. [French]

ricotta *n.* a soft Italian cheese. [Italian, literally 'recooked']

ricrac *n.* (also **rickrack**) ▶ a zigzag braided trimming for garments. [reduplication of RACK[1]]

RICRAC

rictus *n.* **1** *Anat. & Zool.* the expanse or gape of a mouth or beak. **2** a fixed grimace or grin. [Latin, literally 'open mouth'] □ **rictal** *adj.*

rid *v.tr.* (**ridding**; *past* and *past part.* **rid** or *archaic* **ridded**) (foll. by *of*) make (a person or place) free of something unwanted. □ **be** (or **get**) **rid of** be freed or relieved of (something unwanted); dispose of. [earlier in sense 'to clear (land etc.)': from Old Norse *rythja*]

riddance *n.* the act of getting rid of something. □ **good riddance** welcome relief from an unwanted person or thing.

ridden *past part.* of RIDE.

riddle[1] ● *n.* **1** a question or statement testing ingenuity in divining its answer or meaning. **2** a

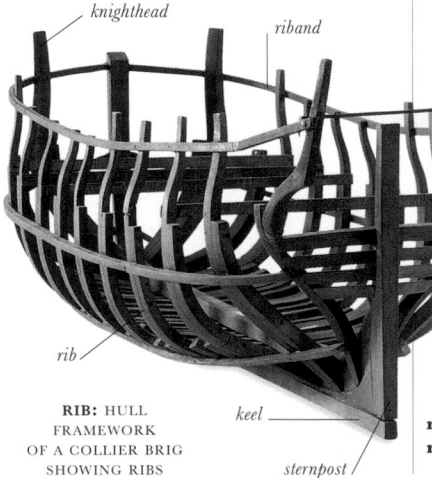

RIB: HULL FRAMEWORK OF A COLLIER BRIG SHOWING RIBS

knighthead

riband

rib

keel

sternpost

R

puzzling fact or thing or person. ● *v.intr.* speak in or propound riddles. [Old English] □ **riddler** *n.*

riddle² ● *v.tr.* (usu. foll. by *with*) **1** make many holes in, esp. with gunshot. **2** (in *passive*) permeate (*riddled with errors*). **3** pass through a riddle. ● *n.* a coarse sieve. [Old English]

ride ● *v.* (*past* **rode**; *past part.* **ridden**) **1** *tr.* travel or be carried on (a bicycle etc.) or esp. *N. Amer.* in (a vehicle). **2** *intr.* (often foll. by *on, in*) travel or be conveyed (on a bicycle or in a vehicle). **3** *tr.* sit on and control or be carried by (a horse etc.). **4** *intr.* (often foll. by *on*) be carried on (a horse etc.). **5** *tr.* be carried over or supported by (*the ship rides the waves*). **6** *tr.* **a** traverse on horseback etc. (*rode the prairie*). **b** compete or take part in on horseback etc. (*rode a good race*). **7** *intr.* **a** lie at anchor; float buoyantly. **b** (of the moon) seem to float. **8** *intr.* (foll. by *in, on*) rest in or on while moving. **9** *tr.* yield to (a blow) so as to reduce its impact. **10** *tr.* give a ride to; cause to ride (*rode the child on his back*). **11** *tr.* (of a rider) cause (a horse etc.) to move forward (*rode their horses at the fence*). **12** *tr.* **a** (in *passive*; foll. by *by, with*) be dominated by; be infested with (*ridden with guilt*). **b** (in *comb.* as **ridden** *adj.*) infested or afflicted (*a rat-ridden cellar*). ● *n.* **1** an act or period of travel in a vehicle. **2** a spell of riding on a horse, bicycle, etc. **3** *Brit.* a path (esp. through woods) for riding on. **4** the quality of sensations when riding (*gives a bumpy ride*). **5** a roller coaster etc., ridden at an amusement park or fairground. □ **ride down** overtake or trample on horseback. **ride for a fall** act recklessly risking defeat or failure. **ride out** come safely through (a storm etc., or a danger or difficulty). **ride roughshod over** see ROUGHSHOD. **ride shotgun** esp. *N. Amer.* **1** travel as a guard in the seat next to the driver of a vehicle. **2** ride in the passenger seat of a vehicle. **3** act as a protector. **ride up** (of a garment, carpet, etc.) work or move out of its proper position. **take for a ride** *colloq.* hoax or deceive. [Old English] □ **rideable** *adj.* (also **ridable**).

ride-on *attrib.adj.* (esp. of a lawnmower) on which one rides while operating it.

rider *n.* **1** a person who rides (esp. a horse). **2** an additional clause amending or supplementing a document. □ **riderless** *adj.*

ridge ● *n.* **1** the line of the junction of two surfaces sloping upwards towards each other (*the ridge of a roof*). ▷ ROOF. **2** a long narrow hilltop, mountain range, or watershed. **3** any narrow elevation across a surface. **4** *Meteorol.* an elongated region of high barometric pressure. **5** a raised strip of arable land, usu. one of a set separated by furrows. ● *v.tr.* **1** mark with ridges. **2** break up (land) into ridges. [Old English] □ **ridgy** *adj.*

ridge pole *n.* the horizontal pole of a long tent.

ridge tile *n.* a tile used in making a roof-ridge.

ridgeway *n.* a road or track along a ridge.

ridicule ● *n.* derision or mockery. ● *v.tr.* make fun of; subject to ridicule; laugh at. [from Latin *ridiculum* 'laughable (thing)']

ridiculous *adj.* **1** deserving or inviting ridicule. **2** unreasonable, absurd. [from Latin *ridiculosus*] □ **ridiculously** *adv.* **ridiculousness** *n.*

riding¹ *n.* **1** in senses of RIDE *v.* **2** the practice or skill of riders of horses. **3** = RIDE *n.* 3.

riding² *n.* **1** each of three former administrative divisions (**East Riding**, **North Riding**, **West Riding**) of Yorkshire. **2** an electoral division of Canada. [from Old Norse *thrithjungr* 'third part']

riding habit see HABIT *n.* 5b.

riding light *n.* a light shown by a ship at anchor.

rife *predic.adj.* **1** of common occurrence; widespread. **2** (foll. by *with*) abounding in; teeming with. [Old English] □ **rifeness** *n.*

riff ● *n.* a short repeated phrase in jazz etc. ● *v.intr.* play riffs. [20th-century coinage]

riffle ● *v.* **1** *tr.* **a** turn (pages) in quick succession. **b** shuffle (playing cards) esp. by flexing and

---

RIGGING

There are two types of rigging on a ship: standing rigging consists of the ropes, wires, and chains that fix the mast and yards into place; running rigging includes blocks, tackle, halyards, and sheets, which are used to hoist, lower, or trim the sails.

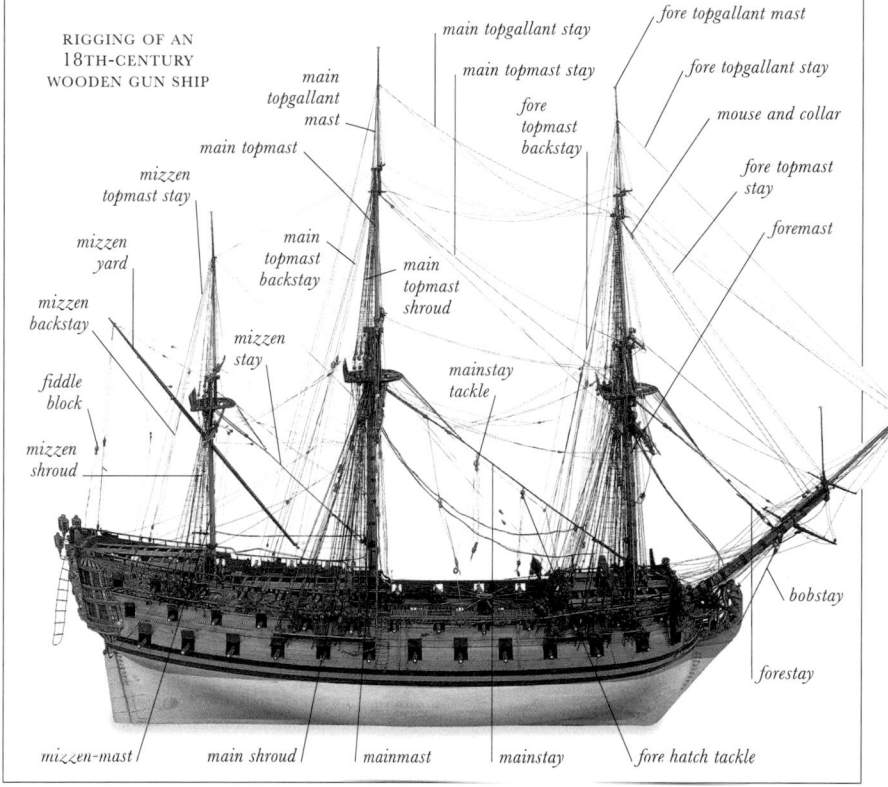

RIGGING OF AN 18TH-CENTURY WOODEN GUN SHIP

main topgallant stay · main topmast stay · fore topgallant mast · fore topgallant stay · mouse and collar · main topgallant mast · main topmast · fore topmast backstay · fore topmast stay · mizzen topmast stay · main topmast backstay · main topmast shroud · foremast · mizzen yard · main topmast backstay · main topmast shroud · mizzen backstay · mizzen stay · mainstay tackle · fiddle block · mizzen shroud · bobstay · forestay · mizzen-mast · main shroud · mainmast · mainstay · fore hatch tackle

---

combining the two halves of a pack. **2** *intr.* (often foll. by *through*) leaf quickly (through pages). ● *n.* the act or an instance of riffling.

riff-raff *n.* (often prec. by *the*) rabble; disreputable or undesirable persons. [from Old French *rif et raf*]

rifle¹ ● *n.* **1** a gun with a long rifled barrel, esp. one fired from shoulder level. ▷ GUN. **2** (in *pl.*) riflemen. ● *v.tr.* make spiral grooves in (a gun or its barrel or bore) to make a bullet spin. [from Old French *rifler* 'to graze, scratch']

rifle² *v.* **1** *intr.* (foll. by *through*) search through. **2** *tr.* search and rob, esp. of all that can be found. [from Old Dutch *riffelen*]

rifleman *n.* (*pl.* **-men**) a soldier armed with a rifle.

rifle range *n.* a place for rifle practice.

rifle shot *n.* **1** the distance coverable by a shot from a rifle. **2** a shot fired with a rifle.

rifling *n.* ▼ the arrangement of grooves on the inside of a gun's barrel.

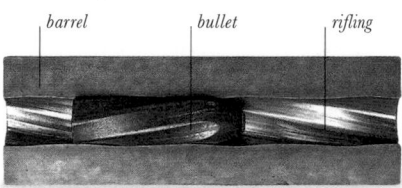

barrel · bullet · rifling

RIFLING: CROSS-SECTION OF A GUN BARREL SHOWING RIFLING

rift ● *n.* **1 a** a crack or split. **b** an opening in a cloud etc. **2** a cleft or fissure in earth or rock. **3** a breach in friendly relations. ● *v.tr.* tear or burst apart. [Middle English] □ **riftless** *adj.*

rift valley *n.* ▼ a steep-sided valley formed by subsidence of the Earth's crust between nearly parallel faults.

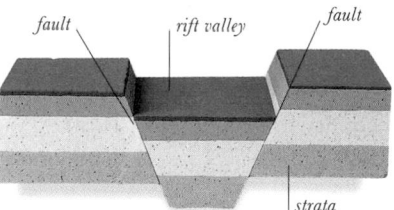

fault · rift valley · fault · strata

RIFT VALLEY: MODEL OF THE EARTH'S CRUST SHOWING A RIFT VALLEY

rig¹ ● *v.tr.* (**rigged**, **rigging**) **1 a** provide (a sailing ship) with sails, rigging, etc. **b** prepare ready for sailing. **2** (often foll. by *out, up*) fit with clothes or other equipment. **3** (foll. by *up*) set up hastily or as a makeshift. **4** assemble and adjust the parts of (an aircraft). ● *n.* **1** the arrangement of masts, sails, rigging, etc., of a sailing ship. **2** equipment for a special purpose, e.g. a radio transmitter. **3** = OIL RIG, DRILLING RIG. [Middle English] □ **rigged** *adj.* (also in *comb.*).

rig² *v.tr.* (**rigged**, **rigging**) manage or conduct fraudulently (*they rigged the election*). [18th-century coinage] □ **rigger** *n.*

rigger *n.* **1 a** a person who rigs or who arranges rigging. **b** a person who erects and maintains scaffolding etc. **2** *Rowing* = OUTRIGGER 4. **3** a ship rigged in a specified way. **4** a worker on an oil rig.

rigging *n.* ▲ a ship's ropes supporting the masts or supporting and controlling the sails. ▷ SHIP

R

right ● *adj.* **1** (of conduct etc.) just, morally or socially correct (*do the right thing*). **2** true, correct (*the right time*). **3** less wrong or not wrong (*which is the right way?*). **4** more or most suitable or preferable (*the right person for the job*). **5** in a sound or normal condition (*the engine doesn't sound right*). **6 a** on or towards the side of the human body which is to the east when facing north. **b** on or towards that part of an object which is analogous to a person's right side or (with opposite sense) which is nearer to the right hand of a person facing it. **7** esp. *Brit. colloq.* or *archaic* real; properly so called (*made a right mess of it*). **8** (also **Right**) *Polit.* of the Right. ● *n.* **1** that which is morally or socially correct or just; fair treatment (often in *pl.*: *the rights and wrongs of the case*). **2** (often foll. by *to*, or *to* + infin.) a justification or fair claim (*has no right to speak like that*). **3** a thing one may legally or morally claim; authority to act (*a right of reply*; *human rights*). **4** the right-hand part or region or direction. **5** *Boxing* **a** the right hand. **b** a blow with this. **6** (often **Right**) *Polit.* **a** a group or section favouring conservatism. **b** such conservatives collectively. **7** (in full **stage right**) the side of a stage which is to the right of a person facing the audience. ● *v.tr.* **1** (often *refl.*) restore to a proper or straight or vertical position. **2 a** correct (mistakes etc.); set in order. **b** avenge (a wrong or a wronged person); make reparation for or to. ● *adv.* **1** straight (*go right on*). **2** *colloq.* immediately; without delay (*do it right now*). **3 a** (foll. by *to*, *round*, *through*, etc.) all the way (*right to the bottom*). **b** (foll. by *off*, *out*, etc.) completely (*am right out of butter*). **4** exactly, quite (*right in the middle*). **5** justly, properly, correctly, truly, satisfactorily (*not holding it right*; *if I remember right*). **6** on or to the right side. **7** *archaic* very; to the full (*dined right royally*). ● *int. colloq.* expressing agreement or assent. □ **as right as rain** perfectly sound and healthy. **at right angles** placed to form a right angle. **by right** (or **rights**) if right were done. **do right by** act dutifully towards (a person). **in one's own right** through one's own position or effort etc. **in the right** having justice or truth on one's side. **in one's right mind** sane; competent to think and act. **of** (or **as of**) **right** having legal or moral etc. entitlement. **put** (or **set**) **right 1** restore to order, health, etc. **2** correct the mistaken impression etc. of (a person). **put** (or **set**) **to rights** make correct or well ordered. **right and left** (or **right, left, and centre**) on all sides. **right away** (or **off**) immediately. **right oh!** (or **ho!**) = RIGHTO. **right on!** *slang* an expression of strong approval or encouragement (cf. RIGHT-ON). **right you are!** *colloq.* an exclamation of assent. **too right** *colloq.* an expression of agreement. **within one's rights** not exceeding one's authority or entitlement. [Old English] □ **righter** *n.* **rightish** *adj.* **rightless** *adj.* **rightness** *n.*

right about *n.* (also **right about-face** or *Brit.* **right about-turn**) **1** esp. *Mil.* a right turn continued to face the rear. **2** a reversal of policy. **3** a hasty retreat.

right angle *n.* an angle of 90°, as formed by dividing a circle into quarters. □ **right-angled** *adj.*

right arm *n.* one's most reliable helper.

right-back *n.* (in football, hockey, etc.) a back who plays primarily on the right of the pitch. ▷ FOOTBALL

right bank *n.* the bank of a river on the right facing downstream.

righteous *adj.* (of a person or conduct) morally right; virtuous, law-abiding. [Old English] □ **righteously** *adv.* **righteousness** *n.*

right-footed *adj.* **1** using the right foot by preference as more serviceable than the left. **2** (of a kick etc.) done or made with the right foot.

rightful *adj.* **1 a** (of a person) legitimately entitled to (a position etc.). **b** (of status or property etc.) that one is entitled to. **2** (of an action etc.)

equitable, fair. [Old English] □ **rightfully** *adv.* **rightfulness** *n.*

right-hand *adj.* **1** on or towards the right side of a person or thing. **2** done with the right hand. **3** (of a screw) = RIGHT-HANDED 4b.

right hand *n.* **1** = RIGHT-HAND MAN. **2** the most important position next to a person.

right-handed *adj.* **1** using the right hand by preference as more serviceable than the left. **2** (of a tool etc.) made to be used with the right hand. **3** (of a blow) struck with the right hand. **4 a** turning to the right; towards the right. **b** (of a screw) advanced by turning clockwise. □ **right-handedly** *adv.* **right-handedness** *n.*

right-hander *n.* **1** a right-handed person. **2 a** right-handed blow.

right-hand man *n.* an indispensable or chief assistant.

Right Honourable *adj. Brit.* a title given to certain high officials, e.g. Privy Counsellors.

rightism *n. Polit.* the principles or policy of the right. □ **rightist** *n. & adj.*

rightly *adv.* justly, properly, correctly, justifiably.

right-minded *adj.* having sound views and principles.

rightmost *adj.* furthest to the right.

righto *int.* (also **righty-ho**) *Brit. colloq.* expressing agreement or assent.

right of abode *n. Brit.* a person's right to take up residence or remain resident in a country.

right of primogeniture see PRIMOGENITURE 2.

right of way *n.* **1** a right established by usage to pass over another's ground. **2** a path subject to such a right. **3** the right of a vehicle to precedence.

right-on *adj. slang* excellent; fashionable; politically correct (cf. *right on*).

Right Reverend *adj.* the title of a bishop.

right side *n.* the better or desirable, or usable side of something, esp. fabric. □ **on the right side of 1** in favour with (a person). **2** somewhat less than (a specified age). **right side out** with the right side outwards; not inside out.

right-thinking *adj.* = RIGHT-MINDED.

right-to-life *adj.* = PRO-LIFE.

rightward ● *adv.* (also **rightwards**) towards the right. ● *adj.* going towards or facing the right.

right whale *n.* ▼ any large-headed whale of the family Balaenidae, rich in whalebone and easily captured. ▷ WHALE

callosity

rotund body

paddle-shaped flippers

RIGHT WHALE: SOUTHERN RIGHT WHALE (*Eubalaena australis*)

right-wing *adj.* **1** conservative; reactionary. **2** of or relating to the right wing in football etc. ▷ RUGBY

right wing *n.* **1** the conservative section of a political party or system. **2** the right side of a football etc. team on the field. □ **right-winger** *n.*

righty-ho var. of RIGHTO.

rigid *adj.* **1** not flexible; that cannot be bent. **2** (of a person, conduct, etc.) inflexible, strict, punctilious. [from Latin *rigidus*] □ **rigidity** *n.* **rigidly** *adv.* **rigidness** *n.*

rigidify *v.tr. & intr.* (**-ies**, **-ied**) make or become rigid.

rigmarole *n.* **1** a lengthy and complicated procedure. **2 a** a rambling or meaningless account or tale. **b** such talk. [originally *ragman roll* 'a catalogue']

rigor[1] *n. Med.* **1** a sudden feeling of cold with shivering accompanied by a rise in temperature. **2** rigidity of the body caused by shock or poisoning etc. [Latin]

rigor[2] *US* var. of RIGOUR.

rigor mortis *n.* stiffening of the body after death. [Latin, literally 'stiffness of death']

rigorous *adj.* **1** characterized by or showing rigour; strict, severe. **2** strictly exact or accurate. □ **rigorously** *adv.* **rigorousness** *n.*

rigour *n.* (*US* **rigor**) **1 a** severity, strictness, harshness. **b** (in *pl.*) harsh measures or conditions. **2** logical exactitude. **3** strict enforcement of rules etc. (*the utmost rigour of the law*). [from Latin *rigor*]

rig-out *n. Brit. colloq.* an outfit of clothes.

rile *v.tr. colloq.* anger, irritate. [variant of dialect *roil* 'to stir up (a liquid)']

Riley *n.* (also **Reilly**) □ **the life of Riley** *colloq.* a carefree existence. [20th-century coinage]

rilievo var. of RELIEVO.

rill *n.* a small stream. [from Low German *ril*]

rim ● *n.* **1 a** a raised edge or border. **b** a margin or verge, esp. of something circular. **2** the part of a pair of spectacles surrounding the lenses. **3** the outer edge of a wheel, on which the tyre is fitted. ● *v.tr.* (**rimmed**, **rimming**) **1 a** provide with a rim. **b** be a rim for or to. **2** edge, border. [Old English] □ **rimless** *adj.* **rimmed** *adj.* (also in *comb.*).

rime[1] ● *n.* **1** frost, esp. formed from cloud or fog. **2** *poet.* hoar frost. ● *v.tr.* cover with rime. [Old English] □ **rimy** *adj.*

rime[2] *archaic* var. of RHYME.

rind ● *n.* **1** the tough outer layer or covering of fruit, cheese, bacon, etc. **2** the bark of a tree or plant. ● *v.tr.* strip the bark from. [Old English] □ **rinded** *adj.* (also in *comb.*). **rindless** *adj.*

rinderpest *n.* a virulent infectious viral disease of ruminants (esp. cattle). [German, from *Rinder* 'cattle' + *Pest* 'plague']

ring[1] ● *n.* **1** a circular band, usu. of precious metal, worn on a finger. **2** a circular band of any material. **3** the rim of a cylindrical or circular object, or a line or band round it. **4** a mark or part having the form of a circular band (*smoke rings*). **5** = ANNUAL RING. **6 a** an enclosure for a circus performance, boxing, the showing of cattle, etc. **b** (prec. by *the*) bookmakers collectively. **7 a** a group of people or things arranged in a circle. **b** such an arrangement. **8 a** combination of traders, spies, politicians, etc. acting together usu. illicitly for profit etc. **9** a circular or spiral course. **10** = GAS RING. **11** *Chem.* a group of atoms each bonded to two others in a closed sequence. ● *v.tr.* **1** make or draw a circle round. **2** (often foll. by *round*, *about*, *in*) encircle or hem in (game or cattle). **3** put a ring on (a bird etc.) or through the nose of (a pig, bull, etc.). □ **run** (or **make**) **rings round** *colloq.* outclass or outwit (another person). [Old English] □ **ringed** *adj.* (also in *comb.*). **ringless** *adj.*

ring[2] ● *v.* (*past* **rang**; *past part.* **rung**) **1** *intr.* (often foll. by *out* etc.) give a clear resonant or vibrating sound or as of as of a bell (*a shot rang out*). **2** *tr.* **a** make (esp. a bell) ring. **b** (*absol.*) call for service or attention by ringing a bell. **3** *tr.* (also *absol.*; often foll. by *up*) esp. *Brit.* call by telephone. **4** *intr.* (usu. foll. by *with*, *to*) resound or be permeated with a sound, or an attribute (*the theatre rang with applause*). **5** *intr.* (of the ears) be filled with a sensation of ringing. **6** *tr.* **a** sound (a peal etc.) on bells. **b** (of a bell) sound (the hour etc.). **7** *tr.* (foll. by *in*, *out*) usher in or out with bell-ringing (*rang out the Old Year*). **8** *intr.* (of sentiments etc.) convey a specified impression

R

(words rang hollow). ● *n.* **1** a ringing sound or tone. **2 a** the act of ringing a bell. **b** the sound caused by this. **3** *colloq.* a telephone call. **4** a specified feeling conveyed by an utterance *(had a melancholy ring).* **5** a set of esp. church bells. □ **ring back** make a return telephone call to. **ring a bell** see BELL. **ring the changes (on)** see CHANGE. **ring down** (or **up**) **the curtain 1** *Theatr.* cause the curtain to be lowered or raised. **2** (foll. by *on*) mark the end or the beginning of (an enterprise etc.). **ring in** *Brit.* report or make contact by telephone. **ring in one's ears** (or **heart** etc.) linger in the memory. **ring off** *Brit.* end a telephone call by replacing the receiver. **ring true** (or **false**) convey an impression of truth or falsehood. **ring up 1** *Brit.* call by telephone. **2** record (an amount etc.) on a cash register. [Old English] □ **ringed** *adj.* (also in *comb.*). **ringer** *n.* **ringing** *adj.* **ringingly** *adv.*

ring-binder *n.* a loose-leaf binder with ring-shaped clasps that can be opened to pass through holes in the paper.

ring circuit *n.* an electrical circuit serving a number of power points with one fuse in the supply to the circuit.

ringed plover *n.* ► either of two small plovers, *Charadrius hiaticula* and *C. dubius.*

ringer *n.* **1** *slang* **a** esp. *US* an athlete or horse entered in a competition by fraudulent means, esp. as a substitute. **b** a person's or thing's double, esp. an impostor. **2** a person who rings, esp. a bell-ringer. □ **be a ringer** (or **dead ringer**) **for** resemble (a person) exactly.

RINGED PLOVER
(Charadrius hiaticula)

ring-fence ● *n.* a fence completely enclosing a piece of land. ● *v.tr.* **1** enclose with a ring-fence. **2 a** guard securely. **b** *Finance* protect or guarantee (funds).

ring finger *n.* the finger next to the little finger, esp. of the left hand, on which the wedding ring is usu. worn.

ringing tone *n.* a sound heard by a telephone caller when the number dialled is being rung.

ringleader *n.* a leading instigator in an illicit or illegal activity.

ringlet *n.* a lock of hair hanging in a corkscrew-shaped curl. □ **ringletted** *adj.* (*US* **ringleted**).

ring main *n.* *Brit.* **1** an electrical supply serving a series of consumers and returning to the original source, so that each consumer has an alternative path in the event of a failure. **2** = RING CIRCUIT.

ringmaster *n.* the person directing a circus performance.

ring ouzel *n.* a thrush, *Turdus torquatus*, with a white crescent across its breast.

ring-pull *n.* a ring on a tin for pulling to break its seal.

ring road *n.* esp. *Brit.* a bypass encircling a town.

ringside *n.* the area immediately beside a boxing ring or circus ring etc. (often *attrib.: a ringside seat*). □ **ringsider** *n.*

ringworm *n.* any of various fungal infections of the skin causing circular inflamed patches, esp. on the scalp.

rink *n.* **1** an area of ice for skating or the game of curling etc. **2** an enclosed area for roller skating. **3** a building containing either of these. **4** *Bowls* a strip of the green used for playing a match. [Middle English, originally Scots in sense 'jousting-ground']

rinse ● *v.tr.* (often foll. by *through*, *out*) **1** wash with clean water. **2** apply liquid to. **3** wash lightly. **4** put (clothes etc.) through water to remove soap or detergent. **5** (foll. by *out*, *away*) clear (impurities) by rinsing. ● *n.* **1** the act or an instance of rinsing. **2** a

solution for cleansing the mouth. **3** a dye for temporary tinting of hair. [from Old French *rincer*] □ **rinser** *n.*

Rioja /ri-o-hă/ *n.* wine produced in Rioja, a district in northern Spain.

riot ● *n.* **1 a** a disturbance of the peace by a crowd. **b** (*attrib.*) involved in suppressing riots (*riot police*). **2** uncontrolled revelry; noisy behaviour. **3** (foll. by *of*) a lavish display or enjoyment (*a riot of colour and sound*). **4** *colloq.* a very amusing thing or person. ● *v.intr.* **1** make or engage in a riot. **2** live wantonly; revel. □ **read the riot act** put a firm stop to insubordination etc.; give a severe warning. **run riot 1** throw off all restraint. **2** (of plants) grow or spread uncontrolled. [from Old French] □ **rioter** *n.*

riot gear *n.* protective clothing, helmets, etc., worn by police or prison officers in situations of violence or potential violence.

riotous *adj.* **1** marked by or involving rioting. **2** characterized by wanton conduct. **3** wildly profuse. □ **riotously** *adv.* **riotousness** *n.*

RIP *abbr.* may he or she or they rest in peace. [Latin *requiescat* (pl. *requiescant*) *in pace*]

rip[1] ● *v.* (**ripped**, **ripping**) **1** *tr.* tear or cut (a thing) quickly or forcibly away or apart. **2** *tr.* **a** make (a hole etc.) by ripping. **b** make a long tear or cut in. **3** *intr.* come violently apart. **4** *intr.* rush along. ● *n.* **1** a long tear or cut. **2** an act of ripping. □ **let rip** *colloq.* **1** act or proceed without restraint. **2** speak violently. **3** not check the speed of or interfere with (a person or thing). **rip into** attack (a person) verbally. **rip off** *colloq.* defraud, steal. [Middle English]

rip[2] *n.* **1** a dissolute person. **2** a rascal. **3** a worthless horse. [18th-century coinage]

riparian *adj.* esp. *Law* of or on a river bank. [based on Latin *ripa* 'river bank']

ripcord *n.* a cord for releasing a parachute from its pack.

ripe *adj.* **1** (of grain, cheese, etc.) ready to be reaped or picked or eaten. **2** mature; fully developed. **3** (of a person's age) advanced. **4** (often foll. by *for*) fit or ready (*when the time is ripe*). [Old English] □ **ripely** *adv.* **ripeness** *n.*

ripen *v.tr. & intr.* make or become ripe.

rip-off *n.* *colloq.* **1** a fraud or swindle. **2** financial exploitation.

riposte /ri-posst/ ● *n.* **1** a quick sharp reply or retort. **2** a quick return thrust in fencing. ● *v.intr.* deliver a riposte. [French]

ripper *n.* **1** a person or thing that rips. **2** a murderer who rips or mutilates victims' bodies.

ripple ● *n.* **1** a ruffling of the water's surface, a small wave or series of waves. **2** a gentle lively sound that rises and falls, e.g. of applause. **3** a wavy appearance in hair, material, etc. ● *v.* **1 a** *intr.* form ripples; flow in ripples. **b** *tr.* cause to do this. **2** *intr.* show or sound like ripples. [17th-century coinage] □ **ripply** *adj.*

rip-roaring *adj.* **1** wildly noisy or boisterous. **2** excellent, first-rate. □ **rip-roaringly** *adv.*

ripsaw *n.* a coarse saw for sawing wood along the grain.

ripsnorter *n.* *colloq.* an energetic, remarkable, or excellent person or thing. □ **ripsnorting** *adj.* **ripsnortingly** *adv.*

ripstop ● *attrib.adj.* (of fabric, clothing, etc.) woven so that a tear will not spread. ● *n.* ripstop fabric.

RISC /risk/ *n.* **1** a computer designed to perform a limited set of operations at high speed. **2** computing using this kind of computer. [acronym from *r*educed *i*nstruction *s*et *c*omputer (or *c*omputing)]

rise ● *v.intr.* (*past* **rose**; *past part.* **risen**) **1** come or go up. **2** grow, project, expand, or incline upwards; become higher. **3** appear above the horizon. **4 a** get up from lying or sitting or kneeling. **b** get out of bed, esp. in the morning. **5** become erect. **6** esp.

Brit. (of a meeting etc.) cease to sit for business. **7** reach a higher position or level or amount (*the flood has risen*). **8** develop greater intensity, strength, volume, or pitch (*their voices rose*). **9** make progress; reach a higher social position (*rose from the ranks*). **10 a** come to the surface of liquid. **b** (of a person) react to provocation (*rise to the bait*). **11** become or be visible above the surroundings etc. **12 a** (of buildings etc.) undergo construction from the foundations (*office blocks were rising*). **b** (of a tree etc.) grow to a (usu. specified) height. **13** come to life again (*rise from the ashes*). **14** (of dough) swell by the action of yeast etc. **15** (often foll. by *up*) rebel (*rose up against the despot*). **16** originate (*the river rises in the mountains*). **17** (of wind) start to blow. **18** (of a person's spirits) become cheerful. **19** (of a barometer) show a higher atmospheric pressure. ● *n.* **1** an act or manner or amount of rising. **2** an upward slope or hill or movement (*the house stood on a rise*). **3** an increase in sound or pitch. **4 a** an increase in amount, extent, etc. (*a rise in unemployment*). **b** *Brit.* an increase in salary, wages, etc. **5** an increase in status or power. **6** social, commercial, or political advancement. **7** the movement of a fish to the surface. **8** origin. **9 a** the vertical height of a step, arch, etc. **b** = RISER 2. □ **get** (or **take**) **a rise out of** *colloq.* provoke an emotional reaction from (a person), esp. by teasing. **on the rise** on the increase. **rise above** be superior to (petty feelings, difficulties, etc.). **rise to** develop or reveal powers appropriate to (an event). [Old English]

riser *n.* **1** a person who rises esp. from bed (*an early riser*). **2** a vertical section between the treads of a staircase. **3** a vertical pipe for the flow of liquid or gas.

rishi *n.* (*pl.* **rishis**) a Hindu sage or saint. [from Sanskrit *ṛṣi*]

risible *adj.* **1** laughable, ludicrous. **2** inclined to laugh. [from Late Latin *risibilis*] □ **risibility** *n.* **risibly** *adv.*

rising ● *adj.* **1** going up; getting higher. **2** increasing (*rising costs*). **3** advancing to maturity or high standing (*a rising young lawyer*). **4** *Brit.* approaching a specified age (*the rising fives*). **5** (of ground) sloping upwards. ● *n.* a revolt or insurrection.

rising damp *n.* *Brit.* moisture absorbed from the ground into a wall.

risk ● *n.* **1** a chance or possibility of danger, loss, injury, etc. (*a health risk*). **2** a person or thing causing a risk or regarded in relation to risk. ● *v.tr.* **1** expose to risk. **2** accept the chance of (*risk getting wet*). **3** venture on. □ **at risk** exposed to danger. **at one's (own) risk** accepting responsibility, agreeing to make no claims. **at the risk of** with the possibility of (an adverse consequence). **put at risk** expose to danger. **risk one's neck** put one's own life in danger. **run a** (or **the**) **risk** (often foll. by *of*) expose oneself to danger, loss, etc. **take** (or **run**) **a risk** chance the possibility of danger etc. [from Italian *risco* 'danger']

risky *adj.* (**riskier**, **riskiest**) **1** involving risk. **2** = RISQUÉ. □ **riskily** *adv.* **riskiness** *n.*

risotto *n.* (*pl.* **-os**) an Italian savoury rice dish cooked in stock. [Italian, from *riso* 'rice']

risqué /reess-kay/ *adj.* (of a story etc.) slightly indecent. [French, literally 'risked']

rissole *n.* a compressed mixture of meat and spices, coated in breadcrumbs and fried. [based on Late Latin *russeolus* 'reddish']

ritardando *adv., adj., & n.* (*pl.* **-os** or **ritardandi**) *Mus.* = RALLENTANDO. [Italian]

rite *n.* **1** a religious or solemn observance or act. **2** an action or procedure required or usual in this. **3** a body of customary observances characteristic of a Church or a part of it (*the Latin rite*). [from Latin *ritus* 'religious' usage']

rite of passage *n.* (often in *pl.*) a ritual or event marking a stage of a person's advance through life, e.g. marriage.

R

ritual ● *n.* **1** a prescribed order of performing rites. **2** a procedure regularly followed. ● *adj.* of or done as a ritual or rites. [from Latin *ritualis*] □ **ritualize** *v.tr.* & *intr.* (also **-ise**). **ritualization** *n.* (also **-isation**). **ritually** *adv.*

ritualism *n.* the regular or excessive practice of ritual. □ **ritualist** *n.* **ritualistic** *adj.* **ritualistically** *adv.*

ritzy *adj.* (**ritzier, ritziest**) *colloq.* **1** high-class, luxurious. **2** ostentatiously smart. [from C. *Ritz*, Swiss hotel-owner, 1850–1918] □ **ritzily** *adv.* **ritziness** *n.*

rival ● *n.* **1** a person competing with another for the same objective. **2** a person or thing that equals another in quality. ● *v.tr.* (**rivalled, rivalling**; *US* **rivaled, rivaling**) **1** be the rival of or comparable to. **2** seem or claim to be as good as. [from Latin *rivalis*, originally in sense 'using the same stream']

rivalry *n.* (*pl.* **-ies**) the state or an instance of being rivals; competition.

rive *v.tr.* (*past* **rived**; *past part.* **riven**) *archaic* or *poet.* (except in *passive* or as **riven** *adj.*) **1** split or tear apart violently (*a country riven by conflict*). **2** split (wood or stone) (*riven paving*). [from Old Norse *rifa*]

river *n.* **1** ▼ a copious natural stream of water flowing in a channel to the sea or a lake etc. **2** a copious flow. [based on Latin *ripa* 'river bank'] □ **rivered** *adj.* (also in *comb.*). **riverless** *adj.*

riverboat *n.* a boat designed for use on rivers. ▷ BOAT

riverine *adj.* of or on a river or river bank; riparian.

riverside *n.* the ground along a river bank.

rivet ● *n.* a nail or bolt for holding together metal plates etc., its headless end being beaten out flat when in place. ● *v.tr.* (**riveted, riveting**) **1 a** join or fasten with rivets. **b** beat out flat or press down the end of (a nail or bolt). **c** fix; make immovable. **2 a** (foll. by *on, upon*) direct intently (one's eyes or attention etc.). **b** (esp. as **riveting** *adj.*) engross (a person or the attention). [from Old French *river* 'to clench'] □ **riveter** *n.*

riviera /ri-vi-**air**-ă/ *n.* a coastal region with a subtropical climate, vegetation, etc., esp. that of SE France and NW Italy. [Italian, literally 'sea-shore']

rivulet *n.* a small stream. [alteration of archaic French *riveret* 'little river']

RM *abbr.* (in the UK) Royal Marines.

RN *abbr.* (in the UK) Royal Navy.

Rn *symb. Chem.* the element radon.

RNA *abbr.* ribonucleic acid.

RNZAF *abbr.* Royal New Zealand Air Force.

RNZN *abbr.* Royal New Zealand Navy.

roach[1] *n.* (*pl.* same) ▼ a small freshwater fish, esp. *Rutilus rutilus*, allied to the carp. [from Old French *roc(h)e*]

ROACH
(*Rutilus rutilus*)

roach[2] *n.* **1** *N. Amer. colloq.* a cockroach. **2** *slang* the butt of a marijuana cigarette. [abbreviation]

roach[3] *n. Naut.* **1 a** a curved part of a fore-and-aft sail extending beyond a straight line between its corners, esp. on the leech side. **b** the breadth of this. **2** an upward curve in the foot of a square sail. [18th c.: origin unknown]

road *n.* **1 a** a path or way with a specially prepared surface, used by vehicles, pedestrians, etc. **b** the part of this used by vehicles (*don't step in the road*). **2** esp. *Brit.* one's way or route (*our road took us through unexplored territory*). **3** (usu. in *pl.*) a partly sheltered piece of water near the shore in which ships can ride at anchor. □ **get out of the** (or **my** etc.) **road** *colloq.* cease to obstruct a person.

in the (or **my** etc.) **road** *colloq.* obstructing a person or thing. **on the road** travelling, esp. as a firm's representative, itinerant performer, or vagrant. [Old English] □ **roadless** *adj.*

roadbed *n.* **1** the foundation structure of a railway. **2** the material laid down to form a road. **3** *US* the part of a road on which vehicles travel.

roadblock *n.* a barrier set up on a road in order to stop and examine traffic.

road fund licence *n. Brit.* a disc displayed on a vehicle certifying payment of road tax.

road hog *n. colloq.* a reckless or inconsiderate road user, esp. a motorist.

road-holding *n.* the capacity of a moving vehicle to remain stable when cornering at high speeds etc.

roadhouse *n.* an inn or club on a major road.

road hump *n.* = SLEEPING POLICEMAN.

roadie *n. colloq.* an assistant employed by a touring band of musicians to erect and maintain equipment.

road manager *n.* the organizer and supervisor of a musicians' tour.

road map *n.* a map showing the roads of a country or area.

road metal *n. Brit.* broken stone used in road-making or for railway ballast.

road-pricing *n.* the practice of charging motorists to use busy roads at certain times.

road rage *n.* anger towards other road users, experienced by a person when driving.

roadroller *n.* a motor vehicle with a heavy roller, used in road-making.

roadrunner *n.* ▼ a fast-running bird of Mexican and US deserts, *Geococcyx californianus*, related to the cuckoo.

ROADRUNNER:
GREATER ROADRUNNER
(*Geococcyx californianus*)

road sense *n. Brit.* a person's capacity for safe behaviour on the road, esp. in traffic.

roadshow *n.* **1 a** a performance given by a touring company, esp. a group of pop musicians. **b** a company giving such performances. **2** a radio or television programme made on location, esp. a series of programmes each from a different venue.

roadside *n.* the strip of land beside a road (often *attrib.: roadside café*).

road sign *n.* a sign giving information or instructions to road users.

roadstead *n.* = ROAD 3.

roadster *n.* **1** an open two-seater motor car. **2** a bicycle or (formerly) a horse for use on the road.

road tax *n. Brit.* a periodic tax payable on road vehicles.

road test ● *n.* a test of the performance of a vehicle on the road. ● *v.tr.* (**road-test**) test (a vehicle) on the road.

roadway *n.* **1** a road. **2** = ROAD 1b. **3** the part of a bridge or railway used for traffic.

roadwork *n.* **1** (in *pl.*) *Brit.* the construction, repair, etc. of roads. **2** athletic exercise or training involving running on roads.

roadworthy *adj.* fit to be used on the road. □ **roadworthiness** *n.*

roam ● *v.* **1** *intr.* ramble, wander. **2** *tr.* travel unsystematically over, through, or about. ● *n.* an act of roaming; a ramble. [Middle English] □ **roamer** *n.*

RIVER

At its source, a river is usually steep, eroding downwards to cut deep valleys and gorges. Rapids and waterfalls may form where the river flows from hard to softer rock. As it looses its steep gradient, the river slows down and deposits silt; sideways erosion increases and the river begins to meander, forming a floodplain. Strong erosion in tight meanders can cut off sections, forming oxbow lakes.

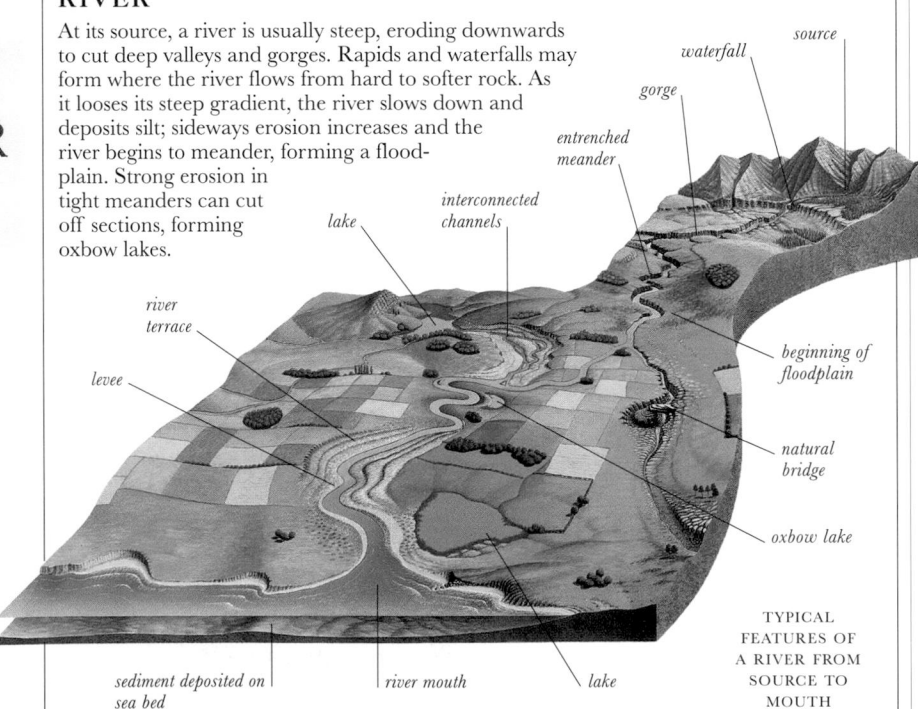

waterfall

source

gorge

entrenched meander

interconnected channels

lake

river terrace

levee

beginning of floodplain

natural bridge

oxbow lake

sediment deposited on sea bed

river mouth

lake

TYPICAL FEATURES OF A RIVER FROM SOURCE TO MOUTH

BLUE
ROAN

STRAWBERRY
ROAN

ROAN: EXAMPLES OF ROAN HORSES

roan ● *adj.* ▲ (of esp. a horse) having a coat of which the prevailing colour is thickly interspersed with hairs of another colour. ● *n.* a roan animal. [from Old French]

roar ● *n.* **1** a loud deep hoarse sound, as made by a lion. **2** a loud laugh. ● *v.* **1** *intr.* **a** utter or make a roar. **b** utter loud laughter. **2** *intr.* travel in a vehicle at high speed, esp. with the engine roaring. **3** *tr.* (often foll. by *out*) say, sing, or utter (words, an oath, etc.) in a loud tone. [Old English] □ **roarer** *n.*

roaring *adj.* in senses of ROAR *v.* □ **roaring drunk** *colloq.* very drunk and noisy. **roaring trade** (or **business**) *colloq.* very brisk trade or business. □ **roaringly** *adv.*

roast ● *v.* **1** *tr.* **a** cook (food, esp. meat) in an oven or by exposure to open heat. **b** heat (coffee beans) before grinding. **2** *tr. & refl.* expose (oneself etc.) to warmth. **3** *tr.* criticize severely, denounce. **4** *intr.* undergo roasting. ● *attrib.adj.* (of meat or a potato, chestnut, etc.) roasted. ● *n.* **1 a** roast meat. **b** a dish of this. **c** a piece of meat for roasting. **2** the process of roasting. **3** *US* a party where roasted food is eaten. [from Old French *rost*]

roaster *n.* **1** a person or thing that roasts. **2 a** an oven or dish for roasting food in. **b** a coffee-roasting apparatus. **3** something fit for roasting, e.g. a fowl, a potato, etc.

roasting ● *adj.* very hot and dry. ● *n.* **1** in senses of ROAST *v.* **2** a severe criticism or denunciation.

rob *v.tr.* (**robbed**, **robbing**) (often foll. by *of*) **1** take unlawfully from, esp. by force or threat of force. **2** deprive of what is due or normal (*was robbed of my sleep*). **3** (*absol.*) commit robbery. [from Old French *rob(b)er*] □ **robber** *n.*

robbery *n.* (*pl.* **-ies**) **1 a** the act or process of robbing, esp. with force or threat of force. **b** an instance of this. **2** excessive financial demand or cost.

robe ● *n.* **1** a long loose outer garment. **2** esp. *N. Amer.* a dressing gown. **3** (often in *pl.*) a long outer garment worn as an indication of the wearer's rank, profession, etc. **4** *N. Amer.* a blanket or wrap of fur. ● *v.* **1** *tr.* clothe (a person) in a robe; dress. **2** *intr.* put on one's robes or vestments. [Middle English]

robin *n.* **1** (also **robin redbreast**) a small brown European bird, *Erithacus rubecula*, the adult of which has a red throat and breast. **2** *N. Amer.* a red-breasted thrush, *Turdus migratorius*. [from Old French, pet form of the name *Robert*]

robinia *n.* ▶ any N. American tree or shrub of the genus *Robinia*, e.g. a locust tree or false acacia. [named after J. *Robin*, 17th-century French gardener]

robot *n.* **1** a machine with a human appearance or functioning like a human. **2** ▼ a machine capable of carrying out a complex series of actions automatically. **3** a person who works mechanically and efficiently but insensitively. **4** *S.Afr.* an automatic traffic signal. [from Czech *robota* 'forced labour', used in K. Čapek's play *R.U.R.* ('Rossum's Universal Robots'), 1920] □ **robotic** *adj.* **robotically** *adv.* **robotize** *v.tr.* (also **-ise**). **robotization** *n.* (also **-isation**).

robotics *n.pl.* (usu. treated as *sing.*) the study of robots; the art or science of their design and operation.

robust *adj.* (**robuster**, **robustest**) **1** strong and sturdy, esp. in physique or construction. **2** (of exercise, discipline, etc.) vigorous, requiring strength. **3** (of intellect or mental attitude) straightforward. **4** (of a statement, reply, etc.) bold, firm, unyielding. **5** (of wine etc.) full-bodied. [from Latin *robustus* 'firm and hard'] □ **robustly** *adv.* **robustness** *n.*

robusta *n.* **1** coffee or coffee beans from a widely grown African species of coffee plant, *Coffea canephora* (formerly *robusta*). **2** this plant. [modern Latin]

ROC *abbr.* (in the UK) Royal Observer Corps.

roc *n.* a gigantic bird of Eastern legend. [from Arabic *rukh*]

rock[1] *n.* **1 a** the hard material of the Earth's crust, exposed on the surface or underlying the soil. **b** a

pinnate leaf

ROBINIA
(*Robinia pseudoacacia*)

pendent raceme

similar material on other planets. **2** a mass of rock projecting and forming a hill, cliff, reef, etc. **3** a large detached stone. **4** *US* a stone of any size. **5** a firm and dependable support or protection. **6** *Brit.* a kind of hard confectionery usu. made in cylindrical peppermint-flavoured sticks. **7** *slang* a precious stone, esp. a diamond. □ **on the rocks** *colloq.* **1** short of money. **2** (esp. of a marriage) in danger of breaking up. **3** (of a drink) served undiluted with ice cubes. [from medieval Latin *rocca*] □ **rockless** *adj.* **rocklet** *n.* **rocklike** *adj.*

rock[2] ● *v.* **1** *tr.* move gently to and fro in or as if in a cradle; set or maintain such motion. **2** *intr.* be or continue in such motion (*sat rocking in his chair*). **3 a** *intr.* sway from side to side; shake, oscillate, reel. **b** *tr.* cause to do this (*an earthquake rocked the house*). **4** *tr.* distress, perturb. **5** *intr.* dance to or play rock music. ● *n.* **1** a rocking movement. **2** a spell of rocking. **3 a** = ROCK AND ROLL. **b** any of a variety of types of modern popular music with a rocking or swinging beat, derived from rock and roll. □ **rock the boat** *colloq.* disturb the equilibrium of a situation. [Old English]

rockabilly *n.* a type of popular music combining elements of rock and roll and hill-billy music.

rock and roll *n.* (also **rock 'n' roll**) a type of popular dance music originating in the 1950s, characterized by a heavy beat and simple melodies, often with a blues element. □ **rock and roller** *n.*

rock-bottom ● *adj.* (of prices etc.) the very lowest. ● *n.* the very lowest level.

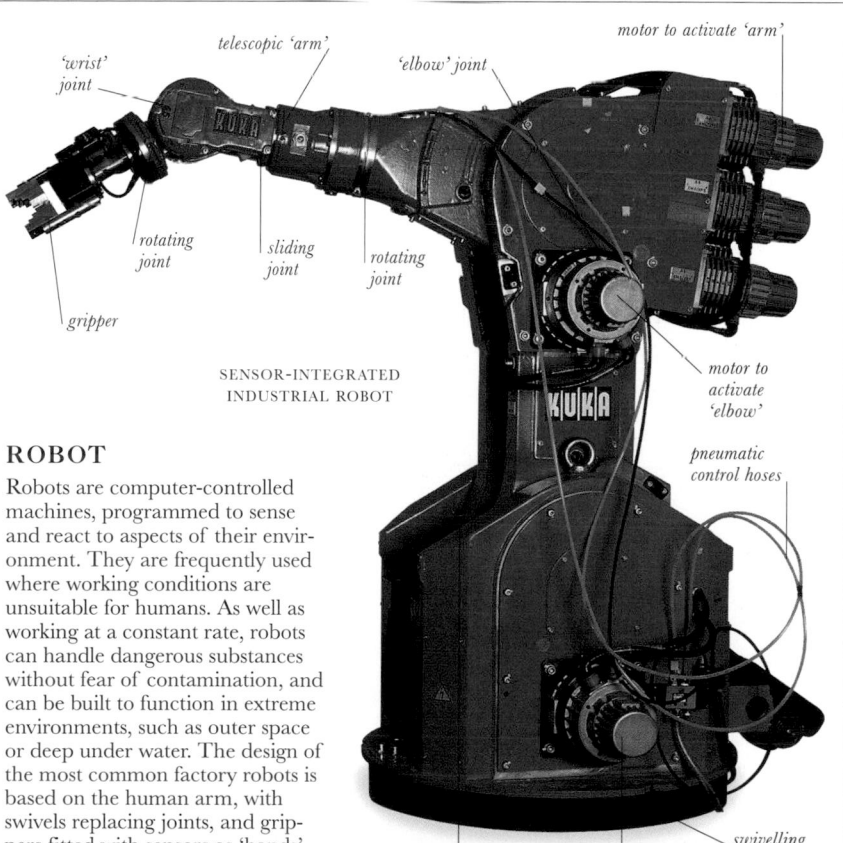

motor to activate 'arm'

telescopic 'arm'

'elbow' joint

'wrist' joint

rotating joint

sliding joint

rotating joint

gripper

motor to activate 'elbow'

SENSOR-INTEGRATED
INDUSTRIAL ROBOT

pneumatic control hoses

ROBOT

Robots are computer-controlled machines, programmed to sense and react to aspects of their environment. They are frequently used where working conditions are unsuitable for humans. As well as working at a constant rate, robots can handle dangerous substances without fear of contamination, and can be built to function in extreme environments, such as outer space or deep under water. The design of the most common factory robots is based on the human arm, with swivels replacing joints, and grippers fitted with sensors as 'hands'.

'shoulder'   *motor*   *swivelling base*

R

ROCK-CLIMBING

The sport of rock-climbing involves specialized safety equipment. Ropes stretch slightly to absorb the shock of a fall; anchors such as friends and nuts secure ropes and runners to the rock face; karabiners are secure coupling links; belay devices allow the climber to control the rope in the event of a fall; and descenders help safe abseiling. On a two-person climb (shown right), the first climber (leader) climbs to the first stage (pitch), putting in anchors on the way. The second follows the same route, collecting the equipment as he or she climbs.

BASIC EQUIPMENT

DESCENDEUR   BELAY DEVICE   SCREWGATE KARABINER   FRIEND   NUT

leader

anchor

SINGLE-PITCH CLIMB

runner

standard helmet

second

6 any rocking device forming part of a mechanism. □ **off one's rocker** *slang* crazy.

rockery *n.* (*pl.* **-ies**) a heaped arrangement of rough stones with soil between them for growing rock plants on.

rocket[1] ● *n.* **1** a cylindrical projectile that can be propelled to a great height or distance by combustion of its contents. **2** an engine using a similar principle but not dependent on air intake for its operation. **3** ▼ a rocket-propelled missile, spacecraft, etc. ▷ SPACECRAFT. **4** *Brit. colloq.* a severe reprimand. ● *v.* (**rocketed, rocketing**) **1** *tr.* bombard with rockets. **2** *intr.* **a** move rapidly upwards or away. **b** increase rapidly (*prices rocketed*). [from Italian *rochetto* 'little rock', with reference to its cylindrical shape]

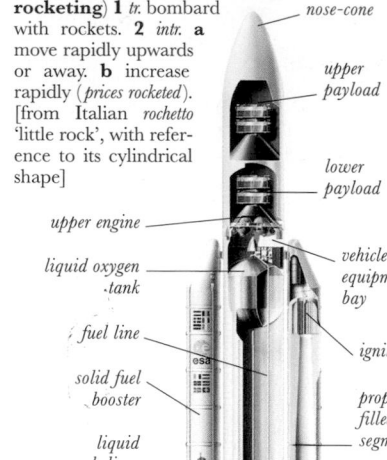

nose-cone

upper payload

lower payload

upper engine

liquid oxygen -tank

fuel line

solid fuel booster

liquid helium

Vulcain engine

vehicle equipment bay

igniter

propellant-filled segment

steel casing

exhaust duct

ROCKET: ARIANE SPACE ROCKET

---

rock-bound *adj.* (of a coast) rocky and inaccessible.

rock cake *n.* esp. *Brit.* a small currant cake with a hard rough surface.

rock candy *n. N. Amer.* = ROCK[1] *n.* 6.

rock-climbing *n.* ▲ the sport of climbing rock faces, esp. with the aid of ropes etc. □ **rock-climber** *n.*

rock crystal *n.* transparent colourless quartz usu. in hexagonal prisms. ▷ CRYSTAL, GEM, QUARTZ

rock cycle *n.* ▼ a cycle of geological processes

involving intrusion of igneous rock, uplift, erosion, transportation, deposition as sedimentary rock, metamorphism, remelting, and further igneous intrusion.

rocker *n.* **1** a person or thing that rocks. **2** a curved bar or similar support, on which something can rock. **3** a rocking chair. **4 a** *Brit.* a devotee of rock music, esp. a leather-clad motorcyclist. **b** a rock musician. **5** a switch constructed on a pivot mechanism operating between the 'on' and 'off' positions.

ROCK CYCLE

All types of rock are constantly being generated and transformed. Igneous rock forms when magma rises from the Earth's mantle, cooling and solidifying below or above the surface. Crustal movements can thrust rock to the surface or bury it deeper. Below ground, any rock subjected

to significant heat and pressure may turn into metamorphic rock or be remelted. At the surface, rock is eventually eroded by wind, water, or ice. Compression and cementation of the eroded particles forms sedimentary rock, which may be uplifted and eroded once again, metamorphosed, or remelted.

TYPES OF ROCK

SEDIMENTARY sandstone ▷ SEDIMENTARY

IGNEOUS basalt ▷ IGNEOUS

METAMORPHIC gneiss ▷ METAMORPHIC

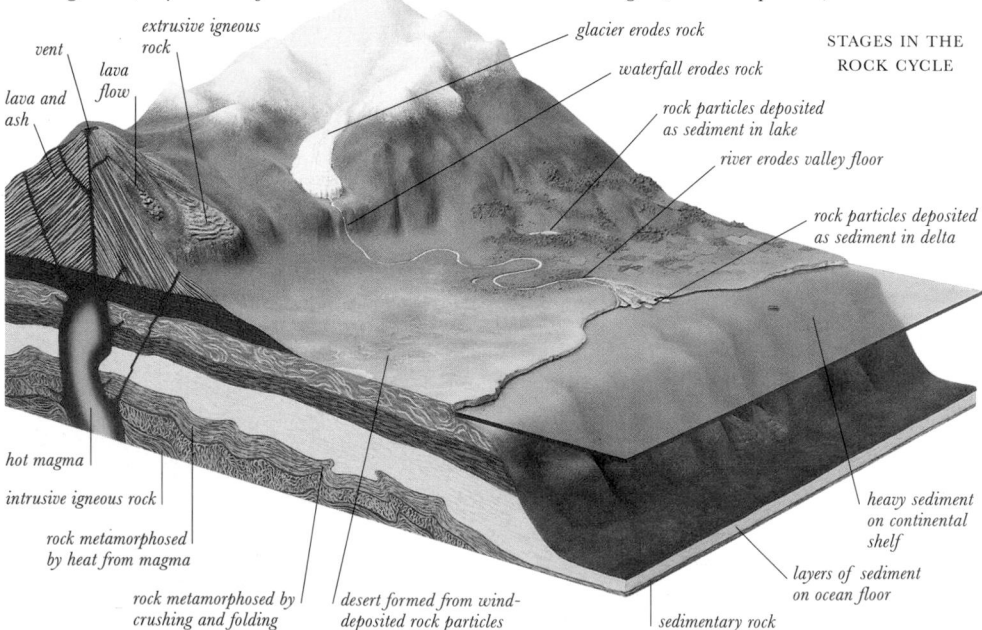

vent

extrusive igneous rock

lava flow

lava and ash

glacier erodes rock

waterfall erodes rock

rock particles deposited as sediment in lake

river erodes valley floor

rock particles deposited as sediment in delta

STAGES IN THE ROCK CYCLE

hot magma

intrusive igneous rock

rock metamorphosed by heat from magma

rock metamorphosed by crushing and folding

desert formed from wind-deposited rock particles

sedimentary rock

layers of sediment on ocean floor

heavy sediment on continental shelf

R

rocket[2] *n.* **1** a variety of the cruciferous annual plant *Eruca vesicaria* grown for salad. **2** (also **sweet rocket**) any of various fast-growing plants, esp. of the genus *Hesperis* or *Sisymbrium*. [based on Latin *eruca* 'downy-stemmed plant']

rocketry *n.* the science or practice of rocket propulsion.

rock face *n.* a vertical surface of natural rock.

rockfall *n.* **1** a descent of loose rocks. **2** a mass of fallen rock.

rock garden *n.* an artificial mound or bank of earth and stones planted with rock plants etc.

rockhopper *n.* a small penguin, *Eudyptes crestatus*, with a crest of feathers on the forehead.

rocking chair *n.* a chair mounted on rockers or springs for gently rocking in.

rocking horse *n.* a model of a horse on rockers or springs for a child to rock on.

rocking-stone *n.* a poised boulder easily rocked; a logan-stone.

rock 'n' roll var. of ROCK AND ROLL.

rock plant *n.* any plant growing on or among rocks.

rock pool *n.* a pool of water among rocks.

rock rose *n.* any plant of the genus *Cistus*, *Helianthemum*, etc., with roselike flowers.

rock salmon *n.* any of several fishes, esp. *Brit.* (as a commercial name) the catfish and dogfish.

rock salt *n.* common salt as a solid mineral.

rock-solid *adj.* very solid or firm.

rock-wool *n.* inorganic material made into matted fibre esp. for insulation or soundproofing.

rocky[1] *adj.* (**rockier**, **rockiest**) **1** of or like rock. **2** full of or abounding in rock or rocks (*a rocky shore*). □ **rockiness** *n.*

rocky[2] *adj.* (**rockier**, **rockiest**) *colloq.* unsteady, tottering. □ **rockily** *adv.* **rockiness** *n.*

Rocky Mountain goat see MOUNTAIN GOAT 2.

rococo /rŏ-**koh**-koh/ ● *adj.* ▼ of a late baroque style of decoration prevalent in 18th-c. continental Europe, with asymmetrical patterns. ● *n.* the rococo style. [French, jocular alteration of *rocaille* ornamentation based on shell etc. motifs]

ROCOCO: 18TH-CENTURY BAVARIAN ROCOCO CHURCH

rod *n.* **1** a slender straight bar esp. of wood or metal. **2** this as a symbol of office. **3 a** a stick or bundle of twigs used in caning or flogging. **b** (prec. by *the*) the use of this. **4 a** = FISHING ROD. **b** an angler using a rod. **5** esp. *Brit. hist.* (as a measure) a perch or square perch (see PERCH[1] 3). **6** *Anat.* any of numerous rod-shaped structures in the eye, detecting dim light. [Old English] □ **rodless** *adj.* **rodlet** *n.* **rodlike** *adj.*

rode past of RIDE.

rodent *n.* ▶ a mammal of the order Rodentia, with strong incisors and no canine teeth, e.g. rat, mouse,

squirrel, beaver, porcupine. [from Latin *rodent-* 'gnawing'] □ **rodential** *adj.*

rodenticide *n.* a poison used to kill rodents.

rodeo *n.* (*pl.* **-os**) **1** an exhibition or entertainment involving cowboys' skills in handling animals. **2** an exhibition of other skills, e.g. in motorcycling. **3 a** a round-up of cattle on a ranch for branding etc. **b** an enclosure for this. [Spanish]

roe[1] *n.* **1** (also **hard roe**) the mass of eggs in a female fish's ovary. **2** (also **soft roe**) the milt of a male fish. [from Middle Dutch *roge(n)*] □ **roed** *adj.* (also in *comb.*).

roe[2] *n.* (*pl.* same or **roes**) (also **roe-deer**) a small European and Asian deer, *Capreolus capreolus*. [Old English]

roebuck *n.* a male roe-deer.

roentgen /**runt**-yĕn/ *n.* (also **röntgen**) a unit of ionizing radiation. [named after W. C. *Röntgen*, German physicist, 1845–1923, discoverer of X-rays]

roentgen rays *n.pl. hist.* X-rays.

rogation *n.* (usu. in *pl.*) *Eccl.* a solemn supplication consisting of the litany of the saints chanted on the three days before Ascension Day. [from Latin *rogatio*] □ **rogational** *adj.*

Rogation Days *n.pl.* the three days before Ascension Day.

Rogation Sunday *n.* the Sunday preceding the Rogation Days.

roger ● *int.* **1** your message has been received and understood (used in radio communication etc.). **2** *slang* I agree. ● *v. Brit. coarse slang* **1** *intr.* have sexual intercourse. **2** *tr.* have sexual intercourse with (a woman). [the name *Roger*, code for R]

rogue *n.* **1** a dishonest or unprincipled person. **2** *joc.* a mischievous person, esp. a child. **3** (usu. *attrib.*) **a** a wild animal driven away or living apart from the herd and of fierce temper (*rogue elephant*). **b** a stray, irresponsible, or undisciplined person or thing

RODENT

Rodents constitute the largest order of mammals, with up to 2,000 species. There are three suborders: Sciuromorpha (squirrel-like), Myomorpha (mouselike), and Cavimorpha (cavy-like). All rodents have only one pair of incisors in each jaw. Although these grow constantly, they are worn down and kept sharp by continual gnawing.

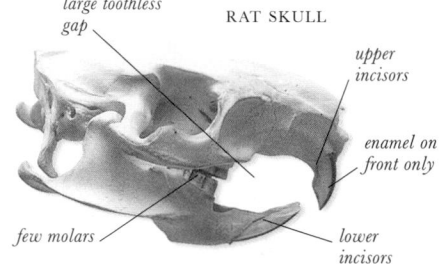

RAT SKULL

large toothless gap

upper incisors

enamel on front only

few molars

lower incisors

TYPES OF RODENT

SCIUROMORPHA

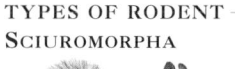

GREY SQUIRREL
(*Sciurus carolinensis*)

CHIPMUNK
(*Eutamias* species)

BEAVER
(*Castor fiber*)

MYOMORPHA

YELLOW-NECKED WOODMOUSE
(*Apodemus flavicollis*)

HAMSTER
(*Mesocricetus auratus*)

BROWN RAT (*Rattus norvegicus*)

PALLID GERBIL
(*Gerbillus* species)

CAVIMORPHA

NAKED MOLE RAT
(*Heterocephalus glaber*)

CAPYBARA
(*Hydrochoerus hydrochaeris*)

MALAYAN PORCUPINE
(*Hystrix brachyura*)

GUINEA PIG
(*Cavia porcellus*)

R

(*rogue trader*). **4** an inferior or defective specimen among many acceptable ones. [16th-century coinage]

roguery *n.* (*pl.* **-ies**) conduct or an action characteristic of rogues.

rogues' gallery *n.* a collection of photographs of known criminals etc., used for identification of suspects.

roguish *adj.* **1** playfully mischievous. **2** characteristic of rogues. □ **roguishly** *adv.* **roguishness** *n.*

roister *v.intr.* (esp. as **roistering** *adj.*) revel noisily; be uproarious. [from obsolete *roister* 'roisterer': from French *rustre* 'ruffian'] □ **roisterer** *n.* **roistering** *n.* **roisterous** *adj.*

role *n.* (also **rôle**) **1** an actor's part in a play, film, etc. **2** a person's or thing's characteristic or expected function. [from obsolete French *roule* 'roll']

role model *n.* a person looked to by others as an example in a particular role or situation.

role-playing *n.* (also **role-play**) an exercise or game in which each participant acts the part of another character, used in psychotherapy, language-teaching, etc. □ **role-play** *v.intr. & tr.*

role reversal *n.* the assumption of a role which is the reverse of that normally performed.

roll ● *v.* **1 a** *intr.* move or go in some direction by turning over and over on an axis (*the ball rolled under the table*). **b** *tr.* cause to do this (*rolled the barrel into the cellar*). **2** *tr.* make revolve between two surfaces (*rolled the clay between his palms*). **3 a** *intr.* (foll. by *along*, *by*, etc.) move or advance on or (of time etc.) as if on wheels etc. (*the years rolled by*). **b** *tr.* cause to do this (*rolled the trolley into the kitchen*). **c** *intr.* (of a person) be conveyed in a vehicle (*rolled by on his tractor*). **4 a** *tr.* turn over and over on itself to form a more or less cylindrical or spherical shape (*rolled a newspaper*). **b** *tr.* make by forming material into a cylinder or ball (*rolled a cigarette*). **c** *tr.* accumulate into a mass (*rolled the dough into a ball*). **d** *intr.* (foll. by *into*) make a specified esp. rounded shape of itself (*the hedgehog rolled into a ball*). **5** *tr.* flatten or form by passing a roller etc. over or by passing between rollers (*roll pastry*). **6** *intr. & tr.* change or cause to change direction by rotatory movement (*his eyes rolled*). **7** *intr.* wallow, turn about in a fluid or a loose medium (*the dog rolled in the dust*). **8** *intr.* **a** (of a moving ship, aircraft, or vehicle) sway to and fro on an axis parallel to the direction of motion. **b** walk with an unsteady swaying gait (*they rolled out of the pub*). **9** *intr.* undulate, show or go with an undulating surface or motion (*rolling hills*). **10 a** *intr.* (of machinery) start functioning or moving (*the cameras rolled*). **b** *tr.* cause (machinery) to do this. **11 a** *tr.* display (credits for a film or television programme) moving as if on a roller up the screen. **b** *intr.* (of credits) be displayed in this way. **12** *intr. & tr.* sound or utter with a vibratory or trilling effect (*he rolls his r*s). ● *n.* **1** a rolling motion or gait; undulation (*the roll of the hills*). **2 a** a spell of rolling (*a roll in the mud*). **b** a gymnastic exercise in which the body is rolled into a tucked position and turned in a forward or backward circle. **3** the continuous rhythmic sound of thunder or a drum. **4** *Aeron.* a complete revolution of an aircraft about its longitudinal axis. **5 a** a cylinder formed by turning flexible material over and over on itself without folding (*a roll of carpet*). **b** a filled cake or pastry of similar form (*sausage roll*). **6 a** a small portion of bread individually baked. **b** this with a specified filling (*ham roll*). **7** a more or less cylindrical or semicylindrical straight or curved mass of something (*rolls of fat*). **8 a** an official list or register. **b** the total numbers on this (*the schools' rolls have fallen*). **c** a document, esp. an official record, in scroll form. **9** a cylinder or roller, esp. to shape metal in a rolling mill. □ **be rolling** *colloq.* be very rich. **be rolling in** *colloq.* have plenty of (esp. money). **on a roll** *N. Amer. slang* experiencing a bout of success or progress; engaged in a period of intense activity. **rolled into one** combined in one

person or thing. **roll in** arrive in great numbers or quantity. **rolling drunk** swaying or staggering from drunkenness. **roll of honour** a list of those honoured. **roll on 1** put on or apply by rolling. **2** (in *imper.*) *colloq.* come quickly (*roll on Friday!*). **roll over 1** send (a person) sprawling or rolling. **2** *Econ.* finance the repayment of (maturing stock etc.) by an issue of new stock. **roll up 1** *colloq.* arrive in a vehicle; appear on the scene. **2** make into or form a roll. **roll up one's sleeves** see SLEEVE. **strike off the rolls** debar from practising. [from Latin *rotulus* 'little wheel'] □ **rollable** *adj.*

roll bar *n.* an overhead metal bar strengthening the frame of a vehicle (esp. in racing) and protecting the occupants if the vehicle overturns.

roll-call *n.* a process of calling out a list of names to establish who is present.

rolled gold *n.* gold in the form of a thin coating applied to a baser metal by rolling.

rolled oats *n.pl.* oats that have been husked and crushed.

roller *n.* **1** a hard revolving cylinder for smoothing the ground, spreading ink or paint, crushing or stamping, rolling cloth around, hanging a towel on, etc., used alone or as a rotating part of a machine. ▷ PRINTING. **2** a small cylinder on which hair is rolled for setting. **3** a long swelling wave.

roller bearing *n.* ▼ a bearing like a ball-bearing but with small cylinders instead of balls.

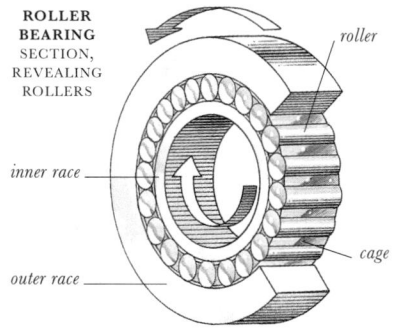

ROLLER BEARING SECTION, REVEALING ROLLERS

roller

inner race

cage

outer race

Rollerblade ● *n. propr.* each of a pair of boots fitted with small wheels, one behind the other, for roller skating in the manner of ice-skating. ● *v.intr.* (**rollerblade**) skate using such boots. □ **rollerblader** *n.*

roller blind *n.* a blind fitted on a roller.

roller coaster *n.* a switchback at a fair etc.

roller skate ● *n.* each of a pair of metal frames with small wheels, fitted to shoes for gliding across a hard surface. ● *v.intr.* move on roller skates. □ **roller skater** *n.*

roller towel *n.* a towel with the ends joined, hung on a roller.

rollick *v.intr.* (esp. as **rollicking** *adj.*) be jovial or exuberant. [19th-century coinage]

rolling mill *n.* a machine or factory for rolling metal into shape.

rolling pin *n.* a cylinder for rolling out pastry, dough, etc.

rolling stock *n.* **1** the locomotives, carriages, or other vehicles, used on a railway. **2** *US* the road vehicles of a company.

rolling stone *n.* a person who is unwilling to settle for long in one place.

rollmop *n.* a rolled uncooked pickled herring fillet. [from German *Rollmops*]

roll-neck ● *n.* **1** a high loosely turned-over neck. **2** a sweater etc. having this. ● *attrib.adj.* having a roll-neck.

roll-on ● *attrib.adj.* (of deodorant etc.) applied by means of a rotating ball in the neck of the container. ● *n. Brit.* a light elastic corset.

roll-on roll-off *adj. Brit.* (usu. *attrib.*) (of a ship, a

method of transport, etc.) in which vehicles are driven directly on and off.

roll-out *n.* **1 a** the official wheeling out of a new aircraft or spacecraft. **b** the official launch of a new product. **2** the part of a landing during which an aircraft travels along the runway losing speed.

rollover *attrib.adj.* (of a lottery jackpot) that (not having been won) is carried over and added to the jackpot for the next draw.

roll-top desk *n.* ▼ a desk with a flexible cover sliding in curved grooves.

sliding cover

ROLL-TOP DESK

roll-up *n.* (also **roll-your-own**) *Brit.* a hand-rolled cigarette.

roly-poly ● *n.* (*pl.* **-ies**) (also **roly-poly pudding**) *Brit.* a pudding made of a sheet of suet pastry covered with jam etc., formed into a roll, and steamed or baked. ● *adj.* (usu. of a child) podgy, plump.

ROM /rom/ *n. Computing* read-only memory.

romaine *n. N. Amer.* a cos lettuce. [French fem. of *romain* 'Roman']

Roman ● *adj.* **1** of ancient Rome or its territory or people. **2** of medieval or modern Rome. **3** = ROMAN CATHOLIC. **4** surviving from a period of ancient Roman rule (*Roman road*). **5** (**roman**) (of type) of a plain upright kind used in ordinary print. **6** (of the alphabet etc.) based on the ancient Roman system with letters A–Z. ● *n.* **1 a** a citizen of the ancient Roman Republic or Empire. **b** a soldier of the Roman Empire. **2** a citizen of modern Rome. **3** = ROMAN CATHOLIC. **4** (**roman**) roman type. [from Latin *Romanus*]

Roman candle *n.* a firework discharging flaming coloured balls.

Roman Catholic ● *adj.* of the part of the Christian Church acknowledging the Pope as its head. ● *n.* a member of this Church. [17th-century translation of Latin *(Ecclesia) Romana Catholica (et Apostolica)* 'Catholic (and Apostolic) (Church) of Rome'] □ **Roman Catholicism** *n.*

romance ● *n.* **1** an atmosphere or tendency characterized by a sense of remoteness from or idealization of everyday life. **2 a** a sentimental or idealized love. **b** a love affair. **3 a** a literary genre with romantic love or highly imaginative unrealistic episodes forming the central theme. **b** a work of this genre. **4** a medieval tale of some hero of chivalry. **5 a** an exaggeration or picturesque falsehood. **b** an instance of this. **6** (**Romance**) the languages descended from Latin. ● *adj.* (**Romance**) of any of the languages descended from Latin. ● *v.* **1** *intr.* exaggerate or distort the truth. **2** *tr.* **a** court, woo. **b** seek the attention or custom of. [based on Latin *Romanicus* 'Romanic']

romancer *n.* **1** a writer of romances. **2** a liar who resorts to fantasy.

Romanesque ● *n.* ▶ a style of architecture prevalent in Europe *c.*900–1200, with massive vaulting and round arches. ● *adj.* of or relating to the Romanesque style of architecture. [French, based on *roman* 'romance']

Romanian (also **Rumanian**, **Roumanian**) ● *n.*
1 a a native or national of Romania in E. Europe.
b a person of Romanian descent. **2** the language of
Romania. ● *adj.* of or relating to Romania or its
people or language.

Romanic ● *n.* = ROMANCE *n.* 6. ● *adj.* **1 a** of or relating
to Romance. **b** Romance-speaking. **2** descended
from the ancient Romans or inheriting aspects of
their social or political life. [from Latin *Romanicus*]

romanize *v.tr.* (also **-ise**) **1** make Roman or Roman
Catholic in character. **2** put into the Roman alphabet or into roman type. □ **romanization** *n.*

Roman nose *n.* one with a high bridge; an aquiline
nose.

Roman numeral *n.* any of the Roman letters
representing numbers: I = 1, V = 5, X = 10, L = 50,
C = 100, D = 500, M = 1,000.

Romano- *comb. form* Roman; Roman and (*Romano-
British*).

romantic ● *adj.* **1** of, characterized by, or suggestive
of an idealized, sentimental, or fantastic view of
reality (*a romantic picture; a romantic setting*). **2** inclined
towards or suggestive of romance in love (*a romantic
woman; a romantic evening*). **3** (of a person) imaginative, visionary, idealistic. **4** (of style in art, music,
etc.) concerned more with feeling and emotion
than with form and aesthetic qualities. **5** (of a
project etc.) unpractical, fantastic. ● *n.* **1** a romantic person. **2** a romanticist. [based on Old French
romanz 'romance'] □ **romantically** *adv.*

romanticism *n.* (also **Romanticism**) adherence
to a romantic style in art, music, etc.

romanticist *n.* (also **Romanticist**) a writer or
artist of the romantic school.

romanticize *v.* (also **-ise**) **1** *tr.* **a** make romantic.
b describe or portray in a romantic fashion. **2** *intr.*
indulge in romantic thoughts or actions. □ **roman-
ticization** *n.*

Romany ● *n.* (*pl.* **-ies**) **1** a gypsy. **2** the language of
the gypsies. ● *adj.* of or relating to gypsies or their
language. [from Romany *Romani*]

romp ● *v.intr.* **1** play roughly and energetically.
2 *colloq.* proceed without effort. ● *n.* a spell of romp-
ing. □ **romp in** (or **home**) *colloq.* finish as the easy
winner.

romper *n.* (usu. in *pl.*) (also **romper suit**) a young
child's one-piece garment covering legs and trunk.

rondeau /ron-doh/ *n.* (*pl.* **rondeaux** *pronunc.*
same or /-dohz/) a poem of ten or thirteen lines
with only two rhymes throughout and the
opening words used twice as a refrain. [French]

rondel *n.* a rondeau, esp. one of special form.
[based on Old French *rond* 'round']

rondo *n.* (*pl.* **-os**) *Mus.* a form with a recurring leading theme. [Italian]

röntgen var. of ROENTGEN.

roo *n.* (also **'roo**) *Austral. colloq.* a kangaroo. [abbre-
viation]

roo bar *n.* = BULL BAR.

rood *n.* **1** a crucifix, esp. one raised on a screen or
beam at the entrance to the chancel. **2** a quarter of
an acre. [Old English]

rood-screen *n.* ▶ a
carved screen sep-
arating nave and
chancel. ▷ CHURCH

roof ● *n.* (*pl.* **roofs**
or *disp.* **rooves**)
1 a ▲ the upper
covering of a build-
ing. **b** the top of
a covered vehicle.
c the top inner
surface of an oven,
refrigerator, etc. **2**
the overhead rock
in a cave or mine
etc. ▷ CAVE. ● *v.tr.*
1 cover with or
as with a roof.

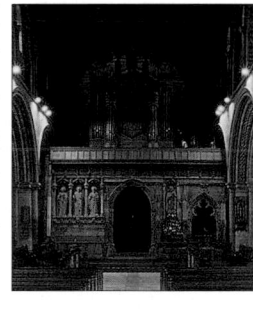

ROOD-SCREEN
IN A 12TH-CENTURY
CATHEDRAL, WALES

2 be the roof of. □ **go through the roof** *colloq.*
(of prices etc.) reach extreme or unexpected
heights. **hit** (or **go through** or **raise**) **the roof**
colloq. become very angry. [Old English] □ **roofed**
adj. (also in *comb.*). **roofless** *adj.*

roofer *n.* a person who constructs or repairs roofs.

roof garden *n.* a garden on the flat roof of a building.

roofing *n.* **1** material for constructing a roof. **2** the
process of constructing a roof or roofs.

roof of the mouth *n.* the palate.

roof-rack *n.* a framework for luggage etc. on the
roof of a vehicle.

ROOF

Most roofs are pitched and consist of a
wooden frame and some form of covering,
such as tiles, slates, thatch, or lead. The
inclined part of the frame is formed by
rafters. To prevent sagging or bowing, these
need to be supported by curved or diagonal
beams (braces) or horizontal beams (e.g.
purlins), which together form strong trusses.

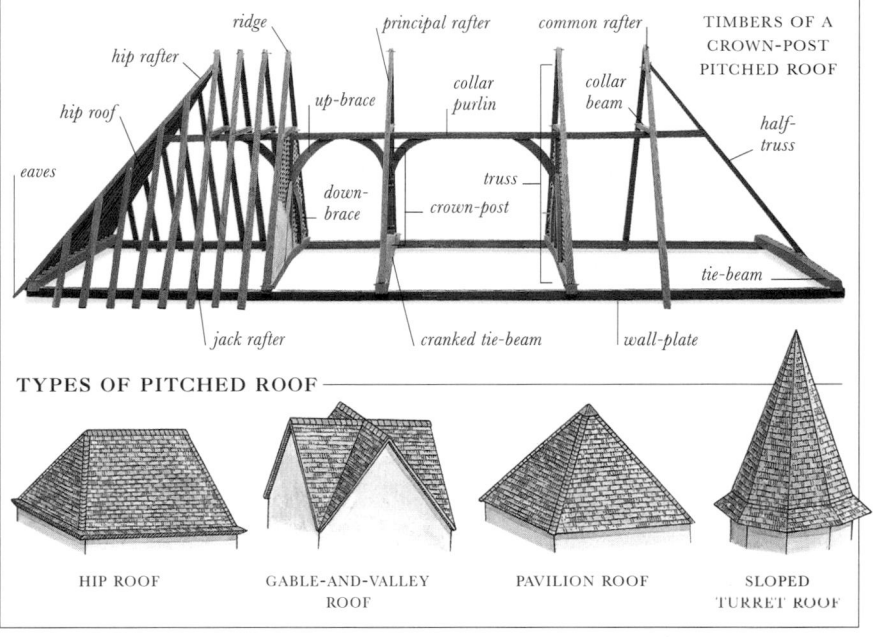

TIMBERS OF A
CROWN-POST
PITCHED ROOF

ridge · principal rafter · common rafter · hip rafter · hip roof · collar purlin · collar beam · half-truss · eaves · up-brace · down-brace · truss · crown-post · tie-beam · jack rafter · cranked tie-beam · wall-plate

TYPES OF PITCHED ROOF

HIP ROOF   GABLE-AND-VALLEY ROOF   PAVILION ROOF   SLOPED TURRET ROOF

ROMANESQUE

While the main inspiration for Romanesque
architecture was classical Rome, the ornamentation of the Byzantine
and Islamic worlds was also
a strong influence, especially
in the Mediterranean. The
style's wide distribution
led to local variation, but
common features were
large vaults, round arches,
and massive stonework.

CUTAWAY VIEW OF
A 12TH-CENTURY
ROMANESQUE
CATHEDRAL, ITALY

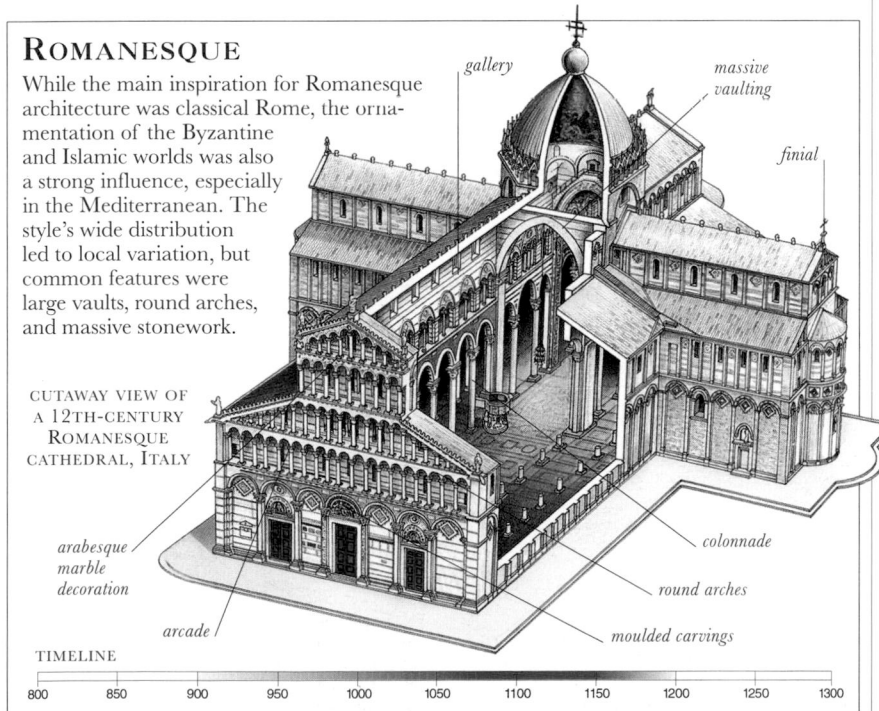

gallery · massive vaulting · finial · colonnade · round arches · moulded carvings · arcade · arabesque marble decoration

TIMELINE
800   850   900   950   1000   1050   1100   1150   1200   1250   1300

R

rooftop *n.* **1** the outer surface of a roof (often *attrib.*: *rooftop terrace*). **2** (esp. in *pl.*) the level of a roof. □ **shout it from the rooftops** make a thing embarrassingly public.

roof-tree *n.* a beam along the ridge of a roof.

rook[1] • *n.* a black European and Asiatic bird, *Corvus frugilegus*, of the crow family, nesting in colonies. • *v.tr. slang* **1** charge (a customer) extortionately. **2** win money from (a person) at cards etc., esp. by swindling. [Old English]

rook[2] *n.* ◀ a chess piece with its top in the shape of a battlement. ▷ CHESS. [from Arabic *rukk*]

rookery *n.* (*pl.* **-ies**) **1 a** a colony of rooks. **b** a clump of trees having rooks' nests. **2** a colony of seabirds (esp. penguins) or seals.

rookie *n. slang* **1** a new recruit. **2** *N. Amer.* a member of a sports team in his or her first full season. [corruption of RECRUIT]

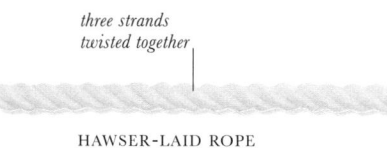

ROOK

room • *n.* **1 a** space that is occupied by something; capaciousness or ability to accommodate contents (*it takes up too much room; there is plenty of room; we have no room here for idlers*). **b** space in or on (*houseroom; shelf room*). **2 a** part of a building enclosed by walls, floor, and ceiling. **b** (in *pl.*) apartments or lodgings. **c** persons present in a room (*the room fell silent*). **3** (in *comb.*) a room or area for a specified purpose (*auction room*). **4** (foll. by *for*, or *to* + infin.) opportunity or scope (*room to improve things; no room for dispute*). • *v.intr.* have a room or rooms; lodge, board. [Old English] □ **-roomed** *adj.* (in *comb.*). **roomful** *n.* (*pl.* **-fuls**).

roomer *n. N. Amer.* a lodger occupying a room or rooms without board.

rooming house *n.* a lodging house.

room-mate *n.* (*US* usu. **roommate**) a person occupying the same room as another.

room service *n.* (in a hotel etc.) service of food or drink taken to a guest's room.

roomy *adj.* (**roomier**, **roomiest**) having much room, spacious. □ **roominess** *n.*

roost • *n.* a branch or other support on which a bird perches, esp. a place where birds regularly settle to sleep. • *v.intr.* settle for rest or sleep. □ **come home to roost** (of a scheme etc.) recoil unfavourably upon the originator. [Old English]

rooster *n.* esp. *N. Amer., Austral.*, etc. a domestic cock.

root[1] • *n.* **1 a** the part of a plant normally below the ground, taking in nourishment from the soil. ▷ SUCCULENT. **b** (in *pl.*) such a part divided into branches or fibres. **c** any small plant with a root for transplanting. **2 a** any plant with an edible root. **b** (also **root vegetable**) such a root. ▷ VEGETABLE. **3** (in *pl.*) social, ethnic, or cultural origins, esp. as the reasons for one's long-standing emotional attachment to a place, community, etc. **4 a** the embedded part of a bodily organ or structure, e.g. hair, tooth, nail, etc. ▷ NAIL, TOOTH. **b** the part of a thing attaching it to a greater whole. **5 a** the basic cause, source, or origin (*love of money is the root of all evil*). **b** (*attrib.*) (of an idea etc.) from which the rest originated. **6** the essential substance or nature of something (*get to the root of things*). **7** *Math.* **a** a number or quantity that when multiplied by itself a usu. specified number of times gives a specified number or quantity (*the cube root of eight is two*). **b** a square root. **c** a value of an unknown quantity satisfying a given equation. **8** *Philol.* a basis on which words are made by the addition of prefixes or suffixes or by other modification. • *v.* **1 a** *intr.* take root or grow roots. **b** *tr.* cause to do this (*take care to root the cuttings firmly*). **2** *tr.* **a** fix firmly; establish (*fear rooted him to the spot*). **b** (as **rooted** *adj.*) firmly established (*her affection was deeply rooted; rooted objection to*). **3** *tr.* (usu. foll. by *out*, *up*) drag or dig up by the roots. **4** *tr. Austral.* & *NZ coarse slang* **a** have sexual intercourse with. **b** exhaust, frustrate. □ **pull up by the roots 1** uproot. **2** eradicate, destroy. **put down roots 1** begin to draw nourishment from the soil. **2** become settled or established. **root and branch** thorough(ly), radical(ly). **root out** find and get rid of. **strike** (or **take**) **root 1** begin to grow and draw nourishment from the soil. **2** become fixed or established. [from Old Norse *rót*] □ **rootedness** *n.* **rootless** *adj.* **rootlet** *n.* **rootlike** *adj.* **rooty** *adj.*

root[2] • *v.* **1** *intr.* turn up the ground with the snout, beak, etc., in search of food. **b** *tr.* (foll. by *up*) turn up (the ground) by rooting. **2 a** *intr.* (foll. by *around, in*, etc.) rummage. **b** *tr.* (foll. by *out* or *up*) find or extract by rummaging. **3** *intr.* (foll. by *for*) orig. *US slang* encourage by applause or support. [from Old Norse *róta*] □ **rooter** *n.* (in sense 3).

root beer *n. N. Amer.* an effervescent soft drink made from an extract of roots.

root canal *n. Dentistry* **1** the pulp-filled cavity in the root of a tooth. **2** *US* a procedure to replace infected pulp with an inert material.

rootle *v.intr.* & *tr. Brit.* = ROOT[2] 1, 2.

rootstock *n.* **1** a rhizome. **2** a plant into which a graft is inserted. **3** a primary form from which offshoots have arisen.

rootsy *adj. colloq.* (of music) uncommercialized, full-blooded, esp. showing traditional origins.

root vegetable see ROOT[1] *n.* 2b.

rooves see ROOF.

rope • *n.* **1 a** ▼ stout cord made by twisting together strands of hemp, sisal, flax, cotton, nylon, wire, or similar material. **b** a piece of this. **c** *US* a lasso. **2** (foll. by *of*) a quantity of onions, ova, or pearls strung together. **3** (in *pl.*; prec. by *the*) **a** the conditions in some sphere of action (*know the ropes; show a person the ropes*). **b** the ropes enclosing a boxing or wrestling ring or cricket ground. **4** (prec. by *the*) **a** a halter for hanging a person. **b** execution by hanging. • *v.* **1** *tr.* fasten, secure, or catch with rope. **2** *tr.* (usu. foll. by *off*, *in*) enclose (a space) with rope. **3** *Mountaineering* **a** *tr.* connect (a party) with a rope; attach (a person) to a rope. **b** (*absol.*) put on a rope. **c** *intr.* (foll. by *down*, *up*) climb down or up using a rope. □ **on the ropes 1** *Boxing* forced against the ropes by the opponent's attack. **2** near defeat. **rope in** persuade to take part. **rope into** persuade to take part in (*was roped into doing the washing-up*). [Old English]

rope ladder *n.* two long ropes connected by short crosspieces, used as a ladder.

roping *n.* a set or arrangement of ropes.

ropy *adj.* (also **ropey**) (**ropier**, **ropiest**) **1** *Brit. colloq.* poor in quality. **2** like a rope.

Roquefort /rok-for/ *n. propr.* a soft blue cheese made from ewes' milk. ▷ CHEESE. [from *Roquefort*, a village in S. France]

ro-ro *adj. Brit.* roll-on roll-off. [abbreviation]

rorqual *n.* any baleen whale of the family Balaenopteridae, with a small dorsal fin. [from Norwegian *røyrkval*]

Rorschach test *n. Psychol.* a type of personality test in which a standard set of ink-blots is presented one by one to the subject, who is asked to describe what they suggest or resemble. [named after H. *Rorschach*, Swiss psychiatrist, 1884–1922]

rosaceous *adj. Bot.* of the large plant family Rosaceae, which includes the rose, apple, plum, blackberry, hawthorn, etc. [from Latin *rosaceus*]

rosary *n.* (*pl.* **-ies**) **1** *RC Ch.* **a** a form of devotion in which five (or fifteen) decades of Hail Marys are repeated, each decade preceded by an Our Father and followed by a Glory Be. **b** ▶ a string of 55 (or 165) beads for keeping count in this. ▷ HABIT. **2** a similar form of bead-string used in other religions. [from Latin *rosarium* 'rose garden']

rose[1] • *n.* **1** ▶ any prickly bush or shrub of the genus *Rosa* (family Rosaceae), bearing usu. fragrant flowers generally of a red, pink, yellow, or white colour. **2** this flower. **3** any flowering plant resembling this (*Christmas rose; rock rose*). **4 a** a light crimson colour, pink. **b** (usu. in *pl.*) a rosy complexion (*roses in her cheeks*). **5** a rose-shaped design. **6** the sprinkling-nozzle of a watering can or hose. **7** a circular mounting on a ceiling through which the wiring of an electric light passes. • *adj.* = ROSE-COLOURED 1. □ **under the rose** in confidence. [from Latin *rosa*] □ **roselike** *adj.*

beads

ROSARY

crucifix

rose[2] past of RISE.

R

ROPE

Although there are variations, there are two main constructions of rope: hawser-laid and kernmantle. Together with the construction, the material used to make a rope determines properties such as durability, strength, and flexibility. Natural materials are increasingly giving way to synthetic ones, resulting in stronger, lighter, and more reliable ropes.

three strands twisted together

HAWSER-LAID ROPE

mantle of plaited nylon fibres

kern (core) of hawser-laid cords

KERNMANTLE ROPE   *nylon filaments*

EXAMPLES OF ROPE MATERIALS

NATURAL

SISAL   COTTON   HEMP   COIR

SYNTHETIC

BRAIDED POLYESTER   NYLON MULTIPLAIT   STAPLE-SPUN POLYPROPYLENE

ROSE

There are approximately 150 species of rose. Cross-breeding, selection, and hybridization have led to the development of many thousands of cultivars from these species. They are valued mainly for the fragrance and colour of their flowers, although some are also grown for the ornamental value of their fruit (hips). Cultivars can be divided into Old Garden and Modern roses, and these into the well-recognized sub-groups shown below.

EXAMPLES OF SPECIES ROSES

Rosa eglanteria   *Rosa rugosa*   *Rosa moschata*

OLD GARDEN ROSES

BOURBON
(*Rosa* 'Variegata di Bologna')

HYBRID PERPETUAL
(*Rosa* 'Baron Girod de l'Ain')

DAMASK
(*Rosa* 'Ispahan')

NOISETTE
(*Rosa* 'Alister Stella Gray')

ALBA
(*Rosa* 'Great Maiden's Blush')

SEMPERVIRENS
(*Rosa* 'Félicité Perpétue')

CHINA
(*Rosa* 'Perle d'Or')

CENTIFOLIA
(*Rosa* 'Tour de Malakoff')

TEA
(*Rosa* 'Duchesse de Brabant')

SCOTS
(*Rosa* 'Grandiflora')

MOSS
(*Rosa* 'Henri Martin')

PORTLAND
(*Rosa* 'Marchesa Boccella')

GALLICA
(*Rosa* 'Charles de Mills')

BOURSAULT
(*Rosa* 'Mme de Sancy de Parabère')

MODERN ROSES

CLUSTER-FLOWERED BUSH
(*Rosa* 'Arthur Bell')

MINIATURE BUSH
(*Rosa* 'Blue Peter')

RAMBLER
(*Rosa* 'Wedding Day')

CLIMBER
(*Rosa* 'Climbing Iceberg')

SHRUB
(*Rosa* 'Abraham Darby')

DWARF CLUSTER-FLOWERED
(*Rosa* 'Gentle Touch')

POLYANTHA
(*Rosa* 'Ballerina')

RUGOSA
(*Rosa* 'Yellow Dagmar Hastrup')

LARGE-FLOWERED BUSH
(*Rosa* 'Cherry Brandy')

MINIATURE CLIMBER
(*Rosa* 'Laura Ford')

GROUND COVER
(*Rosa* 'Hertfordshire')

R

rosé /roh-zay/ *n.* any light pink wine, coloured by only brief contact with red grape skins. [French, literally 'pink']

rose-apple *n.* **1** a tropical tree of the genus *Syzygium*, cultivated for its foliage and fragrant fruit. **2** this fruit.

roseate *adj.* **1** = ROSE-COLOURED 1, 2. **2** having a partly pink plumage. [based on Latin *roseus* 'rosy']

rosebay *n.* **1 a** the oleander. **b** a N. American azalea. **2** (in full **rosebay willowherb**) a tall willowherb, *Chamerion angustifolium*, with pink flowers.

rosebowl *n.* a bowl for displaying cut roses.

rosebud *n.* **1** a bud of a rose. **2** *Brit.* a pretty young woman.

rose bush *n.* a rose plant.

rose colour *n.* the colour of a pale red rose; warm pink.

rose-coloured *adj.* **1** of a warm pink colour. **2** optimistic, cheerful (*takes rose-coloured views*).

rose-hip *n.* = HIP[2].

rosemary *n.* an evergreen fragrant shrub, *Rosmarinus officinalis*, with leaves used as a culinary herb, in perfumery, etc. ▷ HERB. [from Latin *ros marinus* 'dew of the sea']

rose of Sharon *n.* **1** a species of hypericum, *Hypericum calycinum*, with dense foliage and golden-yellow flowers. **2** *Bibl.* a flowering plant of unknown identity.

rose pink ● *n.* = ROSE COLOUR. ● *adj.* (hyphenated when *attrib.*) = ROSE-COLOURED 1.

rose-tinted *adj.* = ROSE-COLOURED.

rose tree *n.* a rose plant, esp. a standard rose.

rosette *n.* **1** ◄ a rose-shaped ornament made usu. of ribbon and worn esp. as a supporter's badge, or as an award or the symbol of an award in a competition. **2** *Archit.* **a** a carved or moulded ornament resembling or representing a rose. **b** a rose window. **3** an object or symbol or arrangement of parts resembling a rose. **4** *Biol.* **a** a roselike cluster of parts. **b** markings resembling a rose. [French, literally 'little rose'] □ **rosetted** *adj.*

ROSETTES

rose water *n.* perfume made from roses.

rose window *n.* ▼ a circular window with roselike tracery.

ROSE WINDOWS IN NOTRE-DAME CATHEDRAL, FRANCE

R

718

ROTATION

The systematic rotation of crops helps to prevent pests and diseases taking hold and, by varying the demands made on the soil, avoids exhaustion. Each phase is beneficial in a different way. Legumes (e.g. clover) fix nitrogen into the soil, preparing it for more demanding cereals or root crops. Digging up the soil to plant and harvest root crops uproots weeds. Leaving the land under pasture rests and naturally fertilizes the soil.

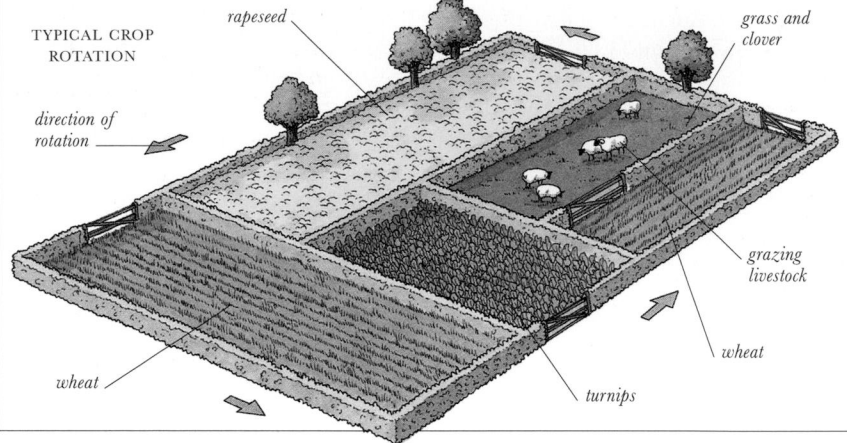

TYPICAL CROP ROTATION

rapeseed

direction of rotation

grass and clover

grazing livestock

wheat

wheat

turnips

---

rosewood *n.* **1** any of several fragrant close-grained woods used in making furniture. **2** a tree yielding such wood.

Rosh Hashana *n.* (also **Rosh Hashanah**) the Jewish New Year. [Hebrew, literally 'beginning of the year']

rosin ● *n.* resin, esp. the solid residue after distillation of oil of turpentine from crude turpentine. ● *v.tr.* (**rosined, rosining**) **1** rub (esp. the bow of a violin etc.) with rosin. **2** smear or seal up with rosin. [Middle English alteration of RESIN]

RoSPA /ross-pă/ *abbr.* (in the UK) Royal Society for the Prevention of Accidents.

roster ● *n.* **1** a list or plan showing turns of duty or leave. **2** a list usu. of names, esp. *N. Amer.* of sports players available for team selection. ● *v.tr.* place on a roster. [from Dutch *rooster* 'list']

rostra *pl.* of ROSTRUM.

rostrum *n.* (*pl.* **rostra** or **rostrums**) **1 a** a platform for public speaking. **b** a conductor's platform facing the orchestra. **c** a similar platform for other purposes. **2** *Zool.* & *Bot.* a beak, stiff snout, or beaklike part, esp. of an insect or arachnid. [Latin, literally 'beak']

rosy *adj.* (**rosier, rosiest**) **1 a** coloured like a pink or red rose (*rosy lips, rosy sky*). **b** pink as an indication of health or youth (*rosy cheeks*). **2** optimistic, hopeful (*a rosy future; a rosy attitude to life*). □ **rosily** *adv.* **rosiness** *n.*

rot ● *v.* (**rotted, rotting**) **1** *intr.* **a** (of animal or vegetable matter) lose its original form by the chemical action of bacteria, fungi, etc.; decay. **b** (foll. by *off, away*) crumble or drop from a stem etc. through decomposition. **2** *intr.* **a** (of society, institutions, etc.) gradually perish from lack of vigour or use. **b** (of a prisoner etc.) waste away (*left to rot in prison*); (of a person) languish. **3** *tr.* cause to rot, make rotten. ● *n.* **1** the process or state of rotting. **2** *colloq.* nonsense. **3** *Brit.* a rapid decline in standards etc. (*a rot set in; we must try to stop the rot*). ● *int. colloq.* expressing incredulity or ridicule. [Old English]

rota *n.* esp. *Brit.* a list of persons acting, or duties to be done, in rotation. [Latin, literally 'wheel']

Rotarian ● *n.* a member of Rotary. ● *adj.* of Rotary.

rotary ● *adj.* acting by rotation (*rotary drill; rotary pump*). ● *n.* (*pl.* **-ies**) **1** a rotary machine. **2** *N. Amer.* a traffic roundabout. **3** (**Rotary**) (in full **Rotary International**) a worldwide charitable society of businessmen and professional men, originally named from members entertaining in rotation. [from medieval Latin *rotarius*]

Rotary club *n.* a local branch of Rotary.

rotate *v.* **1** *intr.* & *tr.* move round an axis or centre, revolve. **2 a** *tr.* take or arrange in rotation. **b** *intr.* act or take place in rotation (*the chairmanship will rotate*). [based on Latin *rotatus* 'rotated'] □ **rotatable** *adj.* **rotative** *adj.* **rotatory** *adj.*

rotation *n.* **1** the act or an instance of rotating or being rotated. **2** a recurrence; a recurrent series or period; a regular succession. **3** ▲ a system of growing different crops in regular order to avoid exhausting the soil. [from Latin *rotatio*] □ **rotational** *adj.* **rotationally** *adv.*

rotator *n.* **1** a machine or device for causing something to rotate. **2** *Anat.* a muscle that rotates a limb etc. **3** a revolving apparatus or part.

Rotavator *n.* (also **Rotovator**) *Brit. propr.* a machine with a rotating blade for breaking up or tilling the soil. [blend of ROTARY and CULTIVATOR] □ **rotavate** *v.tr.*

rote *n.* (usu. prec. by *by*) mechanical or habitual repetition. [Middle English]

rot-gut *n. slang* cheap harmful alcoholic liquor.

rotisserie /rŏ-tis-ĕ-ri/ *n.* **1** a restaurant etc. where meat is roasted or barbecued. **2** a cooking appliance with a rotating spit for roasting and barbecuing meat. [from French *rôtisserie*]

rotor *n.* **1** a rotary part of a machine. ▷ DISTRIBUTOR. **2** a set of radiating aerofoils round a hub on a helicopter, providing lift. ▷ HELICOPTER. [formed irregularly from ROTATOR]

Rotovator var. of ROTAVATOR.

rotten *adj.* (**rottener, rottenest**) **1** rotting or rotted; falling to pieces or liable to break or tear from age or use. **2** morally or politically corrupt. **3** *colloq.* **a** disagreeable, unpleasant (*had a rotten time*). **b** (of a plan etc.) ill-advised, unsatisfactory (*a rotten idea*). **c** disagreeably ill (*feel rotten today*). [from Old Norse *rotinn*] □ **rottenness** *n.*

rotten apple *n. colloq.* a bad or esp. a morally corrupt person in a group etc.

rotten borough *n. hist.* (before 1832) an English borough able to elect an MP though having very few voters.

rotter *n.* esp. *Brit. colloq.* an objectionable, unpleasant, or reprehensible person.

ROTTWEILER

Rottweiler /rot-vy-ler/ ▲ *n.* a large powerful dog of a tall black and tan breed. [German, from *Rottweil*, a town in SW Germany]

rotund *adj.* **1 a** circular, round. **b** (of a person) plump, podgy. **2** (of speech, literary style, etc.) sonorous, grandiloquent. [from Latin *rotundus*] □ **rotundity** *n.* **rotundly** *adv.*

rotunda *n.* **1** ▼ a circular building, esp. one with a dome. **2** a circular hall or room. [from Italian *rotonda (camera)* 'round (chamber)']

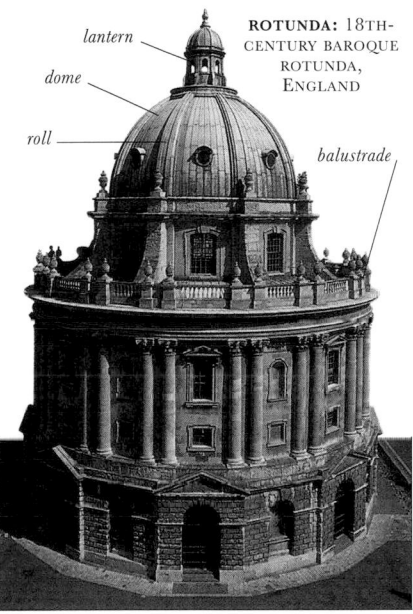

ROTUNDA: 18TH-CENTURY BAROQUE ROTUNDA, ENGLAND

lantern
dome
roll
balustrade

rouble *n.* (also **ruble**) the chief monetary unit of Russia and some other former republics of the USSR. [from Russian *rubl'*]

roué /roo-ay/ *n.* a debauchee, esp. an elderly one. [French, literally 'broken on a wheel', used to mean 'one deserving such punishment']

rouge ● *n.* **1** a red powder or cream used for colouring the cheeks. **2** powdered ferric oxide etc. as a polishing agent. ● *v.* **1** *tr.* colour with rouge. **2** *intr.* apply rouge to one's cheeks. [French, literally 'red']

rough ● *adj.* **1** having an uneven or irregular surface, not smooth or level or polished. **2** (of ground, country, etc.) having many bumps, obstacles, etc. **3 a** hairy, shaggy. **b** (of cloth) coarse in texture. **4 a** (of a person or behaviour) not mild or quiet or gentle; boisterous, unrestrained (*rough manners; rough play*). **b** (of language etc.) coarse, indelicate. **c** (of wine etc.) sharp or harsh in taste. **5** (of the sea, weather, etc.) violent, stormy. **6** disorderly, riotous (*a rough part of town*). **7** harsh, insensitive (*rough words; rough treatment*). **8 a** unpleasant, severe, demanding (*had a rough time*). **b** *Brit.* unfortunate, undeserved (*had rough luck*). **c** (foll. by *on*) hard or unfair towards. **9** lacking finish, elaboration, comfort, etc. (*rough lodgings; a rough welcome*). **10** incomplete, rudimentary (*a rough attempt; a rough makeshift*).

11 a inexact, approximate, preliminary (*a rough estimate; a rough sketch*). **b** (of stationery etc.) for use in writing rough notes etc. **12** *colloq.* **a** ill, unwell (*am feeling rough*). **b** depressed, dejected. ● *adv.* in a rough manner (*play rough*). ● *n.* **1** (usu. prec. by *the*) a hard part or aspect of life; hardship (*take the rough with the smooth*). **2** rough ground (*over rough and smooth*). **3** esp. *Brit.* a rough or violent person (*met a bunch of roughs*). **4** *Golf* rough ground off the fairway between tee and green. **5** an unfinished or provisional or natural state (*have written it in rough; shaped from the rough*). ● *v.tr.* **1** (foll. by *up*) ruffle (feathers, hair, etc.) by rubbing in the wrong direction. **2 a** (foll. by *out*) shape or plan roughly. **b** (foll. by *in*) sketch roughly. □ **rough it** do without basic comforts. **rough up** *colloq.* attack violently. **sleep rough** *Brit.* sleep outdoors, or not in a proper bed. [Old English] □ **roughness** *n.*

roughage *n.* **1** fibrous indigestible material in vegetable foodstuffs which aids the passage of food etc. through the gut. **2** coarse fodder.

rough-and-ready *adj.* crude but effective; not elaborate or over-particular.

rough-and-tumble ● *adj.* irregular, scrambling, disorderly. ● *n.* a haphazard fight; a scuffle.

roughcast ● *n.* plaster of lime and gravel, used on outside walls. ● *v.tr.* (*past* and *past part.* **-cast**) **1** coat (a wall) with roughcast. **2** prepare (a plan, essay, etc.) in outline.

rough copy *n.* **1** a first or original draft. **2** a copy of a picture etc. showing only the essential features.

rough deal *n.* hard or unfair treatment.

rough diamond *n.* **1** ▶ an uncut diamond. **2** a person of good nature but rough manners.

rough-dry *v.tr.* (**-dries**, **-dried**) dry (clothes) without ironing.

roughen *v.tr. & intr.* make or become rough.

rough-handle *v.tr.* treat or handle roughly.

rough-hewn *adj.* **1** formed or shaped out roughly. **2** uncouth, unrefined.

rough-house *v. slang* **1** *tr.* handle (a person) roughly. **2** *intr.* make a disturbance; act violently.

rough justice *n.* **1** treatment that is approximately fair. **2** treatment that is not at all fair.

roughly *adv.* **1** in a rough manner. **2** approximately (*roughly 20 people attended*). □ **roughly speaking** in an approximate sense (*it is, roughly speaking, a square*).

roughneck *n. colloq.* **1** a rough or rowdy person. **2** a worker on an oil rig.

rough passage *n.* **1** a crossing over rough sea. **2** a difficult time or experience.

rough ride *n.* a difficult time or experience.

roughshod *adj.* (of a horse) having shoes with nail heads projecting to prevent slipping. □ **ride roughshod over** treat inconsiderately or arrogantly.

rough stuff *n. colloq.* boisterous or violent behaviour.

roulade /roo-lahd/ *n.* a dish cooked or served in the shape of a roll, esp. a rolled piece of meat or sponge with a filling. [French]

roulette /roo-let/ *n.* a gambling game using a table in which a ball is dropped on to a revolving wheel with numbered compartments. [French]

Roumanian var. of ROMANIAN.

round ● *adj.* **1** shaped like or approximately like a circle, sphere, or cylinder; having a convex or circular outline or surface; curved, not angular. **2** done with or involving circular motion. **3 a** entire, continuous, complete (*a round dozen*). **b** (of a sum of money) considerable. **4** genuine, candid, outspoken; (of a statement etc.) categorical, unmistakable. **5** (usu. *attrib.*) (of a number) expressed for convenience or as an estimate in fewer significant numerals

ROUGH DIAMOND

or with a fraction removed (*spent £297.32, or in round figures £300*). ● *n.* **1** a round object or form. **2 a** a revolving motion, a circular or recurring course (*the earth in its yearly round*). **b** a regular recurring series of activities or functions (*one's daily round; a continuous round of pleasure*). **3 a** esp. *Brit.* a fixed route on which things are regularly delivered (*milk round*). **b** (often in *pl.*) a route or sequence by which people or things are regularly supervised or inspected (*a watchman's round; a doctor's rounds*). **4** an allowance of something distributed or measured out, esp.: **a** a single provision of drinks etc. to each member of a group. **b** ammunition to fire one shot; the act of firing this. **5 a** *Brit.* a slice across a loaf of bread. **b** *Brit.* a sandwich made from whole slices of bread. **6** each of a set or series, a sequence of actions by each member of a group in turn, esp.: **a** one spell of play in a game etc. **b** one stage in a competition. **7** *Golf* the playing of all the holes in a course once. **8** (**the round**) a form of sculpture in which the figure stands clear of any ground (cf. RELIEF 6a). **9** *Mus.* a canon for three or more unaccompanied voices singing at the same pitch or in octaves. **10** a rung of a ladder. ● *adv.* esp. *Brit.* **1** with circular motion (*wheels go round*). **2** with return to the starting point or an earlier state (*summer soon comes round*). **3 a** with change to an opposite position (*he turned round to look*). **b** with change to an opposite opinion etc. (*they were angry but I soon won them round*). **4** to, at, or affecting all or many points of a circumference or an area or the members of a company etc. (*tea was then handed round; may I look round?*). **5** in every direction from a centre or within a radius (*spread destruction round; everyone for a mile round*). **6** by a circuitous way (*will you jump over or go round?; go a long way round*). **7** to a person's house etc. (*ask him round; will be round soon*). **b** to a more prominent or convenient position (*brought the car round*). **8** measuring a (specified distance) in girth. ● *prep.* esp. *Brit.* **1** so as to encircle or enclose (*tour round the world; has a blanket round him*). **2** at or to points on the circumference of (*sat round the table*). **3** with successive visits to (*hawks them round the cafés*). **4** in various directions from or with regard to (*towns round Birmingham; shells bursting round them*). **5** having as an axis of revolution or as a central point (*turns round its centre of gravity; write a book round an event*). **6 a** so as to double or pass in a curved course (*go round the corner*). **b** having passed in this way (*be round the corner*). **c** in the position that would result from this (*find them round the corner*). **7** so as to come close from various sides but not into contact. ● *v.* **1 a** *tr.* give a round shape to. **b** *intr.* assume a round shape. **2** *tr.* pass round (a corner, cape, etc.). **3** *tr.* express (a number) in a less exact but more convenient form (also foll. by *down* when the number is decreased and *up* when it is increased). **4** *tr. Phonet.* pronounce (a vowel) with rounded lips. □ **go the round** (or **rounds**) (of news etc.) be passed on from person to person. **in the round 1** with all features shown; all things considered. **2** *Theatr.* with the audience round at least three sides of the stage. **3** (of sculpture) with all sides shown. **round about 1** all round; on all sides (of). **2** with a change to an opposite position. **3** approximately (*cost round about £50*). **round and round** several times round. **round the bend** see BEND[1]. **round down** see sense 3 of *v.* **round off 1** bring to a complete or symmetrical or well-ordered state. **2** smooth out; blunt the corners or angles of. **round on a person** make a sudden verbal attack on or unexpected retort to a person. **round out 1** = *round off* 1. **2** provide more detail about. **round peg in a square hole** = *square peg in a round hole* (see PEG). **round the twist** see TWIST. **round up** collect or bring together (see also sense 3 of *v.*). [from Latin *rotundus* 'rotund'] □ **roundish** *adj.* **roundness** *n.*

roundabout ● *n.* **1** *Brit.* a road junction at which traffic moves in one direction round a central island. **2** *Brit.* **a** a large revolving device in a play-

ROW

Rowing can be functional or recreational. As a sport, it includes two main types of competition: regattas and head-of-the river races. Regattas are knock-out events held on a straight stretch of water divided into lanes; international regattas are held over 2,000 m (1¼ miles). In head-of-the-river races, boats set off at intervals and are timed over the course. Rowing crews may include a coxwain (cox), who coordinates the rhythm of the strokes and steers. In coxless crews, the rower at the front steers using a foot-operated rudder, while the one at the back (the stroke) sets the rhythm. Racing boats use a sliding seat, while recreational rowing boats have a fixed seat.

COXLESS FOUR

narrow competition boat · oar · bow (front rower) · rowlock · stroke

angle of blade · line of shoulder · line of chest

STROKE CYCLE WITH A FIXED SEAT

oars forward · catch · pull through · finish · feather · square · oars forward

rudder indicator · blade

ground, for children to ride on. **b** = MERRY-GO-ROUND 1. ● *adj.* circuitous.

round brackets *n.pl. Brit.* brackets of the form ( ).

round dance *n.* **1** a dance in which couples move in circles round the ballroom. **2** a dance in which the dancers form one large circle.

roundel *n.* **1** a small disc, esp. a decorative medallion. **2** a circular identifying mark painted on military aircraft, esp. the red, white, and blue of the RAF. [from Old French *rondel(le)*]

roundelay *n.* a short simple song with a refrain. [from French *rondelet*]

rounder *n.* **1** (in *pl.*; treated as *sing.*) a game with a bat and ball in which players after hitting the ball run through a round of bases. **2** a complete run of a player through all the bases as a unit of scoring in rounders.

Roundhead *n. hist.* ▼ a member of the Parliamentary party in the English Civil War. [from their custom of wearing the hair cut short]

R

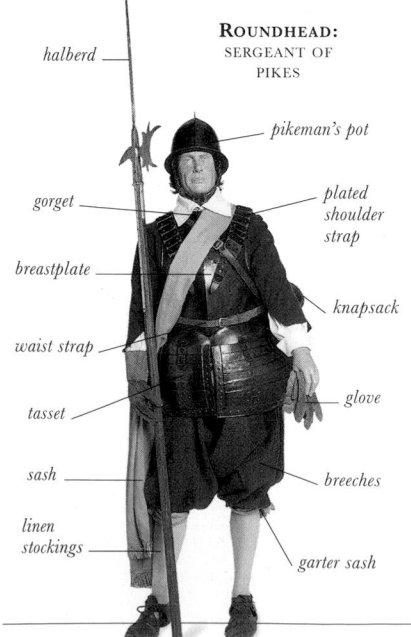

ROUNDHEAD: SERGEANT OF PIKES

halberd · pikeman's pot · gorget · plated shoulder strap · breastplate · knapsack · waist strap · tasset · glove · sash · breeches · linen stockings · garter sash

roundhouse *n.* **1** a repair shed for railway locomotives, built round a turntable. **2** *slang* a blow given with a wide sweep of the arm. **3** *hist.* a prison; a place of detention. **4** *Naut.* a cabin or set of cabins on the after part of the quarterdeck, esp. on a sailing ship.

roundhouse kick *n.* (esp. in karate) a kick made with a wide sweep of the leg and rotation of the body.

roundly *adv.* **1** bluntly, severely (*was roundly criticized; told them roundly that he refused*). **2** in a thoroughgoing manner (*go roundly to work*).

round robin *n.* **1** a petition esp. with signatures written in a circle to conceal the order of writing. **2** *N. Amer.* a tournament in which each competitor plays in turn against every other.

round-shouldered *adj.* with shoulders bent forward so that the back is rounded.

roundsman *n.* (*pl.* **-men**) **1** *Brit.* a trader's employee going round delivering and taking orders. **2** *US* a police officer in charge of a patrol. **3** *Austral.* a journalist covering a specified subject (*political roundsman*).

Round Table *n.* **1** an international charitable association which holds discussions, debates, etc., and undertakes community service. **2** (**round table**) an assembly for discussion, esp. at a conference (often *attrib.*: *round-table talks*). [alluding to the one at which King Arthur and his knights sat so that none should have precedence]

round-the-clock *attrib.adj.* lasting or covering all day and (usu.) all night (*round-the-clock care*). Cf. *round the clock* (CLOCK¹).

round trip *n.* a trip to one or more places and back again.

round-up *n.* **1** a systematic rounding up of people or things. **2** a summary; a résumé of facts or events.

roundworm *n.* a nematode worm.

rouse *v.* **1 a** *tr.* (often foll. by *from, out of*) bring out of sleep, wake. **b** *intr.* cease to sleep, wake up. **2 a** *tr.* stir up, make active or excited (*roused them from their complacency; was roused to protest*). **b** *intr.* become active. **3** *tr.* provoke to anger (*is terrible when roused*). **4** *tr.* evoke (feelings). □ **rouse oneself** overcome one's indolence. [originally a hawking and hunting term] □ **rouser** *n.*

rouseabout *n. Austral. & NZ* an unskilled labourer or odd jobber.

rousing *adj.* **1** exciting, stirring (*a rousing cheer; a rousing song*). **2** (of a fire) blazing strongly. □ **rousingly** *adv.*

roust *v.tr.* **1 a** rouse, stir up. **b** root out. **2** *N. Amer. slang* jostle, harass, rough up. □ **roust around** rummage.

roustabout *n.* **1** a labourer on an oil rig. **2** an unskilled or casual labourer. **3** *US* **a** a dock labourer or deckhand. **b** a circus labourer. **4** *Austral.* = ROUSEABOUT.

rout¹ ● *n.* **1** a disorderly retreat of defeated troops. **2** a decisive defeat. ● *v.tr.* cause to retreat in disorder; defeat. [based on Latin *ruptus* 'broken']

rout² *v.* **1** *intr. & tr.* = ROOT². **2** *tr.* cut a groove, or any pattern not extending to the edges, in (a wooden or metal surface). □ **rout out** force or fetch out of bed or from a house or hiding place. [variant of ROOT²]

route ● *n.* **1** a way or course taken (esp. regularly) in getting from a starting point to a destination. **2** *N. Amer.* a round travelled in delivering, selling, or collecting goods. ● *v.tr.* (**routeing** or **routing**) send or forward or direct to be sent by a particular route. [from Old French *r(o)ute* 'road']

route march *n.* a training march for troops.

router *n.* a type of plane with two handles or esp. a power tool used in routing.

routine ● *n.* **1** a regular course or procedure, an unvarying performance of certain acts. **2** a set sequence in a dance, comedy act, etc. **3** *Computing* a sequence of instructions for performing a task. ● *adj.* **1** performed as part of a routine (*routine duties*). **2** of a customary or standard kind. [French] □ **routinely** *adv.*

roux /roo/ *n.* (*pl.* same) a mixture of fat and flour used in making sauces etc. [French, literally 'browned (butter)']

rove¹ *v.* **1** *intr.* wander without a settled destination, roam, ramble. **2** *intr.* (of eyes) look in changing directions. **3** *tr.* wander over or through. [originally in Archery sense 'to shoot at a casual mark of undetermined range': Middle English]

rove² *past* of REEVE².

rover¹ *n.* **1** a wanderer. **2** (**Rover**) *Brit.* a senior Scout (now called *Venture Scout*).

rover² *n.* a pirate. [Middle Dutch, based on *rōven* 'to rob']

rover ticket *n.* a ticket permitting unlimited bus or railway travel in an area for a specified period.

roving commission *n. Brit.* authority given to a

person or persons conducting an inquiry to travel as may be necessary.

roving eye n. a tendency to flirt or to be fickle sexually.

row[1] /roh/ n. **1** a number of persons or things in a more or less straight line. **2** a line of seats across a theatre etc. (*in the front row*). **3** a street with a continuous line of houses along one or each side. **4** a line of plants in a field or garden. **5** a horizontal line of entries in a table etc. □ **in a row 1** forming a row. **2** colloq. in succession (*two Sundays in a row*). [Old English]

row[2] /roh/ • v. **1** tr. ◀ propel (a boat) with oars. **2** tr. convey (a passenger) in a boat in this way. **3** intr. propel a boat in this way. **4** tr. make (a stroke) or achieve (a rate of striking) in rowing. **5** tr. compete in (a race) by rowing. • n. **1** a spell of rowing. **2** an excursion in a rowing boat. [Old English] □ **rower** n.

row[3] /rhymes with cow/ colloq. • n. **1** esp. Brit. a loud noise or commotion. **2** a fierce quarrel or dispute. **3** Brit. **a** a severe reprimand. **b** the condition of being reprimanded (*shall get into a row*). • v. **1** intr. make or engage in a row. **2** tr. Brit. reprimand. □ **make** (or **kick up**) **a row 1** esp. Brit. make a noise or commotion. **2** make a vigorous protest. [18th-century slang]

rowan n. **1** (also **rowan tree**) **a** Brit. the mountain ash, *Sorbus aucuparia*. **b** US a similar tree, *Sorbus americana*, native to America. **2** (in full **rowan-berry**) the scarlet berry of either of these trees. [Scandinavian]

rowboat n. N. Amer. = ROWING BOAT.

rowdy • adj. (**rowdier**, **rowdiest**) noisy and disorderly. • n. (pl. **-ies**) a rowdy person. [19th-century US coinage, in sense 'lawless backwoodsman'] □ **rowdily** adv. **rowdiness** n. **rowdyism** n.

rowel n. ▼ spiked revolving disc at the end of a spur. [from Late Latin *rotella* 'little wheel']

rowel   *heel grip*

ROWEL ON A
SOUTH AMERICAN
BRASS SPUR

row house n. N. Amer. a terrace house.

rowing boat n. Brit. a small boat propelled by oars. ▷ ROW

rowing machine n. a device for exercising the muscles used in rowing.

rowlock /rol-ŏk/ n. ▶ a device on a boat's gunwale serving as a fulcrum for an oar and keeping it in place. [alteration of earlier *oarlock*, influenced by ROW[2]]

jaw

crutch

crutch plate

captive socket   *shaft*

ROWLOCK

royal • adj. **1** of or suited to or worthy of a king or queen. **2** in the service or under the patronage of a king or queen. **3** belonging to the king or queen (*the royal hands; the royal anger*). **4** of the family of a king or queen. **5** majestic, stately, splendid. **6** on a great scale, of exceptional size or quality, first-rate (*gave us royal entertainment; in royal spirits; had a royal time*). • n. colloq. a member of the royal family. [Middle English via Old French *roial* from Latin *regalis* 'regal'] □ **royally** adv.

royal assent n. assent of the sovereign to a bill passed by Parliament.

royal blue • n. a deep vivid blue. • adj. (hyphenated when attrib.) of this colour.

Royal British Legion n. (in the UK) an association of ex-servicemen (and now women) formed in 1921.

Royal Engineers n.pl. the engineering branch of the British army.

royal family n. the family to which a sovereign belongs.

royal icing n. esp. Brit. a hard white icing made from icing sugar and egg whites.

royalist n. **1** a supporter of monarchy. **2** hist. a supporter of the King against Parliament in the English Civil War. □ **royalism** n.

royal jelly n. a substance secreted by honey bee workers and fed by them to future queen bees.

royal prerogative see PREROGATIVE 2.

Royal Society n. (in full **Royal Society of London**) a society founded in 1662 to promote scientific discussion.

royalty n. (pl. **-ies**) **1** the office or dignity or power of a king or queen. **2 a** royal persons. **b** a member of a royal family. **3** a sum paid to a patentee for the use of a patent or to an author etc. for each copy of a book etc. sold or for each public performance of a work. **4 a** a royal right (now esp. over minerals) granted by the sovereign. **b** a payment made by a producer of minerals, oil, or natural gas to the owner of the site or of the mineral rights over it. [from Old French *roialté*]

royal warrant n. a warrant authorizing a tradesperson to supply goods to a specified royal person.

royal 'we' n. the use of 'we' instead of 'I' by a single person.

rozzer n. Brit. slang a police officer. [19th-century coinage]

RP abbr. received pronunciation.

RPI abbr. retail price index.

r.p.m. abbr. revolutions per minute.

rpt abbr. repeat.

RSI abbr. repetitive strain injury.

RSM abbr. Brit. Regimental Sergeant Major.

RSPB abbr. (in the UK) Royal Society for the Protection of Birds.

RSPCA abbr. (in the UK) Royal Society for the Prevention of Cruelty to Animals.

RSV abbr. Revised Standard Version.

RSVP abbr. please answer. [French *répondez s'il vous plaît*]

rt. abbr. right.

Rt. Hon. abbr. Brit. Right Honourable.

Rt. Revd abbr. (also **Rt. Rev.**) Right Reverend.

Ru symb. Chem. the element ruthenium.

rub • v. (**rubbed**, **rubbing**) **1** tr. move one's hand or another object with firm pressure over the surface of. **2** tr. (usu. foll. by against, in, on, over) apply (one's hand etc.) in this way. **3** tr. clean or polish or make dry or bare by rubbing. **4** tr. apply (polish, ointment, etc.) by rubbing. **5** tr. (foll. by in, into, through) use rubbing to make (a substance) go into or through something. **6** tr. move or slide (objects) against each other. **7** intr. (foll. by against, on) move with contact or friction. **8** tr. chafe or make sore by rubbing. **9** intr. (of cloth, skin, etc.) become frayed or worn or sore or bare with friction. **10** tr. reproduce the design of (a sepulchral brass or a stone) by rubbing paper laid on it with heelball or coloured chalk etc. **11** tr. (foll. by to) reduce to powder etc. by rubbing. • n. **1** a spell or an instance of rubbing (*give it a rub*). **2** an impediment or difficulty (*there's the rub*). □ **rub along** Brit. colloq. cope or manage without undue difficulty. **rub down** dry or smooth or clean by rubbing. **rub elbows with** US = rub shoulders with. **rub one's hands** rub one's hands together usu. as a sign of keen satisfaction, or for warmth. **rub it in** (or **rub a person's nose in it**) emphasize or repeat an embarrassing fact etc. **rub off 1** (usu. foll. by on) be transferred by contact, be transmitted (*some of his attitudes have rubbed off on me*).

2 remove by rubbing. **rub out 1** erase with a rubber. **2** esp. N. Amer. slang kill, eliminate. **rub shoulders with** associate or come into contact with. **rub up 1** polish. **2** Brit. brush up (a subject or one's memory). **rub** (or Brit. **rub up**) **the wrong way** irritate or repel as by stroking a cat against the lie of its fur. [Middle English]

rubato /ruu-bah-toh/ n. (pl. **-os** or **rubati**) Mus. the temporary disregarding of strict tempo. [Italian, literally 'robbed']

rubber[1] n. **1** a tough elastic substance made from the latex of plants or synthetically. **2** esp. Brit. a piece of this or another substance for rubbing out pencil or ink marks. **3** colloq. a condom. **4** (in pl.) US galoshes. [based on RUB, from its early use to rub out pencil marks] □ **rubbery** adj. **rubberiness** n.

rubber[2] n. **1** a match of three or five successive games between the same sides or persons at whist, bridge, cricket, tennis, etc. **2** (prec. by the) **a** the act of winning a majority of games in a rubber. **b** a deciding game when scores are level. [used as a term in bowls from c.1600]

rubber band n. a loop of rubber for holding papers etc. together.

rubber bullet n. a baton round made of rubber.

rubberize v.tr. (also **-ise**) treat or coat with rubber.

rubberneck colloq. • n. a person who cranes and stares inquisitively or stupidly. • v.intr. act in this way.

rubber plant n. **1** an evergreen plant, *Ficus elastica*, often cultivated as a house plant. **2** (also **rubber tree**) any of various tropical trees yielding latex, esp. *Hevea brasiliensis*.

rubber solution n. a liquid drying to a rubber-like material, used esp. as an adhesive in mending rubber articles.

rubber stamp • n. **1** a device for inking and imprinting on a surface. **2 a** a person who mechanically agrees to others' actions. **b** an indication of such agreement. • v.tr. (**rubber-stamp**) approve automatically.

rubbing n. **1** in senses of RUB v. **2** an impression or copy made by rubbing (see RUB v. 10).

rubbish • n. esp. Brit. **1** waste material; refuse, litter. **2** worthless material or articles; junk. **3** (often as int.) nonsense. • v.tr. Brit. colloq. **1** criticize severely. **2** reject as worthless. [from Anglo-French *rubbous*] □ **rubbishy** adj.

rubble n. rough fragments of stone or brick etc. [Middle English] □ **rubbly** adj.

rub-down n. an instance of rubbing down.

rube n. N. Amer. colloq. a country bumpkin. [abbreviation of the name *Reuben*]

rubella n. Med. an acute infectious virus disease with a red rash; German measles. [Latin, literally 'reddish things']

Rubicon n. a boundary which once crossed signifies irrevocable commitment; a point of no return. [ancient name of a boundary stream crossed by Julius Caesar (49 BC) as the start of a war with Pompey]

rubicund adj. (of a face, complexion, or person) ruddy, high-coloured. [from Latin *rubicundus*]

rubidium n. Chem. a soft silvery metallic element. [based on Latin *rubidus* 'red', with reference to its spectral lines]

Rubik's cube n. propr. a puzzle in which the aim is to restore the faces of a composite cube to single colours by rotating layers of constituent smaller cubes. [named after E. *Rubik*, born 1944, its Hungarian inventor]

ruble var. of ROUBLE.

rubric n. **1** a direction for the conduct of divine service in a liturgical book. **2** a heading or passage in red or special lettering. **3** explanatory words. [from Latin *rubrica (terra)* 'red (earth or ochre)', as writing material]

rub-up n. the act or an instance of rubbing up.

R

RUBY

ruby • *n.* (*pl.* **-ies**) **1** ◄ a rare precious stone consisting of corundum with a colour varying from deep crimson or purple to pale rose. ▷ GEM. **2** a glowing purplish-red colour. • *adj.* of this colour. [from medieval Latin *rubinus (lapis)* 'red (stone)']

ruby wedding *n.* the fortieth anniversary of a wedding.

RUC *abbr.* Royal Ulster Constabulary.

ruche /roosh/ *n.* a frill or gathering of lace etc. as a trimming. [from medieval Latin *rusca* 'tree-bark'] □ **ruched** *adj.* **ruching** *n.*

ruck[1] • *n.* **1** (prec. by *the*) the main body of competitors not likely to overtake the leaders. **2** an undistinguished crowd of persons or things. **3** *Rugby* a loose scrum with the ball on the ground. **4** *Austral. Rules* a group of three players who follow the play without fixed positions. • *v.intr. Rugby & Austral. Rules* participate in a ruck. [Middle English in sense 'stack of fuel, rick']

ruck[2] • *v.tr. & intr.* make or become creased or wrinkled. • *n.* a crease or wrinkle. [from Old Norse *hrukka*]

ruckle *v. & n. Brit.* = RUCK[2].

rucksack *n.* a bag slung by straps from both shoulders and resting on the back. [German, from dialect *rucken* 'back' + *Sack* 'sack']

ruckus *n. esp. N. Amer.* a row or commotion. [19th-century coinage]

ruction *n. colloq.* **1** a disturbance or tumult. **2** (in *pl.*) unpleasant arguments or reactions. [19th-century coinage]

rudd *n.* (*pl.* same) a freshwater fish, *Scardinius erythrophthalmus*, resembling a roach and having red fins.

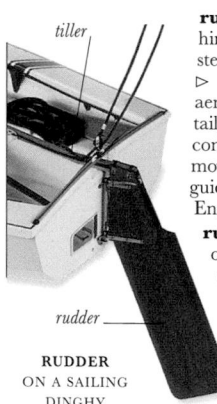

tiller

rudder

RUDDER
ON A SAILING
DINGHY

R

rudder *n.* **1 a** ◄ a flat piece hinged vertically to the stern of a ship for steering. ▷ MAN-OF-WAR. **b** a vertical aerofoil pivoted from the tailplane of an aircraft, for controlling its horizontal movement. ▷ AIRCRAFT. **2** a guiding principle etc. [Old English] □ **rudderless** *adj.*

ruddle *n.* a red ochre, esp. of a kind used for marking sheep.

ruddy *adj.* (**ruddier, ruddiest**) **1 a** (of a person or complexion) freshly or healthily red. **b** (of health, youth, etc.) marked by this. **2** reddish. **3** *Brit. colloq.* bloody, damnable. [Old English] □ **ruddiness** *n.*

ruddy duck *n.* an American duck, *Oxyura jamaicensis*, naturalized in Britain etc., the male of which has deep red-brown plumage.

rude *adj.* **1** impolite or offensive. **2** roughly made or done (*a rude plough*). **3 a** primitive or unsophisticated (*rude simplicity*). **b** *archaic* uneducated. **4** abrupt, sudden, startling (*a rude awakening*). **5** *colloq.* indecent, lewd (*a rude joke*). **6** *esp. Brit.* vigorous or hearty (*rude health*). [from Latin *rudis* 'unwrought'] □ **rudely** *adv.* **rudeness** *n.* **rudery** *n.*

rudiment *n.* **1** (in *pl.*) the elements or first principles of a subject. **2** (in *pl.*) an imperfect beginning of something undeveloped or yet to develop. **3** *Biol.* an undeveloped or immature part or organ. [French]

rudimentary *adj.* **1** involving basic principles; fundamental. **2** incompletely developed; vestigial.

rue[1] *v.tr.* (**rues, rued, rueing** or **ruing**) repent of; bitterly feel the consequences of; wish to be undone or non-existent (esp. *rue the day*). [Old English]

RUGBY

There are two forms of rugby: Rugby Union and Rugby League. Each has a slightly different style of play, but in both, points are scored by placing the ball over the goal line (a try) or kicking it over the goal crossbar. Both forms use scrummaging as one way to restart play.

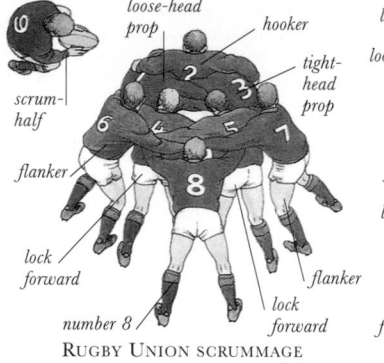

loose-head prop — hooker — tight-head prop — scrum-half — flanker — flanker — lock forward — lock forward — number 8

RUGBY UNION SCRUMMAGE

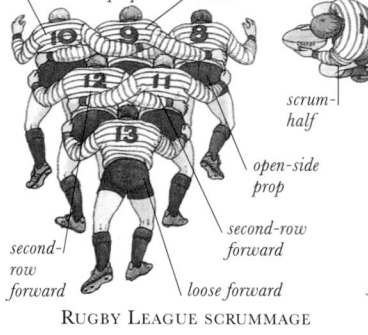

blind-side prop — hooker — scrum-half — open-side prop — second-row forward — second-row forward — loose forward

RUGBY LEAGUE SCRUMMAGE

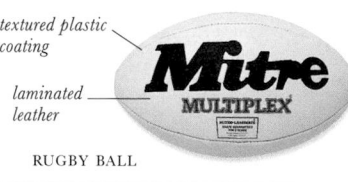

textured plastic coating — laminated leather

RUGBY BALL

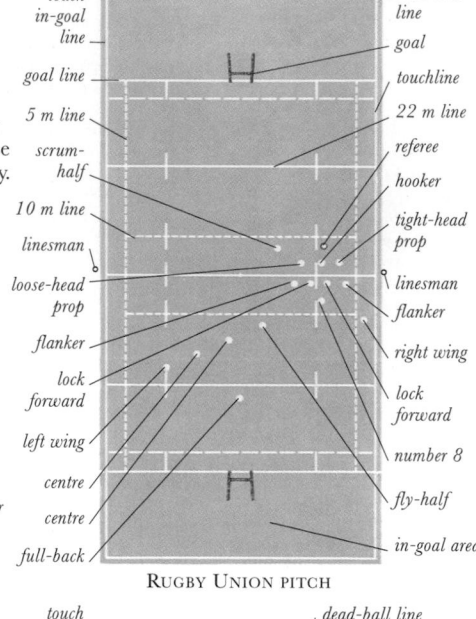

touch in-goal line — dead-ball line — goal — goal line — touchline — 5 m line — 22 m line — scrum-half — referee — hooker — 10 m line — tight-head prop — linesman — loose-head prop — linesman — flanker — flanker — lock forward — right wing — left wing — lock forward — centre — number 8 — centre — fly-half — full-back — in-goal area

RUGBY UNION PITCH

touch in-goal — dead-ball line — goal line — touch in-goal line — 10 m line — touchline — referee — hooker — linesman — open-side prop — blind-side prop — linesman — second-row forward — second-row forward — scrum-half — loose forward — stand-off half — left wing — right wing — centre — centre — full-back — goal

RUGBY LEAGUE PITCH

---

rue[2] *n.* a perennial evergreen shrub, *Ruta graveolens*, with bitter strong-scented leaves. [from Greek *rhuté*]

rueful *adj.* expressing sorrow or regret in a genuine or humorous way. □ **ruefully** *adv.* **ruefulness** *n.*

ruff[1] • *n.* **1** ▶ a projecting starched frill worn round the neck esp. in the 16th c. **2** a projecting or conspicuously coloured ring of feathers or hair round a bird's or animal's neck. **3** (*fem.* **reeve**) a wading bird, *Philomachus pugnax*, of which the male has a ruff and ear-tufts in the breeding season.

ruff[2] • *v.intr. & tr.* trump at cards. • *n.* an act of ruffing. [Middle English]

ruffian *n.* a violent lawless person. [from French *ruf(f)ian*] □ **ruffianism** *n.* **ruffianly** *adj.*

ruffle • *v.* **1** *tr.* disturb the smoothness or tranquillity of. **2** *tr.* upset the calmness of (a person). **3** *tr.* gather (lace etc.) into a ruffle. **4** *tr.* (of a bird) erect (its feathers) in anger, display, etc. **5** *intr.* undergo ruffling. • *n.* **1** an ornamental frill of lace etc. worn at the opening of a garment esp. round the wrist, breast, or neck. **2** perturbation, bustle. **3** a rippling effect on water. [Middle English]

rufous *adj.* (esp. of animals) reddish brown. [from Latin *rufus* 'red, reddish']

rug *n.* **1** a floor-mat of shaggy material or thick pile. **2** esp. *Brit.* a thick woollen coverlet or wrap. □ **pull the rug from under** deprive of support; weaken, unsettle. [related to RAG[1]]

rugby *n.* (also **Rugby**) (in full **rugby football**) ▲ a team game played with an oval ball that may be kicked, carried, and passed from hand to hand. [from *Rugby* School in the Midlands]

Rugby League *n.* a form of rugby with teams of 13. ▷ RUGBY

Rugby Union *n.* a form of rugby with teams of 15. ▷ RUGBY

rugged *adj.* **1** (of ground or terrain)

ruff

RUFF: LATE 16TH-
CENTURY RUFF

having a rough uneven surface. **2** (of features) strongly marked; irregular in outline. **3 a** unpolished; lacking refinement (*rugged grandeur*). **b** harsh in sound. **c** austere, unbending (*rugged honesty*). **d** involving hardship (*a rugged life*). **4** (esp. of a machine) robust, sturdy. [Middle English] □ **ruggedly** *adv.* **ruggedness** *n.*

ruggedized *adj.* (also **-ised**) esp. *US* made hardwearing or shock-resistant. □ **ruggedization** *n.*

rugger *n. Brit. colloq.* rugby.

ruin ● *n.* **1** a destroyed or wrecked state. **2** a person's or thing's downfall or elimination (*the ruin of my hopes*). **3 a** the complete loss of one's property or position (*bring to ruin*). **b** a person who has suffered ruin. **4** (in *sing.* or *pl.*) the remains of a building etc. that has suffered ruin (*an old ruin; ancient ruins*). **5** a cause of ruin (*will be the ruin of us*). ● *v.tr.* **1 a** bring to ruin (*your extravagance has ruined me*). **b** utterly impair or wreck (*the rain ruined my hat*). **2** (esp. as **ruined** *adj.*) reduce to ruins. □ **in ruins 1** in a state of ruin. **2** completely wrecked (*their hopes were in ruins*). [from Latin *ruina*]

ruination *n.* **1** the act of bringing to ruin. **2** the act of ruining or the state of being ruined.

ruinous *adj.* **1** bringing ruin; disastrous (*at ruinous expense*). **2** dilapidated. □ **ruinously** *adv.*

rule ● *n.* **1** a principle to which an action conforms or is required to conform. **2** a prevailing custom or standard; the normal state of things. **3** government or dominion (*under British rule; the rule of law*). **4** a graduated straight measure used in carpentry etc.; a ruler. **5** *Printing* **a** a thin strip of metal for separating headings, columns, etc. **b** a thin line or dash. **6** a code of discipline of a religious order. **7** *Law* an order made by a judge or court with reference to a particular case only. ● *v.* **1 a** keep under control. **2** *tr.* & (often foll. by *over*) *intr.* have sovereign control of (*rules over a vast kingdom*). **3** *tr.* (often foll. by *that* + clause) pronounce authoritatively (*was ruled out of order*). **4** *tr.* **a** make parallel lines across (paper). **b** make (a straight line) with a ruler etc. □ **as a rule** usually **by rule** in a regulation manner; mechanically. **rule in** pronounce as included. **rule out** exclude; pronounce irrelevant or ineligible. **rule the roost** be in control. **run the rule over** *Brit.* examine cursorily for correctness or adequacy. [from Latin *regula* 'straight stick']

rule of thumb *n.* a rule for general guidance, based on experience or practice rather than theory.

ruler *n.* **1** a person exercising government or dominion. **2** a straight usu. graduated strip or cylinder of wood, metal, etc., used to draw lines or measure distance. □ **rulership** *n.*

ruling ● *n.* an authoritative decision or announcement. ● *adj.* dominant, prevailing; currently in force (*ruling prices*).

ruling passion *n.* a motive that habitually directs one's actions.

rum[1] *n.* **1** a spirit distilled from sugar cane residues or molasses. **2** *N. Amer.* intoxicating liquor. [17th-century coinage]

rum[2] *adj.* (**rummer, rummest**) *Brit. colloq.* odd, strange, queer. [18th-century coinage]

Rumanian var. of ROMANIAN.

rumba *n.* (also **rhumba**) **1** a dance originating among Cuban blacks. **2 a** a ballroom dance imitative of this. **b** the music for it. [Latin American Spanish]

rum baba *n.* a small sponge cake soaked in rum-flavoured syrup. [baba: from Polish]

rumble ● *v.* **1** *intr.* make a continuous deep resonant sound as of distant thunder. **2** *intr.* (foll. by *along, by, past*, etc.) move with a rumbling noise. **3** *tr.* utter or say with a rumbling sound. **4** *tr. Brit. slang* find out about (esp. something illicit), discover the misbehaviour of (a person). ● *n.* **1** a rumbling sound. **2** *N. Amer. slang* a street fight between gangs. [Middle English]

rumble strip *n.* a series of raised strips across a road or along its edge to make vehicles vibrate, warning drivers of speed restrictions or of the edge of the road.

rumblings *n.pl.* early indications of some state of things or incipient change (*rumblings of discontent*).

rumbustious *adj.* esp. *Brit. colloq.* boisterous, noisy, uproarious.

rum butter *n.* an accompaniment to hot puddings, made from rum, butter, and sugar.

ruminant ● *n.* ▼ an animal that chews the cud. ● *adj.* **1** of or belonging to ruminants. **2** contemplative; given to or engaged in meditation. [from Latin *ruminant-* 'chewing over']

ruminate *v.* **1** *tr.* & (foll. by *over, on*, etc.) *intr.* meditate, ponder. **2** *intr.* chew the cud. [based on Latin *ruminatus* 'chewed over'] □ **rumination** *n.* **ruminative** *adj.* **ruminatively** *adv.*

rummage ● *v.* **1** *tr.* & (foll. by *in, through, among*) *intr.* search, esp. unsystematically. **2** *tr.* (foll. by *out, up*) find among other things. **3** *tr.* (foll. by *about*) disarrange; make untidy in searching. ● *n.* **1** an instance of rummaging. **2** things found by rummaging; a miscellaneous accumulation. [earlier in sense 'arranging of casks etc. in a hold': from Old French *arrumage*]

rummage sale *n.* esp. *N. Amer.* a jumble sale.

rummy *n.* a card game played usu. with two packs. [20th-century coinage]

rumour (*US* **rumor**) ● *n.* **1** general talk or hearsay of doubtful accuracy. **2** a current but unverified statement or assertion (*heard a rumour that you are leaving*). ● *v.tr.* (usu. in *passive*) report by way of rumour (*it is rumoured that you are leaving; you are rumoured to be leaving*). [from Latin *rumor* 'noise']

rumour-monger *n.* (*US* **rumormonger**) a spreader of rumours. □ **rumour-mongering** *n.*

rump *n.* **1** the hind part of a mammal, esp. the buttocks. **2** a small or contemptible remnant. [Middle English]

rumple *v.tr.* & *intr.* make or become creased or ruffled. [based on Middle Dutch *rompel* 'a wrinkle']

rump steak *n.* a cut of beef from the rump.

rumpus *n.* (*pl.* **rumpuses**) *colloq.* a disturbance, brawl, row, or uproar. [18th-century coinage]

rumpus room *n. N. Amer., Austral., & NZ* a room usu. in the basement of a house for games and play.

run ● *v.* (**running**; *past* **ran**; *past part.* **run**) **1** *intr.* go with quick steps on alternate feet, never having both or all feet on the ground at the same time. **2** *intr.* flee, abscond. **3** *intr.* go or travel hurriedly, briefly, etc. **4** *intr.* **a** advance by or as by rolling or on wheels, or smoothly or easily. **b** be in action or operation (*left the engine running*). **5** *intr.* be current or operative (*the lease runs for 99 years*). **6** *intr.* travel or be travelling on its route (*the train is running late*). **7** *intr.* (of a play, exhibition, etc.) be staged or presented (*is now running at the Apollo*). **8** *intr.* extend; have a course or order or tendency (*the road runs by the coast; prices are running high*). **9 a** *intr.* compete in a race. **b** *intr.* finish a race in a specified position. **c** *tr.* compete in (a race). **10** *intr.* (often foll. by *for*) seek election (*ran for president*). **11 a** *intr.* (of a liquid etc.) flow, drip profusely. **b** *tr.* flow with. **c** *intr.* (foll. by *with*) flow or be wet; drip (*his face ran with sweat*). **12** *tr.* **a** cause (water etc.) to flow. **b** fill (a bath) with water. **13** *intr.* spread or pass rapidly (*a shiver ran down my spine*). **14** *intr. Cricket* (of a batsman) run from one wicket to the other in scoring a run. **15** *tr.* traverse (a course, race, or distance). **16** *tr.* perform (an errand). **17** *tr.* publish (an article etc.) in a newspaper or magazine. **18 a** *tr.* cause to operate. **b** *intr.*

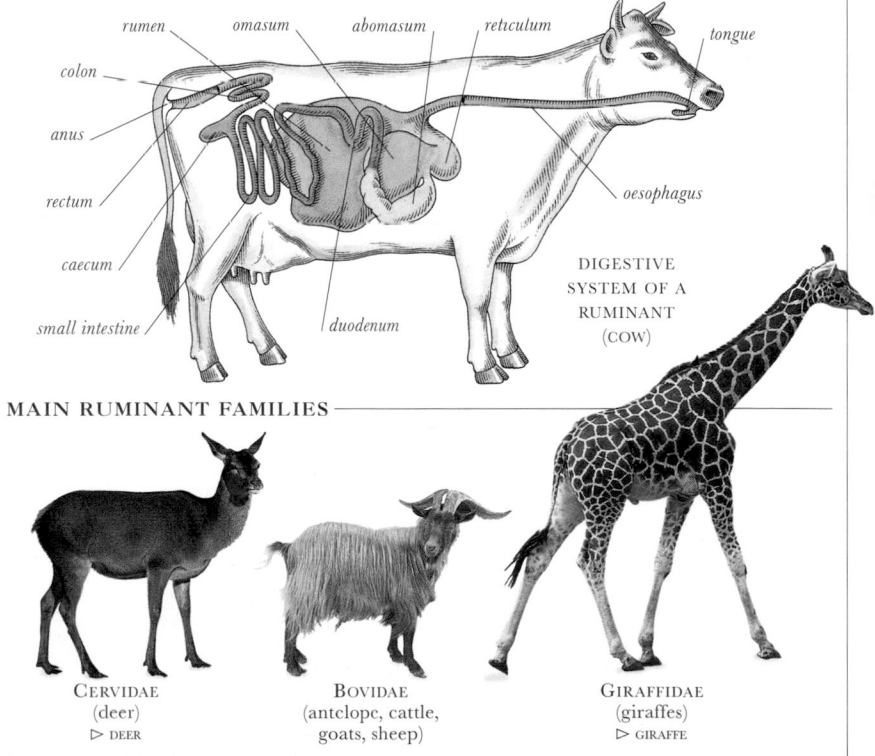

RUMINANT

Ruminants are even-toed mammals that have three- or four-chambered stomachs and perform rumination. Fibrous food material (cud) from the largest chamber (rumen) is formed into masses in the reticulum, and then regurgitated and rechewed. When it returns to the rumen, it is digested further before entering the other chambers.

rumen   omasum   abomasum   reticulum   tongue

colon

anus

rectum

oesophagus

caecum

small intestine   duodenum

DIGESTIVE SYSTEM OF A RUMINANT (COW)

MAIN RUMINANT FAMILIES

CERVIDAE (deer) ▷ DEER

BOVIDAE (antelope, cattle, goats, sheep)

GIRAFFIDAE (giraffes) ▷ GIRAFFE

R

(of a mechanism or component etc.) move or work freely. **19** *tr.* direct or manage (a business etc.). **20** *tr.* own and drive (a vehicle) regularly. **21** *tr.* take (a person) for a journey in a vehicle (*shall I run you to the shops?*). **22** *tr.* cause to run or go in a specified way (*ran the car into a tree*). **23** *tr.* enter (a horse etc.) for a race. **24** *tr.* smuggle (guns etc.). **25** *tr.* chase or hunt. **26** *intr.* (of a colour in a fabric) spread from the dyed parts. **27 a** *intr.* (of a thought, the eye, the memory, etc.) pass in a transitory or cursory way (*ideas ran through my mind*). **b** *tr.* cause (one's eye) to look cursorily (*ran my eye down the page*). **28** *intr.* (of hosiery) ladder. **29** *intr.* (of a candle) gutter. **30** *intr.* (of the eyes or nose) exude liquid matter. **31** *tr.* sew (fabric) loosely or hastily with running stitches. ● *n.* **1** an act or spell of running. **2** a short excursion. **3** a distance travelled. **4** a general tendency. **5** a rapid motion. **6** a regular route. **7** a continuous or long stretch or spell or course (*a metre's run of wiring; had a run of bad luck*). **8** (often foll. by *on*) **a** a high general demand (for a commodity, currency, etc.) (*a run on the dollar*). **b** a sudden demand for repayment by a large number of customers (of a bank). **9** a quantity produced in one period of production (*a print run*). **10** a general or average type or class (*not typical of the general run*). **11 a** *Cricket* a point scored by the batsmen each running to the other's wicket, or an equivalent point awarded for some other reason. **b** *Baseball* a point scored usu. by the batter returning to the plate after touching the other bases. **12** (foll. by *of*) free use of or access to (*had the run of the house*). **13 a** an animal's regular track. **b** an enclosure for fowls, rabbits, etc. **c** a range of pasture. **14** a ladder in hosiery. □ **at a** (or **the**) **run** running. **on the run 1** escaping, running away. **2** hurrying about. **run about 1** bustle; hurry from one person or place to another. **2** (esp. of children) play without restraint. **run across 1** happen to meet. **2** (foll. by *to*) make a brief journey or a flying visit (to a place). **run after 1** pursue with attentions; seek the society of. **2** pursue at a run. **run against** compete against, esp. in a political contest. **run along** *colloq.* depart. **run around 1** *Brit.* take from place to place by car etc. **2** deceive or evade repeatedly. **3** *colloq.* engage in sexual relations. **run at** attack by charging or rushing. **run away 1** flee, abscond. **2** elope. **3** (of a horse) bolt. **run away with 1** carry off. **2** win easily. **3** accept (a notion) hastily. **4** (of expense etc.) consume (money etc.). **5** (of a horse) bolt with (a rider, a carriage or its occupants). **6** leave home to have a relationship with. **7** deprive of self-control or common sense (*let his ideas run away with him*). **run a blockade** see BLOCKADE. **run down 1** knock down. **2** reduce the strength or numbers of. **3** (of an unwound clock etc.) stop. **4** (esp. as **run down** *adj.*) (of a person or a person's health) become feeble from overwork or undernourishment. **5** discover after a search. **6** disparage. **run dry** cease to flow. **run for it** seek safety by fleeing. **a run** (or **a good run**) **for one's money 1** vigorous competition. **2** pleasure derived from an activity. **3** return for outlay or effort. **run foul** (*N. Amer.* also **afoul**) **of 1** *Naut.* collide or become entangled with. **2** act contrary to; go against (*ran foul of their code of practice*). **run the gauntlet** see GAUNTLET[2]. **run high 1** (of the sea) have a strong current with a high tide. **2** (of feelings) be strong. **run in 1** *Brit.* run (a new engine or vehicle) carefully in the early stages. **2** *colloq.* arrest. **run in the family** (of a trait) be common in a family. **run into 1** collide with. **2** encounter. **3** reach as many as (a specified figure). **4** fall into (a practice, absurdity, etc.). **5** be continuous or coalesce with. **run into the ground** *colloq.* bring (a person) to exhaustion etc. **run it fine** see FINE[1]. **run its course** follow its natural progress. **run low** (or **short**) become depleted, have too little (*our tea ran low; we ran short of sugar*). **run off 1** flee. **2** produce (copies etc.) on a machine. **3** decide (a race or other contest) after a series of heats or in the event of a tie. **4** flow or cause to flow away. **5** write or recite fluently. **run**

off one's feet *Brit.* very busy. **run on 1** (of written characters) be joined together. **2** continue in operation. **3** elapse. **4** speak volubly. **5** talk incessantly. **6** *Printing* continue on the same line as the preceding matter. **run out 1** come to an end. **2** (foll. by *of*) exhaust one's stock of. **3** *Cricket* put down the wicket of (a batsman who is running). **4** escape from a container. **5** (foll. by *past*) pass out; be paid out. **run out on** *colloq.* desert (a person). **run over 1** overflow. **2** study or repeat quickly. **3** (of a vehicle or its driver) pass over, knock down, or crush. **run rings round** see RING[1]. **run riot** see RIOT. **run a** (or **the**) **risk** see RISK. **the runs** *colloq.* diarrhoea. **run the show** *colloq.* dominate in an undertaking etc. **run a temperature** be feverish. **run through 1** examine or rehearse briefly. **2** peruse. **3** deal successively with. **4** consume (an estate etc.) by reckless or quick spending. **5** pass through by running. **6** pervade. **7** pierce with a sword etc. **8** draw a line through (written words). **run to 1** have the money or ability for. **2** reach (an amount or number). **3** (of a person) show a tendency to (*runs to fat*). **4 a** be enough for (some expense or undertaking). **b** have the resources or capacity for. **5** fall into (ruin). **run to earth** (or **to ground**) **1** *Hunting* chase to its lair. **2** discover after a long search. **run to meet** anticipate (one's troubles etc.). **run to seed** see SEED. **run up 1** accumulate (a debt etc.) quickly. **2** build or make hurriedly. **3** raise (a flag). **4** grow quickly. **run up against** meet with (a difficulty or difficulties). **run wild** grow or stray unchecked or undisciplined or untrained. [Old English] □ **runnable** *adj.*

runabout *n.* a light car, aircraft, or (esp. *US*) motor boat.

run-around *n.* (esp. in phr. **give a person the run-around**) deceit or evasion.

runaway *n.* **1** a fugitive. **2** an animal or vehicle that is running out of control. **3** (*attrib.*) **a** that is running away or out of control (*runaway inflation; had a runaway success*). **b** done or performed after running away (*a runaway wedding*).

rundown ● *n.* **1** a reduction in numbers. **2** a detailed analysis. ● *adj.* (**run-down**) **1** decayed after prosperity. **2** enfeebled through overwork etc.

rune *n.* **1** any of the letters of the earliest Germanic alphabet used by Scandinavians and Anglo-Saxons from about the 3rd c. **2** ▼ a similar mark of mysterious or magic significance. **3** a Finnish poem or a division of it. [from Old Norse *rúnar* 'magic signs'] □ **runic** *adj.*

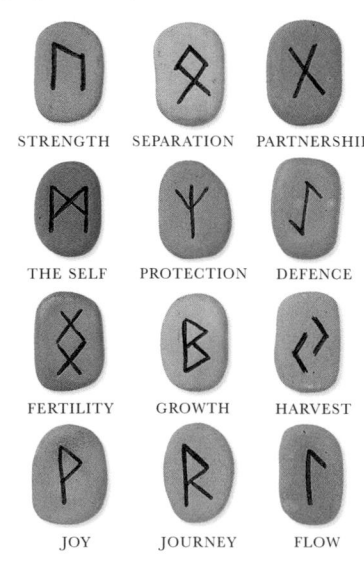

STRENGTH	SEPARATION	PARTNERSHIP
THE SELF	PROTECTION	DEFENCE
FERTILITY	GROWTH	HARVEST
JOY	JOURNEY	FLOW

RUNES WRITTEN ON PEBBLES
USED FOR DIVINATION

rung[1] *n.* **1** each of the horizontal supports of a ladder. **2** a strengthening crosspiece in a chair etc. [Old English]

rung[2] *past part.* of RING[2].

run-in *n.* **1** the approach to an action or event. **2** *colloq.* a quarrel.

runnel *n.* **1** a brook. **2** a gutter. [later form of Old English *rynel*]

runner *n.* **1** a person, horse, etc., that runs, esp. in a race. **2 a** a creeping plant stem that can take root. **b** a twining plant. **3** a rod or groove or blade on which a thing slides. **4** a sliding ring on a rod etc. **5** a messenger, scout, collector, or agent for a bank etc. **6** *slang* a smuggler of a specified kind (*drug runner*). **7** (in full **runner bean**) **a** a twining bean plant, *Phaseolus coccineus*, with red flowers and long green seed pods. **b** the bean from this. ▷ VEGETABLE. **8** each of the long pieces on the underside of a sledge etc. that form the contact in sliding. ▷ SLEDGE. **9** a long narrow ornamental cloth or rug. □ **do a runner** *Brit. slang* leave hastily; abscond.

runner-up *n.* (*pl.* **runners-up** or **runner-ups**) the competitor or team taking second place.

running ● *n.* **1 a** the action of a runner. **b** the sport of racing on foot. **2** the way a race etc. proceeds. ● *adj.* **1** continuing on an essentially continuous basis though changing in detail (*a running battle*). **2** consecutive (*three days running*). **3** done with a run (*a running jump*). □ **in** (or **out of**) **the running** (of a competitor) with a good (or poor) chance of winning. **make** (or **take up**) **the running** take the lead; set the pace. **take a running jump** (esp. as *int.*) *colloq.* go away.

running-board *n.* ▼ a footboard on either side of a vehicle.

RUNNING-BOARD ON A 1940s
MG TC MIDGET

running commentary *n.* an oral description of events as they occur.

running gear *n.* **1** the moving parts of a machine, esp. the wheels, steering, and suspension of a vehicle. **2** the rope and tackle used in handling a boat.

running head *n.* (also **running headline**) a heading printed at the top of a number of consecutive pages of a book etc.

running knot *n.* a knot that slips along the rope etc. and changes the size of a noose.

running light *n.* each of a set of small lights on a motor vehicle that remain illuminated while the vehicle is running.

running mate *n.* esp. *US* a candidate for a secondary position in an election.

running repairs *n.pl.* minor or temporary repairs etc. to machinery while in use.

running sore *n.* a suppurating sore.

running stitch *n.* **1** a line of small non-overlapping stitches for gathering etc. ▷ STITCH. **2** one of these stitches.

running water *n.* water flowing in a stream or from a tap etc.

runny *adj.* (**runnier, runniest**) **1** tending to run or flow. **2** excessively fluid.

run-off *n.* **1** an additional competition, election, race, etc., after a tie or inconclusive result. **2** an amount of rainfall that is carried off an area by streams and rivers.

run-of-the-mill *adj.* ordinary, undistinguished.

R

run-out *n. Cricket* the dismissal of a batsman by being run out.

runt *n.* **1** a small pig or other animal, esp. the smallest in a litter. **2** a weakling; an undersized person. [16th-century coinage] □ **runty** *adj.*

run-through *n.* **1** a rehearsal. **2** a brief survey.

run-up *n.* the period preceding an important event.

runway *n.* **1** a specially prepared surface along which aircraft take off and land. **2** a raised gangway in a theatre, fashion show, etc.

rupee *n.* the chief monetary unit of India, Pakistan, Sri Lanka, Nepal, Mauritius, and the Seychelles. [from Sanskrit *rūpya* 'wrought silver']

rupture ● *n.* **1** the act or an instance of breaking; a breach. **2** a breach of harmonious relations; a disagreement and parting. **3** *Med.* an abdominal hernia. ● *v.* **1** *tr.* break or burst (a cell or membrane etc.). **2** *tr.* sever (a connection). **3** *intr.* undergo a rupture. **4** *tr. & intr.* affect with or suffer a hernia. [from Latin *ruptura*]

rural *adj.* in, of, or suggesting the country; pastoral or agricultural (*in rural seclusion; a rural constituency*). [from Late Latin *ruralis*] □ **ruralism** *n.* **ruralist** *n.* **rurality** *n.* **ruralize** *v.tr. & intr.* (also **-ise**). **rurally** *adv.*

rural dean see DEAN[1] 1b.

ruse *n.* a stratagem or trick. [based on Old French *ruser* 'to drive back']

rush[1] ● *v.* **1** *intr.* go, move, or act precipitately or with great speed. **2** *tr.* move or transport with great haste (*was rushed to hospital*). **3** *intr.* (foll. by *at*) **a** move suddenly towards. **b** begin impetuously. **4** *tr.* perform or deal with hurriedly (*don't rush your dinner; the bill was rushed through Parliament*). **5** *tr.* force (a person) to act hastily. **6** *tr.* attack or capture by sudden assault. **7** *tr. Brit. slang* overcharge (a customer). **8** *tr.* pass (an obstacle) with a rapid dash. ● *n.* **1 a** an act of rushing; a violent advance or attack. **b** a sudden flow or flood. **2** a period of great activity. **3** (*attrib.*) done with great haste or speed (*a rush job*). **4** a sudden migration of large numbers. **5** (foll. by *on*, *for*) a sudden strong demand for a commodity. **6** a sudden feeling of euphoria such as that experienced after taking certain drugs. **7** (in *pl.*) *colloq.* the first prints of a film. □ **rush one's fences** *Brit.* act with undue haste. [from Anglo-French *russher*]

rush[2] *n.* **1** ► any marsh or waterside plant of the family Juncaceae, with slender tapering pith-filled stems (properly leaves) used for making chair-bottoms and plaiting baskets etc. **2** a stem of this. **3** (*collect.*) rushes as a material. [Old English] □ **rushlike** *adj.* **rushy** *adj.*

RUSH:
WOODRUSH
(*Luzula*
species)

rush hour *n.* (often hyphenated when *attrib.*) time(s) each day when traffic is at its heaviest.

rushlight *n.* a candle made by dipping the pith of a rush in tallow.

rusk *n.* a slice of bread rebaked usu. as a light biscuit, esp. as food for babies. [from Spanish & Portuguese *rosca* 'coil, roll of bread']

russet ● *adj.* reddish brown. ● *n.* **1** a reddish-brown colour. **2** a kind of rough-skinned russet-coloured apple. [from Old French *rosset*]

Russian ● *n.* **1 a** a native or national of Russia, or of the former Soviet Union. **b** a person of Russian descent. **2** the language of Russia. ● *adj.* **1** of or relating to Russia. **2** of or in Russian. [from medieval Latin *Russianus*] □ **Russianize** *v.tr.* (also **-ise**). **Russianness** *n.*

Russian roulette *n.* an act of daring in which one squeezes the trigger of a revolver held to one's head with one chamber loaded, having first spun the chamber.

Russian salad *n. Brit.* a salad of mixed diced vegetables with mayonnaise.

Russify *v.tr.* (**-ies**, **-ied**) make Russian in character. □ **Russification** *n.*

Russki *n.* (also **Russky**) (*pl.* **Russkis** or **-ies**) *slang offens.* a Russian; *hist.* (loosely) a Soviet citizen. [from Russian *russkiĭ* 'Russian']

Russo- *comb. form* Russian; Russian and.

rust ● *n.* **1 a** a reddish- or yellowish-brown coating formed on iron or steel by oxidation, esp. as a result of moisture. **b** a similar coating on other metals. **2 a** any of various plant diseases with rust-coloured spots caused by fungi of the class Urediniomycetes or genus *Albugo*. **b** the fungus causing this. **3** a reddish-brown or brownish-red colour. ● *v.* **1** *tr. & intr.* affect or be affected with rust. **2** *intr.* (of bracken etc.) become rust-coloured. **3** *intr.* (of a plant) be attacked by rust. **4** *intr.* lose quality or efficiency by disuse or inactivity. [Old English] □ **rustless** *adj.*

rust belt *n. colloq.* an area of once profitable industry, esp. in the American Midwest and north-eastern states.

rustic ● *adj.* **1** having the characteristics of or associations with the country or country life. **2** unsophisticated. **3** of rude workmanship. **4** made of untrimmed branches or rough timber (*a rustic bench*). ● *n.* a person from or living in the country, esp. a simple unsophisticated one. [from Latin *rusticus*] □ **rusticity** *n.*

rusticate *v.* **1** *tr. Brit.* send down (a student) temporarily from university. **2** *intr.* retire to or live in the country. **3** *tr.* make rural. [based on Latin *rusticatus* 'having lived in the country'] □ **rustication** *n.*

rustle ● *v.* **1** *intr. & tr.* make or cause to make a gentle sound as of dry leaves blown in a breeze. **2** *intr.* move with a rustling sound. **3** *tr.* (also *absol.*) steal (cattle, horses, or sheep). **4** *intr. US colloq.* move or act quickly or energetically. ● *n.* a rustling sound or movement. □ **rustle up** *colloq.* produce quickly when needed. [Middle English] □ **rustler** *n.* (esp. in sense 3 of *v.*).

rustproof ● *adj.* (of a metal) not susceptible to corrosion by rust. ● *v.tr.* make rustproof.

rusty *adj.* (**rustier**, **rustiest**) **1** rusted or affected by rust. **2** stiff with age or disuse. **3** (of knowledge etc.) impaired by neglect (*my French is a bit rusty*). **4** rust-coloured. **5** (of black clothes) discoloured by age. □ **rustily** *adv.* **rustiness** *n.*

rut[1] ● *n.* **1** a deep track made by the passage of wheels. **2** an established mode of practice or procedure. ● *v.tr.* (**rutted**, **rutting**) mark with ruts. □ **in a rut** following a fixed pattern of behaviour that is difficult to change. □ **rutty** *adj.*

rut[2] ● *n.* the periodic sexual excitement of a male deer, goat, sheep, etc. ● *v.intr.* (**rutted**, **rutting**) be affected with rut. [based on Latin *rugire* 'to roar'] □ **ruttish** *adj.*

rutabaga *n. N. Amer.* a swede. [from Swedish dialect *rotabagge*]

ruthenium *n. Chem.* a rare hard white metallic element, occurring naturally in platinum ores, and used as a chemical catalyst and in certain alloys. [based on medieval Latin *Ruthenia* 'Russia', as first found in ores from the Urals]

rutherfordium *n. Chem.* a name variously proposed for the artificial radioactive elements of atomic number 104 and 106. [named after E. *Rutherford*, New Zealand-born physicist, 1871–1937]

ruthless *adj.* having no pity or compassion. [Middle English, based on *ruth* 'compassion'] □ **ruthlessly** *adv.* **ruthlessness** *n.*

RV *abbr.* **1** Revised Version (of the Bible). **2** *US* recreational vehicle.

rye *n.* **1 a** a cereal plant, *Secale cereale*, with spikes bearing florets which yield wheatlike grains. **b** ◄ the grain of this used for bread and fodder. **2** (in full **rye whisky**) whisky distilled from fermented rye. [Old English *ryge*, from Germanic]

RYE
(*Secale cereale*)

ryegrass *n.* any forage or lawn grass of the genus *Lolium*, esp. *L. perenne*. [from obsolete *ray-grass*]

R

S

S[1] *n.* (also **s**) (*pl.* **Ss** or **S's**) **1** the nineteenth letter of the alphabet. **2** an S-shaped object or curve.

S[2] *abbr.* (also **S.**) **1** Saint. **2** South, Southern.

S[3] *symb.* **1** *Chem.* the element sulphur. **2** siemens.

s *abbr.* (also **s.**) **1** second(s). **2** shilling(s). **3** singular. **4** son. [sense 2: originally from Latin *solidus*, a gold coin]

's *abbr. colloq.* **1** is, has (*he's arrived*; *it's raining*; *John's late*). **2** us (*let's*). **3** does (*what's he say?*).

SA *abbr.* **1** Salvation Army. **2 a** South Africa. **b** South America. **c** South Australia. **3** *hist.* *Sturmabteilung* (the paramilitary force of the Nazi party).

Sabbatarian ● *n.* **1** a strict sabbath-keeping Jew. **2** a Christian who favours observing Sunday strictly as the sabbath. **3** a Christian who observes Saturday as the sabbath. ● *adj.* relating to or holding the tenets of Sabbatarians. [based on Latin *sabbatum* 'sabbath'] □ **Sabbatarianism** *n.*

sabbath *n.* **1** (in full **sabbath day**) a day of rest and religious observance kept by Jews on Saturday. **2** Sunday as a day of Christian religious observance and abstinence from work and play. **3** (in full **witches' sabbath**) a supposed general midnight meeting of witches with the Devil. [from Hebrew *šabbāt*]

sabbatical ● *adj.* **1** of or appropriate to the sabbath. **2** (of leave) granted at intervals to a university teacher for study or travel. ● *n.* a period of sabbatical leave.

saber *US var.* of SABRE.

sable[1] *n.* **1 a** ▼ a small brown-furred flesh-eating mammal, *Martes zibellina*, of N. Europe and parts of N. Asia, related to the marten. **b** its skin or fur. **2 a** fine paintbrush made of sable fur. [from medieval Latin *sabelum*]

SABLE
(*Martes zibellina*)

sable[2] ● *n.* **1** esp. *poet.* black. **2** (in *pl.*) mourning garments. **3** (in full **sable antelope**) a large African antelope, *Hippotragus niger*, with long curved horns, the male of which has a black coat with a white belly. ● *adj.* esp. *poet.* dark, gloomy. [from Old French (in Heraldry)]

sabot /**sab**-oh/ *n.* **1** a kind of simple shoe hollowed out from a block of wood. **2** a wooden-soled shoe. [French, blend of *savate* 'shoe' and *botte* 'boot']

sabotage /**sab**-ŏ-tah*zh*/ ● *n.* deliberate damage to productive capacity. ● *v.tr.* **1** commit sabotage on. **2** destroy, spoil (*sabotaged my plans*). [French, from *saboter* 'to make a noise with sabots, wilfully destroy']

saboteur /sab-ŏ-**ter**/ *n.* a person who commits sabotage.

sabra *n.* an Israeli born in Israel. [from modern Hebrew *sābrāh* 'prickly pear', common in coastal regions of Israel]

SABRE: FENCING SABRE

sabre *n.* (*US* **saber**) **1** a cavalry sword with a curved blade. **2** a cavalry soldier and horse. **3** ▲ a light fencing-sword with a tapering blade. ▷ FENCING. [from Polish *szabla*]

sabre-rattling *n.* a display or threat of military force.

sabre saw *n.* a portable electric jigsaw.

sabre-toothed tiger *n.* (also **sabre-toothed cat**) ▼ an extinct mammal of the cat family with long curved upper canine teeth.

SABRE-TOOTHED TIGER
(*Smilodon* species)

SAC *abbr.* Senior Aircraftman.

sac *n.* a bag-like cavity, enclosed by a membrane, in an animal or plant. [French]

saccharide /**sak**-ă-ryd/ *n. Chem.* = SUGAR *n.* 2.

saccharin /**sak**-ă-rin/ *n.* a substance used as a substitute for sugar. [German]

saccharine /**sak**-ă-ryn/ *adj.* **1** sugary. **2** of, containing, or like sugar. **3** unpleasantly over-polite, sentimental, etc.

saccharo- /**sak**-ă-roh/ *comb. form* sugar; sugar and. [from Greek *sakkharon* 'sugar']

sacerdotal /sak-er-**doh**-tăl/ *adj.* of priests or the priestly office; priestly. [from Old French] □ **sacerdotalism** *n.*

sachet /**sash**-ay/ *n.* **1** esp. *Brit.* a small usu. sealed and airtight bag or packet. **2** a small scented bag. **3 a** dry perfume for laying among clothes etc. **b** a packet of this. [based on Latin *saccus* 'sack']

sack[1] ● *n.* **1 a** a large strong bag, usu. made of hessian, paper, or plastic, for storing or conveying goods. **b** (usu. foll. by *of*) this with its contents (*a sack of potatoes*). **c** a quantity contained in a sack. **2** (prec. by *the*) *colloq.* dismissal from employment. **3** (prec. by *the*) *N. Amer. slang* bed. **4** a woman's short loose dress with a sacklike appearance. **5** a man's or woman's loose-hanging coat not shaped to the back. ● *v.tr.* **1** put into a sack or sacks. **2** *colloq.* dismiss from employment. □ **hit the sack** *colloq.* go to bed. [from Greek *sakkos*] □ **sackable** *adj.* **sackful** *n.* (*pl.* **-fuls**) **sacklike** *adj.*

sack[2] ● *v.tr.* **1** plunder and destroy (a captured town etc.). **2** steal valuables from (a place). ● *n.* the sacking of a captured place. [from French *sac* in phrase *mettre à sac* 'to put to sack']

sack[3] *n. hist.* a white wine formerly imported into Britain from Spain and the Canaries (*sherry sack*). [from 16th-century *wyne seck*, from French *vin sec* 'dry wine']

sackbut *n.* an early form of trombone. [from French *saqueb(o)ute* 'hook for pulling a man off a horse']

sackcloth *n.* **1** a coarse fabric of flax or hemp. **2** clothing made of this, formerly worn as a penance or in mourning (esp. *sackcloth and ashes*).

sacking *n.* material for making sacks; sackcloth.

sack race *n.* a race between competitors in sacks up to the waist or neck.

sacra *pl.* of SACRUM.

sacral /**say**-krăl/ *adj.* **1** *Anat.* of or relating to the sacrum. **2** *Anthropol.* of or for sacred rites.

sacrament *n.* **1** a religious ceremony or act of the Christian Churches regarded as an outward and visible sign of inward and spiritual grace, esp. baptism and the Eucharist. **2** a thing of mysterious and sacred significance; a sacred influence, symbol, etc. **3** (also **Blessed** or **Holy Sacrament**) (prec. by *the*) **a** the Eucharist. **b** the consecrated elements, esp. the bread or Host. [from Latin *sacramentum* 'solemn oath']

sacramental ● *adj.* **1** of or of the nature of a sacrament. **2** (of a doctrine etc.) attaching great importance to the sacraments. ● *n.* an observance analogous to but not reckoned among the sacraments, e.g. the use of holy water or the sign of the cross. □ **sacramentally** *adv.*

sacred /**say**-krid/ *adj.* **1 a** (often foll. by *to*) exclusively dedicated or appropriated (to a god or to some religious purpose). **b** made holy by religious association. **c** connected with religion (*sacred music*). **2 a** safeguarded or required by religion, reverence, or tradition. **b** sacrosanct. **3** (of writings etc.) embodying the laws or doctrines of a religion. [based on Latin *sacrare* 'to consecrate'] □ **sacredly** *adv.* **sacredness** *n.*

Sacred College *n. RC Ch.* the body of cardinals.

sacred cow *n. colloq.* an idea or institution unreasonably held to be above criticism (with reference to the Hindus' respect for the cow as a holy animal).

sacrifice ● *n.* **1 a** the act of giving up something valued for the sake of something else more important or worthy. **b** a thing given up in this way. **c** the loss entailed in this. **2 a** the slaughter of an animal or person or the surrender of a possession as an offering to a deity. **b** an animal, person, or thing offered in this way. **3** an act of prayer, thanksgiving, or penitence as propitiation. **4** (in games) a loss incurred deliberately to avoid a greater loss or to obtain a compensating advantage. ● *v.tr.* **1** give up (a thing) as a sacrifice. **2** (foll. by *to*) devote or give over to. **3** (also *absol.*) offer or kill as a sacrifice. [from Latin *sacrificium*] □ **sacrificial** *adj.* **sacrificially** *adv.*

sacrilege /**sak**-ri-lij/ *n.* the violation or misuse of what is regarded as sacred. [from Latin *sacrilegium*] □ **sacrilegious** *adj.* **sacrilegiously** *adv.*

sacristan *n.* a person in charge of a sacristy and its contents. [from medieval Latin *sacristanus*]

sacristy *n.* (*pl.* **-ies**) a room in a church, where the vestments, sacred vessels, etc., are kept. ▷ CATHEDRAL. [from medieval Latin *sacristia*]

sacroiliac *adj. Anat.* relating to the sacrum and the ilium, esp. designating the rigid joint between them at the back of the pelvis.

sacrosanct *adj.* most sacred; inviolable. [from Latin *sacrosanctus*, literally 'inviolable by sacred rite'] □ **sacrosanctity** *n.*

sacrum /**say**-krŭm/ *n.* (*pl.* **sacra** or **sacrums**) *Anat.* a triangular bone formed from fused vertebrae and situated between the two hip bones of the pelvis. ▷ SKELETON, SPINE. [from Late Latin *os sacrum* 'sacred bone', supposed site of the soul]

SACW *abbr.* Senior Aircraftwoman.

SAD *abbr.* seasonal affective disorder.

sad *adj.* (**sadder, saddest**) **1** unhappy. **2** causing or suggesting sorrow (*a sad story*). **3** regrettable. **4** shameful, deplorable (*is in a sad state*). **5** *slang* contemptible, pathetic, unfashionable. [Old English] □ **saddish** *adj.* **sadly** *adv.* **sadness** *n.*

sadden *v.tr. & intr.* make or become sad.

saddle ● *n.* **1** ▲ a seat of leather etc. fastened on a horse etc. for riding. ▷ SIDE-SADDLE. **2** a seat for the rider of a bicycle etc. ▷ BICYCLE. **3** a joint of meat consisting of the two loins. **4** a ridge rising to a summit at each end. **5** the part of a draught horse's harness to which the shafts are attached. **6** a part of an animal's back resembling a saddle in shape or

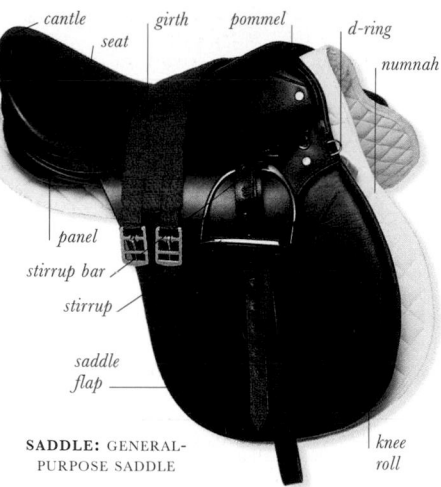

SADDLE: GENERAL-PURPOSE SADDLE

marking. • *v.tr.* **1** put a saddle on (a horse etc.). **2 a** (foll. by *with*) burden (a person) with a task, responsibility, etc. **b** (foll. by *on, upon*) impose (a burden) on a person. □ **in the saddle 1** mounted. **2** in office or control. [Old English] □ **saddleless** *adj.*

saddlebag *n.* **1** each of a pair of bags laid across a horse etc. behind the saddle. **2** a bag attached behind the saddle of a bicycle or motorcycle.

saddler *n.* a maker of or dealer in saddles and other equipment for horses.

saddlery /sad-lĕ-ri/ *n.* (*pl.* **-ies**) **1** the saddles and other equipment of a saddler. **2** a saddler's business or premises.

saddle-sore *adj.* chafed by riding on a saddle.

saddle stitch • *n.* a stitch of thread or a wire staple passed through the centre of a magazine or booklet. • *v.tr.* (**saddle-stitch**) sew with this stitch.

Sadducee *n.* a member of a Jewish sect or party of the time of Christ that denied the resurrection of the dead, the existence of spirits, and the obligation of the traditional oral law. [from Hebrew *ṣᵉdúḳî*] □ **Sadducean** *adj.*

sadhu *n.* (in India) a holy man, sage, or ascetic. [Sanskrit, literally 'holy man']

sadism /say-dizm/ *n.* **1** a form of sexual perversion characterized by the enjoyment of inflicting pain or suffering on others (cf. MASOCHISM 1). **2** *colloq.* the enjoyment of cruelty to others. [from French *sadisme*, named after the Count or 'Marquis' de Sade, French writer, 1740–1814] □ **sadist** *n.* **sadistic** *adj.* **sadistically** *adv.*

sadomasochism /say-doh-**mas**-ŏ-kizm/ *n.* the combination of sadism and masochism in one person. □ **sadomasochist** *n.* **sadomasochistic** *adj.*

sad sack *n. US colloq.* a very inept person.

sae *abbr. Brit.* stamped addressed envelope.

safari *n.* (*pl.* **safaris**) **1** a hunting or scientific expedition, esp. in E. Africa (*go on safari*). **2** a sightseeing trip to see African animals in their natural habitat. [based on Arabic *safara* 'to travel']

safari park *n.* an enclosed area where lions etc. are kept in relatively open spaces for public viewing from vehicles driven through.

safari suit *n.* a lightweight suit usu. with short sleeves and four pleated pockets in the jacket.

safe • *adj.* **1 a** free of danger or injury. **b** out of or not exposed to danger (*safe from their enemies*). **2** affording security or not involving danger or risk (*put it in a safe place*). **3** reliable, certain (*a safe catch; a safe method; is safe to win*). **4** prevented from escaping or doing harm (*have got him safe*). **5** (also **safe and sound**) uninjured; with no harm done. **6** cautious and unenterprising. • *n.* **1** a strong lockable cabinet etc. for valuables. **2** = MEAT SAFE. □ **on the safe side** with a margin of security against risks. [from Latin *salvus* 'uninjured'] □ **safely** *adv.* **safeness** *n.*

safe bet *n.* a bet that is certain to succeed.

safe-breaker *n.* (also **safe-blower** or *US* **safe-cracker**) a person who breaks open and robs safes.

safe conduct *n.* **1** a privilege of immunity from arrest or harm, esp. on a particular occasion. **2** a document securing this.

safe deposit *n.* a strongroom or safe for the safe keeping of valuables, usu. within a bank, hotel, etc. (also *attrib.: safe deposit box*).

safeguard • *n.* **1** a proviso, stipulation, quality, or circumstance, that tends to prevent something undesirable. **2** a safe conduct. • *v.tr.* guard or protect (rights etc.).

safe house *n.* a place of refuge or rendezvous for spies, criminals, etc.

safe keeping *n.* preservation in a safe place.

safe sex *n.* sexual activity in which precautions are taken to reduce the risk of spreading sexually transmitted diseases.

safety *n.* (*pl.* **-ies**) **1** the condition of being safe; freedom from danger or risks. **2** (*attrib.*) **a** designating any of various devices for preventing injury from machinery (*safety bar; safety lock*). **b** designating items of protective clothing (*safety helmet*). **3** *Amer. Football* a defensive back who plays in a deep position. □ **safety first** a motto advising caution. [from medieval Latin *salvitas*]

safety belt *n.* **1** = SEAT BELT. **2** a belt or strap securing a person to prevent injury.

safety catch *n.* a contrivance for locking a gun trigger or preventing the accidental operation of machinery. ▷ GUN

safety curtain *n.* a fireproof curtain that can be lowered to cut off the auditorium in a theatre from the stage. ▷ THEATRE

safety factor *n.* **1** the ratio of a material's strength to an expected strain. **2** a margin of security against risks.

safety glass *n.* glass that will not splinter when broken.

safety harness *n.* ▼ a system of belts or restraints to hold a person to prevent falling or injury.

SAFETY HARNESS: ROCK CLIMBER'S SIT HARNESS

safety lamp *n.* a miner's lamp so protected as not to ignite firedamp.

safety match *n.* a match igniting only on a specially prepared surface.

safety net *n.* **1** a net placed to catch an acrobat etc. in case of a fall. **2** a safeguard against possible hardship or adversity.

safety pin *n.* a pin with a point that is held in a guard when closed.

safety razor *n.* a razor with a guard to reduce the risk of cutting the skin.

safety valve *n.* **1** (in a steam boiler) a valve opening automatically to relieve excessive pressure. **2** a means of giving harmless vent to excitement etc.

safflower *n.* **1** an orange-flowered thistle-like plant, *Carthamus tinctorius*, whose seeds yield an edible oil. **2 a** its dried petals. **b** a red dye made from these. [based on Arabic *aṣfar*]

saffron • *n.* **1** ▶ an orange-yellow flavouring and food colouring made from the dried stigmas of the crocus, *Crocus sativus*. ▷ SPICE. **2** the colour of this. **3** = MEADOW SAFFRON. • *adj.* of an orange-yellow colour. [from Arabic *zaʿfarā*]

SAFFRON: STIGMAS OF SAFFRON CROCUS (*Crocus sativus*)

sag • *v.intr.* (**sagged, sagging**) **1** sink or subside, esp. unevenly. **2** have a downward bulge or curve in the middle. **3** fall in price. • *n.* **1 a** the amount that a rope etc. sags. **b** the distance from the middle of its curve to a straight line between its supports. **2** a sinking condition; subsidence. **3** a fall in price. [from Dutch *zakken* 'to subside'] □ **saggy** *adj.*

saga *n.* **1** a long story of heroic achievement, esp. a medieval Icelandic or Norwegian prose narrative. **2** a series of connected books giving the history of a family etc. **3** a long involved story. [Old Norse, literally 'narrative']

sagacious *adj.* **1** mentally penetrating; gifted with discernment; having practical wisdom. **2** acuteminded, shrewd. **3** (of a saying, plan, etc.) showing wisdom. [from Latin *sagax sagacis*] □ **sagaciously** *adv.* **sagacity** *n.*

sage[1] *n.* **1** an aromatic herb, *Salvia officinalis*, with dull greyish-green leaves. ▷ HERB. **2** its leaves used in cookery. [from Latin *salvia* 'healing plant']

sage[2] • *n.* **1** often *iron.* a wise man. **2** any of the ancients traditionally regarded as the wisest of their time. • *adj.* **1** wise, esp. from experience. **2** of or indicating wisdom. **3** often *iron.* wise-looking; solemn-faced. [based on Latin *sapere* 'to be wise'] □ **sagely** *adv.*

sagebrush *n.* **1** an area covered by shrubby aromatic plants of the genus *Artemisia* found in some semi-arid regions of western N. America. **2** ▶ this plant.

sage Derby *n.* (also **sage Derby cheese**) a cheese made with an infusion of sage which flavours and mottles it.

sage green • *n.* the colour of sage leaves. • *adj.* (hyphenated when *attrib.*) of this colour.

Sagittarius /saj-i-**tair**-iŭs/ *n.* **1** ▼ *Astron.* a large constellation (the Archer), said to represent a centaur carrying a bow and arrow, and in which the centre of the Galaxy is situated. **2** *Astrol.* **a** the ninth sign of the zodiac, which the Sun enters about 22 Nov. ▷ ZODIAC. **b** a person born when the Sun is in this sign. [Latin, literally 'archer'] □ **Sagittarian** *adj. & n.*

SAGEBRUSH (*Artemisia tridentata*)

S

SAGITTARIUS: FIGURE FORMED FROM THE STARS OF SAGITTARIUS

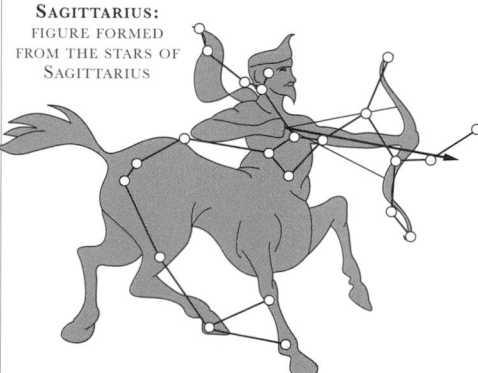

S

sagittate *adj.* ◄ *Bot.* & *Zool.* shaped like an arrowhead.

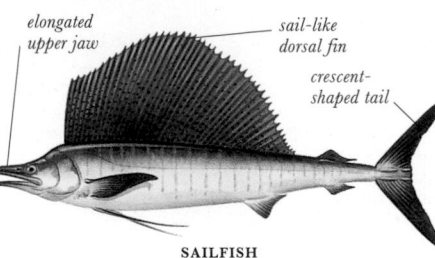

sago *n.* (*pl.* **-os**) **1** a kind of starch, made from the powdered pith of the sago palm and used in puddings etc. **2** (in full **sago palm**) any of several tropical palms and cycads, esp. *Cycas circinalis* and *Metroxylon sagu*, from which sago is made. [from Malay *sāgū*]

sahib /**sah**-ib, sabh/ *n.* **1** (in India) a polite form of address, often placed after a person's name or title. **2** a gentleman (*pukka sahib*). [from Arabic *ṣāḥib* 'friend, lord']

SAGITTATE LEAF

said *past* and *past part.* of SAY.

sail ● *n.* **1** a piece of material extended on rigging to catch the wind and propel a boat or ship. ▷ SAILING BOAT, SHIP. **2** a ship's sails collectively. **3 a** a voyage or excursion in a sailing ship. **b** a voyage of specified duration. **4** a ship, esp. as discerned from its sails. **5** a wind-catching apparatus attached to the arm of a windmill. ● *v.* **1** *intr.* travel on water by the use of sails or engine power. **2** *tr.* **a** navigate (a ship etc.). **b** travel on (a sea). **3** *tr.* set (a toy boat) afloat. **4** *intr.* glide or move smoothly or in a stately manner. **5** *intr. colloq.* succeed easily (*sailed through the exams*). □ **sail close to** (or **near**) **the wind 1** sail as nearly against the wind as possible. **2** come close to indecency or dishonesty. **take in sail 1** furl the sail or sails of a vessel. **2** moderate one's ambitions. **under sail** with sails set. [Old English] □ **sailable** *adj.* **sailed** *adj.* (also in comb.). **sailless** *adj.*

sailboard *n.* a board with a mast and sail, used in windsurfing. ▷ WINDSURFING. □ **sailboarder** *n.* **sailboarding** *n.*

sailboat *n.* US = SAILING BOAT.

sailcloth *n.* **1** canvas or other material for sails. **2** a canvas-like dress material.

sailfish *n.* (*pl.* usu. same) ▼ any large marine fish of the genus *Istiophorus*, with a tall dorsal fin and a spearlike snout.

elongated upper jaw

sail-like dorsal fin

crescent-shaped tail

SAILFISH
(*Istiophorus platypterus*)

sailing boat *n.* ▼ esp. *Brit.* a boat driven by sails. ▷ BOAT

sailing orders *n.pl.* instructions to a captain regarding departure, destination, etc.

sailing ship *n.* = SAILING BOAT.

sailor *n.* **1** a member of the crew of a ship or boat, esp. one below the rank of officer. **2** a person considered as liable or not liable to seasickness (*a good sailor*). □ **sailorly** *adj.*

sailor hat *n.* **1** a straw hat with a straight narrow brim and flat top. **2** a hat with a turned-up brim in imitation of a sailor's, worn by women and children.

sailor suit *n.* a suit like that of an ordinary seaman, worn esp. by small boys.

sailplane *n.* a glider designed for sustained flight.

sainfoin /**sayn**-foyn/ *n.* a pink-flowered leguminous plant, *Onobrychis viciifolia*, grown for fodder. [from modern Latin *sanum foenum* 'wholesome hay', because of its medicinal properties]

saint ● *n.* (*abbr.* **St** or **S**; *pl.* **Sts** or **SS**) **1** a holy or (in some Churches) a canonized person regarded as having a place in heaven. **2** (**Saint** or **St**) the title of a saint or archangel, hence used in the names of churches etc. (*St Paul's*), sometimes without reference to a saint (*St Cross*; *St Saviour's*), or (often with the loss of the apostrophe) in the names of places. (*St Andrews*; *St Albans*). **3** a very virtuous person (*would try the patience of a saint*). ● *v.tr.* **1** canonize; admit to the calendar of saints. **2** call or regard as a saint. **3** (as **sainted** *adj.*) sacred; of a saintly life; worthy to be regarded as a saint. □ **my sainted aunt** see AUNT. [from Latin *sanctus* 'holy, consecrated'] □ **sainthood** *n.* **saintlike** *adj.*

St Bernard *n.* (in full **St Bernard dog**) ▼ a very large dog of a breed originally kept to rescue travellers by the monks of the hospice on the Great St Bernard pass in the Alps.

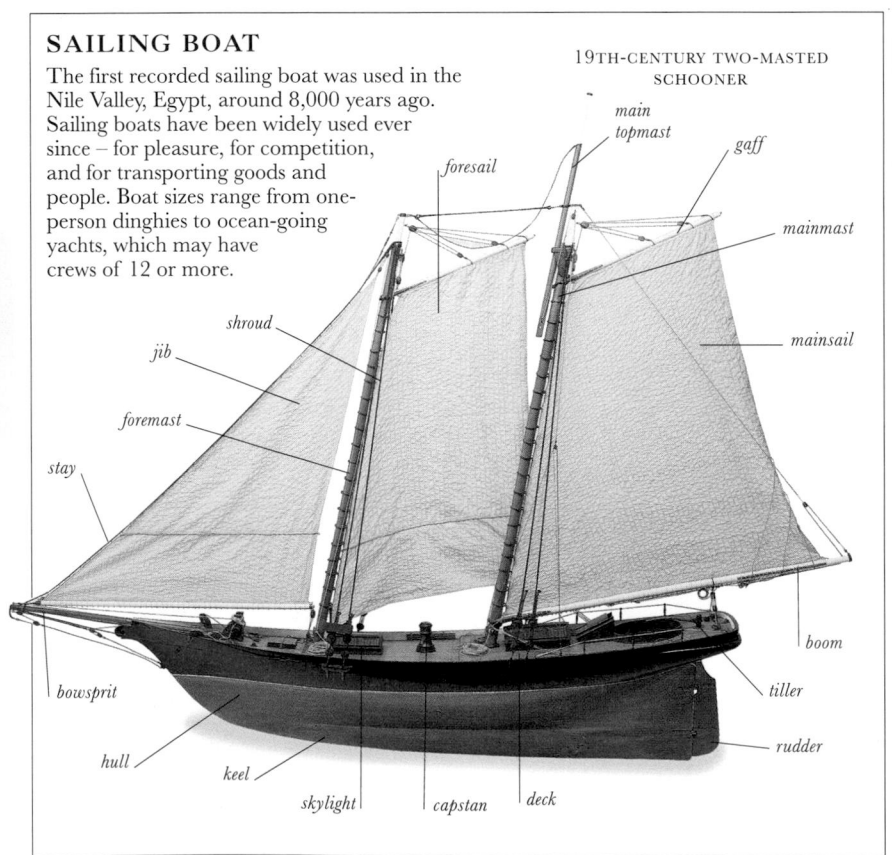

ST BERNARD

St John's wort *n.* any yellow-flowered plant of the genus *Hypericum*, esp. *H. androsaemum*. [so named because some species come into flower near the feast day of St John the Baptist (24 June)]

St Leger *n.* a horse race at Doncaster in England for three-year-olds.

saintly *adj.* (**saintlier**, **saintliest**) very holy or virtuous. □ **saintliness** *n.*

saintpaulia *n.* = AFRICAN VIOLET. [named after Baron W. von *Saint Paul*, German soldier, 1860–1910, its discoverer]

saint's day *n.* a Church festival in memory of a saint.

St Vitus's dance *n.* chorea esp. in children as one of the manifestations of rheumatic fever.

saith *archaic 3rd sing. present* of SAY.

saithe *n.* a codlike edible fish, *Pollachius virens*, with skin that soils fingers like wet coal. [from Old Norse *seithr*]

sake[1] *n.* □ **for Christ's** (or **God's** or **goodness'** or **heaven's** or **Pete's** etc.) **sake** an expression of urgency, impatience, supplication, anger, etc. **for old times' sake** in memory of former times. **for the sake of** (or **for a person's sake**) **1** out of consideration for; in the interest of; because of; owing to (*for my own sake as well as yours*). **2** in order to please, honour, get, or keep (*for the sake of uniformity*). [Old English *sacu* 'charge, fault, sake']

sake[2] /**sah**-ki/ *n.* a Japanese alcoholic drink made from rice. [Japanese]

salaam /să-**lahm**/ ● *n.* **1** the oriental salutation 'Peace'. **2** an obeisance, often consisting of a low bow of the head and body with the right palm on the forehead. **3** (in *pl.*) respectful compliments. ● *v.* **1** *tr.* make a salaam to (a person). **2** *intr.* make a salaam. [Arabic *salām*]

salable var. of SALEABLE.

salacious *adj.* **1** lustful; lecherous. **2** (of writings, pictures, talk, etc.) tending to arouse sexual desire. [from Latin *salax salacis*] □ **salaciously** *adv.* **salaciousness** *n.*

salad *n.* **1** a cold dish of various mixtures of raw or cooked vegetables, usu. seasoned with oil, vinegar, etc. **2** a vegetable or herb suitable for eating raw. [from Provençal *salada*]

salad cream *n.* *Brit.* creamy salad dressing.

salad days *n.pl.* a period of youthful inexperience.

salad dressing *n.* a mixture of oil, vinegar, etc., used with salad.

SAILING BOAT

The first recorded sailing boat was used in the Nile Valley, Egypt, around 8,000 years ago. Sailing boats have been widely used ever since – for pleasure, for competition, and for transporting goods and people. Boat sizes range from one-person dinghies to ocean-going yachts, which may have crews of 12 or more.

19TH-CENTURY TWO-MASTED SCHOONER

main topmast

gaff

foresail

mainmast

mainsail

shroud

jib

foremast

stay

boom

bowsprit

tiller

hull

rudder

keel

skylight

capstan

deck

salamander n. **1** ▶ Zool. any tailed newtlike amphibian of the order Urodela, esp. the genus Salamandra, once thought able to endure fire. **2** a mythical lizard-like creature credited with this property. **3** a metal plate heated and placed over food to brown it. [from Greek salamandra] □ **salamandrine** adj.

salami n. (pl. **salamis**) a highly-seasoned originally Italian sausage. [Italian]

sal ammoniac n. ammonium chloride, a white crystalline salt. [from Latin sal ammoniacus 'salt of Ammon']

salariat n. the salaried class. [French]

salary ● n. (pl. **-ies**) a fixed regular payment, usu. monthly or quarterly, made by an employer to an employee, esp. a white-collar worker (cf. WAGE n. 1). ● v.tr. (**-ies**, **-ied**) (usu. as **salaried** adj.) pay a salary to. [from Latin salarium, originally a soldier's salt-money]

salaryman n. (pl. **salarymen**) (in Japan) a white-collar worker.

sale n. **1** the exchange of a commodity for money etc.; an act or instance of selling. **2** the amount sold (the sales were enormous). **3** the rapid disposal of goods at reduced prices for a period. **4 a** an event at which goods are sold. **b** a public auction. □ **on** (or **for** or **up for**) **sale** offered for purchase. [from Old Norse]

saleable adj. (also **salable**) fit to be sold. □ **saleability** n.

sale of work n. Brit. an event where goods made by parishioners etc. are sold for charity.

sale or return n. (often hyphenated when attrib.) Brit. an arrangement by which a purchaser takes a quantity of goods to sell with the right of returning unsold goods without payment.

saleroom n. esp. Brit. a room in which items are sold at auction.

sales clerk n. N. Amer. a salesman or saleswoman in a shop.

salesgirl n. a saleswoman.

saleslady n. (pl. **-ies**) a saleswoman.

salesman n. (pl. **-men**; fem. **saleswoman**, pl. **-women**) **1** a person employed to sell goods. **2** US a commercial traveller.

salesmanship n. **1** skill in selling. **2** the techniques used in selling.

salesperson n. (pl. **-persons** or **people**) a salesman or saleswoman.

salesroom n. US = SALEROOM.

sales talk n. persuasive talk to promote the sale of goods or the acceptance of an idea etc.

sales tax n. a tax on sales or on the receipts from sales.

saleswoman SEE SALESMAN.

Salic law n. hist. a law excluding females from dynastic succession.

salicylic acid /sal-i-sil-ik/ n. a bitter chemical used as a fungicide and in the manufacture of aspirin and dyestuffs. [based on French salicyle] □ **salicylate** n.

salient ● adj. **1** prominent; conspicuous. **2** (of an angle, esp. in fortification) pointing outwards. ● n. **1** a salient angle or part of a work in fortification. **2** an outward bulge in a line of military attack or defence. [from Latin salient- 'leaping'] □ **salience** n. **saliency** n. **saliently** adv.

salient point n. **1** an important or significant point. **2** archaic the initial stage, origin, or first beginning.

saline ● adj. **1** (of natural waters, springs, etc.) impregnated with or containing salt or salts. **2** tasting of salt. **3** of chemical salts. **4** of the nature of a salt. **5** Med. containing a salt or salts of alkaline metals or magnesium. ● n. **1** a solution of salt in water. **2** a saline substance. [based on Latin sal 'salt'] □ **salinity** n. **salinization** n. (also **-isation**). **salinometer** n.

saliva n. liquid secreted into the mouth by glands to provide lubrication, facilitate chewing and swallowing, and aid digestion. ▷ DIGESTION. [Latin] □ **salivary** adj.

salivate v.intr. secrete or discharge saliva esp. in excess or in greedy anticipation. □ **salivation** n.

Salk vaccine n. a vaccine developed against polio. [named after J. E. Salk, American scientist, born 1914]

sallow[1] adj. (**sallower**, **sallowest**) (of the skin or complexion, or of a person) of a sickly yellow or pale brown. [Old English] □ **sallowness** n.

sallow[2] n. **1** a willow tree, esp. one of a low-growing kind. **2** the wood or a shoot of this. [Old English]

sally[1] (pl. **-ies**) ● n. **1** a sudden charge from a fortification upon its besiegers; a sortie. **2** a going forth; an excursion. **3** a witticism; a piece of banter; a lively remark. **4** a sudden start into activity; an outburst. ● v.intr. (**-ies**, **-ied**) **1** (usu. foll. by out, forth) go for a walk, set out on a journey etc. **2** (usu. foll. by out) make a military sally. [from Latin salire 'to leap']

sally[2] n. Brit. (pl. **-ies**) the part of a bell rope prepared with inwoven wool for holding.

salmi n. (pl. **salmis**) a ragout or casserole esp. of partly roasted game birds. [French]

salmon /sam-ŏn/ ● n. (pl. same or (esp. of types) **salmons**) **1** ▼ a migratory fish of the family Salmonidae, esp. of the genus Salmo, much prized for its pink flesh. **2** any of various similar but unrelated fishes, including: **a** Austral. & NZ (in full **Australian salmon**) a large green and silver marine fish, Arripis trutta. **b** US an American sea trout of the genus Cynoscion. **3** salmon pink. ● adj. salmon pink. [from Latin salmo] □ **salmonoid** adj. & n. (in sense 1 of n.). **salmony** adj.

SALMON: ATLANTIC SALMON
(Salmo salar)

salmonella /sal-mon-el-ă/ n. (pl. **salmonellae** /-lee/) **1** any bacterium of the genus Salmonella, esp. any of various types causing food poisoning. **2** food poisoning caused by infection with salmonellae. [named after D. E. Salmon, American veterinary surgeon, 1850–1914] □ **salmonellosis** n.

salmon pink ● n. the colour of salmon flesh. ● adj. (hyphenated when attrib.) of this colour.

salmon trout n. = SEA TROUT 1.

salon n. **1** the reception room of a large, esp. continental, house. **2** a room or establishment where a hairdresser, beautician, etc., conducts trade. **3 a** hist. a meeting of eminent people in the reception room of a lady of fashion. **b** US a meeting of esp. intellectuals at the invitation of usu. a celebrity or socialite. [French]

saloon n. **1** esp. Brit. **a** a large room or hall, esp. in a hotel or public building. **b** a public room or gallery for a specified purpose (billiard saloon; shooting saloon). **2** (in full **saloon car**) Brit. a motor car with a closed body, boot, and no partition behind the driver. ▷ CAR. **3** a public room on a ship. **4** US colloq. or joc. a drinking bar. **5** (in full **saloon bar**) Brit. the more comfortable bar in a public house. [from Italian salone 'great hall']

saloon deck n. a deck for passengers using the saloon.

saloon-keeper n. US a publican or bartender.

Salopian ● n. a native or inhabitant of Shropshire. ● adj. of or relating to Shropshire. [based on Anglo-French Salopesberia 'Shrewsbury']

salsa n. **1** a kind of dance music of Latin American origin, incorporating jazz and rock elements. **2** a dance performed to this music. **3** (esp. in Latin American cookery) a usu. spicy sauce, esp. one served with meat. [Spanish]

salsify /sal-si-fi/ n. (pl. **-ies**) a plant with long fleshy edible roots. [from French salsifis]

SALT /sawlt/ abbr. Strategic Arms Limitation Talks (or Treaty).

salt n. **1** (also **common salt**) sodium chloride; the substance that gives sea water its characteristic taste, obtained in crystalline form by mining or by the evaporation of sea water, and used for seasoning or preserving food, or for other purposes. **2** a chemical

---

SALAMANDER

Salamanders have small, regenerative limbs, a well-developed tail, webbed feet, and thin, rubbery skin. They are predominantly terrestrial, and breathe through their skin as well as their lungs. Salamanders generally prefer damp, dark habitats, such as under logs or rocks. Salamander species range in length from 2.5 cm (1 in.) to around 1.8 m (6 ft).

EXAMPLES OF OTHER SALAMANDERS

EUROPEAN FIRE SALAMANDER
(Salamandra salamandra)

NORTH AMERICAN TIGER SALAMANDER
(Ambystoma tigrinum)

eye
head
warning coloration
four-fingered forelimb
costal (rib) groove
cylindrical tail

EXTERNAL FEATURES OF A SPOTTED SALAMANDER
(Ambystoma maculatum)

S

compound formed from the reaction of an acid with a base, with all or part of the hydrogen of the acid replaced by a metal or metal-like radical. **3** piquancy; wit (*added salt to the conversation*). **4** (in *sing.* or *pl.*) **a** a substance resembling salt in taste, form, etc. (*bath salts; Epsom salts; smelling salts*). **b** (esp. in *pl.*) this type of substance used as a laxative. **5** (in full **salt marsh**) a marsh, esp. one flooded by the tide, often used as a pasture or for collecting water for salt-making. **6** (also **old salt**) an experienced sailor. ● *adj.* **1** impregnated with, containing, or tasting of salt; cured or preserved or seasoned with salt. **2** (of a plant) growing in the sea or in salt marshes. **3** (of tears etc.) bitter. **4** (of wit) pungent. ● *v.tr.* **1** cure or preserve with salt or brine. **2** season with salt. **3** make (a narrative etc.) piquant. **4** sprinkle (the ground etc.) with salt. **5** treat with a solution of salt or mixture of salts. □ **eat salt with** *Brit.* be a guest of. **salt away** (or **down**) *slang* put (money etc.) by. **salt a mine** *slang* introduce extraneous ore, material, etc., to make the source seem rich. **the salt of the earth** a person or people of great worthiness, reliability, honesty, etc. (Matt. 5:13). **take with a pinch** (or **grain**) **of salt** regard as exaggerated; be incredulous about; believe only part of. **worth one's salt** efficient, capable. [Old English] □ **saltish** *adj.* **saltless** *adj.* **saltness** *n.*

salt-and-pepper *adj.* with light and dark colours mixed together.

salt cellar *n.* a container for salt at the table. [based on obsolete *saler* 'salt cellar', assimilated to CELLAR]

salter *n.* a manufacturer or dealer in salt.

salting *n.* (esp. in *pl.*) a marsh overflowed by the sea.

saltire *n.* ◀ esp. *Heraldry* an X-shaped cross. [from medieval Latin *saltatorium*]

salt lake *n.* a lake of salt water.

salt lick *n.* **1** a place where animals go to lick salt from the ground. **2** a block of this salt.

salt marsh see SALT *n.* 5.

salt meadow *n.* a meadow subject to flooding with salt water.

SALTIRE

salt mine *n.* a mine yielding rock salt.

salt pan *n.* a vessel, or a depression near the sea, used for getting salt by evaporation.

saltpetre *n.* (*US* **saltpeter**) potassium nitrate, a white crystalline salty substance used in preserving meat and as a constituent of gunpowder. [from medieval Latin *salpetra*]

salt shaker *n.* *N. Amer.* a container of salt for sprinkling on food.

salt spoon *n.* a small spoon usu. with a short handle and a roundish deep bowl for taking table salt.

salt water ● *n.* **1** sea water. **2** *slang* tears. ● *attrib.adj.* (**salt-water**) of or living in the sea.

salt well *n.* a bored well yielding brine.

salty *adj.* (**saltier**, **saltiest**) **1** tasting of, containing, or preserved with salt. **2** (of humour etc.) racy, risqué. **3** *slang* tough or aggressive. □ **saltiness** *n.*

salubrious *adj.* **1** health-giving; healthy. **2** (of surroundings etc.) pleasant; agreeable. [based on Latin *salus* 'health'] □ **salubriously** *adv.* **salubriousness** *n.* **salubrity** *n.*

saluki *n.* (*pl.* **salukis**) ▼ **1** a tall slender dog of a silky-coated breed with large drooping ears and fringed feet. **2** this breed. [from Arabic *salūkī*]

SALUKI

salutary *adj.* producing good effects; beneficial. [from Latin *salutaris*]

salutation *n.* **1** a sign or expression of greeting or recognition of another's arrival or departure. **2** (usu. in *pl.*) words spoken or written to enquire about another's health or well-being. [from Old French] □ **salutatory** *adj.*

salute ● *n.* **1** a gesture of respect, homage, or courteous recognition. **2 a** *Mil.* & *Naut.* a prescribed or specified movement of the hand or of weapons or flags as a sign of respect or recognition. **b** (prec. by *the*) the attitude taken by an individual soldier, sailor, police officer, etc., in saluting. **3** the discharge of a gun or guns as a ceremonial sign of respect or celebration. ● *v.* **1 a** *tr.* make a salute to. **b** *intr.* perform a salute. **2** *tr.* greet; make a salutation to. **3** *tr.* (foll. by *with*) receive or greet with (a smile etc.). □ **take the salute 1** (of the highest officer present) acknowledge it by gesture as meant for him. **2** receive ceremonial salutes by members of a procession. [from Latin *salus -utis* 'health, welfare, greeting']

Salvadorean ● *adj.* of or relating to El Salvador, a republic in Central America. ● *n.* a native or national of El Salvador.

salvage ● *n.* **1** the rescue of a ship, its cargo, or other property, from loss at sea, destruction by fire, etc. **2** the property etc. saved in this way. **3 a** the saving and utilization of waste paper, scrap material, etc. **b** the materials salvaged. ● *v.tr.* **1** save from a wreck, fire, etc. **2** retrieve or preserve in adverse circumstances (*tried to salvage some dignity*). [based on Latin *salvare* 'to save'] □ **salvageable** *adj.* **salvager** *n.*

salvation *n.* **1** the act of saving or being saved; preservation from loss, calamity, etc. **2** *Theol.* deliverance from sin and its consequences and admission to heaven. **3** a religious conversion. **4** a person or thing that saves (*was the salvation of*). [from ecclesiastical Latin *salvatio*] □ **salvationism** *n.* **salvationist** *n.* (both nouns esp. with reference to the Salvation Army).

Salvation Army *n.* a worldwide evangelical organization on quasi-military lines for the revival of Christianity and helping the poor.

salve¹ ● *n.* **1** a healing ointment. **2** a thing that is soothing or consoling for wounded feelings, an uneasy conscience, etc. ● *v.tr.* soothe (pride, self-love, conscience, etc.). [Old English]

salve² *v.tr.* **1** save (a ship or its cargo) from loss at sea. **2** save (property) from fire. [back-formation from SALVAGE] □ **salvable** *adj.*

salver *n.* a tray usu. of gold, silver, brass, or electroplate, on which drinks, letters, etc., are offered. [from French *salve* 'tray for presenting food to the king']

salvia *n.* ▶ any plant of the genus *Salvia*, esp. *S. splendens* with scarlet flowers. [Latin, literally 'sage']

Salvo *n.* (*pl.* **-os**) *Austral. slang* a member of the Salvation Army. [abbreviation]

salvo *n.* (*pl.* **-oes** or **-os**) **1** the simultaneous firing of artillery or other guns esp. as a salute, or in a sea-fight. **2** a number of bombs released from aircraft at the same moment. **3** a round of applause. [from Italian *salva* 'salutation']

SALVIA: SCARLET SAGE (*Salvia splendens*)

sal volatile /sal vŏ-**lat**-i-li/ *n.* ammonium carbonate, esp. in the form of a scented solution in alcohol used as smelling salts. [modern Latin, literally 'volatile salt']

Samaritan ● *n.* **1** (in full **good Samaritan**) a charitable or helpful person (with reference to Luke

10:33 etc.). **2** (in the UK) a member of an organization which counsels people in distress by telephone or face to face. **3** a native or inhabitant of Samaria, a region west of the Jordan. **4** the language of the people of Samaria. **5** an adherent of the Samaritan religious system, accepting only the Samaritan Pentateuch. ● *adj.* of or relating to Samaria or the Samaritans. [from Greek *Samareitēs*] □ **Samaritanism** *n.*

samarium *n.* *Chem.* a hard silvery metallic element of the lanthanide series, occurring naturally in monazite etc. and used in making ferromagnetic alloys. [based on *samarskite*, mineral in which its spectrum was first observed]

samba ● *n.* **1** a Brazilian dance of African origin. **2** a ballroom dance imitative of this. **3** the music for this. ● *v.intr.* (**sambas**, **sambaed** or **samba'd**, **sambaing**) dance the samba. [Portuguese]

Sam Browne *n.* (in full **Sam Browne belt**) an army officer's belt and the strap supporting it. [named after Sir *Samuel* J. *Browne*, British military commander, 1824–1901]

same ● *adj.* **1** identical; not different; unchanged (*everyone was looking in the same direction; the same car was used in another crime; saying the same thing over and over*). **2** unvarying, uniform, monotonous (*the same old story*). **3** (usu. prec. by *this, these, that, those*) previously alluded to, just mentioned, aforesaid (*this same man was later my husband*). ● *pron.* (prec. by *the*) **1** the same person or thing (*the others asked for the same*). **2** *Law* or *archaic* the person or thing just mentioned (*detected the youth breaking in and apprehended the same*). ● *adv.* (usu. prec. by *the*) similarly; in the same way (*we all feel the same; I want to go, the same as you do*). See Usage Note. □ **all** (or **just**) **the same 1** emphatically the same. **2** in spite of changed conditions, adverse circumstances, etc. (*but you should offer, all the same*). **at the same time 1** simultaneously. **2** notwithstanding. **be all** (or **just**) **the same to** an expression of indifference or impartiality (*it's all the same to me what we do*). **by the same token** see TOKEN. **same here** *colloq.* the same applies to me. **the same to you!** may you do, have, find, etc., the same thing. **the very same** emphatically the same. [from Old Norse *sami, sama*] □ **sameness** *n.*

■ **Usage** The use of (*the*) same as an adverb, as exemplified by *I want to go*, (*the*) same as you do and *he worked his way through university*, (*the*) same as I did, is considered non-standard by some people. It can be avoided by using *in the same way as* or *just as*.

samey *adj.* (**samier**, **samiest**) *Brit. colloq.* lacking in variety; monotonous. □ **sameyness** *n.*

samizdat *n.* **1** the clandestine copying and distribution of literature, esp. in the former Communist countries of eastern Europe. **2** literature so produced. [Russian, literally 'self-publishing house']

Samoan ● *n.* **1** a native of Samoa, a group of islands in the Pacific. **2** the language of the Samoans. ● *adj.* of or relating to Samoa or its people or language.

samosa *n.* a triangular pasty fried in ghee or oil, containing spiced vegetables or meat. [Hindi]

samovar *n.* ▶ a Russian tea urn, with an internal heating device to keep the water at boiling point. [Russian, literally 'self-boiler']

Samoyed /sam-ŏ-yed/ *n.* **1** a member of a people of northern Siberia. **2** the language of this people. **3** (also **samoyed**) a dog of a white Arctic breed. [from Russian *samoed*]

carrying handle
chimney
water container
spigot   air vents

SAMOVAR

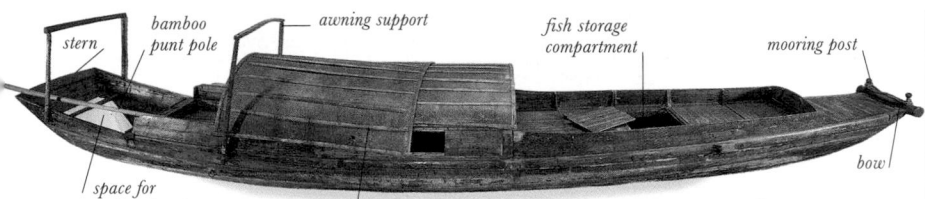

stern · bamboo punt pole · awning support · fish storage compartment · mooring post · bow · space for outboard motors · sliding canopy

SAMPAN: CHINESE SAMPAN

sampan *n.* ▲ a small boat used in the Far East. [from Chinese *san* 'three' + *ban* 'board']

samphire *n.* **1** an umbelliferous maritime rock plant, *Crithmum maritimum*, with aromatic fleshy leaves used in pickles. **2** a glasswort of the genus *Salicornia*. [earlier *samp(i)ere*: from French *(herbe de) Saint Pierre* 'St Peter('s herb)']

sample ● *n.* **1** (also *attrib.*) a small part or quantity intended to show what the whole is like. **2** a small amount of fabric, food, or other commodity, esp. given to a prospective customer. **3** a specimen, esp. one taken for scientific testing or analysis. **4** an illustrative or typical example. **5** *Electronics* a sound created by sampling. ● *v.tr.* **1** take or give samples of. **2** try the qualities of. **3** get a representative experience of. [from Old French *essample* 'example']

sampler[1] *n.* a piece of embroidery worked in various stitches as a specimen of proficiency. [from Old French, related to EXEMPLAR]

sampler[2] *n.* **1** a person who samples. **2** an electronic device for sampling music and sound. **3** *US* a collection of representative items etc.

sampling *n.* **1** the taking of a sample or samples. **2** *Mus.* the technique of digitally encoding sound and reusing it as part of a composition or recording.

Samson *n.* a person of great strength. [from Hebrew *šimšôn* (Judg. 13–16)]

samurai /sam-yuu-ry/ *n.* (*pl.* same) **1** ▶ a Japanese army officer. **2** *hist.* a member of a military caste in feudal Japan. [Japanese]

sanatorium *n.* (*pl.* **sanatoriums** or **sanatoria**) **1** an establishment for the treatment of invalids, esp. of convalescents and the chronically sick. **2** *Brit.* a room or building for sick people in a school etc. [modern Latin]

sanctify *v.tr.* (**-ies**, **-ied**) **1** consecrate; treat as holy. **2** free from sin. **3** make legitimate or binding by religious sanction; justify. **4** make productive of or conducive to holiness. [from ecclesiastical Latin *sanctificare*] □ **sanctification** *n.* **sanctifier** *n.*

sanctimonious *adj.* making a show of piety. [based on Latin *sanctimonia* 'sanctity'] □ **sanctimoniously** *adv.* **sanctimoniousness** *n.* **sanctimony** *n.*

sanction ● *n.* **1** approval by custom or tradition; express permission. **2** confirmation of a law etc. **3 a** a penalty for disobeying a law or rule, or a reward for obeying it. **b** a clause containing this. **4** *Ethics* a consideration operating to enforce obedience to any rule of conduct. **5** (esp. in *pl.*) (esp. economic) action by a state to coerce another to conform to an international agreement or norms of conduct. ● *v.tr.* **1** authorize or agree to (an action etc.). **2** ratify; make binding. [from Latin *sanctio*] □ **sanctionable** *adj.*

sanctity *n.* (*pl.* **-ies**) **1** holiness of life; saintliness. **2** sacredness. **3** inviolability. **4** (in *pl.*) sacred obligations, feelings, etc. [from Latin *sanctitas*]

sanctuary *n.* (*pl.* **-ies**) **1** a holy place; a church, temple, etc. **2 a** the inmost recess or holiest part of a temple etc. **b** the part of the chancel containing the high altar. **3** a place where birds, wild animals, etc., breed and are protected. **4** a place of refuge, esp. for political refugees. **5 a** immunity from arrest. **b** the right to offer this. **6** *hist.* a sacred place where a fugitive from the law or a debtor was secured by medieval Church law against arrest or violence. □ **take sanctuary** resort to a place of refuge. [from Latin *sanctuarium*]

sanctum *n.* (*pl.* **sanctums**) **1** a holy place. **2** *colloq.* a person's private room, study, or den. [Latin, literally 'consecrated (thing)']

sanctus *n.* (also **Sanctus**) **1** the prayer or hymn beginning 'Holy, holy, holy' said or sung at the end of the Eucharistic preface. **2** the music for this. [Latin, literally 'holy']

sand ● *n.* **1** a loose granular substance resulting from the wearing down of esp. siliceous rocks and found on the seashore, river beds, deserts, etc. **2** (in *pl.*) grains of sand. **3** (in *pl.*) an expanse or tracts of sand. **4** a light yellow-brown colour like that of sand. **5** (in *pl.*) a sandbank. ● *v.tr.* **1** smooth with sand or sandpaper, or a mechanical sander. **2** sprinkle or overlay with sand. □ **the sands are running out** the allotted time is nearly at an end. [Old English] □ **sandlike** *adj.*

sandal[1] *n.* a shoe with an openwork upper or no upper, attached to the foot usu. by straps. [from Greek *sandalion* 'little wooden shoe']

sandal[2] *n.* = SANDALWOOD. [from Sanskrit *candana*]

sandal tree *n.* any tree yielding sandalwood, esp. the white sandalwood.

sandalwood *n.* **1** the scented wood of a tree of the genus *Santalum*, esp. (in full **white sandalwood**) *S. Album*. **2** a perfume derived from this.

sandbag ● *n.* a bag filled with sand for use: **1** for making temporary defences or for the protection of a building etc. against blast and splinters or flood waters. **2** as ballast esp. for a boat or balloon. **3** as a weapon to inflict a heavy blow without leaving a mark. **4** to stop a draught from a window or door. ● *v.tr.* (**-bagged**, **-bagging**) **1** barricade or defend. **2** place sandbags against (a window, chink, etc.). **3** fell with a blow from a sandbag. **4** *N. Amer.* coerce by harsh means. □ **sandbagger** *n.*

sandbank *n.* a deposit of sand forming a shallow place in the sea or a river.

sandbar *n.* a sandbank at the mouth of a river or *US* on the coast.

sandblast ● *v.tr.* roughen, treat, or clean with a jet of sand driven by compressed air or steam. ● *n.* this jet. □ **sandblaster** *n.*

sandboy *n.* □ **happy as a sandboy** extremely happy or carefree.

sandcastle *n.* a shape like a castle made in sand, usu. on the seashore.

sand dollar *n.* any flat asymmetrical sea urchin of the order Clypeasteroida.

sand dune *n.* a mound or ridge of sand formed by the wind.

SAMURAI: 19TH-CENTURY SAMURAI ARMOUR

sander *n.* a power tool for smoothing surfaces.

sandfly *n.* (*pl.* **-flies**) **1** any biting blackfly of the genus *Simulium*. **2** any tropical biting fly of the genus *Phlebotomus*, transmitting the disease leishmaniasis.

sandhill *n.* = SAND DUNE.

sandlot *n.* *US* a piece of unoccupied sandy land used for children's games.

sandman *n.* the personification of tiredness causing children's eyes to smart towards bedtime.

sand martin *n.* a swallow-like bird, *Riparia riparia*, nesting in the side of a sandy bank etc.

sandpaper *n.* paper with sand or another abrasive stuck to it for smoothing or polishing.

sandpiper *n.* any of various wading birds of the family Scolopacidae, frequenting moorland and coastal areas.

sandpit *n.* *Brit.* a hollow or box partly filled with sand, usu. for children to play in.

sand-shoe *n.* a shoe with a canvas, rubber, hemp, etc. sole for use on sand.

sandstone *n.* ▶ any of various sedimentary rocks composed of sand grains cemented together. ▷ ROCK CYCLE, SEDIMENT

SANDSTONE

sandstorm *n.* a desert storm of wind with clouds of sand.

sandwich ● *n.* **1** two or more slices of usu. buttered bread with a filling of meat, cheese, etc. between them. **2** *Brit.* a cake of two or more layers with jam or cream between (*sponge sandwich*). ● *v.tr.* **1** put (a thing, statement, etc.) between two of another character. **2** squeeze in between others (*sat sandwiched in the middle*). [named after the 4th Earl of *Sandwich*, English nobleman, 1718–92, said to have eaten such food (*n.* sense 1) by the gaming table]

sandwich-board *n.* one of two advertisement boards carried by a sandwich-man.

sandwich course *n.* *Brit.* a course of training with alternate periods of practical experience and theoretical instruction.

sandwich-man *n.* (*pl.* **-men**) a man who walks the streets with sandwich-boards hanging before and behind.

sandy *adj.* (**sandier**, **sandiest**) **1** having the texture of sand. **2** having much sand. **3 a** (of hair) yellowish red. **b** (of a person) having sandy hair. □ **sandiness** *n.* **sandyish** *adj.*

sane *adj.* **1** of sound mind; not mad. **2** (of views etc.) moderate; sensible. [from Latin *sanus* 'healthy'] □ **sanely** *adv.* **saneness** *n.*

sang *past of* SING.

sang-froid /song-frwah/ *n.* composure, coolness, etc., in danger or under agitating circumstances. [French, literally 'cold blood']

sangria *n.* a Spanish drink of red wine with lemonade, fruit, etc. [Spanish, literally 'bleeding']

sanguinary *adj.* **1** accompanied by or delighting in bloodshed. **2** bloody; bloodthirsty.

sanguine /sang-gwin/ *adj.* **1** optimistic; confident. **2** (of the complexion) florid; ruddy. [from Old French *sanguin(e)* 'blood red'] □ **sanguinely** *adv.* **sanguineness** *n.* (both in sense 1).

Sanhedrin *n.* (also **Sanhedrim**) the highest court of justice and the supreme council in ancient Jerusalem. [from Greek *sunedrion*]

sanitarium *n.* (*pl.* **sanitariums** or **sanitaria**) *US* = SANATORIUM. [based on Latin *sanitas* 'health']

sanitary *adj.* **1** of the conditions that affect health. **2** hygienic. [from French *sanitaire*] □ **sanitarian** *n.* & *adj.* **sanitarily** *adv.*

sanitary engineer *n.* a person dealing with systems needed to maintain public health.

sanitary towel *n.* (*N. Amer.* **sanitary napkin**) an absorbent pad used during menstruation.

sanitary ware *n.* porcelain for lavatories etc.

S

sanitation n. **1** sanitary conditions. **2** the maintenance or improving of these. **3** the disposal of sewage and refuse from houses etc.

sanitize v.tr. (also **-ise**) **1** make sanitary; disinfect. **2** US colloq. render (information etc.) more acceptable by removing improper or disturbing material. □ **sanitization** n. **sanitizer** n.

sanity n. **1 a** the state of being sane. **b** mental health. **2** the tendency to avoid extreme views. [from Latin *sanitas*]

sank past of SINK.

sans prep. archaic or joc. without. [from Latin *sine*]

Sanskrit ● n. the ancient and sacred language of the Hindus in India. ● adj. of or relating to this language. [from Sanskrit *saṃskṛta* 'composed, elaborated'] □ **Sanskritic** adj. **Sanskritist** n.

sans serif (also **sanserif**) Printing ● n. a form of type without serifs. ▷ TYPEFACE. ● adj. without serifs.

Santa Claus n. (also colloq. **Santa**) a person said to bring children presents on the night before Christmas. [originally US, from Dutch dialect *Sante Klaas* 'St Nicholas']

sap[1] ● n. **1** the vital juice circulating in plants. **2** vigour; vitality. **3** = SAPWOOD. **4** US slang a bludgeon. ● v.tr. (**sapped**, **sapping**) **1** drain or dry (wood) of sap. **2** remove the sapwood from (a log). **3** US slang hit with a sap. [Old English] □ **sapful** adj. **sapless** adj.

sap[2] ● n. a tunnel or trench to conceal assailants' approach to a fortified place. ● v. (**sapped**, **sapping**) **1** intr. **a** dig a sap or saps. **b** approach by a sap. **2** tr. undermine; make insecure by removing the foundations. **3** tr. weaken or destroy insidiously (*his confidence has been sapped*). [from Italian *zappa* 'spade, spadework']

sap[3] n. slang a foolish person. [abbreviation of (now dialect) *sapskull*]

sapid adj. literary **1** having flavour; palatable; not insipid. **2** literary (of talk, writing, etc.) not vapid or uninteresting. [from Latin *sapidus*]

sapient adj. literary **1** wise. **2** aping wisdom. [from Latin *sapient-* 'being wise'] □ **sapience** n. **sapiently** adv.

sapling n. **1** a young tree. **2** a youth. **3** a greyhound in its first year.

sapodilla n. a large evergreen tropical American tree, *Manilkara zapota*, with sap from which chicle is obtained. [based on Aztec *tzápotl*]

saponify v. (**-ies**, **-ied**) **1** tr. turn (fat or oil) into soap by reaction with an alkali. **2** tr. convert (an ester) to an acid and alcohol. **3** intr. become saponified. [based on Latin *sapo -onis* 'soap'] □ **saponifiable** adj. **saponification** n.

sapper n. **1** a person who digs saps. **2** Brit. a soldier of the Royal Engineers (esp. as the official term for a private).

Sapphic /saf-ik/ ● adj. **1** of or relating to Sappho, poetess of Lesbos c.600 BC, or her poetry. **2** lesbian. ● n. (in pl.) (**sapphics**) verse in a metre associated with Sappho. [from Greek *Sapphikos*]

sapphire /sa-fyr/ ● n. **1** ◀ a transparent blue precious stone; a variety of corundum. ▷ GEM. **2** precious corundum of any colour. **3** = SAPPHIRE BLUE. **4** a hummingbird with bright blue colouring. ● adj. = SAPPHIRE BLUE adj. [from Greek *sappheiros*] □ **sapphirine** adj.

SAPPHIRE

sapphire blue ● n. a bright blue colour. ● adj. (hyphenated when attrib.) of this colour.

sappy adj. (**sappier**, **sappiest**) **1** full of sap. **2** young and vigorous. **3** N. Amer. colloq. over-sentimental; mawkish. □ **sappily** adv. **sappiness** n.

sapro- comb. form Biol. rotten, putrefying. [from Greek *sapros* 'putrid']

saprogenic adj. causing or produced by putrefaction.

---

saprophyte n. ▶ any plant or micro-organism living on dead or decayed organic matter. □ **saprophytic** adj.

sapwood n. the soft outer layers of recently formed wood between the heartwood and the bark. ▷ WOOD

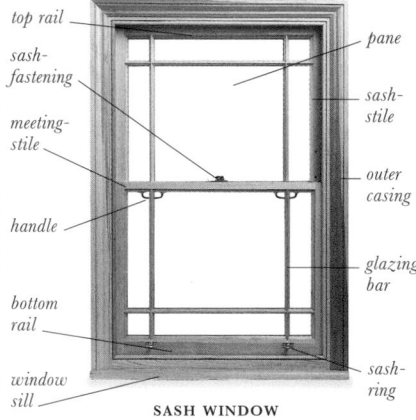
SAPROPHYTE: HONEY FUNGUS ON DEAD WOOD

saraband n. **1** a stately Spanish dance. **2** music for or the rhythm of this. [French *sarabande* from Spanish & Italian *zarabanda*]

Saracen hist. ● n. **1** an Arab or Muslim at the time of the Crusades. **2** a nomad of the Syrian and Arabian desert. ● adj. of the Saracens. [from late Greek *Sarakēnos*] □ **Saracenic** adj.

sarcasm n. **1** the use of bitter or wounding, esp. ironic, remarks; language consisting of such remarks (*suffered from constant sarcasm about his work*). **2** such a remark. [based on Greek *sarkazein* 'to tear flesh', later 'to speak bitterly'] □ **sarcastic** adj. **sarcastically** adv.

sarcenet var. of SARSENET.

sarcoma n. (pl. **sarcomas** or **sarcomata**) a malignant tumour of connective tissue. [Greek, based on *sarx sarkos* 'flesh'] □ **sarcomatosis** n. **sarcomatous** adj.

sarcophagus /sar-kof-ă-gŭs/ n. (pl. **sarcophagi** /-gy/) a stone coffin. [Latin, from Greek *sarkophagos* 'flesh-consuming']

sard n. a yellow or orange-red cornelian. [from Greek *sardios*]

sardine n. a young pilchard or similar young or small herring-like marine fish. □ **like sardines** crowded close together (as sardines are in tins). [from Greek]

Sardinian ● n. **1** a native or inhabitant of Sardinia, a Mediterranean island now administratively part of Italy. **2** the Romance language of Sardinia. ● adj. of or relating to Sardinia or its people or language.

sardonic adj. **1** grimly jocular. **2** (of laughter etc.) bitterly mocking or cynical. [from Greek *sardonios* 'of Sardinia'] □ **sardonically** adv. **sardonicism** n.

sardonyx n. ▶ onyx in which white layers alternate with sard. ▷ GEM. [from Greek *sardonux*]

saree var. of SARI.

sargasso n. (also **sargassum**) any seaweed of the genus *Sargassum*, with berry-like air-vessels, found floating in island-like masses. [from Portuguese *sargaço*]

sarge n. slang sergeant.

sari n. (also **saree**) (pl. **saris** or **sarees**) a length of cotton or silk draped round the body, traditionally worn as a main garment by Indian women. [from Hindi *sār(h)ī*]

SARDONYX

sarky adj. (**sarkier**, **sarkiest**) Brit. slang sarcastic. □ **sarkily** adv. **sarkiness** n.

sarnie n. Brit. colloq. a sandwich.

sarong n. **1** a Malay and Javanese garment consisting of a long strip of cloth worn by both sexes tucked round the waist or under the armpits. **2** a woman's garment resembling this. [Malay, literally 'sheath']

sarsaparilla n. **1** a preparation of the dried roots of various plants, used to flavour some drinks and medicines and formerly as a tonic. **2** any of the plants yielding this. [from Spanish *zarzaparilla*]

sarsen n. Geol. a silicified sandstone boulder as found on the chalk downs of southern England.

sarsenet n. (also **sarcenet**) a soft silk material used esp. for linings. [from Anglo-French *sarzinett*]

sartorial adj. **1** of or relating to a tailor or tailoring. **2** of or relating to clothes. [based on Latin *sartor* 'tailor'] □ **sartorially** adv.

SAS abbr. (in the UK) Special Air Service.

s.a.s.e. abbr. (also **SASE**) US self-addressed stamped envelope.

sash[1] n. a strip or loop of cloth worn over one shoulder or round the waist. [earlier *shash*, from Arabic *šāš* 'muslin, turban'] □ **sashed** adj.

sash[2] n. **1** a frame holding the glass in a window, esp. a sash window. ▷ SASH WINDOW. **2** the glazed sliding light of a glasshouse or garden frame. [from corruption of CHASSIS, mistaken for pl.] □ **sashed** adj.

sashay v.intr. esp. N. Amer. colloq. walk or move ostentatiously, casually, or diagonally. [corruption of CHASSÉ]

sash cord n. a strong cord attaching weights to a window sash.

sashimi /sash-i-mi/ n. a Japanese dish of small pieces of raw fish eaten with soy sauce and horseradish paste. [Japanese]

sash window n. ▼ a window with one or two sashes of which one or either can be slid vertically over the other to make an opening.

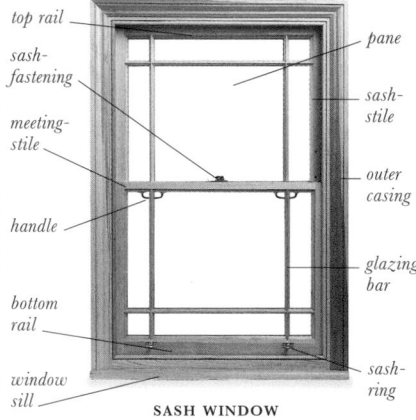

top rail
pane
sash-fastening
sash-stile
meeting-stile
outer casing
handle
glazing bar
bottom rail
sash-ring
window sill
SASH WINDOW

sass N. Amer. colloq. ● n. impudence, cheek. ● v.tr. be impudent to. [variant of SAUCE]

sassafras n. **1** ▶ a small tree, *Sassafras albidum*, native to N. America, with aromatic leaves and bark. **2** a preparation of oil extracted from the leaves or bark, used medicinally or in perfumery. [from Spanish *sasafrás*]

Sassenach /sas-ĕ-nak/ Sc. & Ir. usu. derog. ● n. an English person. ● adj. English. [from Latin *Saxones* 'Saxons']

sassy adj. (**sassier**, **sassiest**) esp. N. Amer. colloq. = SAUCY. [variant of SAUCY] □ **sassily** adv. **sassiness** n.

three-lobed leaf

bark

SASSAFRAS (*Sassafras albidum*)

SAT /sat/ abbr. standard assessment task.

Sat. abbr. Saturday.

sat past and past part. of SIT.

Satan n. the Devil; Lucifer. [from Hebrew *śāṭān*, literally 'adversary']

satanic /să-tan-ik/ adj. **1** of, like, or befitting Satan. **2** diabolical, hellish. □ **satanically** adv.

Satanism n. **1** the worship of Satan, with a travesty of Christian forms. **2** the pursuit of evil for its own sake; deliberate wickedness. □ **Satanist** n. **Satanize** v.tr. (also **-ise**).

satay n. (also **satai**, **saté**) an Indonesian and Malaysian dish consisting of small pieces of meat grilled on a skewer and usu. served with spiced sauce. [from Malay *satai*]

S

satchel *n.* a small bag usu. hung from the shoulder with a strap, for carrying books etc. esp. to and from school. [from Latin *saccellus*]

sate *v.tr.* **1** gratify to the full. **2** cloy, surfeit (*sated with pleasure*). [probably alteration of dialect *sade* 'to satiate']

sateen *n.* cotton fabric woven like satin with a glossy surface. [from *satin*, on the pattern of *velveteen*]

satellite ● *n.* **1** a celestial body orbiting the Earth or another planet. **2** ▼ an artificial body placed in orbit round the Earth or another planet. ▷ ORBIT. **3** a follower; a hanger-on. **4** a member of an important person's staff or retinue. **5** (in full **satellite state**) a small country etc. nominally independent but controlled by or dependent on another. ● *adj.* transmitted by satellite (*satellite communications*; *satellite television*). [from Latin *satelles satellitis* 'attendant']

satellite dish *n.* ◀ a dish-shaped aerial for receiving broadcasting signals transmitted by satellite.

satellite town *n.* a small town dependent on a nearby larger town.

sati var. of SUTTEE.

satiate /**say**-shi-ayt/ ● *adj.* archaic satiated. ● *v.tr.* = SATE. [from Latin *satiatus* 'satiated'] □ **satiable** *adj.* archaic. **satiation** *n.*

satiety /să-**ty**-iti/ *n.* **1** the state of being glutted or satiated. **2** the feeling of having too much of something. □ **to satiety** to an extent beyond what is desired. [from Latin *satietas*]

satin ● *n.* a fabric of silk etc., with a glossy surface on one side. ● *adj.* made of or smooth as satin. [from Arabic *zaytūnī* 'of *Tsinkiang*', a town in China] □ **satinized** *adj.* (also **-ised**). **satiny** *adj.*

satinette *n.* (also **satinet**) a satin-like fabric made partly or wholly of cotton or synthetic fibre.

satin finish *n.* **1** a polish given to silver etc. with a metallic brush. **2** any effect resembling satin in texture produced on materials in various ways.

satin stitch *n.* a long straight embroidery stitch, giving the appearance of satin.

satinwood *n.* **1 a** (in full **Ceylon** or **Sri Lanka satinwood**) a tree, *Chloroxylon swietenia*, native to central and southern India and Sri Lanka. **b** (in full **West Indian** or **Jamaican satinwood**) a tree, *Fagara flava*, native to the W. Indies, Bermuda, and southern Florida. **2** the yellow glossy timber of either of these trees.

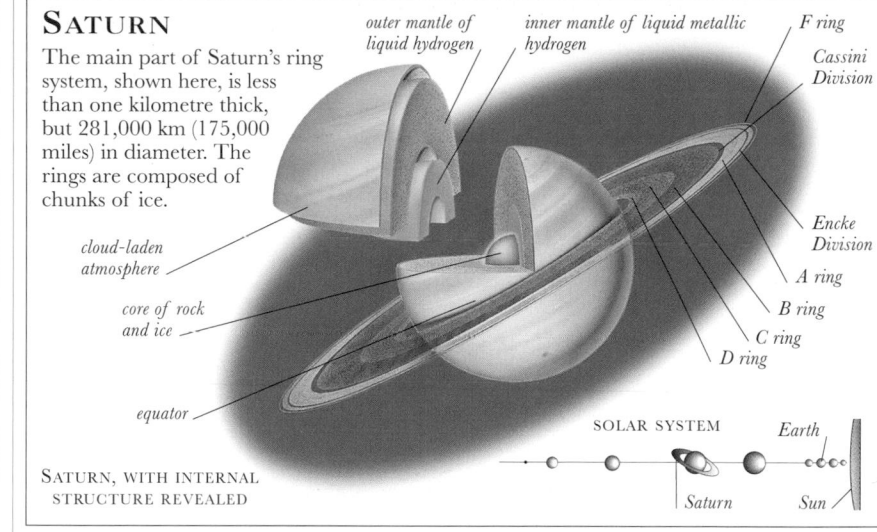

SATURN

The main part of Saturn's ring system, shown here, is less than one kilometre thick, but 281,000 km (175,000 miles) in diameter. The rings are composed of chunks of ice.

outer mantle of liquid hydrogen — *inner mantle of liquid metallic hydrogen* — *F ring* — *Cassini Division* — *cloud-laden atmosphere* — *core of rock and ice* — *equator* — *Encke Division* — *A ring* — *B ring* — *C ring* — *D ring*

SOLAR SYSTEM   *Earth*   *Saturn*   *Sun*

SATURN, WITH INTERNAL STRUCTURE REVEALED

SATELLITE DISH:
DOMESTIC TELEVISION
SATELLITE DISH

mounting bracket — *reflector* — *horn with weather shield* — *low-noise block*

satire *n.* **1** the use of ridicule, irony, sarcasm, etc. to expose folly or vice or to lampoon an individual. **2** a work using satire. **3** this branch of literature. [French]

satiric /să-**ti**-rik/ *adj.* **1** of satire or satires. **2** containing satire (*wrote a satiric review*). **3** writing satire (*a satiric poet*).

satirical /să-**ti**-ri-kăl/ *adj.* **1** = SATIRIC. **2** given to the use of satire in speech or writing or to cynical observation of others; sarcastic; humorously critical. □ **satirically** *adv.*

satirist /**sat**-i-rist/ *n.* **1** a writer of satires. **2** a satirical person.

satirize /**sat**-i-ryz/ *v.tr.* (also **-ise**) **1** assail or ridicule with satire. **2** write a satire upon. **3** describe satirically. □ **satirization** *n.*

satisfaction *n.* **1** the act or an instance of satisfying; the state of being satisfied (*derived great satisfaction*). **2** a thing that satisfies desire or gratifies feeling (*is a great satisfaction to me*). **3** a thing that settles an obligation or pays a debt. **4** (foll. by *for*) atonement; compensation (*demanded satisfaction*). □ **to one's satisfaction** so that one is satisfied. [from Latin *satisfactio*]

satisfactory *adj.* adequate; giving satisfaction (*was a satisfactory pupil*). □ **satisfactorily** *adv.* **satisfactoriness** *n.*

satisfy *v.* (**-ies**, **-ied**) **1** *tr.* **a** meet the expectations or desires of; comply with (a demand). **b** be accepted by (a person, his taste) as adequate; be equal to (a preconception etc.). **2** *tr.* put an end to (an appetite or want) by supplying what was required. **3** *tr.* rid (a

person) of an appetite or want in a similar way. **4** *intr.* give satisfaction; leave nothing to be desired. **5** *tr.* pay (a debt or creditor). **6** *tr.* adequately fulfil or comply with (conditions, obligations, etc.) (*has satisfied all the legal conditions*). **7** *tr.* provide with adequate information or proof, convince (*satisfied the others that they were right*; *satisfy the court of their innocence*). **8** *tr. Math.* (of a quantity) make (an equation) true. **9** *tr.* (in *passive*) **a** (foll. by *with*) contented or pleased with. **b** (foll. by *to*) demand no more than or consider it enough to do. [from Latin *satisfacere*] □ **satisfying** *adj.* **satisfyingly** *adv.*

satnav *n.* esp. *Naut.* **1** navigation assisted by information from satellites. **2** a navigation system capable of receiving such information. [from *satellite navigation*]

satsuma *n.* **1** a variety of tangerine originally grown in Japan. ▷ CITRUS FRUIT. **2** (**Satsuma**) (in full **Satsuma ware**) cream-coloured Japanese pottery. [from *Satsuma*, a province in Japan]

saturate *v.tr.* **1** fill with moisture, soak thoroughly. **2** fill to capacity. **3** cause (a substance) to absorb, hold, or combine with the greatest possible amount of another substance, or of moisture, magnetism, electricity, etc. **4** supply (a market) beyond the point at which the demand for a product is satisfied. **5** (foll. by *with*, *in*) imbue with or steep in (learning, tradition, prejudice, etc.). **6** overwhelm by concentrated bombing. **7** (as **saturated** *adj.*) **a** (of colour) full; rich; free from an admixture of white. **b** *Chem.* (of fat molecules) containing the greatest possible number of hydrogen atoms. [based on Latin *saturatus* 'saturated'] □ **saturable** *adj.*

saturation *n.* the act or an instance of saturating; the state of being saturated.

saturation point *n.* the stage beyond which no more can be absorbed or accepted.

Saturday ● *n.* the seventh day of the week, following Friday. ● *adv. colloq.* **1** on Saturday. **2** (**Saturdays**) on Saturdays; each Saturday. [from Latin *Saturni dies* 'day of Saturn']

Saturn *n.* ▲ the sixth planet from the Sun, circled by a system of broad flat rings, and the most distant of the five planets known in the ancient world. ▷ SOLAR SYSTEM. [Latin *Saturnus*]

saturnalia *n.* (*pl.* same or **saturnalias**) **1** (usu. **Saturnalia**) *Rom.Hist.* the festival of Saturn in December, characterized by unrestrained merry-making for all, the predecessor of Christmas. **2** (treated as *sing.* or *pl.*) a scene of wild revelry. [Latin] □ **saturnalian** *adj.*

saturnine *adj.* **1** of a sluggish gloomy temperament. **2** (of looks etc.) dark and brooding. [from medieval Latin *Saturninus* 'of Saturn', identified with lead by the alchemists and associated with gloom by astrologers]

S

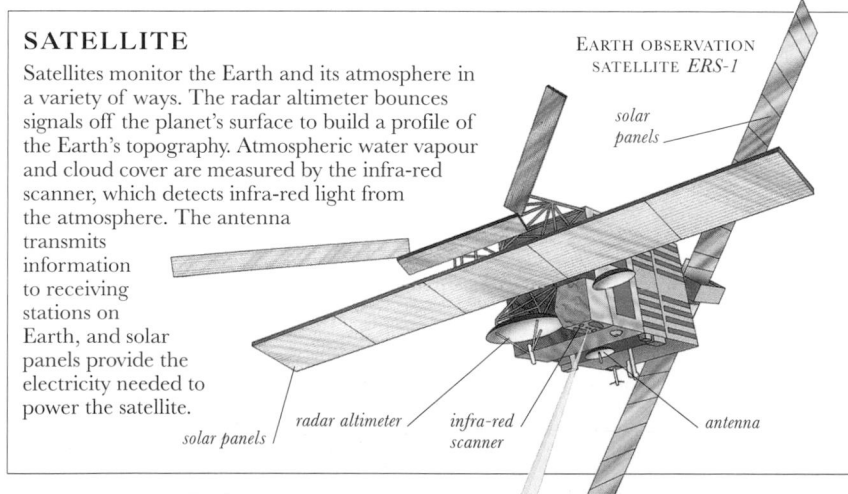

SATELLITE

Satellites monitor the Earth and its atmosphere in a variety of ways. The radar altimeter bounces signals off the planet's surface to build a profile of the Earth's topography. Atmospheric water vapour and cloud cover are measured by the infra-red scanner, which detects infra-red light from the atmosphere. The antenna transmits information to receiving stations on Earth, and solar panels provide the electricity needed to power the satellite.

EARTH OBSERVATION
SATELLITE *ERS-1*

solar panels — *solar panels* — *radar altimeter* — *infra-red scanner* — *antenna*

satyr /sat-er/ n. **1** ◄ (in Greek mythology) one of a class of Greek woodland gods with a horse's ears and tail, or (in Roman representations) with a goat's ears, tail, legs, and budding horns. **2** a lustful or sensual man. [from Greek *saturos*]

satyriasis n. Med. excessive sexual desire in men. [from Greek *saturiasis*]

sauce ● n. **1** a liquid or semi-solid accompaniment to food; the liquid constituent of a dish (*mint sauce*; *tomato sauce*; *chicken in a lemon sauce*). **2** something adding piquancy or excitement. **3** esp. Brit. colloq. impudence, impertinence, cheek. **4** N. Amer. stewed fruit esp. apples, eaten as dessert or used as a garnish. ● v.tr. **1** colloq. be impudent to; cheek. **2** archaic **a** season with sauce or condiments. **b** add excitement to. [based on Latin *salsus* 'salted'] □ **sauceless** adj.

SATYR: GREEK GOD PAN

sauce-boat n. a kind of jug or dish used for serving sauces etc.

saucepan n. a cooking pan, usu. round with a lid and a long handle at the side, used on top of a cooker. □ **saucepanful** n. (pl. **-fuls**)

saucer n. **1** a shallow circular dish used for standing a cup on. **2** any similar dish used to stand a plant pot etc. on. [Middle English in sense 'condiment-dish': from Old French *saussier(e)* 'sauce-boat'] □ **saucerful** n. (pl. **-fuls**). **saucerless** adj.

saucy adj. (**saucier**, **sauciest**) **1** impudent, cheeky. **2** colloq. smart-looking (*a saucy hat*). **3** colloq. smutty, suggestive. [earlier in sense 'savoury'] □ **saucily** adv. **sauciness** n.

Saudi /rhymes with rowdy/ (also **Saudi Arabian**) ● n. (pl. **Saudis**) **1 a** a native or national of Saudi Arabia. **b** a person of Saudi descent. **2** a member of the dynasty founded by King Saud. ● adj. of or relating to Saudi Arabia or the Saudi dynasty. [from A. Ibn-*Saud*, Arabic king, 1880–1953]

sauerkraut /sow-er-krowt; rhymes with our out/ n. a German dish of pickled cabbage. [German, from *sauer* 'sour' + *Kraut* 'vegetable']

sauna n. **1** a special room heated to a high temperature to clean and refresh the body. **2** a period spent in such a room. [Finnish]

saunter ● v.intr. **1** walk slowly; stroll. **2** proceed without hurry or effort. ● n. **1** a leisurely ramble. **2** a slow gait. [Middle English in sense 'to muse'] □ **saunterer** n.

saurian adj. of or like a lizard. [based on Greek *saura* 'lizard']

sauropod n. any of a group of large plant-eating dinosaurs with a long neck and tail, small head, and massive limbs. ▷ DINOSAUR. [from Greek *saura* 'lizard' + *pous podos* 'foot']

sausage n. **1** a short length of minced meat seasoned and often mixed with other ingredients, encased in a cylindrical skin, sold to be cooked before eating. **2 a** minced meat seasoned and preserved and encased in a cylindrical skin, sold mainly to be eaten cold in slices or as a spread. **b** a length of this. **3** a sausage-shaped object. □ **not a sausage** Brit. colloq. nothing at all. [from medieval Latin *salsicia*]

sausage dog n. Brit. colloq. a dachshund.

sausage machine n. **1** a sausage-making machine. **2** Brit. a relentlessly uniform process.

sausage meat n. minced meat used in sausages or as a stuffing etc.

sausage roll n. Brit. sausage meat enclosed in a pastry roll and baked.

sauté /soh-tay/ ● adj. (esp. of potatoes) quickly fried in a little hot fat. ● n. food cooked in this way.

● v.tr. (**sautéd** or **sautéed**) cook in this way. [French, literally 'made to jump']

Sauternes n. a sweet white wine from Sauternes in the Bordeaux region of France.

savage ● adj. **1** fierce; cruel (*savage persecution*; *a savage blow*). **2** wild; primitive (*savage tribes*; *a savage animal*). **3** colloq. angry; bad-tempered (*in a savage mood*). ● n. **1** archaic offens. a member of a primitive tribe. **2** a cruel or barbarous person. ● v.tr. **1** (csp. of a dog, wolf, etc.) attack and bite or trample. **2** (of a critic etc.) attack fiercely. [from Latin *silvaticus* 'of woodland'] □ **savagely** adv. **savageness** n. **savagery** n. (pl. **-ies**).

savannah n. (also **savanna**) ▼ a grassy plain in tropical and subtropical regions. [from Spanish *zavana*]

SAVANNAH: SERENGETI PLAIN, TANZANIA

savant /sav-ănt/ n. (fem. **savante** pronunc. same) a learned person. [French, literally 'knowing']

save[1] ● v. **1** tr. rescue, preserve, protect, or deliver from danger, harm, discredit, etc. (*saved my life*; *saved me from drowning*). **2** tr. keep for future use (*saved up £150 for a new bike*; *likes to save plastic bags*). **3** tr. (often refl.) **a** relieve (another person or oneself) from spending (money, time, trouble, etc.) (*saved myself £50*; *a word processor saves time*). **b** obviate the need or likelihood of (*soaking saves scrubbing*; *will save me a lot of bother*). **4** tr. preserve from damnation; convert (*saved her soul*). **5** tr. & refl. husband or preserve (one's strength, health, etc.) (*saving himself for the last lap*; *save your energy*). **6** intr. save money for future use. **7** tr. **a** avoid losing (a game, match, etc.). **b** prevent an opponent from scoring (a goal etc.). **c** stop (a ball etc.) from entering the goal. ● n. Football etc. the act of preventing an opponent's scoring etc. □ **save appearances** present a prosperous, respectable, etc. appearance. **save-as-you-earn** Brit. a method of saving by regular deduction from earnings at source. **save one's breath** not waste time speaking to no effect. **save face** see FACE. **save the situation** (or **day**) find or provide a solution to difficulty or disaster. **save one's skin** (or **neck** or **bacon**) avoid loss, injury, or death; escape from danger. [from Late Latin *salvare*] □ **savable** adj. (also **saveable**).

save[2] archaic or poet. ● prep. except; but (*all save him*). ● conj. (often foll. by for) unless; but; except (*happy save for one want*; *is well save that he has a cold*). [based on Latin *salvus* 'safe']

saveloy /sav-ĕ-loy/ n. Brit. a seasoned red pork sausage, dried and smoked. [from Italian *cervellata*]

saver n. **1** a person who saves esp. money. **2** (often in comb.) a device for economical use (of time etc.) (*found the short cut a time-saver*).

saving ● adj. (often in comb.) making economical use of (*labour-saving*). ● n. **1** anything that is saved. **2** an economy (*a saving in expenses*). **3** (usu. in pl.) money saved. ● prep. **1** except (*all saving that one*). **2** without offence to (*saving your presence*).

saving grace n. **1** the redeeming grace of God. **2** a redeeming quality.

savings account n. a deposit account.

savings and loan n. (in the US) a cooperative association which accepts savings at interest and lends money to savers for house or other purchases (also attrib.: *savings and loan bailout*).

savings bank n. a bank receiving small deposits at interest and returning the profits to the depositors.

savings certificate n. Brit. an interest-bearing document issued by the Government for the benefit of savers.

saviour n. (US **savior**) **1** a person who saves from danger, harm, etc. (*the saviour of the nation*). **2** (**Saviour**) (prec. by the, our) Christ. [from ecclesiastical Latin *salvator*]

savoir faire /sav-wah fair/ n. the ability to act suitably in any situation; tact. [French, literally 'to know how to do']

savor US var. of SAVOUR.

savory[1] n. (pl. **-ies**) any herb of the genus *Satureja*, esp. *S. hortensis* and *S. montana*, used esp. in cookery. [Middle English]

savory[2] US var. of SAVOURY.

savour (US **savor**) ● n. **1** a characteristic taste, flavour, etc. **2** a quality suggestive of or containing a small amount of another. **3** archaic a characteristic smell. ● v. **1** tr. **a** appreciate and enjoy the taste of (food). **b** enjoy or appreciate (an experience etc.). **2** intr. (foll. by of) **a** suggest by taste, smell, etc. (*savours of mushrooms*). **b** imply or suggest a specified quality (*savours of impertinence*). [from Latin *sapor*] □ **savourless** adj.

savoury (US **savory**) ● adj. **1** (of food) salty or piquant, not sweet (*a savoury omelette*). **2** having an appetizing taste or smell. **3** pleasant; acceptable. ● n. (pl. **-ies**) Brit. a savoury dish, esp. one served as an appetizer or at the end of dinner. [from Old French *savouré* 'savoured'] □ **savouriness** n.

savoy n. ► a hardy variety of cabbage with wrinkled leaves. [from *Savoy*, a region in SE France]

savvy slang ● v.intr. & tr. (**-ies**, **-ied**) know. ● n. knowingness; understanding. ● adj. (**savvier**, **savviest**) US knowing; wise.

saw[1] ● n. **1** ► a hand tool having a toothed blade used to cut esp. wood with a to-and-fro movement. **2** ► any of several power-driven devices with a toothed rotating disc or moving band, for cutting. ● v. (past part. **sawn** or **sawed**) **1** tr. **a** cut (wood etc.) with a saw. **b** make (logs etc.) with a saw. **2** intr. use a saw. **3 a** intr. move to and fro with a motion as of a saw or person sawing (*sawing away on his violin*). **b** tr. divide (the air etc.) with gesticulations. [Old English] □ **sawlike** adj.

SAVOY CABBAGE (*Brassica oleracea* cultivar)

saw[2] past of SEE[1].

saw[3] n. a proverb; a maxim. [Old English]

sawbill n. a merganser.

sawbones n. slang a doctor or surgeon.

sawbuck n. US **1** a sawhorse. **2** slang a $10 note.

sawdust n. powdery particles of wood produced in sawing.

saw-edged adj. with a jagged edge like a saw.

sawed-off US var. of SAWN-OFF.

sawfish n. (pl. usu. same) ▼ any large marine fish of the family Pristidae, with a flat toothed snout.

vertically flattened, toothed snout

asymmetric tail

large pectoral fin

SAWFISH: SMALL-TOOTH SAWFISH (*Pristis pectinata*)

SAW

Saws were probably first used in the Bronze Age. Today they are one of the most versatile cutting implements, used widely in the home and in industry. Saws are designed to perform specific tasks: for example, fretsaws have a short, narrow blade for cutting elaborate shapes in thin wood; hacksaws have fine teeth for cutting harder substances such as metal.

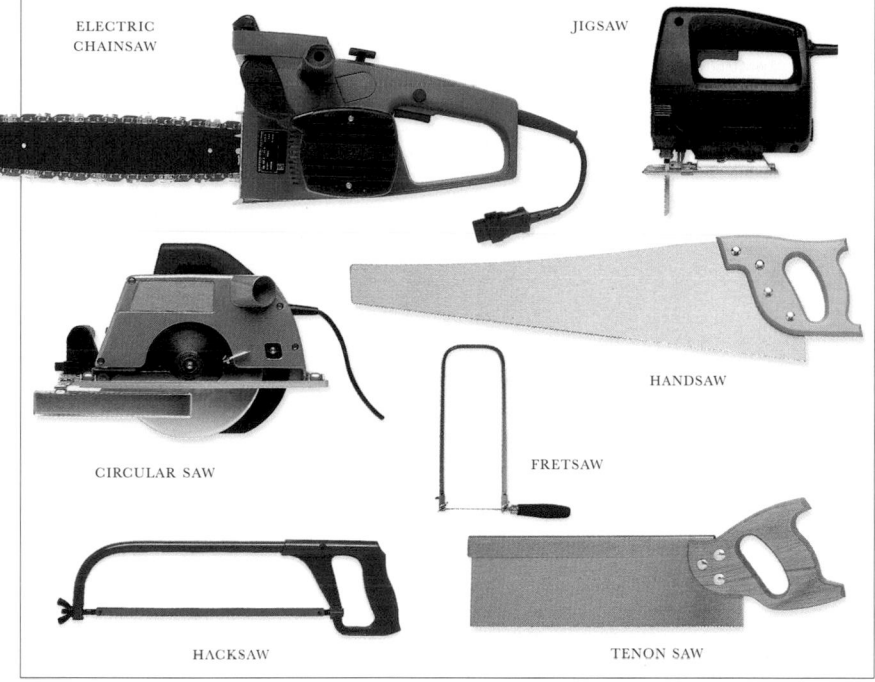

ELECTRIC CHAINSAW

JIGSAW

HANDSAW

CIRCULAR SAW

FRETSAW

HACKSAW

TENON SAW

sawfly *n.* (*pl.* **-flies**) any insect of the superfamily Tenthredinoidea, with a serrated ovipositor, the larvae of which are injurious to plants.

sawhorse *n.* a rack supporting wood for sawing.

sawmill *n.* a factory in which wood is sawn mechanically into planks.

sawn *past part.* of SAW[1].

sawn-off *adj.* (*US* **sawed-off**) (of a gun) having a specially shortened barrel.

sawtooth *adj.* (also **sawtoothed**) serrated.

sawyer /**soy**-er/ *n.* a person who saws timber professionally. [Middle English]

sax *n. colloq.* **1** a saxophone. **2** a saxophone-player. □ **saxist** *n.*

saxe *n. & adj.* = SAXE BLUE. [French, literally 'Saxony', source of a dye of this colour]

saxe blue ● *n.* a lightish blue colour with a greyish tinge. ● *adj.* (hyphenated when *attrib.*) of this colour.

saxhorn *n.* any of a series of different-sized brass instruments with valves and a funnel-shaped mouthpiece. [from *Sax*, name of its Belgian inventors]

saxifrage /**sak**-si-frayj/ *n.* any plant of the genus *Saxifraga*, growing on rocky or stony ground and usu. bearing small white, yellow, or red flowers. [from Old French]

Saxon ● *n.* **1** *hist.* **a** a member of a Germanic people that conquered parts of England in 5th–6th c. **b** (usu. **Old Saxon**) the language of the Saxons. **2** = ANGLO-SAXON. ● *adj.* **1** *hist.* of or concerning the Saxons. **2** belonging to or originating from the Saxon language or Old English. [from Greek *Saxones* 'Saxons'] □ **Saxonize** *v.tr. & intr.* (also **-ise**).

saxophone *n.* ▶ a metal woodwind reed instrument in several sizes and registers, used esp. in jazz and dance music. ▷ ORCHESTRA,

WOODWIND. [based on *Sax* (see SAXHORN)] □ **saxophonic** *adj.* **saxophonist** *n.*

say ● *v.* (*3rd sing. present* **says**; *past* and *past part.* **said**) **1** *tr.* **a** utter (specified words) in a speaking voice; remark (*said 'Damn!'*; *said that he was satisfied*). **b** express (*that was well said*; *cannot say what I feel*). **2** *tr.* **a** state; promise or prophesy (*says that there will be war*). **b** have specified wording; indicate (*says here that he was killed*; *the clock says ten to six*). **3** *tr.* (in *passive*; usu. foll. by *to* + infin.) be asserted or described (*is said to be 93 years old*). **4** *tr.* (foll. by *to* + infin.) *colloq.* tell a person to do something (*he said to bring the car*). **5** *tr.* convey (information) (*spoke for an hour but said little*). **6** *tr.* put forward as an argument or excuse (*much to be said in favour of it*; *what have you to say for yourself?*). **7** *tr.* (often *absol.*) give an opinion or decision as to (*who did it I cannot say*; *do say which you prefer*). **8** *tr.* select, assume, or take as an example or as near enough (*shall we say this one?*; *paid, say, £20*). **9** *tr.* **a** speak the words of (prayers, Mass, a grace, etc.). **b** repeat (a lesson etc.); recite (*can't say his tables*). **10** *tr. Art* etc. convey (inner meaning or intention) (*what is the director saying in this film?*). **11** *tr.* (as **the said** *adj.*) *Law* or *joc.* the previously mentioned (*the said witness*). **12** *intr.* (as *int.*) *N. Amer.* an exclamation of surprise, to attract attention, etc. ● *n.* **1 a** an opportunity for stating one's opinion etc. (*let him have his say*). **b** a stated opinion. **2** a share in a decision etc. (*had no

say in the matter*). □ **how say you?** *Law* how do you find? (addressed to the jury requesting its verdict). **I** etc. **cannot** (or **could not**) **say** I etc. do not know. **I'll say** *colloq.* yes indeed. **I say!** *Brit.* an exclamation expressing surprise, drawing attention, etc. **it is said** the rumour is that. **not to say** and indeed; or possibly even (*his language was rude not to say offensive*). **said he** (or **I** etc.) esp. *Brit. colloq.* or *poet.* he etc. said. **say for oneself** say by way of conversation etc. **say much** (or **something**) **for** indicate the high quality of. **say no** refuse or disagree. **says I** (or **he** etc.) esp. *Brit. colloq.* I, he, etc., said. **says you!** *colloq.* I disagree. **say when** *colloq.* indicate when enough drink or food has been given. **say the word 1** indicate that you agree or give permission. **2** give the order etc. **say yes** agree. **that is to say 1** in other words, more explicitly. **2** at least. **they say** it is rumoured. **to say nothing of** = *not to mention* (see MENTION). **what do** (or **would**) **you say to …?** would you like …? **when all is said and done** after all, in the long run. **you can say that again!** (or **you said it!**) *colloq.* I agree emphatically. **you don't say so** *colloq.* an expression of amazement or disbelief. [Old English] □ **sayable** *adj.* **sayer** *n.*

SAYE *abbr. Brit.* save-as-you-earn.

saying *n.* **1** the act or an instance of saying. **2** a maxim, proverb, etc. □ **as the saying goes** (or **is**) an expression used in introducing a proverb, cliché, etc. **go without saying** be too obvious to need mention. **there is no saying** it is impossible to know.

say-so *n.* **1** the power of decision. **2** mere assertion (*cannot proceed merely on his say-so*).

Sb *symb. Chem.* the element antimony. [Latin *stibium*]

Sc *symb. Chem.* the element scandium.

sc. *abbr.* scilicet.

scab ● *n.* **1** a dry rough protective crust over a cut, sore, etc., formed in healing. **2** (often *attrib.*) *colloq. derog.* a person who refuses to strike or join a trade union, or who tries to break a strike by working; a blackleg. **3** a skin disease esp. in animals. **4** a fungous plant disease causing scablike roughness. **5** a dislikeable person. ● *v.intr.* (**scabbed**, **scabbing**) **1** act as a scab. **2** (of a wound etc.) form a scab; heal over. [from Old Norse *skabb*] □ **scabbed** *adj.* **scabbiness** *n.* **scabby** *adj.* (**scabbier**, **scabbiest**). **scablike** *adj.*

scabbard *n.* **1** ▶ a sheath for a sword, bayonet, etc. **2** *US* a sheath for a revolver etc. [from Anglo-French]

scabies *n.* a contagious skin disease with severe itching. [Latin, based on *scabere* 'to scratch']

scabious *n.* any plant of the genus *Scabiosa*, *Knautia*, etc., with pink, white, or esp. blue pincushion-shaped flowers. [from medieval Latin *scabiosa* (*herba*), formerly regarded as a cure for skin disease]

scabrous *adj.* **1** having a rough surface; bearing short stiff hairs, scales, etc.; scurfy. **2** (of a subject, situation, etc.) requiring tactful treatment; hard to handle with decency. **3 a** indecent, salacious. **b** behaving licentiously. [from Latin *scaber* 'rough'] □ **scabrously** *adv.* **scabrousness** *n.*

■ **Usage** Note that *scabrous* does not mean 'scathing', 'scurrilous', or 'abusive'.

scads *n.pl. US colloq.* large quantities. [19th-century coinage]

scaffold ● *n.* **1** *hist.* a raised wooden platform used for the execution of criminals. **2** = SCAFFOLDING 1. **3** (prec. by *the*) death by execution. ● *v.tr.* attach scaffolding to (a building). [from Old French *escadafaut*] □ **scaffolder** *n.*

scaffolding *n.* **1** a temporary structure formed of poles, planks, etc., erected by workmen and used by

SAXOPHONE: TENOR SAXOPHONE

octave key
mouthpiece with single reed
main body
flared bell
bell brace
thumb holder
key
key rod

SCABBARD: 19TH-CENTURY INDIAN SWORD SCABBARD

S

them while building or repairing a house etc. **2** materials used for this.

scag var. of SKAG.

scalable *adj.* **1** capable of being scaled or climbed. **2** *Computing* able to be used or produced at different ranges of size, capability, etc. □ **scalability** *n.*

scalar *Math. & Physics* ● *adj.* (of a quantity) having only magnitude, not direction. ● *n.* a scalar quantity. [from Latin *scalaris*]

scalawag var. of SCALLYWAG.

scald[1] ● *v.tr.* **1** burn (the skin etc.) with hot liquid or steam. **2** heat (esp. milk) to near boiling point. **3** (usu. foll. by *out*) clean (a pan etc.) by rinsing with boiling water. ● *n.* a burn etc. caused by scalding. □ **like a scalded cat** unusually fast. [based on Latin *calidus* 'hot']

scald[2] var. of SKALD.

scale[1] ● *n.* **1** each of the small thin overlapping plates protecting the skin of fish and reptiles. ▷ FISH, REPTILE. **2** something resembling a fish scale, e.g. a flake of skin. **3** a thick white deposit formed in a kettle, boiler, etc. by the action of heat on water. **4** plaque formed on teeth. ● *v.* **1** *tr.* remove scale or scales from (fish etc.). **2** *tr.* remove plaque from (teeth) by scraping. **3** *intr.* (of skin etc.) form, come off in, or drop, scales. □ **scales fall from a person's eyes** a person is no longer deceived (cf. Acts 9:18). [from Old French *escale*] □ **scaled** *adj.* (also in *comb.*). **scaleless** *adj.* **scaler** *n.*

scale[2] *n.* **1 a** (often in *pl.*) ▼ a weighing machine or device (*bathroom scales*). **b** (also **scale-pan**) each of the dishes on a simple scale balance. **2** (**the Scales**) the zodiacal sign or constellation Libra. ▷ LIBRA. □ **throw into the scale** cause to be a factor in a contest, debate, etc. **tip** (or **turn**) **the scales 1** (usu. foll. by *at*) outweigh the opposite scale-pan (at a specified weight); weigh. **2** (of a motive, circumstance, etc.) be decisive. [from Old Norse *skál* 'bowl']

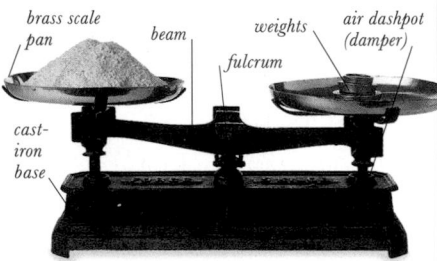

brass scale pan   *beam*   *weights*   *air dashpot (damper)*

fulcrum

cast-iron base

SCALE: TRADITIONAL KITCHEN SCALES

scale[3] ● *n.* **1** a series of degrees; a graded classification system (*a scale of fees; high on the social scale; 5.7 on the Richter scale*). **2 a** (often *attrib.*) *Geog. & Archit.* a ratio of size in a map, model, picture, etc. (*on a scale of one centimetre to the kilometre; a scale model*). **b** relative dimensions or degree (*generosity on a grand scale*). **3** *Mus.* an arrangement of the notes in any system of music in ascending or descending order of pitch. ▷ NOTATION. **4 a** a set of marks on a line used in measuring, reducing, enlarging, etc. **b** a rule determining the distances between these. **c** a piece of metal, apparatus, etc. on which these are marked. **5** (in full **scale of notation**) *Math.* the ratio between units in a numerical system (*decimal scale*). ● *v.* **1** *tr.* **a** climb (a wall, height, etc.) esp. with a ladder. **b** climb (the social scale, heights of ambition, etc.). **2** *tr.* represent in proportional dimensions; reduce to a common scale. **3** *intr.* (of quantities etc.) have a common scale; be commensurable. □ **in scale** (of drawing etc.) in proportion to the surroundings etc. **scale down** make smaller in proportion; reduce in size. **scale up** make larger in proportion; increase in size. **to scale** with a uniform reduction or enlargement. [from Latin *scala* 'ladder, staircase'] □ **scaler** *n.*

scale insect *n.* a homopterous bug of the family Coccidae, clinging to plants and secreting a shield-like scale as covering.

scale-leaf *n.* a modified leaf resembling a scale.

scalene *adj.* (esp. of a triangle) having sides unequal in length. [from Greek *skalēnos* 'unequal']

scale of notation see SCALE[3] *n.* 5.

scaling-ladder *n. hist.* a ladder used to climb esp. fortress walls.

scallawag var. of SCALLYWAG.

scallion *n.* a shallot or spring onion; any long-necked onion with a small bulb. [from Latin *Ascalonia (caepa)* '(onion) of *Ascalon*', a port in ancient Palestine]

scallop (also **scollop**) ● *n.* **1** ▶ any of various bivalve molluscs of the family Pectinidae, esp. of the genus *Chlamys* or *Pecten*, used as food. ▷ BIVALVE. **2** (in full **scallop shell**) a single valve from the shell of a scallop often used for cooking or serving food. **3** (in *pl.*) an ornamental edging cut in material in imitation of the edge of a scallop shell. ● *v.tr.* (**scalloped**, **scalloping**) **1 a** ornament (an edge or material) with scallops or scalloping. **b** cut or shape in the form of a scallop. **2** cook in a scallop. [from Old French *escalope*] □ **scalloper** *n.* **scalloping** *n.* (in sense 3 of *n.*).

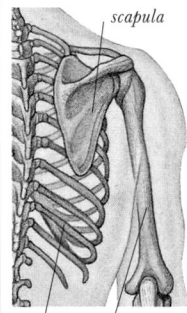

sensory tentacles   *paired shell valves*

SCALLOP (*Chlamys* species)

scallywag *n.* (also **scalawag**, **scallawag**) a scamp; a rascal. [19th-century US slang]

scalp ● *n.* **1** the skin covering the top of the head, with the hair etc. attached. ▷ HEAD. **2** *hist.* the scalp of an enemy cut or torn away as a trophy esp. by an American Indian. ● *v.tr.* **1** *hist.* take the scalp of (an enemy). **2** *US* defeat; humiliate. **3** *N. Amer. colloq.* resell (shares, tickets, etc.) at a high or quick profit. [Middle English] □ **scalper** *n.* **scalpless** *adj.*

scalpel *n.* a surgeon's small sharp knife. [French]

scaly *adj.* (**scalier**, **scaliest**) covered in or having many scales or flakes. □ **scaliness** *n.*

scam *US slang* ● *n.* **1** a trick or swindle; a fraud. **2** a story or rumour. ● *v.* (**scammed**, **scamming**) **1** *intr.* commit fraud. **2** *tr.* swindle. [20th-century coinage] □ **scammer** *n.*

scamp[1] *n. colloq.* a rascal; a rogue. [from archaic *scamp* 'highway robber'] □ **scampish** *adj.*

scamp[2] *v.tr.* do (work etc.) in a perfunctory or inadequate way.

scamper ● *v.intr.* (usu. foll. by *about, through*) run and skip impulsively or playfully. ● *n.* the act or an instance of scampering. [earlier in sense 'to run away, decamp']

scampi *n.pl.* Norway lobsters. [Italian]

scan ● *v.* (**scanned**, **scanning**) **1** *tr.* look at intently or quickly (*scanned the horizon; scanned the speech for errors*). **2** *intr.* (of a verse etc.) be metrically correct (*this line doesn't scan*). **3** *tr.* **a** examine all parts of (a surface etc.) to detect radioactivity etc. **b** cause (a particular region) to be traversed by a radar etc. beam. **4** *tr.* resolve (a picture) into its elements of light and shade in a pre-arranged pattern for the purposes esp. of television transmission. **5** *tr.* test the metre of (a line of verse etc.) by reading with the emphasis on its rhythm, or by examining the number of feet etc. **6** *tr.* make an image of (the body or part of it) with a scanner. ● *n.* **1** the act or an instance of scanning. **2** an image obtained by scanning or with a scanner. [from Latin *scandere* 'to climb', later 'to scan (verses)'] □ **scannable** *adj.*

scandal *n.* **1 a** a thing or a person causing public outrage or indignation. **b** the outrage etc. so caused. **2** *archaic* malicious gossip or backbiting. [earlier in sense 'discredit to religion': from Greek *skandalon* 'snare, stumbling block'] □ **scandalous** *adj.* **scandalously** *adv.* **scandalousness** *n.*

scandalize *v.tr.* (also **-ise**) offend the moral feelings, sensibilities, etc. of; shock.

scandalmonger *n.* a person who spreads malicious scandal.

Scandinavian ● *n.* **1 a** a native or inhabitant of Scandinavia (Denmark, Norway, Sweden, and Iceland). **b** a person of Scandinavian descent. **2** the family of languages of Scandinavia. ● *adj.* of or relating to Scandinavia or its people or languages. [from Latin *Scandinavia*]

scandium *n. Chem.* a rare soft silver-white metallic element occurring naturally in lanthanide ores. [based on *Scandia*, contraction of *Scandinavia*, source of the minerals containing it]

scannable see SCAN.

scanner *n.* **1** a device for scanning, systematically examining, or monitoring something. ▷ RADAR. **2** a machine for measuring the intensity of radiation, ultrasound reflections, etc. from the body as a diagnostic aid. ▷ MRI

scanning electron microscope *n.* an electron microscope in which the surface of a specimen is scanned by a beam of electrons which are reflected to form an image.

scansion *n.* **1** the metrical scanning of verse. **2** the way a verse etc. scans. [from Latin *scansio*]

scant *adj.* barely sufficient; deficient (*scant regard for the truth*). [from Old Norse *skamt* (neut.) 'short'] □ **scantly** *adv.* **scantness** *n.*

scanty *adj.* (**scantier**, **scantiest**) **1** of small extent or amount. **2** meagre; barely sufficient. [based on SCANT] □ **scantily** *adv.* **scantiness** *n.*

scapegoat *n.* a person blamed for the sins, shortcomings, etc. of others. ● *v.tr.* make a scapegoat of. [based on archaic *scape* 'to escape'] □ **scapegoater** *n.*

scapegrace *n.* a rascal; a scamp, esp. a young person or child. [literally, 'a person who escapes the grace of God']

scapula *n.* (*pl.* **scapulae** /-lee/ or **scapulas**) ◀ the shoulder blade. [Late Latin]

scapular ● *adj.* of or relating to the shoulder or shoulder blade. ● *n.* a short monastic cloak.

scar[1] ● *n.* **1** a usu. permanent mark on the skin left after the healing of a wound, burn, or sore. **2** the lasting effect of grief etc. on a person. **3** a mark left by damage etc. (*the table bore many scars*). **4** a mark left at the point of separation of a leaf etc. from a plant. ● *v.* (**scarred**, **scarring**) **1** *tr.* (esp. as **scarred** *adj.*) mark with a scar or scars (*was scarred for life*). **2** *intr.* heal over; form a scar. **3** *tr.* form a scar on. [from Greek *eskhara* 'scab'] □ **scarless** *adj.*

scar[2] *n.* (also **scaur**) a steep craggy outcrop of a mountain or cliff. [from Old Norse *sker* 'low reef in the sea']

scarab /ska-răb/ *n.* **1** a large dung-beetle, *Scarabaeus sacer*, regarded as sacred in ancient Egypt. **2** ▶ an ancient Egyptian gem cut in the form of a beetle and engraved with symbols on its flat side, used as a signet etc. [Latin *scarabaeus* from Greek *skarabeios*]

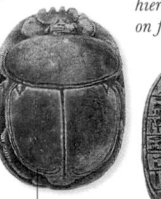

hieroglyphics on flat side

beetle shape

SCARAB: ANCIENT EGYPTIAN SCARAB

scapula

SCAPULA: HUMAN SKELETON SHOWING THE SCAPULA

ribcage   *humerus*

scarce ● *adj.* **1** (usu. *predic.*) (esp. of food, money, etc.)

S

insufficient for the demand. **2** hard to find; rare. ● *adv. archaic* or *literary* scarcely. □ **make oneself scarce** *colloq.* keep out of the way; surreptitiously disappear. [from Old Northern French *scars*] □ **scarceness** *n.*

scarcely *adv.* **1** barely; only just (*I scarcely know him*). **2** surely not (*he can scarcely have said so*). **3** a mild, apologetic, or ironical substitute for 'not' (*I scarcely expected to be insulted*).

scarcity /**skair**-si-ti/ *n.* (*pl.* **-ies**) (often foll. by *of*) a lack or inadequacy, esp. of food.

scare ● *v.* **1** *tr.* frighten, esp. suddenly. **2** *tr.* (as **scared** *adj.*) (usu. foll. by *of*, or *to* + infin.) frightened; terrified. **3** *tr.* (usu. foll. by *away*, *off*, *up*, etc.) drive away by frightening. **4** *intr.* become scared (*they don't scare easily*). ● *n.* **1** a sudden attack of fright (*gave me a scare*). **2** a general, esp. baseless, fear of war, invasion, epidemic, etc. (*a measles scare*). □ **scare up** (or **out**) esp. *N. Amer.* **1** frighten (game etc.) out of cover. **2** *colloq.* manage to find (*see if we can scare up a meal*). [from Old Norse *skirra* 'to frighten'] □ **scarer** *n.*

scarecrow *n.* **1** an object resembling a human figure dressed in old clothes and set up in a field to scare birds away. **2** *colloq.* a badly dressed, grotesque-looking, or very thin person.

scaredy-cat *n. colloq.* a timid person.

scaremonger *n.* a person who spreads frightening reports or rumours. □ **scaremongering** *n.*

scarf[1] *n.* (*pl.* **scarves** or **scarfs**) a square, triangular, or esp. long narrow strip of material worn round the neck, over the shoulders, or tied round the head (of a woman), for warmth or ornament. □ **scarfed** *adj.*

scarf[2] ● *v.tr.* join the ends of (pieces of esp. timber, metal, or leather) by bevelling or notching them to fit and then bolting, brazing, or sewing them together. ● *n.* a joint made by scarfing. [Middle English]

scarf pin *n. Brit.* an ornamental pin for fastening a scarf.

scarf ring *n. Brit.* an ornamental ring through which the ends or corners of a scarf are threaded and held in position.

scarifier *n.* **1** an implement for cutting and removing debris from the turf of a lawn. ▷ RAKE. **2** a spiked road-breaking machine. **3** esp. *Austral.* a machine with prongs for loosening soil without turning it.

scarify[1] *v.tr.* (**-ies**, **-ied**) **1 a** make superficial incisions in. **b** cut off skin from. **2** hurt by severe criticism etc. **3** cut and remove (debris from a lawn) with a scarifier. **4** esp. *Austral.* loosen (soil) with a scarifier. [from Greek *skariphasthai* 'to scratch an outline'] □ **scarification** *n.*

scarify[2] *v.tr. & intr.* (**-ies**, **-ied**) *colloq.* scare; terrify. [based on SCARE]

scarlatina *n.* = SCARLET FEVER. [from Italian *scarlattina* (*febbre*), literally 'lesser scarlet (fever)']

scarlet ● *n.* **1** a brilliant red colour tinged with orange. **2** clothes or material of this colour (*dressed in scarlet*). ● *adj.* of a scarlet colour. [from Old French *escarlate*]

scarlet fever *n.* an infectious bacterial disease affecting esp. children, and causing fever and a scarlet rash.

scarlet pimpernel *n.* ► a small annual wild plant, *Anagallis arvensis*, with small esp. scarlet flowers.

SCARLET PIMPERNEL
(*Anagallis arvensis*)

scarlet runner *n.* esp. *Brit.* **1** a runner bean. **2** a scarlet-flowered climber bearing this bean.

scarlet woman *n. derog.* a notoriously promiscuous woman, a prostitute.

scarp ● *n.* **1** the inner wall or slope of a ditch in a fortification. **2** a steep slope. ● *v.tr.* make (a slope) perpendicular or steep. [from Italian *scarpa*]

scarper *v.intr. Brit. slang* run away; escape.

Scart *n.* (also **SCART**) (usu. *attrib.*) a 24-pin socket used to connect video equipment (*Scart socket*; *Scart connector*). [acronym from *S*yndicat des *C*onstructeurs des *A*ppareils *R*adiorécepteurs et *T*éléviseurs, the designers]

scarves *pl.* of SCARF[1].

scary *adj.* (**scarier**, **scariest**) *colloq.* scaring, frightening. □ **scarily** *adv.* **scariness** *n.*

scat[1] *colloq.* ● *v.intr.* (**scatted**, **scatting**) depart quickly. ● *int.* go!

scat[2] ● *n.* improvised jazz singing using sounds imitating instruments, instead of words. ● *v.intr.* (**scatted**, **scatting**) sing scat.

scathe ● *v.tr.* **1** *poet.* injure esp. by blasting or withering. **2** (as **scathing** *adj.*) witheringly scornful (*scathing sarcasm*). ● *n.* (usu. with *neg.*) *archaic* harm; injury (*without scathe*). [from Old Norse] □ **scatheless** *predic.adj.* **scathingly** *adv.*

scatology *n.* **1** a morbid interest in excrement. **2 a** a preoccupation with obscene literature, esp. that concerned with the excretory functions. **b** such literature. [based on Greek *skōr skatos* 'dung'] □ **scatological** *adj.*

scatter ● *v.* **1** *tr.* **a** throw here and there; strew (*scattered gravel on the road*). **b** cover by scattering (*scattered the road with gravel*). **2** *tr. & intr.* **a** move or cause to move in flight etc.; disperse (*scattered to safety at the sound*). **b** disperse or cause (hopes, clouds, etc.) to disperse. **3** *tr.* (as **scattered** *adj.*) not clustered together; wide apart; sporadic (*scattered villages*). **4** *tr. Physics* deflect or diffuse (light, particles, etc.). **5 a** *intr.* (of esp. a shotgun) fire a charge of shot diffusely. **b** *tr.* fire (a charge) in this way. ● *n.* **1** the act or an instance of scattering. **2** a small amount scattered. **3** the extent of distribution of esp. shot. [Middle English] □ **scatterer** *n.*

scatterbrain *n.* a person given to silly or disorganized thought with lack of concentration. □ **scatterbrained** *adj.*

scatter cushion *n.* (also **scatter rug** etc.) any of a number of small cushions, rugs, etc. placed here and there for effect.

scatter-gun *n.* esp. *N. Amer.* a shot gun.

scatty *adj.* (**scattier**, **scattiest**) *Brit. colloq.* scatterbrained, disorganized. □ **scattily** *adv.* **scattiness** *n.*

scaur var. of SCAR[2].

scavenge *v.* **1** *tr. & intr.* (usu. foll. by *for*) search for and collect (discarded items). **2** *intr.* (foll. by *on*) (of an animal or bird) feed on (carrion). [based on Old Northern French *escauwer* 'to inspect'] □ **scavenger** *n.* **scavengery** *n.*

Sc.D. *abbr.* Doctor of Science. [Latin *scientiae doctor*]

SCE *abbr.* Scottish Certificate of Education.

scenario *n.* (*pl.* **-os**) **1** an outline of the plot of a play, film, opera, etc., with details of the scenes, situations, etc. **2** a postulated sequence of imagined (usu. future) events. [Italian] □ **scenarist** *n.* (in sense 1).

■ **Usage** *Scenario* should not be used in standard English as a loose synonym for 'situation' or 'scene', as in *it was an unpleasant scenario.*

scene *n.* **1** a place in which events in real life, drama, or fiction occur; the locality of an event etc. (*the scene was set in India*; *the scene of the disaster*). **2 a** an incident in real life, fiction, etc. (*distressing scenes occurred*). **b** a description or representation of an incident etc. (*scenes of clerical life*). **3** a public incident displaying emotion, temper, etc. (*made a scene in the restaurant*). **4 a** a continuous portion of a play in a fixed setting and usu. without a change of personnel; a subdivision of an act. **b** a similar section of a film, book, etc. **5 a** any of the pieces of scenery used in a play. **b** these collectively. **6** a landscape or view (*a desolate scene*). **7** *colloq.* **a** an area of action or interest (*not my scene*). **b** a way of life; a milieu (*well known on the jazz scene*). □ **behind the scenes 1** *Theatr.* among the actors, scenery, etc. off stage. **2** unknown to the public; secretly. **behind-the-scenes** (*attrib.*) secret, using secret information (*a behind-the-scenes investigation*). **change of scene** a move to different surroundings esp. through travel. **come on** (or *colloq.* **hit** or *US* **make**) **the scene** arrive; appear. **quit the scene** die; leave. **set the scene 1** describe the location of events. **2** give preliminary information. [from Greek *skēnē* 'tent, stage']

scenery *n.* **1** the general appearance of the natural features of a landscape, esp. when picturesque. **2** *Theatr.* the painted representations of landscape, rooms, etc., used as the background in a play etc. □ **change of scenery** = *change of scene* (see SCENE).

scene-shifter *n.* esp. *Brit.* a person who moves scenery in a theatre. □ **scene-shifting** *n.*

scenic *adj.* **1 a** picturesque; impressive or beautiful (*took the scenic route*). **b** of or concerning natural scenery (*flatness is the main scenic feature*). **2** (of a picture etc.) representing an incident. □ **scenically** *adv.*

scenic railway *n.* **1** a miniature railway running through artificial scenery at funfairs etc. **2** *Brit.* = BIG DIPPER 1.

scent ● *n.* **1** a distinctive, esp. pleasant, smell. **2 a** a scent trail left by an animal perceptible to hounds etc. **b** clues etc. that can be followed like a scent trail (*lost the scent in Paris*). **c** the power of detecting or distinguishing smells etc. or of discovering things (*some dogs have little scent*; *the scent for talent*). **3** *Brit.* = PERFUME 2. ● *v.tr.* **1 a** discern by scent (*the dog scented game*). **b** sense the presence of; detect (*scent treachery*). **2** make fragrant or foul-smelling. **3** (as **scented** *adj.*) having esp. a pleasant smell (*scented soap*). □ **on the scent** in possession of a useful clue in an investigation. **put** (or **throw**) **off the scent** deceive by false clues etc. **scent out** discover by smelling or searching. [from Latin *sentire* 'to perceive'] □ **scentless** *adj.*

scepter *US* var. of SCEPTRE.

sceptic /**skep**-tik/ (*US* **skeptic**) ● *n.* **1** a person inclined to doubt all accepted opinions; a cynic. **2** a person who doubts the truth of Christianity and other religions. ● *adj.* = SCEPTICAL. [from Greek *skeptikos*] □ **scepticism** *n.*

sceptical /**skep**-ti-kăl/ *adj.* (*US* **skeptical**) inclined to question the truth or soundness of accepted ideas, facts, etc.; critical; incredulous. □ **sceptically** *adv.*

sceptre *n.* (*US* **scepter**) ► a staff borne esp. at a coronation as a symbol of sovereignty. [from Greek *skēptron*] □ **sceptred** *adj.*

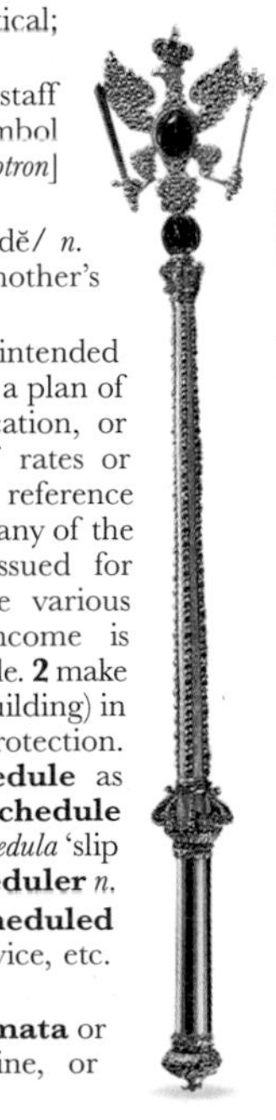

SCEPTRE:
PRUSSIAN SCEPTRE

schadenfreude /**shah**-dĕn-froi-dĕ/ *n.* the malicious enjoyment of another's misfortunes.

schedule ● *n.* **1 a** a list or plan of intended events, times, etc.; a timetable. **b** a plan of work. **2** any list, form, classification, or tabular statement, e.g. a list of rates or prices, an inventory, etc. **3** (with reference to the British income tax system) any of the forms (named 'A', 'B', etc.) issued for completion and relating to the various classes into which taxable income is divided. ● *v.tr.* **1** include in a schedule. **2** make a schedule of. **3** *Brit.* include (a building) in a list for preservation or protection. □ **according to** (or **on**) **schedule** as planned; on time. **behind schedule** behind time. [from Late Latin *schedula* 'slip of paper'] □ **schedular** *adj.* **scheduler** *n.*

scheduled flight *n.* (also **scheduled service** etc.) a public flight, service, etc. keeping to a regular timetable.

schema /**skee**-mă/ *n.* (*pl.* **schemata** or **schemas**) **1** a synopsis, outline, or diagram. **2** a proposed arrangement. [from Greek *skhēma* 'form, figure']

schematic ● *adj.* **1** of or concerning a scheme or schema. **2** representing objects by symbols etc. ● *n.* a schematic diagram, esp. of an electronic circuit. □ **schematically** *adv.*

schematize *v.tr.* (also **-ise**) **1** put in a schematic form; arrange. **2** represent by a scheme or schema. □ **schematization** *n.*

scheme ● *n.* **1** a systematic plan or arrangement (*a scheme of work*; *a colour scheme*). **2** an artful or deceitful plot. **3** a timetable, outline, syllabus, etc. ● *v.* **1** *intr.* (often foll. by *for*, or *to* + infin.) plan esp. secretly or deceitfully. **2** *tr.* plan to bring about, esp. artfully or deceitfully (*schemed their downfall*). [from Greek *skhēma* 'form, figure'] □ **schemer** *n.*

scheming ● *adj.* artful, cunning, or deceitful. ● *n.* plots; intrigues. □ **schemingly** *adv.*

schemozzle var. of SHEMOZZLE.

scherzo /skairt-soh/ *n.* (*pl.* **-os** or **scherzi**) *Mus.* a vigorous, light, or playful composition, usu. as a movement in a symphony, sonata, etc. [Italian, literally 'jest']

schism /skizm/ *n.* **1** the division of a group (esp. a Church) into opposing sections or parties. **2** any of the sections so formed. [from Greek *skhisma* 'cleft']

schismatic /skiz-**mat**-ik/ (also **schismatical**) ● *adj.* of, concerning, or inclining to, schism. ● *n.* **1** a holder of schismatic opinions. **2** a member of a schismatic faction etc. □ **schismatically** *adv.*

schist /shist/ *n.* ▼ a foliated metamorphic rock composed of layers of different minerals and splitting into thin irregular plates. ▷ METAMORPHIC. [from Greek *skhistos* 'split'] □ **schistose** *adj.*

schistosome /shis-tŏ-sohm/ *n.* a parasitic tropical flatworm of the genus *Schistosoma*, carried by freshwater snails and causing bilharzia in humans. [from Greek *skhistos* 'split' + *sōma* 'body']

SCHIST

schistosomiasis /shis-tŏ-sŏ-my-ă-sis/ *n.* = BILHARZIA 1.

schizo /skit-soh/ *colloq. offens.* ● *adj.* schizophrenic. ● *n.* (*pl.* **-os**) a schizophrenic.

schizoid /skit-soid/ ● *adj.* **1** (of a person or personality etc.) tending to schizophrenia, but usu. without delusions. **2** having inconsistent or contradictory elements (*a schizoid musical arrangement*). ● *n.* a schizoid person.

schizophrenia /skit-sŏ-**free**-niă/ *n.* **1** a mental disease marked by a breakdown in the relation between thoughts, feelings, and actions, frequently accompanied by delusions and retreat from social life. **2** *colloq.* a mentality or approach characterized by inconsistent or contradictory elements (*political schizophrenia*). [based on Greek *skhizein* 'to split' + *phrēn* 'mind'] □ **schizophrenic** *adj. & n.*

schlemiel /shlĕ-**meel**/ *n. US colloq.* a foolish or unlucky person. [from Yiddish]

schlep (also **schlepp**) *colloq.* ● *v.* (**schlepped**, **schlepping**) **1** *tr.* carry, drag. **2** *intr.* go or work tediously or effortfully. ● *n. US* **1** a tedious journey; a trek. **2** an inept or stupid person. [from Yiddish]

schlock *n. N. Amer. colloq.* inferior goods; trash. [from Yiddish *shlak*, *schlog* 'an apoplectic stroke']

schlump *n.* esp. *US slang* a slow or slovenly person.

schmaltz *n.* esp. *US colloq.* sentimentality, esp. in music, drama, etc. [Yiddish, from German *Schmalz* 'dripping, lard'] □ **schmaltzy** *adj.* (**schmaltzier**, **schmaltziest**).

schmuck *n.* esp. *US slang* a foolish or contemptible person. [from Yiddish *shmok* 'penis']

schnapps *n.* any of various strong spirits resembling Dutch gin. [German, literally 'dram of liquor']

schnitzel *n.* an escalope of veal. [German, literally 'slice']

schnorkel var. of SNORKEL.

scholar *n.* **1** a learned person, esp. in language, literature, etc.; an academic. **2** *Brit.* the holder of a scholarship. **3** a person with specified academic ability (*is a poor scholar*). [based on Latin *schola* 'school'] □ **scholarly** *adj.* **scholarliness** *n.*

scholarship *n.* **1 a** academic achievement; learning of a high level. **b** the methods and standards characteristic of a good scholar (*shows great scholarship*). **2** a payment from the funds of a school, university, local government, etc., to maintain an able student in education.

scholastic *adj.* of or concerning universities, schools, education, teachers, etc. [from Greek *skholastikos* 'studious'] □ **scholastically** *adv.* **scholasticism** *n.*

school[1] ● *n.* **1 a** an institution for educating or giving instruction, esp. *Brit.* for children under 19 years, or *N. Amer.* including college or university. **b** (*attrib.*) associated with or for use in school (*a school bag*; *school dinners*). **2 a** the buildings used by such an institution. **b** the pupils, staff, etc. of a school. **c** the time during which teaching is done, or the teaching itself (*no school today*). **3** a university department or faculty (*the history school*). **4 a** the disciples, imitators, or followers of a philosopher, artist, etc. **b** a group of artists etc. whose works share distinctive characteristics. **c** a group of people sharing a cause, principle, method, etc. (*school of thought*). **5** *Brit.* a group of gamblers or of persons drinking together (*a poker school*). **6** *colloq.* instructive or disciplinary circumstances, occupation, etc. (*the school of adversity*; *learnt in a hard school*). ● *v.tr.* **1** send to school; provide for the education of. **2** (often foll. by *to*) discipline; train; control. **3** (as **schooled** *adj.*) (foll. by *in*) educated or trained (*schooled in humility*). □ **at** (*US* **in**) **school** attending lessons etc. **go to school 1** begin one's education. **2** attend lessons. **leave school** finish one's education. **of the old school** according to former and esp. better tradition. **school of hard knocks** experience gained from adversity. [from Greek *skholē* 'leisure, philosophy, lecture-place']

school[2] ● *n.* (often foll. by *of*) a shoal of fish, porpoises, whales, etc. ● *v.intr.* form schools. [from Middle Dutch *schōle*]

schoolable *adj.* liable by age etc. to compulsory education.

school board *n. N. Amer.* or *hist.* a board or authority for local education.

schoolboy *n.* a boy attending school.

schoolchild *n.* (*pl.* **-children**) a child attending school.

schooldays *n.* the time of being at school, esp. in retrospect.

schoolfellow *n.* a past or esp. present member of the same school.

schoolgirl *n.* a girl attending school.

schoolhouse *n. Brit.* **1** a building used as a school, esp. in a village. **2** a dwelling house adjoining a school.

schoolie *n. Austral. slang* & *dial.* a schoolteacher.

schooling *n.* **1** education, esp. at school. **2** training or discipline, esp. of an animal.

school inspector *n.* (in the UK) a government official reporting on the efficiency, teaching standards, etc. of schools.

school leaver *n. Brit.* a teenager who is about to leave or has just left school.

school-marm *n.* (also **school-ma'm**) esp. *colloq.* a schoolmistress.

school-marmish *adj.* esp. *US colloq.* prim and fussy.

schoolmaster *n.* a male teacher. □ **schoolmasterly** *adj.*

schoolmastering *n.* teaching as a profession.

schoolmate *n.* = SCHOOLFELLOW.

schoolmistress *n.* a female teacher.

schoolmistressy *adj. colloq.* prim and fussy.

schoolroom *n.* a room used for lessons in a school or in the large private home of a wealthy family.

schoolteacher *n.* a person who teaches in a school. □ **schoolteaching** *n.*

school year *n.* = ACADEMIC YEAR.

schooner *n.* **1** ▼ a fore-and-aft rigged ship with two or more masts, the foremast being smaller than the other masts. ▷ SAILING BOAT. **2 a** *Brit.* a measure or glass for esp. sherry. **b** *US & Austral.* a tall beer glass. [18th-century coinage]

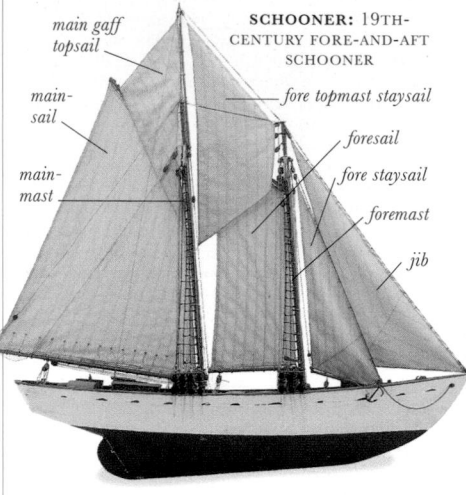

SCHOONER: 19TH-CENTURY FORE-AND-AFT SCHOONER

main gaff topsail
main-sail
main-mast
fore topmast staysail
foresail
fore staysail
foremast
jib

schottische /shŏ-**teesh**/ *n.* **1** a kind of slow polka. **2** the music for this. [from German *der schottische Tanz* 'the Scottish dance']

schuss /shuuss/ ● *n.* a straight downhill run on skis. ● *v.intr.* make a schuss. [German, literally 'shot']

sciatic /sy-**at**-ik/ *adj.* **1** of the hip. **2** of or affecting the sciatic nerve. **3** suffering from or liable to sciatica. [based on Greek *iskhion* 'hip joint'] □ **sciatically** *adv.*

sciatica /sy-**at**-i-kă/ *n.* neuralgia of the hip and thigh; a pain in the sciatic nerve. [from Late Latin *sciatica* (*passio*) 'sciatic (affliction)']

sciatic nerve *n.* the largest nerve in the body, running from the pelvis to the thigh. ▷ NERVOUS SYSTEM

science *n.* **1** a branch of knowledge involving the systematized observation of and experiment with phenomena (see also NATURAL SCIENCE). **2 a** systematic and formulated knowledge, esp. of a specified type or on a specified subject (*political science*). **b** the pursuit or principles of this. [from Latin *scientia*]

science fiction *n.* fiction based on imagined future scientific or technological advances etc., frequently portraying space or time travel, life on other planets, etc.

science park *n.* an area devoted to scientific research or the development of science-based industries.

scientific *adj.* **1 a** (of an investigation etc.) according to rules laid down in exact science for performing observations and testing the soundness of conclusions. **b** systematic, accurate. **2** used in, engaged in, or relating to (esp. natural) science (*scientific discoveries*; *scientific terminology*). [from Late Latin *scientificus*] □ **scientifically** *adv.*

scientist *n.* an expert in, or a student of, a (usu. physical or natural) science.

Scientology *n. propr.* a religious system based on self-improvement and promotion through grades of esp. self-knowledge. [based on Latin *scientia* 'knowledge'] □ **Scientologist** *n.*

sci-fi *n.* (often *attrib.*) *colloq.* science fiction.

scilicet /**sy**-li-set/ *adv.* that is to say; namely (introducing a word to be supplied or an explanation of an ambiguity). [Latin, from *scire licet* 'one is permitted to know']

Scillonian ● *adj.* of or relating to the Scilly Isles off the coast of Cornwall. ● *n.* a native of the Scilly Isles.

scimitar *n.* a curved oriental sword usu. broadening towards the point. [from Italian *scimitarra*]

scintilla /sin-til-ă/ *n.* **1** a trace. **2** a spark. [Latin]

scintillate *v.intr.* **1** (esp. as **scintillating** *adj.*) talk cleverly or wittily; be brilliant. **2** sparkle; twinkle; emit sparks. [based on Latin *scintillatus* 'sparked'] □ **scintillant** *adj.* **scintillatingly** *adv.* **scintillation** *n.*

scion /sy-ŏn/ *n.* **1** (*US* also **cion**) a shoot of a plant etc., esp. one cut for grafting or planting. **2** a descendant; a younger member of (esp. a noble) family. [from Old French *sion* 'shoot, twig']

scirocco var. of SIROCCO.

scissor *v.tr.* **1** (usu. foll. by *off*, *up*, *into*, etc.) cut with scissors. **2** (usu. foll. by *out*) clip out (a newspaper cutting etc.).

scissors *n.pl.* **1** (also **pair of scissors** *sing.*) an instrument for cutting fabric, paper, hair, etc., having two pivoted blades with finger and thumb holes in the handles, operating by closing on the material to be cut. **2** (treated as *sing.*) a hold in wrestling in which the opponent's body or esp. head is gripped between the legs. [from Late Latin *cisoria* 'cutting instruments'] □ **scissorwise** *adv.*

sclera /skleer-ă/ *n.* the white of the eye; a white membrane coating the eyeball. ▷ EYE. [based on Greek *sklēros* 'hard'] □ **scleral** *adj.* **scleritis** *n.* **sclerotomy** *n.* (*pl.* **-ies**)

sclerosed /skleer-rohst/ *adj.* affected by sclerosis.

sclerosis *n.* **1** an abnormal hardening of body tissue. **2** (in full **multiple sclerosis**) a chronic and progressive disease of the nervous system resulting in symptoms such as numbness, severe fatigue, and impairment of muscular coordination. [based on Greek *sklēroun* 'to harden']

sclerotic ● *adj.* **1** of or having sclerosis. **2** of or relating to the sclera. ● *n.* = SCLERA. □ **sclerotitis** *n.*

scoff[1] ● *v.intr.* (usu. foll. by *at*) speak derisively, esp. of serious subjects; mock; be scornful. ● *n.* **1** mocking words; a taunt. **2** an object of ridicule. □ **scoffer** *n.* **scoffingly** *adv.*

scoff[2] esp. *Brit. colloq.* ● *v.tr. & intr.* eat greedily. ● *n.* food; a meal. [from Afrikaans *skof* (n.)]

scold ● *v.* **1** *tr.* rebuke or chide (esp. a child). **2** *intr.* find fault noisily; rail. ● *n. archaic* a nagging or grumbling woman. [Middle English] □ **scolder** *n.* **scolding** *n.*

scollop var. of SCALLOP.

sconce[1] *n.* **1** a flat candlestick with a handle. **2** ► a bracket candlestick to hang on a wall. [from Latin *absconsa* (*laterna*) 'dark (lantern)']

sconce[2] *n.* **1** a small fort or earthwork usu. defending a ford, pass, etc. **2** *archaic* a shelter or screen. [from Dutch *schans* 'brushwood']

scone /skon, skohn/ *n.* a small baked sweet or savoury cake of flour, fat, and milk. [originally Scots]

scoop ● *n.* **1** any of various objects resembling a spoon, esp.: **a** a short-handled deep shovel used for transferring grain, sugar, coal, coins, etc. **b** the excavating part of a digging machine etc. **c** an instrument used for serving mashed potato, ice cream, etc. **2** a quantity taken up by a scoop. **3** a movement of or resembling scooping. **4** a piece of news published by a newspaper etc. before its rivals. **5** a large profit made quickly or by anticipating one's competitors. ● *v.tr.* **1** (usu. foll. by *out*) hollow out with or as if with a scoop. **2** (usu. foll. by *up*) lift with or as if with a scoop. **3** forestall (a rival newspaper, reporter, etc.) with a scoop. **4** secure (a large profit etc.) esp. suddenly. [from Middle Dutch *schōpe* 'bucket'] □ **scooper** *n.* **scoopful** *n.* (*pl.* **-fuls**).

SCONCE: SHAKER TIN SCONCE

scoop neck *n.* the rounded low-cut neck of a garment.

scoot *colloq.* ● *v.intr.* run or dart away, esp. quickly. ● *n.* the act or an instance of scooting. [18th-century US coinage]

scooter ● *n.* **1** a child's toy consisting of a footboard mounted on two wheels and a steering column with handles. **2** (in full **motor scooter**) a light motorcycle with a shieldlike protective front. ● *v.intr.* travel or ride on a scooter. □ **scooterist** *n.*

scope[1] *n.* **1** **a** the extent to which it is possible to range (*this is beyond the scope of our research*). **b** the sweep or reach of mental activity, observation, or outlook (*an intellect limited in its scope*). **2** space or freedom to act (*doesn't leave us much scope*). [from Greek *skopos* 'target']

scope[2] *n. colloq.* a telescope, microscope, or other device ending in *-scope*. [abbreviation]

scopolamine /skŏ-pol-ăm-een/ *n.* = HYOSCINE. [from G. A. *Scopoli*, Italian naturalist, 1723–88]

scorbutic /skor-bew-tik/ ● *adj.* relating to, resembling, or affected with scurvy. ● *n.* a person affected with scurvy. [based on medieval Latin *scorbutus* 'scurvy']

scorch ● *v.* **1** *tr.* **a** burn the surface of with flame or heat so as to discolour, parch, injure, or hurt. **b** affect with the sensation of burning. **2** *intr.* become discoloured etc. with heat. **3** *tr.* (as **scorching** *adj.*) *colloq.* **a** (of the weather) very hot. **b** (of criticism etc.) stringent; harsh. ● *n.* a mark made by scorching. [Middle English] □ **scorchingly** *adv.*

scorched earth policy *n.* the burning of crops etc. and the removing or destroying of anything that might be of use to an enemy force occupying a country.

scorcher *n.* **1** a person or thing that scorches. **2** a very hot day.

score ● *n.* **1** **a** the number of points, goals, runs, etc., made by a player, side, etc., in some games. **b** the respective numbers of points etc. made by each player etc. during a whole game (*the score was 5–0*). **c** the act of gaining esp. a goal. **2** (*pl.* same or **scores**) twenty or a set of twenty. **3** (in *pl.*) a great many (*scores of people arrived*). **4** **a** a reason or motive (*rejected on the score of absurdity*). **b** topic, subject (*no worries on that score*). **5** *Mus.* **a** a usu. printed copy of a composition. **b** the music composed for a film or play, esp. for a musical. **6** a notch, line, etc. cut or scratched into a surface. ● *v.* **1** *tr.* **a** win or gain (a goal, run, points, success, etc.). **b** count for a score of (points in a game etc.) (*a bull's-eye scores most points*). **c** make a record of (a point etc.). **2** *intr.* **a** make a score in a game. **b** keep the tally of points, runs, etc. in a game. **3** *tr.* mark with notches, incisions, lines, etc.; slash; furrow (*scored his name on the desk*). **4** *intr.* have an advantage (*that is where he scores*). **5** *tr. Mus.* **a** orchestrate (a piece of music). **b** (usu. foll. by *for*) arrange for an instrument or instruments. **6** *intr. slang* **a** obtain drugs illegally. **b** (of a man) make a sexual conquest. □ **keep score** (or **the score**) register the score as it is made. **know the score** *colloq.* be aware of the essential facts. **on the score of** *Brit.* for the reason that. **on that score** so far as that is concerned. **pay** (or **settle**) **a** (or **the**) **score 1** require an obligation. **2** avenge an injury. **score off** (or **score points off**) *Brit. colloq.* humiliate, esp. verbally in repartee etc. **score out** draw a line through (words etc.). **score points** outdo another person; make a more favourable impression. **score under** underline. [*n.*: Old English; *v.*: partly based on Old Norse *skor* 'notch, tally, twenty'] □ **scoreless** *adj.* **scorer** *n.* **scoring** *n. Mus.*

scoreboard *n.* a large board for publicly displaying the score in a game or match.

scorebook *n.* (also **scorecard** or **score sheet**) a book etc. prepared for entering esp. cricket scores in.

score draw *n.* a draw in football in which goals are scored.

scoreline *n.* the number of points, goals, etc. scored in a match; the score; the result. [originally the line in a newspaper etc. giving the score in a sports contest]

scoria *n.* (*pl.* **scoriae** /-ri-ee/) **1** cellular lava, or fragments of it. **2** the slag or dross of metals. [from Greek *skōria* 'refuse'] □ **scoriaceous** *adj.*

scorify *v.tr.* (**-ies**, **-ied**) **1** reduce to dross. **2** assay (precious metal) by treating a portion of its ore fused with lead and borax. □ **scorification** *n.* **scorifier** *n.*

scorn ● *n.* **1** disdain, contempt, derision. **2** an object of contempt etc. (*the scorn of all onlookers*). ● *v.tr.* **1** hold in contempt or disdain. **2** (often foll. by *to* + infin.) abstain from or refuse to do as unworthy (*scorns lying; scorns to lie*). □ **pour scorn on** express contempt or disdain for. **think scorn of** *Brit. archaic* despise. [from Old French *esc(h)arn(ir)*] □ **scorner** *n.*

scornful *adj.* (often foll. by *of*) full of scorn; contemptuous. □ **scornfully** *adv.* **scornfulness** *n.*

Scorpio *n.* (*pl.* **-os**) **1** (usu. **Scorpius**) *Astron.* ◄ a large constellation (the Scorpion), said to represent the scorpion which killed Orion. **2** *Astrol.* **a** the eighth sign of the zodiac, which the Sun enters about 23 Oct. ▷ ZODIAC. **b** a person born when the Sun is in this sign. [Middle English from Latin, literally 'scorpion'] □ **Scorpian** *adj. & n.*

SCORPIO: FIGURE FORMED FROM THE STARS OF SCORPIUS

Shaula

Antares

scorpion *n.* **1** ▼ an arachnid of the order Scorpiones, with lobster-like pincers and a jointed tail that can be bent over and inflict a poisoned sting. **2** (**the Scorpion**) the zodiacal sign Scorpio or the constellation Scorpius. [from Greek *skorpios*]

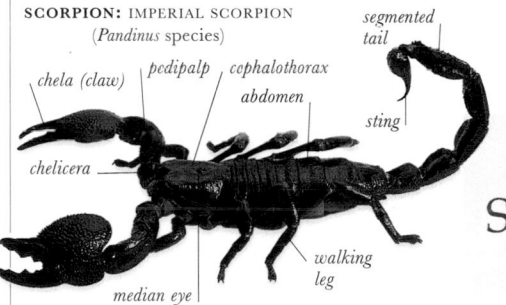

SCORPION: IMPERIAL SCORPION (*Pandinus* species)

chela (claw)

pedipalp

cephalothorax

abdomen

segmented tail

sting

chelicera

median eye

walking leg

scorzonera /skor-zŏ-neer-ă/ *n.* **1** a plant of the daisy family, *Scorzonera hispanica*, with long tapering purple-brown roots. **2** the root used as a vegetable. [Italian]

Scot *n.* **1** a native of Scotland. **2** a person of Scottish descent. [from Late Latin *Scottus*]

■ **Usage** See Usage Note at SCOTCHMAN.

Scotch ● *adj.* var. of SCOTTISH or SCOTS. ● *n.* **1** var. of SCOTTISH or SCOTS. **2** Scotch whisky. [contraction of SCOTTISH]

■ **Usage** The use of *Scotch* as an alternative to *Scottish* or *Scots* is generally regarded as offensive or old-fashioned by Scottish people. It should be avoided except to mean 'Scotch whisky' and in the special compounds (*Scotch broth* etc.) listed below.

scotch *v.tr.* **1** put an end to; frustrate (*injury scotched his attempt*). **2** *archaic* wound without killing. [Middle English]

S

Scotch broth *n.* a soup made from beef or mutton with pearl barley etc.

Scotch cap *n.* = BONNET *n.* 1b.

Scotch egg *n.* a hard-boiled egg enclosed in sausage meat and fried.

Scotch fir *n.* = SCOTS PINE.

Scotchman *n.* (*pl.* **-men**; *fem.* **Scotchwoman**, *pl.* **-women**) = SCOTSMAN.

■ **Usage** *Scotchman* and *Scotchwoman*, like *Scotch*, are old-fashioned and may be regarded as offensive by Scottish people. *Scot*, *Scotsman*, or *Scotswoman* should be used instead.

Scotch mist *n.* **1** a thick drizzly mist common in the Highlands. **2** *Brit.* a retort made to a person implying that he or she has imagined or failed to understand something.

Scotch tape *n.* esp. *US propr.* adhesive transparent tape.

Scotch whisky *n.* whisky distilled in Scotland, esp. from malted barley.

scot-free *adv.* unharmed; unpunished.

Scoticism var. of SCOTTICISM.

Scoticize var. of SCOTTICIZE.

Scotland Yard *n.* **1** the headquarters of the London Metropolitan Police. **2** its Criminal Investigation Department. [from Great and New *Scotland Yard*, streets where sited until 1967]

Scots esp. *Sc.* ● *adj.* **1** = SCOTTISH *adj.* **2** in the dialect, accent, etc., of (esp. Lowlands) Scotland. ● *n.* **1** = SCOTTISH *n.* **2** the form of English spoken in (esp. Lowlands) Scotland. [Middle English]

Scots fir *n.* = SCOTS PINE.

Scotsman *n.* (*pl.* **-men**; *fem.* **Scotswoman**, *pl.* **-women**) **1** a native of Scotland. **2** a person of Scottish descent.

Scots pine *n.* a pine tree, *Pinus sylvestris*, native to Europe and much planted for its wood. ▷ CONIFER

Scotticism *n.* (also **Scoticism**) a Scottish phrase, word, or idiom.

Scotticize *v.tr.* (also **Scoticize**, **-ise**) imbue with or model on Scottish ways etc.

Scottie *n. colloq.* **1** (also **Scottie dog**) a Scottish terrier. **2** a Scot.

Scottish ● *adj.* of or relating to Scotland or its inhabitants. ● *n.* (prec. by *the*; treated as *pl.*) the people of Scotland. See also SCOTS. □ **Scottishness** *n.*

Scottish terrier *n.* a small terrier of a rough-haired short-legged breed.

scoundrel *n.* an unscrupulous villain; a rogue. [16th-century coinage] □ **scoundrelism** *n.* **scoundrelly** *adj.*

S

scour[1] ● *v.tr.* **1 a** cleanse or brighten (esp. metal) by rubbing, esp. with soap, chemicals, sand, etc. **b** (usu. foll. by *away*, *off*, etc.) clear (rust, stains, reputation, etc.) by rubbing, hard work, etc. (*scoured the slur from his name*). **2** clear out (a pipe, channel, etc.) by flushing through with or by the natural action of water. ● *n.* the act or an instance of scouring. [from Late Latin *excurare* 'to clean (off)'] □ **scourer** *n.*

scour[2] *v.tr.* hasten over (an area etc.) searching thoroughly (*scoured the streets for him*; *scoured the newspaper*). [Middle English]

scourge /skurj/ ● *n.* **1** a whip used for punishment, esp. of people. **2** a person or thing seen or regarded as causing suffering (*Genghis Khan, the scourge of Asia*). ● *v.tr.* **1** whip. **2** punish; afflict; oppress. [from Old French *escorge* (n.), *escorgier* (v.)] □ **scourger** *n.*

Scouse /skowss/ *colloq.* ● *n.* **1** the dialect of Liverpool. **2** (also **Scouser**) a native of Liverpool. **3** (**scouse**) = LOBSCOUSE. ● *adj.* of or relating to Liverpool. [abbreviation of LOBSCOUSE]

scout ● *n.* **1** a person, esp. a soldier, sent out to get information about the enemy's position, strength, etc. **2** the act of seeking (esp. military) information (*on the scout*). **3** = TALENT SCOUT. **4** (**Scout**) a member of the Scout Association, an international youth organization (originally for boys) intended to develop character esp. by open-air activities. **5** a ship or aircraft designed for reconnoitring, esp. a small fast aircraft. ● *v.* **1** *intr.* act as a scout. **2** *intr.* (foll. by *about*, *around*, *for*) make a search. **3** *tr.* (often foll. by *out*) *colloq.* explore to get information about (territory etc.). [based on Latin *auscultare* 'to listen'] □ **scouter** *n.* **scouting** *n.*

Scouter *n.* an adult leader in the Scout Association.

Scoutmaster *n.* a person in charge of a group of Scouts.

scow *n.* esp. *US* a flat-bottomed boat used as a lighter etc. [from Dutch *schouw* 'ferry boat']

scowl ● *n.* a sullen, bad-tempered, or threatening frown. ● *v.intr.* make a scowl. [Middle English] □ **scowler** *n.*

scrabble ● *v.intr.* (often foll. by *about*, *at*) scratch or grope to find or collect or hold on to something. ● *n.* **1** an act of scrabbling. **2** (**Scrabble**) *propr.* a game in which players build up words from letter-blocks on a board. [from Middle Dutch *schrabbelen*]

scrag esp. *Brit.* ● *n.* **1** (also **scrag-end**) the inferior end of a neck of mutton. **2** a skinny person or animal. **3** *colloq.* a person's neck. ● *v.tr.* (**scragged**, **scragging**) *slang* **1** strangle, hang. **2** handle roughly; beat up.

scraggly *adj.* sparse and irregular.

scraggy *adj.* (**scraggier**, **scraggiest**) thin and bony. □ **scraggily** *adv.* **scragginess** *n.*

scram *v.intr.* (**scrammed**, **scramming**) (esp. in *imper.*) *colloq.* go away. [20th-century coinage]

scramble ● *v.* **1** *intr.* make one's way over rough ground, rocks, etc., by clambering, crawling, etc. **2** *intr.* (foll. by *for*, *at*) struggle with competitors (for a thing or share of it). **3** *intr.* move with difficulty, hastily, or awkwardly. **4** *tr.* **a** mix together indiscriminately. **b** jumble or muddle. **5** *tr.* cook (eggs) by heating them when broken and well mixed with butter, milk, etc. **6** *tr.* change the speech frequency of (a broadcast transmission or telephone conversation) so as to make it unintelligible without a corresponding decoding device. **7** *intr.* (of fighter aircraft or their pilots) take off quickly in an emergency or for action. ● *n.* **1** an act of scrambling. **2** a difficult climb or walk. **3** (foll. by *for*) an eager struggle or competition. **4** *Brit.* a motorcycle race over rough ground. **5** an emergency take-off by fighter aircraft. [16th-century coinage]

scrambler *n.* a device for scrambling telephone conversations.

scrap[1] ● *n.* **1** a small detached piece; a fragment or remnant. **2** rubbish or waste material. **3** discarded metal for reprocessing (often *attrib.*: *scrap metal*). **4** (with *neg.*) the smallest piece or amount (*not a scrap of food left*). **5** (in *pl.*) **a** odds and ends. **b** bits of uneaten food. ● *v.tr.* (**scrapped**, **scrapping**) discard as useless. [from Old Norse *skrap*]

scrap[2] *colloq.* ● *n.* a fight or rough quarrel, esp. a spontaneous one. ● *v.tr.* (**scrapped**, **scrapping**) (often foll. by *with*) have a scrap. □ **scrapper** *n.*

scrapbook *n.* a book of blank pages for sticking cuttings, drawings, etc. in.

scrape ● *v.* **1** *tr.* **a** move a hard or sharp edge across (a surface), esp. to make something smooth. **b** apply (a hard or sharp edge) in this way. **2** *tr.* (foll. by *away*, *off*, etc.) remove (a stain, projection, etc.) by scraping. **3** *tr.* **a** rub (a surface) harshly against another. **b** scratch or damage by scraping. **4** *tr.* (often foll. by *out*) make (a hollow) by scraping. **5 a** *tr.* draw or move with a sound of, or resembling, scraping. **b** *intr.* emit or produce such a sound. **c** *tr.* produce such a sound from. **6** *intr.* (often foll. by *along*, *by*, *through*, etc.) move or pass along while almost touching close or surrounding features, obstacles, etc. (*the car scraped through the narrow lane*). **7** *tr.* just manage to achieve (a living, an examination pass, etc.). **8** *intr.* (often foll. by *by*, *through*) **a** barely manage. **b** pass an examination etc. with difficulty. **9** *tr.* (foll. by *together*, *up*) contrive to bring or provide; amass with difficulty. **10** *intr.* be economical. **11** *intr.* draw back a foot in making a clumsy bow. ● *n.* **1** the act or sound of scraping. **2** a scraped place (on the skin etc.). **3** *Brit.* a thinly applied layer of butter etc. on bread. **4** the scraping of a foot in bowing. **5** *colloq.* an awkward predicament, esp. resulting from an escapade. □ **scrape acquaintance with** contrive to get to know (a person). **scrape the barrel** *colloq.* be reduced to one's last resources. [from Old Norse *skrapa*]

scraper *n.* a device used for scraping, esp. for removing dirt or paint from a surface.

scrap heap *n.* **1** a pile of scrap materials. **2** a state of uselessness (esp. in phr. **on the scrap heap**).

scrapie *n.* a disease of sheep involving the central nervous system, characterized by lack of coordination and thought to be caused by a virus-like agent.

scraping *n.* **1** in senses of SCRAPE. **2** (esp. in *pl.*) a fragment produced by scraping off, up, or together.

scrap merchant *n.* a dealer in scrap.

scrappy *adj.* (**scrappier**, **scrappiest**) **1** consisting of scraps. **2** incomplete; carelessly arranged or put together. □ **scrappily** *adv.* **scrappiness** *n.*

scrapyard *n.* a place where (esp. metal) scrap is collected.

scratch ● *v.* **1** *tr.* score or mark the surface of with a sharp or pointed object. **2** *tr.* make a long narrow superficial wound in (the skin). **3** *tr.* (also *absol.*) scrape without marking, esp. with the hand to relieve itching. **4** *tr.* make or form by scratching. **5** *tr.* (foll. by *together*, *up*, etc.) obtain (a thing) by scratching or with difficulty. **6** *tr.* (foll. by *out*, *off*, *through*) cancel or strike (out) with a pencil etc. **7** *tr.* (also *absol.*) withdraw (a competitor, candidate, etc.) from a race or competition. **8** *intr.* (often foll. by *about*, *around*, etc.) **a** scratch the ground etc. in search. **b** look around haphazardly (*they were scratching about for evidence*). ● *n.* **1** a mark or wound made by scratching. **2** a sound of scratching. **3** a spell of scratching oneself (*had a scratch*). **4** *Golf* a handicap of zero. ● *attrib.adj.* **1** collected by chance. **2** collected or made from whatever is available (*a scratch crew*). **3** with no handicap given (*a scratch race*). □ **from scratch** **1** from the beginning. **2** without help or advantage. **scratch along** make a living etc. with difficulty. **scratch one's head** be perplexed. **scratch the surface** gain a superficial insight (into a problem, matter, etc.). **up to scratch** up to the required standard. [Middle English] □ **scratcher** *n.*

scratch card *n.* a game card having one or several sections coated in a waxy substance which may be scratched away to reveal a possible prize.

scratch pad *n.* **1** esp. *N. Amer.* a pad of paper for scribbling. **2** *Computing* a small fast memory for the temporary storage of data.

scratchy *adj.* (**scratchier**, **scratchiest**) **1** tending to make scratches or a scratching noise. **2** (esp. of a garment) tending to cause itchiness. **3** (of a drawing etc.) done in scratches or carelessly. □ **scratchily** *adv.* **scratchiness** *n.*

scrawl ● *v.* **1** *tr.* & *intr.* write in a hurried untidy way. **2** *tr.* (foll. by *out*) cross out by scrawling over. ● *n.* **1** a piece of hurried writing. **2** a scrawled note. □ **scrawly** *adj.*

scrawny *adj.* (**scrawnier**, **scrawniest**) lean, scraggy. [variant of dialect *scranny* 'lean'] □ **scrawniness** *n.*

scream ● *n.* **1** a loud high-pitched piercing cry expressing fear, pain, extreme fright, etc. **2** a similar sound, e.g. of sirens. **3** *colloq.* an irresistibly funny occurrence or person. ● *v.* **1** *intr.* emit a scream. **2** *tr.* speak or sing (words etc.) in a screaming tone. **3** *intr.* **a** move with a shrill sound like a scream (*a train screamed past*). **b** make a noise like a scream. **4** *intr.* laugh uncontrollably. **5** *intr.* be blatantly obvious or conspicuous. [Old English]

screamer *n.* **1** a person or thing that screams. **2** *US colloq.* a sensational headline.

scree *n.* small loose stones. ▷ ERODE. [from Old Norse *skritha* 'landslip']

screech ● *n.* a harsh high-pitched scream. ● *v.tr.* & *intr.* utter with or make a screech. [16th-century

variant of Middle English *scritch*] □ **screecher** *n.*
screechy *adj.* (**screechier**, **screechiest**).

screech owl *n.* an owl with a screeching rather
than a hooting call, esp. the barn owl.

screed *n.* **1** a long usu. tiresome piece of writing or
speech. **2** a levelled layer of material (e.g. cement)
applied to a floor or other surface. [Middle
English]

screen ● *n.* **1** a fixed or movable upright partition
for separating, concealing, or sheltering from
draughts or excessive heat or light. **2** a thing used as
a shelter, esp. from observation. **3 a** a measure
adopted for concealment. **b** the protection afforded
by this (*under the screen of night*). **4 a** a blank usu.
white or silver surface on which a photographic
image is projected. **b** (prec. by *the*) the cinema
industry. **5** the surface of a cathode ray tube or
similar electronic device, esp. of a television, VDU,
etc., on which images appear. ▷ MONITOR, TELEVISION.
6 = SIGHT-SCREEN. **7** = WINDSCREEN. **8** a frame with fine
wire netting to keep out flies, mosquitoes, etc. **9** a
large sieve or riddle, esp. for sorting grain, coal,
etc., into sizes. **10** a system of checking for the
presence or absence of a disease, ability, attribute,
etc. **11** *Printing* a transparent finely ruled plate or
film used in half-tone reproduction. ▷ PRINTING.
● *v.tr.* **1** (often foll. by *from*) **a** afford shelter to; hide.
b protect from detection, censure, etc. **2** (foll. by
off) conceal behind a screen. **3** show (a film, television programme, etc.). **4** prevent from causing, or
protect from, electrical interference. **5** test (a
person or group) for a disease, reliability, loyalty,
etc. **6** pass (grain, coal, etc.) through a screen. [from
Old Northern French *escren*] □ **screenable** *adj.*
screener *n.* **screening** *n.*

screenings *n.pl.* refuse separated by sifting.

screenplay *n.* the script of a film, with acting
instructions, scene directions, etc.

screen printing *n.* a process like stencilling
with ink forced through a prepared sheet of fine
material (originally silk). □ **screen print** *n.*
screen-print *v.tr.* (usu. as **screen-printed** *adj.*).

screen test *n.* an audition for a part in a cinema
film.

screenwriter *n.* a person who writes a screenplay.
□ **screenwriting** *n.*

screw ● *n.* **1** a thin cylinder or cone with a spiral
ridge or thread running round the outside (**male
screw**) or the inside (**female screw**). **2** (in full
woodscrew) a metal male screw with a slotted
head and a sharp point. **3** (in full **screw-bolt**) a
metal male screw with a blunt end on which a nut
is threaded to bolt things together. **4** a wooden or
metal straight screw used to exert pressure. **5** (in
sing. or *pl.*) an instrument of torture
acting in this way. **6** (in full **screw
propeller**) ◄ a form of propeller
with twisted blades acting like a
screw on the water or air. **7** one
turn of a screw. **8** (foll. by *of*) *Brit.*
a small twisted-up paper (of
tobacco etc.). **9** *Brit.* (in billiards
etc.) an oblique curling
motion of the ball.
10 *slang offens.* a prison
warder. **11** *Brit. slang*
an amount of
salary or wages.
12 *coarse slang* **a** an act
of sexual intercourse. **b** a
partner in this. ● *v.* **1** *tr.* fasten or
tighten with a screw or screws.
2 *tr.* turn (a screw). **3** *intr.* twist or
turn round like a screw. **4** *tr.* **a** put
psychological etc. pressure on to
achieve an end. **b** oppress.
5 *tr.* **a** (foll. by *out of*) extort
(consent, money, etc.) from (a
person). **b** swindle. **6** *tr.* (also *absol.*)
coarse slang have sexual intercourse
with. **7** *Brit. intr.* (esp. of a billiard

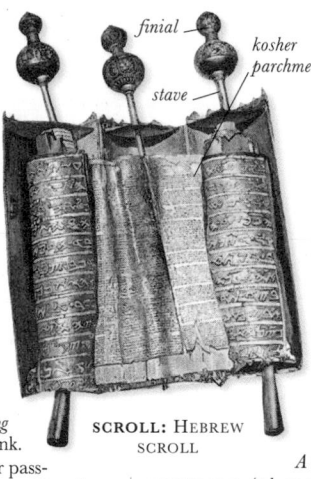

*shaft
keyway*

boss

*twisted
blade*

**SCREW
PROPELLER**

ball) take a curling course. **8** *tr.* = *screw up*. □ **have
one's head screwed on the right way** *colloq.*
have common sense. **have a screw loose** *colloq.*
be slightly crazy. **put the screws on** (also *absol.*)
colloq. exert pressure on (a person), esp. to extort
something or to intimidate. **screw around** *coarse
slang* be sexually promiscuous. **screw up**
1 contract or contort (one's face
etc.). **2** contract and crush into a
tight mass (a piece of paper etc.).
3 summon up (one's courage etc.).
4 *slang* a bungle. **b** spoil (an event,
opportunity, etc.). **5** *slang* disturb
mentally. [from French *escroue*
'female screw, nut'] □ **screw-
able** *adj.* **screwer** *n.*

screwball *N. Amer. slang* ● *n.* a
crazy or eccentric person.
● *adj.* crazy.

screw cap *n.* = SCREW TOP.

screw-coupling *n.* a female screw
with threads at both ends for joining lengths of pipes or rods.

screwdriver *n.* **1** a tool with a
shaped tip to fit into the head of a
screw to turn it. **2** a cocktail made
from vodka and orange juice.

screwed *adj.* **1** twisted. **2** *slang*
a ruined; rendered ineffective. **b** drunk.

screw eye *n.* a screw with a loop for passing cord etc. through instead of a slotted head.

screw propeller see SCREW *n.* 6.

screw top *n.* (hyphenated when *attrib.*) a cap or lid
that can be screwed on to a bottle, jar, etc.

screw-up *n. slang* a bungle, muddle, or mess.

screwy *adj.* (**screwier**, **screwiest**) *slang* **1** crazy or
eccentric. **2** absurd. □ **screwiness** *n.*

scribble ● *n.* **1** *tr. & intr.* write carelessly or hurriedly.
2 *intr.* often *derog.* be an author or writer. **3** *intr. & tr.*
draw carelessly or meaninglessly. ● *n.* **1** a scrawl.
2 a hasty note etc. **3** careless handwriting. [from
medieval Latin *scribillare*] □ **scribbler** *n.* **scribbly**
adj.

scribe ● *n.* **1** a person who writes out documents,
esp. *hist.* an ancient or medieval copyist of manuscripts. **2** *Jewish Hist.* an ancient Jewish record-
keeper or, later, a professional theologian and jurist.
3 (in full **scribe-awl**) a pointed instrument for
making marks on wood, bricks, etc. **4** *N. Amer. colloq.*
a writer, esp. a journalist. ● *v.tr.* mark (wood etc.)
with a scribe (see sense 3 of *n.*). [from Latin *scriba*]
□ **scribal** *adj.*

scriber *n.* = SCRIBE *n.* 3.

scrim *n.* open-weave fabric for lining or upholstery
etc. [18th-century coinage]

scrimmage ● *n.* **1** a struggle; a brawl. **2** *Amer. Football* a sequence of play beginning with the placing
of the ball on the ground with its longest axis at
right angles to the goal line. ● *v.* **1** *intr.* engage in a
scrimmage. **2** *tr. Amer. Football* put (the ball) into a
scrimmage. [variant of SKIRMISH] □ **scrimmager** *n.*

scrimp *v.* **1** *intr.* be sparing or parsimonious. **2** *tr.* use
sparingly. [17th-century coinage, originally Scots]
□ **scrimpy** *adj.*

scrip *n.* **1** a provisional certificate of money
subscribed to a bank etc. entitling the holder to
dividends. **2** (*collect.*) such certificates. **3** an extra
share or shares instead of a dividend. [abbreviation
of *subscription receipt*]

script ● *n.* **1** handwriting as distinct from print;
written characters. **2** type imitating handwriting.
3 an alphabet or system of writing. **4** the text of a
play, film, or broadcast. **5** an examinee's set of written answers. ● *v.tr.* write a script for (a film etc.).
[from Latin *scriptum* '(thing) written']

scripture *n.* **1** sacred writings. **2** (**Scripture** or **the
Scriptures**) **a** the Bible as a collection of sacred
writings in Christianity. **b** the sacred writings of
any other religion. [from Latin *scriptura*] □ **script-
ural** *adj.* **scripturally** *adv.*

scriptwriter *n.* a person who writes a script for a
film, broadcast, etc. □ **scriptwriting** *n.*

scrivener *n. hist.* **1** a copyist or drafter of documents. **2** a notary. [from Old French *escrivein*]

scrofula /skrof-yuu-lă/ *n. archaic* a disease with
glandular swellings, probably a form of tuberculosis. [from Late Latin *scrofulae* 'scrofulous
swellings'] □ **scrofulous** *adj.*

scroll ● *n.* **1** ◄ a roll of
parchment or paper esp.
with writing on it. **2** a book
in the ancient roll form.
3 an ornamental design or
carving imitating a roll of
parchment. ● *v.* **1** *tr.* (often
foll. by *down*, *up*) move (a
display on a VDU screen) in
order to view new material.
2 *tr.* inscribe in or like a scroll.
3 *intr.* curl up like paper.
[Middle English *scrowle*, alteration of *rowle* 'roll'] □ **scroller**
n. (in sense 1 of *v.*).

scrolled *adj.* having a scroll
ornament.

scrollwork *n.* decoration of
spiral lines.

Scrooge *n.* a mean or miserly
person. [character in Dickens's
A Christmas Carol]

finial

*kosher
parchment*

stave

SCROLL: HEBREW
SCROLL

scrotum *n.* (*pl.* **scrota** or **scrotums**) a pouch of
skin containing the testicles. ▷ REPRODUCTIVE ORGANS.
[Latin] □ **scrotal** *adj.*

scrounge *colloq.* ● *v.* **1** *tr.* (also *absol.*) obtain (things)
illicitly or by cadging. **2** *intr.* search about to find
something at no cost. ● *n.* an act of scrounging.
□ **on the scrounge** *Brit.* engaged in scrounging.
[variant of dialect *scrunge* 'to steal'] □ **scrounger** *n.*

scrub[1] ● *v.* (**scrubbed**, **scrubbing**) **1** *tr.* rub hard
so as to clean, esp. with a hard brush. **2** *intr.* use a
brush in this way. **3** *intr.* (often foll. by *up*) (of a
surgeon etc.) thoroughly clean the hands and arms
by scrubbing, before operating. **4** *tr. colloq.* scrap or
cancel. ● *n.* the act or an instance of scrubbing; the
process of being scrubbed. □ **scrub round** *Brit.*
colloq. circumvent, avoid [Middle English]

scrub[2] *n.* **1 a** vegetation consisting mainly of brushwood or stunted forest growth. **b** an area of land
covered with this. **2** *N. Amer.* an animal of inferior
breed or physique (often *attrib.*: *scrub horse*). **3** a small
or dwarf variety (often *attrib.*: *scrub pine*). [Middle
English variant of SHRUB[1]] □ **scrubby** *adj.*

scrubber *n.* **1** an apparatus using water or a solution for purifying gases etc. **2** *Brit. slang offens.* a
sexually promiscuous woman.

scrubbing-brush *n.* (*N. Amer.* **scrub-brush**) a
hard brush for scrubbing floors.

scrubland *n.* land consisting of scrub vegetation.

scruff[1] *n.* the back of the neck (esp. *scruff of the neck*).
[alteration of *scuff* 'hair']

scruff[2] *n. Brit. colloq.* an untidy or scruffy person.
[originally in sense 'scurf', later 'worthless thing']

scruffy *adj.* (**scruffier**, **scruffiest**) *colloq.* shabby,
slovenly, untidy. □ **scruffily** *adv.* **scruffiness** *n.*

scrum *n.* **1** *Rugby* an arrangement of the forwards
of each team in two opposing groups, each with
arms interlocked and heads down, with the ball
thrown in between them to restart play. ▷ RUGBY.
2 *Brit. colloq.* a disorderly crowd. [abbreviation of
SCRUMMAGE]

scrum-half *n. Rugby* a half-back who puts the ball
into the scrum. ▷ RUGBY

scrummage *n. Rugby* = SCRUM *n.* 1. [variant of SCRIM-
MAGE] □ **scrummager** *n.*

scrump *v.tr. Brit. colloq.* steal (fruit) from an orchard
or garden.

scrumple *v.tr. Brit.* crumple, wrinkle.

scrumptious *adj. colloq.* **1** delicious. **2** pleasing,
delightful. [19th-century coinage] □ **scrump-
tiously** *adv.* **scrumptiousness** *n.*

S

SCUBA-DIVING

When breathing underwater, a scuba-diver draws compressed air from a tank worn on the back. On top of the tank is the regulator first-stage, which reduces the air pressure to just above that of the surrounding water. The air then travels down a tube to the regulator second-stage (which includes the mouthpiece). This part of the apparatus lowers the air pressure to exactly that of the external water, making the air safe to breathe.

SCUBA DIVERS

mask

regulator second-stage

buoyancy compensator

buoyancy compensator mouthpiece

octopus rig

regulator first-stage

protective mesh

air tank

wetsuit

instrument console

scrumpy *n. Brit. colloq.* rough cider, esp. as made in the West Country of England. [from dialect *scrump* 'small apple']

scrunch ● *v.* **1** *tr. & intr.* (usu. foll. by *up*) make or become crushed or crumpled. **2** *intr. & tr.* make or cause to make a crunching sound. **3** *tr.* style (hair) by squeezing or crushing in the hands to give a tousled look. ● *n.* the act or an instance of scrunching. [variant of CRUNCH]

scrunch-dry *v.tr.* dry (hair) while scrunching it.

scrunchy *n.* (*pl.* **-ies**) (also **scrunchie**) a circular band of fabric-covered elastic used for fastening the hair.

scruple ● *n.* **1** (in *sing.* or *pl.*) **a** regard to the morality or propriety of an action. **b** a feeling of doubt or hesitation caused by this. **2** *hist.* an apothecaries' weight of 20 grains. **3** *archaic* a very small quantity. ● *v.intr.* **1** (foll. by *to* + infin.; usu. with *neg.*) be reluctant because of scruples (*did not scruple to stop their allowance*). **2** feel or be influenced by scruples. [based on Latin *scrupus* 'rough pebble, anxiety']

scrupulous *adj.* **1** conscientious; thorough. **2** careful to avoid doing wrong. **3** punctilious; overattentive to details. [from Latin *scrupulosus*, related to SCRUPLE] □ **scrupulosity** *n.* **scrupulously** *adv.* **scrupulousness** *n.*

scrutineer *n.* a person who scrutinizes or examines something, esp. *Brit.* the conduct and result of a ballot.

scrutinize *v.tr.* (also **-ise**) look closely at; examine with close scrutiny. □ **scrutinizer** *n.*

scrutiny *n.* (*pl.* **-ies**) **1** a critical gaze. **2** a close investigation or examination of details. **3** an official examination of ballot papers to check their validity or accuracy of counting. [based on Latin *scrutinari*, literally 'to sort rubbish']

scuba *n.* (*pl.* **scubas**) an aqualung. [acronym from *s*elf-*c*ontained *u*nderwater *b*reathing *a*pparatus]

scuba-diving *n.* ▲ swimming underwater using a scuba, esp. as a sport. □ **scuba-dive** *v.intr.* **scuba-diver** *n.*

scud ● *v.intr.* (**scudded**, **scudding**) **1** fly or run straight, fast, and lightly. **2** *Naut.* run before the wind. ● *n.* **1** a spell of scudding. **2** a scudding motion. **3** vapoury driving clouds. **4** a driving shower; a gust. **5** wind-blown spray. **6** (usu. **Scud**) a type of long-range surface-to-surface guided missile originally developed in the former USSR.

scuff ● *v.* **1** *tr.* graze or brush against. **2** *tr.* mark or wear down (shoes) in this way. **3** *intr.* walk with dragging feet; shuffle. ● *n.* a mark made by scuffing.

scuffle ● *n.* a confused struggle or disorderly fight at close quarters. ● *v.intr.* engage in a scuffle. [probably of Scandinavian origin: cf. Swedish *skuffa* 'to push', related to SHOVE]

sculduggery var. of SKULDUGGERY.

scull ● *n.* **1** either of a pair of small oars used by a single rower. **2** an oar placed over the stern of a boat to propel it, usu. by a twisting motion. **3** ► a small boat propelled with a scull or a pair of sculls. ▷ ROW. **4** (in *pl.*) a race between boats with single pairs of oars. ● *v.tr.* propel (a boat) with sculls. [Middle English]

sculler *n.* **1** a user of sculls. **2** a boat intended for sculling.

scullery *n.* (*pl.* **-ies**) a small kitchen or room at the back of a house for washing dishes etc. [from Old French *escuelerie*]

scullion *n. archaic* **1** a cook's boy. **2** a person who washes dishes etc. [Middle English]

sculpt *v.tr. & intr.* (also **sculp**) sculpture. [from French *sculpter*]

sculptor *n.* (*fem.* **sculptress**) an artist who makes sculptures.

sculpture ● *n.* **1** the art of making forms, often representational, in the round or in relief by chiselling, carving, modelling, casting, etc. **2** a work or works of sculpture. ● *v.* **1** *tr.* represent in or adorn with sculpture. **2** *intr.* practise sculpture. □ **sculptural** *adj.* **sculpturally** *adv.* **sculpturesque** *adj.*

scum ● *n.* **1** a layer of dirt, froth, etc. forming at the top of liquid. **2** (foll. by *of*) the most worthless part of something. **3** *colloq.* a worthless person or group. ● *v.tr.* (**scummed**, **scumming**) **1** remove scum from. **2** be or form a scum on. [from

SCULL:
SINGLE SCULL
(WITH DECKING
REMOVED) AND
OARS

bowball

bowpost

internal frame

diagonal deck support

breakwater

hatch

sliding seat

slide track

outrigger

gate

stretcher

keel

blade

sculls (oars)

Middle Dutch *schūm*] □ **scummy** *adj.* (**scummier**, **scummiest**).

scumbag *n. slang* a contemptible or disgusting person.

scupper[1] *n.* a hole in a ship's side to carry off water from the deck. [from Old French *escopir*]

scupper[2] *v.tr. Brit. slang* **1** sink (a ship or its crew). **2** defeat or ruin (a plan etc.). **3** kill. [19th-century coinage]

scurf *n.* **1** flakes on the surface of the skin, cast off as fresh skin develops below, esp. those of the head; dandruff. **2** any scaly matter on a surface. [Old English] □ **scurfy** *adj.*

scurrilous *adj.* **1** (of a person or language) grossly or indecently abusive. **2** given to or expressed with low humour. [from Latin *scurrilus*] □ **scurrility** *n.* (*pl.* **-ies**). **scurrilously** *adv.* **scurrilousness** *n.*

scurry ● *v.intr.* (**-ies**, **-ied**) run or move hurriedly, esp. with short quick steps; scamper. ● *n.* (*pl.* **-ies**) **1** the act or sound of scurrying. **2** a flurry of rain or snow.

scurvy ● *n.* a disease caused by a deficiency of vitamin C. ● *adj.* (**scurvier**, **scurviest**) *archaic* dishonourable, contemptible. [based on SCURF] □ **scurvied** *adj.* **scurvily** *adv.*

scut *n.* a short tail, esp. of a hare, rabbit, or deer. [Middle English]

scutcheon *n.* **1** = ESCUTCHEON. **2** an ornamented brass etc. plate round or over a keyhole. **3** a plate for a name or inscription. [Middle English]

scutter esp. *Brit.* ● *v.intr. colloq.* scurry. ● *n.* the act or an instance of scuttering.

scuttle[1] *n.* **1** a receptacle for carrying and holding a small supply of coal. **2** *Brit.* the part of a motor car body between the windscreen and the bonnet. [from Latin *scutella* 'dish']

scuttle[2] ● *v.intr.* **1** scurry; hurry along. **2** run away. ● *n.* **1** a hurried gait. **2** a precipitate flight.

scuttle[3] ● *n.* a hole with a lid in a ship's deck or side. ● *v.tr.* let water into (a ship) to sink it.

scuzzy *adj. slang* abhorrent or disgusting.

Scylla and Charybdis /sil-ă, kă-**rib**-dis/ *n.pl.* two dangers such that avoidance of one increases the risk from the other. [names of a sea monster and whirlpool in Greek mythology]

scyphozoan /sy-fŏ-zoh-ăn/ ● *n.* any marine jellyfish of the class Scyphozoa, with tentacles bearing stinging cells. ● *adj.* of or relating to this class. ▷ CNIDARIAN. [based on Greek *skuphos* 'drinking cup' + *zōion* 'animal']

scythe /syth/ ● *n.* ► a mowing and reaping implement with a long curved blade swung over the ground by a long pole with two short handles projecting from it. ● *v.tr.* cut with a scythe. [Old English]

SDI *abbr.* strategic defence initiative.

SDLP *abbr.* (in N. Ireland) Social Democratic and Labour Party.

SDP *abbr. hist.* (in the UK) Social Democratic Party.

SE *abbr.* **1** south-east. **2** south-eastern.

Se *symb. Chem.* the element selenium.

sea *n.* **1** the expanse of salt water that covers most of the Earth's surface. **2** any part of this. **3** a particular (usu. named) tract of salt water partly or wholly enclosed by land (*the North Sea*). **4** a large inland lake (*the Caspian Sea*). **5** the waves of the sea, esp. with reference to their local motion or state (*a choppy sea*). **6** (foll. by *of*) a vast quantity or expanse (*a sea of faces*). **7** (*attrib.*) living or used in, on, or near the sea (often prefixed to the name of a marine animal, plant, etc., having a superficial resemblance to what it is named after) (*sea lettuce*). □ **at sea 1** in a ship on the sea. **2** (also **all at sea**) perplexed,

SCYTHE:
EARLY 20TH-
CENTURY
ENGLISH
SCYTHE

S

SEABED

The seabed consists of a number of distinctive geologic features. Mid-ocean ridges (underwater mountain ranges) form when tectonic plates pull apart and magma rises to fill the space. Seamounts are underwater volcanoes; when flat-topped they are known as guyots. Deep-sea trenches form when one tectonic plate is forced under another (subduction).

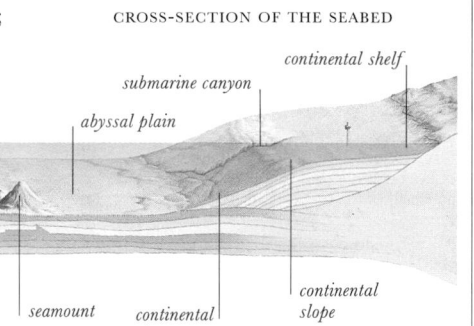

CROSS-SECTION OF THE SEABED

continental shelf
submarine canyon
abyssal plain
guyot
deep-sea trench
subducted tectonic plate
movement of tectonic plate
mid-ocean ridges
rising magma
seamount
continental rise
continental slope

---

confused. **by sea** in a ship or ships. **go to sea** become a sailor. **on the sea 1** in a ship at sea. **2** situated on the coast. **put** (or **put out**) **to sea** leave land or port. [Old English]

sea anchor *n.* a device such as a heavy bag dragged in the water to retard the drifting of a ship.

sea anemone *n.* any of various cnidarians of the order Actiniaria having a polypoid body bearing a ring of tentacles around the mouth. ▷ CNIDARIAN, SYMBIOSIS

sea bass see BASS² 2.

seabed *n.* ▲ the ground under the sea; the ocean floor.

seabird *n.* ▼ a bird frequenting the sea or the land near the sea.

seaboard *n.* **1** the seashore or coastal region. **2** the line of a coast.

seaborne *adj.* transported by sea.

sea bream see BREAM 2.

sea breeze *n.* a breeze blowing towards the land from the sea, esp. during the day.

sea change *n.* a notable or unexpected transformation.

sea-chest *n.* a sailor's storage-chest.

seacock *n.* a valve below a ship's water-line for letting water in or out.

sea cow *n.* a sirenian, esp. a manatee.

sea cucumber *n.* ▶ a type of echinoderm with a wormlike body.

ring of tentacles
row of tube feet
tough skin

SEA CUCUMBER
(*Stichopus chloronotus*)

sea dog *n.* an old or experienced sailor.

sea eagle *n.* any fish-eating eagle esp. of the genus *Haliaeetus*.

sea fan *n.* any colonial coral of the order Gorgonacea supported by a fanlike horny skeleton.

seafarer *n.* **1** a sailor. **2** a traveller by sea.

seafaring *adj. & n.* travelling by sea, esp. regularly.

seafood *n.* edible sea fish or shellfish.

seafront *n.* the part of a coastal town etc. directly facing the sea.

seagoing *adj.* **1** (of ships) fit for crossing the sea. **2** (of a person) seafaring.

sea green ● *n.* a bluish green (as of the sea). ● *adj.* (hyphenated when *attrib.*) of this colour.

seagull *n.* = GULL¹.

sea holly *n.* a spiny-leaved blue-flowered evergreen plant, *Eryngium maritimum*.

sea horse *n.* **1** ▶ any of various small upright marine fish of the family Syngnathidae, having a body suggestive of the head and neck of a horse. **2** a mythical creature with a horse's head and fish's tail.

seakale *n.* a cruciferous maritime plant, *Crambe maritima*, having coarsely toothed leaves and used as a vegetable.

seakale beet *n.* = CHARD.

seal¹ ● *n.* **1** a piece of wax, lead, paper, etc., with a stamped design, attached to a document as a guarantee of authenticity. **2** a similar material attached to a receptacle, envelope, etc., affording security by having to be broken to allow access to the contents. **3** an engraved piece of metal, gemstone, etc., for stamping a design on a seal. **4 a** a substance or device used to close an aperture or act as a fastening. **b** an amount of water standing in the trap of a drain to prevent foul air from rising. **5** an act, gesture, or event regarded as a confirmation or guarantee (*gave her seal of approval to the venture*). **6** a significant or prophetic mark (*has the seal of death in his face*). **7** a decorative adhesive stamp. **8** esp. *Eccl.* a vow of secrecy; an obligation to silence. ● *v.tr.* **1** close securely or hermetically. **2** stamp or fasten with a seal. **3** fix a seal to. **4** certify as correct with a seal or stamp. **5** (often foll. by *up*) confine or fasten securely. **6** settle or decide (*their fate is sealed*). **7** (foll. by *off*) put barriers round (an area) to prevent entry and exit, esp. as a security measure. **8** apply a non-porous coating to (a surface) to make

tubular snout
reduced fin
prehensile tail

SEA HORSE
(*Hippocampus* species)

S

SEABIRD

Birds living near the sea have special adaptations, including waterproof feathers, webbed feet, and facial glands that dispose of excess salt. Seabirds hunt prey in a variety of ways: surface feeders such as albatrosses grab food while flying near the ocean's surface; aerial divers such as gannets plummet into the water from a height; surface divers such as puffins swim on the surface and plunge underwater to feed. Almost all seabirds nest in colonies, in places predators cannot reach, such as cliffs.

WANDERING ALBATROSS
(*Diomedea exulans*)

NORTHERN GANNET
(*Sula bassana*)

KELP GULL
(*Larus dominicanus*)

MAGNIFICENT FRIGATE BIRD
(*Fregata magnificens*)

ARCTIC TERN
(*Sterna paradisea*)

GIANT PETREL
(*Macronectes giganteus*)

ATLANTIC PUFFIN
(*Fratercula arctica*)

it impervious. □ **one's lips are sealed** one is obliged to keep a secret. **set one's seal to** (or **on**) authorize or confirm. [from Latin *sigillum* 'little sign'] □ **sealable** *adj.*

seal² ● *n.* ▶ any fish-eating amphibious sea mammal of the family Phocidae or Otariidae, with flippers and webbed feet. ▷ PINNIPED. ● *v.intr.* hunt for seals. [Old English]

sealant *n.* material for sealing, esp. to make something airtight or watertight.

sea lavender *n.* any maritime plant of the genus *Limonium*, with small brightly coloured funnel-shaped flowers.

sealed-beam *attrib.adj.* designating a vehicle headlamp with a sealed unit consisting of the light source, reflector, and lens.

sealed book *n.* = CLOSED BOOK.

sealed orders *n.pl.* orders for procedure not to be opened before a specified time.

sea legs *n.pl.* the ability to keep one's balance and avoid seasickness when at sea.

sealer¹ *n.* **1** a device or substance used for making esp. a hermetic or an impervious seal. **2** (in full **sealer jar**) *Canad.* a jar designed to preserve fruit etc.

sealer² *n.* a ship or person engaged in hunting seals.

sea level *n.* the mean level of the sea's surface, used in reckoning the height of hills etc. and as a barometric standard.

sea lily *n.* any sessile echinoderm of the class Crinoidea, with long jointed stalks and feather-like arms for trapping food.

sealing wax *n.* a mixture of shellac and rosin with turpentine and pigment, softened by heating and used to make seals.

sea lion *n.* any large, eared seal of the Pacific, esp. of the genus *Zalophus* or *Otaria*. ▷ PINNIPED

sea loch *n.* = LOCH 2.

Sea Lord *n.* (in the UK) either of two senior naval officers (**First Sea Lord**, **Second Sea Lord**) serving as members of the Ministry of Defence.

seal ring *n.* a finger ring with a seal.

sealskin *n.* **1** the skin or prepared fur of a seal. **2** (often *attrib.*) a garment made from this.

seals of office *n.pl.* (in the UK) seals (see SEAL¹ *n.* 3) held during tenure, esp. by the Lord Chancellor or a Secretary of State, and symbolizing the office held.

Sealyham *n.* (in full **Sealyham terrier**) ▼ a terrier of a wire-haired short-legged breed. [from *Sealyham*, a village in SW Wales, where first bred]

S

SEALYHAM TERRIER

seam ● *n.* **1** a line where two edges join, esp. of two pieces of cloth etc. turned back and stitched together, or of boards fitted edge to edge. **2** a fissure between parallel edges. **3** a wrinkle or scar. **4** a stratum of coal etc. ● *v.tr.* **1** join with a seam. **2** (esp. as **seamed** *adj.*) mark or score with or as with a seam. [Old English] □ **seamer** *n.*

seaman *n.* (*pl.* **-men**) **1** a sailor, esp. one below the rank of officer. **2** a person regarded in terms of skill in navigation (*a poor seaman*). □ **seamanlike** *adj.* **seamanly** *adj.*

seamanship *n.* skill in managing a ship or boat.

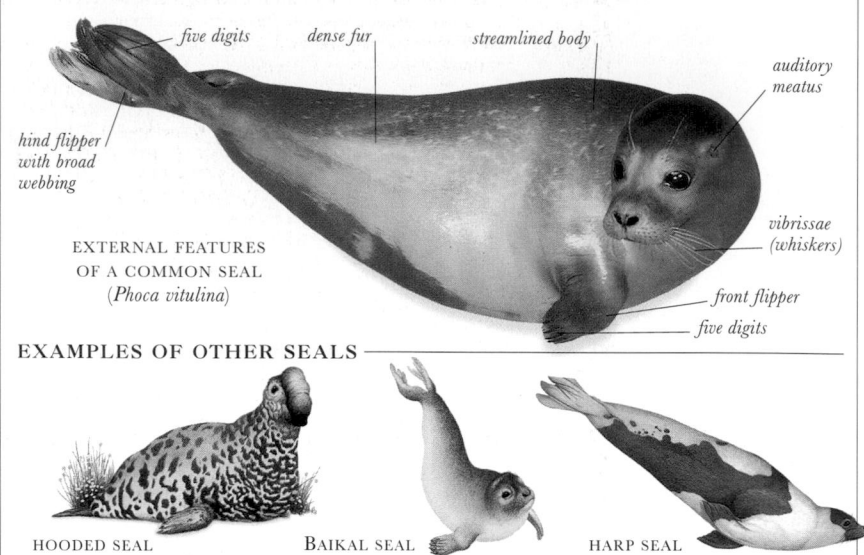

SEAL

True seals (shown below), as opposed to sea lions and fur seals, have no external ear flap (pinna). When underwater, these seals use their webbed hind flippers for propulsion, and the front flippers to steer. They can stay underwater for more than 30 minutes, surviving on oxygen stored in the blood. The Weddell seal can dive to depths of 600 m (1,950 ft).

five digits   *dense fur*   *streamlined body*   *auditory meatus*

hind flipper with broad webbing

EXTERNAL FEATURES OF A COMMON SEAL (*Phoca vitulina*)

vibrissae (whiskers)

front flipper

five digits

EXAMPLES OF OTHER SEALS

HOODED SEAL (*Cystophora cristata*)   BAIKAL SEAL (*Phoca sibirica*)   HARP SEAL (*Phoca groenlandica*)

---

seam bowler *n.* *Cricket* a bowler who makes the ball deviate by bouncing off its seam.

sea mile *n.* a unit of length varying between approx. 2,014 yards (1,842 metres) at the equator and 2,035 yards (1,861 metres) at the pole.

seamless *adj.* **1** without a seam or seams. **2** uninterrupted, smooth. □ **seamlessly** *adv.* (in sense 2).

seamstress *n.* (also **sempstress**) a woman who sews, esp. professionally. [Old English]

seamy *adj.* (**seamier**, **seamiest**) **1** marked with or showing seams. **2** sordid, disreputable (esp. *the seamy side*). □ **seaminess** *n.*

seance /**say**-ahnss/ *n.* (also **séance**) a meeting at which spiritualists attempt to make contact with the dead. [from French *séance*]

sea pink *n.* a maritime plant, *Armeria maritima*, with bright pink flowers.

seaplane *n.* an aircraft designed to take off from and land and float on water.

seaport *n.* a town with a harbour for seagoing ships.

sear /seer/ ● *v.tr.* **1 a** scorch, esp. with a hot iron; cauterize. **b** (as **searing** *adj.*) burning (*searing pain*). **2** cause (esp. emotional) pain or great anguish to. **3** brown (meat) quickly at a high temperature so that it will retain its juices in cooking. ● *adj.* (also **sere**) *literary* (esp. of a plant etc.) withered, dried up. [Old English]

search ● *v.* **1** *tr.* look through or go over thoroughly to find something. **2** *tr.* examine or feel over (a person) to find anything concealed. **3** *tr.* **a** probe or penetrate into. **b** examine (one's mind etc.) thoroughly. **4** *intr.* (often foll. by *for*) make a search or investigation. **5** *intr.* (as **searching** *adj.*) (of an examination) thorough. **6** *tr.* (foll. by *out*) look probingly for. ● *n.* **1** an act of searching. **2** an investigation. □ **in search of** trying to find. **search me!** *colloq.* I do not know. [from Late Latin *circare* 'to go round'] □ **searchable** *adj.* **searcher** *n.* **searchingly** *adv.*

searchlight *n.* **1** a powerful outdoor electric light with a concentrated beam that can be turned in any direction. **2** the light or beam from this.

search party *n.* a group of people organized to look for a lost person or thing.

search warrant *n.* an official authorization to enter and search a building.

sea room *n.* clear space at sea for a ship to turn or manoeuvre in.

sea salt *n.* salt produced by evaporating sea water.

seascape *n.* a picture or view of the sea.

Sea Scout *n.* (esp. in the UK) a member of the maritime branch of the Scout Association.

sea serpent *n.* **1** an enormous legendary serpent-like sea monster. **2** = SEA SNAKE 1.

sea shanty see SHANTY².

seashell *n.* the shell of a salt-water mollusc.

seashore *n.* land close to or bordering on the sea.

seasick *adj.* suffering from sickness or nausea from the motion of a ship at sea. □ **seasickness** *n.*

seaside *n.* (often *attrib.*) the sea coast, esp. as a holiday resort.

sea slug *n.* a shell-less marine gastropod mollusc, esp. of the order Nudibranchia, with external gills.

sea snail *n.* **1** a small slimy fish of the family Cyclopteridae, with a ventral sucker. **2** any spiral-shelled marine mollusc, e.g. a whelk.

sea snake *n.* **1** a venomous tropical marine snake of the family Hydrophidae. **2** = SEA SERPENT 1.

season ● *n.* **1** ▶ each of the four divisions of the year (spring, summer, autumn, and winter). **2** a time of year characterized by climatic or other features (*the dry season*). **3 a** the time of year when a plant is flowering etc. **b** the time of year when an animal breeds or is hunted. **4** a proper or suitable time. **5** a time when something is plentiful or active or in vogue. **6** (usu. prec. by *the*) = HIGH SEASON. **7** the time of year regularly devoted to an activity, social life, etc. (*the football season; up to London for the season*). **8** a period of indefinite or varying length. **9** *Brit. colloq.* = SEASON TICKET. ● *v.* **1** *tr.* flavour (food) with salt, herbs, etc. **2** *tr.* enhance with wit etc. **3** *tr.* temper or moderate. **4** *tr.* & *intr.* **a** make or become suitable, esp. by exposure to the air or weather. **b** make or become experienced (*seasoned soldiers*). □ **in season 1** (of foodstuff) available in plenty and in good condition. **2** (of an animal) on heat. **3** timely. [from Latin *satio -onis* 'sowing']

seasonable *adj.* **1** (of weather) suitable to or usual

SEASON

In relation to the Sun, the Earth spins on a tilted axis. Thus, as the Earth orbits the Sun over the course of a year, the Earth's two hemispheres are alternately nearer to, then further from, the Sun's warmth. This produces four distinct weather phases, called seasons. If the Earth's axis was at right angles to the Sun, there would be only one 'season'.

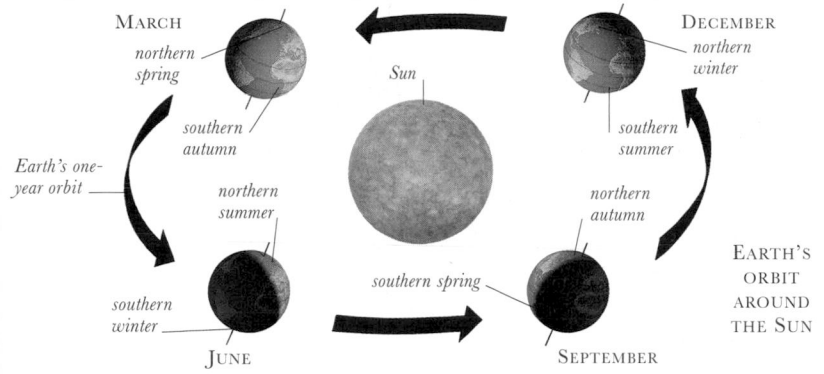

MARCH
northern spring
southern autumn

Sun

DECEMBER
northern winter
southern summer

Earth's one-year orbit

northern summer

northern autumn

southern winter

southern spring

JUNE

SEPTEMBER

EARTH'S ORBIT AROUND THE SUN

---

in the season (*the rain was seasonable if unwelcome*). **2** coming at the right time, opportune; meeting the needs of the occasion (*seasonable advice*). □ **seasonableness** n. **seasonably** adv.

■ **Usage** *Seasonable*, meaning 'suitable; opportune', should not be confused with the (more common) word *seasonal* meaning, 'of or relating to the seasons'.

seasonal adj. of or relating to the seasons of the year or some other temporal cycle; characteristic of or dependent on a particular season. □ **seasonality** n. **seasonally** adv.

■ **Usage** See Usage Note at SEASONABLE.

seasonal affective disorder n. a depressive state associated with late autumn and winter and thought to be caused by a lack of light.

seasoning n. condiments added to food.

season ticket n. a ticket entitling the holder to any number of journeys, admittances, etc., in a given period.

sea squirt n. any marine tunicate of the class Ascidiacea, having a bag-like body with orifices through which water flows into and out of a central pharynx.

seat ● n. **1** a thing made or used for sitting on; a chair, stool, saddle, etc. **2** the buttocks. **3** the part of the trousers etc. covering the buttocks. **4** the part of a chair etc. on which the sitter's weight directly rests. **5** the part of a thing on which it rests; the base. **6** a place for one person in a theatre etc. **7** esp. *Brit.* **a** the right to occupy a seat, esp. as a Member of the House of Commons. **b** a member's constituency. **8** the part of a machine that supports or guides another part. **9** a site or location of something specified (*a seat of learning*; *the seat of the emotions*). **10** a country mansion, esp. with large grounds. **11** the manner of sitting on a horse etc. ● v.tr. **1** cause to sit. **2 a** provide sitting accommodation for (*the cinema seats 500*). **b** provide with seats. **3** (as **seated** adj.) sitting **4** put or fit in position. □ **be seated** sit down. **by the seat of one's pants** *colloq.* by instinct rather than logic or knowledge. **take a** (or **one's**) **seat** sit down. [from Old Norse *sæti*] □ **seatless** adj.

seat belt n. a belt securing a person in the seat of a motor vehicle or aircraft.

seating n. **1** seats collectively. **2** sitting accommodation.

sea trout n. **1** a large silvery fish of a migratory race of the trout, *Salmo trutta*. **2** *US* an unrelated marine fish of the genus *Cynoscion*.

sea urchin n. ▶ a small marine echinoderm of the class Echinoidea, with a spherical or flattened spiny shell.

poisonous spines

SEA URCHIN
(*Sterechinus neumayer*)

sea wall n. a wall or embankment erected to prevent encroachment by the sea.

seaward ● adv. (also **seawards**) towards the sea. ● adj. going or facing towards the sea. ● n. such a direction or position.

sea wasp n. an Indo-Pacific jellyfish of the order Cubomedusae, with a dangerous sting.

sea water n. water in or taken from the sea.

seaway n. **1** an inland waterway open to seagoing ships. **2** a ship's progress. **3** a ship's path across the sea.

seaweed n. ▼ any large alga growing in the sea or on rocks below the high water mark; such plants collectively.

seaworthy adj. (esp. of a ship) fit to put to sea. □ **seaworthiness** n.

sebaceous adj. fatty; secreting oily matter. [from Latin *sebaceus*]

sebaceous gland n. (also **sebaceous follicle** or **sebaceous duct**) a gland etc. secreting or conveying oily matter to lubricate the skin and hair. ▷ SKIN

sebum n. the oily secretion of the sebaceous glands. ▷ FOLLICLE. [Latin, literally 'grease']

Sec. abbr. secretary.

sec[1] abbr. secant.

sec[2] n. *colloq.* (in phrs.) a second (of time).

sec[3] adj. (of wine) dry. [French, from Latin *siccus*]

sec. abbr. second(s).

secant *Math.* ● adj. cutting (*secant line*). ● n. **1** a line cutting a curve at one or more points. **2** the ratio of the hypotenuse to the shorter side adjacent to an acute angle (in a right-angled triangle). [from Latin *secant-* 'cutting']

secateurs /sek-ă-**terz**/ n.pl. esp. *Brit.* a pair of pruning clippers for use with one hand. [from French *sécateur* 'cutter']

secede v.intr. (usu. foll. by *from*) withdraw formally from membership of a political federation or a religious body. [from Latin *secedere*] □ **seceder** n.

secession n. the act or an instance of seceding. [from Latin *secessio*] □ **secessional** adj. **secessionism** n. **secessionist** n.

seclude v.tr. (also *refl.*) **1** keep (a person or place) retired or away from company. **2** (esp. as **secluded** adj.) hide or screen from view. [from Latin *secludere*]

seclusion n. **1** a secluded state; retirement, privacy. **2** a secluded place. [from medieval Latin *seclusio*] □ **seclusionist** n. **seclusive** adj.

second[1] /**sek**-ŏnd/ ● n. **1** the position in a sequence corresponding to that of the number 2 in the sequence 1–2. **2** something occupying this position. **3** the second person etc. in a race or competition. **4** = SECOND GEAR. **5** an additional person or thing (*the policeman was joined by a second*). **6** (in *pl.*) goods of a second or inferior quality. **7** (in *pl.*) *colloq.* **a** a second helping of food at a meal. **b** the second course of a meal. **8** an attendant assisting a combatant in a duel etc. **9** esp. *Brit.* **a** a place in the second class of an examination. **b** a person having this. ● adj. **1** that is the second; next after first. **2** additional, further (*ate a second cake*). **3** subordinate; inferior. **4** *Mus.* performing a lower or subordinate part (*second violins*). **5** such as to be comparable to (*a second*

S

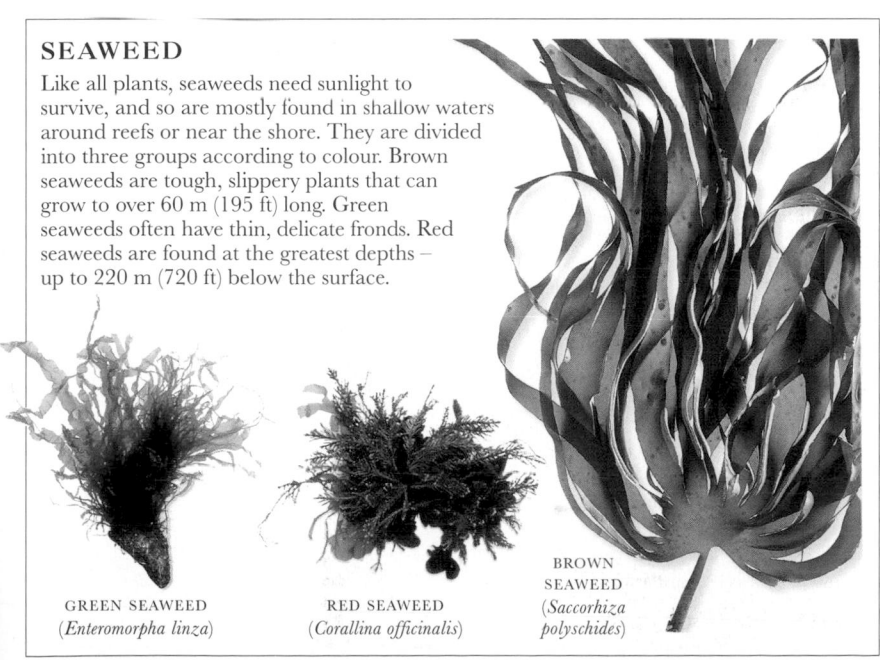

GREEN SEAWEED
(*Enteromorpha linza*)

RED SEAWEED
(*Corallina officinalis*)

BROWN SEAWEED
(*Saccorhiza polyschides*)

Callas). ● *v.tr.* **1** supplement, support; back up. **2** formally support or endorse (a nomination or resolution etc., or its proposer). □ **at second hand** by hearsay, not direct observation etc. **in the second place** as a second consideration etc. **second to none** surpassed by no other. [from Latin *secundus*] □ **seconder** *n.* (esp. in sense 2 of *v.*).

second[2] /sek-ŏnd/ *n.* **1** a sixtieth of a minute of time. **2** *colloq.* a very short time (*wait a second*). **3** a sixtieth of a minute of angular distance. [from medieval Latin *secunda (minuta)* 'secondary (minute)', result of redividing by sixty]

second[3] /si-kond/ *v.tr. Brit.* transfer (a military officer or other official or worker) temporarily to other employment or to another position. [from French *en second* 'in the second rank'] □ **secondee** *n.* **secondment** *n.*

secondary ● *adj.* **1** coming after or next below what is primary. **2** derived from or depending on or supplementing what is primary. **3** (of education, a school, etc.) for those who have had primary education, usu. from 11 to 18 years. ● *n.* (*pl.* **-ies**) a secondary thing. □ **secondarily** *adv.* **secondariness** *n.*

secondary colour *n.* ◄ a colour resulting from the mixing of two primary colours. ▷ COLOUR

secondary feather *n.* a feather growing from the second joint of a bird's wing.

secondary picketing *n. Brit.* the picketing of premises of a firm not otherwise involved in the dispute in question.

secondary sexual characteristics *n.pl.* physical characteristics developed at puberty.

SECONDARY COLOURS FORMED BY OVERLAPPING PRIMARY PIGMENTS

second-best ● *adj.* next after best. ● *n.* a less adequate or desirable alternative.

second chamber *n.* the upper house of a bicameral parliament.

second-class ● *adj.* **1** of or belonging to or travelling by the second class. **2** inferior in quality, status, etc. ● *adv.* by second class (*travelled second-class*).

second class *n.* **1** a set of persons or things grouped together as second-best. **2** the second-best accommodation in a train etc. **3 a** (in the UK) the class of mail not given priority in handling. **b** (in N. America) a class of mail for the handling of newspapers and periodicals. **4 a** the second highest division in a list of examination results. **b** a place in this.

second coming *n. Theol.* the future return of Christ to Earth.

second cousin see COUSIN.

second-degree *adj. Med.* denoting burns that cause blistering but not permanent scars.

second fiddle see *play second fiddle* (FIDDLE).

second floor *n.* **1** *Brit.* the floor two levels above the ground floor. **2** *N. Amer.* the floor above the ground floor.

second gear *n.* the second (and next to lowest) in a sequence of gears.

second-generation *adj.* denoting the offspring of a first generation, esp. of immigrants.

second-guess *v.tr. colloq.* **1** anticipate or predict by guesswork. **2** judge or criticize with hindsight.

second-hand ● *adj.* **1 a** (of goods) having had a previous owner; not new. **b** (of a shop etc.) where such goods can be bought. **2** (of information etc.) accepted on another's authority and not from original investigation. ● *adv.* **1** on a second-hand basis. **2** at second hand; not directly.

second hand *n.* an extra hand in some watches and clocks, recording seconds. ▷ WATCH

second in command *n.* the officer next in rank to the commanding or chief officer.

second lieutenant *n.* an army officer next below lieutenant or *US* first lieutenant.

secondly *adv.* **1** furthermore; in the second place. **2** as a second item.

second name *n. Brit.* a surname.

second nature *n.* (often foll. by *to*) an acquired tendency that has become instinctive (*is second nature to him*).

second officer *n.* an assistant mate on a merchant ship.

second-rate *adj.* of mediocre quality; inferior.

second sight *n.* the supposed power of being able to perceive future or distant events.

second string *n.* **1** an alternative course of action etc. **2** *US* a reserve, esp. for a sports team.

second thoughts *n.pl.* a new opinion or resolution reached after further consideration.

second wind *n.* **1** recovery of the power of normal breathing during exercise after initial breathlessness. **2** renewed energy to continue an effort.

secrecy *n.* **1** the keeping of secrets as a fact, habit, or faculty. **2** a state in which all information is withheld (*done in secrecy*). □ **sworn to secrecy** having promised to keep a secret. [Middle English]

secret ● *adj.* **1** kept or meant to be kept private, unknown, or hidden. **2** acting or operating secretly. **3** fond of, prone to, or able to preserve secrecy. **4** (of a place) completely secluded. ● *n.* **1** a thing kept or meant to be kept secret. **2** a thing known only to a few. **3** a mystery. **4** a valid but not commonly known method (*what's their secret?*). □ **in secret** secretly. **in** (or **in on**) **the secret** among the number of those who know the secret. **keep a secret** not reveal information given in confidence. [from Latin *secretus* 'separate, set apart'] □ **secretly** *adv.*

secret agent *n.* a spy acting for a country.

secretaire *n.* an escritoire. [from French]

secretariat *n.* **1** a permanent administrative office or department, esp. a governmental one. **2** its members or premises. [from medieval Latin *secretariatus*]

secretary *n.* (*pl.* **-ies**) **1** an employee who assists with correspondence, keeps records, makes appointments, etc. **2** an official appointed by a society etc. to conduct its correspondence, organize its affairs, etc. **3** (in some organizations) the chief executive. **4** (in the UK) the principal assistant of a government minister, ambassador, etc. [earlier in sense 'a person entrusted with a secret': from Late Latin *secretarius*] □ **secretarial** *adj.* **secretaryship** *n.*

secretary bird *n.* ► a long-legged snake-eating African bird, *Sagittarius serpentarius*, with a crest likened to a quill pen stuck over a writer's ear.

Secretary-General *n.* (*pl.* **Secretary-Generals**) the principal administrator of an organization.

Secretary of State *n.* **1** (in the UK) the head of a major government department. **2** (in the US) the chief government official responsible for foreign affairs.

secret ballot *n.* a ballot in which votes are cast in secret.

secrete[1] *v.tr. Biol.* (of a cell, organ, etc.) produce by secretion. [back-formation from SECRETION] □ **secretor** *n.* **secretory** *adj.*

secrete[2] *v.tr.* conceal; put into hiding. [from obsolete verb *secret*]

secretion *n.* **1** *Biol.* **a** a process by which substances are produced and

SECRETARY BIRD
(*Sagittarius serpentarius*)

discharged from a cell, gland, or organ for a function in the organism or for excretion. **b** the secreted substance. **2** the act or an instance of concealing. [from Latin *secretio* 'separation']

secretive /see-krĕt-iv/ *adj.* inclined to make or keep secrets; uncommunicative. □ **secretively** *adv.* **secretiveness** *n.*

secret police *n.* a police force operating in secret for political purposes.

secret service *n.* **1** a government department concerned with espionage. **2** (**Secret Service**) (in the US) a branch of the Treasury Department dealing with counterfeiting and providing protection for the President etc.

secret society *n.* a society whose members are sworn to secrecy about it.

sect *n.* **1 a** a body of people subscribing to religious doctrines different from those of others within the same religion. **b** a religious denomination. **2** the followers of a particular philosopher or philosophy, or school of thought in politics etc. [from Latin *secta*]

sectarian ● *adj.* **1** of or concerning a sect. **2** bigoted or narrow-minded in following the doctrines of one's sect. ● *n.* **1** a member of a sect. **2** a bigot. □ **sectarianism** *n.* **sectarianize** *v.tr.* (also **-ise**).

section ● *n.* **1** a part cut off or separated from something. **2** each of the parts into which a thing is divided or divisible or out of which a structure can be fitted together. **3** a distinct group or subdivision of a larger body of people (*the wind section*). **4** a subdivision of a book, document, etc. **5** a *N. Amer.* one square mile of land. **b** *US* a particular district of a town (*residential section*). **6** a subdivision of an army platoon. **7** esp. *Surgery* a separation by cutting. **8** *Biol.* ▲ a thin slice of tissue etc., cut off for microscopic examination. **9 a** the cutting of a solid by or along a plane. **b** the resulting figure or the area of this. ● *v.tr.* **1** arrange in or divide into sections. **2** (esp. as **sectioned** *adj.*) *Brit.* compulsorily commit to a psychiatric hospital. **3** *Biol.* cut into thin slices for microscopic examination. [French]

SECTION: MICROGRAPH OF A ROOT SECTION

sectional *adj.* **1 a** relating to a section, esp. of a community. **b** partisan. **2** made in sections. **3** local rather than general. □ **sectionalism** *n.* **sectionalist** *n. & adj.* **sectionalize** *v.tr.* (also **-ise**). **sectionally** *adv.*

section-mark *n.* the sign (§) used as a reference mark to indicate the start of a section of a book etc.

sector *n.* **1** a distinct part or branch of an enterprise, or of society, the economy, etc. **2** a military subdivision of an area. **3** the plane figure enclosed by two radii of a circle, ellipse, etc., and the arc between them. ▷ CIRCLE [later technical use of Latin *sector* 'cutter'] □ **sectoral** *adj.*

secular ● *adj.* **1** concerned with the affairs of this world; not spiritual or sacred. **2** (of education etc.) not concerned with religion or religious belief. **3 a** not ecclesiastical or monastic. **b** (of clergy) not bound by a religious rule. **4** occurring once in an age or century. ● *n.* a secular priest. [from Latin *saecularis*] □ **secularism** *n.* **secularist** *n.*

S

secularity n. **secularize** v.tr. (also **-ise**). **secularization** n. **secularly** adv.

secure ● adj. **1** untroubled by danger or fear. **2** safe against attack. **3** certain not to fail (*the plan is secure*). **4** fixed or fastened so as not to give way or get loose or be lost (*made the door secure*). **5 a** (foll. by *of*) certain to achieve (*secure of victory*). **b** (foll. by *against, from*) protected (*secure against attack*). **6** (of a prison etc.) difficult to escape from. ● v.tr. **1** make secure or safe; fortify. **2** fasten, close, or confine securely. **3** succeed in obtaining (*secured front seats*). **4** guarantee against loss (*a loan secured by property*). [from Latin *securus*] □ **securable** adj. **securely** adv. **securement** n.

securitize v.tr. (also **-ise**) (often in *passive*) convert (an asset) into securities, usu. in order to raise cash. □ **securitization** n.

security n. (pl. **-ies**) **1** a secure condition or feeling. **2** a thing that guards or guarantees. **3 a** safety against espionage, theft, etc. **b** an organization for ensuring this. **4** a thing deposited or pledged as a guarantee of an undertaking or loan, to be forfeited in case of default. **5** (often in *pl.*) a certificate attesting credit or the ownership of stock, bonds, etc. □ **on security of** using as a guarantee. [from Latin *securitas*]

security blanket n. **1** *Brit.* an official sanction on information in the interest of security. **2** a blanket etc. given as a comfort to a child.

Security Council n. a permanent body of the United Nations seeking to maintain peace and security.

security guard n. a person employed to protect the security of buildings, vehicles, etc.

security risk n. a person, situation, etc. posing a possible threat to security.

sedan n. **1** (in full **sedan chair**) *hist.* an enclosed chair for conveying one person, carried between horizontal poles by two porters. **2** *N. Amer.* an enclosed motor car for four or more people.

sedate[1] adj. tranquil and dignified; equable, serious. [from Latin *sedatus* 'settled'] □ **sedately** adv. **sedateness** n.

sedate[2] v.tr. put under sedation. [back-formation from SEDATION]

sedation n. a state of rest or sleep esp. produced by a sedative drug. [from Latin *sedatio*]

sedative /sed-ă-tiv/ ● n. a drug, influence, etc., that tends to calm or soothe. ● adj. calming, soothing; inducing sleep.

sedentary adj. **1** sitting (*a sedentary posture*). **2** (of work etc.) characterized by much sitting and little physical exercise. **3** (of a person) spending much time seated. [based on Latin *sedēre* 'to sit'] □ **sedentarily** adv. **sedentariness** n.

sedge n. **1** ◄ any grasslike plant of the genus *Carex* with triangular stems, usu. growing in wet areas. **2** an expanse of this plant. [Old English] □ **sedgy** adj.

sediment ● n. **1** matter that settles to the bottom of a liquid; dregs. **2** *Geol.* ▶ matter that is carried by water or wind and deposited on the surface of the land or the seabed. ▷ ROCK CYCLE. ● v.tr. (as **sedimented** adj.) **1 a** *Geol.* deposited as sediment. **b** deep-rooted (*sedimented radicalism*). **2** (of beer) having a sediment. [from Latin *sedimentum*] □ **sedimentary** adj. **sedimentation** n.

sedition n. **1** conduct or speech inciting to rebellion. **2** agitation against the authority of a state. [from Latin *seditio*] □ **seditious** adj. **seditiously** adv.

seduce v.tr. **1** tempt or entice into sexual activity. **2 a** tempt, lure (*seduced by the smell of coffee*). **b** (often foll. by *into*) lead astray (*seduced into a life of crime*). **c** (often as **seduced** adj.) beguiled (*seduced by outward appearances*). [from Latin *seducere*] **seducer** n. **seducible** adj.

SEDGE: GREAT POND SEDGE (*Carex riparia*)

seduction n. **1** the act or an instance of seducing; the process of being seduced. **2** something that tempts or allures. [from Latin *seductio*]

seductive adj. tending to seduce; alluring, enticing. □ **seductively** adv. **seductiveness** n.

seductress n. a female seducer. [from obsolete *seductor* 'male seducer']

sedulous adj. **1** persevering, diligent, assiduous. **2** (of an action etc.) deliberately and consciously continued. [from Latin *sedulus* 'zealous'] □ **sedulity** n. **sedulously** adv. **sedulousness** n.

sedum n. any plant of the genus *Sedum*, with fleshy leaves and star-shaped yellow, pink, or white flowers. [Latin, literally 'houseleek']

see[1] v. (past **saw**; past part. **seen**) **1** tr. discern by use of the eyes; observe; look at. **2** intr. have or use the power of discerning objects with the eyes (*sees best at night*). **3** tr. discern mentally; understand (*I see what you mean*). **4** tr. watch; be a spectator of (a film, game, etc.). **5** tr. ascertain or establish by inquiry or research or reflection (*see if the door opens*). **6** tr. consider; deduce from observation (*I see you are brave*). **7** tr. contemplate; foresee mentally (*we saw that no good would come of it*). **8** tr. look at for information (usu. in *imper.*: *see page 15*). **9** tr. meet or be near and recognize (*I saw your mother in town*). **10** tr. **a** meet socially (*sees her sister most weeks*). **b** meet regularly as a boyfriend or girlfriend (*is still seeing that man*). **11** tr. give an interview to (*the doctor will see you now*). **12** tr. visit to consult (*went to see the doctor*). **13** tr. find out, esp. from a visual source (*I see the match has been cancelled*). **14** intr. reflect; wait until one knows more (*we shall have to see*). **15** tr. interpret (*I see things differently now*). **16** tr. experience (*I never thought I would see this day*). **17** tr. recognize as acceptable; foresee (*do you see your daughter marrying this man?*). **18** tr. observe without interfering (*stood by and saw them squander my money*). **19** tr. find attractive (*can't think what she sees in him*). **20** intr. (usu. foll. by *to*, or *that* + infin.) ensure; attend to (*shall see to your request*) (cf. *see to it*). **21** tr. escort or conduct (to a place etc.) (*saw them home*). **22** tr. be a witness of (an event etc.) (*see the New Year in*). **23** tr. supervise (an action etc.) (*will stay and see the doors locked*). **24** tr. **a** (in gambling, esp. poker) equal (a bet). **b** equal the bet of (a player), esp. to see the player's cards. □ **as far as I can see** to the best of my understanding or belief. **as I see it** in my opinion. **do you see?** do you understand? **has seen better days** has declined from former prosperity, good condition, etc. **I see** I understand (referring to an explanation etc.). **let me see** an appeal for time to think before speaking etc. **see about** attend to. **see after 1** take care of. **2** = *see about*. **see the back of** *Brit. colloq.* be rid of (an unwanted person or thing). **see a person damned first** *Brit. colloq.* refuse categorically and with hostility to do what a person wants. **see eye to eye** see EYE. **see fit** see FIT[1]. **see into** investigate. **see life** gain experience of the world, often by enjoying oneself. **see the light 1** realize one's mistakes etc. **2** suddenly see the way to proceed. **3** undergo religious conversion. **see the light of day** (usu. with *neg.*) come into existence. **see off 1** be present at the departure of (a person). **2** *Brit. colloq.* ward off, get the better of (*managed to see off the proposed investigation*). **see out 1** accompany out of a building etc. **2** *Brit.* finish (a project etc.) completely. **3** *Brit.* remain awake, alive, etc., until the end of (a period). **4** *Brit.* last longer than; outlive. **see over** inspect; tour and examine. **see reason** see REASON. **see red** become suddenly enraged. **see a person right** *Brit. colloq.* make sure that a person is rewarded, safe, etc. **see service** see SERVICE[1]. **see stars** *colloq.* see lights before one's eyes as a result of a blow on the head. **see things** have hallucinations or false imaginings. **see through 1** not be deceived by; detect the true nature of. **2** penetrate visually. **see a person through** support a person during a difficult time. **see a thing through** persist with it until it is completed. **see to it** (foll. by *that* + clause) ensure (*see to it that I am not disturbed*) (cf. sense 20 of *v.*). **see one's way clear to** feel able or entitled to. **see you** or **see you later**) *colloq.* an expression on parting. **we shall see 1** let us await the outcome. **2** a formula for declining to act at once. **will see about it** a formula for declining to act at once. **you see 1** you understand. **2** you will understand when I explain. [Old English] □ **seeable** adj

see[2] n. **1** the area under the authority of a bishop or archbishop, a diocese. **2** the office or jurisdiction of a bishop or archbishop. [from Latin *sedes* 'seat']

SEDIMENT

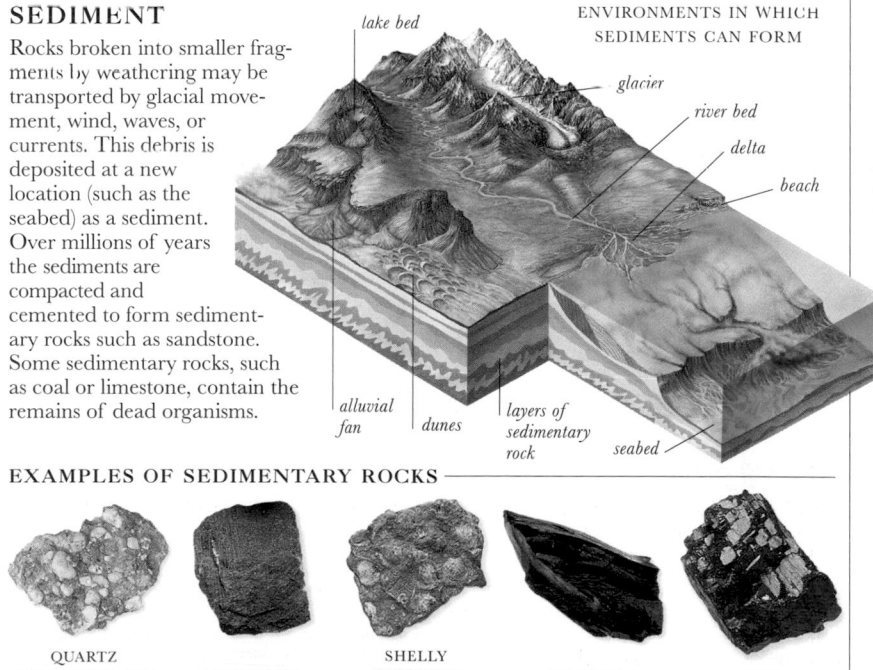

Rocks broken into smaller fragments by weathering may be transported by glacial movement, wind, waves, or currents. This debris is deposited at a new location (such as the seabed) as a sediment. Over millions of years the sediments are compacted and cemented to form sedimentary rocks such as sandstone. Some sedimentary rocks, such as coal or limestone, contain the remains of dead organisms.

ENVIRONMENTS IN WHICH SEDIMENTS CAN FORM

lake bed · glacier · river bed · delta · beach · alluvial fan · dunes · layers of sedimentary rock · seabed

EXAMPLES OF SEDIMENTARY ROCKS

QUARTZ CONGLOMERATE — SANDSTONE — SHELLY LIMESTONE — OIL-SHALE — COAL

S

SEED

A seed contains an embryonic plant together with a store of food, and is surrounded by a protective outer covering or testa. In cereal grains, the food is stored primarily in a tissue called the endosperm. In many other seeds, such as beans, it is held in fleshy seed leaves called cotyledons. In flowering plants, seeds develop inside fruits, which help the seeds to disperse. Conifer seeds form on the surface of cone scales.

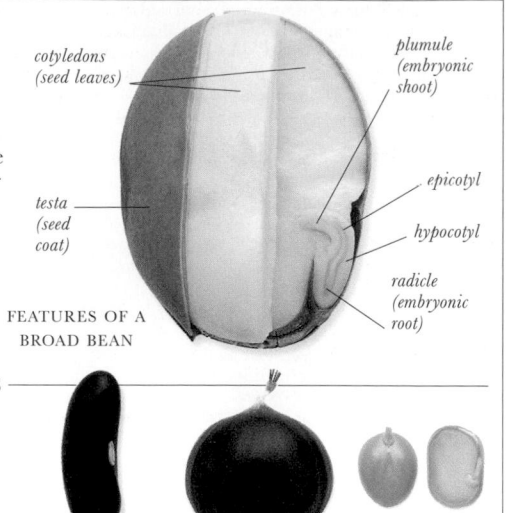

cotyledons (seed leaves)

plumule (embryonic shoot)

epicotyl

hypocotyl

testa (seed coat)

radicle (embryonic root)

FEATURES OF A BROAD BEAN

EXAMPLES OF OTHER SEEDS

CONIFER SEEDS   WHEAT GRAINS   BLACK BEAN   SWEET CHESTNUT   PEAS

APPLE SEEDS   POPPY SEEDS

LOVE-IN-A-MIST SEEDS (ENLARGED)

STRAWBERRY SEEDS (ENLARGED)

HONESTY SEEDS

seed ● *n.* **1 a** ▲ a unit of reproduction (esp. in the form of grain) formed by flowering plants and gymnosperms capable of developing into another such plant. **b** seeds collectively, esp. as collected for sowing (*kept for seed*). **2 a** semen. **b** milt. **3** (foll. by *of*) the beginning or initial germ of development (*seeds of doubt*). **4** *archaic* offspring, descendants (*the seed of Abraham*). **5** *Sport* a seeded player. ● *v.* **1** *tr.* **a** place seeds in. **b** sprinkle with or as with seed. **2** *intr.* sow seeds. **3** *intr.* produce or drop seed. **4** *tr.* remove seeds from (fruit etc.). **5** *tr.* place a crystal or crystalline substance in (a solution etc.) to cause crystallization or condensation. **6** *tr.* *Sport* **a** assign to a list position in a knockout competition so that strong competitors do not meet each other in early rounds. **b** arrange (the order of play) in this way. **7** *intr.* go to seed. □ **go** (or **run**) **to seed 1** cease flowering as seed develops. **2** become degenerate, unkempt, ineffective, etc. [Old English] □ **seedless** *adj.*

seedbed *n.* **1** a bed of fine soil in which to sow seeds. **2** a place of development.

seed cake *n.* cake containing whole seeds esp. of caraway as flavouring.

seedcorn *n.* **1** good-quality corn kept for seed. **2** *Brit.* assets reused for future profit or benefit.

seeder *n.* **1** a person or thing that seeds. **2** a machine for sowing seed, esp. a drill.

seed-head *n.* a flower head in seed.

seedling *n.* a young plant, esp. one raised from seed and not from a cutting etc. ▷ GERMINATE

seedpearl *n.* a very small pearl.

seed potato *n.* a potato kept for seed.

seedsman *n.* (*pl.* **-men**) a dealer in seeds.

seed-time *n.* the sowing season.

seed vessel *n.* a pericarp.

seedy *adj.* (**seedier**, **seediest**) **1** full of seed. **2** going to seed. **3** shabby-looking, in worn clothes. **4** *colloq.* unwell. □ **seedily** *adv.* **seediness** *n.*

seeing *conj.* (usu. foll. by *that* + clause) considering that, inasmuch as, because (*seeing that you do not know it yourself*).

seek *v.* (*past* and *past part.* **sought**) **1 a** *tr.* make a search or inquiry for. **b** *intr.* (foll. by *for*, *after*) make a search or inquiry. **2** *tr.* **a** try or want to find or get. **b** ask for; request (*seeks my aid*). **3** *tr.* (foll. by *to* + infin.) endeavour or try. **4** *tr.* make for or resort to (*sought his bed*; *sought a fortune-teller*). **5** *tr.* *archaic* aim at, attempt. □ **seek out 1** search for and find. **2** single out for companionship, etc. **to seek** (or **much to seek** or **far to seek**) esp. *Brit.* deficient, lacking, or not yet found (*the reason is not far to seek*). [Old English] □ **seeker** *n.* (also in *comb.*).

seem *v.intr.* **1** give the impression or sensation of being. **2** (foll. by *to* + infin.) appear or be perceived or ascertained (*they seem to have left*). □ **can't seem to** *colloq.* seem unable to. **do not seem to** *colloq.* somehow do not (*I do not seem to like him*). **it seems** (or **would seem**) (often foll. by *that* + clause) it appears to be true or the fact (in a hesitant, guarded, or ironical statement). [originally in sense 'to suit, befit': based on Old Norse *sæma* 'honour']

seeming[1] *adj.* **1** apparent but perhaps not real. **2** apparent only; ostensible (usu. in *comb.*: *seeming-virtuous*). □ **seemingly** *adv.*

seeming[2] *n.* *literary* **1** appearance, aspect. **2** deceptive appearance.

seemly *adj.* (**seemlier**, **seemliest**) conforming to propriety or good taste; decorous, suitable. [from Old Norse *sæmiligr*, related to SEEM] □ **seemliness** *n.*

seen *past part.* of SEE[1].

seep *v.intr.* ooze out; percolate slowly.

seepage *n.* **1** the act of seeping. **2** the quantity that seeps out.

seer *n.* **1** a person who sees. **2** a prophet; a person who sees visions; a person of supposed supernatural insight.

seersucker *n.* ► material of linen, cotton, etc., with a puckered surface. [from Persian *šir o šakar*, literally 'milk and sugar']

see-saw ● *n.* **1 a** a device consisting of a long plank balanced on a central support for children to sit on at each end and move up and down by pushing the ground with their feet. **b** a game played on this. **2** an up-and-down or to-and-fro motion. **3** a contest in which the advantage repeatedly changes from one side to the other. ● *v.intr.* **1** play on a see-saw. **2** move up and down as on a see-saw. **3** vacillate in policy, emotion, etc. ● *adj.* & *adv.* with up-and-down or backward-and-forward motion (*see-saw motion*). [reduplication of SAW[1]]

seethe *v.intr.* **1** boil, bubble over. **2** be very agitated, esp. with anger. [Old English] □ **seethingly** *adv.*

see-through *adj.* (esp. of clothing) translucent.

segment ● *n.* **1** each of several parts into which a thing is or can be divided or marked off. **2** *Geom.* a part of a figure cut off by a line or plane intersecting it. ▷ CIRCLE. **3** *Zool.* each of the series of similar anatomical units of which the body and limbs are composed in various animals. ● *v.intr.* & *tr.* divide into segments. [from Latin *segmentum*] □ **segmental** *adj.* **segmentally** *adv.* **segmentary** *adj.* **segmentation** *n.*

segregate *v.* **1** *tr.* put apart from the rest; isolate. **2** *tr.* enforce racial segregation on (persons) or in (a community etc.). **3** *intr.* separate from a mass and collect together. **4** *intr.* *Biol.* (of alleles) be transmitted independently of each other. [based on Latin *segregatus* 'separated from the flock']

segregation *n.* **1** enforced separation of racial groups in a community etc. **2** the act or an instance of segregating; the state of being segregated. □ **segregational** *adj.* **segregationist** *n.* & *adj.*

segue /seg-way/ esp. *Mus.* ● *v.intr.* (**segues**, **segued**, **segueing**) (usu. foll. by *into*) go on without a pause. ● *n.* an uninterrupted transition from one song or melody to another. [Italian, literally 'follows']

seigneur /sayn-yer/ *n.* (also **seignior** /sayn-yer/) a feudal lord; the lord of a manor. [from Old French] □ **seigneurial** *adj.* **seigniorial** *adj.*

seine /sayn/ ● *n.* (also **seine-net**) ▼ a fishing net for encircling fish, with floats at the top and weights at the bottom edge, and usu. hauled ashore. ● *v.intr.* & *tr.* fish or catch with a seine. [from Greek *sagēnē*] □ **seiner** *n.*

floats

SEINE: PURSE SEINE

weighted net

seise var. of SEIZE 9.

seismic /syz-mik/ *adj.* **1** of or relating to an earthquake or earthquakes or other vibrations of the Earth and its crust. ▷ EARTHQUAKE. **2** of enormous proportions or effect. [based on Greek *seismos* 'earthquake'] □ **seismal** *adj.* **seismical** *adj.* **seismically** *adv.*

seismicity /syz-mis-iti/ *n.* seismic activity; esp. the frequency of earthquakes per unit area in a region.

seismo- /syz-moh/ *comb. form* earthquake. [from Greek *seismos*]

seismogram /syz-mō-gram/ *n.* a record given by a seismograph. ▷ SEISMOGRAPH

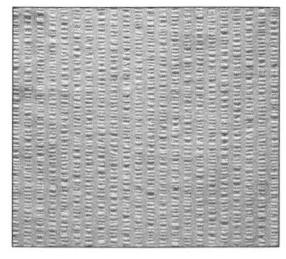

SEERSUCKER

S

seismograph /syz-mŏ-grahf/ *n.* ▼ an instrument that records the force, direction, etc., of earthquakes. □ **seismographic** *adj.* **seismographical** *adj.*

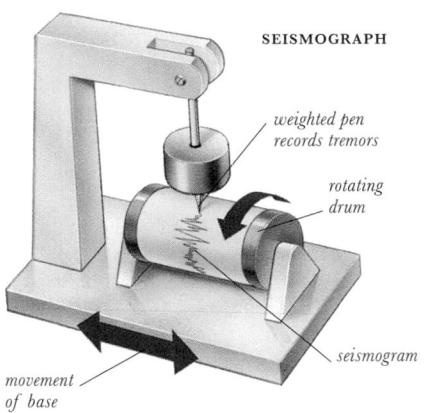

SEISMOGRAPH

weighted pen records tremors

rotating drum

seismogram

movement of base

seismology /syz-mol-ŏji/ *n.* the scientific study and recording of earthquakes and related phenomena. □ **seismological** *adj.* **seismologically** *adv.* **seismologist** *n.*

seize *v.* **1** *tr.* take hold of forcibly or suddenly. **2** *tr.* take possession of forcibly (*seized power*). **3** *tr.* take possession of by warrant or legal right. **4** *tr.* affect suddenly (*panic seized us*). **5** *tr.* take advantage of (an opportunity). **6** *tr.* comprehend quickly or clearly. **7** *intr.* (usu. foll. by *on, upon*) **a** take hold forcibly or suddenly. **b** take advantage eagerly (*seized on a pretext*). **8** *intr.* (usu. foll. by *up*) **a** (of a moving part in a machine) become jammed. **b** (of part of the body etc.) become stiff. **9** *tr.* (also **seise**) (usu. foll. by *of*) *Law* put in possession of. **10** *tr. Naut.* ▶ fasten or attach (two ropes) by binding with turns of yarn etc. □ **seized** (or **seised**) **of 1** possessing legally. **2** aware or informed of. [from Latin *sacire* 'to appropriate'] □ **seizable** *adj.* **seizer** *n.*

flat seizing

block

rope loop

SEIZE: NAUTICAL BLOCK HELD IN A SEIZED ROPE LOOP

seizure *n.* **1** the act or an instance of seizing; the state of being seized. **2** a sudden fit or attack of apoplexy etc., a stroke.

seldom ● *adv.* rarely, not often. ● *adj.* rare, uncommon. [Old English]

select ● *v.tr.* choose, esp. as the best or most suitable. ● *adj.* **1** chosen for excellence or suitability; choice. **2** (of a society etc.) exclusive, cautious in admitting members. [from Latin *selectus* 'selected'] □ **selectable** *adj.* **selectness** *n.*

selectee *n. US* a conscript.

selection *n.* **1** the act or an instance of selecting; the state of being selected. **2** a selected person or thing. **3** things from which a choice may be made. **4** *Biol.* the evolutionary process in which environmental and genetic influences determine which types of organism thrive better than others. □ **selectional** *adj.* **selectionally** *adv.*

selective *adj.* **1** using or characterized by selection. **2** (of the memory etc.) selecting what is convenient. □ **selectively** *adv.* **selectiveness** *n.* **selectivity** *n.*

selector *n.* **1** a person who selects, esp. a representative team in a sport. **2** a device that selects, esp. the required gear in a vehicle.

selenium *n. Chem.* a non-metallic element occurring naturally in various metallic sulphide ores. [based on Greek *selēnē* 'moon']

selenium cell *n.* a piece of selenium used as a photoelectric device.

self ● *n.* (*pl.* **selves**) **1** a person's or thing's own individuality or essence (*his true self*). **2** a person or thing as the object of introspection or reflexive action (*the consciousness of self*). **3 a** one's own interests or pleasure. **b** concentration on these. **4** *Commerce* or *colloq.*

myself, yourself, himself, etc. (*cheque drawn to self*). **5** used in phrs. equivalent to *myself, yourself, himself,* etc. (*your good selves*). ● *adj.* **1** of the same colour as the rest or throughout. **2** (of a flower) of the natural wild colour. **3** (of colour) uniform, the same throughout. ● *v.tr.* (usu. in *passive*) *Bot.* self-fertilize. □ **one's better self** one's nobler impulses. **one's former** (or **old**) **self** oneself as one formerly was. [Old English]

self- *comb. form* expressing reflexive action: **1** of or directed towards oneself or itself (*self-respect; self-cleaning*). **2** by oneself or itself, esp. without external agency (*self-evident*). **3** on, in, for, or relating to oneself or itself (*self-confident*).

self-abasement *n.* the abasement or humiliation of oneself; cringing.

self-abhorrence *n.* the abhorrence of oneself; self-hatred.

self-abnegation *n.* = SELF-DENIAL.

self-absorption *n.* absorption in oneself. □ **self-absorbed** *adj.*

self-abuse *n.* **1** the reviling or abuse of oneself. **2** masturbation.

self-accusation *n.* the accusing of oneself. □ **self-accusatory** *adj.*

self-acting *adj.* acting without external influence or control; automatic.

self-addressed *adj.* (of an envelope etc.) having one's own address on for return communication.

self-adhesive *adj.* (of an envelope, label, etc.) adhesive, esp. without being moistened.

self-adjusting *adj.* (of machinery etc.) adjusting itself. □ **self-adjustment** *n.*

self-advancement *n.* the advancement of oneself.

self-advertisement *n.* the advertising or promotion of oneself. □ **self-advertiser** *n.*

self-aggrandizement *n.* (also **-isement**) the act or process of trying to make oneself more powerful. □ **self-aggrandizing** *adj.*

self-analysis *n. Psychol.* the analysis of oneself, one's motives, character, etc.

self-appointed *adj.* designated so by oneself, not authorized by another (*a self-appointed guardian*).

self-assembly *n.* (often *attrib.*) the construction of furniture etc. from materials sold in kit form.

self-assertion *n.* the aggressive promotion of oneself, one's views, etc. □ **self-assertive** *adj.* **self-assertiveness** *n.*

self-assurance *n.* confidence in one's own abilities etc. □ **self-assured** *adj.* **self-assuredly** *adv.*

self-aware *adj.* conscious of one's character, feelings, motives, etc. □ **self-awareness** *n.*

self-betrayal *n.* **1** the betrayal of oneself. **2** the inadvertent revelation of one's true thoughts etc.

self-build *n.* (often *attrib.*) the building of homes by their future owners (*self-build cooperative*). □ **self-builder** *n.*

self-catering *Brit.* ● *adj.* (esp. of a holiday or holiday premises) providing rented accommodation with cooking facilities but without food. ● *n.* the activity of catering for oneself in rented temporary or holiday accommodation.

self-censorship *n.* the censoring of oneself.

self-centred *adj.* preoccupied with one's own personality or affairs; selfish. □ **self-centredly** *adv.* **self-centredness** *n.*

self-certify *v.tr. Brit.* **1** attest to in writing (a thing concerning oneself). **2** (as **self-certified** *adj.*) acquired as a result of such attestation (*self-certified loan*). □ **self-certification** *n.*

self-cleaning *adj.* (esp. of an oven) cleaning itself when heated etc.

self-closing *adj.* (of a door etc.) closing automatically.

self-cocking *adj.* (of a gun) with the hammer raised by the trigger, not by hand.

self-collected *adj.* composed, self-assured.

self-coloured *adj.* (*US* **self-colored**) **1 a** having the same colour throughout. **b** (of material) natural; undyed. **2 a** ▶ (of a flower) of uniform colour. **b** having its colour unchanged by cultivation or hybridization.

self-command *n.* = SELF-CONTROL.

self-conceit *n.* = SELF-SATISFACTION. □ **self-conceited** *adj.*

SELF-COLOURED DAHLIA

self-condemnation *n.* **1** the blaming of oneself. **2** the inadvertent revelation of one's own sin, crime, etc.

self-confessed *adj.* openly admitting oneself to be (*a self-confessed thief*).

self-confidence *n.* = SELF-ASSURANCE. □ **self-confident** *adj.* **self-confidently** *adv.*

self-congratulation *n.* = SELF-SATISFACTION. □ **self-congratulatory** *adj.*

self-conscious *adj.* **1** unduly aware of one's appearance or actions through embarrassment or shyness. **2** *Philos.* having knowledge of one's own existence; self-contemplating. □ **self-consciously** *adv.* **self-consciousness** *n.*

self-consistent *adj.* (of parts of the same whole etc.) consistent; not conflicting. □ **self-consistency** *n.*

self-constituted *adj.* (of a person, group, etc.) assuming a function without authorization or right.

self-contained *adj.* **1** (of a person) uncommunicative; independent. **2** *Brit.* (of accommodation) complete in itself. □ **self-containment** *n.*

self-contempt *n.* contempt for oneself. □ **self-contemptuous** *adj.*

self-contradiction *n.* internal inconsistency. □ **self-contradictory** *adj.*

self-control *n.* the power of controlling one's behaviour, emotions, etc. □ **self-controlled** *adj.*

self-correcting *adj.* correcting itself without external help.

self-created *adj.* created by oneself or itself. □ **self-creation** *n.*

self-critical *adj.* critical of oneself, one's abilities, etc. □ **self-criticism** *n.*

self-deception *n.* deceiving oneself esp. concerning one's true feelings etc. □ **self-deceit** *n.* **self-deceiver** *n.* **self-deceiving** *adj.* **self-deceptive** *adj.*

self-defeating *adj.* (of an attempt, action, etc.) doomed to failure because of internal inconsistencies etc.

self-defence *n.* **1** a defence of oneself, one's rights or position (*hit him in self-defence*). **2** an instance of aggression in such defence (*it was self-defence*). □ **the noble art of self-defence** boxing. □ **self-defensive** *adj.*

self-delusion *n.* the act or an instance of deluding oneself.

self-denial *n.* the denial of one's own interests, needs, etc.; self-sacrifice. □ **self-denying** *adj.*

self-deprecation *n.* the act of disparaging or belittling oneself. □ **self-deprecating** *adj.* **self-deprecatingly** *adv.* **self-deprecatory** *adj.*

■ **Usage** See Usage Note at DEPRECATE.

self-depreciation *n.* = SELF-DEPRECATION. □ **self-depreciatory** *adj.*

■ **Usage** See Usage Note at DEPRECATE.

self-destroying *adj.* destroying oneself or itself.

self-destruct orig. *N. Amer.* ● *v.intr.* (of a spacecraft, bomb, etc.) explode or disintegrate automatically, esp. when pre-set to do so. ● *attrib.adj.* enabling a thing to self-destruct (*a self-destruct device*).

self-destruction *n.* **1** the process or an act of destroying oneself or itself. **2** orig. *N. Amer.* the process or an act of self-destructing. □ **self-destructive** *adj.* **self-destructively** *adv.*

self-determination *n.* **1** a nation's right to determine its own allegiance, government, etc. **2** the ability to act with free will. □ **self-determined** *adj.* **self-determining** *adj.*

self-development *n.* the development of oneself, one's abilities, etc.

self-discipline *n.* the act of or ability to apply oneself; self-control. □ **self-disciplined** *adj.*

self-discovery *n.* the process of acquiring insight into one's character, desires, etc.

self-disgust *n.* disgust with oneself.

self-doubt *n.* lack of confidence in oneself.

self-drive *adj. Brit.* (of a hired vehicle) driven by the hirer.

self-educated *adj.* educated by oneself by reading etc., without formal instruction. □ **self-education** *n.*

self-effacing *adj.* retiring; modest. □ **self-effacement** *n.* **self-effacingly** *adv.*

self-employed *adj.* working as a freelance or owner of a business etc. □ **self-employment** *n.*

self-esteem *n.* a good opinion of oneself.

self-evident *adj.* obvious; without the need of evidence or further explanation. □ **self-evidence** *n.* **self-evidently** *adv.*

self-examination *n.* **1** the study of one's own conduct, reasons, etc. **2** the examining of one's body for signs of illness etc.

self-existent *adj.* existing without prior cause.

self-explanatory *adj.* not needing explanation.

self-expression *n.* the expression of one's feelings, thoughts, etc. □ **self-expressive** *adj.*

self-fertile *adj.* (of a plant etc.) self-fertilizing. □ **self-fertility** *n.*

self-fertilization *n.* the fertilization of plants and some invertebrate animals by their own pollen or sperm. □ **self-fertilized** *adj.* **self-fertilizing** *adj.*

self-financing *adj.* that finances itself, esp. (of a project or undertaking) that pays for its own implementation or continuation. □ **self-financed** *adj.*

self-flagellation *n.* **1** the flagellation of oneself, esp. as a form of religious discipline. **2** excessive self-criticism.

self-forgetful *adj.* unselfish. □ **self-forgetfulness** *n.*

self-fulfilling *adj.* (of a prophecy, forecast, etc.) bound to come true as a result of its being made.

self-fulfilment *n.* (*US* -**fulfillment**) the fulfilment of one's own hopes and ambitions.

self-generating *adj.* generated by itself or oneself.

self-glorification *n.* the proclamation of oneself, one's abilities, etc.; boasting.

self-governing *adj.* **1** (of a British hospital or school) having opted out of local authority control. **2** (esp. of a former colony etc.) administering its own affairs.

self-government *n.* **1** (esp. of a former colony etc.) government by its own people. **2** = SELF-CONTROL. □ **self-governed** *adj.*

self-hate *n.* = SELF-HATRED.

self-hatred *n.* hatred of oneself, esp. of one's actual self when contrasted with one's imagined self.

self-help *n.* (often *attrib.*) **1** the theory that individuals should provide for their own support and improvement in society. **2** the act or faculty of providing for or improving oneself (*self-help groups*).

selfhood *n.* personality; separate and conscious existence.

self-image *n.* one's own idea or picture of oneself, esp. in relation to others.

self-immolation *n.* the offering of oneself as a sacrifice.

self-importance *n.* a high opinion of oneself; pompousness. □ **self-important** *adj.* **self-importantly** *adv.*

self-imposed *adj.* (of a task or condition etc.) imposed on and by oneself (*self-imposed exile*).

self-improvement *n.* the improvement of one's own position or disposition by one's own efforts.

self-induced *adj.* induced by oneself or itself.

self-indulgent *adj.* **1** indulging oneself in pleasure, idleness, etc. **2** (of a work of art etc.) lacking economy and control. □ **self-indulgence** *n.* **self-indulgently** *adv.*

self-inflicted *adj.* inflicted by and on oneself.

self-interest *n.* one's personal interest or advantage. □ **self-interested** *adj.*

self-involved *adj.* wrapped up in oneself or one's own thoughts. □ **self-involvement** *n.*

selfish *adj.* **1** concerned chiefly with one's own profit or pleasure; actuated by self-interest. **2** (of a motive etc.) appealing to self-interest. □ **selfishly** *adv.* **selfishness** *n.*

self-justification *n.* the justification or excusing of oneself. □ **self-justifying** *adj.*

self-knowledge *n.* the understanding of oneself, one's motives, etc.

selfless *adj.* unselfish. □ **selflessly** *adv.* **selflessness** *n.*

self-loading *adj.* (esp. of a gun) loading itself. □ **self-loader** *n.*

self-locking *adj.* locking itself.

self-love *n.* **1** selfishness; self-indulgence. **2** *Philos.* regard for one's own well-being and happiness.

self-made *adj.* **1** successful or rich by one's own effort. **2** made by oneself.

self-mocking *adj.* mocking oneself or itself.

self-motivated *adj.* acting on one's own initiative. □ **self-motivation** *n.*

self-murder *n.* = SUICIDE 1a. □ **self-murderer** *n.*

self-mutilation *n.* the mutilation of oneself.

self-neglect *n.* neglect of oneself.

self-opinionated *adj.* **1** stubbornly adhering to one's own opinions. **2** arrogant. □ **self-opinion** *n.*

self-parody *n.* the act or an instance of parodying oneself. □ **self-parodying** *adj.*

self-perpetuating *adj.* perpetuating itself or oneself without external agency. □ **self-perpetuation** *n.*

self-pity *n.* extreme sorrow for one's own troubles etc. □ **self-pitying** *adj.* **self-pityingly** *adv.*

self-pollination *n.* the pollination of a flower by pollen from the same plant. □ **self-pollinated** *adj.* **self-pollinating** *adj.* **self-pollinator** *n.*

self-portrait *n.* ▶ a portrait or description of an artist, writer, etc., by himself or herself.

self-possessed *adj.* calm and composed. □ **self-possession** *n.*

self-preservation *n.* **1** the preservation of one's own life, safety, etc. **2** this as a basic instinct of human beings and animals.

self-proclaimed *adj.* proclaimed by oneself or itself to be such.

self-propagating *adj.* able to propagate itself.

self-propelled *adj.* (esp. of a motor vehicle etc.) propelled by its own power. □ **self-propelling** *adj.*

self-protection *n.* protecting oneself or itself. □ **self-protective** *adj.*

self-raising *adj. Brit.* (of flour) having a raising agent already added.

self-realization *n.* **1** the development of one's faculties, abilities, etc. **2** this as an ethical principle.

self-referential *adj.* characterized by or making reference to oneself or itself. □ **self-referentiality** *n.*

self-regard *n.* **1** a proper regard for oneself. **2 a** selfishness. **b** conceit. □ **self-regarding** *adj.*

self-regulating *adj.* regulating oneself or itself without intervention. □ **self-regulation** *n.* **self-regulatory** *adj.*

self-reliance *n.* reliance on one's own resources etc.; independence. □ **self-reliant** *adj.* **self-reliantly** *adv.*

self-renewal *n.* the act or process of renewing oneself or itself.

self-reproach *n.* reproach directed at oneself. □ **self-reproachful** *adj.*

self-respect *n.* respect for oneself. □ **self-respecting** *adj.*

self-restraint *n.* = SELF-CONTROL. □ **self-restrained** *adj.*

self-revealing *adj.* revealing one's character, motives, etc. □ **self-revelation** *n.*

self-righteous *adj.* excessively conscious of or insistent on one's rectitude, correctness, etc. □ **self-righteously** *adv.* **self-righteousness** *n.*

self-righting *adj.* (of a boat) righting itself when capsized.

self-rising *adj. US* = SELF-RAISING.

self-rule *n.* = SELF-GOVERNMENT 1.

self-sacrifice *n.* the negation of one's own interests, wishes, etc., in favour of those of others. □ **self-sacrificing** *adj.*

selfsame *attrib.adj.* (prec. by *the*) the very same (*the selfsame village*).

self-satisfaction *n.* excessive satisfaction with oneself; complacency. □ **self-satisfied** *adj.*

self-sealing *adj.* **1** (of a tyre, fuel tank, etc.) automatically able to seal small punctures. **2** (of an envelope) self-adhesive.

self-seed *v.intr.* (of a plant) propagate itself by seed. □ **self-seeder** *n.* **self-seeding** *adj.*

self-seeking ● *adj.* seeking one's own welfare before that of others. ● *n.* the activity of doing this. □ **self-seeker** *n.*

self-selection *n.* the act of selecting oneself or itself. □ **self-selecting** *adj.*

self-service ● *adj.* (often *attrib.*) **1** (of a shop, restaurant, garage, etc.) where customers serve themselves and pay at a checkout etc. **2** (of a machine) serving goods after the insertion of coins. ● *n. colloq.* a self-service store, garage, etc.

self-serving *adj. & n.* = SELF-SEEKING.

self-slaughter *n.* = SUICIDE *n.* 1a.

self-sown *adj.* grown from seed scattered naturally.

self-starter *n.* **1** an electric appliance for starting a motor vehicle engine without the use of a crank. **2** an ambitious person who needs no external motivation.

self-sterile *adj. Biol.* not self-fertilizing. □ **self-sterility** *n.*

self-styled *adj.* called so by oneself (*a self-styled artist*).

self-sufficient *adj.* **1 a** needing nothing; independent. **b** able to supply one's needs from one's own resources. **2** content with one's own opinion; arrogant. □ **self-sufficiency** *n.* **self-sufficiently** *adv.*

self-supporting *adj.* **1** capable of maintaining oneself

SELF-PORTRAIT BY
VINCENT VAN GOGH (1887)

S

SEMAPHORE

Semaphore may have originated from the ancient Greeks and Romans, who used flags to signal over short distances. The invention of the telescope around 1600 increased the range of semaphore systems, and until the early 1900s semaphore was widely used by the navy as a means of communication between ships. Even with today's sophisticated technology, ships sailing close to each other still occasionally use semaphore. The system can be used to express letters or numbers: the signals for the first nine letters of the alphabet double for the numbers one to nine ('J' is zero) when preceded by the 'numbers follow' signal. Messages can be sent at a rate of around 25 words per minute.

THE SEMAPHORE ALPHABET

or itself financially. **2** staying up or standing without external aid. □ **self-support** *n.*

self-sustaining *adj.* sustaining oneself or itself. □ **self-sustained** *adj.*

self-tapping *adj.* ◀ (of a screw) able to cut its own thread.

self-taught *adj.* educated or trained by oneself, not externally.

self-torture *n.* the inflicting of pain, esp. mental, on oneself.

self-understanding *n.* **1** the act or an instance of comprehending one's actions and reactions. **2** sympathetic tolerance or awareness of oneself.

self-willed *adj.* obstinately pursuing one's own wishes. □ **self-will** *n.*

self-winding *adj.* (of a watch etc.) having an automatic winding apparatus.

self-worth *n.* = SELF-ESTEEM.

non-tapered edge

SELF-TAPPING SCREW

sell ● *v.* (*past* and *past part.* **sold**) **1** *tr.* make over or dispose of in exchange for money. **2** *tr.* keep a stock of for sale (*do you sell candles?*). **3 a** *intr.* (of goods) be purchased (*these are selling well*). **b** *tr.* (of a publication or recording) attain sales of (a specified number of copies) (*the book has sold 10,000 copies*). **4** *intr.* (foll. by *at, for*) have a specified price (*sells at £5*). **5** *tr.* **a** betray for money or other reward (*sell one's country*). **b** offer dishonourably for money or other reward; make a matter of corrupt bargaining (*sell justice; sell one's honour*). **6** *tr.* **a** advertise or publish the merits of. **b** inspire with a desire to buy or acquire or agree to something. **7** *tr.* cause to be sold (*the author's name alone will sell many copies*). ● *n. colloq.* **1** a manner of selling (*soft sell*). **2** a deception or disappointment. □ **sell off** sell the remainder of (goods) at reduced prices. **sell oneself 1** promote one's own abilities. **2 a** offer one's services dishonourably for money or other reward. **b** be a prostitute. **sell out 1 a** sell all one's stock of a commodity (*the shop sold out of bread*). **b** be completely or all sold (*tickets are quickly selling out*). **c** (of a performance etc.) sell all its tickets (*the Christmas pantomime always sells out*). **d** (also *absol.*) dispose of the whole of (one's property, shares, etc.) by sale. **2 a** abandon one's principles, honourable aims, etc. for personal gain. **b** betray (a person etc.). **sell the pass** see PASS². **sell short** disparage, underestimate. **sell up** *Brit.* **1** sell one's business, house, etc. **2** sell the goods of (a debtor). **sold on** *colloq.* enthusiastic about. [Old English] □ **sellable** *adj.*

sell-by date *n. Brit.* the latest recommended date of sale.

seller *n.* **1** a person who sells. **2** a commodity that sells well or badly. □ **seller's** (or **sellers'**) **market** an economic position in which goods are scarce and expensive.

selling point *n.* an advantageous feature.

selling race *n.* a horse race after which the winning horse must be auctioned.

sell-off *n.* **1** the privatization of a state company by a sale of shares. **2** esp. *US Stock Exch.* a sale or disposal of bonds, shares, etc. **3** a sale, esp. to dispose of property.

Sellotape *Brit.* ● *n. propr.* adhesive usu. transparent cellulose or plastic tape. ● *v.tr.* (**sellotape**) fix with Sellotape. [based on alteration of CELLULOSE]

sell-out *n.* **1** a commercial success, esp. the selling of all tickets for a show. **2** a betrayal.

selvedge *n.* (also **selvage**) **1** an edging that prevents cloth from unravelling (either an edge along the warp or a specially woven edging). **2** a border of different material or finish intended to be removed or hidden. [Middle English]

selves *pl.* of SELF.

semantic *adj.* relating to meaning in language. [from Greek *sēmantikos* 'significant'] □ **semantically** *adv.*

semantics *n.pl.* (usu. treated as *sing.*) the branch of linguistics concerned with meaning. □ **semanticist** *n.*

semaphore ● *n.* **1** *Mil.* etc. ◀ a system of sending messages by holding the arms or two flags in certain positions according to an alphabetic code. **2** a signalling apparatus consisting of a post with a movable arm or arms, lanterns, etc. ▷ SIGNAL. ● *v.intr. & tr.* signal or send by semaphore. [from French *sémaphore*] □ **semaphoric** *adj.* **semaphorically** *adv.*

semblance *n.* **1** the outward or superficial appearance of something (*put on a semblance of anger*). **2** resemblance. [from Old French]

semeiology var. of SEMIOLOGY.

semeiotics var. of SEMIOTICS.

semen *n.* the reproductive fluid of male animals. [Latin, literally 'seed']

semester /si-mes-ter/ *n.* a half-year course or term in (esp. German and US) universities. [German]

semi *n.* (*pl.* **semis**) *colloq.* **1** *Brit.* a semi-detached house. **2** a semi-final. **3** *N. Amer. & Austral.* a semi-trailer.

semi- *prefix* **1** half (*semicircle*). **2** partly (*semi-official*; *semi-detached*). **3** almost (*a semi-smile*). **4** occurring or appearing twice in a specified period (*semi-annual*).

semiaquatic *adj.* **1** (of an animal) living partly on land and partly in water. **2** (of a plant) growing in very wet ground.

semi-automatic *adj.* **1** partially automatic. **2** (of a firearm) having a mechanism for continuous loading but not for continuous firing.

semi-autonomous *adj.* **1** partly self-governing. **2** acting to some degree independently or having the partial freedom to do so.

semi-basement *n.* a storey partly below ground level.

semibreve *n.* esp. *Brit. Mus.* the longest note now in common use, having the time value of two minims or four crotchets, and represented by a ring with no stem. ▷ NOTATION

semicircle *n.* **1** half of a circle or of its circumference. ▷ CIRCLE. **2** a set of objects ranged in, or an object forming, a semicircle.

semicircular *adj.* **1** forming or shaped like a semicircle. **2** arranged as or in a semicircle.

semicircular canal *n.* each of three fluid-filled channels in the ear giving information to the brain to help maintain balance. ▷ INNER EAR

semi-civilized *adj.* partially civilized.

semicolon *n.* a punctuation mark (;) of intermediate value between a comma and full stop.

semiconducting *adj.* having the properties of a semiconductor.

semiconductor *n.* a solid substance that is a non-conductor when pure or at a low temperature but has a conductivity between that of insulators and that of most metals when containing a suitable impurity or at a higher temperature.

semi-conscious *adj.* partially conscious.

semi-darkness *adj.* (esp. in phr. **in the semi-darkness**) partial darkness.

semi-detached ● *adj.* (of a house) joined to another on one side only. ● *n. Brit.* a semi-detached house.

S

semi-final *n.* a match or round immediately preceding the final. □ **semi-finalist** *n.*

semi-fluid *adj.* of a consistency between solid and liquid.

semi-independent *adj.* **1 a** partially independent of control or authority. **b** partially self-governing. **2** partially independent of financial support from public funds.

semi-invalid *n.* a partially disabled or somewhat infirm person.

semi-liquid *adj.* = SEMI-FLUID.

semi-literate *adj.* **1** unable to read or write with ease or fluency; poorly educated. **2** *derog.* having little interest in literature. **3** *derog.* (of a text) displaying a lack of literacy on the part of the author. □ **semi-literacy** *n.*

semi-lunar *adj.* shaped like a half-moon or crescent.

seminal *adj.* **1 a** of or relating to semen. **b** of or relating to the seeds of plants. **2 a** (of ideas etc.) providing the basis for future development. **b** (of a person, literary work, etc.) central to the understanding of a subject; influential. [from Latin *seminalis*] □ **seminally** *adv.*

seminal fluid *n.* semen.

seminar *n.* **1** a small class at a university etc. for discussion and research. **2** a short intensive course of study. **3** a conference of specialists. [German]

seminary *n.* (*pl.* **-ies**) **1** a training college for priests, rabbis, etc. **2** a place of education or development. [from Latin *seminarium* 'seedbed'] □ **seminarian** *n.* **seminarist** *n.*

semi-official *adj.* **1** partly official. **2** (of communications) made by an official with the stipulation that the source should not be revealed. □ **semi-officially** *adv.*

semiology *n.* (also **semeiology**) = SEMIOTICS. [based on Greek *sēmeion* 'sign'] □ **semiological** *adj.* **semiologist** *n.*

semi-opaque *adj.* partially transparent.

semiotics *n.* (also **semeiotics**) the study of signs and symbols in various fields, esp. language. [based on Greek *sēmeiōtikos* 'of signs'] □ **semiotic** *adj.* **semiotical** *adj.* **semiotically** *adv.* **semiotician** *n.*

semi-permanent *adj.* rather less than permanent.

semi-permeable *adj.* (of a membrane etc.) selectively permeable, esp. allowing passage of a solvent but not of certain solutes.

semi-precious *adj.* (of a gem) less valuable than a precious stone.

semi-pro *adj.* & *n.* (*pl.* **-os**) *US colloq.* = SEMI-PROFESSIONAL.

semi-professional ● *adj.* **1** receiving payment for an activity but not relying on it for a living. **2** involving semi-professionals. ● *n.* a semi-professional musician, sportsman, etc.

semiquaver *n.* esp. *Brit. Mus.* a note having the time value of half a quaver and represented by a large dot with a two-hooked stem. ▷ NOTATION

semi-retired *adj.* having partially retired from employment. □ **semi-retirement** *n.*

semi-skilled *adj.* (of work or a worker) having or needing some training but less than for a skilled worker.

semi-skimmed *adj.* (of milk) from which some cream has been skimmed.

semi-solid *adj.* viscous, semi-fluid.

semi-sweet *adj.* slightly sweetened.

Semite *n.* a member of any of the peoples supposed to be descended from Shem, son of Noah (Gen. 10:21 ff.), including esp. the Jews, Arabs, Assyrians, Babylonians, and Phoenicians. [based on Greek *Sēm* 'Shem'] □ **Semitism** *n.* **Semitize** *v.tr.* (also **-ise**). **Semitization** *n.*

Semitic *adj.* **1** of or relating to the Semites, esp. the Jews. **2** of or relating to the languages of the family including Hebrew and Arabic.

semitone *n. Mus.* the smallest interval used in classical European music; half a tone.

semi-trailer *n.* a trailer having wheels at the back but supported at the front by a towing vehicle.

semi-transparent *adj.* partially or imperfectly transparent.

semivowel *n.* **1** a sound intermediate between a vowel and a consonant (e.g. *w*, *y*). **2** a letter representing this. [after Latin *semivocalis*]

semolina *n.* **1** the hard grains left after the milling of flour, used in puddings etc. and in pasta. **2** a pudding etc. made of this. [based on Latin *simila* 'flour']

sempstress var. of SEAMSTRESS.

Semtex *n.* a very pliable, odourless plastic explosive.

SEN *abbr.* (in the UK) State Enrolled Nurse.

Sen. *abbr.* **1** Senior. **2** *US* **a** Senator. **b** Senate.

senate *n.* (often **Senate**) **1** a legislative body, esp. the smaller upper assembly in the US, France, and other countries, in states of the US, etc. **2** the governing body of a university or (in the US) of a college. **3** *Rom.Hist.* the State council of the republic and empire. [from Latin *senatus*]

senator *n.* **1** a member of a senate. **2** (in Scotland) a Lord of Session. □ **senatorial** *adj.* **senatorship** *n.*

send *v.* (*past* and *past part.* **sent**) **1** *tr.* order or cause to go or be conveyed (*send a message to headquarters*; *sent me a book*; *sends goods all over the world*). **b** propel; cause to move (*send a bullet*; *sent him flying*). **c** cause to become (*send into raptures*; *send to sleep*). **d** dismiss with or without force (*sent her away*; *sent him about his business*). **2** *intr.* send a message or letter (*he sent to warn me*). **3** *tr.* (of God, providence, etc.) grant or bestow or inflict; bring about; cause to be (*send rain*; *send a judgement*; *send her victorious!*). **4** *tr. slang* put into ecstasy. □ **send away for** send an order to a dealer for (goods). **send down** *Brit.* **1** rusticate or expel from a university. **2** sentence to imprisonment. **send for 1** summon. **2** order by post. **send in 1** cause to go in. **2** submit (an entry etc.) for a competition etc. **send off 1** get (a letter, parcel, etc.) dispatched. **2** attend the departure of (a person) as a sign of respect etc. **3** *Sport* (of a referee) order (a player) to leave the field. **send off for** = *send away for*. **send on** transmit to a further destination or in advance of one's own arrival. **send a person to Coventry** see COVENTRY. **send up 1** cause to go up. **2** transmit to a higher authority. **3** *colloq.* satirize or ridicule, esp. by mimicking. **4** *US* sentence to imprisonment. **send word** send information. [Old English] □ **sender** *n.*

send-off *n.* a demonstration of goodwill etc. at the departure of a person, the start of a project, etc.

send-up *n. colloq.* a satire or parody.

senesce *v.intr.* grow old. [from Latin *senescere*] □ **senescence** *n.* **senescent** *adj.*

seneschal *n. hist.* the steward or major-domo of a medieval great house. [from medieval Latin *seniscalus*]

senhor /sen-**yor**/ *n.* a title used of or to a Portuguese or Brazilian man. [Portuguese]

senhora /sen-**yor**-ă/ *n.* a title used of or to a Portuguese woman or a Brazilian married woman. [Portuguese]

senhorita /sen-yŏ-**ree**-tă/ *n.* a title used of or to a young Brazilian esp. unmarried woman. [Portuguese]

senile *adj.* **1** of or characteristic of old age (*senile apathy*; *senile decay*). **2** having the weaknesses or diseases of old age. [from Latin *senilis*] □ **senility** *n.*

senile dementia *n.* a severe form of mental deterioration in old age, characterized by loss of memory and control of bodily functions.

senior ● *adj.* **1** more or most advanced in age or standing. **2** of high or highest position. **3** (placed after a person's name) senior to another of the same name. **4** *Brit.* (of a school) having pupils in an older age range. **5** *US* of the final year at a university, high school, etc. ● *n.* **1** a person of advanced age or comparatively long service etc. **2** one's elder, or one's superior in length of service, membership,

etc. (*is my senior*). **3** a senior student. [Latin, literally 'older, older man'] □ **seniority** *n.*

senior aircraftman *n.* (*fem.* **senior aircraftwoman**) the rank above leading aircraftman in the RAF.

senior citizen *n.* an old-age pensioner.

senior high school *n. N. Amer.* a secondary school comprising usu. the three highest grades.

senior management *n.* **1** the highest level of management in an organization, immediately below the board of directors. **2** the managers at this level.

senior nursing officer *n. Brit.* the person in charge of nursing services in a hospital.

senior officer *n.* an officer to whom a junior is responsible.

senior partner *n.* the head of a firm.

senior registrar *n.* a hospital doctor undergoing specialist training, one grade below that of consultant.

senior service *n. Brit.* the Royal Navy as opposed to the Army.

senna *n.* **1** ▶ a cassia tree. **2** a laxative prepared from the dried pods of this. [from Arabic *sanā*]

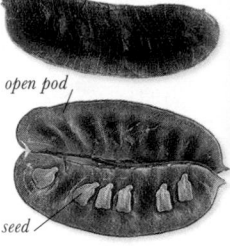
closed pod
open pod
seed
SENNA: DRIED PODS OF THE CASSIA TREE (*Cassia senna*)

señor /sen-**yor**/ *n.* (*pl.* **señores** /-ez/) a title used of or to a Spanish-speaking man. [Spanish]

señora /sen-**yor**-ă/ *n.* a title used of or to a Spanish-speaking married woman. [Spanish]

señorita /sen-yŏ-**ree**-tă/ *n.* a title used of or to a young Spanish-speaking esp. unmarried woman. [Spanish]

sensation *n.* **1** the consciousness of perceiving or seeming to perceive some state or condition of one's body or its parts or of the senses; an instance of such consciousness (*lost all sensation in my left arm*; *the sensation of falling*; *a burning sensation in his leg*). **2** an awareness or impression (*created the sensation of time passing*; *a sensation of being watched*). **3 a** a stirring of emotions or intense interest esp. among a large group of people (*the news caused a sensation*). **b** a person, event, etc., causing such interest. [from medieval Latin *sensatio*]

sensational *adj.* **1** causing or intended to cause great public excitement etc. **2** of or causing sensation. □ **sensationalize** *v.tr.* (also **-ise**). **sensationally** *adv.*

sensationalism *n.* the use of or interest in the sensational. □ **sensationalist** *n.* & *adj.* **sensationalistic** *adj.*

sense ● *n.* **1 a** any of the special bodily faculties by which sensation is roused (*has keen senses*; *has a dull sense of smell*). **b** sensitiveness of all or any of these. **2** the ability to perceive or feel. **3** (foll. by *of*) consciousness (*sense of having done well*; *sense of one's own importance*). **4 a** quick or accurate appreciation, understanding, or instinct regarding a specified matter (*sense of the ridiculous*; *road sense*; *the moral sense*). **b** the habit of basing one's conduct on such instinct. **5** practical wisdom or judgement; common sense; conformity to these (*has plenty of sense*; *what is the sense of talking like that?*; *has more sense than to do that*). **6 a** a meaning; the way in which a word etc. is to be understood (*the sense of the word is clear*; *I mean that in the literal sense*). **b** intelligibility or coherence. **7** the prevailing opinion among a number of people (*take the sense of the meeting*). **8** (in *pl.*) a person's sanity or normal state of mind. ● *v.tr.* **1** perceive by a sense or senses. **2** be vaguely aware of. **3** realize. **4** (of a machine etc.) detect. **5** *US* understand. □ **bring a person to his** or **her senses 1** cure a person of folly. **2** restore a person to consciousness. **come to one's senses 1** regain consciousness. **2** become sensible after acting foolishly. **in a** (or **one**) **sense** if the statement is understood in a particular way (*what you say is true in a sense*). **in one's senses** sane. **make sense** be intelligible or practicable. **make sense of** show or find the meaning of. **out of one's senses** in or into a state of madness (*is out of her senses; frightened him out of his senses*). **take leave of one's senses** go mad. [from Latin *sensus* 'faculty of feeling, thought, meaning']

senseless *adj.* **1** unconscious. **2** wildly foolish. **3** without meaning or purpose. **4** incapable of sensation. □ **senselessly** *adv.* **senselessness** *n.*

sense of direction *n.* the ability to know without guidance the direction in which one is or should be moving.

sense of humour see HUMOUR *n.* 2.

sense organ *n.* a bodily organ conveying (esp. external) stimuli to the sensory system.

sensibility *n.* (*pl.* -**ies**) **1 a** openness to emotional impressions; susceptibility, sensitiveness (*sensibility to kindness*). **b** *archaic* an exceptional or excessive degree of this (*sense and sensibility*). **2 a** (in *pl.*) emotional capacities or feelings (*was limited in his sensibilities*). **b** (in *sing.* or *pl.*) a person's moral, emotional, or aesthetic ideas or standards (*offended the sensibilities of believers*). **3** sensitivity to sensory stimuli (*sensibility in the retina*). [from Late Latin *sensibilitas*]

■ **Usage** *Sensibility* should not be used in standard English as a noun corresponding to sense 1 of *sensible*, i.e. it does not mean 'possession of common sense'. The correct noun to use is *sensibleness*; alternatively, a phrase such as *good sense* can be used.

sensible *adj.* **1** having or showing wisdom or common sense (*a sensible person; a sensible compromise*). **2 a** perceptible by the senses (*sensible phenomena*). **b** great enough to be perceived (*a sensible difference*). **3** (of clothing etc.) practical. **4** (foll. by *of*) aware; not unmindful (*was sensible of his peril*). [from Old French] □ **sensibleness** *n.* **sensibly** *adv.*

■ **Usage** See Usage Note at SENSIBILITY.

sensitive *adj.* **1** (often foll. by *to*) very open to or acutely affected by external stimuli or mental impressions; having sensibility. **2** (of a person) easily offended or emotionally hurt. **3** (often foll. by *to*) (of an instrument etc.) responsive to or recording slight changes. **4** (often foll. by *to*) **a** (of photographic materials) prepared so as to respond (esp. rapidly) to the action of light. **b** (of any material) readily affected by or responsive to external action. **5** (of a topic etc.) subject to restriction of discussion to prevent embarrassment, ensure security, etc. [from medieval Latin *sensitivus*] □ **sensitively** *adv.* **sensitiveness** *n.*

SENSITIVE PLANT
(*Mimosa pudica*)

sensitive plant *n.* **1** ◀ a plant whose leaves curve downwards and leaflets fold together when touched, esp. *Mimosa pudica*. **2** a sensitive person.

sensitivity *n.* (*pl.* -**ies**) **1** the quality or degree of being sensitive. **2** (in *pl.*) fine differences of feeling, attitude, or reaction.

sensitize *v.tr.* (also -**ise**) **1** make sensitive. **2** *Photog.* make sensitive to light. **3** make (an organism etc.) abnormally sensitive to a foreign substance. □ **sensitization** *n.* **sensitizer** *n.*

sensor *n.* a device which detects or measures a physical property.

sensory *adj.* of sensation or the senses. [based on Latin *sentire sens-* 'to feel'] □ **sensorily** *adv.*

sensual *adj.* **1 a** of or depending on the senses only and not on the intellect or spirit; carnal, fleshly (*sensual pleasures*). **b** given to the pursuit of sensual pleasures or the gratification of the appetites; self-indulgent sexually or in regard to food and drink; voluptuous, licentious. **c** indicative of a sensual nature (*sensual lips*). **2** of sense or sensation, sensory. [from Late Latin *sensualis*] □ **sensualism** *n.* **sensualist** *n.* **sensualize** *v.tr.* (also -**ise**). **sensually** *adv.*

■ **Usage** *Sensual* is sometimes confused with *sensuous*. While *sensual* is used to describe things that are gratifying to the body, and has sexual overtones, *sensuous* is used to mean 'affecting or appealing to the senses' in an aesthetic sense.

sensuality *n.* gratification of the senses.

sensuous *adj.* of or derived from or affecting the senses, esp. aesthetically. [based on Latin *sensus* 'sense'] □ **sensuously** *adv.* **sensuousness** *n.*

■ **Usage** See Usage Note at SENSUAL.

sent *past* and *past part.* of SEND.

sentence ● *n.* **1 a** a set of words complete in itself as the expression of a thought, containing or implying a subject and predicate, and conveying a statement, question, exclamation, or command. **b** a piece of writing or speech between two full stops or equivalent pauses, often including several grammatical sentences (e.g. *I went; he came*). **2 a** a decision of a law court, esp. the punishment allotted to a person convicted in a criminal trial. **b** the declaration of this. ● *v.tr.* **1** declare the sentence of (a convicted criminal etc.). **2** (foll. by *to*) declare (such a person) to be condemned to a specified punishment. □ **under sentence of** having been condemned to (*under sentence of death*). |originally in sense 'way of thinking, opinion': from Latin *sententia*]

sententious *adj.* **1** fond of pompous moralizing. **2** affectedly formal. **3** aphoristic, pithy, given to the use of maxims, affecting a concise impressive style. [from Latin *sententiosus*] □ **sententiously** *adv.* **sententiousness** *n.*

sentient *adj.* having the power of perception by the senses. [from Latin *sentient-* 'feeling'] □ **sentience** *n.* **sentiently** *adv.*

sentiment *n.* **1** the sum of what one feels on some subject; an opinion or point of view. **2** an opinion or feeling as distinguished from the words meant to convey it; an emotional feeling conveyed in literature, art, etc. (*the sentiment is good though the words are injudicious*). **3 a** emotional or tender feelings collectively, esp. mawkish tenderness. **b** the display of this. **4** a mental feeling (*the sentiment of pity*). [from medieval Latin *sentimentum*]

sentimental *adj.* **1** of or characterized by sentiment. **2** showing or affected by emotion rather than reason. **3** appealing to sentiment. □ **sentimentalism** *n.* **sentimentalist** *n.* **sentimentality** *n.* **sentimentalize** *v.intr.* & *tr.* (also -**ise**). **sentimentalization** *n.* **sentimentally** *adv.*

sentimental value *n.* the value of a thing to a particular person because of its associations.

sentinel *n.* a sentry or lookout. [from Italian *sentinella*]

sentry *n.* (*pl.* -**ies**) a soldier etc. stationed to keep guard.

sentry box *n.* ▶ a wooden cabin intended to shelter a standing sentry.

sentry-go *n.* *Brit.* the duty of pacing up and down as a sentry.

SENTRY BOX AND GUARD, **BUCKINGHAM PALACE,** **ENGLAND**

calyx

petal *sepal*

SEPAL: NASTURTIUM FLOWER SHOWING SEPALS

sepal *n.* ◀ *Bot.* each of the divisions or leaves of the calyx. ▷ FLOWER. [from Greek *skepē* 'covering', influenced by French *pétale* 'petal']

separable *adj.* able to be separated. [from Latin *separabilis*] □ **separability** *n.* **separably** *adv.*

separate ● *adj.* forming a unit that is apart or by itself; physically disconnected, distinct, or individual (*living in separate rooms; the two questions are essentially separate*). ● *n.* **1** (in *pl.*) separate articles of clothing suitable for wearing together in various combinations. **2** an offprint. ● *v.* **1** *tr.* make separate, sever. **2** *tr.* prevent union or contact of. **3** *intr.* go different ways. **4** *intr.* cease to live together as a married couple. **5** *intr.* (foll. by *from*) secede. **6** *tr.* **a** divide or sort (milk, ore, fruit, light, etc.) into constituent parts or sizes. **b** extract or remove (an ingredient, waste product, etc.) by such a process for use or rejection. [from Latin *separatus* 'separated'] □ **separately** *adv.* **separateness** *n.*

separation *n.* **1** the act or an instance of separating; the state of being separated. **2** (in full **judicial separation** or **legal separation**) an arrangement by which a husband and wife remain married but live apart.

separatist *n.* a person who favours separation, esp. for political independence. □ **separatism** *n.*

separator *n.* a machine for separating, e.g. cream from milk.

Sephardi *n.* (*pl.* **Sephardim**) a Jew of Spanish or Portuguese descent (cf. ASHKENAZI). [modern Hebrew, from sᵉ*p̄arad*, a country mentioned in Obad. 20 and taken to be Spain] □ **Sephardic** *adj.*

sepia ● *n.* **1** a dark reddish-brown colour. **2 a** a brown pigment prepared from a black fluid secreted by cuttlefish, used in monochrome drawing and in watercolours. **b** ▼ a brown tint used in photography.

SEPIA PHOTOGRAPH

3 a drawing done in sepia. **4** the fluid secreted by cuttlefish. ● *adj.* of a dark reddish-brown colour. [from Greek *sēpia* 'cuttlefish']

sepoy *n.* *hist.* a native Indian soldier under European, esp. British, discipline. [from Urdu & Persian *sipāhī* 'soldier']

sepsis *n.* **1** the state of being septic. **2** blood poisoning. [modern Latin, from Greek *sēpsis*]

Sept. *abbr.* **1** September. **2** Septuagint.

sept *n.* a clan, esp. in Ireland. [probably alteration of SECT]

sept- var. of SEPTI-.

September *n.* the ninth month of the year. [originally the seventh month of the Roman year: Latin, based on *septem* 'seven']

septennial *adj.* **1** lasting for seven years. **2** recurring every seven years. [from Late Latin *septennis*]

septet *n.* (also **septette**) **1** *Mus.* **a** a composition for seven performers. **b** the performers of such a composition. **2** any group of seven. [from German *Septett*]

septi- *comb. form* (also **sept-** before a vowel) seven. [from Latin *septem* 'seven']

S

septic *adj.* contaminated with bacteria from a festering wound etc., putrefying. [from Greek *sēptikos*]

septicaemia /sep-ti-**see**-miă/ *n.* (*US* **septicemia**) blood poisoning. [from Greek *sēptikos* 'septic' + *haima* 'blood'] □ **septicaemic** *adj.*

septic tank *n.* a tank in which the organic matter in sewage is decomposed through bacterial activity.

septuagenarian ● *n.* a person from 70 to 79 years old. ● *adj.* of this age. [from Latin *septuagenarius*]

Septuagesima *n.* (in full **Septuagesima Sunday**) the Sunday before Sexagesima. [Latin, literally 'seventieth (day)']

Septuagint *n.* a Greek version of the Old Testament including the Apocrypha. [from Latin *septuaginta* 'seventy']

septum *n.* (*pl.* **septa**) a partition such as that between the nostrils or the chambers of a poppy-fruit or of a shell. ▷ HEART. [Latin]

septuple ● *adj.* **1** sevenfold, having seven parts. **2** being seven times as many or as much. ● *n.* a sevenfold number or amount. ● *v.tr. & intr.* multiply by seven. [from Late Latin *septuplus*]

sepulchral *adj.* **1** of a tomb or interment (*sepulchral mound*; *sepulchral customs*). **2** suggestive of the tomb, gloomy, dismal (*sepulchral look*). □ **sepulchrally** *adv.*

sepulchre /sep-ŭl-ker/ (*US* **sepulcher**) ● *n.* ▼ a tomb esp. cut in rock or built of stone or brick. ● *v.tr.* **1** lay in a sepulchre. **2** serve as a sepulchre for. [from Latin *sepulc(h)rum*]

SEPULCHRE:
ETRUSCAN TOMB, ITALY

seq. *abbr.* (*pl.* **seqq.**) the following. [Latin *sequens*]

sequel *n.* **1** what follows (esp. as a result). **2** a novel, film, etc., that continues the story of an earlier one. [from Latin *sequel(l)a*]

sequence ● *n.* **1** succession, coming after or next. **2** order of succession (*in historical sequence*). **3** a set of things belonging next to one another on some principle of order. **4** a part of a film dealing with one scene or topic. ● *v.tr.* arrange in a definite order. [from Late Latin *sequentia*]

sequencer *n.* **1** *Mus.* a programmable electronic device for storing sequences of musical notes, chords, etc. and transmitting them when required to an electronic musical instrument. **2** an apparatus esp. forming part of a computer control system, for performing or initiating operations in the correct sequence.

sequential *adj.* forming a sequence or consequence. □ **sequentiality** *n.* **sequentially** *adv.*

sequester *v.tr.* **1** (esp. as **sequestered** *adj.*) seclude, isolate, set apart (*a sequestered cottage*). **2** = SEQUESTRATE. [based on Latin *sequester* 'trustee']

sequestrate *v.tr.* **1** confiscate, appropriate. **2** *Law* take temporary possession of (a debtor's estate etc.). [based on Late Latin *sequestratus* 'committed for safe keeping'] □ **sequestrable** *adj.* **sequestration** *n.* **sequestrator** *n.*

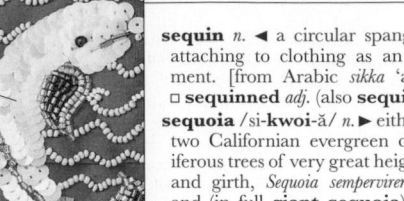

SEQUIN AND BEAD
DESIGN ON A PURSE

sequins

beads

sequin *n.* ◄ a circular spangle for attaching to clothing as an ornament. [from Arabic *sikka* 'a die'] □ **sequinned** *adj.* (also **sequined**).

sequoia /si-**kwoi**-ă/ *n.* ► either of two Californian evergreen coniferous trees of very great height and girth, *Sequoia sempervirens* and (in full **giant sequoia**) *Sequoiadendron giganteum*. [from *Sequoiah*, name of a Cherokee]

sera *pl.* of SERUM.

seraglio /se-**rahl**-yoh/ *n.* (*pl.* **-os**) **1** a harem. **2** *hist.* a Turkish palace. [based on Persian *sarāy* 'palace']

serai /sĕ-**ry**/ *n.* a caravanserai. [Turkish]

seraph *n.* (*pl.* **seraphim** or **seraphs**) an angelic being, one of the highest order of the ninefold celestial hierarchy. [back-formation from *seraphim*, from Hebrew]

seraphic *adj.* **1** of or like the seraphim. **2** ecstatically adoring, fervent, or serene. □ **seraphically** *adv.*

Serb ● *n.* **1** a native of Serbia, part of former Yugoslavia. **2** a person of Serbian descent. ● *adj.* = SERBIAN. [from Serbian *Srb*]

Serbian ● *n.* **1** the dialect of the Serbs. **2** = SERB. ● *adj.* of or relating to the Serbs or their dialect.

Serbo-Croat (also **Serbo-Croatian**) ● *n.* the main official language of former Yugoslavia, combining Serbian and Croatian. ● *adj.* of or relating to this language.

sere[1] *var.* of SEAR *adj.*

sere[2] *n. Ecol.* a natural succession of plant (or animal) communities. [based on Latin *serere* 'to join in a series']

serenade ● *n.* a piece of music performed at night, esp. by a lover under his lady's window. ● *v.tr.* sing or play a serenade to. [from Italian *serenata*] □ **serenader** *n.*

serendipity /se-rĕn-**dip**-iti/ *n.* the faculty of making happy and unexpected discoveries by accident. [coined by Horace Walpole (1754) after *The Three Princes of Serendip*, a fairy tale] □ **serendipitous** *adj.* **serendipitously** *adv.*

serene *adj.* (**serener**, **serenest**) **1** placid, tranquil, unperturbed. **2 a** (of the sky etc.) clear and calm. **b** (of the sea etc.) unruffled. [from Latin *serenus*] □ **serenely** *adv.* **sereneness** *n.*

serenity *n.* (*pl.* **-ies**) tranquillity, being serene. [from Latin *serenitas*]

serf *n.* **1** *hist.* a labourer not allowed to leave the land on which he worked. **2** an oppressed person, a drudge. [from Latin *servus* 'slave'] □ **serfdom** *n.*

serge *n.* a durable twilled worsted etc. fabric. [from Latin *serica (lana)* 'silken (wool)']

sergeant /**sar**-jĕnt/ *n.* **1** a non-commissioned Army or Air Force officer ranking above corporal. **2** a police officer ranking below (*Brit.*) inspector or (*US*) lieutenant. [from Latin *serviens -entis* 'servant']

sergeant major *n. Mil.* **1** (in full **regimental sergeant major**) *Brit.* a warrant officer assisting the adjutant of a regiment or battalion. **2** *US* the highest-ranking non-commissioned officer.

serial ● *n.* **1** a story, play, etc. which is published, broadcast, or shown in regular instalments. **2** a periodical. ● *adj.* **1** of or in or forming a series. **2** (of a story etc.) in the form of a serial. **3** *Mus.* using transformations of a fixed series of notes. [based on SERIES] □ **seriality** *n.* **serially** *adv.*

serialize *v.tr.* (also **-ise**) **1** publish or produce in

instalments. **2** arrange in a series. **3** *Mus.* compose according to a serial technique. □ **serialization** *n.*

serial killer *n.* a person who commits a sequence of murders with no apparent motive.

serial number *n.* a number showing the position of an item in a series. ▷ BANKNOTE

serial rights *n.pl.* the right to publish a story or book as a serial.

sericulture *n.* **1** silkworm-breeding. **2** the production of raw silk. [from French *sériculture*] □ **sericultural** *adj.* **sericulturist** *n.*

series *n.* (*pl.* same) **1** a number of things of which each is similar to the preceding or in which each successive pair are similarly related; a succession, row, or set. **2** a set of successive games between the same teams. **3** a set of programmes with the same actors etc. or on related subjects but each complete in itself. **4** a set of lectures by the same speaker or on the same subject. **5 a** a set of successive issues of a periodical, of articles on one subject or by one writer, etc., esp. when numbered separately from a preceding or following set (*second series*). **b** a set of independent books in a common format or under a common title or supervised by a common general editor. **6** *Geol.* a set of related strata. **7** *Mus.* an arrangement of the twelve notes of the chromatic scale as a basis for serial music. **8** *Electr.* **a** a set of circuits or components arranged so that the current passes through each successively. **b** a set of batteries etc. having the positive electrode of each connected with the negative electrode of the next. □ **in series 1** in ordered succession. **2** *Electr.* (of a set of circuits or components) arranged so that the current passes through each successively. [Latin, literally 'row, chain']

SEQUOIA: COAST
REDWOOD
(*Sequoia sempervirens*)

serif *n.* ► a slight projection finishing off a stroke of a letter as in T contrasted with T. ▷ TYPEFACE. □ **seriffed** *adj.*

serif

serif

serif

SERIF LETTER

serine *n. Biochem.* a hydrophilic amino acid present in proteins. [based on Latin *sericum* 'silk']

serio-comic *adj.* combining the serious and the comic, jocular in intention but simulating seriousness or vice versa. □ **serio-comically** *adv.*

serious *adj.* **1** thoughtful, earnest, not reckless or given to trifling (*a serious young person*). **2** important (*a serious matter*). **3** not slight or negligible (*a serious injury*). **4** sincere, not ironical or joking (*are you serious?*). **5** (of music and literature) not merely for amusement. **6** not perfunctory (*serious thought*). **7** not to be trifled with (*a serious opponent*). **8** *colloq.* (of price or value) high; (of an amount of money) large. [from Latin *serius*] □ **seriousness** *n.*

seriously *adv.* **1** in a serious manner (esp. introducing a sentence, implying that irony etc. is now to cease). **2** to a serious extent. **3** *colloq.* very (*seriously rich*).

serjeant *n. Brit.* **1** (in full **serjeant-at-law**, *pl.* **serjeants-at-law**) *hist.* a barrister of the highest rank. **2** (in official lists) a sergeant in the Army. [variant of SERGEANT]

serjeant-at-arms *n.* (*pl.* **serjeants-at-arms**) *Brit.* an official of a court or city or parliament, with ceremonial duties.

sermon *n.* **1** a spoken or written discourse on a religious or moral subject, esp. one delivered in a service by way of religious instruction or exhortation. **2** a piece of admonition, a lecture. **3** a moral reflection suggested by natural objects etc. (*sermons in stones*). [from Latin *sermo* 'discourse, talk']

sermonize *v.* (also **-ise**) **1** *tr.* deliver a moral lecture to. **2** *intr.* deliver a moral lecture. □ **sermonizer** *n.*

seronegative *adj. Med.* giving a negative result in a test of blood serum e.g. for presence of a virus.

seropositive *adj. Med.* giving a positive result in a test of blood serum e.g. for presence of a virus.

serous *adj.* of or like or producing serum; watery. [from medieval Latin *serosus*]

serous gland *n.* (also **serous membrane**) a gland or membrane with a serous secretion.

serpent *n.* **1** usu. *literary* a scaly limbless reptile; a snake. **2** a sly or treacherous person, esp. one who exploits a position of trust to betray it. **3** *Mus.* ► an old bass wind instrument made from leather-covered wood, roughly in the form of an S. **4** (**the Serpent**) *Bibl.* Satan. [from Latin *serpent-* 'creeping']

serpentine ● *adj.* **1** of or like a serpent. **2** coiling, tortuous, sinuous, meandering, writhing. **3** cunning, subtle, treacherous. ● *n.* a dark green mineral consisting of hydrated magnesium silicate, sometimes mottled like a serpent's skin.

serpentine verse *n.* a metrical line beginning and ending with the same word.

serpentinite *n.* ◄ a soft, dark, usu. greenish metamorphic rock consisting largely of serpentine or related minerals.

SERPS /serps/ *abbr.* (in the UK) State earnings-related pension scheme.

serrate ● *v.tr.* (usu. as **serrated** *adj.*) provide with a sawlike edge. ● *adj.* esp. *Anat., Bot.,* & *Zool.* ► notched like a saw. [based on Latin *serra* 'saw'] □ **serration** *n.*

SERPENTINITE

serried *adj.* (of ranks of soldiers etc.) pressed together; without gaps; close. [from military term *serry* 'to press close']

serum *n.* (*pl.* **sera** or **serums**) **1 a** the amber-coloured protein-rich liquid in which blood cells are suspended and which separates out when blood coagulates. **b** whey. **2** *Med.* the blood serum of an animal used esp. as a diagnostic agent etc. **3** a watery fluid in animal bodies. [Latin, literally 'whey']

servant *n.* **1** a person who has undertaken to carry out the orders of an individual or corporate employer, esp. a person employed in a house on domestic duties. **2** a devoted follower (*a servant of Jesus Christ*). [from Old French]

serve ● *v.* **1** *tr.* do a service for (a person, community, etc.). **2** *tr.* (also *absol.*) be a servant to. **3** *intr.* carry out duties (*served on six committees*). **4** *intr.* (foll. by *in*) be employed in (an organization, esp. the armed forces, or a place, esp. a foreign country). **b** be a member of the armed forces. **5 a** *tr.* be useful to or serviceable for; meet the needs of; do what is required for (*serve a purpose*). **b** *intr.* perform a function (*a sofa serving as a bed*). **c** *intr.* (foll. by *to* + infin.) avail, suffice (*served only to postpone the inevitable*). **6** *tr.* **a** go through a due period of (office, apprenticeship, a prison sentence, etc.). **b** go through (a due period) of imprisonment etc. **7** *tr.* set out or present (food)

for those about to eat it (*dinner is served*). **8** *intr.* (in full **serve at table**) act as a waiter. **9** *tr.* **a** attend to (a customer in a shop). **b** (foll. by *with*) supply with (goods) (*served the town with gas*). **10** *tr.* treat or act towards (a person) in a specified way (*has served me shamefully*). **11** *tr.* **a** (often foll. by *on*) deliver (a writ etc.) to the person concerned in a legally formal manner. **b** (foll. by *with*) deliver a writ etc. to (a person) in this way (*served her with a summons*). **12** *tr. Tennis* etc. **a** (also *absol.*) deliver (a ball etc.) to begin or resume play. **b** produce (a fault etc.) in doing this. **13** *tr. Mil.* keep (a gun, battery, etc.) firing. **14** *tr.* (of an animal, esp. a stallion etc. hired for the purpose) copulate with (a female). **15** *tr. Brit.* distribute (*served the rations round*). **16** *tr.* render obedience to (a deity etc.). ● *n. Tennis* etc. **1** the act or an instance of serving. **2** a manner of serving. **3** a person's turn to serve. □ **it will serve** it will be adequate. **serve one's needs** (or **need**) be adequate. **serve the purpose of** take the place of, be used as. **serve a person right** be a person's deserved punishment or misfortune. **serve** (or esp. *US* **serve out**) **one's time 1** hold office for the normal period. **2** (also **serve time**) undergo imprisonment, apprenticeship, etc. **serve one's** (or **the**) **turn** be adequate. **serve up** offer for acceptance. [from Latin *servire*]

server *n.* **1** a person who serves. **2** (in tennis etc.) the player who serves the ball. **3** *Eccl.* a person assisting the celebrant at a service. **4** *Computing* **a** a program which manages shared access to a centralized resource or service in a network. **b** a device on which such a program is run.

servery *n.* (*pl.* **-ies**) *Brit.* a room from which meals etc. are served and in which utensils are kept.

service[1] ● *n.* **1** the act of helping or doing work for another or for a community etc. **2** work done in this way. **3** assistance or benefit given to someone. **4 a** *Brit.* the provision or system of supplying a public need, e.g. transport, or (often in *pl.*) the supply of water, gas, electricity, telephone, etc. **b** (in *pl.*) — SERVICE AREA 1. **5 a** the fact or status of being a servant. **b** employment or a position as a servant. **6** a state or period of employment doing work for an individual or organization (*resigned after 15 years' service*). **7 a** a public or Crown department or organization (*civil service*). **b** employment in this. **8** (in *pl.*) the armed forces. **9** (*attrib.*) of the kind issued to the armed forces (*a service revolver*). **10 a** a ceremony of worship according to prescribed forms. **b** a form of liturgy for this. **11 a** the provision of what is necessary for the installation and maintenance of a machine etc. or operation. **b** a periodic routine maintenance of a motor vehicle etc. **12** assistance or advice given to customers after the sale of goods. **13 a** the act or process of serving food, drinks, etc. **b** an extra charge nominally made for this. **14** a set of dishes, plates, etc., used for serving meals (*a dinner service*). **15** *Tennis* etc. **a** the act or an instance of serving. **b** a person's turn to serve. ● *v.tr.* **1** provide service or services for, esp. maintain. **2** maintain or repair (a car, machine, etc.). **3** pay interest on (a debt). **4** supply with a service. □ **at a person's service** ready to serve or assist a person. **be of service** be available to assist. **in service 1** employed as a servant. **2** available for use. **on active service** serving in the armed forces in wartime. **out of service** not available for use. **see service 1** have experience of service, esp. in the armed forces. **2** (of a thing) be much used. [from Old French]

service[2] *n.* **1** (in full **service tree**) a southern European tree of the rose family, *Sorbus domestica*, with toothed leaves, cream-coloured flowers, and small round or pear-shaped fruit eaten when over-ripe. **2** (in full **wild service tree**) a related small

Eurasian tree, *Sorbus torminalis*, with lobed leaves and bitter fruit. [based on Latin *sorbus*]

serviceable *adj.* **1** useful or usable. **2** able to render service. **3** durable. **4** suited for ordinary use rather than ornament. □ **serviceability** *n.* **serviceableness** *n.* **serviceably** *adv.*

service area *n.* **1** an area beside a major road for the supply of petrol, refreshments, etc. **2** the area served by a broadcasting station.

service book *n.* a book of authorized forms of worship of a Church.

service charge *n.* an additional charge for service in a restaurant, hotel, etc.

service dress *n. Brit.* ordinary military etc. uniform.

service flat *n.* a flat in which domestic service and sometimes meals are provided by the management.

service industry *n.* one providing services not goods.

serviceman *n.* (*pl.* **-men**) **1** a man serving in the armed forces. **2** a man providing service or maintenance.

service road *n.* a road parallel to a main road, serving houses, shops, etc.

service station *n.* an establishment beside a road selling petrol and oil etc. to motorists and often able to carry out maintenance.

service tree see SERVICE[2].

servicewoman *n.* (*pl.* **-women**) a woman serving in the armed forces.

serviette *n.* esp. *Brit.* a napkin for use at table. [from Old French]

servile *adj.* **1** of or being or like a slave or slaves. **2** slavish, fawning. [from Latin *servilis*] □ **servilely** *adv.* **servility** *n.*

serving *n.* a quantity of food served to one person.

servitor *n.* **1** *archaic* a servant. **2** an attendant. [from Late Latin] □ **servitorship** *n.*

servitude *n.* **1** slavery. **2** subjection (esp. involuntary); bondage. [from Latin *servitudo*]

servo *n.* (*pl.* **-os**) **1** (in full **servo-mechanism**) a powered mechanism producing motion or forces at a higher level of energy than the input level. **2** (in full **servo-motor**) the motive element in a servo-mechanism. **3** (in *comb.*) of or involving a servo-mechanism (*servo-assisted*). [from Latin *servus* 'slave']

sesame /ses-ă-mi/ *n.* **1** an African herbaceous plant, *Sesamum indicum*, with seeds yielding an edible oil. **2** ► its seeds. □ **open sesame** a means of acquiring or achieving what is normally unattainable. [from Greek *sēsamon*]

sesqui- *comb. form* denoting one and a half. [Latin]

sesquicentenary *n.* (*pl.* **-ies**) a one-hundred-and-fiftieth anniversary.

sesquicentennial ● *n.* = SESQUICENTENARY. ● *adj.* of or relating to a sesquicentennial.

sessile *adj.* **1** *Bot.* & *Zool.* (of a flower, leaf, eye, etc.) attached directly by its base without a stalk or peduncle. **2 a** (of a barnacle etc.) fixed in one spot. **b** immobile. [from Latin *sessilis* 'sitting, stunted']

session *n.* **1** the process of assembly of a deliberative or judicial body to conduct its business. **2** a single meeting for this purpose. **3** a period during which such meetings are regularly held. **4 a** an academic year. **b** the period during which a school etc. has classes. **5** a period devoted to an activity (*poker session*). **6** the governing body of a Presbyterian Church. □ **in session** assembled for business; not on vacation. [from Latin *sessio*] □ **sessional** *adj.*

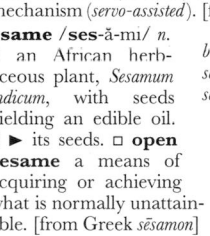

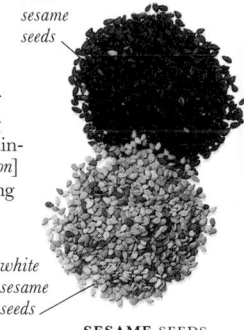

black sesame seeds

white sesame seeds

SESAME SEEDS (*Sesamum indicum*)

S

SERPENT: 19TH-CENTURY FRENCH SERPENT

mouthpiece

key

left-hand fingerholes

key

bell

right-hand fingerholes

serrated edge

SERRATE: SHARK'S TOOTH WITH A SERRATED EDGE

sestet *n.* **1** the last Six lines of a sonnet. **2** a sextet. [from Latin *sextus* 'a sixth']

set[1] *v.* (**setting**; *past* and *past part.* **set**) **1** *tr.* put, lay, or stand (a thing) in a certain position or location (*set it upright*). **2** *tr.* (foll. by *to*) apply (one thing) to (another) (*set pen to paper*). **3** *tr.* **a** fix ready or in position. **b** dispose suitably for use, action, or display. **4** *tr.* **a** adjust the hands of (a clock or watch) to show the right time. **b** adjust (an alarm clock) to sound at the required time. **5** *tr.* **a** fix, arrange, or mount. **b** insert (a jewel) in a ring etc. **6** *tr.* make (a device) ready to operate. **7** *tr.* lay (a table) for a meal. **8** *tr.* arrange (the hair) while damp. **9** *tr.* (foll. by *with*) ornament or provide (a surface, esp. a precious item) (*gold set with gems*). **10** *tr.* cause to be (*set things in motion*). **11** *intr.* & *tr.* harden or solidify (*the jelly is set*). **12** *intr.* (of the Sun, Moon, etc.) appear to move towards and below the Earth's horizon. **13** *tr.* represent (a scene etc.) as happening in a certain time or place. **14** *tr.* **a** (foll. by *to* + infin.) cause or instruct (a person) to perform a specified activity (*set them to work*). **b** (foll. by pres. part.) start (a person or thing) doing something (*set the ball rolling*). **15** *tr.* present or impose as work to be done or a matter to be dealt with (*set them an essay*). **16** *tr.* exhibit as a type or model (*set a good example*). **17** *tr.* initiate; take the lead in (*set the pace*). **18** *tr.* establish (a record etc.). **19** *tr.* determine or decide (*the itinerary is set*). **20** *tr.* appoint or establish (*set them in authority*). **21** *tr.* join, attach, or fasten. **22** *tr.* **a** put parts of (a broken bone etc.) into the correct position for healing. **b** deal with (a fracture etc.) in this way. **23** *tr.* (in full **set to music**) provide (words etc.) with music for singing. **24** *tr.* (often foll. by *up*) *Printing* **a** arrange or produce (type or film etc.) as required. **b** arrange the type or film etc. for (a book etc.). **25** *intr.* (of a tide etc.) have a certain motion or direction. **26** *intr.* (of a face) assume a hard expression. **27** *tr.* **a** cause (a hen) to sit on eggs. **b** place (eggs) for a hen to sit on. **28** *tr.* put (a seed etc.) in the ground to grow. **29** *tr.* give the teeth of (a saw) an alternate outward inclination. **30** *tr.* esp. *US* start (a fire). **31** *intr.* (of eyes etc.) become motionless. **32** *intr.* feel or show a certain tendency (*opinion is setting against it*). **33** *intr.* **a** (of blossom) form into fruit. **b** (of fruit) develop from blossom. **c** (of a tree) develop fruit. **34** *intr.* (of a hunting dog) take a rigid attitude indicating the presence of game. □ **set about 1** begin or take steps towards. **2** *Brit. colloq.* attack. **set against 1** consider or reckon as a counterpoise or compensation for. **2** cause (a person or persons) to oppose (a person or thing). **set apart** separate, reserve, differentiate. **set aside** see ASIDE. **set back 1** place further back in place or time. **2** impede or reverse the progress of. **3** *colloq.* cost (a person) a specified amount. **set by** *archaic* or *US* save for future use. **set down 1** record in writing. **2** allow to alight from a vehicle. **3** (foll. by *to*) attribute to. **4** (foll. by *as*) explain or describe to oneself as. **set eyes on** see EYE. **set one's face against** see FACE. **set foot on** (or **in**) see FOOT. **set forth 1** begin a journey. **2** make known; expound. **set forward** begin to advance. **set free** release. **set one's hand to** see HAND. **set one's heart** (or **hopes**) **on** want or hope for eagerly. **set in 1** (of weather etc.) begin, become established. **2** insert (esp. a sleeve etc. into a garment). **set a person's mind at rest** see MIND. **set much by** consider to be of much value. **set off 1** begin a journey. **2** detonate (a bomb etc.). **3** initiate, stimulate. **4** cause (a person) to start laughing, talking, etc. **5** adorn; enhance. **6** (foll. by *against*) use as a compensating item. **set on** (or **upon**) **1** attack violently. **2** cause or urge to attack. **set out 1** begin a journey. **2** (foll. by *to* + infin.) aim or intend. **3** demonstrate, arrange, or exhibit. **4** mark out. **5** declare. **set sail 1** hoist the sails. **2** begin a voyage. **set the scene** see SCENE. **set the stage** see STAGE. **set store by** (or **on**) see STORE. **set one's teeth 1** clench them. **2** summon one's resolve. **set to** begin vigorously, esp. fighting, arguing, or eating. **set up 1** place in position or view. **2** organize or start (a business etc.). **3** establish in some capacity. **4** supply the needs of. **5** begin making (a loud sound). **6** cause or make arrangements for (a condition or situation). **7** prepare (a task etc. for another). **8** restore or enhance the health of (a person). **9** establish (a record). **10** propound (a theory). **11** *colloq.* frame or cause (a person) to look foolish. **set oneself up as** make pretensions to being. [Old English]

set[2] *n.* **1** a number of things or persons that belong together or resemble one another or are usually found together. **2** a collection or group. **3** a section of society consorting together or having similar interests etc. **4** a collection of implements etc. needed for a specified purpose (*cricket set*; *teaset*). **5** a radio or television receiver. **6** (in tennis, darts, etc.) a group of games counting as a unit towards a match for the player or side that wins a defined number or proportion of the games. **7** *Math.* & *Logic* a collection of distinct entities forming a unit. **8** a group of pupils or students having the same average ability. **9 a** a slip, shoot, bulb, etc., for planting. **b** a young fruit just set. **10 a** a habitual posture or conformation; the way the head etc. is carried or a dress etc. flows. **b** (also **dead set**) a setter's pointing in the presence of game. **11** the way, drift, or tendency (of public opinion etc.) (*the set of public feeling is against it*). **12** the way in which a machine, device, etc., is set or adjusted. **13** a setting, stage furniture etc., for a play or film etc. **14** a sequence of songs or pieces performed in jazz or popular music. **15** the setting of the hair when damp. **16** var. of SETT 1. **17** var. of SETT 2. **18** a number of people making up a square dance. □ **make a dead set at** *Brit.* **1** make a determined attack on. **2** seek to win the affections of. [late Middle English]

set[3] *adj.* **1** in senses of SET[1]. **2** prescribed or determined in advance. **3** fixed, unchanging, unmoving. **4** (of a phrase or speech etc.) having invariable or predetermined wording. **5** prepared for action. **6** (foll. by *on*, *upon*) determined to acquire or achieve etc. **7** (of a book etc.) specified for reading in preparation for an examination. [past participle of SET[1]]

set-aside *n.* **1** the action of setting something aside for a special purpose. **2** the policy of taking land out of production to reduce crop surpluses.

setback *n.* **1** a reversal or arrest of progress. **2** a relapse.

set fair *adj. Brit.* (of the weather) fine without a sign of breaking.

set menu *n.* a limited menu of a set number of courses.

set-off *n.* **1** a thing set off against another. **2** a thing of which the amount or effect may be deducted from that of another or opposite tendency. **3** a counterpoise. **4** a counter-claim. **5** a thing that embellishes; an adornment to something. **6** *Printing* = OFFSET 7.

set phrase *n.* an invariable or usual arrangement of words.

set piece *n.* **1** a formal or elaborate arrangement, esp. in art or literature (hyphenated when *attrib.*: *set-piece occasions*). **2** a pre-arranged movement in a team game. **3** an arrangement of fireworks composing a picture or design.

set point *n. Tennis* etc. **1** the state of a game when one side needs only one more point to win the set. **2** this point.

set scrum *n. Rugby* a scrum ordered by the referee.

set square *n.* ◄ a right-angled triangular plate for drawing lines, esp. at 90°, 45°, 60°, or 30°.

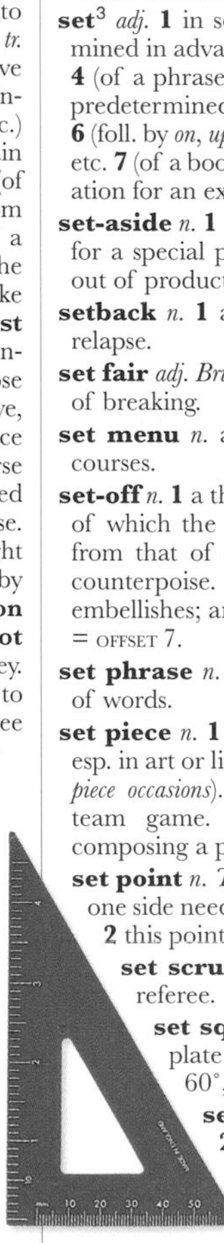

SET SQUARE

sett *n.* (also **set**) **1** a badger's burrow. **2** a granite paving block.

settee *n.* a seat (usu. upholstered), with a back and usu. arms, for more than one person. [18th-century coinage]

SETTER: IRISH SETTER

setter *n.* **1** ▲ a dog of a large long-haired breed trained to stand rigid when scenting game. **2** a person or thing that sets.

set theory *n.* the branch of mathematics which deals with the properties of sets (without regard to the nature of their individual constituents).

setting *n.* **1** the position or manner in which a thing is set. **2** the immediate surroundings (of a house etc.). **3** the surroundings of any object regarded as its framework. **4** the place and time etc. of a drama etc. **5** a frame in which a jewel is set. **6** the music to which words are set. **7** a set of cutlery and other accessories for one person at a table. **8** the way in which or level at which a machine is set to operate.

setting lotion *n.* lotion used to prepare the hair for being set.

settle[1] *v.* **1** *tr.* & *intr.* (often foll. by *down*) establish or become established in a more or less permanent abode or way of life. **2** *intr.* & *tr.* (often foll. by *down*) **a** cease or cause to cease from disturbance, movement, etc. **b** adopt a regular or secure style of life. **c** (foll. by *to*) apply oneself (*settled down to writing letters*). **3 a** *intr.* sit or come down to stay for some time. **b** *tr.* cause to do this. **4** *tr.* & *intr.* bring to or attain fixity, certainty, composure, or quietness. **5** *tr.* determine or decide or agree upon. **6** *tr.* resolve (a dispute, matter, etc.). **7** *tr.* terminate (a lawsuit) by mutual agreement. **8** *intr.* **a** (foll. by *for*) accept or agree to (esp. an alternative not one's first choice). **b** (foll. by *on*) decide on. **9** *tr.* (also *absol.*) pay (a debt, an account, etc.). **10** *intr.* (as **settled** *adj.*) not likely to change for a time (*settled weather*). **11** *tr.* **a** aid the digestion of (food). **b** remedy the disordered state of (nerves etc.). **12** *tr.* **a** colonize. **b** establish colonists in. **13** *intr.* subside; fall to the bottom or on to a surface (*the dust will settle*). □ **settle one's affairs** make any necessary arrangements (e.g. write a will) when death is near. **settle a person's hash** see HASH[1]. **settle in** become established in a place. **settle up 1** (also *absol.*) pay (an account etc.). **2** finally arrange (a matter). **settle with 1** pay all or part of an amount due to (a creditor). **2** get revenge on. [Old English] □ **settleable** *adj.*

settle[2] *n.* a bench with a high back and arms and often with a box fitted below the seat. [Old English *setl* 'a place to sit']

settlement *n.* **1** the act or an instance of settling; the process of being settled. **2 a** the colonization of a region. **b** a place or area occupied by settlers. **c** a small village. **3 a** a political or financial etc. agreement. **b** an arrangement ending a dispute. **4 a** the terms on which property is given to a person. **b** a deed stating these. **c** the amount of property given. **d** = MARRIAGE SETTLEMENT. **5** subsidence of a wall, house, soil, etc.

settler *n.* a person who goes to settle in a new country or place; an early colonist.

set-to *n.* (*pl.* **-tos**) *colloq.* a fight or argument.

set-up *n.* **1 a** the way in which something is organized or arranged. **b** an organization or arrangement. **2** *colloq.* a conspiracy or trick whereby a person is caused to incriminate himself or herself or to look foolish.

seven ● *n.* **1** one more than six. **2** a symbol for this (7, vii, VII). **3** a size etc. denoted by seven. **4** a set or team of seven individuals. **5** the time of seven

SEWING MACHINE

Producing a stitch on a sewing machine requires thread from two sources: the needle and the bobbin (a small reel beneath the needle plate). As the needle pushes through the fabric, the needle's thread forms a loop that is grabbed by the bobbin hook, a circular catch surrounding the bobbin. The bobbin hook then spins, taking the loop around the bobbin. As the needle moves upwards, the loop tightens and pulls the bobbin thread to form a stitch.

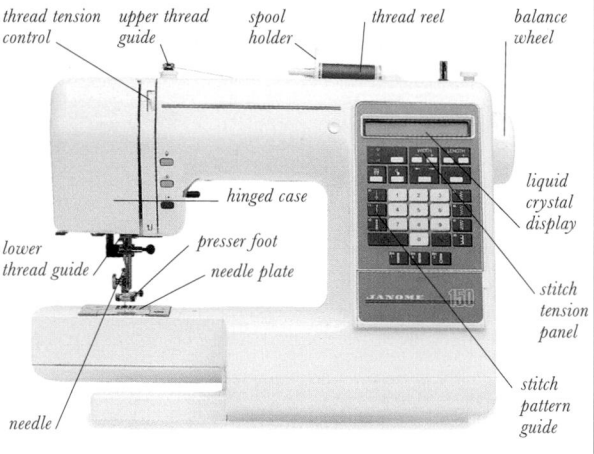

thread tension control · upper thread guide · spool holder · thread reel · balance wheel · hinged case · liquid crystal display · lower thread guide · presser foot · needle plate · stitch tension panel · needle · stitch pattern guide

ELECTRIC SEWING MACHINE

o'clock. **6** a playing card with seven pips. ● *adj.* that amount to seven. [Old English]

seven deadly sins *n.pl.* (prec. by *the*) the sins of pride, covetousness, lust, anger, gluttony, envy, and sloth.

sevenfold *adj. & adv.* **1** seven times as much or as many. **2** consisting of seven parts.

seven seas *n.pl.* (prec. by *the*) the oceans of the world: the Arctic, Antarctic, N. Pacific, S. Pacific, N. Atlantic, S. Atlantic, and Indian Oceans.

seventeen ● *n.* **1** one more than sixteen. **2** a symbol for this (17, xvii, XVII). **3** a size etc. denoted by seventeen. ● *adj.* that amount to seventeen. [Old English] □ **seventeenth** *adj. & n.*

seventh ● *n.* **1** the position in a sequence corresponding to the number 7 in the sequence 1–7. **2** something occupying this position. **3** one of seven equal parts of a thing. **4** *Mus.* **a** an interval or chord spanning seven consecutive notes in the diatonic scale. **b** a note separated from another by this interval. ● *adj.* that is the seventh. □ **seventhly** *adv.*

Seventh-Day Adventist *n.* a member of a strict protestant sect preaching the imminent return of Christ to Earth, and observing the sabbath on Saturday.

seventy ● *n.* (*pl.* **-ies**) **1** the product of seven and ten. **2** a symbol for this (70, lxx, LXX). **3** (in *pl.*) the numbers from 70 to 79, esp. the years of a century or of a person's life. ● *adj.* that amount to seventy. [Old English] □ **seventieth** *adj. & n.* **seventyfold** *adj. & adv.*

seven year itch *n.* a supposed tendency to infidelity after seven years of marriage.

sever *v.* **1** *tr. & intr.* (often foll. by *from*) divide, break, or make separate, esp. by cutting. **2** *tr. & intr.* break off or away (*severed our friendship*). **3** *tr.* end the employment contract of (a person). [from Latin *separare* 'to separate'] □ **severable** *adj.*

several ● *det. & pron.* more than two but not many. ● *adj.* separate or respective; distinct (*all went their several ways*). [from Latin *separ* 'separate'] □ **severally** *adv.*

severance *n.* **1** the act or an instance of severing. **2** a severed state.

severance pay *n.* an amount paid to an employee on the early termination of a contract.

severe *adj.* **1** rigorous, strict, and harsh in attitude or treatment (*a severe critic*). **2** serious, critical (*a severe shortage*). **3** vehement or forceful (*a severe storm*). **4** extreme (in an unpleasant quality) (*a severe winter*). **5** exacting (*severe competition*). **6** plain in style (*severe dress*). [from Latin *severus*] □ **severely** *adv.* **severity** *n.*

Seville orange /sev-il/ *n.* a bitter orange used for marmalade. [from *Seville*, a city and province in Spain]

sew /soh/ *v.tr.* (*past part.* **sewn** or **sewed**) **1** (also *absol.*) fasten, join, etc., by making stitches with a needle and thread or a sewing machine. ▷ STITCH. **2** make (a garment etc.) by sewing. **3** (often foll. by *on*, *in*, etc.) attach by sewing. □ **sew up 1** join or enclose by sewing. **2** (esp. in *passive*) *colloq.* bring to a desired conclusion or condition; complete satisfactorily; ensure the favourable outcome of (a thing). [Old English] □ **sewer** *n.*

sewage /soo-ij/ *n.* waste matter conveyed in sewers.

sewage farm *n.* (also **sewage works**) a place where sewage is treated, esp. to produce manure.

sewer /soo-er/ *n.* a conduit, usu. underground, for carrying off drainage water and sewage. [from Old Northern French *se(u)wiere* 'channel to carry off the overflow from a fishpond']

sewerage /soo-er-ij/ *n.* a system of or drainage by sewers.

sewer rat *n.* the common brown rat.

sewing *n.* material or work to be sewn.

sewing machine *n.* ▲ a machine for sewing or stitching.

sewn *past part.* of SEW.

sex ● *n.* **1** either of the main divisions (male and female) into which living things are placed on the basis of their reproductive functions. **2** the fact of belonging to one of these. **3** males or females

collectively. **4** sexual desires etc., or their manifestation. **5** *colloq.* sexual intercourse. ● *adj.* **1** of or relating to sex (*sex education*). **2** arising from a difference or consciousness of sex (*sex antagonism*). ● *v.tr.* **1** determine the sex of. **2** (as **sexed** *adj.*) **a** having a sexual appetite (*highly sexed*). **b** having sexual characteristics. [from Latin *sexus*]

sex act *n.* (usu. prec. by *the*) the (or an) act of sexual intercourse.

sexagenarian ● *n.* a person from 60 to 69 years old. ● *adj.* of this age. [from Latin *sexagenarius*]

Sexagesima *n.* the Sunday before Quinquagesima. [from ecclesiastical Latin, literally 'sixtieth (day)']

sex appeal *n.* sexual attractiveness.

sex change *n.* an apparent change of sex by surgical means and hormone treatment.

sex chromosome *n.* a chromosome concerned in determining the sex of an organism.

sex hormone *n.* a hormone affecting sexual development or behaviour.

sexism *n.* prejudice or discrimination, esp. against women, on the grounds of sex. □ **sexist** *adj. & n.*

sexless *adj.* **1** *Biol.* neither male nor female. **2** lacking in sexual desire or attractiveness. □ **sexlessly** *adv.* **sexlessness** *n.*

sex life *n.* a person's activity related to sexual instincts.

sex-linked *adj. Genetics* carried on or by a sex chromosome.

sex maniac *n. colloq.* a person needing or seeking excessive gratification of the sexual instincts.

sex object *n.* a person regarded mainly in terms of sexual attractiveness.

sex offender *n.* a person who commits a sexual crime.

sexology *n.* the study of sexual life or relationships, esp. in human beings. □ **sexological** *adj.* **sexologist** *n.*

sexploitation *n. colloq.* the exploitation of sex, esp. commercially.

sexpot *n. colloq.* a sexy person (esp. a woman).

sex-starved *adj.* lacking sexual gratification.

sex symbol *n.* a person widely noted for sex appeal.

sext *n. Eccl.* the office of the fourth canonical hour of prayer, originally said at the sixth hour of the day (i.e. noon). [from Latin *sexta hora* 'sixth hour']

sextant *n.* ▼ an instrument with a graduated arc of 60° used in navigation and surveying for measuring the angular distance of objects by means of mirrors. [from Latin *sextans* *sextant-* 'sixth part']

sextet *n.* (also **sextette**) **1** *Mus.* a composition for six voices or instruments. **2** the performers of such

S

SEXTANT

Sextants are commonly used to measure the angle between the Earth's horizon and a celestial body. The image of the star (for example) is reflected from the index mirror on to the horizon mirror and into the telescope. Next, the index arm is adjusted until the horizon and the star's image align. The angle between the horizon and the star can then be read on the arc. After a series of calculations, the sextant user's latitude and longitude can be worked out.

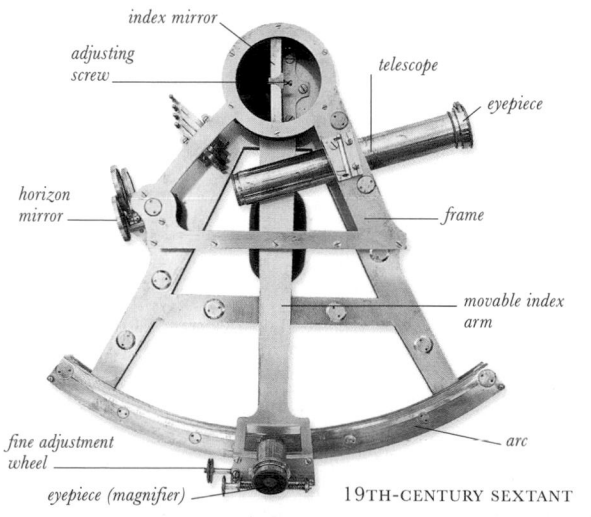

index mirror · adjusting screw · telescope · eyepiece · horizon mirror · frame · movable index arm · fine adjustment wheel · arc · eyepiece (magnifier)

19TH-CENTURY SEXTANT

a piece. **3** any group of six. [alteration of SESTET, suggested by Latin *sex* 'six']

sexton *n.* a person who looks after a church and churchyard, often acting as bell-ringer and grave-digger. [from medieval Latin *sacristanus* 'sacristan']

sextuple ● *adj.* **1** sixfold. **2** having six parts. **3** being six times as many or much. ● *n.* a sixfold number or amount. ● *v.tr. & intr.* multiply by six; increase sixfold. [from medieval Latin *sextuplus*]

sextuplet *n.* **1** each of six children born at one birth.

sexual *adj.* **1** of or relating to sex, or to the sexes or the relations between them. **2** *Biol.* having a sex. □ **sexuality** *n.* **sexually** *adv.*

sexual intercourse *n.* mutual sexual stimulation, esp. the insertion of a man's erect penis into a woman's vagina, usu. followed by the ejaculation of semen.

sexy *adj.* (**sexier**, **sexiest**) **1** sexually attractive or stimulating. **2** sexually aroused. **3** concerned with sex. **4** *colloq.* (of a project etc.) exciting, appealing. □ **sexily** *adv.* **sexiness** *n.*

sez *slang* says (*sez you*). [phonetic representation]

SF *abbr.* science fiction.

sf *abbr. Mus.* sforzando.

SFA *abbr.* Scottish Football Association.

sforzando /sfort-**san**-doh/ (also **sforzato** /sfort-**sah**-toh/) *Mus.* ● *adj. & adv.* with sudden emphasis. ● *n.* (*pl.* **-os** or **sforzandi**) **1** a note or group of notes especially emphasized. **2** an increase in emphasis and loudness. [Italian]

sgd. *abbr.* signed.

SGML *abbr. Computing* Standard Generalized Mark-up Language, a form of generic coding used for producing printed material in electronic form.

Sgt. *abbr.* Sergeant.

sh *int.* calling for silence. [variant of HUSH]

shabby *adj.* (**shabbier**, **shabbiest**) **1** in bad repair or condition; faded and worn. **2** dressed in old or worn clothes. **3** of poor quality. **4** contemptible, dishonourable (*a shabby trick*). [from Old Norse, related to SCAB] □ **shabbily** *adv.* **shabbiness** *n.*

shack ● *n.* a roughly built hut or cabin. ● *v.intr.* (foll. by *up*) *slang* cohabit, esp. as lovers.

shackle ● *n.* **1** ◄ a metal loop or link, closed by a bolt, to connect chains etc. **2** a fetter enclosing the ankle or wrist. **3** (usu. in *pl.*) a restraint or impediment. ● *v.tr.* fetter, impede, restrain. [Old English *sc(e)acul* 'fetter']

shackle

shackle pin (bolt)

SHACKLE

shad *n.* (*pl.* same or **shads**) any deep-bodied edible marine fish of the genus *Alosa*, spawning in fresh water. [Old English]

shaddock *n.* **1** the largest citrus fruit, with a thick yellow skin and bitter pulp. ▷ CITRUS FRUIT. **2** the tree, *Citrus grandis*, bearing these. [named after Capt. *Shaddock*, who introduced it to the W. Indies (17th c.)]

shade ● *n.* **1** comparative darkness (and usu. coolness) caused by shelter from direct light and heat. **2** a place or area sheltered from the Sun. **3** a darker part of a picture etc. **4** a colour, esp. as darker or lighter than one similar. **5** a slight amount (*a shade better*). **6** a translucent cover for a lamp etc. **7** a screen excluding or moderating light. **8** an eye-shield. **9** (in *pl.*) orig. *US colloq.* sunglasses. **10** a slightly differing variety (*all shades of opinion*). **11** *literary* **a** a ghost. **b** (in *pl.*) Hades. **12** (in *pl.*; foll. by *of*) suggesting, reminiscent of (*shades of Dr Johnson!*). ● *v.* **1** *tr.* screen from light. **2** *tr.* cover, moderate, or exclude the light of. **3** *tr.* darken, esp. with parallel pencil lines, to represent shadow etc. **4** *intr. & tr.* (often foll. by *away*, *off*, *into*) pass or change by degrees. □ **put in the shade** appear or be very superior to. [Old English] □ **shadeless** *adj.*

shading *n.* **1** the representation of light and shade, e.g. by pencilled lines, on a map or drawing. **2** the

graduation of tones from light to dark to create a sense of depth.

shadow ● *n.* **1** shade or a patch of shade. **2** a dark figure projected by a body intercepting rays of light. **3** an inseparable attendant or companion. **4** a person secretly following another. **5** the slightest trace (*not a shadow of doubt*). **6** a weak or insubstantial remnant (*a shadow of his former self*). **7** (*attrib.*) *Brit.* denoting members of a political party in opposition holding responsibilities parallel to those of the government (*shadow Cabinet*). **8** the shaded part of a picture. **9** a substance used to colour the eyelids. **10** gloom or sadness. ● *v.tr.* **1** cast a shadow over. **2** secretly follow and watch the movements of. **3** accompany (a person) at work either as training or to obtain insight into a profession. [Old English] □ **shadower** *n.* **shadowless** *adj.*

shadow-boxing *n.* boxing against an imaginary opponent as a form of training.

shadowgraph *n.* **1** an image or photograph made by means of X-rays; = RADIOGRAM 2. **2** a picture formed by a shadow cast on a lighted surface. **3** an image formed by light refracted differently by different densities of a fluid.

shadow theatre *n.* a display in which shadows of puppets are projected onto the rear of a translucent screen and viewed from the front.

shadowy *adj.* **1** like or having a shadow. **2** full of shadows. **3** vague, indistinct. □ **shadowiness** *n.*

shady *adj.* (**shadier**, **shadiest**) **1** giving shade. **2** situated in shade. **3** (of a person or behaviour) disreputable; of doubtful honesty. □ **shadily** *adv.* **shadiness** *n.*

shaft ● *n.* **1 a** an arrow or spear. **b** the long slender stem of these. **2** a remark intended to hurt or provoke (*shafts of wit*). **3** (foll. by *of*) **a** a ray (of light). **b** a bolt (of lightning). **4** the stem or handle of a tool etc. **5** a column, esp. between the base and capital. **6** a long narrow space, usu. vertical, for a lift, ventilation, etc. **7** a long and narrow part supporting or connecting or driving a part or parts of greater thickness etc. **8** each of the pair of poles between which a horse is harnessed to a vehicle. ▷ TRACE. **9** *Mech.* a large axle or revolving bar transferring force by belts or cogs. **10** *N. Amer. colloq.* harsh or unfair treatment. ● *v.tr.* **1** fit (a weapon, tool, or arrowhead) with a shaft. **2** *N. Amer. colloq.* treat unfairly. [Old English]

shafting *n. Mech.* **1** a system of connected shafts for transmitting motion. **2** material from which shafts are cut.

shag¹ *n.* **1 a** a rough growth or mass of hair etc. **b** (*attrib.*) (of a carpet) with a long rough pile. **c** (*attrib.*) (of a pile) long and rough. **2** a coarse kind of cut tobacco. **3** ◄ a cormorant with greenish-black plumage and a curly crest. [Old English]

shag² *v.tr.* (**shagged**, **shagging**) *coarse slang* **1** *Brit.* have sexual intercourse with. **2** (usu. in *passive*; often foll. by *out*) exhaust; tire out. [18th-century coinage] □ **shagger** *n.* (in sense 1 of *v.*; often as a term of abuse).

SHAG: IMPERIAL SHAG (*Phalacrocorax atriceps*)

shaggy *adj.* (**shaggier**, **shaggiest**) **1** hairy, rough-haired. **2** unkempt. **3** (of the hair) coarse and abundant. □ **shaggy-dog story** a long rambling story amusing only by its being inconsequential. □ **shaggily** *adv.* **shagginess** *n.*

shagreen *n.* **1** a kind of untanned leather with a rough granulated surface. **2** a sharkskin rough with natural papillae, used for rasping and polishing. [variant of archaic *chagrin* 'rough skin']

shah *n. hist.* a title of the former monarch of Iran. [from Old Persian *k͟sāytiya* 'king'] □ **shahdom** *n.*

shaikh var. of SHEIKH.

shake ● *v.* (*past* **shook**; *past part.* **shaken**) **1** *tr. & intr.* move forcefully or quickly up and down or to and

fro. **2 a** *intr.* tremble or vibrate markedly. **b** *tr.* cause to do this. **3** *tr.* **a** agitate or shock. **b** *colloq.* upset the composure of. **4** *tr.* weaken or impair; make less convincing or firm or courageous (*shook his confidence*). **5** *intr.* (of a voice, note, etc.) make tremulous or rapidly alternating sounds (*his voice shook with emotion*). **6** *tr.* make a threatening gesture with (one's fist etc.). **7** *intr. colloq.* shake hands. **8** *tr.* esp. *US colloq.* = *shake off*. ● *n.* **1** the act or an instance of shaking; the process of being shaken. **2** a jerk or shock. **3** (in *pl.*; prec. by *the*) a fit of or tendency to trembling or shivering. **4** = MILK SHAKE. □ **in two shakes** (**of a lamb's** or **dog's tail**) very quickly. **no great shakes** *colloq.* not very good or significant. **shake a person by the hand** = *shake hands*. **shake down 1** settle or cause to fall by shaking. **2** settle down. **3** get into harmony with circumstances, surroundings, etc. **4** *N. Amer. slang* extort money from. **shake the dust off one's feet** depart indignantly or disdainfully. **shake hands** (often foll. by *with*) clasp right hands at meeting or parting, in reconciliation or congratulation, or over a concluded bargain. **shake one's head** turn one's head from side to side in refusal, denial, disapproval, or concern. **shake in one's shoes** tremble with apprehension. **shake a leg** *colloq.* **1** begin dancing. **2** make a start. **shake off 1** get rid of (something unwanted). **2** manage to evade (a person). **shake out 1** empty by shaking. **2** spread or open by shaking. **shake up 1** mix (ingredients) by shaking. **2** restore to shape by shaking. **3** disturb or make uncomfortable. **4** rouse from lethargy, conventionality, etc. [Old English] □ **shakeable** *adj.* (also **shakable**).

shakedown *n.* **1** a makeshift bed. **2** a period or process of adjustment or change. **3** esp. *US slang* a swindle; a piece of extortion. **4** esp. (*attrib.*) *colloq.* denoting a voyage, flight, etc., to test a new ship, aircraft, etc., and its crew.

shaken *past part.* of SHAKE.

shake-out *n.* an upheaval or reorganization, esp. in a business and involving streamlining, redundancies, etc.

shaker *n.* **1** a person or thing that shakes. **2** a container for shaking together the ingredients of cocktails etc. **3** (**Shaker**) ▼ a member of an American religious sect living austerely in celibate mixed communities. They made furniture noted for the elegant functionalism of its style. [Middle English; sense 3: from religious dances]

SHAKER FURNITURE (WALL-MOUNTED CUPBOARD AND BOXES)

Shakespearean (also **Shakespearian**) ● *adj.* **1** of or relating to William Shakespeare, English dramatist d. 1616. **2** in the style of Shakespeare. ● *n.* a student of Shakespeare's works etc.

shake-up *n.* an upheaval or drastic reorganization.

shako *n.* (*pl.* **-os**) ▼ a cylindrical peaked military hat with a plume. [from Hungarian *csákó (süveg)* 'peaked (cap)']

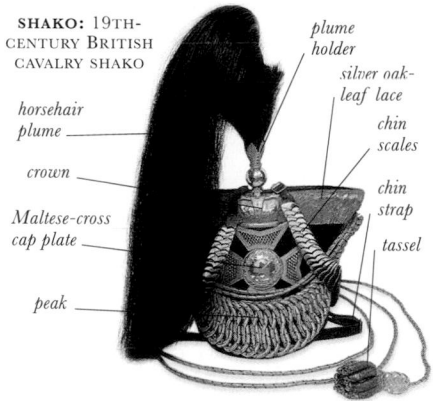

SHAKO: 19TH-CENTURY BRITISH CAVALRY SHAKO

plume · plume holder · silver oak-leaf lace · chin scales · chin strap · tassel · horsehair plume · crown · Maltese-cross cap plate · peak

shaky *adj.* (**shakier**, **shakiest**) **1** unsteady; apt to shake; trembling. **2** unsound, infirm. **3** unreliable, wavering (*a shaky start*). □ **shakily** *adv.* **shakiness** *n.*

shale *n.* ◀ soft finely stratified rock that splits easily, consisting of consolidated mud or clay. □ **shaly** *adj.* ▷ SEDIMENT

shall *v.aux.* (*3rd sing. present* **shall**; *archaic 2nd sing. present* **shalt**; *past* **should**) (foll. by *infin.* without *to*, or *absol.*; *present and past only in use*) **1** (in the 1st person) expressing the future tense (*I shall return soon*) or (with *shall* stressed) emphatic intention (*I shall have a party*). **2** (in the 2nd and 3rd persons) expressing a strong assertion or command rather than a wish (cf. WILL[1]) (*you shall not catch me again*). **3** expressing a command or duty (*thou shalt not steal*). **4** (in 2nd-person questions) expressing an enquiry, esp. to avoid the form of a request (cf. WILL[1]) (*shall you go to France?*). □ **shall I?** do you want me to? [Old English]

SHALE: OIL-SHALE

■ **Usage** There is considerable confusion about when to use *shall* and *will*. The traditional rule in standard British English is that *shall* is used for the first person singular and plural (*I* and *we*) to form the future tense, while *will* is used for the second and third persons e.g. *I shall be late; She will not be there.* In informal usage, *I will* and *we will* are quite often used for the future tense, e.g. *We will try to help*, but this is unacceptable in formal usage. Conversely, *shall* is also used with *you* in polite questions (see sense 4 above), and this is quite acceptable. When expressing a strong assertion or command the traditional rule is that *will* is used with the first person singular and plural, and *shall* for the second and third persons, e.g. *I will not tolerate this; Competitors shall arrive by 8 a.m.* In practice, however, *shall* is often used for the first person singular and plural in emphatic contexts (e.g. *I shall have a new car*), and *will* for the second and third persons (e.g. *You will go to bed early*). These usages are now fully acceptable.

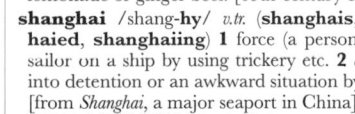

SHALLOT BULB (*Allium ascalonicum*)

shallot /shă-lot/ *n.* ◀ an onion-like plant, *Allium ascalonicum*, with a cluster of small bulbs. [from French *eschalotte*]

shallow ● *adj.* **1** of little depth. **2** superficial, trivial (*a shallow mind*). ● *n.* (often in *pl.*) a shallow place. [Middle English, related to SHOAL[2]] □ **shallowly** *adv.* **shallowness** *n.*

shalom /shă-lom/ *n. & int.* a Jewish salutation at meeting or parting. [from Hebrew *šālôm* 'peace']

shalt *archaic 2nd person sing.* of SHALL.

sham ● *v.* (**shammed**, **shamming**) **1** *intr.* feign, pretend. **2** *tr.* **a** pretend to be. **b** simulate. ● *n.* **1** imposture, pretence. **2** a bogus or false person or thing. ● *adj.* pretended, counterfeit. □ **shammer** *n.*

shaman /sham-ăn/ *n.* ▶ a person regarded as having access to the world of good and evil spirits, esp. among some peoples of northern Asia and North America. [from Tungus (language of E. Siberia) *samán*] □ **shamanic** *adj.* **shamanism** *n.* **shamanist** *n. & adj.* **shamanistic** *adj.*

shamateur *n. Brit. derog.* a sports player who makes money from sporting activities though classed as an amateur. □ **shamateurism** *n.*

shamble ● *v.intr.* walk or run with a shuffling or awkward gait. ● *n.* a shambling gait.

shambles *n.pl.* (usu. treated as *sing.*) **1** *colloq.* a mess or muddle. **2** a butcher's slaughterhouse. **3** a scene of carnage. [pl. of archaic *shamble* 'stool, stall': from Latin *scamellum* 'little bench']

shambolic *adj. Brit. colloq.* chaotic, unorganized. [related to SHAMBLES]

shame ● *n.* **1** a feeling of distress or humiliation caused by consciousness of the guilt or folly of oneself or an associate. **2** a capacity for experiencing this feeling (*have you no shame?*). **3** a state of disgrace, discredit, or intense regret. **4 a** a person or thing that brings disgrace etc. **b** a thing or action that is wrong or regrettable. ● *v.tr.* **1** bring shame on; make ashamed; put to shame. **2** (foll. by *into, out of*) force by shame. □ **for shame!** a reproof to a person for not showing shame. **put to shame** humiliate by revealing superior qualities etc. **shame on you!** you should be ashamed. **what a shame!** how unfortunate! [Old English]

shamefaced *adj.* **1** showing shame. **2** bashful, diffident. [16th-century alteration of archaic *shamefast* 'bashful'] □ **shamefacedly** *adv.* **shamefacedness** *n.*

shameful *adj.* **1** that causes or is worthy of shame. **2** disgraceful, scandalous. □ **shamefully** *adv.* **shamefulness** *n.*

shameless *adj.* **1** having or showing no sense of shame. **2** impudent. □ **shamelessly** *adv.* **shamelessness** *n.*

shammy *n.* (*pl.* **-ies**) (in full **shammy leather**) *colloq.* = CHAMOIS 2. [representing corrupted pronunciation]

shampoo ● *n.* **1** liquid or cream used to lather and wash the hair. **2** a similar substance for washing a car or carpet etc. **3** an act or instance of washing with shampoo. ● *v.tr.* (**shampoos**, **shampooed**) wash with shampoo. [based on Hindi *chhāmpnā* 'to press']

shamrock *n.* any of various plants with trifoliate leaves used as the national emblem of Ireland. [from Irish *seamróg* 'trefoil']

shandy *n.* (*pl.* **-ies**) a drink of beer mixed with lemonade or ginger beer. [19th-century coinage]

shanghai /shang-hy/ *v.tr.* (**shanghais**, **shanghaied**, **shanghaiing**) **1** force (a person) to be a sailor on a ship by using trickery etc. **2** *colloq.* put into detention or an awkward situation by trickery. [from *Shanghai*, a major seaport in China]

shank *n.* **1 a** the leg. **b** the lower part of the leg.

c the shin bone. **2 a** *archaic* part of an animal's hind leg as a cut of meat. **b** *US* = SHIN *n.* 2. **3** a shaft or stem. **4 a** the long narrow part of a tool etc. joining the handle to the working end. **b** the stem of a key, spoon, anchor, etc. [Old English] □ **shanked** *adj.* (also in *comb.*).

shanks's pony *n.* (also **shanks's mare**) one's own legs as a means of conveyance.

shan't *contr.* shall not.

shantung *n.* soft undressed Chinese silk. [from *Shantung*, Chinese province]

shanty[1] *n.* (*pl.* **-ies**) **1** a hut or cabin. **2** a crudely built shack. [19th-century coinage, originally North American]

shanty[2] *n.* (also **chanty**) (*pl.* **-ies**) (in full **sea shanty**) a song of a kind originally sung by sailors while hauling ropes etc.

shanty town *n.* a poor or depressed area of a town, consisting of shanties.

shape ● *n.* **1** the total effect produced by the outlines of a thing. **2** the external form or appearance of a person or thing. **3** a specific form or guise. **4** a description or sort or way (*not on offer in any shape or form*). **5** a definite or proper arrangement (*get our ideas into shape*). **6 a** a condition, as qualified in some way (*in good shape*). **b** (when unqualified) good condition (*back in shape*). **7** a person or thing seen indistinctly or in the imagination (*a shape emerged from the mist*). **8** a mould or pattern. **9** a piece of material, paper, etc., made or cut in a particular form. ● *v.* **1** *tr.* give a certain shape or form to; fashion. **2** *tr.* (foll. by *to*) adapt or make conform. **3** *intr.* give signs of a future shape or development. **4** *tr.* frame mentally. **5** *intr.* assume or develop into a shape. **6** *tr.* direct (one's life etc.). □ **lick** (or **knock**) **into shape** make presentable or efficient. **shape up** **1** take a (specified) form. **2** show promise; make good progress. [Old English *gesceap* 'creation'] □ **shapable** *adj.* (also **shapeable**). **shaped** *adj.* (also in *comb.*). **shaper** *n.*

shapeless *adj.* lacking definite or attractive shape. □ **shapelessly** *adv.* **shapelessness** *n.*

shapely *adj.* (**shapelier**, **shapeliest**) **1** well formed or proportioned. **2** of elegant or pleasing shape or appearance. □ **shapeliness** *n.*

shard *n.* **1** a broken piece of pottery or glass etc. **2** = POTSHERD. [Old English]

share[1] ● *n.* **1** a portion that a person receives from or gives to a common amount. **2 a** a part contributed by an individual to an enterprise or commitment. **b** a part received by an individual from this (*share of the credit*). **3** each of the equal parts into which a company's capital is divided entitling its owner to a proportion of the profits. ● *v.* **1** *tr.* get or have or give a share of. **2** *tr.* use or benefit from jointly with others. **3** *tr.* have in common (*I share your opinion*). **4** *intr.* have a share (*shall I share with you?*). **5** *intr.* (foll. by *in*) participate. **6** *tr.* (often foll. by *out*) *Brit.* **a** divide and distribute. **b** give away part of. □ **share and share alike** make an equal division. [Old English *scearu* 'division'] □ **shareable** *adj.* (also **sharable**). **sharer** *n.*

share[2] *n.* = PLOUGHSHARE. [Old English]

sharecropper *n.* esp. *US* a tenant farmer who gives a part of each crop as rent. □ **sharecrop** *v.tr. & intr.* (**-cropped**, **-cropping**).

share-farmer *n. Austral. & NZ* a tenant farmer who receives a share of the profits from the owner.

shareholder *n.* an owner of shares in a company. □ **shareholding** *n.*

share-out *n.* an act of sharing out; a distribution.

shareware *n. Computing* software that is available free of charge and often distributed informally for evaluation, after which a fee is requested for continued use.

sharia /shă-ree-ă/ *n.* the Muslim code of religious law. [from Arabic *šarī'a*]

sharif *n.* /shĕ-reef/ (also **shereef**, **sherif**) **1** a descendant of Muhammad through his daughter

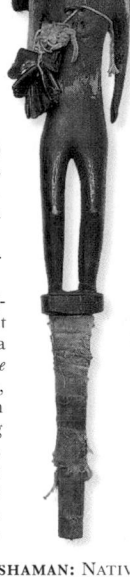

SHAMAN: NATIVE AMERICAN SHAMAN'S CARVING OF A SPIRIT

S

SHARK

Sharks can be classified by the way in which they capture prey. Filter-feeders, such as the whale shark, strain plankton with mesh-like filters in their gills. Bottom-dwellers, such as the wobbegong, use flat back teeth to grind crustaceans found on the seabed. Pursuit feeders, such as the great white shark, commonly eat smaller fish, and have sharp teeth for tearing flesh. Sharks have adaptations that help them hunt, including ampullae of Lorenzini (sensory pores that detect electrical signals) and a lateral line (a series of pressure-sensitive organs down both sides of the head and body that detect the movement of prey).

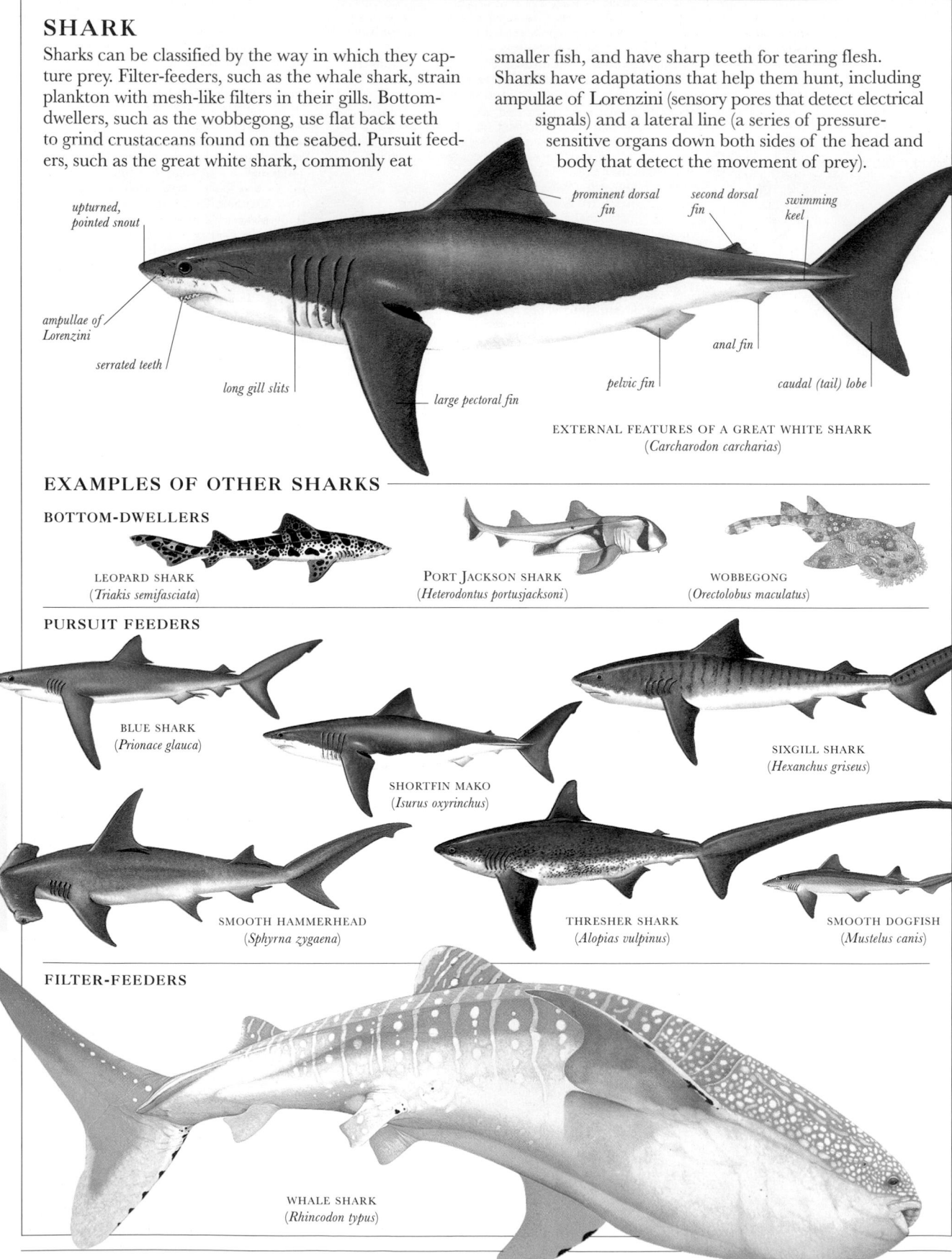

upturned, pointed snout

ampullae of Lorenzini

serrated teeth

long gill slits

large pectoral fin

prominent dorsal fin

second dorsal fin

swimming keel

anal fin

pelvic fin

caudal (tail) lobe

EXTERNAL FEATURES OF A GREAT WHITE SHARK
(*Carcharodon carcharias*)

EXAMPLES OF OTHER SHARKS

BOTTOM-DWELLERS

LEOPARD SHARK
(*Triakis semifasciata*)

PORT JACKSON SHARK
(*Heterodontus portusjacksoni*)

WOBBEGONG
(*Orectolobus maculatus*)

PURSUIT FEEDERS

BLUE SHARK
(*Prionace glauca*)

SHORTFIN MAKO
(*Isurus oxyrinchus*)

TIGER SHARK / SIXGILL SHARK
(*Hexanchus griseus*)

SMOOTH HAMMERHEAD
(*Sphyrna zygaena*)

THRESHER SHARK
(*Alopias vulpinus*)

SMOOTH DOGFISH
(*Mustelus canis*)

FILTER-FEEDERS

WHALE SHARK
(*Rhincodon typus*)

S

Fatima, entitled to wear a green turban or veil. **2** a Muslim leader. [from Arabic, literally 'noble']

shark[1] *n.* ◀ any of various large usu. voracious marine fish with a long body, cartilaginous skeleton, and prominent dorsal fin. ▷ CARTILAGINOUS FISH, ELASMOBRANCH, FISH. [Middle English]

shark[2] *n. colloq.* a person who unscrupulously exploits or swindles others. [16th-century coinage]

sharkskin *n.* **1** the rough scaly skin of a shark. **2** a smooth slightly lustrous fabric.

sharon fruit *n.* a persimmon, esp. of an orange variety grown in Israel. [from *Sharon*, a plain in Israel]

sharp ● *adj.* **1** having an edge or point able to cut or pierce. **2** tapering to a point or edge. **3** abrupt, steep, angular (*a sharp turn*). **4** well defined. **5 a** intense (*has a sharp temper*). **b** (of flavour) pungent, acid. **c** keen (*a sharp appetite*). **d** (of a frost) severe, hard. **6** (of a voice or sound) shrill and piercing. **7** (of sand etc.) composed of angular grains. **8** (of words, temper, etc.) harsh or acrimonious. **9** (of a person) acute; quick to perceive or comprehend. **10** *derog.* quick to take advantage; unscrupulous, dishonest. **11** vigorous or brisk. **12** *Mus.* **a** above the normal pitch. **b** (of a key) having a sharp or sharps in the signature. **c** (as **C sharp**, **F sharp**, etc.) a semitone higher than C, F, etc. ▷ NOTATION. **13** *colloq.* stylish or flashy with regard to dress. ● *n.* **1** *Mus.* a note raised a semitone above natural pitch. **b** the sign (♯) indicating this. **2** *colloq.* a swindler or cheat. **3** a fine sewing-needle. ● *adv.* **1** punctually (*at nine o'clock sharp*). **2** suddenly (*pulled up sharp*). **3** at a sharp angle. **4** *Mus.* above the true pitch (*sings sharp*). [Old English] □ **sharply** *adv.* **sharpness** *n.*

sharpen *v.tr. & intr.* make or become sharp. □ **sharpener** *n.*

sharp end *n.* **1** *Brit. joc.* the bow of a ship. **2** *colloq.* the scene of direct action or decision.

sharper *n.* a swindler, esp. at cards.

sharpish *colloq.* ● *adj.* fairly sharp. ● *adv.* **1** fairly sharply. **2** quite quickly.

sharp practice *n.* dishonest or barely honest dealings.

sharpshooter *n.* a skilled marksman. □ **sharpshooting** *n. & adj.*

sharp-witted *adj.* keenly perceptive or intelligent. □ **sharp-wittedly** *adv.* **sharp-wittedness** *n.*

shat *past* and *past part.* of SHIT.

shatter *v.* **1** *tr. & intr.* break suddenly in pieces. **2** *tr.* severely damage or utterly destroy. **3** *tr.* greatly upset or discompose. **4** *tr.* (usu. as **shattered** *adj.*) *colloq.* exhaust. [Middle English, related to SCATTER] □ **shatterer** *n.* **shattering** *adj.* **shatteringly** *adv.* **shatter-proof** *adj.*

shave ● *v.tr.* (*past part.* **shaved** or (as *adj.*) **shaven**) **1** remove (bristles or hair) from the face etc. with a razor. **2** (also *absol.*) remove bristles or hair with a razor from (the face, leg, etc.). **3 a** reduce by a small amount. **b** take (a small amount) away from. **4** pare (wood etc.) to shape it. **5** pass close to without touching. ● *n.* **1** an act of shaving or the process of being shaved. **2** a close approach without contact. **3** a narrow miss or escape. **4** a tool for shaving wood etc. [Old English]

shaven see SHAVE.

shaver *n.* **1** a person or thing that shaves. **2** an electric razor. **3** *colloq.* a young lad.

Shavian ● *adj.* of or in the manner of G. B. Shaw, Irish-born dramatist d. 1950, or his ideas. ● *n.* an admirer of Shaw. [from *Shavius*, Latinized form of *Shaw*]

shaving *n.* **1** a thin strip cut off the surface of wood etc. **2** (*attrib.*) used in shaving the face (*shaving-cream*).

shawl *n.* a piece of fabric, usu. rectangular and often folded into a triangle, worn over the shoulders or head or wrapped round a baby. [from Persian *šāl*] □ **shawled** *adj.*

she ● *pron.* (*obj.* **her**; *poss.* **her**; *pl.* **they**) **1** the woman or girl or female animal previously named or in

question. **2** a thing regarded as female, e.g. a vehicle or ship. ● *n.* **1** a female; a woman. **2** (in *comb.*) female (*she-goat*). [Middle English]

s/he *pron.* a written representation of 'he or she' used to indicate both sexes.

sheaf ● *n.* (*pl.* **sheaves**) ▶ a group of things held lengthways together, esp. a bundle of cornstalks or papers. ● *v.tr.* make into sheaves. [Old English]

SHEAF OF WHEAT

shear ● *v.* (*past* **sheared**, *archaic* **shore**; *past part.* **shorn** or **sheared**) **1** *tr.* clip the wool off (a sheep etc.). **2** *tr.* remove or take off by cutting. **3** *tr.* cut with scissors or shears etc. **4** *tr.* (foll. by *of*) **a** strip bare. **b** deprive. **5** *tr. & intr.* (often foll. by *off*) distort or be distorted, or break, from a structural strain. ● *n.* **1** *Mech. & Geol.* a strain produced by pressure in the structure of a substance. **2** (in *pl.*) (also **pair of shears** *sing.*) a large clipping or cutting instrument shaped like scissors for use in gardens etc. [Old English] □ **shearer** *n.*

shearwater *n.* ▶ any long-winged seabird of the family Procellariidae, related to petrels, often flying low over the surface of the water.

sheath /sheeth/ *n.* (*pl.* **sheaths**) **1** a close-fitting cover, esp. for the blade of a knife or sword. **2** a condom. **3** *Bot., Anat., & Zool.* an enclosing case or tissue. **4** the protective covering round an electric cable. **5** a woman's close-fitting dress. [Old English] □ **sheathless** *adj.*

sheathe /sheeth/ *v.tr.* **1** put into a sheath. **2** encase; protect with a sheath. [Middle English]

sheathing *n.* a protective casing or covering.

sheath knife *n.* a dagger-like knife carried in a sheath.

sheave *v.tr.* make into sheaves.

sheaves *pl.* of SHEAF.

shebang /shi-**bang**/ *n. N. Amer. slang* a matter or affair (esp. *the whole shebang*). [19th-century coinage]

shebeen /shi-**been**/ *n.* (esp. in Ireland, Scotland, and S. Africa) an unlicensed house selling alcoholic liquor. [from Anglo-Irish *síbín*]

shed[1] *n.* **1** a one-storeyed structure usu. of wood for storage or shelter for animals etc., or as a workshop. **2** a large roofed structure often with one or more sides open, for storing or maintaining machinery, vehicles, etc. (*bicycle shed*). **3** *Austral. & NZ* an open-sided building for shearing sheep or milking cattle.

shed[2] *v.tr.* (**shedding**; *past* and *past part.* **shed**) **1** let or cause to fall off (*trees shed their leaves*). **2** take off (clothes). **3** reduce (an electrical power load) by disconnection etc. **4** cause to fall or flow (*shed blood; shed tears*). **5** disperse, diffuse, radiate (*shed light*). **6** (of a business) reduce its number of (jobs or employees) through redundancy, natural wastage, etc. □ **shed light on** see LIGHT[1]. [Old English]

she'd *contr.* **1** she had. **2** she would.

she-devil *n.* a malicious or spiteful woman.

sheen *n.* **1** a gloss or lustre. **2** radiance, brightness. [from obsolete *sheen* 'beautiful, resplendent'] □ **sheeny** *adj.*

sheep *n.* (*pl.* same) **1** any ruminant mammal of the genus *Ovis* with a thick woolly coat, esp. kept in flocks for its wool or meat, and proverbial for its timidity. **2** a bashful, defenceless, or easily-led

person. **3** (usu. in *pl.*) **a** a member of a minister's congregation. **b** a parishioner. [Old English] □ **sheeplike** *adj.*

sheep-dip *n.* **1** a preparation for cleansing sheep of vermin. **2** the place where sheep are dipped in this.

sheepdog *n.* **1** a dog trained to guard and herd sheep. **2** a dog of a breed suitable for this.

sheepfold *n.* an enclosure for penning sheep.

sheepish *adj.* **1** bashful, shy, reticent. **2** embarrassed through shame. □ **sheepishly** *adv.* **sheepishness** *n.*

sheepshank *n.* ▶ a knot used to shorten a rope temporarily. ▷ KNOT

sheepskin *n.* **1** a garment or rug of sheep's skin with the wool on. **2** leather from a sheep's skin.

sheer[1] ● *adj.* **1** no more or less than; mere, unqualified, absolute (*sheer luck; sheer determination*). **2** (of a cliff or ascent etc.) perpendicular; very steep. **3** (of a textile) diaphanous. ● *adv.* **1** directly, outright. **2** perpendicularly. [Middle English] □ **sheerly** *adv.* **sheerness** *n.*

sheer[2] *v.intr.* **1** esp. *Naut.* swerve or change course. **2** (foll. by *away, off*) go away, esp. from a person or topic one dislikes or fears.

SHEEPSHANK

sheet[1] ● *n.* **1** a large rectangular piece of cotton or other fabric, used esp. in pairs as inner bedclothes. **2 a** a broad usu. thin flat piece of material (e.g. paper or metal). **b** (*attrib.*) made in sheets (*sheet steel*). **3** a wide continuous surface or expanse of water, ice, flame, falling rain, etc. **4** a set of unseparated postage stamps. **5** *derog.* a newspaper. **6** a complete piece of paper of the size in which it was made, for printing and folding as part of a book. ● *v.* **1** *tr.* provide or cover with sheets. **2** *tr.* form into sheets. **3** *intr.* (of rain etc.) fall in sheets. [Old English]

sheet[2] *n.* a rope or chain attached to the lower corner of a sail for securing or controlling it. [from Old Norse *skaut*]

sheet anchor *n.* **1** a second anchor for use in emergencies. **2** a person or thing depended on in the last resort.

sheet bend *n.* a method of temporarily fastening one rope through the loop of another. ▷ KNOT

sheeting *n.* material for making bed linen.

sheet lightning *n.* lightning with its brightness diffused by reflection in clouds etc.

sheet metal *n.* metal formed into thin sheets by rolling, hammering, etc.

sheet music *n.* **1** printed music, as opposed to performed or recorded music and books about music. **2** music published in single or interleaved sheets, not bound.

sheikh /shayk/ *n.* (also **shaikh**, **sheik**) **1** a chief or head of an Arab tribe, family, or village. **2** a Muslim leader. [from Arabic *šayk* 'old man, sheikh'] □ **sheikhdom** *n.*

sheila *n. Austral. & NZ slang* a girl or young woman. [originally *shaler*, assimilated to the name *Sheila*]

shekel *n.* **1** the chief monetary unit of modern Israel. **2** *hist.* a silver coin and unit of weight used in ancient Israel and the Middle East. **3** (in *pl.*) *colloq.* money; riches. [from Hebrew *šeķel*]

shelduck *n.* (*pl.* same or **shelducks**; *masc.* **sheldrake**, *pl.* same or **sheldrakes**) ▶ any large bright-plumaged gooselike duck of the genus *Tadorna*, esp. *T. tadorna* of Eurasian and N. African coasts. [Middle English]

shelf *n.* (*pl.* **shelves**) **1 a** a thin flat piece of wood or metal etc. projecting from a wall, or as part of a unit, used to support books etc. **b** the flat bottom surface of a recess in a wall

SHELDUCK (*Tadorna tadorna*)

SHEARWATER: MANX SHEARWATER (*Puffinus puffinus*)

S

etc. used similarly. **2 a** a projecting horizontal ledge in a cliff face etc. **b** a reef or sandbank. □ **on the shelf 1** (of a woman) past the age when she might expect to be married. **2** (esp. of a retired person) no longer active or of use. [Middle English] □ **shelved** *adj.* **shelfful** *n.* (*pl.* **-fuls**). **shelf-like** *adj.*

shelf-life *n.* (*pl.* **-lives**) the length of time for which a stored item remains usable.

shelf mark *n.* a notation on a book showing its place in a library.

shelf room *n.* available space on a shelf.

shell ● *n.* **1 a** ▶ the hard outer case of many molluscs. ▷ MOLLUSC. **b** the hard but fragile outer covering of an egg. ▷ EGG. **c** the usu. hard outer case of a nut-kernel, seed, etc. **d** the carapace of a tortoise, turtle, etc. **e** the wing-case or pupa-case of many insects etc. **2 a** an explosive projectile for use in a big gun or mortar. **b** a hollow container for fireworks, explosives, cartridges, etc. **c** *US* a cartridge. **3** a mere semblance or outer form without substance. **4** any of several things resembling a shell in being an outer case, esp.: **a** a light racing boat. **b** a hollow pastry case. **c** the metal framework of a vehicle body etc. **d** the walls of an unfinished or gutted building, ship, etc. ● *v.tr.* **1** remove the shell or pod from. **2** bombard with shells. □ **come out of one's shell** cease to be shy. **shell out** (also *absol.*) *colloq.* **1** pay (money). **2** hand over (a required sum). [Old English] □ **shelled** *adj.* **shell-less** *adj.* **shell-like** *adj.* **shellproof** *adj.* (in sense 2a of *n.*). **shelly** *adj.*

she'll *contr.* she will; she shall.

shellac ● *n.* lac resin in thin flakes, used for making varnish (cf. LAC¹). ● *v.tr.* (**shellacked, shellacking**) **1** varnish with shellac. **2** *US slang* defeat or thrash soundly. [SHELL + LAC¹, translation of French *laque en écailles* 'lac in thin plates']

shellfire *n.* the firing of shells.

shellfish *n.* (*pl.* same) **1** an aquatic shelled mollusc. **2** a crustacean.

shell pink ● *n.* a delicate pale pink. ● *adj.* (hyphenated when *attrib.*) of this colour.

shell-shock *n.* a nervous breakdown or other psychological disturbance resulting from exposure to battle. □ **shell-shocked** *adj.*

shell suit *n.* a tracksuit with a soft lining and a weatherproof nylon outer 'shell', used for leisure wear.

Shelta *n.* an ancient secret language used by Irish tinkers, gypsies, etc. and based largely on altered Irish or Gaelic words. [19th-century coinage]

shelter ● *n.* **1** anything serving as a shield or protection from danger, bad weather, etc. **2 a** a place of refuge. **b** *N. Amer.* an animal sanctuary. **3** a shielded condition; protection (*took shelter under a tree*). ● *v.* **1** *tr.* act or serve as shelter to; protect; conceal; defend (*sheltered them from the storm; had a sheltered upbringing*). **2** *intr. & refl.* find refuge; take cover (*sheltered under a tree; sheltered themselves behind the wall*). [16th-century coinage] □ **shelterer** *n.* **shelterless** *adj.*

shelve¹ *v.tr.* **1 a** abandon or defer (a plan etc.). **b** remove (a person) from active work etc. **2** put (books etc.) on a shelf. **3** fit (a cupboard etc.) with shelves. [from *shelves*, pl. of SHELF] □ **shelver** *n.* **shelving** *n.*

shelve² *v.intr.* (of ground etc.) slope (*ground shelved away to the horizon*).

shelves *pl.* of SHELF.

shemozzle *n.* (also **schemozzle**) *slang* **1** a brawl or commotion. **2** a muddle. [Yiddish]

shenanigan *n.* (esp. in *pl.*) *colloq.* **1** high-spirited behaviour; nonsense. **2** trickery; dubious manoeuvres. [19th-century coinage]

shepherd ● *n.* **1** (*fem.* **shepherdess**) a person employed to tend sheep. **2** a member of the clergy etc. who cares for and guides a congregation. ● *v.tr.* **1 a** tend (sheep etc.). **b** guide (followers etc.). **2** marshal or drive (a crowd etc.) like sheep. [Old English]

shepherd's pie *n.* a dish of minced meat under a layer of mashed potato.

sherbet *n.* **1 a** *Brit.* a flavoured sweet effervescent powder or drink. **b** *N. Amer.* a water ice. **2** a drink of sweet diluted fruit juices. [from Arabic *šarba* 'drink']

sherd *n.* = POTSHERD. [variant of SHARD]

sheriff *n.* **1** *Brit.* **a** (also **High Sheriff**) the chief executive officer of the Crown in a county, administering justice etc. **b** an honorary officer elected annually in some towns. **2** *US* an elected officer in a county, responsible for keeping the peace. [Old English]

sheriff court *n. Sc.* a county court.

Sherpa *n.* (*pl.* same or **Sherpas**) a member of a Himalayan people living on the borders of Nepal and Tibet. [native name]

sherry *n.* (*pl.* **-ies**) **1** a fortified wine originally from southern Spain. **2** a glass of this. [earlier *sherris*, from Spanish *(vino de) Xeres*, now Jerez de la Frontera in Andalusia]

she's *contr.* **1** she is. **2** she has.

Shetlander *n.* a native of the Shetland Islands, NNE of the mainland of Scotland.

Shetland pony *n.* ◀ a pony of a small hardy rough-coated breed.

SHETLAND PONY

Shetland wool *n.* a fine loosely twisted wool from Shetland sheep.

shew *archaic* var. of SHOW.

Shia (also **Shi'a**) ● *n.* (*pl.* same or **Shias**) **1** one of the two main branches of Islam, esp. in Iran, that rejects the first three Sunni caliphs and regards Ali, the fourth caliph, as Muhammad's first successor (cf. SUNNI 1). **2** a Shi'ite. ● *adj.* of or relating to Shia. [from Arabic *šī'a* 'party' (of Ali, Muhammad's cousin and son-in-law)]

shiatsu *n.* a kind of therapy of Japanese origin, in which pressure is applied with the thumbs, palms, etc. to certain points of the body. [Japanese, literally 'finger pressure']

shibboleth *n.* a custom, doctrine, phrase, etc., distinguishing a particular group of people. [from Hebrew *šibbōlet* 'ear of corn', used as a test of nationality for its difficult pronunciation (Judg. 12:6)]

shied *past* and *past part.* of SHY².

shield ● *n.* **1 a** esp. *hist.* ▶ a piece of armour carried on the arm or in the hand to deflect blows from the head or body. ▷ QUARTERING. **b** a thing serving to protect (*insurance is a shield against disaster*). **2** a thing resembling a shield, esp.: **a** a trophy in the form of a shield. **b** a protective plate or screen in machinery etc. **c** a shieldlike part of an animal, esp. a shell. **d** a similar part of a plant. ● *v.tr.* protect or screen. [Old English]

shift ● *v.* **1** *intr. & tr.* change or move or cause to change or move from one position to another. **2** *tr. Brit.* remove, esp. with effort (*washing won't shift the stains*). **3** *Brit. slang* **a** *intr.* hurry (*we'll have to shift!*). **b** *tr.* consume (food or drink) hastily or in bulk. **c** *tr. colloq.* sell, esp. quickly, in large quantities, or dishonestly. **4** *intr.* contrive or manage as best one can. **5** *N. Amer.* **a** *tr.* change (gear) in a vehicle. **b** *intr.* change gear. **6** *intr.* (of cargo) get shaken out of place. **7** *intr. archaic* be evasive or indirect. ● *n.* **1 a** the act or an instance of shifting. **b** the

watered steel

chiselled and gilded decoration

boss

SHIELD: 19TH-CENTURY INDIAN SHIELD

substitution of one thing for another. **2 a** a relay of workers (*the night shift*). **b** the time for which they work (*an eight-hour shift*). **3 a** a device, stratagem, or expedient. **b** a trick or evasion. **4 a** a woman's straight unwaisted dress. **b** *archaic* a loose-fitting undergarment. **5** a displacement of spectral lines (see also RED SHIFT). **6** a key on a keyboard used to switch between lower and upper case etc. **7** *N. Amer.* **a** a gear lever in a vehicle. **b** a mechanism for this. □ **make shift** manage or contrive; get along somehow (*made shift without it*). **shift for oneself** rely on one's own efforts. **shift one's ground** take up a new position in an argument etc. **shift off** get rid of (responsibility etc.) to another. [Old English *sciftan* 'to arrange, divide', etc.] □ **shiftable** *adj.* **shifter** *n.*

shiftless *adj.* lacking resourcefulness; lazy. □ **shiftlessly** *adv.* **shiftlessness** *n.*

shifty *adj.* (**shiftier, shiftiest**) *colloq.* evasive; deceitful. □ **shiftily** *adv.* **shiftiness** *n.*

shiitake /shi-tah-kay/ *n.* (in full **shiitake mushroom**) an edible mushroom, *Lentinus edodes*, cultivated in Japan and China on oak logs etc. [Japanese, from *shii* (a kind of oak) + *take* 'mushroom']

Shi'ite /shee-It/ (also **Shiite**) ● *n.* an adherent of the Shia branch of Islam. ● *adj.* of or relating to Shia. □ **Shi'ism** *n.* (also **Shiism**).

shiksa *n. offens.* (used by Jews) a gentile girl or woman. [from Hebrew *šiqsâ*]

shillelagh /shi-lay-lă/ *n.* a thick stick of blackthorn or oak used in Ireland esp. as a weapon. [from *Shillelagh* in Co. Wicklow, Ireland]

shilling *n.* **1** *hist.* a former British coin and monetary unit equal to one-twentieth of a pound. **2** a monetary unit in Kenya, Tanzania, and Uganda. □ **take the King's** (or **Queen's**) **shilling** *Brit. hist.* enlist as a soldier (formerly a soldier was paid a shilling on enlisting). [Old English]

shilly-shally ● *v.intr.* (**-ies, -ied**) be undecided; vacillate. ● *adj.* vacillating. ● *n.* indecision; vacillation. [originally *shill I, shall I*, reduplication of *shall I?*] □ **shilly-shallyer** *n.* (also **-shallier**).

shim ● *n.* a thin strip of material used in machinery etc. to make parts fit. ● *v.tr.* (**shimmed, shimming**) fit or fill up with a shim. [18th-century coinage]

shimmer ● *v.intr.* shine with a tremulous or faint light. ● *n.* such a light. [Old English] □ **shimmeringly** *adv.* **shimmery** *adj.*

shimmy ● *n.* (*pl.* **-ies**) *hist.* a kind of ragtime dance in which the whole body is shaken. ● *v.intr.* (**-ies, -ied**) **1** *hist.* dance a shimmy. **2** move in a similar manner. [20th-century coinage]

shin ● *n.* **1** the front of the leg below the knee. **2** a cut of beef from the lower part of the animal's leg. ● *v.tr. & (usu.* foll. by *up, down*) *intr.* (**shinned, shinning**) climb quickly by clinging with the arms and legs. [Old English]

shin bone *n.* = TIBIA.

shindig *n. colloq.* **1** a festive, esp. noisy, party. **2** = SHINDY 1.

shindy *n.* (*pl.* **-ies**) *colloq.* **1** a brawl, disturbance, or noise (*kicked up a shindy*). **2** = SHINDIG 1.

shine ● *v.* (*past* and *past part.* **shone** or **shined**) **1** *intr.* emit or reflect light; be bright; glow (*the lamp was shining; his face shone with gratitude*). **2** *intr.* (of the Sun, a star, etc.) be visible. **3** *tr.* cause (a lamp etc.) to shine. **4** *tr.* (*past* and *past part.* **shined**) polish (*shined his shoes*). **5** *intr.* be brilliant; excel (*does not shine in conversation; is a shining example*). ● *n.* **1** light; brightness, esp. reflected. **2** a high polish; lustre. **3** *US* the act or an instance of shining esp. shoes. □ **shine up to** *US* seek to ingratiate oneself with. **take the shine out of 1** spoil the brilliance or newness of. **2** throw into the shade by surpassing. **take a shine to** *colloq.* take a fancy to. [Old English] □ **shiningly** *adv.*

S

SHELL

A mollusc's shell consists of layers of a hard mineral (calcium carbonate) laid down within a framework of protein. It is produced by a soft tissue called the mantle, which surrounds the animal's internal organs. Some terrestrial molluscs have shells, but the greatest variation in shell size and shape is shown by marine species. The two main groups are gastropods and bivalves, while tusk shells, chitons, and cephalopods form minor groups. Gastropods usually have a spiral shell, typically with a right-hand coil. Bivalves' shells have paired valves connected by a hinge.

FEATURES OF A NEAPOLITAN TRITON
(*Cymatium parthenopeum*)

CROSS-SECTION OF A NEAPOLITAN TRITON

EXAMPLES OF SHELLS

GASTROPODS

TOWER SCREW SHELL
(*Turritella terebra*)

COMMON SPIDER CONCH
(*Lambis lambis*)

CALIFORNIA FROG SHELL
(*Crossata californica*)

JAPANESE WONDER SHELL
(*Thatcheria mirabilis*)

COMMERCIAL TROCHUS
(*Trochus niloticus*)

WIDE-MOUTHED PURPURA
(*Purpura patula*)

WEST INDIAN WORM SHELL
(*Vermicularia spirata*)

FLEA-BITE CONE
(*Conus pulicarius*)

STRAWBERRY DRUPE
(*Drupa rubusidaeus*)

COMMON EGG COWRIE
(*Ovula ovum*)

FOOL'S CAP
(*Capulus ungaricus*)

BIVALVES

COCKSCOMB OYSTER
(*Lopha cristagalli*)

GIANT RAZOR SHELL
(*Ensis siliqua*)

SPECKLED TELLIN
(*Tellina listeri*)

FAN MUSSEL
(*Pinna rudis*)

DOG COCKLE
(*Glycymeris glycymeris*)

LION'S PAW
(*Lyropecten nodosus*)

TRUE HEART COCKLE
(*Corculum cardissa*)

TUSK SHELLS

ELEPHANT TUSK
(*Dentalium elephantinum*)

CHITONS

BUTTERFLY CHITON
(*Chaetopleura papilio*)

CEPHALOPODS

PEARLY NAUTILUS
(*Nautilus pompilius*)

shiner *n.* **1** a thing that shines. **2** *colloq.* a black eye.

shingle[1] *n.* (in *sing.* or *pl.*) small rounded pebbles, esp. on a seashore. [Middle English] □ **shingly** *adj.*

shingle[2] ● *n.* **1** a rectangular wooden tile used on roofs, spires, or esp. walls. **2** *archaic* **a** shingled hair. **b** the act of shingling hair. **3** *N. Amer.* a small signboard. ● *v.tr.* **1** roof or clad with shingles. **2** *archaic* **a** cut (a woman's hair) short. **b** cut the hair of (a person or head) in this way. [Middle English]

shingles *n.pl.* (usu. treated as *sing.*) an acute painful inflammation of the nerve ganglia, with a skin eruption often forming a girdle around the middle of the body, caused by the same virus as chickenpox. [based on Latin *cingulum* 'girdle']

shin-guard *n.* = SHIN-PAD.

shinny *v.intr.* (**-ies**, **-ied**) (usu. foll. by *up*, *down*) *N. Amer. colloq.* shin (up or down a tree etc.).

shin-pad *n.* a protective pad for the shins, worn when playing football etc.

Shinto *n.* a religion incorporating the worship of ancestors and nature spirits, until 1945 the state religion of Japan. [from Chinese *shen dao* 'way of the gods'] □ **Shintoism** *n.* **Shintoist** *n.*

shinty *n.* (*pl.* **-ies**) *Brit.* **1** a game like hockey played with a ball and curved sticks, and taller goalposts. **2** a stick or ball used in shinty. [earlier *shinny*, apparently from a cry used in the game]

shiny *adj.* (**shinier**, **shiniest**) **1** having a shine; glistening; polished; bright. **2** (of clothing) having the nap worn off. □ **shinily** *adv.* **shininess** *n.*

ship ● *n.* **1 a** ▼ any large seagoing vessel. **b** a sailing vessel with a bowsprit and three, four, or five square-rigged masts. **2** *US* an aircraft. **3** a space-

ship. **4** *colloq.* a boat, esp. a racing boat. ● *v.* (**shipped**, **shipping**) **1** *tr.* put, take, or send away on board ship. **2** *tr.* **a** take in (water) over the side of a ship, boat, etc. **b** take (oars) from the rowlocks and lay them inside a boat. **c** fix (a rudder etc.) in its place. **d** step (a mast). **3** *intr.* **a** embark. **b** (of a sailor) take service on a ship (*shipped for Africa*). **4** *tr.* deliver (goods) to a forwarding agent for conveyance. □ **ship off 1** send or transport by ship. **2** *colloq.* send (a person) away. **ship a sea** *Brit.* be flooded by a wave. **take ship** embark. **when a person's ship comes home** (or **in**) when a person's fortune is made. [Old English] □ **shippable** *adj.*

shipboard *n.* (usu. *attrib.*) used or occurring on board a ship (*a shipboard romance*). □ **on shipboard** on board ship.

shipbuilder *n.* a person, company, etc., that constructs ships. □ **shipbuilding** *n.*

ship canal *n.* a canal large enough for ships.

ship chandler *n.* (also **ship's chandler**) a dealer in ropes, canvas, etc.

shipload *n.* a quantity of goods forming a cargo.

shipmate *n.* a fellow member of a ship's crew.

shipment *n.* **1** an amount of goods shipped. **2** the act or an instance of shipping goods etc.

ship of the desert *n.* the camel.

ship of the line *n. hist.* a ship of sufficient size for the front line of battle.

shipowner *n.* a person owning a ship or ships or shares in ships.

shipper *n.* a person or company that sends or receives goods by ship, or *US* by land or air.

shipping *n.* **1** the act or an instance of shipping goods etc. **2** ships.

shipping agent *n.* a person acting for a ship or ships at a port etc.

ship's biscuit *n. hist.* a hard coarse kind of biscuit kept and eaten on board ship.

ship's boat *n.* a small boat carried on board a ship.

ship's chandler var. of SHIP CHANDLER.

ship's company *n.* a ship's crew.

shipshape *adv. & predic.adj.* in good order; trim and neat.

ship-to-shore ● *adj.* from a ship to land. ● *n.* a radio-telephone for such use.

shipwreck ● *n.* **1 a** the destruction of a ship by a storm, foundering, etc. **b** a ship so destroyed. **2** (often foll. by *of*) the destruction of hopes, dreams, etc. ● *v.* **1** *tr.* inflict shipwreck on. **2** *intr.* suffer shipwreck.

shipwright *n.* **1** a shipbuilder. **2** a ship's carpenter.

shipyard *n.* a place where ships are built, repaired, etc.

shire *n. Brit.* **1** a county. **2** (**the Shires**) **a** a group of English counties with names ending or formerly ending in *-shire*, extending NE from Hampshire and Devon. **b** the midland counties of England. **3** *Austral.* a rural area with its own elected council. [from Old High German *scīra* 'care, official charge']

-shire /shĕ/ *suffix* forming the names of counties (*Derbyshire; Hampshire*).

shire-horse *n.* a heavy powerful type of draught horse. ▷ HORSE

shirk *v.tr.* (also *absol.*) avoid; get out of (duty, work,

SHIP

Throughout history, ships have been used to transport goods and people around the globe. In times of war they are employed in both defence and attack. From the 15th to the mid-19th century, sailing ships like the one shown here were widely used for exploration and trading, but by the 1880s their dominance was ended by the rise of steamships. Today, ships are mainly turbine- or diesel-powered, and include ocean liners, some of which can accommodate over 1,000 passengers; warships such as frigates and aircraft carriers; cargo-carrying container ships; and supertankers, which can carry 300,000 tonnes of oil.

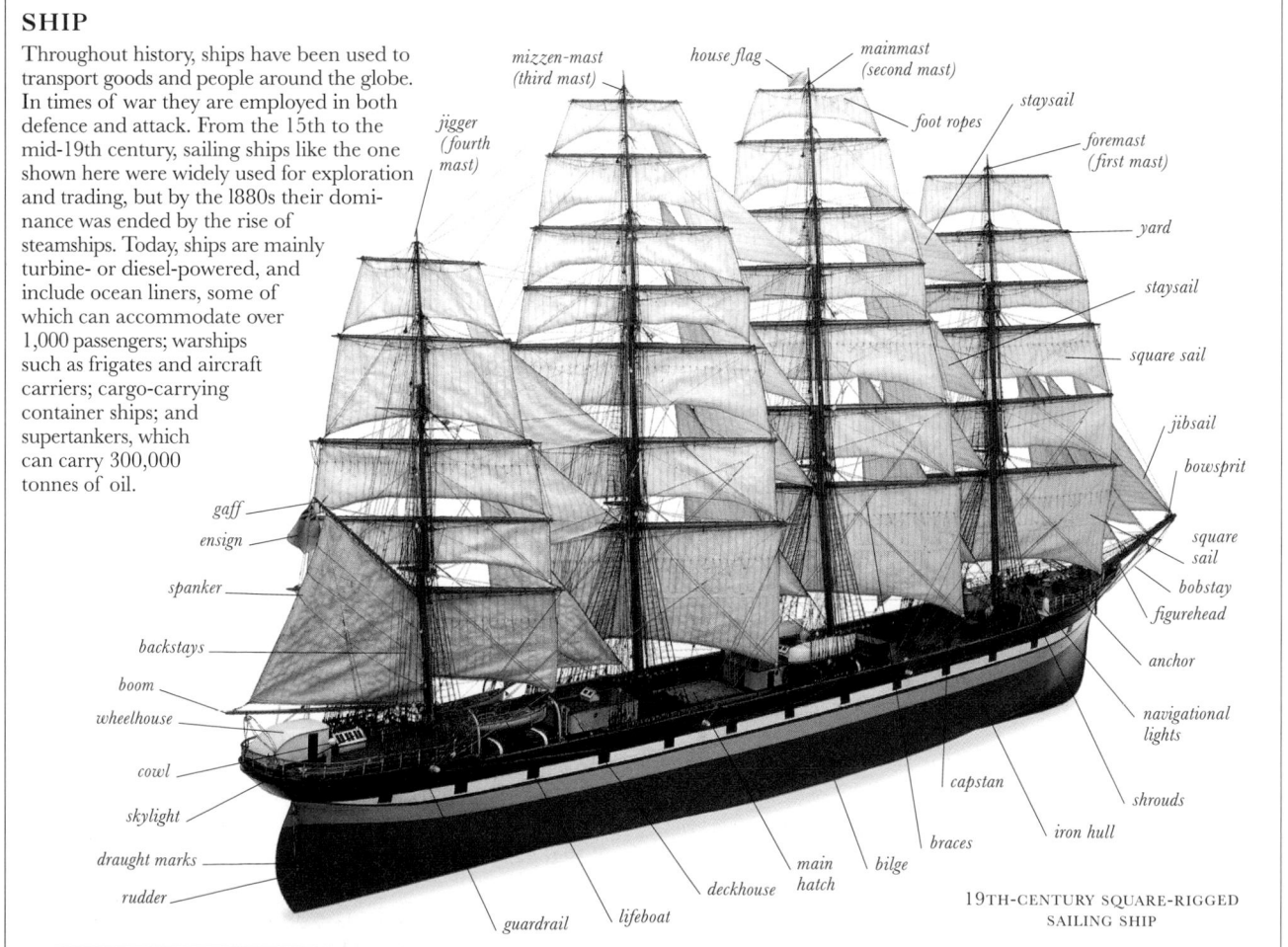

19TH-CENTURY SQUARE-RIGGED SAILING SHIP

mizzen-mast (third mast) · *house flag* · *mainmast (second mast)* · *staysail* · *foot ropes* · *foremast (first mast)* · *jigger (fourth mast)* · *yard* · *staysail* · *square sail* · *jibsail* · *bowsprit* · *square sail* · *bobstay* · *figurehead* · *anchor* · *navigational lights* · *gaff* · *ensign* · *spanker* · *backstays* · *boom* · *wheelhouse* · *cowl* · *skylight* · *draught marks* · *rudder* · *guardrail* · *lifeboat* · *deckhouse* · *main hatch* · *bilge* · *braces* · *iron hull* · *capstan* · *shrouds*

responsibility, fighting, etc.). [from obsolete *shirk* 'sponger'] □ **shirker** *n.*

shirr ● *n.* **1** two or more rows of esp. elastic gathered threads in a garment etc. forming smocking. **2** elastic webbing. ● *v.tr.* **1** gather (material) with parallel threads. **2** *US* bake (eggs) without shells. [19th-century coinage] □ **shirring** *n.*

shirt *n.* **1** a man's upper-body garment of cotton etc., having a collar and sleeves. **2** a similar garment worn by a woman; a blouse. □ **keep one's shirt on** *colloq.* keep one's temper. **lose one's shirt** *colloq.* lose all one's possessions. **put one's shirt on** *Brit. colloq.* bet all one has on. **the shirt off one's back** *colloq.* one's last remaining possessions. [Old English] □ **shirted** *adj.* **shirting** *n.* **shirtless** *adj.*

shirt-dress *n.* = SHIRTWAISTER.

shirt-front *n.* the breast of a shirt, esp. of a stiffened evening shirt.

shirtsleeve *n.* (usu. in *pl.*) the sleeve of a shirt. □ **in shirtsleeves** wearing a shirt with no jacket etc. over it.

shirt-tail *n.* the curved part of a shirt below the waist.

shirtwaist *n.* esp. *US* a woman's blouse resembling a shirt.

shirtwaister *n.* a woman's dress with a bodice like a shirt.

shirty *adj.* (**shirtier**, **shirtiest**) *Brit. colloq.* angry; annoyed. □ **shirtily** *adv.* **shirtiness** *n.*

shish kebab *n.* a dish of pieces of marinated meat and vegetables cooked and served on skewers. [from Turkish *şiş kebabı*]

shit *coarse slang* ● *v.intr. & tr.* (**shitting**; *past* and *past part.* **shitted** or **shit** or **shat**) expel faeces from the body or cause (faeces etc.) to be expelled. ● *n.* **1** faeces. **2** an act of defecating. **3** a contemptible or worthless person or thing. **4** rubbish; nonsense. **5** an intoxicating drug, esp. cannabis. ● *int.* an exclamation of disgust, anger, etc. □ **in the shit** in trouble; in a difficult situation. **not give a shit** not care at all. **up shit creek** in a predicament. [Old English]

shite *n. & int. coarse slang* – SHIT *n. & int.*

shithouse *n. coarse slang* **1** a lavatory. **2** a contemptible place.

shitless *predic.adj. coarse slang* □ **be scared shitless** be extremely frightened.

shit-scared *predic.adj. coarse slang* terrified.

shitty *adj.* (**shittier**, **shittiest**) *coarse slang* **1** disgusting, contemptible. **2** covered with excrement.

shiver[1] ● *v.intr.* **1** tremble with cold, fear, etc. **2** suffer a quick trembling movement of the body; shudder. ● *n.* **1** a momentary shivering movement. **2** (in *pl.*; prec. by *the*) an attack of shivering, esp. from fear or horror (*got the shivers in the dark*). [Middle English] □ **shiveringly** *adv.* **shivery** *adj.*

shiver[2] ● *n.* (esp. in *pl.*) each of the small pieces into which esp. glass is shattered when broken; a splinter. ● *v.tr. & intr.* break into shivers. □ **shiver my timbers** a reputed piratical curse. [Middle English]

shoal[1] ● *n.* **1** a great number of fish swimming together. **2** esp. *Brit.* a multitude; a crowd (*shoals of letters*). ● *v.intr.* (of fish) form shoals.

shoal[2] ● *n.* **1 a** an area of shallow water. **b** a submerged sandbank visible at low water. **2** (esp. in *pl.*) hidden danger. ● *v.intr.* (of water) get shallower. ● *adj.* archaic or *Sc. & N. Amer. dial.* (of water) shallow. [Old English] □ **shoaly** *adj.*

shock[1] ● *n.* **1** a violent collision, impact, tremor, etc. **2** a sudden and disturbing effect on the emotions, physical reactions, etc. (*the news was a great shock*). **3** an acute state of prostration following a wound, pain, etc. (*in shock*). **4** = ELECTRIC SHOCK. **5** esp. *N. Amer.* = SHOCK ABSORBER. ● *v.* **1** *tr.* **a** affect with shock; horrify; outrage. **b** (*absol.*) cause shock. **2** *tr.* (esp. in *passive*) affect with an electric or pathological shock. **3** *intr.* experience shock (*I don't*

shock easily). [from French *choc* (n.), *choquer* (v.)] □ **shockability** *n.* **shockable** *adj.*

shock[2] ● *n.* a group of corn-sheaves stood up with their heads together in a field. ● *v.tr.* arrange (corn) in shocks. [Middle English]

shock[3] *n.* (usu. foll. by *of*) an unkempt or shaggy mass of hair.

shock absorber *n.* ▶ a device on a vehicle etc. for absorbing shocks, vibrations, etc. ▷ CAR

shocker *n. colloq.* **1** a shocking person or thing. **2** *hist.* a sordid or sensational novel etc.

shocking ● *adj.* **1** causing indignation or disgust. **2** *Brit. colloq.* very bad (*shocking weather*). ● *adv. colloq.* shockingly; extremely (*shocking bad manners*). □ **shockingly** *adv.* **shockingness** *n.*

shocking pink ● *n.* a vibrant shade of pink. ● *adj.* of this colour.

shock jock *n. colloq.* a disc jockey who expresses opinions on a talk radio show in a deliberately provocative way, esp. as a means of highlighting a controversial issue.

shockproof *adj.* resistant to the effects of shock.

shock therapy *n.* (also **shock treatment**) *Psychol.* a method of treating depressive patients by electric shock or drugs inducing coma and convulsions.

shock troops *n.pl.* troops specially trained for assault.

shock wave *n.* ▼ a sharp change of pressure in a narrow region travelling through air etc. caused by explosion or by a body moving faster than sound.

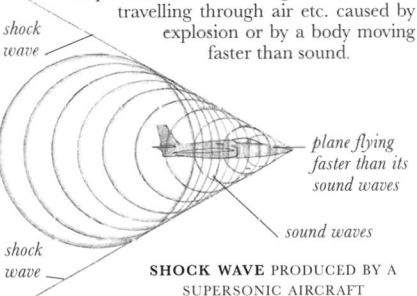

SHOCK WAVE PRODUCED BY A SUPERSONIC AIRCRAFT

shod *past* and *past part.* of SHOE.

shoddy ● *adj.* (**shoddier**, **shoddiest**) **1** poorly made. **2** counterfeit. ● *n.* (*pl.* **-ies**) **1 a** an inferior cloth made partly from the shredded fibre of old woollen cloth. **b** such fibre. **2** any thing of shoddy quality. [19th-century coinage, originally dialect] □ **shoddily** *adv.* **shoddiness** *n.*

shoe ● *n.* **1** ▼ either of a pair of protective foot-coverings of leather, plastic, etc., having a sturdy sole and not reaching above the ankle. **2** a metal rim nailed to the hoof of a horse etc. **3** anything resembling a shoe in shape or use, esp.: **a** a drag for a wheel. **b** = BRAKE SHOE. **c** a socket. ● *v.tr.* (**shoes**, **shoeing**; *past* and *past part.* **shod**) **1** fit (esp. a horse etc.) with a shoe or shoes. **2** (as **shod** *adj.*) (in *comb.*)

having shoes etc. of a specified kind (*dry-shod*; *roughshod*). □ **be in a person's shoes** be in his or her situation, difficulty, etc. **dead men's shoes** property or a position etc. coveted by a prospective successor. [Old English] □ **shoeless** *adj.*

shoeblack *n.* esp. *Brit.* a person who cleans the shoes of passers-by for payment.

shoebox *n.* **1** a box for packing shoes. **2** *colloq.* a very small space or dwelling.

shoehorn ● *n.* a curved piece of horn, metal, etc., for easing the heel into a shoe. ● *v.tr.* force into an inadequate space.

shoelace *n.* a cord for lacing up shoes.

shoe leather *n.* leather for shoes, esp. for the soles when worn through by walking.

shoemaker *n.* a maker of boots and shoes. □ **shoemaking** *n.*

shoeshine *n.* esp. *N. Amer.* a polish given to shoes.

shoestring *n.* **1** a shoelace. **2** *colloq.* a small esp. inadequate amount of money (*living on a shoestring*). **3** (*attrib.*) barely adequate; precarious (*a shoestring majority*).

shoe-tree *n.* a shaped block for keeping a shoe in shape.

shogun *n. hist.* any of a succession of hereditary commanders-in-chief in feudal Japan whose regime dominated Japan from 1192–1867. [Japanese, from Chinese *jiang jun* 'general'] □ **shogunate** *n.*

shone *past* and *past part.* of SHINE.

shoo ● *int.* an exclamation used to frighten away birds, children, etc. ● *v.* (**shoos**, **shooed**) **1** *intr.* utter the word 'shoo'. **2** *tr.* (usu. foll. by *away*) drive (birds etc.) away by shooing.

shoo-in *n. N. Amer.* something easy or certain to succeed.

shook *past* of SHAKE. ● *predic.adj. colloq.* **1** (foll. by *up*) emotionally or physically disturbed; upset. **2** (foll. by *on*) *Austral. & NZ* keen on; enthusiastic about (*not too shook on the English climate*).

shoot ● *v.* (*past* and *past part.* **shot**) **1** *tr.* **a** cause (a gun, etc.) to fire. **b** discharge (a bullet, arrow, etc.) from a gun, bow, etc. **c** kill or wound with a bullet, arrow, etc. from a gun, bow, etc. **2** *intr.* discharge a gun etc. (*shoots well*). **3** *tr.* send out, discharge, propel, etc., swiftly (*shot out the contents*; *shot a glance at his neighbour*). **4** *intr.* come or go swiftly or vigorously. **5** *intr.* **a** (of a plant etc.) put forth buds etc. **b** (of a bud etc.) appear. **6** *intr.* hunt game etc. with a gun. **7** *tr.* film or photograph. **8** esp. *Football* **a** *intr.* take a shot at the goal. **b** *tr.* score (a goal). **9** *tr.* (of a boat) sweep swiftly down or under (a bridge, rapids, falls, etc.). **10** *tr.* move (a door bolt) to fasten or unfasten a door etc. **11** *tr.* (also, *absol.*, foll. by *up*) *slang* inject esp. oneself with (a drug). **12** *tr. N. Amer. colloq.* **a** play a game of (craps, pool, etc.). **b** throw (a die or dice). **13** *tr. Golf* colloq. make (a specified score) for a round or hole. **14** *tr. colloq.* pass (traffic lights at red). ● *n.* **1** the act or an instance of shooting. **2 a** a young branch or sucker. **b** the new growth of a plant. **3** *Brit.* **a** a hunting party, expedition, etc. **b** land shot over for game. **4** = CHUTE[1]. ● *int. N. Amer. slang euphem.* an exclamation of disgust, anger, etc. (see SHIT). □ **shoot ahead** come quickly to the front of competitors etc. **shoot down 1** kill by shooting. **2** cause (an aircraft, its pilot, etc.) to crash by shooting. **3** argue effectively against. **shoot it out** *slang* engage in a decisive gun battle. **shoot a line** *Brit. slang* talk pretentiously. **shoot one's mouth off** *slang* talk too much or indiscreetly. **shoot through** *Austral. & NZ slang* depart; escape; abscond. **shoot up 1** grow rapidly. **2** rise suddenly. **3** terrorize (a district) by indiscriminate shooting. [Old English] □ **shootable** *adj.*

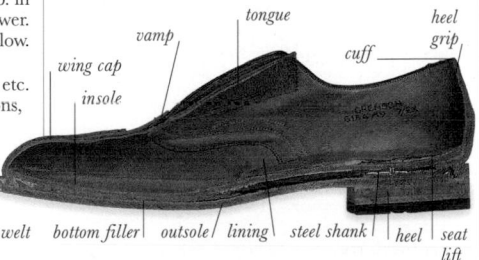

SHOE: CROSS-SECTION OF A LEATHER SHOE

SHOCK ABSORBER: CUTAWAY VIEW OF A CAR'S SHOCK ABSORBER

S

shooter *n.* **1** a person or thing that shoots. **2 a** (in *comb.*) a gun or other device for shooting (*pea-shooter*; *six-shooter*). **b** *slang* a pistol etc. **3** a player who shoots or is able to shoot a goal in football, netball, etc.

shooting ● *n.* **1** the act or an instance of shooting. **2 a** the right of shooting over an area of land. **b** an estate etc. rented to shoot over. ● *adj.* moving, growing, etc. quickly (*a shooting pain in the arm*). □ **the whole shooting match** *colloq.* everything.

shooting box *n.* *Brit.* a lodge used by sportsmen in the shooting season.

shooting brake *n.* (also **shooting break**) *Brit.* an estate car.

shooting gallery *n.* a place used for shooting at targets with rifles etc.

shooting iron *n.* esp. *US colloq.* a firearm.

shooting range *n.* a ground with butts for rifle practice.

shooting star *n.* a small meteor moving rapidly and burning up on entering the Earth's atmosphere.

shooting stick *n.* a walking stick with a handle that unfolds to form a seat.

shooting war *n.* a war in which there is shooting (opp. COLD WAR, WAR OF NERVES, etc.).

shoot-out *n.* *colloq.* **1** a decisive gun battle. **2** (in full **penalty shoot-out**) *Football* a tie-breaker decided by each side taking a specified number of penalty shots.

shop ● *n.* **1** a building, room, etc., for the retail sale of goods or services (*chemist's shop*; *betting shop*). **2** *colloq.* an act of going shopping (*our big weekly shop*). **3** a place in which manufacture or repairing is done (*engineering shop*). **4** a profession, trade, business, etc., esp. as a subject of conversation (*talk shop*). **5** *colloq.* an institution, establishment, place of business, etc. ● *v.* (**shopped**, **shopping**) **1** *intr.* **a** go to a shop or shops to buy goods. **b** *US* = WINDOW-SHOP. **2** *tr.* esp. *Brit.* *slang* inform against (a criminal etc.). □ **all over the shop** *Brit. colloq.* **1** in disorder (*scattered all over the shop*). **2** in every place (*looked for it all over the shop*). **3** wildly (*hitting out all over the shop*). **set up shop** establish oneself in business etc. **shop around** look for the best bargain. [from Old High German *scopf* 'porch']

shopaholic *n.* *colloq.* a compulsive shopper.

shop assistant *n.* *Brit.* a person who serves in a shop.

shopfitter *n.* a person whose job is fitting shops with counters, shelves, etc. □ **shopfitting** *n.*

shop floor *n.* (hyphenated when *attrib.*) *Brit.* **1** workers in a factory etc. as distinct from management. **2** their area or place of work.

shopfront *n.* the façade of a shop.

shop girl *n.* a female assistant in a shop.

shopkeeper *n.* the owner and manager of a shop. □ **shopkeeping** *n.*

shoplifter *n.* a person who steals goods while appearing to shop. □ **shoplift** *v.tr.* (also *absol.*). **shoplifting** *n.*

shopman *n.* (*pl.* **-men**) **1** *Brit.* a shopkeeper or shop assistant. **2** a workman in a repair shop.

shopper *n.* **1** a person who makes purchases in a shop. **2** *Brit.* a shopping bag or trolley. **3** a small-wheeled bicycle with a basket.

shopping *n.* **1** (often *attrib.*) the purchase of goods etc. (*shopping expedition*). **2** goods purchased (*put the shopping on the table*).

shopping centre *n.* an area or complex of shops.

shop-soiled *adj.* *Brit.* **1** soiled or faded by display in a shop. **2** (of a person, idea, etc.) grubby; tarnished; no longer fresh or new.

shop steward *n.* a person elected by workers in a factory etc. to represent them in dealings with management.

shopwalker *n.* *Brit.* an attendant in a large shop who directs customers, supervises assistants, etc.

shop window *n.* **1** a display window in a shop. **2** an opportunity for displaying skills, talents, etc.

shopworker *n.* a person who works in a shop.

shopworn *adj.* esp. *US* = SHOP-SOILED.

shore[1] *n.* **1** the land that adjoins the sea or a large body of water. **2** (usu. in *pl.*) a country; a sea coast (*often visits these shores*; *on a distant shore*). □ **in shore** on the water near or nearer to the shore (cf. INSHORE). **on shore** ashore. [from Middle Dutch *schore* 'shore, sea marsh'] □ **shoreless** *adj.* **shoreward** *adj. & adv.* **shorewards** *adv.*

shore[2] ● *n.* a prop or beam set against a ship, wall, tree, etc., as a support. ● *v.tr.* support with or as if with a shore or shores; hold up. [from Middle Dutch *schōre* 'prop'] □ **shoring** *n.*

shore[3] see SHEAR.

shore-based *adj.* operating from a base on shore.

shore leave *n.* *Naut.* **1** permission to go ashore. **2** a period of time ashore.

shoreline *n.* the line along which a stretch of water meets the shore.

shorn *past part.* of SHEAR.

short ● *adj.* **1 a** measuring little from end to end in space or time (*a short distance*; *a short time ago*; *had a short life*). **b** seeming less than the stated amount (*a few short years of happiness*). **c** consisting of a small number of items (*a short list*). **2** not tall (*a short square tower*; *was shorter than average*). **3 a** (usu. foll. by *of*, (*colloq.*) *on*) having a partial or total lack; deficient; scanty (*short of spoons*; *is rather short on sense*). **b** not far-reaching; acting or being near at hand (*within short range*). **4 a** concise; brief (*kept his speech short*). **b** curt; uncivil (*was short with her*). **5** (of a person's memory) unable to retain things for long. **6** *Phonet.* & *Prosody* of a vowel or syllable: **a** having the lesser of the two recognized durations. **b** (of a vowel) categorized as short with regard to quality and length (cf. LONG[1] *adj.* 7). **7** (of pastry) crumbly; not holding together. **8** esp. *Stock Exch.* (of stocks, a stockbroker, crops, etc.) sold or selling when the amount is not in hand, with reliance on getting the deficit in time for delivery. **9** *Brit.* (of a spirit) undiluted (see also SHORT DRINK). ● *adv.* **1** before the natural or expected time or place; abruptly (*pulled up short*; *cut short the celebrations*). **2** rudely (*spoke to him short*). ● *n.* **1** *Brit. colloq.* = SHORT DRINK. **2** a short circuit. **3** a short film. **4** *Stock Exch.* **a** a person who sells short. **b** (in *pl.*) short-dated stocks. ● *v.tr. & intr.* short-circuit. □ **be caught** (or *Brit.* **taken**) **short 1** be put at a disadvantage. **2** *Brit. colloq.* urgently need to urinate or defecate. **bring up** (or **pull up**) **short** check or pause abruptly. **come short of** fail to reach or amount to. **for short** as a short name (*Tom for short*). **get** (or **have**) **by the short and curlies** *colloq.* be in complete control of (a person). **go short** not have enough. **in short** briefly. **in short order** *US* immediately, rapidly. **in the short run** over a short period of time. **in short supply** scarce. **in the short term** = *in the short run*. **make short work of** accomplish, dispose of, destroy, consume, etc. quickly. **short and sweet** esp. *iron.* brief and pleasant. **short for** an abbreviation for ('*Bob*' *is short for* '*Robert*'). **short of** see sense 3a of *adj.* **2** less than (*nothing short of a miracle*). **3** distant from; before reaching (*two miles short of home*). **4** without going so far as; except (*did everything short of destroying it*). **short on** *colloq.* see sense 3a of *adj.* [Old English] □ **shortish** *adj.* **shortness** *n.*

shortage *n.* a deficiency; an amount lacking (*a shortage of 100 tons*).

short back and sides *n.* *Brit.* a haircut in which the hair is cut short at the back and the sides.

shortbread *n.* a rich type of biscuit made with butter, flour, and sugar.

shortcake *n.* **1** = SHORTBREAD. **2** a cake made of short pastry and filled with fruit and cream.

short change ● *n.* insufficient money given as change. ● *v.tr.* (**short-change**) rob or cheat by giving short change.

short circuit ● *n.* an electric circuit through small resistance, esp. instead of the resistance of a normal circuit. ● *v.* (**short-circuit**) **1** *intr. & tr.* cause a short circuit; cause a short circuit in. **2** *tr.* shorten or avoid (a journey, work, etc.) by taking a more direct route etc.

shortcoming *n.* failure to come up to a standard; a defect.

shortcrust *n.* (in full **shortcrust pastry**) *Brit.* a type of crumbly pastry made with flour, fat, and a little water.

short cut *n.* **1** a route shortening the distance travelled. **2** a quick way of accomplishing something.

short-dated *adj.* due for early payment or redemption.

short division *n.* *Math.* division in which the quotient is written directly without being worked out in writing.

short drink *n.* *Brit.* a strong alcoholic drink served in small measures.

shorten *v.* **1** *intr. & tr.* become or make shorter or short. **2** *tr.* *Naut.* reduce the amount of (sail spread).

shortening *n.* fat used for making pastry.

shortfall *n.* a deficit.

short fuse *n.* *colloq.* a quick temper.

shorthand *n.* **1** (often *attrib.*) a method of rapid writing in abbreviations and symbols. **2** an abbreviated or symbolic mode of expression.

short-handed *adj.* understaffed.

shorthand typist *n.* *Brit.* a typist qualified to take and transcribe shorthand.

short haul *n.* **1** the transport of goods over a short distance (hyphenated when *attrib.* short-haul routes). **2** a short-term effort.

short head *n.* *Brit. Racing* ● *n.* a distance less than the length of a horse's head. ● *v.tr.* (**short-head**) beaten by a short head.

shorthold *adj.* (of a tenancy or lease) whereby a tenant agrees to rent a property for a short fixed term, at the end of which the landlord may recover it.

shorthorn *n.* an animal of a breed of cattle with short horns.

shortlist ● *n.* a list of selected candidates from which a final choice is made. ● *v.tr.* put on a short-list.

short-lived *adj.* ephemeral.

shortly *adv.* **1** (often foll. by *before*, *after*) before long; soon (*will arrive shortly*; *arrived shortly after him*). **2** in a few words; briefly. **3** curtly. [Old English]

short measure *n.* less than the professed amount.

short notice *n.* a small, esp. insufficient, length of warning time.

short odds *n.pl.* nearly equal stakes or chances in betting.

short order *n.* *N. Amer.* an order for quickly cooked food (hyphenated when *attrib.*: short-order chef).

short-range *adj.* **1** having a short range. **2** relating to a fairly immediate future time (*short-range possibilities*).

shorts *n.pl.* **1** trousers reaching only to the knees or higher. **2** *US* underpants.

short shrift *n.* curt treatment.

short sight *n.* the inability to focus except on comparatively near objects. ▷ SIGHT

short-sighted *adj.* **1** having short sight. **2** lacking imagination or foresight. □ **short-sightedly** *adv.* **short-sightedness** *n.*

short-sleeved *adj.* with sleeves not reaching below the elbow.

short-staffed *adj.* having insufficient staff.

shortstop *n.* a baseball fielder between second and third base. ▷ BASEBALL

short story *n.* a story with a fully developed theme but shorter than a novel.

short temper *n.* a tendency to lose one's temper quickly. □ **short-tempered** *adj.*

short-term *adj.* occurring in or relating to a short period of time.

short-termism *n.* concentration on short-term

S

projects etc. for immediate profit at the expense of long-term security.

short time *n.* the condition of working fewer than the regular hours per day or days per week.

short ton see TON 2.

short view *n.* a consideration of the present only, not the future.

short waist *n.* **1** a high or shallow waist of a dress. **2** a short upper body.

short wave *n.* a radio wave of frequency greater than 3 MHz.

short weight *n.* weight less than it is alleged to be.

short wind *n.* breathing power that is quickly exhausted.

short-winded *adj.* **1** having short wind. **2** incapable of sustained effort.

shorty *n.* (also **shortie**) (*pl.* **-ies**) *colloq.* **1** a person shorter than average. **2** a short garment.

shot[1] *n.* **1** the act or an instance of firing a gun etc. (*several shots were heard*). **2** an attempt to hit by shooting or throwing etc. (*took a shot at him*). **3 a** a single non-explosive missile for a gun etc. **b** (*pl.* same or **shots**) a small lead pellet used in quantity in a single charge or cartridge in a shotgun. ▷ SHOTGUN. **c** (treated as *pl.*) these collectively. **4 a** a photograph. **b** a film sequence photographed continuously by one camera. **5 a** a stroke; a kick in a ball game. **b** a kick etc. made with the aim of scoring. **c** *colloq.* an attempt to guess or do something (*let him have a shot at it*). **6** *colloq.* a person having a specified skill with a gun etc. (*is not a good shot*). **7** a heavy ball thrown by a shot-putter. ▷ SHOT-PUT. **8** the launch of a space rocket. **9** the range, reach, or distance to or at which a thing will carry or act. **10** a remark aimed at a person. **11** *colloq.* **a** a drink of esp. spirits. **b** an injection of a drug, vaccine, etc. □ **like a shot** *colloq.* without hesitation; willingly. **shot across the bows** see BOW[3]. **shot in the arm** *colloq.* **1** stimulus or encouragement. **2** *Brit.* an alcoholic drink. **shot in the dark** a mere guess. [Old English]

shot[2] *past* and *past part.* of SHOOT. ● *adj.* **1** (of coloured material) woven so as to show different colours at different angles. **2** *colloq.* **a** exhausted; finished; ruined. **b** drunk. □ **bc** (or **gct**) **shot of** *Brit. slang* be (or get) rid of. **shot through** permeated or suffused.

shot[3] *n. Brit. colloq.* a reckoning, a bill (*paid his shot*). [Middle English]

shotgun *n.* ▼ a smooth-bore gun for firing small shot at short range.

SHOTGUN: OVER-AND-UNDER SHOTGUN AND CARTRIDGE

shotgun marriage *n.* (also **shotgun wedding**) *colloq.* an enforced or hurried wedding, esp. because of the bride's pregnancy.

shot-put *n.* ▶ an athletic contest in which a shot is thrown. □ **shot-putter** *n.*

SHOT-PUT: ATHLETE PUTTING A SHOT

should *v.aux.* (3rd *sing.* **should**) *past* of SHALL, used esp.: **1** in reported speech, esp. with the reported element in the 1st person (cf. WOULD) (*I said I should be home by evening*). **2 a** to express a duty, obligation, or likelihood (*I should tell you; you should have been more careful; they should have arrived by now*). **b** (in

the 1st person) to express a tentative suggestion (*I should like to say something*). **3 a** expressing the conditional mood in the 1st person (cf. WOULD) (*I should have been killed if I had gone*). **b** forming a conditional clause (*if you should see him; should they arrive, tell them where to go*). **4** expressing purpose (*in order that we should not worry*).

■ **Usage** In senses 1, 2b, and 3a, *would* is now more often used with *I* and *we* than *should*, i.e. *I said I would be late; I would have given it to her if I had seen her*, in order to avoid the sense of obligation or duty implied by *should* (see sense 2a above). In senses 2a, 3b, and 4 *should* and not *would* is used with all the persons.

shoulder ● *n.* **1 a** the part of the body at which the arm, foreleg, or wing is attached. **b** (in full **shoulder joint**) the end of the upper arm joining with the collarbone and scapula. ▷ JOINT. **c** either of the two projections below the neck from which the arms hang. **2** the upper foreleg and shoulder blade of a pig, lamb, etc. when butchered. **3** (often in *pl.*) **a** the upper part of the back and arms. **b** this part of the body regarded as capable of bearing a burden or blame, providing comfort, etc. (*needs a shoulder to cry on*). **4** a strip of land next to a road (*pulled over on to the shoulder*). **5** a part of a garment covering the shoulder. **6** a part of anything resembling a shoulder in form or function, as in a bottle, mountain, tool, etc. ● *v.* **1 a** *tr.* push with the shoulder; jostle. **b** *intr.* make one's way by jostling (*shouldered through the crowd*). **2** *tr.* take (a burden etc.) on one's shoulders (*shouldered the family's problems*). □ **put** (or **set**) **one's shoulder to the wheel** set to work vigorously. **shoulder arms** hold a rifle with the barrel against the shoulder and the butt in the hand. **shoulder to shoulder 1** side by side. **2** with closed ranks or united effort. [Old English] □ **shouldered** *adj.* (also in *comb.*).

shoulder bag *n.* a bag that can be hung from the shoulder.

shoulder-belt *n.* a bandolier or other strap passing over one shoulder and under the opposite arm.

shoulder blade *n. Anat.* either of the large flat bones of the upper back.

shoulder joint see SHOULDER *n.* 1b.

shoulder-length *adj.* (of hair etc.) reaching to the shoulders.

shoulder pad *n.* a pad sewn into a garment to bulk out the shoulder.

shoulder strap *n.* **1** a strip of cloth going over the shoulder from front to back of a garment. **2** a strap suspending a bag etc. from the shoulder.

shouldn't *contr.* should not.

shout ● *v.* **1** *intr.* make a loud cry or vocal sound; speak loudly (*shouted for attention*). **2** *tr.* say or express loudly (*shouted that the coast was clear*). **3** *tr.* (also *absol.*) *Austral.* & *NZ colloq.* treat (another person) to drinks etc. ● *n.* **1** a loud cry expressing joy etc. or calling attention. **2** *Brit. colloq.* one's turn to order and pay for a round of drinks etc. □ **all over bar** (or **but**) **the shouting** *colloq.* the contest is virtually decided. **shout down** reduce to silence by shouting. **shout for** call for by shouting. [Middle English] □ **shouter** *n.*

shove ● *v.* **1** *tr.* (also *absol.*) push vigorously (*shoved him out of the way*). **2** *intr.* (usu. foll. by *along, past, through,* etc.) make one's way by pushing (*shoved through the crowd*). **3** *tr. colloq.* put somewhere (*shoved it in the drawer*). ● *n.* an act of shoving or of prompting a person into action □ **shove off 1** start from the shore

in a boat. **2** *slang* depart (*told him to shove off*). [Old English]

shove-halfpenny *n.* a form of shovelboard played with coins etc. on a table.

shovel ● *n.* **1 a** a spadelike tool for shifting quantities of coal, earth, etc., esp. having the sides curved upwards. **b** the amount contained in a shovel; a shovelful. **2** a machine or part of a machine having a similar form or function. ● *v.tr.* (**shovelled**, **shovelling**; *US* **shoveled**, **shoveling**) **1** shift or clear (coal etc.) with or as if with a shovel. **2** *colloq.* move in large quantities or roughly (*shovelled peas into his mouth*). [Old English] □ **shovelful** *n.* (*pl.* **-fuls**).

shovelboard *n. Brit.* a game played esp. on a ship's deck by pushing discs with the hand or with a long-handled shovel over a marked surface. [alteration of obsolete *shoveboard*]

shoveller *n.* (*US* **shoveler**) **1** a person or thing that shovels. **2** (usu. **shoveler**) ▼ a duck, *Anas clypeata*, with a broad shovel-like beak. ▷ DUCK.

SHOVELLER: NORTHERN SHOVELLER
(*Anas clypeata*)

show ● *v.* (*past part.* **shown** or **showed**) **1** *intr.* & *tr.* be, or allow or cause to be, visible; manifest; appear (*the buds are beginning to show; white shows the dirt*). **2** *tr.* offer, exhibit, or produce (a thing) for scrutiny etc. (*show your tickets please; showed him my poems*). **3** *tr.* demonstrate (kindness, rudeness, etc.) to a person (*showed respect towards him; showed him no mercy*). **4** *intr.* (of feelings etc.) be manifest (*his dislike shows*). **5** *tr.* **a** point out; prove (*has shown it to be false; showed that he knew the answer*). **b** (usu. foll. by *how to* + infin.) cause (a person) to understand or be capable of doing (*showed them how to knit*). **6** *tr.* (*refl.*) **a** exhibit oneself as being (*showed herself a generous host*). **b** (foll. by *to be*) exhibit oneself to be (*showed herself to be fair*). **7** *tr.* & *intr.* (with reference to a film) be presented or cause to be presented. **8** *tr.* exhibit in a show. **9** *tr.* conduct or lead (*showed them to their rooms*). **10** *intr.* = *show up* 3 (*waited but he didn't show*). ● *n.* **1** the act or an instance of showing; the state of being shown. **2 a** a spectacle, display, exhibition, etc. (*a fine show of blossom*). **b** a collection of things etc. shown for public entertainment or in competition (*dog show; flower show*). **3 a** a play etc., esp. a musical. **b** a light entertainment programme on television etc. **c** any public entertainment or performance. **4 a** an outward appearance or display (*made a show of agreeing; a show of strength*). **b** empty appearance; mere display (*did it for show; that's all show*). **5** esp. *Brit. colloq.* an opportunity of acting, defending oneself, etc. (*gave him a fair show; made a good show of it*). **6** *Med.* a discharge of blood etc. from the vagina at the onset of childbirth. □ **give the show** (or **whole show**) **away** demonstrate the inadequacies or reveal the truth. **good** (or **bad** or **poor**) **show!** esp. *Brit. colloq.* **1** that was well (or badly) done. **2** that was lucky (or unlucky). **nothing to show for** no visible result of (effort etc.). **on show** being exhibited. **show one's cards** = *show one's hand*. **show a person** etc. **a clean pair of heels** *colloq.* retreat speedily from a person etc.; run away. **show one's colours** make one's opinion clear. **show a person the door** dismiss or eject a person. **show one's face** make an appearance; let oneself be seen. **show fight** be persistent or belligerent. **show forth** *archaic* exhibit; expound. **show one's hand 1** disclose one's plans. **2** reveal one's cards. **show a leg** *Brit. colloq.* **1** get out of bed. **2** make one's appearance. **show off 1** display to advantage. **2** *colloq.* act pretentiously; display one's

S

SHOWJUMPING

Although equestrian events were recorded at the Olympic Games of 642 BC, the first showjumping contests were not staged until the early 1900s. A horse and rider in a showjumping competition must negotiate a set course that includes fences and water hazards. Faults are incurred when the horse or rider falls, when a jump is refused, or when an obstacle is knocked down. Jumping fences in the wrong order results in elimination. Depending on the type of competition, the winning horse and rider have either the fewest faults or the quickest time. Most fences consist of planks or poles supported by wooden stands called standards or wings. To prevent injury, parts of these fences collapse on impact.

SHOWJUMPING HORSE AND RIDER

SHOWJUMPING FENCES

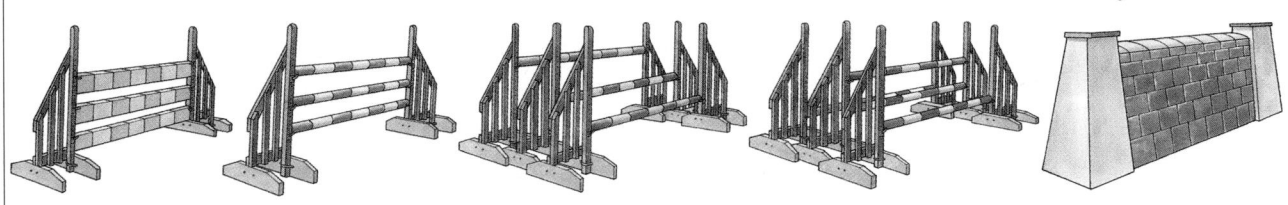

UPRIGHT PLANKS   UPRIGHT POLES   TRIPLE BAR (STAIRCASE)   HOG'S-BACK   WALL

wealth, knowledge, etc. **show oneself 1** be seen in public. **2** see sense 6 of v. **show round** (*US* **around**) take (a person) to places of interest; act as guide for (a person) in a building etc. **show one's teeth** *Brit.* reveal one's strength; be aggressive. **show through 1** be visible through a covering. **2** (of real feelings etc.) be revealed inadvertently. **show up 1** make or be conspicuous or clearly visible. **2** expose (a fraud, impostor, inferiority, etc.). **3** *colloq.* appear; arrive. **4** *colloq.* embarrass or humiliate (*don't show me up by wearing jeans*). **show the way 1** indicate what has to be done etc. by attempting it first. **2** show others which way to go etc. **show willing** display a willingness to help etc. [Old English]

showbiz *n. colloq.* = SHOW BUSINESS.

showboat *n. US* a river steamer on which theatrical performances are given.

show business *n. colloq.* the theatrical profession.

showcase ● *n.* **1** a glass case used for exhibiting goods etc. **2** a place or medium for presenting something to general attention. ● *v.tr.* display in or as if in a showcase.

showdown *n.* **1** a final test or confrontation; a decisive situation. **2** the laying down face up of the players' cards in poker.

shower ● *n.* **1** a brief fall of rain, snow, etc. **2 a** a brisk flurry of arrows, dust, sparks, etc. **b** a flurry of gifts, praise, etc. **3** (in full **shower-bath**) **a** a cubicle, bath, etc. in which one stands under a spray of water. **b** the apparatus etc. used for this. **c** the act of bathing in a shower. **4** *N. Amer.* a party for giving presents to a prospective bride, etc. **5** *Brit. slang* a contemptible or unpleasant person or group of people. ● *v.* **1** *tr.* discharge (water, missiles, etc.) in a shower. **2** *intr.* use a shower-bath. **3** *tr.* (usu. foll. by *on, upon*) lavishly bestow (gifts etc.). **4** *intr.* descend in a shower (*it showered on and off all day*). [Old English] □ **showery** *adj.*

showerproof ● *adj.* resistant to light rain. ● *v.tr.* make showerproof.

showgirl *n.* an actress who sings and dances in musicals, variety shows, etc.

showground *n.* an area of land on which a show takes place.

show house *n.* (also **show home**) *Brit.* a furnished and decorated house on a new estate shown to prospective buyers.

showing *n.* **1** the act or an instance of showing. **2** a usu. specified quality of performance (*a poor showing*). **3** the presentation of a case; evidence (*on present showing*).

showjumping *n.* ▲ the sport of riding horses competitively over a course of fences etc. □ **showjump** *v.intr.* **showjumper** *n.*

showman *n.* (*pl.* **-men**) **1** the proprietor or manager of a circus etc. **2** a person skilled in self-advertisement or publicity. □ **showmanship** *n.*

shown *past part.* of SHOW.

show-off *n. colloq.* a person who shows off.

show of force *n.* a demonstration of one's readiness to use force.

show of hands *n.* raised hands indicating a vote for or against.

showpiece *n.* **1** an item of work presented for exhibition or display. **2** an outstanding example or specimen.

showplace *n.* a house etc. that tourists go to see.

showroom *n.* a room used to display goods for sale.

show-stopper *n. colloq.* a performance receiving prolonged applause. □ **show-stopping** *adj.*

show trial *n.* esp. *hist.* a judicial trial designed by the state to terrorize or impress the public.

show-window *n.* a window for exhibiting goods etc.

showy *adj.* (**showier, showiest**) **1** brilliant; gaudy, esp. vulgarly so. **2** striking. □ **showily** *adv.* **showiness** *n.*

shrank *past* of SHRINK.

shrapnel *n.* **1** fragments of a bomb etc. thrown out by an explosion. **2** a shell containing pieces of metal etc. timed to burst short of impact. [named after Gen. H. *Shrapnel*, British soldier, 1761–1842, inventor of the shell]

shred ● *n.* **1** a scrap, fragment, or strip. **2** the least amount, remnant (*not a shred of evidence*). ● *v.tr.* (**shredded, shredding**) tear or cut into shreds. □ **tear to shreds** completely refute (an argument etc.). [Old English *scrēad* 'piece cut off', *scrēadian* 'to trim, prune']

shredder *n.* **1** a machine used to reduce documents to shreds. **2** any device used for shredding.

shrew *n.* **1** ▼ any small usu. insect-eating mouselike mammal of the family Soricidae, with a long pointed snout. **2** a bad-tempered or scolding woman. [Old English] □ **shrewish** *adj.* (in sense 2). **shrewishly** *adv.* **shrewishness** *n.*

SHREW: COMMON SHREW
(*Sorex araneus*)

shrewd *adj.* **1** showing astute powers of judgement; clever and judicious. **2** (of a face etc.) shrewd-looking. [Middle English in sense 'malignant': from obsolete *shrew* 'to curse'] □ **shrewdly** *adv.* **shrewdness** *n.*

shriek ● *v.* **1** *intr.* **a** utter a shrill screeching sound or words. **b** (foll. by *of*) provide a clear or blatant indication of. **2** *tr.* **a** utter by shrieking (*shrieked his name*). **b** indicate clearly or blatantly. ● *n.* a high-pitched piercing cry or sound. □ **shriek out** say in shrill tones. **shriek with laughter** laugh uncontrollably. □ **shrieker** *n.*

shrift *n. archaic* **1** confession to a priest. **2** confession and absolution. [Old English, from SHRIVE]

shrike *n.* any bird of the family Laniidae that impales its prey of small birds and insects on thorns.

shrill ● *adj.* **1** piercing and high-pitched in sound. **2** *derog.* (esp. of a protester) sharp, unrestrained. ● *v.* **1** *intr.* (of a cry etc.) sound shrilly. **2** *tr.* utter (a song, complaint, etc.) shrilly. [Middle English] □ **shrillness** *n.* **shrilly** *adv.*

shrimp ● *n.* **1** (*pl.* same or **shrimps**) ▼ any of various small (esp. marine) edible crustaceans, with ten legs, grey-green when alive and pink when cooked. **2** *colloq.* a very small slight person. ● *v.intr.* go catching shrimps. [Middle English] □ **shrimper** *n.*

SHRIMP: COMMON SHRIMP
(*Crangon crangon*)

shrine ● *n.* **1** esp. *RC Ch.* **a** a chapel, church, altar, etc., sacred to a saint, relic, etc. **b** the tomb of a saint etc. **c** a reliquary. **d** a niche containing a holy statue etc. **2** a place associated with or containing memorabilia of a particular person, event, etc. **3** ▼ a Shinto place of worship. ● *v.tr. poet.* enshrine. [from Latin *scrinium* 'case for books']

SHRINE: 19TH-CENTURY SHINTO
SHRINE, JAPAN

shrink ● *v.* (*past* **shrank**; *past part.* **shrunk** or (esp. as *adj.*) **shrunken**) **1** *tr. & intr.* make or become smaller; contract, esp. by the action of moisture, heat, or cold. **2** *intr.* (usu. foll. by *from*) **a** recoil; flinch; cower (*shrank from her touch*). **b** be averse from doing (*shrinks from meeting them*). **3** *intr.* (as **shrunken** *adj.*) (esp. of a person etc.) having grown smaller because of age, illness, etc. ● *n.* **1** the act or an instance of shrinking. **2** *slang* a psychiatrist (from 'head-shrinker'). □ **shrink into oneself** become

withdrawn. [Old English] □ **shrinkable** *adj.* **shrinker** *n.* **shrinkingly** *adv.* **shrink-proof** *adj.*

shrinkage *n.* **1 a** the process or fact of shrinking. **b** the degree of shrinking. **2** an allowance made for the reduction in takings due to wastage, theft, etc.

shrinking violet *n.* an exaggeratedly shy person.

shrink-resistant *adj.* (of textiles etc.) resistant to shrinkage when wet etc.

shrink-wrap *v.tr.* (**-wrapped**, **-wrapping**) enclose (an article) in (esp. transparent) film that shrinks tightly on to it.

shrive *v.tr.* (*past* **shrove**; *past part.* **shriven**) *Eccl. archaic* **1** (of a priest) hear the confession of, assign penance to, and absolve. **2** (*refl.*) (of a penitent) submit oneself to a priest for confession etc. [Old English *scrīfan* 'to impose as penance']

shrivel *v.tr. & intr.* (**shrivelled**, **shrivelling**; *US* **shriveled**, **shriveling**) contract or wither into a wrinkled, folded, rolled-up, contorted, or dried-up state.

shriven *past part.* of SHRIVE.

shroud ● *n.* **1** a sheetlike garment for wrapping a corpse for burial. **2** anything that conceals like a shroud (*shroud of mystery*). **3** (in *pl.*) *Naut.* a set of ropes forming part of the standing rigging and supporting the mast or topmast. ▷ **DINGHY, RIGGING**. ● *v.tr.* **1** clothe (a body) for burial. **2** cover, conceal, or disguise (*shrouded in mist*). [Old English] □ **shroudless** *adj.*

shrove *past* of SHRIVE.

Shrove Tuesday *n.* the day before Ash Wednesday.

shrub[1] *n.* a woody plant smaller than a tree and having a very short stem with branches near the ground. [Old English] □ **shrubby** *adj.*

shrub[2] *n.* a cordial made of sweetened fruit juice and spirits, esp. rum. [from Arabic *šurb*]

shrubbery *n.* (*pl.* **-ies**) an area planted with shrubs.

shrug ● *v.* (**shrugged**, **shrugging**) **1** *intr.* slightly and momentarily raise the shoulders to express indifference, ignorance, contempt, etc. **2** *tr.* **a** raise (the shoulders) in this way. **b** shrug the shoulders to express (indifference etc.) (*shrugged his consent*). ● *n.* the act or an instance of shrugging. □ **shrug off** dismiss as unimportant etc. by or as if by shrugging. [Middle English]

shrunk (also **shrunken**) *past part.* of SHRINK.

shuck *US* ● *n.* **1** a husk or pod. **2** the shell of an oyster or clam. **3** (in *pl.*) *colloq.* an expression of contempt or regret or self-deprecation in response to praise. ● *v.tr.* **1** remove the shucks of; shell. **2** (often foll. by *off*) remove, throw or strip off (clothes etc.). [17th-century coinage] □ **shucker** *n.*

shudder ● *v.intr.* **1** shiver esp. convulsively from cold, repugnance, etc. **2** feel strong repugnance etc. (*shudder to think*). **3** (of a machine etc.) vibrate or quiver. ● *n.* **1** the act or an instance of shuddering. **2** (in *pl.*; prec. by *the*) *colloq.* a state of shuddering. [from Middle Dutch *schūderen*] □ **shudderingly** *adv.* **shuddery** *adj.*

shuffle ● *v.* **1** *tr. & intr.* move with a scraping, sliding, or dragging motion. **2** *tr.* **a** (also *absol.*) rearrange (a pack of cards) by sliding them over each other quickly. **b** rearrange; intermingle (*shuffled the documents*). **3** *tr.* (usu. foll. by *on*, *off*, *into*) assume or remove esp. clumsily or evasively (*shuffled on his clothes*; *shuffled off responsibility*). **4** *intr.* **a** equivocate; prevaricate. **b** continually shift one's position; fidget. ● *n.* **1** a shuffling movement. **2** the act or an instance of shuffling cards. **3** a change of relative positions. **4** a quick scraping movement of the feet in dancing. □ **shuffler** *n.*

shuffle-board *n. N. Amer.* = SHOVELBOARD.

shufti *n.* (*pl.* **shuftis**) *Brit. colloq.* a look or glimpse. [based on Arabic *šaffa* 'to try to see']

shul /shool/ *n.* a synagogue.

shun *v.tr.* (**shunned**, **shunning**) avoid; keep clear of (*shuns human company*). [Old English]

shunt ● *v.* **1** *intr. & tr.* diverge or cause (a train) to be diverted esp. on to a siding. **2** *tr.* divert (a decision etc.) on to another person etc. ● *n.* **1** the act or an

instance of shunting on to a siding. **2** *Electr.* a conductor joining two points of a circuit, through which more or less of a current may be diverted. **3** *Brit. slang* a motor accident, esp. a collision of vehicles travelling one close behind another. [Middle English] □ **shunter** *n.*

shush ● *int.* = HUSH *int.* ● *v.* **1** *intr.* **a** call for silence by saying *shush*. **b** be silent (*they shushed at once*). **2** *tr.* make or attempt to make silent.

shut *v.* (**shutting**; *past* and *past part.* **shut**) **1** *tr.* **a** move (a door, lid, lips, etc.) into position so as to block an aperture. **b** close or seal (a room, window, box, eye, mouth, etc.) by moving a door, lid, etc. **2** *intr.* become or be capable of being closed or sealed (*shuts automatically*). **3** *intr. & tr.* esp. *Brit.* become or make (a shop etc.) closed for trade. **4** *tr.* bring (a book, hand, etc.) into a folded-up or contracted state. **5** *tr.* (usu. foll. by *in*, *out*) keep (a person, sound, etc.) in or out of a room etc. by shutting a door etc. (*shut out the noise*). **6** *tr.* (usu. foll. by *in*) catch (a finger, dress, etc.) by shutting something on it (*shut her finger in the door*). □ **be** (or **get**) **shut of** *slang* be (or get) rid of. **shut the door on** refuse to consider; make impossible. **shut down 1** stop (a factory etc.) from operating. **2** (of a factory etc.) stop operating. **shut one's eyes** (or **ears** or **heart** or **mind**) **to** pretend not, or refuse, to see (or hear or feel sympathy for or think about). **shut in** (of hills, houses, etc.) encircle, prevent access etc. to or escape from (*shut in on three sides*) (see also sense 5). **shut off 1 a** stop the flow of (water, gas, etc.) by shutting a valve. **b** switch off (a machine etc.). **2** separate from society etc. **shut out 1** exclude. **2** screen from view. **3** prevent (a possibility etc.). **4** block from the mind. **shut up 1** close all doors and windows of; bolt and bar. **2** imprison (a person). **3** close (a box etc.) securely. **4** *colloq.* reduce to silence by rebuke etc. **5** put (a thing) away in a box etc. **6** (esp. in *imper.*) *colloq.* stop talking. **shut up shop 1** close a business, shop, etc. **2** cease business etc. permanently. [Old English]

shutdown *n.* the closure of a factory etc.

shut-eye *n. colloq.* sleep.

shut-off *n.* **1** something used for stopping an operation. **2** a cessation of flow, supply, or activity.

shutter ● *n.* **1** a person or thing that shuts. **2 a** each of a pair or set of panels fixed inside or outside a window for security, privacy, or shade. **b** a structure of slats on rollers used for the same purpose. **3** a device that exposes the film in a photographic camera. ▷ **CAMERA**. ● *v.tr.* **1** put up the shutters of. **2** provide with shutters. □ **put up the shutters 1** cease business for the day. **2** cease business etc. permanently. □ **shutterless** *adj.*

shuttle ● *n.* **1 a** a bobbin used for carrying the weft-thread across between the warp-threads in weaving. ▷ **WEAVE**. **b** a bobbin carrying the lower thread in a sewing machine. **2** a train, bus, etc., going to and fro over a short route continuously. **3** = SHUTTLE-COCK. **4** = SPACE SHUTTLE. ● *v.* **1** *intr. & tr.* move or cause to move to and fro like a shuttle. **2** *intr.* travel in a shuttle. [Old English *scytel* 'dart']

shuttlecock *n.* **1** ▶ a cork with a ring of feathers, or a similar device of plastic, struck between players in esp. badminton. ▷ **BADMINTON**. **2** a thing passed repeatedly back and forth.

goose feathers

cork base

SHUTTLECOCK

shuttle diplomacy *n.* negotiations conducted by a mediator who travels successively to several countries.

shuttle service *n.* a train or bus etc. service operating to and fro over a short route.

shy[1] ● *adj.* (**shyer**, **shyest**) **1 a** diffident or uneasy in company; timid. **b** (of an animal, bird, etc.) easily startled; timid. **2** (foll. by *of*) avoiding; chary of (*shy of his aunt*). **3** (in *comb.*) showing fear of or distaste for (*work-shy*). ● *v.intr.* (**shies**, **shied**) **1** (usu. foll. by *at*) (esp. of a horse) start

compound eye
antenna
cephalothorax
leg
swimmeret
abdomen
telson

sudenly aside in fright. **2** (usu. foll. by *away from*, *at*) avoid accepting or becoming involved in (a proposal etc.) in alarm. ● *n.* a sudden startled movement, esp. of a horse. [Old English] □ **shyly** *adv.* **shyness** *n.*

shy² ● *v.tr.* (**shies**, **shied**) (also *absol.*) fling or throw (a stone etc.). ● *n.* (*pl.* **shies**) the act or an instance of shying. [18th-century coinage] □ **shyer** *n.*

shyster *n.* esp. *N. Amer. colloq.* a person, esp. a lawyer, who uses unscrupulous methods. [19th-century coinage]

SI *abbr.* **1** (Order of the) Star of India. **2** the international system of units of measurement (French *Système International*).

Si *symb. Chem.* the element silicon.

si *n. Mus.* = TE. [French]

Siamese ● *n.* (*pl.* same) **1 a** a native of Siam (now Thailand) in SE Asia. **b** the language of Siam. **2** (in full **Siamese cat**) ▼ a cat of a lightly-built short-haired breed characterized by slanting blue eyes. ▷ CAT. ● *adj.* of or concerning Siam, its people, or language.

Siamese twins *n.pl.* **1** twins joined at any part of the body and sometimes sharing organs etc. **2** any closely associated pair.

sib *n.* esp. *Genetics* a brother or sister; a sibling. [Old English]

Siberian ● *n.* **1** a native of Siberia in the north-eastern part of the Russian Federation. **2** a person of Siberian descent. ● *adj.* of or relating to Siberia.

sibilant ● *adj.* **1** (of a letter or set of letters) sounded with a hiss, e.g. *s*, *sh*. **2** hissing. ● *n.* a sibilant letter or letters. [from Latin *sibilant-* 'hissing'] □ **sibilance** *n.*

SIAMESE CAT

sibling *n.* each of two or more children having one or both parents in common.

sibyl *n.* a pagan prophetess. [from Greek *Sibulla*]

sibylline *adj.* **1** of or from a sibyl. **2** oracular; prophetic.

sic *adv.* (usu. in brackets) used, spelt, etc., as written (confirming, or calling attention to, the form of quoted or copied words).

■ **Usage** The word *sic* is placed in brackets after a word that appears erroneous to show that the word is exactly as it stands in the original, e.g. *They say they will take measures to insure* (sic) *compliance*.

S

sick¹ ● *adj.* **1** (often in *comb.*) esp. *Brit.* vomiting or tending to vomit (*feels sick*; *seasick*). **2** ill; affected by illness (*has been off sick*). **3 a** (often foll. by *at*) esp. mentally perturbed (*a sick mind*). **b** (often foll. by *for*, or in *comb.*) pining; longing (*lovesick*). **4** (often foll. by *of*) *colloq.* **a** disgusted; surfeited (*sick of chocolates*). **b** angry, esp. because of surfeit (*sick of being teased*). **5** *colloq.* (of humour etc.) jeering at misfortune, illness, death, etc.; morbid (*sick joke*). ● *n. Brit. colloq.* vomit. ● *v.tr.* (usu. foll. by *up*) *Brit. colloq.* vomit (*sicked up his dinner*). □ **go sick** report oneself as ill. **look sick** *colloq.* be unimpressive or embarrassed. **sick at** (or **to**) **one's stomach** *US* vomiting or tending to vomit. **take sick** *colloq.* be taken ill. [Old English] □ **sickish** *adj.*

■ **Usage** In British English, the predicative use of the adjective *sick* in sense 2, to mean 'ill', as in *He had to cancel his holiday because he was sick*, is still considered non-standard by some people, although it is standard in American English. The exception to this is its use in the phrase *off sick* ('away on sick leave') which is acceptable in British English. See also Usage Note at ILL.

sick² *v.tr.* (usu. in *imper.*) (esp. to a dog) set upon, attack. [19th-century coinage, dialect variant of SEEK]

sickbay *n.* **1** part of a ship used as a hospital. **2** any room etc. for sick people.

sickbed *n.* **1** an invalid's bed. **2** the state of being an invalid.

sick benefit *n.* = SICKNESS BENEFIT.

sick building syndrome *n.* a high incidence of illness in office workers, attributed to the immediate working surroundings.

sicken *v.* **1** *tr.* affect with loathing or disgust. **2** *intr.* **a** (often foll. by *for*) *Brit.* show symptoms of illness (*is sickening for measles*). **b** (often foll. by *at*, or *to* + infin.) feel nausea or disgust (*he sickened at the sight*). **3** *tr.* (as **sickening** *adj.*) **a** loathsome, disgusting. **b** *colloq.* very annoying. □ **sickeningly** *adv.*

sickener *n.* **1** something causing nausea, disgust, or severe disappointment. **2** a red toadstool of the genus *Russula*, esp. the poisonous *R. emetica*.

sick headache *n.* = MIGRAINE.

sickie *n. Austral. & NZ colloq.* a period of sick leave, esp. taken with insufficient medical reason.

sickle *n.* ◄ a short-handled farming tool with a semicircular blade, used for cutting corn, lopping, or trimming. [from Latin *secula*]

sick leave *n.* leave of absence granted because of illness.

sickle-cell anaemia *n.* (*US* **sickle-cell anemia**) a severe hereditary form of anaemia, affecting mainly black people.

sick list *n.* a list of the sick, esp. in a regiment, ship, etc.

sickly *adj.* (**sicklier**, **sickliest**) **1 a** of weak health; apt to be ill. **b** (of a person's complexion etc.) languid, faint, or pale, suggesting sickness. **c** (of light or colour) faint, feeble. **2** causing ill health (*a sickly climate*). **3** (of a book etc.) sentimental or mawkish. **4** inducing or connected with nausea (*a sickly taste*). □ **sickliness** *n.*

SICKLE: 19TH-CENTURY SICKLE

sick-making *adj. colloq.* sickening.

sickness *n.* **1** the state of being ill; disease. **2** a specified disease (*sleeping sickness*). **3** vomiting or a tendency to vomit.

sickness benefit *n.* (in the UK) benefit paid by the State for sickness interrupting paid employment.

sicko *n.* (*pl.* **-os**) *N. Amer. slang* a mentally ill or perverted person.

sick pay *n.* pay given to an employee etc. on sick leave.

sickroom *n.* **1** a room occupied by a sick person. **2** a room adapted for sick people.

side ● *n.* **1 a** each of the more or less flat surfaces bounding an object (*this side up*). **b** a more or less vertical inner or outer plane or surface (*a mountain-side*). **c** such a vertical lateral surface or plane as distinct from the top or bottom, front or back, or ends (*at the side of the house*). **2 a** the half of a person or animal that is on the right or the left, esp. of the torso (*pain in his right side*). **b** the left or right half or a specified part of a thing, area, etc. (*put it on that side*). **c** (often in *comb.*) a position next to a person or thing (*graveside*). **d** a specified direction relating to a person or thing (*came from all sides*). **e** half of a butchered carcass (*a side of bacon*). **3 a** either surface of a thing regarded as having two surfaces. **b** the amount of writing needed to fill one side of a sheet of paper (*write three sides*). **4** any of several aspects of a question, character, etc. (*look on the bright side*). **5 a** each of two sets of opponents in war, politics, games, etc. (*the side that bats first*). **b** a cause or philosophical position etc. regarded as being in conflict with another (*on the side of right*). **6 a** a part or region near the edge and remote from the centre (also *attrib.*: *side door*). **b** (*attrib.*) a subordinate, peripheral, or detached part (*a side road*). **7 a** each of the bounding lines of a plane rectilinear figure (*a hexagon has six sides*). **b** each of two quantities stated to be equal in an equation. **8** a position nearer or farther than, or

right or left of, a given dividing line (*on this side of the Alps*). **9** a line of hereditary descent through the father or the mother. **10** *Brit. slang* boastfulness; conceit (*has no side about him*). **11** *Brit. colloq.* a television channel, considered as one of a selection (*shall we try another side?*). ● *v.intr.* (usu. foll. by *with*) take part or be on the same side as a disputant etc. (*sided with his father*). □ **by the side of 1** close to. **2** compared with. **from side to side 1** right across. **2** alternately each way from a central line. **let the side down** *Brit.* fail one's colleagues, esp. by frustrating their efforts or embarrassing them. **on one side 1** not in the main or central position. **2** aside (*took him on one side*). **on the … side** fairly, somewhat (qualifying an adjective: *on the high side*). **on the side 1** as a sideline; in addition to one's regular work etc. **2** secretly or illicitly. **3** *N. Amer.* as a side dish. **side by side** standing close together, esp. for mutual support. **take sides** support one or other cause etc. [Old English] □ **sideless** *adj.*

side-bet *n.* a bet between opponents, esp. in card games, over and above the ordinary stakes.

sideboard *n.* **1** a table or esp. a flat-topped cupboard at the side of a dining room for supporting and containing dishes, table linen, etc. **2** (usu. in *pl.*) *Brit. colloq.* hair grown by a man down each side of his face; side-whisker.

sideburn *n.* (usu. in *pl.*) = SIDEBOARD 2. [originally *burnside*, from General *Burnside*, 1824–81, who affected this style]

sidecar *n.* ▼ a small car for a passenger or passengers, attached to the side of a motorcycle.

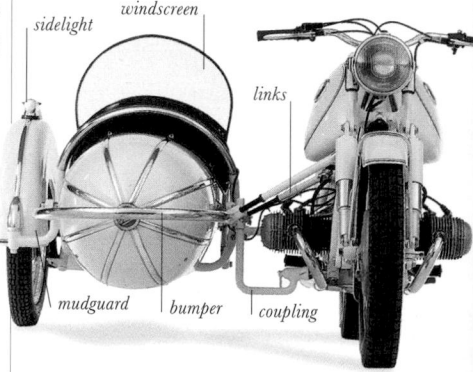

SIDECAR: 1960s MOTORCYCLE WITH SIDECAR

side chapel *n.* a chapel in the aisle or at the side of a church.

sided *adj.* **1** having sides. **2** (in *comb.*) having a specified side or number of sides (*flat-sided*; *three-sided*). □ **-sidedly** *adv.* **sidedness** *n.* (also in *comb.*).

side dish *n.* an extra dish subsidiary to the main course.

side door *n.* **1** a door in or at the side of a building. **2** an indirect means of access.

side drum *n.* a small double-headed drum (originally hung at the drummer's side). ▷ PERCUSSION

side effect *n.* a secondary, usu. undesirable, effect.

side issue *n.* a point that distracts attention from what is important.

sidekick *n. colloq.* a close associate.

sidelamp *n.* a lamp placed at the side of something, esp. on a motor vehicle.

sidelight *n.* **1** a light from the side. **2** incidental information etc. **3** *Brit.* a light at the side of the front of a motor vehicle. ▷ SIDECAR. **4** *Naut.* the red port or green starboard light on a ship under way.

sideline *n.* **1** an activity done in addition to one's main work etc. **2** (usu. in *pl.*) **a** a line bounding the side of a hockey pitch etc. ▷ TENNIS. **b** the space next to these where spectators etc. sit. □ **on** (or **from**) **the sidelines** in (or from) a position removed from the main action.

sidelong ● *adj.* inclining to one side; oblique (*a sidelong glance*). ● *adv.* obliquely (*moved sidelong*).

side note *n.* a marginal note.

side-on ● *adv.* from the side. ● *adj.* **1** from or towards one side. **2** (of a collision) involving the side of a vehicle.

side plate *n.* a plate of approximately 15–20 cm diameter, used for bread etc.

sidereal /sy-**deer**-iăl/ *adj.* of or concerning the constellations or fixed stars. [from Latin *sidereus*]

sidereal day *n.* the time between successive meridional transits of a star or csp. of the first point of Aries, about four minutes shorter than the solar day.

side road *n.* a minor or subsidiary road, esp. branching from a main road.

side-saddle ● *n.* ▶ a saddle for a woman rider who rides with both feet on the same side of the horse. ● *adv.* sitting in this position.

side salad *n.* a salad served as a side dish.

sideshow *n.* **1** a small show or stall in an exhibition, fair, etc. **2** a minor incident or issue.

sidesman *n.* (*pl.* **-men**) *Brit.* a churchwarden's assistant, who shows worshippers to their seats, takes the collection, etc.

side-splitting *adj.* causing violent laughter.

sidestep ● *n.* a step taken sideways. ● *v.tr.* (**-stepped**, **-stepping**) **1** csp. *Football* avoid (esp. a tackle) by stepping sideways. **2** evade. □ **sidestepper** *n.*

side street *n.* a minor or subsidiary street.

sidestroke *n.* **1** a stroke towards or from a side. **2** an incidental action. **3** a swimming stroke in which the swimmer lies on his or her side.

sideswipe ● *n.* **1** a glancing blow along the side. **2** an incidental critical remark. ● *v.tr.* hit with or as if with a sideswipe.

sidetrack ● *n.* a railway siding. ● *v.tr.* **1** turn into a siding; shunt. **2 a** postpone, evade, or divert treatment or consideration of. **b** divert (a person) from considering etc.

side view *n.* **1** a view obtained sideways. **2** a profile.

sidewalk *n.* *N. Amer.* a pedestrian path at the side of a road; a pavement.

sideways ● *adv.* (also **sidewards**) **1** to or from a side (*moved sideways*). **2** with one side facing forward (*sat sideways*). ● *adj.* **1** to or from a side (*a sideways movement*). **2** unconventional, unorthodox (*a sideways look at recent events*). □ **sidewise** *adv. & adj.*

side-whiskers *n.pl.* whiskers growing on the cheeks.

side wind *n.* wind from the side.

siding *n.* **1** a short track at the side of and opening on to a railway line, used for shunting trains. **2** *N. Amer.* cladding material for the outside of a building.

sidle ● *v.intr.* (usu. foll. by *along*, *up*) walk in a timid, furtive, stealthy, or cringing manner. ● *n.* the act or an instance of sidling. [back-formation from archaic *sideling* 'sidelong']

SIDS *abbr.* sudden infant death syndrome; = COT DEATH.

siege *n.* **1 a** a military operation to compel the surrender of a fortified place by surrounding it and cutting off supplies etc. **b** a similar operation by police etc. to force the surrender of an armed person. **c** the period during which a siege lasts. **2** a persistent attack or campaign of persuasion etc. □ **lay siege to** esp. *Mil.* conduct the siege of. **raise the siege of** abandon or cause the abandonment of an attempt to take (a place) by siege. [from Old French *sege* 'seat']

siemens /**see**-mĕnz/ *n.* (*pl.* same) *Electr.* the SI unit of conductance. [named after W. von *Siemens*, German electrical engineer, 1816–92]

---

sienna *n.* **1** a kind of earth used as a pigment in paint. ▷ RAW SIENNA. **2** its colour of yellowish brown (**raw sienna**) or reddish brown (**burnt sienna**). [Italian *(terra di) Sienna* 'earth (of) *Siena*', a city and province in Tuscany]

sierra *n.* a long jagged mountain chain, esp. in Spain, Spanish America, or the western US. [Spanish]

siesta *n.* an afternoon sleep or rest esp. in hot countries. [Spanish]

sieve /siv/ ● *n.* a utensil having a perforated or meshed bottom for separating solids or coarse material from liquids or fine particles, or for pulping. ● *v.tr.* **1** put through or sift with a sieve. **2** examine (evidence etc.) to select or separate. [Old English] □ **sievelike** *adj.*

sievert /**see**-vĕrt/ *n.* an SI unit of dosage of ionizing radiation, defined as that which delivers a joule of energy per kilogram of recipient mass. [named after R. M. *Sievert*, Swedish radiologist, 1896–1966]

sift *v.tr.* **1** sieve (material), esp. to separate finer and coarser parts. **2** (usu. foll. by *from*, *out*) separate (finer or coarser parts) from material. **3** sprinkle (esp. sugar) from a perforated container. **4** examine (evidence, facts, etc.). □ **sift through** examine by sifting. [Old English] □ **sifter** *n.* (also in *comb.*).

sigh ● *v.intr.* **1** emit a long deep audible breath expressive of sadness, weariness, relief, etc. **2** (foll. by *for*) yearn for. **3** (of the wind etc.) make a sighing sound. ● *n.* **1** the act or an instance of sighing. **2** a sound made in sighing (*a sigh of relief*). [Middle English]

sight ● *n.* **1 a** ▼ the faculty of seeing with the eyes. ▷ EYE. **b** the act or an instance of seeing; the state of being seen. **2** a thing seen; a display or spectacle (*not a pretty sight*). **3** a way of considering a thing (*in my sight he can do no wrong*). **4** a range of space within which a person etc. can see or an object be seen (*coming into sight*). **5** (usu. in *pl.*) noteworthy features of a town etc. (*see the sights*). **6 a** a device on a gun or optical instrument used for assisting the precise aim or observation. ▷ GUN. **b** the aim or observation so gained (*got a sight of him*). **7** *colloq.* a person or thing having a ridiculous, repulsive, or dishevelled appearance (*looked a perfect sight*). **8** *colloq.* a great quantity (*cost a sight of money*). ● *v.tr.* **1** get sight of, esp. by approaching (*they sighted land*). **2** observe the presence of (esp. aircraft, animals, etc.) (*sighted buffalo*). **3** take observations of (a star etc.) with an instrument. **4** aim (a gun etc.) with sights. □ **at first sight** on first glimpse or impression. **at** (or **on**) **sight** as soon as a person or a thing has been seen. **catch** (or **lose**) **sight of** begin (or cease) to see or be aware of. **get a sight of** glimpse. **have lost sight of** no longer know the whereabouts of. **in sight 1** visible. **2** near at hand (*salvation is in sight*). **in** (or **within**) **sight of** so as to see or be seen from. **lower one's sights** become less ambitious. **out of my sight!** go at once! **out of sight 1** not visible. **2** *colloq.* excellent; delightful. **set one's sights on** aim at (*set her sights on a directorship*). [Old English] □ **sighter** *n.*

sighted *adj.* **1** capable of seeing; not blind. **2** (in *comb.*) having a specified kind of sight (*long-sighted*).

sightless *adj.* **1** blind. **2** *poet.* invisible. □ **sightlessly** *adv.* **sightlessness** *n.*

sight line *n.* a hypothetical line from a person's eye to what is seen.

sightly *adj.* attractive to the sight; not unsightly. □ **sightliness** *n.*

sight-read *v.tr.* (*past* and *past part.* **-read**) (also *absol.*) read and perform (music) at sight. □ **sight-reader** *n.*

sight-screen *n. Cricket* a large usu. movable white screen placed near the boundary in line with the wicket to help the batsman see the ball. ▷ CRICKET

sightseer *n.* a person who visits places of interest; a tourist. □ **sightsee** *v.intr. & tr.* **sightseeing** *n.*

sight-sing *v.tr. & intr.* sing (music) at sight.

sight unseen *adv.* without previous inspection.

sigma *n.* the eighteenth letter of the Greek alphabet (Σ, σ, or, when final, ς; also, in uncial form, Ϲ, ϲ). [Latin, from Greek]

sigmoidoscopy *n.* (*pl.* **-ies**) an examination of the lower intestine by means of a flexible tube inserted through the anus. □ **sigmoidoscope** *n.*

sign ● *n.* **1 a** a thing indicating or suggesting a quality or state etc.; a thing perceived as indicating a future state or occurrence (*a sign of weakness*). **b** a

---

fixed head (top pommel)

leaping head (lower pommel)

suede seat

nearside flap

safe

nearside single stirrup

SIDE-SADDLE

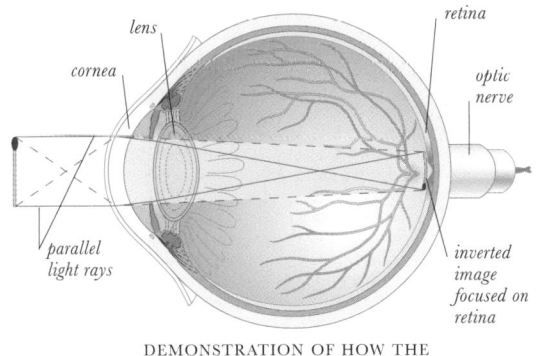

SIGHT

During the process of seeing an object, incoming light rays are focused on to the retina by the cornea and lens, forming an inverted image. The retina then transmits signals to the brain's visual cortex, where the image is reinverted and interpreted. One cause of short-sightedness is when the eyeball is elongated, and the focus falls short of the retina. If the eyeball is shortened, the focus is behind the retina, causing long-sightedness.

lens

retina

cornea

optic nerve

parallel light rays

inverted image focused on retina

DEMONSTRATION OF HOW THE HUMAN EYE SEES AN IMAGE

COMMON SIGHT PROBLEMS

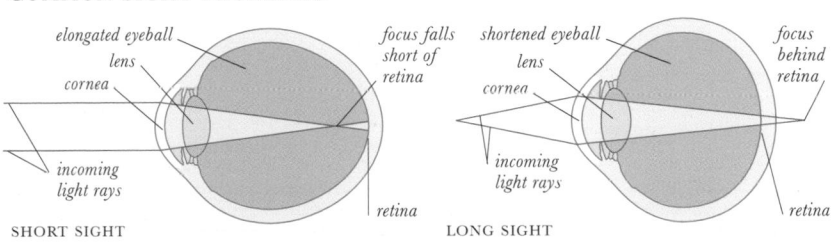

elongated eyeball

lens

focus falls short of retina

cornea

incoming light rays

retina

SHORT SIGHT

shortened eyeball

lens

focus behind retina

cornea

incoming light rays

retina

LONG SIGHT

S

miracle evidencing supernatural power (*wrought signs and wonders*). **2 a** a mark, symbol, or device used to represent something or to distinguish the thing on which it is put (*marked the jar with a sign*). **b** a technical symbol used in algebra, music, etc. **3 a** a gesture or action used to convey information, an order, request, etc. (*conversed by signs*). **b** a gesture used in a system of sign language. **4** a publicly displayed board etc. giving information; a signboard or signpost. **5** a password (*advanced and gave the sign*). **6** each of the twelve divisions of the zodiac, named from constellations (*the sign of Cancer*). ● *v.* **1** *tr.* **a** (also *absol.*) write (one's name, initials, etc.) on a document etc. indicating that one has authorized it. **b** write one's name etc. on (a document) as authorization. **2** *intr. & tr.* **a** communicate by gesture (*signed their assent*). **b** communicate in a sign language. **3** *tr. & intr.* engage or be engaged by signing a contract etc. (see also *sign on, sign up*). **4** *tr.* mark with a sign (esp. with the sign of the cross in baptism). □ **sign away** convey (one's right, property, etc.) by signing a deed etc. **sign for** acknowledge receipt of by signing. **sign in 1** sign a register on arrival in a hotel etc. **2** authorize the admittance of (a person) by signing a register. **sign off 1** end work, a letter, broadcasting, etc., esp. by writing or speaking one's name. **2 a** end a period of employment etc. **b** end the period of employment or contract of (a person). **3** *Brit.* register to stop receiving unemployment benefit after finding work. **sign on 1** agree to a contract, employment, etc. **2** begin work, broadcasting, etc., esp. by writing or announcing one's name. **3** employ (a person). **4** *Brit.* register as unemployed. **sign out** sign a register to record departure. **sign up 1** engage or employ (a person). **2** enlist in the armed forces. **3 a** commit (another person or oneself) by signing etc. (*signed you up for dinner*). **b** enrol (*signed up for evening classes*). [from Latin *signum*] □ **signable** *adj.* **signer** *n.*

signage *n.* signs collectively, esp. commercial or public display signs.

signal[1] ● *n.* **1 a** a usu. prearranged sign conveying information, guidance, etc. esp. at a distance (*waved as a signal to begin*). **b** a message made up of such signs (*signals made with flags*). **2** an immediate occasion for, or cause, of movement, action, etc. (*the uprising was a signal for repression*). **3** *Electr.* **a** an electrical impulse or impulses or radio waves transmitted or received. **b** a sequence of these. **4** ▶ a light, semaphore, etc., on a railway giving instructions or warnings to train drivers etc. ● *v.* (**signalled**, **signalling**; *US* **signaled**, **signaling**) **1** *intr.* make signals. **2** *tr.* **a** (often foll. by *to* + infin.) make signals to; direct. **b** transmit (an order, information, etc.) by signal; announce (*signalled her agreement*). [from Latin *signum* 'sign'] □ **signaller** *n.*

signal[2] *adj.* remarkably good or bad; noteworthy (*a signal victory*). [from Italian *segnalato* 'distinguished'] □ **signally** *adv.*

signal box *n. Brit.* a building beside a railway track from which signals, points, etc., are controlled.

signalize *v.tr.* (also **-ise**) **1** make noteworthy or remarkable. **2** indicate.

signalman *n.* (*pl.* **-men**) **1** a railway employee responsible for operating signals and points. **2** a person who displays or receives naval etc. signals.

signal-to-noise ratio *n.* the ratio of the strength

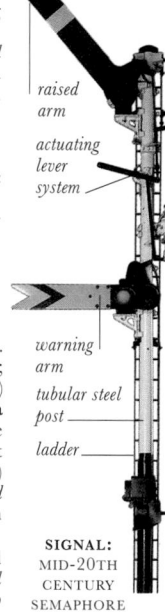

raised arm

actuating lever system

warning arm

tubular steel post

ladder

SIGNAL: MID-20TH CENTURY SEMAPHORE SIGNAL

of an electrical or other signal carrying information to that of unwanted interference, usu. expressed in decibels.

signatory ● *n.* (*pl.* **-ies**) a party or esp. a state that has signed an agreement or esp. a treaty. ● *adj.* having signed such an agreement etc. [from Latin *signatorius* 'of sealing']

signature *n.* **1 a** a person's name, initials, or mark used in signing a letter, document, etc. **b** the act of signing a document etc. **2** a distinctive pattern or characteristic by which something can be identified. **3** *Mus.* **a** = KEY SIGNATURE. **b** = TIME SIGNATURE. [from medieval Latin *signatura*]

signature dish *n.* a speciality dish created by and associated with a particular chef.

signature tune *n.* esp. *Brit.* a distinctive tune used to introduce a particular broadcast or performer.

signboard *n.* a board with a name or symbol etc. displayed outside a shop or hotel etc.

signee *n.* a person who has signed a contract, register, etc.

signet *n.* a seal used instead of or with a signature as authentication. [from medieval Latin *signetum*]

signet ring *n.* ▶ a ring with a seal set in it.

significance *n.* **1** importance; noteworthiness (*of no significance*). **2** a concealed or real meaning (*what is the significance?*). **3** the state of being significant. **4** *Statistics* the extent to which a result deviates from that expected to arise simply from random variation or errors in sampling.

significant *adj.* **1** having a meaning; indicative. **2** having an unstated or secret meaning (*refused it with a significant gesture*). **3** noteworthy; important (*a significant figure in history*). [from Latin *significant-* 'signifying'] □ **significantly** *adv.*

significant figure *n. Math.* a digit conveying information about a number containing it.

signification *n.* **1** the act of signifying. **2** (usu. foll. by *of*) exact meaning or sense, esp. of a word or phrase.

signify *v.* (**-ies**, **-ied**) **1** *tr.* be a sign or indication of (*a yawn signifies boredom*). **2** *tr.* mean; have as its meaning (*'Dr' signifies 'doctor'*). **3** *tr.* make known (*signified their agreement*). **4** *intr.* be of importance; matter (*it signifies little*). [from Latin *significare*] □ **signifier** *n.*

signing *n. Brit.* a person who has recently signed a contract, esp. to join a professional sports team.

sign language *n.* a system of communication by visual gestures, used esp. by the deaf.

sign of the cross *n.* a Christian sign made in blessing or prayer, by tracing a cross from the forehead to the chest and to each shoulder, or in the air.

sign of the times *n.* a portent etc. showing a likely trend.

signor /seen-yor/ *n.* (*pl.* **signori** /seen-yor-i/) **1** a title or form of address used of or to an Italian-speaking man, corresponding to Mr or sir. **2** an Italian man. [Italian]

signora /seen-yor-ă/ *n.* **1** a title or form of address used of or to an Italian-speaking married woman, corresponding to Mrs or madam. **2** a married Italian woman. [Italian]

signorina /seen-yŏ-ree-nă/ *n.* **1** a title or form of address used of or to an Italian-speaking unmarried woman. **2** an Italian unmarried woman. [Italian]

signpost ● *n.* **1** a sign indicating the direction to and sometimes also the distance from various places, esp. a post with arms at a road junction. **2** a means of guidance; an indication. ● *v.tr.* **1** provide with a signpost or signposts. **2** esp. *Brit.* indicate (a course of action etc.).

signwriter *n.* (also **sign-painter**) a person who paints signboards etc. □ **signwriting** *n.*

Sikh /seek/ ● *n.* a member of an Indian monotheistic religion founded in the 16th c. ● *adj.* of or relating to Sikhs or Sikhism. [from Sanskrit *śiṣya* 'disciple']

Sikhism /seek-izm/ *n.* the religious tenets of the Sikhs.

silage ● *n.* **1** storage in a silo. **2** green fodder preserved by pressure in a silo. ● *v.tr.* put into a silo. [alteration of *ensilage*, in same sense]

sild *n.* a small immature herring, esp. one caught in N. European seas. [Danish & Norwegian]

silence ● *n.* **1** absence of sound. **2** abstinence from speech or noise. **3** the avoidance of betraying a secret etc. **4** oblivion; the state of not being mentioned. ● *v.tr.* **1** make silent by coercion, argument, etc. **2** (usu. as **silenced** *adj.*) fit (a gun, exhaust system, etc.) with a silencer. □ **in silence** without speech or other sound. [from Latin *silentium*]

silencer *n.* any of various devices for reducing the noise emitted by a gun or *Brit.* the exhaust of a motor vehicle. ▷ STEN GUN

silent *adj.* **1** not speaking; not uttering or making or accompanied by any sound. **2** (of a letter) written but not pronounced, e.g. *b* in *doubt*. **3** (of a person) taciturn. **4** saying or recording nothing on some subject (*the records are silent on the incident*). [from Latin *silent-* 'being silent'] □ **silently** *adv.*

silent majority *n.* those of moderate opinions who rarely assert them.

silent partner *n. N. Amer.* = SLEEPING PARTNER.

silhouette /sil-oo-et/ ● *n.* **1** a representation of a person or thing showing the outline only, usu. done in solid black on white or cut from paper. **2** a dark shadow or outline against a lighter background. ● *v.tr.* represent or (usu. in *passive*) show in silhouette. [named, for an obscure reason, after Étienne de *Silhouette*, French author and politician, 1709–67]

SIGNET RING

silica *n.* silicon dioxide, occurring as quartz etc. and as a principal constituent of sandstone and other rocks. [based on Latin *silex -icis* 'flint'] □ **siliceous** *adj.* (also **silicious**).

silica gel *n.* hydrated silica in a hard granular hygroscopic form used as a drying agent.

silicate *n.* any of the many insoluble compounds of a metal combined with silicon and oxygen. ▷ MINERAL

silicic *adj. Chem.* of silica or silicon.

silicify *v.tr.* (**-ies**, **-ied**) convert into or impregnate with silica. □ **silicification** *n.*

silicon /sil-i-kŏn/ *n. Chem.* ▶ a metalloid element occurring widely in silica and silicates. [based on Latin *silex -icis* 'flint']

silicon carbide *n.* = CARBORUNDUM.

silicon chip *n.* a silicon microchip.

silicone /sil-i-kohn/ ● *n.* any organic compound of silicon, with high resistance to cold, heat, water, etc. ● *v.tr.* treat with silicone.

Silicon Valley *n.* an area with a high concentration of electronics industries.

SILICON CRYSTAL USED FOR MAKING MICROCHIPS

silicosis *n.* lung fibrosis caused by the inhalation of dust containing silica.

silk *n.* **1** a fine strong soft lustrous fibre produced by silkworms. **2** a similar fibre spun by some spiders etc. **3 a** thread or cloth made from silk fibre. **b** a fine soft thread (*embroidery silk*). **4** (in *pl.*) kinds of silk cloth or garments made from it, esp. as worn by a jockey. ▷ JOCKEY. **5** *Brit. colloq.* Queen's (or King's) Counsel, as having the right to wear a silk gown. **6** (*attrib.*) made of silk (*silk blouse*). □ **take silk** *Brit.* become a Queen's (or King's) Counsel. [based on Greek *Sēres*, an oriental people] □ **silklike** *adj.*

silken *adj.* **1** made of silk. **2** wearing silk. **3** soft or lustrous as silk. **4** (of a person's manner etc.) suave or insinuating.

S

silk-fowl *n.* a breed of fowl with a silky plumage.

silk screen ● *n.* a screen of fine mesh used in screen printing. ● *v.tr.* (**silk-screen**) print, decorate, or reproduce using a silk screen.

silkworm *n.* ▼ the caterpillar of the moth *Bombyx mori*, which spins a cocoon of silk.

SILKWORM:
CHINESE
SILKWORM
(*Bombyx mori*)

— *silkworm*

— *beginnings of a silk cocoon*

silky *adj.* (**silkier**, **silkiest**) **1** like silk in smoothness, softness, fineness, or lustre. **2** (of a person's manner etc.) suave, insinuating. □ **silkily** *adv.* **silkiness** *n.*

sill *n.* (also esp. *Building* **cill**) **1** a shelf or slab of stone, wood, or metal at the foot of a window or doorway. **2** a horizontal timber at the bottom of a dock or lock entrance, against which the gates close. [Old English]

sillabub var. of SYLLABUB.

silly ● *adj.* (**sillier**, **silliest**) **1** lacking sense; foolish, imprudent. **2** weak-minded. **3** *Cricket* very close to the batsman (*silly mid-off*). ▷ CRICKET. ● *n.* (*pl.* **-ies**) *colloq.* a foolish person. [later form of Middle English *sely* (dialect *seely*) 'happy'] □ **sillily** *adv.* **silliness** *n.*

silly season *n.* high summer as the season when newspapers often publish trivial material for lack of important news.

silo ● *n.* (*pl.* **-os**) **1** a pit or airtight structure in which green crops are kept for fodder. **2** ▶ a pit or tower for the storage of grain, cement, etc. **3** an underground storage chamber for a guided missile. ● *v.tr.* (**-oes**, **-oed**) make silage of. [from Greek *siros* 'corn pit']

silo

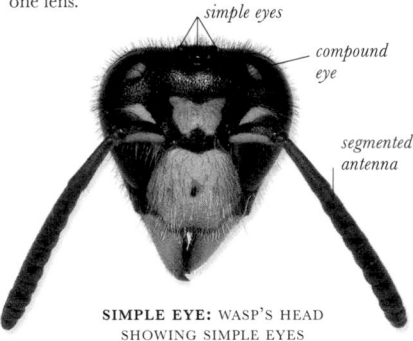

SILO: GRAIN SILO ATTACHED TO A BARN

silt ● *n.* sediment in a channel, harbour, etc. ● *v.tr. & intr.* (often foll. by *up*) choke or be choked with silt. [Middle English] □ **siltation** *n.* **silty** *adj.*

Silurian *Geol.* ● *adj.* of or relating to the third period of the Palaeozoic era. ● *n.* this period or system. [based on Latin *Silures*, a people of ancient SE Wales]

silvan var. of SYLVAN.

silver ● *n. Chem.* **1** ▼ a greyish-white lustrous malleable ductile precious metallic element. **2** the colour of silver. **3** silver or cupro-nickel coins. **4** silver vessels or implements, esp. cutlery. **5** = SILVER MEDAL. ● *adj.* **1** made wholly or chiefly of silver. **2** coloured like silver. ● *v.* **1** *tr.* coat or plate with silver. **2** *tr.* provide (mirror glass) with a backing of tin amalgam etc. **3** *tr.* (of the moon or a white light) give a silvery appearance to. **4 a** *tr.* turn (the hair) grey or white. **b** *intr.* (of the hair) turn grey or white. [Old English]

SILVER:
TYPICAL
NATIVE SILVER

silver age *n.* a period regarded as inferior to a golden age.

silver band *n. Brit.* a band playing silver-plated instruments.

silver birch *n.* ▶ a common birch, *Betula pendula*, with silver-coloured bark.

SILVER BIRCH
BARK
(*Betula pendula*)

silver fern *n.* **1** a New Zealand tree fern, *Cyathea dealbata*. **2** a stylized silver fern leaf as an emblem of New Zealand.

silverfish *n.* (*pl.* usu. same) any small silvery wingless insect of the order Thysanura, esp. *Lepisma saccharina* found in houses and other buildings.

silver jubilee *n.* **1** the 25th anniversary of a sovereign's accession. **2** any other 25th anniversary.

silver-leaf *n.* a fungal disease of fruit trees.

silver lining *n.* a consolation or hopeful feature in misfortune.

silver medal *n.* a silver-coloured medal, usu. awarded as second prize.

silver paper *n.* esp. *Brit.* aluminium or occasionally tin foil.

silver plate *n.* vessels, spoons, etc., of copper etc. plated with silver.

silver sand *n. Brit.* a fine pure sand used in gardening.

silver screen *n.* (usu. prec. by *the*) motion pictures collectively.

silverside *n. Brit.* the upper side of a round of beef from the outside of the leg.

silversmith *n.* a worker in silver; a manufacturer of silver articles. □ **silversmithing** *n.*

silver spoon *n.* a sign of future prosperity.

silver tongue *n.* eloquence.

silverware *n.* articles made of or coated with silver.

silver wedding *n.* the 25th anniversary of a wedding.

silvery *adj.* **1** like silver in colour or appearance. **2** having a clear gentle ringing sound. **3** (of the hair) white and lustrous. □ **silveriness** *n.*

silviculture *n.* (also **sylviculture**) the growing and tending of trees as a branch of forestry. [from Latin *silva* 'a wood' + French *culture* 'culture'] □ **silvicultural** *adj.* **silviculturist** *n.*

simian ● *adj.* **1** of or concerning the anthropoid apes. **2** like an ape or monkey (*a simian walk*). ● *n.* an ape or monkey. [based on Latin *simia* 'ape']

similar *adj.* **1** (often foll. by *to*) like, alike; of the same kind, nature, or amount; having a resemblance. **2** *Geom.* shaped alike. [from Latin *similis* 'like'] □ **similarity** *n.* (*pl.* **-ies**). **similarly** *adv.*

■ **Usage** In sense 1, similar should be followed by *to*, not *as*. The following is non-standard: *I have had similar problems as yourself.* This can be reworded as follows: *I have had problems similar to yours.*

simile /sim-i-li/ *n.* **1** a figure of speech involving the comparison of one thing with another of a different kind (*as brave as a lion*). **2** the use of such comparison. [Latin, literally 'like (thing)']

similitude *n.* **1** the likeness, guise, or outward appearance of a thing or person. **2** a comparison or the expression of a comparison. [from Latin *similitudo*]

simmer ● *v.* **1** *intr. & tr.* be or keep bubbling or boiling gently. **2** *intr.* be in a state of suppressed anger or excitement. ● *n.* a simmering condition. □ **simmer down** become less agitated. [alteration of Middle English (now dialect) *simper*]

simnel cake *n. Brit.* a rich fruit cake, usu. with a marzipan layer and decoration, eaten esp. at Easter. [based on Latin *simila* 'fine flour']

simony *n.* the buying or selling of ecclesiastical privileges. [from Late Latin *simonia*, from *Simon* Magus (Acts 8:18)] □ **simoniac** *adj. & n.* **simoniacal** *adj.*

simoom *n.* (also **simoon**) a hot dry dust laden wind blowing at intervals esp. in the Arabian desert. [from Arabic *samūm*]

simpatico *adj.* congenial, likeable. [Italian & Spanish]

simper ● *v.intr.* smile in a silly or affected way. ● *n.* a silly or affected smile. [16th-century coinage] □ **simperingly** *adv.*

simple *adj.* (**simpler**, **simplest**) **1** easily understood or done; presenting no difficulty. **2** not complicated or elaborate; without luxury or sophistication. **3** not compound; consisting of or involving only one element or operation etc. **4** absolute, unqualified, straightforward (*the simple truth*). **5** foolish or ignorant; gullible (*am not so simple as to agree to that*). **6** plain in appearance or manner; unsophisticated, ingenuous, artless. [from Latin *simplus*] □ **simpleness** *n.*

simple eye *n.* ▼ an eye of an insect etc. having only one lens.

simple eyes

compound eye

segmented antenna

SIMPLE EYE: WASP'S HEAD
SHOWING SIMPLE EYES

simple fracture *n.* a fracture of the bone only, without a skin wound.

simple interest *n.* interest payable on a capital sum only.

simple machine *n.* any of the basic mechanical devices for applying a force (e.g. an inclined plane, wedge, or lever).

simple-minded *adj.* **1** feeble-minded; foolish. **2** unsophisticated; ingenuous. □ **simple-mindedly** *adv.* **simple-mindedness** *n.*

simple sentence *n.* a sentence with a single subject and predicate.

simpleton *n.* a gullible or half-witted person.

simplex *adj.* simple; not compounded. [Latin, literally 'single']

simplicity *n.* the fact or condition of being simple. □ **be simplicity itself** be extremely easy. [from Latin *simplicitas*]

simplify *v.tr.* (**-ies**, **-ied**) make easy or easier to do or understand. [from medieval Latin *simplificare*] □ **simplification** *n.*

simplistic *adj.* **1** excessively or affectedly simple. **2** oversimplified so as to conceal or distort difficulties. □ **simplistically** *adv.*

simply *adv.* **1** in a simple manner. **2** absolutely; without doubt (*simply astonishing*). **3** merely (*simply trying to please*).

simulacrum /sim-yoo-lay-krŭm/ *n.* (*pl.* **simulacra**) **1** an image of something. **2 a** a deceptive substitute. **b** mere pretence. [Latin]

simulate *v.tr.* **1** pretend to be, have, or feel. **2** imitate or counterfeit. **3 a** imitate the conditions of (a situation etc.), e.g. for training. **b** produce a computer model of (a process). **4** (as **simulated** *adj.*) made to resemble the real thing (*simulated fur*). [based on Latin *simulatus* 'imitated'] □ **simulation** *n.*

S

SIMULATOR

Simulators are employed widely by military forces and the transport industry, particularly to train pilots. They are also used to instruct aircraft engineers, and for entertainment. In flight simulators, powerful hydraulic actuators recreate the forces experienced when flying, while computer graphics simulate the view from the cockpit window.

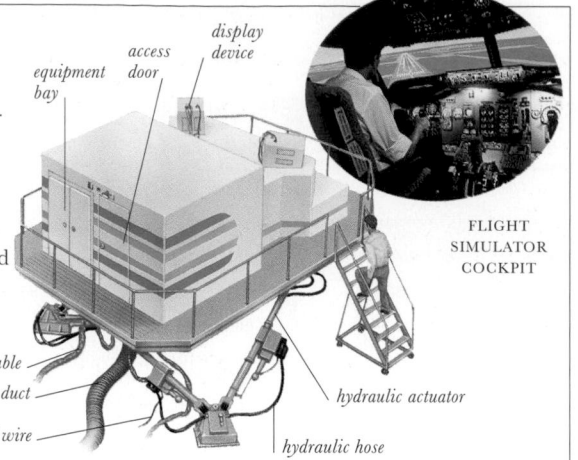

equipment bay
access door
display device
control cable
ventilation duct
control wire
hydraulic hose
hydraulic actuator

FLIGHT SIMULATOR COCKPIT

EXTERNAL VIEW OF A FLIGHT SIMULATOR

---

simulator *n.* **1** a person or thing that simulates. **2 ▲** a device designed to simulate the operations of a complex system, used esp. in training (*flight simulator*).

simulcast *n.* simultaneous transmission of the same programme on radio and television.

simultaneous *adj.* (often foll. by *with*) occurring or operating at the same time. [from medieval Latin *simultaneus*] □ **simultaneity** *n.* **simultaneously** *adv.*

simultaneous equations *n.pl.* equations involving two or more unknowns that are to have the same values in each equation.

sin[1] *n.* **1 a** the breaking of divine or moral law, esp. by a conscious act. **b** such an act. **2** an offence against good taste or propriety etc. ● *v.* (**sinned**, **sinning**) **1** *intr.* commit a sin. **2** *intr.* (foll. by *against*) offend. **3** *tr. archaic* commit (a sin). □ **as sin** *colloq.* extremely (*ugly as sin*). **for one's sins** esp. *Brit. joc.* as a judgement on one for something or other. **live in sin** *colloq.* live together without being married. [Old English] □ **sinless** *adj.* **sinlessly** *adv.* **sinlessness** *n.*

sin[2] *abbr.* sine.

sin bin *n. colloq.* **1** *Ice Hockey* an area reserved for penalized players and some officials. **2** *Brit.* a place set aside for offenders of various kinds.

since ● *prep.* throughout, or at a point in, the period between (a specified time, event, etc.) and the time present or being considered (*going on since June; the greatest since Beethoven*). ● *conj.* **1** during or in the time after (*have you seen him since we met?*). **2** for the reason that; inasmuch as (*since you are drunk I will drive*). **3** (*ellipt.*) as being (*more useful, since better designed*). ● *adv.* **1** from that time or event until now or the time being considered (*has since been cut down*). **2** ago (*happened many years since*). [Middle English, reduced form of obsolete *sithence*]

sincere *adj.* (**sincerer**, **sincerest**) **1** free from pretence or deceit. **2** genuine, honest, frank. [from Latin *sincerus* 'clean, pure'] □ **sincereness** *n.* **sincerity** *n.*

sincerely *adv.* in a sincere manner. □ **yours sincerely** a formula for ending a usu. informal letter.

sine *n. Math.* the trigonometric function that is equal to the ratio of the side opposite a given angle (in a right-angled triangle) to the hypotenuse. [from Latin *sinus* 'curve, fold of a toga']

sinecure /sy-ni-kewr/ *n.* a position that requires little or no work but usu. yields profit or honour. [from Latin *sine cura* 'without care'] □ **sinecurism** *n.* **sinecurist** *n.*

sine die /sy-ni dy-ee/ *adv.* (of business etc.) adjourned indefinitely with no appointed date.

sine qua non /sin-ay kwah nohn/ *n.* an indispensable condition or qualification. [Latin, literally 'without which not']

sinew *n.* **1** tough fibrous tissue uniting muscle to bone; a tendon. **2** (in *pl.*) muscles; bodily strength. **3** (in *pl.*) the strength or framework of a plan, city, organization, etc. [Old English] □ **sinewless** *adj.* **sinewy** *adj.*

sinful *adj.* **1** (of a person) committing sin, esp. habitually. **2 a** (of an act) involving or characterized by sin. **b** *colloq.* reprehensible. □ **sinfully** *adv.* **sinfulness** *n.*

sing ● *v.* (*past* **sang**; *past part.* **sung**) **1** *intr.* utter musical sounds with the voice, esp. words with a set tune. **2** *tr.* utter or produce by singing. **3** *intr.* (of the wind, a kettle, etc.) make melodious, humming, or whistling sounds. **4** *intr.* (of the ears) be affected as with a buzzing sound. **5** *intr. slang* turn informer; confess. ● *n.* **1** an act or spell of singing. **2** *US* a meeting for amateur singing. □ **sing along** sing in accompaniment to a song or piece of music. **sing out** call out loudly; shout. **sing the praises of** see PRAISE. **sing up** sing more loudly. [Old English] □ **singable** *adj.* **singer** *n.* **singingly** *adv.*

■ **Usage** The use of *sung* instead of *sang* for the past tense as in *She sung three songs* is non-standard.

sing. *abbr.* singular.

singalong *n.* **1** a tune etc. to which one can sing in accompaniment (also *attrib.: a singalong chorus*). **2** an occasion of community singing (also *attrib.: a singalong evening*).

singe ● *v.* (**singeing**) **1** *tr. & intr.* burn superficially or lightly. **2** *tr.* burn the bristles or down off (the carcass of a pig or fowl) to prepare it for cooking. ● *n.* a superficial burn. [Old English]

singer-songwriter *n.* a person who sings and writes songs, esp. professionally.

Singhalese var. of SINHALESE.

single ● *adj.* **1** one only, not double or multiple. **2** united or undivided. **3 a** designed or suitable for one person (*single room*). **b** used or done by one person etc. **4** one by itself (*a single tree*). **5** regarded separately (*every single thing*). **6** not married; not involved in a sexual relationship. **7** *Brit.* (of a ticket) valid for an outward journey only. **8** (with *neg.* or *interrog.*) even one (*did not see a single person*). **9** (of a flower) having only one circle of petals. ● *n.* **1** a single thing, or item in a series. **2** *Brit.* a single ticket. **3** a short record with one piece of music etc. on each side. **4 a** *Cricket* a hit for one run. **b** *Baseball* a one-base hit. **5** (usu. in *pl.*) a game with one player on each side. **6** an unmarried person (*young singles*). ● *v.tr.* (foll. by *out* and often by *for, as*) select from a group as worthy of special attention etc. [from Latin *singulus*, related to SIMPLE] □ **singleness** *n.* **singly** *adv.*

single-breasted *adj.* (of a jacket etc.) having only one set of buttons and buttonholes, not overlapping.

single combat *n.* a duel.

single cream *n. Brit.* thin cream with a relatively low fat content.

single-decker *n.* esp. *Brit.* a bus having only one deck.

single file ● *n.* a line of people or things arranged one behind another. ● *adv.* one behind another.

single-handed ● *adv.* **1** without help from another. **2** with one hand. ● *adj.* **1** done etc. single-handed. **2** for one hand. □ **single-handedly** *adv.*

single market *n.* an association of countries trading without restrictions.

single-minded *adj.* having or intent on only one purpose. □ **single-mindedly** *adv.* **single-mindedness** *n.*

single parent *n.* a person bringing up a child or children without a partner.

singles bar *n.* a bar for single people seeking company.

singlet *n.* esp. *Brit.* a garment worn under or instead of a shirt; a vest. [originally a man's short jacket, based on SINGLE, the garment being unlined (cf. DOUBLET)]

singleton *n.* **1** one card only of a suit, esp. as dealt to a player. **2** a single person or thing.

sing-song ● *adj.* uttered with a monotonous rhythm or cadence. ● *n.* **1** a sing-song manner. **2** *Brit.* an informal gathering for singing. ● *v.intr. & tr.* (*past* and *past part.* **sing-songed**) speak or recite in a sing-song manner.

singular ● *adj.* **1** unique; much beyond the average; extraordinary. **2** eccentric or strange. **3** *Gram.* (of a word or form) denoting or referring to a single person or thing. **4** single, individual. ● *n. Gram.* **1** a singular word or form. **2** the singular number. [from Latin *singularis*] □ **singularly** *adv.*

singularity *n.* (*pl.* **-ies**) **1** the state or condition of being singular. **2** an odd trait or peculiarity.

sinh *abbr. Math.* hyperbolic sine. [from *sine* + hyperbolic]

Sinhalese (also **Singhalese**) ● *n.* (*pl.* same) **1** a member of a N. Indian people now forming the majority of the population of Sri Lanka. **2** a language spoken by this people. ● *adj.* of or relating to this people or language. [based on Sanskrit *sinhalam* 'Sri Lanka' (Ceylon)]

sinister *adj.* **1** suggestive of evil; looking villainous. **2** wicked or criminal (*a sinister motive*). **3** of evil omen. **4** *Heraldry* of or on the left-hand side of a shield etc. (i.e. to the observer's right). **5** *archaic* left-hand. [Latin, literally 'left'] □ **sinisterly** *adv.* **sinisterness** *n.*

sink ● *v.* (*past* **sank** or **sunk**; *past part.* **sunk** or as *adj.* **sunken**) **1** *intr.* fall or come slowly downwards. **2** *intr.* disappear below the horizon. **3** *intr.* **a** go or penetrate below the surface esp. of a liquid. **b** (of a ship) go to the bottom of the sea etc. **4** *intr.* settle comfortably (*sank into a chair*). **5** *intr.* **a** gradually lose strength or value or quality etc. (*my heart sank*). **b** (of the voice) descend in pitch or volume. **6** *tr.* send (a ship) to the bottom of the sea etc. **7** *tr.* cause or allow to sink or penetrate (*sank its teeth into my leg*). **8** *tr.* cause (a plan, person, etc.) to fail. **9** *tr.* dig (a well) or bore (a shaft). **10** *tr.* engrave (a die) or inlay (a design). **11** *tr.* **a** invest (money). **b** lose (money) by investment. **12** *tr.* cause (a ball) to enter a pocket in billiards, a hole at golf, etc. **13** *intr.* (of a price etc.) become lower. **14** *intr.* (of a storm or river) subside. **15** *intr.* (of ground) slope down, or reach a lower level by subsidence. **16** *intr.* (foll. by *on, upon*) (of darkness) descend (on a place). **17** *tr.* lower the level of. **18** *tr.* (usu. in *passive*; foll. by *in*) absorb; hold the attention of (*sunk in thought*). ● *n.* **1** a fixed basin with a water supply and outflow pipe. **2** a place where foul liquid collects. **3** a place of vice or corruption. □ **sink in 1** penetrate or make its way in. **2** become gradually comprehended. **sink or swim** even at the risk of complete failure. [Old English] □ **sinkable** *adj.* **sinkage** *n.*

■ **Usage** In the past tense either *sank* or *sunk* is acceptable in standard English, as in *It sank* or *sunk its teeth into her hand*.

SINKER: DISC
WEIGHT USED
FOR FISHING

sinker *n.* ◄ a weight used to sink a fishing line or plumb line.

sinking feeling *n.* a bodily sensation, esp. in the abdomen, caused by hunger or apprehension.

sinking fund *n.* money set aside for the gradual repayment of a debt.

sinner *n.* a person who sins, esp. habitually.

Sinn Fein /shin **fayn**/ *n.* a political movement and party seeking a united republican Ireland, now linked to the IRA. [Irish *sinn féin* 'we ourselves'] □ **Sinn Feiner** *n.*

Sino- *comb. form* Chinese; Chinese and (*Sino-British*). [from Greek *Sinai* 'the Chinese']

sinologue *n.* an expert in sinology.

sinology *n.* the study of Chinese language, history, customs, etc. □ **sinological** *adj.* **sinologist** *n.*

sinter ● *n.* **1** ▶ a siliceous or calcareous rock formed by deposition from hot springs. **2** a substance formed by sintering. ● *v.intr. & tr.* coalesce or cause to coalesce from powder into solid by heating. [German, literally 'cinder']

sinuate *adj.* esp. *Bot.* wavy-edged; with distinct inward and outward bends along the edge. [from Latin *sinuatus*]

SINTER:
TRAVERTINE

sinuous *adj.* with many curves; undulating. [from Latin *sinuosus*] □ **sinuosity** *n.* **sinuously** *adv.* **sinuousness** *n.*

sinus /sy-nŭs/ *n.* ◄ a cavity of bone or tissue, esp. in the skull connecting with the nostrils. ▷ ABSCESS, HEAD. [Latin, literally 'bosom, recess']

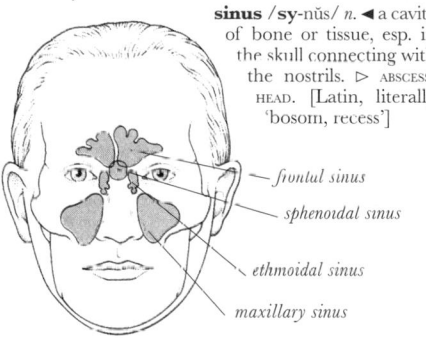

— *frontal sinus*

— *sphenoidal sinus*

— *ethmoidal sinus*

— *maxillary sinus*

SINUS: LOCATION OF SINUSES

sinusitis *n.* inflammation of a sinus.

Sion var. of ZION.

Sioux /soo/ ● *n.* (*pl.* same) **1** a member of a group of N. American Indian peoples chiefly inhabiting the upper Mississippi and Missouri river basins. **2** the language of these peoples. ● *adj.* of or relating to these peoples or language. [N. American French]

sip ● *v.tr. & intr.* (**sipped**, **sipping**) drink in one or more small amounts or by spoonfuls. ● *n.* **1** a small mouthful of liquid (*a sip of brandy*). **2** the act of taking this. [Middle English] □ **sipper** *n.*

siphon var. of SYPHON.

sir *n.* **1** a polite form of address or mode of reference to a man. **2** (**Sir**) a titular prefix to the forename of a knight or baronet. [Middle English]

sire ● *n.* **1** the male parent of an animal, esp. a stallion. **2** *archaic* a respectful form of address, esp. to a king. **3** *archaic poet.* a father or male ancestor. ● *v.tr.* (esp. of an animal) beget. [from Latin *senior* 'older, older man']

siren *n.* **1 a** a device for making a loud prolonged signal or warning sound. **b** the sound made by this. **2** (in Greek mythology) each of a number of women or winged creatures whose singing lured unwary sailors on to rocks. **3 a** a temptress. **b** a tempting pursuit etc. [from Greek *Seirēn*]

sirenian ● *adj.* of the order Sirenia of large aquatic plant-eating mammals. ● *n.* any mammal of this order.

siren suit *n.* a one-piece garment for the whole body, originally for use in air-raid shelters.

sirloin *n.* the upper and choicer part of a loin of beef. [from Old French]

sirocco *n.* (also **scirocco**) (*pl.* **-os**) a hot, oppressive, often dusty or rainy wind blowing from N. Africa across the Mediterranean to southern Europe. [from Arabic *Šarūk* 'east wind']

sirree *int. US colloq.* as an emphatic, esp. after *yes* or *no*.

sirup *US* var. of SYRUP.

sis *n. colloq.* a sister.

sisal /sy-zǎl/ *n.* **1** a Mexican plant, *Agave sisalana*, with large fleshy leaves. **2** the fibre made from this plant. ▷ ROPE. [from *Sisal*, a port in Yucatán, Mexico]

siskin *n.* ◄ a dark-streaked yellowish-green songbird, *Carduelis spinus*. [from Middle Dutch *siseken*]

sissy (also **cissy**) *colloq.* ● *n.* (*pl.* **-ies**) an effeminate or cowardly person. ● *adj.* (**sissier**, **sissiest**) effeminate; cowardly. [based on SIS] □ **sissified** *adj.* **sissiness** *n.* **sissyish** *adj.*

sister *n.* **1** a woman or girl in relation to sons and other daughters of her parents. **2 a** a close female friend or associate. **b** a female fellow member of a trade union, class, sect, or the human race. **c** a fellow feminist. **3** *Brit.* a senior female nurse. **4** a member of a female religious order. **5** (often *attrib.*) of the same type or design or origin etc. (*sister ship*; *prose, the younger sister of verse*). [from Old Norse] □ **sisterless** *adj.* **sisterly** *adj.* **sisterliness** *n.*

sister city *n.* a city that is twinned with another.

sister german see GERMAN 1.

sisterhood *n.* **1** the relationship between sisters. **2 a** a society or association of women, esp. when bound by monastic vows or devoting themselves to religious or charitable work or the feminist cause. **b** its members collectively. **3** community of feeling and mutual support between women.

sister-in-law *n.* (*pl.* **sisters-in-law**) **1** the sister of one's wife or husband. **2** the wife of one's brother. **3** the wife of one's brother-in-law.

sister uterine see UTERINE 2.

Sisyphean /si-si-fee-ǎn/ *adj.* (of toil) endless and fruitless like that of Sisyphus in Greek mythology (whose task in Hades was to push uphill a stone that at once rolled down again).

sit *v.* (**sitting**; past and past part. **sat**) **1** *intr.* adopt or be in a position in which the body is supported more or less upright by the buttocks resting on the ground or a raised seat etc. **2** *tr.* cause to sit; place in a sitting position. **3** *intr.* **a** (of a bird) perch. **b** (of an animal) rest with the hind legs bent and the body close to the ground. **4** *intr.* (of a bird) remain on its nest to hatch its eggs. **5** *intr.* **a** be engaged in an occupation in which sitting position is usual. **b** (of a committee, legislative body, etc.) be engaged in business. **6** *intr.* (usu. foll. by *for*) pose, usu. in a sitting position (for a portrait). **7** *intr.* (foll. by *for*) be a Member of Parliament for (a constituency). **8** *tr. & (foll. by for) intr. Brit.* take (an examination). **9** *intr.* be in a more or less permanent position or condition (esp. of inactivity or being out of use or out of place). **10** *intr.* (of clothes etc.) fit or hang in a certain way. **11** *tr.* keep or have one's seat on (a horse etc.). **12** *intr.* act as a babysitter. □ **be sitting pretty** be comfortably or advantageously placed. **make a person sit up** *colloq.* surprise or interest a person. **sit at a person's feet** be a person's pupil. **sit back** relax one's efforts. **sit by** look on without interfering. **sit down 1** sit after standing. **2** cause to sit. **3** (foll. by *under*) *Brit.* submit tamely to (an insult etc.). **sit heavy on the stomach** take a long time

to be digested. **sit in 1** occupy a place as a protest. **2** (foll. by *for*) take the place of. **3** (foll. by *on*) be present as a guest or observer at (a meeting etc.). **sit in judgement** be censorious. **sit on 1** be a member of (a committee etc.). **2** hold a session or inquiry concerning. **3** *colloq.* delay action about (*the government has been sitting on the report*). **4** *colloq.* repress or rebuke or snub (*felt rather sat on*). **sit on the fence** see FENCE. **sit on one's hands 1** take no action. **2** refuse to applaud. **sit out 1** take no part in (a dance etc.). **2** stay till the end of (esp. an ordeal). **3** sit outdoors. **4** outstay (other visitors). **sit tight** *colloq.* **1** remain firmly in one's place. **2** not be shaken off or move away or yield to distractions. **sit up 1** rise from a lying to a sitting position. **2** sit firmly upright. **3** go to bed later. **4** *colloq.* become interested or aroused etc. **sit well** have a good seat in riding. **sit well on** suit or fit. [Old English]

sitar *n.* ▶ a long-necked Indian lute. ▷ STRINGED. [from Hindi *sitār*] □ **sitarist** *n.*

sitcom *n. colloq.* a situation comedy.

sit-down *adj.* **1** (of a meal) eaten sitting at a table. **2** (of a protest etc.) in which demonstrators occupy their workplace or sit down on the ground in a public place.

site ● *n.* **1** the ground chosen or used for a town or building. **2** a place where some activity is or has been conducted (*camping site*; *launching site*). ● *v.tr.* **1** locate or place. **2** provide with a site. [from Latin *situs* 'local position']

sit-in *n.* a protest involving sitting in.

Sitka *n.* (in full **Sitka spruce**) a fast-growing spruce, *Picea sitchensis*, native to N. America and yielding timber. [named after *Sitka*, a town in Alaska]

sitter *n.* **1** a person who sits, esp. for a portrait. **2** = BABYSITTER (see BABYSIT). **3** *colloq.* **a** an easy catch or shot. **b** an easy task.

sitting ● *n.* **1** a continuous period of being seated, esp. engaged in an activity (*finished the book in one sitting*). **2** a time during which an assembly is engaged in business. **3** a session in which a meal is served (*dinner will be served in two sittings*). **4** a clutch of eggs. ● *adj.* **1** having sat down. **2** (of an animal or bird) not running or flying. **3** (of a hen) engaged in hatching. □ **sitting pretty** see PRETTY.

sitting duck *n.* (also **sitting target**) *colloq.* a vulnerable person or thing.

sitting room *n.* esp. *Brit.* a room in a house for relaxed sitting in.

sitting tenant *n. Brit.* a tenant already in occupation of premises.

situate ● *v.tr.* (usu. in *passive*) **1** put in a certain position or circumstances (*is situated at the top of a hill*; *how are you situated at the moment?*). **2** establish or indicate the place of; put in a context. ● *adj. Law* or *archaic* situated. [based on medieval Latin *situatus* 'situated']

situation *n.* **1** a place and its surroundings (*the house stands in a fine situation*). **2** a set of circumstances; a position in which one finds oneself; a state of affairs (*came out of a difficult situation with credit*). **3** an employee's position or job. [from medieval Latin *situatio*] □ **situational** *adj.* **situationally** *adv.*

■ **Usage** In sense 2, *situation* can be preceded by an adjective as shown above. The substitution of an attributive noun should be avoided where possible

SISKIN
(*Carduelis spinus*)

tuning peg

inlaid finger-board

arched metal fret

bridge

sound box

end pins

SITAR

S

since the result is usually ugly (e.g. *the rainforest situation*) and often tautologous (e.g. *in a crisis situation*).

situation comedy *n.* a comedy, esp. as part of a television or radio series, in which the humour derives from the situations the characters are placed in.

situationism *n.* the theory that human behaviour is determined by surrounding circumstances rather than by personal qualities. □ **situationist** *n. & adj.*

sit-up *n.* a physical exercise in which a person sits up from a supine position without using the arms for leverage.

sit-upon *n. Brit. colloq.* the buttocks.

sitz-bath *n.* a hip bath. [partial translation of German *Sitzbad*]

six ● *n.* **1** one more than five. **2** a symbol for this (6, vi, VI). **3** a size etc. denoted by six. **4** a set or team of six individuals. **5** *Cricket* a hit scoring six runs by clearing the boundary without bouncing. **6** the time of six o'clock. **7** a card etc. with six pips. ● *adj.* that amount to six. □ **at sixes and sevens** in confusion or disagreement. **knock for six** *Brit. colloq.* utterly surprise or overcome. [Old English]

Six Counties *n.pl.* the counties of N. Ireland.

sixer *n.* **1** *Brit.* the leader of a group of six Brownies or Cubs. **2** *Cricket* a hit for six runs.

sixfold *adj. & adv.* **1** six times as much or as many. **2** consisting of six parts.

six-gun *n.* = SIX-SHOOTER.

six-pack *n.* a pack of six cans of beer held together with a plastic fastener.

sixpence *n. Brit.* **1** the sum of six pence, esp. before decimalization. **2** *hist.* a coin worth six old pence (2½ p). □ **on a sixpence 1** within a small area or short distance. **2** quickly and with ease.

sixpenny *adj. Brit.* costing or worth six pence, esp. before decimalization.

six-shooter *n.* a revolver with six chambers. ▷ REVOLVER

sixteen ● *n.* **1** one more than fifteen. **2** a symbol for this (16, xvi, XVI). **3** a size etc. denoted by sixteen. ● *adj.* that amount to sixteen. [Old English] □ **sixteenth** *adj. & n.*

sixth ● *n.* **1** the position in a sequence corresponding to that of the number 6 in the sequence 1–6. **2** something occupying this position. **3** any of six equal parts of a thing. **4** *Mus.* **a** an interval or chord spanning six consecutive notes in the diatonic scale (e.g. C to A). **b** a note separated from another by this interval. ● *adj.* that is the sixth. □ **sixthly** *adv.*

sixth form *n. Brit.* a form in a secondary school for pupils over 16.

sixth-form college *n. Brit.* a college for pupils over 16.

sixth sense *n.* **1** a supposed faculty giving intuitive or extrasensory knowledge. **2** such knowledge.

sixty ● *n.* (*pl.* **-ies**) **1** the product of six and ten. **2** a symbol for this (60, lx, LX). **3** (in *pl.*) the numbers from 60 to 69, esp. the years of a century or of a person's life. **4** a set of sixty persons or things. ● *adj.* that amount to sixty. [Old English] □ **sixtieth** *adj. & n.* **sixtyfold** *adj. & adv.*

sixty-four thousand dollar question *n.* (also **sixty-four dollar question**) a difficult and crucial question (from the top prize in a broadcast quiz show).

sizable var. of SIZEABLE.

size¹ ● *n.* **1** the relative bigness or extent of a thing, dimensions, magnitude (*is of vast size; size matters less than quality*). **2** each of the classes into which things otherwise similar are divided according to size (*is made in several sizes; takes size 7 in gloves; is three sizes too big*). ● *v.tr.* sort in sizes or according to size. □ **of a size** having the same size. **of some size** fairly large. **the size of** as big as. **the size of it** *colloq.* a true account of the matter (*that is the size of it*). **size up 1** estimate the size of. **2** *colloq.* form a judgement of. **what size?** how big? [from Old French *sise*] □ **sized** *adj.* (also in *comb.*). **sizer** *n.*

size² ● *n.* a gelatinous solution used in glazing paper, stiffening textiles, preparing plastered walls for decoration, etc. ● *v.tr.* glaze or stiffen or treat with size. [Middle English]

sizeable *adj.* (also **sizable**) large or fairly large. □ **sizeably** *adv.*

size-stick *n.* a shoemaker's measure for taking the length of a foot.

sizzle ● *v.* **1 a** *intr.* make a sputtering or hissing sound when or as if frying. **b** *tr.* fry or burn. **2** *intr. colloq.* **a** be in a state of great heat or excitement (*Britain sizzled in the heatwave; articles sizzling with the news*). **b** be salacious. ● *n.* **1** a sizzling sound. **2** *colloq.* a state of great heat or excitement. □ **sizzler** *n.*

sizzling *adj. & adv.* (*sizzling hot*).

SJ *abbr.* Society of Jesus.

sjambok /**sham**-bok/ ● *n.* (in S. Africa) a long stiff whip, originally made of rhinoceros hide. ● *v.tr.* flog with a sjambok. [from Urdu *chābuk*]

ska *n.* a style of fast popular music with a strong offbeat, originating in Jamaica. [20th-century coinage]

skag *n.* (also **scag**) esp. *US slang* **1** a cigarette; a cigarette stub. **2** heroin. [20th-century coinage]

skald *n.* (also **scald**) (in ancient Scandinavia) a composer and reciter of poems honouring heroes and their deeds. [from Old Norse *skáld*] □ **skaldic** *adj.*

skat /skaht/ *n.* a three-handed card game with bidding. [from Italian *scarto* 'a discard']

SKELETON

The human skeleton supports the body, protects the internal organs, and provides anchorage for the muscles. It consists of bones and connective tissue called cartilage. Although an individual bone is around five times stronger than a steel bar of similar weight, the many joints in a skeleton allow a wide range of movement. The human skeleton contains 206 bones (about half of which are in the hands and feet) and consists of two main groups: the axial skeleton (skull, vertebral column, and ribcage) and the appendicular skeleton (the bones of the arms and legs). To allow for childbirth, the female pelvic cavity is shallower and wider than the male cavity.

SKELETON OF A HUMAN MALE

cranium · zygomatic bone · maxilla · mandible · clavicle · sternum · coracoid process · humerus · ribcage · vertebral column · epicondyles · ulna · radius · sacrum · ilium · carpals · metacarpals · phalanges · pubis · femur · patella · condyles · tibia · fibula · lateral malleolus · medial malleolus · talus · navicular · cuneiform bones · tarsals · meta-tarsals · calcaneus · phalanges

SEXUAL DIFFERENCES IN THE PELVIS

longer superior pubic ramus · larger pelvic cavity · wider subpubic arch

FEMALE PELVIS

shorter superior pubic ramus · smaller pelvic cavity · narrower subpubic arch

MALE PELVIS

S

skate[1] ● n. **1** ► each of a pair of steel blades (or of boots with blades attached) for gliding on ice. ▷ HOCKEY. **2** = ROLLER SKATE n. **3** a device on which a heavy object moves. ● v. **1 a** intr. move on skates. **b** tr. perform (a specified figure) on skates. **2** intr. (foll. by over) refer fleetingly to, disregard. □ **get one's skates on** Brit. colloq. make haste. **skate on thin ice** colloq. behave rashly, risk danger, esp. by dealing with a subject needing tactful treatment. [from Old French eschasse 'stilt'] □ **skater** n.

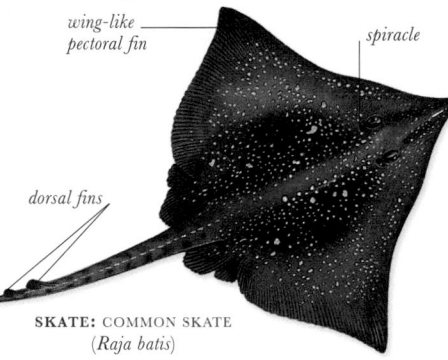

SKATE: ICE HOCKEY SKATE

ankle support
boot
blade   *safety heel tip*

skate[2] n. (pl. same or **skates**) ▼ any cartilaginous marine fish of the family Rajidae, esp. *Raja batis*, a large flat rhomboidal fish used as food. [from Old Norse *skata*]

wing-like pectoral fin   *spiracle*
dorsal fins

SKATE: COMMON SKATE
(*Raja batis*)

skate[3] n. slang a contemptible, mean, or dishonest person (esp. *cheapskate*). [19th-century coinage]

skateboard ● n. ▲ a short narrow board mounted on two wheeled trucks, used for riding on while standing. ● v.intr. ride on a skateboard. □ **skateboarder** n.

board   *truck*

SKATEBOARD

skatepark n. a park with ramps etc. for skateboarding.

skating rink n. **1** a piece of ice artificially made, or a floor used, for skating. **2** a building containing this.

skedaddle colloq. ● v.intr. run away, depart quickly, flee. ● n. a hurried departure or flight. [19th-century coinage]

skeeter[1] n. esp. N. Amer. & Austral. colloq. & dial. a mosquito. [abbreviation]

skeeter[2] var. of SKITTER.

skein /skayn/ n. **1** a loosely-coiled bundle of yarn or thread. **2** a flock of wild geese etc. in flight. **3** a tangle or confusion. [from Old French *escaigne*]

skeletal adj. **1** of, forming, or resembling a skeleton. **2** very thin, emaciated. **3** consisting of only a bare outline or minimum. □ **skeletally** adv.

skeleton n. **1 a** ◄ a hard framework of bones, cartilage, shell, woody fibre, etc., supporting or containing the body of an animal or plant. **b** the dried bones of a human being or other animal fastened together in the same relative positions as in life. **2** the supporting framework or structure of a thing. **3** a very thin person or animal. **4** the remaining part of anything after its life or usefulness is gone. **5** an outline sketch, an epitome or abstract. **6** (attrib.) having only the essential or minimum number of persons, parts, etc. (*skeleton plan*; *skeleton staff*). [from

Greek, literally 'dried-up (thing)'] □ **skeletonize** v.tr. (also **-ise**).

skeleton in the cupboard n. (US **skeleton in the closet**) a discreditable or embarrassing fact kept secret.

skeleton key n. a key designed to fit many locks.

skep n. **1 a** a wooden or wicker basket of any of various forms. **b** the quantity contained in this. **2 ►** a straw or wicker beehive. [from Old Norse *skeppa*]

skeptic US var. of SCEPTIC.

skeptical US var. of SCEPTICAL.

skepticism US var. of SCEPTICISM (see SCEPTIC).

skerry n. (pl. **-ies**) Sc. a reef or rocky island. [Orkney dialect, from Old Norse *sker*]

sketch ● n. **1** a rough, slight, merely outlined, or unfinished drawing or painting, often made to assist in making a more finished picture. **2** a brief account; a rough draft or general outline. **3** a very short usu. humorous play or performance, often limited to one scene in a revue, comedy programme, etc. **4** a short descriptive piece of writing. ● v. **1** tr. make or give a sketch of. **2** intr. draw sketches (*went out sketching*). **3** tr. (often foll. by in, out) indicate briefly or in outline. [from Italian *schizzo*] □ **sketcher** n.

sketch map n. a roughly drawn map with few details.

sketchy adj. (**sketchier**, **sketchiest**) **1** giving only a rough outline, like a sketch. **2** colloq. unsubstantial or imperfect, esp. through haste. □ **sketchily** adv. **sketchiness** n.

skew ● adj. oblique, slanting, set askew. ● v. **1** tr. make skew. **2** tr. distort. **3** intr. move obliquely. **4** intr. twist. □ **on the skew** askew. [from Old Northern French *eskiu(w)er* 'to eschew'] □ **skewness** n.

skewbald ● adj. ► (of an animal) with irregular patches of white and another colour (properly not black). ● n. a skewbald animal. [Middle English *skued* 'skewbald', on the pattern of *piebald*]

skewer ● n. a long pin designed for holding meat etc. compactly together, or the pieces of meat etc. of a kebab, while cooking. ● v.tr. **1** fasten together or pierce with or as with a skewer. **2** esp. N. Amer. criticize sharply. [Middle English]

skew-whiff adj. & adv. Brit. colloq. askew.

ski ● n. (pl. **skis**) **1** each of a pair of long narrow pieces of wood etc., fastened under the feet for travelling over snow. **2** a similar device under a vehicle or aircraft. **3** = WATER-SKI. **4** (attrib.) for wear when skiing (*ski boots*). ● v. (**skis**, **skied**, **skiing** or **ski-ing**) **1** intr. ▼ travel on skis. ▷ SLALOM. **2** tr. ski at (a place). [from Old Norse *skíth* 'billet, snowshoe'] □ **skiable** adj.

ski-bob ● n. a machine like a bicycle with skis instead of wheels. ● v.intr. (**-bobbed**, **-bobbing**) ride a ski-bob. □ **ski-bobber** n.

skid ● v. (**skidded**, **skidding**) **1** intr. (of a vehicle, a wheel, or a driver) slide on slippery ground, esp. sideways or obliquely. **2** tr. cause (a vehicle etc.) to skid. **3** intr. slip, slide. ● n. **1** the act or an instance of skidding. **2** a piece of wood etc. serving as a support, ship's fender, inclined plane, etc. **3** a braking device. **4** a runner beneath an aircraft for use when landing. □ **hit the skids** colloq. enter a rapid decline or deterioration. **on the skids** colloq. **1** about to be discarded or defeated. **2** ready for launching. **put the skids under** colloq. **1** hasten the downfall or failure of. **2** cause to hasten. [17th-century coinage]

skid-pan n. Brit. **1** a slippery surface prepared for vehicle-drivers to practise control of skidding. **2** a braking device.

skid row n. N. Amer. colloq. a part of a town frequented by vagrants, alcoholics, etc.

skier n. a person who skis.

skiff n. a light rowing boat or sculling boat. [from Italian *schifo*]

skiffle n. **1** Brit. a kind of folk music with a blues or jazz flavour,

SKEP

SKEWBALD
PONY

SKI

There are three types of competitive skiing: Alpine (downhill and slalom), Nordic (cross-country and ski jumping), and biathlon (cross-country with rifle shooting). All forms of skiing require specialized equipment. The skis, which are usually made of synthetic materials, vary in length and weight according to use. Slalom skis, for example, are shorter to aid manoeuvrability, while cross-country skis are light and narrow, with a toe fastening that allows the heel to move up and down with each stride. The ski boots support the ankles and ensure the skier is leaning forward at the correct angle. Safety bindings fasten the boot to the ski, but release under pressure. Ski poles assist with balance and turning.

wind- and waterproof jacket
ski pole
basket
ski boot
safety binding
afterbody of ski
forebody of ski

DOWNHILL SKIER

S

popular in the 1950s and played by a small group, mainly with a rhythmic accompaniment to a singing guitarist or banjoist, often incorporating improvised instruments. **2** *US* a style of 1920s and 30s jazz deriving from blues, ragtime, and folk music, and using improvised as well as conventional instruments.

ski jump *n.* **1** a steep slope levelling off before a sharp drop to allow a skier to leap through the air. **2** a jump made from this. □ **ski jumper** *n.* **ski jumping** *n.*

skilful *adj.* (*US* **skillful**) having or showing skill; practised, expert, adroit, ingenious. □ **skilfully** *adv.* **skilfulness** *n.*

ski lift *n.* ◀ a device for carrying skiers up a slope, usu. on seats hung from an overhead cable.

skill *n.* expertness, practised ability, facility in an action; dexterity or tact. [from Old Norse *skil* 'distinction']

skilled *adj.* **1** (often foll. by *in*) having or showing skill; skilful. **2** (of a worker) highly trained or experienced. **3** (of work) requiring skill or special training.

skillet *n.* **1** *Brit.* a small metal cooking pot with a long handle and usu. legs. **2** *N. Amer.* a frying pan. [Middle English]

skillful *US* var. of SKILFUL.

pole to overhead cable

SKI LIFT

skim ● *v.* (**skimmed, skimming**) **1** *tr.* **a** take scum or cream or a floating layer from the surface of (a liquid). **b** take (cream etc.) from the surface of a liquid. **2** *tr.* **a** keep touching lightly or nearly touching (a surface) in passing over. **b** deal with or treat (a subject) superficially. **3** *intr.* **a** go lightly over a surface, glide along in the air. **b** (foll. by *over*) = sense 2b of *v.* **4** *a tr.* read superficially, look over cursorily. **b** *intr.* (usu. foll. by *through*) read or look over cursorily. ● *n.* **1** the act or an instance of skimming. **2** a thin covering on a liquid (*skim of ice*). [back-formation from SKIMMER]

skimmer *n.* **1** a device for skimming liquids. ▷ UTENSIL. **2** a person who skims. **3** a flat hat, esp. a broad-brimmed straw hat. [from Old French *escumoir*]

skim milk *n.* (also **skimmed milk**) milk from which the cream has been skimmed.

skimp *v.* **1** *tr.* supply (a person etc.) meagrely with food, money, etc. **2** *tr.* use a meagre or insufficient amount of, stint (material, expenses, etc.). **3** *tr.* do hastily or carelessly. **4** *intr.* be parsimonious. [18th-century coinage]

skimpy *adj.* (**skimpier, skimpiest**) meagre; insufficient. □ **skimpily** *adv.* **skimpiness** *n.*

skin ● *n.* **1** ▲ the thin layer of tissue forming the natural outer covering of the body. **2 a** the skin of a flayed animal with or without the hair etc. **b** a material prepared from skins esp. of smaller animals. **3** a person's skin with reference to its colour or complexion (*has a fair skin*). **4** an outer layer or covering, esp. the coating of a plant, fruit, or sausage. **5** a film like skin on a liquid etc. **6** a container for liquid, made of an animal's whole skin. **7 a** the planking or plating of a ship or boat, inside or outside the ribs. **b** the outer covering of any craft or vehicle, esp. an aircraft or spacecraft. ● *v.* (**skinned, skinning**) **1** *tr.* **a** remove the skin from. **b** graze (a part of the body). **2 a** *tr.* cover (a sore etc.) with or as with skin. **b** *intr.* (of a wound etc.) become covered with new skin. **3** *tr. slang* swindle. □ **by** (or **with**) **the skin of one's teeth** by a very narrow margin. **get under a person's skin** *colloq.* interest or annoy a person intensely. **have a thick** (or **thin**) **skin** be insensitive (or sensitive) to criticism etc. **no skin off one's nose** *colloq.* a matter of indifference or even benefit to one. **to the skin** through all one's clothing (*soaked to the skin*). [from Old Norse *skinn*] □ **skinless** *adj.* **skinned** *adj.* (also in *comb.*). **skinner** *n.*

S

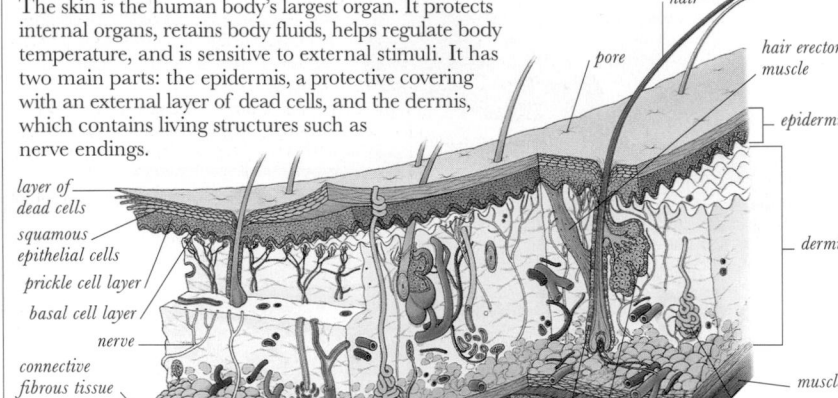

SKIN

The skin is the human body's largest organ. It protects internal organs, retains body fluids, helps regulate body temperature, and is sensitive to external stimuli. It has two main parts: the epidermis, a protective covering with an external layer of dead cells, and the dermis, which contains living structures such as nerve endings.

hair
pore
hair erector muscle
epidermis
dermis
layer of dead cells
squamous epithelial cells
prickle cell layer
basal cell layer
nerve
connective fibrous tissue
arteriole
venule
hair follicle
sebaceous gland
muscle
sweat gland

SECTION THROUGH HUMAN SKIN

skincare *n.* care of the skin by using cosmetics.

skin-deep ● *adj.* (of a wound, or of an emotion, an impression, a quality, etc.) superficial, not deep or lasting. ● *adv.* superficially, slightly.

skin diver *n.* a person who swims underwater without a diving suit, usu. in deep water with an aqualung and flippers. □ **skin diving** *n.*

skinflint *n.* a miserly person.

skinful *n.* (*pl.* **-fuls**) *Brit. colloq.* enough alcoholic liquor to make one drunk.

skin graft *n.* **1** the surgical transplanting of skin. **2** a piece of skin transferred in this way.

skinhead *n.* **1** a person, esp. a youth, characterized by close-cropped hair and heavy boots, esp. one of an aggressive gang. **2** *US* a recruit in the Marines.

skinny *adj.* (**skinnier, skinniest**) **1** thin or emaciated. **2** (of clothing) tight-fitting. **3** made of or like skin. □ **skinniness** *n.*

skint *adj. Brit. colloq.* having no money left. [literally 'skinned']

skin test *n.* a test to determine whether an immune reaction is elicited when a substance is applied to or injected into the skin.

skintight *adj.* (of a garment) very close-fitting.

skip¹ ● *v.* (**skipped, skipping**) **1** *intr.* **a** move along lightly, esp. by taking two steps with each foot in turn. **b** jump lightly from the ground, esp. so as to clear a skipping rope. **c** gambol, caper, frisk. **2** *intr.* move quickly from one point, subject, or occupation to another. **3** *tr.* (also *absol.*) omit in dealing with a series or in reading (*skip every tenth row*; *always skips the small print*). **4** *tr. colloq.* not participate in. **5** *tr. colloq.* depart quickly from; leave hurriedly. ● *n.* **1** a skipping movement or action. **2** *Computing* the action of passing over part of a sequence of data or instructions. □ **skip it** *slang* **1** abandon a topic etc. **2** make off, disappear. [Middle English]

skip² *n.* **1** *Brit.* a large container for builders' refuse etc. **2** a cage, bucket, etc., in which men or materials are lowered and raised in mines and quarries. **3** = SKEP 1. [variant of SKEP]

skipjack *n.* (in full **skipjack tuna**) ▼ a small striped Pacific tuna, *Katsuwonus* (or *Euthynnus*) *pelamis*, used as food.

SKIPJACK TUNA (*Katsuwonus pelamis*)

skipper ● *n.* **1** a sea captain. **2** the captain of an aircraft. **3** the captain of a side in a game or sport. ● *v.tr.* act as captain of.

skipping rope *n.* a length of rope held at each end and swung over the head and under the feet while jumping.

skirl ● *n.* the shrill sound characteristic of bagpipes. ● *v.intr.* make a skirl.

skirmish ● *n.* **1** a piece of irregular or unpremeditated fighting, esp. between small or outlying parts of armies or fleets; a slight engagement. **2** a short argument or contest of wit etc. ● *v.intr.* engage in a skirmish. [from Old French *eskirmir*] □ **skirmisher** *n.*

skirt ● *n.* **1** a woman's outer garment hanging from the waist. **2** the part of a coat, dress, etc. that hangs below the waist. **3** a hanging part round the base of a hovercraft. ▷ HOVERCRAFT. **4** (in *sing.* or *pl.*) an edge, border, or extreme part. **5** (in full **skirt of beef** etc.) **a** the diaphragm and other membranes as food. **b** *Brit.* a cut of meat from the lower flank. ● *v.tr.* **1** go along or round or past the edge of. **2** be situated along. **3** avoid dealing with (an issue etc.). [from Old Norse *skyrta* 'shirt'] □ **skirted** *adj.* (also in *comb.*).

skirting *n.* (in full **skirting board**) *Brit.* a narrow board etc. along the base of an interior wall.

ski run *n.* a slope prepared for skiing.

skit *n.* a light, usu. short, piece of satire or burlesque. [related to (now rare) *skit* 'to satirize']

skite ● *v.intr. Austral. & NZ colloq.* boast, brag. ● *n.* **1** *Austral. & NZ colloq.* a boaster. **2** boasting; boastfulness. [from Scots & northern English dialect in sense 'a person regarded with contempt']

skitter *v.intr.* (also **skeeter**) **1** (usu. foll. by *along, across*) move lightly or hastily. **2** (usu. foll. by *about, off*) hurry about, dart off.

skittery *adj.* skittish, restless.

skittish *adj.* **1** lively, playful. **2** (of a horse etc.) nervous, inclined to shy. [Middle English] □ **skittishly** *adv.* **skittishness** *n.*

skittle ● *n.* **1** a pin used in the game of skittles. **2** (in *pl.*; usu. treated as *sing.*) a game played with wooden pins set up at the end of an alley to be bowled down. ● *v.tr. Cricket* get (batsmen) out in rapid succession. [17th-century coinage]

skive ● *v.* (often foll. by *off*) **1** *tr.* split or pare (hides, leather, etc.). **2** *intr. Brit. colloq.* **a** evade a duty, shirk. **b** avoid work by absenting oneself, play truant. ● *n. colloq.* **1** an instance of shirking. **2** an easy option. [from Old Norse *skifa*] □ **skiver** *n.*

skivvy ● *n.* (*pl.* **-ies**) **1** *Brit. colloq. derog.* a female domestic servant. **2** a person doing work considered menial or poorly paid. ● *v.intr.* (**-ies**, **-ied**) *colloq.* work as a skivvy. [20th-century coinage]

SKUA: GREAT SKUA (*Catharacta skua*)

skua /skew-ă/ *n.* ◄ any large brownish predatory seabird of the family Stercorariidae. [from Old Norse *skúfr*]

skulduggery *n.* (also **sculduggery**, **skullduggery**) trickery; unscrupulous behaviour. [earlier *sculduddery*, originally Scots (18th c.) in sense 'unchastity']

skulk *v.intr.* **1** move stealthily, lurk, or keep oneself concealed, esp. in a cowardly or sinister way. **2** stay or sneak away in time of danger. **3** *Brit.* shirk duty. [from Scandinavian] □ **skulker** *n.*

skull *n.* **1** the bony case of the brain of a vertebrate. **2 a** ▼ the part of the skeleton corresponding to the head. ▷ HEAD. **b** this with the skin and soft internal parts removed. **3** the head as the seat of intelligence. [Middle English] □ **skulled** *adj.* (also in *comb.*).

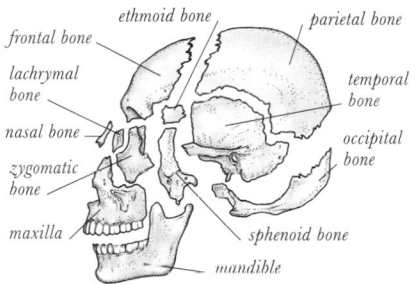

SKULL: EXPLODED VIEW OF THE HUMAN SKULL

Labels: ethmoid bone, parietal bone, frontal bone, temporal bone, lachrymal bone, nasal bone, occipital bone, zygomatic bone, maxilla, sphenoid bone, mandible

skull and crossbones *n.pl.* ► a representation of a skull with two thigh bones crossed below it as an emblem of piracy or death.

skullcap *n.* **1** a small close-fitting peakless cap. **2** the top part of the skull. ▷ HEAD. **3** any plant of the genus *Scutellaria*, having a helmet-shaped calyx after flowering

skunk *n.* **1** ◄ any of various cat-sized flesh-eating mammals of the family Mustelidae, esp. *Mephitis mephitis* having distinctive black and white striped fur and able to emit a powerful stench from a liquid secreted by its anal glands as a defence. ▷ MUSTELID. **2** *colloq.* a contemptible person. [Algonquian]

SKULL AND CROSSBONES ON A POISON-WARNING SIGN

sky ● *n.* (*pl.* **skies**) (in *sing.* or *pl.*) **1** the region of the atmosphere and outer space seen from the Earth. **2** the weather or climate evidenced by this. ● *v.tr.* (**skies**, **skied**) **1** *Cricket* etc. hit (a ball) high. **2** hang (a picture) high on a wall. □ **to**

SKUNK: STRIPED SKUNK (*Mephitis mephitis*)

the skies without reserve (*praised to the skies*). **under the open sky** out of doors. [from Old Norse *ský*] □ **skyey** *adj.* **skyless** *adj.*

skydiving *n.* the sport of performing acrobatic manoeuvres under free fall with a parachute. □ **skydiver** *n.*

sky-high *adv. & adj.* very high.

skyjack *v.tr. slang* hijack (an aircraft). □ **skyjacker** *n.*

skylark ● *n.* a lark, *Alauda arvensis* of Eurasia and N. Africa, that sings while hovering in flight. ● *v.intr.* play tricks, frolic.

skylight *n.* a window set in the plane of a roof or ceiling. ▷ SHIP

skyline *n.* the outline of hills, buildings, etc., defined against the sky.

sky pilot *n. slang* a clergyman.

skyrocket ● *n.* a rocket exploding high in the air. ● *v.intr.* (**-rocketed**, **-rocketing**) (esp. of prices etc.) rise very rapidly.

skyscraper *n.* a very tall building.

skywalk *n.* = SKYWAY 2.

skyward ● *adv.* (also **skywards**) towards the sky. ● *adj.* moving skyward.

skyway *n.* **1** a route used by aircraft. **2** the sky as a medium of transport. **3** a covered overhead walkway between buildings.

slab *n.* **1** a flat broad fairly thick usu. square or rectangular piece of solid material, esp. stone. **2** a large flat piece of cake, chocolate, etc. **3** (of timber) an outer piece sawn from a log. **4** *Brit.* a mortuary table. [Middle English]

slack[1] ● *adj.* **1** not taut; not held tensely (*slack rope; slack muscles*). **2** inactive or sluggish. **3** negligent or remiss. **4** (of tide etc.) neither ebbing nor flowing. **5** (of trade or business or a market) with little happening. ● *n.* **1** the slack part of a rope (*haul in the slack*). **2** a slack time in trade etc. **3** *colloq.* a spell of inactivity or laziness. **4** (in *pl.*) full-length loosely-cut trousers for informal wear. ● *v.* **1 a** *tr. & intr.* slacken. **b** *tr.* loosen (rope etc.). **2** *intr. Brit. colloq.* take a rest; be lazy; shirk. □ **slack off 1** loosen. **2** lose or cause to lose vigour. **slack up** reduce the speed of a train etc. before stopping. **take up the slack** use up a surplus or make up a deficiency; avoid an undesirable lull. [Old English] □ **slackly** *adv.* **slackness** *n.*

slack[2] *n.* coal dust or small pieces of coal. [Middle English]

slacken *v.tr. & intr.* make or become slack. □ **slacken off** = *slack off* (see SLACK[1]).

slacker *n.* a shirker.

slag ● *n.* **1** refuse left after ore has been smelted. ▷ BLAST FURNACE. **2** *Brit. slang offens.* a prostitute or promiscuous woman. ● *v.* (**slagged**, **slagging**) **1** *intr.* **a** form slag. **b** cohere into a mass like slag. **2** *tr.* (often foll. by *off*) *Brit. slang* criticize, insult. [from Middle Low German *slagge*]

slag heap *n.* a hill of refuse from a mine etc.

slain *past part.* of SLAY.

slake *v.tr.* **1** assuage or satisfy (thirst, revenge, etc.). **2** disintegrate (quicklime) by chemical combination with water. [Old English]

slaked lime see LIME[1] *n.* 2.

slalom *n.* **1** ► a ski race down a zigzag course defined by artificial obstacles. **2** an obstacle race in canoes or cars or on skateboards or waterskis. [Norwegian, literally 'sloping track']

slam[1] ● *v.* (**slammed**, **slamming**) **1** *tr. & intr.* shut forcefully and loudly. **2** *tr.* put down (an object) with a similar sound. **3** *intr.* move

violently (*he slammed out of the room*). **4** *tr. & intr.* put or come into action suddenly or forcefully (*slam the brakes on*). **5** *tr. slang* criticize severely. **6** *tr. slang* hit. **7** *tr. slang* gain an easy victory over. ● *n.* **1** a sound of or as of a slammed door. **2** the shutting of a door etc. with a loud bang. **3** (usu. prec. by *the*) *N. Amer. slang* prison.

slam[2] *n. Cards* the winning of every trick in a game. [originally the name of a card game]

slam dunk *n.* (also **slamdunk**) *Basketball* ► a play in which a player jumps and thrusts the ball forcefully down into the basket.

slammer *n.* (usu. prec. by *the*) *slang* prison.

slander ● *n.* **1** a malicious, false, and injurious statement spoken about a person. **2** the uttering of such statements. **3** *Law* false oral defamation. ● *v.tr.* utter slander about. [from Late Latin *scandalum*] □ **slanderer** *n.* **slanderous** *adj.*

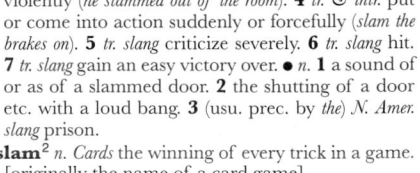

SLAM DUNK

slang ● *n.* words, phrases, and uses that are regarded as very informal and are often restricted to special contexts or are peculiar to a specified profession, class, etc. (*racing slang; schoolboy slang*). ● *v.* **1** *tr.* use abusive language to. **2** *intr.* use such language. [18th-century coinage]

slanging match *n. Brit.* a prolonged exchange of insults.

slangy *adj.* (**slangier**, **slangiest**) **1** of the character of slang. **2** fond of using slang. □ **slangily** *adv.*

slant ● *v.* **1** *intr.* slope; lie or go obliquely. **2** *tr.* cause to do this. **3** *tr.* (often as **slanted** *adj.*) present (information) from a particular angle esp. in a biased or unfair way. ● *n.* **1** a slope; an oblique position. **2** a point of view, esp. a biased one. ● *adj.* sloping, oblique. □ **on a** (or **the**) **slant** aslant. [Middle English; *v.*: from Old Norse]

slantwise *adv.* aslant.

slap ● *v.* (**slapped**, **slapping**) **1** *tr. & intr.* strike with the palm of the hand or a flat object, or so as to make a similar noise. **2** *tr.* lay forcefully (*slapped the money on the table; slapped a writ on the offender*). **3** *tr.* put hastily or carelessly (*slap some paint on the walls*). **4** *tr.* (often foll. by *down*) *colloq.* reprimand or snub. ● *n.* **1** a blow with the palm of the hand or a flat object. **2** a slapping sound. ● *adv.* **1** suddenly, fully, directly (*ran slap into him; hit me slap in the eye*). **2** = SLAP BANG. □ **slap on the back** ● *n.* congratulations. ● *v.tr.* congratulate. [from Low German *slapp*]

slap and tickle *n. Brit. colloq.* light-hearted amorous amusement.

slap bang *adv.* **1** exactly, precisely (*slap bang in the middle of the town*). **2** violently, noisily, headlong. **3** conspicuously, prominently.

slapdash ● *adj.* hasty and careless. ● *adv.* in a slapdash manner.

slap-happy *adj. colloq.* **1** cheerfully casual or flippant. **2** punch-drunk.

slaphead *n. slang derog.* a person with very short hair or very little hair.

slap in the face *n.* a rebuff or affront.

slapper *n. Brit. slang offens.* a promiscuous woman.

slapstick *n.* boisterous knockabout comedy.

slap-up *attrib.adj.* esp. *Brit. colloq.* excellent, lavish (*slap-up meal*).

slash ● *v.* **1** *intr.* make a sweeping or random cut or cuts with a knife, sword, whip, etc. **2** *tr.* make such a cut or cuts

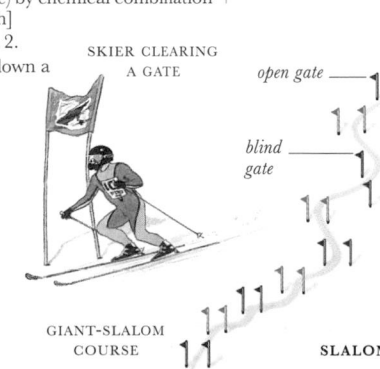

SKIER CLEARING A GATE

open gate, blind gate

SLALOM

GIANT-SLALOM COURSE

at. **3** *tr.* make a long narrow gash or gashes in. **4** *tr.* reduce (prices etc.) drastically. **5** *tr.* censure vigorously. **6** *tr.* make (one's way) by slashing. **7** *tr.* **a** lash (a person etc.) with a whip. **b** crack (a whip). ● *n.* **1 a** a slashing cut or stroke. **b** a wound or slit made by this. **2** an oblique stroke; a solidus. **3** *Brit. slang* an act of urinating. **4** *N. Amer.* debris resulting from the felling or destruction of trees. [Middle English]

slasher *n.* **1** a person or thing that slashes. **2** (in full **slasher film, slasher movie**) a film depicting violent assault with a knife etc.

slat *n.* a thin narrow piece of wood or plastic or metal, esp. used in an overlapping series as in a fence or venetian blind. [from Old French *esclat* 'splinter']

slate ● *n.* **1** ◀ a fine-grained grey, green, or bluish-purple metamorphic rock easily split into flat smooth plates. ▷ METAMORPHIC. **2** a piece of such a plate used as roofing-material. **3** a piece of such a plate used for writing on, usu. framed in wood. **4** a bluish-grey colour. **5** *N. Amer.* a list of nominees for office etc. ● *v.tr.* **1** cover with slates esp. as roofing. **2** *Brit. colloq.* criticize severely. **3** *N. Amer.* make arrangements for (an event etc.). **4** *N. Amer.* nominate for office etc. ● *adj.* made of slate. □ **on the slate** *Brit.* recorded as a debt to be paid. **wipe the slate clean** forgive or cancel the record of past offences. [Middle English, from Old French *esclate* 'slat'] □ **slating** *n.* **slaty** *adj.*

SLATE

slate-pencil *n.* a small rod of soft slate used for writing on slate.

slather ● *n.* **1** (usu. in *pl.*) *US colloq.* a large amount. **2** (often **open slather**) *Austral. & NZ slang* unrestricted scope for action. ● *v.tr. N. Amer. colloq.* **1** spread thickly. **2** squander. [19th-century coinage]

slatted *adj.* having slats.

slattern *n.* a slovenly woman. [17th-century coinage, related to *slattering* 'slovenly'] □ **slatternly** *adj.*

slaughter ● *n.* **1** the killing of an animal or animals. **2** the killing of many persons or animals at once or continuously. ● *v.tr.* **1** kill (people) in a ruthless manner or on a great scale. **2** kill (animals) esp. in large numbers. **3** *colloq.* defeat utterly. [based on Old Norse *slátr* 'butcher's meat'] □ **slaughterer** *n.*

slaughterhouse *n.* **1** a place for the slaughter of animals for food. **2** a place of carnage.

Slav ● *n.* a member of a group of peoples in central and eastern Europe speaking Slavonic languages. ● *adj.* **1** of or relating to the Slavs. **2** = SLAVONIC *adj.* 1. [from late Greek *Sklabos*]

slave ● *n.* **1** a person who is the legal property of another and is bound to absolute obedience. **2** a drudge; a person working very hard. **3** (foll. by *of, to*) a helpless victim of some dominating influence (*slave of fashion; slave to duty*). **4** a machine, or part of one, directly controlled by another. ▷ HYDRAULIC. ● *v.intr.* work very hard. [from Old French *esclave*]

slave-driver *n.* **1** an overseer of slaves. **2** a person who works others hard, esp. excessively so. □ **slave-drive** *v.tr.* (*past* **-drove**; *past part.* **-driven**).

slave labour *n.* forced labour.

slaver[1] *n. hist.* a ship or person engaged in the slave trade.

slaver[2] ● *n.* **1** saliva running from the mouth. **2 a** fulsome flattery. **b** drivel, nonsense. ● *v.intr.* **1** let saliva run from the mouth; dribble. **2** (foll. by *over*) show excessive sentimentality over, or desire for.

slavery *n.* **1** the condition of a slave. **2** drudgery. **3** the custom of having slaves.

slave trade *n. hist.* the procuring, transporting, and selling of human beings, esp. African blacks, as slaves. □ **slave trader** *n.*

Slavic *adj. & n.* = SLAVONIC.

slavish *adj.* **1** of, like, or as of slaves. **2** showing no attempt at originality. **3** abject, servile, base. □ **slavishly** *adv.*

Slavonic ● *adj.* **1** of or relating to the group of Indo-European languages including Russian, Polish, and Czech. **2** of or relating to the Slavs. ● *n.* the Slavonic language group. [from medieval Latin *S(c)lavonicus*]

slaw *n. N. Amer.* coleslaw. [from Dutch *sla*]

slay *v.tr.* (*past* **slew**; *past part.* **slain**) **1** *literary or N. Amer.* kill. **2** *colloq.* overwhelm with delight; convulse with laughter. [Old English] □ **slayer** *n.*

sleaze *colloq.* ● *n.* **1** sleaziness; sleazy material or conditions. **2** a person of low moral standards. ● *v.intr.* move in a sleazy fashion. [back-formation from SLEAZY]

sleazeball *n.* (also **sleazebag**) *slang* a sordid or despicable person.

sleazy *adj.* (**sleazier, sleaziest**) **1** squalid, tawdry. **2** slatternly. **3** (of textiles etc.) flimsy. [17th-century coinage] □ **sleazily** *adv.* **sleaziness** *n.*

sled *N. Amer.* ● *n.* = SLEDGE[1] *n.* ● *v.intr. & tr.* (**sledded, sledding**) = SLEDGE[1] *v.* [from Middle Low German *sledde*, related to SLIDE]

sledge[1] ● *n.* **1** ▼ a vehicle on runners for conveying loads or passengers esp. over snow, drawn by horses, dogs, or reindeer, or pushed or pulled by one or more persons. **2** *Brit.* a toboggan. ● *v.intr. & tr.* ride or convey on a sledge. [from Middle Dutch *sleedse*]

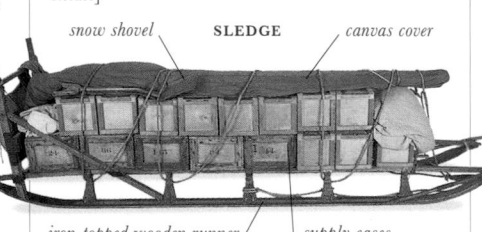

snow shovel   **SLEDGE**   canvas cover

iron-topped wooden runner /   \ supply cases

sledge[2] *n.* = SLEDGEHAMMER 1.

sledgehammer *n.* **1** a large heavy hammer used to break stone etc. **2** (*attrib.*) heavy or powerful (*a sledgehammer blow*). [15th-century coinage, from earlier *slecg* 'sledgehammer']

sleek ● *adj.* **1** (of hair, fur, or skin, or of an animal or person with such hair etc.) smooth and glossy. **2** looking well-fed and comfortable. **3** ingratiating. **4** (of a thing) smooth and polished. ● *v.tr.* make sleek. [later variant of SLICK] □ **sleekly** *adv.* **sleekness** *n.* **sleeky** *adj.*

sleep ● *n.* **1** the condition of body and mind which normally recurs for several hours every night, in which the nervous system is inactive, the eyes closed, the postural muscles relaxed, and consciousness practically suspended. **2** a period of sleep (*shall try to get a sleep*). **3** a state like sleep, such as rest, quiet, or death. **4** the prolonged inert condition of hibernating animals. **5** *colloq.* a substance found in the corners of the eyes after sleep. ● *v.* (*past and past part.* **slept**) **1** *intr.* **a** be in a state of sleep. **b** fall asleep. **2** *intr.* (foll. by *at, in,* etc.) spend the night. **3** *tr.* provide sleeping accommodation for (*the house sleeps six*). **4** *intr.* (foll. by *with, together*) have sexual intercourse, esp. in bed. **5** *intr.* (foll. by *on, over*) not decide (a question) until the next day. **6** *intr.* (foll. by *through*) fail to be woken by. **7** *intr.* be inactive or dormant. **8** *intr.* be dead; lie in the grave. □ **go to sleep 1** enter a state of sleep. **2** (of a limb) become numbed by pressure. **in one's sleep** while asleep. **put to sleep 1** anaesthetize. **2** *euphem.* kill (an animal) painlessly. **sleep around** *colloq.* be sexually promiscuous. **sleep in 1** remain asleep later than usual in the morning. **2** sleep by night at one's place of work. **sleep out** sleep by night out of doors, or not at one's place of work. [Old English]

sleeper *n.* **1** a person or animal that sleeps. **2** a wooden or concrete beam laid horizontally as a support, esp. *Brit.* for railway track. ▷ RAIL. **3 a** a

sleeping car. b a berth in this. **4** *Brit.* a ring worn in a pierced ear to keep the hole from closing. **5** a thing that is suddenly successful after being undistinguished.

sleeping bag *n.* a lined or padded bag to sleep in.

sleeping car *n.* (also *Brit.* **sleeping carriage**) a railway coach with beds or berths.

sleeping draught *n. Brit.* a drink to induce sleep.

sleeping partner *n. Brit.* a partner not sharing in the actual work of a firm.

sleeping pill *n.* a pill to induce sleep.

sleeping policeman *n. Brit.* a ramp etc. in the road intended to cause traffic to reduce speed.

sleeping sickness *n.* any of several tropical diseases with extreme lethargy.

sleeping suit *n. Brit.* a young child's one-piece garment, worn esp. as nightwear.

sleepless *adj.* **1** characterized by lack of sleep. **2** unable to sleep. **3** continually active or moving. □ **sleeplessly** *adv.* **sleeplessness** *n.*

sleepwalk *v.intr.* walk or perform other actions while asleep. □ **sleepwalker** *n.*

sleepy *adj.* (**sleepier, sleepiest**) **1** drowsy; about to fall asleep. **2** lacking activity (*a sleepy town*). **3** habitually indolent, unobservant, etc. □ **sleepily** *adv.* **sleepiness** *n.*

sleepyhead *n.* (esp. as a form of address) a sleepy or inattentive person.

sleepy sickness *n. Brit.* an infection of the brain with drowsiness and sometimes a coma.

sleet ● *n.* **1** a mixture of snow and rain falling together. **2** hail or snow melting as it falls. **3** *US* a thin coating of ice. ● *v.intr.* (prec. by *it* as subject) sleet falls (*if it sleets*). [Middle English] □ **sleety** *adj.*

sleeve *n.* **1** the part of a garment that wholly or partly covers an arm. **2** the cover of a gramophone record. **3** a tube enclosing a rod or smaller tube. **4** a windsock. □ **roll up one's sleeves** prepare to fight or work. **up one's sleeve** in reserve. [Old English] □ **sleeved** *adj.* (also in *comb.*). **sleeveless** *adj.*

sleigh ● *n.* a sledge, esp. one for riding on, drawn by horses or reindeer. ● *v.intr.* travel on a sleigh. [originally US, from Dutch *slee*]

sleigh bell *n.* any of a number of tinkling bells attached to the harness of a sleigh-horse etc.

sleight /slyt/ *n. archaic* **1** a deceptive trick or device or movement. **2** dexterity. **3** cunning. [based on Old Norse *slœgr* 'sly']

sleight of hand *n.* **1** dexterity esp. in conjuring or fencing. **2** a display of dexterity, esp. a conjuring trick.

slender *adj.* (**slenderer, slenderest**) **1 a** of small girth or breadth (*a slender pillar*). **b** gracefully thin (*a slender waist*). **2** slight, meagre, inadequate (*slender hopes; slender resources*). [Middle English] □ **slenderize** *v.tr. & intr.* (also **-ise**). **slenderly** *adv.* **slenderness** *n.*

slept *past and past part.* of SLEEP.

sleuth /slooth/ *colloq.* ● *n.* a detective. ● *v.* **1** *intr.* act as a detective. **2** *tr.* investigate. [Middle English in sense 'trail', originally in SLEUTH-HOUND]

sleuth-hound *n.* **1** a bloodhound. **2** *colloq.* a detective, an investigator.

slew[1] (also **slue**) ● *v.tr. & intr.* (often foll. by *round*) turn or swing forcibly or with effort out of the forward or ordinary position. ● *n.* such a change of position. [18th-century nautical coinage]

slew[2] *past* of SLAY.

slew[3] *n.* esp. *N. Amer. colloq.* a large number or quantity. [from Irish *sluagh*]

slice ● *n.* **1** a thin broad piece or wedge cut off or out esp. from meat or bread or a cake, pie, or large fruit. **2** a share; a part taken or allotted or gained (*a slice of the profits*). **3** a kitchen utensil with a broad flat blade for serving fish, cake, etc. **4** *Golf, Tennis, etc.* a slicing stroke. ● *v.* **1** *tr.* (often foll. by *up*) cut into slices. **2** *tr.* (foll. by *off*) cut (a piece) off. **3** *intr.* (foll. by *into, through*) cut with or like a knife. **4** *tr.* (also *absol.*) **a** *Golf* strike (the ball) so that it deviates away from the striker. **b** (in other sports) propel (the ball) forward at an angle. **5** *tr.* go through (air etc.) with a cutting motion. [from Old French *esclice* 'splinter'] □ **sliceable** *adj.* **slicer** *n.* (also in *comb.*).

slick ● *adj.* **1 a** (of a person or action) skilful or efficient (*slick performance*). **b** superficially or pretentiously smooth and dexterous. **c** glib. **2 a** sleek, smooth. **b** slippery. ● *n.* a smooth patch of oil etc., esp. on the sea. ● *v.tr.* **1** make sleek or smart. **2** (usu. foll. by *down*) flatten (one's hair etc.). [Middle English] □ **slickly** *adv.* **slickness** *n.*

slicker *n. N. Amer.* **1** *colloq.* **a** a plausible rogue. **b** = CITY SLICKER 1. **2** a raincoat of smooth material.

slide ● *v.* (*past* and *past part.* **slid**) **1 a** *intr.* move along a smooth surface with continuous contact on the same part of the thing moving. **b** *tr.* cause to do this. **2** *intr.* move quietly; glide. **3** *intr.* pass gradually or imperceptibly. **4** *intr.* glide over ice without skates. **5** *intr.* (foll. by *over*) barely touch upon (a delicate subject etc.). **6** *intr.* & *tr.* (often foll. by *into*) move or cause to move quietly or unobtrusively (*slid his hand into mine*). **7** *intr.* take its own course (*let it slide*). ● *n.* **1 a** the act or an instance of sliding. **b** a rapid decline. **2** an inclined plane down which children, goods, etc., slide; a chute. **3** a track made by or for sliding, esp. on or of ice. **4** a part of a machine or instrument that slides, esp. to open or close a valve. ▷ BRASS, HARMONICA. **5 a** a piece of glass holding an object for a microscope. **b** a mounted transparency for projection on to a screen. **6** *Brit.* = HAIRSLIDE. **7** a part or parts of a machine on or between which a sliding part works. [Old English] □ **slidable** *adj.* **slider** *n.*

slide fastener *n. US* a zip fastener.

slide rule *n.* ▼ a ruler with a sliding central strip, graduated logarithmically for making rapid calculations, esp. multiplication and division.

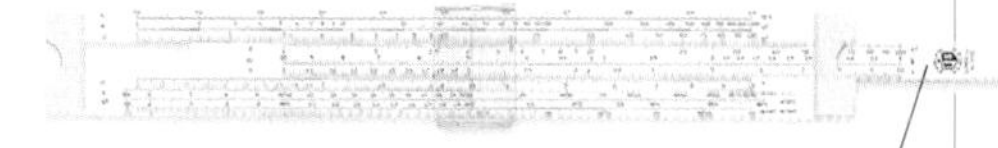

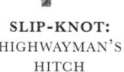

SLIDE RULE

sliding scale *n.* a scale of fees, taxes, wages, etc., that varies as a whole in accordance with variation of some standard.

slight ● *adj.* **1 a** inconsiderable; of little significance (*a slight cold*). **b** barely perceptible (*a slight smell of gas*). **c** not much or great or thorough; inadequate, scanty (*paid him slight attention*). **2** slender, frail-looking. **3** (in *superl.*, with *neg.* or *interrog.*) any whatever (*paid not the slightest attention*). ● *v.tr.* treat or speak of (a person etc.) as not worth attention; fail in courtesy or respect towards. ● *n.* a marked piece of neglect; a failure to show due respect. [originally in sense 'smooth, sleek': from Old Norse *sléttr* 'level, smooth'] □ **slightingly** *adv.* **slightish** *adj.* **slightly** *adv.* **slightness** *n.*

slily var. of SLYLY (see SLY).

slim ● *adj.* (**slimmer**, **slimmest**) **1 a** of small girth or thickness; of long narrow shape. **b** gracefully thin; slenderly built. **c** not fat or overweight. **2** small, insufficient (*a slim chance of success*). ● *v.* (**slimmed**, **slimming**) **1** *intr. Brit.* make oneself slimmer by dieting, exercise, etc. **2** *tr.* make slim or slimmer. [from Dutch] □ **slimly** *adv.* **slimmer** *n.* **slimming** *n.* & *adj.* **slimness** *n.*

slime ● *n.* thick slippery mud or a substance of similar consistency. ● *v.tr.* cover with slime. [Old English]

slimline *adj.* of slender design.

slimy *adj.* (**slimier**, **slimiest**) **1** of the consistency of slime. **2** covered, smeared with, or full of slime. **3** *colloq.* disgustingly dishonest, meek, or flattering. **4** slippery; hard to hold. □ **slimily** *adv.* **sliminess** *n.*

sling[1] ● *n.* **1** a strap, belt, etc., used to support or raise a hanging weight. **2** a bandage looped round the neck to support an injured arm. **3** a strap or string used with the hand to give impetus to a small missile. **4** a pouch or frame supported by a strap round the neck or shoulders for carrying a young child. ● *v.tr.* (*past* and *past part.* **slung**) **1** (also *absol.*) hurl (a stone etc.) from a sling. **2** *colloq.* throw. **3** allow to swing suspended; arrange so as to be supported from above; suspend, hoist, or transfer with a sling. □ **sling one's hook** see HOOK. [Middle English]

sling[2] *n.* a sweetened drink of spirits (esp. gin) and water. [18th-century coinage]

sling-back *n.* ◀ a shoe held in place by a strap above the heel.

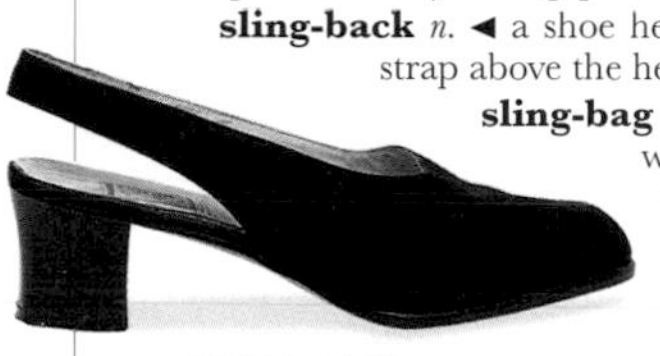

SLING-BACK

sling-bag *n. Brit.* a bag with a long strap which may be hung from the shoulder.

slinger *n.* a person who slings, esp. the user of a sling.

slingshot *n. US* a catapult.

slink *v.intr.* (*past* and *past part.* **slunk**) (often foll. by *off, away, by*) move in a stealthy or guilty or sneaking manner. [Old English *slincan* 'to crawl']

slinky *adj.* (**slinkier**, **slinkiest**) **1** stealthy. **2** (of a garment) close-fitting and flowing; sinuous. **3** gracefully slender. □ **slinkily** *adv.* **slinkiness** *n.*

slip[1] ● *v.* (**slipped**, **slipping**) **1** *intr.* slide unintentionally esp. for a short distance; lose one's footing or balance or place by unintended sliding. **2** *intr.* go or move with a sliding motion (*slipped into her nightdress*). **3** *intr.* escape restraint or capture by being slippery or hard to hold or by not being grasped. **4** *intr.* make one's or its way unobserved or quietly or quickly. **5** *intr.* **a** make a careless or casual mistake. **b** fall below the normal standard; deteriorate, lapse. **6** *tr.* insert or transfer stealthily or casually or with a sliding motion (*slipped a coin into his hand*). **7** *tr.* **a** release from restraint (*slipped the dog from the leash*). **b** release (the clutch of a motor vehicle) for a moment. **8** *tr.* move (a stitch) to the other needle without knitting it. **9** *tr.* (foll. by *on, off*) pull (a garment) hastily on or off. **10** *tr.* escape from; give the slip to (*slipped its collar*). ● *n.* **1** the act or an instance of slipping. **2** an accidental or slight mistake. **3** a loose covering or garment, e.g. a pillowcase. **4 a** a reduction in the movement of a pulley etc. due to slipping of the belt. **b** a reduction in the distance travelled by a ship or aircraft arising from the nature of the medium in which its propeller revolves. **5** (in *sing.* or *pl.*) an incline on which boats are landed, built, etc. **6** *Cricket* **a** a player stationed for fielding any ball glancing off the bat to the off side. ▷ CRICKET. **b** (in *sing.* or *pl.*) the position of such a fielder. □ **give a person the slip** escape from or evade him or her. **let slip 1** release accidentally or deliberately. **2** miss (an opportunity). **3** utter inadvertently. **slip away** (or **off**) depart without leave-taking etc. **slip up** *colloq.* make a mistake. [Middle English]

slip[2] *n.* **1** a small piece of paper, esp. for writing on. **2** a cutting taken from a plant for grafting or planting; a scion. [Middle English]

slip[3] *n.* clay in a creamy mixture with water, used mainly for decorating earthenware. [Old English *slipa* 'slime']

slip case *n.* a close-fitting case for a book etc.

slip cover *n.* **1** a detachable cover for a chair, sofa, etc., esp. when out of use; a loose cover. **2** a jacket or slip case for a book.

slip-knot *n.* **1** ▶ a knot that can be undone by a pull. **2** a running knot.

slip of the pen *n.* (also **slip of the tongue**) a small mistake in which something is written (or said) unintentionally.

slip-on ● *adj.* (of shoes or clothes) that can be easily slipped on and off. ● *n.* a slip-on shoe or garment.

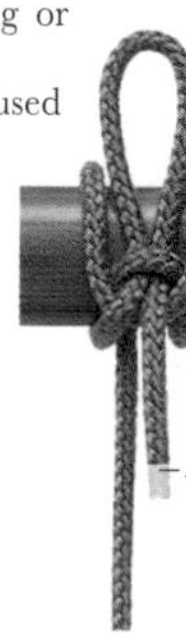

SLIP-KNOT: HIGHWAYMAN'S HITCH

slipover ● *n.* a pullover, usu. without sleeves. ● *adj.* (**slip-over**) (of a garment) to be slipped over the head.

slippage *n.* **1** the act or an instance of slipping. **2 a** a decline, esp. in popularity or value. **b** failure to meet a deadline or fulfil a promise.

slipped disc *n.* a cartilaginous disc between vertebrae that has become displaced, pinching the spinal nerve and causing lumbar pain.

slipper *n.* **1** a light loose comfortable indoor shoe. **2** a light slip-on shoe for dancing etc. □ **slippered** *adj.*

slippery *adj.* **1** difficult to hold firmly because of smoothness, wetness, sliminess, or elusive motion. **2** (of a surface) difficult to stand on, causing slips by its smoothness or muddiness. **3** unreliable, shifty. **4** (of a subject) requiring tactful handling. [Old English *slipor* 'slippery, morally repugnant'] □ **slipperily** *adv.* **slipperiness** *n.*

slippery slope *n.* a course leading to disaster.

slippy *adj.* (**slippier**, **slippiest**) *colloq.* slippery. □ **look** (or **be**) **slippy** *Brit.* look sharp; make haste. □ **slippiness** *n.*

slip road *n. Brit.* a road for entering or leaving a motorway etc.

slipshod *adj.* **1** careless, unsystematic; loose in arrangement. **2** slovenly. **3** having shoes down at heel.

slip stitch ● *n.* **1** a loose stitch joining layers of fabric and not visible externally. ▷ STITCH. **2** a stitch moved to the other needle without being knitted. ● *v.tr.* (**slip-stitch**) sew with slip stitches.

slipstream ● *n.* **1** a current of air or water driven back by a revolving propeller or a moving vehicle. **2** an assisting force regarded as drawing something along with or behind something else. ● *v.tr.* **1** (also *absol.*) follow closely behind (another vehicle). **2** pass after travelling in another's slipstream.

slip-up *n. colloq.* a mistake, a blunder.

slipway *n.* a slip for building ships or landing boats.

slit ● *n.* **1** a long straight narrow incision. **2** a long narrow opening comparable to a cut. ● *v.tr.* (**slitting**; *past* and *past part.* **slit**) **1** make a slit in; cut or tear lengthwise. **2** cut into strips. [Middle English] □ **slitted** *adj.* **slitty** *adj.* (**slittier**, **slittiest**) usu. *derog.*

slither ● *v.intr.* slide unsteadily; go with an irregular slipping motion. ● *n.* an instance of slithering. [Middle English] □ **slithery** *adj.*

sliver ● *n.* a long thin piece cut or split off. ● *v.tr.* & *intr.* **1** break off as a sliver. **2** break up into slivers. **3** form into slivers. [Middle English]

Sloane *n.* (in full **Sloane Ranger**) *Brit. slang* a fashionable and conventional upper-class young person. [from *Sloane* Square, London (+ Lone *Ranger*, a cowboy hero)] □ **Sloaney** *adj.*

slob *n. colloq.* a stupid, careless, coarse, or fat person. [from Irish *slab* 'mud'] □ **slobbish** *adj.*

slobber ● *v.intr.* **1** slaver. **2** (foll. by *over*) show excessive sentiment. ● *n.* slaver. [Middle English] □ **slobbery** *adj.*

sloe *n.* **1** = BLACKTHORN 1. **2** the small bluish-black fruit of this, with a sharp sour taste. [Old English]

sloe gin *n.* a liqueur of sloes steeped in gin.

slog ● *v.* (**slogged**, **slogging**) **1** *intr.* & *tr.* hit hard and usu. wildly, esp. in boxing or cricket. **2** *intr.* (often foll. by *away, on*) walk or work doggedly. ● *n.* **1** a hard random hit. **2 a** a hard steady work or walking. **b** a spell of this. [19th-century coinage] □ **slogger** *n.*

slogan *n.* **1** a short catchy phrase used in advertising etc. **2** a party cry; a watchword or motto. **3** *hist.* a Scottish Highland war cry. [from Gaelic *sluagh-ghairm*]

sloop *n.* a small one-masted fore-and-aft rigged vessel with mainsail and jib. [from Dutch *sloep(e)*]

S

sloosh *Brit. colloq.* • *n.* a pouring or pouring sound of water. • *v.intr.* **1** flow with a rush. **2** make a heavy splashing or rushing noise.

slop • *v.* (**slopped, slopping**) **1** (often foll. by *over*) **a** *intr.* spill or flow over the edge of a vessel. **b** *tr.* allow to do this. **2** *tr.* make (the floor, clothes, etc.) wet or messy by slopping. **3** *intr.* (usu. foll. by *over*) gush; be effusive or maudlin. • *n.* **1** a quantity of liquid spilled or splashed. **2** weakly sentimental language. **3** (in *pl.*) waste liquid. **4** (in *sing.* or *pl.*) unappetizing weak liquid food. □ **slop about** esp. *Brit.* move about in a slovenly manner. **slop out** esp. *Brit.* carry slops out (in prison etc.). [originally in sense 'a mudhole']

slop basin *n. Brit.* a basin for the dregs of cups at table.

slop bucket *n.* a bucket for removing bedroom or kitchen slops.

slope • *n.* **1** an inclined position or direction; a state in which one end or side is at a higher level than another; a position in a line neither parallel nor perpendicular to level ground or to a line serving as a standard. **2** a piece of rising or falling ground. **3 a** a difference in level between two ends or sides (*a slope of 5 metres*). **b** the rate at which this increases with distance etc. **4** a place for skiing on the side of a hill or mountain. **5** (prec. by *the*) the position of a rifle when sloped. • *v.* **1** *intr.* have or take a slope; slant esp. up or down; lie or tend obliquely. **2** *tr.* place or arrange or make in or at a slope. □ **slope arms** place one's rifle in a sloping position against one's shoulder. **slope off** *colloq.* go away, esp. to evade work etc. [shortening of *aslope* 'inclined']

sloppy *adj.* (**sloppier, sloppiest**) **1 a** (of the ground) wet with rain; full of puddles. **b** (of food etc.) watery and disagreeable. **c** (of a floor, table, etc.) wet with slops, having water etc. spilt on it. **2** careless, not thorough. **3** (of a garment) ill-fitting or untidy. **4** (of sentiment or talk) weakly emotional. □ **sloppily** *adv.* **sloppiness** *n.*

slosh • *v.* **1** *intr.* (often foll. by *about*) splash or flounder about; move with a splashing sound. **2** *tr. Brit. slang* hit esp. heavily. **3** *tr. colloq.* **a** pour (liquid) clumsily. **b** pour liquid on. • *n.* **1** slush. **2 a** an instance of splashing. **b** the sound of this. **3** *Brit. slang* a heavy blow. **4** a quantity of liquid. [variant of SLUSH]

sloshed *adj. slang* drunk.

sloshy *adj.* (**sloshier, sloshiest**) **1** slushy. **2** sloppy, sentimental.

slot • *n.* **1** a slit or other aperture in a machine etc. for something (esp. a coin) to be inserted. **2** a slit, groove, channel, or long aperture into which something fits. **3** an allotted place in a scheme or schedule. • *v.* (**slotted, slotting**) **1** *tr. & intr.* place or be placed into or as if into a slot. **2** *tr.* provide with a slot or slots. [Middle English in sense 'hollow of the breast': from Old French *esclot*]

sloth /slohth/ *n.* **1** laziness or indolence; reluctance to make an effort. **2** ▼ any slow-moving nocturnal mammal of the family Bradypodidae or Megalonychidae of S. America, having long limbs and hooked claws for hanging upside down from branches of trees. ▷ EDENTATE. [Middle English, based on SLOW]

downward-pointing fur

SLOTH: TWO-TOED SLOTH (*Choloepus didactylus*)

large, hooked claws

slothful *adj.* lazy; characterized by sloth. □ **slothfully** *adv.* **slothfulness** *n.*

slot machine *n.* a machine worked by the insertion of a coin, esp. for selling small articles or providing amusement.

slouch • *v.* **1** *intr.* stand or move or sit in a drooping ungainly fashion. **2** *tr.* bend one side of the brim of (a hat) downwards. **3** *intr.* droop; hang down loosely. • *n.* **1** a slouching posture or movement. **2** a downward bend of a hat-brim. **3** *colloq.* an incompetent or slovenly worker, operator, or performance. [16th-century coinage] □ **slouchy** *adj.*

slouch hat *n.* a hat with a wide flexible brim.

slough[1] /rhymes with cow/ *n.* a swamp; a miry place; a quagmire. [Old English] □ **sloughy** *adj.*

slough[2] /sluf/ • *n.* a part that an animal casts or moults, esp. a snake's cast skin. • *v.* **1** *tr.* ◀ cast off as a slough. **2** *intr.* (often foll. by *off*) drop off as a slough. **3** *intr.* cast off a slough. [Middle English] □ **sloughy** *adj.*

sloughed skin

SLOUGH: SNAKE CASTING OFF ITS SKIN

Slough of Despond /*first word rhymes with* cow/ *n.* a state of hopeless depression. [with reference to Bunyan's *Pilgrim's Progress*]

Slovak • *n.* **1** a member of a Slavonic people inhabiting Slovakia, an independent republic in central Europe. **2** the West Slavonic language of this people. • *adj.* of or relating to the Slovaks or their language. [related to SLOVENE]

sloven /sluv-ĕn/ *n.* a person who is habitually untidy or careless. [Middle English]

Slovene (also **Slovenian**) • *n.* **1** a member of a Slavonic people inhabiting Slovenia in south-east central Europe. **2** the language of this people. • *adj.* of or relating to Slovenia, its people, or its language. [from a Slavonic root shared with SLOVAK]

slovenly • *adj.* careless and untidy; unmethodical. • *adv.* in a slovenly manner. □ **slovenliness** *n.*

slow • *adj.* **1 a** taking a relatively long time to do a thing or cover a distance (also foll. by *of*: *slow of speech*). **b** acting or moving or done without speed. **2** gradual (*slow growth*). **3** not producing, allowing, or conducive to speed (*in the slow lane*). **4** (of a clock etc.) showing a time earlier than is the case. **5** (of a person) not understanding readily; not learning easily. **6** dull; uninteresting; tedious. **7** sluggish (*business is slow*). **8** (of a fire or oven) giving little heat. **9** *Photog.* **a** (of a film) needing long exposure. **b** (of a lens) having a small aperture. **10 a** reluctant; tardy (*not slow to defend himself*). **b** not hasty or easily moved (*slow to take offence*). • *adv.* **1** at a slow pace; slowly (see Usage Note). **2** (in *comb.*) *slow-moving traffic*). • *v.* (usu. foll. by *down*, *up*) **1** *intr. & tr.* reduce one's speed or the speed of (a vehicle etc.). **2** *intr.* reduce one's pace of life; live or work less actively or intensely. [Old English] □ **slowish** *adj.*

slowly *adv.* **slowness** *n.*

■ **Usage** The use of *slow* as an adverb is chiefly confined to compounds such as *slow-acting*, *slow-moving*. It is also established in the expression *go slow* and the noun *go-slow*. In sentences such as *he drives too slow* and *go as slow as you can*, *slowly* is preferable in formal contexts. Compare *fast* which is fully acceptable as an adverb in standard English.

slowcoach *n. Brit.* **1** a slow or lazy person. **2** a dull-witted person. **3** a person behind the times in opinions etc.

slowdown *n.* the action of slowing down; a go-slow.

slow handclap *n.* slow clapping by an audience as a sign of displeasure or boredom.

slow march *n.* the marching time adopted by troops in a funeral procession etc.

slow motion *n.* **1** the operation or speed of a film using slower projection or more rapid exposure so that actions etc. appear much slower than usual. **2** the simulation of this in real action.

slow-worm *n.* a small European legless lizard, *Anguis fragilis.* [Old English]

slub • *n.* **1** a lump or thick place in yarn or thread. **2** fabric woven from thread etc. with slubs. • *adj.* (of material etc.) with an irregular appearance caused by uneven thickness of the warp. [19th-century coinage]

sludge *n.* **1** thick greasy mud. **2** muddy or slushy sediment. **3** sewage. **4** *Mech.* an accumulation of dirty oil, esp. in the sump of an internal-combustion engine. [17th-century coinage] □ **sludgy** *adj.*

slue var. of SLEW[1].

slug[1] *n.* **1** a small shell-less mollusc of the class Gastropoda often destructive to plants. ▷ GASTROPOD. **2 a** a bullet esp. of irregular shape. **b** a missile for an airgun. **3** orig. *US* a tot of usu. liquor. [Middle English]

slug[2] esp. *N. Amer.* • *v.tr.* (**slugged, slugging**) strike with a hard blow. • *n.* a hard blow. □ **slug it out 1** fight it out. **2** endure; stick it out. [19th-century coinage] □ **slugger** *n.*

sluggard *n.* a lazy sluggish person. [Middle English, from *slug* 'to be slothful'] □ **sluggardly** *adj.*

sluggish *adj.* inert; inactive; slow-moving; torpid; indolent. □ **sluggishly** *adv.* **sluggishness** *n.*

sluice /sloos/ • *n.* **1** (also **sluice-gate, sluice-valve**) a sliding gate etc. for controlling the volume or flow of water. **2** (also **sluice-way**) an artificial water channel esp. for washing ore. **3** a place for rinsing. **4** the act or an instance of rinsing. **5** the water above, below, or issuing through a floodgate. • *v.* **1** *tr.* provide or wash with a sluice or sluices. **2** *tr.* rinse, throw water freely upon. **3** *tr.* (foll. by *out*, *away*) wash out or away with a flow of water. **4** *tr.* flood with water from a sluice. **5** *intr.* (of water) rush out from a sluice, or as if from a sluice. [based on Latin *excludere* 'to exclude']

slum • *n.* **1** an overcrowded and squalid backstreet, district, etc., usu. in a city. **2** a house or building unfit for human habitation. • *v.intr.* (**slummed, slumming**) **1** live in slumlike conditions. **2** go about the slums through curiosity or for charitable purposes. □ **slum it** *colloq.* put up with conditions less comfortable than usual. [19th-century coinage, originally slang] □ **slummy** *adj.* (**slummier, slummiest**). **slumminess** *n.*

slumber *poet. literary* • *v.intr.* **1** sleep, esp. in a specified manner. **2** be idle, drowsy, or inactive. • *n.* a sleep, esp. of a specified kind (*fell into a fitful slumber*). [Middle English] □ **slumberer** *n.* **slumberous** *adj.* **slumbrous** *adj.*

slump • *n.* **1** a sudden severe or prolonged fall in prices or values of commodities or securities. **2** a sharp or sudden decline in business. **3** a lessening of interest in a subject or undertaking. • *v.intr.* **1** undergo a slump; fail; fall in price. **2** sit or fall heavily or limply. **3** lean or subside. [17th-century coinage, originally in sense 'to sink in a bog']

slung *past* and *past part.* of SLING[1].

slunk *past* and *past part.* of SLINK.

slur • *v.* (**slurred, slurring**) **1** *tr. & intr.* pronounce or write indistinctly so that the sounds or letters run into one another. **2** *tr. Mus.* **a** perform (notes) legato. **b** mark (notes) with a slur. **3** *tr. archaic* or *US* put a slur on (a person or a person's character). **4** *tr.* (usu. foll. by *over*) pass over (a fact, fault, etc.) lightly. • *n.* **1** an imputation of wrongdoing; stigma (*a slur on my reputation*). **2** the act or an instance of slurring. **3** *Mus.* a curved line to show that two or more notes are to be sung to one syllable or played or sung legato. ▷ NOTATION. [17th-century coinage]

slurp • *v.tr.* eat or drink noisily. • *n.* the sound of this; a slurping gulp. [from Dutch *slurpen, slorpen*]

slurry *n.* (*pl.* **-ies**) **1** a semi-liquid mixture of fine particles and water; thin mud. **2** thin liquid cement. **3** a fluid form of manure. [Middle English]

slush *n.* **1** watery mud or thawing snow. **2** silly sentiment. [17th-century coinage]

slush fund *n.* reserve funding esp. as used for political bribery.

slushy *adj.* (**slushier**, **slushiest**) like slush; watery. □ **slushiness** *n.*

slut *n. offens.* a slovenly or promiscuous woman. [Middle English] □ **sluttish** *adj.* **sluttishness** *n.*

sly *adj.* (**slyer**, **slyest**) **1** cunning; wily. **2 a** (of a person) practising secrecy or stealth. **b** (of an action etc.) done etc. in secret. **3** hypocritical; ironical. **4** knowing; arch; insinuating. **5** *Austral.* & *NZ slang* (esp. of liquor) illicit. □ **on the sly** privately; covertly; without publicity. [from Old Norse *slœgr* 'cunning'] □ **slyly** *adv.* (also **slily**). **slyness** *n.*

slyboots *n. colloq.* a sly person.

Sm *symb. Chem.* the element samarium.

smack[1] ● *n.* **1** a sharp slap or blow esp. with the palm of the hand or a flat object. **2** a hard hit at cricket etc. **3** a loud kiss. **4** a loud sharp sound. ● *v.* **1** *tr.* strike with the open hand etc. **2** *tr.* part (one's lips) noisily in eager anticipation or enjoyment of food etc. **3** *tr.* crack (a whip). **4** *tr.* & *intr.* move, hit, etc., with a smack. ● *adv. colloq.* **1** with a smack. **2** suddenly; violently (*landed smack on my desk*). **3** exactly (*hit it smack in the centre*). □ **have a smack at** *colloq.* make an attempt at or attack on. **a smack in the eye** (or **face**) *colloq.* a rebuff. [from Middle Dutch *smack(en)*]

smack[2] (foll. by *of*) ● *v.intr.* **1** have a flavour of; taste of (*smacked of garlic*). **2** suggest the effects of (*it smacks of nepotism*). ● *n.* **1** a taste that suggests the presence of something. **2** (in a person's character etc.) a barely discernible quality (*just a smack of disdain*). [Old English]

smack[3] *n.* a single-masted sailing boat for coasting or fishing. [from Dutch *smak*]

smack[4] *n. slang* a hard drug, esp. heroin.

smacker *n. colloq.* **1** a loud kiss. **2** a resounding blow. **3 a** *Brit. slang* £1. **b** *N. Amer.* $1.

small ● *adj.* **1** not large or big. **2** slender; thin. **3** not great in importance, amount, number, strength, or power. **4** trifling (*a small token*). **5** insignificant; unimportant (*a small matter*). **6** consisting of small particles (*small gravel*). **7** doing something on a small scale (*a small farmer*). **8** socially undistinguished. **9** petty; paltry (*a small spiteful nature*). **10** young; not fully developed (*a small child*). ● *n.* **1** the slenderest part of something (esp. in phr. **small of the back**). **2** (in *pl.*) *Brit. colloq.* small items of laundry, esp. underwear. ● *adv.* into small pieces (*chop it small*). □ **in a small way** unambitiously; on a small scale. **no small** considerable (*no small achievement*). **small potatoes** an insignificant person or thing. [Old English] □ **smallish** *adj.* **smallness** *n.*

small arms *n.pl.* portable firearms, esp. rifles, pistols, light machine-guns, sub-machine guns, etc.

small calorie see CALORIE 1.

small change *n.* **1** money in the form of coins as opposed to notes. **2** trivial remarks.

small circle *n.* a circle on the surface of a sphere whose plane does not pass through the sphere's centre.

small craft *n.* a general term for small boats and fishing vessels.

small fry *n.pl.* **1** young children or the young of various species. **2** small or insignificant things or people.

smallholder *n. Brit.* a person who farms a smallholding.

smallholding *n. Brit.* an agricultural holding smaller than a farm.

small hours *n.pl.* the early hours of the morning after midnight.

small intestine *n.* the duodenum, jejunum, and ileum collectively. ▷ DIGESTION, INTESTINE

small letter *n.* (in printed material) a lower-case letter.

small-minded *adj.* petty; of rigid opinions or narrow outlook. □ **small-mindedly** *adv.* **small-mindedness** *n.*

smallpox *n. hist.* an acute contagious viral disease, with fever and pustules usu. leaving permanent scars.

small print *n.* **1** printed matter in small type. **2** inconspicuous and usu. unfavourable limitations etc. in a contract.

small-scale *adj.* made or occurring in small amounts or to a lesser degree.

small talk *n.* light social conversation.

small-time *attrib.adj. colloq.* unimportant or petty.

small-town *attrib.adj.* relating to or characteristic of a small town; unsophisticated; provincial.

smarm *v.tr.* (often foll. by *down*) *Brit. colloq.* smooth, plaster down (hair etc.) usu. with cream or oil. [originally dialect]

smarmy *adj.* (**smarmier**, **smarmiest**) esp. *Brit. colloq.* ingratiating; flattering; obsequious. □ **smarmily** *adv.* **smarminess** *n.*

smart ● *adj.* **1 a** clever; ingenious; quick-witted (*a smart answer*). **b** keen in bargaining. **c** (of transactions etc.) unscrupulous to the point of dishonesty. **2** well-groomed; bright and fresh in appearance (*a smart suit*). **3** in good repair; showing bright colours etc. (*a smart red bicycle*). **4** stylish; fashionable; prominent in society (*the smart set*). **5** brisk (*set a smart pace*). **6** painfully severe; sharp; vigorous (*a smart blow*). ● *v.intr.* **1** feel or give acute pain or distress (*my eye smarts*). **2** (of a grievance etc.) rankle. **3** (foll. by *for*) suffer the consequences of (*you will smart for this*). ● *n.* a bodily or mental sharp pain; a stinging sensation. ● *adv.* smartly; in a smart manner. [Old English] □ **smartingly** *adv.* **smartish** *adj.* & *adv. Brit.* **smartly** *adv.* **smartness** *n.*

smart alec *n.* (also **smart aleck**, **smart alick**) *colloq.* a person displaying ostentatious or smug cleverness. □ **smart-alecky** *adj.*

smart-arse *n.* (*US* **smart-ass**) *slang* = SMART ALEC.

smart bomb *n.* a radio-controlled or laser-guided bomb, often with an inbuilt computer.

smart card *n.* a plastic card with a built-in microprocessor, esp. as a credit or other bank card for the instant transfer of funds etc.

smarten *v.tr.* & *intr.* (usu. foll. by *up*) make or become smart or smarter.

smart money *n.* **1** money paid or exacted as a penalty or compensation. **2** money invested by persons with expert knowledge.

smarty *n.* (*pl.* **-ies**) *colloq.* **1** a know-all; a smart alec. **2** a smartly-dressed person; a member of a smart set.

smarty-pants *n.pl.* (also *Brit.* **smarty-boots**) = SMARTY 1.

smash ● *v.* **1** *tr.* & *intr.* (often foll. by *up*) **a** break into pieces; shatter. **b** bring or come to sudden or complete destruction, defeat, or disaster. **2** *tr.* (foll. by *into*, *through*) move with great force and impact. **3** *tr.* & *intr.* (foll. by *in*) break in with a crushing blow (*smashed in the window*). **4** *tr.* (in tennis, squash, etc.) hit (a ball etc.) with great force, esp. downwards. **5** *intr. colloq.* (of a business etc.) go bankrupt; come to grief. **6** *tr.* (as **smashed** *adj.*) *slang* intoxicated. ● *n.* **1** the act or an instance of smashing; a violent fall, collision, or disaster. **2** the sound of this. **3** (in full **smash hit**) a very successful play, performer, etc. **4** a stroke in tennis etc. in which the ball is hit esp. downwards with great force. **5** a violent blow with a fist etc. **6** *colloq.* bankruptcy; a series of commercial failures. ● *adv.* with a smash (*fell smash on the floor*). [18th-century coinage]

smash-and-grab *adj.* (of a robbery etc.) in which the thief smashes a shop window and seizes goods.

smasher *n.* **1** *Brit. colloq.* a very beautiful or pleasing person or thing. **2** a person or thing that smashes.

smashing *adj.* esp. *Brit. colloq.* superlative; excellent; wonderful; beautiful. □ **smashingly** *adv.*

smash-up *n. colloq.* a violent collision; a complete smash.

smatter *n.* (also **smattering**) a slight superficial knowledge of a language or subject. [Middle English in sense 'to talk ignorantly, prate']

smear ● *v.tr.* **1** daub or mark with a greasy or sticky substance or with something that stains. **2** blot; smudge (writing, artwork, etc.). **3** defame the character of; slander publicly. ● *n.* **1** the act or an instance of smearing. **2** *Med.* **a** material smeared on a microscopic slide etc. for examination. **b** a specimen of this. [Old English] □ **smearer** *n.* **smeary** *adj.*

smear campaign *n.* a planned effort to slander and so discredit a public figure.

smear test *n.* = CERVICAL SMEAR.

smell ● *n.* **1** the faculty of perceiving odours or scents. **2** the quality in substances that is perceived by this (*the smell of thyme*). **3** an unpleasant odour. **4** the act of inhaling to ascertain smell. ● *v.* (*past* and *past part.* **smelt** or **smelled**) **1** *tr.* perceive the smell of; examine by smell. **2** *intr.* emit odour. **3** *intr.* seem by smell to be (*smells sour*). **4** *intr.* (foll. by *of*) **a** be redolent of (*smells of fish*). **b** be suggestive of (*smells of dishonesty*). **5** *intr.* have a strong or unpleasant odour. **6** *tr.* perceive as if by smell; detect, discern (*smell a bargain*; *smell blood*). **7** *intr.* have or use a sense of smell. **8** *intr.* (foll. by *about*) sniff or search about. **9** *intr.* (foll. by *at*) inhale the smell of. □ **smell out** detect by smell; find out by investigation. **smell a rat** begin to suspect trickery etc. [Middle English] □ **smellable** *adj.* **smeller** *n.* **smell-less** *adj.*

smelling salts *n.pl.* ammonium carbonate mixed with scent to be sniffed as a restorative in faintness etc.

smelly *adj.* (**smellier**, **smelliest**) having a strong or unpleasant smell. □ **smelliness** *n.*

smelt[1] *v.tr.* **1** extract metal from (ore) by melting. **2** extract (metal) from ore by melting. [from Middle Dutch *smelten*] □ **smelter** *n.* **smeltery** *n.* (*pl.* **-ies**).

smelt[2] *past* and *past part.* of SMELL.

smelt[3] *n.* (*pl.* same or **smelts**) any small green and silver fish of the genus *Osmerus* etc. allied to salmon and used as food. [Old English]

smidgen *n.* (also **smidgeon**, **smidgin**) *colloq.* a small bit or amount.

smile ● *v.* **1** *intr.* have or assume a pleased or kind or gently sceptical expression, with the corners of the mouth turned up. **2** *tr.* express by smiling (*smiled their consent*). **3** *tr.* give (a smile) of a specified kind (*smiled a sardonic smile*). **4** *intr.* (foll. by *on*, *upon*) adopt a favourable attitude towards (*fortune smiled on me*). **5** *intr.* (foll. by *at*) **a** show amused indifference to; show indulgent amusement towards (*smiled at my feeble attempts*). **b** favour; smile on. ● *n.* **1** the act or an instance of smiling. **2** a smiling expression or aspect. [Middle English] □ **smiler** *n.* **smiley** *adj.* **smilingly** *adv.*

smirch ● *v.tr.* mark, soil, or smear (a thing, a person's reputation, etc.). ● *n.* **1** a spot or stain. **2** a blot (on one's character etc.). [Middle English]

smirk ● *n.* an affected, conceited, or silly smile. ● *v.intr.* put on or wear a smirk. [Old English] □ **smirker** *n.* **smirkingly** *adv.* **smirky** *adj.*

smite *v.tr.* (*past* **smote**; *past part.* **smitten**) esp. *archaic* or *literary* **1** strike or hit. **2** chastise; defeat. **3** (in *passive*) **a** have a sudden strong effect on (*smitten by his conscience*). **b** infatuate, fascinate (*smitten by her beauty*). [Old English *smītan* 'to smear'] □ **smiter** *n.*

smith ● *n.* (esp. in *comb.*) **1** a worker in metal (*goldsmith*). **2** a person who forges iron; a blacksmith. **3** a craftsman (*wordsmith*). ● *v.tr.* make or treat by forging. [Old English]

smithereens *n.pl.* (also **smithers**) small fragments.

smithy /**smi***th*-i/ *n.* (*pl.* **-ies**) a blacksmith's workshop; a forge. [from Old Norse *smithja*]

smitten *past part.* of SMITE.

smock ● *n.* **1** a loose shirtlike garment with the upper part closely gathered in smocking. **2** (also **smock-frock**) a loose overall, esp. *hist.* a field-labourer's outer linen garment. ● *v.tr.* adorn with smocking. [Old English]

smocking *n.* ► an ornamental effect on cloth made by gathering the material tightly into pleats, often with stitches in a honeycomb pattern.

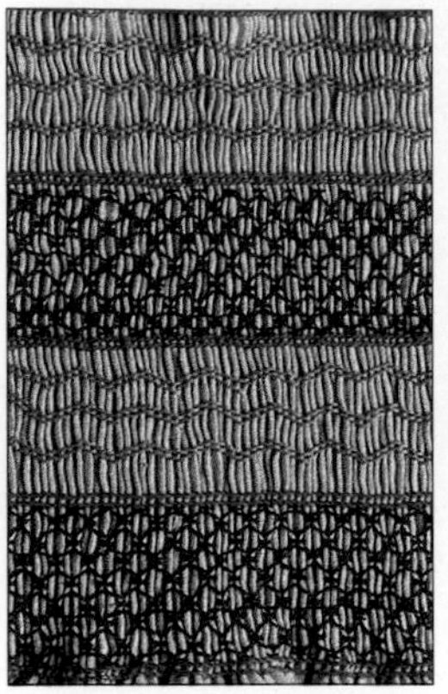

SMOCKING

smog *n.* fog intensified by atmospheric pollutants esp. smoke. [blend of SMOKE and FOG] □ **smoggy** *adj.* (**smoggier**, **smoggiest**).

smoke ● *n.* **1** a visible suspension of carbon etc. in air, emitted from a burning substance. **2** an act or period of smoking tobacco. **3** *colloq.* a cigarette or cigar (*got a smoke?*). **4** (**the Smoke**) *Brit.* & *Austral. colloq.* a big city, esp. London. ● *v.* **1** *intr.* **a** emit smoke or visible vapour. **b** (of a lamp etc.) burn badly with the emission of smoke. **c** (of a chimney or fire) discharge smoke into the room. **2 a** *intr.* inhale and exhale the smoke of a cigarette etc. **b** *intr.* do this habitually. **c** *tr.* use (a cigarette etc.) in this way. **3** *tr.* cure or darken by the action of smoke (*smoked salmon*). □ **go up in smoke** *colloq.* **1** be destroyed by fire. **2** (of a plan etc.) come to nothing. **smoke out 1** drive out by means of smoke. **2** drive out of hiding or secrecy etc. [Old English] □ **smokable** *adj.* (also **smokeable**).

smoke bomb *n.* a bomb that emits dense smoke on exploding.

smoked glass *n.* glass darkened by exposure to smoke.

smoke-free *adj.* **1** free from smoke. **2** where smoking is not permitted.

smokeless *adj.* having or producing little or no smoke.

smokeless zone *n. Brit.* a district in which it is illegal to create smoke and where only smokeless fuel may be used.

smoker *n.* **1** a person or thing that smokes, esp. a person who habitually smokes tobacco. **2** a compartment on a train, in which smoking is allowed. **3** esp. *US* an informal social gathering of men.

smoke ring *n.* smoke from a cigarette etc. exhaled in the shape of a ring.

smokescreen *n.* **1** a cloud of smoke diffused to conceal (esp. military) operations. **2** a device or ruse for disguising one's activities.

smokestack *n.* **1** a chimney or funnel for discharging the smoke of a locomotive or steamer. ▷ STEAM ENGINE. **2** a tall chimney.

smoking gun *n.* (also **smoking pistol**) a piece of incontrovertible incriminating evidence.

smoking room *n.* a room in a hotel or house, kept for smoking in.

S

smoky *adj.* (**smokier**, **smokiest**) **1** emitting, veiled or filled with, or obscured by, smoke (*smoky fire*; *smoky room*). **2** stained with or coloured like smoke (*smoky glass*). **3** having the taste or flavour of smoked food (*smoky bacon*). □ **smokily** *adv.* **smokiness** *n.*

smolder *US* var. of SMOULDER.

smooch *colloq.* ● *n.* **1** *Brit.* a period of slow dancing close together. **2** a spell of kissing and caressing; a kiss. ● *v.intr.* engage in a smooch. [from dialect *smouch*] □ **smoocher** *n.* **smoochy** *adj.*

smooth ● *adj.* **1** having a relatively even and regular surface; free from perceptible projections, lumps, indentations, and roughness. **2** not wrinkled, pitted, scored, or hairy. **3** that can be traversed without check. **4** (of liquids) of even consistency; without lumps. **5** (of the sea etc.) without waves or undulations. **6** (of a journey, progress, etc.) untroubled by difficulties or adverse conditions. **7** having an easy flow or correct rhythm (*smooth breathing*). **8 a** not harsh in sound or taste. **b** (of wine etc.) not astringent. **9** (of a person, his or her manner, etc.) suave, conciliatory, flattering (*a smooth talker*). **10** (of movement etc.) not suddenly varying; not jerky. ● *v.* (also **smoothe**) **1** *tr.* & *intr* (often foll. by *out*, *down*) make or become smooth. **2** (often foll. by *out*, *down*, *over*, *away*) **a** *tr.* reduce or get rid of (differences, difficulties, etc.) in fact or appearance. **b** *intr.* (of difficulties etc.) diminish. **3** *tr.* modify (a graph, curve, etc.) so as to lessen irregularities. **4** *tr.* free from impediments or discomfort (*smooth the way*). ● *n.* **1** a smoothing touch or stroke. **2** the easy part of life (*take the rough with the smooth*). ● *adv.* smoothly (*true love never did run smooth*). [Old English] □ **smoothable** *adj.* **smoother** *n.* **smoothish** *adj.* **smoothly** *adv.* **smoothness** *n.*

smoothie *n. colloq.* a person who is smooth (see SMOOTH *adj.* 9).

smooth talk *colloq.* ● *n.* bland specious language. ● *v.tr.* (**smooth-talk**) address or persuade with this.

smooth-tongued *adj.* insincerely flattering.

smorgasbord *n.* **1** open sandwiches served with delicacies as hors d'oeuvres or a buffet. **2** = BUFFET[1] 2. **3** a medley; a miscellany. [Swedish, from *smörgas* '(slice of) bread and butter' + *bord* 'table']

smote *past* of SMITE.

smother ● *v.* **1** *tr.* suffocate; stifle. **2** *tr.* (foll. by *with*) overwhelm with (kisses, gifts, kindness, etc.). **3** *tr.* (foll. by *in*, *with*) cover entirely in or with (*smothered in mayonnaise*). **4** *tr.* extinguish or deaden (a fire or flame) by covering it. **5** *intr.* **a** die of suffocation. **b** have difficulty breathing. **6** *tr.* (often foll. by *up*) keep from notice or publicity. **7** *tr. US* defeat rapidly or utterly. ● *n.* **1** a cloud of dust or smoke. **2** obscurity caused by this. [Middle English]

smoulder (*US* **smolder**) ● *v.intr.* **1** burn slowly with smoke but without a flame. **2** (of emotions etc.) exist in a suppressed or concealed state. **3** (of a person) show silent anger, hatred, etc. ● *n.* a smouldering or slow-burning fire. [Middle English]

smudge ● *n.* **1** a blurred or smeared line or mark; a blot; a smear of dirt. **2** a stain or blot on a person's character etc. ● *v.* **1** *tr.* make a smudge on. **2** *intr.* become smeared or blurred (*smudges easily*). **3** *tr.* smear or blur the lines of (writing etc.) (*smudge the outline*). **4** *tr.* defile, sully, stain, or disgrace (a person's name etc.). [Middle English]

smudgy *adj.* (**smudgier**, **smudgiest**) **1** smudged. **2** likely to produce smudges. □ **smudgily** *adv.* **smudginess** *n.*

smug *adj.* (**smugger**, **smuggest**) self-satisfied; complacent. [originally in sense 'neat': from Low German *smuk* 'pretty'] □ **smugly** *adv.* **smugness** *n.*

smuggle *v.tr.* **1** (also *absol.*) import or export (goods) illegally, esp. without payment of customs duties. **2** (foll. by *in*, *out*) convey secretly. **3** (foll. by *away*) put into concealment. [from Low German *smukkeln*, *smuggelen*] □ **smuggler** *n.* **smuggling** *n.*

smut ● *n.* **1** a small flake of soot etc. **2** a spot or smudge made by this. **3** obscene or lascivious talk, pictures, or stories. **4** a fungal disease of cereals. ● *v.* (**smutted**, **smutting**) **1** *tr.* mark with smuts. **2** *tr.* infect (a plant) with smut. **3** *intr.* (of a plant) contract smut. [related to Low German *smutt*] □ **smutty** *adj.* (**smuttier**, **smuttiest**) (esp. in sense 3 of *n.*). **smuttily** *adv.* **smuttiness** *n.*

Sn *symb. Chem.* the element tin. [Late Latin *stannum*]

snack ● *n.* **1** a light, casual, or hurried meal. **2** a small amount of food eaten between meals. ● *v.intr.* (often foll. by *on*) eat a snack. [from Middle Dutch *snac(k)* 'a bite']

snack bar *n.* a place where snacks are sold.

snaffle ● *n.* (in full **snaffle-bit**) (on a bridle) a simple bit without a curb and usu. with a single rein. ● *v.tr.* **1** put a snaffle on. **2** *colloq.* steal; seize; appropriate.

snafu *slang* ● *adj.* in utter confusion or chaos. ● *n.* this state. [acronym from *s*ituation *n*ormal: *a*ll *f*ouled (or *f*ucked) *u*p]

snag ● *n.* **1** an unexpected or hidden obstacle or drawback. **2** a jagged or projecting point or broken stump. **3** a tear in material etc. ● *v.tr.* (**snagged**, **snagging**) **1** catch or tear on a snag. **2** clear (land, a waterway, a tree trunk, etc.) of snags. □ **snagged** *adj.* **snaggy** *adj.*

snaggle-tooth *n.* (*pl.* **snaggle-teeth**) an irregular or projecting tooth. □ **snaggle-toothed** *adj.*

snail *n.* any slow-moving gastropod mollusc with a spiral shell. ▷ GASTROPOD, MOLLUSC. [Old English] □ **snail-like** *adj.*

snail's pace *n.* a very slow movement.

snake ● *n.* **1 a** ► any long limbless reptile of the suborder Ophidia, including boas, pythons, cobras, and vipers. **b** a limbless lizard or amphibian. **2** (also **snake in the grass**) a treacherous person or secret enemy. **3** (in full **plumber's snake**) a long flexible wire for clearing obstacles in piping. ● *v.intr.* move or twist like a snake. [Old English] □ **snakelike** *adj.*

snakeboard ● *n.* a flexible type of skateboard. ● *v.intr.* ride on a snakeboard. □ **snakeboarder** *n.* **snakeboarding** *n.*

snake charmer *n.* a person appearing to make snakes move by music etc.

snakeroot *n.* any of various N. American plants with roots reputed to contain an antidote to snake's poison, e.g. *Aristolochia serpentaria*.

snakes and ladders *n.pl.* a game with counters moved along a board with advances up 'ladders' or returns down 'snakes' depicted on the board.

snakeskin ● *n.* the skin of a snake. ● *adj.* made of or resembling snakeskin.

snaky *adj.* **1** of or like a snake. **2** winding; sinuous. **3** showing coldness, ingratitude, venom, or guile. **4** *Austral. slang* angry; irritable. □ **snakily** *adv.* **snakiness** *n.*

snap ● *v.* (**snapped**, **snapping**) **1** *intr.* & *tr.* break suddenly or with a snap. **2** *intr.* & *tr.* emit or cause to emit a sudden sharp sound or crack. **3** *intr.* & *tr.* open or close with a snapping sound (*snapped shut*). **4 a** *intr.* (often foll. by *at*) speak irritably or spitefully (*snapped at the child*). **b** *tr.* say irritably or spitefully. **5** *intr.* (often foll. by *at*) (esp. of a dog etc.) make a sudden audible bite. **6** *tr.* & *intr.* move quickly (*snap into action*). **7** *tr.* take a snapshot of. ● *n.* **1** an act or sound of snapping. **2** a crisp biscuit or cake (*brandy snap*). **3** a snapshot. **4** (in full **cold snap**) a sudden brief spell of cold weather. **5** *Brit.* **a** a card game in which players call 'snap' when two similar cards are exposed. **b** (as *int.*) on noticing the (often unexpected) similarity of two things. **6** crispness of style; zest; dash; spring. **7** *N. Amer. slang* an easy task (*it was a snap*). ● *adv.* with the sound of a snap (*went snap*). ● *adj.* done or taken on the spur of the moment (*snap decision*). □ **snap off** break off or bite off. **snap one's fingers 1** make an audible fillip, esp. in rhythm to music etc. **2** (often foll. by *at*) defy; show contempt for. **snap out** say irritably. **snap out of** *colloq.* get rid of (a mood etc.) by a sudden effort. **snap up 1** accept (an offer) quickly or eagerly. **2** pick up or catch hastily or smartly.

snap bean *n. US* a bean grown for its pods which are broken into pieces and eaten.

snap-brim *adj.* (of a hat) with a brim that can be turned up and down at opposite sides.

snapdragon *n.* a plant, *Antirrhinum majus*, with an irregular flower which gapes like a mouth when a bee lands on the lower part.

snap-fastener *n.* = PRESS STUD.

snap-hook *n.* (also **snap-link**) a hook or link with a spring allowing the entrance but barring the escape of a cord, link, etc.

snapper *n.* **1** a person or thing that snaps. **2** any of several edible marine fish of the family Lutjanidae.

snappish *adj.* **1** (of a person's manner or a remark) curt; ill-tempered; sharp. **2** (of a dog etc.) inclined to snap. □ **snappishly** *adv.* **snappishness** *n.*

SNAKE

There are around 2,700 snake species, most of which belong to the four main families set out below. All snakes are carnivorous vertebrates, with jaws that can dislocate to swallow relatively large animals whole. Constrictor snakes such as pythons and boas kill their prey by squeezing; venomous snakes such as the coral snake inject their victims with poison from their fangs. Other snakes simply crush prey in their jaws. Although snakes have no ears, they can detect vibrations, and their tongues are sensitive to smell, taste, and touch.

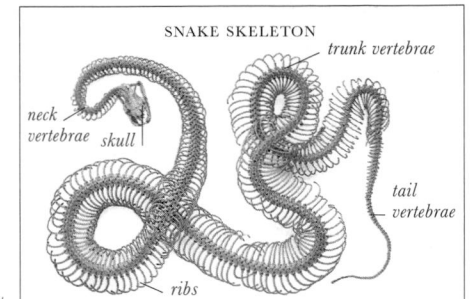

SNAKE SKELETON

neck vertebrae

skull

trunk vertebrae

ribs

tail vertebrae

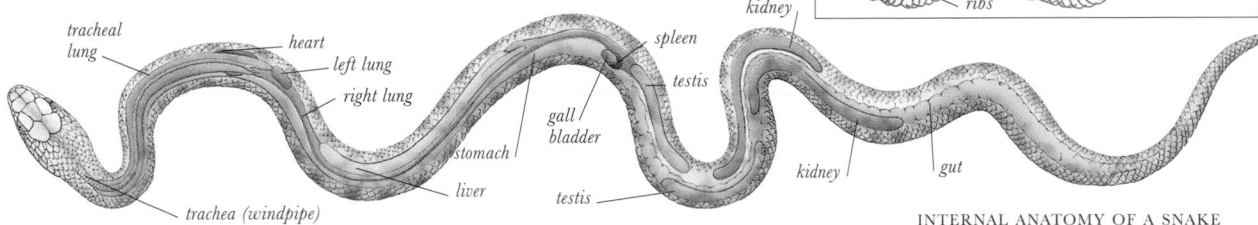

tracheal lung

heart

left lung

right lung

trachea (windpipe)

liver

stomach

gall bladder

spleen

testis

testis

kidney

kidney

gut

INTERNAL ANATOMY OF A SNAKE

EXAMPLES OF SNAKES

FAMILY BOIDAE

BOA CONSTRICTOR
(*Boa constrictor*)

INDIAN PYTHON
(*Python molurus*)

ANACONDA
(*Eunectes murinus*)

FAMILY COLUBRIDAE

FLYING TREE SNAKE
(*Chrysopelea pelias*)

CORN SNAKE
(*Elaphe guttata*)

CALIFORNIAN KING SNAKE
(*Lampropeltis getulus*)

VINE SNAKE
(*Oxybelis fulgidus*)

FAMILY VIPERIDAE

WESTERN DIAMONDBACK
RATTLESNAKE
(*Crotalus atrox*)

FAMILY ELAPIDAE

BLACK-NECKED
COBRA
(*Naja nigricollis*)

PUFF-ADDER
(*Bitis arietans*)

CORAL SNAKE
(*Micrurus nigrocinctus*)

S

snappy *adj.* (**snappier**, **snappiest**) *colloq.* **1** brisk; full of zest. **2** neat and elegant (*a snappy dresser*). **3** snappish. □ **make it snappy** be quick about it. □ **snappily** *adv.* **snappiness** *n.*

snapshot *n.* a casual photograph taken quickly with a small hand camera.

snare ● *n.* **1** a trap for catching birds or animals, esp. with a noose. **2** a thing that acts as a temptation. **3** a device for tempting an enemy etc. into danger, capture, defeat, etc. **4** (in *sing.* or *pl.*) *Mus.* twisted strings of gut, hide, or wire stretched across the lower head of a side drum to produce a rattling sound. **5** (in full **snare drum**) ▼ a drum fitted with snares. ▷ DRUM KIT, ORCHESTRA. **6** *Surgery* a wire loop for extracting polyps etc. ● *v.tr.* catch in a snare; trap. [from Old Norse *snara*] □ **snarer** *n.* (also in *comb.*).

snare
mounting   snare

lug   damper

snare
release lever

sticks   drumhead

SNARE DRUM
(VIEWED FROM BELOW)

snarl¹ ● *v.* **1** *intr.* (of a dog) make an angry growl with bared teeth. **2** *intr.* (of a person) speak cynically; make bad-tempered complaints. **3** *tr.* (often foll. by *out*) **a** utter in a snarling tone. **b** express (discontent etc.) by snarling. ● *n.* the act or sound of snarling. [earlier *snar*, from Middle High German *snarren*] □ **snarler** *n.* **snarlingly** *adv.* **snarly** *adj.* (**snarlier**, **snarliest**).

snarl² ● *v.* **1** *tr.* (often foll. by *up*) twist; entangle; confuse and hamper the movement of (traffic etc.). **2** *intr.* (often foll. by *up*) become entangled, congested, or confused. **3** *tr.* adorn the exterior of (a narrow metal vessel) with raised work. ● *n.* a knot or tangle. [Middle English]

snarling iron *n.* an implement used for snarling metal.

snarl-up *n. colloq.* a traffic jam; a muddle; a mistake.

snatch ● *v.tr.* **1** seize quickly, eagerly, or unexpectedly. **2** steal (a wallet etc.). **3** secure with difficulty (*snatched an hour's rest*). **4** (foll. by *away*, *from*) take away or from, esp. suddenly (*snatched away my hand*). **5** (foll. by *from*) rescue narrowly. **6** (foll. by *at*) **a** try to seize by stretching or grasping suddenly. **b** take (an offer etc.) eagerly. ● *n.* **1** an act of snatching (*made a snatch at it*). **2** a fragment of a song or talk etc. **3** orig. *US colloq.* a kidnapping. □ **in** (or **by**) **snatches** in fits and starts. [Middle English] □ **snatcher** *n.* (esp. in sense 3 of *n.*). **snatchy** *adj.*

snazzy *adj.* (**snazzier**, **snazziest**) *colloq.* smart or attractive esp. in an ostentatious way. [20th-century coinage] □ **snazzily** *adv.* **snazziness** *n.*

sneak ● *v.* (*past* and *past part.* **sneaked** or *colloq.* **snuck**) **1** *intr.* & *tr.* (foll. by *in*, *out*, *past*, *away*, etc.) go or convey furtively; slink. **2** *tr. colloq.* steal unobserved. **3** *intr. Brit. school slang* tell tales. **4** *intr.* (as **sneaking** *adj.*) **a** furtive; undisclosed (*a sneaking affection for him*). **b** persistent in one's mind (*a sneaking feeling*). ● *n.* **1** a mean-spirited cowardly underhand person. **2** *Brit. school slang* a tell-tale. ● *adj.* acting or done without warning; secret. [16th-century coinage] □ **sneakingly** *adv.*

■ **Usage** The form *snuck* for the past or past participle should not be used in formal contexts. It arose in American English in the 19th century and remains non-standard in both American and British English.

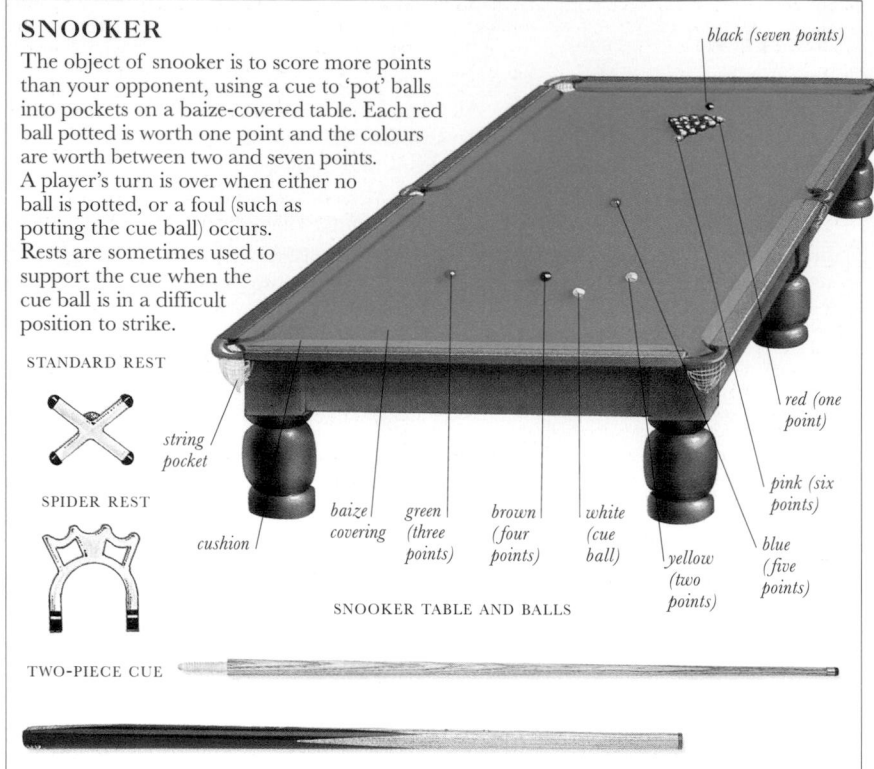

SNOOKER

The object of snooker is to score more points than your opponent, using a cue to 'pot' balls into pockets on a baize-covered table. Each red ball potted is worth one point and the colours are worth between two and seven points. A player's turn is over when either no ball is potted, or a foul (such as potting the cue ball) occurs. Rests are sometimes used to support the cue when the cue ball is in a difficult position to strike.

STANDARD REST

black (seven points)

red (one point)

pink (six points)

blue (five points)

yellow (two points)

SPIDER REST

string pocket

cushion   baize covering   green (three points)   brown (four points)   white (cue ball)

SNOOKER TABLE AND BALLS

TWO-PIECE CUE

sneaker *n.* esp. *N. Amer.* each of a pair of soft-soled canvas etc. shoes.

sneak thief *n.* a thief who steals without breaking in.

sneaky *adj.* (**sneakier**, **sneakiest**) given to or characterized by sneaking; furtive, mean. □ **sneakily** *adv.* **sneakiness** *n.*

sneer ● *n.* a derisive smile or remark. ● *v.* **1** *intr.* (often foll. by *at*) smile derisively. **2** *tr.* say sneeringly. **3** *intr.* (often foll. by *at*) speak derisively. [Middle English] □ **sneerer** *n.* **sneering** *adj.* **sneeringly** *adv.*

sneeze ● *n.* **1** a sudden involuntary expulsion of air from the nose and mouth caused by irritation of the nostrils. **2** the sound of this. ● *v.intr.* make a sneeze. □ **not to be sneezed at** *colloq.* not to be underrated; considerable. [Middle English] □ **sneezer** *n.* **sneezy** *adj.*

snick ● *v.tr.* **1** make a small notch or incision in. **2** *Cricket* deflect (the ball) slightly with the bat. ● *n.* **1** a small notch or cut. **2** *Cricket* a slight deflection of the ball by the bat. [17th-century coinage]

snicker ● *v.intr.* **1** = SNIGGER *v.* **2** whinny, neigh. ● *n.* **1** = SNIGGER *n.* **2** a whinny; a neigh.

snide ● *adj.* **1** sneering; slyly derogatory; insinuating. **2** counterfeit; bogus. **3** *US* mean; underhand. ● *n.* a snide person or remark. [19th-century coinage, originally cant] □ **snidely** *adv.* **snideness** *n.*

sniff ● *v.* **1** *intr.* draw up air audibly through the nose. **2** *tr.* (often foll. by *up*) draw in through the nose. **3** *tr.* draw in the scent of (food, flowers, etc.) through the nose. ● *n.* **1** an act or sound of sniffing. **2** the amount of air etc. sniffed up. □ **sniff at** try the smell of. **2** show contempt for. **sniff out** detect; discover by investigation. [Middle English] □ **sniffingly** *adv.*

sniffer *n.* **1** a person who sniffs, esp. one who sniffs a drug or toxic substances (often in *comb.*: *glue-sniffer*). **2** *slang* the nose. **3** *colloq.* any device for detecting gas, radiation, etc.

sniffer dog *n. colloq.* a dog trained to sniff out drugs or explosives.

sniffle ● *v.intr.* sniff slightly or repeatedly. ● *n.* **1** the act of sniffling. **2** (in *sing.* or *pl.*) a cold in the head causing a running nose and sniffling. □ **sniffler** *n.* **sniffly** *adj.*

sniffy *adj.* (**sniffier**, **sniffiest**) *colloq.* **1** inclined to sniff. **2** disdainful. □ **sniffily** *adv.* **sniffiness** *n.*

snifter *n.* **1** *colloq.* a small drink of alcohol. **2** esp. *N. Amer.* a balloon glass for brandy. [from dialect *snift* 'sniff']

snigger ● *n.* a half-suppressed secretive laugh. ● *v.intr.* utter such a laugh. [variant of SNICKER] □ **sniggerer** *n.* **sniggeringly** *adv.*

snip ● *v.tr.* (**snipped**, **snipping**) (also *absol.*) cut with scissors or shears, esp. in small quick strokes. ● *n.* **1** an act of snipping. **2** a piece of material etc. snipped off. **3** *colloq.* **a** something easily achieved. **b** *Brit.* a bargain. [from Dutch *snippen*] □ **snipping** *n.*

snipe ● *n.* (*pl.* same or **snipes**) any of various wading birds, with a long straight bill and frequenting marshes. ● *v.tr.* **1** fire shots from hiding, usu. at long range. **2** (foll. by *at*) make a sly critical attack. [Middle English] □ **sniper** *n.*

snippet *n.* **1** a small piece cut off. **2** (usu. in *pl.*; often foll. by *of*) **a** a fragment of information etc. **b** a short extract from a book etc. □ **snippety** *adj.*

snitch *slang* ● *v.* **1** *tr.* steal. **2** *intr.* (often foll. by *on*) inform on a person. ● *n.* an informer. [17th-century coinage]

snivel ● *v.intr.* (**snivelled**, **snivelling**; *US* **sniveled**, **sniveling**) **1** weep with sniffling. **2** run at the nose; sniffle. **3** show tearful sentiment. ● *n.* **1** running mucus. **2** hypocritical talk. [Middle English] □ **sniveller** *n.* **snivelling** *adj.* **snivellingly** *adv.*

snob *n.* **1 a** a person with an exaggerated respect for social position or wealth and who despises people considered socially inferior. **b** a person who seeks to cultivate people considered socially superior. **2** a person who despises others whose (usu. specified) tastes or attainments are considered inferior (*an intellectual snob*). [18th-century coinage, originally in

S

sense 'cobbler'] □ **snobbery** *n.* (*pl.* **-ies**). **snobbish** *adj.* **snobbishly** *adv.* **snobbishness** *n.* **snobby** *adj.* (**snobbier, snobbiest**).

snog *Brit. slang.* ● *v.intr. & tr.* (**snogged, snogging**) kiss and caress. ● *n.* a spell of snogging. [20th-century coinage] □ **snogger** *n.*

snood *n.* **1** an ornamental hairnet usu. worn at the back of the head. **2** a ring of woollen etc. material worn as a hood. [Old English]

snook *n. esp. Brit. slang* a contemptuous gesture with the thumb to the nose and the fingers spread out. □ **cock a snook** (often foll. by *at*) **1** make this gesture. **2** register one's contempt. [18th-century coinage]

snooker ● *n.* **1** ◄ a game played with cues on a rectangular baize-covered table using a cue ball (white) to pocket the other balls (15 red and 6 coloured). **2** a position in this game in which a direct shot at a permitted ball is impossible. ● *v.tr.* **1** (also *refl.*) subject to a snooker. **2** (esp. as **snookered** *adj.*) *colloq.* thwart. [19th-century coinage]

snoop *colloq.* ● *v.intr.* **1** pry into matters one need not be concerned with. **2** (often foll. by *about, around*) investigate transgressions of the law etc. ● *n.* **1** an act of snooping. **2** a person who snoops; a detective. [from Dutch *snœpen* 'to eat on the sly'] □ **snooper** *n.* **snoopy** *adj.*

snooty *adj.* (**snootier, snootiest**) *colloq.* supercilious; conceited. □ **snootily** *adv.* **snootiness** *n.*

snooze *colloq.* ● *n.* a short sleep, esp. in the daytime. ● *v.intr.* take a snooze. [18th-century slang] □ **snoozer** *n.* **snoozy** *adj.* (**snoozier, snooziest**).

snore ● *n.* a snorting or grunting sound in breathing during sleep. ● *v.intr.* make this sound. [Middle English] □ **snorer** *n.*

snorkel (also **schnorkel**) ● *n.* **1** ◄ a breathing tube for an underwater swimmer. **2** a device for supplying air to a submerged submarine. ● *v.intr.* (**snorkelled, snorkelling**; *US* **snorkeling**) use a snorkel. [from German *Schnorchel*] □ **snorkeller** *n.*

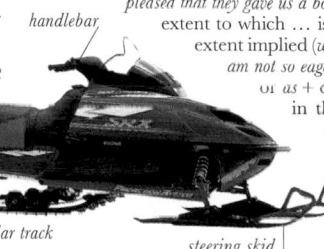

mask
snorkel
mouthpiece

SNORKEL

snort ● *n.* **1** an explosive sound made by the sudden forcing of breath through the nose, expressing indignation, incredulity, etc. **2** a similar sound made by an engine etc. **3** *colloq.* a small drink of liquor. **4** *slang* an inhaled dose of a (usu. illegal) powdered drug. ● *v.* **1** *intr.* make a snort. **2** *tr.* (also *absol.*) *slang* inhale (esp. cocaine or heroin). [Middle English]

snorter *n. Brit. colloq.* **1** something very impressive or difficult. **2** something vigorous or violent.

snot *n. slang* **1** nasal mucus. **2** a term of contempt for a person. [related to SNOUT]

snot-rag *n. slang* a handkerchief.

snotty *adj.* (**snottier, snottiest**) *slang* **1** running or foul with nasal mucus. **2** contemptible. **3** supercilious. □ **snottily** *adv.* **snottiness** *n.*

snout *n.* **1** the projecting nose and mouth of an animal. **2** *derog.* a person's nose. **3** the pointed front of a thing; a nozzle. **4** *Brit. slang* tobacco or a cigarette. [from Middle Dutch *snūt*] □ **snouted** *adj.* (also in *comb.*). **snouty** *adj.*

snow ● *n.* **1** atmospheric water vapour frozen into ice crystals and falling to earth in light white flakes. **2** a fall of this, or a layer of it. **3** a thing resembling snow in whiteness or texture etc. **4** a mass of flickering white spots on a television or radar screen. **5** *slang* cocaine. ● *v.* **1** *intr.* (prec. by *it* as subject) snow falls (*if it snows*). **2** *tr.* (foll. by *in, over, up*, etc.) block with large quantities of snow. **3** *tr. & intr.* sprinkle, scatter, or fall as or like snow. **4** *intr.*

come in large numbers or quantities. **5** *tr. US slang* deceive or charm with plausible words. □ **be snowed under** be overwhelmed, esp. with work. [Old English] □ **snowless** *adj.* **snowlike** *adj.*

snowball ● *n.* snow pressed together into a ball, esp. for throwing in play. ● *v.* **1** *intr. & tr.* throw or pelt with snowballs. **2** *intr.* increase rapidly.

snow-blind *adj.* temporarily blinded by the glare of light reflected by large expanses of snow.

snowboard *n.* ► a wide ski used for sliding downhill on snow. □ **snowboarder** *n.* **snowboarding** *n.*

snowbound *adj.* prevented by snow from going out or travelling.

snowdrift *n.* a bank of snow heaped up by the action of the wind.

snowdrop *n.* a bulbous plant, *Galanthus nivalis*, with white drooping flowers in the early spring.

snowfall *n.* **1** a fall of snow. **2** *Meteorol.* the amount of snow that falls within a given area or time.

snowfield *n.* a permanent wide expanse of snow in mountainous or polar regions.

snowflake *n.* a flake of snow, esp. a feathery ice crystal, often displaying delicate sixfold symmetry.

snowline *n.* the level above which snow never melts entirely.

snowmaking *n.* the production of artificial snow (often *attrib.*: *snowmaking machine*).

snowman *n.* (*pl.* **-men**) a figure resembling a man, made of compressed snow.

snowmobile *n.* ► a motor vehicle, esp. with runners or caterpillar tracks, for travelling over snow.

snow pea *n. esp. N. Amer.* — MANGETOUT.

snowplough *n.* (*US* **snowplow**) **1** a device, or a vehicle equipped with one, for clearing roads of thick snow **2** *Skiing* an act of turning the points of the skis inwards to slow down.

snowscape *n.* **1** a snowy landscape. **2** a picture of this.

snowshoe *n.* a flat device like a racket attached to a boot for walking on snow without sinking in.

snowshoe hare *n.* (also **snowshoe rabbit**) a N. American hare, *Lepus americanus*, with large hind feet and a white coat in winter.

snow-slip *n. Brit.* an avalanche.

snowstorm *n.* a heavy fall of snow, esp. with a high wind.

snow white ● *n.* a pure white colour. ● *adj.* (hyphenated when *attrib.*) of this colour.

snowy *adj.* (**snowier, snowiest**) **1 a** of or like snow. **b** pure white. **2** (of the weather etc.) with much snow. □ **snowily** *adv.*

SNP *abbr.* Scottish National Party.

Snr. *abbr.* Senior.

snub ● *v.tr.* (**snubbed, snubbing**) **1** rebuff or humiliate with sharp words or coldness. **2** check the movement of (a boat, horse, etc.), esp. by a rope wound round a post etc. ● *n.* an act of snubbing; a rebuff. ● *adj.* short and blunt in shape. [from Old Norse *snubba* 'to chide, check the growth of']

snub nose *n.* a short turned-up nose. □ **snub-nosed** *adj.*

snuck *colloq. past* and *past part.* of SNEAK.

snuff¹ ● *n.* the charred part of a candle-wick. ● *v.tr.* trim the snuff from (a candle). □ **snuff it** *Brit.*

boot
binding
tail
tip

SNOWBOARD AND **SNOWBOARDER**

handlebar
seat
YAMAHA
caterpillar track
steering skid

SNOWMOBILE

slang die. **snuff out 1** extinguish, (a candle etc.). **2** *slang* kill; put an end to. [Middle English]

snuff² ● *n.* powdered tobacco or medicine taken by sniffing. ● *v.intr.* take snuff. □ **up to snuff** *colloq.* **1** *Brit.* knowing; not easily deceived. **2** up to standard. [from Middle Dutch *snuffen* 'to snuffle']

snuffbox *n.* a small box for holding snuff.

snuffer *n.* **1** ► a small hollow cone with a handle used to extinguish a candle. **2** (in *pl.*) an implement like scissors used to extinguish a candle or trim its wick.

snuffle ● *v.* **1** *intr.* make sniffing sounds. **2 a** *intr.* speak nasally, whiningly, or like one with a cold. **b** *tr.* say in this way. **3** *intr.* breathe noisily as through a partially blocked nose. **4** *intr.* sniff. ● *n.* **1** a snuffling sound or tone. **2** (in *pl.*) a partial blockage of the nose causing snuffling. **3** a sniff. □ **snuffly** *adj.*

snuff movie *n.* (also **snuff video** etc.) *slang* a pornographic film depicting an actual murder.

SNUFFER

snug ● *adj.* (**snugger, snuggest**) **1 a** cosy, comfortable, sheltered; well enclosed or placed or arranged. **b** cosily protected from the weather or cold. **2** (of an income etc.) allowing comfort and comparative ease. ● *n. Brit.* a small room in a pub. [16th-century nautical coinage] □ **snugly** *adv.* **snugness** *n.*

snuggery *n.* (*pl.* **-ies**) *Brit.* **1** a snug place, esp. a person's private room or den. **2** = SNUG *n.*

snuggle *v.intr. & tr.* settle or draw into a warm comfortable position. [based on SNUG]

so¹ ● *adv.* **1** to such an extent, or to the extent implied (*why are you so angry?*; *do stop complaining so*; *were so pleased that they gave us a bonus*). **2** (with *neg.*) to the extent to which … is or does etc., or to the extent implied (*was not so late as I expected*; *am not so eager as you*). **3** (foll. by *that* or *as* + *clause*) to the degree or in the manner implied (*so expensive that few can afford it*; *so small as to be invisible*; *am not so foolish as to agree to that*). **4** (adding emphasis) to that extent; in that or a similar manner (*I want to leave and so does she*; *you said it was good, and so it is*). **5** to a great or notable degree (*I am so glad*). **6** (with verbs of state) in the way described (*am not very fond of it but may become so*). **7** (with verb of saying or thinking etc.) as previously mentioned or described (*I think so*; *so he said*; *so I should hope*). ● *conj.* **1** with the result that (*there was none left, so we had to go without*). **2** in order that (*came home early so that I could see you*). **3** and then; as the next step (*so then the car broke down*; *and so to bed*). **4 a** (introducing a question) then; after that (*so what did you tell them?*). **b** (*absol.*) = *so what?* □ **and so on** (or **forth**) **1** and others of the same kind. **2** and in other similar ways. **so as** (foll. by *to* + infin.) in order to (*did it so as to get it finished*). **so be it** an expression of acceptance or resignation. **so far** see FAR. **so far as** see FAR. **so far so good** see FAR. **so long!** *colloq.* goodbye till we meet again. **so long as** see LONG¹. **so much 1** a certain amount (of). **2** a great deal of (*is so much nonsense*). **3** (with *neg.*) **a** less than; to a lesser extent (*not so much forgotten as ignored*). **b** not even (*didn't give me so much as a penny*). **so much for** that is all that need be done or said about. **so so** *adj.* (usu. *predic.*) indifferent; not very good. ● *adv.* indifferently; only moderately well. **so to say** (or **speak**) an expression of reserve or apology for an exaggeration or neologism etc. **so what?** *colloq.* why should that be considered significant? [Old English]

so² var. of SOH.

S

soak ● *v.* **1** *tr. & intr.* make or become thoroughly wet through saturation. **2** *tr.* (of rain etc.) drench. **3** *tr.* (foll. by *in*, *up*) **a** absorb (liquid). **b** acquire (knowledge etc.) copiously. **4** *refl.* steep (oneself) in a subject of study etc. **5** *intr.* (foll. by *in*, *into*, *through*) (of liquid) make its way or penetrate by saturation. **6** *tr. colloq.* extract money from by an extortionate charge, taxation, etc. (*soak the rich*). **7** *intr. colloq.* drink persistently. **8** *tr.* (as **soaked** *adj.*) very drunk. ● *n.* **1** the act of soaking or the state of being soaked. **2** a drinking bout. **3** *colloq.* a hard drinker. [Old English, related to SUCK] □ **soakage** *n.*

soakaway *n. Brit.* an arrangement for disposing of waste water by letting it percolate through the soil.

soaking ● *adj.* (in full **soaking wet**) very wet; wet through. ● *n.* the act of soaking; an instance of being soaked.

so-and-so *n.* (*pl.* **so-and-sos**) **1** a particular person or thing not needing to be specified (*told me to do so-and-so*). **2** *colloq.* a person disliked or regarded with disfavour (*the so-and-so left me behind*).

soap ● *n.* **1** a cleansing agent which when rubbed in water yields a lather used in washing. **2** *colloq.* = SOAP OPERA. ● *v.tr.* **1** apply soap to. **2** scrub or rub with soap. **3** [Old English]

soapbox *n.* **1** a box for holding soap. **2** a makeshift stand for a public speaker.

soap opera *n.* a broadcast drama, usu. serialized in many episodes, dealing with esp. domestic themes. [so called because originally sponsored in the US by soap manufacturers]

soap powder *n.* powdered soap esp. with additives.

soapstone *n.* **1** ▼ a soft easily worked rock consisting largely of talc. **2** the mineral talc occurring in massive deposition.

SOAPSTONE: VIKING FORGE STONE
MADE OF SOAPSTONE

soapsuds *n.pl.* = SUDS 1.

S

soapy *adj.* (**soapier**, **soapiest**) **1** of or like soap. **2** containing or smeared with soap. **3** unctuous or flattering.

soar *v.intr.* **1** fly or rise high. **2** reach a high level or standard. **3** maintain height in the air without flapping the wings or using power. [from Old French *essorer*] □ **soaringly** *adv.*

sob ● *v.* (**sobbed**, **sobbing**) **1** *intr.* **a** draw breath in convulsive gasps when weeping or from distress, physical exhaustion, etc. **b** weep in this way. **2** *tr.* (usu. foll. by *out*) utter with sobs. ● *n.* a convulsive drawing of breath, esp. in weeping. [Middle English] □ **sobbingly** *adv.*

sober ● *adj.* (**soberer**, **soberest**) **1** not under the influence of alcohol. **2** not given to excessive drinking of alcohol. **3** moderate, tranquil, sedate. **4** not fanciful or exaggerated (*the sober truth*). **5** (of a colour etc.) quiet and inconspicuous. ● *v.tr. & intr.* make or become sober (*a sobering thought*). [from Latin *sobrius*] □ **soberly** *adv.*

sobriety *n.* the state of being sober. [from Latin *sobrietas*]

sobriquet /**soh**-bri-kay/ *n.* (also **soubriquet** /**soo**-bri-kay/) **1** a nickname. **2** an assumed name. [French, originally in sense 'a tap under the chin']

sob sister *n. colloq.* **1** a female journalist writing sentimental reports or answering readers' problems. **2** an actress who plays sentimental roles.

sob story *n. colloq.* a story or explanation appealing mainly to the emotions.

Soc. *abbr.* **1** Socialist. **2** Society.

soca *n.* a kind of calypso music with elements of soul, originally from Trinidad. [blend of SOUL and CALYPSO]

so-called *adj.* commonly designated or known as, often incorrectly.

soccer *n.* Association Football. ▷ FOOTBALL. [based on *Assoc.*, short for *Association*]

sociable *adj.* **1** fitted for or liking the society of other people; ready and willing to talk and act with others. **2** (of a person's manner or behaviour etc.) friendly. **3** (of a meeting etc.) marked by friendliness, not stiff or formal. [from Latin *sociabilis*] □ **sociability** *n.* **sociably** *adv.*

social ● *adj.* **1** of or relating to society or its organization. **2** concerned with the mutual relations of human beings or of classes of human beings. **3** living in organized communities (*man is a social animal*). **4** needing companionship; gregarious. **5 a** (of insects) living together in organized communities. **b** (of animals or birds) breeding or nesting near each other in communities. ● *n.* a social gathering, esp. one organized by a club, congregation, etc. [from Latin *socialis* 'allied'] □ **sociality** *n.* **socially** *adv.*

social anthropology *n.* the comparative study of peoples through their culture and kinship systems.

social climber *n. derog.* a person anxious to gain a higher social status.

social conscience *n.* a sense of responsibility or concern for the problems and injustices of society.

social democracy *n.* a socialist system achieved by democratic means. □ **social democrat** *n.*

social engineering *n.* the use of sociological principles in approaching social problems.

socialism *n.* **1** a political and economic theory which advocates that the community as a whole should own and control the means of production, distribution, and exchange. **2** policy or practice based on this theory. □ **socialist** *n. & adj.* **socialistic** *adj.*

socialite *n.* a person prominent in fashionable society.

socialize *v.* (also **-ise**) **1** *intr.* mix socially with others. **2** *tr.* make social. **3** *tr.* organize on socialistic principles. □ **socialization** *n.*

socialized medicine *n. US* often *derog.* the provision of medical services for all from public funds.

social order *n.* the network of human relationships in society.

social realism *n.* the realistic depiction of social conditions or political views in art.

social science *n.* **1** the scientific study of human society and social relationships. **2** a branch of this. □ **social scientist** *n.*

social security *n.* State assistance to those lacking in economic security and welfare, e.g. the aged and *Brit.* the unemployed.

social service *n.* **1** philanthropic activity. **2** (in *pl.*) services provided by the State for the community, esp. education, health, and housing.

social war *n.* a war fought between allies.

social work *n.* work of benefit to those in need of help or welfare, esp. done by specially trained personnel. □ **social worker** *n.*

society *n.* (*pl.* **-ies**) **1** the sum of human conditions and activity regarded as a whole functioning interdependently. **2** a social community (*all societies must have firm laws*). **3 a** a social mode of life. **b** the customs and organization of an ordered community. **4** *Ecol.* a plant or animal community. **5 a** the socially advantaged or prominent members of a community (*society would not approve*). **b** this, or a part of it, qualified in some way (*is not done in polite society*). **6** participation in hospitality; other people's homes or company (*avoids society*). **7** companionship, company (*avoids the society of such people*). **8** an

association of persons united by a common aim or interest or principle (*formed a music society*). [from Latin *societas*] □ **societal** *adj.* (esp. in sense 1).

Society of Friends see QUAKER.

Society of Jesus see JESUIT.

socio- *comb. form* **1** of society (and). **2** of or relating to sociology (and). [from Latin *socius* 'companion']

sociobiology *n.* the scientific study of the biological aspects of social behaviour in animals and humans. □ **sociobiological** *adj.* **sociobiologist** *n.*

socio-economic *adj.* relating to or concerned with the interaction of social and economic factors. □ **socio-economically** *adv.*

sociolinguistic *adj.* relating to or concerned with language in its social aspects. □ **sociolinguist** *n.* **sociolinguistically** *adv.*

sociolinguistics *n.* the study of language in relation to social factors.

sociology *n.* **1** the study of the development, structure, and functioning of human society. **2** the study of social problems. [from French *sociologie*] □ **sociological** *adj.* **sociologically** *adv.* **sociologist** *n.*

socio-political *adj.* combining social and political factors.

sock[1] *n.* (*pl.* **socks** or *Commerce* **sox**) **1** a short knitted covering for the foot. **2** a removable inner sole put into a shoe for warmth etc. □ **knock** (or **blow**) **one's socks off** astound, amaze. **pull one's socks up** *colloq.* make an effort to improve. **put a sock in it** *colloq.* be quiet. [from Greek *sukkhos*]

sock[2] *colloq.* ● *v.tr.* hit forcefully. ● *n.* a hard blow. □ **sock it to** attack or address (a person) vigorously. [17th-century coinage]

socket *n.* **1** a natural or artificial hollow for something to fit into or stand firm or revolve in. **2** *Electr.* a device receiving a plug, light bulb, etc., to make a connection. [from Anglo-French]

sockeye *n.* ▼ a blue-backed salmon of Alaska etc., *Oncorhynchus nerka*. [from N. American Indian *sukai* 'fish of fishes']

SOCKEYE
(*Oncorhynchus nerka*)

Socratic *adj.* of or relating to the Greek philosopher Socrates (*c.*470 – 399 BC) or his philosophy. [from Greek *Sōkratikos*]

sod[1] *n.* **1** turf or a piece of turf. **2** the surface of the ground. □ **under the sod** in the grave. [from Middle Dutch *sode*]

sod[2] esp. *Brit. coarse slang* ● *n.* **1** an unpleasant or awkward person or thing. **2** a person of a specified kind; a fellow (*the lucky sod*). ● *v.tr.* (**sodded**, **sodding**) **1** (often *absol.* or as *int.*) an exclamation of annoyance (*sod them, I don't care!*). **2** (as **sodding** *adj.*) a general term of contempt. □ **sod off** go away. [abbreviation of SODOMITE]

soda *n.* **1** any of various compounds of sodium in common use (*washing soda*; *caustic soda*). **2** (in full **soda water**) water made effervescent by impregnation with carbon dioxide under pressure. **3** esp. *US* a sweet effervescent drink. [medieval Latin]

soda bread *n.* bread leavened with baking soda.

soda fountain *n.* esp. *US* **1** a device supplying soda water or soft drinks. **2** a shop or counter featuring this.

soda syphon *n.* a bottle from which carbonated water is dispensed by allowing the gas pressure to force it out.

soda water see SODA 2.

sodden *adj.* **1** saturated; soaked through. **2** rendered dazed or dull etc. with drunkenness. □ **soddenly** *adv.*

sodium *n. Chem.* a soft silver-white reactive metallic element, occurring naturally in soda, salt, etc. [based on SODA] □ **sodic** *adj.*

sodium bicarbonate *n.* a soluble white powder used as a raising agent in baking.

sodium chloride *n.* a colourless crystalline compound occurring naturally in sea water and halite; common salt.

sodium hydroxide *n.* a deliquescent compound which is strongly alkaline.

sodium vapour lamp *n.* (also **sodium lamp**) ▶ a lamp using sodium vapour and giving a yellow light.

sodomite *n.* a person who practises sodomy. [from Greek *Sodomitēs* 'inhabitant of Sodom']

sodomy *n.* = BUGGERY. [based on Late Latin *peccatum Sodomiticum* 'sin of Sodom'] □ **sodomize** *v.tr.* (also **-ise**).

Sod's Law *n.* = MURPHY'S LAW.

sofa *n.* a long upholstered seat with a back and arms. [from Arabic *ṣuffa*]

sofa bed *n.* a sofa that can be converted into a bed.

soffit *n.* the undersurface of an arch, a balcony, overhanging eaves, etc. [from Latin *suffixus* 'fixed underneath']

soft ● *adj.* **1** lacking hardness or firmness; yielding to pressure; easily cut. **2** (of cloth etc.) having a smooth surface or texture; not rough or coarse. **3** (of air etc.) mellow, mild, balmy; not noticeably cold or hot. **4** (of water) free from mineral salts and therefore good for lathering. **5** (of a light or colour etc.) not brilliant or glaring. **6** (of a voice or sounds) gentle and pleasing. **7** *Phonet.* **a** (of a consonant) sibilant or palatal (as *c* in *ice*, *g* in *age*). **b** voiced or unaspirated. **8** (of an outline etc.) not sharply defined. **9** (of an action or manner etc.) gentle, conciliatory; amorous. **10** (of the heart or feelings etc.) compassionate, sympathetic. **11** feeble, lenient, silly, sentimental. **12** *colloq.* (of a job etc.) easy. **13** (of drugs) mild; not likely to cause addiction. **14** (also **soft-core**) (of pornography) not explicit. **15** *Stock Exch.* (of currency, prices, etc.) likely to fall in value. **16** *Polit.* moderate; willing to compromise (*the soft left*). **17** *Brit.* (of the weather etc.) rainy or moist or thawing. ● *adv.* softly (*play soft*). □ **be soft on** *colloq.* **1** be lenient towards. **2** be infatuated with. **have a soft spot for** be fond of or affectionate towards (a person). [Old English *sōfte* 'agreeable'] □ **softish** *adj.* **softness** *n.*

softball *n.* **1** ▼ a ball like a baseball but larger. **2** a modified form of baseball using this.

SOFTBALL AND BASEBALL

soft-boiled *adj.* (of an egg) lightly boiled leaving the yolk soft or liquid.

soft-centred *adj.* **1** (of a sweet) having a soft filling or centre. **2** soft-hearted, sentimental.

soft drink *n.* a non-alcoholic drink.

soften *v.* **1** *tr. & intr.* make or become soft or softer. **2** *tr.* **a** reduce the strength of (defences) by preliminary attack. **b** reduce the resistance of (a person). □ **softener** *n.*

soft focus *n. Photog.* the deliberate slight blurring of a picture.

soft fruit *n. Brit.* small stoneless fruit.

soft furnishings *n.pl. Brit.* curtains, rugs, etc.

soft-headed *adj.* feeble-minded. □ **soft-headedness** *n.*

soft-hearted *adj.* tender, compassionate. □ **soft-heartedness** *n.*

softie *n.* (also **softy**) (*pl.* **-ies**) *colloq.* a weak or silly or soft-hearted person.

soft landing *n.* a landing by a spacecraft without its suffering major damage.

    softly *adv.* in a soft, gentle, or quiet manner.

    softly-softly *attrib.adj.* (of an approach or strategy) cautious; discreet and cunning.

    soft option *n.* the easier alternative.

    soft palate *n.* the rear part of the palate. ▷ HEAD

    soft pedal ● *n.* a pedal on a piano that makes the tone softer. ▷ UPRIGHT. ● *v.tr.* & (often foll. by *on*) *intr.* (**soft-pedal**) (**-pedalled, pedalling**; *US* **-pedaled, pedaling**) **1** refrain from emphasizing; be restrained (about). **2** *Mus.* play with the soft pedal down.

    soft roe see ROE[1] 2.

    soft sell *n.* restrained or subtly persuasive salesmanship.

    soft soap ● *n.* **1** a semi-fluid soap. **2** *colloq.* persuasive flattery. ● *v.tr.* (**soft-soap**) *colloq.* persuade (a person) with flattery.

    soft-spoken *adj.* speaking with a gentle voice.

    soft target *n.* a relatively vulnerable or unprotected target.

soft tissues *n.pl.* tissues of the body that are not bony or cartilaginous.

soft-top *n.* **1** a motor vehicle roof that is soft and can be folded back. **2** a vehicle having such a roof.

soft touch *n. slang* = EASY TOUCH.

software *n.* the programs and other operating information used by a computer.

softwood *n.* the wood of pine, spruce, or other conifers, easily sawn. ▷ WOOD

softy var. of SOFTIE.

soggy *adj.* (**soggier, soggiest**) sodden, saturated, dank. [from dialect *sog* 'swamp'] □ **soggily** *adv.* **sogginess** *n.*

soh *n.* (also **so, sol**) *Mus.* **1** (in tonic sol-fa) the fifth note of a major scale. **2** the note G in the fixed-doh system. [variant of Middle English *sol*]

soigné /swahn-yay/ *adj.* (*fem.* **soignée** *pronunc.* same) well-groomed. [French]

soil[1] *n.* **1** ▼ the upper layer of earth in which plants grow. **2** ground belonging to a nation; territory (*on British soil*). [from Anglo-French] □ **soil-less** *adj.*

soil[2] ● *v.tr.* **1** make dirty; smear or stain (*soiled linen*). **2** defile; bring discredit to (*would not soil my hands with it*). ● *n.* **1** a dirty mark; a stain, smear, or defilement. **2** filth; refuse. [based on Latin *sucula* 'little pig']

soil pipe *n.* a sewage or waste water pipe.

soirée /swah-ray/ *n.* an evening party for conversation or music. [French]

sojourn /soj-ŭn/ ● *n.* a temporary stay. ● *v.intr.* stay temporarily. [from Old French *sojorn*] □ **sojourner** *n.*

sol[1] var. of SOH.

sol[2] *n. Chem.* a fluid colloidal suspension of a solid in a liquid. [abbreviation of SOLUTION]

sola *n.* a pithy-stemmed E. Indian swamp plant, *Aeschynomene indica.* [from Hindi *sholā*]

solace /sol-ǎs/ ● *n.* comfort in distress, disappointment, or tedium. ● *v.tr.* give solace to. [from Latin *solatium*]

solan *n.* (in full **solan goose**) a gannet, *Sula bassana.*

solar *adj.* of, relating to, or reckoned by the Sun (*solar eclipse; solar time*). [based on Latin *sol* 'sun']

solar battery *n.* (also **solar cell**) a device converting solar radiation into electricity.

solar day *n.* the interval between meridian transits of the Sun.

solar eclipse *n.* an eclipse in which the Sun is obscured by the Moon. ▷ ECLIPSE

solar energy *n.* **1** radiant energy emitted by the Sun. **2** = SOLAR POWER.

solarium *n.* (*pl.* **solariums** or **solaria**) a room equipped with sunlamps or fitted with extensive

S

SODIUM VAPOUR LAMP

cap —
electrode supports —
inner envelope —
outer envelope —
sodium vapour —

SOIL

Soil is an ecosystem comprising weathered rock, organic matter, animals, plants, and micro-organisms. Various horizontal layers (horizons) are discernible, including: humus, the topmost layer of rotting organic matter; topsoil, which is rich in minerals and humus; subsoil, which has less humus but plentiful minerals (leached from above); a layer of rock fragments with little organic content; and bedrock, the underlying solid rock.

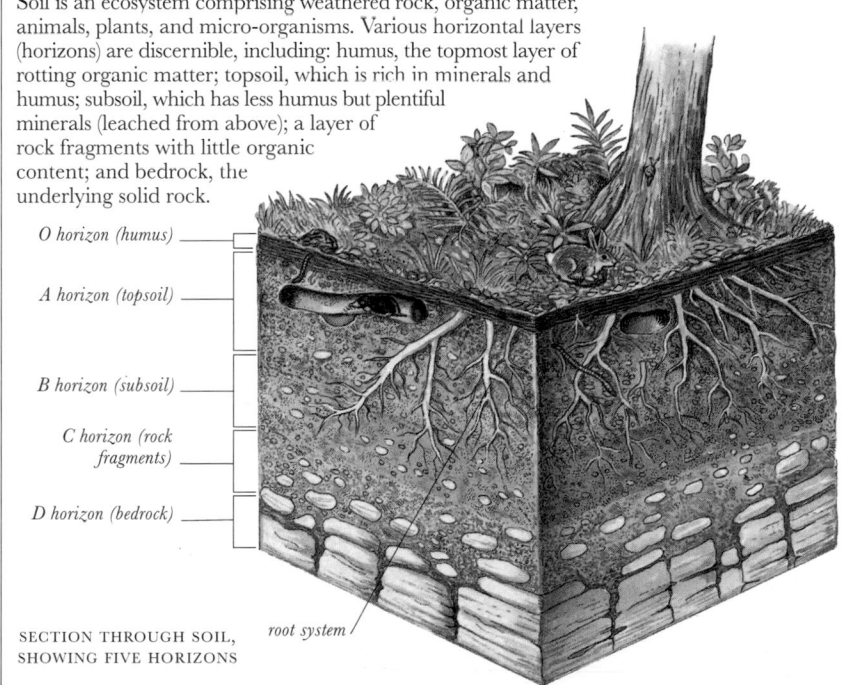

O horizon (humus)
A horizon (topsoil)
B horizon (subsoil)
C horizon (rock fragments)
D horizon (bedrock)
root system

SECTION THROUGH SOIL,
SHOWING FIVE HORIZONS

SOLAR SYSTEM

The solar system, which is more than 12 billion km (7.5 billion miles) across, consists of nine planets; 61 known moons; vast numbers of comets, asteroids, and meteoroids; and interplanetary gas and dust. Latest theories suggest that the solar system began 4.6 billion years ago as a spinning cloud of gas and dust that condensed to create the Sun. The rocky planets (Mercury, Venus, Earth, and Mars) formed from leftover material nearest the Sun, while in the colder outer reaches, the gas giants (Jupiter, Saturn, Uranus, and Neptune) developed from ice, gas, and dust. The smallest planet – Pluto – is neither gas giant nor rocky planet; it is composed of rock and ice. The planets all orbit the Sun, following elliptical paths that are on roughly the same plane. Pluto's orbit is not only the most eccentric (elongated), but also the most tilted (17°).

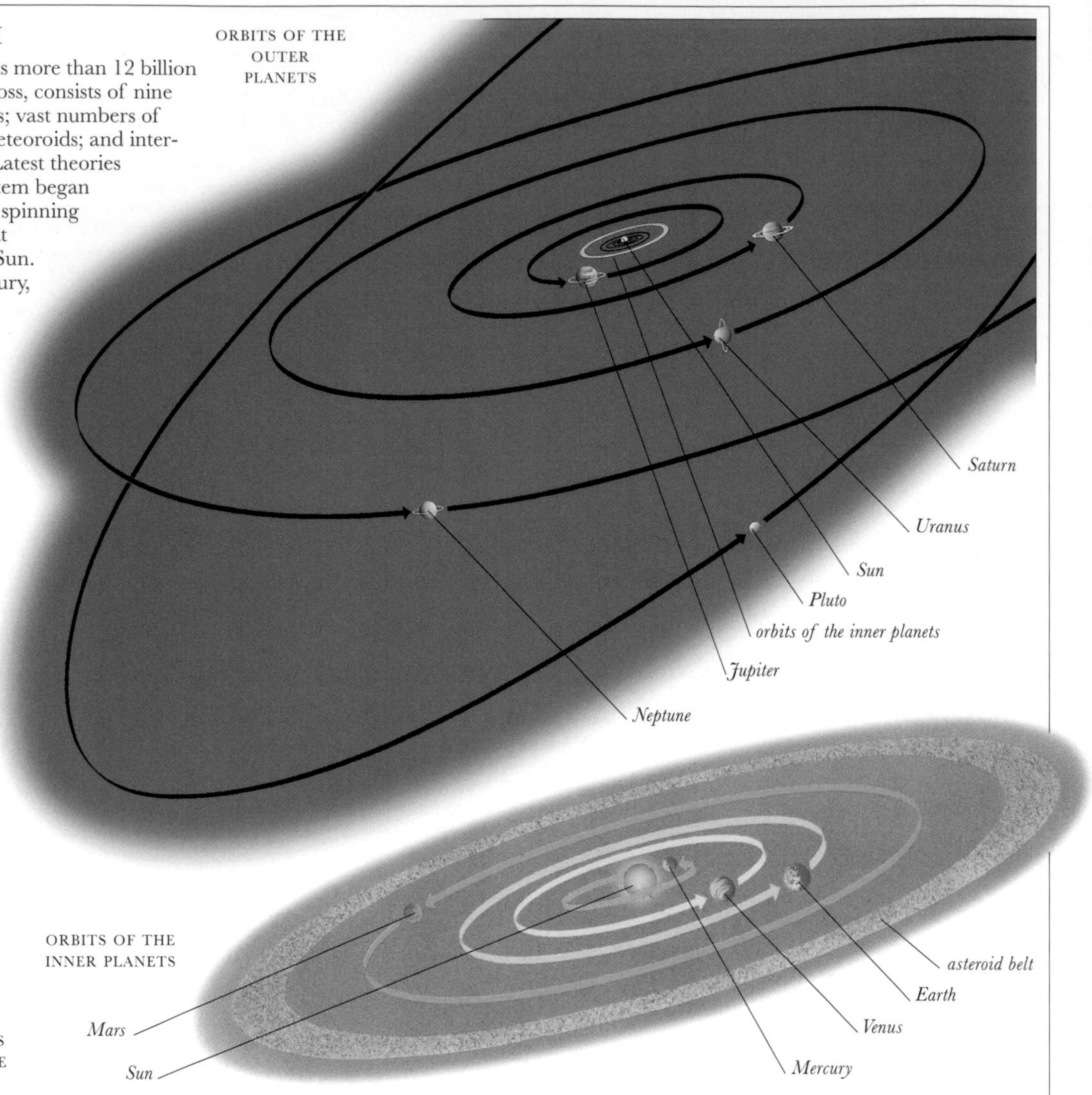

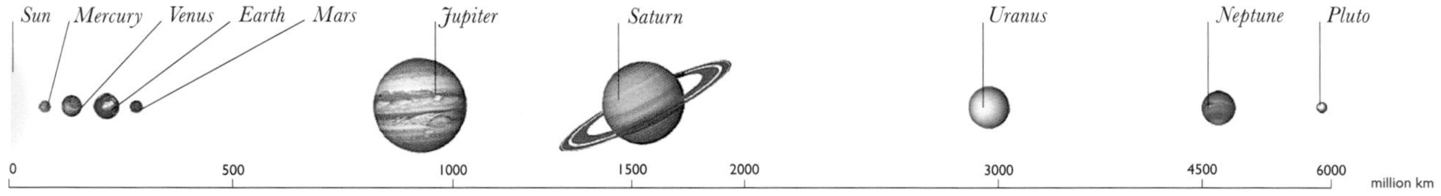

ORBITS OF THE OUTER PLANETS

Saturn

Uranus

Sun

Pluto

orbits of the inner planets

Jupiter

Neptune

ORBITS OF THE INNER PLANETS

asteroid belt

Earth

Venus

Mars

Mercury

Sun

ORDER OF THE PLANETS AND RELATIVE DISTANCE FROM THE SUN

Sun | Mercury | Venus | Earth | Mars   Jupiter   Saturn   Uranus   Neptune   Pluto

S

0   500   1000   1500   2000   3000   4500   6000

million km

---

areas of glass for exposure to the Sun. [Latin, literally 'sundial, sunning-place']

solar panel *n.* ▼ a panel that absorbs the Sun's rays as an energy source. ▷ HOUSE, SATELLITE, SPACECRAFT

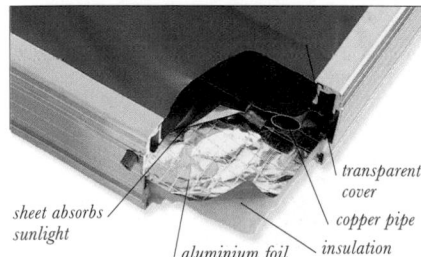

sheet absorbs sunlight

transparent cover

copper pipe

aluminium foil   *insulation*

SOLAR PANEL: INTERNAL STRUCTURE

solar plexus *n.* a complex of nerves at the pit of the stomach.

solar power *n.* power obtained by harnessing the energy of the Sun's rays.

solar system *n.* ▲ the Sun and the celestial bodies whose motion it governs. ▷ ORRERY

solar year *n.* the time taken for the Earth to travel once round the Sun, equal to 365 days, 5 hours, 48 minutes, and 46 seconds.

sola topi *n.* an Indian sun-helmet made from the pith of the sola.

sold *past* and *past part.* of SELL.

solder ● *n.* a fusible alloy used to join less fusible metals or wires etc. ● *v.tr.* join with solder. [from Latin *solidare* 'to fasten'] □ **solderable** *n.*

soldering iron *n.* a tool used for applying solder.

soldier ● *n.* **1** a person serving in an army. **2** (in full

common soldier) a private or NCO in an army. **3** a military commander of specified ability (*a great soldier*). **4** *colloq.* a finger of bread for dipping into a soft-boiled egg. ● *v.intr.* serve as a soldier (*was off soldiering*). □ **soldier on** *colloq.* persevere doggedly. [based on Old French *soude* 'soldier's pay'] □ **soldierly** *adj.*

soldier of fortune *n.* an adventurous person ready to take service under any state or person; a mercenary.

soldiery *n.* (*pl.* **-ies**) **1** soldiers, esp. of a specified character. **2** a group of soldiers.

sole[1] ● *n.* **1** the undersurface of the foot. **2** the part of a shoe, sock, etc., corresponding to this (esp. excluding the heel). **3** the lower surface or base of a plough, golf club head, etc. ● *v.tr.* provide (a shoe etc.) with a sole; replace the sole of. [from Latin *solum* 'bottom, pavement, sole'] □ **-soled** *adj.* (in *comb.*).

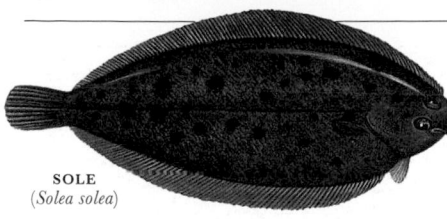

SOLE
(*Solea solea*)

sole[2] *n.* ▲ any flatfish of the family Soleidae, esp. *Solea solea* used as food. [from Latin *solea* 'sole', from its shape]

sole[3] *attrib.adj.* one and only; single, exclusive (*the sole reason*; *has the sole right*). [from Latin *sola* (fem.) 'alone'] □ **solely** *adv.*

solecism /sol-i-sizm/ *n.* **1** a mistake of grammar or idiom. **2** a piece of bad manners or incorrect behaviour. [based on Greek *soloikos* 'speaking incorrectly']

solemn *adj.* **1** serious and dignified (*a solemn occasion*). **2** formal; accompanied by ceremony (*a solemn oath*). **3** mysteriously impressive. **4** serious or cheerless in manner (*looks rather solemn*). **5** full of importance; weighty (*a solemn warning*). **6** grave, sober, deliberate (*a solemn promise*; *solemn music*). [from Latin *sol(l)emnis* 'customary, celebrated at a fixed date'] □ **solemnly** *adv.*

solemnity *n.* (*pl.* **-ies**) **1** the state of being solemn; a solemn character or feeling; solemn behaviour. **2** a rite or celebration; a piece of ceremony.

solemnize *v.tr.* (also **-ise**) **1** duly perform (a ceremony esp. of marriage). **2** celebrate (a festival etc.). **3** make solemn. □ **solemnization** *n.*

solenoid *n.* ◄ a cylindrical coil of wire acting as a magnet when carrying electric current. [based on Greek *sōlēn* 'channel, pipe'] □ **solenoidal** *adj.*

sol-fa *n.* = SOLMIZATION (cf. TONIC SOL-FA).

soli *pl.* of SOLO.

solicit *v.* (**solicited**, **soliciting**) **1** *tr.* & (foll. by *for*) *intr.* ask repeatedly or earnestly for or seek or invite (business etc.). **2** *tr.* make a request or petition to (a person). **3** *tr.* (also *absol.*) accost (a person) and offer one's services as a prostitute. [from Latin *sollicitare* 'to agitate'] □ **solicitation** *n.*

solicitor *n.* **1** *Brit.* a member of the legal profession qualified to advise clients and instruct barristers, and represent clients in the lower courts. **2** a person who solicits. **3** *US* a canvasser.

solicitous *adj.* **1** showing interest or concern. **2** (foll. by *to* + infin.) eager, anxious. [from Latin *sollicitus* 'anxious'] □ **solicitously** *adv.*

solicitude *n.* **1** the state of being solicitous; solicitous behaviour. **2** anxiety or concern. [from Latin *sollicitudo*]

solid ● *adj.* (**solider**, **solidest**) **1** firm and stable in shape; not liquid or fluid (*solid food*; *water becomes solid at 0°C*). ▷ MATTER. **2** of such material throughout, not hollow (*a solid sphere*). **3** of the same substance throughout (*solid silver*). **4** of strong material or construction or build, not flimsy or slender etc. **5 a** having three dimensions. **b** concerned with solids (*solid geometry*). **6 a** sound and reliable (*solid arguments*). **b** dependable (*a solid Tory*). **7** sound but without any special flair etc. (*a solid piece of work*). **8** financially sound. **9** (of time) uninterrupted (*spend four solid hours on it*). **10 a** unanimous, undivided (*support has been pretty solid so far*). **b** (foll. by *for*) united in favour of. ● *n.* **1** a solid substance or body. **2** (in

pl.) solid food. **3** *Geom.* a body or magnitude having three dimensions. ● *adv.* so as to become solid; solidly (*jammed solid*; *set solid*). [from Latin *solidus*] □ **solidly** *adv.* **solidness** *n.*

solidarity *n.* **1** unity or agreement of feeling or action. **2** mutual dependence. [from French *solidarité*]

solidi *pl.* of SOLIDUS.

solidify *v.tr.* & *intr.* (**-ies**, **-ied**) make or become solid. □ **solidification** *n.*

solidity *n.* the state of being solid; firmness.

solid-state *adj.* using the electronic properties of solids (e.g. a semiconductor) to replace those of valves.

solidus *n.* (*pl.* **solidi** /-dy/) esp. *Brit.* an oblique stroke (/) used in writing fractions (¾), to separate other figures and letters, or to denote alternatives (*and/or*) and ratios (*miles/day*). [Latin]

soliloquy *n.* (*pl.* **-ies**) **1** the act of talking when alone or regardless of any hearers, esp. in drama. **2** part of a play involving this. [from Late Latin *soliloquium*] □ **soliloquize** *v.intr.* (also **-ise**).

solipsism /sol-ip-sizm/ *n. Philos.* the view that the self is all that exists or can be known. [based on Latin *solus* 'alone' + *ipse* 'self'] □ **solipsist** *n.* **solipsistic** *adj.*

titanite gem

SOLITAIRE

solitaire *n.* **1** a diamond or other gem set by itself. **2** ◄ a ring having a single gem. **3** a game for one player played by removing pegs etc. one at a time from a board by jumping others over them until only one is left. **4** *N. Amer.* = PATIENCE 4. [French]

solitary ● *adj.* **1** living alone; not gregarious; lonely (*a solitary existence*). **2** (of a place) secluded. **3** single or sole (*a solitary instance*). **4** (of an insect) not living in communities. **5** *Bot.* growing singly, not in a cluster. ● *n.* (*pl.* **-ies**) **1** a recluse or hermit. **2** *colloq.* = SOLITARY CONFINEMENT. [from Latin *solitarius*] □ **solitarily** *adv.* **solitariness** *n.*

solitary confinement *n.* isolation of a prisoner in a separate cell.

solitude *n.* **1** the state of being solitary. **2** a lonely place. [from Latin *solitudo*]

solmization *n.* (also **-isation**) *Mus.* a system of associating each note of a scale with a particular syllable, now usu. *doh ray me fah soh lah te*, with doh as C in the fixed-doh system and as the keynote in the movable-doh or tonic sol-fa system. [from French *solmisation*]

solo ● *n.* (*pl.* **-os**) **1** (*pl.* **-os** or **soli**) **a** a vocal or instrumental piece or passage, or a dance, performed by one person with or without accompaniment. **b** (*attrib.*) performed or performing as a solo (*solo passage*; *solo violin*). **2 a** an unaccompanied flight by a pilot in an aircraft. **b** anything done by one person unaccompanied, alone. **3** (in full **solo whist**) a card game like whist in which one player may oppose the others. ● *v.* (**-oes**, **-oed**) **1** *intr.* perform a solo. **2** *tr.* perform or achieve as a solo. ● *adv.* unaccompanied, alone (*flew solo for the first time*). [Italian]

solo climbing *n.* the sport of climbing alone unaided by ropes etc. and without assistance from other people. □ **solo climber** *n.*

soloist *n.* a performer of a solo, esp. in music.

Solomon *n.* a very wise person. [from *Solomon*, King of Israel in the 10th c. BC, famed for his wisdom] □ **Solomonic** *adj.*

solo whist see SOLO 3.

solstice *n.* either of the two times in the year when the Sun reaches its highest or lowest point in the sky

at noon, marked by the longest and shortest days. [from Latin *solstitium*] □ **solstitial** *adj.*

soluble *adj.* **1** that can be dissolved, esp. in water. **2** that can be solved. [from Late Latin *solubilis*, related to SOLVE] □ **solubility** *n.*

solute *n.* a dissolved substance. [from Latin *solutum* '(thing) released']

solution *n.* **1** the act or a means of solving a problem or difficulty. **2 a** the conversion of a solid or gas into a liquid by mixture with a liquid. **b** the state resulting from this (*held in solution*). **3** the act of dissolving or the state of being dissolved. **4** the act of separating or breaking. [from Latin *solutio*]

solve *v.tr.* find an answer to, or a means of removing or effectively dealing with (a problem). [Middle English in sense 'to loosen': from Latin *solvere* 'to release'] □ **solvable** *adj.* **solver** *n.*

solvent ● *adj.* **1** able to dissolve or form a solution with something. **2** having enough money to meet one's liabilities. ● *n.* a solvent liquid etc. [from Latin *solvent-* 'releasing, dissolving'] □ **solvency** *n.* (in sense 2 of *adj.*).

solvent abuse *n.* the use of volatile organic solvents as intoxicants by inhalation, e.g. glue-sniffing.

Somali ● *n.* **1** (*pl.* same or **Somalis**) a member of a Hamitic Muslim people of Somalia in NE Africa. **2** the language of this people. ● *adj.* of or relating to this people or language. [native name] □ **Somalian** *adj.* & *n.*

somatic *adj.* of or relating to the body, esp. as distinct from the mind. [based on Greek *sōma sōmat-* 'body'] □ **somatically** *adv.*

sombre *adj.* (*US* also **somber**) **1** dark, gloomy (*a sombre sky*). **2** oppressively solemn or sober. **3** dismal, foreboding (*a sombre prospect*). [from Old French] □ **sombrely** *adv.* **sombreness** *n.*

sombrero *n.* (*pl.* **-os**) ◄ a broad-brimmed hat worn esp. in Mexico and the south-western US. [Spanish, based on *sumbra* 'shade']

some ● *det.* **1** an unspecified amount or number of (*some water*; *some apples*; *some of them*). **2** that is unknown or unnamed (*will return some day*; *some fool has locked the door*; *to some extent*). **3** denoting an approximate number (*waited some twenty minutes*). **4** a considerable amount or number of (*went to some trouble*). **5** (usu. stressed) **a** at least a small amount of (*do have some consideration*). **b** such to a certain extent (*that is some help*). **c** *colloq.* notably such (*I call that some story*). ● *pron.* some people or things, some number or amount (*I have some already*; *would you like some more?*). ● *adv. colloq.* to some extent (*we talked some*; *do it some more*). [Old English]

SOMBRERO

somebody ● *pron.* some person. ● *n.* (*pl.* **-ies**) a person of importance (*is really somebody now*).

some day *adv.* (also **someday**) at some time in the future.

somehow *adv.* **1** for some reason or other (*somehow I never liked them*). **2** in some unspecified or unknown way (*he somehow dropped behind*). **3** no matter how (*must get it finished somehow*).

someone *n.* & *pron.* = SOMEBODY.

someplace *adv. N. Amer. colloq.* = SOMEWHERE.

somersault (also **summersault**) ● *n.* an acrobatic movement in which a person turns head over heels in the air or on the ground and lands on the feet. ● *v.intr.* perform a somersault. [from Latin *supra* 'above' + *saltus* 'leap']

something *n.* & *pron.* **1 a** some unspecified or unknown thing (*have something to tell you*; *something has happened*). **b** (in full **something or other**) as a substitute for an unknown or forgotten description (*a student of something or other*). **2** a known or understood but unexpressed quantity, quality, or extent (*there is something about it I do not like*; *is something of a fool*). **3** *colloq.* a notable person or thing (*the party was quite something*). □ **or something** or some unspecified

SOLENOID: DOORBELL MECHANISM USING A SOLENOID

bell

contact breaker

iron bar   *solenoid*

S

SONGBIRD

Songbirds form the largest sub-group of the passerines (perching birds). They are characterized by their highly developed song, which is generated in the syrinx, a voice-box with thin walls that vibrate to create complex sounds. During the breeding season, male songbirds use their song to deter competing males from their territory, and to attract females (who usually do not sing). The song is only recognized by members of the same species, and is ignored by other birds.

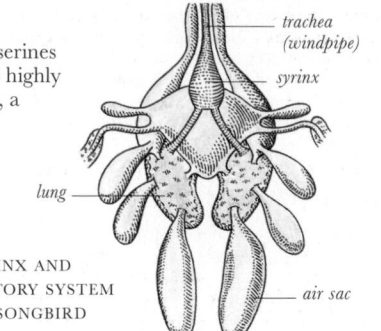

SYRINX AND
RESPIRATORY SYSTEM
OF A SONGBIRD

trachea
(windpipe)

syrinx

lung

air sac

EXAMPLES OF SONGBIRDS

GOULDIAN FINCH
(*Chloebia gouldiae*)

SONG THRUSH
(*Turdus philomelos*)

NIGHTINGALE
(*Luscinia megarhynchos*)

BALTIMORE ORIOLE
(*Icterus galbula*)

---

alternative possibility (*must have run away or something*). **see something of** encounter (a person) briefly or occasionally. **something else 1** something different. **2** *colloq.* something exceptional. **something like 1** an amount in the region of (*left something like a million pounds*). **2** somewhat like (*shaped something like a cigar*). **3** *colloq.* impressive; a fine specimen of. **something of** to some extent (*is something of an expert*). [Old English]

sometime ● *adv.* **1** at some unspecified time. **2** *archaic* formerly. ● *attrib.adj.* former (*the sometime mayor*).

sometimes *adv.* occasionally.

somewhat *adv.* to some extent (*behaviour that was somewhat strange; answered somewhat hastily*).

somewhen *adv. colloq.* at some time.

somewhere ● *adv.* in or to some place. ● *pron.* some unspecified place. □ **get somewhere** *colloq.* achieve success. **somewhere about** approximately.

somnambulism *n.* sleepwalking. [based on Latin *somnus* 'sleep' + *ambulare* 'to walk'] □ **somnambulant** *adj.* **somnambulist** *n.* **somnambulistic** *adj.* **somnambulistically** *adv.*

somnolent *adj.* **1** sleepy, drowsy. **2** inducing drowsiness. [from Latin *somnolentus*] □ **somnolence** *n.* **somnolently** *adv.*

son *n.* **1** a boy or man in relation to either or both of his parents. **2 a** a male descendant. **b** (foll. by *of*) a male member of a family, nation, etc. **3** a person regarded as inheriting an occupation, quality, etc., or associated with a particular attribute (*sons of freedom; sons of the soil*). **4** (in full **my son**) a form of address esp. to a boy. **5** (**the Son**) (in Christian belief) the second person of the Trinity. [Old English] □ **sonship** *n.*

sonar *n.* **1** a system for the underwater detection of objects by reflected sound. ▷ ECHOLOCATION. **2** an apparatus for this. [from *so*und *na*vigation and *r*anging]

sonata *n.* a composition for one instrument or two, usu. in several movements. [Italian, literally 'sounded']

son et lumière /son ay loom-**yair**/ *n.* an entertainment by night at a historic monument, building, etc., using lighting effects and recorded sound to give a dramatic narrative of its history.

song *n.* **1** a short poem or other set of words set to music or meant to be sung. **2** singing or vocal music (*burst into song*). **3** a musical composition suggestive of a song. **4** the musical call of some birds or insects. □ **for a song** *colloq.* very cheaply. **on song** *Brit. colloq.* performing exceptionally well. [Old English]

song and dance *n. colloq.* a fuss or commotion.

songbird *n.* **1** a bird with a musical call. **2** *Zool.* ▲ a perching bird of the group Oscines, possessing a syrinx. ▷ PASSERINE

songbook *n.* a collection of songs with music.

song cycle *n.* a set of musically linked songs.

songster *n.* (*fem.* **songstress**) **1** a singer. **2** a songbird. **3** a poet.

song thrush *n.* a thrush, *Turdus philomelos*, of Europe and W. Asia.

songwriter *n.* a writer of songs or the music for them. □ **songwriting** *n.*

sonic *adj.* of or relating to or using sound or sound waves. [based on Latin *sonus* 'sound'] □ **sonically** *adv.*

sonic boom *n.* (also **sonic bang**) a loud explosive noise caused by the shock wave from an aircraft when it passes the speed of sound.

son-in-law *n.* (*pl.* **sons-in-law**) the husband of one's daughter.

sonnet *n.* a poem of 14 lines using any of a number of formal rhyme schemes, in English usu. having ten syllables per line. [French]

sonny *n. colloq.* a familiar form of address to a young boy.

son of a bitch *n.* (*pl.* **sons of bitches**) *slang* a general term of contempt or abuse.

son of a gun *n.* (*pl.* **sons of guns**) *colloq.* a jocular or affectionate form of address or reference.

sonogram *n.* **1** a graph representing a sound, showing the distribution of energy at different

frequencies. **2** esp. *Med.* a visual image produced from an ultrasound examination. [based on Latin *sonus* 'sound'] □ **sonograph** *n.*

sonorous *adj.* **1** having a loud, full, or deep sound; resonant. **2** (of a speech, style, etc.) imposing, grand. [from Latin *sonorus*] □ **sonority** *n.* (*pl.* **-ies**). **sonorously** *adv.*

sool *v.tr.* esp. *Austral.* & *NZ* **1** (of a dog) attack or worry (an animal). **2** urge or goad. [variant of 17th-century (now dialect) *sowl* 'to seize by the ears'] □ **sooler** *n.*

soon *adv.* **1** after a short interval of time (*shall soon know the result*). **2** relatively early (*must you go so soon?*). **3** (prec. by *how*) early (*how soon will it be ready?*). **4** readily or willingly (in expressing choice or preference: *which would you sooner do?*; *would as soon stay behind*). □ **as** (or **so**) **soon as** at the moment that; not later than; as early as (*came as soon as I heard about it*; *disappears as soon as it's time to pay*). **no sooner ... than** at the very moment that (*we no sooner arrived than the rain stopped*). **sooner or later** at some future time; eventually. [Old English] □ **soonish** *adv.*

■ **Usage** *No sooner* should be followed by *than* as shown above, and not by *when*.

soot ● *n.* a black substance rising in fine flakes in smoke, and deposited on the sides of a chimney etc. ● *v.tr.* cover with soot. [Old English]

sooth *n. archaic* truth, fact. □ **in sooth** really, truly. [Old English, originally as adj. in sense 'true']

soothe *v.tr.* **1** calm (a person or feelings). **2** soften or mitigate (pain). [Old English *sōthian* 'to verify'] □ **soother** *n.* **soothing** *adj.* **soothingly** *adv.*

soothsayer *n.* a diviner or seer. [Middle English, literally 'truth sayer']

sooty *adj.* (**sootier**, **sootiest**) **1** covered with or full of soot. **2** black or brownish black.

sop ● *n.* **1** a thing given or done to pacify or bribe. **2** a piece of bread etc. dipped in gravy etc. ● *v.* (**sopped**, **sopping**) **1** *intr.* (usu. as **sopping** *adj.*) be drenched (*came home sopping*; *sopping wet clothes*). **2** *tr.* (foll. by *up*) absorb (liquid) in a towel etc. **3** *tr.* wet thoroughly; soak. [Old English]

sophism *n.* a false argument, esp. one intended to deceive. [from Greek *sophisma* 'clever device']

sophist *n.* a person who reasons with clever but fallacious arguments. [from Greek *sophistēs*] □ **sophistic** *adj.* **sophistical** *adj.*

sophisticate ● *v.tr.* **1** make (a person etc.) educated, cultured, or refined. **2** make (equipment or techniques etc.) highly developed or complex. **3** deprive (a person or thing) of natural simplicity. ● *adj.* sophisticated. ● *n.* a sophisticated person. [based on medieval Latin *sophisticatus* 'tampered with'] □ **sophistication** *n.*

sophisticated *adj.* **1 a** (of a person) cultured and refined; discriminating in taste and judgement. **b** appealing to sophisticated people or sophisticated taste. **2** (of a thing, idea, etc.) highly developed and complex. □ **sophisticatedly** *adv.*

sophistry *n.* (*pl.* **-ies**) **1** the use of sophisms. **2** a sophism.

sophomore *n. N. Amer.* a second-year university or high school student. [based on *sophum*, obsolete variant of SOPHISM] □ **sophomoric** *adj.*

soporific ● *adj.* tending to produce sleep. ● *n.* a soporific drug or influence. [based on Latin *sopor* 'sleep'] □ **soporifically** *adv.*

sopping see SOP.

soppy *adj.* (**soppier**, **soppiest**) **1** *Brit. colloq.* **a** silly or foolish in a feeble or self-indulgent way. **b** mawkishly sentimental. **2** (foll. by *on*) *Brit. colloq.* foolishly infatuated with. **3** soaked with water. [based on SOP] □ **soppily** *adv.* **soppiness** *n.*

soprano ● *n.* (*pl.* **-os**) **1 a** the highest singing voice. **b** a female or boy singer with this voice. **c** a part written for it. **2** an instrument of a high or the highest pitch in its family. ● *adj.* highest in musical pitch. [Italian]

soprano recorder *n. N. Amer.* = DESCANT RECORDER.

S

sorbet /sor-bay/ n. **1** a water ice. **2** sherbet. [based on Arabic *šarba* 'to drink']

sorbitol n. a sweet-tasting crystalline alcohol found in some fruit, used in industry and as a food additive. [based on *sorb* 'service-tree']

sorcerer n. (fem. **sorceress**) a magician or wizard. [from Old French *sorcier*] □ **sorcerous** adj. **sorcery** n. (pl. **-ies**).

sordid adj. **1** dirty or squalid. **2** ignoble, mercenary. **3** mean or niggardly. [from Latin *sordidus*] □ **sordidly** adv. **sordidness** n.

sore ● adj. **1** (of a part of the body) painful (*has a sore arm*). **2** suffering pain. **3** aggrieved or vexed. **4** *archaic* grievous or severe (*in sore need*). ● n. **1** a raw or tender place on the body. **2** a source of distress or annoyance (*reopen old sores*). ● adv. *archaic* grievously, severely. [Old English] □ **soreness** n.

sorehead n. *N. Amer. colloq.* a touchy or disgruntled person.

sorely adv. **1** extremely, badly (*am sorely tempted; sorely in need of repair*). **2** severely (*am sorely vexed*).

sore point n. a subject causing distress or annoyance.

sore throat n. an inflammation of the lining membrane at the back of the mouth etc.

sorghum n. any tropical cereal grass of the genus *Sorghum*. [from Italian *sorgo*]

soroptimist n. a member of an international association of clubs for professional and business women. [based on Latin *soror* 'sister']

sorority n. (pl. **-ies**) *N. Amer.* a female students' society in a university or college. [from medieval Latin *sororitas*]

sorrel[1] n. any acid-leaved plant of the dock family, esp. *Rumex acetosa*, used in salads and for flavouring. [from Old French *sorele*]

sorrel[2] ● adj. of a light reddish-brown colour. ● n. **1** this colour. **2** ▼ a sorrel animal, esp. a horse. [from Old French *sorel*]

SORREL
HORSE

sorrow ● n. **1** mental distress caused by loss or disappointment etc. **2** a cause of sorrow. **3** lamentation. ● v.intr. **1** feel sorrow. **2** mourn. [Old English] □ **sorrowing** adj.

sorrowful adj. **1** feeling or showing sorrow. **2** distressing, lamentable. □ **sorrowfully** adv.

sorry adj. (**sorrier**, **sorriest**) **1** (*predic.*) pained or regretful or penitent (*were sorry for what they had done; am sorry that you have to go*). **2** (*predic.*; foll. by *for*) feeling pity or sympathy for. **3** as an expression of apology. **4** wretched (*a sorry sight*). □ **sorry for oneself** dejected. [Old English] □ **sorriness** n.

sort ● n. **1** a group of things etc. with common attributes; a class or kind. **2** (foll. by *of*) roughly of the kind specified (*is some sort of doctor*). **3** *colloq.* a person of a specified kind (*a good sort*). **4** *Printing* a letter or piece in a fount of type. **5** *Computing* the arrangement of data in a prescribed sequence. ● v.tr. **1** arrange systematically or according to type, class, etc. **2** = *sort out* 3, 4. □ **after a sort** after a fashion. **in some sort** to a certain extent. **of a sort** (or **of sorts**) *derog.* not fully deserving the name (*a holiday of sorts*). **out of sorts 1** slightly unwell. **2** in low spirits; irritable. **sort of** *colloq.* as it

were; to some extent (*I sort of expected it*). **a sort of** used to imply looseness, vagueness, exaggeration, etc., in the term used (*it's a sort of dull brick red*). **sort out 1** separate into sorts. **2** select from a miscellaneous group. **3** disentangle or put into order. **4** resolve (a problem or difficulty). **5** *colloq.* deal with or reprimand. [from Latin *sors sortis* 'lot, condition'] □ **sorter** n. **sorting** n.

■ **Usage** See Usage Note at KIND[1].

sorted adj. *Brit. colloq.* **1** fixed up, arranged, provided for. **2** (of a person) confident, at ease.

sortie /sor-ti/ ● n. **1** a sally, esp. from a besieged garrison. **2** an operational flight by a single military aircraft. ● v.intr. (**sorties**, **sortied**, **sortieing**) make a sortie. [French]

sorting office n. an office in which mail is sorted according to its destination.

sort-out n. an act of sorting out or putting something in order.

SOS n. (pl. **SOSs**) **1** an international code-signal of extreme distress. **2** an urgent appeal for help. **3** *Brit.* a message broadcast to an untraceable person in an emergency. [chosen as easily transmitted in Morse code; popularly supposed to be an abbreviation of *save our souls*]

sostenuto /sos-tĕ-**noo**-toh/ *Mus.* ● adv. & adj. in a sustained or prolonged manner. ● n. (pl. **-os**) a passage to be played in this way. [Italian]

sot n. a habitual drunkard. [from medieval Latin *sottus*] □ **sottish** adj.

sotto voce /sot-oh **voh**-chi/ adv. in an undertone or aside. [Italian]

sou /soo/ n. **1** *hist.* a former French coin of low value. **2** (usu. with *neg.*) *colloq.* a very small amount of money. [French]

soubrette /soo-**bret**/ n. a pert maidservant or similar female character in a comedy. [from Provençal *soubreto* 'coy (female)']

soubriquet var. of SOBRIQUET.

souffle /soo-fĕl/ n. *Med.* a low murmur heard in the auscultation of various organs etc. [French, from *souffler* 'to blow']

soufflé /soo-flay/ ● n. a light spongy sweet or savoury dish usu. made with flavoured egg yolks added to stiffly beaten whites of eggs and baked (*cheese soufflé*). ● adj. (placed after noun) light and frothy or spongy (*omelette soufflé*). [French, literally 'blown']

sough /rhymes with either cow or cuff/ ● v.intr. make a moaning, whistling, or rushing sound, as of the wind in trees etc. ● n. this sound. [Old English *swōgan* 'to resound']

sought past and past part. of SEEK.

sought after adj. (hyphenated when *attrib.*) much in demand; generally desired or courted.

souk /sook/ n. (also **suk**, **sukh**, **suq**) an Arab market or market place; a bazaar. [from Arabic *sūk*]

soul n. **1** the spiritual or immaterial part of a human being or animal, often regarded as immortal. **2** the moral, emotional, or intellectual nature of a person. **3** the personification or pattern of something (*the very soul of discretion*). **4** a person, an individual (*not a soul in sight; the poor soul was confused*). **5** a person regarded as the animating or essential part of something (*the life and soul of the party*). **6** emotional or intellectual energy or intensity, esp. as revealed in a work of art (*pictures that lack soul*). **7** = SOUL MUSIC. □ **upon my soul** an exclamation of surprise. [Old English] □ **-souled** adj. (in *comb.*).

soul-destroying adj. (of an activity etc.) deadeningly monotonous.

soul food n. the traditional food of American blacks.

soulful adj. **1** having or expressing or evoking deep feeling. **2** *colloq.* over-emotional. □ **soulfully** adv. **soulfulness** n.

soulless adj. **1** lacking sensitivity or noble qualities. **2** undistinguished or uninteresting. □ **soullessly** adv. **soullessness** n.

soulmate n. a person ideally suited to another.

soul music n. a kind of music incorporating elements of rhythm and blues and gospel music, popularized by American blacks.

soul-searching ● n. the examination of one's emotions and motives. ● adj. characterized by such examination.

sound[1] ● n. **1** a sensation caused in the ear by the vibration of the surrounding air or other medium. **2** vibrations causing this sensation. **3** what is or may be heard. **4** an idea or impression conveyed by words (*don't like the sound of that*). **5** mere words. **6** (in full **musical sound**) sound produced by continuous and regular vibrations (cf. NOISE n. 3). **7** any of a series of articulate utterances (*vowel and consonant sounds*). **8** music, speech, etc., accompanying a film or other visual presentation. **9** (often *attrib.*) broadcasting by radio as distinct from television. ● v. **1** *intr. & tr.* emit or cause to emit sound. **2** *tr.* utter or pronounce (*sound a note of alarm*). **3** *intr.* convey an impression when heard (*you sound worried*). **4** *tr.* give an audible signal for (an alarm etc.). **5** *tr.* test (the lungs etc.) by noting the sound produced. **6** *tr.* cause to resound; make known (*sound their praises*). □ **sound off** talk loudly or express one's opinions forcefully. [from Latin *sonus*] □ **soundless** adj. **soundlessly** adv. **soundlessness** n.

sound[2] ● adj. **1** healthy; not diseased or injured. **2** (of an opinion or policy etc.) correct, orthodox, well-founded, judicious. **3** financially secure (*a sound investment*). **4** undisturbed; tending to sleep deeply and unbrokenly (*sound sleep; a sound sleeper*). ● adv. soundly (*sound asleep*). [Middle English] □ **soundly** adv. **soundness** n.

sound[3] v.tr. **1** test the depth or quality of the bottom of (the sea or a river etc.). **2** (often foll. by *out*) inquire (esp. cautiously or discreetly) into the opinions or feelings of (a person). [from Old French *sonder*] □ **sounder** n.

sound[4] n. **1** a strait. **2** a sea inlet. [Old English]

sound barrier n. the high resistance of air to aircraft etc. moving at speeds near that of sound.

sound bite n. a short extract from a recorded interview, chosen for its pungency or appropriateness.

soundcheck n. a test of sound equipment before a musical performance or recording to check that the desired sound is being produced.

sound effect n. a sound other than speech or music made artificially for use in a play, film, etc.

sounding[1] n. **1 a** the action or process of measuring the depth of water, now usu. by means of echo. **b** an instance of this (*took a sounding*). **2** (in *pl.*) cautious investigation (*made soundings as to his suitability*).

sounding[2] adj. giving forth (esp. loud or resonant) sound (*sounding brass*).

sounding board n. **1** a canopy over a pulpit etc. to direct sound towards the congregation. **2** a means of causing opinions etc. to be more widely known (*used his students as a sounding board*).

soundproof ● adj. impervious to sound. ● v.tr. make soundproof.

soundtrack n. **1** the recorded sound element of a film. **2** this recorded on the edge of a film in optical or magnetic form.

sound wave n. a wave of compression and rarefaction, by which sound is propagated in an elastic medium, e.g. air. ▷ DOPPLER EFFECT

soup ● n. a usu. savoury liquid dish made by boiling meat, fish, or vegetables etc. in stock or water. ● v.tr. (foll. by *up*) (usu. as **souped-up** adj.) *colloq.* **1** increase the power and efficiency of (an engine). **2** increase the power or impact of (writing, music, etc.). □ **in the soup** *colloq.* in difficulties. [from (Old) French *soupe* 'sop, broth']

soupçon /soop-son/ n. a very small quantity; a dash. [French, from medieval Latin *suspectio* 'suspicion']

soup kitchen n. a place dispensing soup etc. to the poor.

S

soupy *adj.* (**soupier, soupiest**) **1** resembling soup. **2** *colloq.* sentimental; mawkish. □ **soupily** *adv.* **soupiness** *n.*

sour ● *adj.* **1** having an acid taste like lemon or vinegar, esp. because of unripeness (*sour apples*). **2 a** (of food, esp. milk or bread) bad because of fermentation. **b** smelling or tasting rancid or unpleasant. **3** (of a person, temper, etc.) harsh; morose; bitter. **4** (of a thing) unpleasant; distasteful. ● *n.* *N. Amer.* an alcoholic drink with lemon juice or lime juice (*whisky sour*). ● *v.tr. & intr.* make or become sour. □ **go** (or **turn**) **sour 1** (of food etc.) become sour. **2** turn out badly (*the job went sour on him*). **3** lose one's keenness. [Old English] □ **sourish** *adj.* **sourly** *adv.* **sourness** *n.*

source ● *n.* **1** a spring or fountain from which a stream issues. **2** a place, person, or thing from which something originates (*the source of all our troubles*). **3** a person or document etc. providing evidence (*reliable sources of information*). **4** a body emitting radiation etc. ● *v.tr.* obtain (esp. components) from a specified source. □ **at source** at the point of origin or issue. [from Old French *sourse*]

sour cream *n.* cream deliberately fermented by adding bacteria.

sourdough *n. N. Amer.* **1** a leaven for making bread etc., consisting of fermenting dough, originally that left over from a previous baking. **2** bread made from this. [Middle English, now dialect]

sour grapes *n.pl.* resentful disparagement of something one cannot personally acquire.

sourpuss *n. colloq.* a sour-tempered person.

sousaphone /soo-ză-fohn/ *n.* ▼ a large brass bass wind instrument encircling the player's body. ▷ BRASS. [named after J. P. *Sousa*, American bandmaster, 1854–1932] □ **sousaphonist** *n.*

souse ● *v.* **1** *tr.* put (gherkins, fish, etc.) in pickle. **2** *tr. & intr.* plunge into liquid. **3** *tr.* (as **soused** *adj.*) *colloq.* drunk. ● *n.* **1 a** pickle made with salt. **b** *US* food, esp. a pig's head etc., in pickle. **2** a dip, plunge, or drenching in water. **3** *colloq.* **a** a drinking bout. **b** a drunkard. [from Old French *sous* 'pickle']

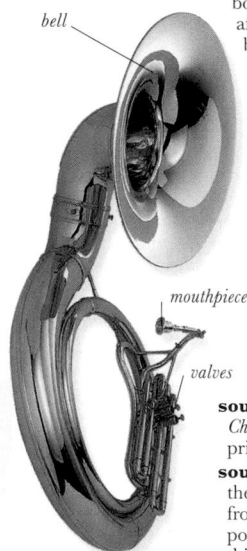

SOUSAPHONE

bell

mouthpiece

valves

soutane /soo-**tahn**/ *n. RC Ch.* a cassock worn by a priest. [from Italian *sottana*]

south ● *n.* **1** the point of the horizon 90° clockwise from east. **2** the compass point corresponding to this. ▷ COMPASS. **3** the direction in which this lies. **4** (usu. **the South**) **a** the part of the world or a country or a town lying to the south. **b** the southern states of the US. **5** *Bridge* a player occupying the position designated 'south'. ● *adj.* **1** towards, at, near, or facing the south (*a south wall; south country*). **b** coming from the south (*south wind*). ● *adv.* **1** towards, at, or near the south (*they travelled south*). **2** (foll. by *of*) further south than. □ **to the south** (often foll. by *of*) in a southerly direction. [Old English]

South African ● *adj.* of or relating to the Republic of South Africa. ● *n.* **1** a native or national of South Africa. **2** a person of South African descent.

South American ● *adj.* of or relating to South America. ● *n.* a native or citizen of South America.

southbound *adj.* travelling or leading southwards.

South-East *n.* the part of a country or town lying to the south-east.

south-east ● *n.* **1** the point of the horizon midway between south and east. **2** the compass point

corresponding to this. **3** the direction in which this lies. ● *adj.* of, towards, or coming from the south-east. ● *adv.* towards, at, or near the south-east.

southeaster *n.* a south-east wind.

south-easterly *adj. & adv.* = SOUTH-EAST.

south-eastern *adj.* lying on the south-east side.

south-eastward *adj. & adv.* (also **south-eastwards**) towards the south-east.

southerly ● *adj. & adv.* **1** in a southern position or direction. **2** (of a wind) blowing from the south. ● *n.* (*pl.* **-ies**) a southerly wind.

southern *adj.* of, in, or towards, the south. [Old English] □ **southernmost** *adj.*

Southern Cross *n.* a small but prominent constellation of the southern hemisphere, in the shape of a cross.

southerner *n.* a native or inhabitant of the south.

southern hemisphere *n.* the half of the earth below the equator.

southern lights *n.pl.* the aurora australis.

Southern Ocean *n.* the expanse of ocean surrounding Antarctica. ▷ OCEAN

Southern States *n.pl.* the states in the south, esp. the south-east, of the US.

southpaw *colloq.* ● *n.* a left-handed person, esp. in boxing. ● *adj.* left-handed.

South Pole see POLE[2] 1.

South Sea *n.* the southern Pacific Ocean.

south-south-east *n.* the point or direction midway between south and south-east.

south-south-west *n.* the point or direction midway between south and south-west.

southward ● *adj. & adv.* (also **southwards**) towards the south. ● *n.* a southward direction or region.

■ **Usage** In nautical use *southward* is often pronounced /**su**th-ĕd/.

South-West *n.* the part of a country or town lying to the south-west.

south-west ● *n.* **1** the point of the horizon midway between south and west. **2** the compass point corresponding to this. **3** the direction in which this lies. ● *adj.* of, towards, or coming from the south-west. ● *adv.* towards, at, or near the south-west.

southwester *n.* a south-west wind.

south-westerly *adj. & adv.* = SOUTH-WEST.

south-western *adj.* lying on the south-west side.

south-westward *adj. & adv.* (also **south-westwards**) towards the south west.

south wind *n.* a wind blowing from the south.

souvenir *n.* (often foll. by *of*) a memento of an occasion, place, etc. [French]

sou'wester *n.* **1** = SOUTHWESTER. **2** a waterproof hat with a broad flap covering the neck.

sovereign ● *n.* **1** a supreme ruler, esp. a monarch. **2** *Brit. hist.* a gold coin nominally worth £1. ● *adj.* **1 a** supreme (*sovereign power*). **b** unmitigated (*sovereign contempt*). **2** excellent; effective (*a sovereign remedy*). **3** possessing sovereign power (*a sovereign state*). **4** royal (*our sovereign lord*). [from Old French *so(u)verain*] □ **sovereignly** *adv.*

sovereign pontiff see PONTIFF.

sovereignty *n.* (*pl.* **-ies**) **1** supremacy. **2** self-government. **3** a self-governing state.

soviet *hist.* ● *n.* **1** an elected local, district, or national council in the former USSR. **2** (**Soviet**) a citizen of the former USSR. **3** *hist.* a revolutionary council of workers, peasants, etc., in Russia before 1917. ● *adj.* (usu. **Soviet**) of or concerning the former Soviet Union. [from Russian *sovet* 'council'] □ **Sovietize** *v.tr.* (also **-ise**). **Sovietization** *n.*

sow[1] /soh/ *v.tr.* (*past* **sowed**; *past part.* **sown** or **sowed**) **1** (also *absol.*) **a** scatter or put (seed) on or in the earth. **b** (often foll. by *with*) plant (a field etc.) with seed. **2** initiate; arouse (*sowed doubt in her mind*). **3** (foll. by *with*) cover thickly with. □ **sow the seed**

(or **seeds**) **of** first give rise to; implant (an idea etc.). [Old English] □ **sower** *n.* **sowing** *n.*

sow[2] /rhymes with cow/ *n.* **1** a female adult pig, esp. after farrowing. **2** a female guinea pig. **3** the female of some other species. [Old English]

sown *past part.* of SOW[1].

sox *Commerce pl.* of SOCK[1].

soy *n.* **1** (also **soy sauce**) a sauce made in Japan and China with fermented soya beans. **2** = SOYA 1. [from Chinese *shi-you*, from *shi* 'salted beans' + *you* 'oil']

soya *n.* **1 a** a leguminous plant, *Glycine max*, originally of SE Asia, cultivated for its seeds. **b** (in full **soya bean**) ◀ the seed of this, used as a replacement for animal protein in certain foods, and as flour, oil, tofu, soy sauce, etc. **2** (in full **soya sauce**) = SOY 1. [from Malay *soi*]

soybean *n.* = SOYA 1.

sozzled *adj. colloq.* very drunk. [from dialect *sozzle* 'to mix sloppily']

spa *n.* **1** a curative mineral spring. **2** a place or resort with this. [from *Spa*, a town and resort in Belgium]

space ● *n.* **1 a** a continuous unlimited area or expanse which may or may not contain objects etc. **b** an interval between one, two, or three-dimensional points or objects (*a space of 10 metres*). **c** an empty area; room (*clear a space in the corner*). **d** any of a limited number of places for a person or thing (*no spaces left at the table*). **2** a large unoccupied region (*the wide open spaces*). **3 a** (also **outer space**) the physical universe beyond the earth's atmosphere. **b** the near-vacuum extending between the planets and stars, containing small amounts of gas and dust. **4** an interval of time (*in the space of an hour*). **5** the amount of paper used in writing etc. (*hadn't the space to discuss it*). **6 a** a blank between printed, typed, or written words, etc. **b** *Printing* a piece of metal providing this. **7** *Mus.* each of the blanks between the lines of a staff. **8** freedom to think, be oneself, etc. (*need my own space*). ● *v.tr.* **1** set or arrange at intervals. **2** put spaces between (esp. words, letters, lines, etc. in printing, typing, or writing). **3** (as **spaced** *adj.*) (often foll. by *out*) *slang* in a state of euphoria or disorientation, esp. from taking drugs. □ **space out** spread out with more or wider spaces or intervals between. [from Latin *spatium*] □ **spacer** *n.* **spacing** *n.* (esp. in sense 2 of *v.*).

space age ● *n.* the era when space travel has become possible. ● *attrib.adj.* (**space-age**) very modern.

space bar *n.* a long key on a typewriter or computer keyboard for making a space between words etc.

space blanket *n.* a light metal-coated sheet designed to retain heat.

space capsule *n.* a small spacecraft.

spacecraft *n.* ▶ a vehicle used for travelling in space.

space flight *n.* **1** a journey through space. **2** = SPACE TRAVEL.

Space Invaders *n. propr.* a computer game in which a player shoots at alien spaceships.

space junk *n.* debris from space missions, usu. comprising damaged or ejected material from spacecraft.

spaceman *n.* (*pl.* **-men**; *fem.* **spacewoman**, *pl.* **-women**) a person who travels in space.

space probe *n.* see PROBE *n.* 4.

space rocket *n.* a rocket travelling through space, or used to launch a spacecraft.

space-saving *adj.* **1** occupying little space. **2** that saves space.

spaceship *n.* a spacecraft, esp. one controlled by its crew.

space shuttle *n.* a rocket for repeated use, esp. between the earth and a space station. ▷ SPACECRAFT

space station *n.* an artificial satellite used as a base for operations in space.

black soya beans

yellow soya beans

SOYA BEANS
(*Glycine max*)

SPACECRAFT

Spacecraft have been used to collect data from around the solar system since 1959. Some craft, such as Giotto, fly by their target and record information as they pass. Others, such as Galileo, go into orbit around a planet. Sometimes a spacecraft may send a 'lander' to a planet in order to obtain detailed information. In 1969, Apollo 11 became the first crewed spacecraft to land on the Moon. The first reusable spacecraft, the space shuttle, was launched 12 years later. Spacecraft employ a variety of specialized components, including thrusters, which make directional corrections, and solar panels, which convert sunlight into electricity used to power on-board systems.

MAIN TYPES OF SPACECRAFT

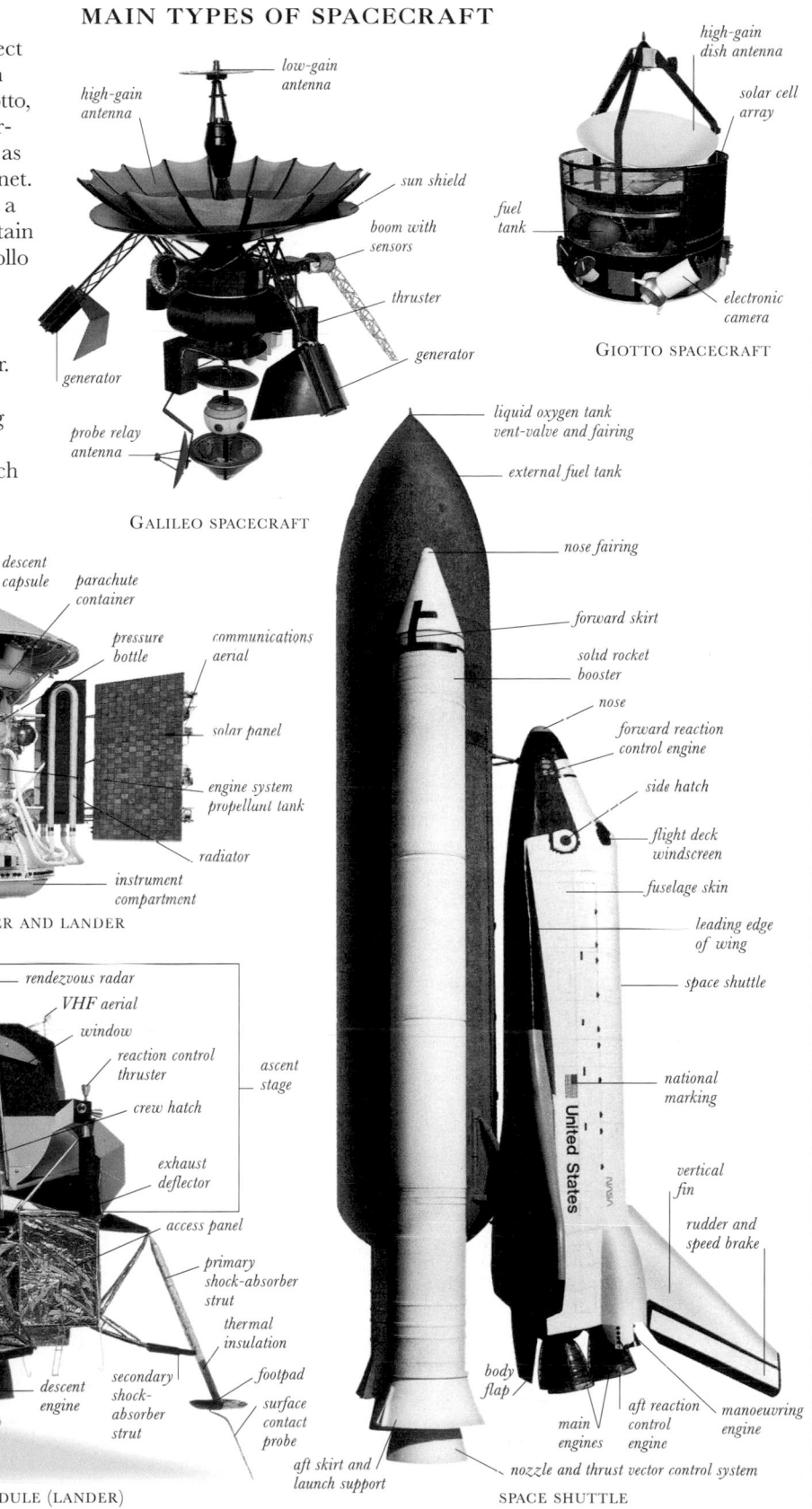

low-gain antenna
high-gain antenna
sun shield
boom with sensors
thruster
generator
generator
probe relay antenna

GALILEO SPACECRAFT

high-gain dish antenna
solar cell array
fuel tank
electronic camera

GIOTTO SPACECRAFT

research apparatus aerial
heat shield
descent capsule
parachute container
pressure bottle
communications aerial
high-gain parabolic aerial
low-gain aerial
solar panel
magnetometer
engine system propellant tank
automatic navigation system
radiator
astro-orientation sensor
instrument compartment

MARS 3 ORBITER AND LANDER

window
upper hatch
steerable aerial
rendezvous radar
VHF aerial
window
tracking light
reaction control thruster
reaction control thruster
crew hatch
ascent stage
entrance/exit platform
exhaust deflector
descent stage
access panel
primary shock-absorber strut
thermal insulation
thermal insulation
footpad
ladder
descent engine
secondary shock-absorber strut
surface contact probe
forward landing leg

APOLLO 16 LUNAR MODULE (LANDER)

liquid oxygen tank vent-valve and fairing
external fuel tank
nose fairing
forward skirt
solid rocket booster
nose
forward reaction control engine
side hatch
flight deck windscreen
fuselage skin
leading edge of wing
space shuttle
national marking
United States
vertical fin
rudder and speed brake
body flap
main engines
aft reaction control engine
manoeuvring engine
aft skirt and launch support
nozzle and thrust vector control system

SPACE SHUTTLE

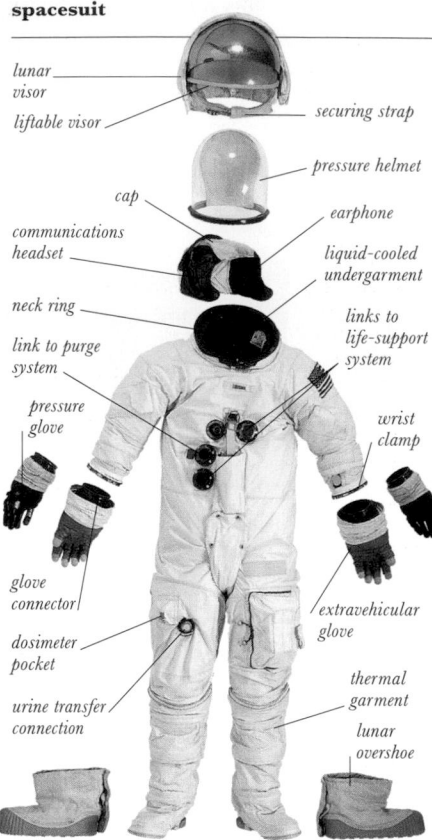

lunar visor
liftable visor
securing strap
pressure helmet
cap
earphone
communications headset
liquid-cooled undergarment
neck ring
links to life-support system
link to purge system
pressure glove
wrist clamp
glove connector
extravehicular glove
dosimeter pocket
thermal garment
urine transfer connection
lunar overshoe

SPACESUIT WORN ON APOLLO 9 MISSION

spacesuit *n.* ▲ a garment designed to allow an astronaut to survive in space.

space-time *n.* (also **space-time continuum**) the fusion of the concepts of space and time, esp. as a four-dimensional continuum.

space travel *n.* travel through outer space. □ **space traveller** *n.*

space walk *n.* any physical activity by an astronaut in space outside a spacecraft.

spacewoman see SPACEMAN.

spacial var. of SPATIAL.

spacious *adj.* having ample space; covering a large area; roomy. [from Latin *spatiosus*] □ **spaciously** *adv.* **spaciousness** *n.*

spade[1] ● *n.* **1** a tool used for digging or cutting the ground etc., with a sharp-edged metal blade and a long handle. **2** a tool of a similar shape for any of various purposes. ● *v.tr.* dig over (ground) with a spade. □ **call a spade a spade** speak plainly or bluntly. [Old English] □ **spadeful** *n.* (*pl.* **-fuls**).

spade[2] *n.* **1 a** a playing card of a suit denoted by black inverted heart-shaped figures with small stalks. **b** (in *pl.*) this suit. **2** *slang offens.* a black person. □ **in spades** *slang* to a high degree, with great force. [from Greek *spathē* 'sword, wooden blade']

spadework *n.* hard or routine preparatory work.

spaghetti *n.* pasta made in solid strings, between macaroni and vermicelli in thickness. ▷ PASTA. [Italian, literally 'little strings']

spaghetti Bolognese *n.* spaghetti served with a sauce of minced beef, tomato, onion, etc. [Italian; *Bolognese*: literally 'of Bologna']

spaghetti junction *n. Brit. colloq.* a multi-level road junction, esp. on a motorway.

spaghetti western *n. colloq.* a western film made by Italians, esp. cheaply.

spam *n. propr.* a tinned meat product made mainly from ham. [from *sp*iced h*am*]

span[1] ● *n.* **1** the full extent from end to end in space

or time (*the span of a bridge*; *the whole span of history*). **2** each arch or part of a bridge between piers or supports. ▷ ARCH. **3** the maximum lateral extent of an aeroplane, its wings, a bird's wings, etc. **4 a** the maximum distance between the tips of the thumb and little finger. **b** this as a measurement, equal to 9 inches. ● *v.tr.* (**spanned**, **spanning**) **1 a** (of a bridge, arch, etc.) stretch from side to side of; extend across (*the bridge spanned the river*). **b** (of a builder etc.) bridge (a river etc.). **2** extend across (space or a period of time etc.). [Old English]

span[2] see SPICK AND SPAN.

span[3] *past of* SPIN.

spangle ● *n.* a small thin piece of glittering material, esp. used in quantity to ornament a dress etc.; a sequin. ● *v.tr.* (esp. as **spangled** *adj.*) cover with or as with spangles (*star-spangled*; *spangled costume*). [from Old Norse *spöng* 'brooch'] □ **spangly** *adj.*

Spaniard *n.* **1 a** a native or national of Spain in southern Europe. **b** a person of Spanish descent. **2** *NZ* a spear grass. [from Old French *Espaignart*]

spaniel *n.* **1** a dog of any of various breeds with a long silky coat and drooping ears. **2** an obsequious or fawning person. [from Old French *espaigneul* 'Spanish (dog)']

Spanish ● *adj.* of or relating to Spain, its people, or its language. ● *n.* **1** the language of Spain and Spanish America. **2** (prec. by *the*; treated as *pl.*) the people of Spain. [Middle English]

Spanish fly *n.* **1** a bright green beetle, *Lytta vesicatoria*. **2** a toxic preparation of the dried bodies of these beetles, formerly used to raise blisters, and supposedly aphrodisiac.

Spanish guitar *n.* the standard six-stringed acoustic guitar, used esp. for classical and folk music.

Spanish Main *n. hist.* the NE coast of South America between the Orinoco river and Panama, and adjoining parts of the Caribbean Sea.

Spanish omelette *n.* an omelette containing chopped vegetables in the mix.

Spanish onion *n.* a large mild-flavoured onion.

spank ● *v.* **1** *tr.* slap esp. on the buttocks. **2** *intr.* (of a horse etc.) move briskly, esp. between a trot and a gallop. ● *n.* a slap esp. on the buttocks.

spanker *n.* **1** a person or thing that spanks. **2** *Naut.* a fore-and-aft sail set on the after side of the mizzen-mast. ▷ SHIP

spanking ● *adj.* **1** (esp. of a horse's pace) brisk. **2** *colloq.* striking; excellent. ● *adv. colloq.* very, exceedingly (*spanking clean*). ● *n.* the act or an instance of slapping, esp. on the buttocks as a punishment for children.

spanner *n.* esp. *Brit.* a tool for turning or gripping a nut on a screw etc. (cf. WRENCH *n.* 2). □ **spanner in the works** *Brit.* a drawback or impediment. [based on German *spannen* 'to draw tight']

spar[1] *n.* **1** a stout pole esp. used for the mast, yard, etc., of a ship. **2** the main longitudinal beam of an aeroplane wing. [from Old Norse]

spar[2] ● *v.intr.* (**sparred**, **sparring**) **1** (often foll. by *at*) make the motions of boxing without landing heavy blows. **2** engage in argument. ● *n.* **1** a sparring motion. **2** a boxing match. [Old English]

spar[3] *n.* any crystalline, easily cleavable, and non-lustrous mineral, e.g. calcite or fluorspar. [Middle Low German] □ **sparry** *adj.*

spare ● *adj.* **1 a** not required for ordinary use; extra (*have no spare cash*). **b** reserved for emergency or occasional use (*slept in the spare room*). **c** *colloq.* not wanted or used by others (*a spare seat in the front row*). **2** lean; thin. **3** scanty; frugal; not copious (*a spare diet*; *a spare prose style*). ● *n.* a spare part; a duplicate. ● *v.tr.* **1** afford to give or do

without; dispense with (*cannot spare him just now*). **2 a** abstain from killing, hurting, wounding, etc. (*spared his feelings*; *spared her life*). **b** abstain from inflicting or causing; relieve from (*spare me this talk*; *spare my blushes*). **3** be frugal or grudging of (*no expense spared*). □ **go spare** *Brit. colloq.* **1** become extremely angry or distraught. **2** be unwanted by others. **not spare oneself** exert one's utmost efforts. **to spare** left over; additional (*an hour to spare*). [Old English] □ **sparely** *adv.* **spareness** *n.*

spare part *n.* a duplicate part to replace a lost or damaged part of a machine etc.

spare rib *n.* (usu. in *pl.*) closely trimmed ribs of esp. pork.

spare time ● *n.* time which is not taken up by one's usual activities; leisure time. ● *attrib.adj.* (**spare-time**) relating to such time (*spare-time activity*).

spare tyre *n.* **1** an extra tyre carried in a motor vehicle for emergencies. **2** *colloq.* a roll of fat round the waist.

sparing *adj.* **1** inclined to save; economical. **2** restrained; limited. □ **sparingly** *adv.*

spark ● *n.* **1** a fiery particle thrown off from a fire, or alight in ashes, or produced by a flint, match, etc. **2** (often foll. by *of*) a particle of a quality etc. (*not a spark of life*; *a spark of interest*). **3** *Electr.* **a** a light produced by a sudden disruptive discharge through the air etc. **b** such a discharge serving to ignite the explosive mixture in an internal-combustion engine. **4 a** a flash of wit etc. **b** anything causing interest, excitement, etc. ● *v.* **1** *intr.* emit sparks of fire or electricity. **2** *tr.* (often foll. by *off*) stir into activity; initiate (a process) suddenly. **3** *intr. Electr.* produce sparks at the point where a circuit is interrupted. [Old English] □ **sparkless** *adj.* **sparky** *adj.*

sparking plug *n. Brit.* = SPARK PLUG.

sparkle ● *v.intr.* **1 a** emit or seem to emit sparks; glitter; glisten (*her eyes sparkled*). **b** be witty; scintillate (*sparkling repartee*). **2** (usu. as **sparkling** *adj.*) (of wine etc.) effervesce (cf. STILL[1] *adj.* 4). ● *n.* a gleam, spark. [Middle English] □ **sparklingly** *adv.* **sparkly** *adj.*

sparkler *n.* **1** a person or thing that sparkles. **2** a hand-held sparkling firework. **3** *colloq.* a diamond or other gem.

spark plug *n.* (also **sparking plug**) ▶ a device for firing the explosive mixture in an internal-combustion engine. ▷ INTERNAL-COMBUSTION ENGINE

high-tension connector
porcelain insulator
metal body
spark gap

SPARK PLUG

sparling *n.* a European smelt, *Osmerus eperlanus*. [from Old French *esperlinge*]

sparring partner *n.* **1** a boxer employed to engage in sparring with another as training. **2** a person with whom one enjoys arguing.

sparrow *n.* **1** any small finchlike Old World bird of the family Ploceidae, with brown and grey plumage, esp. (in full **house sparrow**) *Passer domesticus*. **2** a bird resembling this in size or colour, esp. a New World bird of the bunting family (*song sparrow*). [Old English]

sparrowhawk *n.* ◀ a small hawk, *Accipiter nisus*, preying on small birds.

SPARROWHAWK WITH PREY (*Accipiter nisus*)

sparse *adj.* thinly dispersed or scattered; not dense (*sparse population*; *sparse greying hair*). [from Latin *sparsus* 'scattered'] □ **sparsely** *adv.* **sparseness** *n.* **sparsity** *n.*

S

Spartan ● *adj.* **1** of or relating to Sparta in ancient Greece. **2 a** courageous, hardy, frugal. **b** (of a regime, conditions, etc.) lacking comfort; austere. ● *n.* a citizen of Sparta. [from Latin *Spartanus*]

spasm *n.* **1** a sudden involuntary muscular contraction. **2** a sudden convulsive movement or emotion etc. **3** (usu. foll. by *of*) *colloq.* a brief spell of an activity. [based on Greek *span* 'to draw, pull']

spasmodic *adj.* **1** of, caused by, or subject to, a spasm or spasms (*a spasmodic jerk*; *spasmodic asthma*). **2** occurring or done by fits and starts (*spasmodic efforts*). [from Greek *spasmōdēs*] □ **spasmodically** *adv.*

spastic ● *adj.* **1** often *offens.* suffering from cerebral palsy. **2** *slang offens.* weak, feeble, incompetent. **3** spasmodic. ● *n.* **1** often *offens.* a person suffering from cerebral palsy. **2** *slang offens.* a stupid or incompetent person. [from Greek *spastikos* 'pulling'] □ **spasticity** *n.*

■ **Usage** The use of the word *spastic* in the medical sense may be considered offensive as a result of its use as an offensive slang term. To avoid offence, the term *cerebral palsy* can be used, e.g. *She suffers from cerebral palsy* rather than *She is a spastic*.

spat[1] *past* and *past part.* of SPIT[1].

spat[2] *n.* (usu. in *pl.*) *hist.* a short gaiter reaching from over the instep to just above the ankle. [abbreviation of *spatterdash* 'a long gaiter']

spat[3] orig. *US* esp. *dial,* & *colloq.* ● *n.* a petty quarrel. ● *v.intr.* (**spatted, spatting**) quarrel pettily.

spat[4] ● *n.* the spawn of shellfish, esp. the oyster. ● *v.* (**spatted, spatting**) **1** *intr.* (of an oyster) spawn. **2** *tr.* shed (spawn). [from Anglo-French]

spatchcock ● *n.* a chicken or esp. game bird split open and grilled. ● *v.tr.* treat (poultry) in this way. [originally in Irish use]

spate *n.* **1** *Brit.* a river flood (*the river is in spate*). **2** a large or excessive amount. [Middle English, Scots & northern English]

spathe *n. Bot.* ► a large bract or pair of bracts enveloping a flower cluster. [from Greek *spathē* 'broad blade']

spatial *adj.* (also **spacial**) of or concerning space (*spatial extent*). [based on Latin *spatium* 'space'] □ **spatiality** *n.* **spatialize** *v.tr.* (also **-ise**). **spatially** *adv.*

spatio-temporal *adj. Physics* & *Philos.* belonging to both space and time or to space-time. □ **spatio-temporally** *adv.*

spatter ● *v.* **1** *tr.* **a** (often foll. by *with*) splash (a person etc.) (*spattered him with mud*). **b** scatter or splash (liquid, mud, etc.) here and there. **2** *intr.* (of rain etc.) fall here and there (*glass spattered down*). ● *n.* **1** (usu. foll. by *of*) a splash (*a spatter of mud*). **2** a quick pattering sound. [from Dutch *spatten* 'to burst, spout']

spatula *n.* a tool or implement with a broad, blunt, often flexible blade, used for spreading, scraping, mixing (paints), etc. ▷ UTENSIL. [Latin, literally 'little blade']

spavin *n.* a disease of a horse's hock with a hard bony swelling or excrescence. [from Old French *espavin*] □ **spavined** *adj.*

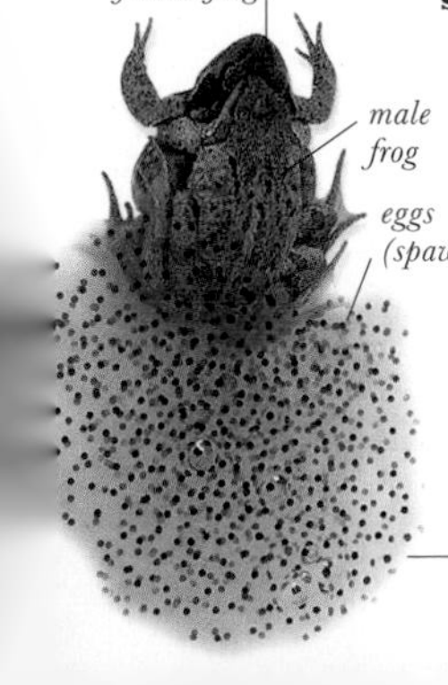

SPAWN: COMMON FROG SPAWNING

spawn ● *v.* **1 a** *tr.* (also *absol.*) ◄ (of a fish, frog, mollusc, or crustacean) release or deposit (eggs). **b** *intr.* be produced as eggs or young. **2** *tr. derog.* (of people) produce (offspring). **3** *tr.* produce or generate, esp. in large numbers. ● *n.* **1** ◄ the eggs of fish, frogs, etc. **2** the mycelium of a fungus, esp. of a cultivated mushroom. [from Old French *espandre* 'to expand'] □ **spawner** *n.*

spay *v.tr.* sterilize (a female animal) by removing the ovaries. [from Old French *espeer* 'to cut with a sword']

speak *v.* (*past* **spoke**; *past part.* **spoken**) **1** *intr.* make articulate verbal utterances in an ordinary (not singing) voice. **2** *tr.* **a** utter (words). **b** make known or communicate (one's opinion, the truth, etc.) in this way. **3** *intr.* **a** (foll. by *to*, *with*) hold a conversation. **b** (foll. by *of*) mention in writing etc. **c** (foll. by *for*) articulate the feelings of (another person etc.) in speech or writing (*speaks for our generation*). **4** *intr.* (foll. by *to*) **a** address (a person etc.). **b** speak in confirmation of or with reference to (*spoke to the resolution*; *can speak to his innocence*). **c** *colloq.* reprove (*spoke to them about their lateness*). **5** *intr.* make a speech before an audience etc. **6** *tr.* use or be able to use (a specified language) (*cannot speak French*). □ **not** (or **nothing**) **to speak of** not (or nothing) worth mentioning; practically not (or nothing). **speak for itself** need no supporting evidence. **speak for oneself 1** give one's own opinions. **2** not presume to speak for others. **speak one's mind** speak bluntly or frankly. **speak out** speak loudly or freely; give one's opinion. **speak up** = *speak out*. **speak volumes** (of a fact etc.) be very significant. [Old English] □ **speakable** *adj.*

speakeasy *n.* (*pl.* **-ies**) *US hist. slang* an illicit liquor shop or drinking club during Prohibition.

speaker *n.* **1** a person who speaks, esp. in public. **2** a person who speaks a specified language (esp. in *comb.*: *a French-speaker*). **3** (**Speaker**) the presiding officer in a legislative assembly. **4** = LOUDSPEAKER. □ **speakership** *n.*

speaking ● *n.* the act or an instance of uttering words etc. ● *adj.* **1** that speaks; capable of articulate speech. **2** (of a portrait) lifelike; true to its subject (*a speaking likeness*). **3** (in *comb.*) speaking a specified foreign language (*French-speaking*). **4** with a reference or from a point of view specified (*roughly speaking*; *professionally speaking*). □ **on speaking terms** (foll. by *with*) **1** slightly acquainted. **2** on friendly terms.

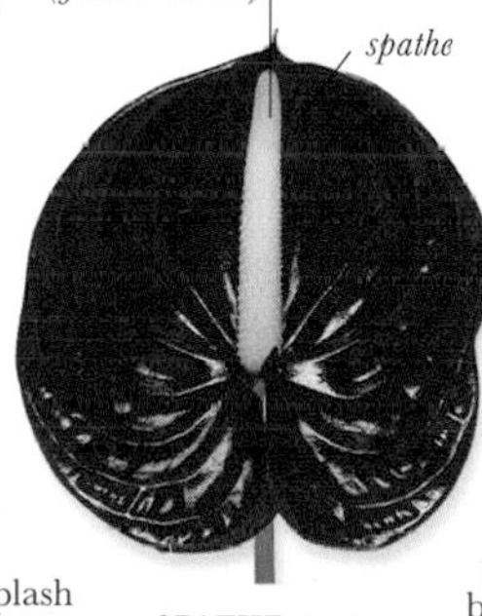

SPATHE AND FLOWER OF *Anthurium andreanum*

speaking acquaintance *n.* **1** a person one knows slightly. **2** this degree of familiarity.

speaking clock *n. Brit.* a telephone service giving the correct time in recorded speech.

spear ● *n.* **1** a thrusting or throwing weapon with a pointed usu. steel tip and a long shaft. **2** a similar barbed instrument used for catching fish etc. **3** a plant shoot, esp. a stem of asparagus or broccoli. ● *v.tr.* pierce or strike with or as if with a spear. [Old English]

speargun *n.* a gun used to propel a spear in underwater fishing.

spearhead ● *n.* **1** the point of a spear. **2** an individual or group chosen to lead a thrust or attack. ● *v.tr.* act as the spearhead of (an attack etc.).

spearmint *n.* a common garden mint, *Mentha spicata*, used in cookery and to flavour chewing gum.

spec[1] *n.* □ **on spec** *colloq.* in the hope of success; on the off chance.

spec[2] *n. colloq.* a detailed working description; a specification.

special ● *adj.* **1 a** particularly good; exceptional; out of the ordinary. **b** peculiar; specific; not general. **2** for a particular purpose (*sent on a special assignment*). **3** in which a person specializes (*statistics is his special field*). **4** relating to or denoting education for children with particular needs, e.g. the handicapped. ● *n.* a special person or thing, e.g. a special constable, train, edition of a newspaper, dish on a menu, etc. [from Latin *specialis* 'individual'] □ **specially** *adv.* **specialness** *n.*

Special Branch *n.* (in the UK) a police department dealing with political security.

special constable *n. Brit.* an officer trained to assist the police, esp. in times of emergency etc.

special correspondent *n. Brit.* a journalist writing on special events or a special area of interest.

special delivery *n.* **1** (in the UK) guaranteed delivery of a letter within the UK the day after posting. **2** (in the US) delivery of mail by a special messenger.

special edition *n.* an extra edition of a newspaper including later news than the ordinary edition.

special effects *n.pl.* scenic illusions created for films and television by props, camerawork, computer graphics, etc.

specialist *n.* (usu. foll. by *in*) **1** a person who is trained in a particular branch of a profession, esp. medicine. **2** a person who specially or exclusively studies a subject or a particular branch of a subject (opp. GENERALIST). □ **specialism** *n.*

speciality *n.* (*pl.* **-ies**) **1** a special pursuit, product, operation, etc., to which a company or a person gives special attention. **2** a special feature, characteristic, or skill. [from Late Latin *specialitas*]

specialize *v.* (also **-ise**) **1** *intr.* (often foll. by *in*) **a** be or become a specialist (*specializes in optics*). **b** devote oneself to an area of interest, skill, etc. (*specializes in insulting people*). **2** *Biol.* **a** *tr.* (esp. in *passive*) adapt or set apart (an organ etc.) for a particular purpose. **b** *intr.* (of an organ etc.) become adapted etc. in this way. **3** *tr.* make specific or individual. □ **specialization** *n.*

special licence *n. Brit.* a marriage licence allowing immediate marriage without banns, or at an unusual time or place.

special pleading *n.* **1** *Law* pleading with reference to new facts in a case. **2** (in general use) a specious or unfair argument favouring the speaker's point of view.

specialty *n.* (*pl.* **-ies**) esp. *N. Amer.* = SPECIALITY.

speciation *n. Biol.* the formation of new species in the course of evolution. □ **speciate** *v.intr.*

specie /spee-shee/ *n.* coin money as opposed to paper money. [from Latin phrase *in specie* 'in the actual form']

species *n.* (*pl.* same) **1** a class of things having some common characteristics. **2** *Biol.* a group of living organisms consisting of related similar individuals capable of exchanging genes or interbreeding. **3** a kind or sort. [Latin, literally 'appearance, kind, beauty']

specific ● *adj.* **1** clearly defined; definite (*has no specific name*; *told me so in specific terms*). **2** relating to a particular subject; peculiar (*a style specific to that*). ● *n.* a specific aspect or factor (*shall we discuss specifics?*). [from Late Latin *specificus*] □ **specifically** *adv.* **specificity** *n.*

specification *n.* **1** the act or an instance of specifying; the state of being specified. **2 a** (esp. in *pl.*) a detailed description of the construction, workmanship, materials, etc. of work done or to be done. **b** a specified standard of workmanship, materials, etc. (*built to a high specification*).

specific gravity *n.* = RELATIVE DENSITY.

specify *v.tr.* (**-ies, -ied**) **1** (also *absol.*) name or mention expressly (*specified the type he needed*). **2** (usu. foll. by *that* + clause) name as a condition (*specified that he must be paid at once*). **3** include in specifications (*a French window was not specified*). [from Late Latin *specificare*] □ **specifiable** *adj.* **specifier** *n.*

specimen *n.* **1** an individual or part taken as an example of a class or whole, esp. when used for investigation or scientific examination. **2** *Med.* a sample of urine for testing. **3** *colloq.* a person or animal of a specified sort (*a fine specimen*). [Latin]

specious *adj.* **1** superficially plausible but actually wrong (*a specious argument*). **2** misleadingly attractive in appearance. [Middle English in sense 'beautiful': from Latin *speciosus* 'fair'] □ **speciously** *adv.* **speciousness** *n.*

speck ● *n.* **1** a small spot, dot, or stain. **2** (foll. by *of*) a particle (*speck of dirt*). **3** a rotten spot in fruit. ● *v.tr.* (esp. as **specked** *adj.*) mark with specks. [Old English] □ **speckless** *adj.*

SPECKLED
SNIPE'S EGG

speckle ● *n.* a small spot, mark, or stain, esp. in quantity on the skin, a bird's egg, etc. ● *v.tr.* (esp. as **speckled** *adj.*) ◄ mark with speckles or patches. [from Middle Dutch *spekkel*]

specs *n.pl. colloq.* a pair of spectacles.

spectacle *n.* **1** a public show, ceremony, etc. **2** anything attracting public attention (*a charming spectacle; a disgusting spectacle*). □ **make a spectacle of oneself** make oneself an object of ridicule. [from Latin *spectaculum*]

spectacled *adj.* **1** wearing spectacles. **2** (of an animal) having markings resembling spectacles.

spectacles *n.pl.* (*US* usu. *joc.*) a pair of lenses in a frame resting on the nose and ears, used to correct defective eyesight or protect the eyes.

spectacular ● *adj.* **1** of or like a public show; striking, lavish. **2** strikingly large or obvious (*a spectacular increase in output*). ● *n.* an event intended to be spectacular, esp. a musical. □ **spectacularly** *adv.*

spectate *v.intr.* be a spectator, esp. at a sporting event. [back-formation from SPECTATOR]

spectator *n.* a person who looks on at a show, game, incident, etc. [Latin] □ **spectatorial** *adj.*

spectator sport *n.* a sport providing popular entertainment for spectators.

spectra *pl.* of SPECTRUM.

spectral *adj.* **1 a** of or relating to spectres or ghosts. **b** ghostlike. **2** of or concerning spectra or the spectrum (*spectral colours*). □ **spectrally** *adv.*

spectral analysis *n.* **1** chemical analysis using a spectroscope. **2** analysis of light, sound, etc. into a spectrum.

spectre *n.* (*US* **specter**) **1** a ghost. **2** a haunting presentiment or preoccupation (*the spectre of war*). [French]

spectro- *comb. form* a spectrum.

spectrogram *n.* a record obtained with a spectrograph.

spectrograph *n.* an apparatus for photographing or otherwise recording spectra. □ **spectrographic** *adj.* **spectrographically** *adv.* **spectrography** *n.*

spectrometer /spek-**trom**-i-ter/ *n.* an instrument used for the measurement of observed spectra. □ **spectrometric** *adj.* **spectrometry** *n.*

spectroscope *n.* an instrument for producing and recording spectra for examination. □ **spectroscopic** *adj.* **spectroscopically** *adv.* **spectroscopist** *n.* **spectroscopy** *n.*

spectrum *n.* (*pl.* **spectra**) **1** a band of colours, as seen in a rainbow etc. ▷ LIGHT. **2** the entire range of wavelengths of electromagnetic radiation. ▷ ELECTROMAGNETIC RADIATION. **3** an image or distribution of components of any electromagnetic radiation arranged in a progressive series according to wavelength. **4** a similar image or distribution of components of sound, particles, etc., arranged according to frequency, charge, energy, etc. **5** the entire range or a wide range of anything arranged by degree or quality etc. [Latin, literally 'image, apparition']

spectrum analysis *n.* = SPECTRAL ANALYSIS.

specula *pl.* of SPECULUM.

specular iron ore *n.* lustrous haematite.

speculate *v.* **1** *intr.* (usu. foll. by *on, upon, about*) form a theory or conjecture, without a firm factual basis; meditate (*speculated on their prospects*). **2** *tr.* (foll. by *that, how*, etc. + clause) conjecture, consider (*speculated how he might achieve it*). **3** *intr.* invest in stocks etc. in the hope of gain but with the possibility of loss. [based on Latin *speculatus* 'observed'] □ **speculation** *n.* **speculative** *adj.* **speculatively** *adv.* **speculator** *n.*

speculum *n.* (*pl.* **specula**) **1** *Surgery* an instrument for dilating the cavities of the human body for inspection. **2** a mirror, usu. of polished metal, esp. (formerly) in a reflecting telescope. [Latin, literally 'mirror']

sped *past* and *past part.* of SPEED.

speech *n.* **1** the faculty or act of speaking. **2** a usu. formal address or discourse delivered to an audience or assembly. **3** a manner of speaking (*a man of blunt speech*). **4** the language of a nation, region, group, etc. [Old English] □ **speechful** *adj.*

speech day *n.* *Brit.* an annual prize-giving day in many schools, usu. marked by speeches etc.

speechify *v.intr.* (**-ies, -ied**) *joc.* or *derog.* make esp. boring or long speeches. □ **speechifier** *n.*

speechless *adj.* **1** temporarily unable to speak because of emotion etc. (*speechless with rage*). **2** dumb. □ **speechlessly** *adv.* **speechlessness** *n.*

speech therapy *n.* treatment to improve defective speech. □ **speech therapist** *n.*

speed ● *n.* **1** rapidity of movement (*with all speed; at full speed*). **2** a rate of progress or motion over a distance in time. **3 a** each of the possible gear ratios of a bicycle. **b** esp. *US* or *archaic* such a gear in a motor vehicle. **4** *Photog.* **a** the sensitivity of film to light. **b** the light-gathering power or f-number of a lens. **c** the duration of an exposure. **5** *slang* an amphetamine drug, esp. methamphetamine. ● *v.* (*past* and *past part.* **sped**) **1** *intr.* go fast. **2** (*past* and *past part.* **speeded**) *intr.* (of a motorist etc.) travel at an illegal or dangerous speed. **3** *tr.* send fast or on its way (*speed an arrow from the bow*). **4** *intr.* & *tr. archaic* be or make prosperous or successful. □ **at speed** moving quickly. **speed up** move or work at greater speed. [Old English] □ **speeder** *n.*

speedboat *n.* a motor boat designed for high speed.

speed bump *n.* (also *Brit.* **speed hump**) a transverse ridge in the road to control the speed of vehicles.

speed limit *n.* the maximum permitted speed for a road vehicle, boat, etc., in a particular area etc.

speed merchant *n. colloq.* a motorist who enjoys driving fast.

speedo *n.* (*pl.* **-os**) *Brit. colloq.* = SPEEDOMETER.

speedometer *n.* an instrument on a motor vehicle etc. indicating its speed.

speed-up *n.* an increase in the speed or rate of working.

speedway *n.* **1 a** motorcycle racing. **b** a stadium or track used for this. **2** *N. Amer.* **a** a road or track used for motor car racing. **b** a highway for fast motor traffic.

speedwell *n.* ► any small herbaceous plant of the genus *Veronica*, with tiny blue or pink flowers.

speedy *adj.* (**speedier, speediest**) **1** moving quickly. **2** done without delay; prompt (*a speedy answer*). □ **speedily** *adv.* **speediness** *n.*

speleology *n.* **1** the scientific study of caves. **2** the exploration of caves. [based on Greek *spēlaion* 'cave'] □ **speleological** *adj.* **speleologist** *n.*

spell[1] *v.tr.* (*past* and *past part.* **spelled** or esp. *Brit.* **spelt**) **1** (also *absol.*) write or name the letters that form (a word etc.) in correct sequence (*spell 'exaggerate'; cannot spell properly*). **2 a** (of letters) make up or form (a word etc.). **b** (of circumstances, a scheme, etc.) result in; involve (*spell ruin*). □ **spell out** make out (words, writing, etc.) letter by letter. **2** explain in detail (*spelled out what the change would mean*). [from Old French *espel(l)er*]

spell[2] *n.* **1** a form of words used as a magical charm or incantation. **2** an attraction or fascination exercised by a person, activity, quality, etc. □ **under a spell** mastered by or as if by a spell. [Old English]

spell[3] ● *n.* **1** a short or fairly short period (*a cold spell*

SPEEDWELL:
GERMANDER
SPEEDWELL
(*Veronica
chamaedrys*)

in April). **2** a turn of work (*did a spell of woodwork*). **3** *Austral.* a period of rest from work. ● *v.intr. Austral.* take a brief rest. [Old English]

spellbind *v.tr.* (*past* and *past part.* **spellbound**) **1** bind with or as if with a spell; entrance. **2** (as **spellbound** *adj.*) entranced, fascinated, esp. by a speaker, activity, quality, etc. □ **spellbinder** *n.* **spellbindingly** *adv.*

spell-check *Computing* ● *n.* a check of the spelling in a file of text, using a spelling checker. ● *v.tr.* check the spelling in (a text) using a spelling checker.

spell-checker *n.* = SPELLING CHECKER.

speller *n.* a person who spells esp. in a specified way (*is a poor speller*).

spellican var. of SPILLIKIN.

spelling *n.* **1** the process or activity of writing or naming the letters of a word etc. **2** the way a word is spelled. **3** the ability to spell (*his spelling is weak*).

spelling-bee *n.* a spelling competition.

spelling checker *n.* a computer program which checks the spelling of words in files of text, usually by comparison with a stored list of words.

spelt[1] *past* and *past part.* of SPELL[1].

spelt[2] *n.* a kind of wheat, *Triticum spelta*, formerly cultivated. [from Old Saxon *spelta*]

spelunker *n. N. Amer.* a person who explores caves, esp. as a hobby. [based on Latin *spelunca* 'cave'] □ **spelunking** *n.*

spencer *n.* **1** a short close-fitting jacket. **2** a woman's thin usu. woollen under-bodice.

spend ● *v.tr.* (*past* and *past part.* **spent**) **1** (usu. foll. by *on*) **a** (also *absol.*) pay out (money) in making a purchase etc. **b** pay out (money) for a particular person's benefit or for the improvement of a thing (*had to spend £200 on the car*). **2 a** use or consume (time or energy). **b** (also *refl.*) use up; exhaust; wear out. **3** (as **spent** *adj.*) having lost its original force or strength; exhausted (*the storm is spent; spent bullets*). ● *n.* **1** the action or an act of spending money. **2** an amount spent, expenditure. □ **spend a penny** *Brit. colloq.* urinate or defecate. [from Latin *expendere*] □ **spendable** *adj.* **spender** *n.*

spending money *n.* pocket money.

spendthrift ● *n.* an extravagant person; a prodigal. ● *adj.* extravagant; prodigal.

spent *past* and *past part.* of SPEND.

sperm *n.* (*pl.* same or **sperms**) **1** = SPERMATOZOON. **2** the male reproductive fluid containing spermatozoa; semen. [from Greek *sperma* 'seed']

spermaceti /sper-mă-**see**-ti/ *n.* a white waxy substance produced by the sperm whale to aid buoyancy, and used in the manufacture of candles, ointments, etc. [from Late Latin *sperma* 'sperm' + *ceti* 'of a whale', from the belief that it was whale spawn] □ **spermacetic** *adj.*

spermatic cord *n. Anat.* a bundle of nerves, ducts, and blood vessels connecting the testicles to the abdominal cavity. ▷ REPRODUCTIVE ORGANS

spermatozoon /sper-mă-tŏ-**zoh**-ŏn/ *n.* (*pl.* **spermatozoa**) ► the mature motile male sex cell in animals. [from Greek *sperma* 'seed' + *zōion* 'animal'] □ **spermatozoal** *adj.* **spermatozoan** *adj.*

sperm bank *n.* a supply of semen stored for use in artificial insemination.

sperm count *n.* the number of spermatozoa in one ejaculation or a measured amount of semen.

spermicide *n.* a substance able to kill spermatozoa. □ **spermicidal** *adj.*

sperm oil *n.* an oil obtained from the head of a sperm whale and used as a lubricant.

acrosome

head

neck

mid-piece

*flagellum
(tail)*

SPERMATOZOON

S

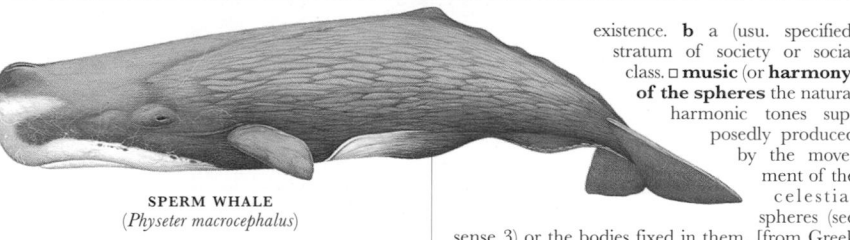

SPERM WHALE
(*Physeter macrocephalus*)

sperm whale *n.* ▲ a large whale, *Physeter macrocephalus*, hunted for spermaceti, sperm oil, and ambergris. ▷ CETACEAN, WHALE

spew *v.* (also **spue**) **1** *tr. & intr.* (often foll. by *up*) vomit. **2** (often foll. by *out*) **a** *tr.* expel (contents) rapidly and forcibly. **b** *intr.* (of contents) be expelled in this way. [Old English] □ **spewer** *n.*

SPF *abbr.* sun protection factor (indicating the effectiveness of protective creams etc.).

sphagnum *n.* (*pl.* **sphagna**) (in full **sphagnum moss**) any moss of the genus *Sphagnum*, growing in bogs and peat, and used as fertilizer etc. [from Greek *sphagnos*, name of a moss]

sphere *n.* **1** ◄ a solid figure, or its surface, with every point on its surface equidistant from its centre. **2** an object having this shape; a ball or globe. **3** *hist.* each of a series of revolving concentrically arranged spherical shells in which celestial bodies were formerly thought to be set in a fixed relationship. **4 a** a field of action, influence, or

SPHERE

existence. **b** a (usu. specified) stratum of society or social class. □ **music** (or **harmony**) **of the spheres** the natural harmonic tones supposedly produced by the movement of the celestial spheres (see sense 3) or the bodies fixed in them. [from Greek *sphaira* 'ball'] □ **spheral** *adj.*

sphere of influence *n.* the claimed or recognized area of a state's interests, an individual's control, etc.

spheric *adj.* = SPHERICAL. □ **sphericity** *n.*

spherical *adj.* **1** shaped like a sphere; globular. **2 a** of or relating to the properties of spheres (*spherical geometry*). **b** formed inside or on the surface of a sphere (*spherical triangle*). □ **spherically** *adv.*

spherical angle *n.* an angle formed by the intersection of two great circles of a sphere.

spheroid *n.* a spherelike but not perfectly spherical body. □ **spheroidal** *adj.* **spheroidicity** *n.*

sphincter *n. Anat.* a ring of muscle surrounding and serving to guard or close an opening or tube, esp. the anus. [from Greek *sphigktēr*] □ **sphincteral** *adj.* **sphincteric** *adj.*

sphinx *n.* **1** (**Sphinx**) (in Greek mythology) the winged monster of Thebes, having a woman's head and a lion's body. **2** *Antiq.* **a** any of several ancient Egyptian stone figures having a lion's body and a human or animal head. **b** (**the Sphinx**) the huge sphinx near the Pyramids at Giza. **3** an enigmatic or inscrutable person. [from Greek *Sphigx*]

sphygmomanometer *n.* ▼ an instrument for measuring blood pressure. [based on Greek *sphugmos* 'pulse'] □ **sphygmomanometric** *adj.*

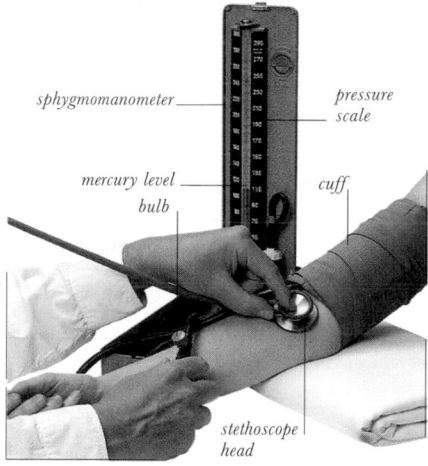

sphygmomanometer — pressure scale
mercury level — cuff
bulb
stethoscope head

SPHYGMOMANOMETER BEING USED TO MEASURE BLOOD PRESSURE

spic *n. US slang offens.* a Spanish-speaking person from Central or S. America or the Caribbean, esp. a Mexican. [abbreviation of *spiggoty*, in same sense]

spice ● *n.* **1** ▼ an aromatic or pungent vegetable substance used to flavour food, e.g. cloves, pepper, or mace. **2** spices collectively (*a dealer in spice*). **3** an

---

SPICE

In the past, spices were often used to mask the taste of an unpalatable meal, and were usually so expensive that only the wealthy could afford them. Today, spices are a common feature of everyday meals, and can be divided into three groups. Hot spices, such as pepper, stimulate the palate and increase perspiration. Fragrant spices, such as mace, add a pungent, sweet taste, and can be used in a variety of dishes. Colouring spices, such as turmeric, give meals a distinctive, often vibrant, hue.

COLOURING SPICES

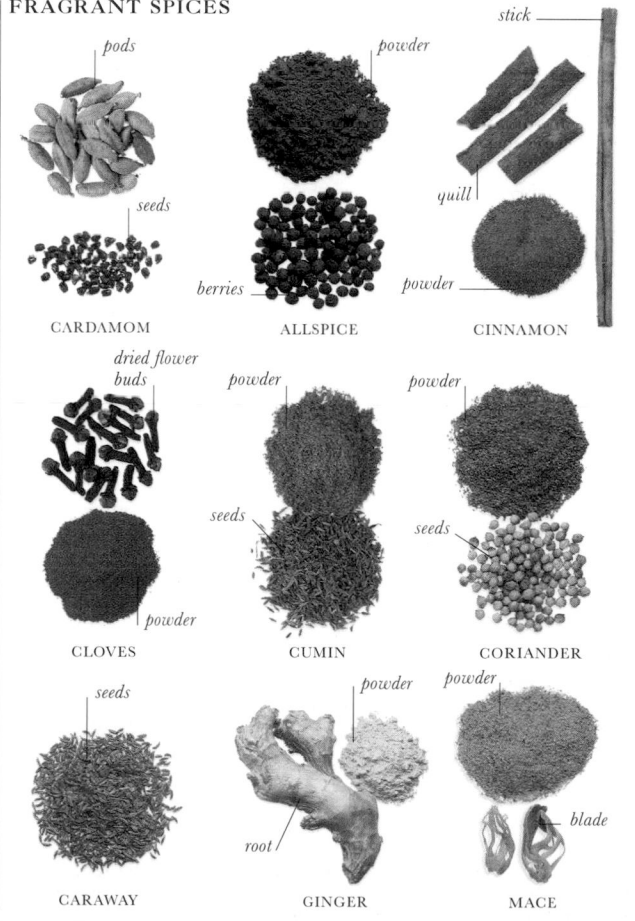

powder

PAPRIKA

dried stigmas
SAFFRON

powder
root
TURMERIC

HOT SPICES

powder
CAYENNE

seeds
MUSTARD

powder
flakes

pepper-corns
powder
PEPPER

powder
CHILLI

FRAGRANT SPICES

stick

pods
seeds
CARDAMOM

powder
berries
powder
ALLSPICE

quill
powder
CINNAMON

dried flower buds
powder
CLOVES

powder
seeds
powder
CUMIN

powder
seeds
CORIANDER

seeds
CARAWAY

root
powder
GINGER

powder
blade
MACE

S

SPIDER

There are 40,000 known species of spider, most of which can be divided into the suborders Mygalomorphae (spiders with fangs that bite downwards) and Araneomorphae (spiders with fangs that bite sideways). Spiders' victims are either ensnared in a web (made of silk produced by the spider's spinnerets), or pounced on. Captured prey is injected with paralysing venom from the spider's fangs, which are connected to poison glands.

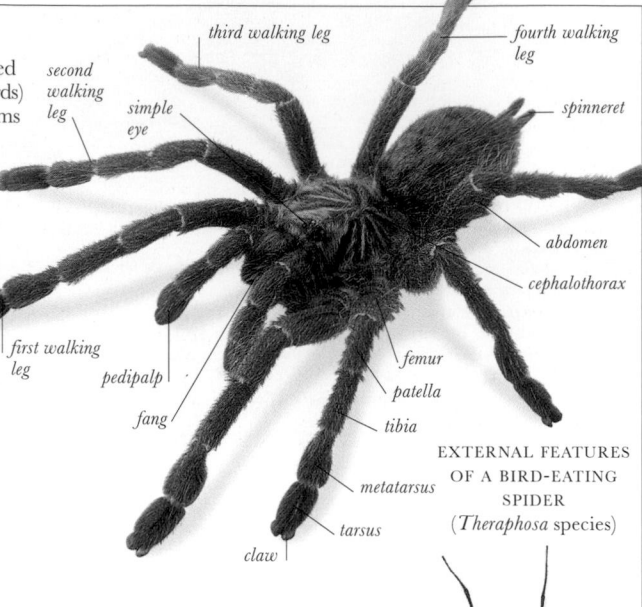

EXTERNAL FEATURES OF A BIRD-EATING SPIDER (*Theraphosa* species)

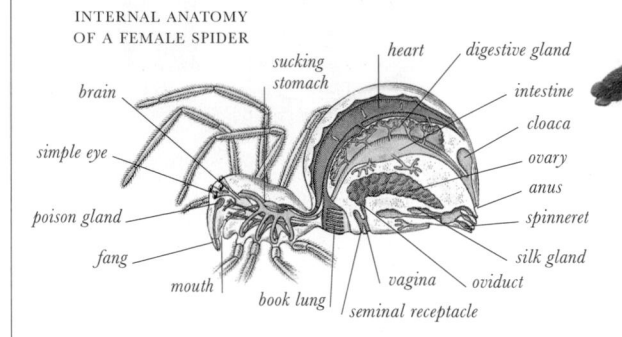

INTERNAL ANATOMY OF A FEMALE SPIDER

EXAMPLES OF OTHER SPIDERS

MYGALOMORPHAE

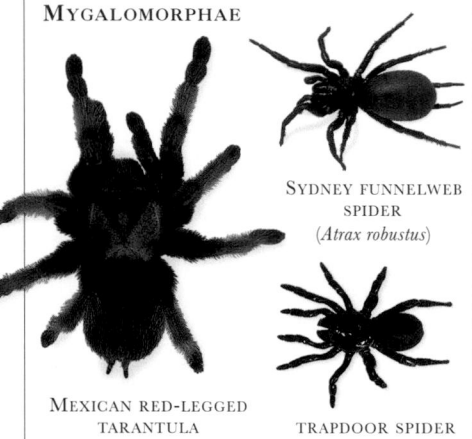

MEXICAN RED-LEGGED TARANTULA (*Euathlus emilia*)

SYDNEY FUNNELWEB SPIDER (*Atrax robustus*)

TRAPDOOR SPIDER (*Ummidia* species)

ARANEOMORPHAE

JUMPING SPIDER (*Plexippus paykulli*)

ORB SPIDER (*Nuctenea umbratica*)

DADDY LONGLEGS SPIDER (*Pholcus phalangioides*)

BLACK WIDOW SPIDER (*Latrodectus mactans*)

GIANT CRAB SPIDER (*Olios* species)

HOUSE SPIDER (*Tegenaria gigantea*)

WOLF SPIDER (*Lycosa* species)

S

interesting or piquant quality. ● *v.tr.* **1** flavour with spice. **2** add an interesting or piquant quality to (*a book spiced with humour*). [from Latin *species* 'specific kind']

spick and span *adj.* (also **spic and span**) **1** neat and clean. **2** smart and new. [from *spick and span new*, emphatic extension of Middle English *span new* 'completely new']

spicy *adj.* (also **spicey**) (**spicier**, **spiciest**) **1** of, flavoured with, or fragrant with spice. **2 a** piquant, pungent. **b** sensational or improper (*a spicy story*). □ **spicily** *adv.* **spiciness** *n.*

spider ● *n.* **1 a** ▲ any eight-legged arthropod of the order Araneae with a round unsegmented body, many of which spin webs for the capture of insects as food. **b** any of various similar or related arachnids. **2** any object comparable to a spider, esp. as having numerous or prominent legs or radiating spokes. ● *v.* **1** *intr.* move in a scuttling manner suggestive of a spider. **2** *tr.* cause to move or appear in this way. [Old English, related to SPIN] □ **spiderish** *adj.*

spider crab *n.* any of various crabs of the family Majidae with a pear-shaped body and long thin legs. ▷ CRAB

spiderman *n.* (*pl.* **-men**) *Brit. colloq.* a person who works at great heights in building construction.

spider mite *n.* (in full **red spider mite**) a plant-eating mite of the family Tetranychidae, esp.

Tetranychus urticae, a serious garden and hothouse pest.

spider monkey *n.* ▶ any S. American monkey of the genera *Ateles* and *Brachyteles*, with long limbs and a prehensile tail. ▷ PRIMATE

spider plant *n.* a southern African plant, *Chlorophytum comosum* (lily family), with long narrow striped leaves.

spidery *adj.* elongated and thin (*spidery handwriting*).

spiel /shpeel/ *slang* ● *n.* a glib speech or story, esp. a salesman's patter. ● *v.* **1** *intr.* speak glibly; hold forth. **2** *tr.* reel off (patter etc.). [German, literally 'play, game']

spieler /shpee-ler/ *n. slang* **1** esp. *US* a person who spiels. **2** *Austral.* & *NZ* a gambler; a swindler.

spigot *n.* **1** a small peg or plug, esp. for insertion into the vent of a cask. **2 a** *US* a tap. **b** a device for controlling the flow of liquid in a tap. [Middle English]

spike[1] ● *n.* **1 a** a sharp point. **b** a pointed piece of metal, esp. the top of an iron railing etc. **2 a** any of several metal points on the sole of a

SPIDER MONKEY: BLACK-HANDED SPIDER MONKEY (*Ateles geoffroyi*)

running shoe to prevent slipping. **b** (in *pl.*) a pair of running shoes with spikes. **3 a** *Brit.* a pointed metal rod standing on a base and used for filing rejected news items. **b** a similar spike used for bills etc. ● *v.tr.* **1 a** fasten or provide with spikes. **b** fix on or pierce with spikes. **2** (of a newspaper editor etc.) reject (a story) by filing it on a spike. **3** *colloq.* **a** lace (a drink) with alcohol, a drug, etc. **b** contaminate (a substance) with something added. **4** *hist.* plug up the vent of (a gun) with a spike. □ **spike a person's guns** spoil his or her plans. [Middle English]

spike[2] *n. Bot.* a flower cluster formed of many flower heads attached closely on a long stem. ▷ INFLORESCENCE. [from Latin *spica* 'ear of corn, spike']

spike heel *n.* a high tapering heel of a shoe.

spikelet *n.* a small spike; esp. the basic unit of a grass flower, with two bracts at the base.

spikenard *n.* **1** *hist.* a costly perfumed ointment. **2** the plant from whose rhizome this was prepared, probably the Himalayan *Nardostachys grandiflora*. [from medieval Latin *spica nardi*]

spiky *adj.* (**spikier**, **spikiest**) **1** like a spike; having many spikes. **2** *colloq.* easily offended; prickly. □ **spikily** *adv.* **spikiness** *n.*

spill[1] ● *v.* (*past* and *past part.* **spilt** or **spilled**) **1** *intr. & tr.* fall or run or cause (a liquid, powder, etc.) to fall or run out of a vessel, esp. unintentionally. **2 a** *tr. & intr.* throw from a vehicle, saddle, etc. **b** *intr.* (esp. of a crowd) tumble out quickly from a place etc. **3** *tr. slang* disclose (information etc.). ● *n.* **1 a** the act or an instance of spilling or being spilt. **b** a quantity spilt. **2** a tumble or fall, esp. from a horse etc. (*had a nasty spill*). □ **spill the beans** *colloq.* divulge information etc. **spill blood** be guilty of bloodshed. **spill the blood of** kill or injure (a person). **spill over 1** overflow. **2** (of a surplus population) be forced to move. [Old English *spillan* 'to kill'] □ **spillage** *n.* **spiller** *n.*

spill[2] *n.* a thin strip of wood, folded or twisted paper, etc., used for lighting a fire, a pipe, etc. [Middle English]

spillikin *n.* (also **spellican**) **1** a splinter of wood, bone, etc. **2** (in *pl.*) a game in which a heap of spillikins is to be removed one at a time without moving the others.

spillover *n.* **1 a** the process or an instance of spilling over. **b** a thing that spills over. **2** a consequence, repercussion, or by-product.

spillway *n.* a passage for surplus water from a dam.

spilt *past* and *past part.* of SPILL[1].

spin ● *v.* (**spinning**; *past* **spun** or **span**; *past part.* **spun**) **1** *intr. & tr.* turn or cause (a person or thing) to turn or whirl round quickly. **2** *tr.* (also *absol.*) **a** draw out and twist (wool, cotton, etc.) into threads. **b** make (yarn) in this way. **3** *tr.* (of a spider, silkworm, etc.) make (a web, a cocoon, etc.) by extruding a fine viscous thread. **4** *tr.* tell or write (a story etc.) (*spins a good tale*). **5** *tr.* impart spin to (a ball). **6** *intr.* (of a person's head etc.) be dizzy through excitement, astonishment, etc. **7** *intr.* esp. *Cricket* (of a ball) move through the air with spin. **8** *tr.* (as **spun** *adj.*) converted into threads (*spun sugar*). **9** *tr.* toss (a coin). **10** *tr.* = *spin-dry* (see SPIN-DRYER). ● *n.* **1** a spinning motion; a whirl. **2** an aircraft's diving descent combined with rotation. **3 a** a revolving motion through the air, e.g. of a ball in flight. **b** *Cricket* a twisting motion given to the ball in bowling. **4** *colloq.* a brief drive in a vehicle etc., esp. for pleasure. **5** esp. *US Polit.* a bias in information to give a favourable impression. □ **spin off** throw off by centrifugal force in spinning. **spin out 1** prolong (a discussion etc.). **2** make (a story, money, etc.) last as long as possible. **3** consume (time etc., by discussion or in an occupation etc.). [Old English]

spina bifida /spy-nă bif-i-dă/ *n.* a congenital defect of the spine, in which part of the spinal cord protudes. [modern Latin]

spinach *n.* **1** a green garden vegetable, *Spinacia oleracea*, with succulent leaves. **2** the leaves of this plant used as food. ▷ VEGETABLE. □ **spinachy** *adj.*

spinach beet *n.* a variety of beetroot cultivated for its edible leaves.

spinal *adj.* of or relating to the spine. [from Late Latin *spinalis*] □ **spinally** *adv.*

spinal column *n.* the spine.

spinal cord *n.* ◀ a cylindrical structure of the central nervous system enclosed in the spine. ▷ HEAD, NERVOUS SYSTEM, PERIPHERAL NERVOUS SYSTEM

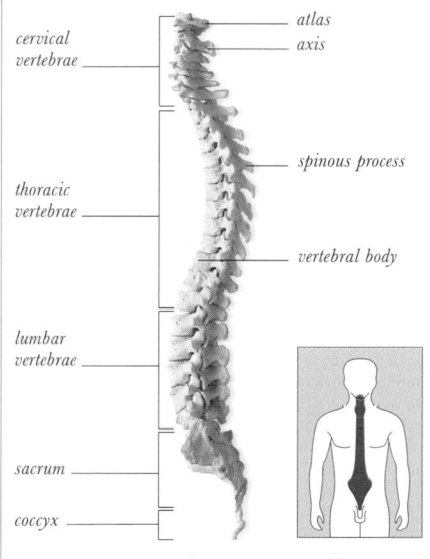

SPINAL CORD: CROSS-SECTION OF THE HUMAN SPINAL CORD

(labels: skull, cerebrum, cerebellum, vertebra, spinal cord, filum terminale, sacrum)

spin bowler *n. Cricket* an expert at bowling with spin.

spindle *n.* **1 a** a pin in a spinning wheel used for twisting and winding the thread. **b** a small bar with tapered ends used for the same purpose in hand-spinning. **c** a pin bearing the bobbin of a spinning machine. **2** a pin or axis that revolves or on which something revolves. **3** *US* = SPIKE[1] *n.* 3a. **4** a turned piece of wood used as a banister, chair leg, etc. [Old English]

spindle-shaped *adj.* having a circular cross-section and tapering towards each end.

spindle tree *n.* a small tree of the genus *Euonymus*, having hard wood formerly used for spindles.

spindly *adj.* (**spindlier**, **spindliest**) long or tall and thin; thin and weak.

spin doctor *n. colloq.* a political spokesperson employed to give a favourable interpretation of events to the media.

spindrift *n.* spray on the surface of the sea. [Scots variant of *spoondrift* from obsolete *spoon* 'to scud']

spin-dryer *n.* (also **spin-drier**) a machine for drying wet clothes etc. centrifugally in a revolving drum. □ **spin-dry** *v.tr.*

spine *n.* **1** ▼ a series of vertebrae extending from the skull to the small of the back; the backbone. ▷ SKELETON, VERTEBRA. **2** *Zool. & Bot.* any hard pointed process or structure. ▷ SEA URCHIN, SUCCULENT. **3** a sharp ridge or projection of a mountain range etc. **4** a central feature, main support, or source of strength. **5** the part of a book's jacket or cover that encloses the inner edges of the pages. [from Latin *spina* 'thorn, backbone'] □ **spined** *adj.*

SPINE OF A HUMAN

(labels: cervical vertebrae, atlas, axis, thoracic vertebrae, spinous process, vertebral body, lumbar vertebrae, sacrum, coccyx)

spine-chiller *n.* a frightening story, film, etc. □ **spine-chilling** *adj.*

spineless *adj.* **1 a** having no spine; invertebrate. **b** (of an animal or plant) having no spines. **2** (of a person) weak and purposeless. □ **spinelessly** *adv.* **spinelessness** *n.*

spinet *n. hist.* ▼ a small harpsichord with oblique strings. [from Italian *spinetta* 'virginal, spinet']

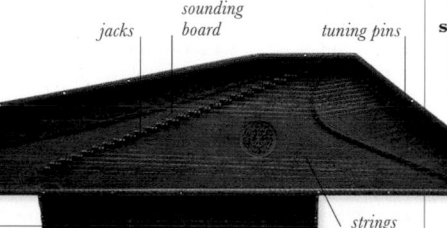

(labels: jacks, sounding board, tuning pins, four-octave keyboard, strings)

SPINET: 16TH-CENTURY ITALIAN SPINET

spinnaker *n.* a large triangular sail carried opposite the mainsail of a racing yacht. [fanciful from *Sphinx*, name of the yacht first using it]

spinner *n.* **1** a person or thing that spins. ▷ AIRCRAFT. **2** *Cricket* **a** a spin bowler. **b** a spun ball. **3** a spin-dryer. **4 a** a fly for esp. trout-fishing. **b** revolving bait. **5** a manufacturer or merchant engaged in (esp. cotton-) spinning.

spinneret *n.* **1** the spinning-organ in a spider etc. ▷ SPIDER. **2** a device for forming filaments of synthetic fibre.

spinney *n.* (*pl.* **-eys**) *Brit.* a small wood; a thicket. [from Latin *spinetum* 'thicket']

spinning *n.* the act or an instance of spinning.

spinning jenny *n. hist.* a machine for spinning with more than one spindle at a time.

spinning top *n.* = TOP[2].

spinning wheel *n.* a household machine for spinning yarn or thread with a spindle driven by a wheel attached to a crank or treadle.

spin-off *n.* an incidental result or results esp. as a side benefit from industrial technology.

spinster *n.* **1** an unmarried woman. **2** a woman, esp. elderly, thought unlikely to marry. [Middle English, originally in sense 'woman who spins'] □ **spinsterhood** *n.* **spinsterish** *adj.*

spiny *adj.* (**spinier**, **spiniest**) **1** full of spines; prickly. **2** perplexing, troublesome, thorny. □ **spininess** *n.*

spiny anteater *n.* = ECHIDNA.

spiny lobster *n.* ▼ any of various large edible crustaceans of the family Palinuridae, esp. *Palinuris vulgaris*, with a spiny shell and no large anterior claws.

(labels: cephalothorax, spiny shell, telson, abdomen, swimmeret, leg, antenna)

SPINY LOBSTER
(*Palinurus vulgaris*)

spiraea /spy-ree-ă/ *n.* (*US* **spirea**) any shrub of the genus *Spiraea* (rose family), with clusters of small white or pink flowers. [from Greek *speiraia*]

spiral ● *adj.* **1** winding about a centre in an enlarging or decreasing continuous circular motion, either on a plane or rising in a cone. **2** winding continuously along or as if along a cylinder, like the thread of a screw. ● *n.* **1** a plane or three-dimensional spiral curve. **2** a spiral spring. **3** a spiral formation in a shell etc. **4** a progressive rise or fall of prices etc., each responding to an upward or downward stimulus provided by the other. ● *v.* (**spiralled**, **spiralling**; *US* **spiraled**, **spiraling**) **1** *intr.* move in a spiral course, esp. upwards or downwards. **2** *tr.* make spiral. **3** *intr.* esp. *Econ.* (of prices, wages, etc.) rise or fall, esp. rapidly. [from medieval Latin *spiralis*] □ **spirally** *adv.*

spiral galaxy *n.* ▼ a galaxy in which the matter is concentrated mainly in one or more spiral arms. ▷ GALAXY

(labels: spiral arm, nucleus)

SPIRAL GALAXY

spiral staircase *n.* a staircase rising in a spiral round a central axis.

spirant *Phonet.* ● *adj.* (of a consonant) uttered with a continuous expulsion of breath, esp. fricative. ● *n.* such a consonant. [from Latin *spirare spirant-* 'breathing']

S

spire ● *n.* **1** a tapering conical or pyramidal structure built esp. on a church tower. ▷ CATHEDRAL. **2** any tapering thing, e.g. the spike of a flower. ● *v.tr.* provide with a spire. [Old English]

spirea *US* var. of SPIRAEA.

spirillum /spy-**rill**-ŭm/ *n.* (*pl.* **spirilla**) any bacterium with a rigid spiral structure, esp. one of the genus *Spirillum*. [based on Latin *spira* 'coil']

spirit ● *n.* **1 a** the vital animating essence of a person or animal (*broken in spirit*). **b** the soul. **2 a** a rational or intelligent being without a material body. **b** a ghost, fairy, etc. **3** a prevailing mental or moral condition or attitude (*took it in the wrong spirit*). **4** (usu. in *pl.*) esp. *Brit.* strong distilled liquor, e.g. brandy, whisky, gin, rum. **5** (*US* esp. in *pl.*) **a** a distilled liquid essence (*spirit of turpentine*). **b** a distilled alcohol (*methylated spirit*). **c** a solution of a volatile principle in alcohol (*spirit of ammonia*). **6 a** a person's character (*has an unbending spirit*). **b** a person characterized in a specified way (*is an ardent spirit*). **c** courage, energy, vivacity (*played with spirit*). **7** the real meaning as opposed to lip-service or verbal expression (*the spirit of the law*). ● *v.tr.* (**spirited**, **spiriting**) (usu. foll. by *away*, *off*, etc.) convey rapidly and secretly by or as if by spirits. □ **in** (or **in the**) **spirit** sensed psychologically as giving support though not present physically. [from Latin *spiritus* 'breath, spirit']

spirited *adj.* **1** full of spirit; animated, courageous (*a spirited attack*). **2** having a spirit or spirits of a specified kind (*high-spirited*). □ **spiritedly** *adv.* **spiritedness** *n.*

spirit gum *n.* a quick-drying solution of gum used esp. for attaching false hair.

spirit lamp *n.* a lamp burning methylated or other volatile spirits instead of oil.

spiritless *adj.* lacking courage, vigour, or vivacity. □ **spiritlessly** *adv.* **spiritlessness** *n.*

SPIRIT LEVEL

spirit level *n.* ◄ a device consisting of a sealed glass tube nearly filled with usu. alcohol, containing an air bubble whose position is used to test horizontality and verticality.

spiritual ● *adj.* **1** of or concerning the spirit as opposed to matter. **2** concerned with sacred or religious things (*spiritual songs*). **3** (of the mind etc.) refined, sensitive. **4** concerned with the spirit etc., not with external reality (*his spiritual home*). ● *n.* = NEGRO SPIRITUAL. [from Latin *spiritualis*] □ **spirituality** *n.* **spiritually** *adv.* **spiritualness** *n.*

spiritualism *n.* **1** the belief that the spirits of the dead can communicate with the living, esp. through mediums. **2** the practice of this. □ **spiritualist** *n.* **spiritualistic** *adj.*

spiritualize *v.tr.* (also **-ise**) **1** make (a person, thoughts, etc.) spiritual; elevate. **2** attach a spiritual as opposed to a literal meaning to. □ **spiritualization** *n.*

spirituous *adj.* **1** containing much alcohol. **2** distilled, as whisky, rum, etc. (*spirituous liquor*).

spirochaete /**spyr**-ŏ-keet/ *n.* (*US* **spirochete**) any flexible spirally twisted bacterium of the order Spirochaetales. [from Greek *speira* 'a coil' + *khaitē* 'long hair']

spirogyra *n.* any filamentous freshwater alga of the genus *Spirogyra*, with cells containing spiral bands of chlorophyll. [modern Latin]

spirt var. of SPURT.

spit[1] ● *v.* (**spitting**; *past* and *past part.* **spat** or **spit**) **1** *intr.* **a** eject saliva from the mouth. **b** do this as a sign of hatred or contempt (*spat at him*). **2** *tr.* (usu. foll. by *out*) **a** eject from the mouth (*spat the meat out*). **b** utter vehemently (*'Damn you!' he spat*). **3** *intr.* (of a fire, pan, etc.) send out sparks, hot fat, etc. **4** *intr.* (of rain) fall lightly (*it's only spitting*). **5** *intr.* (esp. of a cat) make a spitting or hissing noise in anger or hostility. ● *n.* **1** spittle. **2** the act or an instance of spitting. □ **the spit** (or **very spit**) **of** *colloq.* the exact double of. **spit it out** *colloq.* say what is on one's mind. [Old English] □ **spitter** *n.*

spit[2] ● *n.* **1** a slender rod on which meat is skewered before being roasted on a fire etc. **2 a** a small point of land projecting into the sea. ▷ LONGSHORE DRIFT. **b** a long narrow underwater bank. ● *v.tr.* (**spitted**, **spitting**) pierce with or as with a spit. [Old English] □ **spitty** *adj.*

spit[3] *n.* (*pl.* same or **spits**) a spade-depth of earth. [from Middle Dutch]

spit and polish *n.* **1** the cleaning and polishing duties of a soldier etc. **2** exaggerated neatness and smartness.

spitball ● *n. N. Amer.* a ball of chewed paper etc. used as a missile. ● *v.intr.* throw out suggestions for discussion. □ **spitballer** *n.*

spite ● *n.* **1** ill will or malice towards a person. **2** a grudge. ● *v.tr.* thwart, annoy (*does it to spite me*). □ **in spite of** notwithstanding. **in spite of oneself** etc. though one would rather have done otherwise. [from Old French *despit* 'scorn']

spiteful *adj.* motivated by spite; malevolent. □ **spitefully** *adv.* **spitefulness** *n.*

spitfire *n.* a person of fiery temper.

spit-roast *v.tr.* cook on a spit.

spitting distance *n.* a very short distance.

spitting image *n.* (foll. by *of*) *colloq.* the exact double of (another person or thing).

spittle *n.* saliva, esp. as ejected from the mouth. [alteraton of Middle English (now dialect) *spattle*]

spittoon *n.* a metal or earthenware pot with esp. a funnel-shaped top, used for spitting into.

spiv *n. Brit. colloq.* a man, often characterized by flashy dress, living from illicit or unscrupulous dealings. [20th-century coinage] □ **spivvish** *adj.* **spivvy** *adj.*

splash ● *v.* **1** *intr.* & *tr.* spatter or cause (liquid) to spatter in small drops. **2** *tr.* cause (a person) to be spattered with liquid etc. **3** *intr.* **a** (of a person) cause liquid to spatter (*was splashing about*). **b** (usu. foll. by *across*, *along*, etc.) move while spattering liquid etc. **c** step, fall, or plunge etc. into a liquid etc. so as to cause a splash. **4** *tr.* display (news) prominently. **5** *tr.* decorate with scattered colour. **6** *tr.* spend (money) ostentatiously. ● *n.* **1** the act or an instance of splashing. **2 a** a quantity of liquid splashed. **b** the resulting noise. **3** a spot of dirt etc. splashed on to a thing. **4** a prominent news feature etc. **5** a daub or patch of colour. **6** *colloq.* a small quantity of liquid, esp. of soda water etc. to dilute spirits. □ **make a splash** attract much attention, esp. by extravagance. **splash out** *Brit. colloq.* spend money freely. [alteration of PLASH[1]] □ **splashy** *adj.* (**splashier**, **splashiest**).

splashback *n.* a panel behind a sink etc. to protect the wall from splashes.

splashdown *n.* the alighting of a spacecraft on the sea.

splat[1] *n.* a flat piece of thin wood in the centre of a chair back. [from obsolete *splat* 'to split up']

splat[2] ● *n.* a sharp cracking or slapping sound. ● *adv.* with a splat (*fell splat on his head*). ● *v.intr.* & *tr.* (**splatted**, **splatting**) fall or hit with a splat. [abbreviation of SPLATTER]

splatter ● *v.* **1** *tr.* (often foll. by *with*) make wet or dirty by splashing. **2** *tr.* & *intr.* splash, esp. with a continuous noisy action. ● *n.* a noisy splashing sound.

splay ● *v.* **1** *tr.* (usu. foll. by *out*) spread (the feet etc.) out. **2** *intr.* (of an aperture or its sides) diverge in shape or position. **3** *tr.* construct (a window, aperture, etc.) so that it diverges or is wider at one side of the wall than at the other. ● *n.* a surface making an oblique angle with another. ● *adj.* **1** wide and flat. **2** turned outward. [Middle English, from DISPLAY]

splay-foot *n.* a broad flat foot turned outward.

spleen *n.* **1** an abdominal organ involved in the production and removal of blood cells in most vertebrates and forming part of the immune system. ▷ LYMPHATIC SYSTEM. **2** lowness of spirits; ill temper, spite (from the earlier belief that the spleen was the seat of such feelings) (*vented their spleen*). [from Greek *splēn*] □ **spleeny** *adj.*

splendid *adj.* **1** magnificent, gorgeous, brilliant, sumptuous. **2** dignified; impressive (*splendid isolation*). **3** excellent; fine (*a splendid chance*). [from Latin *splendidus*] □ **splendidly** *adv.* **splendidness** *n.*

splendiferous *adj. colloq.* or *joc.* splendid.

splendour *n.* (*US* **splendor**) **1** great or dazzling brightness. **2** magnificence; grandeur. [from Latin *splendor*]

splenetic *adj.* **1** ill-tempered; peevish. **2** of or concerning the spleen. [from Late Latin *spleneticus*] □ **splenetically** *adv.*

splenic *adj.* of or in the spleen. □ **splenoid** *adj.*

splice ● *v.tr.* **1** join the ends of (ropes) by interweaving strands. **2** join (pieces of timber, film, etc.) in an overlapping position. **3** (esp. as **spliced** *adj.*) *colloq.* join in marriage. ● *n.* ► a joint made by splicing, e.g. the handle and blade of a cricket bat. □ **splice the main brace** *Naut. hist.* issue an extra tot of rum. □ **splicer** *n.*

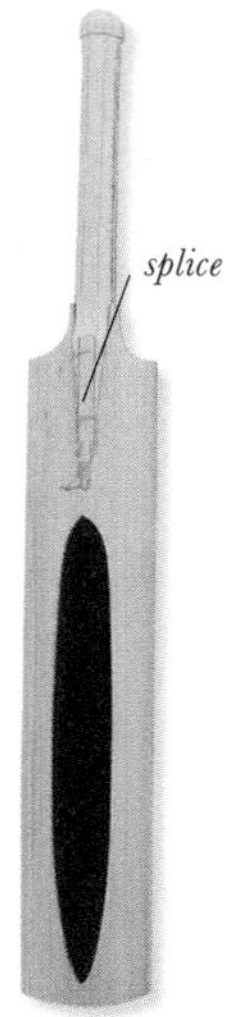

SPLICE: CRICKET BAT WITH HANDLE SPLICED TO BLADE

spliff *n.* (also **splif**) *slang* a cannabis cigarette. [20th-century coinage]

splint ● *n.* **1 a** a strip of rigid material used for holding a broken bone etc. when set. **b** a strip of esp. wood used in basketwork etc. **2** a thin strip of wood etc. used to light a fire, pipe, etc. ● *v.tr.* secure with a splint or splints. [from Middle Dutch *splinte* 'metal plate or pin']

splinter ● *v.tr.* & *intr.* break into fragments. ● *n.* a small thin sharp-edged piece broken off from wood, stone, etc. [from Middle Dutch, related to SPLINT] □ **splintery** *adj.*

splinter group *n.* (also **splinter party**) a group or party that has broken away from a larger one.

split ● *v.* (**splitting**; *past* and *past part.* **split**) **1 a** *intr.* & *tr.* break or cause to break forcibly into parts, esp. into halves or along the grain. **b** *intr.* & *tr.* (often foll. by *up*) divide into parts (*split into groups*). **c** *tr.* (also *absol.*) *slang* divide (money) between usu. accomplices. **2** *tr.* & *intr.* (often foll. by *off*, *away*) remove or be removed by breaking, separating, or dividing (*split away from the group*). **3** *intr.* & *tr.* **a** (usu. foll. by *up*) *colloq.* separate, esp. through discord. **b** (foll. by *with*) *colloq.* quarrel or cease association with (another person etc.). **c** (often as **split** *adj.*) (usu. foll. by *on*, *over*) separate or divide as a result of opposing views (*opinion is split over Europe*). **4** *tr.* cause the fission of (an atom). **5** *intr.* & *tr. slang* leave, esp. suddenly. **6** *intr.* (usu. foll. by *on*) *Brit. slang* betray secrets; inform. **7** *intr.* **a** (as **splitting** *adj.*) (esp. of a headache) very painful; acute. **b** (of the head) suffer great pain from a headache, noise, etc. ● *n.* **1** the act or an instance of splitting; the state of being split. **2** a fissure, crack, cleft, etc. **3** a separation into parties; a schism. **4** (in *pl.*) the athletic feat of leaping in the air or sitting down with the legs at right angles to the body in front and behind, or on either side. **5 a** a half a bottle of mineral water. **b** half a glass of liquor. **6** *slang* a division of money, esp. the proceeds of crime. □ **split the difference** take the average of two proposed amounts. **split hairs** make insignificant distinctions. **split one's sides** be convulsed with laughter. **split the vote** *Brit.* (of a candidate or minority party) attract votes from another so that both are defeated by a third. [originally nautical, from Middle Dutch *splitten*] □ **splitter** *n.*

split end *n.* (usu. in *pl.*) a hair which has split at the end from dryness etc.

S

split infinitive *n.* a phrase consisting of an infinitive with an adverb etc. inserted between *to* and the verb, e.g. *seems to really like it.*

■ **Usage** It is often said that an infinitive should never be split. However, this is an artificial rule and can produce clumsy or ambiguous sentences. In many cases a split infinitive sounds more natural than its avoidance, e.g. *What is it like to actually live in France?* On other occasions, it is better to place the adverb before or after the infinitive, e.g. *He wanted to completely give up his business* reads better as *He wanted to give up his business completely.*

split-level *adj.* (of a building) having a room or rooms a fraction of a storey higher than other parts.

split pea *n.* a pea dried and split in half for cooking.

split personality *n.* the alteration or dissociation of personality occurring in some mental illnesses, esp. schizophrenia and hysteria.

split pin *n.* a metal cotter pin passed through a hole and held in place by its gaping split end.

split ring *n.* a small steel ring with two spiral turns, such as a keyring.

split-screen *n.* a screen on which two or more separate images are displayed.

split second ● *n.* a very brief moment of time. ● *attrib.adj.* (**split-second**) **1** very rapid. **2** (of timing) very precise.

split shift *n.* a shift comprising two or more separate periods of duty.

splodge *colloq.* ● *n.* a daub, blot, or smear. ● *v.tr.* make a large, esp. irregular, spot or patch on. □ **splodgy** *adj.*

splosh *colloq.* ● *v.tr. & intr.* move with a splashing sound. ● *n.* **1** a splashing sound. **2** a splash of water etc. **3** *slang* money.

splotch *n. & v.tr.* = SPLODGE. □ **splotchy** *adj.*

splurge *colloq.* ● *n.* **1** an ostentatious display or effort. **2** an instance of sudden great extravagance. ● *v.intr. & tr.* **1** (usu. foll. by *on*) spend (effort or esp. large sums of money). **2** splash heavily. [19th-century US coinage]

splutter ● *v.* **1** *intr.* **a** speak in a hurried, vehement, or choking manner. **b** emit spitting sounds. **2** *tr.* **a** speak or utter rapidly or incoherently. **b** emit (food, sparks, etc.) with a spitting sound. ● *n.* spluttering speech or sound. □ **splutterer** *n.* **splutteringly** *adv.*

spoil ● *v.* (*past* and *past part.* **spoilt** (esp. *Brit.*) or **spoiled**) **1** *tr.* **a** damage; diminish the value of (*spoilt by the rain*). **b** reduce a person's enjoyment etc. of (*the news spoiled his dinner*). **2** *tr.* injure the character of (a child, pet, etc.) by excessive indulgence. **3** *intr.* **a** (of food) go bad, decay. **b** (usu. in *neg.*) (of a joke, secret, etc.) become stale through long keeping. **4** *tr.* render (a ballot paper) invalid by improper marking. ● *n.* **1** (usu. in *pl.*) **a** plunder taken from an enemy in war, or seized by force. **b** profit or advantage from success or position. **2** earth etc. thrown up in excavating, dredging, etc. □ **be spoiling for** aggressively seek (a fight etc.). **spoilt for choice** *Brit.* having so many choices that it is difficult to choose. [from Latin *spoliare* 'to despoil']

spoilage *n.* **1** paper spoilt in printing. **2** the spoiling of food etc. by decay.

spoiler *n.* **1** a person or thing that spoils something. **2 a** a device on an aircraft to retard its speed by interrupting the airflow. **b** a similar device on a vehicle to improve road-holding at speed. **3** a news item or new product used to divert attention from another.

spoilsport *n.* a person who spoils others' pleasure or enjoyment.

spoilt *past* and *past part.* of SPOIL.

spoke[1] ● *n.* **1** each of the bars running from the hub to the rim of a wheel. ▷ BICYCLE. **2** a rung of a ladder. **3** each radial handle of the wheel of a ship etc. ● *v.tr.* **1** provide with spokes. **2** obstruct (a wheel etc.) by thrusting a spoke in. □ **put a spoke in a**

person's wheel *Brit.* thwart or hinder a person. [Old English] □ **spoked** *adj.* **spokewise** *adv.*

spoke[2] *past* of SPEAK.

spoken *past part.* of SPEAK. ● *adj.* (in *comb.*) speaking in a specified way (*smooth-spoken; well-spoken*). □ **spoken for** claimed, requisitioned.

spokeshave *n.* ▼ a blade set transversely between two handles, used for shaping spokes and other esp. curved work.

handle   adjusting screw   blade   handle

SPOKESHAVE

spokesman *n.* (*pl.* **-men**; *fem.* **spokeswoman**, *pl.* **-women**) **1** a person who speaks on behalf of others, esp. in the course of public relations. **2** a person deputed to express the views of a group etc.

spokesperson *n.* (*pl.* **-persons** or **-people**) a spokesman or spokeswoman.

spoliation *n.* plunder or pillage, esp. of neutral vessels in war. [from Latin *spoliatio*]

spondee *n. Prosody* a foot consisting of two long (or stressed) syllables. [from Greek *spondē* 'libation', as being characteristic of music accompanying libations]

spondulicks /spon-**dew**-liks/ *n.pl. slang* money. [19th-century coinage]

sponge ● *n.* **1** any sessile aquatic animal of the phylum Porifera, with a porous bag-like body structure and a rigid or elastic internal skeleton. **2 a** ▶ the skeleton of a sponge, esp. the soft light elastic absorbent kind used in bathing etc. **b** a piece of porous rubber or plastic etc. used similarly. **c** a piece of sponge or similar material inserted in the vagina as a contraceptive. **3** a thing of spongelike absorbency or consistency, e.g. a sponge pudding, porous metal, etc. **4** = SPONGER. **5** cleansing with or as with a sponge (*give it a sponge*). ● *v.* (**sponging** or **spongeing**) **1** *tr.* wipe or cleanse with a sponge. **2** *tr.* (also *absol.*; often foll. by *down, over*) sluice water over (the body, a car, etc.). **3** *tr.* (often foll. by *out, away*, etc.) wipe off or efface (writing etc.) with or as with a sponge. **4** *tr.* (often foll. by *up*) absorb with or as with a sponge. **5** *intr.* (often foll. by *on, off*) live as a parasite. **6** *tr.* obtain (drink etc.) by sponging. **7** *intr.* gather sponges. **8** *tr.* apply paint with a sponge to (walls, furniture, etc.). [from Greek *spoggia*] □ **spongeable** *adj.* **spongiform** *adj.* (esp. in senses 1, 2a of *n.*).

sponge bag *n. Brit.* a waterproof bag for toilet articles.

sponge cake *n.* a very light cake with a spongelike consistency.

sponge cloth *n.* **1** soft, lightly-woven cloth with a slightly wrinkled surface. **2** a thin spongy material used for cleaning.

sponge pudding *n. Brit.* a steamed or baked pudding of fat, flour, and eggs with a usu. specified flavour.

sponger *n.* a person who contrives to live at another's expense.

sponge rubber *n.* liquid rubber latex processed into a spongelike substance.

spongiform encephalopathy *n.* any of several diseases of the brain, believed to be caused by prions, in which the brain tissue becomes spongy.

spongy *adj.* (**spongier**, **spongiest**) like a sponge, esp. in being

SPONGE: SKELETON
OF A SPONGE
(*Spongia officinalis*)

porous, compressible, elastic, or absorbent. □ **spongily** *adv.* **sponginess** *n.*

sponsor ● *n.* **1** a person who supports an activity done for charity by pledging money in advance. **2 a** a person or organization that promotes or supports an artistic or sporting activity etc. **b** esp. *US* a business organization that promotes a broadcast programme in return for advertising time. **3** an organization lending support to an election candidate. **4** a person who introduces a proposal for legislation. **5 a** a godparent at baptism. **b** esp. *RC Ch.* a person who presents a candidate for confirmation. **6** a person who makes himself or herself responsible for another. ● *v.tr.* be a sponsor for. [Latin] □ **sponsorial** *adj.* **sponsorship** *n.*

spontaneous *adj.* **1** acting or done or occurring without external cause. **2** voluntary, without external incitement. **3** (of style or manner) gracefully natural and unconstrained. **4** (of sudden movement etc.) involuntary. **5** growing naturally without cultivation. [based on Latin *sponte* 'of one's own accord'] □ **spontaneity** *n.* **spontaneously** *adv.* **spontaneousness** *n.*

spontaneous combustion *n.* the ignition of a substance from heat engendered within itself.

spoof *colloq.* ● *n.* **1** a parody. **2** a hoax or swindle. ● *v.tr.* **1** parody. **2** hoax, swindle. [coined by A. Roberts, English comedian, 1852–1933] □ **spoofer** *n.* **spoofery** *n.*

spook ● *n.* **1** *colloq.* a ghost. **2** *US slang* a spy. ● *v. N. Amer. slang* **1** *tr.* frighten, unnerve, alarm. **2** *intr.* take fright, become alarmed. [Dutch]

spooky *adj.* (**spookier**, **spookiest**) **1** *colloq.* ghostly, eerie. **2** *N. Amer. slang* nervous. **3** *US slang* of spies or espionage. □ **spookily** *adv.* **spookiness** *n.*

spool ● *n.* **1 a** a reel for winding magnetic tape, photographic film, etc., on. **b** a reel for winding thread, wire, etc. on. **c** a quantity of tape etc., wound on a spool. **2** the revolving cylinder of an angler's reel. ▷ REEL. ● *v.tr.* wind on a spool. [from Old French *espole*]

spoon ● *n.* **1 a** a utensil consisting of an oval or round bowl and a handle for conveying food (esp. liquid) to the mouth, for stirring, etc. **b** a spoonful, esp. of sugar. **2** a spoon-shaped thing, esp.: **a** (in full **spoon-bait**) a bright revolving piece of metal used as a lure in fishing. **b** an oar with a broad curved blade. ● *v.* **1** *tr.* (often foll. by *up, out*) take (liquid etc.) with a spoon. **2** *tr.* hit (a ball) feebly upwards. **3** *intr. colloq.* behave in an amorous way, esp. foolishly. **4** *intr.* fish with a spoon-bait. □ **born with a silver spoon in one's mouth** born in affluence. [Old English *spōn* 'chip of wood'] □ **spooner** *n.* (in sense 3 of *v.*). **spoonful** *n.* (*pl.* **-fuls**).

spoonbill *n.* **1** ◀ any large mainly white wading bird of the family Threskiornithidae, related to ibises, having a bill with a very broad flat tip. **2** a shoveler duck.

spoon-bread *n. US* soft maize bread.

spoonerism *n.* a transposition, usu. accidental, of the initial letters etc. of two or more words, e.g. *you have hissed the mystery lectures.* [named after Revd W. A. *Spooner*, English scholar, 1844–1930, reputed to make such errors in speaking]

spoon-feed *v.tr.* (*past* and *past part.* **-fed**) **1** feed (a baby etc.) with a spoon. **2** provide help, information, etc., to (a person etc.) without requiring any effort on the recipient's part.

spoor ● *n.* the track or scent of an animal. ● *v.tr. & intr.* follow by the spoor. [from Middle Dutch *spo(o)r*]

sporadic *adj.* occurring only here and there or occasionally; scattered. [from Greek *sporadikos*] □ **sporadically** *adv.*

SPOONBILL:
EURASIAN SPOONBILL
(*Platalea leucorodia*)

S

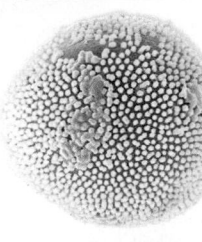

SPORE: MICROGRAPH OF A MOSS SPORE (*Funaria hygrometrica*)

spore *n.* **1** ◄ a specialized reproductive cell of many plants and micro-organisms. **2** these collectively. [from Greek *spora* 'sowing, seed', from *speirō* 'sow']

sporran *n.* a pouch worn in front of the kilt. [from Gaelic *sporan*]

sport ● *n.* **1 a** a game or competitive activity, esp. an outdoor one involving physical exertion, e.g. cricket, football, racing, hunting. **b** such activities collectively (*the world of sport*). **2** (in *pl.*) *Brit.* **a** a meeting for competing in sports, esp. athletics (*school sports*). **b** athletics. **3** amusement, fun. **4** *colloq.* **a** a fair or generous person. **b** a person with a specified attitude to games, rules, etc. (*a bad sport at tennis*). **c** *Austral. & US* a form of address, esp. between males. **5** *Biol.* an animal or plant deviating from the parent type. **6** a plaything or butt (*the sport of Fortune*). ● *v.* **1** *intr.* divert oneself, take part in a pastime. **2** *tr.* wear or exhibit, esp. ostentatiously. **3** *intr. Biol.* become or produce a sport. □ **in sport** jestingly. **make sport of** make fun of. [Middle English, from DISPORT] □ **sporter** *n.*

sporting *adj.* **1** interested in sport (*a sporting man*). **2** sportsmanlike, generous (*a sporting offer*). **3** concerned with sport (*sporting news*). □ **sportingly** *adv.*

sporting chance *n.* some possibility of success.

sportive *adj.* playful. □ **sportively** *adv.* **sportiveness** *n.*

sports car *n.* a usu. open, low-built fast car. ▷ CAR

sportscast *n. N. Amer.* a broadcast of a sports event or information about sport. □ **sportscaster** *n.*

sports coat *n.* (also **sports jacket**) a man's jacket for informal wear.

sports ground *n.* a piece of land used for sports.

sportsman *n.* (*pl.* **-men**; *fem.* **sportswoman**, *pl.* **-women**) **1** a person who takes part in sport, esp. professionally. **2** a person who behaves fairly and generously. □ **sportsmanlike** *adj.* **sportsmanly** *adj.* **sportsmanship** *n.*

sportsperson *n.* (*pl.* **-persons** or **-people**) a sportsman or sportswoman.

sportswear *n.* clothes worn for sport or for casual outdoor use.

sports writer *n.* a person who writes (esp. as a journalist) on sports.

sporty *adj.* (**sportier**, **sportiest**) *colloq.* **1 a** fond of sport. **b** (esp. of clothes) suitable for wearing for sport or for casual outdoor use. **2** rakish, showy. □ **sportily** *adv.* **sportiness** *n.*

spot ● *n.* **1 a** a small part of the surface of a thing distinguished by colour, texture, etc., usu. round or less elongated than a streak or stripe. **b** a small mark or stain. **c** a pimple. **d** a small circle or other shape used in various numbers to distinguish playing cards in a suit etc. **e** a moral blemish or stain. **2 a** a particular place; a definite locality (*on this precise spot*). **b** a place used for a particular activity (often in *comb.*: *nightspot*). **c** (in full **the penalty spot**) *Football* the place from which a penalty kick is taken. **3** a particular part of one's body or aspect of one's character. **4 a** *colloq.* one's (esp. regular) position in an organization, programme, etc. **b** a portion of a show etc. (*did the spot before the interval*). **5** *Brit. colloq.* a small quantity of anything (*a spot of lunch*). **b** a drop (*a spot of rain*). **6** = SPOTLIGHT *n.* 1, 2. **7** (usu. *attrib.*) money paid or goods delivered immediately after a sale (*spot cash*). ● *v.* (**spotted**, **spotting**) **1** *tr.* **a** *colloq.* single out beforehand (the winner of a race etc.). **b** *colloq.* recognize the identity etc. of. **c** watch for and take note of (trains, talent, etc.). **d** *colloq.* catch sight of. **e** *Mil.* locate (an enemy's position), esp. from the air. **2 a** *tr. & intr.* mark or become marked with spots. **b** *tr.* stain (a

person's character etc.). **3** *intr.* rain slightly (*it was spotting with rain*). □ **hit the spot** *colloq.* be exactly what is required. **in a spot** (or **in a tight** etc. **spot**) *colloq.* in difficulty. **on the spot 1** at the scene of an action or event. **2** *colloq.* in a position such that response or action is required. **3** then and there. **put on the spot** *colloq.* force to make a difficult decision, answer an awkward question, etc. **running on the spot** *Brit.* raising the feet alternately as in running but without moving forwards or backwards. [Middle English]

spot check ● *n.* a test made on the spot or on a randomly-selected subject. ● *v.tr.* (**spot-check**) subject to a spot check.

spotlamp *n.* = SPOTLIGHT *n.* 2.

spotless *adj.* immaculate; absolutely clean or pure. □ **spotlessly** *adv.* **spotlessness** *n.*

spotlight ● *n.* **1** a beam of light directed on a small area. **2** a lamp projecting this. **3** full attention or publicity. ● *v.tr.* (*past* and *past part.* **-lighted** or **-lit**) **1** direct a spotlight on. **2** make conspicuous, draw attention to.

spot on *Brit. colloq.* ● *adj.* precise; on target. ● *adv.* precisely.

spotted *adj.* marked or decorated with spots. □ **spottedness** *n.*

spotted dick *n. Brit.* a suet pudding containing currants.

spotted dog *n.* **1** a Dalmatian dog. **2** *Brit.* = SPOTTED DICK.

spotter *n.* **1** (often in *comb.*) a person who spots people or things (*train-spotter*). **2** an aviator or aircraft employed in locating enemy positions etc.

spotty *adj.* (**spottier**, **spottiest**) **1** marked with spots. **2** patchy, irregular. □ **spottily** *adv.* **spottiness** *n.*

spot-weld *v.tr.* join (two metal surfaces) by welding at discrete points. □ **spot-welder** *n.* **spot-welding** *n.*

spouse *n.* a husband or wife. [from Latin *sponsa* (fem.) 'betrothed']

spout ● *n.* **1 a** a projecting tube or lip through which a liquid etc. is poured from a teapot, kettle, jug, etc., or issues from a fountain, pump, etc. **b** a sloping trough down which a thing may be shot into a receptacle. **2** a jet or column of liquid, grain, etc. **3** (in full **spout-hole**) a whale's blowhole (see BLOWHOLE 1). ● *v.tr. & intr.* **1** discharge or issue forcibly in a jet. **2** utter (verses etc.) or speak in a declamatory manner, speechify. □ **up the spout** *Brit. slang* **1** useless, ruined, hopeless. **2** pawned. **3** pregnant. [from Middle Dutch *spouten*] □ **spouter** *n.*

sprain ● *v.tr.* wrench (an ankle, wrist, etc.) violently so as to cause pain and swelling but not dislocation. ● *n.* **1** such a wrench. **2** the resulting inflammation and swelling. [17th-century coinage]

sprang *past* of SPRING.

sprat *n.* **1** a small European herring-like fish, *Sprattus sprattus*, much used as food. **2** a similar fish, e.g. a sand eel or a young herring. [Old English] □ **spratting** *n.*

sprawl ● *v.* **1 a** *intr.* sit or lie or fall with limbs flung out or in an ungainly way. **b** *tr.* spread (one's limbs) in this way. **2** *intr.* (of handwriting, a plant, a town, etc.) be of irregular or straggling form. ● *n.* **1** a sprawling movement or attitude. **2** a straggling group or mass. **3** the straggling expansion of an urban or industrial area. [Old English] □ **sprawlingly** *adv.*

spray[1] ● *n.* **1** water or other liquid flying in small drops from the force of the wind or waves, the action of an atomizer, etc. **2** a liquid preparation to be applied in this form with an atomizer etc., esp. for medical purposes. **3** an instrument or apparatus for such application. ● *v.tr.* (also *absol.*) **1** throw (liquid) in the form of spray. **2** sprinkle (a plant etc.) with small drops or particles. **3** (*absol.*) (of a male animal, esp. a cat) mark its environment with the smell of its urine. [earlier *spry*] □ **sprayable** *adj.* **sprayer** *n.*

spray[2] *n.* **1** a sprig of flowers or leaves, or a branch of a tree with branchlets or flowers. **2** a bunch of flowers decoratively arranged. **3** an ornament in a similar form (*a spray of diamonds*). [from Old English *(e)sprei*, recorded in personal and place names] □ **sprayey** *adj.*

spray-dry *v.tr.* (**-dries**, **-dried**) dry (milk etc.) by spraying into hot air etc.

spray-gun *n.* ▼ a gunlike device for spraying paint etc.

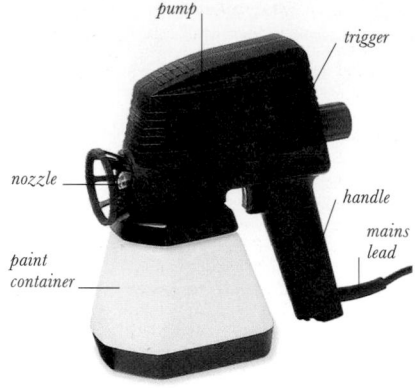

pump

trigger

nozzle

handle

mains lead

paint container

SPRAY-GUN

spray-paint *v.tr.* paint (a surface) by means of a spray.

spread ● *v.* (*past* and *past part.* **spread**) **1** *tr.* (often foll. by *out*) **a** open or extend the surface of. **b** cause to cover a larger surface. **c** display to the eye or the mind (*the view spread before us*). **2** *intr.* (often foll. by *out*) have a wide or specified or increasing extent (*spreading trees*). **3** *intr. & tr.* become or make widely known, felt, etc. (*rumours are spreading*). **4** *tr.* **a** cover the surface of. **b** lay (a table). ● *n.* **1** the act or an instance of spreading. **2** capability of expanding (*has a large spread*). **3** diffusion (*spread of learning*). **4** breadth, compass (*arches of equal spread*). **5** an aircraft's wingspan. **6** increased bodily girth (*middle-aged spread*). **7** the difference between two rates, prices, etc. **8** *colloq.* an elaborate meal. **9** a sweet or savoury paste for spreading on bread etc. **10** a bedspread. **11** printed matter spread across more than one column. **12** *US* a ranch with extensive land. □ **spread one's wings** see WING. [Old English] □ **spreadable** *adj.* **spreader** *n.*

spread eagle ● *n.* ▼ a representation of an eagle with legs and wings extended as an emblem. ● *v.tr.* (**spreadeagle**; usu. as **spreadeagled** *adj.*) **1** place (a person) with arms and legs spread out. **2** defeat utterly.

SPREAD EAGLE: EMBLEM OF THE FRENCH 105TH REGIMENT

S

spreadsheet *n.* a computer program allowing manipulation and flexible retrieval of esp. tabulated numerical data.

spree *colloq.* ● *n.* **1** a lively extravagant outing (*shopping spree*). **2** a bout of fun or drinking etc. ● *v.intr.* (**sprees, spreed**) have a spree. □ **on the spree** engaged in a spree. [18th-century coinage]

sprig¹ ● *n.* **1** a small branch and shoot. **2** an ornament resembling this, esp. on fabric. ● *v.tr.* (**sprigged, sprigging**) ornament with sprigs (*a dress of sprigged muslin*). [Middle English]

sprig² *n.* a small tapering headless tack. [Middle English]

sprightly *adj.* (also **spritely**) (**-lier, -liest**) vivacious, lively, brisk. [based on *spright*, variant of SPRITE] □ **sprightliness** *n.*

spring ● *v.* (*past* **sprang** or *US* **sprung**; *past part.* **sprung**) **1** *intr.* jump; move rapidly or suddenly. **2** *intr.* move rapidly as from a constrained position or by the action of a spring. **3** *intr.* (usu. foll. by *from*) originate or arise. **4** *intr.* (usu. foll. by *up*) come into being; appear, esp. suddenly (*a breeze sprang up*). **5** *tr.* cause to act suddenly, esp. by means of a spring (*spring a trap*). **6** *tr.* (often foll. by *on*) produce or develop or make known suddenly or unexpectedly (*loves to spring surprises*). **7** *tr.* *slang* contrive the escape or release of. **8** *tr.* rouse (game) from earth or covert. **9** *intr.* become warped or split. **10** *tr.* (usu. as **sprung** *adj.*) provide (a motor vehicle etc.) with springs. ● *n.* **1** a jump. **2** a backward movement from a constrained position; a recoil. **3** elasticity; ability to spring back strongly. **4** a resilient device usu. of bent or coiled metal used esp. to drive clockwork or for cushioning in furniture or vehicles. **5 a** the season in which vegetation begins to appear, in the northern hemisphere from March to May and in the southern hemisphere from September to November. ▷ SEASON. **b** *Astron.* the period from the vernal equinox to the summer solstice. **c** (often foll. by *of*) the early stage of life etc. **d** = SPRING TIDE. **6** a place where water, oil, etc., wells up from the earth; the basin or flow so formed. **7** the motive or origin of an action, custom, etc. (*the springs of human action*). □ **spring a leak** develop a leak (orig. *Naut.*, from timbers springing out of position). [Old English] □ **springless** *adj.* **springlike** *adj.*

■ **Usage** The use of *sprung* instead of *sprang* for the past tense, as in *I sprung out of bed*, is non-standard in British English, but acceptable along with *sprang* in American English.

spring balance *n.* ◀ a balance that measures weight by the tension of a spring.

SPRING BALANCE

— *eye*
— *scale*
— *spring inside*
— *hook*
— *ring*
— *weight*

springboard *n.* **1** a flexible board for leaping or diving from. **2** a source of impetus.

springbok *n.* **1** a southern African gazelle, *Antidorcas marsupialis*, with the ability to run with high springing jumps. **2** (**Springbok**) a South African, esp. one who has competed in international sport for South Africa. [Afrikaans]

spring chicken *n.* **1** a young fowl for eating (originally available only in spring). **2** a youthful person.

spring-clean ● *n.* *Brit.* a thorough cleaning of a house or room, esp. in spring. ● *v.tr.* clean (a house or room) in this way.

spring equinox *n.* **1** the equinox in spring, on about 20 March in the northern hemisphere and 22 Sept. in the southern hemisphere. **2** *Astron.* the equinox in March. Also called *vernal equinox*.

springer *n.* **1** a person or thing that springs. **2** a small spaniel of a breed used to spring game.

spring fever *n.* a restless or lethargic feeling sometimes associated with spring.

spring greens *n.pl.* the leaves of young cabbage plants of a variety that does not develop a heart.

spring-loaded *adj.* containing a compressed or stretched spring pressing one part against another.

spring onion *n.* *Brit.* an onion taken from the ground before the bulb has formed, eaten raw.

spring roll *n.* a Chinese fried pancake filled with vegetables.

springtail *n.* ◀ any wingless insect of the order Collembola, leaping by means of a springlike caudal part.

SPRINGTAIL
(*Orchesella* species)

springtime *n. poet.* = SPRINGTIME.

spring tide *n.* a tide just after new and full moon when there is the greatest difference between high and low water. ▷ TIDE

springtime *n.* **1** the season of spring. **2** a time compared to this.

spring water *n.* water from a spring, as opposed to river water or rainwater.

springy *adj.* (**springier, springiest**) **1** springing back quickly when squeezed or stretched; elastic. **2** (of movements) as of a springy substance. □ **springily** *adv.* **springiness** *n.*

sprinkle ● *v.tr.* **1** scatter in small drops or particles. **2** (often foll. by *with*) subject to sprinkling with liquid etc. **3** (of liquid etc.) fall on in this way. **4** distribute in small amounts. ● *n.* (usu. foll. by *of*) **1** a light shower. **2** = SPRINKLING. [Middle English]

sprinkler *n.* a device for sprinkling water on a lawn or for extinguishing fires.

sprinkling *n.* (usu. foll. by *of*) a small thinly distributed number or amount.

sprint ● *v.* **1** *intr.* run a short distance at full speed. **2** *tr.* run (a specified distance) in this way. ● *n.* **1 a** such a run **b** *Sport* a running race over a distance of 400 metres or less. **2** a similar short spell of maximum effort in cycling, swimming, motor racing, etc. [from Old Norse]

sprinter *n.* **1** an athlete who specializes in short distance races. **2** a vehicle, esp. a train, designed for rapid travel over short distances.

sprit *n.* a small spar reaching diagonally from the mast to the upper outer corner of the sail. [Old English *sprēot* 'pole']

sprite *n.* an elf, fairy, or goblin. [from Old French *esprit* 'spirit']

spritely var. of SPRIGHTLY.

spritsail *n.* **1** a sail extended by a sprit. **2** *hist.* a sail extended by a yard set under the bowsprit.

spritzer *n.* a mixture of wine and soda water. [German, literally 'a splash']

sprocket-wheel —

sprocket roller chain —

SPROCKET-WHEEL AND CHAIN OF A BICYCLE

sprocket *n.* **1** ◀ each of several teeth on a wheel engaging with links of a chain. ▷ DERAILLEUR. **2** (also **sprocket-wheel**) ◀ a wheel with sprockets. [16th-century coinage]

sprog *n.* *Brit.* *slang* a child; a baby. [originally services' slang in sense 'new recruit']

sprout ● *v.* **1** *tr.* put forth, produce (shoots, hair, etc.). **2** *intr.* begin to grow, put forth shoots. **3** *intr.* spring up, grow to a height. ● *n.* **1** a shoot of a plant. **2** = BRUSSELS SPROUT. [Old English]

spruce¹ ● *adj.* neat in dress and appearance; smart. ● *v.tr.* & *intr.* (also *refl.*; usu. foll. by *up*) make or become smart. □ **sprucely** *adv.* **spruceness** *n.*

spruce² *n.* **1** ▶ any coniferous tree of the genus *Picea*, with dense foliage growing in a conical shape. **2** the wood of this tree. [alteration of obsolete *Pruce* 'Prussia']

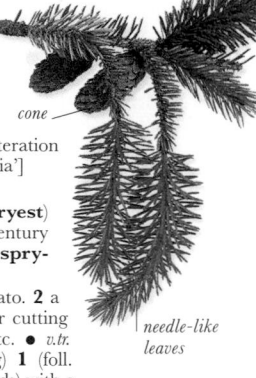

cone

needle-like leaves

SPRUCE
(*Picea sitchensis*)

sprung see SPRING.

spry *adj.* (**spryer, spryest**) active, lively. [18th-century coinage] □ **spryly** *adv.* **spryness** *n.*

spud ● *n.* **1** *slang* a potato. **2** a small narrow spade for cutting the roots of weeds etc. ● *v.tr.* (**spudded, spudding**) **1** (foll. by *up, out*) remove (weeds) with a spud. **2** (also *absol.*; often foll. by *in*) make the initial drilling for (an oil well). [Middle English]

spue var. of SPEW.

spumante /spoo-**man**-ti/ *n.* an Italian sparkling white wine. [Italian, literally 'sparkling']

spume *n.* & *v.intr.* froth, foam. [from Latin *spuma*] □ **spumous** *adj.* **spumy** *adj.*

spun *past* and *past part.* of SPIN.

spunk *n.* **1** touchwood. **2** *colloq.* courage, mettle. **3** *Brit. coarse slang* semen. **4** *Austral. slang* a sexually attractive person. [16th-century coinage]

spunky *adj.* (**spunkier, spunkiest**) **1** *colloq.* brave, spirited. **2** *Austral. slang* sexually attractive. □ **spunkily** *adv.*

spur ● *n.* **1** ▶ a device with a small spike or a spiked wheel worn on a rider's heel for urging a horse forward. **2** a stimulus or incentive. **3** a spur-shaped thing, esp.: **a** a projection from a mountain or mountain range. **b** a branch road or railway. **c** a hard projection on a cock's leg. ● *v.* (**spurred, spurring**) **1** *tr.* prick (a horse) with spurs. **2** *tr.* **a** (often foll. by *on*) incite (a person). **b** stimulate (interest etc.). **3** *intr.* (often foll. by *on, forward*) ride a horse hard. **4** *tr.* (esp. as **spurred** *adj.*) provide with spurs. □ **on the spur of the moment** on a momentary impulse; impromptu. [Old English, related to SPURN] □ **spurless** *adj.* **spurred** *adj.* (esp. in sense 1 of *n.*).

spiked wheel

SPUR: AMERICAN HAND-FORGED SPUR

spurge *n.* any plant of the genus *Euphorbia*, exuding an acrid milky juice. [based on Latin *expurgare* 'to purify']

spurious *adj.* **1** not genuine, not being what it purports to be, not proceeding from the pretended source (*a spurious excuse*). **2** having an outward similarity of form or function only. **3** (of offspring) illegitimate. [from Latin *spurius* 'false'] □ **spuriously** *adv.* **spuriousness** *n.*

spurn *v.tr.* **1** reject with disdain; treat with contempt. **2** repel or thrust back with one's foot. [Old English, related to SPUR]

spurt ● *v.* **1** (also **spirt**) **a** *intr.* gush out in a jet. **b** *tr.* cause (liquid etc.) to do this. **2** *intr.* make a sudden effort. ● *n.* **1** (also **spirt**) a sudden gushing out. **2** a short sudden effort or increase of pace. [16th-century coinage]

sputnik *n.* ▶ each of a series of Russian artificial satellites launched from 1957. [Russian, literally 'fellow-traveller']

aluminium sphere

antenna

SPUTNIK

S

sputter ● *v.* **1** *intr.* emit spitting sounds, esp. when being heated. **2** *intr.* (often foll. by *at*) speak in a hurried or vehement fashion. **3** *tr.* emit with a spitting sound. **4** *tr.* speak or utter rapidly or incoherently. ● *n.* a sputtering sound, esp. sputtering speech. [from Dutch *sputteren*] □ **sputterer** *n.*

sputum *n.* (*pl.* **sputa**) **1** saliva, spittle. **2** an expectorated mixture of saliva and mucus, used for diagnosis. [Latin]

spy ● *n.* (*pl.* **spies**) **1** a person who secretly collects and reports information on the activities etc., of an enemy, competitor, etc. **2** a person who keeps watch on others, esp. furtively. ● *v.* (**spies**, **spied**) **1** *tr.* discern or make out, esp. by careful observation. **2** *intr.* (often foll. by *on*) act as a spy, keep a close and secret watch. **3** *intr.* (often foll. by *into*) pry. □ **spy out** explore or discover, esp. secretly. [from Old French *espier* 'to espy']

spyglass *n.* a small telescope.

spyhole *n. Brit.* a peephole.

spymaster *n. colloq.* the head of an organization of spies.

sq. *abbr.* square.

Sqn. Ldr. *abbr.* Squadron Leader.

squab ● *n.* **1** a short fat person. **2** a very young bird, esp. an unfledged pigeon. **3** a stuffed cushion. **b** *Brit.* the padded back or side of a car-seat. **4** a sofa or ottoman. ● *adj.* squat. [17th-century coinage]

squabble ● *n.* a petty or noisy quarrel. ● *v.intr.* engage in a squabble. □ **squabbler** *n.*

squabby *adj.* (**squabbier**, **squabbiest**) short and fat; squat.

squad *n.* **1** a small group of people sharing a task etc. **2** *Mil.* a small number of men assembled for drill etc. **3** *Sport* a group of players forming a team. **4 a** (often in *comb.*) a specialized unit within a police force (*drug squad*). **b** = FLYING SQUAD. [from Italian *squadra* 'square']

squad car *n.* a police car having a radio link with headquarters.

squaddie *n.* (also **squaddy**) (*pl.* **-ies**) *Brit. Mil. slang* **1** a recruit. **2** a private.

squadron *n.* **1** an organized body of persons. **2** a principal division of a cavalry regiment or armoured formation, consisting of two troops. **3 a** a detachment of warships employed on a particular duty. **b** a division of a naval fleet under the command of a flag-officer. **4** a unit of the Royal Air Force with 10 to 18 aircraft. [from Italian *squadrone*]

squadron leader *n.* the commander of a squadron of the Royal Air Force, the officer next below wing commander.

squalid *adj.* **1** filthy, repulsively dirty. **2** mean or poor in appearance. **3** wretched, sordid. [from Latin *squalidus*] □ **squalidity** *n.* **squalidly** *adv.* **squalidness** *n.*

squall ● *n.* **1** a sudden or violent gust or storm of wind, esp. with rain or snow or sleet. **2** a discordant cry; a scream (esp. of a baby). **3** (esp. in *pl.*) trouble, difficulty. ● *v.* **1** *intr.* utter a squall; scream. **2** *tr.* utter in a screaming or discordant voice. □ **squally** *adj.*

squall line *n. Meteorol.* a narrow band of high winds along a cold front.

squalor *n.* the state of being filthy or squalid. [Latin]

squander *v.tr.* spend wastefully. [16th-century coinage] □ **squanderer** *n.*

square ● *n.* **1** an equilateral rectangle. **2 a** an object of this shape or approximately this shape. **b** a small square area on a game-board. **c** a square scarf. **3 a** an open (usu. four-sided) area surrounded by buildings. **b** an open area at the meeting of streets. **c** *Cricket* a closer-cut area at the centre of a ground. **d** an area within barracks etc. for drill. **e** *US* a block of buildings bounded by four streets. **4** the product of a number multiplied by itself (*81 is the square of 9*). **5** an L-shaped or T-shaped instrument

for obtaining or testing right angles. **6** *slang* a conventional or old-fashioned person. **7** a square arrangement of letters, figures, etc. **8** a body of infantry drawn up in rectangular form. ● *adj.* **1** having the shape of a square. **2** having or in the form of a right angle (*table with square corners*). **3** angular and not round (*has a square jaw*). **4** designating a unit of measure equal to the area of a square whose side is one of the unit specified (*square metre*). **5** (often foll. by *with*) esp. *Brit.* **a** level, parallel. **b** on a proper footing; even, quits. **6** (usu. foll. by *to*) at right angles. **7** broad, sturdy (*a man of square frame*). **8** properly arranged; settled (*get things square*). **9** (also **all square**) **a** not in debt, with no money owed. **b** having equal scores. **c** (of scores) equal. **10** fair and honest. **11** uncompromising, direct (*a square refusal*). **12** *slang* conventional or old-fashioned. ● *adv.* **1** squarely (*sat square on his seat*). **2** fairly, honestly (*play square*). ● *v.* **1** *tr.* make square or rectangular; give a rectangular cross-section to (timber etc.). **2** *tr.* multiply (a number) by itself (*3 squared is 9*). **3** *tr.* & *intr.* (usu. foll. by *to*, *with*) make or be suitable or consistent (*the results do not square with your conclusions*). **4** *tr.* mark out in squares. **5** *tr.* settle or pay (a bill etc.). **6** *tr.* place (one's shoulders etc.) squarely facing forwards. **7** *tr. colloq.* **a** pay or bribe. **b** secure the acquiescence etc. of (a person) in this way. **8** *tr.* (also *absol.*) make the scores of (a match etc.) all square. □ **back to square one** *colloq.* back to the starting point with no progress made. **get square with** pay or compound with (a creditor). **on the square** *adj.* **1** *colloq.* honest, fair. **2** having membership of the Freemasons. ● *adv. colloq.* honestly, fairly. **out of square** not at right angles. **square peg in a round hole** see PEG. **square up** settle an account etc. **square up to 1** move towards (a person) in a fighting attitude. **2** face and tackle (a difficulty etc.) resolutely. [from Old French *esquare*] □ **squarely** *adv.* **squareness** *n.* **squarish** *adj.*

square-bashing *n. Brit. Mil. slang* drill on a barrack square.

square brackets *n.pl.* brackets of the form [ ].

square-built *adj.* comparatively broad; broadly-built.

square dance *n.* a dance with usu. four couples facing inwards from four sides.

square deal *n.* a fair bargain, fair treatment.

square-eyed *adj. joc.* affected by or given to excessive viewing of television.

square leg *n. Cricket* the fielding position at some distance on the batsman's leg side and nearly opposite the stumps. ▷ CRICKET

square meal *n.* a substantial and satisfying meal.

square measure *n.* measure expressed in square units.

square number *n.* the square of an integer e.g. 1, 4, 9, 16, 25, etc.

square-rigged *adj.* ▼ (of a vessel) with the principal sails at right angles to the length of the ship. ▷ SHIP

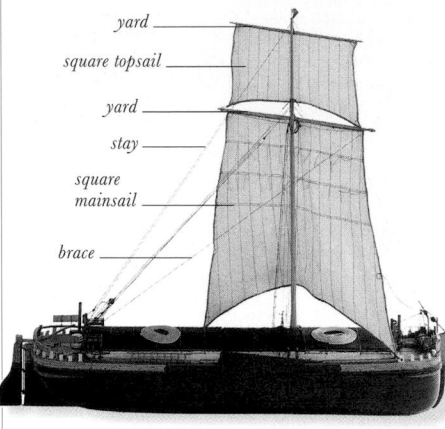

yard
square topsail
yard
stay
square mainsail
brace

SQUARE-RIGGED 19TH-CENTURY ENGLISH BARGE

square root *n.* the number that multiplied by itself gives a specified number.

square-shouldered *adj.* with broad and not sloping shoulders (cf. ROUND-SHOULDERED).

square wave *n. Physics* a wave with periodic sudden alternations between only two values of quantity.

squash[1] ● *v.* **1** *tr.* crush or squeeze flat or into pulp. **2** *intr.* (often foll. by *into*) make one's way by squeezing. **3** *tr.* pack tight, crowd. **4** *tr.* **a** silence (a person) with a crushing retort etc. **b** dismiss (a proposal etc.). **c** quash (a rebellion). ● *n.* **1** a crowd. **2** a sound of or as of something being squashed. **3** *Brit.* a concentrated drink made of crushed fruit etc. **4** (in full **squash rackets**) ▼ a game played with rackets and a small fairly soft ball against the walls of a

SQUASH

Squash players take turns to hit a rubber ball against the front of a four-walled court. The ball is allowed to bounce on the floor only once, but may rebound off any of the walls. It is in play only when below the out lines and above the board. To serve, a player stands with at least part of one foot in the service box and hits the ball above the cut line. The ball must then bounce beyond the short line on the opponent's side of the half-court line.

INTERNATIONAL SQUASH COURT

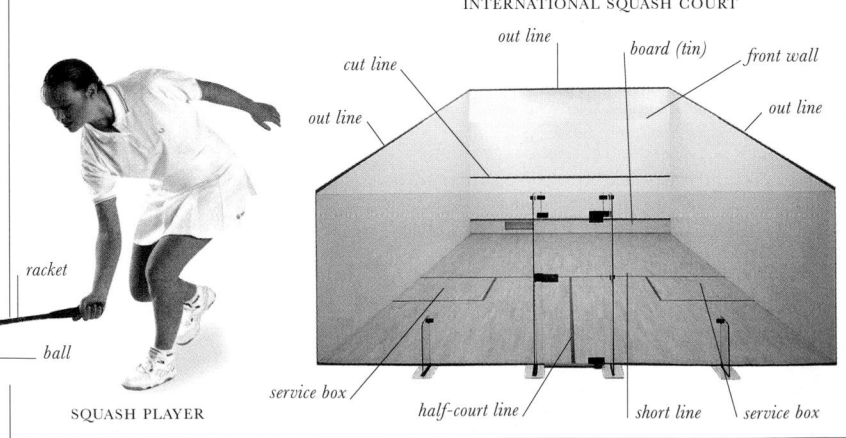

out line
cut line
board (tin)
front wall
out line
out line
racket
ball
service box
half-court line
short line
service box

SQUASH PLAYER

SQUASH: ACORN
SQUASH
(*Cucurbita pepo*)

closed court. **5** a squashed thing or mass. [alteration of QUASH] □ **squashy** *adj.* (**squashier, squashiest**). **squashily** *adv.* **squashiness** *n.*

squash² *n.* (*pl.* same or **squashes**) **1** any of various trailing gourd plants of the genus *Cucurbita* having pumpkin-like fruits. **2** ◀ the fruit of this cooked and eaten as a vegetable. [abbreviation of Algonquian *asquutasquash*]

squat ● *v.* (**squatted, squatting**) **1** *intr.* **a** crouch with the hams resting on the backs of the heels. **b** sit on the ground etc. with the knees drawn up and the heels close to or touching the hams. **2** *intr. colloq.* sit down. **3 a** *intr.* act as a squatter. **b** *tr.* occupy (a building) as a squatter. **4** *intr.* (of an animal) crouch close to the ground. ● *adj.* (**squatter, squattest**) **1** (of a person etc.) dumpy. **2** in a squatting posture. ● *n.* **1** a squatting posture. **2 a** a place occupied by a squatter or squatters. **b** being a squatter. [from Old French *esquatir* 'to flatten'] □ **squatness** *n.*

squatter *n.* **1** a person who takes unauthorized possession of unoccupied premises. **2** *Austral.* a sheep farmer esp. on a large scale. **3** a person who squats.

squat thrust *n.* an exercise in which the legs are thrust backwards starting from a squatting position with the hands on the floor.

squaw *n. offens.* a N. American Indian woman or wife. [from Algonquian *squa* 'woman']

squawk ● *n.* **1** a loud harsh cry esp. of a bird. **2** a complaint. ● *v.tr. & intr.* utter with or make a squawk. □ **squawker** *n.*

squawk-box *n. colloq.* a loudspeaker or intercom.

squeak ● *n.* **1 a** a short shrill cry as of a mouse. **b** a slight high-pitched sound as of an unoiled hinge. **2** (also **narrow squeak**) a narrow escape, a success barely attained. ● *v.* **1** *intr.* make a squeak. **2** *tr.* utter shrilly. **3** *intr.* (foll. by *by, through*) *colloq.* pass narrowly. **4** *intr. slang* turn informer. [Middle English] □ **squeaker** *n.*

squeaky *adj.* (**squeakier, squeakiest**) making a squeaking sound. □ **squeakily** *adv.* **squeakiness** *n.*

squeaky clean *adj.* **1** completely clean. **2** above criticism; beyond reproach.

squeal ● *n.* a prolonged shrill sound, esp. a cry of a child or a pig. ● *v.* **1** *intr.* make a squeal. **2** *tr.* utter (words) with a squeal. **3** *intr. slang* turn informer. **4** *intr. slang* protest loudly or excitedly. [Middle English, imitative] □ **squealer** *n.*

squeamish *adj.* **1** easily nauseated or disgusted. **2** fastidious. [Middle English variant of (now dialect) *squeamous*] □ **squeamishly** *adv.* **squeamishness** *n.*

squeegee ● *n.* a rubber-edged implement set on a handle and used for cleaning windows etc. ● *v.tr.* (**squeegees, squeegeed**) clean or scrape with a squeegee. [from archaic *squeege*, strengthened form of SQUEEZE]

squeeze ● *v.* **1** *tr.* **a** exert pressure on from opposite or all sides, esp. in order to extract moisture or reduce size. **b** compress with one's hand or between two bodies. **c** reduce the size of or alter the shape of by squeezing. **2** *tr.* (often foll. by *out*) extract (moisture) by squeezing. **3 a** *tr.* force into or through a small or narrow space. **b** *intr.* make one's way by squeezing. **c** make (one's way) by squeezing. **4** *tr.* **a** harass by exactions; extort money etc. from. **b** bring pressure to bear on. **c** (usu. foll. by *out*

of) obtain (money etc.) by extortion, entreaty, etc. **5** *tr.* press (a person's hand) with one's own as a sign of sympathy etc. **6** *tr.* (often foll. by *out*) produce with effort. ● *n.* **1** an instance of squeezing; the state of being squeezed. **2** a close embrace. **3** a crush. **4** a small quantity produced by squeezing (*a squeeze of lemon*). **5** *Econ.* a restriction on borrowing, investment, etc., in a financial crisis. □ **put the squeeze on** *colloq.* coerce or pressure (a person). [earlier *squise*, intensive of obsolete *queise*] □ **squeezable** *adj.* **squeezer** *n.*

squeeze bottle *n.* a flexible container whose contents are extracted by squeezing it.

squeeze-box *n. colloq.* an accordion or concertina.

squeezy *adj.* (esp. of a bottle) flexible and able to be squeezed to force out the contents.

squelch ● *v.* **1** *intr.* **a** make a sucking sound as of treading in thick mud. **b** move with a squelching sound. **2** *tr. N. Amer.* **a** disconcert, silence. **b** stamp on, crush flat, put an end to. ● *n.* an instance of squelching. □ **squelchy** *adj.*

squib *n.* **1** a small firework that hisses and then usu. explodes. **2** a short satirical composition, a lampoon. [16th-century coinage]

squid *n.* ▼ any elongated fast-swimming cephalopod mollusc of the order Teuthoidea, with eight arms and two long tentacles, esp. a common edible one of the genus *Loligo*. ▷ CEPHALOPOD. [16th-century coinage]

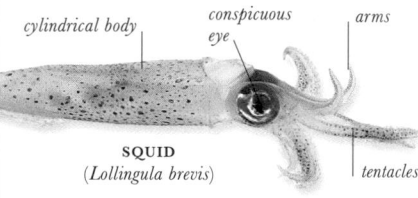

cylindrical body   conspicuous eye   arms

SQUID
(*Lollingula brevis*)

tentacles

squidgy *adj.* (**squidgier, squidgiest**) *colloq.* squashy, soggy.

squiffed *adj. slang* = SQUIFFY.

squiffy *adj.* (**squiffier, squiffiest**) esp. *Brit. slang* slightly drunk. [19th-century coinage]

squiggle ● *n.* a short curly line, esp. in handwriting or doodling. ● *v.* **1** *tr.* write in a squiggly manner; scrawl. **2** *intr.* wriggle, squirm. □ **squiggly** *adj.*

squill *n.* **1** ◀ a bulbous plant of the genus *Scilla* (hyacinth family), typically with star-shaped blue flowers. **2 a** a white-flowered Mediterranean plant, *Drimia maritima* (hyacinth family). **b** an extract of the bulb of this, used in cough mixtures etc. [from Greek *skilla*]

squinch *v.* esp. *US* **1** (usu. foll. by *up*) **a** *tr.* screw up one's eyes, face, etc. **b** *intr.* (of the eyes etc.) screw up, squint. **2** *intr. & tr.* (often foll. by *up, down*) squeeze or squash compactly.

SQUILL: SIBERIAN SQUILL
(*Scilla siberica*)

squint ● *v.* **1** *intr.* have the eyes turned in different directions, have a squint. **2** *intr.* (often foll. by *at*) look obliquely or with half-closed eyes. **3** *tr.* hold (one's eyes) half-shut. ● *n.* **1** = STRABISMUS. **2** a stealthy or sidelong glance. **3** *colloq.* a glance or look (*had a squint at it*). **4** an oblique opening through the wall of a church affording a view of the altar. ● *adj.* **1** squinting. **2** looking different ways. [from obsolete adverb *asquint*] □ **squinty** *adj.*

squint-eyed *adj.* **1** squinting. **2** malignant, ill-willed.

squire ● *n.* **1** a country gentleman, esp. the chief landowner in a district. **2** *hist.* a knight's attendant. **3** *Brit. colloq.* a jocular form of address to a man. ● *v.tr.* (of a man) attend upon or escort (a woman). [from Old French *esquier* 'esquire'] □ **squireling** *n.* **squirely** *adj.* **squireship** *n.*

squirearch *n.* a member of the squirearchy. □ **squirearchical** *adj.* (also **squirarchical**).

squirearchy *n.* (also **squirarchy**) (*pl.* **-ies**) landowners collectively, esp. as a class having political or social influence; a class or body of squires. [on the pattern of *hierarchy*]

squirl *n. colloq.* a flourish or twirl, esp. in handwriting.

squirm ● *v.intr.* **1** wriggle, writhe. **2** show or feel embarrassment or discomfiture. ● *n.* a squirming movement. □ **squirmer** *n.* **squirmy** *adj.* (**squirmier, squirmiest**).

squirrel ● *n.* **1** any rodent of the family Sciuridae, often living in trees, with a bushy tail. ▷ RODENT. **2** the fur of this animal. **3** a person who hoards objects, food, etc. ● *v.tr.* (**squirrelled, squirrelling;** *US* **squirreled, squirreling**) (often foll. by *away*) hoard (objects, food, time, etc.). [from Greek *skiouros*]

squirrelly *adj.* **1** like a squirrel. **2** (of a person) unpredictable, nervous, demented.

squirrel monkey *n.* ▶ a small yellow-haired monkey, *Saimiri sciureus*, native to S. America.

squirt ● *v.* **1** *tr.* eject (liquid or powder) in a jet as from a syringe. **2** *intr.* (of liquid or powder) be discharged in this way. **3** *tr.* splash with liquid or powder ejected by squirting. ● *n.* **1 a** a jet of water etc. **b** a small quantity produced by squirting. **2** a syringe. **3** *colloq.* an insignificant but presumptuous person. [Middle English] □ **squirter** *n.*

squish ● *n.* a slight squelching sound. ● *v.* **1** *intr.* move with a squish. **2** *tr. colloq.* squash, squeeze. □ **squishy** *adj.* (**squishier, squishiest**).

SQUIRREL
MONKEY
(*Saimiri sciureus*)

squit *n. Brit.* **1** *slang* a small or insignificant person. **2** *dial.* nonsense. **3** (**the squits**) *dial. & colloq.* diarrhoea.

Sr *symb. Chem.* the element strontium.

Sr. *abbr.* **1** Senior. **2** Señor. **3** Signor. **4** *Eccl.* Sister.

Sri Lankan ● *n.* **1** a native or national of Sri Lanka. **2** a person of Sri Lankan descent. ● *adj.* of or relating to Sri Lanka or its people.

SRN *abbr.* (in the UK) State Registered Nurse.

SS *abbr.* **1** Saints. **2** steamship. **3** *hist.* Nazi special police force. [sense 3: German *SchutzStaffel*]

SSE *abbr.* south-south-east.

SSI *abbr.* (in the UK) Site of Special Scientific Interest.

SSW *abbr.* south-south-west.

St *abbr.* Saint.

St. *abbr.* Street.

st. *abbr.* **1** stone (in weight). **2** *Cricket* stumped by.

stab ● *v.* (**stabbed, stabbing**) **1** *tr.* pierce or wound with a pointed tool or weapon. **2** *intr.* (often foll. by *at*) aim a blow with such a weapon. **3** *intr.* cause a sensation like being stabbed (*stabbing pain*). **4** *tr.* hurt or distress (a person, feelings, conscience, etc.). **5** *intr.* (foll. by *at*) aim a blow at a person's reputation etc. ● *n.* **1 a** an instance of stabbing. **b** a blow or thrust with a knife etc. **2** a wound made in this way. **3** a sharply painful physical or mental sensation. **4** *colloq.* an attempt, a try. [Middle English] □ **stabber** *n.* **stabbing** *n.*

stabilator *n.* a combined stabilizer and elevator at the tail of an aircraft.

stability *n.* the quality or state of being stable. [from Latin *stabilitas*]

stabilize *v.tr. & intr.* (also **-ise**) make or become stable. □ **stabilization** *n.*

stabilizer *n.* (also **-iser**) a device or substance used to keep something stable, esp.: **1** a gyroscopic

S

S

device to prevent rolling of a ship. **2** *N. Amer.* the horizontal tailplane of an aircraft. **3** (in *pl.*) *Brit.* a pair of small wheels fitted adjacent to the rear wheel of a child's bicycle. **4** a substance which prevents the breakdown of emulsions, esp. as a food additive maintaining texture.

stab in the back ● *n.* a treacherous or slanderous attack. ● *v.tr.* slander or betray.

stable[1] *adj.* (**stabler**, **stablest**) **1** firmly fixed or established; not easily adjusted, destroyed, or altered (*a stable structure; a stable government*). **2 a** firm, resolute; not wavering or fickle (*a stable and steadfast friend*). **b** mentally and emotionally sound, sane and sensible. **3** *Chem.* (of a compound) not readily decomposing. **4** *Physics* (of an isotope) not subject to radioactive decay. **5** in a stable medical condition after an injury, operation, etc. [from Latin *stabilis*] □ **stably** *adv.*

stable[2] ● *n.* **1** a building for keeping horses. **2** an establishment where racehorses are kept and trained. **3** the racehorses of a particular stable. **4** persons, products, etc., having a common origin or affiliation. **5** such an origin or affiliation. ● *v.tr.* put or keep (a horse) in a stable. [from Latin *stabulum*] □ **stableful** *n.* (*pl.* **-fuls**).

stable boy *n.* a boy employed in a stable.

stable companion *n.* **1** a horse of the same stable. **2** a person or product from the same source; a member of the same organization.

stable door *n.* a door divided into two parts horizontally allowing one half to be shut and the other left open.

stable equilibrium *n.* a state in which a body when disturbed tends to return to equilibrium.

stable girl *n.* a girl or woman employed in a stable.

stable lad *n. Brit.* a person employed in a stable.

stablemate *n.* = STABLE COMPANION.

stabling *n.* accommodation for horses.

staccato esp. *Mus.* ● *adv. & adj.* with each sound or note sharply detached or separated from the others. ● *n.* (*pl.* **-os**) **1** a staccato passage in music etc. **2** staccato delivery or presentation. [Italian, literally 'detached']

stack ● *n.* **1** a pile or heap, esp. in orderly arrangement. **2** a circular or rectangular pile of hay, straw, etc., or of grain in sheaf, often with a sloping thatched top. **3** (often in *pl.*) *colloq.* a large quantity. **4 a** = CHIMNEY STACK. **b** = SMOKESTACK. **c** a tall factory chimney. **5** esp. *Brit.* a stacked group of aircraft. **6** (also **stack-room**) a part of a library where books are compactly stored. **7** a vertical arrangement of hi-fi or public-address equipment. **8** *Brit.* a tall column of rock esp. off the coast of Scotland and the Orkneys. ● *v.tr.* **1** pile in a stack or stacks. **2 a** arrange (cards) secretly for cheating. **b** manipulate (circumstances etc.) to one's advantage. **3** cause (aircraft) to fly round the same point at different levels while waiting to land at an airport. □ **stack up** *N. Amer. colloq.* present oneself, measure up. [from Old Norse *stakkr* 'haystack'] □ **stackable** *adj.* **stacker** *n.*

stack-yard *n.* an enclosure for stacks of hay, straw, etc.

staddle *n.* a platform or framework supporting a rick etc. [Old English *stathol* 'base']

staddle-stone *n.* a usu. mushroom-shaped stone supporting a staddle or rick etc.

stadium *n.* (*pl.* **stadiums**) an athletic or sports ground with tiers of seats for spectators. [from Greek *stadion*]

staff ● *n.* **1 a** a stick or pole for use in walking or climbing or as a weapon. **b** a stick or pole as a sign of office or authority. **c** a flagstaff. **2 a** a body of persons employed in a business etc. (*editorial staff of a*

newspaper). **b** those in authority within an organization, esp. the teachers in a school. **c** *Mil.* etc. a body of officers assisting an officer in high command and concerned with an army, regiment, fleet, or air force as a whole (*general staff*). **d** (usu. **Staff**) *Mil.* = STAFF SERGEANT. **3** (*pl.* **staffs** or **staves**) *Mus.* a set of usu. five parallel lines on or between which notes are placed to indicate their pitch. ▷ NOTATION. ● *v.tr.* provide (an institution etc.) with staff. [Old English] □ **staffed** *adj.* (also in *comb.*).

staff college *n. Brit. Mil.* etc. a college at which officers are trained for staff duties.

staffer *n. US* a member of a staff, esp. of a newspaper.

staff notation *n. Mus.* notation by means of a staff, esp. as distinct from tonic sol-fa.

staff nurse *n. Brit.* a nurse ranking just below a sister.

staff officer *n. Mil.* an officer serving on the staff of an army etc.

Staffordshire bull terrier *n.* a dog of a small stocky breed of terrier, with a short broad head and dropped ears.

staffroom *n.* a common room for staff, esp. in a school.

staff sergeant *n.* **1** *Brit.* the senior sergeant of a non-infantry company. **2** *US* a non-commissioned officer ranking just above sergeant.

stag ● *n.* **1** an adult male deer, esp. one with a set of antlers. **2** *Brit. Stock Exch.* a person who applies for shares of a new issue with a view to selling at once for a profit. **3** a man who attends a social gathering unaccompanied by a woman. ● *v.tr.* (**stagged**, **stagging**) *Brit. Stock Exch.* deal in (shares) as a stag. [Middle English]

stag beetle *n.* ◀ any beetle of the family Lucanidae, the male of which has large branched mandibles resembling a stag's antlers. ▷ BEETLE

antler-like jaws

STAG BEETLE (*Lucanus cervus*)

stage ● *n.* **1** a point or period in a process or development (*reached a critical stage; is in the larval stage*). **2 a** a raised floor or platform, esp. one on which plays etc. are performed before an audience. ▷ AUDITORIUM, THEATRE. **b** (prec. by *the*) the acting or theatrical profession; the art of writing or presenting plays. **c** the scene of action (*the stage of politics*). **d** = LANDING STAGE. **3 a** a regular stopping place on a route. **b** the distance between two stopping places. **c** *Brit.* = FARE STAGE. **4** a section of a rocket with a separate engine, jettisoned when its propellant is exhausted. **5** *Geol.* a range of strata forming a subdivision of a series. **6** *Electronics* a single amplifying transistor or valve with the associated equipment. **7** a raised plate on which an object is placed for inspection through a microscope. ● *v.tr.* **1** present (a play etc.) on stage. **2** arrange the occurrence of (*staged a demonstration; staged a comeback*). □ **go on the stage** become an actor. **hold the stage** dominate a conversation etc. **set the stage** (usu. foll. by *for*) prepare the way or conditions for (an event etc.). [based on Latin *stare* 'to stand'] □ **stageable** *adj.* **stageability** *n.* **stager** *n.*

stagecoach *n. hist.* ▼ a large closed horse-drawn coach running regularly by stages between two places.

STAGECOACH: 19TH-CENTURY AMERICAN STAGECOACH

driver   *roll-up leather curtains*   *guard*   *rear trunk*   *brake lever*   *step*

stagecraft *n.* skill or experience in writing or staging plays.

stage direction *n.* an instruction in the text of a play as to the movement, position, tone, etc. of an actor, or sound effects etc.

stage door *n.* an actors' and workmen's entrance from the street to a theatre behind the stage.

stage effect *n.* **1** an effect produced in acting or on the stage. **2** an artificial or theatrical effect produced in real life.

stage fright *n.* nervousness before or during an appearance before an audience.

stagehand *n.* a person handling scenery etc. during a performance on stage.

stage left *adv.* on the left side of the stage, facing the audience.

stage-manage *v.tr.* **1** be the stage manager of. **2** arrange and control for effect.

stage manager *n.* the person responsible for lighting and other mechanical arrangements for a play etc. □ **stage management** *n.*

stage name *n.* a name assumed for professional purposes by an actor.

stage play *n.* a play performed on stage rather than broadcast etc.

stage right *adv.* on the right side of the stage, facing the audience.

stage-struck *adj.* filled with an inordinate desire to go on the stage.

stage whisper *n.* **1** an aside. **2** a loud whisper meant to be heard by people other than the one addressed.

stagey var. of STAGY.

stagflation *n. Econ.* a state of inflation without a corresponding increase of demand and employment.

stagger ● *v.* **1 a** *intr.* walk unsteadily, totter. **b** *tr.* cause to totter (*was staggered by the blow*). **2 a** *tr.* shock, confuse; cause to hesitate or waver (*the question staggered them; they were staggered at the suggestion*). **b** *intr.* hesitate; waver in purpose. **3** *tr.* arrange (events, hours of work, etc.) so that they do not coincide. **4** *tr.* arrange (objects) so that they are not in line. ● *n.* **1** a tottering movement. **2** an overhanging or zigzag arrangement of like parts in a structure etc. [from Old Norse *stakra*] □ **staggerer** *n.*

staggering *adj.* **1** astonishing, bewildering. **2** that staggers. □ **staggeringly** *adv.*

staggers *n.* **1** any of various parasitic or deficiency diseases of farm animals marked by staggering or loss of balance. **2** giddiness.

staghound *n.* any large dog of a breed used for hunting deer by sight or scent.

staging *n.* **1** the presentation of a play etc. **2 a** a platform or support or scaffolding, esp. temporary. **b** *Brit.* shelves for plants in a greenhouse.

staging post *n.* a regular stopping place, esp. on an air route.

stagnant *adj.* **1** (of liquid) motionless, having no current. **2** (of life, action, the mind, business, a person) showing no activity, dull, sluggish. [from Latin *stagnant-* 'stagnating'] □ **stagnancy** *n.* **stagnantly** *adv.*

stagnate *v.intr.* be or become stagnant. □ **stagnation** *n.*

stag-night *n.* (also **stag-party**) an all-male celebration, esp. in honour of a man about to marry.

stagy *adj.* (also **stagey**) (**stagier**, **stagiest**) theatrical, artificial, exaggerated. □ **stagily** *adv.* **staginess** *n.*

staid *adj.* of quiet

and steady character; sedate. variant of past participle *stayed* □ **staidly** *adv.* **staidness** *n.*

stain ● *v.* **1** *tr. & intr.* discolour or be discoloured by the action of liquid sinking in. **2** *tr.* sully, blemish, spoil, damage (a reputation, character, etc.). **3** *tr.* colour (wood, glass, etc.) by a process other than painting or covering the surface. **4** *tr.* impregnate (a specimen) for microscopic examination with colouring matter that makes the structure visible. ● *n.* **1** a discoloration, spot, or mark. **2 a** a blot or blemish. **b** damage to a reputation etc. (*a stain on one's character*). **3** a substance used in staining. [from Old French *desteindre* 'to deprive of brightness'] □ **stainable** *adj.* **stainer** *n.*

stained glass *n.* ● dyed or coloured glass, esp. in a lead framework in a window (also, with hyphen, *attrib.*: *stained-glass window*).

stainless *adj.* **1** (esp. of a reputation) without stains. **2** not liable to stain.

stainless steel *n.* an iron alloy containing chromium and resistant to tarnishing and rust.

stair *n.* **1** each of a set of fixed steps, esp. in a building. **2** (usu. in *pl.*) a set of such steps. [Old English]

staircase *n.* **1** a flight of stairs and the supporting structure. **2** *Brit.* a part of a building containing a staircase.

stairhead *n.* esp. *Brit.* a level space at the top of stairs.

stairlift *n.* a lift in the form of a chair carrying a person up and down stairs.

stair-rod *n.* a rod for securing a carpet in the angle between two steps.

stairway *n.* a staircase.

stairwell *n.* the shaft in which a staircase is built.

staithe *n. Brit.* a wharf, esp. a waterside coal depot. [from Old Norse *stöth* 'landing stage']

stake[1] ● *n.* **1** a stout stick or post sharpened at one end and driven into the ground as a support, boundary mark, etc. **2** *hist.* **a** the post to which a person was tied to be burnt alive. **b** (prec. by *the*) death by burning as a punishment (*was condemned to the stake*). **3** a long vertical rod in basket-making. ● *v.tr.* **1** fasten, secure, or support with a stake or stakes. **2** (foll. by *off*, *out*) mark off (an area) with stakes. **3** state or establish (a claim). □ **stake out** *colloq.* **1** place under surveillance. **2** place (a person) to maintain surveillance. [Old English]

stake[2] ● *n.* **1** a sum of money etc. wagered on an event, esp. deposited with a stakeholder. **2** (often foll. by *in*) an interest or concern, esp. financial. **3** (in *pl.*) **a** money offered as a prize esp. in a horse race. **b** such a race (*maiden stakes; trial stakes*). ● *v.tr.* wager (*£5 on the next race*). □ **at stake 1** risked, to be won or lost (*life itself is at stake*). **2** at issue, in question. [Middle English]

stake-boat *n.* a boat anchored to mark the course for a boat race etc.

stakeholder *n.* **1** an independent party with whom wagered money etc. is deposited. **2** a person with an interest or concern in something, esp. a business.

stake-out *n. colloq.* a period of surveillance.

Stakhanovite *n.* a worker (esp. in the former USSR) who is exceptionally productive or zealous. [from A. G. *Stakhanov*, Russian coal miner, 1906–77]

stalactite *n.* a tapering deposit of calcite hanging from the roof of a cave etc., formed by dripping water. ▷ CAVE. [based on Greek *stalaktos* 'dripping'] □ **stalactitic** *adj.*

stalagmite *n.* a mound or tapering column of calcite rising from the floor of a cave etc., deposited by dripping water. ▷ CAVE. [based on Greek *stalagma* 'a drop'] □ **stalagmitic** *adj.*

stale[1] ● *adj.* (**staler, stalest**) **1 a** not fresh, not quite new (*stale bread*). **b** musty, insipid, or otherwise the worse for age or use. **2** trite or unoriginal (*a stale joke*). **3** (of an athlete or other performer) having ability impaired by excessive exertion or practice. ● *v.tr. & intr.* make or become stale. [Middle English] □ **staleness** *n.*

stale[2] ● *n.* the urine of horses and cattle. ● *v.intr.* (esp. of horses and cattle) urinate. [Middle English]

stalemate ● *n.* **1** *Chess* a position counting as a draw, in which a player is not in check but cannot move except into check. **2** a deadlock or drawn contest. ● *v.tr.* **1** *Chess* bring (a player) to a stalemate. **2** bring to a standstill.

stalk[1] *n.* **1** the main stem of a herbaceous plant. **2** the slender attachment or support of a leaf, flower, fruit, etc. **3** a similar support for an organ etc. in an animal. **4** a slender support or linking shaft in a machine, object, etc., e.g. the stem of a wineglass. [Middle English] □ **stalked** *adj.* (also in *comb.*). **stalkless** *adj.* **stalklike** *adj.* **stalky** *adj.*

stalk[2] ● *v.* **1** *tr.* pursue or approach (game, prey, or an enemy) stealthily. **2** *intr.* stride, walk in a stately or haughty manner. **3** *tr. formal* or *literary* move silently or threateningly through (a place) (*fear stalked the streets*). ● *n.* **1** the stalking of game. **2** an imposing gait. [Old English, related to STEAL] □ **stalker** *n.* (also in *comb.*).

stalking-horse *n.* **1** a horse or screen behind which a hunter is concealed. **2** a pretext concealing one's real intentions or actions. **3** a weak political candidate who forces an election in the hope of a more serious contender coming forward.

stall[1] ● *n.* **1** a trader's stand or booth in a market etc. **2 a** a stable or cowshed. **b** a compartment for one animal in this. **3** a fixed seat in the choir or chancel of a church, more or less enclosed at the back and sides and often canopied. **4** (usu. in *pl.*) *Brit.* each of a set of seats in a theatre, usu. on the ground floor. ▷ AUDITORIUM. **5 a** a compartment for one person in a shower-room, lavatory, etc. **b** a compartment for one horse at the start of a race. **6 a** the stalling of an engine or aircraft. **b** the condition resulting from this. **7** a receptacle or sheath for one object (*finger-stall*). ● *v.* **1 a** *intr.* (of a motor vehicle or its engine) stop because of an overload on the engine or an inadequate supply of fuel to it. **b** *intr.* (of an aircraft) reach a condition where the speed is too low to allow effective operation of the controls. **c** *tr.* cause (an engine or vehicle or aircraft) to stall. **2** *tr.* put or keep (cattle etc.) in a stall or stalls. [Old English]

stall[2] *v.* **1** *intr.* play for time when being questioned etc. **2** *tr.* delay, obstruct, block. [originally in sense 'to act as a pickpocket's accomplice', from Anglo-French]

stallholder *n. Brit.* a person in charge of a stall at a market etc.

stallion *n.* an uncastrated adult male horse, esp. one kept for breeding. [from Old French *estalon*]

stalwart ● *adj.* **1** strongly built, sturdy. **2** courageous, resolute, determined (*stalwart supporters*). ● *n.* a stalwart person, esp. a loyal uncompromising partisan. [Old English] □ **stalwartly** *adv.*

stamen *n.* the male fertilizing organ of a flowering plant, including the anther containing pollen. ▷ FLOWER. [Latin, literally 'warp in an upright loom, thread'] □ **staminiferous** *adj.*

stamina *n.* the ability to endure prolonged physical or mental strain. [Latin pl. of STAMEN, in sense 'threads spun by the Fates']

stammer ● *v.* **1** *intr.* speak with halting articulation, esp. with pauses or rapid repetitions of the same syllable. **2** *tr.* (often foll. by *out*) utter (words) in this way. ● *n.* **1** a tendency to stammer. **2** an instance of stammering. [Old English] □ **stammerer** *n.* **stammeringly** *adv.*

stamp ● *v.* **1 a** *tr.* bring down (one's foot) heavily on the ground etc. **b** *tr.* crush, flatten, or bring into a specified state in this way (*stamped down the earth round the plant*). **c** *intr.* bring down one's foot heavily; walk with heavy steps. **2** *tr.* **a** impress (a pattern, mark, etc.) on metal, paper, butter, etc., with a die or similar instrument of metal, wood, rubber, etc. **b** impress (a surface) with a pattern etc. in this way. **3** *tr.* affix a postage or other stamp to (an envelope or document). **4** *tr.* assign a specific character to; characterize; mark out (*stamps the story an invention*). ● *n.* **1** an instrument for stamping a pattern or mark. **2 a** a mark or pattern made by this. **b** the impression of an official mark required to be made on deeds, bills of exchange, etc., as evidence of payment of tax. **3** a small adhesive piece of paper indicating that a price, fee, or tax has been paid, esp. a postage stamp. **4** a mark impressed on or label etc. affixed to a commodity as evidence of quality etc. **5 a** a heavy downward blow with the foot. **b** the sound of this. **6 a** a characteristic mark or impress (*bears the stamp of genius*). □ **stamp on 1** impress (an idea etc.) on (the memory etc.). **2** suppress. **stamp out 1** produce by cutting out with a die etc. **2** put an end to, crush, destroy. [influenced by Old French *estamper* (v.), French *estampe* (n.)] □ **stamper** *n.*

stamp collector *n.* a person engaged in stamp collecting; a philatelist. □ **stamp collecting** *n.*

stamp duty *n.* a duty imposed on certain kinds of legal document.

stampede ● *n.* **1** a sudden flight and scattering of a number of horses, cattle, etc. **2** a sudden flight or hurried movement of people due to interest or panic. **3** *US* the spontaneous and simultaneous response of many persons to a common impulse. ● *v.* **1** *intr.* take part in a stampede. **2** *tr.* cause to do this. **3** *tr.* cause to act hurriedly or unreasonably. [from Spanish *estampida* 'crash, uproar'] □ **stampeder** *n.*

stamp hinge *n.* a small piece of gummed transparent paper used for fixing postage stamps in an album etc.

stamping ground *n.* a favourite haunt or place of action.

stance *n.* **1** an attitude or position of the body esp. when hitting a ball etc. **2** a standpoint; an attitude of mind. [from Italian *stanza*]

stanch[1] var. of STAUNCH[2].

stanch[2] var. of STAUNCH[1].

stanchion /stan-shŏn/ *n.* **1** a post or pillar, an upright support, a vertical strut. **2** an upright bar, pair of bars, or frame, for confining cattle in a stall. [from Old French *estanchon*]

stand ● *v.* (*past* and *past part.* **stood**) **1** *intr.* have or take or maintain an upright position, esp. on the feet or a base. **2** *intr.* be situated or located. **3** *intr.* be of a specified height (*stands six foot three*). **4** *intr.* be in a specified condition (*stands accused; the thermometer stood at 90°*). **5** *tr.* place or set in an upright or specified position (*stood it against the wall*). **6** *intr.* **a** move to and remain in a specified position (*stand aside*). **b** take a specified attitude (*stand aloof*). **7** *intr.* maintain a position; avoid falling or moving or being moved. **8** *intr.* assume a stationary position; cease to move. **9** *intr.* remain valid or unaltered; hold good. **10** *intr. Naut.* hold a specified course (*you are standing into danger*). **11** *tr.* endure; tolerate (*cannot stand the pain; how can you stand him?*). **12** *tr.* provide for another or others at one's own expense (*stood him a drink*). **13** *intr.* (often foll. by *for*) *Brit.* be a candidate (for an office,

STAR

Stars are created from clouds of gas and dust called nebulae. Regions of higher density inside these clouds collapse under the action of gravity to form protostars. A protostar becomes a main sequence star (like our Sun) when nuclear reactions – hydrogen fusing and being converted to helium – begin in the star's core. Low-mass and high-mass stars then develop differently. When all the hydrogen in a low-mass star's core has been used, the star expands and its surface cools.

It is then called a red giant, and begins to 'burn' helium. When an ageing red giant blows its outer layer of gas into space, it becomes a planetary nebula. As its core dims and cools, the star first becomes a white dwarf, then eventually a black dwarf (when the star stops shining). High-mass stars develop from main sequence stars more quickly, becoming red supergiants. These explode into supernovas, their cores collapsing to form neutron stars or, if sufficiently massive, black holes.

LIFE CYCLE OF A STAR

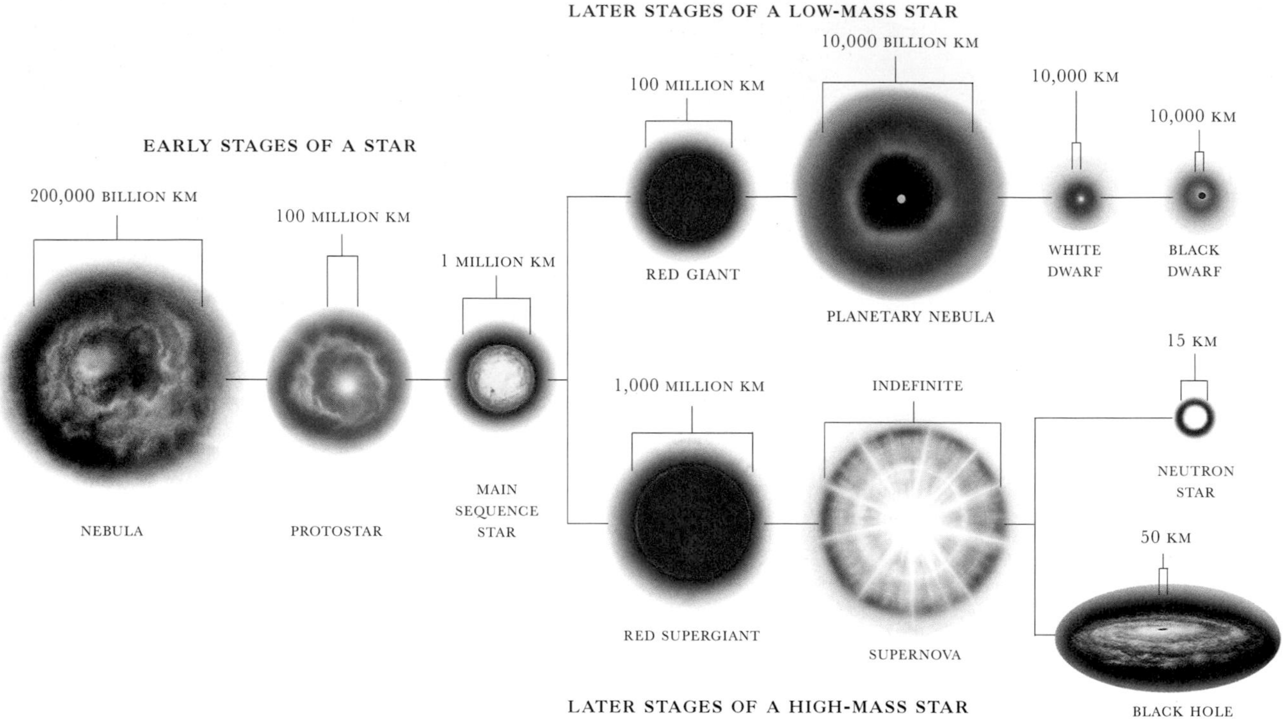

LATER STAGES OF A LOW-MASS STAR

10,000 BILLION KM

100 MILLION KM

10,000 KM

10,000 KM

EARLY STAGES OF A STAR

200,000 BILLION KM

100 MILLION KM

1 MILLION KM

RED GIANT

WHITE DWARF

BLACK DWARF

PLANETARY NEBULA

NEBULA

PROTOSTAR

MAIN SEQUENCE STAR

1,000 MILLION KM

INDEFINITE

15 KM

NEUTRON STAR

50 KM

RED SUPERGIANT

SUPERNOVA

BLACK HOLE

LATER STAGES OF A HIGH-MASS STAR

RELATIVE STAR SIZES

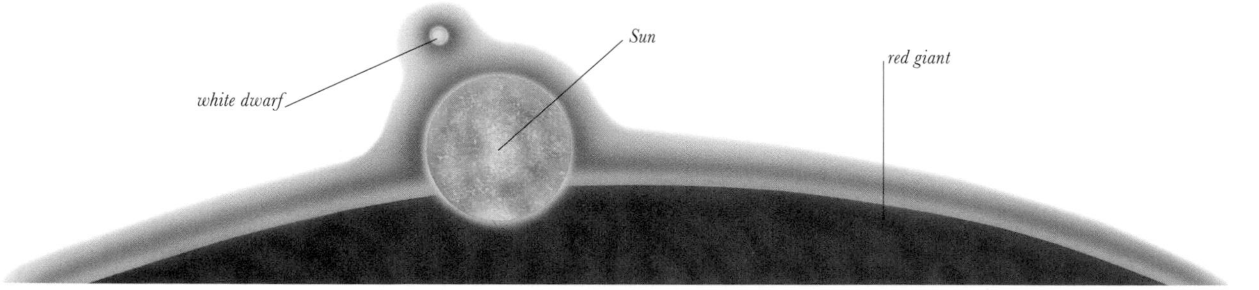

white dwarf

Sun

red giant

legislature, or constituency). **14** *intr.* act in a specified capacity (*stood proxy*). **15** *tr.* undergo (trial). ● *n.* **1** a cessation from motion or progress, a stoppage (*was brought to a stand*). **2 a** a halt made for the purpose of resistance. **b** resistance to attack or compulsion (esp. *make a stand*). **c** *Cricket* a prolonged period at the wicket by two batsmen. **3 a** a position taken up (*took his stand near the door*). **b** an attitude adopted. **4** a rack, set of shelves, table, etc., on or in which things may be placed. **5 a** a small open-fronted structure for a trader outdoors or in a market etc. **b** esp. *Brit.* a structure occupied by an organization at an exhibition. **6** a standing place for vehicles. **7 a** a raised structure for spectators, performers, etc. to sit or stand on. **b** *US* a witness box. **8** *Theatr.* etc. each halt made on a tour to give one or more performances. **9** a group of growing

plants (*stand of trees*). □ **as it stands 1** in its present condition, unaltered. **2** (also **as things stand**) in the present circumstances. **it stands to reason** see REASON. **stand alone** be unequalled. **stand and deliver!** *hist.* a highwayman's order to hand over valuables etc. **stand back 1** withdraw; take up a position further from the front. **2** withdraw emotionally in order to take an objective view. **stand by 1** stand nearby; look on without interfering (*will not stand by and see him ill-treated*). **2** uphold, support, side with (a person). **3** adhere to, abide by (terms or promises). **4 a** *Naut.* stand ready to take hold of or operate (an anchor etc.). **b** be ready to act or assist. **stand a chance** see CHANCE. **stand corrected** accept correction. **stand down 1** withdraw from a team, election, etc. **2** leave the witness box. **3** *Mil.* go off duty; relax after a state

of alert. **stand easy!** see EASY. **stand for 1** represent, signify, imply ('*US*' *stands for* '*United States*'; *democracy stands for a great deal more than that*). **2** (often with *neg.*) *colloq.* endure, tolerate, acquiesce in. **stand one's ground** maintain one's position, not yield. **stand in** (usu. foll. by *for*) deputize; act in place of another. **stand a person in good stead** see STEAD. **stand off** move or keep away, keep one's distance. **stand on** insist on, observe scrupulously (*stand on ceremony*; *stand on one's dignity*). **stand on one's own feet** (or **own two feet**) be self-reliant or independent. **stand out 1** be prominent or conspicuous or outstanding. **2** (usu. foll. by *against*, *for*) hold out; persist in opposition or support or endurance. **stand over 1** stand close to (a person) to watch, control, threaten, etc. **2** be postponed, be left for later settlement etc. **stand**

S

pat see PAT[2]. **stand to 1** *Mil.* stand ready for an attack (esp. before dawn or after dark). **2** be likely or certain to (*stands to lose everything*). **stand up 1 a** rise to one's feet from a sitting or other position. **b** come to or remain in or place in a standing position. **2** (of an argument etc.) be valid. **3** *colloq.* fail to keep an appointment with. **stand up for** support, side with, maintain (a person or cause). **stand upon** = *stand on*. **stand up to 1** meet or face (an opponent) courageously. **2** be resistant to the harmful effects of (wear, use, etc.). **stand well** (usu. foll. by *with*) be on good terms or in good repute. **take one's stand on** base one's argument etc. on, rely on. [Old English]

stand-alone *adj.* (of a computer) operating independently of a network or other system.

standard ● *n.* **1** an object or quality or measure serving as a basis or example or principle to which others conform or should conform or by which others are judged. **2 a** the degree of excellence etc. required for a particular purpose (*not up to standard*). **b** average quality (*of a low standard*). **3** the ordinary procedure, or quality or design of a product, without added or novel features. **4 ▼** a distinctive flag. **5** an upright support. **b** an upright water or gas pipe. **6 a** a tree or shrub that grows on an erect stem of full height and stands alone without support. **b** a shrub grafted on an upright stem and trained in tree form. **7** a document specifying nationally or internationally agreed properties for manufactured goods etc. (*British Standard*). **8** a thing recognized as a model for imitation etc. **9** a tune or song of established popularity. ● *adj.* **1** serving or used as a standard (*a standard size*). **2** of a normal or prescribed quality or size etc. **3** having recognized and permanent value; authoritative (*the standard book on the subject*). **4** (of language) conforming to established educated usage (*standard English*). □ **raise a standard** take up arms; rally support (*raised the standard of revolt*). [from Old French *estendart*]

STANDARD: 17TH-CENTURY NORWEGIAN
CAVALRY STANDARD

standard assessment task *n.* a standard test given to school children to assess their progress in a core subject of the national curriculum.

standard-bearer *n.* **1** a soldier who carries a standard. **2** a prominent leader in a cause.

standard deviation *n.* *Statistics* a quantity calculated to indicate the extent of deviation for a group as a whole.

standardize *v.* (also **-ise**) **1** *tr.* cause to conform to a standard. **2** *intr.* (foll. by *on*) adopt as one's standard or model. □ **standardizable** *adj.* **standardization** *n.* **standardizer** *n.*

standard lamp *n.* *Brit.* a lamp set on a tall upright with its base standing on the floor.

standard of living *n.* the degree of material comfort available to a person or class or community.

standby ● *n.* (*pl.* **-bys**) **1** a person or thing ready if needed in an emergency etc. **2** readiness for duty (*on standby*). ● *adj.* **1** ready for immediate use. **2** (of air travel, theatre seats, etc.) not booked in advance but allocated on the basis of earliest availability.

standee *n.* *colloq.* a person who stands, esp. when all seats are occupied.

stand-in *n.* a deputy or substitute, esp. for an actor when the latter's acting ability is not needed.

standing ● *n.* **1** esteem or repute, esp. high; status, position (*people of high standing*; *is of no standing*). **2** duration (*a dispute of long standing*). ● *adj.* **1** that stands, upright. **2 a** established, permanent (*a standing rule*). **b** not made, raised, etc. for the occasion (*a standing army*). **3** (of a jump, start, race, etc.) performed from rest or from a standing position. **4** (of water) stagnant. **5** (of corn) unreaped. □ **leave a person standing** make far more rapid progress than he or she.

standing joke *n.* an object of permanent ridicule.

standing order *n.* esp. *Brit.* an instruction to a banker to make regular payments, or to a newsagent etc. for a regular supply of a periodical etc.

standing orders *n.pl.* the rules governing procedure in a parliament, council, society, etc.

standing ovation *n.* a period of prolonged applause during which the crowd or audience rise to their feet.

standing room *n.* space to stand in.

standing wave *n.* *Physics* the vibration of a system in which some particular points remain fixed while others between them vibrate with the maximum amplitude.

stand-off half *n.* (also **stand-off**) *Rugby* a half-back who forms a link between the scrum-half and the three-quarters.

stand-offish *adj.* cold or distant in manner. □ **stand-offishly** *adv.* **stand-offishness** *n.*

standpipe *n.* a vertical pipe extending from a water supply, esp. one connecting a temporary tap to the mains.

standpoint *n.* **1** the position from which a thing is viewed. **2** a mental attitude.

standstill *n.* a stoppage; an inability to proceed.

stand-to *n.* *Mil.* the action or state of standing to; readiness for action or attack.

stand-up *attrib.adj.* **1** (of a meal) eaten standing. **2** (of a fight) violent, thorough, or fair and square. **3** (of a collar) upright, not turned down. **4** (of a comedian) performing by standing before an audience and telling jokes.

stank *past* of STINK.

Stanley knife *n.* *Brit. propr.* a type of very sharp knife with a replaceable blade. [from *Stanley*, proprietary name for hand tools]

stannary *n.* (*pl.* **-ies**) (usu. in *pl.* prec. by *the*) any of several tin-mining districts in Cornwall and Devon. [from medieval Latin *stannaria* (pl.)]

stanza *n.* the basic metrical unit in a poem or verse consisting of a recurring group of lines. [Italian, literally 'standing place, chamber, stanza'] □ **stanza'd** *adj.* (also **stanzaed**) (also in *comb.*). **stanzaic** *adj.*

staphylococcus *n.* (*pl.* **staphylococci**) any bacterium of the genus *Staphylococcus*, occurring in grapelike clusters, and sometimes causing pus formation usu. in the skin and mucous membranes of animals. [from Greek *staphulē* 'bunch of grapes' + *kokkos* 'berry'] □ **staphylococcal** *adj.*

staple[1] ● *n.* a U-shaped metal bar or piece of wire with pointed ends for driving through and clenching papers, fastening netting or electric cable, etc. ● *v.tr.* provide or fasten with a staple. [Old English] □ **stapler** *n.*

staple[2] ● *n.* **1** the principal or an important article of commerce (*the staples of British industry*). **2** the chief element or a main component, e.g. of a diet. **3** a raw material. **4** the fibre of cotton or wool etc. as determining its quality (*cotton of fine staple*). ● *adj.* **1** main or principal (*staple commodities*).

2 important as a product or an export. ● *v.tr.* sort or classify (wool etc.) according to fibre. [from Middle Dutch *stapel* 'pillar, emporium']

staple gun *n.* a hand-held device for driving in staples.

star ● *n.* **1** a celestial body appearing as a luminous point in the night sky. **2** (in full **fixed star**) such a body, being so far from the Earth as to appear motionless (except for the diurnal rotation of the heavens), in contrast to planets, comets, etc. **3** *Astron.* ◄ a large gaseous body (such as the Sun), naturally luminous from internal nuclear reactions. ▷ SUN. **4** a celestial body regarded as influencing a person's fortunes etc. (*born under a lucky star*). **5** a thing resembling a star or having the conventional shape of a star, with five or more radiating lines. **6** a figure or object with radiating points esp. as a mark of rank or excellence. **7 a** a famous or brilliant person; the principal or most prominent performer in a play, film, etc. (*the star of the show*). **b** (*attrib.*) outstanding; particularly brilliant (*star pupil*). ● *v.* (**starred**, **starring**) **1 a** *tr.* (of a film etc.) feature as a principal performer. **b** *intr.* (of a performer) be featured in a film etc. **2** *tr.* (esp. as **starred** *adj.*) **a** mark, set, or adorn with a star or stars. **b** put an asterisk or star beside (a name, an item in a list, etc.). [Old English] □ **stardom** *n.* **starless** *adj.* **starlike** *adj.*

starboard *Naut. & Aeron.* ● *n.* the right-hand side (looking forward) of a ship, boat, or aircraft (cf. PORT[3]). ● *v.tr.* (also *absol.*) turn (the helm) to starboard. [Old English *stēorbord* 'rudder side', early Teutonic ships being steered with a paddle over the right side]

starboard tack see TACK[1] *n.* 4.

starboard watch see WATCH *n.* 3b.

starburst *n.* **1 a** a pattern of radiating lines or rays around a central object, light source, etc. **b** an explosion or *Photog.* a lens attachment producing this effect (*starburst filter*). **2** *Astron.* a period of intense activity, apparently star formation, in certain galaxies.

starch ● *n.* **1** an odourless tasteless polysaccharide occurring widely in plants as a carbohydrate store and obtained chiefly from cereals and potatoes. **2** a preparation of this for stiffening fabric. **3** stiffness of manner; formality. ● *v.tr.* stiffen (clothing) with starch. [Old English] □ **starcher** *n.*

starchy *adj.* (**starchier**, **starchiest**) **1 a** of or like starch. **b** containing much starch. **2** (of a person) precise, prim. □ **starchily** *adv.* **starchiness** *n.*

star-crossed *adj.* *archaic* ill-fated.

stardust *n.* **1** a twinkling mass. **2** an illusory or insubstantial substance. **3** a multitude of stars looking like dust.

stare ● *v.* **1** *intr.* (usu. foll. by *at*) look fixedly with eyes open, esp. as the result of curiosity, surprise, bewilderment, admiration, horror, etc. **2** *intr.* (of eyes) be wide open and fixed. **3** *tr.* (foll. by *into*) reduce (a person) to a specified condition by staring (*stared me into silence*). ● *n.* a staring gaze. □ **stare down** (or **out**) outstare. **stare a person in the face** be evident or imminent. [Old English]

starfish *n.* (*pl.* usu. same) ◄ an echinoderm of the class Asteroidea with five or more radiating arms. ▷ ECHINODERM

star fruit *n.* = CARAMBOLA.

stargazer *n.* *colloq.* usu. *derog.* or *joc.* an astronomer or astrologer. □ **stargaze** *v.intr.*

stark ● *adj.* **1** desolate, bare (*a stark landscape*). **2** sharply evident; brutally simple (*in stark contrast*; *the stark reality*). **3** downright, sheer (*stark madness*). ● *adv.* completely (*stark naked*). [Old English] □ **starkly** *adv.* **starkness** *n.*

starkers *adj.* *Brit. colloq.* stark naked.

arm —

madreporite

anus

STARFISH:
SCARLET STARFISH
(*Henricia sanguinolenta*)

S

starlet *n.* **1** a promising young performer, esp. a woman. **2** a little star.

starlight *n.* **1** the light of the stars (*walked home by starlight*). **2** (*attrib.*) = STARLIT (*a starlight night*).

starling *n.* a small gregarious partly migratory bird, *Sturnus vulgaris*, with blackish-brown speckled lustrous plumage. ▷ PREEN. [Old English]

symbol of Elephantine Jews

starlit *adj.* **1** lit by stars. **2** with stars visible.

Star of David *n.* ◀ a figure consisting of two interlaced equilateral triangles used as a Jewish and Israeli symbol.

STAR OF DAVID

starry *adj.* (**starrier**, **starriest**) **1** covered with or full of stars. **2** resembling a star. □ **starrily** *adv.* **starriness** *n.*

starry-eyed *adj. colloq.* **1** visionary; enthusiastic but impractical. **2** euphoric.

Stars and Stripes *n.pl.* ▼ the national flag of the US.

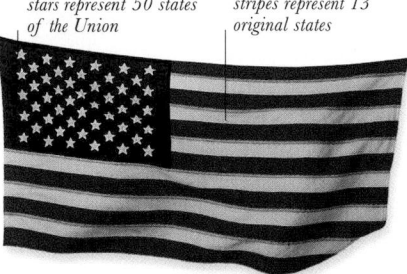

stars represent 50 states of the Union   *stripes represent 13 original states*

STARS AND STRIPES

star shell *n.* an explosive projectile designed to burst in the air and light up the enemy's position.

starship *n.* (in science fiction) a large usu. manned spacecraft for interstellar space travel.

star-spangled *adj.* (esp. of the US national flag) covered or glittering with stars.

star-struck *adj.* fascinated or greatly impressed by stars in entertainment or stardom.

star-studded *adj.* containing or covered with many stars, esp. featuring many famous performers.

start ● *v.* **1** *tr. & intr.* begin; commence. **2** *tr.* set (proceedings, an event, etc.) in motion (*start the meeting*; *started a fire*). **3** *intr.* (often foll. by *on*) make a beginning (*started on a new project*). **4** *intr.* (often foll. by *after, for*) set oneself in motion or action (*'wait!' he shouted, and started after her*). **5** *intr.* set out; begin a journey etc. **6** (often foll. by *up*) **a** *intr.* (of a machine) begin operating. **b** *tr.* cause (a machine etc.) to begin operating. **7** *tr.* **a** cause or enable (a person) to make a beginning (with something) (*started me in business with £10,000*). **b** (foll. by pres. part.) cause (a person) to begin (doing something) (*the smoke started me coughing*). **8** *tr.* (often foll. by *up*) found or establish; originate. **9** *intr.* (foll. by *at, with*) have as the first of a series of items, e.g. in a meal (*we started with soup*). **10** *tr.* give a signal to (competitors) to start in a race. **11** *intr.* (often foll. by *up, from,* etc.) make a sudden movement from surprise, pain, etc. (*started at the sound of my voice*). **12** *intr.* (foll. by *out, up, from,* etc.) spring out, up, etc. (*started up from the chair*). **13** *tr.* conceive (a baby). **14** *tr.* rouse (game etc.) from its lair. **15** *intr.* be displaced by pressure or shrinkage; come loose. ● *n.* **1** a beginning of an event, action, journey, etc. **2** the place from which a race etc. begins. **3** an advantage given at the beginning of a race etc. (*a 15-second start*). **4** an advantageous initial position in life, business, etc. (*a good start in life*). **5** a sudden movement of surprise, pain, etc. (*you gave me a start*). **6** an intermittent or spasmodic effort or movement (esp. *in* or *by fits and starts*). □ **for a start**

colloq. as a beginning; in the first place. **start a hare** see HARE. **start in** *colloq.* **1** begin. **2** (foll. by *on*) *US* make a beginning on. **start off 1** begin; commence. **2** begin to move. **start on** *colloq.* attack; nag; bully. **start out 1** begin a journey. **2** (foll. by *to* + infin.) *colloq.* proceed as intending (to do something). **start over** *N. Amer.* begin again. **start up** arise; occur. **to start with 1** in the first place; before anything else is considered. **2** at the beginning. [Old English]

starter *n.* **1** a person or thing that starts. **2** an esp. automatic device for starting the engine of a motor vehicle etc. **3** a person giving the signal for the start of a race. **4** a horse or competitor starting in a race. **5** esp. *Brit.* the first course of a meal. □ **for starters** *colloq.* to start with. **under starter's orders** (of racehorses etc.) in a position to start a race and awaiting the starting signal.

starting block *n.* (usu. in *pl.*) ▼ a shaped rigid block for bracing the feet of a runner at the start of a race.

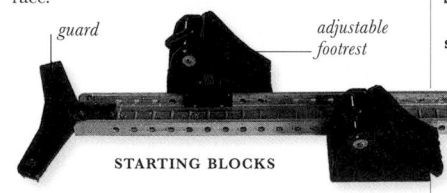

guard   *adjustable footrest*

STARTING BLOCKS

starting gate *n.* a movable barrier for securing a fair start in horse races.

starting pistol *n.* ▶ a pistol used to give the signal for the start of a race.

starting point *n.* the point from which a journey, process, argument, etc. begins.

starting post *n.* the post from which competitors start in a race.

STARTING PISTOL

starting price *n.* the odds ruling at the start of a horse race.

startle *v.tr.* give a shock or surprise to; cause (a person etc.) to start with surprise or sudden alarm. [Old English] □ **startler** *n.*

startling *adj.* **1** surprising. **2** alarming (*startling news*). □ **startlingly** *adv.*

start-up *n.* the action or an instance of starting up, esp. the starting up of a business, machine, or series of operations (often *attrib.*: *start-up costs*).

star turn *n. Brit.* the principal item in an entertainment or performance.

starve *v.* **1** *intr.* die of hunger; suffer from malnourishment. **2** *tr.* cause to die of hunger or suffer from lack of food. **3** *intr.* (esp. as **starved** *adj.* or **starving** *adj.*) *colloq.* feel very hungry (*I'm starving*). **4** *intr.* **a** suffer from spiritual or mental want. **b** (foll. by *for*) feel a strong craving for (sympathy, amusement, knowledge, etc.). **5** *tr.* (foll. by *of, US for*) deprive of; keep scantily supplied with (*starved of affection*). **b** cause to suffer from mental or spiritual want. **6** *tr.* **a** (foll. by *into*) compel by starving (*starved into submission*). **b** (foll. by *out*) compel to surrender etc. by starving (*starved them out*). [Old English *steorfan* 'to die'] □ **starvation** *n.*

starveling *archaic* ● *n.* a starving or ill-fed person or animal. ● *adj.* starving.

stash *colloq.* ● *v.tr.* (often foll. by *away*) **1** conceal; put in a safe or hidden place. **2** hoard, stow, store. ● *n.* **1** a hiding place or hideout. **2** a thing hidden; a cache. [18th-century coinage]

stasis *n.* (*pl.* **stases**) **1** inactivity; stagnation; a state of equilibrium. **2** a stoppage of circulation of any of the body fluids. [modern Latin]

stat[1] *n. colloq.* a thermostat.

stat[2] *n.* (usu. in *pl.*) esp. *N. Amer.* a statistic.

state ● *n.* **1** the existing condition or position of a person or thing. **2** *colloq.* **a** an excited, anxious, or

agitated mental condition (esp. *in a state*). **b** an untidy condition. **3** (also **State**) **a** an organized political community under one government; a nation. **b** such a community forming part of a federal republic, esp. the United States of America. **c** (**the States**) the US. **4** (also **State**) (*attrib.*) **a** of, for, or concerned with the State (*State documents*). **b** reserved for or done on occasions of ceremony (*state apartments*; *state visit*). **c** involving ceremony (*state opening of Parliament*). **5** (usu. **State**) civil government (*Church and State*; *Secretary of State*). ● *v.tr.* **1** express, esp. fully or clearly, in speech or writing (*have stated my opinion*). **2** fix, specify (*at stated intervals*). □ **in state** with all due ceremony. **of state** concerning politics or government. **state of things** (or **affairs** or **play**) the circumstances; the current situation. [Middle English: partly from STATE, partly from STATUS] □ **statable** *adj.* **statehood** *n.*

statecraft *n.* the art of conducting affairs of State.

State Department *n.* (in the US) the department of foreign affairs.

state house *n.* **1** *US* the building where the legislature of a state meets. **2** *NZ* a private house built at the government's expense.

stateless *adj.* having no nationality or citizenship. □ **statelessness** *n.*

stately *adj.* (**statelier**, **stateliest**) dignified; imposing; grand. □ **stateliness** *n.*

stately home *n. Brit.* a large magnificent house, esp. one open to the public.

statement *n.* **1** the act or an instance of stating or being stated; expression in words. **2** a thing stated; a declaration. **3** a formal account of facts, esp. to the police or in a court of law (*make a statement*). **4** a record of transactions in a bank account etc. **5** a formal notification of the amount due to a tradesman etc.

state of emergency *n.* a condition of danger or disaster affecting a country, esp. with normal constitutional procedures suspended.

state of grace *n.* the condition of being free from grave sin.

state of life *n.* rank and occupation.

state of the art *n.* **1** the current stage of development of a practical or technological subject. **2** (usu. **state-of-the-art**) (*attrib.*) using the latest techniques or equipment (*state-of-the-art weaponry*).

state of war *n.* the situation when war has been declared or is in progress.

state pension see PENSION[1] *n.* 1a.

state prisoner see PRISONER OF STATE.

stateroom *n.* **1** a state apartment in a palace, hotel, etc. **2** a private compartment in a passenger ship or *US* train.

state school *n. Brit.* a school managed and funded by the public authorities.

state's evidence *n.* = QUEEN'S EVIDENCE.

stateside *adj.* esp. *US colloq.* of, in, or towards the United States.

statesman *n.* (*pl.* **-men**; *fem.* **stateswoman**, *pl.* **-women**) **1** a person skilled in affairs of state, esp. one taking an active part in politics. **2** a distinguished and capable politician. [from *state's man*, translating French *homme d'état*] □ **statesmanlike** *adj.* **statesmanly** *adj.* **statesmanship** *n.*

statesperson *n.* a statesman or stateswoman.

statewide *adj. US* so as to include or cover a whole state.

static ● *adj.* **1** stationary; not acting or changing; passive. **2** *Physics* **a** concerned with bodies at rest or forces in equilibrium (opp. DYNAMIC *adj.* 2a). **b** acting as weight but not moving (*static pressure*). **c** of statics. ● *n.* **1** static electricity. **2** atmospherics. [from Greek *statikos*]

static electricity *n.* ► electricity not flowing as a current.

statics *n.pl.* (usu. treated as *sing.*) **1** the science of bodies at rest or of forces in equilibrium (opp. DYNAMICS 1a). **2** = STATIC *n.*

station ● *n.* **1 a** a regular stopping place on a railway line. **b** the buildings at this (see also BUS STATION, COACH STATION). **2** a place or building etc. where a person or thing stands or is placed, esp. habitually or for a definite purpose. **3** a designated point or establishment where a particular service or activity is based or organized (*police station; polling station*). **4** an establishment involved in radio or television broadcasting. **5** a military or naval base. **6** position in life; rank or status (*ideas above your station*). **7** *Austral.* & *NZ* a large sheep or cattle farm. ● *v.tr.* **1** assign a station to. **2** put in position. [from Latin *statio*]

stationary *adj.* **1** not moving (*hit a stationary car*). **2** not meant to be moved; not portable (*stationary engine*). **3** not changing in magnitude, number, quality, efficiency, etc. (*stationary temperature*). [Middle English] □ **stationariness** *n.*

stationer *n.* a person who sells writing materials etc. [from medieval Latin *stationarius* 'established bookseller', as opposed to an itinerant tradesman]

stationery *n.* writing materials etc. sold by a stationer.

Stationery Office *n.* (in the UK) the Government's publishing house which also provides stationery for Government offices.

station house *n.* *US* a police station.

stationmaster *n.* the official in charge of a railway station.

station of the cross *n.* *RC Ch.* each of a series of usu. 14 images or pictures representing the events in Christ's passion.

station wagon *n.* esp. *US* an estate car.

statism *n.* centralized State administration and control of social and economic affairs. □ **statist** *n.*

statistic ● *n.* a statistical fact or item. ● *adj.* = STATISTICAL. [from German *statistisch, Statiskik*]

statistical *adj.* of or relating to statistics. □ **statistically** *adv.*

statistical significance *n.* = SIGNIFICANCE 4.

statistics *n.pl.* **1** (usu. treated as *sing.*) the science of collecting and analysing numerical data. **2** any systematic collection or presentation of such facts. □ **statistician** *n.*

statuary ● *adj.* of or for statues (*statuary art*). ● *n.* (*pl.* **-ies**) **1** statues collectively. **2** making statues.

statue *n.* a sculptured, cast, carved, or moulded figure of a person or animal, esp. life-size or larger (cf. STATUETTE). [from Latin *statua*] □ **statued** *adj.*

statuesque *adj.* like, or having the dignity or beauty of, a statue. □ **statuesquely** *adv.*

statuette *n.* a small statue; a statue less than life-size. [French]

stature *n.* **1** the height of a (esp. human) body. **2** a degree of eminence, social standing, or advancement; mental or moral calibre. [from Latin *statura*] □ **statured** *adj.* (also in *comb.*).

status *n.* **1** rank, social position, relation to others, relative importance. **2** a superior social etc. position. **3** the position of affairs (*let me know if the status changes*). [Latin, literally 'standing']

status quo *n.* the existing state of affairs. [Latin, literally 'the state in which']

status symbol *n.* a possession etc. taken to indicate a person's high status.

statute *n.* **1** a written law passed by a legislative body, e.g. an Act of Parliament. **2** a rule of a corporation, founder, etc., intended to be permanent. [from Late Latin *statutum* '(thing) set up']

statute book *n.* **1** a book or books containing the statute law. **2** the body of a country's statutes.

statute law *n.* **1** (*collect.*) the body of principles and rules of law laid down in statutes (cf. COMMON LAW, CASE LAW). **2** a statute.

statute mile see MILE 1.

The build up of charged particles in one location is called static electricity. When, for example, a polythene rod is rubbed against a jersey, the rod picks up electrons (the negatively charged particles in an atom) from the jersey, and becomes charged with static electricity. Touching the rod to the top of an electroscope, as shown below, causes the electricity to discharge: electrons flow down the central strip. Because like charges repel, the rod's electrons and the gold leaf's electrons move apart, causing the gold leaf to lift.

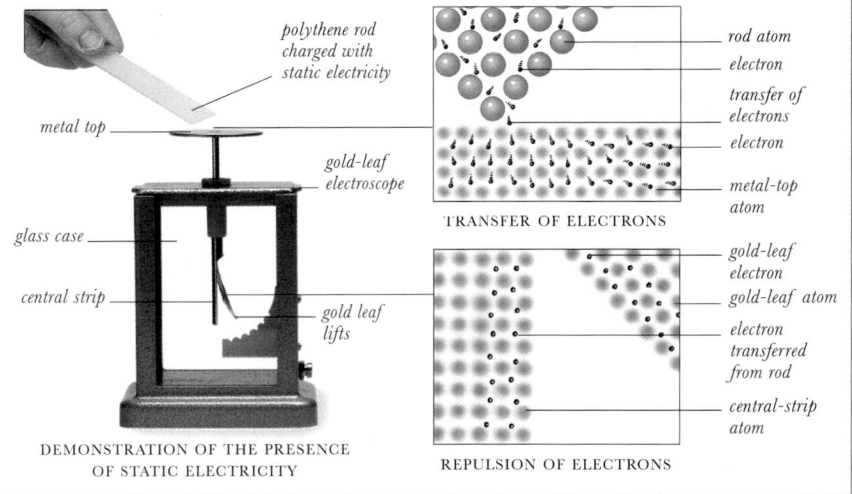

DEMONSTRATION OF THE PRESENCE OF STATIC ELECTRICITY

TRANSFER OF ELECTRONS

REPULSION OF ELECTRONS

statutory *adj.* required, permitted, or enacted by statute. □ **statutorily** *adv.*

statutory rape *n.* *US* the act of sexual intercourse with a minor.

staunch[1] *adj.* (also **stanch**) **1** trustworthy, loyal. **2** (of a ship, joint, etc.) strong, watertight, airtight, etc. [from Old French *estanche* (fem.) 'watertight'] □ **staunchly** *adv.* **staunchness** *n.*

staunch[2] *v.tr.* (also **stanch**) **1** restrain the flow of (esp. blood). **2** restrain the flow from (esp. a wound). [from Old French *estanchier*]

stave ● *n.* **1** each of the curved pieces of wood forming the sides of a cask, pail, etc. **2** = STAFF *n.* 3. **3** a stanza or verse. ● *v.tr.* (*past* and *past part.* **stove** or **staved**) **1** break a hole in. **2** crush or knock out of shape. □ **stave in** crush by forcing inwards. **stave off** (*past* and *past part.* **staved**) avert or defer (esp. danger or misfortune). [back-formation from *staves*, pl. of STAFF]

staves pl. of STAFF *n.* 3.

stay[1] ● *v.* **1** *intr.* continue to be in the same place or condition; not depart or change. **2** *intr.* **a** have temporary residence as a visitor etc. (*stayed with them for Christmas*). **b** *Sc.* & *S.Afr.* dwell permanently. **3** *tr. archaic* or *literary* stop or check (progress, the inroads of a disease, etc.). **4** *tr.* postpone (judgement, decision, etc.). **5 a** *intr.* show endurance. **b** *tr.* show endurance to the end of (a race etc.). **6** *intr.* (foll. by *for, to*) wait long enough to share or join in an activity etc. (*stay to supper; stay for the film*). ● *n.* **1 a** the act or an instance of staying or dwelling in one place. **b** the duration of this. **2** a suspension or postponement of a sentence, judgement, etc. (*was granted a stay of execution*). **3** a prop or support. **4** (in *pl.*) *hist.* a corset esp. with whalebone etc. stiffening, and laced. □ **has come** (or **is here**) **to stay** *colloq.* must be regarded as permanent. **stay the course** pursue a course of action or endure a struggle etc. to the end. **stay in** remain indoors or at home, esp. in school after hours as a punishment. **stay the night** remain until the next day. **stay put** remain where it is placed or where one is. **stay up** not go to bed (until late at night). [from Latin *stare* 'to stand'] □ **stayer** *n.*

stay[2] ● *n.* **1 a** *Naut.* a rope supporting a mast. ▷ RIGGING, SHIP. **b** a guy or rope supporting a flagstaff or other pole. **2** a tie-piece in an aircraft etc. ● *v.tr.* support (a mast etc.) by stays. [Old English *stæg* 'to be firm']

stay-at-home ● *adj.* remaining habitually at home. ● *n.* a person who does this.

staying power *n.* endurance, stamina.

staysail *n.* a triangular fore-and-aft sail extended on a stay. ▷ SCHOONER, SHIP

STD *abbr.* **1** *Brit.* subscriber trunk dialling. **2** sexually transmitted disease.

stead *n.* □ **in a person's** (or **thing's**) **stead** as a substitute; instead of him or her or it. **stand a person in good stead** be advantageous or serviceable to him or her. [Old English *stede* 'place']

steadfast *adj.* constant, firm, unwavering. [Old English] □ **steadfastly** *adv.* **steadfastness** *n.*

steading *n.* *Sc.* & *N.Engl.* a farmstead.

steady ● *adj.* (**steadier, steadiest**) **1** firmly fixed or supported or standing or balanced. **2** done or operating or happening in a uniform and regular manner (*a steady pace; a steady increase*). **3 a** constant in mind or conduct; not changeable. **b** persistent. **4** (of a person) serious and dependable in behaviour. **5** regular, established (*a steady girlfriend*). **6** accurately directed; not faltering; controlled (*a steady hand; a steady eye; steady nerves*). ● *v.tr.* & *intr.* (**-ies, -ied**) make or become steady (*steady the boat*). ● *adv.* steadily (*hold it steady*). ● *int.* as a command or warning to take care. ● *n.* (*pl.* **-ies**) *colloq.* a regular boyfriend or girlfriend. □ **go steady** (often foll. by *with*) *colloq.* have as a regular boyfriend or girlfriend. **steady on!** *Brit.* take care! [based on STEAD] □ **steadier** *n.* **steadily** *adv.* **steadiness** *n.*

steady state *n.* an unvarying condition in a physical process etc., esp. as in the (now rarely held) theory that the universe is eternal and maintained by constant creation of matter.

steak *n.* **1** a thick slice of meat (esp. beef) or fish, often cut for grilling, frying, etc. **2** beef cut for stewing or braising. ▷ CUT. [from Old Norse *steik*]

steakhouse *n.* a restaurant specializing in serving beefsteaks.

steak knife *n.* a knife with a serrated steel blade for eating steak.

steal ● *v.* (*past* **stole**; *past part.* **stolen**) **1** *tr.* (also *absol.*) **a** take (another person's property) illegally. **b** take (property etc.) without right or permission,

STEAM ENGINE

To power a steam locomotive, coal is burnt in a firebox, producing hot gases (mainly carbon dioxide and carbon monoxide). These gases then heat water in a boiler to produce steam.

When the steam is at a high pressure, it is fed into cylinders. The steam expands and forces pistons back and forth, which turn the locomotive's wheels (via a rod and crank).

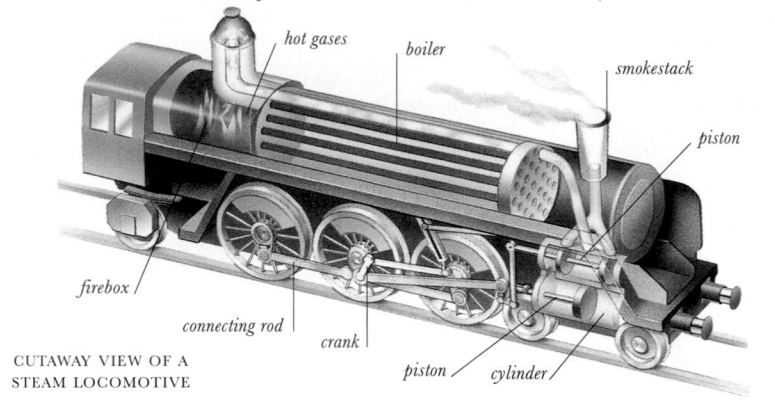

CUTAWAY VIEW OF A STEAM LOCOMOTIVE

hot gases, *boiler*, *smokestack*, *piston*, *firebox*, *connecting rod*, *crank*, *piston*, *cylinder*

esp. in secret with the intention of not returning it. **2** *tr.* obtain surreptitiously or by surprise (*stole a kiss*). **3** *tr.* **a** gain insidiously or artfully. **b** (often foll. by *away*) win or get possession of (a person's affections etc.), esp. insidiously. **4** *intr.* move, esp. silently or stealthily. **5** *tr.* **a** (in various sports) gain (a run, the ball, etc.) surreptitiously or by luck. **b** *Baseball* run to (a base) while the pitcher is in the act of delivery. ● *n.* **1** *US colloq.* the act or an instance of stealing or theft. **2** *colloq.* an unexpectedly easy task or good bargain. □ **steal a march on** get an advantage over by surreptitious means; anticipate. **steal the show** outshine other performers, esp. unexpectedly. **steal a person's thunder** use another person's idea, policy, etc., and spoil the effect the originator hoped to achieve. [Old English] □ **stealer** *n.* (also in *comb.*).

stealth *n.* **1** secrecy, a secret procedure. **2** (*attrib.*) designed in accordance with or designating the technology which makes detection by radar or sonar difficult. □ **by stealth** surreptitiously. [Middle English]

stealth bomber *n.* an aircraft designed to make detection by radar or sonar difficult. ▷ BOMBER

stealthy *adj.* (**stealthier**, **stealthiest**) done, acting, or moving with stealth. □ **stealthily** *adv.* **stealthiness** *n.*

steam ● *n.* **1 a** the gas into which water is changed by boiling. **b** a mist of liquid particles of water produced by the condensation of this gas. **2** any similar vapour. **3 a** energy or power provided by a steam engine or other machine. **b** *colloq.* power or energy generally. ● *v.* **1** *tr.* **a** cook (food) in steam. **b** soften or make pliable (timber etc.) or otherwise treat with steam. **2** *intr.* give off steam or other vapour, esp. visibly. **3** *intr.* **a** move under steam power (*the ship steamed down the river*). **b** (foll. by *ahead*, *away*, etc.) *colloq.* proceed or travel fast or with vigour. **4** *tr.* & *intr.* (usu. foll. by *up*) **a** cover or become covered with condensed steam. **b** (as **steamed up** *adj.*) *colloq.* angry or excited. **5** *tr.* (foll. by *open* etc.) apply steam to the gum of (a sealed envelope) to get it open. **6** *intr. slang* (of a gang) pass rapidly through a public place, robbing bystanders by force of numbers. □ **get up steam 1** generate enough power to work a steam engine. **2** work oneself into an energetic or angry state. **let off steam** relieve one's pent up feelings or energy. **run out of steam** lose one's impetus or energy. **under one's own steam** without assistance; unaided. [Old English]

steam bath *n.* a room etc. filled with steam for bathing in.

steamboat *n.* a boat propelled by a steam engine.

steam engine *n.* **1** an engine which uses the expansion or rapid condensation of steam to generate power. **2** ▲ a locomotive powered by this.

steamer *n.* **1** a person or thing that steams. **2** a vessel propelled by steam, esp. a ship. **3** a receptacle in which things are steamed, esp. cooked by steam. **4** *slang* a member of a gang involved in steaming (see STEAM *v.* 6).

steamer rug *n. US* a travelling rug.

steam hammer *n.* a forging-hammer powered by steam.

steam iron *n.* an electric iron that emits steam to improve its pressing ability.

steam power *n.* the force of steam applied to machinery etc.

steamroll *v.tr.* esp. *US* = STEAMROLLER *v.*

steamroller ● *n.* **1** a heavy slow-moving vehicle with a roller, used to flatten new-made roads. **2** a crushing power or force. ● *v.tr.* **1** crush forcibly or

indiscriminately. **2** (foll. by *through*) force (a measure etc.) through a legislature by overriding opposition.

steamship *n.* a ship propelled by a steam engine.

steam train *n.* a train driven by a steam engine. ▷ TRAIN

steam turbine *n.* ▼ a turbine in which a high-velocity jet of steam rotates a bladed disc or drum.

steamy *adj.* (**steamier**, **steamiest**) **1** like or full of steam. **2** *colloq.* erotic. □ **steamily** *adv.*

stearic *adj.* derived from stearin. [based on Greek *stear* 'tallow'] □ **stearate** *n.*

stearic acid *n.* a solid saturated fatty acid obtained from animal or vegetable fats.

stearin *n.* **1** a glyceryl ester of stearic acid. **2** a mixture of fatty acids used in candle-making. [based on Greek *stear* 'tallow']

steatite /steer-tyt/ *n.* = SOAPSTONE. [from Greek *steatitēs*]

steed *n. archaic* or *poet.* a horse. [Old English *stēda* 'stallion']

steel ● *n.* **1** any of various grey or greyish-blue alloys of iron with carbon and usu. other elements, much used as structural materials and in manufacturing. **2** hardness of character; strength, firmness (*nerves of steel*). **3 a** a rod of steel on which knives are sharpened. ▷ UTENSIL. **b** a strip of steel for expanding a skirt or stiffening a corset. **4** (not in *pl.*) *literary* a sword, lance, etc. (*warriors worthy of their steel*). ● *adj.* **1** made of steel. **2** like steel. ● *v.tr.* & *refl.* harden or make resolute (*steeled myself for a shock*). [Old English]

steel band *n.* a band of musicians who play (chiefly calypso-style) music on steel drums.

steel-clad *adj.* wearing armour.

steel wool *n.* ▶ an abrasive substance consisting of a mass of fine steel shavings.

steelworks *n.pl.* (usu. treated as *sing.*) a place where steel is manufactured. □ **steelworker** *n.*

steely *adj.* (**steelier**, **steeliest**) **1** of, or hard as, steel. **2** severe; ruthless (*steely composure*; *steely-eyed glance*). □ **steeliness** *n.*

STEEL WOOL

STEAM TURBINE

Steam turbines provide most of the world's power. To operate a turbine, high-pressure steam is directed on to moving metal blades connected to a central shaft. Fixed blades with slanting slots ensure the steam hits the moving blades at the correct angle. As the steam expands, the blades spin, causing the turbine shaft to rotate. This turning shaft can be used to drive a range of devices, including an electric generator or a ship's propeller.

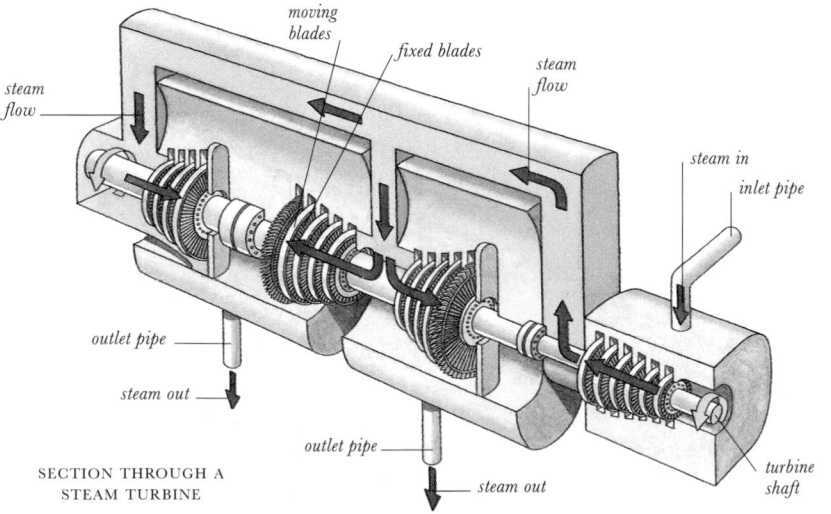

moving blades, *fixed blades*, *steam flow*, *steam flow*, *steam in*, *inlet pipe*, *outlet pipe*, *steam out*, *outlet pipe*, *steam out*, *turbine shaft*

SECTION THROUGH A STEAM TURBINE

steelyard *n.* a kind of balance with a short arm to take the item to be weighed and a long graduated arm along which a weight is moved until it balances.

steep[1] ● *adj.* **1** sloping sharply (*a steep hill; steep stairs*). **2** (of a rise or fall) rapid (*a steep drop in share prices*). **3** (*predic.*) *colloq.* **a** (of a demand, price, etc.) exorbitant; unreasonable (esp. *a bit steep*). **b** (of a story etc.) exaggerated; incredible. ● *n.* a steep slope; a precipice. [Old English] □ **steepen** *v.intr.* & *tr.* **steepish** *adj.* **steeply** *adv.* **steepness** *n.*

steep[2] ● *v.tr.* **1** (often foll. by *in*) soak or bathe in liquid. **2** (foll. by *in*; usu. in *passive*) **a** pervade or imbue with (*steeped in misery*). **b** make deeply acquainted with (a subject etc.) (*steeped in the classics*). ● *n.* **1** the act or process of steeping. **2** the liquid for steeping. [Middle English]

steeple *n.* ◀ a tall tower, esp. one surmounted by a spire, above the roof of a church. [Old English] □ **steepled** *adj.*

steeplechase *n.* **1** a horse race (originally with a steeple as the goal) across the countryside or on a racecourse with ditches, hedges, etc. to jump. **2** a cross-country foot race. □ **steeplechaser** *n.* **steeplechasing** *n.*

steeplejack *n.* a person who climbs tall chimneys, steeples, etc., to do repairs etc.

steer[1] *v.* **1** *tr.* **a** guide (a vehicle, aircraft, etc.) by a wheel etc. **b** guide (a vessel) by a rudder or helm. **2** *intr.* guide a vessel or vehicle in a specified direction (*tried to steer left*). **3** *tr.* direct (one's course). **4** *intr.* direct one's course in a specified direction (*steered for the railway station*). **5** *tr.* guide the movement or trend of (*steered them into the garden; steered the conversation away from that subject*). □ **steer clear of** take care to avoid. [Old English] □ **steerable** *adj.* **steerer** *n.* **steering** *n.* (esp. in senses 1, 2).

spire — *steeple*

STEEPLE OF SALISBURY CATHEDRAL, ENGLAND

steer[2] *n.* = BULLOCK. [Old English]

steerage *n.* **1** the act of steering. **2** esp. *hist.* the part of a ship allotted to passengers travelling at the cheapest rate. **3** *hist.* (in a warship) quarters assigned to midshipmen etc. just forward of the wardroom.

steerage-way *n.* the amount of headway required by a vessel to enable it to be controlled by the helm.

steering column *n.* the shaft or column which connects the steering wheel, handlebars, etc. of a vehicle to the rest of the steering gear.

steering committee *n.* a committee deciding the priorities or order of business, or managing the general course of operations.

steering wheel *n.* a wheel by which a vehicle etc. is steered. ▷ CAR

steersman *n.* (*pl.* **-men**) a person who steers a vessel.

stegosaur *n.* ▼ a plant-eating dinosaur of the genus *Stegosaurus* or related genera, with a double row of large bony plates (or spines) along the back. ▷ DINOSAUR. [from Greek *stegē* 'covering' + *sauros* 'lizard']

STEGOSAUR (*Kentrosaurus* species)

stein /styn/ *n.* a large mug, esp. for beer. [German, literally 'stone']

stellar *adj.* **1** of or relating to a star or stars. **2** esp. *N. Amer.* **a** having star performers (*stellar cast*). **b** *colloq.* outstanding (*stellar performance by the team*). [based on Latin *stella* 'star']

stellate *adj.* (also **stellated**) arranged like a star; radiating. [from Latin *stellatus*]

stem[1] ● *n.* **1** ▼ the main body or stalk of a plant. **2** the stalk supporting a fruit, flower, or leaf, and attaching it to a larger branch, twig, or stalk. **3** a stem-shaped part of an object esp.: **a** the slender part of a wineglass. **b** the tube of a tobacco pipe. **c** a vertical stroke in a letter or musical note. **4** *Gram.* the root or main part of a noun, verb, etc. to which inflections are added. **5** *Naut.* the main upright timber or metal piece at the bow of a ship (*from stem to stern*). ● *v.* (**stemmed**, **stemming**) **1** *intr.* (foll. by *from*) spring or originate from (*stems from a desire to win*).

2 *tr.* remove the stem or stems from (fruit, tobacco, etc.). **3** *tr.* (of a vessel etc.) hold its own or make headway against (the tide etc.). [Old English] □ **stemless** *adj.* **stemmed** *adj.* (also in *comb.*).

stem[2] ● *v.* (**stemmed**, **stemming**) **1** *tr.* check or stop. **2** *tr.* dam up (a stream etc.). **3** *intr.* slide the tail of one ski or both skis outwards usu. in order to turn or slow down. ● *n.* an act of stemming on skis. [from Old Norse *stemma*]

stem cell *n. Biol.* an undifferentiated cell from which specialized cells develop.

stem stitch *n.* an embroidery stitch used for narrow stems etc.

stem turn *n.* a turn on skis made by stemming with one ski.

stench *n.* a foul smell. [Old English]

stencil ● *n.* **1** (in full **stencil-plate**) ▼ a thin sheet of plastic, metal, card, etc. in which a pattern or lettering is cut, used to produce a corresponding pattern on the surface beneath it by applying ink, paint, etc. **2** the pattern, lettering, etc., produced by a stencil-plate. ● *v.tr.* (**stencilled, stencilling;** *US* **stenciled, stenciling**) **1** produce (a pattern) with a stencil. **2** decorate or mark (a surface) in this way. [from Old French *estanceler* 'to sparkle, cover with stars']

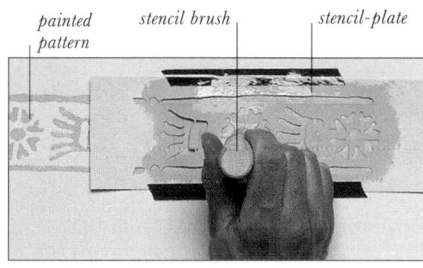

painted pattern   *stencil brush*   *stencil-plate*

STENCIL-PLATE

Sten gun *n.* ▼ a type of lightweight sub-machine gun. [from the initials of the inventors' surnames, *Sh*epherd and *T*urpin, on the pattern of *Bren*]

foresight   *magazine release catch*   *cocking handle*   *rear sight*   *skeleton butt*   *silencer*   *magazine*   *magazine housing*   *trigger*   *trigger guard*

STEN GUN

steno *n.* (*pl.* **-os**) *N. Amer. colloq.* a stenographer. [abbreviation]

stenography *n.* shorthand or the art of writing this. [based on Greek *stenos* 'narrow'] □ **stenographer** *n.* **stenographic** *adj.*

stentorian *adj.* (of a voice or something uttered) loud and powerful. [based on Greek *Stentōr*, herald in the Trojan War (Homer, *Iliad* v. 785)]

step ● *n.* **1 a** the complete movement of one leg in walking or running (*took a step forward*). **b** the distance covered by this. **2** a unit of movement in dancing. **3** a measure taken, esp. one of several in a course of action (*took steps to prevent it; considered it a wise step*). **4 a** a flat-topped structure used singly or as one of a series, for passing from one level to another. **b** the rung of a ladder. **c** a platform etc. in a vehicle provided for stepping up or down. **5** a short distance (*only a step from my door*). **6** the sound or mark made by a foot in walking etc. (*heard a step on the stairs*). **7** the manner of walking etc. as seen or heard (*know her by her step*). **8 a** a degree in the scale of promotion, advancement, or precedence. **b** one of a series of fixed points on a payscale etc.

STEM

The stem is a plant's above-ground support structure, bearing its leaves, buds, and flowers. It also forms part of a plant's transport system. Xylem tissue carries minerals and water from the roots to the rest of the plant, while phloem tissue conveys nutrients produced in the leaves. There are two types of stem: herbaceous (non-woody) stems, which die at the end of each growing season; and woody stems, which develop continuously, adding a ring consisting of secondary xylem and secondary phloem every growing season.

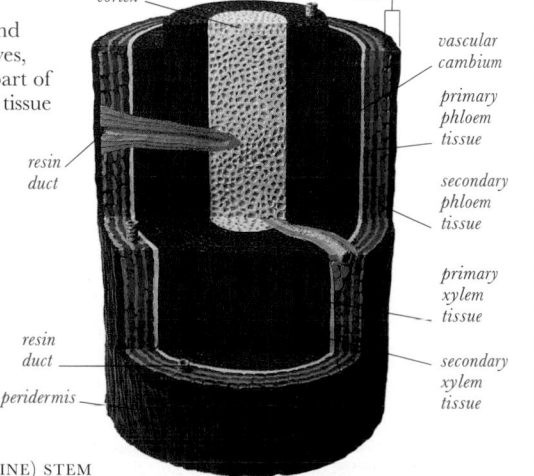

cortex   *bark*   *vascular cambium*   *primary phloem tissue*   *secondary phloem tissue*   *resin duct*   *primary xylem tissue*   *resin duct*   *secondary xylem tissue*   *peridermis*

SECTION THROUGH A WOODY (PINE) STEM

S

9 (in *pl.*) (also **pair of steps** *sing.*) *Brit.* = STEPLADDER. ● *v.* (**stepped, stepping**) **1** *intr.* lift and set down one's foot or alternate feet in walking. **2** *intr.* come or go in a specified direction by stepping. **3** *intr.* make progress in a specified way (*stepped into a new job*). **4** *tr.* (foll. by *off, out*) measure (distance) by stepping. **5** *tr.* perform (a dance). □ **in step 1** stepping in time with music or other marchers. **2** conforming with others. **in a person's steps** following a person's example. **keep step** remain in step. **mind** (or **watch**) **one's step** be careful. **out of step** not in step. **step by step** gradually; cautiously. **step down 1** resign. **2** *Electr.* decrease (voltage) by using a transformer. **step in 1** enter a room, house, etc. **2 a** intervene. **b** act as a substitute for an indisposed colleague etc. **step on it** (or **on the gas**) *colloq.* **1** accelerate a motor vehicle. **2** hurry up. **step out 1** leave a room, house, etc. **2** be active socially. **3** take large steps. **step out of line** behave inappropriately or disobediently. **step up 1 a** increase, intensify (*must step up production*). **b** *Electr.* increase (voltage) using a transformer. **2** come forward for some purpose. **turn one's steps** go in a specified direction. [Old English] □ **stepped** *adj.* **stepwise** *adv. & adj.*

step- *comb. form* denoting a relationship resulting from a remarriage (*step-grandchild*). [Old English *stēop-* 'orphan']

step aerobics *n.pl.* a type of aerobics involving stepping up on to and down from a portable block.

stepbrother *n.* a son of a step-parent by a marriage other than with one's father or mother.

stepchild *n.* (*pl.* **-children**) a child of one's husband or wife by a previous marriage.

stepdaughter *n.* a female stepchild.

stepfamily *n.* (*pl.* **-ies**) a family that includes a stepchild or stepchildren.

stepfather *n.* a male step-parent.

stephanotis *n.* any climbing tropical plant of the genus *Stephanotis*, cultivated for its fragrant waxy flowers. [from Greek, literally 'fit for a wreath']

stepladder *n.* a short ladder with flat steps and a folding prop, used without being leant against a surface.

stepmother *n.* a female step-parent.

step-parent *n.* a mother's or father's later husband or wife.

steppe *n.* a level grassy unforested plain. [from Russian *step'*]

stepping stone *n.* **1** a raised stone in a stream, muddy place, etc. to help in crossing. **2** a means or stage of progress to an end.

stepsister *n.* a daughter of a step-parent by a marriage other than with one's father or mother.

stepson *n.* a male stepchild.

stereo ● *n.* (*pl.* **-os**) **1 a** a stereophonic record player, tape recorder, etc. **b** stereophony. **2** = STEREOSCOPE. ● *adj.* **1** = STEREOPHONIC. **2** stereoscopic.

stereo- *comb. form* solid; having three dimensions. [from Greek *stereos* 'solid']

stereophonic *adj.* (of sound reproduction) using two or more channels so that the sound has the effect of being distributed and of coming from more than one source. □ **stereophonically** *adv.* **stereophony** *n.*

stereoscope *n.* a device by which two photographs of the same object taken at slightly different angles are viewed together, giving an impression of depth and solidity. □ **stereoscopic** *adj.* **stereoscopically** *adv.* **stereoscopy** *n.*

stereotype ● *n.* **1 a** a person or thing that conforms to an unjustifiably fixed mental picture. **b** such an impression or attitude. **2** a printing-plate cast from a mould of composed type. ● *v.tr.* **1** (esp. as **stereotyped** *adj.*) standardize; cause to conform to a type. **2 a** print from a stereotype. **b** make a stereotype of. [from French adj. *stéréotype*] □ **stereotypic** *adj.* **stereotypical** *adj.* **stereotypically** *adv.* **stereotypy** *n.*

sterile *adj.* **1** not able to produce crop or fruit or young; barren. **2** unproductive (*sterile discussions*). **3** free from living micro-organisms etc. **4** lacking originality or emotive force. [from Latin *sterilis*] □ **sterility** *n.*

sterilize *v.tr.* (also **-ise**) **1** make sterile. **2** deprive of the power of reproduction. □ **sterilizable** *adj.* **sterilization** *n.* **sterilizer** *n.*

sterling ● *adj.* **1** of or in British money (*pound sterling*). **2** (of a coin or precious metal) genuine; of standard value or purity. **3** (of a person or qualities etc.) of solid worth; genuine, reliable (*sterling work*). ● *n.* British money (*paid in sterling*). [originally the English silver penny of the Norman dynasty]

sterling area *n.* a group of countries with currencies tied to British sterling and holding reserves mainly in sterling.

sterling silver *n.* silver of 92¼ per cent purity.

stern[1] *adj.* severe, grim; enforcing discipline or submission (*a stern expression; stern treatment*). [Old English] □ **sternly** *adv.* **sternness** *n.*

stern[2] *n.* **1** the rear part of a ship or boat. **2** any rear part. [Middle English] □ **sternward** *adj. & adv.* **sternwards** *adv.*

sternal *adj.* of or relating to the sternum.

sternpost *n.* *Naut.* the central upright support at the stern.

sternum *n.* (*pl.* **sternums** or **sterna**) ◄ the breastbone. ▷ SKELETON. [from Greek *sternon* 'chest']

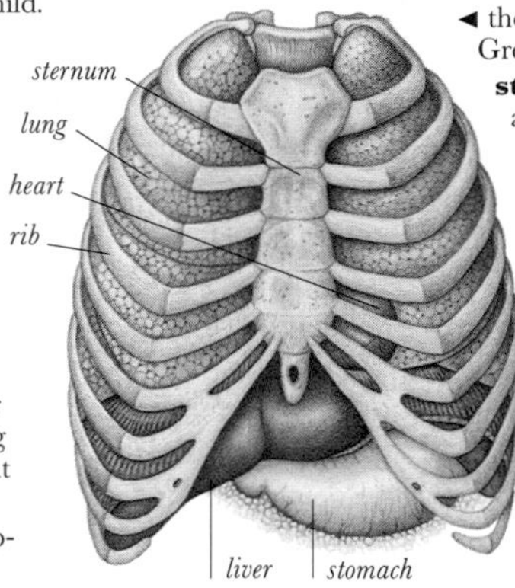
sternum
lung
heart
rib
liver
stomach

STERNUM: HUMAN RIBCAGE SHOWING THE STERNUM

steroid /**steer**-oid/ *n.* *Biochem.* any of a group of organic compounds with a characteristic structure of four rings of carbon atoms, including many hormones, alkaloids, and vitamins. [based on STEROL] □ **steroidal** *adj.*

sterol /**steer**-ol/ *n.* *Chem.* any of a group of naturally occurring steroid alcohols.

stertorous *adj.* (of breathing etc.) laboured and noisy. [based on Latin *stertere* 'to snore'] □ **stertorously** *adv.*

stet *v.* (**stetted, stetting**) **1** *intr.* (usu. written on a proof-sheet etc.) ignore or cancel the correction or alteration; let the original form stand. **2** *tr.* write 'stet' against; cancel the correction of. [Latin, literally 'let it stand']

stethoscope *n.* ► an instrument used in listening to the action of the heart, lungs, etc., usu. consisting of a circular piece placed against the chest, with tubes leading to earpieces. ▷ SPHYGMOMANOMETER. [from French *stéthoscope*]

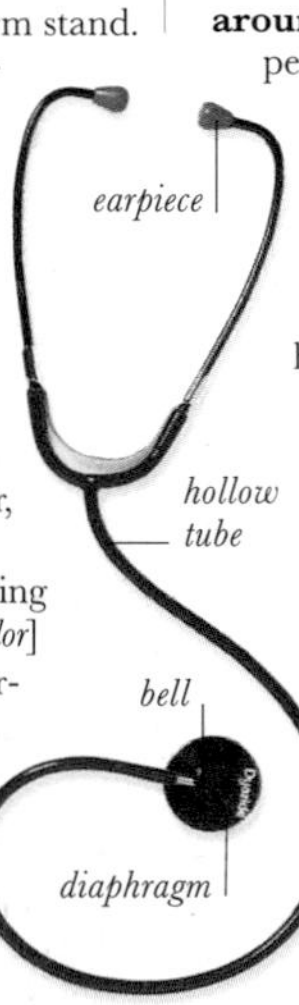
earpiece
hollow tube
bell
diaphragm

STETHOSCOPE

stetson *n.* a slouch hat with a very wide brim and a high crown. ▷ HAT. [named after J. B. *Stetson*, American hat-maker, 1830–1906]

stevedore *n.* a person employed in loading and unloading ships. [from Spanish *estivador*]

stew ● *v.* **1** *tr. & intr.* cook slowly in simmering liquid in a closed dish, saucepan, etc. **2** *intr. colloq.* be oppressed by heat or humidity. **3** *intr. colloq.* **a** suffer prolonged embarrassment, anxiety, etc. **b** (foll. by *over*) fret or be anxious. **4** *intr. Brit.* (of tea) become bitter or strong with prolonged brewing. **5** *tr.* (as **stewed** *adj.*) *colloq.* drunk. ● *n.* **1** a dish of stewed meat etc. **2** *colloq.* an agitated or angry state (*be in a stew*). □ **stew in one's own juice** be left to suffer the consequences of one's own actions. [from Old French *estuve*]

steward ● *n.* **1** a passengers' attendant on a ship or aircraft or train. **2** an official appointed to keep order or supervise arrangements at a meeting or show or demonstration etc. **3** = SHOP STEWARD. **4** a person responsible for supplies of food etc. for a college or club etc. **5** a person employed to manage another's property. **6** *Brit.* the title of several officers of state or the royal household (*Lord High Steward*). ● *v.tr.* act as a steward of (*will steward the meeting*). [Old English] □ **stewardship** *n.*

stewardess *n.* a female steward, esp. on a ship or aircraft.

stick[1] *n.* **1 a** a short slender length of wood broken or cut from a tree. **b** this trimmed for use as a support or weapon. **2** a thin rod or spike of wood etc. for a particular purpose (*cocktail stick*). **3** an implement used to propel the ball in hockey or polo etc. ▷ HOCKEY, POLO STICK. **4** a gear lever. **5** a conductor's baton. **6 a** a slender piece of celery, dynamite, deodorant, etc. **b** a number of bombs or paratroops released rapidly from aircraft. **7** punishment, esp. by beating. **8** esp. *Brit. colloq.* adverse criticism (*took a lot of stick*). **9** *colloq.* a piece of wood as part of a house or furniture (*a few sticks of furniture*). **10** *colloq.* a person, esp. one who is dull or unsociable (*a funny old stick*). **11** (in *pl.*; prec. by *the*) *colloq.* remote rural areas. **12** (in *pl.*) *Austral. slang* goalposts. □ **up sticks** *Brit. colloq.* go to live elsewhere. [Old English]

stick[2] *v.* (*past* and *past part.* **stuck**) **1** *tr.* (foll. by *in, into, through*) insert or thrust (a thing or its point) (*stuck a finger in my eye; stick a pin through it*). **2** *tr.* insert a pointed thing into; stab. **3** *tr. & intr.* (foll. by *in, into, on*, etc.) **a** fix or be fixed on a pointed thing. **b** fix or be fixed by or as by a pointed end. **4** *tr. & intr.* fix or become or remain fixed by or as by adhesive etc. (*stick a label on it; the label won't stick*). **5** *intr.* endure; make a continued impression (*the scene stuck in my mind; the name stuck*). **6** *intr.* lose or be deprived of the power of motion or action through adhesion or jamming or other impediment. **7** *colloq.* **a** *tr.* put in a specified position or place (*stick it in your pocket*). **b** *intr.* remain in a place (*stuck indoors*). **8** *colloq.* **a** *intr.* (of an accusation etc.) be convincing or regarded as valid (*could not make the charges stick*). **b** *tr.* (foll. by *on*) place the blame for (a thing) on (a person). **9** *tr. Brit. colloq.* endure, tolerate (*could not stick it any longer*). **10** *tr.* (foll. by *at*) *colloq.* persevere with. □ **be stuck 1** be unable to progress. **2** be confined in a place (*was stuck in the house*). **be stuck for** be at a loss for or in need of. **be stuck on** *colloq.* be infatuated with. **be stuck with** *colloq.* be unable to get rid of. **get stuck in** (or **into**) *colloq.* begin in earnest. **stick around** *colloq.* linger; remain. **stick at it** *colloq.* persevere. **stick at nothing** allow nothing, esp. no scruples, to deter one. **stick by** (or **with** or **to**) stay loyal or close to. **stick 'em up!** *colloq.* hands up! **stick fast** adhere or become firmly fixed or trapped in a position or place. **stick in one's throat** be against one's principles. **stick it on** *colloq.* **1** make high charges. **2** tell an exaggerated story. **stick it out** *colloq.* put up with or persevere with a burden etc. to the end. **stick one's neck** (or **chin**) **out** expose oneself to censure etc. by acting or speaking boldly. **stick out** protrude or cause to protrude or project (*stuck his tongue out; stick out your chest*). **stick out for** persist in demanding. **stick out a mile** (or **like a sore thumb**) *colloq.* be very obvious or incongruous. **stick to 1** remain close to or fixed on or to. **2** remain faithful to. **3** keep to (a subject etc.) (*stick to the point*). **stick to a person's fingers** *colloq.* (of money) be embezzled by a person. **stick together** *colloq.* remain united or mutually loyal. **stick to one's guns** see GUN. **stick to it** persevere. **stick up 1** be or make erect or

S

protruding upwards. **2** fasten to an upright surface. **3** *colloq.* rob or threaten with a gun. **stick up for** support or defend. **stick with** *colloq.* remain in touch with or faithful to; persevere with. [Old English]

stickability *n. colloq.* perseverance; staying power.

sticker *n.* **1** an adhesive label or notice etc. **2** a person or thing that sticks. **3** a persistent person.

sticking plaster *n. Brit.* an adhesive plaster for wounds etc.

sticking point *n.* the place where obstacles arise to progress or to an agreement etc.

stick insect *n.* ▶ any insect of the family Phasmidae with a twiglike body.

STICK INSECT:
GIANT SPINY
STICK INSECT
(*Acrophylla titan*)

antenna

real leaf

spiny abdomen

flattened, leaf-like legs

stick-in-the-mud *n. colloq.* an unprogressive or old-fashioned person.

stickleback *n.* ▶ any small fish of the family Gasterosteidae, esp. *Gasterosteus aculeatus*, with sharp spines along the back. [Old English *sticel* 'thorn, sting' + *bæc* 'back']

stickler *n.* (foll. by *for*) a person who insists on something (*a stickler for accuracy*). [from obsolete *stickle* 'to be umpire']

stickpin *n. N. Amer.* an ornamental tiepin.

stick-up *n. colloq.* a robbery using a gun.

sticky *adj.* (**stickier**, **stickiest**) **1** tending or intended to stick or adhere. **2** glutinous, viscous. **3 a** humid. **b** damp with sweat. **4** *colloq.* awkward or uncooperative; intransigent (*was very sticky about giving me leave*). **5** *colloq.* difficult, awkward (*a sticky problem*). □ **come to a sticky end** *Brit.* die or come to grief in an unpleasant or painful way. □ **stickily** *adv.* **stickiness** *n.*

stickybeak *Austral. & NZ slang* ● *n.* an inquisitive person. ● *v.intr.* pry.

sticky wicket *n. colloq.* difficult circumstances.

stiff ● *adj.* **1** rigid; not flexible. **2** hard to bend or move or turn etc. **3** hard to cope with; needing strength or effort (*a stiff test*; *a stiff climb*). **4** severe or strong (*a stiff breeze*; *a stiff penalty*). **5** formal, constrained. **6** (of a muscle or limb etc., or a person affected by these) aching when used, owing to previous exertion, injury, etc. **7** (of an alcoholic or medicinal drink) strong. **8** (*predic.*) *colloq.* to an extreme degree (*bored stiff*; *scared stiff*). **9** (foll. by *with*) *colloq.* abounding in (*a place stiff with tourists*). ● *n. slang* a corpse. [Old English] □ **stiffish** *adj.* **stiffly** *adv.* **stiffness** *n.*

stiffen *v.tr. & intr.* make or become stiff. □ **stiffener** *n.* **stiffening** *n.*

stiff neck *n.* a rheumatic condition in which the head cannot be turned without pain.

stiff-necked *adj.* obstinate or haughty.

stiff upper lip *n.* firmness, fortitude.

stifle *v.* **1** *tr.* smother, suppress (*stifled a yawn*). **2** *intr. & tr.* experience or cause to experience constraint of breathing (*stifling heat*). **3** *tr.* kill by suffocating. □ **stifling** *adj. & adv.* **stiflingly** *adv.*

stigma *n.* (*pl.* **stigmas** or esp. in sense 4 **stigmata**) **1** a mark or sign of disgrace or discredit. **2** (foll. by *of*) a distinguishing mark or characteristic. **3** the part of a pistil that receives the pollen in pollination. ▷ FLOWER. **4** (in *pl.*) *Eccl.* (in Christian belief) marks corresponding to those left on Christ's body by the Crucifixion, said to have been impressed by divine favour on the bodies of St Francis of Assisi and others. [Greek, literally 'a mark made by a pointed instrument; a brand']

stigmatize *v.tr.* (also **-ise**) describe as unworthy or disgraceful. [from Greek *stigmatizein* 'to mark with a brand'] □ **stigmatization** *n.*

spines

STICKLEBACK: THREE-SPINED
STICKLEBACK
(*Gasterosteus aculeatus*)

stile *n.* an arrangement of steps allowing people but not animals to climb over a fence or wall. [Old English]

stiletto *n.* (*pl.* **-os**) **1** a short dagger. **2** a pointed instrument for making eyelets etc. **3** (in full **stiletto heel**) **a** a long tapering heel of a shoe. **b** a shoe with such a heel. [Italian, literally 'little dagger']

still[1] ● *adj.* **1** not or hardly moving. **2** with little or no sound; calm and tranquil (*a still evening*). **3** (of sounds) hushed, stilled. **4** (of a drink) not effervescent. ● *n.* **1** deep silence (*in the still of the night*). **2** an ordinary static photograph (as opposed to a motion picture), esp. a single shot from a cinema film. ● *adv.* **1** without moving (*stand still*). **2** even

now or at a particular time (*they still did not understand*; *why are you still here?*). **3** nevertheless. **4** (with *compar.* etc.) even, yet, increasingly (*still greater efforts*; *still another explanation*). ● *v.tr. & intr.* make or become still; quieten. [Old English] □ **stillness** *n.*

still[2] *n.* ▼ an apparatus for distilling spirituous liquors etc. [from obsolete Middle English verb *still* 'to distill']

stillbirth *n.* the birth of a dead child.

stillborn *adj.* **1** born dead. **2** (of an idea, plan, etc.) abortive; not able to succeed.

still life *n.* (*pl.* **still lifes**) (hyphenated when *attrib.*) a painting or drawing of inanimate objects such as fruit or flowers.

Stillson *n.* (in full **Stillson wrench**) a large wrench with jaws that tighten as pressure is increased. ▷ WRENCH. [named after D. C. *Stillson*, 1830–99, its inventor]

stilt *n.* **1** either of a pair of poles with supports for the feet enabling the user to walk at a distance above the ground. **2** ▼ each of a set of piles or posts supporting a building etc. **3** any wading bird of the genus *Himantopus*, with long slender legs. [Middle English]

STILT HOUSE, THAILAND

stilted *adj.* **1** (of a literary style etc.) stiff and unnatural; bombastic. **2** standing on stilts. □ **stiltedly** *adv.* **stiltedness** *n.*

Stilton *n. propr.* a kind of strong rich cheese, often with blue veins, originally made in Leicestershire and formerly sold at a coaching inn in Stilton (now in Cambridgeshire). ▷ CHEESE

stimulant ● *adj.* that stimulates, esp. bodily or mental activity. ● *n.* **1** a stimulant substance. **2** a stimulating influence. [from Latin *stimulant-* 'urging, goading']

stimulate *v.tr.* **1** apply or act as a stimulus to. **2** animate, excite, arouse. **3** be a stimulant to. □ **stimulating** *adj.* **stimulation** *n.* **stimulative** *adj.* **stimulator** *n.* **stimulatory** *adj.*

stimulus *n.* (*pl.* **stimuli** /-ly/) **1** a thing that rouses to activity. **2** a stimulating or rousing effect. [Latin, literally 'goad, spur']

stimy var. of STYMIE.

sting ● *n.* **1** a sharp wounding organ of an insect, nettle, etc. **2 a** the act of inflicting a wound with this. **b** the wound itself or the pain caused by it. **3** a painful quality or effect (*the sting of hunger*; *stings of remorse*). **4** pungency, sharpness, vigour (*a sting in the voice*). **5** *slang* **a** a swindle or robbery. **b** a police undercover operation. ● *v.* (*past* and *past part.* **stung**) **1 a** *tr.* wound or pierce with a sting. **b** *intr.* be able to sting. **2** *intr. & tr.* feel or cause to feel a tingling physical or sharp mental pain. **3** *tr.* (foll. by *into*) incite by a strong or painful mental effect (*was stung into replying*). **4** *tr. slang* swindle or charge exorbitantly. □ **sting in the tail** an unpleasant or problematic end to something, occurring unexpectedly. [Old English] □ **stingingly** *adv.* **stingless** *adj.*

stinger *n.* **1** a stinging insect, snake, nettle, etc. **2** a sharp painful blow.

stinging nettle *n.* a nettle, *Urtica dioica*, having stinging hairs.

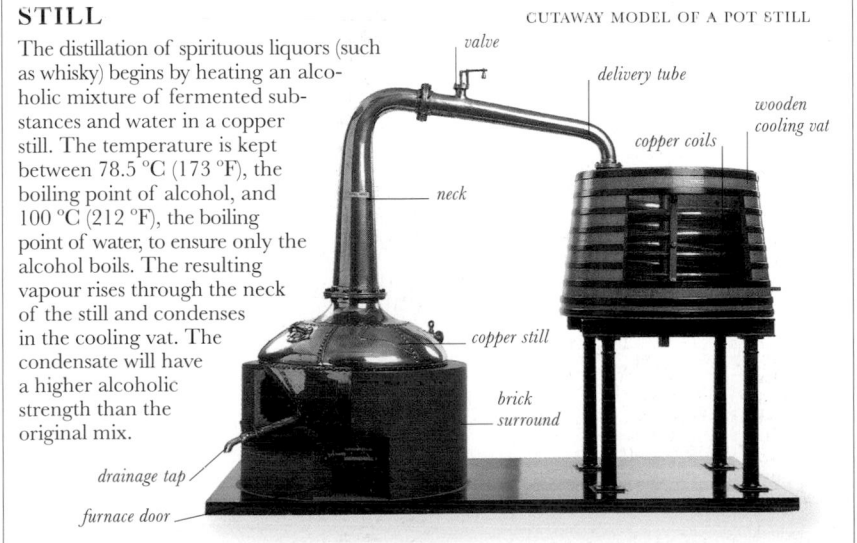

STILL

The distillation of spirituous liquors (such as whisky) begins by heating an alcoholic mixture of fermented substances and water in a copper still. The temperature is kept between 78.5 °C (173 °F), the boiling point of alcohol, and 100 °C (212 °F), the boiling point of water, to ensure only the alcohol boils. The resulting vapour rises through the neck of the still and condenses in the cooling vat. The condensate will have a higher alcoholic strength than the original mix.

CUTAWAY MODEL OF A POT STILL

valve

delivery tube

wooden cooling vat

copper coils

neck

copper still

brick surround

drainage tap

furnace door

S

stingray

tail
poisonous spine
pectoral fin
pelvic fin

STINGRAY
(*Dasyatis* species)

stingray *n.* ▶ any cartilaginous fish of the family Dasyatidae or Urolophidae, having a flattened diamond-shaped body and a poisonous spine at the base of the tail. ▷ RAY

stingy /**stin**-ji/ *adj.* (**stingier**, **stingiest**) niggardly, mean. □ **stingily** *adv.* **stinginess** *n.*

stink ● *v.* (*past* **stank** *or* **stunk**; *past part.* **stunk**) **1** *intr.* emit a strong offensive smell. **2** *tr.* (often foll. by *out*) fill (a place) with a stink. **3** *tr.* (foll. by *out* etc.) drive (a person) out etc. by a stink. **4** *intr. colloq.* be or seem very unpleasant, contemptible, or scandalous. ● *n.* **1** a strong or offensive smell. **2** *colloq.* a row or fuss (*the affair caused quite a stink*). □ **like stink** *colloq.* intensely; extremely hard or fast etc. (*working like stink*). [Old English]

foul-smelling spore mass

STINKHORN:
COMMON STINKHORN
(*Phallus impudicus*)

stink bomb *n.* a device emitting a stink when exploded.

stinker *n.* **1** a person or thing that stinks. **2** *slang* an objectionable person or thing.

stinkhorn *n.* ◀ any foul-smelling fungus of the order Phallales.

stinking ● *adj.* **1** that stinks. **2** *slang* very objectionable. ● *adv. slang* extremely and usu. objectionably (*stinking rich*). □ **stinkingly** *adv.*

stinky *adj.* (**stinkier**, **stinkiest**) *colloq.* having a strong or unpleasant smell.

stint ● *v.* **1** *tr.* supply (food or aid etc.) in a niggardly amount or grudgingly. **2** *tr.* (often *refl.*) supply (a person etc.) in this way. **3** *intr.* (foll. by *on*) be grudging or mean about. ● *n.* **1** a limitation of supply or effort (*without stint*). **2** an allotted amount of work (*do one's stint*). **3** a small sandpiper, esp. a dunlin. [Old English *styntan* 'to blunt, dull']

stipend /**sty**-pend/ *n.* a salary, esp. *Brit.* one paid to a clergyman. [from Latin *stipendium*]

stipendiary /sty-**pend**-yă-ri/ ● *adj.* **1** receiving a stipend. **2** working for pay. ● *n.* (*pl.* **-ies**) a person receiving a stipend.

stipendiary magistrate *n.* a paid professional magistrate.

stipple ● *v.* **1** *tr. & intr.* draw or paint or engrave etc. with dots instead of lines. **2** *tr.* roughen the surface of (paint, cement, etc.). ● *n.* **1** the process or technique of stippling. **2** the effect of stippling. [from Dutch *stippelen* 'to keep pricking'] □ **stippler** *n.* **stippling** *n.*

stipulate *v.tr.* **1** demand or specify as part of a bargain or agreement. **2** (foll. by *for*) mention or insist upon as an essential condition. **3** (as **stipulated** *adj.*) laid down in the terms of an agreement. [based on

Latin *stipulatus* 'having exacted a guarantee'] □ **stipulation** *n.*

stir[1] ● *v.* (**stirred**, **stirring**) **1** *tr.* move a spoon or other implement round and round in (a liquid etc.), esp. to mix the ingredients or constituents. **2 a** *tr.* cause to move or be disturbed, esp. slightly (*a breeze stirred the lake*). **b** *intr.* be or begin to be in motion (*not a creature was stirring*). **c** *refl.* rouse (oneself). **3** *intr.* rise from sleep (*is still not stirring*). **4** *intr.* (foll. by *out of*) leave; go out of. **5** *tr.* arouse or inspire or excite (the emotions etc., or a person) (*was stirred to anger*; *stirred the imagination*). ● *n.* **1** an act of stirring (*give it a good stir*). **2** commotion or excitement (*caused quite a stir*). **3** the slightest movement (*not a stir*). □ **stir the blood** inspire enthusiasm etc. **stir in** mix (an added ingredient) with a substance by stirring. **stir one's stumps** *colloq.* **1** begin to move. **2** become active. **stir up 1** mix thoroughly by stirring. **2** incite (trouble etc.) (*loved stirring things up*). **3** stimulate, excite, arouse (*stirred up their curiosity*). [Old English]

stir[2] *n. slang* a prison (esp. *in stir*). [19th-century coinage]

stir-crazy *adj. slang* deranged from long imprisonment.

stir-fry ● *v.tr.* (**-ies**, **-ied**) fry rapidly while stirring. ● *n.* a stir-fried dish.

stirrer *n.* **1** a thing or a person that stirs. **2** *Brit. colloq.* a troublemaker; an agitator.

stirring ● *adj.* **1** stimulating, exciting, rousing. **2** *archaic* actively occupied (*lead a stirring life*). ● *n.* (in *pl.*) **1** initial activity or indications of such activity (*stirrings of a new culture*). **2** initial feelings (*stirrings of sympathy*).

stirrup *n.* each of a pair of devices attached to each side of a horse's saddle, in the form of a loop with

---

STITCH

Sewing stitches have a variety of uses, including creating a seam (when two or more pieces of material are joined by a line of stitches), neatening a raw edge, making a buttonhole, or producing a hem (a cloth's edge that has been turned under and then sewn down). Hand stitches are often used to sew areas a machine cannot easily reach. Machine stitches perform the same functions as hand stitches, but are created much more quickly. Some stitches have decorative and practical uses. The zigzag stitch, for example, can be used as decoration on dress shirts, or as an edging stitch (to prevent fraying). Stitches are also utilized in embroidery, crochet, and knitting.

HAND SEWING STITCHES

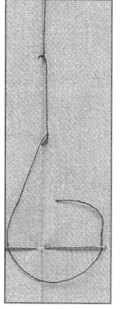
LOCK STITCH

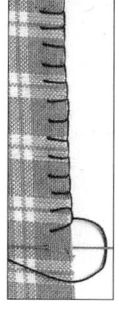
BLANKET STITCH

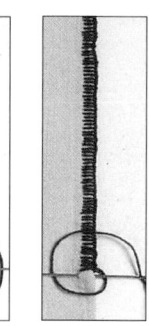
BUTTONHOLE STITCH

MACHINE STITCHES

FEATHER STITCH

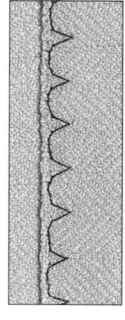
BLIND HEMMING STITCH

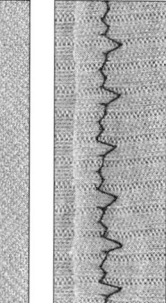
ZIGZAG BLIND HEMMING STITCH

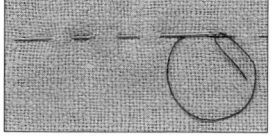
RUNNING STITCH

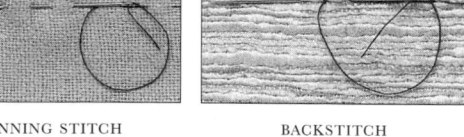
BACKSTITCH

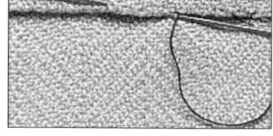
SLIPSTITCH

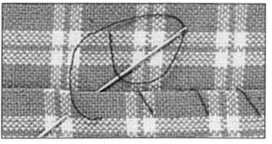
SLANTING HEMSTITCH

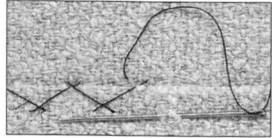
HERRINGBONE STITCH

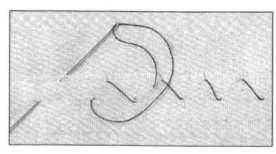
OVERCAST STITCH

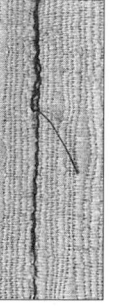
STRAIGHT STITCH

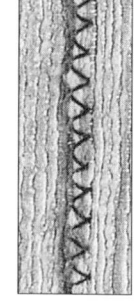
ZIGZAG STITCH

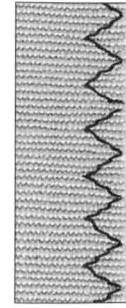
THREE-STEP ZIGZAG STITCH

S

a flat base to support the rider's foot. ▷ SADDLE, SHOWJUMPING. [Old English]

stirrup cup *n.* a cup of wine etc. offered to a person about to depart, originally on horseback.

stirrup pump *n.* a hand-operated water pump with a footrest, used to extinguish small fires.

stitch ● *n.* **1 a** ◀ (in sewing or knitting or crocheting etc.) a single pass of a needle or the thread or loop etc. resulting from this. ▷ KNITTING. **b** a particular method of sewing or knitting etc. (*am learning a new stitch*). **2** (usu. in *pl.*) *Surgery* each of the loops of material used in sewing up a wound. **3** the least bit of clothing (*hadn't a stitch on*). **4** an acute pain in the side of the body induced by running etc. ● *v.tr.* **1** (also *absol.*) sew; make stitches (in). **2** join or close with stitches. □ **in stitches** *colloq.* laughing uncontrollably. **stitch up 1** join or mend by sewing or stitching. **2** *Brit. slang* cause (a person) to be charged with a crime, esp. by informing or manufacturing evidence; cheat. [Old English] □ **stitcher** *n.* **stitchery** *n.*

stitch in time *n.* a timely remedy.

stitch-up *n. slang* **1** an act of incriminating a person for a crime. **2** often *derog.* an act of securing the outcome of something to one's advantage.

stoat *n.* a small long-bodied carnivorous mammal, *Mustela erminea*, of the weasel family, having reddish-brown upper parts and a black-tipped tail, and in northern areas turning white in winter. ▷ MUSTELID. [Middle English]

stock ● *n.* **1** a store of goods etc. ready for sale or distribution etc. **2** a supply or quantity of anything for use (*lay in winter stocks of fuel; a great stock of information*). **3** equipment or raw material for manufacture or trade etc. (*rolling stock; paper stock*). **4 a** farm animals or equipment. **b** = FATSTOCK. **5 a** the capital of a business. **b** shares in this. **6** one's reputation or popularity (*his stock is rising*). **7 a** money lent to a government at fixed interest. **b** the right to receive such interest. **8** a line of ancestry (*comes of Cornish stock*). **9** liquid made by stewing bones, vegetables, fish, etc., as a basis for soup, gravy, sauce, etc. **10** ▶ any of various fragrant-flowered cruciferous plants of the genus *Matthiola* or *Malcolmia* (originally *stock-gillyflower*, so called because it had a stronger stem than the clove gillyflower). **11** a plant into which a graft is inserted. **12** the main trunk of a tree etc. **13** (in *pl.*) *hist.* a timber frame with holes for the feet, and occasionally the hands and head, in which offenders were locked as a public punishment. **14** *US* **a** = STOCK COMPANY. **b** the repertory of this. **15** (in *pl.*) the supports for a ship during building. **16** a band of material worn round the neck. ▷ REDCOAT. **17** hard solid brick pressed in a mould. ● *adj.* **1** kept in stock and so regularly available (*stock sizes*). **2** perpetually repeated; hackneyed, conventional (*a stock answer*). ● *v.tr.* **1** have or keep (goods) in stock. **2 a** provide (a shop or a farm etc.) with goods, equipment, or livestock. **b** fill with items needed (*shelves well-stocked with books*). □ **in stock** available immediately for sale etc. **on the stocks** in construction or preparation. **out of stock** not immediately available for sale. **stock up 1** provide with or get stocks or supplies. **2** (foll. by *with*) get in or gather a stock of (food, fuel, etc.). **take stock 1** make an inventory of one's stock. **2** (often foll. by *of*) make a review or estimate (of a situation etc.). [Old English] □ **stocker** *n.*

stockade ● *n.* **1** a line or enclosure of upright stakes. **2** esp. *N. Amer.* a prison. ● *v.tr.* fortify with a stockade. [from Spanish *estacada*]

stockbreeder *n.* a farmer who raises livestock. □ **stockbreeding** *n.*

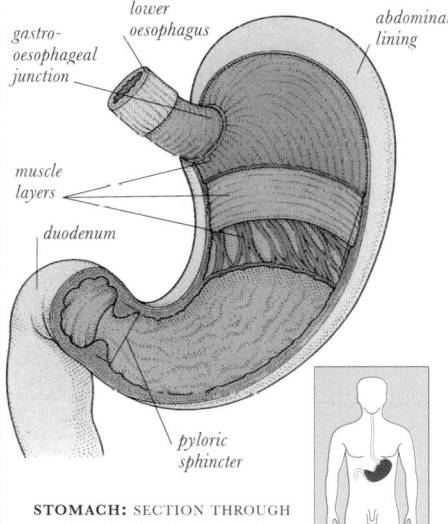

STOCK: VIRGINIA STOCK
(*Malcolmia maritima*)

stockbroker *n.* = BROKER 2. □ **stockbrokerage** *n.* **stockbroking** *n.*

stockbroker belt *n. Brit.* an affluent residential area.

stock car *n.* **1** a specially strengthened car for use in racing in which collision occurs. **2** *N. Amer.* a railway truck for transporting livestock.

stock company *n. US* a repertory company performing mainly at a particular theatre.

Stock Exchange *n.* (also **stock exchange**) **1** a place where stocks and shares are bought and sold. **2** the dealers working there.

stockholder *n.* an owner of stocks or shares. □ **stockholding** *n.*

stockinet *n.* (also **stockinette**) an elastic knitted material.

stocking *n.* **1 a** either of a pair of long separate usu. knitted coverings for the legs and feet. **b** esp. *US* = SOCK[1] 1. **2** any close-fitting garment resembling a stocking (*bodystocking*). **3** a differently coloured, usu. white, lower part of the leg of a horse etc. □ **in one's stocking** (or **stockinged**) **feet** without shoes. [from archaic *stock* 'to strengthen (hose)'] □ **stockinged** *adj.* (also in *comb.*).

stocking stitch *n. Knitting* a stitch of alternate rows of plain and purl. ▷ KNITTING

stock-in-trade *n.* **1 a** all the requisites of a trade or profession. **b** the goods kept on sale by a dealer or shopkeeper. **2** a ready supply of characteristic phrases, attitudes, etc.

stockist *n. Brit.* a dealer who stocks goods of a particular type.

stockjobber *n.* **1** *Brit.* = JOBBER 1. **2** *US* = JOBBER 2b.

stocklist *n. Brit.* a regular publication stating a dealer's stock of goods with current prices etc.

stockman *n.* (*pl.* **-men**) **1 a** *Austral.* a man in charge of livestock. **b** *US* an owner of livestock. **2** *US* a person in charge of a stock of goods in a warehouse etc.

stock market *n.* **1** = STOCK EXCHANGE. **2** transactions on this.

stockpile ● *n.* an accumulated stock of goods, materials, weapons, etc., held in reserve. ● *v.tr.* accumulate a stockpile of.

stockpot *n.* a pot for cooking stock for soup etc.

stockroom *n.* a room for storing goods in stock.

stock-still *adv.* completely motionless.

stocktaking *n.* **1** the process of making an inventory of stock. **2** a review of one's position and resources. □ **stocktake** *n.*

stocky *adj.* (**stockier**, **stockiest**) short and strongly built; thickset. □ **stockily** *adv.*

stockyard *n.* an enclosure for the sorting or temporary keeping of cattle.

stodge *n.* esp. *Brit. colloq.* **1** food esp. of a thick heavy kind. **2** an unimaginative person or idea.

stodgy *adj.* (**stodgier**, **stodgiest**) **1** *Brit.* (of food) heavy and indigestible. **2** dull and uninteresting. **3** (of a literary style etc.) turgid and dull. □ **stodginess** *n.*

stoep /stoop/ *n. S.Afr.* a terraced veranda in front of a house. [Dutch]

Stoic /stoh-ik/ ● *n.* **1** a member of the ancient Greek school of philosophy founded by Zeno *c.*308 BC, which sought virtue as the greatest good and taught control of one's feelings and passions. **2** (**stoic**) a stoical person. ● *adj.* **1** of or like the Stoics. **2** (**stoic**) = STOICAL. [from Greek *stōikos*]

stoical /stoh-i-kăl/ *adj.* having or showing great self-control in adversity. □ **stoically** *adv.*

Stoicism /stoh-i-sizm/ *n.* **1** the philosophy of the Stoics. **2** (**stoicism**) a stoical attitude.

stoke *v.* **1 a** *tr.* feed and tend (a fire or furnace etc.). **b** *intr.* act as a stoker. **2** *intr. colloq.* consume food, esp.

steadily and in large quantities. [back-formation from STOKER]

stokehold *n.* a compartment in a steamship, containing its boilers and furnace.

stokehole *n.* a space for stokers in front of a furnace.

stoker *n.* a person who tends the furnace on a steamship. [based on Middle Dutch *stoken* 'to push, poke']

STOL *abbr. Aeron.* short take-off and landing.

stole[1] *n.* **1** a woman's long garment like a scarf, worn over the shoulders. **2** a strip of silk etc. worn similarly by a priest. ▷ VESTMENT. [from Greek *stolē* 'equipment, clothing']

stole[2] *past* of STEAL.

stolen *past part.* of STEAL.

stolid *adj.* **1** lacking or concealing emotion or animation. **2** not easily excited or moved. [from Latin *stolidus*] □ **stolidity** *n.* **stolidly** *adv.* **stolidness** *n.*

stoma *n.* (*pl.* **stomas** or **stomata**) **1** *Surgery* an artificial orifice made in the abdominal wall. **2** *Bot.* a minute pore in the epidermis of a leaf. [Greek, literally 'mouth']

stomach ● *n.* **1 a** ▼ the internal organ in which the first part of digestion occurs. ▷ DIGESTION. **b** any of several such organs in animals, esp. ruminants, in which there are four. **2 a** the belly, abdomen, or lower front of the body (*pit of the stomach*). **b** a protuberant belly (*what a stomach he has got!*). **3** (usu. foll. by *for*) **a** an appetite. **b** liking, readiness, or inclination (for controversy, conflict, danger, or an undertaking) (*had no stomach for the fight*). ● *v.tr.* **1** find sufficiently palatable to swallow or keep down. **2** submit to or endure (an affront etc.) (usu. with *neg.: cannot stomach it*). [from Greek *stomakhos* 'gullet']

STOMACH: SECTION THROUGH THE HUMAN STOMACH

(labels: *lower oesophagus*; *abdominal lining*; *gastro-oesophageal junction*; *muscle layers*; *duodenum*; *pyloric sphincter*)

stomach-ache *n.* a pain in the belly or bowels.

stomach pump *n.* a syringe for forcing liquid etc. into or out of the stomach.

stomach upset *n.* a slight temporary disorder of the digestive system.

stomatal *adj. Bot.* of or relating to a stoma or stomata.

stomp ● *v.intr.* tread or stamp heavily. ● *n.* **1** a lively jazz dance with heavy stamping. **2** a tune or song suitable for such a dance. [US dialect variant of STAMP] □ **stomper** *n.*

stone ● *n.* **1 a** solid non-metallic mineral matter, of which rock is made. **b** a piece of this, esp. a small piece. **2** *Building* **a** = LIMESTONE (*Portland stone*). **b** = SANDSTONE (*Bath stone*). **3** *Mineral.* = PRECIOUS STONE. **4** a stony meteorite. **5** (often in *comb.*) a piece of stone of a definite shape or for a particular purpose

S

(*stepping stone*). **6 a** a thing resembling stone in hardness or form, e.g. the hard case of the kernel in some fruits. **b** *Med.* (often in *pl.*) a hard concretion in the body (*gallstones*). **7** (*pl.* same) *Brit.* a unit of weight equal to 14 lb (6.35 kg). **8** a brownish-grey colour. ● *adj.* **1** made of stone. **2** of a brownish-grey colour. ● *v.tr.* **1 a** pelt with stones. **b** put to death by pelting with stones. **2** remove the stones from (fruit). □ **cast** (or **throw**) **stones** make aspersions on a person's character etc. **cast** (or **throw**) **the first stone** be the first to make an accusation. **leave no stone unturned** try all possible means. **a stone's throw** a short distance. [Old English] □ **stoned** *adj.* (also in *comb.*). **stoneless** *adj.* **stoner** *n.*

Stone Age *n.* a prehistoric period when weapons and tools were made of stone.

stonechat *n.* ◄ any small brown bird of the thrush family with black and white markings, esp. *Saxicola torquata* with a call like stones being knocked together.

stone circle *n. Archaeol.* = CIRCLE *n.* 7.

stone-cold *adj.* completely cold.

stone-cold sober *predic. adj.* completely sober.

stonecrop *n.* ► any succulent plant of the genus *Sedum*, usu. growing amongst rocks or in walls.

STONECHAT
(*Saxicola torquata*)

stonecutter *n.* a person or machine that cuts or carves stone.

stoned *adj. slang* under the influence of alcohol or drugs.

stone-dead *adj.* completely dead.

stone-deaf *adj.* completely deaf.

stone fruit *n.* a fruit with flesh enclosing a stone.

stoneground *adj.* (of flour) ground with millstones.

stonemason *n.* a person who cuts, prepares, and builds with stone. □ **stonemasonry** *n.*

stonewall *v.* **1** *tr. & intr.* obstruct (discussion or investigation) or be obstructive with evasive answers or denials etc. **2** *intr. Cricket* bat with excessive caution. □ **stonewalling** *n.*

stoneware *n.* a type of pottery which is impermeable and partly vitrified but opaque.

stonewashed *adj.* (of a garment or fabric, esp. denim) washed with abrasives to produce a worn or faded appearance.

stonework *n.* **1** masonry. **2** the parts of a building made of stone.

stonkered *adj. Austral. & NZ slang* utterly defeated or exhausted. [based on *stonk* 'a game of marbles, an artillery bombardment']

stonking *Brit. slang* ● *adj.* considerable; exciting. ● *adv.* extremely. [based on *stonk* (see STONKERED)]

stony *adj.* (**stonier**, **stoniest**) **1** full of or covered with stones (*stony soil*; *a stony road*). **2 a** hard, rigid. **b** unfeeling, uncompromising (*a stony stare*; *a stony silence*). □ **stonily** *adv.* **stoniness** *n.*

stony-broke *adj. Brit. slang* entirely without money.

stony-hearted *adj.* unfeeling, obdurate.

stood *past* and *past part.* of STAND.

stooge *colloq.* ● *n.* **1** a butt or foil, esp. for a comedian. **2** an assistant or subordinate, esp. for routine or unpleasant work. **3** a compliant person; a puppet. ● *v.intr.* **1** (foll. by *for*) act as a stooge for. **2** (foll. by *about*, *around*, etc.) *Brit.* move about aimlessly. [20th-century coinage]

stook *Brit.* ● *n.* a group of sheaves of grain stood on

end in a field. ● *v.tr.* arrange in stooks. [Middle English]

stool ● *n.* **1** a seat without a back or arms, usu. for one person. **2** = FOOTSTOOL. **3** (usu. in *pl.*) = FAECES. **4** the root or stump of a tree or plant from which the shoots spring. ● *v.intr.* (of a plant) throw up shoots from the root. □ **fall between two stools** fail from vacillation between two courses etc. [Old English]

stoolball *n.* a team game resembling cricket, played in the UK chiefly by children.

stoolie *n. N. Amer. slang* a person acting as a stoolpigeon.

stool-pigeon *n.* **1** a person acting as a decoy. **2** a police informer.

stoop[1] ● *v.* **1** *tr.* bend (one's head or body) forwards and downwards. **2** *intr.* carry one's head and shoulders bowed forward. **3** *intr.* (foll. by *to* + infin.) deign or condescend. **4** *intr.* (foll. by *to*) descend or lower oneself to (some conduct) (*has stooped to crime*). ● *n.* a stooping posture. [Old English]

stoop[2] *n. N. Amer.* a porch or small veranda or set of steps in front of a house. [from Dutch *stoep*]

stoop[3] var. of STOUP.

stop ● *v.* (**stopped**, **stopping**) **1** *tr.* **a** put an end to (motion etc.); completely check the progress or motion or operation of. **b** effectively hinder or prevent (*stopped them playing so loudly*). **c** discontinue (an action or sequence of actions) (*stopped playing*; *stopped my visits*). **2** *intr.* come to an end; cease (*supplies suddenly stopped*). **3** *intr.* cease from motion or speaking or action; make a halt or pause. **4** *tr.* cause to cease action; defeat. **5** *tr. colloq.* receive (a blow etc.). **6** *intr.* remain; stay for a short time. **7** *tr.* (often foll. by *up*) block or close up (a hole or leak etc.). **8** *tr.* not permit or supply as usual; discontinue or withhold (*shall stop their wages*). **9** *tr.* (in full **stop payment of** or **on**) instruct a bank to withhold payment on (a cheque). **10** *tr. Brit.* put a filling in (a tooth). **11** *tr.* obtain the required pitch from (the string of a violin etc.) by pressing at the appropriate point with the finger. **12** *tr. Boxing* **a** parry (a blow). **b** knock out (an opponent). **13** *tr.* pinch back (a plant). ● *n.* **1** the act or an instance of stopping; the state of being stopped. **2** a place designated for a bus or train etc. to stop. **3** *Brit.* a punctuation mark, esp. = FULL STOP 1. **4** a device for stopping motion at a particular point. **5** a change of pitch effected by stopping a string. **6 a** (in an organ) a row of pipes of one character. ▷ ORGAN. **b** a knob etc. operating these. **7 a** the effective diameter of a lens. **b** a device for reducing this. **c** a unit of change of relative aperture or exposure. **8** a plosive consonant. □ **pull all the stops out** see PULL. □ **put a stop to** cause to end, esp. abruptly. **stop at nothing** be ruthless. **stop by** (also *absol.*) call at (a place). **stop dead** (or **short**) cease abruptly. **stop down** *Photog.* reduce the aperture of (a lens) with a diaphragm. **stop one's ears 1** put one's fingers in one's ears to avoid hearing. **2** refuse to listen. **stop a person's mouth** induce a person by bribery or other means to keep silent about something. **stop off** (or **over**) break one's journey. [from Late Latin *stuppare* 'to stuff'] □ **stoppable** *adj.*

stopcock *n.* an externally operated valve regulating the flow of a liquid or gas through a pipe etc.

stopgap *n.* (often *attrib.*) a temporary substitute.

stop-go *n.* **1** alternate stopping and restarting of progress. **2** *Brit.* the alternate restriction and stimulation of economic demand.

stop-knob *n. Mus.* a knob controlling an organ stop.

stop lamp *n. Brit.* a light on the rear of a vehicle showing when the brakes are applied.

stop light *n.* **1** a red traffic light. **2** = STOP LAMP.

stopoff *n.* a break in one's journey.

stopover *n.* = STOPOFF.

stoppage *n.* **1** the condition of being blocked or stopped. **2** a stopping (of pay). **3** a stopping or interruption of work in a factory etc.

stopper ● *n.* **1** a plug for closing a bottle etc. **2** a person or thing that stops something. ● *v.tr.* close or secure with a stopper. □ **put a stopper on 1** put an end to (a thing). **2** keep (a person) quiet.

stopping *n. Brit.* a filling for a tooth.

stop press *n. Brit.* (often *attrib.*) late news inserted in a newspaper after printing has begun.

stop-volley *n. Tennis* a checked volley close to the net, dropping the ball dead on the other side.

stopwatch *n.* ► a watch with a mechanism for recording elapsed time, used to time races etc.

storage *n.* **1 a** the storing of goods etc. **b** a particular method of storing or the space available for it. **2** the cost of storing. **3** the electronic retention of data in a computer etc.

storage battery *n.* (also **storage cell**) a battery (or cell) for storing electricity.

lap reset *mode* *start/stop*
button *button* *button*

liquid / crystal display

STOPWATCH

storage heater *n. Brit.* an electric heater accumulating heat outside peak hours for later release.

store ● *n.* **1** a quantity of something kept available for use (*a store of wine*; *a store of wit*). **2** (in *pl.*) **a** articles for a particular purpose accumulated for use (*naval stores*). **b** a supply of these or the place where they are kept. **3 a** = DEPARTMENT STORE. **b** esp. *N. Amer.* any retail outlet or shop. **c** (in *sing.* or *Brit. pl.*) a shop selling basic necessities (*general stores*). **4** esp. *Brit.* a warehouse for the temporary keeping of furniture etc. **5** *Brit.* a device in a computer for storing retrievable data; a memory. ● *v.tr.* **1** put (furniture etc.) in store. **2** (often foll. by *up*, *away*) accumulate (stores, energy, electricity, etc.) for future use. **3** stock or provide with something useful (*a mind stored with facts*). **4** *Computing* enter or retain (data) for retrieval. □ **in store 1** kept in readiness. **2** coming in the future. **3** (foll. by *for*) destined or intended. **set** (or **lay** or **put**) **store by** (or **on**) consider important or valuable. [from Latin *instaurare* 'to renew'] □ **storable** *adj.* **storer** *n.*

store card *n.* a credit card issued by a store to its customers.

storefront *n.* esp. *N. Amer.* **1** the side of a shop facing the street. **2** a room at the front of a shop.

storehouse *n.* a place where things are stored.

storekeeper *n.* **1** esp. *Brit.* a storeman. **2** *N. Amer.* a shopkeeper.

storeman *n.* (*pl.* **-men**) *Brit.* a person responsible for stored goods.

storeroom *n.* a room in which items are stored.

storey *n.* (*US* also **story**) (*pl.* **-eys** or **-ies**) **1** the whole of the rooms in a building having a continuous floor. **2** a thing forming a horizontal division. [from Anglo-Latin *historia*, an architectural term] □ **-storeyed** *adj.* (in *comb.*) (also **-storied**).

storied *adj. literary* celebrated in or associated with stories or legends.

stork *n.* any long-legged large wading bird of the family Ciconiidae, esp. *Ciconia ciconia* with white plumage, black wing-tips, and a long reddish beak, nesting esp. on tall buildings in Europe. [Old English]

storm ● *n.* **1** a violent disturbance of the atmosphere with strong winds and usu. with thunder and rain or snow etc. **2** a violent disturbance of the

S

established order in human affairs. **3** (foll. by *of*) **a** a violent shower of missiles or blows. **b** an outbreak of applause, indignation, hisses, etc. (*they were greeted by a storm of abuse*). **4 a** a direct assault by troops on a fortified place. **b** the capture of a place by such an assault. ● *v.* **1** *intr.* (often foll. by *at, away*) talk violently, rage, bluster. **2** *intr.* (usu. foll. by *in, out of*, etc.) move violently or angrily (*stormed out of the meeting*). **3** *tr.* attack or capture by storm. **4** *intr.* (of wind, rain, etc.) rage; be violent. □ **storm in a teacup** *Brit.* great excitement over a trivial matter. **take by storm 1** capture by direct assault. **2** rapidly captivate (a person, audience, etc.). [Old English] □ **stormproof** *adj.*

stormbound *adj.* prevented by storms from leaving port.

storm centre *n.* **1** the point to which the wind blows spirally inward in a cyclonic storm. **2** a subject etc. upon which agitation or disturbance is concentrated.

storm cloud *n.* **1** a heavy rain cloud. **2** a threatening state of affairs (*storm clouds were gathering over Europe*).

storm-door *n.* an additional outer door for protection in bad weather or winter.

storming *adj.* **1** that storms. **2** esp. *Sport slang* displaying outstanding vigour, speed, or skill.

storm lantern *n. Brit.* a hurricane lamp.

storm petrel *n.* **1** a small mainly black seabird of the family Hydrobatidae, in particular *Hydrobates pelagicus* of the North Atlantic. **2** a person causing unrest.

storm troops *n.pl.* **1** = SHOCK TROOPS. **2** *hist.* the Nazi political militia. □ **storm trooper** *n.*

storm window *n.* an additional outer sash window for protection in bad weather or winter.

stormy *adj.* (**stormier, stormiest**) **1** of or affected by storms. **2** (of a wind etc.) violent, raging, vehement. **3** full of angry feeling or outbursts; lively, boisterous (*a stormy meeting*). □ **stormily** *adv.* **storminess** *n.*

stormy petrel *n.* = STORM PETREL.

story[1] *n.* (*pl.* **-ies**) **1** an account of imaginary or past events. **2** the past course of the life of a person or institution etc. **3** = STORYLINE. **4** facts or experiences that deserve narration. **5** *colloq.* a fib or lie. **6** a narrative or descriptive item of news. □ **the old** (or **same old**) **story** the familiar or predictable course of events. **the story goes** it is said. **to cut** (or **make**) **a long story short** a formula excusing the omission of details. [from Latin *historia* 'narrative, history']

story[2] *US* var. of STOREY.

storyboard *n.* a displayed sequence of pictures etc. outlining the plan of a film, television advertisement, etc.

story book *n.* (hyphenated when *attrib.*) **1** a book of stories for children. **2** (*attrib.*) unreal, romantic (*a story-book ending*).

storyline *n.* the narrative or plot of a novel or play etc.

storyteller *n.* **1** a person who tells stories. **2** *colloq.* a liar. □ **storytelling** *n. & adj.*

stoup /stoop/ *n.* (also **stoop**) **1** a holy-water basin. **2** *archaic* a flagon, beaker, or drinking vessel. [from Old Norse *staup*]

stout ● *adj.* **1** rather fat; corpulent. **2** of considerable thickness or strength (*a stout stick*). **3** brave, resolute, vigorous (*a stout fellow; put up stout resistance*). ● *n.* a strong dark beer brewed with roasted malt or barley. [from Old French dialect word] □ **stoutish** *adj.* **stoutly** *adv.* **stoutness** *n.*

stout heart *n.* courage, resolve.

stout-hearted *adj.* courageous. □ **stout-heartedly** *adv.* **stout-heartedness** *n.*

stove[1] *n.* a closed apparatus burning fuel or electricity for heating or cooking. [Middle English in sense 'sweating-room', from Middle Dutch]

stove[2] *past* and *past part.* of STAVE *v.*

stove-enamel *Brit.* ● *n.* a heatproof enamel. ● *v.tr.*

(usu. as **stove-enamelled** *adj.*) treat in a stove to produce this.

stove-pipe *n.* a pipe conducting smoke and gases from a stove to a chimney.

stow *v.tr.* **1** pack (goods etc.) tidily and compactly. **2** *Naut.* place (a cargo or provisions) in its proper place and order. **3** fill (a receptacle) with articles compactly arranged. **4** (usu. in *imper.*) *slang* abstain or cease from (*stow the noise!*). □ **stow away 1** place (a thing) where it will not cause an obstruction. **2** be or become a stowaway on a ship etc. [Middle English, from BESTOW]

stowage *n.* **1** the act or an instance of stowing. **2** a place for this.

stowaway *n.* a person who hides on board a ship or aircraft etc. to get free passage.

strabismus *n. Med.* the condition of having one or both eyes not correctly aligned in direction; a squint. [from Greek *strabismos*] □ **strabismal** *adj.* **strabismic** *adj.*

straddle ● *v.tr.* **1 a** sit or stand across (a thing) with the legs wide apart. **b** be situated across or on both sides of (*the town straddles the border*). **2** part (one's legs) widely. **3** drop shots or bombs short of and beyond (a target). ● *n.* an act or an instance of straddling. [alteration of *striddle*, back-formation from *striddlings* 'astride'] □ **straddler** *n.*

strafe ● *v.tr.* **1** bombard; harass with gunfire, esp. from aircraft. **2** abuse. ● *n.* an act of strafing. [jocular adaptation of German catchword (1914) *Gott strafe England* 'may God punish England']

straggle ● *v.intr.* **1** lack or lose compactness or tidiness. **2** be or become dispersed or sporadic. **3** trail behind others in a march or race etc. **4** (of a plant, beard, etc.) grow long and loose. ● *n.* a body or group of straggling or scattered persons or things. [Middle English] □ **straggler** *n.* **straggly** *adj.* (**stragglier, straggliest**)

straight ● *adj.* **1** extending uniformly in the same direction; without a curve or bend etc. **2** successive, uninterrupted (*three straight wins*). **3** in proper order or place or condition; duly arranged (*is the picture straight?; put things straight*). **4** honest, candid, not evasive. **5** (of thinking etc.) logical, unemotional. **6** (of drama etc.) serious as opposed to popular or comic; employing conventional techniques. **7 a** unmodified. **b** (of a drink) undiluted. **8** *colloq.* **a** (of a person etc.) conventional or respectable. **b** heterosexual. **9** (of a person's back) not bowed. **10** (of the hair) not curly or wavy. **11** (of a knee) not bent. **12** (of a garment) not flared. **13** coming direct from its source. **14** (of an aim, look, blow, or course) going direct to the mark. ● *n.* **1** the straight part of something, esp. a racecourse. ▷ RACECOURSE. **2** a straight condition. **3** a sequence of five cards in poker. **4** *colloq.* **a** a conventional person. **b** a heterosexual. ● *adv.* **1** in a straight line; direct; without deviation or hesitation or circumlocution (*came straight from Paris; I told them straight*). **2** in the right direction, with a good aim (*shoot straight*). **3** correctly (*can't see straight*). □ **go straight** live an honest life after being a criminal. **the straight and narrow** morally correct behaviour. **straight away** at once; immediately. **straight from the shoulder 1** (of a blow) well delivered. **2** (of a verbal attack) frank or direct. **straight off** (or **out**) *colloq.* without hesitation, deliberation, etc. (*cannot tell you straight off*). **straight up** *colloq.* **1** truthfully, honestly. **2** esp. *N. Amer.* unmixed, undiluted. [Middle English, past participle of STRETCH] □ **straightish** *adj.* **straightly** *adv.* **straightness** *n.*

straightaway *adv.* = *straight away.*

straight-edge *n.* a bar with one edge accurately straight, used for testing.

straighten *v.tr. & intr.* **1** (often foll. by *out*) make or become straight. **2** (foll. by *up*) stand erect after bending. □ **straightener** *n.*

straight face *n.* an intentionally expressionless face, esp. avoiding a smile though amused. □ **straight-faced** *adj.*

straight fight *n. Brit.* a simple contest between two opponents, esp. in an election.

straightforward *adj.* **1** honest or frank. **2** esp. *Brit.* (of a task etc.) uncomplicated. □ **straightforwardly** *adv.* **straightforwardness** *n.*

straightjacket var. of STRAITJACKET.

straight-laced var. of STRAIT-LACED.

straight man *n.* a comedian's stooge.

straight-out *adj.* esp. *US* **1** uncompromising. **2** straightforward, genuine.

straight-up *adj. colloq.* **1** true; trustworthy. **2** esp. *N. Amer.* unmixed, undiluted, unmodified. See also *straight up.*

strain[1] ● *v.* **1** *tr. & intr.* stretch tightly; make or become taut or tense. **2** *tr.* exercise (oneself, one's senses, a thing, etc.) intensely or excessively, press to extremes. **3** *intr.* **a** make an intensive effort. **b** (foll. by *after*) strive intensely for. **4** *intr.* (foll. by *at*) tug, pull. **5** *intr.* hold out with difficulty under pressure (*straining under the load*). **6** *tr.* distort from the true intention or meaning. **7** *tr.* impair or injure by overuse or excessive demands (*strain a muscle; strained their loyalty*). **8 a** *tr.* clear (a liquid) of solid matter by passing it through a sieve etc. **b** *tr.* (foll. by *out*) filter (solids) out from a liquid. **9** *tr.* use (one's ears, eyes, voice, etc.) to the best of one's power. ● *n.* **1 a** the act or an instance of straining. **b** the force exerted in this. **2** an injury caused by straining a muscle etc. **3 a** a severe demand on physical strength or resources. **b** the exertion needed to meet this (*is suffering from strain*). **4** (in *sing.* or *pl.*) a snatch or spell of music or poetry. **5** a tone or tendency in speech or writing (*more in the same strain*). □ **strain oneself 1** injure oneself by effort. **2** make undue efforts. [from Latin *stringere* 'to draw tight']

strain[2] *n.* **1** a breed or stock of animals, plants, etc. **2** a tendency or characteristic (*a strain of aggression*). [Old English]

strained *adj.* **1** constrained, forced, artificial. **2** (of a relationship) mutually distrustful or tense. **3** (of an interpretation) involving an unreasonable assumption; far-fetched, laboured.

strainer *n.* a device for straining liquids etc.

strain gauge *n. Engin.* a device for indicating the strain of a material or structure at the point of attachment.

strait *n.* **1** (in *sing.* or *pl.*) ▼ a narrow passage of water connecting two large bodies of water. **2** (usu. in *pl.*) difficulty, trouble, or distress (usu. *in dire* or *desperate straits*). [from Latin *strictus* 'strict']

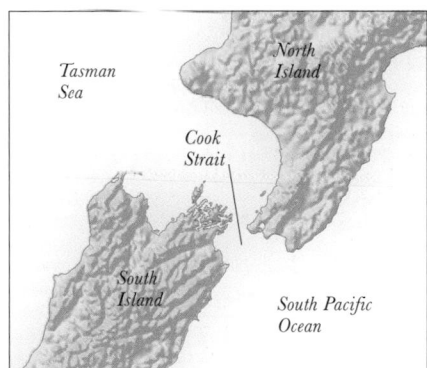

STRAIT: MAP SHOWING THE STRAIT BETWEEN NORTH AND SOUTH ISLANDS, NEW ZEALAND

straiten *v.* **1** *tr.* restrict in range or scope. **2** *tr.* (as **straitened** *adj.*) (esp. of circumstances) characterized by poverty.

straitjacket (also **straightjacket**) ● *n.* **1** a strong garment with long sleeves for confining the arms of a violent prisoner, mental patient, etc. **2** restrictive measures. ● *v.tr.* (**-jacketed, -jacketing**) **1** restrain with a straitjacket. **2** severely restrict.

strait-laced *adj.* (also **straight-laced**) severely virtuous; morally scrupulous; puritanical.

strand[1] ● *v.tr.* **1** run aground. **2** (as **stranded** *adj.*) in difficulties, esp. without money or means of transport. ● *n. esp. poet.* the margin of a sea, lake, or river, esp. the foreshore. [Old English]

strand² *n.* **1** each of the threads or wires twisted round each other to make a rope or cable. **2 a** a single thread or strip of fibre. **b** a constituent filament. **3** an element or strain in any composite whole. [Middle English]

strange ● *adj.* **1** unusual, peculiar, surprising, eccentric, novel. **2** (often foll. by *to*) unfamiliar, alien, foreign (*lost in a strange land*). **3** (foll. by *to*) (of a person) unaccustomed to; unfamiliar with. **4** not at ease; out of one's element. ● *adv. colloq.* in a strange manner; strangely. □ **feel strange** be unwell. [based on Latin *extraneus* 'extraneous'] □ **strangely** *adv.*

strangeness *n.* **1** the state or fact of being strange or unfamiliar etc. **2** *Physics* a property of certain quarks.

stranger *n.* **1** a person who does not know or is not known in a particular place or company. **2** (often foll. by *to*) a person one does not know (*was a complete stranger to me*). **3** (foll. by *to*) a person entirely unaccustomed to (a feeling, experience, etc.) (*no stranger to controversy*). [Middle English]

strangle *v.tr.* **1** squeeze the windpipe or neck of, esp. so as to kill. **2** hamper or suppress (a movement, impulse, cry, etc.). [from Greek *straggalan*] □ **strangler** *n.*

stranglehold *n.* **1** a wrestling hold that throttles an opponent. **2** a deadly grip. **3** complete and exclusive control.

strangulate *v.tr.* **1** *Med.* prevent circulation through (a vein, intestine, etc.) by compression. **2** (as **strangulated** *adj.*) (of a voice) sounding as though the speaker's throat is constricted. [based on Latin *strangulatus* 'strangled']

strangulated hernia *n. Med.* a hernia in which the protruding part is constricted, preventing circulation.

strangulation *n.* **1** the act of strangling or the state of being strangled. **2** the act of strangulating.

strap ● *n.* **1** a strip of leather or other flexible material, often with a buckle or other fastening for holding things together etc. **2** a thing like this for keeping a garment in place. **3** a loop for grasping to steady oneself in a moving vehicle. ● *v.tr.* (**strapped**, **strapping**) **1** (often foll. by *down*, *up*, etc.) secure or bind with a strap. **2** beat with a strap. **3** (esp. as **strapped** *adj.*) (usu. foll. by *for*) *colloq.* subject to a shortage (*strapped for cash*). **4** (often foll. by *up*) *Brit.* close (a wound) or bind (a part) with adhesive plaster. [dialect form of STROP] □ **strappy** *adj.*

straphanger *n. colloq.* a standing passenger in a bus or train. □ **strap-hang** *v.intr.*

strapless *adj.* (of a garment) without straps, esp. shoulder straps.

strapping *adj.* (esp. of a young person) large and sturdy.

strata *pl.* of STRATUM.

■ **Usage** See Usage Note at STRATUM.

stratagem *n.* **1** a cunning plan or scheme, esp. for deceiving an enemy. **2** trickery. [from Greek *stratēgēma*]

stratal see STRATUM.

strategic *adj.* **1** of or serving strategy (*strategic considerations*; *strategic move*). **2** (of materials) essential in fighting a war. **3** (of bombing or weapons) done or for use against an enemy's home territory as a longer-term military objective (opp. TACTICAL 2). [from Greek *stratēgikos*] □ **strategical** *adj.* **strategically** *adv.* **strategics** *n.pl.* (usu. treated as *sing.*).

strategic defence initiative *n.* a projected US system of defence against nuclear weapons, using satellites armed with lasers.

strategy *n.* (*pl.* **-ies**) **1** the art of war. **2 a** the art of moving troops, ships, aircraft, etc. into favourable positions (cf. TACTICS 1). **b** an instance of this or a plan formed according to it. **3** a plan of action or

policy in business or politics etc. (*economic strategy*). [from Greek *stratēgia* 'generalship'] □ **strategist** *n.*

strath *n. Sc.* a broad mountain valley. [from Gaelic *srath*]

strathspey *n.* **1** a slow Scottish dance. **2** the music for this. [from *Strathspey*, valley of the river Spey]

stratify *v.tr.* (**-ies**, **-ied**) **1** (esp. as **stratified** *adj.*) arrange, deposit, or form, in strata. **2** arrange in a hierarchical way. [from French *stratifier*] □ **stratification** *n.*

stratigraphy *n. Geol.* & *Archaeol.* **1** the order and relative position of strata. **2** the study of this. □ **stratigrapher** *n.* **stratigraphic** *adj.* **stratigraphical** *adj.*

stratosphere *n.* a layer of atmospheric air above the troposphere (cf. IONOSPHERE). ▷ ATMOSPHERE. □ **stratospheric** *adj.*

stratum *n.* (*pl.* **strata**) **1** esp. *Geol.* ▼ a layer or set of successive layers of any deposited substance. **2** an atmospheric layer. **3** a layer of tissue etc. **4** a social grade, class, etc. (*the various strata of society*). [Latin, literally 'something spread or laid down'] □ **stratal** *adj.*

■ **Usage** It is incorrect (though a common error) to use *strata*, the plural form, for the singular *stratum*, i.e. it is correct to say *This stratum* (not *strata*) *of society has always exercised power.*

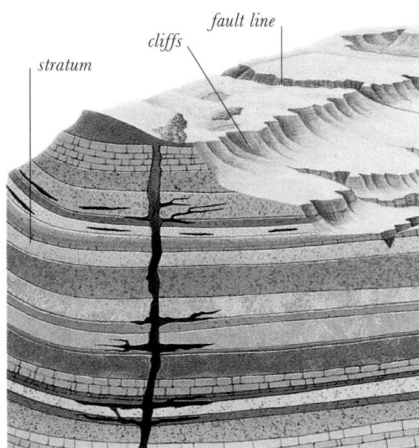

STRATUM: SECTION THROUGH THE GRAND CANYON, USA, SHOWING STRATA

stratus *n. Meteorol.* cloud formed as a continuous horizontal grey sheet. ▷ CLOUD. [Latin, literally 'spread or laid down']

straw ● *n.* **1** dry cut stalks of grain for use as fodder or for bedding, thatching, etc. **2** a single stalk of straw. **3** a thin tube for sucking drink from a glass etc. **4** the pale yellow colour of straw. **5** a straw hat. ● *adj.* **1** made of straw. **2** pale yellow. □ **catch** (or **clutch** or **grasp**) **at a straw** (or **straws**) resort in desperation to an utterly inadequate expedient. **draw the short straw** be chosen by lot, esp. for some disagreeable task. [Old English, related to STREW] □ **strawy** *adj.*

strawberry ● *n.* (*pl.* **-ies**) **1 a** any plant of the genus *Fragaria*, esp. any of various cultivated varieties, with white flowers, and runners. **b** the pulpy red edible fruit of this, having a seed-studded surface. ▷ FRUIT, SEED. **2** a deep pinkish-red colour. ● *adj.* of a deep pinkish-red colour. [Old English]

strawberry blonde ● *n.* **1** pinkish-blonde hair. **2** a woman with such hair. ● *adj.* (hyphenated when *attrib.*) of a pinkish-blonde colour.

strawberry mark *n.* a soft reddish birthmark.

straw in the wind *n.* a slight hint of future developments.

straw vote *n.* (also **straw poll**) an unofficial ballot as a test of opinion.

stray ● *v.intr.* **1** wander from the right place; become

separated from one's companions etc.; go astray. **2** deviate morally. **3** (as **strayed** *adj.*) that has gone astray. ● *n.* a person or thing that has strayed, esp. a domestic animal. ● *adj.* **1** strayed or lost. **2** isolated; found or occurring occasionally (*a stray customer or two*; *hit by a stray bullet*). [from Old French *estrayer*]

streak ● *n.* **1** a long thin usu. irregular line or band, esp. distinguished by colour. **2** a strain or element in a person's character (*has a streak of mischief*). **3** a spell or series (*a winning streak*). ● *v.* **1** *tr.* mark with streaks. **2** *intr.* move very rapidly. **3** *intr. colloq.* run naked in a public place as a stunt. [Old English *strica* 'pen-stroke'] □ **streaker** *n.* **streaking** *n.*

streak of lightning *n.* a sudden prominent flash of lightning.

streaky *adj.* (**streakier**, **streakiest**) **1** full of streaks. **2** *Brit.* (of bacon) with alternate streaks of fat and lean. □ **streakily** *adv.* **streakiness** *n.*

stream ● *n.* **1** a flowing body of water, esp. a small river. **2 a** the flow of a fluid or of a mass of people (*a stream of lava*). **b** (in *sing.* or *pl.*) a large quantity of something that flows or moves along. **3** a current or direction in which things are moving or tending (*against the stream*). **4** *Brit.* a group of schoolchildren taught together as being of similar ability for a given age. ● *v.* **1** *intr.* flow or move as a stream. **2** *intr.* run with liquid (*my eyes were streaming*). **3** *intr.* (of a banner or hair etc.) wave or be blown behind in the wind. **4** *tr.* emit a stream of (blood etc.). **5** *tr. Brit.* arrange (schoolchildren) in streams. □ **on stream** (of a factory etc.) in operation. [Old English] □ **streamlet** *n.*

streamer *n.* **1** a long narrow flag. **2** a long narrow strip of ribbon or paper, esp. in a coil that unrolls when thrown.

streamline ● *v.tr.* **1** give (a vehicle, an object) a smooth shape which minimizes its resistance to the flow of a surrounding fluid (e.g. air, water). **2** make (an organization, process, etc.) simple or more efficient or better organized. ● *adj.* **1** (of flow) free from turbulence. **2** ▼ (of an object) streamlined in shape. □ **streamlined** *adj.*

STREAMLINE: TESTING A CAR'S STREAMLINED SHAPE IN A WIND TUNNEL

stream of consciousness *n.* **1** *Psychol.* a person's thoughts and conscious reactions to events perceived as a continuous flow. **2** a literary style depicting events in such a flow in the mind of a character.

street *n.* **1** a public road in a city, town, or village. **2** this with the houses or other buildings on each side. □ **on the streets 1** living by prostitution. **2** homeless. **streets ahead** (often foll. by *of*) *Brit. colloq.* much superior (to). **up** (or **right up**) **one's street** esp. *Brit. colloq.* **1** within one's range of interest or knowledge. **2** to one's liking. [from Late Latin *strata (via)* 'paved (way)'] □ **streeted** *adj.* (also in *comb.*).

streetcar *n. N. Amer.* a tram.

street credibility *n.* (also *colloq.* **street cred**) *Brit.* acceptability among young fashionable urban people.

street door *n.* a main outer house-door opening on the street.

street entertainer *n.* a person who entertains people in the street for money, esp. with music, acting, or juggling. □ **street entertainment** *n.*

street furniture *n.* postboxes, road signs, litter bins, and other objects placed in the street for public use.

street lamp *n.* = STREET LIGHT.

street light *n.* a light or lamp esp. on a lamp-post, serving to illuminate a road etc. □ **street lighting** *n.*

street trader *n.* a person who trades in the street from a stall, van, etc.

street value *n.* the value of esp. drugs sold illicitly.

streetwalker *n.* a prostitute seeking customers in the street. □ **streetwalking** *n.* & *adj.*

streetwise *adj.* esp. *N. Amer.* familiar with the ways of modern urban life.

strelitzia *n.* a southern African plant of the genus *Strelitzia*, with showy irregular flowers having a long projecting tongue. [named after Charlotte of Mecklenburg-*Strelitz*, 1744–1818, queen of George III]

strength *n.* **1** the state of being strong; the degree to which, or respect in which, a person or thing is strong. **2 a** a person or thing affording strength or support. **b** an attribute making for strength of character (*patience is your great strength*). **3** the number of persons present or available. **4** a full complement (*below strength*). □ **from strength** from a strong position. **from strength to strength** with ever-increasing success. **in strength** in large numbers. **on the strength of** relying on; on the basis of. **the strength of** the essence or main features of. [Old English] □ **strengthless** *adj.*

strengthen *v.tr.* & *intr.* make or become stronger. □ **strengthen a person's hand** (or **hands**) encourage a person to vigorous action. □ **strengthener** *n.*

strenuous *adj.* **1** requiring or using great effort. **2** energetic or unrelaxing. [from Latin *strenuus* 'brisk'] □ **strenuously** *adv.* **strenuousness** *n.*

streptococcus *n.* (*pl.* **streptococci**) any bacterium of the genus *Streptococcus*, usu. found joined in chains, some of which cause infectious diseases. [based on Greek *streptos* 'twisted', taken as 'twisted chain'] □ **streptococcal** *adj.*

streptomycin *n.* an antibiotic produced by the bacterium *Streptomyces griseus*, effective against many disease-producing bacteria. [based on Greek *streptos* 'twisted' + *mukēs* 'fungus']

stress ● *n.* **1 a** pressure or tension exerted on a material object. **b** a quantity measuring this. **2 a** demand on physical or mental energy. **b** distress caused by this (*suffering from stress*). **3 a** emphasis (*the stress was on the need for success*). **b** accentuation; emphasis laid on a syllable or word. **c** an accent, esp. the principal one in a word (*the stress is on the first syllable*). **4** *Mech.* force per unit area exerted between continuous bodies or parts of a body. ● *v.tr.* **1** lay stress on; emphasize. **2** subject to mechanical or physical or mental stress. □ **lay stress on** indicate as important. [based on Latin *strictus* 'tightened'] □ **stressless** *adj.*

stress disease *n.* a disease resulting from continuous mental stress.

stressed out *adj. colloq.* debilitated or exhausted as a result of stress.

stressful *adj.* causing stress; mentally tiring (*had a stressful day*). □ **stressfully** *adv.* **stressfulness** *n.*

stretch ● *v.* **1** *tr.* & *intr.* draw or be drawn or admit of being drawn out into greater length or size. **2** *tr.* & *intr.* make or become taut. **3** *tr.* & *intr.* place or lie at full length or spread out (*with a canopy stretched over them*). **4 a** *tr.* extend (an arm, leg, etc.). **b** *intr.* & *refl.* thrust out one's limbs and tighten one's muscles after being relaxed. **5** *intr.* have a specified length or extension; extend (*farmland stretches for many miles*). **6** *tr.* strain or exert extremely or excessively; exaggerate (*stretch the truth*). **7** *tr.* (as **stretched** *adj.*) elongated or extended. ● *n.* **1** a continuous extent or expanse or period (*a stretch of open road*). **2** the act or an instance of stretching; the state of being stretched. **3** (*attrib.*) able to stretch; elastic (*stretch fabric*). **4 a** *colloq.* a period of imprisonment. **b** a period of service. **5** (usu. *attrib.*) *colloq.* an aircraft or motor vehicle modified so as to have extra seating or storage capacity (*stretch limousine*). □ **at full stretch** working to capacity. **at a stretch 1** in one continuous period. **2** with much effort. **stretch one's legs** exercise oneself by walking. **stretch out 1** extend (a hand or foot etc.). **2** last for a longer period; prolong. **3** make (money etc.) last for a sufficient time. **stretch a point** agree to something not normally allowed. [Old English] □ **stretchable** *adj.* **stretchability** *n.* **stretchy** *adj.* **stretchiness** *n.*

stretcher ● *n.* **1** a framework of two poles with canvas etc. between, for carrying a person in a lying position. **2** a brick or stone laid with its long side along the face of a wall. ▷ BRICK. **3** ▶ a wooden frame over which a canvas is stretched ready for painting. ● *v.tr.* (often foll. by *off*) convey (a sick or injured person) on a stretcher.

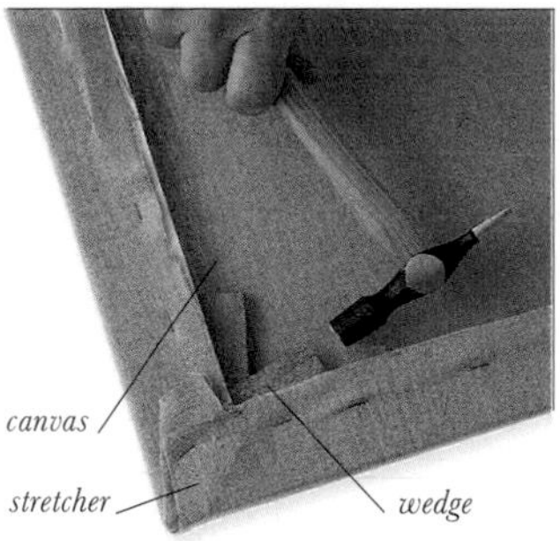

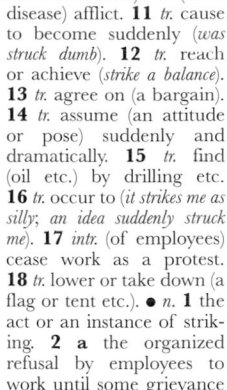

STRETCHER WITH CANVAS FITTED

stretch marks *n.pl.* marks on the skin resulting from a gain of weight, or on the abdomen after pregnancy.

strew *v.tr.* (*past part.* **strewn** or **strewed**) **1** scatter or spread about over a surface. **2** (usu. foll. by *with*) spread (a surface) with scattered things. [Old English] □ **strewer** *n.*

strewth *int.* (also **struth**, **'str-**) esp. *Brit. colloq.* a mild oath. [from *God's truth*]

stria /stry-ă/ *n.* (*pl.* **striae** /-ee/) **1** *Anat.*, *Zool.*, *Bot.*, & *Geol.* **a** a linear mark on a surface. **b** a slight ridge, furrow, or score. **2** *Archit.* a fillet between the flutes of a column. [Latin]

striate ● *adj.* (also **striated**) *Anat.*, *Zool.*, *Bot.*, & *Geol.* marked with striae. ● *v.tr.* mark with striae. □ **striation** *n.*

striated muscle *n. Anat.* muscle with the contractile fibrils in the cells aligned to form stripes visible in a microscope, attached to bones by tendons and under voluntary control.

stricken *adj.* **1** affected or overcome with illness or misfortune etc. (*stricken with measles; grief-stricken*). **2** (often foll. by *from* etc.) *US Law* deleted. □ **stricken in years** *archaic* enfeebled by age. [archaic past participle of STRIKE]

strict *adj.* **1** precisely limited or defined; without exception or deviation (*lives in strict seclusion*). **2** requiring complete compliance or exact performance (*gave strict orders*). [from Latin *strictus* 'tightened'] □ **strictness** *n.*

strictly *adv.* **1** in a strict manner. **2** (also **strictly speaking**) applying words in their strict sense (*he is, strictly, an absconder*). **3** esp. *N. Amer. colloq.* definitely.

stricture *n.* (usu. in *pl.*; often foll. by *on*, *upon*) a critical or censorious remark. [from Latin *strictura*] □ **strictured** *adj.*

stride ● *v.* (*past* **strode**; *past part.* **stridden**) **1** *intr.* & *tr.* walk with long firm steps. **2** *tr.* cross with one step. **3** *tr.* bestride; straddle. ● *n.* **1 a** a single long step. **b** the length of this. **2** a person's gait as determined by the length of stride. **3** (usu. in *pl.*) progress (*has made great strides*). **4** a settled rate of progress (*get into one's stride; be thrown out of one's stride*). **5** (in *pl.*) *Brit. slang* trousers. □ **take in one's stride 1** clear (an obstacle) without changing one's gait to jump. **2** manage without difficulty. [Old English] □ **strider** *n.*

strident *adj.* loud and harsh. [from Latin *strident-* 'creaking'] □ **stridency** *n.* **stridently** *adv.*

stridulate *v.intr.* (of insects, esp. the cicada and grasshopper) make a shrill sound by rubbing esp. the legs or wing-cases together. [from French *striduler*] □ **stridulation** *n.*

strife *n.* **1** conflict; struggle between opposed persons or things. **2** *Austral. colloq.* trouble of any kind. [from Old French *estrif*]

strike ● *v.* (*past* **struck**; *past part.* **struck** or *archaic* **stricken**) **1 a** *tr.* subject to an impact. **b** *tr.* deliver (a blow) or inflict a blow on (also with double object: *struck him a blow*). **2** *tr.* come or bring sharply into contact with. **3** *tr.* propel with a blow. **4** *intr.* (foll. by *at*) try to hit. **5** *tr.* cause to penetrate (*struck terror into him*). **6** *tr.* ignite (a match) or produce (sparks etc.) by rubbing. **7** *tr.* make (a coin) by stamping. **8** *tr.* produce (a musical note) by striking. **9 a** *tr.* (also *absol.*) (of a clock) indicate (the time) by the sounding of a chime etc. **b** *intr.* (of time) be indicated in this way. **10** *tr.* **a** attack or affect suddenly (*was struck with sudden terror*). **b** (of a disease) afflict. **11** *tr.* cause to become suddenly (*was struck dumb*). **12** *tr.* reach or achieve (*strike a balance*). **13** *tr.* agree on (a bargain). **14** *tr.* assume (an attitude or pose) suddenly and dramatically. **15** *tr.* find (oil etc.) by drilling etc. **16** *tr.* occur to (*it strikes me as silly; an idea suddenly struck me*). **17** *intr.* (of employees) cease work as a protest. **18** *tr.* lower or take down (a flag or tent etc.). ● *n.* **1** the act or an instance of striking. **2 a** the organized refusal by employees to work until some grievance is remedied. **b** a similar refusal to participate. **3 a** a discovery of oil, ore, etc. by drilling, mining, etc. **b** a sudden find or success (*a lucky strike*). **4** an attack, esp. from the air. **5** *Baseball* a batter's unsuccessful attempt to hit a pitched ball, or another event counting equivalently against a batter. □ **on strike** taking part in an industrial etc. strike. **strike back** strike or attack in return. **strike down 1** knock down. **2** bring low; afflict (*struck down by a virus*). **strike home 1** deal an effective blow. **2** have an intended effect (*my words struck home*). **strike it rich** *colloq.* find a source of abundance or success. **strike a light 1** produce a light by striking a match. **2** (as *int.*) *Brit. colloq.* an expression of surprise, disgust, etc. **strike lucky** (or **strike it lucky**) *Brit.* have a lucky success. **strike off 1** remove with a stroke. **2** delete (a name etc.) from a list. **strike out 1** hit out. **2** act vigorously. **3** delete (an item or name etc.). **4** set off or begin (*struck out eastwards*). **5** use the arms and legs in swimming. **6** *Baseball* **a** dismiss (a batter) by means of three strikes. **b** be dismissed in this way. **strike through** delete (a word etc.) with a stroke of one's pen. **strike up 1** start (an acquaintance, conversation, etc.) esp. casually. **2** (also *absol.*) begin playing (a tune etc.). **strike upon 1** have (an idea etc.) luckily occur to one. **2** (of light) illuminate. **strike while the iron is hot** act promptly at a good opportunity. **struck on** *Brit. colloq.* infatuated with. [Old English *strīcan* 'to go, stroke'] □ **strikable** *adj.*

strike-bound *adj.* immobilized or closed by a strike.

strike-breaker *n.* a person working in place of others who are on strike. □ **strike-break** *v.intr.* (usu. as **strike-breaking** *n.*).

strike call *n.* an invitation to workers by union representatives to go on strike.

strike force *n.* a military or police force ready for rapid effective action.

strike-out *n. Baseball* an out called when a batter has made three strikes.

strike pay *n.* an allowance paid to strikers by their trade union.

striker *n.* **1** a person or thing that strikes. **2** an employee on strike. **3** *Sport* the player who is to strike, or who is to be the next to strike, the ball. **4** *Football* an attacking player positioned well forward in order to score goals. ▷ FOOTBALL

strike rate *n.* success rate, esp. in scoring goals or runs.

striking *adj.* impressive; attracting attention. □ **within striking distance** near enough to hit or achieve. □ **strikingly** *adv.* **strikingness** *n.*

striking-circle *n.* (in hockey) an elongated semicircle in front of the goal, from within which the ball must be hit in order to score.

strimmer *n. Brit. propr.* a grass trimmer with a rapidly rotating nylon cutting cord.

STRINGED

Most stringed instruments are characterized by a set of stretched strings attached to a hollow body, which amplifies the strings' vibrations. To produce these vibrations a string can be: plucked, as with a guitar; bowed, as with a cello; or struck, as with a piano. The thinner and shorter the string, the higher the note it will produce. Larger instruments are capable of creating lower notes: a double bass, for example, with its sizeable body and long strings, can generate much deeper sounds than a violin.

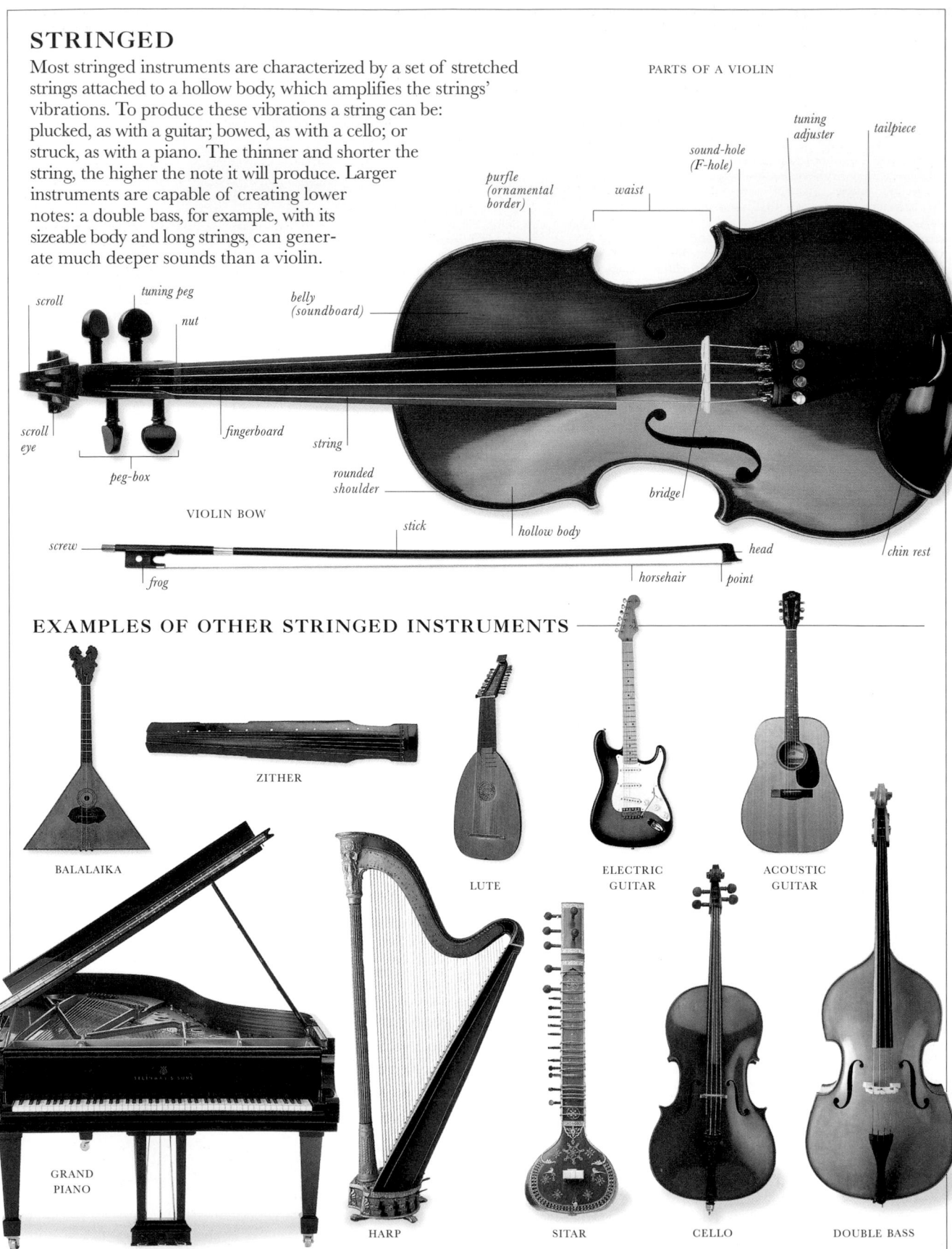

PARTS OF A VIOLIN

tuning adjuster

tailpiece

sound-hole (F-hole)

purfle (ornamental border)

waist

belly (soundboard)

scroll

tuning peg

nut

scroll eye

fingerboard

string

peg-box

rounded shoulder

VIOLIN BOW

bridge

hollow body

chin rest

screw

stick

head

frog

horsehair

point

EXAMPLES OF OTHER STRINGED INSTRUMENTS

S

BALALAIKA

ZITHER

LUTE

ELECTRIC GUITAR

ACOUSTIC GUITAR

GRAND PIANO

HARP

SITAR

CELLO

DOUBLE BASS

Strine *n.* **1** a comic transliteration of Australian speech, e.g. *Emma Chissitt* = 'How much is it?'. **2** (esp. uneducated) Australian English. [transliteration of *Australian*]

string ● *n.* **1** twine or narrow cord. **2** a piece of this or of similar material used for tying or holding together, pulling, etc. **3** a length of catgut or wire etc. on a musical instrument, producing a note by vibration. ▷ STRINGED. **4 a** (in *pl.*) the stringed instruments in an orchestra etc. **b** (*attrib.*) relating to or consisting of stringed instruments (*string quartet*). **5** (in *pl.*) an awkward condition or complication (*the offer has no strings*). **6** a set of things strung together; a series or line of persons or things (*a string of beads*; *a string of oaths*). **7** a tough piece connecting the two halves of a bean-pod etc. **8** a piece of catgut etc. interwoven with others to form the head of a tennis etc. racket. **9** *Computing* a linear sequence of characters, records, or data. ● *v.tr.* (*past* and *past part.* **strung**) **1** supply with a string or strings. **2** tie with string. **3** thread (beads etc.) on a string. **4** arrange in or as a string. **5** remove the strings from (a bean). □ **have two** (or **many**) **strings to one's bow** see BOW[1]. **on a string** under one's control or influence. **string along** *colloq.* **1** deceive, esp. by appearing to comply with (a person). **2** (often foll. by *with*) keep company (with). **string out** extend; prolong (esp. unduly). **string up 1** hang up on strings etc. **2** kill by hanging. **3** (usu. as **strung up** *adj.*) *Brit.* make tense. [Old English] □ **stringless** *adj.* **stringlike** *adj.*

string bass *n. Mus.* a double bass.

string bean *n.* any of various beans eaten in their fibrous pods, esp. runner beans or French beans.

string-course *n.* a slightly projecting horizontal band or course of bricks etc. on a building.

stringed *adj.* ◀ (of musical instruments) having strings (also in *comb.*: *twelve-stringed guitar*). ▷ ORCHESTRA

stringent *adj.* (of rules etc.) strict, precise; requiring exact performance; leaving no loophole or discretion. [from Latin *stringent-* 'drawing tight'] □ **stringency** *n.* **stringently** *adv.*

stringer *n.* **1** a longitudinal structural member in a framework, esp. of a ship or aircraft. **2** *colloq.* a newspaper correspondent not on the regular staff.

string vest *n.* a vest with large meshes.

stringy *adj.* (**stringier**, **stringiest**) **1** (of food etc.) fibrous, tough. **2** of or like string. **3** (of a person) tall, wiry, and thin. □ **stringily** *adv.* **stringiness** *n.*

strip[1] ● *v.* (**stripped**, **stripping**) **1** *tr.* (often foll. by *of*) remove the clothes or covering from (a person or thing). **2** *intr.* (often foll. by *off*) undress oneself. **3** *tr.* (often foll. by *of*) deprive (a person) of property or titles. **4** *tr.* leave bare of accessories or fittings. **5** *tr.* remove bark and branches from (a tree). **6** *tr.* (often foll. by *down*) remove the accessory fittings of or take apart (a machine etc.) to inspect or adjust it. **7** *tr.* sell off (the assets of a company) for profit. **8** *tr.* tear the thread from (a screw). **9** *tr.* remove (paint) or remove paint from (a surface) with solvent. **10** *tr.* (often foll. by *from*) pull or tear (a covering or property etc.) off (*stripped the masks from their faces*). ● *n.* **1** an act of stripping, esp. of undressing in striptease. **2** *Brit.* the identifying outfit worn by a sports team. ▷ FOOTBALL. [Old English *bestrīepan* 'to plunder']

strip[2] *n.* **1** a long narrow piece (*a strip of land*). **2** (in full **strip cartoon**) = COMIC STRIP. □ **tear a person off a strip** *colloq.* angrily rebuke a person. [Middle English]

stripagram *n.* (also **strippergram**) a greetings message delivered by a person who performs a striptease for the recipient.

strip club *n.* a club at which striptease performances are given.

stripe ● *n.* **1** a long narrow band or strip differing in colour or texture from the surface on either side of it (*black with a red stripe*). **2** *Mil.* a chevron etc. denoting military rank. **3** *N. Amer.* a category of character, opinion, etc. (*a man of that stripe*). **4** (usu. in *pl.*) *archaic* a blow with a scourge or lash. **5** (in *pl.*; treated as *sing.*) *colloq.* a tiger. ● *v.tr.* mark with stripes.

striped *adj.* marked with stripes (also in *comb.*: *red-striped*).

strip light *n. Brit.* a tubular fluorescent lamp.

stripling *n.* a youth not yet fully grown. [Middle English]

stripper *n.* **1** a person or thing that strips something. **2** a device or solvent for removing paint etc. **3** a striptease performer.

strippergram var. of STRIPAGRAM.

strip-search ● *n.* a search of a person involving the removal of all clothes. ● *v.tr.* search in this way.

striptease ● *n.* an entertainment in which the performer gradually undresses before the audience. ● *v.intr.* perform a striptease.

stripy *adj.* (**stripier**, **stripiest**) striped; having many stripes.

strive *v.intr.* (*past* **strove** or **strived**; *past part.* **striven** or **strived**) **1** (often foll. by *for*, or *to* + infin.) try hard, make efforts. **2** (often foll. by *with*, *against*) struggle or contend. [from Old French *estriver*] □ **striver** *n.*

strobe *colloq.* ● *n.* **1** a stroboscope. **2** a stroboscopic lamp. **3** *US* an electronic flash for a camera. ● *v.* **1** *tr.* light as if with a stroboscope. **2** *intr.* flash intermittently. **3** *intr.* exhibit or give rise to strobing.

strobing *n.* **1** *Telev.* an irregular movement and loss of continuity sometimes seen in lines and stripes in a television picture. **2** *Cinematog.* jerkiness in what should be a smooth movement on the screen.

stroboscope *n.* **1** *Physics* an instrument for determining speeds of rotation etc. by shining a bright light at intervals so that a rotating object appears stationary. **2** a lamp made to flash intermittently, esp. for this purpose. [based on Greek *strobos* 'whirling'] □ **stroboscopic** *adj.*

strode *past* of STRIDE.

Stroganoff *adj.* (of meat) cut into strips and cooked in sour-cream sauce (*beef Stroganoff*). [named after P. *Stroganoff*, Russian diplomat, 1772–1817]

stroke ● *n.* **1** the act or an instance of striking; a blow or hit (*with a single stroke*; *a stroke of lightning*). **2** a sudden disabling attack or loss of consciousness caused by an interruption in the flow of blood to the brain, esp. through thrombosis; apoplexy. **3 a** an action or movement esp. as one of a series. **b** the slightest such action (*has not done a stroke of work*). **4** the whole of the motion (of a wing, oar, etc.) until the starting position is regained. ▷ ROW. **5** (in rowing) the mode or action of moving the oar (*row a fast stroke*). **6** the whole motion (of a piston) in either direction. **7** a mode of moving the arms and legs in swimming. **8** a method of striking with the bat etc. in games etc. (*played some unorthodox strokes*). **9** a specially successful or skilful effort (*a stroke of diplomacy*). **10 a** a mark made by the movement in one direction of a pen or pencil or paintbrush. **b** a similar mark printed. **11** a detail contributing to the general effect in a description. **12** the sound made by a striking clock. **13** (in full **stroke oar**) the oar or oarsman nearest the stern, setting the time of the stroke. **14** the act or a spell of stroking. ● *v.tr.* **1** pass one's hand gently along the surface of (hair or fur etc.); caress lightly. **2** act as the stroke of (a boat or crew). □ **at a stroke** by a single action. **off one's stroke** not performing as well as usual. **on the stroke** punctually. **on the stroke of nine** etc. with the clock about to strike nine etc. **stroke of genius** an original or strikingly successful idea. **stroke of luck** or **good luck** an unforeseen opportune occurrence. [Old English]

stroke play *n. Golf* play in which the score is reckoned by counting the number of strokes taken for the round (cf. MATCHPLAY).

stroll ● *v.intr.* **1** saunter or walk in a leisurely way. **2** achieve something easily, without effort. ● *n.* **1** a short leisurely walk (*go for a stroll*). **2** something easily achieved; a walkover. [originally of a vagrant, probably based on German *Strolch* 'vagabond']

stroller *n.* **1** a person who strolls. **2** *US* a pushchair.

strolling players *n.pl.* actors etc. going from place to place to give performances.

strong ● *adj.* (**stronger**, **strongest**) **1** having the power of resistance; not easily damaged or overcome (*strong material*; *strong faith*; *a strong character*). **2** (of a patient) restored to health. **3** (of a market) having steadily high or rising prices. **4** capable of exerting great force or of doing much; muscular, powerful. **5** forceful or powerful in effect (*a strong wind*; *a strong protest*). **6** decided or firmly held (*a strong suspicion*; *strong views*). **7** (of an argument etc.) convincing or striking. **8** powerfully affecting the senses or emotions (*a strong light*; *strong acting*). **9** powerful in terms of size or numbers or quality (*a strong army*). **10** capable of doing much when united (*a strong combination*). **11** formidable; likely to succeed (*a strong candidate*). **12** (of a solution or drink etc.) concentrated; containing a large proportion of a substance in water or another solvent (*strong tea*). **13** (of a group) having a specified number (*200 strong*). **14** (of a voice) loud or penetrating. **15** (of food or its flavour) pungent. **16** (of a measure) drastic. **17** *Gram.* in Germanic languages: **a** (of a verb) forming inflections by change of vowel within the stem rather than by the addition of a suffix (e.g. *swim*, *swam*). **b** (of a noun or adjective) belonging to a declension in which the stem originally ended otherwise than in *-n*. ● *adv.* strongly (*the tide is running strong*). □ **come it strong** *Brit. colloq.* go to great lengths; use exaggeration. **come on strong** behave aggressively or assertively. **going strong** *colloq.* continuing action vigorously; continuing to flourish; in good health or trim. [Old English] □ **strongish** *adj.* **strongly** *adv.*

strong-arm *attrib.adj.* using force (*strong-arm tactics*).

strongbox *n.* a strongly made small chest for valuables.

stronghold *n.* **1** a fortified place. **2** a secure refuge. **3** a centre of support for a cause etc.

strong language *n.* forceful language; swearing.

strongman *n.* (*pl.* **-men**) **1** *Polit.* a forceful leader who exercises firm control over a state, group, etc. **2** a performer (at a fair, circus, etc.) of feats of strength.

strong meat *n. Brit.* a doctrine or action acceptable only to vigorous or instructed minds.

strong-minded *adj.* having determination.

strong point *n.* **1** a thing at which one excels. **2** a specially fortified defensive position.

strongroom *n.* a room designed to protect valuables against fire and theft.

strong stomach *n.* a stomach not easily affected by nausea.

strong suit *n.* **1** a suit at cards in which one can take tricks. **2** a thing at which one excels.

strontia *n. Chem.* strontium oxide. [from *Strontian*, Scottish parish where strontium carbonate was discovered]

strontium *n. Chem.* a soft silver-white metallic element occurring naturally in various minerals. [based on STRONTIA]

strontium-90 *n.* a radioactive isotope of strontium concentrated selectively in bones and teeth when taken into the body.

strontium oxide *n.* a white compound used in the manufacture of fireworks.

strop ● *n.* **1** a device, esp. a strip of leather, for sharpening razors. **2** *Naut.* a collar of leather or spliced rope or iron used for handling cargo. ● *v.tr.* (**stropped**, **stropping**) sharpen on or with a strop. [from Latin *stroppus*]

stroppy *adj.* (**stroppier**, **stroppiest**) *Brit. colloq.* bad-tempered; awkward to deal with. [20th-century coinage] □ **stroppily** *adv.* **stroppiness** *n.*

strove *past* of STRIVE.

strow *v.tr.* (*past part.* **strown** or **strowed**) *archaic* = STREW. [variant of STREW]

struck *past* and *past part.* of STRIKE.

structural *adj.* of, concerning, or having a structure. □ **structurally** *adv.*

structuralism *n.* **1** the doctrine that structure rather than function is important. **2** structural linguistics. **3** structural psychology. □ **structuralist** *n.* & *adj.*

structural linguistics *n.* the study of language as a system of interrelated elements.

structural psychology *n.* the study of the arrangement and composition of mental states and conscious experiences.

structure ● *n.* **1 a** a whole constructed unit, esp. a building. **b** the way in which a building etc. is constructed (*has a flimsy structure*). **2** a set of interconnecting parts of any complex thing; a framework (*the structure of a sentence*; *a new wages structure*). ● *v.tr.* give structure to; organize. [from Latin *structura*] □ **structured** *adj.* (also in *comb.*). **structureless** *adj.*

strudel /stroo-dĕl/ *n.* a confection of thin pastry rolled up round a filling and baked (*apple strudel*). [German]

struggle ● *v.intr.* **1** make forceful or violent efforts to get free of restraint or constriction. **2** (often foll. by *for*, or *to* + infin.) make violent or determined efforts under difficulties (*struggled to get the words out*). **3** (foll. by *with*, *against*) contend; fight strenuously. **4** make one's way with difficulty (*struggled to my feet*). **5** (esp. as **struggling** *adj.*) have difficulty in gaining recognition or a living (*a struggling artist*). ● *n.* **1** the act or a spell of struggling. **2** a hard or confused contest. **3** a determined effort under difficulties. [Middle English] □ **struggler** *n.*

strum ● *v.tr.* (**strummed**, **strumming**) **1** play on (a stringed or keyboard instrument), esp. carelessly or unskilfully. **2** play (a tune etc.) in this way. ● *n.* the sound made by strumming. □ **strummer** *n.*

strumpet *n. archaic* or *literary* a prostitute. [Middle English]

strung *past* and *past part.* of STRING.

strut ● *n.* **1** a bar forming part of a framework and designed to resist compression. **2** a strutting gait. ● *v.* (**strutted**, **strutting**) **1** *intr.* walk with a pompous or affected stiff erect gait. **2** *tr.* brace with a strut or struts. [Old English *strūtian* 'to protrude stiffly'] □ **strutter** *n.* **struttingly** *adv.*

struth var. of STREWTH.

strychnine /strik-neen/ *n.* a bitter and highly poisonous vegetable alkaloid obtained from plants of the genus *Strychnos* (esp. nux vomica). [based on Greek *strukhnos*, a kind of nightshade] □ **strychnic** *adj.*

stub ● *n.* **1** the remnant of a pencil or cigarette etc. after use. **2** the counterfoil of a cheque or receipt etc. **3** a stunted tail etc. ● *v.tr.* (**stubbed**, **stubbing**) **1** strike (one's toe) against something. **2** (usu. foll. by *out*) extinguish (a lighted cigarette) by pressing the lighted end against something. [Old English]

stubble *n.* **1** the cut stalks of cereal plants left sticking up after the harvest. **2 a** cropped hair or a cropped beard. **b** a short growth of unshaven hair. [based on Latin *stipula* 'straw'] □ **stubbled** *adj.* **stubbly** *adj.*

stubborn *adj.* **1** unreasonably obstinate. **2** unyielding, obdurate, inflexible. **3** refractory, intractable. [Middle English] □ **stubbornly** *adj.* **stubbornness** *n.*

stubby ● *adj.* (**stubbier**, **stubbiest**) short and thick. ● *n.* (*pl.* **-ies**) *Austral. colloq.* a small squat bottle of beer. □ **stubbiness** *n.*

stucco ● *n.* (*pl.* **-oes**) ▶ plaster or cement used for coating wall surfaces or moulding into architectural decorations. ● *v.tr.* (**-oes**, **-oed**) coat with stucco. [Italian]

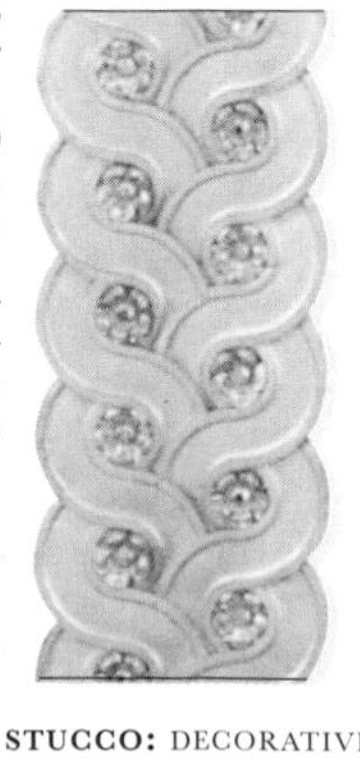

STUCCO: DECORATIVE MOULDED STUCCO

stuck *past* and *past part.* of STICK[2].

stuck-up *adj. colloq.* affectedly superior and aloof, snobbish.

stud[1] ● *n.* **1** a large-headed nail, boss, or knob, projecting from a surface esp. for ornament. **2** a small piece of jewellery for wearing in pierced ears or nostrils. **3** a double button, esp. for use with two buttonholes in a shirt-front. **4** a small object projecting slightly from a road surface as a marker etc. ● *v.tr.* (**studded**, **studding**) **1** set with or as with studs. **2** (as **studded** *adj.*) (foll. by *with*) thickly set or strewn (*studded with diamonds*). **3** be scattered over or about (a surface). [Old English *studu* 'post, prop']

stud[2] *n.* **1 a** a number of horses kept for breeding etc. **b** a place where these are kept. **2** (in full **stud-horse**) a stallion. **3** *colloq.* a young man (esp. one noted for sexual prowess). **4** (in full **stud poker**) a form of poker with betting after the dealing of successive rounds of cards face up. □ **at stud** (of a male horse) publicly available for breeding on payment of a fee. [Old English]

stud book *n.* a book containing the pedigrees of horses.

student *n.* **1 a** a person who is studying, esp. at university or another place of higher education. **b** *N. Amer.* a school pupil. **2** (*attrib.*) studying in order to become (*a student nurse*). **3** a person of studious habits. [from Latin *student-* 'studying']

stud farm *n.* a place where horses are bred.

stud-horse see STUD[2] 2.

studio *n.* (*pl.* **-os**) **1** the workroom of a painter or photographer etc. **2** a place where cinema films or recordings are made or where television or radio programmes are made or produced. [Italian]

studio couch *n.* a couch that can be converted into a bed.

studio flat *n. Brit.* a flat containing a room suitable as an artist's studio, or only one main room.

studious *adj.* **1** devoted to or assiduous in study or reading. **2** studied, deliberate, painstaking (*with studious care*). **3** (foll. by *to* + infin. or *in* + verbal noun) showing care or attention. [from Latin *studiosus*] □ **studiously** *adv.* **studiousness** *n.*

study ● *n.* (*pl.* **-ies**) **1** the devotion of time and attention to acquiring information or knowledge, esp. from books. **2** (in *pl.*) the pursuit of academic knowledge (*continued their studies abroad*). **3** a room used for reading, writing, etc. **4** a piece of work, esp. a drawing, done for practice or as an experiment (*a study of a head*). **5** the portrayal in literature or another art form of an aspect of behaviour or character etc. **6** a musical composition designed to develop a player's skill. **7** a thing worth observing closely (*your face was a study*). **8** a thing that is or deserves to be investigated. ● *v.* (**-ies**, **-ied**) **1** *tr.* make a study of; investigate or examine (a subject) (*study law*). **2** *intr.* (often foll. by *for*) apply oneself to study. **3** *tr.* scrutinize or earnestly contemplate (*studied their faces*; *studied the problem*). **4** *tr.* (as **studied** *adj.*) deliberate, intentional, affected (*with studied politeness*). □ **make a study of** investigate carefully. [from Latin *studium* 'zeal, study'] □ **studiedly** *adv.* **studiedness** *n.*

study-bedroom *n.* a room serving both as a bedroom and as a study, esp. as student accommodation.

study group *n.* a group of people meeting from time to time to study a particular subject or topic.

stuff ● *n.* **1** the material that a thing is made of; material that may be used for some purpose. **2** a substance or things or belongings of an indeterminate kind (*there's a lot of stuff about it in the newspapers*). **3** a particular knowledge or activity (*know one's stuff*). **4** *Brit.* woollen fabric (esp. as distinct from silk, cotton, and linen). **5** valueless matter, trash, nonsense (*take that stuff away*). **6** (prec. by *the*) **a** *colloq.* an available supply of something, esp. drink or drugs. **b** *slang* money. ● *v.* **1** *tr.* pack (a receptacle) tightly. **2** *tr.* (foll. by *in*, *into*) force or cram (a thing). **3** *tr.* fill out the skin of (an animal or bird etc.) with material to restore the original shape. **4** *tr.* fill (poultry etc.) with a savoury or sweet mixture, esp. before cooking. **5 a** *tr.* & *refl.* fill (a person or oneself) with food. **b** *tr.* & *intr.* eat greedily. **6** *tr.* push, esp. hastily or clumsily (*stuffed the note behind the cushion*). **7** *tr.* (usu. in *passive*; foll. by *up*) block up (a person's nose etc.). **8** *tr. slang* (esp. as an expression of contemptuous dismissal) dispose of as unwanted (*you can stuff the job*). □ **do one's stuff** *colloq.* do what one has to. **get stuffed** *Brit. slang* an exclamation of dismissal, contempt, etc. **stuff and nonsense** *Brit.* an exclamation of incredulity or ridicule. **stuff it** *slang* an expression of rejection or disdain. **that's the stuff** *colloq.* that is what is wanted. [from Greek *stuphein* 'to draw together'] □ **stuffer** *n.* (also in *comb.*).

stuffed shirt *n. colloq.* a pompous person.

stuffing *n.* **1** padding used to stuff cushions etc. **2** a mixture used to stuff poultry etc., esp. before cooking. □ **knock** (or **take**) **the stuffing out of** *colloq.* make feeble or weak; defeat.

stuffy *adj.* (**stuffier**, **stuffiest**) **1** (of a room or the atmosphere in it) lacking fresh air or ventilation; close. **2** dull or uninteresting. **3** (of a person) dull and conventional. □ **stuffily** *adv.* **stuffiness** *n.*

stultify *v.tr.* (**-ies**, **-ied**) make ineffective, useless, or futile, esp. as a result of tedious routine (*stultifying boredom*). [based on Late Latin *stultus* 'stupid'] □ **stultification** *n.*

stumble ● *v.intr.* **1** lurch forward or have a partial fall from catching or striking or misplacing one's foot. **2** (often foll. by *along*) walk with repeated stumbles. **3** make a mistake or repeated mistakes in speaking etc. **4** (foll. by *on*, *upon*, *across*) find or encounter by chance. ● *n.* an act of stumbling. [Middle English]

stumbling block *n.* an obstacle or circumstance causing difficulty or hesitation.

stump ● *n.* **1** the projecting remnant of a cut or fallen tree. **2** the similar remnant of anything else (e.g. a branch or limb) cut off or worn down. **3** *Cricket* each of the three uprights of a wicket. ▷ CRICKET. **4** (in *pl.*) *joc.* the legs. ● *v.* **1** *tr.* (of a question etc.) be too hard for; puzzle. **2** *tr.* (as **stumped** *adj.*) at a loss; baffled. **3** *tr. Cricket* (esp. of a wicketkeeper) put (a batsman) out by touching the stumps with the ball while the batsman is out of the crease. **4** *intr.* walk stiffly or noisily. **5** *tr.* (also *absol.*) *US* traverse (a district) making political speeches. □ **on the stump** *colloq.* engaged in political speech-making or agitation. **stump up** *Brit. colloq.* pay or produce (the money required). **up a stump** *US* in difficulties. [from Middle Dutch *stomp*]

stumpy *adj.* (**stumpier**, **stumpiest**) short and thick.

stun *v.tr.* (**stunned**, **stunning**) **1** knock senseless; stupefy. **2** bewilder or shock. [from Old French *estoner* 'to astonish']

stung *past* and *past part.* of STING.

stun gun *n.* a gun which stuns through an electric shock, ultrasound, etc., without causing serious injury.

stunk *past* and *past part.* of STINK.

stunner *n. colloq.* a stunning person or thing.

stunning *adj. colloq.* extremely impressive or attractive. □ **stunningly** *adv.*

stunt[1] *v.tr.* retard the growth or development of. [originally as adj. in sense 'foolish'] □ **stuntedness** *n.*

stunt[2] *n.* **1** something unusual done to attract attention. **2** a trick or daring manoeuvre. [19th-century US coinage, first used in college athletics]

stuntman *n.* (*pl.* **-men**) a man employed to take an actor's place in performing dangerous stunts.

stupa *n.* ▶ a round usu. domed building erected as a Buddhist shrine. [Sanskrit *stūpa*]

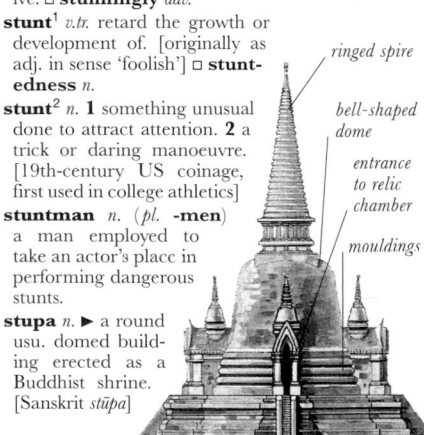

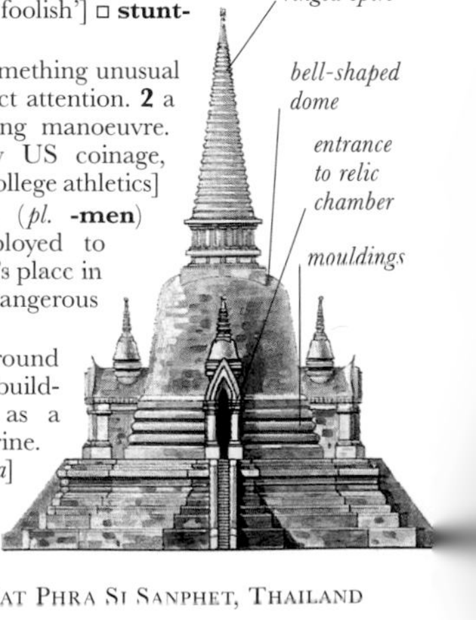
ringed spire
bell-shaped dome
entrance to relic chamber
mouldings

STUPA: WAT PHRA SI SANPHET, THAILAND

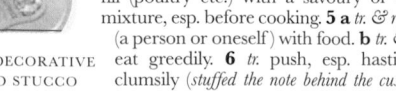

stupefy *v.tr.* (**-ies**, **-ied**) **1** make stupid or insensible. **2** stun with astonishment. [from Latin *stupefacere*] □ **stupefacient** *adj. & n.* **stupefaction** *n.* **stupefying** *adj.* **stupefyingly** *adv.*

stupendous *adj.* amazing or prodigious, esp. in size or degree (*a stupendous achievement*). [from Latin *stupendus* 'to be wondered at'] □ **stupendously** *adv.* **stupendousness** *n.*

stupid *adj.* (**stupider**, **stupidest**) **1** unintelligent, slow-witted, foolish (*a stupid fellow*). **2** typical of stupid persons (*put it in a stupid place*). **3** uninteresting or boring. **4** in a state of stupor or lethargy. **5** obtuse; lacking in sensibility. **6** *colloq.* a general term of disparagement (*all you do is read your stupid books*). [from Latin *stupidus*] □ **stupidity** *n.* (*pl.* **-ies**). **stupidly** *adv.*

stupor *n.* a dazed, torpid, or helplessly amazed state. [Latin] □ **stuporous** *adj.*

sturdy *adj.* (**sturdier**, **sturdiest**) **1** robust; strongly built. **2** vigorous and determined (*sturdy resistance*). [Middle English in sense 'reckless': from Old French *esturdi* 'stunned'] □ **sturdily** *adv.* **sturdiness** *n.*

sturgeon *n.* ▼ any large mailed sharklike fish of the family Acipenseridae etc., used as food and a source of caviar and isinglass. [from Old French *esturgeon*]

narrow snout   *plate-like scales*

STURGEON: ATLANTIC STURGEON
(*Acipenser sturio*)

stutter ● *v.* **1** *intr.* stammer, esp. by involuntarily repeating the first consonants of words. **2** *tr.* utter (words) in this way. ● *n.* **1** the act or habit of stuttering. **2** an instance of stuttering. [from obsolete (now dialect) *stut*] □ **stutterer** *n.*

sty[1] *n.* (*pl.* **sties**) **1** a pen or enclosure for pigs. **2** a filthy room or dwelling. **3** a place of debauchery. [Old English]

sty[2] *n.* (also **stye**) (*pl.* **sties** or **styes**) an inflamed swelling on the edge of an eyelid. [back-formation from obsolete *styany*, in same sense]

Stygian /stij-iăn/ *adj.* **1** (in Greek mythology) of or relating to the Styx, a river in Hades. **2** *literary* dark, gloomy, indistinct. [based on Greek *stugnos* 'gloomy']

style ● *n.* **1** a kind or sort, esp. in regard to appearance and form (*an elegant style of house*). **2** a manner of writing or speaking or performing (*written in a florid style; started off in fine style*). **3** the distinctive manner of a person or school or period, esp. in relation to painting, architecture, furniture, dress, etc. **4** the correct way of designating a person or thing. **5** a superior quality or manner (*do it in style*). **6** a particular make, shape, or pattern (*in all sizes and styles*). **7** a method of reckoning dates (*Old Style; New Style*). **8** *Bot.* the narrow extension of the ovary supporting the stigma. ▷ FLOWER. ● *v.tr.* **1** design or make etc. in a particular style. **2** designate in a specified way. [from Latin *stilus*] □ **styleless** *adj.* **styler** *n.*

styli *pl.* of STYLUS.

stylish *adj.* **1** fashionable; elegant. **2** having a superior quality, manner, etc. □ **stylishly** *adv.* **stylishness** *n.*

stylist *n.* **1 a** a designer of fashionable styles etc. **b** a hairdresser. **2 a** a writer noted for or aspiring to good literary style. **b** (in sport or music) a person who performs with style.

stylistic *adj.* of or concerning style. □ **stylistically** *adv.*

stylistics *n.* the study of literary style.

stylize *v.tr.* (also **-ise**) (esp. as **stylized** *adj.*) paint, draw, etc. (a subject) in a conventional non-realistic style. □ **stylization** *n.*

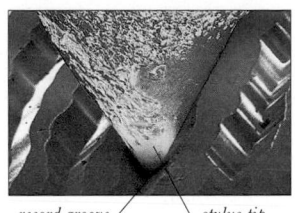

record groove   *stylus tip*

STYLUS: MICROGRAPH OF THE TIP OF A STYLUS IN A RECORD GROOVE

stylus *n.* (*pl.* **-li** or **-luses**) **1** ◀ a hard point following a groove in a gramophone record and transmitting the recorded sound for reproduction. **2** a similar point producing such a groove when recording sound. [erroneous spelling of Latin *stilus*]

stymie (also **stimy**) ● *n.* (*pl.* **-ies**) **1** *Golf* a situation where an opponent's ball lies between the player and the hole (*lay a stymie*). **2** a difficult situation. ● *v.tr.* (**stymies, stymied, stymying** or **stymieing**) **1** obstruct; thwart. **2** *Golf* block with a stymie. [19th-century coinage]

styptic ● *adj.* that checks bleeding. ● *n.* a styptic substance. [from Greek *stuptikos*]

styptic pencil *n.* a stick of a styptic substance used to treat small cuts.

styrene *n. Chem.* a liquid hydrocarbon easily polymerized and used in making plastics etc.

styrofoam *n.* esp. *N. Amer.* a kind of expanded polystyrene.

suasion *n. formal* persuasion (*moral suasion*). [from Latin *suasio*]

suave /swahv/ *adj.* smooth; polite; sophisticated. [French, literally 'agreeable'] □ **suavely** *adv.* **suaveness** *n.* **suavity** *n.* (*pl.* **-ies**).

sub *colloq.* ● *n.* **1** a submarine. **2** a subscription. **3** a substitute. **4** a sub-editor. **5** *Brit.* an advance or loan against expected income. ● *v.* (**subbed, subbing**) **1** *intr.* (usu. foll. by *for*) act as a substitute. **2** *tr. Brit. colloq.* lend or advance (a sum) to (a person) against expected income. **3** *tr.* sub-edit.

sub- *prefix* (also **suc-** before *c*, **suf-** before *f*, **sug-** before *g*, **sup-** before *p*, **sur-** before *r*, **sus-** before *c, p, t*) **1** at or to or from a lower position (*subordinate; submerge; subtract; subsoil*) **2** secondary or inferior in rank or position (*subclass; subcommittee; sub lieutenant; subtotal*). **3** somewhat, nearly; more or less (*subacid; subarctic*). **4** (forming verbs) denoting secondary action (*subdivide; sub-let*). **5** denoting support (*subvention*). **6** *Chem.* (of a salt) basic (*subacetate*). [from Latin *sub* 'under, close to, towards']

subacid *adj.* moderately acid or tart. [from Latin *subacidus*]

subadult *Zool.* ● *adj.* (of an animal) not fully adult. ● *n.* a subadult animal.

subalpine *adj.* of or situated in the higher slopes of mountains just below the timberline.

subaltern /sub-ăl-tĕn/ *n. Brit. Mil.* an officer below the rank of captain, esp. a second lieutenant. [from Late Latin *subalternus*]

subantarctic *adj.* of or like regions immediately north of the Antarctic Circle.

sub-aqua *adj.* of or concerning underwater swimming or diving.

subaquatic *adj.* **1** of more or less aquatic habits or kind. **2** underwater.

subaqueous *adj.* existing, formed, or taking place under water.

subarctic *adj.* of or like regions immediately south of the Arctic Circle.

subatomic *adj.* occurring in or smaller than an atom.

sub-basement *n.* a storey below a basement.

sub-branch *n.* a secondary or subordinate branch.

subcategory *n.* (*pl.* **-ies**) a secondary or subordinate category. □ **subcategorize** *v.tr.* (also **-ise**). **subcategorization** *n.*

subclass *n.* **1** a secondary or subordinate class. **2** *Biol.* a taxonomic category below a class.

sub-clause *n.* **1** esp. *Law* a subsidiary section of a clause. **2** *Gram.* a subordinate clause.

subcommittee *n.* a secondary committee.

subconscious ● *adj.* of or concerning the part of the mind which is not fully conscious but influences actions etc. ● *n.* this part of the mind. □ **subconsciously** *adv.* **subconsciousness** *n.*

subcontinent *n.* **1** a large land mass, smaller than a continent. **2** a large geographically or politically independent part of a continent. □ **subcontinental** *adj.*

subcontract ● *v.* **1** *tr.* employ a firm etc. to do (work) as part of a larger project. **2** *intr.* make or carry out a subcontract. ● *n.* a secondary contract. □ **subcontractor** *n.*

subculture *n.* a cultural group within a larger culture. □ **subcultural** *adj.*

subcutaneous *adj.* under the skin. □ **subcutaneously** *adv.*

subdivide *v.tr. & intr.* divide again after a first division [Middle English]

subdominant *n. Mus.* the fourth note of the diatonic scale of any key.

subduction *n. Geol.* ▼ the sideways and downward movement of the edge of a plate of the Earth's crust into the mantle beneath another plate (*subduction zone*). ▷ PLATE TECTONICS, TRENCH. [from Latin *subductio* 'drawing away']

subdue *v.tr.* (**subdues, subdued, subduing**) **1** conquer, subjugate, or tame. **2** (as **subdued** *adj.*) softened; lacking in intensity; toned down (*subdued*

S

SUBDUCTION

Subduction usually occurs when a thin oceanic plate collides with a thick continental plate, forcing the oceanic plate into the asthenosphere and forming an ocean trench in the process. Magma, which forms as the heat of the asthenosphere melts the subducted plate, rises through the shattered edge of the overlying plate and may erupt as a volcano. Subduction may also occur at the point where two continental plates meet.

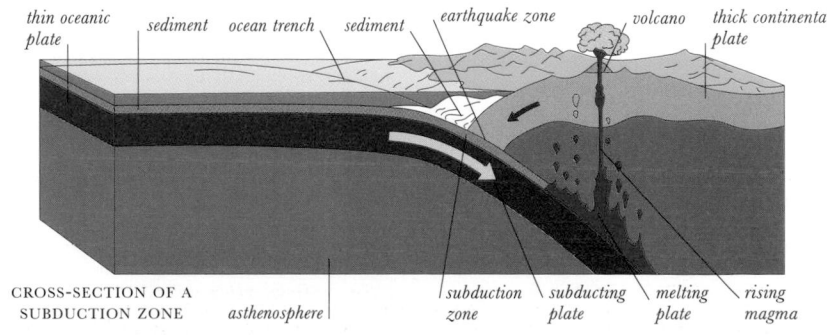

thin oceanic plate   *sediment*   *ocean trench*   *sediment*   *earthquake zone*   *volcano*   *thick continental plate*

CROSS-SECTION OF A SUBDUCTION ZONE   *asthenosphere*   *subduction zone*   *subducting plate*   *melting plate*   *rising magma*

SUBMARINE

To remain submerged for extended periods, a submarine must have a steel hull strong enough to resist the high water pressure. Upright partitions called bulkheads divide the vessel into compartments, which can be sealed off in the event of the hull leaking. Submarines have engines for surface and underwater use, and these run on either nuclear power or a combination of electric and diesel motors. When a submarine dives, valves are opened in ballast tanks located on each side of the hull. Water enters the tanks and the extra weight causes the craft to sink. To surface, water is ejected from the tanks. Today, there are two main types of military submarine: patrol submarines, which attack enemy vessels; and missile submarines, which carry long-range nuclear missiles.

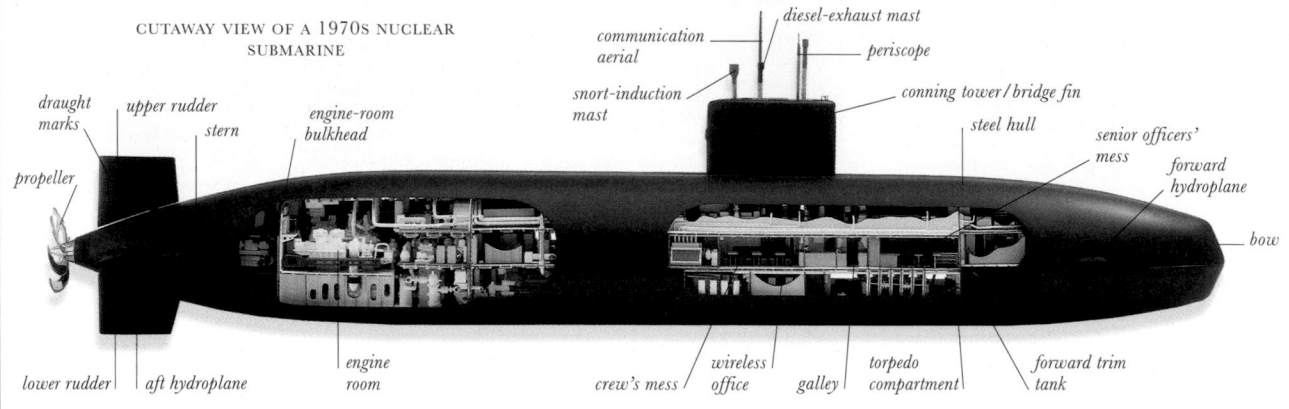

CUTAWAY VIEW OF A 1970s NUCLEAR SUBMARINE

communication aerial · diesel-exhaust mast · periscope · snort-induction mast · conning tower/bridge fin · steel hull · senior officers' mess · forward hydroplane · bow · draught marks · upper rudder · stern · engine-room bulkhead · propeller · lower rudder · aft hydroplane · engine room · crew's mess · wireless office · galley · torpedo compartment · forward trim tank

light; *in a subdued mood*). [from Old French *so(u)duire* 'to deceive', influenced by Latin *subdere* 'to conquer']

sub-editor *n.* **1** an assistant editor. **2** *Brit.* a person who edits material for printing. □ **sub-edit** *v.tr.* (**-edited, -editing**).

subfamily *n.* (*pl.* **-ies**) **1** *Biol.* a taxonomic category below a family. **2** any subdivision of a group.

subfloor *n.* a foundation for a floor in a building.

subform *n.* a subordinate or secondary form.

sub-frame *n.* a supporting frame.

subfusc ● *adj.* formal dull; dusky; gloomy. ● *n. Brit.* formal clothing at some universities.

subgenus *n.* (*pl.* **subgenera**) *Biol.* a taxonomic category below a genus. □ **subgeneric** *adj.*

sub-group *n.* (also *Math.* **subgroup**) a subdivision of a group.

sub-head *n.* (also **sub-heading**) **1** a subordinate heading or title. **2** a subordinate division in a classification.

subhuman *adj.* **1** (of an animal) closely related to man. **2** (of behaviour, intelligence, etc.) less than human.

subject ● *n.* /ˈsub-jikt/ **1 a** a matter, theme, etc. to be discussed, described, represented, etc. **b** (foll. by *for*) a person, circumstance, etc., giving rise to specified feeling, action, etc. (*a subject for congratulation*). **2** a field of study (*his best subject is geography*). **3** *Gram.* a noun or its equivalent about which a sentence is predicated and with which the verb agrees. **4 a** any person except a monarch living under a government (*the ruler and his subjects*). **b** any person owing obedience to another. **5** *Mus.* a theme of a fugue or sonata; a leading phrase or motif. **6** a person of specified tendencies (*a hysterical subject*). ● *adj.* /ˈsub-jikt/ **1** owing obedience to a government, colonizing power, force, etc.; in subjection. **2** (foll. by *to*) liable, exposed, or prone to (*is subject to infection*). **3** (foll. by *to*) conditional upon (*the arrangement is subject to your approval*). ● *adv.* /ˈsub-jikt/ (foll. by *to*) conditionally upon (*subject to your consent, I propose to try again*). ● *v.tr.* /sub-ˈjekt/ **1** (foll. by *to*) make liable; expose (*subjected us to hours of waiting*). **2** (usu. foll. by *to*) subdue (a nation, person, etc.) to one's sway etc. □ **on the subject of** concerning, about. [from Latin *subjectus* 'thrown below'] □ **subjection** *n.* **subjectless** *adj.*

subjective *adj.* **1** (of art, literature, written history, a person's views, etc.) proceeding from personal idiosyncrasy or individuality; not impartial or literal. **2** *Gram.* of or concerning the subject. [from Latin *subjectivus*] □ **subjectively** *adv.* **subjectivity** *n.*

subject matter *n.* the matter treated of in a book, lawsuit, etc.

subjoin *v.tr.* add (an illustration, anecdote, etc.) at the end. [from obsolete French *subjoindre*]

sub judice /sub ˈjoo-di-si/ *adj. Law* under judicial consideration and therefore prohibited from public discussion elsewhere. [Latin, literally 'under a judge']

subjugate *v.tr.* bring into subjection; vanquish. [based on Late Latin *subjugatus* 'brought under the yoke'] □ **subjugation** *n.*

subjunctive *Gram.* ● *adj.* (of a mood) denoting what is imagined or wished or possible (e.g. *if I were you, God help you, be that as it may*). ● *n.* **1** the subjunctive mood. **2** a verb in this mood. [from Late Latin *subjunctivus*]

subkingdom *n. Biol.* a taxonomic category below a kingdom.

sub-lease ● *n.* a lease of a property by a tenant to a subtenant. ● *v.tr.* lease to a subtenant.

sub-lessee *n.* a person who holds a sub-lease.

sub-lessor *n.* a person who grants a sub-lease.

sub-let ● *n.* = SUB-LEASE *n.* ● *v.tr.* (**-letting**; *past* and *past part.* **-let**) = SUB-LEASE *v.*

sub lieutenant *n. Brit.* a naval officer ranking next below lieutenant.

sublimate ● *v.tr.* **1** (also *absol.*) divert (the energy of a primitive impulse, esp. sexual) into a culturally higher, or socially more acceptable, activity. **2** *Chem.* convert (a substance) from the solid state directly to its vapour by heat, and usu. allow it to solidify again. ▷ MATTER. **3** refine; purify; idealize. ● *adj.* **1** *Chem.* (of a substance) sublimated. **2** purified, refined. ● *n. Chem.* a sublimated substance. [based on Latin *sublimatus* 'sublimed'] □ **sublimation** *n.*

sublime ● *adj.* (**sublimer, sublimest**) **1** of the most exalted or noble kind; awe-inspiring (*sublime genius*). **2** (of indifference, impudence, etc.) arrogantly unruffled; extreme. ● *v.* **1** *tr.* & *intr. Chem.* = SUBLIMATE *v.* 2. **2** *tr.* purify or elevate by or as if by sublimation; make sublime. **3** *intr.* become pure by or as if by sublimation. [from Latin *sublimis*] □ **sublimely** *adv.* **sublimity** *n.*

subliminal *adj. Psychol.* (of a stimulus etc.) below the threshold of sensation or consciousness. [based on Latin *limen -inis* 'threshold'] □ **subliminally** *adv.*

subliminal advertising *n.* the use of subliminal images in advertising on television etc. to influence the viewer at an unconscious level.

Sub-Lt. *abbr. Brit.* Sub Lieutenant.

sublunary *adj.* **1** beneath the Moon. **2** *Astron.* **a** within the Moon's orbit. **b** subject to the Moon's influence. **3** of this world; earthly. [from Late Latin *sublunaris*]

sub-machine gun *n.* a hand-held lightweight machine-gun. ▷ GUN

submarine ● *n.* ▲ a vessel, esp. a warship, capable of operating under water. ● *adj.* existing, occurring, done, or used under the sea (*submarine cable*). □ **submariner** *n.*

submerge *v.* **1** *tr.* **a** place under water; flood; inundate. **b** inundate with work, problems, etc. **2** *intr.* dive below the surface of water. [from Latin *submergere*] □ **submergence** *n.*

submersible ● *n.* ▶ a submarine operating under water for short periods. ● *adj.* capable of being submerged.

submersion *n.* the act or an instance of submerging; the state of being submerged.

submicroscopic *adj.* too small to be seen by an ordinary microscope.

subminiature *adj.* **1** of greatly reduced size. **2** (of a camera) very small and using 16-mm film.

submission *n.* **1 a** the act or an instance of submitting; the state of being submitted. **b** anything that is submitted. **2** humility, meekness, obedience, submissiveness (*showed great submission of spirit*). **3** *Law* a theory etc. submitted by counsel to a judge or jury. **4** (in wrestling) the surrender of a participant yielding to the pain of a hold. [from Latin *submissio*]

submissive *adj.* **1** humble; obedient. **2** yielding to power or authority; willing to submit. □ **submissively** *adv.* **submissiveness** *n.*

submit *v.* (**submitted, submitting**) **1** (usu. foll. by *to*) **a** *intr.* cease resistance; yield (*had to submit to defeat; will never submit*). **b** *refl.* surrender (oneself) to the control of another etc. **2** *tr.* present for consideration or decision. **3** *tr.* (usu. foll. by *to*) subject (a person or thing) to a process, treatment, etc. (*submitted it to the flames*). **4** *tr.* esp. *Law* urge or represent esp. deferentially (*that, I submit, is a misrepresentation*). [from Latin *submittere*] □ **submitter** *n.*

submodifier *n. Gram.* a word which modifies an adjective or adverb (e.g. *very* in *he approached very slowly*, and *rather* in *I was rather upset*).

subnormal *adj.* **1** (esp. as regards intelligence) below normal. **2** less than normal. □ **subnormality** *n.*

suboptimal *adj.* less than optimal; not of the best quality, type, etc.

suborder *n. Biol.* a taxonomic category ranked below an order.

subordinate ● *adj.* (usu. foll. by *to*) of inferior importance or rank; secondary, subservient. ● *n.* a person working under another. ● *v.tr.* (usu. foll. by *to*) **1** make subordinate; treat or regard as of minor importance. **2** make subservient. [from medieval Latin *subordinatus* 'placed in a lower order'] □ **subordination** *n.*

subordinate clause *n.* a clause that functions like a noun, adjective, or adverb, and qualifies a main clause (e.g. 'when it rang' in 'she answered the phone when it rang') (cf. MAIN CLAUSE).

suborn *v.tr.* induce by bribery etc. to commit perjury or any other unlawful act. [from Latin *subornare* 'to incite secretly']

subphylum *n.* (*pl.* **subphyla**) *Biol.* a taxonomic category below a phylum.

sub-plot *n.* a subordinate plot in a play etc.

subpoena /sŭb-pee-nă/ ● *n.* a writ ordering a person to attend a law court. ● *v.tr.* (*past* and *past part.* **subpoenaed** or **subpoena'd**) serve a subpoena on. [from Latin *sub poena* 'under penalty', first words of the writ]

sub-postmaster *n.* (*fem.* **sub-postmistress**) a person in charge of a sub-post office.

sub-post office *n.* a small local post office offering fewer services than a main post office.

sub rosa *adj. & adv.* in secrecy or confidence. [Latin, literally 'under the rose', as an emblem of secrecy]

subroutine *n. Computing* a routine designed to perform a frequently used operation within a program.

sub-Saharan *attrib.adj.* from or forming part of the African regions south of the Sahara desert.

subscribe *v.* **1** *tr. & intr.* (usu. foll. by *to*, *for*) contribute (a specified sum) or make or promise a contribution to a fund, project, charity, etc., esp. regularly. **2** *intr.* (usu. foll. by *to*) express one's agreement with an opinion, resolution, etc. (*cannot subscribe to that*). □ **subscribe to** arrange to receive (a periodical etc.) regularly. [from Latin *subscribere* 'to write below']

subscriber *n.* **1 a** a contributor to a fund etc.; a person subscribing to a periodical etc. **b** esp. *Brit.* a person paying for the hire of a telephone line. **2** a person who subscribes to an idea etc.

subscriber trunk dialling *n. Brit.* the automatic connection of trunk calls by dialling.

subscript ● *adj.* written or printed below the line. ● *n.* a subscript number or symbol. [from Latin *subscriptus* 'written below']

subscription *n.* **1 a** the act or an instance of subscribing. **b** money subscribed. **2** *Brit.* a fee for the membership of a society etc. **3 a** an agreement to take and pay for usu. a specified number of issues of a newspaper, magazine, etc. **b** the money paid by this.

subscription concert *n.* each of a series of concerts for which tickets are sold in advance.

subsection *n.* a division of a section.

subsequent *adj.* (usu. foll. by *to*) following a specified event etc. in time, esp. as a consequence. [from Old French] □ **subsequently** *adv.*

subserve *v.tr.* serve as a means in furthering (a purpose, action, etc.).

subservient *adj.* **1** cringing; obsequious. **2** (usu. foll. by *to*) instrumental. **3** (usu. foll. by *to*) subordinate. [from Latin *subservient-* 'lending support'] □ **subservience** *n.* **subserviency** *n.*

subset *n.* **1** a secondary part of a set. **2** *Math.* a set all the elements of which are contained in another set.

subside *v.intr.* **1** become tranquil; abate (*excitement subsided*). **2** (of water, suspended matter, etc.) sink. **3** (of the ground) cave in; sink. **4** (of a building, ship, etc.) sink lower in the ground or water. **5** (of a swelling etc.) become less. **6** usu. *joc.* (of a person) sink into a sitting, kneeling, or lying posture. [from Latin *subsidere* 'to settle down'] □ **subsidence** *n.*

subsidiary ● *adj.* **1** serving to assist or supplement; auxiliary. **2** (of a company) controlled by another. ● *n.* (*pl.* **-ies**) **1** a subsidiary thing or person; an accessory. **2** a subsidiary company. [from Latin *subsidiarius*] □ **subsidiarity** *n.*

subsidize *v.tr.* (also **-ise**) **1** pay a subsidy to. **2** reduce the cost of by subsidy (*subsidized lunches*). □ **subsidization** *n.*

subsidy *n.* (*pl.* **-ies**) **1** money granted by the state or a public body etc. to keep down the price of commodities etc. (*housing subsidy*). **2** money granted to a charity or other undertaking held to be in the public interest. **3** any grant of money. [from Latin *subsidium* 'assistance']

subsist *v.tr.* **1** (often foll. by *on*) keep oneself alive; be kept alive (*subsists on vegetables*). **2** remain in being; exist. **3** (foll. by *in*) be attributable to (*its excellence subsists in its freshness*). [from Latin *subsistere* 'to stand firm'] □ **subsistent** *adj.*

subsistence *n.* **1** the state or an instance of subsisting. **2 a** the means of supporting life; a livelihood. **b** a minimal level of existence or the income providing this (*a bare subsistence*).

subsistence allowance *n.* (also **subsistence money**) esp. *Brit.* an allowance or advance on pay granted esp. as travelling expenses.

subsistence farming *n.* farming which directly supports the farmer's household without producing a significant surplus for trade.

subsistence level *n.* (also **subsistence wage**) a standard of living (or wage) providing only the bare necessities of life.

subsoil *n.* soil lying immediately under the surface soil (opp. TOPSOIL). ▷ SOIL

subsonic *adj.* relating to speeds less than that of sound.

subspecies *n.* (*pl.* same) *Biol.* a taxonomic category below a species, usu. a fairly permanent geographically isolated variety. □ **subspecific** *adj.*

substance *n.* **1 a** the essential material forming a thing (*the substance was transparent*). **b** a particular kind of material having uniform properties (*this substance is salt*). **2 a** reality; solidity (*ghosts have no substance*). **b** seriousness or steadiness of character (*there is no substance in him*). **3** the theme or subject of a work of art, argument, etc. (*prefer the substance to the style*). **4** the real meaning or essence of a thing. **5** wealth and possessions (*a woman of substance*). **6** *Philos.* the essential nature underlying phenomena, which is subject to changes and accidents. **7** an intoxicating or narcotic chemical or drug, esp. an illegal one (*substance abuse*). □ **in substance** generally; apart from details. [from Latin *substantia*]

sub-standard *adj.* **1** of less than the required or normal quality or size. **2** (of language) not conforming to standard usage.

substantial *adj.* **1 a** of real importance, value, or validity (*made a substantial contribution*). **b** of large size or amount (*awarded substantial damages*). **2** of solid material or structure; stout (*a man of substantial build; a substantial house*). **3** commercially successful; wealthy. **4** essential; true in large part (*substantial truth*). **5** having substance; real. [from Late Latin *substantialis*] □ **substantiality** *n.* **substantially** *adv.*

substantiate *v.tr.* prove the truth of (a charge, statement, claim, etc.); give good grounds for. [based on medieval Latin *substantiatus* 'given substance to'] □ **substantiation** *n.*

substantive /sub-stăn-tiv/ ● *adj.* also sub-**stan**-tiv **1** having separate and independent existence. **2** having a firm or solid basis; important, substantial. **3** *Gram.* expressing existence. **4** *Mil.* (of a rank etc.) permanent, not acting or temporary. ● *n. Gram.* = NOUN. [from Late Latin *substantivus*] □ **substantival** *adj.* **substantively** *adv.*

sub-station *n.* a subordinate station, esp. one reducing the high voltage of electric power transmission to that suitable for supply to consumers.

substitute ● *n.* **1** (also *attrib.*) a person or thing acting or serving in place of another. **2** an artificial alternative to a natural substance (*butter substitute*). ● *v.* **1** *intr. & tr.* act or cause to act as a substitute; put or serve in exchange (*substituted for her mother; substituted it for the broken one*). **2** *tr.* (usu. foll. by *by*, *with*) *colloq.* replace (a person or thing) with another

---

SUBMERSIBLE

Submersibles are designed to operate at great depths, sometimes over 4 km (2.5 miles) beneath the ocean's surface. The umbilical cable, which is attached to a vessel on the surface, provides power, control signals, and video lines. Submersibles have a variety of functions, including marine research, the repair of ocean pipelines, salvage, and the exploration of undersea wrecks. External mechanical arms, and sensors such as video cameras, are fitted to help with these specialized tasks

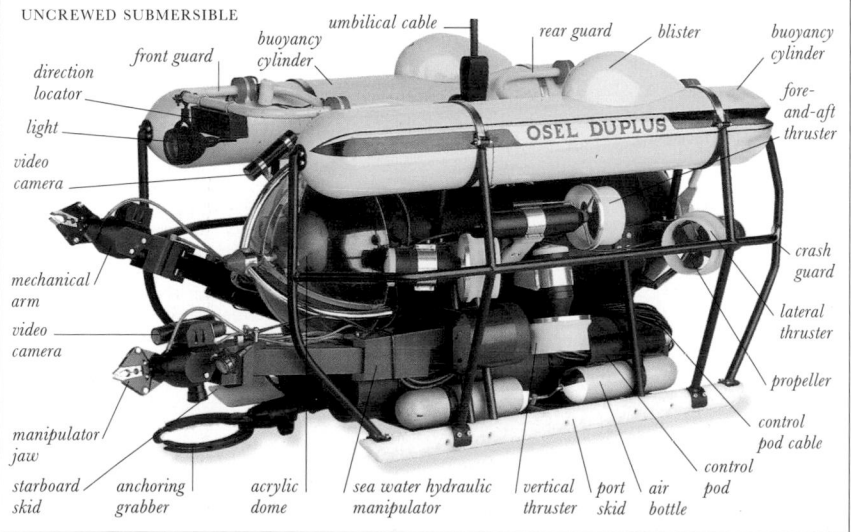

UNCREWED SUBMERSIBLE

umbilical cable · direction locator · front guard · buoyancy cylinder · rear guard · blister · buoyancy cylinder · light · fore-and-aft thruster · video camera · OSEL DUPLUS · mechanical arm · video camera · crash guard · lateral thruster · propeller · control pod cable · manipulator jaw · control pod · starboard skid · anchoring grabber · acrylic dome · sea water hydraulic manipulator · vertical thruster · port skid · air bottle

S

(*substitute dairy milk with soya milk*). [from Latin *substitutus* 'put in place of'] □ **substitutable** *adj.* **substitutability** *n.* **substitution** *n.* **substitutive** *adj.*

■ **Usage** The use of *substitute* with the prepositions *by* or *with*, as illustrated in sense 2 of the verb above, is highly informal and should be avoided in standard English. The example *substitute dairy milk with soya milk* can be reworded as *substitute soya milk for dairy milk* (see sense 1 of the verb above).

substrate *n.* **1** = SUBSTRATUM. **2** a surface to be painted, printed on, etc. **3** *Biol.* **a** the substance upon which an enzyme acts. **b** the surface or material on which any particular organism grows. [Anglicized from SUBSTRATUM]

substratum *n.* (*pl.* **substrata**) **1** an underlying layer or substance. **2** a layer of rock or soil beneath the surface. **3** a foundation or basis (*there is a substratum of truth in it*). [Latin, literally '(thing) spread beneath']

substructure *n.* an underlying or supporting structure.

subsume *v.tr.* (usu. foll. by *under*) include (an instance, idea, term, etc.) in a rule, class, category, etc. [from medieval Latin *subsumere*] □ **subsumption** *n.*

subsurface ● *n.* the stratum or strata below the Earth's surface. ● *adj.* **1** relating to the subsurface. **2** below the ground.

subsystem *n.* a self-contained system within a larger system.

subtenant *n.* a person who leases a property from a tenant. □ **subtenancy** *n.*

subtend *v.tr.* **1** (usu. foll. by *at*) (of a line, arc, figure, etc.) form (an angle) at a particular point when its extremities are joined at that point. **2** (of an angle or chord) have bounding lines or points that meet or coincide with those of (a line or arc). [from Latin *subtendere* 'to stretch under']

subterfuge *n.* **1 a** an attempt to avoid blame or defeat esp. by lying or deceit. **b** a statement etc. resorted to for such a purpose. **2** this as a practice or policy. [based on Latin *subterfugere* 'to escape secretly']

subterranean *adj.* **1** existing, occurring, or done under the Earth's surface. **2** secret, underground, concealed. [from Latin *subterraneus*]

subtext *n.* an underlying theme.

subtitle ● *n.* **1** a secondary or additional title of a book etc. **2** a caption at the bottom of a film etc., esp. translating dialogue. ● *v.tr.* provide with a subtitle or subtitles.

subtle /**sut**-ĕl/ *adj.* (**subtler**, **subtlest**) **1** evasive or mysterious; hard to grasp (*subtle charm*; *a subtle distinction*). **2** (of scent, colour, etc.) faint, delicate, elusive (*subtle perfume*). **3 a** capable of making fine distinctions; perceptive; acute (*subtle intellect*; *subtle senses*). **b** ingenious (*a subtle device*). [from Latin *subtilis*] □ **subtleness** *n.* **subtly** *adv.*

S

subtlety *n.* (*pl.* **-ies**) **1** the quality or state of being subtle. **2** an instance of this; a fine distinction; a subtle argument.

subtopia *n.* *Brit. derog.* unsightly and sprawling suburban development. [blend of SUBURB and UTOPIA] □ **subtopian** *adj.*

subtotal *n.* the total of one part of a group of figures to be added.

subtract *v.tr.* deduct (a part, quantity, or number) from another. [based on Latin *subtractus* 'drawn under'] □ **subtraction** *n.* **subtractive** *adj.*

subtropics *n.pl.* the regions adjacent to the tropics. □ **subtropical** *adj.*

subunit *n.* a distinct component, esp. each of two or more polypeptide chains in a large protein.

suburb *n.* an outlying district of a city. [from Latin *suburbium*]

suburban *adj.* **1** of or characteristic of suburbs. **2** *derog.* provincial, narrow-minded, uncultured, or naive. □ **suburbanite** *n.* **suburbanize** *v.tr.* (also **-ise**). **suburbanization** *n.*

suburbia *n.* often *derog.* the suburbs, their inhabitants, and their way of life.

subvention *n.* a subsidy. [from Late Latin *subventio* 'assistance']

subversive ● *adj.* seeking to subvert (esp. a government). ● *n.* a subversive person. [from medieval Latin *subversivus*] □ **subversion** *n.* **subversively** *adv.* **subversiveness** *n.*

subvert *v.tr.* esp. *Polit.* overturn, overthrow, or upset (religion, government, the monarchy, morality, etc.). [from Latin *subvertere*] □ **subverter** *n.*

subway *n.* **1** *Brit.* **a** a tunnel beneath a road etc. for pedestrians. **b** an underground passage for pipes, cables, etc. **2** esp. *N. Amer.* an underground railway.

subwoofer *n.* a loudspeaker component designed to reproduce very low bass frequencies.

sub-zero *adj.* (esp. of temperature) lower than zero.

succeed *v.* **1** *intr.* **a** have success (*succeeded in his ambition*). **b** (of a plan etc.) be successful. **2 a** *tr.* follow in order; come next after (*night succeeded day*). **b** *intr.* (foll. by *to*) come next, be subsequent. **3** *intr.* (often foll. by *to*) become the rightful or subsequent holder of an inheritance, office, title, property, etc. (*succeeded to the throne*). **4** *tr.* take over an office, throne, inheritance, etc. from (*succeeded his father*; *succeeded the manager*). [from Latin *succedere* 'to come after']

success *n.* **1** the accomplishment of an aim; a favourable outcome (*their efforts met with success*). **2** the attainment of wealth, fame, or position (*spoilt by success*). **3** a thing or person that turns out well. [from Latin *successus* 'advance, happy outcome']

successful *adj.* **1** having or resulting in success. **2** prosperous; having wealth or status. □ **successfully** *adv.* **successfulness** *n.*

succession *n.* **1 a** the process of following in order; succeeding. **b** a series of things or people in succession. **2 a** the right of succeeding to an office, inheritance, the throne, etc. **b** the act or process of so succeeding. **c** those having such a right. **3** *Ecol.* the process by which each of a series of plant or animal communities gives way to the next until a stable climax community is reached. □ **in succession** one after another. **in succession to** as the successor of. [from Latin *successio*] □ **successional** *adj.*

successive *adj.* following one after another; consecutive. □ **successively** *adv.*

successor *n.* a person or thing that succeeds another.

succinct /sŭk-**sinkt**/ *adj.* briefly expressed; terse, concise. [from Latin *succinctus* 'tucked up'] □ **succinctly** *adv.* **succinctness** *n.*

succor *US* var. of SUCCOUR.

succotash *n.* *US* a dish of green maize and beans boiled together. [from Algonquian *msiquatash*]

Succoth *n.* the Jewish autumn thanksgiving festival commemorating the sheltering of the Israelites in the wilderness. [from Hebrew *sukkôt* 'thickets']

succour /**suk**-er/ (*US* **succor**) ● *n.* aid; assistance, esp. in time of need. ● *v.tr.* assist or aid (esp. a person in danger or distress). [from Latin *succurrere*]

succulent ● *adj.* **1** juicy; palatable. **2** *colloq.* desirable. **3** *Bot.* (of a plant, its leaves, or stems) thick and fleshy. ● *n.* *Bot.* ► a succulent plant. [based on Latin *succus* 'juice'] □ **succulence** *n.* **succulently** *adv.*

succumb *v.intr.* (usu. foll. by *to*) **1** be forced to give way; be overcome (*succumbed to temptation*). **2** be overcome by death (*succumbed to his injuries*). [from Latin *succumbere* 'to lie below']

succussion *n.* vigorous shaking, esp. in the preparation of a homoeopathic remedy. [from Latin *succussio*] □ **succuss** *v.tr.*

such ● *predet.* **1** (often foll. by *as*) of the kind or degree in question or under consideration (*such a person*; *such people*). **2** (usu. foll. by *as to* + infin. or *that* + clause) so great; in such high degree (*not such a fool as to believe them*; *had such a fright that he fainted*). **3** of a more than normal kind or degree (*we had such an enjoyable evening*; *such horrid language*). **4** of the kind or degree already indicated, or implied by the context (*there are no such things*). ● *pron.* **1** the thing or action in question or referred to (*such were his words*; *such was not my intention*). **2 a** *Commerce* or *colloq.* the aforesaid thing or things (*those without tickets should purchase such*). **b** similar things; suchlike (*brought sandwiches and such*). □ **as such** as being what has been indicated or named (*a stranger is welcomed as such*; *there is no theatre as such*). **such-and-such** *adj.* of a particular kind but not needing to be specified. ● *n.* a person or thing of this kind. **such-and-such a person** someone; so-and-so. **such as 1** for example (*insects, such as moths and bees*). **2** of a kind that (*a person such as we all admire*). **3** those who (*such as don't need help*). **such as it is** despite its shortcomings (*you are welcome to it, such as it is*). **such a one 1** (usu. foll. by *as*) such a person or such a thing. **2** *archaic* some person or thing unspecified. [Old English]

■ **Usage** See Usage Note at LIKE[1].

suchlike (usu. prec. by *and*) ● *pron.* things, people, etc., of such a kind (*ghosts and suchlike*). ● *det.* of such a kind (*shopping and suchlike chores*).

suck ● *v.* **1** *tr.* draw (a fluid) into the mouth by contracting the lip muscles etc. to make a partial vacuum. **2** *tr.* (also *absol.*) **a** draw milk or other fluid from or through (the breast etc. or a container). **b** extract juice from (a fruit) by sucking. **3** *tr.* **a** draw sustenance, knowledge, or advantage from (a book etc.). **b** imbibe or gain (knowledge, advantage, etc.) as if by sucking. **4** *tr.* roll the tongue round (a sweet, teeth, one's thumb, etc.). **5** *intr.* make a sucking action or sound (*sucking at his pipe*). **6** *intr.* *N. Amer. slang* be very bad, disagreeable, or disgusting. ● *n.* **1** the act or an instance of sucking. **2** (in *pl.*; esp. as *int.*) *Brit. colloq.* **a** an expression of disappointment. **b** an expression of derision or amusement at another's discomfiture. □ **give suck** *archaic* (of a mother, dam, etc.) suckle. **suck dry 1** exhaust the contents of by sucking. **2** exhaust (a person's sympathy, resources, etc.) as if by sucking. **suck in 1** absorb. **2** involve (a person) in an activity etc., esp. against his or her will. **suck up 1** (often foll. by *to*) *colloq.* behave obsequiously esp. for one's own advantage. **2** absorb. [Old English]

sucker ● *n.* **1 a** a person or thing that sucks. **b** a sucking pig, newborn whale, etc. **2** *colloq.* **a** a gullible person. **b** (foll. by *for*) a person especially susceptible to. **3** esp. *US colloq. euphem.* a thing not specified by name (*I can't mend the sucker!*). **4 a** a rubber cup etc. that adheres by suction. **b** an organ enabling an organism to cling by suction. ▷ OCTOPUS. **5** *Bot.* a shoot springing from the rooted part of a stem, from the root at a distance from the main stem, from an axil, or occasionally from a branch. **6** *N. Amer. colloq.* a lollipop. ● *v.* **1** *Bot.* **a** *tr.* remove suckers from. **b** *intr.* produce suckers. **2** *tr.* esp. *N. Amer. colloq.* fool, trick.

sucking *adj.* not yet weaned.

suckle *v.* **1** *tr.* **a** feed (young) from the breast or udder. **b** nourish (*suckled his talent*). **2** *intr.* feed by sucking the breast etc. [Middle English] □ **suckler** *n.*

suckling *n.* an unweaned child or animal.

sucrose /**s'yook**-rohz/ *n.* *Chem.* common sugar, a disaccharide of glucose and fructose units obtained from sugar cane, sugar beet, etc. [based on French *sucre* 'sugar']

suction *n.* **1** the act or an instance of sucking. **2 a** the production of a partial vacuum by the removal of air etc. in order to force in liquid etc. or procure adhesion. **b** the force produced by this process (*suction keeps the lid on*). [from Late Latin *suctio*]

suction pump *n.* a pump for drawing liquid through a pipe into a chamber emptied by a piston.

Sudanese ● *adj.* of or relating to Sudan, a republic in NE Africa, or the Sudan region south of the Sahara. ● *n.* (*pl.* same) **1** a native, national, or inhabitant of Sudan. **2** a person of Sudanese descent.

sudden *adj.* occurring or done unexpectedly or without warning; abrupt, hurried, hasty (*a sudden storm*; *a sudden departure*). □ **all of a sudden**

SUCCULENT

Succulents live in harsh environments,
usually where water is scarce. Their
distinctive appearance is due to fleshy
water-storing tissue, which expands
when moisture is plentiful and contracts
during droughts. Succulents generally
show one of two growth forms. In
leaf succulents, the leaves act as
water-storage organs, and are small
but plump. In stem succulents, the
stem is swollen and the leaves are
reduced or absent. Most cacti are
stem succulents.

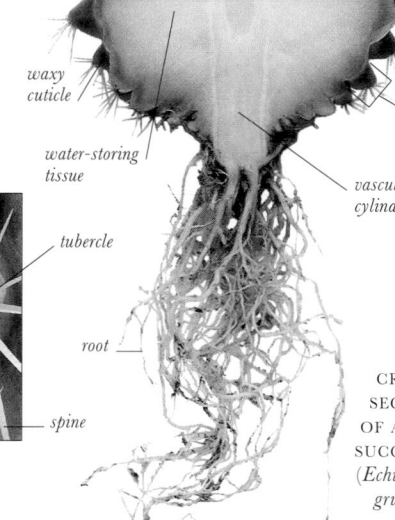

trichome
(hair)

spine

areole

waxy
cuticle

tubercle

water-storing
tissue

vascular
cylinder

tubercle

root

spine

CROSS-
SECTION
OF A STEM
SUCCULENT
(*Echinocactus
grusonii*)

areole

STEM SURFACE ENLARGED

EXAMPLES OF OTHER SUCCULENTS

LEAF SUCCULENTS

HAWORTHIA
(*Haworthia coarctata*)

COCOON PLANT
(*Senecio haworthii*)

LIVING STONE
(*Lithops salicola*)

STEM SUCCULENTS

BASKETBALL EUPHORBIA
(*Euphorbia obesa*)

CLARET CUP CACTUS
(*Echinocereus triglochidiatus*)

Rebutia canigueralii

---

suddenly. [from Latin *subitus*] □ **suddenly** *adv.*
suddenness *n.*

sudden death *n. colloq.* a means of deciding the
winner in a tied game etc., by allowing a further
period of play until one side scores.

sudden infant death syndrome *n. Med.* = COT
DEATH.

sudorific ● *adj.* causing sweating. ● *n.* a sudorific
drug. [based on Latin *sudor* 'sweat']

suds ● *n.pl.* **1** froth of soap and water. **2** *N. Amer.
colloq.* beer. ● *v.* **1** *intr.* form suds. **2** *tr.* lather, cover, or
wash in soapy water. [originally in sense 'fen
waters'] □ **sudsy** *adj.*

sue *v.* (**sues**, **sued**, **suing**) **1** *tr.* (also *absol.*) *Law* institute legal proceedings against (a person). **2** *intr. Law*
make application to a law court for redress. **3** *intr.*
make entreaty to a person for a favour. [based on
Latin *sequi* 'to follow']

suede /swayd/ *n.* (often *attrib.*) **1** leather with the
flesh side rubbed to make a velvety nap. **2** (also
suede-cloth) a woven fabric resembling suede.
[from French *(gants de) Suède* '(gloves of) Sweden']

suet *n.* the hard white fat on the kidneys or loins of
oxen, sheep, etc., used to make dough etc. [based
on Latin *sebum* 'tallow'] □ **suety** *adj.*

suet pudding *n.* a pudding of suet etc., usu. boiled
or steamed.

suffer *v.* **1** *intr.* undergo pain, grief, damage, etc.
(*suffers acutely*; *your reputation will suffer*; *suffers from
neglect*). **2** *tr.* undergo, experience, or be subjected to
(pain, loss, grief, defeat, change, etc.) (*suffered banishment*). **3** *tr.* tolerate (*does not suffer fools gladly*). **4** *intr.
archaic* or *literary* undergo martyrdom. **5** *tr.* (foll. by *to*
+ infin.) *archaic* allow. [from Latin *sufferre* 'to bear']
□ **sufferer** *n.* **suffering** *n.*

sufferance *n.* tacit consent. □ **on sufferance** with
toleration implied by lack of consent or objection.
[from Old French *suffraunce*, related to SUFFER]

suffice *v.* **1** *intr.* be enough or adequate (*that will
suffice for our purpose*; *suffices to prove it*). **2** *tr.* satisfy (*six
sufficed him*). □ **suffice it to say** I shall content
myself with saying. [from Latin *sufficere* 'to supply']

sufficiency *n.* (*pl.* **-ies**) an adequate amount or
adequate resources.

sufficient *adj. & det.* good enough, large enough, or
powerful enough; adequate, enough (*sufficient food to
feed her family*; *sufficient reason for action*). [from Latin
sufficient- 'supplying'] □ **sufficiently** *adv.*

suffix ● *n.* **1** a verbal element added at the end of a
word to form a derivative (e.g. *-fy*, *-ing*, *-itis*). **2** *Math.*
= SUBSCRIPT. ● *v.tr.* append, esp. as a suffix. [from
Latin *suffixum* '(thing) fastened beneath'] □ **suffix-
ation** *n.*

suffocate *v.* **1** *tr.* choke or kill by stopping breathing.
2 *tr.* (often foll. by *by*, *with*) produce a choking or
breathless sensation in. **3** *intr.* be or feel suffocated
or breathless. [based on Latin *suffocatus* 'narrowed
up'] □ **suffocating** *adj.* **suffocatingly** *adv.* **suffocation** *n.*

suffragan *n.* (in full **suffragan bishop** or **bishop
suffragan**) **1** a bishop appointed to help a diocesan bishop in the administration of a diocese. **2** a
bishop in relation to his archbishop or metropolitan. [from Old French]

suffrage *n.* the right of voting in political elections
(*full adult suffrage*). [from Latin *suffragium*]

suffragette *n. hist.* a woman seeking the right to
vote through organized protest.

suffragist *n.* esp. *hist.* a person who advocates the
extension of the suffrage, esp. to women. □ **suf-
fragism** *n.*

suffuse *v.tr.* **1** (of colour, moisture, etc.) spread from
within to colour or moisten (*a blush suffused her cheeks*).
2 cover with colour etc. [based on Latin *suffusus*
'poured underneath or upon'] □ **suffusion** *n.*

Sufi *n.* (*pl.* **Sufis**) a Muslim mystic. [from Arabic
ṣūfī] □ **Sufic** *adj.* **Sufism** *n.*

sug *v.tr.* (**sugged**, **sugging**) *slang* (attempt to) sell (a
person) a product under the guise of conducting

S

market research. [acronym from *sell* *u*nder the *g*uise]

sugar ● *n.* **1** a sweet crystalline substance obtained from various plants, esp. the sugar cane and sugar beet, used in cookery, confectionery, brewing, etc.; sucrose. **2** *Chem.* any of a group of soluble usu. sweet-tasting crystalline carbohydrates found especially in plants, e.g. glucose. **3** esp. *US colloq.* darling, dear (used as a term of address). **4** sweet words; flattery. **5** anything comparable to sugar encasing a pill in reconciling a person to what is unpalatable. ● *v.tr.* **1** sweeten with sugar. **2** make (one's words, meaning, etc.) more pleasant or welcome. **3** coat with sugar (*sugared almond*). **4** spread a sugar mixture on (a tree) to catch moths. □ **sugar the pill** see PILL. [from Italian *zucchero*] □ **sugarless** *adj.*

sugar beet *n.* a beet, *Beta vulgaris*, from which sugar is extracted.

sugar-candy see CANDY *n.* 1.

sugar cane *n.* ◄ any perennial tropical grass of the genus *Saccharum*, esp. *S. officinarum*, with tall stout jointed stems from which sugar is made.

sugar-coated *adj.* **1** (of food) enclosed in sugar. **2** made superficially attractive. **3** excessively sentimental.

sugar daddy *n.* (*pl.* **-ies**) *slang* an elderly man who lavishes gifts etc. on a young woman.

sugar loaf *n.* a conical moulded mass of sugar.

SUGAR CANE
(*Saccharum
officinarum*)

sugar maple *n.* ► a N. American maple, *Acer saccharum*, from the sap of which maple sugar and maple syrup are made.

sugar snap *n.* (also **sugar pea**) (in full **sugar snap pea**) = MANGETOUT.

sugar soap *n. Brit.* an alkaline preparation used for cleaning or removing paint.

sugary *adj.* **1** containing or resembling sugar. **2** excessively sweet or sentimental. **3** falsely sweet or pleasant (*sugary compliments*). □ **sugariness** *n.*

suggest *v.tr.* **1** (often foll. by *that* + clause) propose (a theory, plan, or hypothesis) (*suggested to them that they should wait*; *suggested a different plan*). **2 a** cause (an idea, memory, association, etc.) to present itself; evoke (*this poem suggests peace*). **b** hint at (*his behaviour suggests guilt*). □ **suggest itself** (of an idea etc.) come into the mind. [based on Latin *suggestus* 'suggested, brought up']

suggestible *adj.* **1** capable of being suggested. **2** open to suggestion; easily swayed. □ **suggestibility** *n.*

suggestion *n.* **1** the act or an instance of suggesting; the state of being suggested. **2** a theory, plan, etc., suggested (*made a helpful suggestion*). **3** a slight trace; a hint (*a suggestion of garlic*). **4** *Psychol.* **a** the insinuation of a belief etc. into the mind. **b** such a belief etc.

suggestive *adj.* **1** (usu. foll. by *of*) conveying a suggestion; evocative. **2** (esp. of a remark, joke, etc.) indecent or improper by suggestion. □ **suggestively** *adv.* **suggestiveness** *n.*

suicidal *adj.* **1** inclined to commit suicide. **2** of or concerning suicide. **3** self-destructive; fatally or disastrously rash. □ **suicidally** *adv.*

suicide ● *n.* **1 a** the intentional killing of oneself. **b** a person who commits suicide. **2** a self-destructive action or course (*political suicide*). ● *v.intr.* commit suicide. [based on Latin *sui* 'of oneself' (see -CIDE)]

suicide pact *n.* an agreement between two or more people to commit suicide together.

sui generis /soo-I jen-ĕ-ris/ *adj.* of its own kind; unique.

suit ● *n.* **1 a** ► a set of outer clothes of matching material for men, consisting usu. of a jacket, trousers, and sometimes a waistcoat. **b** a similar set of clothes for women usu. having a skirt instead of trousers. **c** (esp. in *comb.*) a set of clothes for a special occasion, occupation, etc. (*playsuit*; *swimsuit*). **2** any of the four sets (spades, hearts, diamonds, clubs) into which a pack of cards is divided. **3** (in full **suit at law**) a lawsuit (*criminal suit*). **4 a** a petition esp. to a person in authority. **b** the process of courting a woman (*paid suit to her*). **5** (usu. foll. by *of*) a set of sails, armour, etc. **6** *slang* a person wearing a suit; a business executive. ● *v.tr.* **1** go well with (a person's figure, features, etc.); become. **2** (also *absol.*) meet the demands or requirements of (*does not suit all tastes*). **3** make fitting or appropriate (*suited his style to his audience*). **4** (as **suited** *adj.*) appropriate; well fitted (*not suited to the job*). □ **suit oneself 1** do as one chooses. **2** find something that satisfies one. [from Old French *si(e)ute*]

suitable *adj.* (usu. foll. by *to*, *for*) well fitted for the purpose; appropriate. □ **suitability** *n.* **suitableness** *n.* **suitably** *adv.*

suitcase *n.* a usu. oblong case for carrying clothes etc., having a handle and a flat hinged lid. □ **suitcaseful** *n.* (*pl.* **-fuls**).

suite /sweet/ *n.* **1** a set of things belonging together, esp.: **a** a set of rooms in a hotel etc. **b** a sofa, armchairs, etc., of the same design. **2** *Mus.* **a** a set of instrumental compositions to be played in succession. **b** a set of selected pieces from an opera, etc., to be played as one instrumental work. **3** a set of people in attendance; a retinue. [French]

suiting *n.* cloth used for making suits.

suitor *n.* **1** a man seeking to marry a specified woman; a wooer. **2** a plaintiff or petitioner in a lawsuit. **3** a prospective buyer of a business or corporation; the maker of a takeover bid. [from Latin *secutor* 'follower']

sukiyaki *n.* a Japanese dish of sliced meat fried rapidly with vegetables and sauce. [Japanese]

sulcus *n.* (*pl.* **sulci**) *Anat.* a groove or furrow, esp. on the surface of the brain. [Latin]

sulfa *US* var. of SULPHA.

sulfate etc. *US* var. of SULPHATE etc.

sulfur etc. *US* var. of SULPHUR etc.

sulk ● *v.intr.* indulge in a sulk; be sulky. ● *n.* (also in *pl.*; prec. by *the*) a period of sullen esp. resentful silence or aloofness from others (*having a sulk*; *got the sulks*). □ **sulker** *n.*

sulky ● *adj.* (**sulkier, sulkiest**) sullen, morose, or silent, esp. from resentment or ill temper. ● *n.* (*pl.* **-ies**) a light two-wheeled horse-drawn vehicle for one, esp. used in trotting races. ▷ TROTTING. □ **sulkily** *adv.* **sulkiness** *n.*

sullen ● *adj.* **1** morose, resentful, sulky, unsociable. **2 a** (of a thing) slow-moving. **b** dismal (*a sullen sky*).

● *n.* (in *pl.*, usu. prec. by *the*) *archaic* a sullen frame of mind; depression. [from Anglo-French, based on *sol* 'single'] □ **sullenly** *adv.* **sullenness** *n.*

sully *v.tr.* (**-ies, -ied**) **1** disgrace or tarnish (a person's reputation or character, a victory, etc.). **2** *poet.* dirty; soil.

sulpha *n.* (*US* **sulfa**) any drug derived from sulphanilamide (often *attrib.*: *sulpha drug*).

sulphamic acid *n.* (*US* **sulfamic acid**) a strong acid used in weedkiller, an amide of sulphuric acid. □ **sulphamate** *n.*

sulphate *n.* (*US* **sulfate**) a salt or ester of sulphuric acid. [from French *sulfate*]

sulphide *n.* (*US* **sulfide**) *Chem.* a binary compound of sulphur.

sulphite *n.* (*US* **sulfite**) *Chem.* a salt or ester of sulphurous acid. [from French *sulfite*]

sulphonamide *n.* (*US* **sulfonamide**) a substance derived from an amide of a sulphonic acid, able to prevent the multiplication of some pathogenic bacteria.

sulphur *n.* (*US* **sulfur**) **1 a** ► a pale yellow non-metallic element having crystalline and amorphous forms, burning with a blue flame and a suffocating smell. **b** (*attrib.*) like or containing sulphur. **2** the material of which hellfire and lightning were believed to consist. **3** any yellow butterfly of the family Pieridae. **4** a pale greenish-yellow colour. [from Latin *sulfur, sulp(h)ur*] □ **sulphury** *adj.*

SULPHUR CRYSTALS

sulphur candle *n.* a candle burnt to produce sulphur dioxide for fumigating.

sulphur dioxide *n.* a colourless pungent toxic gas formed by burning sulphur in air and used as a food preservative. ▷ ACID RAIN

sulphureous *adj.* (*US* **sulfureous**) **1** of, like, or suggesting sulphur. **2** sulphur-coloured; yellow.

sulphuric /sul-**fewr**-ik/ *adj.* (*US* **sulfuric**) *Chem.* containing hexavalent sulphur.

sulphuric acid *n.* a dense oily colourless highly acid and corrosive liquid.

sulphurous *adj.* (*US* **sulfurous**) **1** /sul-fer-ŭs/ relating to or suggestive of sulphur, esp. in colour. **2** /sul-**fewr**-ŭs/ *Chem.* containing tetravalent sulphur.

sulphurous acid *n.* an unstable weak acid used as a reducing and bleaching acid.

sultan *n.* a Muslim sovereign. [from Arabic *sulṭān* 'power, ruler'] □ **sultanate** *n.*

sultana *n.* **1 a** a seedless raisin used in puddings, cakes, etc. **b** the small pale yellow grape producing this. **2** the mother, wife, concubine, or daughter of a sultan. [Italian fem. of *sultano* 'sultan']

sultry *adj.* (**sultrier, sultriest**) **1** (of the weather etc.) hot or oppressive; close. **2** (of a person etc.) passionate; sensual. [from obsolete *sulter* 'to swelter'] □ **sultrily** *adv.* **sultriness** *n.*

sum ● *n.* **1** the total amount resulting from the addition of two or more items etc. **2** a particular amount of money. **3 a** an arithmetical problem. **b** (esp. *pl.*) *colloq.* arithmetic work (*good at sums*). ● *v.tr.* (**summed, summing**) find the sum of. □ **in sum** in brief. **sum up 1** (esp. of a judge) recapitulate or review the evidence in a case etc. **2** form or express an idea of the character of (a person etc.). **3** collect into or express as a total or whole. [from Latin *summa* 'main part']

SUGAR MAPLE
(*Acer saccharum*)

SUIT: TWO-PIECE SUIT

silk lining
collar
sleeve
notched lapel
breast pocket
cuff
cuff buttons
three-button front fastening
waistband
hip flap pocket
hemmed trousers

S

SUMAC:
STAG HORN SUMAC
(*Rhus typhina*)
fruit cluster

sumac *n.* (also **sumach**) **1 ▲** any shrub or small tree of the genus *Rhus* or *Cotinus*, having conical clusters of reddish fruit used as a spice in cooking. **2** the dried and ground leaves of *R. coriaria* used in tanning and dyeing. [from Arabic *summāk*]

summarize *v.tr.* (also **-ise**) make or be a summary of; sum up. □ **summarist** *n.* **summarizable** *adj.* **summarization** *n.* **summarizer** *n.*

summary ● *n.* (*pl.* **-ies**) a brief account. ● *adj.* **1** without details or formalities; brief (*a summary account*). **2** *Law* without the customary legal formalities (*summary justice*). [from Latin *summarium*] □ **summarily** *adv.* **summariness** *n.*

summation *n.* **1** the finding of a total. **2** a summing-up. □ **summational** *adj.* **summative** *adj.*

summer ● *n.* **1** the warmest season of the year. ▷ SEASON. **2** *Astron.* the period from the summer solstice to the autumnal equinox. **3** the hot weather typical of summer. **4** (often foll. by *of*) the mature stage of life; the height of achievement etc. **5** (esp. in *pl.*) *poet.* a year (esp. of a person's age) (*a child of ten summers*). **6** (*attrib.*) characteristic of or suitable for summer. ● *v.intr.* (usu. foll. by *at, in*) pass the summer. [Old English] □ **summerless** *adj.* **summery** *adj.*

summer house *n.* a light building in a garden etc. used for sitting in in fine weather.

summer pudding *n. Brit.* a pudding of soft summer fruit encased in bread or sponge.

summer school *n.* **1** esp. *Brit.* a course of lectures etc. held during the summer vacation, esp. at a university. **2** esp. *US* a course of remedial or accelerating classes held in the summer.

summer solstice *n.* the solstice at midsummer, at the time of the longest day.

summertime *n.* the season or period of summer (cf. SUMMER TIME).

summer time *n. Brit.* the period from March to October when clocks are advanced an hour.

summing-up *n.* **1** a review of evidence and a direction given by a judge to a jury. **2** a recapitulation of the main points of an argument, case, etc.

summit *n.* **1** the highest point, esp. of a mountain; the apex. **2** the highest degree of power, ambition, etc. **3** (in full **summit meeting, talks**, etc.) a discussion, esp. on disarmament etc., between heads of government. [from Latin *summum* 'highest (thing)']

summiteer *n.* **1** a participant in a summit meeting. **2** a climber who has completed an ascent to a summit.

summon *v.tr.* **1** call upon to appear, esp. as a defendant or witness in a law court. **2** (usu. foll. by *to* + infin.) call upon (*summoned her to assist*). **3** call together for a meeting or some other purpose. **4** (often foll. by *up* and *to, for*) gather (courage, resources, etc.). [from Latin *summonēre* 'to hint', later 'to call'] □ **summonable** *adj.* **summoner** *n.*

summons ● *n.* (*pl.* **summonses**) **1** an authoritative or urgent call to attend on some occasion or do something. **2 a** a call to appear before a judge or magistrate. **b** the writ containing such a summons. ● *v.tr.* esp. *Law* serve with a summons. [from Old French *somonce*]

sumo *n.* ▶ a style of Japanese heavyweight wrestling, in which a participant is defeated by touching the ground with any part of the body except the soles of the feet or by moving outside the marked area. [Japanese]

SUMO WRESTLERS

SUN

The Sun, a main sequence star, is about five billion years old. Around 1.4 million km (870,000 miles) across, it is composed almost entirely of helium and hydrogen. The Sun's surface, the photosphere, has a temperature of 5,500 °C (9,950 °F). During a solar eclipse, when the Moon obscures the Sun, both the Sun's inner atmosphere (chromosphere) and its outer atmosphere (corona) are visible. The corona extends millions of kilometres into space.

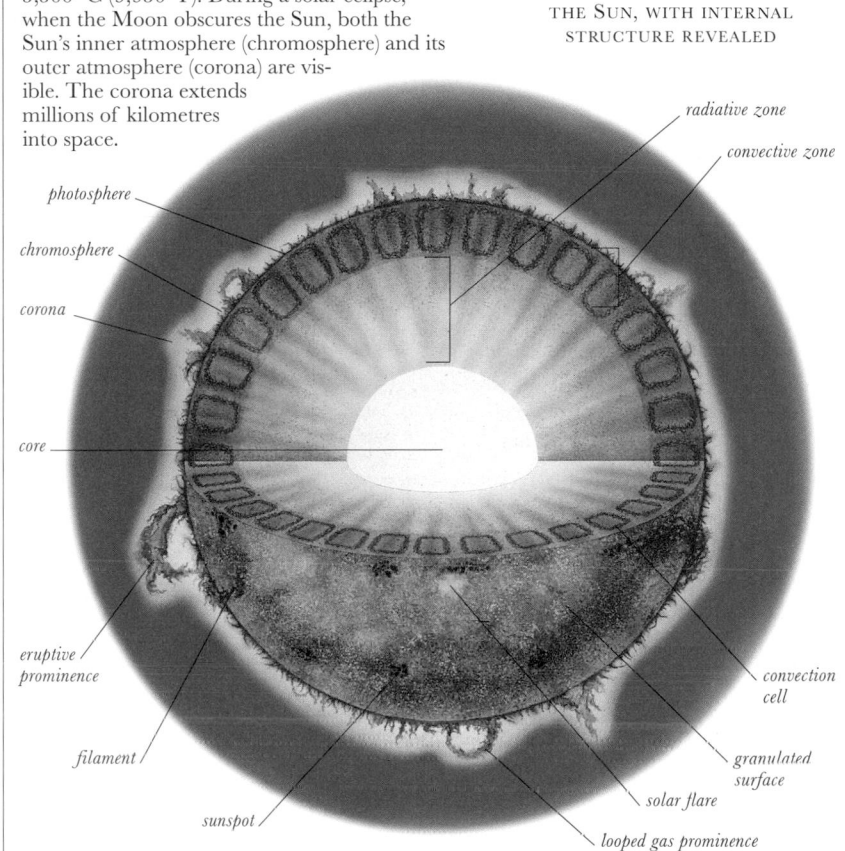

SOLAR SYSTEM *Earth*
Sun

THE SUN, WITH INTERNAL
STRUCTURE REVEALED

radiative zone
convective zone
photosphere
chromosphere
corona
core
eruptive prominence
filament
sunspot
convection cell
granulated surface
solar flare
looped gas prominence

sump *n.* **1** a pit, well, hole, etc., in which superfluous liquid collects in mines, machines, etc. **2** a cesspool. [Middle English in sense 'marsh', from Middle Dutch]

sumptuary *adj.* **1** regulating expenditure. **2** (of a law etc.) limiting private expenditure in the interests of the State. [based on Latin *sumptus* 'cost']

sumptuous *adj.* rich, lavish, costly. [from Latin *sumptuosus*] □ **sumptuosity** *n.* **sumptuously** *adv.* **sumptuousness** *n.*

sum total *n.* = SUM *n.* 1.

Sun. *abbr.* Sunday.

sun ● *n.* **1 a** (also **Sun**) ▲ the star round which the Earth orbits and from which it receives light and warmth. ▷ SOLAR SYSTEM. **b** any similar star in the universe with or without planets. **2** the light or warmth received from the Sun (*keep out the sun*). ● *v.* (**sunned, sunning**) **1** *refl.* bask in the sun. **2** *tr.* expose to the sun. **3** *intr.* sun oneself. □ **beneath** (or **under**) **the sun** anywhere in the world. [Old English] □ **sunless** *adj.* **sunlike** *adj.* **sunward** *adj. & adv.* **sunwards** *adv.*

sun and planet *n.* a system of gearing cogwheels.

sunbathe *v.intr.* bask in the sun, esp. to tan the body. □ **sunbather** *n.*

sunbeam *n.* a ray of sunlight.

sunbed *n. Brit.* **1** a lightweight usu. folding chair with a seat long enough to support the legs, used for sunbathing. **2** a bed for lying on under a sunlamp.

sunbelt *n.* a strip of territory receiving a high amount of sunshine.

sunblind *n. Brit.* a window awning.

sunblock *n.* a cream or lotion for protecting the skin from the sun.

sun-bonnet *n.* a bonnet of cotton etc. covering the neck and shading the face, esp. for children.

sunburn ● *n.* reddening and inflammation of the skin caused by over-exposure to the sun. ● *v.intr.* **1** suffer from sunburn. **2** (as **sunburnt** or **sunburned** *adj.*) suffering from sunburn; brown or tanned.

sunburst *n.* **1** something resembling the Sun and its rays, esp.: **a** ▶ an ornament, brooch, etc. **b** a firework. **2** the sun shining suddenly from behind clouds.

SUNBURST: SYMBOL
OF THE RISEN
CHRIST, SIENA
CATHEDRAL, ITALY

S

833

sun cream *n.* cream for protecting the skin from sunburn and for promoting suntanning.

sundae /**sun**-day/ *n.* a dish of ice cream with fruit, nuts, syrup, etc.

Sunday ● *n.* **1** the first day of the week, a Christian holiday and day of worship. **2** a newspaper published on a Sunday. ● *adv. colloq.* **1** on Sunday. **2** (**Sundays**) on Sundays; each Sunday. [Old English]

Sunday best *n.* often *joc.* a person's best clothes, kept for Sunday use.

Sunday driver *n.* a person who drives chiefly at weekends, esp. slowly or unskilfully.

Sunday letter *n.* = DOMINICAL LETTER.

Sunday school *n.* a school for the religious instruction of children on Sundays.

sun deck *n.* **1** the upper deck of a steamer. **2** *N. Amer.* a terrace or balcony positioned to catch the sun.

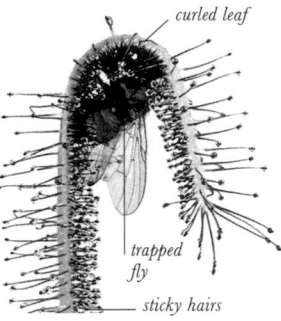

curled leaf

trapped fly

sticky hairs

SUNDEW: FLY CAPTURED IN SUNDEW LEAF (*Drosera* species)

sunder *v.tr. & intr. archaic* or *literary* separate, sever. □ **in sunder** apart. [Old English]

sundew *n.* ◀ any small insect-consuming bog plant of the family Droseraceae, esp. of the genus *Drosera*, with hairs secreting drops of moisture.

sundial *n.* ▼ an instrument showing the time by the shadow of a pointer cast by the Sun on to a graduated plate.

sundown *n.* sunset.

sundress *n.* a dress without sleeves and with a low neck.

sun-dried *adj.* dried by the sun, not by artificial heat.

sundry ● *adj.* various; several (*sundry items*). ● *n.* (*pl.* **-ies**) **1** (in *pl.*) items or oddments not mentioned individually. **2** *Austral. Cricket* = EXTRA *n.* **5**. [Old English *syndrig* 'separate']

sunflower *n.* ▼ any very tall plant of the genus *Helianthus*, esp. *H. annuus* with very large showy golden-rayed flowers, grown also for its seeds which yield an edible oil.

sung *past part.* of SING.

sunglasses *n.pl.* glasses tinted to protect the eyes from sunlight or glare.

sun-god *n.* the Sun worshipped as a deity.

sunhat *n.* a hat designed to protect the head from the sun.

sun-helmet *n.* a helmet of cork etc. formerly worn by white people in the tropics.

SUNFLOWER (*Helianthus annuus*)

sunk *past* and *past part.* of SINK.

sunken *adj.* **1** that has been sunk. **2** beneath the surface; submerged. **3** (of the eyes etc.) hollow, depressed.

sun-kissed *adj.* warmed or affected by the sun.

sunlamp *n.* **1** a lamp giving ultraviolet rays for an artificial suntan, therapy, etc. **2** *Cinematog.* a large lamp with a parabolic reflector used in film-making.

sunlight *n.* light from the Sun. □ **sunlit** *adj.*

sun lounge *n. Brit.* a room with large windows, designed to receive sunlight.

sunlounger *n. Brit.* = SUNBED 1.

Sunna *n.* a traditional portion of Muslim law based on Muhammad's words or acts, accepted (together with the Koran) as authoritative by Muslims. [Arabic, literally 'form, course, rule']

Sunni ● *n.* (*pl.* same or **Sunnis**) **1** one of the two main branches of Islam, commonly described as orthodox, and differing from the Shia in its understanding of the Sunna. **2** an adherent of this branch of Islam. ● *adj.* of or relating to Sunni.

sunny *adj.* (**sunnier, sunniest**) **1 a** bright with sunlight. **b** exposed to or warmed by the sun. **2** cheery in temperament. □ **sunnily** *adv.* **sunniness** *n.*

sunrise *n.* **1** the Sun's rising at dawn. **2** the coloured sky associated with this. **3** the time at which sunrise occurs.

sunrise industry *n.* any newly established industry regarded as signalling prosperity.

sunroof *n.* a hinged or sliding panel in the roof of a car.

sunroom *n.* **1** = SUN LOUNGE. **2** esp. *N. Amer.* a solarium.

sunscreen *n.* a cream or lotion rubbed on to the skin to protect it from the sun.

sunset *n.* **1** the Sun's setting in the evening. **2** the coloured sky associated with this. **3** the time at which sunset occurs.

sunshade *n.* **1** a parasol. **2** an awning.

sunshine *n.* **1 a** the light of the Sun. **b** an area lit by the Sun. **2** fine weather. **3** cheerfulness; joy. □ **sunshiny** *adj.*

sunshine roof *n. Brit.* = SUNROOF.

sunspot *n.* one of the dark patches observed on the Sun's surface. ▷ SUN

gnomon

12 midday

hour mark

shadow marks the time

SUNDIAL

sunstroke *n.* acute prostration or collapse from the excessive heat of the sun.

suntan ● *n.* the brownish colouring of skin caused by exposure to the sun. ● *v.intr.* (**-tanned, -tanning**) colour the skin with a suntan.

suntrap *n. Brit.* a place sheltered from the wind and suitable for catching the sunshine.

sunup *n.* esp. *N. Amer.* sunrise.

sup[1] ● *v.tr.* (**supped, supping**) **1** take (soup, tea, etc.) by sips or spoonfuls. **2** esp. *N.Engl. colloq.* drink (alcohol). ● *n.* a sip of liquid. [Old English]

sup[2] *v.intr.* (**supped, supping**) (usu. foll. by *off, on*) *archaic* take supper. [from Old French *super*]

super ● *adj.* (also **super-duper**) (also as *int.*) *colloq.* exceptional; splendid. ● *n. colloq.* **1** *Theatr.* a supernumerary actor. **2** a superintendent.

super- *comb. form* forming nouns, adjectives, and verbs, meaning: **1** above, beyond, or over (*superstructure; superimpose*). **2** to a great or extreme degree (*superabundant*). **3** extra good or large of its kind (*supertanker*). **4** of a higher kind (*superclass*). [from Latin *super* 'above, beyond']

superable *adj.* able to be overcome. [from Latin *superabilis*]

superabundant *adj.* abounding beyond what is normal or right. [from Late Latin *superabundant-* 'being too abundant'] □ **superabundance** *n.* **superabundantly** *adv.*

superannuate *v.tr.* **1** retire (a person) with a pension. **2** dismiss or discard as too old. **3** (as **superannuated** *adj.*) too old for work or use. **4 a** make (a post) pensionable. **b** make pensionable the post of (an employee). [based on medieval Latin *superannuatus* 'more than a year old'] □ **superannuable** *adj.*

superannuation *n.* **1** a pension paid to a retired person. **2** a regular payment made towards this by an employed person. **3** the process or an instance of superannuating.

superb *adj.* **1** of the most impressive, splendid, etc., kind. **2** excellent; fine. [from Latin *superbus* 'proud'] □ **superbly** *adv.* **superbness** *n.*

supercargo *n.* (*pl.* **-oes** or **-os**) an officer in a merchant ship managing sales etc. of cargo. [from Spanish *sobrecargo*]

supercede var. of SUPERSEDE.

supercharge *v.tr.* **1** (usu. foll. by *with*) charge (the atmosphere etc.) with energy, emotion, etc. **2** use a supercharger on.

supercharger *n.* a device supplying air or fuel to an internal-combustion engine at above normal pressure to increase efficiency. ▷ TURBOCHARGER

supercilious *adj.* assuming an air of contemptuous indifference or superiority. [from Latin *superciliosus*] □ **superciliously** *adv.* **superciliousness** *n.*

superclass *n.* a taxonomic category between class and phylum.

supercomputer *n.* an exceptionally powerful mainframe computer capable of dealing with complex problems. □ **supercomputing** *n.*

superconductivity *n. Physics* ▶ the property of zero electrical resistance in some substances at very low absolute temperatures. □ **superconducting** *adj.* **superconductive** *adj.*

superconductor *n. Physics* a substance having superconductivity. ▷ SUPERCONDUCTIVITY

supercool ● *v. Chem.* **1** *tr.* cool (a liquid) below its freezing point without solidification or crystallization. **2** *intr.* (of a liquid) be cooled in this way. ▷ MATTER. ● *adj. slang* very cool, relaxed, etc.

super-duper var. of SUPER *adj.*

superego *n.* (*pl.* **-os**) *Psychol.* the part of the mind that acts as a conscience and responds to social rules.

supererogation *n.* the performance of more than duty requires. [from Late Latin *supererogatio*] □ **supererogatory** *adj.*

superfamily *n.* (*pl.* **-ies**) a taxonomic category between family and order.

superficial *adj.* **1** of or on the surface; lacking depth. **2** swift or cursory. **3** apparent but not real (*a superficial resemblance*). **4** (esp. of a person) having no depth of character or knowledge. [from Late Latin *superficialis*] □ **superficiality** *n.* (*pl.* **-ies**). **superficially** *adv.*

superficies *n.* (*pl.* same) *Geom.* a surface. [Latin]

superfine *adj.* **1** *Commerce* of extra quality. **2** pretending great refinement. [from medieval Latin *superfinus*]

superfluidity *n.* the property of flowing without friction or viscosity, as in liquid helium below about 2.18 kelvins. □ **superfluid** *n. & adj.*

superfluity *n.* (*pl.* **-ies**) **1** the state of being superfluous. **2** a superfluous amount or thing.

superfluous /soo-**per**-floo-ŭs/ *adj.* more than enough, redundant, needless. [from Latin *superfluus*] □ **superfluously** *adv.* **superfluousness** *n.*

supergiant *n.* a star of very great luminosity and size.

superglue ● *n.* any of various adhesives with an exceptional bonding capability. ● *v.tr.* (**-glues, -glued, -gluing** or **-glueing**) stick with superglue.

supergrass *n. Brit. colloq.* a police informer who implicates a large number of people.

superheat *v.tr. Physics* **1** heat (a liquid) above its boiling point without vaporization. **2** heat (a vapour) above its boiling point. □ **superheater** *n.*

superhero *n.* (*pl.* **-oes**) a person or fictional character with extraordinary heroic attributes.

superhighway *n.* **1** *N. Amer.* a dual carriageway with two or more lanes in each direction. **2** (in full **information superhighway**) a means of rapid transfer of information in different digital forms (e.g. video, sound, and graphics) via an extensive electronic network.

S

SUPERCONDUCTIVITY

A metal cooled to just above absolute zero (−273.15 °C, −459.67 °F) loses its electrical resistance and therefore carries current more efficiently. Materials cooled in this way are called superconductors, and are used in electrical cables and scientific equipment.

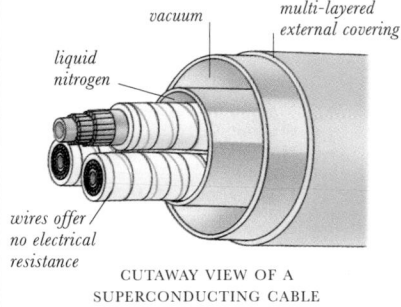

vacuum

multi-layered external covering

liquid nitrogen

wires offer no electrical resistance

CUTAWAY VIEW OF A SUPERCONDUCTING CABLE

superhuman adj. **1** beyond normal human capability. **2** higher than man. [from Late Latin *superhumanus*] □ **superhumanly** adv.

superimpose v.tr. (usu. foll. by on) lay (a thing) on something else. □ **superimposition** n.

superintend v.tr. & intr. supervise and inspect. [from ecclesiastical Latin *superintendere*] □ **superintendence** n. **superintendency** n.

superintendent ● n. **1 a** a person who superintends. **b** a director of an institution etc. **2 a** (in the UK) a police officer above the rank of inspector. **b** (in the US) a high-ranking official, often the chief of a police department. **3** *US* the caretaker of a building. ● adj. superintending.

superior ● adj. **1** in a higher position; of higher rank. **2 a** above average in quality etc. (*superior leather*) **b** supercilious (*superior air*). **3** (often foll. by *to*) **a** better or greater in some respect. **b** above yielding, making concessions, etc. (*superior to bribery*). **4** *Printing* (of figures or letters) placed above the line. ● n. **1** a person superior to another in rank, character, etc. **2** (*fem.* **superioress**) *Eccl.* the head of a monastery or other religious institution (*Mother Superior; Father Superior*). **3** *Printing* a superior letter or figure. [Latin, literally 'higher'] □ **superiorly** adv.

superiority n. the state of being superior.

superiority complex n. *Psychol.* an undue conviction of one's own superiority to others.

superlative /soo-per-la-tiv/ ● adj. **1** of the highest quality or degree (*superlative wisdom*). **2** *Gram.* (of an adjective or adverb) expressing the highest or a very high degree of a quality (e.g. *bravest, most fiercely*). ● n. **1** *Gram.* **a** the superlative expression or form of an adjective or adverb. **b** a word in the superlative. **2** something embodying excellence. **3** (usu. in *pl.*) a hyperbolical expression, esp. of praise. [from Late Latin *superlativus* 'exaggerated'] □ **superlatively** adv. **superlativeness** n.

superlunary adj. **1** situated beyond the Moon. **2** celestial. [from medieval Latin *superlunaris*]

superman n. (*pl.* **-men**) **1** esp. *Philos.* the ideal superior man of the future. **2** *colloq.* a man of exceptional strength or ability.

supermarket n. a large self-service store selling foods, household goods, etc.

supermodel n. a highly-paid model employed in high-profile glamour modelling.

supernatural ● adj. attributed to or thought to reveal some force above the laws of nature; magical, occult, mystical. ● n. (prec. by *the*) supernatural forces, effects, etc. □ **supernaturalism** n. **supernaturally** adv. **supernaturalness** n.

supernormal adj. beyond what is normal or natural. □ **supernormality** n.

supernova n. (*pl.* **-novae** /-vee/ or **-novas**) *Astron.* a star that suddenly increases very greatly in brightness because of an explosion ejecting most of its mass. ▷ STAR

supernumerary ● adj. **1** in excess of the normal number; extra. **2** engaged for extra work. **3** (of an actor) appearing on stage but not speaking. ● n. (*pl.* **-ies**) **1** a supernumerary person or thing. **2** a person engaged for extra work. [from Late Latin *supernumerarius* '(soldier) added to a legion already complete']

superorder n. *Biol.* a taxonomic category between order and class.

superphosphate n. a fertilizer made by treating phosphate rock with sulphuric or phosphoric acid.

superpower n. a state of supreme power and influence, esp. the US and, formerly, the USSR.

supersaturate v.tr. add to (esp. a solution) beyond saturation point. □ **supersaturation** n.

superscribe v.tr. **1** write (an inscription) at the top of or on the outside of a document etc. **2** write an inscription over or on (a thing). [from Latin *superscribere*] □ **superscription** n.

superscript ● adj. written or printed above. ● n. a superscript number or symbol. [from Latin *superscriptus*]

supersede v.tr. (also *disp.* **supercede**) **1 a** adopt or appoint another person or thing in place of. **b** set aside; cease to employ. **2** (of a person or thing) take the place of. [from Latin *supersedēre* 'to be superior to'] □ **supersession** n.

supersonic adj. designating or having a speed greater than that of sound. □ **supersonically** adv.

supersonics n.pl. (treated as *sing.*) = ULTRASONICS.

superstar n. an extremely famous or renowned actor, musician, etc. □ **superstardom** n.

superstate n. a powerful political state, esp. one formed from a federation of nations.

superstition n. **1** credulity regarding the supernatural. **2** an irrational fear of the unknown. **3** misdirected reverence. **4** a practice, opinion, or religion based on these tendencies. **5** a widely held but unjustified idea. [from Latin *superstitio*] □ **superstitious** adj. **superstitiously** adv. **superstitiousness** n.

superstore n. a large supermarket selling a wide range of goods.

superstructure n. **1** the part of a building above its foundations. **2** a structure built on top of something else. **3** a concept or idea based on others. □ **superstructural** adj.

supertanker n. a very large tanker ship.

supertax n. a higher rate of tax on incomes above a certain level.

supervene v.intr. occur as an interruption or a change. [from Latin *supervenire* 'to come on top of'] □ **supervenient** adj. **supervention** n.

supervise v.tr. superintend, oversee. [based on medieval Latin *supervisus* 'surveyed'] □ **supervision** n. **supervisor** n. **supervisory** adj.

superwoman n. (*pl.* **-women**) *colloq.* a woman of exceptional strength or ability.

supine adj. **1** lying face upwards (cf. PRONE 1a). **2** inert, indolent. [from Latin *supinus* 'turned backward'] □ **supinely** adv. **supineness** n.

supper n. an evening meal, esp. a light or informal one. □ **sing for one's supper** do something in return for a benefit. [from Old French *super*]

supplant v.tr. dispossess and take the place of, esp. by underhand means. [from Latin *supplantare* 'to trip up'] □ **supplanter** n.

supple adj. (**suppler**, **supplest**) flexible, pliant. [from Latin *supplex* 'submissive'] □ **suppleness** n.

supplely var. of SUPPLY[2].

supplement ● n. **1** a thing or part added to remedy deficiencies (*dietary supplement*). **2** a part added to a book etc. to provide further information. **3** a separate section, esp. a colour magazine, added to a newspaper etc. **4** an additional charge payable.

● v.tr. provide a supplement for. [from Latin *supplementum*] □ **supplemental** adj. **supplementally** adv. **supplementation** n.

supplementary adj. forming or serving as a supplement; additional. □ **supplementarily** adv.

supplementary benefit n. *hist.* (in the UK) a weekly allowance formerly paid by the state to those with an income below a certain level, now replaced by INCOME SUPPORT.

suppliant /sup-li-ănt/ ● adj. **1** supplicating. **2** expressing supplication. ● n. a supplicating person. [French, literally 'beseeching'] □ **suppliantly** adv.

supplicate v. *formal* **1** tr. petition humbly to (a person) or for (a thing). **2** intr. (foll. by *to, for*) make a petition. [based on Latin *supplicatus* 'beseeched'] □ **supplicant** adj. & n. **supplication** n. **supplicatory** adj.

supply[1] ● v.tr. (**-ies, -ied**) **1** provide or furnish (a thing needed). **2** (often foll. by *with*) provide (a person etc. with a thing needed). **3** meet or make up for (a deficiency, need, etc.). **4** fill (a vacancy etc.) as a substitute. ● n. (*pl.* **-ies**) **1** the act or an instance of providing what is needed. **2** a stock, amount, etc., of something provided or obtainable. **3** (in *pl.*) the provisions and equipment for an army, expedition, etc. **4** (often *attrib.*) a person, e.g. a schoolteacher, acting as a temporary substitute for another. □ **in short supply** scarce. [from Latin *supplēre* 'to fill up'] □ **supplier** n.

supply[2] adv. (also **supplely**) in a supple manner.

supply and demand n. *Econ.* the amount or quantity of a product available and required, as factors regulating its price.

supply-side n. *Econ.* denoting a policy of low taxation and other incentives to produce goods and invest.

support ● v.tr. **1** carry all or part of the weight of. **2** keep from falling or sinking or failing. **3** provide with a home and the necessities of life. **4** enable to last out; give strength to. **5** tend to substantiate or corroborate (a statement, theory, etc.). **6** back up; second. **7** speak in favour of (a resolution etc.). **8** be actively interested in (a particular team or sport). **9** (often as **supporting** adj.) take a part that is secondary to (a principal actor etc.). **10** endure, tolerate (*cannot support the noise*). ● n. **1** the act or an instance of supporting; the process of being supported. **2** a person or thing that supports. **3** a secondary act at a pop concert etc. □ **in support of** in order to support. [from Latin *supportare* 'to convey, carry'] □ **supportable** adj. **supportability** n. **supportably** adv. **supportingly** adv.

supporter n. a person or thing that supports, esp. a person supporting a cause, team, or sport.

supporting film n. a less important film in a cinema programme.

supportive adj. providing support or encouragement. □ **supportively** adv. **supportiveness** n.

suppose v.tr. (often foll. by *that* + clause) **1** assume, esp. in default of knowledge; be inclined to think. **2** take as a possibility or hypothesis (*let us suppose you are right*). **3** (in *imper.*) as a formula of proposal (*suppose we try harder*). **4** (of a theory or result etc.) require as a condition (*design supposes a creator*). **5** in the circumstances that; if (*supposing we stay*). **6** (as **supposed** adj.) generally accepted as being so (*his supposed brother*). **7** (in *passive*; foll. by *to* + infin.) **a** be expected or required (*was supposed to write to you*). **b** (with *neg*) ought not; not be allowed to (*not supposed to smoke*). □ **I suppose so** an expression of hesitant agreement. [from Old French *supposer*] □ **supposable** adj.

supposedly adv. as is generally supposed.

supposition n. **1** a fact or idea etc. supposed. **2** the act or an instance of supposing. □ **suppositional** adj.

suppositious adj. hypothetical, assumed.

supposititious adj. spurious; substituted for the genuine.

suppository n. (*pl.* **-ies**) a medical preparation designed to be inserted into the rectum or vagina to

S

dissolve. ▷ DRUG. [from medieval Latin *suppositorium* '(thing) placed underneath']

suppress *v.tr.* **1** end the activity or existence of, esp. forcibly. **2** prevent (information, feelings, etc.) from being seen, heard, or known. **3 a** partly or wholly eliminate (electrical interference etc.). **b** equip (a device) to reduce such interference due to it. [based on Latin *suppressus* 'pressed down'] □ **suppressible** *adj.* **suppression** *n.* **suppressive** *adj.* **suppressor** *n.*

suppressant *n.* a suppressing or restraining agent, esp. a drug that suppresses the appetite.

suppurate ● *v.intr.* **1** form pus. **2** fester. [based on Latin *pus puris* 'pus'] □ **suppuration** *n.* **suppurative** *adj.*

supra *adv.* above or earlier on (in a book etc.).

supra- *prefix* **1** above. **2** beyond, transcending (*supranational*) (opp. INFRA-). [from Latin *supra* 'above, beyond, before in time']

supranational *adj.* transcending national limits. □ **supranationalism** *n.* **supranationality** *n.*

supremacist ● *n.* an advocate of the supremacy of a particular group. ● *adj.* relating to or advocating such supremacy. □ **supremacism** *n.*

supremacy *n.* the state of being supreme in authority, power, rank, or importance.

supreme *adj.* **1** highest in authority or rank. **2** greatest; most important. **3** (of a penalty or sacrifice etc.) involving death. [from Latin *supremus* 'highest'] □ **supremely** *adv.*

Supreme Being *n.* (prec. by *the*) a name for God.

Supreme Court *n.* the highest judicial court in a country etc., or *US* (often **supreme court**) in a state.

supreme pontiff see PONTIFF.

supremo *n.* (*pl.* **-os**) *Brit.* **1** a supreme leader or ruler. **2** a person in overall charge. [Spanish, literally 'supreme']

surcease *literary* ● *n.* a cessation. ● *v.intr. & tr.* cease. [from Latin *supersedere* 'to supersede']

surcharge ● *n.* **1** an additional charge or payment. **2** a mark printed on a postage stamp changing its value. **3** an additional or excessive load. ● *v.tr.* **1** exact a surcharge from. **2** exact (a sum) as a surcharge. **3** mark (a postage stamp) with a surcharge. **4** overload. **5** fill or saturate to excess.

surcoat *n.* **1** *hist.* a loose robe worn over armour. **2** a similar sleeveless garment worn as part of the insignia of an order of knighthood. **3** *hist.* an outer coat of rich material. [Middle English from Old French *surcot*]

surculose *adj. Bot.* producing suckers. [based on Latin *surculus* 'twig']

surd ● *adj.* **1** *Math.* (of a number) irrational. **2** *Phonet.* (of a sound) uttered with the breath and not the voice (e.g. *f*, *k*, *p*, *s*, *t*). ● *n.* **1** *Math.* a surd number. **2** *Phonet.* a surd sound. [from Latin *surdus* 'deaf, mute']

sure ● *adj.* **1** having or seeming to have adequate reason for a belief or assertion. **2** (often foll. by *of*, or *that* + clause) convinced. **3** (foll. by *of*) confident in anticipation or knowledge of. **4** reliable or unfailing (*a sure way to find out*). **5** (foll. by *to* + infin.) certain. **6** undoubtedly true or truthful. ● *adv. & int. colloq.* certainly. □ **as sure as fate** quite certain. **be sure** (in *imper.* or *infin.*; foll. by *that* + clause or *to* + infin.) take care to; not fail to. **for sure** *colloq.* without doubt. **make sure 1** make or become certain, ensure. **2** (foll. by *of*) establish the truth or ensure the existence or happening of. **sure enough** *colloq.* **1** in fact; certainly. **2** with near certainty. **sure thing** *n. N. Amer. colloq.* a certainty. ● *int.* certainly!, yes, indeed! **to be sure 1** it is undeniable or admitted. **2** it must be admitted. [from Latin *securus* 'secure'] □ **sureness** *n.*

sure-fire *attrib.adj. colloq.* certain to succeed.

sure-footed *adj.* never stumbling or making a mistake. □ **sure-footedly** *adv.* **sure-footedness** *n.*

surely *adv.* **1** with certainty (*the time approaches slowly but surely*). **2** as an appeal to likelihood or reason (*surely that can't be right*). **3** with safety; securely (*the goat plants its feet surely*).

surety /**shoor**-i-ti/ *n.* (*pl.* **-ies**) **1** a person who takes responsibility for another's performance of an undertaking, e.g. to appear in court, or payment of a debt. **2 a** money given as a guarantee. **b** a guarantee. **3** certainty. □ **stand surety** become a surety, go bail. [from Latin *securitas* 'security'] □ **suretyship** *n.*

surf ● *n.* **1** the swell of the sea breaking on the shore or a reef. **2** the foam produced by this. ● *v.* **1** *intr.* go surf-riding. **2** *intr. slang* ride illicitly on the roof or outside of a train. **3** *tr.* browse (the Internet) for information or entertainment. □ **surfer** *n.* **surfing** *n.* **surfy** *adj.*

surface ● *n.* **1 a** the outside of a material body. **b** the area of this. **2** any of the limits of a solid. **3** the upper boundary of a liquid or of the ground etc. **4** the outward aspect of anything (*quiet on the surface*). **5** *Geom.* a set of points that has length and breadth but no thickness. **6** (*attrib.*) **a** of or on the surface. **b** superficial (*surface politeness*). ● *v.* **1** *tr.* give the required surface to (a road, paper, etc.). **2** *intr. & tr.* rise or bring to the surface. **3** *intr.* become visible or known. **4** *intr. colloq.* wake up. □ **come to the surface** become perceptible after being hidden. [from French] □ **surfaced** *adj.* (usu. in *comb.*). **surfacer** *n.*

surface mail *n.* mail carried over land and by sea, and not by air.

surface tension *n.* ▶ the tension of the surface-film of a liquid, tending to minimize its surface area.

surface-to-air *attrib.adj.* (of a missile) designed to be fired from the ground or at sea at an aircraft etc.

surface-to-surface *attrib.adj.* (of a missile) designed to be fired from one point on the ground or at sea to another such point.

surfactant *n.* a substance which reduces surface tension. [based on *surface-active*]

surfboard *n.* ◀ a long narrow board used in surf-riding.

surfeit /**ser**-fit/ ● *n.* **1** an excess esp. in eating or drinking. **2** a feeling of satiety or disgust resulting from this. ● *v.* (**surfeited**, **surfeiting**) **1** *tr.* overfeed. **2** *intr.* overeat. **3** *intr. & tr.* (foll. by *with*) be or cause to be wearied through excess. [from Old French *surfe(i)t*]

surf-riding *n.* the sport of being carried over the surf to the shore on a surfboard.

surge ● *n.* **1** a sudden or impetuous onset (*a surge of anger*). **2** the swell of the waves at sea. **3** a heavy forward or upward motion. **4** a rapid increase in price, activity, etc. **5** a sudden marked increase in voltage in an electric circuit. ● *v.intr.* **1** (of waves etc.) rise and fall or move heavily forward. **2** (of a crowd etc.) move suddenly and powerfully forwards. **3** (of an electric current etc.) increase suddenly. [from Latin *surgere* 'to rise']

surgeon *n.* **1** a medical practitioner qualified to practise surgery. **2** a naval or military medical officer. [from Old French *serurgien*]

surgeon general *n.* (*pl.* **surgeons general**) (in the US) the head of a public health service or of an army etc. medical service.

surgery *n.* (*pl.* **-ies**) **1** the branch of medicine concerned with treatment of injuries or disorders of the body by incision or manipulation. **2** *Brit.* **a** a place where a

doctor, dentist, etc., treats patients. **b** the occasion of this. **3** *Brit.* **a** a place where an MP, lawyer, etc. gives advice. **b** the occasion of this. [from Greek *kheirourgia* 'handiwork, surgery']

surgical *adj.* **1** of or relating to or done by surgeons or surgery. **2** resulting from surgery. **3 a** used in surgery. **b** worn to correct a deformity etc. **4** (esp. of military action) swift and precise. [based on Old French *sirurgie* 'surgery'] □ **surgically** *adv.*

surgical spirit *n. Brit.* methylated spirit used in surgery for cleansing etc.

suricate *n.* a grey meerkat, *Suricata suricatta*. [French]

surly *adj.* (**surlier**, **surliest**) bad-tempered and unfriendly. [alteration of obsolete *sirly* 'haughty'] □ **surlily** *adv.* **surliness** *n.*

surmise ● *n.* a conjecture. ● *v.* **1** *tr.* (often foll. by *that* + clause) infer doubtfully; make a surmise about. **2** *tr.* suspect the existence of. **3** *intr.* make a guess. [from Old French *surmis(e)* 'accused']

surmount *v.tr.* **1** overcome or get over (a difficulty or obstacle). **2** (usu. in *passive*) cap or crown. [from Old French *surmonter*] □ **surmountable** *adj.*

surname ● *n.* a hereditary name common to all members of a family. ● *v.tr.* **1** give a surname to. **2** give (a person a surname). **3** (as **surnamed** *adj.*) having as a family name. [from Anglo-French]

surpass *v.tr.* **1** outdo, be greater or better than. **2** (as **surpassing** *adj.*) pre-eminent, matchless. [from French *surpasser*] □ **surpassingly** *adv.*

surplice *n.* a loose white linen vestment worn over a cassock by clergy and choristers. ▷ VESTMENT. [from medieval Latin *superpellicium*] □ **surpliced** *adj.*

surface-film   *paper clip*

SURFACE TENSION DEMONSTRATED BY A PAPER CLIP FLOATING ON WATER

surplus ● *n.* **1** an amount left over. **2 a** an excess of revenue over expenditure. **b** the excess value of a company's assets over the face value of its stock. ● *adj.* exceeding what is needed or used. [from medieval Latin *superplus*]

surprise ● *n.* **1** an unexpected or astonishing event or circumstance. **2** the emotion caused by this. **3** the act of catching a person etc. unawares, or the process of being caught unawares. **4** (*attrib.*) unexpected (*a surprise visit*). ● *v.tr.* **1** affect with surprise; turn out contrary to the expectations of (*your answer surprised me*). **2** (usu. in *passive*; foll. by *at*) shock (*I am surprised at you*). **3** capture or attack by surprise. **4** come upon (a person) unawares (*surprised him napping*). **5** (foll. by *into*) startle (a person) by surprise into an action etc. (*surprised them into consenting*). □ **take by surprise** affect with surprise, esp. by an unexpected encounter or statement. [from Middle French *surprise* 'a taking unawares'] □ **surprisedly** *adv.* **surprising** *adj.* **surprisingly** *adv.* **surprisingness** *n.*

surreal *adj.* **1** having the qualities of surrealism. **2** strange, bizarre. □ **surreality** *n.* **surreally** *adv.*

surrealism *n.* ▶ a 20th-c. movement in art and literature aiming at expressing the subconscious mind, e.g. by the irrational juxtaposition of images. [from French *surréalisme*] □ **surrealist** *n. & adj.* **surrealistic** *adj.* **surrealistically** *adv.*

surrender ● *v.* **1** *tr.* hand over; relinquish possession of; give into another's power or control. **2** *intr.* **a** accept an enemy's demand for submission. **b** give oneself up; submit. **3** *intr. & refl.* (foll. by *to*) give oneself over to a habit, emotion, etc. **4** *tr.* give up rights under (a life-insurance policy) in return for a smaller sum received immediately. ● *n.* the act or an instance of surrendering. [from Old French *surrendre*]

surrender value *n.* the amount payable to a person who surrenders a life-insurance policy.

surreptitious *adj.* **1** covert; kept secret. **2** done by stealth; clandestine. [from Latin *surrepticius*

SURFBOARD

S

SURREALISM

Surrealism was influenced by the ideas of Freud, and sought to express the imagination as shown in dreams, unshackled by reason or convention. This idea was given literary voice almost exclusively in France, by writers such as Jean Cocteau. In art, the movement spread throughout Europe. Artists such as Salvador Dali used disturbing, dream-like symbols. Others, such as Max Ernst, juxtaposed incongruous images, depicted in a realistic style.

The Sublime Moment (1938), SALVADOR DALI

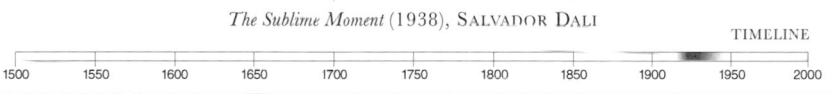

TIMELINE

1500 1550 1600 1650 1700 1750 1800 1850 1900 1950 2000

'fraudulently obtained'] □ **surreptitiously** *adv.* **surreptitiousness** *n.*

surrey *n.* (*pl.* **-eys**) *US* a light four-wheeled carriage with two seats facing forwards. [from *Surrey cart*, made in *Surrey* in England]

surrogate *n.* **1** a substitute, esp. for a person in a specific role or office. **2** *Brit.* a deputy, esp. of a bishop in granting marriage licences. [from Latin *surrogatus* 'elected as a substitute'] □ **surrogacy** *n.* **surrogateship** *n.*

surrogate mother *n.* **1** a person taking on the role of mother. **2** a woman who bears a child on behalf of another woman, either from her own egg fertilized by the other woman's partner, or from the implantation in her womb of a fertilized egg from the other woman.

surround ● *v.tr.* **1** come or be all round; encircle, enclose. **2** (in *passive*; foll. by *by*, *with*) have on all sides. ● *n.* **1** *Brit.* **a** a border or edging, esp. an area between the walls and carpet of a room. **b** a floor covering for this. **2** an area or substance surrounding something. [Middle English in sense 'to overflow': from Late Latin *superundare*] □ **surrounding** *adj.*

surroundings *n.pl.* the things in the neighbourhood of, or the conditions affecting, a person or thing.

surtax ● *n.* **1** an additional tax on something already taxed. **2** a higher rate of tax levied on incomes above a certain level. ● *v.tr.* impose a surtax on. [from French *surtaxe*]

surtitle *n.* (esp. in opera) each of a sequence of captions projected above the stage, translating the text being sung.

surveillance /ser-**vay**-lănss/ *n.* close observation, esp. of a suspected person. [French]

survey ● *v.tr.* /sŭ-**vay**/ **1** take or present a general view of. **2** examine the condition of (a building etc.), esp. on behalf of a prospective buyer. **3** determine the boundaries, ownership, etc., of (a district etc.). ● *n.* /**ser**-vay/ **1** a general view or consideration of something. **2 a** the act of surveying property. **b** the result or findings of this. **3** an inspection or investigation. **4** a map or plan made by surveying an area. [from medieval Latin *supervidere*]

surveyor *n.* **1** a person who surveys land and buildings, esp. professionally. **2** a person who carries out surveys.

survival *n.* **1** the process or an instance of surviving. **2** a relic. **3** the practice of coping with harsh conditions, as a leisure activity or training exercise. □ **survival of the fittest** the process or result of natural selection.

survivalism *n.* **1** a policy of trying to ensure one's own survival or that of one's social or national group. **2** the practising of outdoor survival skills as a sport or hobby. □ **survivalist** *n.* & *adj.*

survival kit *n.* emergency rations etc., esp. as carried by servicemen.

survive *v.* **1** *intr.* continue to live or exist. **2** *tr.* live or exist longer than. **3** *tr.* remain alive after, or continue to exist in spite of (a danger, accident, etc.). [from Latin *supervivere*] □ **survivable** *adj.* (in sense 3).

survivor *n.* a person who survives or has survived.

sus var. of SUSS.

---

susceptibility *n.* (*pl.* **-ies**) **1** the state of being susceptible. **2** (in *pl.*) a person's sensitive feelings.

susceptible *adj.* **1** impressionable, sensitive; easily moved by emotion. **2** (*predic.*) **a** (foll. by *to*) liable or vulnerable to (*susceptible to pain*). **b** (foll. by *of*) admitting of (*facts not susceptible of proof*). [from Late Latin *susceptibilis*] □ **susceptibly** *adv.*

sushi *n.* ► a Japanese dish in which various ingredients such as raw fish are added to vinegar-flavoured cold rice and formed into balls or rolls. [Japanese]

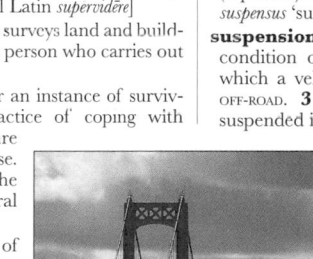

red ginger   cucumber
seaweed   rice
raw fish   raw fish

SUSHI

suspect ● *v.tr.* /sŭs-**pekt**/ **1** have an impression of the existence or presence of. **2** (foll. by *to be*) believe tentatively, without clear grounds. **3** (foll. by *that* + clause) be inclined to think. **4** (often foll. by *of*) be inclined to accuse mentally (*suspect him of complicity*). **5** doubt the genuineness or truth of. ● *n.* /**sus**-pekt/ a suspected person. ● *adj.* /**sus**-pekt/ subject to or deserving suspicion or distrust. [from Latin *suspectus* 'suspected']

suspend *v.tr.* **1** hang up. **2** keep inoperative or undecided for a time; defer. **3** debar temporarily from a function, office, from attending school, etc. **4** (as **suspended** *adj.*) (of solid particles or a body in a fluid medium) sustained somewhere between top and bottom. [from Latin *suspendere*]

suspended animation *n.* a temporary cessation of the vital functions without death.

suspended sentence *n.* a judicial sentence left unenforced subject to good behaviour during a specified period.

suspender *n.* **1** *Brit.* an attachment to hold up a stocking or sock by its top. **2** (in *pl.*) *N. Amer.* a pair of braces.

suspender belt *n.* a woman's undergarment consisting of a belt and suspenders.

suspense *n.* a state of anxious uncertainty or expectation. □ **keep in suspense** delay informing (a person) of urgent information. [based on Latin *suspensus* 'suspended'] □ **suspenseful** *adj.*

suspension *n.* **1** the act of suspending or the condition of being suspended. **2** the means by which a vehicle is supported on its axles. ▷ CAR, OFF-ROAD. **3** a substance consisting of particles suspended in a medium. [from Latin *suspensio*]

suspension bridge *n.* ◄ a bridge with a roadway suspended from cables supported by structures at each end. ▷ BRIDGE

suspicion *n.* **1** the feeling or thought of a person who suspects. **2** the act or an instance of suspecting; the state of being suspected. **3** (foll. by *of*) a slight trace of. □ **above suspicion** too obviously good etc. to be suspected. **under suspicion** suspected. [from medieval Latin *suspectio*]

suspicious *adj.* **1** prone to or feeling suspicion. **2** indicating suspicion (*a suspicious glance*). **3** inviting suspicion (*a suspicious lack of surprise*). □ **suspiciously** *adv.* **suspiciousness** *n.*

suss (also **sus**) *Brit. slang* ● *v.tr.* (**sussed**, **sussing**) **1** suspect of a crime. **2** (usu. foll. by *out*) **a** investigate, inspect. **b** work

SUSPENSION BRIDGE:
MACKINAC BRIDGE, USA

S

out; grasp (*had the market sussed*). ● *n.* **1** a suspect. **2** a suspicion; suspicious behaviour. □ **on suss** on suspicion (of having committed a crime). [abbreviation]

sustain *v.tr.* **1** support, bear the weight of, esp. for a long period. **2** encourage, support. **3** (of food) give nourishment to. **4** endure, stand. **5** undergo or suffer (defeat etc.). **6** (of a court etc.) uphold (an objection etc.). **7** substantiate (a statement or charge). **8** maintain or keep (a sound, effort, etc.) going continuously. [from Latin *sustinēre* 'to hold from beneath'] □ **sustainedly** *adv.* **sustainer** *n.* **sustainment** *n.*

sustainable *adj.* **1** *Ecol.* (esp. of development) which conserves an ecological balance by avoiding depletion of natural resources. **2** that can be sustained. □ **sustainably** *adv. Ecol.* **sustainability** *n. Ecol.*

sustenance *n.* **1** nourishment, food. **2** a means of support. [from Old French *so(u)stenance*]

sutler *n. hist.* a person following an army and selling provisions etc. to the soldiers. [from obsolete Dutch *soeteler*]

Sutra /soo-tră/ *n.* **1** an aphorism or set of aphorisms in Hindu literature. **2** a narrative part of Buddhist literature. **3** Jainist scripture. [from Sanskrit *sūtra* 'thread, rule']

suttee *n.* (also **sati** *pronunc.* same) (*pl.* **suttees** or **satis**) **1** the former Hindu practice of a widow immolating herself on her husband's funeral pyre. **2** a widow who underwent this. [from Sanskrit *satī* 'faithful wife']

suture /soo-cher/ ● *n.* **1** *Surgery* **a** the joining of the edges of a wound or incision by stitching. **b** the thread or wire used for this. **2** ▼ the seamlike junction of two bones, esp. in the skull. ● *v.tr. Surgery* stitch up with a suture. [French] □ **sutural** *adj.* **sutured** *adj.*

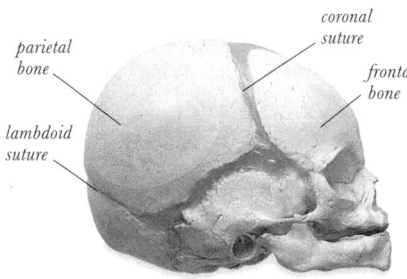

parietal bone

lambdoid suture

coronal suture

frontal bone

SUTURE: SKULL OF A HUMAN FOETUS SHOWING SUTURES

S

suzerain *n.* **1** *hist.* a feudal overlord. **2** a sovereign or state having some control over another state that is internally autonomous. [French] □ **suzerainty** *n.*

svelte *adj.* slender, lissom, graceful. [from Italian *svelto*]

Svengali /sven-**gah**-li/ *n.* (*pl.* **Svengalis**) a person who exercises a controlling, often sinister, influence on another. [a character in George Du Maurier's *Trilby* (1894)]

SW *abbr.* **1** south-west. **2** south-western.

swab (also **swob**) ● *n.* **1** a mop or other absorbent device for cleaning or mopping up. **2 a** an absorbent pad used in surgery or for applying medication. **b** a specimen of a possibly morbid secretion taken with a swab for examination. ● *v.tr.* (**swabbed, swabbing**) **1** clean with a swab. **2** (foll. by *up*) absorb (moisture) with a swab. [from early modern Dutch *zwabber* 'a mop']

swaddle /swod-ĕl/ *v.tr.* swathe (esp. an infant) in garments or bandages etc. [Middle English, based on SWATHE]

swaddling-clothes *n.pl. hist.* narrow bandages formerly wrapped round a newborn child to restrain its movements and quieten it.

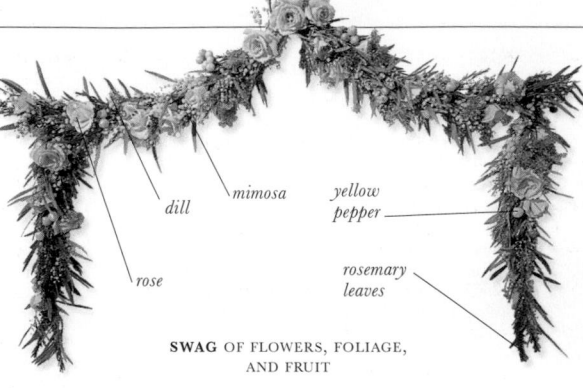

dill   *mimosa*   *yellow pepper*

rose   *rosemary leaves*

SWAG OF FLOWERS, FOLIAGE, AND FRUIT

swag ● *n.* **1** *slang* **a** the booty carried off by burglars etc. **b** illicit gains. **2** ▲ an ornamental festoon of flowers, fruit, drapery, etc. **3** *Austral. & NZ* a traveller's or miner's bundle. ● *v.* (**swagged, swagging**) **1** *tr.* arrange (a curtain etc.) in swags. **2** *intr.* **a** hang heavily. **b** sway from side to side. **3** *tr.* cause to sway or sag. [Middle English]

swagger ● *v.intr.* **1** walk arrogantly or self-importantly. **2** behave arrogantly; be domineering. ● *n.* **1** a swaggering gait or manner. **2** swaggering behaviour. **3** a dashing or confident air or way of doing something. **4** *Brit.* smartness. □ **swaggerer** *n.* **swaggeringly** *adv.*

swagger stick *n.* a short cane carried by a military officer.

swagman *n.* (*pl.* **-men**) *Austral. & NZ* a tramp carrying a swag (see SWAG *n.* 3).

Swahili ● *n.* (*pl.* same) **1** a member of a Bantu-speaking people of Zanzibar and adjacent coasts. **2** their language, used widely as a lingua franca in E. Africa. ● *adj.* of or relating to the Swahili or their language. [from Arabic *sawāḥil* 'coasts']

swain *n.* **1** *archaic* a country youth. **2** *poet.* a young lover or suitor. [from Old Norse *sveinn* 'lad']

swallow[1] ● *v.* **1** *tr.* cause or allow (food etc.) to pass down the throat. **2** *intr.* perform the muscular movement of the oesophagus required to do this. **3** *tr.* accept meekly or credulously. **4** *tr.* resist the expression of (*swallow one's pride*). **5** *tr.* articulate (words etc.) indistinctly. **6** *tr.* (often foll. by *up*) engulf or absorb; exhaust. ● *n.* **1** the act of swallowing. **2** an amount swallowed in one action. [Old English]

swallow[2] *n.* any of various migratory swift-flying insect-eating birds of the family Hirundinidae, with a forked tail and long pointed wings. ▷ PASSERINE. [Old English]

swallow-dive *n. Brit.* a dive with the arms outspread until close to the water.

SWALLOWTAIL: GIANT SWALLOWTAIL (*Papilio cresphontes*)

swallowtail *n.* **1** a deeply forked tail. **2** anything resembling this shape. **3** ◄ any butterfly of the family Papilionidae with wings extended at the back to this shape. ▷ BUTTERFLY, LARVA. □ **swallow-tailed** *adj.*

swam *past* of SWIM.

swami *n.* (*pl.* **swamis**) a Hindu male religious teacher. [from Hindi *swāmī* 'master, prince']

swamp ● *n.* a piece of water-logged ground; a bog or marsh. ● *v.* **1 a** *tr.* overwhelm, flood, or soak with water. **b** *intr.* become swamped. **2** *tr.* overwhelm or make invisible etc. with an excess or large amount of something. [17th-century coinage] □ **swampy** *adj.* (**swampier, swampiest**).

swampland *n.* land consisting of swamps.

swan ● *n.* a large usu. white waterbird of the genus *Cygnus* etc., having a long flexible neck and webbed feet. ▷ WATERFOWL. ● *v.intr.* (**swanned, swanning**)

(usu. foll. by *about, off,* etc.) *Brit. colloq.* move or go aimlessly or casually or with a superior air. □ **Swan of Avon** *literary* Shakespeare. [Old English]

swank *colloq.* ● *n.* ostentation, swagger, bluff. ● *v.intr.* behave with swank; show off. ● *adj.* esp. *US* ostentatiously smart or showy. [19th-century coinage] □ **swanky** *adj.* (**swankier, swankiest**). **swankily** *adv.*

swankpot *n. Brit. colloq.* a person behaving with swank.

swan-neck *n.* a curved structure shaped like a swan's neck.

swannery *n.* (*pl.* **-ies**) a place where swans are bred.

swansdown *n.* **1** the fine down of a swan, used esp. in powder puffs. **2** a kind of thick cotton cloth with a soft nap on one side.

swansong *n.* **1** a person's last work or act before death or retirement etc. **2** a song like that fabled to be sung by a dying swan.

swan-upping *n. Brit.* the annual taking up and marking of Thames swans.

swap (also **swop**) ● *v.tr. & intr.* (**swapped, swapping**) exchange or barter (one thing for another). ● *n.* **1** an act of swapping. **2** a thing swapped or for swapping. [Middle English in sense 'to hit'] □ **swapper** *n.*

swap meet *n.* esp. *N. Amer.* **1** a gathering at which enthusiasts or collectors trade or exchange items. **2** a flea market.

Swapo *abbr.* South-West Africa People's Organization.

sward *n.* esp. *literary* **1** an expanse of short grass. **2** turf. [Old English *sweard* 'skin'] □ **swarded** *adj.*

swarf *n.* **1** fine chips or filings of stone, metal, etc. **2** wax etc. removed in cutting a gramophone record. [from Old Norse *svarf* 'file-dust']

swarm[1] ● *n.* **1** a cluster of bees leaving the hive with a queen to establish a new colony. **2** a large number of insects or birds moving in a cluster. **3** a large group of people, esp. moving over or filling a large area. **4** (in *pl.*; foll. by *of*) great numbers. ● *v.intr.* **1** move in or form a swarm. **2** (foll. by *with*) (of a place) be overrun, crowded, or infested. [Old English]

swarm[2] *v.intr.* (foll. by *up*) & *tr.* climb (a rope or tree etc.), esp. in a rush, by clasping or clinging with the hands and knees etc. [16th-century coinage]

swarthy *adj.* (**swarthier, swarthiest**) dark, dark-complexioned. [variant of obsolete *swarty*] □ **swarthily** *adv.* **swarthiness** *n.*

swash ● *v.* **1** *intr.* (of water etc.) wash about; make the sound of washing or rising and falling. **2** *tr. archaic* strike violently. **3** *intr. archaic* swagger. ● *n.* the motion or sound of swashing water.

swashbuckler *n.* **1** a swaggering adventurer or blustering ruffian. **2** a film, book, etc. portraying swashbuckling characters. □ **swashbuckling** *adj. & n.*

swash-plate *n.* an inclined disc revolving on an axle and giving reciprocating motion to a part in contact with it.

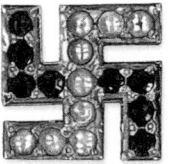

SWASTIKA (1)

swastika *n.* **1** ► an ancient symbol formed by an equal-armed cross with each arm continued at a right angle. **2** ► this with clockwise continuations as the symbol of Nazi Germany. [from Sanskrit, based on *svasti* 'well-being']

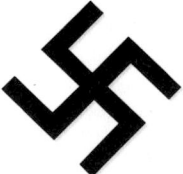

swat ● *v.tr.* (**swatted, swatting**) **1** crush (a fly etc.) with a sharp blow. **2** hit hard and abruptly. ● *n.* a swatting blow. [originally in sense 'to sit down': northern English dialect & US variant of SQUAT]

SWASTIKA (2)

swatch *n.* **1** ◄ a sample, esp. of cloth or fabric. **2** a collection of samples. [16th-century coinage]

swath /swawth/ *n.* (also **swathe**) (*pl.* **swaths** or **swathes**) **1** a ridge of grass or corn etc. lying after being cut. **2** a space left clear after the passage of a mower etc. **3** a broad strip. [Old English]

SWATCHES
OF WOVEN FABRIC

swathe ● *v.tr.* bind or enclose in bandages or garments etc. ● *n.* a bandage or wrapping. [Old English]

swatter *n.* an implement for swatting flies.

sway ● *v.* **1** *intr. & tr.* lean or cause to lean unsteadily in different directions alternately. **2** *intr.* oscillate irregularly; waver. **3** *tr.* **a** control the motion or direction of. **b** have influence or rule over. ● *n.* **1** rule, influence, or government. **2** a swaying motion or position. [Middle English]

swear *v.* (*past* **swore**; *past part.* **sworn**) **1** *tr.* **a** (often foll. by *to* + infin. or *that* + clause) state or promise solemnly or on oath. **b** take (an oath). **2** *tr. colloq.* say emphatically; insist. **3** *tr.* cause to take an oath (*swore them to secrecy*). **4** *intr.* (often foll. by *at*) use profane or indecent language. **5** *tr.* (often foll. by *against*) make a sworn affirmation of (*swear treason against*). **6** *intr.* (foll. by *by*) **a** appeal to as a witness in taking an oath (*swear by Almighty God*). **b** *colloq.* have or express great confidence in (*swears by yoga*). **7** *intr.* (foll. by *to*; usu. in *neg.*) admit the certainty of (*could not swear to it*). □ **swear blind** *Brit. colloq.* affirm emphatically. **swear in** induct into office etc. by administering an oath. **swear off** *colloq.* promise to abstain from (drink etc.). [Old English, related to ANSWER] □ **swearer** *n.*

swear word *n.* a profane or indecent word, esp. uttered as an expletive.

sweat ● *n.* **1** moisture exuded through the pores of the skin, esp. from heat or nervousness. **2** a state or period of sweating. **3** *colloq.* a state of anxiety (*in a sweat about it*). **4** *colloq.* drudgery, effort. **b** a laborious task or undertaking. **5** condensed moisture on a surface. ● *v.* (*past* and *past part.* **sweated** or *US* **sweat**) **1** *intr.* exude sweat; perspire. **2** *intr.* be terrified, suffering, etc. **3** *intr.* (of a wall etc.) exhibit surface moisture. **4** *intr.* drudge, toil. **5 a** *intr. & tr.* exude or cause to exude or condense moisture in the form of drops on a surface, esp. as part of a manufacturing process. **b** *tr.* heat (meat or vegetables) slowly in fat or water to extract the juices. **6** *tr.* emit (blood, gum, etc.) like sweat. **7** *tr.* make (a horse, athlete, etc.) sweat by exercise. **8** *tr.* (as **sweated** *adj.*) (of goods, workers, or labour) produced by or subjected to long hours under poor conditions. □ **by the sweat of one's brow** by one's own hard work. **no sweat** *colloq.* there is no need to worry. **sweat blood** *colloq.* **1** work strenuously. **2** be extremely anxious. **sweat it out** *colloq.* endure a difficult experience to the end. [Old English]

sweatband *n.* a band of absorbent material inside a hat or round a wrist etc. to soak up sweat.

sweater *n.* = PULLOVER.

sweat gland *n.* a spiral tubular gland below the skin secreting sweat. ▷ HAIR, SKIN

sweatpants *n.pl.* loose thick esp. cotton trousers with an elasticated or drawstring waist, worn for sports or leisurewear.

sweatshirt *n.* a loose long-sleeved thick esp. cotton sweater, fleecy on the inside.

sweatshop *n.* a workshop where sweated labour is used.

sweat sock *n. N. Amer.* a thick absorbent calf-length sock worn with trainers.

sweatsuit *n.* a suit of a sweatshirt and sweatpants, as worn by athletes etc.

sweaty *adj.* (**sweatier**, **sweatiest**) **1** sweating; covered with sweat. **2** causing sweat. □ **sweatily** *adv.* **sweatiness** *n.*

Swede *n.* **1 a** a native or national of Sweden. **b** a person of Swedish descent. **2** (**swede**) (in full **swede turnip**) *Brit.* **a** a cruciferous plant, *Brassica napus*, with a large yellow-fleshed root, originally from Sweden. **b** this root as a vegetable. [from Middle Dutch *Swēde*]

Swedish ● *adj.* of or relating to Sweden or its people or language. ● *n.* the language of Sweden.

sweep ● *v.* (*past* and *past part.* **swept**) **1** *tr.* clean or clear (a room or area etc.) with or as with a broom. **2** *intr.* (often foll. by *up*) clean a room etc. in this way. **3** *tr.* (often foll. by *up*) collect or remove (dirt etc.) by sweeping. **4** *tr.* (foll. by *aside*, *away*, etc.) **a** push with or as with a broom. **b** dismiss or reject abruptly. **5** *tr.* (foll. by *along*, *down*, etc.) carry or drive along with force. **6** *tr.* (foll. by *off*, *away*, etc.) remove or clear forcefully. **7** *tr.* traverse swiftly or lightly. **8** *tr.* impart a sweeping motion to. **9** *tr.* swiftly cover or affect (*fear swept the country*). **10** *intr.* **a** glide swiftly; speed along. **b** go majestically. ● *n.* **1** the act or motion or an instance of sweeping. **2** a curve in the road, a sweeping line of a hill, etc. **3** range or scope (*beyond the sweep of the human mind*). **4** = CHIMNEY SWEEP. **5** a sortie by aircraft. **6** *colloq.* = SWEEPSTAKE 1, 2. □ **make a clean sweep of 1** completely abolish or expel. **2** win all the prizes etc. in (a competition etc.).

sweep away 1 abolish swiftly. **2** (usu. in *passive*) powerfully affect, esp. emotionally. **sweep the board** win all the money or possible prizes etc. **sweep under the carpet** see CARPET. [Old English *swāpan* 'to sweep']

sweeper *n.* **1** a person who cleans by sweeping. **2** a device for sweeping carpets etc. **3** *Football* a defensive player usu. playing behind the other defenders across the width of the field.

sweeping ● *adj.* **1** wide in range or effect (*sweeping changes*). **2** taking no account of particular cases or exceptions (*a sweeping statement*). ● *n.* (in *pl.*) dirt etc. collected by sweeping.

sweepstake *n.* **1** a form of gambling on horse races etc. in which all competitors' stakes are paid to the winners. **2** a race with betting of this kind. **3** a prize or prizes won in a sweepstake.

sweet ● *adj.* **1** having a taste like that of sugar. **2** smelling pleasant like roses or perfume etc.; fragrant. **3** (of sound etc.) melodious or harmonious. **4** a not salt, sour, or bitter. **b** fresh, with flavour unimpaired by rottenness. **c** (of water) fresh and readily drinkable. **5** highly gratifying or attractive. **6** amiable, pleasant (*has a sweet nature*). **7** *colloq.* (of a person or thing) pretty, charming, endearing. **8** (foll. by *on*) *colloq.* fond of; in love with. ● *n.* **1** *Brit.* a small shaped piece of confectionery usu. made with sugar or sweet chocolate. **2** *Brit.* a sweet dish forming a course of a meal. [Old English] □ **sweetish** *adj.* **sweetly** *adv.* **sweetness** *n.*

sweet and sour *attrib.adj.* cooked in a sauce containing sugar and vinegar or lemon etc.

sweet basil see BASIL.

sweetbread *n.* the pancreas or thymus of an animal, esp. as food.

sweet chestnut *n.* = CHESTNUT *n.* 1a, 2.

sweet cicely *n.* a white-flowered aromatic umbelliferous plant, *Myrrhis odorata*.

sweetcorn *n.* **1** a kind of maize with kernels having a high sugar content. **2** these kernels, eaten as a vegetable when young.

sweeten *v.* **1** *tr. & intr.* make or become sweet or sweeter. **2** *tr.* make agreeable or less painful. □ **sweeten the pill** see PILL. □ **sweetening** *n.*

sweetener *n.* **1** a substance used to sweeten food or drink. **2** *colloq.* a bribe or inducement.

sweet fennel see FENNEL 3.

sweetheart *n.* **1** a lover or darling. **2** a term of endearment.

sweetheart agreement *n.* (also **sweetheart contract** or **deal**) *colloq.* an industrial agreement reached privately by employers and trade unions in their own interests.

sweetie *n. colloq.* **1** *Brit.* a sweet. **2** (also **sweetie-pie**) a term of endearment.

sweetmeal *n. Brit.* sweetened wholemeal.

sweetmeat *n. archaic* **1** a sweet (see SWEET *n.* 1). **2** a small fancy cake.

sweet pea *n.* ► any climbing plant of the genus *Lathyrus*, esp. *L. odoratus* with fragrant flowers in many colours.

SWEET PEA
(*Lathyrus odoratus*)

sweet pepper *n.* a pepper (capsicum) with a relatively mild taste.

sweet potato *n.* **1** ◄ a tropical climbing plant, *Ipomoea batatas*, with sweet tuberous roots used for food. **2** the root of this.

sweet rocket see ROCKET² 2.

sweetshop *n. Brit.* a shop selling sweets as its main item.

sweet talk *colloq.* ● *n.* flattery, blandishment. ● *v.tr.* (**sweet-talk**) flatter in order to persuade.

sweet-tempered *adj.* amiable.

sweet tooth *n.* a liking for sweet-tasting things.

sweet violet *n.* a sweet-scented violet, *Viola odorata*.

sweet william *n.* a garden pink, *Dianthus barbatus*, with clusters of vivid fragrant flowers.

tuberous root

SWEET POTATO
(*Ipomoea batatas*)

swell ● *v.* (*past part.* **swollen** or **swelled**) **1** *intr. & tr.* grow or cause to grow bigger or louder or more intense. **2** *intr.* (often foll. by *up*) & *tr.* rise or raise up from the surrounding surface. **3** *intr.* (foll. by *out*) bulge. **4** *intr.* (of the heart) feel full of joy, pride, relief, etc. **5** *intr.* (foll. by *with*) be hardly able to restrain (pride etc.). ● *n.* **1** an act or the state of swelling. **2** the heaving of the sea with waves that do not break. **3 a** a crescendo. **b** a mechanism in an organ etc. for obtaining a crescendo or diminuendo. ▷ ORGAN. **4** *archaic colloq.* a dandy. ● *adj.* **1** esp. *N. Amer. colloq.* fine, splendid, excellent. **2** *archaic colloq.* smart, fashionable. [Old English]

swelled head *n.* (also **swollen head**) *colloq.* conceit.

swelling *n.* an abnormal protuberance on or in the body.

swelter ● *v.intr.* be uncomfortably hot. ● *n.* a sweltering atmosphere or condition. [Old English *sweltan* 'to perish'] □ **swelteringly** *adv.*

swept *past* and *past part.* of SWEEP.

swept-back *adj.* (of an aircraft wing) fixed at an acute angle to the fuselage, inclining outwards towards the rear.

swept-wing *adj.* (of an aircraft) having swept-back wings.

swerve ● *v.intr. & tr.* change or cause to change direction, esp. abruptly. ● *n.* **1** a swerving movement. **2** divergence from a course. [Old English *sweorfan* 'to depart, leave']

SWG *abbr.* standard wire gauge.

swift ● *adj.* **1** quick, rapid; soon coming or passing. **2** speedy, prompt (*swift to act*). ● *adv.* (*archaic* except in *comb.*) swiftly (*swift-moving*). ● *n.* ► any swift-flying insect-eating bird of the family Apodidae, with long wings and a superficial resemblance to a swallow. [Old English] □ **swiftly** *adv.* **swiftness** *n.*

SWIFT:
COMMON SWIFT
(*Apus apus*)

S

swig *colloq.* ● *v.tr. & intr.* (**swigged, swigging**) drink in large draughts. ● *n.* a large draught or swallow of drink. [16th-century coinage, originally in sense 'liquor'] □ **swigger** *n.*

swill ● *v.* **1** *tr.* (often foll. by *out*) *Brit.* rinse or flush; pour water over or through. **2** *tr. & intr.* drink greedily. ● *n.* **1** *Brit.* an act of rinsing. **2** mainly liquid usu. kitchen refuse as pig-food. **3** inferior liquor. [Old English] □ **swiller** *n.*

swim ● *v.* (**swimming**; *past* **swam**; *past part.* **swum**) **1** *intr.* propel the body through water by working the arms and legs, or (of a fish etc.) the fins and tail. **2** *tr.* **a** traverse by swimming. **b** compete in (a race) by swimming. **c** use (a particular stroke) in swimming. **3** *intr.* float on or at the surface of a liquid. **4** *intr.* appear to undulate or reel or whirl. **5** *intr.* have a dizzy effect or sensation. **6** *intr.* (foll. by *in, with*) be flooded. ● *n.* **1** a spell or the act of swimming. **2** a deep pool frequented by fish in a river. □ **in the swim** involved in or acquainted with what is going on. [Old English] □ **swimmable** *adj.* **swimmer** *n.*

■ **Usage** The use of *swum* instead of *swam* for the past tense, as in *He swum for the shore*, is non-standard.

swim-bladder *n.* a gas-filled sac in fishes used to maintain buoyancy. ▷ FISH

swimming bath *n. Brit.* a swimming pool, esp. a public indoor one.

swimming costume *n. Brit.* a garment worn for swimming.

swimmingly *adv.* with easy and unobstructed progress.

swimming pool *n.* an artificial indoor or outdoor pool for swimming.

swimming trunks see TRUNK 6.

swimsuit *n.* a one-piece swimming costume worn by women. □ **swimsuited** *adj.*

swimwear *n.* clothing worn for swimming.

swindle ● *v.tr.* (often foll. by *out of*) **1** cheat (a person) of money, possessions, etc. **2** cheat a person of (money etc.) (*swindled his savings out of him*). ● *n.* **1** an act of swindling. **2** a person or thing represented as what it is not. **3** a fraudulent scheme. [based on German *Schwindler* 'extravagant maker of schemes, swindler'] □ **swindler** *n.*

swine *n.* (*pl.* same) **1** *formal* or *US* a pig. **2** (*pl.* **swine** or **swines**) *colloq.* **a** a term of contempt or disgust for a person. **b** a very unpleasant or difficult thing. [Old English] □ **swinish** *adj.* (esp. in sense 2). **swinishly** *adv.* **swinishness** *n.*

swine fever *n.* an intestinal viral disease of pigs.

swine vesicular disease *n.* an infectious viral disease of pigs causing mild fever and blisters around the mouth and feet.

swing ● *v.* (*past* and *past part.* **swung**) **1** *intr. & tr.* move or cause to move with a to-and-fro or curving motion, as of an object attached at one end and hanging free at the other. **2** *intr. & tr.* sway. **b** hang so as to be free to sway. **c** oscillate or cause to oscillate. **3** *intr. & tr.* revolve or cause to revolve. **4** *intr.* move by gripping something and leaping etc. while hanging from the object gripped. **5** *intr.* go with a swinging gait. **6** *intr.* (foll. by *round*) move round to the opposite direction. **7** *intr.* change one's opinion or mood. **8** *intr.* (foll. by *at*) attempt to hit or punch. **9 a** *intr.* (also **swing it**) play music with swing. **b** *tr.* play (a tune or passage) with swing. **c** *intr.* (of music) be played with swing. **10** *intr. colloq.* **a** be lively or up to date; enjoy oneself. **b** be promiscuous. **11** *intr. colloq.* (of a party etc.) be lively etc.

12 *tr.* have a decisive influence on (esp. voting etc.). **13** *tr. colloq.* deal with or achieve; manage. **14** *intr. colloq.* be executed by hanging. ● *n.* **1** the act or an instance of swinging. **2** the motion of swinging. **3** the extent of swinging. **4** a swinging or smooth gait or rhythm or action. **5 a** a seat slung by ropes or chains etc. for swinging on or in. **b** a spell of swinging on this. **6** an easy but vigorous continued action. **7 a** jazz or dance music with an easy flowing but vigorous rhythm. **b** the rhythmic feeling or drive of this music. **8** a discernible change in opinion, esp. as shown by voting. □ **swing the lead** *Brit. colloq.* malinger; shirk one's duty. **swings and roundabouts** *Brit.* a situation affording no eventual gain or loss. [Old English *swingan* 'to beat'] □ **swinger** *n.* (esp. in sense 10 of *v.*).

swingbin *n.* a plastic rubbish bin with a lid that swings open and shut.

swingboat *n.* esp. *Brit.* a boat-shaped swing at fairs.

swing bowler *n. Cricket* a bowler who swings the ball. □ **swing bowling** *n.*

swing-bridge *n.* a bridge that can be swung to one side to allow the passage of ships.

swing-door *n. Brit.* a door able to open in either direction and close itself when released.

swingeing *adj.* esp. *Brit.* **1** (of a blow) forcible. **2** huge or far-reaching, esp. in severity. [from archaic *swinge* 'to strike hard'] □ **swingeingly** *adv.*

swinging *adj.* **1** (of gait, melody, etc.) vigorously rhythmical. **2** *colloq.* **a** lively; up to date. **b** promiscuous. □ **swingingly** *adv.*

swing-wing *n.* an aircraft wing that can move from a right-angled to a swept-back position.

swipe *colloq.* ● *v.* **1** *tr. & intr.* (often foll. by *at*) hit hard and recklessly with a sweeping motion. **2** *tr.* steal. **3** *tr.* pass (a swipe card) over the electronic device that reads it. ● *n.* an act of swiping, esp. a reckless hard hit or attempted hit. □ **swiper** *n.*

swipe card *n.* a credit card etc. on which magnetically encoded information is stored to be read by an electronic device.

swirl ● *v.intr. & tr.* move or flow or carry along with a whirling motion. ● *n.* **1** a swirling motion of or in water, air, etc. **2** the act of swirling. **3** a twist or curl, esp. as part of a pattern or design. [Middle English, originally Scots] □ **swirly** *adj.*

swish ● *v.* **1** *tr.* swing (a scythe or stick etc.) audibly through the air, grass, etc. **2** *intr.* move with or make a swishing sound. **3** *tr.* (foll. by *off*) cut (a flower etc.) in this way. ● *n.* a swishing action or sound. ● *adj. Brit. colloq.* smart, fashionable.

swishy *adj.* **1** making a swishing sound. **2** *slang* effeminate.

Swiss ● *adj.* of or relating to Switzerland in western Europe or its people. ● *n.* (*pl.* same) **1** a native or national of Switzerland. **2** a person of Swiss descent. [from Middle High German *Swīz*]

Swiss chard see CHARD.

Swiss cheese plant *n.* ◀ a climbing house plant, *Monstera deliciosa*, with aerial roots and holes in the leaves.

Swiss roll *n. Brit.* a cylindrical cake with a spiral cross-section, made from a flat piece of sponge cake spread with jam etc. and rolled up.

switch ● *n.* **1** ▶ a device for making and breaking the connection in an electric circuit. **2 a** a transfer, changeover, or deviation. **b** an exchange. **3** a slender flexible shoot cut from a tree. **4** a light tapering rod. **5** *US* = POINT *n.* 17. **6** a tress of false or detached hair tied at one end, used in hairdressing. **7 a** a computer system which

manages the transfer of funds between point-of-sale terminals and institutions. **b** (**Switch** *propr.*) an EFTPOS system in the UK. **c** the transfer of funds by such a system. ● *v.* **1** *tr. & absol.* (foll. by *on, off*) turn (an electrical device) on or off. **2** *intr.* (often foll. by *over*) change or transfer position, subject, etc. **3** *tr.* (often foll. by *over*) change or transfer. **4** *tr.* (often foll. by *over*) reverse the positions of; exchange. **5** *tr.* beat or flick with a switch. □ **switch off** *colloq.* cease to pay attention. **switch over** = senses 2, 3, 4 of the *v.* [earlier *swits, switz*] □ **switchable** *adj.* **switcher** *n.*

switchback *n.* **1** *Brit.* a railway at a fair etc., in which the train's ascents are effected by the momentum of its previous descents. **2** (often *attrib.*) a railway or road with alternate sharp ascents and descents.

switchblade *n.* a pocket knife with the blade released by a spring.

switchboard *n.* an apparatus for varying connections between electric circuits, esp. in telephony.

switched-on *adj. Brit.* **1** *colloq.* up to date; aware of what is going on. **2** *slang* excited; under the influence of drugs.

switchgear *n.* **1** the switching equipment used in the transmission of electricity. **2** the switches or electrical controls in a motor vehicle.

switch-over *n.* an instance of switching over; a changeover.

swivel ● *n.* a coupling between two parts enabling one to revolve without turning the other. ● *v.tr. & intr.* (**swivelled, swivelling**; *US* **swiveled, swiveling**) turn on or as on a swivel. [Middle English]

swivel chair *n.* a chair with a seat able to be turned horizontally.

swizz *n.* (also **swiz**) (*pl.* **swizzes**) *Brit. colloq.* **1** something unfair or disappointing. **2** a swindle. [abbreviation of SWIZZLE]

swizzle *n. Brit. colloq.* = SWIZZ. [20th-century coinage]

swizzle-stick *n.* a stick used for frothing or flattening drinks.

swob var. of SWAB.

swollen *past part.* of SWELL.

swollen head var. of SWELLED HEAD.

swoon *literary* ● *v.intr.* faint; fall into a fainting-fit, esp. from excitement. ● *n.* an occurrence of fainting. [Middle English]

swoop ● *v.* **1** *intr.* (often foll. by *down*) descend rapidly like a bird of prey. **2** *intr.* (often foll. by *on*) make a sudden attack. **3** *tr.* (often foll. by *up*) *colloq.* snatch the whole of at one swoop. ● *n.* a swooping or snatching movement or action. □ **at** (or **in**) **one fell swoop** see FELL[4].

swoosh *n.* the noise of a sudden rush of liquid, air, etc.

swop var. of SWAP.

sword *n.* **1** ▶ a weapon usu. of metal with a long blade and hilt with a handguard. **2** (prec. by *the*) **a** war. **b** military power. □ **put to the sword** kill, esp. in war. [Old English] □ **swordlike** *adj.*

sword dance *n.* a dance in which the performers brandish swords or step about swords laid on the ground.

SWISS CHEESE PLANT
(*Monstera deliciosa*)

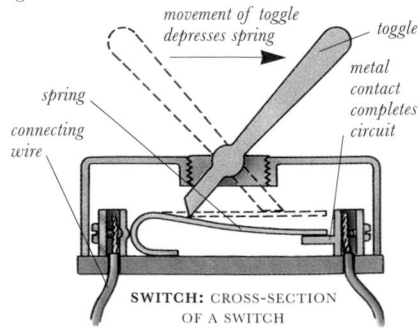

SWITCH: CROSS-SECTION OF A SWITCH

S

SWORD

There are two main types of sword: cutting swords, such as a medieval knight's two-handed sword, which have heavy blades with sharp edges; and stabbing swords, such as a rapier, which are much lighter and have a sharp point. One of humankind's oldest weapons, swords evolved from the dagger early in the Bronze Age, and were used in combat until as recently as the First World War (1914–18). From the 16th to the 19th century, broad-bladed cutting swords were widely used by the cavalry, especially when charging an enemy. Swords are rarely used by modern military forces, except as part of dress uniforms or in ceremonies. However, fencing, which developed in the 14th century, remains a popular sport today.

PARTS OF A 17TH-CENTURY GERMAN RAPIER

sharp point

double-edge

knuckle guard

guard rings

ricasso

grip

pommel

blade

vertically recurved quillon

hilt

EXAMPLES OF OTHER SWORDS

BRONZE AGE SWORD (9TH CENTURY BC)

ROMAN *GLADIUS* (1ST CENTURY AD)

VIKING SWORD (10TH CENTURY)

FRENCH MEDIEVAL KNIGHT'S SWORD (14TH CENTURY)

ENGLISH TWO-HANDED SWORD (15TH CENTURY)

INDIAN GAUNTLET SWORD (17TH CENTURY)

SAMURAI SHORT SWORD (17TH CENTURY)

GERMAN CAVALRY SWORD (17TH CENTURY)

FRENCH HUNTING SWORD (18TH CENTURY)

FRENCH INFANTRY SHORT SWORD (18TH CENTURY)

ENGLISH SMALL SWORD (19TH CENTURY)

INDIAN *SHAMSHIR* (19TH CENTURY)

SCOTTISH BROADSWORD (19TH CENTURY)

FENCING FOIL (MODERN)

S

SWORDFISH
(*Xiphias gladius*)

swordfish *n.* (*pl.* usu. same) ▲ a large marine fish, *Xiphias gladius*, with an extended swordlike upper jaw.

sword of Damocles *n.* an imminent danger. [from *Damokles* (4th c. BC), made to feast while a sword hung by a hair over him]

swordplay *n.* **1** fencing. **2** repartee.

swordsman *n.* (*pl.* **-men**) a person of (usu. specified) skill with a sword. □ **swordsmanship** *n.*

swordstick *n.* a hollow walking stick containing a blade that can be used as a sword.

swore *past* of SWEAR.

sworn *past part.* of SWEAR. ● *adj.* bound by or as by an oath (*sworn enemies*).

swot *Brit. colloq.* ● *v.* (**swotted**, **swotting**) **1** *intr.* study assiduously. **2** *tr.* (often foll. by *up*) study (a subject) hard or hurriedly. ● *n.* **1** a person who swots. **2** hard study. [dialect variant of SWEAT]

swum *past part.* of SWIM.

swung *past* and *past part.* of SWING.

sybarite ● *n.* a person who is self-indulgent or devoted to sensuous luxury. ● *adj.* fond of luxury or sensuousness. [from Greek *subarītēs* 'inhabitant of *Sybaris*', ancient Greek city noted for luxury] □ **sybaritic** *adj.* **sybaritical** *adj.* **sybaritically** *adv.* **sybaritism** *n.*

wing-like
fruit wall   *flower stalk*

seed inside

seed

SYCAMORE MAPLE
FRUITS
(*Acer pseudoplatanus*)

sycamore *n.* **1** (in full **sycamore maple**) ◀ a large maple, *Acer pseudoplatanus*, with seeds in winged fruits. **b** its wood. **2** *N. Amer.* the plane tree or its wood. [from Greek *sukomoros*]

sycophant *n.* a servile flatterer; a toady. [from Greek *sukophantē* 'informer'] □ **sycophancy** *n.* **sycophantic** *adj.* **sycophantically** *adv.*

syllabary *n.* (*pl.* **-ies**) a list of characters representing syllables. [from modern Latin *syllabarium*]

syllabi *pl.* of SYLLABUS.

syllabic *adj.* **1** of, relating to, or based on syllables. **2** (of a symbol) representing a whole syllable. [from Greek *sullabikos*] □ **syllabically** *adv.*

syllable *n.* **1** a unit of pronunciation uttered without interruption, forming the whole or a part of a word and usu. having one vowel sound often with a consonant or consonants before or after: there are two syllables in *water* and three in *inferno*. **2** a character or characters representing a syllable. **3** (usu. with *neg.*) the least important of speech or writing (*did not utter a syllable*). [from Greek *sullabē*] □ **syllabled** *adj.* (also in *comb.*).

syllabub *n.* (also **sillabub**) a dessert made of cream or milk flavoured, sweetened, and whipped to thicken it. [16th-century coinage]

syllabus *n.* (*pl.* **syllabuses** or **syllabi** /-by/) **1** the programme or outline of a course of study, teaching, etc. **2** a statement of the requirements for a particular examination. [from a misreading, based on Greek *sittuba* 'title-slip, label']

syllepsis /sil-**ep**-sis/ *n.* (*pl.* **syllepses**) a figure of speech in which a word is applied to two others in different senses (e.g. *caught the train and a bad cold*) or to two others of which it grammatically suits one only (e.g. *neither they nor it is working*) (cf. ZEUGMA). [from Greek *sullēpsis* 'taking together'] □ **sylleptic** *adj.* **sylleptically** *adv.*

syllogism *n.* a form of reasoning in which a conclusion is drawn from two given or assumed

propositions (premisses). [from Greek *sullogismos*] □ **syllogistic** *adj.*

sylph *n.* **1** an elemental spirit of air. **2** a slender graceful woman or girl. [coined by Paracelsus from modern Latin *pl. sylphes*] □ **sylphlike** *adj.*

sylvan *adj.* (also **silvan**) esp. *poet.* **1 a** of the woods. **b** having woods; wooded. **2** rural. [based on Latin *Silvanus* 'woodland deity']

sylviculture var. of SILVICULTURE.

symbiont *n.* an organism living in symbiosis. [from Greek *sumbion -ountos* 'living together']

symbiosis *n.* (*pl.* **symbioses**) **1 a** ▼ an interaction between two different organisms living in close physical association, usu. to the advantage of both. **b** an instance of this. **2 a** a mutually advantageous association between persons. **b** an instance of this. [from Greek *sumbiōsis* 'a living together'] □ **symbiotic** *adj.* **symbiotically** *adv.*

symbol *n.* **1** a thing conventionally regarded as typifying, representing, or recalling something, esp. an idea or quality. **2** a mark or character taken as the conventional sign of some object, idea, function, or process. [from Greek *sumbolon* 'mark, token'] □ **symbology** *n.*

symbolic *adj.* (also **symbolical**) **1** of or serving as a symbol. **2** involving the use of symbols or symbolism. □ **symbolically** *adv.*

symbolic logic *n.* the use of symbols to denote propositions etc. in order to assist reasoning.

symbolism *n.* **1 a** the use of symbols to represent ideas. **b** symbols collectively. **2** an artistic and poetic movement or style using symbols and indirect suggestion to express ideas, emotions, etc. □ **symbolist** *n.*

symbolize *v.tr.* (also **-ise**) **1** be a symbol of. **2** represent by means of symbols. □ **symbolization** *n.*

symmetry *n.* (*pl.* **-ies**) **1 a** correct proportion of the parts of a thing; balance, harmony. **b** beauty resulting from this. **2 a** a structure that allows an object to be divided into parts of an equal shape and size. **b** the possession of such a structure. **c** approximation to such a structure. **3** the repetition of exactly similar parts facing each other or a centre. [from Latin *summetria*] □ **symmetric** *adj.* **symmetrical** *adj.* **symmetrically** *adv.*

sympathetic *adj.* **1** of, showing, or expressing sympathy. **2** due to sympathy. **3** likeable or capable of evoking sympathy. **4** (of a person) friendly and cooperative. **5** (foll. by *to*) inclined to favour (*sympathetic to the idea*). **6** designating the part of the

autonomic nervous system consisting of nerves arising from ganglia near the middle part of the spinal cord. ▷ AUTONOMIC NERVOUS SYSTEM. □ **sympathetically** *adv.*

sympathize *v.intr.* (also **-ise**) (often foll. by *with*) **1** feel or express sympathy; share a feeling or opinion. **2** agree with a sentiment or opinion. [from French *sympathiser*] □ **sympathizer** *n.*

sympathy *n.* (*pl.* **-ies**) **1 a** the state of being simultaneously affected with a feeling similar to that of another person. **b** the capacity for this. **2** (often foll. by *with*) **a** the act of or capacity for sharing in an emotion, sensation, or condition of another person or thing. **b** (in *sing.* or *pl.*) compassion or commiseration; condolences. **3** (often foll. by *for*) a favourable attitude; approval. **4** (in *sing.* or *pl.*; often foll. by *with*) agreement (with a person etc.) in opinion or desire. **5** (*attrib.*) in support of another cause (*sympathy strike*). □ **in sympathy** (often foll. by *with*) **1** having or showing or resulting from sympathy (with another). **2** by way of sympathetic action (*working to rule in sympathy*). [from Greek *sumpatheia*]

sympatric *adj.* *Biol.* occurring within the same geographical area (cf. ALLOPATRIC). [based on Greek *patra* 'fatherland']

symphonic *adj.* (of music) relating to or having the form or character of a symphony. □ **symphonically** *adv.*

symphonic poem *n.* an extended orchestral piece, usu. in one movement, on a descriptive or rhapsodic theme.

symphonist *n.* a composer of symphonies.

symphony *n.* (*pl.* **-ies**) **1** an elaborate composition usu. for full orchestra and in several movements with one or more in sonata form. **2** an interlude for orchestra alone in a large-scale vocal work. **3** ▷ SYMPHONY ORCHESTRA. [Middle English in sense 'harmony of sound': from Greek *sumphōnia*]

symphony orchestra *n.* a large orchestra suitable for playing symphonies etc. ▷ ORCHESTRA

symposium *n.* (*pl.* **symposia** or **symposiums**) **1 a** a conference or meeting to discuss a particular subject. **b** a collection of essays or papers for this purpose. **2** a philosophical or other friendly discussion. **3** a drinking party, esp. of the ancient Greeks with conversation etc. after a banquet. [Latin]

symptom *n.* **1** *Med.* a physical or mental sign of disease. **2** a sign of the existence of something. [from Greek *sumptōma* 'chance, symptom'] □ **symptomless** *adj.*

symptomatic *adj.* serving as a symptom. □ **symptomatically** *adv.*

S

SYMBIOSIS

Partnerships between pairs of species are a common feature of the living world. The great majority are either mutualistic, where both partners benefit, or parasitic, where one species (the parasite) lives at the expense of the other (the host). Commensal partnerships, where one species gains and the other is unaffected, are rarer and more difficult to verify. In the partnership between a clownfish and a sea anemone, for example, the fish gains protection, but it is unclear whether the anemone benefits.

poisonous tentacles of sea anemone

sheltering clownfish

coral

CLOWNFISH AND SEA ANEMONE IN A SYMBIOTIC RELATIONSHIP

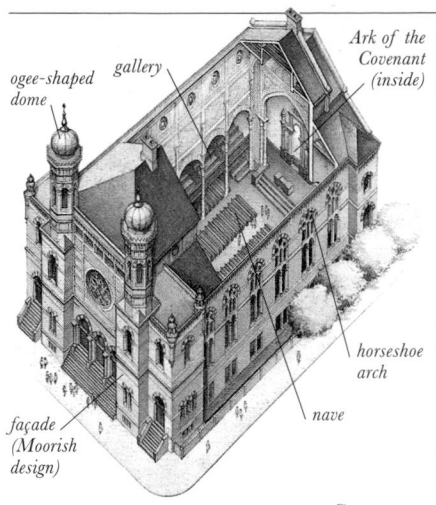

synagogue *n.* **1** ▲ the building for Jewish religious observance and instruction. **2** the assembly itself. [from Greek *sunagōgē* 'meeting'] □ **synagogal** *adj.* **synagogical** *adj.*

synapse *n. Anat.* ▼ a junction of two nerve cells. [from Greek *synapsis*]

sync (also **synch**) *colloq.* ● *n.* synchronization. ● *v.tr. & intr.* synchronize. □ **in** (or **out of**) **sync** (often foll. by *with*) according or agreeing well (or badly).

synchromesh ● *n.* ▲ a system of gear-changing, esp. in motor vehicles, in which the driving and driven gearwheels are made to revolve at the same speed during engagement. ● *adj.* relating to or using this system. [abbreviation of *synchronized mesh*]

synchronic *adj.* describing a subject (esp. a language) as it exists at one point in time. [from Late Latin *synchronus*] □ **synchronically** *adv.*

synchronicity *n.* **1** the simultaneous occurrence of events which appear significantly related but have no discernible connection. **2** = SYNCHRONY 1.

synchronism *n.* **1** = SYNCHRONY. **2** the process of synchronizing sound and picture in cinematography, television, etc. □ **synchronistic** *adj.* **synchronistically** *adv.*

synchronize *v.* (also **-ise**) **1 a** *tr.* cause to occur at the same time. **b** *intr.* (often foll. by *with*) occur at the same time. **2** *tr. disp.* coordinate, combine. **3** *tr.* carry out the synchronism of (a film). **4** *tr.* ascertain or set forth the correspondence in the date of (events). **5 a** *tr.* cause (clocks etc.) to show a standard or uniform time. **b** *intr.* (of clocks etc.) be synchronized. **6** *intr.* operate in unison. □ **synchronization** *n.* **synchronizer** *n.*

■ **Usage** The use of *synchronize* to mean 'coordinate' or 'combine' (see sense 2 above), as in *We must synchronize our efforts*, is considered incorrect by some people and should be avoided in standard English.

synchronized swimming *n.* a form of swimming in which participants make coordinated leg and arm movements in time to music.

synchronous *adj.* (often foll. by *with*) existing or occurring at the same time. [from Greek *sugkhronos*] □ **synchronously** *adv.*

synchronous motor *n. Electr.* a motor having a speed exactly proportional to the current frequency.

synchrony *n.* **1** the state of being synchronic or synchronous. **2** the treatment of events etc. as being synchronous. [from Greek *sugkhronos*]

syncopate *v.tr.* **1** *Mus.* displace the beats or accents in (a passage) so that strong beats become weak and vice versa. **2** shorten (a word) by dropping interior sounds or letters. [based on Late Latin *syncopatus* 'swooned'] □ **syncopation** *n.* **syncopator** *n.*

syncope *n.* **1** *Gram.* the omission of interior sounds or letters in a word. **2** *Med.* a temporary loss of consciousness caused by a fall in blood pressure. [from Greek *sugkopē*] □ **syncopal** *adj.*

syncretize *v.tr.* (also **-ise**) *Philos. & Theol.* attempt, esp. inconsistently, to unify or reconcile differing schools of thought. □ **syncretic** *adj.* **syncretism** *n.* **syncretist** *n.*

syndic *n.* **1** a government official in various countries. **2** (in the UK) a business agent of certain universities and corporations. [from Greek *sundikos*] □ **syndical** *adj.*

syndicalism *n. hist.* a movement for transferring industrial ownership and control to workers' unions. [from French *syndicalisme*] □ **syndicalist** *n.*

syndicate ● *n.* **1** a combination of individuals or commercial firms to promote some common interest. **2** an agency supplying material simultaneously to a number of newspapers or periodicals. **3** a group of people who combine to buy or rent property, gamble, etc. **4** a committee of syndics. ● *v.tr.* **1** form into a syndicate. **2** publish (material) through a syndicate. [from medieval Latin *syndicatus*] □ **syndication** *n.*

syndrome *n.* **1** a group of concurrent symptoms of a disease. **2** a characteristic combination of opinions, behaviour, etc. [from Greek *sundromē*]

syne *Sc.* since. [contraction of Middle English *sithen* 'since']

synecdoche /sin-ek-dŏ-ki/ *n.* a figure of speech in which a part is made to represent the whole or vice versa (e.g. *new faces at the meeting*). [from Greek *sunekdokhē*] □ **synecdochic** *adj.*

synergy *n.* (also **synergism**) **1** the interaction or cooperation of two or more drugs, agents, organizations, etc., to produce a new or enhanced effect compared to their separate effects. **2** an instance of this. [from Greek *sunergia* 'working together'] □ **synergetic** *adj.* **synergistic** *adj.* **synergistically** *adv.*

synod *n.* **1** a Church council attended by delegated clergy and sometimes laity. **2** a Presbyterian ecclesiastical court above the presbyteries and subject to the General Assembly. [from Greek *sunodos* 'meeting'] □ **synodal** *adj.* **synodical** *adj.*

synonym *n.* a word or phrase that means exactly or nearly the same as another in the same language (e.g. *shut* and *close*). [from Greek *sunōnumon*] □ **synonymity** *n.*

synonymous *adj.* (often foll. by *with*) **1** having the same meaning; being a synonym (of). **2** suggestive of or associated with another (*his name is synonymous with fear*). □ **synonymously** *adv.*

synonymy *n.* (*pl.* **-ies**) **1** the state of being synonymous. **2** the collocation of synonyms for emphasis (e.g. *in any shape or form*). **3 a** a system or collection of synonyms. **b** a treatise on synonyms.

synopsis *n.* (*pl.* **synopses**) **1** a summary or outline. **2** a brief general survey. [from Greek] □ **synopsize** *v.tr.* (also **-ise**)

SYNCHROMESH

In a modern synchromesh gearbox, each pair of gearwheels that produces a gear ratio (for example, 'first gear') is constantly meshing together, making it easier to change gear. One of each pair is fixed to the input shaft, which is driven round by the engine. The other spins freely on the output shaft, which is connected to the road wheels. As the driver selects a gear ratio, a sliding collar meshes with the teeth (dogs) at the side of the free-spinning gearwheel, which locks the gear to the output shaft. This gear then turns the output shaft, which propels the car.

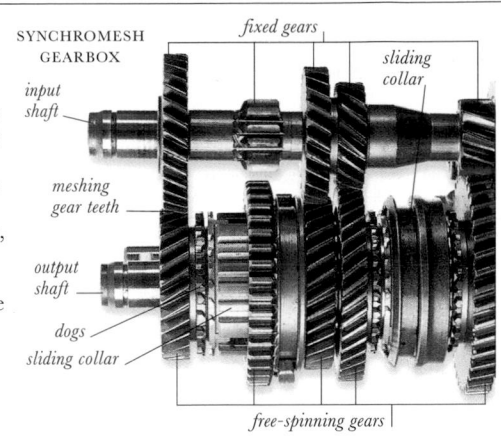

SYNAPSE

The function of the synapse is to relay messages from a neurone (nerve cell) to a target tissue (either another neurone or other tissue, such as muscle). It consists of a synaptic knob, a synaptic cleft, and a target site. A stimulus received by the neurone is transmitted as an electrical impulse along the axon to the synaptic knob. Here, the impulse prompts the synaptic vesicles to release neurotransmitters into the synaptic cleft. The neurotransmitters then attach to receptor sites in the target tissue and relay the message.

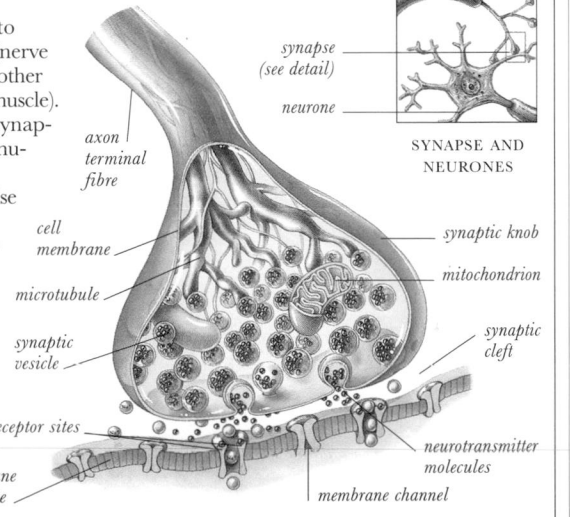

DETAIL (SECTION THROUGH A SYNAPSE)

synoptic ● *adj.* **1** of, forming, or giving a synopsis. **2** of or relating to the Synoptic Gospels. ● *n.* **1** a Synoptic Gospel. **2** the writer of a Synoptic Gospel. [from Greek *sunoptikos*] □ **synoptical** *adj.* **synoptically** *adv.*

Synoptic Gospel *n.* each of the Gospels of Matthew, Mark, and Luke.

synovial *adj. Physiol.* denoting or relating to a viscous fluid lubricating joints and tendon sheaths. [based on modern Latin *synovia* 'synovial fluid']

synovial membrane *n.* ▶ a dense membrane of connective tissue secreting synovial fluid.

synovitis *n.* inflammation of the synovial membrane.

syntactic *adj.* of or according to syntax. □ **syntactical** *adj.* **syntactically** *adv.*

syntax *n.* **1** the grammatical arrangement of words, showing their connection and relation. **2** a set of rules for or an analysis of this. [from Greek *suntaxis*]

SYNOVIAL MEMBRANE
IN A HUMAN SYNOVIAL JOINT

bone
cartilage
synovial fluid
synovial membrane
joint capsule

synth *n. colloq.* = SYNTHESIZER.

synthesis *n.* (*pl.* **syntheses**) **1** the process or result of building up separate elements, esp. ideas, into a connected whole, esp. into a theory or system. **2** a combination or composition. **3** *Chem.* the artificial production of compounds from their constituents as distinct from extraction from plants etc. **4** the joining of divided parts in surgery. [from Greek *sunthesis*] □ **synthesist** *n.*

synthesize *v.tr.* (also **synthetize** , **-ise**) **1** make a synthesis of. **2** combine into a coherent whole.

synthesizer *n.* (also **-iser**) an electronic, usu. keyboard, instrument producing a wide variety of sounds by generating and combining signals of different frequencies.

synthetic ● *adj.* **1** made by chemical synthesis, esp. to imitate a natural product (*synthetic rubber*). **2** (of emotions etc.) affected, insincere. ● *n. Chem.* a synthetic substance. [from Greek *sunthetikos*] □ **synthetical** *adj.* **synthetically** *adv.*

synthetic resin see RESIN *n.* 2.

syphilis *n.* a contagious venereal disease caused by the spirochaete *Treponema*. [from *Syphilus*, a character in a Latin poem (1530), supposed first sufferer from the disease] □ **syphilitic** *adj.*

syphon (also **siphon**) ● *n.* **1** ▶ a pipe or tube used to convey liquid upwards from a container and then down to a lower level by gravity, the liquid being made to enter the pipe by atmospheric pressure. **2** = SODA SYPHON. ● *v.tr. & intr.* (often foll. by *off*) **1** conduct or flow through a syphon. **2** divert or set aside (funds etc.). [from Greek *siphōn* 'pipe']

Syrian ● *n.* **1** a native or national of the modern state of Syria in the Middle East; a person of Syrian descent. **2** a native or inhabitant of the region of Syria in antiquity or later. ● *adj.* of or relating to the region or state of Syria.

syringa /si-**ring**-gǎ/ *n.* **1** = MOCK ORANGE. **2** any plant of the genus *Syringa*, esp. the lilac. [modern Latin]

syringe ● *n.* **1** *Med.* **a** a tube with a nozzle and piston or bulb for sucking in and ejecting liquid in a fine stream. **b** (in full **hypodermic syringe**) ▶ a similar device with a hollow needle for insertion under the skin. ▷ DRUG. **2** any similar device used in cooking etc. ● *v.tr.* (**syringing**) sluice or spray (the ear, a plant, etc.) with a syringe. [from medieval Latin *syringa*]

syrinx *n.* (*pl.* **syrinxes** or **syringes** /si-**rin**-jeez/) a set of pan pipes. [from Greek *surigx* 'pipe, channel']

syrup *n.* (*US* also **sirup**) **1 a** a thick sweet liquid made by dissolving sugar in boiling water, often used for preserving fruit etc. **b** a similar thick liquid of a specified flavour as a drink, medicine, etc. **2** condensed sugar cane juice; molasses, treacle. **3** excessive sweetness of style or manner. [from Arabic *šarāb* 'beverage'] □ **syrupy** *adj.*

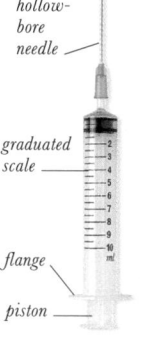

SYPHON:
DEMONSTRATION
OF THE ACTION
OF A SYPHON

syphon tube
difference in height of liquids

hollow-bore needle
graduated scale
flange
piston

SYRINGE:
HYPODERMIC
SYRINGE

systaltic *adj.* (esp. of the heart) contracting and dilating rhythmically. [from Greek *sustaltikos*]

system *n.* **1** a complex whole; a set of connected things or parts; an organized body of things. **2** a set of devices (e.g. pulleys) functioning together. **3** *Physiol.* **a** a set of organs in the body with a common structure or function. **b** the human or animal body as a whole. **4 a** method; considered principles of procedure. **b** classification. **5** orderliness. **6 a** body of theory or practice relating to or prescribing a particular form of government, religion, etc. **b** (prec. by *the*) the prevailing political or social order. **7** a method of choosing one's procedure in gambling etc. **8** *Computing* a group of related hardware units or programs or both. **9** a major group of geological strata (*the Devonian system*). □ **get a thing out of one's system** *colloq.* be rid of a preoccupation or anxiety. [from Greek *sustēma*]

systematic *adj.* **1** methodical; done or conceived according to a plan or system. **2** regular, deliberate (*a systematic liar*). □ **systematically** *adv.* **systematist** *n.*

systematic theology *n.* a form of theology in which the aim is to arrange religious truths in a self-consistent whole.

systematize *v.tr.* (also **-ise**) **1** make systematic. **2** devise a system for. □ **systematization** *n.* **systematizer** *n.*

systemic *adj.* **1** *Physiol.* **a** of or concerning the whole body (*systemic infection*). **b** (of blood circulation) other than pulmonary. **2** (of an insecticide etc.) entering the plant via the roots or shoots and passing through the tissues. □ **systemically** *adv.*

systemize *v.tr.* (also **-ise**) = SYSTEMATIZE. □ **systemization** *n.* **systemizer** *n.*

systems analysis *n.* the analysis of a complex process or operation in order to improve its efficiency, esp. by applying a computer system. □ **systems analyst** *n.*

systems operator *n. Computing* a person who controls or monitors the operation of complex esp. electronic systems.

systole *n. Physiol.* the contraction of the heart, when blood is pumped into the arteries. (cf. DIASTOLE). [from Greek *sustolē*] □ **systolic** *adj.*

S

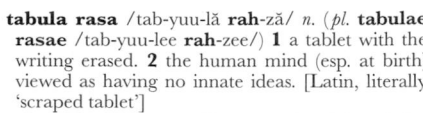

T

T¹ *n.* (also **t**) (*pl.* **Ts** or **T's**) **1** the twentieth letter of the alphabet. **2** a T-shaped thing (esp. *attrib.*: *T-joint*). □ **to a T** exactly; to a nicety.

T² *symb.* tesla.

t *abbr.* (also **t.**) **1** ton(s). **2** tonne(s).

't *pron.* = IT (*'tis*).

TA *abbr.* (in the UK) Territorial Army.

Ta *symb. Chem.* the element tantalum.

ta *int. Brit. colloq.* thank you. [childish form]

TAB *abbr.* typhoid-paratyphoid A and B vaccine.

tab¹ ● *n.* **1** a small flap or strip of material attached for grasping, fastening, or hanging up, or for identification. **2** esp. *N. Amer. colloq.* a bill or price (*picked up the tab*). **3 a** a stage curtain. **b** a loop for suspending this. ● *v.tr.* (**tabbed**, **tabbing**) provide with a tab or tabs. □ **keep tabs** (or **a tab**) **on** *colloq.* **1** keep account of. **2** have under observation or in check. [Middle English]

tab² *n.* = TABULATOR 2.

tabard *n.* **1** a herald's official coat emblazoned with royal arms. **2** a woman's or girl's sleeveless jerkin. **3** *hist.* ◄ a knight's short emblazoned garment worn over armour. [from Old French *tabart*]

Tabasco *n. propr.* a pungent sauce made from the fruit of *Capsicum frutescens*. [from *Tabasco*, a river and state in Mexico]

tabbouleh *n.* an Arab vegetable salad made with cracked wheat. [from Arabic *tabbūla*]

tabby *n.* (*pl.* **-ies**) **1** (in full **tabby cat**) a grey or brownish cat mottled or streaked with dark stripes. ▷ CAT. **2** a kind of watered silk. **3** a plain weave. [sense 2: from Arabic *al-'attabiya*, the quarter of Baghdad where manufactured]

tabernacle *n.* **1** *hist.* a tent used as a sanctuary for the Ark of the Covenant by the Israelites during the Exodus. **2** *Eccl.* a canopied niche or receptacle esp. for the Eucharistic elements. **3** a place of worship in nonconformist creeds. [from Latin *tabernaculum* 'tent']

tabla *n.* (in Indian music) a pair of small drums played with the hands. ▷ PERCUSSION. [from Arabic *ṭabl* 'drum']

table ● *n.* **1** a piece of furniture with a flat top and one or more legs, providing a level surface for eating, working at, etc. **2** a flat surface serving a specified purpose (*bird table*). **3 a** food provided in a household (*keeps a good table*). **b** a group seated at table for dinner etc. **4 a** a set of facts or figures systematically displayed, esp. in columns (*a table of contents*). **b** matter contained in this. **c** = MULTIPLICATION TABLE. **5 a** a slab of wood or stone etc. for bearing an inscription. **b** matter inscribed on this. ● *v.tr.* **1** *Brit.* bring forward for discussion or consideration at a meeting. **2** esp. *US* postpone consideration of

TABARD: KNIGHT WEARING A TABARD

tabard

heraldic arms

armour

(a matter). □ **at table** taking a meal at a table. **on the table** offered for discussion. **turn the tables** (often foll. by *on*) reverse one's relations (with), esp. by turning an inferior into a superior position. **under the table 1** *colloq.* very drunk. **2** = *under the counter* (see COUNTER¹). [from Latin *tabula* 'plank, tablet, list'] □ **tableful** *n.* (*pl.* **-fuls**).

tableau /**tab**-loh/ *n.* (*pl.* **tableaux** /-lohz/) **1** a picturesque presentation. **2** = TABLEAU VIVANT. [French, literally 'picture']

tableau vivant /vee-**von**/ *n.* (*pl.* **tableaux vivants** *pronunc.* same) *Theatr.* a silent and motionless group of people arranged to represent a scene.

tablecloth *n.* a cloth spread over the top of a table, esp. for meals.

table d'hôte /tabhl **doht**/ *n.* a meal consisting of a set menu at a fixed price, esp. in a hotel. [French, literally 'host's table']

tableland *n.* a plateau.

table licence *n. Brit.* a licence to serve alcoholic drinks only with meals.

table linen *n.* tablecloths, napkins, etc.

table mat *n.* a mat for protecting a table top from hot dishes etc.

table napkin see NAPKIN 1.

table salt *n.* salt that is ground or easy to grind for use at meals.

tablespoon *n.* **1** a large spoon for serving food. **2** an amount held by this. □ **tablespoonful** *n.* (*pl.* **-fuls**).

tablet *n.* **1** a small solid dose of a medicine etc. ▷ DRUG. **2** a bar of soap etc. **3** ► a flat slab of stone or wood, esp. for display or an inscription. **4** *N. Amer.* a writing pad. [from Old French *tablete*]

table tennis *n.* ◄ an indoor game based on tennis, played with small bats and a ball bounced on a table divided by a net.

table top *n.* **1** the top or surface of a table. **2** (**table-top**) (*attrib.*) that can be placed or used on a table top.

tableware *n.* dishes, plates, implements, etc., for use at meals.

table wine *n.* ordinary wine for drinking with a meal.

tabloid *n.* a newspaper, usu. popular in style, having pages half the size of those of the average broadsheet. [originally the proprietary name of a medicine sold in tablets]

taboo (also **tabu**) ● *n.* (*pl.* **taboos** or **tabus**) **1** a system or the act of setting a person or thing apart as sacred, prohibited, or accursed. **2** a prohibition imposed by social custom. ● *adj.* **1** avoided or prohibited (*taboo words*). **2** designated as sacred and prohibited. ● *v.tr.* (**taboos**, **tabooed** or **tabus**, **tabued**) **1** put under taboo. **2** exclude or prohibit by authority or social influence. [from Polynesian *tabu*]

tabor /**tay**-ber/ *n. hist.* ► a small drum, esp. one used to accompany a pipe. [from Old French *tabour*]

tabouret /**tab**-ŏ-ret/ *n.* (*US* **taboret**) a low seat usu. without arms or a back. [French, literally 'stool']

tabular *adj.* **1** of or arranged in tables or lists. **2** broad and flat like a table. **3** (of a crystal) having two broad flat faces. [from Latin *tabularis*] □ **tabularly** *adv.*

TABLE TENNIS BAT AND BALL

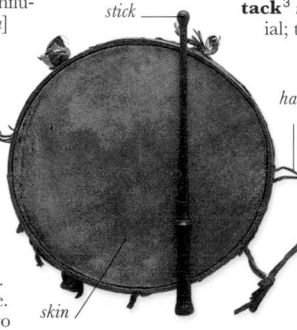

TABOR: MEDIEVAL TABOR AND DRUMSTICK

stick

hanging strap

skin

tabula rasa /tab-yuu-lǎ **rah**-zǎ/ *n.* (*pl.* **tabulae rasae** /tab-yuu-lee **rah**-zee/) **1** a tablet with the writing erased. **2** the human mind (esp. at birth) viewed as having no innate ideas. [Latin, literally 'scraped tablet']

tabulate *v.tr.* arrange (figures or facts) in tabular form. [based on Latin *tabula* 'table'] □ **tabulation** *n.*

tabulator *n.* **1** a person or thing that tabulates. **2** a device on a typewriter for advancing to a sequence of set positions in tabular work. **3** *Computing* a machine that produces lists or tables from a data storage medium such as punched cards.

tabun *n.* an organic phosphorus compound used as a nerve gas.

tacet /**tas**-it/ *v.intr. Mus.* (as an instruction for a particular voice or instrument) be silent. [Latin, literally 'is silent']

tach *n. N. Amer. colloq.* = TACHOMETER.

tache var. of TASH.

tachism /**tash**-izm/ *n.* (also **tachisme**) a form of action painting with dabs of colour arranged randomly. [from French *tachisme*]

tacho *n.* (*pl.* **-os**) *Brit. colloq.* **1** = TACHOMETER. **2** = TACHOGRAPH.

tacho- *comb. form* speed. [from Greek *takhos*]

tachograph *n.* a device used esp. in heavy goods vehicles and coaches etc. for automatically recording speed and travel time.

tachometer *n.* an instrument for measuring the rate of rotation of a shaft and hence the speed or velocity of a vehicle. ▷ INSTRUMENT PANEL

tachy- *comb. form* swift. [from Greek *takhus*]

tachycardia *n. Med.* an abnormally rapid heart rate. [based on Greek *kardia* 'heart']

cuneiform inscription

ocean

Babylon

TABLET SHOWING BABYLONIAN VIEW OF THE WORLD

tacit *adj.* understood or implied without being stated. [from Latin *tacitus* 'silent'] □ **tacitly** *adv.*

taciturn *adj.* reserved in speech; uncommunicative. [from Latin *taciturnus*] □ **taciturnity** *n.* **taciturnly** *adv.*

tack¹ ● *n.* **1** a small sharp broad-headed nail. **2** *N. Amer.* a drawing pin. **3** a long stitch used in fastening fabrics etc. lightly or temporarily together. **4** the direction in which a ship moves, esp. a temporary change of direction to take advantage of a side wind etc. **5** a course of action or policy (*try another tack*). **6** a sticky condition of varnish etc. ● *v.* **1** *tr.* (often foll. by *down*) fasten with tacks. **2** *tr.* stitch (pieces of cloth etc.) lightly together. **3** *tr.* (foll. by *to, on*) annex (a thing). **4** *intr.* (often foll. by *about*) **a** change a ship's course by turning its head to the wind. **b** make a series of tacks. **5** *intr.* change one's conduct or policy etc. **6** *tr. Brit.* append (a clause) to a bill. [Middle English] □ **tacker** *n.*

tack² *n.* the saddle, bridle, etc., of a horse. [shortened from TACKLE]

tack³ *n. colloq.* cheap, shoddy, or tasteless material; tat, kitsch. [back-formation from TACKY²]

tackle ● *n.* **1** equipment for a task or sport. **2** a mechanism, esp. of ropes, hooks, etc., for lifting weights, managing sails, etc. ▷ RIGGING. **3 a** a windlass with its ropes and hooks. **b** an act of tackling in football etc. ● *v.* **1** try to deal with (a problem or difficulty). **2** *Sport* grapple with or try to overcome (an opponent). **3** (often foll. by *on, about*) initiate discussion with (a person), esp. with regard to a disputed issue. **4** obstruct, intercept, or seize and stop (a player running with the ball). **5** secure by means of tackle. [Middle English] □ **tackler** *n.* **tackling** *n.*

stick

T

tackle-block *n.* ► a pulley over which a rope runs.

tacky[1] *adj.* (**tackier, tackiest**) slightly sticky. □ **tackiness** *n.*

tacky[2] *adj.* (**tackier, tackiest**) *colloq.* **1** showing poor taste or style. **2** tatty or seedy. [19th-century coinage] □ **tackily** *adv.* **tackiness** *n.*

taco *n.* (*pl.* **-os**) a Mexican dish of meat etc. in a folded or rolled tortilla. [Mexican Spanish]

tact *n.* **1** skill in dealing with others, esp. in delicate situations. **2** intuitive perception of the right thing to do or say. [from Latin *tactus* 'touch, sense of touch']

tactful *adj.* having or showing tact. □ **tactfully** *adv.* **tactfulness** *n.*

tactic *n.* **1** a tactical manoeuvre. **2** = TACTICS. [from Greek *taktikē* (*tekhnē*) '(art) of tactics']

tactical *adj.* **1** of, relating to, or constituting tactics (*a tactical retreat*). **2** (of bombing or weapons) done or for use in immediate support of military or naval operations (opp. STRATEGIC 3). **3** adroitly planning or planned. □ **tactically** *adv.*

tactics *n.pl.* **1** (also treated as *sing.*) the art of disposing armed forces in order of battle and of organizing operations. **2** the plans and means adopted in carrying out a scheme or achieving some end. □ **tactician** *n.*

tactile *adj.* **1** of or connected with the sense of touch. **2** perceived by touch. **3** tangible. [from Latin *tactilis*] □ **tactual** *adj.* (in senses 1, 2). **tactility** *n.*

tactless *adj.* having or showing no tact. □ **tactlessly** *adv.* **tactlessness** *n.*

tad *n.* esp. *N. Amer. colloq.* a small amount (often used adverbially: *a tad too salty*). [19th-century coinage]

tadpole *n.* ◄ a larva of an amphibian, esp. a frog, toad, or newt in its aquatic stage. [Middle English]

tail
gills

TADPOLES

tae kwon do *n.* ▼ a modern Korean martial art similar to karate. [Korean]

foot raised to strike
arm used for balance

TAE KWON DO:
AXE KICK

taffeta *n.* a fine lustrous silk or silklike fabric. [from Persian *tāfta* 'twisted']

taffrail *n. Naut.* a rail round a ship's stern. [from Dutch *taffereel* 'panel']

Taffy *n.* (*pl.* **-ies**) *Brit. colloq.* often *offens.* a Welshman. [supposed Welsh pronunciation of *Davy* = *David* (Welsh *Dafydd*)]

taffy *n.* (*pl.* **-ies**) **1** *N. Amer.* a confection like toffee.

TACKLE-BLOCK
USED TO HOIST
SAILS ON A SHIP

pulley

2 *US slang* insincere flattery. [19th-century coinage]

tafia *n. W.Ind.* rum distilled from molasses etc.

tag[1] ● *n.* **1** a label, esp. one for tying on an object to show its address, price, etc. **2** a metal or plastic point at the end of a lace etc. to assist insertion. **3** a loop at the back of a boot used in pulling it on. **4** an electronic device that can be attached to a person or thing for monitoring purposes. **5** a loose or ragged end of anything. **6** a trite quotation or stock phrase. ● *v.tr.* (**tagged, tagging**) **1** provide with a tag or tags. **2** (often foll. by *on, on to*) join or attach. **3** *Brit. colloq.* follow closely or trail behind. **4** *Computing* identify (an item of data) by its type for later retrieval. **5** label radioactively (see LABEL *v.* 3). □ **tag along** (often foll. by *with*) go along or accompany passively. [Middle English]

tag[2] ● *n.* **1** a children's chasing game. **2** *Baseball* the act of tagging a runner. ● *v.tr.* (**tagged, tagging**) **1** touch in a game of tag. **2** (often foll. by *out*) *Baseball* put (a runner) out by touching with the ball or with the hand holding the ball. [18th-century coinage]

tag end *n.* esp. *US* the last remnant of something.

tagliatelle /tal-yă-**tel**-i/ *n.* a form of pasta in narrow ribbons. ▷ PASTA. [Italian]

Tahitian ● *n.* **1** a native or national of Tahiti in the S. Pacific. **2** the language of Tahiti. ● *adj.* of or relating to Tahiti or its people or language.

t'ai chi ch'uan /ty chee **chwahn**/ *n.* (also **t'ai chi**) ▼ a Chinese martial art and system of callisthenics consisting of sequences of very slow controlled movements. [Chinese, literally 'great ultimate boxing']

right arm at shoulder level
eyes on left arm
palm turned inwards
weight on right leg

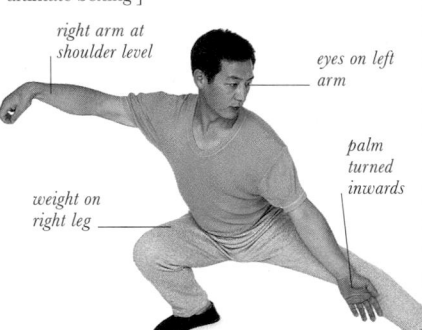

T'AI CHI CH'UAN: LAST POSITION OF THE
DESCENDING SINGLE WHIP MOVE

taiga /ty-gă/ *n.* coniferous forest lying between tundra and steppe, esp. in Siberia. [Russian]

tail[1] ● *n.* **1** the hindmost part of an animal, esp. when prolonged beyond the rest of the body. **2 a** a thing like a tail in form or position. **b** the rear end of anything, e.g. of a procession. **c** a long train or line of people, vehicles, etc. **3** the rear part of an aeroplane, with the tailplane and rudder, or of a rocket, or vehicle. **4** the luminous trail of particles following a comet. **5** the inferior or weaker part of anything, esp. in a sequence. **6 a** the part of a shirt below the waist. **b** the hanging part of the back of a coat. **7** (in *pl.*) *colloq.* **a** a tailcoat. **b** evening dress including this. **8** (in *pl.*) the reverse of a coin as a choice when tossing. **9** *colloq.* a person following or shadowing another. **10** an extra strip attached to the lower end of a kite. **11** the stem of a note in music. **12** the part of a letter (e.g. *y*) below the line. ● *v.* **1** *tr.* remove the stalks of (fruit). **2** *tr.* & (foll. by *after*) *intr. colloq.* shadow or follow closely. **3** *tr.* provide with a tail. **4** *tr.* dock the tail of (a lamb etc.). **5** *tr.* (often foll. by *on to*) join (one thing to another). □ **on a person's tail** closely following a person. **tail back** *Brit.* (of traffic) form a tailback. **tail off** (or **away**) **1** become fewer, smaller, or slighter. **2** fall behind or away in a scattered line.

with one's tail between one's legs in a state of dejection or humiliation. **with one's tail up** in good spirits; cheerful. [Old English] □ **tailed** *adj.* (also in *comb.*). **tailless** *adj.*

tail[2] *Law* ● *n.* limitation of ownership, esp. of an estate limited to a person and that person's heirs. ● *adj.* so limited (*estate tail*). □ **in tail** under such a limitation. [from Latin *talea* 'twig, cutting']

tailback *n. Brit.* a long line of traffic extending back from an obstruction.

tailboard *n. Brit.* a hinged or removable flap at the rear of a lorry etc.

tailcoat *n. Brit.* ◄ a man's morning or evening coat with a long divided flap at the back, worn as part of formal dress.

tailcoat

TAILCOAT: EARLY
20TH-CENTURY
TAILCOAT

tail-end *n.* **1** the hindmost or lowest or last part. **2** = TAIL[1] *n.* 5. □ **tail-ender** *n.*

tail feather *n.* a strong flight feather of a bird's tail. ▷ BIRD, OWL

tailgate ● *n.* **1** esp. *US* **a** = TAILBOARD. **b** ▼ the tail door of an estate car or hatchback. **2** the lower end of a canal lock. ● *v.* *US colloq.* **1** *intr.* drive too closely behind another vehicle. **2** *tr.* follow (a vehicle) too closely. □ **tailgater** *n.*

tailgate

tail light *n.* (also **tail lamp**) a light at the rear of a train, motor vehicle, or bicycle.

tail-off *n.* a decline or gradual reduction, esp. in demand.

tailor ● *n.* a maker of clothes, esp. of men's outer garments to measure. ● *v.* **1** *tr.* make (clothes) as a tailor. **2** *tr.* make or adapt for a special purpose. **3** *intr.* work as or be a tailor. **4** *tr.* (as **tailored** *adj.*) = TAILOR-MADE. [from Old French *tailleur* 'cutter'] □ **tailoring** *n.*

TAILGATE
ON A HATCHBACK

tailor-bird *n.* any small Asian etc. warbler of the genus *Orthotomus* that stitches leaves together to form a nest.

tailored *adj.* (of clothing) well or closely fitted.

tailor-made ● *adj.* **1** (of clothing) made to order by a tailor. **2** made or suited for a particular purpose. ● *n.* a tailor-made garment.

tailpiece *n.* **1** an appendage at the rear of anything. **2** the final part of a thing. **3** a decoration in a blank space at the end of a chapter etc. in a book.

tailpipe *n.* the rear section of the exhaust pipe of a motor vehicle.

tailplane *n. Brit.* a horizontal aerofoil at the tail of an aircraft. ▷ AIRCRAFT

tailspin ● *n.* **1** a spin by an aircraft with the tail spiralling. **2** a state of chaos or panic. ● *v.intr.* (**-spinning**; *past* and *past part.* **-spun**) perform a tailspin.

tailwheel *n.* a wheel supporting the tail of an aircraft. ▷ BIPLANE

tailwind *n.* a wind blowing in the direction of travel of a vehicle or aircraft etc.

taint ● *n.* **1** a spot or trace of decay, infection, or some bad quality. **2** an unpleasant scent or smell. **3** a corrupt condition or infection. ● *v.* **1** *tr.* affect with a taint. **2** *tr.* (foll. by *with*) affect slightly. **3** *intr.* become tainted. [Middle English] □ **taintless** *adj.*

taipan /ty-**pan**/ *n.* the head of a foreign business in China. [Chinese]

take ● *v.* (*past* **took**; *past part.* **taken**) **1** *tr.* lay hold of; get into one's hands. **2** *tr.* acquire, get possession of,

T

capture, earn, or win. **3** *tr.* get the use of by purchase or formal agreement (*take lodgings*). **4** *tr.* (in a recipe) avail oneself of; use. **5** *tr.* use as a means of transport (*took a taxi*). **6** *tr.* regularly buy (a particular newspaper etc.). **7** *tr.* obtain after fulfilling the required conditions (*take a degree*). **8** *tr.* occupy (*take a chair*). **9** *tr.* make use of (*take the next left*). **10** *tr.* consume as food or medicine. **11** *intr.* **a** be successful or effective (*the inoculation did not take*). **b** (of a seed etc.) begin to grow. **12** *tr.* require or use up (*will take time*). **13** *tr.* wear (a particular size of garment etc.) (*takes size six*). **14** *tr.* cause to come or go with one; convey (*take the book home*). **15** *tr.* remove; steal. **16** *tr.* catch or be infected with (fire or fever etc.). **17** *tr.* **a** experience or be affected by (*take fright*). **b** receive (*take comfort*). **c** exert (*take courage*). **18** *tr.* find out and note (details, a temperature, etc.) by enquiry or measurement. **19** *tr.* grasp mentally; understand (*I take your point*). **20** *tr.* treat or regard in a specified way (*took it badly*). **21** *tr.* (foll. by *for*) regard as being (*do you take me for an idiot?*). **22** *tr.* **a** accept (*take the offer*). **b** hold (*takes two pints*). **c** tolerate (*take a joke*). **23** *tr.* choose or assume (*took a job*; *took the initiative*). **24** *tr.* derive (*takes its name from the inventor*). **25** *tr.* (foll. by *from*) subtract. **26** *tr.* execute, make, or undertake; perform or effect (*take notes*; *take an oath*). **27** *tr.* occupy or engage oneself in; indulge in (*take a rest*; *take exercise*). **28** *tr.* conduct (*took the school assembly*). **29** *tr.* deal with in a certain way (*took the corner too fast*). **30** *tr.* **a** teach or be taught (a subject). **b** be examined in (a subject). **31** *tr.* make (a photograph) with a camera; photograph (a person or thing). **32** *tr.* use as an instance (*let us take Napoleon*). **33** *tr. Gram.* have or require as part of the appropriate construction. **34** *tr.* have sexual intercourse with (a woman). **35** *tr.* (in *passive*; foll. by *by*, *with*) be attracted or charmed by. • *n.* **1** an amount taken or caught in one session or attempt etc. **2** a scene or sequence of film photographed continuously at one time. **3** esp. *US* takings, esp. money received at a theatre for seats. □ **be taken ill** become ill, esp. suddenly. **have what it takes** *colloq.* have the necessary qualities etc. for success. **take account of** see ACCOUNT. **take action** see ACTION. **take advantage of** see ADVANTAGE. **take after** resemble. **take against** *Brit.* begin to dislike, esp. impulsively. **take aim** see AIM. **take apart 1** dismantle. **2** *colloq.* beat or defeat conclusively. **3** *colloq.* criticize severely. **take aside** see ASIDE. **take as read** *Brit.* accept without reading or discussing. **take away 1** remove or carry elsewhere. **2** subtract. **3** *Brit.* buy (food etc.) at a shop or restaurant for eating elsewhere. **take back 1** retract (a statement). **2** convey (a person or thing) to his or her or its original position. **3** carry (a person) in thought to a past time. **4** *Printing* transfer to the previous line. **take the biscuit** (or **bun** or **cake**) *colloq.* be the most remarkable. **take one's breath away** see BREATH. **take care of** see CARE. **take a chance** etc. see CHANCE. **take charge** see CHARGE. **take down 1** write down (spoken words). **2** remove (a structure) by dismantling. **3** humiliate. **4** lower (a garment worn below the waist). **take effect** see EFFECT. **take for granted** see GRANT. **take fright** see FRIGHT. **take from** diminish; weaken; detract from. **take heart** be encouraged. **take hold** see HOLD[1]. **take ill** (*US* **sick**) *colloq.* be taken ill. **take in 1** receive as a lodger etc. **2** undertake (work) at home. **3** make (a garment etc.) smaller. **4** understand. **5** cheat, dupe. **6** include or comprise. **7** *colloq.* visit (a place) on the way to another. **8** furl (a sail). **take in hand 1** undertake; start doing or dealing with. **2** undertake the control or reform of (a person). **take into account** see ACCOUNT. **take it 1** (often foll. by *that* + clause) assume. **2** *colloq.* endure a difficulty or hardship in a specified way (*took it badly*). **take it easy** see EASY. **take it from me** (or **take my word for it**) I can assure you. **take it ill** resent it. **take it into one's head** see HEAD. **take it on one** (or **oneself**) (foll. by *to* + infin.) venture or presume. **take it or leave it** (esp. in *imper.*) an expression of indifference or impatience about another's decision after making an offer. **take it out of 1** exhaust the strength of. **2** *Brit.* have revenge on. **take it out on** relieve one's frustration by attacking or treating harshly. **take a thing kindly** see KINDLY[1]. **take kindly to** see KINDLY[1]. **take one's leave of** see LEAVE[2]. **take leave of one's senses** see SENSE. **take leave to** see LEAVE[2]. **take a lot of** (or **some**) **doing** be hard to do. **take lying down** see LIE[1]. **take a person's name in vain** see VAIN. **take off 1 a** remove (clothing). **b** remove or lead away. **c** withdraw (transport, a show, etc.). **2** deduct (part of an amount). **3** depart, esp. hastily (*took off in a fast car*). **4** *colloq.* mimic humorously. **5** jump from the ground. **6** become airborne. **7** (of a scheme etc.) become successful or popular. **8** have (a period) away from work. **take oneself off** go away. **take on 1** undertake (work etc.). **2** engage (an employee). **3** be willing or ready to meet (an adversary in sport, argument, etc.). **4** acquire (a new meaning etc.). **5** esp. *Brit. colloq.* show strong emotion. **take on the chin** see CHIN. **take out 1** remove from within a place; extract. **2** escort on an outing. **3** get (a licence or summons etc.) issued. **4** *US* = *take away* 3. **5** *slang* murder or destroy. **take a person out of himself** or **herself** make a person forget his or her worries. **take over 1** succeed to the management or ownership of. **2** take control (of). **take part** see PART. **take the part of** see PART. **take place** see PLACE. **take one's place** see PLACE. **take the place of** see PLACE. **take a person's point** see POINT. **take root** see ROOT[1]. **take shape** assume a distinct form; develop into something definite. **take sides** see SIDE. **take stock** see STOCK. **take that!** an exclamation accompanying a blow etc. **take one's time** not hurry. **take to 1** fall into the habit of (*took to smoking*). **2** have recourse to. **3** adapt oneself to. **4** form a liking for. **take to the cleaners** see CLEANER. **take to heart** see HEART. **take to one's heels** see HEEL[1]. **take to pieces** see PIECE. **take to task** see TASK. **take the trouble** see TROUBLE. **take up 1** become interested or engaged in (a pursuit). **2** adopt as a protégé. **3** occupy (time or space). **4** begin (residence etc.). **5** resume after an interruption. **6** interrupt or question (a speaker). **7** accept (an offer etc.). **8** shorten (a garment). **9** lift up. **10** absorb (*sponges take up water*). **11** take (a person) into a vehicle. **12** pursue (a matter etc.) further. **take a person up on** accept (a person's offer etc.). **take up the gauntlet** accept a challenge. **take up with** begin to associate with. [from Old Norse *taka*] □ **takable** *adj.* (also **takeable**).

takeaway *Brit.* • *attrib.adj.* (of food) bought at a shop or restaurant for eating elsewhere. • *n.* **1** an establishment selling such food. **2** the food itself.

take-home pay *n.* the pay received by an employee after the deduction of tax etc.

take-off *n.* **1** the act of becoming airborne. **2** an act of mimicking. **3** a place from which one jumps.

take-out *attrib.adj.* & *n.* esp. *N. Amer.* = TAKEAWAY.

takeover *n.* the assumption of control (esp. of a business); the buying-out of one company by another.

taker *n.* **1** a person who takes a bet. **2** a person who accepts an offer.

take-up *n.* acceptance of something offered.

taking • *adj.* **1** attractive or captivating. **2** catching or infectious. • *n.* (in *pl.*) an amount of money taken in business. □ **takingly** *adv.*

talc • *n.* **1** talcum powder. **2** ▼ any crystalline form of magnesium silicate that occurs in soft flat plates, used as a lubricator etc. • *v.tr.* (**talced, talcing** or **talcked, talcking**) powder or treat (a surface) with talc to lubricate or dry it. [from Persian *ṭalk*] □ **talcy** *adj.* (in sense 1 of *n.*).

TALC

talcum • *n.* **1** (in full **talcum powder**) powdered talc for toilet and cosmetic use, usu. perfumed. **2** = TALC *n.* 2. • *v.tr.* (**talcumed, talcuming**) powder with talcum. [medieval Latin]

tale *n.* **1** a narrative or story, esp. fictitious and imaginatively treated. **2** a report of an alleged fact, often malicious or in breach of confidence (*all sorts of tales will get about*). [Old English]

talebearer *n.* a person who maliciously gossips or reveals secrets. □ **talebearing** *n.* & *adj.*

talent *n.* **1** a special aptitude or faculty. **2** high mental ability. **3 a** a person or persons of talent. **b** *Brit. colloq.* attractive members of the opposite sex. **4** an ancient weight and unit of currency, esp. among the Greeks. [from Greek *talanton* 'balance, weight, sum of money'] □ **talented** *adj.* **talentless** *adj.*

talent scout *n.* a person looking for talented performers, esp. in sport and entertainment.

talent spotter *n. Brit.* = TALENT SCOUT.

taleteller *n.* **1** a person who tells stories. **2** a person who spreads malicious reports.

talisman *n.* (*pl.* **talismans**) **1** an object, esp. an inscribed ring or stone, supposed to be endowed with magic powers esp. of bringing good luck. **2** ► a charm or amulet. [from Greek *telesma* 'completion, religious rite'] □ **talismanic** *adj.*

TALISMAN: MAORI TALISMAN

talk • *v.* **1** *intr.* (often foll. by *to*, *with*) converse or communicate ideas by spoken words. **2** *intr.* have the power of speech. **3** *intr.* (foll. by *about*) **a** have as the subject of discussion. **b** (in *imper.*) *colloq.* as an emphatic statement (*talk about expense!*). **4** *tr.* express or utter in words; discuss (*talked cricket*). **5** *tr.* use (a language) in speech (*talking Spanish*). **6** *intr.* (foll. by *at*) address pompously. **7** *tr.* (usu. foll. by *into*, *out of*) bring into a specified condition etc. by talking (*talked himself hoarse*). **8** *intr.* reveal (esp. secret) information; betray secrets. **9** *intr.* gossip (*people are beginning to talk*). **10** *intr.* have influence (*money talks*). • *n.* **1** conversation or talking. **2** a particular mode of speech (*baby talk*). **3** an informal address or lecture. **4 a** a rumour or gossip (*there is talk of a merger*). **b** its theme (*their success was the talk of the town*). **5** (often in *pl.*) extended discussions or negotiations. □ **know what one is talking about** be expert or authoritative. **now you're talking** *colloq.* I like what you say, suggest, etc. **talk back 1** reply defiantly. **2** respond on a two-way radio system. **talk big** *colloq.* talk boastfully. **talk down to** speak patronizingly or condescendingly to. **talk a person down 1** silence a person by greater loudness or persistence. **2** bring (a pilot or aircraft) to landing by radioed instructions. **talk the hind leg off a donkey** talk incessantly. **talk nineteen to the dozen** see DOZEN. **talk of 1** discuss. **2** (often foll. by verbal noun) express some intention of (*talked of moving to London*). **talk out** *Brit.* block the course of (a bill in Parliament) by prolonging discussion to the time of adjournment. **talk over** discuss at length. **talk a person over** (or **round** or *US* **around**) gain a person's agreement by talking. **talk shop** talk about one's occupation, etc. **talk through** discuss thoroughly. **talk a person through** guide a person in (a task) with continuous instructions. **talk through one's hat** (or *Brit.* **neck**) *colloq.* **1** exaggerate. **2** bluff. **3** talk wildly or nonsensically. **talk to** reprove. **talk to oneself** soliloquize. **talk turkey** see TURKEY. **talk up** discuss (a subject) in order to arouse interest in it. **you can't** (or **can**) **talk** *colloq.* a reproof that the person addressed is just as culpable etc. in the matter at issue. [Middle English] □ **talker** *n.*

T

talkathon *n. colloq.* a prolonged session of talking or discussion.

talkative *adj.* fond of or given to talking. □ **talkatively** *adv.* **talkativeness** *n.*

talkback *n.* **1** (often *attrib.*) a system of two-way communication by loudspeaker. **2** = PHONE-IN.

talkie *n. archaic esp. US colloq.* a film with a soundtrack, as distinct from a silent film.

talking ● *adj.* **1** that talks. **2** having the power of speech. **3** expressive (*talking eyes*). ● *n.* in senses of TALK *v.* □ **talking of** *esp. Brit.* while we are discussing (*talking of food, what time is lunch?*).

talking book *n.* a recorded reading of a book, esp. for the blind.

talking film *n.* (also **talking picture**) a film with a soundtrack.

talking head *n. colloq.* a presenter etc. on television, speaking to the camera and viewed in close-up.

talking point *n.* a topic for discussion or argument.

talking shop *n. Brit. derog.* an institution regarded as a place of argument rather than action.

talking-to *n. colloq.* a reproof or reprimand.

talk radio *n.* a radio format in which the disc jockey chats to listeners over the phone about controversial issues, rather than playing records.

talk show *n.* = CHAT SHOW.

tall ● *adj.* **1** of more than average height. **2** of a specified height (*six feet tall*). **3** higher than the surrounding objects (*a tall building*). **4** *colloq.* extravagant or excessive; fanciful (*tall tale*). ● *adv.* as if tall; proudly (*sit tall*). [Middle English in sense 'ready, active'] □ **tallish** *adj.* **tallness** *n.*

tallboy *n. Brit.* a tall chest of drawers sometimes in lower and upper sections or mounted on legs.

tall hat *n.* = TOP HAT.

tall order *n.* an exorbitant or unreasonable demand.

tallow *n.* the harder kinds of (esp. animal) fat melted down for use in making candles, soap, etc. [from Middle Low German *talg*] □ **tallowish** *adj.* **tallowy** *adj.*

tall ship *n.* a sailing ship with a high mast.

tally ● *n.* (*pl.* **-ies**) **1** the reckoning of a debt or score. **2** a total score or amount. **3 a** a mark registering a fixed number of objects delivered or received. **b** such a number as a unit. **4** *hist.* **a** ▶ a piece of wood scored across with notches for the items of an account and then split into halves, each party keeping one. **b** an account kept in this way. **5** a ticket or label for identification. **6** a corresponding thing, counterpart, or duplicate. ● *v.* (**-ies**, **-ied**) (often foll. by *with*) **1** *intr.* agree or correspond. **2** *tr.* record or reckon by tally. [from Latin *talea*] □ **tallier** *n.*

TALLY: HALF OF A TALLY STICK

notches

tally-ho ● *int.* a huntsman's cry to the hounds on sighting a fox. ● *n.* (*pl.* **-hos**) an utterance of this. ● *v.* (**-hoes, -hoed**) **1** *intr.* utter a cry of 'tally-ho'. **2** *tr.* indicate (a fox) or urge (hounds) with this cry.

tallyman *n.* (*pl.* **-men**) **1** a person who keeps a tally. **2** *Brit.* a person who sells goods on credit, esp. from door to door.

Talmud *n.* the body of Jewish civil and ceremonial law and legend. [from late Hebrew *talmūd* 'instruction'] □ **Talmudic** *adj.* **Talmudical** *adj.* **Talmudist** *n.*

talon *n.* **1** ◀ a claw, esp. of a bird of prey. **2** the cards left after the deal in a card game. ▷ RAPTOR. [from Latin *talus* 'heel'] □ **taloned** *adj.* (also in *comb.*).

tam *n.* a tam-o'-shanter.

TALONS ON THE FOOT OF A SPARROWHAWK

talon

toe

---

tamarind *n.* **1** a tropical evergreen tree, *Tamarindus indica.* **2** the fruit of this, containing an acid pulp used as food and in drinks. [from Arabic *tamr-hindī* 'Indian date']

tamarisk *n.* ◀ any shrub of the genus *Tamarix*, usu. with long slender branches and small pink or white flowers. [from Latin *tamarix*]

TAMARISK (*Tamarix ramosissima* 'Pink Cascade')

tambour /tam-boor/ ● *n.* **1** a drum. **2 a** a circular frame for holding fabric taut while it is being embroidered. **b** material embroidered in this way. ● *v.tr.* (also *absol.*) decorate or embroider on a tambour. [French]

tambourine *n.* a percussion instrument consisting of a hoop with a parchment stretched over one side and jingling discs in slots round the hoop. ▷ ORCHESTRA, PERCUSSION. [French, literally 'little tambour'] □ **tambourinist** *n.*

tame ● *adj.* **1** (of an animal) domesticated; not wild or shy. **2** insipid; lacking spirit or interest (*tame acquiescence*). **3** *colloq.* (of a person) amenable or cooperative and available (*you need a tame accountant*). **4** *US* **a** (of land) cultivated. **b** (of a plant) produced by cultivation. ● *v.tr.* **1** make tame; domesticate. **2** subdue, curb. [Old English] □ **tamely** *adv.* **tameness** *n.* **tamer** *n.* (also in *comb.*).

tameable *adj.* capable of being tamed.

Tamil ● *n.* **1** a member of a people inhabiting South India and Sri Lanka. **2** the language of this people. ● *adj.* of or relating to this people or their language. [Tamil]

tammy *n.* (*pl.* **-ies**) = TAM-O'-SHANTER.

tam-o'-shanter *n.* a round woollen or cloth cap of Scottish origin fitting closely round the brows but large and full above. [named after the hero of Burns's *Tam o' Shanter* (1791)]

tamp *v.tr.* ram down hard or tightly. □ **tamper** *n.*

tamper *v.intr.* (foll. by *with*) **1 a** meddle or interfere with; make unauthorized changes in. **b** interfere with (a food product etc.), esp. by contamination and for blackmail purposes. **2** exert a secret or corrupt influence upon; bribe. [variant of TEMPER] □ **tamperer** *n.*

tamper-proof *adj.* made so that it cannot be tampered with.

tampon *n.* a plug of soft material used to stop a wound or absorb secretions, esp. one inserted into the vagina to absorb menstrual blood. [French]

tam-tam *n.* a large metal gong. [Hindi]

tan[1] ● *n.* **1** = SUNTAN. **2** a yellowish-brown colour. **3** bark, esp. of oak, bruised and used to tan hides. ● *adj.* of a yellowish-brown colour. ● *v.* (**tanned, tanning**) **1** *tr. & intr.* make or become brown by exposure to ultraviolet light. **2** *tr.* convert (raw hide) into leather. **3** *tr. slang* beat, thrash. [Old English] □ **tanning** *n.* **tannish** *adj.*

tan[2] *abbr.* tangent.

tanager *n.* ▶ any small American bird of the subfamily Thraupinae, the male usu. having brightly coloured plumage. [from Tupi (Brazilian) *tangará*]

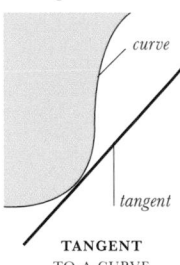

TANAGER: SCARLET TANAGER (*Piranga olivacea*)

TANDEM: OFF-ROAD TANDEM

tandem ● *n.* **1** ▲ a bicycle or tricycle with two or more seats one behind another. **2** a group of two persons etc. with one behind or following the other. **3** a carriage driven tandem. ● *adv.* with two or more horses harnessed one behind another (*drive tandem*). □ **in tandem 1** one behind another. **2** alongside each other, together. [Latin, literally 'at length (of time)']

tandoor /second part rhymes with poor/ *n.* a clay oven. [Hindi]

tandoori *n.* food cooked over charcoal in a tandoor (often *attrib.*: *tandoori chicken*). [Hindi]

tang[1] *n.* **1** a strong taste or flavour or smell. **2** a characteristic quality. **3** the projection on the blade of a tool, esp. a knife, by which the blade is held firm in the handle. [from Old Norse *tange* 'point, tang of a knife']

tang[2] ● *v.tr. & intr.* ring, clang; sound loudly. ● *n.* a tanging sound.

tanga *n. Brit.* a pair of briefs consisting of small panels connected with strings. [Portuguese]

tangelo /tan-jĕ-loh/ *n.* (*pl.* **-os**) a hybrid of the tangerine and grapefruit. [blend of TANGERINE and POMELO]

tangent *n.* **1** ◀ a straight line, curve, or surface that meets another curve or curved surface at a point, but does not intersect it at that point. **2** the ratio of the sides (other than the hypotenuse) opposite and adjacent to an angle in a right-angled triangle. □ **at a tangent** diverging from a previous course of action or thought etc. [from Latin *tangent-* 'touching'] □ **tangency** *n.*

TANGENT TO A CURVE

curve

tangent

tangential *adj.* **1** of or along a tangent. **2** divergent. **3** peripheral. □ **tangentially** *adv.*

tangerine ● *n.* **1** a small sweet orange-coloured citrus fruit with a thin skin; a mandarin. ▷ CITRUS FRUIT. **2** a deep orange-yellow colour. ● *adj.* of this colour. [based on *Tangier*, a seaport in Morocco]

tangible /tan-ji-bŭl/ *adj.* **1** perceptible by touch. **2** definite; clearly intelligible; not elusive (*tangible proof*). [from Late Latin *tangibilis*] □ **tangibility** *n.* **tangibleness** *n.* **tangibly** *adv.*

tangle ● *v.* **1 a** *tr.* intertwine (threads or hairs etc.) in a confused mass; entangle. **b** *intr.* become tangled. **2** *intr.* (foll. by *with*) *colloq.* become involved (esp. in conflict or argument) with (*don't tangle with me*). **3** *tr.* complicate (*a tangled affair*). ● *n.* **1** a confused mass of intertwined threads etc. **2** a confused or complicated state. [Middle English]

tangly *adj.* (**tanglier, tangliest**) tangled.

tango ● *n.* (*pl.* **-os**) **1** a slow ballroom dance originating in Buenos Aires, characterized by gliding movements and abrupt pauses. **2** the music for this. ● *v.intr.* (**-oes, -oed**) dance the tango. [Latin American Spanish]

tangram *n.* a Chinese puzzle square cut into seven

T

pieces to be combined into various figures. [19th-century coinage]

tangy adj. (**tangier**, **tangiest**) having a strong usu. piquant tang. □ **tanginess** n.

tanh abbr. hyperbolic tangent.

tank ● n. **1** a large receptacle or storage chamber usu. for liquid or gas. **2** ▼ a heavy armoured fighting vehicle moving on a tracked carriage. **3** a container for the fuel supply in a motor vehicle. ● v. **1** tr. (usu. foll. by up) fill the tank of (a vehicle etc.) with fuel. **2** colloq. **a** intr. (foll. by up) drink heavily; become drunk. **b** tr. & refl. (often as **tanked up** adj.) inebriate oneself with alcoholic drink or drugs. [from Gujarati *tānkh*] □ **tankful** n. (pl. **-fuls**). **tankless** adj.

    tankard n. **1** ◀ a tall beer mug (esp. of silver or pewter) with a handle. **2** the contents of or an amount held by a tankard. [Middle English]

    tank engine n. a steam locomotive carrying fuel and water receptacles in its own frame, not in a tender.

    tanker ● n. a ship, aircraft, or road vehicle for carrying liquids, esp. mineral oils, in bulk. ● v.tr. (usu. in passive; often foll. by in) transport by tanker.

    tank top n. a sleeveless close-fitting upper garment with a scoop neck.

    tanner n. a person who tans hides.

    tannery n. (pl. **-ies**) a place where hides are tanned.

TANKARD: LIDDED PEWTER TANKARD

tannic adj. of or produced from tan. [from French *tannique*] □ **tannate** n.

tannic acid n. a complex natural organic compound of a yellowish colour used as a mordant and astringent.

tannin n. any of a group of complex organic compounds found in certain tree barks and oak-galls, used in leather production. [from French *tanin*]

tannish see TAN[1].

tannoy n. Brit. propr. a type of public address system. [from *tantalum* alloy (rectifier)]

    tansy n. (pl. **-ies**) ◀ any plant of the genus *Tanacetum*, esp. *T. vulgare* with yellow button-like flowers and aromatic leaves. [based on medieval Latin *athanasia* 'immortality']

    tantalize v.tr. (also **-ise**) **1** torment or tease by the sight or promise of what is unobtainable. **2** raise and then dash the hopes of. [based on Greek *Tantalos*, mythical Phrygian king condemned to be tempted by water and fruit seemingly within reach but ever elusive] □ **tantalization** n. **tantalizer** n. **tantalizingly** adv.

    tantalum n. Chem. a rare hard white metallic element used in surgery and for electronic components. [based on TANTALIZE, with reference to its frustrating insolubility in acids] □ **tantalic** adj.

    tantalus n. Brit. a stand in which spirit-decanters may be locked up though still visible.

TANSY (*Tanacetum vulgare*)

tantamount predic.adj. (foll. by to) equivalent to (was tantamount to a denial). [based on Italian *tanto montare* 'to amount to so much']

tantra n. any of a class of Hindu or Buddhist mystical and magical writings. [Sanskrit, literally 'loom, doctrine'] □ **tantric** adj. **tantrism** n.

tantrum n. an outburst of bad temper or petulance. [18th-century coinage]

Taoiseach /tee-shĕk/ n. the Prime Minister of the Irish Republic. [Irish, literally 'chief, leader']

Taoism /first part rhymes with cow/ n. a Chinese philosophy based on the writings of Laozc (c.500 BC), advocating humility and religious piety. [based on Chinese *dao* '(right) way'] □ **Taoist** n.

tap[1] ● n. **1** ▶ a device by which a flow of liquid or gas from a pipe or vessel can be controlled. **2 a** an act of tapping a telephone etc. **b** a device used for this. **3** Brit. a taproom. **4** an instrument for cutting the thread of a female screw. ● v.tr. (**tapped**, **tapping**) **1 a** provide (a cask) with a tap. **b** let out (a liquid) by means of, or as if by means of, a tap. **2** draw sap from (a tree) by cutting into it. **3 a** obtain information or supplies or resources from. **b** extract or obtain; discover and exploit (tap the nation's skills). **4** connect a listening device to (a telephone etc.). **5** cut a female screw-thread in. □ **on tap 1** ready to be drawn off by tap. **2** colloq. freely available. [Old English] □ **tapless** adj. **tappable** adj.

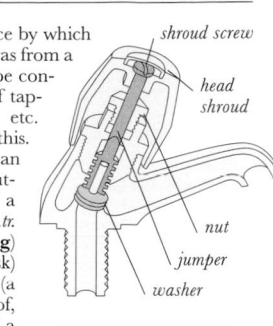

TAP: CROSS-SECTION OF A TAP

(labels: shroud screw, head shroud, nut, jumper, washer)

tap[2] ● v. (**tapped**, **tapping**) **1** intr. (foll. by at, on) strike a gentle but audible blow. **2** tr. strike lightly (tapped me on the shoulder). **3** tr. (foll. by against etc.) cause (a thing) to strike lightly (tapped a stick against it). **4** tr. (often foll. by out) make a tap or taps (tapped out the rhythm). ● n. **1 a** a light blow; a rap. **b** the sound of this. **2 a** tap-dancing. **b** ▲ a metal attachment to a tap-dancer's shoe. [Middle English] □ **tapper** n.

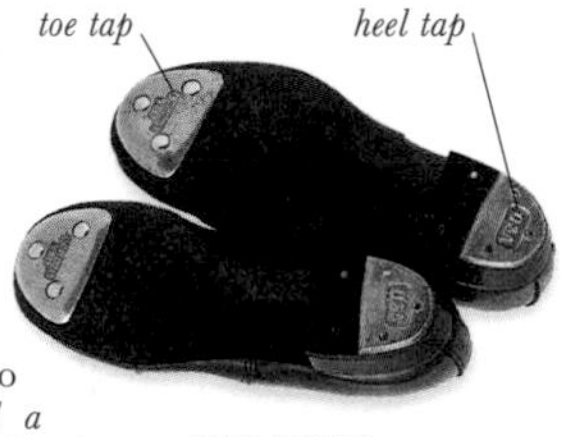

TAP SHOES (UNDERSIDE)

(labels: toe tap, heel tap)

tapas n.pl. (often attrib.) small savoury dishes esp. in Spanish style. [Spanish]

tap-dance ● n. a dance or form of display dancing performed wearing shoes fitted with metal taps,

---

TANK

Tanks were first used in battle in 1916, but were greatly improved in the Second World War (1939–45). Although their basic design has changed little since then, technological advances have meant they now carry a more sophisticated and diverse array of weapons.

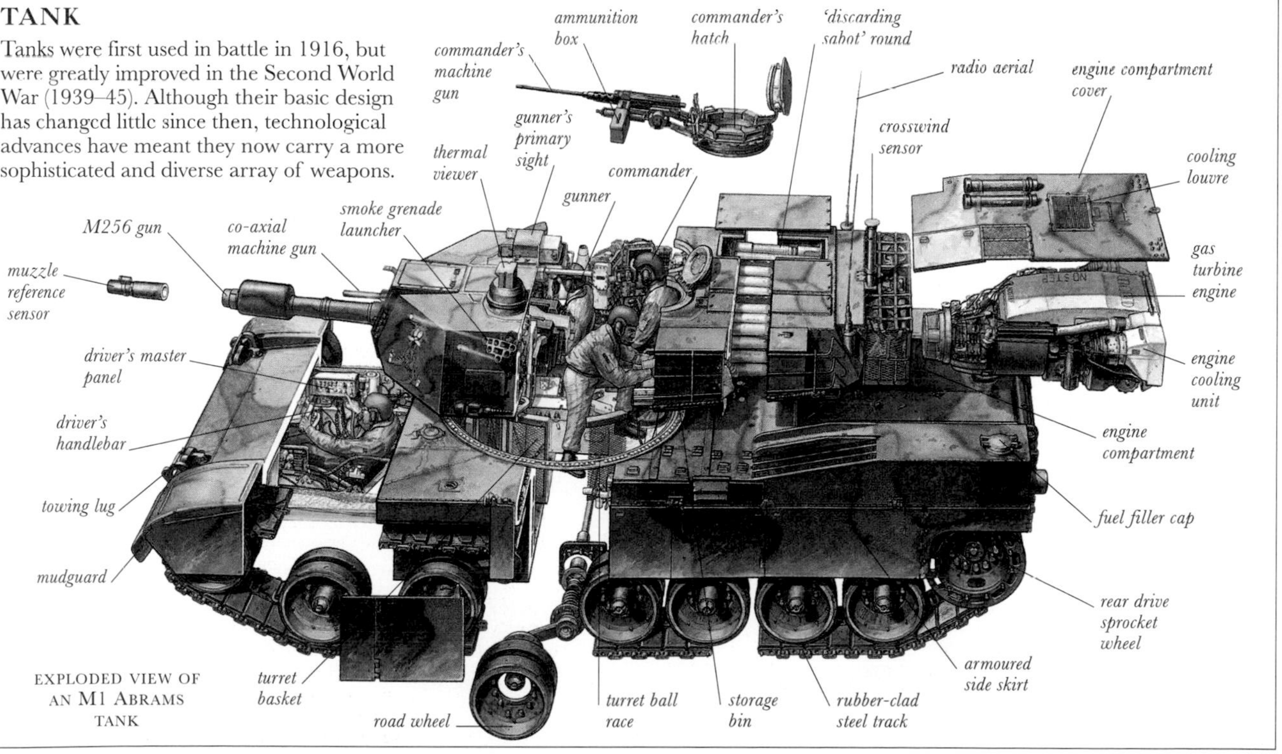

(labels: ammunition box, commander's hatch, 'discarding sabot' round, radio aerial, engine compartment cover, commander's machine gun, gunner's primary sight, commander, crosswind sensor, cooling louvre, thermal viewer, gunner, M256 gun, co-axial machine gun, smoke grenade launcher, gas turbine engine, muzzle reference sensor, driver's master panel, driver's handlebar, engine cooling unit, engine compartment, towing lug, fuel filler cap, mudguard, rear drive sprocket wheel, armoured side skirt, EXPLODED VIEW OF AN M1 ABRAMS TANK, turret basket, road wheel, turret ball race, storage bin, rubber-clad steel track)

T

with rhythmical tapping of the toes and heels. ● *v.intr.* perform a tap-dance. □ **tap-dancer** *n.* **tap-dancing** *n.*

tape ● *n.* **1** a narrow strip of woven material for tying up, fastening, etc. **2 a** a strip of material stretched across the finishing line of a race. **b** a similar strip for marking off an area. **3** (in full **adhesive tape**) a strip of adhesive plastic etc. for masking, insulating, etc. **4 a** ▼ long narrow flexible material with magnetic properties used for recording sound or pictures or data. **b** a length, reel, or cassette of this. **5** = TAPE-MEASURE. ● *v.tr.* **1 a** tie up or join etc. with tape. **b** apply tape to. **2** (foll. by *off*) seal or mark off an area or thing with tape. **3** record on magnetic tape. □ **breast the tape** *Brit.* win a race. **have** (or **get**) **a person** or **thing taped** *Brit. colloq.* understand a person or thing fully. **on tape** recorded on magnetic tape. [Old English]

tape deck *n.* a piece of equipment for playing audiotapes, esp. as part of a stereo system.

tape machine *n.* a machine for receiving and recording telegraph messages.

tape-measure *n.* a strip of tape or thin flexible metal marked for measuring lengths.

taper ● *n.* **1** a wick coated with wax etc. for conveying a flame. **2** a slender candle. ● *v.* (often foll. by *off*) **1** *intr.* & *tr.* diminish or reduce in thickness towards one end. **2** *tr.* & *intr.* make or become gradually less. [from Latin *papyrus* 'papyrus', whose pith was used for candle wicks]

tape recorder *n.* an apparatus for recording sounds on magnetic tape and afterwards reproducing them. □ **tape-record** *v.tr.* **tape recording** *n.*

tapestry *n.* (*pl.* **-ies**) **1 a** a thick textile fabric in which coloured weft threads are woven to form pictures or designs. **b** embroidery imitating this, usu. in wools on canvas. **c** ▶ a piece of such embroidery. **2** events or circumstances etc. compared with a tapestry in being interwoven etc. (*life's rich tapestry*). [from Old French *tapisserie*] □ **tapestried** *adj.*

tapeworm *n.* any parasitic intestinal flatworm of the class Cestoda. ▷ PARASITE

tapioca *n.* a starchy substance in hard white grains obtained from cassava and used for puddings etc. [from Tupi-Guarani (a S. American language) *tipioca*]

TAPIR: MALAYAN TAPIR (*Tapirus indicus*)

flexible snout

tapir /**tay**-peer/ *n.* ▲ any nocturnal hoofed mammal of the genus *Tapirus*, native to Central and S. America and Malaysia, having a short flexible protruding snout. [from Tupi (Brazilian) *tapira*]

tapper see TAP[2].

tappet *n.* a lever or projecting part used in machinery to give intermittent motion.

taproom *n.* a room in which alcoholic drinks (esp. beer) are available on tap.

tap root *n.* ▶ a tapering root growing vertically downwards.

tapster *n.* a person who draws and serves alcoholic drinks at a bar. [Old English]

tap water *n.* water from a piped supply.

tar[1] ● *n.* **1** a dark thick inflammable liquid distilled from wood or coal etc. and used as a preservative of wood and iron, in making roads, as an antiseptic, etc. **2** a similar substance formed in the combustion of tobacco etc. ● *v.tr.* (**tarred**, **tarring**) cover with tar. □ **tar and feather** smear with tar and then cover with feathers as a punishment. **tarred with the same brush** having the same faults. [Old English]

tar[2] *n. colloq.* a sailor. [abbreviation of TARPAULIN]

taradiddle *n.* (also **tarradiddle**) esp. *Brit. colloq.* **1** a petty lie. **2** pretentious nonsense. [18th-century coinage]

taramasalata /ta-ră-mă-să-**lah**-tă/ *n.* (also **tarama** /ta-ră-mă/) a pinkish pâté made from the roe of mullet or other fish with olive

tap root

TAP ROOT OF A CARROT

tap root

oil, seasoning, etc. [from modern Greek *taramas* 'roe' + *salata* 'salad']

tarantella *n.* (also **tarantelle**) **1** a rapid whirling dance of southern Italy. **2** the music for this. [Italian, from *Taranto*, a town in S. Italy]

tarantula *n.* **1** any large hairy tropical spider of the family Theraphosidae. ▷ SPIDER. **2** a large black S. European spider, *Lycosa tarentula*. [from Italian *tarantola*, related to TARANTELLA (dance once thought to be a cure for a tarantula bite)]

tarboosh *n.* a cap like a fez. [from Persian *sar-būš* 'head-cover']

tardy *adj.* (**tardier**, **tardiest**) **1** slow to act or come or happen. **2** delaying or delayed beyond the right or expected time. [from Latin *tardus* 'slow'] □ **tardily** *adv.* **tardiness** *n.*

tare[1] *n.* **1** vetch, esp. as corn-weed or fodder. **2** (in *pl.*) *Bibl.* an injurious weed resembling corn when young (Matt. 13:24–30). [Middle English]

tare[2] *n.* **1** an allowance made for the weight of the packing or wrapping around goods. **2** the weight of a motor vehicle without its fuel or load. [from Arabic *ṭarḥa* 'what is rejected']

targa *n.* (often *attrib.*) a type of convertible sports car with a roof hood or panel that can be removed. [Italian, literally 'shield', originally the name of a model of Porsche]

target ● *n.* **1** ▶ a mark or point fired or aimed at, esp. a round or rectangular object marked with concentric circles. **2** a person or thing aimed at, or exposed to gunfire etc. (*they were an easy target*). **3** (also *attrib.*) an objective or result aimed at (*target date*). **4** a person or thing against whom criticism, abuse, etc., is or may be directed. **5** *archaic* a shield or buckler, esp. a small round one. ● *v.tr.* (**targeted**, **targeting** or *Brit.* **targetted**, **targetting**) **1** identify or single out (a person or thing) as an object of attention or attack. **2** aim or direct (*targeted on major cities*). [Middle English in sense 'little shield'] □ **targetable** *adj.*

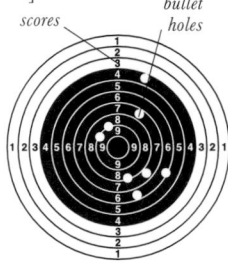

scores   *bullet holes*

TARGET USED IN FREE PISTOL SHOOTING

tariff ● *n.* **1** a table of fixed charges (*a hotel tariff*). **2 a** a duty on a particular class of imports or exports. **b** a list of duties or customs to be paid. **3** *Brit.* standard charges agreed between insurers etc. ● *v.tr.* subject (goods) to a tariff. [from Arabic *ta'rīf(a)*]

tarlatan *n.* a thin stiff open-weave muslin. [from French *tarlatane*]

tarmac ● *n. propr.* **1** = TARMACADAM. **2** a surface made of this, e.g. a runway. ● *v.tr.* (**tarmacked, tarmacking**) apply tarmacadam to.

tarmacadam *n.* a material of stone or slag bound with tar, used in paving roads etc.

tarn *n.* a small mountain lake. ▷ LAKE. [from Old Norse]

tarnish ● *v.* **1** *tr.* lessen or destroy the lustre of (metal etc.). **2** *tr.* impair (one's reputation etc.). **3** *intr.* (of metal etc.) lose lustre. ● *n.* **1 a** a loss of lustre. **b** a film of colour formed on an exposed surface of a mineral or metal. **2** a blemish; a stain. [based on French *terne* 'dark'] □ **tarnishable** *adj.*

taro /**tar**-oh/ *n.* (*pl.* **-os**) a tropical plant, *Colocasia esculenta*, with tuberous roots used as food. [Polynesian]

tarot /**ta**-roh/ *n.* **1** (in *sing.* or *pl.*) **a** any of several games played with a pack of cards having five suits, one of which is a set of permanent trumps. **b** ▲ a similar pack used in fortune-telling. **2 a** any of the trump cards. **b** any card from a fortune-telling pack. [French]

tarpaulin *n.* **1** heavy-duty waterproof cloth, originally of tarred canvas. **2** a sheet or covering of this.

tarradiddle var. of TARADIDDLE.

TAPESTRY CUSHION

TAPE

Recording tape is a thin plastic strip coated with tiny magnetic grains. It is usually carried on spools inside a cassette. On a blank tape, these grains are randomly ordered. When recording sound, a tape head on a tape recorder arranges the grains to represent the sound. To wipe the tape, an erase head disrupts the pattern.

erase protection hole
tape spool
outer case
pinch roller
capstan
arranged magnetic grains
pressure pad
tape head
erase head
feed roller
randomly arranged magnetic grains
direction of tape movement

TAPE CASSETTE RECORDING FROM A TAPE HEAD

T

TAROT

Most tarot decks have 78 cards. These are divided into the major and the minor arcanas. The major arcana consists of 22 unique cards, such as The Lovers and The Moon. The minor arcana consists of four suits: pentacles, swords, cups, and wands, each suit having four court cards and ten number cards.

EXAMPLES OF TAROT CARDS

THE LOVERS

THE MOON

PENTACLES

SWORDS

CUPS

WANDS

COURT CARD

NUMBER CARD

TARRAGON
(*Artemisia dracunculus*)

tarragon *n.* ◄ a bushy aromatic herb, *Artemisia dracunculus*, used in salads, vinegar, etc. [from medieval Greek *tarkhōn*]

tarry[1] *adj.* (**tarrier**, **tarriest**) of or like or smeared with tar. □ **tarriness** *n.*

tarry[2] *v.intr.* (**-ies**, **-ied**) *archaic* delay, linger, stay, wait. [Middle English] □ **tarrier** *n.*

tarsal ● *adj.* of or relating to the bones in the ankle. ● *n.* a tarsal bone. ▷ ANKLE, SKELETON

tarsi *pl.* of TARSUS.

tarsier *n.* any small large-eyed arboreal nocturnal primate of the genus *Tarsius*, native to Borneo, the Philippines, etc., with a long tail and long hind legs. [French]

tarsus *n.* (*pl.* **tarsi**) **1** *Anat.* the group of bones forming the ankle and upper foot. **2** *Zool.* the shank of a bird's leg. [from Greek *tarsos* 'flat of the foot, rim of the eyelid']

tart[1] *n.* **1** an open pastry case containing jam etc. **2** *esp. Brit.* a pie with a fruit or sweet filling. [from Old French *tarte*] □ **tartlet** *n.*

tart[2] *n. slang* **1** a prostitute; a promiscuous woman. **2** *slang offens.* a girl or woman. ● *v.* (foll. by *up*) *esp. Brit. colloq.* **1** *tr.* (usu. *refl.*) smarten (oneself or a thing) up, esp. gaudily. **2** *intr.* dress up gaudily. [probably abbreviation of SWEETHEART]

tart[3] *adj.* **1** sharp or acid in taste. **2** (of a remark etc.) cutting, bitter. [Old English] □ **tartly** *adv.* **tartness** *n.*

tartan *n.* **1** ◄ a pattern of coloured stripes crossing at right angles, esp. denoting a Scottish Highland clan. **2** woollen cloth woven in this pattern (often *attrib.: a tartan scarf*).

Tartar /tar-tǎ/ (also **Tatar** (*pronunc.* same) except in sense 2 of *n.*) ● *n.* **1 a** a member of a group of central Asian peoples including Mongols and Turks. **b** the Turkic language of these peoples. **2** (**tartar**) a violent-tempered or intractable person. ● *adj.* of or relating to the Tartars or their language. [from medieval Latin *Tartarus*] □ **Tartarian** *adj.*

tartar *n.* **1** a hard deposit that forms on the teeth. **2** a deposit that forms a hard crust on the inside of a wine cask during fermentation. See also CREAM OF TARTAR. [from medieval Greek *tartaron*] □ **tartarize** *v.tr.* (also **-ise**).

tartare sauce *n.* (also **tartar sauce**) a sauce of mayonnaise and chopped gherkins, capers, etc.

tartaric *adj. Chem.* of or produced from tartar.

tartaric acid *n.* a natural carboxylic acid found esp. in unripe grapes, used in baking powders.

tartrate *n. Chem.* any salt or ester of tartaric acid.

tartrazine *n. Chem.* a brilliant yellow dye derived from tartaric acid and used to colour food etc.

tarty *adj.* (**tartier**, **tartiest**) *colloq.* (esp. of a woman) vulgarly provocative; gaudy; promiscuous. □ **tartily** *adv.* **tartiness** *n.*

Tarzan *n.* a man of great agility and powerful physique. [name of the hero of stories by E. R. Burroughs, American writer, 1875–1950]

tash *n.* (also **tache**) *colloq.* a moustache. [abbreviation]

task ● *n.* a piece of work to be done. ● *v.tr.* make great demands on (a person's powers etc.). □ **take to task** rebuke, scold. [from medieval Latin *tasca*]

task force *n.* (also **task group**) *Mil.* an armed force or other group organized for a special operation or task.

TARTAN

For hundreds of years, the clans of the Scottish Highlands have expressed their strong individual identities through the wearing of tartans. Each clan has developed its own distinctive styles and colours.

EXAMPLES OF TARTANS

THE MACLEODS

THE STEWARTS

THE FRASERS

THE GORDONS

taskmaster *n.* (*fem.* **taskmistress**) a person who imposes a task or burden, esp. regularly or severely.

Tasmanian ● *n.* **1** a native of Tasmania, an island state of Australia. **2** a person of Tasmanian descent. ● *adj.* of or relating to Tasmania.

Tasmanian devil *n.* a small bearlike nocturnal flesh-eating marsupial, *Sarcophilus harrisi*, now found only in Tasmania.

Tass *n.* the official news agency of the former Soviet Union, renamed ITAR-Tass in 1992. [initials of Russian *Telegrafnoe agentstvo Sovetskogo Soyuza* 'Telegraphic Agency of the Soviet Union']

tassel *n.* **1** a tuft of loosely hanging threads or cords etc. attached for decoration to a cushion, scarf, cap, etc. ▷ SHAKO. **2** a tassel-like head of some plants. [from Old French *tas(s)el* 'clasp']

taste ● *n.* **1 a** the sensation characteristic of a soluble substance caused in the mouth and throat by contact with that substance. **b** the faculty of perceiving this sensation. **2** a small portion of food or drink taken as a sample. **3** a slight experience (*a taste of success*). **4** (often foll. by *for*) a liking or predilection (*expensive tastes*). **5** aesthetic discernment in art etc., esp. of a specified kind (*a person of taste*). ● *v.* **1** *tr.* sample or test the flavour of (food etc.) by taking it into the mouth. **2** *tr.* (also *absol.*) perceive the flavour of (*could taste the lemon*). **3** *tr.* (esp. with *neg.*) eat or drink a small portion of (*had not tasted food for days*). **4** *tr.* have experience of (*tasted failure*). **5** *intr.* (often foll. by *of*) have a specified flavour (*tastes bitter*). □ **a bad** (or **bitter** etc.) **taste** *colloq.* a strong feeling of regret or unease following an experience etc. **to taste** in the amount needed for a pleasing result. [from Old French *tast* (n.), *taster* (v.)]

taste bud *n.* ▼ any of the cells or nerve endings on the surface of the tongue by which things are tasted. ▷ TONGUE

tasteful *adj.* having, or done in, good taste. □ **tastefully** *adv.* **tastefulness** *n.*

tasteless *adj.* **1** lacking flavour. **2** having, or done in, bad taste. □ **tastelessly** *adv.* **tastelessness** *n.*

taster *n.* **1** a person employed to test food or drink by tasting it. **2** a small cup used by a wine taster. **3** an instrument for extracting a small sample from within a cheese.

TASTE BUD

A taste bud consists of receptor cells and supporting cells in the epithelium of the tongue. When a substance is chewed, it mixes with saliva, which enters the taste pores. This stimulates taste hairs on the receptor cells, which in turn transmit an impulse to the brain via nerve fibres.

T

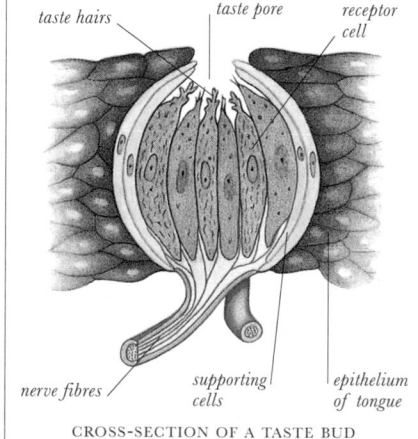

taste hairs　　*taste pore*　　*receptor cell*

nerve fibres　　*supporting cells*　　*epithelium of tongue*

CROSS-SECTION OF A TASTE BUD

tasting *n.* a gathering at which food or drink (esp. wine) is tasted and evaluated.

tasty *adj.* (**tastier, tastiest**) **1** (of food) pleasing in flavour; appetizing. **2** *colloq.* attractive. □ **tastily** *adv.* **tastiness** *n.*

tat[1] *n. Brit. colloq.* **1** tatty or tasteless clothes; worthless goods. **2** rubbish, junk.

tat[2] *v.* (**tatted, tatting**) **1** *intr.* do tatting. **2** *tr.* make by tatting.

tat[3] see TIT[2].

ta-ta *int.* esp. *Brit. colloq.* goodbye. [19th-century coinage]

tatami /tă-**tah**-mi/ *n.* (in full **tatami mat**) a rush-covered straw mat forming a traditional Japanese floor covering.

Tatar var. of TARTAR.

tater *n.* (also *Brit.* **tatie**) *colloq.* = POTATO. [abbreviation]

tatter *n.* (usu. in *pl.*) a rag; an irregularly torn piece of cloth or paper etc. □ **in tatters** *colloq.* **1** torn in many places. **2** (of an argument etc.) ruined. [from Old Norse *tötrar* 'rags'] □ **tattery** *adj.*

tattered *adj.* = in tatters (see TATTER).

tatting *n.* **1** ▼ a kind of knotted lace made by hand with a small shuttle and used for trimming etc. **2** the process of making this. [19th-century coinage]

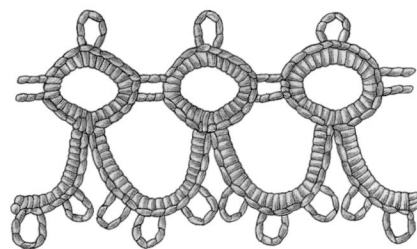

TATTING: CHAIN AND RING TATTING

tattle ● *v.* **1** *intr.* prattle, chatter; gossip idly. **2** *tr.* utter (words) idly. ● *n.* gossip; idle talk. [from Middle Flemish *tatelen*]

tattle-tale *n. N. Amer.* a tell-tale, esp. a child.

tattoo[1] *n.* (*pl.* **tattoos**) **1** an evening drum or bugle signal recalling soldiers to their quarters. **2** an elaboration of this with music and marching, presented as an entertainment. **3** a rhythmic tapping or drumming. [from Dutch *taptoe*, literally 'close the tap (of the cask)!']

tattoo[2] ● *v.tr.* (**tattoos, tattooed**) **1** mark (the skin) with an indelible design by puncturing it and inserting pigment. **2** make (a design) in this way. ● *n.* (*pl.* **tattoos**) a design made by tattooing. [Polynesian] □ **tattooer** *n.* **tattooist** *n.*

tatty *adj.* (**tattier, tattiest**) esp. *Brit. colloq.* **1** tattered; worn and shabby. **2** inferior. **3** tawdry. [originally Scots, literally 'shaggy'] □ **tattily** *adv.* **tattiness** *n.*

tau /taw/ *n.* the nineteenth letter of the Greek alphabet (Τ, τ). [Greek]

tau cross *n.* a T-shaped cross.

taught *past* and *past part.* of TEACH.

taunt ● *n.* an insult; a provocation. ● *v.tr.* **1** assail with taunts. **2** reproach (a person) contemptuously. [from French phrase *tant pour tant* 'tit for tat', hence a smart rejoinder] □ **taunter** *n.* **tauntingly** *adv.*

tau particle *n.* an unstable, heavy, and charged subatomic particle.

taupe /tohp/ ● *n.* a grey with a tinge of another colour, usu. brown. ● *adj.* of this colour. [French, literally 'mole']

taurine[1] /**tor**-een/ *n. Biochem.* a sulphur-containing amino acid important in the metabolism of fats. [based on Greek *tauros* 'bull']

taurine[2] /**tor**-In/ *adj.* of or like a bull; bullish. [from Latin *taurinus*]

Taurus *n.* **1** *Astron.* ▶ a constellation (the Bull). **2** *Astrol.* **a** the second sign of the zodiac. ▷ ZODIAC. **b** a person born when the Sun is in this sign. [Latin, literally 'bull'] □ **Taurean** *adj. & n.*

taut *adj.* **1** (of a rope, muscles, etc.) tight; not slack. **2** (of nerves) tense. [Middle English] □ **tauten** *v.tr. & intr.* **tautly** *adv.* **tautness** *n.*

tautology *n.* (*pl.* **-ies**) the saying of the same thing twice over in different words (e.g. *arrived one after the other in succession*). [based on Greek *to auto* 'the same'] □ **tautological** *adj.* **tautologically** *adv.* **tautologist** *n.* **tautologous** *adj.*

tavern *n.* esp. *archaic* or *literary* an inn or public house. [from Latin *taberna* 'hut, tavern']

taverna *n.* a Greek restaurant. [modern Greek]

tawdry *adj.* (**tawdrier, tawdriest**) **1** showy but worthless. **2** over-ornamented, gaudy, vulgar. [from *tawdry lace*, corruption of *St Audrey's lace*] □ **tawdrily** *adv.* **tawdriness** *n.*

tawny ● *adj.* (**tawnier, tawniest**) of an orange- or yellow-brown colour. ● *n.* this colour. [from Old French *tané*] □ **tawniness** *n.*

tawny owl *n.* **1** a reddish-brown European owl, *Strix aluco.* ▷ OWL. **2** (**Tawny Owl**) *colloq.* the assistant adult leader of a pack of Brownie Guides, officially termed *Assistant Brownie Guider* since 1968.

tax ● *n.* **1** a contribution to state revenue compulsorily levied on individuals, property, or businesses (often foll. by *on*: *a tax on luxury goods*). **2** (usu. foll. by *on, upon*) a strain or heavy demand; an oppressive or burdensome obligation. ● *v.tr.* **1** impose a tax on (persons or goods etc.). **2** deduct tax from (income etc.). **3** make heavy demands on (a person's powers or resources etc.) (*you tax my patience*). **4** (foll. by *with*) confront (a person) with a wrongdoing etc. [from Latin *taxare* 'to censure, charge'] □ **taxable** *adj.* **taxer** *n.* **taxless** *adj.*

taxa *pl.* of TAXON.

taxation *n.* the imposition or payment of tax.

tax avoidance *n. Brit.* the arrangement of financial affairs to minimize payment of tax.

tax break *n. colloq.* a tax concession or advantage allowed by government.

tax-deductible *adj.* (of expenditure) that may be paid out of income before the deduction of income tax.

tax disc *n. Brit.* a paper disc displayed on the windscreen of a motor vehicle, certifying payment of excise duty.

tax evasion *n.* the illegal non-payment or underpayment of income tax.

tax-free *adj.* (of goods, income, etc.) exempt from being taxed.

tax haven *n.* a country etc. where taxes are levied at a low rate.

taxi ● *n.* (*pl.* **taxis**) **1** a motor car licensed to ply for hire and usu. fitted with a taximeter. **2** a boat etc. similarly used. ● *v.* (**taxies, taxied, taxiing** or **taxying**) **1 a** *intr.* (of an aircraft or pilot) move along the ground under the machine's own power before take-off or after landing. **b** *tr.* cause (an aircraft) to taxi. **2** *intr. & tr.* go or convey in a taxi. [abbreviation of *taximeter cab*]

taxicab *n.* = TAXI *n.* 1.

taxidermy *n.* the art of preparing, stuffing, and mounting the skins of animals. [based on Greek *taxis* 'arrangement' + *derma* 'skin'] □ **taxidermal** *adj.* **taxidermic** *adj.* **taxidermist** *n.*

taximeter *n.* an automatic device fitted to a taxi, recording the distance travelled and the fare payable.

taxi rank *n.* (*US* **taxi stand**) a place where taxis wait to be hired.

taxiway *n.* a route along which an aircraft taxies to or from a runway.

taxman *n.* (*pl.* **-men**) *colloq.* **1** an inspector or collector of taxes. **2** the personification of the government department dealing with tax.

taxon *n.* (*pl.* **taxa**) any taxonomic group. [back-formation from TAXONOMY]

taxonomy *n.* **1** the science of classification, esp. of living and extinct organisms. **2** a scheme of classification. [from French *taxonomie*] □ **taxonomic** *adj.* **taxonomical** *adj.* **taxonomically** *adv.* **taxonomist** *n.*

taxpayer *n.* a person who pays taxes.

tax return *n.* a declaration of income for taxation purposes.

tax shelter *n.* a means of organizing business affairs to minimize payment of tax.

tax year see FINANCIAL YEAR.

tayberry *n.* (*pl.* **-ies**) a dark red soft fruit produced by crossing a blackberry and a raspberry. [named after the River *Tay* in Scotland]

TB *abbr.* tuberculosis.

Tb *symb. Chem.* the element terbium.

t.b.a. *abbr.* to be announced.

T-bar *n.* **1** (in full **T-bar lift**) a type of ski lift in the form of a series of inverted T-shaped bars for towing skiers uphill. **2** (often *attrib.*) a T-shaped fastening on a shoe or sandal.

T-bone *n.* a T-shaped bone, esp. in steak from the thin end of a loin.

tbsp *abbr.* (also **tbs**) (*pl.* same or **tbsps**) tablespoonful.

Tc *symb. Chem.* the element technetium.

TCCB *abbr.* (in the UK) Test and County Cricket Board.

T-cell *n.* a lymphocyte of a type produced or processed by the thymus gland and active in the immune response.

TCP *abbr. Brit. propr.* a disinfectant and germicide. [from *t*richloro*p*henylmethyliodasalicyl]

TD *abbr. Ir.* Teachta Dála, Member of the Dáil.

Te *symb. Chem.* the element tellurium.

te /tee/ *n.* (*US* **ti**) **1** (in tonic sol-fa) the seventh note of a major scale. **2** the note B in the fixed-doh system. [earlier *si*: from Italian]

tea *n.* **1 a** (in full **tea plant**) ◀ an evergreen shrub or small tree, *Camellia sinensis*, of India, China, etc. **b** ◀ its dried leaves. **2 a** drink made by infusing tea leaves in boiling water. **3** a similar drink made from the leaves of other plants or from another substance (*beef tea*). **4 a** esp. *Brit.* a light afternoon meal consisting of tea, bread, cakes, etc. **b** *Brit.* a cooked evening meal. **c** esp. *US* an afternoon reception at which tea is served. [17th-century coinage]

fresh leaves

dried leaves

TEA (*Camellia sinensis*)

tea bag *n.* a small porous bag of tea for infusion.

tea break *n. Brit.* a pause in work etc. to drink tea.

tea caddy *n.* a container for tea.

teacake *n. Brit.* a light usu. sweet bun eaten at tea, often toasted.

teach *v.tr.* (*past* and *past part.* **taught**) **1 a** give systematic information to (a person) or about (a subject or skill). **b** (*absol.*) practise this professionally. **c** enable (a person) to do something by instruction

T

and training (*taught me to swim*; *taught me how to dance*). **2 a** advocate as a moral etc. principle (*my parents taught me forgiveness*). **b** communicate, instruct in (*suffering taught me patience*). **3** (foll. by *to* + infin.) **a** induce (a person) by example or punishment to do or not to do a thing (*that will teach you to sit still*; *that will teach you not to laugh*). **b** *colloq.* make (a person) disinclined to do a thing (*I will teach you to interfere*). □ **teach a person a lesson** see LESSON. **teach school** *US* be a teacher in a school. [Old English]

teachable *adj.* **1** apt at learning. **2** (of a subject) that can be taught. □ **teachability** *n.* **teachableness** *n.*

teacher *n.* a person who teaches, esp. in a school. □ **teacherly** *adj.*

tea chest *n.* a light metal-lined wooden box in which tea is transported.

teach-in *n.* an informal lecture and discussion on a subject of public interest.

teaching *n.* **1** the profession of a teacher. **2** (often in *pl.*) what is taught; a doctrine.

teaching hospital *n.* a hospital where medical students are taught.

tea cloth *n.* = TEA TOWEL.

tea cosy *n.* a cover to keep a teapot warm.

teacup *n.* **1** a cup from which tea is drunk. **2** an amount held by this, about 150 ml. □ **teacupful** *n.* (*pl.* **-fuls**).

tea dance *n.* an afternoon tea with dancing.

teak *n.* **1** a large deciduous tree, *Tectona grandis*, native to India and SE Asia. **2** its hard durable timber. [from Portuguese *teca*]

teal ● *n.* (*pl.* same or **teals**) **1** any of various small freshwater ducks of the genus *Anas*, esp. *A. crecca*. **2** a dark greenish-blue colour. ● *adj.* (in full **teal blue**; hyphenated when *attrib.*) of this colour. [Middle English]

tea lady *n. Brit.* a woman employed to make tea in offices etc.

tea leaf *n.* a dried leaf of tea, esp. after infusion.

team ● *n.* **1** a set of players forming one side in a game. **2** two or more persons working together. **3** a set of draught animals. ● *v.* **1** *intr.* & *tr.* (usu. foll. by *up*) join in a team or in common action (*decided to team up with them*). **2** *tr.* (foll. by *with*) match or co-ordinate (clothes). [Old English *tēam* 'offspring']

team-mate *n.* a fellow member of a team or group.

team player *n.* a person who plays or works well as a member of a team and is not solely concerned with his or her own glory.

team spirit *n.* willingness to act as a member of a group rather than as an individual.

teamster *n.* **1** *N. Amer.* a lorry driver, esp. a member of the Teamsters Union. **2** a driver of a team of animals.

team-teaching *n.* teaching by a team of teachers working together.

teamwork *n.* the combined action of a team, group, etc., esp. when effective and efficient.

tea party *n.* a party at teatime.

tea plant see TEA *n.* 1a.

teapot *n.* a pot with a handle, spout, and lid, in which tea is brewed and from which it is poured.

tear[1] /tair/ ● *v.* (*past* **tore**; *past part.* **torn**) **1** *tr.* (often foll. by *up*) pull apart or to pieces with some force. **2** *tr.* **a** make a hole or rent in by tearing. **b** make (a hole or rent). **3** *tr.* (foll. by *away*, *off*, etc.) & *intr.* (foll. by *at* etc.) pull violently or with some force. **4** *tr.* violently disrupt or divide (*the country was torn by civil war*). **5** *intr. colloq.* go or travel hurriedly or impetuously. **6** *intr.* undergo tearing (*the curtain tore down the middle*). ● *n.* **1** a hole or other damage caused by tearing. **2** a torn part of cloth etc. □ **be torn between** have difficulty in choosing between. **tear apart 1** destroy, divide utterly; distress greatly. **2** search (a place) exhaustively. **3** criticize forcefully. **tear one's hair out** behave with extreme desperation or anger. **tear into 1** attack verbally; reprimand. **2** make a vigorous start on (an activity). **tear oneself away** leave despite a strong desire to stay.

tear to shreds *colloq.* refute or criticize thoroughly. **that's torn it** *Brit. colloq.* that has spoiled things, caused a problem, etc. [Old English] □ **tearable** *adj.* **tearer** *n.*

tear[2] /teer/ *n.* **1** a drop of clear salty liquid secreted by glands to moisten and wash the eye and shed from it in grief etc. **2** a tearlike thing; a drop. □ **in tears** crying; shedding tears. [Old English] □ **tearlike** *adj.*

tearaway /ˈtair-ă-way/ *n. Brit.* **1** an impetuous or reckless young person. **2** a hooligan.

teardrop *n.* a single tear.

tear duct *n.* ▼ a passage through which tears pass to the eye or from the eye to the nose.

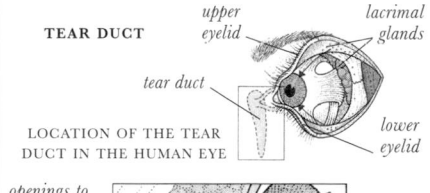

TEAR DUCT

upper eyelid   *lacrimal glands*

tear duct

lower eyelid

LOCATION OF THE TEAR DUCT IN THE HUMAN EYE

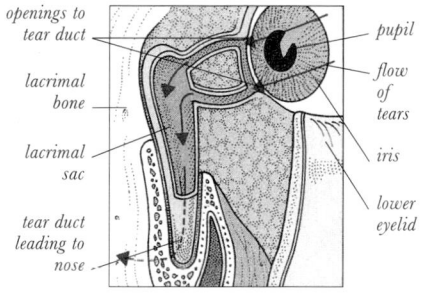

openings to tear duct

pupil

flow of tears

lacrimal bone

iris

lacrimal sac

lower eyelid

tear duct leading to nose

DETAIL OF A TEAR DUCT

tearful *adj.* **1** crying or inclined to cry. **2** causing or accompanied with tears; sad (*a tearful event*). □ **tearfully** *adv.* **tearfulness** *n.*

tear gas *n.* gas that disables by causing severe irritation to the eyes (often hyphenated when *attrib.*: *tear-gas canister*).

tearing *adj.* extreme, overwhelming, violent (*in a tearing hurry*).

tear-jerker *n. colloq.* a story, film, etc. evoking sadness or sympathy. □ **tear-jerking** *n.* & *attrib.adj.*

tearless *adj.* not shedding tears. □ **tearlessly** *adv.*

tearoom *n.* a small restaurant or café where tea is served.

tea rose *n.* a hybrid shrub, *Rosa odorata*, with a scent resembling that of tea.

tear-stained *adj. poet.* **1** wet with tears. **2** sorrowful.

tease ● *v.tr.* (also *absol.*) **1 a** make fun of (a person or animal) playfully or unkindly or annoyingly. **b** tempt or allure, esp. sexually, while refusing to satisfy the desire aroused. **2** pick (wool, hair, etc.) into separate fibres. **3** (also **teaze**) esp. with teasels. ● *n.* **1** *colloq.* a person fond of teasing. **2** an instance of teasing. □ **tease out** separate by disentangling. [Old English] □ **teasingly** *adv.*

teasel (also **teazel**, **teazle**) ● *n.* ▶ any plant of the genus *Dipsacus*, with large prickly heads that were formerly dried and used to raise the nap on woven cloth. **2** a device used as a substitute for teasels. ● *v.tr.* dress (cloth) with teasels. [Old English]

teaser *n.* **1** *colloq.* a hard question or task. **2** a teasing person. **3** esp. *US* a short introductory advertisement, trailer for a film, etc.

teaset *n.* a set of crockery for serving tea.

tea shop *n.* esp. *Brit.* = TEAROOM.

teaspoon *n.* **1** a small spoon for stirring tea. **2** an amount held by this. □ **teaspoonful** *n.* (*pl.* **-fuls**).

teat *n.* **1** a mammary nipple, esp. of an animal. **2** *Brit.* a thing resembling this, esp. a device made of rubber etc. for sucking milk from a bottle. [from Old French *tete*]

teatime *n.* esp. *Brit.* the time in the afternoon when tea is served.

tea towel *n.* esp. *Brit.* a towel for drying washed crockery etc.

tea tray *n.* a tray from which tea is served.

teazel (also **teazle**) var. of TEASEL.

TEC /tek/ *abbr.* Training and Enterprise Council.

tec *n. colloq.* a detective.

tech *n.* (also **tec**) esp. *Brit. colloq.* **1** a technical college. **2** (esp. in phr. **high-tech**) technology.

techie /ˈtek-i/ *n.* (also **techy**) (*pl.* **-ies**) *colloq.* an expert in or enthusiast for (esp. computing) technology.

technetium /tek-nee-shŭm/ *n. Chem.* an artificially produced radioactive metallic element occurring in the fission products of uranium. [based on Greek *tekhnētos* 'artificial']

technical *adj.* **1** of or involving or concerned with the mechanical arts and applied sciences (*technical college*; *a technical education*). **2** of or relating to a particular subject or craft etc. or its techniques. **3** (of a book or discourse etc.) using technical language. **4** due to mechanical failure (*a technical hitch*). **5** legally such; such in strict interpretation (*technical assault*; *lost on a technical point*). [based on Greek *tekhnē* 'art'] □ **technically** *adv.*

technical hitch *n.* **1** a temporary breakdown or problem in machinery etc. **2** an unexpected snag or problem.

technicality *n.* (*pl.* **-ies**) **1** the state of being technical. **2** a technical expression. **3** a technical point or detail (*was acquitted on a technicality*).

technical knockout *n. Boxing* a referee's ruling that a contestant has lost because he is not fit to continue.

technician *n.* **1** an expert in practical science. **2** a person skilled in artistic technique. **3** a person employed to look after technical equipment and do practical work in a laboratory etc.

Technicolor *n.* (often *attrib.*) **1** *propr.* a process of colour cinematography. **2** (usu. **technicolor**, *Brit.* also **technicolour**) *colloq.* **a** vivid colour. **b** artificial brilliance. □ **technicolored** *adj.*

technique *n.* **1** mechanical skill in an art. **2** a means or method of achieving one's purpose, esp. skilfully. **3 a** a manner of performance. **b** a manner of esp. artistic execution in relation to formal details. [French]

techno *n.* a style of popular music making extensive use of electronic instruments and synthesized sound (also in *comb.*: *techno-funk*; *techno-rock*).

technobabble *n. colloq.* incomprehensible technical jargon.

technocracy *n.* (*pl.* **-ies**) **1** the government or control of society or industry by technical experts. **2** an instance or application of this. [based on Greek *tekhnē* 'art']

technocrat *n.* an exponent or advocate of technocracy. □ **technocratic** *adj.* **technocratically** *adv.*

technological *adj.* of or using technology. □ **technologically** *adv.*

technology *n.* (*pl.* **-ies**) **1** the study or use of the mechanical arts and applied sciences. **2** these subjects collectively. [from Greek *tekhnologia* 'systematic treatment'] □ **technologist** *n.*

techy[1] var. of TETCHY.

techy[2] var. of TECHIE.

tectonic *adj.* **1** of or relating to building or construction. **2** *Geol.* relating to the deformation of the Earth's crust or to the structural changes caused by this (see PLATE TECTONICS). ▷ PLATE TECTONICS. [based on Greek *tektōn* 'carpenter'] □ **tectonically** *adv.*

TEASEL: COMMON TEASEL (*Dipsacus fullonum*)

T

tectonics *n.pl.* (usu. treated as *sing.*) *Geol.* the study of large-scale structural features (cf. PLATE TECTONICS).

Ted *n.* (also **ted**) *Brit. colloq.* a Teddy boy.

teddy *n.* (*pl.* **-ies**) **1** (in full **teddy bear**) a soft toy bear. **2** a woman's undergarment combining vest and panties. [sense 1: from pet form of *Theodore* Roosevelt, US president, 1858–1919, famous as a bear-hunter]

Teddy boy *n. Brit. colloq.* a youth, esp. of the 1950s, affecting an Edwardian style of dress and appearance, usu. a long jacket and drainpipe trousers.

tedious *adj.* tiresomely long; wearisome. [from Late Latin *taediosus*] □ **tediously** *adv.* **tediousness** *n.*

tedium *n.* the state of being tedious; boredom. [from Latin *taedium*]

tee[1] *n.* = T[1]. [phonetic spelling]

tee[2] ● *n. Golf* **1** a cleared space from which a golf ball is struck at the beginning of play for each hole. ▷ GOLF. **2** ◄ a small support of wood or plastic from which a ball is struck at a tee. ● *v.tr.* (**tees, teed**) (often foll. by *up*) *Golf* place (a ball) on a tee. □ **tee off 1** *Golf* play a ball from a tee. **2** *colloq.* start, begin. [from earlier (17th c.) *teaz*]

TEE: GRADUATED TEE PEGS

tee-hee (also **te-hee**) ● *n.* **1** a titter. **2** a restrained or contemptuous laugh. ● *v.intr.* (**tee-hees, tee-heed**) titter or laugh in this way.

teem[1] *v.intr.* **1** be abundant (*fish teem in these waters*). **2** (foll. by *with*) be full of or swarming with (*teeming with fish*). [Old English *tēman* 'to give birth to']

teem[2] *v.intr.* (often foll. by *down*) (of water etc.) flow copiously; pour (*it was teeming with rain*). [from Old Norse *tœma*]

teen ● *adj.* = TEENAGE. ● *n.* = TEENAGER.

teenage *adj.* relating to or characteristic of teenagers. □ **teenaged** *adj.*

teenager *n.* a person from 13 to 19 years of age.

teens *n.pl.* the years of one's age from 13 to 19 (*in one's teens*).

teensy *adj.* (**teensier, teensiest**) *colloq.* = TEENY.

teensy-weensy *adj.* = TEENY-WEENY.

teeny *adj.* (**teenier, teeniest**) *colloq.* tiny.

teeny-bopper *n. colloq.* a young teenager, usu. a girl, who keenly follows the latest fashions.

teeny-weeny *adj.* very tiny.

teepee var. of TEPEE.

tee shirt var. of T-SHIRT.

teeter *v.intr.* **1** totter; stand or move unsteadily. **2** hesitate; be indecisive. [variant of dialect *titter*]

teeth *pl.* of TOOTH.

teethe *v.intr.* grow or cut teeth, esp. milk teeth. □ **teething** *n.*

teething ring *n.* ► a small ring for an infant to bite on while teething.

teething troubles *n.pl.* initial difficulties in an enterprise etc., regarded as temporary.

teetotal *adj.* advocating or characterized by total abstinence from alcoholic drink. [reduplication of TOTAL] □ **teetotalism** *n.*

teetotaller *n.* (*US* **teetotaler**) a teetotal person.

TEETHING RING

TEFL *abbr.* teaching of English as a foreign language.

Teflon *n. propr.* polytetrafluoroethylene, esp. used as a non-stick coating for kitchen utensils.

te-hee var. of TEE-HEE.

telco *n.* (*pl.* **-os**) *US* a telecommunications company. [abbreviation]

tele- *comb. form* **1** at or to a distance (*telekinesis*). **2** forming names of instruments for operating over long distances (*telescope*). **3** television (*telecast*). **4** done by

---

TELEPHONE

A telephone transforms sound into electrical signals and back again. When a number is dialled, signals are sent to an exchange, which routes the call. When the caller speaks, a microphone in the handset produces electrical signals. These are sent – as electric currents along wires or as radio waves through the air – to the receiver of the other telephone, where a loudspeaker reproduces the sound.

circuit board

amplifier chip

ribbon cable

wires to receiver

keypad contacts

wires to transmitter

transmitter (microphone)

transmitter housing

connecting lead

back of keypad

base

receiver (loudspeaker)

diaphragm

handset

INTERNAL MECHANISM OF A DIGITAL TELEPHONE

---

means of the telephone (*telesales*). [from Greek *tēle* 'far off']

tele-ad *n.* an advertisement placed in a newspaper etc. by telephone.

telecamera *n.* **1** a television camera. **2** a camera with a telephoto lens.

telecast ● *n.* a television broadcast. ● *v.tr.* transmit by television. □ **telecaster** *n.*

telecommunication *n.* **1** communication over a distance by cable, telegraph, telephone, or broadcasting. **2** (usu. in *pl.*) the branch of technology concerned with this.

telecommute *v.intr.* work from home, communicating by telephone, telex, modem, etc. □ **telecommuter** *n.*

telecoms *n.* (also **telecomms**) (also *attrib.*) telecommunications (see TELECOMMUNICATION 2).

teleconference *n.* a conference with participants in different locations linked by telecommunication devices. □ **teleconferencing** *n.*

telecottage *n.* a centre fitted with office equipment (computer, photocopier, fax machine, etc.) for people working freelance or at a distance from an employer etc.

tele-evangelist var. of TELEVANGELIST.

telefax *n. propr.* facsimile transmission (see FACSIMILE *n.* 2).

telegram *n.* a message sent by telegraph and then usu. delivered in written form.

telegraph ● *n.* **1** a system of or device for transmitting messages or signals esp. by making and breaking an electrical connection. **2** (*attrib.*) used in this system (*telegraph wire*). ● *v.* **1** *tr.* send a message by telegraph to. **2** *tr.* send by telegraph. **3** *tr.* give an advance indication of. **4** *intr.* make signals (*telegraphed to me to come up*). [from French *télégraphe*] □ **telegrapher** *n.*

telegraphic *adj.* **1** of or by telegraphs or telegrams. **2** economically worded. □ **telegraphically** *adv.*

telegraphist *n.* a person skilled or employed in telegraphy.

telegraph pole *n.* a pole used to carry telegraph or telephone wires.

telegraphy *n.* the science or practice of communicating by telegraph.

telekinesis *n. Psychol.* movement of objects at a distance supposedly by paranormal means. [based on Greek *kinēsis* 'motion'] □ **telekinetic** *adj.*

telemarketing *n.* the marketing of goods etc. by means of telephone calls. □ **telemarketer** *n.*

telemessage *n.* a message sent by telephone or telex and delivered in written form.

telemeter /ti-**lem**-i-ter/ ● *n.* an apparatus for recording the readings of an instrument and transmitting them by radio. ● *v.* **1** *intr.* record readings in this way. **2** *tr.* transmit (readings etc.) to a distant receiving set or station. □ **telemetric** *adj.* **telemetry** *n.*

teleology *n.* (*pl.* **-ies**) *Philos.* **1** the explanation of phenomena by the purpose they serve rather than by postulated causes. **2** *Theol.* the doctrine of design and purpose in the material world. [based on Greek *telos teleos* 'end'] □ **teleological** *adj.* **teleologically** *adv.* **teleologism** *n.*

telepath *n.* a telepathic person. [back-formation from TELEPATHY]

telepathy /ti-**lep**-ă-thi/ *n.* the supposed communication of thoughts or ideas otherwise than by the known senses. □ **telepathic** *adj.* **telepathically** *adv.* **telepathist** *n.*

telephone ● *n.* **1** ▲ an apparatus for transmitting sound (esp. speech) to a distance, esp. as electrical signals. **2** a transmitting and receiving instrument used in this. **3** a system of communication using a network of telephones. ● *v.* **1** *tr.* speak to (a person) by telephone. **2** *tr.* send (a message) by telephone. **3** *intr.* make a telephone call. □ **on the telephone 1** having a telephone. **2** by use of or using the telephone. **over the telephone** by use of or using the telephone. □ **telephoner** *n.* **telephonic** *adj.* **telephonically** *adv.*

telephone book *n.* = TELEPHONE DIRECTORY.

telephone booth *n.* a public booth or enclosure from which telephone calls can be made.

telephone box *n. Brit.* = TELEPHONE BOOTH.

telephone call *n.* = CALL *n.* 4.

telephone directory *n.* a book listing telephone subscribers and numbers in a particular area.

telephone exchange *n.* = EXCHANGE *n.* 3.

telephone kiosk *n. Brit.* = TELEPHONE BOOTH.

telephone number *n.* **1** a number assigned to a particular telephone and used in making connections to it. **2** (often in *pl.*) *colloq.* a number with many digits, esp. representing a large sum of money.

telephone operator *n.* esp. *US* an operator in a telephone exchange.

telephonist /ti-**lef**-ŏ-nist/ *n. Brit.* an operator in a telephone exchange or at a switchboard.

telephony /ti-**lef**-ŏ-ni/ *n.* the use, or a system, of telephones.

T

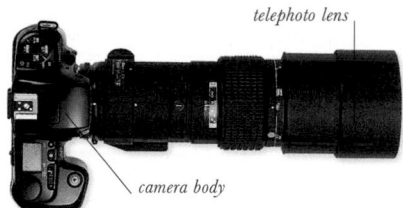

TELEPHOTO LENS ON AN **SLR** CAMERA

telephoto *n.* (*pl.* **-os**) (in full **telephoto lens**) ▲ a lens giving a narrow field of view and a magnified image.

telepoint *n.* **1** a place where a cordless telephone may be connected to the telephone network. **2** a system providing or using such places.

telepresence *n.* **1** the use of virtual reality technology esp. for remote control of machinery or for apparent participation in distant events. **2** a sensation of being elsewhere created in this way.

teleprinter *n. Brit.* a device for transmitting telegraph messages as they are keyed, and for printing messages received.

teleprompter *n.* a device beside a television or cinema camera that slowly unrolls a speaker's script out of sight of the audience.

telesales *n.pl.* selling by means of the telephone.

telescope ● *n.* **1** ▶ an optical instrument using lenses or mirrors or both to make distant objects appear nearer and larger. ▷ OBSERVATORY, SEXTANT. **2** = RADIO TELESCOPE. ● *v.* **1** *tr.* press or drive (sections of a tube, colliding vehicles, etc.) together so that one slides into another. **2** *intr.* close or be driven or be capable of closing in this way. **3** *tr.* compress so as to occupy less space or time. [from modern Latin *telescopium*]

telescopic *adj.* **1 a** of, relating to, or made with a telescope. **b** visible only through a telescope. **2** (esp. of a lens) able to focus on and magnify distant objects. **3** consisting of sections that telescope. □ **telescopically** *adv.*

telescopic sight *n.* ▼ a telescope used for sighting on a rifle etc.

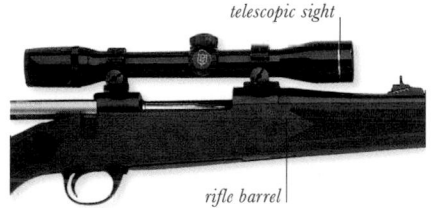

TELESCOPIC SIGHT ON A BIG-BORE
HUNTING RIFLE

teleshopping *n.* the ordering of goods by customers using a telephone or direct computer link.

telesoftware *n. Brit* software transmitted or broadcast to receiving terminals.

teletext *n.* a news and information service, in the form of text and graphics, from a computer source transmitted to televisions with appropriate receivers.

telethon *n.* an exceptionally long television programme, esp. to raise money for a charity.

teletype ● *n. propr.* a kind of teleprinter. ● *v.* **1** *intr.* operate a teleprinter. **2** *tr.* send by means of a teleprinter.

televangelist *n.* (also **tele-evangelist**) esp. *US* an evangelical preacher who appears regularly on television to promote beliefs and appeal for funds. □ **televangelism** *n.*

televiewer *n.* a person who watches television. □ **televiewing** *n.*

televise *v.tr.* transmit by television. [back-formation from TELEVISION] □ **televisable** *adj.*

TELESCOPE

There are two types of optical telescope: reflectors and refractors. In a refractor, light passes through the objective lens to form an image, which is magnified by the eyepiece. In a reflector, the light bounces off a curved primary mirror and on to a flat secondary mirror that reflects it into an eyepiece lens.

SMALL
ASTRONOMICAL
REFRACTOR
TELESCOPE

TYPES OF TELESCOPE

objective lens cell
telescope tube
declination setting circle
attachment cradle
finder scope
illuminator
equatorial mount
right ascension setting circle
polar axis scope
focusing knob
balance weight
azimuth fine-adjustment knob
spirit level
star diagonal
eyepiece
tripod
tripod brace

objective lens
incident light ray
telescope tube
refracted light ray
eyepiece lens
REFRACTOR

incident light ray
eyepiece lens
primary mirror
telescope tube
secondary mirror
reflected light ray
REFLECTOR

television *n.* **1** a system for reproducing on a screen visual images transmitted (usu. with sound) by radio signals. ▷ ELECTROMAGNETIC RADIATION. **2** (in full **television set**) ▼ a device with a screen for receiving these signals. **3** television broadcasting generally.

televisual *adj.* relating to or suitable for television. □ **televisually** *adv.*

telex (also **Telex**) ● *n.* an international system of telegraphy with printed messages transmitted and received by teleprinters using the public telecommunications network. ● *v.tr.* send or communicate with by telex. [blend of TELEPRINTER and EXCHANGE]

tell *v.* (*past* and *past part.* **told**) **1** *tr.* relate or narrate in speech or writing (*tell me a story*). **2** *tr.* make known; express in words; divulge (*tell me your name*). **3** *tr.* reveal or signify to (a person) (*your face tells me everything*). **4** *tr.* utter (*don't tell lies*). **5** *intr.* **a** (often foll. by *of*, *about*) divulge information or a description; reveal a secret. **b** (foll. by *on*) *colloq.* inform against. **6** *tr.* (foll. by *to* + infin.) give (a person) a direction or order. **7** *tr.* assure (*it's true, I tell you*). **8** *tr.* decide, determine, distinguish (*cannot tell which button to press*). **9** *intr.* **a** (often foll. by *on*) produce a noticeable effect (*the strain began to tell on me*). **b** have an influence (*the evidence tells against you*). **10** *tr.* (often *absol.*) count (votes) at a meeting, election, etc. □ **tell apart** distinguish between (*could not tell them apart*).

TELEVISION SET

A television set uses electromagnetic waves to produce a picture; a colour picture is made up of three colour signals. These are usually sent to three electron guns in a cathode ray tube. The guns fire electron beams through deflection coils, which scan them on to the screen. A shadow mask allows only one beam to hit any one phosphor spot, which then glows in red, green, or blue. Together, the three colour images make a full-colour picture.

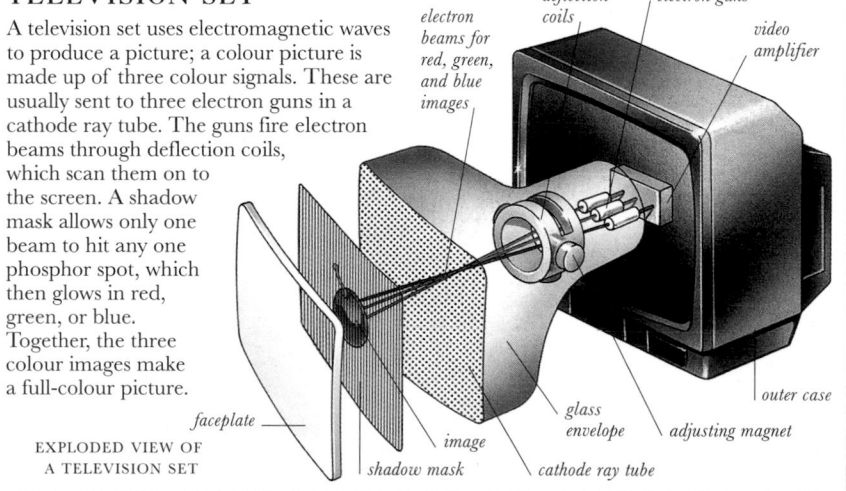

deflection coils
electron guns
electron beams for red, green, and blue images
video amplifier
outer case
glass envelope
adjusting magnet
faceplate
image
shadow mask
cathode ray tube

EXPLODED VIEW OF
A TELEVISION SET

T

TEMPLE

The structure of a temple is often symbolic. In the Aztec temple of Tenochtitlan in Mexico, shown here, two shrines dedicated to the gods were built at the top of a structure symbolizing a mountain. By climbing it, priests came closer to the gods, to whom human sacrifices were made.

sanctuary
shrine to god of sun and war
sacrificial stone
shrine to god of rain
remains of former temples
division between 'mountains'
small altar
base
frog altar
brazier
stone head of serpent god
stairway

MODEL OF THE
AZTEC TEMPLE OF
TENOCHTITLAN, MEXICO

tell off 1 *colloq.* reprimand, scold. **2** count off or detach for duty. **tell tales** report a discreditable fact about another. **tell the time** determine the time from the face of a clock or watch. **that would be telling** *colloq.* that would be to reveal too much (esp. secret or confidential) information. **there is no telling** it is impossible to know (*there's no telling what may happen*). **you're telling me** *colloq.* I agree wholeheartedly. [Old English] □ **tellable** *adj.*

teller *n.* **1** a person employed to receive and pay out money in a bank etc. **2** a person who counts (votes). **3** a person who tells esp. stories (*a teller of tales*).

telling *adj.* **1** having a marked effect; striking. **2** significant. □ **tellingly** *adv.*

telling-off *n.* (*pl.* **tellings-off**) esp. *Brit. colloq.* a reproof or reprimand.

tell-tale *n.* **1** a person who reveals (esp. discreditable) information about another. **2** (*attrib.*) that reveals or betrays (*a tell-tale smile*).

tellurium *n. Chem.* a rare brittle lustrous silver-white element occurring naturally in ores of gold and silver, used in semiconductors. [based on Latin *tellus -uris* 'earth'] □ **telluride** *n.* **tellurite** *n.* **tellurous** *adj.*

telly *n.* (*pl.* **-ies**) esp. *Brit. colloq.* **1** television. **2** a television set.

telophase *n. Biol.* the final stage of cell division, in which the nuclei of the daughter cells are formed. [based on Greek *telos* 'end']

temerity *n.* **1** rashness. **2** audacity, impudence. [from Latin *temeritas*]

temp *colloq.* ● *n.* a temporary employee, esp. a secretary. ● *v.intr.* work as a temp.

temper *n.* **1** habitual or temporary disposition of mind esp. as regards composure (*a person of a placid temper*). **2** irritation or anger (*in a fit of temper*). **3** a tendency to have fits of anger (*have a temper*). **4** composure or calmness (*keep one's temper; lose one's temper*). **5** the condition of metal as regards hardness and elasticity. ● *v.tr.* **1** bring (metal or clay) to a proper hardness or consistency. **2** (foll. by *with*) moderate or mitigate (*temper justice with mercy*). □ **in a bad temper** angry, peevish. **in a good temper** in an amiable mood. **out of temper** angry, peevish. [from Latin *temperare* 'to mingle'] □ **temperative** *adj.* **-tempered** *adj.* (in *comb.*).

tempera *n.* **1** a method of painting using an emulsion e.g. of pigment with egg. **2** this emulsion. [Italian, from *pingere a tempera* 'to paint in distemper']

temperament *n.* **1** a person's distinct nature and character (*a nervous temperament; the artistic tempera-*

ment). **2** a creative or spirited personality (*was full of temperament*). [from Latin *temperamentum*, related to TEMPER]

temperamental *adj.* **1** of or having temperament. **2 a** (of a person) liable to erratic or moody behaviour. **b** (of a thing, e.g. a machine) working unpredictably; unreliable. □ **temperamentally** *adv.*

temperance *n.* **1** moderation or self-restraint esp. in eating and drinking. **2 a** total or partial abstinence from alcoholic drink. **b** (*attrib.*) advocating or concerned with abstinence. [from Anglo-French *temperaunce*]

temperate *adj.* **1** avoiding excess; self-restrained. **2** moderate. **3** (of a region or climate) characterized by mild temperatures. [from Latin *temperatus* 'mingled'] □ **temperately** *adv.* **temperateness** *n.*

temperature *n.* **1** the degree or intensity of heat of a body, esp. as shown by a thermometer or perceived by touch etc. **2** *colloq.* a body temperature above the normal (*have a temperature*). **3** the degree of excitement in a discussion etc. [from Latin *temperatura*]

temperature inversion *n. Meteorol.* = INVERSION 3.

-tempered *comb. form* having a specified temper or disposition (*bad-tempered; hot-tempered*). □ **-temperedly** *adv.* **-temperedness** *n.*

tempest *n.* a violent windy storm. [from Latin *tempestas* 'season, storm']

tempestuous *adj.* **1** stormy. **2** (of a person, emotion, etc.) turbulent, violent, passionate. [from Late Latin *tempestuosus*] □ **tempestuously** *adv.* **tempestuousness** *n.*

tempi *pl.* of TEMPO.

template *n.* (also **templet**) **1** a pattern or gauge, usu. a piece of thin board or metal, used as a guide in cutting or drilling. **2** a flat card or plastic pattern esp. for cutting cloth for patchwork etc. [originally *templet*]

temple[1] *n.* ▲ a building devoted to the worship, or regarded as the dwelling place, of a god or gods or other objects of religious reverence. [Old English]

temple[2] *n.* (often in *pl.*) the flat part of either side of the head between the forehead and the ear. [from Old French]

templet var. of TEMPLATE.

tempo *n.* (*pl.* **-os** or **tempi**) **1** *Mus.* the speed at which music is or should be played, esp. as characteristic (*waltz tempo*). **2** the rate of motion or activity (*the tempo of the war is quickening*). [Italian]

temporal *adj.* **1** of worldly as opposed to spiritual affairs; secular. **2** of or relating to time. **3** *Gram.*

relating to or denoting time or tense (*temporal conjunction*). [based on Latin *tempus -oris* 'time'] □ **temporally** *adv.*

temporal lobe *n.* ► each of the paired lobes of the brain lying beneath the temples, including areas concerned with the understanding of speech.

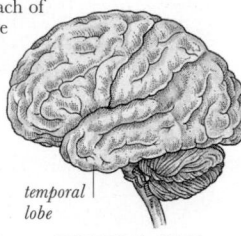

temporal lobe

TEMPORAL LOBE
IN THE
HUMAN BRAIN

temporary ● *adj.* lasting or meant to last only for a limited time. ● *n.* (*pl.* **-ies**) a person employed temporarily. [from Latin *temporarius*] □ **temporarily** *adv.* **temporariness** *n.*

temporize *v.intr.* (also **-ise**) **1** avoid committing oneself so as to gain time. **2** comply temporarily, adopt a time-serving policy. [from medieval Latin *temporizare* 'to delay']

tempt *v.tr.* **1** entice or incite (a person) to do a wrong or forbidden thing (*tempted him to steal it*). **2** allure, attract. **3** risk provoking (fate etc.). □ **be tempted to** be strongly disposed to (*I am tempted to question this*). [from Latin *temptare* 'to handle, test, try'] □ **temptable** *adj.* **tempter** *n.* **temptress** *n.*

temptation *n.* **1** the act or an instance of tempting; the state of being tempted. **2** an attractive thing or course of action.

tempting *adj.* **1** attractive, inviting. **2** enticing to evil. □ **temptingly** *adv.*

tempura *n.* a Japanese dish of fish, shellfish, or vegetables, fried in batter. [Japanese]

ten ● *n.* **1** one more than nine. **2** a symbol for this (10, x, X). **3** a size etc. denoted by ten. **4** ten o'clock. **5** a card with ten pips. **6** a set of ten. ● *adj.* that amount to ten. □ **ten to one** very probably. [Old English]

tenable *adj.* **1** that can be maintained or defended against attack or objection (*a tenable position*). **2** (foll. by *for, by*) (of an office etc.) that can be held for (a specified period) or by (a specified class of person). [French, literally 'holdable'] □ **tenability** *n.*

tenacious *adj.* **1** (often foll. by *of*) keeping a firm hold of property, principles, life, etc.; not readily relinquishing. **2** (of memory) retentive. **3** holding fast. **4** persistent, resolute. **5** adhesive, sticky. [from Latin *tenax -acis*] □ **tenaciously** *adv.* **tenaciousness** *n.* **tenacity** *n.*

tenancy *n.* (*pl.* **-ies**) **1** the status of a tenant; possession as a tenant. **2** the duration or period of this.

tenant ● *n.* **1** a person who rents land or property from a landlord. **2** (often foll. by *of*) the occupant of a place. ● *v.tr.* occupy as a tenant. [from Old French, literally 'holding'] □ **tenantless** *adj.*

tenant farmer *n.* a person who farms rented land.

tenantry *n.* the tenants of an estate etc.

tench *n.* (*pl.* same) ▼ a European freshwater fish, *Tinca tinca*, of the carp family. [from Late Latin *tinca*]

TENCH
(*Tinca tinca*)

tend[1] *v.intr.* **1** (usu. foll. by *to*) be apt or inclined (*tends to lose his temper*). **2** serve, conduce. **3** be moving; be directed; hold a course (*tends in our direction; tends to the same conclusion*). [from Latin *tendere*]

tend[2] *v.* **1** *tr.* take care of, look after (an invalid, a flock, a machine, etc.). **2** *intr.* (foll. by *to*) esp. *US* give attention to. [Middle English]

tendency *n.* (*pl.* **-ies**) **1** (often foll. by *to, towards*) a

T

leaning or inclination, a way of tending. **2** a group within a larger political party or movement. [from medieval Latin *tendentia*]

tendentious *adj. derog.* (of writing etc.) calculated to promote a particular cause or viewpoint. □ **tendentiously** *adv.* **tendentiousness** *n.*

tender¹ *adj.* (**tenderer**, **tenderest**) **1** easily cut or chewed, not tough (*tender steak*). **2** easily touched or wounded, susceptible to pain or grief (*a tender heart*). **3** easily hurt, sensitive (*tender skin*). **4** delicate, fragile (*a tender reputation*). **5** loving, affectionate, fond (*tender parents*). **6** requiring tact or careful handling, ticklish (*a tender subject*). **7** (of age) early, immature (*of tender years*). [from Latin *tener*] □ **tenderly** *adv.* **tenderness** *n.*

tender² ● *v.* **1** *tr.* **a** offer, present (one's services, apologies, resignation, etc.). **b** offer (money etc.) as payment. **2** *intr.* (often foll. by *for*) make a tender for the supply of a thing or the execution of work. ● *n.* an offer, esp. an offer in writing to execute work or supply goods at a fixed price. □ **put out to tender** seek tenders in respect of (work etc.). [from Old French *tendre*] □ **tenderer** *n.*

tender³ *n.* **1** a person who looks after people or things. **2** a vessel attending a larger one to supply stores, convey passengers, etc. **3** ▼ a special truck closely coupled to a steam locomotive to carry fuel and water. [Middle English]

TENDER: CUTAWAY VIEW OF A MID-20TH-CENTURY TENDER

tender-eyed *adj.* **1** having gentle eyes. **2** weak-eyed.

tenderfoot *n.* (*pl.* **-s** or **-feet**) a newcomer or novice, esp. in the bush or in the Scouts or Guides.

tender-hearted *adj.* having a tender heart, easily moved by pity etc. □ **tender-heartedness** *n.*

tenderize *v.tr.* (also **-ise**) make tender, esp. make (meat) tender by beating etc. □ **tenderizer** *n.*

tenderloin *n.* **1** the tenderest part of a loin of beef, pork, etc. **2** *US* the undercut of a sirloin.

tender mercies *n.pl. iron.* attention or treatment which is not in the best interests of its recipient.

tender spot *n.* a subject on which a person is touchy.

tendon *n.* **1** ▼ a cord of strong fibrous tissue attaching a muscle to a bone etc. **2** (in a quadruped) = HAMSTRING *n.* 2. [from Greek *tenōn* 'sinew'] □ **tendinitis** *n.* (also **tendonitis**). **tendinous** *adj.*

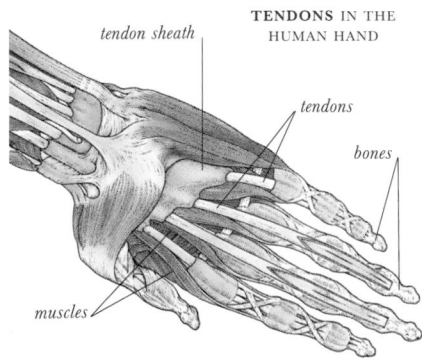

TENDONS IN THE HUMAN HAND

tendon sheath

tendons

bones

muscles

---

tendril *n.* **1** ▶ a slender leafless shoot by which some climbing plants cling for support. **2** a slender curl of hair etc.

tenement *n.* **1** a room or a set of rooms forming a residence within a house or block of flats. **2** (in full **tenement house**) *US* & *Sc.* a house divided into and let in tenements. [from medieval Latin *tenementum*]

tenet *n.* a doctrine, dogma, or principle. [Latin, literally 'he etc. holds']

tenfold *adj.* & *adv.* **1** ten times as much or as many. **2** consisting of ten parts.

ten-gallon hat *n.* a cowboy's large broad-brimmed hat.

tenner *n.* esp. *Brit. colloq.* a ten-pound or ten-dollar note.

tennis *n.* ▲ a game in which two or four players strike a ball with rackets over a net stretched across a court. ▷ BACKHAND, FOREHAND, OVERARM. [Middle English]

tennis ball *n.* a ball used in playing tennis. ▷ TENNIS

tennis court *n.* a court used in playing tennis. ▷ TENNIS

tennis elbow *n.* a painful inflammation of the tendons in the elbow caused by or as by playing tennis.

tennis racket *n.* a racket used in playing tennis. ▷ TENNIS

tennis shoe *n.* a light canvas or leather soft-soled shoe suitable for tennis or general casual wear.

tenon *n.* a wooden projection made for insertion into a corresponding cavity (esp. a mortise) in another piece. ▷ DOVETAIL. [based on French *tenir* 'to hold']

tenon saw *n.* a small saw with a strong brass or steel back for fine work. ▷ SAW

tenor /ten-er/ *n.* **1 a** a singing voice between baritone and alto or counter-tenor, the highest of the ordinary adult male range. **b** a singer with this voice. **c** a part written for it. **2** an instrument, esp. a viola, recorder, or saxophone, of which the range is roughly that of a tenor voice. **3** (usu. foll. by *of*) the general purport or drift of a document or speech. **4** (usu. foll. by *of*) a prevailing course, esp. of a person's life or habits. [Latin, literally 'continuous course']

tenor clef *n. Mus.* a clef placing middle C on the second highest line of the staff.

tenorist *n.* a person who sings a tenor part or esp. who plays a tenor instrument.

tenosynovitis *n.* inflammation and swelling of a tendon, usu. in the wrist, often caused by repeti-

---

TENNIS

TENNIS PLAYER, RACKET, AND BALL

racket

felt-covered ball

Tennis is played on various surfaces, both indoors and outdoors. The aim is to hit the ball over the net so that it cannot be properly returned. Players must win at least six games for a set, and need two sets (women) or three sets (men) for the match.

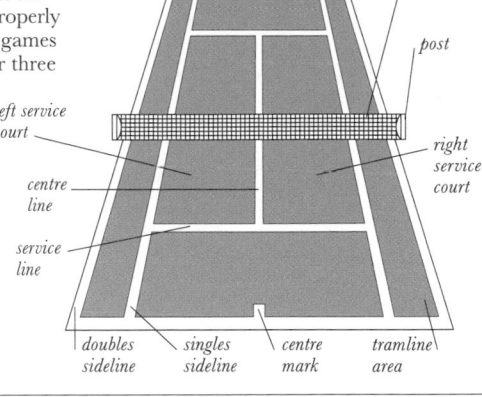

TENNIS COURT

baseline

net

post

left service court

right service court

centre line

service line

doubles sideline

singles sideline

centre mark

tramline area

---

tendril

TENDRIL OF A GOURD PLANT

---

tive movements such as typing. [based on Greek *tenōn* 'tendon']

tenpin *n.* **1** ▶ a pin used in tenpin bowling. **2** (in *pl.*) *US* = TENPIN BOWLING.

tenpin bowling *n.* a game in which ten pins are bowled at in an alley with hard rubber or plastic balls.

tense¹ ● *adj.* **1** stretched tight, strained (*tense muscle*; *tense emotion*). **2** causing tenseness (*a tense moment*). ● *v.tr.* & *intr.* make or become tense. □ **tense up** become tense. [from Latin *tensus* 'stretched'] □ **tensely** *adv.* **tenseness** *n.*

tense² *n. Gram.* **1** a form taken by a verb to indicate the time (also the continuance or completeness) of the action etc. (*present tense*; *imperfect tense*). **2** a set of such forms for the various persons and numbers. [from Latin *tempus* 'time'] □ **tenseless** *adj.*

TENPIN

tensile *adj.* **1** of or relating to tension. **2** capable of being drawn out or stretched. [from medieval Latin *tensilis*] □ **tensility** *n.*

tensile strength *n.* resistance to breaking under tension.

tension ● *n.* **1** the act or an instance of stretching; the state of being stretched; tenseness. **2** mental strain or excitement. **3** a strained (political, social, etc.) state or relationship. **4** electromagnetic force (*high tension*; *low tension*). ● *v.tr.* subject to tension. [French] □ **tensional** *adj.* **tensioner** *n.* **tensionless** *adj.*

tent ● *n.* **1** ▼ a portable shelter or dwelling of canvas, cloth, etc., supported by a pole or poles and stretched by cords or loops attached to pegs in the ground. **2** *Med.* = OXYGEN TENT. ● *v.tr.* **1** cover with or as with a tent. **2** (as **tented** *adj.*) composed of or provided with tents (*tented village*; *tented field*). [from Old French *tente*]

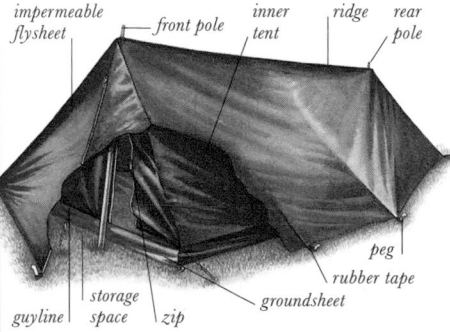

impermeable flysheet

front pole

inner tent

ridge

rear pole

peg

rubber tape

groundsheet

guyline

storage space

zip

TENT: CUTAWAY VIEW OF A RIDGE TENT AND FLYSHEET

T

mud tube

tentacles

**TENTACLES OF
A PEACOCK WORM**

tentacle *n.* **1** ◄ a long slender flexible appendage of an (esp. invertebrate) animal, used for feeling, grasping, or moving. ▷ CEPHALOPOD, CNIDARIAN. **2** a thing used like a tentacle as a feeler etc. [based on Latin *temptare* 'to handle, try'] □ **tentacled** *adj.* (also in *comb.*). **tentacular** *adj.* **tentaculate** *adj.*

tentage *n.* tents; tenting equipment.

tentative *adj.* **1** done by way of trial, experimental. **2** hesitant, not definite. [from medieval Latin *tentativus*] □ **tentatively** *adv.* **tentativeness** *n.*

tenterhook *n.* □ **on tenterhooks** in a state of suspense or mental agitation due to uncertainty.

tenth ● *n.* **1** the position in a sequence corresponding to the number 10 in the sequence 1-10. **2** something occupying this position. **3** one of ten equal parts of a thing. ● *adj.* that is the tenth. [alteration of Old English *teogotha*] □ **tenthly** *adv.*

tent stitch *n.* **1** a series of parallel diagonal stitches. **2** such a stitch.

tenuous *adj.* **1** slight, of little substance (*tenuous connection*). **2** (of a distinction etc.) oversubtle. **3** thin, slender, small. **4** rarefied. [from Latin *tenuis*] □ **tenuously** *adv.* **tenuousness** *n.*

tenure *n.* **1** a condition, or form of right or title, under which (esp. real) property is held. **2** (often foll. by *of*) **a** the holding or possession of an office or property. **b** the period of this. **3** guaranteed permanent employment, esp. as a teacher or lecturer after a probationary period. [from Old French]

tenured *adj.* **1** (of an official position) carrying a guarantee of permanent employment. **2** (of a teacher, lecturer, etc.) having guaranteed tenure of office.

tepee /tee-pee/ *n.* (also **teepee**, **tipi**) ► a N. American Indian's conical tent. [from Sioux *típî*]

poles bound together

smoke flap

TEPEE

wooden pin

buffalo hides

entrance

tepid *adj.* **1** slightly warm. **2** unenthusiastic. [from Latin *tepidus*] □ **tepidity** *n.* **tepidly** *adv.* **tepidness** *n.*

tequila /tĕ-kee-lă/ *n.* a Mexican liquor made from an agave. [from *Tequila*, a town in Mexico]

tera- *comb. form* denoting a factor of 10^{12}. [from Greek *teras* 'monster']

teraflop *n. Computing* a unit of computing speed equal to one million million floating-point operations per second.

teratogen *n. Med.* an agent or factor causing malformation of an embryo. □ **teratogenic** *adj.* **teratogeny** *n.*

terawatt *n.* a unit of power equal to 10^{12} watts or a million megawatts.

terbium *n. Chem.* a silvery metallic element of the lanthanide series. [named after *Ytterby*, a village in Sweden where it was discovered]

terce *n. Eccl.* the office of the third canonical hour of prayer, originally said at the third hour of the day (i.e. 9 a.m.). [variant of TIERCE].

tercel var. of TIERCEL.

tercentenary ● *n.* (*pl.* **-ies**) **1** a three-hundredth anniversary. **2** a celebration of this. ● *adj.* of this anniversary.

terebinth *n.* a small southern European tree, *Pistacia terebinthus*, yielding resin formerly used as a source of turpentine. [from Greek *terebinthos*]

teredo /tĕ-ree-doh/ *n.* (*pl.* **-os**) ▼ any bivalve mollusc of the genus *Teredo*, esp. *T. navalis*, that bores into wooden ships etc. [based on Greek *terein* 'to bore']

terete *adj. Biol.* smooth and rounded; cylindrical. [from Latin *teres -etis*]

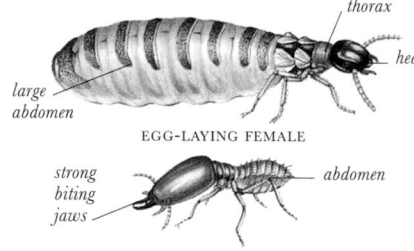

TEREDO: SHELLY TUBES LEFT
IN WOOD BY TEREDO WORMS

tergiversate /ter-jiv-er-sayt/ *v.intr.* **1** be apostate; change one's party or principles. **2** equivocate; make conflicting or evasive statements. [based on Latin *tergiversatus* 'having one's back turned'] □ **tergiversation** *n.* **tergiversator** *n.*

term ● *n.* **1** a word used to express a definite concept, esp. in a particular branch of study etc. (*a technical term*). **2** (in *pl.*) language used; mode of expression (*answered in no uncertain terms*). **3** (in *pl.*) a relation or footing (*we are on familiar terms*). **4** (in *pl.*) **a** conditions or stipulations. **b** charge or price. **5 a** a limited period of some state or activity (*for a term of five years*). **b** a period over which operations are conducted or results contemplated (*in the short term*). **c** a period of some weeks, alternating with holiday or vacation, during which instruction is given in a school, college, or university, or during which a law court holds sessions. **6** *Logic* a word or words that may be the subject or predicate of a proposition. **7** *Math.* **a** each of the two quantities in a ratio. **b** each quantity in a series. **c** a part of an expression joined to the rest by + or − (e.g. *a*, *b*, *c* in *a* + *b* − *c*). **8** the completion of a normal length of pregnancy. ● *v.tr.* denominate, call (*the music termed classical*). □ **bring to terms** cause to accept conditions. **come to terms** yield, give way. **come to terms with 1** reconcile oneself to (a difficulty etc.). **2** conclude an agreement with. **in terms of** in the language peculiar to, using as a basis of expression or thought. **make terms** conclude an agreement. **on terms** on terms of friendship or equality. [from Latin *terminus* 'end, limit'] □ **termless** *adj.* **termly** *adj. & adv.*

termagant *n.* an overbearing or brawling woman. [from Italian *Trivigante*, a deity often appearing in morality plays]

terminable *adj.* **1** that may be terminated. **2** coming to an end after a certain time.

terminal ● *adj.* **1 a** (of a disease) ending in death, fatal. **b** (of a patient) in the last stage of a fatal disease. **c** *colloq.* ruinous, very great (*terminal laziness*). **2** of or forming a limit or terminus (*terminal station*). ● *n.* **1** a terminating thing; an extremity. **2** a terminus for trains or long-distance buses. **3** a departure and arrival building for air passengers at an airport. **4** a point of connection for closing an electric circuit. ▷ BATTERY, CIRCUIT. **5** an apparatus for transmission of messages between a user and a computer, communications system, etc. **6** an installation where oil is stored at the end of a pipeline or at a port. [from Latin *terminalis*] □ **terminally** *adv.*

terminate *v.* **1** *tr. & intr.* bring or come to an end. **2** *tr.* end (a pregnancy) before term by artificial means. [based on Latin *terminatus* 'ended'] □ **terminator** *n.*

termination *n.* **1** the act or an instance of terminating; the state of being terminated. **2** *Med.* an induced abortion. **3** an ending or result of a specified kind (*a happy termination*). □ **put a termination to** (or **bring to a termination**) make an end of.

termini *pl.* of TERMINUS.

terminological *adj.* relating to terminology. □ **terminologically** *adv.*

terminological inexactitude *n. joc.* a lie.

terminology *n.* (*pl.* **-ies**) **1** the system of terms used in a particular subject. **2** the science of the proper use of terms. [from German *Terminologie*] □ **terminologist** *n.*

terminus *n.* (*pl.* **termini** /-ny/ or **terminuses**) **1 a** the end of a railway or bus route. **b** *Brit.* a station at this point. **2** a point at the end of a pipeline etc. **3** a final point, a goal. [Latin, literally 'end, limit, boundary']

termitary *n.* (*pl.* **-ies**) a nest of termites, usu. a large mound of earth. ▷ NEST

termite *n.* ▼ a small social insect of the order Isoptera, chiefly tropical and destructive to timber. [based on Latin *tarmes*]

thorax

head

large abdomen

EGG-LAYING FEMALE

strong biting jaws

abdomen

SOLDIER TERMITE

TERMITES (*Macrotermes* species)

terms of reference *n.pl. Brit.* the definition of the scope of an inquiry etc.

terms of trade *n.pl. Brit.* the ratio between prices paid for imports and those received for exports.

term-time ● *n.* (esp. in phr. **in** or **during term-time**) the period when school is in session. ● *attrib.adj.* relating to this period.

tern *n.* ◄ any seabird of the family Sternidae, like a gull but usu. smaller and with a forked tail. ▷ SEABIRD. [of Scandinavian origin]

ternary *adj.* **1** composed of three parts. **2** *Math.* using three as a base (*ternary scale*). [from Latin *ternarius*]

terrace ● *n.* **1** each of a series of flat areas formed on a slope and used for cultivation. **2** a level paved area next to a house. **3** *Brit.* a row of houses built in one block of uniform style. **4** *Brit.* a flight of wide shallow steps as for spectators at a sports ground. **5** *Geol.* a raised beach, or a similar formation beside a river etc. ● *v.tr.* form into or provide with a terrace or terraces. [from Old French]

TERN:
LITTLE TERN
(*Sterna albifrons*)

terrace house *n.* (also **terraced house**) *Brit.* a house in a terrace.

terracotta ● *n.* **1 a** unglazed usu. brownish-red earthenware used chiefly as an ornamental building material and in modelling. **b** ► a statuette of this. **2** the brownish-red colour of terracotta. ● *adj.* of a brownish-red colour. [Italian, literally 'baked earth']

terra firma *n.* dry land, firm ground. [Latin, literally 'firm land']

terrain *n.* **1** esp. *Geog. & Mil.* a tract of land esp. as regarded by a physical geographer or the military

TERRACOTTA FIGURE OF AN
ASSYRIAN HOUSEHOLD GOD

T

tactician. **2** a particular area of knowledge; a sphere of influence or action. [from Latin *terrenum* 'terrene (thing)']

terra incognita /in-kog-**nee**-tă/ *n.* an unknown or unexplored region. [Latin, literally 'unknown land']

terrapin *n.* **1** any of various small freshwater turtles of the family Emydidae. ▷ CHELONIAN. **2** (**Terrapin**) *Brit. propr.* a type of prefabricated one-storey building. [Algonquian]

terrarium *n.* (*pl.* **terrariums** or **terraria**) **1** a vivarium for small land animals. **2** ▶ a sealed transparent globe etc. containing growing plants. [based on Latin *terra* 'earth']

terrazzo /tĕ-**rat**-soh/ *n.* (*pl.* **-os**) a flooring material of stone chips set in concrete and given a smooth surface. [Italian, literally 'terrace']

terrene *adj.* **1** of the Earth; earthly, worldly. **2** of earth, earthy. **3** of dry land; terrestrial. [based on Latin *terra* 'earth']

terrestrial ● *adj.* **1** of or on or relating to the Earth; earthly. **2 a** of or on dry land. **b** *Zool.* living on or in the ground. **c** *Bot.* growing in the soil. **3** (of broadcasting) not using satellites. **●** *n.* an inhabitant of the Earth. [from Latin *terrestris*] □ **terrestrially** *adv.*

terrestrial globe *n.* a globe representing the Earth.

terrible *adj.* **1** *colloq.* **a** dreadful, awful (*the accident was terrible*). **b** (as an intensifier) very great or bad (*a terrible bore*). **2** *colloq.* very incompetent (*terrible at tennis*). **3** (*predic.*) *colloq.* ill (*he ate too much and feels terrible*). **4** (*predic.*; often foll. by *about*) *colloq.* full of remorse (*I feel terrible about it*). **5** causing terror; fit to cause terror; formidable. [from Latin *terribilis*] □ **terribleness** *n.*

terribly *adv.* **1** *colloq.* very, extremely (*he was terribly nice about it*). **2** in a terrible manner.

terrier *n.* **1** a small dog of various breeds originally used for turning out foxes etc. from their earths. **2** an eager or tenacious person or animal. [from Old French (*chien*) *terrier*, literally 'dog of the (fox etc.) earth']

terrific *adj.* **1** *colloq.* **a** of great size or intensity. **b** excellent (*did a terrific job*). **c** excessive (*making a terrific noise*). **2** causing terror. [from Latin *terrificus* 'frightening'] □ **terrifically** *adv.*

terrify *v.tr.* (**-ies**, **-ied**) fill with terror (*terrified them into submission*; *is terrified of dogs*). [from Latin *terrificare*] □ **terrifyingly** *adv.*

terrine /tĕ-**reen**/ *n.* **1** a kind of pâté. **2** an earthenware container, esp. one in which such food is cooked or sold. [earlier as variant of TUREEN]

territorial ● *adj.* **1** of territory (*territorial possessions*). **2** limited to a district (*the right was strictly territorial*). **3** tending to defend an area of territory. **4** (usu. **Territorial**) of any of the Territories of the US or Canada. **●** *n.* (**Territorial**) (in the UK) a member of the Territorial Army. □ **territoriality** *n.* **territorially** *adv.*

Territorial Army *n.* (in the UK) a volunteer force locally organized to provide a reserve of trained and disciplined manpower for use in an emergency.

territorial waters *n.pl.* the waters under the jurisdiction of a state, esp. the part of the sea within a stated distance of the shore.

territory *n.* (*pl.* **-ies**) **1** the extent of the land under the jurisdiction of a ruler, state, city, etc. **2** (**Territory**) an organized division of a country, esp. one not yet admitted to the full rights of a state. **3** a sphere of action or thought; a province. **4** the area over which a commercial traveller or goods-distributor operates. **5** *Zool.* an area defended by an animal or animals against others of the same species. **6** an area defended by a team or player in a game. [from Latin *territorium*]

terror *n.* **1** extreme fear. **2 a** a person or thing that causes terror. **b** (also **holy terror**) *colloq.* a formidable person; a troublesome person or thing (*the twins are little terrors*). **3** the use of organized intimidation; terrorism. [based on Latin *terrēre* 'to frighten']

terrorist *n.* a person who uses violent and intimidating methods of coercing a government or community. □ **terrorism** *n.* **terroristic** *adj.*

terrorize *v.tr.* (also **-ise**) **1** fill with terror. **2** use terrorism against. □ **terrorizer** *n.*

terror-stricken *adj.* (also **terror-struck**) affected with terror.

terry ● *n.* (*pl.* **-ies**) a pile fabric with the loops uncut, used esp. for towels. **●** *adj.* of this fabric. [18th-century coinage]

terse *adj.* (**terser**, **tersest**) **1** brief, concise. **2** curt, abrupt. [originally in sense 'polished, refined': from Latin *tersus* 'polished'] □ **tersely** *adv.* **terseness** *n.*

tertiary /**ter**-sher-i **●** *adj.* **1** third in order or rank etc. **2** (**Tertiary**) *Geol.* of or relating to the first period in the Cenozoic era. **●** *n.* (**Tertiary**) *Geol.* this period or system. [based on Latin *tertius* 'third']

tertiary education *n.* esp. *Brit.* education, esp. in a college or university, that follows secondary education.

Terylene *n. Brit. propr.* a synthetic polyester used as a textile fibre.

TESL *abbr.* teaching of English as a second language.

tesla *n.* the SI unit of magnetic flux density. [named after N. *Tesla*, Croatian-born American scientist, 1856–1943]

TESSA *n.* (also **Tessa**) (in the UK) tax exempt special savings account.

tessellate *v.tr.* **1** make from tesserae. **2** *Math.* cover (a plane surface) by repeated use of a single shape. [based on Latin *tessella* 'small tessera']

TESSELLATION IN ISLAMIC MOSAIC

tessellated *adj.* **1** of or resembling mosaic. **2** *Bot.* & *Zool.* regularly chequered.

tessellation *n.* **1** the act or an instance of tessellating; the state of being tessellated. **2** ◀ an arrangement of polygons without gaps or overlapping, esp. in a repeated pattern.

tessera /**tes**-ĕ-ră/ *n.* (*pl.* **tesserae** /-ree/) **1** a small square block used in mosaic. **2** *Gk* & *Rom Antiq.* a small square of bone etc. used as a token, ticket etc. [Greek, literally 'four'] □ **tesseral** *adj.*

tessitura *n. Mus.* the range within which most tones of a voice part fall. [Italian, literally 'texture']

test[1] **●** *n.* **1** a critical examination or trial of a person's or thing's qualities. **2** the means of so examining; a standard for comparison or trial; circumstances suitable for this (*success is not a fair test*). **3** a minor examination, esp. in school (*spelling test*). **4** *Brit.* a test match. **5** a ground of admission or rejection (*is excluded by our test*). **6** *Chem.* a reagent or a procedure employed to reveal the presence of another in a compound. **●** *v.tr.* **1** put to the test; make trial of (a person or thing or quality). **2** try severely; tax a person's powers of endurance etc. **3** *Chem.* examine by means of a reagent. □ **put to the test** cause to undergo a test. **test out** put to a practical test. [from Latin *testu(m)* 'earthen pot'] □ **testable** *adj.* **testability** *n.* **testee** *n.*

test[2] *n.* ▶ the shell of some invertebrates. [from Latin *testa* 'tile, jug, shell']

testa *n.* (*pl.* **testae** /-tee/) *Bot.* the protective outer covering of a seed. ▷ SEED. [Latin]

testaceous *adj.* **1** *Biol.* having a hard continuous outer covering. **2** *Bot.* & *Zool.* of a brick-red colour. [related to TEST[2]]

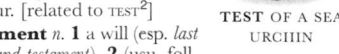

TEST OF A SEA URCHIN

testament *n.* **1** a will (esp. *last will and testament*). **2** (usu. foll. by *to*) evidence, proof (*is testament to his loyalty*). **3** *Bibl.* **a** a covenant or dispensation. **b** (**Testament**) a division of the Christian Bible (see OLD TESTAMENT, NEW TESTAMENT). **c** (**Testament**) a copy of the New Testament. [from Latin *testamentum* 'a will']

testamentary *adj.* of or by or in a will.

testate ● *adj.* having left a valid will at death. **●** *n.* a testate person. [from Latin *testatus* 'testified']

testator *n.* (*fem.* **testatrix**) a person who has made a will.

test bed *n.* equipment for testing aircraft engines before acceptance for general use.

test card *n. Brit.* a still television picture transmitted outside normal programme hours and designed for use in judging the quality and position of the image.

test case *n.* a case setting a precedent for other cases involving the same question of law.

test drive *n.* a drive taken to determine the qualities of a motor vehicle. □ **test-drive** *v.tr.* (*past* **-drove**; *past part.* **-driven**).

tester[1] *n.* **1** a person or thing that tests. **2** a sample of a cosmetic etc., allowing customers to try it before purchase.

tester[2] *n.* a canopy, esp. over a four-poster bed. [based on Latin *testa* 'tile, shell']

testes *pl.* of TESTIS.

test flight *n.* a flight during which the performance of an aircraft is tested. □ **test-fly** *v.tr.* (**-flies**, *past* **-flew**; *past part.* **-flown**).

testicle *n.* ▼ a male organ that produces spermatozoa etc., esp. one of a pair enclosed in the scrotum of a man and most mammals. [from Latin *testiculus* 'little witness (of virility)'] □ **testicular** *adj.*

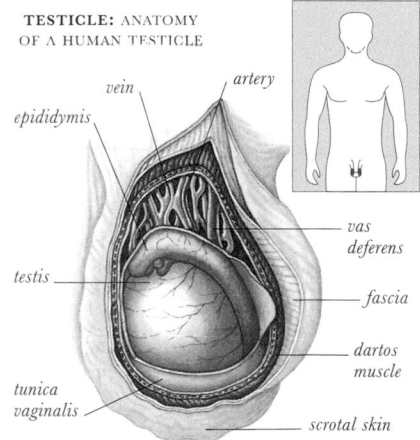

TESTICLE: ANATOMY OF A HUMAN TESTICLE

vein
artery
epididymis
vas deferens
testis
fascia
dartos muscle
tunica vaginalis
scrotal skin

testify *v.* (**-ies**, **-ied**) **1** *intr.* bear witness (*testified to the facts*). **2** *intr. Law* give evidence. **3** *tr.* affirm or declare (*testified his regret*; *testified that she had been present*). **4** *tr.* be evidence of; evince. [from Latin *testificari*] □ **testifier** *n.*

testimonial *n.* **1** a formal letter etc. testifying to a person's character, conduct, or qualifications. **2** a gift presented to a person as a mark of esteem etc. [from Old French *testimoignal*]

T

testimony *n.* (*pl.* **-ies**) **1** *Law* a statement under oath or affirmation. **2** declaration or statement of fact. **3** evidence, demonstration (*called him in testimony*; *produce testimony*). [from Latin *testimonium*]

testing ground *n.* **1** a means of experimenting, or of testing reaction, worth, etc. **2** a site for testing esp. new weapons.

testis *n.* (*pl.* **testes**) *Anat.* & *Zool.* a testicle. ▷ ENDOCRINE, REPRODUCTIVE ORGANS. [Latin, literally 'a witness']

test match *n.* a cricket or rugby match between teams of certain countries.

testosterone *n. Biochem.* a steroid hormone that stimulates development of male secondary sexual characteristics, produced mainly in the testes.

test paper *n.* **1** a minor examination paper. **2** *Chem.* a paper impregnated with a substance changing colour under known conditions.

test pilot *n.* a pilot who test-flies aircraft.

test tube *n.* (hyphenated when *attrib.*) a thin glass tube closed at one end used for chemical tests etc. ▷ FLUORESCENCE

test-tube baby *n. colloq.* a baby conceived by *in vitro* fertilization.

testy *adj.* (**testier**, **testiest**) irritable, touchy. [originally in sense 'headstrong': based on Old French *teste* 'head'] □ **testily** *adv.* **testiness** *n.*

tetanus *n.* a disease caused by the bacterium *Clostridium tetani*, marked by rigidity and spasms of the voluntary muscles. [from Greek *tetanos* 'muscular spasm'] □ **tetanic** *adj.*

tetany *n.* a disease with intermittent muscular spasms caused by malfunction of the parathyroid glands and a consequent deficiency of calcium. [from French *tétanie*]

tetchy *adj.* (also **techy**) (**-ier**, **-iest**) peevish, irritable. □ **tetchily** *adv.* **tetchiness** *n.*

tête-à-tête /tayt-ah-**tayt**/ ● *n.* a private conversation usu. between two persons. ● *adv.* together in private (*dined tête-à-tête*). ● *adj.* **1** private, confidential. **2** concerning only two persons. [French, literally 'head-to-head']

tether ● *n.* a rope etc. by which an animal is tied to confine it to the spot. ● *v.tr.* tie (an animal) with a tether. □ **at the end of one's tether** having reached the limit of one's patience, resources, abilities, etc. [from Old Norse *tjóthr*]

tetra *n.* any of various small, often brightly coloured tropical fish of the family Characidae, frequently kept in aquaria. [abbreviation of modern Latin *Tetragonopterus* 'tetragonal finned', former genus name]

tetra- *comb. form* (also **tetr-** before a vowel) **1** four (*tetrapod*). **2** *Chem.* containing four atoms or groups of a specified kind (*tetroxide*). [from Greek *tettares* 'four']

tetrad *n.* **1** a group of four. ▷ MEIOSIS. **2** the number four. [from Greek *tetras -ados*]

tetragon *n.* a plane figure with four angles and four sides. [Greek, literally 'quadrangle']

tetragonal *adj.* of or like a tetragon.

tetrahedron *n.* (*pl.* **tetrahedra** or **tetrahedrons**) ▶ a four-sided solid; a triangular-based pyramid. [from late Greek *tetraedron* 'four-sided (thing)'] □ **tetrahedral** *adj.*

tetralogy /ti-**tral**-ŏji/ *n.* (*pl.* **-ies**) a group of four related literary or operatic works.

tetrameter /ti-**tram**-i-ter/ *n. Prosody* a verse of four measures. [from Greek *tetrametros*]

tetraplegia *n. Med.* = QUADRIPLEGIA. [based on Greek *plēgē* 'blow, stroke'] □ **tetraplegic** *adj.* & *n.*

tetraploid /**tet**-ră-ployd/ *Biol.* ● *adj.* (of an organism or cell) having four times the haploid set of chromosomes. ● *n.* a tetraploid organism or cell.

tetrapod *n.* **1** *Zool.* an animal with four feet. **2** a structure supported by four feet radiating from a centre. [from Greek *tetrapous*]

tetrathlon *n.* an athletic or sporting contest comprising four events for each competitor, esp. riding, shooting, swimming, and running. [based on Greek *athlon* 'contest']

tetravalent *adj. Chem.* having a valency of four.

tetrode *n.* a thermionic valve having four electrodes. [based on Greek *hodos* 'way']

Teuton *n.* a member of a Teutonic nation, esp. a German. [from Latin *pl.* *Teutones*]

Teutonic *adj.* **1** relating to or characteristic of the Germanic peoples or their languages. **2** German.

Texan ● *n.* a native of Texas in the US. ● *adj.* of or relating to Texas.

Tex-Mex ● *n.* the Texan variety of Mexican cookery, music, Spanish, etc. ● *adj.* relating to one such variety. [blend of TEXAN and MEXICAN]

text *n.* **1** the main body of a book as distinct from notes, appendices, pictures, etc. **2** the original words of an author or document, esp. as distinct from a paraphrase of or commentary on them. **3** a passage quoted from Scripture, esp. as the subject of a sermon. **4** a subject or theme. **5** (in *pl.*) books prescribed for study. **6** a textbook. **7** data in textual form, esp. as stored, processed, or displayed in a word processor etc. [from Latin *textus* 'tissue, literary style'] □ **textless** *adj.*

textbook ● *n.* a book for use in studying, esp. a standard account of a subject. ● *attrib.adj.* **1** exemplary, accurate. **2** instructively typical. □ **textbookish** *adj.*

text editor *n. Computing* a system or program allowing the user to enter and edit text.

textile ● *n.* **1** a woven or bonded fabric; a cloth. **2** a fibre, filament, or yarn used for weaving cloth etc. ● *adj.* **1** of or relating to textiles or weaving (*textile industry*). **2** woven (*textile fabrics*). **3** suitable for weaving (*textile materials*). [from Latin *textilis*]

text processing *n. Computing* the manipulation of text, esp. transforming it from one format to another.

textual *adj.* of, in, or concerning a text (*textual errors*). □ **textually** *adv.*

textual criticism *n.* the process of attempting to ascertain the correct reading of a text.

textualist *n.* a person who adheres strictly to a text. □ **textualism** *n.*

textuality *n.* **1** the medium of textual language. **2** strict adherence to a text; textualism.

texture ● *n.* **1** the feel or appearance of a surface or substance. **2** the arrangement of threads etc. in textile fabric. **3** the arrangement of small constituent parts. ● *v.tr.* (usu. as **textured** *adj.*) provide with a texture. [from Latin *textura* 'weaving'] □ **textural** *adj.* **texturally** *adv.* **textureless** *adj.*

textured vegetable protein see TVP.

texturize *v.tr.* (also **-ise**) (usu. as **texturized** *adj.*) impart a particular texture to (fabrics or food).

Th *symb. Chem.* the element thorium.

Thai /ty/ ● *n.* (*pl.* same or **Thais**) **1 a** a native or national of Thailand in SE Asia; a member of the largest ethnic group in Thailand. **b** a person of Thai descent. **2** the language of Thailand. ● *adj.* of or relating to Thailand or its people or language. [Thai, literally 'free']

thalamus *n.* (*pl.* **thalami**) *Anat.* either of two masses of grey matter in the forebrain, serving as relay stations for sensory tracts. ▷ BRAIN. [from Greek *thalamos*] □ **thalamic** *adj.* (in senses 1 and 2).

thalassaemia *n.* (*US* **thalassemia**) *Med.* any of a group of hereditary diseases caused by faulty haemoglobin synthesis and widespread in Mediterranean, African, and Asian countries. [based on Greek *thalassa* 'sea', because first known around the Mediterranean]

thalassic *adj.* of the sea or seas, esp. small or inland seas. [French *thalassique* from Greek *thalassa* 'sea']

thalidomide *n.* a drug formerly used as a sedative but found in 1961 to cause foetal malformation when taken early in pregnancy. [from ph*thali*mido-glutar*imide*]

thalli *pl.* of THALLUS.

thallium *n. Chem.* a rare soft white metallic element. [formed as THALLUS, from the green line in its spectrum]

thallus *n.* (*pl.* **thalli**) ◀ a plant-body without vascular tissue and not differentiated into root, stem, and leaves. ▷ BRYOPHYTE. [from Greek *thallos* 'green shoot'] □ **thalloid** *adj.*

archegoniophore

thallus

rhizoid

THALLUS OF A LIVERWORT

than *conj.* & *prep.* **1** introducing the second element in a comparison (*you are older than he is*; *you are older than he*). **2** (prec. by *other*, *otherwise*, *rather*) introducing the second element in a statement of difference (*anyone other than me could have done it*; *a preference for watching rather than participating*; *has no aim other than to win*). [Old English]

■ **Usage** The treatment of *than* as a preposition makes it acceptable to say *You are older than him* (see sense 1) or *anyone other than me* in less formal contexts. See also Usage Notes at DIFFERENT and OTHER.

thanatology *n.* the scientific study of death and its associated phenomena and practices. [based on Greek *thanatos* 'death']

thane *n. hist.* **1** (in Anglo-Saxon England) a man who held land from the king or other superior by military service, ranking between ordinary freemen and hereditary nobles. **2** a man who held land from a Scottish king and ranked with an earl's son; the chief of a clan. [Old English *theg(e)n* 'servant, soldier']

thank ● *v.tr.* **1** express gratitude to (*thanked him for the present*). **2** hold responsible (*you can thank yourself for that*). ● *n.* (in *pl.*) **1** gratitude (*expressed his heartfelt thanks*). **2** an expression of gratitude (*give thanks to Heaven*). **3** (as a formula) thank you (*thanks for your help*; *thanks very much*). □ **give thanks** say grace at a meal. **no** (or **small**) **thanks to** despite. **thank goodness** (or **God** or **heavens** etc.) **1** *colloq.* an expression of relief or pleasure. **2** an expression of pious gratitude. **thanks to** as the result of (*thanks to my foresight*; *thanks to your obstinacy*). **thank you** a polite formula acknowledging a gift or service or an offer accepted or refused (see also THANK-YOU). [Old English, related to THINK]

thankful *adj.* **1** grateful, pleased. **2** expressive of thanks. □ **thankfulness** *n.*

thankfully *adv.* **1** in a thankful manner. **2** (qualifying a whole sentence) *disp.* let us be thankful; fortunately (*thankfully, nobody was hurt*).

■ **Usage** The use of *thankfully* in sense 2 is extremely common, but it is still considered incorrect by some people. The main reason is that other such adverbs, e.g. *regrettably*, *fortunately*, etc., can be converted to the form *it is regrettable*, *it is fortunate*, etc., but *thankfully* converts to *one is thankful (that)*. Its use is best restricted to informal contexts.

thankless *adj.* **1** not expressing or feeling gratitude. **2** (of a task etc.) giving no pleasure or profit; unappreciated. **3** not deserving thanks. □ **thanklessly** *adv.* **thanklessness** *n.*

thank-offering *n.* an offering made as an act of thanksgiving.

thanksgiving *n.* **1 a** the expression of gratitude, esp. to God. **b** a form of words for this. **2** (**Thanksgiving** or **Thanksgiving Day**) a national holiday for giving thanks to God, the fourth Thursday in November in the US, usu. the second Monday in October in Canada.

thank-you *n. colloq.* an instance or means of

TETRAHEDRON

T

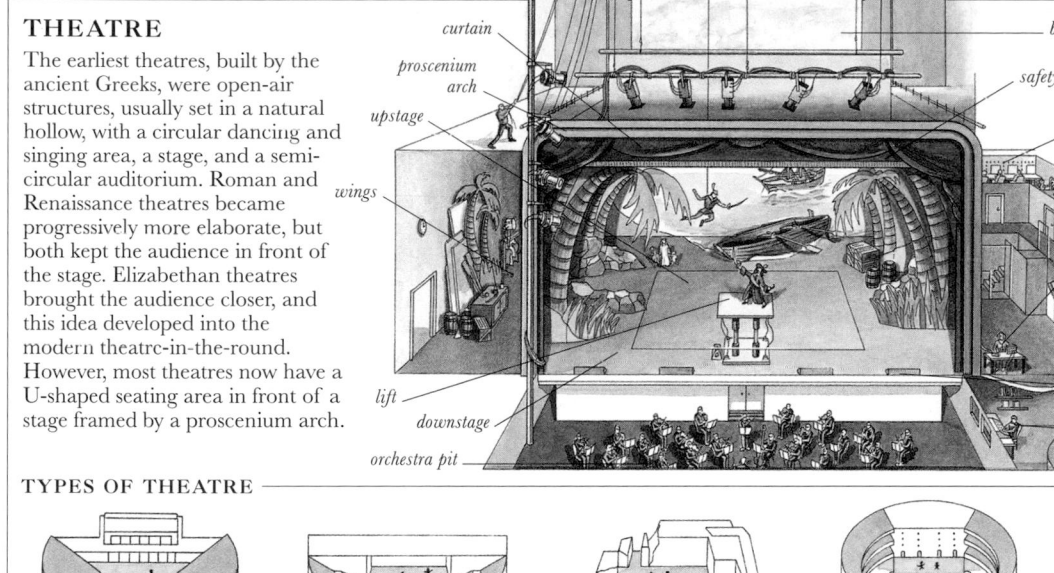

THEATRE

The earliest theatres, built by the ancient Greeks, were open-air structures, usually set in a natural hollow, with a circular dancing and singing area, a stage, and a semi-circular auditorium. Roman and Renaissance theatres became progressively more elaborate, but both kept the audience in front of the stage. Elizabethan theatres brought the audience closer, and this idea developed into the modern theatre-in-the-round. However, most theatres now have a U-shaped seating area in front of a stage framed by a proscenium arch.

LAYOUT OF A MODERN THEATRE

curtain · proscenium arch · upstage · wings · lift · downstage · orchestra pit · backcloth · safety curtain · dressing room · green room · stage manager · wardrobe department · scenery workshop · footlight · lighting operator

TYPES OF THEATRE

ANCIENT GREEK   ROMAN   RENAISSANCE   ELIZABETHAN ENGLISH   THEATRE-IN-THE-ROUND

---

expressing thanks (also *attrib.*: *a thank-you letter*) (cf. *thank you* (see THANK)).

that ● *pron.* (*pl.* **those**) **1** the person or thing indicated, named, or understood (*I heard that*; *who is that in the garden?*; *I knew all that before*; *that is not fair*). **2** (contrasted with *this*) the further or less immediate or obvious of two (*this bag is much heavier than that*). **3** the action, behaviour, or circumstances just observed or mentioned (*don't do that again*). **4** *Brit.* (on the telephone etc.) the person spoken to (*who is that?*). **5** esp. *Brit. colloq.* referring to a strong feeling just mentioned (*'Are you glad?' 'I am that'*). **6** (usu. *pl.*, esp. in relative constructions) the one, the person, etc., described or specified in some way (*those who have cars can take the luggage*; *those unfit for use*; *a table like that described above*). **7** (*pl.* **that**) used instead of *which* or *whom* to introduce a defining clause (*the book that you sent me*; *there is nothing here that matters*). ● *det.* (*pl.* **those**) **1** designating the person or thing indicated, named, understood, etc. (cf. sense 1 of *pron.*) (*look at that dog*; *what was that noise?*; *things were easier in those days*). **2** contrasted with *this* (cf. sense 2 of *pron.*) (*this bag is heavier than that one*). **3** expressing strong feeling (*shall not easily forget that day*). ● *adv.* **1** to such a degree; so (*have done that much*; *will go that far*). **2** *colloq.* very (*not that good*). **3** at which, on which, etc. (*at the speed that he was going he could not stop*; *the day that I first met her*). ● *conj.* introducing a subordinate clause indicating: **1** a statement or hypothesis (*they say that he is better*; *there is no doubt that he meant it*). **2** a purpose (*we live that we may eat*). **3** a result (*am so sleepy that I cannot keep my eyes open*). **4** a reason or cause (*it is rather that he lacks the time*). **5** a wish (*Oh, that summer were here!*). □ **all that** (foll. by an adj.) very (*not all that good*). **and all that** (or **and that** *colloq.*) and all or various things associated with or similar to what has been mentioned; and so forth. **like that 1** of that kind (*is fond of books like that*). **2** in that manner, as you are doing, as he has been doing, etc. (*wish they would not talk like that*). **3** *colloq.* without effort (*did the job like that*). **4** of that character (*he would not accept any payment — he is like that*). **that is** (or **that is to say**) a formula introducing or following an explanation of a preceding word or words. **that's** *colloq.* you are (by virtue of present or future obedience etc.) (*that's a good boy*). **that's more like it** an acknowledgement of improvement. **that's**

right an expression of approval or *colloq.* assent. **that's that** a formula concluding a narrative or discussion or indicating completion of a task. **that will do** no more is needed or desirable. [Old English]

■ **Usage** In sense 7 of the pronoun, *that* usually specifies or identifies something referred to, whereas *who* or *which* need not; compare *The book that you sent me is lost* with *The book, which you sent me, is lost. That* is often omitted in sense 3 of the adverb and senses 1 and 3 of the conjunction, e.g. *the day I first met her*; *They say he is better.*

thatch ● *n.* **1** ▶ a roof covering of straw, reeds, palm leaves, or similar material. **2** *Brit. colloq.* the hair of the head. ● *v.tr.* (also *absol.*) cover with thatch. [Old English] □ **thatcher** *n.*

Thatcherism *n.* the political and economic policies of Margaret Thatcher, former UK prime minister.

thaw ● *v.* **1** *intr.* (of ice or snow or a frozen thing) pass into a liquid or unfrozen state. **2** *intr.* (usu. prec. by *it* as subject) (of the weather) become warm enough to melt ice etc. (*it began to thaw*). **3** *intr.* become warm enough to lose numbness etc. **4** *intr.* become genial. **5** *tr.* cause to thaw. **6** *tr.* make cordial or animated. ● *n.* **1** the act or an instance of thawing. **2** warm weather that thaws (*a thaw has set in*). **3** *Polit.* a relaxation of control or restriction. [Old English]

the ● *det.* (called the *definite article*) **1** denoting one or more persons or things already mentioned or assumed to be familiar (*gave the man a wave*; *shall let the matter drop*; *hurt myself in the arm*; *went to the theatre*). **2** serving to describe as unique (*the Queen*; *the Thames*). **3 a** (foll. by a defining adj.) which is, who are, etc. (*ignored the embarrassed Mr Smith*; *Edward the Seventh*). **b** (foll. by an adj. used as a noun) denoting a class described (*from the sublime to the ridiculous*). **4** (with *the* stressed) best known or best entitled to the name (*no relation to the Kipling*; *this is the book on this*

subject). **5** used to point forward to a following qualifying or defining clause or phrase (*the book that you borrowed*; *the best I can do for you*; *the bottom of a well*). **6 a** used to indicate that a singular noun represents a species, class, etc. (*the cat loves comfort*; *has the novel a future?*). **b** used with a noun which figuratively represents an occupation, pursuit, etc. (*went on the stage*; *too fond of the bottle*). **c** (foll. by the name of a unit) a, per (*5p in the pound*; *£5 the square metre*; *allow 8 minutes to the mile*). **d** *colloq.* or *archaic* designating a disease, affliction, etc. (*the measles*; *the toothache*; *the blues*). **7** (foll. by a unit of time) the present, the current (*man of the moment*; *questions of the day*; *book of the month*). **8** *colloq.* my, our (*the dog*; *the fridge*). ● *adv.* (preceding comparatives in expressions of proportional variation) in or by that (or such a) degree; on that account (*the more the merrier*; *the more he gets the more he wants*). □ **all the** in the full degree to be expected (*that makes it all the worse*). **so much the** in that degree (*so much the worse for him*). [Old English]

■ **Usage** In sense 2 of the determiner, *the* is dropped from a proper noun when it is used attributively, e.g. *The Thames is popular among tourists for its riverboats*; *Thames riverboats are popular tourist attractions.*

THATCH: STRUCTURE OF A THATCHED ROOF

thatch · hazel rod · rafter · lath · tie-beam

theatre *n.* (*US* **theater**) **1 a** ▲ a building or outdoor area for dramatic performances. ▷ AUDITORIUM. **b** (in full **picture theatre**) esp. *N. Amer., Austral., & NZ* a cinema. **2 a** the writing and production of plays. **b** effective material for the stage (*makes good theatre*). **3** (in full **lecture theatre**) a room or hall for lectures etc. with seats in tiers. **4** *Brit.* an operating theatre. **5 a** a scene or field of action (*the theatre of war*). **b** (*attrib.*) designating weapons intermediate between tactical and strategic (*theatre nuclear missiles*). **6** a natural land formation in a gradually rising part circle like ancient Greek and Roman theatres. [from Greek *theatron*]

theatregoing *adj.* (*US* **theatergoing**) frequenting theatres. □ **theatregoer** *n.*

theatre-in-the-round *n.* a dramatic performance on a stage surrounded by spectators. ▷ THEATRE

Theatre of the Absurd *n.* a drama portraying the futility of human struggle in a senseless world.

theatre sister *n. Brit.* a nurse supervising the nursing team in an operating theatre.

theatric ● *adj.* = THEATRICAL. ● *n.* (in *pl.*) theatrical actions.

theatrical ● *adj.* **1** of or for the theatre; of acting or actors. **2** (of a manner, speech, gesture, or person) calculated for effect; showy. ● *n.* **1** (in *pl.*) dramatic performances (*amateur theatricals*). **2** (in *pl.*) theatrical actions. **3** (usu. in *pl.*) a professional actor or actress. □ **theatricalism** *n.* **theatricality** *n.* **theatricalization** *n.* **theatricalize** *v.tr.* (also **-ise**). **theatrically** *adv.*

thee *pron. objective case* of THOU[1]. [Old English]

theft *n.* the act or an instance of stealing. [Old English, related to THIEF]

their *poss.det.* **1** of or belonging to them (*their house*; *their own business*). **2** *disp.* as a third person sing. indefinite meaning 'his or her' (*has anyone lost their purse?*). [from Old Norse *their(r)a*]

■ **Usage** See Usage Note at THEY.

theirs *poss.pron.* the one or ones belonging to or associated with them (*it is theirs*; *theirs are over here*). □ **of theirs** of or belonging to them (*a friend of theirs*). [Middle English]

theism /th'ee-izm/ *n.* belief in the existence of gods or a god, esp. a God supernaturally revealed to man. [based on Greek *theos* 'god'] □ **theist** *n.* **theistic** *adj.*

them ● *pron.* **1** *objective case* of THEY (*I saw them*). **2** *colloq.* they (*it's them again*; *is older than them*). ● *det.* slang or dial. those (*them bones*). [from Old Norse]

■ **Usage** See Usage Note at HER.

thematic *adj.* of or relating to subjects or topics (*thematic philately*; *the arrangement of the anthology is thematic*). [from Greek *thematikos*] □ **thematically** *adv.*

thematic catalogue *n. Mus.* a catalogue giving the opening themes of works as well as their names and other details.

theme ● *n.* **1** a subject or topic on which a person speaks, writes, or thinks. **2** *Mus.* a prominent or frequently recurring melody or group of notes in a composition. **3** *US* a school exercise on a given subject. ● *v.tr.* (as **themed** *adj.*) **1** (of a leisure park, restaurant, event, etc.) designed around a theme to unify ambience, decor, etc. **2** (often in *comb.*) having a particular theme (*war-themed computer game*). [from Greek *thema*]

theme park *n.* an amusement park organized round a unifying idea.

theme song *n.* (also **theme tune**) **1** a recurrent melody in a musical. **2** a signature tune.

themselves *pron.* **1 a** *emphat. form* of THEY or THEM. **b** *refl. form* of THEM; (cf. HERSELF). **2** in their normal state of body or mind (*are quite themselves again*). **3** (also **themself**) *disp.* (referring back to an indefinite pronoun) himself, herself; himself or herself (*everyone kept it to themselves*). □ **be themselves** act in their normal, unconstrained manner.

■ **Usage** The use of *themselves* in sense 3 is considered erroneous by some people. See Usage Note at THEY.

then ● *adv.* **1** at that time (*was then too busy*; *then comes the trouble*; *the then existing laws*). **2 a** next; after that (*then he told me to come in*). **b** and also (*then, there are the children to consider*). **c** after all (*it is a problem, but then that is what we are here for*). **3 a** in that case; therefore; it follows that (*then you should have said so*). **b** if what you say is true (*but then why did you take it?*). **c** (implying grudging or impatient concession) if you must have it so (*all right then, have it your own way*). **d** used parenthetically to resume a narrative etc. (*the policeman, then, knocked on the door*). ● *attrib.adj.* that or who

was such at the time in question (*the then Duke*). ● *n.* that time (*until then*). □ **then and there** immediately and on the spot. [Old English]

■ **Usage** *Then* should not be used as an adjective if it would sound equally well in its usual position, e.g. *Harold Wilson was the then Prime Minister* could equally well be *Harold Wilson was then the Prime Minister*.

thence *adv.* (also **from thence**) *archaic* or *literary* **1** from that place or source. **2** for that reason. [Middle English]

thenceforth *adv.* (also **from thenceforth**) *archaic* or *literary* from that time onward.

thenceforward *adv. archaic* or *literary* thenceforth.

theo- *comb. form* God or gods. [from Greek *theos* 'god']

theobromine *n.* a bitter white alkaloid obtained from cacao seeds. [from *Theobroma*, name of the cacao genus]

theocentric *adj.* having God as its centre.

theocracy *n.* (*pl.* **-ies**) a form of government by God or a god directly or through a priestly order etc. □ **theocrat** *n.* **theocratic** *adj.*

theodolite *n.* ▼ a surveying instrument for measuring horizontal and vertical angles with a rotating telescope. [16th-century coinage]

theologian *n.* a person trained in theology.

theological *adj.* of theology. □ **theologically** *adv.*

theology *n.* (*pl.* **-ies**) **1** the study of theistic religion. **2** a system of theistic religion. [from Latin *theologia*] □ **theologist** *n.* **theologize** *v.tr. & intr.* (also **-ise**).

theorem *n.* esp. *Math.* **1** a general proposition not self-evident but proved by a chain of reasoning. **2** a rule in algebra etc., esp. one expressed by symbols or formulae (*Pythagoras' theorem*). [from Greek *theōrēma* 'speculation, proposition']

theoretic ● *adj.* = THEORETICAL. ● *n.* (in *sing.* or *pl.*) the theoretical part of a science etc. [from Greek *theōrētikos*]

theoretical *adj.* **1** concerned with knowledge but not with its practical application. **2** based on theory rather than experience. □ **theoretically** *adv.*

theoretician *n.* a person concerned with the theoretical aspects of a subject.

theorist *n.* a holder or inventor of a theory.

theorize *v.* (also **-ise**) **1** *intr.* evolve or indulge in theories. **2** *tr.* consider or devise in theory. □ **theorization** *n.* **theorizer** *n.*

theory *n.* (*pl.* **-ies**) **1** a supposition or system of ideas explaining something, esp. one based on general principles independent of the particular things to be explained (*atomic theory*; *theory of evolution*). **2** a speculative view (*one of my pet theories*). **3** the sphere of abstract knowledge or speculative

thought (*this is all very well in theory, but how will it work in practice?*). **4** the exposition of the principles of a science etc. (*the theory of music*). [from Greek *theōria*]

theosophy *n.* (*pl.* **-ies**) any of various philosophies professing to achieve a knowledge of God by spiritual ecstasy, direct intuition, or special individual relations, esp. a modern movement following Hindu and Buddhist teachings and seeking universal brotherhood. [based on Greek *theosophos* 'wise concerning God'] □ **theosopher** *n.* **theosophic** *adj.* **theosophical** *adj.* **theosophist** *n.*

therapeutic /th'e-ră-**pew**-tik/ *adj.* **1** of, for, or contributing to the cure of disease. **2** contributing to general, esp. mental, well-being (*she finds walking therapeutic*). [originally a form of THERAPEUTICS] □ **therapeutically** *adv.*

therapeutics *n.pl.* (usu. treated as *sing.*) the branch of medicine concerned with the treatment of disease and the action of remedial agents. [from Greek *therapeutika*]

therapy *n.* (*pl.* **-ies**) **1** the treatment of physical or mental disorders, other than by surgery. **2** a particular type of such treatment. [from Greek *therapeia* 'healing'] □ **therapist** *n.*

there ● *adv.* **1** in, at, or to that place or position (*lived there for some years*; *goes there every day*). **2** at that point (in speech, performance, writing, etc.) (*there he stopped*). **3** in that respect (*I agree with you there*). **4** used for emphasis in calling attention (*you there!*; *there goes the bell*). **5** used to indicate the fact or existence of something (*there is a house on the corner*). ● *n.* that place (*lives somewhere near there*). ● *int.* **1** expressing confirmation, triumph, dismay, etc. (*there! what did I tell you?*). **2** used to soothe a child etc. (*there, there, never mind*). □ **have been there before** *colloq.* know all about it. **so there** *colloq.* that is my final decision (whether you like it or not). **there and then** immediately and on the spot. **there it is 1** that is the trouble. **2** nothing can be done about it. **there you are** (or **go**) *colloq.* **1** this is what you wanted etc. **2** expressing confirmation, triumph, resignation, etc. [Old English]

thereabouts *adv.* (also **thereabout**) **1** near that place (*ought to be somewhere thereabouts*). **2** near that number, quantity, etc. (*two litres or thereabouts*).

thereafter *adv. formal* after that.

thereat *adv. archaic* **1** at that place. **2** on that account. **3** after that.

thereby *adv.* by that means; as a result of that. □ **thereby hangs a tale** much could be said about that.

therefore *adv.* for that reason; accordingly, consequently.

therefrom *adv. archaic* from that or it.

therein *adv. formal* **1** in that place etc. **2** in that respect.

thereinafter *adv. formal* later in the same document etc.

thereof *adv. formal* of that or it.

thereon *adv. archaic* on that or it (of motion or position).

there's *contr.* **1** there is. **2** esp. *Brit. colloq.* you are (by virtue of present or future obedience etc.) (*there's a dear*).

thereto *adv. formal* **1** to that or it. **2** in addition.

thereupon *adv.* **1** in consequence of that. **2** soon or immediately after that. **3** *archaic* upon that (of motion or position).

therewith *adv. archaic* **1** with that. **2** soon or immediately after that.

therm *n.* a unit of heat, esp. as the former statutory unit of gas supplied in the UK equivalent to 100,000 British thermal units or 1.055×10^8 joules. [from Greek *thermē* 'heat']

thermal ● *adj.* **1** of, for, or producing heat. **2** promoting the retention of heat (*thermal underwear*). ● *n.* **1** ▲ a rising current of heated air (used by gliders, balloons, and birds to gain height). **2** (in *pl.*) thermal underwear. □ **thermalize** *v.tr. & intr.* (also **-ise**). **thermalization** *n.* **thermally** *adv.*

THEODOLITE

A theodolite is an instrument that enables the height and position of distant objects to be calculated by measuring the angles between a baseline (formed by two known positions of the theodolite) and a direct line to the object concerned.

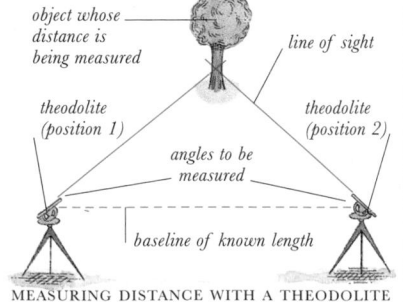

object whose distance is being measured

line of sight

theodolite (position 1)

theodolite (position 2)

angles to be measured

baseline of known length

MEASURING DISTANCE WITH A THEODOLITE

T

THERMAL

Air warmed by the sun expands and becomes less dense than the surrounding air. This creates upcurrents called thermals. Birds use these to gain height in an energy-efficient way, soaring to the top of one then gliding to the base of the next.

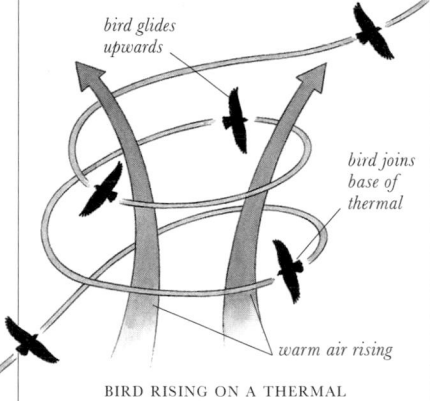

bird glides upwards

bird joins base of thermal

warm air rising

BIRD RISING ON A THERMAL

thermal capacity *n.* the number of heat units needed to raise the temperature of a body by one degree.

thermal springs *n.pl.* springs of naturally hot water.

thermal unit *n.* a unit for measuring heat.

thermic *adj.* of or relating to heat.

thermionic *adj.* of or relating to electrons emitted from a substance at very high temperature.

thermionic valve *n.* (*US* **thermionic tube**) a device giving a flow of thermionic electrons in one direction, used esp. in the rectification of a current and in radio reception.

thermistor *n. Electr.* a resistor whose resistance is greatly reduced by heating, used for measurement and control. ▷ RESISTOR. [from *thermal resistor*]

thermo- *comb. form* denoting heat. [from Greek *thermos* 'hot', *thermē* 'heat']

thermocline *n.* **1** a temperature gradient, esp. an abrupt one in a body of water. **2** a layer of water marked by an abrupt temperature change. [based on Greek *klinein* 'to slope']

thermocouple *n.* a thermoelectric device for measuring temperature, consisting of two wires of different metals connected at two points, a voltage being developed between the two junctions in proportion to the temperature difference.

yellow shows hot area

black shows cold area

THERMOGRAM OF A MAN WEARING GLASSES

thermodynamics *n.pl.* (usu. treated as *sing.*) the science of the relations between heat and other forms of energy. □ **thermodynamic** *adj.* **thermodynamically** *adv.* **thermodynamicist** *n.*

thermoelectric *adj.* relating to electricity produced by a temperature difference. □ **thermoelectrically** *adv.* **thermoelectricity** *n.*

thermogram *n.* ◄ a record made by a thermograph.

thermograph *n.* **1** an instrument that gives a continuous record of temperature. **2** an apparatus used to obtain an

image produced by infra-red radiation from a human or animal body. □ **thermographic** *adj.*

thermography *n. Med.* the taking or use of infra-red thermograms.

thermoluminescence *n.* the property of becoming luminescent when pretreated and subjected to high temperatures, used as a means of dating ancient artefacts. □ **thermoluminescent** *adj.*

thermometer *n.* ► an instrument for measuring temperature, esp. a graduated glass tube containing mercury or alcohol which expands when heated. ▷ MERCURY. [from French *thermomètre*] □ **thermometric** *adj.* **thermometry** *n.*

thermonuclear *adj.* **1** relating to or using nuclear reactions that occur only at very high temperatures. **2** of, relating to, or involving weapons in which explosive force is produced by thermonuclear reactions (*thermonuclear war*).

thermopile *n.* a set of thermocouples esp. arranged for measuring small quantities of radiant heat.

thermoplastic ● *adj.* that becomes plastic on heating and hardens on cooling, and is able to repeat these processes. ● *n.* a thermoplastic substance. ▷ PLASTIC

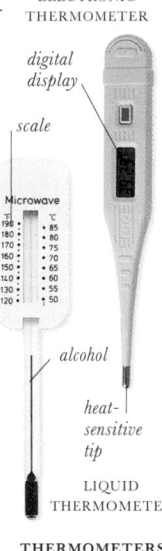

ELECTRONIC THERMOMETER

digital display

scale

Microwave

alcohol

heat-sensitive tip

LIQUID THERMOMETER

THERMOMETERS

thermos *n.* (in full **thermos flask**, *N. Amer.* **thermos bottle**) *propr.* a vacuum flask. [Greek, literally 'hot']

thermosetting *adj.* (of plastics) setting permanently when heated. □ **thermoset** *adj.* ▷ PLASTIC

thermosphere *n.* the region of the atmosphere beyond the mesosphere. ▷ ATMOSPHERE

thermostat *n.* ▼ a device that automatically regulates temperature, or that activates a device when the temperature reaches a certain point. [based on Greek *statos* 'standing'] □ **thermostatic** *adj.* **thermostatically** *adv.*

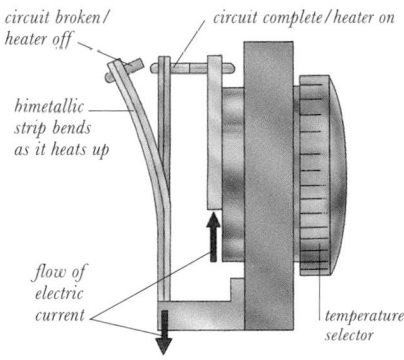

circuit broken/ heater off

circuit complete/ heater on

bimetallic strip bends as it heats up

flow of electric current

temperature selector

THERMOSTAT USED TO CONTROL A HEATING SYSTEM

thesaurus *n.* (*pl.* **thesauri** /-ry/ or **thesauruses**) a book that lists words in groups of synonyms and related concepts. [from Greek *thēsauros* 'treasure']

these *pl.* of THIS.

thesis *n.* (*pl.* **theses**) **1** a proposition to be maintained or proved. **2** a dissertation, esp. by a candidate for a degree. [Greek, literally 'putting, placing, a proposition']

thespian ● *adj.* of or relating to drama. ● *n.* an actor or actress. [based on Greek *Thespis*, traditional originator of Greek tragedy]

Thess. *abbr.* Thessalonians (New Testament).

theta /'thee-tă/ *n.* the eighth letter of the Greek alphabet (Θ, θ). [Greek]

thew /'th'yoo/ *n.* (often in *pl.*) *literary* **1** muscular

strength. **2** mental or moral vigour. [Old English *thēaw* 'usage, conduct']

they *pron.* (*obj.* **them**; *poss.* **their**, **theirs**) **1** the people, animals, or things previously named or in question (*pl.* of HE, SHE, IT). **2** people in general (*they say we are wrong*). **3** those in authority (*they have raised the fees*). **4** *disp.* as a third person sing. indefinite pronoun meaning 'he or she' (*anyone can come if they want to*; *if you have a friend you want to invite, feel free to bring them along*). [from Old Norse *their*]

■ **Usage** The use of *they* instead of 'he or she' (see sense 4 above) is common in spoken English and increasingly so in written English, although still deplored by some people. It is particularly useful when the sex of the person is unspecified or unknown. Similarly, *their* can replace 'his' or 'his or her' and *themselves* 'himself' or 'himself or herself', e.g. *Everyone must provide their own lunch*; *Did anyone hurt themselves in the accident?*

they'd *contr.* **1** they had. **2** they would.

they'll *contr.* **1** they will. **2** they shall.

they're *contr.* they are.

they've *contr.* they have.

thiamine *n.* (also **thiamin**) a vitamin of the B complex, found in unrefined cereals, beans, and liver.

thick ● *adj.* **1 a** of great or specified extent between opposite surfaces (*a thick wall*; *a wall two metres thick*). **b** of large diameter (*a thick rope*). **2 a** (of a line etc.) broad; not fine. **b** (of script or type, etc.) consisting of thick lines. **3** arranged closely; crowded together; dense. **4** (usu. foll. by *with*) densely covered or filled (*air thick with snow*). **5 a** firm in consistency; containing much solid matter (*a thick paste*; *thick soup*). **b** made of thick material (*a thick coat*). **6** muddy, cloudy; impenetrable by sight (*thick darkness*). **7** *colloq.* stupid. **8 a** (of a voice) indistinct. **b** (of an accent) very marked. **9** *colloq.* intimate or very friendly (esp. *thick as thieves*). ● *n.* a thick part of anything. ● *adv.* thickly (*snow was falling thick*; *blows rained down thick and fast*). □ **a bit thick** *Brit. colloq.* unreasonable or intolerable. **in the thick of 1** at the busiest part of. **2** heavily occupied with. **through thick and thin** under all conditions; in spite of all difficulties. [Old English] □ **thickish** *adj.* **thickly** *adv.*

thick ear *n. Brit. slang* the external ear swollen as a result of a blow (esp. *give a person a thick ear*).

thicken *v.* **1** *tr. & intr.* make or become thick or thicker. **2** *intr.* become more complicated (*the plot thickens*). □ **thickener** *n.*

thickening *n.* **1** the process of becoming thick or thicker. **2** a substance used to thicken liquid. **3** a thickened part.

thicket *n.* a tangle of shrubs or trees. [Old English]

thickhead *n. colloq.* a stupid person. □ **thickheaded** *adj.* **thickheadedness** *n.*

thickness *n.* **1** the state of being thick. **2** the extent to which a thing is thick. **3** a layer of material (*three thicknesses of cardboard*). **4** a part that is thick or lies between opposite surfaces (*steps cut in the thickness of the wall*).

thickset *adj.* **1** heavily or solidly built. **2** set or growing close together.

thick-skinned *adj.* not sensitive to criticism.

thief *n.* (*pl.* **thieves**) a person who steals, esp. secretly and without violence. [Old English]

thieve *v.* **1** *intr.* be a thief. **2** *tr.* steal (a thing). [Old English]

thievery *n.* the act or practice of stealing.

thieves *pl.* of THIEF.

thievish *adj.* given to stealing. □ **thievishly** *adv.* **thievishness** *n.*

thigh *n.* **1** the part of the human leg between the hip and the knee. ▷ FEMUR. **2** a corresponding part in other animals. [from Old Norse *thjó*] □ **-thighed** *adj.* (in *comb.*).

thigh bone *n.* = FEMUR.

T

THIMBLE

thimble *n.* ◀ a metal or plastic cap, usu. with a closed end, worn to protect the finger when pushing the needle in sewing. [Old English]

thimbleful *n.* (*pl.* **-fuls**) a small quantity, esp. of liquid to drink.

thin ● *adj.* (**thinner, thinnest**) **1** having the opposite surfaces close together; of small thickness or diameter. **2** (of a line) narrow or fine. **3** made of thin material (*a thin dress*). **4** lean; not plump. **5** not dense or copious (*thin hair*). **6** of slight consistency (*a thin paste*). **7** weak (*a thin voice*). **8** (of an excuse, disguise, etc.) flimsy or transparent. ● *adv.* thinly (*cut it thin*). ● *v.* (**thinned, thinning**) **1** *tr. & intr.* make or become thin or thinner. **2** *tr. & intr.* (often foll. by *out*) make or become less dense or crowded or numerous. **3** *tr.* (often foll. by *out*) remove some of a crop of (seedlings etc.) or some young fruit from (a vine or tree) to improve the growth of the rest. □ **have a thin time** *Brit. colloq.* have a wretched or uncomfortable time. **on thin ice** see ICE. **thin end of the wedge** see WEDGE. **thin on top** balding. [Old English] □ **thinly** *adv.* **thinness** *n.* **thinnish** *adj.*

thin air *n.* a state of invisibility or non-existence (*vanished into thin air*).

thine *archaic* or *dial.* ● *poss.pron.* of or belonging to thee (*it is thine*). ● *poss.det.* (before a vowel) = THY (*lift up thine eyes*). [Old English]

thing *n.* **1** a material or non-material entity, idea, action, etc., that is or may be thought about or perceived. **2** an inanimate material object. **3** an unspecified object or item (*have a few things to buy*). **4** an act, idea, or utterance (*a silly thing to do*). **5** an event (*an unfortunate thing to happen*). **6** a quality (*patience is a useful thing*). **7** expressing pity, affection, etc. (*poor thing!*). **8** a specimen or type (*the latest thing in hats*). **9** one's special interest (*not my thing*). **10** esp. *Brit. colloq.* something remarkable (*now there's a thing!*). **11** (prec. by *the*) *colloq.* **a** what is conventionally proper or fashionable. **b** what is needed or required (*just the thing*). **c** what is to be considered (*the thing is, shall we go or not?*). **d** what is important (*the thing about them is their reliability*). **12** (in *pl.*) personal belongings or clothing. **13** (in *pl.*) equipment (*painting things*). **14** (in *pl.*) affairs in general (*not in the nature of things*). **15** (in *pl.*) circumstances or conditions (*things look good*). **16** (in *pl.* with a following adjective) all that is so describable (*all things Greek*). □ **do one's own thing** *colloq.* pursue one's own interests or inclinations. **do things to** *colloq.* affect remarkably. **have a thing about** *colloq.* be obsessed or prejudiced about. **make a thing of** *colloq.* **1** regard as essential. **2** cause a fuss about. **one** (or **just one**) **of those things** *colloq.* something unavoidable or to be accepted. [Old English]

thingummy *n.* (*pl.* **-ies**) (also **thingamy**, **thingamabob** or **thingumabob**, **thingamajig** or **thingumajig**) *colloq.* a person or thing whose name one has forgotten or does not know or does not wish to mention.

thingy *n.* (*pl.* **-ies**) = THINGUMMY.

think ● *v.* (*past* and *past part.* **thought**) **1** *tr.* (foll. by *that* + clause) be of the opinion. **2** *tr.* (foll. by *that* + clause or *to* + infin.) judge or consider (*is thought to be a fraud*). **3** *intr.* exercise the mind (*let me think for a moment*). **4** *intr.* (foll. by *of* or *about*) **a** consider; be or become aware of (*think of you constantly*). **b** form or entertain the idea of (*couldn't think of such a thing*). **c** choose mentally (*think of a number*). **5** *tr.* have a half-formed intention (*I think I'll stay*). **6** *tr.* form a conception of (*cannot think how*). **7** *tr.* reduce by thinking (*cannot think away a toothache*). **8** *tr.* recognize the presence or existence of (*the child thought no harm*). **9** *tr.* (foll. by *to* + infin.) intend or expect (*thinks to deceive us*). **10** *tr.* (foll. by *to* + infin.) remember (*did not think to lock the door*). ● *n. colloq.* an act of thinking (*have a think*). □ **think again** revise one's plans or opinions. **think aloud** utter one's thoughts as soon as they occur. **think back to** recall (a past event or

time). **think better of** change one's mind about (an intention) after reconsideration. **think fit** see FIT¹. **think for oneself** have an independent mind or attitude. **think little** (or **nothing**) **of** consider to be insignificant or unremarkable. **think much** (or **highly**) **of** have a high opinion of. **think on** (or **upon**) *archaic* think of or about. **think out** **1** consider carefully. **2** produce (an idea etc.) by thinking. **think over** reflect upon in order to reach a decision. **think through** reflect fully upon (a problem etc.). **think twice** use careful consideration, avoid hasty action, etc. **think up** *colloq.* devise. [Old English] □ **thinkable** *adj.*

thinker *n.* **1** a person who thinks, esp. in a specified way (*an original thinker*). **2** a person with a skilled or powerful mind.

thinking ● *adj.* using thought or rational judgement. ● *n.* **1** opinion or judgement. **2** (in *pl.*) thoughts; courses of thought.

think-tank *n.* a body of experts providing advice and ideas on specific national and commercial problems.

thinner *n.* a volatile liquid used to dilute paint etc.

thinnings *n.pl.* plants, trees, etc. which have been removed to improve the growth of those remaining.

thin-skinned *adj.* (of a person) sensitive to reproach or criticism; easily upset.

thio- *comb. form* sulphur, esp. replacing oxygen in compounds (*thio-acid*). [from Greek *theion*]

thiopentone *n. Pharm.* a barbiturate drug used, usu. as the sodium salt, as a general anaesthetic and a hypnotic.

thiosulphate *n.* a sulphate in which one oxygen atom is replaced by sulphur.

third ● *n.* **1** the position in a sequence corresponding to that of the number 3 in the sequence 1–3. **2** something occupying this position. **3** each of three equal parts of a thing. **4** = THIRD GEAR. **5** *Mus.* **a** an interval or chord spanning three consecutive notes in the diatonic scale (e.g. C to E). **b** a note separated from another by this interval. **6** *Brit.* **a** a place in the third class in an examination. **b** a person having this. ● *adj.* that is the third. [Old English] □ **thirdly** *adv.*

third age *n.* the period in life of active retirement; old age.

third-class ● *adj.* **1** belonging to or travelling by the third class. **2** of lower quality; inferior. ● *adv.* by the third class.

third class *n.* **1** the third-best group or category, esp. of hotel and train accommodation. **2 a** the third highest division in an examination test. **b** a place in this.

third degree ● *n.* (usu. prec. by *the*) long and severe questioning esp. by police to obtain information or a confession. ● *adj.* (**third-degree**) denoting burns of the most severe kind, affecting lower layers of tissue.

third force *n.* a political group or party acting as a check on conflict between two opposing parties.

third gear *n.* the third lowest in a set of gears.

third man *n. Cricket* **1** a fielder positioned near the boundary behind the slips. **2** this position. ▷ CRICKET

third party ● *n.* **1** another party besides the two principals. **2** a bystander etc. ● *adj.* (**third-party**) *Brit.* (of insurance) covering damage or injury suffered by a person other than the insured.

third person *n.* **1** = THIRD PARTY. **2** see PERSON 3.

third-rate *adj.* inferior; very poor in quality.

Third Reich *n.* the Nazi regime, 1933–45.

Third World *n.* (usu. prec. by *the*) the developing countries of Asia, Africa, and Latin America.

thirst ● *n.* **1** a physical need to drink liquid, or the

discomfort caused by this. **2** a strong desire or craving. ● *v.intr.* (often foll. by *for* or *after*) **1** feel thirst. **2** have a strong desire. [Old English]

thirsty *adj.* (**thirstier, thirstiest**) **1** feeling thirst. **2** (of land, a season, etc.) dry or parched. **3** (often foll. by *for* or *after*) eager. **4** *colloq.* causing thirst (*thirsty work*). □ **thirstily** *adv.* **thirstiness** *n.*

thirteen ● *n.* **1** one more than twelve. **2** a symbol for this (13, xiii, XIII). **3** a size etc. denoted by thirteen. ● *adj.* that amount to thirteen. [Old English] □ **thirteenth** *adj. & n.*

thirty ● *n.* (*pl.* **-ies**) **1** the product of three and ten. **2** a symbol for this (30, xxx, XXX). **3** (in *pl.*) the numbers from 30 to 39, esp. the years of a century or of a person's life. ● *adj.* that amount to thirty. [Old English] □ **thirtieth** *adj. & n.* **thirtyfold** *adj. & adv.*

Thirty-nine Articles *n.pl.* a series of points of doctrine historically accepted as representing the teaching of the Church of England.

thirty-something *n.* (often *attrib.*) *colloq.* an unspecified age between thirty and forty.

thirty-year rule *n.* a rule that public records may be open to inspection after a lapse of thirty years.

this ● *pron.* (*pl.* **these**) **1** the person or thing close at hand or indicated or already named or understood (*this is my cousin*). **2** (contrasted with *that*) the person or thing nearer to hand or more immediately in mind. **3** the action, behaviour, or circumstances under consideration (*this won't do at all*). **4** (on the telephone): **a** *Brit.* the person speaking (*this is Jane*). **b** *US* the person spoken to (*who is this?*). ● *det.* (*pl.* **these**) **1** designating the person or thing close at hand etc. (cf. senses 1, 2 of *pron.*). **2** (of time): **a** the present or current (*all this week*). **b** relating to today (*this morning*). **c** just past or to come (*gone these three weeks*). **3** *colloq.* (in narrative) designating a person or thing previously unspecified (*then up came this policeman*). ● *adv.* to the degree or extent indicated (*did not reach this far*). □ **this and that** *colloq.* various unspecified examples of things (esp. trivial). **this here** *slang* this particular (person or thing). **this much** the amount or extent about to be stated (*I know this much, that he was not there*). **this world** mortal life. [Old English]

thistle *n.* **1** ◀ any of various prickly herbaceous plants of the genus *Cirsium, Carlina,* or *Carduus* etc. (daisy family), usu. with globular heads of purple flowers. **2** this as the Scottish national emblem. [Old English]

thistledown *n.* a light fluffy down attached to thistle seeds and blown about in the wind.

thistly *adj.* overgrown with thistles.

thither *adv. archaic* or *formal* to or towards that place. [Old English]

tho' *var. of* THOUGH.

thole *n.* (in full **thole-pin**) **1** a pin in the gunwale of a boat as the fulcrum for an oar. **2** each of two such pins forming a rowlock. [Old English *thol* 'fir-tree, peg']

thong *n.* **1** a narrow strip of hide or leather. **2** *Austral., NZ, & N. Amer.* = FLIP-FLOP 1. **3** a skimpy bathing garment like a G-string. [Old English]

thorax *n.* (*pl.* **thoraces** /**thor**-ă-seez/ or **thoraxes**) *Anat. & Zool.* the part of the trunk between the neck and the abdomen. ▷ BEETLE. [Greek] □ **thoracal** *adj.* **thoracic** *adj.* ▷ VERTEBRA

thorium *n. Chem.* a radioactive metallic element. [named after *Thor*, Scandinavian god of thunder]

thorn *n.* **1** a stiff sharp-pointed projection on a plant. **2** (also **thorn bush, thorn tree**) a thorn-bearing shrub or tree. □ **a thorn in one's flesh** (or **side**) a constant annoyance. **on thorns** continuously uneasy, esp. in fear of being detected. [Old English] □ **thornless** *adj.* **thornproof** *adj.*

flower head

spiny bract

THISTLE: WOOLLY
THISTLE
(*Cirsium eriophorum*)

thorn apple *n.* **1** ▶ a poisonous plant of the nightshade family, *Datura stramonium.* **2** the prickly fruit of this.

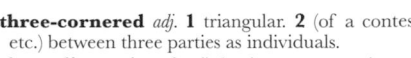

THORN APPLE
(*Datura stramonium*)

thorny *adj.* (**thornier, thorniest**) **1** having many thorns. **2** (of a subject) hard to handle without offence; problematic. □ **thornily** *adv.* **thorniness** *n.*

thorough *adj.* **1** complete and unqualified; not superficial (*a thorough change*). **2** acting or done with great care and completeness (*the report is most thorough*). **3** absolute (*a thorough nuisance*). [originally in sense 'through': Old English] □ **thoroughly** *adv.* **thoroughness** *n.*

thoroughbred ● *adj.* **1** of pure breed. **2** of outstanding quality; first-class. ● *n.* **1** a thoroughbred animal, esp. a horse. **2** (**Thoroughbred**) a breed of racehorses originating from English mares and Arab stallions. ▷ HORSE

thoroughfare *n.* a road or path open at both ends, esp. for traffic.

thoroughgoing *adj.* **1** uncompromising; not superficial. **2** (usu. *attrib.*) extreme; out and out.

thorp *n.* (also **thorpe**) *archaic* a village or hamlet. [Old English]

■ **Usage** *Thorp(e)* is now usually found only in place names, e.g. *Scunthorpe*.

those *pl.* of THAT.

thou[1] *pron.* (*obj.* **thee**; *poss.* **thy** or **thine**; *pl.* **ye** or **you**) second person singular pronoun. [Old English]

■ **Usage** *Thou* has now been replaced by *you* except in some formal, liturgical, dialect, and poetic uses.

thou[2] *n.* (*pl.* same or **thous**) *colloq.* **1** a thousand. **2** one-thousandth.

though (also **tho'**) ● *conj.* **1** despite the fact that (*though it was early we went to bed*). **2** (introducing a possibility) even if (*ask him though he may refuse*). **3** and yet; nevertheless (*she read on, though not to the end*). **4** in spite of being (*ready though unwilling*). ● *adv. colloq.* however; all the same. [from Old Norse *thó*]

thought[1] *n.* **1** the process or power of thinking; the faculty of reason. **2** a way of thinking characteristic of or associated with a particular time, people, etc. (*medieval European thought*). **3** sober reflection or consideration. **4** an idea or piece of reasoning produced by thinking. **5** (foll. by *of* + verbal noun, or *to* + infin.) a partly formed intention or hope (*gave up all thoughts of winning*). **6** (usu. in *pl.*) what one is thinking; one's opinion (*any thoughts on this?*). **7** the subject of one's thinking (*my one thought was to get away*). **8** (prec. by *a*) somewhat (*seems to me a thought arrogant*). □ **give thought to** consider; think about. **in thought** thinking, meditating. **take thought** consider matters. [Old English] □ **-thoughted** *adj.* (in *comb.*).

thought[2] *past* and *past part.* of THINK.

thoughtful *adj.* **1** engaged in or given to meditation. **2** (of a book, writer, etc.) giving signs of serious thought. **3** (often foll. by *of*) (of a person or conduct) considerate. □ **thoughtfully** *adv.* **thoughtfulness** *n.*

thoughtless *adj.* **1** careless of consequences or of others' feelings. **2** due to lack of thought. □ **thoughtlessly** *adv.* **thoughtlessness** *n.*

thought-provoking *adj.* stimulating serious thought.

thought-reader *n.* a person supposedly able to perceive another's thoughts. □ **thought-reading** *n.*

thought transference *n.* telepathy.

thought-wave *n.* an undulation of the supposed medium of thought transference.

thousand ● *n.* (*pl.* **thousands** or (in sense 1) **thousand**) (in *sing.* prec. by *a* or *one*) **1** the product of a hundred and ten. **2** a symbol for this (1,000, m,

M). **3** a set of a thousand things. **4** (in *sing.* or *pl.*) *colloq.* a large number. ● *adj.* that amount to a thousand. [Old English] □ **thousandfold** *adj.* & *adv.* **thousandth** *adj.* & *n.*

thrall *n. literary* **1** (often foll. by *of, to*) a slave (of a person, or a power or influence). **2** a state of slavery (*in thrall*). [from Old Norse *thréll*] □ **thraldom** *n.* (also **thralldom**).

thrash ● *v.* **1** *tr.* beat severely, esp. with a stick or whip. **2** *tr.* defeat thoroughly in a contest. **3** *intr.* act like a flail. **4** *intr.* (foll. by *about, around*) move or fling the limbs about violently or in panic. ● *n.* **1** an act of thrashing. **2** *Brit. colloq.* a party; a lavish one. □ **thrash out** discuss to a conclusion. [Old English] □ **thrasher** *n.* **thrashing** *n.*

thread ● *n.* **1 a** a spun-out filament of cotton, silk, glass, etc.; yarn. **b** a length of this. **2** ▶ a thin cord of twisted yarns used esp. in sewing and weaving. **3** anything regarded as thread-like with reference to continuity (*the thread of life*). **4** the spiral ridge of a screw. **5** (in *pl.*) *slang* clothes. ● *v.tr.* **1 a** pass a thread through the eye of (a needle). **b** (often foll. by *through*) pass (a thread etc.) through a hole or series of holes. **2** put (beads) on a thread. **3** arrange (material in a strip form, e.g. film or magnetic tape) in the proper position on equipment. **4** make (one's way) carefully through a crowded place etc. **5** form a screw thread on. □ **hang by a thread** be in a precarious state, position, etc. [Old English] □ **threader** *n.* **threadlike** *adj.*

threadbare *adj.* **1** (of cloth) so worn that the nap is lost and the thread visible. **2** (of a person) wearing such clothes. **3 a** hackneyed. **b** feeble (*a threadbare excuse*).

thread vein *n.* a very slender vein visible through the skin.

threadworm *n.* any of various esp. parasitic threadlike nematode worms.

thready *adj.* (**threadier, threadiest**) **1** of or like a thread. **2** (of a person's pulse) scarcely perceptible.

threat *n.* **1 a** a declaration of an intention to punish or hurt. **b** *Law* a menace of bodily hurt or injury, such as may restrain a person's freedom of action. **2** an indication of something undesirable coming (*the threat of war*). **3** a person or thing as a likely cause of harm etc. [Old English *threat* 'affliction']

threaten *v.tr.* **1** make a threat or threats against. **2** be a sign or indication of (something undesirable). **3** (foll. by *to* + infin.) announce one's intention to do an undesirable or unexpected thing. **4** (also *absol.*) give warning of (harm etc.) (*the clouds were threatening rain*). **5** (as **threatened** *adj.*) (of a species etc.) in danger of becoming rare or extinct. [Old English] □ **threatener** *n.* **threateningly** *adv.*

three ● *n.* **1 a** one more than two. **b** a symbol for this (3, iii, III). **2** a size etc. denoted by three. **3** three o'clock. **4** a set of three. **5** a card with three pips. ● *adj.* that amount to three. [Old English]

three-cornered *adj.* **1** triangular. **2** (of a contest etc.) between three parties as individuals.

three-dimensional *adj.* having or appearing to have length, breadth, and depth.

threefold *adj.* & *adv.* **1** three times as much or as many. **2** consisting of three parts.

three-handed *adj.* **1** having or using three hands. **2** involving three players.

three-legged race *n.* a running race between pairs, one member of each pair having the left leg tied to the right leg of the other.

three-line whip *n.* (in the UK) a written notice, underlined three times to denote urgency, to members of a political party to attend a parliamentary vote.

three parts *n.pl.* & *adv.* (as *adv.* often hyphenated) three-quarters.

threepence *n. Brit.* the sum of three pence, esp. before decimalization.

threepenny /threp-ĕ-ni/ *adj. Brit.* costing three pence, esp. before decimalization.

threepenny bit *n. hist.* a former coin worth three old pence.

three-piece *attrib.adj.* (esp. of a suit or suite) consisting of three items.

three-ply ● *adj.* of three strands, webs, or thicknesses. ● *n.* **1** three-ply wool. **2** three-ply wood.

three-point turn *n.* a method of turning a vehicle round in a narrow space by moving forwards, backwards, and forwards again in a sequence of arcs.

three-pronged *adj.* having three parts, goals, or lines of attack (*three-pronged strategy*).

three-quarter ● *n.* (also **three-quarter back**) *Rugby* any of three or four players just behind the half-backs. ● *adj.* **1** consisting of three-quarters of something. **2** (of a portrait) going down to the hips or showing three-fourths of the face.

three-quarters ● *n.pl.* three parts out of four; the greater part. ● *adv.* to the extent of three quarters; almost, very nearly.

three Rs *n.pl.* (prec. by *the*) reading, writing, and arithmetic, regarded as the fundamentals of learning.

threescore *n. archaic* sixty.

threesome *n.* a group of three persons.

threnody *n.* (also **threnode**) (*pl.* **-ies** or **threnodes**) **1** a lamentation, esp. on a person's death. **2** a song of lamentation. [based on Greek *thrēnos* 'wailing'] □ **threnodial** *adj.* **threnodic** *adj.* **threnodist** *n.*

threonine *n. Biochem.* an amino acid, considered essential for growth. [based on *threose*, name of a sugar]

thresh *v.* **1** *tr.* beat out or separate grain from (corn etc.). **2** *intr.* = THRASH *v.* 4. □ **thresh out** = *thrash out.* [variant of THRASH]

thresher *n.* **1** ▼ a person or machine that threshes. ▷ COMBINE HARVESTER. **2** a shark, *Alopias vulpinus*, with a long upper lobe to its tail. ▷ SHARK

T

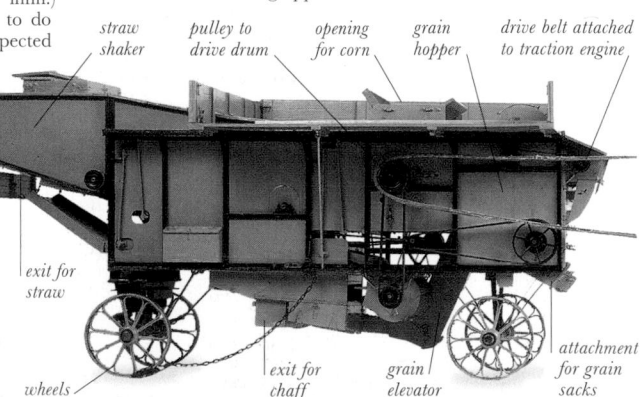

straw shaker   pulley to drive drum   opening for corn   grain hopper   drive belt attached to traction engine

exit for straw

exit for chaff   grain elevator   attachment for grain sacks

wheels

THRESHER: 19TH-CENTURY STEAM-DRIVEN THRESHER

threshing floor *n.* a hard level floor for threshing esp. with flails.

threshold *n.* **1** a strip of wood or stone forming the bottom of a doorway and crossed in entering a house or room etc. **2** a point of entry or beginning. **3** *Physiol.* & *Psychol.* a limit below which a stimulus causes no reaction (*pain threshold*). **4** (often *attrib.*) esp. *Brit.* a step in a scale of wages or taxation. [Old English, related to THRASH in earlier sense 'to tread']

threw past of THROW.

thrice *adv. archaic* or *literary* **1** three times. **2** (esp. in *comb.*) highly (*thrice-blessed*). [Old English]

thrift *n.* **1** frugality; economical management. **2** ◄ a plant of the genus *Armeria*, esp. the sea pink. [from Old Norse, related to THRIVE]

thriftless *adj.* wasteful, improvident. □ **thriftlessness** *n.*

thrift shop *n.* (also **thrift store**) esp. *US* a shop selling second-hand items usu. for charity.

thrifty *adj.* (**thriftier**, **thriftiest**) **1** economical, frugal. **2** thriving, prosperous. □ **thriftily** *adv.* **thriftiness** *n.*

THRIFT
(*Armeria maritima*)

thrill ● *n.* **1** a wave or nervous tremor of emotion or sensation (*a thrill of joy; a thrill of recognition*). **2** a throb or pulsation. ● *v.* **1** *intr.* feel a thrill (*thrilled to the sound*). **2** *tr.* **a** cause to feel a thrill of excitement or emotion. **b** (as **thrilled** *adj.*) *colloq.* delighted, pleased. **3** *intr.* quiver or throb with or as with emotion. [Old English *thyrlian* 'to pierce'] □ **thrilling** *adj.* **thrillingly** *adv.*

thriller *n.* an exciting or sensational story or play etc., esp. one involving crime or espionage.

thrips *n.* (*pl.* same) a minute black insect of the order Thysanoptera, some members of which are injurious to plants. [Greek, literally 'woodworm']

thrive *v.intr.* (*past* **throve** or **thrived**; *past part.* **thriven** or **thrived**) **1** prosper or flourish. **2** grow rich. **3** (of a child, animal, or plant) grow vigorously. [from Old Norse *thrifask*, literally 'to grasp oneself']

thro' var. of THROUGH.

throat *n.* **1 a** the windpipe or gullet. **b** the front part of the neck containing this. **2** *literary* **a** a voice, esp. of a songbird. **b** a thing compared to a throat, esp. a narrow passage, entrance, or exit. □ **cut one's own throat** bring about one's own downfall. **ram** (or **thrust**) **down a person's throat** force (a thing) on a person's attention. [Old English] □ **-throated** *adj.* (in *comb.*).

throaty *adj.* (**throatier**, **throatiest**) **1** (of a voice) hoarsely resonant. **2** guttural; uttered in the throat. □ **throatily** *adv.* **throatiness** *n.*

throb ● *v.intr.* (**throbbed**, **throbbing**) **1** palpitate or pulsate, esp. with more than the usual force or rapidity. **2** vibrate or quiver with a persistent rhythm or with emotion. ● *n.* **1** a throbbing. **2** a palpitation or (esp. violent) pulsation. [Middle English]

throe *n.* (usu. in *pl.*) **1** a violent pang, esp. of childbirth or death. **2** anguish. □ **in the throes of** struggling with the task of. [Middle English]

thrombosis *n.* (*pl.* **thromboses**) the formation of a blood clot in the vascular system. [Greek, literally 'curdling'] □ **thrombotic** *adj.*

throne ● *n.* **1** ► a chair of State for a sovereign or bishop etc. **2** sovereign power (*came to the throne*). ● *v.tr.* place on a throne. [from Greek *thronos* 'high seat']

THRONE: GOLD-PLATED THRONE FROM TUTANKHAMEN'S TOMB, EGYPT

throng ● *n.* **1** a crowd of people. **2** (often foll. by *of*) a multitude, esp. in a small space. ● *v.* **1** *intr.* come in great numbers. **2** *tr.* fill with or as with a crowd (*crowds thronged the streets*). [Old English]

throstle *n. Brit.* a song thrush. [Old English]

throttle ● *n.* **1 a** (in full **throttle-valve**) ▼ a valve controlling the flow of fuel or steam etc. in an engine. **b** (in full **throttle-lever**) a lever or pedal operating this valve. ▷ OUTBOARD. **2** the throat, gullet, or windpipe. ● *v.tr.* **1** choke or strangle. **2** prevent the utterance etc. of. **3** control (an engine or steam etc.) with a throttle. □ **throttle back** (or **down**) reduce the speed of (an engine or vehicle) by throttling. [Middle English]

THROTTLE-VALVE: CARBURETTOR OF A CAR SHOWING THROTTLE-VALVES

fuel inlet — *jet* — *throttle flap* — *throttle-valve* — *choke*

through (also **thro'**, *US* **thru**) ● *prep.* **1 a** from end to end or from side to side of. **b** going in one side or end and out the other of. **2** between or among (*swam through the waves*). **3** from beginning to end of (*read through the letter*). **4** because of; by the agency, means, or fault of (*through carelessness*). **5** *N. Amer.* up to and including (*Monday through Friday*). ● *adv.* **1** through a thing; from side to side, end to end, or beginning to end (*would not let us through*). **2** having completed (esp. successfully) (*are through their exams*). **3** so as to be connected by telephone (*will put you through*). ● *attrib.adj.* **1** (of a route etc.) done without a change of line or vehicle etc. or with one ticket. **2** (of traffic) going through a place to its destination. **3** (of a road) open at both ends. □ **be through** *colloq.* **1** (often foll. by *with*) have finished. **2** (often foll. by *with*) cease to have dealings. **3** have no further prospects (*is through as a politician*). **through and through 1** thoroughly, completely. **2** through again and again. [Old English]

throughout ● *prep.* right through; from end to end of. ● *adv.* in every part or respect (*rotten throughout*).

throughput *n.* the amount of material put through a process, esp. in manufacturing or computing.

throve past of THRIVE.

throw ● *v.tr.* (*past* **threw**; *past part.* **thrown**) **1** propel with some force through the air or in a particular direction. **2** force violently into a specified position or state (*thrown on to the rocks*). **3** compel suddenly to be in a specified condition (*was thrown out of work*). **4** turn or move (part of the body) quickly or suddenly (*threw an arm out*). **5** project or cast (a shadow, a spell, etc.). **6 a** bring to the ground in wrestling. **b** (of a horse) unseat (its rider). **7** *colloq.* disconcert (*the question threw me*). **8** (foll. by *on*, *off*, etc.) put (clothes etc.) hastily on or off etc. **9 a** cause (dice) to fall on a table. **b** obtain (a specified number) by throwing dice. **10** cause to pass or extend suddenly to another state or position (*threw a bridge across*).

11 move (a switch or lever) so as to operate it. **12** form (ceramic ware) on a potter's wheel. **13** have (a fit etc.). **14** give (a party). **15** *colloq.* lose (a contest or race etc.) intentionally. ● *n.* **1** an act of throwing. **2** the distance a thing is or may be thrown (*a record throw*). **3** the act of being thrown in wrestling. **4** esp. *N. Amer.* **a** a light cover for furniture. **b** (in full **throw rug**) a light rug. **5** (prec. by *a*) *colloq.* each; per item (*sold at £10 a throw*). □ **throw about** (or **around**) **1** throw in various directions. **2** spend (one's money) ostentatiously. **throw away 1** discard as useless or unwanted. **2** waste or fail to make use of (an opportunity etc.). **3** discard (a playing card). **4** *Theatr.* speak (lines) with deliberate underemphasis. **5** (in *passive*; often foll. by *on*) be wasted (*the advice was thrown away on him*). **throw back 1** revert to ancestral character. **2** (usu. in *passive*; foll. by *on*) compel to rely on (*was thrown back on his savings*). **throw cold water on** see COLD. **throw down** cause to fall. **throw down the gauntlet** (or **glove**) issue a challenge. **throw one's hand in 1** abandon one's chances in a card game. **2** withdraw from a contest. **throw in 1** interpose (a word or remark). **2** include at no extra cost. **3** throw (a football) from the edge of the pitch where it has gone out of play. **4** *Cricket* etc. return (the ball) from the outfield. **throw in one's lot with** see LOT. **throw in the towel** admit defeat. **throw light on** see LIGHT[1]. **throw off 1** discard; contrive to get rid of. **2** write or utter in an offhand manner. **throw oneself at** seek blatantly as a spouse or sexual partner. **throw oneself into** engage vigorously in. **throw oneself on** (or **upon**) **1** rely completely on. **2** attack. **throw open** (often foll. by *to*) **1** cause to be suddenly or widely open. **2** make accessible. **3** invite general discussion or participation in. **throw out 1** put out forcibly or suddenly. **2** discard as unwanted. **3** expel (a troublemaker etc.). **4** put forward tentatively. **5** reject (a proposal or bill in Parliament). **throw over** desert or abandon. **throw stones** cast aspersions. **throw together 1** assemble hastily. **2** bring into casual contact. **throw up 1** abandon. **2** resign from. **3** *colloq.* vomit. **4** erect hastily. **5** bring to notice. **throw one's weight about** (or **around**) *colloq.* act in a domineering or over-assertive manner. [Old English *thrāwan* 'to twist, turn'] □ **throwable** *adj.* **thrower** *n.* (also in *comb.*).

throwaway ● *adj.* **1** meant to be thrown away after (one) use. **2** (of spoken lines etc.) deliberately underemphasized. **3** wasteful (*throwaway society*). ● *n.* a thing to be thrown away after (one) use.

throwback *n.* **1** reversion to ancestral character. **2** an instance of this.

throw-in *n.* the throwing in of a ball during a match, from the sideline to restart play, from a fielding position in the outfield, etc.

throw-over *attrib.adj.* that can be thrown over (esp. a bed, sofa) as a decorative cover.

throw rug see THROW *n.* 4b.

thru *US* var. of THROUGH.

thrum[1] ● *v.* (**thrummed**, **thrumming**) **1** *tr.* play (a stringed instrument) monotonously or unskilfully. **2** *intr.* (often foll. by *on*) drum idly. ● *n.* **1** such playing. **2** the resulting sound.

thrum[2] ● *n.* **1** (in weaving) the unwoven end of a warp thread, or the whole of such ends, left when the finished web is cut away. **2** any short loose thread. ● *v.tr.* (**thrummed**, **thrumming**) make of or cover with thrums. [Old English] □ **thrummer** *n.* **thrummy** *adj.*

thrush[1] *n.* ► any small or medium-sized songbird of the family Turdidae, esp. a song thrush or mistle thrush. [Old English]

THRUSH:
SONG THRUSH
(*Turdus philomelos*)

T

thrush[2] *n.* **1 a** infection by the yeastlike fungus *Candida albicans*, causing white patches in the mouth and throat. **b** similar infection of the vagina. **2** inflammation affecting the frog of a horse's foot. [17th-century coinage]

thrust ● *v. (past* and *past part.* **thrust**) **1** *tr.* push with a sudden impulse or with force (*thrust the letter into my pocket*). **2** *tr.* (foll. by *on*) impose (a thing) forcibly; enforce acceptance of (a thing) (*had it thrust on me*). **3** *intr.* (foll. by *at, through*) stab; make a sudden lunge. **4** *tr.* make (one's way) forcibly. **5** *intr.* (as **thrusting** *adj.*) aggressive, ambitious. ● *n.* **1** a sudden or forcible push or lunge. **2** the propulsive force developed by a jet or rocket engine. **3** a strong attempt to penetrate an enemy's line or territory. **4** a remark aimed at a person. **5** the stress between the parts of an arch etc. **6** (often foll. by *of*) the chief theme or gist of remarks etc. **7** an attack with the point of a weapon. **8** *Geol.* a reverse fault of low angle, with older strata displaced horizontally over newer. □ **thrust oneself** (or **one's nose**) **in** obtrude, interfere. [from Old Norse *thrýsta*]

thruster *n.* **1** a person or thing that thrusts. **2** a small rocket engine used to provide extra or correcting thrust on a spacecraft. ▷ SPACECRAFT

thrust stage *n.* a stage extending into the audience.

thud ● *n.* a low dull sound as of a blow on a non-resonant surface. ● *v.intr.* (**thudded, thudding**) make or fall with a thud. □ **thuddingly** *adv.*

thug *n.* **1** a vicious or brutal ruffian. **2** (**Thug**) *hist.* a member of a religious organization of robbers and assassins in India. [from Hindi *thag* 'swindler'] □ **thuggery** *n.* **thuggish** *adj.* **thuggishly** *adv.* **thuggishness** *n.*

thuja *n.* (also **thuya**) ▶ any evergreen coniferous tree of the genus *Thuja*, with small leaves closely pressed to the branches; arbor vitae.

thulium *n. Chem.* a soft metallic element of the lanthanide series. [based on Latin *Thule*, name of a region in the remote north]

thumb ● *n.* **1 a** a short thick terminal projection on the human hand, set lower and apart from the other four and opposable to them. ▷ HAND. **b** a digit of other animals corresponding to this. **2** the part of a glove etc. intended to cover the thumb. ● *v.* **1** *tr.* wear or soil (pages etc.) with a thumb (*a well-thumbed book*). **2** *intr.* turn over pages with or as with a thumb (*thumbed through the directory*). **3** *tr.* request or obtain (a lift in a passing vehicle) by signalling with a raised thumb. **4** *tr.* use the thumb in a gesture. □ **be all thumbs** be clumsy with one's hands. **thumb one's nose** = *cock a snook* (see SNOOK). **thumbs down** an indication of rejection or failure. **thumbs up** an indication of satisfaction or approval. **under a person's thumb** completely dominated by a person. [Old English] □ **thumbed** *adj.* (also *in comb.*). **thumbless** *adj.*

thumb index ● *n.* a set of lettered grooves cut down the side of a dictionary etc. for easy reference. ● *v.tr.* (**thumb-index**) (esp. as **thumb-indexed** *adj.*) provide (a book etc.) with these.

thumbnail *n.* **1** the nail of a thumb. **2** (*attrib.*) denoting conciseness (*a thumbnail sketch*).

thumbprint *n.* an impression of a thumb, esp. as used for identification.

thumbscrew *n.* (usu. in *pl.*) ▶ an instrument of torture for crushing the thumbs.

THUJA: AMERICAN ARBOR VITAE (*Thuja occidentalis*)

wing nut   *screw*

thumb hole

THUMBSCREW: 16TH- TO 17TH-CENTURY THUMBSCREWS

thumbtack *n. N. Amer.* a drawing pin.

thump ● *v.* **1** *tr.* beat or strike heavily, esp. with the fist (*threatened to thump me*). **2** *intr.* throb or pulsate strongly. **3** *intr.* (foll. by *at, on*, etc.) deliver blows, esp. to attract attention. **4** *tr.* (often foll. by *out*) play (a tune on a piano etc.) with a heavy touch. **5** *intr.* tread heavily. ● *n.* **1** a heavy blow. **2** the sound of this. □ **thumper** *n.*

thumping *adj. colloq.* big, prominent (*a thumping majority*).

thunder ● *n.* **1** a loud rumbling or crashing noise heard after a lightning flash and due to the expansion of rapidly heated air. **2** a resounding loud deep noise (*thunders of applause*). **3** strong censure or denunciation. ● *v.* **1** *intr.* (prec. by *it* as subject) thunder sounds (*it is thundering; if it thunders*). **2** *intr.* make or proceed with a noise suggestive of thunder (*the traffic thundered past*). **3** *tr.* utter or communicate loudly or impressively. **4** *intr.* (foll. by *against* etc.) make violent threats etc. against. □ **steal a person's thunder** see STEAL. [Old English] □ **thunderer** *n.* **thundery** *adj.*

thunderbolt *n.* **1 a** a flash of lightning with a simultaneous crash of thunder. **b** a stone etc. imagined to be a destructive bolt. **2** a sudden or unexpected occurrence or item of news. **3** a supposed bolt or shaft as a destructive agent, esp. as an attribute of a god.

thunderclap *n.* **1** a crash of thunder. **2** something startling or unexpected.

thundercloud *n.* a cumulus cloud with a tall diffuse top, charged with electricity and producing thunder and lightning.

thunderflash *n.* a noisy but harmless explosive used esp. in military exercises.

thunderfly *n.* = THRIPS.

thunderhead *n.* esp. *US* a rounded cumulus cloud projecting upwards and heralding thunder.

thundering *adj. colloq.* very big or great (*a thundering nuisance*). □ **thunderingly** *adv.*

thunderous *adj.* **1** like thunder. **2** very loud. □ **thunderously** *adv.* **thunderousness** *n.*

thunderstorm *n.* a storm with thunder and lightning and usu. heavy rain or hail.

thunderstruck *adj.* amazed; overwhelmingly surprised or startled.

thunk[1] *n. & v.intr. colloq.* = THUD.

thunk[2] *colloq.*, esp. *joc. past* and *past part.* of THINK.

Thur. *abbr.* Thursday.

thurible *n.* a censer. [from Latin *t(h)uribulum*]

thurifer *n.* an acolyte carrying a censer. [Late Latin, based on *thus thuris* 'incense']

Thurs. *abbr.* Thursday.

Thursday ● *n.* the fifth day of the week, following Wednesday. ● *adv. colloq.* **1** on Thursday. **2** (**Thursdays**) on Thursdays; each Thursday. [Old English *thunresdæg* 'day of thunder']

thus *adv. formal* **1 a** in this way. **b** as indicated. **2 a** accordingly. **b** as a result or inference. **3** to this extent; so (*thus far*). [Old English]

thuya var. of THUJA.

thwack ● *v.tr.* hit with a heavy blow; whack. ● *n.* a heavy blow.

thwart ● *v.tr.* frustrate or foil (a person or purpose etc.). ● *n.* a rower's seat placed across a boat. [from Old Norse *thvert*]

thy *poss.pron.* (*attrib.*) (also **thine** before a vowel) of or belonging to thee. [Middle English]

■ **Usage** *Thy* has now been replaced by *your* except in some formal, liturgical, dialectal, and poetic uses.

thyme /tym/ *n.* any herb or shrub of the genus *Thymus* with aromatic leaves, esp. *T. vulgaris* grown for culinary use. ▷ HERB. [from Greek *thumon*] □ **thymy** *adj.*

thymi *pl.* of THYMUS.

thymine *n. Biochem.* a pyrimidine found in all living tissue as a component base of DNA.

thymol /'th'y-mol/ *n. Chem.* a white crystalline phenol obtained from oil of thyme and used as an antiseptic.

thymus /'th'y-mŭs/ *n.* (*pl.* **thymi** /-my/) (in full **thymus gland**) *Anat.* a lymphoid organ situated in the neck of vertebrates. [from Greek *thumos*]

thyroid *n.* (in full **thyroid gland**) a large ductless gland in the neck of vertebrates secreting hormones which regulate growth and development through the rate of metabolism. ▷ ENDOCRINE, NECK. [based on Greek *thureoeidēs*]

thyroxine *n.* the main hormone produced by the thyroid gland, acting to increase metabolic rate.

thyself *pron. archaic & dial. emphat. & refl.* form of THEE.

Ti *symb. Chem.* the element titanium.

ti var. of TE.

tiara *n.* **1** a jewelled ornamental band worn on the front of a woman's hair. **2** a three-crowned diadem worn by a pope. [Greek]

Tibetan *n.* **1 a** a native of Tibet in SW China. **b** a person of Tibetan descent. **2** the language of Tibet. ● *adj.* of or relating to Tibet, its people, or its language.

tibia *n.* (*pl.* **tibiae** /-i-ee/) *Anat.* ▶ the inner and usu. larger of two bones extending from the knee to the ankle. ▷ SKELETON. [Latin] □ **tibial** *adj.*

tibiotarsus *n.* (*pl.* **tibiotarsi** /-sy/) the bone in a bird corresponding to the tibia fused at the lower end with some bones of the tarsus. [TIBIA + TARSUS]

tic *n.* a habitual spasmodic contraction of the muscles esp. of the face. [French]

tich var. of TITCH.

tick[1] ● *n.* **1** a slight recurring click, esp. that of a watch or clock. **2** esp. *Brit. colloq.* a moment. **3** a mark (✓) to denote correctness, check items in a list, etc. ● *v.* **1** *intr.* **a** (of a clock etc.) make ticks. **b** (foll. by *away*) (of time etc.) pass. **2** *intr.* (of a mechanism) function (*take it apart to see how it ticks*). **3** *tr.* **a** mark (a written answer etc.) with a tick. **b** (often foll. by *off*) mark (an item in a list etc.) with a tick in checking. □ **in two ticks** *Brit. colloq.* in a very short time. **tick off** *colloq.* reprimand. **tick over 1** (of an engine etc.) idle. **2** (of a person, project, etc.) be functioning at a basic or minimum level. **what makes a person tick** *colloq.* a person's motivation. [Middle English]

tick[2] *n.* **1** ◀ any of various arachnids of the order Acarina, parasitic on the skin of dogs and cattle etc. **2** any of various insects of the family Hippoboscidae, parasitic on sheep and birds etc. [Old English]

tick[3] *n. colloq.* credit (*buy goods on tick*).

tick[4] *n.* **1** the cover of a mattress or pillow. **2** = TICKING. [from Greek *thēkē* 'case']

ticker *n. colloq.* **1** the heart. **2** a watch. **3** *N. Amer.* a tape machine.

TIBIA: HUMAN LOWER LEG SHOWING THE TIBIA

tibia

TICK: SOFT TICK

ticker tape *n.* **1** a paper strip from a tape machine. **2** this or similar material thrown from windows etc. to greet a celebrity.

ticket ● *n.* **1 a** a written or printed piece of paper or card entitling the holder to enter a place, participate in an event, travel by public transport, etc. **b** a receipt for an item left temporarily for safe keeping. **2** an official notification of a traffic offence etc. (*parking ticket*). **3** *Brit.* a certificate of discharge from the army. **4** a certificate of qualification as a ship's master, pilot, etc. **5** a label attached to a thing and giving its price or other details. **6** *esp. US* **a** a list of candidates put forward by one group, esp. a political party. **b** the principles of a party. **7** (prec. by *the*) *colloq.* what is correct or needed (*it was just the ticket*). ● *v.tr.* (**ticketed**, **ticketing**) attach a ticket to. [from Old French *estiquet(te)*] □ **ticketed** *adj.* **ticketless** *adj.*

ticket collector *n.* a person who is employed to collect tickets, esp. from rail passengers.

ticket-day *n. Stock Exch.* (in the UK) the day before settling day, when the names of actual purchasers are handed to stockbrokers.

ticket-holder *n.* a person who has purchased a ticket (for a match, concert, etc.).

ticket office *n.* an office or kiosk where tickets are sold for transport, entertainment, etc.

ticket tout *n.* a person who buys up tickets for an event to resell them at a profit.

tickety-boo *adj. Brit. colloq.* all right; in order. [20th-century coinage]

ticking *n.* a stout usu. striped material used to cover mattresses etc.

tickle ● *v.* **1 a** *tr.* apply light touches or strokes to (a person or part of a person's body) so as to excite the nerves and usu. produce laughter and spasmodic movement. **b** *intr.* be subject to this sensation (*my foot tickles*). **c** *intr.* produce this sensation (*this jumper tickles*). **2** *tr.* excite agreeably; amuse or divert (a person, a sense of humour, etc.) (*tickled at the idea*). **3** *tr.* catch (a trout etc.) by rubbing it so that it moves backwards into the hand. ● *n.* **1** an act of tickling. **2** a tickling sensation. □ **tickled pink** (or **to death**) *colloq.* extremely amused or pleased. [Middle English] □ **tickler** *n.* **tickly** *adj.*

ticklish *adj.* **1** sensitive to tickling. **2** (of a matter or person) difficult; requiring careful handling. □ **ticklishly** *adv.* **ticklishness** *n.*

tick-tack *n.* (also **tic-tac**) *Brit.* a kind of manual semaphore signalling used by racecourse bookmakers.

tick-tack-toe *n. N. Amer.* noughts and crosses.

tick-tock *n.* the ticking of a large clock etc.

tidal *adj.* relating to, like, or affected by tides. □ **tidally** *adv.*

tidal bore *n.* a large wave or bore caused by constriction of the spring tide as it enters a long narrow shallow inlet.

tidal flow *n.* the regulated movement of traffic in opposite directions on the same stretch of road at different times of the day.

tidal wave *n.* **1** *Geog.* an exceptionally large ocean wave, esp. a tsunami. **2** a widespread manifestation (of feeling etc.).

tidbit *N. Amer.* var. of TITBIT.

tiddledywink *US* var. of TIDDLYWINK.

tiddler *n. Brit. colloq.* **1** a small fish, esp. a stickleback or minnow. **2** an unusually small thing or person.

tiddly[1] *adj.* (**tiddlier**, **tiddliest**) esp. *Brit. colloq.* slightly drunk. [originally (19th c.) in sense 'a drink']

tiddly[2] *adj.* (**tiddlier**, **tiddliest**) *Brit. colloq.* little.

tiddlywink *n.* (*US* also **tiddledywink**) **1** a counter flicked with another into a cup etc. **2** (in *pl.*) this game. [19th-century coinage]

tide *n.* **1 a** ▲ the periodic rise and fall of the sea due to the attraction of the Moon and Sun. **b** the water as affected by this. **2** a time or season (usu. in *comb.*: *Whitsuntide*). **3** a marked trend of opinion, fortune,

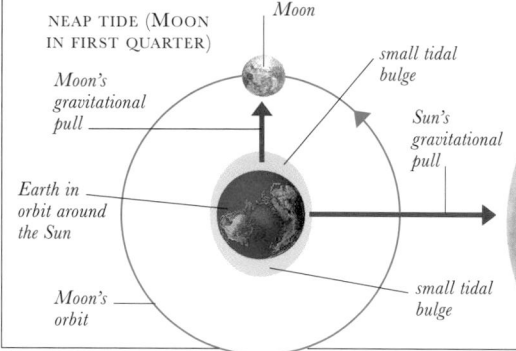

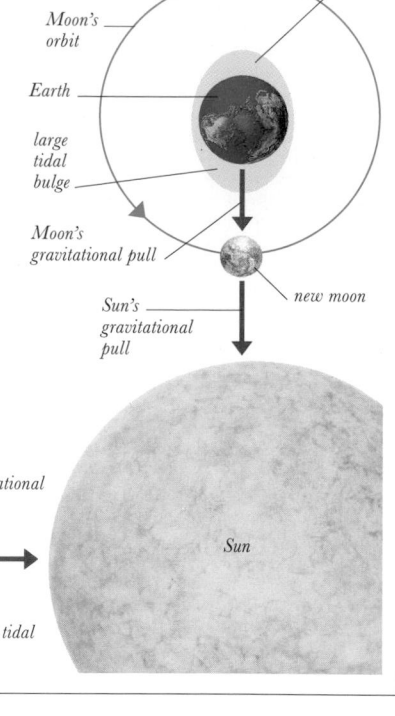

TIDE

The gravitational pull of the Moon and, to a lesser degree, that of the Sun cause the tides. The pull is strongest on the side of the Earth facing the Moon, causing the oceans on that side to bulge out. The pull affects the solid Earth slightly less, but still enough to cause it to pull away from the ocean on the other side, creating a second ocean bulge. As the Earth rotates, each part of the ocean rises and falls twice a day, causing two high tides and two low tides. When the Sun and Moon form a right angle with the Earth, their pulls counteract, causing small, or neap, tides. When they are in line, their pull is combined, creating large, or spring, tides.

SPRING TIDE (NEW MOON)

large tidal bulge

Moon's orbit

Earth

large tidal bulge

Moon's gravitational pull

new moon

Sun's gravitational pull

NEAP TIDE (MOON IN FIRST QUARTER)

Moon

small tidal bulge

Moon's gravitational pull

Sun's gravitational pull

Earth in orbit around the Sun

Sun

small tidal bulge

Moon's orbit

or events. □ **tide over** enable or help (a person) to deal with a difficult period etc. [Old English] □ **tideless** *adj.*

tideland *n. N. Amer.* land that is submerged at high tide.

tideline *n.* the edge defined by the tide on the shore.

tidemark *n.* **1** a mark made by the tide at high water. **2** esp. *Brit.* **a** a mark left round a bath at the level of the water in it. **b** a line on a person's body marking the extent to which it has been washed.

tidemill *n.* a mill with a waterwheel driven by the tide.

tide-rip *n.* **1** rough water caused esp. by opposing tides. **2** a patch of such water.

tide-table *n.* a table indicating the times of high and low tides at a place.

tidewater *n.* **1** water brought by or affected by tides. **2** (*attrib.*) *US* affected by tides.

tidewave *n.* an undulation of water passing round the Earth and causing high and low tides.

tideway *n.* **1** the tidal part of a river. **2** the ebb or flow in a tidal channel.

tidings *n.pl.* esp. *literary* news, information. [Old English]

tidy ● *adj.* (**tidier**, **tidiest**) **1** neat, orderly. **2** (of a person) methodically inclined. **3** *colloq.* considerable (*a tidy sum*). ● *n.* (*pl.* **-ies**) **1** a receptacle for holding small objects or waste scraps, esp. in a kitchen sink. **2** an act or spell of tidying. **3** esp. *US* a cover for a chair back etc. ● *v.tr.* (**-ies**, **-ied**) (also *absol.*; often foll. by *up*) put in good order; make tidy. [earlier in sense 'timely, seasonable': Middle English] □ **tidily** *adv.* **tidiness** *n.*

tie ● *v.* (**tying**) **1** *tr.* attach or fasten with string or cord etc. **2** *tr.* **a** form (a string, ribbon, etc.) into a knot or bow. **b** form (a knot or bow) in this way. **3** *tr.* restrict or limit (a person) (*is tied to his family*).

crown plate

collar

rafter

crown post

tie-beam

TIE-BEAM HOLDING TOGETHER RAFTERS IN A ROOF

4 *intr.* (often foll. by *with*) achieve the same score or place as another competitor (*tied at ten games each*). **5** *tr.* hold (rafters etc.) together by a crosspiece etc. **6** *tr. Mus.* **a** unite (written notes) by a tie. ▷ NOTATION. **b** perform (two notes) as one unbroken note. ● *n.* **1** a cord or chain etc. used for fastening. **2** a strip of material worn round the collar and tied in a knot at the front with the ends hanging down. **3** a thing that unites or restricts persons (*family ties*). **4** a draw, dead heat, or equality of score among competitors. **5** *Brit.* a match between any pair from a group of competing players or teams. **6** (also **tie-beam** etc.) ◄ a rod or beam holding parts of a structure together. ▷ ROOF. **7** *Mus.* a curved line above or below two notes of the same pitch indicating that they are to be played for the combined duration of their time values. **8** *N. Amer.* a railway sleeper. □ **tie in** (foll. by *with*) bring into or have a close association or agreement. **tie up 1** bind securely with cord etc. **2** invest or reserve (capital etc.) so that it is not immediately available for use. **3** prevent from acting freely. **4** secure or complete (an undertaking etc.). **5** (often foll. by *with*) = *tie in*. **6** (usu. in *passive*) fully occupy (a person). [Old English] □ **tieless** *adj.*

tie-back *n.* ► a decorative strip of fabric or cord for holding a curtain back from the window.

tie-break *n.* (also **tie-breaker**) a means of deciding a winner from competitors who have tied.

tie-clip *n.* an ornamental clip for holding a tie in place.

curtain

tie-back

TIE-BACK

T

tied *adj. Brit.* **1** (of a house) occupied subject to the tenant's working for its owner. **2** (of a public house) that is owned by a brewery and is bound to supply the products produced or specified by that brewery.

tie-dye ● *n.* a method of producing dyed patterns by tying string etc. to shield parts of the fabric from the dye. ● *v.tr.* dye by this process.

tie-in *n.* **1** a connection or association. **2** (often *attrib.*) esp. *N. Amer.* a form of sale or advertising that offers or requires more than a single purchase. **3** the joint promotion of related commodities etc. (e.g. a book and a film).

tiepin *n.* an ornamental pin for holding a tie in place.

tier /teer/ *n.* a row or rank or unit of a structure, as one of several placed one above another (*tiers of seats*). ▷ AMPHITHEATRE, AUDITORIUM. [earlier *tire*: based on French *tirer* 'to draw, elongate'] □ **tiered** *adj.* (also in *comb.*).

tierce *n. Eccl.* = TERCE. [from Latin *tertia* (fem.) 'third']

tiercel *n.* (also **tercel**) the male of the hawk, esp. (in falconry) a peregrine or goshawk. [from Old French *tercel*]

tie-up *n.* a connection, an association.

tiff *n. colloq.* a slight or petty quarrel. [18th-century coinage]

tiffin *n. Anglo-Ind.* a light meal, esp. lunch.

tig *n.* = TAG[2] 1. [variant of TICK[1]]

tiger *n.* **1** a large Asian flesh-eating feline, *Panthera tigris*, having a yellow-brown coat with black stripes. **2** a fierce, energetic, or formidable person. [from Greek *tigris*] □ **tigerish** *adj.*

tiger-cat *n.* any moderate-sized striped feline, e.g. the ocelot or margay.

tiger lily *n.* ▶ a tall garden lily, *Lilium lancifolium*, with flowers of dull orange spotted with black or purple.

tiger moth *n.* any moth of the family Arctiidae, esp. *Arctia caja*, having richly spotted and streaked wings ▷ MOTH.

tight ● *adj.* **1** closely held, drawn, fastened, fitting, etc. **2** closely and firmly put together (*a tight joint*). **3** (of clothes etc.) too closely fitting. **4** impermeable, impervious, esp. (in *comb.*) to a specified thing (*watertight*). **5** tense; stretched. **6** *colloq.* drunk. **7** *colloq.* (of a person) stingy. **8 a** (of money or materials) not easily obtainable. **b** (of a money market) in which money is tight. **9 a** (of a programme etc.) stringent, demanding. **b** presenting difficulties (*a tight situation*). **10** produced by or requiring great exertion or pressure (*a tight squeeze*). **11** (of control etc.) strictly imposed. ● *adv.* tightly (*hold tight!*). □ **tight corner** (or **place** or **spot**) a difficult situation. □ **tightly** *adv.* **tightness** *n.*

tighten *v.tr. & intr.* make or become tight or tighter. □ **tighten one's belt** see BELT.

tight-fisted *adj.* stingy.

tight-fitting *adj.* (of a garment) fitting (often too) close to the body.

tight-knit *adj.* (also **tightly-knit**) = CLOSE-KNIT.

tight-lipped *adj.* with or as with the lips compressed to restrain emotion or speech.

tightrope *n.* a rope stretched tightly high above the ground, on which acrobats perform.

tights *n.pl.* **1** a thin close-fitting wool or nylon etc. garment covering the legs and the lower part of the torso, worn by women in place of stockings. **2** a similar garment worn by a dancer, acrobat, etc.

tigress *n.* **1** a female tiger. **2** a fierce or passionate woman.

tike var. of TYKE.

tikka *n.* an Indian dish of kebabs marinated in a spice mixture (often in *comb.*: *chicken tikka*). [from Punjabi *ṭikkā*]

TILAPIA: TIGER TILAPIA (*Tilapia mariae*)

tilapia /ti-**lay**-piă/ *n.* ▲ a freshwater cichlid fish of the African genus *Tilapia* or a related genus, widely introduced for food. [modern Latin]

tilde *n.* a mark (̃), put over a letter, e.g. over a Spanish *n* when pronounced *ny* (as in *señor*) or a Portuguese *a* or *o* when nasalized (as in *São Paulo*). [Spanish, from Latin *titulus* 'title']

tile ● *n.* **1** ▶ a thin slab of concrete or baked clay etc. used in series for covering a roof or pavement etc. **2** a similar slab of glazed pottery, cork, linoleum, etc., for covering a floor, wall, etc. ▷ DELFTWARE. **3** a thin flat piece used in a game (esp. mah-jong). ● *v.tr.* cover with tiles. □ **on the tiles** *Brit. colloq.* having a spree. [from Latin *tegula*]

tiler *n.* a person who makes or lays tiles.

tiling *n.* **1** the process of fixing tiles. **2** an area of tiles.

till[1] ● *prep.* **1** up to or as late as (*wait till six o'clock*). **2** up to the time of (*faithful till death*). ● *conj.* **1** up to the time when (*wait till I return*). **2** so long that (*laughed till I cried*). [from Old Norse *til* 'to']

■ **Usage** In all senses, *till* can be replaced by *until* which is more formal in style.

till[2] *n.* a drawer for money in a shop or bank etc., esp. with a device recording the amount of each purchase. [Middle English]

till[3] *v.tr.* prepare and cultivate (land) for crops. [Old English *tilian* 'to strive for, cultivate'] □ **tillable** *adj.* **tiller** *n.*

tillage *n.* **1** the preparation of land for crop-bearing. **2** tilled land.

TIGER LILY
(*Lilium lancifolium*)

tiller *n.* a horizontal bar fitted to the head of a boat's rudder to turn it in steering. ▷ DINGHY, SAILING BOAT

tilt ● *v.* **1** *intr. & tr.* assume or cause to assume a sloping position. **2** *intr.* (foll. by *at*) strike, thrust, or run at, with a weapon, esp. *hist.* in jousting. **3** *intr.* (foll. by *with*) engage in a contest. ● *n.* **1** the act or an instance of tilting. **2** a sloping position. **3** *hist.* (of medieval knights etc.) the act of charging with a lance against an opponent or at a mark, for exercise or sport. **4** an attack esp. with argument or satire (*have a tilt at*). □ **full** (or **at full**) **tilt 1** at full speed. **2** with full force. [Middle English] □ **tilter** *n.*

tilth *n.* **1** tillage, cultivation. **2** the condition of tilled soil (*in good tilth*). [Old English]

timbale /tam-**bahl**/ *n.* a drum-shaped dish of minced meat or fish cooked in a pastry shell or in a mould. [French]

timber *n.* **1** esp. *Brit.* wood prepared for building, carpentry, etc. **2** a piece of wood or beam, esp. as the rib of a ship. **3** large standing trees suitable for timber. **4** (esp. as *int.*) a warning cry that a tree is about to fall. [Old English in sense 'a building'] □ **timbering** *n.*

timbered *adj.* **1** (esp. of a building) made wholly or partly of timber. **2** (of country) wooded.

---

timberland *n. US* land covered with forest yielding timber.

timberline *n.* (on a mountain) the line or level above which no trees grow.

timber wolf *n.* a type of large N. American grey wolf.

timbre /tambr/ *n.* the distinctive character of a musical sound or voice apart from its pitch and intensity. [French, from Greek *tumpanon* 'drum']

time ● *n.* **1** the indefinite continued progress of existence, events, etc., in past, present, and future regarded as a whole. **2** the progress of this as affecting persons or things (*stood the test of time*). **3** a more or less definite portion of time belonging to particular events or circumstances (*prehistoric times*). **4** an allotted, available, or measurable portion of time; the period of time at one's disposal (*had no time to visit*). **5** a point of time esp. in hours and minutes (*the time is 7.30*). **6** (prec. by *a*) an indefinite period (*waited for a time*). **7** time or an amount of time as reckoned by a conventional standard (*eight o'clock New York time*). **8 a** an occasion (*last time I saw you*). **b** an event or occasion qualified in some way (*had a good time*). **9** a moment or definite portion of time destined or suitable for a purpose etc. (*shall we fix a time?*). **10** (in *pl.*) expressing multiplication (*five times six is thirty*). **11** a lifetime (*will last my time*). **12** (in *sing.* or *pl.*) **a** the conditions of life or a period (*hard times*). **b** (prec. by *the*) the present age, or that being considered. **13** *colloq.* a prison sentence (*is doing time*). **14** an apprenticeship (*served his time*). **15** a period of gestation. **16** the date or expected date of childbirth (*is near her time*) or of death (*my time is near*). **17** measured time spent in work (*on short time*). **18 a** any of several rhythmic patterns of music (*in waltz time*). **b** the duration of a note as indicated by a crotchet, minim, etc. **19** (esp. in phr. **call time**) *Brit.* the moment at which the opening hours of a public house end. ● *v.tr.* **1** choose the time or occasion for (*time your remarks carefully*). **2** do at a chosen or correct time. **3** arrange the time of arrival of. **4** ascertain the time taken by (a process or activity, or a person doing it). **5** regulate the duration or interval of (*timed to arrive hourly*). □ **against time** with utmost speed, so as to finish by a specified time. **ahead of time** earlier than expected. **ahead of one's time** having ideas too enlightened or advanced to be accepted by one's contemporaries. **all the time 1** during the whole of the time referred to (often despite some contrary expectation etc.). **2** constantly (*nags all the time*). **3** at all times (*leaves a light on all the time*). **at one time 1** in or during a known but unspecified past period. **2** simultaneously. **at the same time 1** simultaneously; at a time that is the same for all. **2** nevertheless (*at the same time, I do not want to offend you*). **at a time** separately in the specified groups or numbers (*came three at a time*). **at times** occasionally, intermittently. **before time** (usu. prec. by *not*) before the due or expected time. **before one's time** prematurely. **for the time being** for the present; until some other arrangement is made. **have no time for 1** be unable or unwilling to spend time on. **2** dislike. **have the time 1** be able to spend the time needed. **2** know from a watch etc. what time it is. **have a time of it** undergo trouble or difficulty. **in no** (or **less than no**) **time 1** very soon. **2** very quickly. **in one's own good time** at a time and a rate decided by oneself. **in** (or *US* **on**) **one's own time** outside working hours. **in time 1** not late, punctual. **2** eventually (*in time you may agree*). **3** in accordance with a given rhythm or tempo, esp. of music. **in one's time** at or during some previous period of one's life. **keep good** (or **bad**) **time 1** (of a clock etc.) record time accurately (or inaccurately). **2** be habitually punctual (or not punctual). **keep time** move or sing etc. in time. **know the**

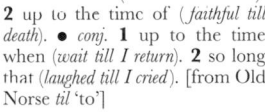
hole for fixing peg

TILE: CLAY ROOFING TILES

T

time of day be well informed. **lose no time** (often foll. by *in* + verbal noun) act immediately. **not before time** not too soon; timely. **no time** *colloq.* a very short interval. **out of time** unseasonable; unseasonably. **pass the time of day** *colloq.* exchange a greeting or casual remarks. **time after time 1** repeatedly; on many occasions. **2** in many instances. **time and** (or **time and time**) **again** on many occasions. **time and a half** a rate of payment for work at one and a half times the normal rate. **the time of day** the hour by the clock. **the time of one's life** a period or occasion of exceptional enjoyment. **time was** there was a time (*time was when I could do that*). [Old English]

time-and-motion *adj.* (usu. *attrib.*) concerned with measuring the efficiency of industrial and other operations.

time bomb *n.* a bomb designed to explode at a pre-set time.

time capsule *n.* a box etc. containing objects typical of the present time, buried for discovery in the future.

time clock *n.* **1** a clock with a device for recording workers' hours of work. **2** a switch mechanism activated at pre-set times by a built-in clock.

time-consuming *adj.* using much or too much time.

time exposure *n.* ▼ the exposure of photographic film for longer than the maximum normal shutter setting.

TIME EXPOSURE: PHOTOGRAPH OF CARS AT NIGHT TAKEN WITH A LONG TIME EXPOSURE

time factor *n.* the passage of time as a limitation on what can be achieved.

time frame *n.* **1** a specific period of time in which something occurs or is planned. **2** *colloq.* a period of time.

time-fuse *n.* a fuse calculated to burn for or explode at a given time.

time-honoured *adj.* esteemed by tradition or through custom.

time immemorial *n.* a longer time than anyone can remember or trace.

timekeeper *n.* **1** a person who records time, esp. of workers or in a game. **2 a** a watch or clock as regards accuracy (*a good timekeeper*). **b** a person as regards punctuality. □ **timekeeping** *n.*

time lag *n.* an interval of time between an event, a cause, etc. and its effect.

time-lapse *attrib.adj.* (of photography) using frames taken at long intervals to photograph a slow process, and shown continuously as if at normal speed.

timeless *adj.* not affected by the passage of time; eternal. □ **timelessly** *adv.* **timelessness** *n.*

time limit *n.* the limit of time within which a task must be done.

time lock ● *n.* **1** a lock that is operated by a timing device. **2** a device built into a computer program to stop it operating after a certain time. ● *v.tr.* (as **time-locked** *adj.*) **1** inextricably linked to a certain period of time. **2** secured by a time lock.

timely *adj.* (**timelier**, **timeliest**) opportune; coming at the right time. □ **timeliness** *n.*

time off *n.* time for rest or recreation etc.

time-out *n.* esp. *N. Amer.* **1** a brief intermission in a game etc. **2** (as **time out**) = TIME OFF.

time out of mind *n.* = TIME IMMEMORIAL.

timepiece *n.* an instrument, such as a clock or watch, for measuring time.

timer *n.* **1** a person or device that measures or records time taken. **2** an automatic mechanism for activating a device etc. at a pre-set time.

timescale *n.* the time allowed for or taken by a sequence of events in relation to a broader period of time.

time-served *adj. Brit.* having completed a period of apprenticeship or training.

time-server *n.* a person who changes his or her views to suit the prevailing circumstances, fashion, etc. □ **time-serving** *adj.*

timeshare *n.* a share in a property under a time-sharing scheme.

time-sharing *n.* **1** the operation of a computer system by several users for different operations at one time. **2** the use of a holiday home at agreed different times by several joint owners.

time sheet *n.* a sheet of paper for recording hours of work etc.

time-shift ● *v.tr.* move from one time to another, esp. record (a television programme) for later viewing. ● *n.* a movement from one time to another.

time signal *n.* an audible (esp. broadcast) signal or announcement of the exact time of day.

time signature *n. Mus.* an indication of rhythm following a clef, usu. expressed as a fraction with the denominator defining the beat as a division of a semibreve and the numerator giving the number of beats in each bar. ▷ NOTATION

time-span *n.* a period spanning a duration of time.

time switch *n.* a switch acting automatically at a pre-set time.

timetable ● *n.* a list of times at which lessons, bus departures, etc. are scheduled to take place. ● *v.tr.* include in or arrange to a timetable; schedule.

time travel *n.* (in science fiction) travel through time into the past or the future. □ **time traveller** *n.*

time trial *n.* a race in which participants are individually timed.

time warp *n.* **1** (in science fiction) an imaginary distortion of space in relation to time, whereby persons or objects of one age can be moved to another. **2** a state in which the styles, attitudes, etc. of a past period are retained.

time-wasting ● *n.* **1** the tactic of slowing down play towards the end of a match to prevent further scoring by the opposition. **2** the act of wasting time. ● *adj.* that wastes time. □ **time-waster** *n.*

time-worn *adj.* impaired by age.

time zone see ZONE *n.* 4.

timid *adj.* (**timider**, **timidest**) easily frightened; apprehensive, shy. [based on Latin *timēre* 'to fear'] □ **timidity** *n.* **timidly** *adv.* **timidness** *n.*

timing *n.* the way an action or process is timed, esp. in relation to others.

timorous *adj.* **1** timid; easily alarmed. **2** frightened. [from medieval Latin *timorosus*] □ **timorously** *adv.* **timorousness** *n.*

timpani /tim-pă-ni/ *n.pl.* (also **tympani**) kettledrums. ▷ ORCHESTRA, PERCUSSION. [Italian] □ **timpanist** *n.*

tin ● *n.* **1** *Chem.* ▶ a silvery-white malleable metallic element, used esp. in alloys and in forming tin plate. ▷ METAL. **2 a** a vessel or container made of tin or tinned iron. **b** esp. *Brit.* an airtight sealed container made of tin plate or aluminium for preserving food. **3** = TIN PLATE. ● *v.tr.* (**tinned**, **tinning**) **1** *Brit.* seal (food) in an airtight tin for preservation. **2** cover or coat with tin. □ **put the tin lid on** see LID. [Old English]

tin can *n.* a tin container (see TIN *n.* 2), esp. an empty one.

tinctorial *adj.* **1** of or relating to colour or dyeing. **2** producing colour. [based on Latin *tinctorius* from *tinctor* 'dyer']

tincture ● *n.* (often foll. by *of*) **1** a slight flavour or trace. **2** a tinge (of a colour). **3** a medicinal solution (of a drug) in alcohol (*tincture of quinine*). ● *v.tr.* **1** colour slightly; tinge, flavour. **2** (often foll. by *with*) affect slightly (with a quality). [from Latin *tinctura* 'dyeing']

tinder *n.* a dry substance such as wood that readily catches fire from a spark. [Old English] □ **tindery** *adj.*

tinderbox *n. hist.* ▼ a box containing tinder, flint, and steel, formerly used for kindling fires.

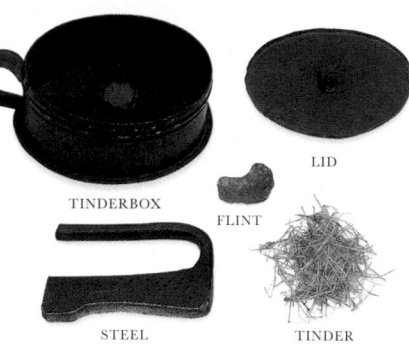

LID

TINDERBOX

FLINT

STEEL

TINDER

TINDERBOX: 19TH-CENTURY METAL TINDERBOX AND CONTENTS

tine *n.* a prong or tooth or point of a fork, comb, antler, etc. [Old English] □ **tined** *adj.* (also in *comb.*).

tinea *n. Med.* ringworm or athlete's foot. [Latin, literally 'moth, worm']

tinfoil *n.* foil made of tin, aluminium, or tin alloy, used for wrapping food.

ting *n.* a tinkling sound as of a bell. ● *v.intr. & tr.* emit or cause to emit this sound.

tinge ● *v.tr.* (**tinging** or **tingeing**) (often foll. by *with*; often in *passive*) **1** colour slightly (*is tinged with red*). **2** affect slightly (*regret tinged with satisfaction*). ● *n.* **1** a tendency towards or trace of some colour. **2** a slight admixture of a feeling or quality. [from Latin *tingere* 'to dye, stain']

tin-glaze ● *n.* a glaze made white and opaque by the addition of tin oxide.

tingle ● *v.* **1** *intr.* feel a slight prickling, stinging, or throbbing sensation. **2** *tr.* make (the ear etc.) tingle. ● *n.* a tingling sensation. [Middle English]

tingly *adj.* (**tinglier**, **tingliest**) causing or characterized by tingling.

tin god *n.* **1** an object of unjustified veneration. **2** a self-important person.

tin hat *n. colloq.* a military steel helmet.

tinker *n.* **1** an itinerant mender of kettles and pans etc. **2** *Sc. & Ir.* a gypsy. **3** a spell of tinkering. ● *v.* **1** *intr.* (foll. by *at*, *with*) work in an amateurish or desultory way, esp. to adjust or mend machinery etc. **2 a** *intr.* work as a tinker. **b** *tr.* repair (pots and pans). [Middle English] □ **tinkerer** *n.*

tinkle ● *v.intr. & tr.* make or cause to make a succession of short light ringing sounds. ● *n.* **1** a tinkling sound. **2** *Brit. colloq.* a telephone call (*will give you a tinkle on Monday*). [Middle English, from obsolete *tink* 'to chink'] □ **tinkly** *adj.*

tinnitus *n. Med.* a ringing in the ears. [Latin]

TIN

tinny ● *adj.* (**tinnier**, **tinniest**) **1** of or like

T

tin. **2** (of a metal object) flimsy, insubstantial. **3** (of reproduced sound) thin and metallic, lacking low frequencies. **4** *Austral. colloq.* lucky. ● *n.* (also **tinnie**) (*pl.* **-ies**) *Austral. colloq.* a can of beer. □ **tinnily** *adv.* **tinniness** *n.*

tin-opener *n. Brit.* a tool for opening tins. ▷ UTENSIL.

Tin Pan Alley *n.* the world of composers and publishers of popular music.

tin plate ● *n.* sheet iron or sheet steel coated with tin. ● *v.tr.* (**tin-plate**) coat with tin.

tinpot *attrib.adj. Brit.* cheap, inferior.

tinsel ● *n.* **1** glittering metallic strips, threads, etc., used as decoration. **2** superficial brilliance or splendour. **3** (*attrib.*) showy, gaudy, flashy. ● *v.tr.* (**tinselled, tinselling**; *US* **tinseled, tinseling**) adorn with or as with tinsel. [based on Latin *scintilla* 'spark'] □ **tinselled** *adj.* **tinselly** *adj.*

tinsmith *n.* a worker in tin and tin plate.

tinsnips *n.pl.* a pair of clippers for cutting sheet metal.

tin soldier *n.* a toy soldier made of metal.

tint ● *n.* **1** a variety of a colour, esp. one made lighter by adding white. **2** a tendency towards or admixture of a different colour (*red with a blue tint*) **3** a faint colour spread over a surface, esp. as a background for printing on. **4** artificial colouring for the hair. ● *v.tr.* apply a tint to; colour. [alteration of earlier *tinct*, from Latin *tinctus* 'dyeing'] □ **tinter** *n.*

tin-tack *n. Brit.* a tack coated with tin.

tintinnabulation *n.* a ringing or tinkling of bells. [based on Latin *tintinnabulum* 'bell']

tin whistle *n.* = PENNY WHISTLE.

tiny ● *adj.* (**tinier, tiniest**) very small or slight. ● *n.* (*pl.* **-ies**) (usu. in *pl.*) a very young child. [Middle English] □ **tinily** *adv.* **tininess** *n.*

tip[1] ● *n.* **1** an extremity or end, esp. of a small or tapering thing (*tips of the fingers*). **2** a small piece or part attached to the end of a thing, e.g. a ferrule on a stick. **3** a leaf bud of tea. ● *v.tr.* (**tipped, tipping**) provide with a tip. □ **on the tip of one's tongue** about to be said, esp. after difficulty in recalling to mind. **the tip of the iceberg** a small evident part of something much larger or more significant. [from Old Norse] □ **tipless** *adj.*

tip[2] ● *v.* (**tipped, tipping**) **1** (often foll. by *over, up*) **a** *intr.* lean or slant. **b** *tr.* cause to do this. **2** *tr.* (foll. by *into* etc.) **a** overturn or cause to overbalance (*was tipped into the pond*). **b** empty the contents from (a container etc.) in this way. **c** pour out (the contents of a container) in this way. **3** *tr.* strike or touch lightly. ● *n.* **1 a** a slight push or tilt. **b** a glancing stroke, esp. in baseball. **2** *Brit.* a place where material (esp. refuse) is tipped. □ **tip the balance** make the critical difference. **tip the scales** see SCALE[2]. [Middle English]

tip[3] ● *v.tr.* (**tipped, tipping**) **1** make a small present of money to, esp. for a service given. **2** *Brit.* name as the likely winner of a race or contest etc. ● *n.* **1** a small money present, esp. for a service given. **2** a piece of private or special information, esp. regarding betting or investment. **3** a small or casual piece of advice. □ **tip off** *colloq.* give (a person) a hint or piece of special information or warning, esp. discreetly or confidentially. **tip a person the wink** *Brit. colloq.* give a person private information. [17th-century coinage] □ **tipper** *n.*

tipi var. of TEPEE.

tip-off *n.* a hint or warning etc. given discreetly or confidentially.

tipper *n.* (often *attrib.*) a road haulage vehicle that tips at the back to discharge its load.

tippet *n.* **1** a covering of fur etc. for the shoulders formerly worn by women. **2** a similar official garment worn esp. by some clergy. [Middle English]

Tipp-Ex (also **Tippex**) ● *n. Brit. propr.* a type of correction fluid. ● *v.tr.* delete with Tipp-Ex. [from German *tippen* 'to type' + Latin *ex* 'out']

tipple ● *v.* **1** *intr.* drink intoxicating liquor habitually.

---

2 *tr.* drink (liquor) repeatedly in small amounts. ● *n. colloq.* a drink, esp. a strong one. [Middle English] □ **tippler** *n.*

tipstaff *n.* **1** a sheriff's officer. **2** a metal-tipped staff carried as a symbol of office. [contraction of *tipped staff*, i.e. tipped with metal]

tipster *n.* a person who gives tips, esp. about betting at horse races.

tipsy *adj.* (**tipsier, tipsiest**) **1** slightly intoxicated. **2** caused by or showing intoxication (*a tipsy leer*). □ **tipsily** *adv.* **tipsiness** *n.*

tiptoe ● *n.* the tips of the toes. ● *v.intr.* (**tiptoes, tiptoed, tiptoeing**) walk on tiptoe, or very stealthily. □ **on tiptoe** with the heels off the ground.

tip-top *colloq.* ● *adj.* highest in excellence, very best. ● *n.* the highest point of excellence.

tip-up *adj.* able to be tipped, e.g. of a folding theatre seat.

TIR *abbr.* international road transport (esp. with reference to EC regulations). [French *transport international routier*]

tirade *n.* a long vehement denunciation or declamation. [French, literally 'long speech']

tire[1] *v.* **1** *tr. & intr.* make or grow weary. **2** *tr.* exhaust the patience or interest of; bore. **3** *tr.* (in *passive*; foll. by *of*) have had enough of; be fed up with (*was tired of arguing*). [Old English]

tire[2] *n.* **1** a band of metal placed round the rim of a wheel to strengthen it. **2** *US* var. of TYRE. [Middle English]

tired *adj.* **1** weary, exhausted; ready for sleep. **2** (of an idea etc.) hackneyed. □ **tiredly** *adv.* **tiredness** *n.*

tireless *adj.* having inexhaustible energy. □ **tirelessly** *adv.* **tirelessness** *n.*

tiresome *adj.* **1** wearisome, tedious. **2** *Brit. colloq.* annoying (*how tiresome of you!*). □ **tiresomely** *adv.* **tiresomeness** *n.*

tiro var. of TYRO.

'tis *archaic* it is.

tisane *n.* a nourishing drink, usu. a herbal tea. [from Greek *ptisanē* 'peeled barley']

tissue *n.* **1** any of the coherent collections of specialized cells of which animals or plants are made (*muscular tissue; nervous tissue*). **2** = TISSUE PAPER. **3** a disposable piece of soft absorbent paper for wiping, drying, etc. **4** fine woven esp. gauzy fabric.

TIT

Tits are small, very active birds. They belong mainly to the Paridae family, but include birds from other families, such as the penduline tit (Remizidae) and the long-tailed tit (Aegithalidae). The majority of tits live in woodland, nesting in holes in trees or banks, and feed on nuts, seeds, and insects. They have small, stout bills, short, rounded wings, and square-ended tails.

EXAMPLES OF TITS

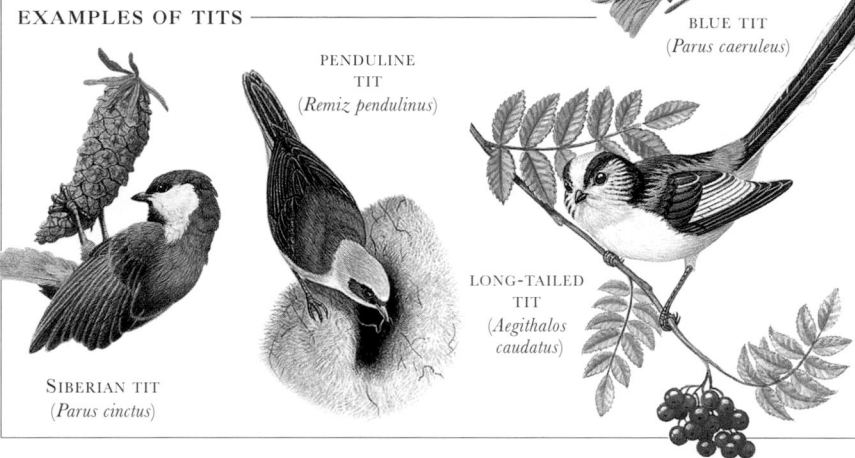

PENDULINE TIT
(*Remiz pendulinus*)

BLUE TIT
(*Parus caeruleus*)

LONG-TAILED TIT
(*Aegithalos caudatus*)

SIBERIAN TIT
(*Parus cinctus*)

---

5 (foll. by *of*) a connected series (*a tissue of lies*). [from Old French *tissu* 'rich material']

tissue paper *n.* thin soft unsized paper for wrapping or protecting fragile or delicate articles.

tit[1] *n.* ▲ any of various small songbirds esp. of the family Paridae.

tit[2] *n.* □ **tit for tat** blow for blow; retaliation (hyphenated when *attrib.*: *tit-for-tat attacks*). [earlier *tip for tap*]

tit[3] *n.* **1** *colloq.* a nipple. **2** *coarse slang* a woman's breast. [Old English]

Titan *n.* **1** (often **titan**) a person of very great strength, intellect, or importance. **2** (in Greek mythology) a member of a family of gigantic gods. [from Greek]

titanic *adj.* **1** of or like the Titans. **2** gigantic, colossal. [from Greek *titanikos*] □ **titanically** *adv.*

titanium /ti-**tay**-ni-ŭm/ *n. Chem.* ◀ a grey metallic element occurring naturally in many clays etc., and used to make strong light alloys that are resistant to corrosion. ▷ METAL. [Greek]

titbit (*N. Amer.* **tidbit**) **1** a dainty morsel. **2** a piquant item of news etc.

titch *n.* (also **tich**) *Brit. colloq.* a small person. [from *Tich*, stage name of Harry Relph, 1868–1928, English music-hall comedian]

titchy *adj.* (**titchier, titchiest**) *Brit. colloq.* very small.

tithe ● *n.* one-tenth of the annual produce of land or labour, formerly taken as a tax for the Church and clergy. ● *v.* **1** *tr.* subject to tithes. **2** *intr.* pay tithes. [Old English *teogotha* 'tenth'] □ **tithable** *adj.*

TITANIUM: ARTIFICIAL HIP JOINT MADE FROM TITANIUM

tithe barn *n.* a barn built to hold tithes paid in kind.

Titian /**tish**-ăn/ *adj.* (of hair) bright golden auburn. [based on *Tiziano* Vecelli, Italian painter, *c.*1488–1576]

titillate *v.tr.* **1** excite pleasantly. **2** tickle. [based on Latin *titillatus* 'tickled'] □ **titillatingly** *adv.* **titillation** *n.*

titivate *v.tr.* (also **tittivate**) *colloq.* **1** adorn, smarten. **2** (often *refl.*) put the finishing touches to. [earlier *tidivate*] □ **titivation** *n.*

T

TOAD

Toads generally differ from frogs in having dry warty skin, short stout legs for walking, and reduced webbing on their feet. They have defensive poison-secreting parotid glands behind the eyes. Although the majority of toads prefer to live on dry land, most enter water during the breeding season; some species also hibernate in water.

nostril
parotid (poison) gland
dry warty skin
short leg
squat body
reduced webbing on foot

EXTERNAL FEATURES OF A
GREEN TOAD (*Bufo viridis*)

EXAMPLES OF TOADS

NATTERJACK TOAD
(*Bufo calamita*)

RED-SPOTTED TOAD
(*Bufo punctatus*)

CANE TOAD
(*Bufo marinus*)

EUROPEAN COMMON TOAD
(*Bufo bufo*)

title ● *n.* **1** the name of a book, work of art, piece of music, etc. **2** the heading of a chapter, poem, document, etc. **3** a book regarded in terms of its title (*published 20 new titles*). **4** a caption or credit in a film, broadcast, etc. **5** a form of nomenclature indicating a person's status (e.g. *professor, queen*) or used as a form of address or reference (e.g. *Lord, Mr, Your Grace*). **6** a championship in sport. **7** *Law* **a** the right to ownership of property with or without possession. **b** the facts constituting this. **c** (foll. by *to*) a just or recognized claim. ● *v.tr.* give a title to. [from Latin *titulus* 'placard, title']

titled *adj.* having a title of nobility or rank.

title deed *n.* a legal instrument as evidence of a right, esp. to property.

title-page *n.* a page at the beginning of a book stating its title, author, etc.

title role *n.* the part in a play etc. that gives it its name (e.g. Othello).

titmouse *n.* (*pl.* **titmice**) any of various small tits, esp. of the genus *Parus*. [Middle English]

titrate *v.tr. Chem.* ascertain the amount of a constituent in (a solution) by measuring the volume of a known concentration of reagent required to complete a reaction with it, often using an indicator. □ **titratable** *adj.* **titration** *n.*

titter ● *v.intr.* laugh in a furtive or restrained way; giggle. ● *n.* a furtive or restrained laugh. □ **titterer** *n.* **titteringly** *adv.*

tittivate var. of TITIVATE.

tittle *n.* a particle; a whit (esp. in phr. **not one jot or tittle**). [from Latin *titulus* 'placard, title']

tittle-tattle ● *n.* petty gossip. ● *v.intr.* gossip, chatter. [reduplication of TATTLE]

tittup ● *v.intr.* (**tittuped, tittuping** or **tittupped, tittupping**) esp. *Brit.* bob up and down; canter. ● *n.* such a gait or movement.

titty *n.* (*pl.* **-ies**) *colloq.* or *joc.* = TIT[3].

titular *adj.* **1** of or relating to a title (*the book's titular hero*). **2** existing, or being what is specified, in name or title only (*titular ruler; titular sovereignty*). [from French *titulaire*] □ **titularly** *adv.*

tizzy *n.* (*pl.* **-ies**) (also **tizz, tiz**) *colloq.* a state of nervous agitation (*in a tizzy*). [20th-century coinage]

T-junction *n.* a road junction at which one road joins another at right angles without crossing it.

Tl *symb. Chem.* the element thallium.

TLC *abbr. colloq.* tender loving care.

TM *abbr.* **1** trade mark. **2** Transcendental Meditation.

Tm *symb. Chem.* the element thulium.

TN *abbr. US* Tennessee (in official postal use).

tn *abbr. US* ton(s).

TNT *abbr.* trinitrotoluene, a high explosive formed from toluene.

to ● *prep.* **1** introducing a noun: **a** expressing what is reached, approached, or touched (*fell to the ground; went to Paris; five minutes to six*). **b** expressing what is aimed at: often introducing the indirect object of a verb (*throw it to me; explained the problem to them*). **c** as far as; up to (*went on to the end; have to stay from Tuesday to Friday*). **d** to the extent of (*were all drunk to a man; was starved to death*). **e** expressing what is followed (*according to instructions; made to order*). **f** expressing

what is considered or affected (*am used to that; that is nothing to me*). **g** expressing what is caused or produced (*turn to stone*). **h** expressing what is compared (*nothing to what it once was; equal to the occasion*). **i** expressing what is increased (*add it to mine*). **j** expressing what is involved or composed as specified (*there is nothing to it*). **2** introducing the infinitive: **a** as a verbal noun (*to get there is the priority*). **b** expressing purpose, consequence, or cause (*we eat to live; left him to starve; am sorry to hear that*). **c** as a substitute for *to* + infinitive (*wanted to come but was unable to*). ● *adv.* **1** in the normal or required position or condition (*come to; heave to*). **2** (of a door) in a nearly closed position. □ **to and fro 1** backwards and forwards. **2** repeatedly between the same points. [Old English]

toad *n.* **1** ◄ any froglike amphibian of the family Bufonidae, esp. of the genus *Bufo*, breeding in water but living chiefly on land. ▷ EGG, FROG, MIDWIFE TOAD. **2** a repulsive or detestable person. [Old English] □ **toadish** *adj.*

toadfish *n.* (*pl.* usu. same) any marine fish of the family Batrachoididae, with a large head and wide mouth, making grunting noises by vibrating the walls of its swim-bladder.

toadflax *n.* **1** ► any plant of the genus *Linaria* or *Chaenorrhinum* (figwort family), esp. *L. vulgaris* (**yellow toadflax**), with narrow leaves like flax and spurred yellow flowers. **2** a related plant, *Cymbalaria muralis*, with lilac flowers and ivy-shaped leaves.

toad-in-the-hole *n. Brit.* sausages or other meat baked in batter.

toadlet *n.* a small or young toad.

toadstone *n.* a stone, sometimes precious, supposed to resemble or to have been formed in the body of a toad, formerly used as an amulet etc.

toadstool *n.* ▼ the spore-bearing body of various fungi, usu. with a round top and slender stalk, esp. one that is poisonous or inedible (cf. MUSHROOM *n.* 1). ▷ FUNGUS

TOADFLAX:
YELLOW TOADFLAX
(*Linaria vulgaris*)

TOADSTOOL

Toadstools, like mushrooms, are fungi belonging to the divisions Ascomycota and Basidiomycota; most produce umbrella-shaped fruiting bodies. Inedible or poisonous types tend to be called 'toadstools', whereas edible ones are 'mushrooms', although the distinction is not truly scientific.

EXAMPLES OF TOADSTOOLS

FLY AGARIC
(*Amanita muscaria*)

STOUT AGARIC
(*Amanita spissa*)

SMOOTH PARASOL
(*Leucoagaricus leucothites*)

YELLOW-GIRDLED WEB CAP
(*Cortinarius triumphans*)

SAW-GILLED BLUE-CAP
(*Entoloma serrulatum*)

COMMON INK-CAP
(*Coprinus atramentarius*)

WOOD WOOLLY-FOOT
(*Collybia peronata*)

T

toady ● *n.* (*pl.* **-ies**) a sycophant; an obsequious hanger-on. ● *v.tr.* & (foll. by *to*) intr. (**-ies, -ied**) behave servilely to; fawn upon. [contraction of *toad-eater*, a charlatan's attendant who ate toads (regarded as poisonous)] □ **toadyish** *adj.* **toady-ism** *n.*

toast ● *n.* **1** bread in slices browned on both sides by radiant heat. **2 a** a person or thing in whose honour a company is requested to drink. **b** a call to drink or an instance of drinking in this way. ● *v.* **1** *tr.* cook or brown (bread, a teacake, cheese, etc.) by radiant heat. **2** *intr.* (of bread etc.) become brown in this way. **3** *tr.* warm (one's feet, oneself, etc.) at a fire etc. **4** *tr.* drink to the health or in honour of (a person or thing). [from Latin *tostus* 'parched'; *n.* sense 2: from the notion that a woman's name flavours the drink as spiced toast would]

toaster *n.* ▼ an electrical device for making toast.

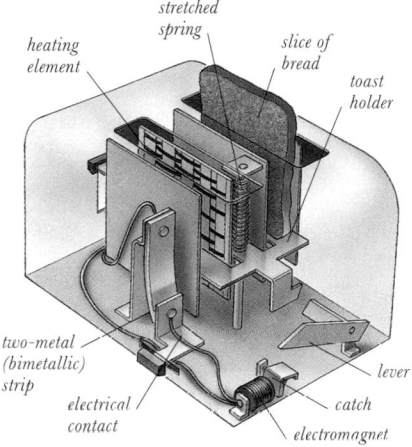

TOASTER: INTERNAL MECHANISM OF A TOASTER

heating element
stretched spring
slice of bread
toast holder
two-metal (bimetallic) strip
lever
electrical contact
catch
electromagnet

toastie *n. colloq.* a toasted sandwich or snack.

toasting-fork *n.* a long handled fork for making toast before a fire.

toastmaster *n.* (*fem.* **toastmistress**) an official responsible for announcing toasts at a public occasion.

tobacco *n.* (*pl.* **-os**) **1** the nicotine-rich leaves of a plant of the genus *Nicotiana*, prepared esp. for smoking or chewing. **2** this plant (cf. TOBACCO PLANT). [from Spanish *tabaco*]

tobacconist *n.* a retailer of tobacco and cigarettes etc.

tobacco pipe see PIPE *n.* 2a.

tobacco plant *n.* ▶ any plant of the genus *Nicotiana*, of American origin, grown for its narcotic leaves (see TOBACCO) or for its night-scented flowers.

toboggan ● *n.* a long light narrow sledge for sliding down-hill esp. over compacted snow or ice. ● *v.intr.* ride on a toboggan. [from Algonquian] □ **toboggan-er** *n.* **tobogganing** *n.*

toby jug *n.* a jug or mug for ale etc., usu. in the form of a stout old man wearing a three-cornered hat. [from *Toby*, pet form of *Tobias*]

toccata *n.* a musical composition for a keyboard instrument designed to exhibit the performer's touch and technique. [Italian, literally 'touched']

tocopherol /to-**kof**-er-ol/ *n.* any of several closely related vitamins, found in wheatgerm oil, egg yolk, and leafy vegetables, and important in the stabil-

TOBACCO PLANT: COMMON TOBACCO (*Nicotiana tabacum*)

---

ization of cell membranes etc. [based on Greek *tokos* 'offspring' + *pherein* 'to bear']

tocsin *n.* an alarm bell or signal. [from Provençal *tocasenh*]

tod *n. Brit. slang* □ **on one's tod** alone; on one's own. [20th-century coinage]

today ● *adv.* **1** on or in the course of this present day. **2** nowadays; in modern times. ● *n.* **1** this present day. **2** modern times. □ **today week** (or **fortnight** etc.) *Brit.* a week (or fortnight etc.) from today. [Old English *tō dæg* 'on (this) day']

toddle ● *v.intr.* **1** walk with short unsteady steps like those of a small child. **2** *colloq.* **a** (often foll. by *round, to,* etc.) take a leisurely walk. **b** (usu. foll. by *off*) depart. ● *n.* **1** a toddling walk. **2** *colloq.* a leisurely walk. [16th-century coinage, originally Scots & northern English]

toddler *n.* a child who is just beginning to walk. □ **toddlerhood** *n.*

toddy *n.* (*pl.* **-ies**) **1** a drink of spirits with hot water and sugar or spices. **2** the sap of some kinds of palm, fermented to produce alcoholic spirit. [based on Sanskrit *tāla* 'palmyra', an Asian palm]

to-do *n.* (*pl.* **to-dos**) a commotion or fuss.

toe ● *n.* **1** any of the five terminal projections of the human foot. **2** the corresponding part of an animal. **3** the part of an item of footwear that covers the toes. **4** the lower end or tip of an implement etc. ● *v.tr.* (**toes, toed, toeing**) **1** touch (a starting line etc.) with the toes before starting a race. **2** mend the toe of (a sock etc.). □ **on one's toes** alert, eager. **toe the line** conform to a general policy or principle, esp. unwillingly or under pressure. **turn up one's toes** *colloq.* die. [Old English] □ **toed** *adj.* (also in *comb.*). **toeless** *adj.*

toecap *n.* the (usu. strengthened) outer covering of the toe of a boot or shoe.

toe clip *n.* ▶ a clip on a bicycle pedal to prevent the foot from slipping. ▷ BICYCLE

toecurling *adj. colloq.* distasteful or regarded as unpleasant, often because of excessive sentimentality.

toehold *n.* **1** a small foothold. **2** a small beginning or advantage.

toenail *n.* the nail at the tip of each toe.

toe clip

TOE CLIP ON A MOUNTAIN BIKE

toe-rag *n. Brit. slang* a term of contempt for a person. [earlier in sense 'tramp, vagrant', from the use of a rag as a sock]

toff ● *n.* an upper-class person; a smart or well-dressed person. ● *v.tr.* (foll. by *up*) dress up smartly.

toffee *n.* **1** a kind of firm or hard sweet made by boiling sugar, butter, etc. **2** *Brit.* a small piece of this. □ **for toffee** (prec. by *can't* etc.) *Brit. colloq.* (denoting incompetence) at all (*they couldn't sing for toffee*). [later variant of TAFFY]

toffee apple *n. Brit.* an apple with a thin coating of toffee, mounted on a stick.

toffee-nosed *adj.* esp. *Brit. colloq.* snobbish, pretentious.

tofu *n.* (esp. in China and Japan) a curd made from mashed soya beans. [from Chinese *dòufu* 'rotten beans']

tog[1] *colloq.* ● *n.* (usu. in *pl.*) an item of clothing. ● *v.tr.* & *intr.* (**togged, togging**) (foll. by *out, up*) dress, esp. elaborately.

tog[2] *n. Brit.* a unit of thermal resistance used to express the insulating properties of clothes and quilts. [from TOG[1], on the pattern of an earlier unit, the *clo* (from *clothes*)]

toga *n. hist.* ▶ an ancient Roman citizen's flowing outer garment. [Latin] □ **toga'd** *adj.* (also **togaed**).

---

together ● *adv.* **1** in company or conjunction (*walking together; built it together*). **2** simultaneously; at the same time (*both shouted together*). **3** one with another (*were talking together*). **4** into conjunction; so as to unite (*tied them together*). **5** into company or companionship (*came together in friendship*). **6** uninterruptedly (*could talk for hours together*). ● *adj. colloq.* well organized or controlled. □ **together with** as well as; and also. [Old English]

togetherness *n.* **1** the condition of being together. **2** a feeling of comfort from being together.

toggle ● *n.* **1** a device for fastening (esp. a garment), consisting of a crosspiece which is passed through a hole or loop. ▷ DUFFEL COAT. **2** *Computing* a key or command that is operated the same way but with opposite effect on successive occasions. ● *v.* **1** *tr.* provide or fasten with a toggle. **2** *intr. Computing* switch from one state to another by using a toggle. [18th-century nautical coinage]

toil ● *v.intr.* **1** work laboriously or incessantly. **2** make slow painful progress (*toiled along the path*). ● *n.* prolonged or intensive labour; drudgery. [from Latin *tudiculare* 'to stir about'] □ **toiler** *n.*

toilet *n.* **1** = LAVATORY. **2 a** the process of washing oneself, dressing, etc. (*make one's toilet*). **b** (*attrib.*) for or to enable this process (*toilet requisites*). [from French *toilette* 'cloth, wrapper']

toilet paper *n.* paper for cleaning oneself after excreting.

toilet roll *n.* a roll of toilet paper.

toiletry *n.* (*pl.* **-ies**) (usu. in *pl.*) any of various articles or cosmetics used in washing, dressing, etc.

toilet soap *n.* soap for washing oneself.

toilette *n.* = TOILET 2. [French]

toilet tissue *n.* = TOILET PAPER.

toilet-training *n.* the training of a young child to use the lavatory. □ **toilet-train** *v.tr.*

toilet water *n.* a dilute form of perfume used after washing.

toils *n.pl. archaic* or *literary* a net or snare. [from Latin *tela* 'web']

toilsome *adj.* involving toil; laborious.

toil-worn *adj.* worn or worn out by toil.

toing and froing *n.* (*pl.* **toings and froings**) constant movement to and fro; bustle; dispersed activity.

token ● *n.* **1** a thing serving as a symbol, reminder, or distinctive mark of something (*as a token of affection*). **2** a thing serving as evidence of authenticity or as a guarantee. **3** a voucher exchangeable for goods (often of a specified kind), given as a gift. **4** anything used to represent something else, esp. a metal disc etc. used instead of money in coin-operated machines etc. ● *attrib.adj.* **1** nominal or perfunctory (*token effort*). **2** conducted briefly to demonstrate strength of feeling (*token resistance; token strike*). **3** serving to acknowledge a principle only (*token payment*). **4** chosen by way of tokenism to represent a particular group (*the token woman on the committee*). □ **by this** (or **the same**) **token 1** similarly. **2** moreover. [Old English]

tokenism *n.* **1** esp. *Polit.* the principle or practice of granting minimum concessions, esp. to appease radical demands etc. (cf. TOKEN *adj.* 4). **2** making only a token effort. □ **tokenistic** *adj.*

told *past* and *past part.* of TELL.

tolerable *adj.* **1** able to be endured. **2** fairly good; mediocre. [from Latin *tolerabilis*] □ **tolerability** *n.* **tolerably** *adv.*

tunic
toga
purple band of an official
leather sandal
TOGA

T

tolerance *n.* **1** a willingness or ability to tolerate; forbearance. **2** the capacity to tolerate something, esp. a drug, transplant, antigen, environmental condition, etc., without adverse reaction. **3** an allowable variation in any measurable property. **4** diminution in response to a drug after continued use. [from Latin *tolerantia*]

tolerant *adj.* **1** disposed or accustomed to tolerate others or their acts or opinions. **2** (foll. by *of*) enduring or patient. [from Latin *tolerant-* 'enduring'] □ **tolerantly** *adv.*

tolerate *v.tr.* **1** allow the existence or occurrence of without authoritative interference. **2** leave unmolested. **3** endure or permit, esp. with forbearance. **4** endure (suffering etc.). **5** be capable of continued subjection to (a drug, radiation, etc.) without harm. [based on Latin *toleratus* 'endured'] □ **tolerator** *n.*

toleration *n.* the process or practice of tolerating, esp. the allowing of differences in religious opinion without discrimination.

toll[1] *n.* **1** a charge payable for permission to pass a barrier or use a bridge or road etc. **2** the cost or damage caused by a disaster, battle, etc. (*death toll*). **3** *N. Amer.* a charge for a long distance telephone call. □ **take its toll** be accompanied by loss or injury etc. [from Greek *telōnion* 'toll-house']

toll[2] ● *v.* **1 a** *intr.* (of a bell) sound with a slow uniform succession of strokes. **b** *tr.* ring (a bell) in this way. **c** *tr.* (of a bell) announce or mark (a death etc.) in this way. **2** *tr.* strike (the hour). ● *n.* **1** the act of tolling. **2** a stroke of a bell. [Middle English, special use of (now dialect) *toll* 'to entice, pull']

toll bridge *n.* a bridge at which a toll is charged.

toll gate *n.* a gate preventing passage until a toll is paid.

toll-house *n.* a house at a toll gate or toll bridge, used by a toll collector.

tollroad *n.* a road maintained by the tolls collected on it.

Toltec *n.* **1** a member of an American Indian people that flourished in Mexico before the Aztecs. **2** the language of this people. [Nahuatl] □ **Toltecan** *adj.*

tolu /tŏ-loo, toh-loo/ *n.* a fragrant brown balsam obtained from either of two S. American trees, *Myroxylon balsamum* or *M. toluifera*, and used in perfumery and medicine. [from Santiago de *Tolu*, in Colombia]

toluene /tol-yoo-een/ *n.* a colourless aromatic liquid hydrocarbon derivative of benzene, used in the manufacture of explosives etc. □ **toluic** *adj.*

tom *n.* a male of various animals, esp. (in full **tom-cat**) a male cat. [abbreviation of the name *Thomas*]

tomahawk ● *n.* **1** ◄ a N. American Indian axe with a stone or iron head, esp. one used as a weapon. **2** *Austral.* a hatchet. ● *v.tr.* strike, cut, or kill with a tomahawk. [American Indian word]

tomato *n.* (*pl.* **-oes**) **1** ▲ a glossy red or yellow pulpy edible fruit. **2** a plant of the nightshade family, *Lycopersicon esculentum*, bearing this. [from Mexican *tomatl*] □ **tomatoey** *adj.*

tomb *n.* **1** ► a large esp. underground vault for the burial of the dead. **2** an enclosure cut in the earth or in rock to receive a dead body. **3** a sepulchral monument. **4** (prec. by *the*) the state of death. [from Greek *tumbos*]

tombola *n. Brit.* a kind of lottery with tickets drawn from a turning drum-shaped container for immediate prizes, esp. at a fête or fair. [based on Italian *tombolare* 'to tumble']

iron axe-head

shaft

T

TOMAHAWK: CEREMONIAL DAKOTA TOMAHAWK

TOMATO

Originally native to South America, the tomato is related to the potato; its fruit is botanically classed as a berry. Many shapes, varieties, and sizes of tomato are available for purchase throughout the year, and are consumed either cooked or raw.

placenta
seed
pulp (endocarp)
fleshy wall (mesocarp)
glossy skin (exocarp)
flower stalk (pedicel)
whorl of sepals (calyx)

STANDARD TOMATO

EXAMPLES OF TOMATOES

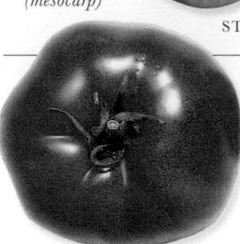

CHERRY TOMATO   BEEFSTEAK TOMATO   PLUM TOMATO

---

tomboy *n.* a girl who behaves in a usu. boyish boisterous way. □ **tomboyish** *adj.* **tomboyishness** *n.*

tombstone *n.* a stone standing or laid over a grave, usu. with an epitaph.

tom-cat SEE TOM.

Tom, Dick, and Harry *n.* (usu. prec. by *any*, *every*) usu. *derog.* ordinary people taken at random.

tome *n.* a large heavy book or volume. [from Greek *tomos* 'section, volume']

tomfool *n.* **1** a foolish person. **2** (*attrib.*) silly, foolish (*a tomfool idea*).

tomfoolery *n.* (*pl.* **-ies**) **1** foolish behaviour; nonsense. **2** an instance of this.

Tommy *n.* (*pl.* **-ies**) *colloq.* a British private soldier. [from *Tommy (Thomas) Atkins*, used in specimens of completed official forms]

tommy bar *n.* a short bar inserted into a hole in a screw etc. to help turn it.

tommy-gun *n.* a type of sub-machine gun. [named after J. T. *Thompson*, US Army officer, 1860–1940, its co-inventor]

tommyrot *n. slang* nonsense.

tomogram *n.* a record obtained by tomography.

tomography *n.* a scanning technique which displays details of a plane cross-section, esp. through the body. [based on Greek *tomē* 'a cutting']

tomorrow ● *adv.* **1** on the day after today. **2** at some future time. ● *n.* **1** the day after today. **2** the near future. □ **tomorrow morning** (or **afternoon** etc.) in the morning (or afternoon etc.) of tomorrow. **tomorrow week** esp. *Brit.* a week from tomorrow. [Middle English]

Tom Thumb *n.* (also **tom thumb**) **1** a dwarf variety of a cultivated flower or vegetable. **2** a small

earth mound
beehive-shaped tomb (tholos)
open-air corridor (dromos)
ossuary
resting-place of king's body

TOMB: RECONSTRUCTION OF A MYCENAEAN ROYAL 'BEEHIVE' TOMB, *c.*1400 BC

---

wild flower, esp. bird's-foot trefoil. [name of the tiny hero of a nursery tale]

tomtit *n.* a tit, esp. a blue tit.

tom-tom *n.* **1** a simple drum beaten with the hands. **2** a tall drum beaten with the hands and used in jazz bands etc. ▷ DRUM KIT. [from Hindi *tamtam*]

-tomy *comb. form* forming nouns denoting cutting, esp. in surgery (*laparotomy*). [from Greek *-tomia* 'cutting']

ton *n.* **1** (in full **long ton**) a unit of weight equal to 2,240 lb avoirdupois (1016.05 kg). **2** (in full **short ton**) esp. *N. Amer.* a unit of weight equal to 2,000 lb avoirdupois (907.19 kg). **3** = METRIC TON. **4** (in full **displacement ton**) a unit of measurement of a ship's weight or volume, equal to 2,240 lb or 35 cu. ft (0.99 cubic metres). **5** (usu. in *pl.*) *colloq.* a large number or amount (*tons of money*). **6** esp. *Brit. slang* **a** a speed of 100 m.p.h. **b** a sum of £100. **c** a score of 100. □ **weigh a ton** *colloq.* be very heavy. [differentiated in the 17th century from TUN]

tonal *adj.* **1** of or relating to tone or tonality. **2** *Mus.* (of a fugue etc.) having repetitions of the subject at different pitches in the same key. [from medieval Latin *tonalis*] □ **tonally** *adv.*

tonality *n.* (*pl.* **-ies**) **1** *Mus.* **a** the relationship between the tones of a musical scale. **b** the observance of a single tonic key as the basis of a composition. **2** the tone or colour scheme of a picture.

tone ● *n.* **1** a musical or vocal sound, esp. with reference to its pitch, quality, and strength. **2** (often in *pl.*) modulation of the voice expressing a particular feeling or mood (*a cheerful tone*). **3** a manner of expression in writing. **4** *Mus.* **a** a musical sound, esp. of a definite pitch and character. **b** an interval of a major second, e.g. C–D. **5 a** the general effect of colour or of light and shade in a picture. **b** the tint or shade of a colour. **6 a** the prevailing character of the morals and sentiments etc. in a group. **b** an attitude or sentiment expressed esp. in a letter etc. **7** the proper firmness or functioning of bodily organs or tissues. **8** a state of good or specified health or quality. **9** *Phonet.* an accent on one syllable of a word. ● *v.* **1** *tr.* give the desired tone to. **2** *tr.* modify the tone of. **3** *intr.* (often foll. by *to*) attune. **4** *intr.* (foll. by *with*) be in harmony (esp. of colour). □ **tone down 1** make or become softer in tone of sound or colour. **2** make (a statement etc.) less harsh or emphatic. **tone up 1** make or become stronger in tone of sound or colour. **2** make (a statement etc.) more emphatic. [from Greek *tonos* 'tension, tone'] □ **toneless** *adj.* **tonelessly** *adv.*

tone arm *n.* the movable arm supporting the pick-up of a record player.

tone control *n.* a switch for varying the proportion of high and low frequencies in reproduced sound.

tone-deaf *adj.* unable to perceive differences of musical pitch accurately. □ **tone-deafness** *n.*

tone poem *n.* = SYMPHONIC POEM.

toner *n.* **1** a chemical bath for toning a photographic print. **2** a powder used in xerographic copying processes. **3** a cosmetic preparation for toning the skin.

tone-row *n.* = SERIES 7.

tongs *n.pl.* (also **pair of tongs** *sing.*) ◀ an instrument with two hinged or sprung arms for grasping and holding. [pl. of obsolete *tong* 'prong']

tongue *n.* **1** ▼ the fleshy muscular organ in the mouth used in tasting, licking, and swallowing, and (in humans) for speech. ▷ DIGESTION, HEAD, TASTE BUD. **2** the tongue of an ox etc. as food. **3** the faculty of or a tendency in speech (*a sharp tongue*). **4** a particular language (*the German tongue*). **5** a thing like a tongue, esp.: **a** a long low promontory. **b** a strip of leather etc., attached at one end only, under the laces in a shoe. ▷ SHOE. **c** the clapper of a bell. **d** the pin of a buckle. **e** the projecting strip on a wooden etc. board fitting into the groove of another. **f** a jet of flame. □ **find** (or **lose**) **one's tongue** be able (or unable) to express oneself after a shock etc. **the gift of tongues** the power of speaking in unknown languages, regarded as one of the gifts of the Holy Spirit (Acts 2). **with one's tongue hanging out** eagerly or expectantly. **with one's tongue in one's cheek** insincerely or ironically. **keep a civil tongue in one's head** avoid rudeness. [Old English] □ **tongued** *adj.* (also in *comb.*). **tongueless** *adj.*

tongue-and-groove ● *n.* (often *attrib.*) planking etc. with a projecting strip down one side and a groove down the other.

tongue-in-cheek ● *adj.* ironic; slyly humorous. ● *adv.* insincerely or ironically.

tongue-lashing *n.* a severe scolding or reprimand.

tongue-tied *adj.* too shy or embarrassed to speak.

tongue-twister *n.* a sequence of words difficult to pronounce quickly and correctly.

tonguing *n.* *Mus.* the technique of playing a wind instrument using the tongue to articulate certain notes.

tonic ● *n.* **1** an invigorating medicine. **2** anything serving to invigorate. **3** = TONIC WATER. **4** *Mus.* the first degree of a scale, forming the keynote of a piece (see KEYNOTE 3). ● *adj.* **1** serving as a tonic; invigorating. **2** *Mus.* denoting the first degree of

a scale. **3** producing tension, esp. of the muscles. [from Greek *tonikos*] □ **tonically** *adv.*

tonicity *n.* **1** the state of being tonic. **2** a healthy elasticity of muscles etc.

tonic sol-fa *n.* *Mus.* a system of notation used esp. in teaching singing, with doh as the keynote of all major keys and lah as the keynote of all minor keys.

tonic water *n.* a carbonated soft drink containing quinine.

tonight ● *adv.* on the present or approaching evening or night. ● *n.* the evening or night of the present day. [Old English]

tonnage *n.* **1** a ship's internal cubic capacity or freight-carrying capacity measured in tons. **2** a charge per ton on freight or cargo. [originally in sense 'duty on a tun of wine': Old French]

tonne *n.* = METRIC TON. [French]

tonsil *n.* either of two small masses of lymphoid tissue, one on each side of the root of the tongue. ▷ TONGUE. [from Latin pl. *tonsillae*] □ **tonsillar** *adj.*

tonsillectomy *n.* (*pl.* **-ies**) the surgical removal of the tonsils.

tonsillitis *n.* inflammation of the tonsils.

tonsorial *adj.* usu. *joc.* of or relating to a hairdresser or hairdressing. [based on Latin *tonsor* 'barber']

tonsure ● *n.* **1** the shaving of the crown of the head or the entire head, esp. of a person entering a priesthood or monastic order. **2** a bare patch made in this way. ● *v.tr.* give a tonsure to. [from Latin *tonsura*]

ton-up *attrib.adj.* *slang* (of a motorcyclist) achieving a speed of 100 m.p.h., esp. habitually.

too *adv.* **1** to a greater extent than is desirable or permissible (*too large*). **2** *colloq.* extremely (*you're too kind*). **3** in addition (*are they coming too?*). □ **none too 1** rather less than (*feeling none too good*). **2** barely. **too bad** see BAD. **too much, too much for** see MUCH. **too right** see RIGHT. [stressed form of TO]

toodle-oo *int.* *colloq.* goodbye.

took *past* of TAKE.

tool ● *n.* **1** any device or implement used to carry out mechanical functions whether manually or by a machine. **2** a thing used in an occupation or pursuit (*the tools of one's trade; literary tools*). **3** a person used as a mere instrument by another. ● *v.tr.* **1** dress (stone) with a chisel. **2** impress a design on (a leather book cover). **3** *slang* drive or ride, esp. in a casual or leisurely manner. **4** (often foll. by *up*) equip with tools. □ **tool up 1** *slang* arm oneself. **2** equip oneself. [Old English] □ **tooler** *n.*

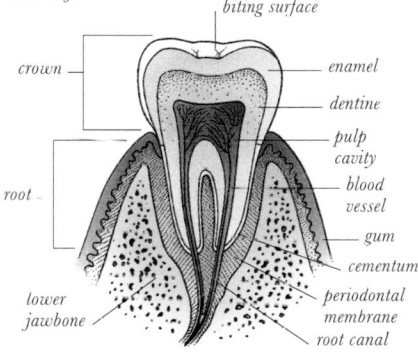

gold tooling

toolbar *n.* a strip of icons on a computer screen, used to initiate commands.

tooling *n.* **1** the process of dressing stone with a chisel. **2** ◀ the ornamentation of a leather book cover with designs impressed by heated tools.

toolmaker *n.* a person who makes precision tools, esp. tools used in a press. □ **toolmaking** *n.*

tool-pusher *n.* a worker directing the drilling on an oil rig.

toolshed *n.* a shed in which tools etc. are stored.

toot ● *n.* **1** a short sharp sound as made by a horn, trumpet, or whistle. **2** *US slang* cocaine or a snort (see SNORT *n.* 4) of cocaine. ● *v.* **1** *tr.* sound (a horn etc.) with a short sharp sound. **2** *intr.* give out such a sound. □ **tooter** *n.*

tooth ● *n.* (*pl.* **teeth**) **1** ▼ each of a set of hard bony enamel-coated structures in the jaws of most vertebrates, used for biting and chewing. **2** a toothlike part or projection, e.g. the cog of a gearwheel, the point of a saw or comb, etc. **3** (often foll. by *for*) one's sense of taste; an appetite. **4** (in *pl.*) force or effectiveness (*the penalties give the contract teeth*). ● *v.* **1** *tr.* provide with teeth. **2** *intr.* (of cogwheels) engage, interlock. □ **armed to the teeth** completely and elaborately armed or equipped. **fight tooth and nail** fight very fiercely. **get one's teeth into** devote oneself seriously to. **in the teeth of 1** in spite of (opposition or difficulty etc.). **2** contrary to (instructions etc.). **3** directly against (the wind etc.). **set a person's teeth on edge** see EDGE. [Old English] □ **toothed** *adj.* (also in *comb.*). **toothless** *adj.* **toothlike** *adj.*

biting surface
crown
enamel
dentine
pulp cavity
root
blood vessel
gum
cementum
lower jawbone
periodontal membrane
root canal

TOOTH: CROSS-SECTION OF
A HUMAN MOLAR

toothache *n.* a pain in a tooth or teeth.

toothbrush *n.* a brush for cleaning the teeth.

toothcomb *n.* *Brit.* = FINE-TOOTH COMB.

■ **Usage** Although *toothcomb* and *fine toothcomb* arose from a misunderstanding of *fine-tooth comb*, they are now accepted as established expressions.

toothed whale *n.* ▶ a whale of the suborder Odontoceti, having teeth rather than baleen plates. ▷ WHALE

tooth fairy *n.* (in nursery tales) a fairy who takes children's milk teeth after they fall out and leaves a coin.

projecting snout (rostrum)
tooth
lower jaw (mandible)

TOOTHED WHALE: KILLER
WHALE (*Orcinus orca*)

toothing *n.* projecting bricks or stones left at the end of a wall to allow for its continuation.

TONGS FOR
KITCHEN USE

TONGUE

The tongue is a fleshy organ rooted within the lower jaw; in humans, it is unique in forming part of the system that produces speech. Its other functions include shaping food into a readily swallowed bolus and the ability to taste. Most taste buds (taste-receptor cells) are sited in papillae on the surface of the tongue; others lie on the palate, throat, and epiglottis. Taste buds respond only to bitter, sour, salty, or sweet flavours, passing signals to the brain, which are enhanced by perceptions such as smell.

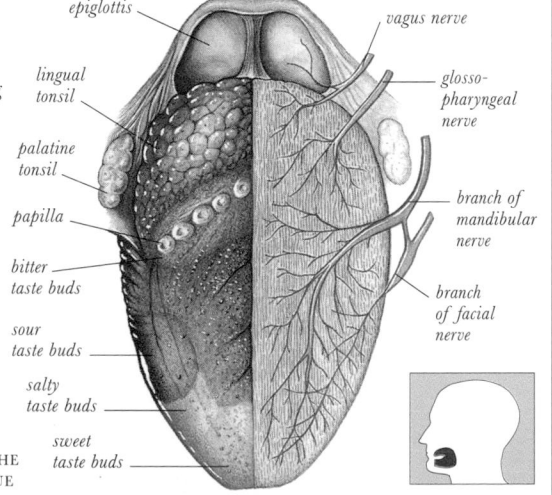

epiglottis
vagus nerve
lingual tonsil
glosso-pharyngeal nerve
palatine tonsil
papilla
branch of mandibular nerve
bitter taste buds
sour taste buds
branch of facial nerve
salty taste buds
sweet taste buds

ANATOMY OF THE
HUMAN TONGUE

toothpaste *n.* a paste for cleaning the teeth.

toothpick *n.* a small sharp instrument for removing pieces of food lodged between the teeth.

tooth powder *n.* powder for cleaning the teeth.

toothsome *adj.* (of food) delicious, appetizing. □ **toothsomely** *adv.* **toothy** *adj.* (**toothier, toothiest**) having or showing numerous or prominent teeth (*a toothy grin*). □ **toothily** *adv.*

tootle *v.intr.* **1** toot gently or repeatedly. **2** *colloq.* move casually or aimlessly. ● *n.* an act of tootling.

too-too *adj. & adv. colloq.* extreme, excessive(ly).

tootsy *n.* (also **tootsie**) (*pl.* **-ies**) (usu. in *pl.*) *colloq.* usu. *joc.* a foot; a toe. [diminutive, from alteration of FOOT]

top¹ ● *n.* **1** the highest point or part (*the top of the house*). **2 a** the highest rank or place (*at the top of the school*). **b** a person occupying this (*was top in maths*). **c** *esp. Brit.* the upper end or head (*the top of the table*). **3** the upper surface of a thing, esp. of the ground, a table, etc. **4 a** the upper part of pyjamas, a track suit, etc. (*pyjama top*). **b** a garment for the upper body, e.g. a T-shirt or blouse. **5 a** the stopper of a bottle. **b** the lid of a jar. **6** *esp. Brit.* the creamy part of milk. **7** the folding roof of a car, pram, or carriage. **8** the utmost degree; height (*called at the top of his voice*). **9** (in *pl.*) *colloq.* a person or thing of the best quality (*he's tops at cricket*). **10** (esp. in *pl.*) the leaves etc. of a plant grown esp. for its root (*turnip-tops*). **11** *Brit.* = TOP GEAR (*climbed the hill in top*). **12** = TOPSPIN. ● *adj.* **1** highest in position (*the top shelf*). **2** highest in degree or importance (*at top speed; the top job*). ● *v.tr.* (**topped, topping**) **1** provide with a top, cap, etc. (*cake topped with icing*). **2** remove the top of (a plant, fruit, etc.). **3** be higher or better than; surpass; be at the top of (*topped the list*). **4** *slang* **a** execute esp. by hanging, kill. **b** (*refl.*) commit suicide. **5** reach the top of (a hill etc.). **6** *Golf* **a** hit (a ball) above the centre. **b** make (a stroke) in this way. □ **at the top** (or **at the top of the tree**) in the highest touch of a profession etc. **come to the top** win distinction. **from top to toe** from head to foot; completely. **off the top of one's head** see HEAD. **on top 1** in a superior position; above. **2** on the upper part of the head (*bald on top*). **on top of 1** fully in command of. **2** in close proximity to. **3** in addition to. **on top of the world** *colloq.* exuberant. **over the top 1** *esp. hist.* over the parapet of a trench (and into battle); into action. **2** (hyphenated when *attrib.*) to excess, beyond reasonable limits; outrageous (*that joke was over the top*). **top off** (or **up**) put an end or the finishing touch to (a thing). **top out** put the highest stone on (a building). **top ten** (or **twenty** etc.) the first ten (or twenty etc.) records in the charts. **top up 1 a** complete (an amount or number). **b** fill up (a glass or other partly full container). **2** top up something for (a person) (*may I top you up with sherry?*). [Old English] □ **topmost** *adj.*

top² *n.* a wooden or metal toy, typically conical, spinning on a point when set in motion by hand, string, etc. [Old English]

topaz *n.* **1** ◄ a transparent or translucent aluminium silicate mineral, usu. yellow, used as a gem. **2** any S. American hummingbird of the genus *Topaza*. [from Greek *topazos*]

topazolite *n.* a yellow or green kind of garnet.

top brass see BRASS *n.* 6.

topcoat *n.* **1** an overcoat. **2** an outer coat of paint etc. ▷ UNDERCOAT

topaz crystal

pegmatite groundmass

TOPAZ

top dog *n. colloq.* a victor or master.

top-down *attrib.adj.* **1** proceeding from the general to the particular, or from the top downwards. **2** hierarchical.

---

top drawer ● *n.* **1** the uppermost drawer in a chest etc. **2** *colloq.* high social position or origin. ● *attrib.adj.* (**top-drawer**) *colloq.* of the highest quality or esp. social level.

top dressing *n.* **1** the application of manure or fertilizer to the top of the earth instead of ploughing it in. **2** manure so applied. □ **top dress** *v.tr.*

tope *n.* ▼ a small shark, *Galeorhinus galeus*. [from Tamil *tōppu*]

TOPE
(*Galeorhinus galeus*)

topee var. of TOPI.

top-flight *adj.* in the highest rank of achievement.

top fruit *n. Brit.* fruit grown on trees, not bushes.

topgallant *n. Naut.* the mast, sail, yard, or rigging immediately above the topmast and topsail. ▷ BATTLESHIP, RIGGING

top gear *n. Brit.* the highest gear in a motor vehicle or bicycle.

top hat *n.* a man's formal hat with a high cylindrical crown. ▷ HAT

top-heavy *adj.* **1** disproportionately heavy at the top so as to be in danger of toppling. **2** (of an organization, business, etc.) having a disproportionately large number of people in senior positions. □ **top-heaviness** *n.*

topi /toh-pee/ *n.* (also **topee**) (*pl.* **topis** or **topees**) *Anglo-Ind.* a hat, esp. a sola topi. [from Hindi *ṭopī*]

topiary /toh-pi-ări/ ● *adj.* concerned with or formed by clipping shrubs, trees, etc. into ornamental shapes. ● *n.* (*pl.* **-ies**) **1** topiary art. **2** ◄ an example of this. [based on Latin *topiarius* 'landscape gardener']

topic *n.* **1** a theme for a book, discourse, essay, sermon, etc. **2** the subject of a conversation or argument. [from Greek *ta topika*, literally 'matters concerning commonplaces', title of a treatise by Aristotle]

topical *adj.* **1** dealing with the news, current affairs, etc. (*a topical song*). **2** dealing with a place; local. □ **topicality** *n.* **topically** *adv.*

topknot *n.* **1** *esp. hist.* a decorative knot or bow of ribbon worn on the head. **2** a tuft or crest growing on the head.

topless *adj.* **1** without a top. **2 a** (of clothes) having no upper part. **b** (of a person) wearing such clothes; bare-breasted. **c** (of a place, esp. a beach) where women go topless. □ **toplessness** *n.*

TOPIARY:
CLIPPED
BOX TREE

top-level *adj.* of the highest level of importance, prestige, etc.

topmast *n. Naut.* the mast next above the lower mast. ▷ RIGGING, SCHOONER

top-notch *adj. colloq.* first-rate.

topography *n.* **1** a detailed description, representation on a map, etc., of the features of a town, district, etc. ▷ MAP. **2** such features. [based on Greek *topos* 'place'] □ **topographer** *n.* **topographic** *adj.* **topographical** *adj.* **topographically** *adv.*

topology *n. Math.* the study of geometrical properties and spatial relations unaffected by the continuous change of shape or size of figures. [based on Greek *topos* 'place'] □ **topological** *adj.* **topologically** *adv.* **topologist** *n.*

toponymy *n.* the study of the place names of a region. [based on Greek *topos* 'place' + *onoma* 'name'] □ **toponymic** *adj.*

---

topper *n. colloq.* = TOP HAT.

topping *n.* anything that tops something else, esp. cream etc. on a dessert.

topple *v.intr. & tr.* **1** (often foll. by *over*) totter and fall (over), or cause to do so. **2** overthrow or be overthrown (*the government was toppled by a coup*). [based on TOP¹]

topsail *n.* **1** the square sail, or each of two such sails, next above the lowest. **2** a fore-and-aft sail above the gaff. ▷ MAN-OF-WAR, SCHOONER

top secret *adj.* of the highest secrecy.

topside *n.* **1** *Brit.* the outer side of a round of beef. **2** the side of a ship above the waterline.

topsoil *n.* the top layer of soil (opp. SUBSOIL). ▷ SOIL

topspin *n.* a fast forward spinning motion imparted to a ball in tennis etc.

topsy-turvy ● *adv. & adj.* **1** upside down. **2** in utter confusion. ● *n.* utter confusion. □ **topsy-turvily** *adv.* **topsy-turviness** *n.*

top-up *n. Brit.* an addition; something that serves to top up (esp. a partly full glass).

toque /tohk/ *n.* a woman's small brimless hat. [French]

tor *n.* a hill or rocky peak, esp. in Devon or Cornwall. [Old English]

Torah *n.* **1** (usu. prec. by *the*) **a** the Pentateuch. **b** ▼ a scroll containing this. **2** the will of God as revealed in Mosaic law. [Hebrew, literally 'instruction']

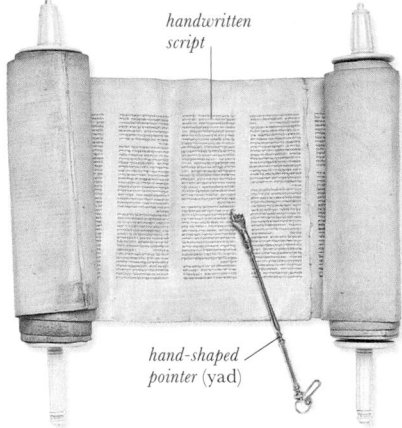

handwritten script

hand-shaped pointer (yad)

TORAH: TRADITIONAL SCROLL CONTAINING THE JEWISH TORAH

torc *n.* (also **torque**) *hist.* ► a necklace of twisted metal, esp. of the ancient Gauls and Britons.

torch ● *n.* **1** (also **electric torch**) *Brit.* a portable battery-powered electric lamp. **2** a piece of wood, cloth, etc., soaked in tallow and lit for illumination. **3** a source of heat, illumination, or enlightenment (*bore aloft the torch of freedom*). **4** *esp. N. Amer.* a blowlamp. **5** *US slang* an arsonist. ● *v.tr. esp. N. Amer. slang* set alight with a torch. □ **carry a torch for** suffer from unrequited love for. **put to the torch** destroy by burning. [from Latin *torqua*]

TORC: ANCIENT CELTIC TORC

twisted bronze

torchlight *n.* the light of a torch or torches. □ **torchlit** *adj.*

torch song *n.* a popular song of unrequited love. □ **torch singer** *n.*

tore past of TEAR¹.

toreador /to-riă-dor/ *n.* a bullfighter, esp. on horseback. [Spanish]

T

TORNADO

Of all types of storm, a tornado (or 'twister') is the most violent. It occurs when moist air rises, heated over warm land or sea; it cools at high altitudes and condenses into water droplets, forming a thundercloud. The suction of the rising air draws up a spiral of air from below, and strong winds begin to blow. The tornado formed beneath the thundercloud may produce winds of 400 k.p.h. (250 m.p.h.) or more, and the low air pressure at its centre can cause buildings to explode. A waterspout occurs when a tornado passes over water.

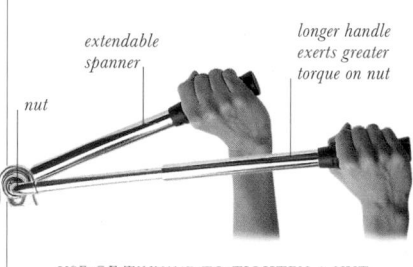

air funnel

spiral of rising air

narrow base, usually less than 1.6 km (1 mile) across

debris left in wake of tornado

FEATURES OF A TORNADO

toreador pants *n.pl.* women's close-fitting calf-length trousers.

torero *n.* (*pl.* **-os**) a bullfighter. [Spanish]

torgoch *n.* /taw-gokh/ a kind of red-bellied char found in some Welsh lakes.

tori *pl.* of TORUS.

toric *adj.* *Geom.* having the form of a torus or part of a torus.

torment ● *n.* /tor-ment/ **1** severe physical or mental suffering (*was in torment*). **2** a cause of this. ● *v.tr.* /tor-**ment**/ **1** subject to torment (*tormented with worry*). **2** tease or worry excessively (*enjoyed tor-*

TORQUE

Torque is a force that makes an object rotate. A nut turns because of the torque applied by a spanner. The size of the torque is found by multiplying the applied force by its distance from the axis, so that a longer spanner exerts greater torque.

extendable spanner

longer handle exerts greater torque on nut

nut

USE OF TORQUE TO TIGHTEN A NUT

menting the teacher). [from Latin *tormentum* 'instrument of torture'] □ **tormentedly** *adv.* **tormentingly** *adv.* **tormentor** *n.*

torn *past part.* of TEAR[1].

tornado *n.* (*pl.* **-ocs** or **-os**) ◄ a violent storm of small extent with whirling winds. □ **tornadic** *adj.*

toroid *n.* a figure of toroidal shape.

toroidal *adj.* *Geom.* of or resembling a torus. □ **toroidally** *adv.*

torpedo ● *n.* (*pl.* **-oes**) **1 a** a cigar-shaped self-propelled underwater missile that explodes on impact with a ship. **b** (in full **aerial torpedo**) a similar device dropped from an aircraft. ▷ WARHEAD. **2** *Zool.* an electric ray. **3** *US* a type of explosive device or firework. ● *v.tr.* (**-oes**, **-oed**) **1** destroy or attack with a torpedo. **2** make (a policy, institution, plan, etc.) ineffective or inoperative. [Latin, literally 'numbness, electric ray']

torpedo boat *n.* a small fast lightly armed warship for carrying or discharging torpedoes.

torpid *adj.* **1** sluggish, inactive, dull, apathetic. **2** numb. **3** (of a hibernating animal) dormant. [from Latin *torpidus*] □ **torpidity** *n.* **torpidly** *adv.* **torpidness** *n.*

torpor *n.* torpidity. [Latin]

torque *n.* **1** *Mech.* ▼ the moment of a system of forces tending to cause rotation. **2** var. of TORC. [based on Latin *torquēre* 'to twist'] □ **torquey** *adj.*

torque converter *n.* a device to transmit the correct torque from the engine to the axle in a motor vehicle. ▷ GEARBOX

torrefy *v.tr.* (**-ies**, **-ied**) **1** roast or dry (metallic ore, a drug, etc.). **2** parch or scorch with heat. [based on Latin *torrēre* 'to scorch'] □ **torrefaction** *n.*

torrent *n.* **1** a rushing stream of water, lava, etc. **2** (in *pl.*) a great downpour of rain (*came down in torrents*). **3** (usu. foll. by *of*) a violent or copious flow (*uttered a torrent of abuse*). [from Latin *torrent-* 'scorching, boiling, roaring'] □ **torrential** *adj.* **torrentially** *adv.*

torrid *adj.* **1 a** (of the weather) very hot and dry. **b** (of land etc.) parched by such weather. **2** (of language or actions) emotionally charged; passionate, intense. [from Latin *torridus*] □ **torridity** *n.* **torridly** *adv.*

torsion *n.* twisting, esp. of one end of a body while the other is held fixed. [from Late Latin *torsio*] □ **torsional** *adj.* **torsionally** *adv.* **torsionless** *adj.*

torsion bar *n.* a bar forming part of a vehicle suspension, twisting in response to the motion of the wheels and absorbing their vertical movement.

torso *n.* (*pl.* **-os** or *US* also **torsi**) **1** the trunk of the human body. **2** a statue of this. [Italian, literally 'stalk, stump']

tort *n.* *Law* a breach of duty (other than under contract) leading to liability for damages. [from medieval Latin *tortum* 'wrong']

torte /tor-tĕ/ *n.* (*pl.* **torten** /tor-tĕn/ or **tortes**) an elaborate sweet cake or tart. [German]

tortilla /tor-tee-yă/ *n.* a thin flat originally Mexican maize cake. [Spanish, literally 'little cake']

tortoise /tor-tŏs/ *n.* ▼ any slow-moving plant-eating land reptile of the family Testudinidae, encased in a domed shell, and having a retractile head. ▷ CHELONIAN. [from medieval Latin *tortuca*]

domed shell (carapace)

horny plate (scute)

clawed foot

retractile head

scaly skin

TORTOISE:
HERMANN'S TORTOISE
(*Testudo hermanni*)

tortoiseshell ● *n.* **1** the yellowish-brown mottled or clouded outer shell of some turtles. **2 a** = TORTOISESHELL CAT. **b** = TORTOISESHELL BUTTERFLY. ● *adj.* **1** having the colouring or appearance of tortoiseshell. **2** ▶ made of tortoiseshell or a synthetic substitute.

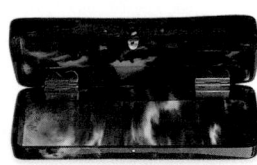

TORTOISESHELL:
EARLY 20TH-CENTURY
TORTOISESHELL BOX

tortoiseshell butterfly *n.* ▼ any of various butterflies of the genus *Aglais* or *Nymphalis* with wings mottled like tortoiseshell.

LARGE TORTOISESHELL
(*Nymphalis polychloros*)

SMALL TORTOISESHELL
(*Aglais urticae*)

TORTOISESHELL BUTTERFLIES

tortoiseshell cat *n.* a domestic cat with markings resembling tortoiseshell. ▷ CAT

tortuous *adj.* **1** full of twists and turns. **2** devious, circuitous (*tortuous mind*). [from Latin *tortuosus*] □ **tortuosity** *n.* (*pl.* **-ies**). **tortuously** *adv.* **tortuousness** *n.*

■ **Usage** *Tortuous*, meaning 'full of twists and turns; devious, crooked' should not be confused with *torturous* meaning 'involving torture, excruciating'.

torture ● *n.* **1** the infliction of severe bodily pain esp. as a punishment or a means of persuasion. **2** severe physical or mental suffering. ● *v.tr.* **1** subject to physical or mental torture. **2** force out of a natural position or state; deform; pervert. [from Late Latin *tortura* 'twisting'] □ **torturer** *n.* **torturous** *adj.* **torturously** *adv.*

■ **Usage** See Usage Note at TORTUOUS.

torus *n.* (*pl.* **tori** /-ry/ or **toruses**) **1** *Geom.* ▶ a surface or solid formed by rotating a closed curve, esp. a circle, about a line in its plane but not intersecting it. **2** a thing of this shape, esp. a large ring-shaped chamber used in physical research. [Latin, literally 'swelling, bulge, cushion']

axis

closed curve (circle)

TORUS

Tory ● *n.* (*pl.* **-ies**) **1** esp. *Brit. colloq.* = CONSERVATIVE *n.* 2. **2** *hist.* (in England) a member of the party that opposed the exclusion of James II and later gave rise to the Conservative Party (opp. WHIG). ● *adj. colloq.* = CONSERVATIVE *adj.* 3. [originally in sense 'Irish outlaw'] □ **Toryism** *n.*

tosh *n. Brit. colloq.* rubbish, nonsense. [19th-century coinage]

toss ● *v.* **1** *tr.* throw up (a ball etc.), esp. with the hand. **2** *tr. & intr.* roll about, throw, or be thrown, restlessly or from side to side. **3** *tr.* (usu. foll. by *to, away, aside, out,* etc.) throw (a thing) lightly or carelessly. **4** *tr.* **a** throw (a coin) into the air to decide a choice etc. by the side on which it lands.

T

b (also *absol.*; often foll. by *for*) settle a question or dispute with (a person) in this way. **5** *tr.* **a** (of a bull etc.) throw (a person etc.) up with the horns. **b** (of a horse etc.) throw (a rider) off its back. **6** *tr.* coat (food) with dressing etc. by shaking it. ● *n.* **1** the act or an instance of tossing (a coin, the head, etc.). **2** *Brit.* a fall, esp. from a horse. □ **toss one's head** throw it back esp. in anger, impatience, etc. **tossing the caber** the Scottish sport of throwing a tree trunk. **toss off 1** drink off at a draught. **2** dispatch (work) rapidly or without effort (*tossed off an omelette*). **toss a pancake** throw it up so that it flips to the other side in the frying pan. **toss up** toss a coin to decide a choice etc. [16th-century coinage]

tosser *n.* **1** *Brit. coarse slang* an unpleasant or contemptible person. **2** a person or thing that tosses.

toss-up *n.* **1** a doubtful matter; a close thing (*it's a toss-up whether he wins*). **2** the tossing of a coin.

tot[1] *n.* **1** a small child (*a tiny tot*). **2** *Brit.* a dram of liquor. [18th-century coinage, of dialect origin]

tot[2] *v.* (**totted**, **totting**) esp. *Brit.* **1** *tr.* (usu. foll. by *up*) add (figures etc.). **2** *intr.* (foll. by *up*) (of items) mount up. □ **tot up to** amount to. [abbreviation of TOTAL]

total ● *adj.* **1** complete, comprising the whole. **2** absolute, unqualified (*total abstinence*). ● *n.* a total number or amount. ● *v.* (**totalled, totalling**; *US* **totaled, totaling**) **1** *tr.* **a** amount in number to. **b** find the total of (things, a set of figures, etc.). **2** *intr.* (foll. by *to*, *up to*) amount to. **3** *tr. N. Amer. slang* wreck (a car etc.) completely. [from medieval Latin *totalis*] □ **totally** *adv.*

total abstinence *n.* abstaining completely from alcohol.

total eclipse *n.* an eclipse in which the whole disc (of the Sun, Moon, etc.) is obscured. ▷ ECLIPSE

totalitarian ● *adj.* of or relating to a centralized dictatorial form of government requiring complete subservience to the State. ● *n.* a person advocating such a system. □ **totalitarianism** *n.*

totality *n.* **1** the complete amount or sum. **2** *Astron.* the time during which an eclipse is total.

totalizator *n.* (also **-isator**) **1** a device showing the number and amount of bets staked on a race, to facilitate the division of the total among those backing the winner. **2** a system of betting based on this.

totalize *v.tr.* (also **-ise**) collect into a total; find the total of. □ **totalization** *n.*

totalizer *n.* (also **-iser**) = TOTALIZATOR.

Total Quality Management *n.* (in industry) a systematic approach to improving the quality of products and customer service etc., while reducing costs.

total recall *n.* the ability to remember every detail of one's experience clearly.

total war *n.* a war in which all available weapons and resources are employed.

tote[1] *n. colloq.* **1** a totalizator. **2** *Brit., Austral., & NZ* a lottery.

tote[2] *v.tr.* esp. *N. Amer. colloq.* carry, convey, or wield. [17th-century US coinage] □ **toter** *n.* (also in *comb.*).

tote bag *n.* a large bag for shopping etc.

totem *n.* **1** a natural object, esp. an animal, adopted among some tribal peoples as an emblem. **2** an image of this. [Algonquian] □ **totemic** *adj.* **totemism** *n.* **totemist** *n.* **totemistic** *adj.*

totem pole *n.* ▶ a pole on which totems are carved or hung.

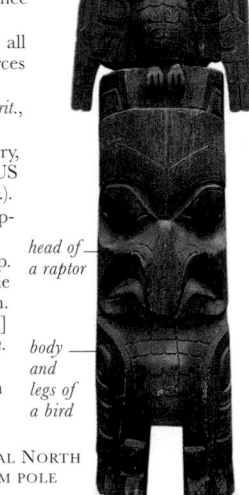

owl —

head of
a raptor

body
and
legs of
a bird

TOTEM POLE: TRADITIONAL NORTH
AMERICAN HAIDA TOTEM POLE

totter ● *v.intr.* **1** stand or walk unsteadily or feebly. **2 a** (of a building etc.) shake or rock as if about to collapse. **b** (of a system of government etc.) be about to fall. ● *n.* an unsteady or shaky movement or gait. [from Middle Dutch *touteren* 'to swing'] □ **totterer** *n.* **tottery** *adj.*

totting-up *n.* **1** the adding of separate items. **2** *Brit.* the adding of convictions for driving offences to cause disqualification.

toucan *n.* ▶ a tropical American fruit-eating bird of the family Ramphastidae, with an immense beak. [from Tupi (Brazilian) *tucana*]

touch ● *v.* **1** *tr.* come into or be in physical contact with (another thing) at one or more points. **2** *tr.* (often foll. by *with*) bring the hand etc. into contact with (*touched her arm*). **3** *a intr.* (of two things etc.) be in or come into contact with one another (*the balls were touching*). **b** *tr.* bring (two things) into mutual contact (*they touched hands*). **4** *tr.* rouse tender or painful feelings in. **5** *tr.* strike lightly. **6** *tr.* (usu. with *neg.*) **a** disturb or interfere with (*don't touch my things*). **b** have any dealings with (*won't touch bricklaying*). **c** consume; make use of (*need not touch your savings*). **d** cope with; affect (*soap won't touch this dirt*). **7** *tr.* **a** deal with (a subject) lightly or in passing (*touched the issue*). **b** concern (*it touches you closely*). **8** *tr.* **a** reach or rise as far as, esp. momentarily (*touched 90˚*). **b** (usu. with *neg.*) approach in excellence etc. (*can't touch him for style*). **9** *tr.* affect slightly; modify (*pity touched with fear*). **10** *tr.* (as **touched** *adj.*) *colloq.* slightly mad. **11** *tr.* (often foll. by *in*) esp. *Art* mark lightly, put in (features etc.) with a brush, pencil, etc. **12** *tr.* **a** strike (the keys etc. of a musical instrument). **b** strike the keys or strings of. **13** *tr.* (usu. foll. by *for*) *slang* ask for and get money etc. from (a person) as a loan or gift (*touched him for £5*). **14** *tr.* injure slightly (*blossom touched by frost*). ● *n.* **1** the act or an instance of touching, esp. with the body or hand. **2 a** the faculty of perception through physical contact, esp. with the fingers (*has no sense of touch*). **b** the qualities of an object etc. as perceived in this way (*the soft touch of silk*). **3** a small amount (*a touch of irony*). **4 a** a musician's manner of playing keys or strings. **b** the manner in which the keys or strings respond to touch. **c** an artist's or writer's style (*has a delicate touch*). **5** a distinguishing quality or trait (*a rather amateur touch*). **6** (esp. in *pl.*) **a** a light stroke with a pen, pencil, etc. **b** a slight alteration or improvement (*needs a few touches*). **7** (prec. by *a*) slightly (*is a touch too arrogant*). **8** *slang* **a** the act of asking for and getting money etc. from a person. **b** a person from whom money etc. is so obtained. **9** *Football* the part of the field outside the side limits. □ **at a touch** if touched, however lightly (*opened at a touch*). **in touch** (often foll. by *with*) **1** in communication (*keeps in touch with events*). **3** aware, conscious (*not in touch with her own feelings*). **lose touch** (often foll. by *with*) **1** cease to be informed. **2** cease to correspond with or be in contact with another person. **lose one's touch** not show one's customary skill. **out of touch** (often foll. by *with*) **1** not in correspondence. **2** not up to date or modern. **3** lacking in awareness or sympathy (*out of touch with his son's beliefs*). **to the touch** when touched. **touch bottom 1** reach the bottom of water with one's feet. **2** be at the lowest or worst point. **3** *Brit.* be in possession of the full facts. **touch down 1 a** *Rugby* touch the ground with the ball behind the goal line. **b** *Amer. Football* score by being in possession of the ball behind

TOUCAN:
CUVIER'S TOUCAN
(*Ramphastos tucanus*)

the opponents' goal line. **2** (of an aircraft or spacecraft) make contact with the ground in landing. **touch off 1** represent exactly (in a portrait etc.). **2** explode by touching with a match etc. **3** initiate (a process) suddenly. **touch on** (or **upon**) **1** treat (a subject) briefly, refer to casually. **2** verge on (*that touches on impudence*). **touch up 1** give finishing touches to or retouch (a picture, writing, etc.). **2** *Brit. slang* **a** caress so as to excite sexually. **b** sexually molest. **touch wood** esp. *Brit.* touch something wooden with the hand to avert ill luck. **would not touch with a bargepole** see BARGEPOLE. [from Old French *tochier*] □ **touchable** *adj.* **toucher** *n.*

touch-and-go *adj.* uncertain regarding a result; risky.

touchdown *n.* **1** the act or an instance of an aircraft or spacecraft making contact with the ground during landing. **2** *Rugby* & *Amer. Football* the act or an instance of touching down.

touché /too-shay/ *int.* **1** the acknowledgement of a hit by a fencing opponent. **2** the acknowledgement of a justified accusation, a witticism, or retort. [French, literally 'touched']

touch football *n.* a form of American football with touching in place of tackling.

touching ● *adj.* moving; pathetic. ● *prep. literary* concerning; about. □ **touchingly** *adv.* **touchingness** *n.*

touch judge *n. Rugby* a linesman.

touchline *n.* (in various sports) either of the lines marking the side boundaries of the pitch. ▷ RUGBY

touchpaper *n.* paper impregnated with nitre, for firing fireworks etc.

touch screen *n.* ▲ a computer screen displaying data, esp. information to customers, that responds to touch.

touchstone *n.* **1** a fine-grained dark schist or jasper used for testing alloys of gold etc. **2** a standard or criterion.

touch-type *v.tr. & intr.* type without looking at the keys. □ **touch-typist** *n.*

touch-up *n.* a quick restoration or improvement (of paintwork, a piece of writing, etc.).

touchwood *n.* readily inflammable wood, esp. when made soft by fungi, used as tinder.

touchy *adj.* (**touchier, touchiest**) **1** apt to take offence; oversensitive. **2** requiring careful handling (*a touchy subject*). □ **touchily** *adv.* **touchiness** *n.*

tough ● *adj.* **1** hard to break, cut, tear, or chew; durable. **2** (of a person) able to endure hardship. **3** unyielding, difficult (*a tough job*). **4** *colloq.* **a** acting sternly; hard (*get tough with*). **b** (of circumstances, luck, etc.) severe, hard, unjust. **5** *colloq.* criminal or violent (*tough guys*). ● *n.* a tough person, esp. a ruffian or criminal. □ **tough it** (or **tough it out**) *colloq.* endure or withstand difficult conditions. [Old English] □ **toughen** *v.tr. & intr.* **toughener** *n.* **toughish** *adj.* **toughly** *adv.* **toughness** *n.*

tough guy *n. colloq.* **1** a hard unyielding person. **2** a violent aggressive person.

tough-minded *adj.* realistic, not sentimental.

toupee /too-pay/ *n.* (also **toupet** *pronunc.* same) a wig or artificial hairpiece to cover a bald spot. [from French *toupet* 'hair-tuft']

tour ● *n.* **1 a** a journey from place to place, esp. as a holiday. **b** an excursion, ramble, or walk. **2 a** a spell of duty on military or diplomatic service. **b** the time to be spent at a particular post. **3** a series of performances, matches, etc., at different places. ● *v.* **1** *intr.* (usu. foll. by *through*) make a tour. **2** *tr.* make a tour of (a country etc.). □ **on tour** (esp. of a team, theatre company, etc.) touring. [from Greek *tornos* 'lathe']

tour de force *n.* (*pl.* **tours de force** *pronunc.* same) a feat of strength or skill. [French]

tourer *n.* a vehicle, esp. a car, for touring.

Tourette's syndrome *n. Med.* a neurological disorder characterized by involuntary tics and the

T

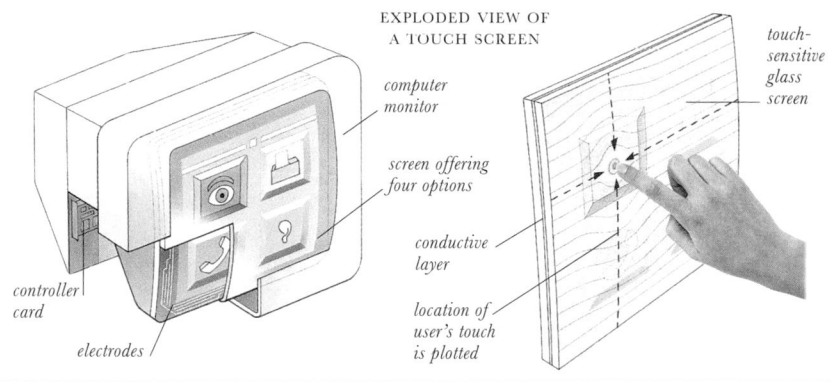

TOUCH SCREEN

Multimedia kiosks in museums, retail outlets, and public information displays offer easy-access information. The software displays graphical buttons or numbered options on a screen, and users move through the system by touching a chosen button or option. The pressure of their touch affects the electric current in a conductive layer beneath the screen. A controller card detects the location of the changes, activating the selected option.

EXPLODED VIEW OF A TOUCH SCREEN

computer monitor

screen offering four options

touch-sensitive glass screen

conductive layer

location of user's touch is plotted

controller card

electrodes

---

compulsive utterance of obscenities. [named after G. de la *Tourette*, French neurologist, 1857–1904]

tourism *n.* the organization and operation of (esp. foreign) holidays, esp. commercially.

tourist *n.* **1** a person making a visit or tour as a holiday; a traveller, esp. abroad (often *attrib.*: *tourist accommodation*). **2** a member of a touring sports team. □ **touristic** *adj.* **touristically** *adv.*

tourist class *n.* the lowest class of passenger accommodation in a ship, aircraft, etc.

touristy *adj.* usu. *derog.* appealing to or visited by many tourists

tourmaline *n.* ► a boron aluminium silicate mineral of various colours, possessing unusual electrical properties, and used in electrical and optical instruments and as a gemstone. ▷ AGGREGATE, MINERAL. [from Sinhalese *toramalli* 'porcelain']

tournament *n.* **1** any contest of skill between a number of competitors, esp. played in heats. **2** a display of military exercises etc. (*Royal Tournament*). **3** *hist.* **a** a pageant with jousting. **b** a meeting for jousting. [from Old French *torneiement*]

TOURMALINE

tournedos /toor-nĕ-doh/ *n.* (*pl.* same) a small round thick cut from a fillet of beef. [French]

tourney ● *n.* (*pl.* **-eys**) a tournament. ● *v.intr.* (**-eys**, **-eyed**) take part in a tournament. [from Latin *tornus* 'a turn']

tourniquet /toor-ni-kay/ *n.* a device for stopping the flow of blood through an artery by constriction. [French]

tour operator *n.* a travel agent specializing in package holidays.

tousle *v.tr.* **1** make (esp. the hair) untidy. **2** handle roughly. [Middle English]

tout ● *v.* **1** *intr.* (usu. foll. by *for*) solicit custom persistently. **2** *tr.* solicit the custom of (a person) or for (a thing). **3** *intr.* **a** *Brit.* spy out the movements and condition of racehorses in training. **b** *US* offer racing tips for a share of the resulting profit. ● *n.* **1** a person employed in touting. **2** = TICKET TOUT. [Middle English *tūte* 'to look out']

tout de suite /toot **sweet**/ *adv.* immediately; at once. [French]

tow[1] /toh/ ● *v.tr.* pull (a boat, vehicle, etc.) along by a rope etc. ● *n.* the act or an instance of towing; the state of being towed. □ **have in** (or **on**) **tow 1** be towing. **2** be accompanied by and often in charge of (a person). [Old English] □ **towable** *adj.* **towage** *n.*

tow[2] /toh/ *n.* **1** the coarse and broken part of flax or hemp prepared for spinning. **2** a loose bunch of rayon etc. strands. [Old English] □ **towy** *adj.*

toward *prep.* = TOWARDS.

towards *prep.* **1** in the direction of (*set out towards town*). **2** as regards; in relation to (*his attitude towards death*). **3** as a contribution to (*put this towards your expenses*). **4** near (*towards the end of our journey*). [Old English]

tow bar *n.* a bar for towing esp. a trailer or caravan.

tow-coloured *adj.* (of hair) very light in colour.

towel ● *n.* **1 a** a piece of rough-surfaced absorbent cloth used for drying oneself or a thing after washing. **b** absorbent paper etc. used for this. **c** a tea towel. **2** *Brit.* = SANITARY TOWEL. ● *v.* (**towelled, towelling;** *US* **toweled, toweling**) **1** *tr.* (often *refl.*) wipe or dry with a towel. **2** *intr.* wipe or dry oneself with a towel. [from Old French *toail(l)e*] □ **towelling** *n.*

towel-horse *n.* a wooden frame for hanging towels on.

towel rail *n.* a rail, esp. in a bathroom, for hanging towels on.

tower ● *n.* **1** a tall esp. square or circular structure, often part of a church, castle, etc. ▷ CASTLE, CHURCH. **2** a fortress etc. comprising or including a tower. **3** a tall structure housing machinery, operators, etc. (*cooling tower; control tower*). ▷ CONTROL TOWER. ● *v.intr.* **1** (usu. foll. by *above, high*) reach or be high or above; be superior. **2** (of a bird, esp. a falcon) soar or hover. **3** (as **towering** *adj.*) **a** high, lofty (*towering intellect*). **b** violent (*towering rage*). [Old English] □ **towered** *adj.*

tower block *n. Brit.* a tall building containing offices or flats.

tower of strength *n.* a person who gives strong and reliable support.

tow-headed *adj.* having very light-coloured or unkempt hair.

towing-net var. of TOW-NET.

towing-path var. of TOWPATH.

towing-rope var. of TOW ROPE.

towline *n.* = TOW ROPE.

town *n.* **1 a** an urban area with a name, defined boundaries, and local government, being larger than a village and usu. not created a city. **b** any densely populated area, esp. as opposed to the country or suburbs. **c** the people of a town (*the whole town knows*). **2 a** *Brit.* London or the chief city or town in one's neighbourhood (*went up to town*). **b** the

central shopping area in a neighbourhood (*just going into town*). **3** *N. Amer.* = TOWNSHIP 2. □ **go to town** *colloq.* act or work with energy or enthusiasm. **on the town** *colloq.* enjoying the entertainments, esp. the nightlife, of a town; celebrating. [Old English *tūn* 'enclosure'] □ **townish** *adj.* **townlet** *n.* **townward** *adj. & adv.* **townwards** *adv.*

town clerk *n.* **1** *US & hist.* the officer of the corporation of a town in charge of records etc. **2** *Brit. hist.* the secretary and legal adviser of a town corporation until 1974.

town council *n.* (esp. in the UK) the elective governing body in a municipality. □ **town councillor** *n.*

town crier *n. hist.* an officer employed by a town council etc. to make public announcements in the streets or market place.

townee var. of TOWNIE.

tow-net *n.* (also **towing-net**) a net used for dragging through water to collect specimens.

town gas *n. Brit.* manufactured gas for domestic and commercial use.

town hall *n.* a building for the administration of local government, having public meeting rooms etc.

town house *n.* **1** a town residence, esp. of a person with a house in the country. **2** a terrace house, esp. of a stylish modern type.

townie *n.* (also **townee**) *derog.* a person living in a town, esp. as opposed to a country dweller.

town planning *n.* the planning of the construction and growth of towns. □ **town planner** *n.*

townscape *n.* **1** the visual appearance of a town or towns. **2** a picture of a town.

townsfolk *n.* (treated as *pl.*) the inhabitants of a particular town or towns.

township *n.* **1** *S.Afr.* **a** *hist.* an urban area set aside for black occupation. **b** (usu. in phr. **proclaim a new township**) a new area being developed by speculators. **2** *N. Amer.* **a** a division of a county with some corporate powers. **b** a district six miles square. **3** *Austral. & NZ* a small town; a town site.

townsman *n.* (*pl.* **-men**; *fem.* **townswoman**, *pl.* **-women**) an inhabitant of a town; a fellow citizen.

townspeople *n.pl.* the people of a town.

towpath *n.* (also **towing-path**) a path beside a river or canal, originally used for towing barges by horse.

tow rope *n.* (also **towing-rope**) a line etc. used in towing.

toxaemia /tok-see-miă/ *n.* (*US* **toxemia**) **1** blood poisoning. **2** a condition in pregnancy characterized by increased blood pressure. □ **toxaemic** *adj.*

toxic ● *adj.* **1** of or relating to poison (*toxic symptoms*). **2** poisonous (*toxic gas*). **3** caused by poison (*toxic anaemia*). ● *n.* (in *pl.*) toxic substances. [from Greek *toxikon (pharmakon)* '(poison) for arrows'] □ **toxically** *adv.* **toxicity** *n.*

toxicology *n.* the scientific study of poisons. □ **toxicological** *adj.* **toxicologist** *n.*

toxic shock syndrome *n. Med.* acute septicaemia in women, typically caused by bacterial infection from a retained tampon, IUD, etc.

toxin *n.* a poison produced by a living organism.

toxocara *n.* any nematode worm of the genus *Toxocara*, esp. one found in dogs or cats. [based on Greek *kara* 'head'] □ **toxocariasis** *n.*

toxoplasmosis *n. Med.* a disease caused by infection with the protozoan *Toxoplasma gondii*, transmitted esp. through poorly prepared food or in cat faeces.

toy ● *n.* **1 a** a plaything, esp. for a child. **b** (often *attrib.*) a model or miniature replica of a thing (*toy gun*). **2 a** a thing regarded as providing amusement. **b** a task or undertaking regarded in an unserious way. **3** (usu. *attrib.*) a diminutive breed or variety of dog etc. ● *v.intr.* (usu. foll. by *with*) **1** trifle, flirt (*toyed with the idea of going to Africa*). **2 a** move a material object idly (*toyed with her necklace*). **b** nibble at food etc. unenthusiastically (*toyed with a peach*). [Middle English] □ **toylike** *adj.*

T

toyboy *n. Brit. colloq.* a woman's much younger male lover.

toyshop *n.* a shop which sells toys.

toy soldier *n.* **1** a miniature figure of a soldier. **2** *colloq.* a soldier in a peacetime army.

TQM *abbr.* Total Quality Management.

trace[1] ● *v.tr.* **1 a** observe, discover, or find vestiges or signs of by investigation. **b** (often foll. by *along, through, to,* etc.) follow or mark the track or position of (*traced their footprints in the mud*). **c** (often foll. by *back*) follow to its origins (*traced back to you*). **2** ▼ (often foll. by *over*) copy (a drawing etc.) by drawing over its lines on a superimposed piece of translucent paper, or by using carbon paper. **3** (often foll. by *out*) mark out, delineate, sketch, or write esp. laboriously (*traced out his vision of the future*). **4** pursue one's way along (a path etc.). ● *n.* **1 a** a sign or mark or other indication of something having existed; a vestige (*no trace remains*). **b** a very small quantity. **2** a track or footprint left by a person or animal. **3** a track left by the moving pen of an instrument etc. **4** a line on the screen of a cathode ray tube showing the path of a moving spot. [based on Latin *tractus* 'drawing, draught'] □ **traceability** *n.* **traceable** *adj.* **traceless** *adj.*

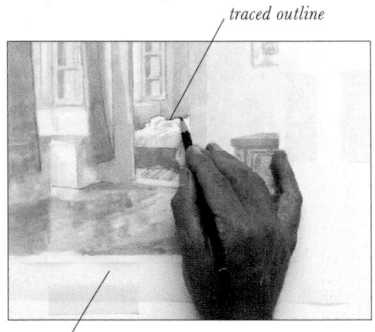

traced outline

tracing paper

TRACE: USING TRACING PAPER TO COPY AN IMAGE

trace[2] *n.* ▼ each of the two side straps, chains, or ropes by which a horse draws a vehicle. □ **kick over the traces** become insubordinate or reckless. [from Old French *trais* 'traits']

afterwale

shaft

trace chain

TRACE: HORSE HARNESSED WITH A TRACE CHAIN TO THE SHAFTS OF A WAGON

trace element *n.* **1** a chemical element occurring in minute amounts. **2** a chemical element required only in minute amounts by living organisms for normal growth.

tracer *n.* **1** a person or thing that traces. **2** *Mil.* **a** a bullet etc. whose course is made visible in flight because of flames etc. emitted. **b** such bullets etc. collectively, used to assist in aiming. **3** an artificially produced radioactive isotope capable of being followed through the body by the radiation it produces.

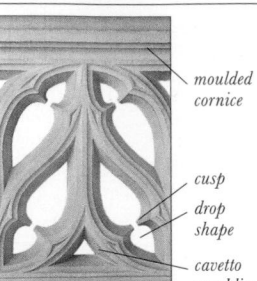

moulded cornice

cusp

drop shape

cavetto moulding

TRACERY IN A 14TH–15TH CENTURY GOTHIC BALUSTRADE

tracery *n.* (*pl.* **-ies**) **1** ◄ ornamental stone openwork esp. in the upper part of a Gothic window. ▷ MASONRY, ROSE WINDOW. **2** a fine decorative pattern. □ **traceried** *adj.*

trachea /tră-kee-ă/ *n.* (*pl.* **tracheae** /-kee-ee/ or **tracheas**) the passage, reinforced by rings of cartilage, through which air reaches the bronchial tubes from the larynx. ▷ ADAM'S APPLE, LUNG, RESPIRATION. [from Greek *trakheia (artēria)* 'rough (artery)'] □ **tracheal** *adj.* **tracheate** *adj.*

tracheotomy /trak-i-ot-ŏmi/ *n.* (also **tracheostomy**) (*pl.* **-ies**) an incision made in the trachea to relieve an obstruction to breathing.

tracheotomy tube *n.* a breathing tube inserted into a tracheotomy.

tracing *n.* **1** a copy of a drawing etc. made by tracing. **2** = TRACE[1] *n.* 3. **3** the act or an instance of tracing.

tracing paper *n.* translucent paper used for making tracings. ▷ TRACE

track ● *n.* **1 a** ▶ a mark or marks left by a person, animal, or thing in passing. **b** (in *pl.*) such marks, esp. footprints. **2** a rough path, esp. one beaten by use. **3** a continuous railway line. **4 a** a racecourse for horses, dogs, etc. **b** ▼ a prepared course for runners etc. **5 a** a groove on a gramophone record. **b** a section of a gramophone record, cassette tape, etc., containing one song etc. **c** a lengthwise strip of magnetic tape containing one sequence of signals. **6** = SOUNDTRACK. **7 a** a line of travel, passage, or motion (*the track of the hurricane*). **b** the path travelled by a ship,

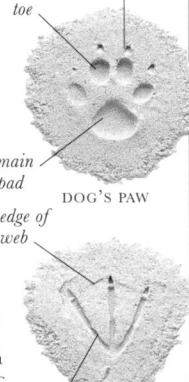

pad of toe

claw

main pad

edge of web

DOG'S PAW

toe

DUCK'S FOOT

TRACKS MADE BY ANIMALS

aircraft, etc. **8** *US Education* = STREAM *n.* 4. **9** a continuous band around the wheels of a tank, tractor, etc. **10 a** a course of action or conduct; a way of proceeding (*America followed in the same track*). **b** a line of reasoning or thought (*this track proved fruitless*). ● *v.* **1** *tr.* follow the track of. **2** *tr.* make out (a course, development, etc.); trace by vestiges. **3** *intr.* (often foll. by *back, in,* etc.) (of a film or television camera) move in relation to the subject being filmed. **4** *intr.* (of a stylus) follow a groove in a record. **5** *tr. US Education* assign (a pupil) to a course of study according to ability. **6** *tr. N. Amer.* **a** make a track with (dirt etc.) from the feet. **b** leave such a track on (a floor etc.). □ **in one's tracks** *colloq.* where one stands, there and then. **keep** (or **lose**) **track of** follow (or fail to follow) the course or development of. **make tracks** *colloq.* go or run away. **make tracks for** *colloq.* go in pursuit of or towards. **off the track** away from the subject. **on a person's track 1** in pursuit of a person. **2** in possession of a clue to a person's conduct, plans, etc. **on the wrong** (or **right**) **track** following the wrong (or right) line of inquiry. **track down** reach or capture by tracking. **the wrong side of the tracks** *colloq.* a poor or less prestigious part of town. [from Old French *trac*] □ **trackage** *n. US.* **trackless** *adj.*

trackball *n. Computing* a small ball that is rotated in a holder to move a cursor on a screen. ▷ MOUSE

tracker *n.* **1** a person or thing that tracks. **2** a police dog tracking by scent.

track events *n.pl.* running races as opposed to jumping etc. ▷ TRACK

tracking *n. Electr.* the formation of a conducting path over the surface of an insulating material.

tracking station *n.* an establishment set up to track objects in the sky.

track record *n.* a person's past performance or achievements.

track shoe *n.* ▶ a spiked shoe worn by a runner.

tracksuit *n.* a loose warm suit worn by an athlete etc., esp. for exercising or jogging.

trackway *n.* a beaten path; an ancient roadway.

spiked sole

TRACK SHOE

TRACK

An athletics track is marked for running events – sprinting, relay running, middle- and long-distance running, hurdling, and walking. Field events such as the long jump, triple jump, and pole vault are often sited in the outfield, beyond the track area, while the javelin, shot-put, hammer, and discus are thrown inside the perimeter, in the infield.

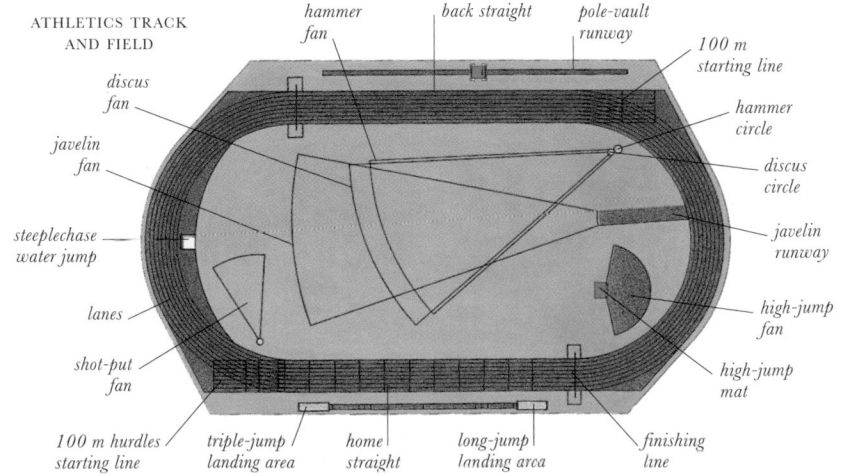

ATHLETICS TRACK AND FIELD

hammer fan · *back straight* · *pole-vault runway* · *100 m starting line* · *hammer circle* · *discus circle* · *javelin runway* · *discus fan* · *javelin fan* · *steeplechase water jump* · *high-jump fan* · *high-jump mat* · *lanes* · *shot-put fan* · *100 m hurdles starting line* · *triple-jump landing area* · *home straight* · *long-jump landing area* · *finishing line*

T

tract[1] *n.* **1** a region or area of indefinite, esp. large, extent (*pathless desert tracts*). **2** *Anat.* an area of an organ or system (*respiratory tract*). [from Latin *tractus* 'dragging']

tract[2] *n.* a short treatise in pamphlet form esp. on a religious subject.

tractable *adj.* **1** (of a person) easily handled; manageable. **2** (of material etc.) malleable. [from Latin *tractabilis*] □ **tractability** *n.* **tractableness** *n.* **tractably** *adv.*

tractate *n.* a treatise. [from Latin *tractatus* 'handled']

traction *n.* **1** the act of drawing or pulling a thing over a surface, esp. a road or track. **2 a** a sustained therapeutic pulling on a limb etc. by means of pulleys, weights etc. **b** contraction, e.g. of a muscle. [based on Latin *trahere tract-* 'to draw, pull'] □ **tractional** *adj.* **tractive** *adj.*

traction engine *n.* ▼ a steam or diesel engine for drawing heavy loads on roads, fields, etc.

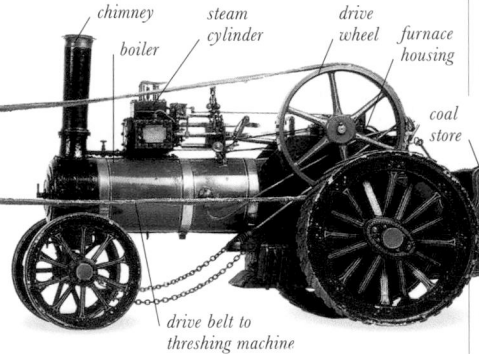

chimney   steam cylinder   drive wheel   furnace housing
boiler   coal store
drive belt to threshing machine

TRACTION ENGINE: 19TH-CENTURY STEAM-DRIVEN TRACTION ENGINE

traction wheel *n.* the driving wheel of a locomotive etc.

tractor *n.* **1** a motor vehicle used for hauling esp. farm machinery, heavy loads, etc. **2** a traction engine. [from Late Latin]

trad esp. *Brit. colloq.* ● *n.* traditional jazz. ● *adj.* traditional.

trade ● *n.* **1 a** buying and selling. **b** buying and selling conducted between nations etc. **c** business conducted for profit (esp. as distinct from a profession) (*a butcher by trade*). **d** business of a specified nature or time (*tourist trade*). **2** a skilled handicraft esp. requiring an apprenticeship (*learnt a trade*). **3** (usu. prec. by *the*) the people engaged in a specific trade (*trade enquiries only*). **4** *US* a transaction, esp. a swap. **5** (usu. in *pl.*) a trade wind. ● *v.* **1** *intr.* (often foll. by *in*, *with*) engage in trade; buy and sell. **2** *tr.* **a** exchange in commerce; barter (goods). **b** exchange (insults, blows, etc.). **c** esp. *N. Amer.* (foll. by *for*) swap, exchange. **3** *intr.* (usu. foll. by *with*, *for*) have a transaction with a person for a thing. **4** *intr.* (usu. foll. by *to*) carry goods to a place. □ **trade in** (often foll. by *for*) exchange (esp. a used car etc.) in part payment for another. **trade off** exchange, esp. as a compromise. **trade on** take advantage of (a person's credulity, one's reputation, etc.). [from Old High German *trata* 'track'] □ **tradable** *adj.* **tradeable** *adj.*

trade cycle *n. Brit.* recurring periods of boom and recession.

trade deficit *n.* the extent by which a country's imports exceed its exports.

trade gap *n.* = TRADE DEFICIT.

trade-in *n.* a thing, esp. a car, exchanged in part payment for another.

trade journal *n.* a periodical containing news etc. concerning a particular trade.

trade mark ● *n.* (also **trademark**) **1** a device, word, or words, secured by legal registration or established by use as representing a company,

product, etc. **2** a distinctive characteristic etc. ● *v.tr.* (**trademark**) provide with a trade mark.

trade name *n.* **1** a name by which a thing is called in a trade. **2** a name given to a product. **3** a name under which a business trades.

trade-off *n.* a balance achieved between two desirable but incompatible features.

trade paper *n.* = TRADE JOURNAL.

trade plates *n.pl. Brit.* number plates used by a car-dealer etc. on unlicensed cars.

trade price *n.* a wholesale price charged to the dealer before goods are retailed.

trader *n.* **1** a person engaged in trade. **2** a merchant ship.

tradescantia *n.* ► any often trailing plant of the genus *Tradescantia*, with large blue, white, or pink flowers. [named after J. *Tradescant*, English naturalist, 1570–1638]

trade secret *n.* **1** a secret device or technique used esp. in a trade. **2** *joc.* any secret.

tradesman *n.* (*pl.* **-men**; *fem.* **tradeswoman**, *pl.* **-women**) a person engaged in trade, esp. *Brit.* a shopkeeper.

   tradespeople *n.pl.* people engaged in trade and their families.

   Trades Union Congress *n. Brit.* the official representative body of British trade unions, meeting annually.

trade union *n.* (also *Brit.* **trades union**) an organized association of workers in a trade, group of trades, or a profession, formed to protect and further their rights and interests. □ **trade unionism** *n.*

trade unionist *n.* (also *Brit.* **trades unionist**) a member of a trade union.

trade-weighted *adj.* (esp. of exchange rates) weighted according to the importance of the trade with the various countries involved.

trade wind *n.* ► a wind blowing continually towards the equator and deflected westward.

trading *n.* the act of engaging in trade.

trading estate *n.* esp. *Brit.* a specially designed industrial and commercial area.

trading post *n.* a store etc. established in a remote or unsettled region.

trading stamp *n.* a stamp given to customers by some stores which is exchangeable in large numbers for various articles.

trading station *n.* esp. *hist.* a place established or visited for trade.

tradition *n.* **1 a** a custom, opinion, or belief handed down to posterity esp. orally or by practice. **b** this process of handing down. **2** artistic, literary, etc., principles based on experience and practice; any one of these (*stage tradition*; *traditions of the Dutch School*). [from Latin *traditio*] □ **traditionary** *adj.* **traditionist** *n.*

traditional *adj.* **1** of, based on, or obtained by tradition. **2** (of jazz) in the style of the early 20th c. □ **traditionally** *adv.*

traditionalism *n.* respect, esp. excessive, for tradition, esp. in religion. □ **traditionalist** *n. & adj.* **traditionalistic** *adj.*

traduce *v.tr.* speak ill of; misrepresent. [from Latin *traducere* 'to disgrace'] □ **traducement** *n.* **traducer** *n.*

traffic ● *n.* **1** (often *attrib.*) **a** vehicles moving in a public highway, esp. of a specified kind, density, etc. (*heavy traffic on the M1*; *traffic accident*). **b** such movement in the air or at sea. **2** (usu. foll. by *in*) trade, esp. illegal. **3 a** the transportation of goods, the coming and going of people or goods by road, air, etc. **b** the persons or goods so transported.

4 dealings or communication between people etc. (*had no traffic with them*). **5** the messages, signals, etc., transmitted through a communications system; the volume of this. ● *v.* (**trafficked**, **trafficking**) **1** *intr.* (usu. foll. by *in*) deal in something, esp. illegally. **2** *tr.* deal in; barter. [from Italian *traffico*] □ **trafficker** *n.* **trafficless** *adj.*

traffic calming *n.* (often *attrib.*) the deliberate slowing of traffic, esp. along residential streets, by building road humps, obstructions, etc. [translation of German *Verkehrsberuhigung*]

traffic island *n.* a paved or grassed area in a road to divert traffic and provide a refuge for pedestrians.

TRADESCANTIA
(*Tradescantia* × *andersoniana* 'Blue and Gold')

traffic jam *n.* a line or lines of traffic at a standstill because of roadworks, an accident, etc.

traffic light *n.* (also **traffic lights**, **traffic signal**) a usu. automatic signal controlling road traffic esp. at junctions by coloured lights.

traffic warden *n. Brit.* an official employed to help control road traffic and esp. parking.

tragacanth *n.* a white or reddish gum from a plant, *Astragalus gummifer*, used in pharmacy, printing on calico, etc., as a vehicle for drugs, dye, etc. [from Greek *tragakantha*, name of a shrub]

tragedian *n.* **1** a writer of tragedies. **2** an actor in tragedy.

tragedienne *n.* an actress in tragedy.

tragedy *n.* (*pl.* **-ies**) **1** a serious accident, crime, or natural catastrophe. **2** a sad event; a calamity. **3 a** a play in verse or prose dealing with tragic events and with an unhappy ending. **b** tragic plays as a genre. [from Greek *tragoidia*]

tragic *adj.* **1** (also **tragical**) sad; calamitous; greatly distressing. **2** of, or in the style of, tragedy. [from Greek *tragikos*] □ **tragically** *adv.*

tragic irony *n.* a device, originally in Greek tragedy, by which words carry a tragic, esp. prophetic, meaning to the audience.

tragicomedy *n.* (*pl.* **-ies**) **1 a** a play etc. having a mixture of comedy and tragedy. **b** plays etc. of this

---

TRADE WIND

The trade winds were so named when transport of cargo relied on strong winds to propel sailing ships. Flowing from the mid-latitudes towards the equator, the trade winds blow reliably from east to west as a result of the Earth rotating faster than the atmosphere at the equator. The converse is true at mid-latitudes, where westerly winds prevail.

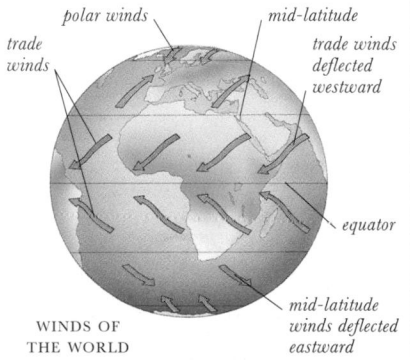

polar winds   mid-latitude
trade winds   trade winds deflected westward
equator
WINDS OF THE WORLD   mid-latitude winds deflected eastward

T

TRAIN

Invented in the early nineteenth century, trains were drawn by steam locomotives until the first use of electricity in the 1880s and diesel power in the 1940s. Many modern trains have diesel-electric locomotives: these transmit power from a diesel engine to the wheels via a generator and electric motors. Electric trains are driven by electric motors on one or more of their coaches and receive electricity from an overhead cable or from electrified rails.

EXPLODED VIEW OF
BRITISH CLASS 73 ELECTRO-DIESEL
LOCOMOTIVE ENGINE (1962)

Labels: brake control reservoirs; main generator case; turbocharger; guard over engine exhaust manifold; engine crankshaft; warning horns; cab cupboard; driver's desk; windscreen wiper; power controller; cab telephone stand; route indicator panel; main wheel spring (two per wheel); buffer; yaw damper; headlight; traction motor field winding; handbrake wheel; electric traction control frame; bogie damper; axle box; sand box; main air reservoir; fuel tank; axle; 73

OTHER TYPES OF TRAIN

STEAM TRAIN
British 'Lady of Lynn' (1908)

DIESEL-ELECTRIC TRAIN
American 'Deltic' (1956)

ELECTRIC TRAIN
French 'TGV' (1983)

---

kind as a genre. **2** an event etc. having tragic and comic elements. [from Latin *tragico-comoedia*] □ **tragicomic** *adj.* **tragicomically** *adv.*

trail ● *n.* **1 a** a track left by a thing, person, etc., moving over a surface (*left a trail of wreckage; a slug's slimy trail*). **b** a track or scent followed in hunting, seeking, etc. **2** a beaten path or track, esp. through a wild region. **3** a part dragging behind a thing or person (*a trail of smoke*). ● *v.* **1** *tr.* & *intr.* draw or be drawn along behind, esp. on the ground. **2** *intr.* (often foll. by *behind*) walk wearily; lag. **3** *tr.* follow the trail of (*trailed him to his home*). **4** *intr.* be losing in a game or other contest. **5** *intr.* (usu. foll. by *away, off*) peter out; tail off. **6** *intr.* **a** (of a plant etc.) grow or hang over a wall, along the ground, etc. **b** (of a garment etc.) hang loosely. **7** *tr.* (often *refl.*) drag (oneself, one's limbs, etc.) along wearily etc. **8** *tr.* advertise (a film, programme, etc.) in advance by showing extracts etc. □ **trail arms** *Mil.* let a rifle etc. hang balanced in one hand and, *Brit.*, parallel to the ground. [from Latin *tragula* 'dragnet']

trail bike *n.* a light motorcycle for use in rough terrain. ▷ MOTORCYCLE

trailblazer *n.* **1** a person who marks a new track through wild country. **2** an innovator. □ **trailblazing** *n.* & *attrib.adj.*

trailer ● *n.* **1** a vehicle towed by another, esp.: **a** the rear section of an articulated lorry. **b** an open cart. **c** a platform for transporting a boat etc. **d** *N. Amer.* a caravan. **2** a series of brief extracts from a film etc., used to advertise it in advance. **3** a person or thing that trails. **4** a trailing plant. ● *v.tr.* **1** transport by trailer. **2** advertise (a film etc.) in advance by trailer.

trailing edge *n.* the rear edge of an aircraft's wing etc.

train ● *v.* **1 a** *tr.* (often foll. by *to* + infin.) teach (a person, animal, oneself, etc.) a specified skill esp. by practice. **b** *intr.* undergo this process (*trained as a teacher*). **2** *tr.* & *intr.* bring or come into a state of physical efficiency by exercise, diet, etc. **3** *tr.* cause (a plant) to grow in a required shape. **4** *tr.* (usu. as **trained** *adj.*) make (the mind, eye, etc.) sharp or discerning as a result of instruction, practice, etc.

5 *tr.* (often foll. by *on*) point or aim (a gun, camera, etc.) at an object etc. **6** *colloq.* **a** *intr.* go by train. **b** *tr.* (foll. by *it* as object) *Brit.* make a journey by train (*trained it to Aberdeen*). ● *n.* **1 ▲** a series of railway carriages or trucks moved by a locomotive or powered carriage. ▷ LOCOMOTIVE. **2** something dragged along behind or forming the back part of a dress, robe, etc. **3** a succession or series of people, things, events, etc. (*train of camels; train of thought*). **4** a body of followers; a retinue (*a train of admirers*). **5** a succession of military vehicles etc., including artillery, supplies, etc. (*baggage train*). **in train** properly arranged or directed. **in a person's train** following behind a person. **in the train of** as a sequel of. [based on Latin *trahere* 'to pull, draw'] □ **trainability** *n.* **trainable** *adj.* **trainless** *adj.*

trainee *n.* (often *attrib.*) a person undergoing training. □ **traineeship** *n.*

trainer *n.* **1** a person who trains. **2** a person who trains horses, athletes, footballers, etc., as a profession. **3** *Brit.* a soft sports or running shoe of leather, canvas, etc.

training *n.* the act or process of teaching or learning a skill, discipline, etc. □ **in training 1** undergoing physical training. **2** physically fit as a result of this. **out of training 1** no longer training. **2** physically unfit.

training college *n.* (in the UK) a college or school for training esp. prospective teachers.

trainload *n.* a number of people, or quantity of goods etc., transported by train.

trainman *n.* (*pl.* **-men**) a railway employee working on trains.

train-shed *n.* a roof supported by posts to shelter railway platforms etc.

train-spotter *n.* *Brit.* a person who collects locomotive numbers as a hobby. □ **train-spotting** *n.*

traipse (also **trapes**) *colloq.* ● *v.intr.* **1** tramp or trudge wearily. **2** (often foll. by *about*) esp. *Brit.* go on errands. ● *n.* a tedious journey on foot. [16th-century coinage]

trait *n.* a distinguishing feature or characteristic, esp. of a person. [French]

traitor *n.* (*fem.* **traitress**) (often foll. by *to*) a person who is treacherous or disloyal, esp. to his or her country. [from Latin *traditor*] □ **traitorous** *adj.* **traitorously** *adv.*

trajectory *n.* (*pl.* **-ies**) the path described by a projectile flying or an object moving under the action of given forces. [originally as *adj.*: from medieval Latin *trajectorius*]

tram *n.* *Brit.* ▼ an electrically powered passenger vehicle running on rails laid in a public road. [from Middle Dutch *trame* 'beam, barrow-shaft']

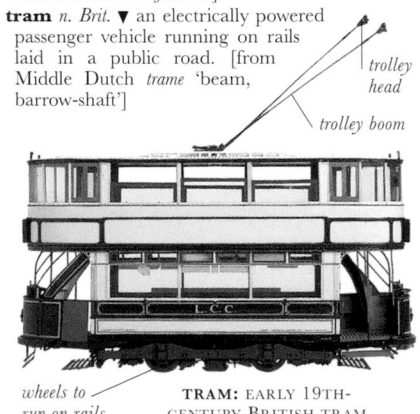

Labels: trolley head; trolley boom; wheels to run on rails

TRAM: EARLY 19TH-CENTURY BRITISH TRAM

tramcar *n.* *Brit.* = TRAM.

tramline *n.* (usu. in *pl.*) *Brit.* **1** a rail for a tramcar. **2** *colloq.* each of a pair of parallel lines, esp. either of two sets of long lines at the sides of a tennis court or at the side or back of a badminton court. **3** an inflexible principle or course of action etc.

trammel ● *n.* **1** (usu. in *pl.*) an impediment to free movement; a hindrance (*the trammels of domesticity*). **2** a triple dragnet for fish. ● *v.tr.* (**trammelled**, **trammelling**; *US* **trammeled**, **trammeling**) confine or hamper with or as if with trammels. [from medieval Latin *tramaculum*]

tramp ● *v.* **1** *intr.* **a** walk heavily and firmly. **b** go on foot, esp. a distance. **2** *tr.* **a** cross on foot, esp. wearily or reluctantly. **b** cover (a distance) in this way. **3** *tr.* (often foll. by *down*) tread on; trample. ● *n.* **1** an itinerant vagrant or beggar. **2** the sound of horses' hoofs, people marching, etc. **3** a journey on foot, esp. a protracted one. **4** esp. *US slang offens.* a promiscuous woman. [Middle English] □ **tramper** *n.* **trampish** *adj.*

trample ● *v.tr.* **1** tread underfoot. **2** press down or crush in this way. ● *n.* the sound or act of trampling. □ **trample on 1** tread heavily on. **2** treat roughly or with contempt; disregard (a person's feelings etc.). [Middle English] □ **trampler** *n.*

trampoline ● *n.* a strong fabric sheet connected by springs to a horizontal frame, used by gymnasts etc. for somersaults, as a springboard, etc. ● *v.intr.* use a trampoline. [from Italian *trampolino*] □ **trampolinist** *n.*

tramway *n. Brit.* **1** rails for a tramcar. **2** a tramcar system.

trance ● *n.* **1 a** a sleeplike or half-conscious state without response to stimuli. **b** a hypnotic or cataleptic state. **2** such a state as entered into by a medium. **3** ecstasy. ● *v.tr. poet.* = ENTRANCE². [based on Old French *transir* 'to depart, fall into a trance'] □ **trance-like** *adj.*

tranche /trahnsh/ *n.* a portion, esp. of income or of a block of shares. [French, literally 'slice']

tranny *n.* (*pl.* **-ies**) esp. *Brit. colloq.* a transistor radio.

tranquil *adj.* calm, serene, unruffled. [from Latin *tranquillus*] □ **tranquillity** *n.* (also **tranquility**). **tranquilly** *adv.*

tranquillize *v.tr.* (also **-ise**; *US* **tranquilize**) make tranquil, esp. by a drug etc.

tranquillizer *n.* (also **-iser**; *US* **tranquilizer**) a drug used to diminish anxiety.

trans- *prefix* **1** across, beyond (*transcontinental*). **2** on or to the other side of (*transatlantic*) (opp. CIS-). **3** through (*transonic*). **4** into another state or place (*transcribe*). **5** surpassing, transcending (*transpersonal*).

transact *v.tr.* perform or carry through (business). [based on Latin *transactus* 'accomplished'] □ **transactor** *n.*

transaction *n.* **1** a piece of esp. commercial business done; a deal. **2** (in *pl.*) published reports of discussions, papers read, etc., at the meetings of a learned society. □ **transactional** *adj.* **transactionally** *adv.*

transalpine *adj.* beyond the Alps.

transatlantic *adj.* **1** beyond the Atlantic, esp.: **a** *Brit.* American. **b** *US* European. **2** crossing the Atlantic.

transceiver *n.* a combined radio transmitter and receiver.

transcend *v.tr.* **1** be beyond the range or grasp of (human experience, belief, etc.). **2** excel; surpass. [from Latin *transcendere*]

transcendent *adj.* **1** excelling, surpassing. **2** transcending human experience. **3** (esp. of the supreme being) existing apart from the material universe. □ **transcendence** *n.* **transcendency** *n.* **transcendently** *adv.*

transcendental *adj.* **1** = TRANSCENDENT. **2 a** presupposed in and necessary to experience; a priori. **b** explaining matter and objective things as products of the subjective mind. **3 a** visionary, abstract. **b** vague, obscure. □ **transcendentally** *adv.*

transcendentalism *n.* **1** transcendental philosophy. **2** exalted or visionary language. □ **transcendentalist** *n.* **transcendentalize** *v.tr.* (also **-ise**).

Transcendental Meditation *n.* a method of detaching oneself from problems, anxiety, etc., by silent meditation and repetition of a mantra.

transcontinental *adj.* (of a railway etc.) extending across a continent. □ **transcontinentally** *adv.*

transcribe *v.tr.* **1** make a copy of, esp. in writing. **2** transliterate. **3** write out (shorthand etc.) in ordinary characters or continuous prose. **4** arrange (music) for a different instrument etc. [from Latin *transcribere*] □ **transcriber** *n.* **transcriptional** *adj.* **transcriptive** *adj.*

TRANSFORMER

A transformer consists of two wire coils wrapped around an iron core. An alternating current passed through the primary coil creates a fluctuating magnetic field in the core, inducing a new voltage in the secondary coil. While step-up transformers have a greater number of coils in the secondary coil and increase voltage, step-down transformers have more coils in the primary coil and reduce voltage.

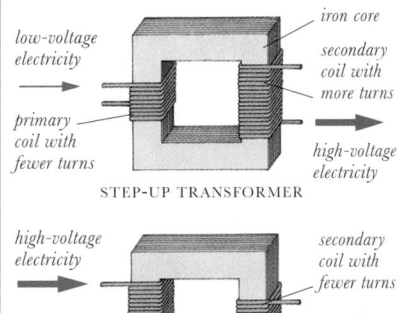

STEP-UP TRANSFORMER

STEP-DOWN TRANSFORMER

transcript *n.* **1** a written or recorded copy. **2** any copy. [from Latin *transcriptum* '(thing) transcribed']

transcription *n.* **1 a** the action or process of transcribing something. **b** an instance of this. **2** a transcript or copy. **3** *Biol.* the process by which a sequence of nucleotides is copied from a DNA template during the synthesis of a molecule of RNA.

transducer *n.* any device for converting a signal from one medium of transmission to another. [based on Latin *transducere* 'to lead across'] □ **transduce** *v.tr.* **transduction** *n.*

transept *n.* **1** either arm of the part of a cross-shaped church at right angles to the nave. ▷ CATHEDRAL. **2** this part as a whole. [based on Latin *septum* 'partition'] □ **transeptal** *adj.*

transexual var. of TRANSSEXUAL.

transfer ● *v.* (**transferred**, **transferring**) **1** *tr.* (often foll. by *to*) **a** convey, remove, or hand over (a thing etc.). **b** make over the possession of (property, a ticket, rights, etc.) to a person. **2** *tr. & intr.* change or move to another group, club, department, etc. **3** *intr.* change from one station, route, etc., to another on a journey. **4** *tr.* convey (a drawing etc.) from one surface to another. **5** *tr.* change (the sense of a word etc.) by extension or metaphor. ● *n.* **1** the act or an instance of transferring or being transferred. **2** a design etc. conveyed or to be conveyed from one surface to another. **3** a football player etc. who is or is to be transferred. **4 a** the conveyance of property, a right, etc. **b** a document effecting this. [from Latin *transferre*] □ **transferee** *n.* **transferor** *n.* esp. *Law.* **transferrer** *n.*

transferable *adj.* capable of being transferred. □ **transferability** *n.*

transferable vote *n.* a vote that can be transferred to another candidate if the first choice is eliminated.

transfer-book *n.* a register of transfers of property, shares, etc.

transference *n.* **1** the act or an instance of transferring; the state of being transferred. **2** *Psychol.* the redirection of childhood emotions to a new object, esp. to a psychoanalyst.

transfer fee *n. Brit.* a fee paid for the transfer of esp. a professional footballer.

transfer list *n. Brit.* a list of footballers available for transfer.

transferral *n.* = TRANSFER *n.* 1.

transfer RNA *n.* RNA conveying an amino acid molecule from the cytoplasm to a ribosome for use in protein synthesis.

transfiguration *n.* **1** a change of form or appearance. **2 a** Christ's appearance in radiant glory to three of his disciples (Matt. 17:2, Mark 9:2–3). **b** (**Transfiguration**) the festival of Christ's transfiguration, 6 Aug.

transfigure *v.tr.* change in form or appearance, esp. so as to elevate or idealize. [from Latin *transfigurare*]

transfix *v.tr.* **1** pierce with a sharp implement or weapon. **2** root (a person) to the spot with horror or astonishment. [based on Latin *transfixus* 'fixed by piercing'] □ **transfixion** *n.*

transform *v.* **1 a** *tr.* make a thorough or dramatic change in the form, character, etc., of. **b** *intr.* (often foll. by *into*, *to*) undergo such a change. **2** *tr. Electr.* change the voltage etc. of (a current). [from Latin *transformare*] □ **transformable** *adj.* **transformation** *n.* **transformative** *adj.*

transformational *adj.* relating to or involving transformation. □ **transformationally** *adv.*

transformer *n.* ◀ an apparatus for reducing or increasing the voltage of an alternating current. ▷ HYDROELECTRIC, NUCLEAR POWER

transfuse *v.tr.* **1** permeate. **2 a** transfer (blood) from one person or animal to another. **b** inject (liquid) into a blood vessel to replace lost fluid. [based on Latin *transfusus* 'poured across'] □ **transfusion** *n.*

transgress *v.tr.* (also *absol.*) go beyond the bounds or limits set by (a commandment, law, etc.); violate; infringe. [based on Latin *transgressus* 'stepped across'] □ **transgression** *n.* **transgressive** *adj.* **transgressor** *n.*

tranship var. of TRANS-SHIP.

transient ● *adj.* of short duration; momentary; passing; impermanent. ● *n.* a temporary visitor, worker, etc. [from Latin *transeunt-* 'going across'] □ **transience** *n.* **transiency** *n.* **transiently** *adv.*

transistor *n.* **1** ▼ a semiconductor device with three connections, capable of amplification in addition to rectification. **2** (in full **transistor radio**) a portable radio with transistors. ▷ RADIO. [blend of TRANSFER and RESISTOR]

TRANSISTOR

A transistor is an electric component used to control electric current and to provide amplification. A small change in the voltage applied between its base and emitter causes a large change in the current flowing from the collector to the emitter. In a radio, transistors amplify small voltages from the aerial to create the large currents needed to operate the loudspeaker.

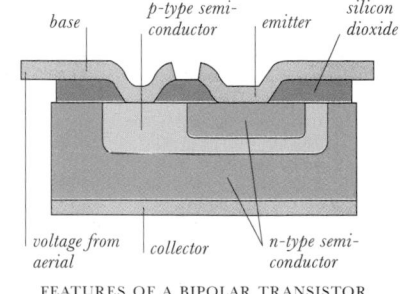

FEATURES OF A BIPOLAR TRANSISTOR

T

transistorize *v.tr.* (also **-ise**) design or equip with, or convert to, transistors rather than valves. □ **transistorization** *n.*

transit ● *n.* **1** the act or process of going, conveying, or being conveyed, esp. over a distance. **2** a passage or route. **3** the apparent passage of a celestial body across the meridian of a place, or across the Sun or a planet. ● *v.* (**transited, transiting**) **1** *tr.* make a transit across. **2** *intr.* make a transit. □ **in transit** while going or being conveyed. [from Latin *transitus*]

transit camp *n.* a camp for the temporary accommodation of soldiers, refugees, etc.

transition *n.* **1** a passing or change from one place, state, condition, etc., to another. **2** (in the arts) a change from one style to another, esp. *Archit.* from Norman to Early English. [from Latin *transitio*] □ **transitional** *adj.* **transitionally** *adv.* **transitionary** *adj.*

transitive *adj. Gram.* (of a verb or sense of a verb) that takes a direct object (whether expressed or implied), e.g. *saw* in *saw the donkey; saw that she was ill.* [from Late Latin *transitivus*] □ **transitively** *adv.* **transitiveness** *n.* **transitivity** *n.*

transit lounge *n.* a lounge at an airport for passengers waiting between flights.

transitory *adj.* not permanent, brief, transient. [from Latin *transitorius*] □ **transitorily** *adv.* **transitoriness** *n.*

transit visa *n.* a visa allowing only passage through a country.

translate *v.* **1** *tr.* (also *absol.*) **a** (often foll. by *into*) express the sense of (a word, speech, etc.) in another language. **b** do this as a profession etc. **2** *intr.* (of a literary work etc.) be translatable, bear translation (*does not translate well*). **3** *tr.* express (an idea, book, etc.) in another, esp. simpler, form. **4** *tr.* interpret (*translated his silence as dissent*). **5** *tr.* move or change, esp. from one person, place, or condition, to another (*was translated by joy*). **6** *intr.* (foll. by *into*) result in; manifest itself as. [based on Latin *translatus* 'carried across'] □ **translatable** *adj.* **translatability** *n.*

translation *n.* **1** the act or an instance of translating. **2** a written or spoken rendering of the meaning of a word, speech, book, etc., in another language. □ **translational** *adj.* **translationally** *adv.*

translator *n.* **1** a person who translates from one language into another. **2** a television relay transmitter. **3** a program that translates from one (esp. programming) language into another.

transliterate *v.tr.* represent (a word etc.) in the closest corresponding letters of a different alphabet or language. [based on Latin *littera* 'letter'] □ **transliteration** *n.* **transliterator** *n.*

translocate *v.tr.* move from one place to another. □ **translocation** *n.*

translucent *adj.* **1** allowing light to pass through diffusely. **2** transparent. [from Latin *translucent-* 'shining through'] □ **translucence** *n.* **translucency** *n.* **translucently** *adv.*

transmigrate *v.intr.* **1** (of the soul) pass, esp. at or after death, into a different body. **2** migrate. □ **transmigration** *n.* **transmigrator** *n.* **transmigratory** *adj.*

transmission *n.* **1** the act or an instance of transmitting; the state of being transmitted. **2** a broadcast radio or television programme. **3** the mechanism by which power is transmitted from an engine to the axle in a motor vehicle.

transmit *v.tr.* (**transmitted, transmitting**) **1 a** pass or hand on; transfer. **b** communicate (ideas, emotions, etc.). **2 a** allow (heat, light, etc.) to pass through; be a medium for. **b** be a medium for (ideas, emotions, etc.). **3** broadcast (a radio or television programme). [from Latin *transmittere*] □ **transmissible** *adj.* **transmissive** *adj.* **transmittable** *adj.* **transmittal** *n.*

transmitter *n.* **1** a person or thing that transmits. **2** a set of equipment used to generate and transmit electromagnetic waves carrying messages, signals, etc., esp. those of radio or television.

transmogrify *v.tr.* (**-ies, -ied**) esp. *joc.* transform, esp. in a magical or surprising manner. [17th-century coinage] □ **transmogrification** *n.*

transmute *v.tr.* **1** change the form, nature, or substance of. **2** subject (base metals) to alchemical transmutation. [from Latin *transmutare*] □ **transmutable** *adj.* **transmutation** *n.* **transmutational** *adj.* **transmuter** *n.*

transnational ● *adj.* extending beyond national boundaries. ● *n.* a transnational company.

transoceanic *adj.* situated beyond or crossing the ocean.

transom /tran-sŏm/ *n.* **1** a horizontal bar of wood or stone across a window or the top of a door. ▷ WINDOW. **2** *US* = TRANSOM WINDOW. [from Old French *traversin*] □ **transomed** *adj.*

transom window *n.* **1** a window divided by a transom. ▷ WINDOW. **2** a fanlight.

transonic *adj.* (also **trans-sonic**) relating to speeds close to that of sound.

transpacific *adj.* **1** beyond the Pacific. **2** crossing the Pacific.

transparence *n.* = TRANSPARENCY 1.

transparency *n.* (*pl.* **-ies**) **1** the condition of being transparent. **2** *Photog.* a positive transparent photograph on glass or in a frame to be viewed using a slide projector etc. **3** a picture, inscription, etc., made visible by a light behind it. [from medieval Latin *transparentia*]

transparent *adj.* **1** allowing light to pass through so that bodies can be distinctly seen. **2 a** (of a pretext etc.) easily seen through. **b** (of a motive, quality, etc.) easily discerned; evident; obvious. **3** (of a person etc.) easily understood. [from Latin *transparent-* 'appearing through'] □ **transparently** *adv.*

transpersonal *adj.* **1** *Literature* transcending the personal. **2** *Psychol.* (esp. in psychotherapy) of or relating to the exploration of transcendental states of consciousness beyond personal identity.

transpire *v.* **1** *intr.* **a** (of a secret or something unknown) leak out; come to be known. **b** (prec. by *it* as subject) turn out; prove to be the case. **2** *intr. disp.* occur; happen (*nobody knows what transpired between them*). **3** *tr. & intr.* emit (vapour, sweat, etc.), or be emitted, through the skin or lungs; perspire. **4** *intr.* ▼ (of a plant or leaf) release water vapour.

TRANSPIRE

Water vapour transpires (evaporates) constantly through pores (stomata) in the surface of a plant's leaves. Fresh supplies of moisture enter the plant's roots from the soil. Root pressure forces the water up the stem, where capillary action draws it further in a continuous 'transpiration stream'.

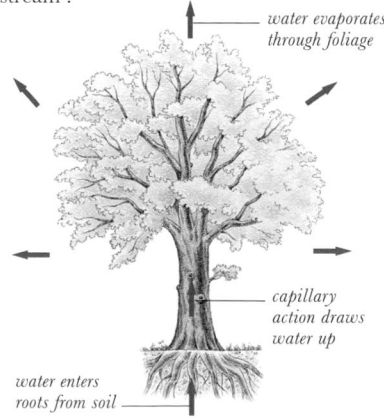

water evaporates through foliage

capillary action draws water up

water enters roots from soil

TRANSPIRATION STREAM WITHIN A TREE

[from medieval Latin *transpirare*] □ **transpirable** *adj.* **transpiration** *n.*

■ **Usage** The use of *transpire* in sense 2 is considered incorrect by some people and should be restricted to informal contexts.

transplant ● *v.tr.* **1 a** plant in another place (*transplanted the daffodils*). **b** move to another place (*whole nations were transplanted*). **2** *Surgery* transfer (living tissue or an organ) and implant in another part of the body or in another body. ● *n.* **1** *Surgery* **a** the transplanting of an organ or tissue. **b** such an organ etc. **2** a thing, esp. a plant, which is transplanted. □ **transplantable** *adj.* **transplantation** *n.* **transplanter** *n.*

transponder *n.* a device for receiving a radio signal and automatically transmitting a different signal. ▷ RADAR. [from blend of TRANSMIT and RESPOND]

transpontine *adj.* **1** on the other side of a bridge. **2** on or from the other side of the ocean (esp. in relation to N. America).

transport ● **1** take or carry (a person, goods, etc.) from one place to another. **2** *hist.* take (a criminal) to a penal colony. **3** (as **transported** *adj.*) (usu. foll. by *with*) affected with strong emotion. ● *n.* **1 a** a system of conveying people, goods, etc., from place to place. **b** esp. *Brit.* the means of this. **2** a ship, aircraft, etc. used to carry soldiers, stores, etc. **3** (esp. in *pl.*) vehement emotion (*transports of joy*). [from Latin *transportare*] □ **transportable** *adj.* **transportability** *n.*

transportation *n.* **1** the act of conveying or the process of being conveyed. **2 a** a system of conveying. **b** esp. *N. Amer.* the means of this. **3** *hist.* removal to a penal colony.

transport café *n. Brit.* a roadside café for drivers.

transporter *n.* **1** a person or device that transports. **2** a vehicle used to transport other vehicles or large pieces of machinery etc. by road.

transporter bridge *n.* a bridge carrying vehicles etc. across water on a suspended moving platform.

transpose *v.tr.* **1 a** cause (two or more things) to change places. **b** change the position of (a thing) in a series. **2** change the order or position of (words or a word) in a sentence. **3** (also *absol.*; often followed by *up, down*) *Mus.* write or play in a different key from the original. **4** *Algebra* transfer (a term) with a changed sign to the other side of an equation. [from Old French *transposer*] □ **transposable** *adj.* **transposer** *n.*

transposition *n.* the act or an instance of transposing; the state of being transposed.

transputer *n.* a microprocessor with integral memory designed for parallel processing. [blend of TRANSISTOR and COMPUTER]

transsexual (also **transexual**) ● *adj.* having the physical characteristics of one sex and the supposed psychological characteristics of the other. ● *n.* **1** a transsexual person. **2** a person whose sex has been changed by surgery. □ **transsexualism** *n.*

trans-ship *v.tr.* (also **tranship**) *intr.* (**-shipped, -shipping**) transfer from one ship or form of transport to another. □ **trans-shipment** *n.*

trans-sonic var. of TRANSONIC.

transubstantiation *n. Theol. & RC Ch.* the conversion of the Eucharistic elements wholly into the body and blood of Christ, only the appearance of bread and wine still remaining.

transuranic *adj. Chem.* (of an element) having a higher atomic number than uranium.

transverse *adj.* situated, arranged, or acting in a crosswise direction. [from Latin *transversus* 'turned across'] □ **transversely** *adv.*

transverse flute see FLUTE *n.* 1.

transvestism *n.* the practice of wearing the clothes of the opposite sex, esp. as a sexual stimulus. [based on Latin *vestire* 'to clothe']

transvestite *n.* a person, esp. a man, given to transvestism.

trap[1] ● *n.* **1 a** an enclosure or device, for catching animals. **b** a device with bait for killing vermin, esp. = MOUSETRAP 1. **2** a trick betraying a person into speech or an act (*is this question a trap?*). **3** an arrangement to catch an unsuspecting person. **4** a device for hurling an object such as a clay pigeon into the air to be shot at. **5** a compartment from which a greyhound is released at the start of a race. **6 a** a curve in a downpipe etc. that fills with liquid and forms a seal against the upward passage of gases. **b** a device for preventing the passage of steam etc. **7** a two-wheeled carriage (*a pony and trap*). **8** = TRAPDOOR. **9** *slang* the mouth (esp. *shut one's trap*). **10** (esp. in *pl.*) *slang* a percussion instrument. ● *v.tr.* (**trapped**, **trapping**) **1** catch (an animal) in a trap. **2** catch or catch out (a person) by means of a trick, plan, etc. **3** stop and retain in or as in a trap. [Old English] □ **traplike** *adj.*

trap[2] *v.tr.* (**trapped**, **trapping**) **1** provide with trappings. **2** adorn. [based on Old French *drap* 'drape']

trap[3] *n.* (in full **trap-rock**) any dark-coloured igneous rock, fine-grained and columnar in structure. [from Swedish *trappa* 'stair', from the often stairlike appearance of its outcroppings]

trapdoor *n.* a door or hatch in a floor, ceiling, or roof, usu. made flush with the surface.

trapes var. of TRAIPSE.

trapeze *n.* a crossbar or set of crossbars suspended by ropes and used as a swing for acrobatics etc. [from Late Latin *trapezium*]

trapezium *n.* (*pl.* **trapezia** or **trapeziums**) **1** *Brit.* ◄ a quadrilateral with only one pair of sides parallel. **2** *N. Amer.* = TRAPEZOID 1. [from Greek *trapezion*]

TRAPEZIUM

trapezius *n.* (*pl.* **trapezii** /-zi-I/) *Anat.* either of a pair of large triangular muscles extending over the back of the neck and shoulders. ▷ MUSCULATURE

trapezoid *n.* **1** *Brit.* ► a quadrilateral with no two sides parallel. **2** *N. Amer.* = TRAPEZIUM 1. [from Greek *trapezoeidēs*] □ **trapezoidal** *adj.*

TRAPEZOID

trapper *n.* a person who traps wild animals, esp. to obtain furs.

trappings *n.pl.* **1** ornamental accessories (*the trappings of office*). **2** the harness of a horse esp. when ornamental. [Middle English, related to TRAP[2]]

Trappist ● *n.* a member of a branch of the Cistercian order of monks founded in 1664 at La Trappe in Normandy and noted for an austere rule including a vow of silence. ● *adj.* of or relating to this order. [from French *trappiste*]

trap-rock see TRAP[3].

traps *n.pl. Brit. colloq.* personal belongings; baggage.

trap-shooting *n.* the sport of shooting at objects released from a trap.

trash ● *n.* **1** esp. *US* rubbish, refuse. **2** things of poor workmanship, quality, or material; worthless stuff. **3** esp. *US* nonsense (*talk trash*). **4** a worthless person or persons. ● *v.tr.* **1** esp. *N. Amer. colloq.* wreck. **2** esp. *US colloq.* expose the worthless nature of; disparage. [Middle English]

trash can *n. N. Amer.* a dustbin.

trashy *adj.* (**trashier**, **trashiest**) worthless; poorly made. □ **trashily** *adv.* **trashiness** *n.*

trattoria /trat-ŏ-ree-ă/ *n.* an Italian restaurant. [Italian]

trauma *n.* (*pl.* **traumas**) **1 a** *Psychol.* emotional shock following a stressful event, sometimes leading to longterm neurosis. **b** a distressing or emotionally disturbing experience etc. **2** any physical wound or injury. **3** physical shock following this, characterized by a drop in body temperature, mental confusion, etc. [from Greek *trauma traumatos* 'wound'] □ **traumatize** *v.tr.* (also **-ise**). **traumatization** *n.*

traumatic *adj.* **1** of or causing trauma. **2** *colloq.* distressing (*a traumatic experience*). **3** of or for wounds. □ **traumatically** *adv.*

travail *literary* ● *n.* **1** painful or laborious effort. **2** the pangs of childbirth. ● *v.intr.* undergo a painful effort, esp. in childbirth. [from Old French]

travel ● *v.intr. & tr.* (**travelled**, **travelling**; *US* usu. **traveled**, **traveling**) **1** *intr.* go from one place to another; make a journey, esp. a long one or abroad. **2** *tr.* **a** journey along or through (a country). **b** cover (a distance) in travelling. **3** *intr. colloq.* withstand a long journey (*wines that do not travel*). **4** *intr.* go from place to place as a salesman. **5** *intr.* move or proceed in a specified manner or at a specified rate (*light travels faster than sound*). **6** *intr. colloq.* move quickly. **7** *intr.* pass esp. in a deliberate manner from point to point (*the photographer's eye travelled over the scene*). ● *n.* **1** the act of travelling, esp. in foreign countries. **2** (often in *pl.*) a spell of this (*have returned from their travels*). [Middle English, originally in sense 'travail']

travel agency *n.* (also **travel bureau**) an agency that makes the necessary arrangements for travellers. □ **travel agent** *n.*

travelled *adj.* experienced in travelling (also in comb.: *much-travelled*).

traveller *n.* (*US* **traveler**) **1** a person who travels or is travelling. **2** *Brit.* = COMMERCIAL TRAVELLER. **3** a gypsy. **4** (also **New Age traveller**) a person who embraces New Age values and leads an itinerant and unconventional lifestyle. **5** *Austral.* an itinerant workman; a swagman.

traveller's cheque *n.* a cheque for a fixed amount that may be cashed on signature, usu. internationally.

traveller's joy *n.* ► a wild clematis, *Clematis vitalba.*

travelling crane *n.* a crane able to move on rails, esp. along an overhead support.

travelling salesman *n.* a male commercial traveller.

travelogue *n.* a film or illustrated lecture about travel.

travel-sick *adj.* suffering from nausea caused by motion in travelling. □ **travel-sickness** *n.*

traverse ● *v.tr.* **1** travel or lie across (*traversed the country; a pit traversed by a beam*). **2** consider or discuss the whole extent of (a subject). ● *n.* **1** a sideways movement. **2** an act of traversing. **3** a thing, esp. a part of a structure, that crosses another. **4** the sideways movement of a part in a machine. **5 a** a sideways motion across a rock face from one practicable line of ascent or descent to another. **b** a place where this is necessary. [from Late Latin *traversare*] □ **traversable** *adj.* **traversal** *n.* **traverser** *n.*

travesty ● *n.* (*pl.* **-ies**) a grotesque misrepresentation or imitation (*a travesty of justice*). ● *v.tr.* (**-ies**, **-ied**) make or be a travesty of. [originally as adj.: from French *travesti* 'disguised, dressed up']

trawl ● *v.* **1** *intr.* fish with a trawl or seine. **2** *tr.* **a** catch by trawling. **b** search thoroughly through (*trawled the schools for new trainees*). ● *n.* **1** an act of trawling. **2** (in full **trawl net**) ▼ a large wide-mouthed fishing net dragged by a boat along the bottom. **3** (in full **trawl line**) *US* a long sea-fishing line buoyed and supporting short lines with baited hooks.

TRAVELLER'S JOY
(*Clematis vitalba*)

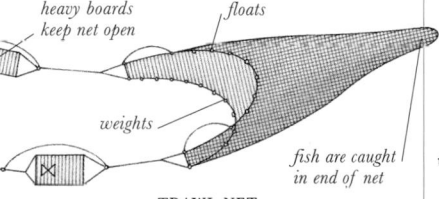

heavy boards keep net open   *floats*

weights

fish are caught in end of net

TRAWL NET

trawler *n.* **1** a boat used for trawling. **2** a person who trawls.

trawlerman *n.* (*pl.* **-men**) a man who works on a trawler.

tray *n.* **1** a flat shallow vessel usu. with a raised rim for carrying dishes etc. or containing small articles, papers, etc. **2** a shallow lidless box forming a compartment of a trunk. [Old English] □ **trayful** *n.* (*pl.* **-fuls**)

treacherous *adj.* **1** guilty of or involving treachery. **2** (of the weather, ice, the memory, etc.) not to be relied on; likely to fail or give way. [from Old French *trecherous*] □ **treacherously** *adv.* **treacherousness** *n.*

treachery *n.* (*pl.* **-ies**) **1** violation of faith or trust; betrayal. **2** an instance of this.

treacle *n.* **1** esp. *Brit.* **a** a syrup produced in refining sugar. **b** molasses. **2** cloying sentimentality or flattery. [from Greek *thēriakē* 'antidote against venom'] □ **treacly** *adj.*

tread ● *v.* (*past* **trod**; *past part.* **trodden** or **trod**) **1** *intr.* set down one's foot; walk or step (*do not tread on the grass; trod on a snail*). **b** (of the foot) be set down. **2** *tr.* **a** walk on. **b** (often foll. by *down*) press or crush with the feet. **3** *tr.* perform (steps etc.) by walking (*trod a few paces*). ▷ TYRE. **4** *tr.* make (a hole etc.) by treading. **5** *intr.* (foll. by *on*) suppress; subdue mercilessly. **6** *tr.* make a track with (dirt etc.) from the feet. **7** *tr.* press down into the ground with the feet (*trod dirt into the carpet*). **8** *tr.* (also *absol.*) (of a male bird) copulate with (a hen). ● *n.* **1** a manner or sound of walking (*recognized the heavy tread*). **2** (in full **tread-board**) the top surface of a step or stair. **3** the thick moulded part of a vehicle tyre for gripping the road. ▷ TYRE. **4** the part of a wheel that touches the ground or rail. **5** the part of the sole of a shoe that rests on the ground. **6** (of a male bird) copulation. □ **tread the boards** (or **stage**) be an actor. **tread on air** see AIR. **tread on a person's toes** offend a person or encroach on a person's privileges etc. **tread out 1** stamp out (a fire etc.). **2** press out (wine or grain) with the feet. **tread water** maintain an upright position in the water by moving the feet and the hands. [Old English]

treadle ● *n.* a lever worked by the foot and imparting motion to a machine. ● *v.intr.* work a treadle. [Old English *tredel* 'stair']

treadmill *n.* **1** a device for producing motion by the weight of persons or animals stepping on steps on the inner surface of a revolving upright wheel. **2** a similar device used for exercise. **3** monotonous routine work.

treadwheel *n.* = TREADMILL 1.

treason *n.* **1** (in full **high treason**: see note below) violation by a subject of allegiance to the sovereign or to the State, esp. by attempting to kill or overthrow the sovereign or to overthrow the government. **2** (in full **petty treason**) *hist.* murder of one's master or husband, regarded as a form of treason. [from Latin *traditio* 'handing over'] □ **treasonous** *adj.*

■ **Usage** The crime of *petty treason* was abolished in 1828; this is why the term *high treason*, originally distinguished from *petty treason*, now has the same meaning as *treason*.

treasonable *adj.* involving or guilty of treason. □ **treasonably** *adv.*

treasure ● *n.* **1 a** a precious metals or gems. **b** a hoard of these. **c** accumulated wealth. **2** a thing valued for its rarity, workmanship, associations, etc. (*art treasures*). **3** *colloq.* a much loved or highly valued person. ● *v.tr.* **1** (often foll. by *up*) store up as valuable. **2** value (esp. a long-kept possession) highly. [from Greek *thēsauros*]

treasure hunt *n.* **1** a search for treasure. **2** a game in which players seek a hidden object from a series of clues.

T

TREE

Trees are adapted for growth in a wide range of conditions. Conifers typically occupy habitats that have cold winters, although a few grow in the Tropics. Their slender profile minimizes snow damage, while their small evergreen leaves withstand drying winds. Broadleaves generally grow in regions with warmer climates and regular rainfall. Temperate species are often deciduous, although in the Tropics many are evergreen. Representatives of some major tree families are shown here.

EXAMPLES OF CONIFEROUS TREES

CUPRESSACEAE
sawara cypress
(*Chamaecyparis pisifera*)

PINACEAE
bishop pine
(*Pinus muricata*)

TAXODIACEAE
Japanese cedar
(*Cryptomeria japonica*)

EXAMPLES OF BROADLEAVED TREES

ACERACEAE
sycamore
(*Acer pseudoplatanus*)

BETULACEAE
grey birch
(*Betula populifolia*)

BIGNONIACEAE
western catalpa
(*Catalpa speciosa*)

ERICACEAE
madroña
(*Arbutus menziesii*)

FAGACEAE
black oak
(*Quercus velutina*)

LAURACEAE
California laurel
(*Umbellularia californica*)

LEGUMINOSAE
black locust
(*Robinia pseudoacacia*)

MAGNOLIACEAE
magnolia
(*Magnolia kobus*)

MELIACEAE
toona
(*Toona sinensis*)

MYRTACEAE
mountain gum
(*Eucalyptus dalrympleana*)

OLEACEAE
white ash
(*Fraxinus americana*)

PALMAE
Chusan palm
(*Trachycarpus fortunei*)

PLATANACEAE
American sycamore
(*Platanus occidentalis*)

ROSACEAE
spring cherry
(*Prunus* ✕ *subhirtella*)

RUTACEAE
hop tree
(*Ptelea trifoliata*)

SALICACEAE
Chinese weeping willow
(*Salix babylonica*)

STYRACACEAE
snowdrop tree
(*Halesia carolina*)

THEACEAE
silky camellia
(*Stewartia malacodendron*)

TILIACEAE
silver lime
(*Tilia tomentosa*)

ULMACEAE
hackberry
(*Celtis occidentalis*)

T

treasurer *n.* **1** a person appointed to administer the funds of a society or municipality etc. **2** an officer authorized to receive and disburse public revenues.

treasure trove *n.* **1** *Law* treasure of unknown ownership which is found hidden in the ground etc. and is declared the property of the Crown. **2** a collection of valuable or delightful things.

treasury *n.* (*pl.* **-ies**) **1** a place or building where treasure is stored. **2** the funds or revenue of a state, institution, or society. **3** (**Treasury**) **a** the department managing the public revenue of a country. **b** the offices and officers of this. **c** the place where the public revenues are kept. [from Old French *tresorie*]

Treasury bench *n.* (in the UK) the front bench in the House of Commons occupied by the Prime Minister, Chancellor of the Exchequer, etc.

treasury bill *n.* a bill of exchange issued by the government to raise money for temporary needs.

treasury note *n. US & hist.* a note issued by the Treasury for use as currency.

treat ● *v.* **1** *tr.* act or behave towards or deal with (a person or thing) in a certain way (*treated me kindly; treat it as a joke*). **2** *tr.* deal with or apply a process to (*treat it with acid*). **3** *tr.* apply medical care or attention to. **4** *tr.* present or deal with (a subject) in literature or art. **5** *tr.* provide with food or drink or entertainment at one's own expense (*treated us to dinner*). **6** *intr.* (often foll. by *with*) negotiate terms (with a person). **7** *intr.* (often foll. by *of*) give a spoken or written exposition. ● *n.* **1** an event or circumstance (esp. when unexpected or unusual) that gives great pleasure. **2** a meal, entertainment, etc., provided by one person for the enjoyment of another or others. **3** (prec. by *a*) *Brit.* extremely good or well (*they looked a treat; has come on a treat*). [from Latin *tractare* 'to handle'] □ **treatable** *adj.* **treating** *n.*

treatise /**tree**-tis/ *n.* a written work dealing formally and systematically with a subject. [based on Old French *traitier* 'to treat']

treatment *n.* **1** a process or manner of behaving towards or dealing with a person or thing (*received rough treatment*). **2** the application of medical care or attention to a patient. **3** a manner of treating a subject in literature or art. **4** subjection to the action of a chemical, physical, or biological agent. **5** (prec. by *the*) *colloq.* the customary way of dealing with a person, situation, etc. (*got the full treatment*).

treaty *n.* (*pl.* **-ies**) **1** a formally concluded and ratified agreement between states. **2** an agreement between individuals or parties, esp. for the purchase of property. [from Latin *tractatum* 'a tractate']

treble ● *adj.* **1 a** threefold. **b** triple. **c** three times as much or many (*treble the amount*). **2** high-pitched. **3** *Mus.* = SOPRANO *adj.* (esp. of an instrument or with reference to a boy's voice). ● *n.* **1** a treble quantity or thing. **2** *Darts* a hit on the narrow ring enclosed by the two middle circles of a dartboard, scoring treble. **3 a** *Mus.* = SOPRANO *n.* (esp. a boy's voice or part, or an instrument). **b** a high-pitched voice. **4** the high-frequency output of a radio, record player, etc. **5** *Brit.* a system of betting in which the winnings and stake from the first bet are transferred to a second and then (if successful) to a third. **6** *Brit. Sport* three victories or championships in the same season, event, etc. ● *v. tr. & intr.* make or become three times as much or many; increase threefold; multiply by three. [from Latin *triplus* 'triple'] □ **trebly** *adv.* (in sense 1 of *adj.*).

treble chance *n. Brit.* a form of football pool in which different numbers of points are awarded for a draw, an away win, and a home win.

treble clef *n.* a clef placing G above middle C on the second lowest line of the staff. ▷ NOTATION

tree ● *n.* **1 a** ◀ a perennial plant with a woody self-supporting main stem or trunk when mature and usu. unbranched for some distance above the ground. **b** any similar plant having a tall erect usu. single stem, e.g. palm tree. **2** a piece or frame of wood etc. for various purposes (*shoe-tree*). **3** (in full **tree diagram**) *Math.* a diagram with a structure of branching connecting lines. **4** = FAMILY TREE. ● *v.tr.* (**trees**, **treed**) **1** force to take refuge in a tree. **2** esp. *US* put into a difficult position. **3** stretch on a shoe-tree. □ **grow on trees** (usu. with *neg.*) be plentiful. **up a tree** esp. *N. Amer.* cornered; nonplussed. [Old English] □ **treeless** *adj.* **treelessness** *n.* **treelike** *adj.*

treecreeper *n.* ◀ any small creeping bird, esp. of the family Certhiidae, feeding on insects in the bark of trees.

TREECREEPER: COMMON TREECREEPER (*Certhia familiaris*)

tree diagram see TREE *n.* 3.

tree fern *n.* ▶ a large fern with an upright trunklike stem.

tree house *n.* a structure in a tree for children to play in.

tree line *n.* = TIMBERLINE.

tree of knowledge *n.* **1** *Bibl.* the tree in the Garden of Eden bearing the forbidden fruit. **2** the branches of knowledge as a whole.

tree ring *n.* a ring in a cross-section of a tree, from one year's growth. ▷ DENDROCHRONOLOGY

tree surgeon *n.* a person who treats decayed trees in order to preserve them. □ **tree surgery** *n.*

tree tomato *n.* a S. American shrub, *Cyphomandra betacea*, with egg-shaped red fruit.

treetop *n.* the topmost part of a tree.

tree trunk *n.* the trunk of a tree.

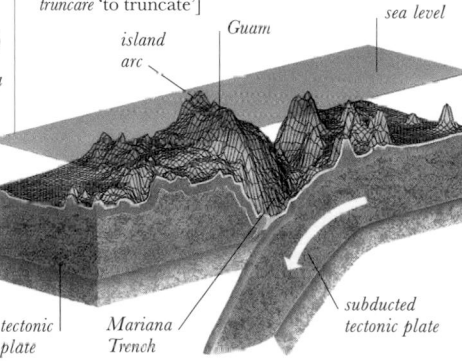
TREE FERN (*Dicksonia antarctica*)

trefoil ● *n.* **1** any leguminous plant of the genus *Trifolium*, with leaves of three leaflets, esp. clover. **2** any plant with similar leaves. **3** a three-lobed ornamentation, esp. in tracery windows. ▷ ARCH. **4** a thing arranged in or with three lobes. ● *adj.* of or concerning a three-lobed plant, window tracery, etc. [from Latin *trifolium*] □ **trefoiled** *adj.* (also in *comb.*).

trek ● *v.intr.* (**trekked**, **trekking**) **1** travel or make one's way arduously (*trekking through the forest*). **2** esp. *S.Afr. hist.* migrate or journey with one's belongings by ox-wagon. **3** *S.Afr.* (of an ox) draw a vehicle or pull a load. ● *n.* **1 a** a journey or walk made by trekking (*it was a trek to the nearest launderette*). **b** each stage of such a journey. **2** an organized migration of a body of persons. [Afrikaans] □ **trekker** *n.*

trellis ● *n.* (in full **trellis-work**) ◀ a lattice of light wooden or metal bars used esp. as a support for fruit trees or creepers. ● *v.tr.* (**trellised**, **trellising**) **1** provide with a trellis. **2** support (a vine etc.) with a trellis. [from Latin *trilix* 'three-ply']

trematode *n.* any parasitic flatworm of the class Trematoda. [from Greek *trēmatōdēs* 'perforated']

tremble ● *v.intr.* **1** shake involuntarily from fear, excitement, weakness, etc. **2** be in a state of extreme apprehension (*trembled at the very thought of it*). **3** quiver (*leaves trembled in the breeze*). ● *n.* a trembling state or movement; a quiver

TRELLIS-WORK SUPPORTING A CLIMBER

(*couldn't speak without a tremble*). □ **all of a tremble** *colloq.* **1** trembling all over. **2** extremely agitated. [from medieval Latin *tremulare*] □ **tremblingly** *adv.*

trembler *n. Brit.* an automatic vibrator for making and breaking an electrical circuit.

trembly *adj.* (**tremblier**, **trembliest**) *colloq.* trembling; agitated.

tremendous *adj.* **1** awe-inspiring, fearful, overpowering. **2** *colloq.* remarkable, considerable, excellent (*a tremendous explosion; gave a tremendous performance*). [from Latin *tremendus* 'to be trembled at'] □ **tremendously** *adv.*

tremolo *n.* (*pl.* **tremolos**) *Mus.* **1** a tremulous effect produced on musical instruments or in singing: **a** by rapid reiteration of a note. **b** by rapid alternation between two notes. **c** by rapid repeated slight variation in the pitch of a note. Cf. VIBRATO. **2 a** a device in an organ producing a tremolo. **b** (in full **tremolo arm**) a lever on an electric guitar, used to produce a tremolo. [Italian]

tremor ● *n.* **1** a shaking or quivering. **2** a thrill (of fear or exultation etc.). **3** (in full **earth tremor**) a slight earthquake. ● *v.intr.* undergo a tremor or tremors. [from Latin *tremere* 'tremble']

tremulous *adj.* **1** trembling or quivering (*in a tremulous voice*). **2** drawn by a tremulous hand. **3** timid or vacillating. [based on Latin *tremere* 'to tremble'] □ **tremulously** *adv.* **tremulousness** *n.*

trench ● *n.* **1** a long narrow usu. deep ditch. **2** *Mil.* **a** this dug by troops to stand in and be sheltered from enemy fire. **b** (in *pl.*) a defensive system of these. **3** ▼ a long narrow deep depression in the ocean bed. ▷ SEABED, SUBDUCTION. ● *v.tr.* **1** dig a trench or trenches in (the ground). **2** turn over the earth of (a field, garden, etc.) by digging a succession of adjoining ditches. [based on Latin *truncare* 'to truncate']

island arc   *Guam*   *sea level*

tectonic plate   *Mariana Trench*   *subducted tectonic plate*

TRENCH: FORMATION OF THE MARIANA TRENCH IN THE PACIFIC OCEAN

trenchant *adj.* (of a style or language etc.) incisive, terse, vigorous. [from Old French] □ **trenchancy** *n.* **trenchantly** *adv.*

trench coat *n.* **1** a soldier's lined or padded waterproof coat. **2** ▶ a loose belted raincoat.

trencher *n. hist.* **1** a wooden or earthenware platter for serving food. **2** (in full **trencher cap**) a stiff square academic cap; a mortarboard. [from Old French *trencheoir*]

trencherman *n.* (*pl.* **-men**) a person who eats well, or in a specified manner (*a good trencherman*).

TRENCH COAT

T

trench warfare *n.* hostilities carried on from trenches.

trend ● *n.* a general direction and tendency (esp. of events, fashion, or opinion). ● *v.intr.* **1** bend or turn away in a specified direction. **2** have a general tendency. [Old English *trendan* 'to revolve, rotate']

trendsetter *n.* a person who leads the way in fashion etc. □ **trendsetting** *adj.*

trendy *colloq.* ● *adj.* (**trendier**, **trendiest**) often *derog.* fashionable; following fashionable trends. ● *n.* (*pl.* **-ies**) a fashionable person. □ **trendily** *adv.* **trendiness** *n.*

trepan /tri-pan/ ● *n.* a cylindrical saw formerly used by surgeons for removing part of the bone of the skull. ● *v.tr.* (**trepanned**, **trepanning**) perforate (the skull) with a trepan. [from Greek *trupanon*] □ **trepanation** *n.* **trepanning** *n.*

trepidation *n.* **1** a feeling of fear or alarm; perturbation of the mind. **2** tremulous agitation. [based on Latin *trepidus* 'alarmed']

trespass ● *v.intr.* **1** (usu. foll. by *on*, *upon*) make an unlawful or unwarrantable intrusion (esp. on land or property). **2** (foll. by *on*) make unwarrantable claims (*shall not trespass on your hospitality*). **3** (foll. by *against*) *literary* or *archaic* offend. ● *n.* **1** *Law* a voluntary wrongful act against the person or property of another, esp. unlawful entry to a person's land or property. **2** *archaic* a sin or offence. [from Old French *trespasser* 'to pass over, trespass'] □ **trespasser** *n.*

tress *n.* **1** a long lock of human (esp. female) hair. **2** (in *pl.*) a woman's or girl's head of hair. [from Old French *tresse*] □ **tressed** *adj.* (also in *comb.*).

trestle *n.* **1** a supporting structure for a table etc., consisting of two frames fixed at an angle or hinged or of a bar supported by two divergent pairs of legs. **2** (in full **trestle-table**) a table consisting of a board or boards laid on trestles or other supports. **3** (in full **trestle-work**) an open braced framework to support a bridge etc. [from Latin *transtrum* 'beam']

trevally /tri-val-i/ *n.* (*pl.* **-ies**) ▼ any sporting fish of the genus *Caranx* or of a related genus found in the Indo-Pacific and used as food.

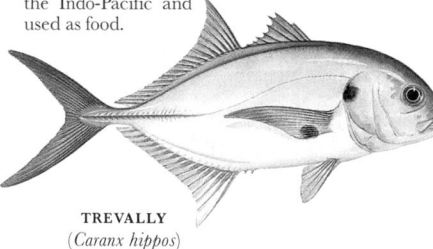

TREVALLY
(*Caranx hippos*)

trews *n.pl.* esp. *Brit.* trousers, esp. close-fitting tartan trousers. [from Gaelic *triubhas* (sing.)]

trey /tray/ *n.* (*pl.* **treys**) the three on dice or cards. [from Latin *tres* 'three']

tri- *comb. form* forming nouns and adjectives meaning: **1** three or three times. **2** *Chem.* containing three atoms or groups of a specified kind (*triacetate*). [Latin & Greek]

triacetate /try-**ass**-i-tayt/ *n.* a cellulose derivative containing three acetate groups, esp. as a base for man-made fibres.

triad *n.* **1** a group of three (esp. notes in a chord). **2** the number three. **3 a** any of various Chinese secret societies in various countries, usu. involved in criminal activities. **b** a member of such a society. [from Greek *trias -ados*] □ **triadic** *adj.*

triage /try-ij/ *n.* **1** the act of sorting according to quality. **2** the assignment of degrees of urgency to decide the order of treatment of wounds, illnesses, etc. [French]

trial ● *n.* **1** a judicial examination and determination of issues between parties by a judge with or without a jury (*stood trial for murder*). **2 a** a process or mode of testing qualities. **b** experimental treatment. **c** a test (*will give you a trial*). **3** a trying thing or experience or person (*the trials of old age*). **4** a sports match to test the ability of players eligible for selection to a team. **5** a test of individual ability on a motorcycle over rough ground or on a road. **6** any of various contests involving performance by horses, dogs, or other animals. ● *v.tr. & intr.* (**trialled**, **trialling**; *US* **trialed**, **trialing**) subject to or undergo a test to assess performance. □ **on trial 1** being tried in a court of law. **2** being tested; to be chosen or retained only if suitable. [from Anglo-French]

trialist *n.* (also *Brit.* **triallist**) **1** a person who takes part in a sports trial, motorcycle trial, etc. **2** a person involved in a judicial trial.

trial run *n.* a preliminary test of a vehicle, vessel, machine, etc.

triangle *n.* **1** ▼ a plane figure with three sides and angles. ▷ HYPOTENUSE. **2** any three things not in a straight line, with imaginary lines joining them. **3** an implement of this shape. **4** a musical instrument consisting of a steel rod bent into a triangle and sounded by striking it with a small steel rod. ▷ ORCHESTRA, PERCUSSION. **5** a situation, esp. an emotional relationship, involving three people. **6** a right-angled triangle of wood etc. as a drawing implement. [from Old French]

acute angle (less than 90°)

TRIANGLE: OBTUSE-ANGLED TRIANGLE

acute angle

obtuse angle (more than 90°)

triangular *adj.* **1** triangle-shaped, three-cornered. **2** between three persons or parties. **3** (of a pyramid) having a three-sided base. [from Late Latin *triangularis*] □ **triangularity** *n.* **triangularly** *adv.*

triangulate *v.tr.* **1** divide (an area) into triangles for surveying purposes. **2 a** measure and map (an area) by the use of triangles with a known base length and base angles. **b** determine (a height, distance, etc.) in this way. [based on Latin *triangulatus* 'triangular'] □ **triangulation** *n.*

Triassic *Geol.* ● *adj.* of or relating to the earliest period of the Mesozoic era. ● *n.* this period or system. [based on Late Latin *trias* 'the number 3']

triathlon *n.* an athletic contest consisting of three different events. □ **triathlete** *n.*

triatomic *adj. Chem.* **1** having three atoms (of a specified kind) in the molecule. **2** having three replacement atoms or radicals.

tribal *adj.* of, relating to, or characteristic of a tribe or tribes. □ **tribally** *adv.*

tribalism *n.* **1** tribal organization. **2** loyalty to one's own tribe or social group. □ **tribalist** *n.* **tribalistic** *adj.*

tribe *n.* **1** a group of (esp. primitive) families or communities, linked by social, economic, religious, or blood ties, and usu. having a common culture and dialect and a recognized leader. **2** any similar natural or political division. **3** usu. *derog.* a set or number of persons esp. of one profession etc. or family (*the whole tribe of actors*). [from Latin *tribus*]

tribesman *n.* (*pl.* **-men**; *fem.* **tribeswoman**, *pl.* **-women**) a member of a tribe or of one's own tribe.

tribespeople *n.pl.* the members of a tribe.

tribology *n.* the study of friction, wear, lubrication, and the design of bearings. [based on Greek *tribos* 'rubbing'] □ **tribologist** *n.*

tribulation *n.* **1** great affliction. **2** a cause of this (*was a real tribulation to me*). [based on Latin *tribulare* 'to press, oppress']

tribunal *n.* **1** *Brit.* a board appointed to adjudicate in some matter, esp. one appointed by the government to investigate a matter of public concern. **2** a court of justice. **3** a seat or bench for a judge or judges. **4** a place of judgement. **b** judicial authority (*the tribunal of public opinion*). [French]

tribune[1] *n.* **1** a popular leader or demagogue. **2** *Rom.Hist.* **a** (in full **tribune of the people**) an official in ancient Rome chosen by the people to protect their interests. **b** (in full **military tribune**) a Roman legionary officer. [from Latin *tribunus*] □ **tribunate** *n.*

tribune[2] *n.* **1 a** a bishop's throne in a basilica. **b** an apse containing this. **2** a dais or rostrum. **3** a raised area with seats. [from medieval Latin *tribuna* 'tribunal']

tributary ● *n.* (*pl.* **-ies**) **1** a river or stream flowing into a larger river or lake. **2** *hist.* a person or state paying or subject to tribute. ● *adj.* **1** (of a river etc.) that is a tributary. **2** *hist.* **a** paying tribute. **b** serving as tribute. [from Latin *tributarius*]

tribute *n.* **1** a thing said or done or given as a mark of respect or affection etc. (*paid tribute to their achievements*; *floral tributes*). **2** *hist.* **a** a payment made periodically by one state or ruler to another, esp. as a sign of dependence. **b** an obligation to pay this (*was laid under tribute*). **3** (foll. by *to*) an indication of (some praiseworthy quality) (*their success is a tribute to their perseverance*). [from Latin *tributum* '(thing) assigned']

trice *n.* □ **in a trice** in a moment; instantly. [based on Middle Dutch *trīsen* 'to pull, haul']

triceps ● *adj.* (of a muscle) having three heads or points of attachment. ● *n.* ▶ any triceps muscle, esp. the large muscle at the back of the upper arm. [Latin, literally 'three-headed']

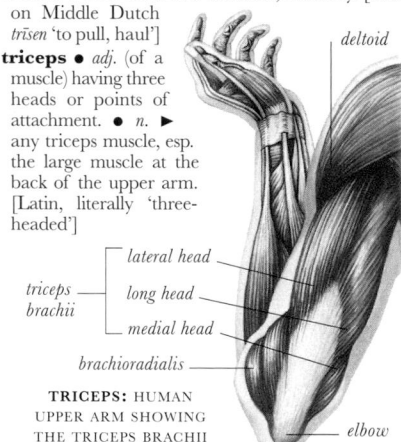

deltoid

lateral head
long head
medial head

triceps brachii

brachioradialis

elbow

TRICEPS: HUMAN UPPER ARM SHOWING THE TRICEPS BRACHII

triceratops *n.* ▼ a large quadrupedal plant-eating dinosaur of the late Cretaceous genus *Triceratops*, with two large horns, a smaller horn on the snout, and a bony frill above the neck. ▷ DINOSAUR. [from Greek *trikeratos* 'three-horned' + *ōps* 'face']

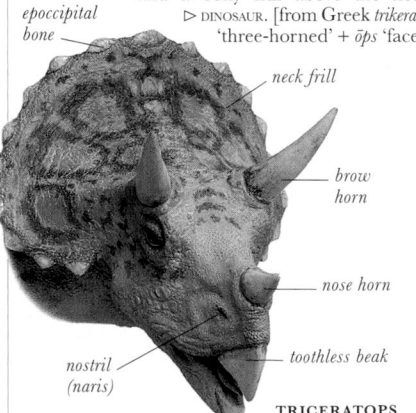

epoccipital bone

neck frill

brow horn

nose horn

toothless beak

nostril (naris)

TRICERATOPS

trichina /trik-i-nă/ *n.* (*pl.* **trichinae** /-nee/) any hairlike parasitic nematode worm of the genus *Trichinella*, esp. *T. spiralis*, whose larvae live in the muscle tissue of humans and other mammals. [modern Latin]

T

trichinosis /trik-i-**noh**-sis/ *n.* a disease caused by trichinae, usu. ingested in meat, and characterized by digestive disturbance, fever, and muscular rigidity.

trichology /tri-**kol**-ŏji/ *n.* the study of the structure, functions, and diseases of the hair. [based on Greek *thrix trikhos* 'hair'] □ **trichologist** *n.*

trichromatic *adj.* **1** having or using three colours. **2** (of vision) having the normal three colour-sensations, i.e. red, green, and purple. □ **trichromatism** *n.*

trick ● *n.* **1** an action or scheme intended to fool, outwit, or deceive. **2** an illusion (*a trick of the light*). **3** a special technique; a knack. **4 a** a feat of skill or dexterity. **b** an unusual action (e.g. begging) learnt by an animal. **5** a mischievous, foolish, or discreditable act; a practical joke (*a mean trick to play*). **6** a peculiar or characteristic habit or mannerism (*has a trick of repeating himself*). **7 a** the cards played in a single round of a card game. **b** such a round. **c** a point gained as a result of this. **8** (*attrib.*) done to deceive or mystify or to create an illusion (*trick photography*; *trick question*). ● *v.tr.* **1** deceive by a trick; outwit. **2** cheat; treat deceitfully so as to deprive (*were tricked into agreeing*; *were tricked out of their savings*). □ **do the trick** *colloq.* achieve the required result. **how's tricks?** *colloq.* how are you? **trick of the trade** a special technique or method of achieving a result in an industry or profession etc. **trick or treat** esp. *N. Amer.* a children's custom of calling at houses at Hallowe'en with the threat of pranks if they are not given a small gift. **trick out** (or **up**) dress, decorate, or deck out. **up to one's tricks** *colloq.* misbehaving. **up to a person's tricks** aware of what a person is likely to do by way of mischief. [from Old French *triche*]

trick cyclist *n.* **1** a cyclist who performs tricks. **2** *Brit. slang* a psychiatrist.

trickery *n.* (*pl.* **-ies**) **1** the practice or an instance of deception. **2** the use of tricks.

trickle ● *v.* **1** *intr. & tr.* flow or cause to flow in drops or a small stream (*water trickled through the crack*). **2** *tr.* come or go slowly or gradually (*information trickles out*). ● *n.* a trickling flow. [Middle English]

trickle charger *n.* an electrical charger for batteries that works at a steady slow rate.

trickster *n.* a deceiver or rogue.

tricksy *adj.* (**tricksier**, **tricksiest**) full of tricks; playful. □ **tricksily** *adv.* **tricksiness** *n.*

tricky *adj.* (**trickier**, **trickiest**) **1** difficult or intricate; requiring care and adroitness (*a tricky job*). **2** crafty or deceitful. **3** resourceful or adroit. □ **trickily** *adv.* **trickiness** *n.*

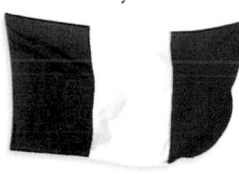

TRICOLOUR: FRENCH NATIONAL FLAG

tricolour /**trik**-ŏ-lŏ/ (*US* **tricolor**) ● *n.* ◄ a flag of three colours, esp. the French national flag of blue, white, and red. ● *adj.* (also **tricoloured**) having three colours. [from French *tricolore*]

tricorne /**try**-korn/ (also **tricorn**) ● *adj.* **1** having three horns. **2** (of a hat) having a brim turned up on three sides. ● *n.* a tricorne hat. [from Latin *tricornis*]

tricot /**trik**-oh/ *n.* a fine knitted fabric made of natural or man-made fibres. [French, literally 'knitting']

tricycle ● *n.* **1** a vehicle having three wheels, two on an axle at the back and one at the front, driven by pedals in the same way as a bicycle. **2** a three-wheeled motor vehicle for a disabled driver. ● *v.intr.* ride on a tricycle. □ **tricyclist** *n.*

trident *n.* a three-pronged spear. [from Latin *tridens trident-* 'three-toothed']

Tridentine *adj.* of or relating to the Council of Trent, held at Trento in Italy 1545–63, esp. as the basis of Roman Catholic doctrine. [based on Latin *Tridentum* 'Trent']

Tridentine mass *n.* the Latin Eucharistic liturgy used by the Roman Catholic Church from 1570 to 1964.

tried *past* and *past part.* of TRY.

triennial *adj.* **1** lasting three years. **2** recurring every three years. [from Late Latin *triennis*] □ **triennially** *adv.*

triennium *n.* (*pl.* **trienniums** or **triennia**) a period of three years. [Latin]

trier *n.* **1** a person who perseveres (*is a real trier*). **2** a tester, esp. of foodstuffs.

trifid *adj.* esp. *Biol.* partly or wholly split into three divisions or lobes. [from Latin *trifidus*]

trifle ● *n.* **1** a thing of slight value or importance. **2 a** a small amount esp. of money (*was sold for a trifle*). **b** (prec. by *a*) somewhat (*seems a trifle annoyed*). **3** *Brit.* a dessert of sponge cake with custard, jelly, fruit, cream, etc. ● *v.* **1** *intr.* talk or act frivolously. **2** *intr.* (foll. by *with*) **a** treat or deal with frivolously; flirt heartlessly with. **b** refuse to take seriously. **3** *tr.* (foll. by *away*) waste frivolously. [from Old French *truf(f)le*] □ **trifler** *n.*

trifling *adj.* **1** unimportant, petty. **2** frivolous.

trifocal ● *adj.* having three focuses, esp. of a lens with different focal lengths. ● *n.* (in *pl.*) trifocal spectacles.

trifoliate *adj.* ▶ (of a compound leaf) having three leaflets.

triforium *n.* (*pl.* **triforia**) ▼ a gallery or arcade above the arches of the nave, choir, and transepts of a church. [medieval Latin]

leaflet

TRIFOLIATE
LEAF OF A
LABURNUM TREE

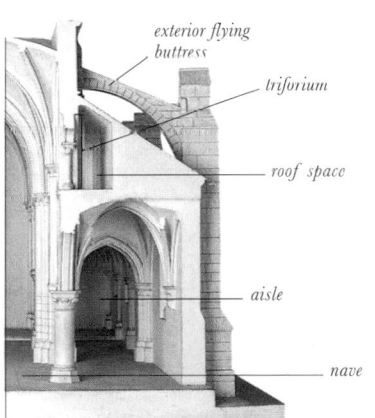

exterior flying buttress

triforium

roof space

aisle

nave

TRIFORIUM IN A LATE 12TH-CENTURY FRENCH GOTHIC CHURCH

trigger ● *n.* **1** a movable device for releasing a spring or catch and so setting off a mechanism (esp. that of a gun). ▷ GUN. **2** an event, occurrence, etc., that sets off a chain reaction. ● *v.tr.* **1** set (an action or process) in motion; precipitate. **2** fire (a gun) by the use of a trigger. □ **quick on the trigger** quick to respond. [based on Dutch *trekken* 'to pull']

triggerfish *n.* (*pl.* usu. same) ▶ any marine fish of the family Balistidae with a first dorsal fin-spine which can be depressed by pressing on the second.

trigger-happy *adj.* apt to shoot without or with slight provocation.

trigonometry *n.* the branch of mathematics dealing with the relations of the sides and angles of triangles and with the relevant functions of any angles. [from modern Latin *trigonometria*] □ **trigonometric** *adj.* **trigonometrical** *adj.*

trigraph *n.* (also **trigram**) **1** a group of three letters representing one sound. **2** a figure of three lines.

trigynous *adj. Bot.* having three pistils.

trike *n. & v.intr. colloq.* a tricycle.

trilateral *adj.* ● **1** of, on, or with three sides. **2** shared by or involving three parties, countries, etc. (*trilateral negotiations*). ● *n.* a figure having three sides.

trilby *n.* (*pl.* **-ies**) *Brit.* a soft felt hat with a narrow brim and indented crown. [from the name of the heroine in G. du Maurier's novel *Trilby* (1894)] □ **trilbied** *adj.*

trilingual *adj.* **1** able to speak three languages. **2** spoken or written in three languages. □ **trilingualism** *n.*

trill ● *n.* **1** a quavering sound, esp. a rapid alternation of sung or played notes. **2** a bird's warbling sound. **3** the pronunciation of *r* with a vibration of the tongue. ● *v.* **1** *intr.* produce a trill. **2** *tr.* warble (a song) or pronounce (*r* etc.) with a trill. [from Italian]

trillion *n.* (*pl.* same or (in sense 3) **trillions**) **1** a million million (1,000,000,000,000 or 10^{12}). **2** (formerly, esp. *Brit.*) a million million million (1,000,000,000,000,000,000 or 10^{18}). **3** (in *pl.*) *colloq.* a very large number (*trillions of times*). [French, on the pattern of *billion*] □ **trillionth** *adj. & n.*

■ **Usage** Senses 1–2 correspond to the change in sense of *billion*.

trilobite *n.* ▶ any fossil marine arthropod of the subphylum Trilobita of Palaeozoic times, characterized by a three-lobed body. [based on Greek *lobos* 'lobe']

trilogy *n.* (*pl.* **-ies**) a group of three related literary or operatic works.

trim ● *v.* (**trimmed**, **trimming**) **1** *tr.* make neat or of the required size or form, esp. by cutting away irregular or unwanted parts. **2** *tr.* (foll. by *off*, *away*) cut off (such parts). **3** *tr.* **a** make (a person) neat in dress and appearance. **b** ornament or decorate by adding ribbons, lace, etc. **4** *tr.* adjust the balance of (a ship or aircraft) by the arrangement of its cargo etc. **5** *tr.* arrange (sails) to suit the wind. **6** *intr.* associate oneself with currently prevailing views, esp. to advance oneself. **7** *tr. colloq.* **a** rebuke sharply. **b** thrash. **c** get the better of in a bargain etc. ● *n.* **1** the state or degree of readiness or fitness (*found everything in perfect trim*). **2** ornament or decorative material. **3** dress or equipment. **4** the act of trimming a person's hair. ● *adj.* (**trimmer**, **trimmest**) **1** neat or spruce. **2** in good order; well arranged or equipped. □ **in trim 1** looking smart, healthy, etc. **2** *Naut.* in good order. □ **trimly** *adv.* **trimmer** *n.* **trimness** *n.*

trimaran *n.* a vessel like a catamaran, with three hulls side by side.

trimer /**try**-mer/ *n. Chem.* a polymer comprising three monomer units. □ **trimeric** *adj.*

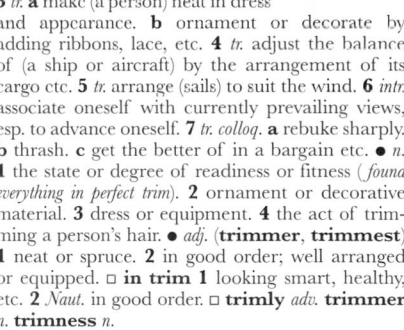

head shield

thorax

tail shield

TRILOBITE
(*Paradoxides* species)

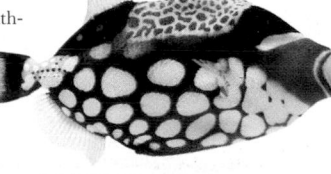

first dorsal fin

TRIGGERFISH: CLOWN TRIGGERFISH
(*Balistoides conspicillum*)

trimester /tri-**mes**-ter/ *n.* a period of three months, esp. of human gestation or *N. Amer.* as a university term. [from Latin *trimestris*]

trimer *n. Chem.* a polymer comprising three monomer units. □ **trimeric** *adj.*

trimeter /**trim**-i-ter/ *n. Prosody* a verse of three measures. [from Greek *trimetros*] □ **trimetric** *adj.*

T

trimming *n.* **1** ornamentation or decoration, esp. for clothing. **2** (in *pl.*) *colloq.* the usual accompaniments, esp. of the main course of a meal. **3** (in *pl.*) pieces cut off in trimming.

trimorphism ● *n. Bot., Zool.,* & *Crystallog.* existence in three distinct forms. □ **trimorphic** *adj.* **trimorphous** *adj.*

Trinidadian ● *n.* a native or inhabitant of Trinidad, an island in the W. Indies. ● *adj.* of or relating to Trinidad or its people.

Trinitarian ● *n.* a person who believes in the doctrine of the Trinity. ● *adj.* of or relating to this belief. □ **Trinitarianism** *n.*

trinitrotoluene *n.* (also **trinitrotoluol**) = TNT.

trinity *n.* (*pl.* **-ies**) **1** the state of being three. **2** a group of three. **3** (**the Trinity** or **the Holy Trinity**) *Theol.* the three persons of the Christian Godhead (Father, Son, and Holy Spirit). [from Latin *trinitas* 'triad']

Trinity House *n. Brit.* an association concerned with the licensing of pilots, the erection and maintenance of buoys, lighthouses, etc. on the coasts of England and Wales.

Trinity Sunday *n.* the next Sunday after Whit Sunday.

Trinity term *n. Brit.* the university and law term beginning after Easter.

trinket *n.* a trifling ornament, jewel, etc., esp. one worn upon the person. [16th-century coinage] □ **trinketry** *n.*

trinomial *adj.* consisting of three terms.

trio *n.* (*pl.* **-os**) **1** a set or group of three. **2** *Mus.* **a** a composition for three performers. **b** a group of three performers. **c** the central, usu. contrastive, section of a minuet, scherzo, or march. **3** (in piquet) three aces, kings, queens, or jacks in one hand. [French & Italian]

triode *n.* **1** a thermionic valve having three electrodes. **2** a semiconductor rectifier having three connections.

trioxide *n. Chem.* an oxide containing three oxygen atoms.

trip ● *v.* (**tripped**, **tripping**) **1** *intr.* **a** walk or dance with quick light steps. **b** (of a rhythm etc.) run lightly. **2** *intr.* & *tr.* (often foll. by *up*) stumble or cause to stumble, esp. by catching or entangling the feet. **b** *intr.* & *tr.* (foll. by *up*) make or cause to make a slip or blunder. **3** *intr.* make an excursion to a place. **4** *tr.* release (part of a machine) suddenly by knocking aside a catch etc. **5** *tr.* **a** release and raise (an anchor) from the bottom by means of a cable. **b** turn (a yard etc.) from a horizontal to a vertical position for lowering. **6** *intr. colloq.* have a drug-induced experience, esp. from taking LSD. ● *n.* **1** a journey or excursion, esp. for pleasure. **2 a** a stumble or blunder. **b** the act of tripping or the state of being tripped up. **3** a nimble step. **4** *colloq.* a drug-induced experience, esp. from taking LSD. **5** a contrivance for a tripping mechanism etc. □ **trip the light fantastic** *joc.* dance. [from Middle Dutch *trippen* 'to skip, hop']

tripartite *adj.* **1** consisting of three parts. **2** shared by or involving three parties. **3** *Bot.* (of a leaf) divided into three segments almost to the base. [from Latin *tripartitus*]

tripe *n.* **1** the first or second stomach of a ruminant, esp. an ox, as food. **2** *colloq.* nonsense, rubbish (*don't talk such tripe*). [from Old French]

triple ● *adj.* **1** consisting of three usu. equal parts or things; threefold. **2** involving three parties. **3** three times as much or many . ● *n.* **1** a threefold number or amount. **2** a set of three. **3** (in *pl.*) a peal of changes on seven bells. ● *v.tr.* & *intr.* multiply by three; increase threefold. [from Greek *triplous*] □ **triply** *adv.*

triple bond *n. Chem.* a set of three bonds between two atoms in a molecule.

triple crown *n.* **1** *RC Ch.* the Pope's tiara. **2** the act of winning all three of a group of important events in horse racing, rugby, etc.

triple jump *n.* an athletic exercise or contest comprising a hop, a step, and a jump.

triple play *n. Baseball* the act of putting out three players (two runners and the batter) from one batted ball.

triplet *n.* **1** each of three children or animals born at one birth. **2** a set of three things, esp. of equal notes played in the time of two.

triple time *n.* musical time with three beats to the bar; waltz time.

triplex *adj.* triple or threefold. [Latin]

triplicate ● *adj.* **1** existing in three examples or copies. **2** having three corresponding parts. **3** tripled. ● *n.* each of a set of three copies or corresponding parts. ● *v.tr.* **1** make in three copies. **2** multiply by three. □ **in triplicate** consisting of three exact copies. [from Latin *triplicatus* 'folded three times'] □ **triplication** *n.*

triploid /trip-loid/ *Biol.* ● *n.* an organism or cell having three times the haploid set of chromosomes. ● *adj.* of or being a triploid. [from Greek]

triploidy *n.* the condition of being triploid.

tripmeter *n.* a vehicle instrument that can be set to record the distance of individual journeys.

tripod *n.* **1** ◄ a three-legged stand for supporting a camera etc. **2** a stool, table, or utensil resting on three feet or legs. **3** *Gk Antiq.* a bronze altar at Delphi on which a priestess sat to utter oracles. [from Greek *tripous*] □ **tripodal** *adj.*

tripos *n.* (at Cambridge University) the honours examination for the BA degree. [from Greek *tripous* 'tripod', referring to the stool from which a satirical speech was made at graduation]

tripper *n.* **1** *Brit.* a person who goes on a pleasure trip. **2** *colloq.* a person experiencing hallucinatory effects from taking a drug.

triptych /trip-tik/ *n.* **1** a picture or relief carving on three panels, usu. hinged vertically together and often used as an altarpiece. **2** a set of three artistic works.

tripwire *n.* a wire stretched close to the ground, operating an alarm etc. when disturbed.

trireme *n.* ▼ a galley with three banks of oars. [from Latin *triremis*]

trisaccharide /try-sak-ă-ryd/ *n. Chem.* a sugar consisting of three linked monosaccharides.

trisect *v.tr.* cut or divide into three (usu. equal) parts. [based on Latin *sectus* 'cut'] □ **trisection** *n.* **trisector** *n.*

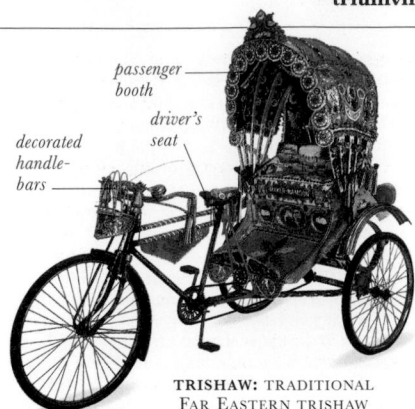

TRISHAW: TRADITIONAL FAR EASTERN TRISHAW

trishaw *n.* ▲ a light three-wheeled pedalled vehicle used in the Far East.

triskaidekaphobia *n.* fear of the number thirteen.

trismus *n. Med.* a variety of tetanus with continuous contraction of the jaw muscles causing the mouth to remain tightly closed. [based on Greek *trigmos* 'a scream, grinding']

trisyllable *n.* a word or metrical foot of three syllables. □ **trisyllabic** *adj.*

trite *adj.* (of a phrase, opinion, etc.) hackneyed, worn out by constant repetition. [from Latin *tritus* 'worn'] □ **tritely** *adv.* **triteness** *n.*

tritium *n. Chem.* a radioactive isotope of hydrogen with a mass about three times that of ordinary hydrogen. [based on Greek *tritos* 'third']

triumph ● *n.* **1 a** the state of being victorious or successful (*returned home in triumph*). **b** a great success or achievement. **2** a supreme example (*a triumph of engineering*). **3** joy at success; exultation. ● *v.intr.* **1** (often foll. by *over*) gain a victory; be successful; prevail. **2** ride in triumph. **3** (often foll. by *over*) exult. [from Latin *triump(h)us*]

triumphal *adj.* of or used in celebrating a triumph.

■ **Usage** *Triumphal*, meaning 'of or used in celebrating a triumph', e.g. *triumphal arch*, should not be confused with *triumphant* meaning 'victorious' or 'exultant', e.g. *the triumphant army; a triumphant laugh.*

triumphant *adj.* **1** victorious or successful. **2** exultant. □ **triumphantly** *adv.*

■ **Usage** See Usage Note at TRIUMPHAL.

triumvir *n.* (*pl.* **triumvirs** or **triumviri** /-ry/) **1** each of three men holding a joint office. **2** a member of a triumvirate. [Latin, from *trium virorum* 'of three men'] □ **triumviral** *adj.*

---

camera

pan-and-tilt head

extendable braced legs

adjustable centre column

TRIPOD: BRACED CAMERA TRIPOD

T

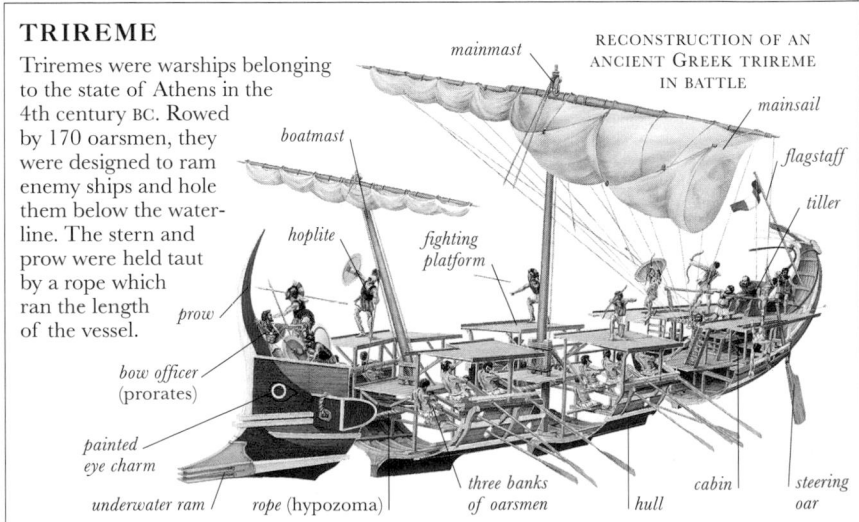

TRIREME

Triremes were warships belonging to the state of Athens in the 4th century BC. Rowed by 170 oarsmen, they were designed to ram enemy ships and hole them below the waterline. The stern and prow were held taut by a rope which ran the length of the vessel.

RECONSTRUCTION OF AN ANCIENT GREEK TRIREME IN BATTLE

passenger booth

driver's seat

decorated handlebars

mainmast

mainsail

flagstaff

tiller

boatmast

hoplite

fighting platform

prow

bow officer (prorates)

painted eye charm

underwater ram

rope (hypozoma)

three banks of oarsmen

hull

cabin

steering oar

triumvirate *n.* **1** a board or ruling group of three men, esp. in ancient Rome. **2** the office of triumvir.

triune *adj.* three in one, esp. with reference to the Trinity. [based on Latin *unus* 'one'] □ **triunity** *n.* (*pl.* **-ies**)

trivalent *adj.* *Chem.* having a valency of three. □ **trivalency** *n.*

trivet *n.* an iron tripod or bracket for a cooking pot or kettle to stand on. [Middle English]

trivia *n.pl.* trifles or trivialities. [modern Latin]

trivial *adj.* **1** of small value or importance; trifling. **2** (of a person etc.) concerned only with trivial things. [from Latin *trivialis* 'commonplace'] □ **triviality** *n.* (*pl.* **-ies**). **trivially** *adv.*

trivialize *v.tr.* (also **-ise**) make trivial or apparently trivial; minimize. □ **trivialization** *n.*

tri-weekly *adj.* produced or occurring three times a week or every three weeks.

tRNA *abbr.* transfer RNA.

trochaic /trŏ-**kay**-ik/ *Prosody* ● *adj.* of or using trochees. ● *n.* (usu. in *pl.*) trochaic verse.

trochee /**troh**-kee/ *n.* *Prosody* a foot consisting of one long or stressed syllable followed by one short or unstressed syllable. [from Greek *trokhaios* (*pous*) 'running (foot)']

trod *past* and *past part.* of TREAD.

trodden *past part.* of TREAD.

troglodyte *n.* **1** a cave dweller. **2** a hermit. **3** *derog.* a wilfully obscurantist or old-fashioned person. [from Greek *trōglodutēs*, based on the name of an Ethiopian people] □ **troglodytic** *adj.*

troika *n.* **1 a** a Russian vehicle with a team of three horses abreast. **b** this team. **2** a group of three people, esp. as an administrative council. [Russian, from *troe* 'set of three']

troilism *n.* sexual activity involving three participants.

Trojan ● *adj.* of or relating to ancient Troy in Asia Minor. ● *n.* **1** a native or inhabitant of Troy. **2** a person who works, fights, etc. courageously (*works like a Trojan*). [from Latin *Troianus*]

Trojan Horse *n.* **1** a hollow wooden horse said to have been used by the Greeks to enter Troy. **2** a person or device planted to bring about an enemy's downfall.

troll[1] *n.* (in Scandinavian folklore) a fabulous being, esp. a giant or dwarf dwelling in a cave. [from Old Norse]

troll[2] ● *v.* **1** *intr.* sing out in a carefree jovial manner. **2** *tr. & intr.* **a** fish by drawing bait along in the water. **b** (often foll. by *for*) search, seek. **3** *intr.* esp. *Brit.* walk, stroll. ● *n.* **1** the act of trolling for fish. **2** a line or bait used in this. [Middle English] □ **troller** *n.*

trolley *n.* (*pl.* **-eys**) **1** esp. *Brit.* a table, stand, or basket on wheels or castors for serving food, transporting luggage or shopping, gathering purchases in a supermarket, etc. **2** esp. *Brit.* a low truck running on rails. **3** (in full **trolley-wheel**) a wheel attached to a pole etc. used for collecting current from an overhead electric wire to drive a vehicle. ▷ TRAM. **4 a** *US* = TROLLEY-CAR. **b** *Brit.* = TROLLEYBUS. □ **off one's trolley** *slang* crazy. [of dialect origin]

trolleybus *n.* ◀ a bus powered by electricity obtained from an overhead cable by means of a trolley-wheel.

trolley-car *n.* *US* a tram powered by electricity obtained from an overhead cable by means of a trolley-wheel.

trollop *n.* **1** a disreputable or promiscuous girl or woman. **2** a prostitute. [17th-century coinage]

TROLLEYBUS: MODERN GREEK TROLLEYBUS

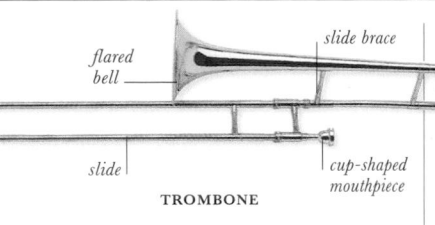

flared bell   *slide brace*
slide   *cup-shaped mouthpiece*

TROMBONE

trombone *n.* **1** ▲ a large brass wind instrument with a sliding tube. ▷ BRASS, ORCHESTRA. [based on Italian *tromba* 'trumpet'] □ **trombonist** *n.*

trompe l'œil /tromp **lŏ**'i/ *n.* (*pl.* **trompe l'œils** *pronunc.* same) a painting etc. designed to give an illusion of reality. [French, literally 'deceives the eye']

troop ● *n.* **1** an assembled company; an assemblage of people or animals. **2** (in *pl.*) soldiers or armed forces. **3** a cavalry unit commanded by a captain. **4** a unit of artillery and armoured formation. **5** a grouping of three or more Scout patrols. ● *v.intr.* (foll. by *in*, *out*, *off*, etc.) come together or move in large numbers. □ **troop the colour** esp. *Brit.* show a flag ceremonially at a public mounting of garrison guards. [from French *troupe*]

troop carrier *n.* a large aircraft, armoured vehicle, etc., for carrying troops.

trooper *n.* **1** a private soldier in a cavalry or armoured unit. **2** *Austral. & US* a mounted or motor-borne police officer. **3** a cavalry horse. **4** esp. *Brit.* a troopship. □ **swear like a trooper** swear extensively or forcefully.

troopship *n.* a ship used for transporting troops.

trope *n.* a figurative (e.g. metaphorical or ironical) use of a word. [from Greek *tropos* 'turn, way, trope']

trophy *n.* (*pl.* **-ies**) **1** a cup or other decorative object awarded as a prize in a contest. **2** a memento or souvenir, e.g. a deer's antlers, taken in hunting. **3** *Gk & Rom. Antiq.* the weapons etc. of a defeated army set up as a memorial of victory. [from Greek *tropaion*] □ **trophied** *adj.* (also in *comb.*).

tropic ● *n.* **1** ▶ the parallel of latitude 23°26' north (**tropic of Cancer**) or south (**tropic of Capricorn**) of the equator. **2** each of two corresponding circles on the celestial sphere where the Sun appears to turn after reaching its greatest declination. **3** (**the Tropics**) ▶ the region between the tropics of Cancer and Capricorn. ● *adj.* **1** = TROPICAL 1. **2** of tropism. [from Greek *tropikos*]

tropical *adj.* **1** of, peculiar to, or suggesting the Tropics (*tropical fish*; *tropical diseases*). **2** very hot; passionate, luxuriant. **3** of or by way of a trope. □ **tropically** *adv.*

tropical cyclone see CYCLONE 2.

tropical storm *n.* = CYCLONE 2.

tropical year see YEAR 1.

tropic of Cancer see TROPIC *n.* 1.

tropic of Capricorn see TROPIC *n.* 1.

tropism *n.* *Biol.* the turning of all or part of an organism in a particular direction in response to an external stimulus. [based on Greek *tropos* 'turning']

troposphere *n.* the lowest region of the atmosphere (cf. STRATOSPHERE, IONOSPHERE). ▷ ATMOSPHERE. [based on Greek *tropos* 'turning'] □ **tropospheric** *adj.*

trot ● *v.* (**trotted**, **trotting**) **1** *intr.* (of a person) run at a moderate pace esp. with short strides. **2** *intr.* (of a horse) proceed at a steady pace faster than a walk lifting each diagonal pair of legs alternately. **3** *intr. colloq.* walk or go. **4** *tr.* cause (a horse or person) to trot. **5** *tr.* traverse (a distance) at a trot. ● *n.* **1** the action or exercise of trotting. **2** (**the trots**) *slang* an attack of diarrhoea. **3** (in *pl.*) *Austral. colloq.* **a** trotting races. ▷ TROTTING. **b** a meeting for these. □ **on the trot** *colloq.* **1** continually busy (*kept them on the trot*). **2** *Brit.* in succession (*five weeks on the trot*). **trot out 1** cause (a horse) to trot to show its paces. **2** *colloq.* produce or introduce (an opinion etc.). [from medieval Latin *trottare*]

troth /trohth/ *n.* *archaic* **1** faith, loyalty. **2** truth. □ **pledge** (or **plight**) **one's troth** pledge one's word esp. in marriage or betrothal. [Old English *trēowth* 'truth']

Trotskyism *n.* the political or economic principles of L. Trotsky, Russian politician d. 1940, esp. as urging worldwide socialist revolution. □ **Trotskyist** *n.* **Trotskyite** *n. derog.*

trotter *n.* **1** a horse bred or trained for trotting. **2** (usu. in *pl.*) an animal's foot as food.

trotting *n.* ▼ racing for trotting horses pulling a two-wheeled vehicle and driver.

troubadour /**troo**-bă-door; *last part rhymes with poor*/ *n.* **1** a French medieval lyric poet composing and singing on the theme of courtly love. **2** a singer or poet. [French]

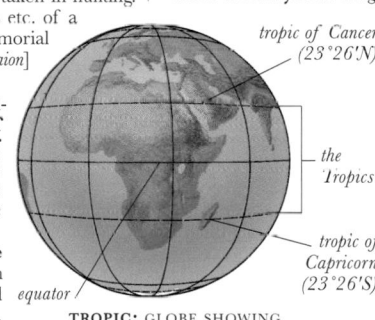

tropic of Cancer (23°26'N)
the Tropics
equator
tropic of Capricorn (23°26'S)

TROPIC: GLOBE SHOWING LOCATION OF THE TROPICS

TROTTING

In many regions, including North America, Australia, and New Zealand, the trotting (or harness) race is as popular as flat racing. Modern trotting races resemble ancient chariot races, except that they are run with single horses equipped with restraining reins and overshoes; these hobbles permit only trotting or pacing gaits.

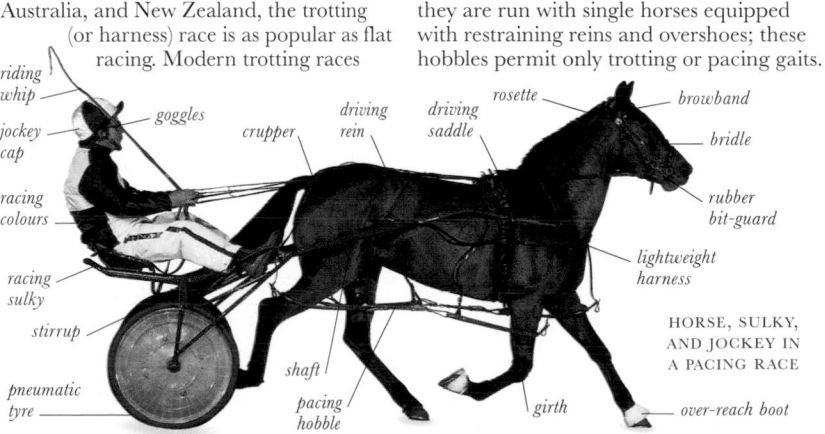

riding whip
jockey cap
goggles
crupper
driving rein
driving saddle
rosette
browband
bridle
racing colours
rubber bit-guard
racing sulky
lightweight harness
stirrup
shaft
pacing hobble
pneumatic tyre
girth
over-reach boot

HORSE, SULKY, AND JOCKEY IN A PACING RACE

T

trouble ● *n.* **1** difficulty or distress; vexation, affliction (*am having trouble with my car*). **2 a** inconvenience; unpleasant exertion; bother (*went to a lot of trouble*). **b** a cause of this (*the child was no trouble*). **3** a cause of annoyance or concern (*the trouble with you is that you can't say no*). **4** a faulty condition or operation (*engine trouble*). **5 a** fighting, disturbance (*crowd trouble*). **b** (in *pl.*) political or social unrest, public disturbances. **6** disagreement, strife (*is having trouble at home*). ● *v.* **1** *tr.* cause distress or anxiety to; disturb (*troubled by their debts*). **2** *intr.* be disturbed or worried (*don't trouble about it*). **3** *tr.* afflict; cause pain etc. to (*am troubled with arthritis*). **4** *tr.* & *intr.* (often *refl.*) subject or be subjected to inconvenience or unpleasant exertion (*sorry to trouble you; don't trouble yourself*). □ **ask for trouble** *colloq.* invite trouble or difficulty by rash or indiscreet behaviour etc. **be no trouble** cause no inconvenience etc. **go to the trouble** (or **some trouble** etc.) exert oneself to do something. **in trouble 1** involved in a matter likely to bring censure or punishment. **2** *colloq.* pregnant while unmarried. **look for trouble** *colloq.* **1** aggressively seek to cause trouble. **2** invite trouble. **take trouble** (or **the trouble**) exert oneself to do something. [from Old French *truble* (n.), *trubler* (v.)]

troubled *adj.* showing, experiencing, or reflecting trouble, anxiety, etc. (*a troubled mind*).

troublemaker *n.* a person who habitually causes trouble. □ **trouble-making** *n.* & *attrib.adj.*

troubleshooter *n.* **1** a mediator in industrial or diplomatic etc. disputes. **2** a person who traces and corrects faults in machinery etc. □ **troubleshoot** *v.intr.* & *tr.* (*past* and *past part.* **-shot**). **troubleshooting** *n.*

troublesome *adj.* **1** causing or full of trouble. **2** vexing, annoying. □ **troublesomely** *adv.* **troublesomeness** *n.*

trouble spot *n.* a place where difficulties regularly occur.

troublous *adj. archaic* or *literary* full of troubles; agitated, disturbed (*troublous times*).

trough *n.* **1** a long narrow open receptacle for water, animal feed, etc. **2** a channel for conveying a liquid. **3** ▼ an elongated region of low barometric pressure. **4** a hollow between two wave crests. **5** the time of lowest economic performance etc. **6** a low point or depression. [Old English]

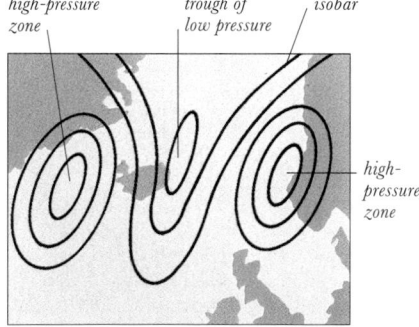

high-pressure zone   *trough of low pressure*   *isobar*   *high-pressure zone*

TROUGH OF LOW PRESSURE ON
A WEATHER CHART

trounce *v.tr.* **1** defeat heavily. **2** beat, thrash. **3** punish severely. [16th-century coinage, originally in sense 'to afflict'] □ **trouncer** *n.* **trouncing** *n.*

troupe /troop/ *n.* a company of actors or acrobats etc. [French, literally 'troop']

trouper /troop-er/ *n.* **1** a member of a theatrical troupe. **2** a staunch colleague.

trouser-clip *n.* = BICYCLE CLIP.

trousers *n.pl.* **1** (also **pair of trousers** *sing.*) an outer garment reaching from the waist usu. to the ankles, divided into two parts to cover the legs. **2** (**trouser**) (*attrib.*) designating parts of this (*trouser leg*). □ **wear the trousers** be the dominant part-

ner in a marriage etc. [from Irish *triubhas* 'trews'] □ **trousered** *adj.* **trouserless** *adj.*

trouser suit *n. Brit.* a woman's suit of trousers and jacket.

trousseau /troo-soh/ *n.* (*pl.* **trousseaus** or **trousseaux** /-sohz/) the clothes collected by a bride for her marriage. [French, literally 'bundle']

trout *n.* (*pl.* same or **trouts**) **1** ▼ any of various freshwater fishes of the genus *Salmo* or *Salvelinus* of the northern hemisphere, esp. *Salmo trutta* of Europe, valued as food. **2** *Brit. slang derog.* a woman, esp. an old or ill-tempered one (usu. *old trout*). [from Late Latin *tructa*]

TROUT: BROWN TROUT
(*Salmo trutta*)

trove *n.* = TREASURE TROVE. [from Anglo-French]

trowel ● *n.* **1** ◄ a small hand-held tool with a flat pointed blade, used to apply and spread mortar etc. **2** a similar tool with a curved scoop for lifting plants or earth. ● *v.tr.* (**trowelled**, **trowelling**; *US* **troweled**, **troweling**) apply (plaster etc.). [from Latin *trulla* 'scoop']

troy *n.* (in full **troy weight**) a system of weights used for precious metals and gems, with a pound of 12 ounces or 5,760 grains. [Middle English]

truant ● *n.* **1** a child who stays away from school without leave or explanation. **2** a person missing from work etc. ● *adj.* (of a person, conduct, thoughts, etc.) shirking, idle, wandering. ● *v.intr.* (also **play truant**) stay away as a truant. [from Old French] □ **truancy** *n.*

truce *n.* **1** a temporary agreement to cease hostilities. **2** a suspension of private feuding or bickering. [Old English] □ **truceless** *adj.*

TROWEL:
MASON'S
TROWEL

truck[1] ● *n.* **1** *Brit.* an open railway wagon for carrying freight. **2** a large road vehicle for carrying heavy goods, troops, etc.; a lorry. ● *v.* **1** *tr.* convey on or in a truck. **2** *intr. N. Amer.* drive a truck. **3** *intr. N. Amer. slang* proceed; go, stroll. □ **truckage** *n.*

truck[2] *n.* dealings; exchange, barter. □ **have no truck with** avoid dealing with. [from Old French]

trucker *n.* a long-distance lorry driver.

truckie *n. Austral. colloq.* a lorry driver; a trucker.

trucking *n. US* conveyance of goods by lorry.

truckle *n.* (in full **truckle-bed**) *esp. Brit.* a low bed on wheels that can be stored under a larger bed. ● *v.intr.* (foll. by *to*) submit obsequiously. [originally in sense 'wheel, pulley': from Latin *trochlea* 'pulley']

truckload *n.* **1** a quantity of goods etc. that can be transported in a truck. **2** *colloq.* a large quantity or number. □ **by the truckload** in large quantities or numbers.

truculent *adj.* **1** aggressively defiant. **2** aggressive, pugnacious. **3** fierce, savage. [from Latin *truculentus*] □ **truculence** *n.* **truculency** *n.* **truculently** *adv.*

trudge ● *v.* **1** *intr.* go on foot esp. laboriously. **2** *tr.* traverse (a distance) in this way. ● *n.* a trudging walk. [16th-century coinage]

true ● *adj.* (**truer**, **truest**) **1** in accordance with fact or reality (*a true story*). **2** genuine; rightly or strictly so called (*the true heir to the throne*). **3** (often foll. by *to*) loyal or faithful. **4** (foll. by *to*) accurately conforming (to a standard or expectation etc.) (*true to form*). **5** correctly positioned or balanced; upright, level. **6** exact, accurate (*a true aim; a true copy*). **7** (*absol.*) (also **it is true**) certainly, admittedly (*true, it would cost more*). ● *adv.* **1** truly (*tell me true*). **2** accurately (*aim*

true). **3** without variation (*breed true*). ● *v.tr.* (**trues**, **trued**, **truing** or **trueing**) bring (a tool, wheel, frame, etc.) into the exact position or form required. □ **come true** actually happen or be the case. **out of true** (or **the true**) not in the correct or exact position. **true to form** (or **type**) being or behaving etc. as expected. **true to life** accurately representing life. [Old English] □ **trueness** *n.*

true-blue ● *adj.* extremely loyal or orthodox. ● *n.* such a person, esp. a Conservative.

true coral see CORAL *n.* 2.

true love *n.* a sweetheart.

true north *n.* north according to the Earth's axis, not magnetic north.

truffle *n.* **1** ▶ any strong-smelling underground fungus of the order Tuberales, used as a culinary delicacy and found esp. in France by trained dogs or pigs. ▷ FUNGUS. **2** a usu. round sweet made of chocolate mixture covered in cocoa etc.

TRUFFLE:
SUMMER TRUFFLE
(*Tuber aestivum*)

trug *n. Brit.* ◄ a shallow oblong garden basket usu. of wood strips.

truism *n.* an obviously true or hackneyed statement. □ **truistic** *adj.*

truly *adv.* **1** sincerely, genuinely (*am truly grateful*). **2** really, indeed (*truly, I do not know*). **3** faithfully, loyally (*served them truly*). **4** accurately, truthfully (*is not truly depicted*). **5** rightly, properly (*well and truly*).

TRUG:
GARDENER'S
TRUG

trump[1] ● *n.* **1 a** a playing card of a suit ranking above the others. **b** (in *pl.*) this suit (*hearts are trumps*). **2** *colloq.* **a** a helpful or admired person. **b** *Austral.* & *NZ* a person in authority. ● *v.tr.* **1** defeat (a card or its player) with a trump. **2** *colloq.* gain a surprising advantage over (a person, proposal, etc.). □ **trump up** fabricate or invent (an accusation, excuse, etc.) (*on a trumped-up charge*). **turn up trumps** *Brit. colloq.* **1** turn out better than expected. **2** be greatly successful or helpful. [corruption of TRIUMPH, in same (now obsolete) sense]

trump[2] *n. archaic* a trumpet-blast. [from Old French *trompe*]

trump card *n.* **1** a card belonging to, or turned up to determine, a trump suit. **2** *colloq.* a valuable resource.

trumpery ● *n.* (*pl.* **-ies**) **1 a** worthless finery. **b** a worthless article. **2** rubbish. ● *adj.* **1** showy but worthless. **2** delusive, shallow. [from Old French *tromperie*]

trumpet ● *n.* **1** a brass instrument with a flared bell and a bright penetrating tone. ▷ BRASS, ORCHESTRA. **2 a** the tubular corona of a daffodil etc. **b** a trumpet-shaped thing (*ear-trumpet*). **3** a sound of or like a trumpet. ● *v.* (**trumpeted**, **trumpeting**) **1** *intr.* **a** blow a trumpet. **b** (of an elephant etc.) make a loud sound as of a trumpet. **2** *tr.* proclaim loudly (a person's or thing's merit). [from Old French *trompette*]

trumpet call *n.* an urgent summons to action.

trumpeter *n.* a person who plays a trumpet.

trumpet major *n.* the chief trumpeter of a cavalry regiment.

truncate *v.tr.* cut the top or the end from (a tree, a body, a piece of writing, etc.). [based on Latin *truncatus* 'maimed'] □ **truncation** *n.*

truncheon *n.* **1** *esp. Brit.* a short club or cudgel, esp. carried by a police officer. **2** a staff or baton as a symbol of authority. [from Latin *truncus* 'trunk']

T

trundle *v.tr. & intr.* roll or move heavily or noisily esp. on or as on wheels. [Old English *trendel* 'circle']

trundle-bed *n.* esp. *US* = TRUCKLE *n.*

trunk *n.* **1** the main stem of a tree as distinct from its branches and roots. **2** a person's or animal's body apart from the limbs and head. **3** a large box with a hinged lid for transporting luggage, clothes, etc. **4** *N. Amer.* the luggage compartment of a motor car. **5** ▶ an elephant's elongated prehensile nose. ▷ ELEPHANT. **6** (in *pl.*) men's shorts worn for swimming, boxing, etc. [from Latin *truncus*] □ **trunkful** *n.* (*pl.* **-fuls**). **trunkless** *adj.*

TRUNK: SECTION THROUGH AN ELEPHANT'S TRUNK

epidermis

longitudinal muscle

radiating muscle

nerve

nostril

septum

blood vessel

trunk call *n.* esp. *Brit.* a telephone call on a trunk line with charges made according to distance.

trunking *n.* **1** a system of shafts or conduits for cables, ventilation, etc. **2** the use or arrangement of trunk lines.

trunk line *n.* a main line of a railway, telephone system, etc.

trunk road *n.* esp. *Brit.* an important main road.

truss ● *n.* **1** a framework, e.g. of rafters and struts, supporting a roof or bridge etc. ▷ BRIDGE, HOUSE, QUEEN POST, ROOF. **2** a surgical appliance worn to support a hernia. **3** *Brit.* a bundle of hay or straw. **4** ▶ a compact terminal cluster of flowers or fruit. ● *v.tr.* **1** tie up (a fowl) compactly for cooking. **2** (often foll. by *up*) tie (a person) up with the arms to the sides. **3** support (a roof or bridge etc.) with a truss or trusses. [from Old French *trusse* (n.), *trusser* (v.)] □ **trusser** *n.*

TRUSS OF TOMATOES

trust ● *n.* **1 a** a firm belief in the reliability or truth or strength etc. of a person or thing. **b** the state of being relied on. **2** a confident expectation. **3** obligation or responsibility (*am in a position of trust*; *have fulfilled my trust*). **4** reliance on the truth of a statement etc. without examination. **5** *Law* confidence placed in a person by making that person the nominal owner of property to be used for another's benefit. **6 a** a body of trustees. **b** an organization managed by trustees. **c** an organized association of several companies for the purpose of reducing or defeating competition etc. ● *v.* **1** *tr.* place trust in; believe in; rely on the character or behaviour of. **2** *tr.* (foll. by *with*) allow (a person) to have or use (a thing) from confidence in its proper use (*I can trust him with my keys*). **3** *tr.* (often foll. by *that* + clause) have faith or confidence or hope that a thing will take place (*I trust you will come*). **4** *tr.* (foll. by *to*) consign (a thing) to (a person) with trust. **5** *intr.* (foll. by *in*) place reliance in (*we trust in you*). **6** *intr.* (foll. by *to*) place (esp. undue) reliance on (*shall have to trust to luck*). □ **in trust** *Law* held on the basis of trust (see sense 5 of *n.*). **on trust** on the basis of trust or confidence. **take on trust** accept (an assertion, claim, etc.) without evidence or investigation. [from Old Norse *traust*] □ **trustable** *adj.*

trust company *n.* a company formed to act as a trustee or to deal with trusts.

trustee *n.* *Law* a person or member of a board given control or powers of administration of property in trust with a legal obligation to administer it solely for the purposes specified. □ **trusteeship** *n.*

trustful *adj.* full of trust or confidence. □ **trustfully** *adv.* **trustfulness** *n.*

trust fund *n.* a fund of money etc. held in trust.

trustie var. of TRUSTY *n.*

trusting *adj.* having trust, esp. being trustful by nature. □ **trustingly** *adv.* **trustingness** *n.*

trust territory *n.* a territory under the trusteeship of the United Nations or of a state designated by them.

trustworthy *adj.* deserving of trust; reliable. □ **trustworthily** *adv.* **trustworthiness** *n.*

trusty ● *adj.* (**trustier, trustiest**) **1** *archaic* or *joc.* trustworthy (*a trusty steed*). **2** *archaic* loyal (to a sovereign) (*my trusty subjects*). ● *n.* (also **trustie**) (*pl.* **-ies**) a prisoner who is given special privileges for good behaviour.

truth *n.* (*pl.* **truths**) **1** the quality or a state of being true or truthful. **2** what is true. □ **in truth** *literary* truly, really. **to tell the truth** (or **truth to tell**) to be frank. [Old English]

truthful *adj.* **1** habitually speaking the truth. **2** (of a story etc.) true. **3** (of a likeness etc.) corresponding to reality. □ **truthfully** *adv.* **truthfulness** *n.*

try ● *v.* (**-ies, -ied**) **1** *intr.* make an effort with a view to success (often foll. by *to* + infin.; *colloq.* foll. by *and* + infin.: *tried to be on time*; *try and be early*; *I shall try hard*). **2** *tr.* make an effort to achieve (*tried my best*; *had better try something easier*). **3** *tr.* **a** test (the quality of a thing) by use or experiment. **b** test the qualities of (a person or thing) (*try it before you buy*). **4** *tr.* make severe demands on (a person, quality, etc.) (*my patience has been sorely tried*). **5** *tr.* examine the effectiveness or usefulness of for a purpose (*try cold water*; *have you tried kicking it?*). **6** *tr.* **a** investigate and decide (a case or issue) judicially. **b** subject (a person) to trial (*will be tried for murder*). **7** *intr.* (foll. by *for*) **a** apply or compete for. **b** seek to reach or attain (*am going to try for a gold medal*). ● *n.* (*pl.* **-ies**) **1** an effort to accomplish something; an attempt (*give it a try*). **2** *Rugby* the act of touching the ball down behind the opposing goal line, scoring points and entitling the scoring side to a kick at goal. **3** *Amer. Football* an attempt to score an extra point in various ways after a touchdown. □ **try for** try out or test for suitability. **try one's hand** see how skilful one is, esp. at the first attempt. **try it on** *Brit. colloq.* **1** test another's patience. **2** (often foll. by *with*) attempt to outwit, deceive, or seduce another person. **try on** put on (clothes etc.) to see if they fit or suit the wearer. **try out 1** put to the test. **2** test thoroughly. [Middle English in sense 'to separate, distinguish': from Old French *trier* 'to sift']

■ **Usage** Use of the verb *try* with *and* (see sense 1 above) is uncommon in the past tense and in negative contexts (except in the imperative, e.g. *Don't try and get the better of me*)

trying *adj.* annoying, vexatious; hard to endure. □ **tryingly** *adv.*

try-on *n. Brit. colloq.* **1** an act of trying it on. **2** an attempt to fool or deceive.

try-out *n.* an experimental test of efficiency, popularity, etc.

tryst *archaic* ● *n.* **1** a time and place for a meeting, esp. of lovers. **2** such a meeting (*keep a tryst*; *break one's tryst*). ● *v.intr.* (often foll. by *with*) make a tryst. [Middle English variant of obsolete *trist* 'an appointed station in hunting'] □ **tryster** *n.*

tsar /zar/ *n.* (also **czar, tzar**) **1** *hist.* the title of the former emperors of Russia. **2** a person with great authority. [Russian, from Latin *Caesar*] □ **tsardom** *n.* **tsarism** *n.* **tsarist** *n. & adj.*

tsarevich /zar-i-vich/ *n.* (also **czarevich**) *hist.* the eldest son of an emperor of Russia. [Russian, literally 'son of a tsar']

tsarina /zar-ree-nă/ *n.* (also **czarina, tzarina**) *hist.* the title of the former empress of Russia. [from German *Czarin*]

tsetse /tset-si/ *n.* any fly of the genus *Glossina* native to Africa, that feeds on human and animal blood. [Tswana (a Bantu language)]

TSUNAMI

A tsunami is a great wave of sea water, formed by shock waves emanating from an earthquake or volcanic eruption on the ocean floor. On open sea, the swiftly moving wave normally remains less than 0.5 m (1 ft 8 in.) high. Near the shoreline, however, it rises up to 60 m (200 ft) high, causing catastrophic coastal flooding.

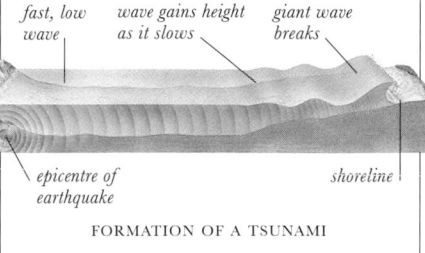

fast, low wave

wave gains height as it slows

giant wave breaks

epicentre of earthquake

shoreline

FORMATION OF A TSUNAMI

T-shirt *n.* (also **tee shirt**) a short-sleeved casual top having the form of a T when spread out.

tsk *int., n., & v.* (also **tsk tsk**) = TUT (see TUT-TUT).

tsp *abbr.* (*pl.* **tsps** or same) teaspoonful.

T-square *n.* a T-shaped instrument for drawing or testing right angles.

TSS *abbr.* toxic shock syndrome.

tsunami /tsoo-nah-mi/ *n.* (*pl.* **tsunamis**) ▲ a long high sea wave caused by an underwater earthquake or other disturbance. [Japanese, from *tsu* 'harbour' + *nami* 'wave']

TT *abbr.* **1** Tourist Trophy. **2** tuberculin-tested. **3 a** teetotal. **b** teetotaller.

tub ● *n.* **1** an open flat-bottomed usu. round container for various purposes. **2** the amount a tub will hold. **3** *colloq.* a bath. **4** *colloq.* a clumsy slow boat. ● *v.tr. & intr.* (**tubbed, tubbing**) plant, bathe, or wash in a tub. [Middle English] □ **tubful** *n.* (*pl.* **-fuls**).

tuba *n.* (*pl.* **tubas**) **a** ▶ a low-pitched brass wind instrument. **b** its player. ▷ BRASS, ORCHESTRA. [Italian]

flared bell

piston valves

mouthpiece

tube

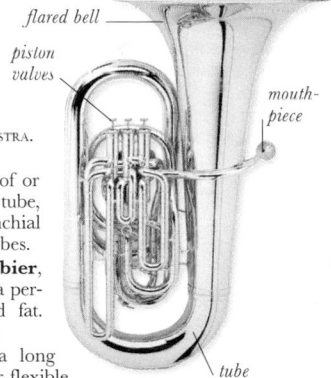

TUBA

tubal *adj. Anat.* of or relating to a tube, esp. the bronchial or Fallopian tubes.

tubby *adj.* (**tubbier, tubbiest**) (of a person) short and fat. □ **tubbiness** *n.*

tube ● *n.* **1** a long hollow rigid or flexible cylinder, esp. for holding or carrying air, liquids, etc. **2** a soft metal or plastic cylinder sealed at one end and having a cap at the other, for holding a semi-liquid substance ready for use (*a tube of toothpaste*). **3** *Anat. & Zool.* a hollow cylindrical organ (*bronchial tubes*; *Fallopian tubes*). **4** *Brit. colloq.* **a** (often prec. by *the*) an underground railway system, esp. the one in London (*went by tube*). **b** (in full **tube train**) a train running on such a system. **5 a** a cathode ray tube esp. in a television set. **b** (prec. by *the*) esp. *US colloq.* television. **6** *US* a thermionic valve. **7** = INNER TUBE. **8** *Austral. slang* a can of beer. ● *v.tr.* **1** equip with tubes. **2** enclose in a tube. [from Latin *tubus*] □ **tubeless** *adj.* (esp. in sense 7 of *n.*). **tubelike** *adj.*

tubectomy *n.* (*pl.* **-ies**) the surgical removal of a Fallopian tube.

T

tuber *n.* **1** ► the short thick rounded part of a stem or rhizome, usu. found underground and covered with modified buds, e.g. in a potato. **2** the similar root of a dahlia etc. [Latin, literally 'hump, swelling']

TUBERS OF A DAHLIA

tubercle *n.* **1** a small rounded protuberance esp. on a bone. **2** a small rounded inflamed swelling, esp. one characteristic of tuberculosis in the lungs etc. [from Latin *tuberculum* 'little lump'] □ **tuberculate** *adj.* **tuberculous** *adj.*

tubercle bacillus *n.* a bacterium causing tuberculosis.

tubercular ● *adj.* of or having tubercles or tuberculosis. ● *n.* a person with tuberculosis.

tuberculin *n.* a sterile protein extract from cultures of tubercle bacillus, used in the diagnosis and (formerly) the treatment of tuberculosis.

tuberculin test *n.* a hypodermic injection of tuberculin to detect infection with or immunity from tuberculosis.

tuberculin-tested *adj.* (of milk) from cows giving a negative response to a tuberculin test.

tuberculosis *n.* an infectious disease caused by the bacillus *Mycobacterium tuberculosis*, characterized by tubercles, esp. in the lungs.

tuberose[1] *adj.* **1** covered with tubers; knobby. **2** of or resembling a tuber. **3** bearing tubers. [from Latin *tuberosus*] □ **tuberosity** *n.*

tuberose[2] *n.* a plant, *Polianthes tuberosa*, native to Mexico, having heavily scented white funnel-like flowers and strap-shaped leaves. [from Latin *tuberosa* (fem.) 'covered with tubers']

tuberous *adj.* = TUBEROSE[1]. [from Latin *tuberosus*]

tuberous root *n.* a thick and fleshy root like a tuber but without buds.

tube train see TUBE *n.* 4b.

tubifex *n.* ► any red annelid worm of the genus *Tubifex*, found in mud at the bottom of rivers and lakes and used as food for aquarium fish. [based on Latin *tubus* 'tube' + *facere* 'to make']

tubiform *adj.* tube-shaped.

tubing *n.* **1** a length of tube. **2** a quantity of tubes.

tub-thumper *n. colloq.* a ranting preacher or orator. □ **tub-thumping** *adj. & n.*

tubular *adj.* **1** tube-shaped. **2** having or consisting of tubes.

tubular bells *n.pl.* ▼ an orchestral instrument consisting of a row of vertically suspended metal tubes that are struck with a hammer. ▷ ORCHESTRA, PERCUSSION

TUBIFEX WORMS

T

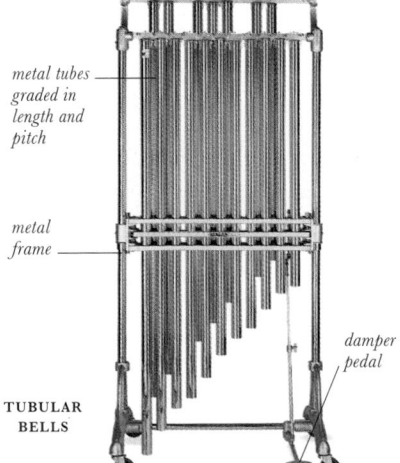

metal tubes graded in length and pitch

metal frame

damper pedal

TUBULAR BELLS

tubule *n.* a small tube in a plant or an animal body. [from Latin *tubulus* 'little tube']

TUC *abbr.* (in the UK) Trades Union Congress.

tuck ● *v.tr.* **1** (often foll. by *in*) **a** draw, fold, or turn the outer or end parts of (cloth or clothes etc.) close together so as to be held; thrust in the edge of (a thing) so as to confine it (*tucked his shirt into his trousers*). **b** (often foll. by *up*) thrust in the edges of bedclothes around (a person) (*came to tuck me in*). **2** draw together into a small space (*tucked her legs under her*). **3** stow (a thing) away in a specified place or way (*tucked it in a corner*). **4 a** make a stitched fold in (material, a garment, etc.). **b** shorten, tighten, or ornament with stitched folds. ● *n.* **1** a flattened usu. stitched fold in material, a garment, esp. for shortening, tightening, or ornament. **2** *Brit. colloq.* food, esp. cakes and sweets eaten by children (also *attrib.*: *tuck box*). **3** (in full **tuck position**) (in diving, gymnastics, etc.) a position with the knees bent upwards into the chest and the hands clasped round the shins. □ **tuck in** *Brit. colloq.* eat food heartily. **tuck into** (or **away**) *colloq.* eat (food) heartily (*tucked into their dinner*; *could really tuck it away*). [from Middle Dutch *tucken*]

tucker ● *n.* **1** *hist.* a piece of lace or linen etc. in or on a woman's bodice. **2** *Austral. colloq.* food. ● *v.tr.* (esp. in *passive*; often foll. by *out*) *N. Amer. colloq.* tire, exhaust.

tucker-bag *n.* (also **tucker-box**) *Austral. & NZ colloq.* a container for food.

tuck-in *n. Brit. colloq.* a large meal.

tucking *n.* a series of usu. stitched tucks in material or a garment.

tuck position see TUCK *n.* 3.

tuck shop *n. Brit.* a small shop, esp. near or in a school, selling food to children.

Tudor *hist.* ● *adj.* **1** of, characteristic of, or associated with the royal family of England ruling 1485–1603 or this period. **2** of or relating to the architectural style of this period, esp. with half-timbering. ▷ ARCH. ● *n.* a member of the Tudor royal family. [from Owen Tudor of Wales, grandfather of Henry VII]

Tudor rose *n.* ► a figure of a rose, esp. a combination of the red and white roses of Lancaster and York adopted as a badge by Henry VII. ▷ EMBOSS

Tues. *abbr.* (also **Tue.**) Tuesday.

Tuesday ● *n.* the third day of the week, following Monday. ● *adv. colloq.* **1** on Tuesday. **2** (**Tuesdays**) on Tuesdays; each Tuesday. [Old English, from *Tīw*, Germanic god identified with Roman Mars]

tufa *n.* **1** ► a porous rock composed of calcium carbonate and formed round mineral springs. **2** = TUFF. [Italian] □ **tufaceous** *adj.*

tuff *n.* rock formed by the consolidation of volcanic ash. [from Late Latin *tofus*] □ **tuffaceous** *adj.*

tuffet *n.* **1** = TUFT. **2** a low seat. [variant of TUFT]

TUFA

tuft *n.* **1** a bunch or collection of threads, grass, feathers, hair, etc., held or growing together at the base. **2** *Anat.* a bunch of small nerves. [Middle English] □ **tufty** *adj.*

tufted *adj.* having or growing in a tuft or tufts.

tufted duck *n.* a small freshwater duck, *Aythya fuligula*, of the Old World, with black or brown plumage and a drooping crest.

tug ● *v.tr. & (foll. by at)* intr. (**tugged, tugging**) pull hard or violently; jerk (*tugged it from my grasp*; *tugged at my sleeve*). ● *n.* **1** a hard, violent, or jerky pull. **2** a sudden strong emotional feeling (*felt a tug as I watched them go*). **3** a small powerful boat for towing larger boats and ships. [Middle English] □ **tugger** *n.*

tugboat *n.* = TUG *n.* 3.

tug of love *n. Brit. colloq.* a dispute over the custody of a child.

tug-of-war *n.* **1** a trial of strength between two sides pulling against each other on a rope. **2** a decisive or severe contest.

tuition *n.* teaching or instruction, esp. if paid for. [from Latin *tuitio*] □ **tuitional** *adj.*

tulip *n.* any bulbous spring-flowering plant of the genus *Tulipa*, esp. one of the many cultivated forms with showy cup-shaped flowers of various colours and markings. [from Persian *dulband* 'turban', from the shape of the flower]

tulip tree *n.* ► any of various N. American trees of the genus *Liriodendron*, with tulip-like flowers and lobed leaves.

tulle /tewl/ *n.* a soft fine silk etc. net for veils and dresses. [from *Tulle*, a town in SW France]

TULIP TREE: FLOWER AND LEAVES (*Liriodendron tulipifera*)

tum *n. Brit. colloq.* stomach.

tumble ● *v.* **1** *intr. & tr.* fall or cause to fall suddenly, clumsily, or headlong. **2** *intr.* fall rapidly in amount etc. (*prices tumbled*). **3** *intr.* (often foll. by *about, around*) roll or toss erratically or helplessly to and fro. **4** *intr.* move or rush in a headlong or blundering manner (*the children tumbled out of the car*). **5** *intr.* (often foll. by *to*) *colloq.* grasp the meaning or hidden implication of an idea, circumstance, etc. (*they quickly tumbled to our intentions*). **6** *tr.* overturn; fling or push roughly or carelessly. **7** *intr.* perform acrobatic feats, esp. somersaults. **8** *tr.* dry (washing) in a tumble-dryer. ● *n.* **1** a sudden or headlong fall. **2** a somersault or other acrobatic feat. **3** an untidy or confused state. [from Old High German *tumalōn*]

tumbledown *adj.* falling or fallen into ruin; dilapidated.

tumble-dryer *n.* (also **tumble-drier**) a machine for drying washing in a heated rotating drum. □ **tumble-dry** *v.tr. & intr.* (**-dries, -dried**).

tumbler *n.* **1** a drinking glass with no handle or foot. **2** an acrobat, esp. one performing somersaults. **3** a pivoted piece in a lock that holds the bolt until lifted by a key. □ **tumblerful** *n.* (*pl.* **-fuls**).

tumbleweed *n. N. Amer. & Austral.* a plant of arid areas, esp. *Amaranthus albus*, forming a globular bush that breaks off in late summer and is tumbled about by the wind.

TUDOR ROSE: 16TH-CENTURY ENGLISH CARVED EMBLEM

tumbril *n.* (also **tumbrel**) *hist.* an open cart in which condemned persons were conveyed to their execution, esp. to the guillotine during the French Revolution. [from Old French *tumberel*]

tumefy *v.* (**-ies, -ied**) **1** *intr.* swell, inflate; be inflated. **2** *tr.* cause to do this.

tumescent *adj.* **1** becoming tumid; swelling. **2** swelling as a response to sexual stimulation. [from Latin *tumescent-* 'swelling'] □ **tumescence** *n.* **tumescently** *adv.*

tumid *adj.* **1** (of parts of the body etc.) swollen, inflated. **2** (of a style etc.) inflated, bombastic. [from Latin *tumidus*] □ **tumidity** *n.* **tumidly** *adv.*

tummy *n.* (*pl.* **-ies**) *colloq.* the stomach. [childish pronunciation of STOMACH]

tummy button *n. colloq.* the navel.

tumour *n.* (*US* **tumor**) a swelling, esp. from an abnormal growth of tissue, whether benign or malignant. [from Latin *tumor*] □ **tumorous** *adj.*

tumult *n.* **1** an uproar or din, esp. of a disorderly crowd. **2** an angry demonstration by a mob; a riot;

TUNDRA

The tundra is a cold treeless plain located in the Arctic Circle. Worn smooth by huge ice sheets in past ages, the region is an open landscape of shallow lakes, barren outcrops, and hillocks. Vegetation is sparse as the subsoil remains frozen all year with permafrost, and wildlife is largely restricted to small, hardy species. Unique ground features such as stone polygons and pingos are caused by freezing and thawing of subterranean ice.

SECTION THROUGH A TUNDRA LANDSCAPE

stone polygons · marshy land · lake · sparse vegetation · pingo (hillock over ice core) · gravel-filled ice wedge · involution of thawed and refrozen sediments (cryoturbation) · crack formed as sediments freeze and expand · subsoil frozen with permafrost

a public disturbance. **3** a conflict of emotions in the mind. [from Latin *tumultus*]

tumultuous *adj.* **1** noisily vehement; uproarious; making a tumult (*a tumultuous welcome*). **2** disorderly. **3** agitated. □ **tumultuously** *adv.* **tumultuousness** *n.*

tumulus *n.* (*pl.* **tumuli**) an ancient burial mound or barrow. [Latin]

tun *n.* **1** a large beer or wine cask. **2** a brewer's fermenting-vat. [from medieval Latin *tunna*]

tuna *n.* (*pl.* same or **tunas**) **1** any marine fish of the family Scombridae native to tropical and warm waters, having a round body and pointed snout, and used for food. ▷ SKIPJACK. **2** (in full **tuna fish**) the flesh of the tuna. [from Spanish *atún* 'tunny']

tundra *n.* ▲ a vast level treeless Arctic region usu. with a marshy surface and underlying permafrost. [Lappish]

tune ● *n.* a melody with or without harmony. ● *v.tr.* **1** put (a musical instrument) in tune. **2** *tr.* (often foll. by *in*; also *absol.*) adjust (a radio receiver etc.) to the particular frequency of the required signals (*he tuned the radio*; *she tuned in to Radio 2*). **3** adjust (an engine etc.) to run smoothly and efficiently. **4** (foll. by *to*) adjust or adapt to a required or different purpose, situation, etc. □ **in tune 1** having the correct pitch or intonation (*sings in tune*). **2** (usu. foll. by *with*) harmonizing with one's company, surroundings, etc. **out of tune 1** not having the correct pitch or intonation (*always plays out of tune*). **2** (usu. foll. by *with*) clashing with one's company etc. **to the tune of** *colloq.* to the considerable sum or amount of. **tuned in** (often foll. by *to*) *colloq.* acquainted; in rapport; up to date (with). **tune up 1** (of a musician) bring one's instrument to the proper or uniform pitch. **2** bring to the most efficient condition. [Middle English] □ **tunable** *adj.* (also **tuneable**).

tuneful *adj.* melodious, musical. □ **tunefully** *adv.* **tunefulness** *n.*

tuneless *adj.* **1** unmelodious, unmusical. **2** out of tune. □ **tunelessly** *adv.* **tunelessness** *n.*

tuner *n.* **1** a person who tunes musical instruments, esp. pianos. **2** a device for tuning a radio receiver.

tungsten *n.* *Chem.* a steel-grey dense metallic element with a very high melting point, occurring naturally in scheelite and used for the filaments of electric lamps and for alloying steel etc. [Swedish, from *tung* 'heavy' + *sten* 'stone'] □ **tungstate** *n.*

tungsten carbide *n.* a very hard black substance used in making dies and cutting tools.

tunic *n.* **1** a close-fitting short coat of police or military etc. uniform. **2** a loose often sleeveless garment usu. reaching to about the knees, as worn in ancient Greece and Rome. ▷ TOGA. **3** a gymslip. **4** any of various similar loose often mid-thigh length garments, usu. worn over a skirt, blouse, or trousers. [from Latin *tunica*]

tunicate *n.* any marine animal of the subphylum Urochordata, having a rubbery or hard outer coat, and including sea squirts.

tuning *n.* the process or a system of putting a musical instrument in tune.

tuning fork *n.* ▶ a two-pronged steel fork that gives a particular note when struck, used in tuning.

tunnel ● *n.* **1** an artificial underground passage through a hill or under a road or river etc., esp. for a railway or road to pass through, or in a mine. **2** an underground passage dug by a burrowing animal. ● *v.* (**tunnelled, tunnelling,** *US* **tunneled, tunneling**) **1** *intr.* (foll. by *through, into,* etc.) make a tunnel through (a hill etc.). **2** *tr.* make (one's way) by tunnelling. [from Old French *tonel* 'little cask'] □ **tunneller** *n.*

tunnel vision *n.* **1** vision that is defective in not adequately including objects away from the centre

prong

TUNING FORK

of the field of view. **2** *colloq.* **a** concentration focused on a limited or single objective, perception, etc. **b** inability to be diverted or swayed from this.

tunny *n.* (*pl.* same or **-ies**) esp. *Brit.* = TUNA. [from Greek *thunnos*]

tup esp. *Brit.* ● *n.* **1** a male sheep; a ram. **2** the striking-head of a piledriver, etc. ● *v.tr.* (**tupped, tupping**) (of a ram) copulate with (a ewe). [Middle English]

tuppence *n. Brit.* = TWOPENCE.

tuppenny *adj. Brit.* = TWOPENNY.

Tupperware *n. propr.* a range of plastic containers for storing food. [from *Tupper*, name of the US manufacturer]

tuque /rhymes with spook/ *n.* a Canadian stocking cap. [Canadian French form of TOQUE]

turban *n.* **1** a man's headdress of cotton or silk wound round a cap or the head, worn esp. by Muslims and Sikhs. **2** ▶ a woman's headdress or hat resembling this. [from Persian *dulband*] □ **turbaned** *adj.*

TURBAN: CEREMONIAL WEST AFRICAN TURBAN

turbid *adj.* **1** (of a liquid or colour) muddy, thick; not clear. **2** (of a style etc.) confused, disordered. [based on Latin *turba* 'a crowd, a disturbance'] □ **turbidity** *n.* **turbidly** *adv.* **turbidness** *n.*

■ **Usage** *Turbid* is sometimes confused with *turgid*, which means (of language) 'inflated, pompous', or (of objects) 'swollen, distended'. The confusion arises because, as well as sounding similar, both words are used (in different senses) of rivers etc. on the one hand, and of literary style on the other.

turbine *n.* a rotary motor or engine driven by a flow of water, steam, gas, wind, etc., esp. to produce electrical power. ▷ HYDROELECTRIC, JET ENGINE, NUCLEAR POWER, STEAM TURBINE. [from Latin *turbo -binis* 'spinning top, whirlwind']

turbo *n.* (*pl.* **-os**) **1** = TURBOCHARGER. **2** a motor vehicle equipped with this.

turbocharger *n.* ▼ a supercharger driven by a turbine powered by the engine's exhaust gases. □ **turbocharge** *v.tr.* (esp. as **turbocharged** *adj.*).

turbofan *n. Aeron.* **1** a jet engine in which a turbine-driven fan provides additional thrust. ▷ JET ENGINE. **2** an aircraft powered by this.

TURBOCHARGER

A turbocharger is a form of supercharger – a device that increases an engine's power and efficiency by forced induction of compressed air and fuel (the charge) into the cylinders, providing a greater explosion on the power stroke. The compressor, powered by an exhaust-driven turbine, impels pressurized air into the cylinders, while a fuel injector introduces a metered dose of fuel into this airstream.

TURBOCHARGER ON A MODERN V6 ENGINE

inlet passage · air and fuel vapour fed to fuel injector · air compressor · distributor · engine · exhaust turbine · exhaust gases diverted into turbocharger · outlet for exhaust gases · oil pipe · air inlet · air filter

T

turbojet *n. Aeron.* **1** a jet engine in which the jet also operates a turbine-driven compressor for the air drawn into the engine. ▷ JET ENGINE. **2** an aircraft powered by this.

turboprop *n. Aeron.* **1** a jet engine in which a turbine is used as in a turbojet and also to drive a propeller. ▷ JET ENGINE. **2** an aircraft powered by this.

turboshaft *n.* a gas turbine that powers a shaft for driving heavy vehicles, generators, pumps, etc.

turbot *n.* (*pl.* same or **turbots**) **1** ▼ a flatfish, *Scophthalmus maximus*, prized as food. **2** any of various similar fishes including halibut. [from Old Swedish *törnbut*]

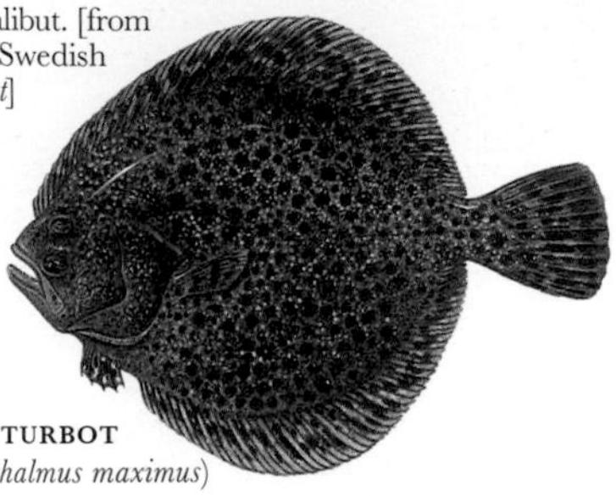

TURBOT
(*Scophthalmus maximus*)

turbulence *n.* **1** an irregularly fluctuating flow of air or fluid. **2** *Meteorol.* stormy conditions as a result of atmospheric disturbance. **3** a disturbance, commotion, or tumult.

turbulent *adj.* **1** disturbed; in commotion. **2** (of a flow of air etc.) varying irregularly; causing disturbance. **3** tumultuous. **4** insubordinate, riotous. [from Latin *turbulentus*] □ **turbulently** *adv.*

turd *n. coarse slang* **1** a lump of excrement. **2** a term of contempt for a person. [Old English]

tureen *n.* a deep covered dish for serving soup etc. [from French *terrine* 'earthenware dish']

turf ● *n.* (*pl.* **turfs** or **turves**) **1 a** a layer of grass etc. with earth and matted roots as the surface of grassland. **b** a piece of this cut from the ground. **2** a slab of peat for fuel. **3** (prec. by *the*) **a** horse racing generally. **b** a general term for racecourses. ● *v.tr.* **1** cover (ground) with turf. **2** (foll. by *out*) esp. *Brit. colloq.* expel or eject (a person or thing). [Old English]

turf accountant *n. Brit.* a bookmaker.

turfman *n.* (*pl.* **-men**) esp. *US* a devotee of horse racing.

turfy *adj.* (**turfier, turfiest**) like turf; grassy.

turgescent *adj.* becoming turgid; swelling. □ **turgescence** *n.*

turgid *adj.* **1** (of language) pompous, bombastic (*the film was spoilt by a turgid script*). **2** swollen, distended, puffed out (*sat by the turgid Thames*). [based on Latin *turgēre* 'to swell'] □ **turgidity** *n.* **turgidly** *adv.* **turgidness** *n.*

■ **Usage** See Usage Note at TURBID.

turion *n. Bot.* **1** a young shoot or sucker arising from an underground bud. **2** a bud formed by certain aquatic plants. [from Latin *turio -onis* 'shoot']

Turk *n.* **1 a** a native or national of Turkey in SE Europe and Asia Minor. **b** a person of Turkish descent. **2** a member of a central Asian people from whom the Ottomans derived, speaking Turkic languages. **3** *offens.* a ferocious, wild, or unmanageable person. [Middle English]

turkey *n.* (*pl.* **-eys**) **1** a large mainly domesticated game bird, *Meleagris gallopavo*, originally of N. America, having a bald head and (in the male) red wattles, prized as food esp. on festive occasions including Christmas and (in the US) Thanksgiving. ▷ WATTLE. **2** the flesh of the turkey as food. **3** esp. *N. Amer. slang* **a** a theatrical failure; a flop. **b** a stupid or inept person. □ **talk turkey** *N. Amer. colloq.* talk frankly and straightforwardly; get down to business. [short for *turkeycock* or *turkeyhen*, originally applied to guinea fowl imported through Turkey]

Turkey carpet *n.* = TURKISH CARPET.

turkeycock *n.* **1** a male turkey. **2** a pompous or self-important person.

Turkic ● *adj.* of or relating to a large group of Altaic languages including Turkish, Azerbaijani, and Kyrgyz, or the peoples speaking them. ● *n.* the Turkic languages collectively.

Turkish ● *adj.* of or relating to Turkey in SE Europe and Asia Minor, or to the Turks or their language. ● *n.* this language.

Turkish bath *n.* **1** a hot-air or steam bath followed by washing, massage, etc. **2** (in *sing.* or *pl.*) a building for this.

Turkish carpet *n.* a wool carpet with a thick pile and traditional bold design.

Turkish coffee *n.* a strong black coffee.

Turkish delight *n.* a sweet of flavoured gelatin cubes coated in powdered sugar.

Turkish towel *n.* a towel made of cotton terry.

turmeric *n.* **1** ► a tropical Asian plant, *Curcuma longa*, of the ginger family, yielding aromatic rhizomes used as a spice and for yellow dye. **2** this rhizome powdered and used as a spice esp. in curry powder. ▷ SPICE

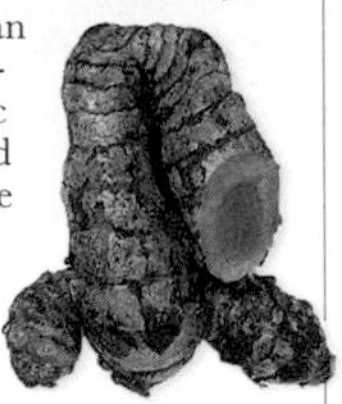

TURMERIC ROOT
(*Curcuma longa*)

turmoil *n.* **1** violent confusion; agitation. **2** din and bustle. [16th-century coinage]

turn ● *v.* **1** *tr.* & *intr.* move around a point or axis so that the point or axis remains in a central position; give a rotary motion to or receive a rotary motion (*turned the wheel; the wheel turns; the key turns in the lock*). **2** *tr.* & *intr.* change in position so that a different side, end, or part becomes outermost or uppermost etc.; invert or reverse or cause to be inverted or reversed (*turned inside out; turned it upside down*). **3 a** *tr.* give a new direction to (*turn your face this way*). **b** *intr.* take a new direction (*turn left here; my thoughts have often turned to you*). **4** *tr.* aim in a certain way (*turned the hose on them*). **5** *intr.* & *tr.* (foll. by *into*) change in nature, form, or condition to (*turned into a dragon; turned the book into a play*). **6** *intr.* (foll. by *to*) **a** apply oneself to; set about (*turned to doing the ironing*). **b** have recourse to; begin to indulge in habitually (*turned to drink; turned to me for help*). **c** go on to consider next (*let us now turn to your report*). **7** *intr.* & *tr.* become or cause to become (*turned hostile; has turned informer; your comment turned them angry*). **8 a** *tr.* & *intr.* (foll. by *against*) make or become hostile to (*has turned them against us*). **b** *intr.* (foll. by *on, upon*) become hostile to; attack (*suddenly turned on them*). **9** *intr.* (of hair or leaves) change colour. **10** *intr.* (of milk) become sour. **11** *intr.* (of the stomach) be nauseated. **12** *tr.* twist or sprain (an ankle). **13** *intr.* (of the head) become giddy. **14** *tr.* cause (milk) to become sour, (the stomach) to be nauseated, or (the head) to become giddy. **15** *tr.* translate (*turn it into French*). **16** *tr.* move to the other side of; go round (*turned the corner*). **17** *tr.* pass the age or time of (*he has turned 40; it has now turned 4 o'clock*). **18** *intr.* (foll. by *on*) depend on; be determined by (*it all turns on the weather tomorrow*). **19** *tr.* send or put into a specified place or condition; cause to go (*was turned loose; turned the water out into a basin*). **20** *tr.* perform (a somersault etc.) with rotary motion. **21** *tr.* make (a profit). **22** *tr.* shape (an object) on a lathe. **23** *intr.* (of the tide) change from flood to ebb or vice versa. ● *n.* **1** the act or process or an instance of turning; rotary motion (*a single turn of the handle*). **2 a** a changed or a change of direction or tendency (*took a sudden turn to the left*). **b** a deflection or deflected part (*full of twists and turns*). **3** a point at which a turning or change occurs. **4** a turning of a road. **5** a change of the tide from flood to ebb or vice versa. **6** a change in the course of events. **7** a tendency or disposition (*is of a mechanical turn of mind*). **8** an opportunity or obligation etc. that comes successively to each of several persons etc. (*your turn will come; my turn to read*). **9** a short walk or ride (*shall take a turn in the garden*). **10** a short performance on stage or in a circus etc. **11** service of a specified kind (*did me a good turn*). **12** purpose (*served my turn*). **13** *colloq.* a momentary nervous shock or ill feeling (*gave me quite a turn*). **14** *Mus.* an ornament consisting of the principal note with those above and below it. □ **at every turn** continually; at each new stage etc. **by turns** in rotation of individuals or groups. **in turn** in succession; one by one. **in one's turn** when one's turn or opportunity comes. **not know which way** (or **where**) **to turn** be completely at a loss, unsure how to act, etc. **not turn a hair** see HAIR. **on the turn 1** changing. **2** (of milk) becoming sour. **3** at the turning point. **out of turn 1** at a time when it is not one's turn. **2** inappropriately; inadvisedly or tactlessly. **take turns** (or **take it in turns**) act or work alternately or in succession. **to a turn** (esp. cooked) to exactly the right degree etc. **turn about** move so as to face in a new direction. **turn and turn about** esp. *Brit.* alternately. **turn around** esp. *N. Amer.* = *turn round*. **turn away 1** turn to face in another direction. **2** refuse to accept; reject. **3** send away. **turn back 1** begin or cause to retrace one's steps. **2** fold back. **turn one's back on** see BACK. **turn the corner 1** pass round it into another street. **2** pass the critical point in an illness, difficulty, etc. **turn a deaf ear** see DEAF. **turn down 1** reject (a proposal, application, etc.). **2** reduce the volume or strength of (sound, heat, etc.) by turning a knob etc. **3** fold down. **4** place downwards. **turn one's hand to** see HAND. **turn a person's head** see HEAD. **turn in 1** hand in or return. **2** achieve or register (a performance, score, etc.). **3** *colloq.* go to bed in the evening. **4** fold inwards. **5** incline inwards. **6** hand over (a suspect etc.) to the authorities. **7** *colloq.* abandon (a plan etc.). **turn off 1 a** stop the flow or operation of (water etc.) by means of a tap etc. **b** operate (a tap etc.) to achieve this. **2 a** enter a side road. **b** (of a side road) lead off from another road. **3** *colloq.* repel; cause to lose interest. **4** dismiss from employment. **turn of speed** the ability to go fast when necessary. **turn on 1 a** start the flow or operation of (water etc.) by means of a tap etc. **b** operate (a tap etc.) to achieve this. **2** *colloq.* excite; stimulate the interest of, esp. sexually. **3** *tr.* & *intr. slang* intoxicate or become intoxicated with drugs. **turn on one's heel** see HEEL[1]. **turn the other cheek** see CHEEK. **turn out 1** expel. **2** extinguish (an electric light etc.). **3** dress or equip (*well turned out*). **4** produce (manufactured goods etc.). **5** *Brit.* empty or clean out (a room etc.). **6** empty (a pocket) to see the contents. **7** *colloq.* **a** get out of bed. **b** go out of doors. **8** *colloq.* attend a meeting etc. **9** (often foll. by *to* + infin. or *that* + clause) prove to be the case; result (*turned out to be true*). **10** *Mil.* call (a guard) from the guardroom. **turn over 1** reverse or cause to reverse vertical position; bring the under or reverse side into view (*turn over the page*). **2** upset; fall or cause to fall over. **3 a** cause (an engine) to run. **b** (of an engine) start running. **4** consider thoroughly. **5** (foll. by *to*) **a** transfer the care or conduct of (a person or thing) to (a person). **b** = *turn in* 6. **6** do business to the amount of (*turns over £5,000 a week*). **turn over a new leaf** improve one's conduct or performance. **turn round 1** turn so as to face in a new direction. **2 a** *Commerce* unload and reload (a ship, vehicle, etc.). **b** receive, process, and send out again. **3** adopt new opinions or policy. **turn the scales** see SCALE[2]. **turn the tables** see TABLE. **turn tail** turn one's back; run away. **turn the tide** reverse the trend of events. **turn to** set about one's work. **turn to account** see ACCOUNT. **turn turtle** see TURTLE. **turn up 1** increase the volume or strength of by turning a knob etc. **2** discover or reveal. **3** be found, esp. by chance. **4** happen or present itself. **5** shorten (a garment) by increasing the size of the hem. **turn up one's nose** see NOSE. [from Greek *tornos* 'lathe, circular movement']

turnabout *n.* **1** an act of turning about. **2** an abrupt change of policy etc.

turnaround *n.* **1 a** the process of receiving, processing, and sending out again; progress through a system; the time taken for this. **b** the process of unloading and reloading a ship, vehicle, etc.; the time taken for this. **2** an abrupt or unexpected change of fortune, attitude, etc.

turncoat *n.* a person who changes sides in a conflict, dispute, etc.

turndown ● *n.* **1** a rejection or refusal. **2** a downturn. ● *attrib.adj.* (of a collar) turned down.

turner *n.* **1** a person or thing that turns. **2** a person who works with a lathe. [Middle English]

turnery *n.* **1** objects made on a lathe. **2** work with a lathe.

turning *n.* **1 a** a road that branches off another. **b** a place where this occurs. **2 a** use of the lathe. **b** (in *pl.*) chips or shavings from a lathe.

turning circle *n.* the smallest circle in which a vehicle can turn without reversing.

turning point *n.* a point at which a decisive change occurs.

turnip *n.* **1** a cruciferous plant, *Brassica rapa*, with a large white globular root and sprouting leaves. **2** the root of such a plant used as a vegetable. [based on Latin *napus* 'turnip'] □ **turnipy** *adj.*

turnip-tops *n.pl.* (*US* also **turnip greens**) the leaves of the turnip eaten as a vegetable.

turnkey ● *n.* (*pl.* **-eys**) *archaic* a jailer. ● *adj.* (of a contract etc.) providing for a supply of equipment in a state ready for operation.

turn-off *n.* **1** a turning off a main road. **2** *colloq.* something that repels or causes a loss of interest.

turn-on *n. colloq.* a person or thing that causes (esp. sexual) arousal.

turnout *n.* **1** the number of people attending a meeting, voting at an election, etc. **2** the quantity of goods produced in a given time. **3** a set or display of equipment, clothes, etc.

turnover *n.* **1** the act or an instance of turning over. **2** the amount of money taken in a business. **3** the number of people entering and leaving employment etc. **4** a small pie or tart made by folding a piece of pastry over a filling.

turnpike *n.* **1** *hist.* a defensive frame of spikes. **2** *hist.* **a** a toll gate. **b** a road on which a toll was collected at a toll gate. **3** *US* a motorway on which a toll is charged.

turnround *n.* = TURNAROUND.

turnstile *n.* a gate with revolving arms allowing people through singly.

turntable *n.* **1** a circular revolving plate supporting a gramophone record that is being played. **2** a circular revolving platform for turning esp. a railway locomotive.

turn-up *n.* **1** *Brit.* the lower turned-up end of a trouser leg. **2** (esp. in phr. **turn-up for the books**) *Brit. colloq.* an unexpected (esp. welcome) happening; a surprise.

turpentine ● *n.* **1** (in full **crude turpentine** or **gum turpentine**) a sticky fragrant resin secreted by esp. pines. **2** (in full **oil of turpentine**) a volatile pungent oil distilled from gum turpentine or pinewood, and used in mixing paints etc., and in medicine. ● *v.tr.* apply turpentine to. [from Latin *ter(e)binthina (resina)* 'terebinth (resin)']

turpitude *n. formal* baseness, depravity, wickedness. [from Latin *turpitudo*]

turps *n. colloq.* oil of turpentine.

turquoise ● *n.* **1** ◀ a semi-precious stone, usu. opaque and of a greenish-blue or sky-blue colour, consisting of hydrated copper aluminium phosphate. ▷ GEM, MINERAL. **2** a greenish-blue colour. ● *adj.* of this colour. [from Old French *turqueise* 'Turkish (stone)']

turret *n.* **1** a small tower, esp. decorating a building. ▷ CASTLE. **2** a low flat usu. revolving armoured tower for a gun and gunners in a ship, aircraft, fort,

or tank. ▷ WARSHIP. **3** a rotating holder for tools in a lathe etc. [from Old French *to(u)rete*] □ **turreted** *adj.*

turret lathe *n.* = CAPSTAN LATHE.

turtle *n.* **1** ▼ any of various marine or freshwater reptiles of the order Chelonia, encased in a shell of bony plates, and having flippers or webbed toes. ▷ CHELONIAN. **2** the flesh of the turtle, esp. used for soup. **3** *Computing* a directional cursor in a computer graphics system which can be instructed to move around a screen. □ **turn turtle** capsize; turn upside down.

TURTLE:
HAWKSBILL TURTLE
(*Eretmochelys imbricata*)

carapace — bony plate (scute) — beak — flipper

turtle-dove *n.* any wild dove of the genus *Streptopelia*, noted for its soft cooing and its affection for its mate. [based on Latin *turtur*]

turtleneck *n.* **1** *Brit.* a high close-fitting neck on a knitted garment. **2** *US* = POLO NECK.

turtle shell ● *n.* = TORTOISESHELL *n.* 1. ● *adj.* (**turtle-shell**) = TORTOISESHELL *adj.*

turves *pl.* of TURF.

Tuscan ● *n.* an inhabitant of Tuscany in central Italy. ● *adj.* **1** of or relating to Tuscany or the Tuscans. **2** *Archit.* denoting the least ornamented of the classical orders. ▷ COLUMN

tush[1] *int. archaic* expressing strong disapproval or scorn. [Middle English]

tush[2] *n.* esp. *N. Amer. slang* the buttocks.

tusk *n.* ▼ a long pointed tooth, esp. protruding from a closed mouth, as in the elephant, walrus, etc. ▷ ELEPHANT, WALRUS. [Old English] □ **tusked** *adj.* (also in *comb.*). **tusky** *adj.*

point of entry into skull

TUSK OF AN ELEPHANT

tusker *n.* an elephant or wild boar with well-developed tusks.

tussah *US* var. of TUSSORE.

tusser var. of TUSSORE.

tussle ● *n.* a struggle or scuffle. ● *v.intr.* engage in a tussle. [originally Scots & northern English]

tussock *n.* a clump of grass etc. [16th-century coinage] □ **tussocky** *adj.*

tussock grass *n.* a grass which grows in tussocks, esp. of the genus *Poa*, *Nassella*, or *Deschampsia*.

tussore *n.* (also **tusser**, *US* **tussah**) **1** an Indian or Chinese silkworm, *Antheraea mylitta*, yielding strong but coarse brown silk. **2** (in full **tussore-silk**) silk from this. [from Sanskrit *tasara* 'shuttle']

tut var. of TUT-TUT.

tutee *n.* a student or pupil of a tutor.

tutelage *n.* **1** guardianship. **2** the state or duration of being under this. **3** tuition. [based on Latin *tutela* 'keeping']

tutelary *adj.* (also **tutelar**) **1 a** serving as guardian. **b** relating to a guardian. **2** giving protection (*tutelary saint*). [from Latin *tutelarius*]

tutor ● *n.* **1** a private teacher, esp one in general charge of a person's education. **2** *Brit.* a university teacher supervising the studies or welfare of assigned undergraduates. **3** *Brit.* a book of instruction in a subject. ● *v.* **1** *tr.* act as a tutor to. **2** *intr.* work as a tutor. **3** *tr.* restrain, discipline. **4** *intr. US* receive tuition. [Latin] □ **tutorage** *n.* **tutorship** *n.*

tutorial ● *adj.* of or relating to a tutor or tuition. ● *n.* **1** a period of undergraduate tuition given to an individual or a small group. **2** an explanation of a subject, printed or on-screen, intended for private study. □ **tutorially** *adv.*

Tutsi /tuut-si/ *n.* (*pl.* same or **Tutsis**) a member of a Bantu-speaking people forming a minority of the population of Rwanda. [Bantu]

tutti /tuut-i/ *Mus.* ● *adv.* with all voices or instruments together. ● *n.* (*pl.* **tuttis**) a passage to be performed in this way. [Italian]

tutti-frutti /too-ti-**froo**-ti/ *n.* (*pl.* **-fruttis**) a confection, esp. ice cream, of or flavoured with mixed fruits. [Italian, literally 'all fruits']

tut-tut (also **tut**, **tsk**, **tsk tsk**) ● *int.* expressing rebuke, impatience, or contempt. ● *n.* such an exclamation. ● *v.intr.* (**-tutted**, **-tutting**) exclaim this.

tutu *n.* a ballet dancer's short skirt of stiffened projecting frills. [French]

tu-whit tu-whoo *n.* a representation of the cry of an owl.

tux *n. N. Amer. colloq.* = TUXEDO.

tuxedo /tuk-**see**-doh/ *n.* (*pl.* **-os** or **-oes**) *N. Amer.* **1** a dinner jacket. **2** a suit of clothes including this. [after a country club at *Tuxedo* Park, New York]

TV *abbr.* television (the system or a set).

TVEI *abbr.* Technical and Vocational Educational Initiative.

TVP *abbr. propr.* textured vegetable protein, obtained from soya beans and made to resemble meat.

twaddle /twod-ĕl/ *n.* useless, senseless, or dull writing or talk. [alteration of TATTLE] □ **twaddler** *n.*

twain *adj. & n. archaic* two (usu. *in twain*). [Old English]

twang ● *n.* **1** a strong ringing sound made by a plucked string or a released bowstring. **2** the nasal quality of a voice compared to this. ● *v.intr. & tr.* emit or cause to emit this sound. □ **twangy** *adj.*

'twas *archaic* it was.

twat *n. coarse slang* **1** the female genitals. **2** a term of contempt for a person. [17th-century coinage]

tweak ● *v.tr.* **1** pinch and twist sharply; pull with a sharp jerk; twitch. **2** make fine adjustments to (a mechanism). ● *n.* an instance of tweaking.

twee *adj.* (**tweer**, **tweest**) *Brit.* usu. *derog.* affectedly dainty or quaint. [childish pronunciation of SWEET] □ **tweely** *adv.* **tweeness** *n.*

tweed *n.* **1** a rough-surfaced woollen cloth, usu. of mixed flecked colours. **2** (in *pl.*) clothes made of tweed. [originally a misreading of *tweel*, Scots form of TWILL]

tweedy *adj.* (**tweedier**, **tweediest**) **1** of or relating to tweed cloth. **2** characteristic of country gentry; heartily informal. □ **tweedily** *adv.* **tweediness** *n.*

tweet (also **tweet tweet**) ● *n.* the chirp of a small bird. ● *v.intr.* make a chirping noise.

tweeter *n.* a loudspeaker designed to reproduce high frequencies (cf. WOOFER). ▷ LOUDSPEAKER

tweezers *n.pl.* ▶ a small pair of pincers for taking up small objects, plucking out hairs, etc. [extended form from obsolete *tweeze* 'a case for small instruments']

TWEEZERS

twelfth ● *n.* **1** the position in a sequence corresponding to the number 12 in the sequence 1–12. **2** something occupying this position. **3** each of twelve equal parts of a thing. ● *adj.* that is the twelfth. [Old English] □ **twelfthly** *adv.*

Twelfth Day *n.* 6 Jan., the festival of the Epiphany.

twelfth man *n.* a reserve member of a cricket team.

Twelfth Night *n.* **1** the evening of 5 Jan., the eve of the Epiphany. **2** = TWELFTH DAY.

twelve ● *n.* **1** one more than eleven; the product of two units and six units. **2** a symbol for this (12, xii, XII). **3** a size etc. denoted by twelve. **4** twelve o'clock. **5** (**the Twelve**) the Apostles. **6** (**12**) *Brit.* (of films) classified as suitable for persons of 12 years and over. ● *adj.* that amount to twelve. [Old English]

twelvefold *adj. & adv.* **1** twelve times as much or as many. **2** consisting of twelve parts.

twelvemonth *n. archaic* a year; a period of twelve months.

twelve-note *adj.* (also **twelve-tone**) *Mus.* using the twelve chromatic notes of the octave on an equal basis without dependence on a key system.

twenty ● *n.* (*pl.* **-ies**) **1** the product of two and ten. **2** a symbol for this (20, xx, XX). **3** (in *pl.*) the numbers from 20 to 29, esp. the years of a century or of a person's life. ● *adj.* that amount to twenty. [Old English] □ **twentieth** *adj. & n.* **twentyfold** *adj. & adv.*

twenty-twenty *adj.* (also **20/20**) **1** denoting vision of normal acuity. **2** *colloq.* denoting clear perception or hindsight.

twerp *n.* (also **twirp**) *slang* a stupid or objectionable person. [19th-century coinage]

twice *adv.* **1** two times (esp. of multiplication); on two occasions. **2** in double degree or quantity (*twice as good*). [Old English]

twiddle ● *v.* **1** *tr. &* (foll. by *with* etc.) intr. twirl, play idly. **2** *intr.* move twirlingly. ● *n.* **1** an act of twiddling. **2** a twirled mark or sign. □ **twiddle one's thumbs 1** make them rotate round each other. **2** have nothing to do. □ **twiddler** *n.* **twiddly** *adj.*

twig[1] *n.* a small branch or shoot of a tree or shrub. [Old English] □ **twigged** *adj.* (also in *comb.*). **twiggy** *adj.*

twig[2] *v.tr.* (**twigged**, **twigging**) *Brit. colloq.* (also *absol.*) understand; perceive. [18th-century coinage]

twilight *n.* **1** the soft glowing light from the sky when the Sun is below the horizon, esp. in the evening. **2** the period of this. **3** a faint light. **4** a period of decline or destruction. [Middle English]

twilight zone *n.* **1** an urban area that is becoming dilapidated. **2** any physical or conceptual area which is undefined or intermediate.

twilit *adj.* (also **twilighted**) dimly illuminated by or as by twilight.

twill ● *n.* a fabric so woven as to have a surface of diagonal parallel ridges. ● *v.tr.* (esp. as **twilled** *adj.*) weave (fabric) in this way. [Middle English] □ **twilled** *adj.*

twin ● *n.* **1** each of a closely related or associated pair, esp. of children or animals born at the same birth. **2** the exact counterpart of a person or thing. **3** (**the Twins**) the zodiacal sign or constellation Gemini. ● *adj.* forming, or being one of, such a pair (*twin brothers*). ● *v.* (**twinned**, **twinning**) **1** *tr. & intr.* **a** join intimately together. **b** (foll. by *with*) pair. **2** *intr.* bear twins. **3** *intr. & tr. Brit.* link or cause (a town) to link with one in a different country, for the purposes of cultural exchange. [Old English *twinn* 'double'] □ **twinning** *n.*

twin bed *n.* each of a pair of single beds. □ **twin-bedded** *adj.*

twin-cam *attrib.adj.* (esp. of an engine) having two camshafts.

twine ● *n.* **1** a strong thread or string of twisted strands of hemp or cotton etc. **2** a coil or twist. **3** a tangle; an interlacing. ● *v.* **1** *tr.* form (a string or thread etc.) by twisting strands together. **2** *tr.* form (a garland etc.) of interwoven material. **3** *intr.* (often foll. by *round, about, around*) coil or wind. **4** *intr. & refl.* (of a plant) grow in this way. [Old English *twin* 'linen'] □ **twiner** *n.*

twin-engined *adj.* having two engines.

twinge ● *n.* a sharp momentary local pain or pang. ● *v.intr. & tr.* (**twingeing** or **twinging**) experience or cause to experience a twinge. [Old English *twengan* 'to pinch, wring']

twinkle ● *v.* **1** *intr.* (of a star or light etc.) shine with rapidly intermittent gleams. **2** *intr.* (of the eyes) sparkle, **3** *intr.* (of the feet in dancing) move lightly and rapidly. **4** *tr.* emit (a light or signal) in quick gleams. ● *n.* **1 a** a sparkle or gleam of the eyes. **b** a blink or wink. **2** a slight flash of light. **3** a short rapid movement. □ **in a twinkle** (or **a twinkling** or **the twinkling of an eye**) in an instant. [Old English] □ **twinkler** *n.* **twinkly** *adj.*

twin-screw *attrib.adj.* (of a ship) having two propellers on separate shafts with opposite twists.

twinset *n.* esp. *Brit.* a woman's matching cardigan and jumper.

twin town *n. Brit.* a town which is twinned with another.

twirl ● *v.tr. & intr.* spin or swing or twist quickly and lightly round. ● *n.* **1** a twirling motion. **2** a form made by twirling, esp. a flourish made with a pen. [16th-century coinage] □ **twirler** *n.* **twirly** *adj.*

twirp var. of TWERP.

twist ● *v.* **1 a** *tr.* change the form of by rotating one end and not the other or the two ends in opposite directions. **b** *intr.* undergo such a change. **c** *tr.* wrench with a twisting action (*twisted my ankle*). **2** *tr.* **a** wind (strands etc.) about each other. **b** form (a rope etc.) by winding the strands. **c** (foll. by *with, in with*) interweave. **d** form by interweaving or twining. **3 a** *tr.* give a spiral form to (a rod, cord, etc.) as by rotating the ends in opposite directions. **b** *intr.* take a spiral form. **4** *tr.* (foll. by *off*) break off or separate by twisting. **5** *tr.* distort or misrepresent the meaning of (words). **6 a** *intr.* take a curved course. **b** *tr.* make (one's way) in a winding manner. **7** *tr. Brit. slang* cheat. **8** *tr.* (as **twisted** *adj.*) (of a person or mind) emotionally unbalanced. **9** *intr.* dance the twist. ● *n.* **1** the act or an instance of twisting. **2 a** a twisted state. **b** the manner or degree in which a thing is twisted. **3** a thing formed by or as by twisting, esp. a thread or rope etc. **4** the point at which a thing twists or bends. **5** usu. *derog.* a peculiar tendency of mind or character etc. **6** an unexpected development, esp. in a story etc. **7** a fine strong silk thread used by tailors etc. **8** a roll of bread etc., in the form of a twist. **9** *Brit.* a paper packet with screwed-up ends. **10** a curled piece of lemon etc. peel to flavour a drink. **11** (prec. by *the*) a popular 1960s dance with a twisting movement of the body. □ **round the twist** *Brit. colloq.* crazy. **twist a person's arm** *colloq.* apply coercion, esp. by moral pressure. [Old English] □ **twistable** *adj.* **twisty** *adj.* (**twistier, twistiest**).

twister *n.* **1** *Brit. colloq.* a swindler. **2** a twisting ball in cricket, billiards, etc. **3** *N. Amer.* a tornado or waterspout.

twit[1] *n.* esp. *Brit. colloq.* a silly or foolish person. [originally dialect] □ **twittish** *adj.*

twit[2] *v.tr.* (**twitted**, **twitting**) reproach or taunt, usu. good-humouredly. [Old English *ætwītan* 'to reproach with']

twitch ● *v.* **1** *intr.* (of the features etc.) move or contract spasmodically. **2** *tr.* give a short sharp pull at. ● *n.* **1 a** a sudden involuntary contraction or movement. **b** a pang; a twinge. **2** a sudden pull or jerk. [Middle English] □ **twitchy** *adj.* (**twitchier, twitchiest**).

twitcher *n.* **1** *Brit. slang* a birdwatcher who tries to get sightings of rare birds. **2** a person or thing that twitches.

twitter ● *v.* **1** *intr.* **a** (of a bird) emit a succession of light tremulous sounds. **b** talk rapidly in an idle or trivial way. **2** *tr.* utter or express in this way. ● *n.* **1** the act or an instance of twittering. **2** *colloq.* a tremulously excited state. [Middle English, imitative] □ **twitterer** *n.* **twittery** *adj.*

'twixt *prep. archaic* = BETWIXT. [contraction]

twizzle *colloq.* or *dial.* ● *v.tr. & intr.* twist, turn. ● *n.* a twist or turn.

two ● *n.* **1** one more than one. **2** a symbol for this (2, ii, II). **3** a size etc. denoted by two. **4** two o'clock. **5** a set of two. **6** a card with two pips. ● *adj.* that amount to two. □ **in two** in or into two pieces. **in two shakes** (or **ticks**) see SHAKE, TICK[1]. **or two** denoting several (*a thing or two* = several things). **put two and two together** make (esp. an obvious) inference from what is known or evident. **that makes two of us** *colloq.* that is true of me also. **two by two** (or **two and two**) in pairs. **two a penny** see PENNY. [Old English]

two-bit *adj. N. Amer. colloq.* cheap, petty.

two-by-four *n.* a length of timber with a rectangular cross-section nominally 2 in. by 4 in.

two-dimensional *adj.* **1** having or appearing to have length and breadth but no depth. **2** lacking substance; superficial.

two-edged *adj.* double-edged.

two-faced *adj.* **1** having two faces. **2** insincere.

twofold *adj. & adv.* **1** twice as much or as many. **2** consisting of two parts.

two-handed *adj.* **1** having, using, or requiring the use of two hands. **2** (of a card game) for two players.

twoness *n.* the fact or state of being two; duality.

twopence *n. Brit.* **1** the sum of two pence, esp. before decimalization. **2** (esp. with *neg.*) *colloq.* a thing of little value (*don't care twopence*).

twopenn'orth *n.* **1** as much as is worth or costs twopence. **2** a paltry or insignificant amount. □ **add** (or **put in**) **one's twopenn'orth** *colloq.* contribute one's opinion.

twopenny /túp-ĕ-ni/ *adj. Brit.* **1** costing two pence, esp. before decimalization. **2** *colloq.* cheap, worthless.

twopenny-halfpenny *adj.* cheap, insignificant.

two-piece ● *attrib.adj.* (of a suit etc.) consisting of two matching items. ● *n.* a two-piece suit etc.

two-ply ● *attrib.adj.* of two strands, webs, or thicknesses. ● *n.* **1** two-ply wool. **2** two-ply wood made by gluing together two layers with the grain in different directions.

two-seater *n.* **1** a vehicle or aircraft with two seats. **2** a sofa etc. for two people.

two-sided *adj.* **1** having two sides. **2** having two aspects; controversial.

twosome *n.* **1** two persons together. **2** a game, dance, etc., for two persons.

two-step *n.* a round dance with a sliding step in march or polka time.

two-stroke *attrib.adj.* **1** ▼ (of an internal-combustion engine) having its power cycle completed in one up-and-down movement of the piston. **2** (of a vehicle) having a two-stroke engine. ▷ OFF-ROAD

TWO-STROKE

A two-stroke engine has ports in its cylinder which are exposed by the motion of a piston. The rising piston draws fuel and air into the crankcase and compresses fuel and air already in the cylinder. The compressed mixture is ignited by a spark, forcing the piston down and pushing fresh mixture from the crankcase into the cylinder through the transfer port. Exhaust gases are expelled via the exhaust port.

TWO STAGES OF POWER CYCLE

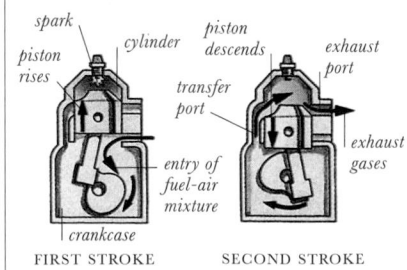

FIRST STROKE SECOND STROKE

TYPE

Type enables text to be read easily and without ambiguity. Standard text is given in roman type, while italic or bold type are often used to emphasize or distinguish terms. Serif faces, based on ancient Roman scripts, have cross-strokes (serifs); sans-serif typefaces lack these.

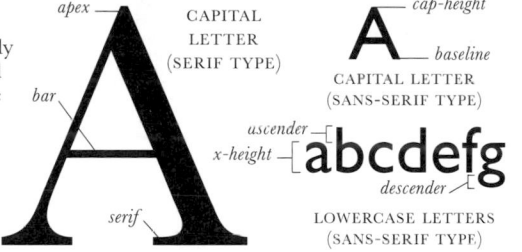

CAPITAL LETTER (SERIF TYPE)

CAPITAL LETTER (SANS-SERIF TYPE)

apex — cap-height — baseline — ascender — x-height — descender — bar — serif

LOWERCASE LETTERS (SANS-SERIF TYPE)

TYPE STYLES

abcdefg   **abcdefg**   *abcdefg*

ROMAN TYPE   BOLD TYPE   ITALIC TYPE

---

two-time *v.tr. colloq.* **1** be unfaithful to (a lover). **2** swindle, double-cross. □ **two-timer** *n.*

two-tone *attrib.adj.* having two colours or sounds.

two-up *n. Austral. & NZ* a gambling game played by tossing two coins with bets placed on a showing of two heads or two tails.

two-way *adj.* **1** involving two ways or participants. **2** (of a switch) permitting a current to be switched on or off from either of two points. **3** (of a radio) capable of transmitting and receiving signals. **4** (of a tap etc.) permitting fluid to flow in either of two channels or directions. **5** (of traffic etc.) moving in two esp. opposite directions.

two-way mirror *n.* a panel of glass that can be seen through from one side and is a mirror on the other.

tychism *n. Philos.* the theory that chance controls the universe. [from Greek *tukhē* 'chance']

tycoon *n.* a business magnate. [from Japanese *taikun* 'great lord']

tying *pres. part.* of TIE.

tyke *n.* (also **tike**) **1** *esp. Brit.* an unpleasant or coarse man. **2** a mongrel. **3** a small child. **4** *Brit. slang* a Yorkshireman. [from Old Norse *tík* 'bitch']

tympana *pl.* of TYMPANUM.

tympani *var.* of TIMPANI.

tympanum /tim-pă-nŭm/ *n.* (*pl.* **tympanums** or **tympana**) **1** *Anat.* the middle ear. ▷ EAR. **2** *Archit.* **a** a vertical triangular space forming the centre of a pediment. **b** a similar space over a door; a carving on this. [from Greek *tumpanon* 'drum']

Tynwald *n.* the parliament of the Isle of Man. [from Old Norse *thing-völlr* 'place of assembly']

type ● *n.* **1 a** a class of things or persons having common characteristics. **b** a kind or sort (*would like a different type of car*). **2** a person, thing, or event serving as an illustration, symbol, or characteristic specimen of another, or of a class. **3** (in *comb.*) made of, resembling, or functioning as (*Cheddar-type cheese*). **4** *colloq.* a person, esp. of a specified character (*not really my type*). **5** an object, conception, or work of art serving as a model for subsequent artists. **6** *Printing* **a** ▲ printed characters or letters. **b** a piece of metal etc. with a raised letter or character on its upper surface, for use in letterpress printing. **c** such pieces collectively. **c** printed characters produced by type. ● *v.* **1** *tr.* be a type or example of. **2** *tr. & intr.* write with a typewriter. **3** *tr.* esp. *Biol. & Med.* assign to a type; classify. **4** *tr.* = TYPECAST. □ **in type** *Printing* composed and ready for printing. [from Greek *tupos* 'impression, figure, type'] □ **typal** *adj.*

typecast *v.tr.* (*past* and *past part.* **-cast**) assign (an actor or actress) repeatedly to the same type of role, esp. one in character.

typeface *n. Printing* **1** a set of types or characters in a particular design. **2** the inked part of type, or the impression made by this.

typescript *n.* a typewritten document.

typesetter *n. Printing* **1** a person who composes type. **2** a composing machine. □ **typeset** *v.tr.* (**-setting**; *past* and *past part.* **-set**) (also *absol.*). **typesetting** *n.* (also *attrib.*).

type site *n. Archaeol.* a site where objects regarded as defining the characteristics of a period etc. are found.

type size *n.* a size of type usu. specified by name, e.g. *pica* etc.

typewriter *n.* ▼ a machine with keys for producing printlike characters one at a time on paper inserted round a roller. □ **typewriting** *n.*

carriage return lever — type bars bearing characters — ruler — platen — paper bail — ribbon — shift lock key — shift key — QWERTY keyboard — space bar

TYPEWRITER: LATE 20TH-CENTURY MANUAL PORTABLE TYPEWRITER

typewritten *adj.* produced with a typewriter.

typhoid *n.* **1** (in full **typhoid fever**) an infectious bacterial fever with an eruption of red spots on the chest and abdomen and severe intestinal irritation. **2** a similar disease of animals. [based on TYPHUS] □ **typhoidal** *adj.*

typhoon *n.* a tropical storm in the western Pacific. [partly from Arabic *ṭūfān*; partly from Chinese dialect *tai fung* 'big wind'] □ **typhonic** *adj.*

typhus *n.* an infectious fever caused by parasitic micro-organisms of the genus *Rickettsia*, characterized by a purple rash, headaches, fever, and usu. delirium. [from Greek *tuphos* 'smoke, stupor'] □ **typhous** *adj.*

typical *adj.* **1** serving as a characteristic example; representative. **2** characteristic of or serving to distinguish a type. **3** (often foll. by *of*) conforming to expected behaviour, attitudes, etc. (*is typical of them to forget*). [from Greek *tupikos*] □ **typicality** *n.* **typically** *adv.*

typify *v.tr.* (**-ies, -ied**) **1** be a representative example of; embody the characteristics of. **2** represent by a type or symbol; serve as a type, figure, or emblem of; symbolize. □ **typification** *n.*

typist *n.* a person who uses a typewriter, esp. professionally.

typo *n.* (*pl.* **-os**) *colloq.* **1** a typographical error. **2** a typographer.

typographer *n.* a person skilled in typography.

typography *n.* **1** printing as an art. **2** the style and appearance of printed matter. □ **typographic** *adj.* **typographical** *adj.* **typographically** *adv.*

typology *n.* the study and interpretation of (esp. biblical) types. □ **typological** *adj.* **typologist** *n.*

tyrannical *adj.* **1** acting like a tyrant; imperious, arbitrary. **2** given to or characteristic of tyranny. [from Greek *turannikos*] □ **tyrannically** *adv.*

tyrannize /ti-ră-nyz/ *v.tr. &* (foll. by *over*) *intr.* (also **-ise**) behave like a tyrant; rule or treat despotically or cruelly. [from French *tyranniser*]

tyrannosaurus *n.* (also **tyrannosaur**) ▼ a very large bipedal flesh-eating dinosaur, *Tyrannosaurus rex*, of the late Cretaceous period, having powerful jaws and hind legs, small clawlike front legs, and a large tail. ▷ DINOSAUR. [from Greek *turannos* 'tyrant' + *sauros* 'lizard']

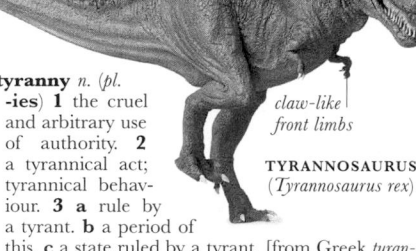

large tail — powerful jaws — claw-like front limbs

TYRANNOSAURUS (*Tyrannosaurus rex*)

tyranny *n.* (*pl.* **-ies**) **1** the cruel and arbitrary use of authority. **2** a tyrannical act; tyrannical behaviour. **3 a** a rule by a tyrant. **b** a period of this. **c** a state ruled by a tyrant. [from Greek *turannia*] □ **tyrannous** *adj.* **tyrannously** *adv.*

tyrant /tyr-ănt/ *n.* **1** an oppressive or cruel ruler. **2** a person exercising power arbitrarily or cruelly. [from Greek *turannos*]

tyre *n.* (*US* **tire**) ▼ a rubber covering, usu. inflated, placed round a wheel to form a soft contact with the road. [Middle English]

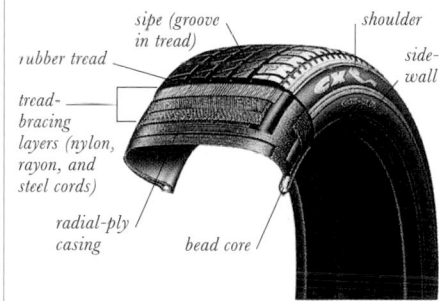

sipe (groove in tread) — shoulder — side-wall — rubber tread — tread-bracing layers (nylon, rayon, and steel cords) — radial-ply casing — bead core

TYRE: SECTION THROUGH A MODERN RADIAL-PLY CAR TYRE

tyre gauge *n.* a portable device for measuring the air pressure in a tyre.

Tyrian purple see PURPLE *n.* 2.

tyro *n.* (also **tiro**) (*pl.* **-os**) a beginner or novice. [from Latin *tiro* 'recruit']

Tyrolean ● *adj.* of or characteristic of the Tyrol in Austria. ● *n.* a native or inhabitant of the Tyrol. □ **Tyrolese** *adj. & n.*

tyrosine /tyr-ŏ-seen/ *n. Chem.* a hydrophilic amino acid present in many proteins and important in the synthesis of some hormones etc. [based on Greek *turos* 'cheese']

tzar *var.* of TSAR.

tzarina *var.* of TSARINA.

tzatziki *n.* a Greek side dish of yogurt with cucumber, garlic, and often mint. [modern Greek]

tzigane /tsi-gahn/ *n.* **1** a Hungarian gypsy. **2** (*attrib.*) characteristic of the tziganes or (esp.) their music. [from Hungarian *c(z)igány*]

T

U

U¹ *n.* (also **u**) (pl. **Us** or **U's**) **1** the twenty-first letter of the alphabet. **2** a U-shaped object or curve (esp. in *comb.*: *U-bolt*).

U² *adj.* esp. *Brit. colloq.* **1** upper class. **2** supposedly characteristic of the upper class. [abbreviation]

U³ *n.* a Burmese title of respect before a man's name.

U⁴ *symb.* **1** *Chem.* the element uranium. **2** *Brit.* universal (of films classified as suitable without restriction).

UB40 *abbr.* (in the UK) a card issued to a person registered as unemployed.

ubiquitous *adj.* **1** present everywhere or in several places simultaneously. **2** often encountered. [based on Latin *ubique* 'everywhere'] □ **ubiquitously** *adv.* **ubiquitousness** *n.* **ubiquity** *n.*

U-boat *n. hist.* ▼ a German submarine used in the First and Second World Wars. ▷ SUBMARINE. [from German *Unterseeboot* 'undersea boat']

U-BOAT: MODEL OF A U-25 SUBMARINE

conning tower

propeller

UCAS /**yoo**-kas/ *abbr.* (in the UK) Universities and Colleges Admissions Service.

UDA *abbr.* Ulster Defence Association (a Loyalist paramilitary organization).

udder *n.* the mammary gland of cattle, sheep, etc., hanging as a bag-like organ with several teats. [Old English] □ **uddered** *adj.* (also in *comb.*).

UDI *abbr.* unilateral declaration of independence.

UFO /**yoo**-foh/ *abbr.* (also **ufo**) (pl. **UFOs** or **ufos**) unidentified flying object.

ufology /yoo-**fol**-ŏji/ *n.* the study of UFOs. □ **ufologist** *n.*

ugh /uuh, uh, er, uukh, ug, *etc.*/ *int.* **1** expressing disgust etc. **2** the sound of a cough or grunt.

ugli fruit *n.* (pl. same) (also **Ugli** *propr.*) ◄ a mottled green and yellow hybrid of a grapefruit and tangerine.

uglify *v.tr.* (**-ies**, **-ied**) make ugly. □ **uglification** *n.*

ugly *adj.* (**uglier**, **ugliest**) **1** unpleasing or repulsive to see or hear. **2** unpleasantly suggestive; discreditable (*ugly rumours*). **3** threatening, dangerous (*the sky has an ugly look*). **4** morally repulsive (*ugly vices*). [from Old Norse *uggligr* 'to be dreaded'] □ **uglily** *adv.* **ugliness** *n.*

UGLI FRUIT (*Citrus* species)

ugly customer *n.* an unpleasantly formidable person.

ugly duckling *n.* a person who turns out to be beautiful or talented etc. against all expectations.

UHF *abbr.* ultra-high frequency.

uh-huh *int. colloq.* expressing assent.

UHT *abbr.* ultra heat-treated (esp. of milk, for long keeping).

UK *abbr.* United Kingdom.

ukase /yoo-**kayz**/ *n.* **1** an arbitrary command. **2** an edict of the Russian government. [from Russian *ukaz* 'ordinance, edict']

Ukrainian ● *n.* **1** a native or inhabitant of Ukraine in eastern Europe. **2** the East Slavonic language of Ukraine. ● *adj.* of or relating to Ukraine, its people, or its language. [based on Russian *ukraina* 'frontier region']

ukulele /yoo-kŭ-**lay**-li/ *n.* ► a small four-stringed Hawaiian guitar. [Hawaiian, literally 'jumping flea']

tuning key

neck

sound-hole

bridge

UKULELE

ulcer *n.* **1** an open sore on an external or internal surface of the body, often forming pus. **2 a** a moral blemish. **b** a corrupting influence etc. [from Latin *ulcus -eris*] □ **ulcered** *adj.* **ulcerous** *adj.*

ulcerate *v.tr. & intr.* form into or affect with an ulcer. □ **ulceration** *n.* **ulcerative** *adj.*

ulna *n.* (pl. **ulnae** /-nee/ or **ulnas**) **1** ► the thinner and longer bone in the forearm, on the side opposite to the thumb. ▷ SKELETON. **2** a corresponding bone in an animal's foreleg or a bird's wing. [Latin] □ **ulnar** *adj.*

ulster *n.* a long loose overcoat of rough cloth. [from *Ulster*, former province of Ireland]

Ulsterman *n.* (pl. **-men**; *fem.* **Ulsterwoman**; pl. **-women**) a native of Ulster.

ult. *abbr.* ultimo.

ulterior *adj.* existing in the background, or beyond what is evident or admitted. [Latin, literally 'further, more distant'] □ **ulteriorly** *adv.*

ulna

fin

ultimata pl. of ULTIMATUM.

ultimate ● *adj.* **1** last, final. **2** beyond which no other is possible. **3** fundamental, primary (*ultimate truths*). **4** maximum (*ultimate tensile strength*). ● *n.* **1** (prec. by *the*) the best achievable or imaginable. **2** a final or fundamental fact or principle. [from Late Latin *ultimatus* 'ended'] □ **ultimacy** *n.* (pl. **-ies**). **ultimately** *adj.* **ultimateness** *n.*

ultima Thule *n.* a faraway unknown region. [Latin = furthest Thule, a remote northern region]

ULNA: HUMAN FOREARM SHOWING THE ULNA

ultimatum *n.* (pl. **ultimatums** or **ultimata**) a final demand or statement of terms by one party, the rejection of which could cause hostility. [Latin, literally '(thing) ended']

ultimo *adj. Commerce* of last month (*the 28th ultimo*). [from Latin *ultimo mense* 'in the last month']

ultra ● *adj.* favouring extreme views or measures, esp. in religion or politics. ● *n.* an extremist. [originally abbreviation of French *ultra-royaliste*]

ultra- *prefix* **1** beyond; on the other side of (opp. CIS-). **2** extreme(ly), excessive(ly) (*ultra-conservative*).

ultra-high *adj.* (of a frequency) in the range 300 to 3000 megahertz.

ultramarine ● *n.* **1** ► a brilliant deep blue pigment originally obtained from lapis lazuli. **2** a brilliant deep blue colour. ● *adj.* of this colour. [from medieval Latin *ultramarinus* 'beyond the sea']

ULTRAMARINE

ultramicroscopic *adj.* too small to be seen by an ordinary optical microscope.

ultramontane ● *adj.* **1** situated on the other side of the Alps. **2** advocating supreme papal authority. ● *n.* **1** a person living on the other side of the Alps. **2** an advocate of supreme papal authority. [from medieval Latin *ultramontanus*]

ultrasonic *adj.* of or involving sound waves with a frequency above the upper limit of human hearing. □ **ultrasonically** *adv.*

ultrasonics *n.pl.* (usu. treated as *sing.*) the science and application of ultrasonic waves.

ultrasound *n.* **1** sound having an ultrasonic frequency. **2** ▼ ultrasonic waves.

ultraviolet *adj. Physics* of or using electromagnetic radiation having a wavelength shorter than that of the violet end of the visible spectrum. ▷ ELECTROMAGNETIC RADIATION

ultra vires /-**vy**-reez/ *adv. & predic.adj.* beyond one's legal power or authority. [Latin]

ululate *v.intr.* howl, wail; make a hooting cry. [based on Latin *ululatus* 'wailed'] □ **ululant** *adj.* **ululation** *n.*

um *int.* expressing hesitation or a pause in speech.

umbel *n. Bot.* a flower cluster in which stalks spring from a common centre and form a flat or curved surface. ▷ INFLORESCENCE. [from Latin *umbella* 'sunshade']

ULTRASOUND

One of the uses of ultrasound is in antenatal assessment. As a probe is passed over the abdomen, a transducer transmits a pulse of ultrasound every millisecond. The pulses are reflected back by tissue in their path and appear as bright spots on a dark screen. The spots form an accurate image of the foetus.

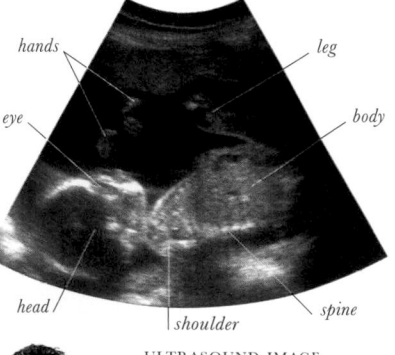

hands

leg

eye

body

head

shoulder

spine

ULTRASOUND IMAGE OF A HUMAN FOETUS

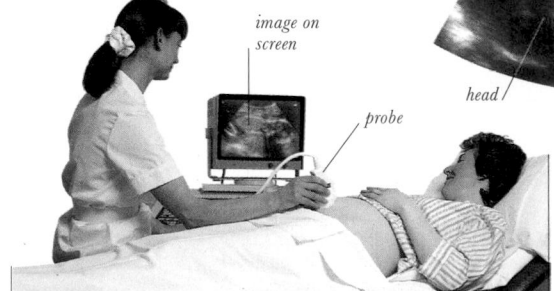

image on screen

probe

ULTRASOUND SCANNING OF AN EXPECTANT MOTHER

umbellifer *n.* ▶ any plant of the family Umbelliferae bearing umbels, including parsley and parsnip. [from obsolete French *umbellifère*]
□ **umbelliferous** *adj.*

umber ● *n.* **1** a natural pigment like ochre but darker and browner. ▷ RAW UMBER. **2** a dark brown colour. ● *adj.* **1** dark brown. **2** dusky. [from Italian *(terra di) ombra*, literally '(earth of) shadow']

umbilical ● *attrib.adj.* of, situated near, or affecting the navel. ● *n.* a flexible supply or control line etc., esp. from a main source to a site otherwise difficult to access. [from obsolete French *umbilical*]

umbilical cord *n.* **1** ▼ a flexible cordlike structure containing blood vessels and attaching a foetus to the placenta. **2** a supply cable linking a missile to its launcher, or an astronaut in space to a spacecraft.

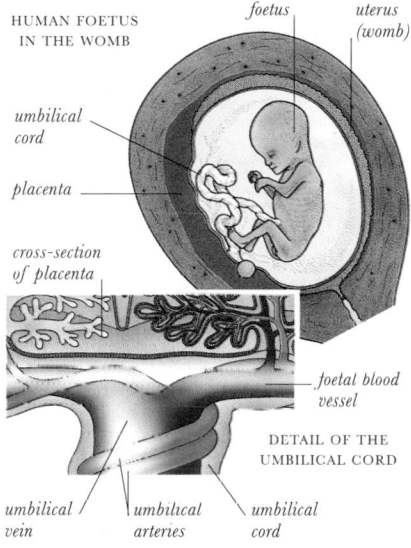

HUMAN FOETUS
IN THE WOMB

foetus

uterus (womb)

umbilical cord

placenta

cross-section of placenta

foetal blood vessel

DETAIL OF THE
UMBILICAL CORD

umbilical vein   *umbilical arteries*   *umbilical cord*

UMBILICAL CORD

umbilicate *adj.* shaped like a navel.

umbilicus *n.* (*pl.* **umbilici** /-sy/ or **umbilicuses**) **1** *Anat.* the navel. **2** *Bot. & Zool.* a navel-like formation. [Latin]

umbles *n.pl. archaic* the edible offal of deer etc. (cf. *eat humble pie*: see HUMBLE). [Middle English]

umbra *n.* (*pl.* **umbras** or **umbrae** /-bree/) **1** the fully shaded inner region of a shadow, esp. *Astron.* the area on the Earth or Moon experiencing the total phase of an eclipse. ▷ ECLIPSE. **2** the dark central part of a sunspot. [Latin, literally 'shade'] □ **umbral** *adj.*

umbrage *n.* offence; a sense of slight or injury (esp. *give* or *take umbrage at*). [from Old French, literally 'shadow']

umbrella *n.* **1** ▶ a light portable device for protection against rain etc., consisting of a usu. circular canopy of cloth mounted by means of a collapsible metal frame on a central stick. **2** protection or patronage. **3** (often *attrib.*) a coordinating agency (*umbrella organization*). [from Italian *ombrella* 'little shade'] □ **umbrellaed** *adj.* **umbrella-like** *adj.*

tip
canopy
rib
tube
tip cup
handle

UMBRELLA

umlaut *n.* **1** a mark (¨) used over a vowel, esp. in Germanic languages, to indicate a vowel change. **2** such a vowel change, e.g. German *Mann, Männer*, English *man, men*. [German, from *um* 'about' + *Laut* 'sound']

ump *n.* esp. *N. Amer. slang* an umpire, esp. in baseball.

umpire ● *n.* **1** a person chosen to enforce the rules and settle disputes in various sports. **2** a person chosen to arbitrate between disputants, or to see fair play. ● *v.* **1** *intr.* (usu. foll. by *for, in*, etc.) act as umpire. **2** *tr.* act as umpire in (a game etc.). [based on Old French *nonper* 'not equal'] □ **umpirage** *n.* **umpireship** *n.*

umpteen *colloq.* ● *adj.* indefinitely many; a lot of. ● *pron.* indefinitely many. [jocular formation]
□ **umpteenth** *adj.* **umpty** *adj.*

UN *abbr.* United Nations.

un-¹ *prefix* **1** added to adjectives and participles and their derivative nouns and adverbs, meaning: **a** not: denoting the absence of (*unusable; uncalled for; uneducated; unhappiness*). **b** the reverse of, esp. with an implication of approval or disapproval (*unselfish; unscientific*). **2** (less often) added to nouns, meaning 'a lack of' (*unrest; untruth*).

■ **Usage** The number of words that can be formed with the prefix *un-¹* (and similarly with *un-²*) is potentially as large as the number of adjectives in use; consequently only a selection, being considered the most current or semantically noteworthy, can be given here. Words meaning 'the reverse of' (see sense 1b above) often have neutral counterparts in *non-* (see NON- 6) and counterparts in *in-* (see IN- 1), e.g. *unadvisable.*

un-² *prefix* added to verbs and (less often) nouns, forming verbs denoting: **1** the reversal or cancellation (*undress; unlock; unsettle*). **2** deprivation or separation (*unmask*). **3** release from (*unburden; uncage*). **4** causing to be no longer (*unman*).

■ **Usage** See Usage Note at UN-¹.

'un *pron. colloq.* one (*that's a good 'un*).

unabashed *adj.* not abashed. □ **unabashedly** *adv.*

unabated *adj.* not abated; undiminished.

unable *adj.* (usu. foll. by *to* + infin.) not able; lacking ability.

unabridged *adj.* (of a text etc.) complete; not abridged.

unabsorbed *adj.* not absorbed.

unacademic *adj.* **1** not academic (esp. not scholarly). **2** (of a person) not suited to academic study.

unaccented *adj.* not accented; not emphasized.

unacceptable *adj.* not acceptable. □ **unacceptability** *n.* **unacceptableness** *n.* **unacceptably** *adv.*

unaccommodating *adj.* not accommodating; disobliging.

unaccompanied *adj.* **1** not accompanied. **2** *Mus.* without accompaniment.

unaccomplished *adj.* **1** uncompleted. **2** lacking accomplishments.

unaccountable *adj.* **1** unable to be explained. **2** strange in behaviour. **3** not responsible. □ **unaccountability** *n.* **unaccountableness** *n.* **unaccountably** *adv.*

unaccounted *adj.* of which no account is given. □ **unaccounted for** unexplained; not included in an account.

unaccustomed *adj.* **1** (usu. foll. by *to*) not accustomed. **2** not customary. □ **unaccustomedly** *adv.*

unacknowledged *adj.* not acknowledged.

unacquainted *adj.* (usu. foll. by *with*) not acquainted.

unadjusted *adj.* (esp. of figures) not adjusted; crude.

unadopted *adj.* **1** not adopted. **2** *Brit.* (of a road) not taken over for maintenance by a local authority.

unadorned *adj.* not adorned; plain.

unadulterated *adj.* **1** not adulterated; pure; concentrated. **2** complete, utter.

unadventurous *adj.* not adventurous. □ **unadventurously** *adv.*

unadvised *adj.* **1** indiscreet; rash. **2** not having had advice. □ **unadvisedly** *adv.* **unadvisedness** *n.*

unaffected *adj.* **1** (usu. foll. by *by*) not affected. **2** free from affectation. □ **unaffectedly** *adv.* **unaffectedness** *n.*

unaffiliated *adj.* not affiliated.

unaffordable *adj.* not affordable.

unafraid *adj.* not afraid.

unaided *adj.* not aided; without help.

unalike *adj.* not alike; different.

unalleviated *adj.* not alleviated; relentless.

unalloyed *adj.* **1** not alloyed; pure. **2** complete; utter (*unalloyed joy*).

unalterable *adj.* not alterable. □ **unalterableness** *n.* **unalterably** *adv.*

unaltered *adj.* not altered; remaining the same.

unambiguous *adj.* not ambiguous; clear or definite in meaning. □ **unambiguity** *n.* **unambiguously** *adv.*

unambitious *adj.* not ambitious; without ambition. □ **unambitiously** *adv.* **unambitiousness** *n.*

unambivalent *adj.* (of feelings etc.) not ambivalent; straightforward. □ **unambivalently** *adv.*

un-American *adj.* **1** not in accordance with American characteristics etc. **2** contrary to US interests; (in the US) treasonable. □ **un-Americanism** *n.*

unamiable *adj.* not amiable.

unamused *adj.* not amused.

unanimous /yoo-**nan**-i-mŭs/ *adj.* **1** all in agreement (*the committee was unanimous*). **2** (of an opinion, vote, etc.) held or given by general consent. [from Latin *unanimus*] □ **unanimity** *n.* **unanimously** *adv.*

unannounced *adj.* not announced; without warning (of arrival etc.).

unanswerable *adj.* **1** unable to be refuted. **2** unable to be answered. □ **unanswerableness** *n.* **unanswerably** *adv.*

unanswered *adj.* not answered.

unanticipated *adj.* not anticipated.

unapologetic *adj.* not apologetic or sorry. □ **unapologetically** *adv.*

unapparent *adj.* not apparent.

unappealing *adj.* not appealing; unattractive. □ **unappealingly** *adv.*

unappeased *adj.* not appeased.

unappetizing *adj.* (also **-ising**) not appetizing. □ **unappetizingly** *adv.*

unappreciated *adj.* not appreciated.

unappreciative *adj.* not appreciative.

unapproachable *adj.* **1** not approachable; remote, inaccessible. **2** (of a person) unfriendly. □ **unapproachability** *n.* **unapproachableness** *n.* **unapproachably** *adv.*

unapproved *adj.* not approved or sanctioned.

unapt *adj.* **1** (usu. foll. by *for*) not suitable. **2** (usu. foll. by *to* + infin.) not apt. □ **unaptly** *adv.* **unaptness** *n.*

unarguable *adj.* not arguable; certain. □ **unarguably** *adv.*

unarmed *adj.* not armed; without weapons.

unarresting *adj.* uninteresting, dull.

unartistic *adj.* not artistic, esp. not concerned with art. □ **unartistically** *adv.*

unashamed *adj.* **1** feeling no guilt, shameless. **2** blatant; bold. □ **unashamedly** *adv.* **unashamedness** *n.*

unasked *adj.* not asked, requested, or invited.

unasked-for *adj.* (usu. *attrib.*) (esp. of advice) not sought or requested.

U

unassailable *adj.* unable to be attacked; impregnable. □ **unassailability** *n.* **unassailableness** *n.* **unassailably** *adv.*

unassertive *adj.* (of a person) not assertive or forthcoming; reticent. □ **unassertively** *adv.* **unassertiveness** *n.*

unassigned *adj.* not assigned.

unassimilated *adj.* not assimilated. □ **unassimilable** *adj.*

unassisted *adj.* not assisted.

unassuaged *adj.* not assuaged. □ **unassuageable** *adj.*

unassuming *adj.* not pretentious or arrogant; modest by nature. □ **unassumingly** *adv.* **unassumingness** *n.*

unattached *adj.* **1** (often foll. by *to*) not attached, esp. to a particular body, organization, etc. **2** single; not married or having an established partner.

unattainable *adj.* not attainable. □ **unattainableness** *n.* **unattainably** *adv.*

unattempted *adj.* not attempted.

unattended *adj.* **1** (usu. foll. by *to*) not attended. **2** (of a person, vehicle, etc.) not accompanied; alone.

unattractive *adj.* not attractive. □ **unattractively** *adv.* **unattractiveness** *n.*

unattributable *adj.* (esp. of information) that cannot or may not be attributed to a source etc. □ **unattributably** *adv.*

unattributed *adj.* (of a painting, quotation, etc.) not attributed to a source etc.

unauthenticated *adj.* not authenticated.

unauthorized *adj.* (also **-ised**) not authorized.

unavailable *adj.* not available. □ **unavailability** *n.* **unavailableness** *n.*

unavailing *adj.* not availing; achieving nothing; ineffectual. □ **unavailingly** *adv.*

unavoidable *adj.* not avoidable; inevitable. □ **unavoidability** *n.* **unavoidably** *adv.*

unaware ● *adj.* **1** (usu. foll. by *of*, or *that* + clause) not aware; ignorant. **2** (of a person) insensitive; unperceptive. ● *adv.* = UNAWARES. □ **unawareness** *n.*

unawares *adv.* **1** unexpectedly. **2** inadvertently. [earlier *unaware(s)*, from Old English]

unbacked *adj.* **1** not supported. **2** (of a horse etc.) having no backers. **3** (of a picture etc.) having no back or backing.

unbalance ● *v.tr.* **1** upset the physical or mental balance of. **2** (as **unbalanced** *adj.*) **a** not balanced. **b** (of a mind or a person) unstable or deranged. ● *n.* lack of balance; instability, esp. mental.

unban *v.tr.* (**unbanned**, **unbanning**) cease to ban; remove a ban from.

unbar *v.tr.* (**unbarred**, **unbarring**) **1** remove a bar or bars from (a gate etc.). **2** unlock.

unbearable *adj.* not bearable. □ **unbearableness** *n.* **unbearably** *adv.*

unbeatable *adj.* not beatable; excelling.

unbeaten *adj.* **1** not beaten. **2** (of a record etc.) not surpassed.

unbecoming *adj.* **1** (esp. of clothing) not flattering or suiting a person. **2** (usu. foll. by *to*, *for*) indecorous or unsuitable. □ **unbecomingly** *adv.*

unbeknown *adj.* (also **unbeknownst**) (foll. by *to*) without the knowledge of. [based on archaic *beknown* 'known']

unbelief *n.* lack of belief, esp. in religious matters. □ **unbeliever** *n.* **unbelieving** *adj.* **unbelievingly** *adv.*

unbelievable *adj.* impossible to believe; incredible. □ **unbelievability** *n.* **unbelievably** *adv.*

unbend *v.* (*past* and *past part.* **unbent**) **1** *tr.* & *intr.* change from a bent position; straighten. **2** *intr.* relax from strain or severity; become affable.

unbending *adj.* **1** not bending; inflexible. **2** firm; austere. **3** relaxing from strain, activity, or formality. □ **unbendingly** *adv.* **unbendingness** *n.*

unbiased *adj.* (also **unbiassed**) not biased; impartial.

unbidden *adj.* not commanded or invited (*arrived unbidden*).

unbind *v.tr.* (*past* and *past part.* **unbound**) release from bonds or binding.

unbirthday *n.* (often *attrib.*) *joc.* any day but one's birthday (*an unbirthday party*).

unbleached *adj.* ► not bleached.

unblemished *adj.* not blemished.

unblinking *adj.* **1** not blinking. **2** steadfast. **3** stolid. □ **unblinkingly** *adv.*

unblock *v.tr.* remove an obstruction from.

unblushing *adj.* **1** not blushing. **2** unashamed; frank. □ **unblushingly** *adv.*

unbolt *v.tr.* release (a door etc.) by drawing back the bolt.

unbolted *adj.* **1** not bolted. **2** (of flour etc.) not sifted.

unborn *adj.* **1** not yet born (*an unborn child*). **2** never to be brought into being (*unborn hopes*).

unbosom *v.tr.* **1** disclose (thoughts, secrets, etc.). **2** (*refl.*; often foll. by *of*) unburden (oneself) of one's thoughts, secrets, etc.

unbothered *adj.* not bothered; unconcerned.

unbound[1] *adj.* **1** not bound or tied up. **2** unconstrained. **3** (of a book) **a** not having a binding. **b** having paper covers. **4** (of a substance or particle) in a loose or free state.

unbound[2] *past* and *past part.* of UNBIND.

unbounded *adj.* infinite (*unbounded optimism*). □ **unboundedly** *adv.* **unboundedness** *n.*

unbowed *adj.* (usu. *predic.*) undaunted.

unbreakable *adj.* not breakable.

unbreathable *adj.* not able to be breathed.

unbridgeable *adj.* not able to be bridged.

unbridle *v.tr.* **1** remove a bridle from (a horse). **2** remove constraints from (one's tongue, a person, etc.). **3** (as **unbridled** *adj.*) unconstrained (*unbridled insolence*).

unbroken *adj.* **1** not broken. **2** not tamed (*an unbroken horse*). **3** not interrupted (*unbroken sleep*). **4** not surpassed (*an unbroken record*). □ **unbrokenly** *adv.* **unbrokenness** *n.*

unbruised *adj.* not bruised.

unbuckle *v.tr.* release the buckle of (a strap, shoe, etc.).

unbuild *v.tr.* (*past* and *past part.* **unbuilt**) **1** demolish or destroy (a building, theory, system, etc.). **2** (as **unbuilt** *adj.*) not yet built or (of land etc.) not yet built on.

unbundle *v.tr.* **1** unpack; remove from a bundle. **2** market (goods or services) separately. **3** split (a company) into separate businesses. □ **unbundler** *n.* (in sense 3).

unburden *v.tr.* **1** relieve of a burden. **2** (esp. *refl.*; often foll. by *to*) relieve (oneself, one's conscience, etc.) by confession etc. □ **unburdened** *adj.*

unburied *adj.* not buried.

unbusinesslike *adj.* not businesslike.

unbutton *v.tr.* **1 a** unfasten (a coat etc.) by taking the buttons out of the buttonholes. **b** unbutton the clothes of (a person). **2** (*absol.*) *colloq.* relax from tension or formality, become communicative. **3** (as **unbuttoned** *adj.*) **a** not buttoned. **b** *colloq.* communicative; informal.

uncalled *adj.* not summoned or invited. □ **uncalled for** (also (hyphenated) *attrib.*) (of an opinion, action, etc.) impertinent or unnecessary (*such extreme measures are entirely uncalled for*; *an uncalled-for remark*).

uncanny *adj.* (**uncannier**, **uncanniest**) seemingly supernatural; mysterious. [originally Scots & northern English] □ **uncannily** *adv.* **uncanniness** *n.*

uncanonical *adj.* not canonical.

uncap *v.tr.* (**uncapped**, **uncapping**) remove the cap from (a jar, bottle, etc.).

uncapped *adj. Sport* (of a player) never having been selected for his or her national team.

uncared-for *adj.* (also **uncared for** *predic.*) disregarded; neglected.

uncaring *adj.* **1** neglectful. **2** lacking compassion.

uncarpeted *adj.* not covered with a carpet or carpeting.

uncashed *adj.* not cashed.

uncaught *adj.* not caught.

unceasing *adj.* not ceasing; continuous (*unceasing effort*). □ **unceasingly** *adv.*

uncensored *adj.* not censored.

uncensured *adj.* not censured.

unceremonious *adj.* **1** lacking ceremony or formality. **2** abrupt; discourteous. □ **unceremoniously** *adv.*

uncertain *adj.* **1** not certainly knowing or known (*uncertain what it means*; *the result is uncertain*). **2** unreliable (*his aim is uncertain*). **3** changeable, erratic (*uncertain weather*). □ **in no uncertain terms** clearly and forcefully. □ **uncertainly** *adv.*

uncertainty *n.* (*pl.* **-ies**) **1** the fact or condition of being uncertain. **2** an uncertain matter or circumstance.

uncertified *adj.* **1** not attested as certain. **2** not guaranteed by a certificate of competence etc. **3** not certified as insane.

unchain *v.tr.* **1** remove the chains from. **2** release.

unchallengeable *adj.* not challengeable; unassailable.

unchallenged *adj.* not challenged.

unchangeable *adj.* not changeable; immutable, invariable. □ **unchangeability** *n.* **unchangeableness** *n.* **unchangeably** *adv.*

unchanged *adj.* not changed; unaltered.

unchanging *adj.* not changing; remaining the same. □ **unchangingly** *adv.*

unchaperoned *adj.* without a chaperone.

uncharacteristic *adj.* not characteristic. □ **uncharacteristically** *adv.*

uncharitable *adj.* censorious, severe in judgement. □ **uncharitableness** *n.* **uncharitably** *adv.*

uncharted *adj.* not charted, mapped, or surveyed.

unchartered *adj.* **1** not furnished with a charter. **2** unauthorized; illegal.

unchaste *adj.* not chaste. □ **unchastity** *n.*

unchecked *adj.* **1** not checked. **2** unrestrained (*unchecked violence*).

unchivalrous *adj.* not chivalrous. □ **unchivalrously** *adv.*

unchosen *adj.* not chosen.

unchristian *adj.* **1** contrary to Christian principles, esp. uncaring or selfish. **2** not Christian. □ **unchristianly** *adv.*

uncial /un-siăl/ ● *adj.* **1** ► of or written in rounded unjoined letters found in manuscripts of the 4th–8th c., from which modern capitals are derived. **2** of or relating to an inch or an ounce. ● *n.* **1** an uncial letter. **2** an uncial style or manuscript. [based on Latin *uncia* 'inch']

uncircumcised *adj.* **1** not circumcised. **2** *archaic* spiritually impure; heathen. □ **uncircumcision** *n.*

uncivil *adj.* **1** ill-mannered; impolite. **2** not public-spirited.

uncivilized *adj.* (also **-ised**) **1** not civilized. **2** rough; uncultured.

unclad *adj.* naked.

unclaimed *adj.* not claimed.

unclasp *v.tr.* **1** loosen the clasp or clasps of. **2** release the grip of (a hand etc.).

unclassifiable *adj.* not classifiable.

unclassified *adj.* **1** not classified. **2** (of State information) not secret.

UNBLEACHED
COTTON T-SHIRT

U

uncle *n.* **1 a** the brother of one's father or mother. **b** an aunt's husband. **2** *colloq.* a name given by children to a male family friend. **3** *slang* a pawnbroker. [from Latin *avunculus* 'maternal uncle']

unclean *adj.* **1** not clean. **2** unchaste. **3** unfit to be eaten, ceremonially impure. **4** *Bibl.* (of a spirit) wicked. [Old English] □ **uncleanly** *adv.* **uncleanness** *n.*

uncleanly *adj.* *archaic* or *formal* unclean. □ **uncleanliness** *n.*

unclear *adj.* **1** not clear or easy to understand. **2** (of a person) doubtful, uncertain (*I'm unclear as to what you mean*). □ **unclearly** *adv.* **unclearness** *n.*

uncleared *adj.* **1** (of a cheque etc.) not cleared. **2** not cleared away or up. **3** (of land) not cleared of trees etc.

unclench *v.* **1** *tr.* release (clenched hands, features, teeth, etc.). **2** *intr.* (of clenched hands etc.) become relaxed or open.

Uncle Sam *n.* *colloq.* the federal government or citizens of the US (*will fight for Uncle Sam*).

Uncle Tom *n.* *offens.* a black man considered to be servile, cringing, etc. [from the hero of H. B. Stowe's *Uncle Tom's Cabin* (1852)]

unclimbed *adj.* (of a peak, rock face, etc.) not previously climbed. □ **unclimbable** *adj.*

unclog *v.tr.* (**unclogged**, **unclogging**) unblock (a drain, pipe, etc.).

unclose *v.* **1** *tr.* & *intr.* open. **2** *tr.* reveal; disclose.

unclothe *v.tr.* **1** remove the clothes from. **2** strip of leaves or vegetation (*trees unclothed by the wind*). **3** expose, reveal. □ **unclothed** *adj.*

unclouded *adj.* **1** clear; bright. **2** untroubled (*unclouded serenity*).

uncluttered *adj.* not cluttered; austere, simple.

uncoil *v.tr.* & *intr.* = UNWIND 1.

uncollected *adj.* **1** left awaiting collection. **2** (of money) not collected in or claimed. **3** (of literary work) not gathered into a collection for publication.

uncoloured *adj.* (*US* **uncolored**) **1** having no colour. **2** not influenced; impartial. **3** not exaggerated.

uncombed *adj.* (of hair or a person) not combed.

uncomfortable *adj.* **1** not comfortable. **2** uneasy; causing or feeling disquiet (*an uncomfortable silence*). □ **uncomfortably** *adv.*

uncommercial *adj.* **1** not commercial. **2** contrary to commercial principles.

uncommitted *adj.* **1** not committed. **2** unattached to any specific political cause or group.

uncommon *adj.* **1** not common; unusual; remarkable. **2** remarkably great etc. (*an uncommon fear of spiders*). □ **uncommonly** *adv.*

uncommunicative *adj.* taciturn. □ **uncommunicatively** *adv.* **uncommunicativeness** *n.*

uncompetitive *adj.* not competitive.

uncomplaining *adj.* not complaining; resigned. □ **uncomplainingly** *adv.*

uncompleted *adj.* not completed; incomplete.

uncomplicated *adj.* simple; straightforward.

uncomplimentary *adj.* insulting.

uncomprehending *adj.* not comprehending. □ **uncomprehendingly** *adv.*

uncompromising *adj.* stubborn; unyielding. □ **uncompromisingly** *adv.* **uncompromisingness** *n.*

unconcealed *adj.* not concealed; obvious.

unconcern *n.* lack of concern; indifference; apathy. □ **unconcerned** *adj.* **unconcernedly** *adv.*

unconditional *adj.* not subject to conditions; complete (*unconditional surrender*). □ **unconditionally** *adv.* **unconditionality** *n.*

unconditioned *adj.* **1** not subject to conditions or to an antecedent condition. **2** (of behaviour etc.) not determined by conditioning.

unconditioned reflex *n.* an instinctive response to a stimulus.

unconfined *adj.* not confined; boundless.

unconfirmed *adj.* not confirmed.

uncongenial *adj.* not congenial.

unconnected *adj.* **1** not physically joined. **2** not connected or associated. **3** (of speech etc.) disconnected; not joined in order or sequence (*unconnected ideas*). **4** not related by family ties. □ **unconnectedly** *adv.* **unconnectedness** *n.*

unconquerable *adj.* not conquerable. □ **unconquerably** *adv.*

unconquered *adj.* not conquered or defeated.

unconscionable /un-kon-shŏn-ăbŭl/ *adj.* **1 a** having no conscience. **b** contrary to conscience. **2 a** excessive (*an unconscionable length of time*). **b** not right or reasonable. [based on obsolete *conscionable* 'permitted by conscience'] □ **unconscionably** *adv.*

unconscious ● *adj.* not conscious (*unconscious of any change; fell unconscious on the floor; an unconscious prejudice*). ● *n.* that part of the mind which is inaccessible to the conscious mind but which affects behaviour, emotions, etc. □ **unconsciously** *adv.* **unconsciousness** *n.*

unconsecrated *adj.* not consecrated.

unconsidered *adj.* **1** not considered; disregarded. **2** (of a response etc.) immediate; not premeditated.

unconstitutional *adj.* not in accordance with the political constitution or with procedural rules. □ **unconstitutionality** *n.* **unconstitutionally** *adv.*

unconstrained *adj.* not constrained or compelled.

unconstricted *adj.* not constricted.

unconsumed *adj.* not consumed.

unconsummated *adj.* not consummated.

uncontaminated *adj.* not contaminated.

uncontested *adj.* not contested.

uncontradicted *adj.* not contradicted.

uncontrollable *adj.* not controllable. □ **uncontrollably** *adv.*

uncontrolled *adj.* not controlled; unrestrained.

uncontroversial *adj.* not controversial. □ **uncontroversially** *adv.*

unconventional *adj.* unusual; unorthodox. □ **unconventionality** *n.* **unconventionally** *adv.*

unconverted *adj.* not converted.

unconvinced *adj.* not convinced.

unconvincing *adj.* not convincing. □ **unconvincingly** *adv.*

uncooked *adj.* not cooked; raw.

uncool *adj.* **1** *slang* not stylish or fashionable; not having street credibility. **2** (of jazz) not cool.

uncooperative *adj.* not cooperative.

uncoordinated *adj.* **1** not coordinated. **2** (of a person's movements etc.) clumsy.

uncork *v.tr.* **1** draw the cork from (a bottle). **2** allow (feelings etc.) to be vented.

uncorrected *adj.* not corrected.

uncorroborated *adj.* not corroborated.

uncorrupted *adj.* not corrupted.

uncountable *adj.* inestimable, immense (*uncountable wealth*). □ **uncountably** *adv.*

uncountable noun *n.* *Gram.* a noun that cannot form a plural or be used with the indefinite article (e.g. *happiness*). Cf. MASS NOUN, COUNTABLE NOUN.

uncounted *adj.* **1** not counted. **2** very many; innumerable.

uncount noun *n.* *Gram.* = UNCOUNTABLE NOUN.

uncouple *v.tr.* **1** unfasten, disconnect, detach. **2** release (wagons) from couplings. □ **uncoupled** *adj.*

uncouth /un-kooth/ *adj.* uncultured, rough (*uncouth voices; behaviour was uncouth*). [Old English *uncūth* 'unknown'] □ **uncouthness** *n.*

uncover *v.* **1** *tr.* **a** remove a cover or covering from. **b** disclose (*uncovered the truth at last*). **2** *intr.* *archaic* remove one's hat, cap, etc. **3** *tr.* (as **uncovered** *adj.*) **a** not covered by a roof, clothing, etc. **b** not wearing a hat.

uncreative *adj.* not creative.

uncredited *adj.* not acknowledged as the author, actor, etc.

uncritical *adj.* **1** not critical; complacently accepting. **2** not in accordance with the principles of criticism. □ **uncritically** *adv.*

uncross *v.tr.* **1** remove from a crossed position. **2** (as **uncrossed** *adj.*) **a** *Brit.* (of a cheque) not crossed. **b** not thwarted or challenged.

UNCIAL

Uncial script developed from Roman square capitals as a quicker, less elaborate hand. The characters are rounded and simply seriffed. In it are found the beginnings of upper- and lower-case script. Artificial uncial, a slightly later variation, is more intricate, with broad diagonal and vertical strokes contrasted with hairlines.

FORMATION OF UNCIAL CHARACTERS

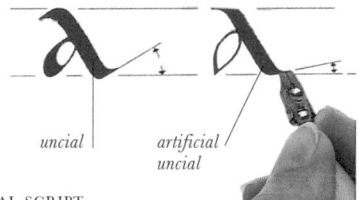

uncial | *artificial uncial*

8TH-CENTURY ENGLISH PSALTER IN ARTIFICIAL UNCIAL SCRIPT

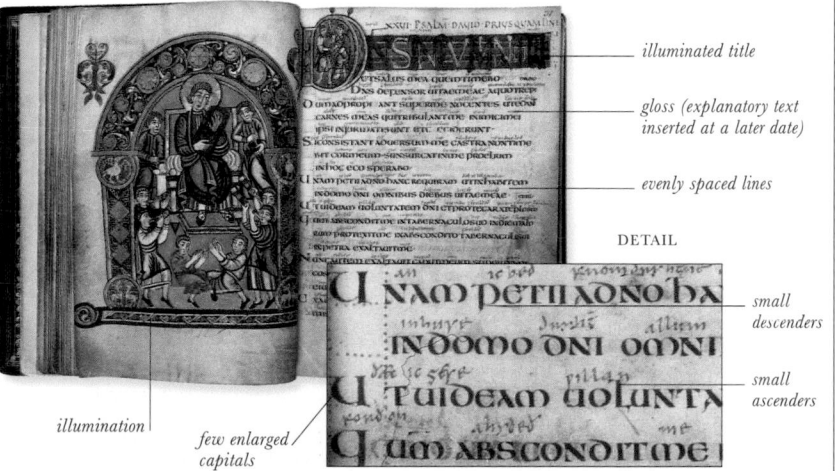

illumination

few enlarged capitals

illuminated title

gloss (explanatory text inserted at a later date)

evenly spaced lines

DETAIL

small descenders

small ascenders

U

uncrowded *adj.* not filled or likely to fill with crowds.

uncrown *v.tr.* **1** deprive (a monarch etc.) of a crown. **2** deprive (a person) of a position. **3** (as **uncrowned** *adj.*) **a** not crowned. **b** having the status but not the name of (*the uncrowned king of boxing*).

uncrushable *adj.* not crushable.

unction *n.* **1 a** the act of anointing with oil etc. as a religious rite. **b** the oil etc. so used. **2 a** a soothing words or thought. **b** excessive or insincere flattery. **3 a** the act of anointing for medical purposes. **b** an ointment so used. **4 a** a fervent or sympathetic quality in words or tone caused by or causing deep emotion. **b** a pretence of this. [from Latin *unctio*]

unctuous *adj.* **1** unpleasantly flattering; oily. **2** having a greasy or soapy feel. [based on Latin *unctus* 'anointing'] □ **unctuously** *adv.* **unctuousness** *n.*

uncultivated *adj.* not cultivated.

uncultured *adj.* **1** not cultured, unrefined. **2** (of soil or plants) not cultivated.

uncured *adj.* **1** not cured. **2** (of pork etc.) not salted or smoked.

uncurl *v.intr. & tr.* relax from a curled position, untwist.

uncurtained *adj.* not curtained.

uncut *adj.* **1** not cut. **2** (of a book) with the pages not cut open or with untrimmed margins. **3** (of a book, film, etc.) complete; uncensored. **4** ◄ (of a stone, a diamond) not shaped by cutting. **5** (of fabric) having its pile-loops intact (*uncut moquette*).

undamaged *adj.* not damaged; intact.

UNCUT DIAMOND

undated *adj.* not provided or marked with a date.

undaunted *adj.* not daunted. □ **undauntedly** *adv.*

undead ● *adj.* (esp. of a vampire etc. in fiction) technically dead but still animate. ● *n.* (prec. by *the*; treated as *pl.*) those who are undead.

undeceive *v.tr.* free (a person) from a misconception, deception, or error.

undecided *adj.* **1** not settled or certain (*the question is undecided*). **2** hesitating; irresolute (*undecided about their relative merits*). □ **undecidedly** *adv.*

undecipherable *adj.* not decipherable.

undeclared *adj.* not declared.

undecorated *adj.* **1** not adorned; plain. **2** not honoured with an award.

undefeated *adj.* not defeated.

undefended *adj.* not defended.

undefiled *adj.* not defiled; pure.

undefined *adj.* **1** not defined. **2** not clearly marked; vague, indefinite. □ **undefinably** *adv.*

undelivered *adj.* not delivered or handed over.

undemanding *adj.* not demanding; easily satisfied.

undemocratic *adj.* not democratic. □ **undemocratically** *adv.*

undemonstrative *adj.* not expressing feelings etc. outwardly; reserved. □ **undemonstratively** *adv.*

undeniable *adj.* **1** unable to be denied or disputed; certain. **2** excellent (*was of undeniable character*). □ **undeniably** *adv.*

undenied *adj.* not denied.

undependable *adj.* not to be depended upon; unreliable.

under ● *prep.* **1 a** in or to a position lower than; below; beneath (*fell under the table; under the left eye*). **b** within, on the inside of (*wore a vest under his shirt*). **2 a** inferior to; less than (*a captain is under a major; is under 18*). **b** at or for a lower cost than (*was under £20*). **3 a** subject or liable to; controlled by (*lives under oppression; under pain of death; born under Saturn; the country prospered under him*). **b** undergoing (*is under repair*). **c** classified or subsumed in (*that book goes under biology; goes under many names*). **4** at the foot of or sheltered by (*hid under the wall; under the cliff*).

5 planted with (a crop). **6** powered by (sail, steam, etc.). ● *adv.* **1** in or to a lower position or condition (*kept him under*). **2** *colloq.* in or into a state of unconsciousness (*put him under for the operation*). ● *adj.* lower (*the under jaw*). □ **under one's arm** see ARM[1]. **under arms** see ARM[2]. **under one's belt** see BELT. **under one's breath** see BREATH. **under canvas** see CANVAS. **under a cloud** see CLOUD. **under control** see CONTROL. **under the counter** see COUNTER[1]. **under cover** under a roof or other shelter (see also COVER *n.* 4). **under fire** see FIRE. **under foot** see FOOT. **under a person's nose** see NOSE. **under the rose** see ROSE[1]. **under separate cover** in another envelope. **under the sun** anywhere in the world. **under water** in and covered by water. **under way** in motion; in progress. **under the weather** see WEATHER. [Old English] □ **undermost** *adj.*

under- *prefix* in senses of UNDER: **1** below, beneath (*undercarriage; underground*). **2** lower in status; subordinate (*under-secretary*). **3** insufficiently, incompletely (*undercook; underdeveloped*).

underachieve *v.intr.* do less well than might normally be expected. □ **underachievement** *n.* **underachiever** *n.*

under age *adj.* (usu. hyphenated when *attrib.*) not old enough.

underarm ● *adj. & adv.* **1** *Sport*, esp. *Cricket* with the arm below shoulder level. **2** under the arm. **3** in the armpit. ● *n.* the armpit.

underbelly *n.* (*pl.* **-ies**) the undersurface of an animal, vehicle, etc., esp. as vulnerable to attack.

underbid ● *v.tr.* (**-bidding**; *past* and *past part.* **-bid**) **1** make a lower bid than. **2** (also *absol.*) *Bridge* etc. bid less on (one's hand) than its strength warrants. ● *n.* **1** such a bid. **2** the act or an instance of underbidding.

underbrush *n.* N. *Amer.* undergrowth in a forest.

undercarriage *n.* **1** ▼ a wheeled retractable structure beneath an aircraft to receive the impact on landing and support the aircraft on the ground etc. **2** the supporting frame of a vehicle.

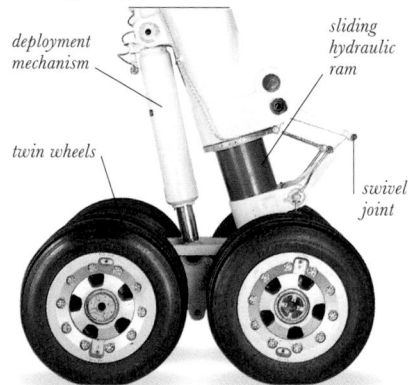

deployment mechanism
sliding hydraulic ram
twin wheels
swivel joint

UNDERCARRIAGE OF A 1950s AVRO VULCAN BOMBER

undercharge *v.tr.* **1** charge (a person) too little. **2** give less than the proper charge to (a gun, an electric battery, etc.).

underclass *n.* a subordinate social class.

undercliff *n.* ► a terrace or lower cliff formed by a landslip.

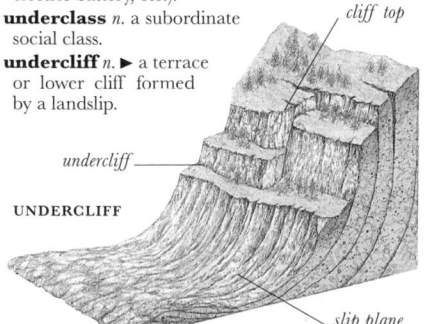

cliff top
undercliff
slip plane

UNDERCLIFF

underclothes *n.pl.* clothes worn under others, esp. next to the skin.

underclothing *n.* underclothes collectively.

undercoat *n.* **1 a** a preliminary layer of paint under the finishing coat. **b** the paint used for this. **2** an animal's under layer of hair or down. □ **undercoating** *n.*

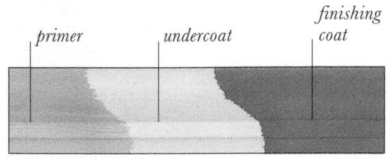

primer   *undercoat*   *finishing coat*

UNDERCOAT APPLIED TO BARE WOOD SAMPLE

undercook *v.tr.* cook insufficiently.

undercover *adj.* (usu. *attrib.*) **1** surreptitious. **2** engaged in spying, esp. by working with or among those to be observed (*undercover agent*).

undercroft *n.* a crypt. [Middle English, based on Latin *crypta* 'crypt']

undercurrent *n.* **1** a current below the surface. **2** an underlying often contrary feeling, activity, or influence (*an undercurrent of protest*).

undercut ● *v.tr.* (**-cutting**; *past* and *past part.* **-cut**) **1** sell or work at a lower price or lower wages than. **2** *Golf* etc. strike (a ball) so as to make it rise high. **3** cut away the part below or under (a thing). **4** undermine. ● *n. Brit.* the underside of a sirloin.

underdeveloped *adj.* **1** not fully developed; immature. **2** (of a country etc.) below its potential economic level. **3** *Photog.* not developed sufficiently to give a normal image. □ **underdevelopment** *n.*

underdog *n.* **1** a competitor thought to have little chance of winning. **2** a downtrodden person.

underdone *adj.* **1** not thoroughly done. **2** lightly or insufficiently cooked.

underdress *v.tr. & intr.* dress too plainly or too lightly.

underemphasis *n.* (*pl.* **-emphases**) an insufficient degree of emphasis. □ **underemphasize** *v.tr.* (also **-ise**).

underemployed *adj.* not fully employed. □ **underemployment** *n.*

underestimate ● *v.tr.* form too low an estimate of. ● *n.* an estimate that is too low. □ **underestimation** *n.*

underexpose *v.tr. Photog.* expose (film) for too short a time or with insufficient light. □ **underexposure** *n.*

underfed *adj.* insufficiently fed.

underfelt *n.* felt for laying under a carpet.

under-fives *n.pl.* children who are less than five years old.

underfloor *attrib.adj.* situated or operating beneath the floor (*underfloor heating*).

underflow *n.* an undercurrent.

underfoot *adv.* **1** under one's feet. **2** on the ground. **3** in a state of subjection. **4** so as to obstruct or inconvenience.

underfund *v.tr.* (esp. as **underfunded** *adj.*) provide insufficient funding for. □ **underfunding** *n.*

undergarment *n.* a piece of underclothing.

undergo *v.tr.* (*3rd sing. present* **-goes**; *past* **-went**; *past part.* **-gone**) be subjected to; suffer; endure. [Old English]

undergrad *n. colloq.* = UNDERGRADUATE.

undergraduate *n.* a student at a university who has not yet taken a first degree.

underground ● *adv.* **1** beneath the surface of the ground. **2** in or into secrecy or hiding. ● *adj.* **1** situated underground. **2** secret, hidden, esp. working secretly to subvert a ruling power. **3** unconventional, experimental (*underground press*). ● *n.* **1** *Brit.* an underground railway. **2** a secret group or activity, esp. aiming to subvert the established order. ● *v.tr.* lay (cables) below ground level.

undergrowth *n.* a dense growth of shrubs etc., esp. under large trees.

underhand ● *adj.* **1** secret, clandestine, not above board. **2** deceptive, crafty. **3** *Sport*, esp. *Baseball* underarm. ● *adv.* in an underhand manner. [Old English]

underhanded *adj. & adv.* = UNDERHAND.

underlay[1] ● *v.tr.* (*past* and *past part.* **-laid**) lay something under (a thing) to support or raise it (*underlaid the tiles with felt*). ● *n.* ▼ a thing laid under another, esp. material laid under a carpet or mattress as protection or support.

■ **Usage** Care should be taken not to confuse *underlay*, a somewhat rare verb, with *underlie*. See also Usage Note at LAY[1].

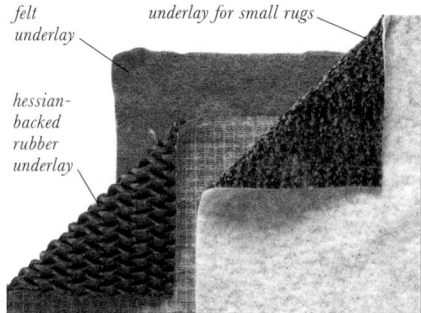

felt underlay

underlay for small rugs

hessian-backed rubber underlay

UNDERLAY TYPES

underlay[2] *past* of UNDERLIE.

underlie *v.tr.* (**-lying**; *past* **-lay**; *past part.* **-lain**) **1** (also *absol.*) lie or be situated under (a stratum etc.). **2** (also *absol.*) (esp. as **underlying** *adj.*) be the basis of (a doctrine, law, conduct, etc.). **3** exist beneath the superficial aspect of.

underline ● *v.tr.* **1** draw a line under (a word etc.) to give emphasis or draw attention or indicate italic or other special type. **2** emphasize, stress. ● *n.* **1** a line drawn under a word etc. **2** a caption below an illustration.

underlinen *n.* underclothes esp. of linen.

underling *n. usu. derog.* a subordinate.

underlip *n.* the lower lip of a person or animal.

underlying *pres. part.* of UNDERLIE.

undermanned *adj.* having too few people as crew or staff.

undermentioned *adj. Brit.* mentioned later in a book etc.

undermine *v.tr.* **1** injure (a person, reputation, influence, etc.) by secret or insidious means. **2** weaken, injure, or wear out (health etc.) imperceptibly or insidiously. **3** wear away the base or foundation of (*rivers undermine their banks*). **4** make an excavation under. [Middle English] □ **underminer** *n.*

underneath ● *prep.* **1** at or to a lower place than, below. **2** on the inside of. ● *adv.* **1** at or to a lower place. **2** inside. ● *n.* the lower surface or part. ● *adj.* lower. [Old English]

undernourished *adj.* insufficiently nourished. □ **undernourishment** *n.*

underpaid *past* and *past part.* of UNDERPAY.

underpants *n.pl.* an undergarment, esp. men's, covering the lower part of the body and usu. part of the legs.

underpart *n.* (usu. in *pl.*) a lower part, esp. a part of the underside of an animal.

underpass *n.* **1** a road etc. passing under another. **2** a crossing of this form.

underpay *v.tr.* (*past* and *past part.* **-paid**) pay too little to (a person) or for (a thing). □ **underpayment** *n.*

underperform *v.* **1** *intr.* perform less well or be less profitable than expected. **2** *tr.* perform less well or be less profitable than. □ **underperformance** *n.*

underpin *v.tr.* (**-pinned**, **-pinning**) **1** support from below with masonry etc. **2** support, strengthen.

underplay *v.* **1** *tr.* play down the importance of. **2** *intr. & tr. Theatr.* perform with deliberate restraint.

underpopulated *adj.* having an insufficient or very small population.

underpowered *adj.* lacking full electrical, mechanical, etc. power; lacking sufficient amplification.

underprice *v.tr.* price lower than what is usual or appropriate.

underprivileged ● *adj.* **1** less privileged than others. **2** not enjoying the normal standard of living or rights in a society. ● *n.* (prec. by *the*; treated as *pl.*) underprivileged people.

underproduction *n.* production of less than is usual or required.

underrate *v.tr.* have too low an opinion of.

under-represent *v.tr.* (usu. as **under-represented** *adj.*) not include (a social group, specimen, type, etc.) in sufficient numbers.

underscore ● *v.tr.* = UNDERLINE *v.* ● *n.* = UNDERLINE *n.* 1.

undersea *adj.* below the sea or the surface of the sea.

underseal *Brit.* ● *v.tr.* seal the underpart of (esp. a motor vehicle against rust etc.). ● *n.* a protective coating for undersealing.

under-secretary *n.* (*pl.* **-ies**) a subordinate official, esp. *Brit.* a junior minister or senior civil servant or *US* the principal assistant to a member of the Cabinet.

undersell *v.tr.* (*past* and *past part.* **-sold**) **1** sell at a lower price than (another seller). **2** sell at less than the true value.

undersexed *adj.* having unusually weak sexual desires.

undershirt *n.* esp. *N. Amer.* an undergarment worn under a shirt; a vest.

undershoot ● *v.tr.* (*past* and *past part.* **-shot**) **1** land short of (a runway etc.). **2** shoot short of or below. ● *n.* the act or an instance of undershooting.

undershorts *n.* *US* short underpants; trunks.

underside *n.* the lower or under side or surface.

undersigned *adj.* whose signature is appended (*we, the undersigned, wish to state …*).

undersized *adj.* (also **undersize**) of less than the usual size.

underskirt *n.* a skirt worn under another; a petticoat.

underslung *adj.* **1** supported from above. **2** (of a vehicle chassis) hanging lower than the axles.

undersold *past* and *past part.* of UNDERSELL.

underspend ● *v.* (*past* and *past part.* **-spent**) **1** *tr.* spend less than (a specified amount). **2** *intr. & refl.* spend too little. ● *n.* **1** the act of underspending. **2** an instance of this. **3** the amount by which a specified amount is underspent.

understaffed *adj.* having too few staff. □ **understaffing** *n.*

understand *v.* (*past* and *past part.* **-stood**) **1** *tr.* perceive the meaning of (words, a person, a language, etc.) (*does not understand what you say; understood you perfectly; cannot understand French*). **2** *tr.* perceive the significance or explanation or cause of (*do not understand why he came; do not understand the point of her remark*). **3** *tr.* be sympathetically aware of the character or nature of, know how to deal with (*quite understand your difficulty; cannot understand him at all; could never understand algebra*). **4** *tr.* **a** infer, take as implied, take for granted (*I understand that it begins at noon; I understand him to be a distant relation*). **b** (*absol.*) believe or assume from knowledge or inference (*she is coming tomorrow, I understand*). **5** *tr.* supply (a word) mentally (*the verb may be either expressed or understood*). **6** *intr.* have understanding. □ **understand each other 1** know each other's views or feelings. **2** be in agreement or collusion. [Old English] □ **understandable** *adj.* **understandability** *n.* **understandably** *adv.* **understander** *n.*

understanding ● *n.* **1 a** the ability to understand or think; intelligence. **b** the power of apprehension; the power of abstract thought. **2** an individual's perception of a situation etc. **3** an agreement; a thing agreed upon, esp. informally (*had an understanding with the rival company; consented only on this understanding*). **4** harmony in opinion or feeling (*disturbed the good understanding between them*). **5** sympathetic awareness or tolerance. ● *adj.* **1** having understanding or insight or good judgement. **2** sympathetic to others' feelings. □ **understandingly** *adv.*

understate *v.tr.* **1** express in greatly or unduly restrained terms. **2** represent as being less than it actually is. □ **understatement** *n.*

understeer ● *n.* a tendency of a vehicle to turn less sharply than was intended. ● *v.intr.* have such a tendency.

understood *past* and *past part.* of UNDERSTAND.

understorey *n.* (*pl.* **-eys**) (also **understory**, *pl.* **-ies**) **1** a layer of vegetation beneath the main canopy of a forest. ▷ RAINFOREST. **2** the plants forming this.

understudy esp. *Theatr.* ● *n.* (*pl.* **-ies**) a person who studies another's role or duties in order to act at short notice in the absence of the other. ● *v.tr.* (**-ies**, **-ied**) **1** study (a role etc.) as an understudy. **2** act as an understudy to (a person).

undersubscribed *adj.* without sufficient subscribers, participants, etc.

undersurface *n.* the lower or under surface.

undertake *v.tr.* (*past* **-took**; *past part.* **-taken**) **1** bind oneself to perform, make oneself responsible for, engage in, enter upon (work, an enterprise, a responsibility). **2** (usu. foll. by *to* + infin.) promise. **3** guarantee, affirm (*I will undertake that he has not heard a word*).

undertaker *n.* a person whose business is to make arrangements for funerals.

undertaking *n.* **1** work etc. undertaken, an enterprise (*a serious undertaking*). **2** a promise. **3** the management of funerals as a profession.

undertenant *n.* a subtenant.

under-the-counter *attrib.adj.* (esp. of illicit goods) obtained surreptitiously (cf. *under the counter* (COUNTER[1])).

underthings *n.pl. colloq.* underclothes.

undertint *n.* a subdued tint.

undertone *n.* **1** a subdued tone of sound or colour. **2** an underlying quality. **3** an undercurrent of feeling.

undertook *past* of UNDERTAKE.

undertow *n.* ▼ a current below the surface of the sea moving in the opposite direction to the surface current.

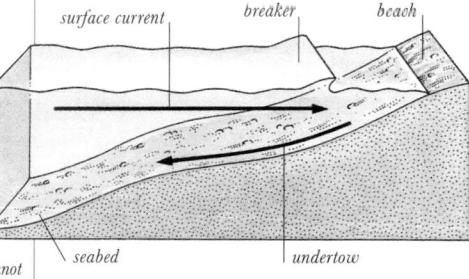

surface current   *breaker*   *beach*

seabed   *undertow*

UNDERTOW

underuse ● *v.tr.* /-yooz/ use below the optimum level. ● *n.* /-yooss/ insufficient use.

undervalue *v.tr.* (**-values**, **-valued**, **-valuing**) **1** value insufficiently. **2** underestimate. □ **undervaluation** *n.*

underwater ● *adj.* situated or done under water. ● *adv.* under water.

underwear *n.* underclothes.

underweight ● *adj.* weighing less than is normal or desirable. ● *n.* insufficient weight.

U

underwent *past* of UNDERGO.

underwhelm *v.tr. joc.* fail to impress. [on the pattern of *overwhelm*]

underwing *n.* the underside of a bird's wing.

underwood *n.* undergrowth.

underwork *v.* **1** *tr.* impose too little work on. **2** *intr.* do too little work.

underworld *n.* **1** those who live by organized crime and immorality. **2** the mythical abode of the dead under the earth.

underwrite *v.* (*past* **-wrote**; *past part.* **-written**) **1 a** *tr.* sign, and accept liability under (an insurance policy). **b** *tr.* accept (liability) in this way. **c** *intr.* practise insurance. **2** *tr.* undertake to finance or support. **3** *tr.* engage to buy all the stock in (a company etc.) not bought by the public. **4** *tr.* write below (*the underwritten names*). □ **underwriter** *n.*

undeserved *adj.* not deserved. □ **undeservedly** *adv.*

undeserving *adj.* not deserving.

undesigned *adj.* unintentional. □ **undesignedly** *adv.*

undesirable ● *adj.* objectionable, unpleasant. ● *n.* an undesirable person. □ **undesirability** *n.* **undesirably** *adv.*

undesired *adj.* not desired.

undetectable *adj.* not detectable. □ **undetectably** *adv.*

undetected *adj.* not detected.

undeterred *adj.* not deterred.

undeveloped *adj.* not developed.

undiagnosed *adj.* not diagnosed.

undid *past* of UNDO.

undies /un-diz/ *n.pl. colloq.* (esp. women's) underclothes.

undifferentiated *adj.* not differentiated; amorphous.

undigested *adj.* **1** not digested. **2** (esp. of information, facts, etc.) not properly arranged or considered.

undignified *adj.* lacking dignity.

undiluted *adj.* **1** not diluted. **2** complete, utter.

undiminished *adj.* not diminished or lessened.

undine /un-deen/ *n.* a female water spirit. [based on Latin *unda* 'a wave']

undiplomatic *adj.* tactless. □ **undiplomatically** *adv.*

undischarged *adj.* (esp. of a bankrupt) not discharged.

undisciplined *adj.* lacking discipline; not disciplined.

undisclosed *adj.* not revealed or made known.

undiscoverable *adj.* that cannot be discovered.

undiscovered *adj.* not discovered.

undiscriminating *adj.* not showing good judgement.

undiscussed *adj.* not discussed.

undisguised *adj.* not disguised. □ **undisguisedly** *adv.*

undismayed *adj.* not dismayed.

undisputed *adj.* not disputed or called in question.

undissolved *adj.* not dissolved.

undistinguished *adj.* not distinguished; mediocre.

undisturbed *adj.* not disturbed or interfered with.

undivided *adj.* not divided or shared; whole, entire (*gave him my undivided attention*).

undo *v.tr.* (*3rd sing. present* **-does**; *past* **-did**; *past part.* **-done**) **1 a** unfasten (a coat, button, parcel, etc.). **b** unfasten the clothing of (a person). **2** annul, cancel (*cannot undo the past*). **3** ruin the prospects, reputation, or morals of. [Old English]

undocumented *adj.* **1** *US* not having the appropriate document. **2** not proved by or recorded in documents.

undoing *n.* **1** ruin or a cause of ruin. **2** the process of reversing what has been done. **3** the action of opening or unfastening.

undomesticated *adj.* not domesticated.

undone *adj.* **1** not done (*left the job undone*). **2** not fastened (*left the buttons undone*). **3** *archaic* ruined.

undoubted *adj.* certain, not questioned. □ **undoubtedly** *adv.*

undraped *adj.* **1** not covered with drapery. **2** naked.

undreamed *adj.* (also **undreamt**) (often foll. by *of*) not dreamed or thought of or imagined.

undress ● *v.* **1** *intr.* take off one's clothes. **2** *tr.* take the clothes off (a person). ● *n.* **1** ordinary dress as opposed to full dress or uniform (also *attrib.*: *undress cap*). **2** casual or informal dress. **3** the state of being naked or only partially clothed.

undressed *adj.* **1** not or no longer dressed. **2** (of leather etc.) not treated. **3** (of food) not having a dressing.

undrinkable *adj.* unfit for drinking.

undue *adj.* (usu. *attrib.*) **1** excessive, disproportionate. **2** not suitable. □ **unduly** *adv.*

undulate /un-dew-layt/ *v.intr. & tr.* have or cause to have a wavy motion or look. [based on Latin *unda* 'a wave']

undulation /un-dew-lay-shŏn/ *n.* **1** a wavy motion or form, a gentle rise and fall. **2** each wave of this. **3** a set of wavy lines.

undulatory /un-dew-lay-tŏri/ *adj.* **1** undulating, wavy. **2** of or due to undulation.

undutiful *adj.* not dutiful.

undyed *adj.* not dyed.

undying *adj.* **1** immortal. **2** unending (*undying love*).

unearned *adj.* not earned.

unearned income *n.* income from interest payments etc. as opposed to salary, wages, or fees.

unearth *v.tr.* **1** discover by searching or in the course of digging or rummaging. **2** dig out of the earth.

unearthly *adj.* **1** supernatural, mysterious. **2** *colloq.* absurdly early or inconvenient (*got up at an unearthly hour*). **3** not earthly. □ **unearthliness** *n.*

unease *n.* lack of ease, discomfort, distress.

uneasy *adj.* (**uneasier**, **uneasiest**) **1** disturbed or uncomfortable in mind or body (*passed an uneasy night*). **2** disturbing (*had an uneasy suspicion*). □ **uneasily** *adv.* **uneasiness** *n.*

uneatable *adj.* not able to be eaten, esp. because of its condition (cf. INEDIBLE).

uneaten *adj.* not eaten; left undevoured.

uneconomic *adj.* not economic; incapable of being profitably operated etc. □ **uneconomically** *adv.*

uneconomical *adj.* not economical; wasteful.

unedifying *adj.* not edifying, esp. uninstructive or degrading. □ **unedifyingly** *adv.*

unedited *adj.* not edited.

uneducated *adj.* not educated. □ **uneducable** *adj.*

unelectable *adj.* holding views likely to bring defeat at an election.

unelected *adj.* not elected.

unembarrassed *adj.* not embarrassed.

unemotional *adj.* not emotional; lacking emotion. □ **unemotionally** *adv.*

unemphatic *adj.* not emphatic. □ **unemphatically** *adv.*

unemployable ● *adj.* unfitted for paid employment. ● *n.* an unemployable person. □ **unemployability** *n.*

unemployed ● *adj.* **1** out of work. **2** not in use. ● *n.* (prec. by *the*; treated as *pl.*) unemployed people.

unemployment *n.* **1** the state of being unemployed. **2** the condition or extent of this in a country or region etc. (*the North has higher unemployment*).

unemployment benefit *n.* a payment made by the state or (in the US) a trade union to an unemployed person.

unencumbered *adj.* **1** (of an estate) not having any liabilities (e.g. a mortgage). **2** having no encumbrance; free.

unending *adj.* having or apparently having no end. □ **unendingly** *adv.*

unendowed *adj.* not endowed.

unendurable *adj.* that cannot be endured. □ **unendurably** *adv.*

unenforceable *adj.* impossible to enforce.

un-English *adj.* **1** not characteristic of the English. **2** not English.

unenjoyable *adj.* not enjoyable.

unenlightened *adj.* not enlightened.

unenterprising *adj.* not enterprising.

unenthusiastic *adj.* not enthusiastic. □ **unenthusiastically** *adv.*

unenviable *adj.* not enviable. □ **unenviably** *adv.*.

unequal *adj.* **1** not equal. **2** of varying quality. **3** lacking equal advantage to both sides (*an unequal bargain*). □ **unequally** *adv.*

unequalled *adj.* (*US* **unequaled**) superior to all others.

unequipped *adj.* not equipped.

unequivocal *adj.* not ambiguous, plain, unmistakable. □ **unequivocally** *adv.*

unerring *adj.* not erring, failing, or missing the mark; true, certain. □ **unerringly** *adv.*

UNESCO /yoo-nes-koh/ *abbr.* (also **Unesco**) United Nations Educational, Scientific, and Cultural Organization.

unessential ● *adj.* **1** not essential. **2** not of the first importance. ● *n.* an unessential part or thing.

unestablished *adj.* not established.

unethical *adj.* not ethical, esp. unscrupulous in business or professional conduct. □ **unethically** *adv.*

uneven *adj.* **1** not level or smooth. **2** not uniform or equable. **3** (of a contest) unequal. □ **unevenly** *adv.* **unevenness** *n.*

uneventful *adj.* not eventful. □ **uneventfully** *adv.* **uneventfulness** *n.*

unexamined *adj.* not examined.

unexceptionable *adj.* entirely satisfactory. □ **unexceptionably** *adv.*

■ **Usage** See Usage Note at EXCEPTIONABLE.

unexceptional *adj.* not out of the ordinary; usual, normal. □ **unexceptionally** *adv.*

■ **Usage** See Usage Note at EXCEPTIONABLE.

unexcitable *adj.* not easily excited. □ **unexcitability** *n.*

unexciting *adj.* not exciting; dull.

unexpected *adj.* not expected; surprising. □ **unexpectedly** *adv.* **unexpectedness** *n.*

unexpired *adj.* that has not yet expired.

unexplainable *adj.* inexplicable. □ **unexplainably** *adv.*

unexplained *adj.* not explained.

unexploded *adj.* (usu. *attrib.*) (of a bomb etc.) that has not exploded.

unexplored *adj.* not explored.

unexposed *adj.* not exposed.

unexpressed *adj.* not expressed or made known (*unexpressed fears*).

unexpurgated *adj.* (esp. of a text etc.) not expurgated; complete.

unfading *adj.* that never fades.

unfailing *adj.* **1** not failing. **2** not running short. **3** constant. **4** reliable. □ **unfailingly** *adv.* **unfailingness** *n.*

unfair *adj.* **1** not equitable or honest (*obtained by unfair means*). **2** not impartial or according to the rules (*unfair play*). [Old English] □ **unfairly** *adv.* **unfairness** *n.*

unfaithful *adj.* **1** not faithful, esp. adulterous. **2** not loyal. **3** treacherous. □ **unfaithfully** *adv.* **unfaithfulness** *n.*

unfaltering *adj.* not faltering; steady, resolute. □ **unfalteringly** *adv.*

unfamiliar *adj.* not familiar. □ **unfamiliarity** *n.*

unfashionable *adj.* not fashionable. □ **unfashionably** *adv.*

U

unfasten v. **1** tr. & intr. make or become loose. **2** tr. open the fastening(s) of. **3** tr. detach.

unfastened adj. **1** that has not been fastened. **2** that has been loosened, opened, or detached.

unfatherly adj. not befitting a father.

unfathomable adj. incapable of being fathomed. □ **unfathomably** adv.

unfathomed adj. **1** of unascertained depth. **2** not fully explored or known.

unfavourable adj. (US **unfavorable**) not favourable; adverse, hostile. □ **unfavourably** adv.

unfavourite adj. (US **unfavorite**) colloq. least favourite; most disliked.

unfazed adj. colloq. untroubled; not disconcerted.

unfeasible adj. not feasible; impractical. □ **unfeasibility** n. **unfeasibly** adv.

unfed adj. not fed.

unfeeling adj. unsympathetic, harsh, not caring about others' feelings. [Old English] □ **unfeelingly** adv.

unfeigned adj. genuine, sincere. □ **unfeignedly** adv.

unfeminine adj. not in accordance with, or appropriate to, female character. □ **unfemininity** n.

unfenced adj. **1** not provided with fences. **2** unprotected.

unfermented adj. not fermented.

unfertilized adj. (also **-ised**) not fertilized.

unfettered adj. unrestrained, unrestricted.

unfilled adj. not filled.

unfiltered adj. **1** not filtered. **2** (of a cigarette) not provided with a filter.

unfinished adj. not finished; incomplete.

unfit ● adj. (often foll. by for, or to + infin.) not fit. ● v.tr. (**unfitted, unfitting**) (usu. foll. by for) make unsuitable. □ **unfitness** n.

unfitted adj. **1** not fit. **2** not fitted or suited. **3** not provided with fittings.

unfitting adj. not fitting or suitable, unbecoming. □ **unfittingly** adv.

unfix v.tr. **1** release or loosen from a fixed state. **2** detach.

unfixed adj. not fixed.

unflagging adj. tireless, persistent. □ **unflaggingly** adv.

unflappable adj. colloq. imperturbable; remaining calm in a crisis. □ **unflappability** n. **unflappably** adv.

unflattering adj. not flattering. □ **unflatteringly** adv.

unfledged adj. **1** (of a person) inexperienced. **2** (of a bird) not yet fledged.

unflinching adj. not flinching. □ **unflinchingly** adv.

unfocused adj. (also **unfocussed**) not focused.

unfold v. **1** tr. open the fold or folds of, spread out. **2** tr. reveal (thoughts etc.). **3** intr. become opened out. **4** intr. develop. [Old English] □ **unfoldment** n. US.

unforced adj. **1** not produced by effort; easy, natural. **2** not compelled or constrained.

unforeseeable adj. not foreseeable.

unforeseen adj. not foreseen.

unforgettable adj. that cannot be forgotten; memorable, wonderful (an unforgettable experience). □ **unforgettably** adv.

unforgivable adj. that cannot be forgiven. □ **unforgivably** adv.

unforgiven adj. not forgiven.

unforgiving adj. not forgiving. □ **unforgivingly** adv. **unforgivingness** n.

unforgotten adj. not forgotten.

unformed adj. **1** not formed. **2** shapeless. **3** not developed.

unforthcoming adj. not forthcoming.

unfortified adj. not fortified.

unfortunate ● adj. **1** having bad fortune;

unlucky. **2** unhappy. **3** regrettable. **4** disastrous. ● n. an unfortunate person.

unfortunately adv. **1** (qualifying a whole sentence) it is unfortunate that. **2** in an unfortunate manner.

unfounded adj. having no foundation (unfounded hopes; unfounded rumour).

unframed adj. (esp. of a picture) not framed.

unfree adj. deprived or devoid of liberty. □ **unfreedom** n.

unfreeze v. (past **unfroze**; past part. **unfrozen**) **1** tr. cause to thaw. **2** intr. thaw. **3** tr. remove restrictions from, make (assets, credits, etc.) realizable.

unfrequented adj. not frequented.

unfriendly adj. (**unfriendlier, unfriendliest**) not friendly. □ **unfriendliness** n.

unfrock v.tr. = DEFROCK.

unfroze past of UNFREEZE.

unfrozen past part. of UNFREEZE.

unfruitful adj. **1** not producing good results, unprofitable. **2** not producing fruit or crops. □ **unfruitfully** adv. **unfruitfulness** n.

unfulfilled adj. not fulfilled. □ **unfulfillable** adj. **unfulfilling** adj.

unfunded adj. (of a debt) not funded.

unfunny adj. (**unfunnier, unfunniest**) not amusing (though meant to be). □ **unfunnily** adv. **unfunniness** n.

unfurl v. **1** tr. spread out (a sail, umbrella, etc.). **2** intr. become spread out.

unfurnished adj. without furniture.

ungainly adj. (of a person, animal, or movement) awkward, clumsy. [based on Old Norse gegn 'straight'] □ **ungainliness** n.

ungallant adj. not gallant. □ **ungallantly** adv.

ungenerous adj. not generous; mean. □ **ungenerosity** adv. **ungenerously** adv.

ungentlemanly adj. not gentlemanly. □ **ungentlemanliness** n.

unget-at-able adj. colloq. inaccessible.

unglamorous adj. **1** lacking glamour or attraction. **2** mundane.

unglazed adj. not glazed.

ungloved adj. not wearing a glove or gloves.

ungodly adj. **1** impious, wicked. **2** colloq. outrageous (an ungodly hour to arrive). □ **ungodliness** n.

ungovernable adj. uncontrollable, violent. □ **ungovernability** n. **ungovernably** adv.

ungraceful adj. not graceful. □ **ungracefully** adv. **ungracefulness** n.

ungracious adj. **1** not kindly or courteous; unkind. **2** unattractive. □ **ungraciously** adv. **ungraciousness** n.

ungrammatical adj. contrary to the rules of grammar. □ **ungrammaticality** n. **ungrammatically** adv. **ungrammaticalness** n.

ungrateful adj. not feeling or showing gratitude. □ **ungratefully** adv. **ungratefulness** n.

ungreen adj. **1** not supporting protection of the environment. **2** harmful to the environment.

ungrounded adj. **1** having no basis or justification; unfounded. **2** Electr. not earthed. **3** (foll. by in a subject) not properly instructed. **4** (of an aircraft, ship, etc.) no longer grounded.

ungrudging adj. not grudging. □ **ungrudgingly** adv.

unguarded adj. **1** incautious, thoughtless (an unguarded remark). **2** not guarded; without a guard. □ **unguardedly** adv. **unguardedness** n.

unguent /ung-gew-ĕnt/ n. a soft substance used as ointment or for lubrication. [from Latin unguentum]

unguessable adj. that cannot be guessed or imagined.

unguided adj. not guided in a particular path or direction; left to take its own course.

ungulate /ung-gew-lăt/ ● adj. hoofed. ● n. ▼ a hoofed mammal. [based on Latin ungula 'little claw']

UNGULATE

Ungulate is a general term applied to the two orders of hoofed mammals: perissodactyls and artiodactyls. Perissodactyls have one or three functional toes, and include horses, rhinoceroses, and tapirs. Artiodactyls have two or four functional toes, and include cattle, sheep, camels, giraffes, pigs, and hippopotamuses. In many two-toed ungulates the narrow gap between the toes forms a cloven hoof. The majority of two-toed ungulates are ruminants.

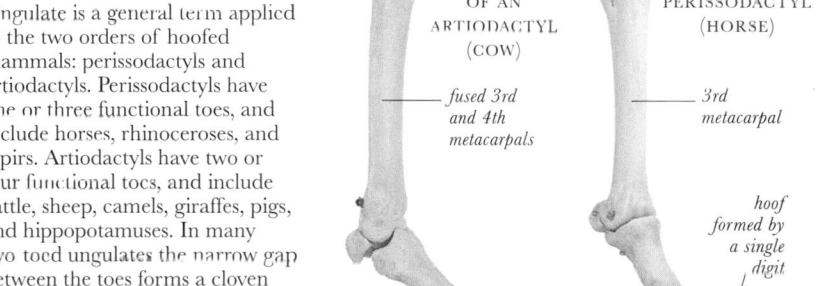

FORELEG OF AN ARTIODACTYL (COW)
fused 3rd and 4th metacarpals
cloven hoof

FORELEG OF A PERISSODACTYL (HORSE)
3rd metacarpal
hoof formed by a single digit

TYPES OF UNGULATE

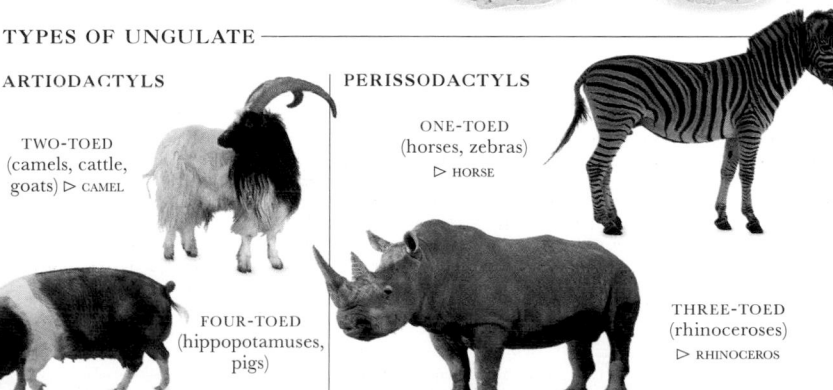

ARTIODACTYLS

TWO-TOED (camels, cattle, goats) ▷ CAMEL

FOUR-TOED (hippopotamuses, pigs)

PERISSODACTYLS

ONE-TOED (horses, zebras) ▷ HORSE

THREE-TOED (rhinoceroses) ▷ RHINOCEROS

U

unhallowed *adj.* **1** not consecrated. **2** not sacred; unholy, wicked.

unhampered *adj.* not hampered.

unhand *v.tr. literary* or *joc.* **1** take one's hands off (a person). **2** release from one's grasp.

unhang *v.tr.* (*past* and *past part.* **unhung**) take down from a hanging position.

unhappy *adj.* (**unhappier, unhappiest**) **1** not happy, miserable. **2** unsuccessful, unfortunate. **3** causing misfortune. **4** disastrous. **5** inauspicious. □ **unhappily** *adv.* **unhappiness** *n.*

unharbour *v.tr. Brit.* dislodge (a deer) from a covert.

unharmed *adj.* not harmed.

unharmful *adj.* not harmful.

unharness *v.tr.* remove a harness from.

unhatched *adj.* (of an egg etc.) not hatched.

unhealed *adj.* not yet healed.

unhealthy *adj.* (**unhealthier, unhealthiest**) **1** not in good health. **2 a** (of a place etc.) harmful to health. **b** unwholesome. **c** *slang* dangerous to life. □ **unhealthily** *adv.* **unhealthiness** *n.*

unheard *adj.* **1** not heard. **2** (usu. **unheard-of**) unprecedented, unknown.

unheated *adj.* not heated.

unheeded *adj.* not heeded; disregarded.

unheeding *adj.* not giving heed; heedless. □ **unheedingly** *adv.*

unhelpful *adj.* not helpful. □ **unhelpfully** *adv.* **unhelpfulness** *n.*

unheralded *adj.* not heralded; unannounced.

unheroic *adj.* not heroic. □ **unheroically** *adv.*

unhesitating *adj.* without hesitation. □ **unhesitatingly** *adv.*

unhindered *adj.* not hindered.

unhinge *v.tr.* **1** take (a door etc.) off its hinges. **2** (esp. as **unhinged** *adj.*) unsettle or disorder (a person's mind etc.), make (a person) crazy.

unhistorical *adj.* not historical. □ **unhistorically** *adv.*

unhitch *v.tr.* **1** release from a hitched state. **2** unhook, unfasten.

unholy *adj.* (**unholier, unholiest**) **1** impious, profane, wicked. **2** *colloq.* dreadful, outrageous (*made an unholy row about it*). **3** not holy. [Old English] □ **unholiness** *n.*

unhook *v.tr.* **1** remove from a hook or hooks. **2** unfasten by releasing a hook or hooks.

unhoped *adj.* (foll. by *for*) not hoped for or expected.

unhorse *v.tr.* **1** throw or drag from a horse. **2** (of a horse) throw (a rider). **3** dislodge, overthrow.

unhoused *v.tr.* not provided with or living in a house; homeless.

unhuman *adj.* **1** not human. **2** superhuman. **3** inhuman, brutal.

unhung *adj.* **1** not (yet) executed by hanging. **2** not hung up (for exhibition).

unhurried *adj.* not hurried. □ **unhurriedly** *adv.*

unhurt *adj.* not hurt.

unhusk *v.tr.* remove a husk or shell from.

unhygienic *adj.* not hygienic. □ **unhygienically** *adv.*

unhyphenated *adj.* not hyphenated.

uni *n.* (*pl.* **unis**) esp. *Austral.* & *NZ colloq.* a university.

uni- *comb. form* one; having or consisting of one. [Latin]

Uniate ● *adj.* of or relating to any community of Christians in E. Europe or the Near East that acknowledges papal supremacy but retains its own liturgy etc. ● *n.* a member of such a community. [based on Latin *unio* 'union']

unicameral *adj.* with a single legislative chamber. [based on Latin *camera* 'chamber']

UNICEF /yoo-ni-sef/ *abbr.* United Nations Children's (originally International Children's Emergency) Fund.

chloroplast

cell wall

UNICELLULAR ORGANISM
(A DESMID, MAGNIFIED)

unicellular *adj.* ◄ (of an organism, organ, tissue, etc.) consisting of a single cell.

unicorn *n.* a fabulous animal usually represented as a horse with a single straight horn. [based on Latin *cornu* 'horn']

unicycle *n.* ► a single-wheeled cycle, esp. as used by acrobats. □ **unicyclist** *n.*

unideal *adj.* not ideal.

unidentifiable *adj.* unable to be identified.

unidentified *adj.* not identified.

unidimensional *adj.* having (only) one dimension.

unidirectional *adj.* having only one direction of motion, operation, etc. □ **unidirectionally** *adv.*

unification *n.* the act or an instance of unifying; the state of being unified. □ **unificatory** *adj.*

Unification Church *n.* a religious organization founded in 1954 in Korea by Sun Myung Moon (cf. MOONIE).

uniform ● *adj.* **1** not changing in form or character; the same, unvarying (*present a uniform appearance; all of uniform size*). **2** conforming to the same standard, rules, or pattern. ● *n.* uniform distinctive clothing worn by members of the same body, e.g. by soldiers, police, and schoolchildren. ● *v.tr.* clothe in uniform (*a uniformed officer*). [from Latin *uniformis*] □ **uniformity** *n.* (*pl.* **-ies**). **uniformly** *adv.*

unify *v.tr.* (**-ies, -ied**) (also *absol.*) reduce to unity or uniformity. [from Late Latin *unificare*] □ **unifier** *n.*

unilateral *adj.* **1** performed by or affecting only one person or party (*unilateral disarmament; unilateral declaration of independence*). **2** one-sided. □ **unilaterally** *adv.*

unilateralism *n.* **1** unilateral disarmament. **2** *US* the pursuit of a foreign policy without allies. □ **unilateralist** *n.* & *adj.*

unilluminated *adj.* not illuminated.

unillustrated *adj.* (esp. of a book) without illustrations.

unimaginable *adj.* impossible to imagine. □ **unimaginably** *adv.*

unimaginative *adj.* lacking imagination; stolid, dull. □ **unimaginatively** *adv.* **unimaginativeness** *n.*

unimpaired *adj.* not impaired.

unimpeachable *adj.* giving no opportunity for censure; beyond reproach or question. □ **unimpeachably** *adv.*

UNICYCLE

unimpeded *adj.* not impeded.

unimportance *n.* lack of importance.

unimportant *adj.* not important.

unimposing *adj.* unimpressive. □ **unimposingly** *adv.*

unimpressed *adj.* not impressed.

unimpressionable *adj.* not impressionable.

unimpressive *adj.* not impressive. □ **unimpressively** *adv.* **unimpressiveness** *n.*

unimproved *adj.* **1** not made better. **2** (of land) not used for agriculture or building; not developed.

uninflected *adj.* **1** *Gram.* (of a language) not having inflections. **2** not changing or varying.

uninfluenced *adj.* (often foll. by *by*) not influenced.

uninfluential *adj.* having little or no influence.

uninformative *adj.* not informative; giving little information.

uninformed *adj.* **1** not informed or instructed. **2** ignorant, uneducated.

uninhabitable *adj.* that cannot be inhabited.

uninhabited *adj.* not inhabited.

uninhibited *adj.* not inhibited. □ **uninhibitedly** *adv.* **uninhibitedness** *n.*

uninitiated *adj.* not initiated; not admitted or instructed.

uninjured *adj.* not injured.

uninspired *adj.* **1** not inspired. **2** (of oratory etc.) commonplace.

uninspiring *adj.* not inspiring. □ **uninspiringly** *adv.*

uninsurable *adj.* that cannot be insured.

uninsured *adj.* not insured.

unintelligent *adj.* not intelligent. □ **unintelligently** *adv.*

unintelligible *adj.* not intelligible. □ **unintelligibility** *n.* **unintelligibly** *adv.*

unintended *adj.* not intended.

unintentional *adj.* not intentional. □ **unintentionally** *adv.*

uninterested *adj.* **1** not interested. **2** unconcerned, indifferent. □ **uninterestedly** *adv.* **uninterestedness** *n.*

uninteresting *adj.* not interesting. □ **uninterestingness** *n.*

uninterrupted *adj.* not interrupted. □ **uninterruptedly** *adv.*

uninvited *adj.* not invited.

UNIFORM

Uniforms make a group of people immediately identifiable, which can be important for members of the emergency services and the armed forces. They also set a clear standard for the wearer in terms of quality and function. Although some uniforms are ceremonial, especially in the military, most are designed to be practical.

EXAMPLES OF UNIFORMS

AMERICAN SUBMARINE CAPTAIN   BRITISH FLIGHT LIEUTENANT   AUSTRALIAN FIREFIGHTER   BRITISH NURSE   AMERICAN POLICEMAN   FRENCH GENDARME

U

uninviting *adj.* not inviting, unattractive, repellent. □ **uninvitingly** *adv.*

uninvolved *adj.* not involved.

union *n.* **1** the act or an instance of uniting; the state of being united. **2 a** a whole resulting from the combination of parts or members. **b** (often **Union**) a political unit formed in this way, esp. the US, the UK, or South Africa. **3** = TRADE UNION. **4** marriage, matrimony. **5** concord, agreement (*lived together in perfect union*). **6** (**Union**) (in the UK) **a** a general social club and debating society at some universities and colleges. **b** the buildings or accommodation of such a society. **7** *Math.* the totality of the members of two or more sets. **8** a joint or coupling for pipes etc. **9** a fabric of mixed materials, e.g. cotton with linen or silk. [from ecclesiastical Latin *unio* 'unity']

Union flag *n.* ▼ the national ensign of the United Kingdom formed by the union of the crosses of St George, St Andrew, and St Patrick.

St Andrew's cross   *St Patrick's cross*

St George's cross

UNION FLAG

unionist *n.* **1 a** a member of a trade union. **b** an advocate of trade unions. **2** (usu. **Unionist**) an advocate of union, esp. a person opposed to the rupture of the parliamentary union between Great Britain and Northern Ireland. □ **unionism** *n.*

unionize *v.tr. & intr.* (also **-ise**) bring or come under trade-union organization or rules. □ **unionization** *n.*

Union Jack *n.* = UNION FLAG.

union suit *n. N. Amer.* a single undergarment for the body and legs; combinations.

uniparous *adj.* **1** producing one offspring at a birth. **2** *Bot.* having one axis or branch

unipersonal *adj.* (of the Deity) existing only as one person.

unique *adj.* **1** of which there is only one; unequalled; having no like, equal, or parallel. **2** *disp.* unusual, remarkable (*a unique opportunity*). [based on Latin *unus* 'one'] □ **uniquely** *adv.* **uniqueness** *n.*

■ **Usage** In sense 1, *unique* should not be qualified by adverbs such as *absolutely*, *most*, and *quite* because it is an absolute concept. The use of *unique* in sense 2 is regarded as incorrect by some people.

unironed *adj.* not ironed.

unisex *adj.* (of clothing, hairstyles, etc.) designed to be suitable for both sexes.

unisexual *adj.* **1 a** of one sex. **b** *Bot.* ▼ having stamens or pistils but not both. **2** unisex. □ **unisexually** *adv.*

UNISEXUAL BEGONIA FLOWERS

stamens

pistil

FEMALE FLOWER   MALE FLOWER

UNIT CELL

A unit cell consists of a set number of atoms in a crystal, kept together in a specific arrangement by bonding forces. The atoms can only be arranged into seven identifiable forms (hexagonal is shown here). The form of the unit cells in a crystal determines that crystal's shape.

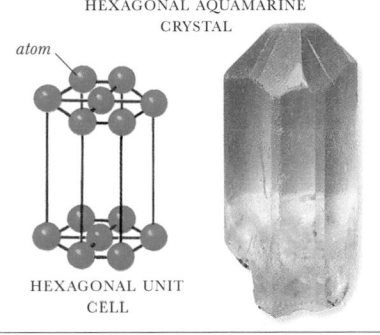

HEXAGONAL AQUAMARINE CRYSTAL

atom

HEXAGONAL UNIT CELL

unison ● *n.* **1** *Mus.* coincidence in pitch of sounds or notes. **2** *Mus.* a combination of voices or instruments at the same pitch or at pitches differing by one or more octaves (*sang in unison*). **3** agreement, concord (*acted in perfect unison*). ● *adj. Mus.* coinciding in pitch. [from Late Latin *unisonus*]

unit *n.* **1 a** an individual thing, person, or group, esp. for calculation. **b** each of the separate individuals or smallest groups into which a complex whole may be analysed (*the family as the unit of society*). **2** a quantity chosen as a standard in terms of which other quantities may be expressed (*unit of heat*; *SI unit*). **3** *Brit.* the smallest share in a unit trust. **4** a part of a mechanism with a specified function. **5** a piece of furniture for fitting with others like it or made of complementary parts. **6** a group with a special function in an organization. **7** a group of buildings, wards, etc., in a hospital. **8** the number 'one'. [based on Latin *unus* 'one']

Unitarian ● *n.* **1** a person who believes that God is not a Trinity but one person. **2** a member of a religious body maintaining this and advocating freedom from formal dogma or doctrine. ● *adj.* of or relating to the Unitarians. [based on Latin *unitas* 'unity'] □ **Unitarianism** *n.*

unitary *adj.* **1** of a unit or units. **2** marked by unity or uniformity. □ **unitarily** *adv.* **unitarity** *n.*

unit cell *n. Crystallog* ◀ the smallest repeating group of atoms, ions, or molecules in a crystal. ▷ CRYSTAL

unit cost *n.* the cost of producing one item of manufacture.

unite *v.* **1** *tr. & intr.* join together; make or become one; combine. **2** *tr. & intr.* join together for a common purpose or action (*united in their struggle against injustice*). **3** *tr. & intr.* join in marriage. **4** *tr.* possess (qualities, features, etc.) in combination (*united anger with mercy*). [based on Latin *unitus* 'united'] □ **unitive** *adj.*

United Brethren *n.pl. Eccl.* the Moravians.

United Kingdom *n.* Great Britain and Northern Ireland (until 1922, Great Britain and Ireland).

United Nations *n.pl.* a supranational peace-seeking organization.

United Reformed Church *n.* a Church formed in 1972 from the English Presbyterian and Congregational Churches.

United States *n.pl.* (in full **United States of America**) ▼ a federal republic of 50 states, mostly in N. America and including Alaska and Hawaii.

UNITED STATES

The United States of America, the fourth largest country in the world, consists of 48 contiguous states and two outlying ones – Alaska to the northwest, and Hawaii, a group of islands in the Pacific Ocean 3,380 km (2,100 miles) southwest of California. In 1787, 13 states on the east coast were united by constitutional law to establish the USA. The last states to join were Hawaii and Alaska, in 1959.

MAP OF THE UNITED STATES

ALASKA

HAWAII

KEY TO SMALLER STATES

1	VERMONT	5	RHODE ISLAND
2	NEW HAMPSHIRE	6	NEW JERSEY
3	MASSACHUSETTS	7	DELAWARE
4	CONNECTICUT	8	MARYLAND

U

unitholder *n. Brit.* a person with a holding in a unit trust.

unit trust *n. Brit.* an investment company investing combined contributions from many persons in various securities and paying them dividends in proportion to their holdings.

unity *n.* (*pl.* **-ies**) **1** oneness; being one, single, or individual; being formed of parts that constitute a whole (*the pictures lack unity; national unity*). **2** harmony or concord between persons etc. (*lived together in unity*). **3** a thing forming a complex whole (*a person regarded as a unity*). **4** *Math.* the number 'one', the factor that leaves unchanged the quantity on which it operates. [from Latin *unitas*]

Univ. *abbr.* University.

universal ● *adj.* of, belonging to, or done etc. by all persons or things in the world or in the class concerned; applicable to all cases (*the feeling was universal; met with universal approval*). ● *n.* a term or concept of general application. [from Old French] □ **universality** *n.* **universally** *adv.*

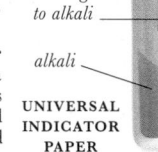

paper

dyes reacting to alkali

alkali

UNIVERSAL INDICATOR PAPER

universal indicator paper *n.* ▶ a paper stained with a mixture of dyes that changes colour over a range of pH and is used as a test for acids and alkalis. ▷ pH

universalize *v.tr.* (also **-ise**) **1** apply universally; give a universal character to. **2** bring into universal use; make available for all. □ **universalization** *n.*

universal joint *n.* (also **universal coupling**) ▼ a coupling or joint which can transmit rotary power by a shaft at any selected angle.

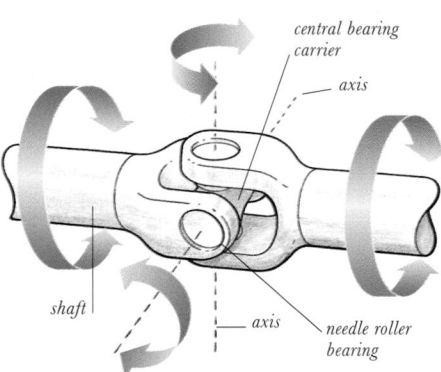

central bearing carrier

axis

shaft

axis

needle roller bearing

UNIVERSAL JOINT

universal language *n.* an artificial language intended for use by all nations.

universal suffrage *n.* a suffrage extending to all adults with minor exceptions.

universe *n.* **1** all existing things; the whole creation; the cosmos. **2** all humankind. [from Latin *universum* '(thing) combined into one, whole']

university *n.* (*pl.* **-ies**) **1** an educational institution of advanced learning and research conferring degrees. **2** the members of this collectively. □ **at university** *esp. Brit.* studying at a university. [from Latin *universitas* 'the whole (world)', later 'college, guild']

Unix *n. Computing propr.* a multi-user operating system.

unjoin *v.tr.* detach from being joined; separate

unjust *adj.* not just, contrary to justice or fairness. □ **unjustly** *adv.* **unjustness** *n.*

unjustifiable *adj.* not justifiable. □ **unjustifiably** *adv.*

unjustified *adj.* not justified.

unkempt *adj.* **1** untidy, of neglected appearance. **2** uncombed, dishevelled. [based on archaic *kempt* 'cobed'] □ **unkemptness** *n.*

unkept *adj.* **1** (of a promise, law, etc.) not observed; disregarded. **2** not tended; neglected.

unkind *adj.* **1** not kind. **2** harsh, cruel. □ **unkindly** *adv.* **unkindness** *n.*

unknit *v.tr.* (**unknitted**, **unknitting**) separate (things joined, knotted, or interocked).

unknot *v.tr.* (**unknotted**, **unknotting**) release the knot or knots of, untie.

unknowable ● *adj.* that cannot be known. ● *n.* an unknowable thing. □ **unknowability** *n.*

unknowing ● *adj.* (often foll. by *of*) not knowing; ignorant, unconscious. ● *n.* ignorance (*cloud of unknowing*). □ **unknowingly** *adv.* **unknowingness** *n.*

unknown ● *adj.* (often foll. by *to*) not known, unfamiliar (*his purpose was unknown to me*). ● *n.* **1** an unknown thing or person. **2** an unknown quantity (*equation in two unknowns*). □ **unknown to** without the knowledge of. □ **unknownness** *n.*

unknown quantity *n.* a person or thing whose nature, significance, etc., cannot be determined.

Unknown Soldier *n.* (also **Unknown Warrior**) an unidentified representative member of a country's armed forces killed in war, given burial with special honours in a national memorial.

unlabelled *adj.* (*US* **unlabeled**) not labelled; without a label.

unlace *v.tr.* **1** undo the lace or laces of. **2** unfasten or loosen in this way.

unladen *adj.* not laden.

unladen weight *n.* the weight of a vehicle etc. when not loaded with goods etc.

unladylike *adj.* not ladylike.

unlamented *adj.* not lamented.

unlatch *v.* **1** *tr.* release the latch of. **2** *tr. & intr.* open or be opened in this way.

unlawful *adj.* not lawful; illegal, not permissible. □ **unlawfully** *adv.* **unlawfulness** *n.*

unleaded *adj.* **1** (of petrol etc.) without added lead. **2** not covered, weighted, or framed with lead. **3** *Printing* not spaced with leads.

unlearn *v.tr.* (*past* and *past part.* **unlearned** or **unlearnt**) **1** discard from one's memory. **2** rid oneself of (a habit, false information, etc.).

unlearned[1] *adj.* not well educated; untaught, ignorant.

unlearned[2] *adj.* (also **unlearnt**) that has not been learnt.

unleash *v.tr.* **1** release from a leash or restraint. **2** set free to engage in pursuit or attack.

unleavened *adj.* not leavened; made without yeast or other raising agent.

unless *conj.* if not; except when (*shall go unless I hear from you; always walked unless I had a bicycle*). [originally *in, upon,* etc. *less*: Middle English]

unlettered *adj.* **1** illiterate. **2** not well educated.

unliberated *adj.* not liberated.

unlicensed *adj.* not licensed, esp. *Brit.* without a licence to sell alcoholic drink.

unlighted *adj.* **1** not provided with light. **2** not set burning.

unlike ● *adj.* **1** not like; different from (*is unlike both his parents*). **2** uncharacteristic of (*such behaviour is unlike him*). **3** dissimilar, different. ● *prep.* differently from (*acts quite unlike anyone else*). □ **unlikeness** *n.*

unlikeable *adj.* (also **unlikable**) not easy to like; unpleasant.

unlikely *adj.* (**unlikelier**, **unlikeliest**) **1** improbable (*unlikely tale*). **2** (foll. by *to* + infin.) not to be expected to do something (*he's unlikely to be available*). **3** unpromising (*an unlikely candidate*). □ **unlikelihood** *n.* **unlikeliness** *n.*

unlimited *adj.* without limit; unrestricted; very great in number or quantity (*has unlimited possibilities; an unlimited expanse of sea*). □ **unlimitedly** *adv.* **unlimitedness** *n.*

unlined[1] *adj.* **1** (of paper etc.) without lines. **2** (of a face etc.) without wrinkles.

unlined[2] *adj.* (of a garment etc.) without lining.

unliquidated *adj.* not liquidated.

unlisted *adj.* not included in a published list, esp. of stock exchange prices or of telephone numbers.

unlit *adj.* not lit.

unlivable *adj.* that cannot be lived or lived in.

unlived-in *adj.* **1** uninhabited. **2** unused by the inhabitants.

unload *v.tr.* **1** (also *absol.*) remove a load from (a vehicle etc.). **2** remove (a load) from a vehicle etc. **3** remove the charge from (a firearm etc.). **4** *colloq.* get rid of. □ **unloader** *n.*

unlock *v.tr.* **1 a** release the lock of (a door, box, etc.). **b** release or disclose by unlocking. **2** release thoughts, feelings, etc. from (one's mind etc.).

unlocked *adj.* not locked.

unlooked-for *adj.* unexpected, unforeseen.

unloose *v.tr.* (also **unloosen**) loose; set free.

unlovable *adj.* (also **unloveable**) not lovable.

unloved *adj.* not loved.

unlovely *adj.* not attractive; unpleasant, ugly. □ **unloveliness** *n.*

unloving *adj.* not loving. □ **unlovingly** *adv.* **unlovingness** *n.*

unlucky *adj.* (**unluckier**, **unluckiest**) **1** not fortunate or successful. **2** wretched. **3** bringing bad luck. **4** ill-judged. □ **unluckily** *adv.* **unluckiness** *n.*

unmade *adj.* **1** not made. **2** destroyed, annulled.

unmake *v.tr.* (*past* and *past part.* **unmade**) undo the making of; destroy, depose, annul.

unman *v.tr.* (**unmanned**, **unmanning**) deprive of supposed manly qualities (e.g. self-control, courage); cause to weep etc., discourage.

unmanageable *adj.* not (easily) managed, manipulated, or kept under control. □ **unmanageableness** *n.* **unmanageably** *adv.*

unmanaged *adj.* **1** not handled or directed in a controlled way. **2** (of land etc.) left wild; in a natural state.

unmanly *adj.* not manly. □ **unmanliness** *n.*

unmanned *adj.* **1** not manned. **2** overcome by emotion etc.

unmannered *adj.* lacking affectation; straightforward.

unmannerly *adj.* **1** without good manners. **2** (of actions, speech, etc.) showing a lack of good manners. □ **unmannerliness** *n.*

unmapped *adj.* **1** not represented on a usu. geographical or chromosome map. **2** unexplored.

unmarked *adj.* **1** not marked. **2** not noticed.

unmarketable *adj.* not marketable.

unmarried *adj.* not married; single.

unmask *v.* **1** *tr.* **a** remove the mask from. **b** expose the true character of. **2** *intr.* remove one's mask. □ **unmasker** *n.*

unmatched *adj.* not matched or equalled.

unmeaning *adj.* having no meaning or significance; meaningless. □ **unmeaningly** *adv.*

unmeant *adj.* not meant or intended.

unmediated *adj.* with no intervention; directly perceived.

unmemorable *adj.* not memorable. □ **unmemorably** *adv.*

unmentionable ● *adj.* that cannot (properly) be mentioned. ● *n.* **1** (in *pl.*) *joc.* undergarments. **2** a person or thing not to be mentioned. □ **unmentionability** *n.* **unmentionableness** *n.* **unmentionably** *adv.*

unmerciful *adj.* merciless. □ **unmercifully** *adv.* **unmercifulness** *n.*

unmerited *adj.* not merited.

unmet *adj.* (of a quota, demand, goal, etc.) not achieved or fulfilled.

unmetalled *adj. Brit.* (of a road etc.) not surfaced with road metal.

unmethodical *adj.* not methodical. □ **unmethodically** *adv.*

U

unmindful *adj.* (often foll. by *of*) not mindful. □ **unmindfully** *adv.* **unmindfulness** *n.*

unmissable *adj.* that cannot or should not be missed.

unmistakable *adj.* (also **unmistakeable**) that cannot be mistaken or doubted, clear. □ **unmistakability** *n.* **unmistakableness** *n.* **unmistakably** *adv.*

unmitigated *adj.* **1** not mitigated or modified. **2** absolute, unqualified (*an unmitigated disaster*). □ **unmitigatedly** *adv.*

unmixed *adj.* not mixed.

unmixed blessing *n.* a thing having advantages and no disadvantages.

unmodernized *adj.* (also **-ised**) (of a house etc.) not modernized; retaining the original features.

unmodified *adj.* not modified.

unmodulated *adj.* not modulated.

unmolested *adj.* not molested.

unmoor *v.tr.* **1** (also *absol.*) release the moorings of (a vessel) **2** weigh all but one anchor of (a vessel).

unmoral *adj.* not concerned with morality (cf. IMMORAL). □ **unmorality** *n.*

unmotherly *adj.* not motherly.

unmotivated *adj.* without motivation; without a motive.

unmounted *adj.* not mounted.

unmourned *adj.* not mourned.

unmoved *adj.* **1** not moved. **2** not changed in one's purpose. **3** not affected by emotion. □ **unmovable** *adj.* (also **unmoveable**).

unmoving *adj.* **1** not moving; still. **2** not emotive.

unmown *adj.* not mown.

unmusical *adj.* **1** not pleasing to the ear. **2** unskilled in or indifferent to music. □ **unmusicality** *n.* **unmusically** *adv.*

unmuzzle *v.tr.* **1** remove a muzzle from. **2** relieve of an obligation to remain silent.

unnameable *adj.* that cannot be named, esp. too bad to be named.

unnamed *adj.* not named.

unnatural *adj.* **1** contrary to nature or the usual course of nature; not normal. **2 a** lacking natural feelings. **b** extremely cruel or wicked. **3** artificial. **4** affected. □ **unnaturally** *adv.* **unnaturalness** *n.*

unnecessary ● *adj.* **1** not necessary. **2** more than is necessary (*with unnecessary care*). ● *n.* (*pl.* **-ies**) (usu. in *pl.*) an unnecessary thing. □ **unnecessarily** *adv.*

unneeded *adj.* not needed.

unneighbourly *adj.* not neighbourly. □ **unneighbourliness** *n.*

unnerve *v.tr.* deprive of strength or resolution. □ **unnerving** *adj.* **unnervingly** *adv.*

unnoticeable *adj.* not easily seen or noticed. □ **unnoticeably** *adv.*

unnoticed *adj.* not noticed.

unnumbered *adj.* **1** not marked with a number. **2** not counted. **3** countless.

UNO /yoo-noh/ *abbr.* United Nations Organization.

unobjectionable *adj.* not objectionable; acceptable. □ **unobjectionably** *adv.*

unobservable *adj.* not observable; imperceptible.

unobservant *adj.* not observant. □ **unobservantly** *adv.*

unobserved *adj.* not observed.

unobstructed *adj.* not obstructed.

unobtainable *adj.* that cannot be obtained.

unobtrusive *adj.* not making oneself or itself noticed. □ **unobtrusively** *adv.* **unobtrusiveness** *n.*

unoccupied *adj.* not occupied.

unoffending *adj.* not offending; harmless, innocent. □ **unoffended** *adj.*

unofficial *adj.* **1** not officially authorized or confirmed. **2** not characteristic of officials. □ **unofficially** *adv.*

unofficial strike *n.* esp. *Brit.* a strike not formally approved by the strikers' trade union.

unopened *adj.* not opened.

unopposed *adj.* not opposed.

unorganized *adj.* (also **-ised**) not organized (cf. DISORGANIZE).

unoriginal *adj.* lacking originality; derivative. □ **unoriginality** *n.* **unoriginally** *adv.*

unorthodox *adj.* not orthodox. □ **unorthodoxly** *adv.* **unorthodoxy** *n.*

unostentatious *adj.* not ostentatious. □ **unostentatiously** *adv.* **unostentatiousness** *n.*

unpack *v.tr.* **1** (also *absol.*) open and remove the contents of (luggage, a package, etc.). **2** take (a thing) out from a package etc. □ **unpacker** *n.*

unpaged *adj.* with pages not numbered.

unpaid *adj.* (of a debt or a person) not paid.

unpainted *adj.* not painted.

unpaired *adj.* **1** not arranged in pairs. **2** not forming one of a pair.

unpalatable *adj.* **1** not pleasant to taste. **2** (of an idea, suggestion, etc.) difficult to accept, distasteful. □ **unpalatability** *n.* **unpalatableness** *n.*

unparalleled *adj.* having no parallel or equal.

unpardonable *adj.* that cannot be pardoned. □ **unpardonably** *adv.*

unparliamentary *adj.* contrary to proper parliamentary usage.

unparliamentary language *n.* oaths or abuse.

unpasteurized *adj.* (also **-ised**) not pasteurized.

unpatented *adj.* not patented.

unpatriotic *adj.* not patriotic. □ **unpatriotically** *adv.*

unpatronizing *adj.* (also **-ising**) not showing condescension.

unpaved *adj.* not paved.

unpeeled *adj.* not peeled.

unperceived *adj.* not perceived; unobserved.

unperceptive *adj.* not perceptive.

unperforated *adj.* not perforated.

unperformed *adj.* not performed.

unperfumed *adj.* not perfumed.

unperson *n.* a person whose name or existence is denied or ignored.

unpersuaded *adj.* not persuaded.

unpersuasive *adj.* not persuasive. □ **unpersuasively** *adv.*

unperturbed *adj.* not perturbed. □ **unperturbedly** *adv.*

unpick *v.tr.* undo the sewing of (stitches, a garment, etc.).

unpicked *adj.* **1** not selected. **2** (of a flower) not plucked.

unpin *v.tr.* (**unpinned**, **unpinning**) unfasten or detach by removing a pin or pins.

unpitied *adj.* not pitied.

unpitying *adj.* not pitying. □ **unpityingly** *adv.*

unplaceable *adj.* that cannot be placed or classified (*his accent was unplaceable*).

unplaced *adj.* not placed, esp. not placed as one of the first three finishing in a race etc.

unplanned *adj.* not planned.

unplayable *adj.* **1** *Sport* (of a ball) that cannot be struck or returned. **2** that cannot be played. □ **unplayably** *adv.*

unpleasant *adj.* not pleasant; displeasing; disagreeable. □ **unpleasantly** *adv.* **unpleasantness** *n.*

unpleasantry *n.* (*pl.* **-ies**) **1** unkindness. **2** (in *pl.*) **a** unpleasant comments. **b** unpleasant problems.

unpleasing *adj.* not pleasing. □ **unpleasingly** *adv.*

unplug *v.tr.* (**unplugged**, **unplugging**) **1** disconnect (an electrical device) by removing its plug from the socket. **2** unstop.

unplumbed *adj.* **1** not plumbed. **2** not fully explored or understood. □ **unplumbable** *adj.*

unpointed *adj.* **1** having no point or points. **2 a** not punctuated. **b** (of written Hebrew etc.) without vowel points. **3** (of masonry or brickwork) not pointed.

unpolished *adj.* **1** ▶ not polished; rough. **2** without refinement; crude.

unpolitic *adj.* impolitic, unwise.

unpolitical *adj.* not concerned with politics. □ **unpolitically** *adv.*

unpolluted *adj.* not polluted.

unpopular *adj.* not popular; not liked by the public or by people in general. □ **unpopularity** *n.* **unpopularly** *adv.*

unpopulated *adj.* not populated.

unposed *adj.* not in a posed position, esp. for a photograph.

UNPOLISHED

POLISHED

UNPOLISHED AND POLISHED AMBER

unpowered *adj.* (of a boat, vehicle, etc.) propelled other than by fuel.

unpractical *adj.* **1** not practical. **2** (of a person) not having practical skill. □ **unpracticality** *n.* **unpractically** *adv.*

unpractised *adj.* (*US* **unpracticed**) **1** not experienced or skilled. **2** not put into practice.

unprecedented *adj.* **1** having no precedent; unparalleled. **2** novel. □ **unprecedentedly** *adv.*

unpredictable *adj.* that cannot be predicted. □ **unpredictability** *n.* **unpredictably** *adv.*

unprejudiced *adj.* not prejudiced.

unpremeditated *adj.* not previously thought over; not deliberately planned; unintentional.

unprepared *adj.* not prepared (in advance); not ready. □ **unpreparedness** *n.*

unprepossessing *adj.* not prepossessing; unattractive.

unpresentable *adj.* not presentable.

unpressed *adj.* not pressed, esp. (of clothing) unironed.

unpressurized *adj.* (also **-ised**) not pressurized.

unpresuming *adj.* not presuming; modest.

unpretending *adj.* unpretentious.

unpretentious *adj.* not making a great display; simple, modest. □ **unpretentiously** *adv.* **unpretentiousness** *n.*

unpriced *adj.* not having a price or prices fixed, marked, or stated.

unprincipled *adj.* lacking or not based on good moral principles.

unprintable *adj.* that cannot be printed, esp. because indecent or libellous or blasphemous. □ **unprintably** *adv.*

unprinted *adj.* not printed.

unprivileged *adj.* not privileged.

unproblematic *adj.* causing no difficulty. □ **unproblematically** *adv.*

unprocessed *adj.* (esp. of food, raw materials) not processed.

unproductive *adj.* not producing much. □ **unproductively** *adv.* **unproductiveness** *n.*

unprofessional *adj.* contrary to professional standards of behaviour etc. □ **unprofessionally** *adv.*

unprofitable *adj.* not profitable. □ **unprofitableness** *n.* **unprofitably** *adv.*

Unprofor /un-prŏ-for/ *abbr.* (also **UNPROFOR**) United Nations Protection Force.

unprogressive *adj.* not progressive.

unpromising *adj.* not likely to turn out well. □ **unpromisingly** *adv.*

unprompted *adj.* spontaneous.

unpronounceable *adj.* that cannot be pronounced. □ **unpronounceably** *adv.*

unpropitious *adj.* not propitious. □ **unpropitiously** *adv.*

unprotected *adj.* **1** not protected. **2** (of sexual intercourse) performed without a condom or other contraceptive. □ **unprotectedness** *n.*

U

unprotesting *adj.* not protesting. □ **unprotestingly** *adv.*

unprovable *adj.* that cannot be proved. □ **unprovability** *n.*

unproved *adj.* (also **unproven**) not proved.

unprovided *adj.* (usu. foll. by *with*) not furnished, supplied, or equipped.

unprovoked *adj.* (of a person or act) without provocation.

unpublicized *adj.* (also **-ised**) not publicized.

unpublished *adj.* not published. □ **unpublishable** *adj.*

unpunctual *adj.* not punctual. □ **unpunctuality** *n.*

unpunctuated *adj.* not punctuated.

unpunished *adj.* not punished.

unpurified *adj.* not purified.

unputdownable *adj. colloq.* (of a book) so engrossing that one has to go on reading it.

unqualified *adj.* **1** not competent (*unqualified to give an answer*). **2** not legally or officially qualified (*an unqualified practitioner*). **3** not modified or restricted; complete (*unqualified assent*; *unqualified success*).

unquantifiable *adj.* impossible to quantify. □ **unquantified** *adj.*

unquenchable *adj.* that cannot be quenched. □ **unquenchably** *adv.*

unquenched *adj.* not quenched.

unquestionable *adj.* that cannot be disputed or doubted. □ **unquestionability** *n.* **unquestionably** *adv.*

unquestioned *adj.* **1** not disputed or doubted; definite, certain. **2** not interrogated.

unquestioning *adj.* **1** asking no questions. **2** done etc. without asking questions. □ **unquestioningly** *adv.*

unquiet *adj.* **1** restless, agitated, stirring. **2** perturbed, anxious. □ **unquietly** *adv.* **unquietness** *n.*

unquotable *adj.* that cannot be quoted.

unquote *v.tr.* (as *int.*) (in dictation, reading aloud, etc.) indicate the presence of closing quotation marks.

unravel *v.* (**unravelled**, **unravelling**; *US* **unraveled**, **unraveling**) **1** *tr.* cause to be no longer ravelled, tangled, or intertwined. **2** *tr.* probe and solve (a mystery etc.). **3** *tr.* undo (a fabric, esp. a knitted one). **4** *intr.* become disentangled or unknitted.

unreachable *adj.* that cannot be reached. □ **unreachably** *adv.*

unread *adj.* **1** (of a book etc.) not read. **2** (of a person) not well read.

unreadable *adj.* **1** too dull or too difficult to be worth reading. **2** illegible. □ **unreadability** *n.* **unreadably** *adv.*

unready *adj.* **1** not ready. **2** not prompt in action. □ **unreadily** *adv.* **unreadiness** *n.*

unreal *adj.* **1** not real. **2** imaginary, illusory. **3** *N. Amer.* & *Austral. slang* incredible, amazing. □ **unreality** *n.* **unreally** *adv.*

unrealism *n.* lack of realism.

unrealistic *adj.* not realistic. □ **unrealistically** *adv.*

unrealizable *adj.* (also **-isable**) that cannot be realized.

unrealized *adj.* (also **-ised**) not realized.

unreason *n.* lack of reasonable thought or action. [Middle English in sense 'injustice']

unreasonable *adj.* **1** going beyond the limits of what is reasonable or equitable (*unreasonable demands*). **2** not guided by or listening to reason. □ **unreasonableness** *n.* **unreasonably** *adv.*

unreasoned *adj.* not reasoned.

unreasoning *adj.* not reasoning. □ **unreasoningly** *adv.*

unreceptive *adj.* not receptive.

unreciprocated *adj.* not reciprocated.

unrecognizable *adj.* (also **-isable**) that cannot be recognized. □ **unrecognizably** *adv.*

unrecognized *adj.* (also **-ised**) not recognized.

unreconciled *adj.* not reconciled.

unreconstructed *adj.* **1** not reconciled or converted to the current political orthodoxy. **2** not rebuilt.

unrecorded *adj.* not recorded. □ **unrecordable** *adj.*

unrectified *adj.* not rectified.

unredeemable *adj.* that cannot be redeemed.

unredeemed *adj.* not redeemed.

unreel *v.tr. & intr.* unwind from a reel.

unrefined *adj.* not refined.

unreflecting *adj.* not engaging in reflection or thought. □ **unreflectingly** *adv.* **unreflectingness** *n.* **unreflective** *adj.*

unreformed *adj.* not reformed.

unregarded *adj.* not regarded.

unregenerate *adj.* not regenerate; obstinately wrong or bad. □ **unregeneracy** *n.* **unregenerately** *adv.*

unregistered *adj.* not registered.

unregulated *adj.* not regulated.

unrehearsed *adj.* not rehearsed.

unrelated *adj.* not related. □ **unrelatedness** *n.*

unrelaxed *adj.* not relaxed.

unreleased *adj.* not released, esp. (of a recording, film, etc.) to the public.

unrelenting *adj.* **1** not relenting or yielding. **2** unmerciful. **3** not abating or relaxing. □ **unrelentingly** *adv.* **unrelentingness** *n.*

unreliable *adj.* not reliable; erratic. □ **unreliability** *n.* **unreliableness** *n.* **unreliably** *adv.*

unrelieved *adj.* lacking the relief given by contrast or variation. □ **unrelievedly** *adv.*

unremarkable *adj.* not remarkable; uninteresting. □ **unremarkably** *adv.*

unremarked *adj.* **1** not mentioned or remarked upon. **2** unnoticed.

unremembered *adj.* not remembered; forgotten.

unremitting *adj.* never relaxing or slackening, incessant. □ **unremittingly** *adv.* **unremittingness** *n.*

unremunerative *adj.* bringing no, or not enough, profit or income. □ **unremuneratively** *adv.*

unrenewable *adj.* that cannot be renewed. □ **unrenewed** *adj.*

unrepeatable *adj.* **1** that cannot be done, made, or said again. **2** too indecent to be said again. □ **unrepeatability** *n.*

unrepentant *adj.* not repentant, impenitent. □ **unrepentantly** *adv.*

unreported *adj.* not reported.

unrepresentative *adj.* not representative. □ **unrepresentativeness** *n.*

unrepresented *adj.* not represented.

unrequited *adj.* (of love etc.) not returned. □ **unrequitedly** *adv.* **unrequitedness** *n.*

unreserved *adj.* **1** not reserved (*unreserved seats*). **2** without reservations; absolute (*unreserved confidence*). **3** free from reserve (*an unreserved nature*). □ **unreservedly** *adv.* **unreservedness** *n.*

unresisting *adj.* not resisting. □ **unresistingly** *adv.*

unresolved *adj.* **1 a** uncertain how to act, irresolute. **b** uncertain in opinion, undecided. **2** (of questions etc.) undetermined, undecided, unsolved. □ **unresolvedly** *adv.* **unresolvedness** *n.*

unresponsive *adj.* not responsive. □ **unresponsively** *adv.* **unresponsiveness** *n.*

unrest *n.* restlessness, disturbance, agitation.

unrestful *adj.* not restful. □ **unrestfully** *adv.*

unrestored *adj.* not restored.

unrestrained *adj.* not restrained. □ **unrestrainedly** *adv.* **unrestrainedness** *n.*

unrestricted *adj.* not restricted. □ **unrestrictedly** *adv.*

unreturned *adj.* **1** not reciprocated or responded to. **2** not having returned or been returned.

unrevealed *adj.* not revealed; secret. □ **unrevealing** *adj.*

unrevised *adj.* not revised; in an original form.

unrevoked *adj.* not revoked or annulled; still in force.

unrewarded *adj.* not rewarded.

unrewarding *adj.* not rewarding or satisfying.

unridden *adj.* not ridden.

unrideable *adj.* (also **unridable**) that cannot be ridden.

unrighteous *adj.* not righteous; unjust, wicked, dishonest. □ **unrighteously** *adv.* **unrighteousness** *n.*

unripe *adj.* not ripe.

unrivalled *adj.* (*US* **unrivaled**) having no equal; peerless.

unroadworthy *adj.* not roadworthy.

unroll *v.tr. & intr.* **1** open out from a rolled-up state. **2** display or be displayed in this form.

unromantic *adj.* not romantic. □ **unromantically** *adv.*

unroof *v.tr.* remove the roof of.

unroofed *adj.* not provided with a roof.

unruffled *adj.* **1** not agitated or disturbed; calm. **2** not physically ruffled.

unruled *adj.* **1** not ruled or governed. **2** not having ruled lines.

unruly *adj.* (**unrulier**, **unruliest**) not easily controlled or disciplined, disorderly. [based on RULE] □ **unruliness** *n.*

unsaddle *v.tr.* **1** remove the saddle from (a horse etc.). **2** dislodge from a saddle.

unsafe *adj.* **1** not safe. **2** *Law* (of a verdict, conviction, etc.) likely to constitute a miscarriage of justice. □ **unsafely** *adv.* **unsafeness** *n.*

unsaid[1] *adj.* not said or uttered.

unsaid[2] *past* and *past part.* of UNSAY.

unsalaried *adj.* not salaried.

unsaleable *adj.* (also **unsalable**) not saleable. □ **unsaleability** *n.*

unsalted *adj.* not salted.

unsanctified *adj.* not sanctified.

unsanctioned *adj.* not sanctioned.

unsanitary *adj.* not sanitary.

unsatisfactory *adj.* **1** not satisfactory; poor, unacceptable. **2** *Law* (of a verdict, conviction, etc.) likely to constitute a miscarriage of justice. □ **unsatisfactorily** *adv.* **unsatisfactoriness** *n.*

unsatisfied *adj.* not satisfied. □ **unsatisfiedness** *n.*

unsatisfying *adj.* not satisfying. □ **unsatisfyingly** *adv.*

unsaturated *adj.* **1** *Chem.* ▼ (of a compound, esp. a fat or oil) having double or triple bonds in its molecule and therefore capable of further reaction. **2** not saturated. □ **unsaturation** *n.*

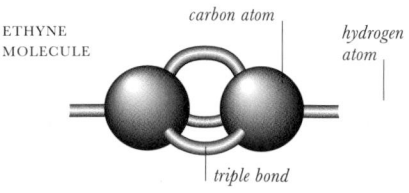

ETHYNE MOLECULE — carbon atom — hydrogen atom — triple bond

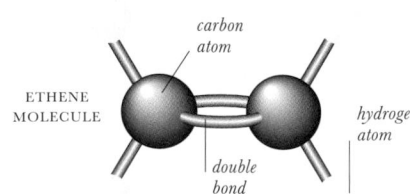

ETHENE MOLECULE — carbon atom — hydrogen atom — double bond

UNSATURATED: MOLECULAR STRUCTURE OF TWO UNSATURATED COMPOUNDS

U

unsavoury adj. (US **unsavory**) **1** disagreeable to the taste, smell, or feelings; disgusting. **2** disagreeable, unpleasant (an unsavoury character). **3** morally offensive. □ **unsavourily** adv. **unsavouriness** n.

unsay v.tr. (past and past part. **unsaid**) retract (a statement).

unsayable adj. that cannot be said.

unscalable adj. that cannot be scaled.

unscarred adj. not scarred or damaged.

unscathed adj. without suffering any injury.

unscented adj. not scented.

unscheduled adj. not scheduled.

unscholarly adj. not scholarly. □ **unscholarliness** n.

unschooled adj. **1** uneducated, untaught. **2** not sent to school. **3** untrained, undisciplined. **4** not made artificial by education.

unscientific adj. **1** not in accordance with scientific principles. **2** not familiar with science. □ **unscientifically** adv.

unscramble v.tr. restore from a scrambled state, esp. interpret (a scrambled transmission etc.). □ **unscrambler** n.

unscrew v. **1** tr. & intr. unfasten or be unfastened by turning or removing a screw or screws or by twisting like a screw. **2** tr. loosen (a screw).

unscripted adj. (of a speech etc.) delivered without a prepared script.

unscrupulous adj. having no scruples, unprincipled. □ **unscrupulously** adv. **unscrupulousness** n.

unseal v.tr. break the seal of; open (a letter, receptacle, etc.).

unsealed adj. not sealed.

unsearched adj. not searched.

unseasonable adj. **1** not appropriate to the season. **2** untimely, inopportune. □ **unseasonableness** n. **unseasonably** adv.

unseasonal adj. not typical of, or appropriate to, the time or season.

unseasoned adj. **1** not flavoured with salt, herbs, etc. **2** (esp. of timber) not matured. **3** not habituated.

unseat v.tr. **1** remove from a seat, esp. in an election. **2** dislodge from a seat, esp. on horseback.

unseaworthy adj. not seaworthy.

unsecured adj. not secured.

unseeded adj. Sport (of a player) not seeded.

unseeing adj. **1** unobservant. **2** blind. □ **unseeingly** adv.

unseemly adj. (**unseemlier**, **unseemliest**) **1** indecent. **2** unbecoming. □ **unseemliness** n.

unseen ● adj. **1** not seen. **2** invisible. **3** esp. Brit. (of a translation) to be done without preparation. ● n. Brit. an unseen translation.

unsegregated adj. not segregated.

unselective adj. not selective.

unselfconscious adj. not self-conscious; natural. □ **unselfconsciously** adv. **unselfconsciousness** n.

unselfish adj. mindful of others' interests. □ **unselfishly** adv. **unselfishness** n.

unsentimental adj. not sentimental. □ **unsentimentally** adv.

unserviceable adj. not serviceable; unfit for use. □ **unserviceability** n.

unsettle v. **1** tr. disturb the settled state or arrangement of; discompose. **2** tr. derange. **3** intr. become unsettled. □ **unsettlement** n.

unsettled adj. **1** not (yet) settled. **2** liable or open to change or further discussion. **3** (of a bill etc.) unpaid. □ **unsettledness** n.

unsex v.tr. deprive (a person) of the typical qualities of one or other (esp. the female) sex.

unsexed adj. having no sexual characteristics.

unsexy adj. (**unsexier**, **unsexiest**) not sexually attractive or stimulating; not appealing.

unshackle v.tr. **1** release from shackles. **2** set free.

unshakeable adj. (also **unshakable**) that cannot be shaken; firm, obstinate. □ **unshakeability** n. **unshakeably** adv.

unshaken adj. not shaken. □ **unshakenly** adv.

unshaven adj. not shaved.

unsheathe v.tr. remove (a knife etc.) from a sheath.

unshell v.tr. (usu. as **unshelled** adj.) extract from its shell.

unsheltered adj. not sheltered.

unshockable adj. that cannot be shocked. □ **unshockability** n. **unshockably** adv.

unshrinkable adj. (of fabric etc.) not liable to shrink. □ **unshrinkability** n.

unshrinking adj. unhesitating, fearless. □ **unshrinkingly** adv.

unsighted adj. **1** not sighted or seen. **2** prevented from seeing, esp. by an obstruction.

unsightly adj. unpleasant to look at, ugly. □ **unsightliness** n.

unsigned adj. not signed.

unsinkable adj. unable to be sunk. □ **unsinkability** n.

unsized[1] adj. **1** not made to a size. **2** not sorted by size.

unsized[2] adj. not treated with size.

unskilful adj. (US **unskillful**) not skilful. □ **unskilfully** adv. **unskilfulness** n.

unskilled adj. lacking or not needing special skill or training.

unsleeping adj. not or never sleeping. □ **unsleepingly** adv.

unsliced adj. (esp. of a loaf of bread) not having been cut into slices.

unsmiling adj. not smiling. □ **unsmilingly** adv.

unsmoked adj. **1** not cured by smoking (unsmoked bacon). **2** not consumed by smoking (an unsmoked cigar).

unsociable adj. not sociable, disliking the company of others. □ **unsociability** n. **unsociableness** n. **unsociably** adv.

■ **Usage** Unsociable is easily confused with unsocial and antisocial because there is some overlap in meanings. Antisocial is sometimes used to mean 'unsociable', and (mistakenly) to mean 'unsocial' (sense 2), while unsocial is sometimes used to mean 'antisocial'. However, these are not the words' primary meanings.

unsocial adj. **1** not social; not suitable for, seeking, or conforming to society. **2** Brit. outside the normal working day (unsocial hours). **3** antisocial. □ **unsocially** adv.

■ **Usage** See Usage Note at UNSOCIABLE.

unsocialist adj. not socialist.

unsoiled adj. not soiled or dirtied.

unsold adj. not sold.

unsolicited adj. not asked for; given or done voluntarily.

unsolvable adj. that cannot be solved, insoluble.

unsolved adj. not solved.

unsophisticated adj. **1** artless, simple, natural. **2** not adulterated or corrupted; not artificial.

unsorted adj. not sorted.

unsought adj. **1** not sought for. **2** without being requested.

unsound adj. **1** unhealthy, diseased. **2** rotten, weak. **3 a** ill-founded, fallacious. **b** unorthodox, heretical. **4** unreliable. **5** wicked. □ **of unsound mind** insane. □ **unsoundness** n.

unsparing adj. **1** lavish. **2** merciless. □ **unsparingly** adv. **unsparingness** n.

unspeakable adj. **1** that cannot be expressed in words. **2** indescribably bad. □ **unspeakableness** n. **unspeakably** adv.

unspecialized adj. (also **-ised**) not specialized.

unspecific adj. not specific; general, inexact.

unspecified adj. not specified.

unspectacular adj. not spectacular; dull. □ **unspectacularly** adv.

unspilled adj. not spilt.

unspilt adj. not spilt.

unspoiled adj. **1** unspoilt. **2** not plundered.

unspoilt adj. not spoilt.

unspoken adj. **1** not expressed in speech. **2** not uttered as speech.

unsponsored adj. not supported or promoted by a sponsor.

unspool v. **1** tr. & intr. unwind from or as if from a spool. **2 a** tr. screen (a film). **b** intr. (of a film) be screened.

unsporting adj. not fair or generous. □ **unsportingly** adv.

unsportsmanlike adj. unsporting.

unspotted adj. **1 a** not marked with a spot or spots. **b** morally pure. **2** unnoticed.

unsprayed adj. not sprayed.

unstable adj. (**unstabler**, **unstablest**) **1** not stable. **2** changeable. **3** showing a tendency to sudden mental or emotional changes. □ **unstableness** n. **unstably** adv.

unstained adj. not stained.

unstamped adj. **1** not marked by stamping. **2** not having a stamp affixed.

unstarched adj. not starched.

unstated adj. not stated or declared.

unsteady adj. (**unsteadier**, **unsteadiest**) **1** not steady or firm. **2** changeable. **3** not uniform or regular. □ **unsteadily** adv. **unsteadiness** n.

unsterile adj. **1** (of a syringe etc.) not sterile. **2** productive.

unstick v.tr. (past and past part. **unstuck**) separate (a thing stuck to another). □ **come unstuck** colloq. come to grief, fail.

unstinted adj. not stinted. □ **unstintedly** adv.

unstinting adj. ungrudging, lavish. □ **unstintingly** adv.

unstitch v.tr. undo the stitches of.

unstop v.tr. (**unstopped**, **unstopping**) **1** free from obstruction. **2** remove the stopper from.

unstoppable adj. that cannot be stopped or prevented. □ **unstoppability** n. **unstoppably** adv.

unstopper v.tr. remove the stopper from.

unstrained adj. **1** not subjected to straining or stretching. **2** not injured by overuse or excessive demands. **3** not forced or produced by effort.

unstreamed adj. Brit. (of schoolchildren) not arranged in streams.

unstressed adj. **1** not pronounced with stress. **2** not subjected to stress.

unstring v.tr. (past and past part. **unstrung**) **1** remove or relax the string or strings of (a bow, harp, etc.). **2** remove from a string. **3** (esp. as **unstrung** adj.) unnerve.

unstructured adj. **1** not structured. **2** informal.

unstuck past and past part. of UNSTICK.

unstudied adj. easy, natural, spontaneous.

unstuffy adj. **1** informal, casual. **2** not stuffy.

unstylish adj. **1** lacking style. **2** unfashionable.

unsubstantial adj. having little or no solidity, reality, or factual basis.

unsubstantiated adj. not substantiated.

unsubtle adj. not subtle; obvious, clumsy. □ **unsubtly** adv.

unsuccessful adj. not successful. □ **unsuccessfully** adv.

unsuitable adj. not suitable. □ **unsuitability** n. **unsuitably** adv.

unsuited adj. **1** (usu. foll. by for) not fit for a purpose. **2** (usu. foll. by to) not adapted.

unsullied adj. not sullied.

unsung adj. **1** not celebrated; unknown. **2** not sung.

unsupervised adj. not supervised.

unsupportable adj. **1** that cannot be endured. **2** indefensible.

U

unsupported *adj.* not supported.

unsupportive *adj.* not giving support.

unsure *adj.* not sure. □ **unsurely** *adv.* **unsureness** *n.*

unsurpassable *adj.* that cannot be surpassed. □ **unsurpassably** *adv.*

unsurpassed *adj.* not surpassed.

unsurprised *adj.* not surprised.

unsurprising *adj.* not surprising. □ **unsurprisingly** *adv.*

unsusceptible *adj.* not susceptible.

unsuspected *adj.* not suspected.

unsuspecting *adj.* not suspecting. □ **unsuspectingly** *adv.*

unsuspicious *adj.* not suspicious.

unsustainable *adj.* not sustainable. □ **unsustainably** *adv.*

unsustained *adj.* not sustained.

unswayed *adj.* uninfluenced, unaffected.

unsweetened *adj.* not sweetened.

unswept *adj.* not swept.

unswerving *adj.* **1** steady, constant. **2** not turning aside. □ **unswervingly** *adv.*

unsymmetrical *adj.* not symmetrical. □ **unsymmetrically** *adv.*

unsympathetic *adj.* not sympathetic. □ **unsympathetically** *adv.*

unsystematic *adj.* not systematic. □ **unsystematically** *adv.*

untack *v.tr.* detach, esp. by removing tacks.

untainted *adj.* not tainted.

untalented *adj.* not talented.

untameable *adj.* (also **untamable**) that cannot be tamed.

untamed *adj.* not tamed, wild.

untangle *v.tr.* **1** free from a tangled state. **2** free from entanglement.

untanned *adj.* not tanned.

untapped *adj.* not (yet) tapped or wired (*untapped resources*).

untarnished *adj.* not tarnished.

untasted *adj.* not tasted.

untaught *adj.* **1** not instructed by teaching. **2** not acquired by teaching; natural, spontaneous.

untaxed *adj.* not required to pay or not attracting taxes.

unteachable *adj.* **1** incapable of being instructed. **2** that cannot be imparted by teaching.

untechnical *adj.* not technical.

untenable *adj.* (of an argument, position, etc.) not tenable. □ **untenability** *n.*

untended *adj.* not tended; neglected.

untested *adj.* not tested or proved. □ **untestable** *adj.*

untether *v.tr.* release (an animal) from a tether.

untethered *adj.* not tethered.

unthankful *adj.* not thankful.

untheorized *adj.* (also **-ised**) not elaborated from a fundamental theory.

unthinkable *adj.* **1** that cannot be imagined or grasped by the mind. **2** *colloq.* highly unlikely or undesirable. □ **unthinkableness** *n.* **unthinkably** *adv.*

unthinking *adj.* **1** thoughtless. **2** unintentional, inadvertent. □ **unthinkingly** *adv.* **unthinkingness** *n.*

unthread *v.tr.* take the thread out of (a needle etc.).

unthreatening *adj.* not threatening or aggressive.

unthrone *v.tr.* dethrone.

untidy *adj.* (**untidier**, **untidiest**) not neat or orderly. □ **untidily** *adv.* **untidiness** *n.*

untie *v.tr.* (*pres. part.* **untying**) **1** undo (a knot etc.). **2** unfasten the cords etc. of (a package etc.). **3** release from bonds or attachment. [Old English]

untied *adj.* not tied.

until *prep. & conj.* = TILL[1]. [from Old Norse *und* 'as far as' + TILL[1]]

U

■ **Usage** *Until*, as opposed to *till*, is used especially at the beginning of a sentence and in formal style, e.g. *Until you told me, I had no idea*; *He resided there until his decease.*

untilled *adj.* not tilled.

untimely ● *adj.* **1** inopportune. **2** (of death) premature. ● *adv. archaic* **1** inopportunely. **2** prematurely. □ **untimeliness** *n.*

untiring *adj.* tireless. □ **untiringly** *adv.*

untitled *adj.* having no title.

unto *prep. archaic* = *prep.* (in all senses except sense 2, introducing the infinitive) (*do unto others*; *faithful unto death*; *take unto oneself*). [Middle English, from UNTIL]

untold *adj.* **1** not told. **2** not (able to be) counted or measured (*untold misery*). [Old English]

untouchable ● *adj.* that may not or cannot be touched. ● *n.* a member of a hereditary Hindu group held to defile members of higher castes on contact. □ **untouchability** *n.*

■ **Usage** The use of the term *untouchable* and the social restrictions accompanying it were declared illegal under the Indian constitution in 1949.

untouched *adj.* **1** not touched. **2** not affected physically; not harmed, modified, used, or tasted. **3** not affected by emotion. **4** not discussed.

untoward *adj.* **1** inconvenient, unlucky. **2** awkward. **3** perverse, refractory. **4** unseemly.

untraceable *adj.* that cannot be traced. □ **untraceably** *adv.*

untraced *adj.* not traced.

untracked *adj.* **1** not marked with tracks from skis etc. **2** having no previously-trodden track; unexplored. **3** not traced or followed.

untraditional *adj.* not traditional; unusual.

untrained *adj.* not trained. □ **untrainable** *adj.*

untrammelled *adj.* (*US* **untrammeled**) not trammelled, unhampered.

untranslatable *adj.* that cannot be translated. □ **untranslatability** *n.* **untranslated** *adj.*

untravelled *adj.* (*US* **untraveled**) **1** that has not travelled. **2** that has not been travelled over or through.

untreatable *adj.* (of a disease etc.) that cannot be treated.

untreated *adj.* not treated.

untried *adj.* **1** not tried or tested. **2** inexperienced. **3** not yet tried by a judge.

untrodden *adj.* not trodden, stepped on, or traversed.

untroubled *adj.* calm, tranquil.

untrue *adj.* **1** not true. **2** not faithful or loyal. **3** deviating from an accepted standard. [Old English] □ **untruly** *adv.*

untrusting *adj.* not trusting; suspicious.

untrustworthy *adj.* not trustworthy. □ **untrustworthiness** *n.*

untruth *n.* (*pl.*) **1** the state of being untrue. **2** a false statement (*told me an untruth*). [Old English]

untruthful *adj.* not truthful. □ **untruthfully** *adv.* **untruthfulness** *n.*

untuck *v.tr.* free (bedclothes etc.) from being tucked in or up.

untuned *adj.* **1** not in tune, not made tuneful. **2** (of a radio receiver etc.) not tuned to any one frequency. **3** not in harmony or concord, disordered.

unturned *adj.* **1** not turned over, round, away, etc. **2** not shaped by turning.

untutored *adj.* uneducated, untaught.

untwine *v.tr. & intr.* untwist, unwind.

untwist *v.tr. & intr.* open from a twisted or spiralled state.

untying *pres. part.* of UNTIE.

untypical *adj.* not typical; unusual. □ **untypically** *adv.*

unusable *adj.* not usable.

unused *adj.* **1 a** not in use. **b** never having been used. **2** (foll. by *to*) not accustomed.

unusual *adj.* **1** not usual. **2** remarkable. □ **unusually** *adv.* **unusualness** *n.*

unutterable *adj.* inexpressible; beyond description (*unutterable torment*; *an unutterable fool*). □ **unutterably** *adv.*

unvaccinated *adj.* not vaccinated.

unvalued *adj.* **1** not regarded as valuable. **2** not having been valued.

unvanquished *adj.* not vanquished.

unvaried *adj.* not varied.

unvarnished *adj.* **1** not varnished. **2** (of a statement or person) plain and straightforward (*the unvarnished truth*).

unvarying *adj.* not varying. □ **unvaryingly** *adv.*

unveil *v.* **1** *tr.* remove a veil from. **2** *tr.* remove a covering from (a statue, plaque, etc.) as part of the ceremony of the first public display. **3** *tr.* disclose, reveal, make publicly known. **4** *intr.* remove one's veil.

unventilated *adj.* **1** not provided with a means of ventilation. **2** not discussed.

unverifiable *adj.* that cannot be verified.

unverified *adj.* not verified.

unversed *adj.* (usu. foll. by *in*) not experienced or skilled.

unviable *adj.* not viable.

unvoiced *adj.* **1** not spoken. **2** *Phonet.* not voiced.

unwaged *adj.* not receiving a wage; out of work.

unwanted *adj.* not wanted.

unwarlike *adj.* not warlike.

unwarrantable *adj.* unjustifiable. □ **unwarrantably** *adv.*

unwarranted *adj.* **1** unauthorized. **2** unjustified.

unwary *adj.* **1** not cautious. **2** not aware of possible danger etc. □ **unwarily** *adv.*

unwashed *adj.* **1** not washed. **2** not usually washed or clean.

unwatchable *adj.* disturbing or not interesting to watch.

unwatered *adj.* not watered.

unwavering *adj.* not wavering. □ **unwaveringly** *adv.*

unweaned *adj.* not weaned.

unwearable *adj.* that cannot be worn.

unwearied *adj.* **1** not wearied or tired. **2** never becoming weary, indefatigable. **3** unremitting. □ **unweariedly** *adv.*

unwearying *adj.* **1** persistent. **2** not causing or producing weariness.

unwed *adj.* unmarried.

unwedded *adj.* unmarried.

unwelcome *adj.* not welcome or acceptable. □ **unwelcomely** *adv.* **unwelcomeness** *n.*

unwelcoming *adj.* **1** having an inhospitable atmosphere. **2** hostile; unfriendly.

unwell *adj.* **1** not in good health; ill. **2** indisposed.

unwholesome *adj.* **1** detrimental to physical or moral health. **2** unhealthy, insalubrious. **3** unhealthy-looking. □ **unwholesomely** *adv.* **unwholesomeness** *n.*

unwieldy *adj.* (**unwieldier**, **unwieldiest**) cumbersome or hard to manage, owing to size, shape, or weight. [Middle English, based on (now dialect) *wieldy* 'active'] □ **unwieldiness** *n.*

unwilling *adj.* not willing or inclined; reluctant. [Old English] □ **unwillingly** *adv.* **unwillingness** *n.*

unwind *v.* (*past* and *past part.* **unwound**) **1 a** *tr.* draw out (a thing that has been wound). **b** *intr.* become drawn out after having been wound. **2** *intr. & tr. colloq.* relax.

unwinking *adj.* **1** not winking. **2** *Brit.* vigilant.

unwinnable *adj.* that cannot be won.

unwisdom *n.* lack of wisdom; folly, imprudence. [Old English]

UPHOLSTERY

The elements of traditional upholstery are webbing, preparing a coil spring platform, judging the amount and shape of stuffing, sculpting it with stitches, tacking, and trimming. Tools include tack lifters, ripping chisels, webbing stretchers, hammers, and various types of needle. Some hammers are magnetized to help pick up the tacks neatly.

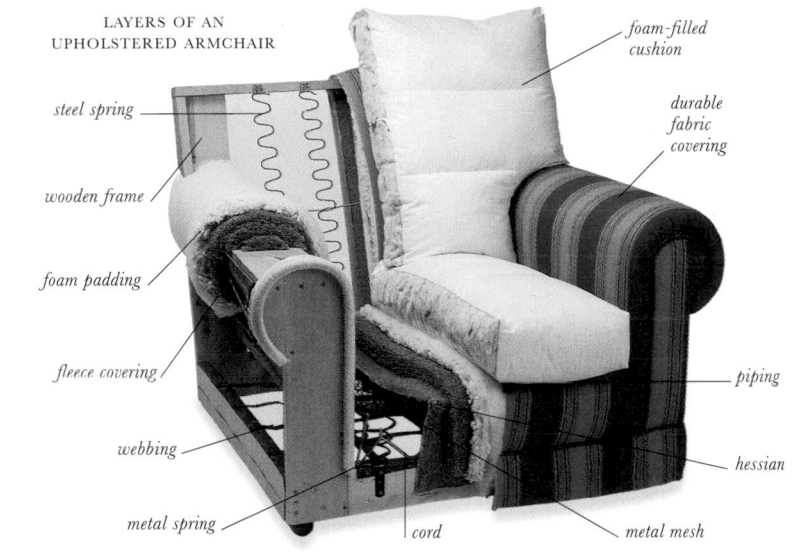

LAYERS OF AN
UPHOLSTERED ARMCHAIR

steel spring

wooden frame

foam padding

fleece covering

webbing

metal spring

cord

foam-filled cushion

durable fabric covering

piping

hessian

metal mesh

unwise *adj.* **1** foolish, imprudent. **2** injudicious. [Old English] □ **unwisely** *adv.*

unwished *adj.* (usu. foll. by *for*) not wished for.

unwitting *adj.* **1** unaware of the state of the case (*an unwitting offender*). **2** unintentional. [Old English] □ **unwittingly** *adv.*

unwomanly *adj.* not womanly; not befitting a woman.

unwonted /un-**wohn**-tid/ *adj.* not customary or usual. □ **unwontedly** *adv.*

unworkable *adj.* not workable; impracticable. □ **unworkably** *adv.* **unworkability** *n.*

unworked *adj.* **1** not wrought into shape. **2** not exploited or turned to account.

unworkmanlike *adj.* badly done or made.

unworldly *adj.* **1** spiritually-minded. **2** spiritual. □ **unworldliness** *n.*

unworn *adj.* not worn or impaired by wear.

unworried *adj.* not worried; calm.

unworthy *adj.* (**unworthier, unworthiest**) **1** not worthy or befitting the character of a person etc. **2** discreditable, unseemly. **3** contemptible, base. □ **unworthily** *adv.* **unworthiness** *n.*

unwound[1] *adj.* not wound or wound up.

unwound[2] *past* and *past part.* of UNWIND.

unwounded *adj.* not wounded, unhurt.

unwoven *adj.* not woven.

unwrap *v.* (**unwrapped, unwrapping**) **1** *tr.* remove the wrapping from. **2** *tr.* open or unfold. **3** *intr.* become unwrapped.

unwritten *adj.* **1** not written. **2** (of a law etc.) resting originally on custom or judicial decision, not on statute.

unyielding *adj.* **1** not yielding. **2** firm, obstinate. □ **unyieldingly** *adv.* **unyieldingness** *n.*

unzip *v.tr.* (**unzipped, unzipping**) unfasten the zip of.

up ● *adv.* **1** at, in, or towards a higher place or position (*jumped up in the air; what are they doing up there?*). **2** to or in a place regarded as higher, esp.: **a** northwards (*up in Scotland*). **b** *Brit.* towards a major city or a university (*went up to London*). **3** *colloq.* ahead etc. as indicated (*went up front*). **4 a** to or in an erect position or condition (*stood it up*). **b** to or in a required

position (*wound up the watch*). **c** in or into a condition of efficiency, activity, or progress (*stirred up trouble; the house is up for sale; the hunt is up*). **5** in a stronger or winning position or condition (*our team was three goals up; am £10 up on the transaction*). **6** (of a computer) running and available for use. **7** to the place or time in question or where the speaker etc. is (*a child came up to me; went straight up to the door; has been fine up till now*). **8** at or to a higher price or value (*our costs are up; shares are up*). **9 a** completely (*burn up; eat up; tear up; use up*). **b** more loudly or clearly (*speak up*). **10** in a state of completion; denoting the end of availability, supply, etc. (*time is up*). **11** into a compact, accumulated, or secure state (*pack up; save up; tie up*). **12** out of bed (*are you up yet?*). **13** (of the sun etc.) having risen. **14** happening, esp. unusually (*something is up*). **15** taught or informed (*is well up in French*). **16** (usu. foll. by *before*) appearing for trial etc. (*was up before the magistrate*). **17** *Brit.* (of a road etc.) being repaired. **18** (of a jockey) in the saddle. **19** towards the source of a river. **20** inland. **21** upstairs, esp. to bed (*are you going up yet?*). **22** (of a theatre curtain) raised etc. to reveal the stage. ● *prep.* **1** upwards along, through, or into (*climbed up the ladder*). **2** from the bottom to the top of. **3** along (*walked up the road*). **4 a** at or in a higher part of (*is situated up the street*). **b** towards the source of (a river). ● *adj.* **1** directed upwards. **2** *Brit.* of travel towards a capital or centre (*the up train; the up platform*). ● *n.* a spell of good fortune. ● *v.* (**upped, upping**) **1** *intr. colloq.* begin abruptly to say or do something (*upped and hit him*). **2** *intr.* (foll. by *with*) raise; pick up (*upped with his stick*). **3** *tr.* increase or raise (*upped all their prices*). □ **be all up with** (with *it* as subject) be hopeless for (a person). **on the up and up** *colloq.* **1** *Brit.* steadily improving. **2** esp. *N. Amer.* honest(ly); on the level. **something is up** *colloq.* something unusual or undesirable is afoot or happening. **up against 1** close to. **2** in or into contact with. **3** *colloq.* confronted with (*up against a problem*). **up against it** *colloq.* in great difficulties. **up and about** (or **doing**) having risen from bed; active. **up and down 1** to and fro (along). **2** in every direction. **3** *colloq.* in varying health or spirits. **up and running** functioning; in operation. **up for** available for or being considered for (office etc.). **up in**

arms see ARM[2]. **up the pole** see POLE[1]. **up the spout** see SPOUT. **up sticks** see STICK[1]. **up to 1** until (*up to the present*). **2** not more than (*you can have up to five*). **3** less than or equal to (*sums up to £10*). **4** incumbent on (*it is up to you to say*). **5** capable of (*am not up to a long walk*). **6** occupied or busy with (*what have you been up to?*). **up to the mark** see MARK[1]. **up to snuff** see SNUFF[2]. **up to one's tricks** see TRICK. **up to a person's tricks** see TRICK. **up with** *int.* expressing support for a stated person or thing. **up yours** *coarse slang* expressing contemptuous defiance or rejection. **what's up?** *colloq.* **1** what is going on? **2** what is the matter? [Old English]

up- *prefix* in senses of UP, added: **1** as an adverb to verbs and verbal derivations, = 'upwards' (*upcurved; update*). **2** as a preposition to nouns forming adverbs and adjectives (*up-country; uphill*). **3** as an adjective to nouns (*upland; upstroke*).

up-and-coming *adj. colloq.* making good progress and likely to succeed.

up-and-over *adj.* (of a door) opened by being raised and pushed back into a horizontal position.

Upanishad *n.* each of a series of philosophical compositions concluding the exposition of the Vedas. [Sanskrit, from *upa* 'near' + *ni-ṣad* 'sit down']

upbeat ● *n.* an unaccented beat in music. ● *adj. colloq.* optimistic or cheerful.

upbraid *v.tr.* chide or reproach. [Old English] □ **upbraiding** *n.*

upbringing *n.* the bringing up of a child. [from obsolete *upbring* 'to rear']

upcoming *adj.* esp. *N. Amer.* forthcoming; about to happen.

up-country *adv. & adj.* inland.

update ● *v.tr.* bring up to date. ● *n.* **1** the act or an instance of updating. **2** an updated version; a set of updated information.

updraught *n.* (*US* **updraft**) an upward draught of air.

upend *v.tr. & intr.* set or rise up on end.

upfield *adv.* in or to a position nearer to the opponents' end of a field.

upfront *colloq.* ● *adv.* (usu. **up front**) **1** at the front; in front. **2** (of payments) in advance. ● *adj.* **1** honest, open, frank. **2** (of payments) made in advance.

upgrade ● *v.tr.* **1** raise in rank etc. **2** improve (equipment, machinery, etc.). ● *n.* **1** the act or an instance of upgrading. **2** an upgraded piece of equipment etc. □ **on the upgrade 1** improving in health etc. **2** advancing, progressing. □ **upgradeable** *adj.* (also **upgradable**) esp. *Computing*.

upheaval *n.* **1** a violent or sudden change or disruption. **2** *Geol.* an upward displacement of part of the Earth's crust. **3** the act or an instance of heaving up.

uphill ● *adv.* up a hill, slope, etc. ● *adj.* **1** sloping up; ascending. **2** arduous (*an uphill task*). ● *n.* an upward slope.

uphold *v.tr.* (*past* and *past part.* **upheld**) **1** confirm (a decision etc.). **2** give support or countenance to. □ **upholder** *n.*

upholster *v.tr.* provide (furniture) with upholstery.

upholsterer *n.* a person who upholsters furniture, esp. professionally. [based on obsolete *uphold* 'to keep in repair']

upholstery *n.* **1** ▲ textile covering, padding, springs, etc., for furniture. **2** an upholsterer's work.

upkeep *n.* **1** maintenance in good condition. **2** the cost or means of this.

upland ● *n.* high or hilly country. ● *adj.* of or relating to this.

uplift ● *v.tr.* **1** esp. *Brit.* raise. **2** elevate morally or spiritually. ● *n.* **1** the act or an instance of being raised. **2** *colloq.* a morally or spiritually elevating influence. **3** support for the bust etc. from a garment. □ **uplifter** *n.* **uplifting** *adj.* (esp. in sense 2 of *v.*).

uplighter *n.* a light placed or designed to throw illumination upwards.

U

upmarket *adj. & adv.* towards or relating to the dearer or more affluent sector of the market.

upon *prep.* = ON. [Middle English]

■ **Usage** *Upon* is sometimes more formal than *on*, but is standard in the phrases *once upon a time* and *upon my word*, and in uses such as *row upon row of seats* and *Christmas is almost upon us*.

upper[1] *adj.* **1** higher in position or status (*the upper class*) **2** situated above another part (*the upper atmosphere; the upper lip*). **3** (**Upper**) situated on higher ground (*Upper Egypt*). ● *n.* the part of a boot or shoe above the sole. □ **on one's uppers** *colloq.* extremely short of money. [Middle English]

upper[2] *n. slang* a stimulant drug, esp. an amphetamine. [based on UP (*v.*)]

upper case *n.* (hyphenated when *attrib.*) capital letters.

upper class ● *n.* the highest class of society, esp. the aristocracy. ● *adj.* (**upper-class**) of the upper class.

upper crust *n.* (prec. by *the*) *colloq.* the aristocracy.

uppercut ● *n.* an upwards blow delivered with the arm bent. ● *v.tr.* hit with an uppercut.

upper hand *n.* (prec. by *the*) dominance or control.

Upper House *n.* the higher house in a legislature, esp. the House of Lords.

uppermost ● *adj.* **1** highest in place or rank. **2** predominant. ● *adv.* at or to the highest or most prominent position.

uppish *adj. esp. Brit. colloq.* self-assertive or arrogant.

uppity *adj. colloq.* uppish, snobbish. [fanciful from UP]

uprate *v.tr.* **1** increase the value of (a pension, benefit, etc.). **2** upgrade.

upright ● *adj.* **1** erect, vertical (*an upright posture; stood upright*). **2** (of a piano) with vertical strings. **3** honourable or honest. **4** (of a picture, book, etc.) greater in height than breadth. ● *n.* **1** a post or rod fixed upright esp. as a structural support. **2** ▼ an upright piano. [Old English] □ **uprightness** *n.*

uprising *n.* a rebellion or revolt.

uproar *n.* a tumult; a violent disturbance. [from Dutch *oproer*]

uproarious *adj.* **1** very noisy. **2** provoking loud laughter. □ **uproariously** *adv.* **uproariousness** *n.*

uproot *v.* **1** *tr.* pull (a plant etc.) up from the ground. **2** *tr.* displace (a person). **3** *tr.* eradicate. **4** *intr.* move away from one's accustomed location or home.

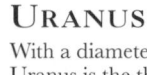

URANUS

With a diameter of about 51,000 km, Uranus is the third largest planet in the solar system. It is a cold gas giant, believed to consist of a mixture of gas and ice around a solid core. Uranus is tilted at 97.9° and so rolls on its side along its orbital path. It has 15 moons, 10 rings made up of boulders, and a broad ring of dust.

URANUS, WITH INTERNAL STRUCTURE REVEALED

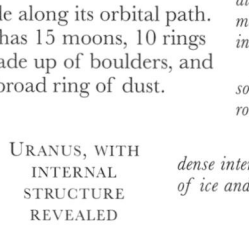

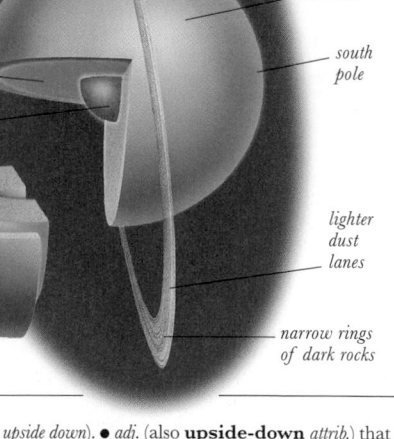

atmosphere merging into interior

solid rocky core

dense interior of ice and gas

Earth
Sun
SOLAR SYSTEM
Uranus

atmosphere of hydrogen, helium, and methane

blue-green hue due to methane

south pole

lighter dust lanes

narrow rings of dark rocks

---

uprush *n.* an upward rush.

ups-a-daisy var. of UPSY-DAISY.

ups and downs *n.pl.* **1** rises and falls. **2** alternate good and bad fortune.

upset ● *v.* (**upsetting**; *past* and *past part.* **upset**) **1** *tr. & intr.* overturn or be overturned. **2** *tr.* disturb the composure or digestion of (*was very upset by the news; ate something that upset me*). **3** *tr.* disrupt. ● *n.* **1** a condition of upsetting or being upset (*a stomach upset*). **2** a surprising result in a game etc. ● *adj.* disturbed (*an upset stomach*). □ **upsetter** *n.* **upsettingly** *adv.*

upshot *n.* the outcome or conclusion.

upside *n.* **1** the positive aspect of something; an advantage. **2** an upward movement of share prices etc.

upside down ● *adv.* **1** with the upper part where the lower part should be; in an inverted position. **2** in or into total disorder (*everything was turned upside down*). ● *adj.* (also **upside-down** *attrib.*) that is positioned upside down; inverted. [Middle English, originally *up so down*]

upsilon /up-sy-lŏn/ *n.* the twentieth letter of the Greek alphabet (Y, υ). [Greek, literally 'slender U']

upstage ● *adj. & adv.* **1** nearer the back of a theatre stage. ▷ THEATRE. **2** snobbish(ly). ● *v.tr.* **1** (of an actor) move upstage to make (another actor) face away from the audience. **2** divert attention from (a person) to oneself.

upstairs ● *adv.* to or on an upper floor. ● *adj.* (also **upstair**) situated upstairs. ● *n.* an upper floor.

upstanding *adj.* **1** standing up. **2** strong and healthy. **3** honest.

upstart ● *n.* a person who has risen suddenly to prominence, esp. one who behaves arrogantly. ● *adj.* **1** that is an upstart. **2** of or characteristic of an upstart.

upstate *US* ● *n.* part of a state remote from its large cities, esp. the northern part. ● *adj.* of or relating to this part. ● *adv.* in or to this part.

upstream ● *adv.* against the flow of a stream etc. ● *adj.* moving upstream.

upsurge *n.* an upward surge.

upswept *adj.* **1** (of the hair) combed to the top of the head. **2** curved or sloped upwards.

upswing *n.* an upward movement or trend.

upsy-daisy *int.* (also **ups-a-daisy**, **oops-a-daisy**) expressing encouragement to a child who is being lifted or has fallen. [alteration of *up-a-daisy*, from extended form of *a-day*]

uptake *n.* **1** *colloq.* understanding; comprehension (esp. *quick* or *slow on the uptake*). **2** the act or an instance of taking up.

upthrust *n.* **1** upward thrust. **2** *Geol.* = UPHEAVAL 2.

uptight *adj. colloq.* **1** nervously tense or angry. **2** rigidly conventional.

up to date *adj.* (hyphenated when *attrib.*) meeting or according to the latest requirements, knowledge, or fashion.

up-to-the-minute *adj.* (usu. *attrib.*) latest; most modern.

uptown *N. Amer.* ● *adj.* of or in the residential part of a town or city. ● *adv.* in or into this part. ● *n.* this part. □ **uptowner** *n.*

upturn ● *n.* **1** an upward trend; an improvement. **2** an upheaval. ● *v.tr.* turn up or upside down.

upward ● *adv.* (also **upwards**) towards what is higher, superior, larger in amount, more important, or earlier. ● *adj.* moving, extending, pointing,

---

UPRIGHT

Developed at the turn of the 19th century, the upright piano has vertical wire strings stretched over a metal frame. When a key is depressed, a damper lifts from the string as a hammer strikes it, making it vibrate. The three pedals vary the quality of the notes.

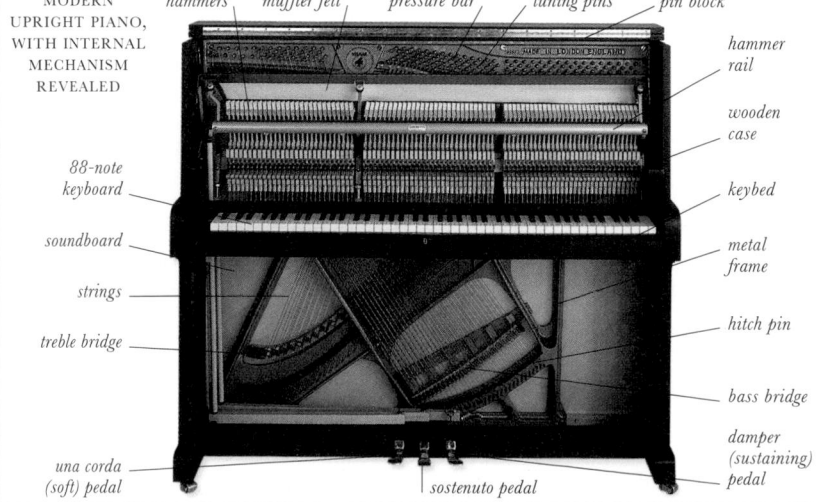

MODERN UPRIGHT PIANO, WITH INTERNAL MECHANISM REVEALED

hammers
muffler felt
pressure bar
tuning pins
pin block
hammer rail
wooden case
keybed
88-note keyboard
soundboard
metal frame
strings
hitch pin
treble bridge
bass bridge
damper (sustaining) pedal
una corda (soft) pedal
sostenuto pedal

U

or leading upward. □ **upwards of** more than (*found upwards of forty specimens*). [Old English]

upwardly *adv.* in an upward direction.

upwardly mobile *adj.* aspiring to advance socially or professionally.

upward mobility *n.* social or professional advancement.

upwind *adj. & adv.* against the direction of the wind.

ur- *comb. form* primitive, original, earliest. [German]

uranium *n. Chem.* a radioactive grey dense metallic element capable of nuclear fission and therefore used as a source of nuclear energy. [based on *Uranus*, the planet] □ **uranic** *adj.*

Uranus *n.* ◄ a planet discovered by Herschel in 1781, the outermost of the solar system except Neptune and Pluto. ▷ SOLAR SYSTEM. [Latin from Greek *Ouranos* 'heaven, Uranus', in Greek Mythol. the son of Gaea (Earth) and father of Kronos (Saturn), the Titans, etc.]

urban *adj.* of, living in, or situated in a town or city (*an urban population*). [based on Latin *urbs urbis* 'city']

urbane *adj.* suave; elegant and refined in manner. [related to URBAN] □ **urbanely** *adv.*

urban guerrilla *n.* a terrorist operating in an urban area.

urbanism *n.* **1** urban character or way of life. **2** a study of urban life. □ **urbanist** *n.*

urbanite *n.* a dweller in a city or town.

urbanity *n.* **1** an urbane quality; refinement of manner. **2** urban life.

urbanize *v.tr.* (also **-ise**) **1** make urban. **2** destroy the rural quality of (a district). □ **urbanization** *n.*

urban myth *n.* a modern old wives' tale.

urchin *n.* **1** a mischievous child, esp. young and raggedly dressed. **2** = SEA URCHIN. [from Latin *(h)ericius* 'hedgehog']

Urdu *n.* a language related to Hindi but with many Persian words, an official language of Pakistan and also used in India. [from Hindi *(zabān i) urdū* 'language of the) camp']

urea /yuu-**ree**-ă/ *n. Biochem.* a soluble nitrogenous compound contained esp. in urine. [based on Greek *ouron* 'urine'] □ **ureal** *adj.*

ureter /yoo-**ree**-ter/ *n.* the duct by which urine passes from the kidney to the bladder or cloaca. ▷ URINARY SYSTEM. [from Greek *ourētēr*] □ **ureteral** *adj.* **ureteric** *adj.* **ureteritis** *n.*

urethane /**yoor**-i-thayn/ *n. Chem.* an amide used in plastics and paints. [from French *uréthane*]

urethra /yoo-**ree**-thră/ *n.* (*pl.* **urethrae** /-ree/ or **urethras**) the duct by which urine is discharged from the bladder. ▷ URINARY SYSTEM. [from Greek *ourēthra*] □ **urethral** *adj.* **urethritis** *n.*

urge ● *v.tr.* **1** drive forcibly; hasten (*urged them on; urged the horses forward*). **2** encourage or entreat earnestly or persistently (*urged them to go; urged them to action; urged that they should go*). **3** (often foll. by *on, upon*) advocate (an action or argument etc.) emphatically (to a person). **4** adduce forcefully as a reason or justification (*urged the seriousness of the problem*). **5** ply (a person etc.) hard with argument or entreaty. ● *n.* **1** an urging impulse or tendency. **2** a strong desire. [from Latin *urgēre* 'to press, drive']

urgent *adj.* **1** requiring immediate action or attention (*an urgent need for help*). **2** importunate. [from Latin *urgent-* 'pressing'] □ **urgency** *n.* **urgently** *adv.*

uric *adj.* of or relating to urine. [from French *urique*]

uric acid *n.* an almost insoluble acid forming the main nitrogenous waste product in birds, reptiles, and insects.

urinal *n.* **1** a sanitary fitting for men to urinate into. **2** a place or receptacle for urination. [from Late Latin *urinal*]

urinary *adj.* **1** of or relating to urine. **2** affecting or occurring in the urinary system (*urinary diseases*).

urinary system *n.* ▲ the system of organs and structures in the body that are concerned with the excretion and discharge of urine.

URINARY SYSTEM

The human urinary system facilitates regulation of the amount and composition of fluids in the body. The kidneys filter blood to form urine for the excretion of waste products. Ureters carry the urine to the bladder where it is stored until it can be discharged. At this time, the bladder contracts, the bladder and urethral outlets (sphincters) relax, and the urine is expelled. A woman's bladder is smaller and lower in the pelvis than a man's, and her urethra is about one-fifth the length of a man's.

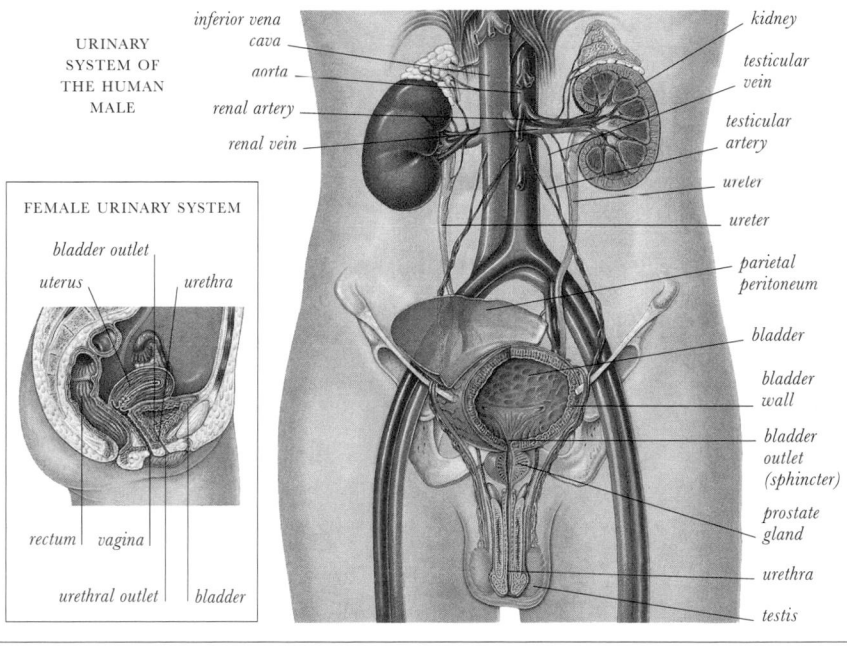

URINARY SYSTEM OF THE HUMAN MALE

inferior vena cava
aorta
renal artery
renal vein
kidney
testicular vein
testicular artery
ureter
ureter
parietal peritoneum
bladder
bladder wall
bladder outlet (sphincter)
prostate gland
urethra
testis

FEMALE URINARY SYSTEM

bladder outlet
uterus
urethra
rectum
vagina
urethral outlet
bladder

---

urinate *v.intr.* discharge urine. [based on medieval Latin *urinatus* 'having passed water'] □ **urination** *n.*

urine *n.* a fluid secreted as waste from the blood by the kidneys, stored in the bladder, and discharged through the urethra. [from Latin *urina*] □ **urinous** *adj.*

urn *n.* **1** a vase with a foot and usu. a rounded body, esp. for storing the ashes of the cremated dead. **2** a large vessel with a tap, in which tea or coffee etc. is made or kept hot. [from Latin *urna*]

uro- *comb. form* urine. [from Greek *ouron*]

urodele *n.* any amphibian of the order Urodela, having a tail when in the adult form, including newts and salamanders. ▷ NEWT, SALAMANDER. [from Greek *oura* 'tail' + *dēlos* 'evident']

urogenital *adj.* of or relating to urinary and genital products or organs.

urology *n.* the scientific study of the urinary system. □ **urologic** *adj.* **urological** *adj.* **urologist** *n.*

Ursa Major *n.* ► a prominent constellation in the northern sky, containing seven bright stars. [Latin, literally 'greater (she-)bear']

Ursa Minor *n.* ▼ a small constellation containing the north celestial pole and the pole star. [Latin, literally 'lesser (she-)bear']

URSA MAJOR: FIGURE OF A BEAR FORMED FROM THE STARS OF URSA MAJOR

Polaris

URSA MINOR: FIGURE OF A SMALL BEAR FORMED FROM THE STARS OF URSA MINOR

---

ursine *adj.* of or like a bear. [based on Latin *ursus* 'bear']

urticaria *n. Med.* nettle-rash. [based on Latin *urtica* 'nettle']

US *abbr.* **1** United States (of America). **2** *Brit.* unserviceable.

us *pron.* **1** objective case of WE (*they saw us*). **2** *colloq.* = ME[1] (*give us a kiss*). [Old English]

■ **Usage** See Usage Note at HER.

USA *abbr.* **1** United States of America. **2** *US* United States Army.

usable *adj.* (also **useable**) that can be used. □ **usability** *n.*

USAF *abbr.* United States Air Force.

usage *n.* **1** a manner of using or treating; use (*damaged by rough usage*). **2** habitual or customary practice. [from Old French]

use ● *v.tr.* /yooz/ **1** cause to act or serve for a purpose; bring into service (*rarely uses the car; use your discretion*). **2** treat in a specified manner (*they used him shamefully*). **3** exploit for one's own ends (*they are just using you*). **4** (in *past*; foll. by *to* + infin.) did or had in the past as a customary practice or state (*I used to be an archaeologist; it used not (or did not use) to rain so often*). **5** (as **used** /yoozd/ *adj.*) second-hand. **6** (as **used** /yoost/ *predic.adj.*) (foll. by *to*) familiar by habit; accustomed (*not used to hard work*). **7** apply (a name or title etc.) to oneself. ● *n.* /yooss/ **1** the act of using or the state of being used (*put it to good use; is in daily use; worn and polished with use*). **2** the right or power of using (*lost the use of my right arm*). **3 a** the ability to be used (*a torch would*

U

UTENSIL

Most households have a basic set of cooking utensils for the preparation of food. Since cooking as a hobby has increased in popularity, the range and quality of utensils available has grown with it. While there have been many innovations, a well-equipped kitchen will still have most of the traditional tools shown here.

CUTTING AND SLICING

KITCHEN KNIVES   TWO-PRONGED FORK   STEEL

MISCELLANEOUS

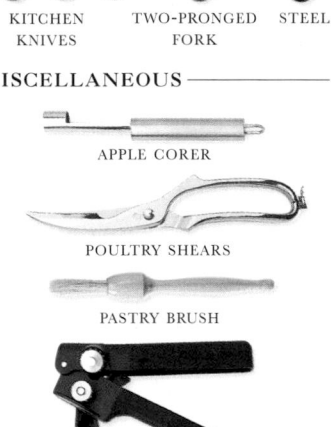

APPLE CORER

POULTRY SHEARS

PASTRY BRUSH

TIN-OPENER

SERVING, STRAINING, AND MIXING

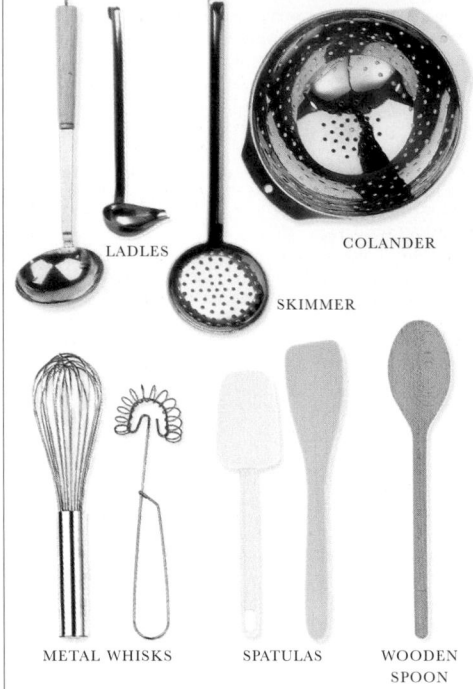

LADLES   COLANDER

SKIMMER

METAL WHISKS   SPATULAS   WOODEN SPOON

MEASURING

SPOONS

CUPS

TRADITIONAL SCALES

---

forgot my keys as usual). **2** (prec. by *the, my,* etc.) *colloq.* a person's usual drink etc. [from Old French] □ **usually** *adv.* **usualness** *n.*

usurer *n.* a person who practises usury. [from Old French *usureor*]

usurp *v.* **1** *tr.* seize (a throne or power etc.) wrongfully. **2** *intr.* (foll. by *on, upon*) encroach. [from Latin *usurpare* 'to seize for use'] □ **usurpation** *n.* **usurper** *n.*

usury *n.* **1** the act or practice of lending money at interest, esp. *Law* at an exorbitant rate. **2** interest at this rate. [from Latin *usura*, related to *use*]

utensil *n.* ◄ an implement or vessel (*cooking utensils*). [medieval Latin, literally 'usable (thing)']

uterine *adj.* **1** of or relating to the uterus. **2** born of the same mother but not the same father (*sister uterine*). [from Late Latin *uterinus*]

uterus *n.* (*pl.* **uteri** /-ry/) the womb. ▷ REPRODUCTIVE ORGANS. [Latin]

utilitarian ● *adj.* **1** designed to be useful rather than attractive; severely practical. **2** of utilitarianism. ● *n.* an adherent of utilitarianism.

utilitarianism *n.* **1** the doctrine that actions are right if they are useful or for the benefit of a majority. **2** the doctrine that the greatest happiness of the greatest number should be the guiding principle of conduct.

utility *n.* (*pl.* **-ies**) **1** the condition of being useful or profitable. **2** a useful thing. **3** = PUBLIC UTILITY. **4** (*attrib.*) **a** severely practical and standardized (*utility furniture*). **b** made or serving for utility. [from Latin *utilitas*]

utility program *n. Computing* a program for carrying out a routine function.

utility room *n.* a room equipped with appliances for washing, ironing, and other domestic work.

utility vehicle *n.* (also **utility truck** etc.) a vehicle capable of serving various functions.

utilize *v.tr.* (also **-ise**) turn to account; use effectively. [from Italian *utilizzare*] □ **utilizable** *adj.* **utilization** *n.*

utmost ● *adj.* furthest, extreme, or greatest (*the utmost limits; showed the utmost reluctance*). ● *n.* (prec. by *the*) the utmost point or degree etc. □ **do one's utmost** do all that one can. [Old English]

Utopia *n.* (also **utopia**) an imagined perfect place or state of things. [title of a book (1516) by Thomas More: based on Greek *ou* 'not' + *topos* 'place']

Utopian (also **utopian**) ● *adj.* characteristic of Utopia; idealistic. ● *n.* an idealistic reformer. □ **Utopianism** *n.*

utter[1] *attrib.adj.* complete, absolute (*utter misery; saw the utter absurdity of it*). [Old English in sense 'outer'] □ **utterly** *adv.* **utterness** *n.*

utter[2] *v.tr.* **1** emit audibly (*uttered a startled cry*). **2** express in words. **3** *Law* put (esp. forged money) into circulation. [from Middle Dutch *ūteren* 'to make known'] □ **utterer** *n.*

utterance *n.* **1** the act or an instance of uttering. **2** a thing spoken. **3** the power of speaking.

uttermost *adj.* furthest, extreme.

U-turn *n.* **1** the turning of a vehicle in a U-shaped course so as to face in the opposite direction. **2** a reversal of policy.

UV *abbr.* ultraviolet.

UVA *abbr.* ultraviolet radiation of relatively long wavelengths.

UVB *abbr.* ultraviolet radiation of relatively short wavelengths.

uvula /yoov-yoo-lă/ *n.* (*pl.* **uvulae** /-lee/) *Anat.* ► a fleshy extension of the soft palate hanging above the throat. [based on Latin *uva* 'grape'] □ **uvular** *adj.*

uxorious *adj.* greatly or excessively fond of one's wife. [based on Latin *uxor* 'wife'] □ **uxoriousness** *n.*

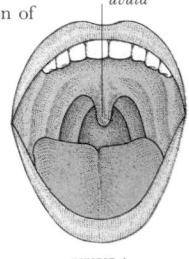

UVULA

U

be of use). **b** the purpose for which a thing can be used (*it's no use talking*). **4** custom or usage (*long use has reconciled me to it*). □ **could use** *colloq.* would be glad to have; would be improved by having. **have no use for 1** be unable to find a use for. **2** dislike or be impatient with. **make use of 1** employ, apply. **2** benefit from. **use up 1** consume completely, use the whole of. **2** find a use for (something remaining). **3** exhaust or wear out. [based on Latin *usus* 'used']

■ **Usage** In sense 4 of the verb, the negative and interrogative can be formed in two ways: (1) **Negative**: *used not/usedn't to*, e.g. *He used not to smoke*. **Interrogative** *used X to?*, e.g. *Used he to smoke?* (2) **Negative** *did not/didn't use to*, e.g. *He didn't use to smoke*. **Interrogative** *did X use to?*, e.g. *Did he use to smoke?* Note the correct spellings of the abbreviated negative forms, *usedn't to, didn't use to*. *Usen't to* and *didn't used to* are incorrect. All the forms given at (1) and (2) are acceptable but those at (1) are more formal. The interrogative form at (1) tends to sound over-formal.

use-by date *n.* esp. *Brit.* a date marked on a perishable product, esp. a foodstuff, recommending the date by which it should be used.

useful *adj.* **1 a** of use; serviceable. **b** producing or able to produce good results (*gave me some useful hints*). **2** *colloq.* highly creditable or efficient (*a useful performance*). □ **make oneself useful** perform useful services. □ **usefully** *adv.* **usefulness** *n.*

useless *adj.* **1** serving no purpose; unavailing. **2** *colloq.* feeble or ineffectual (*am useless at swimming*). □ **uselessly** *adv.* **uselessness** *n.*

user *n.* **1** a person who uses (esp. a particular commodity or service, or a computer). **2** *colloq.* a drug addict.

user-friendly *adj.* esp. *Computing* (of a machine or system) designed to be easy to use.

usher ● *n.* **1** a person who shows people to their seats in a hall or theatre etc. **2** a doorkeeper at a court etc. **3** *Brit.* an officer walking before a person of rank. ● *v.tr.* **1** act as usher to. **2** (usu. foll. by *in*) announce or show in etc. (*ushered us into the room; ushered in a new era*). [based on Latin *ostium* 'door']

usherette *n.* a female usher esp. in a cinema.

USN *abbr.* United States Navy.

USSR *abbr. hist.* Union of Soviet Socialist Republics.

usual *adj.* **1** such as commonly occurs; customary, habitual (*the usual formalities; it is usual to tip them;*

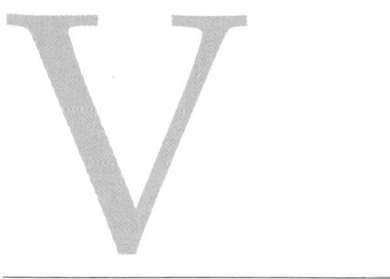

V[1] *n.* (also **v**) (*pl.* **Vs** or **V's**) **1** the twenty-second letter of the alphabet. **2** a V-shaped thing. **3** (as a Roman numeral) five.

V[2] *symb.* **1** *Chem.* the element vanadium. **2 a** volt(s). **b** voltage, potential difference.

v *abbr.* (also **v.**) **1** verse. **2** verso. **3** versus. **4** very. **5** *vide*. **6** velocity.

vac *n. colloq.* **1** *Brit.* vacation. **2** vacuum cleaner.

vacancy *n.* (*pl.* **-ies**) **1** the state of being vacant. **2** an unoccupied job (*there are three vacancies for typists*). **3** an available room in a hotel etc.

vacant *adj.* **1** not filled or occupied. **2** not mentally active; showing no interest (*had a vacant stare*). [from Old French] □ **vacantly** *adv.*

vacant possession *n. Brit.* ownership of a house etc. with any previous occupant having moved out.

vacate *v.tr.* **1** leave vacant or cease to occupy (a house, room, etc.). **2** give up tenure of (a post etc.). [based on Latin *vacatus* 'made empty']

vacation ● *n.* **1** a fixed period of cessation from work, esp. in universities and law courts. **2** *N. Amer.* a holiday. **3** the act of vacating (a house or post etc.). ● *v.intr. US* take a holiday. [from Old

VACUUM CLEANER

Vacuum cleaners suck up dust using a strong current of air and hold it in a bag or container. In a cyclone vacuum cleaner, the air and dust rotates inside a chamber. As it enters an inner cylinder, its speed decreases, and the dust falls into a bin.

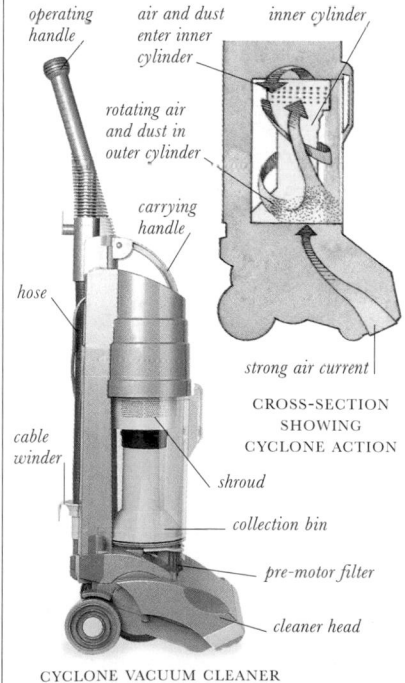

operating handle
air and dust enter inner cylinder
inner cylinder
rotating air and dust in outer cylinder
carrying handle
hose
strong air current
cable winder
shroud
collection bin
pre-motor filter
cleaner head

CROSS-SECTION SHOWING CYCLONE ACTION

CYCLONE VACUUM CLEANER

French, related to VACATE] □ **vacationer** *n.* **vacationist** *n.*

vaccinate *v.tr.* inoculate with a vaccine to provide immunity against a disease. □ **vaccination** *n.* **vaccinator** *n.*

vaccine /vak-seen/ *n.* a preparation used to stimulate the production of antibodies and provide immunity against one or several diseases. [from modern Latin *virus vaccinus* 'cowpox vaccine']

vacillate /vas-i-layt/ *v.intr.* **1** fluctuate in opinion or resolution. **2** move from side to side; oscillate, waver. [based on Latin *vacillatus* 'swayed'] □ **vacillation** *n.*

vacua *pl.* of VACUUM.

vacuole *n. Biol.* a space within the cytoplasm of a cell, enclosed by a membrane and usu. containing fluid. ▷ CELL, DIATOM. [French] □ **vacuolar** *adj.*

vacuous *adj.* **1** lacking expression (*a vacuous stare*). **2** unintelligent (*a vacuous remark*). **3** empty. [from Latin *vacuus* 'empty'] □ **vacuity** *n.* **vacuously** *adv.* **vacuousness** *n.*

vacuum ● *n.* (*pl.* **vacuums** or **vacua**) **1** a space entirely devoid of matter. **2** a space or vessel from which the air has been completely or partly removed by a pump etc. **3 a** the absence of the normal or previous content of a place, environment, etc. **b** the absence of former circumstances, activities, etc. **4** (*pl.* **vacuums**) *colloq.* a vacuum cleaner. ● *v. colloq.* **1** *tr.* clean with a vacuum cleaner. **2** *intr.* use a vacuum cleaner. [modern Latin, literally 'empty (thing)']

vacuum cleaner *n.* ◀ an apparatus for removing dust etc. by suction. □ **vacuum-clean** *v.intr. & tr.*

vacuum flask *n.* esp. *Brit.* ► a vessel with a double wall enclosing a vacuum so that the liquid in the inner receptacle retains its temperature.

vacuum-packed *adj.* sealed after the partial removal of air.

vacuum pump *n.* a pump for producing a vacuum.

vacuum tube *n.* a tube with a near-vacuum for the free passage of electric current.

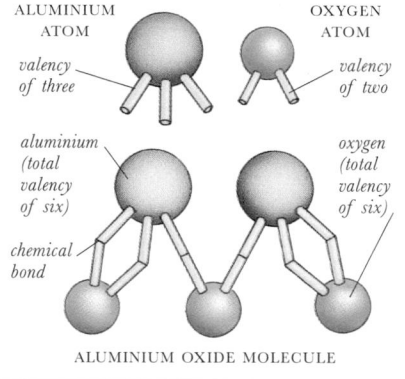

spout
stopper
liquid
vacuum
double wall
silvering reflects heat
cushioning spring

VACUUM FLASK: CROSS-SECTION

vagabond ● *n.* a wanderer, esp. an idle one. ● *adj.* having no fixed habitation; wandering. [from Latin *vagabundus*] □ **vagabondage** *n.*

vagal see VAGUS.

vagary /vay-gă-ri/ *n.* (*pl.* **-ies**) a caprice; an eccentric idea or act (*the vagaries of Fortune*). [based on Latin *vagari* 'to wander']

vagi *pl.* of VAGUS.

vagina *n.* (*pl.* **vaginas** or **vaginae** /-nee/) **1** the canal between the uterus and vulva of a woman or other female mammal. ▷ REPRODUCTIVE ORGANS. [Latin, literally 'sheath, scabbard'] □ **vaginal** *adj.* **vaginitis** *n.*

vagrant ● *n.* **1** a person without a settled home or regular work. **2** *archaic* a wanderer. ● *adj.* characteristic of or relating to a vagrant or vagrancy. [from Anglo-French *vag(a)raunt*] □ **vagrancy** *n.*

vague *adj.* **1** of uncertain or ill-defined meaning or character (*gave a vague answer*; *has some vague idea of emigrating*). **2** inexact in thought, expression, or understanding. [French, literally 'wandering, uncertain'] □ **vaguely** *adv.* **vagueness** *n.*

vagus /vay-gŭs/ *n.* (*pl.* **vagi** /-jy/) *Anat.* either of the tenth pair of cranial nerves, with branches to the heart, lungs, and viscera. ▷ NERVOUS SYSTEM. [Latin, literally 'wandering'] □ **vagal** *adj.*

vain *adj.* **1** excessively proud or conceited. **2** empty, trivial (*vain boasts*; *vain triumphs*). **3** useless; followed

VALENCY

The valency of an atom is the number of chemical bonds it is able to make. Hydrogen has a valency of one, so valency is measured by this standard. To form a compound (as below), the total valencies of the elements present must be equal.

ALUMINIUM ATOM
OXYGEN ATOM
valency of three
valency of two
aluminium (total valency of six)
oxygen (total valency of six)
chemical bond

ALUMINIUM OXIDE MOLECULE

by no good result (*in the vain hope of dissuading them*). □ **in vain** without success (*it was in vain that we protested*). **take a person's name in vain** use it lightly or profanely. [from Latin *vanus* 'empty, without substance'] □ **vainly** *adv.*

vainglory *n. literary* boastfulness; extreme vanity. [Middle English] □ **vainglorious** *adj.* **vaingloriously** *adv.*

valance /val-ănss/ *n.* (also **valence**) a short curtain round the frame or canopy of a bedstead, above a window, or under a shelf. [based on Old French *avaler* 'to descend'] □ **valanced** *adj.*

vale *n. archaic* or *poet.* (except in place names) a valley (*Vale of the White Horse*). [from Latin *vallis*]

valediction /val-i-dik-shŏn/ *n.* **1** the act or an instance of bidding farewell. **2** the words used in this. [based on Latin *valedictus* 'having said farewell']

valedictory /val-i-dik-tŏri/ ● *adj.* serving as a farewell. ● *n.* (*pl.* **-ies**) a farewell address.

valence[1] /vay-lĕnss/ *n. Chem.* = VALENCY.

valence[2] var. of VALANCE.

valency /vay-lĕn-si/ *n.* (*pl.* **-ies**) *Brit. Chem.* ▲ the combining power of an atom measured by the number of hydrogen atoms it can displace or combine with. [from Late Latin *valentia* 'power, competence']

valentine *n.* **1** ► a card or gift sent, often anonymously, as a mark of love on St Valentine's Day (14 Feb.). **2** a sweetheart chosen on this day. [from Latin *Valentinus*, name of two saints]

valerian /vă-leer-iăn/ *n.* **1** a plant of the genus *Valeriana* (family Valerianaceae) with small usu. pink or white flowers and strong-smelling roots, esp. (in full **common valerian**) *Valeriana officinalis*. **2** a drug from the root of this. [from medieval Latin *valeriana (herba)*]

valet /val-ay/ ● *n.* **1** a man's personal attendant who looks after his clothes etc. **2** a hotel etc. employee with similar duties. ● *v.* (**valeted, valet-**

VALENTINE CARD FROM THE VICTORIAN ERA

V

VALLEY

Valleys form through fluvial and glacial erosion or where the land between two faults sinks. Those carved by glaciers have a characteristic U shape, and are often associated with hanging valleys, formed when a glacier slices off the ends of valleys that slope into it. The movement of debris by the ice also leaves very distinctive features.

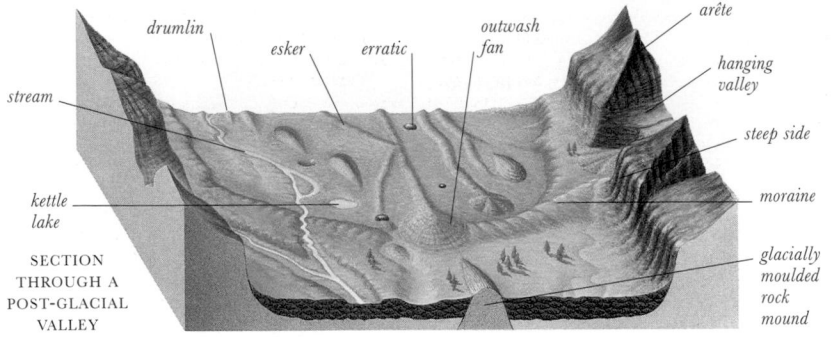

SECTION THROUGH A POST-GLACIAL VALLEY

drumlin · esker · erratic · outwash fan · arête · hanging valley · steep side · moraine · glacially moulded rock mound · kettle lake · stream

ing) **1** *intr.* work as a valet. **2** *tr.* act as a valet to. **3** *tr.* clean or clean out (a car). [French, related to VASSAL.]

valetudinarian ● *n.* a person of poor health or unduly anxious about health. ● *adj.* of or being a valetudinarian. [from Latin *valetudinarius* 'in ill health']

Valhalla *n.* (in Norse mythology) a palace in which the souls of slain heroes feasted for eternity. [from Old Norse *valr* 'the slain' + *höll* 'hall']

valiant *adj.* brave. [from Old French *vaillant*] □ **valiantly** *adv.*

valid *adj.* **1** (of a reason, objection, etc.) sound or defensible. **2 a** executed with the proper formalities (*a valid contract*). **b** legally acceptable (*a valid passport*). **c** not having reached its expiry date. [from Latin *validus* 'strong'] □ **validity** *n.* **validly** *adv.*

validate *v.tr.* make valid; ratify. □ **validation** *n.*

valise /vă-leez/ *n.* **1** a kitbag. **2** *US* a small portmanteau. [from Italian *valigia*]

Valium /val-iŭm/ *n. propr.* the drug diazepam used as a tranquillizer. [20th-century coinage]

Valkyrie /val-keer-i/ *n.* (in Norse mythology) each of Odin's twelve handmaidens who conducted the slain warriors of their choice from the battlefield to Valhalla. [from Old Norse *Valkyrja*, literally 'chooser of the slain']

valley *n.* (*pl.* **-eys**) **1** ▲ a low area between hills and usu. with a stream flowing through it. ▷ GLACIER, RIFT VALLEY. **2** any depression compared to this. **3** *Archit.* an internal valley formed by the intersecting planes of a roof. [from Latin *vallis*]

valor *US* var. of VALOUR.

valour *n.* (*US* **valor**) courage, esp. in battle. [from Late French *valor*] □ **valorous** *adj.*

valuable ● *adj.* of great value, price, or worth (*a valuable property; valuable information*). ● *n.* (usu. in *pl.*) a valuable thing. □ **valuably** *adv.*

valuation *n.* **1 a** an estimation (esp. by a professional valuer) of a thing's worth. **b** the worth estimated. **2** the price set on a thing.

value ● *n.* **1** the worth, desirability, or utility of a thing, or the qualities on which these depend (*the value of regular exercise*). **2** worth as estimated (*set a high value on my time*). **3** the amount for which a thing can be exchanged in the open market. **4** the equivalent of a thing (*paid them the value of their lost property*). **5** (in full **value for money**) something well worth the money spent. **6** the ability of a thing to serve a purpose or cause an effect (*news value; nuisance value*). **7** (in *pl.*) one's principles or standards; one's judgement of what is valuable or important in life. **8** *Mus.* the duration of the sound signified by a note. **9** *Math.* the amount denoted by an algebraic term or expression. **10** the relative rank or importance of a playing card, chess piece, etc. **11** *Physics*

& *Chem.* the numerical measure of a quantity or a number denoting magnitude on some conventional scale (*the value of gravity at the equator*). ● *v.tr.* (**values**, **valued**, **valuing**) **1** estimate the value of; appraise (esp. professionally) (*valued the property at £200,000*). **2** have a high or specified opinion of (*a valued friend*). □ **good** (or **poor** etc.) **value** well worth (or not worth) the money or attention spent. [based on Latin *valēre* 'to be worth'] □ **valueless** *adj.*

value added tax *n.* a tax on the amount by which the value of an article has been increased at each stage of its production.

value judgement *n.* a subjective estimate of quality etc.

valuer *n.* esp. *Brit.* a person who estimates or assesses values, esp. professionally.

valve *n.* **1** a device for controlling the passage of fluid through a pipe etc., esp. an automatic device allowing movement in one direction only. **2** *Anat.* & *Zool.* ▼ a membranous part of an organ etc. allowing a flow of blood etc. in one direction only. **3** *Brit.* = THERMIONIC VALVE. **4** a device to vary the effective length of the tube in a brass musical instrument. ▷ BRASS. **5** each of the two shells of an oyster, mussel, etc. ▷ BIVALVE, OYSTER. [from Latin *valva* 'leaf of a folding door'] □ **valved** *adj.* (also in *comb.*).

VALVE

Valves such as the aortic valve in the human heart ensure unidirectional blood flow. A build-up of pressure in the heart chamber as it fills with blood forces the cusps of the valve to open; once the blood flows out into the aorta, the cusps snap shut and prevent blood from pouring backwards.

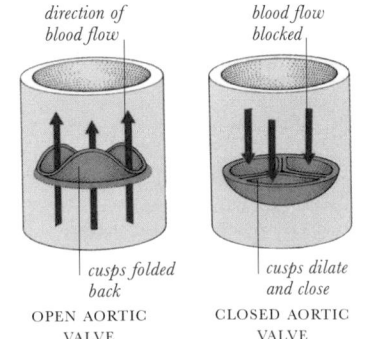

direction of blood flow · blood flow blocked · cusps folded back · cusps dilate and close

OPEN AORTIC VALVE   CLOSED AORTIC VALVE

valvular *adj.* **1** having a valve or valves. **2** having the form or function of a valve.

valvulitis *n.* inflammation of the valves of the heart.

vamoose *v.intr.* (esp. as *int.*) *US slang* depart hurriedly. [from Spanish *vamos* 'let us go']

vamp[1] ● *n.* **1** the upper front part of a boot or shoe. ▷ SHOE. **2** *Mus.* a short simple introductory passage usu. repeated several times until otherwise instructed. ● *v.* **1** *tr.* repair or furbish. **2** *intr.* play a vamp. [from Old French *avantpié*]

vamp[2] *colloq.* ● *n.* a woman who uses sexual attraction to exploit men. ● *v.intr.* act as a vamp. [abbreviation of VAMPIRE] □ **vampish** *adj.* **vampy** *adj.*

vampire *n.* **1** a reanimated corpse supposed to leave its grave at night to suck the blood of persons sleeping. **2** a person who preys ruthlessly on others. **3** (in full **vampire bat**) ▼ any tropical (esp. S. American) bat of the family Desmodontidae, with incisors for piercing flesh and feeding on blood. ▷ BAT. [from Hungarian *vampir*] □ **vampiric** *adj.*

VAMPIRE BAT (*Desmodus rotundus*)

incisors

vampirism *n.* **1** belief in the existence of vampires. **2** the practices of a vampire.

van[1] *n.* **1** a covered vehicle for conveying goods etc. **2** *Brit.* a railway carriage for luggage or for the use of the guard. [abbreviation of CARAVAN]

van[2] *n.* **1** a vanguard. **2** the forefront (*in the van of progress*).

van[3] *n. Brit. Tennis colloq.* = ADVANTAGE *n.* 4. [Middle English, southern & western variant of FAN[1]]

vanadium *n. Chem.* a hard grey metallic element used in small quantities for strengthening some steels. [based on Old Norse *Vanadís*, a name of the Scandinavian goddess Freyja] □ **vanadate** *n.*

vandal ● *n.* **1** a person who wilfully or maliciously destroys or damages property etc. **2** (**Vandal**) a member of a Germanic people that ravaged Gaul, Spain, N. Africa, and Rome in the 4th–5th c. ● *adj.* of or relating to the Vandals. [from Latin *Vandalus*]

vandalism *n.* wilful or malicious destruction or damage to property etc. □ **vandalistic** *adj.*

vandalize *v.tr.* (also **-ise**) destroy or damage wilfully or maliciously.

vandyke ● *n.* **1** each of a series of large points forming a border to lace or cloth etc. **2** a cape or collar etc. with these. ● *adj.* (**Vandyke**) in the style of dress, esp. with pointed borders, common in portraits by Van Dyck. [named after Sir A. *Van Dyck*, Flemish painter, 1599–1641]

Vandyke beard *n.* a neat pointed beard.

Vandyke brown ● *n.* a deep rich brown. ● *adj.* (hyphenated when *attrib.*) of this colour.

vane *n.* **1 a** = WEATHERVANE. **b** an inconstant person or thing. **2** ▶ blade of a screw propeller or a windmill etc. [from Old English *fana* 'banner'] □ **vaned** *adj.*

VANES ON A MODEL POST-MILL

vane

V

vanguard n. **1** the foremost part of an army or fleet advancing or ready to advance. **2** the leaders of a movement or of opinion etc. [from Old French *avan(t)garde*]

vanilla n. **1 a** any tropical climbing orchid of the genus *Vanilla*, esp. *V. planifolia*, with fragrant flowers. **b** (in full **vanilla-pod**) the fruit of these. **2** a substance obtained from the vanilla-pod or synthesized and used to flavour ice cream, chocolate, etc. [from Spanish *vainilla* 'pod']

vanillin n. the fragrant principle of vanilla.

vanish v.intr. **1 a** disappear suddenly. **b** disappear gradually; fade away. **2** cease to exist. [from Latin *evanescere*]

vanishing point n. ▼ the point at which receding parallel lines viewed in perspective appear to meet.

vanishing point — *receding lines*

chessboard viewed in perspective

VANISHING POINT: RECEDING LINES ON A CHESSBOARD EXTENDED TO THE VANISHING POINT

vanity n. (*pl.* **-ies**) **1** conceit and desire for admiration of one's attainments or attractions. **2 a** futility or insubstantiality (*the vanity of human achievement*). **b** an unreal thing. **3** ostentatious display. **4** *N. Amer.* a dressing table. [from Latin *vanitas*]

vanity bag n. (also **vanity case**) a bag or case carried by a woman and containing a small mirror, make-up, etc.

vanity publisher n. a publisher who publishes only at the author's expense. □ **vanity publishing** n.

vanity unit n. a unit consisting of a washbasin set into a flat top with cupboards beneath.

vanquish v.tr. *literary* conquer or overcome. [based on Latin *vincere*] □ **vanquisher** n.

vantage n. (also **vantage point** or **ground**) a place affording a good view. [from Old French *avantage* 'advantage']

vapid /*vap*-id/ adj. insipid; flat, dull (*vapid moralizing*). [from Latin *vapidus*] □ **vapidity** n. **vapidly** adv.

vapor US var. of VAPOUR.

vaporize v.tr. & intr. (also **-ise**) convert or be converted into vapour. □ **vaporization** n.

vaporizer n. (also **-iser**) a device that vaporizes substances, esp. for medicinal inhalation.

vapour (US **vapor**) ● n. **1** moisture or another substance diffused or suspended in air, e.g. mist or smoke. **2** *Physics* a gaseous form of a normally liquid or solid substance. **3** a medicinal agent for inhaling. **4** (in *pl.*) *archaic* a state of depression or melancholy, thought to be caused by exhalations of vapour from the stomach. ● v.intr. **1** rise as vapour. **2** make idle boasts or empty talk. [from Latin *vapor* 'steam, heat'] □ **vaporous** adj. **vapouring** n. **vapoury** adj.

vapour trail n. a trail of condensed water from an aircraft or rocket at high altitude, seen as a white streak against the sky.

var. abbr. variety.

variable ● adj. **1 a** that can be varied or adapted. **b** (of a gear) designed to give varying speeds. **2** apt to vary; not constant. **3** *Math.* (of a quantity) indeterminate; able to assume different numerical values. **4** (of wind or currents) tending to change direction. **5** *Astron.* (of a star) periodically varying in brightness. ● n. **1** a variable thing or quantity. **2** *Math.* a variable quantity. **3** *Naut.* **a** a shifting wind. **b** (in *pl.*) the region between the NE and SE trade winds. [from Latin *variabilis*] □ **variability** n. **variably** adv.

variance n. **1** difference of opinion; dispute, disagreement; lack of harmony (*at variance among*

ourselves; *a theory at variance with all known facts*). **2** *Law* a discrepancy between statements or documents. [from Latin *variantia* 'difference']

variant ● adj. **1** differing in form or details from the main one (*a variant spelling*). **2** having different forms (*forty variant types of pigeon*). **3** variable or changing. ● n. a variant form, spelling, type, reading, etc. [from Old French]

variation n. **1** the act or an instance of varying. **2** departure from a former or normal condition, action, or amount, or from a standard or type (*prices are subject to variation*). **3** the extent of this. **4** a thing that varies from a type. **5** *Mus.* a repetition of a theme in a changed or elaborated form. □ **variational** adj.

varicella n. *Med.* **1** = CHICKENPOX. **2** (in full **varicella zoster**) a herpesvirus causing chickenpox and shingles. [based on VARIOLA]

varicoloured adj. (US **varicolored**) **1** variegated in colour. **2** of various or different colours.

varicose adj. (esp. of the veins of the legs) affected by a condition causing them to become dilated and swollen. [from Latin *varicosus*] □ **varicosity** n.

varied adj. showing variety; diverse.

variegate /*vair*-i-ĕ-gayt/ v.tr. **1** mark with irregular patches of different colours. **2** diversify in appearance, esp. in colour. **3** (as **variegated** adj.) *Bot.* ▶ (of plants) having leaves containing two or more colours. [based on Latin *variegatus* 'made varied'] □ **variegation** n.

varietal /*vă*-ry-ĕ-tăl/ adj. **1** esp. *Bot.* & *Zool.* of, forming, or designating a variety. **2** (of wine) made from a single designated variety of grape. □ **varietally** adv.

variety n. (*pl.* **-ies**) **1** diversity; absence of uniformity; many-sidedness (*not enough variety in our lives*). **2** a quantity or collection of different things (*for a variety of reasons*). **3** a class of things different in some common qualities from the rest of a larger class to which they belong. **4** (foll. by *of*) a different form of a thing, quality, etc. **5** *Biol.* **a** a subspecies. **b** a cultivar. **c** an individual or group usually fertile within the species to which it belongs but differing from the species type in some qualities capable of perpetuation. **6** a mixed sequence of dances, songs, comedy acts, etc. (usu. *attrib.*: *a variety show*). [from Latin *varietas*]

variform adj. having various forms.

variola n. *Med.* smallpox. [medieval Latin, literally 'pustule, pock']

variometer n. **1** a device for varying the inductance in an electric circuit. **2** a device for indicating an aircraft's rate of change of altitude.

variorum ● adj. **1** (of an edition of a text) having notes by various editors or commentators. **2** (of an edition of an author's works) including variant readings. ● n. a variorum edition. [Latin, from *editio cum notis variorum* 'edition with notes by various (commentators)']

various adj. **1** different, diverse (*too various to form a group*). **2** more than one, several (*for various reasons*). [from Latin *varius* 'changing, diverse'] □ **variously** adv. **variousness** n.

■ **Usage** *Various* (unlike *several*) cannot be used with *of* as (wrongly) in *Various of our friends arrived late.*

varlet n. *archaic* or *joc.* **1** a menial or rascal. **2** *hist.* a knight's attendant. [from Old French]

varmint n. *N. Amer.* or *dial.* a mischievous or discreditable person or animal. [variant of *varmin* 'vermin']

varnish ● n. **1** a resinous solution used to give a hard shiny transparent coating to wood, metal, paintings, etc. **2** any other preparation for a similar purpose (*nail varnish*). **3** artificial or natural glossiness. ● v.tr. **1** apply varnish to. **2** gloss over (a fact).

[from medieval Latin *veronix* 'fragrant resin'] □ **varnisher** n.

varsity n. (*pl.* **-ies**) **1** *Brit. colloq.* (esp. with reference to sports) university. **2** *N. Amer.* a university etc. first team in a sport.

vary v. (**-ies**, **-ied**) **1** tr. make different; modify, diversify (*seldom varies the routine; the style is not sufficiently varied*). **2** intr. **a** undergo change; become or be different (*the temperature varies from 30° to 70°*). **b** be of different kinds (*his mood varies*). **3** intr. (foll. by *as*) be in proportion to. [from Latin *variare*] □ **varyingly** adv.

vas n. (*pl.* **vasa**) *Anat.* a vessel or duct. [Latin, literally 'vessel']

vascular adj. of, made up of, or containing vessels for conveying blood or sap etc. (*vascular functions; vascular tissue*). [based on Latin *vasculum* 'little vessel'] □ **vascularity** n.

vascularize v.tr. (also **-ise**) *Med.* & *Anat.* (usu. in *passive*) make vascular, develop vessels in. □ **vascularization** n.

vas deferens /*def*-er-enz/ n. (*pl.* **vasa deferentia** /*def*-er-**ren**-shiă/) *Anat.* the sperm duct from the testicle to the urethra. ▷ REPRODUCTIVE ORGANS. [Latin, literally 'vessel carrying away']

vase n. a vessel used as an ornament or container, esp. for flowers. [from Latin *vas* 'vessel']

vasectomy n. (*pl.* **-ies**) the cutting and sealing of part of each vas deferens, esp. as a means of sterilization. □ **vasectomize** v.tr. (also **-ise**).

Vaseline ● n. *propr.* a type of petroleum jelly used as an ointment, lubricant, etc. ● v.tr. (**vaseline**) treat with Vaseline. [formed irregularly from German *Wasser* 'water' + Greek *elaion* 'oil']

vaso- comb. form a vessel, esp. a blood vessel (*vasoconstrictive*). [from Latin *vas*]

vasoactive adj. = VASOMOTOR.

vasoconstriction n. ▼ the constriction of blood vessels. □ **vasoconstrictive** adj. **vasoconstrictor** n.

vasodilation n. (also **vasodilatation**) ▼ the dilatation of blood vessels. □ **vasodilator** n. **vasodilatory** adj.

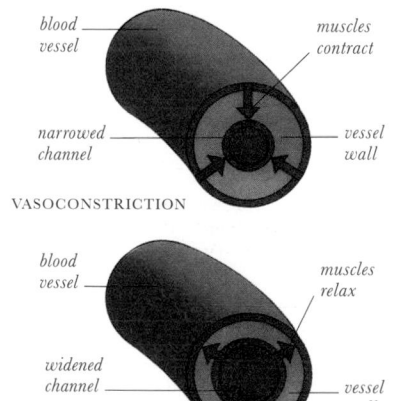

VARIEGATED IVY (*Hedera helix* 'Goldchild')

variegated leaf

VASOCONSTRICTION AND VASODILATION

When the vasomotor centre in the human brain is activated, signals are sent via the autonomic nervous system to muscle fibres in the walls of blood vessels. These signals cause the muscle fibres to contract (vasoconstriction) or relax (vasodilation).

blood vessel — *muscles contract*

narrowed channel — *vessel wall*

VASOCONSTRICTION

blood vessel — *muscles relax*

widened channel — *vessel wall*

VASODILATION

V

VATICAN

The Vatican is the official residence of the Pope and is located within Vatican City, the seat of the central government of the Roman Catholic Church. The first papal residence on the site was built in 1198, but it was not until the 14th century that it became the Pope's principal residence. The palace buildings, few of which are earlier than the 15th century, are now museums that house one of the most important art collections in the world. They also include the Sistine Chapel and the Vatican library.

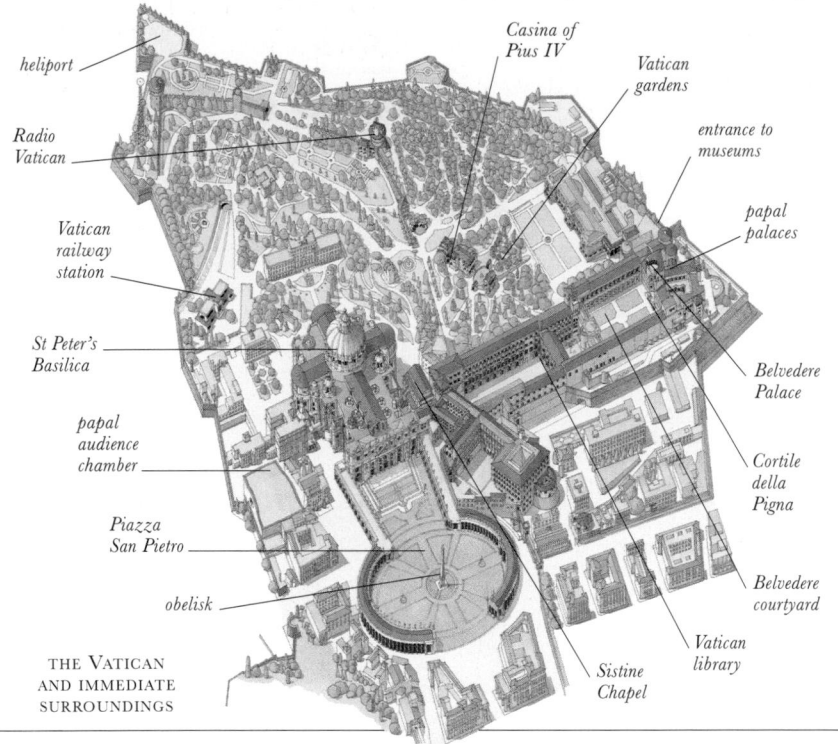

THE VATICAN
AND IMMEDIATE
SURROUNDINGS

heliport

Radio
Vatican

Vatican
railway
station

St Peter's
Basilica

papal
audience
chamber

Piazza
San Pietro

obelisk

Casina of
Pius IV

Vatican
gardens

entrance to
museums

papal
palaces

Belvedere
Palace

Cortile
della
Pigna

Belvedere
courtyard

Vatican
library

Sistine
Chapel

vasomotor *adj.* causing constriction or dilatation of blood vessels.

vassal *n. hist.* a holder of land by feudal tenure on conditions of homage and allegiance. [from medieval Latin *vassallus* 'retainer'] □ **vassalage** *n.*

vast *adj.* immense, huge (*a vast expanse of water*; *a vast crowd*). [from Latin *vastus* 'void, immense'] □ **vastly** *adv.* **vastness** *n.*

VAT *abbr.* (in the UK) value added tax.

vat *n.* ▼ a large tank or other vessel, esp. for holding liquids or something in liquid in the process of brewing, tanning, dyeing, etc. [Middle English, southern & western variant of obsolete *fat*]

metal body

stirring
device

malt and
water

VAT: CUTAWAY VIEW OF
A WHISKY-MAKING VAT

vatic *adj. formal* prophetic or inspired. [based on Latin *vates* 'prophet']

Vatican *n.* **1** ▲ the palace and official residence of the Pope in Rome. **2** papal government. [from Latin *Vaticanus*, name of a hill in Rome]

Vatican City *n.* an independent Papal State in Rome, instituted in 1929.

Vatican Council *n.* an ecumenical council of the Roman Catholic Church, esp. that held in 1869–70 or that held in 1962–5.

vaticinate /vă-**tis**-i-nayt/ *v.tr. & intr. formal* prophesy. [based on Latin *vaticinatus* 'prophesied'] □ **vaticinal** *adj.* **vaticination** *n.*

VATman *n.* (*pl.* **-men**) *Brit. colloq.* a customs and excise officer who administers VAT.

vaudeville *n.* **1** esp. *US* variety entertainment. **2** a stage play on a trivial theme with interspersed songs. **3** a satirical or topical song with a refrain. [name reputedly given to songs by O. Basselin, 15th-century Norman poet born at *Vau de Vire*] □ **vaudevillian** *adj. & n.*

Vaudois /voh-**dwah**/ ● *n.* (*pl.* same) a native of Vaud in W. Switzerland. ● *adj.* of or relating to Vaud. [French]

vault ● *n.* **1 a** ▼ an arched roof. **b** a continuous arch. **c** a set or series of arches whose joints radiate from a central point or line. **2** a vaultlike covering (*the vault of heaven*). **3** an enclosed space, esp. an underground chamber: **a** as a place of storage (*bank vaults*). **b** as a place of interment beneath a church or in a cemetery etc. (*family vault*). **4** an act of vaulting. **5** *Anat.* the arched roof of a cavity. ● *v.* **1** *intr.* leap or spring, esp. while resting on one or both hands or with the help of a pole. **2** *tr.* spring over in this way. **3** *tr.* (esp. as **vaulted**) **a** make in the form of a vault. **b** provide with a vault or vaults. [from Old French *vaute*] □ **vaulter** *n.*

vaulting *n.* **1** arched work in a vaulted roof or ceiling. **2** a gymnastic or athletic exercise in which participants vault over obstacles.

vaulting horse *n.* ▼ a padded wooden block to be vaulted over by gymnasts.

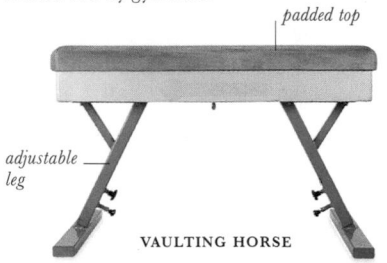

padded top

adjustable
leg

VAULTING HORSE

vaunt *v. literary* **1** *intr.* boast. **2** *tr.* boast of; extol boastfully. [based on Latin *vanus* 'vain']

V-chip *n.* a microchip fitted to television sets, allowing the reception of programmes considered unsuitable for children to be blocked. [initial letter of *violence*]

VCR *abbr.* video cassette recorder.

VD *abbr.* venereal disease.

VDU *abbr.* visual display unit.

VE *abbr.* Victory in Europe (in 1945).

've *abbr. colloq.* (usu. after pronouns) have (*I've*; *they've*).

veal *n.* a calf's flesh as food. [from Latin *vitellus* 'little calf']

veal crate *n.* a partitioned area in which a calf is reared for slaughter, having little light and space with the purpose of ensuring the whiteness of the meat.

vector *n.* **1** *Math. & Physics* a quantity having direction as well as magnitude. **2** a course to be taken by an aircraft. [Latin, literally 'carrier'] □ **vectorial** *adj.* **vectorize** *v.tr.* (also **-ise**) (in sense 1 of *n.*). **vectorization** *n.*

Veda /**vay**-dă/ *n.* (in *sing.* or *pl.*) the most ancient Hindu scriptures. [Sanskrit, literally '(sacred) knowledge']

Vedanta /vi-**dahn**-tă/ *n.* **1** the Upanishads. **2** the Hindu philosophy based on these, esp. in its monistic form. [Sanskrit] □ **Vedantic** *adj.* **Vedantist** *n.*

VAULT

Usually composed of stone, concrete, or brick, vaults are heavy structures that exert downward and outward pressure on to their supports. The simplest form is the barrel vault. Two intersecting barrel vaults form a groin vault. If ribs are added along the groins, a ribbed vault is made. Adding decorative fan patterns creates a fan vault.

TYPES OF VAULT

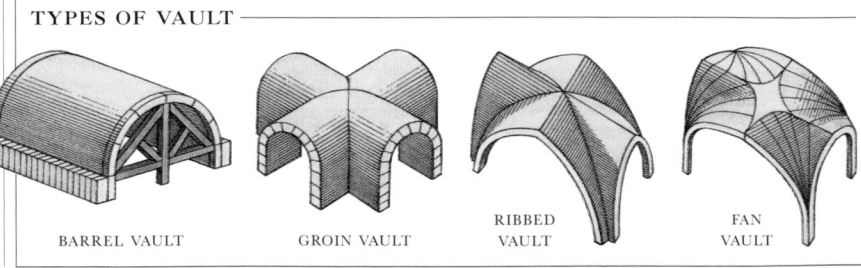

BARREL VAULT

GROIN VAULT

RIBBED
VAULT

FAN
VAULT

V

VEGETABLE

Any edible part of a plant can potentially be used as a vegetable. Derived from wild plants, many of the vegetables we use for food today have been in cultivation since prehistory. This long and extensive cultivation has led to vast diversity (there are over 1,000 varieties of potato alone), but vegetables are generally grouped into leaf, fruiting, flowering, podded, stem, bulb, and root types. Despite their high water content (up to 80 per cent), vegetables are a valuable source of protein, starch, vitamins, and minerals.

LEAF VEGETABLES

CURLY ENDIVE
(*Cichorium endivia*)

SPINACH
(*Spinacia oleracea*)

LETTUCE
(*Lactuca sativa*)

CHARD
(*Beta vulgaris*)

CABBAGE
(*Brassica oleracea*)

FRUITING AND FLOWERING VEGETABLES

CAULIFLOWER
(*Brassica oleracea*)

ARTICHOKE
(*Cynara scolymus*)

SQUASH
(*Caryoka nuciferum*)

MARROW
(*Cucurbita pepo*)

AUBERGINE
(*Solanum melongena*)

PODDED VEGETABLES

MANGETOUT
(*Pisum sativum*)

PEA
(*Pisum sativum*)

GREEN BEAN
(*Phaseolus vulgaris*)

RUNNER BEAN
(*Phaseolus coccineus*)

BLACK-EYED PEA
(*Vigna unguiculata*)

STEM, BULB, AND ROOT VEGETABLES

ASPARAGUS
(*Asparagus officinalis*)

POTATO
(*Solanum tuberosum*)

RADISH
(*Raphanus sativus*)

LEEK
(*Allium porrum*)

CARROT
(*Daucus carota*)

VE day *n.* 8 May, the day marking Victory in Europe in 1945.

Vedic /**vay**-dik/ *adj.* of or relating to the Veda or Vedas. [from French *védique*]

vee *n.* **1** the letter V. **2** a thing shaped like a V. [name of the letter]

veep *n.* esp. *US colloq.* a vice-president. [from the initials *VP*]

veer *v.intr.* **1** change direction, esp. (of the wind) clockwise. **2** change in course, opinion, etc. [French *virer*]

veg /vej/ *n.* (*pl.* same) *Brit. colloq.* a vegetable or vegetables.

vegan /**vee**-găn/ ● *n.* a person who does not eat or use animal products. ● *adj.* using or containing no animal products.

vegetable ● *n.* **1** *Bot.* ▲ any of various plants, esp. a herbaceous plant used for food, e.g. a cabbage, potato, or bean. **2** *colloq. offens.* a person who is incapable of normal intellectual activity, esp. through brain injury etc. ● *adj.* **1** of, derived from, relating to, or comprising plants or plant life. **2** of or relating to vegetables as food. [originally in sense 'living and growing as a plant': from Old French, literally 'animating']

vegetable marrow see MARROW 1.

vegetable oil *n.* an oil derived from plants, e.g. rapeseed oil, olive oil, sunflower oil.

vegetable spaghetti *n. Brit.* a variety of marrow with flesh resembling spaghetti.

vegetal *adj.* **1** of or having the nature of plants (*vegetal growth*). **2** vegetative. [based on Latin *vegetare* 'to animate']

vegetarian ● *n.* a person who abstains from eating meat, and sometimes also fish, eggs, and dairy products. ● *adj.* excluding animal food, esp. meat (*a vegetarian diet*). □ **vegetarianism** *n.*

vegetate *v.intr.* **1** live an uneventful or monotonous life. **2** grow as plants do. [based on Latin *vegetatus* 'animated']

vegetation *n.* **1** plants collectively; plant life. **2** the process of vegetating. □ **vegetational** *adj.*

vegetative *adj.* **1** concerned with growth and development as distinct from sexual reproduction. **2** of or relating to vegetation or plant life. **3** *Med.* alive but without apparent brain activity or responsiveness. □ **vegetatively** *adv.*

veggie /**vej**-i/ *n. & adj.* (also **vegie**) *colloq.* **1** (a) vegetarian. **2** esp. *N. Amer.* (a) vegetable.

vehement *adj.* showing or caused by strong feeling; forceful, ardent (*a vehement protest; vehement desire*). [from Latin *vehemens -entis*] □ **vehemence** *n.* **vehemently** *adv.*

vehicle *n.* **1** any conveyance for transporting people, goods, etc., esp. on land. **2** a medium for thought, feeling, or action (*the stage is the best vehicle for their talents*). **3** a liquid etc. as a medium for suspending pigments, drugs, etc. [from Latin *vehiculum*] □ **vehicular** *adj.*

veil ● *n.* **1** ► a piece of usu. more or less transparent fabric attached to a woman's hat etc., esp. to conceal the face or protect against the sun, dust, etc. **2** a piece of linen etc. as part of a nun's headdress, resting on the head and shoulders. **3** a curtain, esp. that separating the sanctuary in the Jewish Temple. **4** a disguise; a pretext; a thing that conceals (*under the veil of friendship; a veil of mist*). **5** *Photog.* slight fogging. ● *v.tr.* **1** cover with a veil. **2** (esp. as **veiled** *adj.*) partly conceal (*veiled threats*) □ **beyond the veil** in the unknown state of life after death. **take the veil** become a nun. [from Latin *vela* 'curtains, veils, sails']

VEIL:
19TH-CENTURY
WEDDING VEIL

vein ● *n.* **1 a** ▼ any of the tubes carrying blood to the heart. ▷ CARDIOVASCULAR. **b** (in general use) any blood vessel (*has royal blood in his veins*). **2** a nervure of an insect's wing. **3** a rib in the framework of a leaf. **4** a streak of a different colour in wood, marble, cheese, etc. ▷ VEINING. **5** a fissure in rock filled with ore or other deposited material. **6** a source of a particular characteristic (*a rich vein of humour*). **7** a distinctive character or tendency; a cast of mind or disposition; a mood (*spoke in a sarcastic vein*). ● *v.tr.* fill or cover with or as with veins. [from Latin *vena*] □ **veinlet** *n.* **veiny** *adj.* (**veinier**, **veiniest**).

V

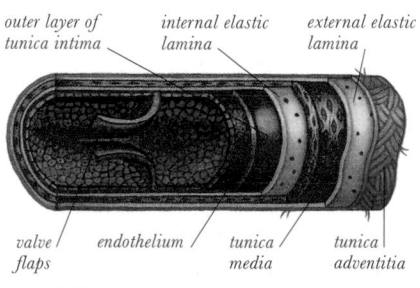

outer layer of
tunica intima

internal elastic
lamina

external elastic
lamina

valve
flaps

endothelium

tunica
media

tunica
adventitia

VEIN: SECTION REVEALING THE LAYERS
OF A HUMAN VEIN

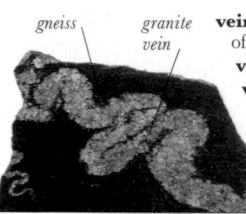

gneiss *granite vein*

VEINING IN
METAMORPHIC ROCK

veining *n.* ◄ a pattern of streaks or veins.

vela *pl.* of VELUM.

velar *adj.* **1** of a veil or velum. **2** *Phonet.* (of a sound) pronounced with the back of the tongue near the soft palate. [from Latin *velaris*]

Velcro *n. propr.* a fastener consisting of two strips of fabric which adhere when pressed together. [from French *velours croché* 'hooked velvet'] □ **Velcroed** *adj.*

veld *n.* (also **veldt**) *S.Afr.* open country; grassland. [Afrikaans, literally 'field']

vellum *n.* **1 a** fine parchment originally from the skin of a calf. **b** a manuscript written on this. **2** smooth writing paper imitating vellum. [from Old French *velin*, related to VEAL]

velocipede *n.* **1** *hist.* an early form of bicycle propelled by pressure from the rider's feet on the ground. **2** *US* a child's tricycle. [from French *vélocipède*]

velociraptor *n.* ▼ a small bipedal carnivorous dinosaur of the genus *Velociraptor*, with an enlarged curved claw on each hind foot. [based on Latin *velox -ocis* 'swift']

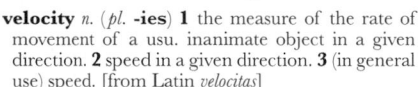

VELOCIRAPTOR
(*Velociraptor* species)

curved claw

velocity *n.* (*pl.* **-ies**) **1** the measure of the rate of movement of a usu. inanimate object in a given direction. **2** speed in a given direction. **3** (in general use) speed. [from Latin *velocitas*]

velour /vě-**loor**/ *n.* (also **velours**) a plush woven fabric or felt resembling velvet. [from Latin *villosus* 'hairy']

velouté /vě-loo-**tay**/ *n.* a sauce made from a roux of butter and flour with white stock. [French, literally 'velvety']

velum /**vee**-lŭm/ *n.* (*pl.* **vela**) a membrane, membranous covering, or flap. [Latin, literally 'sail, curtain, covering, veil']

velvet ● *n.* **1** a closely woven fabric of silk, cotton, etc., with a thick short pile on one side. **2** the furry skin on a deer's growing antler. ● *adj.* of, like, or soft as velvet. [from Latin *villus* 'tuft, down'] □ **velvety** *adj.*

velveteen *n.* a cotton fabric with a pile like velvet.

Ven. *abbr.* Venerable (as the title of an archdeacon).

vena cava /vee-nă **kay**-vă/ *n.* (*pl.* **venae cavae** /vee-nee **kay**-vee/) each of usu. two veins carrying deoxygenated blood into the heart. ▷ CARDIOVASCULAR, HEART. [Latin, literally 'hollow vein']

venal *adj.* **1** able to be bribed or corrupted. **2** characteristic of a venal person. [based on Latin *venum* 'thing for sale'] □ **venality** *n.*

■ **Usage** *Venal* is sometimes confused with *venial*, which means 'pardonable'.

vend *v.tr.* **1** offer (small wares) for sale. **2** *Law* sell. [from Latin *vendere* 'to sell']

vendetta *n.* **1 a** a blood feud in which the family of a murdered person seeks vengeance on the murderer or the murderer's family. **b** this practice as prevalent in Corsica and Sicily. **2** a prolonged bitter quarrel. [Italian]

vendeuse /von-**derz**/ *n.* a saleswoman, esp. in a fashionable dress shop. [French]

vending machine *n.* a machine that dispenses small articles for sale when a coin or token is inserted.

vendor *n.* **1** *Law* the seller in a sale. **2** = VENDING MACHINE.

veneer ● *n.* **1** a thin covering of fine wood or other surface material applied to a coarser wood. **2** a deceptive outward appearance of a good quality etc. ● *v.tr.* apply a veneer to. [earlier *fineer*, from Old French *fournir* 'to furnish']

venerable *adj.* **1** entitled to veneration on account of character, age, associations, etc. (*a venerable priest*; *venerable relics*). **2** as the title of an archdeacon in the Anglican Church. **3** *RC Ch.* as the title of a deceased person who has attained a certain degree of sanctity but has not been fully beatified or canonized. [from Old French] □ **venerability** *n.* **venerably** *adv.*

venerate *v.tr.* **1** regard with deep respect. **2** revere on account of sanctity etc. [based on Latin *veneratus* 'adored, revered'] □ **veneration** *n.*

venereal *adj.* **1** of or relating to sexual desire or intercourse. **2** relating to venereal disease. [based on Latin *venus veneris* 'sexual love']

venereal disease *n.* any of various diseases contracted chiefly by sexual intercourse with a person already infected; a sexually transmitted disease.

venereology *n.* the scientific study of venereal diseases. □ **venereologist** *n.*

Venetian ● *n.* **1** a native or citizen of Venice in NE Italy. **2** the Italian dialect of Venice. ● *adj.* of or relating to Venice. [from Old French *Vénicien*]

venetian blind *n.* a window blind of adjustable horizontal slats.

vengeance *n.* punishment inflicted or retribution exacted for wrong to oneself or to a person etc. whose cause one supports. □ **with a vengeance** in a higher degree than was expected or desired; in the fullest sense (*punctuality with a vengeance*). [from Old French]

■ **Usage** *Vengeance* incorporates the idea of justifiable retribution, as opposed to *revenge* which often implies that the main aim of the retribution is the satisfaction of the injured party's resentment.

vengeful *adj.* vindictive; seeking vengeance. □ **vengefully** *adv.* **vengefulness** *n.*

venial /**vee**-niăl/ *adj.* (of a sin or fault) pardonable; not mortal. [from Late Latin *venialis*] □ **venially** *adv.*

■ **Usage** *Venial* is sometimes confused with *venal*, which means 'corrupt'.

venison *n.* a deer's flesh as food. [based on Latin *venatio -onis* 'hunting']

Venn diagram *n.* ▼ a diagram consisting of a group of intersecting (usually circular) areas which represent logical sets, the areas of overlap representing subsets whose members are common to the sets concerned. [named after J. *Venn*, English logician, 1834–1923]

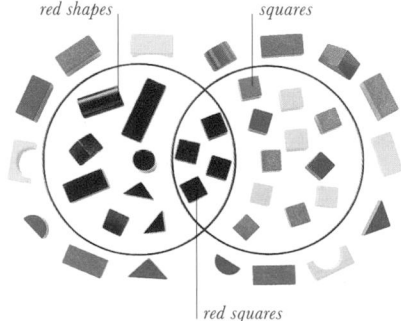

red shapes   *squares*

red squares

VENN DIAGRAM SHOWING LOGICAL SETS
OF COLOURED SHAPES

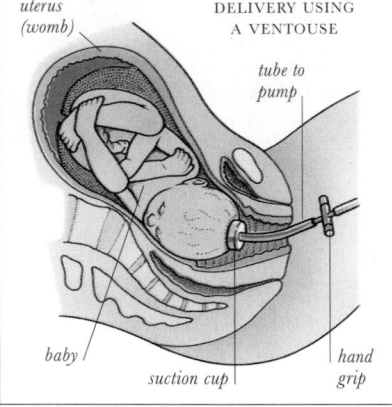

uterus (womb)

DELIVERY USING
A VENTOUSE

tube to pump

baby   *suction cup*   *hand grip*

venom *n.* **1** a poisonous fluid secreted by snakes, scorpions, etc., usu. transmitted by a bite or sting. ▷ FANG. **2** malignity; virulence of feeling, language, or conduct. [from Latin *venenum* 'poison']

venomous *adj.* **1 a** containing, secreting, or injecting venom. **b** (of a snake etc.) inflicting poisonous wounds by this means. **2** (of a person etc.) virulent, spiteful, malignant. □ **venomously** *adv.* **venomousness** *n.*

venose *adj.* having many or very marked veins. [from Latin *venosus*, from *vena* 'vein']

venous /**vee**-nŭs/ *adj.* of, full of, or contained in veins. [based on Latin *vena* 'vein']

vent[1] ● *n.* **1** (also **vent-hole**) an opening allowing motion of air etc. out of or into a confined space. ▷ VOLCANO. **2** an outlet; free passage or play (*gave vent to their indignation*). **3** the anus esp. of a lower animal, serving for both excretion and reproduction. ● *v.tr.* **1 a** make a vent in (a cask etc.). **b** provide (a machine) with a vent. **2** give free expression to (*vented my anger on the cat*). □ **vent one's spleen on** scold or ill-treat without cause. [based on Latin *ventus* 'wind']

vent[2] *n.* a slit in a garment, esp. in the lower edge of the back of a coat. [from Old French *fente* 'slit']

ventilate *v.tr.* **1** cause air to circulate freely in (a room etc.). **2** submit (a question, grievance, etc.) to public consideration and discussion. **3** *Med.* **a** oxygenate (the blood). **b** admit or force air into (the lungs). [based on Latin *ventilatus* 'blown, winnowed'] □ **ventilation** *n.*

ventilator *n.* **1** an appliance or aperture for ventilating a room etc. **2** *Med.* = RESPIRATOR 2.

ventouse *n.* ▲ a vacuum extractor for use in childbirth. [French]

ventral *adj.* **1** *Anat.* & *Zool.* of or on the abdomen (cf. DORSAL 1). **2** *Bot.* of the front or lower surface. [based on Latin *venter ventr-* 'belly'] □ **ventrally** *adv.*

ventral fin *n.* ▼ either of the ventrally placed fins on a fish.

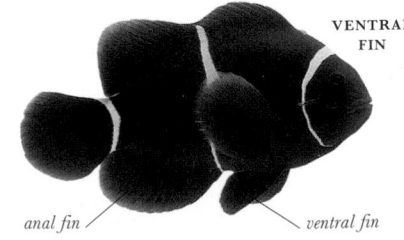

VENTRAL FIN

anal fin   *ventral fin*

V

VENUS

Venus is a rocky planet, slightly smaller than Earth, and probably with a similar internal structure of a partly molten metal core surrounded by a rocky mantle and crust. The planet's cloudy atmosphere reflects sunlight strongly, making Venus the brightest object in the sky after the Sun and Moon. The atmosphere is composed mainly of carbon dioxide, which traps heat and creates a maximum surface temperature of 480 °C (896 °F), making Venus the hottest planet in our solar system.

Akna Montes · Vesta Rupes · Cleopatra Patera · Maxwell Montes · Sif Mons · Dekla Tessera · Nefertiti Corona · Tellus Tessera · Pavlova · Hestia Rupes · semi-solid iron core · Gula Mons · Hathor Mons · Sappho Patera · Eve · rocky mantle · silicate rock crust

VENUS, WITH INTERNAL STRUCTURE REVEALED

Sun · Earth · Venus · SOLAR SYSTEM

ventricle *n. Anat.* **1** a cavity in the body. **2** a hollow part of an organ, esp in the brain or heart. ▷ BRAIN, HEART [from Latin *ventriculus* 'little belly'] □ **ventricular** *adj.*

ventriloquism *n.* the skill of speaking or uttering sounds so that they seem to come from a source other than the speaker. [based on Latin *ventriloquus* 'ventriloquist'] □ **ventriloquial** *adj.* **ventriloquist** *n.* **ventriloquize** *v.intr.* (also **-ise**).

ventriloquy *n.* = VENTRILOQUISM.

venture ● *n.* **1 a** an undertaking of a risk. **b** a risky enterprise. **2** a commercial speculation. ● *v.* **1** *intr.* dare; not be afraid (*did not venture to stop them*). **2** *intr.* dare to go. **3** *tr.* dare to put forward (an opinion, suggestion, etc.). **4** *tr.* expose to risk; stake (a bet etc.). **5** *intr.* (foll. by *on, upon*) dare to engage in etc. (*ventured on a longer journey*). [from ADVENTURE]

venture capital *n.* money put up for speculative business investment.

venturesome *adj.* **1** disposed to take risks. **2** risky.

venue *n.* an appointed site or meeting place, esp. for a sports event, meeting, concert, etc. [French, literally 'a coming']

venule /**ven**-yool/ *n. Anat.* a small vein, esp. one collecting blood from the capillaries. ▷ SKIN. [from Latin *venula*]

Venus *n.* (*pl.* **Venuses**) **1** ▲ the planet second from the Sun in the solar system. ▷ SOLAR SYSTEM. **2** *poet.* **a** a beautiful woman. **b** sexual love; amorous influences or desires. [Old English, from Latin *Venus Veneris*, name of the goddess of love] □ **Venusian** *adj. & n.*

Venus flytrap *n.* ▶ a plant, *Dionaea muscipula*, with hinged leaves that close on and digest insects etc. [based on Latin *Venus*, goddess of love]

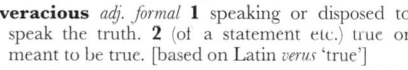
trapped damselfly · marginal teeth

VENUS FLYTRAP
(*Dionaea muscipula*)

veracious *adj. formal* **1** speaking or disposed to speak the truth. **2** (of a statement etc.) true or meant to be true. [based on Latin *verus* 'true']

veracity *n.* **1** truthfulness; honesty. **2** accuracy (of a statement etc.). [from medieval Latin *veracitas*]

veranda *n.* (also **verandah**) **1** a portico or external gallery, usu. with a roof, along the side of a house. **2** *Austral. & NZ* a roof over a pavement in front of a shop. [from Portuguese *varanda* 'railing, balustrade']

veratrine *n.* a poisonous compound obtained from sabadilla etc., and used esp. as a local irritant in the treatment of neuralgia and rheumatism. [via French from Latin *veratrum* 'hellebore']

verb *n. Gram.* a word used to indicate an action, state, or occurrence, and forming the main part of the predicate of a sentence (e.g. *hear*, *be*, *happen*). [from Latin *verbum* 'word, verb']

verbal ● *adj.* **1** of or concerned with words (*made a verbal distinction*). **2** oral, not written (*gave a verbal statement*). **3** *Gram.* of or in the nature of a verb (*verbal inflections*). **4** literal (*a verbal translation*). **5** talkative, articulate. ● *n.* **1** *Gram.* **a** a verbal noun. **b** a word or words functioning as a verb. **2** (usu. in *pl.*) *Brit. slang* a verbal statement, esp. one made to the police. **3** *Brit. slang* an insult; abuse (*gave them a lot of verbals*). [Middle English, related to VERB] □ **verbally** *adv.*

■ **Usage** Some people reject sense 2 of the adjective *verbal* as illogical, and prefer *oral*. However, *verbal* is the usual term in expressions such as *verbal communication*, *verbal contract*, and *verbal evidence*.

verbalism *n.* **1** minute attention to words. **2** merely verbal expression.

verbalize *v.* (also **-ise**) **1** *tr.* express in words. **2** *intr.* be verbose. **3** *tr.* make (a noun etc.) into a verb. □ **verbalization** *n.* **verbalizer** *n.*

verbal noun *n. Gram.* a noun formed as an inflection of a verb and partly sharing its constructions (e.g. *smoking* in *smoking is forbidden*).

verbascum *n.* a plant of the genus *Verbascum*.

verbatim /ver-**bay**-tim/ *adv. & adj.* in exactly the same words; word for word (*copied it verbatim; a verbatim report*). [medieval Latin]

verbena *n.* ▶ any plant of the genus *Verbena*, bearing clusters of fragrant flowers. [Latin, literally 'sacred bough of olive']

VERBENA
(*Verbena × hybrida*
Romance Series)

verbiage *n.* needless accumulation of words. [French]

verbose *adj.* using or expressed in more words than are needed. [from Latin *verbosus*] □ **verbosely** *adv.* **verbosity** *n.*

verboten /vě-**boh**-těn/ *adj.* forbidden, esp. by an authority. [German]

verdant *adj.* **1** (of grass etc.) green, fresh-coloured. **2** (of a field etc.) green with grass and vegetation; lush. [based on Latin *viridis* 'green'] □ **verdancy** *n.* **verdantly** *adv.*

verdict *n.* **1** a decision or finding on an issue submitted in a civil or criminal case or an inquest. **2** a decision; a judgement. [from Old French *voir* 'true' + *dit* 'saying']

verdigris /**ver**-di-gree/ *n.* **1** a green crystallized substance formed on copper by the action of acetic acid. **2** ▶ green rust on copper or brass. [from Old French *vert de Grece* 'green of Greece']

verdure *n.* **1** green vegetation. **2** the greenness of this. [from Old French]

verge[1] ● *n.* **1** an edge or border. **2** an extreme limit beyond which something happens (*on the verge of tears*). **3** *Brit.* a grass edging of a road, flower bed, etc. **4** *Archit.* an edge of tiles projecting over a gable. ● *v.intr.* (foll. by *on*) border on; approach closely (*verging on the ridiculous*). [from Latin *virga* 'rod']

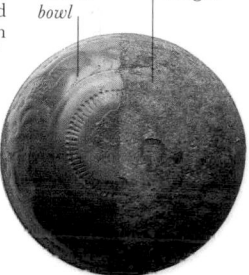
restored bowl · verdigris

VERDIGRIS ON A HALF-RESTORED COPPER BOWL

verge[2] *v.intr.* incline downwards or in a specified direction (*the now verging sun; verge to a close*). [from Latin *vergere* 'to bend, incline']

verger *n.* **1** an official in a church who acts as caretaker and attendant. **2** an officer who bears the staff before a bishop etc. [related to VERGE[1]] □ **vergership** *n.*

verification *n.* **1** the process or an instance of establishing the truth or validity of something. **2** *Philos.* the establishment of the validity of a proposition empirically. **3** the process of verifying procedures laid down in weapons agreements.

verify *v.tr.* (**-ies**, **-ied**) establish the truth or correctness of by examination or demonstration (*must verify the statement; verified my figures*). [from medieval Latin *verificare*] □ **verifiable** *adj.* **verifier** *n.*

verily *adv. archaic* really, truly. [Middle English]

verisimilitude *n.* **1** the appearance of being true or real. **2** a statement etc. that seems true. [based on Latin *verisimilis* 'probable'] □ **verisimilar** *adj.*

verismo *n.* (esp. with reference to opera) realism. [Italian]

veritable *adj.* real; rightly so called (*a veritable feast*). [from Old French] □ **veritably** *adv.*

verity *n.* (*pl.* **-ies**) **1** a true statement, esp. one of fundamental import. **2** truth. **3** a really existent thing. [from Latin *veritas*]

vermi- *comb. form* worm. [from Latin *vermis* 'worm']

vermicelli /ver-mi-**chel**-i/ *n.* **1** pasta made in long slender threads. **2** *Brit.* shreds of chocolate used as cake decoration etc. [Italian, literally 'little worms']

vermicide *n.* a substance that kills worms.

vermicular *adj.* **1** like a worm in form or movement. **2** *Med.* of or caused by intestinal worms. **3** marked with close wavy lines. [based on Latin *vermiculus* 'little worm']

vermiculite *n.* **1** *Mineral.* ◀ a hydrated silicate resulting from the alteration of mica etc., esp. an aluminosilicate of magnesium. **2** this material in flakes used as a medium for growing plants, for insulation, etc.

vermiform *adj.* worm-shaped.

vermiform appendix see APPENDIX 1.

VERMICULITE

vermifuge ● *adj.* that expels intestinal worms. ● *n.* a drug that does this.

vermilion ● *n.* **1** cinnabar. **2 a** ▶ a brilliant red pigment made by grinding this or artificially. **b** the colour of this. ● *adj.* of this colour. [based on Latin *vermiculus* 'little worm']

VERMILION

vermin *n.* (usu. treated as *pl.*) **1** mammals and birds injurious to game, crops, etc., e.g foxes, rodents, and noxious insects. **2** parasitic worms or insects. **3** vile or contemptible persons. [based on Latin *vermis* 'worm'] □ **verminous** *adj.*

vermivorous *adj.* feeding on worms.

vermouth /ver-mŭth/ *n.* a wine flavoured with aromatic herbs. [from German *Wermut* 'wormwood']

vernacular ● *n.* **1** the language or dialect of a particular country (*Latin gave place to the vernacular*). **2** the language of a particular clan or group. **3** homely speech. ● *adj.* **1** (of language) of one's native country; not of foreign origin or of learned formation. **2** (of architecture) concerned with ordinary rather than monumental buildings. [from Latin *vernaculus* 'domestic, native'] □ **vernacularize** *v.tr.* (also **-ise**). **vernacularly** *adv.*

vernal *adj.* of, in, or appropriate to spring (*vernal equinox*; *vernal breezes*). [based on Latin *ver* 'spring']

vernal equinox *n.* = SPRING EQUINOX.

vernal grass *n.* a sweet-scented European grass, *Anthoxanthum odoratum*, grown for hay.

vernalization *n.* (also **-isation**) the cooling of seed before planting, in order to accelerate flowering.

vernation *n.* *Bot.* the arrangement of leaves in a leaf bud.

vernier *n.* ▼ a small movable graduated scale for obtaining fractional parts of subdivisions on a fixed main scale of a barometer, sextant, etc. [from P. *Vernier*, French mathematician, 1580–1637]

V

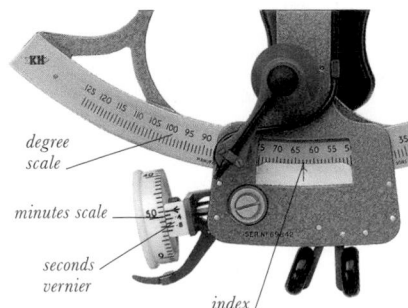

degree scale

minutes scale

seconds vernier

index

VERNIER ON A MODERN SEXTANT

VERTEBRA

There are three major types of vertebra in the human spine: lumbar, thoracic, and cervical. Lumbar vertebrae support a major part of the body's weight and so are comparatively large and strong. Thoracic vertebrae anchor the ribs. Cervical vertebrae support the head and neck.

TYPES OF VERTEBRA

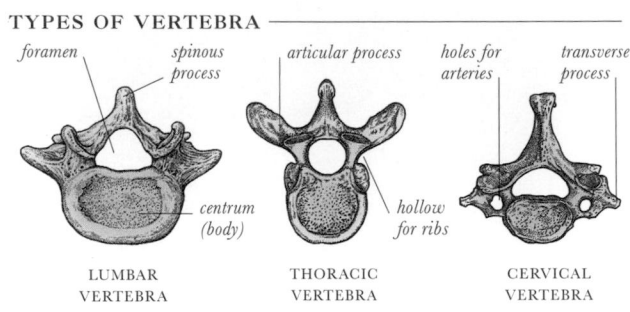

foramen   *spinous process*   *articular process*   *holes for arteries*   *transverse process*

centrum (body)   *hollow for ribs*

LUMBAR VERTEBRA   THORACIC VERTEBRA   CERVICAL VERTEBRA

SPINAL COLUMN

cervical vertebrae

thoracic vertebrae

lumbar vertebrae

sacrum

coccyx

---

veronal *n.* a sedative drug, a derivative of barbituric acid. [German, based on *Verona*, a city in Italy]

veronica *n.* **1** ▶ any plant of the genus *Veronica* or *Hebe*. **2** a cloth supposedly impressed with an image of Christ's face. **3** the movement of a matador's cape away from a charging bull. [medieval Latin, from the name *Veronica*; sense 2: from the association with St Veronica]

VERONICA (*Veronica longifolia*)

verruca /vĕ-**roo**-kă/ *n.* (*pl.* **verrucae** /-kee/ or **verrucas**) a wart or similar growth, esp. a contagious wart on the sole of the foot. [Latin] □ **verrucose** *adj.*

versatile *adj.* **1** turning easily or readily from one subject or occupation to another; capable of dealing with many subjects (*a versatile mind*). **2** having many uses. [French] □ **versatility** *n.*

verse *n.* **1 a** a metrical composition in general (*wrote pages of verse*) (opp. PROSE *n.* 1). **b** a particular type of this (*English verse*). **2 a** a metrical line in accordance with the rules of prosody. **b** a group of a definite number of such lines. **c** a stanza of a poem or song. **3** each of the short numbered divisions of a chapter in the Bible or other scripture. [from Latin *versus* 'a turn of the plough, a line of writing']

versed *adj.* (foll. by *in*) experienced or skilled in; knowledgeable about. [from Latin *versatus* 'engaged in']

versicle *n.* each of the short sentences in a liturgy said or sung by a priest etc. and alternating with responses. [from Latin *versiculus*]

versify *v.* (**-ies**, **-ied**) **1** *tr.* turn into or express in verse. **2** *intr.* compose verses. [from Latin *versificare*] □ **versification** *n.* **versifier** *n.*

version *n.* **1** an account of a matter from a particular point of view (*told them my version of the incident*). **2** a book etc. in a particular edition or translation (*Authorized Version*). **3** a form or variant of a thing as performed, adapted, etc. [French]

vers libre /vair **leebr**/ *n.* irregular or unrhymed verse in which the traditional rules of prosody are disregarded. [French, literally 'free verse']

verso *n.* (*pl.* **-os**) **1 a** the left-hand page of an open book. **b** the back of a printed leaf of paper or manuscript. **2** the reverse of a coin. [from Latin *verso (folio)* 'on the turned (leaf)']

---

verst *n.* a Russian measure of length, about 1.1 km (0.66 mile). [from Russian *versta*]

versus *prep.* against (esp. in legal and sports use). [Latin, literally 'towards']

vertebra *n.* (*pl.* **vertebrae** /-bree/) ▲ each segment of the backbone. ▷ SKELETON. [Latin] □ **vertebral** *adj.*

vertebrate ● *n.* ▶ any animal of the subphylum Vertebrata, having a spinal column. ● *adj.* of or relating to the vertebrates. [from Latin *vertebratus* 'jointed']

vertex *n.* (*pl.* **vertices** or **vertexes**) **1** the highest point; the top or apex. **2** *Geom.* **a** ▼ each angular point of a polygon, polyhedron, etc. **b** ▼ a meeting point of two lines that form an angle. **c** ▼ the point at which an axis meets a curve or surface. **3** *Anat.* the crown of the head. [Latin, literally 'whirlpool, crown of a head']

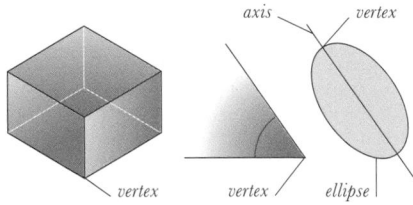

axis   *vertex*

vertex   *vertex*   *ellipse*

VERTEX (2a)   VERTEX (2b)   VERTEX (2c)

vertical ● *adj.* **1** at right angles to a horizontal plane. **2** in a direction from top to bottom of a picture etc. **3** at, or passing through, the zenith. **4** involving all the levels in an organizational hierarchy or stages in the production of a class of goods (*vertical integration*). ● *n.* a vertical line or plane. [French] □ **verticality** *n.* **vertically** *adv.*

vertical take-off *n.* ▼ the take-off of an aircraft directly upwards.

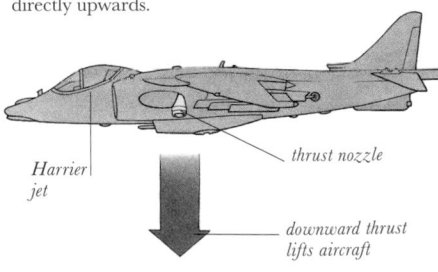

Harrier jet

thrust nozzle

downward thrust lifts aircraft

VERTICAL TAKE-OFF OF A HARRIER JUMP JET

VERTEBRATE

There are five classes of vertebrate: mammals, birds, fish, reptiles, and amphibians. In addition to the main defining feature (a backbone), vertebrates are characterized by an internal skeleton, a brain enclosed in a cranium, a closed circulatory system, and a heart with up to four chambers. Most vertebrates also have two pairs of limbs.

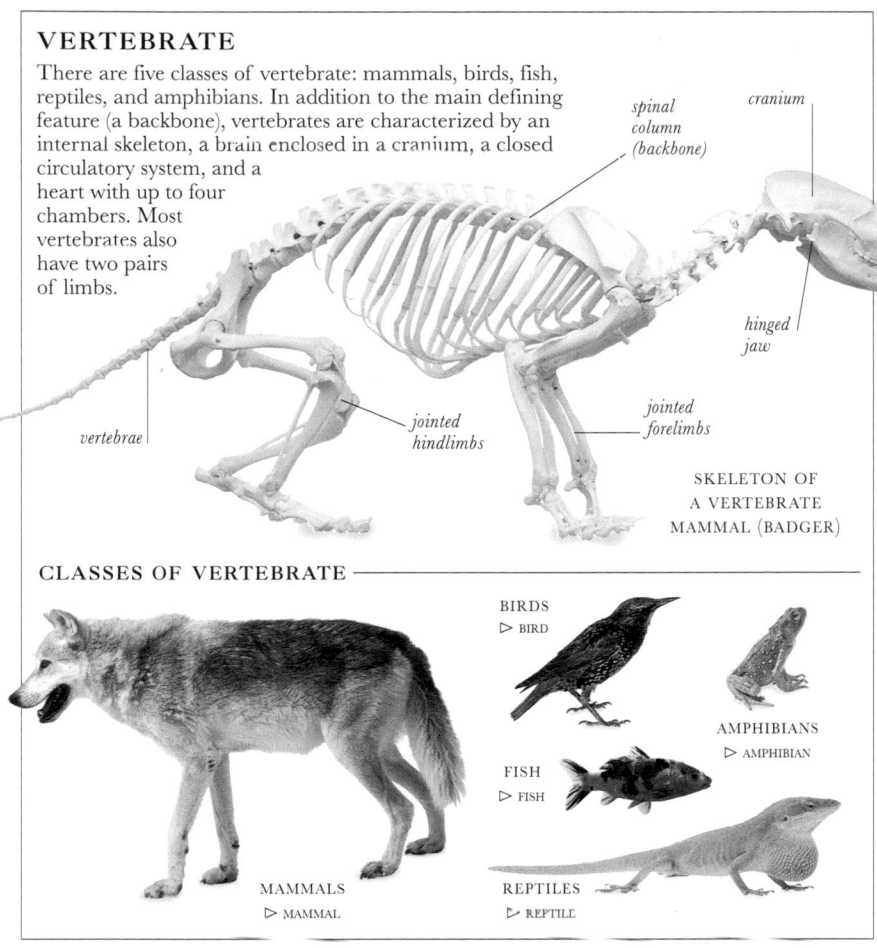

spinal column (backbone) — *cranium* — *hinged jaw* — *jointed forelimbs* — *jointed hindlimbs* — *vertebrae*

SKELETON OF
A VERTEBRATE
MAMMAL (BADGER)

CLASSES OF VERTEBRATE

BIRDS
▷ BIRD

AMPHIBIANS
▷ AMPHIBIAN

FISH
▷ FISH

MAMMALS
▷ MAMMAL

REPTILES
▷ REPTILE

---

vertiginous *adj.* of or causing vertigo. □ **vertiginously** *adv.*

vertigo *n.* a condition with a sensation of whirling and a tendency to lose balance, dizziness, giddiness. [Latin, literally 'whirling']

vervain *n.* any of various herbaceous plants of the genus *Verbena*, esp. *V. officinalis* with small blue, white, or purple flowers. [from Latin *verbena*]

verve *n.* enthusiasm, vigour, spirit. [French, earlier in sense 'a form of expression']

vervet *n.* ◀ a small grey African monkey, *Cercopithecus aethiops*. [French]

very ● *adv.* **1** in a high degree (*did it very easily; had a very bad cough; am very much better*). **2** in the fullest sense (foll. by *own* or superl. adj.: *at the very latest; do your very best; my very own room*). ● *adj.* **1** real, true, actual; truly such (*the very thing we need; those were his very words*). **2** *archaic* real, genuine (*very God*). □ **not very 1** in a low degree. **2** far from being. **very good** (or **well**) a formula of consent or approval. **the very same** see SAME. [based on Latin *verus* 'true']

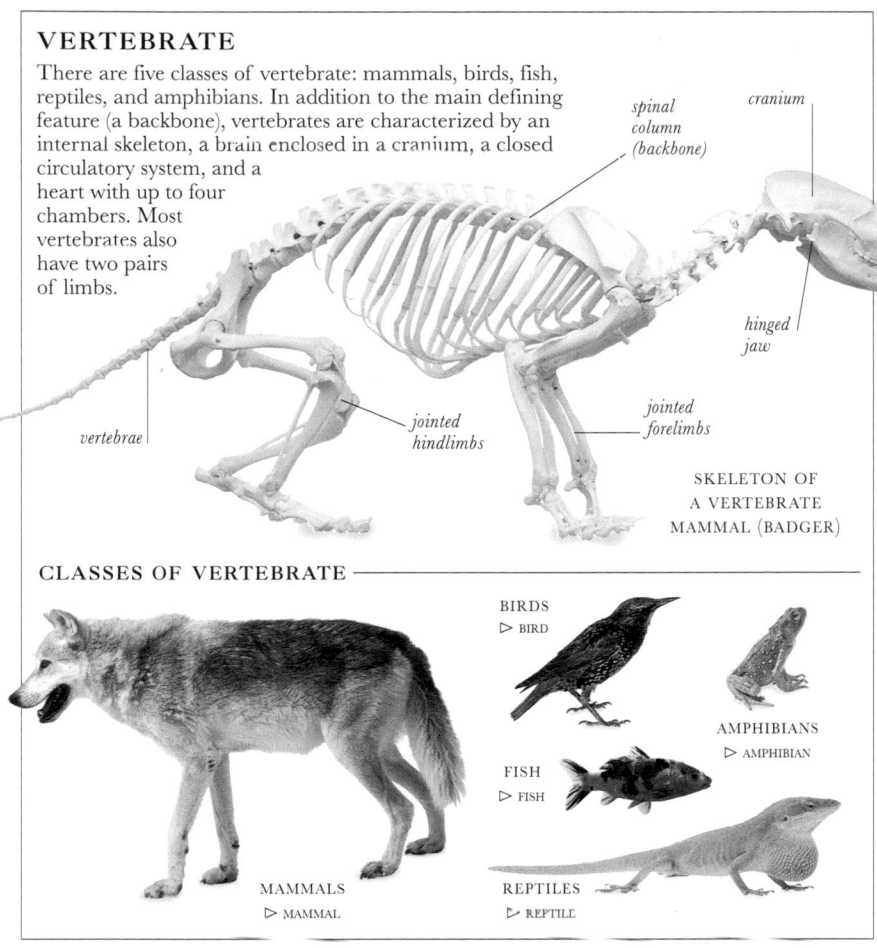

VERVET
(*Cercopithecus aethiops*)

Very light *n.* a flare projected from a pistol for signalling or temporarily illuminating the surroundings. [named after E. W. *Very*, American inventor, 1847–1910]

Very pistol *n.* ◀ a gun for firing a Very light.

Very Reverend *adj.* the title of a dean etc.

chamber — *extractor* — *stirrup* — *hammer* — *stock* — *butt* — *butt lanyard ring* — *trigger guard* — *trigger* — *barrel*

VERY PISTOL:
EARLY 20TH-
CENTURY
VERY PISTOL

vesica /ves-i-kă/ *n.* **1** *Anat.* & *Zool.* a bladder, esp. the urinary bladder. **2** (in full **vesica piscis** /pis-kis/) *Art* a pointed oval used as an aureole in medieval sculpture and painting. [Latin] □ **vesical** *adj.*

vesicle /ves-i-kăl/ *n.* **1** a *Anat.* & *Biol.* a small fluid-filled bladder, sac, or vacuole. **b** *Bot.* an air-filled swelling in a seaweed etc. **2** *Geol.* a small cavity in volcanic rock produced by gas bubbles. **3** *Med.* a blister. [from Latin *vesicula* 'little bladder'] □ **vesicular** *adj.* **vesiculation** *n.*

vesper *n.* **1** *poet.* the planet Venus as the evening star. **2** *poet.* evening. **3** (in *pl.*) **a** the office of the sixth canonical hour of prayer, originally said towards evening. **b** evening prayer. [Latin, literally 'evening (star)']

vespiary *n.* (*pl.* **-ies**) a nest of wasps.

vessel *n.* **1** a hollow receptacle esp. for liquid. **2** a ship or boat, esp. a large one. **3** *Anat.* a duct or canal etc. holding or conveying blood or other fluid; = BLOOD VESSEL. [from Late Latin *vascellum* 'little vessel']

vest ● *n.* **1** *Brit.* an undergarment worn on the upper part of the body. **2** *N. Amer.* & *Austral.* a waistcoat.

● *v.tr.* **1** (esp. in *passive*; foll. by *with*) bestow (powers, authority, etc.) on. **2** (foll. by *in*) confer (property or power) on with an immediate fixed right of immediate or future possession. [from Latin *vestis* 'garment']

vesta *n.* esp. *hist.* a short wooden or wax match. [from *Vesta*, Roman goddess of the hearth and household]

vestal ● *adj.* chaste, pure. ● *n.* **1** a chaste woman. **2** *Rom. Antiq.* a vestal virgin. [from Latin *vestalis*]

vestal virgin *n. Rom. Antiq.* ▶ a virgin consecrated to Vesta and vowed to chastity.

vested interest *n.* **1** *Law* an interest (usu. in land or money held in trust) recognized as belonging to a person. **2** a personal interest in a state of affairs, usu. with an expectation of gain.

vestibule *n.* **1** a an antechamber, hall, or lobby next to the outer door of a building. **b** a porch of a church etc. **2** *US* an enclosed entrance to a railway carriage. **3** *Anat.* a chamber or channel communicating with others. [French] □ **vestibular** *adj.*

vestige *n.* **1** a trace; a sign (*vestiges of an earlier civilization; found no vestige of their presence*). **2** a slight amount; a particle (*without a vestige of clothing; showed not a vestige of decency*). [from Latin *vestigium* 'footprint']

vestigial /ves-tij-iăl/ *adj.* **1** being a vestige or trace. **2** *Biol.* (of an organ etc.) degenerate or atrophied, having become functionless in the course of evolution (*a vestigial wing*). □ **vestigially** *adv.*

vestment *n.* **1** ▼ any of the official robes of clergy, choristers, etc., worn during divine service, esp. a chasuble. **2** a garment, esp. an official or state robe. [from Latin *vestimentum*]

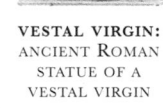

VESTAL VIRGIN:
ANCIENT ROMAN
STATUE OF A
VESTAL VIRGIN

bishop's mitre — *chasuble* — *stole* — *priest's surplice*

VESTMENT: CATHOLIC CEREMONIAL
VESTMENTS

vest-pocket *attrib.adj. N. Amer.* **1** small enough to fit into a waistcoat pocket. **2** very small (*vest-pocket parks in urban areas*).

vestry *n.* (*pl.* **-ies**) **1** a room or building attached to a church for keeping vestments in. ▷ CHURCH. **2** *hist.* a meeting of parishioners, usu. in a vestry for parochial business. [from Latin *vestiarium*]

vet[1] ● *n. colloq.* a veterinary surgeon. ● *v.tr.* (**vetted**, **vetting**) make a careful and critical examination of (a scheme, work, candidate, etc.).

vet[2] *n. N. Amer. colloq.* a veteran.

vetch *n.* any plant of the genus *Vicia*, esp. *V. sativa*, largely used for silage or fodder. [from Latin *vicia*]

V

veteran *n.* **1** a person who has long experience of an occupation (*a war veteran; a veteran of the theatre; a veteran marksman*). **2** *N. Amer.* an ex-serviceman or servicewoman. **3** (*attrib.*) of or for veterans. [based on Latin *vetus -eris* 'old']

veteran car *n. Brit.* a car made before 1916, or (strictly) before 1905.

veterinarian *n. N. Amer.* a veterinary surgeon.

veterinary • *adj.* of or for diseases and injuries of animals, or their treatment. • *n.* (*pl.* **-ies**) a veterinary surgeon. [based on Latin *veterinae* 'cattle']

veterinary surgeon *n. Brit.* a person qualified to treat diseased or injured animals.

vetiver *n.* the aromatic root of an Indian grass, *Vetiveria zizanioides*. [from Tamil]

veto • *n.* (*pl.* **-oes**) **1 a** a constitutional right to reject a legislative enactment. **b** the right of a permanent member of the UN Security Council to reject a resolution. **c** such a rejection. **2** a prohibition (*put one's veto on a proposal*). • *v.tr.* (**-oes, -oed**) **1** exercise a veto against (a measure etc.). **2** forbid authoritatively. [Latin, literally 'I forbid', used in opposing measures of the Senate]

vex *v.tr.* anger by a slight or a petty annoyance; irritate. [from Latin *vexare* 'to shake, disturb'] □ **vexing** *adj.*

vexation *n.* **1** the act or an instance of vexing; the state of being vexed. **2** an annoying or distressing thing.

vexatious *adj.* **1** such as to cause vexation. **2** *Law* not having sufficient grounds for action and seeking only to annoy the defendant. □ **vexatiously** *adv.*

vexed *adj.* **1** irritated, angered. **2** (of a problem, issue, etc.) much discussed; problematic. □ **vexedly** *adv.*

VG *abbr.* **1** very good. **2** Vicar-General.

vgc *abbr.* very good condition.

VHF *abbr.* very high frequency (designating radio waves of frequency *c.*30–300 MHz and wavelength *c.*1–10 metres).

VI *abbr.* Virgin Islands.

via *prep.* by way of; through (*London to Rome via Paris; send it via your secretary*). [Latin, literally 'by the way, by the road']

viable *adj.* **1** (of a plan etc.) feasible; practicable, esp. from an economic standpoint. **2 a** (of a seed or spore) able to germinate. **b** (of a plant, animal, etc.) capable of living or developing normally under particular environmental conditions. **3** *Med.* (of a foetus or unborn child) able to live after birth. [French] □ **viability** *n.*

viaduct *n.* **1** ▼ a long bridgelike structure, esp. a series of arches, carrying a road or railway across a valley or dip in the ground. **2** such a road or railway. [based on Latin *via* 'way']

VIADUCT: Puente Nuevo, Spain

vial *n.* a small (usu. cylindrical glass) vessel esp. for holding medicines. [Middle English, related to phial]

viaticum *n.* (*pl.* **viatica**) the Eucharist as given to a person near or in danger of death. [Latin]

vibes *n.pl. colloq.* **1** vibrations, esp. in the sense of feelings or atmosphere communicated (*the house had bad vibes*). **2** = vibraphone.

vibrant *adj.* **1** vibrating. **2** (of a person or thing) thrilling, quivering (*vibrant with emotion*). **3** (of sound) resonant. **4** (of colour) bright and striking. [from Latin *vibrant-* 'shaking'] □ **vibrancy** *n.* **vibrantly** *adv.*

vibraphone *n.* ▼ a percussion instrument of tuned bars set over motorized rotating vanes in tubular metal resonators, giving a vibrato effect. ▷ orchestra, percussion. □ **vibraphonist** *n.*

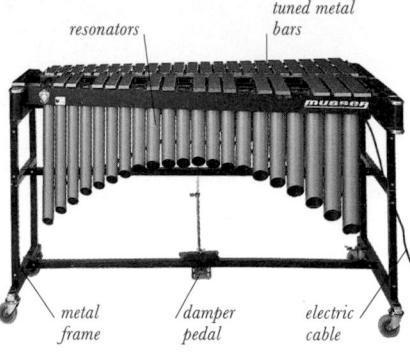

resonators   tuned metal bars

metal frame   damper pedal   electric cable

VIBRAPHONE

vibrate *v.* **1** *intr. & tr.* move or cause to move continuously and rapidly to and fro. **2** *intr. Physics* move unceasingly to and fro. **3** *intr.* (of a sound) throb; continue to be heard. [based on Latin *vibratus* 'shaken, swung']

vibration *n.* **1** the act or an instance of vibrating. **2** *Physics* motion to and fro. **3** (in *pl.*) **a** a mental (esp. occult) influence. **b** a characteristic atmosphere or feeling in a place, regarded as communicable to people present in it. □ **vibrational** *adj.*

vibrato /vi-**brah**-toh/ *n. Mus.* a rapid slight variation in pitch in singing or in playing a stringed or wind instrument, producing a tremulous effect (cf. tremolo 1). [Italian, literally 'vibrated']

vibrator *n.* a device that vibrates or causes vibration, esp. an instrument used in massage or for sexual stimulation. □ **vibratory** *adj.*

viburnum *n.* ▶ any shrub of the genus *Viburnum*, usu. with white flowers. [Latin, literally 'wayfaring tree']

vicar *n.* **1 a** (in the Church of England) an incumbent of a parish where tithes formerly passed to a chapter or religious house or layman (cf. rector 1a). **b** (in other Anglican churches) a member of the clergy deputizing for another. **2** *RC Ch.* a representative or deputy of a bishop. [from Latin *vicarius* 'substitute'] □ **vicariate** *n.*

vicarage *n.* the residence or benefice of a vicar.

vicar-general *n.* (*pl.* **vicars-general**) **1** an Anglican official assisting or representing a bishop esp. in administrative matters. **2** *RC Ch.* a bishop's assistant in matters of jurisdiction etc.

vicarial /vi-**kair**-iăl/ *adj.* of or serving as a vicar.

vicarious /vi-**kair**-iŭs/ *adj.* **1** experienced in the imagination through another person (*vicarious pleasure*). **2** acting or done for another (*vicarious suffering*). **3** deputed, delegated (*vicarious authority*). [from Latin *vicarius*] □ **vicariously** *adv.* **vicariousness** *n.*

vice[1] *n.* **1 a** evil or grossly immoral conduct. **b** a particular form of this, esp. involving prostitution, drugs, etc. **c** an immoral or dissolute habit or practice. **2** a defect or weakness of character or behaviour (*drunkenness was not among his vices*). [from Latin *vitium*]

vice[2] (*US* **vise**) • *n.* ▶ a device usually attached to a workbench, with two jaws between which an object may be clamped by moving one jaw by means of a screw leaving the hands free to work on it. • *v.tr.* secure in a vice. [Middle English in sense 'winding stair, screw': from Latin *vitis* 'vine'] □ **vice-like** *adj.*

vice[3] *n. colloq.* = vice-president, vice admiral, etc. [Latin, literally 'by change']

vice- *comb. form* forming nouns meaning next in rank to, often in the capacity of deputy or substitute for (*vice-chairman; vice-governor*). [Latin, literally 'in place of']

vice admiral *n.* a naval officer ranking below admiral and above rear admiral.

vice-chancellor *n.* a deputy chancellor (esp. of a British university, discharging most of the administrative duties).

vicegerent /vys-**jeer**-ĕnt/ • *adj.* exercising delegated power. • *n.* a vicegerent person; a deputy. [from medieval Latin *vicegerent-* 'deputizing']

vice-president *n.* an official ranking below and deputizing for a president. □ **vice-presidency** *n.* (*pl.* **-ies**). **vice-presidential** *adj.*

viceregal *adj.* of or relating to a viceroy.

vice ring *n.* a group of criminals involved in organizing illegal prostitution.

viceroy *n.* a ruler exercising authority on behalf of a sovereign in a colony, province, etc. [from Old French] □ **viceroyalty** *n.*

vice squad *n.* a police department enforcing laws against prostitution, drug abuse, etc.

vice versa *adv.* with the order of the terms or conditions changed; the other way round (*could go from left to right or vice versa*). [Latin, literally 'the position being reversed']

vichyssoise /vee-shee-**swahz**/ *n.* a creamy soup of leeks and potatoes. [French, fem. of *vichyssois* 'of *Vichy*', a town in France]

Vichy water /**vee**-shee/ *n.* an effervescent mineral water from Vichy in France.

vicinal /**vis**-in-ăl/ *adj.* **1** neighbouring, adjacent. **2** of a neighbourhood; local. [French]

vicinity *n.* (*pl.* **-ies**) **1** a surrounding district. **2** (foll. by *to*) nearness. □ **in the vicinity** (often foll. by *of*) near (to). [from Latin *vicinitas*]

vicious *adj.* **1** bad-tempered, spiteful (*a vicious dog; vicious remarks*). **2** violent (*a vicious attack*). **3** of the nature of or addicted to vice. [from Latin *vitiosus*] □ **viciously** *adv.* **viciousness** *n.*

VIBURNUM
(*Viburnum macrocephalum*)

vicious circle see circle 11.

vicissitude *n.* a change of circumstances. [French]

victim *n.* **1** a person injured or killed (*a road victim; the victims of war*). **2** a person or thing harmed or destroyed in pursuit of an object or in gratification of a passion etc. (*the victim of their ruthless ambition*). **3** a prey; a dupe (*fell victim to a confidence trick*). **4** a living creature sacrificed to a deity or in a religious rite. [from Latin *victima*]

victimize *v.tr.* (also **-ise**) single out for punishment or unfair treatment. □ **victimization** *n.* **victimizer** *n.*

victimless *adj.* orig. *US* (of a crime) in which there is no injured party

V

victor *n.* a winner in battle or in a contest. [Latin]

Victoria *n.* (also **victoria**) **1** a low light four-wheeled carriage with a collapsible top, seats for two passengers, and a raised driver's seat. **2** (in full **Victoria plum**) *Brit.* a large red luscious variety of plum. [named after Queen *Victoria*, 1819–1901]

Victoria Cross *n.* ◄ a decoration awarded for conspicuous bravery in the armed services, instituted by Queen Victoria in 1856.

Victorian ● *adj.* **1** of or characteristic of the time of Queen Victoria. **2** associated with attitudes attributed to this time, esp. of prudery and moral strictness. ● *n.* a person of this time. □ **Victorianism** *n.*

Victoriana *n.pl.* articles, esp. collectors' items, of the Victorian period.

Victoria sandwich *n.* (also **Victoria sponge**) *Brit.* a sponge cake consisting of two layers of sponge with a jam filling.

VICTORIA
CROSS

victorious *adj.* **1** conquering, triumphant. **2** marked by victory (*victorious day*). [from Latin *victoriosus*] □ **victoriously** *adv.*

victor ludorum *n.* (*fem.* **victrix ludorum**) *Brit.* the overall champion in a sports competition. [Latin, literally 'victor of the games']

victory *n.* (*pl.* **-ies**) **1** the process of defeating an enemy in battle or war or an opponent in a contest. **2** an instance of this; a triumph. [from Latin *victoria*]

victory roll *n.* a roll performed by an aircraft as a sign of triumph, esp. after a successful mission.

victrix ludorum SEE VICTOR LUDORUM.

victual /vit-ăl/ ● *n.* (usu. in *pl.*) food, provisions. ● *v.* (**victualled**, **victualling**; *US* **victualed**, **victualing**) **1** *tr.* supply with victuals. **2** *intr.* obtain stores. **3** *intr.* eat victuals. [based on Latin *victus* 'food']

victualler /vit-ler/ *n.* (*US* **victualer**) **1** a person etc. who supplies victuals. **2** (in full **licensed victualler**) *Brit.* a publican etc. licensed to sell alcoholic liquor.

vicuña /vi-koon-yă/ *n.* a S. American mammal, *Vicugna vicugna*, related to the llama, with fine silky wool. [from Quechua]

vide /vid-ay/ *v.tr.* (as an instruction in a reference to a passage in a book etc.) see, consult. [Latin, literally 'see!']

video ● *adj.* **1** relating to the recording, reproducing, or broadcasting of visual images on magnetic tape or disc. **2** relating to the broadcasting of television pictures. ● *n.* (*pl.* **-os**) **1** the process of recording, reproducing, or broadcasting visual images on magnetic tape or disc. **2** the visual element of television broadcasts. **3** *colloq.* = VIDEO RECORDER. **4** (in full **video film**) a film etc. recorded on a videotape. ● *v.tr.* (**-oes, -oed**) make a video recording of. [based on Latin *videre* 'to see']

video camera *n.* a camera for recording images on videotape etc. or for transmitting them to a monitor screen.

video cassette *n.* a cassette of videotape.

video cassette recorder *n.* = VIDEO RECORDER.

videoconference *n.* the use of television sets linked by telephone lines etc. to enable a group of people to communicate with each other in sound and vision. □ **videoconferencing** *n.*

videodisc *n.* a metal-coated disc on which visual material is recorded for reproduction on a television screen.

video film *n.* a film etc. recorded on videotape.

videofit *n.* a reconstructed picture of a person (esp. one sought by the police) built up on a computer screen by selecting and combining facial features according to witnesses' descriptions (cf. PHOTOFIT).

VIDEO RECORDER

A video recorder captures and replays television signals. A capstan feeds a magnetic tape past two heads: a video head to record pictures and an audio head to record sound. When the tape is replayed, the heads turn the signals back into audio and video signals and send them back to the television.

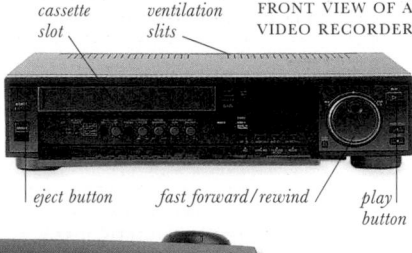

cassette slot   *ventilation slits*   FRONT VIEW OF A VIDEO RECORDER

eject button   *fast forward / rewind*   *play button*

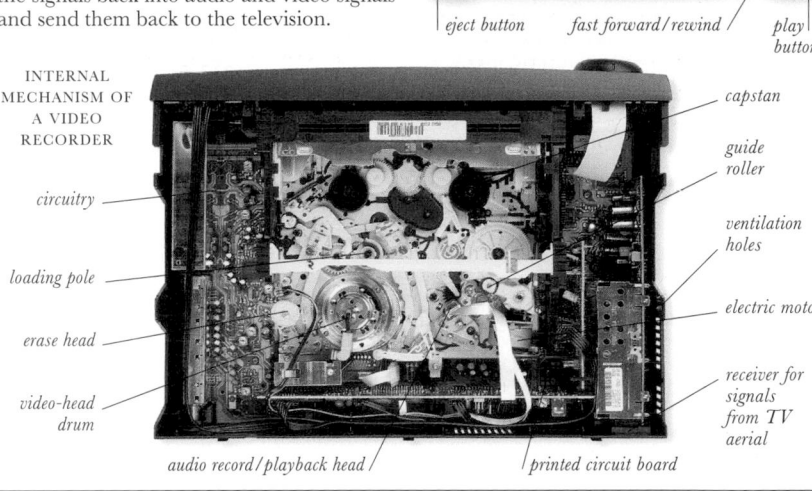

INTERNAL MECHANISM OF A VIDEO RECORDER

circuitry

loading pole

erase head

video-head drum

capstan

guide roller

ventilation holes

electric motor

receiver for signals from TV aerial

audio record / playback head   *printed circuit board*

---

video game *n.* a game played by manipulating images produced by a computer program on a television screen.

video nasty *n. Brit. colloq.* a horrific or pornographic video film.

videophone *n.* a telephone device transmitting a visual image as well as sound.

video recorder *n.* ▲ an apparatus for recording and playing videotapes. □ **video recording** *n.*

videotape ● *n.* **1** magnetic tape for recording television pictures and sound. **2** a length of this; a video cassette. ● *v.tr.* make a recording of (broadcast material etc.) with this.

vie *v.intr.* (**vying**) compete; strive for superiority (*vied with each other for recognition*).

Viennese ● *adj.* of, relating to, or associated with Vienna in Austria. ● *n.* (*pl.* same) a native or citizen of Vienna.

Vietnamese ● *adj.* of or relating to Vietnam in SE Asia. ● *n.* (*pl.* same) **1** a native or national of Vietnam. **2** the language of Vietnam.

view ● *n.* **1** range of vision (*came into view; in full view of the crowd*). **2 a** what is seen from a particular point; a scene or prospect (*a fine view of the downs; a room with a view*). **b** a picture etc. representing this.

3 a visual or mental survey. **4** an opportunity for visual inspection; a viewing (*a private view of the exhibition*). **5 a** an opinion (*holds strong views on morality*). **b** a mental attitude (*took a favourable view of the matter*). **c** a manner of considering a thing (*took a long-term view of it*). ● *v.* **1** *tr.* survey visually; inspect (*we are going to view the house*). **2** *tr.* survey mentally (*different ways of viewing a subject*). **3** *tr.* form a mental impression or opinion of; consider (*does not view the matter in the same light*). **4** *intr.* watch television. □ **have in view 1** have as one's object. **2** bear (a circumstance) in mind in forming a judgement etc. **in view of** considering. **on view** being shown; being exhibited. **with a view to 1** with the hope or intention of. **2** with the aim of attaining (*with a view to marriage*). [based on Latin *videre* 'to see'] □ **viewable** *adj.*

viewdata *n.* a news and information service from a computer source to which a television screen is connected by telephone link.

viewer *n.* **1** a person who views. **2** a person watching television. **3** a device for looking at film transparencies etc.

viewfinder *n.* ▼ a device on a camera showing the area covered by the lens in taking a photograph. ▷ CAMERA

VIEWFINDER

A viewfinder allows the photographer to aim the camera accurately. The image seen through the viewfinder will only be exactly the same as the one seen by the camera if the light travels through the objective lens on its way to the user's eye (as in the SLR). The blue lines on the diagrams show how light travels through different viewfinders.

TYPES OF VIEWFINDER

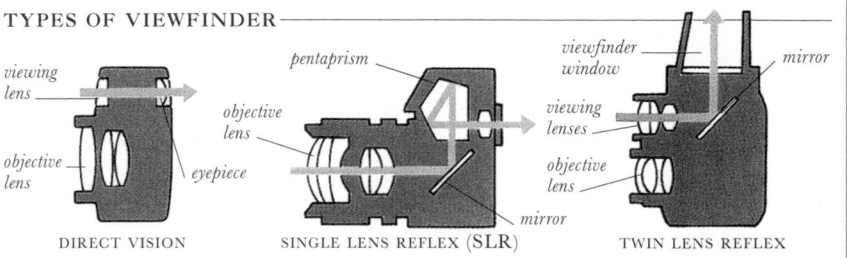

viewing lens

objective lens

eyepiece

DIRECT VISION

pentaprism

objective lens

mirror

SINGLE LENS REFLEX (SLR)

viewfinder window

viewing lenses

objective lens

mirror

TWIN LENS REFLEX

V

viewing *n.* **1** an opportunity or occasion to view; an exhibition. **2** the act or practice of watching television.

viewpoint *n.* a point of view.

vigesimal /vi-jes-i-măl/ *adj.* **1** of twentieths or twenty. **2** reckoning or reckoned by twenties. [based on Latin *viginti* 'twenty']

vigil *n.* **1 a** keeping awake during the time usually given to sleep, esp. to keep watch or pray (*keep vigil*). **b** a period of this. **2** a stationary, peaceful demonstration in support of a particular cause, usu. without speeches. **3** *Eccl.* the eve of a festival or holy day. **4** (in *pl.*) nocturnal devotions. [Latin, literally 'awake']

vigilance *n.* watchfulness, caution. [from Latin *vigilantia*]

vigilance committee *n.* *US* a group of vigilantes.

vigilant *adj.* watchful against danger, difficulty, etc. [from Latin *vigilant-* 'keeping awake'] □ **vigilantly** *adv.*

vigilante /vi-ji-**lan**-ti/ *n.* a member of a self-appointed group undertaking law enforcement but without legal authority. [Spanish, literally 'vigilant'] □ **vigilantism** *n.*

vigneron /vee-n'yĕ-ron/ *n.* a vine-grower. [French]

vignette /veen-**yet**/ ● *n.* **1 a** a short descriptive essay or character sketch. **b** a short evocative episode in a play, film, etc. **2** an illustration or decorative design. **3** a photograph or portrait showing only the head and shoulders with the background gradually shaded off. ● *v.tr.* **1** make a portrait of (a person) in vignette style. **2** shade off (a photograph or portrait). [French, literally 'little vine']

vigor *US* var. of VIGOUR.

vigorous *adj.* **1** strong and active; robust. **2** (of a plant) growing strongly. **3** forceful; acting or done with physical or mental vigour; energetic. **4** showing or requiring physical strength or activity. [from medieval Latin *vigorosus*] □ **vigorously** *adv.* **vigorousness** *n.*

vigour *n.* (*US* **vigor**) **1** physical strength or energy. **2** a flourishing physical condition. **3** healthy growth. **4 a** mental strength or activity. **b** forcefulness; trenchancy, animation. [from Latin *vigor*]

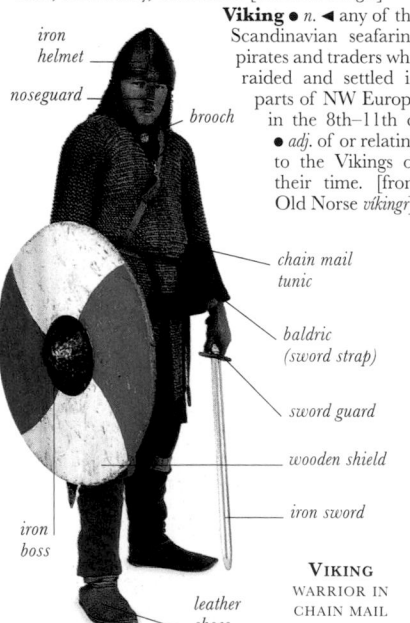

Viking ● *n.* ◄ any of the Scandinavian seafaring pirates and traders who raided and settled in parts of NW Europe in the 8th–11th c. ● *adj.* of or relating to the Vikings or their time. [from Old Norse *víkingr*]

iron helmet
noseguard
brooch
chain mail tunic
baldric (sword strap)
sword guard
wooden shield
iron sword
iron boss
leather shoes

VIKING WARRIOR IN CHAIN MAIL

vile *adj.* **1** disgusting. **2** morally base; depraved, shameful. **3** *colloq.* abominably bad (*vile weather*). [from Latin *vilis* 'cheap, base'] □ **vilely** *adv.* **vileness** *n.*

vilify *v.tr.* (**-ies**, **-ied**) defame; speak evil of. [from Late Latin *vilificare*] □ **vilification** *n.* **vilifier** *n.*

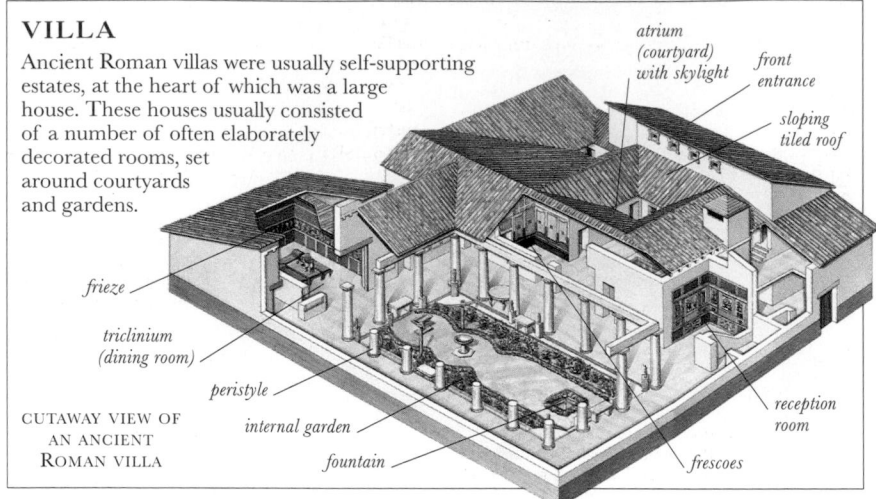

VILLA

Ancient Roman villas were usually self-supporting estates, at the heart of which was a large house. These houses usually consisted of a number of often elaborately decorated rooms, set around courtyards and gardens.

atrium (courtyard) with skylight
front entrance
sloping tiled roof
frieze
triclinium (dining room)
peristyle
internal garden
fountain
reception room
frescoes

CUTAWAY VIEW OF AN ANCIENT ROMAN VILLA

villa *n.* **1** *Rom. Antiq.* ▲ a large country house with an estate. **2** a country residence. **3** a rented holiday home, esp. abroad. [Italian]

village *n.* **1 a** a group of houses and associated buildings, larger than a hamlet and smaller than a town, esp. in a rural area. **b** the inhabitants of a village regarded as a community. **2** *Brit.* a self-contained district or community within a town or city, regarded as having features characteristic of village life. **3** *US* a small municipality with limited corporate powers. **4** *Austral.* a select suburban shopping centre. [from Latin *villa*] □ **villager** *n.* **villagey** *adj.*

village idiot *n.* *offens.* a person of very low intelligence living and well known in a village.

villain *n.* **1** a person guilty or capable of great wickedness. **2** *colloq.* usu. *joc.* a rascal or rogue. **3** (also **villain of the piece**) (in a play etc.) a character whose evil actions or motives are important in the plot. [from Old French *vilein*]

villainous *adj.* wicked. □ **villainously** *adv.*

villainy *n.* (*pl.* **-ies**) **1** villainous behaviour. **2** a wicked act.

-ville *comb. form colloq.* forming the names of fictitious places with reference to a particular quality etc. (*dragsville*; *squaresville*). [from French *ville* 'town']

villein *n.* *hist.* a feudal tenant entirely subject to a lord or attached to a manor. [variant of VILLAIN]

villus *n.* (*pl.* **villi**) *Anat.* ► a small hair-like or finger-like projection, esp. as lining the small intestine in large numbers to form the surface through which nutrients are absorbed into the blood. ▷ DIGESTION. [Latin, literally 'shaggy hair'] □ **villose** *adj.* **villous** *adj.*

epithelial layer
lacteal
mucus cell
vein
artery
lymph vessel
muscle layers

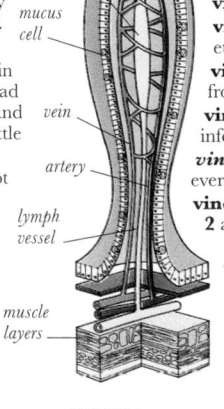

VILLUS: SECTION THROUGH AN INTESTINAL VILLUS

vim *n.* *colloq.* vigour.

vinaigrette /vin-ay-**gret**/ *n.* (in full **vinaigrette sauce**) a salad dressing of oil, wine vinegar, and seasoning. [French, literally 'little vinegar']

vindaloo *n.* a highly-spiced hot Indian curry dish made with meat, fish, or poultry.

vindicate *v.tr.* **1** clear of blame or suspicion. **2** establish the existence, merits, or justice of. **3** justify (a person, oneself, etc.) by evidence or argument. [based on Latin *vindicatus* 'claimed, avenged'] □ **vindication** *n.* **vindicator** *n.*

vindicatory *adj.* tending to vindicate.

vindictive *adj.* **1** tending to seek revenge. **2** spiteful. [based on Latin *vindicta* 'vengeance'] □ **vindictively** *adv.* **vindictiveness** *n.*

vindictive damages *n.pl.* esp. *Brit. Law* damages exceeding simple compensation and awarded to punish the defendant.

vine *n.* **1** ► any climbing or trailing woody stemmed plant, esp. of the genus *Vitis*, bearing grapes. **2** a slender trailing or climbing stem. [from Latin *vinea* 'vineyard'] □ **viny** *adj.*

VINE (*Vitis vinifera*)

grapes

vine-dresser *n.* a person who prunes, trains, and cultivates vines.

vinegar *n.* **1** a sour liquid obtained from wine, cider, etc., by fermentation and used as a condiment or for pickling. **2** sour behaviour or character. [from Old French *vyn egre* 'sour wine'] □ **vinegarish** *adj.* **vinegary** *adj.*

vinery *n.* (*pl.* **-ies**) **1** a greenhouse for grapevines. **2** a vineyard.

vineyard *n.* a plantation of grapevines, esp. for wine-making.

vingt-et-un /vant-ay-**ern**/ *n.* = PONTOON[1]. [French, literally 'twenty-one']

vinho verde *n.* a young Portuguese wine, not allowed to mature. [Portuguese, literally 'green wine']

vini- *comb. form* wine. [from Latin *vinum*]

viniculture *n.* the cultivation of grapevines.

vinification *n.* ► the conversion of grape juice etc. into wine.

vining *n.* the separation of leguminous crops from their vines and pods.

vino /vee-noh/ *n.* esp. *Brit. slang* wine, esp. of an inferior kind. [Spanish, literally 'wine']

vin ordinaire /van or-din-**air**/ *n.* cheap wine for everyday use. [French, literally 'ordinary wine']

vinous *adj.* **1** of, like, or associated with wine. **2** addicted to wine. [based on Latin *vinum* 'wine'] □ **vinosity** *n.*

vintage ● *n.* **1 a** a season's produce of grapes. **b** the wine made from this. **2 a** the gathering of grapes for wine-making. **b** the season of this. **3** a wine of high quality from a single identified year and district. **4 a** the year etc. when a thing was made etc. **b** a thing made etc. in a particular year etc. ● *adj.* of high quality, esp. from the past or characteristic of the best period of a person's work. [alteration of Middle English *vendage*: from Old French *vendange*]

V

vintage car *n. Brit.* a car made between 1917 and 1930.

vintner *n.* a wine-merchant. [based on Latin *vinetum* 'vineyard']

viny see VINE.

vinyl *n.* **1** *Chem.* the radical –CH:CH$_2$, derived from ethylene by removal of a hydrogen atom (usu. *attrib.: vinyl group*). **2** any plastic made by polymerizing a compound containing the vinyl group, esp. polyvinyl chloride. [based on Latin *vinum* 'wine']

viol *n.* ◄ a medieval stringed musical instrument, played with a bow and held vertically on the knees or between the legs. [from Provençal *viola*]

fingerboard

tuning peg

sound-hole

VIOL: 18TH-CENTURY BRITISH VIOL

viola[1] /vi-**oh**-lă/ *n.* **1** an instrument of the violin family, larger than the violin and of lower pitch. **2** a viol. ▷ ORCHESTRA, STRINGED. [Italian & Spanish]

viola[2] /vy-**ŏ**-lă/ *n.* **1** any plant of the genus *Viola*, including the pansy and violet. **2** a cultivated hybrid of this genus. [Latin, literally 'violet']

viola da gamba /vi-**oh**-lă dă **gam**-ba/ *n.* a viol held between the player's legs. [Italian, literally 'viol for the leg']

viola d'amore /vi-**oh**-lă dam-**or**-ay/ *n.* a sweet-toned tenor viol. [Italian, literally 'viol of love']

violate *v.tr.* **1** disregard; fail to comply with (an oath, treaty, law, etc.). **2** treat (a sanctuary etc.) profanely or with disrespect. **3** disturb (a person's privacy etc.). **4** rape. [based on Latin *violatus* 'treated violently'] □ **violation** *n.* **violator** *n.*

violence *n.* **1** the quality of being violent. **2** violent conduct or treatment. **3** *law* **a** the unlawful exercise of physical force. **b** intimidation by the exhibition of this. □ **do violence to** act contrary to; outrage. [from Latin *violenta*]

violent *adj.* **1 a** using or tending to use aggressive physical force (*a violent person*). **b** involving physical force (*a violent storm*). **2 a** vehement, passionate, extreme (*a violent contrast; violent dislike*). **b** vivid, intense (*violent colours*). **3** (of death) resulting from external force or from poison. **4** involving an unlawful exercise of force. [from Latin *violentus*] □ **violently** *adv.*

violet ● *n.* **1** any plant of the genus *Viola*, esp. the sweet violet, with usu. purple, blue, or white flowers. **2** the bluish-purple colour seen at the end of the spectrum opposite red. **3** pigment of this

colour. ● *adj.* of a purplish-blue colour. [from Latin *viola*]

violin *n.* a musical instrument with four strings of treble pitch played with a bow. ▷ ORCHESTRA, STRINGED. [from Italian *violino* 'little viola'] □ **violinist** *n.*

violist *n.* a viol-player or viola-player.

violoncello /vy-ŏ-lŏn-**chel**-oh/ *n.* (*pl.* **-os**) *formal* = CELLO. ▷ ORCHESTRA, STRINGED. [Italian] □ **violoncellist** *n.*

VIP *abbr.* very important person.

viper *n.* **1** ▼ any venomous snake of the family Viperidae, esp. the common viper (see ADDER). ▷ SNAKE. **2** a malignant or treacherous person. [from Latin *vipera*] □ **viperish** *adj.* **viperous** *adj.*

VIPER: GABOON VIPER (*Vipera gabonica*)

viper's bugloss *n.* a stiff bristly blue-flowered plant, *Echium vulgare*.

virago /vi-**rah**-goh/ *n.* (*pl.* **-os**) a fierce or abusive woman. [Latin, literally 'female warrior']

viral /**vy**-răl/ *adj.* of or caused by a virus. □ **virally** *adv.*

Virgilian *adj.* of, or in the style of, the Roman poet Virgil (d. 19 BC). [from P. *Vergilius Maro*, the full name of Virgil]

virgin ● *n.* **1** a person (esp. a woman) who has never had sexual intercourse. **2** (**the Virgin**) Christ's mother the Blessed Virgin Mary. **3** (**the Virgin**) the zodiacal sign or constellation Virgo. ● *adj.* **1** that is a virgin. **2** of or befitting a virgin (*virgin modesty*). **3** not yet used, penetrated, or tried (*virgin soil*). **4** (of olive oil etc.) obtained from the first pressing of olives etc. **5** (of clay) not fired. **6** (of metal) made from ore by smelting. **7** (of wool) not yet, or only once, spun or woven. [from Latin *virgo -ginis*]

virginal ● *adj.* that is or befits or belongs to a virgin. ● *n.* (usu. in *pl.*) (in full **pair of virginals**) an early form of spinet in a box. □ **virginally** *adv.*

virgin birth *n.* **1** (the doctrine of) Christ's birth from a mother who was a virgin. **2** parthenogenesis.

virgin forest *n.* a forest in its untouched natural state.

Virginia *n.* **1** tobacco from Virginia. **2** a cigarette made of this. [from *Virginia*, a US state] □ **Virginian** *n.* & *adj.*

Virginia creeper *n.* a N. American vine, *Parthenocissus quinquefolia*, cultivated esp. for its red autumn foliage.

Virginia stock *n.* (also **Virginian stock**) a cruciferous plant, *Malcolmia maritima*, with white or pink flowers.

virginity *n.* the state of being a virgin.

Virgin Queen *n.* Queen Elizabeth I of England.

Virgo *n.* (*pl.* **-os**) **1** *Astron.* ► a large constellation (the Virgin), said to represent a maiden or goddess associated with the harvest. **2** *Astrol.* **a** the sixth sign of the zodiac, which the Sun enters about 23 Aug. ▷ ZODIAC. **b** a person born when the Sun is in this sign. [Latin, literally 'virgin'] □ **Virgoan** *n.* & *adj.*

Spica

VIRGO: FIGURE OF A MAIDEN FORMED FROM THE STARS OF VIRGO

virgule *n.* **1** a slanting line used to mark division of words or lines. **2** = SOLIDUS 1.

viridescent *adj.* greenish, tending to become green. [from Late Latin *viridescent-* 'becoming green'] □ **viridescence** *n.*

viridian ● *n.* **1** a bluish-green chromium oxide pigment. **2** the colour of this. ● *adj.* bluish green. [based on Latin *viridis* 'green']

virile *adj.* **1** of or characteristic of a man; having masculine (esp. sexual) vigour or strength. **2** of or having procreative power. **3** of a man as distinct from a woman or child. [from Latin *virilis*] □ **virility** *n.*

virology *n.* the scientific study of viruses. □ **virological** *adj.* **virologist** *n.*

virtual *adj.* **1** that is such for practical purposes though not in name or according to strict definition (*is the virtual manager of the business; take this as a virtual promise*). **2** *Optics* relating to the points at which rays would meet if produced backwards (*virtual focus; virtual image*). **3** *Mech.* relating to an infinitesimal displacement of a point in a system. **4** *Computing* not physically existing as such but made by software to appear to do so (*virtual memory*) (see also VIRTUAL REALITY). [from medieval Latin *virtualis*] □ **virtuality** *n.*

virtually *adv.* **1** in effect, to all intents. **2** nearly, almost.

virtual reality *n.* ▼ an image or environment generated by computer software with which a user can interact realistically using a helmet with a screen inside, gloves fitted with sensors, etc.

VINIFICATION

Vinification starts when grapes are crushed or pressed, bringing the juice into contact with yeast cells on the skins. The grapes are macerated (usually only for red wine) to make free-run wine, and then pressed to extract the press wine. The resulting liquid may then be racked to separate out the lees. Final fermentation occurs in vats or casks.

STAGES IN THE VINIFICATION PROCESS

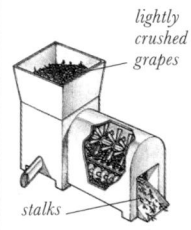

lightly crushed grapes

stalks

CRUSHING

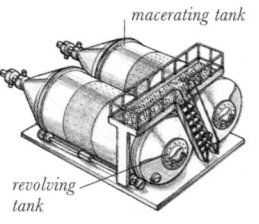

macerating tank

revolving tank

MACERATION

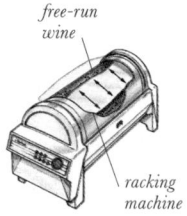

free-run wine

racking machine

RACKING

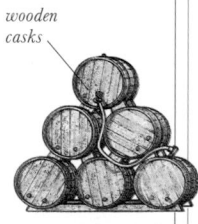

wooden casks

FERMENTATION

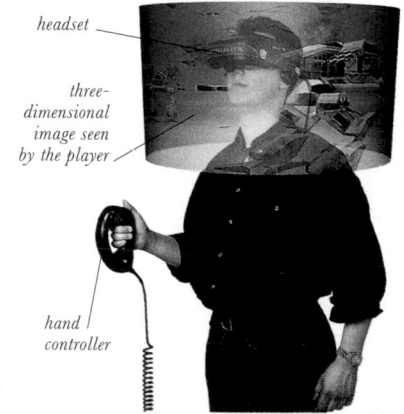

headset

three-dimensional image seen by the player

hand controller

VIRTUAL REALITY: PLAYER USING A HEADSET AND HAND CONTROLLER

V

virtue *n.* **1** moral excellence; goodness. **2** a particular form of this (*patience is a virtue*). **3** chastity, esp. of a woman. **4** a good quality (*has the virtue of being adjustable*). **5** efficacy (*no virtue in such drugs*). □ **by** (or **in**) **virtue of** on the strength or ground of (*got the job by virtue of his experience*). **make a virtue of necessity** derive some credit or benefit from an unwelcome obligation. [from Latin *virtus*]

virtuoso *n.* (*pl.* **virtuosi** or **-os**) **1** a person highly skilled in the technique of a fine art, esp. music. **2** (*attrib.*) displaying the skills of a virtuoso. [Italian, literally 'learned, skilful'] □ **virtuosic** *adj.* **virtuosity** *n.*

virtuous *adj.* **1** possessing or showing moral rectitude. **2** (esp. of a woman) chaste. [from Late Latin *virtuosus*] □ **virtuously** *adv.* **virtuousness** *n.*

virtuous circle *n.* a beneficial recurring cycle of cause and effect (cf. *vicious circle* (CIRCLE *n.* 11)).

virulent *adj.* **1** strongly poisonous. **2** (of a disease) violent. **3** bitterly hostile. [Middle English, originally of a poisoned wound] □ **virulence** *n.* **virulently** *adv.*

virus *n.* **1** ▼ a submicroscopic pathogenic agent usu. consisting of a nucleic acid molecule in a protein coat, and able to multiply only within the living cells of a host. **2** *Computing* = COMPUTER VIRUS. [Latin, literally 'slimy liquid, poison']

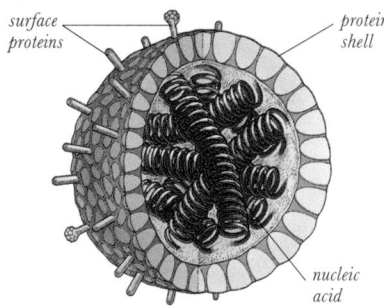

surface proteins

protein shell

nucleic acid

VIRUS: TYPICAL STRUCTURE OF A VIRUS

Vis. *abbr.* Viscount.

visa *n.* an endorsement on a passport etc., esp. as allowing the holder to enter or leave a country. [Latin, literally 'seen']

visage *n. literary* a face. [based on Latin *visus* 'sight'] □ **visaged** *adj.* (also in *comb.*).

vis-à-vis /veez-ah-**vee**/ ● *prep.* in relation to. ● *adv.* facing one another. ● *n.* (*pl.* same) **1** a person or thing facing another. **2** a person occupying a corresponding position in another group. [French, literally 'face to face']

Visc. *abbr.* Viscount.

viscera see VISCUS.

visceral /**vis**-ĕ-răl/ *adj.* **1** of the viscera. **2** relating to inward feelings rather than conscious reasoning. □ **viscerally** *adv.*

viscid /**vis**-id/ *adj.* **1** glutinous, sticky. **2** semi-fluid. [based on Latin *viscum* 'birdlime']

viscometer *n.* an instrument for measuring the viscosity of liquids. □ **viscometric** *adj.* □ **viscometrically** *adv.* □ **viscometry** *n.*

viscose *n.* **1** a form of cellulose in a highly viscous state suitable for drawing into yarn. **2** rayon made from this. [based on Late Latin *viscosus* 'viscous']

viscosity *n.* (*pl.* **-ies**) **1** the quality or degree of being viscous. **2** *Physics* (of a fluid) internal friction, the resistance to flow.

viscount /**vy**-kownt/ *n.* a British nobleman ranking between an earl and a baron. [from medieval Latin *vicecomes -mitis*] □ **viscountcy** *n.* (*pl.* **-ies**).

viscountess /**vy**-kownt-ess/ *n.* **1** a viscount's wife or widow. **2** a woman holding the rank of viscount in her own right.

viscous *adj.* **1** glutinous, sticky. **2** semi-fluid. **3** *Physics*

having a high viscosity; not flowing freely. [from Late Latin *viscosus*] □ **viscously** *adv.*

viscus *n.* (*pl.* **viscera** /**vis**-er-ă/) (usu. in *pl.*) any of the soft internal organs of the body (e.g. the heart and liver). [Latin]

vise *US var.* of VICE².

visibility *n.* **1** the state of being visible. **2** the range or possibility of vision as determined by the conditions of light and atmosphere (*visibility was down to 50 yards*).

visible *adj.* **1 a** that can be seen. **b** (of light) within the range of wavelengths to which the eye is sensitive. **2** that can be perceived or ascertained (*has no visible means of support; spoke with visible impatience*). **3** (of exports etc.) consisting of actual goods (cf. INVISIBLE EXPORTS). [from Latin *visibilis*] □ **visibleness** *n.* **visibly** *adv.*

Visigoth *n.* a West Goth, a member of the branch of the Goths who settled in France and Spain in the 5th c. and ruled much of Spain until 711.

vision ● *n.* **1** the act or faculty of seeing; sight. **2 a** a thing or person seen in a dream or trance. **b** a supernatural or prophetic apparition. **3** a thing or idea perceived vividly in the imagination (*the romantic visions of youth; had visions of warm sandy beaches*). **4** imaginative insight. **5** statesmanlike foresight. **6** a person etc. of unusual beauty. **7** what is seen on a television screen; television images collectively. ● *v.tr.* see or present in or as in a vision. [from Latin *visio*] □ **visionless** *adj.*

visionary ● *adj.* **1** given to seeing visions or to indulging in fanciful theories. **2** having vision or foresight. ● *n.* (*pl.* **-ies**) a visionary person.

vision mixer *n. Brit.* a person whose job is to switch from one image to another in television broadcasting or recording.

visit ● *v.* (**visited, visiting**) **1** *tr.* (also *absol.*) go or come to see (a person, place, etc.). **2** *tr.* reside temporarily with (a person) or at (a place). **3** *tr.* (of a disease, calamity, etc.) come upon, attack. **4** *tr. Bibl.* **a** (foll. by *with*) punish (a person). **b** (often foll. by *upon*) inflict punishment for (a sin). **5** *intr.* **a** (foll. by *with*) *N. Amer.* converse, chat. **b** (usu. foll. by *with*) *US* converse, chat. ● *n.* **1 a** an act of visiting (*was on a visit to some friends; paid him a long visit*). **b** temporary residence. **2** (foll. by *to*) an occasion of going to a doctor, dentist, etc. **3** a formal or official call for the purpose of inspection etc. **4** *US* a chat. [from Latin *visitare* 'to go to see'] □ **visitable** *adj.*

visitant *n.* a visitor, esp. a supposedly supernatural one.

visitation *n.* **1** an official visit of inspection. **2** trouble or difficulty regarded as a divine punishment.

visiting ● *n.* paying a visit or visits. ● *attrib.adj.* (of an academic) spending some time at another institution (*a visiting professor*).

visiting card *n.* esp. *Brit.* a card with a person's name etc., sent or left in lieu of a formal visit.

visiting hours *n.pl.* a designated time when visitors may call, esp. to see a patient in hospital etc.

visitor *n.* **1** a person who visits. **2** esp. *Brit.* a migratory bird present in a locality for part of the year (*winter visitor*).

visitors' book *n.* esp. *Brit.* a book in which visitors to a hotel, church, embassy, etc., write their names and addresses and sometimes remarks.

visor /**vy**-zer/ *n.* (also **vizor**) **1 a** ▶ a movable part of a helmet covering the face. ▷ SPACESUIT. **b** the projecting front part of a cap. **2 a** shield to protect the eyes from unwanted light, esp. one at the top of a vehicle windscreen. [from Old French *visiere*] □ **visored** *adj.*

VISOR: 16TH-CENTURY VISORED HELMET

lifting pin

visor

breathing vents

VISTA IN THE BOBOLI GARDENS, FLORENCE, ITALY

vista *n.* **1** ▲ a long narrow view as between rows of trees. **2** a mental view of a long succession of events (*opened up new vistas to his ambition*). [Italian, literally 'view']

visual ● *adj.* of, concerned with, or used in seeing. ● *n.* (usu. in *pl.*) a visual image or display, a picture. [from Late Latin *visualis*] □ **visually** *adv.*

visual aid *n.* a film, model, etc., as an aid to learning.

visual display unit *n.* esp. *Brit. Computing* a device displaying data on a screen.

visual field *n.* = FIELD OF VISION.

visualize *v.tr.* (also **-ise**) make visible, esp. to one's mind (a thing not visible to the eye). □ **visualization** *n.*

vital ● *adj.* **1 a** essential; indispensable; extremely important (*a vital question; secrecy is vital*). **b** paramount, very great (*of vital importance*). **2** of, concerned with, or essential to organic life (*vital energy; vital functions*). **3** full of life or activity. ● *n.* (in *pl.*) the body's vital organs, e.g. the heart and brain. [based on Latin *vita* 'life']

vital force *n.* **1** (in H. Bergson's philosophy) life-force. **2** any mysterious vital principle. [translation of French *élan vital*]

vitalism *n. Biol.* the doctrine that life originates in a vital principle distinct from chemical and other physical forces. □ **vitalist** *n.* **vitalistic** *adj.*

vitality *n.* **1** liveliness, animation. **2** the ability to sustain life.

vitalize *v.tr.* (also **-ise**) **1** endow with life. **2** infuse with vigour.

vitally *adv.* essentially, indispensably.

vital power *n.* the power to sustain life.

vital statistics *n.pl.* **1** the number of births, marriages, deaths, etc. **2** *colloq. offens.* the measurements of a woman's bust, waist, and hips.

vitamin *n.* ▶ any of a group of organic compounds essential in small amounts for many living organisms to maintain normal health and development. [from Latin *vita* 'life' + AMINE, because originally thought to contain an amino acid]

vitamin A *n.* ▶ = RETINOL.

vitamin B₁ *n.* ▶ = THIAMINE.

vitamin B₂ *n.* ▶ = RIBOFLAVIN.

vitamin B₆ *n.* ▶ = PYRIDOXINE.

vitamin B₁₂ *n.* ▶ = CYANOCOBALAMIN.

vitamin B complex *n.* a group of vitamins which, although not chemically related, are often found together in the same foods.

vitamin C *n.* ▶ = ASCORBIC ACID.

V

vitamin D *n.* ▶ any of a group of vitamins found in liver and fish oils, essential for the absorption of calcium and the prevention of rickets in children and softening of the bones in adults.

vitamin D₂ *n.* = CALCIFEROL.

vitamin D₃ *n.* = CHOLECALCIFEROL.

vitamin E *n.* ▶ = TOCOPHEROL.

vitaminize *v.tr.* (also **-ise**) add vitamins to.

vitamin K *n.* ▶ any of a group of vitamins found mainly in green leaves and essential for the blood-clotting process.

vitamin K₁ *n.* = PHYLLOQUINONE.

vitamin K₂ *n.* = MENAQUINONE.

vitamin M *n.* esp. *US* = FOLIC ACID.

vitiate /vish-i-ayt/ *v.tr.* **1** impair the quality or efficiency of; debase. **2** make invalid or ineffectual. [based on Latin *vitiatus* 'impaired'] □ **vitiation** *n.*

viticulture *n.* the cultivation of grapevines; the science or study of this. [based on Latin *vitis* 'vine'] □ **viticultural** *adj.* **viticulturist** *n.*

vitreous *adj.* **1** of, or of the nature of, glass. **2** like glass in hardness, brittleness, transparency, structure, etc. (*vitreous enamel*). [based on Latin *vitrum* 'glass']

vitreous humour *n.* (also **vitreous body**) *Anat.* a transparent jelly-like tissue filling the eyeball. ▷ EYE

vitrify *v.tr. & intr.* (**-ies**, **-ied**) convert or be converted into glass or a glasslike substance, esp. by heat. [from medieval Latin *vitrificare*] □ **vitrification** *n.*

vitriol *n.* **1** sulphuric acid or a sulphate. **2** caustic or hostile speech, criticism, or feeling. [from Old French]

vitriolic *adj.* caustic or hostile

vituperate *v.tr. & intr.* revile, abuse. [based on Latin *vituperatus* 'censured'] □ **vituperation** *n.* **vituperative** *adj.*

viva¹ /vy-vă/ *Brit. colloq.* ● *n.* = VIVA VOCE *n.* ● *v.tr.* (**vivas**, **vivaed** or **viva'd**, **vivaing**) subject to an oral examination.

viva² /vee-vă/ ● *int.* long live ● *n.* a cry of this as a salute etc. [Italian, literally 'may he or she live']

vivace /vi-vah-chi/ *adv. Mus.* in a lively manner. [Italian]

vivacious *adj.* lively, animated. [from Latin *vivax -acis*] □ **vivaciously** *adv.* **vivaciousness** *n.* **vivacity** *n.*

vivarium *n.* (*pl.* **vivaria**) a place artificially prepared for keeping animals in (nearly) their natural state; an aquarium or terrarium. [Latin, literally 'warren, fishpond']

viva voce /vy-vă voh-chi/ ● *adj.* oral. ● *adv.* orally. ● *n. Brit.* an oral examination for an academic qualification. [medieval Latin, literally 'with the living voice']

vivid *adj.* **1** (of light or colour) strong, intense (*a vivid flash of lightning*; *of a vivid green*). **2** (of a mental faculty, impression, or description) clear, lively, graphic. [from Latin *vividus*] □ **vividly** *adv.* **vividness** *n.*

vivify *v.tr.* (**-ies**, **-ied**) enliven, animate, make lively or living. [from Late Latin *vivificare*] □ **vivification** *n.*

viviparous /vi-vip-ă-rŭs/ *adj. Zool.* bringing forth young alive. [from Latin *viviparus*] □ **viviparity** *n.*

vivisect *v.tr.* perform vivisection on.

vivisection *n.* dissection or other painful treatment of living animals for purposes of scientific research. [based on Latin *vivus* 'living', on the pattern of *dissection*] □ **vivisectionist** *n.* **vivisector** *n.*

vixen *n.* **1** a female fox. **2** a spiteful woman. [Old English] □ **vixenish** *adj.*

viz. *adv.* namely; that is to say; in other words (*came to a firm conclusion, viz. that we were right*). [abbreviation of Latin *videlicet* 'it is permissible to see']

vizier /vi-zeer/ *n. hist.* a high official in some Muslim countries. [from Arabic *wazīr* 'caliph's chief counsellor']

vizor var. of VISOR.

VITAMIN

Vitamins are either fat-soluble (A, D, E, K) or water-soluble (B vitamins, including niacin, folic acid, pantothenic acid, and riboflavin, and vitamin C). They consist mainly of the elements nitrogen, oxygen, carbon, and hydrogen. Fat-soluble vitamins are stored in body fat, while water-soluble vitamins are used or quickly excreted in the urine. Vitamin A is essential for the eyes, skin, hair, and bones; the B vitamins help enzymes to function; C is essential for the formation of collagen; D helps the body absorb calcium; E prevents cell damage; and K helps blood clotting. Most vitamins cannot be produced by the body and so must be obtained directly from food. Examples of food sources are shown below.

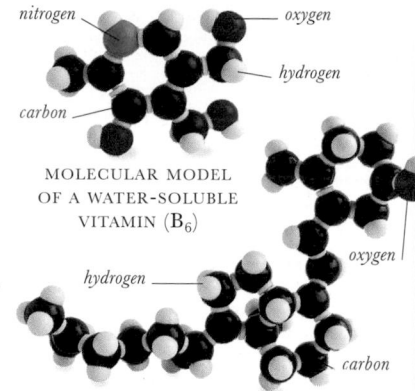

MOLECULAR MODEL OF A WATER-SOLUBLE VITAMIN (B₆)

MOLECULAR MODEL OF A FAT-SOLUBLE VITAMIN (D)

SOURCES OF THE MAIN VITAMINS

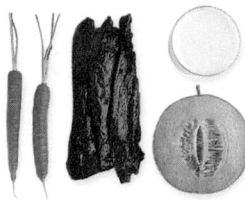

VITAMIN A (RETINOL)
carrots, calf's liver, fortified milk products, melons

VITAMIN B₁ (THIAMINE)
nuts, pork, peas, whole grains

VITAMIN B₂ (RIBOFLAVIN)
meat, eggs, cheese

VITAMIN B₆ (PYRIDOXINE)
fish, vegetables, wholegrain products, fruit

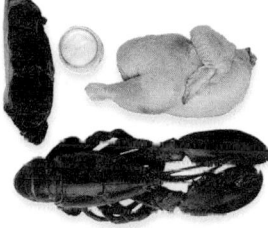

VITAMIN B₁₂ (CYANOCOBALAMIN)
beef, milk, poultry, seafood

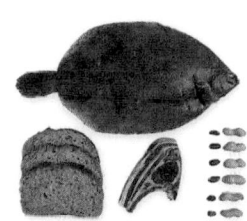

NIACIN (NICOTINIC ACID)
fish, wholegrain products, meat and poultry, peanuts

FOLIC ACID
offal, green leafy vegetables, nuts

VITAMIN C (ASCORBIC ACID)
citrus fruits, broccoli, strawberries, green peppers

VITAMIN D
oily fish, fortified cereals and breads, fortified margarine, eggs

VITAMIN E (TOCOPHEROL)
vegetable oils, green leafy vegetables, seafood, egg yolks

VITAMIN K
green leafy vegetables, pork liver, fruit, grain products, cauliflower

V

933

VJ *abbr.* Victory over Japan (in 1945).

VJ day *n.* 15 August, the day Japan ceased fighting in the Second World War, or 2 September, when Japan formally surrendered.

V-neck *n.* (often *attrib.*) a neck of a pullover etc. with straight sides meeting at an angle in the front to form a V.

vocabulary *n.* (*pl.* **-ies**) **1** the words used in a language or a particular book or branch of science etc. or by a particular author (*scientific vocabulary*; *the vocabulary of Shakespeare*). **2** a list of these, arranged alphabetically with definitions or translations. **3** the range of words known to an individual (*his vocabulary is limited*). [from medieval Latin *vocabularius*]

vocal ● *adj.* **1** of or concerned with or uttered by the voice (*a vocal communication*). **2** outspoken (*was very vocal about his rights*). **3** *Phonet.* voiced. **4** (of music) written for or produced by the voice with or without accompaniment (cf. INSTRUMENTAL *adj.* 2). ● *n.* (in *sing.* or *pl.*) the sung part of a musical composition. [from Latin *vocalis*] □ **vocally** *adv.*

vocal cords *n.pl.* (also **vocal folds**) ▼ folds of the lining membrane of the larynx, with edges vibrating in the airstream to produce the voice.

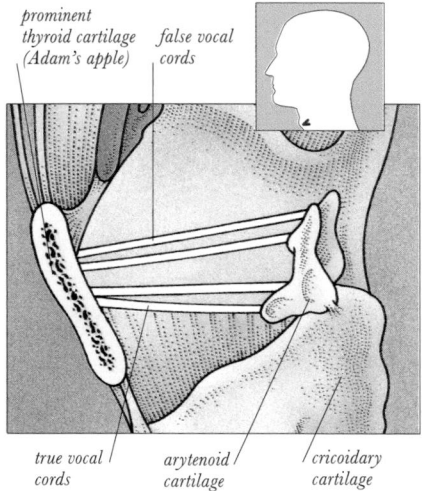

VOCAL CORDS: CROSS-SECTION OF THE LARYNX SHOWING THE VOCAL CORDS

prominent thyroid cartilage (Adam's apple) — false vocal cords — true vocal cords — arytenoid cartilage — cricoidary cartilage

vocalic *adj.* of or consisting of a vowel or vowels.

vocalist *n.* a singer.

vocalize *v.tr.* (also **-ise**) form (a sound) or utter (a word) with the voice. □ **vocalization** *n.*

vocal score *n.* a musical score showing the voice parts in full, but with the accompaniment reduced or omitted.

vocation *n.* **1** a strong feeling of fitness for a particular career (in religious contexts regarded as a divine call). **2** a person's employment, esp. regarded as requiring dedication. [based on Latin *vocare* 'to call']

vocational *adj.* **1** of or relating to an occupation or employment. **2** (of education or training) directed at a particular occupation and its skills. □ **vocationalism** *n.* **vocationally** *adv.*

vocative *Gram.* ● *n.* the case of nouns, pronouns, and adjectives used in addressing a person or thing. ● *adj.* of or in this case. [from Latin *vocativus*]

vociferate *v.* **1** *tr.* utter noisily. **2** *intr.* shout, bawl. [based on Latin *vociferatus* 'carried by voice'] □ **vociferation** *n.*

vociferous *adj.* **1** (of a person, speech, etc.) noisy, clamorous. **2** insistently and forcibly expressing one's views. □ **vociferously** *adv.* **vociferousness** *n.*

Vodafone *n. propr.* a cellular telephone system in the UK. [VOICE + DATA + *fone*, representing PHONE]

vodka *n.* an originally Russian alcoholic spirit made by distillation of rye etc. [Russian, literally 'little water']

VOLCANO

Most volcanoes occur at the edge of tectonic plates, where magma can rise to the surface. A volcano's shape depends mainly on the viscosity of the lava, the shape of the vent, the amount of ash, and the frequency and size of the eruptions. In fissure volcanoes, the magma rises up gently through a crack, forming lava plateaux or plains. In cone-shaped volcanoes, the more viscous the lava, the steeper the cone. Some cones fall in on themselves or are exploded outwards, forming calderas.

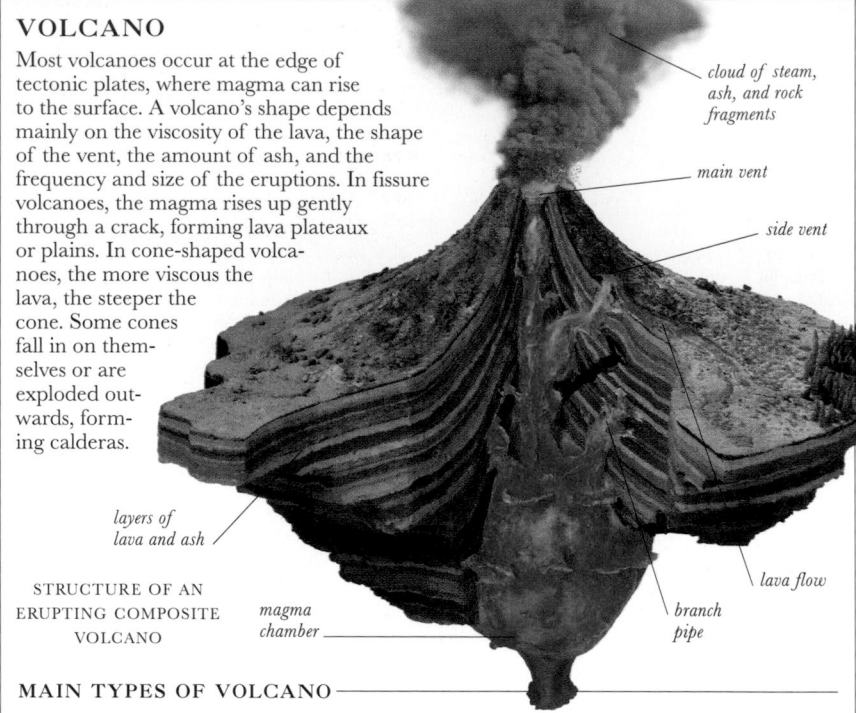

cloud of steam, ash, and rock fragments — main vent — side vent — lava flow — branch pipe — magma chamber — layers of lava and ash

STRUCTURE OF AN ERUPTING COMPOSITE VOLCANO

MAIN TYPES OF VOLCANO

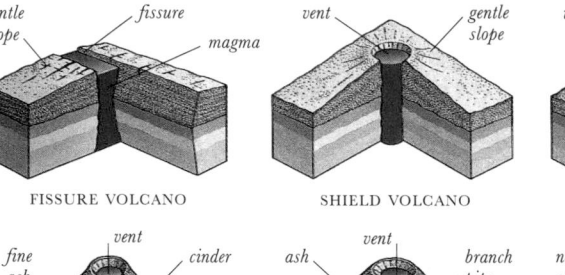

gentle slope — fissure — magma
FISSURE VOLCANO

vent — gentle slope
SHIELD VOLCANO

vent — steep convex slope
DOME VOLCANO

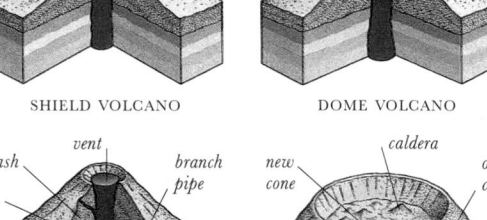

fine ash — vent — cinder
ASH-CINDER VOLCANO

ash — vent — lava — branch pipe
COMPOSITE VOLCANO

new cone — caldera — old cone
CALDERA VOLCANO

vogue *n.* **1** (prec. by *the*) the prevailing fashion. **2** popular use or currency (*has had a great vogue*). □ **in vogue** in fashion. [French] □ **voguish** *adj.*

voice ● *n.* **1 a** sound formed in the larynx etc. and uttered by the mouth, esp. human utterance in speaking, shouting, singing, etc. (*heard a voice*; *spoke in a low voice*). **b** the ability to produce this (*has lost her voice*). **2 a** the use of the voice; utterance, esp. in spoken or written words (*give voice*). **b** an opinion so expressed. **c** the right to express an opinion (*I have no voice in the matter*). **3** *Gram.* a form or set of forms of a verb showing the relation of the subject to the action (*active voice*; *passive voice*). ● *v.tr.* **1** express (*the letter voices our opinion*). **2** (esp. as **voiced** *adj.*) *Phonet.* utter with vibration of the vocal cords (e.g. *b*, *d*, *g*, *v*, *z*). □ **in voice** (or **good voice**) in proper vocal condition for singing or speaking. **with one voice** unanimously. [from Latin *vox vocis*] □ **-voiced** *adj.* (in *comb.*).

voice box *n.* the larynx.

voiceless *adj.* **1** dumb, speechless. **2** *Phonet.* uttered without vibration of the vocal cords (e.g. *f*, *k*, *p*, *s*, *t*). □ **voicelessness** *n.*

voicemail *n.* a central computerized system for storing messages from telephone callers.

voice-over *n.* narration in a film etc. not accompanied by a picture of the speaker.

voiceprint *n.* a visual record of speech, analysed with respect to frequency, duration, and amplitude.

void ● *adj.* **1 a** empty, vacant. **b** (foll. by *of*) free from (*a style void of affectation*). **2** esp. *Law* (of a contract, deed, promise, etc.) invalid, not binding (*null and void*). ● *n.* **1** an empty space, a vacuum (*vanished into the void*; *cannot fill the void made by death*). **2** an unfilled space in a wall or building. ● *v.tr.* **1** render invalid. **2** (also *absol.*) excrete. [from Old French *vuide*] □ **voidable** *adj.* **voidness** *n.*

voidance *n.* **1** *Eccl.* a vacancy in a benefice. **2** the act or an instance of voiding; the state of being voided.

voile *n.* a thin semi-transparent dress material of cotton, wool, or silk. [French, literally 'veil']

vol. *abbr.* volume.

volatile ● *adj.* **1** evaporating rapidly (*volatile salts*). **2** changeable, fickle. **3** lively, light-hearted. **4** apt to break out into violence. **5** transient. ● *n.* a volatile substance. [from Latin *volatilis*] □ **volatileness** *n.* **volatility** *n.*

volatile oil *n.* = ESSENTIAL OIL.

VOL-AU-VENT WITH MUSHROOM FILLING

vol-au-vent /vol-oh-von/ *n.* ◄ a round case of puff pastry filled with meat, fish, etc., and sauce. [French, literally 'flight in the wind']

volcanic *adj.* (also **vulcanic**) of, like, or produced by a volcano. □ **volcanically** *adv.* **volcanicity** *n.*

volcanic bomb *n.* a mass of ejected lava usu. rounded and sometimes hollow.

volcanism *n.* (also **vulcanism**) volcanic activity or phenomena.

volcano *n.* (*pl.* **-oes**) ◄ a mountain or hill having an opening or openings in the Earth's crust through which lava, cinders, steam, gases, etc., are or have been expelled continuously or at intervals. [based on Latin *Volcanus* 'Vulcan', Roman god of fire]

volcanology var. of VULCANOLOGY.

vole *n.* ► any small ratlike or mouselike plant-eating rodent of the family Cricetidae. ▷ RODENT. [originally *vole-mouse*, from Norwegian *voll* 'field' + *mus* 'mouse']

volition *n.* **1** the exercise of the will. **2** the power of willing. □ **of** (or **by**) **one's own volition** voluntarily. [from medieval Latin *volitio*] □ **volitional** *adj.*

volley ● *n.* (*pl.* **-eys**) **1 a** the simultaneous discharge of a number of weapons. **b** the bullets etc. discharged in a volley. **2** (usu. foll. by *of*) a noisy emission of oaths etc. in quick succession. **3** *Tennis* the return of a ball in play before it touches the ground. **4** *Football* the kicking of a ball in play before it touches the ground. **5** *Cricket* a ball pitched right up to the batsman or the stumps without bouncing. ● *v.* (**-eys**, **-eyed**) **1** *tr.* (also *absol.*) *Sport* return, send, or pitch (a ball) by a volley. **2** *tr. & absol.* discharge (bullets, abuse, etc.) in a volley. **3** *intr.* (of bullets etc.) fly in a volley. **4** *intr.* (of guns etc.) sound together. [from French *volée*]

volleyball *n.* ► a game for two teams of six hitting a large ball by hand over a net.

volt *n.* the SI unit of electromotive force, the difference of potential that would carry one ampere of current against one ohm resistance. [named after A. *Volta*, Italian physicist, 1745–1827]

voltage *n.* electromotive force or potential difference expressed in volts.

volte-face /volt-fas/ *n.* (*pl.* same) **1** a complete reversal of position in argument or opinion. **2** the act or an instance of turning round. [French]

voltmeter *n.* an instrument for measuring electric potential in volts.

voluble *adj.* **1** speaking or spoken vehemently, incessantly, or fluently (*voluble spokesman*; *voluble excuses*). **2** *Bot.* twisting around a support, twining. [French] □ **volubility** *n.* **volubly** *adv.*

volume *n.* **1** a set of sheets of paper, usu. printed, bound together and forming part or the whole of a work or comprising several works (*issued in three volumes*; *a library of 12,000 volumes*). **2 a** solid content, bulk. **b** the space occupied by a gas or liquid. **c** (foll. by *of*) an amount or quantity (*large volume of business*). **3 a** quantity or power of sound. **b** fullness of tone. [from Latin *volumen* 'roll']

volumetric *adj.* of or relating to measurement by volume. □ **volumetrically** *adv.*

voluminous *adj.* **1** large in volume; bulky. **2** (of

drapery etc.) loose and ample. □ **voluminously** *adv.* **voluminousness** *n.*

voluntarism *n.* **1** the principle of relying on voluntary action rather than compulsion. **2** *Philos.* the doctrine that the will is a fundamental or dominant factor in the individual or the universe. □ **voluntarist** *n.*

voluntary ● *adj.* **1** done, acting, or able to act of one's own free will; not constrained or compulsory; intentional (*a voluntary gift*). **2** unpaid (*voluntary work*). **3** (of an institution) supported by voluntary contributions. **4** (of a movement, muscle, or limb) controlled by the will. **5** (of a confession by a criminal) not prompted by a promise or threat. ● *n.* (*pl.* **-ies**) **1** an organ solo played before, during, or after a church service. **2** the music for this. [based on Latin *voluntas* 'will'] □ **voluntarily** *adv.*

voluntary-aided *adj.* (usu. *attrib.*) (in the UK) designating a voluntary school funded mainly by the local authority.

voluntary-controlled *adj.* (usu. *attrib.*) (in the UK) designating a voluntary school fully funded by the local authority.

voluntary school *n.* (in the UK) a school which, though not established by the local education authority, is funded mainly or entirely by it, and which encourages a particular set of usu. religious beliefs.

Voluntary Service Overseas *n.* a British organization promoting voluntary work in underdeveloped countries.

volunteer ● *n.* **1** a person who voluntarily takes part in an enterprise or offers to undertake a task. **2** a person who enrols for military service, esp. *hist.* (in the UK) a member of any of the former corps of voluntary soldiers provided with instructors, arms, etc., by the state. **3** (usu. *attrib.*) a self-sown plant. ● *v.* **1** *tr.* (often foll. by *to* + infin.) undertake or offer (one's services, a remark or explanation, etc.) voluntarily. **2** *intr.* (often foll. by *for*) make a voluntary offer of one's services; be a volunteer. **3** *tr.* (usu. in *passive*) assign or commit (a person) to a particular undertaking, esp. without consultation. [from French *volontaire*]

volunteerism *n.* esp. *N. Amer.* the involvement of volunteers, esp. in community service.

voluptuary ● *n.* (*pl.* **-ies**) a person given up to luxury and sensual pleasure. ● *adj.* concerned with luxury and sensual pleasure. [from Latin *volupt(u)arius*]

voluptuous *adj.* **1** of, tending to, occupied with, or derived from sensuous or sensual pleasure. **2** (of a woman) curvaceous and sexually desirable. [from Latin *voluptuosus*] □ **voluptuously** *adv.* **voluptuousness** *n.*

volute ● *n.* **1** *Archit.* a spiral scroll characteristic of Ionic capitals and also used in Corinthian and composite capitals. ▷ ACANTHUS. **2 a** any marine gastropod mollusc of the genus *Voluta*. **b** ◄ the spiral shell of this. ● *adj.* esp. *Bot.* rolled up. [French] □ **voluted** *adj.*

VOLUTE: HEBREW **VOLUTE** (*Voluta ebraea*)

volution *n.* **1** a rolling motion. **2** a spiral turn. **3** a whorl of a spiral shell.

vomer *n.* *Anat.* ► the small thin bone separating the nostrils in man and most vertebrates. [Latin, literally 'ploughshare']

vomit ● *v.tr.* (**vomited**, **vomiting**) **1** (also *absol.*) eject (matter) from the stomach through the mouth. **2** (of a volcano, chimney, etc.) eject violently, belch forth. ● *n.* **1** matter vomited from the stomach. **2** *archaic* an emetic. [based on Latin *vomitus*] □ **vomiter** *n.*

VOMER IN A HUMAN SKULL

vomitorium *n.* (*pl.* **vomitoria**) *Rom. Antiq.* a vomitory. [Latin]

vomitory ● *adj.* emetic. ● *n.* (*pl.* **-ies**) *Rom. Antiq.* each of a series of passages for entrance and exit in an amphitheatre or theatre.

VOLE: BANK VOLE (*Clethrionomys glareolus*)

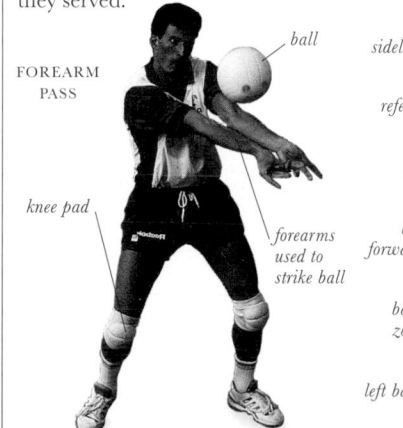

VOLLEYBALL

Volleyball is played on an indoor or outdoor court. The aim of the game is to hit the ball over the net with the hands or arms so that it hits the ground on the opponent's side. Teams may hit the ball up to three times before it crosses the net, and only score if they served.

FOREARM PASS

ball

knee pad

forearms used to strike ball

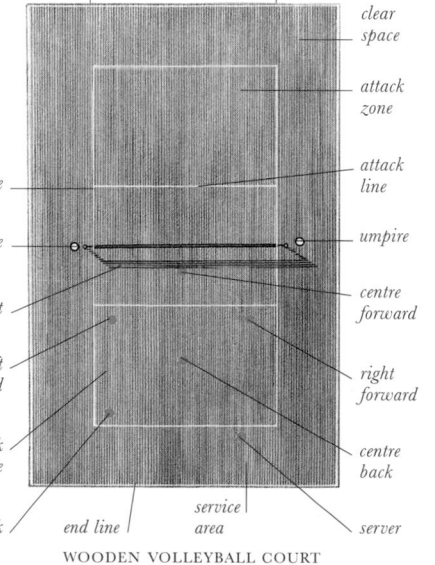

9 m (29 ft 6 in)

clear space

attack zone

attack line

sideline

referee

umpire

net

centre forward

left forward

right forward

back zone

centre back

left back

end line

service area

server

WOODEN VOLLEYBALL COURT

V

voodoo ● *n.* **1** ▶ use of or belief in religious witchcraft as practised among blacks esp. in the W. Indies. **2** a person skilled in this. **3** a voodoo spell. ● *v.tr.* (**voodoos, voodooed**) affect by voodoo; bewitch. [Louisiana French] □ **voodooist** *n.*

voracious *adj.* **1** greedy in eating, ravenous. **2** very eager in some activity (*a voracious reader*). [based on Latin *vorare* 'to devour'] □ **voraciously** *adv.* **voraciousness** *n.* **voracity** *n.*

-vorous *comb. form* forming adjectives meaning 'feeding on' (*carnivorous*). [based on Latin *vorare* 'to devour'] □ **-vora** *comb. form* forming names of groups. **-vore** *comb. form* forming names of individuals.

vortex *n.* (*pl.* **vortexes** or **vortices** /*vor*-ti-seez/) **1** a mass of whirling fluid, esp. a whirlpool or whirlwind. **2** any whirling motion or mass. **3** a system, occupation, pursuit, etc., viewed as swallowing up or engrossing those who approach it (*the vortex of society*). **4** *Physics* a portion of fluid whose particles have rotatory motion. [Latin, literally 'eddy'] □ **vortical** *adj.* **vorticity** *n.*

vorticist *n. Art* ▶ an artist of a British movement *c.*1914–15 influenced by futurism and characterized by machine-like forms. □ **vorticism** *n.*

votary *n.* (*pl.* **-ies**; *fem.* **votaress**) (usu. foll. by *of*) **1** a person vowed to the service of God or a god or cult. **2** a devoted follower, adherent, or advocate of a person, system, occupation, etc. [from Latin, related to VOTE]

vote ● *n.* **1** a formal expression of choice or opinion by means of a ballot, show of hands, etc., concerning a choice of candidate, approval of a motion or resolution, etc. (*let us take a vote on it*; *gave my vote to the independent candidate*). **2** (usu. prec. by *the*) the right to vote, esp. in a state election. **3** an opinion expressed by a majority of votes. **4** the collective votes that are or may be given by or for a particular group (*will lose the Welsh vote*; *the Conservative vote increased*). ● *v.* **1** *intr.* give a vote. **2** *tr.* **a** enact or resolve by a majority of votes. **b** grant (a sum of money) by a majority of votes. **c** cause to be in a specified position by a majority of votes (*was voted off the committee*). **3** *tr. colloq.* pronounce or declare by general consent (*was voted a failure by consumers*). **4** *tr. colloq.* announce one's proposal (*I vote that we all go home*). □ **put to a** (or **the**) **vote** submit to a decision by voting. **vote in** elect by voting. **vote out** dismiss from office etc. by voting. **vote with one's feet** *colloq.* indicate an opinion by one's presence or absence. [based on Latin *votus* 'avowed'] □ **voteless** *adj.*

vote of censure *n.* = VOTE OF NO CONFIDENCE.

vote of no confidence *n.* a vote showing that the majority do not support the policy of the governing body etc.

voter *n.* **1** a person with the right to vote at an election. **2** a person voting.

voting paper *n.* a paper used in voting by ballot.

votive *adj.* offered or consecrated in fulfilment of a vow (*votive offering*; *votive picture*). [from Latin *votivus*]

vouch *v.intr.* (foll. by *for*) answer for, be surety for (*will vouch for the truth of this*; *can vouch for him*; *could not vouch for his honesty*). [from Old French *vo(u)cher* 'to summon']

voucher *n.* a document which can be exchanged for goods or services. [from Anglo-French]

vouchsafe *v.tr. formal* **1** condescend to grant (*vouch-*

safed me no answer). **2** (foll. by *to* + infin.) condescend.

vow ● *n.* **1** *Relig.* a solemn promise esp. in the form of an oath to God or another deity or to a saint. **2** (in *pl.*) the promises by which a monk or nun is bound to poverty, chastity, and obedience. **3** a promise of fidelity (*lovers' vows*; *marriage vows*). **4** (usu. as **baptismal vows**) the promises given at baptism by the baptized person or by sponsors. ● *v.tr.* **1** promise solemnly (*vowed obedience*). **2** dedicate to a deity. [based on Latin *vovēre* 'to pledge'; *v.* sense 2: partly from AVOW]

vowel *n.* **1** a speech sound made with vibration of the vocal cords but without audible friction. **2** a letter or letters representing this, as *a, e, i, o, u, aw, ah.* [from Latin *vocalis (littera)* 'vocal (letter)'] □ **vowelled** *adj.* (*US* **voweled**) (also in *comb.*).

vox pop *n. Brit. Broadcasting colloq.* popular opinion as represented by informal comments from members of the public. [abbreviation of VOX POPULI]

vox populi /*pop*-yuu-lee/ *n.* public opinion; the general verdict. [Latin, literally 'the people's voice']

voyage ● *n.* a journey, esp. a long one by water or in space. ● *v.* **1** *intr.* make a voyage. **2** *tr.* traverse, esp. by water or air. [from Latin *viaticum*] □ **voyager** *n.*

voyeur /vwah-*yer*/ *n.* **1** a person who obtains sexual gratification from observing others' sexual actions or organs. **2** a powerless or passive spectator. [French] □ **voyeurism** *n.* **voyeuristic** *adj.* **voyeuristically** *adv.*

VP *abbr.* Vice-President.

VR *abbr.* virtual reality.

vroom ● *v.* **1** *intr.* (esp. of an engine) make a roaring noise. **2** *intr.* (of a motor vehicle etc.) travel at speed. **3** *tr.* rev (an engine). ● *n.* the roaring sound of an engine. ● *int.* an imitation of such a sound.

vs. *abbr.* versus.

V-sign *n.* **1** *Brit.* a sign of the letter V made with the first two fingers pointing up and the back of the hand facing outwards, as a gesture of abuse,

contempt, etc. **2** a similar sign made with the palm of the hand facing outwards, as a symbol of victory.

VSO *abbr.* Voluntary Service Overseas.

VSOP *abbr.* Very Special Old Pale (brandy).

Vt. *abbr.* Vermont.

VTO *abbr.* vertical take-off.

VTOL /*vee*-tol/ *abbr.* vertical take-off and landing.

vulcanic var. of VOLCANIC.

vulcanism var. of VOLCANISM.

vulcanite *n.* ▶ a hard black vulcanized rubber.

vulcanize *v.tr.* (also **-ise**) treat (rubber or rubber-like material) with sulphur etc. at a high temperature to increase its strength. [based on *Vulcan*, Roman god of fire and metalworking] □ **vulcanization** *n.*

vulcanology *n.* (also **volcanology**) the scientific study of volcanoes. □ **vulcanologist** *n.*

vulgar *adj.* **1 a** of or characteristic of the common people. **b** coarse in manners; low (*vulgar expressions*; *vulgar tastes*). **2** in common use; generally prevalent (*vulgar errors*). [based on Latin *vulgus* 'common people'] □ **vulgarly** *adv.*

vulgar fraction *n. Brit.* a fraction expressed by numerator and denominator, not decimally.

vulgarian *n.* a vulgar (esp. rich) person.

vulgarism *n.* **1** a word or expression in coarse or uneducated use. **2** an instance of coarse or uneducated behaviour.

vulgarity *n.* (*pl.* **-ies**) **1** the quality of being vulgar. **2** an instance of this.

vulgarize *v.tr.* (also **-ise**) **1** make vulgar. **2** spoil (a scene, sentiment, etc.) by making it too common, frequented, or well known. **3** popularize. □ **vulgarization** *n.*

VOODOO STATUE USED TO BIND AN ENEMY

VULCANITE SAXOPHONE MOUTHPIECE

VORTICIST

Vorticism was a short-lived artistic movement, at its height from 1914 to 1915. Led by the British artist Wyndham Lewis, it was essentially cubist in approach, but owed much to Italian futurism. Its theme was modern industrial society, portrayed using strong geometrical shapes and mechanical forms that produced works full of movement and energy. The name comes from a statement made by the futurist artist Boccioni – that all artistic creation must originate in a state of emotional vortex.

The Vorticist (1912), WYNDHAM LEWIS

TIMELINE

| 1500 | 1550 | 1600 | 1650 | 1700 | 1750 | 1800 | 1850 | 1900 | 1950 | 2000 |

V

Vulgate *n*. **1** the Latin version of the Bible prepared mainly by St Jerome in the late fourth century. **2** the official Roman Catholic Latin text as revised in 1592. [from Latin *vulgata (editio)* '(edition) made public']

vulnerable *adj*. **1** that may be wounded or harmed. **2** (foll. by *to*) exposed to damage by a weapon, criticism, etc. **3** *Bridge* having won one game towards rubber and therefore liable to higher penalties. [from Late Latin *vulnerabilis*] □ **vulnerability** *n*. (*pl.* **-ies**). **vulnerably** *adv*.

vulnerary ● *adj*. useful or used for the healing of wounds. ● *n*. (*pl.* **-ies**) a vulnerary drug or plant etc.

vulpine *adj*. of or like a fox. [based on Latin *vulpes* 'fox']

vulture *n*. **1** ▶ any of various large birds of prey of the family Accipitridae or (in the New World) Cathartidae, with the head and neck more or less bare of feathers, feeding chiefly on carrion. **2** a rapacious person. [from Latin *vulturius*] □ **vulturine** *adj*.

vulva *n*. (*pl.* **vulvas**) *Anat.* the external female genitals. ▷ REPRODUCTIVE ORGANS. [Latin, literally 'womb'] □ **vulval** *adj*. **vulvitis** *n*.

vv. *abbr*. **1** verses. **2** volumes.

vying *pres. part*. of VIE.

VULTURE

Found in both temperate and tropical regions, vultures are solitary birds, but gather in crowds to feed. Scavengers, they use their keen eyesight and, in some cases, well-developed sense of smell to locate a carcass. The head and neck of most vultures are bald, allowing them to reach inside a carcass cleanly.

bald head

hooked beak

talons

EXTERNAL
FEATURES OF A
HOODED VULTURE
(*Necrosyrtes monachus*)

EXAMPLES OF OTHER VULTURES

ANDEAN
CONDOR
(*Vultur gryphus*)

TURKEY
VULTURE
(*Cathartes aura*)

EGYPTIAN
VULTURE
(*Neophron percnopterus*)

WHITE-BACKED
VULTURE
(*Gyps africanus*)

V

W

W[1] *n.* (also **w**) (*pl.* **Ws** or **W's**) the twenty-third letter of the alphabet.

W[2] *abbr.* (also **W.**) West; Western.

W[3] *symb.* **1** *Chem.* the element tungsten. **2** watt(s). [sense 1: from WOLFRAM]

w *abbr.* (also **w.**) *Cricket* **1** wicket(s). **2** wide(s).

Waaf /waf/ *n. Brit. hist.* a member of the Women's Auxiliary Air Force (1939–48).

WAC *abbr.* (in the US) Women's Army Corps.

wacko *esp. N. Amer. slang* ● *adj.* crazy. ● *n.* (*pl.* **-os** or **-oes**) a crazy person.

wacky *adj.* (**-ier**, **-iest**) *slang* crazy. [originally dialect in sense 'left-handed', from WHACK] □ **wackily** *adv.* **wackiness** *n.*

wad /wod/ ● *n.* **1** a lump or bundle of soft material used esp. to keep things apart or in place or to stuff up an opening. **2** a disc of felt etc. keeping powder or shot in place in a gun. **3** a number of banknotes or documents placed together. **4** (in *sing.* or *pl.*) a large quantity esp. of money. ● *v.tr.* (**wadded**, **wadding**) **1** stop up (an aperture or a gun barrel) with a wad. **2** keep (powder etc.) in place with a wad. **3** line or stuff with wadding. **4** protect with wadding. **5** press (cotton etc.) into a wad or wadding.

wadding /wod-ing/ *n.* **1** soft pliable material used to line or stuff, or to pack fragile articles. **2** any material from which gun wads are made.

waddle /wod-ĕl/ ● *v.intr.* walk with short steps and a swaying motion. ● *n.* a waddling gait. □ **waddler** *n.*

waddy *n.* (*pl.* **ies**) an Australian Aborigine's war club.

wade ● *v.* **1** *intr.* walk through water or some impeding medium. **2** *intr.* make one's way with difficulty or by force. **3** *intr.* (foll. by *through*) read (a book etc.) in spite of its dullness etc. **4** *intr.* (foll. by *into*) *colloq.* attack vigorously. **5** *tr.* ford on foot. ● *n.* a spell of wading. □ **wade in** *colloq.* make a vigorous attack or intervention. [Old English] □ **wadable** *adj.* (also **wadeable**).

wader *n.* **1 a** a person who wades. **b** a wading bird. **2** (in *pl.*) ◄ high waterproof boots, or a waterproof garment for the legs and body.

wading bird *n.* ► any long-legged waterbird that wades.

WAF *abbr.* (in the US) Women in the Air Force.

wafer ● *n.* **1** a very thin light crisp sweet biscuit. **2** a disc of unleavened bread used in the Eucharist. **3** a disc of red paper stuck on a legal document instead of a seal. **4** *Electronics* a very thin slice of a semiconductor crystal. ● *v.tr.* fasten or seal with a wafer. [from Old Northern French *waufre*] □ **wafery** *adj.*

wafer-thin *adj.* very thin.

fastening strap

high-grip sole

WADERS

waffle[1] /wof-ĕl/ *colloq.* ● *n.* verbose but aimless or ignorant talk or writing. ● *v.intr.* **1** (often foll. by *on*) indulge in waffle. **2** waver, equivocate. [originally dialect, from *waff* 'to yelp, yap'] □ **waffler** *n.* **waffly** *adj.*

waffle[2] /wof-ĕl/ *n.* a small crisp batter cake. [from Dutch *wafel*]

waft ● *v.tr. & intr.* convey or travel easily as through air or over water; sweep smoothly along. ● *n.* **1** (usu. foll. by *of*) a whiff or scent. **2** a transient sensation. [originally in sense 'to convoy': back-formation from obsolete *wafter* 'armed convoy-ship']

wag[1] ● *v.tr. & intr.* (**wagged**, **wagging**) shake or wave energetically to and fro. ● *n.* a single wagging motion (*with a wag of his tail*). [Middle English]

wag[2] *n.* a facetious person, a joker.

wage ● *n.* **1** (in *sing.* or *pl.*) a fixed regular payment, made by an employer to an employee, esp. to a manual or unskilled worker (cf. SALARY). **2** (in *sing.* or *pl.*) requital. ● *v.tr.* carry on (a war or contest). [from Old French *g(u)age*]

wage bill *n.* the amount paid in wages to employees.

waged *adj.* in regular paid employment.

wager *n. & v.* = BET. [from Anglo-French *wageure*]

wages council *n. Brit.* a board of workers' and employers' representatives determining wages where there is no collective bargaining.

waggish *adj.* playful, facetious. □ **waggishly** *adv.* **waggishness** *n.*

waggle *colloq.* ● *v.intr. & tr.* wag. ● *n.* a waggling motion.

waggly *adj.* unsteady.

Wagnerian /vahg-neer-iăn/ *adj.* of or relating to the operas of Richard Wagner, German composer d. 1883, esp. with reference to their large scale.

wagon *n.* (also *Brit.* **waggon**) **1** a four-wheeled vehicle for heavy loads. **2** *Brit.* a railway vehicle for goods, esp. an open truck. **3** *colloq.* a motor car, esp. an estate car. □ **on the wagon** (or *Brit.* **water wagon**) *colloq.* teetotal. [from Dutch *wag(h)en*]

wagoner *n.* (also *Brit.* **waggoner**) the driver of a wagon.

wagon-lit /vag-on-lee/ *n.* (*pl.* **wagons-lits** *pronunc.* same) a sleeping car on a Continental railway. [French]

wagonload *n.* as much as a wagon can carry.

wagtail *n.* any small bird of the genus *Motacilla* with a long tail in frequent motion.

waif *n.* a homeless and helpless person, esp. a child. [from Anglo-French] □ **waifish** *adj.*

wail ● *n.* **1** a prolonged plaintive inarticulate loud high-pitched cry of pain, grief, etc. **2** a sound like this. ● *v.intr.* **1** utter a wail. **2** lament or complain persistently or bitterly. **3** make a sound like a person wailing. [from Old Norse] □ **wailer** *n.* **wailingly** *adv.*

wainscot ● *n.* boarding or wooden panelling on the lower part of a room-wall. ● *v.tr.* (**wainscoted**, **wainscoting** or **wainscotted**, **wainscotting**) line with wainscot. [from Middle Low German *wagenschot*]

wainscoting *n.* (also **wainscotting**) **1** a wainscot. **2** material for this.

waist *n.* **1 a** the part of the human body below the ribs and above the hips. **b** the circumference of this. **2** a similar narrow part in the middle of a violin etc. ▷ STRINGED. **3 a** the part of a garment covering the waist. **b** the narrow middle part of a woman's dress etc. [Middle English] □ **waisted** *adj.* (also in *comb.*). **waistless** *adj.*

waistband *n.* a strip of cloth forming the waist of a garment.

waistcoat *n.* ► *Brit.* a close-fitting waist-length garment, without sleeves or collar but usu. buttoned.

waistline *n.* the outline or the size of a person's waist.

WAISTCOAT: 18TH-CENTURY EMBROIDERED WAISTCOAT

wait ● *v.* **1** *intr.* **a** defer action or departure for a specified time or until some expected event occurs (*wait a minute*; *wait for a fine day*). **b** be expectant or on the watch (*waited to see what would happen*). **2** *tr.* await (an opportunity, one's turn, etc.). **3** *intr.* (usu. as **waiting** *n.*) park a vehicle for a short time at the side of a road etc. (*no waiting*). **4** *intr.* (in full **wait at** (or *N. Amer.* **on**)

WADING BIRD

Wading birds belong to the order Charadriiformes, in which there are some 200 species. They live in a wide range of damp habitats, and are often found by the shore. Thin, long, sensitive beaks are ideally suited to probing for molluscs, worms, or shrimps in mud, while their long legs are adapted for striding in water. Side-facing eyes provide good, all-round vision, allowing wading birds to remain alert to danger.

side-facing eye

slender beak

long legs

EXTERNAL FEATURES OF AN OYSTERCATCHER (*Haematopus ostralegus*)

waterproofed feathers

OTHER EXAMPLES OF WADING BIRDS

EURASIAN CURLEW (*Numenius arquata*)

WATTLED JACANA (*Jacana jacana*)

WHITE-HEADED LAPWING (*Vanellus albiceps*)

PIED AVOCET (*Recurvirostra avosetta*)

table) act as a waiter. **5** *intr.* (foll. by *on, upon*) **a** await the convenience of. **b** serve as an attendant to. ● *n.* **1** a period of waiting (*had a long wait*). **2** (usu. foll. by *for*) watching for an enemy; ambush (*lie in wait*). **3** (in *pl.*) *Brit. archaic* street singers of Christmas carols. □ **cannot wait 1** is impatient. **2** needs to be dealt with immediately. **can wait** need not be dealt with immediately. **wait and see** await the progress of events. **wait for it!** *Brit. colloq.* used to create an interval of suspense before saying something unexpected or amusing. **wait up** (often foll. by *for*) not go to bed until a person arrives or an event happens. **you wait!** used to imply a threat, warning, or promise. [from Old Northern French *waitier*]

waiter *n.* a man or *US* a woman who serves at table in a hotel or restaurant etc.

waiting *n.* **1** in senses of WAIT *v.* **2 a** official attendance at court. **b** one's period of this.

waiting list *n.* a list of people waiting for a thing not immediately available.

waitress *n.* a woman who serves at table in a hotel or restaurant etc.

waitressing *n.* the occupation of working as a waitress.

waive *v.tr.* refrain from insisting on or using (a right, claim, etc.). [from Old French *gaiver* 'to allow to become a waif, abandon']

waiver *n. Law* **1** the act or an instance of waiving. **2** a document recording this.

wake[1] ● *v.intr. & tr.* (*past* **woke** or **waked**; *past part.* **woken** or **waked**) **1** (often foll. by *up*) cease or cause to cease to sleep. **2** (often foll. by *up*) become or cause to become alert or active (*needs something to wake him up*). ● *n.* a watch or vigil beside a corpse before burial. [Old English]

wake[2] *n.* **1** the track left on the water's surface by a moving ship. **2** turbulent air left behind a moving aircraft etc. □ **in the wake of** behind, following, as a result of.

wakeful *adj.* **1** unable to sleep. **2** (of a night etc.) passed with little sleep. **3** vigilant. □ **wakefully** *adv.* **wakefulness** *n.*

waken *v.tr. & intr.* make or become awake.

wale *n.* **1** = WEAL. **2** a ridge on a woven fabric, e.g. corduroy. **3** *Naut.* a broad thick timber along a ship's side. [Old English *walu* 'stripe, ridge']

walk ● *v.* **1** *intr.* **a** (of a person or other biped) progress by lifting and setting down each foot in turn, never having both feet off the ground at once. **b** progress with similar movements (*walked on his hands*). **c** (of a quadruped) go with the slowest gait, always having at least two feet on the ground at once. **2** *intr.* **a** travel or go on foot. **b** take exercise in this way. **3** *tr.* perambulate, traverse on foot at walking speed, tread the floor or surface of. **4** *tr.* **a** cause to walk with one. **b** accompany in walking. **c** ride or lead (a horse, dog, etc.) at walking pace. **5** *intr. N. Amer. slang* be released from suspicion or from a charge. ● *n.* **1 a** an act of walking, the ordinary human gait (*go at a walk*). **b** the slowest gait of an animal. **c** a person's manner of walking. **2 a** (an act or instance of) travelling a specified distance on foot (*only ten minutes' walk from here*). **b** an excursion on foot (*go for a walk*). **3** a place, track, or route intended or suitable for walking. □ **walk all over** *colloq.* **1** defeat easily. **2** take advantage of. **walk away from 1** easily outdistance. **2** refuse to become involved with. **3** survive (an accident etc.) without serious injury. **walk away with** *colloq.* = *walk off with*. **walk off 1** depart (esp. abruptly). **2** get rid of the effects of by walking (*walked off his anger*). **walk off with** *colloq.* **1** steal. **2** win easily. **walk on air** see AIR. **walk out** depart suddenly or angrily. **walk out on** desert, abandon. **walk over** *colloq.* = *walk all over*. **walk the plank** see PLANK. **walk the streets 1** be a prostitute. **2** traverse the streets esp. in search of work. **walk tall** *colloq.* feel justifiable pride. [Old English *wealcan* 'to roll, toss, wander'] □ **walkable** *adj.*

walkabout *n.* **1** esp. *Brit.* an informal stroll among a crowd by a visiting dignitary. **2** *Austral.* a period of wandering in the bush by an Aborigine.

walkathon *n.* an organized fund-raising walk.

walker *n.* **1** a person or animal that walks. **2** a framework in which a baby can learn to walk.

walkie-talkie *n.* ▶ a two-way radio carried on the person.

walk-in *attrib.adj.* (of a storage area) large enough to walk into.

walking frame *n. Brit.* a usu. tubular metal frame used by disabled or old people to help them walk.

walking shoe *n.* a sturdy, practical shoe for walking.

walking stick *n.* a stick carried when walking, esp. for extra support.

walking tour *n.* a holiday journey on foot, esp. of several days.

walking wounded *n.* (*pl.* same) (usu. in *pl.*) **1** a casualty able to walk despite injuries. **2** *colloq.* a person having esp. mental or emotional difficulties.

Walkman *n.* (*pl.* **-mans** or **-men**) *propr.* a type of personal stereo.

walk of life *n.* an occupation or calling.

walk-on *n.* **1** (in full **walk-on part**) a non-speaking dramatic role. **2** an actor playing this.

walkout *n.* a sudden angry departure, esp. as a protest or strike.

walkover *n.* an easy victory or achievement.

walkway *n.* a passage or path for walking along.

wall ● *n.* **1 a** a continuous and usu. vertical structure of usu. brick or stone, esp. for enclosing, protecting, or dividing a space or supporting a roof. **b** the surface of a wall (*pictures on the wall*). **2** anything like a wall in appearance or effect (*a wall of bayonets; a wall of indifference; stomach wall*). ● *v.tr.* **1** surround or protect with a wall (*walled garden*). **2 a** (usu. foll. by *up, off*) block or seal with a wall. **b** (foll. by *up*) enclose (a person) within a sealed space (*walled up in a dungeon*). □ **go to the wall** be defeated or pushed aside. **go up the wall** *colloq.* become crazy or furious. **off the wall** (hyphenated when *attrib.*) esp. *N. Amer. slang* unconventional. **walls have ears** beware of eavesdroppers. [from Latin *vallum* 'rampart'] □ **walling** *n.* **wall-less** *adj.*

wallaby *n.* (*pl.* **-ies**) ▼ any of various marsupials of the family Macropodidae, smaller than kangaroos, and having large hind feet and long tails. [from Aboriginal *walabi*]

wallah *n.* orig. *Anglo-Ind.*, now *slang* **1** a person concerned with or in charge of a usu. specified thing, business, etc. (*asked the ticket wallah*). **2** a bureaucrat. [from Hindi *-wālā*, equivalent of English suffix *-er*]

wall bar *n. Brit.* one of a set of parallel bars, attached to the wall of a gymnasium, on which exercises are performed.

WALLABY:
RED-NECKED WALLABY
(*Macropus rufogriseus*)

WALKIE-TALKIE:
MODERN US HAND-
HELD RADIO SET

earpiece

mouthpiece

handset cable

short aerial

dust cap

speaker

frequency display panel

tuning button

carrying pouch

wallchart *n.* a chart or poster designed for display on a wall as a teaching aid etc.

wallcovering *n.* material used to cover and decorate interior walls.

wallet *n.* a small flat esp. leather case for holding banknotes etc. [Middle English]

wall-eye *n.* **1** an eye with a streaked or opaque white iris. **2** an eye squinting outwards. [from Old Norse *vagleygr*] □ **wall-eyed** *adj.*

wallflower *n.* **1** ▶ a spring-flowering garden plant, *Cheiranthus cheiri*, with yellow, orange, or red flowers. **2** *colloq.* a neglected or socially awkward person, esp. a woman sitting out at a dance for lack of partners.

wall-hung *adj.* (often *attrib.*) = WALL-MOUNTED.

wall-mounted *adj.* (often *attrib.*) attached by a bracket or other support to a wall.

Walloon /wol-oon/ ● *n.* **1** a member of a French-speaking people inhabiting S. and E. Belgium and neighbouring France. **2** the French dialect spoken by this people. ● *adj.* of or concerning the Walloons or their language. [from medieval Latin *Wallo -onis*]

WALLFLOWER
(*Cheiranthus cheiri*)

wallop /wol-ŏp/ *colloq.* ● *v.tr.* (**walloped**, **walloping**) **1 a** thrash; beat. **b** hit hard. **2** (as **walloping** *adj.*) big; thumping (*a walloping profit*). ● *n.* **1** a heavy blow; a thump. **2** *Brit.* beer or any alcoholic drink. [earlier in senses 'to gallop, boil': from Old French *galoper*] □ **walloping** *n.*

wallow /wol-oh/ ● *v.intr.* **1** (esp. of an animal) roll about in mud, water, etc. **2** indulge in unrestrained pleasure, misery, etc. (*wallowing in nostalgia*). ● *n.* **1** the act or an instance of wallowing. **2** a place used by buffalo etc. for wallowing. [Old English *walwian* 'to roll'] □ **wallower** *n.*

wallpaper ● *n.* **1** paper sold in rolls for pasting on to interior walls as decoration. **2** *Brit.* an unobtrusive background, esp. (usu. *derog.*) with reference to sound, music, etc. ● *v.tr.* (often *absol.*) decorate with wallpaper.

wall space *n.* space on the surface of a wall.

Wall Street *n.* the American financial world or money market. [a street in New York City]

wall-to-wall *attrib.adj.* **1** (of carpeting etc.) covering the entire floor area. **2** endless; exclusive of all else (*wall-to-wall coverage of sport*).

wally /wol-i/ *n.* (*pl.* **-ies**) *Brit. slang* a foolish or inept person.

walnut *n.* **1** (also **walnut tree**) ▼ a tree of the genus *Juglans*, having aromatic leaves and drooping catkins. **2** the nut of this tree. ▷ NUT. **3** the timber of this tree, used in cabinetmaking. ▷ WOOD. [Old English]

catkin

W

WALNUT
(*Juglans regia*)

Walpurgis night *n.* the eve of 1 May when witches are alleged to meet on the Brocken mountain in Germany and hold revels with the Devil. [German *Walpurgisnacht* from *Walpurgis* (genitive of *Walpurga*, the name of an 8th c. English woman saint) + *Nacht* NIGHT]

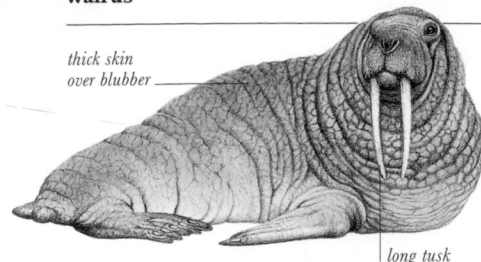

thick skin
over blubber

long tusk

WALRUS
(*Odobenus rosmarus*)

walrus *n.* ▲ a large amphibious long-tusked Arctic mammal, *Odobenus rosmarus*, related to the seal. ▷ PINNIPED

walrus moustache *n.* a long thick drooping moustache.

waltz ● *n.* **1** a dance in triple time. **2** the usu. flowing music for this. ● *v.* **1** *intr.* dance a waltz. **2** *intr.* (often foll. by *in*, *out*, *round*, etc.) *colloq.* move lightly, casually, with deceptive ease, etc. (*waltzed in and took first prize*). **3** *tr.* move (a person) in or as if in a waltz, casually or with ease (*was waltzed off to Paris*). [from German *walzen* 'to revolve'] □ **waltzer** *n.*

wampum /**wom**-pum/ *n.* ▼ beads made from shells and strung together for use as money, decoration, or as aids to memory by N. American Indians. [from Algonquian *wampumpeag*]

WAMPUM: 17TH-CENTURY IROQUOIS
WAMPUM USED AS MONEY

wan /rhymes with don/ *adj.* (**wanner**, **wannest**) **1** pale; exhausted; worn. **2** faint. [Old English *wann* 'dark, black'] □ **wanly** *adv.* **wanness** *n.*

WAN *abbr. n. Computing* wide area network.

wand *n.* **1** a supposedly magic stick used by a fairy, magician, etc. **2** a slender rod carried or used as a marker in the ground. **3** a staff symbolizing authority. [from Old Norse *vendr*]

wander ● *v.* **1** *intr.* go about from place to place aimlessly. **2** *intr.* **a** (of a person, river, etc.) meander; diverge. **b** get lost; leave home; stray from a path etc. **3** *intr.* talk or think incoherently. **4** *tr.* cover while wandering (*wanders the world*). ● *n.* the act or an instance of wandering (*a wander round the garden*). [Old English] □ **wanderer** *n.* **wandering** *n.* (esp. in *pl.*).

wandering Jew *n.* **1 a** a legendary person said to have been condemned by Christ to wander the earth until the second advent. **b** a person who never settles down. **2 a** a climbing plant, *Tradescantia albiflora*, with stemless variegated leaves. **b** a trailing plant, *Zebrina pendula*, with pink flowers.

wanderlust *n.* an eagerness for travelling. [German]

wane ● *v.intr.* **1** (of the moon) decrease in apparent size after the full moon (cf. WAX[2]). **2** decrease in importance, brilliance, size, etc.; decline. ● *n.* the process of waning. □ **on the wane** waning; declining. [Old English *wanian* 'to lessen']

wangle *colloq.* ● *v.tr.* (often *refl.*) obtain (a favour etc.) by scheming etc. (*wangled himself a free trip*). ● *n.* the act or an instance of wangling. [19th-century printers' slang] □ **wangler** *n.*

wank *Brit. coarse slang* ● *v.intr.* & *tr.* masturbate. ● *n.* an act of masturbating. [20th-century coinage]

wanker *n. Brit. coarse slang* **1** a contemptible or ineffectual person. **2** a person who masturbates.

wannabe /**won**-ă-bi; *first part rhymes with* don/ *n. slang* an avid fan who tries to emulate a particular celebrity or type. [representing *want to be*]

want ● *v.* **1** *tr.* **a** (often foll. by *to* + infin.) desire; wish for possession of; need (*wants a toy train*; *wanted to leave*; *wanted him to leave*). **b** need or desire (a person, esp. sexually). **c** esp. *Brit.* require to be attended to in a specified way (*the garden wants weeding*). **d** (foll. by *to* + infin.) *colloq.* ought; should; need (*you want to get a job*). **2** *intr.* (usu. foll. by *for*) lack (*wants for nothing*). **3** *intr.* (foll. by *in*, *out*) esp. *US colloq.* desire to be in, out, etc. (*wants in on the deal*). **4** *tr.* (as **wanted** *adj.*) (of a suspected criminal) sought by the police. ● *n.* **1** (often foll. by *of*) **a** a lack (*shows great want of judgement*). **b** poverty; need (*living in great want*; *in want of necessities*). **2 a** a desire (*meets a long-felt want*). **b** a thing so desired (*can supply your wants*). □ **do not want to** am unwilling to. [from Old Norse *vant* 'thing' lacking']

wanting *adj.* **1** lacking; deficient (*wanting in judgement*). **2** absent, not provided. □ **be found wanting** fail to meet requirements.

wanton *adj.* **1** licentious; lewd; sexually promiscuous. **2** capricious; random (*wanton destruction*). **3** luxuriant (*wanton profusion*). [Middle English] □ **wantonly** *adv.* **wantonness** *n.*

wapiti /**wop**-i-ti/ *n.* (*pl.* **wapitis**) ► a large race of the red deer, *Cervus elaphus*, living in N. America. [from Algonquian *wapitik* 'white deer']

war ● *n.* **1 a** armed hostilities between esp. nations; conflict (*war broke out*). **b** a specific conflict or the time of such conflict (*was before the war*). **2** (as **the War**) a war in progress; the most recent major war. **3 a** hostility or contention (*war of words*). **b** a sustained campaign against crime, poverty, etc. ● *v.intr.* (**warred**, **warring**) **1** (as **warring** *adj.*) **a** a rival; fighting (*warring factions*). **b** conflicting (*warring principles*). **2** make war. □ **at war** engaged in a war. **go to war** declare or begin a war. [Middle English]

warble ● *v.* **1** *intr.* & *tr.* sing in a gentle trilling manner. **2** *tr.* utter in a warbling manner. ● *n.* a warbled song or utterance. [from Frankish *hwirbilōn* 'to whirl, trill']

warble fly *n.* any of various flies of the genus *Hypoderma*, infesting the skin of cattle and horses.

warbler *n.* **1** a person, bird, etc. that warbles. **2** any small insect-eating bird of the family Sylviidae or, in N. America, Parulidae.

war chest *n.* funds for a campaign.

war crime *n.* a crime violating the international laws of war. □ **war criminal** *n.*

war cry *n.* a phrase or name shouted to rally one's troops.

ward *n.* **1** a separate room or division of a hospital etc. **2** an administrative division of a constituency. **3 a** a minor under the care of a guardian appointed by the parents or a court. **b** (in full **ward of court**) a minor or mentally deficient person placed under the protection of a court. □ **ward off 1** parry (a blow). **2** avert (danger etc.). [Old English]

-ward /wĕd/ *suffix* (also **-wards** /wĕdz/) added to nouns of place or destination and to adverbs of direction and forming: **1** adverbs (usu. **-wards**) meaning 'towards the place etc.' (*set off homewards*). **2** adjectives (usu. **-ward**) meaning 'turned or tending towards' (*an onward rush*). **3** (less commonly) nouns meaning 'the region towards or about' (*look to the eastward*).

war damage *n.* damage to property etc. caused by bombing, shelling, etc.

war dance *n.* a dance performed before a battle, ceremonially, or to celebrate victory.

WAPITI
(*Cervus elaphus*)

warden *n.* **1** (usu. in *comb.*) a supervising official (*traffic warden*). **2 a** *Brit.* a president or governor of a college, youth hostel, etc. **b** esp. *US* a prison governor. [from Anglo-French *wardein*] □ **wardenship** *n.*

war department *n. hist.* the State office in charge of the army etc.

warder *n.* **1** *Brit.* (*fem.* **wardress**) a prison officer. **2** a guard.

ward of court see WARD *n.* 3b.

wardrobe *n.* **1** a large cupboard with rails etc., for storing clothes. **2** a person's stock of clothes. **3** the costume department or costumes of a theatre, a film company, etc. [from Old Northern French *warderobe*]

wardrobe mistress *n.* (also **wardrobe master**) a person in charge of a theatrical etc. wardrobe.

wardroom *n.* a room in a warship for the use of commissioned officers.

-wards var. of -WARD.

ware[1] *n.* **1** (esp. in *comb.*) things of the same kind, esp. ceramics, made usu. for sale (*chinaware*; *hardware*). **2** (usu. in *pl.*) articles for sale (*displayed his wares*). **3** ceramics etc. of a specified material, factory, or kind (*Wedgwood ware*). [Old English]

ware[2] *v.tr.* (also **'ware**) (esp. in hunting) look out for; avoid (usu. in *imper.*: *ware hounds!*). [Old English]

warehouse ● *n.* **1** a building in which esp. retail goods are stored. **2** a wholesale or large retail store. ● *v.tr.* store temporarily in a repository. □ **warehouseman** *n.* (*pl.* **-men**)

warfare *n.* a state of war; campaigning, engaging in war (*chemical warfare*).

warfarin *n.* a water-soluble anticoagulant used esp. as a rat poison and in the treatment of thrombosis. [*W*isconsin *A*lumni *R*esearch *F*oundation + *-arin*]

warhead *n.* ► the explosive head of a missile, torpedo, or similar weapon.

warhorse *n.* **1** *hist.* a knight's or trooper's powerful horse. ▷ JOUST. **2** *colloq.* a veteran soldier, politician, etc.; a reliable hack.

warlike *adj.* **1** hostile. **2** soldierly. **3** of or for war (*warlike preparations*).

war loan *n.* stock issued by the British Government to raise funds in wartime.

warlock *n. archaic* a sorcerer or wizard. [Old English *wĕr-loga* 'traitor']

warlord *n.* a military commander or commander-in-chief.

warm ● *adj.* **1** of or at a fairly or comfortably high temperature. **2** (of clothes etc.) affording warmth. **3 a** sympathetic; cordial; loving (*a warm welcome*; *has a warm heart*). **b** enthusiastic; hearty (*was warm in her praise*). **4** animated, heated (*a warm exchange of views*). **5** *colloq. iron.* difficult or hostile (*met a warm reception*). **6** *colloq.* near to guessing (*you're not even warm*). **7** (of a colour, light, etc.) reddish, pink, or yellowish, etc. ● *v.* **1** *tr.* **a** make warm (*warms the room*). **b** make cheerful (*warms the heart*). **2** *intr.* **a** (often foll. by *up*) become warm (*while the dinner was warming up*). **b** (often foll. by *to*) become enthusiastic or sympathetic (*warmed to his subject*). ● *n.* the act of warming; the state of being warmed (*had a nice warm by the fire*). □ **warm up 1** (of an athlete, performer, etc.) prepare by practising. **2** become or cause to become warmer. **3** become enthusiastic etc. **4** (of an appliance etc.) reach a temperature for efficient working. **5** reheat (food). [Old English] □ **warmer** *n.* (also in *comb.*). **warmish** *adj.* **warmly** *adv.* **warmness** *n.* **warmth** *n.*

WARHEAD
ON AN EARLY
20TH-CENTURY
TORPEDO

warhead

torpedo

fin

W

WARSHIP

The introduction of heavily armoured 'dreadnought' warships in the 20th century revolutionized sea warfare. They combined the latest advances in steam propulsion and weaponry, and were protected by belt-armour plating. Modern warships fall into three broad categories: surface ships, which defend carriers and attack enemy ships; search-and-destroy submarines; and ballistic missile submarines, which stay hidden below the sea for months.

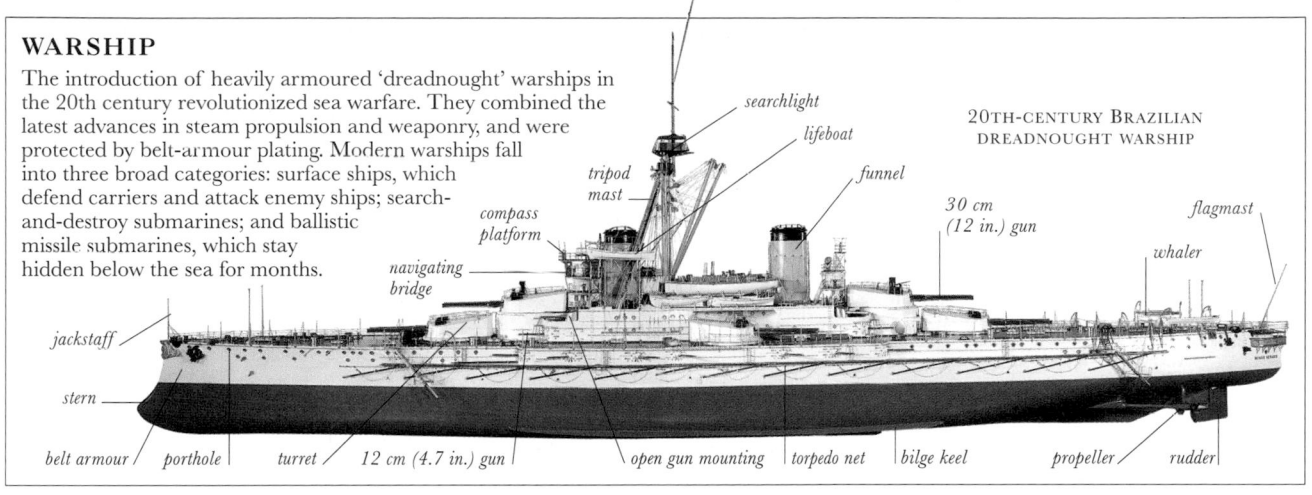

20TH-CENTURY BRAZILIAN DREADNOUGHT WARSHIP

searchlight · lifeboat · funnel · 30 cm (12 in.) gun · flagmast · whaler · tripod mast · compass platform · navigating bridge · jackstaff · stern · belt armour · porthole · turret · 12 cm (4.7 in.) gun · open gun mounting · torpedo net · bilge keel · propeller · rudder

---

warm-blooded *adj.* **1** (of an organism) having warm blood; mammalian. **2** ardent, passionate. □ **warm-bloodedness** *n.*

warmed-up *adj.* (*N. Amer.* **warmed-over**) **1** (of food etc.) reheated. **2** stale; second-hand.

war memorial *n.* a monument etc. commemorating those killed in a war.

warm front *n.* an advancing mass of warm air. ▷ FRONT, WEATHER CHART

warm-hearted *adj.* kind, friendly. □ **warm-heartedly** *adv.* **warm-heartedness** *n.*

warming-pan *n. hist.* a usu. brass container for live coals with a flat body and a long handle, used for warming a bed.

warmonger *n.* a person who seeks to bring about or promote war. □ **warmongering** *n. & adj.*

warm-up *n.* a period of preparatory exercise for a contest or performance etc.

warn *v.tr.* **1** (also *absol.*) **a** (often foll. by *of*, or *that* + clause, or *to* + infin.) inform of danger, unknown circumstances, etc. (*warned them of the danger*). **b** (often foll. by *against*) inform (a person etc.) about a specific danger, hostile person, etc. (*warned her against trusting him*). **2** (usu. with *neg.*) tell forcefully (*was warned not to go*). **3** give (a person) cautionary notice (*shall not warn you again*). □ **warn off** tell (a person) to keep away (from). [Old English] □ **warner** *n.*

warning ● *n.* **1** in senses of WARN *v.* **2** anything that serves to warn. ● *attrib.adj.* serving to warn. □ **warningly** *adv.*

war of attrition *n.* a war in which each side seeks to wear out the other over a long period.

warp ● *v.* **1** *tr. & intr.* **a** make or become bent or twisted out of shape. **b** make or become perverted or strange (*a warped sense of humour*). **2** *tr.* haul (a ship) by a rope attached to a fixed point. ● *n.* **1 a** a state of being warped, esp. of timber. **b** perversion of the mind or character. **2** the threads stretched lengthwise in a loom. ▷ WEFT. **3** a rope used in towing or warping, or attached to a trawl net. [originally in sense 'to throw': Old English *weorpan*] □ **warpage** *n.* (esp. in sense 1a of *v.*).

warpaint *n.* **1** paint used to adorn the body before battle. **2** *colloq.* elaborate make-up.

warpath *n.* **1** a warlike expedition of N. American Indians. **2** *colloq.* any hostile course (*on the warpath*).

warrant ● *n.* **1** anything that authorizes a person or an action. **2 a** a written authorization, money voucher, etc. (*a dividend warrant*). **b** a written authorization allowing police to search premises etc. **3** a document of authorization to counsel in a lawsuit (*warrant of attorney*). ● *v.tr.* **1** justify (*nothing can warrant his behaviour*). **2** guarantee or attest to. □ **I** (or **I'll**) **warrant** I am certain (*he'll be sorry, I'll warrant*). [from Old Northern French *warant*] □ **warrantable** *adj.* **warranter** *n.* **warrantor** *n.*

warrant officer *n.* an officer in the army or RAF ranking between commissioned officers and NCOs.

warranty *n.* (*pl.* **-ies**) **1** an undertaking as to the ownership or quality of a thing sold, hired, etc., often accepting responsibility or liability over a specified period. **2** (usu. foll. by *for* + verbal noun) an authority or justification. **3** an undertaking by an insured person of the truth of a statement or fulfilment of a condition. □ **warrantee** *n.*

warren *n.* **1** a network of interconnecting rabbit burrows. **2** a labyrinthine building or district. [from Old Northern French *warenne*]

warrior *n.* **1** a person experienced or distinguished in fighting in an armed force, tribe, etc. **2** (*attrib.*) **a** of or relating to a warrior. **b** martial (*a warrior nation*). [from Old Northern French *werreior*]

warship *n.* ▲ an armoured ship used in war.

Wars of the Roses *n.pl. hist.* the 15th-c. civil wars between the houses of York and Lancaster, represented by white and red roses respectively.

wart *n.* **1** ▼ a small benign virus-induced growth on the skin, usu. hard and rounded. **2** a protuberance on the skin of an animal, surface of a plant, etc. [Old English] □ **warty** *adj.*

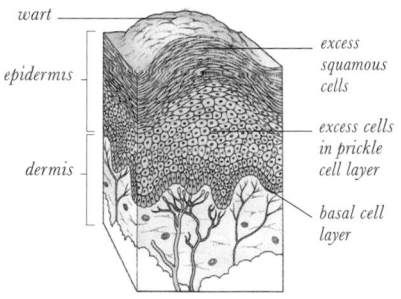

wart · epidermis · dermis · excess squamous cells · excess cells in prickle cell layer · basal cell layer

WART: CROSS-SECTION THROUGH A WART ON HUMAN SKIN

warthog *n.* an African wild pig, *Phacochoerus aethiopicus*, with a large head and warty lumps on its face, and large curved tusks.

wartime *n.* the period during which a war is waged.

war-torn *adj.* racked or devastated by war.

war widow *n.* a woman whose husband has been killed in war.

wary /wair-i/ *adj.* (**warier, wariest**) **1** on one's guard; circumspect. **2** (foll. by *of*) cautious, suspicious (*am wary of using lifts*). **3** showing or done with caution or suspicion (*a wary expression*). [based on WARE²] □ **warily** *adv.* **wariness** *n.*

was *1st* & *3rd sing. past* of BE.

wash ● *v.* **1** *tr.* cleanse with liquid, esp. water. **2** *tr.* (foll. by *out, off, away*, etc.) remove (a stain or dirt) in this way. **3** *intr.* wash oneself or esp. one's hands and face. **4** *intr.* wash clothes etc. **5** *intr.* (of fabric or dye) bear washing without damage. **6** *intr.* (foll. by *off, out*) (of a stain etc.) be removed by washing. **7 a** *tr.* (of moving liquid) carry along in a specified direction (*a wave washed him overboard*). **b** *intr.* be carried in this way (*shells wash up on the beaches*). **8** *intr.* (foll. by *over*) occur all around without affecting (a person). **9** *tr.* brush a thin coat of watery paint or ink over (in watercolour painting, decorating, etc.). ● *n.* **1 a** the act or an instance of washing; the process of being washed (*only needed one wash*). **b** (prec. by *the*) treatment at a laundry etc. (*sent them to the wash*). **2** a quantity of clothes for washing or just washed. **3** the visible or audible motion of agitated water or air, due to the passage of a ship etc. **4** soil swept off by water. ▷ ERODE. **5** kitchen slops given to pigs. **6** liquid food for animals. **7** a liquid to spread over a surface to cleanse, heal, or colour. **8** a thin coating of watercolour, wall colouring, or metal. □ **wash-and-wear** *adj.* (of a fabric or garment) easily and quickly laundered. **wash down 1** wash completely (esp. a large surface). **2** (usu. foll. by *with*) accompany or follow (food) with a drink. **wash one's hands** *euphem.* go to the lavatory. **wash one's hands of** renounce responsibility for (originally with reference to Matt. 27:24). **wash out 1** clean the inside of (a thing) by washing. **2** clean (a garment etc.) by brief washing. **3 a** rain off. **b** *colloq.* cancel. **4** (of a downpour etc.) make a breach in (a road etc.). **wash up 1** wash (crockery and cutlery) after use. **2** *N. Amer.* wash one's face and hands. **won't wash** *colloq.* will not be believed or accepted. [Old English] □ **washy** *adj.*

washable *adj.* that can be washed, esp. without damage. □ **washability** *n.*

washbasin *n.* a basin for washing one's hands, face, etc., esp. fixed to a wall or on a pedestal and connected to a water supply and a drain.

washboard *n.* **1** a board of ribbed wood or a sheet of corrugated zinc on which clothes are scrubbed in washing. **2** this used as a percussion instrument.

washday *n.* a day on which clothes etc. are washed.

washed out *adj.* (hyphenated when *attrib.*) **1** faded by washing. **2** pale. **3** *colloq.* limp, enfeebled.

washed up *adj.* esp. *N. Amer. slang* defeated, having failed.

washer *n.* **1 a** a person or thing that washes. **b** a washing machine. **2** a flat ring of rubber, metal, etc., inserted at a joint to prevent leakage. **3** a similar ring placed under a nut etc. to disperse pressure.

washer-dryer *n.* (also **washer-drier**) a washing machine with an inbuilt tumble-dryer.

washerwoman *n.* (*pl.* **-women**) a laundress.

washeteria *n.* = LAUNDERETTE.

W

washing n. **1** a quantity of clothes for washing or just washed. **2** the act of washing clothes.

washing machine n. a machine for washing clothes and linen etc.

washing powder n. esp. *Brit.* powder of soap or detergent for washing clothes.

washing soda n. sodium carbonate, used dissolved in water for washing and cleaning.

washing-up n. *Brit.* **1** the process of washing dishes etc. after use. **2** used dishes etc. for washing.

wash-out n. **1** *colloq.* a fiasco; a complete failure. **2** a breach in a road etc. caused by flooding.

washroom n. *N. Amer.* a room with washing and toilet facilities.

washstand n. *hist.* a piece of furniture to hold a jug of water, a basin, soap, etc. for washing oneself with.

washtub n. a tub or vessel for washing clothes etc.

wasn't *contr.* was not.

Wasp n. (also **WASP**) *N. Amer.* usu. *derog.* a middle-class American white Protestant descended from early English settlers. [acronym from *white Anglo-Saxon Protestant*] □ **Waspy** *adj.*

wasp n. ▶ a stinging often predatory insect of the order Hymenoptera, esp. a social insect of the common genus *Vespula*, with black and yellow stripes and a very thin waist. ▷ HYMENOPTERAN, NEST. [Old English] □ **wasplike** *adj.*

waspish *adj.* irritable, petulant. □ **waspishly** *adv.* **waspishness** n.

wasp-waist n. a very slender waist. □ **wasp-waisted** *adj.*

wassail /wos-ayl/ *archaic* ● n. **1** a festive occasion; a drinking bout. **2** a kind of liquor drunk on such an occasion. ● *v.intr.* make merry; celebrate with drinking etc. [from Old Norse *ves heill* 'be in good health!'] □ **wassailer** n.

wastage n. **1** an amount wasted. **2** loss by use, wear, or leakage. **3** (also **natural wastage**) loss of employees other than by redundancy.

waste ● v. **1** *tr.* use to no purpose or for inadequate result (*waste time*). **2** *tr.* fail to use (esp. an opportunity). **3** *tr.* (often foll. by *on*) **a** utter (words etc.), without effect. **b** (often in *passive*) fail to be appreciated (*I feel wasted in this job*). **4** *tr. & intr.* (often foll. by *away*) wear gradually away; wither. **5** *tr. literary* ravage. **6** *intr.* be expended without useful effect. **7** *tr.* esp. *N. Amer. slang* beat up, kill, murder. ● *adj.* **1** superfluous. **2** (of a district etc.) not inhabited or cultivated. ● n. **1** the act or an instance of wasting; extravagant or ineffectual use of an asset, time, etc. **2** waste material or food; refuse; unwanted by-products. **3** a waste region, a desert, etc. **4** the state of being used up; diminution by wear and tear. □ **go** (or **run**) **to waste** be wasted. **lay waste** (or **lay waste to** or **lay** (a thing) **to waste**) ravage, devastate. [based on Latin *vastus* 'void, immense']

wastebasket n. esp. *N. Amer.* = WASTE-PAPER BASKET.

waste disposal n. (often *attrib.*) the disposing of waste products, rubbish, etc., esp. as a public or corporate process.

waste disposal unit n. an electrical device fitted to the waste pipe of a kitchen sink etc. for grinding up waste.

wasteful *adj.* **1** extravagant. **2** causing or showing waste. □ **wastefully** *adj.* **wastefulness** n.

waste ground n. an area of unused land, esp. one left undeveloped in an urban area.

wasteland n. **1** an unproductive or useless area of land. **2** a place considered spiritually barren.

waste paper n. used or unwanted paper.

waste-paper basket n. esp. *Brit.* a receptacle for waste paper.

waste pipe n. a pipe to carry off waste water etc.

waster n. **1** a wasteful person. **2** *colloq.* a worthless person; an idler.

wastrel /wayss-trĕl/ n. a wasteful or good-for-nothing person.

watch ● v. **1** *tr.* look at attentively. **2** *tr.* **a** keep under observation. **b** monitor or consider carefully (*have to watch my weight*). **3** *intr.* (often foll. by *for*) be in an alert state; be vigilant (*watch for the holes in the road*). **4** *intr.* (often foll. by *over*) take care of. ● n. **1** ▶ a small portable timepiece for carrying on one's person. **2** a state of alert observation or attention. **3** *Naut.* **a** usu. four-hour spell of duty. **b** (in full **starboard** or **port watch**) each of the halves, divided according to the position of the bunks, into which a ship's crew is divided to take alternate watches. □ **on the watch** waiting for an expected or feared occurrence. **on watch** on lookout duty. **watch it** (or **oneself**) *colloq.* be careful. **watch out 1** (often foll. by *for*) be on one's guard. **2** (as *int.*) a warning of immediate danger. **watch one's step** proceed cautiously. [Old English] □ **watchable** *adj.* **watcher** n. (also in *comb.*).

watch-chain n. a metal chain for securing a pocket watch.

watchdog ● n. **1** a dog kept to guard property etc. **2** a person or body monitoring others' rights, behaviour, etc. ● *v.tr.* (**-dogged**, **-dogging**) maintain surveillance over.

watchful *adj.* **1** accustomed to watching. **2** on the watch. **3** showing vigilance. **4** *archaic* wakeful. □ **watchfully** *adv.* **watchfulness** n.

watch-glass n. *Brit.* a glass disc covering the dial of a watch.

watching brief n. *Brit.* **1** a brief held by a barrister following a case for a client not directly involved.

WATCH: QUARTZ WATCH

2 a state of interest maintained in a proceeding not directly or immediately concerning one.

watchmaker n. a person who makes and repairs watches and clocks. □ **watchmaking** n.

watchman n. (*pl.* **-men**) **1** a man employed to look after an empty building etc. at night. **2** *archaic* or *hist.* a member of a night watch.

watch spring n. the mainspring of a watch.

watchtower n. a tower from which observation can be kept. ▷ CASTLE

watchword n. **1** a phrase summarizing a guiding principle; a slogan. **2** *hist.* a military password.

water ● n. **1** a colourless transparent odourless tasteless liquid compound of oxygen and hydrogen. **2** a liquid consisting chiefly of this and found in seas, lakes, and rivers, in rain, and in the fluids of living organisms. **3** (in *pl.*) part of a sea or river (*in Icelandic waters*). **4** (often as **the waters**) mineral water at a spa etc. **5** the state of a tide (*high water*). **6** a solution of a specified substance in water (*lavender-water*). **7** the quality of the transparency and brilliance of a gem, esp. a diamond. **8** (*attrib.*) **a** found in, on, or near water. **b** of, for, or worked by water. **c** involving, using, or yielding water. **9 a** urine. **b** (usu. in *pl.*) the amniotic fluid discharged before childbirth. ● v. **1** *tr.* sprinkle or soak with water. **2** *tr.* supply (a plant) with water. **3** *tr.* give water to (an animal) to drink. **4** *intr.* (of the mouth or eyes) secrete water as saliva or tears. **5** *tr.* (as **watered** *adj.*) (of silk etc.) having irregular wavy glossy markings. **6** *tr.* adulterate (beer etc.) with water. □ **like water** lavishly, profusely. **like water off a duck's back** see DUCK[1]. **of the first water 1** (of a diamond) of the greatest brilliance and transparency. **2** of the finest quality or extreme degree. **on the water wagon** see WAGON. **water down 1** dilute with water. **2** (often as **watered down** *adj.*) make less vivid, forceful, or horrifying. **water under the bridge** past events accepted as past and irrevocable. [Old English] □ **waterer** n. **waterless** *adj.*

waterbed n. a bed with a mattress of rubber or plastic etc. filled with water.

waterbird n. a bird frequenting esp. fresh water.

water biscuit n. a thin crisp unsweetened biscuit made from flour and water.

water-boatman n. an aquatic bug of the family Notonectidae or Corixidae, swimming with oarlike hind legs. ▷ HEMIPTERA

water buffalo n. the common domestic Indian buffalo, *Bubalus arnee*.

W

WASP (*Vespula vulgaris*)

antenna

thorax

thin waist

black and yellow stripes

wing

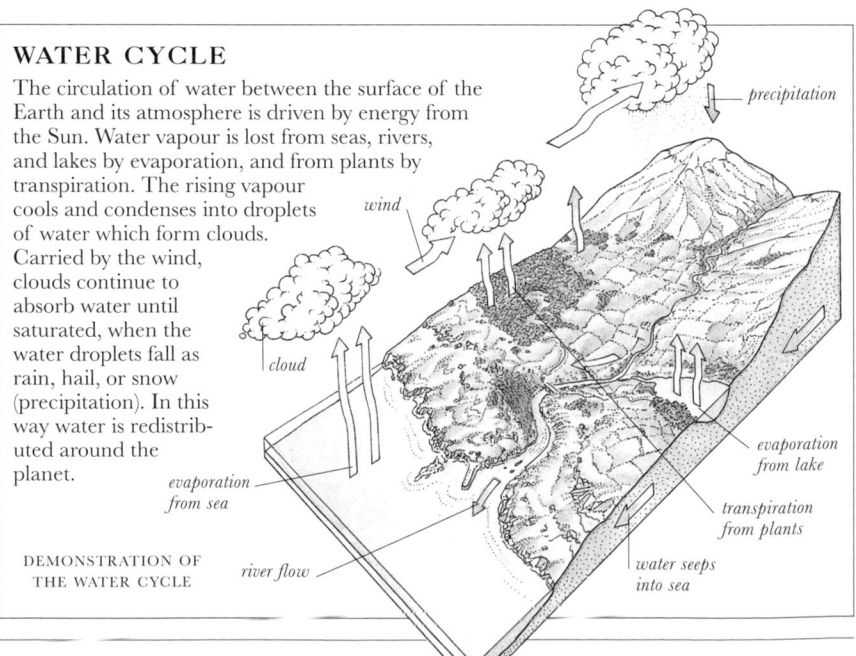

WATER CYCLE

The circulation of water between the surface of the Earth and its atmosphere is driven by energy from the Sun. Water vapour is lost from seas, rivers, and lakes by evaporation, and from plants by transpiration. The rising vapour cools and condenses into droplets of water which form clouds. Carried by the wind, clouds continue to absorb water until saturated, when the water droplets fall as rain, hail, or snow (precipitation). In this way water is redistributed around the planet.

DEMONSTRATION OF THE WATER CYCLE

precipitation

wind

cloud

evaporation from sea

river flow

evaporation from lake

transpiration from plants

water seeps into sea

water-cannon *n.* a device giving a powerful jet of water to disperse a crowd etc.

Water-carrier *n.* (prec. by *the*) the zodiacal sign or constellation Aquarius. ▷ AQUARIUS

water chestnut *n.* **1** an aquatic plant, *Trapa natans*, bearing an edible seed. **2** (in full **Chinese water chestnut**) **a** a sedge, *Eleocharis tuberosa*, with rush-like leaves arising from a corm. **b** this corm used as food.

water closet *n.* **1** a lavatory with the means for flushing the pan with water. **2** a room containing this.

watercolour *n.* (*US* **watercolor**) **1** artists' paint made of pigment to be diluted with water and not oil. **2** ▼ a picture painted with this. **3** the art of painting with watercolours. □ **watercolourist** *n.*

WATERCOLOUR PAINTING

water-cooled *adj.* cooled by the circulation of water.

water-cooler *n.* a vessel in which water is cooled and kept cool, esp. a tank of cooled drinking water in a place of work.

watercourse *n.* **1** a brook, stream, or artificial water channel. **2** the bed along which this flows.

watercress *n.* a hardy perennial cress, *Nasturtium officinale*, growing in running water, with pungent leaves used in salad.

water cycle *n.* ◀ the circulation of water on Earth, in which precipitation returns to the sea via rivers and to the atmosphere by evaporation and transpiration.

water-diviner *n. Brit.* a person who dowses (see DOWSE¹) for water.

waterfall *n.* ▼ a cascade of water from a river or stream falling vertically from a height over a rock, precipice, etc.

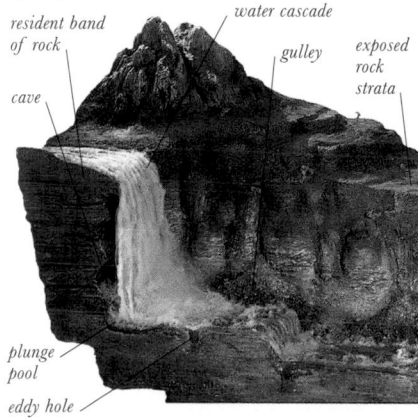

WATERFALL: MODEL OF A WATERFALL

waterfowl *n.* (usu. collect., treated as *pl.*) ▲ birds frequenting water, esp. ducks and geese regarded as game birds. ▷ DUCK

waterfront *n.* the part of a town adjoining a river, lake, harbour, etc.

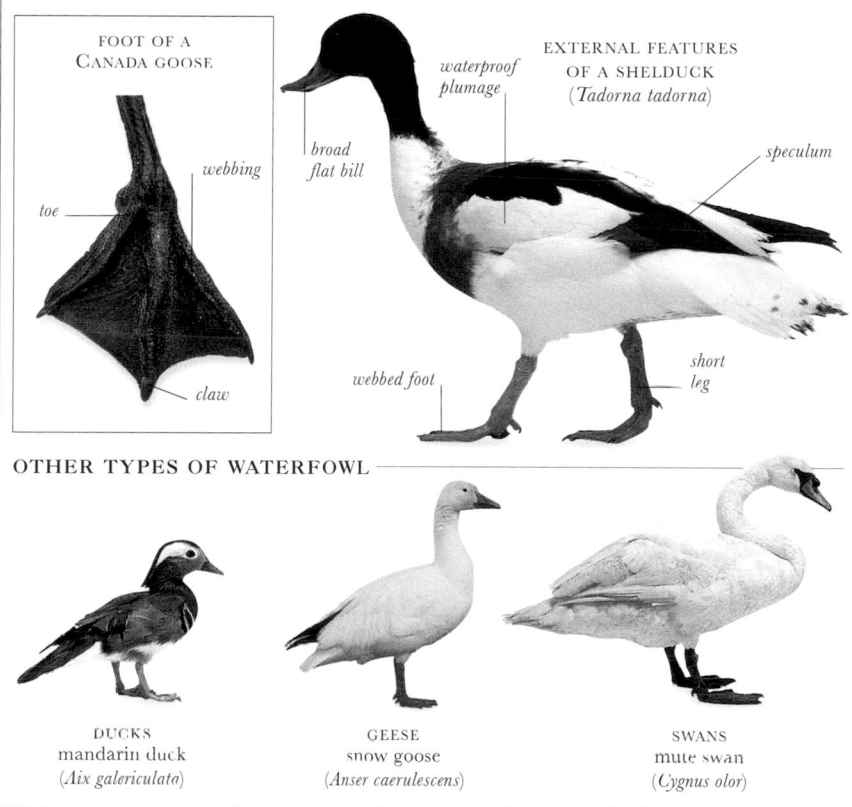

WATERFOWL

Waterfowl form the order Anseriformes, which comprises around 160 swan, goose, duck, and shelduck species. All have short legs with webbed feet, used as paddles to push through the water; their waterproof plumage is so effective that they remain dry when diving underwater. Geese typically feed on dry land, whereas swans and ducks feed in water, either diving for food on the bottom of lakes, rivers, or shallow coastal waters, or using their broad bills to dabble on the surface. Most waterfowl migrate in winter.

FOOT OF A
CANADA GOOSE

webbing

toe

claw

waterproof plumage

broad flat bill

EXTERNAL FEATURES
OF A SHELDUCK
(*Tadorna tadorna*)

speculum

webbed foot

short leg

OTHER TYPES OF WATERFOWL

DUCKS
mandarin duck
(*Aix galericulata*)

GEESE
snow goose
(*Anser caerulescens*)

SWANS
mute swan
(*Cygnus olor*)

watergate *n.* **1** a floodgate **2** a gate giving access to a river etc.

water gauge *n.* a glass tube etc. indicating the height of water in a reservoir, boiler, etc.

water hammer *n.* a knocking noise in a water pipe when a tap is suddenly turned off.

water heater *n.* a device for heating (esp. domestic) water.

waterhole *n.* a shallow depression in which water collects (esp. in the bed of a river otherwise dry).

water ice *n.* a confection of flavoured and frozen water and sugar etc.; a sorbet.

watering can *n.* a hard portable container with a long spout usu. ending in a perforated sprinkler, for watering plants.

watering hole *n.* **1** a pool of water from which animals regularly drink. **2** *slang* a bar.

water lily *n.* ◀ any aquatic plant of the family Nymphaceaceae, with broad flat floating leaves and large usu. cup-shaped floating flowers.

WATER LILY
(*Nymphaea* species)

waterline *n.* the line along which the surface of water touches a ship's side (marked on a ship for use in loading).

waterlogged *adj.* **1** saturated with water. **2** (of a boat etc.) hardly able to float from being filled with water. **3** (of ground) made useless by being saturated with water.

Waterloo *n.* a decisive defeat; an irrevocable end (esp. in phr. **meet one's Waterloo**). [from *Waterloo*, Belgian village where Napoleon was finally defeated (1815)]

water main *n.* the main pipe in a water supply system.

waterman *n.* (*pl.* **-men**) **1** a boatman plying for hire. **2** an oarsman as regards skill in keeping the boat balanced.

watermark ● *n.* ▼ a faint design made in some paper during manufacture, visible when held against the light, identifying the maker etc. ● *v.tr.* mark with this.

W

watermark

CONNOISSEUR
100% COTTON

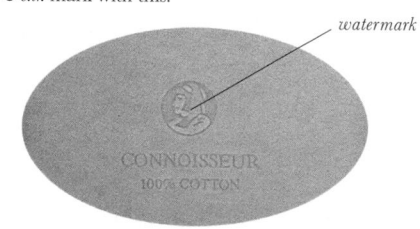

WATERMARK ON PAPER

water-meadow n. a meadow periodically flooded by a stream or river.

water measurer n. ▼ a long thin aquatic bug of the family Hydrometridae which walks slowly on the surface film of water.

WATER MEASURER
(*Hydrometra stagnorum*)

watermelon n. a large smooth green melon, *Citrullus lanatus*, with red pulp and watery juice.

watermill n. a mill worked by a waterwheel.

water meter n. a device for measuring and recording the amount of water supplied to a house etc.

water nymph n. a nymph regarded as inhabiting or presiding over water; a naiad.

water pistol n. a toy pistol shooting a jet of water.

water plantain n. ◄ a plant of the genus *Alisma*, with plantain-like leaves, found esp. in ditches.

water polo n. a game played by swimmers, with a ball like a football.

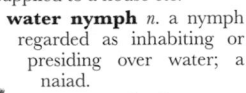

WATER PLANTAIN
(*Alisma plantago-aquatica*)

waterproof ● adj. impervious to water. ● n. Brit. a waterproof garment or material. ● v.tr. make waterproof. □ **waterproofer** n. **waterproofness** n.

WATERWHEEL

Water power was first harnessed around 100 BC for grinding corn, and later in mills and heavy industry. Where slow-moving water falls from a great height, an overshot wheel is used to push the wheel around as the water falls. An undershot wheel is built where fast-moving water passes under the wheel, moving the blades around.

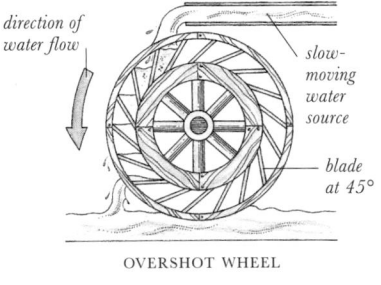

direction of water flow

slow-moving water source

blade at 45°

OVERSHOT WHEEL

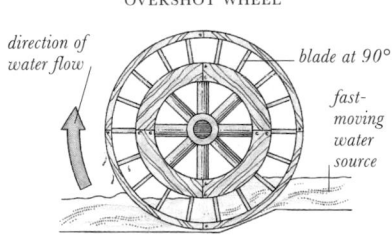

direction of water flow

blade at 90°

fast-moving water source

UNDERSHOT WHEEL

W

---

water rat n. = WATER VOLE.

water rate n. a charge made for the use of the public water supply.

water-resistant adj. (of a fabric, wristwatch, etc.) able to resist, but not entirely prevent, the penetration of water. □ **water-resistance** n.

watershed n. 1 a line of separation between waters flowing to different rivers, basins, or seas. 2 a turning point in affairs. [suggested by German *Wasserscheide*]

water-ski ● n. (pl. **-skis**) each of a pair of skis for skimming the surface of the water when worn by a person towed by a motor boat. ● v.intr. (**-skis, -skied, -skiing**) travel on water-skis. □ **water-skier** n.

waterspout n. a gyrating column of water and spray formed by a whirlwind between sea and cloud.

water-table n. a level below which the ground is saturated with water.

watertight adj. 1 closely fastened or fitted or made so as to prevent the passage of water. 2 (of an argument etc.) unassailable.

water torture n. a form of torture in which the victim is exposed to the incessant dripping of water on the head, or the sound of dripping.

water tower n. a tower with an elevated tank to give pressure for distributing water.

water vole n. a large semiaquatic vole, esp. *Arvicola terrestris*.

water wagon see *on the wagon* (WAGON).

waterway n. 1 a navigable channel. 2 a route for travel by water.

waterweed n. any of various aquatic plants.

waterwheel n. ▼ a wheel driven by water to work machinery, or to raise water.

water wings n.pl. inflated floats fixed on the arms of a person learning to swim.

waterworks n.pl. 1 an establishment for managing a water supply. 2 colloq. the shedding of tears. 3 Brit. colloq. the urinary system.

watery adj. 1 containing too much water. 2 too thin in consistency. 3 of or consisting of water. 4 (of the eyes) suffused with water. 5 (of colour) pale. □ **wateriness** n.

watt /wot/ n. the SI unit of power, equivalent to one joule per second. [named after J. *Watt*, Scots engineer, 1736–1819]

wattage n. an amount of electrical power expressed in watts.

watt-hour n. the energy used when one watt is applied for one hour

wattle[1] /wot-ĕl/ n. 1 a interlaced rods as a material for making fences, walls, etc. b (in sing. or pl.) rods and twigs for this use. 2 an Australian acacia with long pliant branches, with golden flowers used as the national emblem. [Old English]

wattle[2] /wot-ĕl/ n. 1 ► a loose fleshy appendage on the head or throat of a bird. 2 = BARB n. 3. [16th-century coinage] □ **wattled** adj.

wattle

WATTLE
OF A TURKEY

wattle and daub n. ▼ a network of rods and twigs plastered with mud or clay as a building material.

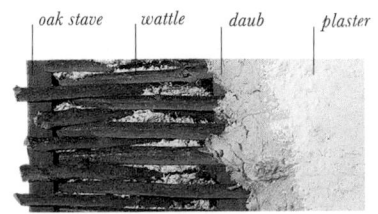

oak stave   wattle   daub   plaster

WATTLE AND DAUB WALL

---

wave ● v. 1 a intr. move a hand etc. to and fro in greeting or as a signal (*waved to me across the street*). b tr. move (a hand etc.) in this way. 2 a intr. show a sinuous motion as of a flag, tree, or cornfield in the wind. b tr. impart a waving motion to. 3 tr. tell or direct (a person) by waving (*waved them away*). 4 tr. express (a greeting etc.) by waving (*waved goodbye to them*). 5 tr. give an undulating form to; make wavy. 6 intr. (of hair etc.) have such a form; be wavy. ● n. 1 a ridge of water between two depressions. 2 ► a long body of water curling into an arched form and breaking on the shore. 3 a body of persons in one of successive advancing groups. 4 a gesture of waving. 5 an undulating form produced in the hair by waving. 6 a temporary occurrence of a condition, emotion, or influence (*a wave of enthusiasm*). 7 Physics a a periodic disturbance of the particles of a substance which may be propagated without net movement of the particles, as in the passage of undulating motion, heat, sound, etc. b a single curve in the course of this motion. 8 Electr. a similar variation of an electromagnetic field in the propagation of light or other radiation through a medium or vacuum. □ **make waves** colloq. 1 cause trouble. 2 create a significant impression. **wave aside** dismiss as intrusive or irrelevant. **wave down** wave to (a vehicle or its driver) as a signal to stop. [Old English] □ **waveless** adj. **wavelike** adj. & adv.

waveband n. a range of wavelengths between certain limits.

wave equation n. a differential equation expressing the properties of motion in waves.

waveform n. Physics a curve showing the shape of a wave at a given time.

wavefront n. Physics a surface containing points affected in the same way by a wave at a given time.

wave function n. a function satisfying a wave equation and describing the properties of a wave.

waveguide n. Electr. a metal tube etc. confining and conveying microwaves.

wavelength n. 1 the distance between successive crests of a wave, esp. as a distinctive feature of radio waves from a transmitter. ▷ ELECTROMAGNETIC RADIATION. 2 colloq. a particular mode or range of thinking and communicating (*we don't seem to be on the same wavelength*).

wavelet n. a small wave on water.

wave machine n. a device for producing waves in a swimming pool.

wave mechanics n. a method of analysis of the behaviour esp. of atomic phenomena with particles represented by wave equations (see QUANTUM MECHANICS).

waver v.intr. 1 be or become unsteady; falter; begin to give way. 2 be undecided between different opinions; be shaken in resolution or belief. 3 (of a light) flicker. [from Old Norse *vafra* 'to flicker'] □ **waverer** n. **waveringly** adv. **wavery** adj.

wave theory n. hist. the theory that light is propagated through the ether by a wave motion imparted to the ether by the molecular vibrations of the radiant body.

wavy adj. (**wavier, waviest**) (of a line or surface) having waves or alternate contrary curves (*wavy hair*). □ **waviness** n.

wax[1] ● n. 1 a sticky mouldable yellowish substance secreted by bees as the material of honeycomb cells. 2 a white translucent material obtained from this by bleaching and purifying and used for candles, in modelling, as a basis of polishes, and for other purposes. 3 any similar substance (*earwax, paraffin wax*). 4 (attrib.) made of wax. ● v.tr. 1 cover or treat with wax or a similar substance. 2 remove unwanted hair from (legs etc.) by applying sticky wax and peeling off the wax and hairs together. [Old English] □ **waxer** n.

wax[2] v.intr. 1 (of the moon between new and full) have a progressively larger part of its visible

---

WAVE

Waves form when the sea's surface is blown by a strong wind across a sufficient 'fetch' (the distance taken to build a wave). The water within the wave remains constant, each level moving in an orbital path, like rollers in a conveyor belt, irrespective of the distance the wave has travelled. In shallow water a wave's path elongates and becomes elliptical, before breaking on a shore.

SECTION THROUGH A WAVE

wave length — *breaking wave* — *beach* — *swash* — *incline* — *elliptical orbital path in shallow water* — *circular orbital path in deep water*

---

surface illuminated, increasing in apparent size. **2** *literary* become larger or stronger (*wax and wane*). **3** *literary* (foll. by compl.) pass into a specified state or mood (*wax lyrical*). [Old English]

wax jacket *n.* an outdoor jacket made of waterproof waxed cotton.

wax paper *n.* paper impregnated with wax to make it waterproof or greaseproof.

waxen *adj.* **1** having a smooth pale translucent surface as of wax. **2** able to receive impressions like wax. **3** *archaic* made of wax.

waxwing *n.* ▶ any bird of the genus *Bombycilla*, with small tips like red sealing wax to some wing feathers.

waxwork *n.* **1** an object, esp. a lifelike dummy, modelled in wax. **2** (in *pl.*) an exhibition of wax dummies.

waxy *adj.* (**waxier**, **waxiest**) resembling wax in consistency or in its surface. □ **waxiness** *n.*

way ● *n.* **1** a road, path, etc., for passing along. **2** a route for reaching a place, esp. the best one (*asked the way to London*). **3** a place of passage into a building etc. (*could not find the way out*). **4 a** a method for attaining an object (*that is not the way to do it*). **b** the ability to obtain one's object (*has a way with him*). **5 a** a person's chosen course of action. **b** a manner of behaving; a personal peculiarity (*has a way of forgetting things*). **6** a specific manner of procedure (*soon got into the way of it*). **7** the normal course of events (*that is always the way*). **8** a distance traversed or to be traversed (*is a long way away*). **9** impetus, progress (*pushed my way through*). **10** movement of a ship etc. (*gather way; lose way*). **11** the state of being engaged in movement from place to place; time spent in this (*met them on the way home*). **12** a specified direction (*step this way; which way are you going?*). **13** (in *pl.*) parts into which a thing is divided (*split it three ways*). **14** a specified condition or state (*in a bad way*). **15** a respect (*useful in some ways*). ● *adv. colloq.* to a considerable extent; far (*you're way off the mark*). □ **across** (or *Brit.* **over**) **the way** opposite. **be on one's way** set off; depart. **by the way** incidentally. **by way of 1** through; by means of. **2** as a substitute for or as a form of (*did it by way of apology*). **come one's way** become available to one; become one's lot. **get** (or **have**) **one's way** (or **have it one's own way** etc.) get what one wants; ensure one's wishes are met. **give way 1 a** make concessions. **b** yield. **2** concede precedence. **3** (of a structure etc.) be dislodged or broken

WAXWING:
BOHEMIAN WAXWING
(*Bombycilla garrulus*)

under a load; collapse. **4** (foll. by *to*) be superseded by. **5** (foll. by *to*) be overcome by (an emotion etc.). **go out of one's way** make a special effort; act gratuitously or without compulsion (*went out of their way to help*). **go one's own way** act independently, esp. against contrary advice. **go one's way** leave, depart. **go a person's way 1** travel in the same direction as a person (*are you going my way?*). **2** (of events, circumstances, etc.) be favourable to a person. **in its way** if regarded from a particular standpoint appropriate to it. **in the** (or **one's**) **way** forming an obstacle or hindrance. **lead the way 1** act as guide or leader. **2** show how to do something. **one way and another** taking various considerations into account. **on the** (or **one's**) **way 1** in the course of a journey etc. **2** having progressed (*is well on the way to completion*). **3** *colloq.* (of a child) conceived but not yet born. **on the way out** *colloq.* **1** going down in status, estimation, or favour. **2** dying. **the other way round** (or *Brit.* **about** or *US* **around**) in an inverted or reversed position. **out of the way 1** no longer an obstacle. **2** disposed of; settled. **3** (of a person) imprisoned or killed. **4** (with *neg.*) unusual or remarkable (*nothing out of the way*). **5** (of a place) remote, inaccessible. **out of one's way** not on one's intended route. **way back** *colloq.* long ago. **way of life** the habits governing all one's actions etc. **ways and means 1** methods of achieving something. **2** methods of raising government revenue. [Old English]

waybill *n.* a list of passengers or parcels on a vehicle.

wayfarer *n.* a traveller. □ **wayfaring** *n. & adj.*

wayfaring tree *n.* a white-flowered European and Asian shrub, *Viburnum lantana*, common along roadsides.

waylay *v.tr.* (*past* and *past part.* **waylaid**) **1** lie in wait for. **2** stop to rob or interview.

way-out *adj. colloq.* **1** unusual, eccentric. **2** avant-garde, progressive. **3** excellent, exciting.

waypoint *n.* **1** a stopping place, esp. on a journey. **2** the computer-checked coordinates of each stage of a flight, sea journey, etc. (also *attrib.*: *waypoint navigation facility*).

-ways *suffix* forming adjectives and adverbs of direction or manner (*sideways*) (cf. -WISE).

wayside *n.* **1** the side of a road. **2** the land at the side of a road. □ **fall by the wayside** fail to continue in an endeavour or undertaking (after Luke 8:5).

wayward *adj.* **1** childishly self-willed or perverse; capricious. **2** unaccountable or freakish. [Middle English] □ **waywardly** *adv.* **waywardness** *n.*

WC *abbr.* **1** *Brit.* water closet. **2** West Central.

WCC *abbr.* World Council of Churches.

W/Cdr. *abbr.* Wing Commander.

we *pron.* (*obj.* **us**; *poss.* **our**, **ours**) **1** (*pl.* of I^2) used by and with reference to more than one person speaking or writing, or one such person and one or more associated persons. **2** used for or by a royal person in a proclamation etc. and by a writer or editor in a formal context. **3** people in general. **4** *colloq.* = I^2 (*give us a chance*). **5** *colloq.* (often implying condescension) you (*how are we feeling today?*). [Old English]

WEA *abbr.* (in the UK) Workers' Educational Association.

weak *adj.* **1** deficient in strength, power, or number; easily broken or bent or defeated. **2** deficient in vigour (*weak health; a weak imagination*). **3 a** deficient in resolution; easily led (*a weak character*). **b** indicating a lack of resolution (*a weak surrender; a weak chin*). **4** unconvincing or logically deficient (*a weak argument*). **5** (of a mixed liquid or solution) watery, thin, dilute (*weak tea*). **6** (of a syllable etc.) unstressed. **7** *Gram.* in Germanic languages: **a** (of a verb) forming inflections by the addition of a suffix to the stem. **b** (of a noun or adjective) belonging to a declension in which the stem originally ended in *-n*. [from Old Norse *veikr*] □ **weaken** *v.tr. & intr.* make or become weak or weaker.

weaker sex *n.* (prec. by *the*) *derog.* women.

weak-kneed *adj. colloq.* lacking resolution.

weakling *n.* a feeble person or animal.

weakly ● *adv.* in a weak manner. ● *adj.* (**weaklier**, **weakliest**) sickly, not robust.

weak-minded *adj.* **1** mentally deficient. **2** lacking in resolution. □ **weak-mindedness** *n.*

weak moment *n.* a time when one is unusually compliant or temptable.

weakness *n.* **1** the state or condition of being weak. **2** a weak point; a defect. **3** the inability to resist a particular temptation. **4** (foll. by *for*) a self-indulgent liking (*have a weakness for chocolate*).

weak point *n.* (also **weak spot**) **1** a place where defences are assailable. **2** a flaw in an argument or character or in resistance to temptation.

weal *n.* a ridge raised on the flesh by a stroke of a rod or whip. [variant of WALE, influenced by obsolete *wheat* 'to suppurate']

wealth *n.* **1** riches; abundant possessions. **2** the state of being rich. **3** (foll. by *of*) an abundance (*a wealth of new material*). [Middle English]

wealthy *adj.* (**wealthier**, **wealthiest**) having an abundance esp. of money.

wean[1] *v.tr.* **1** accustom (a young mammal) to food other than milk. **2** disengage (from a habit etc.) by enforced discontinuance. [Old English *wenian* 'to accustom']

wean[2] *n. Sc.* a young child. [contraction of *wee ane* 'little one']

weapon *n.* **1** a thing designed or used for inflicting bodily harm. **2** a means employed for trying to gain the advantage in a conflict (*irony is a double-edged weapon*). [Old English] □ **weaponless** *adj.*

weaponry *n.* weapons collectively.

wear[1] ● *v.* (*past* **wore**; *past part.* **worn**) **1** *tr.* have on one's person as clothing or an ornament etc. **2** *tr.* exhibit or present (a facial expression or appearance) (*wore a frown; the day wore a different aspect*). **3** *tr. Brit. colloq.* tolerate, accept (*they won't wear that excuse*). **4 a** *tr.* injure the surface of, or partly obliterate or alter, by rubbing, stress, or use. **b** *intr.* undergo such injury or change. **5** *tr. & intr.* (foll. by *off*, *away*) rub or be rubbed off. **6** *tr.* make (a hole etc.) by constant rubbing or dripping etc. **7** *intr.* (foll. by *down*) overcome by persistence. **8** *intr.* (foll. by *well*, *badly*, etc.) endure continued use or life. **9** *intr.* (usu. foll. by *on*) (of time) pass, esp. tediously. ● *n.* **1** the act of wearing or the state of being worn (*suitable for informal wear*). **2** things worn; fashionable or suitable clothing (*sportswear; footwear*). **3** (in full **wear and tear**) damage sustained from continuous use. **4** the capacity for resisting wear and tear (*still a great deal of wear left in it*). □ **in wear** being regularly worn. **wear off** lose effectiveness or intensity. **wear out**

W

WEATHER CHART

Detailed recordings of pressure, wind direction, and temperature are constantly made across the globe. The data is fed into supercomputers to build a picture of atmospheric conditions and to generate forecasts. This information is depicted on charts; a synoptic chart is produced when data is gathered simultaneously. The markings on a weather chart show the position of fronts, which bring the most changeable weather, as well as isobars indicating air pressure and arrows denoting wind direction.

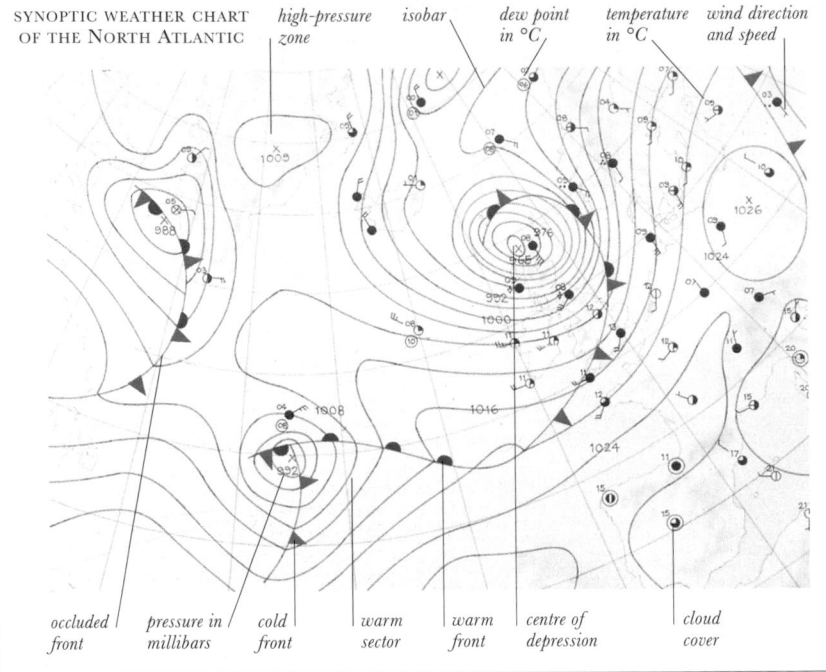

SYNOPTIC WEATHER CHART OF THE NORTH ATLANTIC — high-pressure zone — isobar — dew point in °C — temperature in °C — wind direction and speed

occluded front | pressure in millibars | cold front | warm sector | warm front | centre of depression | cloud cover

1 use or be used until no longer usable. **2** tire out. **wear thin** (of patience, excuses, etc.) begin to fail. **wear the trousers** see TROUSERS. [Old English] □ **wearable** adj. **wearability** n. **wearer** n.

wear[2] v. (past and past part. **wore**) **1** tr. bring (a ship) about by turning its head away from the wind. **2** intr. (of a ship) come about in this way. [17th-century coinage]

wearisome adj. tedious; tiring by monotony or length.

weary ● adj. (**wearier**, **weariest**) **1** disinclined for further exertion or endurance. **2** (foll. by of) dismayed at the continuing of; impatient of. **3** tiring or tedious. ● v. (**-ies**, **-ied**) **1** tr. & intr. make or grow weary. **2** intr. esp. Sc. long. [Old English] □ **wearily** adv. **weariness** n.

weasel ● n. a small brown and white carnivorous mammal, Mustela nivalis, with a slender body. ▷ MUSTELID. ● v.intr. (**weaselled**, **weaselling**; US **weaseled**, **weaseling**) **1** esp. US equivocate or quibble. **2** (foll. by on, out) default on an obligation. [Old English] □ **weaselly** adj.

weasel-faced adj. having thin, sharp features.

weasel word n. (usu. in pl.) a word that is intentionally ambiguous or misleading.

weather ● n. **1** the state of the atmosphere at a place and time as regards heat, cloudiness, dryness, sunshine, wind, and rain etc. **2** (attrib.) Naut. windward (on the weather side). ● v. **1** tr. expose to atmospheric changes (weathered timber). **2 a** tr. discolour or partly disintegrate (rock or stones) by exposure to air. **b** intr. be discoloured or worn in this way. □ **keep a** (or **one's**) **weather eye open** be watchful. **make heavy weather of** colloq. exaggerate the difficulty presented by. **under the weather** colloq. **1** slightly unwell. **2** in low spirits. **3** drunk. [Old English]

weather-beaten adj. affected by exposure to the weather.

weatherboard n. esp. Brit. **1** a sloping board attached to the bottom of an outside door to keep out the rain etc. **2** each of a series of horizontal boards with edges overlapping to keep out the rain etc. □ **weatherboarding** n. (in sense 2).

weather chart n. ▲ a diagram showing the state of the weather over a large area.

weathercock n. ◄ a weathervane in the form of a cock.

weathering n. **1** the action of the weather on materials etc. exposed to it. ▷ OUTCROP. **2** exposure to adverse weather conditions.

weatherman n. (pl. **-men**; fem. **weathergirl**) a meteorologist, esp. one who broadcasts a weather forecast.

weatherproof ● adj. resistant to the effects of bad weather. ● v.tr. make weatherproof. □ **weatherproofed** adj.

weather side n. the side from which the wind is blowing (opp. LEE SIDE).

weather station n. an observation post for recording meteorological data.

weatherstrip n. a piece of material used to make a door or window proof against rain or wind.

W

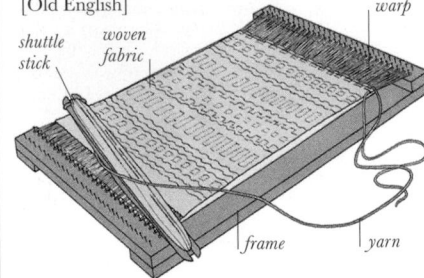

WEAVE: FORMING FABRIC ON A SIMPLE WEAVING FRAME

shuttle stick — woven fabric — warp — frame — yarn

weathervane n. a revolving pointer mounted on a high place to show the direction of the wind. ▷ WEATHERCOCK

weave[1] ● v. (past **wove**; past part. **woven** or **wove**) **1** tr. **a** form (fabric) by interlacing long threads in two directions. **b** ▼ form (thread) into fabric in this way. **2** tr. make fabric in this way. **3** tr. make by interlacing rods or flowers etc. **4** tr. **a** (foll. by into) make (facts etc.) into a story or connected whole. **b** make (a story) in this way. ● n. a style of weaving. [Old English]

weave[2] v.intr. move repeatedly from side to side; take an intricate course to avoid obstructions. □ **get weaving** Brit. slang begin action; hurry.

weaver n. **1** a person whose occupation is weaving. **2** (in full **weaver-bird**) any tropical bird of the family Ploceidae, building elaborately woven nests. ▷ NEST

web n. **1** a network of fine threads constructed by a spider to catch its prey. **2** a complete network or connected series (a web of social problems). **3** a membrane between the toes of a swimming animal or bird. **4** a woven fabric. **5** a large roll of paper used in a continuous printing process. **6** (**the Web**) = WORLD WIDE WEB. [Old English]

webbed adj. (of a bird's foot etc.) having the digits connected by a membrane or fold of skin. ▷ WATERFOWL

webbing n. ▼ strong closely woven fabric used for supporting upholstery, for belts, etc.

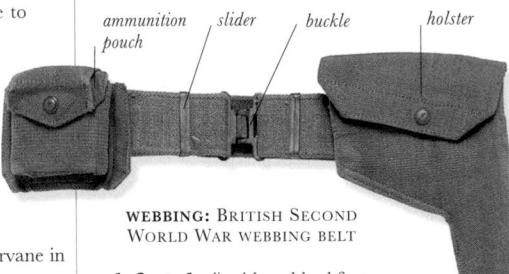

ammunition pouch — slider — buckle — holster

WEBBING: BRITISH SECOND WORLD WAR WEBBING BELT

web-footed adj. with webbed feet.

web offset n. offset printing on a web of paper.

wed v.tr. & intr. (**wedding**; past and past part. **wedded** or **wed**) **1** usu. formal or literary **a** tr. & intr. marry. **b** tr. join in marriage. **2** tr. unite (wed efficiency to economy). **3** tr. (as **wedded** adj.) of or in marriage (wedded bliss). **4** tr. (as **wedded** adj.) (foll. by to) obstinately attached or devoted (to a pursuit etc.). [Old English weddian 'to pledge']

we'd contr. **1** we had. **2** we should; we would.

wedding n. a marriage ceremony.

wedding breakfast n. Brit. a meal etc. usually served between a wedding and the departure for the honeymoon.

wedding night n. the night after a wedding (esp. with reference to its consummation).

wedding ring n. a ring worn by a married person.

wedge ● n. **1** a piece of wood or metal etc. tapering to a thin edge, that is driven between two objects or parts of an object to secure or separate them. **2** anything resembling or acting as a wedge. **3** a golf

wind direction indicator — compass direction indicator

WEATHERCOCK

club with a wedge-shaped head. **4 a** a wedge-shaped heel. **b** a shoe with this. ● *v.tr.* **1** tighten, secure, or fasten by means of a wedge (*wedged the door open*). **2** (foll. by *in*, *into*) pack or thrust (a thing or oneself) tightly in or into. □ **thin end of the wedge** *colloq.* an action or procedure of little importance in itself, but likely to lead to more serious developments. [Old English]

Wedgwood *propr.* ● *n.* **1** ceramic ware made by J. Wedgwood, English potter d. 1795, and his successors, esp. a kind of fine stoneware usu. with a white cameo design. **2** the characteristic blue colour of this stoneware. ● *adj.* of this colour.

wedlock *n.* the married state. □ **born in** (or **out of**) **wedlock** born of married (or unmarried) parents. [Old English *wedlāc* 'marriage vow']

Wednesday ● *n.* the fourth day of the week, following Tuesday. ● *adv. colloq.* **1** on Wednesday. **2** (**Wednesdays**) on Wednesdays; each Wednesday. [Old English *wōdnesdæg* 'day of (the god) Odin']

wee[1] *adj.* (**weer**, **weest**) **1** esp. *Sc.* little; very small. **2** *colloq.* tiny; extremely small (*a wee bit*). [originally Scots noun, from northern Middle English *wei* '(small) quantity']

wee[2] *n.* esp. *Brit. slang* = WEE-WEE.

weed ● *n.* **1** a plant growing where it is not wanted. **2** *colloq.* a thin weak-looking or contemptibly feeble person. **3** (prec. by *the*) *slang* **a** marijuana. **b** tobacco. ● *v.* **1** *tr.* **a** clear (an area) of weeds. **b** remove unwanted parts from. **2** *tr.* (foll. by *out*) sort out (inferior or unwanted parts etc.) for removal. **3** *intr.* cut off or uproot weeds. [Old English] □ **weeder** *n.* **weedless** *adj.*

weedkiller *n.* a substance used to destroy weeds.

weedy *adj.* (**weedier**, **weediest**) **1** having many weeds. **2 a** weak-looking; of poor physique etc. **b** (of a person) feeble; lacking strength of character. □ **weediness** *n.*

week *n.* **1** a period of seven days reckoned usu. from and to 24.00 hours on Saturday. **2** a period of seven days reckoned from any point. **3** the six days between Sundays. **4 a** the five days from Monday to Friday. **b** the time spent working in this period (*a 35-hour week*). **5** (prec. by a specified day) esp. *Brit.* a week after (that day) (*Tuesday week; tomorrow week*). [Old English]

weekday *n.* a day other than Sunday or other than Saturday and Sunday (often *attrib.: a weekday afternoon*).

weekend ● *n.* **1** Saturday and Sunday. **2** this period extended slightly. ● *v.intr.* spend a weekend (*decided to weekend in the country*).

weekender *n.* a person who spends weekends away from home.

week-long *adj.* lasting for a week.

weekly ● *adj.* done, produced, or occurring once a week. ● *adv.* once a week; from week to week. ● *n.* (*pl.* **-ies**) a weekly newspaper or periodical.

weep ● *v.* (*past and past part.* **wept**) **1** *intr.* shed tears. **2 a** *tr.* & (foll. by *for*) *intr.* shed tears for. **b** *tr.* utter or express with tears (*she wept her thanks*). **3** *intr.* & *tr.* come or send forth in drops; exude liquid (*weeping sore*). **4** *intr.* (as **weeping** *adj.*) (of a plant) having drooping branches (*weeping willow*). ● *n.* a fit or spell of weeping. [Old English] □ **weeper** *n.*

weepie *n.* (also **weepy**) (*pl.* **-ies**) *colloq.* a sentimental film, play, etc.

weepy *adj.* (**weepier**, **weepiest**) *colloq.* inclined to weep; tearful.

weever *n.* ▼ any marine fish of the genus *Trachinus*, with sharp venomous dorsal spines.

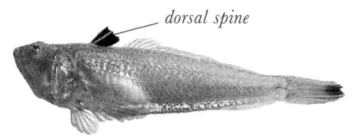

WEEVER
(*Trachinus* species)

weevil *n.* **1** ► any beetle of the large family Curculionidae or a related family. ▷ BEETLE. **2** any insect damaging stored grain. [Middle English] □ **weevily** *adj.*

wee-wee *slang* ● *n.* **1** the act or an instance of urinating. **2** urine. ● *v.intr.* (**-wees**, **-weed**) urinate. [20th-century coinage]

weft *n.* **1** ▼ the threads woven across a warp to make fabric. **2** yarn for these. **3** a thing woven. [Old English]

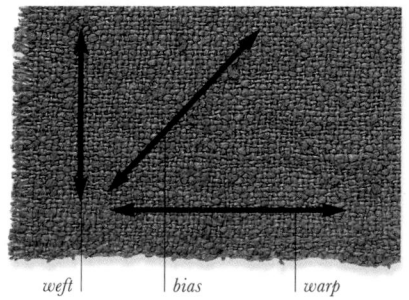

weft   *bias*   *warp*

WEFT ON A PIECE OF FABRIC

weigh *v.* **1** *tr.* find the weight of. **2** *tr.* balance in the hands to guess or as if to guess the weight of. **3** *tr.* (often foll. by *out*) **a** take a definite weight of; take a specified weight from a larger quantity. **b** distribute in exact amounts by weight. **4** *tr.* **a** estimate the relative importance or desirability of (*weighed the consequences; weighed the merits of the candidates*). **b** (foll. by *with*, *against*) compare (one consideration with another). **5** *tr.* be equal to (a specified weight) (*weighs three kilos; weighs very little*). **6** *intr.* **a** have importance; exert an influence. **b** (foll. by *with*) be regarded as important by (*the point that weighs with me*). **7** *intr.* (often foll. by *on*) be heavy or burdensome (to); be depressing (to). □ **weigh anchor** see ANCHOR. **weigh down 1** bring or keep down by exerting weight. **2** be oppressive or burdensome to (*weighed down with worries*). **weigh in** (of a boxer before a contest, or a jockey after a race) be weighed. **weigh into** *colloq.* attack (physically or verbally). **weigh in with** *colloq.* advance (an argument etc.) assertively or boldly. **weigh up** *colloq.* form an estimate of; consider carefully. **weigh one's words** carefully choose the way one expresses something. [Old English] □ **weigher** *n.*

weighbridge *n.* a weighing machine for vehicles.

weigh-in *n.* the weighing of a boxer before a fight.

weight ● *n.* **1** *Physics* **a** the force experienced by a body as a result of the Earth's gravitation. **b** any similar force with which a body tends to a centre of attraction. **2** the heaviness of a body regarded as a property of it; its relative mass or the quantity of matter contained in it by giving rise to a downward force (*is twice your weight; kept in position by its weight*). **3** the quantitative expression of a body's weight (*has a weight of three pounds*). **4** a body of a known weight for use in weighing. **5** a heavy body (*a clock worked by weights*). **6** a load or burden (*a weight off my mind*). **7 a** influence, importance (*carried weight with the public*). **b** preponderance (*the weight of evidence was against them*). **8 a** a heavy object thrown as an athletic exercise; = SHOT[1] 7. **b** (in *pl.*) blocks or discs used in weightlifting or weight training. **9** the surface density of cloth etc. as a measure of its suitability. ● *v.tr.* **1 a** attach a weight to. **b** hold down with a weight or weights. **2** (foll. by *with*) impede or burden. **3** *Statistics* multiply the components of (an average) by factors to take account of their importance. **4** assign a handicap weight to (a horse). □ **throw one's weight about** (or **around**) *colloq.* be unpleasantly self-assertive. [Old English]

WEEVIL: NUT WEEVIL
(*Curculio nucum*)

proboscis   thorax   abdomen

antenna   hind leg

weighting *n.* *Brit.* an extra allowance paid in special cases (*London weighting*).

weightless *adj.* not apparently acted on by gravity. □ **weightlessly** *adv.* **weightlessness** *n.*

weightlifting *n.* the sport of lifting a heavy weight, esp. a barbell. □ **weightlifter** *n.*

weight training *n.* physical training involving the use of weights.

weighty *adj.* (**weightier**, **weightiest**) **1** weighing much; heavy. **2** momentous, important. **3** (of utterances etc.) deserving consideration; careful and serious. □ **weightily** *adv.* **weightiness** *n.*

weir /weer/ *n.* **1** a dam built across a river to raise the level of water upstream or regulate its flow. **2** an enclosure of stakes etc. set in a stream as a trap for fish. [Old English]

weird /weerd/ *adj.* **1** uncanny, supernatural. **2** *colloq.* strange, queer, incomprehensible. [earlier as noun: Old English *wyrd* 'destiny'] □ **weirdly** *adv.* **weirdness** *n.*

weirdo /weerd-oh/ *n.* (*pl.* **-os**) *colloq.* an odd or eccentric person.

welch var. of WELSH.

welcome ● *n.* the act or an instance of greeting or receiving gladly; a kind or glad reception (*gave them a warm welcome*). ● *int.* expressing such a greeting. ● *v.tr.* receive with a welcome. ● *adj.* **1** that one receives with pleasure. **2** (foll. by *to*, or *to* + infin.) **a** cordially allowed or invited (*you are welcome to use my car*). **b** *iron.* gladly given (an unwelcome task, thing, etc.) (*here's my work and you are welcome to it*). □ **outstay one's welcome** stay too long as a visitor etc. **you are welcome** there is no need for thanks. [originally Old English *wilcuma* 'a person whose coming is pleasing'] □ **welcomer** *n.* **welcomingly** *adv.*

weld ● *v.tr.* **1 a** hammer or press (pieces of metal) into one piece. **b** join by fusion with an electric arc etc. **2** fashion into an effectual or homogeneous whole. ● *n.* a welded joint. [alteration of obsolete *well* 'to melt or weld (heated metal)'] □ **weldable** *adj.* **weldability** *n.* **welder** *n.*

welfare *n.* **1** well-being, happiness; health and prosperity. **2** (**Welfare**) **a** the maintenance of persons in such a condition esp. by statutory procedure or social effort. **b** financial support given for this purpose. [Middle English]

welfare state *n.* **1** a system whereby the state undertakes to protect the health and well-being of its citizens by means of grants, pensions, etc. **2** a country practising this system.

welfare work *n.* organized effort for the welfare of the poor, disabled, etc.

well[1] ● *adv.* (**better**, **best**) **1** in a satisfactory way. **2** in the right way (*well said; you did well to tell me*). **3** with some talent or distinction. **4** in a kind way. **5** thoroughly, extensively, soundly. **6** with heartiness or approval. **7** probably, reasonably, advisably (*you may well be right; we might well take the risk*). **8** to a considerable extent (*is well over forty*). **9** successfully, fortunately (*it turned out well*). **10** luckily, opportunely (*well met!*). **11** comfortably, abundantly, liberally (*we live well here; the job pays well*). ● *adj.* (**better**, **best**) **1** (usu. *predic.*) in good health (*are you well?; was not a well person*). **2** (*predic.*) **a** in a satisfactory state or position (*all is well*). **b** advisable (*it would be well to enquire*). ● *int.* expressing surprise, resignation, insistence, etc., or used merely to introduce a remark (*well I never!; well, I suppose so; well, who was it?*). □ **as well 1** in addition; to an equal extent. **2** (also **just as well**) with equal reason; with no loss of advantage or need for regret (*may as well give up; it would be just as well to stop now*). **as well as** in addition to. **leave** (or **let**) **well alone** avoid needless change or disturbance. **well and truly** decisively, completely. **well away 1** having made considerable progress. **2** *Brit. colloq.* fast asleep or drunk. [Old English] □ **wellness** *n.*

W

■ **Usage** A hyphen is normally used in combinations of *well-* when used attributively, but not when used predicatively, e.g. *a well-made coat* but *the coat is well made.*

well² ● *n.* **1** ▶ a shaft sunk into the ground to obtain water, oil, etc. **2** an enclosed space like a well-shaft, e.g. in the middle of a building for stairs or a lift, or for light or ventilation. **3** (foll. by *of*) a source, esp. a copious one (*a well of information*). **4 a** a mineral spring. **b** (in *pl.*) a spa. ● *v.intr.* (foll. by *out, up*) spring as from a fountain; flow copiously. [Old English]

we'll *contr.* we shall; we will.

well-adjusted *adj.* (**well adjusted** when *predic.*) **1** mentally and emotionally stable. **2** in a good state of adjustment.

well advised *predic.adj.* (usu. foll. by *to* + infin.) (of a person) prudent (*would be well advised to wait*).

well-appointed *adj.* (**well appointed** when *predic.*) having all the necessary equipment.

well aware *predic.adj.* (often foll. by *of*) certainly aware (*well aware of the danger*).

well-balanced *adj.* (**well balanced** when *predic.*) **1** sane, sensible. **2** equally matched.

well-behaved *adj.* (**well behaved** when *predic.*) having good manners or conduct.

well-being *n.* a state of being well, healthy, contented, etc.

well-born *adj.* (**well born** when *predic.*) of noble or *US* wealthy family.

well-bred *adj.* (**well bred** when *predic.*) having or showing good breeding or manners.

well-built *adj.* (**well built** when *predic.*) **1** of good construction. **2** (of a person) big and strong and well-proportioned.

well-chosen *adj.* (**well chosen** when *predic.*) carefully selected, esp. for effect.

well-connected *adj.* associated, esp. by birth, with persons of good social position.

well-defined *adj.* (**well defined** when *predic.*) clearly indicated or determined.

well-deserved *adj.* (**well deserved** when *predic.*) rightfully merited or earned.

well-developed *adj.* (**well developed** when *predic.*) **1** fully developed, fully grown. **2** of generous size.

well disposed *adj.* (hyphenated when *attrib.*; often foll. by *towards*) having a good disposition or friendly feeling (for).

well done *adj.* (hyphenated when *attrib.*) **1** (of meat etc.) thoroughly cooked. **2** (of a task etc.) performed well (also as *int.*).

well-dressed *adj.* fashionably smart.

well-earned *adj.* (**well earned** when *predic.*) fully deserved.

well-educated *adj.* (**well educated** when *predic.*) educated to a high level; with a wide knowledge.

well-endowed *adj.* (**well endowed** when *predic.*) **1** (often foll. by *with*) well provided with money, a resource, etc. **2** *colloq.* **a** (of a man) having large genitals. **b** (of a woman) large-breasted.

well-equipped *adj.* (**well equipped** when *predic.*) having a plentiful supply of equipment.

well-established *adj.* (**well established** when *predic.*) well-authenticated; long-standing.

well-fed *adj.* (**well fed** when *predic.*) having or having had plenty to eat.

well-founded *adj.* (**well founded** when *predic.*) (of suspicions etc.) based on good evidence.

well-groomed *adj.* (**well groomed** when *predic.*) (of a person) with carefully tended hair, clothes, etc.

well-grounded *adj.* (**well grounded** when *predic.*) **1** = WELL-FOUNDED. **2** having a good training in or knowledge of the groundwork of a subject.

well-head *n.* a source.

well-heeled *adj. colloq.* wealthy.

well-hung *adj.* (**well hung** when *predic.*) *colloq.* (of a man) having large genitals.

wellie var. of WELLY.

well-informed *adj.* (**well informed** when *predic.*) having much knowledge or information about a subject.

wellington *n.* (in full **wellington boot**) *Brit.* a waterproof rubber or plastic boot usu. reaching the knee. [named after the 1st Duke of *Wellington*, British general and statesman, 1769–1852]

well-intentioned *adj.* (**well intentioned** when *predic.*) having or showing good intentions.

well-judged *adj.* (**well judged** when *predic.*) opportunely, skilfully, or discreetly done.

well-kept *adj.* (**well kept** when *predic.*) kept in good order or condition.

well-known *adj.* (**well known** when *predic.*) **1** known to many. **2** known thoroughly.

well-liked *adj.* (**well liked** when *predic.*) (esp. of a person) liked; popular.

well-loved *adj.* (**well loved** when *predic.*) regarded with great affection or approval.

well-made *adj.* (**well made** when *predic.*) **1** strongly or skilfully manufactured. **2** (of a person or animal) having a good build.

well-mannered *adj.* (**well mannered** when *predic.*) having good manners.

well-meaning *adj.* (also **well-meant**) (**well meaning, well meant** when *predic.*) well-intentioned (but ineffective or unwise).

well-off *adj.* (**well off** when *predic.*) **1** having plenty of money. **2** in a fortunate situation or circumstances.

well-oiled *adj.* (**well oiled** when *predic.*) *colloq.* **1** drunk. **2** (of an organization etc.) running smoothly.

well-paid *adj.* (**well paid** when *predic.*) **1** (of a job) that pays well. **2** (of a person) amply rewarded for a job.

well placed *adj.* (hyphenated when *attrib.*) **1** set in a good place or position. **2** holding a good social position. **3** (foll. by *to* + infin.) easily able (*you are well placed to know*).

well-prepared *adj.* (**well prepared** when *predic.*) **1** prepared with care. **2** having prepared thoroughly (for an interview etc.).

well-preserved *adj.* (**well preserved** when *predic.*) (of an elderly person) showing little sign of ageing.

well-qualified *adj.* (**well qualified** when *predic.*) **1** holding many or prestigious qualifications. **2** (foll. by *to* + infin.) able through acquired expertise.

well-read *adj.* (**well read** when *predic.*) knowledgeable through much reading.

well received *adj.* (hyphenated when *attrib.*) welcomed; favourably received.

well-rounded *adj.* (**well rounded** when *predic.*) **1** complete and symmetrical. **2** (of a phrase etc.) complete and well expressed.

well spent *adj.* (hyphenated when *attrib.*) (esp. of money or time) used profitably.

well-spoken *adj.* articulate or refined in speech.

wellspring *n.* a source.

well-stocked *adj.* (**well stocked** when *predic.*) (of a shop, garden, etc.) plentifully filled with goods etc.

well-structured *adj.* (**well structured** when *predic.*) (esp. of a text) having a clear structure.

well thought of *adj.* (hyphenated when *attrib.*) having a good reputation; esteemed; respected.

well-thumbed *adj.* (**well thumbed** when *predic.*) bearing marks of frequent handling.

well-timed *adj.* (**well timed** when *predic.*) opportune, timely.

well-to-do *adj.* prosperous.

well-travelled *adj.* (*US* **well-traveled**) **1** having travelled widely. **2** (of a path etc.) much frequented.

well-tried *adj.* (**well tried** when *predic.*) often tested with good results.

well-trodden *adj.* much frequented.

well-turned *adj.* (**well turned** when *predic.*) **1** (of a compliment, phrase, or verse) elegantly expressed. **2** (of a leg, etc.) elegantly shaped or displayed.

well-used *adj.* **1** much frequented. **2** much handled or worn.

well-wisher *n.* a person who wishes one well.

well-worn *adj.* (**well worn** when *predic.*) **1** damaged by use or wear. **2** (of a phrase, joke, etc.) trite, hackneyed; stale.

welly *n.* (also **wellie**) (*pl.* **-ies**) *colloq.* = WELLINGTON.

Welsh ● *adj.* of or relating to Wales or its people or language. ● *n.* **1** the Celtic language of Wales. **2** (prec. by *the*; treated as *pl.*) the people of Wales. [from Latin *Volcae*, name of a Celtic people] □ **Welshness** *n.*

welsh *v.intr.* (also **welch** /welsh/) **1** (of a loser of a bet) decamp without paying. **2** evade an obligation. **3** (foll. by *on*) **a** fail to carry out a promise to (a person). **b** fail to honour (an obligation). [19th-century coinage] □ **welsher** *n.*

Welsh corgi SEE CORGI.

Welsh dresser *n.* a type of dresser with open shelves above a cupboard.

Welshman *n.* (*pl.* **-men**) a man who is Welsh by birth or descent.

Welsh rabbit *n.* (also **Welsh rarebit**) a dish of melted cheese etc. on toast.

Welshwoman *n.* (*pl.* **-women**) a woman who is Welsh by birth or descent.

welt *n.* **1** a leather rim sewn round the edge of a shoe-upper for the sole to be attached to. ▷ SHOE. **2** a ribbed or reinforced border of a garment; a trimming. [Middle English]

Weltanschauung /velt-an-show-uung; *third part rhymes with* cow/ *n.* (*pl.* **Weltanschauungen**) a particular philosophy or view of life; a conception of the world. [German, from *Welt* 'world' + *Anschauung* 'perception']

welter *n.* (foll. by *of*) a disorderly mixture or contrast of beliefs, policies, etc. [from Middle Dutch *welteren*]

welterweight *n.* **1** a weight in certain sports intermediate between lightweight and middleweight, in the amateur boxing scale 63.5–67 kg. **2** a sportsman of this weight.

wen *n.* a benign tumour on the skin esp. of the scalp. [Old English]

wench ● *n. joc.* a girl or young woman. ● *v.intr. archaic* (of a man) consort with prostitutes. [Old English *wencel* 'child'] □ **wencher** *n.*

wend *v.tr. & intr. literary* or *archaic* go. □ **wend one's way** make one's way. [Old English *wendan* 'to turn']

went *past of* GO¹.

wept *past of* WEEP.

were *2nd sing. past, pl. past, and past subjunctive of* BE.

we're *contr.* we are.

weren't *contr.* were not.

werewolf /wair-wuulf/ *n.* (also **werwolf**) (*pl.* **-wolves**) a mythical being who at times changes from a person to a wolf. [Old English]

Wesleyan ● *adj.* of or relating to a Protestant denomination founded by the English evangelist John Wesley (d. 1791) (cf. METHODIST). ● *n.* a member of this denomination. □ **Wesleyanism** *n.*

west ● *n.* **1 a** the point of the horizon where the sun sets at the equinoxes (cardinal point 90° to the left of north). ▷ COMPASS. **b** the direction in which this lies. **2** (usu. **the West**) **a** European in contrast to

---

WELL: CROSS-SECTION OF AN OIL WELL

(labels: *sea*, *offshore rig*, *rock strata*, *well*, *oil*)

W

oriental civilization. **b** *hist.* the states of Europe and N. America. **c** the western part of a country, town, etc. ● *adj.* **1** towards, at, near, or facing west. **2** coming from the west (*west wind*). ● *adv.* **1** towards, at, or near the west. **2** (foll. by *of*) further west than. □ **go west** *Brit. slang* be killed or destroyed etc. [Old English]

westbound *adj.* travelling or leading westwards.

West Country *n.* the south-western counties of England.

West End *n.* the entertainment and shopping area of London to the west of the City.

westerly ● *adj. & adv.* **1** in a western position or direction. **2** (of a wind) blowing from the west. ● *n.* (*pl.* **-ies**) a wind blowing from the west. ▷ TRADE WIND

western ● *adj.* **1** of, in, or towards, the west. **2** (**Western**) of or relating to the West (see WEST *n.* 2). ● *n.* a film, television drama, or novel about cowboys in western North America. □ **westerner** *n.*

Western Church *n.* the branch of the Christian Church which originated in Western Europe (opp. EASTERN CHURCH), esp. the Roman Catholic Church.

western hemisphere *n.* the half of the earth containing the Americas.

westernize *v.tr.* (also **Westernize, -ise**) influence with or convert to the ideas and customs etc. of the West. □ **westernization** *n.* **westernizer** *n.*

West Indian ● *adj.* of or relating to the West Indies. ● *n.* **1** a native or national of any island of the West Indies. **2** a person of West Indian descent.

West Indian satinwood see SATINWOOD 1b.

west-north-west *n.* the direction or compass point midway between west and north-west.

West Side *n.* *US* the western part of Manhattan.

west-south-west *n.* the direction or compass point midway between west and south-west.

westward ● *adj. & adv.* (also **westwards**) towards the west. ● *n.* a westward direction or region.

wet ● *adj.* (**wetter, wettest**) **1** soaked, covered, or dampened with water or other liquid (*a wet sponge; a wet surface; got my feet wet*). **2** (of the weather etc.) rainy (*a wet day*). **3** (of paint, ink, etc.) not yet dried. **4** *Brit. colloq.* feeble, inept. **5** *Brit. Polit. colloq.* Conservative with liberal tendencies, esp. as regarded by right-wing Conservatives. ● *v.tr.* (**wetting**; *past* and *past part.* **wet** or **wetted**) **1** make wet. **2 a** urinate in or on (*wet the bed*). **b** *refl.* urinate involuntarily. ● *n.* **1** moisture. **2** rainy weather; a time of rain. **3** *Brit. colloq.* a feeble or inept person. **4** *Brit. Polit. colloq.* a Conservative with liberal tendencies (see sense 6 of *adj.*). □ **wet behind the ears** immature, inexperienced. **wet through** with one's clothes soaked. **wet one's whistle** *colloq.* drink. [Old English] □ **wetly** *adv.* **wetness** *n.* **wettable** *adj.* **wetting** *n.* **wettish** *adj.*

wet blanket *n. colloq.* a gloomy person preventing the enjoyment of others.

wet dream *n.* an erotic dream with involuntary ejaculation of semen.

wether *n.* a castrated ram. [Old English]

wet-nurse ● *n.* a woman employed to suckle another's child. ● *v.tr.* **1** act as a wet-nurse to. **2** *colloq.* treat as if helpless.

wetsuit *n.* ▶ a close-fitting rubber garment worn for warmth in water sports, diving, etc. ▷ DIVER

wetting agent *n.* a substance that helps water etc. to spread or penetrate.

we've *contr.* we have.

Wg. Cdr. *abbr.* Wing Commander.

whack *colloq.* ● *v.tr.* **1** strike or beat forcefully. **2** (as **whacked** *adj.*) esp. *Brit.* tired out; exhausted. ● *n.* **1** a sharp or resounding blow. **2** *slang* a turn; an attempt. **3** *Brit. slang* a share or portion. □ **out of whack** esp. *N. Amer. & Austral. slang* out of order; malfunctioning.

whacking *Brit. colloq.* ● *adj.* very large. ● *adv.* very.

whacko *int. Brit. slang* expressing delight or enjoyment.

whacky var. of WACKY.

whale *n.* (*pl.* same or **whales**) ▼ any of the larger marine mammals of the order Cetacea. ▷ CETACEAN. □ **a whale of a** *colloq.* an exceedingly good or fine etc. [Old English]

WETSUIT

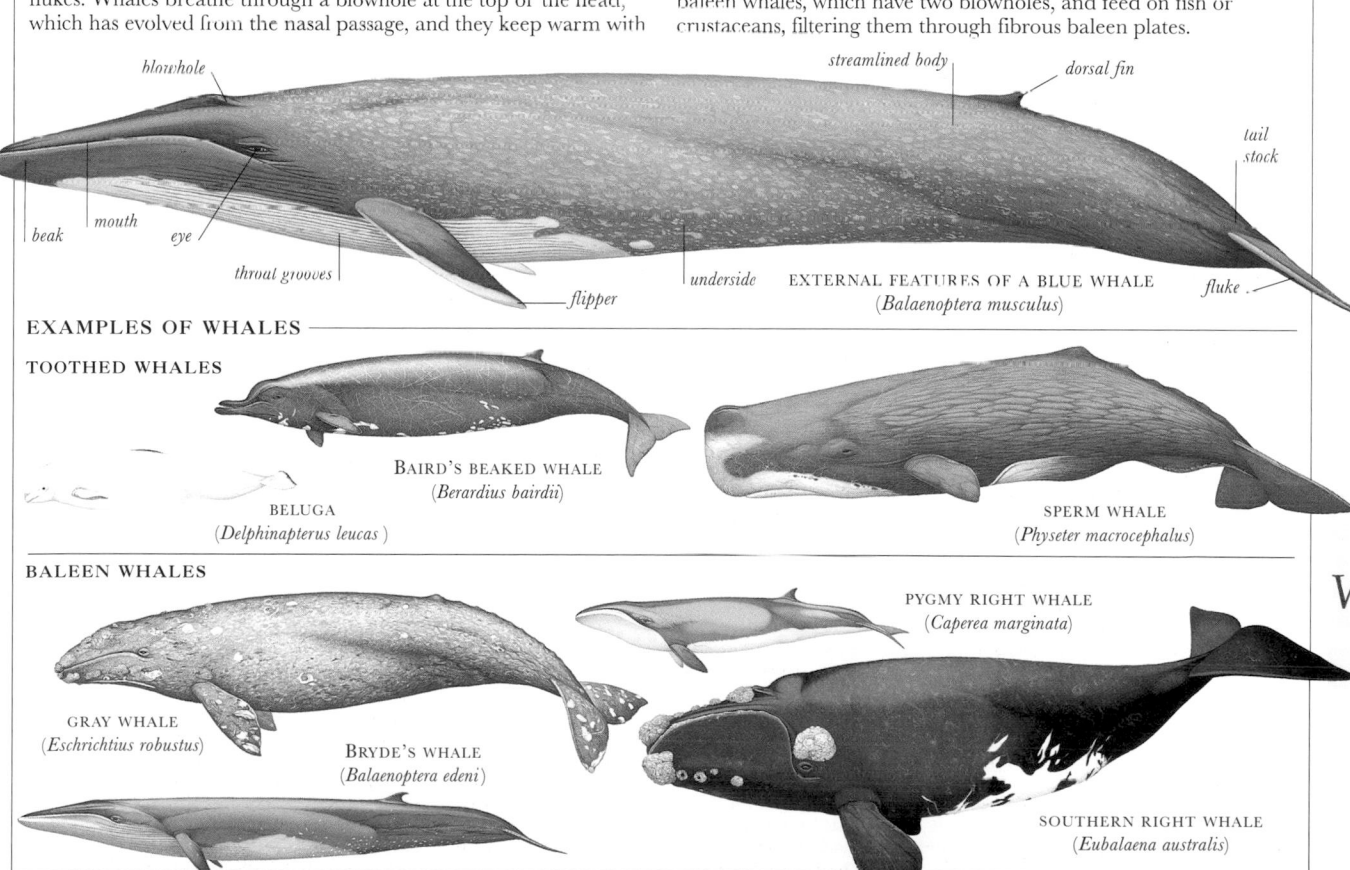

WHALE

Some 78 species of whale inhabit the world's oceans. Their streamlined bodies now show little trace of their terrestrial ancestry, with front limbs converted into flippers and hindlimbs replaced by flukes. Whales breathe through a blowhole at the top of the head, which has evolved from the nasal passage, and they keep warm with an insulating layer of blubber. Whales form two groups: the toothed whales, including sperm whales and dolphins, which hunt fish, squid and seals, and have a single blowhole; and the baleen whales, which have two blowholes, and feed on fish or crustaceans, filtering them through fibrous baleen plates.

blowhole
streamlined body
dorsal fin
tail stock
beak
mouth
eye
throat grooves
flipper
underside
EXTERNAL FEATURES OF A BLUE WHALE
(*Balaenoptera musculus*)
fluke

EXAMPLES OF WHALES

TOOTHED WHALES

BELUGA
(*Delphinapterus leucas*)

BAIRD'S BEAKED WHALE
(*Berardius bairdii*)

SPERM WHALE
(*Physeter macrocephalus*)

BALEEN WHALES

PYGMY RIGHT WHALE
(*Caperea marginata*)

GRAY WHALE
(*Eschrichtius robustus*)

BRYDE'S WHALE
(*Balaenoptera edeni*)

SOUTHERN RIGHT WHALE
(*Eubalaena australis*)

W

whalebone *n.* ◄ an elastic horny substance growing in thin parallel plates in the upper jaw of some whales, used as stiffening etc.

whaler *n.* a whaling ship or a seaman engaged in whaling.

whaling *n.* the practice or industry of hunting and killing whales.

wham *colloq.* ● *int.* expressing the sound of a forcible impact. ● *n.* such a sound. ● *v.* (**whammed, whamming**) **1** *intr.* make such a sound or impact. **2** *tr.* strike forcibly.

whammy *n.* (*pl.* **-ies**) esp. *US colloq.* **1** an evil or unlucky influence. **2** (esp. in phr. **double whammy**) a blow or setback.

WHALEBONE: FRINGED PLATE OF BALEEN

wharf *n.* (*pl.* **wharves** or **wharfs**) ▼ a level quayside area to which a ship may be moored to load and unload. [Old English]

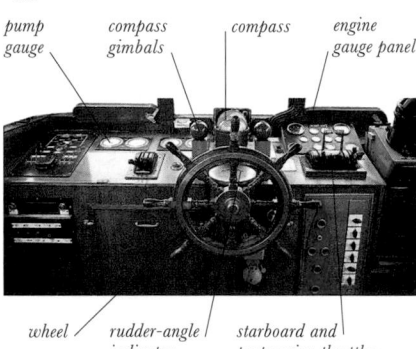

WHARF: FINGER WHARF IN SYDNEY, AUSTRALIA

wharves *pl.* of WHARF.

what ● *pron.* **1** *interrog. & rel.pron.* asking for a statement representing a choice from a number of possibilities (*what have you been reading?; she asked what his name was*) (cf. WHICH *pron.*). **2** *rel.pron.* that which, anything that (*will do what I can*). **3** asking for a remark to be repeated (*what?*). **4** asking for confirmation or agreement of something not completely understood (*what, you really mean it?*). **5** how much (*what you must have suffered!*) ● *det.* **1** *interrog. & rel.det.* corresponding to the functions of senses 1 and 2 of the pronoun (*what books have you read? she asked what thoughts he had*). **2** (in exclamations) how great or remarkable (*what luck!*). **3** *rel.det.* as much … as; any … that (*will give you what help I can*). ● *interrog.adv.* to what extent (*what does it matter?*). □ **what about** what is the news or position or your opinion of (*what about me?*). **what-d'you-call-it** (or **what's-its-name**) a substitute for a name not recalled. **what ever** what at all or in any way (*what ever do you mean?*) (see also WHATEVER). **what for** *colloq.* **1** for what reason? **2** a severe reprimand (esp. *give a person what for*). **what have you** (prec. by *or*) *colloq.* anything else similar. **what if? 1** what would result etc. if? **2** what would it matter if? **what is more** and as an additional point; moreover. **what not** (prec. by *and*) other similar things. **what of?** what is the news concerning? **what of it?** why should that be considered significant? **what's-his** (or **-its**) **-name** = *what-d'you-call-it.* **what's what** *colloq.* what is useful or important etc. **what with** *colloq.* because of (usu. several things). [Old English]

whate'er *poet.* var. of WHATEVER.

whatever *det. & pron.* **1** = WHAT (in relative uses) with the emphasis on indefiniteness (*lend me whatever (money) you have*). **2** though anything (*we are safe whatever happens*). **3** (with *neg.* or *interrog.*) at all; of any kind (*there is no doubt whatever*). **4** *colloq.* = *what ever.* □ **or whatever** *colloq.* or anything similar.

■ **Usage** See Usage Note at EVER.

whatnot *n.* an indefinite or trivial thing.

whatsoever *det. & pron.* = WHATEVER 1, 2, 3.

wheat *n.* **1** any cereal plant of the genus *Triticum.* **2** its grain, used in making flour etc. ▷ GRAIN. [Old English, related to WHITE.]

wheatear *n.* any small migratory bird of the genus *Oenanthe.*

wheaten *adj.* made of wheat.

wheatgerm *n.* the embryo of the wheat grain, extracted as a source of vitamins.

wheatgrass *n.* = *couch grass* (see COUCH[2]).

wheatmeal *n.* flour made from wheat with some of the bran and germ removed.

whee *int.* expressing delight, excitement, or exhilaration.

wheedle *v.tr.* **1** coax by flattery or endearments. **2** (foll. by *out*) get (a thing) out of a person by wheedling. □ **wheedler** *n.* **wheedling** *adj.* **wheedlingly** *adv.*

wheel ● *n.* **1** a circular frame or disc that revolves on an axle and is used to facilitate the motion of a vehicle or for various mechanical purposes. **2** a wheel-like thing (*Catherine wheel; potter's wheel; steering wheel*). **3** (in *pl.*) *slang* a car. **4** = STEERING WHEEL. **5** *US slang* = BIG WHEEL 2. **6** a set of short lines concluding a stanza. ● *v.* **1** *intr. & tr.* **a** turn on an axis or pivot. **b** swing round in line with one end as a pivot. **2 a** *intr.* (often foll. by *about, round, US around*) change direction or face another way. **b** *tr.* cause to do this. **3** *tr.* push or pull (a wheeled thing, esp. a barrow, bicycle, or pram, or its load or occupant). **4** *intr.* go in circles or curves (*seagulls wheeling overhead*). □ **at the wheel 1** driving a vehicle. **2** directing a ship. **wheel and deal** engage in political or commercial scheming. **wheels within wheels** *Brit.* **1** intricate machinery. **2** *colloq.* indirect or secret agencies. [Old English] □ **wheeled** *adj.* (also in *comb.*). **wheelless** *adj.*

wheelbarrow *n.* a small cart with one wheel and two shafts for carrying garden loads etc.

wheelbase *n.* the distance between the front and rear axles of a vehicle.

wheelchair *n.* a chair on wheels for an invalid or disabled person.

wheel clamp *n.* = CLAMP[1] *n.* 2.

wheeler-dealer *n.* a person who wheels and deals (see WHEEL). □ **wheeler-dealing** *n.*

wheelhouse *n.* ▼ a steersman's shelter. ▷ FACTORY SHIP

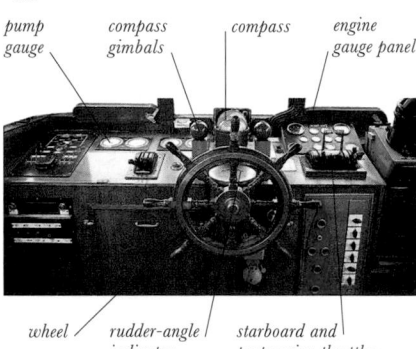

pump gauge   compass gimbals   compass   engine gauge panel

wheel   rudder-angle indicator   starboard and port engine throttles

WHEELHOUSE OF FIRE-FIGHTING BOAT

wheelie *n. Brit. slang* the stunt of riding a bicycle or motorcycle for a short distance with the front wheel off the ground.

wheelsman *n.* (*pl.* **-men**) *US* a steersman.

wheelspin *n.* rotation of a vehicle's wheels without traction.

wheel well *n.* the recess into which a wheel of a vehicle fits.

wheelwright *n.* a person who makes or repairs esp. wooden wheels.

wheeze ● *v.* **1** *intr.* breathe with an audible chesty

whistling sound. **2** *tr.* (often foll. by *out*) utter in this way. ● *n.* **1** a sound of wheezing. **2** *colloq. Brit.* a clever scheme. □ **wheezer** *n.* **wheezy** *adj.* **wheezily** *adv.* **wheeziness** *n.*

whelk *n.* ► any predatory marine gastropod mollusc of the family Buccinidae. [Old English]

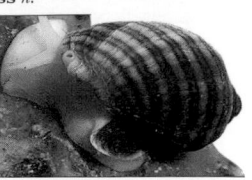

WHELK: DOG WHELK (*Nucella lapillus*)

whelp ● *n.* **1** a young dog; a puppy. **2** an ill-mannered child or youth. ● *v.tr.* (also *absol.*) bring forth (a whelp or whelps). [Old English]

when ● *interrog.adv.* **1** at what time? **2** on what occasion? ● *rel.adv.* (prec. by *time* etc.) at or on which (*there are times when I could cry*). ● *conj.* **1** at the or any time that; as soon as (*come when you like; when I was your age*). **2** although; considering that (*why stand up when you could sit down?*). **3** after which; and then; but just then (*I had just fallen asleep when the bell rang*). ● *pron.* what time?; which time (*till when can you stay?; since when it has been better*). ● *n.* (prec. by *the*) the time, occasion, or date (*fixed the where and when*). [Old English]

whence *formal* ● *adv.* from what place? (*whence did they come?*). ● *conj.* **1** to the place from which (*return whence you came*). **2** (often prec. by *place* etc.) from which (*the source whence these errors arise*). **3** and thence (*whence it follows that*). [Middle English]

■ **Usage** The use of *from whence* rather than simply *whence* (as in *the place from whence they came*), though common, is generally considered incorrect.

whenever *conj. & adv.* **1** at whatever time; on whatever occasion. **2** every time that. □ **or whenever** *colloq.* or at any similar time.

■ **Usage** See Usage Note at EVER.

where ● *interrog.adv.* **1** in or to what place or position? (*where is the milk?; where are you going?*). **2** in what direction or respect? (*where does the argument lead?; where does it concern us?*). **3** in what book etc.?; from whom? (*where did you read that?; where did you hear that?*). **4** in what situation or condition? (*where does that leave us?*). ● *rel.adv.* (prec. by *place* etc.) in or to which (*places where they meet*). ● *conj.* **1** in or to the or any place, direction, or respect in which (*go where you like; that is where you are wrong*). **2** and there (*reached Crewe, where the car broke down*). ● *pron.* what place? (*where do you come from?*). ● *n.* (prec. by *the*) the place; the scene of something (see WHEN *n.*). [Old English]

whereabouts ● *adv.* where or approximately where? (*whereabouts are they?; show me whereabouts to look*). ● *n.* (treated as *sing.* or *pl.*) a person's or thing's approximate location.

whereafter *conj. formal* after which.

whereas *conj.* **1** in contrast or comparison with the fact that. **2** (esp. in legal preambles) taking into consideration the fact that.

whereby *conj.* by what or which means.

wherefore ● *adv. archaic* **1** for what reason? **2** for which reason. ● *n. colloq.* a reason (*the whys and wherefores*).

wherein *formal* ● *conj.* in what or which place or respect. ● *adv.* in what place or respect?

whereof *formal* ● *conj.* of what or which (*the means whereof*). ● *adv.* of what?

wheresoever *conj. & adv. formal* or *literary* = WHERESEVER

whereupon *conj.* immediately after which.

wherever ● *adv.* in or to whatever place. ● *conj.* in every place that. □ **or wherever** *colloq.* or in any similar place.

■ **Usage** See Usage Note at EVER.

wherewithal *n. colloq.* money etc. needed for a purpose (*has not the wherewithal to do it*).

whet *v.tr.* (**whetted, whetting**) **1** sharpen (a tool or weapon) by grinding. **2** stimulate (the appetite or a desire, interest, etc.). [Old English]

whether *conj.* introducing the first or both of alternative possibilities (*I do not know whether they have arrived or not*). □ **whether or no** see NO². [Old English]

whetstone *n.* a fine-grained stone used esp. with water to sharpen cutting tools (cf. OILSTONE).

whew *int.* expressing surprise, consternation, or relief.

whey /way/ *n.* ▶ the watery liquid left when milk forms curds. [Old English]

whey-faced *adj.* pale esp. with fear.

which ● *pron.* **1** *interrog.pron.* asking for choice from a definite set of alternatives (*which do you prefer?*) (cf. WHAT *pron.* 1). **2** *rel.pron.* (*poss.* **of which**, **whose**) being the thing or things just referred to (*the house, which is empty, has been damaged*) (cf. THAT *pron.* 7). **3** *rel.pron.* used in place of *that* after a preposition or after *that* (*there is the house in which I was born; that which you have just seen*). ● *interrog. & rel.det.* corresponding to the functions of senses 1 and 2 of the pronoun (*which book do you prefer?*; *three days, during all of which time he said nothing*). □ **which is which** a phrase used when two or more persons or things are difficult to distinguish from each other. [Old English]

whichever *det. & pron.* **1** any which (*take whichever you like; whichever one you like*). **2** no matter which (*whichever one wins, they both get a prize*).

whiff ● *n.* **1** a puff or breath of air, smoke, etc. (*went outside for a whiff of fresh air*). **2** a smell (*caught the whiff of a cigar*). ● *v.* **1** *tr. & intr.* blow or puff lightly. **2** *intr. Brit. colloq.* smell (esp. unpleasant). **3** *tr.* get a slight smell of.

whiffle ● *v.* **1** *intr.* (of a flame, leaves, etc.) flicker, flutter. **2** *intr.* make the sound of a light wind in breathing etc. ● *n.* a slight movement of air.

whiffy *adj.* (**whiffier**, **whiffiest**) *Brit. colloq.* having an unpleasant smell.

Whig *n. hist. Polit.* a member of the British reforming and constitutional party that was succeeded in the 19th c. by the Liberal Party (opp. TORY 2). □ **Whiggery** *n.* **Whiggish** *adj.* **Whiggism** *n.*

while ● *n.* **1** a space of time, time spent in some action (*a long while ago; waited a while; all this while*). **2** (prec. by *the*) during some other process. ● *conj.* **1** during the time that; at the same time as (*while I was away, the house was burgled; fell asleep while reading*). **2** although, whereas (*while I want to believe it, I cannot*). **3** *N.Engl.* until (*wait while Monday*). ● *v.tr.* (foll. by *away*) pass (time etc.) in a leisurely or interesting manner. □ **all the while** during the whole time (that). **for a long while** for a long time past. **for a while** for some time. **in a while** (or **little while**) soon, shortly. **worth while** (or **worth one's while**) worth the time or effort spent. [Old English]

■ **Usage** See Usage Note at WORTHWHILE.

whilst *adv. & conj.* esp. *Brit.* while. [Middle English]

whim *n.* **1** a sudden fancy; a caprice. **2** capriciousness. [17th-century coinage]

whimper ● *v.* **1** *intr.* make feeble, querulous, or frightened sounds; cry and whine softly. **2** *tr.* utter whimperingly. ● *n.* a whimpering sound. □ **whimperer** *n.* **whimperingly** *adv.*

whimsical *adj.* **1** odd or quaint; fanciful, humorous. **2** capricious. □ **whimsicality** *n.* **whimsically** *adv.*

whimsy *n.* (also **whimsey**) (*pl.* **-ies** or **-eys**) **1** a whim; a capricious notion or fancy. **2** capricious or quaint humour.

whinchat *n.* a small brownish songbird, *Saxicola rubetra*.

whine ● *n.* **1** a complaining long-drawn wail as of a dog. **2** a similar shrill prolonged sound. **3 a** a querulous tone. **b** an instance of feeble or undignified complaining. ● *v.* **1** *intr.* emit or utter a whine. **2** *intr.* complain in a querulous tone or in a feeble or undignified way. **3** *tr.* utter in a whining tone. [Old English] □ **whiner** *n.* **whiningly** *adv.* **whiny** *adj.* (**whinier**, **whiniest**).

whinge *Brit. colloq.* ● *v.intr.* (**whingeing**) whine; grumble peevishly. ● *n.* a whining complaint; a peevish grumbling. [Old English] □ **whinger** *n.* **whingeingly** *adv.*

whinny ● *n.* (*pl.* **-ies**) a gentle or joyful neigh. ● *v.intr.* (**-ies**, **-ied**) give a whinny.

whip ● *n.* **1** ▼ a lash attached to a stick for urging on animals or punishing etc. **2 a** a member of a political party in Parliament appointed to control its parliamentary discipline and tactics, esp. ensuring voting in debates. **b** *Brit.* the whips' written notice requesting or requiring attendance for voting at a division etc. **c** (prec. by *the*) party discipline and instructions (*asked for the Labour whip*). ● *v.* (**whipped**, **whipping**) **1** *tr.* beat or urge on with a whip. **2** *tr.* beat (cream or eggs etc.) into a froth. **3** *tr. & intr.* take or move suddenly, unexpectedly, or rapidly (*whipped out a knife; whipped behind the door*). **4** *tr. Brit. colloq.* steal (*who's whipped my pen?*). **5** *tr. slang* **a** excel. **b** defeat. □ **whip in** bring (hounds) together. **whip on** urge into action. **whip up 1** excite or stir up (feeling etc.). **2** summon (attendance). [Middle English] □ **whipless** *adj.* **whiplike** *adj.* **whipper** *n.*

whipcord *n.* **1** a tightly twisted cord such as is used for making whiplashes. **2** a closely woven worsted fabric.

whip graft *n.* (in horticulture) a graft with the tongue of the scion in a slot in the stock and vice versa.

whip hand *n.* (usu. prec. by *the*) the advantage or control in any situation.

whiplash ● *n.* **1** the flexible end of a whip. **2** a blow with a whip. **3** a sharp reaction (*whiplash against the status quo*). ● *v.* **1** *tr.* jerk causing a whiplash effect. **2** *intr.* flick or move like a whip flashing.

whiplash injury *n.* an injury to the neck caused by a severe jerk of the head, esp. in a motor accident.

whipper-in *n.* (*pl.* **whippers-in**) a huntsman's assistant who manages the hounds.

whippersnapper *n.* **1** a small child. **2** an insignificant but presumptuous or intrusive (esp. young) person.

whippet *n.* ▼ a dog of a small slender breed originally a cross between the greyhound and the terrier or spaniel, bred for racing.

WHIPPET

whipping *n.* **1** a beating, esp. with a whip. **2** cord wound round in binding.

whippoorwill /wip-ŏ-wil/ *n.* ▶ an American nightjar, *Caprimulgus vociferus*.

whippy *adj.* flexible, springy. □ **whippiness** *n.*

WHIP: LATE 19TH-CENTURY AUSTRALIAN STOCKWHIP

WHEY SEPARATED FROM CURDS

WHIPPOORWILL
(*Caprimulgus vociferus*)

whip-round *n.* esp. *Brit. colloq.* an informal collection of money from a group of people.

whip snake *n.* any of various long slender snakes of the family Colubridae.

whir var. of WHIRR.

whirl ● *v.* **1** *tr. & intr.* swing round and round; revolve rapidly. **2** *tr. & intr.* (foll. by *away*) convey or go rapidly in a vehicle etc. **3** *tr. & intr.* send or travel swiftly in an orbit or a curve. **4** *intr.* **a** (of the brain, senses, etc.) seem to spin round. **b** (of thoughts etc.) be confused; follow each other in bewildering succession. ● *n.* **1** a whirling movement (*vanished in a whirl of dust*). **2** a state of intense activity (*the social whirl*). **3** a state of confusion (*my mind is in a whirl*). **4** *colloq.* a try (*give it a whirl*). [from Old Norse *hvirfill* 'circle'] □ **whirler** *n.*

whirligig *n.* **1** a spinning or whirling toy. **2** a merry-go-round. **3** any freshwater beetle of the family Gyrinidae that circles about on the surface. [Middle English, based on obsolete *gig* 'whipping-top']

whirling dervish *n.* (also **howling dervish**) a dervish performing a wild dance, or howling, according to which sect he belongs to.

whirlpool *n.* a powerful circular eddy in the sea etc. often causing suction to its centre.

whirlwind *n.* **1** a mass or column of air whirling rapidly round and round. **2** (*attrib.*) very rapid (*a whirlwind romance*). □ **reap the whirlwind** suffer worse results of a bad action.

whirlybird *n. colloq.* a helicopter.

whirr (also **whir**) ● *n.* a continuous rapid buzzing or softly clicking sound as of a bird's wings or of cogwheels in constant motion. ● *v.intr.* (**whirred**, **whirring**) make this sound. [Middle English]

whisht *v.* (also **whist**) esp. *Sc. & Ir. dial.* **1** *intr.* (esp. as *int.*) be quiet; hush. **2** *tr.* quieten.

whisk ● *v.* **1** *tr.* (foll. by *away*, *off*) brush with a sweeping movement. **2** *tr.* whip (cream, eggs, etc.). ▷ UTENSIL. **3** *tr. & intr.* convey or go (esp. out of sight) lightly or quickly (*whisked me off to the doctor; the mouse whisked into its hole*). ● *n.* **1** a whisking action or motion. **2** a utensil for whisking eggs or cream etc. **3** a bunch of grass, twigs, bristles, etc., for removing dust or flies. [Middle English]

whisker *n.* **1** (usu. in *pl.*) the hair growing on a man's face, esp. on the cheek. **2** ▶ each of the bristles on the face of a cat etc. **3** *colloq.* a small distance (*within a whisker of; won by a whisker*). □ **have** (or **have grown**) **whiskers** *colloq.* (esp. of a story etc.) be very old. □ **whiskered** *adj.* **whiskery** *adj.*

whiskers

WHISKERS ON A CAT

whisky *n.* (*US & Ir.* **whiskey**) (*pl.* **-ies** or **-eys**) **1** a spirit distilled esp. from malted barley. **2** a drink of this. [abbreviation of obsolete *whiskybae*]

whisper ● *v.* **1** *intr. & tr.* speak or say very softly, esp. without vibration of the vocal cords. **2** *intr.* speak privately or conspiratorially. ● *n.* **1** whispering speech (*talking in whispers*). **2** a whispering sound. [Old English] □ **whisperer** *n.* **whispering** *n.*

whispering gallery *n.* a gallery esp. under a dome with acoustic properties such that a whisper may be heard round its entire circumference.

whist *n.* a card game usu. for two pairs of players, with the winning of tricks. [earlier *whisk*]

whist drive *n. Brit.* a social occasion with the playing of progressive whist.

whistle ● *n.* **1** a clear shrill sound made by forcing breath through a small hole between nearly closed lips, or between the teeth. **2** a similar sound made by a bird, the wind, a missile, etc. **3** an instrument used to produce such a sound, esp. for giving a signal. ● *v.* **1** *intr.* emit a whistle. **2 a** *intr.* give a signal or express surprise or derision by whistling. **b** *tr.* (often foll. by *up*) summon or give a signal to (a dog etc.) by whistling. **3** *tr.* (also *absol.*) produce (a tune) by whistling. **4** *intr.* (foll. by *for*) vainly seek or desire. □ **as clean** (or **clear** or **dry**) **as a whistle** very clean or clear or dry. **blow the whistle on** *colloq.* bring (an activity) to an end; inform on (those responsible). **wet one's whistle** see WET. [Old English] □ **whistler** *n.*

whistle-blower *n.* a person who blows the whistle on someone or something (see WHISTLE).

whistle-stop *n.* **1** *US* a small unimportant town on a railway. **2** a politician's brief pause for an electioneering speech on tour. **3** (*attrib.*) with only brief pauses; very fast (*a whistle-stop tour*).

whistling kettle *n.* a kettle fitted with a whistle sounded by steam when the kettle is boiling.

Whit *attrib.adj.* connected with, belonging to, or following Whit Sunday (*Whit Monday*; *Whit weekend*). [Old English *Hwīta Sunnandæg*, literally 'white Sunday']

whit *n.* a particle; a least possible amount (*not a whit better*).

white ● *adj.* **1** resembling a surface reflecting sunlight without absorbing any of the visible rays; of the colour of milk or fresh snow. **2** approaching such a colour; pale esp. in the face (*turned as white as a sheet*). **3** (also **White**) **a** of the human group having light-coloured skin. **b** of or relating to white people. **4** (of a person) white-haired, esp. in old age. **5** (of wine) made from white grapes or dark grapes with the skins removed. **6** *Brit.* (of coffee) with milk or cream added. **7** colourless (*white glass*). ● *n.* **1** a white colour or pigment. **2 a** white clothes or material (*dressed in white*). **b** (in *pl.*) white garments as worn in cricket, tennis, etc. **c** (in *pl.*) white clothing etc. for washing. **3** the white part or albumen round the yolk of an egg. ▷ EGG. **4** the visible part of the eyeball round the iris. **5** (also **White**) a member of a light-skinned race. □ **bleed white** drain (a person, country, etc.) of wealth etc. [Old English] □ **whitely** *adv.* **whiteness** *n.* **whitish** *adj.*

white ant *n.* a termite.

whitebait *n.* (*pl.* same) (usu. *pl.*) the small silvery-white young of herrings, sprats, and similar fish esp. as food.

whiteboard *n.* a board with a white surface, used esp. for classroom presentations using felt-tip pens.

white cell *n.* (also **white blood cell**) = LEUCOCYTE.

white Christmas *n.* Christmas with snow on the ground.

white-collar *attrib.adj.* (of a worker or work) clerical or administrative rather than manual.

white dwarf *n.* a small very dense star. ▷ STAR

white elephant *n.* an item or property that is no longer useful or wanted, esp. one that is difficult to maintain or dispose of.

whitefish *n.* (*pl.* usu. same) ▼ any freshwater fish of the genus *Coregonus* etc., of the trout family, and used esp. for food.

white fish *n.* fish with pale flesh, e.g. plaice, cod, etc.

white flag *n.* a symbol of surrender or a period of truce.

whitefly *n.* (*pl.* **-flies**) any small insect of the family Aleyrodidae, having wings covered with white powder and feeding on sap.

WHITEFISH: LARGE WHITEFISH
(*Coregonus clupeaformis*)

White Friar *n.* a Carmelite. [from their white habits]

white gold *n.* any of various silver-coloured alloys of gold used in jewellery.

white goods *n.pl.* large domestic electrical equipment that is conventionally white, e.g. refrigerators and washing machines.

Whitehall *n.* **1** the British Government. **2** its offices or policy. [a street in London, site of Government offices]

whitehead *n. colloq.* a white or white-topped skin-pustule.

white heat *n.* **1** the temperature at which metal emits white light. **2** a state of intense passion or activity.

white horses *n.pl.* white-crested waves at sea.

white-hot *adj.* at white heat.

White House *n.* the official residence of the US President in Washington, DC.

white-knuckle *attrib.adj.* (esp. of a fairground ride) designed to cause excitement or tension.

white lie *n.* a harmless or trivial untruth.

white light *n.* apparently colourless light, e.g. ordinary daylight.

white magic *n.* magic used only for beneficent purposes.

white meat *n.* poultry, veal, rabbit, and pork.

white metal *n.* a white or silvery alloy.

whiten *v.tr.* & *intr.* make or become white. □ **whitener** *n.* **whitening** *n.*

white noise *n.* noise containing many frequencies with equal intensities.

white-out *n.* **1** a dense blizzard esp. in polar regions. **2** a weather condition in which the features, horizon, etc. of snow-covered country are indistinguishable due to uniform light diffusion.

White Paper *n.* (in the UK) a Government report giving information or proposals on an issue.

white pepper *n.* the ripe or husked ground or whole berries of *Piper nigrum* as a condiment.

white sauce *n.* a sauce of flour, melted butter, and milk or cream.

white slave *n.* a woman tricked or forced into prostitution, usu. abroad.

white spirit *n. Brit.* light petroleum as a solvent.

whitethorn *n.* the hawthorn.

whitethroat *n.* ► any white-throated Eurasian warbler of the genus *Sylvia*, esp. the common *S. communis.*

white tie *n.* a man's white bow tie as part of full evening dress.

whitewash ● *n.* **1** a solution of quicklime or of ground chalk and size for whitening walls etc. **2** a means employed to conceal mistakes or faults. ● *v.tr.* **1** cover with whitewash. **2** attempt by concealment to clear the reputation of. **3** defeat (an opponent) without allowing any opposing score.

white water *n.* a shallow or foamy stretch of water.

white wedding *n. Brit.* a wedding at which the bride wears a formal white dress.

white whale *n.* a northern cetacean, *Delphinapterus leucas*, white when adult.

whitey *n.* (also **Whitey**) (*pl.* **-eys**) *slang offens.* **1** a white person. **2** white people collectively.

whither *archaic* ● *adv.* **1** to what place, position, or state? **2** (prec. by *place* etc.) to which (*the house whither we were walking*). ● *conj.* **1** to the or any place to which (*go whither you will*). **2** and thither (*we saw a house, whither we walked*). [Old English]

WHITETHROAT
(*Sylvia communis*)

whiting *n.* (*pl.* same) a small white-fleshed fish, *Merlangus merlangus*, used as food. [from Middle Dutch *wijting*]

whitlow *n.* an inflammation near a fingernail or toenail. [Middle English]

Whitsun ● *n.* = WHITSUNTIDE. ● *adj.* = WHIT. [Middle English, from *Whitsun Day* 'Whit Sunday']

Whit Sunday *n.* the seventh Sunday after Easter, commemorating the descent of the Holy Spirit at Pentecost (Acts 2).

Whitsuntide *n.* the weekend or week including Whit Sunday.

whittle *v.* **1** *tr.* & (foll. by *at*) *intr.* pare (wood etc.) with repeated slicing with a knife. **2** *tr.* (often foll. by *away*, *down*) reduce by repeated subtractions. [earlier as noun, variant of Middle English *thwitel* 'long knife']

whiz-bang *n.* (also **whizz-bang**) *colloq.* **1** a high-velocity shell from a small-calibre gun, whose passage is heard before the gun's report. **2** a jumping kind of firework.

whizz (also **whiz**) *colloq.* ● *n.* **1** the sound made by the friction of a body moving through the air at great speed. **2** (also **wiz**) *colloq.* a person who is remarkable or skilful in some respect (*is a whiz at chess*). ● *v.intr.* (**whizzed**, **whizzing**) move with or make a whizz. [sense 2: influenced by WIZARD]

whizz-kid *n.* (also **whiz-kid**) *colloq.* a brilliant or highly successful young person.

WHO *abbr.* World Health Organization.

who *pron.* (*obj.* **whom** or (informally) **who**; *poss.* **whose**) **1** *interrog.pron.* what or which person or persons? (*who called?*; *you know who it was?*; *whom* or *who did you see?*). **2** *rel.pron.* (a person) that (*anyone who wishes can come*; *the man whom* or *who you saw*). **3** and (or but) he, she, they, etc. (*gave it to Tom, who sold it to Jim*). □ **who goes there?** see GO¹. [Old English]

■ **Usage** In the last examples of senses 1 and 2, *whom* is correct, but *who* is common in less formal contexts.

whoa *int.* used as a command to stop or slow a horse etc.

who'd *contr.* **1** who had. **2** who would.

whodunnit *n.* (*US* **whodunit**) *colloq.* a story or play about the detection of a crime etc., esp. murder.

whoever *pron.* (*obj.* **whomever** or (informally) **whoever**; *poss.* **whosever**) **1** the or any person or persons who (*whoever comes is welcome*). **2** though anyone (*whoever else objects, I do not*; *whosever it is, I want it*). **3** *colloq.* (as an intensive) who ever; who at all (*whoever heard of such a thing?*).

■ **Usage** The use of *whomever* for the objective case can sound stilted nowadays, and *whoever* is generally acceptable in its place, e.g. *I ask whoever I meet*. See also Usage Note at EVER.

whole ● *adj.* **1** in an uninjured, unbroken, intact, or undiminished state (*swallowed it whole*; *there is not a plate left whole*). **2** not less than; all there is of; entire, complete (*waited a whole year*; *the whole school knows*). ● *n.* **1** a thing complete in itself. **2 a** (foll. by *of*) all there is of a thing (*the whole of the summer*). **b** all members, inhabitants, etc., of (*the whole of London knows it*). □ **as a whole** as a unity; not as separate parts. **go the whole hog** see HOG. **on the whole** taking everything relevant into account; in general. [Old English] □ **wholeness** *n.*

wholefood *n. Brit.* food which has not been processed or refined more than necessary (often *attrib.*: *wholefood diet*).

wholegrain *adj.* made with or containing whole grains (*wholegrain bread*).

wholehearted *adj.* **1** (of a person) completely devoted or committed. **2** (of an action etc.) done with all possible effort or sincerity; thorough. □ **wholeheartedly** *adv.* **wholeheartedness** *n.*

W

whole lot see LOT.

wholemeal n. (usu. attrib.) Brit. meal or flour with none of the bran or germ removed.

whole number n. a number without fractions; an integer.

wholesale ● n. the selling of things in large quantities to be retailed by others (cf. RETAIL). ● adj. & adv. **1** by wholesale; at a wholesale price. **2** on a large scale (wholesale destruction occurred). ● v.tr. sell wholesale. [Middle English: originally by whole sale] □ **wholesaler** n.

wholesome adj. **1** promoting or indicating physical, mental, or moral health. **2** prudent (wholesome respect). [Middle English] □ **wholesomely** adv. **wholesomeness** n.

whole-tone scale n. Mus. a scale consisting entirely of tones, with no semitones.

wholewheat n. (usu. attrib.) wheat with none of the bran or germ removed.

wholism var. of HOLISM.

wholly /hohl-li/ adv. entirely; without limitation or diminution.

whom objective case of WHO.

whomever objective case of WHOEVER.

whomsoever objective case of WHOSOEVER.

whoop (also **hoop**) ● n. a loud cry of or as of excitement etc. ● v.intr. utter a whoop. □ **whoop it up** colloq. **1** engage in revelry. **2** US make a stir. [Middle English]

whoopee colloq. ● int. /wuu-**pee**/ expressing exuberant joy. ● n. /**wuup**-i/ exuberant enjoyment or revelry. □ **make whoopee** colloq. **1** rejoice noisily or hilariously. **2** make love.

whooper /hoo-per, woo-per/ n. (in full **whooper swan**) a large migratory swan, Cygnus cygnus, with a black and yellow bill and a loud whooping call.

whooping cough /hoop-ing/ n. an infectious bacterial disease, esp. of children, with a series of short violent coughs followed by a rasping indrawn breath.

whoops int. (also **whoops-a-daisy**) colloq. expressing surprise or apology, esp. on making an obvious mistake. [variant of OOPS]

whoosh (also **woosh**) ● v.intr. & tr. move or cause to move with a rushing sound. ● n. a sudden movement accompanied by a rushing sound.

whopper n. slang **1** something big of its kind. **2** a blatant or gross lie.

whopping adj. slang very big.

whore ● n. a prostitute. ● v. **1** intr. **a** (of a man) use the services of prostitutes. **b** work as a prostitute. **2** tr. prostitute (a person or oneself). [Old English]

whorehouse n. a brothel.

whorl /worl/ n. **1** ▶ a ring of leaves or other organs round a stem of a plant. **2** one turn of a spiral, esp. on a shell. ▷ SHELL. **3** a complete circle in a fingerprint. [Middle English] □ **whorled** adj.

whose ● pron. of or belonging to which person (whose is this book?). ● det. of whom or which (whose book is this?; the man, whose name was Tim).

whosever poss. of WHOEVER.

whosoever pron. (obj. **whomsoever**; poss. **whosesoever**) archaic = WHOEVER.

whump n. a dull thud.

why ● adv. **1** for what reason or purpose; on what grounds (why did you do it?). **2** (prec. by reason etc.) for which (the reasons why I did it). ● int. expressing: **1** surprised discovery or recognition (why, it's you!). **2** impatience (why, of course I do!). **3** reflection (why, yes, I think so). **4** objection (why, what is wrong with it?). ● n. (pl. **whys**) a reason or explanation (esp. whys and wherefores). [Old English]

whorl

WHORL:
CLEAVER LEAVES
IN WHORLS

WI abbr. **1** West Indies. **2** Brit. Women's Institute.

Wicca n. the religious cult of modern witchcraft. [Old English wicca 'witch'] □ **Wiccan** adj. & n.

wick n. a strip or thread of fibrous or spongy material feeding a flame with fuel in a candle etc. [Old English]

wicked adj. (**wickeder**, **wickedest**) **1** sinful. **2** spiteful. **3** playfully malicious. **4** colloq. very bad (a wicked cough). **5** slang excellent. [Middle English] □ **wickedly** adv. **wickedness** n.

wicker n. plaited twigs or osiers etc. as material for baskets etc. [Middle English]

wickerwork n. **1** wicker. **2** ▼ things made of wicker.

WICKERWORK BASKET

wicket n. **1** Cricket **a** a set of three stumps with the bails in position defended by a batsman. ▷ CRICKET. **b** the ground between two wickets. **2** (in full **wicket-door** or **-gate**) a small door or gate esp. beside or in a larger one or closing the lower part only of a doorway. **3** US an aperture in a door or wall usu. closed with a sliding panel. □ **on a good** (or **sticky**) **wicket** colloq. in a favourable (or unfavourable) position. [from Old Northern French wiket]

wicketkeeper n. Cricket the fieldsman stationed close behind a batsman's wicket. ▷ CRICKET. □ **wicketkeeping** n.

widdershins adv. (also **withershins**) esp. Sc. in a direction contrary to the Sun's course (considered as unlucky); anticlockwise. [from Middle High German wider 'against' + sin 'direction']

wide ● adj. **1** measuring much or more than other things of the same kind across or from side to side. **2** (following a measurement) in width (a metre wide). **3** extending far; embracing much. **4** not tight or close or restricted; loose. **5** open to the full extent (staring with wide eyes). **6 a** (foll. by of) not within a reasonable distance of. **b** at a considerable distance from a point or mark. **7** (in comb.) extending over the whole of (nationwide). ● adv. **1** widely. **2** to the full extent (wide awake). **3** far from the target etc. (is shooting wide). ● n. Cricket a ball judged beyond the batsman's reach and so scoring a run. □ **give a wide berth to** see BERTH. **wide of the mark** see MARK[1]. [Old English] □ **wideness** n. **widish** adj.

wide-angle attrib.adj. (of a lens) having a short focal length and hence a field covering a wide angle.

wide boy n. Brit. slang a man skilled in dishonest practices; a spiv.

wide-eyed adj. surprised or naive.

widely adv. **1** far apart (widely spaced). **2** extensively (widely read). **3** by many people (widely thought). **4** to a large degree (a widely different view).

widen v.tr. & intr. make or become wider. □ **widener** n.

wide open adj. **1** open wide. **2** stretching over an outdoor expanse (wide open spaces). **3** (esp. of a contest) of which the outcome is not predictable. **4** (predic.: often foll. by to) vulnerable (esp. to attack).

wide-ranging adj. covering an extensive range.

wide-screen attrib.adj. designed with or for a screen presenting a wide field of vision in relation to its height.

widespread adj. widely distributed or disseminated.

widget n. colloq. any gadget or device. [perhaps an alteration of GADGET]

widow ● n. **1** a woman who has lost her husband by death and has not married again. **2** a woman whose husband is often away on a specified activity (golf widow).

3 extra cards dealt separately and taken by the highest bidder. **4** Printing the short last line of a paragraph at the top of a page or column. ● v.tr. make into a widow or widower. [Old English] □ **widowhood** n.

widower n. a man who has lost his wife by death and has not married again.

widow's mite n. a small money contribution (see Mark 12:42).

widow's peak n. a V-shaped growth of hair towards the centre of the forehead.

width n. **1** measurement or distance from side to side. **2** a large extent. **3** breadth or liberality of views etc. **4** a strip of material of full woven width. [17th-century coinage] □ **widthways** adv. **widthwise** adv.

wield v.tr. **1** hold and use (a weapon or tool). **2** exert or command (power etc.). [Old English] □ **wielder** n.

Wiener schnitzel /**vee**-ner/ n. a breaded, fried, and garnished schnitzel.

wife n. (pl. **wives**) a married woman esp. in relation to her husband. □ **have** (or **take**) **to wife** archaic marry (a woman). [Old English wíf 'woman'] □ **wifely** adj.

wig n. ▶ an artificial head of hair esp. to conceal baldness or as a disguise, or worn by a judge or barrister or as period dress. [abbreviation of PERIWIG] □ **wigged** adj. (also in comb.). **wigless** adj.

wigging n. Brit. colloq. a reprimand.

wiggle colloq. ● v.intr. & tr. move or cause to move quickly from side to side etc. ● n. an act of wiggling. [from Middle Dutch wiggelen] □ **wiggler** n. **wiggly** adj. (**wigglier**, **wiggliest**).

WIG:
18TH-CENTURY
MAN'S WIG

wigwam n. a N. American Indian's domed hut or tent of skins, mats, or bark on poles; (loosely) a tepee. [from Algonquian wikiwam 'their house']

wild ● adj. **1** (of an animal or plant) in its original natural state; not domesticated or cultivated. **2** not civilized; barbarous. **3** (of scenery etc.) having a conspicuously desolate appearance. **4** unrestrained, disorderly (a wild youth; wild hair). **5** tempestuous (a wild night). **6 a** excited, frantic (wild with excitement). **b** (of looks etc.) indicating distraction. **c** (foll. by about) colloq. enthusiastically devoted to. **7** colloq. infuriated (makes me wild). **8** haphazard, ill-aimed, rash (a wild guess; a wild shot). **10** colloq. exciting, delightful. **11** (of a card) having any rank chosen (the joker is wild). ● adv. in a wild manner (shooting wild). ● n. a wild tract. □ **in the wild** in an uncultivated etc. state. **in** (or **out in**) **the wilds** colloq. far from normal habitation. [Old English] □ **wildish** adj. **wildly** adv. **wildness** n.

wild boar see BOAR 1.

wild card n. **1** see WILD adj. 11. **2** Computing a character that will match any character or sequence of characters in a file name etc. **3** Sport an extra player or team chosen to enter a competition at the selectors' discretion.

wildcat ● n. **1** a hot-tempered or violent person. **2** ◀ any of various smallish non-domesticated animals of the cat family, esp. (usu. **wild cat**) Felis sylvestris of Eurasia and Africa, with a grey and black coat and a bushy tail, or (US) a bobcat. **3** an exploratory oil well. ● adj. (attrib.) **1** esp. US reckless; financially unsound. **2** (of a strike) sudden and unofficial.

WILD CAT:
SCOTTISH WILD CAT
(Felis sylvestris)

W

wildebeest /wil-dĕ-beest/ *n.* (*pl.* same or **wilde-beests**) = GNU. [Afrikaans]

wilderness *n.* a desert; an uncultivated and uninhabited area. [Old English *wildēornes*, from *wild dēor* 'wild deer']

wildfire *n.* **1** *hist.* a combustible liquid formerly used in warfare. **2** = WILL-O'-THE-WISP.

wildfowl *n.* (*pl.* same) (usu. in *pl.*) a game bird, esp. an aquatic one. ▷ DUCK, WATERFOWL

wild-goose chase *n.* a foolish or hopeless and unproductive quest.

wilding *n.* *US slang* an instance of going on a violent rampage through the streets in a group.

wildlife *n.* wild animals collectively.

wild oat *n.* a grass, *Avena fatua*, related to the cultivated oat and found as a weed in cornfields.

wild rice *n.* any tall grass of the genus *Zizania*, yielding edible grains. ▷ GRAIN

wild silk *n.* **1** silk from wild silkworms. **2** an imitation of this from short silk fibres.

wild type *n.* *Genetics* a strain or characteristic which prevails in natural conditions, as distinct from an atypical mutant.

Wild West *n.* the western US in a time of lawlessness in its early history.

wildwood *n.* *poet.* uncultivated or unfrequented woodland.

wile ● *n.* (usu. in *pl.*) a trick or cunning procedure. ● *v.tr.* (foll. by *away*, *into*, etc.) lure or entice. [Middle English]

wilful *adj.* (*US* **willful**) **1** (of an action or state) intentional, deliberate (*wilful murder*; *wilful neglect*; *wilful disobedience*). **2** (of a person) obstinate, headstrong. [Middle English] □ **wilfully** *adv.* **wilfulness** *n.*

wiliness see WILY.

will[1] *v.aux. & tr.* (*3rd sing. present* **will**; *past* **would**) (foll. by infin. without *to*, or *absol.*; present and past only in use) **1** (in the 2nd and 3rd persons, and often in the 1st: see SHALL) expressing the future tense in statements, commands, or questions (*you will regret this*; *they will leave at once*; *will you go to the party?*). **2** (in the 1st person) expressing a wish or intention (*I will return soon*). **3** expressing desire, consent, or inclination (*will you have a sandwich?*; *come when you will*; *the door will not open*). **4** expressing a request as a question (*will you please open the window?*). **5** expressing ability or capacity (*the jar will hold a kilo*). **6** expressing habitual or inevitable tendency (*accidents will happen*; *will sit there for hours*). **7** expressing probability or expectation (*that will be my wife*). □ **will do** *colloq.* expressing willingness to carry out a request. [Old English]

▪ **Usage** See Usage Note at SHALL.

will[2] ● *n.* **1** the faculty by which a person decides and initiates action (*the mind consists of the understanding and the will*). **2** (also **will-power**) control exercised by deliberate purpose over impulse; self-control (*has a strong will*). **3** a deliberate or fixed desire or intention (*a will to live*). **4** the power of effecting one's intentions or dominating others. **5** directions in legal form for the disposition of one's property after death (*make your will*). **6** disposition towards others (*good will*). **7** *archaic* what one desires or ordains (*thy will be done*). ● *v.tr.* **1** have as the object of one's will (*what God wills*; *willed that we should succeed*). **2** instigate or impel or compel by the exercise of will-power (*willed herself into contentment*). **3** bequeath by the terms of a will (*shall will my money to charity*). □ **at will 1** whenever one pleases. **2** *Law* able to be evicted without notice (*tenant at will*). **have one's will** obtain what one wants. **with the best will in the world** however good one's intentions. **with a will** energetically or resolutely. [Old English] □ **willed** *adj.* (also in *comb.*).

willful *US* var. of WILFUL.

willie var. of WILLY.

willies *n.pl. colloq.* nervous discomfort (esp. *give* or *get the willies*). [19th-century coinage]

willing ● *adj.* **1** ready to consent or undertake (*a willing ally*; *am willing to go*). **2** given or done etc. by a willing person (*willing hands*). ● *n.* cheerful intention (*show willing*). □ **willingly** *adv.* **willingness** *n.*

will-o'-the-wisp *n.* **1** a phosphorescent light seen on marshy ground, perhaps resulting from the combustion of gases. **2** an elusive person. **3** a delusive hope or plan. [originally *Will with the wisp*; *wisp*: literally 'handful of (lighted) hay'

willow *n.* **1** (also **willow tree**) ◀ a tree or shrub of the genus *Salix*, growing usu. near water in temperate climates, with small flowers borne on catkins, and pliant branches. **2** a cricket bat. [Old English]

willowherb *n.* any plant of the genus *Epilobium* etc.

catkin

willow-pattern *n.* ▶ a conventional design representing a Chinese scene, often with a willow tree, of blue on white porcelain, stoneware, or earthenware.

WILLOW:
WHITE WILLOW
(*Salix alba*)

willow warbler *n.* (also **willow wren**) a small woodland bird, *Phylloscopus trochilus*, with a tuneful song.

willowy *adj.* **1** having or bordered by willows. **2** lithe and slender.

will-power *n.* var. of WILL[2] *n.* 2.

willy *n.* (also **willie**) (*pl.* -ies) *Brit. slang* the penis. [pet form of the name *William*]

willy-nilly ● *adv.* whether one likes it or not. ● *adj.* existing or occurring willy-nilly. [later spelling of *will I, nill I* 'I am willing, I am unwilling']

wilt ● *v.intr.* **1** (of a plant) wither, droop. **2** (of a person) lose one's energy. ● *n.* a plant disease causing wilting. [originally dialect]

wily *adj.* (**wilier, wiliest**) crafty, cunning. □ **wilily** *adv.* **wiliness** *n.*

wimp *n. colloq.* a feeble or ineffectual person. [20th-century coinage] □ **wimpish** *adj.* **wimpishly** *adv.* **wimpishness** *n.* **wimpy** *adj.*

wimple *n.* a linen or silk headdress covering the neck and the sides of the face, formerly worn by women and still worn by some nuns. [Old English]

win ● *v.* (**winning**; *past* and *past part.* **won**) **1** *tr.* acquire or secure as a result of a contest, bet, litigation, or some other effort (*won some money*; *won my admiration*). **2** *tr.* be victorious in (a fight etc.). **3** *intr.* **a** be the victor (*who won?*). **b** (foll. by *through*, *free*, etc.) make one's way or become by successful effort. **4** *tr.* reach by effort (*win the summit*). **5** *tr.* obtain (ore) from a mine. ● *n.* a victory in a game, contest, bet, etc. □ **win over** persuade, gain the support of. **win through** (or **out**) overcome obstacles. **you can't win** *colloq.* there is no way to succeed. [Old English *winnan* 'to toil, endure'] □ **winnable** *adj.*

wince ● *n.* a start or involuntary shrinking movement showing pain or distress. ● *v.intr.* give a wince. [from Old French *guenchir* 'to turn aside'] □ **wincingly** *adv.*

winceyette *n. Brit.* a lightweight napped flannelette used esp. for nightclothes.

winch ● *n.* **1** the crank of a wheel or axle. **2** a windlass. ● *v.tr.* lift with a winch. [Old English] □ **wincher** *n.*

Winchester *n. propr.* a breech-loading repeating rifle. [named after O. F. *Winchester*, 1810–80, US manufacturer of the rifle]

wind[1] /wind/ ● *n.* **1 a** air in more or less rapid natural motion, esp. between areas of high and low pressure. **b** a current of wind blowing from a specified direction or otherwise defined (*north wind*;

contrary wind). **2 a** breath as needed in physical exertion or in speech. **b** the power of breathing without difficulty (*let me recover my wind*). **3** mere empty words; meaningless rhetoric. **4** flatulence. **5** the wind instruments of an orchestra collectively. ▷ WOODWIND. ● *v.tr.* **1** exhaust the wind of by exertion or a blow. **2** renew the wind of by rest (*stopped to wind the horses*). **3** *Brit.* make (a baby) bring up wind after feeding. **4** detect the presence of by a scent. **5** (*past* and *past part.* **winded** or **wound**) *poet.* sound (a bugle or call) by blowing. □ **close to** (or **near**) **the wind 1** sailing as nearly against the wind as is consistent with using its force. **2** *colloq.* verging on indecency or dishonesty. **get wind of** *colloq.* **1** smell out. **2** hear a rumour of. **get** (or **have**) **the wind up** *colloq.* be alarmed or frightened. **how** (or **which way**) **the wind blows** (or **lies**) **1** what the state of opinion is. **2** what developments are likely. **in the wind** happening or about to happen. **like the wind** swiftly. **put the wind up** *colloq.* alarm or frighten. **take the wind out of a person's sails** frustrate a person by anticipating an action or remark etc. **to the winds** (or **four winds**) **1** in all directions. **2** into a state of abandonment or neglect. [Old English] □ **windless** *adj.*

WILLOW-PATTERN
PLATE

wind[2] /wynd/ ● *v.* (*past* and *past part.* **wound** /wownd/) **1** *intr.* go in a circular, spiral, curved, or crooked course (*a winding staircase*). **2** *tr.* make (one's way) by such a course (*wind your way up to bed*). **3** *tr.* wrap closely (*wound the blanket round me*). **4 a** *tr.* turn (wool, thread, etc.) around a thing or itself to produce a compact mass (*wound cotton on a reel*). **b** *intr.* coil (*the creeper winds round the pole*). **5** *tr.* wind up (a clock etc.). **6** *tr.* draw with a windlass etc. (*wound the cable car up the mountain*). ● *n.* **1** a bend or turn in a course. **2** a single turn when winding. □ **wind down 1** lower by winding. **2** (of a mechanism) unwind. **3** (of a person) relax. **4** draw gradually to a close. **wind up 1** coil the whole of (a piece of string etc.). **2** esp. *Brit.* tighten the coiled spring of (a clock etc.). **3** *colloq.* **a** increase the tension of (*wound myself up to fever pitch*). **b** irritate or provoke to the point of anger. **4** end (*wound up his speech*). **5** *Commerce* **a** arrange the affairs of and dissolve (a company). **b** (of a company) cease business and go into liquidation. **6** *colloq.* end in a specified state or circumstance (*you'll wind up in prison*). **wound up** *adj. colloq.* (of a person) excited or tense or angry. [Old English] □ **winder** *n.*

windbag *n. colloq.* a person who talks a lot but says little of any value.

windbreak *n.* a thing serving to break the force of the wind.

windbreaker *n.* *US* = WINDCHEATER.

windburn *n.* inflammation of the skin caused by exposure to the wind.

windcheater *n. Brit.* a kind of wind-resistant outer jacket with close-fitting neck, cuffs, and lower edge.

windfall *n.* **1** an apple or other fruit blown to the ground by the wind. **2** a piece of unexpected good fortune.

wind farm *n.* a group of energy-producing windmills or wind turbines.

windflower *n.* an anemone.

wind-gauge *n.* an anemometer.

windhover /wind-hov-er/ *n. Brit.* a kestrel.

winding-sheet /wynd-ing-/ *n.* a sheet in which a corpse is wrapped for burial.

wind instrument *n.* a musical instrument in which sound is produced by a current of air, esp. the breath. ▷ BRASS, WOODWIND

windlass /wind-lăs/ ● *n.* a machine with a horizontal axle for hauling or hoisting. ● *v.tr.* hoist or haul with a windlass. [from Old Norse *vindáss*]

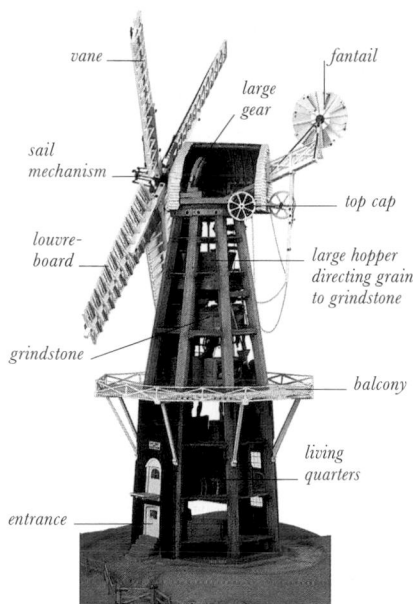

WINDMILL: MODEL OF AN EARLY
19TH-CENTURY BRITISH WINDMILL

vane
fantail
large gear
sail mechanism
top cap
louvre-board
large hopper directing grain to grindstone
grindstone
balcony
living quarters
entrance

windmill ● *n.* **1** ▲ a mill worked by the action of the wind on its sails. **2** esp. *Brit.* a toy consisting of a stick with curved vanes attached that revolve in a wind. **●** *v.tr. & intr.* move like the sails of a windmill.

window *n.* **1 a ▶** an opening in a wall, roof, vehicle, etc., usu. with glass in fixed, sliding, or hinged frames, to admit light or air etc. and allow the occupants to see out. **b** the glass filling this opening (*have broken the window*). **2** a space for display behind the front window of a shop. **3** an aperture in a wall etc. through which customers are served in a bank, ticket office, etc. **4** an opportunity to observe or learn. **5** an opening or transparent part in an envelope to show an address. **6** *Computing* a defined area on a display screen in which a part of a file or image can be displayed. **7** any interval or opportunity for action. [from Old Norse *vindauga*] □ **windowed** *adj.* (also in *comb.*). **windowless** *adj.*

window box *n.* a box placed on an outside window sill for growing flowers.

window dressing *n.* **1** the art of arranging a display in a shop window etc. **2** an adroit presentation of facts etc. to give a deceptively favourable impression.

window frame *n.* a supporting frame for the glass of a window. ▷ SASH WINDOW, WINDOW

windowing *n. Computing* the use of windows for the simultaneous display of parts of different files, images, etc.

window ledge *n.* a sill below a window.

window pane *n.* a pane of glass in a window.

window seat *n.* **1** a seat below a window, esp. in a bay or alcove. **2** a seat next to a window in an aircraft, train, etc.

window-shop *v.intr.* (**-shopped**, **-shopping**) (esp. as **window-shopping** *n.*) look at goods displayed in shop windows, usu. without buying anything. □ **window-shopper** *n.*

windpipe *n.* the air passage from the throat to the lungs; the trachea. ▷ RESPIRATION

windscreen *n. Brit.* a screen of glass at the front of a motor vehicle. ▷ CAR

windscreen wiper *n.* a device consisting of a rubber blade on an arm, moving in an arc, for keeping a windscreen clear of rain etc.

wind shear *n.* a variation in wind velocity at right angles to the wind's direction.

windshield *n. N. Amer.* = WINDSCREEN.

WINDOW

Originally used by the ancient Romans, glazed windows were rare until the Middle Ages, when glass became more available. As a result, the size of windows grew, so that by the Renaissance period they were quite large. Buildings can often be dated by their windows: the segmental head of the window below is distinctive of the Victorian period.

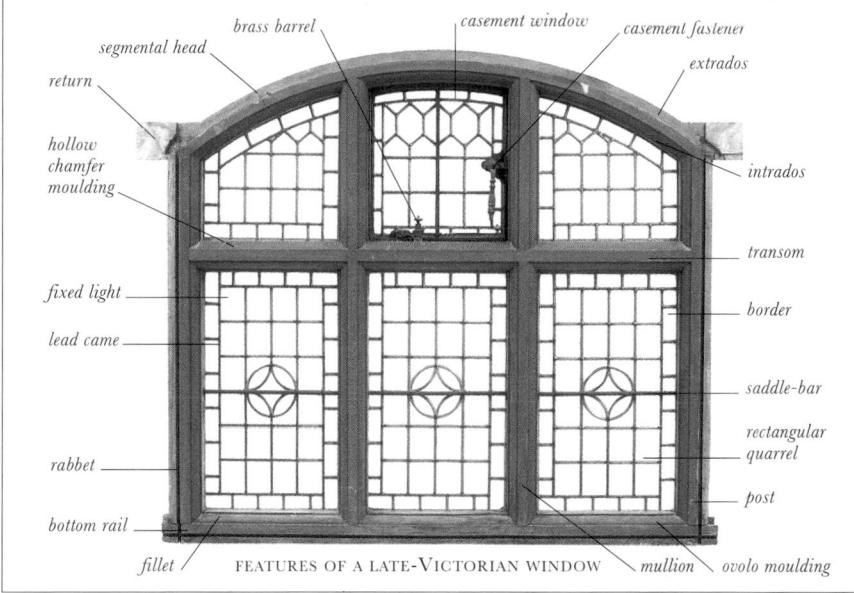

brass barrel
segmental head
casement window
casement fastener
return
extrados
hollow chamfer moulding
intrados
transom
fixed light
border
lead came
saddle-bar
rectangular quarrel
rabbet
post
bottom rail
fillet
mullion
ovolo moulding

FEATURES OF A LATE-VICTORIAN WINDOW

windsock *n.* a canvas cylinder or cone on a mast to show the direction of the wind at an airfield etc.

Windsor chair *n.* a wooden dining chair with a semicircular back supported by upright rods.

windstorm *n.* esp. *N. Amer.* a storm with very strong wind but little or no rain, snow, etc.; a gale.

windsurfing *n.* ▼ the sport of riding on water on a sailboard. □ **windsurf** *v.intr.* **windsurfer** *n.*

windswept *adj.* exposed to or swept back by the wind.

wind tunnel *n.* a tunnel-like device to blow an airstream past models of aircraft etc. for the study of wind effects on them.

wind-up /wynd-up/ *n.* **1** *attrib.* operated by being wound up. **2** *Brit. colloq.* an attempt to provoke someone.

windward ● *adj. & adv.* on the side from which the wind is blowing (opp. LEEWARD). **●** *n.* the windward region, side, or direction (*to windward*).

windy *adj.* (**windier**, **windiest**) **1** stormy with wind (*a windy night*). **2** exposed to the wind; windswept (*a windy plain*). **3** *Brit.* generating or

WINDSURFING

Windsurfing uses the wind's energy as a driving force. Windsurfers stand on a board, and steer by controlling the position of the boom. Beginners can use a funboard, but experienced slalom racers and speed windsurfers often have a custom-built board.

EXAMPLES OF SAILBOARDS

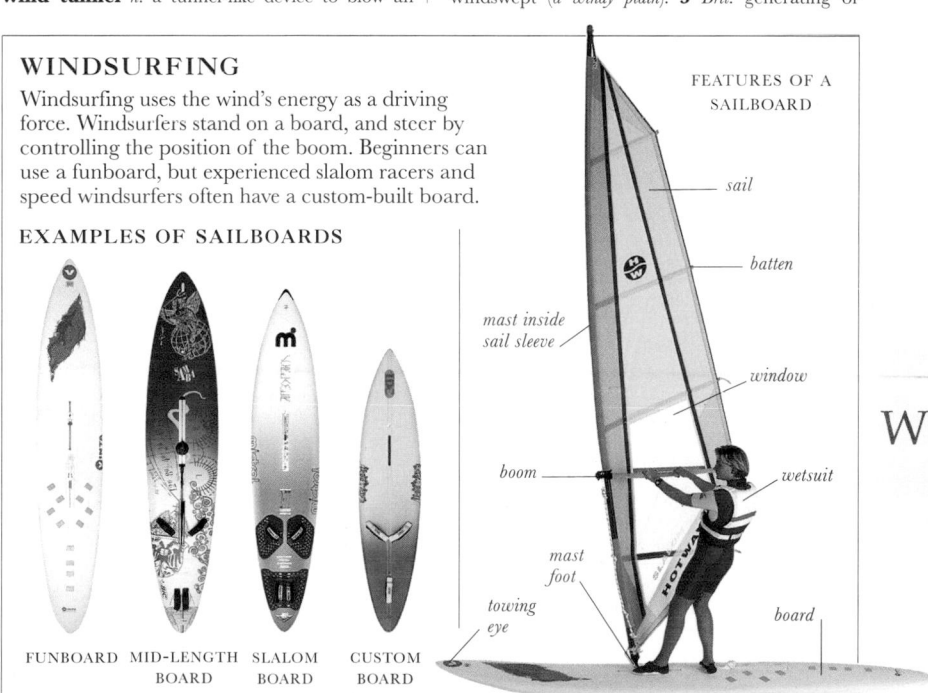

FUNBOARD   MID-LENGTH BOARD   SLALOM BOARD   CUSTOM BOARD

FEATURES OF A SAILBOARD

sail
batten
mast inside sail sleeve
window
boom
wetsuit
mast foot
towing eye
board

W

suffering from flatulence. **4** *Brit. colloq.* nervous, frightened. □ **windiness** *n.*

wine ● *n.* **1** fermented grape juice as an alcoholic drink. ▷ VINIFICATION. **2** a similar drink made from other fruits etc. as specified (*elderberry wine; ginger wine*). **3** = WINE RED. ● *v.tr.* entertain to wine. □ **wine and dine** entertain to or have a meal with wine. [Old English]

wine bar *n.* a bar or small restaurant where wine is the main drink available.

wine bottle *n.* a glass bottle for wine, the standard size holding 75 cl or 26 ⅔ fl.oz.

wine box *n.* a square carton of wine with a dispensing tap.

wine cellar *n.* **1** a cellar for storing wine. **2** the contents of this.

wineglass *n.* **1** a glass for wine, usu. with a stem and foot. **2** a wineglassful.

wineglassful *n.* (*pl.* **-fuls**) **1** the capacity of a small wineglass as a measure of liquid, about 2 fl. oz. **2** the contents of a wineglass.

wine-grower *n.* a cultivator of grapes for wine.

wine list *n.* a list of wines available in a restaurant etc.

winepress *n.* a press in which grapes are squeezed in making wine.

wine red ● *n.* the dark red colour of red wine. ● *adj.* (hyphenated when *attrib.*) of this colour.

winery /**wyn**-ĕ-ri/ *n.* (*pl.* **-ies**) esp. *US* an establishment where wine is made.

wineskin *n.* a whole skin of a goat etc. sewn up and used to hold wine.

wine tasting *n.* **1** judging the quality of wine by tasting it. **2** an occasion for this. □ **wine taster** *n.*

wine vinegar *n.* vinegar made from wine as distinct from malt.

wine waiter *n. Brit.* a waiter responsible for serving wine.

winey *adj.* (also **winy**) (**winier**, **winiest**) resembling wine in taste or appearance.

wing ● *n.* **1** each of the limbs or organs by which a bird, bat, or insect is able to fly. ▷ BAT, BIRD, FEATHER, INSECT. **2** ▼ a rigid horizontal winglike structure forming a supporting part of an aircraft. ▷ AILERON, AIRCRAFT, DELTA WING. **3** part of a building etc. which projects or is extended in a certain direction (*lived in the north wing*). **4 a** a forward player at either end of a line in football, hockey, etc. **b** the side part of a playing area. **5** (in *pl.*) the sides of a theatre stage out of view of the audience. ▷ THEATRE. **6** a section of a political party in terms of the extremity of its views. **7** a flank of a battle array. **8** *Brit.* the part of a motor vehicle extending above a wheel. ● *v.* **1** *intr.* & *tr.* travel or traverse on wings or in an aircraft (*winging through the air; am winging my way home*). **2** *tr.* wound in a wing or an arm. **3** *tr.* enable to fly; send in flight (*fear winged my steps; winged an arrow towards them*). □ **on the wing** flying or in flight. **spread one's wings** develop one's powers fully. **take under one's wing** treat as a protégé. [from Old Norse] □ **winged** *adj.* (also in *comb.*). **wingless** *adj.* **winglet** *n.* **winglike** *adj.*

aileron
flap girder
gouge-type flap
wingtip fairing
main spar
radial engine
outboard fuel tank
propellor

WING OF AN EARLY 20TH-CENTURY FLYING BOAT

wing-beat *n.* one complete set of motions with a wing in flying.

wing-case *n.* the horny cover of an insect's wing. ▷ INSECT

wing collar *n.* a high stiff shirt collar with turned-down corners.

wing commander *n.* an RAF officer next below group captain.

winger *n.* **1** a player on a wing in football, hockey, etc. **2** (in *comb.*) a member of a specified political wing (*left-winger*).

wing nut *n.* a nut with projections for the fingers to turn it on a screw.

wingspan *n.* (also **wingspread**) the measurement right across the wings of a bird or aircraft.

wink ● *v.* **1 a** *tr.* close and open (one eye or both eyes) quickly. **b** *intr.* close and open an eye. **2** *intr.* (often foll. by *at*) wink one eye as a signal of friendship or greeting or to convey a message to a person. **3** *intr.* (of a light etc.) shine or flash intermittently. ● *n.* **1** the act or an instance of winking. **2** *colloq.* a brief moment of sleep (*didn't sleep a wink*). [Old English]

winkle ● *n.* any edible marine gastropod mollusc of the genus *Littorina*; a periwinkle. ▷ GASTROPOD. ● *v.tr.* (foll. by *out*) esp. *Brit.* extract or eject (*winkled the information out of them*). [abbreviation of PERIWINKLE²]

winner *n.* **1** a person, racehorse, etc. that wins. **2** *colloq.* a successful or highly promising idea, enterprise, etc.

winning ● *adj.* **1** having or bringing victory or an advantage. **2** attractive, persuasive (*a winning smile; winning ways*). ● *n.* (in *pl.*) money won, esp. in betting etc. □ **winningly** *adv.*

winning post *n.* a post marking the end of a race.

winnow *v.tr.* **1** blow (grain) free of chaff etc. by an air current. **2** ▼ (foll. by *out, away, from*, etc.) get rid of (chaff etc.) from grain. **3** sift, separate. [Old English] □ **winnower** *n.* (in senses 1, 2).

WINNOW: SEPARATING CHAFF FROM GRAIN BY HAND

wino /**wyn**-oh/ *n.* (*pl.* **-os**) *slang* a habitual excessive drinker of cheap wine.

winsome *adj.* (of a person, looks, or manner) winning, attractive, engaging. [Old English] □ **winsomely** *adv.* **winsomeness** *n.*

winter ● *n.* **1** the coldest season of the year. ▷ SEASON. **2** *Astron.* the period from the winter solstice to the vernal equinox. **3** (*attrib.*) characteristic of or suitable for winter. ● *v.* **1** *intr.* (usu. foll. by *at, in*) pass the winter (*likes to winter in the Canaries*). **2** *tr.* keep or feed (plants, cattle) during winter. [Old English] □ **winterer** *n.*

winter aconite see ACONITE 2.

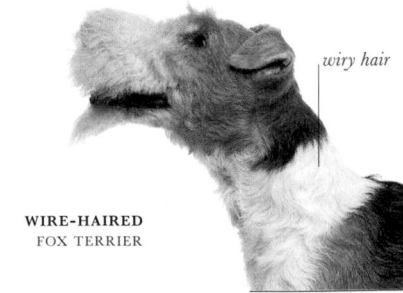

WINTERGREEN (*Gaultheria procumbens*)

winter garden *n.* a garden or conservatory of plants flourishing in winter.

wintergreen *n.* **1** a low-growing plant of the genus *Pyrola*, with drooping spikes of white bell-shaped flowers. **2** *N. Amer.* ◄ a creeping evergreen shrub, *Gaultheria procumbens*. [so called because of remaining green in winter]

winter heliotrope see HELIOTROPE 2.

winterize *v.tr.* (also **-ise**) esp. *N. Amer.* adapt for operation or use in cold weather. □ **winterization** *n.*

winter jasmine *n.* a jasmine, *Jasminum nudiflorum*, with yellow flowers.

winter quarters *n.* a place where soldiers spend the winter.

winter sleep *n.* hibernation.

winter solstice *n.* the solstice at midwinter, about 22 Dec. in the northern hemisphere and 21 June in the southern hemisphere; in *Astron.*, the solstice in December.

winter sports *n.pl.* sports performed on snow or ice (e.g. skiing and ice-skating).

wintertime *n.* the season of winter.

wintry *adj.* (also **wintery**) (**wintrier**, **wintriest**) **1** characteristic of winter (*wintry weather, a wintry sun, a wintry landscape*). **2** (of a smile, greeting, etc.) lacking warmth or enthusiasm. □ **wintrily** *adv.* **wintriness** *n.*

winy var. of WINEY.

wipe ● *v.tr.* **1** clean or dry the surface of by rubbing with the hands or a cloth etc. **2** rub (a cloth) over a surface. **3** spread (a liquid etc.) over a surface by rubbing. **4** (often foll. by *away, off*, etc.) clear or remove by wiping. **5 a** erase (data, a recording, etc., from a magnetic medium). **b** erase data from (the medium). ● *n.* **1** an act of wiping (*give the floor a wipe*). **2** a disposable piece of treated cloth or paper for wiping (*antiseptic wipes*). □ **wipe down** clean (esp. a vertical surface) by wiping. **wipe the floor with** *colloq.* inflict a humiliating defeat on. **wipe out** destroy, annihilate. **wipe the slate clean** see SLATE. **wipe up 1** *Brit.* dry (dishes etc.). **2** take up (a liquid etc.) by wiping. [Old English] □ **wipeable** *adj.*

wipe-out *n.* **1** the obliteration of one radio signal by another. **2** an instance of destruction or annihilation. **3** *slang* a fall from a surfboard.

wiper *n.* = WINDSCREEN WIPER.

wire ● *n.* **1** metal drawn out into a thread or thin flexible rod. **2** a piece of this. **3** (*attrib.*) made of wire. ● *v.tr.* **1** provide, fasten, strengthen, etc., with wire. **2** (often foll. by *up*) *Electr.* install electrical circuits in (a building, piece of equipment, etc.). □ **get one's wires crossed** become confused and have a misunderstanding. [Old English]

wire brush *n.* **1** a brush with tough wire bristles. **2** a brush with wire strands brushed against cymbals to produce a soft metallic sound.

wired *adj. colloq.* **1** making use of information technology to relay information, esp. via the Internet. **2** (usu. *predic.*) **a** in a nervous or tense state. **b** under the influence of drugs or alcohol.

wire-haired *adj.* ▼ (esp. of a dog) having stiff or wiry hair.

wiry hair

WIRE-HAIRED FOX TERRIER

wireless ● *n.* **1** esp. *Brit.* **a** (in full **wireless set**) a radio receiving set. ▷ RADIO. **b** the transmission and reception of radio signals. **2** = RADIO-TELEGRAPHY. ● *adj.* lacking or not requiring wires.

■ **Usage** The term *wireless* is now old-fashioned, esp. with reference to broadcasting, and has been superseded by *radio*.

wire netting *n.* netting of meshed wire.

wire stripper *n.* (often in *pl.*) a tool for removing the insulation from electric wires.

wire-tapping *n.* the practice of tapping (see TAP[1] *v.* 4) a telephone or telegraph line to eavesdrop. □ **wire-tapper** *n.*

wire wheel *n.* a vehicle wheel with spokes of wire.

wire wool *n. Brit.* a mass of fine wire for cleaning.

wireworm *n.* the larva of the click beetle causing damage to crop plants.

wiring *n.* a system of wires providing electrical circuits.

wiry *adj.* (**wirier**, **wiriest**) **1** tough and flexible as wire. **2** (of a person) thin and sinewy; untiring. □ **wirily** *adv.*

wisdom *n.* **1** experience and knowledge together with the power of applying them. **2** prudence; common sense. **3** (also in *pl.*) wise sayings, thoughts, etc. [Old English]

wisdom tooth *n.* each of four hindmost molars not usu. cut before 20 years of age. ▷ MOLAR, TOOTH

wise[1] ● *adj.* **1** having, determined by, or showing wisdom. **2** prudent, sensible. **3** having knowledge. **4** suggestive of wisdom (*a wise nod*). **5** *US colloq.* (often foll. by *to*) having (usu. confidential) information (about). ● *v.tr. & intr.* (foll. by *up*) esp. *US colloq.* put or get wise. □ **be** (or **get**) **wise to** *colloq.* be (or become) aware of. **no** (or **none the** or **not much**) **wiser** knowing no more than before. **put a person wise** (often foll. by *to*) *colloq.* inform a person (about). [Old English] □ **wisely** *adv.*

wise[2] *n.* archaic way, manner, or degree (*on this wise*). □ **in no wise** not at all. [Old English]

-wise *suffix* forming adjectives and adverbs of manner (*crosswise*; *clockwise*; *lengthwise*) or respect (*moneywise*) (cf. -WAYS).

■ **Usage** The use of *-wise* in more fanciful phrase-based combinations, such as *employment-wise* (= as regards employment), is colloquial and should be restricted to informal contexts.

wisecrack *colloq.* ● *n.* a smart pithy remark. ● *v.intr.* make a wisecrack. □ **wisecracker** *n.*

wise guy *n. colloq.* a know-all.

wise man *n.* a wizard, esp. one of the Magi.

wish ● *v.* **1** *intr.* (often foll. by *for*) have or express a desire or aspiration for. **2** *tr.* (often foll. by an implied *that* + clause, or *that* + clause) have as a desire or aspiration (*I wish I could sing*). **3** *tr.* want or demand, usu. so as to bring about what is wanted (*I wish to go*; *I wish you to do it*). **4** *tr.* express one's hopes for (*wish you success*). **5** *tr.* (foll. by *on*, *upon*) *colloq.* foist on a person. ● *n.* **1 a** a desire, request, or aspiration. **b** an expression of this. **2** a thing desired. □ **best** (or **good**) **wishes** hopes felt or expressed for another's happiness etc. [Old English] □ **wisher** *n.* (in sense 4 of *v.*); (also in *comb.*).

wishbone *n.* ◄ a forked bone between the neck and breast of a bird, esp. this bone from a cooked bird, which when broken by two people entitles the holder of the longer portion to make a wish.

neck

wishbone

keel

WISHBONE IN THE SKELETON OF A PENGUIN

wishful *adj.* **1** (often foll. by *to* + infin.) desiring, wishing. **2** having or expressing a wish. □ **wishfully** *adv.* **wishfulness** *n.*

wish-fulfilment *n.* a tendency for subconscious desire to be satisfied in fantasy.

wishful thinking *n.* belief founded on wishes rather than facts.

wishing-well *n.* a well into which coins are dropped and a wish is made.

wish-list *n.* a mental list of wishes or desires.

wishy-washy *adj.* **1** feeble or insipid in quality or character. **2** (of tea, soup, etc.) weak, watery.

wisp *n.* **1** a small bundle or twist of straw etc. **2** a small separate quantity of smoke, hair, etc. [Middle English] □ **wispy** *adj.* (**wispier**, **wispiest**). **wispily** *adv.* **wispiness** *n.*

wisteria /wis-**teer**-iă/ *n.* (also **wistaria** /wis-**tair**-iă/) ▼ any climbing shrub of the genus *Wisteria*, with hanging pale bluish-lilac, sometimes white, flowers. [named after C. *Wistar* (or *Wister*), American anatomist, 1761–1818]

WISTERIA
(*Wisteria floribunda*)

wistful *adj.* (of a person, looks, etc.) yearningly or mournfully expectant or wishful. □ **wistfully** *adv.* **wistfulness** *n.*

wit[1] *n.* **1** (in *sing.* or *pl.*) intelligence; quick understanding. **2 a** the unexpected, quick, and humorous combining or contrasting of ideas or expressions (*conversation sparkling with wit*). **b** the power of giving intellectual pleasure by this. **3** a person possessing such a power. □ **at one's wit's** (or **wits'**) **end** utterly at a loss or in despair. **have** (or **keep**) **one's wits about one** be alert or vigilant or of lively intelligence. **live by one's wits** live by ingenious or crafty expedients, without a settled occupation. **out of one's wits** mad, distracted. [Old English]

wit[2] *v.* □ **to wit** that is to say; namely. [Old English]

witch ● *n.* **1 a** a sorceress, esp. a woman supposed to have dealings with the Devil or evil spirits. **b** a follower or practitioner of modern witchcraft; a Wiccan. **2** an ugly old woman; a hag. ● *v.tr. archaic* **1** bewitch. **2** fascinate, charm, lure. [Old English] □ **witching** *adj.* **witchlike** *adj.* **witchy** *adj.*

witchcraft *n.* the use of magic; sorcery.

witch doctor *n.* a tribal magician of tribal people.

witch elm var. of WYCH ELM.

witchery *n.* witchcraft.

witches' sabbath see SABBATH 3.

witch hazel *n.* (also **wych hazel**)
1 ► any ornamental E. Asian or American shrub of the genus *Hamamelis*, with yellow to orange flowers. **2** an astringent lotion obtained from *H. virginiana* of N. America. [based on *witch*, variant of *wych* (see WYCH ELM)]

orange flower

WITCH HAZEL
(*Hamamelis × intermedia*)

witch-hunt *n.* **1** *hist.* a search for and persecution of supposed witches. **2** a campaign directed against a particular group of those holding dissenting or unorthodox views. □ **witch-hunting** *n.*

with *prep.* expressing: **1** an instrument or means used (*cut with a knife*). **2** association or company (*lives with his mother*; *lamb with mint sauce*). **3** cause or origin (*shiver with fear*). **4** possession, attribution (*the man with dark hair*). **5** circumstances; accompanying conditions (*sleep with the window open*). **6** manner adopted or displayed (*behaved with dignity*; *won with ease*). **7** agreement or harmony (*sympathize with*). **8** disagreement, antagonism, competition (*stop arguing with me*). **9** responsibility for (*the decision rests with you*). **10** reference or regard (*be patient with them*; *how are things with you?*). □ **away** (or **in** or **out** etc.) **with** (as *int.*) take, send, or put (a person or thing) away, in, out, etc. **be with a person 1** agree with and support a person. **2** *colloq.* follow a person's meaning (*are you with me?*). **with that** thereupon. [Old English]

withdraw *v.* (*past* **withdrew**; *past part.* **withdrawn**) **1** *tr.* pull or take aside or back. **2** *tr.* discontinue, cancel, retract (*withdrew my support*). **3** *tr.* remove; take away (*withdrew the child from school*). **4** *tr.* take (money) out of an account. **5** *intr.* move away or back. **6** *intr.* (as **withdrawn** *adj.*) abnormally shy and unsociable. [Middle English]

withdrawal *n.* **1** the act or an instance of withdrawing or being withdrawn. **2** a process of ceasing to take addictive drugs. **3** = COITUS INTERRUPTUS.

wither *v.* **1** *tr. & intr.* (often foll. by *up*) make or become dry and shrivelled. **2** *tr. & intr.* (often foll. by *away*) deprive of or lose vigour or freshness. **3** *tr.* (as **withering** *adj.*) scornful (*a withering look*). [Middle English] □ **witheringly** *adv.*

withers *n.pl.* ▼ the ridge between a horse's shoulder blades. [shortening of *widersome* (16th c.) from *wider-* 'against', as the part that resists the strain of the collar]

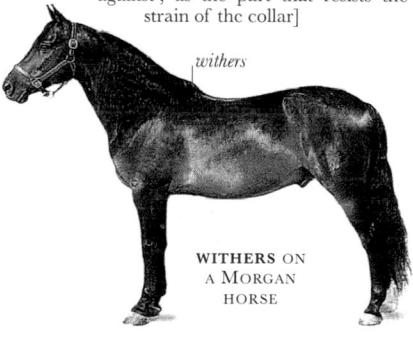

withers

WITHERS ON A MORGAN HORSE

withershins var. of WIDDERSHINS.

withhold *v.tr.* (*past and past part.* **-held**) **1** refuse to give, grant, or allow (*withhold one's consent*). **2** hold back; restrain. [Middle English]

within ● *adv. archaic* or *literary* **1** inside. **2** indoors. **3** in spirit (*make me pure within*). ● *prep.* **1** inside; enclosed or contained by. **2 a** not beyond or exceeding (*within one's means*). **b** not transgressing (*within the law*). **3** not further off than (*within three miles of a station*; *within ten days*). □ **within reach** (or **sight**) **of** near enough to be reached or seen. [Old English]

with it *adj. colloq.* (hyphenated when *attrib.*) up to date; conversant with modern ideas etc.

without ● *prep.* **1** not having, feeling, or showing. **2** with freedom from (*without fear*). **3** in the absence of (*cannot live without you*). **4** with neglect or avoidance of (*do not leave without telling me*). **5** *archaic* outside (*without the city wall*). ● *adv. archaic* or *literary* outside (*seen from without*). □ **without end** infinite, eternal. [Old English]

■ **Usage** The use of *without* as a *conj.*, as in *Do not leave without you tell me*, is non-standard.

withstand *v.tr.* (*past and past part.* **-stood**) resist, hold out against (a person, force, etc.). [Old English, prefixed with *with-* 'against']

W

witless *adj.* **1** lacking wits; foolish, stupid. **2** crazy. □ **witlessly** *adv.* **witlessness** *n.*

witness ● *n.* **1** a person present at some event and able to give information about it (cf. EYEWITNESS). **2 a** a person giving sworn testimony. **b** a person attesting another's signature to a document. **3** (foll. by *to*, *of*) a person or thing whose existence, condition, etc., attests or proves something (*is a living witness to their generosity*). **4** testimony, evidence, confirmation. ● *v.tr.* **1** be a witness of (an event etc.). **2** be witness to the authenticity of (a document or signature). **3** serve as evidence or an indication of. **4** (as *imper.*) introducing an illustration of the preceding statement (*he is a fine musician: witness his performance last week*). □ **bear witness to 1** attest the truth of. **2** state one's belief in. [Old English]

witness box *n.* (*US* **witness-stand**) an enclosure in a law court from which witnesses give evidence.

witter *v.intr.* (often foll. by *on*) *Brit. colloq.* speak tediously on trivial matters. [19th-century coinage]

witticism *n.* a witty remark. [coined by Dryden (1677) from WITTY]

witting *adj.* **1** aware. **2** intentional. [Middle English] □ **wittingly** *adv.*

witty *adj.* (**wittier**, **wittiest**) showing esp. verbal wit. □ **wittily** *adv.* **wittiness** *n.*

wives *pl.* of WIFE.

wiz var. of WHIZZ *n.* 2.

wizard ● *n.* **1** a sorcerer; a magician. **2** a genius. ● *adj.* esp. *Brit. archaic slang* wonderful, excellent. [Middle English, based on WISE¹] □ **wizardly** *adj.* **wizardry** *n.*

wizened /wíz-ĕnd/ *adj.* (also **wizen**) (of a person or face etc.) shrivelled-looking. [literally 'shrivelled': Old English *wisnian* 'to shrivel']

wk. *abbr.* week.

wks. *abbr.* weeks.

WNW *abbr.* west-north-west.

WO *abbr.* Warrant Officer.

wo *int.* = WHOA.

woad *n.* **1** a cruciferous plant, *Isatis tinctoria*, yielding a blue dye. **2** this dye. [Old English]

wobble ● *v.* **1 a** *intr.* sway or vibrate unsteadily from side to side. **b** *tr.* cause to do this. **2** *intr.* stand or go unsteadily. **3** *intr.* waver, vacillate. **4** *intr.* (of the voice or sound) quaver, pulsate. ● *n.* **1** a wobbling movement. **2** an instance of wobbling. [related to WAVE and WAVER] □ **wobbler** *n.*

wobbly ● *adj.* (**wobblier**, **wobbliest**) **1** wobbling or tending to wobble. **2** wavy (*a wobbly line*). **3** weak after illness (*feeling wobbly*). **4** wavering, insecure (*the economy was wobbly*). ● *n.* (in phr. **throw a wobbly**) *Brit. colloq.* have a fit of nerves or temper. □ **wobbliness** *n.*

woe *n. archaic* or *literary* **1** affliction; bitter grief; distress. **2** (in *pl.*) calamities, troubles. □ **woe betide** there will be unfortunate consequences for (*woe betide you if you are late*). [Old English]

woebegone *adj.* dismal-looking. [literally 'beset with woe': from Old English *begān* 'to beset']

woeful *adj.* **1** sorrowful. **2** causing sorrow or affliction. **3** very bad (*woeful ignorance*). □ **woefully** *adv.* **woefulness** *n.*

wog *n. Brit. slang offens.* a foreigner, esp. a non-white one. [20th-century coinage]

wok *n.* ▼ a bowl-shaped frying pan used in esp. Chinese cookery. [Cantonese]

W

chopstick

WOK

bowl

---

woke *past* of WAKE¹.

woken *past part.* of WAKE¹.

wold *n.* a piece of high open uncultivated land or moor. [Old English]

wolf ● *n.* (*pl.* **wolves**) **1** ▶ a wild flesh-eating tawny-grey mammal, *Canis lupus*, related to the dog. **2** *colloq.* a man given to seducing women. ● *v.tr.* (often foll. by *down*) devour (food) greedily. □ **cry wolf** raise repeated false alarms (so that a genuine one is disregarded). **keep the wolf from the door** avert hunger or starvation. [Old English] □ **wolfish** *adj.* **wolfishly** *adv.* **wolflike** *adj. & adv.*

WOLF: GREY WOLF (*Canis lupus*)

wolfhound *n.* ▼ any of several breeds of large dog originally bred to hunt wolves.

WOLFHOUND

wolfram *n.* **1** tungsten. **2** tungsten ore. [German]

wolf whistle ● *n.* a whistle made to indicate sexual admiration. ● *v.intr.* (**wolf-whistle**) make a wolf whistle.

---

wolves *pl.* of WOLF.

woman *n.* (*pl.* **women**) **1** an adult human female. **2** the female sex; any or an average woman (*how does woman differ from man?*). **3** *colloq.* a wife or female sexual partner. **4** (*attrib.*) female (*woman driver*). [Old English]

womanhood *n.* **1** female maturity. **2** womanly instinct. **3** womankind.

womanish *adj.* usu. *derog.* **1** (of a man) effeminate, unmanly. **2** suitable to or characteristic of a woman.

womanize *v.intr.* (also **-ise**) chase after women; philander. □ **womanizer** *n.*

womankind *n.* women in general.

womanly *adj.* (of a woman) having or showing qualities traditionally associated with women. □ **womanliness** *n.*

womb *n.* **1** the organ of conception and gestation in a woman and other female mammals; the uterus. ▷ REPRODUCTIVE ORGANS. **2** a place of origination and development. [Old English] □ **womb-like** *adj.*

wombat *n.* any burrowing plant-eating Australian marsupial of the family Vombatidae. ▷ MARSUPIAL. [Aboriginal]

women *pl.* of WOMAN.

womenfolk *n.* **1** women in general. **2** the women in a family.

womenkind var. of WOMANKIND.

Women's Institute *n.* an organization of women, esp. in rural areas, who meet regularly and participate in crafts, cultural activities, etc.

WOOD

Wood may be divided into two groups – hardwood from broadleaved trees and softwood from conifers. These terms can be misleading, however; yew for example, is classed as a softwood, yet it is as hard as oak. Different woods have different qualities, and are therefore put to different uses: larch is cheap and tough; iroko resists decay in the damp; ash is a great shock absorber; while oak is one of the most durable of woods. Mahogany and walnut are valued for their beautiful grain and rich colour.

heartwood
sapwood
bark
cambium
area of slow growth
area of rapid growth

CROSS-SECTION OF A YEW TREE BRANCH

EXAMPLES OF WOOD

SOFTWOOD   **HARDWOOD**

YEW   CHERRY   MAHOGANY   WALNUT

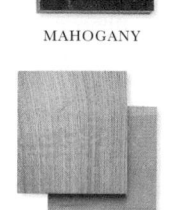

LARCH   IROKO   OAK   ASH

women's lib *n. colloq.* = WOMEN'S LIBERATION. □ **women's libber** *n.*

women's liberation *n.* the liberation of women from inequalities and subservient status in relation to men.

women's rights *n.pl.* rights that promote a position of legal and social equality of women with men.

won *past* and *past part.* of WIN.

wonder ● *n.* **1** surprise mingled with admiration or curiosity. **2** a strange or remarkable person or thing, event, etc. **3** (*attrib.*) having marvellous properties etc. (*a wonder drug*). ● *v.* **1** *intr.* (often foll. by *at*, or *to* + infin.) be filled with wonder or great surprise. **2** *tr.* (foll. by *that* + clause) be surprised to find. **3** *tr.* desire or be curious to know (*I wonder what the time is*). **4** *tr.* expressing a tentative enquiry (*I wonder whether you would mind?*). □ **I wonder** I very much doubt it. **no** (or **small**) **wonder** (often foll. by *that* + clause) one cannot be surprised. **work** (or **do**) **wonders 1** do miracles. **2** succeed remarkably. [Old English] □ **wonderer** *n.*

wonderful *adj.* **1** very remarkable or admirable. **2** arousing wonder. □ **wonderfully** *adv.* **wonderfulness** *n.*

wonderland *n.* **1** a fairyland. **2** a land of surprises or marvels.

wonderment *n.* surprise, awe.

wondrous *poet.* ● *adj.* wonderful. ● *adv.* wonderfully (*wondrous kind*). [alteration of obsolete *wonders* 'of wonder'] □ **wondrously** *adv.*

wonky *adj.* (**wonkier, wonkiest**) *Brit. slang* **1** crooked, off-centre, askew. **2** loose, unsteady. [fanciful formation] □ **wonkily** *adv.* **wonkiness** *n.*

wont /wohnt/ ● *predic.adj.* (foll. by *to* + infin.) *archaic* or *literary* accustomed (*as we were wont to say*). ● *n. formal* or *joc.* what is customary, one's habit (*as is my wont*). [Old English]

won't *contr.* will not.

wonted *attrib.adj.* habitual, accustomed, usual.

wonton *n.* (in Chinese cookery) a small round dumpling or roll with a savoury filling, usu. eaten boiled in soup. [from Cantonese *wān t'ān*]

woo *v.tr.* (**woos, wooed**) **1** court; seek the hand or love of (a woman). **2** try to win (fame, fortune, etc.). **3** seek the favour or support of. [Old English] □ **wooer** *n.*

wood *n.* **1 a** ◄ a hard fibrous material from the trunk or branches of a tree or shrub. **b** this cut for timber or for fuel. **2** (in *sing.* or *pl.*) growing trees densely occupying a tract of land. **3** (prec. by *the*) wooden storage, esp. a cask, for wine etc. (*poured straight from the wood*). **4** a wooden-headed golfclub. ▷ GOLF. **5** = BOWL² *n.* 1. □ **not see the wood for the trees** fail to grasp the main issue from over-attention to details. **out of the wood** (or *US* **woods**) out of danger or difficulty. [Old English]

wood anemone *n.* ◄ a wild spring-flowering anemone, *Anemone nemorosa*.

woodbine *n.* **1** wild honeysuckle. **2** *US* Virginia creeper.

woodblock *n.* a block from which woodcuts are made.

woodcarver *n.* **1** a person who carves designs in relief on wood. **2** a tool for carving wood.

woodcarving *n.* **1** (also *attrib.*) ▶ the act or process of carving wood. **2** a design in wood produced by this art.

woodchip *n.* **1** a chip of

WOOD ANEMONE
(*Anemone nemorosa*)

wood. **2** (in full **woodchip paper**) wallpaper with woodchips etc. embedded in it to give an uneven surface texture.

woodchuck *n.* a reddish-brown and grey N. American marmot, *Marmota monax*.

woodcock *n.* (*pl.* same) ◄ any game bird of the genus *Scolopax*.

woodcraft *n.* esp. *N. Amer.* **1** skill in woodwork. **2** knowledge of woodland esp. in camping, scouting, etc.

woodcut *n.* **1** a relief cut on a block of wood sawn along the grain. **2** a print made from this, esp. as an illustration in a book.

WOODCOCK
(*Scolopax rusticola*)

woodcutter *n.* **1** a person who cuts wood. **2** a maker of woodcuts.

wooded *adj.* having woods or many trees.

wooden *adj.* **1** made of wood. **2** like wood. **3 a** stiff, clumsy, or stilted; without animation or flexibility. **b** expressionless (*a wooden stare*). □ **woodenly** *adv.* **woodenness** *n.*

wood engraving *n.* **1** ◄ a relief cut on a block of wood sawn across the grain. **2** a print made from this.

wooden spoon *n.* **1** a spoon made of wood. **2** (prec. by *the*) esp. *Brit.* a booby prize.

wood fibre *n.* fibre obtained from wood esp. as material for paper.

wood-grain *attrib.adj.* (of a finish) imitating the grain pattern of wood.

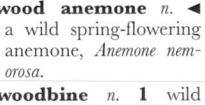

WOOD ENGRAVING ON A
MEDIEVAL GAME COUNTER

woodland *n.* wooded country, woods (often *attrib.: woodland scenery*). □ **woodlander** *n.*

woodlouse *n.* (*pl.* **-lice**) any small terrestrial crustacean of the genus *Oniscus* etc. feeding on rotten wood etc. ▷ CRUSTACEAN

woodman *n.* (*pl.* **-men**) **1** a forester. **2** a woodcutter.

woodnote *n.* (often in *pl.*) a natural or spontaneous note of a bird etc,

wood nymph *n. Mythol.* a nymph inhabiting a tree.

woodpecker *n.* ▼ any bird of the family Picidae that climbs and taps tree trunks in search of insects.

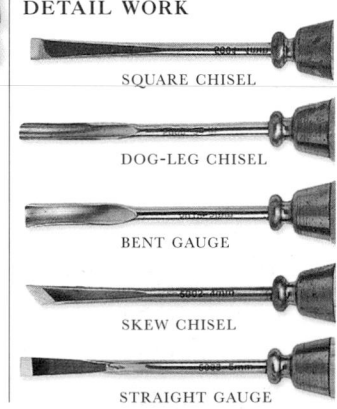

WOODPECKER:
GREAT SPOTTED
WOODPECKER
(*Dendrocopos major*)

wood pigeon *n.* a dove, *Columba palumbus*, having white patches like a ring round its neck.

woodpile *n.* a pile of wood, esp. for fuel.

wood pulp *n.* fibre obtained from wood and reduced chemically or mechanically to pulp as raw material for paper.

wood rat *n.* a rat of the N. American genus *Neotoma*.

woodruff *n.* ◄ a white-flowered plant of the genus *Galium*.

woodscrew see SCREW *n.* 2.

woodshed *n.* a shed where wood for fuel is stored.

woodsman *n.* (*pl.* **-men**) **1** a person who lives in or is familiar with woodland. **2** a person skilled in woodcraft.

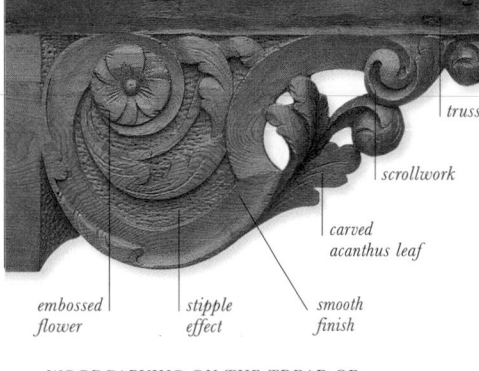

WOODRUFF
(*Galium odoratum*)

woodsmoke *n.* the smoke from a wood fire.

wood sorrel *n.* a small plant, *Oxalis acetosella*, with trifoliate leaves and white flowers streaked with purple.

wood spirit *n.* crude methanol obtained from wood.

wood stain *n.* a commercially produced substance for colouring wood.

woodturning *n.* the shaping of wood with a lathe. □ **woodturner** *n.*

wood warbler *n.* **1** a European woodland bird, *Phylloscopus sibilatrix*, with a trilling song. **2** any American warbler of the family Parulidae. ▷ PASSERINE

WOODCARVING

Woodcarving was a popular way of providing an attractive finish for building interiors and furniture from the Middle Ages through to the 19th century. A highly skilled, labour-intensive craft, large pieces of wood are first removed with a wooden mallet and a chisel; the intricate details and textures are then achieved by using a range of chisels to shave away wood by hand. The tools below are designed for working on a small scale.

truss

scrollwork

carved acanthus leaf

embossed flower   *stipple effect*   *smooth finish*

WOODCARVING ON THE TREAD OF
AN 18TH-CENTURY STAIRCASE

WOOD CHISELS FOR DETAIL WORK

SQUARE CHISEL

DOG-LEG CHISEL

BENT GAUGE

SKEW CHISEL

STRAIGHT GAUGE

W

WOODWIND

Woodwind instruments produce sound when air is blown into them. Originally made of wood, many are now manufactured from metal or plastic. The saxophone is an exception, having always been made of metal, but it appears in this category because it was constructed as a hybrid of the oboe and clarinet. Notes are produced in different ways: by blowing across an open hole in a pipe on a flute or piccolo, or by blowing into one end of a recorder or flageolet; other woodwind instruments have a reed that vibrates when blown.

OTHER WOODWIND INSTRUMENTS

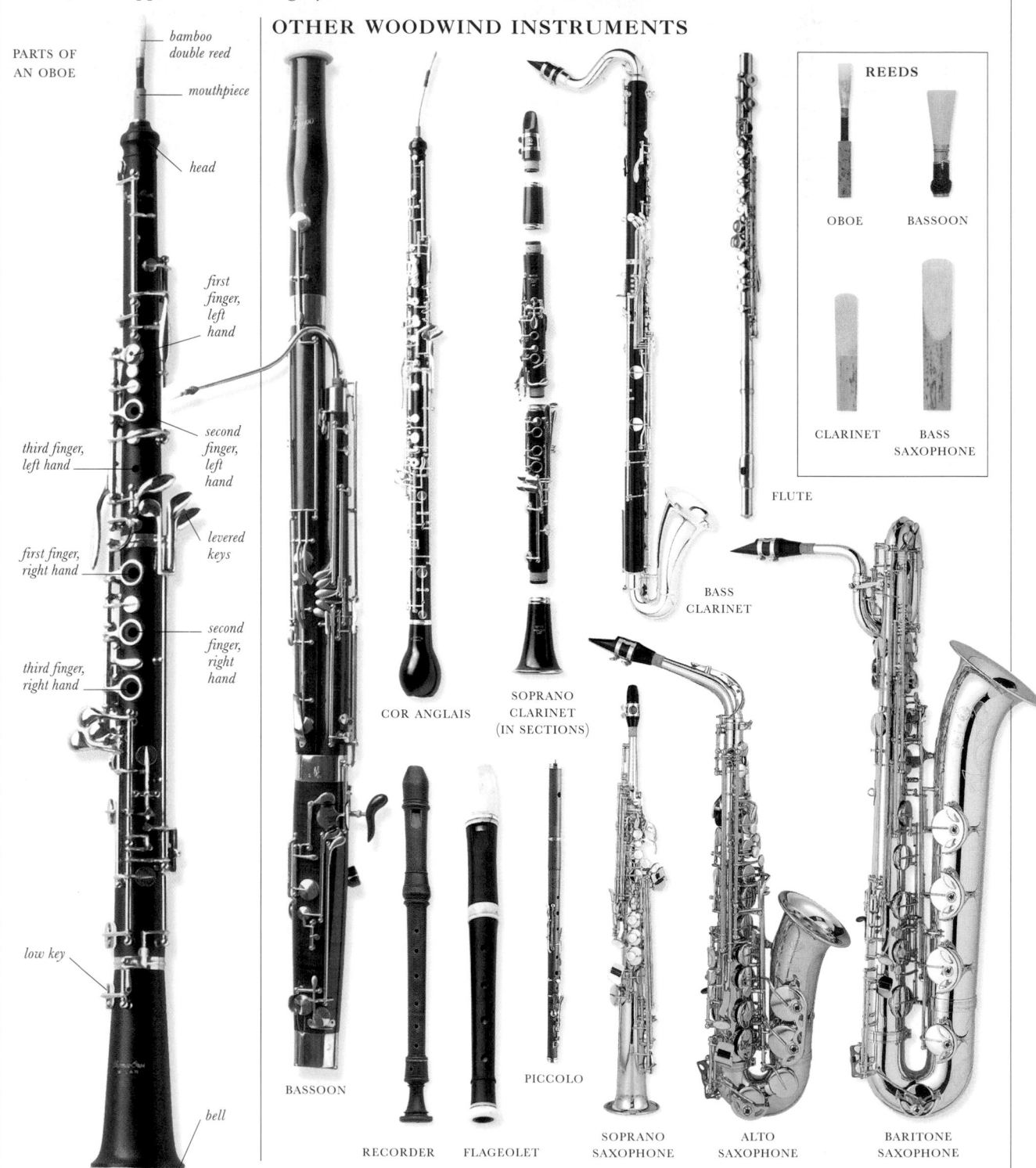

PARTS OF
AN OBOE

bamboo
double reed

mouthpiece

head

first
finger,
left
hand

third finger,
left hand

second
finger,
left
hand

levered
keys

first finger,
right hand

second
finger,
right
hand

third finger,
right hand

low key

bell

REEDS

OBOE

BASSOON

CLARINET

BASS
SAXOPHONE

FLUTE

COR ANGLAIS

SOPRANO
CLARINET
(IN SECTIONS)

BASS
CLARINET

BASSOON

RECORDER

FLAGEOLET

PICCOLO

SOPRANO
SAXOPHONE

ALTO
SAXOPHONE

BARITONE
SAXOPHONE

W

woodwind *n.* (often *attrib.*) **1** (*collect.*) ◄ wind instruments that were (mostly) originally made of wood, e.g. the flute and clarinet. ▷ ORCHESTRA. **2** (usu. in *pl.*) an individual instrument of this kind.

woodwork *n.* **1** the making of things in wood. **2** things made of wood. □ **crawl** (or **come**) **out of the woodwork** *colloq.* (of something unwelcome) appear; become known. □ **woodworker** *n.* **woodworking** *n.*

woodworm *n.* the wood-boring larva of the furniture beetle.

woody *adj.* (**woodier, woodiest**) **1** (of a region) wooded; abounding in woods. **2** like or of wood. □ **woodiness** *n.*

woodyard *n.* a yard where wood is used or stored.

woody nightshade see NIGHTSHADE.

woof[1] /wuuf/ ● *n.* the gruff bark of a dog. ● *v.intr.* give a woof.

woof[2] /rhymes with roof/ *n.* = WEFT[1] 1. [Old English]

woofer /woo-fer/ *n.* a loudspeaker designed to reproduce low frequencies (cf. TWEETER). ▷ LOUDSPEAKER

wool *n.* **1** fine soft wavy hair from the fleece of sheep, goats, etc. **2 a** yarn produced from this hair. **b** cloth or clothing made from it. **3** any of various wool-like substances (*steel wool*). □ **pull the wool over a person's eyes** deceive a person. [Old English] □ **wool-like** *adj.*

wool-gathering *n.* absent-mindedness; dreamy inattention.

woollen (*US* **woolen**) ● *adj.* made wholly or partly of wool. ● *n.* **1** a fabric produced from wool. **2** (in *pl.*) woollen garments.

woolly ● *adj.* (**woollier, woolliest**) **1** bearing or naturally covered with wool. **2** resembling or suggesting wool (*woolly clouds*). **3** made of wool, woollen. **4** (of a sound) indistinct. **5** (of thought) vague or confused. ● *n.* (*pl.* **-ies**) esp. *Brit. colloq.* a woollen garment, esp. a knitted pullover. □ **woolliness** *n.*

woolly-bear *n.* **1** ► a large hairy caterpillar, esp. of the tiger moth. **2** the small hairy larva of a carpet beetle, destructive to textiles etc.

woosh var. of WHOOSH.

woozy *adj.* (**woozier, wooziest**) *colloq.* **1** dizzy or unsteady. **2** dazed or slightly drunk. [19th-century coinage] □ **woozily** *adv.* **wooziness** *n.*

wop *n. slang offens.* an Italian or other S. European. [20th-century coinage]

Worcester sauce *n.* (*N. Amer.* **Worcestershire sauce**) a pungent sauce first made in Worcester.

word ● *n.* **1** a sound or combination of sounds forming a meaningful element of speech, usu. shown with a space on either side of it when written or printed. **2** speech, esp. as distinct from action (*bold in word only*). **3** one's promise or assurance (*gave us their word*). **4** (in *sing.* or *pl.*) a thing said, a remark or conversation. **5** (in *pl.*) the text of a song or an actor's part. **6** (in *pl.*) angry talk (*they had words*). **7** news, intelligence. **8** a command, password, or motto (*gave the word to begin*). ● *v.tr.* put into words; select words to express (*how shall we word that?*). □ **have a word** (often foll. by *with*) speak briefly (to). **in other words** expressing the same thing differently. **in so many words** explicitly or bluntly. **in a** (or **one**) **word** briefly. **my** (or **upon my**) **word** an exclamation of surprise or consternation. **of few words** taciturn. **put into words** express in speech or writing. **take a person at his** (or **her**) **word** interpret a person's words literally or exactly. **take a person's word for it** believe a person's statement without investigation or proof. **Word** (or **Word of God**) **1** the Bible. **2** Jesus Christ (John 1:14). **word for word** in exactly the same or (of translation) corresponding words. [Old English] □ **wordage** *n.* **wordless** *adj.* **wordlessly** *adv.* **wordlessness** *n.*

word game *n.* a game involving the making or selection etc. of words.

wording *n.* **1** a form of words used. **2** the way in which something is expressed.

word of honour *n.* an assurance given upon one's honour.

word of mouth *n.* spoken communication between people as a means of transmitting information.

word order *n.* the sequence of words in a sentence, esp. affecting meaning etc.

word-perfect *adj.* knowing one's part etc. by heart.

wordplay *n.* use of words to witty effect, esp. by punning.

word processor *n.* a purpose-built computer system for electronically storing text entered from a keyboard, incorporating corrections, and providing a printout. □ **word-process** *v.tr.* **word processing** *n.*

wordsearch *n.* a grid-shaped puzzle of letters in columns, containing several hidden words written in any direction.

wordsmith *n.* a skilled user or maker of words.

wordy *adj.* (**wordier, wordiest**) using or expressed in too many words; verbose. □ **wordily** *adv.* **wordiness** *n.*

wore[1] *past* of WEAR[1].

wore[2] *past* and *past part.* of WEAR[2].

work ● *n.* **1** the application of mental or physical effort to a purpose; the use of energy. **2 a** a task to be undertaken. **b** the materials for this. **3** a thing done or made by work; the result of an action; an achievement. **4** a person's employment or occupation etc., esp. as a means of earning income (*looked for work; is out of work*). **5** a literary or musical composition. **6** (in *comb.*) things or parts made of a specified material or with specified tools etc. (*ironwork; needlework*). **7** (in *pl.*) the operative part of a clock or machine. **8** *Physics* the exertion of force overcoming resistance or producing molecular change (*convert heat into work*). **9** (in *pl.*; prec. by *the*) *colloq.* all that is available; everything needed. **10** (in *pl.*) esp. *Brit.* operations of building or repair (*major building works*). **11** (in *pl.*; often treated as *sing.*) esp. *Brit.* a place where manufacture is carried on. ● *v.* (*past* and *past part.* **worked** or (esp. as *adj.*) **wrought**) **1** *intr.* (often foll. by *at, on*) do work; be engaged in bodily or mental activity. **2** *intr.* be employed in certain work (*works in industry; works as a secretary*). **3** *intr.* (often foll. by *for*) make efforts (*works for peace*). **4** *intr.* (foll. by *in*) be a craftsman (in a material). **5** *intr.* operate or function; be effective (*how does this machine work?; your idea will not work*). **6** *tr.* carry on, manage, or control (*cannot work the machine*). **7** *tr.* **a** put or keep in operation or at work (*this mine is no longer worked; works the staff very hard*). **b** cultivate (land). **8** *tr.* **a** bring about; produce as a result (*worked miracles*). **b** *colloq.* arrange (matters) (*worked it so that we could go*). **9** *tr.* knead, hammer; bring to a desired shape or consistency. **10** *intr.* & *tr.* do, or make by, needlework etc. **11** *tr.* & *intr.* (cause to) progress or penetrate, or make (one's way), gradually or with difficulty in a specified way (*worked our way through the crowd; worked the peg into the hole*). **12** *intr.* (foll. by *loose* etc.) gradually become (loose etc.) by constant movement. **13** *tr.* artificially excite (*worked themselves into a rage*). **14** *tr.* **a** purchase with one's labour instead of money (*work one's passage*). **b** obtain by labour the money for (one's way through university etc.). **15** *intr.* (foll. by *on, upon*) have influence. □ **at work** in action or engaged in work. **get worked up** become angry, excited, or tense. **have one's work cut out** be faced with a hard task. **in**

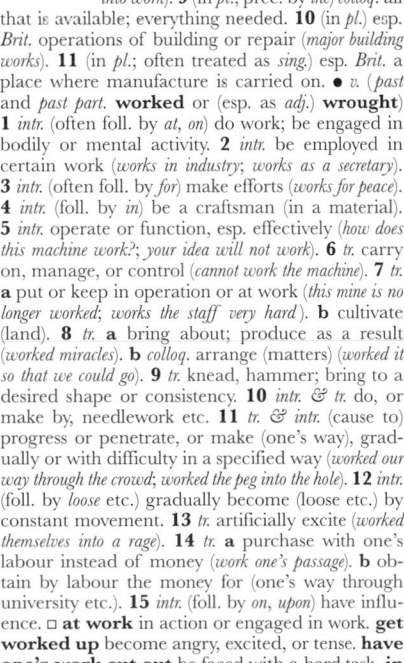

WOOLLY-BEAR: TIGER MOTH CATERPILLAR (*Arctia caja*)

WORKBENCH:
PORTABLE FOLDING WORKBENCH

Labels on figure: stop, vice handle, vice, work surface, footstand, collapsible leg

the works esp. *N. Amer.* being planned, worked on, or produced. **set to work** begin or cause to begin operations. **work in** find a place for. **work off** get rid of by work or activity. **work out 1 a** solve (a sum) or find out (an amount) by calculation. **b** solve or understand (a problem, person, etc.). **2** (foll. by *at*) be calculated (*the total works out at 230*). **3** have a specified result (*the plan worked out well*). **4** provide for the details of (*has worked out a scheme*). **5** engage in physical exercise or training. **work over 1** examine thoroughly. **2** *colloq.* treat with violence. **work to rule** esp. *Brit.* (esp. as industrial action) follow official working rules exactly in order to reduce output. **work up 1** bring gradually to an efficient state. **2** (foll. by *to*) advance gradually to a climax. **3** elaborate or excite by degrees. **work wonders** see WONDER. [Old English] □ **workless** *adj.*

workable *adj.* **1** that can be worked or will work. **2** that is worth working; practicable, feasible (*a workable quarry; a workable scheme*). □ **workability** *n.* **workably** *adv.*

workaday *adj.* ordinary, everyday, practical.

workaholic *n. colloq.* a person addicted to working.

work-basket *n.* (also **work-bag** etc.) a basket or bag etc. containing sewing materials.

workbench *n.* ◄ a bench for doing mechanical or practical work, esp. carpentry.

workbook *n.* a student's book including exercises.

workday *n.* esp. *US* a day on which work is usually done.

worker *n.* **1** a person who works, esp. a manual or industrial employee. **2** a neuter or undeveloped female of various social insects, esp. a bee or ant, that does the basic work of its colony. **3** a person who works hard.

work experience *n.* a scheme intended to give young people short-term experience of employment.

workfare *n.* a welfare system which requires some work from or training of those receiving benefits.

workforce *n.* the workers engaged or available in an industry etc.

workhorse *n.* a horse, person, or machine that performs hard work.

workhouse *n.* **1** *Brit. hist.* a public institution giving the poor of a parish board and lodging in return for work. **2** *US* a house of correction for petty offenders.

working ● *adj.* **1** engaged in work, esp. in manual or industrial labour. **2** functioning or able to function. ● *n.* **1** the activity of work. **2** the act or manner of functioning of a thing. **3 a** a mine or quarry. **b** the part of this in which work is being or has been done (*a disused working*).

working capital *n.* the capital actually used in a business.

working class ● *n.* the class of people who are employed for wages, esp. in manual or industrial work. ● *adj.* (**working-class**) of or relating to the working class.

working day *n.* esp. *Brit.* **1** a workday. **2** the part of the day devoted to work.

working drawing *n.* a drawing to scale, serving as a guide for construction or manufacture.

working hours *n.pl.* hours normally devoted to work.

working hypothesis *n.* a hypothesis used as a basis for action.

working knowledge *n.* knowledge adequate to work with.

W

working lunch *n.* a lunch at which business is conducted.

working order *n.* the condition in which a machine works (satisfactorily or as specified).

working party *n. Brit.* a group of people appointed to study a particular problem or advise on some question.

workload *n.* the amount of work to be done by an individual etc.

workman *n.* (*pl.* **-men**) **1** a man employed to do manual labour. **2** a person having specified skill in a job (*a good workman*).

workmanlike *adj.* characteristic of a good workman; showing practised skill.

workmanship *n.* the degree of skill in doing a task or of finish in the product made.

workmate *n.* esp. *Brit.* a fellow worker.

work of art *n.* a fine picture, poem, or building etc.

workout *n.* a session of physical exercise.

workpiece *n.* a thing worked on with a tool or machine.

workplace *n.* a place at which a person works; an office, factory, etc.

works council *n.* esp. *Brit.* a group of employees representing those employed in a works etc. in discussions with their employers.

worksheet *n.* **1** a paper for recording work done or in progress. **2** a paper listing questions or activities for students etc. to work through.

workshop *n.* **1** a room or building in which goods are manufactured. **2** a meeting for concerted discussion or activity (*a dance workshop*).

work-shy *adj.* disinclined to work.

workspace *n.* space in which to work.

workstation *n.* **1** the location of a stage in a manufacturing process. **2** a computer terminal or the desk etc. where this is located.

work study *n.* a system of assessing methods of working so as to achieve the maximum output and efficiency.

work surface *n.* = WORKTOP.

work table *n.* a table for working at.

worktop *n. Brit.* a flat surface for working on, esp. in a kitchen.

work-to-rule *n.* esp. *Brit.* the act or an instance of working to rule.

workwear *n.* hard-wearing clothes for work.

world *n.* **1 a** the Earth, or a planetary body like it. **b** its countries and their inhabitants. **c** all people. **2** the universe or all that exists; everything. **3 a** the time, state, or scene of human existence. **b** (prec. by *the*, *this*) mortal life. **4** secular interests and affairs. **5** human affairs; active life (*how goes the world with you?*). **6** all that concerns or all who belong to a specified class, time, or sphere of activity (*the medieval world*; *the world of sport*). **7** (foll. by *of*) a vast amount (*that makes a world of difference*). **8** (*attrib.*) affecting many nations, of all nations (*world politics*; *a world champion*). □ **bring into the world** give birth to. **come into the world** be born. **for all the world** (foll. by *like*, *as if*) precisely (*looked for all the world like twins*). **get the best of both worlds** benefit from two incompatible sets of ideas, circumstances, etc. **man** (or **woman**) **of the world** a person experienced and practical in human affairs. **out of this world** *colloq.* extremely good etc. **think the world of** have a very high regard for. **world without end** for ever. [Old English, related to OLD]

world-class *adj.* of a quality or standard regarded as high throughout the world.

World Cup *n.* a competition between football or other sporting teams from various countries.

world-famous *adj.* known throughout the world.

worldly *adj.* (**worldlier**, **worldliest**) **1** temporal or earthly (*worldly goods*). **2** engrossed in temporal affairs, esp. wealth and pleasure. **3** experienced in life, sophisticated, practical. [Old English] □ **worldliness** *n.*

worldly wisdom *n.* prudence as regards one's own interests. □ **worldly-wise** *adj.*

world order *n.* (esp. in phr. **new world order**) a system controlling events in the world, esp. an international set of arrangements for preserving global political stability.

world power *n.* a nation having power and influence in world affairs.

World Series *n.* a series of games between the champions of the two major N. American baseball leagues.

world war *n.* a war involving many important nations.

world-weary *adj.* bored with human affairs. □ **world-weariness** *n.*

worldwide ● *adj.* affecting, occurring in, or known in all parts of the world. ● *adv.* throughout the world.

World Wide Web *n.* (prec. by *the*) **1 a** a set of standards for the representation and distribution of hypertext documents. **b** software operating according to these standards. **2** the information accessible by such means.

worm ● *n.* **1** any of various types of creeping or burrowing invertebrate animals with long slender bodies and no limbs. ▷ ANNELID, NEMATODE. **2** the long slender larva of an insect. **3** (in *pl.*) internal parasites. **4** a maggot supposed to eat dead bodies in the grave. **5** *colloq.* an insignificant or contemptible person. ● *v.* **1** *intr.* & *tr.* move with a crawling motion (*wormed through the bushes*; *wormed our way through the bushes*). **2** *intr.* & *refl.* (foll. by *into*) insinuate oneself into a person's favour, confidence, etc. **3** *tr.* (foll. by *out*) obtain (a secret etc.) by cunning persistence (*managed to worm the truth out of them*). **4** *tr.* rid (a plant or dog etc.) of worms. [Old English] □ **wormer** *n.* **wormlike** *adj.*

worm-cast *n.* a convoluted mass of earth left on the surface by a burrowing earthworm.

worm-eaten *adj.* **1** eaten into by worms. **2** rotten, decayed.

worm-gear *n.* ◄ an arrangement of a toothed wheel worked by a short revolving cylinder bearing a screw thread. ▷ ODOMETER

wormhole *n.* **1** a hole made by a burrowing worm or insect in wood, fruit, etc. **2** *Physics* a hypothetical connection between widely separated regions of space–time.

wormwood *n.* ► any woody shrub of the genus *Artemisia*, with a bitter aromatic taste. ▷ HERB. [Middle English alteration of obsolete *wormod*]

wormy *adj.* (**wormier**, **wormiest**) **1** full of worms. **2** worm-eaten.

bevel gear
toothed sector gear
worm-gear
revolving cylinder

WORM-GEAR IN A STEERING RACK

worn *past part.* of WEAR[1]. ● *adj.* **1** looking tired and exhausted. **2** = WELL-WORN 1. **3** = WELL-WORN 2.

worn out *adj.* **1** exhausted. **2** worn esp. to the point of being no longer usable (hyphenated when *attrib.*: *worn-out engine*).

worriment *n.* esp. *US* **1** the act of worrying or state of being worried. **2** a cause of worry.

worrisome *adj.* causing or apt to cause worry or distress.

worry ● *v.* (**-ies**, **-ied**) **1** *intr.* allow one's mind to dwell on troubles. **2** *tr.* harass, importune; be a trouble to. **3** *tr.* (of a dog etc.) shake or pull about with the teeth. **4** *tr.* (as **worried** *adj.*) **a** uneasy, troubled in the mind. **b** suggesting worry (*a worried look*). ● *n.* (*pl.* **-ies**) **1** a thing that causes anxiety. **2** a disturbed

state of mind. □ **not to worry** *colloq.* there is no need to worry. [Old English *wyrgan* 'to strangle'] □ **worriedly** *adv.* **worrier** *n.* **worryingly** *adv.*

worry beads *n.pl.* a string of beads manipulated with the fingers to occupy or calm oneself.

worse ● *adj.* **1** more bad. **2** (*predic.*) in or into worse health or a worse condition. ● *adv.* more badly or more ill. ● *n.* **1** a worse thing or things (*you might do worse than accept*). **2** (prec. by *the*) a worse condition (*a change for the worse*). □ **none the worse for** not adversely affected by. **or worse** or as an even worse alternative. **the worse for drink** fairly drunk. **the worse for wear 1** damaged by use. **2** injured. **worse luck** see LUCK. **worse off** in a worse position. [Old English]

worsen *v.tr.* & *intr.* make or become worse.

worship ● *n.* **1 a** homage or reverence paid to a deity. **b** the acts, rites, or ceremonies of worship. **2** adoration or devotion shown towards a person or principle (*the worship of wealth*). ● *v.* (**worshipped**, **worshipping**; *US* **worshiped**, **worshiping**) **1** *tr.* adore as divine; honour with religious rites. **2** *tr.* regard with adoration (*worships the ground she walks on*). **3** *intr.* attend public worship. **4** *intr.* be full of adoration. □ **Your** (or **His** or **Her**) **Worship** esp. *Brit.* a title of respect used to or of a mayor, certain magistrates, etc. [Old English] □ **worshipper** *n.* (*US* **worshiper**).

worshipful *adj.* **1** (usu. **Worshipful**) *Brit.* a title given to justices of the peace and to certain old companies or their officers etc. **2** *archaic* entitled to honour or respect.

worst ● *adj.* most bad. ● *adv.* most badly. ● *n.* the worst part, event, circumstance, or possibility (*the worst of the storm is over*; *prepare for the worst*). ● *v.tr.* defeat, outdo. □ **at its** etc. **worst** in the worst state. **at worst** (or **the worst**) in the worst possible case. **get** (or **have**) **the worst of it** be defeated. **if the worst comes to the worst** if the worst happens. [Old English]

worsted /**wuust**-id/ *n.* **1** a fine smooth yarn spun from combed long staple wool. **2** fabric made from this. [from *Worste(a)d*, a parish in Norfolk, England]

wort *n.* **1** *archaic* (except in names) a plant (*St John's wort*). **2** the infusion of malt which after fermentation becomes beer. [Old English]

worth ● *predic.adj.* (governing a noun like a preposition) **1** of a value equivalent to (*is worth £50*). **2** such as to justify or repay (*worth doing*; *not worth the trouble*). **3** possessing or having property amounting to. ● *n.* **1** what a person or thing is worth (*of great worth*; *persons of worth*). **2** the equivalent of money in a commodity (*ten pounds' worth of petrol*). □ **for all one is worth** *colloq.* with one's utmost efforts. **for what it is worth** without a guarantee of its truth or value. **worth one's salt** see SALT. **worth one's while** (or **worth while**) see WHILE. [Old English]

worthless *adj.* without value or merit. □ **worthlessness** *n.*

worthwhile *adj.* that is worth the time or effort spent; of value or importance.

■ **Usage** *Worthwhile* is used both attributively and predicatively, e.g. *a worthwhile cause*, *decided it wasn't worthwhile*, while *worth while* (two words) is used only predicatively, e.g. *thought it worth while to ring the police*.

WORMWOOD: ARCTIC WORMWOOD (*Artemisia borealis*)

worthy ● *adj.* (**worthier**, **worthiest**) **1** estimable; having some moral worth (*lived a worthy life*). **2** (of a person) entitled to recognition (*a worthy old couple*). **3 a** (foll. by *of*, or *to* + infin.) deserving (*worthy of a mention*; *worthy to be remembered*). **b** (foll. by *of*) suitable to the dignity etc. of (*in words worthy of the occasion*). ● *n.* (*pl.* **-ies**)

W

1 a worthy person. **2** a person of some distinction. [Middle English] □ **worthily** adv. **worthiness** n.

-worthy comb. form forming adjectives meaning: **1** deserving of (blameworthy; noteworthy). **2** suitable or fit for (newsworthy; roadworthy).

would v.aux. (3rd sing. **would**) past of WILL¹, used esp.: **1** (in the 2nd and 3rd persons, and often in the 1st: see SHOULD) **a** in reported speech (he said he would be home by evening). **b** to express the conditional mood (they would have been killed if they had gone). **2** to express habitual action (would wait for her every evening). **3** to express a question or polite request (would they like it?; would you come in, please?). **4** to express probability (I guess she would be over fifty by now). **5** (foll. by that + clause) literary to express a wish (would that you were here). **6** to express consent (they would not help). [Old English]

■ **Usage** See Usage Note at SHOULD.

would-be attrib.adj. often derog. desiring or aspiring to be (a would-be politician).

wouldn't contr. would not. □ **I wouldn't know** colloq. (as is to be expected) I do not know.

wound¹ /woond/ ● n. **1** an injury done to living tissue by a cut or blow etc. **2** an injury to a person's reputation or a pain inflicted on a person's feelings. ● v.tr. inflict a wound on (wounded soldiers; wounded feelings). [Old English]

wound² past and past part. of WIND² (cf. WIND¹ v. 5).

wove¹ past of WEAVE¹.

wove² adj. (of paper) made on a wire-gauze mesh and so having a uniform unlined surface.

woven past part. of WEAVE¹.

wow¹ ● int. (also **wowee**) expressing astonishment or admiration. ● n. slang a sensational success. ● v.tr. slang impress or excite greatly. [originally Scots]

wow² n. a slow pitch-fluctuation in sound reproduction, perceptible in long notes.

WP abbr. word processor or processing.

WPC abbr. (in the UK) woman police constable.

w.p.m. abbr. words per minute.

wrack n. **1** seaweed cast up or growing on the shore. ▷ FUCUS. **2** = RACK². [from Middle Dutch wrak]

wraggle-taggle var. of RAGGLE-TAGGLE.

wraith n. **1** a ghost. **2** the spectral appearance of a living person supposed to portend that person's death. [16th-century Scots] □ **wraithlike** adj.

wrangle ● n. a noisy argument or dispute. ● v.intr. engage in a wrangle. [Middle English] □ **wrangling** n.

wrangler n. **1** a person who wrangles. **2** US a cowboy.

wrap ● v.tr. (**wrapped**, **wrapping**) **1** envelop in folded or soft encircling material (wrap it up in paper; wrap up a parcel). **2** arrange or draw (a pliant covering) round (a person) (wrapped the scarf closer around me). ● n. **1** a shawl or scarf or other such addition to clothing. **2** esp. US material used for wrapping. □ **take the wraps off** disclose. **under wraps** in secrecy. **wrapped up in** engrossed in. **wrap up 1** finish off, bring to completion (wrapped up the deal in two days). **2** put on warm clothes (mind you wrap up well). **3** (in imper.) Brit. slang be quiet. [Middle English]

wraparound ● adj. (esp. of clothing) designed to wrap round. ● n. anything that wraps round.

wrap-over attrib.adj. Brit. (of a garment) having no seam at one side but wrapped around the body and fastened.

wrapper n. **1** a cover for a sweet, chocolate, etc. **2** a cover enclosing a newspaper or similar packet for posting.

wrapping n. (esp. in pl.) material used to wrap.

wrapping paper n. strong or decorative paper for wrapping parcels.

wrasse n. ▼ any brightly coloured marine fish of the family Labridae. [from Cornish wrach, variant of gwrach 'old woman']

WRASSE: CUCKOO WRASSE
(Labrus mixtus)

wrath /roth/ n. literary extreme anger. [Old English]

wrathful adj. literary extremely angry. □ **wrathfully** adv.

wreak /reek/ v.tr. **1** put in operation (vengeance or one's anger etc.). **2** cause (damage etc.) (the hurricane wreaked havoc on the crops). [Old English wrecan 'to drive, avenge']

wreath /reeth/ n. (pl. **wreaths**) **1** ◄ flowers or leaves fastened in a ring. **2** a carved representation of a wreath. **3** (foll. by of) a curl or ring of smoke or cloud. [Old English, related to WRITHE]

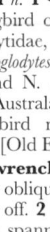

ivy leaf

peony

gilded pomegranate

spray of roses

WREATH

wreathe /reeth/ v.tr. **1** encircle as, with, or like a wreath. **2** (foll. by round) put (one's arms etc.) round (a person etc.). [partly from WRITHE, partly from WREATH]

wreck ● n. **1** the destruction or disablement of a ship. **2** a ship that has suffered a wreck (the shores are strewn with wrecks). **3** a greatly damaged or disabled thing or person (had become a physical and mental wreck). **4** Law goods etc. cast up by the sea. ● v.tr. **1** cause the wreck of (a ship). **2** completely ruin (hopes, chances, etc.). **3** (as **wrecked** adj.) involved in a shipwreck (wrecked sailors). [from Anglo-French wrec]

wreckage n. **1** wrecked material. **2** the remnants of a wreck.

Wren n. hist. (in the UK) a member of the former Women's Royal Naval Service. [originally in pl., from abbreviation WRNS]

wren n. **1** ◄ any short-winged songbird of the family Troglodytidae, esp. the very small Troglodytes troglodytes of Eurasia and N. America. **2** a small Australasian or S. American bird resembling a wren. [Old English]

WREN
(Troglodytes troglodytes)

wrench ● n. **1** a violent twist or oblique pull or act of tearing off. **2** ► an adjustable tool like a spanner for gripping and turning nuts etc. **3** an instance of painful uprooting or parting (leaving home was a great wrench). ● v.tr. **1** twist or pull violently round or sideways. **2** pull off with a wrench. **3** distort (facts) to suit a theory etc. [Old English wrencan 'to twist']

wrest v.tr. **1** force or wrench away from a person's grasp. **2** (foll. by from) obtain by effort or with difficulty. [Old English, related to WRIST]

wrestle ● n. a contest in which two opponents grapple and try to throw each other to the ground. ● v. **1** intr. take part in a wrestle. **2** tr. fight (a person) in a wrestle (wrestled his opponent to the ground). **3** intr. (foll. by with, against) struggle, contend. [Old English] □ **wrestler** n. **wrestling** n.

wretch n. **1** a pitiable person. **2** (often as a playful term) a contemptible person. [Old English]

wretched adj. (**wretcheder**, **wretchedest**) **1** unhappy or miserable. **2** of bad quality or no merit; contemptible. **3** unsatisfactory. □ **feel wretched 1** be unwell. **2** be much embarrassed. [Middle English] □ **wretchedly** adv. **wretchedness** n.

wrick Brit. var. of RICK².

wriggle ● v. **1** intr. **a** (of a worm etc.) twist or turn its body with short writhing movements. **b** (of a person or animal) make similar movements. **2** tr. & intr. move or go in this way (wriggled into the corner; wriggled his hand into the hole). **3** intr. practise evasion. ● n. an act of wriggling. □ **wriggle out of** colloq. avoid on a contrived pretext. [from Middle Low German wriggelen] □ **wriggler** n. **wriggly** adj.

wring ● v.tr. (past and past part. **wrung**) **1 a** squeeze tightly. **b** squeeze and twist. **2** twist forcibly; break by twisting. **3** distress or torture. **4** extract by squeezing. **5** (foll. by out, from) obtain by pressure or importunity; extort. ● n. an act of wringing; a squeeze. □ **wring a person's hand** clasp it forcibly or press it with emotion. **wring one's hands** clasp them as a gesture of great distress. [Old English]

wringer n. a device for wringing water from washed clothes etc.

wringing adj. (in full **wringing wet**) so wet that water can be wrung out.

wrinkle ● n. **1** a slight crease in the skin such as is produced by age. **2** a similar mark in another flexible surface. ● v. **1** tr. make wrinkles in. **2** intr. form wrinkles; become marked with wrinkles. [originally representing Old English gewrinclod 'sinuous']

wrinkly ● adj. (**wrinklier**, **wrinkliest**) having many wrinkles. ● n. (also **wrinklie**) (pl. **-ies**) slang offens. an old or middle-aged person.

wrist n. **1** the part connecting the hand with the forearm. ▷ JOINT. **2** the part of a garment covering the wrist. [Old English]

wristband n. a band forming or concealing the end of a shirtsleeve; a cuff.

wristlet n. a band or ring worn on the wrist to strengthen or guard it or as an ornament, bracelet, handcuff, etc.

wristwatch n. a small watch worn on a strap round the wrist.

writ¹ n. a form of written command in the name of a court, state, sovereign, etc. □ **serve a writ on** deliver a writ to (a person). [Old English, related to WRITE]

writ² archaic past part. of WRITE. □ **writ large** in magnified or emphasized form.

WRENCH: STILLSON PIPE WRENCH

write v. (past **wrote**; past part. **written**) **1** intr. mark a surface by means of a pen, pencil, etc., with symbols, letters, or words. **2** tr. form (such symbols etc.). **3** tr. form the symbols that represent or constitute (a word or sentence, or a document etc.). **4** tr. fill or complete (a sheet, cheque, etc.) with writing. **5** tr. put (data) into a computer store. **6** tr. indicate (a quality or condition) by one's or its appearance (guilt was written on his face). **7** tr. compose (a text, article, novel, etc.) for written or printed reproduction or publication. **8** intr. be engaged in composing a text, article, etc. (writes for the local newspaper).

W

9 *intr.* (foll. by *to*) write and send a letter (to a recipient). **10** *tr. US* or *colloq.* write and send a letter to (a person) (*wrote him last week*). **11** *tr.* convey (news, information, etc.) by letter (*wrote that they would arrive next Friday*). □ **nothing to write home about** *colloq.* of little interest or value. **write down 1** record or take note of in writing. **2** write as if for those considered inferior. **3** disparage in writing. **4** reduce the nominal value of (stock, goods, etc.). **write in** send a suggestion, query, etc., in writing to an organization. **write off 1** write and send a letter. **2** cancel the record of (a bad debt etc.); acknowledge the loss of or failure to recover (an asset). **3** *Brit.* damage (a vehicle etc.) so badly that it cannot be repaired. **write out** write in full or in finished form. **write up 1** write a full account of. **2** praise in writing. **3** make entries to bring (a diary etc.) up to date. [Old English *wrītan* 'to scratch, score, write': originally used of symbols inscribed with sharp tools] □ **writable** *adj.* **writer** *n.*

■ **Usage** The use of *write* as a transitive verb with a person as the direct object, e.g. *He writes me every week*, is best avoided in British English, but is good American English. *He writes me a letter every week* is acceptable because *me* is not the direct object.

write-down *n.* a reduction in the estimated or nominal value of stock, assets, etc.

write-off *n.* a thing written off, esp. a vehicle too badly damaged to be repaired.

writer *n.* **1** a person who writes or has written something. **2** a person who writes books; an author. **3** *Brit.* a clerk, esp. in the Navy or government offices.

writerly *adj.* **1** characteristic of a professional author. **2** consciously literary.

writer's block *n.* a periodic lack of inspiration afflicting creative writers etc.

writer's cramp *n.* a muscular spasm due to excessive writing.

write-up *n. colloq.* a written or published account, a review.

writhe ● *v.intr.* **1** twist or roll oneself about in or as if in acute pain. **2** suffer severe mental discomfort or embarrassment (*writhed with shame; writhed*

at the thought of it). **3** *tr.* twist (one's body etc.) about. ● *n.* an act of writhing. [Old English, related to WREATHE]

writing *n.* **1** a group or sequence of letters or symbols. **2** = HANDWRITING. **3** (usu. in *pl.*) a piece of literary work done; a book, article, etc. □ **in writing** in written form.

writing pad *n.* a pad (see PAD[1] *n.* 2) of paper for writing on.

writing paper *n.* paper for writing (esp. letters) on.

written *past part.* of WRITE.

wrong ● *adj.* **1** mistaken; not true; in error (*gave a wrong answer; we were wrong to think that*). **2** less or least desirable (*the wrong road; a wrong decision*). **3** contrary to law or morality (*it is wrong to steal*). **4** out of order, in or into a bad or abnormal condition (*something wrong with my heart*). ● *adv.* (usually placed last) in a wrong manner or direction; with an incorrect result (*guessed wrong; told them wrong*). ● *n.* **1** what is morally wrong; a wrong action. **2** injustice; unjust action or treatment (*suffer wrong*). ● *v.tr.* **1** treat unjustly. **2** mistakenly attribute bad motives to. □ **get wrong 1** misunderstand (a person, statement, etc.). **2** obtain an incorrect answer to. **get** (or **get hold of**) **the wrong end of the stick** misunderstand completely. **go down the wrong way** (of food) enter the windpipe instead of the gullet. **go wrong 1** take the wrong path. **2** stop functioning properly. **3** depart from virtuous or suitable behaviour. **in the wrong** responsible for a quarrel, mistake, or offence. **wrong way round** in the reverse of the normal or desirable orientation or sequence etc. [from Old Norse *rangr* 'awry, unjust'] □ **wrongly** *adv.* **wrongness** *n.*

wrongdoer *n.* a person who behaves immorally or illegally. □ **wrongdoing** *n.*

wrong-foot *v.tr. Brit. colloq.* (in tennis, football, etc.) play so as to catch (an opponent) off balance.

WROUGHT IRON:
18TH-CENTURY
ORNAMENTAL
RAIL POST

wrongful *adj.* **1** characterized by unfairness or injustice. **2** contrary to law. **3** (of a person) not entitled to the position etc. occupied. □ **wrongfully** *adv.*

wrong-headed *adj.* perverse and obstinate. □ **wrongheadedly** *adv.* **wrong-headedness** *n.*

wrong side *n.* the worse or undesired or unusable side of something, esp. fabric. □ **on the wrong side of 1** out of favour with (a person). **2** somewhat more than (a specified age). **the wrong side of the tracks** see TRACK.

wrote *past* of WRITE.

wrought /rawt/ *archaic past* and *past part.* of WORK. *adj.* (of metals) beaten out or shaped by hammering.

wrought iron *n.* ◀ a tough malleable form of iron suitable for forging or rolling (hyphenated when *attrib.*: *wrought-iron gate*).

wrung *past* and *past part.* of WRING.

WRVS *abbr.* (in the UK) Women's Royal Voluntary Service.

wry *adj.* (**wryer, wryest** or **wrier, wriest**) **1** distorted. **2** (of a smile etc.) contorted in disgust, disappointment, or mockery. **3** (of humour) dry and mocking. [from Old English *wrīgian* 'to tend, incline', later 'to deviate, contort'] □ **wryly** *adv.* **wryness** *n.*

WSW *abbr.* west-south-west.

wt. *abbr.* weight.

wunderkind /vuun-der-kint/ *n.* (*pl.* **wunderkinds** or **wunderkinder** /-kin-der/) *colloq.* a person who achieves great success while relatively young. [German, literally 'wonder child']

WWW *abbr.* = WORLD WIDE WEB.

wych elm *n.* (also **witch elm**) a Eurasian elm, *Ulmus glabra*, with large rough leaves. [based on *wych*, used in names of trees with pliant branches]

wych hazel var. of WITCH HAZEL.

WYSIWYG /wiz-i-wig/ *adj.* (also **wysiwyg**) *Computing* denoting the representation of text on-screen in a form exactly corresponding to its appearance on a printout. [acronym from *what you see is what you get*]

W

X[1] *n.* (also **x**) (*pl.* **Xs** or **X's**) **1** the twenty-fourth letter of the alphabet. **2** (as a Roman numeral) ten. **3** (usu. **x**) *Algebra* the first unknown quantity. **4** (usu. **x**) *Geom.* the first coordinate. **5** an unknown or unspecified number or person etc. **6** a cross-shaped symbol esp. used: **a** to indicate position (*X marks the spot*). **b** to indicate incorrectness. **c** to symbolize a kiss or a vote. **d** as the signature of a person who cannot write.

X[2] *symb. hist.* (of films) classified as suitable for adults only.

xanthate *n.* any salt or ester of xanthic acid.

xanthine /**zan**-th'een/ *n.* (also **xanthin** /**zan**-thin/) *Biochem.* **1** a purine derivative found in blood and urine which is a breakdown product of nucleic acids and is the parent compound of caffeine and other alkaloids. **2** (**xanthin**) any of various orange or yellow pigments found in plants.

X chromosome *n.* a sex chromosome of which the number in female cells is twice that in male cells. [X: arbitrary label]

Xe *symb. Chem.* the element xenon.

xeno- /**zen**-oh/ *comb. form* **1 a** foreign. **b** a foreigner. **2** other. [from Greek *xenos* 'strange, stranger']

xenolith /**zen**-ŏ-lith/ *n. Geol.* ▶ an inclusion within an igneous rock mass.

xenon /**zen**-on/ *n. Chem.* a heavy colourless odourless inert gaseous element occurring in traces in the atmosphere and used in fluorescent lamps. [Greek, literally 'strange (thing)']

xenophobe /**zen**-ŏ-fohb/ *n.* a person given to xenophobia.

xenophobia /zen-ŏ-**foh**-biă/ *n.* a deep dislike of foreigners. □ **xenophobic** *adj.*

xeranthemum /zeer-**ran**-thi-mŭm/ *n.* ▼ a plant of the genus *Xeranthemum* (daisy family), with dry everlasting flowers. [from Greek *xēros* 'dry' + *anthemon* 'flower']

xero- /**zeer**-oh/ *comb. form* dry. [from Greek *xēros*]

xeroderma /zeer-ŏ-**der**-mă/ *n.* any of various diseases characterized by extreme dryness of the skin. [based on Greek *derma* 'skin']

xerograph /**zeer**-ŏ-grahf/ *n.* a copy produced by xerography.

xerography /zeer-**rog**-ră-fi/ *n.* a dry copying process in which powder adheres to parts of a surface remaining electrically charged after exposure to light from an image of the document to be copied. □ **xerographic** *adj.*

xerophyte /**zeer**-ŏ-fyt/ *n.* (also **xerophile** /**zeer**-ŏ-fyl/) ▲ a plant able to grow in very dry conditions.

Xerox /**zeer**-oks/ ● *n. propr.* **1** a machine for copying by xerography. **2** a copy made using this

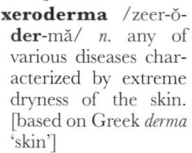

XERANTHEMUM
(*Xeranthemum annuum*)

machine. ● *v.tr.* (**xerox**) reproduce by this process. [invented from XEROGRAPHY]

Xhosa /**koh**-să/ ● *n.* **1** (*pl.* same or **Xhosas**) a member of a Bantu-speaking people of Cape Province, South Africa. **2** the language of this people. ● *adj.* of or relating to this people or language. [native name]

xi /ksy/ *n.* the fourteenth letter of the Greek alphabet (Ξ, ξ). [Greek]

Xmas /**kris**-măs, **eks**-măs/ *n. colloq.* = CHRISTMAS *n.* [abbreviation (X = initial chi of Greek *Khristos* 'Christ')]

X-rated *adj.* (usu. *attrib.*) **1** indecent, pornographic (*X-rated humour*). **2** *hist.* relating to films given an X classification (see X[2]).

X-ray (also **x-ray**) ● *n.* **1** (in *pl.*) electromagnetic radiation of very short wavelength, able to pass through objects opaque to light. ▷ ELECTROMAGNETIC RADIATION. **2** ▼ an image made by the effect of X-rays on a photographic plate. ● *v.tr.* photograph, examine, or treat with X-rays. [from translation of German *x-Strahlen* 'x-rays', so called because when discovered (1895) the nature of the rays was unknown]

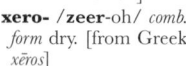

XENOLITH:
LAVA SURROUNDED
BY PINK GRANITE

granite

lava

X-ray tube *n.* a device for generating X-rays by accelerating electrons to high energies and causing them to strike a metal target from which the X-rays are emitted.

xylem /**zy**-lĕm/ *n. Bot.* woody tissue. ▷ STEM. [from Greek *xulon* 'wood']

xylene /**zy**-leen/ *n. Chem.* each of three isomeric liquid hydrocarbons obtained by distilling wood, coal tar, etc.

xylo- /**zy**-loh/ *comb. form* wood. [from Greek *xulon*]

xylophone /**zy**-lŏ-fohn/ *n.* ▼ a musical instrument of wooden or metal bars graduated in length and struck with a small wooden hammer or hammers. ▷ ORCHESTRA, PERCUSSION. □ **xylophonist** *n.*

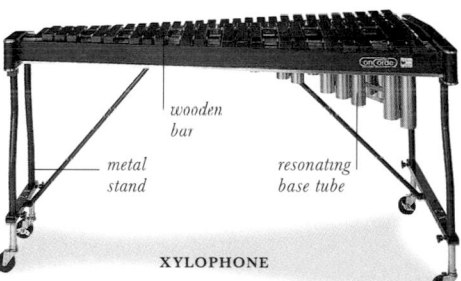

wooden bar

metal stand

resonating base tube

XYLOPHONE

XEROPHYTE

Xerophytes exhibit a range of adaptations that enable them to survive in arid environments. Succulents, such as stonecrops and cacti, store water in their leaves or stems. In cacti, the leaves are much reduced or absent altogether, and the stem is armed with spines to deter browsing animals. Other xerophytes, such as snake plants and yuccas, often have sharp-tipped leaves, and are also protected by an extremely tough leaf surface, or cuticle. As well as deterring animals, this helps to reduce water loss.

EXAMPLES OF XEROPHYTES

STONECROP
(*Sedum obtusatum*)

CLARET-CUP CACTUS
(*Echinocereus triglochidiatus*)

AGAVE
(*Agave pumila*)

X-RAY

X-rays come near the high-energy end of the electromagnetic spectrum. In an X-ray tube, electrons emitted by an electrically heated filament are accelerated towards a heavy metal target by an intense electric field. Because there is no air in the tube, the electrons reach high speeds; when they are rapidly decelerated by hitting the target, their kinetic energy turns into high-frequency electromagnetic radiation (X-rays). Used mostly in medical imaging, X-rays pass through muscle but are absorbed by bone, so that an image recorded on photographic film reveals the bones as shadows.

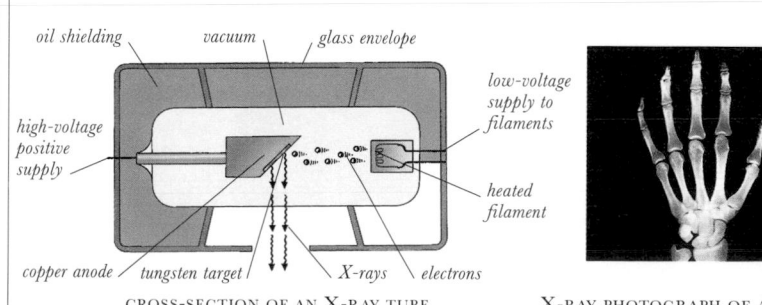

oil shielding

vacuum

glass envelope

high-voltage positive supply

low-voltage supply to filaments

heated filament

copper anode

tungsten target

X-rays

electrons

CROSS-SECTION OF AN X-RAY TUBE

X-RAY PHOTOGRAPH OF A HAND

X

Y[1] *n.* (also **y**) (*pl.* **Ys** or **Y's**) **1** the twenty-fifth letter of the alphabet. **2** (usu. *y*) *Algebra* the second unknown quantity. **3** (usu. *y*) *Geom.* the second coordinate.

Y[2] *symb. Chem.* the element yttrium.

y. *abbr.* year(s).

-y[1] *suffix* forming adjectives: **1** from nouns and adjectives, meaning: full of; having the quality of (*messy*; *icy*; *horsy*). **2** from verbs, meaning 'inclined to', 'apt to' (*runny*; *sticky*).

-y[2] *suffix* (also **-ey**, **-ie**) forming diminutive nouns, pet names, etc. (*granny*; *nightie*; *Mickey*).

-y[3] *suffix* forming nouns denoting: **1** state, condition, or quality (*courtesy*; *orthodoxy*; *modesty*). **2** an action or its result (*colloquy*; *remedy*; *subsidy*).

yacht /yot/ ● *n.* **1** ▼ a light sailing vessel, esp. equipped for racing. **2** a larger usu. power-driven vessel equipped for cruising. ▷ BOAT. **3** a light vessel for travel on sand or ice. ● *v.intr.* race or cruise in a yacht. [from early modern Dutch *jaghte*] □ **yachting** *n.*

yacht club *n.* a sailing club, esp. for yacht racing.

YACHT

By adjusting the position of their sails, yachts can travel in almost any direction, except directly into the wind. Most modern sailing yachts have triangular fore- and aft sails, arranged in a 'Bermuda rig'. Many have an auxiliary engine and can increase speed by setting a spinnaker.

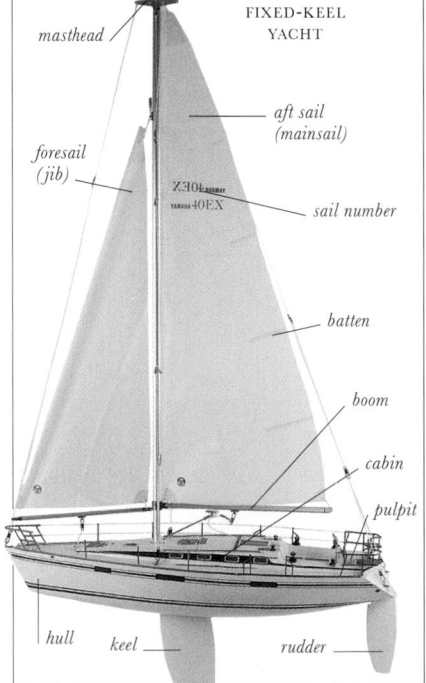

FIXED-KEEL YACHT

masthead

aft sail (mainsail)

foresail (jib)

sail number

batten

boom

cabin

pulpit

hull   keel   rudder

yachtsman *n.* (*pl.* **-men**; *fem.* **yachtswoman**, *pl.* **-women**) a person who sails yachts.

yack var. of YAK[2].

yackety-yack var. of YAK[2].

yah *int.* = YES. [representing affected pronunciation]

yahoo *n.* a coarse person; a lout, a hooligan. [name of an imaginary race of brutish creatures in Swift's *Gulliver's Travels* (1726)]

Yahweh *n.* (also **Yahveh**) the Hebrew name of God in the Old Testament. [Hebrew *YHVH* with added vowels (see JEHOVAH)]

yak[1] *n.* ▼ a long-haired humped Tibetan ox, *Bos grunniens*. [from Tibetan *gyag*]

YAK: WILD YAK (*Bos grunniens*)

yak[2] (also **yack**, **yackety-yack**) *colloq.* often *derog.* ● *n.* trivial or unduly persistent conversation. ● *v.intr.* (**yakked**, **yakking**) (often foll. by *away*, *about*) engage in such conversation; chatter.

yakitori *n.* a Japanese dish of skewered grilled chicken pieces. [Japanese, from *Yaki*, 'grilling, toasting' + *tori* 'bird']

Yale lock *n. propr.* ▲ a type of lock for doors etc. with a cylindrical barrel turned by a flat key with a serrated edge. [named after L. *Yale*, American locksmith, 1821–68, its inventor]

yam *n.* **1 a** any tropical or subtropical climbing plant of the genus *Dioscorea*. **b** ▶ the edible starchy tuber of this. **2** *N. Amer.* a sweet potato. [from Spanish *iñame*]

yammer *colloq.* or *dial.* ● *n.* **1** a lament, wail, or grumble. **2** voluble talk. ● *v.intr.* **1** utter a yammer. **2** talk volubly. [Middle English]

yang *n.* (in Chinese philosophy) the active male principle of the universe.

▷ YIN. [Chinese, literally 'Sun, positive, male genitals']

Yank *n. Brit. colloq.* often *derog.* an American. [abbreviation of YANKEE]

yank *colloq.* ● *v.tr.* pull with a jerk. ● *n.* a sudden hard pull. [19th-century coinage]

Yankee *n. colloq.* **1** often *derog.* = YANK. **2** *US* an inhabitant of New England or one of the northern states. **3** *hist.* ◀ a Federal soldier in the Civil War. **4** a type of bet on four or more horses to

forage cap

sword strap

sergeant's chevrons

waist belt

frock coat

trouser stripe

sword

worsted sash

YANKEE: SERGEANT, 157TH NEW YORK VOLUNTEERS

YALE LOCK

In a Yale lock, pairs of pins block the gap between the cylinder and lock body. Inserting a key raises the pins, and causes the gap between them to line up with the edge of the cylinder and lock body. Turning the key rotates the cylinder and the cam, pulling back the bolt to open the door.

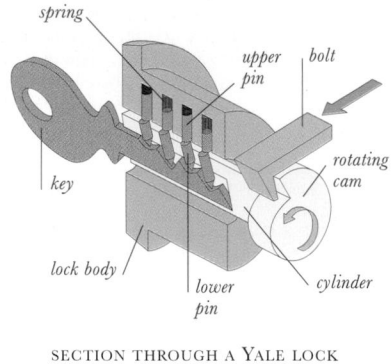

spring

upper pin

bolt

key

rotating cam

lock body

lower pin

cylinder

SECTION THROUGH A YALE LOCK

win (or be placed) in different races. **5** (*attrib.*) of or as of the Yankees. [18th-century coinage]

Yankee Doodle *n.* **1** an American tune and song regarded as a national air. **2** = YANKEE 1, 2, 3.

yap ● *v.intr.* (**yapped**, **yapping**) **1** bark shrilly or fussily. **2** *colloq.* talk noisily, foolishly, or complainingly. ● *n.* a sound of yapping. □ **yappy** *adj.* (**yappier**, **yappiest**).

yapok *n.* a semi-aquatic tropical American opossum, *Chironectes minimus*, with dark-banded grey fur. Also called *water opossum*. [*Oyapok*, *Oiapoque*, the name of a N. Brazilian river]

yard[1] *n.* **1** a unit of linear measure equal to 3 feet (0.9144 metre). **2** a square or cubic yard esp. (in building) of sand etc. **3** a cylindrical spar tapering to each end slung across a mast for a sail to hang from. ▷ RIGGING. **4** (in *pl.*; foll. by *of*) *colloq.* a great length (*yards of spare wallpaper*). □ **by the yard** at great length. [Old English]

yard[2] *n.* **1** esp. *Brit.* a piece of enclosed ground esp. attached to a building or used for a particular purpose. **2** *N. Amer.* the garden of a house. □ **the Yard** *Brit. colloq.* = SCOTLAND YARD. [Old English *geard* 'enclosure, region']

yardage *n.* a number of yards of material etc.

yardarm *n.* the outer extremity of a ship's yard.

yardbird *n. US slang* **1** a new military recruit. **2** a convict.

yard of ale *n. Brit.* **1** a deep slender beer glass, about a yard long and holding two to three pints. **2** the contents of this.

yardstick *n.* **1** a standard used for comparison. **2** a measuring rod a yard long, usu. divided into inches etc.

yarmulke /yar-muul-kě/ *n.* (also **yarmulka**) ▶ a skullcap worn by Jewish men. [Yiddish]

yarn ● *n.* **1** spun thread, esp. for knitting, weaving, rope-making, etc. **2** *colloq.* a long or rambling story or discourse. ● *v.intr. colloq.* tell yarns. [Old English]

YAM: WING-STALKED YAM (*Dioscorea alata*)

Hebrew characters

YARMULKE

YARROW
(*Achillea millefolium*)

yarrow *n.* ◀ any perennial herbaceous plant of the genus *Achillea* (daisy family), esp. milfoil. [Old English]

yashmak *n.* a veil concealing the face except the eyes, worn by some Muslim women when in public. [from Arabic *yašmak*]

yaw ● *v.intr.* (of a ship or aircraft etc.) fail to hold a straight course; go unsteadily, esp. turning from side to side. ● *n.* the yawing of a ship etc. from its course. [16th-century coinage]

yawl *n.* **1** a two-masted fore-and-aft sailing boat with the mizzen-mast stepped far aft. **2** a small kind of fishing boat. [from Dutch *jol*]

yawn ● *v.* **1** *intr.* (as a reflex) open the mouth wide and inhale esp. when sleepy or bored. **2** *intr.* (of a chasm etc.) gape, be wide open. **3** *tr.* utter with a yawn. ● *n.* **1** an act of yawning. **2** *colloq.* a boring or tedious idea, activity, etc. [Old English] □ **yawningly** *adv.*

yaws *n.pl.* (usu. treated as *sing.*) a contagious tropical skin disease with large red swellings, caused by spirochaete bacteria. [17th-century coinage]

Yb *symb. Chem.* the element ytterbium.

Y chromosome *n.* a sex chromosome occurring only in male cells, in humans and other mammals. [Y: arbitrary label]

yd *abbr.* yard (measure).

yds *abbr.* yards (measure).

ye[1] *pron. archaic pl.* of THOU[1].

ye[2] *det. pseudo-archaic* = THE (*ye olde tea-shoppe*). [variant spelling, from a transcription of the runic letter *thorn* (=th)]

yea /yay/ *archaic* or *formal* ● *adv.* **1** yes. **2** indeed, nay (*ready, yea eager*). ● *n.* the word 'yea'. [Old English]

yeah /yaiı/ *adv. colloq.* yes.

year *n.* **1** (also **equinoctial year**, **solar year**, **tropical year**) the time taken by the Earth to revolve once round the Sun, 365 days, 5 hours, 48 minutes, and 46 seconds in length. **2** (also **calendar year**, **civil year**) the period of 365 days (**common year**) or 366 days (see LEAP YEAR) from 1 Jan. to 31 Dec., used for reckoning time in ordinary affairs. **3 a** a period of the same length as this starting at any point (*four years ago*). **b** such a period in terms of a particular activity etc. occupying its duration (*school year; tax year*). **4** (in *pl.*) age or time of life (*young for his years*). **5** (usu. in *pl.*) *colloq.* a very long time (*it took years to get served*). **6** a group of students entering college etc. in the same academic year. □ **in the year of Our Lord** (foll. by the year) in a specified year AD. **the year dot** see DOT. **year in, year out** continually over a period of years. [Old English]

yearbook *n.* an annual publication dealing with events or aspects of the (usu. preceding) year.

yearling ● *n.* **1** an animal between one and two years old. **2** a racehorse in the calendar year after the year of foaling. ● *adj.* a year old; having existed or been such for a year (*a yearling heifer*).

year-long *adj.* lasting a year or the whole year.

yearly ● *adj.* done, produced, or occurring once a year. ● *adv.* once a year; from year to year.

yearn *v.intr.* **1** (usu. foll. by *for, after,* or *to* + infin.) have a strong emotional longing. **2** (usu. foll. by *to, towards*) be filled with compassion or tenderness. [Old English] □ **yearning** *n.* & *adj.* **yearningly** *adv.*

year-round *adj.* existing etc. throughout the year.

years of discretion see DISCRETION.

yeas and nays *n.pl.* affirmative and negative votes.

yeast *n.* **1** ▼ a greyish-yellow fungous substance obtained esp. from fermenting malt liquors and used as a fermenting agent, to raise bread, etc. **2** any of various unicellular fungi in which vegetative reproduction takes place by budding or fission. [Old English] □ **yeastlike** *adj.*

fresh yeast   *dried yeast*

YEAST

yeasty *adj.* (**yeastier**, **yeastiest**) **1** frothy or tasting like yeast. **2** in a ferment. **3** working like yeast.

yell ● *n.* **1** a loud sharp cry of pain, anger, fright, encouragement, delight, etc. **2** a shout. **3** *US* an organized shout, used esp. to support a sports team. ● *v.intr.* & *tr.* make or utter with a yell. [Old English]

yellow ● *adj.* **1** of the colour, between green and orange in the spectrum, of buttercups, lemons, egg yolks, or gold. **2** of the duller colour of faded leaves, ripe wheat, old paper, etc. **3** having a yellow skin or complexion. **4** *colloq.* cowardly. ● *n.* **1** a yellow colour or pigment. **2** yellow clothes or material (*dressed in yellow*). **3 a** a yellow ball, piece, etc., in a game or sport. **b** the player using such pieces. **4** (usu. in *comb.*) a yellow moth or butterfly. ● *v.tr.* & *intr.* make or become yellow. [Old English] □ **yellowish** *adj.* **yellowness** *n.* **yellowy** *adj.*

yellow-belly *n.* **1** *colloq.* a coward. **2** any of various animals with yellow underparts. □ **yellow-bellied** *adj.*

yellow bile *n. hist.* one of the four bodily humours, characterized as hot and dry, and associated with a peevish or irascible temperament (cf. HUMOUR *n.* 4).

yellow card *n. Football* a card shown by the referee to a player being cautioned.

yellow fever *n.* a tropical virus disease with fever and jaundice, transmitted by the mosquito and often fatal.

yellowhammer *n.* ▶ a bunting, *Emberiza citrinella*, of which the male has a yellow head, neck, and breast. [16th-century coinage]

yellow line *n.* (in the UK) a line painted along the side of the road in yellow to denote parking restrictions.

Yellow Pages *n.pl. propr.* a telephone directory on yellow paper and listing business subscribers.

yelp ● *n.* a sharp shrill cry of or as of a dog in pain or excitement. ● *v.intr.* utter a yelp. [Old English *gielp(an)* 'to boast']

YELLOWHAMMER
(*Emberiza citrinella*)

Yemeni /yem-ĕ-ni/ ● *n.* a native or inhabitant of Yemen, a country in southern Arabia. ● *adj.* of or relating to Yemen or its people. [from Arabic *yamanī*]

yen[1] *n.* (*pl.* same) the chief monetary unit of Japan. [from Japanese *en* 'round']

yen[2] *colloq.* ● *n.* a longing or yearning. ● *v.intr.* (**yenned**, **yenning**) feel a longing. [from Chinese *yán*]

yeoman /yoh-măn/ *n.* (*pl.* **-men**) **1** esp. *hist.* a man holding and cultivating a small landed estate. **2** *hist.* a person qualified by possessing free land of an annual value of 40 shillings to serve on juries. **3** *Brit.* a member of the yeomanry force. **4** *hist.* a servant in a royal or noble household. **5** (in full **yeoman of signals**) a petty officer in the Navy, concerned with visual signalling. **6** *US* a petty off-

icer performing clerical duties on board ship. [Middle English]

Yeoman of the Guard *n.* (*pl.* **Yeomen of the Guard**) **1** a member of the British sovereign's bodyguard. **2** (loosely) a Yeoman Warder.

yeomanry *n.* (*pl.* **-ies**) a body of yeomen.

Yeoman Warder *n.* (*pl.* **Yeoman Warders**) a warder at the Tower of London, a 'beefeater'.

yep *int.* & *n.* (also **yup**) *US colloq.* = YES.

yes ● *int.* **1** equivalent to an affirmative sentence: the answer to your question is affirmative, it is as you say or as I have said, the statement etc. made is correct, the request or command will be complied with, the negative statement etc. made is not correct. **2** (in answer to a summons or address) an acknowledgement of one's presence. ● *n.* **1** an utterance of the word *yes*. **2** an affirmation or assent. **3** a vote in favour of a proposition. □ **yes?** **1** indeed? is that so? **2** what do you want? **yes and no** that is partly true and partly untrue. [Old English]

yes-man *n.* (*pl.* **-men**) *colloq.* a weakly acquiescent person, an obsequious subordinate.

yester- *comb. form poet.* or *archaic* of yesterday; that is the last past (*yestereve*). [Old English]

yesterday ● *adv.* **1** on the day before today. **2** in the recent past. **3** *colloq.* extremely urgently; immediately (*they want delivery yesterday!*). ● *n.* **1** the day before today. **2** the recent past. □ **yesterday morning** (or **afternoon** etc.) in the morning (or afternoon etc.) of yesterday. [Old English]

yesteryear *n. literary* **1** last year. **2** the recent past.

yet ● *adv.* **1** as late as now (or then), until now (or then) (*there is yet time; your best work yet*). **2** (with *neg.* or *interrog.*) so soon as now (or then), by now (or then) (*it is not time yet; have you finished yet?*). **3** again; in addition (*more and yet more*). **4** in the remaining time available; before all is over (*I will do it yet*). **5** (foll. by *compar.*) even (*a yet more difficult task*). **6** nevertheless; and in spite of that; but for all that (*it is strange, and yet it is true*). ● *conj.* but at the same time; but nevertheless (*I won, yet what good has it done?*). □ **nor yet** and also not (*won't listen to me nor yet to you*). [Old English]

yeti *n.* = ABOMINABLE SNOWMAN. [Tibetan]

yew *n.* (also **yew tree**) ▶ any dark-leaved evergreen coniferous tree of the genus *Taxus*, bearing berry-like cones. **2** its wood. [Old English]

Y-fronts *n.pl. Brit. propr.* men's or boys' briefs with a Y-shaped seam at the front.

Yggdrasil /ig-dră-sil/ *n.* (in Scandinavian mythology) an ash tree whose roots and branches join heaven, earth, and hell. [from Old Norse *Yggr* 'Odin' + *drasill* 'horse']

YHA *abbr.* (in the UK) Youth Hostels Association.

Yid *n. slang offens.* a Jew.

Yiddish ● *n.* a vernacular used by Jews in or from central and eastern Europe, originally a German dialect with words from Hebrew and several modern languages. ● *adj.* of or relating to this language. [from German *jüdisch* 'Jewish']

yield ● *v.* **1** *tr.* (also *absol.*) produce or return as a fruit, profit, or result (*the land yields crops; the land yields poorly; the investment yields 15%*). **2** *tr.* give up; surrender, concede; comply with a demand for (*yielded the fortress; yielded themselves prisoners*). **3** *intr.* (often foll. by *to*) **a** surrender; make submission. **b** give consent or change one's course of action in deference to; respond as required to (*yielded to persuasion*). **4** *intr.* (foll. by *to*) be inferior or confess

aril (fruit)

YEW:
COMMON YEW
(*Taxus baccata*)

Y

YIN

In Chinese philosophy, yin represents one half of the duality in the universe. Yin is the feminine force, associated with the heavens and the Moon. Yin is complemented by yang, the male force, associated with the Earth and the Sun. The symbol for yin and yang is divided into the dark (yin) and light (yang). The dots in each field represent the potential for change within either force.

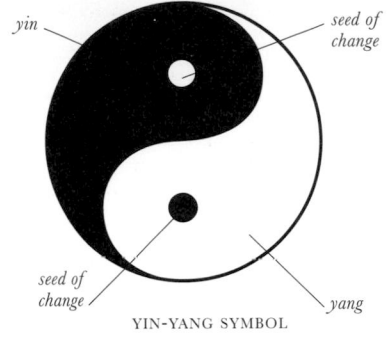

yin   seed of change

seed of change   yang

YIN-YANG SYMBOL

inferiority to (*I yield to none in understanding the problem*). **5** *intr.* (foll. by *to*) give right of way to other traffic. **6** *intr.* US allow another the right to speak in a debate etc. ● *n.* an amount yielded or produced; an output or return. [Old English *g(i)eldan* 'to pay'] □ **yielder** *n.*

yielding *adj.* **1** compliant, submissive. **2** (of a substance) able to bend; soft and pliable, not stiff or rigid.

yield point *n. Physics* the stress beyond which a material becomes plastic.

yin *n.* ▲ (in Chinese philosophy) the passive female principle of the universe (cf. YANG). [Chinese, literally 'shade, feminine, the Moon']

yippee *int.* expressing delight or excitement.

yips *n.pl.* (usu. prec. by *the*) *colloq.* extreme nervousness, esp. causing a golfer to miss an easy putt. [20th-century coinage]

ylang-ylang /ee-lang-**ee**-lang/ *n.* (also **ilang-ilang**) **1** ◄ a Malayan tree, *Cananga odorata*, from the fragrant yellow flowers of which a perfume is distilled. **2** the perfume itself. [from Tagalog (a language of the Philippines) *álang-ilang*]

YLANG-YLANG
(*Cananga odorata*)

YMCA *abbr.* Young Men's Christian Association.

yob *n. Brit. colloq.* a lout or hooligan. [back slang for BOY] □ **yobbish** *adj.* **yobbishness** *n.*

yobbo *n.* (*pl.* **-os** or **-oes**) *Brit. colloq.* = YOB.

yod *n.* **1** the tenth and smallest letter of the Hebrew alphabet. **2** its semivowel sound. [from Hebrew *yōd*]

yodel ● *v.tr. & intr.* (**yodelled**, **yodelling**; US **yodeled**, **yodeling**) sing with melodious inarticulate sounds and frequent changes between falsetto and the normal voice in the manner of the Swiss mountain-dwellers. ● *n.* a yodelling cry. [from German *jodeln*] □ **yodeller** *n.*

Y

yoga *n.* **1** a Hindu system of philosophic meditation and asceticism designed to effect reunion with the universal spirit. **2** ► a system of physical exercises and breathing control used in yoga. [Sanskrit, literally 'union'] □ **yogic** *adj.*

yogi *n.* (*pl.* **yogis**) a person proficient in yoga. [Hindi, from YOGA] □ **yogism** *n.*

yogurt *n.* (also **yoghurt**) a semi-solid sourish food prepared from milk fermented by added bacteria. [from Turkish *yoğurt*]

yoke ● *n.* **1** ▼ a wooden crosspiece fastened over the necks of two oxen etc. and attached to the plough or wagon to be drawn. **2** (*pl.* same or **yokes**) a pair (of oxen etc.). **3** an object like a yoke in form or function, e.g. a wooden shoulder-piece for carrying a pair of pails, the top section of a dress or skirt etc. from which the rest hangs. **4** sway, dominion, or servitude, esp. when oppressive. ● *v.tr* **1** put a yoke on. **2** couple or unite (a pair). **3** (foll. by *to*) link (one thing) to (another). [Old English]

yokel *n.* a rustic; a country bumpkin.

yolk *n.* **1** the yellow inner part of an egg, rich in fat and protein, that nourishes the young before it hatches. ▷ EGG. **2** *Biol.* the corresponding part of any animal ovum. [Old English, from *geolu* 'yellow'] □ **yolked** *adj.* (also in *comb.*).

yolkless *adj.* **yolky** *adj.*

Yom Kippur *n.* = DAY OF ATONEMENT. [Hebrew]

yomp *v.intr. Brit. slang* march with heavy equipment over difficult terrain. [20th-century coinage]

yon *literary & dial.* ● *adv.* yonder. ● *pron.* yonder person or thing. [Old English]

yonder ● *adv.* over there; at some distance in that direction; in the place indicated by pointing etc. ● *det.* situated yonder. [Middle English]

yonks *n.pl. Brit. slang* a long time (*haven't seen them for yonks*). [20th-century coinage]

yoo-hoo *int.* used to attract a person's attention.

Yorkshireman *n.* (*pl.* **-men**; *fem.* **Yorkshirewoman**, *pl.* **-women**) a native of Yorkshire in northern England.

Yorkshire pudding *n.* ◄ a baked batter pudding usu. eaten with roast beef. [from *Yorkshire* in northern England]

Yorkshire terrier *n.* ► a small long-haired blue-grey and tan kind of terrier.

YORKSHIRE PUDDINGS

Yoruba *n.* (*pl.* same) **1** a member of a black African people inhabiting the west coast, esp. Nigeria. **2** the language of this people. [native name]

you *pron.* (*obj.* **you**; *poss.* **your**, **yours**) **1** used with reference to the person or persons addressed or one such person and one or more associated persons. **2** (as *int.* with a noun) in an exclamatory statement (*you fools!*). **3** (in general statements) one, a person, anyone, or everyone (*it's bad at first, but you get used to it*). [Old English]

you and yours *pron.* you together with your family, property, etc.

you'd *contr.* **1** you had. **2** you would.

you-know-what *n.* (also **you-know-who**) a thing or person unspecified but understood.

you'll *contr.* you will; you shall.

young ● *adj.* (**younger**, **youngest**) **1** not far advanced in life, development, or existence; not yet old. **2 a** immature or inexperienced. **b** youthful. **3** felt in or characteristic of youth (*young love*; *young ambition*). **4** representing young people (*Young Conservatives*; *Young England*). **5** (**younger**) distinguishing one person from another of the same name (*the younger Pitt*). ● *n.* (*collect.*) offspring, esp. of animals before or soon after birth. [Old English] □ **youngish** *adj.*

young blood see BLOOD.

young hopeful see HOPEFUL *n.*

young lady *n.* **1** a young (esp. unmarried) woman; a girl. **2** *colloq.* a girlfriend or sweetheart.

young man *n.* **1** a man who is young; a boy. **2** *colloq.* a boyfriend or sweetheart.

young offender *n.* a young criminal, esp.: **1** *Brit. Law* a young criminal between 14 and 17 years of age. **2** *Canad. Law* a young criminal between 12 and 18 years of age.

young person *n. Law* (in the UK) a person generally between 14 and 17 years of age.

youngster *n.* a child or young person.

young thing *n. colloq.* a young person (*bright young things working in the City*).

young 'un *n. colloq.* a youngster.

young woman *n.* **1** a woman who is young. **2** *colloq.* a girlfriend or sweetheart.

your *poss.det.* **1** of or belonging to you (*your house*; *your own business*). **2** *colloq. usu. derog.* much talked of; well known (*none so fallible as your self-styled expert*). [Old English]

you're *contr.* you are.

yours *poss.pron.* **1** the one or ones belonging to or associated with you (*it is yours*; *yours are over there*). **2** your letter (*yours of the 10th*). **3** introducing a formula ending a letter (*yours ever, yours sincerely; yours truly*). □ **of yours** of or belonging to you (*a friend of yours*).

yourself *pron.* (*pl.* **yourselves**) **1 a** *emphat. form* of YOU. **b** *refl. form* of YOU. **2** in your normal state of body or mind (*are quite yourself again*). □ **be yourself** act in your normal, unconstrained manner.

youse /yooz/ *pron.* (also **yous**) *dial.* you (usu. more than one person).

youth *n.* (*pl.* **youths**) **1** the state of being young; the period between childhood and adult age. **2** the vigour or enthusiasm, inexperience, or other characteristic of this period. **3** an early stage of development etc. **4** a young person (esp. male). **5** (*pl.*) young people collectively (*the youth of the country*). [Old English]

youth club *n.* (also **youth centre**) a place or organization provided for young people's leisure activities.

youthful *adj.* **1** young, esp. in appearance or manner. **2** having the characteristics of youth (*youthful impatience*). **3** having the freshness or vigour of youth (*a youthful complexion*). □ **youthfully** *adv.* **youthfulness** *n.*

youth hostel *n.* a place where (esp. young) holidaymakers can put up cheaply for the night. □ **youth hosteller** *n.*

YOGA: THE BOW POSE

YOKE: CURVED OX YOKE

crosspiece

chain ring

oxbow

YORKSHIRE TERRIER

you've *contr.* you have.

yowl ● *n.* a loud wailing cry of or as of a cat or dog in pain or distress. ● *v.intr.* utter a yowl.

yo-yo ● *n.* (*pl.* **yo-yos**) *propr.* **1** ▼ a toy consisting of a pair of joined discs with a deep groove between them in which string is attached and wound, and which can be spun alternately downward and upward by its weight and momentum as the string unwinds and rewinds. **2** a thing that repeatedly falls and rises again. ● *v.intr.* (**yo-yoes**, **yo-yoed**) **1** play with a yo-yo. **2** move up and down; fluctuate. [20th-century coinage]

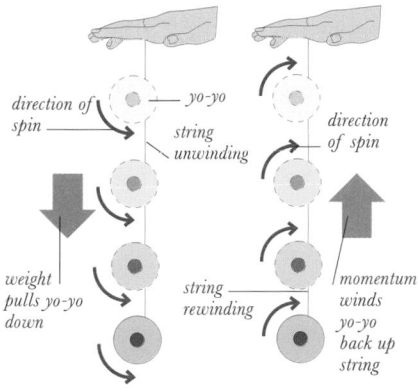

YO-YO: DEMONSTRATION OF A YO-YO'S ACTION

yr. *abbr.* **1** year(s). **2** younger. **3** your.

yrs. *abbr.* **1** years. **2** yours.

YTS *abbr.* Youth Training Scheme.

ytterbium /i-**ter**-bi-ŭm/ *n. Chem.* a silvery metallic element of the lanthanide series occurring naturally as various isotopes. [named after *Ytterby* in Sweden]

yttrium /**it**-ri-ŭm/ *n. Chem.* a greyish metallic element resembling the lanthanides, occurring naturally in uranium ores and used in making superconductors. [formed as YTTERBIUM]

yucca *n.* ▶ any plant of the genus *Yucca* (lily family), with swordlike leaves. [Carib]

yuck (also **yuk**) *slang* ● *int.* an expression of strong distaste or disgust. ● *n.* something messy or repellent.

yucky *adj.* (also **yukky**) (**-ier**, **-iest**) *slang* **1** messy, repellent. **2** sickly, sentimental.

Yugoslav (also **Jugoslav**) ● *n.* **1** a native or national of the former Yugoslavia in SE Europe. **2** a person of Yugoslav descent. ● *adj.* of or relating to Yugoslavia or its people. [based on Serbo-Croat *jug* 'south'] □ **Yugoslavian** *adj. & n.*

yuk var. of YUCK.

yukky var. of YUCKY.

Yule *n.* (in full **Yuletide**) *archaic* the Christmas festi-

YUCCA
(*Yucca elephantipes* 'Variegata')

val. [Old English, originally applied to a heathen festival]

yule log *n.* **1** a large log burnt on Christmas Eve. **2** a log-shaped chocolate cake eaten at Christmas.

yummy *adj.* (**yummier**, **yummiest**) *colloq.* tasty, delicious.

yum-yum *int.* expressing pleasure from eating or the prospect of eating.

yup var. of YEP.

yuppie *n.* (also **yuppy**) (*pl.* **-ies**) *colloq.*, usu. *derog.* a young middle-class professional person working in a city. [from *young urban professional*] □ **yuppiedom** *n.*

yuppify *v.tr.* (**-ies**, **-ied**) (esp. as **yuppified** *adj.*) *colloq.* make typical of or suitable for yuppies. □ **yuppification** *n.*

yurt *n.* **1** ▼ a circular tent of felt, skins, etc., on a collapsible framework, used by nomads in Mongolia and Siberia. **2** a semi-subterranean hut, usu. of timber covered with earth or turf. [from Turkish *jurt*]

YWCA *abbr.* Young Women's Christian Association.

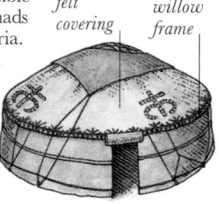

YURT

Y

Z *n.* (also **z**) (*pl.* **Zs** or **Z's**) **1** the twenty-sixth letter of the alphabet. **2** (usu. **z**) *Algebra* the third unknown quantity. **3** (usu. **z**) *Geom.* the third coordinate.

zabaglione /za-băl-**yoh**-ni/ *n.* an Italian sweet of whipped and heated egg yolks, sugar, and wine. [Italian]

zag ● *n.* a sharp change of direction in a zigzag course. ● *v.intr.* (**zagged**, **zagging**) perform a zag.

zander *n.* (*pl.* usu. same) a large pikeperch, *Stizostedion lucioperca*, native to central and N. Europe and introduced in W. Europe. [German]

ZANU /**zah**-noo/ *abbr.* Zimbabwe African National Union.

zany ● *adj.* (**zanier**, **zaniest**) comically idiotic; crazily ridiculous. ● *n.* a buffoon or jester. [based on the Venetian form of *Gianni, Giovanni* 'John', stock name of servants acting as clowns in the *commedia dell'arte*] □ **zanily** *adv.* **zaniness** *n.*

zap *slang* ● *v.* (**zapped**, **zapping**) **1** *tr.* **a** kill or destroy; deal a sudden blow to. **b** hit forcibly (*zapped the ball over the net*). **2** *intr. & tr.* move quickly and vigorously. **3** *tr.* overwhelm emotionally. **4** *tr. Computing* erase or change (an item in a program). **5** *intr.* (foll.

by *through*) fast-forward a videotape to skip a section. ● *n.* **1** energy, vigour. **2** a strong emotional effect. ● *int.* expressing the sound or impact of a bullet, ray gun, etc., or any sudden event.

zappy *adj.* (**zappier**, **zappiest**) *colloq.* **1** lively, energetic. **2** striking.

ZAPU /**zah**-poo/ *abbr.* Zimbabwe African People's Union.

Zarathustrian var. of ZOROASTRIAN.

zarzuela /thar-**thway**-lă/ *n.* **1** a Spanish traditional form of operetta. **2** a Spanish dish of various kinds of seafood cooked in a rich sauce. [Spanish]

zeal *n.* earnestness or fervour in advancing a cause or rendering service.[from Greek *zēlos*]

zealot /**zel**-ŏt/ *n.* **1** an uncompromising or extreme partisan; a fanatic. **2** (**Zealot**) *hist.* a member of an ancient Jewish sect aiming at a world Jewish theocracy and resisting the Romans until AD 70. [from Greek *zēlōtēs*] □ **zealotry** *n.*

zealous /**zel**-ŭs/ *adj.* full of zeal; enthusiastic. □ **zealously** *adv.* **zealousness** *n.*

zebra *n.* (*pl.* same or **zebras**) **1** any of various African quadrupeds, esp. *Equus burchelli*, related to the ass and horse, with black and white stripes. ▷ UNGULATE. **2** (*attrib.*) with alternate dark and pale stripes. [Italian, Spanish, & Portuguese, earlier in sense 'wild ass']

zebra crossing *n. Brit.* a striped street-crossing where pedestrians have precedence over vehicles.

zebu *n.* ▶ a humped ox, *Bos indicus*, of India, E. Asia, and Africa. [from French *zébu*]

zed *n. Brit.* the letter Z. [from Greek *zeta*]

zee *n. US* the letter Z. [17th-century coinage]

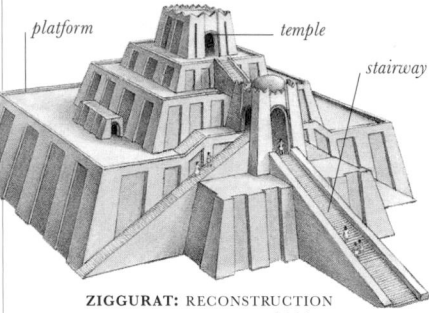

ZEBU
(*Bos indicus*)

Zeitgeist /**tsyt**-gyst/ *n.* **1** the spirit of the times. **2** the trend of thought and feeling in a period. [German, from *Zeit* 'time' + *Geist* 'spirit']

Zen *n.* a Japanese school of Buddhism emphasizing the value of meditation and intuition. [Japanese, literally 'meditation'] □ **Zenist** *n.* (also **Zennist**).

zenith *n.* **1** the part of the celestial sphere directly above an observer (opp. NADIR). **2** the highest point in one's fortunes; a time of great prosperity etc. [from Arabic *samt (ar-ra's)* 'path (over the head)']

zeolite *n.* each of a number of minerals consisting mainly of hydrous silicates of calcium, sodium, and aluminium, able to act as cation exchangers. [based on Greek *zein* 'to boil', from their characteristic swelling and fusing under a blowpipe] □ **zeolitic** *adj.*

zephyr /**zef**-er/ *n. literary* a mild gentle wind or breeze. [from Greek *zephuros* '(god of the) west wind']

Zeppelin *n. hist.* ▼ a large German dirigible airship of the early 20th c., originally for military use. [named after Count F. von *Zeppelin*, German airman, 1838–1917, its first constructor]

ZEPPELIN:
RIGID-FRAMED ZEPPELIN

fabric envelope
stabilizing fin
nose
crew car
registration number
passenger car

zero ● *n.* (*pl.* **-os**) **1 a** the figure 0; nought. **b** no quantity or number; nil. **2** a point on the scale of an instrument from which a positive or negative quantity is reckoned. **3** (*attrib.*) having a value of zero; no, not any (*zero population growth*). **4** (in full **zero hour**) **a** the hour at which a planned, esp. military, operation is timed to begin. **b** a crucial moment. **5** the lowest point; a nullity or nonentity. ● *v.tr.* (**-oes**, **-oed**) **1** adjust (an instrument etc.) to zero point. **2** set the sights of (a gun) for firing. □ **zero in on 1** take aim at. **2** focus one's attention on. [from Arabic *ṣifr* 'cipher']

zero option *n.* a disarmament proposal for the total removal of certain types of weapons on both sides.

zero-rate *v.tr.* (esp. as **zero-rated** *adj.*) *Brit.* rate as not liable to a levy of value added tax.

zero tolerance *n.* non-acceptance of antisocial behaviour, especially by strict and uncompromising application of the law.

zest *n.* **1** piquancy; a stimulating flavour or quality. **2 a** keen enjoyment or interest. **b** (often foll. by *for*) relish. **c** gusto (*entered into it with zest*). **3** fine shreds of the outer coloured part of the peel of citrus

fruit used as flavouring. [from French *zeste* 'orange or lemon peel'] □ **zestful** *adj.* **zestfully** *adv.* **zestfulness** *n.* **zesty** *adj.* (**zestier**, **zestiest**).

zeta /**zee**-tă/ *n.* the sixth letter of the Greek alphabet (Z, ζ). [Greek]

zeugma /**zewg**-mă/ *n.* a figure of speech using a verb or adjective with two nouns, to one of which it is strictly applicable while the word appropriate to the other is not used (e.g. *with weeping eyes and* [sc. *grieving*] *hearts*) (cf. SYLLEPSIS). [based on Greek *zeugnunai* 'to yoke'] □ **zeugmatic** *adj.*

zidovudine /zi-**dov**-yuu-dyn/ *n.* drug used to treat HIV and other viral infections. [arbitrary alteration of chemical name]

zig ● *n.* an abrupt angled movement, esp. in a zigzag course. ● *v.intr.* (**zigged**, **zigging**) perform a zig.

ziggurat *n.* ▼ a rectangular stepped tower in ancient Mesopotamia, surmounted by a temple. [from Semitic *ziqquratu* 'pinnacle']

platform
temple
stairway

ZIGGURAT: RECONSTRUCTION OF A ZIGGURAT FROM *c.*2100 BC

zigzag ● *n.* **1** a line or course having abrupt alternate right and left turns. **2** (often in *pl.*) each of these turns. ● *adj.* having the form of a zigzag; alternating right and left. ● *adv.* with a zigzag course. ● *v.intr.* (**zigzagged**, **zigzagging**) move in a zigzag course. [from German *zickzack*]

zilch *n.* esp. *N. Amer. slang* nothing. [20th-century coinage]

zillion *n. colloq.* an indefinite large number. □ **zillionth** *adj. & n.*

Zimmer *n.* (in full **Zimmer frame**) *propr.* a kind of walking frame. [name of the manufacturer]

zinc ● *n. Chem.* a white metallic element occurring naturally as zinc blende, and used as a component of brass and other alloys, in galvanizing sheet iron, and in electric batteries. ▷ METAL. ● *v.tr.* (usu. as **zinced**) coat (iron etc.) with zinc or a zinc compound to prevent rust. [from German *Zink*]

zinc blende see BLENDE.

zinc oxide *n.* a powder used as a white pigment and in medicinal ointments.

zing *colloq.* ● *n.* vigour, energy. ● *v.intr.* move swiftly or with a shrill sound. □ **zingy** *adj.* (**zingier**, **zingiest**).

zinger *n.* esp. *US slang* **1** a wisecrack. **2** an unexpected turn of events. **3** an outstanding person or thing.

zinnia *n.* ◀ a plant of the genus *Zinnia* (daisy family), with showy rayed flowers of deep red and other colours. [named after J. G. *Zinn*, German physician and botanist, 1727–59]

Zion *n.* (also **Sion**) **1** the hill of Jerusalem on which the city of David was built. **2 a** the Jewish people or religion. **b** the Christian Church. **3** (in Christian thought) the Kingdom of God in Heaven. [from Hebrew *ṣīyôn*]

ZINNIA
(*Zinnia elegans* 'Dreamland Scarlet')

ZODIAC

The zodiac is an imaginary band around the celestial sphere, which is divided into 12 parts known as the constellations of the zodiac. The band contains the ecliptic (the line representing the Sun's apparent path across the sky over the course of the year), and the Sun, Moon, and planets are always to be found within its limits. Each constellation of the zodiac contains a pattern of stars that represents an animal or character from Greek mythology. The zodiac originated as a device for measuring time, but by the 5th century BC it had been incorporated into attempts to determine character and predict the future. Although there is no scientific proof of its validity, astrologers still use the zodiac for assessing trends in people's emotional and physical lives.

CONSTELLATIONS OF THE ZODIAC
SHOWN ON THE CELESTIAL SPHERE

SIGNS OF THE ZODIAC

ARIES (RAM)
21 MAR–20 APR

TAURUS (BULL)
21 APR–20 MAY

GEMINI (TWINS)
21 MAY–20 JUN

CANCER (CRAB)
21 JUN–21 JUL

LEO (LION)
22 JUL–21 AUG

VIRGO (VIRGIN)
22 AUG–21 SEPT

LIBRA (SCALES)
22 SEPT–22 OCT

SCORPIO (SCORPION)
23 OCT–21 NOV

SAGITTARIUS (ARCHER)
22 NOV–20 DEC

CAPRICORN (GOAT)
21 DEC–19 JAN

AQUARIUS (WATER-BEARER)
20 JAN–18 FEB

PISCES (FISH)
19 FEB–20 MAR

Zionism *n.* a movement for the re-establishment and the development of a Jewish nation in what is now Israel. □ **Zionist** *n. & adj.*

zip ● *n.* **1** a light fast sound, as of a bullet passing through air. **2** energy, vigour. **3** esp. *Brit.* (in full **zip fastener**) ◄ a fastening device of two flexible strips with interlocking projections closed or opened by pulling a slide along them. **b** (*attrib.*) having a zip fastener (*zip bag*). ● *v.* (**zipped, zipping**) **1** *tr. & intr.* (often foll. by *up*) fasten with a zip fastener. **2** *intr.* move with zip or at high speed.

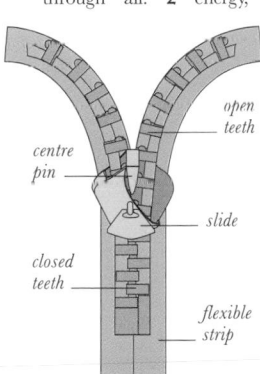

ZIP FASTENER

Zip code *n.* (also **ZIP code, zip code**) *US* a system of postal codes consisting of five-digit or nine-digit numbers. [from *zone improvement plan*]

zipper esp. *US* ● *n.* a zip fastener. ● *v.tr.* (often foll. by *up*) fasten with a zipper. □ **zippered** *adj.*

zippy *adj.* (**zippier, zippiest**) *colloq.* **1** bright, fresh, lively. **2** fast, speedy. □ **zippily** *adv.* **zippiness** *n.*

zip-up *attrib.adj.* able to be fastened with a zip fastener.

zircon *n.* ▶ a zirconium silicate of which some translucent varieties are cut into gems. [from German *Zirkon*]

ZIRCON

zircon crystal

syenite groundmass

zirconium *n. Chem.* a grey metallic element occurring naturally in zircon and used in various industrial applications.

zit *n.* esp. *US slang* a pimple. [20th-century coinage]

zither *n.* ▼ a musical instrument consisting of a flat wooden body with numerous strings stretched across it, placed horizontally and played with the fingers and a plectrum. ▷ STRINGED. [German] □ **zitherist** *n.*

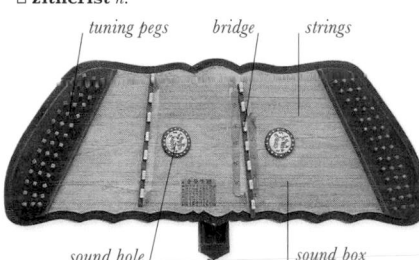

tuning pegs   *bridge*   *strings*

sound hole   *sound box*

ZITHER: 17TH-CENTURY CHINESE ZITHER

zizz *Brit. colloq.* ● *n.* **1** a whizzing or buzzing sound. **2** a short sleep. ● *v.intr.* **1** make a whizzing sound. **2** doze or sleep.

zloty /zlot-i/ *n.* (*pl.* same or **zlotys** or **zloties**) the chief monetary unit of Poland. [Polish, literally 'golden']

Zn *symb. Chem.* the element zinc.

zodiac *n.* **1** ▲ a belt of the heavens within about 8° of the ecliptic, including all apparent positions of the Sun, Moon, and most familiar planets, and divided into twelve parts (signs) named after constellations (Aries, Taurus, Gemini, Cancer, Leo, Virgo, Scorpio, Sagittarius, Capricorn, Aquarius, Pisces) and used in astrology. **2** a representation of the signs of the zodiac or of a similar astrological system. [from Greek *zōidiakos*]

■ **Usage** Owing to precession of the equinoxes, each sign of the zodiac now in fact coincides roughly with the constellation corresponding to the preceding sign.

zodiacal *adj.* of or in the zodiac.

zoetrope /zoh-i-trohp/ *n. hist.* ▶ an optical toy in the form of a cylinder with a series of pictures on the inner surface which give an impression of continuous motion when viewed through slits with the cylinder rotating. [based on Greek *zōē* 'life' + *-tropos* 'turning']

picture   *rotating cylinder*

viewing slit

spindle

fixed base

ZOETROPE

zoic /zoh-ik/ *adj.* **1** of or relating to animals. **2** *Geol.* (of rock etc.) containing fossils; with traces of animal or plant life.

zombie *n.* **1** *colloq.* a dull or apathetic person. **2** a corpse said to be revived by witchcraft. [from West African *zumbi* 'fetish']

zonation *n.* distribution in zones, esp. (*Ecol.*) of plants into zones characterized by the dominant species.

zone ● *n.* **1** an area having particular features, properties, purpose, or use (*danger zone*; *erogenous zone*; *smokeless zone*). **2** any well-defined region of more or less beltlike form. **3 a** an area between two exact or approximate concentric circles. **b** a part of the surface of a sphere enclosed between two parallel planes, or of a cone or cylinder etc. between such planes cutting it perpendicularly to the axis. **4** (in full **time zone**) a range of longitudes where a common standard time is used. **5** *Geol.* etc. a range between specified limits of depth, height, etc., esp. a section of strata distinguished by characteristic fossils. **6** *Geog.* any of five divisions of the Earth bounded by the Arctic and Antarctic Circles and the tropics. ● *v.tr.* **1** encircle as or with a zone. **2** arrange or distribute by zones. **3** assign as or to a particular area. [from Greek *zōnē* 'girdle'] □ **zonal** *adj.* **zoning** *n.* (in sense 3 of *v.*).

zonk *slang* ● *v.* **1** *tr.* hit or strike. **2** (often foll. by *out*) **a** *tr.* overcome with sleep; intoxicate. **b** *intr.* fall heavily asleep. ● *n.* (often as *int.*) the sound of a blow.

zoo *n.* an establishment which maintains a collection of usu. wild animals in a park, gardens, etc., for display to the public, conservation, etc. [abbreviation of ZOOLOGICAL GARDEN]

zoo- /zoo-oh, zoh-oh/ *comb. form* of animals or animal life. [from Greek *zōion* 'animal']

zooid /zoo-oid, zoh-oid/ *n.* **1** a more or less independent invertebrate organism arising by budding or fission. **2** a distinct member of an invertebrate colony. □ **zooidal** *adj.*

zoological /zoo-ŏ-loj-i-kăl, zoh-ŏ-loj-i-kăl/ *adj.* of or relating to zoology. □ **zoologically** *adv.*

zoological garden *n.* (also **zoological gardens** *n.pl.*) = ZOO.

zoology /zoo-ol-ŏji, zoh-ol-ŏji/ *n.* the scientific study of animals, esp. with reference to their structure, physiology, classification, and distribution. □ **zoologist** *n.*

zoom ● *v.* **1** *intr.* move quickly, esp. with a buzzing sound. **2 a** *intr.* cause an aeroplane to mount at high speed and a steep angle. **b** *tr.* cause (an aeroplane) to do this. **3 a** *intr.* (of a camera) close up rapidly from a long shot to a close-up. **b** *tr.* cause (a lens or camera) to do this. ● *n.* **1** an aeroplane's steep climb. **2** a zooming camera shot.

zoom lens *n.* a lens allowing a camera to zoom by varying the focal length. ▷ CAMCORDER

zoomorphic /zoo-ŏ-**mor**-fik, zoh-ŏ-**mor**-fik/ *adj.* **1** dealing with or represented in animal forms. **2** having gods of animal form. [based on Greek *morphē* 'form'] □ **zoomorphism** *n.*

zoonosis /zoo-ŏ-**noh**-sis, zoh-ŏ-**noh**-sis/ *n.* (*pl.* **-noses**) any of various diseases which can be transmitted to humans from animals. [based on Greek *nosos* 'disease']

zoophyte /**zoo**-ŏ-fyt, **zoh**-ŏ-fyt/ *n.* a plantlike animal, esp. a coral, sea anemone, or sponge. □ **zoophytic** *adj.*

Zoroastrian /zo-roh-**ass**-tri-ăn/ (also **Zarathustrian** /za-ră-**thuus**-tri-ăn/) ● *adj.* of or relating to Zoroaster (or Zarathustra) or the religion taught by him or his followers in the Zend-Avesta, sacred writings which portray a conflict between a spirit of light and good and a spirit of darkness and evil. ● *n.* a follower of Zoroaster. [based on *Zarathustra*, name of the Persian founder of the religion (6th c. BC)]

Zouave /zoo-**ahv**/ *n.* **1** a member of a French light-infantry corps originally formed of Algerians and retaining their oriental uniform. **2** (in *pl.*) women's trousers with wide tops, tapering to a narrow ankle. [French, from *Zouaoua*, name of a tribe]

zouk /zook/ *n.* an exuberant style of popular music combining Caribbean and Western elements and having a fast heavy beat. [French]

ZPG *abbr.* zero population growth.

Zr *symb. Chem.* the element zirconium.

zucchetto /tsuu-**ket**-oh/ *n.* (*pl.* **-os**) a Roman Catholic ecclesiastic's skullcap, black for a priest, purple for a bishop, red for a cardinal, and white for a pope. [from Italian *zucchetta* 'little gourd']

zucchini /zuu-**kee**-ni/ *n.* (*pl.* same or **zucchinis**) esp. *N. Amer. & Austral.* a courgette. ▷ VEGETABLE. [Italian, literally 'little gourds']

Zulu ● *n.* **1** a member of a black South African people originally inhabiting Zululand and Natal. **2** the language of this people. ● *adj.* ▶ of or relating to this people or language. [native name]

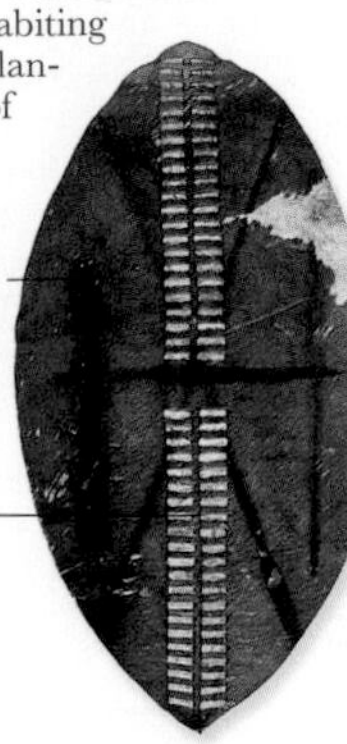

zwieback /**zwee**-bak/ *n.* a kind of biscuit rusk or sweet cake toasted in slices. [German, literally 'twice baked']

zydeco /**zy**-di-koh/ *n.* a kind of Afro-American dance music originally from southern Louisiana. [Louisiana Creole, possibly from French *les haricots* in a dance-tune title]

oxhide

slits

ZULU SHIELD

zygoma *n.* (*pl.* **zygomata**) the bony arch of the cheek formed by connection of the zygomatic and temporal bones. [Greek, based on *zugon* 'yoke'] □ **zygomatic** *adj.*

zygomatic arch *n.* = ZYGOMA.

zygomatic bone *n.* the bone that forms the prominent part of the cheek. ▷ SKELETON, SKULL

zygospore *n.* a thick-walled spore formed by certain fungi.

zygote *n. Biol.* a cell formed by the union of two gametes. ▷ OVARY. [from Greek *zugōtos* 'yoked'] □ **zygotic** *adj.* **zygotically** *adv.*

Z

REFERENCE SECTION

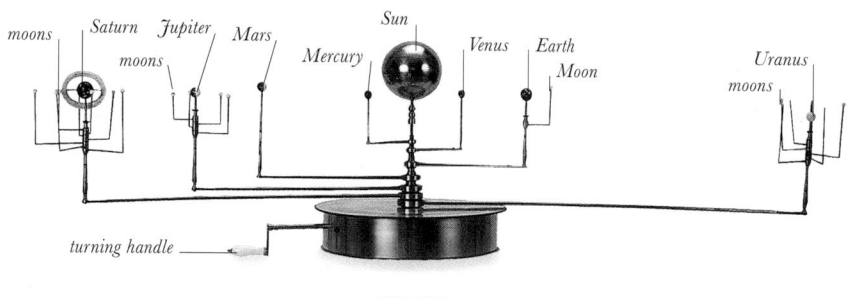

ORRERY

POLITICAL MAP OF THE WORLD *974–975*

PHYSICAL MAP OF THE WORLD *976–977*

COUNTRIES OF THE WORLD *978–985*

THE NIGHT SKY *986–987*

MEASUREMENTS *988–989*

NUMBERS AND SYMBOLS *990–991*

TIME *992–993*

MISCELLANEOUS INFORMATION *994–995*

THE LIVING WORLD *996–997*

THE ANIMAL KINGDOM *998–999*

GEOLOGICAL TIME PERIODS *1000–1001*

GRAMMAR USAGE *1002–1007*

ACKNOWLEDGEMENTS *1008*

POLITICAL MAP OF THE WORLD

THIS MAP depicts the political boundaries of the world's nations. There are currently 192 independent countries in the world – a marked increase from the 82 that existed in 1950. With the trend towards greater fragmentation, this figure is likely to increase. There are also some 60 overseas dependencies still in existence, with various forms of local administration, but all belonging to a sovereign state. The largest country in the world is the Russian Federation, which covers 17,075,400 sq. km (6,592,800 sq. mi.), while the smallest is the Vatican City, covering 0.44 sq. km (0.17 sq. mi.). Under the Antarctic Treaty of 1959, no countries are permitted territorial claims in Antarctica.

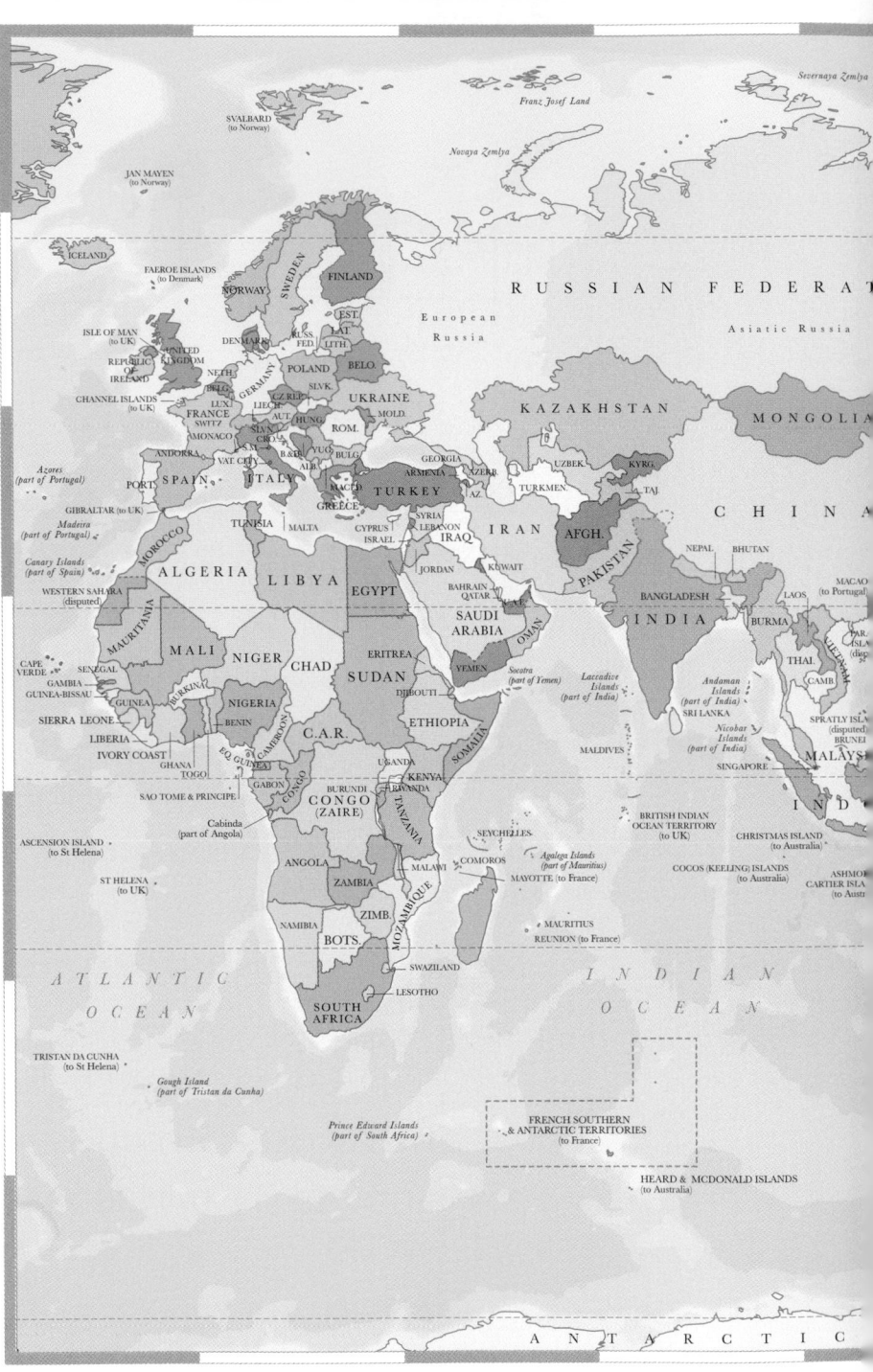

ABBREVIATIONS

AFGH.	Afghanistan
ALB.	Albania
AUT.	Austria
AZ. OR AZERB.	Azerbaijan
B. & H.	Bosnia & Herzegovina
BELG.	Belgium
BULG.	Bulgaria
BOTS.	Botswana
CAMB.	Cambodia
CRO.	Croatia
CZ. REP.	Czech Republic
DOM. REP.	Dominican Republic
EST.	Estonia
HUNG.	Hungary
KYRG.	Kyrgyzstan
LAT.	Latvia
LIECH.	Liechtenstein
LITH.	Lithuania
LUX.	Luxembourg
MACED.	Macedonia
MOLD.	Moldavia
NETH.	Netherlands
NETH. ANT.	Netherland Antilles
PORT.	Portugal
ROM.	Romania
RUSS. FED.	Russian Federation
SLVK.	Slovakia
SLVN.	Slovenia
S. M.	San Marino
SWITZ.	Switzerland
TAJ.	Tajikistan
THAI.	Thailand
TURKMEN.	Turkmenistan
U. A. E.	United Arab Emirates
UZBEK.	Uzbekistan
VAT. CITY	Vatican City
YUG.	Yugoslavia
ZIMB.	Zimbabwe

KEY TO LABEL STYLES

Eg. MEXICO	Independent state
Eg. FAEROE ISLANDS (to Denmark)	Self-governing territory, with parent state indicated
Eg. *Andaman Islands (part of India)*	Non self-governing territory, with parent state indicated

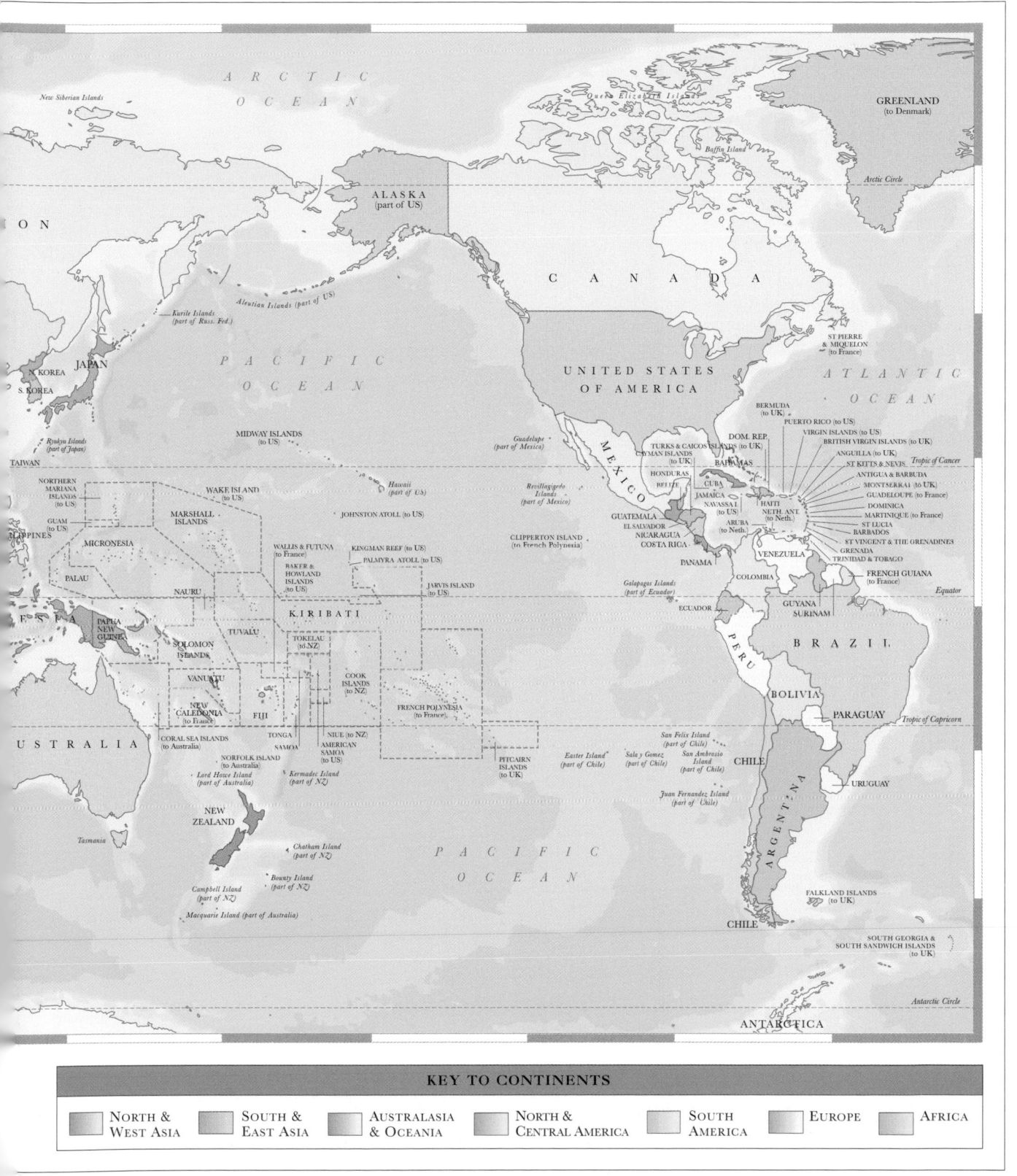

ARCTIC OCEAN

New Siberian Islands

GREENLAND
(to Denmark)

Queen Elizabeth Islands

Baffin Island

Arctic Circle

ALASKA
(part of US)

C A N A D A

Aleutian Islands (part of US)

Kurile Islands
(part of Russ. Fed.)

JAPAN
N. KOREA
S. KOREA

PACIFIC OCEAN

UNITED STATES
OF AMERICA

ST PIERRE
& MIQUELON
(to France)

ATLANTIC OCEAN

Ryukyu Islands
(part of Japan)

TAIWAN

MIDWAY ISLANDS
(to US)

Guadelupe
(part of Mexico)

BERMUDA
(to UK)

PUERTO RICO (to US)

MEXICO

VIRGIN ISLANDS (to US)
BRITISH VIRGIN ISLANDS (to UK)

DOM. REP.

TURKS & CAICOS ISLANDS (to UK)
CAYMAN ISLANDS
(to UK)

ANGUILLA (to UK)

HONDURAS

BAHAMAS

ST KITTS & NEVIS

Tropic of Cancer

ANTIGUA & BARBUDA

NORTHERN
MARIANA
ISLANDS
(to US)

WAKE ISLAND
(to US)

Hawaii
(part of US)

CUBA

BELIZE

MONTSERRAT (to UK)

JAMAICA

GUADELOUPE (to France)

GUAM
(to US)

MARSHALL
ISLANDS

JOHNSTON ATOLL (to US)

Revillagigedo
Islands
(part of Mexico)

GUATEMALA

NAVASSA I.
(to US)

MARTINIQUE (to France)

DOMINICA

PHILIPPINES

MICRONESIA

EL SALVADOR

HAITI
NETH. ANT.
(to Neth.)

ST LUCIA
BARBADOS

PALAU

WALLIS & FUTUNA
(to France)

KINGMAN REEF (to US)

NICARAGUA
COSTA RICA

ARUBA
(to Neth.)

ST VINCENT & THE GRENADINES
GRENADA
TRINIDAD & TOBAGO

CLIPPERTON ISLAND
(to French Polynesia)

VENEZUELA

FRENCH GUIANA
(to France)

BAKER &
HOWLAND
ISLANDS
(to US)

PALMYRA ATOLL (to US)

PANAMA

NAURU

JARVIS ISLAND
(to US)

Galapagos Islands
(part of Ecuador)

COLOMBIA

GUYANA
SURINAM

Equator

KIRIBATI

ECUADOR

PAPUA
NEW
GUINEA

TUVALU

BRAZIL

SOLOMON
ISLANDS

PERU

VANUATU

TOKELAU
(to NZ)

COOK
ISLANDS
(to NZ)

BOLIVIA

NEW
CALEDONIA
(to France)

FIJI

FRENCH POLYNESIA
(to France)

PARAGUAY

Tropic of Capricorn

AUSTRALIA

CORAL SEA ISLANDS
(to Australia)

TONGA
SAMOA

NIUE (to NZ)
AMERICAN
SAMOA
(to US)

San Felix Island
(part of Chile)

San Ambrosio
Islands
(part of Chile)

Sala y Gomez
(part of Chile)

Easter Island
(part of Chile)

NORFOLK ISLAND
(to Australia)

PITCAIRN
ISLANDS
(to UK)

CHILE

URUGUAY

Lord Howe Island
(part of Australia)

Kermadec Island
(part of NZ)

Juan Fernandez Island
(part of Chile)

Tasmania

NEW
ZEALAND

Chatham Island
(part of NZ)

ARGENTINA

Campbell Island
(part of NZ)

Bounty Island
(part of NZ)

PACIFIC OCEAN

FALKLAND ISLANDS
(to UK)

Macquarie Island (part of Australia)

CHILE

SOUTH GEORGIA &
SOUTH SANDWICH ISLANDS
(to UK)

Antarctic Circle

ANTARCTICA

KEY TO CONTINENTS

| NORTH & WEST ASIA | SOUTH & EAST ASIA | AUSTRALASIA & OCEANIA | NORTH & CENTRAL AMERICA | SOUTH AMERICA | EUROPE | AFRICA |

PHYSICAL MAP OF THE WORLD

THIS MAP shows the world's topographic relief both above and below sea level. Seas and oceans occupy around 70% of the Earth's total surface area of 510,000,000 sq. km (197,000,000 sq. mi.), whereas land covers a mere 149,000,000 sq. km (57,500,000 sq. mi.). While most land is found in the northern hemisphere, the only continents located exclusively in this region are North America and Europe. Similarly, only Australia and Antarctica are situated purely in the southern hemisphere. The circumference at the equator is 40,077 km (24,900 miles) and the diameter from pole to pole is 12,714 km (7,900 miles).

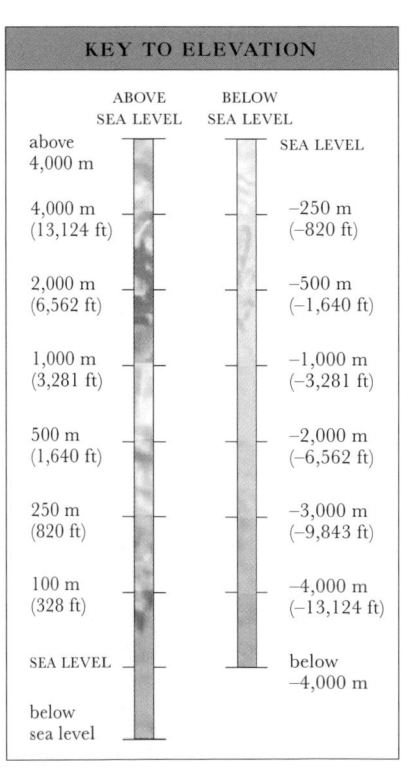

KEY TO ELEVATION

ABOVE SEA LEVEL	BELOW SEA LEVEL
above 4,000 m	SEA LEVEL
4,000 m (13,124 ft)	−250 m (−820 ft)
2,000 m (6,562 ft)	−500 m (−1,640 ft)
1,000 m (3,281 ft)	−1,000 m (−3,281 ft)
500 m (1,640 ft)	−2,000 m (−6,562 ft)
250 m (820 ft)	−3,000 m (−9,843 ft)
100 m (328 ft)	−4,000 m (−13,124 ft)
SEA LEVEL	below −4,000 m
below sea level	

LARGEST CONTINENT	SMALLEST CONTINENT	LARGEST OCEAN	LARGEST ISLAND
ASIA	AUSTRALASIA	PACIFIC OCEAN	GREENLAND
44,485,900 SQ. KM	8,924,100 SQ. KM	165,384,000 SQ. KM	2,175,219 SQ. KM
(17,176,000 SQ. MILES)	(3,445,600 SQ. MILES)	(63,855,000 SQ. MILES)	(839,852 SQ. MILES)

ARCTIC OCEAN

New Siberian Islands

Laptev Sea

East Siberian Sea

Limit of summer pack ice

Beaufort Sea

Ellesmere Island

Greenland

Queen Elizabeth Islands

Chukchi Sea

Baffin Bay

Baffin Island

Arctic Circle

Brooks Range

Lena

Bering Strait

Kamchatka

Mount McKinley Denali 6194m

Great Bear Lake

Hudson Bay

Peninsula d'Ungava

Labrador Sea

Sea of Okhotsk

Bering Sea

Aleutian Basin

Great Slave Lake

Canadian Shield

Sakhalin

Aleutian Islands

Aleutian Trench

Gulf of Alaska

NORTH AMERICA

Lake Winnipeg

Laurentian Highlands

Amur

Kuril Trench

Northwest Pacific Basin

Vancouver Island

Coast Ranges

Great Plains

Great Lakes

Grand Banks of Newfoundland

Hokkaido

Honshu

Emperor Seamounts

Mendocino Fracture Zone

Rocky Mountains

Mississippi

Appalachian Mts.

North American Basin

Sea of Japan

Mid-Atlantic Ridge

Yellow Sea

Kyushu

Ryukyu Islands

Murray Fracture Zone

Hawaiian Islands

Hawaii

Sierra Madre Occidental

Sierra Madre Oriental

Gulf of Mexico

Tropic of Cancer

Taiwan

East China Sea

Philippine Sea

Mid Pacific Mountains

Central Pacific Basin

Yucatan Peninsula

Greater Antilles

West Indies

Caribbean Sea

Lesser Antilles

ATLANTIC OCEAN

Philippine Trench

Mariana Islands

Mariana Trench

PACIFIC OCEAN

Middle America Trench

Caroline Islands

Marshall Islands

Line Islands

Guiana Highlands

New Guinea

Solomon Islands

Phoenix Islands

Galapagos Islands

Equator

Arafura Sea

Timor Sea

Coral Sea

Vanuatu

Fiji

Tonga

Samoa

Marquesas Islands

Tuamotu Islands

Amazon Basin

SOUTH AMERICA

Amazon

Brazil Basin

Great Sandy Desert

Great Barrier Reef

Great Dividing Range

New Caledonia

Cook Islands

Peru Basin

Planalto de Mato Grosso

AUSTRALIA

Great Victoria Desert

Nullarbor Plain

Darling

Tasman Sea

North Island

New Zealand

South Island

Easter Island

Juan Fernandez Islands

East Pacific Rise

Southwest Pacific Basin

Cerro Aconcagua 6960m

Gran Chaco

Pampas

Argentine Basin

Tropic of Capricorn

Bass Strait

Tasmania

Campbell Plateau

Kermadec Trench

Cape Horn

Tierra del Fuego

Falkland Islands

South Georgia

Limit of winter pack ice

Drake Passage

Antarctic Peninsula

South Sandwich Islands

Limit of summer pack ice

Antarctic Circle

DEEPEST OCEAN	TALLEST MOUNTAIN	LARGEST LAKE	LONGEST RIVER
MARIANA TRENCH, PACIFIC OCEAN 11,034 M (36,201 FT)	MT EVEREST, CHINA/NEPAL 8,848 M (29,028 FT)	CASPIAN SEA, ASIA 378,400 SQ. KM (146,111 SQ. MILES)	NILE, AFRICA 6,695 KM (4,160 MILES)

COUNTRIES OF THE WORLD

THE FOLLOWING LIST OF COUNTRIES of the world has been researched from up-to-date sources and includes information correct at the time of publication. Each entry contains the flag of a country, the noun most widely used to describe a person from that country, the related adjective in general use, the country's currency unit, its capital, and its estimated total population. All population statistics were compiled in 1996, with the exception of the following, which are based on 1994 estimates: Andorra, Antigua and Barbuda, Dominica, Grenada, Kiribati, Liechtenstein, Marshall Islands, Micronesia, Monaco, Nauru, Palau, San Marino, São Tome and Principe, the Seychelles, St Kitts and Nevis, St Lucia, St Vincent and the Grenadines, Taiwan, Tonga, Tuvalu, and the Vatican City.

AFGHANISTAN
PERSON: Afghan
RELATED ADJ.: Afghan
CURRENCY: afghani = 100 puls
CAPITAL: Kabul
POPULATION: 21,500,000

ALBANIA
PERSON: Albanian
RELATED ADJ.: Albanian
CURRENCY: new lek = 100 qindarka
CAPITAL: Tirana
POPULATION: 3,500,000

ALGERIA
PERSON: Algerian
RELATED ADJ.: Algerian
CURRENCY: Algerian dinar = 100 centimes
CAPITAL: Algiers
POPULATION: 28,600,000

ANDORRA
PERSON: Andorran
RELATED ADJ.: Andorran
CURRENCY: French franc & Spanish peseta
CAPITAL: Andorra la Vella
POPULATION: 65,000

ANGOLA
PERSON: Angolan
RELATED ADJ.: Angolan
CURRENCY: new kwanza = 100 lwei
CAPITAL: Luanda
POPULATION: 11,500,000

ANTIGUA & BARBUDA
PERSON: Antiguan, Barbudan
RELATED ADJ.: Antiguan, Barbudan
CURRENCY: East Caribbean dollar = 100 cents
CAPITAL: St John's
POPULATION: 65,000

ARGENTINA
PERSON: Argentinian
RELATED ADJ.: Argentine/Argentinian
CURRENCY: Argentine peso = 10,000 australes
CAPITAL: Buenos Aires
POPULATION: 35,000,000

ARMENIA
PERSON: Armenian
RELATED ADJ.: Armenian
CURRENCY: dram = 100 luma
CAPITAL: Yerevan
POPULATION: 3,600,000

AUSTRALIA
PERSON: Australian
RELATED ADJ.: Australian
CURRENCY: Australian dollar = 100 cents
CAPITAL: Canberra
POPULATION: 18,300,000

AUSTRIA
PERSON: Austrian
RELATED ADJ.: Austrian
CURRENCY: Austrian schilling = 100 Groschen
CAPITAL: Vienna
POPULATION: 8,000,000

AZERBAIJAN
PERSON: Azerbaijani
RELATED ADJ.: Azerbaijani
CURRENCY: manat = 100 gopik
CAPITAL: Baku
POPULATION: 7,600,000

BAHAMAS
PERSON: Bahamian
RELATED ADJ.: Bahamian
CURRENCY: Bahamian dollar = 100 cents
CAPITAL: Nassau
POPULATION: 300,000

BAHRAIN
PERSON: Bahraini
RELATED ADJ.: Bahraini
CURRENCY: Bahraini dinar = 100 fils
CAPITAL: Manama
POPULATION: 600,000

BANGLADESH
PERSON: Bangladeshi
RELATED ADJ.: Bangladeshi
CURRENCY: taka = 100 poisha
CAPITAL: Dhaka
POPULATION: 123,100,000

BARBADOS
PERSON: Barbadian
RELATED ADJ.: Barbadian
CURRENCY: Barbadian dollar = 100 cents
CAPITAL: Bridgetown
POPULATION: 300,000

BELGIUM
PERSON: Belgian
RELATED ADJ.: Belgian
CURRENCY: Belgian franc = 100 centimes
CAPITAL: Brussels
POPULATION: 10,100,000

BELIZE
PERSON: Belizian
RELATED ADJ.: Belizian
CURRENCY: Belizian dollar = 100 cents
CAPITAL: Belmopan
POPULATION: 200,000

BELORUSSIA
PERSON: Belorussian/ Byelorussian
RELATED ADJ.: Belorussian/Byelorussian
CURRENCY: Belorussian rouble
CAPITAL: Minsk **POPULATION:** 10,000,000

BENIN
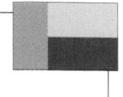
PERSON: Beninese
RELATED ADJ.: Beninese
CURRENCY: African franc
CAPITAL: Porto-Novo
POPULATION : 5,600,000

BHUTAN

PERSON: Bhutanese
RELATED ADJ.: Bhutanese
CURRENCY: ngultrum = 100 chetrum
CAPITAL: Thimphu
POPULATION: 1,700,000

BOLIVIA

PERSON: Bolivian
RELATED ADJ.: Bolivian
CURRENCY: Boliviano = 100 centavos
CAPITALS: La Paz, Sucre
POPULATION: 7,600,000

BOSNIA & HERZEGOVINIA

PERSON: Bosnian
RELATED ADJ.: Bosnian
CURRENCY: Bosnian dinar = 100 paras
CAPITAL: Sarajevo **POPULATION:** 3,500,000

BOTSWANA
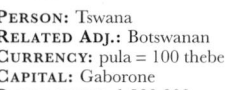
PERSON: Tswana
RELATED ADJ.: Botswanan
CURRENCY: pula = 100 thebe
CAPITAL: Gaborone
POPULATION: 1,500,000

BRAZIL

PERSON: Brazilian
RELATED ADJ.: Brazilian
CURRENCY: real = 100 centavos
CAPITAL: Brasília
POPULATION: 164,400,000

BRUNEI
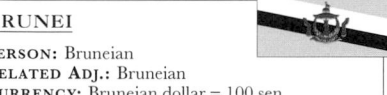
PERSON: Bruneian
RELATED ADJ.: Bruneian
CURRENCY: Bruneian dollar = 100 sen
CAPITAL: Bandar Seri Begawan
POPULATION: 300,000

BULGARIA
PERSON: Bulgarian
RELATED ADJ.: Bulgarian
CURRENCY: lev = 100 stotinki
CAPITAL: Sofia
POPULATION: 8,700,000

BURKINA

PERSON: Burkinese
RELATED ADJ.: Burkinese
CURRENCY: African franc
CAPITAL: Ouagadougou
POPULATION: 10,600,000

BURMA
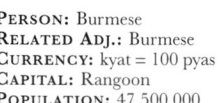
PERSON: Burmese
RELATED ADJ.: Burmese
CURRENCY: kyat = 100 pyas
CAPITAL: Rangoon
POPULATION: 47,500,000

BURUNDI
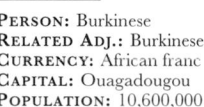
PERSON: Burundian
RELATED ADJ.: Burundian
CURRENCY: Burundian franc = 10 centimes
CAPITAL: Bujumbura
POPULATION: 6,600,000

CAMBODIA
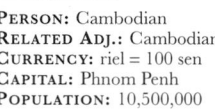
PERSON: Cambodian
RELATED ADJ.: Cambodian
CURRENCY: riel = 100 sen
CAPITAL: Phnom Penh
POPULATION: 10,500,000

CAMEROON
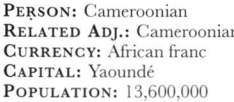
PERSON: Cameroonian
RELATED ADJ.: Cameroonian
CURRENCY: African franc
CAPITAL: Yaoundé
POPULATION: 13,600,000

CANADA
PERSON: Canadian
RELATED ADJ.: Canadian
CURRENCY: Canadian dollar = 100 cents
CAPITAL: Ottawa
POPULATION: 29,800,000

CAPE VERDE

PERSON: Cape Verdean
RELATED ADJ.: Cape Verdean
CURRENCY: Cape Verdean escudo
CAPITAL: Praia
POPULATION: 400,000

CENTRAL AFRICAN REPUBLIC
PERSON: n/a
RELATED ADJ.: n/a
CURRENCY: African franc
CAPITAL: Bangui **POPULATION:** 3,400,000

CHAD
PERSON: Chadian
RELATED ADJ.: Chadian
CURRENCY: African franc
CAPITAL: Ndjamena
POPULATION: 6,500,000

CHILE
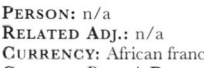
PERSON: Chilean
RELATED ADJ.: Chilean
CURRENCY: Chilean peso = 100 centavos
CAPITAL: Santiago
POPULATION: 14,500,000

CHINA
PERSON: Chinese
RELATED ADJ.: Chinese
CURRENCY: yuan = 10 jiao or 100 fen
CAPITAL: Beijing
POPULATION: 1,234,300,000

COLOMBIA
PERSON: Colombian
RELATED ADJ.: Colombian
CURRENCY: Colombian peso = 100 centavos
CAPITAL: Bogotá
POPULATION: 35,700,000

COMOROS

PERSON: Comoran
RELATED ADJ.: Comoran
CURRENCY: African franc
CAPITAL: Moroni
POPULATION: 700,000

CONGO
PERSON: Congolese
RELATED ADJ.: Congolese
CURRENCY: African franc
CAPITAL: Brazzaville
POPULATION: 2,700,000

CONGO (formerly ZAIRE)
PERSON: Congolese
RELATED ADJ.: Congolese
CURRENCY: new Zaire = 100 makuta
CAPITAL: Kinshasa
POPULATION: 45,300,000

COSTA RICA

PERSON: Costa Rican
RELATED ADJ.: Costa Rican
CURRENCY: colón = 100 centimos
CAPITAL: San José
POPULATION: 3,500,000

CROATIA
PERSON: Croat or Croatian
RELATED ADJ.: Croat or Croatian
CURRENCY: kuna = 100 lipa
CAPITAL: Zagreb
POPULATION: 4,500,000

CUBA
PERSON: Cuban
RELATED ADJ.: Cuban
CURRENCY: Cuban peso = 100 centavos
CAPITAL: Havana
POPULATION: 11,100,000

CYPRUS

PERSON: Cypriot
RELATED ADJ.: Cypriot
CURRENCY: Cypriot pound/Turkish lira
CAPITAL: Nicosia
POPULATION: 800,000

CZECH REPUBLIC
PERSON: Czech
RELATED ADJ.: Czech
CURRENCY: Czech koruna = 100 haleru
CAPITAL: Prague
POPULATION: 10,300,000

DENMARK

PERSON: Dane
RELATED ADJ.: Danish
CURRENCY: Danish krone = 100 øre
CAPITAL: Copenhagen
POPULATION: 5,200,000

DJIBOUTI

PERSON: Djiboutian
RELATED ADJ.: Djiboutian
CURRENCY: Djiboutian franc = 100 centimes
CAPITAL: Djibouti
POPULATION: 600,000

DOMINICA

PERSON: Dominican
RELATED ADJ.: Dominican
CURRENCY: East Caribbean dollar = 100 cents
CAPITAL: Roseau
POPULATION: 71,000

DOMINICAN REPUBLIC

PERSON: Dominican
RELATED ADJ.: Dominican
CURRENCY: Dominican peso = 100 centavos
CAPITAL: Santo Domingo
POPULATION: 8,000,000

ECUADOR

PERSON: Ecuadorean
RELATED ADJ.: Ecuadorean
CURRENCY: sucre = 100 centavos
CAPITAL: Quito
POPULATION: 11,700,000

EGYPT

PERSON: Egyptian
RELATED ADJ.: Egyptian
CURRENCY: Egyptian pound = 100 piastres
CAPITAL: Cairo
POPULATION: 64,200,000

EL SALVADOR

PERSON: Salvadorean
RELATED ADJ.: Salvadorean
CURRENCY: colón = 100 centavos
CAPITAL: San Salvador
POPULATION: 5,900,000

EQUATORIAL GUINEA

PERSON: Equatorial Guinean
RELATED ADJ.: Equatorial Guinean
CURRENCY: African franc
CAPITAL: Malabo
POPULATION: 400,000

ERITREA

PERSON: Eritrean
RELATED ADJ.: Eritrean
CURRENCY: Ethiopean birr = 100 cents
CAPITAL: Asmara
POPULATION: 3,600,000

ESTONIA

PERSON: Estonian
RELATED ADJ.: Estonian
CURRENCY: kroon = 100 sents
CAPITAL: Tallinn
POPULATION: 1,500,000

ETHIOPIA

PERSON: Ethiopian
RELATED ADJ.: Ethiopian
CURRENCY: birr = 100 cents
CAPITAL: Addis Ababa
POPULATION: 56,700,000

FIJI

PERSON: Fijian
RELATED ADJ.: Fijian
CURRENCY: Fijian dollar = 100 cents
CAPITAL: Suva
POPULATION: 800,000

FINLAND

PERSON: Finn
RELATED ADJ.: Finnish
CURRENCY: markka = 100 penniä
CAPITAL: Helsinki
POPULATION: 5,100,000

FRANCE

PERSON: Frenchman/Frenchwoman
RELATED ADJ.: French
CURRENCY: franc = 100 centimes
CAPITAL: Paris
POPULATION: 58,200,000

GABON

PERSON: Gabonese
RELATED ADJ.: Gabonese
CURRENCY: African franc
CAPITAL: Libreville
POPULATION: 1,400,000

GAMBIA

PERSON: Gambian
RELATED ADJ.: Gambian
CURRENCY: dalasi = 100 butut
CAPITAL: Banjul
POPULATION: 1,200,000

GEORGIA

PERSON: Georgian
RELATED ADJ.: Georgian
CURRENCY: coupon
CAPITAL: Tbilisi
POPULATION: 5,500,000

GERMANY

PERSON: German
RELATED ADJ.: German
CURRENCY: Deutschmark = 100 pfennig
CAPITAL: Berlin
POPULATION: 81,800,000

GHANA

PERSON: Ghanaian
RELATED ADJ.: Ghanaian
CURRENCY: cedi = 100 pesewas
CAPITAL: Accra
POPULATION: 18,000,000

GREECE

PERSON: Greek
RELATED ADJ.: Greek
CURRENCY: drachma = 100 leptae
CAPITAL: Athens
POPULATION: 10,500,000

GRENADA
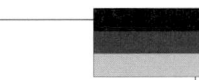

PERSON: Grenadian
RELATED ADJ.: Grenadian
CURRENCY: East Caribbean dollar = 100 cents
CAPITAL: St George's
POPULATION: 92,000

GUATEMALA

PERSON: Guatemalan
RELATED ADJ.: Egyptian
CURRENCY: quetzal = 100 centavos
CAPITAL: Guatemala City
POPULATION: 101,900,000

GUINEA

PERSON: Guinean
RELATED ADJ.: Guinean
CURRENCY: Guinea franc = 100 centimes
CAPITAL: Conakry
POPULATION: 6,900,000

GUINEA-BISSAU

PERSON: Guinean
RELATED ADJ.: Guinean
CURRENCY: Guinean peso = 100 centavos
CAPITAL: Bissau
POPULATION: 1,100,000

GUYANA

PERSON: Guyanese
RELATED ADJ.: Guyanese
CURRENCY: Guyanese dollar = 100 cents
CAPITAL: Georgetown
POPULATION: 800,000

HAITI

PERSON: Haitian
RELATED ADJ.: Haitian
CURRENCY: gourde = 100 centimes
CAPITAL: Port-au-Prince
POPULATION: 7,300,000

HONDURAS

PERSON: Honduran
RELATED ADJ.: Honduran
CURRENCY: lempira = 100 centavos
CAPITAL: Tegucigalpa
POPULATION: 5,800,000

HUNGARY
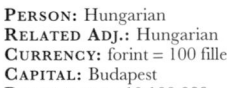

PERSON: Hungarian
RELATED ADJ.: Hungarian
CURRENCY: forint = 100 filler
CAPITAL: Budapest
POPULATION: 10,100,000

ICELAND
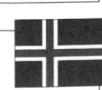

PERSON: Icelander
RELATED ADJ.: Icelandic
CURRENCY: new Icelandic króna = 100 aurar
CAPITAL: Reykjavik
POPULATION: 300,000

INDIA

PERSON: Indian
RELATED ADJ.: Indian
CURRENCY: rupee = 100 paisa
CAPITAL: New Delhi
POPULATION: 953,000,000

INDONESIA

PERSON: Indonesian
RELATED ADJ.: Indonesian
CURRENCY: rupiah = 100 sen
CAPITAL: Jakarta
POPULATION: 200,600,000

IRAN

PERSON: Iranian
RELATED ADJ.: Iranian
CURRENCY: rial = 100 dinars
CAPITAL: Tehran
POPULATION: 68,700,000

IRAQ

PERSON: Iraqi
RELATED ADJ.: Iraqi
CURRENCY: Iraqi dinar = 1,000 fils
CAPITAL: Baghdad
POPULATION: 21,000,000

IRELAND, REPUBLIC OF
PERSON: Irishman/Irishwoman
RELATED ADJ.: Irish
CURRENCY: Irish pound (punt) − 100 pence
CAPITAL: Dublin
POPULATION: 3,600,000

ISRAEL

PERSON: Israeli
RELATED ADJ.: Israeli
CURRENCY: shekel = 100 agora
CAPITAL: Jerusalem
POPULATION: 5,800,000

ITALY
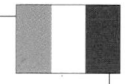
PERSON: Italian
RELATED ADJ.: Italian
CURRENCY: lira = 100 centesemi
CAPITAL: Rome
POPULATION: 57,200,000

IVORY COAST
PERSON: n/a
RELATED ADJ.: n/a
CURRENCY: African franc
CAPITAL: Yamoussoukro
POPULATION: 14,700,000

JAMAICA

PERSON: Jamaican
RELATED ADJ.: Jamaican
CURRENCY: Jamaican dollar = 100 cents
CAPITAL: Kingston
POPULATION: 2,500,000

JAPAN

PERSON: Japanese
RELATED ADJ.: Japanese
CURRENCY: yen = 100 sen
CAPITAL: Tokyo
POPULATION: 125,400,000

JORDAN

PERSON: Jordanian
RELATED ADJ.: Jordanian
CURRENCY: Jordanian dinar = 1,000 fils
CAPITAL: Amman
POPULATION: 5,700,000

KAZAKHSTAN

PERSON: Kazakh
RELATED ADJ.: Kazakh
CURRENCY: tenge = 100 teins
CAPITAL: Akmola
POPULATION: 17,200,000

KENYA

PERSON: Kenyan
RELATED ADJ.: Kenyan
CURRENCY: Kenyan shilling = 100 cents
CAPITAL: Nairobi
POPULATION: 29,100,000

KIRIBATI

PERSON: Kiribati
RELATED ADJ.: Kiribati
CURRENCY: Australian dollar = 100 cents
CAPITAL: Bairiki
POPULATION: 77,000

KUWAIT

PERSON: Kuwaiti
RELATED ADJ.: Kuwaiti
CURRENCY: Kuwaiti dinar = 1,000 fils
CAPITAL: Kuwait
POPULATION: 1,500,000

KYRGYZSTAN

PERSON: Kyrgyz
RELATED ADJ.: Kyrgyz
CURRENCY: som
CAPITAL: Bishkek
POPULATION: 4,800,000

LAOS

PERSON: Laotian
RELATED ADJ.: Laotian
CURRENCY: kip = 100 ats
CAPITAL: Vientiane
POPULATION: 5,000,000

LATVIA
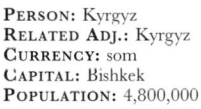
PERSON: Latvian
RELATED ADJ.: Latvian
CURRENCY: lat − 100 santims
CAPITAL: Riga
POPULATION: 2,500,000

LEBANON
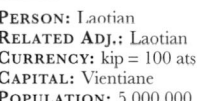
PERSON: Lebanese
RELATED ADJ.: Lebanese
CURRENCY: Lebanese pound = 100 piastres
CAPITAL: Beirut
POPULATION: 3,100,000

LESOTHO

PERSON: Mosotho (*pl.* Bosotho)
RELATED ADJ.: n/a
CURRENCY: loti = 100 lisente
CAPITAL: Maseru
POPULATION: 2,100,000

LIBERIA

PERSON: Liberian
RELATED ADJ.: Liberian
CURRENCY: Liberian dollar = 100 cents
CAPITAL: Monrovia
POPULATION: 3,100,000

LIBYA

PERSON: Libyan
RELATED ADJ.: Libyan
CURRENCY: Libyan dinar = 1,000 dirhams
CAPITAL: Tripoli
POPULATION: 5,600,000

LIECHTENSTEIN

PERSON: Liechtensteiner
RELATED ADJ.: n/a
CURRENCY: Swiss franc = 100 centimes
CAPITAL: Vaduz
POPULATION: 31,000

LITHUANIA
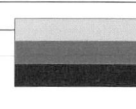
PERSON: Lithuanian
RELATED ADJ.: Lithuanian
CURRENCY: litas = 100 centas
CAPITAL: Vilnius
POPULATION: 3,700,000

LUXEMBOURG

PERSON: Luxembourger
RELATED ADJ.: n/a
CURRENCY: Luxembourg franc = 100 centimes
CAPITAL: Luxembourg
POPULATION: 400,000

MACEDONIA
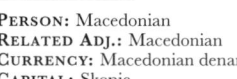
PERSON: Macedonian
RELATED ADJ.: Macedonian
CURRENCY: Macedonian denar
CAPITAL: Skopje
POPULATION: 2,200,000

MADAGASCAR
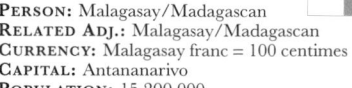
PERSON: Malagasay/Madagascan
RELATED ADJ.: Malagasay/Madagascan
CURRENCY: Malagasay franc = 100 centimes
CAPITAL: Antananarivo
POPULATION: 15,200,000

MALAWI

PERSON: Malawian
RELATED ADJ.: Malawian
CURRENCY: kwacha = 100 tambala
CAPITAL: Lilongwe
POPULATION: 11,400,000

MALAYSIA

PERSON: Malaysian
RELATED ADJ.: Malaysian
CURRENCY: ringgit = 11 sen
CAPITAL: Kuala Lumpur
POPULATION: 20,600,000

MALDIVES

PERSON: Maldivian
RELATED ADJ.: Maldivian
CURRENCY: rufiyaa = 100 laris
CAPITAL: Male
POPULATION: 300,000

MALI

PERSON: Malian
RELATED ADJ.: Malian
CURRENCY: African franc
CAPITAL: Bamako
POPULATION: 11,100,000

MALTA

PERSON: Maltese
RELATED ADJ.: Maltese
CURRENCY: Maltese lira = 100 cents
CAPITAL: Valletta
POPULATION: 400,000

MARSHALL ISLANDS

PERSON: n/a
RELATED ADJ.: n/a
CURRENCY: US dollar
CAPITAL: Majuro
POPULATION: 54,000

MAURITANIA

PERSON: Mauritanian
RELATED ADJ.: Mauritanian
CURRENCY: ouguiya = 5 khoums
CAPITAL: Nouakchott
POPULATION: 2,300,000

MAURITIUS

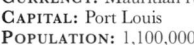

PERSON: Mauritian
RELATED ADJ.: Mauritian
CURRENCY: Mauritian rupee = 100 cents
CAPITAL: Port Louis
POPULATION: 1,100,000

MEXICO

PERSON: Mexican
RELATED ADJ.: Mexican
CURRENCY: Mexican new peso = 100 centavos
CAPITAL: Mexico City
POPULATION: 95,500,000

MICRONESIA

PERSON: Micronesian
RELATED ADJ.: Micronesian
CURRENCY: US dollar
CAPITAL: Kolonia
POPULATION: 104,000

MOLDAVIA

PERSON: Moldovan
RELATED ADJ.: Moldovan
CURRENCY: leu = 100 bani
CAPITAL: Chişinău
POPULATION: 4,400,000

MONACO

PERSON: Monégasque/Monacan
RELATED ADJ.: Monégasque/Monacan
CURRENCY: French franc = 100 centimes
CAPITAL: Monaco
POPULATION: 31,000

MONGOLIA

PERSON: Mongolian
RELATED ADJ.: Mongolian
CURRENCY: tugrik = 100 mongos
CAPITAL: Ulan Bator
POPULATION: 2,500,000

MOROCCO

PERSON: Moroccan
RELATED ADJ.: Moroccan
CURRENCY: Moroccan dirham = 100 centimes
CAPITAL: Rabat
POPULATION: 27,600,000

MOZAMBIQUE

PERSON: Mozambican
RELATED ADJ.: Mozambican
CURRENCY: metical = 100 centavos
CAPITAL: Maputo
POPULATION: 16,500,000

NAMIBIA

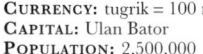

PERSON: Namibian
RELATED ADJ.: Namibian
CURRENCY: South African rand = 100 cents
CAPITAL: Windhoek
POPULATION: 1,600,000

NAURU

PERSON: Nauruan
RELATED ADJ.: Nauruan
CURRENCY: Australian dollar
CAPITAL: No official capital
POPULATION: 11,000

NEPAL

PERSON: Nepalese
RELATED ADJ.: Nepalese
CURRENCY: Nepalese rupee = 100 paisa
CAPITAL: Kathmandu
POPULATION: 22,500,000

NETHERLANDS

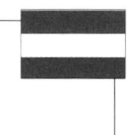

PERSON: Dutchman/Dutchwoman
RELATED ADJ.: Dutch
CURRENCY: guilder = 100 cents
CAPITALS: Amsterdam, The Hague
POPULATION: 15,600,000

NEW ZEALAND

PERSON: New Zealander
RELATED ADJ.: n/a
CURRENCY: New Zealand dollar = 100 cents
CAPITAL: Wellington
POPULATION: 3,600,000

NICARAGUA

PERSON: Nicaraguan
RELATED ADJ.: Nicaraguan
CURRENCY: cordoba = 100 centavos
CAPITAL: Managua
POPULATION: 4,600,000

NIGER

PERSON: Nigerien
RELATED ADJ.: Nigerien
CURRENCY: African franc
CAPITAL: Niamey
POPULATION: 9,500,000

NIGERIA

PERSON: Nigerian
RELATED ADJ.: Nigerian
CURRENCY: naira = 100 kobo
CAPITAL: Abuja
POPULATION: 115,000,000

NORTH KOREA

PERSON: North Korean
RELATED ADJ.: North Korean
CURRENCY: won = 100 jun
CAPITAL: Pyongyang
POPULATION: 24,300,000

NORWAY

PERSON: Norwegian
RELATED ADJ.: Norwegian
CURRENCY: Norwegian krone = 100 øre
CAPITAL: Oslo
POPULATION: 4,400,000

OMAN

PERSON: Omani
RELATED ADJ.: Omani
CURRENCY: rial = 1,000 baiza
CAPITAL: Muscat
POPULATION: 2,300,000

PAKISTAN

PERSON: Pakistani
RELATED ADJ.: Pakistani
CURRENCY: Pakistani rupee = 100 paisa
CAPITAL: Islamabad
POPULATION: 144,500,000

PALAU

PERSON: Palauan
RELATED ADJ.: Palauan
CURRENCY: US dollar
CAPITAL: Oreor
POPULATION: 16,500

PANAMA

PERSON: Panamanian
RELATED ADJ.: Panamanian
CURRENCY: balboa = 100 centésimos
CAPITAL: Panama City
POPULATION: 2,700,000

PAPUA NEW GUINEA

PERSON: Papua New Guinean
RELATED ADJ.: Papua New Guinean
CURRENCY: kina = 100 toea
CAPITAL: Port Moresby
POPULATION: 4,400,000

PARAGUAY

PERSON: Paraguayan
RELATED ADJ.: Paraguayan
CURRENCY: guaraní = 100 centimos
CAPITAL: Asunción
POPULATION: 5,100,000

PERU

PERSON: Peruvian
RELATED ADJ.: Peruvian
CURRENCY: New sol = 100 cents
CAPITAL: Lima
POPULATION: 24,200,000

PHILIPPINES

PERSON: Filipino/Filipina
RELATED ADJ.: Filipino/Philippine
CURRENCY: Philippine peso = 100 centavos
CAPITAL: Manila
POPULATION: 69,000,000

POLAND

PERSON: Pole
RELATED ADJ.: Polish
CURRENCY: zloty = 100 groszy
CAPITAL: Warsaw
POPULATION: 38,400,000

PORTUGAL

PERSON: Portuguese
RELATED ADJ.: Portuguese
CURRENCY: escudo
CAPITAL: Lisbon
POPULATION: 9,800,000

QATAR
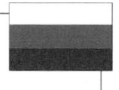
PERSON: Qatari
RELATED ADJ.: Qatari
CURRENCY: Qatar riyal = 100 dirhams
CAPITAL: Doha
POPULATION: 600,000

ROMANIA

PERSON: Romanian
RELATED ADJ.: Romanian
CURRENCY: leu = 100 bani
CAPITAL: Bucharest
POPULATION: 22,800,000

RUSSIAN FEDERATION

PERSON: Russian
RELATED ADJ.: Russian
CURRENCY: rouble = 100 copecks
CAPITAL: Moscow
POPULATION: 146,700,000

RWANDA

PERSON: Rwandan
RELATED ADJ.: Rwandan
CURRENCY: Rwandan franc
CAPITAL: Kigali
POPULATION: 8,200,000

ST KITTS & NEVIS

PERSON: n/a
RELATED ADJ.: n/a
CURRENCY: East Caribbean dollar = 100 cents
CAPITAL: Basseterre
POPULATION: 41,000

ST LUCIA

PERSON: St Lucian
RELATED ADJ.: St Lucian
CURRENCY: East Caribbean dollar = 100 cents
CAPITAL: Castries
POPULATION: 141,000

ST VINCENT & THE GRENADINES

PERSON: Vincentian/Grenadian
RELATED ADJ.: Vincentian/Grenadian
CURRENCY: East Caribbean dollar = 100 cents
CAPITAL: Kingstown **POPULATION:** 111,000

SAMOA

PERSON: Samoan
RELATED ADJ.: Samoan
CURRENCY: tala = 100 sene
CAPITAL: Apia
POPULATION: 200,000

SAN MARINO

PERSON: n/a
RELATED ADJ.: n/a
CURRENCY: Italian lira
CAPITAL: San Marino
POPULATION: 25,000

SÃO TOMÉ & PRINCIPE

PERSON: n/a
RELATED ADJ.: n/a
CURRENCY: dobra = 100 centavos
CAPITAL: São Tomé **POPULATION:** 125,000

SAUDI ARABIA

PERSON: Saudi Arabian/Saudi
RELATED ADJ.: Saudi Arabian/Saudi
CURRENCY: Saudi riyal = 20 qursh
CAPITAL: Riyadh
POPULATION: 18,400,000

SENEGAL

PERSON: Senegalese
RELATED ADJ.: Senegalese
CURRENCY: African franc
CAPITAL: Dakar
POPULATION: 8,500,000

SEYCHELLES

PERSON: Seychellois
RELATED ADJ.: Seychellois
CURRENCY: Seychellois rupee = 100 cents
CAPITAL: Victoria
POPULATION: 74,000

SIERRA LEONE

PERSON: Sierra Leonian
RELATED ADJ.: Sierra Leonian
CURRENCY: leone = 100 cents
CAPITAL: Freetown
POPULATION: 4,600,000

SINGAPORE

PERSON: Singaporean
RELATED ADJ.: Singaporean
CURRENCY: Singaporean dollar = 100 cents
CAPITAL: Singapore
POPULATION: 2,900,000

SLOVAKIA

PERSON: Slovak
RELATED ADJ.: Slovak
CURRENCY: koruna = 100 haleru
CAPITAL: Bratislava
POPULATION: 5,400,000

SLOVENIA
PERSON: Slovene/Slovenian
RELATED ADJ.: Slovene/Slovenian
CURRENCY: tolar = 100 stotins
CAPITAL: Ljubljana
POPULATION: 1,900,000

SOLOMON ISLANDS
PERSON: Solomon Islander
RELATED ADJ.: n/a
CURRENCY: Solomon Islands dollar = 100 cents
CAPITAL: Honiara
POPULATION: 400,000

SOMALIA
PERSON: Somali
RELATED ADJ.: Somali
CURRENCY: Somali shilling = 100 cents
CAPITAL: Mogadishu
POPULATION: 9,500,000

SOUTH AFRICA

PERSON: South African
RELATED ADJ.: South African
CURRENCY: rand = 100 cents
CAPITALS: Pretoria, Cape Town, Bloemfontein
POPULATION: 42,400,000

SOUTH KOREA

PERSON: South Korean
RELATED ADJ.: South Korean
CURRENCY: won = 100 jeon
CAPITAL: Seoul
POPULATION: 45,400,000

SPAIN

PERSON: Spaniard
RELATED ADJ.: Spanish
CURRENCY: peseta = 100 centimos
CAPITAL: Madrid
POPULATION: 39,700,000

SRI LANKA

PERSON: Sri Lankan
RELATED ADJ.: Sri Lankan
CURRENCY: Sri Lankan rupee = 100 cents
CAPITAL: Colombo
POPULATION: 18,600,000

SUDAN

PERSON: Sudanese
RELATED ADJ.: Sudanese
CURRENCY: Sudanese dinar = 10 pounds
CAPITAL: Khartoum
POPULATION: 28,900,000

SURINAM

PERSON: Surinamer/Surinamese
RELATED ADJ.: Surinamer/Surinamese
CURRENCY: Surinamese guilder = 100 cents
CAPITAL: Paramaribo
POPULATION: 400,000

SWAZILAND

PERSON: Swazi
RELATED ADJ.: Swazi
CURRENCY: lilangeni = 100 cents
CAPITAL: Mbabane
POPULATION: 900,000

SWEDEN

PERSON: Swede
RELATED ADJ.: Swedish
CURRENCY: Swedish krona = 100 øre
CAPITAL: Stockholm
POPULATION: 8,800,000

SWITZERLAND

PERSON: Swiss
RELATED ADJ.: Swiss
CURRENCY: Swiss franc = 100 centimes
CAPITAL: Bern
POPULATION: 7,300,000

SYRIA

PERSON: Syrian
RELATED ADJ.: Syrian
CURRENCY: Syrian pound = 100 piastres
CAPITAL: Damascus
POPULATION: 15,200,000

TAIWAN

PERSON: Taiwanese
RELATED ADJ.: Taiwanese
CURRENCY: new Taiwanese dollar = 100 cents
CAPITAL: Taipei
POPULATION: 21,125,792

TAJIKISTAN

PERSON: Tajik/Tadjik
RELATED ADJ.: Tajik/Tadjik
CURRENCY: Russian rouble
CAPITAL: Dushanbe
POPULATION: 6,300,000

TANZANIA

PERSON: Tanzanian
RELATED ADJ.: Tanzanian
CURRENCY: Tanzanian shilling = 100 cents
CAPITAL: Dodoma
POPULATION: 30,500,000

THAILAND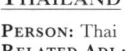

PERSON: Thai
RELATED ADJ.: Thai
CURRENCY: baht = 100 satangs
CAPITAL: Bangkok
POPULATION: 59,400,000

TOGO

PERSON: Togolese
RELATED ADJ.: Togolese
CURRENCY: African franc
CAPITAL: Lomé
POPULATION: 4,300,000

TONGA

PERSON: Tongolese
RELATED ADJ.: Tongolese
CURRENCY: pa'anga = 100 seniti
CAPITAL: Nuku'alofa
POPULATION: 98,000

TRINIDAD & TOBAGO

PERSON: Trinidadian/Tobagonian
RELATED ADJ.: Trinidadian and/or Tobagonian
CURRENCY: Trinidadian dollar = 100 cents
CAPITAL: Port-of-Spain
POPULATION: 1,300,000

TUNISIA

PERSON: Tunisian
RELATED ADJ.: Tunisian
CURRENCY: Tunisian dinar = 1,000 milliemes
CAPITAL: Tunis
POPULATION: 9,100,000

TURKEY

PERSON: Turk
RELATED ADJ.: Turkish
CURRENCY: Turkish lira = 100 kurus
CAPITAL: Ankara
POPULATION: 63,100,000

TURKMENISTAN

PERSON: Turkmen/Turkoman
RELATED ADJ.: Turkmen/Turkoman
CURRENCY: manat = 100 tenge
CAPITAL: Ashgabat
POPULATION: 4,200,000

TUVALU

PERSON: Tuvaluan
RELATED ADJ.: Tuvaluan
CURRENCY: Tuvaluan dollar = 100 cents
CAPITAL: Fongafale
POPULATION: 9,000

UGANDA

PERSON: Ugandan
RELATED ADJ.: Ugandan
CURRENCY: Ugandan shilling = 100 cents
CAPITAL: Kampala
POPULATION: 22,000,000

UKRAINE

PERSON: Ukrainian
RELATED ADJ.: Ukrainian
CURRENCY: karbovanet (coupon)
CAPITAL: Kiev
POPULATION: 51,300,000

UNITED ARAB EMIRATES

PERSON: n/a
RELATED ADJ.: n/a
CURRENCY: UAE dirham = 100 fils
CAPITAL: Abu Dhabi **POPULATION:** 1,900,000

UNITED KINGDOM

PERSON: Briton
RELATED ADJ.: British
CURRENCY: pound sterling = 100 pence
CAPITAL: London
POPULATION: 58,400,000

UNITED STATES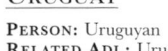

PERSON: American
RELATED ADJ.: American
CURRENCY: dollar = 100 cents
CAPITAL: Washington, DC
POPULATION: 265,800,000

URUGUAY

PERSON: Uruguyan
RELATED ADJ.: Uruguyan
CURRENCY: new Uruguyan peso = 100 centésimos
CAPITAL: Montevideo **POPULATION:** 3,200,000

UZBEKISTAN

PERSON: Uzbek
RELATED ADJ.: Uzbek
CURRENCY: som
CAPITAL: Tashkent
POPULATION: 23,300,000

VANUATU

PERSON: n/a
RELATED ADJ.: n/a
CURRENCY: vatu = 100 centimes
CAPITAL: Port-Vila
POPULATION: 200,000

VATICAN CITY

PERSON: n/a
RELATED ADJ.: Vatican
CURRENCY: lira
CAPITAL: n/a
POPULATION: 1,000

VENEZUELA

PERSON: Venezuelan
RELATED ADJ.: Venezuelan
CURRENCY: bolívar = 100 centimos
CAPITAL: Caracas
POPULATION: 22,300,000

VIETNAM

PERSON: Vietnamese
RELATED ADJ.: Vietnamese
CURRENCY: dong = 10 hao
CAPITAL: Hanoi
POPULATION: 76,200,000

YEMEN

PERSON: Yemeni
RELATED ADJ.: Yemeni
CURRENCY: rial (north), dinar (south)
CAPITAL: Sana
POPULATION: 15,100,000

YUGOSLAVIA (SERBIA & MONTENEGRO)

PERSON: Yugoslav
RELATED ADJ.: Yugoslav
CURRENCY: dinar = 100 paras
CAPITAL: Belgrade **POPULATION:** 10,900,000

ZAMBIA

PERSON: Zambian
RELATED ADJ.: Zambian
CURRENCY: kwacha = 100 ngwee
CAPITAL: Lusaka
POPULATION: 9,700,000

ZIMBABWE

PERSON: Zimbabwean
RELATED ADJ.: Zimbabwean
CURRENCY: Zimbabwean dollar = 100 cents
CAPITAL: Harare
POPULATION: 11,500,000

THE NIGHT SKY

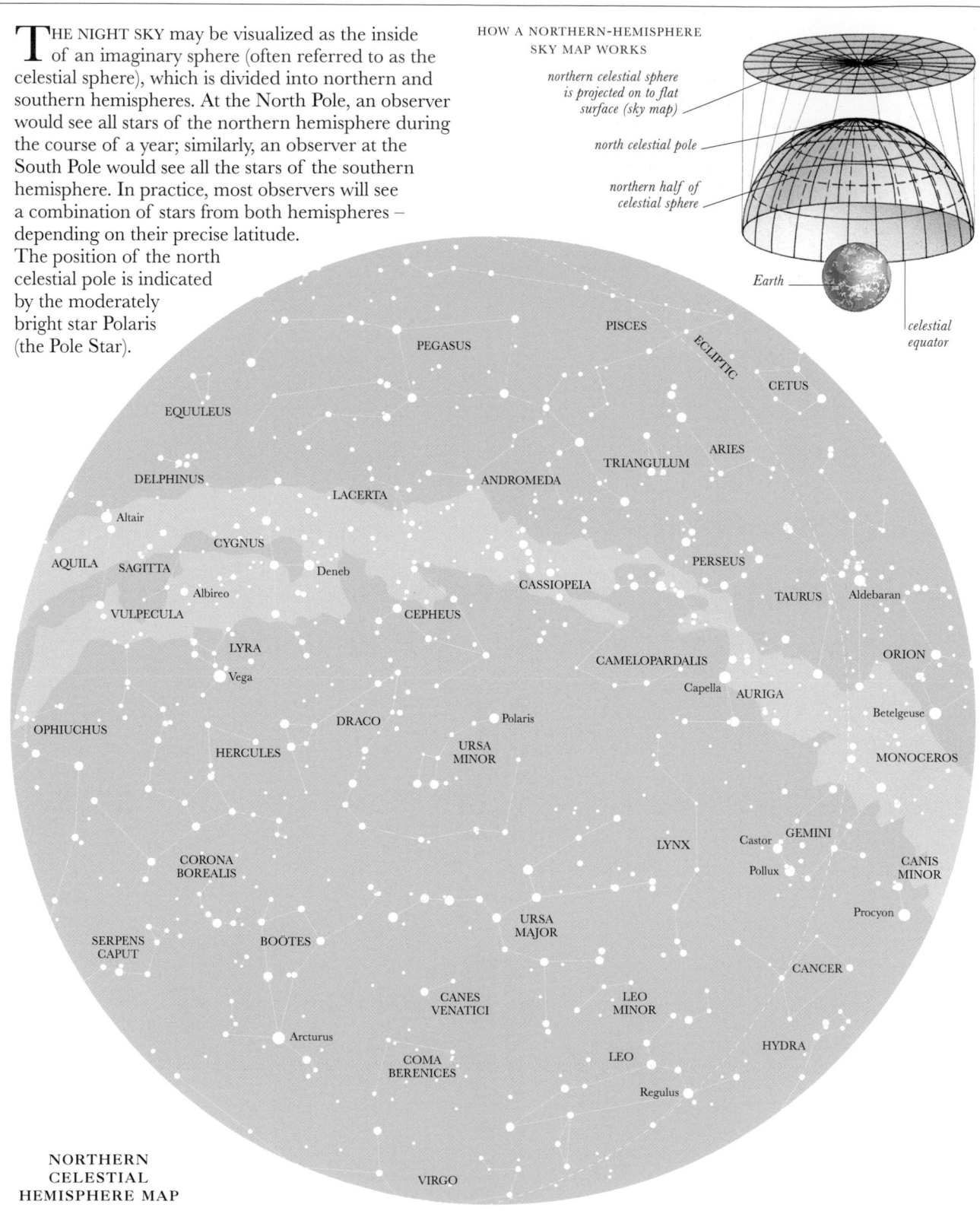

THE NIGHT SKY may be visualized as the inside of an imaginary sphere (often referred to as the celestial sphere), which is divided into northern and southern hemispheres. At the North Pole, an observer would see all stars of the northern hemisphere during the course of a year; similarly, an observer at the South Pole would see all the stars of the southern hemisphere. In practice, most observers will see a combination of stars from both hemispheres – depending on their precise latitude. The position of the north celestial pole is indicated by the moderately bright star Polaris (the Pole Star).

HOW A NORTHERN-HEMISPHERE SKY MAP WORKS

northern celestial sphere is projected on to flat surface (sky map)

north celestial pole

northern half of celestial sphere

Earth

celestial equator

PISCES

PEGASUS

ECLIPTIC

CETUS

EQUULEUS

ARIES

TRIANGULUM

DELPHINUS

ANDROMEDA

LACERTA

Altair

CYGNUS

PERSEUS

AQUILA

SAGITTA

Deneb

TAURUS

Aldebaran

Albireo

CASSIOPEIA

VULPECULA

CEPHEUS

ORION

LYRA

CAMELOPARDALIS

Vega

Capella

AURIGA

Betelgeuse

OPHIUCHUS

DRACO

Polaris

HERCULES

URSA MINOR

MONOCEROS

GEMINI

LYNX

Castor

CANIS MINOR

CORONA BOREALIS

Pollux

Procyon

SERPENS CAPUT

BOÖTES

URSA MAJOR

CANCER

CANES VENATICI

LEO MINOR

Arcturus

HYDRA

COMA BERENICES

LEO

Regulus

NORTHERN CELESTIAL HEMISPHERE MAP

VIRGO

WHILE STARS IN THE southern hemisphere appear to rotate around the south celestial pole, there is no equivalent of Polaris to mark the position of the southern pole. An observer of the southern celestial hemisphere is looking towards the centre of our galaxy. Since stars in that direction are more densely massed, southern skies appear brighter than those in the northern hemisphere. The southern sky includes Crux (the Southern Cross), as well as the brightest star in the sky, Sirius, located in the constellation Canis Major. It also contains Alpha Centauri, one of the stars nearest to the Sun.

HOW A SOUTHERN-HEMISPHERE SKY MAP WORKS

Earth

celestial equator

southern half of celestial sphere

south celestial pole

southern celestial sphere is projected on to flat surface (sky map)

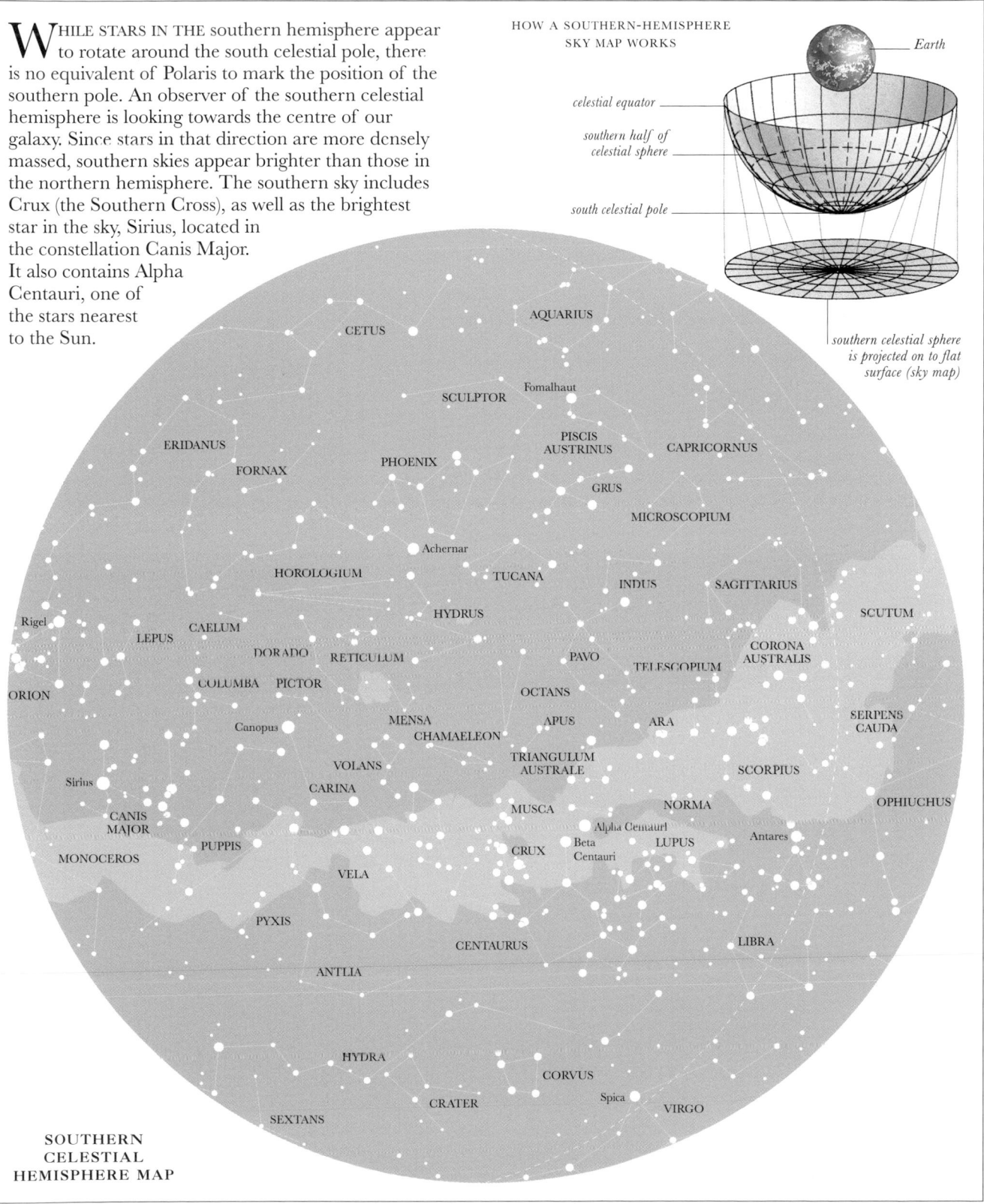

SOUTHERN CELESTIAL HEMISPHERE MAP

MEASUREMENTS

METRIC MEASURES, WITH IMPERIAL EQUIVALENTS

LINEAR MEASURE
1 millimetre = 0.039 inch
1 centimetre = 10 mm = 0.394 inch
1 decimetre = 10 cm = 3.94 inches
1 metre = 100 cm = 1.094 yards
1 kilometre = 1,000 m = 0.6214 mile

SQUARE MEASURE
1 square centimetre = 0.155 sq. inch
1 square metre = 10,000 sq. cm = 1.196 sq. yards
1 acre = 100 sq. m = 119.6 sq. yards
1 hectare = 100 acres = 2.471 acres
1 square kilometre = 100 hectares = 0.386 sq. mile

CUBIC MEASURE
1 cubic centimetre = 0.061 cu. inch
1 cubic metre = 1,000,000 cu. cm = 1.308 cu. yards

CAPACITY MEASURE
1 millilitre = 0.002 pint (British)
1 centilitre = 10 ml = 0.018 pint
1 decilitre = 10 cl = 0.176 pint
1 litre = 1,000 ml = 1.76 pints
1 decalitre = 10 l = 2.20 gallons
1 hectolitre = 100 l = 2.75 bushels
1 kilolitre = 1,000 l = 3.44 quarters

WEIGHT
1 milligram = 0.015 grain
1 centigram = 10 mg = 0.154 grain
1 decigram = 100 mg = 1.543 grains
1 gram = 1,000 mg = 15.43 grains
1 decagram = 10 g = 5.64 drams
1 hectogram = 100 g = 3.527 ounces
1 kilogram = 1,000 g = 2.205 pounds
1 tonne (metric ton) = 1,000 kg = 0.984 (long) ton

BRITISH (IMPERIAL) AND AMERICAN MEASURES, WITH METRIC EQUIVALENTS

LINEAR MEASURE
1 inch = 25.4 millimetres exactly
1 foot = 12 inches = 0.3048 metre exactly
1 yard = 3 feet = 0.9144 metre exactly
1 (statute) mile = 1.609 kilometres = 1,760 yards
1 int. nautical mile = 1.852 kilometres
= 1.150779 miles exactly

SQUARE MEASURE
1 square inch = 6.45 sq. cm
1 square foot = 144 sq. in = 9.29 sq. decimetres
1 square yard = 9 sq. ft = 0.836 sq. metre
1 acre = 4,840 sq. yd = 0.405 hectare
1 square mile = 640 acres = 259 hectares

CUBIC MEASURE
1 cubic inch = 16.4 cu. cm
1 cubic foot = 1,728 cu. in. = 0.0283 cu. metre
1 cubic yard = 27 cu. ft = 0.765 cu. metre

CAPACITY MEASURE
BRITISH
1 fluid oz = 1.8047 cu. in. = 0.0282 litre
1 gill = 5 fluid oz = 0.1421 litre
1 pint = 20 fluid oz = 34.68 cu. in. = 0.568 litre
1 quart = 2 pints = 1.136 litres
1 gallon = 4 quarts = 4.546 litres
1 peck = 2 gallons = 9.092 litres
1 bushel = 4 pecks = 36.4 litres

AMERICAN DRY
1 pint = 33.60 cu. in. = 0.550 litre
1 quart = 2 pints = 1.101 litres
1 peck = 8 quarts = 8.81 litres
1 bushel = 4 pecks = 35.3 litres

AMERICAN LIQUID
1 fluid oz = 0.0296 litre
1 pint = 16 fluid oz = 28.88 cu. in. = 0.473 litre
1 quart = 2 pints = 0.946 litre
1 gallon = 4 quarts = 3.785 litres

AVOIRDUPOIS WEIGHT
1 grain = 0.065 gram
1 dram = 1.772 grams
1 ounce = 16 drams = 28.35 grams
1 pound = 16 ounces = 7,000 grains
= 0.4536 kilogram (0.45359237 exactly)
1 stone = 14 pounds = 6.35 kilograms
1 hundredweight = 112 pounds = 50.80 kilograms
1 short ton = 2,000 pounds = 0.907 tonne
1 (long) ton = 20 hundredweight = 1.016 tonnes

METRIC PREFIXES

NAME	ABBREVIATIONS	FACTORS
deca-	da	10
hecto-	h	10^2
kilo-	k	10^3
mega-	M	10^6
giga-	G	10^9
tera-	T	10^{12}
peta-	P	10^{15}
exa-	E	10^{18}
deci-	d	10^{-1}
centi-	c	10^{-2}
milli-	m	10^{-3}
micro-	μ	10^{-6}
nano-	n	10^{-9}
pico-	p	10^{-12}
femto-	f	10^{-15}
atto-	a	10^{-18}

Pronunciations and derivations of the above are given at their alphabetical places in the illustrated dictionary. They may be applied to any units of the metric system:

hectogram (abbr. hg) = 100 grams
kilowatt (abbr. kW) = 1,000 watts
megahertz (MHz) = 1 million hertz
centimetre (cm) = 1/100 metre
microvolt (μV) = one millionth of a volt
picofarad (pF) = 10^{-12} farad

and are sometimes applied to other units (megabit, microinch).

SI UNITS

BASE UNITS

PHYSICAL QUANTITY	NAME	ABBREVIATION/SYMBOL
length	metre	m
mass	kilogram	kg
time	second	s
electric current	ampere	A
temperature	kelvin	K
amount of substance	mole	mol
luminous intensity	candela	cd

SUPPLEMENTARY UNITS

PHYSICAL QUANTITY	NAME	ABBREVIATION/SYMBOL
plane angle	radian	rad
solid angle	steradian	sr

DERIVED UNITS WITH SPECIAL NAMES

PHYSICAL QUANTITY	NAME	ABBREVIATION/SYMBOL
frequency	hertz	Hz
energy	joule	J
force	newton	N
power	watt	W
pressure	pascal	Pa
electric charge	coulomb	C
electromotive force	volt	V
electric resistance	ohm	Ω
electric conductance	siemens	S
electric capacitance	farad	F
magnetic flux	weber	Wb
inductance	henry	H
magnetic flux density	tesla	T
luminous flux	lumen	lm
illumination	lux	lx

TEMPERATURE

Celsius or Centigrade
water boils at 100° and freezes at 0°.

Fahrenheit
water boils (under standard conditions) at 212° and freezes at 32°.

Kelvin
water boils at 373.15 K and freezes at 273.15 K.

To convert Fahrenheit into Centigrade:
subtract 32, multiply by 5, and divide by 9.

To convert Centigrade into Fahrenheit:
multiply by 9, divide by 5, and add 32.

To convert Centigrade into Kelvin:
add 273.15.

TEMPERATURE CONVERSION

Celsius	–20	–10	0	10	20	30	40	50	60	70	80	90	100
Fahrenheit	–4	14	32	50	68	86	104	122	140	158	176	194	212
Kelvin	253	263	273	283	293	303	313	323	333	343	353	363	373

TEMPERATURE SCALE

°C →	°F	°F →	°C
– 40	– 40	– 40	– 40
– 10	14	– 10	– 23
0	32	0	– 18
10	50	10	– 12
20	68	20	– 7
30	86	30	– 1
40	104	40	4
50	122	50	10
60	140	60	16
70	158	70	21
80	176	80	27
90	194	90	32
100	212	100	38
	(exact)		(approx.)

POWER NOTATION

This expresses concisely any power of 10 (any number that is formed by multiplying or dividing ten by itself), and is sometimes used in the main dictionary.

10^2 (ten squared) = 10 × 10 = 100
10^3 (ten cubed) = 10 × 10 × 10 = 1,000
10^4 = 10 × 10 × 10 × 10 = 10,000
10^{10} = 10,000,000,000
(1 followed by ten noughts)
10^{-2} = 1/10^2 = 1/100 = 0.01
10^{-10} = 1/10^{10} = 1/10,000,000,000 = 0.0000001
6.2 × 10^3 = 6,200
4.7 × 10^{-2} = 0.047

PAPER SIZES

International paper sizes are based upon a rectangle of paper with an area of one square metre, the sides of which are in the proportion 1:√2. This geometrical relationship is used so that any lengthways halving of the original rectangle of paper produces another rectangle of paper with the same geometric relationship. For example, the widely used A series is shown below. All measurements are given in millimetres.

A0	841 × 1189	A6	105 × 148
A1	594 × 841	A7	74 × 105
A2	420 × 594	A8	52 × 74
A3	297 × 420	A9	37 × 52
A4	210 × 297	A10	26 × 37
A5	148 × 210		

A0

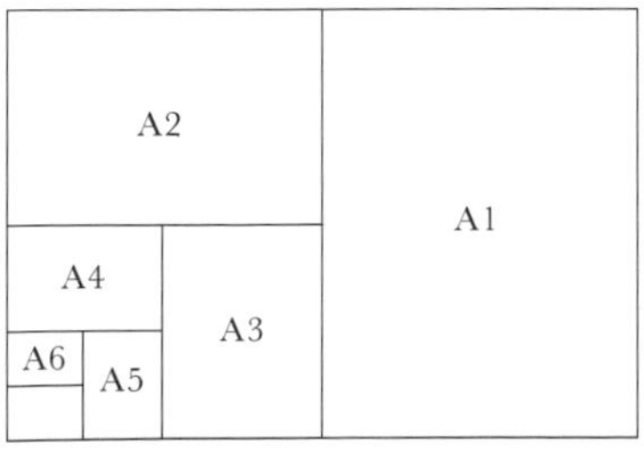

CLOTHING SIZES

MEN'S SHOES

UK	USA	Europe
6½	7	39
7	7½	40
7½	8	41
8	8½	42
8½	9	43
9½	10	44
10	10½	44
10½	11	45

WOMEN'S SHOES

UK	USA	Europe
3½	5	36
4½	6	37
5½	7	38
6½	8	39
7½	9	40

CHILDREN'S SHOES

UK	USA	Europe
0	0	15
1	1	17
2	2	18
3	3	19
4	4	20
4½	4½	21
5	5	22
6	6	23
7	7	24
8	8	25
8½	8½	26
9	9	27
10	10	28
11	11	29
12	12	30
12½	12½	31
13	13	32

MEN'S SUITS/OVERCOATS

UK	USA	Europe
36	36	46
38	38	48
40	40	50
42	42	52
44	44	54
46	46	56

MEN'S SHIRTS

UK	USA	Europe
12	12	30–31
12½	12½	32
13	13	33
13½	13½	34–35
14	14	36
14½	14½	37
15	15	38
15½	15½	39–40
16	16	41
16½	16½	42
17	17	43
17½	17½	44–45

MEN'S SOCKS

UK	USA	Europe
9	9	38–39
10	10	39–40
10½	10½	40–41
11	11	41–42
11½	11½	42–43

WOMEN'S CLOTHING

UK	USA	Europe
8	6	36
10	8	38
12	10	40
14	12	42
16	14	44
18	16	46
20	18	48
22	20	50
24	22	52

CHILDREN'S CLOTHING

UK	USA	Europe
16–18	2	40–45
20–22	4	50–55
24–26	6	60–65
28–30	7	70–75
32–34	8	80–85
36–38	9	90–95

NUMBERS AND SYMBOLS

ROMAN NUMERALS

1	I	24	XXIV	99	XCIX
2	II	25	XXV	100	C
3	III	26	XXVI	101	CI
4	IV	27	XXVII	144	CXLIV
5	V	28	XXVIII	200	CC
6	VI	29	XXIX	400	CD
7	VII	30	XXX		(or CCCC)
8	VIII	31	XXXI	500	D
9	IX	32	XXXII	900	CM
10	X	33	XXXIII		(or DCCCC)
11	XI	34	XXXIV	1000	M
12	XII	35	XXXV	1900	MCM (or
13	XIII	36	XXXVI		MDCCCC)
14	XIV	37	XXXVII	1995	MCMXCV
15	XV	38	XXXVIII	1999	MCMXCIX
16	XVI	39	XXXIX	2000	MM
17	XVII	40	XL	2005	MMV
18	XVIII	49	XLIX	2010	MMX
19	XIX	50	L		
20	XX	60	LX		
21	XXI	70	LXX		
22	XXII	80	LXXX		
23	XXIII	90	XC		

MATHEMATICAL SYMBOLS

$+$	plus, positive	$\geq$	greater than, equal to
$-$	minus, negative	$\leq$	less than, equal to
$\pm$	plus or minus, positive or negative	$\gg$	much greater than
$\times$	multiplied by	$\ll$	much less than
$\div$	divided by	$\sqrt{}$	square root
$=$	equal to	∞	infinity
$\equiv$	identically equal to	$\propto$	proportional to
$\neq$	not equal to	Σ	sum of
$\not\equiv$	not identically equal to	Π	product of
$\approx$	approximately equal to	Δ	difference
$\sim$	of the order of, similar to	$\therefore$	therefore
$>$	greater than	$\angle$	angle
$<$	less than	$\parallel$	parallel to
$\not>$	not greater than	$\perp$	perpendicular to
$\not<$	not less than	$:$	is to

PHYSICS SYMBOLS

α	alpha particle
β	beta ray
γ	gamma ray; photon
ε	electromotive force
η	efficiency; viscosity
λ	wavelength
μ	micro-; permeability
ν	frequency; neutrino
ρ	density; resistivity
σ	conductivity
c	velocity of light
e	electronic charge

CHEMISTRY SYMBOLS

$+$	plus; together with
$-$	single bond
$\cdot$	single bond; single unpaired electron; two separate parts or compounds regarded as loosely joined
$=$	double bond
$\equiv$	triple bond
R	group
X	halogen atom
Z	atomic number

BIOLOGY SYMBOLS

$\bigcirc$	female individual (used in inheritance charts)
$\square$	male individual (used in inheritance charts)
$\female$	female
$\male$	male
$\times$	crossed with; hybrid
$+$	wild type
F_1	offspring of the first generation
F_2	offspring of the second generation

BRAILLE

A	F	K	P	U	Z		
B	G	L	Q	V	AND		
C	H	M	R	W	OF		
D	I	N	S	X	FOR		
E	J	O	T	Y	THE		

LAUNDRY CODES

	machine or hand wash (at temperature shown)
	tumble dry
	do not tumble dry
	iron
	do not iron
	dry-cleanable
	do not dry-clean
	can be bleached
	do not bleach

PERIODIC TABLE OF THE ELEMENTS

An element is a substance that cannot be broken down into a more basic substance by chemical means. It is the basic matter from which all other matter is composed. Each element is made up of only one atom and each element is assigned an atomic number. The periodic table is a conventional presentation of the complete list of known chemical elements in a form that allows easy identification of the relationships between them. The table lays out the chemical elements in order of increasing atomic number, as well as into 'groups' (columns) of elements with similar properties. The rows of elements that arise from this are called 'periods'. The chemical properties of the elements, as well as their atomic number, change gradually along each period.

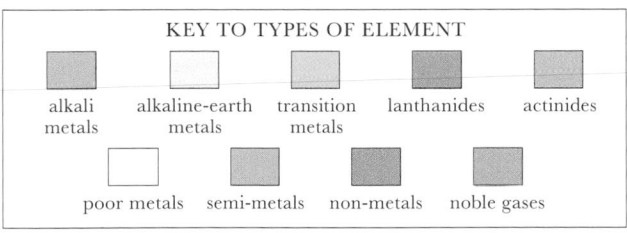

KEY TO TYPES OF ELEMENT

alkali metals · alkaline-earth metals · transition metals · lanthanides · actinides

poor metals · semi-metals · non-metals · noble gases

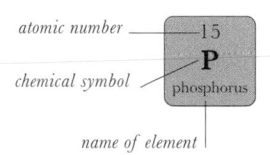

atomic number — 15
chemical symbol — P
name of element — phosphorus

NUMBER, SYMBOL, AND NAME
Every box contains the following basic information about the element:
• its atomic number, which is the number of protons in the nuclei of the element's atoms. This is also the number of orbiting electrons.
• its chemical symbol.
• its chemical name.

GROUPS AND PERIODS

The first element within each period (row) is an extremely reactive alkali metal with one electron in its outer shell. At the far end of the period is a stable noble gas in group 18 (0) that has eight electrons in its outer shell. All the elements in one group (column) have a similar number of electrons in their outer shells.

metallic properties decrease to the right

1	2	3	4	5	6	7	8	9	10	11	12	13	14	15	16	17	18
1 H hydrogen																	2 He helium
3 Li lithium	4 Be beryllium											5 B boron	6 C carbon	7 N nitrogen	8 O oxygen	9 F fluorine	10 Ne neon
11 Na sodium	12 Mg magnesium											13 Al aluminium	14 Si silicon	15 P phosphorus	16 S sulphur	17 Cl chlorine	18 Ar argon
19 K potassium	20 Ca calcium	21 Sc scandium	22 Ti titanium	23 V vanadium	24 Cr chromium	25 Mn manganese	26 Fe iron	27 Co cobalt	28 Ni nickel	29 Cu copper	30 Zn zinc	31 Ga gallium	32 Ge germanium	33 As arsenic	34 Se selenium	35 Br bromine	36 Kr krypton
37 Rb rubidium	38 Sr strontium	39 Y yttrium	40 Zr zirconium	41 Nb niobium	42 Mo molybdenum	43 Tc technetium	44 Ru ruthenium	45 Rh rhodium	46 Pd palladium	47 Ag silver	48 Cd cadmium	49 In indium	50 Sn tin	51 Sb antimony	52 Te tellurium	53 I iodine	54 Xe xenon
55 Cs caesium	56 Ba barium	57–71 lanthanides	72 Hf hafnium	73 Ta tantalum	74 W tungsten	75 Re rhenium	76 Os osmium	77 Ir iridium	78 Pt platinum	79 Au gold	80 Hg mercury	81 Tl thallium	82 Pb lead	83 Bi bismuth	84 Po polonium	85 At astatine	86 Rn radon
87 Fr francium	88 Ra radium	89–103 actinides	104 Rf rutherfordium	105 Db dubnium	106 Sg seaborgium	107 Bh bohrium	108 Hs hassium	109 Mt meitnerium									

GROUP I GROUP II

GROUP III GROUP IV GROUP V GROUP VI GROUP VII GROUP 0

an alternative (roman) numbering system is also used to group the elements

ionization energy decreases down the table

Lanthanides and actinides are positioned away from the rest of the table to make the shape of the table easier to interpret.

LANTHANIDES AND ACTINIDES

57 La lanthanum	58 Ce cerium	59 Pr praseodymium	60 Nd neodymium	61 Pm promethium	62 Sm samarium	63 Eu europium	64 Gd gadolinium	65 Tb terbium	66 Dy dysprosium	67 Ho holmium	68 Er erbium	69 Tm thulium	70 Yb ytterbium	71 Lu lutetium
89 Ac actinium	90 Th thorium	91 Pa protactinium	92 U uranium	93 Np neptunium	94 Pu plutonium	95 Am americium	96 Cm curium	97 Bk berkelium	98 Cf californium	99 Es einsteinium	100 Fm fermium	101 Md mendelevium	102 No nobelium	103 Lr lawrencium

PROVISIONAL NAMES

All the elements heavier than bismuth (no. 83) are radioactive; all those heavier than uranium (no. 92) have only been produced artificially. The names given above for the elements are in standard use.

The elements with atomic numbers 104 to 109 were the subject of controversy until September 1997, when the International Union of Pure and Applied Chemistry (IUPAC) confirmed the names of the elements, which are those given in the table. The focus of the controversy was the disagreement over who discovered these artificial elements, and in particular whether elements should be named after living scientists. During the three years leading up to August 1997, the elements were given temporary names derived from Latin numbers. For example, element 104, rutherfordium, was called unnilquadium, derived from the Latin for one-zero-four.

CHEMICAL NOTATION

The formula for a compound indicates the number of atoms of each element present in each molecule of the compound: e.g. a molecule of water (H_2O) contains two atoms of hydrogen and one of oxygen. The formula for an ionic compound indicates the proportions of the constituent elements: e.g. common salt ($NaCl$) contains equal proportions of sodium and chloride ions. Formulae for more complex compounds may indicate the manner of combination of the atoms in a molecule: e.g. ethanol (ethyl alcohol) may be represented as CH_3CH_2OH.

TIME

TIME PERIODS

NAME	PERIOD	NAME	PERIOD
bicentennial	200 years	quadricentennial	every 400 years
biennial	2 years	quincentennial	every 500 years
century	100 years	quinquennial	every 5 years
decade	10 years	septennial	every 7 years
centennial	every 100 years	sesquicentennial	every 150 years
decennial	every 10 years	sexcentenary	600 years
half-century	50 years	sexennial	every 6 years
half-decade	5 years	tercentenary	300 years
half-millennium	500 years	triennial	every 3 years
leap year	366 days	vicennial	every 20 years
millennium	1,000 years	week	7 days
month	28–31 days	year	365 days
Olympiad	every 4 years	year	12 months
quadrennial	every 4 years	year	52 weeks

TIME INTERVALS

annual	occurring every year
biannual	occurring twice a year
bimonthly	occurring every two months or twice a month
biweekly	occurring every two weeks or twice a week
diurnal	daily, of each day
perennial	lasting through a year or several years
semi-annual	twice a year
semi-diurnal	twice a day
semi-weekly	twice a week
trimonthly	every three months
triweekly	every three weeks or three times a week
thrice weekly	three times a week

TYPES OF CALENDAR

GREGORIAN

The Gregorian calendar was a modification of the Julian calendar and was introduced by Pope Gregory XIII in 1582, adopted in Scotland in 1600, and in England and Wales in 1752, and is now in use throughout most of the Western world. To correct errors which had accumulated because the average Julian calendar year of 365¼ days was 11 min. 10 sec. longer than the solar year, 10 days were suppressed in 1582. As a further refinement, Gregory proclaimed that, of the centenary years, only those exactly divisible by 400 should be counted as leap years.

Below are the names of the months and number of days for a non-leap year.

NAME OF MONTH	NUMBER OF DAYS
January	31
February	28 (29 in leap years)
March	31
April	30
May	31
June	30
July	31
August	31
September	30
October	31
November	30
December	31

JEWISH

The Jewish calendar is a lunar calendar adapted to the solar year, normally consisting of twelve months but having thirteen months in leap years, which occur seven times in every cycle of nineteen years. The years are reckoned from the Creation (which is placed at 3761 BC); the months are Nisan, Iyyar, Sivan, Thammuz, Ab, Elul, Tishri, Hesvan, Kislev, Tebet, Sebat, and Adar, with an intercalary month (First Adar) being added in leap years. The religious year begins with Nisan and ends with Adar, while the civil year begins with Tishri and ends with Elul.

MUSLIM

The Muslim calendar is based on a year of twelve months, each month beginning roughly at the time of the New Moon. The length of a month alternates between 30 and 29 days, except for the twelfth month, the length of which is varied in a 30-year cycle, intended to keep the calendar in step with the true phases of the moon. The months are Muharram, Safar, Rabi'I, Rabi'II, Jumada I, Jumada II, Rajab, Sha'ban, Ramadan, Shawwal, Dhu l-Qa'dah, and Dhu l-Hijja.

CHINESE

The Chinese calendar is a lunar calendar, with a year consisting of twelve months of alternately 29 and 30 days, the equivalent of approximately twelve full lunar months. Intercalary months are added to keep the calendar in step with the solar year of 365 days. Months are referred to by a number within a year, but also by animal names (listed below) that, from ancient times, have been attached to years and hours of the day.

ZODIAC SIGNS

ARIES
Ram
(March 21–April 20)

TAURUS
Bull
(April 21–May 20)

GEMINI
Twins
(May 21–June 20)

CANCER
Crab
(June 21–July 21)

LEO
Lion
(July 22–August 21)

VIRGO
Virgin
(August 22–September 21)

LIBRA
Scales
(September 22–October 22)

SCORPIO
Scorpion
(October 23–November 21)

SAGITTARIUS
Archer
(November 22–December 20)

CAPRICORN
Goat
(December 21–January 19)

AQUARIUS
Water-bearer
(January 20– February 18)

PISCES
Fish
(February 19–March 20)

CHINESE ZODIAC

DOG	SHEEP	DRAGON	OX
1910	1907	1904	1901
1922	1919	1916	1913
1934	1931	1928	1925
1946	1943	1940	1937
1958	1955	1952	1949
1970	1967	1964	1961
1982	1979	1976	1973
1994	1991	1988	1985
2006	2003	2000	1997

CHICKEN	HORSE	RABBIT	RAT
1909	1906	1903	1900
1921	1918	1915	1912
1933	1930	1927	1924
1945	1942	1939	1936
1957	1954	1951	1948
1969	1966	1963	1960
1981	1978	1975	1972
1993	1990	1987	1984
2005	2002	1999	1996

MONKEY	SNAKE	TIGER	PIG
1908	1905	1902	1911
1920	1917	1914	1923
1932	1929	1926	1935
1944	1941	1938	1947
1956	1953	1950	1959
1968	1965	1962	1971
1980	1977	1974	1983
1992	1989	1986	1995
2004	2001	1998	2007

WEDDING ANNIVERSARIES

YEAR	TRADITION
1st	Paper
2nd	Cotton
3rd	Leather
4th	Linen (silk)
5th	Wood
6th	Iron
7th	Wool (copper)
8th	Bronze
9th	Pottery (china)
10th	Tin (aluminium)
11th	Steel
12th	Silk
13th	Lace
14th	Ivory
15th	Crystal
20th	China
25th	Silver
30th	Pearl
35th	Coral (jade)
40th	Ruby
45th	Sapphire
50th	Gold
55th	Emerald
60th	Diamond

BIRTHSTONES

JANUARY (garnet)   FEBRUARY (amethyst)   MARCH (aquamarine)

APRIL (diamond)   MAY (emerald)   JUNE (pearl)

JULY (ruby)   AUGUST (peridot)   SEPTEMBER (sapphire)

OCTOBER (opal)   NOVEMBER (topaz)   DECEMBER (turquoise)

TIME ZONES

The world is divided into 24 time zones, measured in relation to 12 noon Greenwich Mean Time (GMT), on the Greenwich Meridian (0°). Time advances by one hour for every 15° longitude east of Greenwich (and goes back one hour for every 15° west), but the system is adjusted in line with regional administrative boundaries. Numbers on the map below indicate the number of hours that must be added or subtracted in each time zone to reach GMT. Thus, east coast USA (+5) is 5 hours behind GMT.

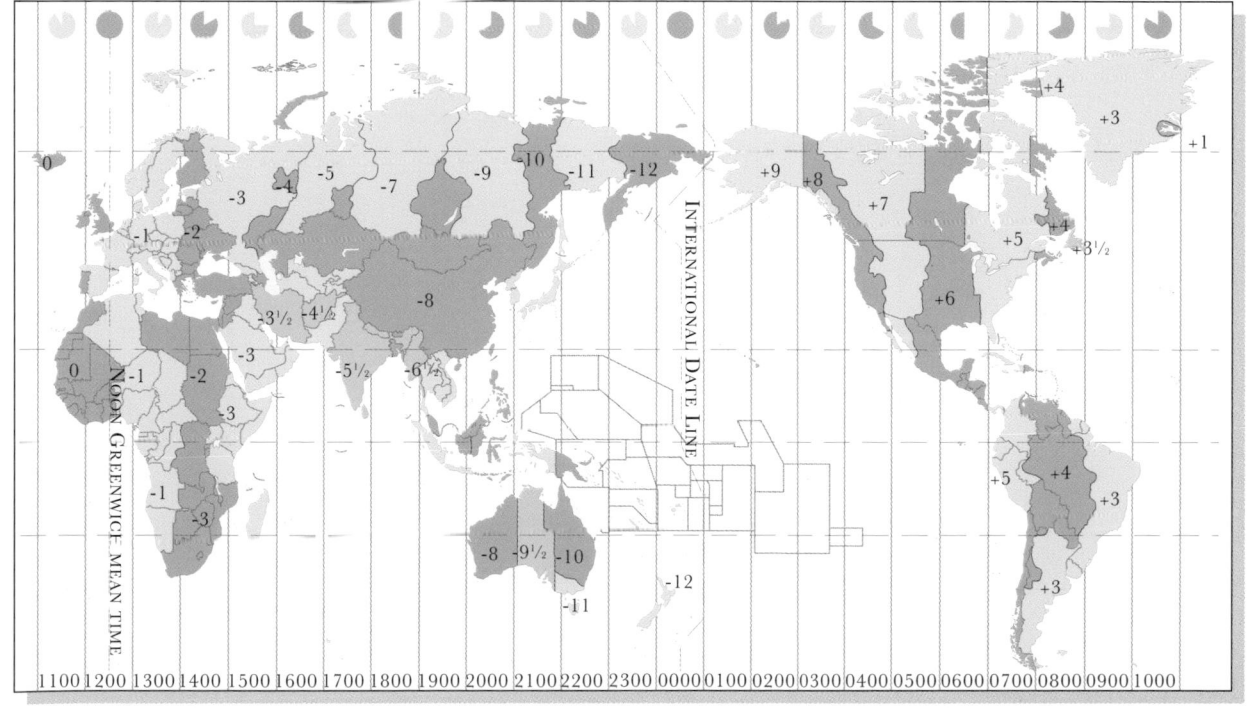

MISCELLANEOUS INFORMATION

COUNTIES OF THE UNITED KINGDOM

ENGLAND
Avon
Bedfordshire (Beds.)
Berkshire (Berks.)
Buckinghamshire (Bucks.)
Cambridgeshire (Cambs.)
Cheshire (Ches.)
Cleveland
Cornwall (Corn.)
Cumbria
Derbyshire (Derbs.)
Devon
Dorset
Durham (Dur.)
East Sussex
Essex
Gloucestershire (Glos.)
Greater London
Greater Manchester
Hampshire (Hants.)
Hereford & Worcester
Hertfordshire (Herts.)
Humberside
Isle of Wight (IOW)
Kent

Lancashire (Lancs.)
Leicestershire (Leics.)
Lincolnshire (Lincs.)
Merseyside
Norfolk
Northamptonshire (Northants.)
Northumberland (Northumb.)
North Yorkshire
Nottinghamshire (Notts.)
Oxfordshire (Oxon.)
Shropshire
Somerset (Som.)
South Yorkshire
Staffordshire (Staffs.)
Suffolk
Surrey
Tyne and Wear
Warwickshire (War.)
West Midlands
West Sussex
West Yorkshire
Wiltshire (Wilts.)

NORTHERN IRELAND
Antrim
Armagh
Down
Fermanagh (Ferm.)
Londonderry
Tyrone

Note: Officially, the counties of Northern Ireland have been abolished and replaced by 26 districts; they are listed here as they are still commonly referred to.

SCOTLAND
Regions
Borders
Central
Dumfries & Galloway
Fife
Grampian
Highland
Lothian
Strathclyde
Tayside

Island Areas
Orkney
Shetland
Western Isles

WALES
Clwyd
Dyfed
Gwent
Gwynedd
Mid Glamorgan
Powys
South Glamorgan
West Glamorgan

COMMONWEALTH COUNTRIES AND STATES

THE COMMONWEALTH
The Commonwealth is a free association of the fifty sovereign independent states listed below, together with their associated states and dependencies.

Antigua and Barbuda
Australia
Bahamas
Bangladesh
Barbados
Belize
Botswana
Brunei
Canada
Cyprus
Dominica
Gambia, the
Ghana
Grenada
Guyana
India
Jamaica
Kenya
Kiribati
Lesotho
Malawi
Malaysia
Maldives
Malta
Mauritius
Nauru
New Zealand
Nigeria
Pakistan
Papua New Guinea
St Kitts and Nevis
St Lucia
St Vincent and the Grenadines
Seychelles
Sierra Leone

Singapore
Solomon Islands
South Africa
Sri Lanka
Swaziland
Tanzania
Tongo
Trinidad and Tobago
Tuvalu
Uganda
United Kingdom
Vanuatu
Western Samoa
Zambia
Zimbabwe

CANADA
Provinces and territories
(with official abbreviations)

Province
Alberta (Alta.)
British Columbia (BC)
Manitoba (Man.)
New Brunswick (NB)
Newfoundland and Labrador (Nfld.)
Nova Scotia (NS)
Ontario (Ont.)
Prince Edward Islnd (PEI)
Quebec (Que.)
Saskatchewan (Sask.)

Northwest Territories (NWT)
Yukon Territory (YT)

THE COMMONWEALTH OF AUSTRALIA
States and territories

State
New South Wales
Northern Territory
Queensland
South Australia
Tasmania
Victoria
Western Australia

Australian Capital Territory

INDIA
States and Union Territories

State
Andhra Pradesh
Arunchal Pradesh
Assam
Bihar
Goa
Gujarat
Haryana
Himachal Pradesh
Jammu and Kashmir
Karnataka
Kerala
Madhya Pradesh
Maharashtra
Manipur
Meghalaya
Mizoram
Nagaland
Orissa
Punjab
Rajastan
Sikkim
Tamil Nadu

Tripura
Uttar Pradesh
West Bengal

Union Territory
Andaman and Nicobar Islands
Chandigargh
Dadra and Nagar Haveli
Daman and Diu
Delhi
Lakshadweep
Pondicherry

KINGS AND QUEENS OF ENGLAND AND BRITAIN

The list below details the monarchs of England from 1042 until 1603. Subsequent monarchs were joint rulers of both England and Scotland following union of the two kingdoms under the Stuarts. From the mid-17th-century, monarchs also ruled the British Commonwealth.

MONARCHS OF ENGLAND

SAXONS

1042–1066	Edward the Confessor
1066	Harold II

NORMANS

1066–1087	William the Conqueror
1087–1100	William II
1100–1135	Henry I
1135–1154	Stephen

PLANTAGENETS

1154–1189	Henry II
1189–1199	Richard I
1199–1216	John
1216–1272	Henry III
1272–1307	Edward I
1307–1327	Edward II
1327–1377	Edward III
1377–1399	Richard II

LANCASTERS

1399–1413	Henry IV
1413–1422	Henry V
1422–1461	Henry VI

YORKS

1461–1483	Edward IV
1483	Edward V
1483–1485	Richard III

TUDORS

1485–1509	Henry VII
1509–1547	Henry VIII
1547–1553	Edward VI
1553–1558	Mary I
1558–1603	Elizabeth I

STUARTS

1603–1625	James I (VI of Scotland)
1625–1649	Charles I

MONARCHS OF SCOTLAND

1306–1329	Robert I, the Bruce
1329–1371	David II
1371–1390	Robert II
1390–1406	Robert III
1406–1437	James I
1437–1460	James II
1460–1488	James III
1488–1513	James IV
1513–1542	James V
1542–1567	Mary, Queen of Scots
1567–1625	James VI

MONARCHS OF BRITAIN AND THE COMMONWEALTH

STUARTS

1660–1685	Charles II
1685–1688	James II
1689–1694	Mary II
1694–1702	William III
1702–1714	Anne

HANOVERS

1714–1727	George I
1727–1760	George II
1760–1820	George III
1820–1830	George IV
1830–1837	William IV

SAXE-COBURG-GOTHAS

1837–1901	Victoria
1901–1910	Edward VII

WINDSORS

1910–1936	George V
1936	Edward VII
1936–1952	George VI
1952–	Elizabeth II

BOOKS OF THE BIBLE

THE OLD TESTAMENT

BOOK	ABBREV.
Genesis	Gen.
Exodus	Exod.
Leviticus	Lev.
Numbers	Num.
Deuteronomy	Deut.
Joshua	Josh.
Judges	Judg.
Ruth	no abbrev.
First Book of Samuel	1 Sam.
Second Book of Samuel	2 Sam.
First Book of Kings	1 Kgs.
Second Book of Kings	2 Kgs.
First Book of Chronicles	1 Chr.
Second Book of Chronicles	2 Chr.
Ezra	no abbrev.
Nehemiah	Neh.
Esther	no abbrev.
Job	no abbrev.
Psalms	Ps.
Proverbs	Prov.
Ecclesiastes	Eccles.
Song of Songs, Song of Solomon, Canticles	S. of S., Cant.
Isaiah	Isa.
Jeremiah	Jer.
Lamentations	Lam.
Ezekiel	Ezek.
Daniel	Dan.
Hosea	Hos.
Joel	no abbrev.

BOOK	ABBREV.
Amos	no abbrev.
Obadiah	Obad.
Jonah	no abbrev.
Micah	Mic.
Nahum	Nah.
Habakkuk	Hab.
Zephaniah	Zeph.
Haggai	Hag.
Zechariah	Zech.
Malachi	Mal.

APOCRYPHA

BOOK	ABBREV.
First Book of Esdras	1 Esd.
Second Book of Esdras	2 Esd.
Tobit	no abbrev.
Judith	no abbrev.
Rest of Esther	Rest of Esth.
Wisdom of Solomon	Wisd.
Ecclesiasticus, Wisdom of Jesus the Son of Sirach	Ecclus., Sir
Baruch	no abbrev.
Song of the Three Children	S. of III Ch.
Susanna	Sus.
Bel and the Dragon	Bel & Dr.
Prayer of Manasses	Pr. of Man.
First Book of Maccabees	1 Macc.
Second Book of Maccabees	2 Macc.

THE NEW TESTAMENT

BOOK	ABBREV.
Gospel according to St Matthew	Matt.
Gospel according to St Mark	Mark
Gospel according to St Luke	Luke
Gospel according to St John	John
Acts of the Apostles	Acts
Epistle to the Romans	Rom.
First Epistle to the Corinthians	1 Cor.
Second Epistle to the Corinthians	2 Cor.
Epistle to the Galatians	Gal.
Epistle to the Ephesians	Eph.
Epistle to the Philippians	Phil.
Epistle to the Colossians	Col.
First Epistle to the Thessalonians	1 Thess.
Second Epistle to the Thessalonians	2 Thess.
First Epistle to Timothy	1 Tim.
Second Epistle to Timothy	2 Tim.
Epistle to Titus	Tit.
Epistle to Philemon	Philem.
Epistle to the Hebrews	Heb.
Epistle of James	Jas.
First Epistle of Peter	1 Pet.
Second Epistle of Peter	2 Pet.
First Epistle of John	1 John
Second Epistle of John	2 John
Third Epistle of John	3 John
Epistle of Jude	Jude
Revelation, Apocalypse	Rev., Apoc.

THE LIVING WORLD

IN THE SYSTEM OF CLASSIFICATION used by most modern biologists, living things are organized into five kingdoms; four are shown here, while the fifth appears overleaf. The smallest kingdom, in terms of species so far identified, is the Kingdom Monera, which contains bacteria – single-celled organisms that are the simplest forms of life. The Kingdom Protista also contains single-celled organisms, together with some multicellular algae, but their cells are larger and more complex than those of monerans. Most members of the Kingdom Fungi are multicellular, and live by absorbing organic matter from their surroundings. All plants (Kingdom Plantae) are multicellular, and live by photosynthesis. This large kingdom contains some 400,000 known species.

TAXONOMY

Taxonomy is the science of classification of living things. It uses a hierarchy of progressively smaller groups, from kingdom to species, and organizes living things in a way that reflects their evolutionary links. This box features the principal groups used in classification. In addition to these, taxonomists use a number of intermediate groups, such as suborders or superfamilies.

KINGDOM
One of the overall categories of life, containing organisms that share fundamental features.

PHYLUM
A major grouping within a kingdom; known as a 'division' in the classification of plants and fungi.

CLASS
A major part of a phylum. For example, mosses (Musci) form a class within the phylum Bryophyta.

ORDER
A part of a class, consisting of one or more families.

FAMILY
A large collection of species that share a number of important physical features.

GENUS
A narrower group containing a small number of species that share many features.

SPECIES
A collection of living things that interbreed in the wild, producing similar offspring.

KINGDOM MONERA

KINGDOM PROTISTA

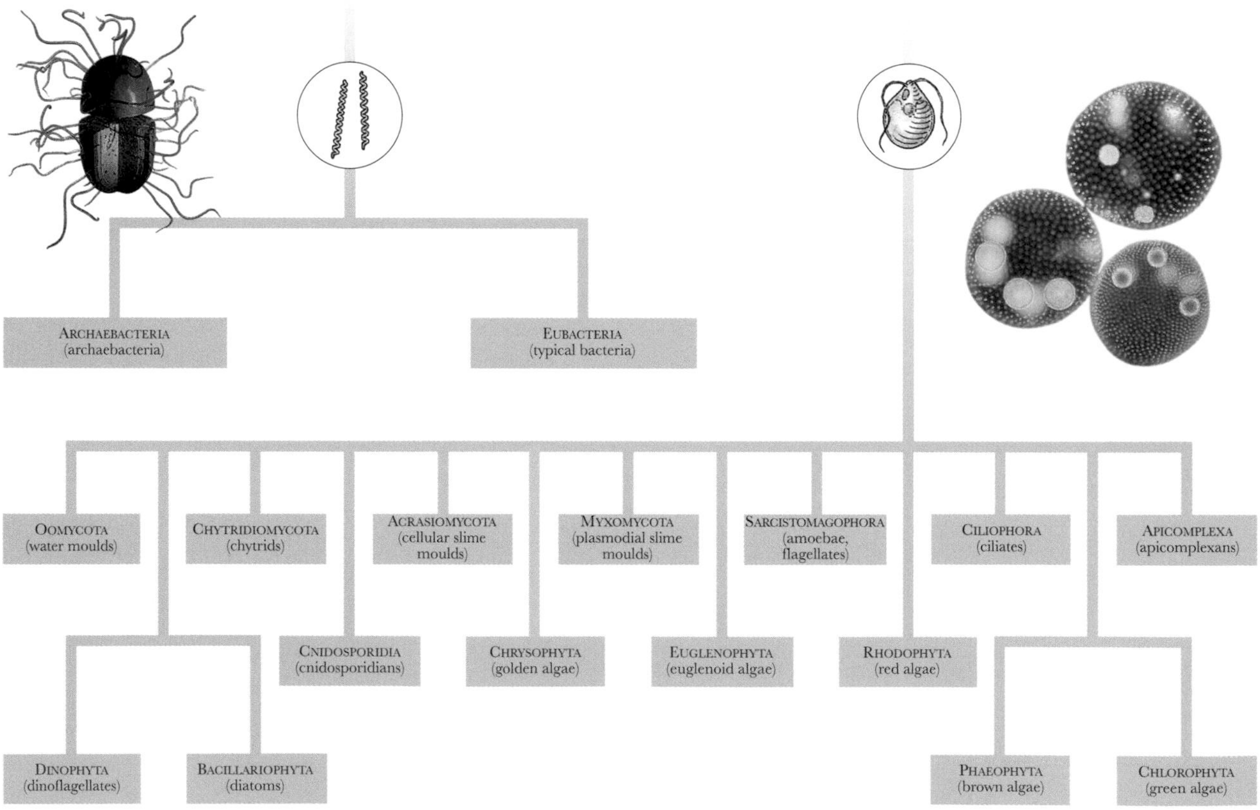

ARCHAEBACTERIA
(archaebacteria)

EUBACTERIA
(typical bacteria)

OOMYCOTA
(water moulds)

CHYTRIDIOMYCOTA
(chytrids)

ACRASIOMYCOTA
(cellular slime moulds)

MYXOMYCOTA
(plasmodial slime moulds)

SARCISTOMAGOPHORA
(amoebae, flagellates)

CILIOPHORA
(ciliates)

APICOMPLEXA
(apicomplexans)

CNIDOSPORIDIA
(cnidosporidians)

CHRYSOPHYTA
(golden algae)

EUGLENOPHYTA
(euglenoid algae)

RHODOPHYTA
(red algae)

DINOPHYTA
(dinoflagellates)

BACILLARIOPHYTA
(diatoms)

PHAEOPHYTA
(brown algae)

CHLOROPHYTA
(green algae)

KEY
These colours indicate the taxonomic levels – from kingdom to family – used in the chart.

KINGDOM PHYLUM OR DIVISION CLASS FAMILY

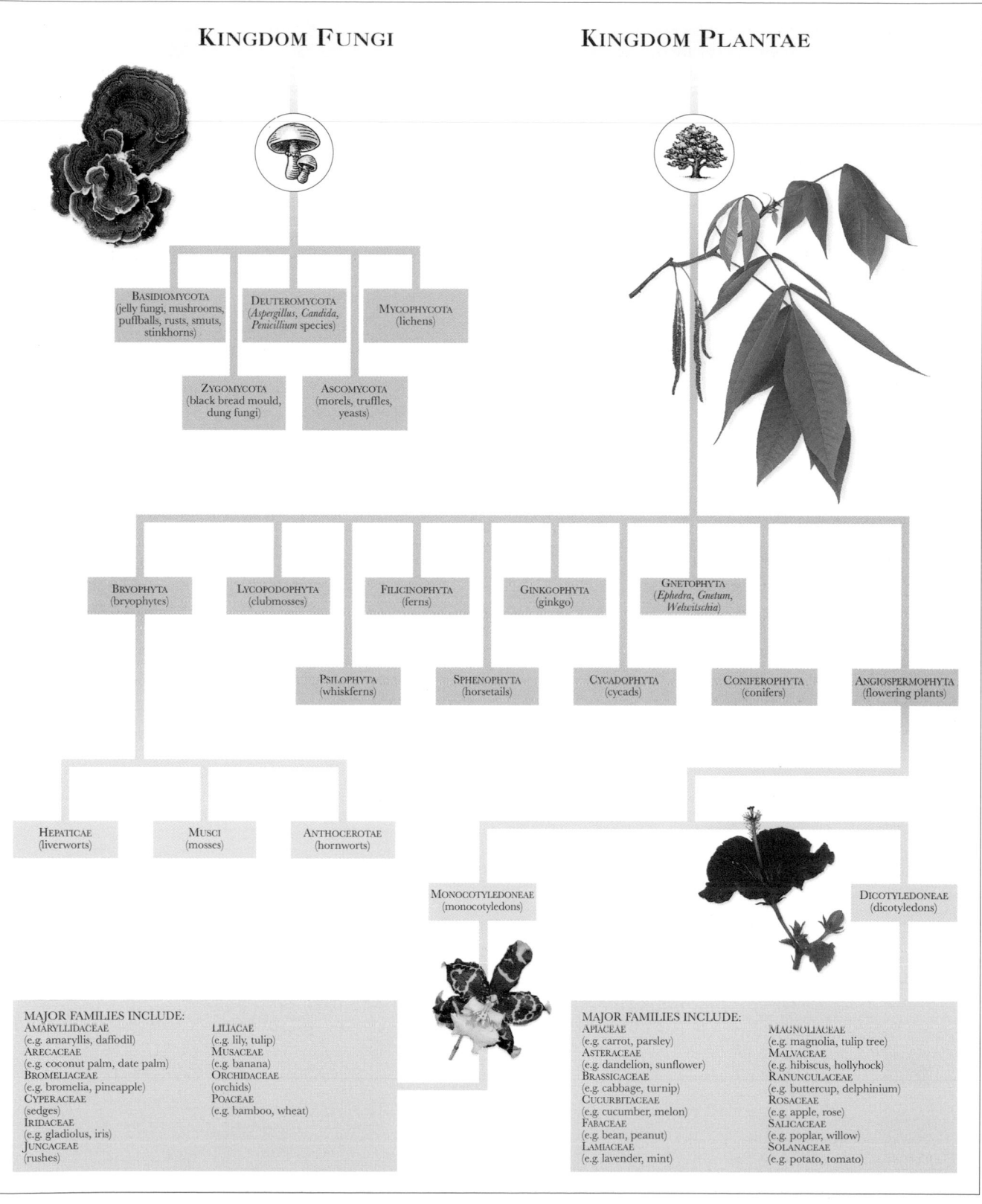

KINGDOM FUNGI

KINGDOM PLANTAE

BASIDIOMYCOTA
(jelly fungi, mushrooms, puffballs, rusts, smuts, stinkhorns)

DEUTEROMYCOTA
(*Aspergillus, Candida, Penicillium* species)

MYCOPHYCOTA
(lichens)

ZYGOMYCOTA
(black bread mould, dung fungi)

ASCOMYCOTA
(morels, truffles, yeasts)

BRYOPHYTA
(bryophytes)

LYCOPODOPHYTA
(clubmosses)

FILICINOPHYTA
(ferns)

GINKGOPHYTA
(ginkgo)

GNETOPHYTA
(*Ephedra, Gnetum, Welwitschia*)

PSILOPHYTA
(whiskferns)

SPHENOPHYTA
(horsetails)

CYCADOPHYTA
(cycads)

CONIFEROPHYTA
(conifers)

ANGIOSPERMOPHYTA
(flowering plants)

HEPATICAE
(liverworts)

MUSCI
(mosses)

ANTHOCEROTAE
(hornworts)

MONOCOTYLEDONEAE
(monocotyledons)

DICOTYLEDONEAE
(dicotyledons)

MAJOR FAMILIES INCLUDE:
AMARYLLIDACEAE
(e.g. amaryllis, daffodil)
ARECACEAE
(e.g. coconut palm, date palm)
BROMELIACEAE
(e.g. bromelia, pineapple)
CYPERACEAE
(sedges)
IRIDACEAE
(e.g. gladiolus, iris)
JUNCACEAE
(rushes)

LILIACAE
(e.g. lily, tulip)
MUSACEAE
(e.g. banana)
ORCHIDACEAE
(orchids)
POACEAE
(e.g. bamboo, wheat)

MAJOR FAMILIES INCLUDE:
APIACEAE
(e.g. carrot, parsley)
ASTERACEAE
(e.g. dandelion, sunflower)
BRASSICACEAE
(e.g. cabbage, turnip)
CUCURBITACEAE
(e.g. cucumber, melon)
FABACEAE
(e.g. bean, peanut)
LAMIACEAE
(e.g. lavender, mint)

MAGNOLIACEAE
(e.g. magnolia, tulip tree)
MALVACEAE
(e.g. hibiscus, hollyhock)
RANUNCULACEAE
(e.g. buttercup, delphinium)
ROSACEAE
(e.g. apple, rose)
SALICACEAE
(e.g. poplar, willow)
SOLANACEAE
(e.g. potato, tomato)

THE ANIMAL KINGDOM

WITH OVER 2 MILLION KNOWN SPECIES, the Kingdom Animalia is the largest grouping in the classification of living things. Its members are divided into approximately 30 phyla, which are featured on these two pages. Over 95 per cent of animal species are invertebrates – an informal term used for any animal that does not have a backbone. Invertebrates include a vast array of varied organisms in many different phyla, from sponges to insects. Many remain poorly known, and it is believed that as many as 10 million species may still await discovery. Vertebrates, or animals with backbones, form part of the Phylum Chordata. Although they total only about 45,000 species, they include the largest and most familiar members of the animal kingdom, and also ourselves.

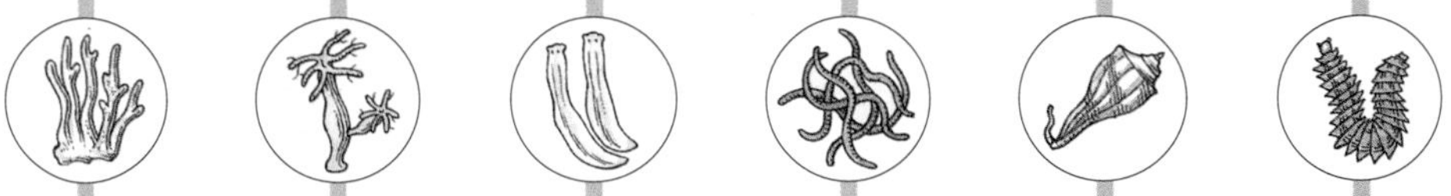

UNIRAMIA (uniramians)

MALACOSTRACA (crabs, lobsters, shrimps, woodlice)

PORIFERA (sponges)	CNIDARIA (cnidarians)	PLATYHELMINTHES (flatworms)	NEMATODA (roundworms)	MOLLUSCA (molluscs)	ANNELIDA (true worms)

HYDROZOA (hydras, hydroids) SCYPHOZOA (jellyfish) ANTHOZOA (anemones, corals)

POLYPLACO-PHORA (chitons) GASTROPODA (slugs, snails) BIVALVIA (clams, mussels, scallops) CEPHALOPODA (octopuses, squid)

TURBELLARIA (free-living flatworms) MONOGENEA (parasitic flukes) TREMATODA (parasitic flukes) CESTODA (tapeworms)

POLYCHAETA (marine worms) OLIGOCHAETA (earthworms, freshwater worms) HIRUDINEA (leeches)

INSECTA (insects) CHILOPODA (centipedes) DIPLOPODA (millipedes) OTHER CLASSES: PAUROPODA (pauropodans) SYMPHYLA (symphylans)

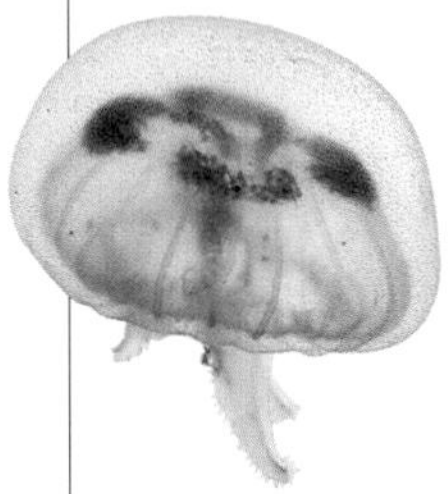

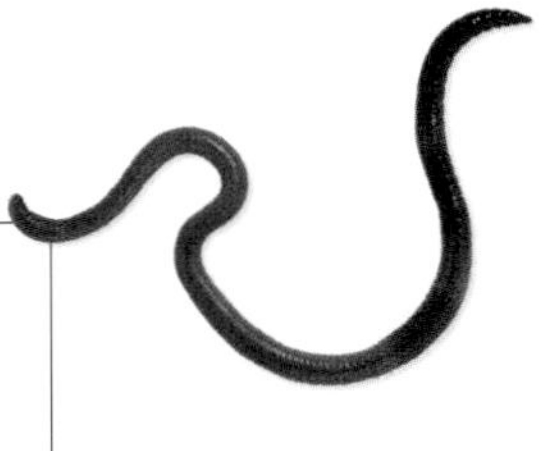

KEY
These colours show the taxonomic levels used in the chart.

KINGDOM		PHYLUM
SUBPHYLUM	SUPERCLASS	CLASS
SUBCLASS	INFRACLASS	ORDER

MAJOR ORDERS INCLUDE:
ANOPLURA (suckling lice)
COLEOPTERA (beetles, weevils)
COLLEMBOLA (springtails)
DERMAPTERA (earwigs)
DIPTERA (gnats, mosquitos, true flies)
EPHEMEROPTERA (mayflies)
HEMIPTERA (true bugs)
HYMENOPTERA (ants, bees, wasps)
ISOPTERA (termites)
LEPIDOPTERA (butterflies, moths)
MALLOPHAGA (birdlice, biting lice)
NEUROPTERA (alder flies, ant lions, dobsonflies, lacewings, snake flies)
ODONATA (damselflies, dragonflies)
ORTHOPTERA (cockroaches, crickets, grasshoppers, locusts, mantids)
PHASMIDA (leaf insects, stick insects)
PSOCOPTERA (barklice, booklice)
SIPHONAPTERA (fleas)
THYSANURA (bristletails, silverfish)

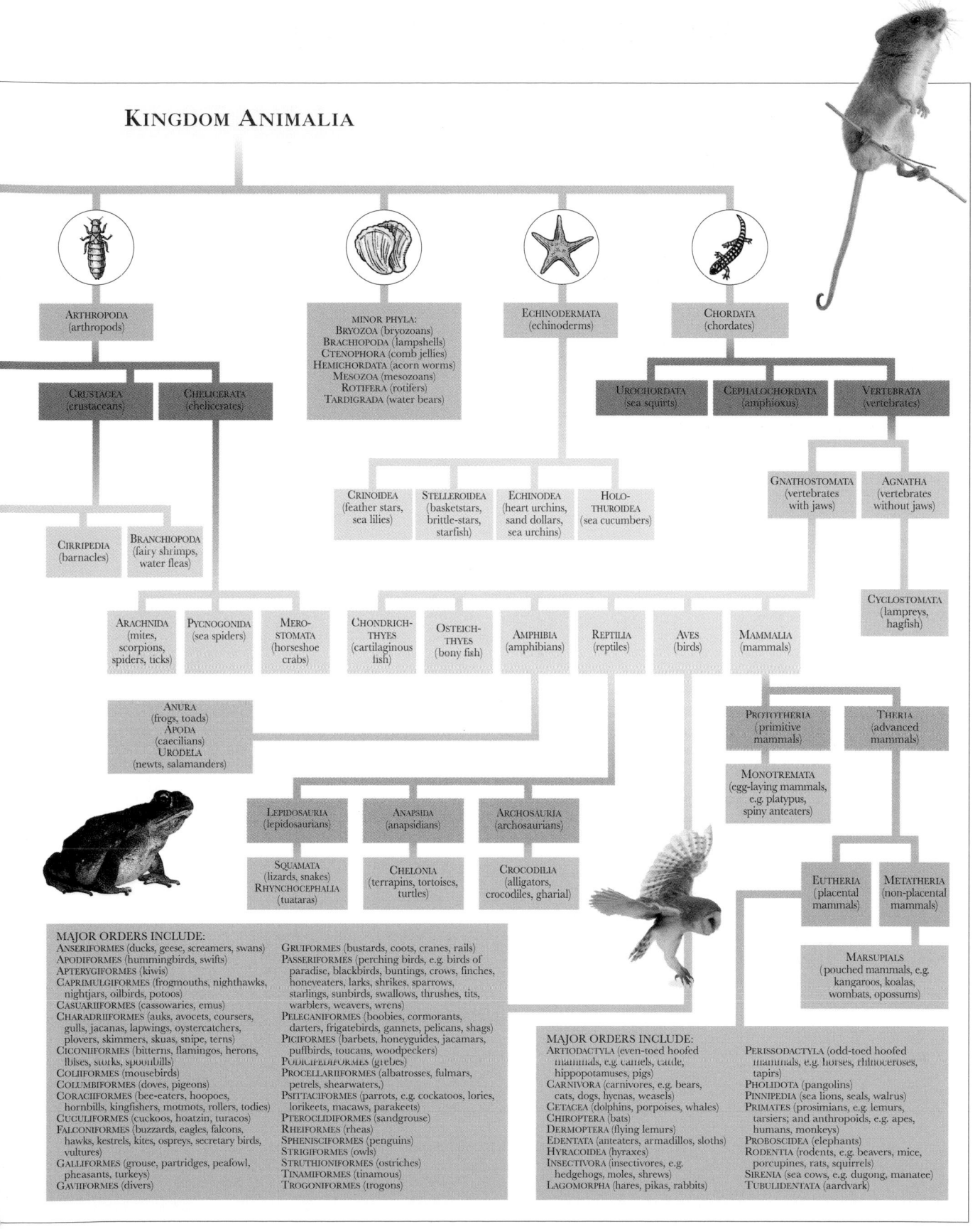

KINGDOM ANIMALIA

ARTHROPODA (arthropods)

MINOR PHYLA:
BRYOZOA (bryozoans)
BRACHIOPODA (lampshells)
CTENOPHORA (comb jellies)
HEMICHORDATA (acorn worms)
MESOZOA (mesozoans)
ROTIFERA (rotifers)
TARDIGRADA (water bears)

ECHINODERMATA (echinoderms)

CHORDATA (chordates)

CRUSTACEA (crustaceans)

CHELICERATA (chelicerates)

UROCHORDATA (sea squirts)

CEPHALOCHORDATA (amphioxus)

VERTEBRATA (vertebrates)

CRINOIDEA (feather stars, sea lilies)

STELLEROIDEA (basketstars, brittle-stars, starfish)

ECHINODEA (heart urchins, sand dollars, sea urchins)

HOLO-THUROIDEA (sea cucumbers)

GNATHOSTOMATA (vertebrates with jaws)

AGNATHA (vertebrates without jaws)

CIRRIPEDIA (barnacles)

BRANCHIOPODA (fairy shrimps, water fleas)

CYCLOSTOMATA (lampreys, hagfish)

ARACHNIDA (mites, scorpions, spiders, ticks)

PYCNOGONIDA (sea spiders)

MERO-STOMATA (horseshoe crabs)

CHONDRICH-THYES (cartilaginous fish)

OSTEICH-THYES (bony fish)

AMPHIBIA (amphibians)

REPTILIA (reptiles)

AVES (birds)

MAMMALIA (mammals)

ANURA (frogs, toads)
APODA (caecilians)
URODELA (newts, salamanders)

PROTOTHERIA (primitive mammals)

THERIA (advanced mammals)

MONOTREMATA (egg-laying mammals, e.g. platypus, spiny anteaters)

LEPIDOSAURIA (lepidosaurians)

ANAPSIDA (anapsidans)

ARCHOSAURIA (archosaurians)

SQUAMATA (lizards, snakes)
RHYNCHOCEPHALIA (tuataras)

CHELONIA (terrapins, tortoises, turtles)

CROCODILIA (alligators, crocodiles, gharial)

EUTHERIA (placental mammals)

METATHERIA (non-placental mammals)

MARSUPIALS (pouched mammals, e.g. kangaroos, koalas, wombats, opossums)

MAJOR ORDERS INCLUDE:
ANSERIFORMES (ducks, geese, screamers, swans)
APODIFORMES (hummingbirds, swifts)
APTERYGIFORMES (kiwis)
CAPRIMULGIFORMES (frogmouths, nighthawks, nightjars, oilbirds, potoos)
CASUARIIFORMES (cassowaries, emus)
CHARADRIIFORMES (auks, avocets, coursers, gulls, jacanas, lapwings, oystercatchers, plovers, skimmers, skuas, snipe, terns)
CICONIIFORMES (bitterns, flamingos, herons, Ibises, storks, spoonbills)
COLIIFORMES (mousebirds)
COLUMBIFORMES (doves, pigeons)
CORACIIFORMES (bee-eaters, hoopoes, hornbills, kingfishers, motmots, rollers, todies)
CUCULIFORMES (cuckoos, hoatzin, turacos)
FALCONIFORMES (buzzards, eagles, falcons, hawks, kestrels, kites, ospreys, secretary birds, vultures)
GALLIFORMES (grouse, partridges, peafowl, pheasants, turkeys)
GAVIIFORMES (divers)

GRUIFORMES (bustards, coots, cranes, rails)
PASSERIFORMES (perching birds, e.g. birds of paradise, blackbirds, buntings, crows, finches, honeyeaters, larks, shrikes, sparrows, starlings, sunbirds, swallows, thrushes, tits, warblers, weavers, wrens)
PELECANIFORMES (boobies, cormorants, darters, frigatebirds, gannets, pelicans, shags)
PICIFORMES (barbets, honeyguides, jacamars, puffbirds, toucans, woodpeckers)
PODICIPEDIFORMES (grebes)
PROCELLARIIFORMES (albatrosses, fulmars, petrels, shearwaters,)
PSITTACIFORMES (parrots, e.g. cockatoos, lories, lorikeets, macaws, parakeets)
PTEROCLIDIFORMES (sandgrouse)
RHEIFORMES (rheas)
SPHENISCIFORMES (penguins)
STRIGIFORMES (owls)
STRUTHIONIFORMES (ostriches)
TINAMIFORMES (tinamous)
TROGONIFORMES (trogons)

MAJOR ORDERS INCLUDE:
ARTIODACTYLA (even-toed hoofed mammals, e.g. camels, cattle, hippopotamuses, pigs)
CARNIVORA (carnivores, e.g. bears, cats, dogs, hyenas, weasels)
CETACEA (dolphins, porpoises, whales)
CHIROPTERA (bats)
DERMOPTERA (flying lemurs)
EDENTATA (anteaters, armadillos, sloths)
HYRACOIDEA (hyraxes)
INSECTIVORA (insectivores, e.g. hedgehogs, moles, shrews)
LAGOMORPHA (hares, pikas, rabbits)

PERISSODACTYLA (odd-toed hoofed mammals, e.g. horses, rhinoceroses, tapirs)
PHOLIDOTA (pangolins)
PINNIPEDIA (sea lions, seals, walrus)
PRIMATES (prosimians, e.g. lemurs, tarsiers; and anthropoids, e.g. apes, humans, monkeys)
PROBOSCIDEA (elephants)
RODENTIA (rodents, e.g. beavers, mice, porcupines, rats, squirrels)
SIRENIA (sea cows, e.g. dugong, manatee)
TUBULIDENTATA (aardvark)

GEOLOGICAL TIME PERIODS

SINCE THE EARTH WAS formed from a massive cloud of dust and gas some 4,600 years ago, layers of igneous, sedimentary, and metamorphic rocks have built up on its crust. The study of the history and formation of these layers has given rise to a system of classification that describes geological time. The largest division is an aeon and divisions of the three aeons are classified as the Archaean (4,600–2,500 million years ago), the Proterozoic (2,500–550 million years ago), and the Phanerozoic (550 million years ago to the present). Aeons are then broken down into smaller hierarchical divisions – eras, periods, epochs, and ages – which provide more precise dating information on the history of the Earth.

GEOLOGICAL HISTORY OF THE EARTH

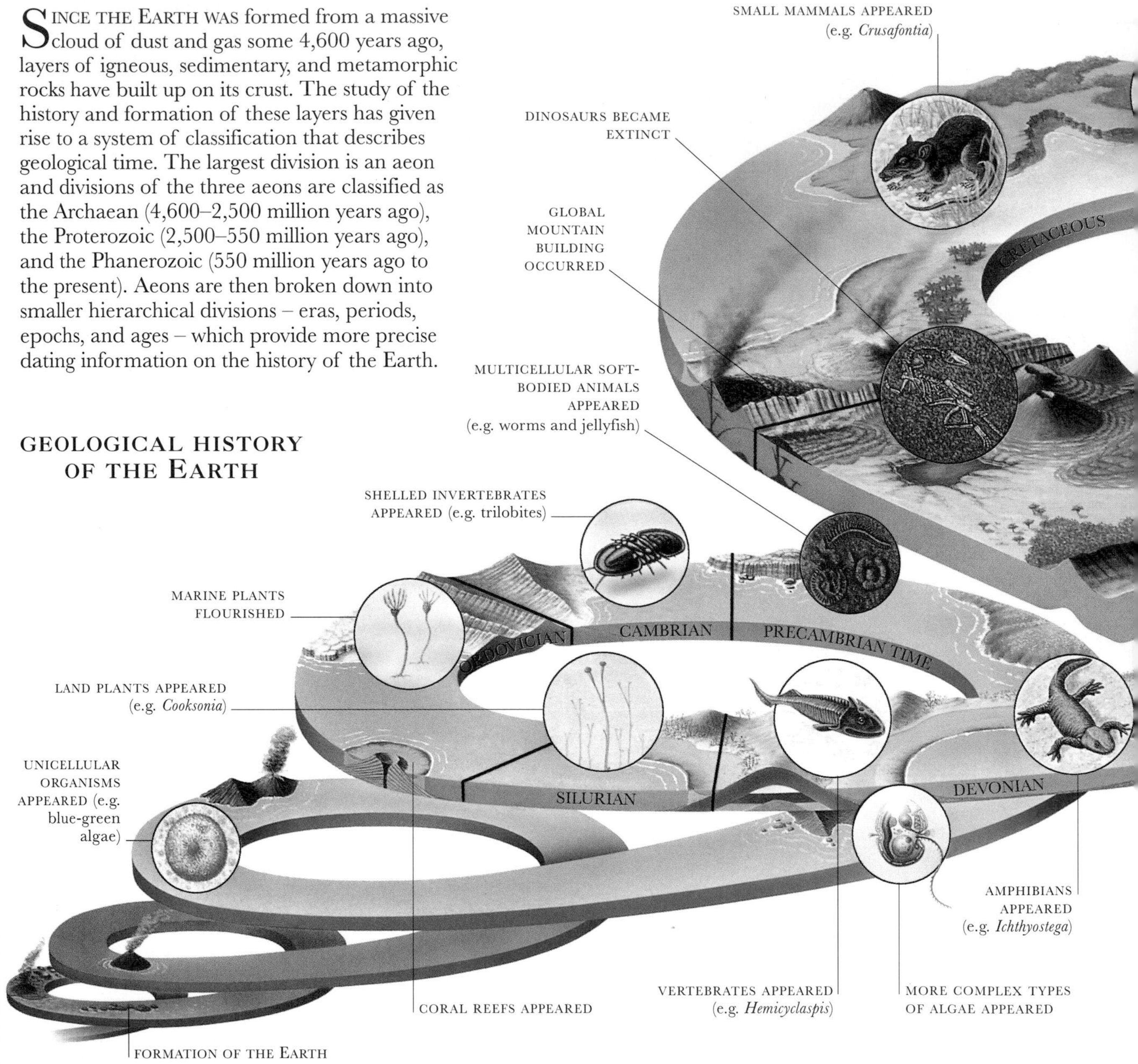

SMALL MAMMALS APPEARED (e.g. *Crusafontia*)

DINOSAURS BECAME EXTINCT

GLOBAL MOUNTAIN BUILDING OCCURRED

MULTICELLULAR SOFT-BODIED ANIMALS APPEARED (e.g. worms and jellyfish)

SHELLED INVERTEBRATES APPEARED (e.g. trilobites)

MARINE PLANTS FLOURISHED

LAND PLANTS APPEARED (e.g. *Cooksonia*)

UNICELLULAR ORGANISMS APPEARED (e.g. blue-green algae)

CRETACEOUS

ORDOVICIAN

CAMBRIAN

PRECAMBRIAN TIME

SILURIAN

DEVONIAN

AMPHIBIANS APPEARED (e.g. *Ichthyostega*)

FORMATION OF THE EARTH

CORAL REEFS APPEARED

VERTEBRATES APPEARED (e.g. *Hemicyclaspis*)

MORE COMPLEX TYPES OF ALGAE APPEARED

THE GEOLOGICAL TIMESCALE

MILLIONS OF YEARS AGO (MYA)

4,600	5,500	2,900	2,500	1,600	900	550	505	438

FORMATION OF THE EARTH	PRECAMBRIAN TIME						CAMBRIAN	ORDOVICIAN
	EARLY ARCHAEAN	MIDDLE ARCHAEAN	LATE ARCHAEAN	EARLY PROTEROZOIC	MIDDLE PROTEROZOIC	LATE PROTEROZOIC		
	ARCHAEAN			PROTEROZOIC				

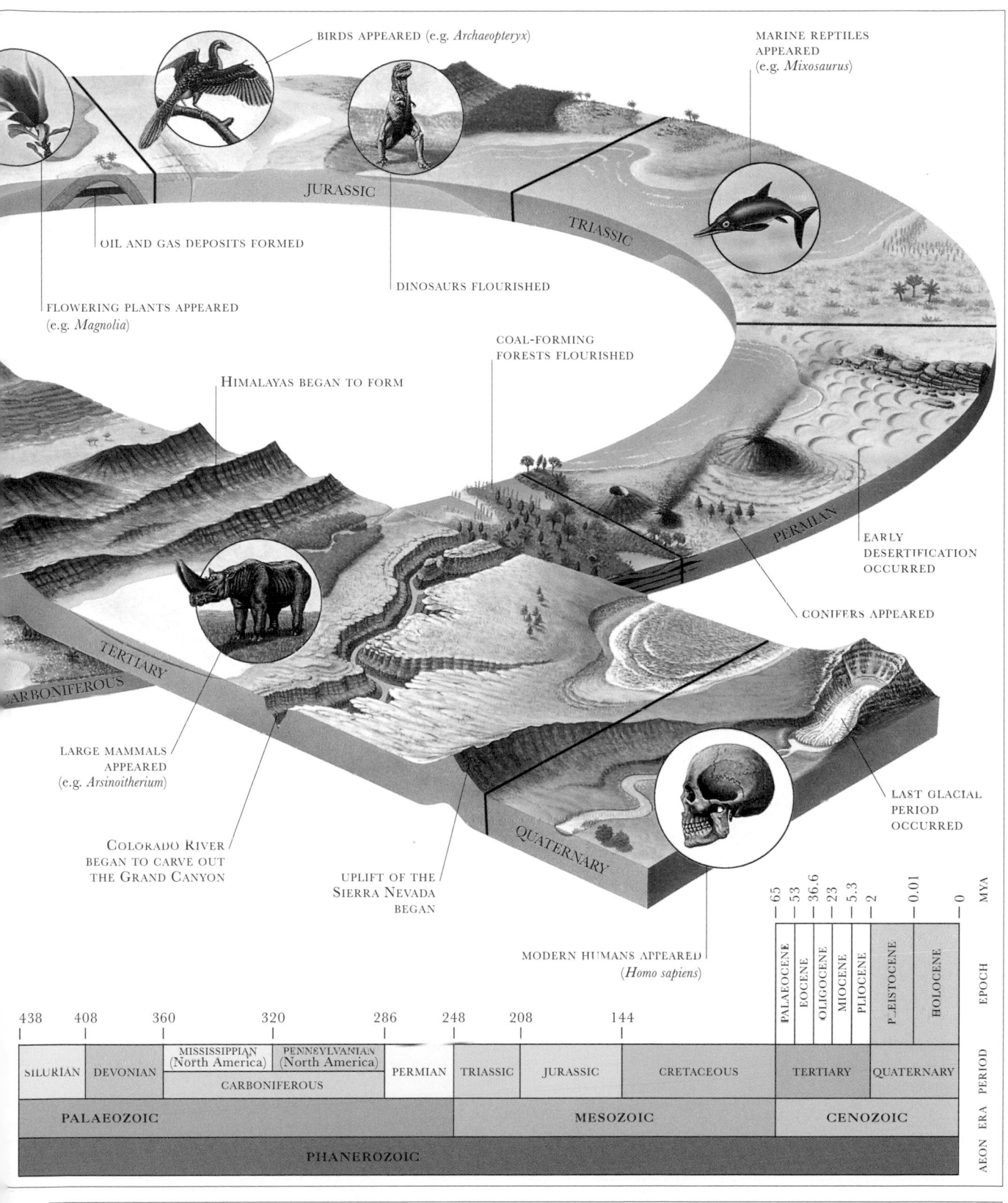

BIRDS APPEARED (e.g. *Archaeopteryx*)

MARINE REPTILES
APPEARED
(e.g. *Mixosaurus*)

JURASSIC

TRIASSIC

OIL AND GAS DEPOSITS FORMED

DINOSAURS FLOURISHED

FLOWERING PLANTS APPEARED
(e.g. *Magnolia*)

COAL-FORMING
FORESTS FLOURISHED

HIMALAYAS BEGAN TO FORM

PERMIAN

EARLY
DESERTIFICATION
OCCURRED

CONIFERS APPEARED

TERTIARY

CARBONIFEROUS

LARGE MAMMALS
APPEARED
(e.g. *Arsinoitherium*)

LAST GLACIAL
PERIOD
OCCURRED

COLORADO RIVER
BEGAN TO CARVE OUT
THE GRAND CANYON

UPLIFT OF THE
SIERRA NEVADA
BEGAN

QUATERNARY

MODERN HUMANS APPEARED
(*Homo sapiens*)

					65	53	36.6	23	5.3	2		0.01		0	MYA
					PALAEOCENE	EOCENE	OLIGOCENE	MIOCENE	PLIOCENE		PLEISTOCENE		HOLOCENE		EPOCH
438	408	360	320	286	248	208		144							
SILURIAN	DEVONIAN	MISSISSIPPIAN (North America) / PENNSYLVANIAN (North America) CARBONIFEROUS			PERMIAN	TRIASSIC	JURASSIC		CRETACEOUS		TERTIARY			QUATERNARY	PERIOD
PALAEOZOIC						MESOZOIC					CENOZOIC				ERA
PHANEROZOIC															AEON

1001

GRAMMAR AND STYLE

Dictionaries of current English, as distinct from historical dictionaries, generally record the language as it is used at the time; usage is constantly changing and the distinction between right and wrong is not always easy to determine. Unlike French – guided by the rulings of the Académie Française – English is not monitored by any single authority, and established usage is the principal criterion. One result of this is that English tolerates many more alternative spellings than other languages. Such alternatives are based on patterns of word formation and variation in the different languages through which they have passed before reaching ours. The following notes offer guidance on difficult and controversial points of grammar usage and style. An asterisk (*) denotes an example of incorrect usage.

ACCENT

1 A person's accent is the way he or she pronounces words. People from different regions and different groups in society have different accents. For instance, most people in northern England say *path* with a 'short' *a*, while most people in southern England say it with a 'long' *a*. In America and Canada the *r* in *far* and *port* is generally pronounced, while in south-eastern England, for example, it is not. Everyone speaks with an accent, although some accents may be regarded as having more prestige, such as 'Received Pronunciation' (RP) in the UK.

2 An accent on a letter is a mark added to it to alter the sound it stands for. French, for example, has

  ´ (acute), as in *état*   ¨ (diaresis), as in *Noël*
  ` (grave), as in *mère*   ↄ (cedilla), as in *français*
  ^ (circumflex), as in *guêpe*

and German has

  ¨ (umlaut), as in *München*.

There are no accents on native English words, but many words borrowed from other languages still have them, such as *façade*.

ADJECTIVE

An adjective is a word that describes a noun or pronoun, e.g.
  red, clever, German, depressed, battered, sticky, shining

Most can be used either before a noun, e.g.
  the red *house*   *a lazy* man   *a clever* woman

or after a verb like *be, seem,* or *call,* e.g.
  The house is red.   *I wouldn't call him* lazy.
  She seems very clever.

Some can be used only before a noun, e.g.
  the chief *reason*
  (one cannot say **the reason is chief*)

Some can be used only after a verb, e.g.
  The ship is still afloat.
  (one cannot say **an afloat ship*)

A few can be used only immediately after a noun, e.g.
  a writer manqué
  (one cannot say either **a manqué writer*
  or **as a writer he is* manqué)

See also notes at COMPARATIVE and SUPERLATIVE.

ADVERB

An adverb is used:

1 with a verb, to say:

  a how something happens, e.g. *He walks* quickly.

  b where something happens, e.g. *I live* here.

  c when something happens, e.g. *They visited us* yesterday.

  d how often something happens, e.g. *We* usually *have coffee.*

2 to strengthen or weaken the meaning of:

  a a verb, e.g. *He* really *meant it*   *I almost fell asleep.*

  b an adjective, e.g. *She is* very *clever.*   *This is a* slightly *better result.*

  c another adverb, e.g.
    It comes off terribly *easily.*   *The boys* nearly *always get home late.*

3 to add to the meaning of a whole sentence, e.g.
  Luckily, *no one was hurt.*   *He is* probably *our best player.*

In writing or in formal speech, it is **incorrect** to use an adjective instead of an adverb. For example, use
  Do it properly.   and not   **Do it* proper.

Note that many words are both an adjective and an adverb, e.g.

ADJECTIVE	ADVERB
a fast *horse*	*He ran* fast.
a long *time*	*Have you been here* long?

APOSTROPHE '

This is used:

1 to indicate possession:

  with a singular noun:
    a boy's book   *a week's work*   *the boss's salary*

  with a plural already ending with *-s*:
    a girls' school   *two weeks' newspapers* *the bosses' salaries*

  with a plural not already ending with *-s*:
    the children's books   *women's literature*

  with a singular name:
    Bill's book   *Nicholas' (or Nicholas's) coat*
    Barnabas' (or Barnabas's) book   *John's coat*

  with a name ending in *-es* that is pronounced /-ɪz/:
    Bridges' poems   *Moses' mother*

  in phrases using *sake*;
    for God's sake   *for goodness' sake*   *for Nicholas' sake*

  but it is often omitted in a business name:
    Barclays Bank.

2 to mark an omission of one or more letters or numbers:
  he's (he is or *he has)*   *haven't (have not)*
  can't (cannot)   *we'll (we shall)*
  won't (will not)   *o'clock (of the clock)*
  the summer of '68 (1968)

3 when letters or numbers are referred to in plural form:
  mind your p's and q's   *find all the number 7's*

  but it is unnecessary in, e.g. *MPs; the 1940s.*

AUXILIARY VERB

An auxiliary verb is used in front of another verb to alter its meaning. Mainly, it expresses:

1 when something happens, by forming a tense of the main verb, e.g. *I shall go.*   *He was going.*

2 permission, necessity, or possibility to do something, e.g.
  They may go.   *You must go.*
  I can't go.   *I might go.*
  She would go if she could.

These auxiliaries (and those listed below except *be*, *do*, and *have*) are sometimes called modal verbs.

The principal auxiliary verbs are:

be	*have*	*must*	*will*
can	*let*	*ought*	*would*
could	*may*	*shall*	
do	*might*	*should*	

BRACKETS ( ) [ ]

Round brackets, also called parentheses, are used mainly to enclose:

1 explanations and extra information or comment, e.g.
Congo (formerly Zaire)   *He is (as he always was) a rebel.*
This is done using integrated circuits (see page 38).

2 in this dictionary, the type of word which can be used with the word being defined, e.g.
crow² ... (of a baby) utter happy cries
backfill ...refill (a hole) with the material dug out of it

Square brackets are used mainly to enclose:

1 words added by someone other than the original writer or speaker, e.g.
Then the man said, 'He [the police officer] can't prove I did it.'

2 various special types of information, such as stage directions, e.g.
HEDLEY: Goodbye! [Exit].

3 in this dictionary, etymologies, e.g.
babushka ... [Russian, literally 'grandmother']

CLAUSE

A clause is a group of words that includes a finite verb. If it makes complete sense by itself, it is known as a main clause, e.g.
The sun came out.

Otherwise, although it makes some sense, it must be attached to a main clause; it is then known as a subordinate clause, e.g.
when the sun came out
(as in *When the sun came out, we went outside.*)

COLON :

This is used:

1 between two main clauses of which the second explains, enlarges on, or follows from the first, e.g.
It was not easy: to begin with I had to find the right house.

2 to introduce a list of items (a dash should not be added), and after expressions such as *namely*, *for example*, *to resume*, *to sum up*, and *the following*, e.g.
You will need: a tent, a sleeping bag, cooking equipment, and a rucksack.

3 before a quotation, e.g.
The poem begins: 'Earth has not anything to show more fair'.

COMMA ,

The comma marks a slight break between words, phrases, etc. In particular, it is used:

1 to separate items in a list, e.g
red, white, and blue (or *red, white and blue*)
We bought some shoes, socks, gloves, and handkerchiefs.

2 to separate adjectives that describe something in the same way, e.g.
It is a hot, dry, dusty place.

but not if they describe it in different ways, e.g.
a distinguished foreign author

or if one adjective adds to or alters the meaning of another, e.g.
a bright red tie.

3 to separate a name or word used to address someone, e.g.
David, I'm here.
Well, Mr Jones, we meet again.
Have you seen this, my friend?

4 to separate a phrase from the rest of the sentence, e.g.
Having had lunch, we went back to work.

especially in order to clarify the meaning, e.g.
In the valley below, the village looked very small.

5 after words that introduce direct speech, or after direct speech where there is no question mark or exclamation mark, e.g.
They answered, 'Here we are.'
'Here we are,' they answered.

6 after *Dear Sir*, *Dear Sarah*, etc., and *Yours faithfully*, *Yours sincerely*, etc. in letters.

7 to separate a word, phrase, or clause that is secondary or adds information or a comment, e.g.
I am sure, however, that it will not happen.
Fred, who is bald, complained of the cold.

but not with a relative clause (one usually beginning with *who*, *which*, or *that*) that restricts the meaning of the noun it follows, e.g.
Men who are bald should wear hats.

(See note at RELATIVE CLAUSE)

No comma is needed between a month and a year in dates, e.g.
in December 1993

or between a number and a road in addresses, e.g.
17 Devonshire Avenue.

COMPARATIVE

The form of an adjective used to compare two people or things in respect of a certain quality is called the comparative. Comparative adjectives are formed in two ways: generally, short words add *-er* to the base form, e.g.
smaller, faster, greater.

Often, the base form alters, e.g.
bigger, finer, easier.

Long words take *more* in front of them, e.g.
more beautiful, more informative.

COMPLEMENT

A complement is a word or phrase that comes after a verb but has the same reference as the subject or object, e.g.
the culprit in *The dog was the culprit.*
president in *They elected him president.*

CONJUNCTION

A conjunction is used to join parts of sentences which usually, but not always, contain their own verbs, e.g.
He found it difficult so I helped him.
They made lunch for Alice and Mary.
I waited until you came.

There are two types of conjunction. **Coordinating conjunctions** (*and*, *or*, *but*) join two equal clauses, phrases, or words. **Subordinating** conjunctions join a subordinate clause to a main clause.

The most common subordinating conjunctions are:

after	*like*	*though*
although	*now*	*till*
as	*once*	*unless*
because	*since*	*until*
before	*so*	*when*
for	*so that*	*where*
if	*than*	*whether*
in order that	*that*	*while*

DASH –

This is used:

1 to mark the beginning and end of an interruption in the structure of a sentence:

My son – where has he gone? – would like to meet you.

2 to show faltering speech in conversation:

Yes – well – I would – only you see – it's not easy.

3 to show other kinds of break in a sentence, often where a comma, semicolon, or colon would traditionally be used, e.g.

Come tomorrow – if you can.
The most important thing is this – don't rush the work.

A dash is not used in this way in formal writing.

DEFINITE ARTICLE

See note at DETERMINER.

DETERMINER

A determiner is a word that starts a noun phrase, determining its role in relation to the rest of the text in which it occurs. The most common determiners are *the* (sometimes called the **definite article**) and *a* or *an* (sometimes called the **indefinite article**). *A* or *an* is used with a singular noun phrase that is introduced as new information in a text; *the* is used with information that is already established (*A* man came in ... *The* man went up to Jim) or that is regarded as common knowledge (*the* Moon, *the* sea).

Other kinds of determiners are:

possessive determiners (sometimes called **possessive adjectives**):

my, your, his, her, its, our, their.

demonstratives:

this, that, these, those.

DIALECT

Everyone speaks a particular dialect: that is, a particular type of English distinguished by its vocabulary and its grammar. Different parts of the world and different groups of people speak different dialects: for example, Australians may say *arvo* while others say *afternoon*, and a London Cockney may say *I done it* while most other people say *I did it*. A dialect is not the same thing as an accent, which is the way a person pronounces words.

See also note at STANDARD ENGLISH.

DIRECT SPEECH

Direct speech is the actual words of a speaker quoted in writing.

1 In a novel etc., speech punctuation is used for direct speech:

a The words spoken are usually put in quotation marks.

b Each new piece of speech begins with a capital letter.

c Each paragraph within one person's piece of speech begins with quotation marks, but only the last paragraph ends with them.

For example:

Christopher looked into the box. 'There's nothing in here,' he said. 'It's completely empty.'

2 In a script (the written words of a play, a film, or a radio or television programme):

a The names of speakers are written in the margin in capital letters.

b Each name is followed by a colon.

c Quotation marks are not needed.

d Any instructions about the way the words are spoken or about the scenery or the actions of the speakers (stage directions) are written in the present tense in brackets or italics.
For example:

CHRISTOPHER: [Looks into box.] There's nothing in here. It's completely empty.

EXCLAMATION MARK !

This is used instead of a full stop at the end of a sentence to show that the speaker or writer is very angry, enthusiastic, insistent, disappointed, hurt, surprised, etc., e.g.

I am not pleased at all!   *I wish I could have gone!*
I just love sweets!   *Ow!*
Go away!   *He didn't even say goodbye!*

FULL STOP .

This is used:

1 at the end of a sentence, e.g.

I am going to the cinema tonight.
The film begins at seven.

The full stop is replaced by a question mark at the end of a question, and by an exclamation mark at the end of an exclamation.

2 after an abbreviation, e.g.

H. G. Wells   *p.19 (= page 19)*
Sun. (= Sunday)   *Ex. 6 (= Exercise 6)*

Full stops are not used with:

a numerical abbreviations, e.g.
1st, 2nd, 15th, 23rd

b acronyms, e.g.
FIFA, NATO

c abbreviations that are used as ordinary words, e.g.
con, demo, recap

d chemical symbols, e.g.
Fe, K, H_2O

Full stops are not essential for:

a abbreviations consisting entirely of capitals, e.g.
BBC, AD, BC, PLC

b C (= Celsius), F (= Fahrenheit)

c measures of length, weight, time, etc., except for
in. (= inch), st. (= stone)

d contractions (i.e. where the last letter is the same as the last letter of the full word), e.g.
Dr, Revd (but note *Rev.*), *Mr, Mrs, Mme, Mlle, St* (= *Saint*)

e certain other conventional abbreviations which are not directly related to the full word, e.g.
Hants, Northants

HYPHEN -

This is used:

1 to join two or more words so as to form a compound or single expression, e.g.
mother-in-law   *non-stick*

This use is growing less common; often you can do without such hyphens:
treelike   *dressing table*

2 to join words in an attributive compound (one put before a noun, like an adjective), e.g.
a well-known man (but *the man is well known*)
an out-of-date list (but *the list is out of date*)

3 to join a prefix etc. to a proper name, e.g.
anti-Darwinian   half-Italian
non-British

4 to make a meaning clear by linking words, e.g.
twenty-odd people or *twenty odd people*

or by separating a prefix, e.g.
re-cover or *recover*
re-present or *represent*
re-sign or *resign*

5 to separate two identical letters in adjacent parts of a word, e.g.

    pre-exist   *Ross-shire*

6 to represent a common second element in the items of a list, e.g.

    two-, three-, or fourfold

7 to divide a word if there is no room to complete it at the end of a line, e.g.

    ... diction-
    ary ...

The hyphen comes at the end of the line, not at the beginning of the next line. In general, words should be divided at the end of a syllable; *dicti-onary* would be quite wrong. In handwriting, typing, and word processing, it is safest (and often neatest) not to divide words at all.

INDEFINITE ARTICLE
See note at DETERMINER.

INTERROGATIVE PRONOUN
Interrogative pronouns (*who, whom, which, what*) introduce direct and indirect questions:

    What did he say?
    She asked him what he had said.
    Who are you?
    She asked him who he was.

A question mark is used after a direct question, but not after an indirect question.

INTRANSITIVE VERB
See note at TRANSITIVE VERB.

MAIN CLAUSE
See note at CLAUSE.

METAPHOR
A metaphor is a figure of speech that goes further than a simile, either by saying that something is something else that it could not normally be called, e.g.

    The moon was a ghostly galleon tossed upon cloudy seas.
    Stockholm, the Venice of the North

or by suggesting that something appears, sounds, or behaves like something else, e.g.

    burning ambition   *blindingly obvious*
    the long arm of the law

NOUN
A noun denotes a person or thing. There are four kinds:

1 common nouns (the words for objects and creatures), e.g.

    The red shoe *was left on the shelf.*
    The large box *stood in the corner.*
    The plant *grew to two metres.*
    A horse *and* rider *galloped by.*

2 proper nouns (the names of people, places, ships, institutions, and animals, which always begin with a capital letter), e.g.

    Jane   *USS Enterprise*   *Bambi*
    London   *Grand Hotel*

3 abstract nouns (the words for qualities, things we cannot see or touch, and things which have no physical reality), e.g.

    truth   *absence*
    explanation   *warmth*

4 collective nouns (the words for groups of things), e.g.

    committee   *squad*   *the Cabinet*
    herd   *swarm*   *the clergy*
    majority   *team*   *the public*

OBJECT
There are two types of object:

1 A direct object refers to a person or thing directly affected by the verb and can usually be identified by asking the question 'whom or what?' after the verb, e.g.

    The electors chose Mr Smith.   *Charles wrote* a letter.

2 An indirect object usually refers to a person or thing receiving something from the subject of the verb, e.g.

    He gave me *the pen.*
    (*me* is the indirect object, and *the pen* is the direct object.)
    I sent my bank *a letter.*
    (*my bank* is the indirect object, and *a letter* is the direct object.)

Sentences containing an indirect object usually contain a direct object as well, but not always, e.g.

    Pay me.

'Object' on its own usually means a direct object.

PARTICIPLE
There are two kinds of participle in English: the **present participle**, which consists of -*ing* added to the base form of a verb, and the **past participle**, which for most verbs consists of -*ed* added to the base form.

There are three main uses of participles:

1 with *be* or *have* to form different tenses:

    She is *relaxing.*   *She* has *relaxed.*

2 to form verbal adjectives:

    a relaxing drink   *a leaving* present

3 to form verbal nouns:

    I don't want your leavings.

PASSIVE
A verb in the passive takes the object or person affected by the action as its subject. Passive verbs are formed by placing a form of the auxiliary verb *be* in front of the past participle:

    This proposal will *probably* be *accepted.*
    Several people were *injured.*
    He was *hit* by a train.

The passive is often used when the writer does not want to say who exactly is responsible for the action in question:

    I'm afraid your ideas have been rejected.

PHRASAL VERB
A phrasal verb is a verb made up of an ordinary verb plus an adverb or preposition, or both. *Give in, set off, take over,* and *look down on* are phrasal verbs. The meaning of a phrasal verb can be quite different from the meanings of the words of which it is composed.

PHRASE
A phrase is a group of words that has meaning but does not have a subject, main verb, or object (unlike a clause or sentence). It can be:

1 a noun phrase, functioning as a noun, e.g.

    I went to see my friend Tom.
    The only ones they have *are too small.*

2 an adjective phrase, functioning as an adjective, e.g.

    I was very pleased *indeed.*   *This one* is better *than mine.*

3 an adverb phrase, functioning as an adverb, e.g.

    They drove off *in their car.*
    I was there *ten days ago.*

POSSESSIVE DETERMINER
See note at DETERMINER.

POSSESSIVE PRONOUN

A possessive pronoun is a word such as *mine, yours,* or *theirs,* functioning as subject, complement, or direct or indirect object in a clause.

This one is mine.   *That one is* yours.
Hers *is no good.*

PREPOSITION

A preposition is used in front of a noun or pronoun to form a phrase. It often describes the position or movement of something, e.g. under *the chair,* or the time at which something happens, e.g. in *the evening.*

Prepositions in common use are:

about	*behind*	*into*	*through*
above	*beside*	*like*	*till*
across	*between*	*near*	*to*
after	*by*	*of*	*towards*
against	*down*	*off*	*under*
along	*during*	*on*	*underneath*
among	*except*	*outside*	*until*
around	*for*	*over*	*up*
as	*from*	*past*	*upon*
at	*in*	*round*	*with*
before	*inside*	*since*	*without*

PRONOUN

A pronoun is used as a substitute for a noun or a noun phrase, e.g.

He was upstairs.   *Did you see* that?
Anything can happen now.   *It*'s lovely weather.

Using a pronoun often avoids repetition, e.g.

I found Jim – he *was upstairs.*
(instead of *I found Jim – Jim was upstairs.*)
Where are your keys? – I've got them.
(instead of *Where are your keys? – I've got my keys.*)

Pronouns are the only words in English which have different forms when used as the subject (*I, we, he, she,* etc.) and as the object (*me, us, him, her,* etc.).

See also notes at INTERROGATIVE PRONOUN, POSSESSIVE PRONOUN, REFLEXIVE PRONOUN, and RELATIVE CLAUSE.

QUANTIFIER

A quantifier is a word such as *some, all,* or *enough,* used to describe the amount of something. Most quantifiers, like numbers, can be used either as determiners or with an 'of' structure:

some dresses   some of the dresses
enough soap   enough of the soap
all students   all of the students

A few quantifiers are also found before *the* or a possessive determiner:

all the dresses   both her shoes

QUESTION MARK ?

This is used instead of a full stop at the end of a sentence to show that it is a question, e.g.

Have you seen the film yet?
You didn't lose my purse, did you?

It is **not** used at the end of a reported question, e.g.

I asked you whether you'd seen the film yet.

QUOTATION MARKS ' ' " "

These are also called inverted commas, and are used:

1 round a direct quotation (closing quotation marks come after any punctuation which is part of the quotation), e.g.

He said, 'That is nonsense.'
'That', he said, 'is nonsense.'
'That, however,' he said, 'is nonsense.'
Did he say, 'That is nonsense'?
He asked, 'Is that nonsense?'

2 round a quoted word or phrase, e.g.

What does 'integrated circuit' mean?

3 round a word or phrase that is not being used in its central sense, e.g.

the 'king' of jazz
He said he had enough 'bread' to buy a car.

4 round the title of a book, song, poem, magazine article, television programme, etc. (but not a book of the Bible), e.g.

'Hard Times' by Charles Dickens

5 as double quotation marks round a quotation within a quotation, e.g.

He asked, 'Do you know what "integrated circuit" means?'

In handwriting, double quotation marks are usual.

REFLEXIVE PRONOUN

Reflexive pronouns (*himself, yourselves,* etc.) are used in two ways:

1 for a direct or indirect object that refers to the same person or thing as the subject of the clause:

They didn't hurt themselves.   *He wanted it for* himself.

2 for emphasis:

She said so herself.   *I* myself *do not believe her.*

RELATIVE CLAUSE

A relative clause is a subordinate clause used to add to the meaning of a noun. A relative clause is usually introduced by a relative pronoun (*who, which, that*).

Restrictive relative clauses are distinguished from non-restrictive relative clauses by punctuation. A non-restrictive relative clause has commas round it, e.g.

Please approach any member of our staff, who will be pleased to help, and discuss your needs.

The shopkeeper who left the commas out turned this into a restrictive relative clause, implying that there were other members of staff who would not be pleased to help!

The relative pronoun *whom* (the objective case of *who*) is now used only in formal writing.

The person whom he hit was a policeman. (formal)
The person who he hit was a policeman. (less formal)

The relative pronoun may be omitted if it is the object of the relative clause:

The person he hit was a policeman.

SEMICOLON ;

This is used:

1 between clauses that are too short or too closely related to be made into separate sentences; such clauses are not usually connected by a conjunction, e.g.

To err is human; to forgive, divine.
You could wait for him here; on the other hand I could wait in your place; this would save you valuable time.

2 between items in a list which themselves contain commas, if it is necessary to avoid confusion, e.g.

The party consisted of three teachers, who had already climbed with the leader; seven pupils; and two parents.

SENTENCE

A sentence is the basic unit of language in use and expresses a complete thought. There are three types of sentence, each starting with a capital letter, and each normally ending with a full stop, a question mark, or an exclamation mark:

Statement: *You're happy.*
Question: *Is it raining?*
Exclamation: *I wouldn't have believed it!*

A sentence, especially a statement, often has no punctuation at the end in a public notice, a newspaper headline, or a legal document, e.g.

> *Government cuts public spending*

A sentence normally contains a subject and a verb, but may not, e.g.

> *What a mess!*   *Where?*   *In the sink.*

SIMILE

A simile is a figure of speech involving the comparison of one thing with another of a different kind, using *as* or *like*, e.g.

> *The water was as clear as glass.*
> *Cherry blossom lay like driven snow upon the lawn.*

Everyday language is rich in similes:

with *as*:	*as like as two peas* *as strong as an ox*
	as poor as a church mouse
	as rich as Croesus
with *like*:	*spread like wildfire* *run like the wind*
	sell like hot cakes
	like a bull in a china shop

STANDARD ENGLISH

Standard English is the dialect of English used by most educated English speakers and is spoken with a variety of accents (see note at ACCENT). While not *in itself* any better than any other dialect, standard English is the form of English normally used for business dealings, legal work, diplomacy, teaching, examinations, and in all formal written contexts.

SUBJECT

The subject of a sentence is the person or thing that carries out the action of the verb and can be identified by asking the question 'who or what' before the verb, e.g.

> The goalkeeper *made a stunning save.*
> Hundreds of books *are now available on CD-ROM.*

In a passive construction, the subject of the sentence is in fact the person or thing to which the action of the verb is done, e.g.

> I *was hit by a ball.*
> Has the programme *been broadcast yet?*

SUBORDINATE CLAUSE

See note at CLAUSE.

SUPERLATIVE

The superlative form of an adjective is used to say that something is the supreme example of its kind. Superlative adjectives are formed in two ways: generally, short words add *-est* to the base form, e.g. *smallest, fastest, greatest.*

Often, the base form alters, e.g. *biggest, finest, easiest.*

Long words take *most* in front of them, e.g. *most beautiful, most informative.*

SYLLABLE

A syllable is the smallest unit of speech that can be pronounced in isolation, such as *a, at, ta,* or *tat.* A word can be made up of one, two, or more syllables:

> *cat, fought,* and *twinge* each have one syllable;
> *rating, deny,* and *collapse* each have two syllables;
> *excitement, superman,* and *telephone* each have three syllables;
> *America* and *complicated* each have four syllables;
> *examination* and *uncontrollable* each have five syllables.

SYNONYM

A synonym is a word that has the same meaning as, or a similar meaning to, another word:

> *cheerful, happy, merry,* and *jolly*

are synonyms that are quite close to each other in meaning, as are

> *lazy, indolent,* and *slothful.*

In contrast, the following words all mean 'a person who works with another', but their meanings vary considerably:

| *colleague* | *conspirator* |
| *ally* | *accomplice* |

TRANSITIVE VERB

A transitive verb is one that has a direct object, e.g.

> *John was reading a book*
> (where *a book* is the direct object).

An intransitive verb is one that does not have a direct object, e.g.

> *John was reading.*

Some verbs are always transitive, e.g. *bury, foresee, rediscover*; others are always intransitive, e.g. *dwell, grovel, meddle.* Many, as *read* in the examples above, are used both transitively and intransitively.

VERB

A verb says what a person or thing does, and can describe:

> an action, e.g. *run, hit*
> an event, e.g. *rain, happen*
> a state, e.g. *be, have, seem, appear*
> a change, e.g. *become, grow*

Verbs occur in different forms, usually in one or other of their tenses. The most common tenses are:

the simple present tense:	*The boy walks down the road.*
the continuous present tense:	*The boy is walking down the road.*
the simple past tense:	*The boy walked down the road.*
the continuous past tense:	*The boy was walking down the road.*
the perfect tense:	*The boy has walked down the road.*
the future tense:	*The boy will walk down the road.*

Each of these forms is a finite verb, which means that it is in a particular tense and that it changes according to the number and person of the subject, as in

> *I am*   *you walk*
> *we are*   *he walks*

An infinitive is the form of a verb that usually appears with to, e.g.

> *to wander, to look, to sleep.*

See also notes at PARTICIPLE, PASSIVE, PHRASAL VERB, TRANSITIVE VERB.

ACKNOWLEDGEMENTS

Dorling Kindersley would like to thank the following:
Clare Double and Lesley Malkin for editorial assistance; Mark Bracey for DTP guidance; Simonne Dearing, Harvey de Roemer, Maite Lantaron, and Sarah Williams for DTP assistance; Neale Chamberlain and Sue Hadley for additional picture research.

Dorling Kindersley would also like to thank the following private individuals and staff at the locations and organizations listed below for their help with research or photography for this dictionary. Unless otherwise stated, all are located in the UK.
Philip Abbot, Royal Armouries Museum, Leeds; P. Adams and Sons for Laurel Keepsake II; Airborne Forces Museum, Aldershot; Chris Alderson; Angels and Bermans, London; Avoncroft Museum of Building, Bromsgrove; Barleylands Farm Museum and Animal Centre, Essex; Brooking Collection, University of Greenwich, London; Château de Saumur, France; Civil War Library and Museum, Philadelphia; Dominic Corr; Detmold Open Air Museum, Germany; Helen Dorey, Sir John Soane's Museum, London; Ermine Street Guard; Exeter Maritime Museum; Fireplace World, Croydon; Kevin Fox; Deane Granoff; Guns & Tackle, Whitton, Twickenham; Andie Laidlaw; Bill Leonard; Lorne Mackillop, MW William Pitters UK Ltd; Carlo Manzi Rentals, London; the staff at Market House Books, Aylesbury, Bucks.; Musée de l'Empéri, Salon de Provence; Museum of English Rural Life, Reading; Naturmuseum, Senckenburg, Frankfurt, Germany; Norfolk Rural Life Museum; Michael Osborn; Potter's Music Shop Ltd, Richmond, Surrey; Royal Museum of Scotland; Royal Tyrrell Museum of Palaeontology, Canada; Kevin Salt, Pegasus Stables, Newmarket; Richmond Music Shop Ltd, Surrey; Bhupinder Singh, Central Gurdwara Resource Centre, London; Alan Turton, English Civil War Society; University Museum of Archaeology and Anthropology, Cambridge; Zoology Department, University College London.

Illustrators While all efforts have been made to acknowledge all illustrators, Dorling Kindersley will be pleased to add any missing credits in future editions.
Julie Anderson; Philip Argent; Steven Biesty; Evelyn Binns; Rick Blakely; Richard Bonson; Peter Bull; Joanna Cameron; Martin Camm; Kyokah G. Chen; Julia Cobbold; Luciano Corbella; Peter Dennis; Richard Draper; Carl Ellis; Angelika Elsebach; Simone End; Chris Forsey; Mark Franklin; Mick Gillah; Kevin Goold; Tony Graham; Andrew Green; Mike Grey; Nick Hall; Nick Hewetson; Sandie Hill; Christian Hook; Roger Hutchins; John Hutchinson; Mike Illey; Kevin Jones Associates; Chris King; Jason Lewis; Richard Lewis; Kenneth Lilly; Ruth Linden; Chris Lyon; Andrew Macdonald; S. Mackay; Janos Marffy; David More; Colin Newman; Richard Orr; Jonathan Potter; John Preston, Maltings Partnership; David Pugh; Dan Pyne; Sebastian Quigley; Sally Alane Reason; Jim Robbins; Eric Robson/Garden Studios; Colin Rose; Colin Salmon; Mustafa Sami; Hamish Simpson; John Temperton; Halli Verinder; Barbara Walker; Richard Ward; Steve Weston; Paul Williams; Philip Wilson; John Woodcock; Debra Woodward; Martin Woodward.

Model-makers Centaur Studios; Richard Davies; Dave Donkin; Will Long; Simon Miles; Chris Reynolds and the team at BBC Special Effects; Steve Schott; Charles Somerville; Ted Taylor; Thorp Modelmakers.

Commissioned photography While all efforts have been made to acknowledge all photographers, Dorling Kindersley will be pleased to add any missing credits in future editions:
Peter Anderson; Sue Barnes; Jon Bouchier; Geoff Brightling; Peter Bull; John Bulmer; Jane Burton; Peter Chadwick; Tina Chambers; Bruce Chisholm, John Cousins; Andy Crawford; Paul Croft; Geoff Dann; Michael Dent; Philip Dowell; Peter Downs; Mike Dunning; Neil Fletcher; Lynton Gardiner; Phillip Gatward; Steve Gorton; Frank Greenaway; Derek Hall; Mark Hamilton; Paul Harris; Marc Henrie; John Heseltine; Chas Howson; Dudley Hubbard; Colin Keates; Gary Kevin; Dave King; Bob Langrish; Cyril Laubscher; Andrew Lawson; Mike Linley; Liz McAuley; Andrew McRob; Kevin Mallet; H. K. Melton; Ray Moller; Tracy Morgan; Stephen Oliver; Gary Ombler; Roger Phillips; Martin Plomer; Laurence Pordes; Rob Reichenfeld; Steve Ridley; Tim Ridley; Dave Rudkin; Kim Sayer; Karl Shone; James Stevenson; Clive Streeter; Jane Stockman; Harry Taylor; Kim Taylor; Andreas Von Einseidel; Matthew Ward; Dave Watts; Linda Whitwam; Alan Williams; Jerry Young.

Agency photography Dorling Kindersley would like to thank the following for their kind permission to reproduce their photographs.

a = above; b = below; c = centre; l = left; r = right; t = top.

Accordions of London Ltd: 174bc. **Action Plus:** 50bc, Chris Barry 935b, Peter Tarry 833bl. **AKG London Ltd:** Solomon R. Guggenheim Museum New York: *Composition in Red, Blue, Yellow and Black* 1929 by Piet Mondrian © Mondrian/Holtzman Trust, c/o Beeldrecht, Amsterdam, Holland/DACS 1998 19c; Hermitage St. Petersburg: *Adoration of the Child c.1480* by Filippino Lippi 544tl; Heinrich Heine Institute, Düsseldorf: 211l; Erich Lessing 809c; Santa Maria Novella, Florence: *The Trinity* by Massachio 669tr; Stuttgart Staatsgalerie: *The Sublime Moment* 1938 by Salvador Dali © DACS 1998 837tl; Uffizi Gallery, Florence/Photo Erich Lessing: *Birth of Venus* by Botticelli 695tr. **Allsport UK Ltd:** 95br, Stephen Dunn 505r, Bob Martin 779tr; Pascal Rondeau 95br. **American Museum of Natural History, New York:** 759c, 874br, 878bl. **Ancient Art and Architecture Collection:** Ronald Sheridan 643bl, 713bl, 812cl, 866bl. **Heather Angel/Biofotos:** 71cr. **Anglo-Australian Observatory:** David Malin 330tl, tcl. **Aquila Photographics:** R. Maier 540t. **Arcaid:** Richard Bryant 639br. **Ardea London Ltd:** S. Meyers 713r; John E. Swedberg 146c; Valerie Taylor 300bla. By courtesy of the visitors of the **Ashmolean Museum, Oxford:** 265bl, 610bc. **Axiom:** Jim Holmes 769bl. By kind permission of **Bentley and Company, Jewellers, New Bond Street, London:** 772c. By kind permission of **Boosey and Hawkes Music Publishers Ltd, London:** 558c. **Bridgeman Art Library, London:** Artemis, Luxembourg: *Les Poseuses* 1888 by George Pierre Seurat 631br; Hermitage, St. Petersburg: *Violin and Guitar* 1913 by Pablo Picasso © Succession Picasso/DACS 1998 201br; Louvre, Paris: *The Oath of Horatii* 1784 by Jacques Louis David 547tr; Musée D'Orsay, Paris: *The Gleaners* 1857 by Jean-François Millet 544tr; National Gallery, London: *An Allegory with Venus and Cupid* 1540–50 by Agnolo Bronzino 34tc; National Gallery London: *Wilton Diptych c.1395* by Anonymous 228tr; National Gallery London: *Waterlily Pond* 1899 by Claude Monet 407br; Phillips, The International Fine Art Auctioneers: *Marilyn*, (silk screen) by Andy Warhol © The Andy Warhol Foundation for the Visual Arts, Inc./ARS, NY and DACS London 1988 635br; Private Collection: *Self Portrait Screaming* 1910 by Egon Schiele 279br; Schloss Charlottenburg, Berlin 737br; Southampton City Art Gallery: *The Vorticist* 1912 by Percy Wyndham Lewis © Estate of Mrs G. A. Wyndham-Lewis 936br; Stapleton Collection: *Italian Instruments* by A. J. Hipkins 824c. **Paul Brierly:** 171tc. **British Council Collection/Bridget Riley:** 572bl. By kind permission of the **British Library, London:** 166cra, 351c, 497tr. By courtesy of the trustees of the **British Museum, London:** 137tl, 203cla, 217cra, 286c, 289cl, 307bcr, 383t, 391br, 540c, 537bc, 693r, 694l, 736br, 845cr, 858br, 890br, 903bl. **Duncan Brown:** 795br. **Building of Bath Museum:** Christopher Woodward 187tl. **Mathewson Ball:** 285cr. **John Bulmer:** 182ca. **Martin Cammin:** 139br. By kind permission of the **Central Gurdwara Resource Centre, London:** 354cla. **Bruce Coleman Collection:** John Cancalosi 713br; Gerald Cubitt 496cl; 481cr; Gordon Langsbury 820l; Dr Scott Neilson 58br; Hans Reinhard 128bcl; Frieder Saver 805cla; Kim Taylor 700tr; 866br; Rod Williams 401cr. **Colorific:** Andre Gelpke 230bl. **Dassault Aviation:** 295tr. **Mark Dennis:** 505r. **Courtesy of Division Ltd:** 931br. **E. T. Archives:** 845l. **The European Space Agency:** 712br. **Ford UK Ltd:** 822r. **The Werner Forman Archive:** Private Collection 431ca, 788l; Ben Heller Collection NY 936tl. **Michael Freeman:** 758br. **The Garden:** T. Sandell 460cr, 611tr. **The Garden Picture Library:** Rex Butcher 482c; Brian Carter 819c. **Geoscience Features:** Dr Basil Booth 209r. **Getty Images:** Bruce Forster 215t. By kind permission of **Glasgow Museums:** 509c, 522cr, 966br. **GKN/Westland Helicopters:** 377r. **The Goldfish Bowl:** 270c. **Sonia Halliday Photographs:** 530bl. **Robert Harding Picture Library:** 511bc, 527t; M. F. Chillmaid 908bcr; Tony Waltham 236br; Adam Woolfit 671cr. **S. C. Hendricks:** 540r. **HMSO:** Crown Copyright with the kind permission of the controller HMSO: 574cr. **Michael Holford:** 195br. **Angelo Hornak Library:** 53tc. **Kit Houghton/ Houghton's Horses:** 501tl. **The Hutchison Library:** Christine Pemberton 215r. **Image Bank:** Guido Alberto Rossi 497tc. **Images Colour Library:** 502b. **Image Select/Anne Ronan:** 614cr, 660b. The Trustees of the **Imperial War Museum, London:** 334tl, 521tl. **Michael Jenner:** 137bc, 472t. **The Jewish Museum, London:** 876cr. **A. F. Kersting:** 282tr, 453c. **Frank Lane Picture Agency:** A. R. Hamblin 202tl; E & D Hosking 768br; L. West 837br; Roger Tidman 938 bcl; D. P. Wilson 525 bcl; T. S. Zylva 803b. **London Transport Museum:** 142bl. **Louisiana National Guard:** 939t. **Lund Observatory:** 517tl. **Hugh McManners:** 751tl. **Microscopix:** Andrew Syred 663br. **Milton Glaser Inc, New York:** 659c. **Ministry of Defence, Pattern Room, Nottingham:** 362cla, 815crb. **Nilesh Mistry/David Higham Associates:** 147bc. **Musée D'Orsay:** *The Italian Woman*, 1888 Vincent Van Gogh. **Museum of Archaeology and Anthropology, Cambridge:** 876crb. **Museum of Artillery in the Rotunda, London:** 707b. **Museum of London:** 157bl, 432cra, 848cl, 870r. **The Museum of the Moving Image:** 971br. **NASA:** 624br; 801br. Courtesy of the Director of the **National Army Museum, London:** 97cr, 804br, 972t. **National Maritime Museum, Greenwich:** 57bc, 75c, 102cla, 124cr, 135cl, 223cl, 243cr, 296tl, 306c, 321c, 437tr, 441b, 456cb, 469tl, 471cl, 479br, 484b, 496br, 511br, 581bc, 681t, 706b, 707tr, 728bl, 731tl, 738tr, 764b, 806cr, 900l, 926br, 927bc, 941tr, 950bc. **National Motor Museum, Beaulieu:** 453br. **National Museums of Scotland, Edinburgh:** 122br, 518br, 679tl, 841bl. **National Railway Museum, York:** 883cl. **National Trust Photographic Library:** Nick Meers 312crb. **Natural History Museum, London:** 228bl, 389tr, 523bl. **Natural History Photographic Agency:** B & C Alexander 943cr; George Bernard 439r; Andy Callow 138tl; Mark Deeble/Victoria Stone 311cl; Ken Griffiths 475crb; Jany Sauvant 38cra; Kevin Schafer 800b; John Shaw 573bc. **Oxford Scientific Films:** Doug Allan 474b, 745tr; Michael Fogden 785bcr; Stan Osolinski 779tl; Steve Littlewood 512bc. **Photographie Giraudon, Paris:** Musée de la Ville de Paris, Musée Carnavalet 360br. **Pictor International:** 30cr, 394c. **Pitt-Rivers Museum, Oxford:** 351br, 847r. **Planet Earth Pictures:** Mary Clay 644r; Beth Davidow 655cr; David George 200bcl; Hans Christian Heap 461bl; David Kjaer 967bc; Doug Perrine 138br, 169tr; David A. Ponton 680trc; Peter Scoones 163tc. **Pontificia Commissione de Archeologia Sacra/IKONA:** 163c. **Powell-Cotton Museum, Leeds:** 436r. **RAF Museum, Hendon:** 929tl. By kind permission of the Board of Trustees of the **Royal Armouries XXVIA.20, Leeds:** 841bl. By kind permission of **Rye Town Hall:** 341tc. **Peter Sanders Photography:** 518tc. **SCALA:** Gipsoteca Canoviana, Possagno 155r. **Science Museum, London:** 741bl. **Science Museum, London:** 741bl. **Science Photo Library:** Alex Bartel 328r; Lawrence Berkeley Laboratory 638b; Biophoto Associates 150b; Dr Jeremy Burgess 593cra, 827t; Simon Fraser, Newcastle University Robotics Dept. 711br; Astrid and Hans Frieder-Richler 328cra; Adam Hart-Davis 863bl; Manfred Kage 996cl; James King Holmes 774tr; NOAD 330tr; Photolibrary International 870l; Stammers Thompson 965br; Alexander Tsiaras 871br. **Science and Society Picture Library:** 125t, 246r. **Sporting Pictures:** 720tl. **Stockmarket:** 773clb. **Surfer Publications:** Tony Servais 836bl. **Telegraph Colour Library:** A. Rye 928bl. **Topham Picturepoint:** 970cl. By kind permission of the Trustees of the **Victoria and Albert Museum, London:** 482bl, 491crb. **Vision Agenzia Fotografica:** 695cra. **Visual Arts Library:** Albright Knox Museum, Buffalo: *Convergence* 1952 Jackson Pollock © ARS, NY and DACS 1998 23br; J. Hay Whitney Collection, New York: *The Open Window at Collioure* 1905 © Succession H. Matisse/ DACS 1988 289tr. **Wallace Collection, London:** 69tr, 488tr. By kind permission of the **Walsall Leather Museum:** 721cl, 805r. **Warwick Castle:** 156bl, 335tl, 932b. **Waterhouse:** Howard Hall 493tl. By kind permission of the **Weald and Downland Open Air Museum:** 706cr, 761tr, 777tr, 968cra. **Robert Wigington, Arbour Antiques, Stratford upon Avon:** 417bl. **Colin Woolf:** 551cr. **Worthing Museum and Art Gallery:** 702c. **Yamaha UK Ltd:** 787c. **Michael Zabe:** 856tl.

Jacket: By courtesy of the trustees of the **British Museum:** back tr. **National Maritime Museum, Greenwich:** spine.